YEARBOOK OF THE UNITED NATIONS 2011

Volume 65

YEARBOOK OF THE UNITED NATIONS, 2011

Volume 65

The United Nations Department of Public Information is dedicated to communicating the ideals and work of the United Nations to the world; to interacting and partnering with diverse audiences; and to building support for peace, development and human rights for all. Based on official documents, although not itself an official record, the *Yearbook of the United Nations* stands as the most authoritative reference work on the Organization and an indispensable tool for anyone seeking information on the UN system.

The *Yearbook of the United Nations* is produced by the Yearbook Unit of the Publications and Editorial Section in the Outreach Division of the Department of Public Information.

Chief Editor: Orrin F. Summerell
Managing Editor: Edoardo Bellando
Senior Editors: Abraham Azubuike, Lawri Moore, John R. Sebesta, Vikram Sura
Associate Editors: Natalie Alexander, Adrian Brune, Raffaella De Lia, Meghan Lynn, Shiyun Sang
Copy Editor: Sunita Chabra
Typesetter: Galina V. Brazhnikova
Researcher: Nilton Sperb
Administrative Assistant: Sheila Poinesette
Copy Coordinator: Melissa Gay
Editorial Assistant: Stanislawa Blaszczyszyn

Yearbook of the United Nations
Room S-927
United Nations
New York, New York 10017
United States of America
e-mail: **unyearbook@un.org**

All volumes of the *Yearbook of the United Nations* can be accessed in full online on the *Yearbook* website: **unyearbook.un.org**.

For more information on the United Nations, please visit the website of the Organization: **un.org**.

YEARBOOK OF THE UNITED NATIONS 2011

Volume 65

Department of Public Information
United Nations, New York

Yearbook of the United Nations, 2011
Volume 65

Published by the United Nations Department of Public Information
New York, New York 10017, United States of America

Copyright © 2015 United Nations
All rights reserved

ISBN: 978-92-1-101277-4
eISBN: 978-92-1-057510-2
ISSN: 0082-8521
United Nations publication
Sales No. E.13.I.4 H

Jacket design: Graphic Design Unit, United Nations, New York

Printed in the United States of America

Foreword

The year 2011 was marked by dramatic events across the Arab world inspired, in part, by the values of democracy, good governance and human rights that are cherished and defended at the United Nations. Described as an "Arab Spring" or "Arab Awakening", demonstrations in many countries, often with younger generations in the lead, demanded peaceful change. Tragically, violent responses by authorities and unresolved social tensions left once-promising movements struggling against new forms of oppression. While the people of Tunisia made encouraging progress, those in Egypt, Libya and elsewhere were plunged into what would prove to be prolonged turmoil. The most deadly conflict of all, in Syria, caused the deaths of many thousands of people, drove millions more from their homes, and destabilized the already volatile region. The United Nations worked urgently to meet rapidly escalating humanitarian needs while exploring avenues for a negotiated end to the conflict.

In July, the United Nations welcomed its 193rd Member State to the community of nations: the Republic of South Sudan, which had gained its independence following a United Nations-led peace process that ended two decades of civil war. The raising of the country's flag at United Nations Headquarters was greeted with global enthusiasm, but that feeling dissipated as political rivalries remained and, in December 2013, triggered an outbreak of armed conflict. The United Nations Mission in South Sudan, originally deployed to promote stability, subsequently opened its gates to tens of thousands of vulnerable people, protecting them from deadly hostilities and saving thousands of lives.

The year also saw the United Nations lead the way in helping save lives in the wake of devastating natural disasters. The Fukushima Daiichi nuclear power plant accident, triggered by an earthquake and tsunami, prompted the United Nations to galvanize international action on nuclear safety and security.

The Organization continued to advance global health, education, the rule of law, gender equality, institution-building and other efforts to achieve the Millennium Development Goals. As the impacts of climate change became more pronounced, the United Nations intensified calls for a global response that would contain emissions while ushering in a new era of low-carbon prosperity. Building on previous visits to climate-vulnerable regions, in September 2011, I travelled to Kiribati, a low-lying island nation where rising sea levels pose a grave risk to the country's way of life and very existence.

I was deeply honoured to be elected in 2011 to a second term as Secretary-General. In thanking the Member States for this renewal of my mandate, I pledged to continue working as a harmonizer and bridge-builder in serving "We the peoples".

This *Yearbook of the United Nations*, like the others in the series since the Organization's inception in 1945, provides a comprehensive account of the action taken by the United Nations to maintain peace and security, protect human rights, promote sustainable development, deliver humanitarian aid and uphold international law. The *Yearbook* is meant to serve not just as a tool to engage public understanding of our work, but also as a reference by which future generations, which we are obligated to protect and empower, may judge the success of our collective efforts.

Ban Ki-moon
Secretary-General of the United Nations
New York, October 2015

Table of contents

Foreword	v
Table of contents	vii
About the 2011 edition of the *Yearbook*	xiv
The *Yearbook* online	xv
Abbreviations commonly used in the *Yearbook*	xvi
Explanatory note on documents	xvii
Report of the Secretary-General on the work of the Organization	3

Part One: Political and security questions

I. International peace and security — 33

PROMOTION OF INTERNATIONAL PEACE AND SECURITY, 33: Maintenance of international peace and security, 33; Peacemaking and peacebuilding, 43; Protection issues, 49; Special political missions, 50. THREATS TO INTERNATIONAL PEACE AND SECURITY, 52: International terrorism, 52. PEACEKEEPING OPERATIONS, 57: General aspects of UN peacekeeping, 58; Comprehensive review of peacekeeping, 61; Operations in 2011, 62; Roster of 2011 operations, 63; Financial and administrative aspects of peacekeeping operations, 65.

II. Africa — 87

PROMOTION OF PEACE IN AFRICA, 90. CENTRAL AFRICA AND GREAT LAKES REGION, 97: Central Africa and Great Lakes, 97; Democratic Republic of the Congo, 102; Burundi, 117; Central African Republic, 121; Central African Republic and Chad, 128; Uganda, 132; Rwanda, 132. WEST AFRICA, 133: Regional issues, 133; Côte d'Ivoire, 140; Liberia, 162; Sierra Leone, 174; Guinea-Bissau, 180; Cameroon–Nigeria, 186; Guinea, 188. HORN OF AFRICA, 189: The Sudan and South Sudan, 189; Chad–Sudan, 232; Somalia, 233; Eritrea, 261; Eritrea–Ethiopia, 265. NORTH AFRICA, 266: Libyan Arab Jamahiriya, 266; Western Sahara, 289. OTHER ISSUES, 296: Egypt and Tunisia, 296; Mauritius–United Kingdom, 296.

III. Americas — 297

CENTRAL AMERICA, 297: Guatemala, 297; Honduras, 298; Nicaragua–Costa Rica, 298. HAITI, 298: Political and security developments, 299; MINUSTAH, 305. OTHER ISSUES, 308: Cuba–United States, 308.

IV. Asia and the Pacific — 310

AFGHANISTAN, 310: Political and security developments, 311; UNAMA, 331; International Security Assistance Force, 331; Children and armed conflict, 335; Sanctions, 336. IRAQ, 351: Political and security developments, 352; UNAMI, 356; Post-Development Fund mechanism, 356; Non-proliferation and disarmament obligations, 357; Children and armed conflict, 358; Oil-for-food programme, 358. IRAQ–KUWAIT, 360: POWs, Kuwaiti property and missing persons, 360; UN Compensation Commission and Fund, 361. TIMOR-LESTE, 362: Political and security developments, 362; UNAMET, 366; UNMIT, 366. DEMOCRATIC PEOPLE'S REPUBLIC OF KOREA, 368: Non-proliferation, 368; Other issues, 369. IRAN, 369: Non-proliferation, 369. NEPAL, 372: Political and security developments, 372. YEMEN, 373: Political and security developments, 373. OTHER ISSUES, 375: India–Pakistan, 375; Pakistan, 375; Sri Lanka, 375; Thailand–Cambodia, 375; United Arab Emirates–Iran, 376.

V. Europe and the Mediterranean — 377

BOSNIA AND HERZEGOVINA, 377: Implementation of Peace Agreement, 378. Kosovo, 384: Political and security developments, 384; EULEX, 386; UNMIK, 387. THE FORMER YUGOSLAV REPUBLIC OF MACEDONIA, 389. GEORGIA, 389: UNOMIG, 391. ARMENIA AND AZERBAIJAN, 392. CYPRUS, 392: Political and security developments, 393; UNFICYP, 394. OTHER ISSUES, 400: Strengthening of security and cooperation in the Mediterranean, 400; Organization for Democracy and Economic Development, 401.

VI. Middle East — 402

PEACE PROCESS, 403: Diplomatic efforts, 403; Occupied Palestinian Territory, 403. ISSUES RELATED TO PALESTINE, 434: General aspects, 434; Assistance to Palestinians, 438. LEBANON, 455: Political and security developments, 455; Implementation of resolution 1559(2004), 456; Implementation of resolution 1701(2006) and UNIFIL activities, 458; Special Tribunal for Lebanon, 466. SYRIAN ARAB REPUBLIC, 468: Political and security developments, 468; The Syrian Golan, 471. UNTSO, 477.

VII. Disarmament — 478

UN MACHINERY, 478. UN ROLE IN DISARMAMENT, 483. NUCLEAR DISARMAMENT, 485: Comprehensive Nuclear-Test-Ban Treaty, 493; Advisory opinion of the International Court of Justice, 498; Prohibition of the use of nuclear weapons, 499. NON-PROLIFERATION, 500: Non-proliferation treaty, 500; Missiles, 505; Non-proliferation of weapons of mass destruction, 506; Multilateralism in disarmament and non-proliferation, 511; IAEA safeguards, 513; Radioactive waste, 516; Nuclear-weapon-free zones, 517. BACTERIOLOGICAL (BIOLOGICAL) AND CHEMICAL WEAPONS, 520: Bacteriological (biological) weapons, 521; Chemical weapons, 522. CONVENTIONAL WEAPONS, 524: Towards an arms trade treaty, 524; Small arms, 524; Convention on excessively injurious conventional weapons and Protocols, 529; Cluster munitions, 532; Anti-personnel mines, 532; Practical disarmament, 533; Transparency, 533. OTHER ISSUES, 538: Prevention of an arms race in outer space, 538; Observance of environmental norms, 539; Science and technology and disarmament, 540. STUDIES, RESEARCH AND TRAINING, 540. REGIONAL DISARMAMENT, 541: Regional centres for peace and disarmament, 545.

VIII. Other political and security questions   551

GENERAL ASPECTS OF INTERNATIONAL PEACE AND SECURITY, 551: Support for democracies, 551. REGIONAL ASPECTS OF INTERNATIONAL PEACE AND SECURITY, 552: Indian Ocean, 552. DECOLONIZATION, 553: Decade for the Eradication of Colonialism, 553; Puerto Rico, 560; Territories under review, 560; Other issues, 572. PEACEFUL USES OF OUTER SPACE, 577: Implementation of UNISPACE III recommendations, 577; Scientific and Technical Subcommittee, 578; Legal Subcommittee, 581; UN system coordination, 582. EFFECTS OF ATOMIC RADIATION, 586. INFORMATION SECURITY, 589. INFORMATION, 590: UN public information, 590.

Part Two: Human rights

I. Promotion of human rights   603

UN MACHINERY, 603: Human Rights Council, 603; Office of High Commissioner for Human Rights, 614; Other aspects, 616. HUMAN RIGHTS INSTRUMENTS, 617: Convention against racial discrimination, 619; Covenant on civil and political rights and optional protocols, 620; Covenant on economic, social and cultural rights and optional protocol, 620; Convention on elimination of discrimination against women and optional protocol, 621; Convention against torture, 621; Convention on the rights of the child, 622; Convention on migrant workers, 633; Convention on rights of persons with disabilities, 633; Convention for protection from enforced disappearance, 634; Convention on genocide, 636; General aspects, 636. OTHER ACTIVITIES, 638: Strengthening action to promote human rights, 638; Human rights education, 645; World Down Syndrome Day, 648; International Day for the Right to the Truth, 649; International Year for People of African Descent, 649; Follow-up to 1993 World Conference, 649.

II. Protection of human rights   650

SPECIAL PROCEDURES, 650. CIVIL AND POLITICAL RIGHTS, 651: Racism and racial discrimination, 651; Human rights defenders, 663; Reprisals for cooperation with human rights bodies, 665; Protection of migrants, 666; Discrimination against minorities, 671; Freedom of religion or belief, 674; Right to self-determination, 680; Rule of law, democracy and human rights, 685; Other issues, 691. ECONOMIC, SOCIAL AND CULTURAL RIGHTS, 704: Realizing economic, social and cultural rights, 704; Right to development, 704; Social Forum, 720; Extreme poverty, 720; Right to food, 721; Right to adequate housing, 726; Right to health, 727; Cultural rights, 730; Right to education, 733; Environmental and scientific concerns, 734; Slavery and related issues, 735; Vulnerable groups, 737.

III. Human rights country situations   753

GENERAL ASPECTS, 753. AFRICA, 754: Burundi, 754; Côte d'Ivoire, 754; Democratic Republic of the Congo, 757; Guinea, 757; Libya, 758; Somalia, 759; Sudan, 760; South Sudan, 761; Tunisia, 761. AMERICAS, 761: Bolivia, 761; Colombia, 762; Guatemala, 762; Haiti, 762. ASIA, 763: Afghanistan, 763; Cambodia, 763; Democratic People's Republic of Korea, 764; Iran, 768; Kyrgyzstan, 771; Myanmar, 772; Nepal, 776; Yemen, 777. EUROPE AND THE MEDITERRANEAN, 778: Belarus, 778; Cyprus, 778. MIDDLE EAST, 779: Syrian Arab Republic, 779; Territories occupied by Israel, 782.

Part Three: Economic and social questions

I. Development policy and international economic cooperation — 789

INTERNATIONAL ECONOMIC RELATIONS, 789: Development and international economic cooperation, 790; Happiness and well-being, 796; People's empowerment and development, 796; Human security, 797; Sustainable development, 797; Eradication of poverty, 805; Science and technology for development, 810. DEVELOPMENT POLICY AND PUBLIC ADMINISTRATION, 821: Committee for Development Policy, 821; Public administration, 823. GROUPS OF COUNTRIES IN SPECIAL SITUATIONS, 825: Least developed countries, 826; Small island developing States, 832; Landlocked developing countries, 834.

II. Operational activities for development — 838

SYSTEM-WIDE ACTIVITIES, 838. TECHNICAL COOPERATION THROUGH UNDP, 843: UNDP/UNFPA/UNOPS Executive Board, 843; UNDP operational activities, 844; Programming arrangements, 847; Financial and administrative matters, 849. OTHER TECHNICAL COOPERATION, 853: Development Account, 853; UN activities, 853; UN Office for Partnerships, 854; UN Office for Project Services, 856; UN Volunteers, 857; Economic and technical cooperation among developing countries, 859; UN Capital Development Fund, 860.

III. Humanitarian and special economic assistance — 861

HUMANITARIAN ASSISTANCE, 861: Coordination, 861; Central Emergency Response Fund, 865; Disaster response, 869; Mine action, 879; Humanitarian action, 881. SPECIAL ECONOMIC ASSISTANCE, 891: African economic recovery and development, 891; Other economic assistance, 899.

IV. International trade, finance and transport — 902

INTERNATIONAL TRADE AND DEVELOPMENT, 902: Multilateral trading system, 902; United Nations Conference on Trade and Development, 905; Commodities, 910; Coercive economic measures, 913. INTERNATIONAL FINANCIAL SYSTEM AND DEVELOPMENT, 914: Debt situation of developing countries, 917; Financing for development, 921; Other matters, 930. TRANSPORT, 932: Maritime transport, 932; Transport of dangerous goods, 933.

V. Regional economic and social activities — 937

REGIONAL COOPERATION, 937. AFRICA, 938: Economic trends, 938; Activities, 938; Programme and organizational questions, 944. ASIA AND THE PACIFIC, 944: Economic trends, 944; Activities, 945; Programme and organizational questions, 950. EUROPE, 951: Economic trends, 951; Activities, 951; Programme and organizational questions, 954. LATIN AMERICA AND THE CARIBBEAN, 954: Economic trends, 954; Activities, 954. WESTERN ASIA, 958: Economic trends, 958; Activities, 958.

VI. Energy, natural resources and cartography — 963

ENERGY AND NATURAL RESOURCES, 963: Energy, 963; Natural resources, 966. CARTOGRAPHY, 967.

VII. Environment and human settlements	**970**

ENVIRONMENT, 970: UN Environment Programme, 970; Global Environment Facility, 976; International conventions and mechanisms, 977; Environmental topics, 984; Other matters, 991. HUMAN SETTLEMENTS, 994: UN-Habitat, 994; Follow-up to the 1996 UN Conference on Human Settlements (Habitat II), 998.

VIII. Population	**1002**

COMMISSION ON POPULATION AND DEVELOPMENT, 1002. INTERNATIONAL MIGRATION AND DEVELOPMENT, 1004. UNITED NATIONS POPULATION FUND, 1005. OTHER POPULATION ACTIVITIES, 1011.

IX. Social policy, cultural development and human resources development	**1013**

SOCIAL POLICY, 1013: Social development, 1013; Ageing persons, 1024; Persons with disabilities, 1029; Youth, 1032; Family, 1039. CULTURAL DEVELOPMENT, 1042: Culture of peace, 1042; Sport for peace and development, 1047; Culture and development, 1049. HUMAN RESOURCES DEVELOPMENT, 1051: UN research and training institutes, 1053; Education, 1056.

X. Women	**1057**

FOLLOW-UP TO THE FOURTH WORLD CONFERENCE ON WOMEN AND BEIJING+5, 1057: Critical areas of concern, 1061. UN MACHINERY, 1090: Convention on the elimination of discrimination against women, 1090; Commission on the Status of Women, 1092; UN-Women, 1093.

XI. Children	**1101**

FOLLOW-UP TO 2002 GENERAL ASSEMBLY SPECIAL SESSION ON CHILDREN, 1101. PROMOTION AND PROTECTION OF THE RIGHTS OF CHILDREN, 1102. UNITED NATIONS CHILDREN'S FUND, 1103.

XII. Refugees and displaced persons	**1112**

OFFICE OF THE UNITED NATIONS HIGH COMMISSIONER FOR REFUGEES, 1112: Programme policy, 1112; Refugee protection and assistance, 1117; Regional activities, 1121; Policy development and cooperation, 1130; Financial and administrative questions, 1131.

XIII. Health, food and nutrition	**1134**

HEALTH, 1134: AIDS prevention and control, 1134; Non-communicable diseases, 1145; Tobacco, 1152; Malaria, 1153; Global public health, 1157; Road safety, 1159. FOOD AND AGRICULTURE, 1160: Food aid, 1160; Food security, 1162. NUTRITION, 1169.

XIV. International drug control and crime prevention	**1170**

UN OFFICE ON DRUGS AND CRIME, 1170. INTERNATIONAL DRUG CONTROL, 1174: Commission on Narcotic Drugs, 1174; Cooperation against the world drug problem, 1176; Conventions, 1183. CRIME PREVENTION AND CRIMINAL JUSTICE, 1188: Commission on Crime Prevention and Criminal Justice, 1188; Follow-up to the Twelfth United Nations Crime Congress, 1189; Crime prevention programme, 1190; Transnational organized crime, 1198.

XV. Statistics	**1215**

STATISTICAL COMMISSION, 1215: Demographic and social statistics, 1215; Economic statistics, 1217; Natural resources and environment statistics, 1220; Other activities, 1221.

Part Four: Legal questions

I. International Court of Justice — 1227

Judicial work of the Court, 1227: Contentious proceedings, 1228; Advisory proceedings, 1240. Other questions, 1240: Functioning and organization of the Court, 1240; Trust Fund to Assist States in the Settlement of Disputes, 1241.

II. International tribunals and court — 1242

International Tribunal for the Former Yugoslavia, 1242: The Chambers, 1242; Office of the Prosecutor, 1246; The Registry, 1247; Financing, 1248. International Tribunal for Rwanda, 1249: The Chambers, 1250; Office of the Prosecutor, 1255; The Registry, 1255; Financing, 1256. Functioning of the Tribunals, 1258: Implementation of completion strategy, 1258. International Criminal Court, 1261: The Chambers, 1261; Office of the Prosecutor, 1263; The Registry, 1264; International cooperation, 1264.

III. International legal questions — 1266

Legal aspects of international political relations, 1266: International Law Commission, 1266; International State relations and international law, 1282; International terrorism, 1284; Diplomatic relations, 1289; Treaties and agreements, 1290. International economic law, 1290: Commission on International Trade Law, 1291. Other questions, 1298: Rule of law at the national and international levels, 1298; Strengthening the role of the United Nations, 1300; Host country relations, 1305.

IV. Law of the sea — 1308

Convention on the Law of the Sea, 1308. Institutions created by the Convention, 1323: International Seabed Authority, 1323; International Tribunal for the Law of the Sea, 1324; Commission on the Limits of the Continental Shelf, 1325. Other developments related to the Convention, 1325: Assessment of global marine environment, 1327; Marine biological resources, 1328; United Nations Open-ended Informal Consultative Process, 1328; Piracy, 1328; Division for Ocean Affairs and the Law of the Sea; 1328.

Part Five: Institutional, administrative and budgetary questions

I. United Nations restructuring and institutional matters — 1351

Restructuring matters, 1351: Programme of reform, 1351. Institutional matters, 1353: Admission to UN of new Member, 1353; General Assembly, 1354; Security Council, 1358; Economic and Social Council, 1359. Coordination, monitoring and cooperation, 1360: Institutional mechanisms, 1360; Other matters, 1362. UN and other organizations, 1362: Cooperation with organizations, 1362; Other cooperation, 1369; Participation in UN work, 1369.

II. United Nations financing and programming — 1375

Financial situation, 1375. UN budget, 1375: Budget for 2010–2011, 1375; Budget for 2012–2013, 1382. Contributions, 1399: Assessments, 1399. Accounts and auditing, 1401: Financial management practices, 1402; Review of UN administrative and financial functioning, 1403. Programme planning, 1404: Programme performance, 1405.

III. **Administrative and staff matters**   1406

ADMINISTRATIVE MATTERS, 1406: Managerial reform and oversight, 1406; Conference management, 1411; UN information systems, 1419; UN premises and property, 1421. STAFF MATTERS, 1427: Appointment of Secretary-General, 1427; Conditions of service, 1428; Staff safety and security, 1435; Other staff matters, 1439; UN Joint Staff Pension Fund, 1447; Travel-related matters, 1448; Administration of justice, 1448.

Appendices

I. Roster of the United Nations   1461

II. Charter of the United Nations and Statute of the International Court of Justice   1464

III. Structure of the United Nations   1482

IV. Agendas of United Nations principal organs in 2011   1495

V. United Nations information centres and services   1506

VI. Intergovernmental organizations related to the United Nations   1508

Indices

Subject index   1513

Index of 2011 resolutions and decisions   1538

Index of 2011 Security Council presidential statements   1541

About the 2011 edition of the *Yearbook*

This sixty-fifth volume of the *Yearbook of the United Nations* continues the tradition of providing the most comprehensive coverage available of the annual activities and concerns of the United Nations.

The present volume recounts the work of the United Nations in 2011 as it responded to large-scale humanitarian crises amid political and social turmoil, especially in North Africa and the Middle East. In addition to detailing the many United Nations contributions worldwide to peacekeeping, supporting national elections, protecting human rights and helping those affected by natural disasters, this *Yearbook* volume articulates how the Organization addressed during the year such issues as sustainable development and poverty eradication; climate change; HIV/AIDS and non-communicable diseases; youth; desertification, land degradation and drought; and nuclear safety and security.

Coverage of economic and social questions in PART THREE of the *Yearbook* has been restructured. Chapter IX now focuses on "Social policy, cultural development and human resources development", including youth and ageing persons; Chapter XI is exclusively devoted to issues of "Children"; and Chapter XIV collectively addresses "International drug control and crime prevention".

Readers can locate information by using the Table of contents, the Subject index, the Index of resolutions and decisions and the Index of Security Council presidential statements. The volume also features six appendices: Appendix I comprises a roster of Member States; Appendix II reproduces the Charter of the United Nations and the Statute of the International Court of Justice; Appendix III presents the structure of the principal organs of the United Nations; Appendix IV provides the agenda for each session of the principal organs in 2011; Appendix V gives the addresses of United Nations information centres and services worldwide; and Appendix VI lists the addresses of the specialized agencies and other related organizations of the UN system with their respective heads as at 2011.

Structure and scope of articles

The *Yearbook* is subject-oriented and divided into five parts covering political and security matters; human rights issues; economic and social questions; legal issues; and institutional, administrative and budgetary matters. Chapters summarize pertinent UN activities, including those of intergovernmental and expert bodies, as well as major reports and, in selected cases, the views of States in written communications.

Activities of UN bodies. The *Yearbook* places the major activities of the principal organs of the United Nations and, on a selective basis, those of their subsidiary bodies in a narrative context of consideration, deliberation and action. The texts of all resolutions and decisions of a substantive nature adopted in 2011 by the General Assembly, the Security Council and the Economic and Social Council are reproduced or summarized under the relevant topic. Such texts are preceded by procedural details giving the date of adoption, meeting number and vote totals (in favour–against–abstaining), if any, and an indication of their approval by a sessional or subsidiary body prior to final adoption. The texts are followed by details of any recorded or roll-call vote. Substantive action by the Security Council is analysed and brief reviews of the Council's deliberations given, particularly in cases where an issue was taken up but no resolution was adopted.

Major reports. Most reports of the Secretary-General in 2011, along with those of main United Nations committees, regional and functional commissions, and Special Rapporteurs, as well as selected reports from other UN sources, such as seminars and expert and working groups, are summarized.

Views of States. Written communications sent to the United Nations by Member States and circulated as documents of the principal organs have been summarized, in selected cases, under the relevant topics.

Multilateral treaties. Information on signatories and parties to multilateral treaties and conventions has been taken from the series *Multilateral Treaties Deposited with the Secretary-General* (ST/LEG/SER/E) (see **treaties.un.org**).

Terminology

Formal titles of bodies, organizational units, conventions, declarations and officials are normally given in full on first mention in each main section. They are also used in resolution/decision texts, as well as in the Subject index under the key word of the title. Short titles, abbreviations or acronyms are used in subsequent references in the main text.

Acknowledgements

The Yearbook Unit would like to express its appreciation to the following persons for their contribution to the *Yearbook of the United Nations, 2011*:

Contributing Editors/Writers: Cate Attwood, Elizabeth Baldwin-Penn, Udy Bell, Kathryn Gordon, Peter Jackson, Kelsey Keech, Christine Koerner, Sandra Rademacher

Copy Editor: Alison Koppelman, Rebecca Wolfe

Proofreaders: Judith Goss, Kathryn Kuchenbrod

Interns: Rochelle Atizado, Simon Callaghan, Lerone Charles, Sara Gärtner, Frank Polizzi, Robin Porsfelt, Hazel Wheldon

Indexer: Maria A. Sullivan

The *Yearbook* online

All published volumes of the *Yearbook of the United Nations*—from the 1946–47 edition onwards—can be accessed and read in full on the *Yearbook* website (**unyearbook.un.org**). The site's multi-option search engine enables readers to quickly find specific information in an individual volume, across a range of volumes or throughout the entire *Yearbook* collection. Visitors to the website can download PDFs of *Yearbook* pages and chapters for offline use. Additional resources include the Yearbook Pre-press and the Yearbook Express, as well as links to the *Yearbook* Twitter account, United Nations databases and other information products.

Pre-press. The Yearbook Pre-press (**unyearbook.un.org/pre-press**) offers draft chapters or detailed and hyperlinked chapter outlines from volumes currently in production. Pre-press material is made available as a service to readers and researchers and reflects the fact that the Yearbook Unit works simultaneously on researching, writing, editing, copyediting and finalizing multiple volumes of the *Yearbook*. The Pre-press is updated on a regular basis. Pre-press chapters do not represent the final edited and proofread versions that will appear in published form, nor do Pre-press chapter outlines represent the final form and content or document scope of the chapter in question.

Express. The Yearbook Express (**unyearbook.un.org/express**) features the chapter introductions of recently published *Yearbooks*, along with the report of the Secretary-General on the work of the Organization in those years, in all six United Nations official languages—Arabic, Chinese, English, French, Russian and Spanish. To provide speakers of those languages with such summary *Yearbook* content, the Yearbook Unit works with teams of volunteer translators. Only the annual report of the Secretary-General represents a United Nations official translation.

Social media. The *Yearbook of the United Nations* can be also found on Twitter (**twitter.com/UNYearbook**), where **@UNYearbook** addresses current United Nations activities and concerns in their historical perspective, linking readers to relevant information in the *Yearbook* collection.

Abbreviations commonly used in the *Yearbook*

ACABQ	Advisory Committee on Administrative and Budgetary Questions	**OCHA**	Office for the Coordination of Humanitarian Affairs
AU	African Union	**ODA**	official development assistance
BNUB	United Nations Office in Burundi	**OECD**	Organization for Economic Cooperation and Development
BINUCA	United Nations Integrated Peacebuilding Office in the Central African Republic	**OHCHR**	Office of the United Nations High Commissioner for Human Rights
CARICOM	Caribbean Community	**OIOS**	Office of Internal Oversight Services
CEB	United Nations System Chief Executives Board for Coordination	**OSCE**	Organization for Security and Cooperation in Europe
CIS	Commonwealth of Independent States	**PA**	Palestinian Authority
CPC	Committee for Programme and Coordination	**UNAIDS**	Joint United Nations Programme on HIV/AIDS
DPKO	Department of Peacekeeping Operations	**UNAMA**	United Nations Assistance Mission in Afghanistan
DPRK	Democratic People's Republic of Korea	**UNAMI**	United Nations Assistance Mission for Iraq
DRC	Democratic Republic of the Congo	**UNAMID**	African Union-United Nations Hybrid Operation in Darfur
ECA	Economic Commission for Africa	**UNCTAD**	United Nations Conference on Trade and Development
ECE	Economic Commission for Europe	**UNDOF**	United Nations Disengagement Observer Force
ECLAC	Economic Commission for Latin America and the Caribbean	**UNDP**	United Nations Development Programme
ECOWAS	Economic Community of West African States	**UNEP**	United Nations Environment Programme
ESCAP	Economic and Social Commission for Asia and the Pacific	**UNESCO**	United Nations Educational, Scientific and Cultural Organization
ESCWA	Economic and Social Commission for Western Asia	**UNFICYP**	United Nations Peacekeeping Force in Cyprus
EU	European Union	**UNFPA**	United Nations Population Fund
FAO	Food and Agriculture Organization of the United Nations	**UN-Habitat**	United Nations Human Settlements Programme
HIV/AIDS	human immunodeficiency virus/acquired immunodeficiency syndrome	**UNHCR**	Office of the United Nations High Commissioner for Refugees
IAEA	International Atomic Energy Agency	**UNICEF**	United Nations Children's Fund
ICC	International Criminal Court	**UNIFIL**	United Nations Interim Force in Lebanon
ICJ	International Court of Justice	**UNIOGBIS**	United Nations Integrated Peacebuilding Office in Guinea-Bissau
ICRC	International Committee of the Red Cross	**UNIPSIL**	United Nations Integrated Peacebuilding Office in Sierra Leone
ICSC	International Civil Service Commission	**UNMIK**	United Nations Interim Administration Mission in Kosovo
ICTR	International Criminal Tribunal for Rwanda	**UNMIL**	United Nations Mission in Liberia
ICTY	International Tribunal for the Former Yugoslavia	**UNMIS**	United Nations Mission in the Sudan
IDPs	internally displaced persons	**UNMISS**	United Nations Mission in South Sudan
IFAD	International Fund for Agricultural Development	**UNMIT**	United Nations Integrated Mission in Timor-Leste
ILO	International Labour Organization	**UNOCA**	United Nations Regional Office for Central Africa
IMF	International Monetary Fund	**UNOCI**	United Nations Operation in Côte d'Ivoire
IMO	International Maritime Organization	**UNODC**	United Nations Office on Drugs and Crime
ITU	International Telecommunication Union	**UNOPS**	United Nations Office for Project Services
JIU	Joint Inspection Unit	**UNOWA**	United Nations Office for West Africa
LDC	least developed country	**UNRWA**	United Nations Relief and Works Agency for Palestine Refugees in the Near East
MDGs	Millennium Development Goals	**UNSMIL**	United Nations Support Mission in Libya
MINURCAT	United Nations Mission in the Central African Republic and Chad	**UNTSO**	United Nations Truce Supervision Organization
MINURSO	United Nations Mission for the Referendum in Western Sahara	**UN-Women**	United Nations Entity for Gender Equality and the Empowerment of Women
MINUSTAH	United Nations Stabilization Mission in Haiti	**UNWTO**	World Tourism Organization
MONUSCO	United Nations Organization Stabilization Mission in the Democratic Republic of the Congo	**WFP**	World Food Programme
NEPAD	New Partnership for Africa's Development	**WHO**	World Health Organization
NGO	non-governmental organization	**WMDs**	weapons of mass destruction
NPT	Treaty on the Non-Proliferation of Nuclear Weapons	**WMO**	World Meteorological Organization
NSGTs	Non-Self-Governing Territories	**WTO**	World Trade Organization
OAS	Organization of American States	**YUN**	Yearbook of the United Nations

Explanatory note on documents

The following principal United Nations document symbols appear in this volume:

A/- refers to documents of the General Assembly, numbered in separate series by session. Thus, A/66/- refers to documents issued for consideration at the sixty-sixth session, beginning with A/66/1. Documents of special and emergency special sessions are identified as A/S and A/ES-, followed by the session number.

A/C.- refers to documents of the Assembly's Main Committees. For example, A/C.1/- identifies documents of the First Committee, A/C.6/- documents of the Sixth Committee. A/BUR/- refers to documents of the General Committee. A/AC.- documents are those of the Assembly's ad hoc bodies and A/CN.- those of its commissions. For example, A/AC.105/- identifies documents of the Assembly's Committee on the Peaceful Uses of Outer Space, A/CN.4/- those of its International Law Commission. Assembly resolutions and decisions since the thirty-first (1976) session have been identified by two Arabic numerals: the first indicates the session of adoption, the second the sequential number in the series. Resolutions are numbered consecutively from 1 at each session. Decisions since the fifty-seventh (2002) session are numbered consecutively from 401 for those concerned with elections and appointments and from 501 for all other decisions. Decisions of special and emergency special sessions are numbered consecutively from 11 for those concerned with elections and appointments and from 21 for all other decisions.

E/- refers to documents of the Economic and Social Council, numbered in separate series by year. Thus, E/2011/- refers to documents issued for consideration by the Council at its 2011 sessions, beginning with E/2011/1. E/AC.-, E/C.- and E/CN.-, followed by identifying numbers, refer to documents of the Council's subsidiary ad hoc bodies, committees and commissions. For example, E/CN.5/- refers to documents of the Council's Commission for Social Development, E/C.2/- to documents of its Committee on Non-Governmental Organizations. E/ICEF/- documents are those of the United Nations Children's Fund (UNICEF). Symbols for the Council's resolutions and decisions since 1978 consist of two Arabic numerals: the first indicates the year of adoption and the second the sequential number in the series. There are two series: one for resolutions, beginning with 1 (e.g. resolution 2011/1), and one for decisions, beginning with 201 (e.g. decision 2011/201).

S/- refers to documents of the Security Council. Its resolutions are identified by consecutive numbers followed by the year of adoption in parentheses, beginning with resolution 1(1946).

ST/-, followed by symbols representing the issuing department or office, refers to documents of the United Nations Secretariat.

Documents of certain bodies bear special symbols, including the following:

CD/-	Conference on Disarmament
CERD/-	Committee on the Elimination of Racial Discrimination
DC/-	Disarmament Commission
DP/-	United Nations Development Programme
HSP/-	United Nations Human Settlements Programme
ITC/-	International Trade Centre
TD/-	United Nations Conference on Trade and Development
UNEP/-	United Nations Environment Programme

Many documents of the regional commissions bear special symbols, which are sometimes preceded by the following:

E/ECA/-	Economic Commission for Africa
E/ECE/-	Economic Commission for Europe
E/ECLAC/-	Economic Commission for Latin America and the Caribbean
E/ESCAP/-	Economic and Social Commission for Asia and the Pacific
E/ESCWA/-	Economic and Social Commission for Western Asia

Various other document symbols include the following:

L.- refers to documents of limited distribution, such as draft resolutions.
CONF.- refers to conference documents.
INF- refers to general information documents.
SR.- refers to summary records and is followed by a meeting number.
PV.- refers to verbatim records and is followed by a meeting number.

United Nations sales publications each carry a sales number with the following components separated by periods: a capital letter indicating the language(s) of the publication; two Arabic numerals indicating the year; a Roman numeral indicating the subject category; a capital letter indicating a subdivision of the category, if any; and an Arabic numeral indicating the number of the publication within the category. Examples: E.11.IX.1; E.11.II.C.1.

All UN official documents cited in the text in square brackets may be obtained through the UN Official Document System website: **documents.un.org**.

Report of the Secretary-General
on the work of the Organization

Report of the Secretary-General on the work of the Organization

Following is the Secretary-General's report on the work of the Organization [A/66/1], *dated 26 July 2011, submitted to the sixty-sixth session of the General Assembly. The Assembly took note of it on 4 October 2011* (**decision 66/505**).

Chapter I
Introduction

1. Since 2007, the world has changed significantly. We have seen the widening and deepening impact of global food, fuel and economic shocks on populations around the world. We have seen revolution and the rebirth of grass-roots-led democratic movements in North Africa and across the Middle East. We have witnessed shifts in economic power as parts of Africa and Asia have emerged as the new engines of global growth. We have experienced the rising incidence of mega-disasters, with their huge costs in terms of lives, livelihoods and development. And we have seen the increasing salience of a set of global challenges that threaten the lives of people around the world and the sustainability of the planet.

2. We are living in a time of global transition. Future generations are likely to describe this period as a pivotal juncture in world history when the status quo was irrevocably weakened and the contours of a new world began to emerge.

3. Throughout this period, the United Nations has striven to put the needs of the poorest and most vulnerable at the centre of the international agenda, attracting billions of dollars in new investments to accelerate progress on the Millennium Development Goals. The United Nations has led global efforts to address the worst natural disasters and man-made complex emergencies, mobilizing resources and providing life-saving assistance to populations in need. The United Nations has taken important steps towards transforming the political landscape to empower women worldwide, adopted institutional changes, and advocated for policy changes that tackle gender discrimination in politics, the workplace and the home. We have delivered on complex peacekeeping mandates and have assisted Member States with numerous difficult political transitions and sensitive elections. We have championed human rights and the rule of law. We have confronted head-on the key global challenges of our generation: addressing climate change and global health; breaking the deadlock on disarmament, arms control and non-proliferation; and mobilizing action against terrorism. In each of these arenas, we have brokered significant agreements or commitments to global strategies and mobilized resources and capacities to implement internationally agreed action plans.

Chapter II
Delivering results for people most in need

4. Large segments of the world's population are challenged by unequal recovery from economic crisis, natural and man-made disasters, and internal conflict. Globally, United Nations staff worked tirelessly to help deliver to the poor and the most vulnerable.

A. Development

5. With global economic recovery uneven and uncertain, many countries are still struggling. The financial crisis, as well as high and volatile food and energy prices, will have an impact for years to come. There is an urgent need to embark on a new era of sustainable development for all. The upcoming United Nations Conference on Sustainable Development (Rio+20 Conference), to be held in Rio de Janeiro in June 2012, will provide a historic opportunity for doing so. At the Conference, the international community must agree on an ambitious and actionable framework that complements the Millennium Development Goals.

1. The Millennium Development Goals and the other internationally agreed development goals

6. Four years away from the agreed target date of 2015, success is within reach for several key Millennium Development Goal targets. In 2015, the global poverty rate is expected to fall below 15 per cent, well below the 23 per cent target level. More than 90 per cent of the world's population will have access to improved sources of drinking water. Major strides have been made in increasing primary school enrolment, even in the poorest countries.

7. The number of deaths in children under 5 years of age worldwide declined from 12.4 million in 1990 to 8.1 million in 2009, with nearly 12,000 fewer children dying each day. Although many countries have demonstrated that progress is possible, efforts must be intensified to target the poorest and most vulnerable.

8. In 2009, nearly one quarter of the children in the developing world were underweight. Maternal death continues to require attention, especially in sub-Saharan Africa and Southern Asia. The developing world's net school enrolment ratio increased by just two percentage points, from 87 per cent to 89 per cent between 2004 and 2009, dimming hope for achieving universal primary education. Half of the population of the developing regions still lacked access to improved sanitation facilities in 2009.

9. In general, persistent and increasing inequalities are emerging within countries between the rich and the poor, and between rural populations and urban populations. This affects in particular those disadvantaged as a result of geographic location, gender, age or conflict.

10. The greatest progress towards the achievement of goals has been made under two sets of circumstances: first, when key health interventions, such as malaria control measures, hiv/aids prevention and treatment and immunization provision and campaigns, have been introduced; and second, when increased funding has translated into an expansion of programmes to deliver services and tools directly to those in need. Far less progress has been made towards targets that require structural changes and strong political commitment to guarantee sustained, predictable funding. This typifies the patterns seen in reducing hunger and maternal mortality and increasing access to education and improved sanitation.

11. Official development assistance reached a record high in 2010 of $128.7 billion, yet this remains well short of the United Nations target of 0.7 per cent of donor country gross national income as aid to developing countries by 2015. The Organization for Economic Cooperation and Development has warned that bilateral aid will decelerate during the next few years, given the global economic slowdown.

12. The Secretary-General has initiated an integrated implementation framework based on an interactive web-based tracking system, accessible to all stakeholders in the global partnership for development. The framework will help to increase transparency and screen pledges and commitments for consistency and clarity, thereby contributing to greater accountability.

13. At the 2010 High-level Plenary Meeting of the General Assembly on the Millennium Development Goals, countries acknowledged the challenges but agreed that the Goals remained achievable and called for the scaling-up of successful approaches and intensified collective action. They also agreed on the need to begin looking ahead to the post-2015 period. Within the United Nations system, the Secretary-General has initiated work to develop ideas on the post-2015 development framework, with a view to producing concrete recommendations in 2012.

14. Important initiatives are under way to address both global and regional challenges in achieving the Millennium Development Goals. In response to the continued threat of high and volatile food prices, the Secretary-General's High-level Task Force on the Global Food Security Crisis has recommended concrete measures to address both the short-term emergency and long-term interventions for sustainable food production and nutrition.

15. The needs and specific challenges of the least developed countries were the focus of the Fourth United Nations Conference on the Least Developed Countries, held in Istanbul in May 2011. In the resulting Programme of Action, Member States committed to addressing the structural challenges faced by the least developed countries by building productive capacities and reducing those countries' vulnerability to economic, natural and environmental shocks.

2. The special needs of Africa

16. Africa remains a key area of focus in the work of the entire United Nations system. Africa has been experiencing solid economic growth. Growth in gross domestic product accelerated to 4.7 per cent on average in 2010, up from 2.4 per cent in 2009. But this masks a great variation in growth across the continent. The sharp increase in food and energy prices in 2011 was especially devastating for the poor. Consequently, the absolute number of people in the region living in extreme poverty continues to increase. Unemployment remains high in the region, while armed conflicts exacerbate poverty, disrupt schooling and fuel sexual and gender-based violence.

17. Africa's population of 1 billion, the overwhelming majority of which comprises young men and women, has been increasingly recognized both as a challenge and as an opportunity. Sixty per cent of Africa's population is under 25 years old. With the increasing youth bulge, greater emphasis must be placed on providing young people with better opportunities for education, training, skills and jobs.

18. In the light of these challenges, development policy and, in particular, efforts to achieve the Millennium Development Goals and the goals set out in the African Union New Partnership for Africa's Development have taken on even greater significance. At the 2010 High-level Plenary Meeting of the General Assembly on the Millennium Development Goals, the international community was called upon to honour its aid commitments to Africa. While net disbursements of official development assistance to Africa increased from $29.5 billion in 2004 to an estimated $46 billion in 2010, this remains $18 billion short of what was committed by donors at the Group of Eight summit held in Gleneagles, United Kingdom of Great Britain and Northern Ireland.

19. The United Nations system continues to improve its operational support for the development efforts of African countries. It is advancing the implementation of the Declaration on Enhancing United Nations-African Union Cooperation: Framework for the Ten-Year Capacity-Building Programme for the African Union. It is partnering with several African Governments to implement projects that boost financing for development in areas such as sustainable forest management and to promote and strengthen the engagement of citizens in governance and public administration.

20. A number of African countries face daunting peace and security challenges. The Secretary-General has devoted a great deal of time and effort to these issues, in close consultation and coordination with the African Union and African regional organizations.

B. Peace and security

21. During the past year, the United Nations and the international community grappled with instability in sub-Saharan Africa, North Africa and the Middle East and beyond. The current environment underlines the need for an agile United Nations equipped with prevention, peacekeeping and peacebuilding tools to prevent and resolve violent conflicts.

1. Preventive diplomacy and support to peace processes

22. The United Nations aims to anticipate potential conflicts and to be proactive in helping to resolve them through preventive diplomacy and mediation efforts.

23. In 2011, the United Nations placed a particular focus on preventing election-related violence by helping Member States, through good offices, strategic advice and technical assistance, to conduct credible and transparent electoral processes in countries including the Central African Republic, the Comoros, Côte d'Ivoire, Guinea, Haiti, Kyrgyzstan, the Niger and the United Republic of Tanzania. Globally, the United Nations provided electoral assistance to about 50 countries, consistently emphasizing impartiality, sustainability and cost-effectiveness in electoral processes.

24. The United Nations played an important role in ensuring the peaceful and successful conduct of the Southern Sudan independence referendum in January 2011. Working closely alongside the African Union High-level Implementation Panel on the Sudan, the United Nations helped align the international community behind a common approach, delivered significant technical and logistical assistance to the referendum process and assisted in facilitating negotiations on post-referendum arrangements. The Secretary-General deployed his Panel on the Referenda in the Sudan to monitor progress and provide high-level good offices. These coordinated efforts led to the independence of South Sudan on 9 July and its admission to the United Nations on 14 July. But the remaining challenges are great and will require the continued engagement of the United Nations system.

25. In response to the popular uprisings in the Middle East and North Africa, the United Nations has encouraged all parties to adhere to relevant international law, in particular the Universal Declaration of Human Rights. It has highlighted the crucial importance of addressing social and economic inequalities and has offered to provide appropriate assistance to facilitate peaceful political transitions. With respect to the Libyan Arab Jamahiriya, the Secretary-General appointed a Special Envoy to engage with the parties on the ground with a view to ending the violence, addressing the humanitarian consequences of the crisis and helping to find a political solution. Contingency planning is ongoing to assist a political process that may emerge as a result of negotiations between the parties to the conflict. The Secretary-General also dispatched several United Nations missions to Yemen to engage with all stakeholders and contribute to the peaceful resolution of the situation.

26. In Côte d'Ivoire, the successful installation of a democratically elected Government has set the tone for numerous upcoming elections in Africa. The United Nations worked to prevent relapse into conflict, including through the activities of integrated peacebuilding missions in Burundi, the Central African Republic, Guinea-Bissau and Sierra Leone. In Kenya, the United Nations maintained support for the review process that led to the adoption of a new constitution with enhanced checks and balances.

27. In Somalia, the United Nations worked closely with the transitional federal institutions to further the implementation of transitional tasks, including constitution-building. The Secretary-General also encouraged the international community to fight piracy off the Somali coast through deterrence, security, the rule of law and development.

28. The United Nations undertook successful efforts to help countries return to constitutional order following unconstitutional changes of Government in Guinea, and the Niger. In Kyrgyzstan, the United Nations contributed to the adoption of a new constitution, the establishment of a credible electoral process and a reconstituted, legitimate Government.

29. In the Middle East, the United Nations explored concrete ways to encourage the resumption of deadlocked negotiations between Israelis and Palestinians, to improve the living conditions of civilians in Gaza, while addressing Israel's legitimate security concerns, and to achieve full implementation of Security Council resolution 1701(2006). As Israel

took some welcome measures to facilitate access to Gaza, the United Nations was able to commence a number of reconstruction and economic recovery projects. The United Nations helped defuse tensions after an armed incident between the Israeli and Lebanese armies along the Blue Line. Following the flotilla incident of 31 May 2010, and in close consultation with Israel and Turkey, the Secretary-General established a panel of inquiry to recommend ways to avoid similar incidents in the future.

30. In Iraq, the United Nations Assistance Mission for Iraq has worked to promote national reconciliation and mutually acceptable solutions to resolve the status of Kirkuk and other disputed areas. It facilitated talks with key stakeholders, in particular with respect to property restitution, minority rights, detainees and language and education rights, and engaged with Iraq and Kuwait to help resolve outstanding issues between them.

31. In Nepal, following the withdrawal of the United Nations Mission in Nepal, the United Nations ensured ongoing support for the peace process. In Sri Lanka, the Secretary-General established an advisory panel of experts, which submitted its report on 12 April, with a view to helping the United Nations and Sri Lanka take meaningful measures towards addressing the issue of accountability as a critical step towards national reconciliation and lasting peace.

32. In Myanmar, the Secretary-General maintained active engagement with all stakeholders to promote national reconciliation, democratic transition and respect for human rights. The new Government's commitment to closer cooperation with the United Nations could provide a basis for more effective engagement. But much remains to be done to usher in real political change in the country.

33. Elsewhere, the United Nations supported efforts towards the peaceful resolution of border disputes, including between Equatorial Guinea and Gabon.

34. With respect to Western Sahara, a series of United Nations-convened rounds of informal talks succeeded in having the parties agree on new ways of approaching the negotiating process and a range of confidence-building measures.

35. In Cyprus, the United Nations continued to facilitate full-fledged negotiations between the leaders of the Greek Cypriot and the Turkish Cypriot communities, in efforts to achieve progress towards a comprehensive settlement.

36. Central America has seen a dramatic rise in violence related to organized crime. The positive experience of the United Nations-sponsored International Commission against Impunity in Guatemala has drawn international interest and the United Nations has received new requests for assistance from El Salvador and Honduras.

2. Peacekeeping

37. After a historical high in the number of uniformed personnel deployments in March 2010, United Nations peacekeeping has entered a period of consolidation in terms of the size of deployments. As of June 2011, United Nations peacekeeping counted more than 120,000 uniformed and civilian personnel, deployed in 14 peacekeeping operations on four continents.

38. In Timor-Leste, the United Nations Integrated Mission in Timor-Leste completed the handover of its policing responsibilities to national authorities in March 2011. In Liberia, the United Nations Mission in Liberia consolidated progress in planning with the Government towards the eventual transfer of its security functions to national institutions and supported preparations for the October 2011 elections. Following the independence of South Sudan on 9 July, a new peacekeeping operation, the United Nations Mission in South Sudan, was established, focusing exclusively on that country.

39. Contributing to the protection of civilians remains the core task of seven peacekeeping operations. In Darfur, the Democratic Republic of the Congo, Côte d'Ivoire and South Sudan, in particular, protecting civilians remained a serious challenge.

40. Peacekeepers contributed to political transitions in Côte d'Ivoire, Haiti and the Sudan through technical and logistical support to national authorities for the holding of elections and referendums. They also contributed to ensuring the necessary political and security conditions for the holding of free and fair polls. The South Sudan self-determination referendum of January 2010, which resulted in a vote for independence, brought an end to the longest civil war in Africa. The North and the South need to continue to work together in order to resolve all outstanding issues peacefully. The instability which followed the elections in Afghanistan, Côte d'Ivoire and Haiti also offered a stark reminder of the fragility of peace gains in post-conflict environments.

41. In Côte d'Ivoire, the acute political and military crisis that followed the round of presidential elections on 28 November 2010 tested the United Nations capacity to protect civilians and to sustain an operation under siege. It also tested the resolve and unity of the international community in staying the course in implementing critical mandated tasks, particularly with regard to elections. The Secretary-General worked closely with the African Union, the Economic Community of West African States and world leaders to find a peaceful solution to the post-election crisis that respected the democratically expressed will of the Ivorian people. Meanwhile, the United Nations Operation in Côte d'Ivoire used, as mandated by the Security Council, all necessary means in self-defence and in defence of its mandate to protect civil-

ians, including through preventing the use of heavy weapons against the civilian population.

42. United Nations peacekeeping provided sustained support for rule-of-law and security institutions in a number of countries emerging from conflict. In this regard, the United Nations strengthened its existing standing police capacity.

43. Over the past year, the United Nations has made significant progress in developing necessary peacekeeping policies and implementing reforms. Initiatives undertaken include the development of an early peacebuilding strategy to guide the prioritization and sequencing of Security Council-mandated tasks executed by peacekeepers in post-conflict settings and comprehensive efforts to develop baseline capability standards, strengthen resource-generation processes and bolster training. Progress was also achieved in the implementation of the five-year global field support strategy. A regional service centre was established in Entebbe, Uganda, with four support functions in full operation. The Secretary-General also submitted to the General Assembly a new, standardized, funding model for the first year of peacekeeping operations.

44. In eight missions, the Secretariat partnered with United Nations agencies, funds and programmes to complete integrated strategic frameworks that set system-wide priorities for United Nations engagement on peace, security and humanitarian issues.

45. The General Assembly approved new, harmonized conditions of service for international staff in field missions which should help field missions to attract and retain qualified staff.

3. Peacebuilding

46. The Peacebuilding Commission helped align relevant actors in support of nationally identified priorities, mobilized resources for such priorities and assisted national actors in staying focused on the development of institutions and capacities critical to resilience against relapse into conflict. There are now six countries on the agenda of the Commission: Burundi, the Central African Republic, Guinea, Guinea-Bissau, Liberia and Sierra Leone. Guinea and Liberia were included within the past nine months.

47. In further support of peacebuilding efforts, in February 2011 the independent report of the Senior Advisory Group on Civilian Capacity in the Aftermath of Conflict was issued. The report presents a series of recommendations aimed at making the United Nations more efficient and effective in providing civilian capacity to countries emerging from conflict. Following an internal review and consultations with Member States and other stakeholders, the Secretary-General will work towards implementing those recommendations that are most likely to help the United Nations deliver on the ground.

48. In 2010, the Peacebuilding Fund, which provides catalytic funding for peacebuilding, also continued a growth trend in terms of additional countries, improved partnerships with stakeholders and closer work with the Peacebuilding Commission. Altogether during 2010, $76 million was allocated, up from $52 million in 2009, to 12 countries, including 4 countries newly declared eligible. The Peacebuilding Fund aims to raise, allocate and spend $100 million per year in the period from 2011 to 2013.

C. Humanitarian affairs

49. 2010/11 was an extremely demanding period for the United Nations humanitarian system, which worked to deliver assistance to tens of millions of people across 30 countries. Droughts, floods and soaring fuel prices contributed to rapid increases in international food prices, affecting millions of poor and vulnerable people worldwide.

50. The United Nations was called on to support national authorities in a wide range of natural disasters and complex emergencies, often in hostile operating environments and with constrained human and financial resources. Sustained monsoon rains in Pakistan affected as many as 20 million people—nearly 10 per cent of the population. Following a devastating earthquake in January 2010, Haitians faced a series of new setbacks, including tropical storms, a cholera outbreak and political unrest. Armed conflict and communal violence in Côte d'Ivoire in the wake of contested presidential elections drove as many as 200,000 refugees across borders and displaced half a million people in Abidjan alone. In the Sudan, tens of thousands of people fled violence ahead of southern independence. In the Horn of Africa, more than 8 million people suffered from food insecurity in 2011 due to the most severe drought in a decade.

51. Crises in the Libyan Arab Jamahiriya and Yemen resulted in a large number of civilian casualties, internal displacements and refugees. More than 630,000 people fled fighting in the Libyan Arab Jamahiriya, of whom 280,000 were third-country nationals. Their return home placed an added burden on already vulnerable communities in the Niger, Chad and elsewhere. Meanwhile, Japan faced a combined natural and nuclear disaster, posing a significant challenge even for a country well prepared for emergencies.

52. These crises provided the United Nations with clear lessons on how to improve the way the international humanitarian system prepares for and responds to humanitarian needs. Under the leadership of the Emergency Relief Coordinator, the Inter-Agency Standing Committee principals, including non-governmental partners, began developing a new strategy, focusing on improving humanitarian leader-

ship and coordination; ensuring that adequate staff and funds are deployed to address large emergencies, especially in their crucial early stages; and improving accountability to both Member States and affected peoples.

53. Donor support grew for the Central Emergency Response Fund, an innovative global tool with low transaction costs designed to provide funds quickly and equitably. The Fund increased from $409 million in 2009 to $428 million in 2010, and in May 2011 it passed $2 billion in total disbursements. Twelve Member States became first-time donors, and 19 Member States substantially increased their contributions.

54. Donations managed by the United Nations through the consolidated appeals process totalled $7 billion, much as in 2009. But that figure represented a declining percentage of the total funds requested to meet needs, from 73 per cent to 63 per cent.

55. The United Nations is improving joint planning efforts, based on a more rigorous assessment of needs; monitoring progress in real time through the better use of technology; reinforcing leadership structures; and improving accountability.

56. Security concerns continued to affect the ability of humanitarian actors to deliver basic services to affected populations. The recent study commissioned by the Office for the Coordination of Humanitarian Affairs, *To Stay and Deliver*, calls upon Member States to refrain from enacting legislation and policies that might undermine humanitarian engagement with non-State armed groups.

57. Looking forward, the Organization will be working to strengthen its efforts to promote effective disaster risk reduction strategies to limit the exposure and vulnerability of communities and nations to natural hazards.

D. Human rights, rule of law, genocide prevention and the responsibility to protect, and democracy and good governance

58. It has been a momentous year for human rights, the rule of law, democracy and good governance, both on the ground, with the "Arab spring" of 2011, and as reflected in the intense debates at Headquarters.

1. Human rights

59. The Secretary-General and the High Commissioner for Human Rights have been speaking out forcefully for the application of international human rights standards in all situations, promptly dispatching assessment missions in response to needs on the ground and assisting the activities of the Human Rights Council and other human rights mechanisms in engaging with urgent situations.

60. The past year saw the review of the Human Rights Council, both by the Council itself and by the General Assembly. The fact that the first cycle of the universal periodic review will be completed by the end of 2011 is lauded as a significant accomplishment of the Council. The true test of this innovative process will come with the second cycle, beginning in mid-2012, when Member States are expected to report on progress made in implementing the recommendations that came out of the first cycle.

61. The Human Rights Council also expanded its coverage of issues, with two new thematic mandates on the right to peaceful assembly and association and on discrimination against women in law and in practice, as well as a new country mandate on the Islamic Republic of Iran.

62. The articulation of the global human rights commitments in the outcome document of the High-level Plenary Meeting of the General Assembly on the Millennium Development Goals was a pivotal achievement. Human rights mainstreaming also achieved important milestones in the field of peace and security through strengthened human rights components in peace and political missions. In Côte d'Ivoire, amid the political crisis in the aftermath of the presidential elections, the steadfast and principled voice and actions of the United Nations underscored the vital importance of protecting civilians, upholding international law and bringing perpetrators of serious violations to account.

2. Rule of law

63. In the Middle East and North Africa, calls for greater accountability, transparency and the rule of law are pushing Government reforms at an unprecedented pace. The United Nations is poised to respond to increased requests for its rule-of-law expertise.

64. Over the past year, United Nations rule-of-law interventions were strengthened through greater emphasis on inter-agency cooperation, which led to joint programming in the Democratic Republic of the Congo, Haiti and Timor-Leste, among other countries. The United Nations supported accountability for international crimes and transitional justice processes through a broad range of mechanisms, including the International Criminal Court, international commissions of inquiry of the Human Rights Council and international ad hoc and hybrid tribunals.

65. Following the success of the ninth session of the Assembly of States Parties to the Rome Statute, efforts towards universality have yielded positive results. Tunisia, in the wake of the Secretary-General's visit there, became the first North African country and the fourth member of the League of Arab States to become a party to the Rome Statute. Egypt has also announced its intention to ratify the Rome Statute and become a party to the International Criminal Court.

66. The General Assembly mandated a high-level event on the rule of law for the opening of the sixty-seventh session of the General Assembly. The event should encourage greater commitments to international coordination as a means of strengthening the impact of rule-of-law activities.

3. Genocide prevention and the responsibility to protect

67. Human protection was a top priority for the Secretary-General, the General Assembly, the Security Council and the Human Rights Council.

68. The Special Advisers on the Prevention of Genocide and the Responsibility to Protect are assisting the General Assembly in its continuing consideration of this concept. They are jointly assessing country situations, issuing statements and preparing advisory notes to the Secretary-General and the United Nations system.

69. The joint office has accelerated its capacity-building activities for Government officials, regional and subregional organizations, civil society and United Nations staff. Calls from parliamentarians, the media, educators and public groups for information and views on the Special Advisers' respective mandates have also grown.

4. Democracy and good governance

70. The peaceful demonstrations forcing the ouster of long-time leaders in Egypt and Tunisia exerted pressure for democratic reforms elsewhere. From the outset, in addition to actively pressing for the respect of human rights in North Africa and the Middle East, the Secretary-General called for the granting of freedom of assembly, speech and information. He appealed for an immediate end to the use of violence against demonstrators and urged leaders in the region to respond to the legitimate aspirations of the people through dialogue and reforms.

71. The United Nations Democracy Fund, which channels support to local non-governmental organizations worldwide, allocated almost $15 million to 64 projects in its fourth round of funding. In 2010, the Fund received almost twice as many project proposals as in previous years, reflecting unprecedented demand from civil society organizations for democracy. This demand is expected to grow further as a result of developments in the Arab world and elsewhere.

Chapter III
Securing global goods

72. Current global challenges are complex in nature, contagious and wide-ranging. Member States have turned to the United Nations to assist them in securing the global good through addressing such challenges as climate change, disease, terrorism and the proliferation of conventional and non-conventional arms.

A. Climate change

73. Climate change is central to global peace and prosperity. Meeting the climate challenge will require sustained global cooperation coupled with accelerated national actions to reduce emissions and strengthen climate resilience. Every year that we delay action costs lives, money and the opportunity to build a safer, greener future for all.

74. 2010 saw progress on a number of fronts, not least in increased transparency, trust and confidence in the multilateral negotiation process.

75. Progress was made at the United Nations Climate Change Conference in Cancun, Mexico. There, Governments agreed to establish a "green climate fund"; formalize their mitigation pledges; take concrete action to prevent deforestation, which accounts for nearly one fifth of global carbon emissions; bolster technology cooperation; and enhance the ability of vulnerable populations to adapt to climate impacts.

76. Steps were also taken to improve the reporting and delivery of $30 billion in fast-start financing to support vulnerable populations in developing countries. The High-level Advisory Group of the Secretary-General on Climate Financing concluded that efforts to meet the $100 billion per annum goal by 2020 would be challenging but feasible, with both public and private revenue sources from developed countries to support mitigation and adaptation efforts in developing countries.

77. Cancun gave the world an important set of tools. The international community must now put them into practice and redouble its efforts in line with the urgent scientific imperative for action. In 2010, extreme weather events consistent with projected climate change trends, including widespread flooding, heat waves, fires and heavy rains, inflicted massive suffering on millions in Pakistan, the Russian Federation and north-western China.

78. Now more than ever, it is clear that the world needs the most accurate, objective and transparent scientific assessments possible to inform policymaking. To that end, in August 2010 the Secretary-General and the Chair of the Intergovernmental Panel on Climate Change launched an independent review of the Organization's processes and management structure and called on Member States to act on the findings.

79. The Secretary-General also launched a High-level Panel on Global Sustainability to provide a practical road map for sustainable, climate-resilient development that addresses poverty eradication, energy, food, water and other key issues. Its recommendations will be released early in 2012 and will provide important inputs for the Rio+20 Conference.

B. Global health

80. With just five years left to achieve the Millennium Development Goals, the Secretary-General launched the Global Strategy for Women's and Children's Health in September 2010. The Strategy marks the first time that women's and children's health has received such a high level of commitment, and brings together leaders from Government, multilateral institutions, including the United Nations, civil society, private foundations, business and academia. New policy and service delivery commitments and more than $40 billion have been pledged to the Strategy. All 192 States Members of the United Nations affirmed their support for the Strategy and for the creation of an accountability framework to ensure that resources are delivered and results achieved.

81. The global aids response has demonstrated results: infections are decreasing. Nevertheless, five new infections occur for every three persons beginning treatment. The high-level meeting of the General Assembly on HIV/AIDS held in June 2011 delivered an ambitious Political Declaration with concrete targets, including the elimination of vertical transmission, for achieving universal access to HIV prevention, treatment, care and support by 2015.

82. Tuberculosis is the greatest killer of those with HIV, and collaborative tuberculosis-HIV actions are advancing; yet most multi-drug-resistant cases of tuberculosis remain untreated.

83. The malaria burden has fallen significantly since 2000. Growing resources and the scale-up of control interventions have contributed to a 50 per cent reduction in malaria cases and deaths in 43 countries in the period from 2008 to 2010. In sub-Saharan Africa, enough insecticide-treated mosquito nets were delivered to cover 76 per cent of people at risk.

84. The Global Polio Eradication Initiative made record progress, with India and Nigeria reducing cases by 95 per cent compared with 2009. To fully exploit this momentum and eradicate polio in the next two years, additional financial and political support is urgently needed.

85. Remarkable progress was also made in reducing measles mortality. Between 2000 and 2008, the number of measles deaths dropped by 78 per cent; these averted deaths represent one quarter of the decline in mortality from all causes among children under 5 years of age.

86. Current and projected non-communicable-disease burdens and their impact on economic development galvanized the international community to call for the holding in 2011 of a high-level meeting of the General Assembly on the prevention and control of non-communicable diseases. Thirty-six million people die annually from non-communicable diseases; 25 per cent of them are under 60 years of age, and most reside in developing countries.

87. Looking forward, the principal challenge is to ensure social protection and the equitable delivery of health services so that all can enjoy improved health outcomes. An important element of this agenda will be a renewed focus on meeting the sanitation challenge. Having access to sanitation not only increases health but has a multiplying impact on well-being and economic productivity. Solutions exist—they simply need to be implemented.

C. Countering terrorism

88. Terrorism remains a major threat to international peace and security. The Secretary-General's principal response mechanism, the Counter-Terrorism Implementation Task Force, consisting of 31 entities within and outside the United Nations system, pushed ahead with implementation of the United Nations Global Counter-Terrorism Strategy. The Task Force worked to enhance interaction with Member States and build in-depth knowledge of the Strategy through regular briefings to the General Assembly, regional workshops and the upgrading of external communications. It produced reports on coordination in the event of nuclear or radiological terrorist attacks, countering the use of the Internet for terrorist purposes, and basic human rights reference guides on the stopping and searching of persons. It established a Working Group on Border Management to provide guidance for the implementation of counter-terrorism-related border-control measures called for within the Strategy. Together with the European Union and United Nations Regional Centre for Preventive Diplomacy in Central Asia, it launched a project to assist Member States in the region in implementing the Strategy in all its pillars.

89. While the primary responsibility of implementing the Strategy rests with Member States, the United Nations system will continue to support the implementation of the Strategy by developing good practices, strengthening collaboration among partners and delivering as one to those countries that request assistance.

D. Disarmament and non-proliferation

90. Following the successful outcome of the 2010 Review Conference of the Parties to the Treaty on the Non-Proliferation of Nuclear Weapons, the States parties have begun translating the commitments made at the Conference into agreed "actions" relating to nuclear disarmament, non-proliferation and the peaceful uses of nuclear energy.

91. The Russian Federation and the United States of America brought into force the new Strategic Arms Reduction Treaty further limiting deployments of their strategic nuclear weapons. The nuclear-weapon States have initiated a process of dialogue on systematic and progressive efforts to accomplish the com-

plete elimination of their nuclear arsenals. Preparations are under way for a conference in 2012 on the establishment of a Middle East zone free of weapons of mass destruction and their delivery systems.

92. States and members of civil society continued to explore the specific requirements for achieving a world free of nuclear weapons, including by means of a universal and effectively verifiable nuclear weapons convention. In August 2010, the Secretary-General became the first in his official capacity to attend the peace memorial ceremony in Hiroshima, Japan. Paying respect to survivors and all those who perished in Hiroshima and Nagasaki 66 years ago, he stressed that the time has come to realize the dream of a world free of nuclear weapons.

93. A source of great concern remains the lack of substantive progress made by the Conference on Disarmament in Geneva. Further work is needed to implement the recommendations made at the high-level meeting on revitalizing the work of the Conference on Disarmament and taking forward multilateral disarmament negotiations, which was convened at the initiative of the Secretary-General on 24 September 2010.

94. There has been no progress on a peaceful and negotiated denuclearization of the Korean peninsula through the six-party talks.

95. Concern persists with respect to the nuclear programme of the Islamic Republic of Iran.

96. New issues have emerged in the context of the nuclear accident at the Fukushima Daiichi nuclear power plant in Japan. In the light of the global ramifications of the crisis, the Secretary-General underscored the role that international organizations can play as well as the importance of joint and coordinated efforts in addressing such challenges. In April 2011, at the Kyiv Summit on the Safe and Innovative Use of Nuclear Energy, the Secretary-General called for concrete measures for strengthening nuclear safety. In this regard, he launched a United Nations system-wide study on the implications of the nuclear accident at Fukushima. The study will be issued as a report of the Secretary-General in an effort to facilitate the high-level meeting on nuclear safety and security to be held on 22 September 2011.

97. With respect to conventional armaments, States must continue making good progress towards an arms trade treaty, which the Secretary-General considers of the utmost importance. The excessive accumulation and the easy availability of small arms and light weapons in zones of conflict and crime remain a profound concern.

98. The Secretary-General attaches importance to the cooperation between the United Nations and regional organizations, as well as to the role of civil society organizations in regions affected by cross-border arms trafficking, unsecured weapons stockpiles and rising armed violence. He believes that the adoption of the Central African Convention for the Control of Small Arms and Light Weapons, Their Ammunition and All Parts and Components That Can Be Used for Their Manufacture, Repair and Assembly represents an important contribution in this regard.

99. The United Nations will continue to work with Member States to maintain and reinvigorate effective disarmament and non-proliferation norms.

Chapter IV
Creating a stronger United Nations

A. The Secretariat, the intergovernmental machinery, system-wide coherence and regional organizations

100. In the context of a struggling global economy—and the subsequent budget reductions in a number of countries worldwide—the United Nations is being asked to do more with less. Various initiatives currently under way regarding reform of the intergovernmental machinery, as well as the process to make the work of the United Nations system more coherent, will enhance the Organization's role in setting and implementing the global agenda.

1. The Secretariat

101. The Secretary-General has launched four complementary processes aimed at delivering a more effective and efficient United Nations. First, he has proposed a budget with a view to reducing the overall United Nations budget by more than 3 per cent. Second, he has asked the United Nations System Chief Executives Board for Coordination to collaborate on a system-wide reform effort. Third, he has mobilized all senior managers to propose specific ideas for changing the way the United Nations works and does business. Fourth, he has established a change management team to deepen reform efforts.

102. Collectively, these efforts will build on the progress made over the past year to strengthen accountability, performance and results, including the development of a framework for implementing results-based management, which will be presented to Member States in the latter part of 2011, and a policy on enterprise risk management that is currently being piloted in selected departments.

103. The Secretariat has made good progress in preparing for the implementation of the International Public Sector Accounting Standards, which will introduce internationally accepted best practices, enhance transparency, in particular in relation to the costs of programmes, improve internal controls and significantly improve the stewardship of assets. With regard to Umoja, the enterprise resource planning

project, efforts to ensure that the potential benefits of increasingly harmonized and streamlined business practices across the Secretariat are delivered will have to be redoubled in the light of challenges resulting from delays in project implementation.

104. Excellence in human resources management is central to achieving the Secretary-General's vision of a global, adaptable Organization that is responsive and flexible, supports a culture of empowerment and performance and allows staff to learn and grow. We have made progress in this area with the recent reforms on contracts and conditions of service. We will continue our work to improve recruitment, career development and the way in which staff members move around the Organization.

2. The intergovernmental machinery

105. Over the past year, the General Assembly addressed crucial issues relating to the global development agenda and beyond, including through the holding of thematic debates on topics such as disaster risk reduction, investment in and financing of productive capacities in the least developed countries, the rule of law, global migration and global governance.

106. A new impetus has been felt in the efforts of Member States to reform the Security Council, particularly in the increasingly concrete and specific proposals being put forth by delegations within the framework of intergovernmental negotiations.

107. The Security Council, in dealing with the upheaval in the Arab world, invoked the responsibility to protect with respect to the Libyan Arab Jamahiriya. Its agenda was otherwise dominated by overseeing peacekeeping and political missions on four continents, with particular attention to the Southern Sudan independence referendums and enforcement action in Côte d'Ivoire. Thematic areas of focus included preventive diplomacy, terrorism, post-conflict peacebuilding, women and peace and security, and the interdependence of security and development. The Council also undertook efforts to ensure the full and fair implementation of existing sanctions regimes, including by the active engagement of the newly created Ombudsman, to ensure that the Organization's counter-terrorism efforts are in compliance with human rights norms.

108. The Economic and Social Council worked in new ways to mobilize the international community to achieve the Millennium Development Goals. Its high-level meeting strengthened the global partnership for development and improved policy coordination among major institutional stakeholders, including the World Bank, the International Monetary Fund, the World Trade Organization and the United Nations Conference on Trade and Development. The annual ministerial review succeeded in advancing the agreed education agenda. The Council also reviewed the United Nations system's approach to gender issues and made recommendations to accelerate progress.

3. System-wide coherence

109. Since the General Assembly adopted its landmark resolution 64/289 on system-wide coherence on 2 July 2010, notable advances have been achieved in its implementation. On 1 January 2011, the United Nations Entity for Gender Equality and the Empowerment of Women (UN-Women), became operational. UN-Women brings together resources and mandates for greater impact by merging and building on the important work of four previously distinct parts of the United Nations system dedicated to gender issues. Combining global norm-setting responsibilities into one entity and giving it the means to provide operational support to countries to implement those norms and standards will allow the United Nations to significantly step up efforts to advance gender equality and women's empowerment worldwide.

110. Efforts continue to be made to improve how the United Nations delivers as one. An independent evaluation is being conducted on the lessons learned from pilot countries. The voluntary adoption of common country programme documents opens up the possibility of eliminating duplication and overlap between agency-specific programmes. This year, the United Nations System Chief Executives Board for Coordination made noteworthy progress in the implementation of the Plan of Action for the Harmonization of Business Practices in the United Nations System and the adoption of a coordinated system approach on a fairer, greener and sustainable globalization.

4. Regional organizations

111. The United Nations carried forward efforts to strengthen its partnerships with regional organizations, illustrated by co-deployments, joint mediation, mediation capacity-building, joint training, the exchange of best practices, desk-to-desk dialogues and the establishment of liaison offices.

112. The establishment of the United Nations Office to the African Union has brought additional focus to strategic partnership with that organization. The United Nations partnership with the Southern African Development Community in conflict prevention, mediation and elections made a qualitative leap forward with the signing of a framework for cooperation and the deployment of a liaison team to Gaborone. The new United Nations Regional Office for Central Africa in Libreville has already ensured enhanced collaboration with the Economic Community of Central African States, helping to strengthen

the regional organization's early warning and mediation capacity.

113. The United Nations established a partnership liaison office in Brussels, further institutionalizing peace and security cooperation with the European Union and the Organization for Security and Cooperation in Europe.

114. The Association of Southeast Asian Nations and the United Nations strongly reaffirmed their ties during their third joint summit, and cooperation with the Caribbean Community was strengthened by the participation of the Secretary-General, for the first time ever, in its thirty-first Conference of Heads of Government.

B. Global constituencies

115. Civil society, the business community and academia make essential contributions towards United Nations goals, in particular the Millennium Development Goals. In the past year, the United Nations has taken steps to increase engagement, learning from experiences with the goal of developing truly transformational partnerships to help tackle pressing challenges.

1. Strengthening partnerships with civil society

116. The Organization expanded and deepened its interaction with civil society, including through the United Nations Academic Impact initiative, which already includes more than 650 institutions of higher education in 104 countries.

117. More than 6,000 non-governmental organization representatives working on the United Nations economic, social and environmental development agenda participated in meetings of the Economic and Social Council and its subsidiary bodies, contributing the voice of grass-roots organizations and communities.

118. United Nations information centres worldwide work with civil society in nearly 50 languages through such high-profile campaigns as those related to the Millennium Development Goals, climate change and sustainable development, Stand-Up and Take Action against Poverty and UNiTE to End Violence against Women. Several United Nations information centres in North Africa and the Middle East played an instrumental role in maintaining an open dialogue with various communities during the tumultuous changes that occurred across the region.

2. Engaging the business community

119. An advanced network of private sector experts from more than 30 United Nations entities are focusing on helping the Organization move towards transformational partnerships that address systemic challenges globally and locally.

120. Work is under way, linked to the Guidelines on Cooperation between the United Nations and the Business Sector, to enhance due diligence and screening mechanisms for partner selection. A new United Nations business website has facilitated dozens of engagements, matching corporate resources with organizational needs, as well as supporting disaster relief linked to crises in Haiti, Japan, the Libyan Arab Jamahiriya and Pakistan.

121. The business community has also worked through the United Nations Global Compact, the world's largest corporate responsibility initiative, with 9,000 participants in over 135 countries. The Global Compact platforms on women's empowerment, anti-corruption, climate and water are bringing business actions to critical areas. The United Nations hosted the third Private Sector Forum in September 2010, with executives and Governments identifying concrete actions by business to help close Millennium Development Goal gaps. The successful integration of the business community through the "private sector track" at the Fourth United Nations Conference on the Least Developed Countries, held in Istanbul, provides a model for closer engagement around United Nations summits such as Rio+20.

Chapter V
Conclusion

122. As we look to the next five years, we recognize that the need for the United Nations has never been greater and that meeting the diversity of needs and demands placed on us will not be easy. We must ensure that this Organization serves its entire membership—from the least developed to the most developed States and all their people. Much of our engagement will need to build on the achievements of the past five years.

123. Achieving sustainable development is imperative. Not only must we redouble our efforts on the Millennium Development Goals so that they can be met by 2015; we will also need to develop a vision and agree on a framework for promoting development post-2015. We will further need to design strategies and adopt action plans to address the 50-50-50 challenge. By the year 2050, the world's population will have reached over 9 billion—50 per cent more than a decade ago—and by that time the world must have cut global greenhouse gas emissions by 50 per cent. A crucial part of addressing this agenda will be forging a sustainable global energy strategy.

124. In the area of peace and security, the past five years have begun to witness the positive impact that a strengthened United Nations prevention capacity can have when it is harnessed by Member States to help them defuse internal and cross-border tensions. We must continue to deepen and expand the preventive services that we are able to provide Member States.

125. During the past five years, we have seen the increasing complexity of peacekeeping operations and have been forced to stretch scarce resources to meet broad mandates. During the past two years, we have begun to rethink and restructure the way in which we support missions. We are thinking creatively about how we can increase our agility and better leverage potential partnerships to ensure that we have the capacities necessary to meet needs on the ground, whether related to peacekeeping missions, peacebuilding efforts or political missions. Our next challenge is to implement additional necessary changes to ensure that we are able to continue to provide peace and security to the people we serve.

126. Haiti, Pakistan and Japan provided us with a glimpse of what the future might hold in terms of the shape and magnitude of disasters. We have entered the era of mega-disasters, and the past few years have shown us that we must be better equipped and configured to adequately address them. We have begun to take steps to modify the way we do business, reshaping our response strategies and placing a much higher premium on disaster risk reduction. In addition, in order to bolster capacities, the United Nations has begun to forge new types of partnerships with the business community and with civil society and is experimenting with new technologies that coordinate responders and link responders to victims. These efforts will need to be accelerated over the next five years if we are to meet the humanitarian challenges that are likely to be coming our way.

127. The events of the past year have reminded us all of the vital importance of the normative standards that our Organization sets for the world. We have supported the call for democracy in the Middle East and North Africa, and we have urged the international community to protect civilians from egregious violations of their rights in Côte d'Ivoire and the Libyan Arab Jamahiriya. We have seen the important positive impact that this advocacy work can have in supporting the people on the front lines fighting for human rights, the rule of law and democracy, as well as the responsibility to protect. Now we must go beyond advocacy and help both Government and non-governmental actors that want to effect change to institutionalize these norms and values. As the next five years will be crucial in determining the path that many transitions will take, it is essential that we rapidly upgrade our abilities to support countries engaged in building democratic structures and processes.

128. The global challenges of the past decades—climate change, weapons proliferation, disease and terrorism—will not disappear. We will need to continue to strengthen and deepen the international collaboration that we have already forged. We must also, however, be ready for new challenges that we will have to face together, not least those posed by demographic patterns.

129. Finally, in order to deliver externally, we must take an honest look inward and work with Member States to ensure that our organizational structures, our work processes and our staff are optimally configured to meet the challenges of the next decade. We have already launched an important change initiative that will introduce greater effectiveness and efficiency throughout the Organization over the next five years.

130. Periods of global transition present huge challenges but also tremendous opportunities for advancing humanity's progress. Together, no challenge is too large. Together, nothing is impossible.

ANNEX

Millennium Development Goals, targets and indicators, 2011: statistical tables

GOAL 1
Eradicate extreme poverty and hunger

Target 1.A
Halve, between 1990 and 2015, the proportion of people whose income is less than one dollar a day

Indicator 1.1
Proportion of population living below $1.25 purchasing power parity (PPP) per day[a,b]
(Percentage)

	1990	1999	2005
Developing regions	45.5	36.1	26.9
Northern Africa	4.5	4.4	2.6
Sub-Saharan Africa	57.5	58.3	50.9
Latin America and the Caribbean	11.3	10.9	8.2
Caribbean	28.8	25.4	25.8
Latin America	10.5	10.2	7.4
Eastern Asia	60.1	35.6	15.9
Southern Asia	49.5	42.2	38.6
Southern Asia excluding India	44.6	35.3	30.7
South-Eastern Asia	39.2	35.3	18.9
Western Asia	2.2	4.1	5.8
Oceania	—	—	—
Caucasus and Central Asia	6.3	22.3	19.2
Least developed countries	63.3	60.4	53.4
Landlocked developing countries	49.1	50.7	42.8
Small island developing States	32.4	27.7	27.5

[a] High-income economies, as defined by the World Bank, are excluded.

[b] Estimates by the World Bank, March 2011.

Indicator 1.2
Poverty gap ratio[a,b]
(Percentage)

	1990	1999	2005
Developing regions	15.4	11.6	8.0
Northern Africa	0.8	0.8	0.5
Sub-Saharan Africa	26.3	25.8	20.7
Latin America and the Caribbean	3.9	3.8	2.8
Caribbean	13.4	12.7	12.8
Latin America	3.5	3.4	2.3
Eastern Asia	20.7	11.1	4.0
Southern Asia	14.5	11.2	9.8
Southern Asia excluding India	14.2	9.9	8.1

	1990	1999	2005
South-Eastern Asia	11.1	9.6	4.2
Western Asia	0.6	1.0	1.5
Oceania	—	—	—
Caucasus and Central Asia	2.1	7.5	5.4
Least developed countries	27.5	24.7	19.9
Landlocked developing countries	21.9	20.2	15.5
Small island developing States	14.4	12.3	11.9

[a] The poverty gap ratio measures the magnitude of poverty. It is the result of multiplying the proportion of people who live below the poverty line (at $1.25 PPP per day) by the difference between the poverty line and the average income of the population living under the poverty line.

[b] High-income economies, as defined by the World Bank, are excluded.

Indicator 1.3
Share of poorest quintile in national consumption

No global or regional data are available.

Target 1.B
Achieve full and productive employment and decent work for all, including women and young people

Indicator 1.4
Growth rate of gross domestic product (GDP) per person employed

(a) Annual growth rate of GDP per person employed
(Percentage)

	2000	2010[a]
World	2.9	3.1
Developing regions	3.9	5.2
Northern Africa	2.5	2.7
Sub-Saharan Africa	0.5	1.8
Latin America and the Caribbean	1.9	3.0
Eastern Asia	6.9	8.5
Southern Asia	2.4	4.8
South-Eastern Asia	4.3	5.0
Western Asia	7.6	3.0
Oceania	-6.0	3.7
Caucasus and Central Asia	5.5	2.7
Developed regions	2.7	3.0
Least developed countries	2.2	2.1
Landlocked developing countries	2.3	2.4
Small island developing States	3.1	4.9

[a] Preliminary data.

(b) GDP per person employed
(2005 United States dollars (PPP))

	2000	2010[a]
World	18 272	21 828
Developing regions	8 163	12 211
Northern Africa	16 528	18 994
Sub-Saharan Africa	4 389	5 294
Latin America and the Caribbean	21 047	23 013
Eastern Asia	6 058	13 431
Southern Asia	5 378	7 978
South-Eastern Asia	7 109	9 774
Western Asia	33 722	39 743
Oceania	5 590	5 883
Caucasus and Central Asia	7 062	12 527
Developed regions	56 565	64 345
Least developed countries	2 174	3 053
Landlocked developing countries	3 398	4 905
Small island developing States	21 611	25 938

[a] Preliminary data.

Indicator 1.5
Employment-to-population ratio

(a) Total
(Percentage)

	1991	2000	2009	2010[a]
World	62.2	61.5	61.2	61.1
Developing regions	64.3	63.2	62.7	62.7
Northern Africa	43.4	43.1	45.8	45.9
Sub-Saharan Africa	62.6	62.6	64.3	64.4
Latin America and the Caribbean	56.4	58.1	60.6	60.7
Eastern Asia	74.4	73.9	70.3	70.2
Southern Asia	58.5	56.9	58.3	58.5
South-Eastern Asia	68.3	67.1	65.9	65.8
Western Asia	48.0	45.3	43.6	43.5
Oceania	65.9	66.3	66.4	66.1
Caucasus and Central Asia	57.4	54.9	59.1	59.8
Developed regions	56.6	55.8	55.4	54.8
Least developed countries	70.2	68.5	69.1	69.1
Landlocked developing countries	67.4	67.1	69.5	69.7
Small island developing States	55.2	56.7	57.9	57.7

[a] Preliminary data.

(b) Men, women and youth, 2009[a]
(Percentage)

	Men	Women	Youth
World	72.9	49.2	44.3
Developing regions	75.8	49.4	45.3
Northern Africa	69.8	22.3	28.5
Sub-Saharan Africa	74.1	54.9	47.4
Latin America and the Caribbean	74.6	47.5	44.3
Eastern Asia	75.9	64.3	54.5
Southern Asia	78.5	37.4	42.7
South-Eastern Asia	77.5	54.5	44.2
Western Asia	66.1	18.9	24.2
Oceania	70.2	62.0	50.7
Caucasus and Central Asia	66.3	53.9	39.4
Developed regions	61.5	48.5	38.1
Least developed countries	78.9	59.5	54.9
Landlocked developing countries	77.6	62.2	57.0
Small island developing States	69.3	46.5	41.5

[a] Preliminary data.

Indicator 1.6
Proportion of employed people living below $1.25 (PPP) per day

(a) Total number
(Millions)

	1991	1999	2009[a]
World	972.8	875.1	631.9
Developing regions	970.9	871.4	631.7
Northern Africa	2.5	2.2	1.3
Sub-Saharan Africa	124.7	155.8	184.0
Latin America and the Caribbean	21.8	26.3	17.4
Eastern Asia	444.4	286.2	73.0
Southern Asia	264.9	285.5	282.3
South-Eastern Asia	104.5	104.9	62.2
Western Asia	3.1	3.1	4.2
Oceania	1.0	1.1	1.5
Caucasus and Central Asia	4.0	6.3	5.9
Developed regions	1.9	3.7	0.2
Least developed countries	151.0	184.7	206.2
Landlocked developing countries	61.9	73.8	77.8
Small island developing States	3.2	4.1	5.4

[a] Preliminary data.

(b) Percentage of total employment

	1991	1999	2009[a]
World	43.0	33.9	20.7
Developing regions	56.1	42.9	25.6
Northern Africa	8.0	5.4	2.5
Sub-Saharan Africa	68.5	67.9	59.1
Latin America and the Caribbean	13.4	13.0	6.9
Eastern Asia	67.4	39.2	9.1
Southern Asia	60.7	54.5	41.9
South-Eastern Asia	53.5	45.2	22.4
Western Asia	8.1	6.4	7.0
Oceania	51.2	44.6	44.6
Caucasus and Central Asia	16.1	24.6	17.7
Developed regions	0.4	0.7	0.0
Least developed countries	71.9	71.3	59.8
Landlocked developing countries	60.1	59.9	46.6
Small island developing States	18.7	20.0	21.8

[a] Preliminary data.

Indicator 1.7
Proportion of own-account and contributing family workers in total employment

(a) Both sexes
(Percentage)

	1991	1999	2008	2009
World	55.5	53.5	50.2	50.1
Developing regions	69.0	64.8	60.0	59.6
Northern Africa	37.2	32.6	33.5	33.3
Sub-Saharan Africa	81.0	80.0	75.0	75.6
Latin America and the Caribbean	34.9	36.1	31.8	32.2
Eastern Asia	69.6	60.6	52.5	51.2
Southern Asia	81.3	79.8	77.5	77.2
South-Eastern Asia	69.4	66.1	62.3	61.6
Western Asia	42.7	37.5	28.4	28.6
Oceania	75.1	76.6	78.4	78.1
Caucasus and Central Asia	46.8	57.0	43.9	43.6
Developed regions	11.2	11.5	9.9	9.7
Least developed countries	86.2	85.0	80.6	80.8
Landlocked developing countries	75.0	78.0	72.9	73.7
Small island developing States	32.6	35.5	36.3	36.5

(b) Men
(Percentage)

	1991	1999	2008	2009
World	53.1	51.8	48.9	48.9
Developing regions	64.7	61.4	57.2	56.9
Northern Africa	33.2	30.0	28.5	29.1
Sub-Saharan Africa	76.4	74.6	68.1	69.1
Latin America and the Caribbean	34.5	35.4	31.3	31.6
Eastern Asia	63.8	56.1	49.2	48.1
Southern Asia	77.9	76.7	74.8	74.4
South-Eastern Asia	65.0	62.4	59.5	58.8
Western Asia	35.7	32.0	25.4	25.4
Oceania	70.6	72.0	73.7	73.4
Caucasus and Central Asia	49.7	56.5	42.9	42.9
Developed regions	11.3	12.0	10.8	10.7
Least developed countries	83.2	81.0	75.6	76.1
Landlocked developing countries	72.2	74.4	68.7	69.8
Small island developing States	32.3	36.1	37.4	37.6

(c) Women
(Percentage)

	1991	1999	2008	2009
World	59.2	56.1	52.1	51.8
Developing regions	75.9	70.3	64.4	63.8
Northern Africa	51.9	41.2	48.9	46.5
Sub-Saharan Africa	87.6	87.4	84.2	84.2
Latin America and the Caribbean	35.8	37.3	32.6	33.2
Eastern Asia	76.7	66.2	56.6	55.0
Southern Asia	89.8	87.6	83.8	83.4
South-Eastern Asia	75.5	71.2	66.2	65.4
Western Asia	67.4	57.6	40.0	40.6
Oceania	81.0	82.0	83.8	83.5
Caucasus and Central Asia	43.5	57.7	45.1	44.4
Developed regions	11.0	10.9	8.7	8.5
Least developed countries	90.2	90.5	87.2	86.9
Landlocked developing countries	78.3	82.4	78.0	78.3
Small island developing States	32.9	34.6	34.8	35.0

Target 1.C
Halve, between 1990 and 2015, the proportion of people who suffer from hunger

Indicator 1.8
Prevalence of underweight children under 5 years of age[a]

(a) Total
(Percentage)

	1990	2009
Developing regions	30	23
Northern Africa	10	6
Sub-Saharan Africa	27	22
Latin America and the Caribbean	10	4
Eastern Asia	15	6
Eastern Asia excluding China	11	5
Southern Asia	52	43
Southern Asia excluding India	59	39
South-Eastern Asia	30	18
Western Asia[b]	11	7
Oceania	—	—
Caucasus and Central Asia	7	5

[a] Data are from 64 countries, covering 73 per cent of the under-5 population in developing regions. Prevalence of underweight children is estimated according to World Health Organization Child Growth Standards. For the Caucasus and Central Asia, the baseline for trend analysis is 1996, since there are not sufficient data for 1990.

[b] Regional aggregate covers only 47 per cent of the regional population, owing to lack of data from Yemen.

(b) By sex, 2003–2009
(Percentage)

	Boys	Girls	Boy-to-girl ratio
Developing regions	24	24	1.01
Northern Africa	7	5	1.29
Sub-Saharan Africa	24	21	1.14
Latin America and the Caribbean	4	4	1.12
Eastern Asia	7	7	1.00
Eastern Asia excluding China	5	5	1.02
Southern Asia	41	42	0.97
Southern Asia excluding India	37	39	0.96
South-Eastern Asia	—	—	—
Western Asia	—	—	—
Oceania	21	15	1.44
Caucasus and Central Asia	6	6	1.11

(c) By residence, 2003–2009
(Percentage)

	Rural	Urban
Developing regions	28	14
Northern Africa	7	5
Sub-Saharan Africa	25	15
Latin America and the Caribbean	7	3
Eastern Asia	8	3
Eastern Asia excluding China	6	4
Southern Asia	45	33
Southern Asia excluding India	41	31
South-Eastern Asia	—	—
Western Asia	—	—
Oceania	20	12
Caucasus and Central Asia	7	4

(d) By household wealth, 2003–2009
(Percentage)

	Poorest quintile	Richest quintile
Developing regions	38	15
Northern Africa	8	4
Sub-Saharan Africa	28	13
Latin America and the Caribbean	—	—
Eastern Asia	—	—
Eastern Asia excluding China	7	3
Southern Asia	55	20
Southern Asia excluding India	48	24
South-Eastern Asia	—	—
Western Asia	—	—
Oceania	—	—
Caucasus and Central Asia	7	4

Indicator 1.9
Proportion of population below minimum level of dietary energy consumption
(Percentage)

	1990–1992	1995–1997	2000–2002	2005–2007
World	16	14	14	13
Developing regions	20	18	16	16
Northern Africa	<5	<5	<5	<5
Sub-Saharan Africa	31	31	30	26
Latin America and the Caribbean	12	11	10	8
Caribbean	26	28	22	24
Latin America	11	10	9	7
Eastern Asia	18	12	10	10
Eastern Asia excluding China	8	11	13	12
Southern Asia	21	19	20	21
Southern Asia excluding India	26	26	23	23
South-Eastern Asia	24	18	17	14
Western Asia	6	8	8	7
Oceania	—	—	—	—
Caucasus and Central Asia	16	13	17	9
Developed regions	<5	<5	<5	<5
Least developed countries	40	41	36	32
Landlocked developing countries	34	34	30	26
Small island developing States	24	25	21	21

GOAL 2
Achieve universal primary education

Target 2.A
Ensure that, by 2015, children everywhere, boys and girls alike, will be able to complete a full course of primary schooling

Indicator 2.1
Net enrolment ratio in primary education[a]

(a) Total

	1991	1999	2009
World	82.7	83.9	89.7
Developing regions	80.5	82.1	89.0
Northern Africa	80.0	86.0	94.3
Sub-Saharan Africa	53.5	57.9	76.2
Latin America and the Caribbean	85.7	93.5	95.0
Caribbean	67.6	78.0	76.1
Latin America	87.2	94.8	96.6
Eastern Asia	97.4	95.1	95.6
Eastern Asia excluding China	97.2	95.9	97.5
Southern Asia	77.0	79.2	90.9
Southern Asia excluding India	67.7	69.1	77.2
South-Eastern Asia	94.0	93.0	94.5
Western Asia	82.0	83.1	88.3
Oceania	—	—	—
Caucasus and Central Asia	—	94.3	92.7
Developed regions	96.3	97.1	95.8
Least developed countries	52.2	57.8	79.6
Landlocked developing countries	55.5	63.8	81.2
Small island developing States	70.4	78.9	76.0

(b) By sex

	1991 Boys	1991 Girls	2000 Boys	2000 Girls	2009 Boys	2009 Girls
World	86.6	78.7	86.8	80.9	90.6	88.8
Developing regions	85.0	75.9	85.4	78.7	90.0	87.9
Northern Africa	86.7	73.0	89.2	82.6	96.0	92.4
Sub-Saharan Africa	58.2	48.8	61.5	54.1	78.0	74.5
Latin America and the Caribbean	87.8	83.6	94.1	92.8	95.1	94.9
Caribbean	67.3	68.0	77.7	78.3	75.5	76.7
Latin America	89.5	84.9	95.5	94.1	96.7	96.4
Eastern Asia	98.9	95.8	94.2	96.0	94.1	97.3
Eastern Asia excluding China	97.6	96.9	96.6	95.3	97.9	97.0
Southern Asia	84.7	68.7	86.3	71.6	92.6	89.1
Southern Asia excluding India	74.2	60.9	74.4	63.6	79.8	74.6
South-Eastern Asia	95.7	92.3	94.2	91.9	95.0	93.9
Western Asia	86.2	77.6	88.0	78.0	91.0	85.5
Oceania	—	—	—	—	—	—
Caucasus and Central Asia	—	—	94.6	94.0	93.2	92.0
Developed regions	96.4	96.1	97.0	97.1	95.3	96.3
Least developed countries	57.8	46.5	61.5	54.0	81.0	78.1
Landlocked developing countries	61.5	49.4	68.6	59.0	83.7	78.6
Small island developing States	71.2	69.7	79.7	78.2	77.0	75.0

[a] Primary- and secondary-level enrolees of official primary school age per 100 children of the same age, defined as the number of pupils of the theoretical school age for primary education enrolled either in primary or secondary school, expressed as a percentage of the total population in that age group. Ratios correspond to school years ending in the years for which data are presented.

Indicator 2.2

Proportion of pupils starting grade 1 who reach last grade of primary school[a,b]

(a) Total

	1991	2000	2009
World	80.1	81.9	88.5
Developing regions	77.2	79.6	87.3
Northern Africa	72.2	81.1	91.7
Sub-Saharan Africa	50.8	51.2	66.9
Latin America and the Caribbean	83.7	96.9	101.0
Caribbean	58.7	71.3	77.0
Latin America	85.4	98.8	102.8
Eastern Asia	106.3	97.9	95.9
Eastern Asia excluding China	95.0	98.3	98.1
Southern Asia	64.4	69.3	86.0
Southern Asia excluding India	55.2	62.3	65.3
South-Eastern Asia	85.7	92.3	100.1
Western Asia	77.6	78.5	84.3
Oceania	60.8	63.6	61.6
Caucasus and Central Asia	—	94.6	95.9
Developed regions	96.7	97.9	97.7
Least developed countries	39.9	45.0	61.0
Landlocked developing countries	52.0	55.2	65.7
Small island developing States	61.9	72.3	75.0

(b) By sex

	1991		2000		2009	
	Boys	Girls	Boys	Girls	Boys	Girls
World	84.0	75.7	84.6	78.9	89.5	87.3
Developing regions	81.9	72.0	82.7	76.2	88.4	86.1
Northern Africa	79.9	64.1	84.2	77.9	93.0	90.3
Sub-Saharan Africa	55.0	45.0	55.3	46.4	70.6	63.0
Latin America and the Caribbean	82.8	84.6	96.5	97.3	100.5	101.6
Caribbean	57.3	60.0	70.4	72.2	76.5	77.4
Latin America	84.5	86.3	98.5	99.2	102.2	103.3
Eastern Asia	—	—	97.9	97.8	94.2	97.8
Eastern Asia excluding China	95.2	94.9	98.6	98.0	98.4	97.8
Southern Asia	73.8	54.3	75.8	62.3	87.5	84.4
Southern Asia excluding India	61.2	48.9	66.5	58.0	68.7	61.6
South-Eastern Asia	86.5	84.9	92.7	92.0	99.8	100.4
Western Asia	83.3	71.7	83.7	73.1	88.0	80.4
Oceania	64.6	56.8	67.5	59.5	65.5	57.6
Caucasus and Central Asia	—	—	95.8	93.4	96.6	95.1
Developed regions	—	—	97.8	97.7	98.1	97.0
Least developed countries	44.9	33.4	48.7	40.5	64.1	57.8
Landlocked developing countries	56.5	47.4	60.5	49.7	69.2	62.0
Small island developing States	61.8	62.0	72.5	72.0	75.8	74.2

[a] Since there are no regional averages for the official indicator, the table displays the gross intake ratio at last grade of primary, which corresponds to the "total number of new entrants in the last grade of primary education, regardless of age, expressed as a percentage of the population of the theoretical entrance age to the last grade" (*Global Education Digest 2009: Comparing Education Statistics Across the World*, Montreal, Canada, United Nations Educational, Scientific and Cultural Organization (UNESCO) Institute for Statistics, 2009), annex B, p. 255.

[b] The primary completion rates correspond to school years ending in the years for which data are presented.

Indicator 2.3

Literacy rate of 15- to 24-year-olds, women and men

(a) Total[a]
(Percentage who can both read and write)

	1990	2000	2009
World	83.2	87.1	89.3
Developing regions	80.1	84.8	87.7
Northern Africa	67.5	79.3	86.6
Sub-Saharan Africa	65.3	68.7	72.0
Latin America and the Caribbean	91.7	96.1	97.0
Caribbean	86.8	—	89.5
Latin America	92.1	96.7	97.6
Eastern Asia	94.6	98.9	99.4
Eastern Asia excluding China	99.4	—	99.6
Southern Asia	60.3	73.7	79.7
Southern Asia excluding India	56.4	67.3	76.7
South-Eastern Asia	94.4	96.3	97.7
Western Asia	87.4	91.7	93.2
Oceania	72.5	74.8	74.9
Caucasus and Central Asia	99.8	99.8	99.9
Developed regions	99.6	99.6	99.6
Least developed countries	55.6	65.3	70.2
Landlocked developing countries	62.1	68.4	71.7
Small island developing States	84.9	86.9	87.6

[a] The regional averages presented in this table are calculated using a weighted average of the latest available observed data point for each country or territory for the reference period. UNESCO Institute for Statistics estimates have been used for countries with missing data.

(b) By sex[a]
(Percentage who can both read and write)

	1990		2000		2009	
	Boys	Girls	Boys	Girls	Boys	Girls
World	87.7	78.6	90.3	83.8	91.9	86.8
Developing regions	85.5	74.5	88.6	80.9	90.7	84.8
Northern Africa	77.2	57.3	85.2	73.3	90.1	83.0
Sub-Saharan Africa	72.8	58.3	75.7	62.4	76.7	67.3
Latin America and the Caribbean	91.4	92.0	95.8	96.5	96.8	97.2
Caribbean	87.3	86.3	—	—	89.6	89.4
Latin America	91.8	92.4	96.3	97.1	97.3	97.8
Eastern Asia	97.1	91.9	99.2	98.6	99.5	99.3
Eastern Asia excluding China	99.3	99.5	—	—	99.4	99.7
Southern Asia	71.6	48.3	81.1	65.6	85.9	73.8
Southern Asia excluding India	66.9	45.9	73.9	60.8	80.5	72.6
South-Eastern Asia	95.4	93.5	96.6	96.1	97.8	97.5
Western Asia	93.4	81.0	95.5	87.8	95.8	90.6
Oceania	77.5	67.4	76.9	72.5	73.3	76.5
Caucasus and Central Asia	99.8	99.8	99.8	99.9	99.8	99.9
Developed regions	99.2	99.6	99.6	99.6	99.6	99.6
Least developed countries	64.0	47.5	72.2	58.9	74.5	65.9
Landlocked developing countries	68.2	56.5	74.8	62.6	77.2	66.5
Small island developing States	86.5	83.3	87.7	86.1	87.6	87.7

[a] The regional averages presented in this table are calculated using a weighted average of the latest available observed data point for each country or territory for the reference period. UNESCO Institute for Statistics estimates have been used for countries with missing data.

GOAL 3
Promote gender equality and empower women

Target 3.A
Eliminate gender disparity in primary and secondary education, preferably by 2005, and in all levels of education no later than 2015

Indicator 3.1
Ratios of girls to boys in primary, secondary and tertiary education

(a) Primary education[a]

	1991	2000	2009
World	0.89	0.92	0.96
Developing regions	0.87	0.91	0.96
Northern Africa	0.82	0.90	0.95
Sub-Saharan Africa	0.83	0.85	0.92
Latin America and the Caribbean	0.98	0.97	0.97
Caribbean	0.99	0.98	0.96
Latin America	0.98	0.97	0.97
Eastern Asia	0.92	1.01	1.04
Eastern Asia excluding China	1.00	0.98	0.98
Southern Asia	0.77	0.83	0.95
Southern Asia excluding India	0.79	0.81	0.92
South-Eastern Asia	0.97	0.96	0.97
Western Asia	0.86	0.86	0.92
Oceania	0.90	0.90	0.89
Caucasus and Central Asia	0.99	0.99	0.98
Developed regions	0.99	1.00	1.00
Least developed countries	0.80	0.83	0.93
Landlocked developing countries	0.83	0.82	0.92
Small island developing States	0.96	0.96	0.94

[a] Using gross enrolment ratios.

(b) Secondary education[a]

	1991	2000	2009
World	0.84	0.91	0.97
Developing regions	0.78	0.88	0.96
Northern Africa	0.79	0.93	0.98
Sub-Saharan Africa	0.76	0.82	0.79
Latin America and the Caribbean	1.07	1.07	1.08
Caribbean	1.12	1.08	1.04
Latin America	1.07	1.07	1.08
Eastern Asia	0.77	0.93	1.06
Eastern Asia excluding China	0.97	0.98	0.98
Southern Asia	0.61	0.75	0.89
Southern Asia excluding India	0.63	0.85	0.92
South-Eastern Asia	0.90	0.95	1.03
Western Asia	0.68	0.74	0.86
Oceania	0.83	0.89	0.88
Caucasus and Central Asia	—	0.98	0.98
Developed regions	1.01	1.01	1.00
Least developed countries	0.60	0.77	0.82
Landlocked developing countries	0.87	0.83	0.85
Small island developing States	1.07	1.04	1.01

[a] Using gross enrolment ratios.

(c) Tertiary education[a]

	1991	2000	2009
World	0.91	0.98	1.08
Developing regions	0.71	0.82	0.97
Northern Africa	0.59	0.74	0.98
Sub-Saharan Africa	0.53	0.67	0.63
Latin America and the Caribbean	0.98	1.17	1.26
Caribbean	1.35	1.38	1.61
Latin America	0.95	1.16	1.23
Eastern Asia	0.53	0.67	1.03
Eastern Asia excluding China	0.54	0.63	0.77
Southern Asia	0.50	0.65	0.74
Southern Asia excluding India	0.36	0.67	0.87
South-Eastern Asia	0.96	0.96	1.09
Western Asia	0.64	0.78	0.87
Oceania	0.56	0.81	0.86
Caucasus and Central Asia	—	0.91	1.07
Developed regions	1.10	1.20	1.30
Least developed countries	0.38	0.59	0.58
Landlocked developing countries	0.82	0.81	0.87
Small island developing States	1.24	1.31	1.50

[a] Using gross enrolment ratios.

Indicator 3.2
Share of women in wage employment in the non-agricultural sector
(Percentage of employees)

	1990	2000	2005	2009
World	35.0	37.5	38.4	39.6
Developing regions	28.8	31.7	32.6	33.8
Northern Africa	19.0	18.8	18.6	18.8
Sub-Saharan Africa	23.5	28.1	30.2	32.6
Latin America and the Caribbean	36.4	40.4	41.5	43.0
Eastern Asia	38.1	39.7	40.9	41.7
Eastern Asia excluding China	40.1	42.3	44.0	44.8
Southern Asia	13.3	17.1	18.1	19.4
Southern Asia excluding India	14.6	18.4	18.0	19.0
South-Eastern Asia	34.6	36.9	36.8	37.6
Western Asia	14.9	16.8	17.5	18.7
Oceania	33.3	35.5	35.2	36.2
Caucasus and Central Asia	43.8	44.2	45.3	45.2
Developed regions	44.3	46.2	47.1	48.3

Indicator 3.3
Proportion of seats held by women in national parliament[a,b]
(Percentage)

	1990	2000	2005	2011[b]
World	12.8	13.7	15.9	19.3
Developing regions	11.6	12.3	14.2	18.0
Northern Africa	2.6	3.3	8.5	11.7
Sub-Saharan Africa	9.6	12.6	14.2	19.6
Latin America and the Caribbean	11.9	15.2	19.0	23.0
Caribbean	22.1	20.6	26.0	31.3
Latin America	8.6	13.2	16.4	20.0
Eastern Asia	20.2	19.9	19.4	19.5
Eastern Asia excluding China	17.8	14.6	17.2	14.5
Southern Asia	5.7	6.8	8.8	18.2
Southern Asia excluding India	5.9	5.9	9.0	20.1
South-Eastern Asia	10.4	12.3	15.5	17.6
Western Asia	4.5	4.2	3.9	9.4
Oceania	1.2	3.6	3.0	2.3
Caucasus and Central Asia	—	7.0	9.9	16.1
Developed regions	16.1	16.3	19.8	22.5
Least developed countries	8.7	9.9	13.0	19.9
Landlocked developing countries	14.2	7.8	13.4	22.9
Small island developing States	15.2	14.0	17.9	21.2

[a] Single or lower house only.
[b] As of 31 January 2011.

GOAL 4
Reduce child mortality

Target 4.A
Reduce by two thirds, between 1990 and 2015, the under-five mortality rate

Indicator 4.1
Under-five mortality rate[a]

	1990	2000	2009
World	89	77	60
Developing regions	99	84	66
Northern Africa	80	46	26
Sub-Saharan Africa	180	160	129
Latin America and the Caribbean	52	33	23
Caribbean	76	58	48
Latin America	50	32	21
Eastern Asia	45	36	19
Eastern Asia excluding China	28	29	17
Southern Asia	122	95	69
Southern Asia excluding India	131	101	78
South-Eastern Asia	73	48	36
Western Asia	68	45	32
Oceania	76	65	59
Caucasus and Central Asia	78	62	37
Developed regions	15	10	7
Least developed countries	178	146	121

[a] Deaths of children before reaching the age of 5 per 1,000 live births.

Indicator 4.2
Infant mortality rate[a]

	1990	2000	2009
World	62	54	44
Developing regions	68	59	48
Northern Africa	61	38	24
Sub-Saharan Africa	109	98	82
Latin America and the Caribbean	41	28	20
Caribbean	54	43	38
Latin America	41	26	18
Eastern Asia	36	29	18
Eastern Asia excluding China	18	22	14
Southern Asia	87	70	55
Southern Asia excluding India	95	76	61
South-Eastern Asia	50	36	27
Western Asia	53	36	27
Oceania	56	49	46
Caucasus and Central Asia	64	52	34
Developed regions	12	8	6
Least developed countries	112	93	79

[a] Deaths of children before reaching age 1, per 1,000 live births.

Indicator 4.3
Proportion of 1-year-old children immunized against measles[a]
(Percentage)

	1990	2000	2009
World	72	71	82
Developing regions	71	69	80
Northern Africa	85	93	94
Sub-Saharan Africa	56	55	68
Latin America and the Caribbean	76	92	93
Eastern Asia	98	84	94
Eastern Asia excluding China	95	87	95
Southern Asia	57	56	75
Southern Asia excluding India	60	68	85
South-Eastern Asia	70	81	88
Western Asia	77	84	82
Oceania	70	66	58
Caucasus and Central Asia	—	93	92
Developed regions	81	92	94
Least developed countries	54	60	77

[a] Children aged 12–23 months who received at least one dose of measles vaccine.

GOAL 5
Improve maternal health

Target 5.A
Reduce by three quarters, between 1990 and 2015, the maternal mortality ratio

Indicator 5.1
Maternal mortality ratio[a]

	1990	2000	2008
World	400	340	260
Developing regions	440	370	290
Northern Africa	230	120	92
Sub-Saharan Africa	870	790	640
Latin America and the Caribbean	140	110	85
Caribbean	320	230	170
Latin America	130	99	80
Eastern Asia	110	63	41
Eastern Asia excluding China	110	110	110
Southern Asia	590	420	280
Southern Asia excluding India	640	490	370
South-Eastern Asia	380	230	160
Western Asia	140	98	70
Oceania	290	260	230
Caucasus and Central Asia	70	69	54
Developed regions	26	17	17
Least developed countries	900	750	590

[a] Maternal deaths per 100,000 live births.

Indicator 5.2
Proportion of births attended by skilled health personnel
(Percentage)

	1990	2009
World	59	68
Developing regions	55	65
Northern Africa	45	81
Sub-Saharan Africa	42	46
Latin America and the Caribbean[a]	70	88
Caribbean[a]	67	69
Latin America[a]	70	90
Eastern Asia	94	99
Eastern Asia excluding China	97	99
Southern Asia	32	50
Southern Asia excluding India	27	42
South-Eastern Asia	49	72
Western Asia	62	78
Oceania	54	56
Caucasus and Central Asia	93	97
Developed regions	99	99

[a] Includes only deliveries in health-care institutions.

Target 5.B
Achieve, by 2015, universal access to reproductive health

Indicator 5.3
Contraceptive prevalence rate[a]
(Percentage)

	1990	2000	2008
World	55.4	61.5	62.9
Developing regions	52.3	59.6	61.3
Northern Africa	44.0	58.8	60.5
Sub-Saharan Africa	13.4	20.1	21.7
Latin America and the Caribbean	62.0	71.2	72.9
Caribbean	53.7	59.9	61.8
Latin America	62.7	72.1	73.8
Eastern Asia	77.7	85.7	84.2
Eastern Asia excluding China	73.9	76.6	76.2
Southern Asia	39.9	46.7	53.9
Southern Asia excluding India	30.2	46.2	48.0
South-Eastern Asia	47.9	57.0	62.3
Western Asia	44.4	50.6	55.2
Oceania	29.4	32.2	36.7
Caucasus and Central Asia	54.3	59.7	55.6
Developed regions	68.8	71.1	72.2
Least developed countries	17.7	28.1	31.4
Landlocked developing countries	24.5	30.7	33.7
Small island developing States	49.7	53.9	55.4

[a] Among women aged 15–49 who are married or in a union.

Indicator 5.4
Adolescent birth rate[a]

	1990	2000	2008
World	59.8	51.5	50.5
Developing regions	64.8	56.0	54.4
Northern Africa	43.0	33.3	29.9
Sub-Saharan Africa	124.1	122.9	122.0
Latin America and the Caribbean	91.1	87.6	80.7
Caribbean	80.9	77.1	68.5
Latin America	91.9	88.4	81.6
Eastern Asia	15.3	5.8	6.0
Eastern Asia excluding China	4.0	3.1	2.5
Southern Asia	89.3	59.4	52.6
Southern Asia excluding India	121.0	77.4	69.0
South-Eastern Asia	53.5	40.3	44.1
Western Asia	63.8	52.7	52.3
Oceania	82.8	63.3	61.2
Caucasus and Central Asia	44.7	28.2	29.3
Developed regions	33.9	25.5	24.0
Least developed countries	133.4	121.2	121.9
Landlocked developing countries	105.8	106.6	107.1
Small island developing States	77.1	71.7	63.9

[a] Births per 1,000 women aged 15–19 years.

Indicator 5.5
Antenatal care coverage
(at least one visit and at least four visits)

(a) At least one visit[a]
(Percentage)

	1990	2009
World	64	81
Developing regions	64	81
Northern Africa	51	79
Sub-Saharan Africa	68	78
Latin America and the Caribbean	78	95
Caribbean	89	93
Latin America	77	95
Eastern Asia	70	91
Southern Asia	51	70
Southern Asia excluding India	22	58
South-Eastern Asia	72	92
Western Asia	62	84
Oceania	77	79
Caucasus and Central Asia	90	96

[a] Proportion of women aged 15–49 years who received antenatal care during pregnancy from skilled health personnel at least once.

(b) At least four visits[a]
(Percentage)

	1990	2009
World	35	51
Developing regions	35	51
Northern Africa	20	57
Sub-Saharan Africa	44	43
Latin America and the Caribbean	69	84
Caribbean	59	72
Latin America	70	85
Southern Asia	23	44
Southern Asia excluding India	10	26
South-Eastern Asia	46	69
Western Asia	32	54

[a] Proportion of women aged 15–49 years who received antenatal care during pregnancy from any provider (skilled or unskilled) at least four times.

Indicator 5.6
Unmet need for family planning[a]
(Percentage)

	1990	2000	2008
World	13.8	11.5	11.1
Developing regions	14.3	11.7	11.3
Northern Africa	19.4	11.2	9.6
Sub-Saharan Africa	26.2	24.1	24.8
Latin America and the Caribbean	15.8	10.3	9.9
Caribbean	19.5	20.4	20.2
Latin America	15.6	9.7	9.3
Eastern Asia	3.3	2.4	2.3
Southern Asia	20.3	17.2	14.7
Southern Asia excluding India	23.6	23.3	20.6
South-Eastern Asia	15.5	10.9	10.9
Western Asia	15.7	13.7	12.3
Caucasus and Central Asia	14.4	12.4	12.5
Least developed countries	25.4	23.9	24.0
Landlocked developing countries	24.3	24.1	23.8

[a] Among women, married or in a union, of reproductive age (aged 15–49 years).

GOAL 6
Combat HIV/AIDS, malaria and other diseases

Target 6.A
Have halted by 2015 and begun to reverse the spread of HIV/AIDS

Indicator 6.1
(a) HIV incidence rates[a]

	1990	2009
World	0.08	0.06
Developing regions	0.09	0.08
Northern Africa	0.01	0.01
Sub-Saharan Africa	0.57	0.40
Latin America and the Caribbean	0.04	0.04

	1990	2009
Caribbean	0.09	0.08
Latin America	0.04	0.03
Eastern Asia	0.01	0.01
Southern Asia	0.04	0.02
South-Eastern Asia (including Oceania)	0.04	0.04
Western Asia	<0.01	<0.01
Caucasus and Central Asia	0.01	0.03
Developed regions	0.05	0.03

[a] "HIV prevalence among population aged 15–24 years" was chosen as a proxy indicator for the incidence rate when the indicators for the Millennium Declaration were developed. However, the estimated incidence rate among people 15–49 years is now available for all regions and 60 countries. Therefore, HIV incidence rate data are presented here together with HIV prevalence data among population aged 15–49 years.

(b) HIV prevalence among population aged 15–24 years
(Percentage)

	1990		2001		2009	
	Estimated adult (15–49) HIV prevalence	Adults (15+) living with HIV who are women	Estimated adult (15–49) HIV prevalence	Adults (15+) living with HIV who are women	Estimated adult (15–49) HIV prevalence	Adults (15+) living with HIV who are women
World	0.3	44	0.8	51	0.8	52
Developing regions	0.3	49	0.9	53	0.9	54
Northern Africa	<0.1	29	<0.1	30	0.1	30
Sub-Saharan Africa	2.1	56	5.5	59	4.7	60
Latin America and the Caribbean	0.3	28	0.5	35	0.5	37
Caribbean	0.6	48	1.1	54	1	53
Latin America	0.3	25	0.4	32	0.4	35
Eastern Asia	<0.1	25	<0.1	28	0.1	29
Eastern Asia excluding China	<0.1	29	<0.1	30	<0.1	31
Southern Asia	<0.1	28	0.3	35	0.3	37
Southern Asia excluding India	<0.1	27	0.1	30	0.1	30
South-Eastern Asia (including Oceania)	0.2	16	0.4	34	0.4	34
Western Asia	<0.1	30	<0.1	30	<0.1	30
Oceania	<0.1	54	0.4	57	0.8	57
Caucasus and Central Asia	<0.1	32	<0.1	37	0.1	37
Developed regions	0.2	18	0.3	31	0.4	35
Least developed countries	1.4	55	2.2	58	2	58
Landlocked developing countries	2.4	57	3.9	58	3	58
Small island developing States	0.4	48	0.8	52	0.8	51

Indicator 6.2
Condom use at last high-risk sex,[a] **2005–2010**[b]

	Women		Men	
	Number of countries covered by surveys	Percentage who used a condom at last high-risk sex	Number of countries covered by surveys	Percentage who used a condom at last high-risk sex
Sub-Saharan Africa	34	34	27	48
Caribbean	3	37	2	56
Southern Asia	1	22	2	38
Oceania	3	34	4	48

[a] Percentage of young women and men aged 15–24 years reporting the use of a condom during sexual intercourse with a non-regular (non-marital and non-cohabiting) sexual partner in the last 12 months, among those who had such a partner in the last 12 months.

[b] Data refer to the most recent year available during the period specified.

Indicator 6.3
Proportion of population aged 15–24 years with comprehensive correct knowledge of HIV/AIDS,[a] **2005–2010**[b]

	Women		Men	
	Number of countries covered by surveys	Percentage who have comprehensive knowledge	Number of countries covered by surveys	Percentage who have comprehensive knowledge
World[c]	91	21	—	—
Developing regions[c]	82	20	—	—
Northern Africa	2	7	1	18
Sub-Saharan Africa	37	26	28	33
Caribbean	5	43	2	37
Southern Asia	5	17	2	36
Southern Asia excluding India	4	10	—	—
South-Eastern Asia	6	24	—	—
Caucasus and Central Asia	8	20	—	—

[a] Percentage of young women and men aged 15–24 years who correctly identify the two major ways of preventing the sexual transmission of HIV (using condoms and limiting sex to one faithful, uninfected partner), who reject two common local misconceptions and who know that a healthy-looking person can transmit the AIDS virus.

[b] Data refer to the most recent year available during the period specified.

[c] Excludes China.

Indicator 6.4
Ratio of school attendance of orphans to school attendance of non-orphans aged 10–14 years,[a] **2005–2010**[b]

	Number of countries with data	School attendance ratio
Developing regions	44	0.81
Sub-Saharan Africa	33	0.92
Caribbean	2	0.82
Southern Asia	2	0.73

[a] Ratio of the current school attendance rate of children aged 10–14 years both of whose biological parents have died, to the current school attendance rate of children aged 10–14 years both of whose parents are still alive and who currently live with at least one biological parent.

[b] Data refer to the most recent year available during the period specified.

Target 6.B
Achieve, by 2010, universal access to treatment for HIV/AIDS for all those who need it

Indicator 6.5
Proportion of population with advanced HIV infection with access to antiretroviral drugs[a,b]
(Percentage)

	2004	2006	2008	2009
World[b]	6	15	28	36
Developing regions	6	16	29	37
Northern Africa	10	21	29	25

	2004	2006	2008	2009
Sub-Saharan Africa	3	14	28	37
Latin America and the Caribbean	34	41	48	50
Caribbean	5	14	30	38
Latin America	39	44	49	51
Eastern Asia	6	16	19	23
Eastern Asia excluding China	<1	<1	<1	<1
Southern Asia	2	7	18	24
Southern Asia excluding India	1	2	4	6
South-Eastern Asia and Oceania	12	24	39	46
Western Asia	44	38	52	57
Caucasus and Central Asia	2	12	22	26
Least developed countries	4	14	30	39
Landlocked developing countries	5	17	35	47
Small island developing States	5	15	31	40

[a] Antiretroviral treatment coverage among people with CD4 counts of less than 350.

[b] Includes only low- and middle-income economies as defined by the World Bank.

Target 6.C
Have halted by 2015 and begun to reverse the incidence of malaria and other major diseases

Indicator 6.6
Incidence and death rates associated with malaria

(a) Incidence[a]

World	69
Northern Africa	0
Sub-Saharan Africa	248
Latin America and the Caribbean	7
Caribbean	14
Latin America	6
Eastern Asia	0
Eastern Asia excluding China	15
Southern Asia	20
Southern Asia excluding India	12
South-Eastern Asia	32
Western Asia	20
Oceania	225
Caucasus and Central Asia	0
Least developed countries	173
Landlocked developing countries	148
Small island developing States	98

[a] Number of new cases per 1,000 population, 2009, in malaria-endemic countries.

(b) Deaths[a]

	All ages	Children under 5
World	24	182
Northern Africa	0	0
Sub-Saharan Africa	96	519
Latin America and the Caribbean	1	3
Caribbean	4	11
Latin America	<0.5	1
Eastern Asia	<0.5	<0.5
Eastern Asia excluding China	0	0
Southern Asia	2	8
Southern Asia excluding India	1	5
South-Eastern Asia	6	18
Western Asia	6	15
Oceania	55	163
Caucasus and Central Asia	<0.5	<0.5
Least developed countries	70	384
Landlocked developing countries	67	351
Small island developing States	30	146

[a] Number of deaths per 100,000 population, 2009, in malaria-endemic countries.

Indicator 6.7
Proportion of children under 5 sleeping under insecticide-treated bednets, 2008–2010

(a) Total
(Percentage)

Sub-Saharan Africa (24 countries)	31[a]

[a] Data for a subset of 24 countries in sub-Saharan Africa with trend data showed that the use of insecticide-treated bednets among children increased from 2 per cent in 2000 to 31 per cent in 2010. Calculation includes data available as at 31 April 2011.

(b) By sex
(Percentage)

	Boys	Girls
Sub-Saharan Africa (21 countries)	27	27

(c) By residence
(Percentage)

	Urban	Rural
Sub-Saharan Africa (23 countries)	28	33

Indicator 6.8
Proportion of children under 5 with fever who are treated with appropriate anti-malarial drugs, 2008–2010

(a) Total
(Percentage)

Sub-Saharan Africa (34 countries)	36

(b) By residence
(Percentage)

	Urban	Rural
Southern Asia (3 countries)	41	36

Indicator 6.9
Incidence, prevalence and death rates associated with tuberculosis

(a) Incidence
(Number of new cases per 100,000 population, including HIV-infected)[a]

	1990	2000	2009
World	128 (114:144)	136 (129:144)	137 (131:145)
Developing regions	155 (135:174)	163 (153:172)	164 (155:173)
Northern Africa	58 (47:69)	48 (43:52)	42 (39:46)
Sub-Saharan Africa	176 (159:194)	316 (300:333)	345 (326:363)
Latin America and the Caribbean	88 (73:103)	61 (56:66)	44 (41:48)
Caribbean	95 (67:122)	91 (78:104)	79 (67:90)
Latin America	87 (71:103)	59 (54:64)	42 (39:45)
Eastern Asia	136 (105:167)	109 (90:128)	100 (88:112)
Southern Asia	172 (117:227)	172 (148:197)	173 (149:196)
South-Eastern Asia	238 (191:284)	226 (205:247)	217 (197:237)
Western Asia	59 (48:70)	49 (44:54)	33 (30:36)
Oceania	202 (131:273)	194 (161:226)	190 (162:219)
Caucasus and Central Asia	116 (92:141)	135 (123:146)	134 (123:146)
Developed regions	39 (33:46)	36 (33:39)	27 (25:29)
Least developed countries	212 (183:240)	272 (258:287)	275 (261:289)

	1990	2000	2009
Landlocked developing countries	167 (148:187)	270 (254:287)	270 (253:287)
Small island developing States	108 (86:129)	104 (94:114)	104 (95:113)

^aLower and upper bounds in brackets.

(b) Prevalence
(Number of existing cases per 100,000 population, including HIV-infected)[a]

	1990	2000	2009
World	253 (200:318)	231 (194:275)	201 (169:239)
Developing regions	310 (233:387)	280 (229:331)	241 (198:284)
Northern Africa	98 (56:139)	65 (40:89)	54 (34:74)
Sub-Saharan Africa	287 (231:344)	456 (377:534)	479 (397:560)
Latin America and the Caribbean	148 (99:198)	90 (67:114)	58 (43:72)
Caribbean	176 (90:263)	139 (81:198)	111 (61:162)
Latin America	146 (93:199)	86 (62:111)	54 (38:69)
Eastern Asia	284 (122:446)	218 (101:334)	141 (63:220)
Southern Asia	359 (167:551)	294 (177:410)	267 (154:380)
South-Eastern Asia	524 (369:679)	465 (349:580)	344 (259:429)
Western Asia	94 (57:131)	74 (50:98)	51 (35:67)
Oceania	416 (163:669)	250 (103:396)	258 (107:408)
Caucasus and Central Asia	224 (139:308)	207 (144:269)	208 (147:269)
Developed regions	66 (42:89)	49 (33:64)	34 (23:45)
Least developed countries	397 (291:502)	460 (378:543)	431 (358:503)
Landlocked developing countries	252 (202:302)	372 (300:445)	385 (305:464)
Small island developing States	202 (131:272)	152 (107:198)	146 (104:187)

^aLower and upper bounds in brackets.

(c) Deaths
(Number of deaths per 100,000 population, excluding HIV-infected)[a]

	1990	2000	2009
World	30 (25:36)	26 (24:29)	20 (17:22)
Developing regions	37 (30:44)	32 (29:35)	23 (21:26)
Northern Africa	6.6 (3.3:9.9)	3 (2.1:4)	2.4 (1.7:3.2)
Sub-Saharan Africa	32 (27:38)	54 (50:59)	53 (48:58)
Latin America and the Caribbean	13 (8.8:17)	6 (5.3:6.8)	3.3 (2.7:4)
Caribbean	21 (12:29)	15 (11:19)	11 (7.3:14)
Latin America	12 (7.9:16)	5.3 (4.6:6.1)	2.8 (2.1:3.4)
Eastern Asia	37 (26:48)	28 (21:34)	12 (7.2:16)
Southern Asia	47 (28:66)	33 (25:41)	26 (18:34)
South-Eastern Asia	52 (39:66)	51 (45:58)	31 (25:37)
Western Asia	8.2 (4.8:12)	6.2 (4.6:7.7)	4.7 (3.6:5.8)
Oceania	53 (28:77)	17 (7.8:25)	20 (10:29)
Caucasus and Central Asia	23 (16:30)	22 (20:23)	20 (17:23)
Developed regions	7.5 (4.7:10)	4.8 (4.5:5.1)	3.7 (2.8:4.6)
Least developed countries	49 (40:59)	57 (52:62)	48 (44:53)
Landlocked developing countries	25 (21:30)	41 (37:46)	42 (37:47)
Small island developing States	24 (17:31)	15 (12:18)	13 (10:16)

^aLower and upper bounds in brackets.

Indicator 6.10
Proportion of tuberculosis cases detected and cured under directly observed treatment short course

(a) New cases detected under directly observed treatment short course (DOTS)
(DOTS smear-positive case detection rate: percentage)[a]

	1990	2000	2009
World	55 (49:62)	45 (43:48)	62 (59:65)
Developing regions	55 (49:63)	43 (41:46)	61 (58:64)
Northern Africa	63 (53:78)	90 (82:98)	89 (82:98)
Sub-Saharan Africa	45 (41:50)	38 (36:40)	48 (46:51)
Latin America and the Caribbean	53 (45:64)	69 (64:75)	73 (68:79)
Caribbean	11 (8.8:16)	51 (45:60)	17 (15:20)
Latin America	56 (47:69)	72 (66:78)	81 (75:88)
Eastern Asia	27 (22:35)	35 (30:43)	76 (68:87)
Southern Asia	85 (65:130)	50 (44:58)	64 (56:74)
South-Eastern Asia	50 (42:62)	34 (31:38)	63 (57:69)
Western Asia	70 (59:87)	64 (58:70)	68 (62:75)
Oceania	31 (23:48)	76 (65:91)	74 (64:87)
Caucasus and Central Asia	42 (34:53)	68 (63:75)	65 (59:71)
Developed regions	58 (50:70)	81 (74:89)	84 (78:92)
Least developed countries	32 (28:37)	35 (33:37)	48 (46:51)
Landlocked developing countries	54 (49:61)	47 (44:50)	49 (46:52)
Small island developing States	22 (19:28)	58 (53:65)	45 (42:50)

^aLower and upper bounds in brackets.

(b) Patients successfully treated under directly observed treatment short course
(Percentage)

	2000	2008
World	69	86
Developing regions	69	87
Northern Africa	88	87
Sub-Saharan Africa	71	80
Latin America and the Caribbean	76	77
Caribbean	72	76
Latin America	77	77
Eastern Asia	92	94
South Asia	42	88
South-Eastern Asia	86	89
Western Asia	77	84
Oceania	76	70
Caucasus and Central Asia	79	74
Developed regions	66	59
Least developed countries	77	85
Landlocked developing countries	75	81
Small island developing States	73	75

GOAL 7
Ensure environmental sustainability

Target 7.A
Integrate the principles of sustainable development into country policies and programmes and reverse the loss of environmental resources

Indicator 7.1
Proportion of land area covered by forest
(Percentage)

	1990	2000	2010
World	32.0	31.4	31.0
Developing regions	29.4	28.2	27.6
Northern Africa	1.4	1.4	1.4
Sub-Saharan Africa	31.2	29.5	28.1
Latin America and the Caribbean	52.0	49.6	47.4
Caribbean	25.8	28.1	30.3
Latin America	52.3	49.9	47.6
Eastern Asia	16.4	18.0	20.5

	1990	2000	2010
Eastern Asia excluding China	15.2	14.0	12.8
Southern Asia	14.1	14.1	14.5
Southern Asia excluding India	7.8	7.3	7.1
South-Eastern Asia	56.9	51.3	49.3
Western Asia	2.8	2.9	3.3
Oceania	67.5	65.1	62.5
Caucasus and Central Asia	3.9	3.9	3.9
Developed regions	36.3	36.6	36.7
Least developed countries	32.7	31.0	29.6
Landlocked developing countries	19.3	18.2	17.1
Small island developing States	64.6	63.7	62.7

Indicator 7.2
Carbon dioxide emissions, total, per capita and per $1 GDP (PPP)

(a) Total[a]
(millions of tons)

	1990	2000	2005	2007
World	21 839	23 839	27 895	30 121
Developing regions	6 760	9 925	13 533	15 955
Northern Africa	232	333	400	453
Sub-Saharan Africa	462	554	648	688
Latin America and the Caribbean	1 019	1 334	1 464	1 652
Caribbean	84	99	105	136
Latin America	934	1 235	1 359	1 516
Eastern Asia	2 988	3 964	6 388	7 670
Eastern Asia excluding China	527	559	598	638
Southern Asia	1 009	1 675	2 061	2 509
Southern Asia excluding India	319	489	650	766
South-Eastern Asia	426	785	1 055	1 173
Western Asia	617	943	1 126	1 325
Oceania	6	7	11	9
Caucasus and Central Asia	485[b]	329	380	477
Developed regions	14 953	13 696	14 100	13 907
Least developed countries	74	110	164	191
Landlocked developing countries	50	399	451	557
Small island developing States	139	158	172	183
ANNEX I countries[c,d,e]	14 968	14 430	14 902	14 652

(b) Per capita
(Tons)

	1990	2000	2005	2008
World	4.1	3.9	4.2	4.4
Developing regions	1.7	2.0	2.6	2.9
Northern Africa	1.9	2.3	2.6	2.8
Sub-Saharan Africa	0.9	0.8	0.9	0.8
Latin America and the Caribbean	2.3	2.6	2.7	2.9
Caribbean	2.7	2.9	2.9	3.6
Latin America	2.3	2.6	2.6	2.8
Eastern Asia	2.5	2.9	4.6	5.4
Eastern Asia excluding China	7.4	7.1	7.4	7.8
Southern Asia	0.8	1.1	1.3	1.5
Southern Asia excluding India	0.9	1.2	1.4	1.6
South-Eastern Asia	1.0	1.5	1.9	2.0
Western Asia	4.8	5.6	6.0	6.6
Oceania	1.0	1.0	1.3	0.9
Caucasus and Central Asia	7.1[b]	4.6	5.1	6.3
Developed regions	12.3	11.4	11.5	11.2
Least developed countries	0.1	0.2	0.2	0.2
Landlocked developing countries	0.3	1.2	1.2	1.4
Small island developing States	3.2	3.1	3.1	3.2
ANNEX I countries[c,d,e]	12.7	11.7	11.8	11.5

(c) Per $1 GDP (PPP)
(kilograms)

	1990	2000	2005	2008
World	0.60	0.50	0.49	0.46
Developing regions	0.64	0.59	0.61	0.58
Northern Africa	0.43	0.50	0.49	0.47
Sub-Saharan Africa	0.55	0.53	0.48	0.43
Latin America and the Caribbean	0.32	0.31	0.30	0.29
Caribbean	0.60	0.58	0.53	0.62
Latin America	0.32	0.30	0.29	0.28
Eastern Asia	1.46	0.87	0.94	0.83
Eastern Asia excluding China	0.44	0.44	0.38	0.36
Southern Asia	0.59	0.61	0.54	0.54
Southern Asia excluding India	0.49	0.51	0.51	0.52
South-Eastern Asia	0.42	0.47	0.49	0.46
Western Asia	0.52	0.59	0.57	0.57
Oceania	0.29	0.25	0.38	0.20
Caucasus and Central Asia	2.31[b]	1.80	1.30	1.22
Developed regions	0.59	0.45	0.41	0.38
Least developed countries	0.18	0.19	0.20	0.19
Landlocked developing countries	0.20	0.93	0.73	0.71
Small island developing States	0.59	0.41	0.37	0.32
ANNEX I countries[c,d,e]	0.59	0.46	0.43	0.39

[a] Total CO_2 emissions from fossil fuels. Includes CO_2 emissions from solid fuel consumption, liquid fuel consumption, gas fuel consumption, cement production and gas flaring (US Carbon Dioxide Information Analysis Center).

[b] 1992 data.

[c] Includes all annex I countries that report to the UN Framework Convention on Climate Change; non-annex I countries do not have annual reporting obligations.

[d] National reporting to the UN Framework Convention on Climate Change that follows the Intergovernmental Panel on Climate Change guidelines is based on national emission inventories and covers all sources of anthropogenic carbon dioxide emissions. It can be calculated as the sum of emissions for the sectors of energy, industrial processes, agriculture and waste.

[e] Excludes emissions/removals from land use, land-use change and forestry.

Indicator 7.3
Consumption of ozone-depleting substances
(Tons of ozone depletion potential)

	1990[a]	2000	2009
Developing regions	236 892	207 991	41 983
Northern Africa	6 203	8 129	1 307
Sub-Saharan Africa	23 449	9 574	1 787
Latin America and the Caribbean	76 048	31 104	5 359
Caribbean	2 177	1 669	159
Latin America	73 871	29 435	5 200
Eastern Asia	103 217	105 762	24 734
Eastern Asia excluding China	12 904	14 885	4 363
Southern Asia	3 338	28 161	1 904
Southern Asia excluding India	3 338	9 466	927
South-Eastern Asia	21 108	16 831	2 940
Western Asia	3 481	8 299	3 939
Oceania	47	129	13
Caucasus and Central Asia	2 738	928	188
Developed regions	828 590	25 364	2 007
Least developed countries	1 457	4 791	1 055
Landlocked developing countries	3 354	2 395	484
Small island developing States	7 162	2 147	434

[a] For years prior to the entry into force of the reporting requirement for a group of substances, missing country consumption values have been estimated at the base year level. This applies to substances in annexes B, C and E, whose years of entry into force are 1992, 1992 and 1994, respectively.

Indicator 7.4
Proportion of fish stocks within safe biological limits
(Percentage)

	1990	2000	2008
Underexploited	9.0	4.1	2.7
Moderately exploited	22.3	21.3	11.8
Fully exploited	50.0	47.2	52.7
Overexploited	8.5	17.7	28.4
Depleted	7.4	8.6	3.3
Recovering	2.7	1.1	1.0

Indicator 7.5
Proportion of total water resources used,[a] around 2005
(Percentage)

Developing regions	9.6
Northern Africa	91.9
Sub-Saharan Africa	3.3
Latin America and the Caribbean	2.0
Eastern Asia	15.2
Eastern Asia excluding China	1.9
Southern Asia	19.7
Southern Asia excluding India	19.7
South-Eastern Asia	57.8
Western Asia	53.4
Oceania	7.7
Caucasus and Central Asia	165.5
Developed regions	0.04
Least developed countries	56.0
Landlocked developing countries	10.1
Small island developing States	4.5

[a] Surface water and groundwater withdrawal as percentage of total actual renewable water resources.

Target 7.B
Reduce biodiversity loss, achieving, by 2010, a significant reduction in the rate of loss

Indicator 7.6
Proportion of terrestrial and marine areas protected
(a) Terrestrial and marine[a,b]
(Percentage)

	1990	2000	2010
World[c]	8.1	10.6	12.0
Developing regions	7.9	10.6	12.2
Northern Africa	3.3	3.7	4.0
Sub-Saharan Africa	10.7	11.0	11.5
Latin America and the Caribbean	9.0	14.7	19.3
Caribbean	3.3	3.8	4.6
Latin America	9.3	15.1	19.9
Eastern Asia	11.5	14.3	15.3
Eastern Asia excluding China	3.9	11.4	11.6
Southern Asia	5.0	5.6	5.9
Southern Asia excluding India	5.4	6.2	6.8
South-Eastern Asia	4.6	7.1	7.8
Western Asia	3.5	14.2	14.3
Oceania	0.5	1.1	3.2
Caucasus and Central Asia	2.7	3.0	3.0
Developed regions	8.3	10.4	11.6
Least developed countries	8.9	9.5	9.8
Landlocked developing countries	8.9	10.9	11.3
Small island developing States	1.5	2.7	4.2

[a] Ratio of protected area (terrestrial and marine combined) to total territorial area. Differences between these figures and those set out in the statistical annex to the *Millennium Development Goals Report 2010* (see http://unstats.un.org/unsd/mdg) are due to the availability of new data and to revised methodologies.

[b] Protected areas with an unknown year of establishment are included in all years.

[c] Includes territories that are not considered in the calculations of aggregates for developed regions and developing regions.

(b) Terrestrial[a,b]
(Percentage)

	1990	2000	2010
World[c]	8.8	11.3	12.7
Developing regions	8.8	11.7	13.3
Northern Africa	3.3	3.7	4.0
Sub-Saharan Africa	11.1	11.3	11.8
Latin America and the Caribbean	9.7	15.3	20.3
Caribbean	9.2	9.9	11.2
Latin America	9.7	15.4	20.4
Eastern Asia	12.0	14.9	15.9
Eastern Asia excluding China	4.0	12.1	12.2
Southern Asia	5.3	5.9	6.2
Southern Asia excluding India	5.8	6.7	7.3
South-Eastern Asia	8.7	13.1	13.8
Western Asia	3.8	15.3	15.4
Oceania	2.0	3.0	4.9
Caucasus and Central Asia	2.7	3.0	3.0
Developed regions	8.7	10.7	11.6
Least developed countries	9.4	10.0	10.2
Landlocked developing countries	8.9	10.9	11.3
Small island developing States	4.0	6.3	7.6

[a] Ratio of terrestrial protected area to total surface area. Differences between these figures and those set out in the statistical annex to the *Millennium Development Goals Report 2010* (see http://unstats.un.org/unsd/mdg) are due to the availability of new data and to revised methodologies.

[b] Protected areas with an unknown year of establishment are included in all years.

[c] Includes territories that are not considered in the calculations of aggregates for the developed regions and developing regions.

(c) Marine[a,b]
(Percentage)

	1990	2000	2010
World[c]	3.1	5.2	7.2
Developing regions	1.0	2.9	4.0
Northern Africa	3.1	3.6	4.6
Sub-Saharan Africa	1.4	3.1	4.0
Latin America and the Caribbean	2.7	8.9	10.8
Caribbean	1.1	1.5	2.2
Latin America	3.3	11.8	14.3
Eastern Asia	0.8	1.4	1.6
Eastern Asia excluding China	2.1	2.1	2.3
Southern Asia	0.9	1.1	1.2
Southern Asia excluding India	0.5	0.6	0.8
South-Eastern Asia	0.6	1.3	2.1
Western Asia	0.7	2.0	2.2
Oceania	0.2	0.6	2.8
Caucasus and Central Asia	0.2	0.4	0.4
Developed regions	5.9	8.5	11.5
Least developed countries	0.9	1.9	3.4
Landlocked developing countries[d]	0.0	0.0	0.0
Small island developing States	0.4	1.2	2.8

[a] Ratio of marine protected area to total territorial waters. Differences between these figures and those set out in the statistical annex to the *Millennium Development Goals Report 2010* (see http://unstats.un.org/unsd/mdg) are due to the availability of new data and to revised methodologies.

^{b} Protected areas with an unknown year of establishment are included in all years.

^{c} Includes territories that are not considered in the calculations of aggregates for the developed regions and developing regions.

^{d} Excludes territorial water claims within inland seas made by some landlocked developing countries.

Indicator 7.7
Proportion of species threatened with extinction^a
(Percentage of species not expected to become extinct in the near future)

	1986	1990	2000	2008
World	85.3	85.0	84.3	83.7
Developing regions	84.9	84.7	84.0	83.4
Northern Africa	94.3	94.1	93.9	93.6
Sub-Saharan Africa	87.6	87.6	87.3	87.1
Latin America and the Caribbean	84.1	83.8	83.1	82.6
Eastern Asia	89.9	89.7	89.0	88.4
Southern Asia	84.9	84.8	84.4	84.1
South-Eastern Asia	87.9	87.6	86.6	86.0
Western Asia	93.5	93.3	92.7	92.2
Oceania	91.2	91.0	90.4	90.0
Caucasus and Central Asia	95.7	95.5	94.9	94.4
Developed regions	90.9	90.6	90.1	89.6

^{a} Red List Index (RLI) of species survival for vertebrate biodiversity (mammals, birds and amphibians). RLI is an index of the proportion of species expected to remain extant in the near future without additional conservation action, ranging from 1.0 (equivalent to all species being categorized as of "least concern" on the International Union for Conservation of Nature Red List) to zero (equivalent to all species having become extinct).

Target 7.C
Halve, by 2015, the proportion of people without sustainable access to safe drinking water and basic sanitation

Indicator 7.8
Proportion of population using an improved drinking water source
(Percentage)

	1990			2008		
	Total	Urban	Rural	Total	Urban	Rural
World	77	95	64	87	96	78
Developing regions	72	93	60	84	94	76
Northern Africa	86	94	78	92	95	87
Sub-Saharan Africa	49	83	36	60	83	47
Latin America and the Caribbean	85	95	63	93	97	80
Eastern Asia	69	97	56	89	98	82
Eastern Asia excluding China	96	97	93	98	100	91
Southern Asia	75	91	69	87	95	83
Southern Asia excluding India	82	95	77	85	93	80
South-Eastern Asia	72	92	63	86	92	81
Western Asia	85	96	70	90	96	78
Oceania	51	92	38	50	92	37
Caucasus and Central Asia	88	96	80	88	97	80
Developed regions	98	100	96	99	100	97

Indicator 7.9
Proportion of population using an improved sanitation facility
(Percentage)

	1990			2008		
	Total	Urban	Rural	Total	Urban	Rural
World	54	77	36	61	76	45
Developing regions	42	65	29	53	68	40
Northern Africa	72	91	55	89	94	83
Sub-Saharan Africa	28	43	21	31	44	24
Latin America and the Caribbean	69	81	39	80	86	55
Eastern Asia	43	53	39	56	61	53
Eastern Asia excluding China	100	100	100	97	99	92
Southern Asia	25	56	13	36	57	26
Southern Asia excluding India	42	74	30	50	65	42
South-Eastern Asia	46	69	36	69	79	60
Western Asia	79	96	53	85	94	67
Oceania	55	85	46	53	81	45
Caucasus and Central Asia	91	96	86	95	96	95
Developed regions	97	99	93	97	99	92

Target 7.D
By 2020, to have achieved a significant improvement in the lives of at least 100 million slum-dwellers

Indicator 7.10
Proportion of urban population living in slums^a
(Percentage)

	1990	2000	2010
Developing regions	46.1	39.3	32.7
Northern Africa	34.4	20.3	13.3
Sub-Saharan Africa	70.0	65.0	61.7
Latin America and the Caribbean	33.7	29.2	23.5
Eastern Asia	43.7	37.4	28.2
Southern Asia	57.2	45.8	35.0
South-Eastern Asia	49.5	39.6	31.0
Western Asia	22.5	20.6	24.6
Oceania	24.1	24.1	24.1

^{a} Represented by the urban population living in households with at least one of the following four characteristics: lack of access to improved drinking water; lack of access to improved sanitation; overcrowding (three or more persons per room); and dwellings made of non-durable material. Half of pit latrines are considered improved sanitation. These new figures are not comparable with previously published estimates in which all households using pit latrines were considered slum households.

GOAL 8
Develop a global partnership for development

Target 8.A
Develop further an open, rule-based, predictable, non-discriminatory trading and financial system

Includes a commitment to good governance, development and poverty reduction—both nationally and internationally

Target 8.B
Address the special needs of the least developed countries

Includes tariff- and quota-free access for least developed countries' exports; enhanced programme of debt relief for heavily indebted poor countries (HIPC) and cancellation of official bilateral debt; and more generous official development assistance (ODA) for countries committed to poverty reduction

Target 8.C
Address the special needs of landlocked developing countries and small island developing States (through the Programme of Action for the Sustainable Development of Small Island Developing States and the outcome of the twenty-second special session of the General Assembly)

Target 8.D
Deal comprehensively with the debt problems of developing countries through national and international measures in order to make debt sustainable in the long term

Official development assistance

Indicator 8.1
Net ODA, total and to the least developed countries, as a percentage of Organization for Economic Cooperation and Development/Development Assistance Committee (OECD/DAC) donors' gross national income

(a) Annual total assistance[a]
(Billions of United States dollars)

	1990	2002	2006	2007	2008	2009	2010[b]
All developing countries	52.8	58.6	104.8	104.2	122.0	119.8	128.7
Least developed countries	15.1	16.7	29.7	32.3	37.8	37.4	

[a] Includes non-ODA debt forgiveness but excluding forgiveness of debt for military purposes.

[b] Preliminary data.

(b) Share of OECD/DAC donors' gross national income
(Percentage)

	1990	2002	2006	2007	2008	2009	2010[a]
All developing countries	0.32	0.23	0.30	0.27	0.30	0.31	0.32
Least developed countries	0.09	0.07	0.08	0.08	0.09	0.10	

[a] Preliminary data.

Indicator 8.2
Proportion of total bilateral, sector-allocable ODA of OECD/DAC donors to basic social services (basic education, primary health care, nutrition, safe water and sanitation)

	1999	2001	2003	2005	2007	2009
Percentage	10.1	14.0	15.7	15.9	19.9	21.0
Billions of United States dollars	3.1	3.5	5.8	8.2	12.4	16.7

Indicator 8.3
Proportion of bilateral official development assistance of OECD/DAC donors that is untied[a]

	1990	2003	2005	2006	2007	2008	2009
Percentage	67.6	91.1	91.4	88.3	83.9	86.6	84.4
Billions of United States dollars	16.3	30.1	49.0	62.2	60.3	80.5	71.1

[a] Excludes technical cooperation and administrative costs as well as ODA whose tying status is not reported. The percentage of bilateral ODA, excluding technical cooperation and administrative costs, with reported tying status was 99.6 in 2008.

Indicator 8.4
ODA received in landlocked developing countries as a proportion of their gross national incomes

	1990	2003	2005	2006	2007	2008	2009
Percentage	10.3	8.1	7.0	6.2	5.6	5.3	4.6
Billions of United States dollars	7.0	12.1	15.0	16.6	18.9	22.6	25.0

Indicator 8.5
ODA received in small island developing States as a proportion of their gross national incomes

	1990	2003	2005	2006	2007	2008	2009
Percentage	2.6	2.2	2.5	2.6	2.7	2.7	2.8
Billions of United States dollars	2.1	1.8	2.5	2.7	3.2	3.7	4.2

Market access

Indicator 8.6
Proportion of total developed country imports (by value and excluding arms) from developing countries and least developed countries, admitted free of duty
(Percentage)

	1996	2000	2005	2007	2009
(a) Excluding arms					
Developing countries[a]	53	63	76	82	82
of which, preferential[b]	16	14	17	16	16
Northern Africa	52	57	97	97	97
Sub-Saharan Africa	78	80	93	96	97
Latin America and the Caribbean	66	75	93	94	94
Eastern Asia	35	52	62	67	67
Southern Asia	47	48	58	72	69
South-Eastern Asia	59	75	77	80	79
Western Asia	34	39	66	96	97
Oceania	85	83	89	91	93
Caucasus and Central Asia	91	84	94	94	98
Least developed countries	68	75	83	89	89
of which, preferential[b]	29	42	28	27	29
(b) Excluding arms and oil					
Developing countries[a]	54	65	76	78	78
of which, preferential[b]	19	16	20	19	19
Northern Africa	20	26	95	95	94
Sub-Saharan Africa	88	83	91	93	95
Latin America and the Caribbean	73	81	93	93	93
Eastern Asia	35	52	62	67	67
Southern Asia	41	46	58	63	62
South-Eastern Asia	60	76	77	79	79
Western Asia	35	44	87	93	93
Oceania	82	79	87	89	92
Caucasus and Central Asia	90	69	84	82	90
Least developed countries	78	70	80	80	80
of which, preferential[b]	35	35	49	52	53

[a] Includes least developed countries.

[b] The true preference margin is calculated by subtracting from the total duty-free access all products receiving duty-free treatment under the most-favoured-nation regime. The indicators are based on the best available treatment, including regional and preferential agreements.

Indicator 8.7
Average tariffs imposed by developed countries on agricultural products and textiles and clothing from developing countries
(Percentage)

	1996	2000	2005	2009
(a) Excluding arms				
Developing countries	10.5	9.2	8.8	7.8

	1996	2000	2005	2009
Northern Africa	6.7	7.4	7.2	6.4
Sub-Saharan Africa	7.4	6.2	6.2	4.5
Latin America and the Caribbean	12.1	10.3	9.8	8.0
Eastern Asia	9.3	9.5	10.8	10.7
Southern Asia	5.4	5.4	4.5	5.5
South-Eastern Asia	11.4	10.2	9.2	9.0
Western Asia	8.2	7.5	5.0	5.3
Oceania	11.5	9.5	8.8	8.4
Caucasus and Central Asia	4.8	3.9	3.4	4.1
Least developed countries	3.8	3.6	3.0	1.2
(b) Textiles				
Developing countries	7.3	6.5	5.2	5.1
Northern Africa	8.0	7.2	4.4	3.9
Sub-Saharan Africa	3.9	3.4	2.9	2.9
Latin America and the Caribbean	4.7	3.5	1.5	1.3
Eastern Asia	7.3	6.7	5.8	5.8
Southern Asia	7.1	6.5	6.1	5.8
South-Eastern Asia	9.2	8.4	6.0	5.6
Western Asia	9.2	8.2	4.6	4.5
Oceania	5.9	5.3	4.9	4.9
Caucasus and Central Asia	7.3	6.3	5.8	5.7
Least developed countries	4.6	4.1	3.2	3.2
(c) Clothing				
Developing countries	11.4	10.8	8.3	8.1
Northern Africa	11.9	11.1	8.0	5.9
Sub-Saharan Africa	8.5	7.9	1.6	1.6
Latin America and the Caribbean	8.8	7.8	1.3	1.3
Eastern Asia	12.0	11.5	11.0	11.1
Southern Asia	10.2	9.6	8.6	8.6
South-Eastern Asia	14.2	13.6	10.5	9.4
Western Asia	12.6	11.8	8.5	8.3
Oceania	8.8	8.3	8.4	8.8
Caucasus and Central Asia	12.9	11.8	11.5	10.8
Least developed countries	8.2	7.8	6.4	6.4

Indicator 8.8
Agricultural support estimate for OECD countries as a percentage of their gross domestic product

	1990	2003	2005	2006	2007	2008	2009[a]
Percentage	1.86	1.12	1.04	0.95	0.87	0.86	0.93
Billions of United States dollars	327	340	369	358	362	379	384

[a] Preliminary data.

Indicator 8.9
Proportion of ODA provided to help build trade capacity[a]

	2001	2003	2005	2007	2008	2009
Trade policy and regulations and trade-related adjustment[b]	1.0	0.8	0.8	0.8	0.8	0.9
Economic infrastructure	21.5	14.8	17.2	13.6	18.7	15.1
Building productive capacity	16.0	13.4	12.8	13.3	14.8	12.9
TOTAL aid for trade	38.5	29.0	30.7	27.7	34.4	28.9

[a] Aid-for-trade proxies as a percentage of bilateral sector-allocable ODA, World.

[b] Reporting of trade-related adjustment data started in 2007. Only Canada and the European Commission reported.

Debt sustainability

Indicator 8.10
Total number of countries that have reached their HIPC decision points and number that have reached their HIPC completion points (cumulative)

	2000[a]	2011[b]
Reached completion point	1	32
Reached decision point but not completion point	21	4
Yet to be considered for decision point	12	4
TOTAL eligible countries	**34**	**40**

[a] Includes only countries that are heavily indebted poor countries in 2011. Data for 2000 reflect status as of end of each year.

[b] As of March 2011.

Indicator 8.11
Debt relief committed under HIPC and Multilateral Debt Relief initiatives[a]
(Billions of United States dollars, cumulative)

	2000	2011
To countries that reached decision or completion point	32	90

[a] Expressed in end-2009 net present value terms; commitment status as of March 2011.

Indicator 8.12
Debt service as a percentage of exports of goods and services[a]

	1990	2000	2008	2009
Developing regions	18.7	12.5	3.4	3.6
Northern Africa	39.8	15.3	6.1	6.9
Sub-Saharan Africa	11.4	9.4	2.0	3.1
Latin America and the Caribbean	20.6	21.8	6.8	7.2
Caribbean	16.8	8.0	11.4	14.6
Latin America	20.7	22.2	6.7	7.1
Eastern Asia	10.5	5.1	0.6	0.6
Southern Asia	17.6	13.7	5.2	3.5
Southern Asia excluding India	9.3	11.5	7.7	9.8
South-Eastern Asia	16.7	6.5	3.0	4.0
Western Asia	26.4	16.2	9.2	9.0
Oceania	14.0	5.9	2.8	1.9
Caucasus and Central Asia	0.62[b]	8.4	0.6	1.0
Least developed countries	16.8	11.4	2.9	5.6
Landlocked developing countries	14.4	8.6	1.3	1.9
Small island developing States	13.7	8.7	7.6	9.5

[a] Includes countries reporting to the World Bank Debtor Reporting System. Aggregates are based on available data, and for some years, might exclude countries that do not have data on exports of goods and services and net income from abroad.

[b] Data are for 1993.

Target 8.E
In cooperation with pharmaceutical companies, provide access to affordable, essential drugs in developing countries

Indicator 8.13
Proportion of population with access to affordable essential drugs on a sustainable basis

No global or regional data are available.

Target 8.F
In cooperation with the private sector, make available the benefits of new technologies, especially information and communications

Indicator 8.14
Number of fixed telephone lines per 100 population

	1990	2000	2009
Word	9.8	15.9	17.5
Developing regions	2.3	7.9	12.2
Northern Africa	2.8	7.1	11.3
Sub-Saharan Africa	1.0	1.4	1.5
Latin America and the Caribbean	6.3	14.7	18.2
Caribbean	7.0	11.2	10.7
Latin America	6.2	15.0	18.8
Eastern Asia	2.4	13.8	24.8
Eastern Asia excluding China	24.8	42.8	43.9
Southern Asia	0.7	3.2	4.3
Southern Asia excluding India	1.0	3.4	7.1
South-Eastern Asia	1.3	4.8	12.4
Western Asia	8.6	16.5	15.3
Oceania	3.3	5.2	5.4
Caucasus and Central Asia	7.9	8.8	12.5
Developed regions	37.0	49.2	41.5
Least developed countries	0.3	0.5	1.0
Landlocked developing countries	2.4	2.8	3.9
Small island developing States	7.9	12.9	12.2

Indicator 8.15
Cellular subscribers per 100 population

	1995	2000	2009
World	1.6	12.1	68.4
Developing regions	0.4	5.4	58.2
Northern Africa	<0.1	2.7	79.7
Sub-Saharan Africa	0.1	1.7	37.3
Latin America and the Caribbean	0.8	12.3	89.4
Caribbean	1.2	7.4	54.2
Latin America	0.8	12.6	92.1
Eastern Asia	0.5	9.9	57.8
Eastern Asia excluding China	3.4	49.9	86.8
Southern Asia	<0.1	0.4	44.7
Southern Asia excluding India	<0.1	0.5	46.7
South-Eastern Asia	0.7	4.3	79.5
Western Asia	0.6	12.7	87.0
Oceania	0.2	2.4	25.2
Caucasus and Central Asia	<0.1	1.3	74.9
Developed regions	6.4	39.8	114.3
Least developed countries	<0.1[a]	0.3	26.2
Landlocked developing countries	<0.1	1.1	34.7
Small island developing States	1.5	11.0	57.5

[a] 1996 data.

Indicator 8.16
Internet users per 100 population

	1995	2000	2009
World	0.8	6.6	26.5
Developing regions	0.1	2.1	18.0
Northern Africa	<0.1	0.7	25.2
Sub-Saharan Africa	0.1	0.5	8.9
Latin America and the Caribbean	0.1	3.9	32.9
Caribbean	0.1	2.9	22.3
Latin America	0.1	4.0	33.7
Eastern Asia	0.1	3.8	31.0
Eastern Asia excluding China	1.1	28.7	57.9
Southern Asia	<0.1	0.5	5.6
Southern Asia excluding India	<0.1[a]	0.3	6.6
South-Eastern Asia	0.1	2.4	15.2
Western Asia	0.1	3.2	27.0
Oceania	0.1	1.8	6.4
Caucasus and Central Asia	<0.1	0.5	18.8
Developed regions	3.2	25.1	64.9
Least developed countries	<0.1[b]	0.1	2.7
Landlocked developing countries	<0.1[a]	0.3	7.1
Small island developing States	0.4	5.2	22.3

[a] 1996 data.
[b] 1998 data.

Notes

Sources: United Nations Inter-Agency and Expert Group on Millennium Development Goals Indicators and Millennium Development Goal Indicators Database (http://mdgs.un.org).

Notes: Except where indicated, regional groupings are based on United Nations geographical regions, with some modifications necessary to create, to the extent possible, homogeneous groups of countries for analysis and presentation. The regional composition adopted for 2011 reporting on Millennium Development Goal indicators is available at http://mdgs.un.org, under "Data".

Where shown, "Developed regions" comprises Europe (including Commonwealth of Independent States—Europe countries), Australia, Canada, Israel, Japan, New Zealand and the United States of America.

Where shown, "Caucasus and Central Asia" comprises Armenia, Azerbaijan, Georgia, Kazakhstan, Kyrgyzstan, Tajikistan, Turkmenistan and Uzbekistan.

PART ONE

Political and security questions

Chapter I

International peace and security

Peacekeeping, peacebuilding, economic recovery in post-conflict countries and counter-terrorism strategies were among the key challenges addressed by the United Nations in 2011. During the year, the Security Council issued statements on post-conflict peacebuilding, the interdependence between security and development, threats to international peace and security caused by terrorist acts, the impact of climate change on maintaining peace and security, and conflict prevention.

At the end of 2011, there were 15 peacekeeping operations served by 119,348 uniformed and civilian personnel, including United Nations Volunteers. On 8 July, the United Nations Mission in South Sudan (UNMISS) was established to succeed the United Nations Mission in the Sudan (UNMIS), which completed its mandate on 9 July. The Council, concerned by the situation in the Abyei Area and recognizing that it constituted a threat to international peace and security, established, for an initial period of six months commencing 27 June, the United Nations Interim Security Force for Abyei (UNISFA).

At year's end, the United Nations was carrying out 13 political or peacebuilding missions, served by 4,284 personnel. The United Nations Mission in Nepal (UNMIN) ended on 15 January.

Acts of international terrorism continued, resulting in the deaths of hundreds of innocent civilians and injuries to many others, including in Afghanistan, Belarus, Burundi, Iraq, Israel, Lebanon, Morocco, Nigeria, Norway, Pakistan, Russian Federation, Somalia, South Sudan and the Syrian Arab Republic. In Nigeria, a 26 August attack on the United Nations House in Abuja caused numerous deaths and injuries. A 19 August suicide attack on a mosque in the Khyber region in Pakistan reportedly killed more than 40 people and injured over 100. The Security Council and the Secretary-General condemned those and other attacks.

Throughout 2011, the United Nations continued to work to prevent and combat all forms of terrorism. In November, the United Nations Counter-Terrorism Centre was established at United Nations Headquarters in New York to promote the implementation of the United Nations Global Counter-Terrorism Strategy through the Counter-Terrorism Implementation Task Force. The General Assembly reiterated its commitment to strengthening international cooperation to prevent and combat terrorism in all its forms and manifestations. In December, the Assembly condemned all acts, methods and practices of terrorism, and reiterated its call on Member States to refrain from financing, encouraging, providing training for or otherwise supporting terrorist activities.

The Assembly adopted resolutions on strengthening the role of mediation in the peaceful settlement of disputes, conflict prevention and resolution, cross-cutting issues, strengthening the capacity of the United Nations to manage and sustain peacekeeping operations, reformed procedures for determining reimbursement to Member States for contingent-owned equipment, closed peacekeeping missions, the comprehensive review of peacekeeping operations in all their aspects, the financing of the United Nations Logistics Base at Brindisi and the criminal accountability of United Nations officials and experts on missions.

Regarding the financial position of UN peacekeeping operations, expenditures decreased by 0.6 per cent, from $7,616.1 million to $7,573.7 million for the 2010/2011 financial year. Unpaid assessed contributions increased by 6.5 per cent, from $907.1 million at the end of 2009/2010 to $965.8 million at the end of 2010/2011.

Promotion of international peace and security

Maintenance of international peace and security

Security sector reform

Special Committee on Peacekeeping Operations consideration. During its 2011 substantive session (New York, 22 February–18 March and 9 May) [A/65/19], the Special Committee on Peacekeeping Operations emphasized the importance of security sector reform in peacekeeping operations and stressed that reform had to take place within the framework of the rule of law. Given increased demands on the Security Sector Reform Unit, the Committee encouraged the UN Secretariat, funds, agencies and programmes to enhance the Unit's capacity and requested the Unit to provide a briefing on its activities. The Committee supported the development of a UN roster of senior security reform experts, but underlined the need for the Unit to ensure that the roster reflected the capacities of developing countries, particularly from unrepresented regions. The Unit was requested to provide an analysis of the roster's performance at its 2012 session.

Security Council consideration. On 12 October, the Council held a high-level open debate [S/PV.6630] on moving forward with security sector reform: prospects and challenges in Africa. It had before it a concept note [S/2011/627] submitted by Nigeria. The Council was briefed by the Under-Secretary-General for Peacekeeping Operations, Hervé Ladsous, who said that over the previous few years, the demand for security sector support had increased exponentially and had become an integral part of the mandate of many new UN missions, several of which were in Africa. There was no single approach to security sector reform, and the United Nations and its partners should be adaptable. The African Union (AU), with the support of regional economic communities and the Security Sector Reform Unit, was at the forefront of developing a specific reform framework; other regions were encouraged to do the same. Many Member States recognized that security sector governance was necessary for early recovery from conflict, economic development and sustainable peacebuilding, as well as regional stability and international peacekeeping. Experience had shown that security sector reform was a crucial preventive tool.

SECURITY COUNCIL ACTION

On 12 October [meeting 6630], following consultations among Security Council members, the President made statement **S/PRST/2011/19** on behalf of the Council:

The Security Council recalls the statements by its President of 20 February 2007 and 12 May 2008, and the report of the Secretary-General entitled "Securing peace and development: the role of the United Nations in supporting security sector reform" of 23 January 2008, and emphasizes that the establishment of an effective, professional and accountable security sector is at the cornerstone of peace and sustainable development. Equally, security sector reform underscores that effectiveness, accountability and good governance are mutually reinforcing elements of security.

The Council notes that the bulk of the international community's assistance in the area of security sector reform takes place in and is directed to countries in Africa. At the same time, a number of African countries are becoming important providers of such assistance. The Council welcomes this intra-African collaboration and emphasizes that there is a need to expand the consideration given to African perspectives on security sector reform. This includes enhancing cooperation with regional and subregional organizations, as well as sharing knowledge and experience with women and members of civil society. Focusing security sector reform efforts on the needs and priorities of populations in post-conflict countries will considerably enhance the legitimacy, viability and sustainability of such support.

The Council recognizes that security sector reform is a long-term process and reiterates the sovereign right and primary responsibility of the country concerned to determine its national approach and priorities for security sector reform. It should be a nationally owned process that is rooted in the particular needs and conditions of the country in question. The successful coordination of security sector reform efforts must be based on national consensus and driven by political leadership and political will to progress reform. In this regard, the Council underlines the responsibility of States to coordinate security sector reform support, including but not limited to establishing a strategic vision and the parameters for reform, identifying gaps and needs, prioritizing areas for technical support and avoiding duplication of donor efforts.

The Council encourages reforming States, while taking into account their capacity constraints, to strive to allocate national resources to security sector reform efforts to ensure the long-term sustainability and viability of such reform. In this context, the Council emphasizes the importance of improving women's participation in discussions pertinent to the prevention and resolution of conflict and the maintenance of peace and security, and encourages women to participate in the national armed and security forces in accordance with relevant international law. In this regard, the Council encourages the development of a security sector that is accessible and responsive to all, including women and other vulnerable groups.

The Council recognizes the importance of regional frameworks as a foundation for multilateral security sector reform efforts. In this regard, the Council welcomes the partnership between the United Nations and the African Union in developing a continental security sector reform policy framework, for its implementation. The Council encourages other regions to consider establishing such partnerships in order to better facilitate the exchange of lessons learned and best practices, as well as develop regional frameworks for security sector reform support, reflecting the participation of regional and subregional organizations. The Council also recognizes the support provided by bilateral actors, as well as regional actors, including the European Union, to security sector reform efforts in Africa and other initiatives in the area of security sector reform in Africa carried out by organizations such as the Economic Community of West African States and the Community of Portuguese-speaking Countries.

The Council recalls the previous statements by its President concerning the need for early and adequate support in priority areas of peacebuilding, including security sector reform, as well as the importance of security sector reform programmes for conflict prevention. In the light of ongoing conflict in Africa, the Council reiterates the link between security sector reform and socioeconomic development, and underlines that such reform efforts should be situated within the broader and more comprehensive spectrum of peacebuilding. In this regard, the Council emphasizes the important role of the Peacebuilding Commission and the Peacebuilding Fund in supporting security sector reform, including in African countries. The Council encourages the Commission to continue to promote coordination among and between national and external actors involved in security sector reform in the countries on its agenda.

The Council underlines that United Nations support to security sector reform must take place within a broad framework of the rule of law and should contribute to the overall strengthening of the United Nations rule of law activities as well as wider reconstruction and development efforts. This will require continued coordination with relevant United Nations actors to ensure an increasingly coherent approach. In this context, the Council stresses the need for security sector reform efforts to be cognizant of the issue of impunity.

The Council notes that peacekeeping has evolved significantly over the past decades from primarily monitoring ceasefires to complex multidimensional operations which seek to undertake peacebuilding tasks and address underlying causes of conflict. In this regard, the Council notes that an increasing number of peacekeeping and special political missions are mandated to support national security sector reform programmes, including those in Africa, through strategic assistance to develop security sector frameworks and capacity-building of the security and law enforcement institutions in key areas, including training in human rights, child protection and protection from sexual and gender-based violence. The Council stresses the need to continue to include, as appropriate, security sector reform aspects as an integral part of the planning of United Nations operations.

The Council recognizes the important role that the United Nations has played in supporting national efforts to build sustainable security institutions, and commends the efforts of the United Nations, in particular the Department of Peacekeeping Operations of the Secretariat, including the Security Sector Reform Unit and the United Nations Inter-Agency Security Sector Reform Task Force, in further strengthening a comprehensive United Nations approach to security sector reform, through the development of guidance and civilian capacities, coordination mechanisms and collaboration with regional and subregional organizations, in particular the African Union.

The Council requests the Secretary-General to submit, by early 2013, an assessment of the United Nations support for security sector reform, including those efforts in Africa, and to make recommendations on how best to strengthen the United Nations comprehensive approach to security sector reform, taking into account the linkages between United Nations assistance and conflict prevention and peacebuilding, and also taking into consideration the views of relevant United Nations organs and actors.

Mediation and settlement of disputes

In June, the General Assembly considered the role of mediation in the peaceful settlement of disputes, conflict prevention and resolution. It had before it the Secretary-General's 2009 report on enhancing mediation and its support activities [YUN 2009, p. 38], which was submitted in response to presidential statement S/PRST/2008/36 [YUN 2008, p. 40].

GENERAL ASSEMBLY ACTION

On 22 June [meeting 102], the General Assembly adopted **resolution 65/283** [draft: A/65/L.79 & Add.1] without vote [agenda item 33].

Strengthening the role of mediation in the peaceful settlement of disputes, conflict prevention and resolution

The General Assembly,

Guided by the purposes and principles enshrined in the Charter of the United Nations,

Reaffirming its commitment to respect the sovereignty, territorial integrity and political independence of all States,

Recalling Chapter VI, including Article 33, paragraph 1, of the Charter, and other Articles relevant to mediation,

Bearing in mind its responsibilities, functions and powers under the Charter, and thus recalling all its relevant resolutions in matters related to the peaceful settlement of disputes, conflict prevention and resolution, including through mediation,

Reaffirming its commitment to uphold the sovereign equality of all States, respect for their territorial integrity and political independence and the duty of Member States to refrain in their international relations from the threat or use of force in any manner inconsistent with the purposes and principles of the United Nations, and to uphold the resolution of disputes by peaceful means and in conformity with the principles of justice and international law, the right to self-determination of peoples which remain under colonial domination or foreign occupation, non-interference in the internal affairs of States, respect for human rights and fundamental freedoms, respect for the equal rights of all without distinction as to race, sex, language or religion, international cooperation in solving international problems of an economic, social, cultural or humanitarian character and the fulfilment in good faith of the obligations assumed in accordance with the Charter,

Bearing in mind that armed and other types of conflicts and terrorism, in all its forms and manifestations, and hostage-taking still persist in many parts of the world,

Recalling its resolution 57/337 of 3 July 2003 on the prevention of armed conflict and the 2005 World Summit Outcome which recognizes the important role of the good offices of the Secretary-General, including in the mediation of disputes, and which supports the efforts of the Secretary-General in strengthening his capacity in this area,

Taking note of the report of the Secretary-General of 8 April 2009 on enhancing mediation and its support activities,

Reaffirming the respective role and authority of the General Assembly and the Security Council in the maintenance of international peace and security in accordance with the Charter,

Recalling all relevant General Assembly resolutions and Security Council presidential statements related to mediation,

Recognizing the growing interest in and the provision of mediation, and its use as a promising and cost-effective tool in the peaceful settlement of disputes, conflict prevention and resolution, without prejudice to other means mentioned in Chapter VI of the Charter, including the use of arbitration and the roles and functions of the International Court of Justice,

Recognizing also the useful role that mediation can play in preventing disputes from escalating into conflicts and conflicts from escalating further, as well as in advancing the resolution of conflicts and thus preventing and/or reducing human suffering and creating conditions conducive to lasting peace and sustainable development, and in this regard, recognizing that peace and development are mutually reinforcing,

Emphasizing that justice is a fundamental building block of sustainable peace,

Reaffirming its commitment to the purposes and principles of the Charter and international law, which are indispensable foundations of a more peaceful, prosperous and just world, and reiterating its determination to foster strict respect for them and to establish a just and lasting peace all over the world,

Recalling that the peaceful settlement of disputes, conflict prevention and resolution, in accordance with the Charter and international law, including through mediation, remain a primary responsibility of Member States without prejudice to Article 36 of the Charter,

Stressing the importance of mediation activities in peacebuilding and recovery processes, in particular in preventing post-conflict countries from relapsing into conflict, and in this regard recognizing the advisory role of the Peacebuilding Commission in supporting peace efforts in countries on its agenda,

Recalling the good offices of the Secretary-General and his efforts, through the Department of Political Affairs of the Secretariat and its Mediation Support Unit, to develop United Nations mediation capacities in accordance with agreed mandates,

Reaffirming the role of regional and subregional organizations in the maintenance of international peace and security as set out in Chapter VIII of the Charter, and taking note of their important role as mediators, in many regions, acting with the consent of parties to a particular dispute or conflict,

Recognizing national and civil society actors active in mediation, and encouraging their contributions, when appropriate, in this regard,

Recognizing also the necessity for cooperation and coordination among the actors involved in a specific mediation context, as well as the need to build capacity for mediation activities,

Welcoming different initiatives for mediation, including the mediation for peace initiative, as a step towards strengthening the role of mediation in the peaceful settlement of disputes, conflict prevention and resolution,

Recognizing the importance of the full and effective participation of women at all levels, at all stages and in all aspects of the peaceful settlement of disputes, conflict prevention and resolution, as well as the provision of adequate gender expertise for all mediators and their teams, noting that further efforts are necessary to address the lack of women as chief or lead peace mediators, and in this context reaffirming the full and effective implementation of all relevant United Nations resolutions and the Beijing Declaration and Platform for Action, and furthermore welcoming the role of the United Nations Entity for Gender Equality and the Empowerment of Women (UN-Women) in this respect,

1. *Reiterates* that all Member States should strictly adhere to their obligations as laid down in the Charter of the United Nations, including in the peaceful settlement of disputes, conflict prevention and resolution;

2. *Invites* Member States, as appropriate, to optimize the use of mediation and other tools mentioned in Chapter VI of the Charter for the peaceful settlement of disputes, conflict prevention and resolution;

3. *Welcomes* the contributions of Member States to mediation efforts, as appropriate, and encourages them, where appropriate, to develop national mediation capacities, as applicable, in order to ensure coherent mediation and responsiveness;

4. *Encourages* Member States, in this regard, to promote equal, full and effective participation of women in all forums and at all levels of the peaceful settlement of disputes, conflict prevention and resolution, particularly the decision-making level;

5. *Also encourages* Member States, as appropriate, to use the mediation capacities of the United Nations as well as those of regional and subregional organizations, where applicable, and to promote mediation in their bilateral and multilateral relations;

6. *Invites* all Member States to consider providing timely and adequate resources for mediation, in order to assure its success, as well as for mediation capacity-building activities of the United Nations and of regional and subregional organizations, with a view to ensuring the sustainability and predictability of all catalytic resources;

7. *Requests* the Secretary-General to continue to offer good offices, in accordance with the Charter and relevant United Nations resolutions, and to continue to provide mediation support, where appropriate, to special representatives and envoys of the United Nations and to enhance partnerships with regional and subregional organizations, as well as Member States;

8. *Stresses* the importance of well-trained, impartial, experienced and geographically diverse mediation process and substance experts at all levels to ensure the timely and highest quality support to mediation efforts, supports the efforts of the Secretary-General in maintaining an updated roster of mediators, and encourages the continuing efforts to improve its gender balance and equitable geographical representation;

9. *Encourages* the Secretary-General to appoint women as chief or lead mediators in United Nations-sponsored peace processes, as well as to ensure adequate gender expertise for all United Nations processes;

10. *Recommends* that the Secretary-General, in accordance with mandates agreed upon by Member States, continue to strengthen the mediation capacities of the United Nations system, in particular the Mediation Support Unit of the Department of Political Affairs, and its responsiveness, in accordance with agreed mandates and fully taking into account existing United Nations activities and structures, including in the fields of rule of law and accountability, so as to avoid duplication;

11. *Requests* the Secretary-General, in consultation with Member States and other relevant actors, to develop guidance for more effective mediation, taking into account, inter alia, lessons learned from past and ongoing mediation processes;

12. *Recognizes* that responsible and credible mediation requires, inter alia, the consent of parties to a particular dispute or conflict, the impartiality of the mediators, their compliance with agreed mandates, respect for national sovereignty, compliance with obligations of States and other relevant actors under international law, including applicable treaties, and the operational preparedness, including process and substantive expertise, of the mediators;

13. *Welcomes* the efforts of the Secretary-General to assist Member States and relevant regional and subregional organizations, upon request, in mediation capacity-building for the peaceful settlement of disputes, conflict prevention and resolution, and calls upon the Secretary-General to continue these efforts, in accordance with agreed mandates;

14. *Stresses* the importance of partnerships and cooperation of international, regional and subregional organizations with the United Nations, with each other and with civil society, and of developing mechanisms to improve information-sharing, cooperation and coordination in order to ensure the coherence and complementarity of efforts of actors involved in a specific mediation context;

15. *Invites* relevant international, regional and subregional organizations, as well as civil society, to develop mediation capacities and structures, as appropriate, as well as resource mobilization, and encourages them to follow United Nations guidance for effective mediation;

16. *Welcomes* the efforts of the African Union in developing its mediation capacities and structures, in particular its early warning assessment systems and prevention and response capabilities;

17. *Requests* the Secretary-General to submit a report on the implementation of the present resolution for consideration by Member States at the sixty-sixth session of the General Assembly and to include the views of Member States and other relevant actors, as well as guidance for more effective mediation, as an annex to the report, and requests the Secretary-General to hold regular briefings on this issue in order to promote closer consultation with Member States and increase transparency;

18. *Decides* to include in the provisional agenda of its sixty-sixth session, under the item entitled "Prevention of armed conflict", a sub-item entitled "Strengthening the role of mediation in the peaceful settlement of disputes, conflict prevention and resolution".

Preventive diplomacy

Pursuant to presidential statement S/PRST/2010/14 [YUN 2010, p. 43], the Secretary-General submitted an August report [S/2011/552] entitled "Preventive diplomacy: delivering results". The report examined opportunities and challenges the United Nations and its partners faced in conducting preventive diplomacy in a changing political and security landscape. Focusing on diplomatic action to prevent or mitigate the spread of armed conflict, the report described the relevance of preventive diplomacy in conflicts and as part of nationally owned strategies to promote peace. It highlighted the growing expectations placed on the UN system in the area of conflict prevention and, in that regard, stressed the importance of partnerships. The report identified six key elements that proved critical in maximizing the success of preventive diplomacy efforts on the ground: early warning, flexibility, partnerships, sustainability, evaluation and resources. It also examined issues related to the roles of the Peacebuilding Commission; the Secretary-General's good offices; envoys appointed by the Secretary-General; regional offices, which served as forward platforms for preventive diplomacy in West Africa, Central Asia and Central Africa; resident political missions; peacekeeping operations; groups of friends and contact groups; fact-finding inquiries and investigations; and UN country teams.

The Secretary-General said that in the face of political tension or escalating crises, preventive diplomacy might be one of few options available to preserve peace. The biggest return of preventive diplomacy came in lives saved, but prevention also made strong economic sense, as armed conflicts imposed great costs on societies. Through its norm-setting capacity and deliberative functions, the General Assembly played a central role in conflict prevention. Its adoption of resolution 65/283 (see, p. 35) positioned the Organization as a setter of standards for mediation, providing a broad framework for collaboration with Member States, regional organizations and other mediation actors. In the past, the Security Council focused largely on dealing with conflicts and emergencies after they occurred, but in recent years, greater engagement and flexibility had been called for in addressing emerging threats before they were placed on the Council's formal agenda. The United Nations had deepened existing or established new conflict-prevention and mediation partnerships with the African Union, the European Union, the Caribbean Community the Organization of Islamic Cooperation and other organizations. Cooperation with the World Bank and other financial institutions had grown, and the United Nations was forging closer links with independent mediators and civil society.

The Secretary-General concluded with recommendations to strengthen international capacity for preventive diplomacy. The establishment of regular and informal early warning dialogues between the United Nations and regional partners in order to pool information would help in anticipating "threshold moments" when actors could decide to use violence. The United Nations had to invest in and better equip "preventive diplomats" to lead efforts to avert violent conflict. The pool of envoys and mediators who could be deployed rapidly to situations of concern needed to be expanded and the number of senior female mediators increased. A longer-term priority was to invest in the training of staff to support senior envoys and mediators. The Secretary-General appealed to Member States to ensure predictable financial support for preventive diplomacy. The United Nations needed to strengthen partnerships with regional and subregional organizations, Member States and civil society in the area of conflict prevention. Internationally led preventive diplomacy might serve only to avert violence in the short term; only national mechanisms and institutions could sustainably prevent conflict in the long term. The Secretary-General concluded that preventive diplomacy was delivering results with modest resources in many parts of the world, saving lives and protecting development gains. He believed that better preventive diplomacy was necessary.

Security Council consideration. On 22 September [S/PV.6621], the Security Council convened a high-level meeting on conflict prevention. It had before it the Secretary-General's August report on preventive diplomacy (see above) and a concept note submitted by Lebanon on 12 September [S/2011/570].

SECURITY COUNCIL ACTION

On 22 September [meeting 6621], following consultations among Security Council members, the President made statement **S/PRST/2011/18** on behalf of the Council:

The Security Council recalls its previous relevant resolutions and the statements by its President on preventive diplomacy, the prevention of armed conflict, and mediation and the peaceful settlement of disputes.

The Council welcomes the report of the Secretary-General entitled "Preventive diplomacy: delivering results", and takes note of the recommendations contained therein.

The Council reaffirms its primary responsibility for the maintenance of international peace and security, acting in accordance with the purposes and principles of the Charter of the United Nations. The Council further expresses its determination to enhance the effectiveness of the United Nations in preventing the eruption of armed conflicts, their escalation or spread when they occur, and their resurgence once they end.

The Council underlines the overriding political, humanitarian and moral imperatives as well as the economic advantages of preventing the outbreak or escalation of or relapse into conflicts.

The Council recalls that the prevention of conflict remains a primary responsibility of States, and further recalls their primary responsibility to respect and ensure the human rights of all individuals within their territory and subject to their jurisdiction, as provided for by relevant international law, and also reaffirms the responsibility of each individual State to protect its population from genocide, war crimes, ethnic cleansing and crimes against humanity.

The Council reaffirms that actions undertaken within the framework of conflict prevention by the United Nations should support and complement, as appropriate, the conflict prevention roles of national Governments.

The Council pays tribute to the efforts undertaken by the Secretary-General in using his good offices, and dispatching representatives, special envoys and mediators, to help to facilitate durable and comprehensive settlements. The Council encourages the Secretary-General to increasingly and effectively use all the modalities and diplomatic tools at his disposal under the Charter for the purpose of enhancing mediation and its support activities, and recalls in this regard General Assembly resolution 65/283 of 22 June 2011, as well as the report of the Secretary-General of 8 April 2009. The Council further encourages concerned parties to act in good faith when engaging with prevention and mediation efforts, including those undertaken by the United Nations.

The Council encourages the Secretary-General to continue improving coherence and consolidation within the United Nations system, with a view to maximizing the impact of swift and timely preventive efforts undertaken by the Organization. The Council underlines the importance of the regular briefings it receives on such efforts and further calls upon the Secretary-General to continue this good practice.

The Council recalls that a comprehensive conflict prevention strategy should include, inter alia, early warning, preventive deployment, mediation, peacekeeping, practical disarmament, accountability measures as well as post-conflict peacebuilding, and recognizes that these components are interdependent, complementary and non-sequential.

The Council recognizes that conflict prevention strategies should address the root causes of armed conflict, and political and social crises in a comprehensive manner, including by promoting sustainable development, poverty eradication, national reconciliation, good governance, democracy, gender equality, end of impunity, the rule of law and respect for and protection of human rights.

The Council encourages the peaceful settlement of local disputes through regional arrangements in accordance with Chapter VIII of the Charter. The Council acknowledges the efforts undertaken to strengthen operational and institutional cooperation between the United Nations and regional and subregional organizations for conflict prevention, and in this regard reiterates the need to continue strengthening strategic dialogue, partnerships and more regular exchange of views and information at the working level, with the aim of building national and regional capacities in relation to the preventive diplomacy tools of, inter alia, mediation, gathering and analysis of information, early warning, prevention and peacemaking.

The Council intends to continue to strengthen its partnerships with all other relevant players, both at the strategic level and on the ground, in particular the General Assembly, the Economic and Social Council, the Peacebuilding Commission and international financial institutions, such as the World Bank. The Security Council further intends to continue to strengthen its partnership with the United Nations regional offices.

The Council emphasizes that an effective preventive diplomacy framework requires the active involvement of civil society, especially youth, and other relevant actors, such as academia and the media. The Council also reaffirms the important role of women in the prevention and resolution of conflicts and in peacebuilding, and reiterates its call to increase the equal participation, representation and full involvement of women in preventive diplomacy efforts in line with resolutions 1325(2000), 1820(2008), 1888(2009) and 1889(2009) and the statements by its President of 13 and 26 October 2010.

The Council recognizes the importance of enhancing efforts, including coordination among relevant bilateral and multilateral donors, to ensure predictable, coherent and timely financial support to optimize the use of preventive diplomacy tools, including mediation, throughout the conflict cycle.

The Council looks forward to further consideration of the report of the Secretary-General entitled "Preventive diplomacy: Delivering results" by the General Assembly and the Economic and Social Council, as well as other actors, including international financial institutions, and supports strengthening the capacity of the United Nations and its partners in the field of preventive diplomacy.

Impact of HIV/AIDS on peace and security

On 7 June, the Security Council held a high-level debate [S/PV.6547] on the impact of the HIV/AIDS epidemic on international peace and security. It had before it a concept note [S/2011/340] submitted by Gabon on 6 June. The Council President said that the debate was intended to consider progress made since the adoption of resolution 1308(2000) [YUN 2000, p. 82], which underscored the threat posed by the disease to the staff of peacekeeping and peacebuilding missions.

SECURITY COUNCIL ACTION

On 7 June [meeting 6547], the Security Council unanimously adopted **resolution 1983(2011)**. The draft [S/2011/341] was submitted by Bosnia and Herzegovina, France, Gabon, Germany, Nigeria, Portugal, the United Kingdom and the United States.

The Security Council,

Deeply concerned that, in the thirty years since the beginning of the HIV epidemic, more than 60 million people have been infected, more than 25 million people have died and more than 16 million children have been orphaned by AIDS,

Recalling its meeting of 10 January 2000 on "The situation in Africa: the impact of AIDS on peace and security in Africa" and its subsequent meetings on "The responsibility of the Security Council in the maintenance of international peace and security: HIV/AIDS and international peacekeeping operations", and reaffirming its commitment to the continuing and full implementation, in a complementary manner, of all its relevant resolutions, including resolutions 1308(2000) of 17 July 2000, 1325(2000) of 31 October 2000, 1820(2008) of 19 June 2008, 1888(2009) of 30 September 2009, 1889(2009) of 5 October 2009, 1894(2009) of 11 November 2009 and 1960(2010) of 16 December 2010 and all relevant statements by its President,

Reaffirming the Declaration of Commitment on HIV/AIDS of 2001 and the Political Declaration on HIV/AIDS of 2006, including its commitment towards the goal of universal access to prevention, treatment, care and support, which will require renewed efforts at the local, national, regional and international levels,

Recalling the outcome document of the High-level Plenary Meeting of the General Assembly on the Millennium Development Goals and the report of the Special Committee on Peacekeeping Operations,

Taking note of the report of the Secretary-General on the implementation of the Declaration of Commitment and the Political Declaration,

Recognizing that HIV poses one of the most formidable challenges to the development, progress and stability of societies and requires an exceptional and comprehensive global response, and noting with satisfaction the unprecedented global response of Member States, public and private partnerships and non-governmental organizations and the important roles of civil society, communities and persons living with and affected by HIV in shaping the response,

Emphasizing the important roles of the General Assembly and the Economic and Social Council in addressing HIV and AIDS and the continuing need for coordinated efforts of all relevant United Nations entities, in line with their respective mandates, to assist in the global efforts against the epidemic,

Commending the efforts of the Joint United Nations Programme on HIV/AIDS to coordinate and intensify the global, regional, national and local response to HIV and AIDS in all appropriate forums, and the pivotal role of the Global Fund to Fight AIDS, Tuberculosis and Malaria in mobilizing and providing international assistance, including resources, to respond to HIV and AIDS,

Recognizing that the spread of HIV can have a uniquely devastating impact on all sectors and levels of society and that, in conflict and post-conflict situations, these impacts may be felt more profoundly,

Recognizing also that conditions of violence and instability in conflict and post-conflict situations can exacerbate the HIV epidemic, inter alia, through large movements of people, widespread uncertainty over conditions, conflict-related sexual violence and reduced access to medical care,

Recognizing further that women and girls are particularly affected by HIV,

Underlining the importance of concerted efforts towards ending conflict-related sexual and gender-based violence, empowering women in an effort to reduce their risk of exposure to HIV, and curbing vertical transmission of HIV from mother to child in conflict and post-conflict situations,

Noting that the protection of civilians by peacekeeping operations, where mandated, can contribute to an integrated response to HIV and AIDS, inter alia, through the prevention of conflict-related sexual violence,

Underlining the continuing negative impact of HIV on the health and fitness of United Nations mission personnel, and concerned that available statistics indicate that health-related issues have become a leading cause of fatality in the field since 2000,

Welcoming the efforts to implement HIV prevention, treatment, care and support, including voluntary and confidential testing and counselling programmes by many Member States for their uniformed personnel and by the United Nations for its civilian staff in preparation for deployment to United Nations missions,

Bearing in mind the primary responsibility of the Council for the maintenance of international peace and security,

1. *Underlines* that urgent and coordinated international action continues to be required to curb the impact of the HIV epidemic in conflict and post-conflict situations;

2. *Notes*, in this context, the need for effective and coordinated action at the local, national, regional and international levels to combat the epidemic and to mitigate its impact and the need for a coherent United Nations response to assist Member States to address this issue;

3. *Also notes* that the disproportionate burden of HIV and AIDS on women is one of the persistent obstacles and challenges to gender equality and empowerment of women, and urges Member States, United Nations entities, international financial institutions and other relevant stakeholders to support the development and strengthening of capacities of national health systems and civil society networks in order to provide sustainable assistance to women living with or affected by HIV in conflict and post-conflict situations;

4. *Recognizes* that United Nations peacekeeping operations can be important contributors to an integrated response to HIV and AIDS, welcomes the incorporation of HIV awareness in mandated activities and outreach projects for vulnerable communities, and encourages further such actions;

5. *Stresses* the importance of strong support by United Nations mission civilian and military leadership for HIV and AIDS prevention, treatment, care and support, as a factor for reducing the stigma and discrimination associated with HIV and AIDS;

6. *Requests* the Secretary-General to consider HIV-related needs of people living with, affected by and vulnerable to HIV, including women and girls, in his activities pertinent to the prevention and resolution of conflict, the maintenance of international peace and security, the prevention and response to sexual violence related to conflict, and post-conflict peacebuilding;

7. *Encourages* the incorporation, as appropriate, of HIV prevention, treatment, care and support, including voluntary and confidential counselling and testing programmes, in the implementation of mandated tasks of peacekeeping operations, including assistance to national institutions, to security sector reform and to disarmament, demobilization and reintegration processes; and the need to ensure the continuation of such prevention, treatment, care and support during and after transitions to other configurations of United Nations presence;

8. *Underlines* the need to intensify HIV prevention activities within United Nations missions, takes note of the "Department of Peacekeeping Operations/Department of Field Support Policy Directive on the Role and Functions of HIV/AIDS Units in United Nations Peacekeeping Operations", and requests the Secretary-General to ensure the implementation of HIV and AIDS awareness and prevention programmes for United Nations missions;

9. *Requests* the Secretary-General to continue and strengthen efforts to implement the policy of zero tolerance of sexual exploitation and abuse in United Nations missions;

10. *Welcomes and encourages* continued cooperation among Member States, through their relevant national bodies, for the development and implementation of sustainable HIV and AIDS prevention, treatment, care and support, capacity-building and programme and policy development for uniformed and civilian personnel to be deployed to United Nations missions;

11. *Invites* the Secretary-General to provide further information to the Security Council as appropriate.

The Secretary-General, addressing the Council following the adoption of resolution 1983(2011), said that the Joint United Nations Programme on HIV/AIDS (UNAIDS), the UN Department of Peacekeeping Operations (DPKO) and a number of Governments were training Blue Helmets (UN peacekeepers) and troops in various countries on HIV/AIDS-related matters. Predeployment HIV training was standard for UN personnel. The United Nations had trained more than 1,500 peacekeepers as peer counsellors. In five years, the number of Blue Helmets seeking voluntary counselling and testing increased from fewer than 2,000 to more than 14,000. The Council entrusted a broader mission to peacekeepers: to stop gender and sexual-based violence, enhance the role of women and protect children. Following the adoption of Council resolution 1308(2000) [YUN 2000, p. 82] concerning HIV/AIDS and peace and security, the United Nations understood that its troops and police were part of prevention, treatment and care. Council members were urged to link efforts against HIV/AIDS with UN campaigns against sexual violence and for the rights of women. Such efforts would include addressing the interaction between AIDS, the international drug trade, sex trafficking and the abuse of women.

The UNAIDS Executive Director, Michel Sidibé, also briefed the Council on the relationship between HIV/AIDS and international peace and security.

Security and development

On 11 February, the Council held a high-level debate [S/PV.6479] on the interdependence of security and development. It had before it a concept note [S/2011/50] submitted by Brazil. The Secretary-General, addressing the Council, said that peace, security and development were interdependent; political stability needed to be anchored in peace, opportunity, decent standards of living and the consent of the governed. He requested UN presences that had both a UN country team and a multidimensional peacekeeping operation or political mission to identify priority areas for peace consolidation and develop integrated strategic frameworks to guide their work in those areas in cooperation with the host countries. Five areas in which the Organization could do more to integrate security and development approaches were highlighted: a "whole of Government" approach applied by Member States across the multilateral system; better management of the process of drawdown and withdrawal of Council-mandated operations, and providing more seamless transitions of tasks to the UN country team and other development actors; finding innovative ways to strengthen national institutions in fragile countries; focusing more on the climate change-security-development nexus; and considering how to reduce criminal violence. The Council might wish to consider advancing strategies with the General Assembly to halt the illicit proliferation of small arms and ammunition, which was a standing threat to the security of ordinary people in many places around the world.

SECURITY COUNCIL ACTION

On 11 February [meeting 6479], following consultations among Security Council members, the President made statement **S/PRST/2011/4** on behalf of the Council:

> The Security Council reaffirms its primary responsibility under the Charter of the United Nations for the maintenance of international peace and security and its readiness to strive for sustainable peace in all situations under its consideration.
>
> The Council underlines that security and development are closely interlinked and mutually reinforcing and key to attaining sustainable peace. The Council recognizes that their relationship is complex, multifaceted and case-specific.
>
> The Council reiterates that, in order to support a country in emerging sustainably from conflict, there is a need for a comprehensive and integrated approach that incorporates and strengthens coherence between political, security, development, human rights and rule of law activities, and addresses the underlying causes of each conflict. In this regard, the Council affirms the necessity to consider relevant economic, political and social dimensions of conflict.
>
> The Council affirms that national ownership and national responsibility are key to establishing sustainable peace. The Council reaffirms the primary responsibility of national authorities in identifying their priorities and strategies for post-conflict peacebuilding, with a view to ensuring national ownership.
>
> The Council re-emphasizes the importance of considering and initiating peacebuilding activities from the earliest stages of planning and implementation of peacekeeping operations, including through clear and achievable mandates. The Council stresses the importance of clarity of roles and responsibilities of the United Nations peacekeeping operation and the United Nations country team and other relevant actors for the delivery of prioritized support to a country consistent with its specific peacebuilding needs and priorities, as outlined by national authorities, in order to ensure effective integration of effort. The Council recommends that particular focus be given to improved integration of United Nations efforts where peacekeeping missions are operating together with peacebuilding activities of other United Nations actors, such as in the Democratic Republic of the Congo and in the Sudan.
>
> The Council notes that successful implementation of the many tasks that peacekeeping operations could be mandated to undertake in the areas of security sector reform; disarmament, demobilization and reintegration; rule of law; and human rights requires an understanding of and acting with a perspective which takes into account the close interlinkage between security and development. In this context, the Council notes with appreciation the contribution that peacekeepers and peacekeeping missions make to early peacebuilding, including by creating a conducive environment which enables economic recovery and the provision of basic services. The Council acknowledges that this contribution can help to establish and build confidence in the mission.
>
> The Council undertakes to consider how peacekeeping operations can best support national authorities, as appropriate, to articulate peacebuilding priorities and, acting in accordance with these priorities, can both support other national and international actors to implement peacebuilding activities and undertake certain early peacebuilding tasks themselves. The Council underlines that reconstruction, economic revitalization and capacity-building constitute crucial elements for the long-term development of post-conflict societies and in generating sustainable peace, and in this regard attaches special importance to national ownership and stresses the significance of international assistance.
>
> The Council notes that, in matters relating to the maintenance of international peace and security under its consideration, conflict analysis and contextual information on, inter alia, social and economic issues is important, when such issues are drivers of conflict, represent a challenge to the implementation of Council mandates or endanger the process of consolidation of peace. In this regard, the Council requests the Secretary-General to ensure that his reporting to the Council contains such contextual information.
>
> The Council stresses the importance it attaches to the sustainability of peace in post-conflict situations. In this regard, it reaffirms that the overarching objective of peacekeeping missions should be to achieve success by creating the conditions for security and sustainable peace on the ground, thereby allowing for reconfiguration or withdrawal of the mission.
>
> The Council recalls the role played by the illegal exploitation of natural resources in fuelling some past and current conflicts. In this regard, it recognizes that the United Nations can play a role in helping the States concerned, as appropriate, upon their request and with full respect for their sovereignty over natural resources and under national ownership, to prevent illegal access to those resources and to lay the basis for their legal exploitation with a view to promoting development, in particular through the empowerment of Governments in post-conflict situations to better manage their resources.
>
> The Council encourages close cooperation within the United Nations system and with regional, subregional and other organizations on the ground and at Headquarters in order to properly engage in conflict and post-conflict situations, in accordance with its responsi-

bilities under the Charter, and expresses its willingness to consider ways to improve such cooperation.

The Council underlines that integrated action on the ground by security and development actors needs to be coordinated with the national authorities and can significantly contribute to stabilizing and improving the security situation and ensuring the protection of civilians. The Council also notes the importance of cooperation with civil society in this context. The Council affirms that sustainable peace and development cannot be achieved without the inclusion of all relevant stakeholders and underlines that women must be included as active participants in all stages of peacebuilding, peace agreements and development programmes. The Council expresses its willingness to engage in dialogue, where necessary, on specific situations on its agenda with other actors, including United Nations agencies, funds and programmes and international financial institutions.

The Council encourages Member States, particularly those represented on the governance structures of the United Nations agencies, funds and programmes, to promote coherence in the work of the United Nations in conflict and post-conflict situations.

The Council reiterates its support for the work of the Peacebuilding Commission and its readiness to make greater use of the advisory role of the Commission. The Council further recognizes the need for coordination and dialogue with the Commission. The Council calls upon the Commission to continue to promote an integrated and coherent approach to peacebuilding and to seek to ensure that development and security-related activities supported by the Commission are mutually reinforcing.

The Council highlights the contribution that the Economic and Social Council can make in addressing economic, social, cultural and humanitarian issues and underlines the importance of close cooperation in accordance with Article 65 of the Charter.

Climate change

On 20 July, the Security Council, in presidential statement **S/PRST/2011/15** (see p. 978), expressed its concern that possible adverse effects of climate change might aggravate certain existing threats to international peace and security, and that there could be security implications of the loss of territory of some States due to sea-level rise, particularly in small low-lying island States.

New challenges to international peace and security

On 23 November, the Council held a high-level debate [S/PV.6668] on new challenges to international peace and security and conflict prevention. It had before it a concept note [S/2011/698] submitted by Portugal on 8 November. The Secretary-General, addressing the Council, said that the threats of transnational organized crime, pandemics and climate change, while not new phenomena, were increasingly transnational and acute, and had ever greater implications for international security, as they undermined state capacity and institutions. The threats also had implications for the United Nations. No country or region could address the threats alone; they could only be dealt with through global and regional cooperation. The United Nations would continue to play a lead role in fostering such cooperation.

The Council was also briefed by the Executive Director of the United Nations Office on Drugs and Crime, Yury Fedotov; the United Nations High Commissioner for Refugees, António Guterres; and the Director-General of the World Health Organization, Margaret Chan.

Conflict prevention

Conflict diamonds

The Kimberley Process [YUN 2000, p. 76], at its ninth annual session (Kinshasa, Democratic Republic of the Congo, 31 October–3 November) continued its work related to the Kimberley Process Certification Scheme (KPCS), which was established in 2003 [YUN 2003, p. 55] to stop the trade in conflict diamonds from fuelling armed conflict, protect the legitimate diamond industry and ensure implementation of UN resolutions on trade in conflict diamonds. Swaziland joined the Kimberley Process in May. As at 3 November, KPCS had 50 members representing 76 countries, including the 27 members of the EU.

In accordance with General Assembly resolution 65/137 [YUN 2010, p. 49], the Democratic Republic of the Congo (DRC), acting in its capacity as chair of the Kimberley Process for 2011, transmitted to the Secretary-General on 6 December the 2011 Kimberley Process report [A/66/593]. The report stated that since its establishment, KPCS had contributed to the improvement of the security situations in several diamond-producing countries. Pursuant to Security Council resolution 1961(2010) [YUN 2010, p. 208], the Kimberley Process continued to monitor progress in the implementation of internal controls in Liberia. In response to Assembly resolution 65/137, the Process monitored the implementation of KPCS in West Africa; the Process stated that Guinea, in particular, had strengthened its certification system.

As at 3 November, 45 participants representing 71 countries had submitted their annual reports on KPCS implementation. Venezuela voluntarily withdrew from the Process in 2008 for two years, suspending its exports and imports of rough diamonds; in 2010, it extended its self-suspension for an additional year. In 2011, Venezuela presented to the Process a letter explaining the current status of its diamond mining operations and its development plans. Given the country's non-compliance with the minimum Kimberley Process requirements and its failure to submit annual reports in 2009 and 2010, however, the plenary decided Venezuela would be removed from the list of Process participants if it did not submit reports by 20 December.

The Working Group on Monitoring conducted a second series of peer review visits to producing countries (Botswana, Lesotho) and industrial countries (Ukraine and, in late 2010, India) to ensure that participants identified and remedied compliance issues, and to facilitate the sharing of best practices. The Process expressed concern regarding the increase in online sales and postal shipments of rough diamonds, given the difficulty of monitoring and analysing shipments of rough diamonds by those means. In such transactions, Kimberley Process certificates were not always transmitted to customs authorities, potentially affecting the quality of statistical data. The Process set up a team of experts coordinated by Canada to research online trading trends of rough diamonds.

The Working Group of Diamond Experts collaborated with the Liberia Kimberley Process authorities and the UN Group of Experts on Liberia on "footprinting" Liberian diamonds. The Working Group also worked on footprinting diamonds produced in the Bria region in the Central African Republic, the Marange region in Zimbabwe, and in Sierra Leone. Kimberley Process authorities in Brazil worked on footprinting Brazilian diamonds.

Civil society representatives decided not to participate in the Kinshasa plenary, despite the Chair's attempt to engage them in dialogue. Kimberley Process participants and other observers appealed to civil society to resume contacts with the Process and to participate in its work. Civil society participation was essential, especially in the light of the reform process and the periodic review being undertaken to improve KPCS. Reform and improvement of the Process, and the periodic review of KPCS, were among the greatest challenges. The United States would succeed the DRC as Kimberley Process Chair, with effect from 1 January 2012; South Africa would serve as Vice-Chair.

(For information on the Security Council Committee established pursuant to resolution 1572(2004), which monitored the embargo on the import of rough diamonds from Côte d'Ivoire, and its Expert Group, see p. 255.)

On 24 December, the Assembly, by **decision 66/557**, decided that the item entitled "The role of diamonds in fuelling conflict" would remain for consideration during its resumed sixty-sixth (2012) session.

Implementation of 1970 Declaration

The General Assembly, by **decision 66/514** of 2 December, included in the provisional agenda of its sixty-eighth (2013) session the item on the review of the implementation of the Declaration on the Strengthening of International Security [YUN 1970, p. 105].

Peacemaking and peacebuilding

Post-conflict peacebuilding

Post-conflict stabilization

On 21 January, the Security Council held a debate [S/PV.6472] on institution-building in a post-conflict context. The Council had before it a 10 January concept paper [S/2011/16] submitted by Bosnia and Herzegovina.

The Secretary-General, addressing the Council, said that institutions could be critical in sustaining peace and reducing the risk of relapse into violence. Building legitimate institutions that respected and promoted human rights had to be a central element of the overall peacebuilding effort. Unfortunately, the record of international support to institution-building had been inconsistent. Experience suggested that three lessons needed to be applied to institution-building. First, national ownership and leadership needed to be reinforced and built on existing institutions. Responsive and inclusive institutions could be built only by national actors using their contextual knowledge. Secondly, one-size-fits-all solutions had to be avoided, as attempts to impose an outside model on a post-conflict country could do more harm than good. Each country's institutions should be allowed to develop incrementally, and institutional change should be pursued in the context of a country's political processes, development and social change. Thirdly, institution-building should start early and be sustained for decades. In the short term, tangible progress needed to be made in a few priority areas, such as increasing access to justice systems or expanding health and education services, to restore confidence and increase the legitimacy of national institutions.

The Chairperson of the Peacebuilding Commission, Peter Wittig (Germany), who also addressed the Council, said that the principle of national ownership should stand at the beginning of any effort to build institutions in countries emerging from conflict; a common institutional understanding within conflict-torn societies should be developed; and community-based organizations, the private sector and civil society were essential to advancing national reconciliation, restoring trust, rebuilding the social fabric and generating economic opportunities in such societies.

SECURITY COUNCIL ACTION

On 21 January [S/PV.6472], following consultations among Security Council members, the President made statement **S/PRST/2011/2** on behalf of the Council:

The Security Council recalls the previous statements by its President on post-conflict peacebuilding. The Council stresses the importance of institution-building as a critical component of peacebuilding and emphasizes the importance of a more effective and coherent national and international response to it, so that countries emerging from conflict can deliver core government functions, including managing political disputes peacefully, providing security and maintaining stability, protecting their population, ensuring respect for the rule of law, revitalizing the economy and providing basic services, which are essential to achieving durable peace. The Council emphasizes the importance of national ownership in this regard.

The Council underlines that the primary responsibility for successful peacebuilding lies with Governments and relevant national actors, including civil society, in countries emerging from conflict and that the United Nations can play a critical role in support of building their national institutions. The Council acknowledges the need for continued improvement in the delivery of support in the immediate aftermath of conflict in order to help to stabilize the situation, while at the same time starting the longer-term process of institution-building, including building those institutions that promote democratic processes and foster economic and social development, with a view to sustainable peace.

The Council emphasizes that the United Nations and the international community need to be more effective and coordinated in assessing needs and planning for effective institution-building, including how to make better use of existing national capacities and perspectives in order to ensure national ownership. The Council stresses the need for mainstreaming support to national capacity development in all United Nations peacebuilding activities as a system-wide priority and underscores that peacebuilding strategies and institution-building should be considered in a country-specific context.

The Council stresses the need for greater integration of effort, as well as predictability and accountability within the United Nations, in helping to build institutions in countries emerging from conflict. The Council highlights the importance of coordinated, sector-wide and context-driven approaches in governance, economic stability, enhancing the rule of law and strengthening the security sector that must be nationally owned.

The Council stresses its willingness to make greater use of the advisory role of the Peacebuilding Commission. The Council notes the potential role that the Commission can play in helping to achieve critical peacebuilding objectives, including the development of viable and accountable institutions in the countries on its agenda. The Council also stresses the importance of focused and well-defined partnerships among the United Nations, development agencies, bilateral partners and all other relevant actors, in particular regional and subregional organizations and the international financial institutions, to implement national strategies aimed at effective institution-building which are based on the achievement of results and mutual accountability.

The Council reaffirms the critical importance of timely, flexible and predictable funding for peacebuilding, including institution- and capacity-building, and urges Member States and other partners to increase efforts towards achieving this goal, including through the replenishment of the Peacebuilding Fund and through multi-donor trust funds, acknowledging contributions already made.

The Council expresses its commitment to continuing to improve its consideration and reflection of early peacebuilding tasks related to institution-building in the mandates and composition of peacekeeping operations, special political missions and integrated peacebuilding offices, with a view to making the necessary adjustments, where appropriate, according to progress achieved, lessons learned or changing circumstances on the ground. In this context, the Council notes with appreciation the contribution that peacekeepers and peacekeeping missions make to early peacebuilding and recognizes the need to integrate mission expertise and experience into the development of peacebuilding strategies.

The Council looks forward to the report of the international review of civilian capacity in early 2011, recognizing the need for improved mechanisms for timely deployment of skilled civilian experts in support of national institution-building needs in post-conflict countries. The Council requests the Secretary-General to include in the next follow-up report on peacebuilding in the immediate aftermath of conflict an assessment of the impact that his agenda for action has had in contributing to building viable institutions in post-conflict countries, as well as additional recommendations to improve the effectiveness of the United Nations contribution to more effective, stable and sustainable institutions that can help to prevent a relapse into conflict.

Civilian capacity in the aftermath of conflict

Report of Senior Advisory Group. On 18 February, the Secretary-General transmitted to the General Assembly and the Security Council the report [A/65/747-S/2011/85] of the independent review on civilian capacity in the aftermath of conflict, conducted by the Senior Advisory Group led by former Under-Secretary-General for Peacekeeping Operations Jean-Marie Guéhenno. The report analysed the challenges facing the international community in responding to the needs of post-conflict societies and put forward recommendations focusing on the immediate aftermath of conflict. It stated that as communities emerged from conflict, they often faced a critical shortage of capacities needed to secure a sustainable peace, including those to run a government, re-establish institutions of justice, reintegrate demobilized fighters, revitalize the economy, and restore basic health care and education. Faced with expanded civilian mandates in a growing number of crises, the United Nations struggled to rapidly deploy the range of expertise required and transfer skills and knowledge to national actors, thus increasing the risk of relapse into conflict. The Advisory Group identified four key principles for addressing capacity-building challenges: ownership, partnership, expertise and nimbleness. With regard to enabling national ownership, the Advisory Group recommended that the United Nations and other actors working in conflict-affected communities prioritize national capacities, ensuring that national actors and institutions were the primary source of capacity; revise wages for locally recruited staff to preserve national capacities; co-locate international capacities with national institutions; prioritize women's needs; design procurement for local economic impact; develop shared guidance on enabling national capacity; and support the United Nations Development Programme (UNDP) and World Bank work on core government functionality. The United Nations should establish a mechanism to enable and manage partnerships, develop a policy framework for partnership, and improve training resources for the global pool of capacity providers. To build expertise, the United Nations should fix core capacities by, among other measures, establishing a cluster system for areas of activity in the aftermath of conflict; creating a culture of accountability; and providing training for leaders. The Advisory Group also recommended that the United Nations take action to enable a more nimble response to conflict. The Secretary-General set up a Steering Committee to facilitate coordinated follow-up action.

Report of Secretary-General. In August, the Secretary-General submitted a report [A/66/311-S/2011/527] that responded to the independent review on civilian capacity in the aftermath of conflict (see above). The report identified actions to be taken by the United Nations over the course of 12 months, including developing guidelines for better use and development of national capacity, and guidance on procurement practices; giving stronger strategic direction to new planning processes; reviewing gender expertise; consulting Member States and regional organizations on strengthening partnerships; establishing an online platform to broadcast civilian needs and available capacities; broadening the scope for deploying personnel; detailing critical capacity gaps and engaging with external partners to address them; pursuing a corporate emergency model in the Secretariat to enable an effective response to situations requiring rapid deployment; ensuring that UN leaders in the field exercised the operational and financial agility to fulfil their mandates; applying the principle of comparative advantage in discharging mandates; and piloting the recommended approaches in the field. The report stated that externally imposed solutions could not replace ownership by, and the capacity of, national communities, their leaders and institutions.

The Secretary-General asked the Steering Committee Chair to ensure that country-specific task forces, mission leadership and UN country teams were engaged to identify opportunities for testing ideas for strengthening civilian capacity in post-conflict countries. The approach emphasized the development of proposals on the issue in partnership with Member States, international financial institutions and the wider group of peacebuilding stakeholders.

Disarmament, demobilization and reintegration

In response to resolution 64/266 [YUN 2010, p. 84], the Secretary-General, in March, submitted a report [A/65/741] on progress made in disarmament, demobilization and reintegration (DDR), which focused on the civilian reintegration of ex-combatants. The Secretary-General introduced revised policy and guidance related to the UN approach to reintegration but noted gaps in their implementation. Worldwide adult ex-combatants typically received up to one year of economic reintegration assistance, most often through vocational training, but the majority of programmes lacked the comprehensive support necessary to achieve sustainable reintegration. Multidimensional reintegration programmes were needed, including economic, psychosocial, political and security components; community-based reintegration approaches; and stronger linkages with other returnees and refugees. Reintegration had to be aligned with larger employment and income generation programmes, private sector development initiatives and poverty reduction strategies to provide a bridge between immediate recovery and longer-term development. Recent experiences suggested that a dedicated capacity at Headquarters had helped in providing operational support and integrated guidance, which ensured the quality of DDR programmes and their alignment with the overall peace process and recovery initiatives. The Inter-Agency Working Group on DDR continued to facilitate an integrated approach to programme planning and implementation, in addition to its work on developing guidance.

The Secretary-General reported that in 2010, UN agencies, funds and programmes were supporting reintegration programmes in 18 countries and territories, assisting an estimated 257,000 ex-combatants, approximately 10 per cent of whom were female; 9,000 women associated with armed forces; and 11,393 children associated with armed forces and groups (8,624 males and 2,769 females). In the previous five years, the United Nations had completed reintegration programmes in Angola, Liberia, the Niger and Timor-Leste, supporting some 234,000 participants. The largest reintegration programme ever supported by the United Nations was being conducted in the Sudan, where some 180,000 ex-combatants would undergo reintegration.

The Secretary-General recommended that easily accessible start-up voluntary funding for reintegration be made available for assessment studies, including through the deployment of integrated assessment teams. He called on Member States to provide timely and sustained funding to longer, multidimensional reintegration programmes. Member States and relevant UN actors should establish multi-year, country-specific funding strategies to support reintegration programmes, which should be aligned with peace processes, recovery and peacebuilding activities. Member States and other partners who might be called on to work alongside the United Nations on DDR programmes should associate themselves with and be guided by the principles contained in the Integrated Disarmament, Demobilization and Reintegration Standards (IDDRS). Member States were also called on to support the Integrated Disarmament, Demobilization and Reintegration Training Group. The international community had to utilize innovative approaches to meet the complex challenges posed by cross-border armed groups, and better links needed to be made with the return and integration of refugees and other returnees to harmonize multiple programmes within a region.

Special Committee on Peacekeeping Operations consideration. The Special Committee, at its 2011 session [A/65/19], stressed that DDR programmes were crucial components of peacekeeping operations, and that their success depended on the political will and concerted effort of all parties. It was important that DDR was firmly established within a political process and that all actors were prepared for a multi-year programme. The Committee recognized that the DDR process was an evolving field and that related programmes should be tailored to specific contexts to ensure consistency with national strategies and address the different needs of female and male ex-combatants and their dependants. In that regard, it emphasized the need to implement IDDRS gender guidelines. The Special Committee also underlined the importance of building synergies between security sector reform and DDR in the planning and implementation of peacekeeping operations, and ensuring that DDR programmes were designed in accordance with national priorities and the specific context of each country.

Rule of law

Special Committee on Peacekeeping Operations consideration. The Special Committee [A/65/19] emphasized the importance of strengthening the rule of law in countries emerging from conflict in order to stabilize the situation, end impunity, tackle the underlying causes of conflict and build lasting peace. It called on the Secretariat and peacekeeping operations to implement the commitments contained in the Secretary-General's 2010 report on women's participation in peacebuilding [YUN 2010, p. 1166], in particular the provision of immediate support for women's and girls' access to justice and law enforcement institutions. The Committee reiterated the need for greater specificity in UN peacekeeping mandates on rule-of-law issues and requested that DPKO continue to ensure that rule of law and transitional justice were integrated into the planning of peacekeeping operations. It urged the Secretariat to implement measures to ensure that UN staff were made available to implement mandates related to the rule of law throughout the life of the mission. The Special Committee called on DPKO and the Department of Field Support (DFS) to consider ways to provide adequate rule-of-law capacities through, among other means, the use of rosters of civilian experts. The Special Committee welcomed the establishment of the rule-of-law team of experts on sexual violence and the development of the Rule of Law Training for Judicial Affairs Officers, and encouraged DPKO to continue to enhance the capacity of its judicial affairs and corrections personnel. It asked the Secretariat to brief Member States on progress in the development of guidance material for operational rule-of-law issues. The Special Committee also requested an analysis of how the work of the Office of Rule of Law and Security Institutions contributed to closer coherence among its sections and between other UN actors; and an update on progress made in the establishment and operations of the Justice and Corrections Standing Capacity. The Secretariat was encouraged to implement the UN Rule of Law Indicators in Peacekeeping Operations and asked for periodic updates on how they supported national justice strategies to strengthen the rule of law and assisted rule-of-law planning and assistance. The Secretariat was requested to provide, prior to its next session, information on the concept developed by DPKO to support national authorities in establishing temporary prison facilities in the immediate aftermath of conflict or in response to natural disasters.

Communications. The Secretary-General, in a 23 June letter [S/2011/396] addressed to the Security Council President, conveyed a request to postpone until 1 November the submission of a progress report on the implementation of recommendations contained in the 2004 report [YUN 2004, p. 65] of the Secretary-General on the rule of law and transitional justice; the Council, in presidential statement S/PRST/2010/11 [YUN 2010, p. 42], had requested the Secretary-General to submit such a report within 12 months. On 27 June 2011 [S/2011/397], the Council stated that it looked forward to the submission of the report by 1 November.

Report of Secretary-General. In October, the Secretary-General submitted to the Security Council his progress report [S/2011/634] on the implementation of the recommendations made in his 2004 report [YUN 2004, p. 65] on the rule of law and transitional justice in conflict and post-conflict societies, and further steps to promote the rule of law. The report discussed the rule of law and the peace and security agenda; promoting the rule of law; ensuring accountability and reinforcing norms; building confidence in national justice and security institutions; promoting gender equality through greater access to justice; emerging threats and root causes of conflict; and delivering more predictable, accountable and effective rule-of-law assistance.

In conflict and post-conflict societies, the United Nations assisted counties in establishing the rule of law by ensuring accountability and reinforcing norms, building confidence in justice and security institutions, and promoting gender equality. The Organization was increasingly focused on emerging threats to the rule of law, such as organized crime and illicit trafficking, and the root causes of conflict, including economic and social justice issues. Greater efforts were needed to ensure a unified approach to the rule of law, address gaps in evidence-based programming and integrate security sector reform into the wider rule-of-law framework. More work was also required to increase national ownership, promote donor coordination and foster political will. Rapidly developing situations in Côte d'Ivoire, Egypt, the Libyan Arab Jamahiriya, South Sudan, Syria and Tunisia were placing significant demands on the Organization's expertise and testing the limits of its capacities.

The Council mandated support for the rule of law in many peacekeeping and special political missions, including in Afghanistan, Burundi, the Central African Republic, Chad, Côte d'Ivoire, the Democratic Republic of the Congo, Guinea-Bissau, Haiti, Iraq, Liberia, Sierra Leone, South Sudan, the Sudan and Timor-Leste. Efforts to build the rule of law required the support and involvement of national stakeholders. National actors were playing a larger role in the promotion, design and implementation of rule-of-law programmes, increasing the prospects for sustainable impact. More programmes were being led by and aligned with national development strategies, as found in Afghanistan, Kenya, Liberia and South Sudan.

Transitional justice initiatives had become well-established components of the wider UN rule-of-law framework and indispensable elements of post-conflict strategic planning. Women and girls increasingly participated in transitional justice processes and highlighted the grave consequences of forced displacement, abduction, sexual and gender-based violence, and violations of economic and social rights.

Transnational organized crime took root in conflict and post-conflict settings, constituting an emerging threat to peace and security, development and the rule of law. In particular, piracy and illicit trafficking fostered violent crime and contributed to cross-border instability. The United Nations was increasingly focused on enhancing transborder intelligence-sharing and law enforcement cooperation.

Greater investment of financial and political capital in the UN rule-of-law initiatives was needed to meet the multidimensional challenge of the peace and security agenda. The Secretary-General encouraged the Security Council to strengthen its support for the International Court of Justice and support the implementation of transitional justice and rule-of-law provisions in peace agreements. Among other measures, the Council should encourage stakeholder implementation of United Nations Rule of Law Indicators and mandate baseline statistical surveys, benchmarking exercises and reporting against progress indicators; incorporation of gender perspectives in rule-of-law programmes and greater investment in women's access to justice initiatives; and increased funding in support of justice and security institutions in the budgets of peacekeeping and special political missions. Member States should be encouraged to nominate civilian justice experts to support UN entities engaged in the rule-of-law sector and accommodate persons acquitted by international criminal tribunals or who had served their sentences and could not return to their countries for security reasons.

Peacebuilding Commission

In response to Security Council resolutions 1645(2005) and 1646(2005) [YUN 2005, p. 94], and General Assembly resolution 60/180 [ibid.], the Peacebuilding Commission submitted a report on its fifth session [A/66/675-S/2012/70], reviewing its activities in 2011. In accordance with Assembly resolution 65/7 [YUN 2010, p. 56] and Council resolution 1947(2010) [ibid.], the report also reflected the Commission's progress in advancing recommendations contained in the 2010 review of the UN peacebuilding architecture [ibid., p. 55].

The country configurations continued to assist the countries on the Commission's agenda: Burundi, the Central African Republic, Guinea (placed on the agenda in February), Guinea-Bissau, Liberia and Sierra Leone. They provided political advocacy and support, fostering coherence among key actors and intensifying efforts at resource mobilization.

The two overarching recommendations of the 2010 review were for the Commission to enhance its impact in the field and strengthen its relations with key actors at Headquarters. The Commission's Organizational Committee (see below) approved in January the Chair's road map for 2011 actions, which addressed those recommendations. The road map prioritized support for national capacity development; resource mobilization; alignment of key actors behind common peacebuilding objectives; and adoption of flexible instruments of engagement. The Commission emphasized strengthening its relationships with UN operational entities. It adopted the statement of mutual commitments as a new instrument of engagement for countries to be placed on its agenda, recognizing the need to build on national frameworks and to pursue mutual accountability for progress between the Commission and those countries. The Commission initiated dialogues with UNDP and DFS to gain a better understanding of the UN system-wide approach to national capacity-building in post-conflict settings. It facilitated the sharing of experiences between countries that had undergone peacebuilding and reconstruction processes and the countries on its agenda. Rwanda, in its capacity as Commission Chair, and in collaboration with the Peacebuilding Support Office and the African Development Bank, convened a high-level meeting on post-conflict peacebuilding: the experience of Rwanda (Kigali, Rwanda, 8–9 November). The Commission explored ways to mobilize resources for the countries on its agenda, including by co-sponsoring donor round tables.

In response to a recommendation of the 2010 review, the West African configurations for Guinea, Guinea-Bissau, Liberia and Sierra Leone met in New York on 6 July to discuss the issue of transnational crime and drug trafficking and its impact on peacebuilding in the four countries. The meeting underlined the need for an approach rooted in the principle of common and shared responsibility. It called on the Commission to collaborate more closely with the Economic Community of West African States and to support international initiatives, including the joint United Nations and International Criminal Police Organization West Africa Coast Initiative [YUN 2009, p. 169].

On 24 December, the Assembly, by **decision 66/557**, decided that the item on the report of the Peacebuilding Commission would remain for consideration during its resumed sixty-sixth (2012) session.

Organizational Committee

The Peacebuilding Commission's Organizational Committee, at its 26 January meeting [PBC/5/OC/SR.1], elected for one year, beginning 1 January, the Chairperson and two Vice-Chairpersons of the Commission, as well as the Chairpersons of its country-specific configurations on Burundi, the Central African Republic, Guinea-Bissau, Liberia and Sierra Leone. The Chairperson said that the 2010 review of the UN peacebuilding architecture [YUN 2010, p. 55] renewed confidence in the future of the Commission. The Commission's role as a platform for building partnerships with international financial institutions, regional and subregional organizations and global initiatives were enhanced. Progress was made, in particular, with the World Bank in some countries on the Commission's agenda. The Commission initiated dialogue with the Peace and Security Council of the African Union.

On 12 December, the General Assembly elected Croatia and El Salvador as members of the Organizational Committee for a two-year term of office, beginning on 1 January 2012, to fill the vacancies occurring on the expiration of the terms of office of the Czech Republic and Peru (**decision 66/415**).

Peacebuilding Fund

In response to General Assembly resolution 63/282 [YUN 2009, p. 49], the Secretary-General submitted its fifth report [A/66/659] on the Peacebuilding Fund, which was established in 2006 [YUN 2006, p. 58] to extend critical support at the early stages of a peace process. The report covered the Fund's operations and activities from 1 July 2010 to 31 December 2011.

The Fund allocated $99.4 million in 2011, consistent with its business plan target for 2011–2013 of $100 million in annual allocations. Income for 2011 of $66.7 million represented a significant improvement from $31.3 million in 2010. Funds carried over were expected to support the same level of activity for 2012, but more funds were required for 2013 and beyond. By December 2011, 18 UN organizations had received funds.

The Fund was an increasingly successful instrument to support countries emerging from conflict, and its strategic position was becoming clearer. Nevertheless, the Fund took steps to improve its performance during the year, including the development of business and performance management plans; the expansion of allocations; a commitment to rapid response; increased synergies with the Commission; better country support and the organization of annual stakeholder forums. The establishment of baselines provided the foundation for measuring the Fund's performance.

By **decision 66/557** of 24 December, the Assembly decided that the item on the report of Secretary-General on the Peacebuilding Fund would remain for consideration during its resumed sixty-sixth (2012) session.

Protection issues

Responsibility to protect

Report of Secretary-General. In response to the 2005 World Summit Outcome [YUN 2005, p. 48], which dealt with, among other issues, the responsibility to protect populations from genocide, war crimes, ethnic cleansing and crimes against humanity [ibid., p. 62], and General Assembly resolution 63/308 on the same topic [YUN 2009, p. 50], the Secretary-General submitted a June report [A/65/877-S/2011/393] on the role of regional and subregional arrangements in implementing the responsibility to protect. The report was issued in anticipation of an informal interactive dialogue to be held in the Assembly on the matter (see below).

The Secretary-General's strategy to fulfil the responsibility to protect was built on three pillars: the protection responsibilities of the State; international assistance and capacity-building to prevent or curb mass atrocities; and timely and decisive response. A key part of the strategy was to foster more effective global-regional collaboration. Over the previous three years, the United Nations had applied principles of the responsibility to protect in addressing threats to populations in around 12 specific situations, and its regional and/or subregional arrangements had made important contributions in each situation.

The responsibility to protect primarily concerned reasserting and reinforcing the sovereign responsibilities of the State. It affirmed that a core function of global and regional organizations was to permit the full and peaceful expression of sovereignty in accordance with the Charter of the United Nations and international law. Preventing mass atrocities was the legal responsibility of the State, but meeting that responsibility required partnering with civil society. The Joint Office of the Secretary-General's Special Advisers on the Prevention of Genocide and the Responsibility to Protect provided training and awareness-raising programmes to Governments, civil society and other organizations that sought to forestall violent upheaval. Regional and subregional organizations could encourage Governments to recognize their obligations under international conventions and to identify and address sources of friction in their societies before they led to violence. Regional and subregional arrangements strengthened the second pillar of the Secretary-General's strategy by developing norms, standards and institutions that promoted tolerance, transparency, accountability and constructive management of diversity. Regarding the provision of timely and decisive responses to crises, the Secretary-General said that the Security Council could make more use of its authority under Article 34 of the Charter to "investigate any dispute, or any situation which might lead to international frictions or give rise to dispute". Discouraging incitement and monitoring statements by national officials and opposition leaders and their supporters could serve as preventive steps. Doctrine for the possible use of peacekeeping and military assets in the context of preventing, deterring or responding to atrocities was not well developed; a deeper discussion of such matters was needed among Governments and independent experts.

Informal dialogue. An informal interactive dialogue in the General Assembly on the role of regional and subregional arrangements in implementing the responsibility to protect, held on 12 July, featured two panel discussions on regional and subregional perspectives and experience and UN perspectives and experience, respectively [GA/11112]. In his opening remarks, the President of the Assembly underscored the responsibility of Member States to protect populations from genocide, war crimes, ethnic cleansing and crimes against humanity, emphasizing the importance of conflict prevention. The Secretary-General highlighted the benefits of information and insights generated by regional and subregional arrangements, as well as from local and international civil society.

Communication. A 9 November note [A/66/551-S/2011/701] from Brazil addressed to Secretary-General contained a concept note on the responsibility to protect.

Protection of civilians in armed conflict

Security Council consideration. On 10 May, the Security Council held an open debate [S/PV.6531] on the protection of civilians in armed conflict. The Under-Secretary-General for Humanitarian Affairs, Valerie Amos, addressing the Council, said that the deliberate targeting of civilians, or other disregard for their well-being in violation of humanitarian law during hostilities, had resulted in hundreds being killed or seriously harmed every week. In the six months since her last briefing [YUN 2010, p. 59], the world had witnessed an unprecedented series of crises in parts of the Middle East and North- and sub-Saharan Africa. Demanding compliance with the law and enforcing such demands through targeted sanctions were important actions the Council could take to enhance compliance. The Council had a key role in promoting accountability for serious violations, and had to be comprehensive and consistent in its approach.

The Under-Secretary-General for Peacekeeping Operations, Alain Le Roy, briefed the Council on DPKO efforts to protect civilians in the framework of the seven peacekeeping operations with such a mandate. The Special Committee on Peacekeeping Operations developed a strategic framework for the protection of civilians that included the use of the political process to protect civilians. DPKO finalized guidance to assist missions in developing protection strategies and created training modules on the protection of civilians. The Under-Secretary-General said that such efforts had to be complemented by the Council's sustained political support. The Assistant Secretary-General for Human Rights, Ivan Šimonović, also addressed the Council.

On 9 November [S/PV.6650], the Security Council held a second debate on the protection of civilians in armed conflict. The Secretary-General said that in conflicts throughout the world, women, girls, boys and men were subjected to blatant and frequent violations of international human rights and humanitarian law, including killing, torture, kidnapping, rape and mutilation. Civilians suffered because they were deliberately targeted. Humanitarian actors could contribute to the survival of affected populations but only political solutions could stop and prevent the majority of conflicts and ensure the safety and well-being of civilians. The Council was also addressed by the United Nations High Commissioner for Human Rights, Navanethem Pillay, and the Assistant Secretary-General for Humanitarian Affairs, Catherine Bragg.

Special political missions

Roster of 2011 political missions and offices

As at 31 December, 13 UN political and peacebuilding missions were in operation: 8 in Africa, 3 in the Asia and the Pacific region, and 2 in the Middle East.

The United Nations Regional Office for Central Africa (unoca) was established on 1 January with a two-year mandate. On the same date, the United Nations Office in Burundi (bnub) succeeded the United Nations Integrated Office in Burundi (binub); on 20 December, the Security Council extended the initial 12-month bnub mandate until 15 February 2013. On 16 September 2011, the Council established the United Nations Support Mission in Libya (unsmil); on 2 December, the Council extended the mission's mandate until 16 March 2012. On 21 December 2011, the Council extended the mandate of the United Nations Integrated Peacebuilding Office in Guinea-Bissau (uniogbis) until 28 February 2013 and the United Nations Integrated Peacebuilding Office in the Central African Republic (binuca) until 31 January 2013. The mandate of the United Nations Mission in Nepal (unmin) ended on 15 January 2011.

In the Asia and the Pacific region, the Council, on 22 March, extended the mandate of the United Nations Assistance Mission in Afghanistan (unama) until 23 March 2012. On 28 July 2011, it renewed the mandate of the United Nations Assistance Mission for Iraq (unami) for a further 12-month period.

(For financing of UN political and peacebuilding missions, see part five, Chapter II.)

UNPOS

United Nations Political Office for Somalia
Established: 15 April 1995.
Mandate: To promote a lasting peace and stability in Somalia through the implementation of the Djibouti Peace Agreement and to facilitate coordination of international support.
Special Representative of the Secretary-General: Augustine Mahiga (Tanzania).
Strength: 57 international civilian staff, 30 local civilian staff, 3 military advisers.

UNSCO

Office of the United Nations Special Coordinator for the Middle East Peace Process
Established: 1 October 1999.
Mandate: To act as the focal point for the UN contribution to the peace process and to enhance UN humanitarian and development assistance.
Special Coordinator for the Middle East Peace Process and Personal Representative of the Secretary-General to the Palestine Liberation Organization and the Palestinian Authority: Robert H. Serry (Netherlands).
Strength: 33 international civilian staff, 29 local civilian staff.

UNOWA

United Nations Office for West Africa
Established: 1 January 2002.
Mandate: To enhance the contribution of the United Nations towards the achievement of peace and security in West Africa.
Special Representative of the Secretary-General: Said Djinnit (Algeria).
Strength: 19 international civilian staff, 16 local civilian staff, 3 military advisers.

UNAMA

United Nations Assistance Mission in Afghanistan
Established: 28 March 2002.
Mandate: To assist the Government and the people of Afghanistan in laying the foundations for sustainable peace and development.
Special Representative of the Secretary-General: Staffan de Mistura (Sweden).
Strength: 421 international civilian staff, 1,730 local civilian staff, 13 military advisers, 2 police, 77 UN Volunteers.

UNAMI

United Nations Assistance Mission for Iraq

Established: 14 August 2003.

Mandate: To promote political dialogue, assist the Government and the Independent High Electoral Commission in electoral processes, promote human rights, regional dialogue, and reconstruction and development.

Special Representative of the Secretary-General: Martin Kobler (Germany).

Strength: (staff based in Iraq, Jordan and Kuwait) 391 international civilian staff, 502 local civilian staff, 353 troops, 8 military advisers, 4 police.

UNMIN

United Nations Mission in Nepal

Established: 23 January 2007.

Mandate: To support the peace process by monitoring the management of arms and armed personnel of the Nepal Army and the Maoist Army; assisting the parties, through a Joint Monitoring Coordinating Committee, in implementing the agreement on the management of arms and armed personnel; assisting in the monitoring of ceasefire agreements; and providing technical assistance to the Election Commission. UNMIN completed its mandate on 15 January.

Representative of the Secretary-General: Karin Landgren (Sweden).

UNSCOL

Office of the United Nations Special Coordinator for Lebanon

Established: 16 February 2007.

Mandate: To represent the Secretary-General politically and coordinate UN work in Lebanon.

Special Coordinator for Lebanon: Derek Plumbly (United Kingdom).

Strength: 19 international civilian staff, 59 local civilian staff.

UNRCCA

United Nations Regional Centre for Preventive Diplomacy for Central Asia

Established: 10 December 2007.

Mandate: To liaise with Governments of the region and other parties on preventive diplomacy issues; monitor and analyse the situation on the ground and provide the Secretary-General with information related to conflict prevention; maintain contact with regional organizations; and support the UN system in promoting an integrated approach to preventive development and humanitarian assistance.

Special Representative of the Secretary-General: Miroslav Jenča (Slovakia).

Strength: 8 international civilian staff, 21 local civilian staff.

UNIPSIL

United Nations Integrated Peacebuilding Office in Sierra Leone

Established: 1 October 2008.

Mandate: To provide political support for resolving tensions and threats of potential conflict; monitor and promote human rights, democratic institutions and the rule of law; consolidate good governance reforms; support decentralization and the enactment of legislation; and support the Peacebuilding Commission and the Peacebuilding Fund.

Executive Representative of the Secretary-General: Michael von der Schulenburg (Germany).

Strength: 37 international civilian staff, 29 local civilian staff, 5 police, 7 UN Volunteers.

BINUCA

United Nations Integrated Peacebuilding Office in the Central African Republic

Established: 1 January 2010.

Mandate: Support the implementation of the transition process, conflict prevention and humanitarian assistance; stabilization of the security situation; extension of State authority; and promotion and protection of human rights.

Special Representative of the Secretary-General: Margaret Vogt (Nigeria).

Strength: 66 international civilian staff, 75 local civilian staff, 2 military advisers, 2 police, 6 UN Volunteers.

UNIOGBIS

United Nations Integrated Peacebuilding Office in Guinea-Bissau

Established: 1 January 2010.

Mandate: To assist the Peacebuilding Commission in its engagement with Guinea-Bissau; strengthen the capacity of national institutions to maintain constitutional order and respect for the rule of law; support an inclusive political dialogue and a national reconciliation process; assist in reforming the security sector, combating human trafficking, mobilizing international assistance and curbing the proliferation of small arms and light weapons; and promote human rights.

Special Representative of the Secretary-General: Joseph Mutaboba (Rwanda).

Strength: 55 international civilian staff, 51 local civilian staff, 2 military advisers, 14 police, 6 UN Volunteers.

BNUB

United Nations Office in Burundi

Established: 1 January 2011.

Mandate: To strengthen key national institutions; promote and facilitate dialogue between national actors; support efforts to fight impunity through the establishment of transitional justice mechanisms; promote and protect human rights; ensure that economic strategies and policies focused on peacebuilding and equitable growth; and support Burundi as Chair of the East African Community in 2011.

Special Representative of the Secretary-General: Karin Landgren (Sweden).

Strength: 50 international civilian staff, 65 local civilian staff, 1 military adviser, 1 police, 6 UN Volunteers.

UNOCA

United Nations Regional Office for Central Africa

Established: 1 January 2011.

Mandate: To assist Member States and subregional organizations in consolidating peace and preventing potential conflicts.

Special Representative of the Secretary-General: Abou Moussa (Chad).

Strength: 14 international civilian staff, 5 local civilian staff, 1 military adviser.

UNSMIL

United Nations Support Mission in Libya

Established: 16 September 2011.

Mandate: To help restore security and promote the rule of law; undertake political dialogue, promote national reconciliation and embark on the constitution-making and electoral process; extend State authority by strengthening accountable institutions and public services; promote and protect human rights, and support transitional justice; initiate economic recovery; coordinate support from multi- and bilateral actors, and assist national efforts against the proliferation of arms.

Special Representative of the Secretary-General: Ian Martin (United Kingdom).

Strength: 14 international civilian staff, 1 police.

Threats to international peace and security

International terrorism

Security Council consideration. On 28 February, the Security Council held a meeting [S/PV.6492] on threats to international peace and security caused by terrorist acts. It had before it a 21 January letter [S/2011/29] containing the first report of the Office of the Ombudsperson, submitted pursuant to Council resolution 1904(2009) [YUN 2009, p. 355]. The report summarized activities of the Office from 14 July 2010 to 15 January 2011. The Council adopted presidential statement **S/PRST/2011/5** (see p. 350), by which it took note of the observations contained in the report in the context of renewal of the Ombudsperson's mandate in June.

Statement by Secretary-General. In a 2 May press statement [SG/SM/13535], the Secretary-General said that the death of Osama bin Laden, announced by United States President Barack Obama on 1 May, marked a watershed moment in the global fight against terrorism. The United Nations would continue to work with Member States to eradicate terrorism, based on the Global Counter-Terrorism Strategy adopted by the General Assembly in 2006 [YUN 2006, p. 66].

SECURITY COUNCIL ACTION

On 2 May [meeting 6526], following consultations among Security Council members, the President made statement **S/PRST/2011/9** on behalf of the Council:

> The Security Council recalls its resolutions regarding Osama bin Laden and its condemnation of the Al-Qaida network and other associated terrorist groups for the multiple criminal terrorist acts aimed at causing the deaths of numerous innocent civilians and the destruction of property.
>
> The Council also recalls the heinous terrorist attacks which took place on 11 September 2001 in New York, Washington, D.C., and Pennsylvania and the other numerous attacks perpetrated by the network throughout the world.
>
> In this regard, the Council welcomes the news on 1 May 2011 that Osama bin Laden will never again be able to perpetrate such acts of terrorism, and reaffirms that terrorism cannot and should not be associated with any religion, nationality, civilization or group.
>
> The Council recognizes this critical development and other accomplishments made in the fight against terrorism and urges all States to remain vigilant and intensify their efforts in the fight against terrorism.
>
> The Council expresses once again its deepest sympathy and condolences to the victims of terrorism and their families.

The Council reaffirms the importance of all its resolutions and the statements by its President on terrorism, in particular resolutions 1267(1999), 1373(2001), 1624(2005), 1904(2009) and 1963(2010), as well as other applicable international counter-terrorism instruments, stresses the need for their full implementation, and calls for enhanced cooperation in this regard.

The Council further reaffirms its call upon all States to work together urgently to bring to justice the perpetrators, organizers and sponsors of terrorist attacks and its determination that those responsible for aiding, supporting or harbouring the perpetrators, organizers and sponsors of these acts will be held accountable.

The Council reaffirms that Member States must ensure that any measures taken to combat terrorism comply with all their obligations under international law, in particular international human rights, refugee and humanitarian law.

The Council stresses that no cause or grievance can justify the murder of innocent people and that terrorism will not be defeated by military force, law enforcement measures and intelligence operations alone, and can only be defeated by a sustained and comprehensive approach involving the active participation and collaboration of all States and relevant international and regional organizations and civil society to address the conditions conducive to the spread of terrorism and to impede, impair, isolate and incapacitate the terrorist threat.

On 17 June, the Council, by **resolutions 1988(2011)** (see p. 337) and **1989(2011)** (see p. 341), adopted measures to combat, through sanctions, the threat to peace in Afghanistan and elsewhere posed by the violent and terrorist activities conducted by the Taliban, Al-Qaida and other illegal armed groups.

Measures to eliminate international terrorism

In 2011, the United Nations strengthened its efforts to combat and eliminate international terrorism. The General Assembly examined the Secretary-General's June report [A/66/96 & Add.1] on measures to eliminate international terrorism and the report [A/66/37] of the Ad Hoc Committee established by Assembly resolution 51/210. It also considered the oral report [A/C.6/66/SR.28] of the Chair of the Working Group established by the Sixth (Legal) Committee at the Assembly's sixty-sixth session to finalize the draft comprehensive convention on international terrorism and discuss the question of convening a high-level conference under the auspices of the United Nations.

In **resolution 66/105** of 9 December (see p. 1285), the Assembly requested that the Terrorism Prevention Branch of the United Nations Office on Drugs and Crime enhance UN capabilities in preventing terrorism. It recognized, in the context of the United Nations Global Counter-Terrorism Strategy [YUN 2006, p. 66] and Security Council resolution 1373(2001) [YUN 2001, p. 61], the Branch's role in assisting States in becoming parties to and implementing the international conventions and protocols relating to terrorism, and in strengthening international cooperation mechanisms in criminal matters related to terrorism.

In **resolution 66/50** of 2 December on measures to prevent terrorists from acquiring weapons of mass destruction (see p. 510), the Assembly urged Member States to strengthen measures to prevent terrorists from acquiring such weapons, their means of delivery, and materials and technologies related to their manufacture.

The Economic and Social Council, in **resolution 2011/31** of 28 July (see p. 1204), recommended to the Assembly a draft resolution on technical assistance for implementing the international conventions and protocols related to counter-terrorism. The draft was adopted by the Assembly in **resolution 66/178** of 19 December (see p. 1204). Member States were urged to strengthen international cooperation in order to prevent and combat terrorism in accordance with international law, including the Charter of the United Nations. In **resolution 66/171** of 19 December (see p. 700), on the protection of human rights and fundamental freedoms while countering terrorism, the Assembly reaffirmed that States had to ensure that any measure taken to combat terrorism complied with international law, in particular international human rights, refugee and humanitarian law.

Communication. By an 8 August letter [A/65/926-S/2011/52], Iran transmitted to the Secretary-General the Chairman's Conclusion of the International Conference on the Global Fight against Terrorism (Tehran, 25–26 June), which was organized by that country. Conference participants underlined the need for a consensual definition of terrorism without prejudicing or affecting the rules and principles of international humanitarian law.

Counter-Terrorism Committee

In 2011, the Committee established pursuant to Security Council resolution 1373(2001) [YUN 2001, p. 61], known as the Counter-Terrorism Committee (CTC), held 13 formal meetings. The CTC Chairman submitted on 25 March its work programme for 2011 [S/2011/223]. CTC was assisted in its work by the Counter-Terrorism Committee Executive Directorate (CTED).

On 28 December [S/2011/812], the Secretary-General informed the Council of his intention to extend the appointment of Mike Smith (Australia) as CTED Executive Director until 31 December 2012. The Council took note of that intention on 30 December [S/2011/813].

Briefing by CTC Chairman (May). Reporting to the Security Council on 16 May [S/PV.6536], the CTC Chairman said that the Committee organized and participated in discussions and workshops on thematic and regional issues. Issues considered by CTC included the control of cash couriers; the abuse of the non-profit sector for terrorist financing; and the application of good practices for the implementation and assessment of resolution 1624(2005) [YUN 2005, p. 102], which called on States to combat terrorism, including incitement to commit terrorist acts. In pursuance of resolution 1963(2010) [YUN 2010, p. 73] concerning the work of CTC and CTED, the Executive Directorate was working towards providing an updated global implementation survey on resolution 1373(2001), as well as a global implementation survey on resolution 1624(2005). CTC adopted a plan of action for the implementation of resolution 1624(2005). The Committee, in collaboration with the Council of Europe, held a special meeting with international, regional and subregional organizations on the prevention of terrorism (Strasbourg, France, 19–21 April) [S/2011/303]. The meeting focused on prevention policies, comprehensive and integrated strategies and the role of law enforcement in preventing terrorism.

Implementation of resolution 1373(2001). On 17 August, the CTC Chairman submitted the updated global survey [S/2011/463] of the implementation of Security Council resolution 1373(2001) [YUN 2001, p. 61], as requested by the Council in resolution 1963(2010) [YUN 2010, p. 73]. The survey assessed the implementation of resolution 1373(2001) along with the evolution of risks and threats and the impact of implementation. It identified gaps in the implementation of the resolution and proposed implementation measures. The survey focused on five major issues: counter-terrorism legislation, counter-financing of terrorism, law enforcement, border control and international cooperation.

Communication. By a 2 November letter [S/2011/689], the CTC Chairman transmitted to the Security Council President the outcome document of the special meeting of the CTC (New York, 28 September), held pursuant to resolution 1963(2010) to commemorate the tenth anniversary of the adoption of resolution 1373(2001) and the establishment of the Committee.

Briefing by CTC Chairman. Briefing the Security Council on 14 November [S/PV.6658], the CTC Chairman said that since May, the Committee had considered, among other issues, the provision of technical assistance to Member States and challenges in adopting and implementing counter-terrorism measures relating to legislation and law enforcement, with an emphasis on prevention and emergency response.

Reports of States. Between May and June, the CTC Chairman transmitted to the Council President reports submitted by Member States on action they had taken or planned to take to implement resolution 1624(2005). Reports were submitted by Cuba [S/2011/352] and the Sudan [S/2011/324].

Global Counter-Terrorism Strategy

Establishment of Counter-Terrorism Centre

On 19 September, the Secretary-General announced that the United Nations had signed an agreement with Saudi Arabia on the creation of the United Nations Counter-Terrorism Centre. Saudi Arabia would contribute $10 million over three years to set up the Centre, which would be based in New York. The Centre would support the implementation of the Global Counter-Terrorism Strategy adopted by the General Assembly in resolution 60/288 [YUN 2006, p. 66] and foster international cooperation, strengthen individual countries' capacity-building efforts and build a database of best practices to counter terrorism.

In accordance with the agreement, Saudi Arabia, addressing the Assembly on 18 November [A/66/PV.60], introduced a draft resolution entitled "United Nations Counter-Terrorism Centre" [A/66/L.5/Rev.1].

GENERAL ASSEMBLY ACTION

On 18 November [meeting 60], the General Assembly adopted **resolution 66/10** [draft: A/66/L.5/Rev.1 & Add.1, as orally revised] without vote [agenda item 118].

United Nations Counter-Terrorism Centre

The General Assembly,

Recalling all General Assembly resolutions on measures to eliminate international terrorism and Security Council resolutions on threats to international peace and security caused by terrorist acts,

Reaffirming its resolutions 60/288 of 8 September 2006, 62/272 of 5 September 2008, 64/235 of 24 December 2009 and 64/297 of 8 September 2010 concerning the United Nations Global Counter-Terrorism Strategy,

Noting with appreciation the contribution agreement to launch the United Nations Counter-Terrorism Centre signed by the United Nations and the Kingdom of Saudi Arabia on 19 September 2011,

1. *Welcomes* the establishment of the United Nations Counter-Terrorism Centre at United Nations Headquarters;

2. *Also welcomes* the decision of the Kingdom of Saudi Arabia to fund for three years the United Nations Counter-Terrorism Centre established within the Counter-Terrorism Implementation Task Force Office, to be funded through voluntary contributions;

3. *Notes* that the United Nations Counter-Terrorism Centre will operate under the direction of the Secretary-General and will contribute to promoting the implementation of the United Nations Global Counter-Terrorism Strategy through the Counter-Terrorism Implementation Task Force;

4. *Encourages* all Member States to collaborate with the United Nations Counter-Terrorism Centre in contributing to the implementation of its activities in support of the United Nations Global Counter-Terrorism Strategy;

 5. *Decides* to review the implementation of the present resolution at its sixty-eighth session within the existing reporting and review framework of the fourth biennial review of the United Nations Global Counter-Terrorism Strategy.

Terrorist attacks in 2011

In 2011, hundreds of innocent civilians were killed and many more were injured in terrorist attacks conducted worldwide. Such attacks were condemned by the Security Council, Member States and the Secretary-General.

In **resolution 66/12** of 18 November (see p. 1288), concerning terrorist attacks on internationally protected persons, the General Assembly reiterated its condemnation of terrorism in all its forms and manifestations, and condemned acts of violence against diplomatic and consular missions and representatives, as well as against missions and representatives of intergovernmental organizations.

Afghanistan

On 1 April [SG/SM/13490], the Secretary-General condemned the attack against the United Nations operations centre in the northern city of Mazar-i-Sharif, Afghanistan, that occurred the same day. Reports indicated that three UN staff and four international security officers were killed in the attack. The Security Council, by a 1 April press statement [SC/10216], also condemned the attack.

On 20 September [SG/SM/13821], the Secretary-General condemned a bomb attack in Kabul, at the house of the former President of Afghanistan and Chairman of the High Peace Council, Professor Burhanuddin Rabbani, who was killed. Minister Masmoom Stanekzai, Head of the Joint Secretariat was injured in the attack; other civilians were killed or injured. On 21 September, the Security Council, by a press statement [SC/10391], also condemned the terrorist attack.

On 31 October, the Security Council issued a press statement [SC/10432] condemning the terrorist attack against the guest house of the Office of the United Nations High Commissioner for Refugees in Kandahar on the same day, which resulted in the death of three UN staff members and the injury of two others. Afghan police officers protecting UN personnel were also killed or injured. The Council called on Afghanistan to bring those responsible to justice.

On 6 December [SG/SM/13997], the Secretary-General condemned the indiscriminate attacks against civilians that took place in Kabul and Mazar-i-Sharif that day. The attacks resulted in the death and injury of dozens of Afghans who had gathered to mourn on the occasion of the Tenth of Muharam. On 7 December, the Security Council, by a press statement [SC/10474], also condemned the attacks.

Burundi

On 19 September [SG/SM/13809], the Secretary-General condemned the armed attack in Bujumbura Rural Province, Burundi, that occurred the previous day, killing and injuring scores of people. He noted that the attack came at a time when Burundi was trying to consolidate recent gains in peace and stability following decades of civil war.

Iraq

On 18 August, the Security Council, by a press statement [SC/10362], condemned the series of terrorist attacks that occurred in Iraq on 15 August, which caused scores of deaths and injuries. The Council underlined the need to bring to justice perpetrators, organizers, financiers and sponsors of the acts of terrorism.

Israel

On 12 March [SG/SM/13442], the Secretary-General condemned the murder of an Israeli family of five, including three children, in a West Bank settlement the previous night. He called for the perpetrators to be brought to justice and for all to act with restraint.

On 23 March [SG/SM/13470], the Secretary-General condemned a bomb attack that occurred adjacent to a bus stop in West Jerusalem that day. The attack reportedly killed one woman and injured over 30 Israeli civilians, some of them seriously.

On 18 August [SG/SM/13748], the Secretary-General condemned the coordinated terror attacks that occurred in southern Israel that day.

Lebanon

On 27 May, the Security Council, by a press statement [SC/10264], condemned the terrorist attack against a United Nations Interim Force in Lebanon (UNIFIL) convoy north of Sidon, Lebanon, that took place the same day. Six UN peacekeepers and two Lebanese civilians were injured in the attack. The Council called on all parties to abide by their obligations to respect the safety of UNIFIL and other UN personnel.

Morocco

On 29 April, the Security Council, by a press statement [SC/10238], condemned the terrorist attack that occurred in Marrakech, Morocco, the previous day. The attack caused numerous deaths and injuries.

Nigeria

In a 26 August press statement [SG/SM/13759], the Secretary-General said that the United Nations House in the Nigerian capital, Abuja, was struck by a car bomb earlier that day. He condemned the attack, in which a number of people were killed and many were injured. The Security Council, by a press statement issued the same day [SC/10370], also condemned the bombing.

On 5 November [SG/SM/13924], the Secretary-General condemned the armed attacks and bombings that took place the previous day in and near the city of Damaturu, causing numerous deaths and injuries. The Council, by a 5 November press statement [SC/10437], also condemned the attacks.

On 25 December, the Council, by a press statement [SC/10507], condemned the terrorist attacks that occurred in Madalla, Jos and Damaturu that day, causing numerous deaths and injuries.

Norway

On 22 July [SG/SM/13717], the Secretary-General condemned acts of violence that took place in Norway that day, including a large explosion in central Oslo and a shooting in Utøya, which caused numerous death and injuries. On 23 July, the Security Council, by a press statement [SC/10337], condemned the terrorist attacks.

Pakistan

On 4 January [SG/SM/13336], the Secretary-General condemned the assassination of the Governor of Punjab Province in Pakistan, Salman Taseer, which occurred that day.

On 10 February [SG/SM/13397], the Secretary-General condemned the suicide bombing that occurred that day at an army recruitment centre in Mardan, killing and injuring numerous people.

On 2 March [SG/SM/13426] the Secretary-General condemned the assassination of Pakistan's Minister for Minority Affairs, Shahbaz Bhatti, which occurred earlier that day.

On 19 August [SG/SM/13751], the Secretary-General condemned the suicide attack that occurred that day at a mosque in the Khyber tribal region, in the north-west of the country. More than 40 people were reported killed and over 100 injured.

On 8 September [SG/SM/13782], the Secretary-General condemned the suicide bombings in Quetta that took place the previous day. The attack, which reportedly targeted officers of the region's Frontier Corps, left scores of people dead, including two children, and wounded many others.

On 13 September [SG/SM/13795], the Secretary-General condemned the terrorist attack conducted that day near Peshawar, on a school bus carrying young children. The attack resulted in a number of deaths and injuries.

Belarus

On 13 April, the Security Council, by a press statement [SC/10225], condemned the apparent terrorist attack that occurred in Minsk, on 11 April, causing numerous deaths and injuries.

Russian Federation

On 24 January [SG/SM/13363], the Secretary-General condemned the bombing that occurred that day at Moscow's Domodedovo Airport, which killed dozens of people and injured more than 100. The Security Council, by a 24 January press statement [SC/10162], also condemned the attack.

Somalia

On 4 October, the Security Council, by a press statement [SC/10402], condemned the terrorist attack that occurred the same day in Mogadishu, resulting in the death and injury of many civilians.

On 23 December [SG/SM/14034], the Secretary-General condemned the killing that day of two World Food Programme staff members and a staff member of a cooperating partner in Mataban, Hiraan Province.

Sudan

On 20 May [SG/SM/13584], the Secretary-General condemned the attack against a convoy of the United Nations Mission in the Sudan (UNMIS) operating in Abyei on 19 May. At the time of the attack, the convoy was escorting 200 troops of the Joint Integrated Units of the Sudan Armed Forces.

Syria

On 23 December, the Security Council, by a press statement [SC/10506], condemned the attacks that occurred in Damascus on that day, causing numerous death and injuries.

Anniversary of 2001 terrorist attacks

On 9 September, on the occasion of the tenth anniversary of the terrorist attacks of 11 September 2001, the Security Council, by a press statement [SC/10378], recalled the attacks that took place that day in New York, Washington, D. C., and Pennsylvania, USA, resulting in the deaths of nearly 3,000 people from over 90 countries, and the other numerous attacks perpetrated by the Al-Qaida network throughout the world. The Council again condemned the attacks, and expressed sympathy and condolences to the victims of terrorism and their families.

Peacekeeping operations

In 2011, the General Assembly and the Security Council continued to oversee the management and operation of UN peacekeeping missions. The Department of Peacekeeping Operations (DPKO) continued to implement the recommendations of the Special Committee on Peacekeeping Operations, whose mandate was to review the whole question of peacekeeping operations in all their aspects.

Security Council consideration. On 26 August, the Security Council held an open debate [S/PV.6603] on peacekeeping. It had before it a concept paper [S/2011/496] submitted by India. The Secretary-General, addressing the Council, said that peacekeeping must have a clear and achievable mandate, unified political support from the Council, and adequate and predictable human, material and financial resources. Since 2001, the number of uniformed personnel had doubled, reaching a peak of 101,000 in early 2010. Peacekeepers were increasingly tasked to protect civilians, placing greater demands on their work and creating need for resources to implement such mandates. Peacekeeping needed to evolve to meet specific demands in a variety of environments and to bring together multiple capabilities. The New Horizon initiative [YUN 2009, p. 74] served to build a common vision and stronger partnership linking the resources of the Secretariat, the Security Council, troop- and police-contributing countries and the wider membership of the Organization, but the financial climate, differing perspectives on mandated tasks and, in some cases, the loss of host Government consent had created tensions in those relationships. The role of civilian peacekeepers was also critical; close to 20,000 civilians within peacekeeping operations were implementing activities in support of peace processes.

SECURITY COUNCIL ACTION

On 26 August [meeting 6603], following consultations among Security Council members, the President made statement **S/PRST/2011/17** on behalf of the Council:

> The Security Council reaffirms its primary responsibility under the Charter of the United Nations for the maintenance of international peace and security.
>
> The Council affirms that respect for the basic principles of peacekeeping, including consent of the parties, impartiality and the non-use of force except in self-defence and the defence of a mandate authorized by the Council, is essential to the success of peacekeeping operations.
>
> The Council stresses the role of the United Nations peacekeepers in supporting efforts to promote political processes and peaceful settlements of disputes. The Council underlines the need for precise, full and effective implementation of mandates and its intention to continue to review and monitor such implementation on a regular basis. The Council recognizes the role of regional organizations in peacekeeping in accordance with Chapter VIII of the Charter.
>
> The Council recognizes the importance of providing peacekeeping operations with clear, credible and achievable mandates. It also recognizes the need for adequate provision, management and efficient and effective use of operational and logistical resources for peacekeeping operations, in congruence with approved mandates and based on a realistic assessment of the situation. The Council also requests that the Secretary-General include a realistic assessment of how available capabilities and logistical planning affect the implementation of the various mandate elements in briefings regarding specific peacekeeping operations.
>
> The Council welcomes efforts by Member States to respond more quickly to requests for the provision of personnel to take part in United Nations peacekeeping operations and underlines the importance of swift force generation in the early stages of mandate formulation.
>
> The Council believes that United Nations peacekeeping is a unique global partnership that draws together the contribution and commitment of the entire United Nations system. The Council stresses the need to improve the communication between the Council, the troop-contributing countries and police-contributing countries and the Secretariat, and other stakeholders, in accordance with resolution 1353(2001), to foster a spirit of partnership, cooperation, confidence and mutual trust and to ensure that the Council has the benefit of the views of those serving in the field when making its decisions about peacekeeping mandates. The Council also underlines the importance of an improved system of consultations among these actors, in order to promote a common understanding of the situation on the ground, of the mandate of the mission and of its implementation. The Council welcomes practical suggestions to improve this relationship and underscores the useful role of its Working Group on Peacekeeping Operations.
>
> The Council reaffirms the recommendations made in its resolutions 1327(2000) and 1353(2001) and in the statements by its President of 3 May and 4 November 1994, 28 March 1996, 31 January 2001, 17 May 2004 and 5 August 2009 and the note by its President of 14 January 2002 and confirms its intention to strengthen further efforts to implement fully those recommendations.
>
> The Council recalls, in particular, the statement by its President of 4 November 1994 and its resolution 1353(2001) and the decision contained therein to circulate an informal paper setting out the agenda, including issues to be covered, and drawing attention to the relevant background documentation to troop-contributing countries and police-contributing countries when they are invited to attend meetings with the Council or the Secretary-General. The Council requests that the Secretariat circulate to troop-contributing countries and police-contributing countries by the fifteenth day of each month notice of and invitations for the upcoming meetings of the Council with troop-contributing countries and police-contributing countries that are

anticipated to take place during the following month on individual peacekeeping mission mandates. This routine notification mechanism shall not constrain the Council from convening additional special, emergency or short-notice meetings with troop-contributing countries and police-contributing countries as circumstances may make appropriate.

The Council recognizes the need to improve its access to military advice, including from troop-contributing countries, and intends to pursue its work on mechanisms to that effect. The Council will continue to review the role of the Military Staff Committee. The Council recognizes the benefit of maintaining regular contact with mission senior leadership, including through an annual briefing by heads of military components. The Council would welcome similar briefings by heads of police components in order to improve understanding of operational challenges.

The Council expresses its commitment to continuing to improve its consideration and reflection of early peacebuilding tasks in the mandates and composition of peacekeeping operations. In this context, the Council notes with appreciation the contribution that peacekeepers and peacekeeping missions make to early peacebuilding and recognizes the need to integrate mission expertise and experience into the development of peacebuilding strategies.

The Council also recognizes the important work conducted by the Special Committee on Peacekeeping Operations and the Fifth Committee of the General Assembly.

The Council commits to making progress on the issue of more meaningful engagement with troop-contributing countries and police-contributing countries and to reviewing progress in 2012.

General aspects of UN peacekeeping

Safety and security

The Special Committee [A/65/19] condemned the killing of UN peacekeeping personnel and all acts of violence against them, as well as restrictions on their freedom of movement. The Committee requested the Secretariat to report on the impact of Joint Operations Centres and Joint Mission Analysis Centres on mission performance before the 2012 regular session, and to submit in 2012 a progress report on the implementation of the Security Level System introduced on 1 January 2011. It requested the Secretary-General to prepare and submit to the General Assembly by the end of November 2011 a further report on the investigation and prosecution of crimes committed against deployed UN peacekeepers. The Special Committee noted with concern that some deployed troop formations continued to be stretched to cover geographic areas that exceeded their capacities. Such practices not only threatened the safety and security of the troops but also adversely affected their performance, discipline, command and control, and capacity to implement the mandate.

Report of Secretary-General. In response to a request (above) made by the Special Committee, the Secretary-General submitted a December report [A/66/598] on all processes involved in the investigation and prosecution of crimes committed against deployed UN peacekeepers. The report provided information on the legal jurisdictional framework for the investigation and prosecution of crimes against peacekeepers, UN practice with regard to cooperation with the States concerned in the investigation and prosecution of such crimes, the investigative procedures set out in the revised model memorandum of understanding between the United Nations and troop-contributing countries, and a comparative summary of investigations, conducted under the revised model memorandum of understanding, of crimes committed against and by peacekeepers.

Conduct and discipline

The Special Committee [A/65/19] reaffirmed the need to ensure that all peacekeeping personnel functioned in a manner that preserved the image, credibility, impartiality and integrity of the United Nations. It emphasized that misconduct was unacceptable and that the reputation of peacekeeping missions in the eyes of the local population could have a direct bearing on operational activities. The same standards of conduct had to be applied to all categories of UN peacekeeping personnel, and such personnel had to be informed of and adhere to all applicable rules, regulations, provisions and guidelines provided by the United Nations for peacekeepers, as well as national laws and regulations. The Special Committee reiterated that troop-contributing countries bore the primary responsibility for maintaining discipline among their contingents deployed in peacekeeping missions.

Sexual exploitation and abuse in UN peacekeeping operations

In response to General Assembly resolution 57/306 [YUN 2003, p. 1237], the Secretary-General, in February, submitted a report [A/65/742] on special measures for protection from sexual exploitation and sexual abuse, presenting data on allegations of such incidents received from 43 UN system entities in 2010. The number of allegations reported by all entities decreased to 116 from 154 in 2009. In 2010, 85 allegations of sexual exploitation and abuse involving personnel deployed in peacekeeping and special political missions supported by the Department of Field Support (DFS) were reported to the Office of Internal Oversight Services (OIOS), a decrease of 24 per cent from the 112 reported in 2009. Of that number, 30 were considered egregious forms of sexual exploitation and abuse, namely the abuse of minors. A total of 13 allegations involved non-consensual sex.

From 2009 to 2010, the number of allegations reported decreased for four missions: the United Nations Integrated Office in Burundi (BINUB), the United Nations Organization Stabilization Mission in the Democratic Republic of the Congo (MONUSCO), the United Nations Mission in Liberia (UNMIL) and the United Nations Operation in Côte d'Ivoire (UNOCI). The most significant decrease occurred in MONUSCO, for which the number of allegations decreased from 59 allegations in 2009 to 36 allegations in 2010. An increase in the number of reported allegations was observed for the following four missions: the United Nations Mission in the Central African Republic and Chad (MINURCAT), the United Nations Stabilization Mission in Haiti (MINUSTAH), the United Nations Mission in the Sudan (UNMIS) and the United Nations Integrated Mission in Timor-Leste (UNMIT). The United Nations Interim Administration Mission in Kosovo (UNMIK) and the African Union-United Nations Hybrid Operation in Darfur (UNAMID) reported no allegations for 2010. At the United Nations Military Observer Group in India and Pakistan (UNMOGIP), no allegations were reported in 2009, but one was reported in 2010.

As at 31 December, investigations into allegations of sexual exploitation and abuse reported in 2010 had been completed in 38 per cent of cases. Of the completed investigations, 55 per cent were substantiated.

The Secretary-General also reported on measures to address the problem, including the activities of the Task Force on Protection from Sexual Exploitation and Abuse and the DFS Conduct and Discipline Unit and Teams.

The Assembly took note of the report in resolution 65/289 of 30 June (see p. 78).

Special Committee on Peacekeeping Operations consideration. The Special Committee [A/65/19] underlined the gravity of all acts of sexual and gender-based violence, including sexual exploitation and abuse, and stressed the importance of addressing the needs of victims. It reaffirmed the importance of implementing the policy of zero tolerance of sexual exploitation and abuse in UN peacekeeping operations. The Committee also stressed the importance of eliminating all forms of misconduct and expressed its concern about new cases of misconduct reported, including sexual exploitation and abuse. The Committee encouraged efforts to address the backlog of outstanding allegations awaiting investigation. The Special Committee called for the continued implementation of the United Nations Comprehensive Strategy on Assistance and Support to Victims of Sexual Exploitation and Abuse by United Nations Staff and Related Personnel, adopted in resolution 62/214 [YUN 2007, p. 1519].

Pilot project on centres of investigation

In March, OIOS submitted a preliminary report [A/65/765] on the implementation of the decision of the General Assembly, in its resolution 63/287 [YUN 2009, p. 84], to designate as a pilot project from 1 July 2009 to 30 June 2012 post-based budget allocations for centres of investigation in Nairobi, Vienna and New York, as well as resident investigators in seven peacekeeping missions. The report indicated an inefficient distribution of resources, with some missions receiving nominal staffing while the centre in Vienna was allocated positions in seniority and number in excess of its management and operational needs. Nevertheless, there appeared to be advantages to locating investigators in missions in terms of facilitating the reporting of wrongdoing and increasing investigator productivity. OIOS was analysing data to provide an improved basis for determining efficient and effective resource allocation and distribution to support operational requirements. The results would be included in a comprehensive report on the project to be submitted to the Assembly in the context of the 2012/13 support account budget.

Strengthening operational capacity

The Special Committee on Peacekeeping Operations [A/65/19] underscored the importance of ensuring that a sound and timely interaction and better understanding were maintained among the Security Council, the Secretariat and the troop-contributing countries in order to devise clear, unambiguous and achievable mandates and to generate and mobilize the necessary political, human, financial and logistical resources and information capacity to achieve the mandates. It reiterated that there should be adequate capabilities and clear operational guidelines for peacekeeping missions to ensure that they were able to carry out their mandated tasks effectively. The Committee was of the view that, whenever the mandate of a mission was changed or amended, the Secretariat should ensure, at the earliest opportunity, that the operational documents conformed with the changed mandate. It reaffirmed that the views of concerned troop- and police-contributing countries should be given due consideration during the process. The Special Committee recommended that the Security Council be advised on the availability of the operational and logistic capabilities that would be necessary for the success of a peacekeeping operation prior to deciding on a change of mandate.

Strategies for complex peacekeeping operations

The Special Committee on Peacekeeping Operations [A/65/19] encouraged the Secretariat to further engage with Member States, particularly troop- and police-contributing countries, on matters relating to peacekeeping operations. It stressed that peacekeeping operations had to be complemented with activities aimed at improving the living conditions of the affected populations, including rapid implementation of projects that helped create jobs and deliver basic social services in the post-conflict phase. The UN system and the international community, cooperating with national authorities, should develop coordination mechanisms that focused on immediate needs as well as long-term reconstruction and poverty reduction. The Special Committee underlined that reconstruction, economic revitalization and capacity-building were crucial to the long-term development of post-conflict societies and for generating sustainable peace.

Cooperation with troop- and police-contributing countries

The Special Committee [A/65/19] underlined the importance of enhancing the triangular cooperation between troop- and police-contributing countries, the Secretariat and the Security Council in addressing peacekeeping challenges. It recommended consulting with troop- and police-contributing countries in order to involve them early on and fully in all stages of operations. It requested that the Secretariat produce pre-deployment threat assessments and make them available to potential troop-contributing countries before such countries presented their pledges to new missions. The Committee urged the Secretariat to consult with the troop- and police-contributing countries when planning any change in military and police tasks, mission-specific rules of engagement, operational concepts or command and control structure that would have an impact on personnel, equipment, training and logistics requirements. The Special Committee recommended that guidelines for pre-deployment visits for military contributions and formed police units be improved.

Cooperation with regional organizations

OIOS evaluation. In February, OIOS submitted the thematic evaluation [A/65/762] of cooperation between DPKO/DFS and regional organizations. The evaluation found, among other things, that the United Nations and some regional organizations were committed to cooperating on peacekeeping issues and activities, but there was no clear strategic vision guiding cooperation. The practice of cooperation lacked measurable objectives and was largely driven by operational needs. The evaluation concluded that cooperation with regional organizations in peacekeeping contributed to the overall capacity of the United Nations to deploy and sustain peacekeeping missions, but organizational differences between the Organization and its partners created multiple challenges in operational cooperation. OIOS recommended a series of measures for strengthening relationships between DPKO/DFS and regional organizations.

Special Committee on Peacekeeping Operations consideration. The Special Committee [A/65/19] reaffirmed the important contribution that regional arrangements and agencies could make to peacekeeping, in accordance with Chapter VIII of the UN Charter, and encouraged the Secretariat to strengthen cooperation with them. It recognized the growing importance of partnership and cooperation between the United Nations and regional arrangements in planning and conducting peacekeeping operations, and encouraged the Secretariat to develop exercise and training policies with regional arrangements aimed at improving interoperability.

Women in peacekeeping

With respect to gender and peacekeeping, the Special Committee [A/65/19] emphasized the importance of full implementation of Security Council resolutions 1325(2000) [YUN 2000, p. 1113], 1820(2008) [YUN 2008, p. 1265] and 1888(2009) [YUN 2009, p. 1137], 1889(2009) [ibid., p. 1141] and 1960(2010) [YUN 2010, p. 1164] on women and peace and security and all General Assembly resolutions on the elimination of all forms of violence against women.

The Special Committee stressed the importance of the equal participation and full involvement of women in all peace and security efforts. It noted the increase in the overall proportion of women, as reported by DPKO and DFS, and welcomed the UN Police Division's intention to raise the participation of female police officers to 20 per cent before 2014. It continued to express its concern, however, at the low proportion of women among UN peacekeeping staff, and encouraged Member States to increase the participation of women among uniformed personnel. The Committee urged DPKO and Member States to continue to develop a comprehensive strategy to increase the participation of women in all aspects and at all levels of UN peacekeeping operations. The Special Committee took note of the gender training strategy developed by DPKO and requested that it be implemented expeditiously. It called for the promotion of gender perspectives by all categories of personnel in multidimensional peacekeeping activities.

On 28 October, the Council, by presidential statement **S/PRST/2011/20** on women and peace and security (see p. 1076), reiterated its condemnation of all violations of international law committed against women and girls in armed conflict and post-conflict situations and urged the cessation by all parties of such acts. It also urged Member States to bring to justice those responsible for crimes of that nature.

Security Council Working Group on Peacekeeping Operations

On 30 December, the Chairman of the Security Council Working Group on Peacekeeping Operations submitted to the Council a report [S/2011/817] covering its work since 29 June. In meetings held on 29 June, 24 August, 2 November, 30 November and 12 December, the Working Group discussed, among other issues, challenges faced by the United Nations in the procurement of helicopters for peacekeeping missions; enhancement of triangular cooperation between troop-contributing countries, the Secretariat and the Security Council; welfare and safety of troops; and capacity gaps in the context of clear and achievable mandates. The report summarized the discussions that took place during the meetings, including the exchange of views and recommendations of the Chair of the Working Group.

Oversight activities

OIOS reported in March [A/65/271 (Part II) & Add.1] on its peacekeeping oversight activities in 2010. The Office issued 195 oversight reports related to peace operations, which accounted for 46 per cent of all OIOS recommendations for the year. OIOS also discussed 92 audit reports issued to various departments and missions in 2010. Those reports contained a total of 852 audit recommendations related to the following audit risk categories: strategy, governance, compliance, finance, operations, human resources and information resources. Of those recommendations, 29 per cent were categorized as high risk, 69 per cent were medium risk, and 2 per cent were low risk. OIOS issued 101 investigation reports concerning peacekeeping operations.

Comprehensive review of peacekeeping

Special Committee on Peacekeeping Operations

As requested by the General Assembly in resolution 64/266 [YUN 2010, p. 84], the Special Committee on Peacekeeping Operations and its Working Group continued their comprehensive review of the question of peacekeeping operations in all their aspects.

The Committee held its 2011 substantive session from 22 February to 18 March and on 9 May [A/65/19]. It discussed guiding principles, definitions and implementation of mandates; restructuring of peacekeeping; safety and security; conduct and discipline; strengthening operational capacity; strategies for complex peacekeeping operations; cooperation with troop-contributing countries; triangular cooperation between the Security Council, the Secretariat and the troop- and police-contributing countries; cooperation with regional arrangements; enhancement of African peacekeeping capabilities; UN field support arrangements; and best practices, training, personnel and financial matters, among other issues.

Report of Secretary-General. In January [A/65/680 & Add.1], the Secretary-General reported on the implementation of the recommendations contained in the Special Committee's 2010 report [YUN 2010, p. 84], as requested by the Committee. The Secretary-General's report set out progress made over the previous year in clarifying and delivering on critical roles in UN peacekeeping; building capabilities; strengthening field support arrangements; and improving mission planning, management and oversight.

The Secretary-General observed that action was needed to ensure that missions were mobile, flexible and had the expertise to discharge complex mandates. The capabilities required for multidimensional peacekeeping should be generated through shared standards, training and attention to resource gaps, along with strengthened partnerships. Arrangements with partners would need to be explored to address requirements for specialized civilian capacity, and to recruit and retain more women. It was imperative to ensure the highest level of integrity and dedication in keeping with the roles entrusted by the international community to UN peacekeeping operations. The Secretary-General also observed that 2010 was one of the most tragic years in UN peacekeeping in terms of loss of civilian and uniformed personnel, which stood at 164 as at 30 November 2010.

GENERAL ASSEMBLY ACTION

On 19 July [meeting 109], the General Assembly, on the recommendation of the Fourth (Special Political and Decolonization) Committee [A/65/424/Add.1], adopted **resolution 65/310** without vote [agenda item 53].

Comprehensive review of the whole question of peacekeeping operations in all their aspects

The General Assembly,

Recalling its resolution 2006(XIX) of 18 February 1965 and all other relevant resolutions,

Recalling in particular its resolution 64/266 of 21 May 2010,

Affirming that the efforts of the United Nations in the peaceful settlement of disputes, including through its peacekeeping operations, are indispensable,

Convinced of the need for the United Nations to continue to improve its capabilities in the field of peacekeeping and to enhance the effective and efficient deployment of its peacekeeping operations,

Considering the contribution that all States Members of the United Nations make to peacekeeping,

Noting the widespread interest in contributing to the work of the Special Committee on Peacekeeping Operations expressed by Member States, in particular troop- and police-contributing countries,

Bearing in mind the continuous necessity of preserving the efficiency and strengthening the effectiveness of the work of the Special Committee,

1. *Welcomes* the report of the Special Committee on Peacekeeping Operations;

2. *Endorses* the proposals, recommendations and conclusions of the Special Committee, contained in paragraphs 15 to 278 of its report;

3. *Urges* Member States, the Secretariat and relevant organs of the United Nations to take all steps necessary to implement the proposals, recommendations and conclusions of the Special Committee;

4. *Reiterates* that those Member States that become personnel contributors to the United Nations peacekeeping operations in years to come or participate in the future in the Special Committee for three consecutive years as observers shall, upon request in writing to the Chair of the Special Committee, become members at the following session of the Special Committee;

5. *Decides* that the Special Committee, in accordance with its mandate, shall continue its efforts for a comprehensive review of the whole question of peacekeeping operations in all their aspects and shall review the implementation of its previous proposals and consider any new proposals so as to enhance the capacity of the United Nations to fulfil its responsibilities in this field;

6. *Requests* the Special Committee to submit a report on its work to the General Assembly at its sixty-sixth session;

7. *Decides* to include in the provisional agenda of its sixty-sixth session the item entitled "Comprehensive review of the whole question of peacekeeping operations in all their aspects".

On 9 December, the Assembly, by **decision 66/521**, took note of the report [A/66/428] of the Fourth (Special Political and Decolonization) Committee on the comprehensive review of peacekeeping.

Operations in 2011

As at 31 December, there were 15 peacekeeping missions in operation—7 in Africa, 1 in the Americas, 2 in Asia, 2 in Europe and the Mediterranean and 3 in the Middle East.

Africa

In Africa, the Security Council extended the mandates of the United Nations Mission for the Referendum in Western Sahara (MINURSO) until 30 April 2012; the United Nations Mission in Liberia (UNMIL) until 30 September 2012; and the African Union-United Nations Hybrid Operation in Darfur (UNAMID) until 31 July 2012. The Council renewed the mandate of the United Nations Operation in Côte d'Ivoire (UNOCI) twice—until 31 July 2011, and until 31 July 2012. It extended the mandate of the United Nations Organization Stabilization Mission in the Democratic Republic of the Congo (MONUSCO) until 30 June 2012. In April, the Council extended the mandate of the United Nations Mission in the Sudan (UNMIS) until 9 July 2011. After considering the request by South Sudan for a continued UN presence in that country, the Council established the United Nations Mission in South Sudan (UNMISS) for an initial period of one year, commencing 8 July. The Council, concerned by the situation in the Abyei area, and recognizing that it demanded an urgent response and constituted a threat to international peace and security, established, for an initial period of six months beginning on 27 June, the United Nations Interim Security Force for Abyei (UNISFA). In December, the Council extended the UNISFA mandate for a further five-month period.

Americas

In the Americas, the Security Council extended the mandate of the United Nations Stabilization Mission in Haiti (MINUSTAH) until 15 October 2012.

Asia

In Asia, the United Nations Military Observer Group in India and Pakistan (UNMOGIP), established in 1949, continued to monitor the ceasefire in Jammu and Kashmir. The Security Council extended the mandate of the United Nations Integrated Mission in Timor-Leste (UNMIT) until 26 February 2012. It extended the authorization of the International Security Assistance Force (ISAF) in Afghanistan until 13 October 2012.

Europe and the Mediterranean

The Council extended the United Nations Peacekeeping Force in Cyprus (UNFICYP) twice—to 15 December 2011 and to 19 July 2012. The United Nations Interim Administration Mission in Kosovo (UNMIK) remained in place. On 16 November, the Council authorized the Member States acting through or in cooperation with the European Union to establish, for a further 12-month period, a multinational stabilization force (EUFOR) in Bosnia and Herzegovina.

Middle East

Three long-standing operations continued in the Middle East. The United Nations Truce Supervision Organization (UNTSO) monitored ceasefires, supervised armistice agreements and assisted other

Chapter I: International peace and security

peacekeeping operations in the region. The Security Council extended the mandate of the United Nations Disengagement Observer Force (UNDOF) twice—until 31 December 2011, and until 30 June 2012—and that of the United Nations Interim Force in Lebanon (UNIFIL) until 31 August 2012.

Roster of 2011 operations

UNTSO

United Nations Truce Supervision Organization
Established: May 1948.
Mandate: To monitor ceasefires, supervise armistice agreements, prevent isolated incidents from escalating and assist other peacekeeping operations in the region.
Strength: 150 military observers, 101 international civilian staff, 132 local civilian staff.

UNMOGIP

United Nations Military Observer Group in India and Pakistan
Established: January 1949.
Mandate: To supervise the ceasefire between India and Pakistan in Jammu and Kashmir.
Strength: 39 military observers, 25 international civilian staff, 51 local civilian staff.

UNFICYP

United Nations Peacekeeping Force in Cyprus
Established: March 1964.
Mandate: To prevent the recurrence of fighting between the two Cypriot communities and to contribute to the maintenance and restoration of law and order and a return to normal conditions.
Strength: 872 troops, 69 police, 38 international civilian staff, 112 local civilian staff.

UNDOF

United Nations Disengagement Observer Force
Established: June 1974.
Mandate: To supervise the ceasefire between Israel and Syria and the disengagement of Israeli and Syrian forces in the Golan Heights.
Strength: 1,043 troops, 41 international civilian staff, 103 local civilian staff.

UNIFIL

United Nations Interim Force in Lebanon
Established: March 1978.

Mandate: To restore peace and security and assist the Lebanese Government in ensuring the return of its effective authority in the area; expanded in 2006 to include monitoring the cessation of hostilities between Hizbullah and Israel, supporting the deployment of the Lebanese armed forces throughout southern Lebanon, helping to ensure humanitarian access to civilian populations and the return of displaced persons, and assisting the Government in securing its borders to prevent the entry of unauthorized arms or materiel.
Strength: 12,017 troops, 353 international civilian staff, 666 local civilian staff.

MINURSO

United Nations Mission for the Referendum in Western Sahara
Established: April 1991.
Mandate: To monitor and verify the implementation of a settlement plan for Western Sahara and assist in the holding of a referendum in the Territory.
Strength: 27 troops, 195 military observers, 6 police, 102 international civilian staff, 165 local civilian staff, 19 UN Volunteers.

UNMIK

United Nations Interim Administration Mission in Kosovo
Established: June 1999.
Mandate: To help ensure conditions for a peaceful and normal life for all inhabitants of Kosovo and advance regional stability in the Western Balkans.
Strength: 9 military observers, 7 police, 150 international civilian staff, 215 local civilian staff, 26 UN Volunteers.

UNMIL

United Nations Mission in Liberia
Established: September 2003.
Mandate: To support the implementation of the 2003 ceasefire agreement and the peace process; protect UN staff, facilities and civilians; support humanitarian and human rights activities; and assist in national security reform, including national police training and formation of a new, restructured military.
Strength: 7,778 troops, 131 military observers, 1,297 police, 477 international civilian staff, 991 local civilian staff, 255 UN Volunteers.

UNOCI

United Nations Operation in Côte d'Ivoire
Established: April 2004.

Mandate: To facilitate the implementation of the 2003 peace agreement; contribute to the consolidation of the stability of the country, to the electoral process and the identification of the population, and to other peace-related tasks.

Strength: 9,416 troops, 197 military observers, 1,386 police, 397 international civilian staff, 743 local civilian staff, 276 UN Volunteers.

MINUSTAH

United Nations Stabilization Mission in Haiti
Established: June 2004.

Mandate: To provide support in ensuring a secure and stable environment; assist in monitoring and reforming the National Police; help with disarmament, demobilization and reintegration programmes; protect civilians as well as UN personnel and property; support the constitutional and political process; assist in maintaining the rule of law, public safety and public order; promote and protect human rights; and promote an inclusive political dialogue and national reconciliation.

Strength: 8,065 troops, 3,546 police, 568 international civilian staff, 1,355 local civilian staff, 236 UN Volunteers.

UNMIS

United Nations Mission in the Sudan
Established: March 2005.

Mandate: To support the implementation of the 2005 Comprehensive Peace Agreement between the Government of the Sudan and the Sudan People's Liberation Movement/Army; facilitate and coordinate humanitarian assistance and the return of refugees and internally displaced persons; assist with demining; and protect and promote human rights. The mandate was expanded in 2006 to support implementation of the 2006 Darfur Peace Agreement and the 2004 N'djamena Agreement on Humanitarian Ceasefire on the Conflict in Darfur. UNMIS completed its mandate on 9 July 2011.

UNMIT

United Nations Integrated Mission in Timor-Leste
Established: August 2006.

Mandate: To build capacity in the governance, justice and security sectors; provide law enforcement and public security; assist the Government in organizing elections; strengthen human rights mechanisms; and complete investigations into cases of serious human rights violations.

Strength: 33 military observers, 1,183 police, 394 international civilian staff, 883 local civilian staff, 211 UN Volunteers.

UNAMID

African Union-United Nations Hybrid Operation in Darfur
Established: July 2007.

Mandate: To contribute to the protection of civilians and to security for humanitarian assistance; monitor and verify implementation of agreements; assist an inclusive political process; contribute to the promotion of human rights and the rule of law; and monitor and report on the situation along the borders with Chad and the Central African Republic.

Strength: 17,778 troops, 262 military observers, 4,950 police, 1,124 international civilian staff, 2,904 local civilian staff, 483 UN Volunteers.

MONUSCO

United Nations Organization Stabilization Mission in the Democratic Republic of the Congo
Established: July 2010.

Mandate: To protect civilians and provide support to the Government in stabilization and peace consolidation.

Strength: 16,854 troops, 703 military observers, 1,371 police, 976 international civilian staff, 2,865 local civilian staff, 614 UN Volunteers.

UNISFA

United Nations Interim Security Force for Abyei
Established: June 2011.

Mandate: To monitor and verify the redeployment of any Sudanese Armed Forces and the Sudan People's Liberation Army or its successor from the Abyei area; facilitate the delivery of humanitarian aid and the free movement of relief workers in the area; provide security for the region's oil infrastructure; protect UN personnel, facilities, installations and equipment; and protect civilians from the threat of violence.

Strength: 3,724 troops, 74 military observers, 20 international civilian staff.

UNMISS

United Nations Mission in South Sudan
Established: July 2011.

Mandate: To support the Government in consolidating peace, thereby fostering longer-term state building and economic development; conflict prevention, mitigation and resolution, and protecting civilians; and developing capacity to provide security, establishing the rule of law, and strengthening the security and justice sectors.

Strength: 4,803 troops, 169 military observers, 485 police, 697 international civilian staff, 1,117 local civilians, 226 UN Volunteers.

Financial and administrative aspects of peacekeeping operations

The General Assembly considered a number of issues related to financial and administrative aspects of UN peacekeeping operations, including the financial performance of UN peacekeeping operations; the support account for peacekeeping operations; funds for closed missions; UN air operations financial reports and audited financial statements; management and financing of the United Nations Logistics Base (UNLB) at Brindisi, Italy; restructuring; UN police capacities; personnel matters; criminal accountability of UN staff and experts on mission; the welfare and recreational needs of peacekeeping staff; death and disability; and training.

Financing

Expenditures for UN peacekeeping operations from 1 July 2010 to 30 June 2011 [A/66/5 (Vol. II)] decreased by 0.6 per cent, from $7,616.1 million in the previous fiscal year to $7,573.7 million. Total assessments decreased by 3.1 per cent, from $7,963.2 million to $7,719.2 million. The decrease was attributable largely to the completion of the MINURCAT mandate in 2010 [YUN 2010, p. 87], and to UNIFIL. The decrease was partially offset by increases in UNAMID, MINUSTAH and UNMIS. Unpaid assessments pertaining to active peacekeeping missions increased by 6.5 per cent, from $907.1 million to $965.8 million at 30 June 2011. Unpaid assessments for closed missions decreased marginally, from $548.3 million to $547.3 million. The overall level of unpaid assessments increased from $1,455.4 million to $1,513.1 million.

Available cash for active peacekeeping missions as at 30 June totalled $1,909.2 million, while liabilities reached $2,416.8 million. For closed missions with cash surpluses, which remained the only source of lending to active missions, available cash totalled $300.9 million, while liabilities amounted to $261.8 million. During the reporting period, the United Nations Peace Forces provided loans of $88.9 million to MONUSCO ($37.0 million), MINURSO ($26.9 million), UNMIK ($21.0 million) and UNFICYP ($4.0 million). Total loans outstanding as at 30 June amounted to $52.3 million.

Notes of Secretary-General. On 7 February, the Secretary-General, in a note [A/C.5/65/15] on approved resources for peacekeeping operations from 1 July 2010 to 30 June 2011, including requirements for UNLB and the support account for peacekeeping operations, provided information on further financing actions taken by the General Assembly at the main part of its sixty-fifth session in respect of MINUSTAH, UNMIS, MINURCAT, MONUSCO and the support account for peacekeeping operations. Approved resources for the period ended 30 June 2011 totalled $7,832,407,000.

On 7 April [A/C.5/65/17], in accordance with Assembly resolution 49/233 A [YUN 1994, p. 1338], the Secretary-General submitted to the Fifth (Administrative and Budgetary) Committee information on the proposed budgetary requirements of each peacekeeping operation, including budget levels for UNLB and the support account for peacekeeping operations, for the period from 1 July 2011 to 30 June 2012, by category. Aggregate total resource requirements amounted to $7,600,439,100.

On 30 June, the Secretary-General submitted to the Fifth Committee a note [A/C.5/65/18] reflecting the resources to be approved by the Assembly in respect of each peacekeeping mission, including the prorated shares of the support account for peacekeeping operations and UNLB.

On 22 July, the Secretary-General submitted information [A/C.5/65/19] on approved resources for peacekeeping operations for 1 July 2011 to 30 June 2012, including requirements for UNLB and the support account for peacekeeping operations, which amounted to $7,060,322,827.

Financial performance

In February, the Secretary-General submitted an overview report [A/65/715] on the financing of UN peacekeeping operations: budget performance for the period from 1 July 2009 to 30 June 2010 and the budget for 1 July 2011 to 30 June 2012. During the former period, total expenditure amounted to $7,576.6 million, against an approved budget of $7,980.3 million, exclusive of voluntary contributions in kind. The budget for peacekeeping operations for the latter period was estimated at $7.6 billion.

Peacekeeping support account

The Secretary-General, in his performance report [A/65/610 & Add.1] on the budget of the support account for peacekeeping operations for the period from 1 July 2009 to 30 June 2010 stated that expenditures for that period amounted to $318,475,800 against approved resources of $322,547,400, resulting in unutilized resources totalling $4,071,600. The unutilized balance was attributable to underexpenditure in respect of post and non-post resources, in particular under general temporary assistance, official travel and other services, supplies and equipment, offset by additional requirements under the post resources, facilities and infrastructure and communications categories of expenditure. The Secretary-General recommended that the General Assembly appropriate and assess an additional amount of $24,444,900 with respect to the period from 1 July 2009 to 30 June 2010; and decide on the treatment of other income amounting to $6,048,000, comprising interest income ($2,161,000), other miscellaneous income ($1,359,000) and cancellations of prior-period obligations ($2,528,000) in respect of the period from 1 July 2009 to 30 June 2010.

The Secretary-General, in his performance report [A/66/610 & Add.1] on the budget of the support account for peacekeeping operations for the period from 1 July 2010 to 30 June 2011, stated that expenditures for that period amounted to $341,421,400 against authorized resources of $363,811,506, resulting in unutilized resources totalling $22,390,100. The unutilized balance was attributable to under-expenditure in respect of post and non-post resources, in particular under the general temporary assistance, information technology and other supplies, services and equipment resource categories. The Secretary-General recommended that the General Assembly decide on the treatment of the unencumbered balance of $22,390,100 in respect of the period from 1 July 2010 to 30 June 2011; and decide on the treatment of other income amounting to $6,098,000, comprising interest income ($1,026,000), other miscellaneous income ($615,000) and cancellations of prior-period obligations ($4,457,000), in respect of the period from 1 July 2010 to 30 June 2011.

In February [A/65/761 & Corr.1,2], the Secretary-General submitted the budget for the support account for peacekeeping operations for the period from 1 July 2011 to 30 June 2012, amounting to $315,362,400. It provided for 1,356 posts, comprising 1,350 continuing posts and 6 new posts.

The Independent Audit Advisory Committee, in February, submitted its comments [A/65/734] on the proposed budget for OIOS under the support account for peacekeeping operations for 1 July 2011 to 30 June 2012.

In April, ACABQ provided its observations and recommendations [A/65/827] on the Secretary-General's performance report on the budget of the support account for peacekeeping operations for 1 July 2009 to 30 June 2010 (see above) and the proposed budget for the support account for peacekeeping operations from 1 July 2011 to 30 June 2012. Its recommendations involved reductions totalling $1,739,900 gross ($2,006,000 net), as detailed in the report. Accordingly, it recommended that the Assembly approve a total amount of $360,807,000 gross ($328,972,700 net) for the support account for the period from 1 July 2011 to 30 June 2012, which included $313,622,500 for the staffing and non-staffing resources for the support account and $47,185,200 for enterprise resource planning. ACABQ also recommended approval of two of the six additional posts proposed by the Secretary-General in his February report on the support account budget.

The Advisory Committee recommended that the Assembly appropriate and assess the additional amount of $24,444,900 with respect to the period from 1 July 2009 through 30 June 2010, as proposed by the Secretary-General in his performance report for that period (see above), and that it apply the amount of $6,048,000, comprising interest income ($2,161,000), other income ($1,359,000) and cancellation of prior-period obligations ($2,528,000), to the support account requirements for the period from 1 July 2011 to 30 June 2012.

ACABQ recommended that the excess of the authorized level of the Peacekeeping Reserve Fund in respect of the financial period ended 30 June 2010 in the amount of $3,377,000 be applied to the support account requirements for the period from 1 July 2011 to 30 June 2012.

GENERAL ASSEMBLY ACTION

On 30 June [meeting 106], the General Assembly, on the recommendation of the Fifth (Administrative and Budgetary) Committee [A/65/890] adopted **resolution 65/290** without vote [agenda item 143].

Strengthening the capacity of the United Nations to manage and sustain peacekeeping operations

The General Assembly,

Recalling its resolutions 45/258 of 3 May 1991, 47/218 A of 23 December 1992, 48/226 A of 23 December 1993, 55/238 of 23 December 2000, 56/241 of 24 December 2001, 56/293 of 27 June 2002, 57/318 of 18 June 2003, 58/298 of 18 June 2004, 59/301 of 22 June 2005, 60/268 of 30 June 2006, 61/245 and 61/246 of 22 December 2006, 61/256 of 15 March 2007, 61/279 of 29 June 2007, 62/250 of 20 June 2008, 63/287 of 30 June 2009 and 64/271 of 24 June 2010, its decisions 48/489 of 8 July 1994, 49/469 of 23 December 1994 and 50/473 of 23 December 1995 and its other relevant resolutions,

Having considered the reports of the Secretary-General on strengthening the capacity of the United Nations to manage and sustain peacekeeping operations, on the budget performance of the support account for peacekeeping operations for the period from 1 July 2009 to 30 June 2010 and on the budget for the support account for peacekeeping operations for the period from 1 July 2011 to 30 June 2012, the preliminary report of the Office of Internal Oversight Services on the implementation of the pilot project designated by the General Assembly in its resolution 63/287, the report of the Independent Audit Advisory Committee on the budget of the Office of Internal Oversight Services under the support account for peacekeeping operations for the period from 1 July 2011 to 30 June 2012 and the related report of the Advisory Committee on Administrative and Budgetary Questions, as well as the report of the Office of Internal Oversight Services on the thematic evaluation of cooperation between, on the one hand, the Department of Peacekeeping Operations and the Department of Field Support of the Secretariat and, on the other, regional organizations,

Recognizing the importance of the United Nations being able to respond and deploy rapidly to a peacekeeping operation upon the adoption of a relevant resolution of the Security Council, within thirty days for traditional peacekeeping operations and ninety days for complex peacekeeping operations,

Recognizing also the need for adequate support during all phases of peacekeeping operations, including the liquidation and termination phases,

Mindful that the level of the support account should broadly correspond to the mandate, number, size and complexity of peacekeeping missions,

1. *Reaffirms* its role in carrying out a thorough analysis and approval of human and financial resources and policies with a view to ensuring the full, effective and efficient implementation of all mandated programmes and activities and the implementation of policies in this regard;

2. *Also reaffirms* that the Fifth Committee is the appropriate Main Committee of the General Assembly entrusted with responsibility for administrative and budgetary matters;

3. *Further reaffirms* rule 153 of its rules of procedure;

4. *Reaffirms* that the support account funds shall be used for the sole purpose of financing human resources and non-human resource requirements for backstopping and supporting peacekeeping operations at Headquarters, and that any changes in this limitation require the prior approval of the General Assembly;

5. *Also reaffirms* the need for adequate funding for the backstopping of peacekeeping operations, as well as the need for full justification for that funding in support account budget submissions;

6. *Emphasizes* the importance of interaction and coordination with troop- and police-contributing countries;

7. *Recalls* section I, paragraph 6, of resolution 55/238, paragraph 11 of resolution 56/241, paragraph 19 of resolution 61/279 and paragraph 22 of resolution 62/250, and requests the Secretary-General to make further concrete efforts to ensure the proper representation of troop-contributing countries in the Department of Peacekeeping Operations and the Department of Field Support of the Secretariat, taking into account their contribution to United Nations peacekeeping;

8. *Recognizes* the significant role of the Police Division of the Department of Peacekeeping Operations in contributing to peacekeeping operations, including their peacekeeping efforts, and the increase in the policing dimension in a number of operations;

9. *Reaffirms* the need for effective and efficient administration and financial management of peacekeeping operations, and urges the Secretary-General to continue to identify measures to increase the productivity and efficiency of the support account;

10. *Requests* the Secretary-General to ensure the full implementation of the relevant provisions of General Assembly resolutions 59/296 of 22 June 2005, 60/266 of 30 June 2006, 61/276 of 29 June 2007, 64/269 of 24 June 2010 and 65/289 of 30 June 2011, and other relevant resolutions;

11. *Endorses* the conclusions and recommendations contained in the report of the Advisory Committee on Administrative and Budgetary Questions, subject to the provisions of the present resolution, and requests the Secretary-General to ensure their full implementation;

12. *Takes note* of the report of the Office of Internal Oversight Services on the thematic evaluation of cooperation between, on the one hand, the Department of Peacekeeping Operations and the Department of Field Support and, on the other, regional organizations;

13. *Reaffirms* its role with regard to the structure of the Secretariat, and stresses that proposals that amend the overall departmental structure, as well as the format of the budgets of the Organization and the biennial programme plan, are subject to review and approval by the General Assembly;

14. *Notes* the overall benefits of the restructuring of the Department of Peacekeeping Operations and the Department of Field Support, and requests the Secretary-General to assess these benefits and to continue to make every effort to enhance the capacity of the Organization to manage and sustain peacekeeping operations;

15. *Underlines* the crucial importance of ensuring that the lessons learned and best practices of peacekeeping missions are adequately captured, processed and incorporated into guidelines and policies, particularly with regard to peacebuilding efforts by peacekeepers and peacekeeping operations in transition, and in this regard recognizes the significant role of the Peacekeeping Best Practices Section and best practices officers on the ground;

16. *Notes* that the strategy for early peacebuilding is still being developed by the Secretariat, and in this regard requests the Secretary-General to consult closely, throughout the process of the preparation of the strategy, with Member States, the Peacebuilding Commission, United Nations agencies, funds and programmes and all other relevant Secretariat entities, and underlines that specific peacebuilding tasks undertaken by peacekeeping missions should be based on the priorities of the country concerned and on the specific context;

17. *Takes note* of the report of the Secretary-General on the budget for the support account for peacekeeping operations for the period from 1 July 2011 to 30 June 2012 and the report of the Independent Audit Advisory Committee on the budget of the Office of Internal Oversight Services under the support account for peacekeeping operations for the period from 1 July 2011 to 30 June 2012;

18. *Decides* to maintain, for the financial period from 1 July 2011 to 30 June 2012, the funding mechanism for the support account used in the period from 1 July 2010 to 30 June 2011, as approved in paragraph 3 of its resolution 50/221 B of 7 June 1996;

19. *Takes note* of paragraphs 44 and 55 of the report of the Advisory Committee on Administrative and Budgetary Questions;

20. *Reiterates its request* to the Secretary-General to review the level of the support account on a regular basis, taking into consideration the number, size and complexity of peacekeeping operations;

21. *Emphasizes* that support functions should be scalable to the size and scope of peacekeeping operations;

22. *Requests* the Secretary-General to fill all vacancies in an expeditious manner;

Financial performance report for the period from 1 July 2009 to 30 June 2010

23. *Takes note* of the report of the Secretary-General on the financial performance of the support account for peacekeeping operations for the period from 1 July 2009 to 30 June 2010;

Budget estimates for the period from 1 July 2011 to 30 June 2012

24. *Approves* the support account requirements in the amount of 344,792,400 United States dollars for the financial period from 1 July 2011 to 30 June 2012, inclusive of the amount of 47,185,200 dollars for the enterprise resource planning project pursuant to its resolution 64/243 of 24 December 2009, including 1,294 continuing posts and 1 new temporary post, as well as the redeployment, reassignment and reclassification of posts as set out in annex I to the present resolution and 151 continuing and 11 new general temporary assistance positions as set out in annex II, as well as their related post and non-post requirements;

Financing of the support account for peacekeeping operations for the periods from 1 July 2009 to 30 June 2010 and from 1 July 2011 to 30 June 2012

25. *Decides* that the requirements for the support account for peacekeeping operations for the financial periods from 1 July 2009 to 30 June 2010 and from 1 July 2011 to 30 June 2012 shall be financed as follows:

(a) An additional amount of 24,444,900 dollars, to be appropriated and assessed in respect of the financial period from 1 July 2009 to 30 June 2010;

(b) The total amount of 6,048,000 dollars, comprising interest income of 2,161,000 dollars, other miscellaneous income of 1,359,000 dollars and the cancellation of prior-period obligations of 2,528,000 dollars, to be applied to the resources required for the financial period from 1 July 2011 to 30 June 2012;

(c) The amount of 3,377,000 dollars, representing the excess of the authorized level of the Peacekeeping Reserve Fund in respect of the financial period ended 30 June 2010, to be applied to the resources required for the financial period from 1 July 2011 to 30 June 2012;

(d) The balance of 359,812,300 dollars, to be prorated among the budgets of the active peacekeeping operations for the financial period from 1 July 2011 to 30 June 2012;

(e) The net estimated staff assessment income of 30,474,500 dollars, comprising the amount of 29,685,000 dollars for the financial period from 1 July 2011 to 30 June 2012 and the increase of 789,500 dollars in respect of the financial period ended 30 June 2010, to be set off against the balance referred to in subparagraph (d) above, to be prorated among the budgets of the individual active peacekeeping operations.

ANNEX I

A. Support account posts to be established for the period from 1 July 2011 to 30 June 2012

Organizational unit		Number	Level	Function	Status
Department of Peacekeeping Operations					
Policy, Evaluation and Training Division	Peacekeeping Best Practices Section	1	P-4	Child Protection Adviser	Conversion from general temporary assistance
	TOTAL	**1**			

B. Redeployment, reassignment, reclassification, restructuring and abolition of posts under the support account for the period from 1 July 2011 to 30 June 2012

Redeployments

Department of Peacekeeping Operations/Office of Operations/Africa I Division/United Nations Mission in the Central African Republic and Chad integrated operational team

Redeployment of 1 post (P-5 Senior Political Affairs Officer) to the Africa II Division, United Nations Mission in Liberia/United Nations Operation in Côte d'Ivoire integrated operational team

Redeployment of 1 post (P-3 Political Affairs Officer) to the Africa I Division, United Nations Mission in the Sudan integrated operational team

Department of Peacekeeping Operations/Office of Military Affairs/Military Planning Service

Redeployment of 2 posts (1 P-4 Capability Development Officer and 1 P-4 Military Policy and Doctrine Officer) to the Office of the Military Adviser, Policy and Doctrine Team

Department of Peacekeeping Operations/Office of Rule of Law and Security Institutions/Police Division

Redeployment of 16 posts (1 P-5 Chief of Section, 6 P-4 Selection and Recruitment Officers, 7 P-3 Selection and Recruitment Officers and 2 General Service (Other level) Administrative Assistants) from the Mission Management and Support Section to the Selection and Recruitment Section

Department of Field Support/Field Budget and Finance Division/Office of the Director/Field Finance Procedures Management Unit

Redeployment of 5 posts (1 P-4 Administrative Management Officer, 2 P-3 Administrative Officers, 1 General Service (Other level) Finance Assistant and 1 General Service (Other level) Team Assistant) to the Front Office/Office of the Director (Field Budget and Finance Division restructuring)

Redeployment of 2 posts (1 P-4 Finance Officer and 1 General Service (Other level) Finance Assistant) to the Budget and Performance Reporting Service (Field Budget and Finance Division restructuring)

Department of Field Support/Field Budget and Finance Division/Office of the Director/Field System Support Unit

Redeployment of 4 posts (1 P-4 Chief, 1 P-3 Systems Analyst, 1 P-2 Associate Programme Analyst and 1 General Service (Other level) Computer Information Systems Assistant) to the Budget and Performance Reporting Service (Field Budget and Finance Division restructuring)

Redeployment of 1 post (P-3 Programme Analyst) to the Office of the Chief/Communications and Information Technology Services (United Nations Logistics Base at Brindisi, Italy)

Department of Field Support/Field Budget and Finance Division/Memorandums of Understanding and Claims Management Section

Redeployment of 1 post (P-3 Finance and Budget Officer) to the Office of the Under-Secretary-General/Programme Implementation Coordination Team (global field support strategy)

Department of Field Support/Field Personnel Division/ Field Personnel Operations Service

Redeployment of 2 posts (2 General Service (Other level) Human Resources Assistants) to the Field Central Review Board (United Nations Logistics Base)

Department of Field Support/Logistics Support Division/ Specialist Support Service/Supply Section

Redeployment of 3 posts (1 P-4 Chief, Contracts Management Unit, 1 P-3 Contracts Officer and 1 P-2 Associate Contracts Officer) to the Office of the Director (United Nations Logistics Base)

Department of Field Support/Information and Communications Technology Division/Field Communications and Information Technology Operations Service

Redeployment of 2 posts (1 P-4 Strategic Deployment Stock Telecommunications Officer and 1 General Service (Other level) Information and Communications Technology Assistant) to the Assets Management Section/ Communications and Information Technology Services (United Nations Logistics Base)

Department of Field Support/Information and Communications Technology Division/Field Communications and Information Technology Operations Service/Logistics and Administration Unit

Redeployment of 1 post (General Service (Other level) Administrative Assistant) to the Office of the Under-Secretary-General/Programme Implementation Coordination Team (global field support strategy)

Office of Internal Oversight Services/Internal Audit Division/ United Nations Interim Administration Mission in Kosovo

Redeployment of 1 post (P-4 Resident Auditor) to the Internal Audit Division/Regional Audit Centre (Entebbe, Uganda)

Office of Internal Oversight Services/Internal Audit Division/United Nations Organization Stabilization Mission in the Democratic Republic of the Congo

Redeployment of 1 post (Field Service Audit Assistant) to the Internal Audit Division/Regional Audit Centre (Entebbe)

Reassignments

Department of Field Support/Logistics Support Division/ Specialist Support Service/Engineering Section

Reassignment of 1 post (P-4 Engineer) to the Office of the Under-Secretary-General/Programme Implementation Coordination Team (P-4 Programme Officer) (global field support strategy)

Department of Field Support/Field Personnel Division/ Field Personnel Operations Services

Reassignment of 1 post (P-4 Human Resources Officer) to the Office of the Under-Secretary-General/Programme Implementation Coordination Team (P-4 Programme Officer) (global field support strategy)

Office of Internal Oversight Services/Internal Audit Division/ United Nations Interim Administration Mission in Kosovo

Reassignment of 1 post (P-5 Chief Resident Officer) to the Inspection and Evaluation Division (P-5 Senior Evaluation Officer)

Reclassifications

Office of the United Nations Ombudsman and Mediation Services/United Nations Mission in the Sudan

Reclassification of 1 post (National General Service Administrative Assistant to Field Service)

Office of the United Nations Ombudsman and Mediation Services/United Nations Organization Stabilization Mission in the Democratic Republic of the Congo

Reclassification of 1 post (National General Service Administrative Assistant to Field Service)

Restructuring

Department of Peacekeeping Operations

Change name from "Peacekeeping Best Practices Section" to "Policy and Best Practices Service"

Establish the Protection Coordination Team in the Policy, Evaluation and Training Division/Policy and Best Practices Service

Establish the Selection and Recruitment Section in the Office of Rule of Law and Security Institutions/Police Division

Department of Field Support

Discontinue the Field Finance Procedures Management Unit and the Field System Support Unit of the Field Budget and Finance Division

Abolition

Department of Peacekeeping Operations/Office of Operations/Africa I Division/United Nations Mission in the Central African Republic and Chad integrated operational team

Abolition of 1 post (P-4 Political Affairs Officer)

Department of Field Support/Field Budget and Finance Division/Office of the Director/Field System Support Unit

Abolition of 1 post (General Service (Other level) Information Management Assistant)

Department of Field Support/Field Personnel Division/ Guidance and Organizational Design Section

Abolition of 1 post (General Service (Other level) Team Assistant)

Department of Field Support/Logistics Support Division/ Operational Support Service

Abolition of 1 post (General Service (Other level) Team Assistant)

Office of Internal Oversight Services/Internal Audit Division/ United Nations Mission in the Central African Republic and Chad

Abolition of 1 post (P-5 Chief Resident Officer)

Abolition of 3 posts (1 P-4 Resident Auditor, 1 P-3 Resident Auditor and 1 Field Service Audit Assistant)

Office of Internal Oversight Services/Internal Audit Division/ United Nations Interim Administration Mission in Kosovo

Abolition of 1 post (National General Service Administrative Assistant)

Annex II

Support account general temporary assistance positions to be established for the period from 1 July 2011 to 30 June 2012

Organizational unit		Number of positions	Position level	Function[a]	Status
Department of Peacekeeping Operations					
Office of the Under-Secretary-General	Front Office	1	P-4	Organizational Resilience Officer	Continuation
		1	GS (OL)	Team Assistant–Organizational Resilience	Continuation
	Executive Office	—	4 months, 3 P-3	Administrative Officer	—
		—	4 months, 3 GS (OL)	Administrative Assistant	—
	Public Affairs Section	1	P-3	Internal Communications Officer	Continuation
Office of Operations	Africa II Division	1	D-1	Principal Officer	Continuation
		1	P-4	Political Affairs Officer	Continuation
		1	P-3	Political Affairs Officer	Continuation
		1	GS (OL)	Team Assistant	Continuation
	Africa I Division	1	GS (OL)	Team Assistant	Continuation
Office of Military Affairs	Military Planning Service	1	GS (OL)	Team Assistant	Continuation
	Current Military Operations Service	1	GS (OL)	Team Assistant	Continuation
Office of Rule of Law and Security Institutions	Criminal Law and Judicial Advisory Service	1	P-4	Judicial Officer (Islamic law)	Continuation
		1	P-3	Corrections Officer (force generation)	Continuation
		1	P-4	Judicial Officer	New
Policy, Evaluation and Training Division	Partnerships Team	1	P-5	Senior Coordination Officer	Continuation
		1	P-4	Coordination Officer	Continuation
		1	GS (OL)	Team Assistant	Continuation
	Peacekeeping Best Practices Section	1	P-4	Coordination Officer (protection of civilians)	New
		2	P-3	Coordination Officer	Continuation
	Integrated Training Service	1	P-4	Training Officer (Senior Mission Administration and Resource Training Programme (SMART))	Continuation
		1	P-3	Training Officer (SMART)	Continuation
		2	P-4	Training Coordination Officer	Continuation
	SUBTOTAL	23			
Department of Field Support					
Office of the Under-Secretary-General	Support to the African Union Mission in Somalia Headquarters support team	1	P-5	Senior Support Officer	Continuation
		1	P-4	Support Officer	Continuation
		1	GS (OL)	Administrative Assistant	Continuation
	Front Office/Programme Implementation Coordination Team	1	D-1	Team Leader	Continuation
Field Personnel Division	Recruitment, Outreach and Career Development Section/Occupational Group	12	P-3	Human Resources Officer	Continuation
		4	GS (OL)	Human Resources Assistant	Continuation
	Quality Assurance and Information Management Section/Administration of Justice	1	P-3	Human Resources Officer	Continuation
Logistics Support Division	Air Transport Section/Airfields and Air Terminals Unit	1	P-3	Air Transport Officer	Continuation
	Specialist Support Service	1	P-3	Water Engineer	Continuation
		1	P-3	Boundary Analyst	Continuation
	SUBTOTAL	24			
Department of Management					
Office of the Under-Secretary-General	Executive Office	—	4 months, 3 P-4	Administrative Officer	—
		—	4 months, 3 GS (OL)	Administrative Assistant	—
	Headquarters Committee on Contracts	1	P-4	Capacity Development Officer	Continuation
		1	GS (OL)	Training and Analysis Assistant	Continuation
Office of Programme Planning, Budget and Accounts	Accounts Division	1	P-4	Policy Guidance and Training Officer	Continuation
		1	P-4	Strategic Deployment Stocks Officer	Continuation
		3	GS (OL)	Finance Assistant (peacekeeping accounts)	Continuation
		1	GS (OL)	Finance Assistant (insurance)	Continuation
		1	P-4	Accounting Policy Analyst (International Public Sector Accounting Standards)	New
		2	P-3	Accounting Policy Analyst (International Public Sector Accounting Standards)	New

Chapter I: International peace and security

Organizational unit		Number of positions	Position level	Function[a]	Status
	Treasury	1	P-3	Finance Officer	Continuation
		1	P-2	Associate Finance Officer	Continuation
	Financial Information Operations Service	1	P-4	Information Systems Officer	Continuation
		1	P-2	Information Systems Officer	Continuation
		1	GS (OL)	Information Systems Assistant	Continuation
	Peacekeeping Financing Division	2	P-3	Finance and Budget Officer	Continuation
Office of Human Resources Management	Human Resources Policy Service	1	P-2	Associate Legal Officer	Continuation
		1	P-3	Legal Officer	Continuation
	Learning, Development and Human Resources Services Division	2	P-3	Human Resources Officer	Continuation
		1	GS (OL)	Human Resources Assistant	Continuation
	Human Resources Information Systems Section (New York)	1	P-4	Data Warehouse Project Manager	Continuation
		1	GS (OL)	Integrated Management Information System Help Desk Assistant	Continuation
	Human Resources Information Systems Section (Bangkok)/ Inspira Centre of Excellence	1	P-4	Chief	Continuation
		1	P-3	Help Desk Manager	New
		1	P-3	Development and Production Support Analyst	Continuation
		1	P-2	Associate Applications Support Officer	Continuation
		1	GS (OL)	Database Administrator	Continuation
		1	GS (OL)	Administrative Assistant	Continuation
		1	GS (PL)	Customer Support Representative	Continuation
		6	GS (OL)	Customer Support Representative	Continuation
	Strategic Planning and Staffing Division	—	6 months, P-4	Human Resources Officer	—
Office of Central Support Services	Office of the Assistant Secretary-General	1	P-3	Administrative Officer	Continuation
	Procurement Division	1	P-3	Procurement Officer (vendor registration)	New
		3	GS (OL)	Procurement Assistant (vendor registration)	Continuation
		3	P-3	Procurement Officer (engineering, logistics, vehicles)	Continuation
	Facilities and Commercial Services Division	1	P-3	Office Space Planning Officer	Continuation
		1	P-2	Associate Information Management Officer	Continuation
	Subtotal	48			
Office of Internal Oversight Services					
Executive Office		—	4 months, P-3	Auditor	—
		—	4 months, P-3	Investigator	—
		—	4 months, 3 GS (OL)	Administrative Assistant	—
Internal Audit Division	New York	1	P-4	Auditor	Continuation
	United Nations support for the African Union Mission in Somalia	1	P-4	Resident Auditor	Continuation
Investigations Division	New York	1	P-5	Senior Investigator	Continuation
		3	P-4	Investigator	Continuation
		1	P-3	Investigator	Continuation
		1	P-3	Administrative Officer	Continuation
		1	GS (OL)	Administrative Assistant	Continuation
		1	GS (OL)	Office Assistant	Continuation
		1	GS (OL)	Information Technology Assistant	Continuation
Investigations Division	Vienna	1	D-1	Deputy Director	Continuation
		1	P-5	Senior Investigator	Continuation
		1	P-4	Forensic Investigator	Continuation
		1	P-4	Investigator	Continuation
		7	P-3	Investigator	Continuation
		1	GS (PL)	Investigation Assistant	Continuation
		1	GS (OL)	Investigation Assistant	Continuation
		1	GS (OL)	Information Technology Assistant	Continuation
Investigations Division	Nairobi	1	D-1	Deputy Director	Continuation
		1	P-5	Senior Investigator	Continuation
		1	P-4	Forensic Investigator	Continuation
		3	P-4	Investigator	Continuation
		1	P-4	Investigator	New

Organizational unit		Number of positions	Position level	Function[a]	Status
		6	P-3	Investigator	Continuation
		1	P-3	Investigator	New
		1	GS (OL)	Administrative Assistant	Continuation
		3	GS (OL)	Investigation Assistant	Continuation
		1	GS (OL)	Investigation Assistant	New
Investigations Division	United Nations Stabilization Mission in Haiti	1	P-4	Resident Investigator	Continuation
	United Nations Organization Stabilization Mission in the Democratic Republic of the Congo	1	P-4	Chief Resident Investigator	Continuation
		1	P-3	Resident Investigator	Continuation
		1	NGS	Administrative Assistant	Continuation
	United Nations Mission in Liberia	1	P-4	Chief Resident Investigator	Continuation
		2	P-3	Resident Investigator	Continuation
		1	NGS	Administrative Assistant	Continuation
	United Nations Mission in the Sudan	1	P-4	Chief Resident Investigator	Continuation
		2	P-3	Resident Investigator	Continuation
	United Nations Operation in Côte d'Ivoire	1	P-4	Resident Investigator	Continuation
	Subtotal	56			
Executive Office of the Secretary-General		—	6 months, 2 GS (OL)	Administrative Assistant	—
	Subtotal	—			
Office of the United Nations Ombudsman and Mediation Services		1	P-4	Case Officer	Continuation
		1	GS (OL)	Administrative Assistant	Continuation
	Subtotal	2			
Ethics Office		1	P-3	Ethics Officer	Continuation
		1	GS (OL)	Administrative Assistant	Continuation
	Subtotal	2			
Office of Legal Affairs					
General Legal Division		1	P-4	Legal Officer	Continuation
		1	P-4	Legal Officer	New
		1	P-3	Legal Officer	New
Office of the Legal Counsel		—	6 months, P-4	Legal Officer	—
	Subtotal	3			
Office of Information and Communications Technology					
Field Systems Section		1	P-4	Project Manager (customer relationship management/troop contributions management)	Continuation
		1	P-3	Information Systems Officer (customer relationship management/troop contributions management)	Continuation
		1	P-4	Project Manager (rations management system)	Continuation
	Subtotal	3			
Advisory Committee on Administrative and Budgetary Questions secretariat		1	P-4	Administrative Management Officer	Continuation
	Subtotal	1			
	Total	**162**	positions (of which 11 are new) and 92 person months (positions of less than 12 months duration)[b]		

Abbreviations: GS (OL), General Service (Other level); GS (PL), General Service (Principal level); NGS, National General Service.

[a] The specific assignment of the general temporary assistance positions is set out in the report of the Secretary-General on the budget for the support account for peacekeeping operations for the period from 1 July 2011 to 30 June 2012 (A/65/761 & Corr.1,2) and referenced in the related report of the Advisory Committee on Administrative and Budgetary Questions (A/65/827), with the exception of 1 P-4 position for the Department of Peacekeeping Operations in the Office of Operations/Africa II Division, 1 P-3 position for the Department of Field Support in the Air Transport Section/Airfields and Air Terminals Unit and 1 P-4, 1 P-3 and 1 General Service (Other level) positions for the Office of Internal Oversight Services in the Investigations Division (Nairobi).

[b] Person months are indicated in the column entitled "Position level".

UN air operations

In response to General Assembly resolution 64/269 [YUN 2010, p. 97], the Secretary-General issued a February report [A/65/738] on air operations. The report reviewed the strategic planning and acquisition strategy, the management of the global UN air fleet, the military aircraft provided to the United Nations under letters of assist, and aviation standards, quality, performance and aviation safety. The UN aircraft fleet increased from 104 aircraft supporting 15 missions in 2000 to 257 aircraft supporting 20 field operations in 2010. During that period, over 4.6 million passengers were transported across missions.

The approved peacekeeping air transportation budgets for the period from 1 July 2009 to 30 June 2010 totalled $927.37 million for DPKO missions and an additional amount of $76.08 million in support of political missions. Troop rotations utilizing short-term aircraft charter, letters of assist and UN long-term aircraft, amounted to a charge of $153.1 million in 2009–2010. The accident rate per 10,000 flight hours dropped from 0.30 in 2005 to 0.08 in 2009 as a result of safety initiatives. The Secretary-General concluded that the UN Secretariat remained committed to achieving operational and cost efficiencies in the conduct of air operations without compromising the support provided to field missions or the safety and security of UN personnel and peacekeepers deployed in field missions.

Funds for closed missions

A report of the Secretary-General [A/65/556] provided information on the updated financial position of 23 closed peacekeeping missions as at 30 June 2010. The net cash surplus in the accounts of 18 closed missions available for credit to Member States as at that date amounted to $230,745,000. That amount did not include loans totalling $22,816,000 owed by two closed missions—the United Nations Support Mission in Haiti/United Nations Transition Mission in Haiti/United Nations Civilian Police Mission in Haiti ($7,366,000) and the United Nations Mission in the Central African Republic ($3,450,000)—and by one active peacekeeping mission—MINURSO ($12,000,000)—which remained unpaid. Five of the 23 closed missions reflected cash deficits totalling $86,720,000, owing to outstanding payments of assessed contributions. Pursuant to General Assembly decision 64/558 [YUN 2010, p. 94], two thirds of the adjusted net credits in the account of the United Nations Iraq-Kuwait Observation Mission (UNIKOM) as at 30 June 2009, in the amount of $291,900, was returned to the Government of Kuwait. As at 30 June 2010, the adjusted net available cash balance for the UNIKOM account was $105,900. The Secretary-General intended to return two-thirds of that amount, totalling $70,600, to Kuwait, and to return $180,745,000 of the cash balances of closed missions available for credit to Member States as at 30 June 2010.

The Secretary-General recommended that the Assembly instruct him to apply available credits against outstanding contributions, and that it consider establishing a time period for the transmission of instructions for the disposition of those credits, after which he would be authorized to apply them, bearing in mind the situation of the closed missions with cash deficits. He recommended that the Assembly approve retention of the balance of $50 million available in four closed peacekeeping missions, in the light of the experience regarding cash requirements of the Organization during the 2009/2010 and 2010/2011 financial periods.

In March [A/65/775], ACABQ provided its comments on the Secretary-General's report. Regarding the proposal that the amount of $50 million be retained to cover the cash requirements of the Organization, the Advisory Committee noted that the level of cross-borrowings had increased from $4 million at the end of 2010 to $44.5 million in February 2011, and that the maximum amount required for cross-borrowings exceeded $50 million three times in 2008. ACABQ therefore recommended that the Assembly authorize the Secretary-General to retain $75 million and return $155,745,000 of the cash balances of closed peacekeeping missions available for credit to Member States as at 30 June 2010. It supported the Secretary-General's approach regarding the application of available credits against outstanding contributions, and recommended that the Assembly authorize the Secretary-General to return to Kuwait the amount of $70,600, reflecting two-thirds of the adjusted net credits in the UNIKOM account. ACABQ also recommended that the Assembly consider requesting the Board of Auditors to conduct an in-depth study on the most appropriate mechanisms for achieving a balance between the interests of Member States to which surplus payments might be owed and Governments providing troops and other resources, and for ensuring sound financial management of cash inflows and outflows.

GENERAL ASSEMBLY ACTION

On 30 June [meeting 106], on the recommendation of the Fifth Committee [A/65/890], the General Assembly adopted **resolution 65/293** without vote [agenda item 143].

Closed peacekeeping missions

The General Assembly,

Having considered the reports of the Secretary-General on the updated financial position of closed peacekeeping missions as at 30 June 2008 and 30 June 2009, and the related reports of the Advisory Committee on Administrative and Budgetary Questions,

Having also considered the report of the Secretary-General on the updated financial position of closed peacekeeping missions as at 30 June 2010 and the related report of the Advisory Committee on Administrative and Budgetary Questions,

1. *Takes note* of the report of the Secretary-General on the updated financial position of closed peacekeeping missions as at 30 June 2010 and the related report of the Advisory Committee on Administrative and Budgetary Questions, subject to the provisions of the present resolution;

2. *Stresses* that all Member States should fulfil their financial obligations as set out in the Charter of the United Nations on time, in full and without conditions;

3. *Urges* Member States that are in arrears in their payments of assessed contributions to closed peacekeeping missions to pay those contributions expeditiously;

4. *Urges* all Member States to make every possible effort to ensure payment of their assessed contributions in full;

5. *Decides* to return the amount of 70,600 United States dollars, reflecting two thirds of the adjusted net credits available in the Special Account for the United Nations Iraq-Kuwait Observation Mission, to the Government of Kuwait;

6. *Requests* the Secretary-General to return 78.01 per cent of the 230,745,000 dollars net cash available for credit to Member States as at 30 June 2010, in the amount of 180 million dollars, based on the scale applicable to each mission's last assessment;

7. *Decides* to consider at the second part of its resumed sixty-sixth session the financial position of closed peacekeeping missions, including the remaining amounts owed to Member States, following the implementation of paragraphs 5 and 6 above, determined to have been 50,674,400 dollars as at 30 June 2010, under the agenda item entitled "Administrative and budgetary aspects of the financing of the United Nations peacekeeping operations", and requests the Secretary-General to submit to it for its consideration and approval concrete proposals and alternatives to address the issue of outstanding dues to Member States from closed peacekeeping missions that are in net cash deficit.

Accounts and auditing

At its resumed sixty-fifth (2011) session, the General Assembly considered the financial report and audited financial statements [A/65/5 (Vol. II)] for UN peacekeeping operations for the period from 1 July 2009 to 30 June 2010, the Secretary-General's report [A/65/719] on the implementation of the recommendations of the Board of Auditors concerning UN peacekeeping operations for the financial period ended 30 June 2010, the ACABQ report [A/65/782] on the report of the Board of Auditors on the accounts of the UN peacekeeping operations and the Secretary-General's report on the implementation of the Board's recommendations for the financial period ended 30 June 2010.

GENERAL ASSEMBLY ACTION

On 30 June [meeting 106], the General Assembly, on the recommendation of the Fifth Committee [A/65/594/Add.1], adopted **resolution 65/243 B** without vote [agenda item 127].

Financial reports and audited financial statements, and reports of the Board of Auditors

B

The General Assembly,

Recalling its resolutions 64/268 of 24 June 2010 and 65/243 A of 24 December 2010,

Having considered the financial report and audited financial statements for the twelve-month period from 1 July 2009 to 30 June 2010 and the report of the Board of Auditors on the United Nations peacekeeping operations and the report of the Secretary-General on the implementation of the recommendations of the Board of Auditors concerning United Nations peacekeeping operations for the financial period ended 30 June 2010, as well as the report of the Advisory Committee on Administrative and Budgetary Questions on the report of the Board of Auditors on the accounts of the United Nations peacekeeping operations for the financial period ended 30 June 2010,

1. *Accepts* the audited financial statements of the United Nations peacekeeping operations for the period from 1 July 2009 to 30 June 2010;

2. *Takes note* of the observations and endorses the recommendations contained in the report of the Board of Auditors;

3. *Also takes note* of the observations and endorses the recommendations contained in the report of the Advisory Committee on Administrative and Budgetary Questions;

4. *Commends* the Board of Auditors for the continued high quality of its report and the streamlined format thereof;

5. *Notes* the enhanced coordination among the Board of Auditors, the Secretary-General and the Advisory Committee, and welcomes the timely submission of the relevant reports on peacekeeping operations;

6. *Notes with encouragement* that there were improvements in the financial and administrative management of peacekeeping operations, and expects that these trends will be sustained in future financial periods;

7. *Takes note* of the report of the Secretary-General on the implementation of the recommendations of the Board of Auditors concerning United Nations peacekeeping operations for the financial period ended 30 June 2010;

8. *Recalls* paragraph 7 of resolution 64/268, and reiterates the need to strengthen administrative and institutional measures to address the root causes of recurring issues and to minimize the ageing of the Board's previous recommendations;

9. *Notes with concern* the recurrence of problems previously identified by the Board of Auditors in regard to the management of expendable and non-expendable property;

10. *Requests* the Secretary-General to ensure the full implementation of the recommendations of the Board of Auditors and the related recommendations of the Advisory Committee in a prompt and timely manner;

11. *Stresses* the importance of the Secretary-General's stewardship of the management of assets for peacekeeping, including expendable and non-expendable property and strategic deployment stocks, and reiterates its requests to the

Secretary-General to strengthen internal controls in the management of those assets to ensure adequate safeguards that would prevent waste and financial loss to the Organization;

12. *Notes* paragraphs 27 to 34 of the report of the Board of Auditors, expresses concern over the creation of a large amount of unliquidated obligations at the end of the financial year and the risk of applying the amount reserved during the current-year budget to the following year, and notes with concern the increase in the cancellation of unliquidated obligations over the previous financial year;

13. *Requests* the Secretary-General to adhere to the criteria for the creation and cancellation of obligations and to strengthen internal controls in the management of these matters, and also requests the Secretary-General to entrust the Office of Internal Oversight Services with assisting in that regard;

14. *Also requests* the Secretary-General to continue to indicate an expected time frame for the implementation of the recommendations of the Board of Auditors and the priorities for their implementation, including the office holders to be held accountable and measures taken in that regard;

15. *Recalls* section D of its resolution 64/259 of 29 March 2010, and requests the Secretary-General to reinforce his efforts to ensure that managers are effectively held accountable for the implementation of the recommendations of the Board of Auditors through the identification of priorities, clear time frames and an assessment of actions taken in that regard, in the context of the assessment of managers' performance mechanisms, including sanctions in case of recurrent non-compliance, and to continue to report thereon in the context of the report of the Secretary-General on the implementation of the recommendations of the Board;

16. *Requests* the Secretary-General to provide, in his next report on the implementation of the recommendations of the Board of Auditors concerning United Nations peacekeeping operations, a full explanation for the delays in the implementation of all outstanding recommendations of the Board, the root causes of the recurring issues and the measures to be taken;

17. *Recalls* paragraph 5 of its resolution 65/243 A, and requests the Secretary-General to ensure that adequate and specific plans for peacekeeping operations are in place to address matters relating to expendable and non-expendable property in order to serve as a basis for preparations for the implementation of the International Public Sector Accounting Standards;

18. *Stresses* that the leadership and commitment of senior managers to the implementation strategy of the enterprise resource planning project, Umoja, will be critical to the successful adoption of the International Public Sector Accounting Standards, and requests the Secretary-General to take all necessary measures to this end;

19. *Recalls* paragraphs 32 and 33 of the report of the Advisory Committee and paragraph 14 of resolution 64/268, and welcomes the willingness of the Board of Auditors to conduct performance audits;

20. *Requests* the Advisory Committee to request the Board of Auditors to submit to the General Assembly at its sixty-sixth session, in coordination with the Office of Internal Oversight Services and the Administration, a comprehensive proposal in this regard, including its impact with respect to the Financial Regulations and Rules of the United Nations.

Reimbursement issues

Reformed procedures for determining reimbursement for contingent-owned equipment

Report of Working Group. On 25 February, the Chairman of the 2011 Working Group on Contingent-Owned Equipment transmitted to the Fifth Committee the report [A/C.5/65/16] on the Group's findings on reimbursement rates for equipment. The Working Group, which was presented with 45 issue papers by various Member States and the Secretariat, addressed issues related to reimbursement procedures in three areas (major equipment, self-sustainment and medical support services), each dealt with by a sub-working group. Consensus was reached regarding an average increase of the self-sustainment rates of 2.1 per cent. Based on the assessment of troop numbers provided by the Secretariat, the overall impact on the self-sustainment portion of the peacekeeping budget was calculated at 1.84 per cent, which would lead to an estimated increase of $7,143,102 per annum. The Working Group conducted a comprehensive review of definitions and reimbursement rates for the categories of major equipment, self-sustainment and medical support services. It recommended the adoption of proposed revised rates, and that triennial reviews be conducted in the form of a comprehensive review, using data provided or elected by troop/police contributors.

Report of Secretary-General. In March, the Secretary-General, in his report [A/65/800] on the subject, set out the cost implications of implementing the Working Group's recommendations with effect from 1 July 2011. Additional resource requirements, estimated at $16.3 million, would be reported in the context of the individual peacekeeping operations' financial performance reports for the 2011–2012 biennium. The Secretary-General said that the proposed revised standards and procedures and other recommendations would benefit the Secretariat by improving the structure of the contingent-owned equipment system, and provide more transparent and enhanced verification tools. The Secretariat requested Member States to submit national cost data no later than two months prior to the next Working Group meeting.

The Secretary-General recommended that the Assembly approve the new reimbursement rates proposed for major equipment, self-sustainment and medical equipment. Regarding "special cases" major equipment, the Assembly should approve the reimbursement rates for new items and new categories of such equipment and adopt the addition to the determination of rates of special cases. It should approve United Nations responsibility for the reimbursement of the cost of ammunition expended for training exercises and the provision of suitable firing ranges for helicopters; take note of the definition and reimbursement rates of police armoured and protected vehicles and police crowd control vehicles; and approve the proposed concepts of consumables and excessive costs of using major equipment. As to authorized accommodation to troops provided by the United Nations, the Assembly should approve the proposed guidelines for provision of accommodation for aviation unit aircrew and the reimbursement of extra and reasonable cost for troop- and police-contributing countries due to the required relocation of base camp. It should approve the proposed guidance document on minor engineering tasks under self-sustainment; the requirement for explosive ordnance disposal self-sustainment to be reviewed 18 months after forces deployed; and the split and reimbursement rates for laundry and cleaning categories. The Assembly should approve an annual comprehensive review of mission factors within the existing mission-factor ceilings; the application of different mission factors to different geographic areas within a mission area; and the obligatory revision of mission factors after a natural disaster. It should also approve the incorporation of a recommended list of special equipment for aviation contingents; the revision to high-frequency radio set requirements for air contingents; the addition of a portable X-ray machine, an ultrasound machine and orthopaedic, gynaecology and internal medicine modules to level II hospitals, and CT scanners as special-case equipment for level III hospitals.

In April [A/65/830], ACABQ recommended approval of the 2011 Working Group's proposals.

GENERAL ASSEMBLY ACTION

On 30 June [meeting 106], the General Assembly, on the recommendation of the Fifth Committee [A/65/890] adopted **resolution 65/292** without vote [agenda item 143].

Reformed procedures for determining reimbursement to Member States for contingent-owned equipment

The General Assembly,

Having considered the report of the Secretary-General on reformed procedures for determining reimbursement to Member States for contingent-owned equipment, the report of the 2011 Working Group on Contingent-Owned Equipment, as transmitted by the Chair of the Working Group to the Chair of the Fifth Committee, and the related report of the Advisory Committee on Administrative and Budgetary Questions,

1. *Takes note* of the report of the Secretary-General and the report of the 2011 Working Group on Contingent-Owned Equipment;

2. *Endorses* the conclusions and recommendations contained in the report of the Advisory Committee on Administrative and Budgetary Questions, and requests the Secretary-General to ensure their full implementation.

Management of peacekeeping assets

UN Logistics Base

The General Assembly, at its resumed sixty-fifth (2011) session, considered the performance report [A/65/642] on the budget of the United Nations Logistics Base (UNLB) at Brindisi, Italy, for the period from 1 July 2009 to 30 June 2010. Expenditure totalled $57,931,200 gross ($53,564,300 net) against an appropriation of $57,954,100 gross ($54,145,500 net), resulting in an unencumbered balance of $22,900.

The value of strategic deployment stock activities for the period from 1 July 2009 to 30 June 2010 amounted to $107.3 million and included the $70.2 million rolled over from the prior period and $37.2 million of strategic deployment stock at replacement values, which was shipped to peacekeeping and special political missions. The amount of $41.1 million was rolled over into the 2010/11 fund balance. The Secretary-General recommended that the Assembly decide on the treatment of the unencumbered balance of $22,900 with respect to the period from 1 July 2009 to 30 June 2010; and on the treatment of other income for the period ended 30 June 2010 amounting to $2,536,300 from interest income ($2,037,200), other/miscellaneous income ($289,700) and cancellation of prior-period obligations ($209,400), and an unutilized balance from the 1996/97 to 2003/04 periods in the amount of $1,149,900.

The Assembly also considered the proposed UNLB budget [A/65/760] for 1 July 2011 to 30 June 2012, which amounted to $60,528,400 and provided for 73 international staff and 278 national staff, including 13 temporary national staff positions.

In May [A/65/743/Add.12], ACABQ recommended that the Assembly approve the amount of $60,528,400 for maintenance of UNLB for the 12-month period from 1 July 2011 to 30 June 2012, and that it prorate that amount among active peacekeeping operation budgets to meet UNLB requirements for that period. The Advisory Committee recommended that the unencumbered balance of $22,900 with respect to the period from 1 July 2009 to 30 June 2010, other income for the period ended 30 June 2010 amounting to $2,536,300 and an unutilized fund balance from the 1996/97 to 2003/04 periods in the amount of $1,149,900 be credited to Member States.

GENERAL ASSEMBLY ACTION

On 30 June [meeting 106], the General Assembly, on the recommendation of the Fifth Committee [A/65/890], adopted **resolution 65/291** without vote [agenda item 143].

Financing of the United Nations Logistics Base at Brindisi, Italy

The General Assembly,

Recalling section XIV of its resolution 49/233 A of 23 December 1994 and its resolution 62/231 of 22 December 2007,

Recalling also its decision 50/500 of 17 September 1996 on the financing of the United Nations Logistics Base at Brindisi, Italy, and its subsequent resolutions thereon, the latest of which was resolution 64/270 of 24 June 2010,

Recalling further its resolution 56/292 of 27 June 2002 concerning the establishment of the strategic deployment stocks and its subsequent resolutions on the status of the implementation of the strategic deployment stocks, the latest of which was resolution 64/270,

Having considered the reports of the Secretary-General on the financing of the United Nations Logistics Base and the related report of the Advisory Committee on Administrative and Budgetary Questions,

Reiterating the importance of establishing an accurate inventory of assets,

1. *Notes with appreciation* the facilities provided by the Government of Italy to the United Nations Logistics Base at Brindisi, Italy, and by the Government of Spain to the secondary active telecommunications facility at Valencia, Spain;

2. *Endorses* the conclusions and recommendations contained in the report of the Advisory Committee on Administrative and Budgetary Questions, subject to the provisions of the present resolution, and requests the Secretary-General to ensure their full implementation;

3. *Takes note* of paragraph 22 of the report of the Advisory Committee and decides not to transfer the airfield and air terminal standards function to the United Nations Logistics Base;

4. *Also takes note* of paragraph 30 of the report of the Advisory Committee;

5. *Requests* the Secretary-General to ensure the full implementation of the relevant provisions of its resolutions 59/296 of 22 June 2005, 60/266 of 30 June 2006, 61/276 of 29 June 2007, 64/269 of 24 June 2010 and 65/289 of 30 June 2011, as well as other relevant resolutions;

Financial performance report for the period from 1 July 2009 to 30 June 2010

6. *Takes note* of the report of the Secretary-General on the financial performance of the United Nations Logistics Base for the period from 1 July 2009 to 30 June 2010;

Budget estimates for the period from 1 July 2011 to 30 June 2012

7. *Approves* the cost estimates for the United Nations Logistics Base amounting to 68,512,500 United States dollars for the period from 1 July 2011 to 30 June 2012;

Financing of the budget estimates

8. *Decides* that the requirements for the United Nations Logistics Base for the period from 1 July 2011 to 30 June 2012 shall be financed as follows:

(a) The unencumbered balance and other income in the total amount of 2,559,200 dollars in respect of the financial period ended 30 June 2010, and an unutilized fund balance from the 1996/97 to 2003/04 periods in the amount of 1,149,900 dollars, to be applied against the resources required for the period from 1 July 2011 to 30 June 2012;

(b) The balance of 64,803,400 dollars to be prorated among the budgets of the active peacekeeping operations for the period from 1 July 2011 to 30 June 2012;

(c) The estimated staff assessment income of 6,808,200 dollars, comprising the amount of 6,249,900 dollars for the period from 1 July 2011 to 30 June 2012 and the increase of 558,300 dollars in respect of the period from 1 July 2009 to 30 June 2010, to be set off against the balance referred to in subparagraph (b) above, to be prorated among the budgets of the individual active peacekeeping operations;

9. *Also decides* to consider at its sixty-sixth session the question of the financing of the United Nations Logistics Base at Brindisi, Italy.

Restructuring issues

The Special Committee on Peacekeeping Operations, at its 2011 session [A/65/19], urged the Secretariat to ensure optimal configuration of integrated operational teams through the enhancement of their flexibility and an effective use of resources. The Committee stressed the importance of effective Departments of Peacekeeping Operations and Field Support that were efficiently structured and adequately staffed, in particular during periods of surge, transition and drawdown of peacekeeping operations; and of strengthening coherence among the various strands of policy development carried out in different areas of DPKO and DFS. The Special Committee reiterated the importance of preserving unity of command in missions at all levels, as well as coherence in policy and strategy and clear command structures in the field and at Headquarters, and requested the Secretariat to provide a briefing on the results of the evaluation on command and control arrangements for peacekeeping. It urged the Secretariat to better develop strategic communication and operational-level public information activities to ensure continued support for UN peacekeeping and to better respond to public perceptions of peacekeeping's role and impact on the ground.

In April [A/65/827], ACABQ recommended that the General Assembly take note of the Secretary-General's 2010 report on strengthening the capacity of the United Nations to manage and sustain peacekeeping operations [YUN 2010, p. 101]. Regarding the proposed structural adjustments contained within the Secretary-General's report, the Committee recommended acceptance of the proposal to establish the Selection and Recruitment Section in the Police Division, on the understanding that no additional resources would be required, and also recommended acceptance of the name change of the Peacekeeping Best Practices Section to Policy and Best Practices Service, on the understanding that no additional resources would be required.

Global field support strategy

In response to General Assembly resolution 64/269 [YUN 2010, p. 99], the Secretary-General submitted a January report [A/65/696 & Corr.1] on the standardized funding model of the global field support strategy. The strategy was developed by the Secretary-General as a five-year process to transform the delivery of services to UN field operations [YUN 2010, p. 97]. The Secretary-General stated that the standardized funding model ensured the pre-eminence of the Assembly's role in the budget process and provided opportunities for improved financial management. He recommended that the Assembly endorse the funding model for the first year of peacekeeping operations, emphasizing that the use of such a model in no way derogated from the legislative role of the Assembly in the approval of budgets; and that it take action, including appropriation and assessment, on peacekeeping budget proposals formulated using the model for the first year. The Secretary-General requested that the Assembly decide, if the Security Council's decision related to the start-up or expansion phase of peacekeeping operations resulted in the need for expenditure, to authorize him to enter into commitments of up to $150 million from the available balance of the Peacekeeping Reserve Fund. In that context, he also asked the Assembly to authorize him to enter into commitments for the available balance of the stores available from the Organization's strategic deployment stocks and draw on those, which were to be replenished when the initial appropriation was received.

In April, ACABQ submitted its comments [A/65/743] on the report.

GENERAL ASSEMBLY ACTION

On 30 June [meeting 106], the General Assembly, on the recommendation of the Fifth Committee [A/65/890], adopted **resolution 65/289** without vote [agenda item 143].

Cross-cutting issues

The General Assembly,

Recalling its resolutions 49/233 A of 23 December 1994, 49/233 B of 31 March 1995, 51/218 E of 17 June 1997, 57/290 B of 18 June 2003, 58/315 of 1 July 2004, 59/296 of 22 June 2005, 60/266 of 30 June 2006, 61/276 and 61/279 of 29 June 2007 and 64/269 of 24 June 2010,

Having considered the report of the Secretary-General entitled "Overview of the financing of the United Nations peacekeeping operations: budget performance for the period from 1 July 2009 to 30 June 2010 and budget for the period from 1 July 2011 to 30 June 2012", the reports of the Secretary-General on the progress of training in peacekeeping, on special measures for protection from sexual exploitation and sexual abuse, on United Nations air operations, on progress in the implementation of the global field support strategy and on its standardized funding model and on the welfare and recreation needs of all categories of personnel and detailed implications, as well as the report of the Office of Internal Oversight Services on peacekeeping operations and the related reports of the Advisory Committee on Administrative and Budgetary Questions,

1. *Reaffirms* its resolutions 57/290 B, 59/296, 60/266, 61/276 and 64/269, and requests the Secretary-General to ensure the full implementation of their relevant provisions;

2. *Appreciates* the efforts of all peacekeeping personnel in the field and at Headquarters;

3. *Takes note* of the report of the Secretary-General entitled "Overview of the financing of the United Nations peacekeeping operations: budget performance for the period from 1 July 2009 to 30 June 2010 and budget for the period from 1 July 2011 to 30 June 2012", the reports of the Secretary-General on the progress of training in peacekeeping, on special measures for protection from sexual exploitation and sexual abuse, on United Nations air operations, on progress in the implementation of the global field support strategy and on its standardized funding model and on the welfare and recreation needs of all categories of personnel and detailed implications, as well as the related reports of the Advisory Committee on Administrative and Budgetary Questions;

4. *Also takes note* of the report of the Office of Internal Oversight Services on peacekeeping operations;

5. *Endorses* the recommendations contained in the report of the Advisory Committee, subject to the provisions of the present resolution, and requests the Secretary-General to ensure their full implementation;

I

Budget presentation and financial management

6. *Takes note* of paragraph 24 of the report of the Advisory Committee;

7. *Reiterates* that the delegation of authority on the part of the Secretary-General should be to facilitate the better management of the Organization, but stresses that the overall responsibility for management of the Organization rests with the Secretary-General as its Chief Administrative Officer;

8. *Affirms* the need for the Secretary-General to ensure that the delegation of authority to the Department of Peacekeeping Operations and the Department of Field Support of the Secretariat and to field missions is in strict compliance with relevant resolutions and decisions, as well as with relevant rules and procedures of the General Assembly on this matter;

9. *Stresses* that heads of departments report and are accountable to the Secretary-General;

10. *Reiterates* the importance of strengthened accountability in the Organization and of ensuring greater accountability of the Secretary-General to Member States, inter alia, for the effective and efficient implementation of legislative mandates and the use of human and financial resources;

11. *Notes* that the compacts with senior managers are meant to improve the management of the Organization, inter alia, by increasing accountability and transparency at the senior level, and in this regard urges the Secretary-

General to implement measures that adequately address the performance of senior managers, especially with regard to achieving goals and targets;

12. *Recalls* paragraph 4 of the report of the Advisory Committee, and emphasizes that all field missions shall be provided with adequate resources for the effective and efficient discharge of their respective mandates and that the transition of peacekeeping operations to peacebuilding may entail a change in resource requirements;

13. *Welcomes* the timely issuance of budget proposals for peacekeeping operations by the Secretary-General;

14. *Recalls* paragraph 10 of section I of resolution 64/269;

15. *Stresses* the importance of further steps by the Secretary-General towards improving budget presentations and making more accurate forecasts;

16. *Takes note* of paragraph 5 of the report of the Advisory Committee, emphasizes that all field missions shall be provided with adequate resources for the effective and efficient discharge of their respective mandates, and stresses that the current level of peacekeeping activity should have scalable implications on resource requirements, taking into consideration the number, size and complexity of peacekeeping operations;

17. *Requests* the Secretary-General to intensify his efforts to achieve economies of scale within and between field missions without undermining their operational requirements and the implementation of their respective mandates and to report thereon in the context of the overview report on the financing of the United Nations peacekeeping operations;

18. *Notes* the establishment of a resource efficiency group in the Department of Field Support, in this regard concurs with the recommendations contained in paragraph 28 of the report of the Advisory Committee, and encourages further such initiatives by the Secretary-General, both at Headquarters and at the mission level;

19. *Recalls* paragraph 59 of the report of the Advisory Committee, and requests the Secretary-General to provide the General Assembly with information in this regard in the context of the next overview report on the financing of the United Nations peacekeeping operations for its consideration;

II

Personnel issues

20. *Expresses its appreciation* to all United Nations personnel performing functions related to peacekeeping, in particular those serving in hardship duty stations under some of the most difficult conditions;

21. *Pays tribute* to all United Nations peacekeepers who have been wounded in the line of duty or who have made the ultimate sacrifice while working in the pursuit of peace;

22. *Requests* the Secretary-General to provide, in the context of the next report on the overview of the financing of the United Nations peacekeeping operations, updates on the implementation in United Nations field missions of human resources management reforms, in particular those contained in its resolution 65/247 of 24 December 2010;

23. *Notes* the variety of human resources management initiatives that the Organization has undertaken since the adoption by the General Assembly of its resolution 63/250 on 24 December 2008, and recognizes that the continued implementation of the reform initiatives will better equip the Organization to address a variable and demanding environment in which integration and harmonization will provide the basis for longer-term efficiencies in productivity and an improved work environment that will, in turn, better enable the Organization to meet its mandates;

24. *Recalls* paragraph 47 of the report of the Advisory Committee;

25. *Recognizes* the importance of welfare and recreation for personnel serving in peacekeeping operations, bearing in mind that welfare and recreation also contribute to strengthening morale and discipline;

26. *Takes note* of paragraph 52 of the report of the Advisory Committee;

27. *Recalls* section VII of resolution 63/250, and reiterates its request contained in paragraph 34 of resolution 65/247;

28. *Recognizes* the need of the Organization for a mechanism to address rapidly changing situations in the field, and in this regard requests comprehensive information regarding the use of the temporary duty assignment mechanism and its implications for the regular recruitment process;

29. *Notes* the use by the Secretary-General of temporary vacancy announcements to address the issue of lengthy recruitment processes, stresses the need to expedite the filling of vacancies through the regular recruitment process, and requests the Secretary-General to provide information on the impact of using temporary vacancy announcements on the regular recruitment process in the field and at Headquarters in the context of his next overview report on the financing of the United Nations peacekeeping operations;

30. *Recalls* paragraph 19 of section C of its resolution 65/248 of 24 December 2010;

31. *Emphasizes* the importance of further steps to make training programmes more relevant and cost-effective through, inter alia, the training of trainers and the use of videoconferencing and e-learning where feasible, and stresses that travel for training purposes should be kept under close review;

32. *Notes* the increasing role of national staff in peacekeeping operations and the need to build national capacities and to provide professional development opportunities for national staff, and emphasizes that national staff should be fully included in all relevant training programmes;

33. *Recalls* paragraph 132 of the report of the Advisory Committee, notes the generally positive findings of the evaluation of the Senior Mission Administration and Resource Training Programme carried out in 2010, and looks forward to additional information on the impact of the training programme on improved performance;

34. *Also recalls* paragraph 4 of section II of resolution 64/269, and requests the Secretary-General to take urgent measures to eliminate the existing backlog of death and disability claims pending for more than three months and to report on the progress made to the General Assembly at the second part of its resumed sixty-sixth session;

35. *Further recalls* paragraph 55 of the report of the Advisory Committee, requests the Secretary-General to ensure cost-effectiveness and a high level of service to troop- and police-contributing countries, without affecting their operational requirements, underscores the need for close coordination with troop- and police-contributing countries, and requests the Secretary-General to include further information in his next overview report on the financing of the United Nations peacekeeping operations;

III

Operational requirements

36. *Underlines* the need for the United Nations to improve the management of its ground transportation in order to achieve maximum operational efficiency, and urges the Secretary-General to accelerate and strengthen his efforts in this regard and to submit concrete proposals in his next overview report on the financing of the United Nations peacekeeping operations;

37. *Notes* that fuel is a major item of expenditure and that its management is vulnerable to serious risk of fraud and abuse;

38. *Requests* the Secretary-General to ensure that all peacekeeping missions are provided with the necessary fuel supplies in an uninterrupted manner to ensure their smooth functioning, without jeopardizing safety, and that measures aimed at increasing efficiencies, including the use of turnkey contracts, must not undermine the operational needs and safety of the mission;

39. *Also requests* the Secretary-General to report to the General Assembly at its resumed sixty-seventh session in the context of his overview report on the financing of the United Nations peacekeeping operations on all aspects of fuel management, including on the implementation of the Department of Field Support Fuel Operations Manual, the feasibility of introducing a global electronic fuel management system, the status of strategic reserve stocks of fuel for contingency purposes, the preparation and application of standard operating procedures for fuel management and the results of the assessment of fuel support costs and performance for several missions, including the comparison of turnkey and in-house models, as well as on efforts aimed at factoring in the cost of fuel when awarding contracts for vehicles and aircraft;

40. *Stresses* that the effective management of rations means ensuring that United Nations peacekeepers receive sufficient rations of appropriate quality for three meals per day, including planning, organizing and controlling the operations from the initial requisition to the final payment to suppliers, as well as accurate and reliable record-keeping and filing;

41. *Requests* the Secretary-General to ensure that all missions monitor and evaluate the quality management systems of rations contractors to ensure that food quality and hygienic conditions are in accordance with established standards;

42. *Urges* the Secretary-General to continue to implement the new standard ratios for personal information and communications technology equipment on the basis of the 2010 review and to ensure the most appropriate level of service with regard to satellite communications and Internet services in each location within missions, taking into account operational requirements;

43. *Recalls* paragraph 61 of the report of the Advisory Committee, and requests the Secretary-General to submit a comprehensive assessment of the efficiencies and effectiveness, including savings achieved and impact, of turnkey arrangements in his next overview report on the financing of the United Nations peacekeeping operations;

44. *Requests* the Secretary-General to continue to ensure that the utilization of systems contracts is subject to prior full analysis of all costs, in accordance with current practice;

45. *Emphasizes* that concerted efforts should be made to identify potential vendors in developing countries and countries with economies in transition and to increase the representation from those countries in the bidding for and award of contracts so as to develop a supplier base that is more representative of the membership of the Organization;

46. *Requests* the Secretary-General to provide the General Assembly at the second part of its resumed sixty-sixth session with a comprehensive analysis of the administrative and budgetary aspects of the role and implementation of the integrated operational teams;

IV

Air operations

47. *Stresses* that efforts to explore possibilities for economies of scale and efficiencies in air operations must not undermine safety and operational requirements or rotation and troop deployment cycles for each peacekeeping operation;

48. *Recalls* paragraph 77 of the report of the Advisory Committee, and stresses the need to evaluate the full range and overall cost efficiency of factors involved in air services, including fuel consumption, maintenance costs and safety and security considerations;

49. *Also recalls* paragraph 13 of the report of the Secretary-General on the budget of the United Nations Logistics Base at Brindisi, Italy, for the period from 1 July 2011 to 30 June 2012, and stresses that the procurement process should ensure that acquired air assets correspond to the operational requirements of missions;

50. *Recognizes* the launch of a pilot project on transition to the request for proposal methodology for the acquisition of air services, notes that best value for money is one of the four key principles for United Nations procurement, along with fairness, integrity and transparency; effective international competition; and the interest of the United Nations, according to the Financial Regulations and Rules of the United Nations, and reiterates its request to the Secretary-General in paragraph 25 of its resolution 62/269 of 20 June 2008 to report to the General Assembly on clear guidelines for the implementation of the best value for money methodology in United Nations procurement, including all specifics of the weighted evaluation techniques, and to submit a report on the results of the pilot project;

51. *Requests* the Secretary-General to ensure full transparency in developing the request for proposal methodology, and emphasizes that the development of requests for proposal shall be driven by the operational requirements of the Organization;

52. *Takes note* of the United Nations Common Aviation Safety Standards, requests the Secretary-General to continue to ensure compliance with the International Civil Aviation Organization Standards and Recommended Practices, with the objective of meeting the operational requirements of mandate delivery in the field, and also requests the Secretary-General to report, in the context of his next overview report on the financing of the United Nations peacekeeping operations, on the differences between the International Civil Aviation Organization Standards and Recommended Practices and the United Nations Common Aviation Safety Standards;

53. *Recalls* paragraph 21 of section VI of resolution 64/269;

54. *Requests* the Secretary-General to provide an update on the status of the Memorandum of Understanding with the World Food Programme and its financial implications, as well as a detailed analysis of the governance of United Nations air operations and overall resource levels, including information on the effective and efficient provision of backstopping functions and information and communications technology support, in the context of his next overview report on the financing of the United Nations peacekeeping operations;

V

Special measures for protection from sexual exploitation

55. *Recalls* section IV of resolution 64/269;

56. *Reaffirms* the need for full implementation of the United Nations policy of zero tolerance of sexual exploitation and abuse in peacekeeping operations;

57. *Stresses* that in the case of any violations of standards, appropriate action will be taken within the authority of the Secretary-General, while criminal and disciplinary responsibility in respect of members of national contingents will depend on the national law of the Member State;

58. *Emphasizes* that all acts of sexual exploitation and abuse should be investigated and punished without delay in accordance with due process of law as well as with memorandums of understanding that have been concluded between the United Nations and Member States;

59. *Confirms* that no payment, including payment under paragraph 72 below, will be made in respect of individual peacekeepers who have been repatriated for disciplinary reasons, such as violation of the United Nations policy of zero tolerance;

60. *Recalls* its resolution 62/214 of 21 December 2007 containing the United Nations Comprehensive Strategy on Assistance and Support to Victims of Sexual Exploitation and Abuse by United Nations Staff and Related Personnel and calls for its continued implementation, and in this regard stresses the importance of addressing, in a comprehensive manner, the needs of all victims of sexual exploitation and abuse;

61. *Takes note* of paragraphs 10 and 18 of the report of the Secretary-General on special measures for protection from sexual exploitation and sexual abuse;

62. *Expresses concern* at the number of investigations that have not been completed, and encourages continued efforts to address the backlog, in accordance with memorandums of understanding, where applicable;

63. *Remains concerned* about the new cases of sexual exploitation and abuse reported, and notes the continuing decline in the number of allegations of sexual exploitation and abuse, but regrets that the proportion of allegations of the most egregious forms of sexual exploitation and abuse has not decreased;

64. *Requests* the Secretary-General to continue his efforts with regard to standardized training and awareness-raising on sexual exploitation and abuse matters;

65. *Welcomes* the efforts of the Conduct and Discipline Unit at Headquarters and of the conduct and discipline teams in the field, and notes with appreciation the regularly updated website dedicated to conduct and discipline, including statistical information, which helps the Department of Field Support to evaluate progress and Member States to gain a better understanding of the policies of the United Nations in dealing with conduct and discipline issues;

66. *Requests* an update on progress in implementing the United Nations Comprehensive Strategy on Assistance and Support to Victims of Sexual Exploitation and Abuse by United Nations Staff and Related Personnel in the next overview report on the financing of the United Nations peacekeeping operations;

67. *Encourages* the Inter-Agency Standing Committee Task Force to strengthen its leadership role in the implementation of the Comprehensive Strategy on Assistance and Support to Victims of Sexual Exploitation and Abuse by United Nations Staff and Related Personnel;

68. *Notes with appreciation* the actions taken to prevent unsubstantiated allegations of misconduct from damaging the credibility of any United Nations peacekeeping mission or troop- or police-contributing country or United Nations peacekeeping personnel, and requests that the Secretary-General take appropriate measures in this regard and that he continue to ensure that prompt actions are taken to restore the image and credibility of any United Nations peacekeeping mission, troop- or police-contributing country or United Nations peacekeeping personnel when allegations of misconduct are, ultimately, legally unproven;

VI

Other issues

69. *Notes with concern* the difficulties experienced by Member States in providing the data requested through the survey questionnaire under the provisions of General Assembly resolution 63/285 of 30 June 2009, and in this regard requests the Secretary-General to intensify the efforts of the Secretariat, in particular the Department of Field Support and the Department of Management, to work closely with troop-contributing countries with a view to facilitating data collection and assisting in the completion of the questionnaire, in order to maintain the process within the envisaged time frame;

70. *Notes* that the last review of troop costs was in 1992, with a subsequent ad hoc increase in 2002, and that troop-contributing countries have expressed concern that this has placed a difficult financial burden on them, which they assert could jeopardize the sustainability of participation in peacekeeping operations;

71. *Recalls* that all United Nations peacekeepers must act in a manner that preserves the image, credibility, impartiality and integrity of the United Nations;

72. *Decides* to provide, on an exceptional basis, a one-time supplemental payment of 85 million United States dollars to troop-contributing countries during the period from 1 July 2011 to 30 June 2012, without prejudice to the integrity of the process set forth in resolution 63/285;

73. *Requests* the Secretary-General to establish, by October 2011, a senior advisory group consisting of five eminent persons of relevant experience appointed by the Secretary-General, five representatives from major troop contributors, five representatives from major financial contributors and one member from each regional group, to consider rates of reimbursement to troop-contributing countries and related issues;

74. *Decides* that the senior advisory group shall complete its work as soon as practicable;

75. *Notes with concern* the recurrence of problems previously identified by the Board of Auditors in regard to the management of expendable and non-expendable property;

76. *Stresses* the importance of the Secretary-General's stewardship of the management of assets for peacekeeping, including expendable and non-expendable property and strategic deployment stocks, and reiterates its requests to the Secretary-General to strengthen internal controls in the management of those assets to ensure adequate safeguards that would prevent waste and financial loss to the Organization;

77. *Recalls* section I, paragraph 14, of resolution 64/269, and requests the Secretary-General to submit the report requested in that paragraph to the General Assembly at the second part of its resumed sixty-sixth session;

78. *Notes* that the strategy for early peacebuilding is still being developed by the Secretariat, and, in this regard, requests the Secretary-General to consult closely with Member States, the Peacebuilding Commission, United Nations agencies, funds and programmes and all relevant Secretariat entities throughout the process of preparing the strategy, and underlines that specific peacebuilding tasks undertaken by peacekeeping missions should be based on priorities of the country concerned and on the specific context, in accordance with the principle of national ownership;

VII

Global field support strategy

79. *Expresses its appreciation* for the inclusive and participatory approach taken by the Secretary-General in developing and implementing the global field support strategy, and encourages the Secretary-General to continue to intensify close consultations with Member States, in particular troop-contributing countries, in the implementation of the global field support strategy;

80. *Recognizes* the challenges faced by the Organization in providing logistical, administrative and information and communications technology support for peacekeeping operations, and expresses its appreciation for the efforts made by the Secretary-General to present an integrated approach to enable more timely mission start-up and deployment and to improve quality, efficiency and economy of scale in the delivery of services to field missions;

81. *Recalls* paragraph 143 of the report of the Advisory Committee;

82. *Also recalls* paragraph 156 of the report of the Advisory Committee, and encourages the Secretary-General to continue to work in close consultation with Member States, in particular troop- and police-contributing countries, in further developing predefined modules and service packages;

83. *Requests* the Secretary-General, in a manner consistent with the objectives of the global field support strategy, to take into account the risks involved in using single-source or multifunctional contracts in developing further proposals related to logistics modules, as well as applicable limitations on the number of United Nations commodities codes per vendor;

84. *Recalls* paragraph 157 of the report of the Advisory Committee, and requests the Secretary-General to include all relevant information regarding the development and implementation of predefined modules and service packages in his next annual progress report;

85. *Emphasizes* the importance of enabling capacities in the effective deployment of service packages in field missions, and requests the Secretary-General to provide the General Assembly with information on various options available for enabling capacities in his next progress report for its consideration;

86. *Recalls* paragraphs 12 and 14 of section VI of resolution 64/269, and emphasizes the role of the Global Service Centre at Brindisi, Italy, in delivering and managing predefined modules and service packages;

87. *Reaffirms* paragraph 16 of section VI of resolution 64/269, in which it stressed that functions primarily involving interactions with Member States, particularly troop-contributing countries, would continue to be located at Headquarters;

88. *Notes with appreciation* the performance of the Transportation and Movements Integrated Control Centre at Entebbe, Uganda;

89. *Notes* the results achieved to date in enhancing effective service delivery through the Regional Service Centre at Entebbe;

90. *Recognizes* the potential of the Peacekeeping Reserve Fund and the strategic deployment stocks in playing a crucial role in rapid mission start-up and expansion, and requests the Secretary-General to provide the General Assembly with information on the implementation of paragraphs 8 and 9 of section VI of resolution 64/269;

91. *Requests* the Secretary-General to provide the General Assembly, on an annual basis and in a consolidated manner, with information on the financial and human resources provided by client missions to the Regional Service Centre at Entebbe and on the shares of the resource requirements for the individual client missions provided in their respective budget proposals, as well as information on the vacancy rates, expenditures and budget performance of the Centre.

Report of Secretary-General. In December, the Secretary-General submitted his progress report [A/66/591 & Add.1] on the implementation of the global field support strategy. The report provided information on the implementation of the four components (pillars) of the strategy: the financial framework, predefined modules and service packages, service centres, and an integrated human resources management framework. Implementation focused on accelerating benefits and introducing efficiencies; introducing, evaluating and reinforcing governance structures; and supporting the shift to the field-focused provision of services.

The Secretary-General stated that 16 months into its implementation, the new service delivery model had shown results in terms of improved and faster delivery of services to the missions. Given the security environment in many missions, the global field support strategy had reduced mission footprints by lowering the number of support staff whose work was not location-dependent. Nevertheless, in order to achieve the optimal use of resources and realize efficiency gains, including reducing staffing requirements, a functional shift was required that refocused the efforts of DFS headquarters, global and regional service centres and field mission support components. The Secretary-General requested the General Assembly to endorse the concept of regional service centres for missions in West Africa and the Middle East, in accordance with the Assembly's directives in its resolution 64/269 [YUN 2010, p. 97], and to ask the Secretary-General to seek proposals from Member States to ensure full transparency and optimal results in the site-selection process, to be presented to the Assembly for its approval in the context of its sixty-seventh (2012) session.

UN police capacities

Special Committee on Peacekeeping Operations consideration. At its 2011 session [A/65/19], the Special Committee requested the Secretariat to present to the Committee before the end of 2011 a report on the functioning of the DPKO Police Division and the challenges faced by the police components in UN peacekeeping missions. The Committee was of the view that the police should be matched with positions that made the best use of their specific areas of expertise. The Secretariat was requested to brief the Special Committee on the implementation of the revised policy on formed police units. The Committee welcomed the increase in the deployment of female police officers and took note of the Police Division's initiative to develop a UN Police training curriculum on investigating and preventing sexual and gender-based crimes.

Report of Secretary-General. Pursuant to the request made by the Special Committee (see above), the Secretary-General submitted, in December, a comprehensive report [A/66/615] on the functioning of the Police Division. The report described progress made since the issuance of the 2008 audit report [AP2007/600/01] of OIOS on the management of UN police operations, internal review of the Police Division, and report of the Panel of Experts on the Standing Police Capacity's first year of operation [YUN 2008, p. 96]. The report addressed the mandates, structure and function of the UN police, and the challenges faced and responses. The Secretary-General said that the presence of the UN police contributed to restoring popular confidence in the host State police and in the role of law structures. The importance of UN police in supporting global security was illustrated in the growth in demand and the increasing complexity of policing mandates. The Secretary-General observed that the Police Division was working to develop the necessary policy and technical guidance; recruit appropriately skilled, equipped and trained personnel; and establish and maintain partnerships to implement mandated tasks. The Division's capacity had not reached the level proposed in its internal review; significant gaps remained in guidance, curriculum development and training, and specialist policing. Overall capacity should be developed for resource management and the administration of funds in missions and at Headquarters.

Personnel matters

The Special Committee on Peacekeeping Operations [A/65/19] requested the Secretary-General to ensure proper representation of troop-contributing countries when selecting personnel for staff positions in DPKO and DFS. The Special Committee expressed concern at the low proportion of women in the Secretariat, especially at the senior levels. It stressed that, in the recruitment process, women from certain countries, in particular developing countries, should be accorded equal opportunities, in conformity with relevant resolutions. The Special Committee requested the Secretary-General to ensure equitable representation of Member States at the senior and policymaking levels of the Secretariat, especially those with inadequate representation.

Concerned about the high number of vacancies in peacekeeping missions, the Special Committee reiterated its request that the Secretariat accelerate the recruitment and approval process for personnel, and its request to the Secretary-General to implement the decisions on contractual arrangements and harmonization of conditions of service, which were addressed in General Assembly resolutions 63/250 [YUN 2008, p. 1616], 65/247 [YUN 2010, p. 1480] and 65/248 [ibid., p. 1468]. The Secretary-General was also asked to ensure greater use of national staff in peacekeeping operations. The Secretariat was urged to expedite the recruitment and selection system for seconded military and police personnel, with a view to filling vacant DPKO positions in a timely manner. The Special Committee urged DPKO and DFS to recruit staff and experts on mission with language skills that were relevant to the mission area to which they were to be deployed.

Criminal accountability of UN staff and experts on mission

In response to General Assembly resolution 65/20 [YUN 2010, p. 102], the Secretary-General submitted a July report [A/66/174 & Add.1] on the criminal accountability of UN officials and experts on mission. The report provided information from Governments on the extent to which their laws established jurisdiction, in particular over serious crimes committed by their nationals while serving as UN officials or experts on mission, as well as information on cooperation among States and with the United Nations in the exchange of information and the facilitation of investigations and prosecution. It also detailed Secretariat activities conducted in implementation of the resolution, focusing on the bringing of credible allegations to the attention of the State against whose nationals such allegations were made, as well as assistance and training activities.

GENERAL ASSEMBLY ACTION

On 9 December [meeting 82], the General Assembly, on the recommendation of the Sixth (Legal) Committee [A/66/470], adopted **resolution 66/93** without vote [agenda item 78].

Criminal accountability of United Nations officials and experts on mission

The General Assembly,

Recalling its resolution 59/281 of 29 March 2005, in which it endorsed the recommendation of the Special Committee on Peacekeeping Operations that the Secretary-General make available to the United Nations membership a comprehensive report on the issue of sexual exploitation and abuse in United Nations peacekeeping operations,

Recalling also that the Secretary-General, on 24 March 2005, transmitted to the President of the General Assembly a report of his Adviser concerning sexual exploitation and abuse by United Nations peacekeeping personnel,

Recalling further its resolution 59/300 of 22 June 2005, in which it endorsed the recommendation of the Special Committee on Peacekeeping Operations that a group of legal experts be established to provide advice on the best way to proceed so as to ensure that the original intent of the Charter of the United Nations can be achieved, namely that United Nations staff and experts on mission would never be effectively exempt from the consequences of criminal acts committed at their duty station, nor unjustly penalized, without due process,

Recognizing the valuable contribution of United Nations officials and experts on mission towards the fulfilment of the purposes and principles of the Charter,

Reaffirming the need to promote and ensure respect for the principles and rules of international law,

Reaffirming also that the present resolution is without prejudice to the privileges and immunities of United Nations officials and experts on mission and the United Nations under international law,

Reaffirming further the obligation of United Nations officials and experts on mission to respect the national laws of the host State, as well as the right of the host State to exercise, where applicable, its criminal jurisdiction, in accordance with the relevant rules of international law and agreements governing operations of United Nations missions,

Deeply concerned by reports of criminal conduct, and conscious that such conduct, if not investigated and, as appropriate, prosecuted, would create the negative impression that United Nations officials and experts on mission operate with impunity,

Reaffirming the need to ensure that all United Nations officials and experts on mission function in a manner that preserves the image, credibility, impartiality and integrity of the United Nations,

Emphasizing that crimes committed by such persons are unacceptable and have a detrimental effect on the fulfilment of the mandate of the United Nations, in particular with respect to the relations between the United Nations and the local population in the host country,

Conscious of the importance of protecting the rights of victims of criminal conduct, as well as of ensuring adequate protection for witnesses, and recalling the adoption of its resolution 62/214 of 21 December 2007 on the United Nations Comprehensive Strategy on Assistance and Support to Victims of Sexual Exploitation and Abuse by United Nations Staff and Related Personnel,

Emphasizing the need to enhance international cooperation to ensure the criminal accountability of United Nations officials and experts on mission,

Recalling its resolution 61/29 of 4 December 2006, by which it established the Ad Hoc Committee on criminal accountability of United Nations officials and experts on mission,

Having considered at its previous sessions the report of the Group of Legal Experts established by the Secretary-General pursuant to its resolution 59/300 and the reports of the Ad Hoc Committee, as well as the note by the Secretariat and the reports of the Secretary-General on criminal accountability of United Nations officials and experts on mission,

Recalling its resolutions 62/63 of 6 December 2007, 63/119 of 11 December 2008, 64/110 of 16 December 2009 and 65/20 of 6 December 2010,

Recalling also its decision that, bearing in mind its resolutions 62/63 and 63/119, the consideration of the report of the Group of Legal Experts, in particular its legal aspects, taking into account the views of Member States and the information contained in the note by the Secretariat, shall be continued during its sixty-seventh session in the framework of a working group of the Sixth Committee,

Convinced of the continuing need for the United Nations and its Member States to urgently take strong and effective steps to ensure the criminal accountability of United Nations officials and experts on mission in the interest of justice,

1. *Takes note* of the report of the Secretary-General;

2. *Strongly urges* States to take all appropriate measures to ensure that crimes by United Nations officials and experts on mission do not go unpunished and that the perpetrators of such crimes are brought to justice, without prejudice to the privileges and immunities of such persons and the United Nations under international law, and in accordance with international human rights standards, including due process;

3. *Strongly urges* all States to consider establishing, to the extent that they have not yet done so, jurisdiction over crimes, particularly those of a serious nature, as known in

their existing domestic criminal laws, committed by their nationals while serving as United Nations officials or experts on mission, at least where the conduct as defined in the law of the State establishing jurisdiction also constitutes a crime under the laws of the host State;

4. *Encourages* all States to cooperate with each other and with the United Nations in the exchange of information and in facilitating the conduct of investigations and, as appropriate, the prosecution of United Nations officials and experts on mission who are alleged to have committed crimes of a serious nature, in accordance with their domestic law and applicable United Nations rules and regulations, fully respecting due process rights, as well as to consider strengthening the capacities of their national authorities to investigate and prosecute such crimes;

5. *Also encourages* all States:

(*a*) To afford each other assistance in connection with criminal investigations or criminal or extradition proceedings in respect of crimes of a serious nature committed by United Nations officials and experts on mission, including assistance in obtaining evidence at their disposal, in accordance with their domestic law or any treaties or other arrangements on extradition and mutual legal assistance that may exist between them;

(*b*) In accordance with their domestic law, to explore ways and means of facilitating the possible use of information and material obtained from the United Nations for purposes of criminal proceedings initiated in their territory for the prosecution of crimes of a serious nature committed by United Nations officials and experts on mission, bearing in mind due process considerations;

(*c*) In accordance with their domestic law, to provide effective protection for victims of, witnesses to and others who provide information in relation to crimes of a serious nature alleged to have been committed by United Nations officials and experts on mission and to facilitate access of victims to victim assistance programmes, without prejudice to the rights of the alleged offender, including those relating to due process;

(*d*) In accordance with their domestic law, to explore ways and means of responding adequately to requests by host States for support and assistance in order to enhance their capacity to conduct effective investigations in respect of crimes of a serious nature alleged to have been committed by United Nations officials and experts on mission;

6. *Requests* the Secretariat to continue to ensure that requests to Member States seeking personnel to serve as experts on mission make States aware of the expectation that persons who serve in that capacity should meet high standards in their conduct and behaviour and be aware that certain conduct may amount to a crime for which they may be held accountable;

7. *Urges* the Secretary-General to continue to take such other practical measures as are within his authority to strengthen existing training on United Nations standards of conduct, including through predeployment and in-mission induction training for United Nations officials and experts on mission;

8. *Reiterates* its decision that, bearing in mind its resolutions 62/63 and 63/119, the consideration of the report of the Group of Legal Experts, in particular its legal aspects, taking into account the views of Member States and the information contained in the note by the Secretariat, shall be continued during its sixty-seventh session in the framework of a working group of the Sixth Committee, and, for that purpose, invites further comments from Member States on that report, including on the question of future action;

9. *Requests* the Secretary-General to bring credible allegations that reveal that a crime may have been committed by United Nations officials or experts on mission to the attention of the States against whose nationals such allegations are made and to request from those States an indication of the status of their efforts to investigate and, as appropriate, prosecute crimes of a serious nature, as well as the types of appropriate assistance that States may wish to receive from the Secretariat for the purposes of such investigations and prosecutions;

10. *Urges* States to provide to the Secretary-General at the appropriate time information on their handling of the credible allegations brought to their attention by the Secretary-General in accordance with paragraph 9 above;

11. *Requests* the United Nations, when its investigations into allegations suggest that crimes of a serious nature may have been committed by United Nations officials or experts on mission, to consider any appropriate measures that may facilitate the possible use of information and material for purposes of criminal proceedings initiated by States, bearing in mind due process considerations;

12. *Encourages* the United Nations, when allegations against United Nations officials or experts on mission are determined by a United Nations administrative investigation to be unfounded, to take appropriate measures, in the interests of the Organization, to restore the credibility and the reputation of such officials and experts on mission;

13. *Urges* the United Nations to continue cooperating with States exercising jurisdiction in order to provide them, within the framework of the relevant rules of international law and agreements governing activities of the United Nations, with information and material for purposes of criminal proceedings initiated by States;

14. *Emphasizes* that the United Nations, in accordance with the applicable rules of the Organization, should take no action that would retaliate against or intimidate United Nations officials and experts on mission who report allegations concerning crimes of a serious nature committed by United Nations officials and experts on mission;

15. *Takes note with appreciation* of the information provided by Governments in response to its resolutions 62/63, 63/119, 64/110 and 65/20, and urges Governments to continue taking the measures necessary for the implementation of those resolutions, including their provisions addressing the establishment of jurisdiction over crimes, particularly those of a serious nature, as known in their existing domestic criminal laws, committed by their nationals while serving as United Nations officials or experts on mission, as well as cooperation among States, and to provide specific details thereon, in particular with respect to paragraph 3 of the present resolution, in the information provided to the Secretary-General;

16. *Reiterates its request* to the Secretary-General to report to the General Assembly at its sixty-seventh session on the implementation of the present resolution, in particular with respect to paragraphs 3, 5, 8 and 9 above, as well as any practical problems in its implementation, on

the basis of information received from Governments and the Secretariat;

17. *Requests* the Secretary-General to include in his report information on the number and types of credible allegations and any actions taken by the United Nations and its Member States regarding crimes of a serious nature committed by United Nations officials and experts on mission, including information on efforts made to ensure the completeness of incident reporting;

18. *Decides* to include in the provisional agenda of its sixty-seventh session the item entitled "Criminal accountability of United Nations officials and experts on mission".

Training

The Secretary-General, in his report [A/65/644 & Corr.1] on the progress of training in peacekeeping, said that the new direction for peacekeeping training outlined in his 2009 report [YUN 2009, p. 98] had been incorporated into the broader framework of peacekeeping reform set out in the New Horizon process [ibid., p. 73]. The report described the improvements made in all phases of the training cycle, including the identification and prioritization of training needs, the setting of standards, ensuring efficient delivery and the outlining of new systems for monitoring and evaluating the impact of training. The achievements showed that peacekeeping training was a strategic investment for the United Nations and the international community that could enable peacekeeping personnel to meet the complex challenges facing UN peacekeeping in its consolidation phase.

The Special Committee [A/65/19] reiterated that troop-contributing countries and the Secretariat shared responsibility in providing adequately trained personnel with the required professional background, expertise and capabilities according to UN standards. The Committee expressed concern over the DPKO decision regarding the allocation of its resources away from training activities, and requested a briefing from the Department regarding the projected impact of its decision on training. The Committee took note of the ongoing efforts referred to in the Secretary-General's report on the progress of training in peacekeeping and requested a consolidated update on predeployment training strategy, regulations and opportunities open to Member States to ensure that troops and police committed to UN peacekeeping operations were properly prepared for their missions. The Special Committee welcomed progress made in translating peacekeeping training materials and asked the Secretariat to strengthen its efforts to make those documents available in the six UN official languages. It requested DPKO to ensure the provision of adequate and updated gender-sensitivity training material to national and regional peacekeeping training centres. While recognizing the important role played by non-United Nations partners in the provision of training, the Special Committee underscored the primary role of the DPKO Division of Policy Evaluation and Training, together with Member States, in developing peacekeeping training standards and advice in their implementation.

Chapter II

Africa

In 2011, the United Nations maintained its commitment to promoting peace, stability and development in Africa through concerted efforts in peacekeeping, peacebuilding and conflict prevention. The Organization supported African peace efforts through seven peacekeeping operations and eight political and peacebuilding missions. The year witnessed the birth of a new nation, South Sudan, which became the 193rd Member State of the United Nations. Political change swept through North Africa, including in Tunisia, Egypt and Libya.

The United Nations continued to address the causes of conflict in Africa and promote sustainable peace and development. The Security Council conducted a mission to Ethiopia, Kenya and the Sudan to support cooperation with the African Union (au) and encourage peace and stability efforts. Cooperation with the au included the annual consultative meeting between the UN Security Council and the au Peace and Security Council. The newly established United Nations Office to the African Union sought to improve coordination, common understanding and comparative advantages on joint peace efforts. The Office of the Special Adviser on Africa worked to enhance international support for the continent's development and security, particularly through the New Partnership for Africa's Development, which commemorated its tenth anniversary in October.

At the subregional level, the United Nations worked with countries in Central Africa and the Great Lakes region to confront threats to peace and security. The United Nations Regional Office for Central Africa (unoca) in Libreville, Gabon, was inaugurated on 2 March. The United Nations Standing Advisory Committee on Security Questions in Central Africa met twice in 2011, adopting the Sao Tome Declaration on a Central African Common Position on the Arms Trade Treaty and a Declaration on a road map for counter-terrorism and non-proliferation of arms.

In the Democratic Republic of the Congo (drc), pre-electoral activities intensified ahead of the presidential and national legislative elections in November. The campaign period was marked by tension and violence, including attacks in February on the presidential residence in Kinshasa and an army camp, resulting in the deaths of eight armed forces elements and 17 assailants. Nonetheless, polling began as scheduled on 28 November, and on 16 December President Joseph Kabila was declared the winner. The United Nations Organization Stabilization Mission in the Democratic Republic of the Congo (monusco) continued to discharge its mandate, including developing and implementing a joint contingency plan to meet protection needs during the electoral period and supporting the Independent National Electoral Commission; its efforts were curtailed, however, by a critical shortage of military helicopters. The security situation in the Kivus deteriorated during the year and the process of integrating armed group elements into the armed forces remained weak, with limited progress made in implementing the Agreements of 23 March 2009. On 4 April, an airplane contracted by monusco crashed while landing in Kinshasa, killing all but one of the 33 passengers and crew.

In Burundi, the political landscape was dominated by the aftermath of the 2010 elections. The Alliance démocratique pour le changement-Ikibiri continued to criticize the country's political governance, and acts of violence and attacks against civilians and security forces continued; most notably, an attack in Gatumba on 18 September left 39 dead. Nonetheless, the nation continued to make progress in peace consolidation, including in establishing independent institutions for human rights and mediation. The United Nations Office in Burundi (bnub), which replaced the United Nations Integrated Office in Burundi on 1 January, provided assistance to the National Independent Human Rights Commission, established in January, and logistical support to the Office of the Ombudsman, whose activities began in February.

In the Central African Republic, legislative and presidential elections were held in January and March. Incumbent President François Bozizé won the presidential election and was sworn in for his final presidential term on 15 March, while the results of the legislative elections confirmed the leadership of Prime Minister Faustin Archange Touadera. The Government launched activities in line with its commitment to complete the disarmament, demobilization and reintegration process by the end of 2011; and on 8 July, the Disarmament, Demobilization and Reintegration Steering Committee endorsed a national strategy for reintegrating former combatants. The nation, supported by the United Nations Integrated Peacebuilding Office in the Central African Republic (binuca), continued to implement the recommendations of the inclusive political dialogue of December 2008.

West Africa witnessed progress towards greater stability and peace, owing to the end of the transition processes in Guinea and the Niger, although the overall political situation was marked by several election-related challenges at the presidential, parliamentary and local levels in Benin, Cape Verde, the Niger and Nigeria. The rise in piracy attacks in the Gulf of Guinea, and the effects of drug trafficking and transnational organized crime, brought heightened insecurity. During the year, the United Nations Office for West Africa (unowa) focused on carrying out good offices and special assignments for conflict prevention; enhancing the subregion's capacity to address threats to peace and security; and promoting good governance, the rule of law and human rights.

Côte d'Ivoire faced significant security, humanitarian and political hurdles following the crisis that ensued after the presidential run-off election of November 2010. While the international community recognized Alassane Dramane Ouattara as the duly elected president, former President Laurent Gbagbo mobilized youth and armed forces against perceived opponents, including the United Nations. On 30 March, the Security Council repeated its call for Mr. Gbagbo to step down and urged an end to the violence against the civilian population. After pro-Gbagbo forces fired heavy weapons in Abidjan, killing many civilians, the Council reaffirmed the mandate of the United Nations Operation in Côte d'Ivoire (unoci) to protect civilians. Progress was made after Mr. Gbagbo was captured on 11 April. On 6 May, Mr. Ouattara took the oath of office one day after the Constitutional Council ratified the election results, reversing its December 2010 decision proclaiming Mr. Gbagbo the winner. A Dialogue, Truth and Reconciliation Commission was inaugurated on 28 September. Legislative elections were held on 11 December, with unoci providing logistical, security and technical support to help secure the vote. The Rassemblement des républicains party of President Ouattara obtained the majority of seats.

In Liberia, the political situation was dominated by the presidential and legislative elections of 11 October. The United Nations Mission in Liberia (unmil) provided support to the elections by coordinating international assistance and providing logistical support. No single presidential candidate won an absolute majority, necessitating a run-off ballot between incumbent President Ellen Johnson Sirleaf of the Unity Party and Winston Tubman of the Congress for Democratic Change (cdc). CDC announced a boycott of the run-off, and an opposition gathering on the eve of the election became violent, resulting in one confirmed death. The run-off election was held on 8 November. Voter turnout was 37.4 per cent, and President Johnson Sirleaf emerged the winner, obtaining more than 90 per cent of the votes cast. International and local observers billed the run-off vote as transparent, fair and credible.

In Sierra Leone, the main political parties intensified their preparations for the 2012 presidential, parliamentary and local council elections, with support from the United Nations Integrated Peacebuilding Office in Sierra Leone (unipsil). The relationship between the ruling All Peoples Congress party and the opposition Sierra Leone People's Party continued to be characterized by mutual distrust. Political tensions increased in the second half of the year, with supporters of both parties being complicit in violence. The Special Court for Sierra Leone continued to try those bearing the greatest responsibility for violations of international humanitarian and Sierra Leonean laws committed in the country since 1996. The Court was in its completion phase, with the trial of former Liberian President Charles Taylor continuing as the sole case before the Court.

The political leadership of Guinea-Bissau sought to improve the political and security environment, as well as the country's relationship with regional and international partners. The national dialogue process initially progressed in anticipation of a national conference later in the year, but the political situation worsened in the second half of the year, when a collective of opposition parties led demonstrations against the country's leadership. On 22 November, President Malam Bacai Sanhá was evacuated from the country for medical reasons, delaying preparations for the national conference. On 26 December, an armed attack occurred on the General Staff armory. The Government denied a coup attempt, although on 30 December Prime Minister Carlos Gomes Júnior said that there had been a plot to kill him and the Chief of Defence Staff. Twenty-four military officers and one civilian were detained. As a result, the national conference was postponed indefinitely.

Cameroon and Nigeria continued to cooperate in implementing the 2002 ruling of the International Court of Justice on their land and maritime boundary through the Cameroon-Nigeria Mixed Commission. The Commission continued to facilitate the process, and by the end of the year more than 1,700 kilometres out of the estimated 2,000 kilometres of the land boundary between the two countries had been demarcated.

On 26 August, a suicide terrorist attack on United Nations House in the Nigerian capital of Abuja killed 23 people, including 13 UN staff members. More than 100 others were wounded.

The political situation in Guinea remained tense as a result of an assassination attempt against President Alpha Condé on 19 July and a lack of consensus on modalities for organizing the country's legislative elections. On 15 September, the President of the Independent National Electoral Commission announced that legislative elections would be held on 29 December. The main opposition coalition rejected the announced date, calling on its members to participate in a demonstration on 27 September, an event that resulted in three deaths, as well as many injuries and arrests. In February, at the request of the Government, the Peacebuilding Commission placed Guinea on its agenda and set up a country-specific configuration.

The successful completion of the Southern Sudan self-determination referendum was a momentous achievement. On 9 January, exactly six years after the Comprehensive Peace Agreement (CPA) had come into effect, voting commenced for the referendum. On 7 February, the official results were announced—with over 98 per cent voting in favour of separation—and accepted by the National Congress Party, the Sudan's ruling party. On 9 July, with the expiration of the interim period under the CPA, South Sudan was formally declared an independent State. It joined the United Nations on 14 July. The transition of South Sudan from decades of war to sustainable peace, however, presented considerable challenges, such as developing governance institutions and addressing multiple security, humanitarian and economic crises. In the second half of the year, relations between the Sudan and South Sudan deteriorated, particularly in the resource-rich border area of Abyei, where the presence of the armed forces of both Governments continued. On 27 June, the Security Council established the United Nations Interim Security Force for Abyei (UNISFA), whose mandate was to monitor the border between north and south and facilitate the delivery of humanitarian aid. The United Nations Mission in the Sudan (UNMIS) wound up its operations on 11 July. In support of the newly created nation, the Security Council established a successor mission—the United Nations Mission in South Sudan (UNMISS).

In the Darfur region of the Sudan, fighting between the Government and armed movements remained a source of insecurity. An All Darfur Stakeholders Conference (Doha, Qatar, 27–31 May) was followed, on 14 July, by the signature of an Agreement between the Sudan and the Liberation and Justice Movement on the adoption of the Doha Document for Peace in Darfur. Meanwhile, the Darfur-based political process, led by the AU and the United Nations, sought to take into account the voice of all Darfurians, complementing the Doha negotiations. The African Union-United Nations Hybrid Operation in Darfur (UNAMID) continued to protect civilians and promote an inclusive political process.

There was improvement in the security situation in eastern Chad, which was positively affected by improved relations between Chad and the Sudan. The Chad-Sudan joint border force, deployed in 2010, increased in size to 5,000 personnel, and its mandate was extended until September. Following the withdrawal of the United Nations Mission in the Central African Republic (MINURCAT) in December 2010, Chad's Détachement intégré de sécurité assumed responsibility for security and for humanitarian operations in and around refugee camps and internally displaced persons sites, while the joint border force secured the border area. The Government made progress in assuming responsibility for the security and protection of the civilian population following the withdrawal of MINURCAT.

In Somalia, the Transitional Federal Government and its allies, with the support of the African Union Mission to Somalia (AMISOM), launched on 19 February a major offensive in Mogadishu and in the south of the country, gaining ground against the Islamic militant group Al-Shabaab. The group continued to receive arms and ammunition through southern Somali ports, however, and acquired financial resources from extortion, illegal exports and taxation. On the political front, President Sheikh Sharif Sheikh Ahmed and the Speaker of the Transitional Federal Parliament, Sharif Hassan Sheikh Adan, ended a political stalemate between the executive and the legislature by signing on 9 June the Kampala Accord. The Accord deferred elections for one year and provided for the establishment of a road map for ending the transitional period in August 2012. The road map was adopted on 6 September in Mogadishu at a Consultative Meeting on Ending the Transition in Somalia facilitated by the United Nations Political Office for Somalia. The humanitarian situation worsened during the year: drought left over 2 million Somalis in need of humanitarian assistance and resulted in higher flows of refugees to neighbouring countries.

The Security Council, in December, expanded the restrictive measures against Eritrea in the area of "diaspora tax", the Eritrean mining sector and financial services. The Council called on Eritrea to resolve its border disputes with its neighbours and to cease all efforts to destabilize other States.

In 2011, as the Organization marked the twentieth anniversary of the United Nations Mission for the Referendum in Western Sahara and the successful maintenance of the ceasefire between Morocco and the Frente Popular para la Liberacíon de Saguía el-Hamra y de Río de Oro (Frente Polisario), the situation of Western Sahara remained unresolved and negotiations towards a peace agreement continued. On the core issues concerning the future status of Western Sahara and the means by which the self-determination of the people of the Territory was to occur, no progress was registered. Frente Polisario maintained that the Territory's final status should be decided in a referendum on self-determination that included independence as an option. Morocco supported regional autonomy.

In 2011, an internal crisis in the Libyan Arab Jamahiriya escalated into a civil conflict. On 15 February, the Government met a peaceful protest, held by families calling for the release of a lawyer who was representing their claims in connection to the 1996 Abu Salim prison massacre, with lethal repression. Subsequently, civilians across Libya took up arms against the Government. On 26 February, the Security Council referred the situation in Libya to the International Criminal Court, imposed an arms embargo, a travel ban and asset freeze on Colonel Muammar Qadhafi and members of his circle and established a sanctions committee tasked with monitoring implementation of the sanctions. On 1 March, the General Assembly suspended the membership of Libya in the Human Rights Council. On 17 March, the Security Council demanded the establishment of a ceasefire and a complete end to violence against civilians, authorized Member States to take all necessary measures to protect civilians and established a ban on all flights within Libya's airspace. On 19 March, United States and European forces began air strikes with the objective of establishing a no-fly zone and protecting civilians. After months of intense fighting between Colonel Qadhafi loyalists and opposition forces, the latter on 20 October took the city of Sirte and Colonel Qadhafi was killed. On 23 October, the National Transitional Council—the political leadership of the anti-Qadhafi movement formed on 27 February—declared Libya fully liberated and took charge of the country, representing Libya both at the United Nations and in other international settings.

Promotion of peace in Africa

In 2011, the United Nations continued to identify and address the causes of conflict in Africa and promote sustainable peace and development on the continent. South Africa chaired the Ad Hoc Working Group on Conflict Prevention and Resolution in Africa, which focused on enhancing its role; improving cooperation between the UN Security Council and the African Union (AU) Peace and Security Council; preventing post-election violence; and addressing the root causes of conflict and emerging threats to peace and security in Africa. The Security Council conducted a mission to Ethiopia, the Sudan and Kenya from 19 to 26 May. The United Nations continued its cooperation with the AU, including the fifth consultative meeting between the UN Security Council and the AU Peace and Security Council in May. The Head of the newly established United Nations Office to the African Union, Zachary Muburi-Muita (Kenya), briefed the Security Council on activities to operationalize the Office, based in Addis Ababa, Ethiopia. The Office of the Special Adviser on Africa, headed by Cheick Sidi Diarra (Mali), promoted international support for Africa's development and security, including through the New Partnership for Africa's Development (NEPAD), and assisted the Secretary-General in providing coherent and coordinated UN system support to Africa. On 12 October, by a presidential statement, the Security Council welcomed intra-African collaboration on security sector reform and called for greater consideration of African perspectives on the issue. In December, the General Assembly adopted a resolution on assistance to refugees, returnees and displaced persons in Africa.

Conflict prevention and resolution

Security Council consideration. On 21 June [S/PV.6561], the Council was briefed by the Special Representative of the Secretary-General and Head of the United Nations Office to the African Union, Zachary Muburi-Muita, on the status of the Office and the cooperation between the United Nations and the AU (see p. 93).

On 12 October [S/PV.6630], the Council held an open debate on security sector reform, focusing on prospects and challenges in Africa. By presidential statement **S/PRST/2011/19** of the same day (see p. 34), the Council welcomed intra-African collaboration on security sector reform and called for greater consideration of African perspectives on the issue.

AU session. On 2 June [S/2011/337], the representative of the AU Chairman transmitted to the Council President the "Declaration on the state of peace and security in Africa", adopted at the extraordinary session of the AU Assembly (Addis Ababa, Ethiopia, 25 May). The Assembly noted that its session was marked by profound changes in Tunisia and Egypt, the conflict in the Libyan Arab Jamahiriya, and the situations in Somalia and the Sudan. It stressed the need to renew efforts to consolidate peace and prevent conflict; affirm and promote African leadership in managing and resolving the crises affecting the continent; strengthen collective action within the AU; and maximize the impact and effectiveness of the AU contribution in the UN Security Council. At the same session, the Assembly adopted a decision on the peaceful resolution of the Libyan crisis (see p. 277).

Working Group. The Ad Hoc Working Group on Conflict Prevention and Resolution in Africa, established in 2002 [YUN 2002, p. 93], continued to monitor the implementation of Security Council recommendations relating to conflict prevention and resolution in the continent. South Africa, in its capacity as Chair, in December, submitted a report [S/2011/820] on the Group's 2011 activities, which focused on enhancing the role of the Working Group; improving cooperation between the UN Security Council and the AU Peace and Security Council; the prevention of post-election violence and early warning tools and indicators for election-related violence; the root causes of conflict and emerging threats to peace and security on the continent; and lessons learned in African conflict prevention and resolution, including coordinating response and supporting local and national capacities for prevention. The report concluded that the Working Group provided a platform for States' representatives to articulate their views on enhancing the work of the United Nations, particularly the Council, in conflict prevention and resolution in Africa. South Africa would continue to chair the Group's work in 2012.

Security Council mission

On 18 May [S/2011/319], the Security Council President informed the Secretary-General that the Council would send a mission to Ethiopia, the Sudan and Kenya from 19 to 26 May. On 6 June [S/PV.6546], the Council was briefed on the mission's activities, which were detailed in a later report [S/2013/221].

The Addis Ababa segment, led by Ambassador Gérard Araud (France), aimed to continue developing the partnership between the AU and the United Nations through an exchange of views on issues of interest to the UN Security Council and the AU Peace and Security Council. On 21 May, Council members met with the Prime Minister of Ethiopia, Meles Zenawi, to discuss relations between Ethiopia and Eritrea, as well as the situation in Somalia, the Sudan and Libya. On the same day, the Security Council met with the AU Peace and Security Council for their fifth consultative meeting to review matters of common interest and assess cooperation on conflict prevention and resolution, peacekeeping and peacebuilding (see p. 92).

(For more information on Ethiopia and Eritrea, see p. 265; on cooperation with the AU, see p. 93.)

The Khartoum, Abyei and Juba segment, co-led by Ambassadors Susan Rice (United States) and Vitaly Churkin (Russian Federation), aimed to congratulate the parties to the Comprehensive Peace Agreement (CPA) [YUN 2005, p. 301] and the people of the Sudan for a peaceful and successful referendum; reaffirm the Council's commitment to the full implementation of the CPA; assess preparations for independence in Southern Sudan; and reiterate the responsibility of the CPA parties to reach agreement on the status of Abyei. The situation in Abyei rapidly deteriorated as the Council members travelled to the region. The mission's overriding purposes were to urge a halt to fighting and restore calm to Abyei; press the North and South to resolve outstanding issues in order to pave the way for two successful States beginning on 9 July; and better understand what an independent South Sudan would need from the United Nations and the international community. On 22 May, Council members visited the Mayo Camp for internally displaced persons, where they heard the concerns of southerners regarding future citizenship arrangements after 9 July, as well as protection, health care, education and job prospects. On the same day, Council members, accompanied by the Secretary-General's Special Representative for the Sudan, Haile Menkerios, met with ministers and advisers of the Sudanese Government, who reassured the Council that the Government was keen to conclude the CPA and efforts were being made to advance negotiations on post-9 July arrangements. The Council mission expressed concern about the situation in Abyei and urged the parties to resume negotiations. Also on 22 May, in Khartoum, the Council was briefed by the Joint AU-United Nations Special Representative for Darfur, Ibrahim Gambari, on political, security and humanitarian developments in Darfur, and the forthcoming Darfur peace process consultations; received a briefing by the Chair of the AU High-level Implementation Panel, Thabo Mbeki, regarding Abyei, the post-9 July arrangements and the Darfur peace process; and met with Misseriya elders on the history of Abyei. On 23 May, in Wau, the Council visited a maternity and childcare health centre, and met with Ngok Dinka representatives regarding the history and security challenges of Abyei. In Juba, the mission met with the President of Southern Sudan, Salva Kiir, and government ministers, congratulating them on the successful conduct of the referendum. Council members noted the challenges of independence and the need for inclusiveness, particularly with regard to the Constitution. That meeting was followed, on 24 May, by a visit to Malau, where the Council was briefed on the security challenges faced in Jonglei State; a visit to the Jebel Kujur way station in Juba, operated by the United Nations High Commissioner for Refugees; and a briefing by the Secretary-General's Special Representative regarding follow-on mission planning in Southern Sudan.

(For more information on the Sudan and South Sudan, see p. 189.)

The visit to Nairobi, led by Ambassadors Baso Sangqu (South Africa) and Mark Lyall Grant (United Kingdom), was intended to reiterate the Council's concern at the continued instability in Somalia and the need for a comprehensive strategy to encourage peace and stability; reaffirm the Council's support for the Djibouti Agreement [YUN 2008, p. 281] as the basis for conflict resolution in Somalia; and reaffirm the Council's support for the work of the Secretary-General's Special Representative for Somalia, the United Nations and the AU in promoting peace and reconciliation in the country. On 25 May, the Council met with representatives of the United Nations Political Office for Somalia (UNPOS), the AU and the

Intergovernmental Authority on Development (IGAD) to discuss the political, security and humanitarian situation in Somalia. On the same day, the Council met with the Vice-President of Kenya, Kalonzo Musyoka, and the Prime Minister of Kenya, Raila Odinga, expressing appreciation for the leadership and actions of the country in helping address the situation. The Council also held a meeting with the President of the Transitional Federal Government of Somalia, Sharif Sheikh Ahmed, and the Speaker of the Transitional Federal Parliament, Sharif Hassan Sheikh, expressing concern at the continuing instability in Somalia and stressing the need for a comprehensive strategy to address terrorism, piracy, hostage-taking and the humanitarian situation. It urged them to participate in forthcoming consultations, with a view to reaching a common understanding on post-transitional arrangements. Also in Nairobi, the mission was briefed by the United Nations Resident Coordinator and Humanitarian Coordinator, Mark Bowden, and the United Nations country team, and met with representatives of Puntland, Galmudug and Somaliland.

(For more information on the situation in Somalia, see p. 233.)

Cooperation with the African Union

In a February report [A/65/716-S/2011/54] on the review of the ten-year capacity-building programme for the AU [YUN 2006, p. 340], the Secretary-General addressed cooperation with the AU, including the activities of the UN Department of Political Affairs and the Departments of Peacekeeping Operations (DPKO) and Field Support (DFS) (see p. 1364). On 18 April, the General Assembly adopted **resolution 65/274** on cooperation between the two organizations (ibid.).

Annual consultative meeting. On 21 May, as part of the Security Council mission to Addis Ababa (see p. 91), the Security Council and the AU Peace and Security Council held their fifth consultative meeting. Members reviewed matters of common interest, particularly ways to strengthen the partnership between the two institutions; assessed their cooperation with regard to conflict prevention and resolution, peacekeeping and peacebuilding; and discussed the crisis in Libya, the post-electoral crisis in Côte d'Ivoire, and the situation in Somalia and the Sudan.

In a joint communiqué of the meeting, transmitted to the Security Council President on 8 June [S/2011/350], members expressed concern at the situation of women and children in conflict and post-conflict situations, and stressed the need to address sexual violence in armed conflicts, investigate crimes committed against women and children, and ensure that perpetrators were brought to justice. They also considered the strengthening of work and cooperation methods, welcoming the establishment of the United Nations Office to the African Union (see below) and the second meeting of the United Nations-AU Joint Task Force on Peace and Security (see p. 93), and reiterated the need to enhance the predictability, sustainability and flexibility of financing of the AU peace and security capability.

United Nations Office to the African Union

Briefing by Head of Office. On 21 June [S/PV.6561], the Head of the United Nations Office to the African Union (UNOAU) and Special Representative of the Secretary-General, Zachary Muburi-Muita (Kenya), gave his first presentation to the Security Council on the work of the Office, established in 2010 [YUN 2010, p. 111]. Mr. Muburi-Muita described the activities designed to operationalize the Office and streamline the United Nations presence in Addis Ababa from four separate entities to one self-sufficient operation. With the engagement of DFS, that transition was nearing completion. A memorandum of understanding had been signed with the Economic Commission for Africa (ECA), allowing the Office to benefit from their common services, and to provide it with adequate office space in the new premises being built at the ECA compound. To help inform UN decision-making, the Office was producing real-time reporting and political analysis on peace and security issues based on daily consultations with senior AU officials. At the strategic level, the Office focused on enhancing coordination, common understanding and comparative advantages on United Nations-AU joint peace efforts. Consultations with the AU had intensified to respond to common challenges on long-standing peace efforts in the continent, as well as recent developments in Egypt, Libya and Tunisia. Mr. Muburi-Muita also noted the Office's role in strengthening coordination with AU institutions and enhancing their capacity to deliver peace on the continent. His regular participation at meetings of the AU Peace and Security Council on country-specific situations, such as Côte d'Ivoire, Somalia, the Sudan and North Africa, had proven instrumental in coordinating action. The Office also strengthened regional coordination activities, particularly regarding peace and security; capacity-building support to the AU; coordination with partners outside the United Nations to provide the AU with specialist assistance and resources; advice for AU planning, including for peace support operations; assistance to the African Union Mission in Somalia; and the facilitation of training activities and workshops for AU regional economic communities on peacekeeping, planning, logistics and operational and administrative issues. He concluded that, while the Office had achieved much in its partnership with the AU, the full potential of that cooperation was still to be achieved. The Office's activities would strengthen that relationship and lead to more effective political coordination between the two organizations.

Support for AU peacekeeping operations

Report of Secretary-General. Following up on his 2010 report on UN support to AU peacekeeping operations [YUN 2010, p. 112], the Secretary-General in December submitted a report on cooperation between the United Nations and the AU in peace and security [S/2011/805], which reviewed joint efforts in the areas of conflict prevention, mediation, peacekeeping, peacebuilding, human rights and humanitarian affairs.

The Secretary-General stated that the partnership between the United Nations and the AU had evolved at the strategic and operational levels; however, while it had led to swift and effective responses to conflict, cooperation had at times been challenged due to divergent positions on certain crises.

In the area of coordination and consultation, the report reviewed the relationship between the UN Security Council and the AU Peace and Security Council; coordination with Member States and regional and subregional actors, particularly in the form of high-level meetings; and coordination between the UN Secretariat and the AU Commission. The United Nations-AU Joint Task Force on Peace and Security, launched in 2010 to enhance the strategic partnership between the two organizations, held its second (Addis Ababa, 1 February) and third (New York, 19 September) meetings, which focused on cooperation in Côte d'Ivoire, Libya, the Sudan, South Sudan and Somalia.

Cooperation in the area of mediation had significantly expanded. The United Nations had worked with the AU and the regional economic communities in mediation processes in Côte d'Ivoire, Guinea, Guinea-Bissau, Kenya, Madagascar, Somalia, the Sudan/Darfur and the Sudan/South Sudan. The two organizations were developing common guidelines for mediation in Africa in order to clarify roles and strengthen cooperation in joint mediation efforts.

On peacekeeping, in addition to cooperation in ongoing operations, the UN Secretariat, through UNOAU (see p. 92), provided operational, planning and capacity-building support to the AU Commission for its peace support operations, including the African Union Mission in Somalia (AMISOM). The United Nations-AU strategic partnership on security sector reform was also progressing, with UNAOU and DPKO providing advice and technical support to the AU Commission in the elaboration of its security sector reform policy. The report also considered lessons learned from peacekeeping partnerships with the AU.

The Secretary-General concluded that while UN cooperation with the AU had expanded significantly, it was a relationship in progress. In his recommendations, he noted the need to develop agreed principles to govern the modalities of cooperation and decision-making; conduct more informal communication between the Security Council and the AU Peace and Security Council to develop a common vision and coordinate action; ensure that the conceptualization, mandates, rules of engagement and institutional arrangements for each peacekeeping operation were based on strategic and operational requirements; and continue efforts to find sustainable financing for AU peace support operations.

African peacekeeping capacities

Special Committee. At its 2011 substantive session (New York, 22 February–18 March) [A/65/19], the Special Committee on Peacekeeping Operations discussed the enhancement of African peacekeeping capacities. It emphasized the importance of a strategic and effective relationship between the United Nations and the AU with regard to peacekeeping operations; of enhancing the capacity of the AU in conflict prevention and resolution, early warning, mediation and peacekeeping operations; and of implementing the ten-year capacity-building programme and the joint action plan for UN support to the AU in peacekeeping in the short, medium and long-terms. The Committee reiterated its request that the multidisciplinary AU peacekeeping support team continue to serve as a coordinating point for all issues in DPKO related to cooperation with the AU, and brief the Committee regularly on its functioning and mandate. To address AU peacekeeping requirements at the continental level, the Committee recommended enhancing cooperation with the AU to improve the planning, deployment and management of African peacekeeping operations. The Committee reaffirmed the need to strengthen training, logistics and other forms of support to the AU. It called for close coordination among international partners and donors supporting AU capacity-building, including through improving the effectiveness of training centres in Africa.

Implementation of Secretary-General's 1998 recommendations on promotion of peace

In 2011, the General Assembly continued its consideration of the implementation of the recommendations contained in the 1998 report of the Secretary-General on the causes of conflict and the promotion of durable peace and sustainable development in Africa [YUN 1998, p. 66], including the 2010 review report of the Secretary-General [YUN 2010, p. 115], which set out proposals for a renewed United Nations engagement with Africa.

GENERAL ASSEMBLY ACTION

On 13 June [meeting 96], the General Assembly adopted **resolution 65/278** [draft: A/65/L.62/Rev.1 & Add.1] without vote [agenda item 62 (*b*)].

Implementation of the recommendations contained in the report of the Secretary-General on the causes of conflict and the promotion of durable peace and sustainable development in Africa

The General Assembly,

Recalling the report of the Open-ended Ad Hoc Working Group on the Causes of Conflict and the Promotion of Durable Peace and Sustainable Development in Africa, its resolution 53/92 of 7 December 1998 and subsequent annual resolutions, including resolutions 60/223 of 23 December 2005, 61/230 of 22 December 2006, 62/275 of 11 September 2008, 63/304 of 23 July 2009 and 64/252 of 8 February 2010, as well as its resolutions 62/179 of 19 December 2007, 63/267 of 31 March 2009 and 64/258 of 16 March 2010 on the New Partnership for Africa's Development, and 59/213 of 20 December 2004, 61/296 of 17 September 2007 and 63/310 of 14 September 2009 on cooperation between the United Nations and the African Union,

Recalling also, in this context, Security Council resolutions 1809(2008) of 16 April 2008 on peace and security in Africa, 1325(2000) of 31 October 2000 and 1820(2008) of 19 June 2008 on women and peace and security, 1366(2001) of 30 August 2001 on the role of the Council in the prevention of armed conflicts, 1612(2005) of 26 July 2005 on children and armed conflict, 1625(2005) of 14 September 2005 on strengthening the effectiveness of the role of the Council in conflict prevention, particularly in Africa, and 1631(2005) of 17 October 2005 on cooperation between the United Nations and regional and subregional organizations in maintaining international peace and security,

Recalling further the 2005 World Summit Outcome, through which world leaders reaffirmed their commitment to addressing the special needs of Africa, and its resolution 60/265 of 30 June 2006,

Reaffirming the political declaration on Africa's development needs adopted at the high-level meeting on Africa's development needs on 22 September 2008,

Recalling the High-level Plenary Meeting of the General Assembly on the Millennium Development Goals and its outcome document,

Recognizing that development, peace, security and human rights are interlinked and mutually reinforcing,

Stressing that the responsibility for peace and security in Africa, including the capacity to address the root causes of conflict and to resolve conflicts in a peaceful manner, lies primarily with African countries, while recognizing the need for support from the international community and the United Nations, taking into account the responsibilities of the United Nations in this regard according to the Charter of the United Nations,

Recognizing, in particular, the importance of strengthening the capacity of the African Union and subregional organizations to address the causes of conflict in Africa,

Noting that, despite the positive trends and advances in obtaining durable peace in Africa, the conditions required for sustainable development have yet to be consolidated throughout the continent and that there is therefore an urgent need to continue developing African human and institutional capacities, particularly in countries emerging from conflict,

Noting also that conflict prevention and the consolidation of peace would benefit from the coordinated, sustained and integrated efforts of the United Nations system and Member States and regional and subregional organizations, as well as international and regional financial institutions,

Reaffirming the need to strengthen the synergy between Africa's economic and social development programmes and its peace and security agenda,

Underlining the need to address the negative implications of the illegal exploitation of natural resources in all its aspects for peace, security and development in Africa, and condemning the illicit trade in natural resources that fuels armed conflict and the illicit trade in and proliferation of arms, especially small arms and light weapons,

Reaffirming the importance of the Peacebuilding Commission as a dedicated mechanism to address, within its existing mandate and in an integrated manner, the special needs of countries emerging from conflict towards recovery, reintegration and reconstruction and to assist them in laying the foundation for peace and sustainable development, taking into consideration the principle of national ownership,

Welcoming the establishment of the United Nations Office to the African Union to enhance the partnership between the United Nations and the African Union, particularly in the areas of peace, security and political and humanitarian affairs, and reaffirming the need to ensure coordination and increase cost-effectiveness among relevant entities of the United Nations system involved in the implementation of the ten-year capacity-building programme, in particular the Economic Commission for Africa and the United Nations Office to the African Union, whose efforts are critical,

1. *Takes note* of the report of the Secretary-General on the review of the implementation of the recommendations contained in his report on the causes of conflict and the promotion of durable peace and sustainable development in Africa, and underlines the progress made and the challenges faced in addressing such causes;

2. *Welcomes* the progress made, in particular by the African Union and subregional organizations, in the prevention, management and resolution of conflict and in post-conflict peacebuilding in a number of African countries, and calls for intensified efforts and a coordinated approach among national Governments, the African Union, subregional organizations, the United Nations system and partners, with a view to achieving further progress towards the goal of a conflict-free Africa;

3. *Also welcomes* the ongoing efforts of the African Union and subregional organizations to strengthen their peacekeeping capacity and to take the lead in peacekeeping operations on the continent, in accordance with Chapter VIII of the Charter of the United Nations and in close coordination with the United Nations, through the Peace and Security Council of the African Union, as well as ongoing efforts to develop a continental early warning system, response capacity, such as the African Standby Force, and enhanced mediation capacity, including through the Panel of the Wise;

4. *Calls upon* the United Nations system and Member States to support the peace consolidation mechanisms

and processes, including the Panel of the Wise, the African Union Post-Conflict Reconstruction and Development Framework and the continental early warning system, including its subregional components, as well as the operationalization of the African Standby Force;

5. *Calls upon* Member States to support relevant United Nations bodies, including the Peacebuilding Commission, and to assist post-conflict countries, at their request, in achieving a smooth transition from relief to development;

6. *Stresses* the importance of creating an environment conducive to national reconciliation and social and economic recovery in countries emerging from conflict;

7. *Invites* the United Nations and the donor community to increase efforts to support ongoing regional efforts to build African mediation and negotiation capacity;

8. *Calls upon* the United Nations system and Member States to support the African Union in its effort to effectively integrate training in international humanitarian law and international human rights law, with particular emphasis on the rights of women and children, into the training of civilian and military personnel of national standby contingents at both the operational and tactical levels, as set out in article 13 of the Protocol Relating to the Establishment of the Peace and Security Council of the African Union;

9. *Recognizes* that international and regional efforts to prevent conflict and consolidate peace in Africa should be channelled towards the sustainable development of Africa and the human and institutional capacity-building of African countries and organizations, particularly in priority areas identified at the continental level;

10. *Recalls* the signing of the declaration on enhancing cooperation between the United Nations and the African Union in Addis Ababa on 16 November 2006 and the ongoing efforts in this regard, underlines the importance of the implementation of the ten-year capacity-building programme for the African Union, in particular the operationalization of the African Standby Force, urges all stakeholders to support the full implementation of the ten-year capacity-building programme in all its aspects, and requests the Secretary-General to report on the progress made in this regard;

11. *Stresses* the critical importance of a regional approach to conflict prevention, in particular with respect to cross-border issues such as transnational organized crime, disarmament, demobilization and reintegration programmes, prevention of the illegal exploitation of natural resources and trafficking in high value commodities and the illicit trade in small arms and light weapons in all its aspects, and emphasizes in this regard the central role of the African Union and subregional organizations in addressing such issues;

12. *Notes with concern* that violence against women and children continues and often increases, even as armed conflicts draw to an end, urges further progress in the implementation of policies and guidelines relating to the protection of and assistance to women and children in conflict and post-conflict situations in Africa, notes the adoption by the Security Council of its resolution 1820(2008) on women and peace and security, welcomes the appointment of the Special Representative of the Secretary-General on Sexual Violence in Conflict, and invites support for the implementation of her mandate in Africa;

13. *Also notes with concern* the tragic plight of children in conflict situations in Africa, in particular the phenomenon of child soldiers, as well as other grave violations against children, and stresses the need for the protection of children in armed conflicts, post-conflict counselling, rehabilitation and education, with due regard for the relevant resolutions of the General Assembly and the Security Council;

14. *Calls for* the enhancement of the role of women in conflict prevention, conflict resolution and post-conflict peacebuilding, consistent with Security Council resolutions 1325(2000) and 1820(2008);

15. *Welcomes* the ongoing efforts of the African Union to ensure the protection of the rights of women in conflict and post-conflict situations, recalls in this regard the adoption and entry into force of the Protocol to the African Charter on Human and Peoples' Rights on the Rights of Women in Africa, and the Solemn Declaration on Gender Equality in Africa and the African Union Gender Policy, as well as the Southern African Development Community Protocol on Gender and Development, stresses the significance of those instruments for all countries in Africa for strengthening the role of women in peace and conflict prevention on the continent, and strongly urges the United Nations and all parties to redouble their efforts and support in this regard;

16. *Takes note* of the African Union Convention for the Protection and Assistance of Internally Displaced Persons in Africa and the Kampala Declaration on Refugees, Returnees and Internally Displaced Persons in Africa;

17. *Calls for* the safeguarding of the principle of refugee protection in Africa and the resolution of the plight of refugees, including through support for efforts aimed at addressing the causes of refugee movement and bringing about the voluntary, dignified, safe and sustainable return and reintegration of those populations, and calls upon the international community, including States and the Office of the United Nations High Commissioner for Refugees and other relevant United Nations organizations, within their respective mandates, to take concrete action to meet the protection and assistance needs of refugees, returnees and displaced persons and to contribute generously to projects and programmes aimed at alleviating their plight, facilitating durable solutions for refugees and displaced persons and supporting vulnerable local host communities;

18. *Welcomes* African-led initiatives to strengthen political, economic and corporate governance such as the African Charter on Democracy, Elections and Governance and the African Peer Review Mechanism and encourages even more African countries to participate in this process, and calls upon the United Nations system and Member States to assist African Member States and regional and subregional organizations in their efforts to enhance good governance, including the promotion of the rule of law and the holding of free and fair elections;

19. *Recognizes* the role of the Peacebuilding Commission in ensuring that national ownership of the peacebuilding process in countries emerging from conflict is observed and that nationally identified priorities are at the core of international and regional efforts in post-conflict peacebuilding in the countries under consideration, notes the important steps taken by the Commission in engaging with Sierra Leone, Burundi, Guinea-Bissau, the Central African Republic and Liberia through integrated peacebuilding strategies, calls for sustained regional and international

commitment to the implementation of those strategies, and looks forward to the development of an integrated peacebuilding strategy for Guinea;

20. *Calls upon* the United Nations system and invites Member States to assist African countries emerging from conflict in their efforts to build national capacities, including through the rehabilitation of the security sector, the disarmament, demobilization and reintegration of ex-combatants, provision for the safe return of internally displaced persons and refugees, the launch of income-generation activities, particularly for youth and women, and the delivery of basic public services;

21. *Stresses* the importance of effectively addressing challenges that continue to hamper the achievement of peace, stability and sustainable development on the continent, inter alia, the food, fuel and financial crises, the increased prevalence of infectious diseases such as HIV/AIDS, the effects of global warming and climate change, the extremely high rates of youth unemployment, social exclusion, corruption, human trafficking, rapid urbanization and city slums, massive displacements of people, the emergence of terrorist networks, maritime security and the increased activity of transnational organized crime, including drug trafficking, and in this regard encourages the United Nations system and Member States to assist African countries in effectively addressing these challenges;

22. *Calls upon* the United Nations system and bilateral and multilateral partners, as well as new partners, to deliver expeditiously on commitments and to ensure the full and speedy implementation of the provisions of the political declaration on Africa's development needs, as well as the implementation of the New Partnership for Africa's Development;

23. *Stresses* the need to promote socio-economic development on the continent, and in this context takes note of the Declaration on Employment and Poverty Alleviation in Africa, adopted by the African Union in 2004, as well as the recommendations of the Millennium Development Goals Africa Steering Group, which were endorsed by the African Union in July 2008 and cover such critical areas as agriculture and food security, education, health, infrastructure and trade facilitation and the national statistical system;

24. *Encourages* African Governments to strengthen structures and policies to create an environment conducive to attracting foreign direct investment and to promote socio-economic development and social justice, calls upon African Member States and regional and subregional organizations to assist the African countries concerned, at their request, by enhancing their capacity to devise and improve their national natural resources and public revenue management structures, and in this regard invites the international community to assist in that process by providing adequate financial and technical assistance, as well as by renewing its commitment to efforts aimed at combating the illegal exploitation of the natural resources of those countries, in conformity with international law;

25. *Notes* the completion of the review of the implementation of the recommendations contained in the 1998 report of the Secretary-General, and requests the Secretary-General to develop, in consultation with relevant partners, policy proposals on issues identified in his report;

26. *Requests* the Secretary-General to continue to monitor and report to the General Assembly on an annual basis on persistent and emerging challenges to the promotion of durable peace and sustainable development in Africa, as well as on the approach and support of the United Nations system.

Report of Secretary-General (August). In response to General Assembly resolution 65/278 (see above), the Secretary-General submitted an August report [A/66/214-S/2011/476] on implementation of the 1998 recommendations, which assessed major developments on the continent during the previous year and examined the implementation by the UN system of priority areas identified in the 2010 review report. It also provided an in-depth analysis and recommendations on emerging challenges in Africa.

Over the previous year, Africa experienced strong economic growth and improvement in social development indicators, especially in health and education. Nevertheless, some parts of Africa continued to endure armed conflict, fragility, erosion of the rule of law and chronic poverty. The increased threat of violent demonstrations and terrorist attacks, unresolved issues regarding electoral processes and human rights violations posed strategic challenges for Africa and its international partners. The Secretary-General particularly noted the revolts in North Africa, some of which had resulted in sustained violence; ongoing violence in the Sudan and South Sudan; a growing number of pirate attacks off the Somali coast in 2010; and rising food and fuel prices in 2011. There was a need to focus on the interlinkages between peace and development, particularly by establishing a more robust and gender-responsive social, political and economic agenda, as well as institutional frameworks to address interconnected challenges. The Secretary-General would engage the Inter-Agency Task Force on Africa to develop indicators and examine progress achieved in the recommendations outlined in the 2010 review report in order to better understand the correlation between peace and development and identify areas requiring attention.

The Secretary-General addressed emerging challenges, providing analysis and recommendations on two of the most pressing issues for the continent: youth, education and employment; and conflict and natural resources. He called on the General Assembly and the Security Council, through its Ad Hoc Working Group on Conflict Prevention and Resolution in Africa, to further engage with the UN system in implementing those recommendations, and to provide guidelines on the most pressing issues.

On youth, education and employment, the Secretary-General noted that access to quality education and decent employment was vital for poverty reduction, political stability, peace, security and sustainable development. He called on the UN system to deepen its engagement with youth and facilitate their participation in decision-making processes, in order to identify and remove sources of social, political and economic discontent among young people. The Secretary-General would consider ways to ensure that social and psychological support to youth groups affected by conflict was included in peacekeeping, peacebuilding and development mandates, and that adequate assistance was provided to governmental and community-based support systems for youth in conflict areas. He reiterated his call to the Regional Coordination Mechanism for Africa to integrate the issue of youth into all clusters and to support sectors that were capable of securing investments and facilitating job creation for young people.

The Secretary-General noted that conflict over natural resources had made Africa the focus of international attention. The complex interplay between politics and economics with regard to the ownership, management and control of natural resources had disrupted communities, fuelled armed conflicts, and increased corruption. He called on the UN system to mainstream its analysis of natural resource management issues, including land reform, water management and environmental challenges, within peacekeeping, peacebuilding and humanitarian assessments. The United Nations should support national dialogue on the role of natural resources revenues, with a view to defining inclusive growth and development strategies, as well as promoting accountable and transparent use of natural resources. The Secretary-General called on international partners and the private sector to uphold corporate responsibility codes and comply with regulatory mechanisms to ensure that natural resource revenues were not diverted to activities exacerbating conflict; on all partners to consider the use of indigenous and women's knowledge and practices in natural resources management, and in the mitigation of and adaption to climate change; and on the Regional Coordination Mechanism for Africa and other partners to build the capacity of river basin institutions and Nubian aquifer system countries so as to make them more responsive to the challenges of climate change and conflict.

On 19 December, the General Assembly adopted **resolution 66/135** (see p. 1123) on assistance to refugees, returnees and displaced persons in Africa, by which it noted the need for African States to address the root causes of forced displacement and to foster peace, stability and prosperity.

Office of the Special Adviser on Africa

In 2011, the Office of the Special Adviser on Africa (osaa), established by General Assembly resolution 57/7 [YUN 2002, p. 910], continued to enhance international support for Africa's development and security through its advocacy and analytical work; assist the Secretary-General in improving coherence and coordination of UN system support to Africa; and facilitate global intergovernmental deliberations on Africa, in particular regarding the New Partnership for Africa's Development (nepad) (see p. 891). The work of the Office focused on its mandate to support the Assembly and the Economic and Social Council in their deliberations on Africa; coordinate and guide the preparation of Africa-related reports and inputs; coordinate the interdepartmental task force on African affairs to ensure a coherent and integrated approach for United Nations support; initiate reports on issues affecting Africa; and coordinate global advocacy in support of nepad. Among other activities, the Office, in October, commemorated the tenth anniversary of nepad, collaborating with other UN entities to raise awareness of the achievements of the New Partnership; organized, in collaboration with the International Organization for Migration, a panel discussion on Africa and international migration (New York, 28 June); and organized an expert group meeting on peace, stability and development in Africa in December. The Inter-Agency Task Force on Africa, convened by osaa, provided a framework for UN system agencies to share expertise and experience, and participated in the preparation of reports of the Secretary-General on UN system support to nepad, and on the causes of conflict and the promotion of durable peace and sustainable development in Africa.

Central Africa and Great Lakes region

Central Africa and Great Lakes

UN Office for Central Africa

Establishment of UNOCA. In 2009, the Secretary-General [YUN 2009, p. 117] informed the Security Council of his intention to establish the United Nations Regional Office for Central Africa (unoca) in Libreville, Gabon. Following the Council's response welcoming the proposal [YUN 2010, p. 118], the Office was established on 1 January and inaugurated on 2 March 2011. The activities of unoca covered the 10 countries of the Central Africa subregion that constituted the Economic Community of Central African States (eccas): Angola, Burundi, Cameroon, the Central African Republic (car), Chad, the Congo, the Democratic Republic of the Congo (drc), Equatorial Guinea, Gabon and Sao Tome and Principe. In May, the Secretary-General transferred the secretariat functions of the United Nations Standing Advisory Committee on Security Questions in Central Africa (see p. 99) from the United Nations Regional Centre for Peace and Disarmament in Africa, in the United Nations Office for Disarmament Affairs, to the Department of Political Affairs, to be assumed by unoca. In a 21 July press statement [SC/10335], the Council President requested UNOCA, in coordination with UNOAU, to facilitate cooperation between the United Nations and the AU in countering the threat posed by the Lord's Resistance Army (LRA).

Appointment of Special Representative. On 11 March [S/2011/130], the Secretary-General informed the Council of his intention to appoint Abou Moussa (Chad) as his new Special Representative for Central Africa and Head of UNOCA. The Council took note of that intention on 14 March [S/2011/131], and Mr. Moussa assumed his functions on 24 May.

Report of Secretary-General (November). The Secretary-General in November presented his first report [S/2011/704] on the activities of UNOCA, which reviewed work following its inauguration in March. The Secretary-General noted that the Office had become fully operational and was working towards implementing its mandate to enhance the contribution of the United Nations towards the achievement of peace and security in the region.

Between July and October, the Special Representative held consultations with ECCAS member States on peace and security priorities, as well as with the AU Commission in Addis Ababa and the Central African Economic and Monetary Community in Bangui, Central African Republic, to explore areas of cooperation. Leaders of the subregion, while highlighting their efforts to strengthen peace and prevent conflicts, appealed for greater international support to confront new and recurrent threats, including piracy, cross-border movements of arms and fighters, drug trafficking and organized crime, youth unemployment, gender-based violence and the illegal exploitation of natural resources. Discussions also covered the threat of piracy in the Gulf of Guinea (see p. 136); the threat posed by LRA to a number of countries (see p. 99); and concerns regarding the potential impact of the Libyan crisis on peace and security, particularly the illegal movement of weapons and fighters from Libya into Central African States, and the social and economic consequences of the return of migrant workers. UNOCA had established strong working relationships with the ECCAS secretariat, with the two offices initiating regular meetings to discuss issues of mutual interest and concern. ECCAS sought institutional cooperation with the United Nations to build the capacity of regional mechanisms, such as the Council for Peace and Security in Central Africa, the Central African Early Warning Mechanism and the Central African multinational force, and requested greater cooperation to tackle growing incidents of election-related violence in the subregion.

The Special Representative also held consultations with other UN presences in Central Africa to determine ways in which the Organization could respond effectively to challenges, including a meeting with the Secretary-General's Special Representative for West Africa to explore areas of possible cooperation on cross-cutting issues, particularly the threat of piracy in the Gulf of Guinea, and consultations with UN country teams from ECCAS member States. He also organized a meeting at UNOCA headquarters (10–11 October) with the heads of the UN country teams and peacekeeping and special political missions. Participants highlighted the role of UNOCA in facilitating a concerted UN response to the threat posed by LRA, and agreed on a coordinated approach, under the auspices of UNOCA, to enhance the effectiveness of UN support in the subregion in the areas of early warning, conflict prevention and peacebuilding. The Office was requested to undertake a mapping of early warning mechanisms in the subregion, and to facilitate awareness of how the United Nations could better support initiatives in that field.

On the issue of women, peace and security, UNOCA had begun working with UN-Women towards the improvement of the status of women in the subregion and the implementation of Security Council resolutions on the situation of women in the context of peace and security. The region faced high levels of unemployment, especially among youth, with Governments increasingly concerned about the risk of unemployed youth falling into illegal and destabilizing activities. UNOCA would increase working relationships with ECCAS member States, intergovernmental institutions and UN system entities to explore ways to reduce the negative impact of such economic pressures on peace and security. Climate change and environmental degradation also posed threats to regional stability. With the Lake Chad basin area facing desertification, land degradation and shrinking water levels, the movement of large numbers of people who depended on the lake's resources could heighten inter-communal tensions. There was a need to support regional efforts to address the impact of a changing climate on peace, security and socioeconomic development, as well as prevent the illegal exploitation of the Congo basin's natural resources to ensure environmental sustainability and avert communal tensions related to competition for resources.

The Secretary-General concluded that continued collaboration between UNOCA and regional stakeholders was vital for the successful operation of the Office. He called for increased voluntary contributions to support the Office's programme of activities. Joint efforts between UNOCA and the United Nations Office for West Africa (UNOWA) to tackle security challenges would continue, and the two Offices would collaborate to promote an integrated UN response to the consequences of the Libyan conflict on West and Central Africa.

Year-end developments. In a later report [S/2012/421], the Secretary-General reviewed further activities of the Office. It held its first consultative meeting with unowa (Dakar, Senegal, 21 December), which focused on security and terrorism, efforts to combat drug trafficking, piracy in the Gulf of Guinea, youth unemployment and the impact of the Libyan crisis on the two subregions. The two Offices agreed to work together on the recommendations of the December assessment mission on the impact of the Libyan crisis on the Sahel region (see p. 286), and to define joint initiatives on terrorism and the illicit flow of weapons across the two subregions. Unoca also organized the thirty-third meeting of the United Nations Standing Advisory Committee on Security Questions in Central Africa (Bangui, Central African Republic, 5–9 December) (see below).

Financing

In December, the General Assembly considered the Secretary-General's October report [A/66/354/Add.3] on estimates in respect of special political missions, good offices and other political initiatives authorized by the Assembly and/or the Security Council, which included resource requirements for unoca totalling $4,424,000 for 2012, and the related report of the Advisory Committee on Administrative and Budgetary Questions (acabq) [A/66/7/Add.12]. On 24 December, in section IX of **resolution 66/247** (see p. 1393), the Assembly endorsed the recommendations of acabq and approved the resource requirements, including those for unoca.

Standing Advisory Committee on Security Questions

The United Nations Standing Advisory Committee on Security Questions in Central Africa met twice in 2011, adopting the Sao Tome Declaration on a Central African Common Position on the Arms Trade Treaty at its thirty-second ministerial meeting (Sao Tome, Sao Tome and Principe, 12–16 March) [A/66/72-S/2011/225], and a Declaration on a road map for counter-terrorism and non-proliferation of arms in Central Africa at its thirty-third ministerial meeting (Bangui, 5–9 December) [A/67/72-S/2012/159].

In July, the Secretary-General presented the outcome of the Committee's thirty-first [YUN 2010, p. 119] and thirty-second meetings to the General Assembly [A/66/163]. In a later report [A/67/359], the Secretary-General provided information on the Committee's thirty-third meeting and the Committee's activities in second half of 2011.

By **resolution 66/55** of 2 December (see p. 544), the Assembly reaffirmed its support for efforts to promote confidence-building measures in order to ease tensions and conflicts in Central Africa and to further sustainable peace, stability and development; welcomed the adoption of the Sao Tome Declaration on a Central African Common Position on the Arms Trade Treaty; and requested unoca, in collaboration with the United Nations Regional Centre for Peace and Disarmament in Africa, to facilitate the efforts of States members of the Standing Advisory Committee, particularly their execution of the Implementation Plan for the Kinshasa Convention [YUN 2010, p. 118].

(For information on the Committee's activities related to disarmament and arms limitation, see p. 543.)

Political and security developments

Lord's Resistance Army

Security Council statement (July). The Council held a private meeting on 21 July [S/PV.6588] to look at the continuing threat posed by the Lord's Resistance Army (lra) to regional security. On the same day, by a press statement [SC/10335], the Council condemned the ongoing attacks carried out by lra across central Africa, and expressed concern at the atrocities committed by lra, which had led to the displacement of over 380,000 people across the region. The Council demanded an end to all attacks on civilians by lra, and urged all lra elements to surrender and disarm. The Council also requested the Secretary-General to provide further information on the UN regional strategic approach to counter the impact of lra.

Report of Secretary-General (November). In response to that press statement, the Secretary-General submitted a November report [S/2011/693] that reviewed developments regarding lra since the previous report on the issue [YUN 2006, p. 169].

The report reviewed the impact of lra activities in the car, the drc, South Sudan and Uganda. The indiscriminate attacks by lra on civilians had caused a humanitarian crisis in the affected countries, with a reported 254 attacks on civilians in the car, the drc and South Sudan between January and August. An estimated 440,000 persons were internally displaced or living as refugees owing to lra attacks, which typically included killings, abductions, the recruitment and use of children as combatants and in other roles, sexual violence, forced marriage, mutilations, looting and the destruction of property. Recent attacks appeared to be aimed at ensuring the group's survival through the pillaging of food, medicine and arms, and the abduction of children.

The report reviewed national, regional and international efforts to tackle the challenge. United Nations actions included initiatives by the Organization's peace operations in the car, the drc, South Sudan and the Sudan to improve information-sharing and coordination, protect civilians and deter lra attacks; and activities by UNOCA, as the Organization's regional focal point for the LRA issue, to support a coordinated UN approach in addressing the LRA threat. From 16 to 27 May, the United Nations conducted a multidisciplinary evaluation mission to the affected countries and held a meeting with the AU in Addis Ababa, during which it assessed developments regarding LRA since the 2008 negotiations [YUN 2008, p. 169], as well as regional, national and international efforts to respond to the challenge.

The Secretary-General called for decisive and timely action to eliminate the LRA threat, arrest leaders indicted by the International Criminal Court, and address the challenges posed by the group's activities. He urged relevant partners to provide support to the Governments of LRA-affected countries in their efforts to lead and coordinate measures to eliminate the group, and noted that any military action against LRA should be carried out in compliance with international humanitarian and human rights law. He urged national authorities in the CAR, the DRC and South Sudan to extend the presence of State authorities in their respective territories, particularly with respect to civilian administration, security forces and rule-of-law institutions. Welcoming the initiative of the AU to develop a regional strategy to address the LRA problem, he noted that the United Nations stood ready to support the AU through the Organization's presences in the region. Furthermore, the humanitarian crisis caused by the armed group had not received adequate international attention. Appropriate rehabilitation needed to be provided to the victims of LRA attacks, and donors should strengthen their commitment to humanitarian partners in affected countries. He encouraged the national security forces in the CAR, the DRC and South Sudan, in collaboration with UN child protection agencies, to adopt standard operating procedures for the release and handover of children; invited Member States and other actors to develop a system of cross-border information-sharing; called on all parties to provide safe and unhindered access for humanitarian organizations to the affected populations; and encouraged Governments of the affected countries to continue their efforts to facilitate defections of LRA combatants and their reintegration, and to take measures to prevent impunity and strengthen the rule of law. The Secretary-General concluded that the United Nations was taking steps to address the LRA problem in a more effective manner through its political, peacekeeping, human rights, humanitarian and development efforts, and through enhanced coordination and synergy among UN entities, including UNOAU and UNOCA. He encouraged the strengthening of UN peacekeeping capacities in LRA-affected areas to help deter attacks against civilians and facilitate humanitarian operations.

Security Council consideration. On 14 November [S/PV.6657], the Council was briefed by the Special Representative for Central Africa, Mr. Moussa, who presented the Secretary-General's report on LRA-affected areas (see above) and his first report on the activities of UNOCA [S/2011/704].

SECURITY COUNCIL ACTION

On 14 November [meeting 6657], following consultations among the Security Council members, the President made statement **S/PRST/2011/21** on behalf of the Council:

The Security Council strongly condemns the ongoing attacks carried out by the Lord's Resistance Army in parts of Central Africa, which pose a continuing threat to regional security. The Council reiterates its grave concern at the atrocities committed by the Lord's Resistance Army, which have serious humanitarian and human rights consequences, including the displacement of over 440,000 people across the region. The Council remains deeply concerned that its previous calls for the Lord's Resistance Army to cease its attacks have not been heeded.

The Council strongly condemns the continued violations of international humanitarian law and the abuses of human rights by the Lord's Resistance Army. The Council condemns further the recruitment and use of children, killing and maiming, rape, sexual slavery and other sexual violence, and abductions. The Council demands an immediate end to all attacks by the Lord's Resistance Army, particularly those on civilians, urges Lord's Resistance Army leaders to release all those abducted, and insists that all Lord's Resistance Army elements put an end to such practices, and surrender and disarm.

The Council encourages the remaining Lord's Resistance Army fighters to leave the Group's ranks and take advantage of offers of reintegration support. Over the course of the existence of the Lord's Resistance Army, more than 12,000 combatants and abductees have left the ranks of the Lord's Resistance Army and have been integrated and reunited with their families through Uganda's Amnesty Commission. The Council emphasizes its support for continued efforts across the affected countries to disarm, demobilize and reintegrate former Lord's Resistance Army fighters back into normal life, and notes the recent successful escape of 30 women and children from two Lord's Resistance Army groups on the border between South Sudan and the Democratic Republic of the Congo. The Council acknowledges the important ongoing efforts of the disarmament, demobilization, repatriation, reintegration and resettlement office of the United Nations Organization Stabilization Mission in the Democratic Republic of the Congo to encourage and facilitate further Lord's Resistance Army defections, and requests that the United Nations work with regional Governments to expand these efforts across the Lord's Resistance Army-affected region.

The Council commends the important efforts undertaken by the militaries of the Central African Republic, the Democratic Republic of the Congo, South Sudan and Uganda to address the threat posed by the Lord's Resistance Army, and urges those militaries to coordinate and concert their efforts to apprehend Mr. Joseph Kony and top Lord's Resistance Army commanders in the coming months and bring them to justice. The Council recognizes the challenges that the Governments in the region face, and welcomes efforts by the international community, in coordination with the African Union and the United Nations, to enhance the capacity of regional militaries to conduct effective operations against top Lord's Resistance Army commanders and better protect civilians; it notes, for example, the efforts of the United States of America to work with regional militaries. The Council underlines the need for all action against the Lord's Resistance Army to be conducted in compliance with applicable international humanitarian, human rights and refugee law.

The Council commends the enhanced engagement of the African Union on this issue through its regional cooperation initiative for the elimination of the Lord's Resistance Army, and its efforts to establish a Regional Intervention Force, a Joint Operations Centre and a Joint Coordination Mechanism. The Council further commends the support provided by the Secretary-General to the African Union Commission through the planning process and encourages the African Union to promote coordination on Lord's Resistance Army issues by sharing its counter-Lord's Resistance Army plans at the earliest opportunity. The Council urges the prompt appointment of the proposed African Union Special Envoy for the Lord's Resistance Army-affected areas, and expresses hope that this official will work quickly to solidify cooperation between regional Governments and promote a regional framework for the defection, disarmament, demobilization and reintegration of Lord's Resistance Army fighters.

The Council underlines the primary responsibility of States in the Lord's Resistance Army-affected region to protect civilians and calls upon them to take all appropriate measures in this regard. The Council notes at the same time the important role being played by United Nations missions in the region, particularly through the adoption of protection measures such as community liaison, and stresses the need for them to play a major role in the coordination among all those engaged in addressing the threat posed by the Lord's Resistance Army. The Council requests that the United Nations Organization Stabilization Mission in the Democratic Republic of the Congo and the United Nations Mission in South Sudan seek, within their mandates and capabilities, to increase protection activities in Lord's Resistance Army-affected areas over the coming months, with a particular focus on the communities which are most vulnerable. The Council also welcomes the increased focus of the United Nations Integrated Peacebuilding Office in the Central African Republic on Lord's Resistance Army issues in the Central African Republic and encourages further action by the United Nations to address the needs of Lord's Resistance Army-affected communities in the Central African Republic. The Council encourages all United Nations offices and missions in the Lord's Resistance Army-affected region to continue to enhance information-sharing and coordination with all relevant actors, and welcomes the preparation of a regional human rights report on the Lord's Resistance Army.

The Council commends efforts by the European Union, the United States and other donors to provide humanitarian assistance to Lord's Resistance Army-affected populations in the Central African Republic, the Democratic Republic of the Congo and South Sudan. The Council stresses the need for an enhanced, comprehensive and more regional approach to the humanitarian situation, including assistance to victims of sexual violence and other attacks, and reiterates the requirement for all parties to promote and ensure safe and unhindered access for humanitarian organizations to the civilian population. The Council calls upon the international community to provide support to capacity-building, good governance and humanitarian efforts in Lord's Resistance Army-affected areas.

The Council welcomes the report of the Secretary-General on the Lord's Resistance Army, and commends the efforts made by the United Nations Regional Office for Central Africa, in coordination with the United Nations Office to the African Union, to engage with the United Nations missions in the Lord's Resistance Army-affected region, the African Union and affected Central African States to facilitate cooperation on issues related to countering the threat posed by the Lord's Resistance Army. The Council encourages the Regional Office to work with the United Nations missions and the African Union to develop a regional strategy for international humanitarian, development and peacebuilding assistance in the Lord's Resistance Army-affected area, enhancing cross-border mechanisms to improve civilian protection, early warning capacity, humanitarian access and response, and appropriate reintegration support for those returning from displacement, abductees and ex-combatants, as well as strengthening the overall capacity of affected States to extend their authority throughout their respective territories.

The Council recalls the arrest warrants issued by the International Criminal Court for three remaining Lord's Resistance Army leaders on charges of, among other things, war crimes and crimes against humanity, including murder, rape and the enlistment of children through abduction, and encourages all States to cooperate with the Ugandan authorities and the Court in order to implement those warrants and to bring to justice those responsible for the atrocities. The Council recalls the statement by its President of 22 June 2006 and reaffirms the vital importance of promoting justice and the rule of law, including respect for human rights, as an indispensable element for lasting peace.

The Council requests that the Secretary-General keep it informed on developments in relation to the Lord's Resistance Army, including through a single report on both the United Nations Regional Office for Central Africa and the Lord's Resistance Army, to be submitted before 31 May 2012, identifying opportunities for improved information-sharing between the African Union, Lord's Resistance Army-affected States and United Nations missions, and outlining the role of the Regional Office in coordinating activity against the Lord's Resistance Army.

Year-end developments. In a further report [S/2012/65], the Secretary-General said that in October, the United States announced the deployment of 100 military advisers to the LRA-affected areas to strengthen the efforts of national armed forces. On 22 November, the AU Peace and Security Council authorized a regional cooperation initiative against LRA for an initial six-month period. On 23 November, the Chairperson of the AU Commission appointed Francisco Madeira (Mozambique) as his Special Envoy on LRA.

Democratic Republic of the Congo

In 2011, pre-electoral activities intensified across the Democratic Republic of the Congo (DRC) ahead of the presidential and national legislative elections in November. The campaign period was marked by tension and violence, including the arrest of 126 people in connection with the attack on 27 February on the presidential residence in Kinshasa and an army camp that resulted in the deaths of 17 assailants and eight members of Forces armées de la République démocratique du Congo (FARDC). Nonetheless, polling began as scheduled on 28 November, and on 16 December the Supreme Court of Justice declared Joseph Kabila the winner. The United Nations Organization Stabilization Mission in the Democratic Republic of the Congo (MONUSCO) continued to discharge its mandate, including developing and implementing, together with UN agencies, funds and programmes, a joint contingency plan to meet protection needs during the electoral period, and providing technical and logistical support to the Independent National Electoral Commission. The Mission's efforts, however, were curtailed by a shortage of military helicopters. The security situation in the Kivus deteriorated during the year, owing to decreased military pressure on armed groups due to the ongoing reconfiguration of FARDC. The process of integrating armed group elements into FARDC remained tenuous, and limited progress was made in implementing the 23 March 2009 Agreements. The Haut- and Bas-Uélé districts in Orientale Province saw an increase in attacks—targeting population centres and in some instances FARDC—attributed to the Lord's Resistance Army (LRA). On 28 June, the Security Council extended until 30 June 2012 the mandate of MONUSCO, and the General Assembly in December approved the financing of the Mission. The year was also marked by an accident on 4 April, when an airplane contracted by MONUSCO crashed while landing in Kinshasa, killing all but one of the 33 passengers and crew.

The Security Council considered the situation in the DRC at meetings held on 7 February [S/PV.6476], 9 June [S/PV.6551] and 8 November [S/PV.6649], during which it was briefed by the Secretary-General's Special Representative for the DRC, Roger A. Meece.

Political and security developments

Report of Secretary-General (January). In response to Security Council resolution 1925(2010) [YUN 2010, p. 123], the Secretary-General in January submitted a report on MONUSCO [S/2011/20] that reviewed major developments between 8 October 2010 and 13 January 2011. According to the report, while the situation in most of the country remained stable, the conflict in the east persisted, with violent, mostly small-scale attacks carried out against civilians by foreign and Congolese armed groups. MONUSCO enhanced its efforts to protect civilians by improving communication with local populations and early warning, and conducting several military operations in coordination with FARDC. President Joseph Kabila reaffirmed his Government's commitment to hold general elections in 2011; however, delays in the voter registration process and in the adoption of essential legislation posed challenges to the timely holding of the polls.

Human rights violations by elements of the national security forces continued to be reported in the context of ongoing military operations. Notably, on the night of 1–2 January, FARDC elements carried out multiple exactions, including lootings, rape, torture, arrests and extortion, against civilians in Fizi town, South Kiwu Province. In response, MONUSCO dispatched a patrol and met with local officials of the national police and FARDC on 2 January; established a mobile operating base in Fizi on 7 January; and deployed a joint protection team mission the following day. Attacks by LRA continued in the Haut Uélé and Bas Uélé districts of Orientale Province. Between 27 December 2010 and 13 January 2011, MONUSCO conducted Operation Kimiana Lombango (Swift Peace) in Ango and the surrounding area to facilitate humanitarian access and deter LRA attacks.

Security Council consideration. On 18 May [S/PV.6539], the Council held a debate on the situation concerning the DRC. It had before it a concept note [S/2011/282] prepared by France, which focused on four key issues for the stabilization of the country: strengthening security; organizing a free and transparent electoral cycle beginning in November; consolidating democratic institutions and State authority, particularly in the east; and fostering long-term economic development. Addressing the debate, the Secretary-General noted that while security had improved in most of the country, foreign and Congolese armed groups posed significant threats. Human rights violations, including murder, sexual violence and the looting and burning of villages, continued to have large-scale humanitarian consequences. He urged all national stakeholders to work together to ensure that the presidential and national elections offered all Congolese the opportunity to participate without fear of harassment or violence. MONUSCO would continue providing logistical and technical support for the elections, for which it would require additional resources. It was also critical to provide the necessary equipment to the Congolese police units being trained on electoral security by MONUSCO, France and the Government. While welcoming the Government's increased leadership in addressing sexual violence, including strengthening the military justice system and prosecuting some of those accused of sexual and gender-based violence, the Secretary-General remained troubled by ongoing reports of widespread sexual violence. He urged the Congolese authorities to put an end to such crimes, and international partners to support the nation's police, army and justice systems.

SECURITY COUNCIL ACTION

On 18 May [meeting 6539], following consultations among the Security Council members, the President made statement **S/PRST/2011/11** on behalf of the Council:

The Security Council welcomes its enhanced dialogue with the Government of the Democratic Republic of the Congo. It reiterates that the challenges the Democratic Republic of the Congo is facing as it enters a phase of stabilization and peace consolidation require a strategic partnership with the United Nations, including with the United Nations Organization Stabilization Mission in the Democratic Republic of the Congo. The Council appreciates and welcomes the constructive approach of the Congolese authorities, and welcomes the efforts made by the Mission in this regard.

The Council stresses the importance of four key issues for the stabilization of the country: peace and security, the forthcoming elections, governance and institution-building, and economic development.

The Council considers that the overall peace and security situation in the Democratic Republic of the Congo has improved in recent years. It acknowledges the results of the action taken to address the threat of foreign and national armed groups, particularly the progress made against the Forces démocratiques de libération du Rwanda, including through the disarmament, demobilization, repatriation, resettlement and reintegration process. The Council underlines that significant security challenges remain, in particular in the Kivus and Orientale Province. The Council is concerned about the difficulties which have been encountered throughout the integration process of the Congrès national pour la défense du peuple into the Armed Forces of the Democratic Republic of the Congo, and the limited progress made in the reform of the security forces, both army and police. It calls upon the Congolese authorities to swiftly adopt the necessary legal framework and implement their long-term vision for the role and structure of the army and the police, and strongly encourages the Mission and international partners to provide coordinated support for these reforms.

The Council reiterates its deep concern about the persistent high levels of violence, especially sexual violence, and human rights abuses against civilians, mostly affecting women and children, including the use and recruitment of children by parties to the conflict, in particular in the eastern part of the country. It reiterates its deep concern about continuing activities of the Lord's Resistance Army. It calls for an urgent end to the attacks against the civilian population by all armed groups. It condemns all violations of human rights, including those committed by some elements of the Congolese security forces. The Council welcomes progress with the recent prosecutions after the incidents in Fizi and other cases. It reiterates the urgent need for the swift prosecution of all perpetrators of human rights abuses, and urges the Congolese authorities, with the support of the Mission, to implement the appropriate responses to address this challenge, including in Walikale. It urges the Government of the Democratic Republic of the Congo to take all necessary steps, including ensuring proper conduct by its armed forces in compliance with international humanitarian and human rights law, to facilitate the return of refugees and displaced persons.

The Council notes with interest the electoral calendar presented by the Congolese authorities and urges the Government of the Democratic Republic of the Congo as well as all relevant parties to ensure an environment conducive to a credible, inclusive, transparent, peaceful, timely, free and fair electoral process. It expresses its thanks to the Mission and the international community for their support to the electoral process to date, and encourages continued support. The Council recalls that ensuring freedom of expression and freedom of movement for all candidates, as well as for journalists, human rights defenders and civil society actors, is of the utmost importance. It calls upon the Government and all Congolese stakeholders to meet their responsibility in this regard, and further calls upon the Mission to support these efforts, in particular through the good offices of the Special Representative of the Secretary-General for the Democratic Republic of the Congo, enhanced and regular dialogue with the National Independent Electoral Commission through the Election Partnership Committee, and follow-up on human rights violations. It also calls upon the Mission and all relevant international actors to swiftly support the training of the Congolese police, and calls for donors to provide support for police equipment. It requests the Secretary-General to keep it regularly informed on the electoral process, including on support by the Mission to this process.

The Council stresses the need for urgent progress with regard to governance and institution-building, judicial reform and support to domestic courts, in order to ensure the rule of law and strengthen the fight against impunity. In this regard, the Council notes the interest of the Congolese authorities for establishing specialized mixed courts to address serious violations of international humanitarian and human rights law, complemented by their existing cooperation with the International Criminal Court. It calls upon the Mission and other relevant international actors to support the efforts of the Government of the Democratic Republic of the Congo in these fields and to assist in the restoration of basic services, including access to justice, road access, priority health and education infrastructures, and security infrastructures, throughout the country, and especially in conflict-affected areas.

The Council underlines the importance of economic development to ensure long-term stabilization and peace consolidation. It stresses that special attention should be placed on women's empowerment and participation in the economy, job creation for youth, and reintegration of former combatants. It also underlines the need for further progress in ensuring that the trade in mineral resources is founded on sound economic governance practices and is therefore transparent, fair and legal. It notes that urgent attention is needed to create an enabling environment to attract the public and private investment necessary to address food security, infrastructure and energy needs. The Council reiterates that regional cooperation with neighbouring countries should play a key role in the economic development of the Democratic Republic of the Congo.

The Council calls upon the international community, the African Union and all relevant subregional organizations to further engage in support of the stabilization efforts in the Democratic Republic of the Congo, notably in the fields of security, the fight against the illicit exploitation of and trade in natural resources and socioeconomic development.

Report of Secretary-General (May). In a May report [S/2011/298], submitted pursuant to resolution 1925(2010), the Secretary-General reported on progress on the ground and on the assessment conducted jointly with the Congolese authorities on the implementation of the objectives set out in paragraph 6 of that resolution. He also informed the Council of the accident which occurred on 4 April, when an airplane contracted by MONUSCO crashed while landing in Kinshasa. All but one of the 33 passengers and crew perished, including staff of MONUSCO, the United Nations Development Programme, the World Food Programme and the United Nations Office for Project Services.

Pre-electoral activities intensified across the DRC ahead of the presidential and national legislative elections of 28 November, announced by the Electoral Commission on 30 April. On 20 January, President Kabila promulgated the draft law on constitutional amendments, adopted by the National Assembly and the Senate on 15 January. Those amendments, inter alia, changed the voting system for the presidential elections from a two-round to a single-round poll. Opposition parties expressed concern about the lack of public debate accompanying their adoption, and noted that a single round of voting could affect the popular legitimacy of the results. On 15 February, Etienne Tshisekedi, leader of the Union pour la démocratie et le progrès social (UDPS), reiterated his intention to run for president. On 7 March, the national police announced that 126 people had been arrested in connection with the attack on 27 February on the presidential residence in Kinshasa and FARDC Camp Kokolo, which resulted in the deaths of eight FARDC members and 17 assailants. The pre-electoral campaign period also saw an increase in politically motivated human rights violations, with MONUSCO documenting more than 100 reported incidents targeting political opposition members and supporters, journalists and human rights defenders. On 5 April, the political parties that formed the Alliance pour la majorité presidentielle (AMP)—with the exception of l'Alliance pour le renouveau du Congo and le Rassemblement congolais pour la démocratie—signed a Charter establishing a new political platform that replaced the AMP with the Majorité présidentielle (MP). The Charter aimed to strengthen the coalition of political parties that had adhered to AMP in advance of the general elections.

Violence persisted in North and South Kivu and in Orientale Province. In the Kivus, the security situation was marked by attacks against civilians by the Forces démocratiques de libération du Rwanda (FDLR) and Congolese armed groups. Operation Amani Leo (Peace Today) [YUN 2010, p. 121] continued as the framework for support provided by MONUSCO to FARDC operations. Between 6 and 15 February, the Mission supported the FARDC operation Mapema Mupya (New Dawn) in North Kivu, aimed at deterring armed group activity and enhancing civilian protection. Despite some developments in the integration of armed group elements into FARDC, the process remained tenuous and limited progress was made in the implementation of the 23 March 2009 Agreements [YUN 2009, p. 120]. The Haut- and Bas-Uélé districts in Orientale Province saw an increase in attacks, attributed to LRA, targeting population centres and in some instances FARDC. The M'bororo pastoralist group was also increasingly targeted, with MONUSCO confirming reports of summary execution, the looting of cattle, sexual violence and other human rights violations. In February and March, FARDC, with the support of MONUSCO, launched a number of military operations in response to attacks in the Faradje and Bamangana areas, and conducted Operation Bokila Ya Nkoyi (Leopard Chase) in Ituri district to neutralize the militia remaining active in southern Irumu territory. In addition, MONUSCO launched Operation Easter Shield in the Doruma area following reports of two LRA attacks. On 17 March, the Ministers of Defence of the DRC and Uganda met in Kasese, Uganda, to review progress made regarding operations against LRA and the Ugandan Allied Democratic Forces (ADF) in the DRC. During that meeting, also attended by the Secretary-General's Special Representative and the MONUSCO Force Commander, the Ministers called for better coordination and cooperation to address the armed groups. In Equateur Province, representatives of the Enyele and Monzaya communities attended a joint ceremony in Monzaya marking the end of a conflict that had erupted in October and November 2009.

The United Nations and the Government continued the joint assessment of the situation on the ground and of progress in implementing the objectives outlined in paragraph 6 of resolution 1925(2010). Since the start of the exercise in June 2010, joint Government and UN teams had visited 124 territories and localities. The assessment results indicated that, where violence and protection challenges remained, there had been a shift from organized and coordinated attacks towards common criminality or acts of banditry by armed group elements. There was a need to secure resources for State institutions and the national security forces to ensure sufficient numbers of trained and equipped personnel, as well as for logistical support and suitable infrastructure to deliver State services. Despite reduced numbers of foreign and Congolese armed groups in Orientale Province, Ituri district and the Kivus, civilians remained victims of foreign and national armed groups, and access, even with the Mission's support, remained difficult.

The Secretary-General concluded that the timely conduct of general elections would be vital for the future legitimacy of the country's democratic institutions, as well as for consolidating peace and stability. He urged the Congolese authorities and relevant stakeholders to take steps to end acts of harassment and violence against opposition members and supporters, journalists and human rights defenders; the Electoral Commission to ensure the timely completion of voter registration; the Congolese authorities to ensure the safety and freedom of movement of all candidates for the general elections, as well as secure conditions for the conduct of polls; and Member States to increase their support for training and equipping FARDC. He recommended that the mandate of MONUSCO be extended by 12 months, and that the Mission continue to provide logistical and technical assistance for the conduct of the elections; assist the Electoral Commission in encouraging and facilitating dialogue among all stakeholders; protect UN personnel; contain violent acts that threatened the protection of civilians during the election period; and continue supporting the Government's Stabilization and Reconstruction Plan for War-Affected Areas through the International Security and Stabilization Support Strategy in eastern DRC.

Extension of MONUSCO mandate. By resolution 1991(2011) (see below), the Security Council extended until 30 June 2012 the mandate of the Mission, with civilian protection remaining the priority.

SECURITY COUNCIL ACTION

On 28 June [meeting 6568], the Security Council unanimously adopted **resolution 1991(2011)**. The draft [S/2011/390] was submitted by France, Gabon, the United Kingdom and the United States.

The Security Council,

Recalling its previous resolutions and the statements by its President concerning the Democratic Republic of the Congo,

Reaffirming its commitment to the sovereignty, territorial integrity and political independence of the Democratic Republic of the Congo,

Stressing the primary responsibility of the Government of the Democratic Republic of the Congo for ensuring security in its territory and protecting its civilians with respect for the rule of law, human rights and international humanitarian law,

Acknowledging that the overall peace and security situation in the Democratic Republic of the Congo has improved in recent years,

Stressing that significant security challenges remain in the Democratic Republic of the Congo, including the continued presence of armed groups in the Kivus and Oriental Province, serious abuses and violations of human rights and acts of violence against civilians, limited progress in building professional and accountable national security and rule of law institutions, and illegal exploitation of natural resources,

Commending the enhanced regional cooperation in the Great Lakes region, and encouraging further efforts to promote peace and stability in the region, including through existing regional mechanisms, and to intensify efforts on regional economic development,

Stressing that the successful holding of timely, inclusive, peaceful, credible and transparent elections, in accordance with the Constitution and international standards, is a key condition for the consolidation of democracy, national reconciliation and the restoration of a stable, peaceful and secure environment in which stabilization and socio-economic development can progress in the Democratic Republic of the Congo, and emphasizing the need to promote the participation of women in the electoral process,

Recognizing the importance of supporting peacebuilding efforts in order to achieve further progress in the stabilization of the country, underlining the importance of economic development to ensure long-term stabilization and peace consolidation, and stressing the need for sustained international support to ensure early recovery activities and lay the foundations for sustainable development,

Remaining greatly concerned by the humanitarian situation and the persistent high levels of violence and human rights abuses and violations against civilians, condemning, in particular, the targeted attacks against civilians, widespread sexual and gender-based violence, the recruitment and use of children by parties to the conflict, forced displacement and extrajudicial executions, reiterating the urgent need for the swift prosecution of all perpetrators of human rights abuses and international humanitarian law violations, and urging the Government of the Democratic Republic of the Congo, in cooperation with the United Nations and other relevant actors, to implement the appropriate responses to address these challenges, including in Walikale, and to provide security, medical, legal, humanitarian and other assistance to victims,

Recalling its resolutions 1325(2000) of 31 October 2000, 1820(2008) of 19 June 2008, 1888(2009) of 30 September 2009, 1889(2009) of 5 October 2009 and 1960(2010) of 16 December 2010 on women and peace and security, its resolution 1894(2009) of 11 November 2009 on the protection of civilians in armed conflict and its resolution 1882(2009) of 4 August 2009 on children and armed conflict, and recalling the conclusions of the Security Council Working Group on Children and Armed Conflict pertaining to parties to the armed conflict in the Democratic Republic of the Congo, especially in relation to the adoption of action plans to put an end to the recruitment and use of children,

Condemning all attacks against United Nations peacekeepers and humanitarian personnel, regardless of the perpetrators, and emphasizing that those responsible for such attacks must be brought to justice,

Recognizing the significant sacrifices made by the United Nations Organization Stabilization Mission in the Democratic Republic of the Congo, and expressing appreciation for its efforts to improve peace and stability in the Democratic Republic of the Congo,

Emphasizing the importance of the continued support of the United Nations and the international community for the long-term security and development of the Democratic Republic of the Congo,

Encouraging relevant international actors to support efforts and to assist in the restoration of basic services, especially in conflict-affected areas of the Democratic Republic of the Congo,

Calling upon the African Union and all relevant subregional organizations to further engage in support of the stabilization efforts in the Democratic Republic of the Congo, notably in the fields of security and combating illicit exploitation of and trade in natural resources,

Taking note of the report of the Secretary-General of 12 May 2011 on the Mission and of the recommendations contained therein,

Determining that the situation in the Democratic Republic of the Congo continues to pose a threat to international peace and security in the region,

Acting under Chapter VII of the Charter of the United Nations,

1. *Decides* to extend until 30 June 2012 the mandate of the United Nations Organization Stabilization Mission in the Democratic Republic of the Congo as set out in paragraphs 2, 11 and 12 (*a*) to (*p*) and (*r*) to (*t*) of resolution 1925(2010) of 28 May 2010, reaffirms that the protection of civilians must be given priority in decisions about the use of available capacity and resources, and encourages further the use of innovative measures implemented by the Mission in the protection of civilians;

2. *Reiterates* that the Government of the Democratic Republic of the Congo bears primary responsibility for security, peacebuilding and development in the country, and encourages the Government to remain fully committed to protecting the civilian population through the establishment of professional and sustainable security forces and the rule of law and respect for human rights, to promote non-military solutions as an integral part of the overall solution for reducing the threat posed by Congolese and foreign armed groups and to restore full State authority in the areas freed from armed groups;

3. *Welcomes* its enhanced dialogue with the Government of the Democratic Republic of the Congo, reiterates that the challenges the Democratic Republic of the Congo is facing as it enters a phase of stabilization and peace consolidation require a strategic partnership with the United Nations, including with the Mission, welcomes the constructive approach of the Congolese authorities and the Mission in this regard, in particular through the joint assessment process, and encourages the continuing of such assessment discussions with a view to enabling the Security Council to continue to make informed decisions regarding any reconfiguration of the Mission, in accordance with the provisions of paragraph 7 of resolution 1925(2010);

4. *Reiterates* that future reconfigurations of the Mission should be determined on the basis of the evolution of the situation on the ground and on the achievement of the following objectives to be pursued by the Government of the Democratic Republic of the Congo and the United Nations Mission:

(*a*) The completion of the ongoing military operations in the Kivus and Orientale Province, resulting in reducing to a minimum the threat from armed groups and restoring stability in sensitive areas;

(*b*) An improved capacity of the Government of the Democratic Republic of the Congo to effectively protect the population through the establishment of professional, accountable and sustainable security forces with a view to progressively taking over the security role of the Mission;

(*c*) The consolidation of State authority throughout the territory through the deployment of Congolese civil administration, in particular the police, territorial administration and rule of law institutions in areas freed from armed groups;

5. *Recognizes* the primary responsibility of the Government of the Democratic Republic of the Congo and its national partners to create propitious conditions for the forthcoming elections, urges the Government as well as all relevant parties to ensure an environment conducive to a free, fair, credible, inclusive, transparent, peaceful and timely electoral process, which includes free and constructive political debate, freedom of expression, freedom of assembly, equitable access to media, including State media, and safety for all candidates as well as for election observers and witnesses, journalists, human rights defenders and civil society actors, including women, calls upon the Congolese authorities to ensure secure conditions for the conduct of and unrestricted access to the polls, including through cooperation with the Mission, consistent with the role of the Mission with regard to the protection of civilians, and calls upon all parties to respect the results of the polls;

6. *Calls upon* the National Independent Electoral Commission, political parties and relevant Congolese authorities to swiftly adopt and implement codes of conduct and ensure timely accreditation of national and international observers;

7. *Decides* that the Mission shall support the organization and conduct of national, provincial and local elections through the provision of technical and logistical support as requested by the Congolese authorities, by facilitating enhanced and regular dialogue with the National Independent Electoral Commission, including through the Election Partnership Committee, by supporting the Commission in facilitating dialogue among various Congolese stakeholders, by monitoring, reporting and following up on human rights violations in the context of the elections, and by using the good offices of the Special Representative of the Secretary-General for the Democratic Republic of the Congo as required;

8. *Calls upon* the Mission and the United Nations country team to collect information on and identify potential threats against the civilian population, as well as reliable information on violations of international humanitarian and human rights law, to bring them to the attention of the Congolese authorities as appropriate, and to take

appropriate action in accordance with the United Nations system-wide protection strategy in harmonization with the Mission's protection strategy, and further requests the Mission, consistent with its mandate and within its current capabilities, to provide assistance and advice to the Congolese authorities with security preparations in relation to the elections;

9. *Calls upon* the international community to remain engaged in supporting the elections in the Democratic Republic of the Congo, and urges donors to swiftly provide equipment and financial support for the training of the Congolese National Police, with a view to enhancing Congolese efforts in this regard;

10. *Requests* the Mission, consistent with the authorization provided by resolution 1925(2010), to keep a reserve force capable of redeploying rapidly in the country within its mandated strength;

11. *Reiterates* the primary responsibility of the Government of the Democratic Republic of the Congo regarding the professionalization of its security sector and urges the Congolese authorities, with the support of the Mission, to develop and implement a comprehensive national security sector development strategy, in order to establish democratic, accountable and professional national security institutions, urges the Government to swiftly adopt the relevant legislation and to coordinate, with the support of the Mission, the efforts of the international community, including all bilateral and multilateral actors working on security sector development issues, and calls upon all Member States and international organizations to fully cooperate with the Congolese authorities in this regard;

12. *Encourages* the Government of the Democratic Republic of the Congo to address the underlying issue of the cohesion of the national army, including by further developing its efforts to ensure proper integration and vetting of former armed groups, in particular the Congrès national pour la défense du peuple, into the Armed Forces of the Democratic Republic of the Congo, and expresses concern at the promotion within the Congolese security forces of well-known individuals responsible for serious human rights abuses;

13. *Demands* that all armed groups, in particular the Forces démocratiques de libération du Rwanda and the Lord's Resistance Army, immediately cease all forms of violence and human rights abuses against the civilian population in the Democratic Republic of the Congo, in particular against women and children, including rape and other forms of sexual abuse, and demobilize;

14. *Takes note* of the respective initiatives taken by the United Nations and the African Union to facilitate regional action against the Lord's Resistance Army and to protect civilians, reiterates the need to enhance cooperation of all relevant parties to help to address the threat to civilians posed by the Lord's Resistance Army, welcomes the steps taken by the Mission to enhance information-sharing and coordination with those conducting military operations against the Lord's Resistance Army, and encourages the Mission to continue to keep close contacts with Lord's Resistance Army-affected communities and to keep under review the deployment of its available resources to ensure maximum effect;

15. *Acknowledges* the results of the action taken to address the threat of foreign and national armed groups, particularly the progress made against the Forces démocratiques de libération du Rwanda, including through the disarmament, demobilization, repatriation, resettlement and reintegration process, urges the international community and donors to support the Government of the Democratic Republic of the Congo and the Mission in disarmament, demobilization, repatriation, resettlement and reintegration activities, calls upon the Government of the Democratic Republic of the Congo and neighbouring States to remain engaged in the process, and urges the Government to make progress on the national programme for the disarmament, demobilization and reintegration of residual Congolese armed elements in eastern Democratic Republic of the Congo, with the support of the Mission;

16. *Encourages* the Government of the Democratic Republic of the Congo to continue to build on its cooperation with the Special Representative of the Secretary-General for Children and Armed Conflict and the Special Representative of the Secretary-General on Sexual Violence in Conflict and to meet, without further delay, its commitments to adopt and implement an action plan to halt the recruitment and use of children by the Armed Forces of the Democratic Republic of the Congo, in close collaboration with the Mission;

17. *Welcomes* the initial steps taken by the mining authorities in the Democratic Republic of the Congo and throughout the region to address the tracing and certification of minerals, encourages further demilitarization of the mining areas in the Democratic Republic of the Congo and the professionalization and deployment of the Congolese Mining Police in these areas, and calls upon the Mission to support the relevant Congolese authorities in preventing the provision of support to armed groups from illicit economic activities and illicit trade in natural resources, including to carry out spot checks and regular visits to mining sites, trade routes and markets in the vicinity of the five pilot trading counters;

18. *Urges* the Government of the Democratic Republic of the Congo to approve the multi-year joint United Nations justice support programme and to implement it, with the support of international partners, welcomes the positive steps taken by the Congolese authorities to try those responsible for human rights violations, including rape, in South Kivu, and encourages the Congolese authorities to promote lasting reconciliation in the Democratic Republic of the Congo by pursuing these efforts to combat impunity against all perpetrators of human rights and international humanitarian law violations, including those committed by any illegal armed groups or elements of the Congolese security forces;

19. *Commends* the Government of the Democratic Republic of the Congo for the apprehension and the transfer to the International Criminal Tribunal for Rwanda of Mr. Bernard Munyagishari, a fugitive from international criminal justice, further stresses the importance of the Government of the Democratic Republic of the Congo actively seeking to hold accountable those responsible for war crimes and crimes against humanity in the country and of regional cooperation to this end, including through cooperation with the International Criminal Court, and calls upon the Mission to use its existing authority to assist the Government in this regard;

20. *Calls upon* the Mission to continue to work with the United Nations country team and the Congolese authorities towards the adoption and implementation of the Peace Consolidation Programme covering provinces not affected by the conflict and to continue to support the implementation of the Government's Stabilization and Reconstruction Plan, including through the implementation of the International Security and Stabilization Support Strategy, and calls upon donors to support these efforts;

21. *Demands* that all parties cooperate fully with the operations of the Mission and that they ensure the security of as well as unhindered and immediate access for United Nations and associated personnel in carrying out their mandate, throughout the territory of the Democratic Republic of the Congo, and requests the Secretary-General to report without delay any failure to comply with these demands;

22. *Commends* the contribution of troop- and police-contributing countries and donors to the Mission, and calls upon Member States to pledge and provide the remaining force enablers required for the Mission;

23. *Requests* the Secretary-General to report in October 2011, in January 2012 and by 23 May 2012 on the progress on the ground, also requests the Secretary-General to regularly brief and inform the Council on the significant events of the electoral process, including on support by the Mission to this process, and to provide a comprehensive assessment of the political, security, humanitarian and human rights environment following the elections, and further requests the Secretary-General to provide in these reports an indication of progress towards achieving a coordinated United Nations approach in-country, and, in particular, on critical gaps to achieving peacebuilding objectives alongside the mission;

24. *Decides* to remain actively seized of the matter.

Communication. In identical letters dated 23 August to the Security Council and the Secretary-General [S/2011/534], the DRC transmitted a Government communiqué regarding the seizure of minerals from a MONUSCO vehicle at the Congolese-Rwandan border on 22 August. The incident was subsequently confirmed by provincial civil and military authorities and MONUSCO officials. The DRC requested the Security Council to mount an inquiry and publish its findings.

Letter of Secretary-General (September). The Secretary-General, on 20 September [S/2011/589], brought to the attention of the Security Council the acute shortage of military helicopters in MONUSCO. The impact of that shortage had become critical, particularly in the run-up to the November presidential and parliamentary elections.

Report of Secretary-General (October). In response to Council resolution 1991(2011) (see p. 105), the Secretary-General in October submitted a report [S/2011/656] reviewing major developments in the electoral process. Preparations for the elections gathered pace with the completion of the voter and candidate registration process. Provisional figures released by the Electoral Commission indicated that over 32 million people had registered to vote. On 25 June, President Kabila promulgated the electoral law governing the presidential, legislative and provincial elections, followed on 17 August by the promulgation of the law on seat distribution for legislative and provincial elections. The Electoral Commission convened the first meeting (Kinshasa, 25 July) of the Forum of Political Parties, which aimed to foster dialogue between the Commission and the political parties and was attended by 275 of the over 400 registered parties. That was followed on 8 September by the Forum's second meeting, also in Kinshasa, during which political parties, with the exception of UDPS and the opposition parties allied to it, signed the code of conduct.

On 24 August, some 70 opposition political parties chose Etienne Tshisekedi, leader of UDPS, as their common presidential candidate. While the MP designated President Kabila as their presidential candidate, Mr. Kabila announced on 21 August his intention to run as an independent. In early September some opposition parties expressed concern about alleged irregularities in the voter registration process. Following public protest marches on 1 September in Kinshasa, Goma, Lubumbashi and Tshikapa, the Electoral Commission announced on 2 September its intention to give experts appointed by political parties access to its central server, as well as the opportunity to verify voter registration data. On 5 September, following Mr. Tshisekedi's registration as a presidential candidate, a branch office of the Parti du peuple pour la reconstruction et le développement was set ablaze, allegedly by supporters of UDPS. Subsequently, on 6 September, armed individuals set fire to the headquarters of Mr. Tshisekedi's party in Kinshasa, reportedly killing one civilian and injuring several others.

The security situation in the Kivus deteriorated, owing to decreased military pressure on armed groups as a result of the reconfiguration of FARDC, which required the withdrawal of the armed forces from a number of areas. In North Kivu, some elements of the former Congrès national pour la défense du peuple (CNDP) and the Patriotes résistants congolais that had integrated into the armed forces and the national police refused to deploy outside their areas of operation. In South Kivu, the reconfiguration process led to significant desertions by former armed group elements that had integrated into the armed forces, particularly from the Patriotes résistants congolais, the CNDP and the Forces républicaines fédéralistes. They, along with some armed forces elements, were involved in increasing incidents of violence throughout the province. Mayi-Mayi Yakutumba elements were reportedly reinforcing their collaboration with the Burundian Forces nationales de liberation and the Forces démocratiques de libération du Rwanda in South Kivu. From May to September, MONUSCO conducted five military operations aimed at filling security vacuums and enhancing civilian protection in Kalehe, Walungu, Mwenga and Uvira territories in South Kivu. In Orientale Province, several reports indicated that LRA elements, including those operating in the DRC, might be regrouping in the Obo area in the Central African Republic. FARDC continued military operations against LRA, with the support of MONUSCO and in coordination with the Ugandan armed forces, including eight operations aimed at protecting the population in Haut-Uélé. With the Mission's support, the armed forces also conducted five operations in Ituri district to address the activities of the Front populaire pour la justice au Congo and the Front de résistance patriotique de l'Ituri, partially curtailing their capacity.

MONUSCO engaged in dialogue with Congolese electoral authorities, Government authorities and political parties in support of election preparations, and provided technical and logistical support to the Electoral Commission. While it continued to prioritize civilian protection, those efforts were curtailed by the shortage of military helicopters. MONUSCO was facing a shortfall of 6 military utility helicopters, 6 attack helicopters and 3 observation helicopters. That resulted in the postponement of joint operations with the armed forces, a delay of investigations into human rights allegations, the deferment of some deployments to protection hotspots, and severe constraints on operations throughout the eastern region, including 11 company and temporary operating bases in North Kivu and 15 such bases in Oriental Province.

The United Nations and the Government continued the joint assessment process to review implementation of the objectives outlined in paragraph 4 of Security Council resolution 1991(2011). From 19 to 23 July, a joint delegation co-led by the Secretary-General's Special Representative and the Congolese Special Adviser of the Head of State for Security Matters visited the Kivus as well as Dungu, Duru and Bunia in Orientale Province. The findings highlighted that, following the decrease in military operations of the armed forces owing to its reconfiguration, activity by armed groups had resumed, resulting in an increased threat to the population, with exactions against civilians including looting, banditry, illegal taxation, rape, kidnapping for ransom and population displacements in the Kivus.

The Secretary-General concluded that, while important steps had been made ahead of the November polls, logistical challenges remained, and the incomplete integration of Congolese armed groups into the armed forces presented challenges. He urged the Electoral Commission and political parties to continue consultations, including through the Forum of Political Parties, and also urged the Commission to intensify its efforts to ensure the timely arrival of electoral material procured from abroad. Concerned about continued violence against civilians and the limited capability of MONUSCO to prevent it, the Secretary-General reiterated his appeal to Member States to provide additional military utility and attack helicopters. Security gaps throughout the Kivus caused by the reconfiguration process needed to be addressed, particularly by ensuring that army troops redeployed in those regions were more cohesive, regularly and better paid, and properly trained and equipped.

Year-end developments. In a later report [S/2012/65], the Secretary-General stated that alongside the 11 presidential candidates, the Electoral Commission registered 18,864 candidates for the 500 seats in the National Assembly. On 26 and 27 October, the Commission, supported by MONUSCO, held a colloquium to foster dialogue between presidential candidates, the Commission and other political leaders, which resulted in the signing of a declaration by President Kabila and several other presidential candidates renouncing all forms of violence, intimidation and statements based on ethnicity, religion or race.

There was mounting tension as the leading presidential candidates campaigned across the country. In the provinces of Kinshasa and Orientale, Kasai Occidentale and Katanga, a number of election-related incidents were reported, resulting in deaths, injuries and the destruction of property, primarily involving supporters of the opposition party UDPS and of the presidential majority. On 26 November, in Kinshasa, clashes between UDPS and presidential coalition supporters, and between UDPS and the national security forces, resulted in several fatalities and injuries, and led to a ban by city authorities of all final campaign rallies scheduled for that day. On 28 November, in Lubumbashi, six people were reportedly killed in two separate armed attacks aimed at disrupting the distribution of electoral material.

The Electoral Commission faced logistical challenges in delivering electoral material to about 17,000 polling centres and 64,000 polling stations. To support the delivery of electoral material, the air assets of the Government and MONUSCO were supplemented by the provision of helicopters and airplanes from the Governments of Angola, the Congo and South Africa. The Mission provided the Commission with technical advice and logistical support for the deployment of 3,977 tons of material to 15 hubs and 210 sub-hubs, and transported material to 400 polling stations in insecure and remote areas. MONUSCO, together with UN agencies, funds and programmes, developed and implemented a joint contingency plan to meet protection needs during the electoral period. The Mission redeployed troops and police, including about 1,400 uniformed personnel deployed in Kinshasa, who conducted patrols prior to, during and after the polls.

From October to December, MONUSCO conducted 13 joint protection team missions in North and South Kivu, Katanga, Ituri and Haut Uélé, bringing the total number of such missions during 2011 to 46. The first pilot phase of 24 Community Alert Networks established in the Kivus and Orientale Province enabled more than 200 communities in isolated areas to contact local authorities and MONUSCO in order to request intervention in the event of threats to their communities. In addition to training six crowd control units in Kinshasa, comprising 3,000 national police personnel, MONUSCO conducted election security training for 15,531 national police officers, as well as 180 other police officers and 50 FARDC personnel.

Despite security and logistical challenges, polling for the presidential and legislative elections began as scheduled on 28 November, and continued in some places until 2 December. Nearly 19 million people—about 59 per cent of the 32 million registered voters—cast their vote. The Electoral Commission on 9 December announced the provisional results of the presidential elections, according to which President Kabila obtained 8,880,944 votes (48.95 per cent), followed by Mr. Tshisekedi with 5,864,775 votes (32.33 per cent) and Vital Kamerhe of the Union pour la nation congolaise with 1,403,372 votes (7.74 per cent). On 16 December, the Supreme Court of Justice validated those results, declaring Mr. Kabila the winner of the presidential election. A number of opposition candidates rejected the results, and on 12 December President Kabila, during a press conference, said that while mistakes had been made in the conduct of the elections, they were not of a nature to put the announced results in question. On 20 December, he was sworn in as President for a second five-year term. The elections were observed by a number of intergovernmental organizations, several of which issued statements expressing regret at the lack of transparency and irregularities in the collection, compilation and publication of the results. Many international partners emphasized the need to enhance the transparency of the vote counting process for the legislative polls, as well as for the upcoming provincial and local elections.

During the reporting period, the FARDC regimentation process in the provinces of North and South Kivu was completed. FARDC units were redeployed to fill security gaps and resume military operations, and MONUSCO conducted 10 military operations to deter armed groups and protect civilians, notably in the Kivus. In North Kivu, FDLR continued to be weakened under military and judicial pressure and efforts to encourage combatants to surrender. While a number of command positions created as part of the regimentation process were given to former CNDP commanders, several CNDP elements continued to maintain parallel command and control structures within FARDC and to resist orders to redeploy outside their areas of operation. In South Kivu, the integration of the Forces républicaines fédéralistes (FRF) into FARDC remained incomplete and some FRF elements continued to carry out militia activities. In Orientale Province, FARDC conducted a number of unilateral operations aimed at containing LRA activities around the Garamba National Park, and MONUSCO launched one unilateral and three joint operations against LRA. The threat posed by militia groups in Ituri district persisted, and on 2 December a militia group attacked a MONUSCO patrol in the Bunia area. In a positive development, MONUSCO and partners completed the development of the second phase of the International Security and Stabilization Support Strategy: the stabilization priority plan for 2012–2014, which identified 37 priority projects aimed at expanding stabilization efforts in the Kivus and Orientale, Maniema and Katanga Provinces.

The General Assembly, on 24 December decided that the item on armed aggression against the DRC would remain for consideration during its resumed sixty-sixth (2012) session (**decision 66/557**).

Arms embargo

The Security Council Committee on the DRC, established pursuant to resolution 1533(2004) [YUN 2004, p. 137] to review and monitor the arms embargo on armed groups imposed by resolution 1493(2003) [YUN 2003, p. 130], reported on its activities in 2011 [S/2012/3]. The Committee held four informal meetings throughout the year, during which it received the workplan and reports of the Group of Experts on the DRC (see below), as well as a briefing by the Secretary-General's Special Representative on Sexual Violence in Conflict, Margot Wallström. In accordance with paragraph 5 of Council resolution 1807(2008) [YUN 2008, p. 136], the Committee received 20 notifications from States in advance of the shipment of arms and related materiel, or the provision of technical training and assistance, to the DRC. On 15 July, the Committee updated the list of individuals and entities subject to the measures imposed by paragraphs 13 and 15 of resolution 1596(2005) [YUN 2005, p. 192], as renewed by paragraph 3 of resolution 1952(2010) [YUN 2010, p. 133], and added two individuals in October and November. During the year, the Committee received reports from Brazil [S/AC.43/2011/5], Colombia [S/AC.43/2011/4], Latvia [S/AC.43/2011/3], Serbia [S/AC.43/2011/1] and the United Kingdom [S/AC.43/2011/2] on action taken to implement the measures imposed by resolution 1952(2010).

Group of Experts

The Group of Experts on the DRC, established pursuant to Council resolution 1533(2004) to gather and analyse information on flows of arms and related materiel as well as networks operating in violation of the measures imposed by paragraph 20 of resolution 1493(2003), submitted during the year an interim report [S/2011/345] and a final report [S/2011/738].

As requested by resolution 1952(2010), the Secretary-General, on 17 February [S/2011/77] and 1 April [S/2011/219], appointed six experts to constitute the Group for a period ending 30 November.

Reports of Group of Experts. On 6 June, pursuant to Council resolution 1533(2004), the Security Council Committee on the DRC submitted to the Council the Group's interim report [S/2011/345]. As requested by Council resolution 1952(2010), the Group's activities focused on areas affected by the presence of illegal armed groups, including the Kivus and Orientale Province, as well as on regional and international networks providing support to illegal armed groups, criminal networks and perpetrators of serious violations of international humanitarian law and human rights abuses operating in the east. The Group conducted field missions in 13 of the 15 territories of North and South Kivu, as well as Ituri and Haut Uélé in Orientale Province. The Group welcomed the political commitment to resolve the issue of armed groups in the Kivus, noting that FARDC in February had launched a plan to form new regiments of 1,200 soldiers throughout the Kivus with the aim of reunifying operational and military region command structures. The absence of a viable national programme of demobilization, disarmament, repatriation, reintegration and resettlement, with a focus on community integration, however, represented a significant impediment to resolving the presence of armed groups. While recognizing the need to control incentives for new mobilization, the Group highlighted the importance of providing managed disarmament, demobilization and reintegration (DDR) options for Congolese armed groups, which could also help to isolate and diminish the strength of foreign armed groups. With regard to arms embargo violations and controls, the Group was working with national authorities to gather and analyse information, particularly relating to cross-border trafficking, risks of diversion, and estimates of stocks of arms controlled by the major armed groups. The Group had begun working with FARDC to review arms and ammunition stockpile management, logistics and accountability practices. On natural resource exploitation, the Group recognized the Government's efforts to demilitarize principal mining sites and to place them under police control, and encouraged similar efforts in smaller, more remote mines. By resolution 1952(2010), the Security Council supported taking forward the Group's recommended guidelines on due diligence for importers, processing industries and consumers of Congolese mineral products, which contained a set of measures by which to mitigate the risk of providing direct or indirect support to armed groups in eastern DRC. The Group of Experts, the Organization for Economic Cooperation and Development (OECD) and the International Conference on the Great Lakes Region jointly hosted a meeting (Paris, 5–6 May) on the implementation of both the OECD and the UN due diligence guidelines, enabling discussion among a wide range of stakeholders on ways to monitor their implementation.

The Group invited the Security Council Committee to review, revise and update its list of individuals and entities designated for targeted sanctions on the basis of information provided by the Group and its predecessors; request Member States to provide more detailed and complete information in their notifications of arms transfers to the DRC; and encourage Member States to convey the due diligence guidelines to importers, processing industries and consumers of mineral products. The Group also made recommendations regarding the activities of MONUSCO; due diligence; weapons marking, stockpile management and accountability; border controls; and army integration and DDR.

In its final report, submitted in November [S/2011/738], the Group of Experts stated that, despite further reorganization, FARDC was still divided by parallel chains of command. The Forces démocratiques de libération du Rwanda (FDLR) remained the most militarily strong and politically significant rebel force in the Kivus, and continued to build alliances with Congolese armed groups. LRA activity decreased in the second half of the year, as most units moved to the Central African Republic, and the group did not appear to be benefiting from external support. The Ugandan Allied Democratic Forces regained control over territory previously lost to FARDC and continued to receive income from money transfers, taxation on gold mines and timber production. Combatants from the Burundian Forces nationales de libération continued to use South Kivu province as a rear base for remobilization efforts, having built a strong alliance with the Congolese rebels of Mai Mai Yakutumba in Fizi territory. Congolese armed groups had been preparing for possible outbreaks of unrest resulting from post-electoral disputes. Those already integrated into FARDC, including the Coalition des patriotes résistants congolais (PARECO), the Congrès national pour la défense du peuple (CNDP) and FRF, sought to consolidate their grip on key command positions and territories, hoping to ensure maximum support for the campaigns of their own candidates and that of President Kabila. Ex-CNDP member General Bosco Ntaganda hijacked the Government's efforts to reform army units in the country's east by placing his most loyal officers in critical positions throughout the Kivus. For their part, non-integrated armed groups, including Mai Mai Yakutumba and PARECO LaFontaine, sought to capitalize on anti-Kabila and anti-CNDP sentiment in the Kivus.

Regarding natural resource exploitation, the Group continued to evaluate the impact of its due diligence guidelines. Since Chinese refiners, smelters and trading companies made up a significant portion of the buyers of tin, tungsten and tantalum from eastern DRC, awareness and implementation of due diligence on the part of such companies was of particular importance. There was strong awareness of the Group's due diligence guidelines among international refiners and smelters belonging to the International Tin Research Institute, while awareness among non-members was weaker. Awareness of the issue of conflict minerals had increased internationally in most affected industries, particularly electronics, vehicle manufacture and aerospace. Congolese gold was in high demand, and the gold trade was among the main sources of financing available to Congolese armed groups and criminal networks within FARDC. Gold *comptoirs* in eastern DRC and neighbouring countries had not demonstrated significant awareness of the Group's due diligence guidelines, and implementation by gold refiners, smelters and jewellers was also weak. On 6 September, the Ministry of Mines of the DRC issued a *note circulaire* obliging all mining operators in the country to exercise due diligence as defined in Council resolution 1952(2010) and OECD guidance. On 10 March, the Government lifted its suspension of all artisanal mining activity in the Kivus and Maniema Province, which had been in place since 11 September 2010. The Group determined that during the ban, the mining of tin, coltan and wolframite had continued in several areas, often under the control of FARDC or armed groups. Furthermore, smuggling was a widespread problem, and the Group had identified a number of illegal border crossings, including a street controlled by General Ntaganda in Goma and a Lake Kivu port north of Bukavu run by FARDC elements. Armed groups continued to obtain most of their arms, ammunition and uniforms from FARDC, and leakage from FARDC stocks was widespread and largely uncontrolled.

The Group recommended, among other measures, that the Security Council urge Member States to incorporate the due diligence guidelines into national legislation, and that MONUSCO enhance its maritime and aerial capacity to deter piracy and fulfil its role in monitoring implementation of the arms embargo. Member States should raise awareness of the guidelines and support the installation of satellite or radar coverage of airports in eastern DRC and the automation of the sharing of flight plans. Customs authorities in the DRC should, in collaboration with their counterparts in Burundi, Kenya, Rwanda, Uganda, the United Arab Emirates and the United Republic of Tanzania, develop enhanced systems for verifying the authenticity of certificates of origin for gold; and the DRC Ministry of Mines should ensure that nationally recognized exploration and exploitation concessions were respected at the provincial and local levels. The Government should mark State-owned firearms as a matter of priority; take a national inventory of arms and ammunition; relaunch a national DDR programme; provide special induction training to officers integrated into FARDC from armed groups; and shut down illegal border crossings controlled by criminal networks within FARDC. Furthermore, MONUSCO and international donors should provide specialist training and logistical support to prosecutors and mining and border police in investigating cases of illegal trade, smuggling and other economic crimes.

SECURITY COUNCIL ACTION

On 29 November [meeting 6671], the Security Council unanimously adopted **resolution 2021(2011)**. The draft [S/2011/737] was submitted by France.

The Security Council,

Recalling its previous resolutions and the statements by its President concerning the Democratic Republic of the Congo,

Reaffirming its commitment to the sovereignty, territorial integrity and political independence of the Democratic Republic of the Congo as well as all States in the region,

Stressing the primary responsibility of the Government of the Democratic Republic of the Congo for ensuring security in its territory and protecting its civilians with respect for the rule of law, human rights and international humanitarian law,

Taking note of the interim report and the final report of the Group of Experts on the Democratic Republic of the Congo ("the Group of Experts") established pursuant to resolution 1771(2007) of 10 August 2007, whose mandate was extended pursuant to resolutions 1807(2008) of 31 March 2008, 1857(2008) of 22 December 2008, 1896(2009) of 30 November 2009 and 1952(2010) of 29 November 2010, and of the recommendations contained therein, and welcoming the ongoing collaboration between the Group of Experts and the Government of the Democratic Republic of the Congo, as well as other Governments in the region and other international forums,

Reiterating its serious concern regarding the presence of armed groups in the Democratic Republic of the Congo, including the provinces of North and South Kivu and Orientale Province, which perpetuates a climate of insecurity in the whole region, and reiterating its concern about the support received by these armed groups from regional and international networks,

Condemning the continuing illicit flow of weapons within and into the Democratic Republic of the Congo in violation of resolutions 1533(2004) of 12 March 2004, 1807(2008), 1857(2008), 1896(2009) and 1952(2010), declaring its determination to continue to monitor closely the implementation of the arms embargo and other measures set out in its resolutions concerning the Democratic Republic of the Congo, and stressing the obligation of all States to abide by the notification requirements set out in paragraph 5 of resolution 1807(2008),

Recalling the linkage between the illegal exploitation of natural resources, illicit trade in such resources and the proliferation of and trafficking in arms as one of the major factors fuelling and exacerbating conflicts in the Great Lakes region of Africa,

Underlining the importance of economic development to ensure long-term stabilization and peace consolidation, expressing in this regard its concern about further rise in unemployment and worsened poverty in some mining areas, and noting at the same time the link between the exercise of due diligence by some *comptoirs*, the improvement of mining sector governance and the rise in minerals production and export in other mining areas, as reported by the Group of Experts,

Welcoming the regional efforts of the countries of the Great Lakes region in the context of the International Conference on the Great Lakes Region against the illegal exploitation of natural resources, noting the commitment of these countries to establish a Regional Initiative against the Illegal Exploitation of Natural Resources and their endorsement of the due diligence guidelines, as defined by the Organization for Economic Cooperation and Development, and encouraging those States to implement the components of the Regional Initiative,

Expressing its concern that armed groups are turning increasingly to new sources of funding through diverse criminal activities, including illicit drug trafficking, illegal taxation and agricultural sales,

Noting with great concern the persistence of human rights abuses and humanitarian law violations against civilians in the eastern part of the Democratic Republic of the Congo, including the killing and displacement of significant numbers of civilians, the recruitment and use of child soldiers and widespread sexual violence, stressing that the perpetrators must be brought to justice, reiterating its firm condemnation of all human rights abuses and international humanitarian law violations in the country, and recalling all its relevant resolutions on women and peace and security, on children and armed conflict and on the protection of civilians in armed conflict,

Determining that the situation in the Democratic Republic of the Congo continues to constitute a threat to international peace and security in the region,

Acting under Chapter VII of the Charter of the United Nations,

1. *Decides* to renew until 30 November 2012 the measures on arms imposed by paragraph 1 of resolution 1807(2008), and reaffirms the provisions of paragraphs 2, 3 and 5 of that resolution;

2. *Decides also* to renew, for the period specified in paragraph 1 above, the measures on transport imposed by paragraphs 6 and 8 of resolution 1807(2008), and reaffirms the provisions of paragraph 7 of that resolution;

3. *Decides further* to renew, for the period specified in paragraph 1 above, the financial and travel measures imposed by paragraphs 9 and 11 of resolution 1807(2008), and reaffirms the provisions of paragraphs 10 and 12 of that resolution regarding the individuals and entities referred to in paragraph 4 of resolution 1857(2008);

4. *Requests* the Secretary-General to extend, for a period expiring on 30 November 2012, the mandate of the Group of Experts established pursuant to resolution 1533(2004) and renewed by subsequent resolutions, and requests the Group of Experts to fulfil its mandate as set out in paragraph 18 of resolution 1807(2008) and expanded by paragraphs 9 and 10 of resolution 1857(2008) and to report to the Security Council in writing, through the Security Council Committee established pursuant to resolution 1533(2004), by 18 May 2012 and again before 19 October 2012;

5. *Reaffirms* the provisions of paragraphs 6 to 13 of resolution 1952(2010), and requests the Group of Experts to include in its evaluation of the impact of due diligence a comprehensive assessment of the economic and social development of the relevant mining areas in the Democratic Republic of the Congo;

6. *Welcomes* the support of the due diligence guidelines, as defined by the Group of Experts and the Organization for Economic Cooperation and Development, by the Democratic Republic of the Congo, welcomes further the measures taken by the Government of the Democratic Republic of the Congo to implement the guidelines, and calls upon all States to assist the Democratic Republic of the Congo and the countries in the Great Lakes region in the implementation of the guidelines;

7. *Encourages* all States, particularly those in the region, to continue to raise awareness of the Group of Experts due diligence guidelines, in particular in the gold sector, as part of broader efforts to mitigate the risk of further financing armed groups and criminal networks within the Armed Forces of the Democratic Republic of the Congo in the Democratic Republic of the Congo;

8. *Encourages* the Democratic Republic of the Congo and the States in the Great Lakes region to require their customs authorities to strengthen their control on exports and imports of minerals from the Democratic Republic of the Congo, and calls upon the international community to assist the Democratic Republic of the Congo and other States in the Great Lakes region, as necessary and requested, to enhance their capacities in this regard;

9. *Recommends* that all States, particularly those in the region, regularly publish full import and export statistics for natural resources, including gold, cassiterite, coltan, wolframite, timber and charcoal, and enhance information-sharing and joint action at the regional level to investigate and combat regional criminal networks and armed groups involved in the illegal exploitation of natural resources;

10. *Recalls* the mandate of the United Nations Organization Stabilization Mission in the Democratic Republic of the Congo to support the relevant Congolese authorities in preventing the provision of support to armed groups from illicit activities, including production of and trade in natural resources, notably by carrying out spot checks and regular visits to mining sites, trade routes and markets, in the vicinity of the five pilot trading counters;

11. *Encourages* the Government of the Democratic Republic of the Congo to enhance stockpile security, accountability and management of arms and ammunition, with the assistance of international partners, as necessary and requested, and to urgently implement a national weapons marking programme, in particular for State-owned firearms, in line with the standards established by the Nairobi Protocol for the Prevention, Control and Reduction of Small Arms and Light Weapons in the Great Lakes Region and the Horn of Africa and the Regional Centre on Small Arms and Light Weapons in the Great Lakes Region, the Horn of Africa and Bordering States;

12. *Also encourages* the Government of the Democratic Republic of the Congo to continue to address the underlying issue of the cohesion of the national army, including by further ensuring proper integration and vetting of former armed groups, in particular the Congrès national pour la défense du peuple, into the Armed Forces of the Democratic Republic of the Congo, to ensure that members of the national army are paid in a timely fashion, operate in accordance with established command and control regulations, and are subject to such disciplinary action as may be appropriate when regulations are violated, and to ensure that the Congolese security forces redeploy to mitigate the threats caused by security vacuums, including those which have arisen during the reconfiguration process of the Armed Forces of the Democratic Republic of the Congo;

13. *Demands* that all armed groups, in particular the Forces démocratiques de libération du Rwanda, the Lord's Resistance Army, Mai Mai Yakutumba, the Forces nationales de libération and the Allied Democratic Forces, lay down their arms and immediately cease all forms of violence, human rights abuses and international humanitarian law violations against the civilian population in the Democratic Republic of the Congo and the Great Lakes region, in particular against women and children, including rape and other forms of sexual abuse, and demobilize;

14. *Welcomes* the ongoing efforts of the Congolese authorities to fight against impunity, and encourages their continuation, including against perpetrators of human rights abuses and international humanitarian law violations, including sexual violence, and against those responsible for illegal exploitation of natural resources, including those committed by any illegal armed groups or elements of the Armed Forces of the Democratic Republic of the Congo;

15. *Stresses* the importance of the Government of the Democratic Republic of the Congo actively seeking to hold accountable those responsible for war crimes and crimes against humanity in the country and of regional cooperation to this end, including through its ongoing cooperation with the International Criminal Court, and encourages the Mission to use its existing authority to assist the Government in this regard;

16. *Encourages* enhanced cooperation between all States, particularly those in the region, the Mission and the Group of Experts, further encourages all parties and all States to ensure cooperation with the Group of Experts by individuals and entities within their jurisdiction or under their control, and reiterates its demand that all parties and all States ensure the safety of its members and unhindered and immediate access, in particular to persons, documents and sites that the Group of Experts deems relevant to the execution of its mandate;

17. *Calls upon* the Group of Experts to cooperate actively with other relevant panels of experts, in particular the Group of Experts on Côte d'Ivoire re-established pursuant to paragraph 13 of resolution 1980(2011) of 28 April 2011 and the Panel of Experts on Liberia re-established pursuant to paragraph 6 of resolution 1961(2010) of 17 December 2010 with respect to natural resources;

18. *Encourages* the Mission to take into account the findings of the Group of Experts regarding armed groups and challenges to the integration of armed groups in the contingency plans of the Mission in the six-month post-electoral period;

19. *Calls upon* all States, particularly those in the region and those in which individuals and entities designated pursuant to paragraph 3 of the present resolution are based, to regularly report to the Committee on the actions they have taken to implement the measures imposed by paragraphs 1, 2 and 3 of the present resolution and recommended in paragraph 8 of resolution 1952(2010);

20. *Encourages* all States to submit to the Committee for inclusion on its list of designees individuals or entities that meet the criteria set out in paragraph 4 of resolution 1857(2008), as well as any entities owned or controlled, directly or indirectly, by the submitted individuals or entities or individuals or entities acting on behalf of or at the direction of the submitted entities;

21. *Decides* that, when appropriate and no later than 30 November 2012, it shall review the measures set forth in the present resolution, with a view to adjusting them, as appropriate, in the light of the security situation in the Democratic Republic of the Congo, in particular progress in security sector reform, including the integration of the armed forces and the reform of the national police, and in disarming, demobilizing, repatriating, resettling and reintegrating, as appropriate, Congolese and foreign armed groups;

22. *Decides also* to remain actively seized of the matter.

Children and armed conflict

On 25 March [S/2011/194], the Council President forwarded to the Secretary-General the conclusions of the Security Council Working Group on Children and Armed Conflict with regard to the DRC [S/AC.51/2011/1], adopted at its twenty-ninth meeting on 25 February. The Working Group stressed the need for MONUSCO to redouble its efforts for long-term reintegration support, and requested the Secretary-General to ensure that action plans with various parties were implemented without delay.

MONUSCO

The United Nations Organization Stabilization Mission in the Democratic Republic of the Congo (MONUSCO), first established as MONUC by Security Council resolution 1279(1999) [YUN 1999, p. 92], continued to discharge its mandate as established in Council resolution 1925(2010) [YUN 2010, p. 123], including the protection of civilians under imminent threat of physical violence, and to support the Government in its stabilization and peace consolidation efforts. By resolution 1991(2011) of 28 June (see p. 105), the Council extended the mandate of MONUSCO until 30 June 2012, and reaffirmed that civilian protection had to be given priority in decisions about the use of available capacity and resources. The Mission was headed by Roger A. Meece (United States), the Special Representative of the Secretary-General in the DRC. Lieutenant General Chander Prakash Wadhwa (India) continued as Force Commander.

Financing

In June, the General Assembly considered the performance report [A/65/682] on the MONUC budget for the period 1 July 2009 to 30 June 2010, showing a total expenditure of $1,345,224,000 gross ($1,317,146,100 net) against an appropriation of $1,346,584,600 ($1,320,348,300 net), and the proposed budget of monusco for the period 1 July 2011 to 30 June 2012 [A/65/744], amounting to $1,423,044,000 gross ($1,391,063,500 net). Acabq in April [A/65/743/Add.8] stated that any request for additional resources to support the elections should be submitted in a timely manner for consideration by the Assembly, urged monusco to make every effort to achieve savings and efficiencies during the course of the 2011–2012 financial period, and recommended approval of the proposed budget.

GENERAL ASSEMBLY ACTION

On 30 June [meeting 106], the General Assembly, on the recommendation of the Fifth (Administrative and Budgetary) Committee [A/65/654/Add.1], adopted **resolution 65/296** without vote [agenda items 147 & 148].

Financing of the United Nations Organization Mission in the Democratic Republic of the Congo and of the United Nations Organization Stabilization Mission in the Democratic Republic of the Congo

The General Assembly,

Having considered the reports of the Secretary-General on the financing of the United Nations Organization Mission in the Democratic Republic of the Congo and the United Nations Organization Stabilization Mission in the Democratic Republic of the Congo and the related report of the Advisory Committee on Administrative and Budgetary Questions,

Recalling Security Council resolutions 1258(1999) of 6 August 1999 and 1279(1999) of 30 November 1999 regarding, respectively, the deployment to the region of the Democratic Republic of the Congo of military liaison personnel and the establishment of the United Nations Organization Mission in the Democratic Republic of the Congo, and the subsequent resolutions by which the Council extended the mandate of the Mission, the latest of which was resolution 1925(2010) of 28 May 2010, by which the Council decided to extend the deployment of the Mission until 30 June 2010,

Recalling also that, by resolution 1925(2010), the Council decided that, as of 1 July 2010, the Mission would bear the title of the United Nations Organization Stabilization Mission in the Democratic Republic of the Congo, and decided that the Stabilization Mission would be deployed until 30 June 2011 and authorized the continuation until that date of up to 19,815 military personnel, 760 military observers, 391 police personnel and 1,050 personnel of formed police units, and recalling further resolution 1991(2011) of 28 June 2011, by which the Council decided to extend the mandate of the Stabilization Mission until 30 June 2012,

Recalling further its resolution 54/260 A of 7 April 2000 on the financing of the Mission and its subsequent resolutions thereon, the latest of which was resolution 65/255 of 24 December 2010,

Recalling its resolution 58/315 of 1 July 2004,

Reaffirming the general principles underlying the financing of United Nations peacekeeping operations, as stated in General Assembly resolutions 1874(S-IV) of 27 June 1963, 3101(XXVIII) of 11 December 1973 and 55/235 of 23 December 2000,

Noting with appreciation that voluntary contributions have been made to the Mission,

Mindful of the fact that it is essential to provide the Mission with the financial resources necessary to enable it to fulfil its responsibilities under the relevant resolutions of the Security Council,

1. *Requests* the Secretary-General to entrust the Head of Mission with the task of formulating future budget proposals in full accordance with the provisions of General Assembly resolutions 59/296 of 22 June 2005, 60/266 of 30 June 2006, 61/276 of 29 June 2007, 64/269 of 24 June 2010 and 65/289 of 30 June 2011, as well as other relevant resolutions;

2. *Takes note* of the status of contributions to the United Nations Organization Stabilization Mission in the Democratic Republic of the Congo as at 30 April 2011, including the contributions outstanding in the amount of 288.1 million United States dollars, representing some 3 per cent of the total assessed contributions, notes with concern that only forty-four Member States have paid their assessed contributions in full, and urges all other Member States, in particular those in arrears, to ensure payment of their outstanding assessed contributions;

3. *Expresses its appreciation* to those Member States which have paid their assessed contributions in full, and urges all other Member States to make every possible effort to ensure payment of their assessed contributions to the Mission in full;

4. *Expresses concern* at the financial situation with regard to peacekeeping activities, in particular as regards the reimbursements to troop contributors that bear additional burdens owing to overdue payments by Member States of their assessments;

5. *Also expresses concern* at the delay experienced by the Secretary-General in deploying and providing adequate resources to some recent peacekeeping missions, in particular those in Africa;

6. *Emphasizes* that all future and existing peacekeeping missions shall be given equal and non-discriminatory treatment in respect of financial and administrative arrangements;

7. *Also emphasizes* that all peacekeeping missions shall be provided with adequate resources for the effective and efficient discharge of their respective mandates;

8. *Requests* the Secretary-General to ensure that proposed peacekeeping budgets are based on the relevant legislative mandates;

9. *Endorses* the conclusions and recommendations contained in the report of the Advisory Committee on Administrative and Budgetary Questions, subject to the provisions of the present resolution, and requests the Secretary-General to ensure their full implementation;

10. *Requests* the Secretary-General to ensure the full implementation of the relevant provisions of resolutions 59/296, 60/266, 61/276, 64/269 and 65/289;

11. *Also requests* the Secretary-General to take all action necessary to ensure that the Mission is administered with a maximum of efficiency and economy;

12. *Decides* not to abolish the child protection posts, requests the Secretary-General to make every effort to fill them, and also requests the Secretary-General to identify an equivalent number of posts at the same level that have been vacant for more than one year to offset the financial impact of retaining the child protection posts, without affecting operational requirements or mandate implementation, and to report thereon in the context of the performance report;

13. *Notes* that the overall level of appropriation has been adjusted in accordance with the terms of resolution 65/289;

**Financial performance report
for the United Nations Organization
Mission in the Democratic Republic of the Congo
for the period from 1 July 2009 to 30 June 2010**

14. *Takes note* of the report of the Secretary-General on the financial performance of the Mission for the period from 1 July 2009 to 30 June 2010;

**Budget estimates for the United Nations
Organization Stabilization Mission
in the Democratic Republic of the Congo
for the period from 1 July 2011 to 30 June 2012**

15. *Decides* to appropriate to the Special Account for the United Nations Organization Stabilization Mission in the Democratic Republic of the Congo the amount of 1,507,538,900 dollars for the period from 1 July 2011 to 30 June 2012, inclusive of 1,416,926,000 dollars for the maintenance of the Mission, 76,783,900 dollars for the support account for peacekeeping operations and 13,829,000 dollars for the United Nations Logistics Base at Brindisi, Italy;

Financing of the appropriation

16. *Also decides* to apportion among Member States the amount of 1,507,538,900 dollars for the period from 1 July 2011 to 30 June 2012, in accordance with the levels updated in General Assembly resolution 64/249 of 24 December 2009, and taking into account the scale of assessments for 2011 and 2012, as set out in Assembly resolution 64/248 of 24 December 2009;

17. *Further decides* that, in accordance with the provisions of its resolution 973(X) of 15 December 1955, there shall be set off against the apportionment among Member States, as provided for in paragraph 16 above, their respective share in the Tax Equalization Fund of the amount of 39,936,800 dollars, comprising the estimated staff assessment income of 31,980,500 dollars approved for the Mission, the prorated share of 6,503,300 dollars of the estimated staff assessment income approved for the support account and the prorated share of 1,453,000 dollars of the estimated staff assessment income approved for the United Nations Logistics Base;

18. *Decides* that, for Member States that have fulfilled their financial obligations to the Mission, there shall be set off against the apportionment, as provided for in paragraph 16 above, their respective share of the unencumbered balance and other income in the total amount of 35,075,700 dollars in respect of the financial period ended 30 June 2010, in accordance with the levels updated in resolution 64/249, and taking into account the scale of assessments for 2010, as set out in resolution 64/248;

19. *Also decides* that, for Member States that have not fulfilled their financial obligations to the Mission, there shall be set off against their outstanding obligations their respective share of the unencumbered balance and other income in the total amount of 35,075,700 dollars in respect of the financial period ended 30 June 2010, in accordance with the scheme set out in paragraph 18 above;

20. *Further decides* that the increase of 1,841,600 dollars in the estimated staff assessment income in respect of the financial period ended 30 June 2010 shall be added to the credits from the amount of 35,075,700 dollars referred to in paragraphs 18 and 19 above;

21. *Emphasizes* that no peacekeeping mission shall be financed by borrowing funds from other active peacekeeping missions;

22. *Encourages* the Secretary-General to continue to take additional measures to ensure the safety and security of all personnel participating in the Mission under the auspices of the United Nations, bearing in mind paragraphs 5 and 6 of Security Council resolution 1502(2003) of 26 August 2003;

23. *Invites* voluntary contributions to the Mission in cash and in the form of services and supplies acceptable to the Secretary-General, to be administered, as appropriate, in accordance with the procedure and practices established by the General Assembly;

24. *Decides* to include in the provisional agenda of its sixty-sixth session the item entitled "Financing of the United Nations Organization Stabilization Mission in the Democratic Republic of the Congo".

In December, the Assembly considered a September note by the Secretary-General [A/66/375] regarding electoral support resource requirements for MONUSCO for the period from 1 July 2011 to 30 June 2012. On the basis of the electoral calendar and in response to the request of the Government, additional resources amounting to $74,560,100 would be required for logistical support for elections scheduled for November 2011 and March and July 2012. ACABQ, in its related report [A/66/545], considered that it should be possible for MONUSCO to absorb some of the cost of logistical support from its current appropriation. It recommended that the Assembly request the Secretary-General to assess an initial amount of $37,280,000 for the 2011–2012 financial period in respect of the requested appropriation of $74,560,100, and to assess the remaining amount following a review of the cash position of the Mission.

GENERAL ASSEMBLY ACTION

On 24 December [meeting 93], the General Assembly, on the recommendation of the Fifth Committee [A/66/584], adopted **resolution 66/251** without vote [agenda item 152].

**Financing of the United Nations Organization
Stabilization Mission in the
Democratic Republic of the Congo**

The General Assembly,

Having considered the note by the Secretary-General on the financing arrangements for the United Nations Organization Stabilization Mission in the Democratic Republic of the Congo for the period from 1 July 2011 to 30 June 2012 and the related report of the Advisory Committee on Administrative and Budgetary Questions,

Recalling Security Council resolution 1991(2011) of 28 June 2011, by which the Council extended the mandate of the Stabilization Mission until 30 June 2012,

Recalling also its resolution 54/260 A of 7 April 2000 on the financing of the Stabilization Mission and its subsequent resolutions thereon, the latest of which was resolution 65/296 of 30 June 2011,

1. *Endorses* the conclusions and recommendations contained in the report of the Advisory Committee on Administrative and Budgetary Questions, subject to the provisions of the present resolution, and requests the Secretary-General to ensure their full implementation;

2. *Emphasizes* the need for the Secretary-General to make every effort to ensure that technical and logistical support is provided for the elections in full and on time in accordance with the mandate given to the United Nations Organization Stabilization Mission in the Democratic Republic of the Congo;

3. *Takes note* of paragraphs 22 and 23 of the report of the Advisory Committee on Administrative and Budgetary Questions;

Financing arrangements for the period from 1 July 2011 to 30 June 2012

4. *Decides* to appropriate to the Special Account for the United Nations Organization Stabilization Mission in the Democratic Republic of the Congo the amount of 69,560,100 United States dollars for the period from 1 July 2011 to 30 June 2012 for the support of elections in the Democratic Republic of the Congo, in addition to the amount of 1,507,538,900 dollars previously appropriated for the Stabilization Mission for the same period under the terms of its resolution 65/296, inclusive of 1,416,926,000 dollars for the maintenance of the Stabilization Mission, 76,783,900 dollars for the support account for peacekeeping operations and 13,829,000 dollars for the United Nations Logistics Base at Brindisi, Italy;

Financing of the appropriation

5. *Also decides*, taking into account the amount of 1,507,538,900 dollars already apportioned under the terms of its resolution 65/296 for the period from 1 July 2011 to 30 June 2012, to apportion among Member States the additional amount of 69,560,100 dollars for the same period, in accordance with the levels updated in General Assembly resolution 64/249 of 24 December 2009, taking into account the scale of assessments for 2011 and 2012, as set out in its resolution 64/248 of 24 December 2009;

6. *Further decides* to keep under review during its sixty-sixth session the item entitled "Financing of the United Nations Organization Stabilization Mission in the Democratic Republic of the Congo".

The Assembly, on 24 December, decided that the item on the financing of monusco would remain for consideration during its resumed sixty-sixth (2012) session (**decision 66/557**).

Burundi

In 2011, the political landscape in Burundi was dominated by the outcome of the 2010 elections. The Alliance démocratique pour le changement-Ikibiri (adc-Ikibiri) continued to challenge the outcome of the elections and to criticize Burundi's political governance. While the country remained free of large-scale violence, acts of violence and attacks against civilians and security and defence forces continued; most notably, an attack in Gatumba on 18 September left 39 people dead. Credible reports were made of the arrest, detention and killing of members of the opposition, as well as of cross-border armed activities, including in areas adjacent to the drc and Tanzania. The country continued to make progress in peace consolidation, including in establishing independent institutions for human rights and reconciliation. The United Nations Office in Burundi (bnub), which replaced the United Nations Integrated Office in Burundi (binub) on 1 January, provided assistance to the National Independent Human Rights Commission, established on 5 January, and logistical support to the Office of the Ombudsman, whose activities started in February. In December, the Security Council extended the mandate of bnub until 15 February 2013. In April and December, the General Assembly approved the financing of the Office.

The Security Council considered the situation in Burundi at public meetings held on 17 May [S/PV.6538] and 7 December [S/PV.6677], during which it was briefed by the Secretary-General's Special Representative for Burundi, Karin Landgren.

Political and security developments

Report of Secretary-General (November). In response to Security Council resolution 1959(2010) [YUN 2010, p. 144], the Secretary-General in November submitted a report [S/2011/751] reviewing major developments in Burundi; peace consolidation challenges and UN activities to help meet those challenges; and the implementation of the mandate of bnub, which replaced binub on 1 January.

The political landscape remained dominated by the aftermath of the 2010 elections [YUN 2010, p. 141], most notably the tensions between the Government and adc-Ikibiri, a coalition of political parties that withdrew from the political process. The coalition continued to challenge the outcome of the elections and to criticize aspects of Burundi's political governance. On 25 July, the First Vice-President, Thérence Sinunguruza, convened a meeting of registered political parties, during which he reiterated a call made by President Pierre Nkurunziza on 30 June urging political party leaders in exile to return, and affirmed that measures were in place to ensure their security.

ADC-Ikibiri did not attend the meeting and boycotted a second meeting on 28 September. On 24 August, the coalition presented detailed demands, including official recognition of ADC-Ikibiri, the creation of an environment conducive to peaceful negotiations, and the reinstatement of Agathon Rwasa as leader of the Forces nationales de libération (FNL) party. Regional, national and international actors, including BNUB, encouraged the Government and the extra-parliamentary opposition to engage in dialogue, normalize relations and avoid resorting to violence. The Special Representative of the Secretary-General held several meetings with senior State officials, representatives of the extra-parliamentary opposition and other stakeholders.

While the overall security situation remained stable, acts of violence continued, including armed robberies, killings, grenade attacks and exchanges of gunfire between security forces and unidentified armed groups. Attacks against civilians and security and defence forces occurred in various parts of the country. Most notably, on 18 September, an attack on a bar in Gatumba, just outside of Bujumbura, resulted in 39 deaths and many injuries. ADC-Ikibiri and Mr. Rwasa issued statements in October denying any involvement in the attack. The National Security Council, chaired by President Nkurunziza, met on 18 and 19 August and again on 20 September. At its second meeting, held after the Gatumba attack, the Council released a communiqué urging the Government to conduct investigations and prosecute the perpetrators. Meanwhile, credible reports were made of the arrest, detention and killing of members of the opposition, particularly persons affiliated with the former FNL of Mr. Rwasa. There were also reports of cross-border armed activities, including in areas adjacent to the DRC and Tanzania.

Burundi made progress in peace consolidation. With assistance from the United Nations and other partners, the Government undertook various initiatives to enhance democratic governance; adopted, in October, a national strategy on good governance and the fight against corruption; and organized workshops for parliamentarians on budget analysis and oversight and on transitional justice mechanisms. BNUB provided logistical support to the Office of the Ombudsman, whose activities started officially in February, and provided assistance to the National Independent Human Rights Commission, established on 5 January. Following the conclusion in December 2010 of the national consultative exercise on the establishment of transitional justice mechanisms [YUN 2010, p. 146], the Government, on 3 May, presented a timeline for the establishment of such mechanisms, including the creation of a technical committee charged with preparing for the establishment of a truth and reconciliation commission in January 2012. The Secretary-General stated that preparations for transitional justice mechanisms would need the commitment and participation of all groups to succeed. He remained concerned about the lack of dialogue between the Government and the parties that had pulled out of the 2010 elections, calling on all parties to renew their renunciation of violence and normalize political relations.

Extension of BNUB mandate. In the same report, the Secretary-General noted that, while the light footprint and mandate of BNUB reflected the nation's progress, continued international support and assistance in peace consolidation, recovery and development remained important, and recommended that the mandate of the Office be extended for one year effective 1 January 2012.

SECURITY COUNCIL ACTION

On 20 December [meeting 6691], the Security Council unanimously adopted **resolution 2027(2011)**. The draft [S/2011/782] was submitted by France.

The Security Council,

Recalling its resolutions and the statements by its President on Burundi,

Reaffirming its strong commitment to the sovereignty, independence, territorial integrity and unity of Burundi,

Welcoming the progress that Burundi has made towards peace, stability and development, and emphasizing the need for the United Nations system and the international community, including the international financial institutions and Burundi's development partners, to maintain their support for peace consolidation and long-term development in Burundi,

Taking note of the smooth transition from the United Nations Integrated Office in Burundi to the United Nations Office in Burundi, and commending the continued contribution of the United Nations to the peace, security and development of the country,

Encouraging the efforts of the Government of Burundi to create a space for all political parties and to continue improving dialogue between all relevant actors, including civil society,

Supporting the renewed commitment of Burundi to "zero tolerance" for corruption,

Welcoming the continued engagement of the Peacebuilding Commission in Burundi and the recent visit of the Chair of the Burundi configuration of the Commission, taking note of the April 2011 outcome document of the fifth review of the implementation of the Strategic Framework for Peacebuilding in Burundi and of the briefing by the Chair of the Burundi configuration of the Commission on 7 December 2011, and acknowledging the contribution that the Peacebuilding Fund has made to peacebuilding in Burundi,

Supporting the commitment of Burundi to regional integration, notably in the Economic Community of the Great Lakes Countries, the East African Community and the International Conference on the Great Lakes Region,

Recognizing the importance of transitional justice in promoting lasting reconciliation among all the people of Burundi, and noting with appreciation the completion of the work of the Technical Committee and the commitment of the Government of Burundi to establishing transitional justice mechanisms, consistent with the results of the 2009 national consultations, Security Council resolution

1606(2005) of 20 June 2005 as well as the Arusha Agreement of 2000,

Welcoming the establishment of the Office of the Ombudsman and the National Independent Human Rights Commission,

Noting with grave concern continued human rights violations, in particular extrajudicial politically motivated killings and torture, and restrictions on civil liberties, including harassment, intimidation and restrictions on the freedom of expression, association and assembly of opposition political parties, media and civil society organizations,

Noting with great concern the attacks against civilians as well as security and defence forces in various parts of the country and the reports of paramilitary activities in neighbouring countries, and calling upon all those involved to put an end to such acts,

Calling upon the Government of Burundi to protect civil liberties and to fight impunity, particularly by ensuring that those responsible for incidents of torture, extrajudicial killings and mistreatment of detainees are brought to justice,

Recalling its resolutions 1325(2000) of 31 October 2000, 1820(2008) of 19 June 2008, 1888(2009) of 30 September 2009 and 1889(2009) of 5 October 2009 on women and peace and security, its resolutions 1674(2006) of 28 April 2006 and 1894(2009) of 11 November 2009 on the protection of civilians in armed conflict and its resolutions 1612(2005) of 26 July 2005, 1882(2009) of 4 August 2009 and 1998(2011) of 12 July 2011 on children and armed conflict,

Having considered the first report of the Secretary-General on the United Nations Office in Burundi,

1. *Decides* to extend until 15 February 2013 the mandate of the United Nations Office in Burundi, as set out in paragraphs 3 (*a*) to (*d*) of resolution 1959(2010) of 16 December 2010;

2. *Decides also* that, in addition to paragraph 1 above, the United Nations Office in Burundi shall also continue to support the Government of Burundi in the following areas:

(*a*) Supporting the efforts of the Government and the international community to focus on the socioeconomic development of women and youth and the socioeconomic reintegration of conflict-affected populations in particular, and advocating for resource mobilization for Burundi;

(*b*) Providing support to Burundi's deepening regional integration, as requested;

3. *Recognizes* the primary responsibility of the Government of Burundi for peacebuilding, security and long-term development in the country, and encourages the Government to pursue its efforts regarding peace consolidation challenges, in particular democratic governance, the fight against corruption, security sector reform, civilian protection, justice and the promotion and protection of human rights, with a special focus on the rights of women and children as well as marginalized and vulnerable minorities;

4. *Encourages* the Government of Burundi, with the support of the United Nations Office in Burundi and other international partners, to redouble its efforts to pursue structural reforms aimed at improving political, economic and administrative governance and tackling corruption, with a view to setting up strong drivers for sustained and equitable social and economic growth;

5. *Also encourages* the Government of Burundi to pursue its efforts of peace consolidation and reconstruction in a regional perspective, especially through projects fostering peace, reconciliation and exchanges within the East African Community, the Economic Community of the Great Lakes Countries and the International Conference on the Great Lakes Region;

6. *Underscores* the importance of security sector reform, and urges all international partners, together with the United Nations Office in Burundi, to continue supporting the efforts of the Government of Burundi to professionalize and enhance the capacity of the national security services and the police, in particular in the fields of training on human rights and sexual and gender-based violence, and with a view to consolidating security sector governance;

7. *Calls upon* the Government of Burundi, with the support of the United Nations Office in Burundi and its national and international partners, to finalize the new poverty reduction strategy paper, with clear peacebuilding priorities and an implementation plan;

8. *Encourages* the Government of Burundi, the Peacebuilding Commission and Burundi's national and international partners to honour their commitments made under the outcome document of the fifth review of the implementation of the Strategic Framework for Peacebuilding in Burundi and to review these commitments when the new poverty reduction strategy paper is finalized to determine how the Commission can best contribute to Burundi's peacebuilding priorities;

9. *Calls upon* the Government of Burundi to take all steps necessary to prevent further human rights violations and to take measures to ensure that those responsible for such violations are swiftly brought to justice;

10. *Stresses* the need for a thorough, credible, impartial and transparent investigation of serious crimes, in particular extrajudicial killings, and calls upon the authorities of Burundi to put an end to such criminal acts and to ensure that those responsible are brought to justice;

11. *Calls upon* the Government of Burundi to pursue its efforts to ensure the promotion and protection of human rights and, together with its international partners, to support the newly established National Independent Human Rights Commission and the Office of the Ombudsman, and further encourages the Government to continue its fight against impunity and to take the measures necessary to ensure that its citizens fully enjoy their civil, political, social, economic and cultural rights as enshrined in the Constitution of Burundi and in accordance with international human rights law;

12. *Encourages* the Government of Burundi, with the support of international partners and the United Nations Office in Burundi as appropriate, to establish transitional justice mechanisms, including the establishment of a Truth and Reconciliation Commission, in accordance with the results of the work of the Technical Committee, the 2009 national consultations, Security Council resolution 1606(2005) as well as the Arusha Agreement of 2000;

13. *Takes note* of the progress reported by the Secretary-General in the development of benchmarks for the future evolution of the United Nations Office in Burundi into a United Nations country team presence, and requests to be updated on these by 31 May 2012;

14. *Requests* the Secretary-General to keep the Council informed on the implementation of the mandate of the United Nations Office in Burundi and the present resolution, with a briefing by the end of July 2012 and a report by 18 January 2013;

15. *Decides* to remain actively seized of the matter.

Peacebuilding Commission

Review of Strategic Framework. In April, the Peacebuilding Commission considered the fifth progress report [PBC/5/BDI/3] on the implementation of the Strategic Framework for Peacebuilding in Burundi [YUN 2007, p. 52], covering developments from February 2010 to January 2011. The report was the last to be prepared before the consolidation of the Strategic Framework and the Government's second Growth and Poverty Reduction Strategy Framework, aimed at applying the experience of peacebuilding to sustainable development. The report analysed progress and trends, and presented recommendations regarding good governance; the 2006 Ceasefire Agreement between the Government and the Forces nationales de libération [YUN 2006, p. 153]; the security sector; justice, promotion of human rights and action to combat impunity; community recovery, socioeconomic reintegration and land issues; regional integration; and mobilization and coordination of international assistance. The period under consideration saw increased attention by Burundi's partners to supporting the 2010 electoral process. The Commission noted that the length and complexity of the electoral process slowed progress in implementing the recommendations of its fourth report [YUN 2010, p. 146]. During that same period, the Secretary-General, the chairpersons of the Burundi configuration of the Commission and the Head of the Peacebuilding Support Office visited the country.

In its outcome document on the fifth review of the Strategic Framework [PBC/5/BDI/2], the Commission welcomed the progress made since the fourth review, including the completion of the 2010 elections and the functioning of the elected institutions; the creation of the institution of the Ombudsman and the appointment of the Ombudsman; the adoption of the law creating the Independent National Human Rights Commission; and the report of the national consultations on the establishment of transitional justice mechanisms. It recognized the support of BNUB to the country's peacebuilding and recovery efforts, and stressed the need for all actors to support national efforts in the political, institutional, social and economic domains. The Commission would organize a stocktaking exercise from the 2010 elections to draw lessons from the Commission's contributions and role, and to discuss support for future electoral processes; support Government efforts to address cases of corruption and implement the zero tolerance policy against corruption; mobilize support for the Independent National Human Rights Commission; and provide a platform for the Government, civil society and victims associations to share the outcome of the national consultations on transitional justice mechanisms with the international community in New York. Noting the Government's intention to integrate peacebuilding into its second poverty reduction strategy paper, the Commission outlined areas in which it would continue to support the nation's peacebuilding efforts. It envisaged aligning its future engagement with the poverty reduction strategy paper, as well as mobilizing resources for capacity-building and strengthening institutions.

The Council took note of the outcome document by resolution 2027(2011) of 20 December (see p. 118). The Chair of the Burundi configuration briefed the Security Council on 7 December [S/PV.6677].

Participation in Burundi configuration. During the year, the Chairperson of the Peacebuilding Commission invited South Africa [PBC/5/OC/1], the Netherlands [PBC/5/OC/3], Mexico [PBC/5/OC/5] and Australia [PBC/5/OC/10] to participate in the Commission's configuration on Burundi.

(For further information on the Peacebuilding Commission, see p. 47.)

BNUB

The United Nations Office in Burundi (BNUB), established by Security Council resolution 1959(2010) [YUN 2010, p. 144], succeeded the United Nations Integrated Office in Burundi (BINUB) on 1 January. All BINUB operations not included in the BNUB mandate ceased on 31 March. By resolution 2027(2011) (see p. 118), the Council extended until 15 February 2013 the BNUB mandate, as set out in resolution 1959(2010). It further mandated BNUB to support the efforts of the Government and the international community to focus on the socioeconomic development of women and youth, and the socioeconomic reintegration of conflict-affected populations; advocate for resource mobilization for the country; and support Burundi's regional integration. BNUB was headed by the Special Representative of the Secretary-General, Karin Landgren (Sweden).

Financing

In April, the General Assembly considered the Secretary-General's report [A/65/328/Add.6 & Corr.1] on proposed resource requirements for BNUB for 2011, totalling $25,075,600 gross ($23,103,200 net), and the related ACABQ report [A/65/602/Add.1].

On 4 April, in section II of **resolution 65/268** (see p. 1378), the Assembly endorsed the conclusions and recommendations of ACABQ; approved the 2011 BNUB budget of $23,989,700 gross ($22,145,800 net); decided to utilize the unencumbered balance for BINUB to offset part of the additional appropriation required for BNUB; and requested the Secretary-General to meet the additional requirements for BNUB from the overall appropriation for special political missions.

Central African Republic

In 2011, the Central African Republic (CAR) continued efforts to implement the recommendations of the December 2008 inclusive political dialogue. The political environment was dominated by legislative and presidential elections held in January and March. Incumbent President François Bozizé received 64 per cent of the votes in the presidential election and was sworn in for his second and final presidential term on 15 March.

Following legislative elections, Faustin Archange Touadera was reconfirmed as Prime Minister and a new Government was announced on 22 April. While observers highlighted the inclusive nature of the elections, they also noted irregularities and shortcomings in the proceedings, including the inaccuracy of voters' lists, insufficient training of electoral staff and the high rate of absentee voting. During the year, the Government launched activities in line with its commitment to complete the disarmament, demobilization and reintegration (DDR) process by year's end. On 8 July, the Disarmament, Demobilization and Reintegration Steering Committee finalized and endorsed a national strategy for the reintegration of former combatants that sought to address the reintegration needs of demobilized combatants and the needs of host communities. While some progress was made in security sector reform, including the resumption of regular ministerial- and technical-level meetings to revive the process, there was limited advancement in the design of a credible national security sector reform strategy. In November, the Peacebuilding Commission presented the conclusions of the second biannual review of the Strategic Framework for Peacebuilding in the CAR, which expired at the end of the year. The United Nations Integrated Peacebuilding Office in the Central African Republic (BINUCA) continued to assist in efforts to implement the 2008 inclusive political dialogue. In December, the Security Council extended until 31 January 2013 the mandate of BINUCA, and the General Assembly approved the financing of the Office.

The Security Council considered the situation in the country at public meetings held on 7 July [S/PV.6575] and 14 December [S/PV.6687], during which it was briefed by the Secretary-General's Special Representative for the CAR, Margaret Vogt.

Political and security developments

Report of Secretary-General (May). In his May report on the situation in the country and the activities of BINUCA [S/2011/311], the Secretary-General reviewed the implementation of the recommendations of the December 2008 inclusive political dialogue [YUN 2008, p. 157], particularly the holding of legislative and presidential elections, the DDR of combatants of politico-military groups, and security sector reform.

The political environment was dominated by the first round of the legislative and presidential elections, held on 23 January, and the second round of legislative elections, held on 27 March. Five candidates contested the presidential election, including the incumbent President, François Bozizé, leader of the Kwa na Kwa (KNK) ruling party. A total of 889 candidates representing 41 parties ran for the 105 seats of the National Assembly. On 4 January, opposition leaders threatened to withdraw from the elections, stating that electoral lists had not been posted early enough to allow for challenges and amendments. Nonetheless, on 7 January, representatives of all political parties, politico-military groups, State institutions and civil society organizations signed a code of good conduct for political life, and all political parties participated in the electoral campaign from 10 to 21 January. There was strong voter turnout for the first round of elections, with the Independent Electoral Commission estimating that 54 per cent of the 1.8 million registered voters had taken part in the polls. On 1 February, the Commission announced the provisional results of the presidential election, which were adjusted by the Constitutional Court on 12 February to take into account additional results from polling stations that had not previously been counted. President Bozizé received 64 per cent of the votes, eliminating the need for a run-off. He was sworn in for a second and final five-year presidential term on 15 March. Former President Ange-Félix Patassé received 21 per cent of the votes, and Martin Ziguélé, leader of the Mouvement pour la libération du peuple centrafricain (MLPC), 6 per cent. While international and national observers highlighted the inclusive nature of the elections, they also noted a number of irregularities and shortcomings in the proceedings, including the inaccuracy of voters' lists, the insufficient training of electoral staff and the high rate of absentee voting. In its ruling of 12 February, the Constitutional Court rejected for lack of evidence the appeals made by three opposition candidates to annul the presidential election, and made recommendations to improve the organization of future polls and enhance their transparency and credibility, including the creation of an independent administrative body. Subsequently, on 29 April, the Government announced its intention to create a permanent administrative body within the Independent Electoral Commission.

The Commission on 6 February issued the results of the legislative elections, which gave KNK 26 seats, the opposition 1 seat and independent candidates 8 seats. That was followed, on 4 March, by the formation of the Front pour l'annulation et la reprise des élections (FARE), comprising former Collectif des forces du changement members and former President Patassé. FARE called for the cancellation of the first round of elections, the withdrawal of opposition candidates and a boycott of the second round of legislative elections. Nonetheless, the second round was held in 67 electoral districts on 27 March, which gave the KNK party 37 more seats, independent candidates a further 18 seats, candidates from parties allied with KNK 11 seats and one other opposition candidate one seat. The incumbent Prime Minister, Faustin Archange Touadera, was subsequently reconfirmed in the post of Prime Minister on 17 April, with a new Government announced on 22 April. While the electoral process took place in a peaceful atmosphere, there were elements of concern, including the detention of some opposition figures and the placement of travel restrictions on some opposition leaders, notably former President Patassé. The United Nations Development Programme (UNDP) electoral assistance project supported the Commission in the provision of expertise, technical assistance and support during the voter registration process and the elections, including by finalizing the transcription of voters' lists, facilitating the transfer of 7,000 ballot boxes from Togo, and preparing a package of corrective measures for the second round of legislative elections to address irregularities noted in the first round.

With regard to the disarmament and demobilization of former combatants, the Working Group on Reintegration [YUN 2010, p. 154] developed a draft national reintegration strategy for former combatants, which was presented to the Disarmament, Demobilization and Reintegration Steering Committee on 22 February.

From 28 February to 9 March, a mission comprising representatives of the armed forces, the Mission for the Consolidation of Peace in the Central African Republic (MICOPAX) [YUN 2008, p. 157], the Union des forces démocratiques pour le rassemblement (UFDR) and the Mouvement des libérateurs centrafricains pour la justice was carried out in the north-east to assess whether conditions were in place to begin the verification of combatants. While noting the fragile security situation in that area, the mission concluded that verification could go ahead. Furthermore, progress was made in security sector reform, including the resumption of regular ministerial- and technical-level meetings to revive the reform process and define a national vision and way forward with support from the BINUCA Security Institutions Unit. The Office also provided training and supported projects aimed at enhancing the professionalism of the police, gendarmerie and armed forces.

Some progress was made on bringing the Convention des patriotes pour la justice et la paix (CPJP), the only politico-military group that did not sign the 2008 Libreville Comprehensive Peace Agreement [YUN 2008, p. 156], into the peace process. Following overtures by President Bozizé, the leadership of CPJP announced on 26 April that it was ready to accept a ceasefire and begin discussions with the Government. Prior to that announcement, there had been numerous clashes between CPJP and the armed forces, UFDR and self-defence militias across the north of the country, resulting in civilian and combatant casualties.

The military and security situation was characterized by frequent, violent attacks perpetrated by CPJP, foreign rebel elements, the Lord's Resistance Army (LRA), and bandits and poachers, particularly in the eastern and northern parts of the country. While the number of LRA attacks decreased by nearly half during the reporting period, about 19,000 Central Africans remained displaced in the south-eastern Haut-Mbomou and Mbomou regions due to LRA activity.

The Secretary-General concluded that the near absence of a political opposition in democratic institutions since the elections represented a challenge to the process of national reconciliation. Building on the lessons learned from the elections, he urged the Government to address the irregularities and shortcomings indicated by the observers and the recommendations of the Constitutional Court. He urged the authorities to begin planning for municipal elections, and the Government to expedite the implementation of outstanding recommendations from the 2008 inclusive political dialogue. He reiterated his call to the Government and politico-military groups to move forward with the DDR process, stating that it must be linked to reform in the security sector to ensure that the defence and security forces had the capacity and capability to provide security across the country.

Security Council statement. Taking note of the Secretary-General's report, the Security Council, by a press statement of 7 July [SC/10313], stressed the need for all parties to work towards national reconciliation. The Council welcomed the engagement of the new Government, as expressed by the Prime Minister in his inaugural declaration on 19 May, to fight corruption, improve governance and the rule of law, reform the Electoral Code and establish a Permanent Technical Secretariat to build technical capacity for future elections.

Report of Secretary-General (November). In November [S/2011/739], the Secretary-General provided an update on the country's political and security environment, which was dominated by the holding of legislative by-elections in September; significant progress in the disarmament and demobilization of former combatants in the north-west; and the deterioration of the security situation in the north-east. Following the legislative elections in January and March, the Constitutional Court overturned close to 20 per cent of the results on the grounds of irregularities, and ruled that 13 reruns and one election which had not taken place in Bouar be held. As the Independent Electoral Commission had been dissolved following the elections, the Minister of Territorial Administration and Decentralization established, on 14 July, a transitional committee for elections responsible for preparing and organizing legislative by-elections in the 14 outstanding constituencies; drafting a legal framework for the establishment of the Permanent Technical Secretariat responsible for organizing future elections; and revising the electoral code. The by-elections were held peacefully on 4 September; however, the opposition, including the FARE coalition, boycotted the process. The election in Bouar was invalidated and would be rerun. Following those elections, the 104-seat National Assembly comprised 62 KNK seats, 28 independent candidate seats, 11 KNK-affiliated seats, 2 MLPC seats and 1 Rassemblement démocratique centrafricain seat.

In the post-electoral period, the Government focused on reforming the electoral code and establishing a permanent electoral management body. From 1 October to 6 November, the UNDP electoral assistance project organized a study tour to Benin, Cameroon, Canada, Ghana and Senegal for the Minister of Territorial Administration and Decentralization and staff of his ministry to learn best practices from the experience of those countries. The Secretary-General's Special Representative, supported by the UN Department of Political Affairs (DPA), held a series of meetings in August with national and international stakeholders, including leaders of the presidential majority and the opposition, the President of the National Assembly, civil society organizations and members of the diplomatic community, to seek their views regarding the electoral process and reforms. While the meetings with FARE confirmed a willingness to take part in dialogue, the coalition continued to demand a rerun of the legislative elections, believing that only a consensus Government would be able to ease political tension and allow for electoral reforms. The relationship between the Government and the opposition remained difficult, with opposition leaders criticizing the Government for not respecting basic democratic principles, including freedom of assembly.

The lack of State authority outside the capital led to a security vacuum in many parts of the country. National security and defence forces were under-resourced and largely incapable of fulfilling their responsibilities, and the Government had yet to assure adequate security in areas where disarmament and demobilization of former combatants and the dismantling of checkpoints had taken place. The presence of armed groups with large numbers of foreign fighters continued to pose a threat to peace and stability. On 23 May, the Presidents of the CAR, Chad and the Sudan signed a tripartite agreement in Khartoum to enhance security in the border areas through joint patrols. To improve information exchange and coordination with the CAR Government and its partners, BINUCA designated a focal point for LRA-related activities and established a working group that included Government officials, representatives of the embassies accredited to the country, regional and subregional organizations, and the UN country team.

The results of the peace process with armed groups were mixed. On 12 June, CPJP, the only armed group that was not party to the Libreville Comprehensive Peace Agreement, signed a ceasefire agreement with the Government. The development was considered a major step towards durable peace. In September, however, UFDR and CPJP clashed in Haute-Kotto and Vakaga provinces, claiming the lives of dozens of belligerents and civilians. On 20 September, BINUCA called for a ceasefire between the armed groups and the protection of civilians, and on 28 September facilitated a visit of the Minister of Territorial Administration and Decentralization to Ndelé and Birao to meet with the leaders of both armed groups. The belligerents signed a ceasefire agreement on 8 October in Bangui under the auspices of the Government and the National Mediator, and with the support of the United Nations, the AU and MICOPAX. DPA deployed a team to Bangui to assist the National Mediator, Archbishop Paulin Pomodimo, during the negotiations between UFDR and CPJP. On 13 June, the Chadian rebel leader, Baba Laddé, of the Front populaire pour le redressement (FPR), an armed group present in the north-western part of the CAR since 2008, signed a communiqué with the National Mediators of Chad and the CAR. In that document, FPR announced its willingness to lay down its weapons and enter into discussions towards the signing of a peace agreement within a month; however, talks stalled with regard to the implementation of the modalities of the communiqué, and FPR reportedly continued to acquire weapons and to recruit in the region, jeopardizing the implementation of outstanding disarmament and demobilization operations in the north-west.

Significant progress was made in the disarmament and demobilization of former combatants. On 25 June, President Bozizé launched related activities in the north-west in line with the Government's commitment to complete the DDR process by the end of the year. The operations started in Ouham-Pendé province on 13 July and concluded on 11 September; some 4,777 combatants of the Armée populaire pour la restauration de la démocratie disarmed and demobilized, and 3,558 arms were collected. On 8 July, following the establishment of the Working Group on Reintegration in December 2010 [YUN 2010, p. 154], the Disarmament, Demobilization and Reintegration Steering Committee finalized and endorsed the national strategy for the reintegration of former combatants, proposed by the Working Group on Reintegration in February. The strategy aimed at addressing the individual reintegration needs of demobilized combatants and the needs of host communities. It also envisaged the integration of demobilized combatants into the security and defence forces and the civil service. The nexus between DDR and security sector reform, however, had yet to be fully developed.

Limited progress was made in security sector reform. The national Permanent Technical Secretariat, established to coordinate and ensure coherence across relevant ministries, had yet to design a credible and viable national security sector reform strategy. At the request of the Secretary-General's Special Representative, an assessment mission in July reviewed the overall DDR and security sector reform programmes for the CAR. The mission recommended that BINUCA enhance its role as political facilitator by expanding engagement with international actors on the ground, so as to develop and leverage international positions on the DDR and security sector reform programmes. In August, the Minister Delegate for Defence, who chaired the Security Sector Reform Steering Committee, requested BINUCA to help revive the security sector reform process. BINUCA responded by proposing a road map for developing strategies for each ministry engaged in security sector reform, culminating in a national strategy.

Year-end developments. In a later report [S/2012/374], the Secretary-General stated that in November, the national authorities launched a dialogue with political parties and civil society organizations to introduce the proposed electoral code and national mechanism for the conduct of elections.

UFDR and CPJP leaders participated, along with 25,000 people, in a peace and reconciliation caravan organized in November by the National Mediator with support from BINUCA. Consequently, many internally displaced persons who had fled as a result of clashes between the two armed groups were able to return to Haute-Kotto.

Extension of BINUCA mandate. The Secretary-General [S/2011/739], noting the leading role of BINUCA in the country's peace consolidation and reconciliation process, as well as the need for continued United Nations support for peacebuilding challenges, recommended that the mandate of the Office be extended until 31 December 2012.

SECURITY COUNCIL ACTION

On 21 December [meeting 6696], the Security Council unanimously adopted **resolution 2031(2011)**. The draft [S/2011/785] was submitted by France, Gabon, Germany, the United Kingdom and the United States.

The Security Council,

Recalling the statements by its President relating to the situation in the Central African Republic, in particular the statements of 7 April, 8 May and 21 December 2009 and 14 and 20 December 2010,

Reaffirming its strong commitment to the sovereignty, independence, territorial integrity and unity of the Central African Republic, and recalling the importance of the principles of good-neighbourliness and regional cooperation,

Welcoming ongoing efforts aimed at national reconciliation in the Central African Republic based on the Libreville Comprehensive Peace Agreement of 21 June 2008, calling upon its signatories to remain committed to the Agreement, and calling upon all remaining armed groups to join the Agreement without delay,

Acknowledging the important role played by the United Nations Integrated Peacebuilding Office in the Central African Republic in support of mediation efforts undertaken by the Government of the Central African Republic and the National Mediator,

Acknowledging also the efforts made by the authorities of the Central African Republic, the Independent Electoral Commission and all Central African stakeholders in organizing peaceful presidential and legislative elections in 2011, and welcoming the establishment by the Government of the Central African Republic on 14 July 2011 of a transitional committee for elections,

Noting with concern that the near absence of a political opposition in the democratic institutions of the Central African Republic, which has added to the atmosphere of tension in the country, may constitute a considerable challenge to the process of national reconciliation and nation-building,

Welcoming the intention of the Government of the Central African Republic to work towards an all-inclusive political approach for the reform of the electoral code and the establishment of a permanent electoral management body, and welcoming in this regard the organization by the Government, with the support of the United Nations Integrated Peacebuilding Office in the Central African Republic, of a workshop on electoral reforms with all national stakeholders from 28 to 30 November 2011,

Expressing deep concern at the precarious security situation in the Central African Republic due to the persisting presence and activities of national and foreign armed groups, including the Lord's Resistance Army and the Front populaire pour le redressement, that threaten peace and security in the Central African Republic and the subregion,

Expressing concern at the lack of State authority outside the capital, which has led to a serious security vacuum in many parts of the Central African Republic,

Welcoming the ceasefire agreement signed between the Government of the Central African Republic and the Convention des patriotes pour la justice et la paix and the ceasefire agreement signed between the Convention des patriotes pour la justice et la paix and the Union des forces démocratiques pour le rassemblement under the auspices of the Government and the National Mediator and with the support of the United Nations, the African Union, the Mission for the Consolidation of Peace in the Central African Republic and the Government of Chad,

Commending the African Union's regional cooperation initiative for the elimination of the Lord's Resistance Army, the appointment in November 2011 of a Special Envoy on the Lord's Resistance Army, and its efforts to establish a Regional Intervention Force, a Joint Operations Centre and a Joint Coordination Mechanism,

Recalling its resolutions 1325(2000) of 31 October 2000, 1820(2008) of 19 June 2008, 1888(2009) of 30 September 2009, 1889(2009) of 5 October 2009 and 1960(2010) of 16 December 2010 on women and peace and security and its resolutions 1612(2005) of 26 July 2005, 1882(2009) of 4 August 2009 and 1998(2011) of 12 July 2011 on children and armed conflict, recalling the conclusions of the Security Council Working Group on Children and Armed Conflict, including the adoption of action plans to put an end to the recruitment and use of children by armed groups, including by self-defence militias, and recalling its resolutions 1265(1999) of 17 September 1999, 1296(2000) of 19 April 2000, 1325(2000), 1612(2005), 1674(2006) of 28 April 2006, 1738(2006) of 23 December 2006, 1820(2008), 1882(2009), 1888(2009) and 1889(2009) on the protection of civilians in armed conflict,

Expressing serious concern at reports of continued human rights violations, in particular cases of extrajudicial executions and restrictions on civil liberties,

Noting the importance of the current dialogue between the Government of the Central African Republic and the International Monetary Fund on economic and financial developments in the Central African Republic,

Welcoming the continued engagement of the Peacebuilding Commission in the Central African Republic and the recent visit of a delegation from the country-specific configuration of the Commission, and acknowledging the contribution of the Peacebuilding Fund to peacebuilding in the Central African Republic,

Having considered the report of the Secretary-General on the situation in the Central African Republic and on the activities of the United Nations Integrated Peacebuilding Office in the Central African Republic,

1. *Decides* to extend the mandate of the United Nations Integrated Peacebuilding Office in the Central African Republic, as recommended by the Secretary-General in his report, until 31 January 2013;

2. *Underlines* the importance of a fully integrated office ensuring effective coordination of strategy and programmes among the United Nations agencies, funds and programmes in the Central African Republic, and emphasizes the role of the Special Representative of the Secretary-General for the Central African Republic in coordinating the country team;

3. *Looks forward* to progress by the Government of the Central African Republic on the creation of a permanent and independent electoral management body responsible for organizing future elections and on the revision of the electoral code, drawing from the lessons learned during the elections held earlier in the year, and calls upon the Government to organize municipal elections as soon as possible;

4. *Encourages* the Government of the Central African Republic to continue to engage in consultations with the opposition in a consensual and inclusive manner, including on the electoral reform;

5. *Urges* the Government of the Central African Republic to ensure that freedom of expression and assembly, including for the opposition parties, as well as the rule of law, which are essential for democracy, are fully respected, and urges the opposition parties and the Government to engage in a constructive dialogue to establish an environment allowing equal chances in the run-up to the next electoral cycle;

6. *Calls upon* the Government of the Central African Republic and all armed groups to remain committed to the national reconciliation process by fully observing the recommendations of the inclusive political dialogue that ended in 2008, and demands that all armed groups cooperate with the Government in the disarmament, demobilization and reintegration process;

7. *Welcomes* the progress that the Central African Republic has made in the disarmament and demobilization of former combatants in the north-west, following the launch of related activities by President Bozizé on 25 June 2011, and encourages the Government of the Central African Republic to pursue the disarmament and demobilization of former combatants, in particular members of the Union des forces démocratiques pour le rassemblement and the Convention des patriotes pour la justice et la paix;

8. *Also welcomes* the finalization on 8 July 2011 of the national strategy for the reintegration of former combatants drafted with the support of the United Nations Integrated Peacebuilding Office in the Central African Republic, and urges the Government of the Central African Republic to redouble its efforts towards ensuring national ownership and full implementation of the strategy, in line with the wider security sector reform, and to define a timeline and draw up specific reintegration programmes in order to be able to seek support from bilateral and multilateral partners;

9. *Underscores* the importance of security sector reform in the Central African Republic, notes with concern the absence of a credible and viable national security sector reform strategy, and in this regard calls upon the Government of the Central African Republic to re-engage in a meaningful dialogue with the United Nations Integrated Peacebuilding Office in the Central African Republic on this issue, in particular by taking into consideration the security sector reform road map drafted by the Office in response to the request by the Government for help to revive the security sector reform process;

10. *Expresses concern* at the security situation in the Central African Republic, which remains precarious, welcomes in this regard the continued efforts of the Mission for the Consolidation of Peace in the Central African Republic in support of durable peace and security in the Central African Republic, and calls upon countries in the subregion and regional and subregional organizations to consider, upon the request of the Central African Republic, the extension of the mandate of the Mission and other measures deemed appropriate to improve the security situation in the Central African Republic and the subregion;

11. *Underscores* the primary responsibility of the Government of the Central African Republic to promote security and protect its civilians with full respect for the rule of law, human rights and international humanitarian law, stresses the importance of bilateral partners' work enhancing the capacity of the Central African Armed Forces, and stresses that such assistance should be in support of the wider security reform process;

12. *Also underscores* the need for Chad, the Sudan and the Central African Republic to implement the tripartite

agreement, signed on 23 May 2011 in Khartoum, to enhance security in their common border areas through joint patrols, and also the need for Chad, the Central African Republic and Cameroon to pursue the tripartite initiative, signed in December 2005, aimed at enhancing security at their borders;

13. *Expresses deep concern* at the extensive recruitment and the acquisition of weapons by the Front populaire pour le redressement, which threaten peace and security in the Central African Republic and the region and constitute violations of the commitments made by the Front populaire pour le redressement to lay down its weapons and enter into discussions towards peace in the final communiqué signed on 13 June 2011 by the leader of the Front populaire pour le redressement, Mr. Baba Laddé, and the national mediators of Chad and the Central African Republic, condemns human rights violations perpetrated by the Front populaire pour le redressement, and encourages the Government of the Central African Republic to continue to liaise with the Government of Chad to reach a solution;

14. *Strongly condemns* the continued violations of international humanitarian and human rights law, including the recruitment and use of children, killing and maiming, rape, sexual slavery and other sexual violence and abductions perpetrated by armed groups, and specifically the Lord's Resistance Army, that threaten the population as well as the peace and stability of the Central African Republic and the subregion, and calls upon the United Nations Integrated Peacebuilding Office in the Central African Republic to report on human rights violations perpetrated by armed groups, particularly against children and women;

15. *Welcomes* the efforts of the Government of the Central African Republic to combat the Lord's Resistance Army on its territory, further welcomes the African Union's regional cooperation initiative for the elimination of the Lord's Resistance Army and the appointment of an African Union Special Envoy to coordinate this activity, and commends States in the region for their increased cooperation and efforts to address this threat;

16. *Also welcomes* the designation by the United Nations Integrated Peacebuilding Office in the Central African Republic of a focal point for Lord's Resistance Army-related activities and the establishment of a working group that includes national and international stakeholders, including the African Union, the European Union, the United States of America, France and the United Nations Regional Office for Central Africa, and calls upon the United Nations Integrated Peacebuilding Office in the Central African Republic to reinforce information-sharing on the Lord's Resistance Army, in particular with the United Nations Regional Office for Central Africa, the United Nations Office to the African Union, the United Nations Organization Stabilization Mission in the Democratic Republic of the Congo, the United Nations Mission in South Sudan and the newly appointed African Union Special Envoy on the Lord's Resistance Army, and to assist the Government of the Central African Republic in developing a strategy and supporting activities to encourage defections from the Lord's Resistance Army, and address the disarmament and demobilization of Lord's Resistance Army escapees and defectors, and their resettlement or repatriation to their countries of origin, within existing resources;

17. *Urges* all parties concerned to provide for unhindered humanitarian access to populations in need;

18. *Welcomes* the recent signature by the Armée populaire pour la restauration de la démocratie and the Convention des patriotes pour la justice et la paix of action plans to halt the recruitment and use of children, calls upon all remaining parties listed in the report of the Secretary-General on children and armed conflict to follow suit as soon as possible, welcomes the work of the Special Representative of the Secretary-General for Children and Armed Conflict in the Central African Republic and encourages the parties to continue engaging with her in this regard, calls upon the international community to support child reintegration efforts, and urges the Government of the Central African Republic to continue to strengthen the protection of children, including through the implementation of pertinent legislation and in the conduct of military operations;

19. *Expresses concern* at persistent incidents of sexual and gender-based violence, and encourages the United Nations Integrated Peacebuilding Office in the Central African Republic to continue engaging with the Government of the Central African Republic and other stakeholders, including the Special Representative of the Secretary-General for the Central African Republic, to address these issues;

20. *Urges* the Government of the Central African Republic to investigate reports of human rights violations in the country, to ensure that those who may be responsible for such violations are brought to justice and to take the steps necessary to prevent further violations;

21. *Encourages* the Government of the Central African Republic to more meaningfully engage the Bretton Woods institutions, especially the International Monetary Fund, as their assistance is critical for the revitalization of the economy and for the development of the country;

22. *Encourages* the Government of the Central African Republic, the Peacebuilding Commission and the country's national and international partners to honour the commitments made under the Strategic Framework for Peacebuilding in the Central African Republic, requests the Commission, with the support of the United Nations Integrated Peacebuilding Office in the Central African Republic, to continue to assist the Government in laying the foundations for sustainable peace and development in the Central African Republic, including by ensuring that progress is made in the enforcement of the rule of law and that peacebuilding objectives are fully taken into account in the future strategic planning processes, and requests the Commission to provide advice to the Security Council on these issues;

23. *Commends* the Government of the Central African Republic for launching its second-generation poverty reduction strategy paper, and calls upon the Government to prioritize its objectives, including those on access to basic services and health care, food security, infrastructure and disarmament, demobilization and reintegration as well as security sector reform, and to tackle the issue of corruption and enhance fiscal transparency;

24. *Decides* to remain actively seized of the matter.

Peacebuilding Commission

Review of Strategic Framework. In November, the Peacebuilding Commission presented the conclusions and recommendations of the second biannual review of the Strategic Framework for Peacebuilding in the CAR [PBC/5/CAF/3], which was adopted in

2009 [YUN 2009, p. 152] and would expire at the end of the year. The Commission noted that the timing of the review coincided with the finalization of the country's second-generation poverty reduction strategy paper; in that context, the review might inform the fine-tuning of that paper in order to incorporate peacebuilding elements of the Strategic Framework.

The review assessed the commitments by the Commission, the Government and civil society in support of national peacebuilding efforts. Notably, in the post-electoral phase, the Commission increased support to national authorities in developing the poverty reduction strategy paper, and maintained its dialogue with the political opposition, civil society and the private sector to support an inclusive peacebuilding process. With respect to the implementation of the recommendations of the December 2008 inclusive political dialogue [YUN 2008, p. 157], the Commission focused on the DDR and the electoral processes, and gave sustained attention to the work of the Disarmament, Demobilization and Reintegration Steering Committee. The commitments of the Government and civil society focused on three priorities: security sector reform and DDR; good governance and rule of law; and the establishment of development hubs. In that context, the Commission noted that the incorporation of those priorities in the new poverty reduction strategy paper was a positive development. Furthermore, those areas should be translated in terms of programmes and projects, and future progress should be monitored through the mechanisms of the strategy paper.

The Commission made several recommendations to the Government, civil society and the Steering Committee. In particular, the Government should implement the remaining recommendations of the 2008 inclusive political dialogue; seek to complete the DDR process by the end of the year, establish a permanent body in charge of organizing future elections, improve good governance and the fight against corruption, and improve national security; and prioritize the activities envisaged in its poverty reduction strategy paper, focusing on those that would improve the living conditions of populations formerly affected by conflict. The Commission itself would extend its engagement with the country beyond the expiration of the Strategic Framework and would, in consultation with the Government and civil society, develop a new tool of engagement, based on the peacebuilding elements of the poverty reduction strategy paper. It would continue working with relevant actors in the country's DDR process, encouraging the development of a reintegration solution that would also benefit host communities. Furthermore, the Commission would press for the start of the development hubs programme, particularly in the area of community development and socioeconomic stabilization, and focus on security sector reform.

The Chair of the CAR configuration briefed the Security Council on 7 July [S/PV.6575].

Commission mission. Reporting in November [PBC/5/CAF/1] on its mission to the CAR (10–15 October), the Peacebuilding Commission stated that the overall objectives of the visit were to continue dialogue and cooperation with the Government and other actors in the country's peacebuilding process; assess the progress made in implementing the key priorities in the Strategic Framework for Peacebuilding and other peacebuilding frameworks, on the basis of the second review of the Framework (see above); and continue discussions on the future engagement between the Commission and the country after the expiration of the Strategic Framework. The Commission highlighted the importance of the regional dimension of peacebuilding, and stated that the engagement of regional and subregional organizations, such as the AU, the Central African Economic and Monetary Community, and the Economic Community of Central African States, must be strengthened. As two of the remaining sources of insecurity, namely, the threat posed by LRA in the south-east and the Chadian group led by Baba Laddé, were regional in nature, cooperation with neighbouring countries facing similar security threats must be strengthened. Furthermore, with a considerable number of disarmed and demobilized combatants waiting, it had become urgent to finalize the reintegration strategy approved by the Disarmament, Demobilization and Reintegration Steering Committee and resolve funding issues. On security sector reform, the delegation noted the lack of an overall medium- to long-term national strategy. It expressed concern about the expiration of the mandate of the Economic Community of Central African States Mission for the Consolidation of Peace in the Central African Republic (MICOPAX) in 2013, encouraged the Government to ensure that the withdrawal of MICOPAX did not result in a security vacuum, and stated that steps should be taken to ensure the extension of the MICOPAX mandate should a situational analysis warrant it.

Participation in CAR configuration. During the year, the Chairperson of the Peacebuilding Commission invited South Africa [PBC/5/OC/1] to participate in the Commission's configuration on the Central African Republic.

(For further information on the Peacebuilding Commission, see p. 47.)

Children and armed conflict

Report of Secretary-General. In April, in response to Security Council resolution 1612(2005) [YUN 2005, p. 863], the Secretary-General submitted his second report on children and armed conflict in the CAR [S/2011/241]. The report covered the period from

December 2008 to December 2010, and focused on grave violations perpetrated against children and progress made to end such violations, in follow-up to the recommendations contained in the first report and the subsequent conclusions of the Working Group on Children and Armed Conflict [YUN 2009, p. 153]. Insecurity continued to hamper progress towards respect for children's rights, with serious violations of international human rights and humanitarian law perpetrated by all parties to the conflict, including the national armed forces, rebel groups and self-defence groups. Sporadic fighting between Government forces and armed groups and widespread banditry had led to a protection crisis, particularly affecting women and children.

Child recruitment by armed groups continued, particularly in the north-east and east of the country. While the disarmament, demobilization and reintegration of 525 children associated with the Armée populaire pour la restauration de la République et la démocratie between June 2008 and December 2010 marked a significant step forward, the United Nations received reports of children remaining with that armed group. In the north, the Union des forces démocratiques pour le rassemblement, the Convention des patriotes pour la justice et la paix (CPJP) and local self-defence militias reportedly continued to use children. It was also reported that the Front démocratique du peuple centrafricain, which had refused to join the DDR process, continued to use children in Ouham prefecture. LRA engaged in the abduction and forced recruitment into its ranks, where children were allegedly used as combatants, spies, servants, sex slaves and carriers.

The killing and maiming of children continued to be reported, particularly in the north-west and southeast. Rape and other sexual violence remained a concern; incidents were severely underreported as victims were reluctant to seek assistance or report violations owing to cultural factors, public stigmatization, fear of reprisal and lack of trust in the judiciary. The education system was affected by the climate of insecurity, with the dropout rate throughout the country estimated at 53 per cent in 2010. In the east, fear of incursions by armed groups, including LRA, prevented parents from sending their children to school. Several villages in Mbomou and Haut-Mbomou prefectures were closed from mid-May to September 2010 owing to LRA activity. Between May and July 2010, several schools in Haute-Kotto prefecture were occupied by CPJP elements.

The Government made efforts to strengthen child protection, including with regard to reinforcing and training defence and security forces, strengthening the national child protection mechanism, ending the use of children in armed groups and forces, and enacting national legislation.

Working Group. The Working Group on Children and Armed Conflict examined the Secretary-General's report at its thirtieth meeting on 2 May [S/2011/485], and adopted conclusions and recommendations at its thirty-first meeting on 22 June [S/AC.51/2011/5].

BINUCA

The United Nations Integrated Peacebuilding Office in the Central African Republic (BINUCA), established pursuant to the Security Council presidential statement S/PRST/2009/5 [YUN 2009, p. 146], continued to implement its mandate, including assisting in efforts to implement the 2008 inclusive political dialogue [YUN 2008, p. 157]. By resolution 2031(2011) (see p. 124), the Security Council extended the mandate of the Office until 31 January 2013.

Appointment of Special Representative. On 6 May [S/2011/291], the Secretary-General informed the Security Council of his intention to appoint Margaret Vogt (Nigeria) as his new Special Representative in the CAR and Head of BINUCA, replacing Sahle-Work Zewde (Ethiopia). The Council took note of the Secretary-General's intention on 10 May [S/2011/292].

Financing

In April, the General Assembly considered the report of the Secretary-General [A/66/354/Add.3] on proposed requirements for special political missions, good offices and other political initiatives authorized by the Assembly and/or the Security Council, which included resource requirements for BINUCA for 2012 totalling $20,881,700, and the related ACABQ report [A/66/7/Add.12], which recommended approval of the requested resources.

On 24 December, in section IX of **resolution 66/247** (see p. 1393), the Assembly reduced the 2012 budget for BINUCA by $350,000, authorizing appropriations for $20,531,700.

Central African Republic and Chad

In 2011, the security situation in the Central African Republic and Chad progressively improved, and was positively affected by improved relations between Chad and the Sudan. The Chad-Sudan joint border force, deployed since April 2010 to end cross-border rebel attacks, increased in size to 5,000 personnel, and its mandate was extended until September. Following the withdrawal of the United Nations Mission in the Central African Republic and Chad (MINURCAT) on 31 December 2010, Chad's Détachement intégré de sécurité assumed responsibility for security in and around refugee camps and internally displaced persons sites and for humanitarian operations, while the joint border force secured the border area. The Government made progress in fulfilling its commitment to assume full responsibility for the security and protection of the civilian population following the withdrawal of MINURCAT. The UN Resident Coordinator assumed senior leadership of the United Nations in Chad.

Political and security developments

Report of Secretary-General (April). In response to Security Council presidential statement S/PRST/2010/29 [YUN 2010, p. 168], the Secretary-General in April reported [S/2011/278] on the progress made in the protection of civilians in eastern Chad and the conclusion of the MINURCAT liquidation phase, due to end on 30 April. The report assessed the situation of civilians and steps taken by the Government, the United Nations and the humanitarian community to address protection concerns.

The Secretary-General stated that the security situation in the east progressively improved and was positively affected by improved relations between Chad and the Sudan. The Chad-Sudan joint border force, deployed since April 2010 [YUN 2010, p. 158], had enforced security along the border with the Sudan; it had increased in size to 5,000 personnel, and its mandate was extended until September 2011. The majority of combatants from Chadian opposition armed groups—an estimated 16,000 persons—had returned to Chad from neighbouring countries. There had been no armed clashes between Chadian security forces and armed groups that had not demobilized. Nonetheless, remnants of armed groups, particularly the Union des forces de la résistance and the Front populaire pour la renaissance nationale, were present in the Sudan and in the northeast of the CAR, and their potential to carry out hit-and-run operations in Chad remained. The Secretary-General reported that the withdrawal of MINURCAT on 31 December 2010 had not adversely affected the security situation, and patrols and escorts by the Détachement intégré de sécurité (DIS) and the deployment of the joint border force had improved security and stability. DIS had assumed responsibility for security in and around refugee camps and internally displaced persons (IDPs) sites and for humanitarian operations.

On 11 January, Chad celebrated its fiftieth year of independence. Animosity between the main political factions had declined and most political parties participated in the legislative elections held on 13 February, in accordance with the political agreement of 13 August 2007 [YUN 2007, p. 155]. The Constitutional Council published the final results, according to which 113 seats out of 188 were won by the ruling party, the Mouvement patriotique du salut. The Council, however, subsequently annulled the results of the vote in three districts, representing 13 seats, in which serious irregularities were found.

The presidential election scheduled for 3 April was postponed to 25 April. Opposition candidates raised concerns about the electoral process, with three candidates suspending their participation on 22 March on the grounds that conditions for a fair election had not been met. The incumbent, President Idriss Déby Itno, was re-elected, winning 88 per cent of the votes.

Despite the improved security situation, the nation's humanitarian needs remained immense, with 2.5 million people in need of assistance. The population continued to be affected by food insecurity and malnutrition, as well as epidemic outbreaks of disease. Furthermore, civilians continued to face the daily threat of banditry carried out by armed actors. With the departure of MINURCAT, the capacity of the United Nations to monitor and report attacks against civilians was severely reduced. The network of local non-governmental organizations (NGOs) in Abéché, previously supported by the Mission, continued to undertake human rights monitoring; however, its ability to investigate and verify specific incidents in the east had been curtailed. Humanitarian access was affected by banditry and criminal activity, including road ambushes and theft of humanitarian supplies, vehicle hijacking, and break-ins into humanitarian compounds and facilities. Nonetheless, humanitarian access had increased in tandem with the country's improved security, owing to the increased DIS operations, the deployment of the joint border force and the renewed engagement of the national authorities in addressing the security of humanitarian operations. Risks remained, however, in the tri-border area in the south-east, where the joint border force was not deployed, as well as in several regions in the north, east and south-east, which were contaminated with landmines and explosive remnants of war. The withdrawal of MINURCAT also reduced the logistical capacity and transport assets available to humanitarian organizations, thereby limiting access to remote areas during the rainy season.

Pursuant to Security Council resolution 1923(2010) [YUN 2010, p. 159], the Government had committed to assuming full responsibility for the security and protection of the civilian population following the withdrawal of MINURCAT. The report reviewed the Government's progress in meeting benchmarks for civilian protection. The Government made progress in fulfilling that commitment with regard to the voluntary return and resettlement of IDPs; the demilitarization of refugee and IDP camps; and security for refugees, IDPs, civilians and humanitarian workers. To assist the Government, the United Nations and its partner organizations carried out various activities in the area of civilian protection. The Office of the United Nations High Commissioner for Refugees (UNHCR) led consultations with UN entities and partners to develop a strategy to address such protection in the east. The strategy helped to clarify the responsibilities of the UN country team following the departure of MINURCAT, and the ways in which the team could assist the Government in meeting its obligations concerning civilian protection. The role of the UN Resident Coordinator had been strengthened to assume senior leadership of the United Nations in Chad and to help facilitate the coordination of UN assistance during the transition phase. On 1 March, UNDP, UNHCR and the Government signed off on the UN assistance programme for DIS, which was aimed at providing administrative and logistical support to the Government in ensuring the continuation of DIS activities and in meeting its obligations in accordance with resolution 1923(2010).

The Secretary-General concluded that, despite continued improvement in the country's security situation, a number of root causes of conflict remained, including competition over scarce resources, poor governance and insufficient respect for human rights. The protection benchmarks to which the Government had committed should remain the clear measure by which progress on civilian protection was judged. It was imperative that the UN country team finalize its strategy for the protection of civilians and develop the means by which to measure progress. The Secretary-General also noted that DIS represented only a temporary solution to the security problem in eastern Chad, and the priority should be a clear plan for security sector reform and the demobilization and reintegration of ex-combatants in Chad.

Children and armed conflict

Report of Secretary-General. In February, pursuant to Security Council resolution 1612(2005) [YUN 2005, p. 863], the Secretary-General presented his third report [S/2011/64] on the situation of children and armed conflict in Chad to the Council and its Working Group on Children and Armed Conflict. The report covered the period from July 2008 to December 2010. It focused on grave violations perpetrated against children and measures undertaken to strengthen the monitoring and reporting mechanisms in the country.

The Task Force on Monitoring and Reporting in Chad documented grave violations against children during the reporting period. The national army and armed groups, including the Justice and Equality Movement (JEM), continued to recruit and use children in the east. While most of those children were between 14 and 17 years old, some cases involved children as young as 12. The Task Force verified one of three allegations of the killing in combat of a child recruited by JEM in June 2009. Contamination from explosive remnants of war continued to exist throughout the country, including in and around the capital, N'Djamena, and there were concerns over the presence of mines and unexploded ordnance in the north. The population did not have the necessary awareness of mine issues to prevent or decrease casualties; with the departure of MINURCAT and the termination of its mine and clearance of explosive remnants of war and road verification programmes, incidents of killing and maiming of children might increase. Sexual and gender-based violence was widespread, including rape, sexual harassment and exploitation, female genital mutilation, early and forced marriages, and mistreatment associated with undesired or early pregnancies. There was a rising trend of such violence reported among refugees; of the 563 cases recorded by UNHCR in the first semester of 2010, nearly 30 per cent affected children.

The report also reviewed actions to end violations and abuses against children, in follow-up to the recommendations of the Working Group [YUN 2007, p. 157 & YUN 2008, p. 852], including progress in developing a national action plan to address the recruitment and use of children; the establishment in 2008 of a Government-led task force to conduct verification and sensitization visits to Government military training centres and sites; a regional conference organized by the Government on ending recruitment and use of children by armed forces and groups (N'Djamena, 7–9 June 2010); and activities by UNHCR, the United Nations Children's Fund (UNICEF) and the Government in response to violations against children.

The Secretary-General stated that, with the withdrawal of MINURCAT, the capacity of the UN system and national partners to monitor, report and respond to violations would decline significantly. As part of the completion and transfer of key MINURCAT activities to the UN country team, it was essential that the monitoring and reporting mechanism on grave violations against children, in accordance with Council resolutions 1612(2005) and 1882(2009) [YUN 2009, p. 739], continue under the leadership of the Resident Coordinator and the UNICEF representative. He urged the Government to engage in dialogue with the United Nations to finalize the preparation and implementation of a time-bound action plan. The Government should issue clear orders to its military chain of command prohibiting the recruitment and use of children; investigate and prosecute perpetrators of rape and other crimes of sexual violence; and ensure that appropriate attention was afforded to child victims of mines and that mine-risk education programmes were in place.

Working Group. The Working Group on Children and Armed Conflict examined the Secretary-General's report at its twenty-ninth meeting on 25 February [S/AC.51/2011/4], and adopted conclusions and recommendations at its thirtieth meeting on 2 May [S/AC.51/2011/5]. On 8 June [S/2011/347],

MINURCAT

The United Nations Mission in the Central African Republic and Chad (MINURCAT) withdrew from Chad on 31 December 2010. Established by Security Council resolution 1778(2007) [YUN 2007, p. 153] to create the security conditions for the return of refugees and displaced persons, and favourable conditions for reconstruction and development, the Mission's mandate was subsequently expanded by resolution 1861(2009) [YUN 2009, p. 154] to include security and protection of civilians and humanitarian workers. The mandate was extended by resolutions 1913(2010) [YUN 2010, p. 157] and 1922(2010) [YUN 2010, p. 159], and extended and revised by resolution 1923(2010) [ibid.], to include training and support to the Chadian Détachement integré de sécurité. The Secretary-General reported in April [S/2011/278] that the technical liquidation of the Mission commenced on 1 January and would end on 30 April.

Financing

In June, the General Assembly considered the performance report on the MINURCAT budget for the period from 1 July 2009 to 30 June 2010 [A/65/638], showing a total expenditure of $540,805,300 gross ($531,979,500 net) against an appropriation of $690,753,100 gross ($683,454,500 net), and the related ACABQ report [A/65/743/Add.11]. ACABQ had no objection to the Secretary-General's proposal to defer action on the unencumbered balance and other income adjustments of the Mission to the sixty-sixth (2011) session of the Assembly.

GENERAL ASSEMBLY ACTION

On 30 June [meeting 106], the General Assembly, on the recommendation of the Fifth Committee [A/65/653/Add.1], adopted **resolution 65/254 B** without vote [agenda item 144].

Financing of the United Nations Mission in the Central African Republic and Chad

The General Assembly,

Having considered the report of the Secretary-General on the financial performance of the United Nations Mission in the Central African Republic and Chad for the period from 1 July 2009 to 30 June 2010 and the related report of the Advisory Committee on Administrative and Budgetary Questions,

Recalling Security Council resolution 1778(2007) of 25 September 2007, by which the Council established in the Central African Republic and Chad a multidimensional presence, including the United Nations Mission in the Central African Republic and Chad, and the subsequent resolutions by which the Council extended the mandate of the Mission, the latest of which was resolution 1923(2010) of 25 May 2010, by which the Council extended the mandate of the Mission until 31 December 2010, decided to reduce the military component of the Mission to 2,200 military personnel and called upon the Secretary-General to complete the withdrawal of all uniformed and civilian components, other than those required for the liquidation of the Mission, by 31 December 2010,

Recalling also its resolution 62/233 A of 22 December 2007 on the financing of the United Nations Mission in the Central African Republic and Chad and its subsequent resolutions thereon, the latest of which was resolution 65/254 A of 24 December 2010,

Reaffirming the general principles underlying the financing of United Nations peacekeeping operations, as stated in General Assembly resolutions 1874(S-IV) of 27 June 1963, 3101(XXVIII) of 11 December 1973 and 55/235 of 23 December 2000,

Noting with appreciation that voluntary contributions have been made to the Mission,

1. *Takes note* of the status of contributions to the United Nations Mission in the Central African Republic and Chad as at 30 April 2011, including the contributions outstanding in the amount of 57.1 million United States dollars, representing some 4 per cent of the total assessed contributions, notes with concern that only ninety-five Member States have paid their assessed contributions in full, and urges all other Member States, in particular those in arrears, to ensure payment of their outstanding assessed contributions;

2. *Expresses its appreciation* to those Member States which have paid their assessed contributions in full, and urges all other Member States to make every possible effort to ensure payment of their assessed contributions to the Mission in full;

3. *Endorses* the conclusions and recommendations contained in the report of the Advisory Committee on Administrative and Budgetary Questions, and requests the Secretary-General to ensure their full implementation;

Financial performance report for the period from 1 July 2009 to 30 June 2010

4. *Takes note* of the report of the Secretary-General on the financial performance of the Mission for the period from 1 July 2009 to 30 June 2010;

5. *Decides* to defer until its sixty-sixth session action on the unencumbered balance of 149,947,800 dollars as well as the other income and adjustments in the amount of 13,466,100 dollars and the increase of 1,527,100 dollars in the estimated staff assessment income, and requests the Secretary-General to report to the General Assembly at its sixty-sixth session updated information on the cash position of the Mission;

6. *Also decides* to include in the provisional agenda of its sixty-sixth session the item entitled "Financing of the United Nations Mission in the Central African Republic and Chad".

The General Assembly on 24 December decided that the item on the financing of MINURCAT would remain for consideration during its resumed sixty-sixth (2012) session (**decision 66/557**).

Uganda

The Secretary-General, reporting in November [S/2011/693] on areas affected by the Lord's Resistance Army (LRA), reviewed the situation in Uganda. Most of the 1.8 million people formerly displaced as a result of LRA activities in the north had returned to their villages or integrated locally elsewhere. Some 80,000 IDPs remained in six camps in the north, unable to return home due to the presence of landmines and land disputes. Steps were being taken to find durable solutions for the former IDPs, and in June the Government announced a five-year extension of the peace, recovery and development plan for northern Uganda beyond its anticipated completion in mid-2012. As at September, 26,130 suspected LRA and other armed group combatants had been granted amnesty under the Uganda Amnesty Act, including former senior LRA commanders. The UN country team had embarked upon a dedicated peacebuilding programme, funded by the United Nations Peacebuilding Fund, to address issues that contributed to conflict and to provide integration assistance for female-headed, IDP, returnee and ex-combatants' households.

(For more information on LRA, see p. 99.)

Rwanda

Assistance to survivors of 1994 genocide

Commemoration. During the week of 4 April, the United Nations held its seventeenth commemoration of the 1994 genocide in Rwanda [YUN 1994, p. 281], during which more than 800,000 innocent persons lost their lives, at Headquarters and at United Nations Information Centres around the world. The commemoration, under the theme "Rebuilding Rwanda: Reconciliation and Education", included memorial services, a student conference at Headquarters and educational activities. The United Nations also continued the programme of information and outreach entitled "The Rwanda Genocide and the United Nations", established by General Assembly resolution 60/225 [YUN 2005, p. 216].

Report of Secretary-General (September). In response to Assembly resolution 64/226 [YUN 2009, p. 166], the Secretary-General in September submitted a report [A/66/331] on assistance to survivors of the 1994 genocide in Rwanda, particularly orphans, widows and victims of sexual violence, which analysed the challenges to the delivery of relief and rehabilitation assistance by the United Nations and its partners to survivors. The report stated that, 17 years after those tragic events, Rwanda had steadily recovered and achieved socioeconomic progress and institutional transformation. The Secretary-General also noted the country's progress in peace and reconciliation, restoration of law and order, and democratization. Similarly, the country had made advances in rebuilding and strengthening national capacity for good governance through institutional capacity-building, public sector reform and decentralization, and anti-corruption measures. Despite that progress, much remained to be done to address the high rates of poverty, population growth, maternal mortality and child malnutrition. Insufficient investment in infrastructure for energy, water and sanitation, and transportation, coupled with the combined pressures of agricultural production, population growth, economic expansion and rising energy needs, were placing an increasing environmental stress on the country.

The United Nations provided support to Rwanda in various initiatives, including assisting the national police in crime prevention programmes; contributing to the work of documenting and honouring the memory of the genocide victims; providing funding to NGOs delivering medical, legal, psychological and social assistance to persons tortured during the genocide and members of their families; supporting the Association of Genocide Widows in training and capacity-building activities; and supporting the association Uyisenga n'Imanzi in addressing mental health problems of child survivors of the genocide.

The Secretary-General concluded that the United Nations would continue to provide advice and support to Government efforts in ensuring peace and reconciliation, the rule of law, human rights and shared economic growth, as well as the provision of and access to basic social services. Among the various areas of support, assisting groups to build sustainable micro, small and medium enterprises and other income-generating activities through capacity-building, microcredit and access to markets remained priorities for self-sufficiency and poverty alleviation. Support for those who had experienced physical injuries resulting in mental and physical disabilities was critical, as was support for ageing genocide survivors.

GENERAL ASSEMBLY ACTION

On 23 December [meeting 92], the General Assembly adopted **resolution 66/228** [draft: A/66/L.31 & Add.1] without vote [agenda item 71].

Assistance to survivors of the 1994 genocide in Rwanda, particularly orphans, widows and victims of sexual violence

The General Assembly,

Guided by the Charter of the United Nations and the Universal Declaration of Human Rights,

Recalling the findings and recommendations of the independent inquiry commissioned by the Secretary-General, with the approval of the Security Council, into the actions of the United Nations during the 1994 genocide in Rwanda,

Recalling also the 2005 World Summit Outcome, particularly its recognition that all individuals, in particular vulnerable people, are entitled to freedom from fear and freedom from want, with an equal opportunity to enjoy all their rights and fully develop their human potential,

Recalling further its resolution 59/137 of 10 December 2004, in which it requested the Secretary-General to encourage relevant agencies, funds and programmes of the United Nations system to continue to work with the Government of Rwanda to develop and implement programmes aimed at supporting vulnerable groups that continue to suffer from the effects of the 1994 genocide,

Recalling its resolution 60/225 of 23 December 2005, in which it urged Member States to develop educational programmes on the lessons of the genocide in Rwanda, and also requested the Secretary-General to establish a programme of outreach for Rwanda genocide victim remembrance and education, in order to prevent future acts of genocide,

Recognizing the numerous difficulties faced by survivors of the 1994 genocide in Rwanda, particularly the orphans, widows and victims of sexual violence, who are poorer and more vulnerable as a result of the genocide, especially the many victims of sexual violence who have contracted HIV and have since either died or become seriously ill with AIDS,

Commending the significant efforts of the Government and people of Rwanda and civil society organizations, as well as international efforts, to provide support for restoring the dignity of the survivors, including the allocation by the Government of Rwanda of 5 per cent of its national budget every year to support genocide survivors,

Recalling Security Council resolution 1966(2010) of 22 December 2010, in which the Council requested the International Criminal Tribunal for Rwanda to take all possible measures to expeditiously complete all its remaining work no later than 31 December 2014, to prepare its closure and to ensure a smooth transition to the International Residual Mechanism for Criminal Tribunals,

Firmly convinced of the necessity of restoring the dignity of the survivors of the 1994 genocide in Rwanda, which would help to promote reconciliation and healing in Rwanda,

Welcoming the report of the Secretary-General,

1. *Requests* the Secretary-General to continue to encourage the relevant agencies, funds and programmes of the United Nations system to implement resolution 59/137 expeditiously, inter alia, by providing assistance in the areas of education for orphans, medical care and treatment for victims of sexual violence, including HIV-positive victims, trauma and psychological counselling, and skills training and microcredit programmes aimed at promoting self-sufficiency and alleviating poverty;

2. *Calls upon* Member States and the United Nations system to urgently implement the recommendations contained in the report of the Secretary-General;

3. *Requests* the Secretary-General to continue the activities of the programme of outreach entitled "The Rwanda Genocide and the United Nations" aimed at Rwanda genocide victim remembrance and education, in order to help to prevent future acts of genocide;

4. *Notes* the importance of residual issues, including witness protection and victim support, the archives of the International Criminal Tribunal for Rwanda and judicial issues and capacity-building for the Rwandan judiciary, and underlines the need for increased and sustained attention to these issues;

5. *Welcomes* the adoption of Security Council resolution 1966(2010), in which the Council decided to establish the International Residual Mechanism for Criminal Tribunals and, in this regard, calls upon the Mechanism to conclude the remaining cases within the initial period set out in resolution 1966(2010), and calls upon Member States to support that effort;

6. *Requests* the Secretary-General, in consultation with the Government of Rwanda, to continue to encourage the relevant agencies, funds and programmes of the United Nations system to take appropriate steps to support, in particular, efforts to enhance judicial capacity-building and victim support in Rwanda;

7. *Also requests* the Secretary-General, in view of the critical situation of the survivors of the 1994 genocide in Rwanda and the International Criminal Tribunal for Rwanda completion strategy, to continue to take all necessary and practicable measures for the implementation of the present resolution and to report thereon to the General Assembly, at its sixty-eighth session, with concrete recommendations for appropriate solutions to the remaining needs of survivors of the Rwandan genocide of 1994;

8. *Decides* to include in the provisional agenda of its sixty-eighth session the item entitled "Assistance to survivors of the 1994 genocide in Rwanda, particularly orphans, widows and victims of sexual violence".

West Africa

Regional issues

Political and security developments

The Secretary-General, as requested by the Security Council in 2007 [YUN 2007, p. 168], reported every six months on the fulfilment of the mandate of the United Nations Office for West Africa (UNOWA). The reports focused on political developments in the subregion; economic, social and humanitarian trends; security trends, including drug trafficking and organized crime; trends on human rights and gender issues; and UNOWA activities (see p. 139). The reports also described developments in the Cameroon-Nigeria Mixed Commission (see p. 186).

Report of Secretary-General (June). Pursuant to a Security Council letter of December 2010 [YUN 2010, p. 177], which extended the mandate of UNOWA until December 2013, the Secretary-General in June reported [S/2011/388] on developments in the subregion and the activities of the Office in the first half of the year. The region witnessed progress towards greater stability and peace, owing to the end of the transition processes in Guinea [YUN 2010, p. 233] and the Niger.

The overall political situation, however, was marked by several election-related challenges, with nine elections held at the presidential, parliamentary and local levels in Benin, Cape Verde, the Niger and Nigeria. While international observers noted improvements in the conduct and management of elections, aspects such as voter registration and the release of results remained contentious and represented potential triggers of violence. As a result, the subregion continued to witness tensions among political parties, which in some instances resulted in deadly confrontations between security forces and activists.

In Benin, the presidential elections scheduled for 27 February were postponed due to delays in the electoral process, particularly the finalization of the permanent computerized voters list. On 3 March, the Economic Community of West African States (ECOWAS), the African Union (AU) and the Special Representative of the Secretary-General for West Africa conducted a joint good offices mission to the country, encouraging national stakeholders to find solutions to the challenges related to the holding of the elections. Following that mission, the Constitutional Court authorized the postponement until 13 March of the presidential elections, which took place under peaceful conditions. The provisional results indicated that 53 per cent of the votes went to President Yayi Boni, and on 29 March, despite appeals by the opposition, the Constitutional Court proclaimed the re-election of President Boni. Observers from ECOWAS and the AU certified the election as generally free and transparent, despite some shortcomings in the process. Subsequently, on 30 April, legislative elections took place under peaceful conditions, and the electoral process ended with the inauguration ceremony of the sixth legislature on 16 May.

The reporting period saw the successful conclusion of the transition process in the Niger and the nation's return to constitutional order a year after President Mamadou Tandja was ousted from power [YUN 2010, p. 174]. Peaceful legislative and presidential elections were held on 31 January, followed by the presidential run-off on 12 March, leading to the election of Mahamadou Issoufou of the Nigerien Party for Democracy and Socialism as President with 58 per cent of the votes. Observers from ECOWAS, the AU, the Organization of the Islamic Conference and the European Union (EU) declared that the elections were conducted in a free, fair and transparent manner. President Issoufou was sworn in for a five-year term at a ceremony in Niamey on 7 April, during which he outlined the main priorities of his mandate, including reducing hunger, alleviating poverty and fighting corruption and insecurity. On 10 May, the Court of Appeals of the Niger cleared former President Tandja, who had been under house arrest since February 2010, of corruption charges and ordered his release from jail.

Growing insecurity, a deteriorating humanitarian situation and concerns about the impact of the Libyan crisis renewed the political drive to increase regional cooperation to stabilize the Sahel area. The Governments of Algeria, Mali, Mauritania and the Niger intensified consultations to strengthen cooperation in the field of security and to ensure economic and social development in the border areas. The four nations convened a conference on development and security in the Sahel (Algiers, Algeria, 7–8 September), during which they expressed concern over the proliferation of a range of weapons originating from Libya into neighbouring countries. The matter was also discussed during the meeting of the Chiefs of Staff of the armies of the four countries (Bamako, Mali, 21 November).

Regarding security and humanitarian challenges, there were indications that weapons had been transferred from Libya and fallen into the hands of terrorists in the Sahel, which risked destabilizing the whole region. Furthermore, there was a significant drop in remittance inflow from migrant workers in Libya, which would place a strain on local livelihoods. The Secretary-General called on Sahel countries to strengthen their collaboration to address those challenges, and in that regard was encouraged by cooperation among the four nations. Furthermore, West African States were taking steps to operationalize the regional plan of action on the implementation of Council resolutions 1325(2000) [YUN 2000, p. 1113] and 1820(2008) [YUN 2008, p. 1265] on women and peace and security, and an increasing number of countries had adopted national action plans. The Secretary-General encouraged Governments of the subregion to develop and adopt similar plans, noting that the United Nations, particularly UN-Women, stood ready to provide assistance.

Security Council statement. On 26 August, by a press statement [SC/10370], the Security Council condemned the bombing on that day of the UN building in Abuja, Nigeria. The attack killed 23 people, including 13 UN staff members.

Report of Secretary-General (December). In a December report covering the second half of the year [S/2011/811], the Secretary-General stated that, despite the fragile security situation in several countries, there was a decline in open conflict in the subregion. At the same time, the period saw an increase in cross-border and structural threats to stability. The post-presidential election crisis in Côte d'Ivoire continued to affect the socioeconomic, humanitarian and security situation of countries in the Mano River Union subregion, and the rise in piracy attacks in the Gulf of Guinea (see below), as well as the negative effects of drug trafficking and transnational organized crime, brought increased insecurity. Furthermore, the conflict in Libya continued to have an impact on the Sahel region. The return of armed elements from Libya to their home countries, particularly Mali and the Niger, raised concerns that those elements could stir up political and security tensions. There were also concerns over the proliferation of a range of weapons originating from Libya—from small arms to surface-to-air missiles—in neighbouring countries, and the possibility that some of those weapons could fall into the hands of criminal and terrorist groups. The presence of armed combatants and mercenary groups along the border between Côte d'Ivoire and Liberia was also a source of instability, including recurrent attacks on local populations by those groups.

By 27 November, some 200,000 migrants had crossed Libya's borders into neighbouring West African countries. To assess the implications of that large-scale migration, the Secretary-General's Special Representative for West Africa visited Burkina Faso, Mali, Mauritania and the Niger in October, where he consulted with the Heads of State, senior Government officials, UN country teams and other international partners, and expressed the willingness of the United Nations to develop a common approach for the Sahel region. Against that background, the Secretary-General dispatched an assessment mission to the region (7–23 December), led by the UN Department of Political Affairs (DPA) and under the supervision of the Special Representative, to develop recommendations for a UN system-wide strategy to respond to the needs of the subregion. The mission visited Chad, Mali, Mauritania, the Niger and Nigeria (see below).

Election-related tensions and risks continued to be of concern in Côte d'Ivoire, the Gambia, Guinea, Liberia and Senegal. In the Gambia, presidential elections were held on 24 November, with the incumbent, President Yahya Jammeh, winning his fourth consecutive term with 72 per cent of the votes. Opposition parties disputed the results; however, observer teams stated that while there were shortcomings in the pre-election environment, the voting process was generally held under free, fair and transparent conditions. On 11 October, the Special Representative visited Mali, meeting with President Amadou Toumani Touré to advocate for the conduct of transparent, peaceful presidential and parliamentary elections in April 2012.

General Assembly action. On 9 December, by **resolution 66/113** (see p. 1372), the Assembly granted observer status to the West African Economic and Monetary Union in the sessions and work of the Assembly.

Assessment mission to Sahel region

The Secretary-General reported [S/2012/42] that he had dispatched an assessment mission from 7 to 23 December to Mali, the Niger, Chad, Mauritania and Nigeria to assess the scope of the threat of the Libyan crisis in the region. As a result of the crisis, millions of economic migrants were forced to flee Libya and return to their communities. Governments of the region were faced with the impact of the crisis on an already challenging humanitarian, development and security situation. The mission, deployed under the guidance of the Special Representative, was led by DPA with assistance from the AU. Its mandate was to collect information on the influx of unemployed returnees and the impact of their return on the socioeconomic and political stability of the host communities; the inflow and proliferation of weapons into the region; the nature and extent of criminal and terrorist activities and regional initiatives to address them; the impact on the security sector; the national operational capacity of the security sector; judicial reform; additional efforts needed to address the root causes of food insecurity and malnutrition, as well as other humanitarian issues; youth unemployment; and disaster risk evaluation. The mission was also mandated to assess national capacities in those areas and to recommend measures that the United Nations and the AU could undertake to support national and international efforts.

The mission noted that the extent and degree of the impact of the crisis differed according to geographical location, as well as political and economic agreements with the Qadhafi regime. Some factors, however, remained consistent across the region. In particular, all of the countries sharing a border with Libya had seen an influx of returnees that had strained social structures. Furthermore, some countries that did not share a border with Libya, including Mali and Mauritania, also registered inflows of returnees.

The Libyan crisis had exacerbated the region's already precarious security situation, with key security concerns relating to the proliferation of arms and weapons, terrorist threats, transnational organized crime, uneven border management and cooperation, and limited police and judicial cooperation. The Governments of the countries visited indicated that, in spite of efforts to control their borders, large quantities of weapons and ammunition from Libyan stockpiles were smuggled into the Sahel region. Certain authorities indicated that some of those weapons were smuggled by returnees, particularly former fighters who had been either members of the Libyan army or mercenaries during the conflict. Officials in Chad, Mauritania and the Niger stated that they had achieved relative success in limiting the inflow of weapons into their territories as a result of security measures, including the deployment of additional troops in strategic locations along their borders. All national and international interlocutors stressed the need to develop better coordinated regional approaches to address the illegal transfer of weapons across borders and prevent them from being used to instigate armed violence in the Sahel or bolster old rebellions in Mali and the Niger. Furthermore, terrorist and criminal activities had increased in the region, and the potential recruitment by terrorist or criminal groups of unemployed youth and returnees and the growing risk of radicalization was of growing concern. The mission was informed that the terrorist group Boko Haram was a source of concern for most countries in the region. The radicalization of youth was also a problem, particularly in the south of the Niger. The mission was informed that Boko Haram had established links with Al-Qaida in the Islamic Maghreb.

The level of protection and control of borders varied widely. In Mali and the Niger, the authorities appealed to the international community for assistance in protecting and securing their borders. The mission was informed that the border authorities of most countries lacked human capacity and modern logistical capabilities. Furthermore, a large number of returnees came without proper identification, and there were also difficulties with the control of the massive and frequent movement of cross-border workers. On police and judicial cooperation, participants noted the lack of national coordination and liaison mechanisms for combating transnational organized crime and terrorism. Without such mechanisms, it would be challenging for countries to address the impact of the Libyan crisis, including the increase in armed violence. Officials from the Ministry of Justice in Mali stressed the need to strengthen regional judicial cooperation, for example, through the regional judicial platform for Sahel countries which was being developed between Burkina Faso, Mali, Mauritania, and the Niger with the support of the United Nations Office on Drugs and Crime (UNODC).

The mission, while noting the determination of the region's Governments to address the challenges before them, particularly the threat posed by Al-Qaida in the Islamic Maghreb, Boko Haram and other criminal groups, as well as the proliferation of weapons, stated that national and regional capacities varied and were limited overall. Most countries could not address the threats in isolation, and while regional mechanisms had been established, they lacked the means to adequately implement their tasks. The mission outlined four main recommendations. At the national level, support was needed to build the capacity of Government initiatives to address immediate crises and to increase the coherence of UN country teams for implementing humanitarian and development programmes. It was necessary to strengthen regional mechanisms and to bolster border control and information-sharing on cross-border activities. At the international level, the United Nations should mobilize greater international support for the Sahel region to address the challenges of human insecurity and underdevelopment. In addition, an overarching framework should be established to bring together all affected countries in an integrated manner to discuss and propose solutions.

Piracy and armed robbery

In his December report on developments in West Africa [S/2011/811] (see p. 134), the Secretary-General provided information on maritime piracy in the Gulf of Guinea. In response to a 27 July request by President Boni Yayi of Benin for assistance from the international community, the Secretary-General's Special Representative for West Africa travelled to Benin to engage with national authorities. In November, the Secretary-General deployed an assessment mission to Benin and the Gulf of Guinea (see p. 138).

Security Council statement (August). On 30 August, following a briefing by the Under-Secretary-General for Political Affairs, B. Lynn Pascoe, the Security Council, by a press statement [SC/10372], expressed concern over the increase in piracy, maritime armed robbery and reports of hostage-taking in the Gulf of Guinea and their damaging impact on security, trade and economic activities. The Council underlined the need for regional coordination and leadership to develop a strategy to address the threat; called on the international community to support securing international navigation along the Gulf of Guinea; and stressed the need for UNOWA and the United Nations Office for Central Africa to work with UNODC and the International Maritime Organization, as well as with concerned countries and regional organizations.

Security Council consideration. On 19 October [S/PV.6633], the Council held an open debate on piracy in the Gulf of Guinea, which was guided by a concept note [S/2011/644] prepared by Nigeria. Briefing the Council, the Secretary-General said that new cases of piracy and armed robbery aboard vessels along the West African coast were being regularly reported, with significant potential consequences for economic development and security. The threat was compounded by the limited capacity of most Gulf States to ensure safe maritime trade, freedom of navigation, protection of marine resources, and safety and security of lives and property. He was encouraged by the initiatives taken by ECOWAS and the Economic Community of Central African States (ECCAS) to coordinate regional responses, and urged the two organizations to work together to develop a comprehensive strategy, in close cooperation with the Commission of the Gulf of Guinea and the Maritime Organization of West and Central Africa. The recent deployment of naval vessels to support anti-piracy operations in the Gulf of Guinea attested to the readiness of States in the region to address the threat, and he called upon other Member States to join those efforts. The ECOWAS Commissioner for Political Affairs, Peace and Security and the Gulf of Guinea Commission's Deputy Executive Secretary for Political Affairs highlighted subregional initiatives to counter piracy.

SECURITY COUNCIL ACTION

On 31 October [meeting 6645], the Security Council unanimously adopted **resolution 2018(2011)**. The draft [S/2011/673] was submitted by France, Gabon, Germany, India, Lebanon, Nigeria, Portugal, South Africa, the United Kingdom and the United States.

The Security Council,

Expressing its deep concern about the threat that piracy and armed robbery at sea in the Gulf of Guinea pose to international navigation, security and the economic development of States in the region,

Recalling its statement to the press of 30 August 2011 on piracy and armed robbery at sea in the Gulf of Guinea,

Expressing its concern about the threat that piracy and armed robbery at sea pose to the safety of seafarers and other persons, including through their being taken as hostages, and deeply concerned by the violence employed by pirates and persons involved in piracy and armed robbery at sea in the Gulf of Guinea,

Affirming its respect for the sovereignty and territorial integrity of the States of the Gulf of Guinea and their neighbours,

Affirming that the provisions of the present resolution apply only with respect to the situation in the Gulf of Guinea,

Affirming also that international law, as reflected in the United Nations Convention on the Law of the Sea of 10 December 1982, in particular articles 100, 101 and 105 thereof, sets out the legal framework applicable to countering piracy and armed robbery at sea, as well as other ocean activities,

Noting that applicable international legal instruments provide for parties to create criminal offences, establish jurisdiction and prosecute or extradite for prosecution persons responsible for or suspected of seizing or exercising control over a ship or fixed platform by force or threat thereof or any other form of intimidation,

Emphasizing the importance of finding a comprehensive solution to the problem of piracy and armed robbery at sea in the Gulf of Guinea,

Noting the efforts of the States of the Gulf of Guinea to address this problem, including joint patrols at sea and the activities of Nigeria and Benin off the coast of Benin,

Noting also the need for international assistance as part of a comprehensive strategy to support national and regional efforts to assist States in the region with their efforts to address piracy and armed robbery at sea in the Gulf of Guinea,

Welcoming the contributions made by some Member States and international organizations in support of the maritime sector, including security, capacity-building and the joint operations of the States of the Gulf of Guinea,

Stressing that the coordination of efforts at the regional level is necessary for the development of a comprehensive strategy to counter the threat of piracy and armed robbery at sea in the Gulf of Guinea,

Noting that States in the region have a leadership role to play in this regard, supported by organizations in the region,

1. *Condemns* all acts of piracy and armed robbery at sea committed off the coast of the States of the Gulf of Guinea;

2. *Welcomes* the intention to convene a summit of Gulf of Guinea Heads of State in order to consider a comprehensive response in the region, and encourages the States members of the Economic Community of West African States, the Economic Community of Central African States and the Gulf of Guinea Commission to develop a comprehensive strategy, including through:

(*a*) The development of domestic laws and regulations, where these are not in place, criminalizing piracy and armed robbery at sea;

(*b*) The development of a regional framework to counter piracy and armed robbery at sea, including information-sharing and operational coordination mechanisms in the region;

(*c*) The development and strengthening of domestic laws and regulations, as appropriate, to implement relevant international agreements addressing the safety and security of navigation, in accordance with international law;

3. *Encourages* the States members of the Economic Community of West African States, the Economic Community of Central African States and the Gulf of Guinea Commission, through concerted action, to counter piracy and armed robbery at sea in the Gulf of Guinea through the conduct of bilateral or regional maritime patrols consistent with relevant international law, and requests the States concerned to take appropriate steps to ensure that the activities they undertake pursuant to the present resolution do not have the practical effect of denying or impairing freedom of navigation on the high seas or the right of innocent passage in the territorial sea to vessels of third States;

4. *Calls upon* States, in cooperation with the shipping industry, the insurance industry and the International Maritime Organization, to issue to ships entitled to fly their flag appropriate advice and guidance, in the context of the Gulf of Guinea, on avoidance, evasion and defensive techniques and measures to take if under the threat of attack or attack when sailing in the waters of the Gulf of Guinea;

5. *Calls upon* the States members of the Economic Community of West African States, the Economic Community of Central African States and the Gulf of Guinea Commission, in conjunction with flag States and States of nationality of victims or of perpetrators of acts of piracy or armed robbery at sea, to cooperate in the prosecution of alleged perpetrators, including facilitators and financiers of acts of piracy and armed robbery at sea committed off the coast of the Gulf of Guinea, in accordance with applicable international law, including human rights law;

6. *Encourages* the international community to assist, upon request, the States concerned in the region, the Economic Community of West African States, the Economic Community of Central African States, the Gulf of Guinea Commission and other relevant organizations and agencies in strengthening their efforts to counter piracy and armed robbery at sea in the Gulf of Guinea;

7. *Welcomes* the intention of the Secretary-General to deploy a United Nations assessment mission to examine the threat of piracy and armed robbery at sea in the Gulf of Guinea and explore options on how best to address the problem, and looks forward to receiving the report of the mission, with recommendations on the matter;

8. *Decides* to remain seized of the matter.

Assessment mission on piracy

The Secretary-General dispatched an assessment mission to Benin, Nigeria, Gabon and Angola from 7 to 24 November, with the aim of assisting Benin to formulate a national programme to address drug trafficking, organized crime and piracy; assessing the scope of the threat of piracy in the Gulf of Guinea; and making recommendations for responses by the United Nations and the international community. A later report [S/2012/45] outlined the work of the mission, co-led by DPA and UNODC. In Benin (7–17 November), the mission met with President Yayi, senior Government officials, representatives of the nation's army, police, navy, port and judiciary institutions, and international partners. It assessed the scope of the threat of piracy; the impact of piracy on the nation's economy, the capacity of the country's legal framework to address the threat; and national, regional and international measures to help combat piracy. The mission also assessed the scope of drug trafficking and transnational organized crime, and the nation's legal framework to fight that threat. The report noted that Benin was one of the most vulnerable countries affected by piracy in the Gulf of Guinea, with 21 attacks in the waters off Benin in 2011, compared with none in 2010 and one in 2009. Benin lacked the capacity to effectively deter or pursue attackers, as pirates generally used more advanced equipment than those operated by the Benin navy. Officials acknowledged that corruption at ports was likely, and that attacks could not occur without the complicity of Benin nationals operating on land. Government efforts to combat piracy included investing in military, maritime and aviation assets to enhance maritime security capabilities, and the establishment of two national coordination mechanisms to address maritime security issues. Furthermore, on 28 September, Benin and Nigeria commenced a six-month joint patrol programme, Operation Prosperity, along Benin's coast. Since the start of the programme, the number of successful pirate attacks had fallen; however, the operation faced major constraints, including the absence of logistical support facilities for vessels conducting patrols.

The mission made several recommendations, including that the Government adopt a national maritime security strategy; establish an interdepartmental national maritime security committee to serve as the main national interlocutor; review the country's legal framework to enable it to effectively prosecute piracy and armed robbery at sea and counter unlawful acts against the security of maritime navigation, port facilities and offshore platforms; make use of the system, tools and services of the International Criminal Police Organization (INTERPOL), utilize existing networks, and coordinate with international bodies to support law enforcement regarding crimes committed at sea; and develop a national maritime security plan that identified current capabilities, gaps, and requirements for maritime security sector governance and reform. International partners should provide funding and support to ensure the presence of adequate patrols off the coast of Benin. The United Nations should help coordinate international assistance in support of Benin's efforts to combat piracy, and assist the country in developing legislation to bring international maritime instruments into national law, as well as a national programme to fight piracy, drug trafficking and organized crime.

The mission subsequently travelled to Nigeria (18–19 November), Gabon (20–22 November) and Angola (23–24 November) to meet with ECOWAS, ECCAS and the Gulf of Guinea Commission, respectively, as well as with national authorities in the three countries. The report noted that no country appeared to have the capacity to tackle maritime security alone, with many pirate attacks occurring beyond national territorial waters. Furthermore, piracy also affected hinterland and landlocked countries, which depended on the sea for exports and imports. The mission also assessed anti-piracy efforts by Central African States and West African States, as well as collective regional concerns on the issue. Regional interlocutors called for the United Nations to play a facilitation and coordination role regarding piracy, particularly in mobilizing leaders, countries and organizations of West and Central Africa towards a joint maritime security framework in the Gulf of Guinea. All interlocutors highlighted the need to involve the AU in any initiative related to maritime security on the continent, as well as the participation of hinterland countries in any regional maritime security strategy. The report also highlighted several joint regional requirements to fight piracy, in particular, a collective surveillance system; a sustainable process for funding maritime security and safety activities; a formal system for information-sharing; and adequate legal frameworks.

The mission made several recommendations for regional stakeholders, international partners and the United Nations. The regional summit of Gulf of Guinea Heads of State, supported by the Security Council in resolution 2018(2011) (see p. 137), should be convened as early as possible in 2012, with a view to developing a regional strategy to combat piracy. ECOWAS, ECCAS, the Gulf of Guinea Commission and regional States should closely coordinate with the AU on efforts to tackle the piracy threat, and ECOWAS and ECCAS member States should consider initiating and intensifying joint patrols at sea. West and Central African States should develop land-based patrolling, surveillance and information-gathering systems, and law enforcement agencies of ECOWAS and ECCAS member States should take steps to be connected to regional and international networks for combating organized crime, including activities at sea. International partners should provide logistical support to ECOWAS and ECCAS to improve their capabilities to counter piracy, particularly relating to infrastructure, radar, communications equipment and the training of maritime security personnel. As requested by the three regional organizations, the United Nations should help mobilize resources to assist in building capacities and in coordinating international assistance for maritime security in the Gulf of Guinea.

UNOWA

Activities

During the year, UNOWA activities, covered in the Secretary-General's reports [S/2011/388, S/2011/811], focused on raising awareness on emerging threats and challenges to regional peace and stability; carrying out good offices and special assignments for conflict prevention; enhancing the subregion's capacity to address threats to peace and security, including with regard to elections and stability, security sector reform, drug trafficking and cross-border organized crime, and maritime piracy; promoting good governance, the rule of law, human rights and gender mainstreaming; cooperating with UN entities and with regional and subregional partners; and assisting the Cameroon-Nigeria Mixed Commission (see p. 186). The Office was headed by the Special Representative of the Secretary-General for West Africa, Said Djinnit, who briefed the Security Council on the Office's activities on 8 July [S/PV.6577].

In light of the growing cross-border challenges to peace and security, UNOWA undertook various joint initiatives with UN peace missions, UN country teams, the Office of the United Nations High Commissioner for Human Rights and the Peacebuilding Commission. During the year, the Secretary-General's Special Representative convened the eighth and ninth meetings of the regional directors and heads of UN agencies based in Dakar, Senegal, the host city of UNOWA. Participants agreed to develop a subregional strategy to address the threats of mercenaries, cross-border movements of weapons and armed groups, and illicit trafficking, as well as to work together to enhance UN efforts in the Sahel region. Meetings of the heads of the UN peace missions in West Africa were held in Dakar on 28 February, 28 May and 28 November, providing a framework to further harmonize action for promoting stability. UNOWA also collaborated with ECOWAS to strengthen regional capacities, particularly in conflict management and prevention.

As election-related tensions and violence continued, UNOWA convened a high-level regional conference on elections and stability (Praia, Cape Verde, 18–20 May) to draw lessons from electoral processes and analyse their implications for crisis prevention and peacebuilding. The conference adopted the Praia Declaration on Elections and Stability in West Africa, which stressed the need to harmonize the normative and institutional arrangements for governing elections at the regional level. In follow-up to that conference, UNOWA and the International Peace Institute organized a round table (New York, 26 September) during which representatives of the ECOWAS Commission, delegates from UN Member States and election practitioners discussed ways to improve the conduct of electoral processes and the provision of international assistance to prevent election-related violence.

Regarding security sector reform, UNOWA cooperated closely with ECOWAS in the context of implementing its political framework and its plan of action on security sector governance and reform. Efforts focused on supporting such reform in Guinea, including the national seminar on security sector reform (Conakry, Guinea, 28–31 March) organized by the Government, which resulted in the launch of the National Security Sector Reform Steering Committee on 20 June. In response to President Alpha Condé's request for UN support in coordinating the country's security sector reform activities, the Secretary-General deployed a senior security sector reform adviser to Guinea to work closely with the UN country team.

UNOWA, UNODC, DPKO and INTERPOL continued to implement the West Africa Coast Initiative in Guinea-Bissau, Liberia and Sierra Leone, which aimed to support the ECOWAS regional action plan to address illicit drug trafficking, organized crime and drug abuse. UNOWA also advocated for national and international political support for the fight against drug trafficking and transnational organized crime.

UNOWA hosted the sixth consultative meeting of Heads of United Nations human rights offices in West Africa (16–17 March), which focused on human rights in electoral processes, the fight against impunity, and gender and human rights. The Office facilitated the activities of the Working Group on Women, Peace and Security in West Africa in the context of implementing Security Council resolutions 1325(2000) [YUN 2000, p. 1113] and 1820(2008) [YUN 2008, p. 1265]. Furthermore, in collaboration with ECOWAS and Guinea, the Office organized a round table (Conakry, 15 April) on the implementation of those resolutions in the 16 countries of the subregion.

Financing

In an October report [A/66/354/Add.3] on estimates in respect of special political missions, good offices and other political initiatives authorized by the General Assembly and/or the Security Council, the Secretary-General proposed resource requirements for UNOWA in the amount of $8,857,500 for 2012. In its related report [A/66/7/Add.12], ACABQ recommended a reduction in that amount, arguing that the mandate of the Office could be effectively carried out without adding two new international posts.

On 24 December, in section IX of **resolution 66/247** (see p. 1393), the Assembly took note of the ACABQ recommendation and approved the resource requirements for UNOWA.

Côte d'Ivoire

In 2011, the political, security and humanitarian situation in Côte d'Ivoire deteriorated following the second round of the presidential elections in November 2010. Diplomatic efforts continued with the aim of finding a peaceful solution to the crisis, including several visits by leaders of the region to hold talks with President Alassane Ouattara and former President Laurent Gbagbo. The Secretary-General dispatched his Special Representative for West Africa and his Principal Deputy Special Representative for Côte d'Ivoire to various African capitals. The AU Peace and Security Council established a High-level Panel to evaluate the situation and propose a political solution to the crisis. The security situation was characterised by escalating violence between forces loyal to Mr. Gbagbo and supporters of President Ouattara, resulting in significant civilian casualties and displacements throughout the country. Consequently, the United Nations Operation in Côte d'Ivoire (UNOCI) adjusted its posture and increased patrols in areas where civilians were under threat. UNOCI also faced direct threats from forces loyal Mr. Gbagbo, and in response the Security Council adopted several resolutions on the composition of the mission, including the temporary redeployment of personnel and capability from the United Nations Mission in Liberia (UNMIL) to UNOCI to provide it with the capacity to meet security challenges. Following the apprehension of Mr. Gbagbo in April, President Ouattara was sworn in on 6 May, and announced his new Government on 1 June. In May, the Secretary-General dispatched an assessment mission to Côte d'Ivoire, which recommended several areas where the United Nations should focus its efforts to support the Government with a view to stabilizing the security situation, preventing a relapse into conflict, and creating space for the Government to regain lost capacity. Subsequently, in July, the Council extended the mandate of UNOCI to 31 July 2012 and outlined the priorities of such mandate. The country's legislative elections were held in a generally calm and peaceful manner on 11 December, with the provisional results giving the winning Rassemblement des républicains party of President Ouattara 127 seats. The Secretary-General's Special Representative welcomed the peaceful conduct of the electoral campaign.

Political and security developments

Post-electoral situation

The political, security and humanitarian situation continued to deteriorate following the outcome of the second round of the presidential election in December 2010 [YUN 2010, p. 191]. Pursuant to Security Council resolution 1962(2010) [ibid., p. 193], the Secretary-General reported [S/2011/211] on the situation on the ground, noting that diplomatic efforts aimed at finding a peaceful solution to the crisis continued. On 3 January, the Presidents of Benin, Cape Verde and Sierra Leone visited Abidjan, Côte d'Ivoire, together with Kenyan Prime Minister Raila Odinga in his capacity as the Special Envoy of the AU to Côte d'Ivoire. The delegation issued a communiqué on 4 January, announcing that it had met with President Ouattara and Mr. Gbagbo. President Ouattara had indicated a willingness to ensure a dignified exit for Mr. Gbagbo, provided that he accepted the election outcome as announced by the Independent Electoral Commission. Further efforts to hold talks with President Ouattara and Mr. Gbagbo were undertaken, including visits to the country by former Nigerian President Olusegun Obasanjo, on behalf of ECOWAS (9–10 January); the AU Special Envoy (17 January); and the outgoing Chair of the AU, President Bingu Wa Mutharika of Malawi (25 January). The Secretary-General maintained contact with key African leaders to encourage them in their efforts, and dispatched his Special Representative for West Africa and his Principal Deputy Special Representative for Côte d'Ivoire to various African capitals to further clarify the role of the United Nations in the Ivorian elections, including certification. From 18 to 25 January, they visited Angola, Burkina Faso, the Gambia, Ghana, Mali and South Africa. The security situation was characterised by escalating violence, with forces loyal to Mr. Gbagbo continuing to use disproportionate force against supporters of President Ouattara. The Forces de défense et de sécurité (FDS) raided the headquarters of the Parti démocratique de Côte d'Ivoire on 4 January, resulting in one death, and conducted further raids in Abidjan on 11 January, killing at least three civilians.

Letter of Secretary-General. The Secretary-General, in a letter of 7 January [S/2011/5] to the Security Council, stated that, following the Council's decisions in 2010 to reinforce UNOCI during the first and second rounds of the presidential election in resolutions 1942(2010) [YUN 2010, p. 189], 1951(2010) [ibid., p. 192] and 1962(2010), the security situation continued to deteriorate and the stalemate remained unresolved. New challenges had emerged, and UNOCI was operating in an openly hostile security environment with direct threats from regular and irregular forces loyal to former President Gbagbo. Logistical threats to the mission included denying customs clearance for vital life-support supplies at the port; instructing vendors not to sell fuel and supplies to UNOCI and its personnel; and obstructing the delivery of supplies to UNOCI personnel and sites through roadblocks and other means. UNOCI had sought to reinforce its troops and police in Abidjan by redeploying more troops and police from the north and east; however, that left the mission unable to respond to any deterioration in the security situation in other areas, particularly in the west. The mission required additional capacity, and the assets deployed from UNMIL to UNOCI remained essential. The Secretary-General requested that the Council authorize several measures to provide the mission with the capacity to meet challenges relating to protecting United Nations personnel and installations; protecting the delivery of vital supplies; deterring threats from forces loyal to Mr. Gbagbo; enhancing the mission's ability to address obstruction and the denial of access; and protecting civilians. The proposed measures would entail an increase, through the end of the mandate period, of 2,000 military personnel in addition to the temporary military and police capabilities from UNMIL authorized in Council resolutions 1942(2010) and 1951(2010). Also proposed were the deployment, on a temporary basis, of three Mi-24 armed helicopters with crews (approximately 200 personnel) from UNMIL to UNOCI; and the extension beyond January of the temporary transfer of the two military utility helicopters from UNMIL to UNOCI.

Security Council press statement (January). In a 10 January press statement [SC/10149], following a 5 January briefing on the situation in Côte d'Ivoire by the Under-Secretary-General for Peacekeeping Operations, Alain Le Roy, the Council expressed concern over continued violence and human rights violations in Côte d'Ivoire, including against United Nations peacekeepers; condemned deliberate attempts to impede UNOCI from fulfilling its mandate; demanded a halt to the use of media to propagate false information to incite hatred and violence, including against the United Nations; demanded that all parties allow for the complete freedom of movement of UNOCI; and urged Mr. Gbagbo to lift the blockade around the Golf Hotel, the temporary seat of President Ouattara's Government.

SECURITY COUNCIL ACTION

On 19 January [meeting 6469], the Security Council unanimously adopted **resolution 1967(2011)**. The draft [S/2011/15] was submitted by Bosnia and Herzegovina, France, Gabon, Germany, Lebanon, Nigeria, South Africa, the United Kingdom and the United States.

The Security Council,

Recalling its previous resolutions, in particular resolutions 1933(2010) of 30 June 2010, 1942(2010) of 29 September 2010, 1946(2010) of 15 October 2010, 1951(2010) of 24 November 2010 and 1962(2010) of 20 December 2010, and the statements by its President relating to the situation in Côte d'Ivoire and in the subregion,

Recalling also the letter dated 7 January 2011 from the Secretary-General to the President of the Security Council, in which the Secretary-General recommended the temporary deployment of an additional 2,000 military personnel to the United Nations Operation in Côte d'Ivoire, until 30 June 2011, in addition to the temporary military and police capabilities authorized by resolution 1942(2010),

Recalling further the inter-mission cooperation arrangements provided for in paragraphs 4 to 6 of its resolution 1609(2005) of 24 June 2005 and in paragraph 6 of its resolution 1938(2010) of 15 September 2010, and recalling paragraph 7 of resolution 1962(2010) and its intention to consider authorizing the Secretary-General to redeploy further troops, as may be needed, between the United Nations Mission in Liberia and the United Nations Operation in Côte d'Ivoire on a temporary basis,

Commending the initiatives of the Secretary-General, and reaffirming its full support for his Special Representative for Côte d'Ivoire in carrying out his mandate in view of resolving the situation peacefully,

Expressing deep concern over the continued violence and human rights violations in Côte d'Ivoire, including against United Nations peacekeepers and civilians, and stressing that those responsible for crimes against United Nations personnel and civilians must be held accountable,

Acting under Chapter VII of the Charter of the United Nations,

1. *Decides* to authorize, as recommended by the Secretary-General in his letter dated 7 January 2011 to the President of the Security Council, the deployment of an additional 2,000 military personnel to the United Nations Operation in Côte d'Ivoire until 30 June 2011;

2. *Decides also* to authorize, as recommended by the Secretary-General in his letter dated 7 January 2011, the extension, until 30 June 2011, of the temporary additional military and police capabilities authorized by resolution 1942(2010);

3. *Decides further* to authorize the Secretary-General, further to resolution 1951(2010) and paragraph 6 of resolution 1962(2010), to extend by up to four additional weeks the temporary redeployment from the United Nations Mission in Liberia to the United Nations Operation in Côte d'Ivoire of 3 infantry companies and 1 aviation unit comprising 2 military utility helicopters;

4. *Decides* to authorize the transfer, on a temporary basis and pursuant to paragraphs 4 and 6 of resolution 1609(2005), of 3 armed helicopters with crews from the United Nations Mission in Liberia to the United Nations Operation in Côte d'Ivoire for a period of four weeks, as recommended by the Secretary-General in his letter dated 7 January 2011, and requests the Secretary-General to keep the Council informed of efforts made in this regard;

5. *Decides also* to authorize the deployment of 60 formed police unit personnel to meet threats posed by unarmed crowds, as recommended by the Secretary-General in his letter dated 7 January 2011, who will replace 60 United Nations police officers;

6. *Requests* the Secretary-General to include a review of the temporary personnel deployments as set out in paragraphs 1, 2 and 5 above in his midterm review, due no later than 31 March 2011;

7. *Decides* to authorize the immediate deployment of the additional capacities as set out in paragraphs 1, 4 and 5 above, and requests the support of troop- and police-contributing countries in that regard;

8. *Reiterates its authorization and its full support* given to the Special Representative of the Secretary-General for Côte d'Ivoire to use all means necessary to carry out the mandate of the United Nations Operation in Côte d'Ivoire, including protection of civilians, and to ensure its freedom of movement, within its capabilities and its areas of deployment;

9. *Demands* that all parties abide scrupulously by their obligation to respect the safety of the United Nations Operation in Côte d'Ivoire and other United Nations personnel and ensure that the freedom of movement of the United Nations Operation in Côte d'Ivoire and the French forces supporting it is fully respected, with unhindered and immediate access throughout the territory of Côte d'Ivoire, including to all the administrative and State bodies, and further urges that the ongoing blockade around the Golf Hotel be lifted without delay;

10. *Demands also*, without prejudice to freedom of expression, an immediate halt to the use of media, especially Radiodiffusion Télévision Ivoirienne, to propagate false information and to incite hatred and violence, including against the United Nations and particularly the United Nations Operation in Côte d'Ivoire;

11. *Reiterates its readiness* to impose measures, including targeted sanctions against those who obstruct the work of the United Nations Operation in Côte d'Ivoire, as underlined in resolutions 1946(2010) and 1962(2010);

12. *Decides* to remain actively seized of the matter.

On 16 February [meeting 6482], the Security Council unanimously adopted **resolution 1968(2011)**. The draft [S/2011/75] was submitted by France.

The Security Council,

Recalling its previous resolutions, in particular resolutions 1933(2010) of 30 June 2010, 1942(2010) of 29 September 2010, 1946(2010) of 15 October 2010, 1951(2010) of 24 November 2010, 1962(2010) of 20 December 2010 and 1967(2011) of 19 January 2011, and the statements by its President relating to the situation in Côte d'Ivoire and in the subregion,

Recalling also the inter-mission cooperation arrangements provided for in paragraphs 4 to 6 of its resolution 1609(2005) of 24 June 2005 and in paragraph 6 of its resolution 1938(2010) of 15 September 2010, and recalling further paragraph 7 of resolution 1962(2010) and paragraphs 3 and 4 of resolution 1967(2011),

Recalling its intention to consider authorizing the Secretary-General to redeploy further troops, as may be needed, between the United Nations Mission in Liberia and the United Nations Operation in Côte d'Ivoire on a temporary basis, and mindful of the need to support the ability of the United Nations Mission in Liberia to carry out its mandate,

Recalling the letter dated 7 January 2011 from the Secretary-General to the President of the Security Council stressing the essential role played by the assets deployed from the United Nations Mission in Liberia to the United Nations Operation in Côte d'Ivoire in the current challenging circumstances in Côte d'Ivoire,

Reaffirming its full support to the Special Representative of the Secretary-General for Côte d'Ivoire in carrying out his mandate,

Acting under Chapter VII of the Charter of the United Nations,

1. *Decides* to authorize the Secretary-General, further to paragraphs 4 and 6 of resolution 1609(2005), resolution 1951(2010), paragraph 6 of resolution 1962(2010) and paragraphs 3 and 4 of resolution 1967(2011), to extend for up to three months the temporary redeployment from the United Nations Mission in Liberia to the United Nations Operation in Côte d'Ivoire of 3 infantry companies, 1 aviation unit comprising 2 military utility helicopters and 3 armed helicopters with crews;

2. *Requests* the support of troop- and police-contributing countries in that regard;

3. *Decides* to remain actively seized of the matter.

Letter of Secretary-General. On 23 February [S/2011/89], the Secretary-General informed the Council that the three Pakistani infantry companies transferred from UNMIL on temporary redeployment had returned to Liberia. The Secretariat was generating additional capacities for UNOCI, approved under Council resolution 1967(2011) (see p. 141), to replace those infantry companies. Furthermore, pursuant to paragraph 4 of that resolution, Ukraine consented to the temporary transfer from UNMIL to UNOCI of three armed helicopters with crew. The Secretary-General reported [S/2011/211] that those helicopters arrived in the country on 1 and 21 March.

Report of Secretary-General (March). In a March report [S/2011/211], submitted pursuant to Council resolution 1962(2010), the Secretary-General described the security situation in the first quarter of the year, as violence continued between forces loyal to Mr. Gbagbo and supporters of President Ouattara. On 19 February, President Ouattara called for further protests by his supporters to demand that Mr. Gbagbo step down. In response, forces loyal to Mr. Gbagbo used excessive force, including heavy weapons, to disperse protesters in Abidjan, Yamoussoukro and Daoukro, resulting in significant civilian fatalities and displacements from the affected neighbourhoods in Abidjan. In the latter part of February, President Ouattara's supporters in Abidjan reportedly became more organized and were reinforced by some elements of the rebel movement Forces nouvelles and individuals who had defected from FDS. Meanwhile, forces loyal to Mr. Gbagbo were reinforced by foreign mercenaries, with some accounts stating that the administration loyal to Mr. Gbagbo had hired an estimated 4,500 mercenaries, the majority of whom were deployed in Abidjan, San-Pédro and Yamoussoukro and along the former zone of confidence [YUN

2007, p. 169], including in Danané, Douékoué, Daloa and Tiébissou. Following a call in February by the leader of the Young Patriots, Blé Goudé, to identify "foreigners" throughout the country, there were reports of attacks targeting nationals of West African countries, with some abducted or burned alive. Foreign-owned businesses in Abidjan were vandalized and looted.

The situation escalated further in March, with violent incidents reported throughout the country. On 3 March in Abobo, supporters of Mr. Gbagbo used heavy weapons against a group of women demonstrating peacefully in support of President Ouattara, killing seven and seriously wounding many others. At a demonstration in Treichville on 8 March by women commemorating the dead, at least four persons were killed when clashes broke out between security forces loyal to Mr. Gbagbo and armed individuals supporting President Ouattara. On 7 March, in Anonkoua-Kouté, the Ebrié ethnic community, thought to support Mr. Gbagbo, was attacked by armed individuals who were allegedly partisans of the anti-Gbagbo group the "invisible commandos", displacing most of the approximately 5,000 inhabitants. Meanwhile, direct armed confrontations between FDS elements loyal to Mr. Gbagbo and the Forces nouvelles were reported in the country's western and central regions, in violation of the comprehensive ceasefire agreement of 2003 [YUN 2003, p. 177], with both sides reportedly using heavy weapons. In response to the deteriorating security situation, UNOCI increased patrols in areas where civilians were under threat. The Operation also devised a mixed-patrol mechanism, which included troops and formed police unit personnel with crowd control capabilities, to better respond to emerging security threats.

Security Council statement (March). On 3 March [SC/10191], following a briefing by the Under-Secretary-General for Peacekeeping Operations, the Security Council expressed concern about the risk of resurgence of civil war, urging all parties to show restraint and to resolve their differences peacefully. The Council urged UNOCI to use all necessary means to carry out its mandate, in particular to protect civilians and to monitor compliance by all parties with the 2003 ceasefire agreement.

High-level Panel on Côte d'Ivoire. The AU Peace and Security Council, on 28 January, established a High-level Panel on Côte d'Ivoire, supported by a team of experts, to evaluate the overall situation in the country and propose a political solution to the crisis. The Panel would report to the Peace and Security Council, and the Council's decisions would be binding. The Secretary-General supported the establishment of the Panel, and, as agreed with the AU, designated his Special Representative for West Africa to participate in the work of the team of experts, which comprised the Presidents of Burkina Faso, Chad, Mauritania, South Africa and the United Republic of Tanzania. The experts conducted a fact-finding mission to the country (6–10 February), during which they sought the views of President Ouattara and Mr. Gbagbo, and consulted with Ivorian stakeholders including Prime Minister Guillaume Soro, representatives of the Independent Electoral Commission, the President of the Constitutional Council, and representatives of political parties, civil society, UNOCI and the diplomatic community. The experts, together with the Chair of the AU Commission and the AU Commissioner for Peace and Security, travelled to Abidjan from 21 to 22 February and met with President Ouattara, Mr. Gbagbo and the President of the Constitutional Council. The Panel, on 9 March, held separate meetings with President Ouattara and Mr. Gbagbo's representatives, during which it proposed a solution to the crisis, which was consistent with the previous decisions of ECOWAS and the AU, and recognized Mr. Ouattara as President-elect. Mr. Gbagbo's representatives, however, declared that they would never accept a proposal that entailed his stepping down, and insisted that he was the nation's elected leader.

On 10 March, the AU Peace and Security Council met at the level of Heads of State to receive a briefing from the Panel on its recommendations. Following the meeting, the Council issued a communiqué in which it recognized Mr. Ouattara as President, endorsed the Panel's recommendations, and requested the Chair of the AU Commission to appoint a high representative for the implementation of those recommendations. While President Ouattara expressed his satisfaction, Mr. Gbagbo's representatives rejected the binding decision. President Ouattara addressed the nation on 15 March, reiterating his acceptance of the Panel's recommendations regarding the formation of a Government of national unity, the continuation of reforms set out in the Ouagadougou Political Agreement [YUN 2007, p. 175], and the holding of legislative elections. He called upon Mr. Gbagbo, the Constitutional Council and the army to accept the opportunity provided by the AU to end the crisis. On 23 March, the Secretary-General transmitted to the Security Council the communiqué of the AU Peace and Security Council meeting, as well as the report of the Panel [S/2011/180].

Communications. In a letter of 24 March [S/2011/182], Nigeria transmitted to the Council a resolution of the same date of the Authority of Heads of State and Government of ECOWAS on the situation in Côte d'Ivoire, adopted at its thirty-ninth summit (Abuja, Nigeria, 23–24 March). On 28 March [S/2011/200], the Secretary-General transmitted to the Council that same resolution, conveyed in a letter from the President of the Commission of ECOWAS. In its resolution, the Authority stated that the time had come to enforce its decisions of December 2010 [YUN 2010, p. 191] in order to protect life and ensure the transfer of the reins of power to President Ouattara. To that end, it requested the Security Council to authorize the implementation of those decisions; strengthen the mandate of UNOCI to enable it to use all necessary means to protect life and property, and facilitate the immediate transfer of power to President Ouattara; and adopt more stringent international targeted sanctions against Mr. Gbagbo and his associates.

SECURITY COUNCIL ACTION

On 30 March [meeting 6508], the Security Council unanimously adopted **resolution 1975(2011)**. The draft [S/2011/202] was submitted by France and Nigeria.

The Security Council,

Recalling its previous resolutions, in particular resolutions 1572(2004) of 15 November 2004, 1893(2009) of 29 October 2009, 1911(2010) of 28 January 2010, 1924(2010) of 27 May 2010, 1933(2010) of 30 June 2010, 1942(2010) of 29 September 2010, 1946(2010) of 15 October 2010, 1951(2010) of 24 November 2010, 1962(2010) of 20 December 2010, 1967(2011) of 19 January 2011 and 1968(2011) of 16 February 2011, and the statements by its President relating to the situation in Côte d'Ivoire, and its resolution 1938(2010) of 15 September 2010 on the situation in Liberia,

Reaffirming its strong commitment to the sovereignty, independence, territorial integrity and unity of Côte d'Ivoire, and recalling the importance of the principles of good-neighbourliness, non-interference and regional cooperation,

Reiterating its strong desire that the post-electoral crisis in Côte d'Ivoire be resolved peacefully and that it requires an overall political solution that preserves democracy and peace and promotes lasting reconciliation among all Ivorians,

Commending the constructive efforts of the African Union High-Level Panel for the Resolution of the Crisis in Côte d'Ivoire, and reiterating its support for the African Union and the Economic Community of West African States for their commitment to resolve the crisis in Côte d'Ivoire,

Welcoming the decision of the Peace and Security Council of the African Union adopted at its two hundred and sixty-fifth meeting, held at the level of Heads of State and Government in Addis Ababa on 10 March 2011, which reaffirms all its previous decisions on the rapidly deteriorating post-electoral crisis facing Côte d'Ivoire since the second round of the presidential election, on 28 November 2010, which recognize the election of Mr. Alassane Dramane Ouattara as the President of Côte d'Ivoire,

Welcoming also the political initiatives and noting the communiqué and the resolution on Côte d'Ivoire adopted by the Authority of Heads of State and Government of the Economic Community of West African States on 24 March 2011,

Expressing grave concern about the recent escalation of violence in Côte d'Ivoire and the risk of relapse into civil war, and urging all parties to show utmost restraint to prevent such outcome and to resolve their differences peacefully,

Condemning unequivocally all provocative action and statements that constitute incitement to discrimination, hostility, hatred and violence made by any party,

Condemning the serious abuses and violations of international law in Côte d'Ivoire, including humanitarian, human rights and refugee law, reaffirming the primary responsibility of each State to protect civilians, and reiterating that parties to armed conflicts bear the primary responsibility to take all feasible steps to ensure the protection of civilians and facilitate the rapid and unimpeded passage of humanitarian assistance and the safety of humanitarian personnel, recalling its resolutions 1325(2000) of 31 October 2000, 1820(2008) of 19 June 2008, 1888(2009) of 30 September 2009 and 1889(2009) of 5 October 2009 on women and peace and security, its resolutions 1612(2005) of 26 July 2005 and 1882(2009) of 4 August 2009 on children and armed conflict and its resolutions 1674(2006) of 28 April 2006 and 1894(2009) of 11 November 2009 on the protection of civilians in armed conflict,

Welcoming Human Rights Council resolution 16/25 of 25 March 2011, including the decision to dispatch an independent international commission of inquiry to investigate the facts and circumstances surrounding the allegations of serious abuses and violations of human rights committed in Côte d'Ivoire following the presidential election of 28 November 2010,

Stressing that those responsible for such serious abuses and violations, including by forces under their control, must be held accountable,

Reaffirming that it is the responsibility of Côte d'Ivoire to promote and protect all human rights and fundamental freedoms, to investigate alleged violations of human rights and international law and to bring to justice those responsible for such acts,

Considering that the attacks currently taking place in Côte d'Ivoire against the civilian population could amount to crimes against humanity and that perpetrators of such crimes must be held accountable under international law, and noting that the International Criminal Court may decide on its jurisdiction over the situation in Côte d'Ivoire on the basis of article 12, paragraph 3, of the Rome Statute of the Court,

Determining that the situation in Côte d'Ivoire continues to constitute a threat to international peace and security,

Acting under Chapter VII of the Charter of the United Nations,

1. *Urges* all the Ivorian parties and other stakeholders to respect the will of the people and the election of Mr. Alassane Dramane Ouattara as President of Côte d'Ivoire, as recognized by the Economic Community of West African States, the African Union and the rest of the international community, expresses its concern at the recent escalation of violence, and demands an immediate end to the violence against civilians, including women, children and internally displaced persons;

2. *Calls upon* all parties to pursue the overall political solution of the African Union, and in this regard welcomes the decision of the Peace and Security Council of the African Union, taken at its summit of 10 March 2011, to appoint a High Representative for the implementation of

the overall political solution, and calls upon all parties to fully cooperate with him;

3. *Condemns* the decision of Mr. Laurent Gbagbo not to accept the overall political solution proposed by the High-Level Panel for the Resolution of the Crisis in Côte d'Ivoire put in place by the African Union, and urges him to immediately step aside;

4. *Urges* all Ivorian State institutions, including the Defence and Security Forces of Côte d'Ivoire, to yield to the authority vested by the Ivorian people in President Alassane Dramane Ouattara, condemns the attacks, threats, and acts of obstruction and violence perpetrated by the Defence and Security Forces, militias and mercenaries against United Nations personnel, obstructing them from protecting civilians and monitoring and helping to investigate human rights violations and abuses, stresses that those responsible for such crimes under international law must be held accountable, and calls upon all parties, in particular Mr. Laurent Gbagbo's supporters and forces, to fully cooperate with the United Nations Operation in Côte d'Ivoire and to cease interfering with its activities in implementation of its mandate;

5. *Reiterates its firm condemnation* of all violence committed against civilians, including women, children, internally displaced persons and foreign nationals, and other violations and abuses of human rights, in particular enforced disappearances, extrajudicial killings, killing and maiming of children and rapes and other forms of sexual violence;

6. *Recalls its authorization and stresses its full support* given to the United Nations Operation in Côte d'Ivoire, while impartially implementing its mandate, to use all means necessary to carry out its mandate to protect civilians under imminent threat of physical violence, within its capabilities and its areas of deployment, including to prevent the use of heavy weapons against the civilian population, and requests the Secretary-General to keep it urgently informed of measures taken and efforts made in this regard;

7. *Calls upon* all parties to cooperate fully in the operation of the United Nations Operation in Côte d'Ivoire and the French forces supporting it, in particular by guaranteeing their safety, security and freedom of movement, with unhindered and immediate access throughout the territory of Côte d'Ivoire, to enable them to fully carry out their mandate;

8. *Also calls upon* all parties to fully cooperate with the independent international commission of inquiry put in place by the Human Rights Council on 25 March 2011 to investigate the facts and circumstances surrounding the allegations of serious abuses and violations of human rights committed in Côte d'Ivoire following the presidential election of 28 November 2010, and requests the Secretary-General to transmit this report to the Security Council and other relevant international bodies;

9. *Condemns* the use of Radiodiffusion Télévision Ivoirienne and other media to incite discrimination, hostility, hatred and violence, including against the United Nations Operation in Côte d'Ivoire, as well as acts of intimidation and violence against journalists, and calls for the lifting of all restrictions placed on the exercise of the right to freedom of expression in Côte d'Ivoire;

10. *Expresses deep concern* about the increasing number of internally displaced persons and Ivorian refugees, especially in Liberia, caused by the crisis in Côte d'Ivoire, and calls upon all Ivorian parties to cooperate fully with United Nations agencies and other actors working to enhance access to humanitarian aid to refugees and internally displaced persons;

11. *Reiterates its longstanding demand* that Mr. Laurent Gbagbo lift the siege of the Golf Hotel without delay;

12. *Decides* to adopt targeted sanctions against those individuals who meet the criteria set out in resolution 1572(2004) and subsequent resolutions, including those individuals who obstruct peace and reconciliation in Côte d'Ivoire, obstruct the work of the United Nations Operation in Côte d'Ivoire and other international actors in Côte d'Ivoire and commit serious violations of human rights and international humanitarian law, and decides, therefore, that the individuals listed in the annex to the present resolution shall be subject to the financial and travel measures imposed by paragraphs 9 and 11 of resolution 1572(2004), and reaffirms its intention to consider further measures, as appropriate, including targeted sanctions against media actors who meet the relevant sanctions criteria, including by publicly inciting hatred and violence;

13. *Decides also* to remain actively seized of the matter.

Annex
Targeted sanctions

1. Laurent Gbagbo
Date of birth: 31 May 1945
Place of birth: Gagnoa, Côte d'Ivoire
Former President of Côte d'Ivoire: obstruction of the peace and reconciliation process, rejection of the results of the presidential election.

2. Simone Gbagbo
Date of birth: 20 June 1949
Place of birth: Moossou, Grand-Bassam, Côte d'Ivoire
Chairperson of the Parliamentary Group of the Ivorian Popular Front (FPI): obstruction of the peace and reconciliation process, public incitement to hatred and violence.

3. Désiré Tagro
Passport number: PD–AE 065FH08
Date of birth: 27 January 1959
Place of birth: Issia, Côte d'Ivoire
Secretary-General in the so-called "presidency" of Mr. Gbagbo: participation in the illegitimate government of Mr. Gbagbo, obstruction of the peace and reconciliation process, rejection of the results of the presidential election, participation in violent repressions of popular movements.

4. Pascal Affi N'Guessan
Passport number: PD–AE 09DD00013
Date of birth: 1 January 1953
Place of birth: Bouadriko, Côte d'Ivoire
Chairman of the Ivorian Popular Front (FPI): obstruction of the peace and reconciliation process, incitement to hatred and violence.

5. Alcide Djédjé
Date of birth: 20 October 1956
Place of birth: Abidjan, Côte d'Ivoire
Close advisor to Mr. Gbagbo: participation in the illegitimate government of Mr. Gbagbo, obstruction of the peace and reconciliation process, public incitement to hatred and violence.

Further developments

The Secretary-General reported [S/2011/387] that the situation in the country continued to deteriorate in late March and early April as Mr. Gbagbo continued to rebuff efforts to find a peaceful solution to the crisis. On 17 March, President Ouattara signed a decree unifying the Ivorian defence and security forces and the Forces nouvelles under one command, named the Forces républicaines de Côte d'Ivoire (FRCI). FCRI continued its military offensive towards Abidjan, capturing towns in the west, centre and east. The former FDS, including police and gendarmerie, fled in large numbers, with some joining the ranks of FRCI, while others surrendered or sought refuge in UNOCI camps. By 30 March, FRCI had encircled Abidjan. President Ouattara ordered the force to hold its positions outside the city, so as to give Mr. Gbagbo a last chance to leave peacefully, and reached out to FDS commanders to join FRCI. On 31 March, UNOCI and the French Operation Licorne force secured the airport, and FDS abandoned its checkpoints around the Golf Hotel, the temporary seat of the legitimate Government.

Letter of Secretary-General. In a letter of 4 April [S/2011/221], the Secretary-General informed the Security Council that forces loyal to Mr. Gbagbo had intensified use of heavy weapons against the civilian population in Abidjan, and had targeted the UNOCI headquarters at the Sebroko Hotel as well as UNOCI patrols dispatched to protect civilians and convoys transporting the wounded in Abidjan. Several peacekeepers were wounded, and one international UNOCI staff member and one national World Health Organization staff member were killed during the fighting. Consequently, pursuant to paragraph 6 of Council resolution 1975(2011) (see p. 144), the Secretary-General had instructed UNOCI to take the necessary measures to prevent the use of heavy weapons against civilians, with the support of French forces pursuant to Council resolution 1962(2010).

Arrest of Mr. Gbagbo. The Secretary-General reported [S/2011/387] that, on 11 April, Mr. Gbagbo and members of his family, staff and "cabinet" were apprehended by FRCI in a bunker in the presidential residence. On 13 April, Mr. Gbagbo was transferred to a location in the north of the country. While fighting abated in Abidjan after 11 April, pro-Gbagbo militias, mercenaries and FDS elements continued to fight in Yopougon district. FRCI dislodged the remaining elements from Yopougon on 4 May, with some FDS elements fleeing towards the Liberian border area, where they continued to kill civilians and loot property in south-western Côte d'Ivoire. In mid-April, UNOCI began joint patrols with FRCI, and assisted in collecting and registering some 500 weapons. UNOCI was also clearing unexploded ordnance in Abidjan.

UNOCI reconfiguration. The Secretary-General, on 12 April [S/2011/247], recommended a temporary reconfiguration of the police component of UNOCI, which would replace 40 individual police officers whose positions were currently unencumbered with 40 formed police unit personnel. The measure would provide the Mission with additional capacity to protect civilians and United Nations personnel and installations. The Council on 14 April [S/2011/248] approved that course of action.

Inauguration of President Ouattara. As the situation slowly began to stabilize, the Government took various initiatives to restore normalcy, the Secretary-General reported [S/2011/387]. On 1 May, the President announced the establishment of the Dialogue, Truth and Reconciliation Commission, to be chaired by former Prime Minister Charles Konan Banny. President Ouattara was sworn in by the Constitutional Council on 6 May, and the Secretary-General attended his inauguration ceremony in Yamoussoukro on 21 May, together with some 20 Heads of State. The President announced his new Government on 1 June, headed by Prime Minister Soro and comprising 36 ministers, including representatives of President Ouattara's Rassemblement des républicains party, the Parti démocratique de Côte d'Ivoire, the Forces nouvelles and civil society. Mr. Gbagbo's Front populaire ivoirien (FPI) party declined the offer to join the inclusive Government, demanding that former President Gbagbo be released from detention first.

Extension of UNOCI mandate

Letters of Secretary-General. By a letter of 9 May [S/2011/295] to the Security Council the Secretary-General referred to Council resolution 1962(2010), which requested him to report on the situation in the country by 31 May and to deploy an assessment mission following the legislative elections scheduled for early 2011. As the crisis following the presidential elections had delayed those elections, as well as the assessment mission, the Secretary-General requested that the issuance of the report be deferred until 30 June, and that the Council authorize a technical rollover of the mandate of UNOCI to 31 July 2011. On 12 May [S/2011/296], the Security Council took note of the Secretary-General's request for an extension of the report's issuance date.

By a letter of 11 May [S/2011/297], the Secretary-General informed the Council that the Government had identified the stabilization of the security situation in Abidjan and in the western part of the country as a priority, and, in that regard, had requested assistance from UNOCI. While the pro-Gbagbo militias and mercenaries had been dislodged from their main base in Abidjan, some remained in the area and others had fled to the west, where security risks were already high owing to tensions over ethnic identity and land ownership. Following Council resolution 1968(2011) (see p. 142), which extended for up to three months the inter-mission cooperation arrangements between UNMIL and UNOCI, the Secretary-General proposed that the Council authorize another extension of those arrangements until 31 July, subject to the extension of UNOCI and the ongoing assessment of the security situation in both Côte d'Ivoire and Liberia.

SECURITY COUNCIL ACTION

On 13 May [meeting 6535], the Security Council unanimously adopted **resolution 1981(2011)**. The draft [S/2011/299] was submitted by France and Lebanon.

The Security Council,

Recalling its previous resolutions, in particular resolutions 1933(2010) of 30 June 2010, 1942(2010) of 29 September 2010, 1951(2010) of 24 November 2010, 1962(2010) of 20 December 2010, 1967(2011) of 19 January 2011, 1968(2011) of 16 February 2011, 1975(2011) of 30 March 2011 and 1980(2011) of 28 April 2011, and the statements by its President relating to the situation in Côte d'Ivoire and in the subregion,

Recalling also the inter-mission cooperation arrangements provided for in paragraphs 4 to 6 of its resolution 1609(2005) of 24 June 2005 and in paragraph 6 of its resolution 1938(2010) of 15 September 2010, and recalling further paragraph 7 of resolution 1962(2010), paragraphs 3 and 4 of resolution 1967(2011) and paragraph 1 of resolution 1968(2011),

Recalling its intention to consider authorizing the Secretary-General to redeploy further troops, as may be needed, between the United Nations Mission in Liberia and the United Nations Operation in Côte d'Ivoire on a temporary basis, and mindful of the need to support the ability of the United Nations Mission in Liberia to carry out its mandate,

Recalling the letter dated 11 May 2011 from the Secretary-General to the President of the Security Council stressing the essential role played by the assets deployed from the United Nations Mission in Liberia to the United Nations Operation in Côte d'Ivoire in the current challenging circumstances in Côte d'Ivoire,

Recalling also the letter dated 9 May 2011 from the Secretary-General to the President of the Security Council stressing the need to postpone the publication of his final report from 31 May to 30 June 2011 and the subsequent need for a technical rollover of the mandate of the United Nations Operation in Côte d'Ivoire to 31 July 2011, following the delay in the deployment of the assessment mission to Côte d'Ivoire,

Acting under Chapter VII of the Charter of the United Nations,

1. *Decides* to extend until 31 July 2011 the mandate of the United Nations Operation in Côte d'Ivoire as set out in resolutions 1933(2010), 1962(2010) and 1975(2011);

2. *Requests* the Secretary-General to submit to the Security Council the final report referred to in paragraphs 18 and 19 of resolution 1962(2010), including the findings and recommendations on the mandate of the United Nations Operation in Côte d'Ivoire following the assessment mission deployed to Côte d'Ivoire, no later than 30 June 2011;

3. *Decides* to authorize the Secretary-General, further to paragraphs 4 and 6 of resolution 1609(2005), resolution 1951(2010), paragraph 6 of resolution 1962(2010), paragraphs 3 and 4 of resolution 1967(2011) and paragraph 1 of resolution 1968(2011), to extend until 30 June 2011 the temporary redeployment from the United Nations Mission in Liberia to the United Nations Operation in Côte d'Ivoire of 3 infantry companies, 1 aviation unit comprising 2 military utility helicopters and 3 armed helicopters with crews, and further requests the Secretary-General to provide the Council with an updated analysis and recommendations on the inter-mission cooperation arrangements by 15 June 2011;

4. *Requests* the support of troop- and police-contributing countries in that regard;

5. *Requests* the Secretary-General, further to paragraph 6 of resolution 1980(2011), to keep the Council informed by 30 June 2011, in the final report referred to in paragraph 2 above and further in his next relevant reports on the United Nations Operation in Côte d'Ivoire and the United Nations Mission in Liberia, of developments, measures taken and efforts made in the coordination of the United Nations Operation in Côte d'Ivoire and the United Nations Mission in Liberia to assist respectively the Governments of Côte d'Ivoire and Liberia in monitoring their border and surrounding areas, including on how the redeployed assets are assisting in this effort, with particular attention to any cross-border movement of combatants or transfer of arms, and in this regard encourages the United Nations Operation in Côte d'Ivoire and the United Nations Mission in Liberia, within their mandates and limits of capabilities and areas of deployment, to assist respectively the Governments of Côte d'Ivoire and of Liberia jointly in disarming those endangering national reconciliation and the consolidation of peace;

6. *Decides* to remain actively seized of the matter.

Letter of Secretary-General. Pursuant to Security Council resolution 1981(2011) (see above), the Secretary-General, on 10 June [S/2011/351], provided an analysis and recommendations on the inter-mission cooperation arrangements between UNMIL and UNOCI, particularly regarding the temporary redeployment from UNMIL of three infantry companies, one aviation unit comprising two military utility helicopters and three armed helicopters with crews. In that regard, the Department of Peacekeeping Operations (DPKO) conducted a military capability study in Côte d'Ivoire (21–29 April) and in Liberia (3–6 May). In addition, the DPKO-led interdepartmental assessment mission to Côte d'Ivoire (see p. 148) conducted a threat assessment that was pertinent to the issue of the redeployed military utility and armed helicopters. The military capability study concluded that, in light of the Liberian national referendum and elections scheduled to take place in August and thereafter, the two military utility helicopters should be returned to UNMIL before 30 June. Both the military capability study and the threat assessment determined that the temporary deployment of the three armed helicopters to Côte d'Ivoire would be required beyond 30 June, as the security situation remained precarious, particularly in Abidjan and the west. There remained a risk of renewed armed conflict and continued attacks against the civilian population, and the three armed helicopters provided high deterrent value and response capacity against the many spoilers in the country, as well as the mobility required for UNOCI to monitor border and surrounding areas and to respond to cross-border incidents. To that end, UNMIL and UNOCI agreed that the three armed helicopters should be retained in Côte d'Ivoire for the time being, on the understanding that those assets would be tasked to operate mainly in the west, as well as to undertake missions in support of specific UNMIL operations. In light of the assessments, the Secretary-General recommended that the Council authorize a further extension of the temporary redeployment of the three armed helicopters, with a further review to be conducted at the end of September.

SECURITY COUNCIL ACTION

On 29 June [meeting 6570], the Security Council unanimously adopted **resolution 1992(2011)**. The draft [S/2011/394] was submitted by France.

The Security Council,

Recalling its previous resolutions, in particular resolutions 1933(2010) of 30 June 2010, 1942(2010) of 29 September 2010, 1951(2010) of 24 November 2010, 1962(2010) of 20 December 2010, 1967(2011) of 19 January 2011, 1968(2011) of 16 February 2011, 1975(2011) of 30 March 2011, 1980(2011) of 28 April 2011 and 1981(2011) of 13 May 2011, and the statements by its President relating to the situation in Côte d'Ivoire and in the subregion,

Recalling also the inter-mission cooperation arrangements provided for in paragraphs 4 to 6 of its resolution 1609(2005) of 24 June 2005 and in paragraph 6 of its resolution 1938(2010) of 15 September 2010, and recalling further paragraph 7 of resolution 1962(2010), paragraphs 3 and 4 of resolution 1967(2011) and paragraph 1 of resolution 1968(2011),

Recalling further the letter dated 10 June 2011 from the Secretary-General to the President of the Security Council stressing the fragile security situation in Côte d'Ivoire and on the border with Liberia, the essential role played by the assets deployed from the United Nations Mission in Liberia to the United Nations Operation in Côte d'Ivoire in the current challenging circumstances in Côte d'Ivoire and the need to support the ability of the United Nations Mission in Liberia to carry out its mandate in view of the elections,

Welcoming the joint operations planning implemented by the United Nations Operation in Côte d'Ivoire and the United Nations Mission in Liberia around the Côte d'Ivoire and Liberia border, taking note of the agreement set out between the two missions to maintain the temporary redeployment from the United Nations Mission in Liberia to the United Nations Operation in Côte d'Ivoire of 3 armed helicopters with crews, and taking note also of the arrangements made by the United Nations Operation in Côte d'Ivoire to task these assets mainly in western Côte d'Ivoire,

Recalling paragraph 1 of resolution 1981(2011), by which it extended until 31 July 2011 the mandate of the United Nations Operation in Côte d'Ivoire as set out in resolutions 1933(2010), 1962(2010) and 1975(2011),

Acting under Chapter VII of the Charter of the United Nations,

1. *Decides* to authorize the Secretary-General, further to paragraphs 4 and 6 of resolution 1609(2005), paragraph 1 of resolution 1951(2010), paragraph 6 of resolution 1962(2010), paragraphs 3 and 4 of resolution 1967(2011) and paragraph 1 of resolution 1968(2011), to extend until 30 September 2011 the redeployment from the United Nations Mission in Liberia to the United Nations Operation in Côte d'Ivoire of 3 armed helicopters with crews;

2. *Requests* the Secretary-General to provide the Security Council with an updated analysis and recommendations on the inter-mission cooperation arrangements by 15 September 2011;

3. *Decides* to extend the deployment of an additional 2,000 military personnel to the United Nations Operation in Côte d'Ivoire, as set out in resolution 1967(2011), as well as the temporary additional military and police capabilities authorized by resolution 1942(2010), until 31 July 2011;

4. *Requests* the support of troop- and police-contributing countries in that regard;

5. *Decides* to remain actively seized of the matter.

Report of Secretary-General (June). In a June report [S/2011/387], submitted pursuant to Security Council resolutions 1962(2010) and 1981(2011), the Secretary-General presented the findings of the assessment mission dispatched to Côte d'Ivoire from 1 to 14 May. The mission received briefings from UNOCI and the UN country team, the World Bank, the African Development Bank and the French Licorne force. The mission recommended several areas on which the United Nations should focus its efforts to support the Government, with a view to stabilizing the security situation, preventing a relapse into conflict, and creating space for the Government to regain lost capacity. UNOCI should play a greater role in helping the national authorities stabilize the security situation, with particular focus on Abidjan and the west, including the border areas; and enhance its support to the Ivorian and Liberian authorities in monitoring and addressing cross-border security challenges, in close coordination with UNMIL. The mission should support the Government in reconstituting and reforming the security and rule-of-law institutions, particularly the armed forces, police, gendarmerie, judiciary and prisons; provide training in human rights, child protection and sexual- and gender-based violence for the security and law enforcement forces; support the development and implementation of a multi-year joint United Nations justice support programme in order to develop the police, judiciary, prisons and access to justice; and deploy an expert to work in the Office of the Prime Minister on security sector reform, as requested by the Prime Minister. UNOCI and the UN country team should assist the Government in developing a new national programme for demobilization, disarmament and reintegration of combatants, and dismantling of militias, as well as in developing and implementing community weapons collection programmes; reinforce their support to the Ivorian authorities for extending and re-establishing State authority, and for implementing the unfinished aspects of the Ouagadougou Agreements [YUN 2007, pp. 174 & 184] relating to the reunification of the country; support the creation of a political environment conducive to the upcoming legislative elections, including enhancing women's participation in political life; and support the organization and conduct of those elections. UNOCI should assist the Government in developing a comprehensive transitional justice approach that included prosecutions, truth-telling, reparations and institutional reforms; ensure systematic monitoring and reporting on sexual- and gender-based violence; assist the national authorities in protecting the civilian population through presence, deterrence and direct intervention; and review the mission's strategy regarding civilian protection to take into account new realities on the ground, enhance coordination and include measures to prevent gender-based violence. Furthermore, both UNOCI and the UN country team should continue to work with the Facilitator, President Blaise Compaoré of Burkina Faso, and his Special Representative in supporting the implementation of the unfinished aspects of the peace process.

In the same report, the Secretary-General recommended that, in light of the continuing security challenges and the impact of the crisis on the national security institutions, the mandate of UNOCI be extended for an additional 12 months. The troop and police strength, configuration and deployment of UNOCI would be reviewed following the legislative elections.

SECURITY COUNCIL ACTION

On 27 July [meeting 6591], the Security Council unanimously adopted **resolution 2000(2011)**. The draft [S/2011/458] was submitted by France and the United States.

The Security Council,

Recalling its previous resolutions, in particular resolutions 1933(2010) of 30 June 2010, 1942(2010) of 29 September 2010, 1951(2010) of 24 November 2010, 1962(2010) of 20 December 2010, 1967(2011) of 19 January 2011, 1968(2011) of 16 February 2011, 1975(2011) of 30 March 2011, 1980(2011) of 28 April 2011, 1981(2011) of 13 May 2011 and 1992(2011) of 29 June 2011, and the statements by its President relating to the situation in Côte d'Ivoire,

and its resolution 1938(2010) of 15 September 2010 on the situation in Liberia,

Reaffirming its strong commitment to the sovereignty, independence, territorial integrity and unity of Côte d'Ivoire, and recalling the importance of the principles of good-neighbourliness, non-interference and regional cooperation,

Welcoming the report of the Secretary-General of 24 June 2011, and taking note of the recommendations contained therein, including those of the assessment mission that deployed to Côte d'Ivoire from 1 to 14 May 2011,

Welcoming also the progress towards restoring stability and peace in Côte d'Ivoire following the inauguration of Mr. Alassane Dramane Ouattara as President of Côte d'Ivoire on 21 May 2011,

Commending President Ouattara's commitment and initiatives to promote dialogue, justice and reconciliation, including the establishment of the Dialogue, Truth and Reconciliation Commission, and calling upon all Ivorian actors to work together in their efforts for the stabilization and reconstruction of the country,

Taking note of the fact that the Prosecutor of the International Criminal Court has requested authorization from the Pre-Trial Chamber to open an investigation into war crimes and crimes against humanity in Côte d'Ivoire since 28 November 2010, on the basis of the declaration lodged by Côte d'Ivoire accepting the jurisdiction of the Court, pursuant to article 12, paragraph 3, of the Rome Statute of the Court,

Taking note also of President Ouattara's request that President Blaise Compaoré of Burkina Faso ("the Facilitator"), continue to assist the Government of Côte d'Ivoire in implementing the unfinished aspects of the peace process and the Ouagadougou Agreements,

Expressing its concern about the continuing precarious and volatile security situation, and recalling that the Government of Côte d'Ivoire bears primary responsibility for ensuring peace, stability and the protection of the civilian population in Côte d'Ivoire,

Taking note of the establishment of the Republican Forces of Côte d'Ivoire by a decree issued by President Ouattara on 17 March 2011, replacing the former Defence and Security Forces of Côte d'Ivoire, and stressing the need for an inclusive process of security sector reform,

Taking note also of the remaining high risk of a relapse into renewed armed conflict and attacks against the civilian population, notably by ex-Republican Guard soldiers, militias, mercenaries, escaped prisoners and other illegal armed elements as referred to in the report of the Secretary-General,

Recalling that the last legislative elections were held on 10 December 2000, and emphasizing that the holding of credible, free and fair legislative elections is critical for the full restoration of constitutional order in Côte d'Ivoire, national reconciliation and inclusive governance,

Stressing the importance of an inclusive participation of Ivorian civil society, men and women alike, in the electoral process and of ensuring the equal protection of and respect for the human rights of all Ivorian stakeholders as they relate to the electoral system, and, in particular, respect for freedom of opinion and expression,

Strongly condemning the atrocities, serious human rights abuses and violations as well as violations of international humanitarian law that occurred throughout the post-election crisis, including extrajudicial killing, maiming, arbitrary arrest and abduction of civilians, enforced disappearances, acts of revenge, sexual and gender-based violence, including against children, and the alleged recruitment and use of children in the conflict throughout the country and particularly in Abidjan and the west,

Strongly condemning also the attacks and harassment against United Nations personnel that occurred during the post-election crisis, and reiterating that these acts constitute violations of international law,

Stressing the importance of investigating alleged human rights abuses and violations committed by all parties, further reaffirming that those responsible for such abuses and violations, regardless of their affiliation, must be held accountable, and welcoming President Ouattara's commitment in this regard,

Taking note of the report and recommendations of the independent international commission of inquiry established pursuant to Human Rights Council resolution 16/25 of 25 March 2011,

Commending the African Union and the Economic Community of West African States for their efforts during the post-election crisis, and encouraging them to remain committed in support of the stabilization of the situation in Côte d'Ivoire and the implementation of the outstanding tasks of the peace process,

Commending also the contribution of troop- and police-contributing countries and donors to the United Nations Operation in Côte d'Ivoire,

Recalling its resolutions 1325(2000) of 31 October 2000, 1820(2008) of 19 June 2008, 1888(2009) of 30 September 2009, 1889(2009) of 5 October 2009 and 1960(2010) of 16 December 2010 on women and peace and security, its resolutions 1612(2005) of 26 July 2005, 1882(2009) of 4 August 2009 and 1998(2011) of 12 July 2011 on children and armed conflict and its resolutions 1674(2006) of 28 April 2006 and 1894(2009) of 11 November 2009 on the protection of civilians in armed conflict, and reiterating the vital role of women in conflict resolution and peacebuilding and their key role in re-establishing the fabric of societies recovering from conflict,

Determining that the situation in Côte d'Ivoire continues to pose a threat to international peace and security in the region,

Acting under Chapter VII of the Charter of the United Nations,

1. *Decides* to extend the mandate of the United Nations Operation in Côte d'Ivoire until 31 July 2012;

2. *Decides also* that the authorized strength of the military component of the United Nations Operation in Côte d'Ivoire shall remain at 9,792 personnel, comprising 9,600 troops and staff officers, including 2,400 additional troops authorized by resolutions 1942(2010) and 1967(2011), and 192 military observers;

3. *Decides further* that the authorized strength of the police component of the United Nations Operation in Côte d'Ivoire shall remain at 1,350 personnel, and decides to maintain the 8 customs officers previously authorized;

4. *Decides* to authorize an increase of the individual police personnel by 205 advisers, with the appropriate skills, who should be experts in the specialized areas identified in the report of the Secretary-General, to be accommodated through appropriate adjustments to the military and police strength of the United Nations Operation in Côte d'Ivoire, within its authorized strength of military and police personnel;

5. *Decides also* that the additional 2,000 troops authorized by resolution 1967(2011) and the additional 400 troops and 100 police authorized by resolution 1942(2010) are necessary for the stabilization of Côte d'Ivoire, including the establishment of a security environment conducive to the legislative elections;

6. *Reiterates* that, pursuant to paragraph 4 of resolution 1933(2010) and previous resolutions, the Special Representative of the Secretary-General for Côte d'Ivoire shall certify that all stages of the upcoming legislative elections provide all the necessary guarantees for open, free, fair and transparent elections, in accordance with international standards and the agreed criteria;

7. *Decides* that the United Nations Operation in Côte d'Ivoire shall have the following mandate:

Protection and security

(*a*) *Protection of civilians*
—To protect, without prejudice to the primary responsibility of the Ivorian authorities, the civilian population from imminent threat of physical violence, within its capabilities and areas of deployment;
—To revise the comprehensive strategy for the protection of civilians and coordinate it with the United Nations protection of civilians strategy in liaison with the United Nations country team, to take into account the new realities on the ground and the specific needs of vulnerable groups, and to include measures to prevent gender-based violence pursuant to resolutions 1960(2010) and 1882(2009);
—To work closely with humanitarian agencies, particularly in relation to areas of tension and areas of return of displaced persons, to collect information on and identify potential threats against the civilian population, as well as reliable information on violations of international humanitarian and human rights law, to bring them to the attention of the Ivorian authorities, as appropriate, and to take appropriate action in accordance with the United Nations system-wide protection strategy in harmonization with the protection strategy of the United Nations Operation in Côte d'Ivoire;
—To monitor and report on violations and abuses against vulnerable populations, including children, in line with resolutions 1612(2005), 1882(2009) and 1998(2011) and contribute to efforts to prevent such violations and abuses;

(*b*) *Addressing remaining security threats and border-related challenges*
—To continue to support, within its existing authorities, capabilities and areas of deployment, the national authorities in stabilizing the security situation in the country;

— To continue to monitor and deter the activities of militias, mercenaries and other illegal armed groups consistent within its existing mandate to protect civilians, and to keep the Security Council regularly informed of developments in this regard;
— To support the Government of Côte d'Ivoire in monitoring and addressing cross-border security and other challenges along the borders and in border areas, notably with Liberia, with particular attention to the cross-border movement of armed elements and weapons and, to this end, to coordinate closely with the United Nations Mission in Liberia with a view to further inter-mission cooperation, such as undertaking joint patrols and contingency planning, where appropriate and within their mandates and capabilities;
— To liaise with the Republican Forces of Côte d'Ivoire in order to promote mutual trust among all elements composing the Republican Forces;
— To support, in coordination with the Government of Côte d'Ivoire, the provision of security for members of the Government and key political stakeholders, including in view of the preparation and the holding of the upcoming legislative elections;

(c) *Monitoring of the arms embargo*
— To monitor the implementation of the measures imposed by paragraph 7 of resolution 1572(2004) of 15 November 2004, in cooperation with the Group of Experts on Côte d'Ivoire established pursuant to resolution 1584(2005) of 1 February 2005, including by inspecting, as they deem it necessary and when appropriate without notice, all weapons, ammunition and related materiel regardless of location, consistent with resolution 1980(2011);
— To collect, as appropriate, arms and any related materiel brought into Côte d'Ivoire in violation of the measures imposed by paragraph 7 of resolution 1572(2004), and to dispose of such arms and related materiel as appropriate;

(d) *Collection of weapons*
— To continue to assist the national authorities, including the National Commission to Fight against the Proliferation and Illicit Traffic of Small Arms and Light Weapons, in collecting, registering, securing and disposing of weapons and in clearing explosive remnants of war, as appropriate, in accordance with resolution 1980(2011);
— To support the Government of Côte d'Ivoire in coordination with other partners to develop and implement community weapons collection programmes, which should be linked to community violence reduction and reconciliation;
— To coordinate with the Government of Côte d'Ivoire in ensuring that the collected weapons are not disseminated or reutilized outside a comprehensive national security strategy, as referred to in point (f) below;

(e) *Disarmament, demobilization and reintegration programme*
— To assist the Government of Côte d'Ivoire, in close coordination with other international and bilateral partners, in developing and implementing without delay a new national programme for the disarmament, demobilization and reintegration of combatants and the dismantling of militias and self-defence groups that includes clear individual criteria and is tailored to the new context, taking into account the rights and needs of the different categories of persons to be disarmed, demobilized and reintegrated, including children and women;
— To continue to support the registration and screening of former combatants;
— To support the disarmament and repatriation of foreign armed elements, where relevant in cooperation with the United Nations Mission in Liberia and United Nations country teams in the region;

(f) *Reconstitution and reform of security and rule of law institutions*
— To assist the Government of Côte d'Ivoire in conducting, without delay and in close coordination with other international partners, a sector-wide review of the security institutions and in developing a comprehensive national security strategy and plans for their reform, taking also into account the national disarmament, demobilization and reintegration programme;
— Under the leadership of the Government of Côte d'Ivoire and in close cooperation with international stakeholders, to support effective coordination, transparency and harmonization of efforts, as well as a clear division of tasks and responsibilities, by all international partners involved in assisting the security sector reform process, and to report to the Security Council, when appropriate, on developments in the security sector reform process;
— To advise the Government of Côte d'Ivoire, as appropriate, on security sector reform and the organization of the future national army, to facilitate the provision, within its current resources, as requested by the Government and in close coordination with other international partners, of training in human rights, child protection and protection from sexual and gender-based violence to the security and law enforcement institutions, as well as support for capacity development through technical assistance, co-location and mentoring programmes for the police, gendarmerie, and justice and corrections officers, to contribute to restoring their presence throughout Côte d'Ivoire and to offer support with regard to the development of a sustainable vetting mechanism for personnel that will be absorbed in security sector institutions;
— To support the development and implementation by the Government of Côte d'Ivoire of a national justice sector strategy as well as the development and implementation of a multi-year joint United Nations justice support programme in order to develop the police, judiciary, prisons and access to justice in Côte d'Ivoire, as well as the initial emergency rehabilitation of relevant infrastructure and the provision of equipment, within existing resources and in coordination with international partners;
— To support, within its current resources and in collaboration with the broader United Nations system, reconciliation, including the establishment and functioning of mechanisms to prevent, mitigate or resolve conflict, in particular at the local level, as well as to foster social cohesion;

(g) *Support for efforts to promote and protect human rights*
— To contribute to the promotion and protection of human rights in Côte d'Ivoire, with special attention to grave violations and abuses committed against children and women, notably sexual and gender-based violence, in close coordination with the independent expert whose mandate was established pursuant to Human Rights Council resolution 17/21 of 17 June 2011;
— To monitor, help to investigate, and report publicly and to the Security Council on human rights and humanitarian law violations with a view to preventing violations, developing a protecting environment and ending impunity, and to this end to strengthen its human rights monitoring, investigation and reporting capacity;
— To bring to the attention of the Security Council all individuals identified as perpetrators of serious human rights violations and to keep the Security Council Committee established pursuant to resolution 1572(2004) regularly informed of developments in this regard;
— To support the efforts of the Government of Côte d'Ivoire in combating sexual and gender-based violence, including by contributing to the development of a nationally owned multisectoral strategy in cooperation with United Nations Action against Sexual Violence in Conflict entities, to appoint women's protection advisers and to ensure gender expertise and training, as appropriate and from within existing resources, in accordance with resolutions 1888(2009), 1889(2009) and 1960(2010);

(h) *Support for humanitarian assistance*
— To continue to facilitate unhindered humanitarian access and to help to strengthen the delivery of humanitarian assistance to conflict-affected and vulnerable populations, notably by contributing to enhancing security conducive to this delivery;
— To support the Ivorian authorities in preparing for the voluntary, safe and sustainable return of refugees and displaced persons in cooperation with relevant humanitarian organizations, and in creating security conditions conducive to it;

Peace and electoral process

(i) *Support for the organization and conduct of open, timely, free, fair and transparent legislative elections*
— To promote an inclusive political process and support the creation of a political environment conducive to the upcoming elections, including in coordination with efforts undertaken by the Economic Community of West African States and the African Union;
— To support the organization and conduct of open, free, fair and transparent legislative elections, provide appropriate logistical and technical assistance and assist the Government of Côte d'Ivoire to put in place effective security arrangements;
— To provide technical and logistical support to assist the Independent Electoral Commission in completing outstanding tasks prior to the holding of the legislative elections and to facilitate, as required, consultations between all political stakeholders as well as with the Commission to this end;
— To undertake the coordination of international observers and to contribute to their security, within its capabilities and areas of deployment;
— To provide the Special Representative of the Secretary-General with the assistance necessary to fulfil his role of certifying the legislative elections consistent with paragraph 6 above, taking into account the specificity of legislative elections;

(j) *Public information*
— To continue to closely monitor the Ivorian media and continue to facilitate providing assistance, as appropriate, to media and regulatory bodies, consistent with its mandate;
— To continue to use the broadcasting capacity of the United Nations Operation in Côte d'Ivoire, through ONUCI FM, to contribute to the overall effort to create a peaceful environment, including for the legislative elections;
— To encourage the Ivorian mass media and the main political actors to fully implement the Code of Good Conduct for Elections that the Ivorian parties have signed under the auspices of the Secretary-General as well as to sign and adhere to the Code of Good Conduct for the Media;
— To monitor any public incidents of incitement to hatred, intolerance and violence and bring to the attention of the Security Council all individuals identified as instigators of political violence, and to keep the Committee established pursuant to resolution 1572(2004) regularly informed of developments in this regard;

(k) *Redeployment of State administration and the extension of State authority throughout the country*
— To support the Ivorian authorities in extending and re-establishing effective State administration and strengthening public administration in key areas throughout the country, at the national and local levels, as well as the implementation of the unfinished aspects of the Ouagadougou Agreements as they relate to the reunification of the country;

(l) *Facilitation*
— To coordinate with the Facilitator and his Special Representative in Abidjan, to assist the Government of Côte d'Ivoire in the implementation of the outstanding tasks of the peace process, as needed and within available means, including by providing logistical support to the office of the Special Representative, as appropriate;

(m) *Protection of United Nations personnel*
— To protect United Nations personnel, installations and equipment and ensure the security and freedom of movement of United Nations personnel;

8. *Decides* to continue its authorization given to the United Nations Operation in Côte d'Ivoire to use all means necessary to carry out its mandate, within its capabilities and its areas of deployment, pursuant to resolutions 1933(2010) and 1962(2010);

9. *Welcomes* the establishment of the Dialogue, Truth and Reconciliation Commission by a decree issued by President Ouattara on 13 May 2011, encourages the Government of Côte d'Ivoire to ensure that the Commission becomes fully operational as soon as possible, and further calls upon the United Nations system to support its work,

with a view to ensuring that it will function in a manner consistent with Côte d'Ivoire's international obligations;

10. *Calls upon* the Government of Côte d'Ivoire to take the steps necessary to re-establish and reinforce relevant institutions, including the judiciary and the police and corrections services, and further to ensure the effective protection of human rights and accountability for all perpetrators of human rights violations and abuses in Côte d'Ivoire;

11. *Also calls upon* the Government of Côte d'Ivoire to ensure that the conditions of protection and detention of the former President, Mr. Laurent Gbagbo, his wife, former officials and any other detainees are in line with international obligations, including with regard to access by relevant organizations with a mandate to monitor detention centres, and to fulfil their prosecutions and trials in accordance with international obligations relating to due process and fair trial requirements;

12. *Calls upon* the United Nations Operation in Côte d'Ivoire, where consistent with its existing authorities and responsibilities, to support national and international efforts to bring to justice perpetrators of grave violations of human rights and international humanitarian law in Côte d'Ivoire;

13. *Urges* all parties to cooperate fully with the operations of the United Nations Operation in Côte d'Ivoire and the French Forces supporting it, in particular by ensuring their safety, security and freedom of movement with unhindered and immediate access throughout the territory of Côte d'Ivoire to enable them to fully carry out their mandates;

14. *Calls upon* the United Nations country team to contribute to the planning and the implementation of microprojects, in consultation with the Government of Côte d'Ivoire and in close collaboration with the United Nations Development Programme and interested international partners, to provide sustainable alternative livelihoods for some former combatants, as part of the socio-economic reintegration component of the national disarmament, demobilization and reintegration programme;

15. *Encourages* the Economic Community of West African States to develop, with the support of the United Nations Office for West Africa, a subregional strategy to address the threat of the cross-border movements of armed groups and weapons as well as illicit trafficking, with the assistance of the United Nations Operation in Côte d'Ivoire and the United Nations Mission in Liberia, as appropriate;

16. *Calls upon* the Government of Côte d'Ivoire and all international partners, including private companies, involved in assisting the Government in the reform of the security sector, to comply with the provisions of resolution 1980(2011) and to coordinate their efforts with a view to promoting transparency and a clear division of labour among all international partners;

17. *Decides* to extend until 31 July 2012 the authorization that the Council provided to the French forces in order to support the United Nations Operation in Côte d'Ivoire, within the limits of their deployment and their capabilities;

18. *Requests* the Secretary-General to provide to the Council a midterm report no later than 31 December 2011 and a final report no later than 30 June 2012 on the situation on the ground and the implementation of the present resolution, and further requests the Secretary-General to regularly brief and inform the Council on the significant events of the electoral process, including on support by the United Nations Operation in Côte d'Ivoire to this process;

19. *Also requests* the Secretary-General to submit to the Council, through the midterm report referred to in paragraph 18 above or through a special report, no later than 31 March 2012, taking into account the holding of the upcoming legislative elections as well as the prevailing security challenges and progress in rebuilding national capacities, recommendations on possible adjustments in the structure and strength of the United Nations Operation in Côte d'Ivoire;

20. *Decides* to remain seized of the matter.

Security situation

Letters of Secretary-General. Pursuant to Security Council resolution 1992(2011) (see p. 148), the Secretary-General, in a 15 September letter to the Council [S/2011/577], provided an analysis and recommendations on inter-mission cooperation between UNOCI and UNMIL. In accordance with Council resolutions 1967(2011) (see p. 141) and 1975(2011) (see p. 144), the temporary transfer of three armed helicopters from UNMIL proved an invaluable asset in preventing the use of heavy weapons against the civilian population in Abidjan. Thereafter, the primary tasking of the armed helicopters shifted to the west and border areas between Côte d'Ivoire and Liberia, in view of the emerging challenges in those areas. The missions were implementing measures to enhance security, including the joint tasking of the three armed helicopters to meet the reconnaissance and deterrence requirements of both missions in the border areas. The patrols on both sides had mitigated cross-border incidents and other militia and mercenary activities in western Côte d'Ivoire. That surveillance, using a combination of air and ground patrols, had also resulted in reduced cross-border movement of Ivorian militia elements and Liberian elements who participated in the conflict in Côte d'Ivoire. In light of the fragile security situation and the upcoming elections in Liberia, the Secretary-General recommended the return of the three armed helicopters to UNMIL by 30 September, in keeping with resolution 1992(2011), and made several recommendations regarding the support that UNMIL required from UNOCI within the framework of inter-mission cooperation provided for in resolution 1609(2005) [YUN 2005, p. 236].

In a letter of 22 November [S/2011/730], the Secretary-General updated the Council on the country's security situation. UNOCI had conducted a threat assessment in preparation for the upcoming legislative elections, which highlighted the risk that spoilers could seek to disrupt the electoral process. The mission anticipated a deterioration of the security situation, particularly in Abidjan and the west, and assessed that it would require reinforcement of its capabilities to deter and respond to security threats. Accordingly, the Secretary-General recommended that the Council authorize the temporary transfer from

UNMIL to UNOCI of the three Mi-24 armed helicopters and the two military utility helicopters; one infantry company, comprising 150 personnel, to reinforce UNOCI in the west; and three formed police unit platoons with supporting elements, comprising 100 personnel, to Abidjan. The duration of the deployment of the personnel and helicopters, from 4 December and up to 31 December, took into account the risk that tensions resulting from the elections could escalate into violence before, during or after polling day.

On 30 November [S/2011/747], the Council approved the Secretary-General's recommendations on the condition that consent was received from troop- and police-contributors and other relevant Governments.

Legislative elections

Report of Secretary-General (December). Pursuant to Security Council resolution 2000(2011) (see p. 149), the Secretary-General, in December, reported [S/2011/807] on the holding of the legislative elections on 11 December. Political stakeholders across the spectrum focused on positioning themselves for the elections. President Ouattara and his Government made considerable efforts to create a political environment conducive to the peaceful conduct of elections, and the authorities undertook steps to ensure that the elections were inclusive by encouraging all parties to participate in the electoral process, particularly the former ruling party, FPI, and parties from the opposition coalition, the Congrès national de la résistance pour la démocratie. On 14 August, President Ouattara appointed 14 members of the Independent Electoral Commission, in accordance with the Pretoria Agreement [YUN 2005, p. 232]; however, FPI suspended its participation in the Commission on 21 September. It maintained its demands for changes to the composition of the Commission, the release of detainees associated with the former regime and the disbursement of funds for political parties as conditions for its participation in the elections. In response, an additional position of a fifth vice-president was created in the Commission on 24 October, which was offered to FPI, and funds were released in early December. After validation by the Constitutional Council, the Commission, on 30 November, published the final list of candidates, which comprised 1,160 candidates representing 34 political parties. The Forces nouvelles announced the participation of their representatives under the umbrella of the Rassemblement des houphouëtistes pour la démocratie et la paix alliance, which included President Ouattara's Rassemblement des républicains (RDR) party and former President Henri Konan Bédié's Parti démocratique de Côte d'Ivoire (PCDI) party. Four parties from the opposition registered candidates for the elections, and although FPI maintained its position of boycotting the elections, some FPI representatives participated as independent candidates. In the lead-up to the elections, the Secretary-General's Special Representative for Côte d'Ivoire worked with the Government and all political stakeholders, including the Facilitator, President Compaoré of Burkina Faso, to promote an inclusive political process and support the creation of a political environment conducive to the elections. The Special Representative urged political parties and independent candidates to participate in the elections and adhere to the Code of Good Conduct signed in 2008 under the auspices of the Secretary-General [YUN 2008, p. 181].

The Electoral Commission was generally successful in overcoming technical and logistical challenges in preparing for the elections, with support from UNOCI and the UN country team. From 24 to 28 November, UNOCI delivered approximately 200 tons of non-sensitive electoral material to all departments countrywide. Campaigning took place in a generally calm atmosphere from 3 to 9 December, although cases of intimidation and tensions were reported across the country. The Forces républicaines de Côte d'Ivoire, the police, the gendarmerie, UNOCI and the French Licorne force worked jointly to develop security arrangements. While the police and gendarmerie, with support from the armed forces, were responsible for securing polling operations, UNOCI focused on providing support in the most sensitive areas, including in the west, while Licorne intensified patrols in Abidjan. The mission also strengthened its civilian presence in many areas around the country to assist in responding to potential challenges.

On 11 December, the elections were held in a generally calm and peaceful manner, with a participation rate of approximately 37 per cent of registered voters. The elections were observed by representatives of the candidates, approximately 3,000 national observers and political party representatives, and 150 international observers. UNOCI and the UN country team were present with some 300 monitoring teams throughout the country. No major security incidents were reported, and international observers positively assessed both the voting and the performance of the national security personnel. On 16 December, the Commission released the provisional results, which gave 127 seats to President Ouattara's RDR party, 77 seats to PCDI, 35 seats to independent candidates, and the remaining seats to smaller parties and coalitions. As part of the certification process, the Special Representative welcomed the peaceful conduct of the electoral campaign and of the voting.

Security and national reconciliation

The Secretary-General also reported [S/2011/807] on the security situation in the country in the second half of the year, as well as the implementation of Security

Council resolution 2000(2011), which outlined the mandate of UNOCI. President Ouattara and his Government took initiatives to consolidate the security situation and to reconstitute security and rule of law institutions across the country. In spite of positive developments, the security environment in Abidjan and in the west remained fragile, with large numbers of weapons present throughout the country. There was an increasing number of disgruntled ex-combatants due to slow progress in disarmament, demobilization and reintegration and in security sector reform. Furthermore, elements loyal to former President Gbagbo continued to have access to arms, while the cross-border movement of armed groups and weapons presented security threats to the country and its neighbours, particularly Liberia. That resulted in a number of security incidents, including an attack by armed elements on the border villages of Zriglo and Nigré in the west, resulting in the death of 21 persons. On 18 December, five people were killed when a group of armed youths clashed with the armed forces in Vavoua. A series of violent intercommunal clashes in villages in the west were reported from October to December, resulting in the death of at least 12 persons and many wounded. In Abidjan, a large number of weapons remained in circulation, and the majority of the 12,000 prisoners who escaped from custody during the post-election crisis remained at large. That contributed to high levels of crime and security incidents involving armed elements.

On national reconciliation and transitional justice, President Ouattara took initiatives to restore normalcy in the country, including appointing a new President of the Constitutional Council on 25 July. The transfer of former President Gbagbo to the International Criminal Court (ICC) in The Hague on 29 November dominated the political discourse and provoked mixed reactions among Ivorians, with some segments of the population welcoming the development as an important step towards ending impunity, and others condemning it for political or procedural reasons. On 30 November, FPI issued a statement claiming that President Gbagbo's extradition was illegal, and that the party would withdraw from the national reconciliation process. While the Government had indicted a number of individuals associated with the former regime, it had been slow in addressing violations committed by its own forces. The President continued to emphasize national reconciliation as a way to restore lasting peace and stability, and called on refugees and members of FPI and the former FDS to return to the country, including during official visits to Ghana in July, September and October. The Commission on Dialogue, Truth and Reconciliation was inaugurated on 28 September, following the nomination of 11 members of the Commission and the appointment of a President, Charles Konan Banny.

UNOCI provided support to the efforts of the national security forces to stabilize the country. In Abidjan and elsewhere, the mission increased joint patrols with the national security forces and the French Licorne forces, and reinforced its presence in the west with the establishment of three new camps in Tabou, Taï and Zouan Hounien. The mission also increased its presence in the east to monitor cross-border movements from Ghana. In accordance with its mandate to protect civilians, the mission sought to improve its quick-reaction capacity by refining its system of mobile and static patrols, and enhanced its visible presence in areas of concern, including approximately 36 camps for internally displaced persons and the routes used by refugees and displaced persons to return to their communities. With the support of UNOCI, the Government held a pre-seminar on security sector reform and disarmament, demobilization and reintegration (Abidjan, 21–23 September) in preparation for a national seminar in 2012. The Mission deployed a senior security sector reform adviser to the Prime Minister, as requested by the Government, and held weekly coordination meetings with international partners interested in supporting security sector reform. Also at the Government's request, UNOCI and the national police conducted a joint audit of police services throughout the country from 22 August to 9 September, which revealed several challenges, including restructuring and professionalizing the national police and increasing its operational ability. While progress in developing a new national disarmament, demobilization and reintegration programme was slow, the mission provided advice on the task to the national authorities and supported the capacity-building of Government personnel.

Sanctions

Security Council Committee. The Security Council Committee established pursuant to resolution 1572(2004) [YUN 2004, p. 187] concerning Côte d'Ivoire continued to monitor implementation of the arms embargo, travel restrictions and an asset freeze on designated individuals and entities, as well as the embargo on the export of diamonds imposed by resolution 1643(2005) [YUN 2005, p. 251]. Those sanctions were renewed by various resolutions, the latest of which was resolution 1946(2010) [YUN 2010, p. 196]. The Committee reported on its activities in 2011 [S/2011/808], during which it held three informal consultations and considered 10 monthly media and arms embargo monitoring reports prepared by UNOCI, seven UNOCI human rights reports and one special human rights report. Following up on the recommendations contained in the April [S/2011/272] and October [S/2011/642] reports of the Group of Experts (see below), the Committee, on 10 May and 11 November, dispatched letters to Burkina Faso, Côte d'Ivoire, Ghana, Guinea, Liberia and Mali, drawing attention to relevant paragraphs in the Group's reports. Pursuant to a request by Côte d'Ivoire, the Committee approved seven exemption requests for the shipment of materiel and provision of military assistance to the country. The Committee also approved a request concerning supplies of non-lethal military equipment intended solely for humanitarian or protective use, and related technical assistance and training, submitted on 4 April by Germany. On 29 November, the Committee approved a request for exemption to the travel ban, submitted by Côte d'Ivoire and the Netherlands, to authorize the transfer of listed individual Laurent Gbagbo to the ICC in The Hague.

Group of Experts

The Group of Experts on Côte d'Ivoire submitted one midterm report and two final reports during the year (see below). Pursuant to Security Council resolution 1946(2010), the Secretary-General, on 5 January, appointed five experts to constitute the Group for a period ending 30 April [S/2011/3]. In response to Council resolution 1980(2011) (see p. 157), he appointed four experts on 7 July for a period ending 30 April 2012 [S/2011/419]; an additional expert on 13 October [S/2011/638]; and one expert on 20 December [S/2011/788] to replace a member who had resigned.

Reports of Group of Experts. On 20 April, pursuant to Council resolution 1893(2009) [YUN 2009, p. 186], the Chair of the Security Council Committee transmitted to the Council the final report of the Group of Experts [S/2011/271], which presented the results of its investigations in 2010. The Group maintained a continuous presence in Côte d'Ivoire and conducted inspections of military equipment and installations in all major regions of the country, as well as field-based investigations on all aspects of the sanctions regime. The Group remained concerned about the impact of the future political trajectory on the sanctions regime; despite the arms embargo, northern and southern Ivorian parties were rearming and re-equipping with weapons and related materiel, and rehabilitating existing military assets. Among its recommendations, the Group encouraged the Council, through the Sanctions Committee, to take a firmer stance against Ivorian parties that breached the embargo or refused to allow inspections of weapons and ammunition, including imposing targeted sanctions on the Minister of Defence and the Forces nouvelles zone commanders if they continued to deny the Group and UNOCI unhindered access to military sites and installations. It recommended that the Kimberley Process [YUN 2000, p. 76] ensure that illicit traders did not use the Certification Scheme of the Process to trade in illegally exported Ivorian rough diamonds, including the implementation of origin control measures. UNOCI personnel in charge of the country's airports should immediately inform the mission's Integrated Embargo Cell and the Group of Experts of any unidentified or unscheduled flights; and UNOCI should deploy customs inspectors to monitor the two primary border-crossing points, Laleraba and Pogo, linking northern Côte d'Ivoire to Burkina Faso and Mali, respectively.

Pursuant to Council resolution 1946(2010), the Chair of the Committee, on 20 April, transmitted to the Council the Group's final report [S/2011/272]. Amid hazardous security and political instability, the Group continued its field-based investigations, which indicated that the country faced continued violations of the sanctions regime. The Group was concerned about increasing levels of armed violence, which had led parties to rearm, deploy foreign mercenaries and rehabilitate military air assets in violation of the sanctions regime. At the time of the report's submission, the post-electoral crisis had developed into an internal armed conflict of political, religious and ethnic dimensions. The south, under the administration of Mr. Gbagbo, and the north, controlled by the Forces nouvelles in support of President Ouattara, had engaged in a rapidly escalating conflict. Both parties sought weapons and ammunition and were willing to violate the embargo. At the same time, the capacity of UNOCI to monitor violations was significantly reduced due to restricted movement, closure of bases and the disinclination of its military command to expose UN troops and personnel to attacks by Ivorian security forces. Furthermore, the conflict had reached a stage where some neighbouring countries, to protect their national interests, had lent assistance to parties in the conflict, including the supply of weapons and materiel in violation of the arms embargo. The crisis had also released a series of fast-changing economic events with a direct impact on finance-related aspects of the sanctions regime in both the north and south. Following the second round of presidential elections in November 2010, the country's financial system had deteriorated to the verge of collapse as a consequence of the unstable security situation and measures imposed by the European Commission, international organizations and President Ouattara in efforts to encourage the exit of Mr. Gbagbo's administration. In February 2011, the Forces nouvelles experienced financial shortages due to a dramatic reduction in all forms of trade, particularly cocoa, compelling the coalition to increase taxes at all road checkpoints across the north in an attempt to reduce the impact of the lost revenues. The Group observed that in the early months of 2011 there were numerous violations of the arms embargo, which benefited both sides in the conflict. The Group also observed several suspicious flights and sea cargoes in the south. In the north, the Forces nouvelles received consistent transfers of weapons and ammunition in breach of the sanctions regime. In the area of customs, the Group reported that its experts as well as UNOCI had encountered restricted access to seaports, airports and the documentation related to imports and exports. Regarding diamonds, the Group observed that the production of rough diamonds was increasing and that diamonds had been illegally exported through neighbouring countries, in violation of the sanctions regime. Ivorian diamonds continued to emerge on international markets, exiting through several conduits, including Abidjan and neighbouring countries. Guinea, Liberia and Mali were major transit points, and ongoing investigations suggested that traders also used Burkina Faso and Senegal as corridors for such trade. Furthermore, there was evidence of diamond cutting and polishing in Abidjan, meaning that traders were also exporting polished stones as a way to circumvent the sanctions. Diamond prospecting and production appeared to have expanded, with newly mined diamond deposits observed in the Séguéla and Tortiya regions, in addition to other others areas in the north.

The Group recommended that the Government of Liberia and the United Nations Mission in Liberia take all necessary measures to apprehend suspected mercenaries who attempted to cross the country's eastern border into Côte d'Ivoire or endeavoured to depart from Liberian seaports. Member States should ensure that multinational companies resident in their territories with businesses in Ivorian cocoa, coffee, oil, metals, minerals and timber sectors refrain from making business deals with the administration of Mr. Gbagbo. International financial institutions should issue alerts warning national financial organizations against supporting enterprises linked to the administration of the former President. The Group recommended that UNOCI hire at least six additional customs agents to provide consistent monitoring capacity to investigate potential violations of the embargo on arms and related materiel; Member States ensure that private companies operating from their territories did not sell, supply, finance, broker or deliver vehicles to Ivorian defence and security forces without a prior authorization from the Sanctions Committee; the UNOCI Integrated Embargo Cell recruit a consultant to follow up on all primary resource extraction activities, including diamonds; and the Ministry of Mines provide the Group with access to all documentation related to diamonds.

SECURITY COUNCIL ACTION

On 28 April [meeting 6525], the Security Council unanimously adopted **resolution 1980(2011)**. The draft [S/2011/273] was submitted by France.

The Security Council,

Recalling its previous resolutions and the statements by its President relating to the situation in Côte d'Ivoire, in particular resolutions 1880(2009) of 30 July 2009, 1893(2009) of 29 October 2009, 1911(2010) of 28 January 2010, 1933(2010) of 30 June 2010, 1946(2010) of 15 October 2010, 1962(2010) of 20 December 2010 and 1975(2011) of 30 March 2011,

Reaffirming its strong commitment to the sovereignty, independence, territorial integrity and unity of Côte d'Ivoire, and recalling the importance of the principles of good-neighbourliness, non-interference and regional cooperation,

Taking note of the report of the Secretary-General of 30 March 2011 and of the final report of 2010 of the Group of Experts on Côte d'Ivoire and the 2011 report of the Group of Experts,

Emphasizing the continued contribution to the stability in Côte d'Ivoire of the measures imposed by resolutions 1572(2004) of 15 November 2004, 1643(2005) of 15 December 2005 and 1975(2011), and stressing that these measures aim at supporting the peace process in Côte d'Ivoire,

Welcoming the fact that President Alassane Dramane Ouattara of Côte d'Ivoire is now able to assume all his responsibilities as Head of State, in accordance with the will of the Ivorian people expressed at the presidential election of 28 November 2010 and as recognized by the international community,

Emphasizing the imperative of sustained efforts by all Ivorians to promote national reconciliation and the consolidation of peace through dialogue and consultation, and welcoming the assistance of the African Union and the Economic Community of West African States in this regard,

Recalling its resolutions 1325(2000) of 31 October 2000, 1820(2008) of 19 June 2008, 1888(2009) of 30 September 2009, 1889(2009) of 5 October 2009 and 1960(2010) of 16 December 2010 on women and peace and security, its resolutions 1612(2005) of 26 July 2005 and 1882(2009) of 4 August 2009 on children and armed conflict and its resolutions 1674(2006) of 28 April 2006 and 1894(2009) of 11 November 2009 on the protection of civilians in armed conflict,

Reiterating its firm condemnation of all violations of human rights and international humanitarian law in Côte d'Ivoire, condemning all violence committed against civilians, including women, children, internally displaced persons and foreign nationals, and other violations and abuses of human rights, in particular enforced disappearances, extrajudicial killings, killing and maiming of children and rapes and other forms of sexual violence, and stressing that the perpetrators must be brought to justice,

Stressing the importance for the Group of Experts, originally established pursuant to paragraph 7 of resolution 1584(2005) of 1 February 2005, to be provided with sufficient resources for the implementation of its mandate,

Determining that the situation in Côte d'Ivoire continues to pose a threat to international peace and security in the region,

Acting under Chapter VII of the Charter of the United Nations,

1. *Decides* to renew until 30 April 2012 the measures on arms and the financial and travel measures imposed by paragraphs 7 to 12 of resolution 1572(2004), paragraph 5

of resolution 1946(2010) and paragraph 12 of resolution 1975(2011), and further decides to renew until 30 April 2012 the measures preventing the importation by any State of all rough diamonds from Côte d'Ivoire imposed by paragraph 6 of resolution 1643(2005);

2. *Decides also* to review the measures renewed in paragraph 1 above in the light of the progress achieved in the stabilization throughout the country, the holding of the parliamentary elections and the implementation of the key steps of the peace process, as referred to in resolution 1933(2010), by the end of the period mentioned in paragraph 1 above, and decides further to carry out a midterm review of the measures renewed in paragraph 1 above no later than 31 October 2011, with a view to possibly modifying, lifting or maintaining, ahead of 30 April 2012, all or part of the measures of the sanctions regime, in accordance with progress in the peace process, the developments related to human rights violations and the developments related to the parliamentary elections;

3. *Calls upon* all Member States, in particular those in the subregion, to fully implement the measures renewed in paragraph 1 above, including, as appropriate, by enforcing the necessary rules and regulations, calls upon the United Nations Operation in Côte d'Ivoire to lend its full support within its capacities and its mandate, and calls upon the French forces to support the United Nations Operation in Côte d'Ivoire in this regard, within the limits of their deployment and their capabilities;

4. *Urges* all illegal armed combatants to lay down their arms immediately, encourages the United Nations Operation in Côte d'Ivoire, within its mandate and the limits of its capabilities and its areas of deployment, to continue to assist the Government of Côte d'Ivoire in collecting and storing those arms, and calls upon the Ivorian authorities, including the National Commission to Fight against the Proliferation and Illicit Traffic of Small Arms and Light Weapons, to ensure that those arms are neutralized or are not illegally disseminated, in accordance with the Economic Community of West African States Convention on Small Arms and Light Weapons, Their Ammunition and Other Related Materials;

5. *Recalls* that the United Nations Operation in Côte d'Ivoire is mandated, within the monitoring of the arms embargo, to collect, as appropriate, arms and any related materiel brought into Côte d'Ivoire in violation of the measures imposed by paragraph 7 of resolution 1572(2004), and to dispose of such arms and related materiel as appropriate;

6. *Expresses its deep concern* about the presence of mercenaries in Côte d'Ivoire, notably from neighbouring countries, and calls upon the authorities of Côte d'Ivoire and Liberia to coordinate their action to solve this issue, and further encourages the United Nations Operation in Côte d'Ivoire and the United Nations Mission in Liberia, within their respective mandates, capabilities and areas of deployment, to assist respectively the Governments of Côte d'Ivoire and Liberia in monitoring their border, with particular attention to any cross-border movement of combatants or transfer of arms;

7. *Reiterates* the necessity for the Ivorian authorities to provide unhindered access to the Group of Experts on Côte d'Ivoire, as well as the United Nations Operation in Côte d'Ivoire and the French forces supporting it, to equipment, sites and installations referred to in paragraph 2 (*a*) of resolution 1584(2005), and to all weapons, ammunition and related materiel of all armed security forces, regardless of location, including the arms issued from the collection referred to in paragraph 4 above, when appropriate without notice, as set out in its resolutions 1739(2007) of 10 January 2007, 1880(2009), 1933(2010) and 1962(2010);

8. *Decides* that the supply of vehicles to the Ivorian security forces shall be subject to the measures imposed by paragraph 7 of resolution 1572(2004);

9. *Decides also* that the exemption procedure set out in paragraph 8 (*e*) of resolution 1572(2004) shall apply only to arms and related materiel, vehicles and the provision of technical training and assistance in support of the Ivorian process of security sector reform, pursuant to a formal request by the Government of Côte d'Ivoire and approved in advance by the Security Council Committee established pursuant to resolution 1572(2004);

10. *Underlines* that it is fully prepared to impose targeted measures against persons to be designated by the Committee in accordance with paragraphs 9, 11 and 14 of resolution 1572(2004) who are determined to be, among other things:

(*a*) A threat to the peace and national reconciliation process in Côte d'Ivoire, in particular by blocking the implementation of the peace process, as referred to in the Ouagadougou Political Agreement;

(*b*) Attacking or obstructing the action of the United Nations Operation in Côte d'Ivoire, the French forces supporting it and the Special Representative of the Secretary-General for Côte d'Ivoire;

(*c*) Responsible for obstacles to the freedom of movement of the United Nations Operation in Côte d'Ivoire and the French forces supporting it;

(*d*) Responsible for serious violations of human rights and international humanitarian law committed in Côte d'Ivoire;

(*e*) Publicly inciting hatred and violence;

(*f*) Acting in violation of the measures imposed by paragraph 1 above;

11. *Reiterates its readiness* to impose sanctions against those who obstruct the electoral process, specifically the action of the Independent Electoral Commission and all other operators involved, and the proclamation and certification of the results of the parliamentary elections;

12. *Requests* all States concerned, in particular those in the subregion, to cooperate fully with the Committee, and authorizes the Committee to request whatever further information it may consider necessary;

13. *Decides* to extend the mandate of the Group of Experts as set out in paragraph 7 of resolution 1727(2006) of 15 December 2006 until 30 April 2012, and requests the Secretary-General to take the measures necessary to support its action;

14. *Requests* the Group of Experts to submit a midterm report to the Committee by 15 October 2011 and to submit a final report, as well as recommendations, to the Council, through the Committee, fifteen days before the end of its mandated period, on the implementation of the measures imposed by paragraphs 7, 9 and 11 of resolution 1572(2004), paragraph 6 of resolution 1643(2005) and paragraph 12 of resolution 1975(2011);

15. *Decides* that the report of the Group of Experts, as referred to in paragraph 7 (*e*) of resolution 1727(2006), may include, as appropriate, any information and recommendations relevant to the possible additional designation by the Committee of the individuals and entities described in paragraphs 9 and 11 of resolution 1572(2004), and further recalls the report of the Informal Working Group of the Security Council on General Issues of Sanctions on best practices and methods, including paragraphs 21, 22 and 23 thereof, which discuss possible steps for clarifying methodological standards for monitoring mechanisms;

16. *Requests* the Secretary-General to communicate, as appropriate, to the Council, through the Committee, information gathered by the United Nations Operation in Côte d'Ivoire and, where possible, reviewed by the Group of Experts, concerning the supply of arms and related materiel to Côte d'Ivoire;

17. *Requests* the Government of France to communicate, as appropriate, to the Council, through the Committee, information gathered by the French forces and, where possible, reviewed by the Group of Experts, concerning the supply of arms and related materiel to Côte d'Ivoire;

18. *Requests* the Kimberley Process to communicate, as appropriate, to the Council, through the Committee, information which, where possible, has been reviewed by the Group of Experts, concerning the production and illicit export of diamonds from Côte d'Ivoire, and further decides to renew the exemptions set out in paragraphs 16 and 17 of resolution 1893(2009) with regard to the securing of samples of rough diamonds for scientific research purposes coordinated by the Kimberley Process;

19. *Encourages* the Ivorian authorities to work with the Kimberley Process Certification Scheme to conduct a review and assessment of Côte d'Ivoire's internal controls system for trade in rough diamonds and a comprehensive geologic study of Côte d'Ivoire's potential diamond resources and production capacity, with a view to possibly modifying or lifting, as appropriate, the measures imposed by paragraph 6 of resolution 1643(2005);

20. *Also encourages* the Ivorian authorities to deploy customs and border control officials throughout the country, particularly in the north and the west, and encourages the United Nations Operation in Côte d'Ivoire, within its mandate, to assist the Ivorian authorities in the reestablishment of normal customs and border control operation;

21. *Urges* all States, relevant United Nations bodies and other organizations and interested parties to cooperate fully with the Committee, the Group of Experts, the United Nations Operation in Côte d'Ivoire and the French forces, in particular by supplying any information at their disposal on possible violations of the measures imposed by paragraphs 7, 9 and 11 of resolution 1572(2004), paragraph 6 of resolution 1643(2005) and paragraph 12 of resolution 1975(2011) as reiterated in paragraph 1 above; and further requests the Group of Experts to coordinate its activities, as appropriate, with all political actors;

22. *Recalls* paragraph 7 of resolution 1960(2010) and paragraph 7 (*b*) of resolution 1882(2009) regarding sexual and gender-based violence and children in armed conflict, and welcomes the information-sharing between the Committee and the Special Representatives of the Secretary-General for Children and Armed Conflict and on Sexual Violence in Conflict, in accordance with their respective mandates and as appropriate;

23. *Urges*, in this context, that all Ivorian parties and all States, particularly those in the region, ensure:
—The safety of the members of the Group of Experts;
—Unhindered access by the Group of Experts, in particular to persons, documents and sites, in order for the Group of Experts to execute its mandate;

24. *Decides* to remain actively seized of the matter.

Midterm report. On 17 October, in accordance with Council resolution 1980(2011), the Chair of the Security Council Committee transmitted the midterm report of the Group of Experts [S/2011/642], which commenced its investigations after the post-electoral crisis, dedicating particular attention to contacting and improving cooperation with the members of the new Ivorian administration. The Group expressed concern about the circulation of large amounts of weapons and ammunition throughout the country that remained unaccounted for following the crisis. Numerous caches of weapons had been found in areas near the border with Liberia, and Liberian mercenaries were active in remote parts of western Côte d'Ivoire. Furthermore, forces loyal to the former Ivorian administration remained active abroad, notably in Liberia and Ghana. The lack of control by State officials over Ivorian territory posed a risk of possible violations of the sanctions regime. On financing the purchase of arms, the Group noted that the former Government of Mr. Gbagbo destroyed, at almost every ministerial agency, multiple records that might have assisted the Group in determining the nature of the diversion of public funds and their use in violation of the arms embargo. Although the Government claimed to have reunified its financial institutions from the former north-south divide, taxes in the north were being collected by deputies appointed by former zone commanders who were not accountable to the central Government, and not by the newly appointed administrative authorities. Diamonds mined from deposits throughout the north continued to be exported through neighbouring countries in violation of the sanctions regime. The Group recommended that the Government continue to improve its cooperation with the Group in order to increase financial and economic transparency and reaffirm its readiness to comply with the sanctions regime; accelerate the process of financial reunification and centralization of the Ivorian financial system; engage with all stakeholders in the diamond sector in order to establish a dialogue that could assist the Government in fighting diamond smuggling; and request the Chair of the Kimberley Process to invite a delegation of experts to assess the measures taken by the Government in establishing an effective system to implement the Certification Scheme. UNOCI should permanently employ a customs consultant for its Integrated Embargo Cell in order to improve its surveillance capacity; and neighbouring countries, particularly Burkina Faso and Mali, should enforce stricter customs controls on all transit shipments destined for or leaving Côte d'Ivoire.

UNOCI

The United Nations Operation in Côte d'Ivoire (UNOCI) was established in 2004 by Security Council resolution 1528(2004) [YUN 2004, p. 173] to replace the United Nations Mission in Côte d'Ivoire and ECOWAS forces, with the mandate to monitor the ceasefire and movement of armed groups; assist in disarmament, demobilization, reintegration, repatriation and resettlement; protect UN personnel and civilians; support implementation of the peace process; and provide assistance in the monitoring of human rights, public information and law and order. The UNOCI mandate was revised in 2007 [YUN 2007, p. 170]. In 2011, by resolution 2000(2011) (see p. 149), the Security Council decided that UNOCI would have the mandate to protect civilians; address remaining security threats and border-related challenges; monitor the implementation of the arms embargo; assist the national authorities in the collection of weapons, the disarmament, demobilization and reintegration of combatants, and the reconstitution and reform of security and rule of law institutions; support efforts to promote and protect human rights and provide humanitarian assistance; support the organization and conduct of legislative elections; monitor public information; support the redeployment of State administration and the extension of State authority throughout the country; assist the Government in implementing the outstanding tasks of the peace process; and protect UN personnel.

Appointments. By a letter of 11 March [S/2011/134], the Secretary-General informed the Council of his intention to appoint Major General Gnakoudè Béréna (Togo) as Force Commander of UNOCI, to replace Major General Abdul Hafiz (Bangladesh). The Council took note of his intention on 14 March [S/2011/135].

In a letter of 26 July [S/2011/468], the Secretary-General informed the Council President that he intended to appoint Albert Gerard Koenders (Netherlands) as his Special Representative for Côte d'Ivoire and Head of UNOCI, to replace Choi Young-jin (Republic of Korea). The Council took note of his intention on 28 July [S/2011/469].

Financing

In June, the General Assembly considered the Secretary-General's performance report on the budget of UNOCI for the period from 1 July 2009 to 30 June 2010 [A/65/615], the proposed budget for the mission for the period from 1 July 2011 to 30 June 2012 [A/65/736 & Corr.1] and the related ACABQ report [A/65/743/Add.14]. The performance report for the 2009–2010 financial period showed actual expenditure at $473,558,600 gross ($463,057,900 net) against an appropriation of $491,774,100 gross ($482,126,200 net). The proposed budget for the 2011–2012 period amounted to $485,839,600 gross ($475,116,200 net), which provided for the deployment of 192 military observers, 7,200 military contingent personnel, 450 United Nations police officers, 800 formed police unit personnel, 414 international staff, 799 national staff, 176 United Nations Volunteers, 16 Government-provided personnel, 14 international temporary positions and 10 national temporary positions. ACABQ, in April, recommended approval of the Secretary-General's proposals.

GENERAL ASSEMBLY ACTION

On 30 June [meeting 106], the General Assembly, on the recommendation of the Fifth Committee [A/65/881], adopted **resolution 65/294** without vote [agenda item 145].

Financing of the United Nations Operation in Côte d'Ivoire

The General Assembly,

Having considered the reports of the Secretary-General on the financing of the United Nations Operation in Côte d'Ivoire and the related report of the Advisory Committee on Administrative and Budgetary Questions,

Recalling Security Council resolution 1528(2004) of 27 February 2004, by which the Council established the United Nations Operation in Côte d'Ivoire for an initial period of twelve months as from 4 April 2004, and the subsequent resolutions by which the Council extended the mandate of the Operation, the latest of which was resolution 1981(2011) of 13 May 2011, by which the Council extended the mandate of the Operation until 31 July 2011,

Recalling also its resolution 58/310 of 18 June 2004 on the financing of the Operation and its subsequent resolutions thereon, the latest of which was resolution 64/273 of 24 June 2010,

Reaffirming the general principles underlying the financing of United Nations peacekeeping operations, as stated in General Assembly resolutions 1874(S-IV) of 27 June 1963, 3101(XXVIII) of 11 December 1973 and 55/235 of 23 December 2000,

Mindful of the fact that it is essential to provide the Operation with the financial resources necessary to enable it to fulfil its responsibilities under the relevant resolutions of the Security Council,

1. *Requests* the Secretary-General to entrust the Head of Mission with the task of formulating future budget proposals in full accordance with the provisions of General Assembly resolutions 59/296 of 22 June 2005, 60/266 of 30 June 2006, 61/276 of 29 June 2007, 64/269 of 24 June 2010 and 65/289 of 30 June 2011, as well as other relevant resolutions;

2. *Takes note* of the status of contributions to the United Nations Operation in Côte d'Ivoire as at 30 April 2011, including the contributions outstanding in the amount of 81.9 million United States dollars, representing some 2 per cent of the total assessed contributions, notes with concern that only fifty-one Member States have paid their assessed contributions in full, and urges all other Member States, in particular those in arrears, to ensure payment of their outstanding assessed contributions;

3. *Expresses its appreciation* to those Member States which have paid their assessed contributions in full, and urges all other Member States to make every possible effort to ensure payment of their assessed contributions to the Operation in full;

4. *Expresses concern* at the financial situation with regard to peacekeeping activities, in particular as regards the reimbursements to troop contributors that bear additional burdens owing to overdue payments by Member States of their assessments;

5. *Also expresses concern* at the delay experienced by the Secretary-General in deploying and providing adequate resources to some recent peacekeeping missions, in particular those in Africa;

6. *Emphasizes* that all future and existing peacekeeping missions shall be given equal and non-discriminatory treatment in respect of financial and administrative arrangements;

7. *Also emphasizes* that all peacekeeping missions shall be provided with adequate resources for the effective and efficient discharge of their respective mandates;

8. *Requests* the Secretary-General to ensure that proposed peacekeeping budgets are based on the relevant legislative mandates;

9. *Endorses* the conclusions and recommendations contained in the report of the Advisory Committee on Administrative and Budgetary Questions, subject to the provisions of the present resolution, and requests the Secretary-General to ensure their full implementation;

10. *Takes note* of paragraphs 1 and 36 of the report of the Advisory Committee;

11. *Requests* the Secretary-General to ensure the full implementation of the relevant provisions of its resolutions 59/296, 60/266, 61/276, 64/269 and 65/289;

12. *Also requests* the Secretary-General to take all action necessary to ensure that the Operation is administered with a maximum of efficiency and economy;

13. *Notes* that the overall level of appropriation has been adjusted in accordance with the terms of resolution 65/289;

Financial performance report for the period from 1 July 2009 to 30 June 2010

14. *Takes note* of the report of the Secretary-General on the financial performance of the Operation for the period from 1 July 2009 to 30 June 2010;

Budget estimates for the period from 1 July 2011 to 30 June 2012

15. *Decides* to appropriate to the Special Account for the United Nations Operation in Côte d'Ivoire the amount of 517,850,700 dollars for the period from 1 July 2011 to 30 June 2012, inclusive of the amount of 486,726,400 dollars for the maintenance of the Operation, 26,374,200 dollars for the support account for peacekeeping operations and 4,750,100 dollars for the United Nations Logistics Base, at Brindisi, Italy;

Financing of the appropriation

16. *Also decides* to apportion among Member States the amount of 43,154,225 dollars for the period from 1 to 31 July 2011, in accordance with the levels updated in General Assembly resolution 64/249 of 24 December 2009, and taking into account the scale of assessments for 2011, as set out in Assembly resolution 64/248 of 24 December 2009;

17. *Further decides* that, in accordance with the provisions of its resolution 973(X) of 15 December 1955, there shall be set off against the apportionment among Member States, as provided for in paragraph 16 above, their respective share in the Tax Equalization Fund of 1,121,350 dollars, comprising the estimated staff assessment income of 893,616 dollars approved for the Operation, the prorated share of 186,142 dollars of the estimated staff assessment income approved for the support account and the prorated share of 41,592 dollars of the estimated staff assessment income approved for the United Nations Logistics Base;

18. *Decides* to apportion among Member States the amount of 474,696,475 dollars for the period from 1 August 2011 to 30 June 2012, at a monthly rate of 43,154,225 dollars, in accordance with the levels updated in resolution 64/249 and taking into account the scale of assessments for 2011 and 2012, as set out in resolution 64/248, subject to a decision of the Security Council to extend the mandate of the Operation;

19. *Also decides* that, in accordance with the provisions of its resolution 973(X), there shall be set off against the apportionment among Member States, as provided for in paragraph 18 above, their respective share in the Tax Equalization Fund of 12,334,850 dollars, comprising the estimated staff assessment income of 9,829,784 dollars approved for the Operation, the prorated share of 2,047,558 dollars of the estimated staff assessment income approved for the support account and the prorated share of 457,508 dollars of the estimated staff assessment income approved for the United Nations Logistics Base;

20. *Further decides* that, for Member States that have fulfilled their financial obligations to the Operation, there shall be set off against the apportionment, as provided for in paragraph 16 above, their respective share of the unencumbered balance and other income in the total amount of 25,042,400 dollars in respect of the financial period ended 30 June 2010, in accordance with the levels updated in resolution 64/249, and taking into account the scale of assessments for 2010, as set out in resolution 64/248;

21. *Decides* that, for Member States that have not fulfilled their financial obligations to the Operation, there shall be set off against their outstanding obligations their respective share of the unencumbered balance and other income in the total amount of 25,042,400 dollars in respect of the financial period ended 30 June 2010, in accordance with the scheme set out in paragraph 20 above;

22. *Also decides* that the increase of 852,800 dollars in the estimated staff assessment income in respect of the financial period ended 30 June 2010 shall be added to the credits from the amount of 25,042,400 dollars referred to in paragraphs 20 and 21 above;

23. *Emphasizes* that no peacekeeping mission shall be financed by borrowing funds from other active peacekeeping missions;

24. *Encourages* the Secretary-General to continue to take additional measures to ensure the safety and security of all personnel participating in the Operation under the auspices of the United Nations, bearing in mind paragraphs 5 and 6 of Security Council resolution 1502(2003) of 26 August 2003;

25. *Invites* voluntary contributions to the Operation in cash and in the form of services and supplies acceptable to the Secretary-General, to be administered, as appropriate, in accordance with the procedure and practices established by the General Assembly;

26. *Decides* to include in the provisional agenda of its sixty-sixth session the item entitled "Financing of the United Nations Operation in Côte d'Ivoire".

Request for additional resources. Following the extension of the UNOCI mandate by Council resolution 2000(2011), the Assembly, in December, considered the Secretary-General's report on the supplementary estimates for the mission's budget for the period from 1 July 2011 to 30 June 2012 [A/66/529], and the related ACABQ report [A/66/612]. To implement the mandate outlined in that resolution, additional funding of $165,735,000 was requested, which ACABQ recommended be reduced by $381,500 to $165,353,500.

GENERAL ASSEMBLY ACTION

On 24 December [meeting 93], the General Assembly, on the recommendation of the Fifth Committee [A/66/633], adopted **resolution 66/242 A** without vote [agenda item 149].

Financing of the United Nations Operation in Côte d'Ivoire

The General Assembly,

Having considered the report of the Secretary-General on the financing of the United Nations Operation in Côte d'Ivoire and the related report of the Advisory Committee on Administrative and Budgetary Questions,

Recalling Security Council resolution 2000(2011) of 27 July 2011, by which the Council extended the mandate of the Operation until 31 July 2012,

Recalling also its resolution 58/310 of 18 June 2004 on the financing of the Operation and its subsequent resolutions thereon, the latest of which was resolution 65/294 of 30 June 2011,

1. *Endorses* the conclusions and recommendations contained in the report of the Advisory Committee on Administrative and Budgetary Questions, subject to the provisions of the present resolution;

Financing arrangements for the period from 1 July 2011 to 30 June 2012

2. *Decides* to appropriate to the Special Account for the United Nations Operation in Côte d'Ivoire the amount of 159,235,000 United States dollars for the period from 1 July 2011 to 30 June 2012 for the maintenance of the Operation, in addition to the amount of 517,850,700 dollars previously appropriated for the Operation for the same period under the terms of its resolution 65/294, inclusive of 486,726,400 dollars for the maintenance of the Operation, 26,374,200 dollars for the support account for peacekeeping operations and 4,750,100 dollars for the United Nations Logistics Base at Brindisi, Italy;

Financing of the appropriation

3. *Also decides*, taking into account the amount of 517,850,700 dollars already apportioned for the period from 1 July 2011 to 30 June 2012 under the terms of its resolution 65/294, to apportion among Member States the additional amount of 159,235,000 dollars for the same period, in accordance with the levels updated in General Assembly resolution 64/249 of 24 December 2009, and taking into account the scale of assessments for 2011 and 2012, as set out in its resolution 64/248 of 24 December 2009;

4. *Further decides* that, in accordance with the provisions of its resolution 973(X) of 15 December 1955, there shall be set off against the apportionment among Member States, as provided for in paragraph 3 above, their respective share in the Tax Equalization Fund of 780,900 dollars, representing the estimated staff assessment income approved for the Operation;

5. *Decides* to keep under review during its sixty-sixth session the item entitled "Financing of the United Nations Operation in Côte d'Ivoire".

On 24 December, the Assembly decided that the item on the financing of UNOCI would remain for consideration during its resumed sixty-sixth (2012) session (**decision 66/557**).

Liberia

In 2011, the political situation in Liberia was dominated by the presidential and legislative elections of 11 October, preceded by a constitutional referendum on 23 August to put in place a revised legal framework for the elections. While the day of the referendum was generally peaceful, voter turnout was low owing to a boycott by the opposition party, and controversy emerged due to an error on the printed ballot. None of the referendum provisions were initially passed. The Supreme Court, however, subsequently ruled in favour of a petition that invalid votes should not count in the referendum outcome, and consequently the amendment providing for a simple rather than absolute majority to determine the outcome of elections, except presidential elections, was passed. While the period leading up to the elections was highly charged, voting proceeded peacefully on 11 October, with a voter turnout of nearly 72 per cent. National and international observers issued positive preliminary statements. Tensions, however, began to rise while the votes were being tallied, and provisional results confirmed the need for a run-off election between President Ellen Johnson Sirleaf and Winston Tubman of the Congress for Democratic Change (CDC). On 7 November, in response to a large gathering of CDC supporters in Monrovia, the security services used tear gas and live ammunition to disperse civilians, resulting in the death of at least one person and several injuries. The President announced on 11 November the establishment of an independent commission of inquiry to investigate the incident. The presidential run-off was held on 8 November with a voter turnout of 38.6 per cent; President Johnson Sirleaf received 90.7 per cent of the vote and Mr. Tubman 9.3 per cent.

The security situation remained fragile, particularly owing to the impact of the post-electoral crisis in Côte d'Ivoire on the border areas of Liberia, ethnic and communal tensions, and disputes over land and resources. The Government and the United Nations Mission in Liberia (UNMIL) worked to address the influx into Liberia of Ivorian combatants and Liberian nationals who fought in Côte d'Ivoire. UNMIL and UNOCI intensified inter-mission cooperation, including joint border activities and coordination of ground and air patrols.

In support of election preparations, UNMIL intensified its work with the authorities to create an atmosphere conducive to peaceful elections. It provided capacity-building for national security institutions, developed plans to provide security support to the national authorities during the elections, and deployed magisterial electoral officers to support National Elections Commission magistrates. The Mission also supported national efforts in security sector reform and in strengthening the capacity of rule-of-law institutions and mechanisms. The development of a joint transition plan for the transfer of responsibility for internal security from UNMIL to the national authorities continued. On 16 September, the Security Council extended the mandate of UNMIL until 30 September 2012.

Political and security developments

Report of Secretary-General (February). The Secretary-General, in his twenty-second progress report on UNMIL [S/2011/72], reviewed the political situation in Liberia ahead of the 2011 elections. Voter registration began as scheduled on 10 January with only minor challenges, including late openings in some remote locations and logistical problems. In view of those challenges, the National Elections Commission extended the registration period, originally closing on 6 February, until 12 February. The UN system in Liberia established a task force to coordinate the Organization's support to the electoral process. UNMIL provided logistical support for the delivery of voter registration materials to remote locations and assisted the national police in developing an integrated security and contingency plan. The United Nations and other partners were also working closely with the National Elections Commission on measures to strengthen women's participation in the electoral process.

Pursuant to Security Council resolution 1938(2010) [YUN 2010, p. 202], the Secretary-General reported on progress in joint planning with the Government for the transfer of security responsibilities from UNMIL to national authorities, and presented the benchmarks necessary for a successful transition. The core benchmarks included the completion and implementation of a strategy and plan for the handover of security responsibilities from UNMIL to national authorities; the institutionalization of the national security architecture in line with the national security strategy; effective maintenance of law and order by national security institutions; enhanced national capacity to secure and control the borders; increased effectiveness of State authority throughout the country; and the conduct of peaceful, credible and accepted national elections.

Report of Secretary-General (August). Pursuant to Council resolution 1938(2010), the Secretary-General in August reported [S/2011/497] on preparations for the presidential and legislative elections, as well as progress in achieving the benchmarks for the transfer of responsibility for internal security from UNMIL to the national authorities. Political developments were dominated by the activities of political parties ahead of the constitutional referendum on 23 August and the elections, scheduled for 11 October. The voter registration exercise concluded in February, with close to 1.8 million registering, representing approximately 89 per cent of the estimated eligible population. Despite a number of party mergers, including additions to the Unity Party, of which President Ellen Johnson Sirleaf was a member, the political landscape remained fluid and fragmented. The Inter-Party Consultative Committee provided an important forum for addressing key issues arising among political parties and the National Elections Commission, and within the framework of the Committee, an agreement was reached to start the political campaign period on 5 July. Nonetheless, disagreements remained regarding the legal framework for the elections, including the electoral districting exercise, the composition of the Commission, and the conduct of the constitutional referendum.

The security situation, while generally stable, remained fragile, particularly owing to the impact of the situation in Côte d'Ivoire on the border areas of Liberia, ethnic and communal tensions, and disputes over land and other resources. The Government and UNMIL worked to address the influx into Liberia of Ivorian combatants and Liberian nationals who fought in Côte d'Ivoire. In April, Government security personnel arrested a known former Liberian warlord for allegedly fighting in Côte d'Ivoire; he reported that other fighters had returned to Liberia through unofficial border-crossing points. In June, 88 suspected Ivorian combatants were interned in a special facility in Bong County after being detained when crossing the border in Maryland County in April. On 14 June, Liberian security agencies retrieved a significant number of weapons and ammunition from a cache in River Gee County, believed to have been hidden by a group of suspected fighters who reportedly entered the county in May. UNMIL destroyed the weapons and ammunition in July, and 37 people were arrested in connection with the cache. The Government, supported by UNMIL, increased its patrolling and presence along the Ivorian border to monitor the presence of militias and armed elements and provide deterrence; however, the 700-kilometre border was difficult to monitor. UNMIL and UNOCI intensified inter-mission cooperation, including joint border activities, increasing joint meetings, coordinating ground and air patrols, and institutionalizing information-sharing. The Governments of the two countries engaged in discussions about border security when the Prime Minister of Côte d'Ivoire led an official delegation to Monrovia on 9 July. Furthermore, tensions related to land and labour disputes, as well as ethnic tensions, threatened the country's long-term stability, with UNMIL and the national police responding to several incidents during the year. Regionally, renewed tensions in Guinea were being monitored closely, as ethnic tensions had led to an influx of Guineans into Liberia, primarily from the Kpelle ethnic group.

In support of election preparations, UNMIL assisted in the dissemination of information on the electoral process through radio programmes and other outreach activities in rural areas. The mission intensified its work with Liberian authorities to create an atmosphere conducive to peaceful elections and strengthened its monitoring of electoral, legal, political, public information, security and human rights issues to mitigate tensions. It also provided capacity-building for national security institutions in the planning and training of personnel, developed plans to provide security support to the national authorities during the elections, and deployed magisterial electoral officers to support magistrates of the National Elections Commission in all counties. Regarding security sector reform, UNMIL supported battalion-level field exercises in April as part of the annual training plan of the armed forces. The army conducted a number of joint operations, including a complex operation in June with other security institutions, the Ministry of Internal Affairs and UNMIL, to transport suspected former combatants from Côte d'Ivoire to the Government-designated internment camp. Nonetheless, while it had been estimated that the army would become fully operational in 2012, factors such as insufficient equipment and delays in the procurement of new assets and in endorsing the national defence strategy would likely delay the army's full operational status until at least 2014. UNMIL also supported the national police in border operations. While the national police had shown increased capacity to execute complex operations, mobility remained an issue, and UNMIL continued to provide air and other logistical support. The Secretary-General noted that coordination and collaboration within the justice sector and between the justice and security sectors had continued to strengthen. UNMIL focused on strengthening the capacity of rule-of-law institutions and mechanisms, supporting efforts to improve delivery and access to justice, and mentoring key justice-sector actors.

Regarding transition planning, the Government and UNMIL initiated a joint transition planning process, led by the National Security Council, which resulted in the establishment of a senior-level core group, a working group and four security task groups covering the areas of border security, law and order, security of assets and logistics. In April, the task groups began assessing the capacity of security agencies to assume responsibility in those four security areas. Progress, however, had slowed, particularly for the national police, which would absorb much of the burden for law and order and security of assets.

The Secretary-General concluded that the success of the coming elections, and the peaceful inauguration of a new administration, were critical to the consolidation of progress the country had made over the previous eight years. He urged all political actors and the population to ensure that the elections would be free, fair and without violence; and encouraged the prompt resolution of the remaining differences between political parties and the National Elections Commission concerning aspects of the legal framework. Furthermore, a number of national security gaps needed to be addressed to enable a smooth handover of security responsibilities from UNMIL to national institutions. The Government's international partners should increase support for the development of the security sector to ensure that UNMIL operations could be progressively scaled down as it handed over security responsibilities to national authorities. The Secretary-General said that following the inauguration of the next Government, a comprehensive technical assessment mission would be deployed to Liberia to develop proposals for the next stages of the mission's drawdown. The Secretary-General recommended that the Security Council extend the mission's mandate until 30 September 2012, and conduct a review of its authorized military and police strength by 30 May 2012.

Extension of UNMIL mandate. By resolution 2008(2011) (see below), the Council extended the mandate of UNMIL until 30 September 2012, reiterating its authorization to the mission to assist the Government with the 2011 presidential and legislative elections.

SECURITY COUNCIL ACTION

On 16 September [meeting 6619], the Security Council unanimously adopted **resolution 2008(2011)**. The draft [S/2011/576] was submitted by Gabon, India, Nigeria, South Africa and the United States.

The Security Council,

Recalling its resolutions and the statements by its President concerning the situation in Liberia and the subregion, in particular resolutions 1509(2003) of 19 September 2003, 1836(2008) of 29 September 2008, 1885(2009) of 15 September 2009, 1938(2010) of 15 September 2010 and 1971(2011) of 3 March 2011,

Welcoming the report of the Secretary-General of 5 August 2011, and taking note of the recommendations contained therein,

Welcoming also the efforts of the Government of Liberia to further national reconciliation and economic recovery and to combat corruption and promote efficiency and good governance, in particular steps taken with regard to strengthening Government control over natural resources, noting with concern the slow progress on the important issue of land reform, and urging intensified efforts towards achieving progress on the transition of security responsibilities from the United Nations Mission in Liberia to the national authorities, particularly with regard to improving the capacity and capability of the Liberia National Police and on the consolidation of State authority throughout the territory,

Recognizing that lasting stability in Liberia and the subregion will require well-functioning and sustainable government institutions, including security and rule of law sectors,

Commending the assistance provided by both the Government of Liberia and the Liberian people to the refugees that have relocated temporarily in eastern Liberia,

Noting that the mandate of the Mission includes assisting the Government of Liberia to consolidate peace and stability with national institutions that are able to maintain security and stability independently of a peacekeeping mission and ensure the future stability of Liberia, recalling the transition benchmarks for the drawdown phase of the Mission, including core benchmarks on the Liberia National Police and the national security strategy, welcoming the progress achieved, and noting the need for accelerated progress in taking forward planning for the security transition, the process of which is expected to commence in mid-2012,

Stressing that the successful holding of timely, credible, inclusive and peaceful elections, in accordance with the Constitution and applicable international standards, is a key condition for the consolidation of democracy, national reconciliation and the restoration of a stable, peaceful and secure environment in which stabilization and socio-economic development can progress in Liberia, and emphasizing the need to promote strong voter turnout and the participation of women in the electoral process,

Taking note of the recommendation of the Secretary-General to deploy a technical assessment mission to Liberia after the inauguration of the elected Government in 2012 that will develop detailed proposals for the next stages of the drawdown of the Mission, as well as for the handover of security responsibilities from the Mission to the national authorities,

Welcoming the contribution of the Peacebuilding Commission to security sector reform, the rule of law and national reconciliation, and noting that challenges still remain in these key areas,

Recognizing the significant challenges that remain across all sectors, including continuing problems with violent crime, and recognizing that the instability in Côte d'Ivoire continues to pose cross-border security challenges for Liberia and Côte d'Ivoire,

Noting with concern the threats to subregional stability, including to Liberia, in particular those posed by illicit drug trafficking, organized crime and illicit arms,

Commending the work of the Mission, under the leadership of the Special Representative of the Secretary-General for Liberia, for its continuing and significant contribution to maintaining peace and stability in Liberia, and noting with satisfaction the close cooperation between the Mission and the United Nations Operation in Côte d'Ivoire, as well as the neighbouring Governments, in coordinating security activities in the border areas in the subregion,

Welcoming the efforts of the Secretary-General to keep all peacekeeping operations, including the Mission, under close review, and reiterating the need for the Security Council to pursue a rigorous, strategic approach to peacekeeping deployments,

Expressing its appreciation for the continuing support of the international community, the Economic Community of West African States and the African Union,

Recalling its resolutions 1325(2000) of 31 October 2000, 1820(2008) of 19 June 2008, 1888(2009) of 30 September 2009, 1889(2009) of 5 October 2009 and 1960(2010) of 16 December 2010 on women and peace and security, concerned about the high incidence of sexual and gender-based violence, welcoming the continuing efforts of the Mission and the Government of Liberia to promote and protect the rights of civilians, in particular women and children, and reaffirming the importance of appropriate gender expertise and training in missions mandated by the Council,

Encouraging the efforts to ensure adequate human rights presence, capacity and expertise within the Mission to carry out human rights promotion, protection and monitoring activities,

Expressing its appreciation for the contribution of military personnel of the Mission to the provision of security for the Special Court for Sierra Leone, which concluded on 7 March 2011, in accordance with resolution 1971(2011),

Determining that the situation in Liberia continues to constitute a threat to international peace and security in the region,

Acting under Chapter VII of the Charter of the United Nations,

1. *Decides* that the mandate of the United Nations Mission in Liberia shall be extended until 30 September 2012;

2. *Reiterates* its authorization to the Mission to continue to assist the Government of Liberia, as requested, with the 2011 general presidential and legislative elections, by providing logistical support, particularly to facilitate access to remote areas, coordinating international electoral assistance and supporting Liberian institutions and political parties in creating an atmosphere conducive to the conduct of peaceful elections;

3. *Recognizes* the primary responsibility of the Government of Liberia and other national actors to create propitious conditions for the forthcoming elections, and in that regard urges the Government, political parties and their constituents, as well as all Liberian people, to help to ensure an environment conducive to a timely, credible, inclusive and peaceful electoral process, which includes free and con-

structive political debate, calls upon the Liberian actors to ensure that any outstanding issues regarding the electoral framework are finalized and ensure secure conditions for the conduct of and unrestricted access to the polls, including through cooperation with the Mission, consistent with the role of the Mission with regard to the protection of civilians, and calls upon all parties to respect the results of the polls;

4. *Recalls* its endorsement of the recommendation of the Secretary-General that the conduct of free, fair and peaceful elections be a core benchmark for the future drawdown of the Mission;

5. *Encourages* the Government of Liberia and the Mission to continue to make progress in the transition planning process, particularly in addressing critical gaps that need to be filled in order to facilitate a successful transition, and requests that the Secretary-General deploy a technical assessment mission to Liberia after the inauguration of the elected Government in 2012 that should focus on the security transition and also develop detailed proposals for the next stages of the drawdown of the Mission, based on a thorough review of progress made towards the transition benchmarks, with a view to providing timelines and recommendations for the further reduction of the military component of the Mission;

6. *Reaffirms* the inter-mission cooperation arrangements provided for in resolution 1609(2005) of 24 June 2005, as needed and on a temporary basis, between the Mission and the United Nations Operation in Côte d'Ivoire, and calls upon troop-contributing countries to support the efforts of the Secretary-General in this regard;

7. *Emphasizes* the need for the Mission and the United Nations Operation in Côte d'Ivoire to regularly coordinate their strategies and operations in areas near the Liberian-Côte d'Ivoire border, in order to contribute to subregional security and to prevent armed groups from exploiting the seam of political boundaries, and requests the Secretary-General to report on them to the Security Council and troop-contributing countries;

8. *Also emphasizes* the need for the donor community to support the Government of Liberia, as well as the United Nations and other humanitarian actors, as appropriate, in their response to the current influx of Ivorian refugees;

9. *Further emphasizes* the need for coherence between, and integration of, peacekeeping, peacebuilding and development to achieve an effective response to post-conflict situations, requests that the Secretary-General continue to coordinate and collaborate with the Peacebuilding Commission, and encourages the Commission, following close consultation with the Government of Liberia, to continue to report on the findings of its missions and its recommendations on how it can accelerate progress first and foremost on security sector reform, the rule of law and national reconciliation;

10. *Underscores* the importance of the military concept of operations and rules of engagement being regularly updated and fully in line with the provisions of the present resolution, and requests the Secretary-General to report on them to the Council and troop-contributing countries;

11. *Calls upon* the Government of Liberia, in coordination with the Mission, the United Nations country team and international partners, to continue to develop national security and rule of law institutions that are fully and independently operational, and to this end continues to encourage coordinated progress on the implementation of all security and justice development plans;

12. *Encourages* the Economic Community of West African States to develop, with the support of the United Nations Office for West Africa, a subregional strategy to address the threat of the cross-border movements of armed groups and weapons as well as illicit trafficking, with the assistance of the Mission and the United Nations Operation in Côte d'Ivoire, as appropriate;

13. *Welcomes* the efforts of the Government of Liberia to combat sexual and gender-based violence and further encourages it, in coordination with the Mission, to continue to combat impunity for perpetrators of such crimes and to provide redress, support and protection to victims;

14. *Requests* the Mission to continue to support the participation of women in conflict prevention, conflict resolution and peacebuilding, including in decision-making roles in post-conflict governance institutions, appointed and elected in Liberia, within existing resources;

15. *Requests* the Secretary-General to keep the Council regularly informed of the situation on the ground as Liberia enters this next critical phase and to provide by 30 April 2012 a report on the issues addressed in paragraphs 2, 5 and 7 above, including recommendations for appropriate action by the Council, and expresses its intention to consider these recommendations in a timely manner;

16. *Decides* to remain seized of the matter.

Reinforcement of UNMIL. In a 15 September letter to the Council [S/2011/577], the Secretary-General stated that the security and humanitarian challenges created in Liberia as a result of the Ivorian post-election crisis had overstretched the capacity of Liberian security institutions and added to the risks posed by elections in a nation emerging from protracted conflict. The priority areas of concern during the elections period were Monrovia and its environs, as well as the eastern counties bordering Côte d'Ivoire. Enhancing the visibility, coverage and robust posture of UNMIL in Monrovia during the electoral period was critical to deterring violence and preventing any escalation of incidents. Furthermore, hotspots where violence could be triggered were identified throughout the country, particularly in the north and east. The Secretary-General therefore recommended that the three armed helicopters deployed to UNOCI be returned to UNMIL by 30 September; that options remain open for the possible use of the helicopters to address security challenges in other areas of Côte d'Ivoire and for the possible relocation of the helicopters to UNOCI during the Ivorian legislative elections; and that the Council authorize the temporary transfer from UNOCI to UNMIL of one infantry company comprising 150 personnel, as well as three formed police unit platoons with supporting elements, totalling 100 personnel, from 1 October to 30 November, to reinforce UNMIL during the elections period. The Council should also authorize UNOCI to place other military units on standby during that period, to be deployed to Liberia if the situation required.

Presidential and legislative elections

Security Council consideration. On 13 September [S/PV.6610], the Special Representative of the Secretary-General and Head of UNMIL, Ellen Margrethe Løj (Denmark), briefed the Council on developments in the preparation of the elections since the issuance of the Secretary-General's August report (see p. 163). The country's 29 political parties were organizing for the vote, negotiating alliance and nominating candidates. Sixteen presidential candidates had been presented, and more than 800 legislative candidates were competing for the 88 House and Senate seats being contested.

Report of Secretary-General. In a special report on UNMIL [S/2012/230], the Secretary-General provided information on the results of both the constitutional referendum on a revised legal framework for the elections [YUN 2010, p. 204] and the presidential and legislative elections. The referendum took place as scheduled on 23 August, and while the day was generally peaceful, voter turnout was low owing to a boycott by the opposition party, the Congress for Democratic Change (CDC). Controversy emerged due to an error on the printed ballot, and a high percentage of ballots cast were spoiled. While none of the referendum provisions were passed, the Supreme Court subsequently ruled in favour of a petition, presented by the Chair of the ruling Unity Party, that invalid votes should not count in determining the referendum outcome. Consequently, the amendment providing for a simple rather than absolute majority to determine the outcome of all elections, except presidential, was passed.

The period leading up to the elections was highly charged, with presidential candidates making allegations of incitement or intimidation against each other. Many opposition parties claimed that the ruling party had an unfair advantage due to access to public resources and preferential treatment from the National Elections Commission and the international community. The inflammatory rhetoric, however, was softened prior to the elections, partially due to the good offices of the Secretary-General's Special Representative and the political engagement of ECOWAS. Voting proceeded peacefully on 11 October, with a voter turnout of nearly 72 per cent. While all national and international observers issued positive preliminary statements about the fairness and transparency of the polls, tensions began to rise while the votes were being tallied. On 15 October, nine opposition parties issued a joint statement claiming that the National Elections Commission had rigged the elections in favour of incumbent President Johnson Sirleaf. Tensions subsided when provisional results confirmed the need for a run-off election between President Johnson Sirleaf and Winston Tubman of CDC; however, CDC announced that it would not participate in the election unless the Elections Commission was reconstituted, among other conditions. While the Chair of the Commission resigned at the end of October, Mr. Tubman announced on 4 November that CDC would boycott the run-off election as the party's conditions had not been met. On 7 November, approximately 1,000 CDC supporters gathered at the party headquarters in Monrovia, and in the process of dispersing the unarmed civilians, elements of the security services used tear gas and live ammunition, resulting in the death of at least one person and several injuries. UNMIL peacekeepers intervened to restore order and prevent further violence. On 11 November, the President announced the establishment of a special independent commission of inquiry to investigate the incident, as well as the establishment of a national peace and reconciliation initiative led by Nobel Peace Prize laureate Leymah Gbowee.

The presidential run-off was held on 8 November, with a voter turnout of 38.6 per cent. The Elections Commission announced the final results on 15 November, with President Johnson Sirleaf receiving 90.7 per cent of the vote and Mr. Tubman 9.3 per cent. While international observers found that the election had been generally free, fair and transparent, many noted that the widening political divisions underlined a need for national healing and reconciliation. Subsequently, the President initiated consultation with Mr. Tubman and other opposition members about their concerns. In the 73-member House of Representatives, 33 per cent of incumbents were successful in their re-election bids, and female representation dropped to 7 per cent from 13 per cent. Of the 30 Senate seats, 15 were contested in 2011, with two incumbents winning re-election and the number of women senators decreasing from five to four. Although no party had an absolute majority in either chamber, the ruling Unity Party was in the strongest position, controlling 22 seats and the leadership of the House, and 11 seats in the Senate.

Sanctions

Security Council Committee. The Security Council Committee established pursuant to resolution 1521(2003) [YUN 2003, p. 208] concerning Liberia monitored implementation of the sanctions imposed on Liberia by that resolution and subsequent resolutions; the sanctions banned arms and related materiel, as well as international travel by designated individuals, and froze the assets of designated individuals who constituted a threat to the peace in Liberia and the subregion. By resolution 1903(2009) [YUN 2009, p. 201], the Council redefined the arms embargo by directing States to prevent the supply, sale or transfer from their territories or by their nationals, or using their vessels or aircraft, of arms and related materiel to non-governmental entities and individuals in Liberia. By resolution 1961(2010) [YUN 2010, p. 208], the Council renewed the arms embargo on all non-governmental entities and individuals operating in the territory of Liberia and the travel ban.

In its report on its 2011 activities [S/2011/804], the Committee stated that it considered four requests for travel-ban waivers, all of which were granted. The Committee received five advance notifications regarding shipment of arms and related material to Liberia, or provision of military assistance, advice or training. It received four reports from UNMIL on the results of the mission's inspections of inventories of weapons and ammunition, and received two de-listing requests in relation to the travel-ban and assets-freeze lists. On 4 August and 23 December, the Committee updated the list of individuals subject to those lists. On 19 August, on the recommendation of the Panel of Experts on Liberia (see below), the Committee consulted with the Special Representative of INTERPOL to the United Nations regarding the possible preparation of INTERPOL-United Nations special notices for the individuals included in the travel-ban list. The Committee, on 15 September, agreed on procedures for cooperation with INTERPOL to create those notices, marking the first time that another sanctions committee would utilize the special notices mechanism since 2005, when the first special notices were issued in the context of Council resolutions 1267(1999) [YUN 1999, p. 265] and 1989(2011) (see p. 341) concerning Al-Qaida and associated individuals [YUN 2005, p. 414].

Panel of Experts

The Panel of Experts on Liberia, established pursuant to resolution 1521(2003), submitted a midterm report and a final report during the year (see below). Pursuant to Council resolution 1961(2010), the Secretary-General, on 17 February [S/2011/78], appointed three experts to the Panel for a period ending 16 December, and on 7 September [S/2011/559] appointed one expert to replace a member who had resigned.

Reports of Panel of Experts. On 15 June [S/2011/367], the Chairman of the Security Council Committee transmitted to the Council the midterm report of the Panel of Experts on Liberia. The Panel identified the crisis in Côte d'Ivoire as a security threat, as armed Ivorian elements, including Liberian mercenaries, attempted to cross into Liberia through official border posts and unofficial crossing points. While there was concern about security forces of former President Gbagbo and Liberian mercenaries entering Liberia with arms and ammunition, the situation was difficult to monitor given the porous border between the two countries. Nonetheless, the Panel was able to confirm, during its field mission (29 March–13 April) and subsequent inquiries, several attempts to bring weapons into Liberia from Côte d'Ivoire from February to April. The Panel also initiated investigations to update its assessments of the Liberian Government's implementation of the Kimberley Process Certification Scheme and the contribution of forestry and other natural resources to peace, security and development. It noted that, as there was a new team of officials in the Ministry of Lands, Mines and Energy, there appeared to have been little action on implementation of the Kimberley Process since December 2010.

On 30 November, the Chairman of the Committee transmitted to the Council the Panel's final report [S/2011/757]. The Panel identified one significant arms embargo violation committed by Liberian mercenaries and Ivorian combatants in River Gee County in May, which involved the discovery of weapons in an arms cache near the Liberian-Ivorian border comprising 74 assault weapons and associated ammunition. The Panel focused on the cross-border movement of Liberian mercenaries and Ivorian militia, and interviewed Liberian mercenaries who fought on both sides of the conflict, as well as one Ivorian militia leader aligned with the former Gbagbo regime. It received anecdotal information that some of those combatants brought small quantities of weapons into Liberia in violation of the arms embargo, and estimated that up to several hundred assault weapons were hidden in remote border locations. Liberian mercenary command structures in the Ivorian conflict were fluid and relied on an alliance of generals who often activated their own recruits. Furthermore, there was substantive overlap between the military operations of Liberian mercenaries and certain pro-Gbagbo Ivorian militias, whose forces were residing in Liberia, intermingled with Ivorian refugees. Those groups might attempt to destabilize areas along the Liberian-Ivorian border, enhancing insecurity and exacerbating land tenure conflicts. The availability of financing would define the future disposition of those groups.

The Panel obtained documentation concerning the assets of eight individuals designated on the assets freeze list, including income generated through companies owned or controlled by those individuals; it also identified several bank accounts of designated individuals and one case of international financial transfer. During the Panel's mandate, however, the Liberian Government did not take action to implement the financial measures imposed by Council resolution 1532(2004) [YUN 2004, p. 204]. The Panel noted that, based on its recommendation, the Security Council Committee had authorized the submission of names of individuals on the travel ban list to INTERPOL for the issuance of INTERPOL-Security Council special notices, a process that would enhance the dissemination of the names cited in the travel ban list to Member States, and especially to security agencies conducting border control. Regarding the export of diamonds and gold, the Kimberley Process Certification Scheme was functioning relatively well for export but internal controls were hampered by a lack of funding for regional officers. Furthermore, artisanal miners had moved out of diamond mines and into gold mines, where a lack of regulation had resulted in considerable losses in potential government revenue. Positive steps were reported in implementing forest reform, including the establishment of community forests, improvements to social agreements between logging companies and affected communities, and a regulation on disbursement of benefit-sharing funds. Liberia also signed a binding trade agreement with the EU to certify timber legality. Reform was at risk, however, due to a lack of compliance in concession allocation and a tax collection rate of just 15 per cent, resulting in production and revenues that were far below government projections. Reforms might also be undermined by the increase in private use permits on deeded land, which constituted almost half the area under concession but contributed little in taxes. Furthermore, while agriculture was a critical sector for the economy and rural livelihood, there was limited donor support or political will for reform, leading to weak compliance with concession allocation laws, lack of commodity and revenue tracking mechanisms, lack of consultation and vague and ad hoc social agreements with affected communities. The situation resulted in land disputes, rubber theft and violence.

Among its recommendations, the Panel stated that the Government should prosecute Liberian mercenary commanders and develop a sustainable strategy for dealing with armed elements, including by establishing an effective screening process for refugees. UNMIL should establish a task force to gather information on the presence, disposition and capabilities of Liberian mercenaries and Ivorian militia present in Liberia; UNMIL and UNOCI should enhance their collaboration, including information-sharing on Liberian mercenaries and other fighters residing in the border region, and reach an agreement on a sustainable stabilization programme and a disarmament, demobilization and reintegration programme targeting former militia. The Governments of Liberia and Côte d'Ivoire should increase their presence in their shared border region and work with local communities to enhance confidence in Government authorities, and develop, with support from UNMIL and UNOCI, a framework for the transfer to Côte d'Ivoire of identified Ivorian militia residing in Liberia. The Ministry of Justice of Liberia should ensure proper oversight of arms and ammunition recovered by the national police, and maintain comprehensive records of all arms and ammunition destroyed. The Government should strengthen the system of internal controls that underpinned the Kimberley Process Certification Scheme, exercise control over the gold sector, and impose a moratorium on allocating further natural resources concessions, as well as private use permits, until the Lands Commission completed its review of ownership of existing concessions. Multi-stakeholder re-engagement was needed in the rubber sector, where rubber theft had become an increasing security problem. UNMIL and donors should pay more attention to the agricultural sector to gauge the risks to peace, development and security from the lack of governance reform in that sector.

SECURITY COUNCIL ACTION

On 14 December [meeting 6684], the Security Council unanimously adopted **resolution 2025(2011)**. The draft [S/2011/769] was submitted by the United States.

The Security Council,

Recalling its previous resolutions and the statements by its President on the situation in Liberia and West Africa,

Welcoming the sustained progress made by the Government of Liberia since January 2006 in rebuilding Liberia for the benefit of all Liberians, with the support of the international community,

Stressing that Liberia's progress in the timber sector must continue with the effective implementation and enforcement of the National Forestry Reform Law signed into law on 5 October 2006 and other new legislation related to revenue transparency (the Liberia Extractive Industries Transparency Initiative Act) and resolution of land and tenure rights (the Community Rights Law with respect to Forest Lands and the Lands Commission Act),

Encouraging the Government of Liberia to reaffirm its commitment and redouble its efforts to ensure the effective implementation of the Kimberley Process Certification Scheme in Liberia and to take all possible measures to prevent rough diamond smuggling,

Also encouraging the Government of Liberia to improve its control over the gold sector and adopt the necessary legislation in this regard, and to focus its efforts on establishing effective governance of the gold production sector,

Stressing the continuing importance of the United Nations Mission in Liberia in improving security throughout Liberia and helping the Government of Liberia to establish its authority throughout the country, particularly in the regions producing diamonds, gold, timber and other natural resources, and border areas,

Taking note of the report of the Panel of Experts on Liberia,

Underlining its determination to support the Government of Liberia in its efforts to meet the conditions of resolution 1521(2003) of 22 December 2003, welcoming the engagement of the Peacebuilding Commission, and encouraging all stakeholders, including donors, to support the Government in its efforts,

Acknowledging the implementation of the guidelines of the Department of Peacekeeping Operations of the Secretariat on cooperation and information-sharing between the United Nations peacekeeping missions and the Security Council sanctions committee expert panels,

Commending the people of Liberia on the completion of their presidential election of 8 November 2011, which was free, fair and transparent, and further commending the successful organization by the National Elections Commission of the electoral process, in accordance with Liberian law,

Expressing concern about the violent events of 7 November 2011, and welcoming the establishment by the Government of Liberia of a special independent commission of inquiry to investigate the events and determine the facts and circumstances through independent and impartial proceedings that meet international standards, in order to hold accountable those responsible,

Calling upon all Liberian leaders to promote meaningful reconciliation and inclusive dialogue to consolidate peace and advance Liberia's democratic development,

Determining that, despite significant progress, the situation in Liberia continues to constitute a threat to international peace and security in the region,

Acting under Chapter VII of the Charter of the United Nations,

1. *Reaffirms* that the measures imposed by paragraph 1 of resolution 1532(2004) of 12 March 2004 remain in force, notes with serious concern the lack of progress with regard to the implementation of the financial measures imposed by paragraph 1 of resolution 1532(2004), and demands that the Government of Liberia make all necessary efforts to fulfil its obligations;

2. *Decides*, for a period of twelve months from the date of adoption of the present resolution:

(*a*) To renew the measures on travel imposed by paragraph 4 of resolution 1521(2003);

(*b*) To renew the measures on arms, previously imposed by paragraph 2 of resolution 1521(2003) and modified by paragraphs 1 and 2 of resolution 1683(2006) of 13 June 2006, by paragraph 1 (*b*) of resolution 1731(2006) of 20 December 2006, by paragraphs 3 to 6 of resolution 1903(2009) of 17 December 2009 and by paragraph 3 of resolution 1961(2010) of 17 December 2010;

(*c*) To review the measures in the present paragraph and in paragraph 1 above in the light of the progress achieved in the stabilization throughout the country and the holding of presidential and parliamentary elections, with a view to possibly modifying or lifting all or part of the measures of the sanctions regime, and decides that such a review shall be carried out at the end of the above-mentioned twelve-month period, with a midterm review no later than 30 April 2012;

3. *Decides also* to review any of the above measures at the request of the Government of Liberia, once the Government reports to the Security Council that the conditions set out in resolution 1521(2003) for terminating the measures have been met and provides the Council with information to justify its assessment;

4. *Directs* the Security Council Committee established pursuant to resolution 1521(2003), in coordination with the Government of Liberia and relevant designating States and with the assistance of the Panel of Experts on Liberia, to, as necessary and without delay, update the publicly available reasons for listing for entries on the travel ban and assets freeze lists as well as the guidelines of the Committee;

5. *Decides* to extend the mandate of the Panel of Experts appointed pursuant to paragraph 9 of resolution 1903(2009) for a period of twelve months from the date of adoption of the present resolution to undertake the following tasks:

(*a*) To conduct two follow-up assessment missions to Liberia and neighbouring States, in order to investigate and compile a midterm report and a final report on the implementation, and any violations, of the measures on arms as amended by resolution 1903(2009), including any information relevant to the designation by the Committee of the individuals described in paragraph 4 (*a*) of resolution 1521(2003) and paragraph 1 of resolution 1532(2004), and including the various sources of financing, such as from natural resources, for the illicit trade in arms;

(*b*) To assess the impact, effectiveness and continued need for the measures imposed by paragraph 1 of resolution 1532(2004), including, in particular, with respect to the assets of former President Charles Taylor;

(*c*) To identify and make recommendations regarding areas where the capacity of Liberia and the States in the region can be strengthened to facilitate the implementation of the measures imposed by paragraph 4 of resolution 1521(2003) and paragraph 1 of resolution 1532(2004);

(*d*) Within the context of Liberia's evolving legal framework, to assess the extent to which forests and other natural resources are contributing to peace, security and development rather than to instability and to what extent relevant legislation (the National Forestry Reform Law, the Lands Commission Act, the Community Rights Law with respect to Forest Lands and the Liberia Extractive Industries Transparency Initiative Act) and other reform efforts are contributing to this transition, and to provide recommendations on how such natural resources could better contribute to the country's progress towards sustainable peace and stability;

(*e*) To cooperate actively with the Kimberley Process and to assess the compliance of the Government of Liberia with the Kimberley Process Certification Scheme;

(*f*) To provide a midterm report to the Council, through the Committee, by 1 June 2012 and a final report to the Council, through the Committee, by 1 December 2012 on all the issues listed in the present paragraph, and to provide informal updates to the Committee, as appropriate, before those dates, especially on progress in the forest sector since the lifting of the measures imposed by paragraph 10 of resolution 1521(2003) in June 2006, and in the diamond sector since the lifting of the measures imposed by paragraph 6 of resolution 1521(2003) in April 2007;

(*g*) To cooperate actively with other relevant panels of experts, in particular the Group of Experts on Côte d'Ivoire re-established by paragraph 13 of resolution 1980(2011) of 28 April 2011 and the Group of Experts on the Democratic Republic of the Congo re-established by paragraph 4 of resolution 2021(2011) of 29 November 2011 with respect to natural resources;

(*h*) To assist the Committee in updating the publicly available reasons for listing for entries on the travel ban and assets freeze lists;

6. *Requests* the Secretary-General to reappoint the Panel of Experts and to make the necessary financial and security arrangements to support the work of the Panel;

7. *Calls upon* all States and the Government of Liberia to cooperate fully with the Panel of Experts in all aspects of its mandate;

8. *Recalls* that responsibility for controlling the circulation of small arms within the territory of Liberia and between Liberia and neighbouring States rests with the relevant governmental authorities in accordance with the Economic Community of West African States Convention on Small Arms and Light Weapons, Their Ammunition and Other Related Materials, of 2006;

9. *Reaffirms* the need for the United Nations Mission in Liberia and the United Nations Operation in Côte d'Ivoire to regularly coordinate their strategies and operations in areas near the Liberian-Côte d'Ivoire border, in order to contribute to subregional security;

10. *Reiterates* the importance of the Mission's continuing assistance to the Government of Liberia, the Committee and the Panel of Experts, within its capabilities and areas of deployment and, without prejudice to its mandate, continuing to carry out its tasks set forth in previous resolutions, including resolution 1683(2006);

11. *Urges* the Government of Liberia to complete implementation of the recommendations of the 2009 Kimberley Process review team to strengthen internal controls over diamond mining and exports;

12. *Encourages* the Kimberley Process to continue to cooperate with the Panel of Experts and to report on developments regarding implementation by Liberia of the Kimberley Process Certification Scheme;

13. *Decides* to remain actively seized of the matter.

Peacebuilding Commission

The Peacebuilding Commission, in the annual report on its fifth (2011) session [A/66/675-S/2012/70], stated that in its first year of engagement with Liberia it drew on a range of expertise to become familiar with the conflict, history and culture of the country. Those insights, in addition to three missions undertaken by the Chair and one by the Liberia configuration, enabled the Commission to form independent recommendations on the country's peacebuilding challenges. One of the main achievements in 2011 was the full alignment of peacebuilding instruments with core country strategies. The statement of mutual commitments was translated into the Liberia peacebuilding programme. The process was inclusive and participatory, enabling improved coherence and coordination among Government officials, national and international stakeholders, donors and the Commission.

Implementation of mutual commitments. The Commission reported [PBC/6/LBR/1] on progress in the implementation of the statement of mutual commitments on peacebuilding in Liberia [YUN 2010, p. 210] over the first nine months of engagement, from 1 November 2010 to 31 July 2011, based on the three peacebuilding priorities: rule of law, security sector reform and national reconciliation. The reporting period witnessed increased political will for judicial reform, significant evolution in the legal framework for the security sector, and progress towards a concerted approach to national reconciliation. On strengthening the rule of law, the Commission stated that a well-crafted approach had evolved, which included measures to expedite the processing of cases, advance legal training, harmonize traditional and statutory systems, increase access, and address conflict drivers. Efforts in the sector were linked with those in the security sector, namely, through the regional justice and security hubs. Nonetheless, due to the scale of the tasks, implementation of that approach was at various stages and fundamental deficiencies were not fully resolved, including an outdated legal system, a limited number of qualified justice officials, limited public access to courts, incipient linkages among rule-of-law actors, weak accountability and oversight mechanisms, and differing views on what the justice system should be. Substantive judicial reform had been initiated; an essential piece of legislation was submitted to the Legislature during the reporting period, which, if enacted, should significantly reduce the backlog of court cases and, in turn, lower the high pre-trial detention rates. The Land and Law Reform Commissions were moving forward in realizing their mandates, including the piloting of an alternative dispute resolution system. The Peacebuilding Commission developed a five-year strategic plan containing proposals to remedy, among other weaknesses, the limited engagement of the public in legal reform. Regarding security sector reform, an effective, accountable security presence was gradually being established throughout the country, and the National Security Reform and Intelligence Act was enacted. The first regional justice and security hub—a core peacebuilding project that would help the Government deliver justice and provide stability throughout the country—became partially operational. Nonetheless, there was disparity between progress in the areas of rule of law and security sector reform and that achieved in national reconciliation efforts. In consultation with national and international stakeholders, the Peacebuilding Commission sought and obtained the President's agreement to prepare a national strategy on reconciliation. The Commission also supported the translation of the statement of mutual commitments into the Liberia peacebuilding programme, which contained a series of projects to support the Government in achieving its commitments. While the statement of mutual commitments remained valid, the report summarized proposed amendments to the commitments and deliverable targets of both the Government and the Commission.

Participation in Liberia configuration. During the year, the Chairperson of the Peacebuilding Commission invited South Africa [PBC/5/OC/1], the United Nations Office on Drugs and Crime [PBC/5/OC/7] and Australia [PBC/5/OC/10] to participate in the Commission's configuration on Liberia.

(For further information on the Peacebuilding Commission, see p. 47.)

UNMIL

The United Nations Mission in Liberia (UNMIL), established by Security Council resolution 1509(2003) [YUN 2003, p. 194], was mandated to support the implementation of the 2003 Agreement on Ceasefire and Cessation of Hostilities [ibid., p. 189] and the peace process; protect UN staff, facilities and civilians; support humanitarian and human rights activities; and assist in national security reform, including national police training and the formation of a new, restructured military. By resolution 1638(2005) [YUN 2005, p. 267], the Council enhanced the mandate to include the apprehension and detention of former President Charles Taylor in the event of his return to Liberia, as well as his transfer to the Special Court for Sierra Leone. By resolution 1750(2007) [YUN 2007, p. 194], the Council included in the Mission's mandate the provision of administrative and related support and security for activities conducted in Liberia by the Special Court for Sierra Leone. By resolution 1971(2011) (see p. 180), the Council requested that UNMIL withdraw, by 7 March 2011, the military personnel providing security for the Special Court for Sierra Leone.

In 2010, when run-off elections were scheduled for 28 November in Côte d'Ivoire, the Council, by resolutions 1951(2010) [YUN 2010, p. 192] and 1962(2010) [ibid., p. 193], authorized the Secretary-General to temporarily redeploy from UNMIL to UNOCI three infantry companies and an aviation unit comprising two military utility helicopters. In 2011, by resolution 1967(2011) (see p. 141), the Council extended that temporary redeployment by up to four additional weeks, and authorized the temporary transfer of three armed helicopters with crews from UNMIL to UNOCI for a period of four weeks. By resolutions 1968(2011) (see p. 142) and 1981(2011) (see p. 147), the Council extended the temporary redeployment of the three infantry companies, two military utility helicopters and three armed helicopters with crews, and further extended the redeployment of the three armed helicopters with crews by resolution 1992(2011) (see p. 148). On 27 September [S/2011/594], ahead of Liberia's presidential and legislative elections, the Council authorized the return to UNMIL by 30 September of the three armed helicopters deployed to UNOCI, as well as the temporary transfer from UNOCI to UNMIL of one infantry company comprising 150 personnel, and three formed police unit platoons with supporting elements from 1 October to 30 November, to reinforce UNMIL during the elections period.

The Mission was headed by the Special Representative of the Secretary-General, Ellen Margrethe Løj.

Financing

In June, the General Assembly considered the performance report on the UNMIL budget for the period from 1 July 2009 to 30 June 2010 [A/65/620], showing a total expenditure of $541,809,500 gross ($530,317,800 net) against an appropriation of $560,978,700 gross ($549,848,900 net). The Assembly also had before it the proposed budget for the Mission for the period from 1 July 2011 to 30 June 2012 [A/65/727], amounting to $540,836,400 gross ($528,436,800 net), together with the related ACABQ report [A/65/743/Add.7], in which the Board recommended a reduction of $18,607,270.

GENERAL ASSEMBLY ACTION

On 30 June [meeting 106], the General Assembly, on the recommendation of the Fifth Committee [A/65/885], adopted **resolution 65/301** without vote [agenda item 155].

Financing of the United Nations Mission in Liberia

The General Assembly,

Having considered the reports of the Secretary-General on the financing of the United Nations Mission in Liberia and the related report of the Advisory Committee on Administrative and Budgetary Questions,

Recalling Security Council resolution 1497(2003) of 1 August 2003, by which the Council declared its readiness to establish a United Nations stabilization force to support the transitional government and to assist in the implementation of a comprehensive peace agreement in Liberia,

Recalling also Security Council resolution 1509(2003) of 19 September 2003, by which the Council decided to establish the United Nations Mission in Liberia for a period of twelve months, and the subsequent resolutions by which the Council extended the mandate of the Mission, the latest of which was resolution 1938(2010) of 15 September 2010, by which the Council extended the mandate of the Mission until 30 September 2011,

Recalling further its resolution 58/315 of 1 July 2004,

Recalling its resolution 58/261 A of 23 December 2003 on the financing of the Mission and its subsequent resolutions thereon, the latest of which was resolution 64/280 of 24 June 2010,

Reaffirming the general principles underlying the financing of United Nations peacekeeping operations, as stated in General Assembly resolutions 1874(S-IV) of 27 June 1963, 3101(XXVIII) of 11 December 1973 and 55/235 of 23 December 2000,

Noting with appreciation that voluntary contributions have been made to the Mission,

Mindful of the fact that it is essential to provide the Mission with the financial resources necessary to enable it to fulfil its responsibilities under the relevant resolutions of the Security Council,

1. *Requests* the Secretary-General to entrust the Head of Mission with the task of formulating future budget proposals in full accordance with the provisions of General Assembly resolutions 59/296 of 22 June 2005, 60/266 of

30 June 2006, 61/276 of 29 June 2007, 64/269 of 24 June 2010 and 65/289 of 30 June 2011, as well as other relevant resolutions;

2. *Takes note* of the status of contributions to the United Nations Mission in Liberia as at 30 April 2011, including the contributions outstanding in the amount of 88 million United States dollars, representing some 2 per cent of the total assessed contributions, notes with concern that only eighty-five Member States have paid their assessed contributions in full, and urges all other Member States, in particular those in arrears, to ensure payment of their outstanding assessed contributions;

3. *Expresses its appreciation* to those Member States which have paid their assessed contributions in full, and urges all other Member States to make every possible effort to ensure payment of their assessed contributions to the Mission in full;

4. *Expresses concern* at the financial situation with regard to peacekeeping activities, in particular as regards the reimbursements to troop contributors that bear additional burdens owing to overdue payments by Member States of their assessments;

5. *Also expresses concern* at the delay experienced by the Secretary-General in deploying and providing adequate resources to some recent peacekeeping missions, in particular those in Africa;

6. *Emphasizes* that all future and existing peacekeeping missions shall be given equal and non-discriminatory treatment in respect of financial and administrative arrangements;

7. *Also emphasizes* that all peacekeeping missions shall be provided with adequate resources for the effective and efficient discharge of their respective mandates;

8. *Requests* the Secretary-General to ensure that proposed peacekeeping budgets are based on the relevant legislative mandates;

9. *Endorses* the conclusions and recommendations contained in the report of the Advisory Committee on Administrative and Budgetary Questions, subject to the provisions of the present resolution, and requests the Secretary-General to ensure their full implementation;

10. *Notes with appreciation* the immediate assistance of the United Nations Mission in Liberia to the mission in Côte d'Ivoire during the post-election crisis;

11. *Also notes with appreciation* that the United Nations entities with field presence in Liberia have advanced in developing coordination mechanisms and in this regard encourages more effective cooperation among the Mission, the United Nations country team and other United Nations entities with field presence, in line with their respective roles and mandates as adopted by the relevant intergovernmental bodies;

12. *Requests* the Secretary-General to implement the initiative "Delivering as one" in accordance with the relevant mandates adopted by the General Assembly, the Economic and Social Council and the executive boards of United Nations funds and programmes and the governing bodies of the specialized agencies;

13. *Recalls* paragraph 24 of the report of the Advisory Committee on Administrative and Budgetary Questions, and encourages the Secretary-General to take all steps necessary to provide the support required for the Liberia National Police to ensure that the capacity-building process is concluded in a proper and timely manner;

14. *Requests* the Secretary-General to ensure the full implementation of the relevant provisions of resolutions 59/296, 60/266, 61/276, 64/269 and 65/289;

15. *Also requests* the Secretary-General to take all action necessary to ensure that the Mission is administered with a maximum of efficiency and economy;

16. *Notes* that the overall level of appropriation has been adjusted in accordance with the terms of resolution 65/289;

Financial performance report for the period from 1 July 2009 to 30 June 2010

17. *Takes note* of the report of the Secretary-General on the financial performance of the Mission for the period from 1 July 2009 to 30 June 2010;

Budget estimates for the period from 1 July 2011 to 30 June 2012

18. *Decides* to appropriate to the Special Account for the United Nations Mission in Liberia the amount of 559,147,030 dollars for the period from 1 July 2011 to 30 June 2012, inclusive of 513,404,030 dollars for the maintenance of the Mission, 12,155,900 dollars for electoral support to be provided by the Mission, 28,461,200 dollars for the support account for peacekeeping operations and 5,125,900 dollars for the United Nations Logistics Base, at Brindisi, Italy;

Financing of the appropriation

19. *Also decides* to apportion among Member States the amount of 136,747,783 dollars for the period from 1 July to 30 September 2011, in accordance with the levels updated in General Assembly resolution 64/249 of 24 December 2009, and taking into account the scale of assessments for 2011, as set out in Assembly resolution 64/248 of 24 December 2009;

20. *Further decides* that, in accordance with the provisions of its resolution 973(X) of 15 December 1955, there shall be set off against the apportionment among Member States, as provided for in paragraph 19 above, their respective share in the Tax Equalization Fund in the amount of 3,806,125 dollars, comprising the estimated staff assessment income of 3,068,850 dollars approved for the Mission, the prorated share of 602,650 dollars of the estimated staff assessment income approved for the support account and the prorated share of 134,625 dollars of the estimated staff assessment income approved for the United Nations Logistics Base;

21. *Decides* to apportion among Member States the amount of 12,155,900 dollars for electoral support to be provided by the Mission, in accordance with the levels updated in General Assembly resolution 64/249, and taking into account the scale of assessments for 2011, as set out in Assembly resolution 64/248;

22. *Also decides* that, in accordance with the provisions of its resolution 973(X), there shall be set off against the apportionment among Member States, as provided for in paragraph 21 above, their respective share in the Tax Equalization Fund in the amount of 40,900 dollars of estimated staff assessment income approved for the Mission;

23. *Further decides* to apportion among Member States the amount of 410,243,347 dollars for the period from 1 October 2011 to 30 June 2012, at a monthly rate of 45,582,593 dollars, in accordance with the levels updated

in resolution 64/249 and taking into account the scale of assessments for 2011 and 2012, as set out in resolution 64/248, subject to a decision of the Security Council to extend the mandate of the Mission;

24. *Decides* that, in accordance with the provisions of its resolution 973(X), there shall be set off against the apportionment among Member States, as provided for in paragraph 23 above, their respective share in the Tax Equalization Fund in the amount of 11,418,375 dollars, comprising the estimated staff assessment income of 9,206,550 dollars approved for the Mission, the prorated share of 1,807,950 dollars of the estimated staff assessment income approved for the support account and the prorated share of 403,875 dollars of the estimated staff assessment income approved for the United Nations Logistics Base;

25. *Also decides* that, for Member States that have fulfilled their financial obligations to the Mission, there shall be set off against the apportionment, as provided for in paragraph 19 above, their respective share of the unencumbered balance and other income in the total amount of 32,775,600 dollars in respect of the financial period ended 30 June 2010, in accordance with the levels updated in resolution 64/249, and taking into account the scale of assessments for 2010, as set out in resolution 64/248;

26. *Further decides* that, for Member States that have not fulfilled their financial obligations to the Mission, there shall be set off against their outstanding obligations their respective share of the unencumbered balance and other income in the total amount of 32,775,600 dollars in respect of the financial period ended 30 June 2010, in accordance with the scheme set out in paragraph 25 above;

27. *Decides* that the increase of 361,900 dollars in the estimated staff assessment income in respect of the financial period ended 30 June 2010 shall be added to the credits from the amount of 32,775,600 dollars referred to in paragraphs 25 and 26 above;

28. *Emphasizes* that no peacekeeping mission shall be financed by borrowing funds from other active peacekeeping missions;

29. *Encourages* the Secretary-General to continue to take additional measures to ensure the safety and security of all personnel participating in the Mission under the auspices of the United Nations, bearing in mind paragraphs 5 and 6 of Security Council resolution 1502(2003) of 26 August 2003;

30. *Invites* voluntary contributions to the Mission in cash and in the form of services and supplies acceptable to the Secretary-General, to be administered, as appropriate, in accordance with the procedure and practices established by the General Assembly;

31. *Decides* to include in the provisional agenda of its sixty-sixth session the item entitled "Financing of the United Nations Mission in Liberia".

On 24 December, by **decision 66/557**, the Assembly decided that the item on the financing of UNMIL would remain for consideration during its resumed sixty-sixth (2012) session.

Sierra Leone

In 2011, Sierra Leone celebrated its fiftieth anniversary of independence. The nation continued to advance good governance and promote socioeconomic development, as outlined in the Government's Agenda for Change. Progress was also made in implementing the joint communiqué of 2 April 2009 on ending political violence, including the launch in June, with support from the United Nations Integrated Peacebuilding Office in Sierra Leone (UNIPSIL), of the All Political Parties Women's Association. UNIPSIL also supported the development of the All Political Parties Youth Association, which became fully operational during the year after establishing chapters in all of the country's 112 constituencies.

The main political parties intensified their preparations for the 2012 presidential, parliamentary and local council elections. The relationship between the ruling All Peoples Congress (APC) party and the opposition Sierra Leone People's Party (SLPP) continued to be characterized by mutual distrust. There were also dissensions within the People's Movement for Democratic Change (PMDC), which announced in April that it was leaving the coalition with the ruling party. Political tensions increased in the second half of the year, and on 9 September, APC supporters in Bo attacked a convoy carrying the SLPP presidential candidate. On the same day, SLPP supporters set fire to the APC district office and two residential properties belonging to APC supporters in Bo. As the police attempted to control the situation, one person was killed and several people were injured. President Ernest Bai Koroma condemned the violence on 10 September, and announced the establishment of an independent investigation panel, which concluded that supporters of both parties were complicit in the violence.

In preparation for the elections, the National Electoral Commission made progress in developing the biometric voter registration system, with support from the United Nations Development Programme (UNDP). The Executive Representative of the Secretary-General and the Minister for Finance and Economic Development co-chaired meetings of the Election Steering Committee, which aimed at ensuring proper coordination of election arrangements. UNIPSIL worked with the Inter-Religious Council, paramount chiefs, youth and women groups, artists, community-based organizations, the media and academic institutions to mobilize key non-State actors to play a constructive role in the 2012 elections, as well as to carry out prevention and mediation tasks.

The Special Court for Sierra Leone was conducting its last trial, against former Liberian President Charles Taylor. In March, upon request from the Government, the Security Council authorized the withdrawal of the guard force from UNMIL that was providing security for the Special Court.

On 14 September, the Council extended the UNIPSIL mandate until 15 September 2012.

Political and security developments

Report of Secretary-General (March). The Secretary-General, in his sixth report [S/2011/119] on UNIPSIL, reviewed developments in Sierra Leone in January and February, during which the country continued to advance good governance and promote socioeconomic development, as outlined in the Government's Agenda for Change. The implementation of the joint communiqué of 2 April 2009 [YUN 2009, p. 208] continued, and following a series of dialogue sessions among the women's wings of Sierra Leone People's Party (SLPP), APC, PMDC and the National Democratic Alliance (NDA) [YUN 2010, p. 217], facilitated by UNIPSIL, the women leaders of those parties on 13 January established the All Political Parties Women's Association to promote gender equality and women's political participation, as well as serve as a forum for inter-party dialogue and conflict prevention. With regard to arrangements for the country's elections in 2012, on 3 February, the UNDP electoral support programme was approved at a meeting jointly chaired by the Minister for Finance and Economic Development and the Secretary-General's Executive Representative.

The security situation remained stable, and Government efforts to enhance the capacity of the armed forces were supplemented with assistance from international partners. Furthermore, a joint training programme for members of the armed forces and the police, funded by the United Nations Peacebuilding Fund and facilitated by UNIPSIL, concluded during the reporting period. The programme, in which 6,247 personnel from security agencies participated, aimed at improving communication and collaboration among security sector personnel, and addressing occasional clashes among members of the armed forces and the police.

Report of Secretary-General (September). The Secretary-General, in his seventh report [S/2011/554] on UNIPSIL, stated that Sierra Leone celebrated its fiftieth anniversary of independence on 29 April. In a speech to mark the occasion, President Koroma recalled the conflict of the 1990s and affirmed that the country was celebrating a new Sierra Leone that would sustain peace, democracy and development. He also emphasized the need for Sierra Leoneans to resolve their political differences through peaceful, civil and constitutional means. As part of the anniversary celebration, UNIPSIL, with financial assistance from the United Nations Peacebuilding Fund and in collaboration with local groups, arranged for a "peace torch" to be carried throughout the country, providing an opportunity for various stakeholders to reaffirm their commitment to peace and unity.

While the overall political situation remained calm, the relationship between the ruling APC and the opposition SLPP continued to be characterized by mutual distrust. The main political parties intensified their preparations for the 2012 presidential, parliamentary and local council elections. President Koroma was nominated as the APC candidate at the party's national conference in 2009 [YUN 2009, p. 209]. From 29 to 31 July, SLPP held a national conference in Freetown and elected retired Brigadier Maada Bio, a former Head of State, as the party's presidential candidate. On 5 August, however, the APC Secretary-General raised questions about the role of Mr. Bio in the military regime of the National Provisional Ruling Council, which overthrew an APC Government in 1992. There were also continued dissensions within the PMDC, the third party represented in Parliament, which, on 7 April, announced that it was leaving the coalition with the ruling party. That position was challenged by three PMDC ministers serving in the Koroma administration, and subsequently, two of them announced their resignation from the party. On 28 May, a crucial by-election was held in Kailahun District, an SLPP stronghold, when the incumbent parliamentarian from SLPP was appointed to a ministerial position in the APC Government and resigned from the party. The political campaign was tense, with clashes between supporters of the two parties, as well as of NDA. To prevent further deterioration of the situation, UNIPSIL facilitated a visit to the district by representatives of the international community in Freetown, and helped mobilize the All Political Parties Youth Association to lead efforts aimed at tackling political violence. The election was held peacefully, and was won by the SLPP candidate.

During the reporting period, the Minister for Finance and Economic Development and the Secretary-General's Executive Representative co-chaired two election steering committee meetings, which were attended by international development partners and key national stakeholders. The National Electoral Commission, with support from UNDP and UNIPSIL, organized an electoral legal reform workshop (29–31 March), which was attended by the political parties and civil society. The workshop submitted its recommendations to a technical committee, comprising the Law Reform Commission and the Law Officers Department, UNIPSIL and representatives of civil society. The committee made recommendations on issues such as the determination of dates for the conduct of elections, the rules for the election of a president, and forfeiture of parliamentary seats. Furthermore, UNIPSIL continued to work with the Inter-Religious Council, paramount chiefs, youth and women's groups, artists, community-based organizations, the media and academic institutions to mobilize key non-State actors to play a constructive role in the 2012 elections. The project was also aimed at building the capacities of those institutions to carry out conflict prevention and mediation tasks in the longer term, particularly when the political presence of the United Nations drew down. To that end, unipsil, in collaboration with the Ministry of Local Government and Community Development, organized a conference of paramount chiefs in Bo City (19–22 April), resulting in the adoption of the Bo Communiqué of 22 April, which, among other things, called on paramount chiefs to remain neutral in politics. The National Security Council Coordinating Group, which included the police, the armed forces and security sector agencies, approved an election security strategy amounting to $11.7 million, covering areas such as training, logistics, and the establishment of a command and control apparatus.

Unipsil continued to help implement the joint communiqué of 2 April 2009. With funding from the United Nations Peacebuilding Fund, the Office facilitated the establishment of the All Political Parties Women's Association, launched by President Koroma in Bo on 12 June. Unipsil also supported the All Political Parties Youth Association, which became fully operational after establishing chapters in all of the country's 112 constituencies, as well as Freetown.

Extension of UNIPSIL mandate. Taking into account planning for the 2012 elections, the Secretary-General recommended [S/2011/554] that the mandate of unipsil be renewed for a further year. The renewal would also allow the Office to continue its peace consolidation and national reconciliation efforts and support for good governance reforms, as well as to address areas such as youth unemployment, corruption, drug trafficking and organized crime.

SECURITY COUNCIL ACTION

On 14 September [meeting 6611], the Security Council unanimously adopted **resolution 2005(2011)**. The draft [S/2011/572] was submitted by the United Kingdom.

The Security Council,

Recalling its previous resolutions and the statements by its President concerning the situation in Sierra Leone, in particular resolution 1941(2010) of 29 September 2010,

Welcoming the report of the Secretary-General of 2 September 2011, and taking note of his recommendation that the mandate of the United Nations Integrated Peacebuilding Office in Sierra Leone be extended for a period of one year, with a view to providing continued peacebuilding assistance to the Government of Sierra Leone, including preparations for the elections in 2012,

Welcoming also the preparations currently under way for the national and local elections to be held in 2012, and underlining the importance of the Government of Sierra Leone and the international community in continuing efforts to foster an environment that is conducive to the holding of peaceful, transparent, free and fair elections by strengthening the national electoral and democratic institutions, providing security, ensuring political access by the contestants to all regions of the country, making available forums for mediation and dialogue and assuring the credibility of the electoral process, and, in doing so, contribute to the institutional development and continued stability of the country,

Mindful of the United Nations efforts in assisting the Government of Sierra Leone to address the capacity challenges of the national electoral institutions, and noting the potential for an increase in tensions during the preparations for, and the period leading up to, the 2012 elections in Sierra Leone due to political, security, socioeconomic and humanitarian challenges,

Welcoming the ongoing implementation of the joint communiqué of 2 April 2009 by the political parties, including efforts to prevent political violence among the youth and to enhance greater political participation of women, and underlining the need for political parties to hasten the full implementation of its provisions and to ensure that their supporters abide by the code of conduct for political parties and remain committed to sustained cessation of the political violence in Sierra Leone,

Welcoming also the steady progress that the Government of Sierra Leone has made in implementing the Agenda for Change, in particular steps taken with regard to strengthening the Government's control over natural resources and to combat corruption, and noting the challenges that remain to be addressed in the Government's national peacebuilding strategy and the efforts being made to address them,

Recognizing the challenges posed by illicit drug trafficking, corruption and youth unemployment, welcoming the progress made under the West Africa Coast Initiative, in particular the establishment of the Transnational Organized Crime Unit to address the growing problem of illicit drug trafficking, organized crime and drug abuse in Sierra Leone, and appreciating the coordinated efforts of the international development partners to address the challenge of youth unemployment,

Emphasizing the importance of the continued integrated support of the United Nations system and the international community for the long-term peace, security and development of Sierra Leone,

Commending the valuable contribution that the United Nations Integrated Peacebuilding Office in Sierra Leone has made to peacebuilding efforts in Sierra Leone, and its continued progress, with the United Nations country team, in achieving the integration of the political, development and humanitarian mandates as set out in the United Nations Joint Vision for Sierra Leone, encouraging all United Nations entities in Sierra Leone to continue the implementation of the Joint Vision, and calling upon Sierra Leone's bilateral and multilateral partners to provide the necessary resources to implement the Joint Vision,

Stressing that the 2012 elections and the wide acceptance of the outcome will be a major milestone indicating the consolidation of peace and security in Sierra Leone, which should help to define the transition of the United Nations Integrated Peacebuilding Office in Sierra Leone into a United Nations country team,

Acknowledging the role that the Peacebuilding Commission and the Peacebuilding Fund play in support of the peacebuilding efforts in Sierra Leone,

Reiterating its appreciation for the work of the Special Court for Sierra Leone, stressing the importance of the trial of former President of Liberia Charles Taylor by the Court, welcoming the completion of all the other cases, as well as effective outreach on the trials at the local level, reiterating its expectation that the Court will finish its work as soon as possible, including any contempt cases, and calling upon

Member States to contribute generously to the Court and the Residual Special Court,

Recalling that the responsibility for controlling the circulation of small arms and light weapons within the territory of Sierra Leone and between Sierra Leone and neighbouring States rests with the relevant governmental authorities in accordance with the Economic Community of West African States Convention on Small Arms and Light Weapons, Their Ammunition and Other Related Materials, of 2006, and welcoming the launch of the national action plan on small arms,

Welcoming the role played by the African Union and the Economic Community of West African States, and encouraging the States members of the Mano River Union and other regional organizations to continue their dialogue aimed at consolidating regional peace and security,

1. *Decides* to extend the mandate of the United Nations Integrated Peacebuilding Office in Sierra Leone, as set out in resolution 1941(2010), until 15 September 2012;

2. *Emphasizes* the importance of the United Nations Integrated Peacebuilding Office in Sierra Leone achieving, jointly with the United Nations country team, the objectives outlined in the United Nations Joint Vision for Sierra Leone within their respective mandates, including focusing on:

  (i) Providing support to the Government of Sierra Leone and its electoral and democratic institutions in the preparations for the 2012 elections as requested, and providing technical assistance to all relevant stakeholders to play a meaningful role, in accordance with relevant national legislation, in achieving peaceful, credible and democratic elections;

  (ii) Providing assistance to conflict prevention and mitigation efforts, and promoting dialogue among political parties, the Government and all relevant stakeholders;

  (iii) Assisting the Government and national institutions in tackling youth unemployment, including by supporting training, education and skills provision;

  (iv) Assisting the Government and national institutions in implementing the Sierra Leone national action plan on women and peace and security; including by advancing the four-pronged approach to addressing gender matters adopted by the Office and the United Nations country team;

  (v) Providing assistance to the Government in promoting good governance, the rule of law and human rights, including institutional reform; combating illicit drug trafficking and organized crime; combating corruption; providing support to the National Human Rights Commission; and assisting in strengthening national capacity-building in the areas of law enforcement, forensics, border management, money-laundering and the strengthening of criminal justice institutions;

3. *Calls upon* the Government of Sierra Leone, all political parties, as well as all other stakeholders, in particular civil society in Sierra Leone, to contribute to an atmosphere of political tolerance and peaceful coexistence and to demonstrate their full commitment to the democratic process, so as to ensure that the 2012 elections are peaceful, transparent, free and fair;

4. *Calls upon* the Sierra Leone authorities to resolve any outstanding issues regarding the electoral legal framework;

5. *Urges* the Government of Sierra Leone to step up its efforts to hold regular, inclusive and constructive party political dialogue on all major national, political, social and economic issues, which are clearly focused on identifying the priorities and milestones necessary for the future peace and development of Sierra Leone;

6. *Encourages* the Executive Representative of the Secretary-General for Sierra Leone to continue with the progress already made to enhance the integration and effectiveness of United Nations efforts on the ground, in support of the implementation of the Joint Vision and the recovery and development priorities of the Government and people of Sierra Leone;

7. *Calls upon* the Secretary-General to continue to report on progress achieved towards meeting the benchmarks, including in supporting the capacity of key national institutions to be able to adequately address the causes of conflict and manage political disputes by themselves, as agreed upon by the Government of Sierra Leone and the United Nations in the Joint Vision for the transition of the United Nations Integrated Peacebuilding Office in Sierra Leone into a United Nations country team;

8. *Emphasizes* that the Government of Sierra Leone bears the primary responsibility for peacebuilding, security and long-term development in the country, and encourages the Government to continue its implementation of the Agenda for Change, and international partners to continue to provide support to the Government;

9. *Calls upon* the Government of Sierra Leone, with the support of the United Nations Integrated Peacebuilding Office in Sierra Leone, development partners and all other stakeholders in the country, to increase its efforts to combat corruption, improve accountability and promote the development of the private sector in order to generate wealth and employment opportunities; to continue good governance reform by supporting the Anti-Corruption Commission and the Ministry of Mines and Mineral Resources to increase the transparency and management of Sierra Leone's natural and mineral resources for the benefit of all Sierra Leoneans and mitigating the risk of resource-based conflict; to intensify efforts against illicit drug trafficking through the strengthening of the Transnational Organized Crime Unit; and to promote human rights, including through the implementation of the recommendations of the Truth and Reconciliation Commission and Sierra Leone's universal periodic review by the Human Rights Council;

10. *Encourages* the Peacebuilding Commission to provide support to the Government of Sierra Leone and the United Nations Integrated Peacebuilding Office in Sierra Leone in preparation for the 2012 elections, including the potential to mobilize support from international partners, and in the implementation of the Government's Agenda for Change and the United Nations Joint Vision strategy and in that regard to advise and keep the Security Council updated, including on progress made in meeting core peacebuilding objectives, as necessary;

11. *Commends* the Government of Sierra Leone for recognizing the important role of women in the prevention and resolution of conflicts and in peacebuilding, reaffirms the importance of appropriate gender expertise and training in missions mandated by the Council in accor-

dance with resolutions 1325(2000) of 31 October 2000 and 1889(2009) of 5 October 2009, underscores that the Government should continue its effort in addressing sexual and gender-based violence, in accordance with resolutions 1820(2008) of 19 June 2008, 1888(2009) of 30 September 2009 and 1960(2010) of 16 December 2010, and encourages the United Nations Integrated Peacebuilding Office in Sierra Leone to continue to work with the Government in this area;

12. *Requests* that the Secretary-General keep the Council informed every six months of progress made in the implementation of the mandate of the United Nations Integrated Peacebuilding Office in Sierra Leone and the present resolution;

13. *Decides* to remain actively seized of the matter.

Year-end developments. In a later report [S/2012/160], the Secretary-General stated that political tensions increased in the lead-up to the 2012 presidential, parliamentary and local council elections. On 9 September, APC supporters in Bo attacked a convoy carrying the SLPP presidential candidate, Mr. Bio. On the same day, SLPP supporters set fire to the APC district office and two residential properties belonging to APC supporters in Bo. As the police attempted to control the situation, one person was killed and several people were injured. President Koroma condemned the violence on 10 September, and announced the establishment of an independent investigation panel, which, on 30 September, concluded that supporters of both parties were complicit in the violence. Shortly after the submission of the panel's report, criminal proceedings were initiated against supporters of both parties who were accused of being involved in the incident. Following the 9 September attack, the Inspector General of Police imposed a ban on all political party processions and rallies. The ban was lifted on 12 December after the signing of a memorandum of understanding by APC, PMDC, the People's Liberation Party and the United Democratic Movement, which committed the political parties to engaging in regular consultations with the police; deploying marshals during political party processions; and adhering to the code of conduct for political parties and the Public Order Act. SLPP and NDA did not sign the memorandum and insisted that the police had no legal authority to ban political party processions and rallies. On 7 October, President Koroma addressed the fifth State Opening of Parliament, during which he outlined his vision for the long-term development and transformation of Sierra Leone. He stated that SLPP, APC and PMDC were all partners in the country's transformation and gave assurances of the Government's determination to ensure free, fair, transparent and peaceful elections. Parliamentarians from SLPP and PMDC, however, boycotted the opening of Parliament in protest against, among other things, the ban on political processions and rallies.

In preparation for the elections, the National Electoral Commission procured approximately 800 biometric voter registration kits, with assistance from UNDP. The upcoming elections would mark the first time voter registration in Sierra Leone would be undertaken using the biometric system, and the Commission conducted a pilot test of the system from 1 to 3 November, and also undertook awareness-raising programmes throughout the country. The United Nations assisted the Commission in developing training manuals and guides for administering the system. The Secretary-General's Executive Representative and the Minister for Finance and Economic Development co-chaired meetings of the Election Steering Committee, which aimed at ensuring proper coordination of election arrangements. At the 15 September meeting, the Government announced that its contribution to the elections would amount to approximately $18 million.

Peacebuilding Commission

In the report of its fifth session [A/66/675-S/2012/70], the Peacebuilding Commission described its activities in Sierra Leone during 2011. The Commission confirmed its engagement with the country on the basis of the peacebuilding elements of the Government's Agenda for Change, namely, good governance and the rule of law, youth employment, and combating drug trafficking [YUN 2009, p. 212]. The configuration focused its engagement in the area of governance on support for national actors to help them prepare the country to hold free and fair elections. The Commission impressed upon the political parties the importance of inter-party dialogue, as well as dialogue with the independent institutions mandated to prepare the elections, notably the National Electoral Commission, in order to bridge disagreements and clarify the rules of engagement. The Peacebuilding Commission conveyed that message in a visit to Sierra Leone in May (see p. 179).

The Commission's engagement in Sierra Leone was also instrumental in fostering United Nations coherence on the ground by supporting the integration of the political mandate of UNIPSIL with the development mandates of the UN agencies; strengthening the role of the Secretary-General's Executive Representative; and endorsing the United Nations Joint Vision for Sierra Leone [YUN 2008, p. 212]. With political support provided by the Commission, the United Nations succeeded in providing integrated and coordinated support to the country through the Joint Vision, which reflected the intention of the funds, programmes and specialized agencies of the UN system to work together towards key objectives in peace and security, humanitarian and development areas.

Delegation visit. The Commission reported [PBC/5/SLE/1] on its visit to Freetown, Sierra Leone, from 22 to 28 May. The delegation was composed of the Permanent Representative of Canada to the United Nations in his capacity as Chair of the Sierra Leone configuration, the Permanent Representative of Ghana, and delegates from Australia, Azerbaijan, Japan and Sierra Leone. During its visit, the delegation reviewed progress on peace consolidation; identified opportunities for future engagement in the areas of good governance and the rule of law, youth employment and empowerment, and drug trafficking and transnational crime; and discussed preparations for the 2012 elections and natural resources management. The delegation met with the President, Government ministers, members of Parliament, the Secretary-General's Executive Representative, the UN country team, representatives of the major political parties, election officials, the Anti-Corruption Commissioner and civil society groups.

The delegation noted that Sierra Leone had taken considerable strides to consolidate peace. The country was in the midst of a transition from the final stages of peacebuilding to a more traditional development approach, and the forthcoming elections were widely viewed as an important indicator of progress. The delegation also noted the Government's continued dedication to fighting corruption and the country's progress in supporting youth employment and empowerment, notably through the appointment of a new National Youth Commissioner. Nonetheless, significant challenges remained in the near and medium term, and the country would require sustained support to accelerate progress towards the Millennium Development Goals. The delegation highlighted the importance of enhancing dialogue and building trust between the major political parties and national institutions charged with managing the 2012 elections; the continuing need for police vehicles to enable the police to respond promptly to election-related disturbances across the country; and the importance of establishing a political, institutional and regulatory framework for managing the country's natural resource wealth.

Participation in Sierra Leone configuration. During the year, the Chairperson of the Peacebuilding Commission invited South Africa [PBC/5/OC/1] and Azerbaijan [PBC/5/OC/6] to participate in the Commission's configuration on Sierra Leone.

(For further information on the Peacebuilding Commission, see p. 47.)

UNIPSIL

The United Nations Integrated Peacebuilding Office in Sierra Leone (UNIPSIL) was established in 2008 by Security Council resolution 1829(2008) [YUN 2008, p. 215] as the successor mission to the United Nations Integrated Office in Sierra Leone, with a mandate focused on strengthening governmental capacities, including assisting the Government in providing political support to national and local efforts for identifying and resolving tensions and threats of conflict; monitoring and promoting human rights, democratic institutions and the rule of law; consolidating good governance reforms, with a focus on anti-corruption efforts; strengthening the Parliament and key governance institutions; and coordinating strategy among UN agencies in Sierra Leone. In resolution 1886(2009) [YUN 2009, p. 210], the Council emphasized the importance of UNIPSIL in supporting the Government in constitutional reform; building police capacity; tackling corruption, illicit drug trafficking and organized crime; addressing youth unemployment; supporting preparations for the 2012 elections; and assisting the work of the Peacebuilding Commission. In 2010, by resolution 1941(2010) [YUN 2010, p. 215], the Council reiterated the importance of the Office's focus on those objectives as outlined in the United Nations Joint Vision for Sierra Leone, in particular supporting the Government in preparations for the 2012 elections.

By resolution 2005(2011), the Council extended the mandate of the mission until 15 September 2012. Michael von der Schulenburg (Germany) continued to serve as the Secretary-General's Executive Representative and Head of UNIPSIL.

Financing

In December, the General Assembly considered the Secretary-General's October report [A/66/354/Add.3] on estimates in respect of special political missions, good offices and other political initiatives authorized by the General Assembly and/or the Security Council, which included resource requirements for UNIPSIL totalling $17,711,600 for 2012, and the related ACABQ report [A/66/7/Add.12], which recommended approval of those resources.

On 24 December, in section IX of **resolution 66/247** (see p. 1393), the Assembly endorsed the recommendations of ACABQ and approved the resource requirements, including those for UNIPSIL.

Special Court for Sierra Leone

The Special Court for Sierra Leone, jointly established by the Government of Sierra Leone and the United Nations in 2002 [YUN 2002, p. 164] pursuant to Security Council resolution 1315(2000) [YUN 2000, p. 205], continued to try those bearing the greatest responsibility for violations of international humanitarian and Sierra Leonean laws committed in Sierra Leone since November 1996.

The Special Court was in its completion phase, the Secretary-General reported in November [A/66/563].

The eight persons convicted by the Court were serving their sentences in Mpagna Prison in Rwanda. The trial of *Prosecutor v. Charles Ghankay Taylor*, the former President of Liberia, continued at The Hague as the sole case before the Court. Trial Chamber II accepted written briefs and heard oral pleadings in February and March, with the final closing arguments made on 11 March. As those arguments were presented two and a half months later than projected, the Special Court judges in May reviewed the completion strategy and established new milestones. The Court expected to issue a judgement on the merits of the Taylor case in December, and a possible appeals judgement was projected for July 2012.

In addition, two unforeseen contempt cases, *Independent Counsel v. Senessie* and *Independent Counsel v. Bangura et. al.*, were ongoing before the Court. On 24 May, by orders in lieu of indictments, Trial Chamber II charged five persons with contempt of the Court. Of the five accused persons, two were serving their sentences in Mpanga Prison in Rwanda. The initial appearances of all accused occurred on 15 July in Freetown. As four of the five accused pleaded not guilty to charges contained in the orders in lieu of indictments, the Court was moving forward with trial. The Court had one fugitive indictee at large, Johnny Paul Koroma. The Prosecutor was negotiating the transfer of the Koroma case to a State that had jurisdiction and was willing and prepared to accept the case.

Financing

Pursuant to General Assembly resolution 65/259 [YUN 2010, p. 1429], the Secretary-General in November reported [A/66/563] on the implementation of that resolution, in which the Assembly authorized the Secretary-General, as an exceptional measure, to enter into commitments in an amount not to exceed $9,882,594 to supplement the voluntary financial resources of the Court for 2011. The report stated that, due to unforeseen circumstances, the Court would not be able to complete its mandate by February 2012, and required additional time and financial support for its activities through July 2012, the anticipated date when the Court would complete its work. The Secretary-General sought approval for funding of $9,066,400 for the period from 1 January to 31 July 2012 to enable the Court to complete its mandate. In December [A/66/7/Add.19], ACABQ recommended that, in view of the importance of the Court's activities and the progress it had made towards achieving its mandate, the Assembly approve that amount.

On 24 December, in section IX of **resolution 66/247** (see p. 1393), the General Assembly authorized the Secretary-General to enter into commitments in an amount not to exceed $9,066,400 for the subvention for the Special Court.

Withdrawal of military guard force

On 11 February [S/2011/74], the Secretary-General informed the Security Council that the Government of Sierra Leone had requested the withdrawal of the military guard force from UNMIL that was providing security for the Special Court, pursuant to Council resolution 1626(2005) [YUN 2005, p. 264], by the end of February/early March. The Registrar of the Court on 13 October 2010 had informed the UN Secretariat that the guard force would no longer be required, since the evidence and archives would be transferred to The Hague in December 2010. Accordingly, the Secretary-General recommended that the guard force be withdrawn in early March.

SECURITY COUNCIL ACTION

On 3 March [meeting 6493], the Security Council unanimously adopted **resolution 1971(2011)**. The draft [S/2011/106] was submitted by the United States.

The Security Council,

Recalling its previous resolutions and the statements by its President concerning the situation in Liberia and in Sierra Leone, in particular resolution 1626(2005) of 19 September 2005, in which it authorized the deployment of military personnel of the United Nations Mission in Liberia to Sierra Leone to provide security for the Special Court for Sierra Leone,

Welcoming the letter dated 11 February 2011 from the Secretary-General to the President of the Security Council,

Expressing its appreciation for the contribution of military personnel of the Mission, particularly the Mongolian contingent, to the provision of security for the Court,

Noting that the Registrar of the Court informed the Secretariat by a letter dated 13 October 2010 that the Mission military guard force would no longer be required beyond February 2011, and the request of the Government of Sierra Leone that withdrawal be postponed to late February or early March 2011,

Acting under Chapter VII of the Charter of the United Nations,

1. *Decides* to discontinue the authorization granted in paragraph 5 of resolution 1626(2005), and requests that the United Nations Mission in Liberia withdraw, by 7 March 2011, the military personnel providing security for the Special Court for Sierra Leone;

2. *Also decides* to discontinue the authorization and request to the Mission, in paragraph 7 of resolution 1626(2005), to evacuate officials of the Court in the event of a serious security crisis affecting those personnel and the Court;

3. *Looks forward* to the successful provision of security for the Court by local security personnel, and requests the United Nations Integrated Peacebuilding Office in Sierra Leone to include, within existing security evacuation contingency arrangements, relevant officials of the Court.

Guinea-Bissau

In 2011, the political leadership of Guinea-Bissau made efforts to improve the political and security environment, as well as the country's relationship with regional and international partners. Progress was made in security sector reform, including the launch of the Angolan security sector reform technical military cooperation mission, and the adoption of the Economic Community of West African States (ecowas)/ Community of Portuguese-speaking Countries (cplp) road map on security sector reform in Guinea-Bissau. In support of the road map, the Secretary-General deployed a technical assessment mission to Guinea-Bissau in April, with the mission's final report approved by ecowas and cplp.

The political situation worsened in the second half of the year, when a collective of opposition parties led demonstrations against the country's leadership, partly triggered by the decision of the Prosecutor General in May to close investigations into a coup plot case allegedly involving two former Government ministers who were killed in June 2009. The opposition parties called for the dismissal of Prime Minister Carlos Gomes Júnior. The Prime Minister, however, denied any involvement in the June 2009 political violence and called on the opposition to engage in dialogue on political issues. On 1 August, President Malam Bacai Sanhá replaced the Prosecutor General with the Deputy Director of the Judiciary Police. The Government urged the newly appointed Prosecutor General to clarify the status of the investigations into the assassinations. The political situation deteriorated further when, on 22 November, the President was medically evacuated from the country. On 26 December, an armed attack occurred on the General Staff Armoury, with 24 military officers and one civilian detained in connection with the attack.

During the year, the United Nations Integrated Peacebuilding Office in Guinea-Bissau (uniogbis) and undp supported the strengthening of national institutions, inclusive political dialogue and national reconciliation, including by providing technical and financial assistance for security sector reform and technical support to the organizing committee of the planned national conference on dialogue and reconciliation. The Special Representative of the Secretary-General pursued his advocacy of the swift implementation of the ecowas/cplp road map for security sector reform, including the operationalization of the pension fund for members of the armed forces and the police. On 21 December, the Security Council extended the uniogbis mandate until 28 February 2013.

Political and security developments

Report of Secretary-General (February). Pursuant to Security Council resolution 1876(2009) [YUN 2009, p. 219] the Secretary-General in February reported [S/2011/73] on developments in Guinea-Bissau and on the activities of uniogbis. In early 2011, the political leadership and Government institutions made noticeable progress to reverse the negative effects of the civil-military events of April 2010 [YUN 2010, p. 223], and to improve the country's relationship with regional and international partners. The national dialogue process had advanced, and was expected to result in a national conference in mid-2011. Uniogbis and undp provided technical support to the organizing committee of the national conference to enhance political dialogue with national stakeholders, including parliamentarians, civil society organizations, and military and security leaders. On 16 January, with assistance from the United Nations Peacebuilding Fund, the organizing committee completed a series of eight regional conferences for defence and security personnel as part of the conference process. Those consultations resulted in a series of recommendations, including on the need for a separation of roles for the defence and security sectors, a career structure, mobility based on merit, and an improvement in conditions of service.

Report of Secretary-General (June). In June [S/2011/370], the Secretary-General reported that in February and March, President Sanhá and the Government undertook diplomatic efforts to advocate for greater understanding by the international community of the challenges facing the country. Prime Minister Gomes Júnior led a delegation to Senegal (14–16 February), and the Minister for Foreign Affairs headed a visit to Lisbon, Paris, Berlin, London and Brussels (13–25 February). At the same time, the Special Representative of the Secretary-General impressed upon the national authorities the need to address during those consultations the issues that had prompted partial suspension of international support to the country.

The ecowas Summit of Heads of State and Government (Abuja, 23–24 March) adopted the ecowas/cplp road map on security sector reform in Guinea-Bissau, and decided to allocate $63 million to the country. The Prime Minister led a high-level delegation to the opening meeting of Guinea-Bissau's consultations with the eu (Brussels, 29 March), where he presented to the eu Council his country's response to the concerns raised by the eu, including on governance and the status of the investigations into the 2009 political assassinations [YUN 2009, p. 216]. The Prime Minister emphasized the commitment of the national authorities to consolidate national stability, and called for support from the eu, the United Nations, the au, ecowas and cplp in reforming the defence, security and justice sectors, enhancing the fight against drug trafficking and organized crime, and reducing poverty. In a communiqué released after the meeting, the eu listed what it saw as the Government's obligations before full cooperation could resume, including the provision of a detailed timetable on the implementation of security sector reform; the renewal of the military hierarchy in keeping with the recommendations of the ECOWAS/CPLP road map on security sector reform; and the conclusion of independent judicial investigations into the 2009 assassinations and the military events of April 2010.

In support of the ECOWAS/CPLP road map, the Secretary-General deployed a technical assessment mission to Bissau and Abuja (11–18 April), led by his Deputy Special Representative in Guinea-Bissau. The mission recommended that ECOWAS establish a joint task force/coordination mechanism, together with CPLP, the AU, the EU and the United Nations, to finalize preparations for implementing the road map. The mission also made recommendations to improve coordination mechanisms and to mobilize resources for the immediate launching of the pension fund for members of the armed forces and the police, as well as related initiatives, such as reinsertion and reintegration. On 4 May the Secretary-General's Special Representative shared the mission's final report with the President of the ECOWAS Commission and the Executive Secretary of CPLP; the report was subsequently endorsed by the two organizations.

UNIOGBIS continued to support the strengthening of national institutions, inclusive political dialogue and national reconciliation. The Office and UNDP provided technical support to the organizing committee of the national conference, which launched preparatory regional conferences in May. On 18 February, UNIOGBIS, in collaboration with the Faculty of Law of Bissau, completed eight training workshops for members of the ad hoc Parliamentary Commission for the Review of the Constitution. In March and April, UNDP supported the creation of three civil conflict prevention brigades in Oio, Biombo and Cachéu regions, areas which were the most affected by chronic local conflicts. The brigades aimed to bring together traditional authorities, youth, women, farmer organizations and representatives from the justice sector and the police to facilitate conflict analysis exercises and regular meetings among ethnic groups and between traditional leaders and the national authorities. Progress was also made in security sector reform. Following a request for assistance from the Government, UNIOGBIS and the United Nations Mine Action Service conducted a technical assessment mission (13–19 February) to review ammunition storage areas and stockpile management mechanisms, and inspect ammunition storage sites in Bissau and the regions of Buba, Quebo, Bafata and Gabú. The mission provided technical support for the identification and destruction of more than 4 tons of unserviceable and dangerous munitions posing an immediate threat to local populations. On 7 April, the Permanent Secretariat of the National Security Sector Reform Steering Committee, with support from UNIOGBIS, convened the first of a series of bimonthly meetings with international partners to exchange information on security sector reform and facilitate the coordination of activities. From March to May, UNDP funded four regional awareness-raising and information workshops on security sector reform with the technical support of UNIOGBIS.

The reporting period marked the second anniversary of the March 2009 assassinations of President João Bernardo Vieira and the Chief of General Staff, General Tagme Na Waie [YUN 2009, p. 216]. In line with Council resolution 1949(2010) [YUN 2010, p. 227], the Secretary-General's Special Representative facilitated a meeting on 25 March in Dakar, Senegal, between members of the diplomatic corps accredited to Guinea-Bissau and the Prosecutor General to receive an update on the criminal investigations. The Prosecutor General disclosed that the judicial process faced political, financial and administrative obstacles, as well as security constraints. In his briefing to the EU on 29 March (see above), the Prime Minister confirmed that while the investigations into the assassinations were ongoing, they remained inconclusive owing to a lack of evidence, the inability to hear key witnesses and little international assistance.

Report of Secretary-General (October). In October [S/2011/655], the Secretary-General provided an update on political, security and military developments. The reporting period was marked by several demonstrations against the country's leadership, particularly Prime Minister Gomes Júnior, launched by a collective of opposition parties led by the interim leader of the Party for Social Renewal (PRS), Ibrahima Sory Djaló. The collective said that their action was triggered by, among other factors, the decision of the Prosecutor General in May to close investigations into a coup plot case allegedly involving former Government ministers Baciro Dabó and Hélder Proença, both of whom were killed in June 2009 [YUN 2009, p. 218]. The Prosecutor General had concluded that allegations of their involvement in the coup attempt were baseless, and had referred the case to the military court. In response to that decision, the collective of opposition parties, which included PRS, the Republican Party for Independence and Development (PRID) and 15 opposition parties without representation in Parliament, called for the dismissal of the Prime Minister. On 11 July 2011, the ruling African Party for the Independence of Guinea and Cape Verde reiterated its support for the Prime Minister, who was the party's leader. At a rally later that day, the Prime Minister denied any involvement in the June 2009 political violence, underlined the need for national reconciliation, and called on the opposition to engage in dialogue. On 25 July 2011, the President embarked on consultations with national and international stakeholders on the evolving political situation. While PRS and PRID continued to insist on the dismissal of the Prime Minister, the Democratic Alliance and the New Democracy Party opposed changing the Government and suggested that the investigations into the 2009 political assassinations be conducted by the international community. The President, on 1 August, issued a decree replacing the Prosecutor General, Amine Saad, with the Deputy Director of the Judiciary Police, Edmundo Mendes; however, that decision did not defuse the tensions with the opposition. On 11 August, the Government urged the newly appointed Prosecutor General to clarify the status of the investigations into the June 2009 assassinations, and stated that the Commission of Inquiry's conclusions regarding the coup plot case had not been officially conveyed to the Government. At the ceremony on 4 October to swear in newly appointed Government ministers following a Cabinet reshuffle, the President reaffirmed his confidence that the Government led by the Prime Minister would serve its term until the end of the legislature in November 2012.

On 18 July, the Council of the EU announced the conclusions of the consultations with the Government of Guinea-Bissau which opened on 29 March (see above), in which it set out a road map for the gradual resumption of development cooperation with the country, based on the Government's compliance with a range of conditions relating to security sector reform; combating drug trafficking and money-laundering; contributions by the Government and ECOWAS to the pension fund for retired military and police personnel; the conclusion of independent judicial investigations into the 2009 political assassinations; improvements in the administrative and financial management of public, civilian and military employees; the commencement of judicial investigations and proceedings into the April 2010 events; and a review of the military hierarchy.

Meanwhile, the preparatory regional meetings for the national conference, anticipated in December, continued across the country in June and July, with discussions focused on the topics of national identity and sovereignty; democracy and the political organization of the State; impunity and the rule of law; the relationship between the people and the armed forces; and justice, human security and development. UNDP and UNIOGBIS provided technical support to the conference organizing committee. The United Nations was also providing technical advice on the next steps of the conference, including the drafting of documents, resource mobilization, and the development of a post-conference follow-up mechanism. Regarding security sector reform, UNIOGBIS provided technical and financial assistance to the first phase of the vetting and certification process targeting police institutions. The first model police station in the Bissau suburb of Bairro Militar, established with the Office's support, was inaugurated on 12 September. The Secretary-General's Special Representative pursued his advocacy of the swift implementation of the ECOWAS/CPLP road map in support of security sector reform, including the operationalization of the pension fund for members of the armed forces and the police, holding consultations with national and international stakeholders, including the President, the Prime Minister, the Minister of Defence, the leadership of the armed forces, and the Chief of General Staff of the Angolan Armed Forces. On 9 August, the Prime Minister opened a meeting of the National Security Sector Reform Steering Committee, during which the national authorities confirmed their intention to gradually contribute up to $4.5 million to the pension fund for the period 2011–2015.

The Secretary-General concluded that the forthcoming national conference offered an opportunity for the people of Guinea-Bissau to move towards a future based on genuine national reconciliation and unity. He welcomed the steps taken to prepare for the demobilization and reintegration of military and police personnel earmarked for retirement, and noted the country's readiness to jump-start the security sector reform process to rejuvenate and professionalize the military and security sectors. The Secretary-General called on the country's regional and international partners to support the reforms by providing financial and material resources. He also called on the Guinea-Bissau authorities to complete a credible judicial process with respect to the 2009 killings, and to implement the commitment to introduce judicial reforms. Following consultations with the Government, the Secretary-General recommended that the mandate of UNIOGBIS be renewed until 31 December 2012.

SECURITY COUNCIL ACTION

On 21 December [meeting 6695], the Security Council unanimously adopted **resolution 2030(2011)**. The draft [S/2011/786] was submitted by Brazil, Nigeria and Portugal.

The Security Council,

Recalling its previous resolutions and the statements by its President concerning the situation in Guinea-Bissau, in particular resolutions 1876(2009) of 26 June 2009 and 1949(2010) of 23 November 2010,

Welcoming the efforts made by the Government of Guinea-Bissau towards the maintenance of stability and constitutional order, including the work of the National Assembly on reconciliation,

Noting the encouraging steps taken by the Government of Guinea-Bissau in achieving economic reform, including public administration and public finance reforms, and welcoming the adoption by the authorities of Guinea-Bissau of the second poverty reduction strategy paper and a national strategic document for action on the social determinants of health, and noting the efforts of bilateral partners to support the development of the health sector,

Stressing the importance of the upcoming legislative election in Guinea-Bissau and the need to have free, fair and transparent elections as a crucial and necessary step towards the consolidation of democracy and national reconciliation, and calling upon all stakeholders to contribute to a peaceful environment during and after the election,

Reaffirming that the Government of Guinea-Bissau and all stakeholders must remain committed to national reconciliation through genuine and inclusive political dialogue, respect for constitutional order, reforms in the defence, security and justice sectors, the promotion of the rule of law, human rights, the promotion of socioeconomic development and the fight against impunity and illicit drug trafficking,

Stressing the importance of security sector reform for the consolidation of peace in Guinea-Bissau and the need for the authorities of Guinea-Bissau to intensify efforts to create the enabling environment for enhanced civilian control over the security forces of Guinea-Bissau, in particular the armed forces,

Noting with deep concern the threats to national and subregional security and stability posed by the growth in illicit drug trafficking and organized crime in Guinea-Bissau, welcoming the approval by the Government of Guinea-Bissau of the 2011–2014 national operational plan to combat illicit drug trafficking and organized crime and the establishment in Guinea-Bissau, within the framework of the West Africa Coast Initiative, of a Transnational Crime Unit, and re-emphasizing the need to tackle the problem of illicit drug trafficking in the countries of origin, transit and final destination through an approach of common and shared responsibility,

Reiterating the importance of the continued support of the United Nations and the international community for the long-term security and development of Guinea-Bissau, particularly in the fields of security sector reform, justice and the fight against illicit drug trafficking and to create the enabling environment to fight impunity and strengthen Guinea-Bissau's institutional capacity,

Welcoming the efforts of the Economic Community of West African States and the Community of Portuguese-speaking Countries to assist in the reforms of the defence and security sectors in Guinea-Bissau, noting the need for further efforts to implement the Economic Community of West African States-Community of Portuguese-speaking Countries road map in support of those reforms, and encouraging the international community to remain engaged in addressing key challenges in the country,

Reiterating the importance of regional and subregional cooperation in addressing the challenges faced by Guinea-Bissau,

Encouraging relevant stakeholders to remain engaged in addressing key governance and peacebuilding challenges in the country,

Re-emphasizing that the Government of Guinea-Bissau bears the primary responsibility for security, the protection of its civilian population, peacebuilding and long-term development in the country,

Recalling its appreciation for the work of the United Nations Integrated Peacebuilding Office in Guinea-Bissau in coordinating the assistance provided by the United Nations and international partners to Guinea-Bissau,

Welcoming the continued engagement of the Peacebuilding Commission in Guinea-Bissau and the recent visit of the Chair of the Guinea-Bissau configuration of the Commission, taking note of the briefing by the Chair of the Guinea-Bissau configuration on 3 November 2011, and acknowledging the contribution of the Peacebuilding Fund to peacebuilding in Guinea-Bissau,

Reaffirming its full commitment to the consolidation of peace and stability in Guinea-Bissau,

1. *Decides* to extend the mandate of the United Nations Integrated Peacebuilding Office in Guinea-Bissau, as established in paragraph 3 of resolution 1876(2009), until 28 February 2013;

2. *Takes note* of the report of the Secretary-General of 21 October 2011 on Guinea-Bissau and of the recommendations contained therein, and welcomes the activities of the United Nations Integrated Peacebuilding Office in Guinea-Bissau;

3. *Takes note also* of the strategic workplan developed pursuant to resolution 1949(2010), emphasizes that the reform of the defence and security sectors, the fight against impunity and the fight against illicit drug trafficking remain priority sectors for peace consolidation in Guinea-Bissau, and further requests the Secretary-General to measure and track progress, in the next reports, on the work of the United Nations Integrated Peacebuilding Office in Guinea-Bissau in support of efforts by the relevant authorities of Guinea-Bissau in those sectors through the appropriate benchmarks, including recommendations to address gaps if there are any, without prejudice to the remaining tasks of the mandate of the Office;

4. *Calls upon* the Government and all political stakeholders in Guinea-Bissau to work together to consolidate peace and stability in the country, to use legal and peaceful means to resolve differences and to intensify efforts for genuine and inclusive political dialogue and national reconciliation, including the national conference on reconciliation, and requests the Secretary-General, including through his Special Representative for Guinea-Bissau, to support such efforts;

5. *Urges* members of the armed forces of Guinea-Bissau, in particular their leaders, to respect constitutional order, civilian rule and oversight, as well as the rule of law and human rights, to refrain from any interference in political issues, to guarantee the security of the national institutions as well as the population in general, and to fully participate in the reform of the defence and security sectors, and further urges Guinea-Bissau's political leaders to refrain from involving the military and the judiciary in politics;

6. *Requests* the Secretary-General, through his Special Representative, to continue to assist the Government of Guinea-Bissau to enhance its coordination of international assistance for credible security sector reform under the principle of national ownership and full civilian control of the military;

7. *Welcomes* the partnership between the Economic Community of West African States and the Community of Portuguese-speaking Countries to support security sector reform in Guinea-Bissau, calls upon the Economic Community of West African States, the Community of Portuguese-speaking Countries and the Government of Guinea-Bissau to continue to fulfil their commitments within the framework of the Economic Community of West African States-Community of Portuguese-speaking Countries road map, especially the operationalization of a pension fund for

members of the armed forces and security services, including their leaders, as well as the rejuvenation and professionalization of the military and security structures, recognizes the importance of contributions to the pension fund to take forward security sector reform, and in this context further welcomes the contribution of the Government to the pension fund, and further calls upon the authorities of Guinea-Bissau to complete the adoption of the basic legislation and framework related to the reform of the defence and security sectors, including the pension fund;

8. *Calls for* the conclusion of the investigations into the political assassinations of March and June 2009 as soon as possible, calls upon the Government of Guinea-Bissau to create the enabling environment to ensure that the work of the national commission of inquiry is credible, transparent and consistent with internationally agreed standards, and requests the Secretary-General to assist in the conclusion of these investigations, and further calls upon the African Union, the Economic Community of West African States, the Community of Portuguese-speaking Countries, the European Union and other partners to support, as appropriate, these and other efforts by the authorities to end impunity;

9. *Calls upon* the authorities of Guinea-Bissau to ensure the prosecution, with full respect for due process, of those responsible for all criminal acts, including illicit drug trafficking;

10. *Urges* the Government of Guinea-Bissau to continue to tackle corruption, including by implementing the United Nations Convention against Corruption;

11. *Encourages* the Government of Guinea-Bissau to continue the implementation of the West Africa Coast Initiative in the country;

12. *Urges* the international community, including the Peacebuilding Commission and regional organizations such as the African Union, the Economic Community of West African States, the Community of Portuguese-speaking Countries and the European Union, as well as bilateral partners as appropriate, to increase their support to the West Africa Coast Initiative to fight transnational organized crime and illicit drug trafficking, which threaten security and stability in Guinea-Bissau and in the subregion; welcomes in this regard the commitment of the Government of Guinea-Bissau to tackle this threat through the implementation of its 2011–2014 national operational plan, and calls upon the Government to allocate the resources necessary to implement the plan and for international partners to assist national authorities in this regard;

13. *Requests* the Peacebuilding Commission to continue to support the implementation of Guinea-Bissau's peacebuilding priorities as well as to continue to provide advice to the Security Council on how to remove critical obstacles to peacebuilding in Guinea-Bissau, in particular security sector reform and illicit drug trafficking, and to keep the Council updated on progress it has made in helping to address these;

14. *Calls upon* all national stakeholders, including political, military and civil society actors, to fully participate in the national conference on reconciliation and to ensure that a follow-up mechanism to implement the recommendations of the national conference is put in place;

15. *Encourages* the Special Representative to continue to pursue efforts to enhance the integration and effectiveness of the United Nations presence on the ground in support of the stabilization, peace and development priorities of the Government and people of Guinea-Bissau and, further, to give special attention to increased interaction with the authorities of Guinea-Bissau in order to strengthen their institutional capacities;

16. *Emphasizes* the important role of women in the prevention and resolution of conflicts and in peacebuilding, as recognized in resolutions 1325(2000) of 31 October 2000, 1820(2008) of 19 June 2008, 1888(2009) of 30 September 2009, 1889(2009) of 5 October 2009 and 1960(2010) of 16 December 2010, underlines that a gender perspective should continue to be taken into account in implementing all aspects of the mandate of the United Nations Integrated Peacebuilding Office in Guinea-Bissau, and encourages the Office to continue to work with national authorities in this regard, and relevant stakeholders to improve women's participation in peacebuilding;

17. *Requests* the Secretary-General to report on progress made in implementing the present resolution and the mandate of the United Nations Integrated Peacebuilding Office in Guinea-Bissau as outlined in resolution 1876(2009), through a briefing in March 2012, a report in July 2012 and every six months thereafter;

18. *Decides* to remain actively seized of the matter.

Year-end developments. In a further report [S/2012/554], the Secretary-General said that President Sanhá had set the date for the much-awaited national conference for 14 to 18 January 2012. On 22 November, however, the President was evacuated for medical reasons, delaying preparations for the event. On 26 December, elements from the military attacked the General Staff armoury and reportedly removed weapons. Following the incident, 24 military officers, including the Navy Chief of Staff, José Américo Bubo Na Tchuto, the Deputy Army Chief of Staff, Gletche Na Gana, a former Army Chief of Staff, General Watna Na Laie, and a civilian were arrested. Rear Admiral Bubo Na Tchuto denied any knowledge of or involvement in the incident. Although the Government denied that there had been a coup attempt, on 30 December the Prime Minister announced that there had been a plot at the time to assassinate him and General António Indjai. The Secretary-General, the AU, ECOWAS and the EU condemned the military actions.

Peacebuilding Commission

The Peacebuilding Commission reviewed its activities in Guinea-Bissau in the report of its fifth session [A/66/675-S/2012/70], covering 2011. The Commission continued to address key peacebuilding priorities, with particular focus on supporting the Government's efforts to implement security sector reform. Conscious that stability was fragile, the Commission engaged with the Government in a dialogue aimed at consolidating the foundations for sustainable peace. The Guinea-Bissau configuration addressed peacebuilding priorities, such as security sector reform, combating drug trafficking and organized crime, and consolidating the rule of law. The report noted that the Government had made important progress in the area of transnational crime and drug trafficking, including the establishment of a transnational crime unit in Bissau as part of the West Africa Coast Initiative, and the adoption of an operational plan to combat drug trafficking.

The Chair of the configuration visited the country (1–3 September), where she met with the Prime Minister, Government ministers, representatives of civil society and the diplomatic corps, the heads of UN agencies and the press. All interlocutors recognized the urgency of focusing on security sector reform; the launching of a pension fund for the armed forces and security forces personnel to be demobilized was regarded as a crucial step in advancing that process. To that end, the configuration's resource mobilization efforts focused on fast-tracking crucial parts of the security sector reform, notably the pension fund. On 28 June, the Secretary-General allocated up to $16.8 million from the Peacebuilding Fund to the implementation of the peacebuilding priority plan. Subsequently, the Peacebuilding Joint Steering Committee approved all four draft projects jointly designed by the Government and the UN country team to implement the plan, which focused on supporting security sector reform, promoting job creation for youth and women, and boosting political dialogue and national reconciliation.

Participation in Guinea-Bissau configuration. During the year, the Chairperson of the Peacebuilding Commission invited South Africa [PBC/5/OC/1], Mexico [PBC/5/OC/5] and the Food and Agriculture Organization of the United Nations [PBC/5/OC/8] to participate in the Commission's configuration on Guinea-Bissau.

(For further information on the Peacebuilding Commission, see p. 47.)

UNIOGBIS

The United Nations Integrated Peacebuilding Office in Guinea-Bissau (UNIOGBIS) was established on 1 January 2010 as the successor to the United Nations Peacebuilding Support Office in Guinea-Bissau by Security Council resolution 1876(2009) [YUN 2009, p. 219]. The original Office was established in 1999 by a decision of the Secretary-General [YUN 1999, p. 140]; the Council expressed support for that decision in resolution 1233(1999) [ibid.]. In 2011, by resolution 2030(2011) (see p. 183), the Council extended the UNIOGBIS mandate until 28 February 2013. Joseph Mutaboba (Rwanda) served as the Special Representative of the Secretary-General and Head of UNIOGBIS.

As per Council resolution 1876(2009), the Office was assigned to the following tasks: strengthening national institutions' capacities to maintain constitutional order, public security and the rule of law; assisting the Peacebuilding Commission in addressing critical peacebuilding needs; supporting law enforcement and criminal justice systems; supporting political dialogue and national reconciliation; providing support to the Government in security sector reform; assisting national efforts to combat drug trafficking, organized crime and human trafficking; supporting efforts to reduce small arms proliferation; promoting human rights; integrating a gender perspective in peacebuilding; and enhancing cooperation with regional organizations and international assistance.

Financing

In an October report [A/66/354/Add.3] on estimates in respect of special political missions, good offices and other political initiatives authorized by the General Assembly and/or the Security Council, the Secretary-General proposed resource requirements for UNIOGBIS in the amount of $18,982,100 for 2012, which ACABQ recommended for approval [A/66/7/Add.12].

On 24 December, in section IX of **resolution 66/247** (see p. 1393), the Assembly endorsed the recommendations of ACABQ and approved the resource requirements, including those for UNIOGBIS.

Cameroon–Nigeria

Cameroon-Nigeria Mixed Commission

Cameroon and Nigeria continued to cooperate in implementing the 2002 ruling of the International Court of Justice (ICJ) on their border dispute [YUN 2002, p. 1265] through the Cameroon-Nigeria Mixed Commission, established by the Secretary-General in 2002 at the request of the Presidents of Cameroon and Nigeria [YUN 2003, p. 8]. The Commission was responsible for the demarcation of the land and maritime boundaries between the two countries; the withdrawal of civil administration, military and police forces and a transfer of authority in relevant areas along the boundary; the demilitarization of the Bakassi peninsula; the protection of the rights of the affected populations; the development of projects to promote joint economic ventures and cross-border cooperation; and the reactivation of the five-member Lake Chad Basin Commission (Cameroon, Central African Republic, Chad, Niger, Nigeria), created in 1964 for the regulation and planning of the uses of the Lake and other natural resources of the conventional basin. By 2007, all four sections of the ICJ ruling had been resolved to the satisfaction of the two parties: the withdrawal and transfer of authority in the Lake Chad area in 2003; the withdrawal and transfer of authority along the land border in 2004; the agreement on the modalities of withdrawal and transfer of authority in the Bakassi peninsula in 2006; and the agreement on the delineation of the maritime boundary in 2007 [YUN 2007, p. 232]. The transfer of authority from Nigeria to Cameroon of the remaining "zone" of the Bakassi peninsula was finalized in 2008, [YUN 2008, p. 231], and in 2009 the emplacement of the boundary demarcation pillars began [YUN 2009, p. 226], a process that continued in 2010 [YUN 2010, p. 231]. The Commission was chaired by the Special Representative of the Secretary-General for West Africa, Said Djinnit (Algeria).

Activities

The Secretary-General reviewed the Commission's achievements and activities in 2011 in a letter to the President of the Security Council [S/2012/28], as well as in his June [S/2011/388] and December [S/2011/811] reports on UNOWA activities. Throughout the year, the Commission continued to facilitate the process, including by helping to maintain open dialogue and communication between the two countries. More than 1,700 kilometres out of the estimated 2,000 kilometres of the land boundary between the two countries had been demarcated, including 99.4 kilometres of inaccessible areas in the Atlantika Mountains through satellite imagery. In November, the United Nations assisted an independent expert team in determining the boundary in the Mount Tosso area, to be examined by the Commission in 2012.

At its twenty-seventh session (Yaoundé, Cameroon, 10–11 March), the parties expressed the desire to assume stronger ownership of the implementation of the ICJ judgment, and resolved to complete the substantial part of the demarcation work by November 2012, including the construction of another 1,056 boundary pillars. The parties agreed on a new structure that would give them a leading role in the management of future demarcation works, as well to carry out joint sensitization missions, accompanied by the United Nations, to facilitate acceptance of the demarcation by local communities. The parties also concluded that the Working Group on the Maritime Boundary had fulfilled its mandate, having implemented the ICJ ruling in respect of the maritime boundary. At its twenty-eighth session (Abuja, 23 July), the Commission stressed the need for comprehensive planning for the completion of the remaining tasks, including the assessment of all boundary lines, the extraction of coordinates and the drawing of final maps. To that end, it agreed that the demarcation work would be concluded with a boundary statement, which would include a series of legally-agreed maps depicting the Cameroon-Nigeria boundary line.

The Follow-up Committee established by the 12 June 2006 Greentree Agreement [YUN 2006, p. 252] continued its work following the final transfer of authority in the "zone" in the Bakassi peninsula from Nigeria to Cameroon in 2008. In its visits to the zone in 2011, the Committee noted considerable improvement of the situation in the peninsula, as evidenced by the significant increase of the population and good relations between the community and the authorities. Nevertheless, the population raised concerns regarding the increased security risk caused by piracy and banditry, which would require enhanced cross-border cooperation between the security forces of both countries. The United Nations was encouraging the parties to conclude a framework agreement to enhance security cooperation in a common effort to combat the threat of piracy and terrorism in the subregion.

The Commission continued to support the formulation of confidence-building measures for the welfare of affected populations, and to promote initiatives aimed at enhancing trust between the two Governments and their peoples. In that regard, the Special Representative continued to work with the UN country teams of Cameroon and Nigeria to pursue an integrated approach towards supporting such confidence-building measures. The Government of Cameroon and the UN country team in Cameroon undertook a needs assessment mission on the border area in May and June, identifying four new confidence-building projects aimed at supporting border communities affected by the demarcation process.

The Secretary-General stated that, after 2012, the activities that would conclude the work of the Commission entailed monitoring the situation in the zone of the Bakassi peninsula for the remainder of the five-year transitional period (August 2008–August 2013); facilitating the boundary pillar emplacement, financed by a trust fund, and promoting the replenishment of the trust fund through voluntary contributions; and implementing the exit strategy by handing over the activities of the Commission to the Joint Bilateral Commission and other subregional structures.

Financing

In an October report [A/66/354/Add.3] on estimates in respect of special political missions, good offices and other political initiatives authorized by the General Assembly and/or the Security Council, the Secretary-General proposed resource requirements for United Nations support for the Cameroon-Nigeria Mixed Commission in the amount of $8,854,600 for 2012. In its related report [A/66/7/Add.12], ACABQ, while reiterating its concern regarding the high unit cost of air travel to support the Commission and expecting that efforts would continue in identifying efficiencies in that regard, recommended approval of the requested resources.

On 24 December, in section IX of **resolution 66/247** (see p. 1393), the Assembly reduced the 2012 budget for the Commission by $250,000.

Guinea

Political and security developments

Reports of Secretary-General. In his June [S/2011/388] and December [S/2011/811] reports on the activities of the United Nations Office for West Africa (UNOWA), the Secretary-General reported on developments in Guinea following the signing of the Ouagadougou Joint Declaration [YUN 2010, p. 233] and the country's first multiparty presidential election [ibid., p. 235]. Following the election of Alpha Condé as President, the International Contact Group on Guinea, established in 2009 at the consultative meeting on the situation in Guinea [YUN 2009, p. 228], and in which the United Nations was represented by the Secretary-General's Special Representative, Said Djinnit, met for the final time on 10 February. Participants agreed on the need to establish a Group of Friends of Guinea, which would follow up on the initiatives undertaken by the International Contact Group.

Nonetheless, the political situation remained tense as a result of an assassination attempt against President Condé and a lack of consensus on modalities for the organization of the legislative elections. On 19 July, a group of heavily armed assailants attacked the President's private residence, resulting in the arrest of several members of the armed forces. Following the incident, the Secretary-General's Special Representative travelled to Conakry, Guinea, to reiterate the United Nations condemnation of the attack, and to call on all Guineans to refrain from any acts that could undermine the consolidation of democratic institutions. Also in July, President Condé instructed the Minister of Territorial Administration and Decentralization to engage all political parties in preparations for the legislative elections. Several issues continued to divide the political class, including revisions to the voters' list, the conduct of a new census, the reform of the Independent National Electoral Commission and representation by the political parties in the decentralized structures of the Commission. On 15 September, the President of the Electoral Commission announced that legislative elections would be held on 29 December. The main opposition coalition rejected the announced date, calling on its members to participate in a demonstration on 27 September, an event that resulted in three deaths, as well as many injuries and arrests. At the request of President Condé, on 26 September, Prime Minister Mohamed Said Fofana proposed the establishment of a consultative framework for political parties to reach consensus on preparations for the elections. On 29 September, the main opposition parties conditioned their participation in consultations on the release of those arrested in connection with the September demonstration, as well as the suspension of all activities of the Electoral Commission until consensus was reached on the modalities for the elections. Subsequently, on 15 November, President Condé convened a meeting with the leaders of the main opposition parties and the ruling party to discuss election preparations. On 17 November and 6 December, he granted amnesty to 40 individuals connected with the demonstration. Nonetheless, on 20 November, the two main opposition coalitions concluded that the Government lacked the political will to facilitate dialogue with a view to organizing credible legislative polls.

The period under review saw limited progress in the implementation of the national reconciliation framework. On 15 August, President Condé nominated the Grand Imam and the Archbishop of Conakry as co-Presidents of the Provisional Commission for National Reconciliation. Subsequently, the co-Presidents began countrywide consultations to obtain preliminary consensus on the framework for national reconciliation. On 15 December, the Secretary-General's Special Representative participated in a session of the Provisional Commission in Conakry. Throughout the reporting period, the Special Representative, in collaboration with the UN country team in Guinea, the AU Special Envoy for Guinea, the President of the ECOWAS Commission, the Guinea configuration of the Peacebuilding Commission and the Group of Friends of Guinea, remained engaged with the country's main political stakeholders to support national reconciliation and promote political inclusiveness.

Peacebuilding Commission

On 23 February, at the request of the Government, the Organizational Committee of the Peacebuilding Commission decided to place Guinea on its agenda and to set up a country-specific configuration. The report of the Peacebuilding Commission on its fifth (2011) session [A/66/675-S/2012/70] stated that the Committee elected as Chair of the configuration the Permanent Representative of Luxembourg to the United Nations, who led the initial mission to Guinea (3–10 April). That was followed in May by a joint United Nations technical mission, led by the Peacebuilding Support Office, which introduced the Peacebuilding Fund and examined how it could be used to support the Commission's engagement in the country. The Chair conducted a second mission to the country (4–6 September), during which she held discussions with the Government and other key actors to define priority actions and mutual commitments on peacebuilding priorities.

Statement of mutual commitments. Following those missions, in a letter of 4 October [A/66/491-S/2011/619], the Chair of the configuration transmitted to the Presidents of the General Assembly, the Security Council and the Economic and Social Council the statement of mutual commitments on peacebuilding in Guinea between the Government and the Peacebuilding Commission [PBC/5/GUI/2], adopted on 23 September in the presence of President Alpha Condé. The statement noted that the post-election period provided an opportunity for the country and its partners to deepen the democratic gains made, address long-standing challenges to peace and security, and deliver improvements in living standards to the population. It outlined the peacebuilding priorities agreed between the Government and the Commission, as proposed by the Government in its request for the Commission's support, namely, the promotion of national reconciliation and unity, reform of the defence and security sector, and youth and women's employment policy. The statement outlined the key actions to be undertaken in each of the priority areas by the Government and the Commission, and noted that a review of the mutual commitments would be undertaken at six-month intervals, with the first review providing an opportunity to revisit and refine those commitments.

Participation in Guinea configuration. During the year, the Chair of the Peacebuilding Commission invited the United Nations Office on Drugs and Crime [PBC/5/OC/7], Burkina Faso [PBC/5/OC/9] and the Czech Republic [PBC/5/OC/11] to participate in the Commission's configuration on Guinea.

(For further information on the Peacebuilding Commission, see p. 47.)

Horn of Africa

The Sudan and South Sudan

In 2011, the successful completion of the Southern Sudan self-determination referendum was a momentous achievement. On 9 January, exactly six years after the Comprehensive Peace Agreement (CPA) came into effect, voting commenced for the referendum. On 7 February, the official results were announced—with over 98 per cent voting in favour of separation—and accepted by the National Congress Party, the Sudan's ruling party. Immediately thereafter, the parties reiterated their commitment to resolving all remaining issues pertaining to the Agreement by 9 July, the date that would mark the end of the interim period set in the Agreement. On that date, South Sudan was formally declared an independent State. During the independence ceremony, the President of South Sudan, Salva Kiir, took the oath of office, promulgated the Transitional Constitution and declared an amnesty for all militia groups. On 14 July, South Sudan joined the United Nations as its 193rd Member. The transition of South Sudan from decades of war to sustainable peace, however, presented considerable challenges, such as developing governance institutions and addressing multiple security, humanitarian and economic crises.

The relations between South Sudan and the Sudan deteriorated in the second half of the year, particularly in the border area of Abyei, where the presence of security forces of both Governments continued. On 27 June, the Security Council established the United Nations Interim Security Force for Abyei (UNISFA), whose mandate was to monitor the border between the north and the south and facilitate the delivery of humanitarian aid.

The United Nations Mission in the Sudan (UNMIS) ended its operations on 9 July as agreed on by the Sudan and the Sudan People's Liberation Movement (SPLM) in the CPA. In support of the newly created nation, the Security Council established a successor mission—the United Nations Mission in South Sudan (UNMISS)—for an initial period of one year.

In Darfur, fighting between the Government and armed movements continued to be a major source of insecurity. An All Darfur Stakeholders Conference held in May in Doha, Qatar, was followed, on 14 July, by the signature of an Agreement between the Sudan and the Liberation and Justice Movement (LJM) on the adoption of the Doha Document for Peace in Darfur. Meanwhile, the Darfur-based political process, led by the AU and the United Nations, was launched. It was intended to take into account the voices of all Darfurians and be complementary to the Doha negotiations. On 29 July, the Security Council extended the mandate of the African Union-United Nations Hybrid Operation in Darfur (UNAMID) until 31 July 2012.

Political and security developments

Voting for the Southern Sudan self-determination referendum commenced on 9 January and lasted until 15 January. It proceeded without incident throughout the Sudan and in the eight countries designated for overseas voting. On 7 February, the official results were announced, with over 98 per cent of voters in favour of separation. The results were immediately accepted by the Sudan's ruling National Congress Party and were later endorsed by the national legislature. Both parties to the CPA—the Government of the Sudan and the Sudan People's Liberation Movement/Army [YUN 2005, p. 301]—reiterated their commitment to resolving all remaining issues pertaining to the Agreement by 9 July, the date that would mark the end of the CPA interim period. The Secretary-General's three-member panel on the referendums, led by former Tanzanian President Benjamin Mkapa, visited the Sudan during the polling, counting, aggregation and transmission period (5–21 January) and during the announcement of the results (5–7 February). The panel found that the referendum reflected the free will of the people of Southern Sudan.

Communication. On 28 January [S/2011/34], the Sudan requested the Security Council to retain the item entitled "Letter dated 20 February 1958 from the representative of the Sudan addressed to the Secretary-General" [YUN 1958, p. 82] on the list of matters of which the Council was seized.

SECURITY COUNCIL ACTION

On 9 February [meeting 6478], following consultations among Security Council members, the President made statement **S/PRST/2011/3** on behalf of the Council:

The Security Council welcomes the announcement on 7 February 2011 by the Southern Sudan Referendum Commission of the final results of the referendum on self-determination for the people of Southern Sudan, which showed that 98.83 per cent of voters chose independence. The Council calls upon the international community to lend its full support to all Sudanese people as they build a peaceful and prosperous future.

The Council congratulates the parties to the Comprehensive Peace Agreement and the people of the Sudan on a peaceful and successful referendum, and commends the United Nations Mission in the Sudan for its contribution to the process.

The Council warmly welcomes the statements of President Omar al-Bashir and Vice President Salva Kiir on 7 February 2011, in which they accept the final results of the referendum. The Council calls upon all Member States to respect the outcome of the referendum and looks forward to welcoming an independent South Sudan as a new member of the international community after 9 July 2011.

The Council welcomes the work of the Secretary-General's Panel on the Referenda in the Sudan led by former President Benjamin Mkapa. The Council praises the parties to the Comprehensive Peace Agreement for their commitment to the Agreement, as illustrated by their support for a timely and credible referendum process. The Council underlines that full and timely implementation of the Agreement is essential to peace and stability in the Sudan and the region and to future cooperation between northern and southern Sudan and the international community.

The Council further acknowledges that the process mandated by the Comprehensive Peace Agreement represents an exceptional case and does not by itself set a precedent.

The Council reaffirms its support for the work of the African Union High-level Implementation Panel on the Sudan and its Chairperson, President Thabo Mbeki, and notes the commitments made by the parties to the Comprehensive Peace Agreement at the Presidency meeting of 27 January 2011, and encourages them to continue to strive for a timely agreement on the implementation of outstanding Agreement issues. The Council urges the parties to reach quickly an agreement on Abyei and other critical issues, including border demarcation, security arrangements, citizenship, debts, assets, currency, wealth-sharing and natural resource management. The Council welcomes the start of the popular consultation process in Blue Nile State and stresses the importance of inclusive, timely and credible popular consultations processes in Blue Nile and Southern Kordofan States, in accordance with the Agreement.

The Council deeply regrets the loss of life in violence in Upper Nile State from 3 to 5 February 2011.

The Council underlines the need for the parties to the Comprehensive Peace Agreement to prevent further clashes and promote calm, including by providing immediate and ongoing reassurance to people of all nationalities in the Sudan, including Southerners in the North and Northerners in the South, that their rights, safety and property will continue to be respected. The Council urges the parties to the Agreement to respect their obligations.

The Council reiterates its deep concern over the increase in violence and insecurity in Darfur, including ceasefire violations, attacks by rebel groups and aerial bombardment by the Sudanese Armed Forces, which recently displaced approximately 43,000 civilians, and the kidnapping on 13 January 2011 of three members of the United Nations Humanitarian Air Service. The Council recalls the importance it attaches to an end to impunity, and to justice for crimes committed in Darfur. The Council reaffirms its support for the African Union-United Nations Hybrid Operation in Darfur and urges all parties to ensure full and unhindered access for the Operation throughout the mission area and to allow humanitarian workers to provide assistance to all populations in need.

The Council reaffirms its support for the African Union-United Nations-led peace process for Darfur, hosted by Qatar, the work of the Joint African Union-United Nations Chief Mediator for Darfur, Mr. Djibril Bassolé, and the principles guiding the negotiations. The Council welcomes the presence of the Justice and Equality Movement and the Liberation and Justice Movement in Doha, and strongly urges all other rebel movements to join the peace process without further delay or preconditions, and all parties to engage with a view to concluding urgently a comprehensive agreement.

The Council requests the Secretary-General to report to the Council by the end of February 2011 on issues related to the Darfur-based political process, including an assessment of the enabling environment.

The Council reiterates the importance of increased participation of women in the Sudanese peace processes.

The Council will continue to follow closely developments in the Sudan, including in Darfur.

Report of Secretary-General (April). In his April report [S/2011/239], submitted pursuant to Security Council resolution 1590(2005) [YUN 2005, p. 304], the Secretary-General reviewed the implementation of the CPA and the activities of the United Nations Mission in the Sudan (UNMIS) since his December 2010 report [YUN 2010, p. 252].

Tensions rose in the South following the referendum. In particular, conflicts between the Sudan People's Liberation Army (SPLA) and a number of insurgents and militia resumed in Jonglei, Upper Nile and Unity States. The situation in the resource-rich Abyei Area remained volatile. The failure of the parties to make progress towards resolving the region's status empowered hard-line elements within the Misseriya and Ngok Dinka communities, contributing to continued violence. An agreement between those two tribes on 13 January in Kadugli was followed on 17 January by an agreement between the Ministers of the Interior of the Sudan and Southern Sudan. The Kadugli agreements provided for arrangements to find solutions to disputes and for the withdrawal of all forces other than the Joint Integrated Units and Joint Integrated Police. They also included the establishment of a standing committee consisting of representatives from each party. Those agreements contributed to containing the situation, even though their full implementation remained a challenge. Following the resurgence of violence in Abyei, Jonglei and Upper Nile, UNMIS responded through political facilitation and increased military presence. Denial of access, however, curtailed the Mission's ability to patrol those areas and deter threats against civilians. Since January and despite persistent attempts, UNMIS patrols were not able to gain access to the sites where fighting had taken place. In addition, UNMIS patrols were frequently harassed. In March, due to SPLA operations against armed militias in Jonglei and Upper Nile States, SPLA requested that UNMIS remain outside of the counties where the operations were occurring. That restriction was revoked in late March, but it severely hampered the UNMIS ability to verify the military and humanitarian situation in those areas. A number of economic questions, such as the ownership of pipelines and transitional financial arrangements for oil revenue-sharing, remained to be solved. The AU High-level Implementation Panel convened the parties in Ethiopia from 1 to 5 March, together with technical experts from UNMIS, the African Development Bank, the United States and Norway, to discuss issues of debt, currency and oil. Some progress was made on the shared management of the border, such as the establishment of a joint mechanism to ensure the implementation of the post-referendum security arrangements, but the physical demarcation had not started and the parties differed on the necessity of a third-party involvement. The popular consultations in Southern Kordofan and Blue Nile States, provided for in the CPA, were lagging behind.

The Secretary-General underscored that the question of Abyei's future status could not be postponed any longer. Further, the popular consultations in Southern Kordofan and Blue Nile States were vital for the development of peaceful North-South relations.

Many difficult questions remained to be addressed before separation. A failure to resolve security issues and the disposition of armed forces along the border could easily spark renewed violence. He urged the parties to resolve those questions quickly, also availing themselves of third-party assistance.

SECURITY COUNCIL ACTION

On 21 April [meeting 6521], following consultations among Security Council members, the President made statement **S/PRST/2011/8** on behalf of the Council:

The Security Council reaffirms its support for the continued negotiations between the parties to the Comprehensive Peace Agreement, including under the auspices of the African Union High-level Implementation Panel on the Sudan and its Chairperson, President Thabo Mbeki. Noting that the conclusion of the Comprehensive Peace Agreement interim period on 9 July 2011 is soon approaching, the Council urges the parties, meeting at the highest level, as necessary, to reach agreement on outstanding Agreement issues and post-Agreement arrangements. The Council also encourages the parties to engage with the United Nations on the future of the United Nations presence in the Sudan.

The Council reiterates its deep concern over increased tensions, violence and displacement in the Abyei Area. The Council calls upon both parties to implement and adhere to recent security agreements by withdrawing from the Abyei Area all forces other than the Joint Integrated Units and Joint Integrated Police Units allowed under those agreements and to urgently reach an agreement on Abyei's post-Comprehensive Peace Agreement status. The Council affirms that it is the responsibility of the parties to the Agreement, including during their negotiations under the auspices of the African Union High-level Implementation Panel and its Chairperson, President Thabo Mbeki, to reach agreement on the status of Abyei. In this regard, the Council acknowledges the ruling of 22 July 2009 by the Permanent Court of Arbitration at The Hague, which defines the borders of Abyei.

The Council welcomes the start of the popular consultations process in Blue Nile State and the rescheduled gubernatorial and state assembly elections on 2 to 4 May 2011 in Southern Kordofan State. The Council expresses its concern about recent violence in Southern Kordofan and underscores the responsibility of all parties to avoid inflammatory rhetoric and to ensure peaceful and credible elections. The Council also stresses the importance of inclusive, timely and credible popular consultations processes, in accordance with the Comprehensive Peace Agreement. The Council urges both parties to reach a security agreement regarding the future of the tens of thousands of troops from the Sudan People's Liberation Army from Southern Kordofan and Blue Nile States. The Council also urges the parties to reach agreement on security arrangements and to determine the future status of Southerners currently serving in the Sudanese Armed Forces.

The Council is deeply concerned about recent violence between the Sudan People's Liberation Army and local militias, specifically in Jonglei, Upper Nile and

Unity States. The Council calls upon the leaders of the Government of Southern Sudan and the Sudan People's Liberation Army to find peaceful solutions to the violence, prevent further clashes and restore calm.

The Council underlines the need for the parties to the Comprehensive Peace Agreement to promote calm, including by providing immediate and ongoing reassurance to people of all nationalities in the Sudan, including Southerners in the North and Northerners in the South, that their rights, safety and property will be respected. The Council urges the parties to the Agreement to respect their obligations in this regard.

The Council reiterates in the strongest terms that any obstruction to the freedom of movement of the United Nations Mission in the Sudan is unacceptable and that the Mission requires full and unfettered access throughout the mission area.

The Council will not tolerate any support to proxy militias by either party to the Comprehensive Peace Agreement.

The Council reiterates its deep concern over the serious increase in violence and insecurity in Darfur, including ceasefire violations, restrictions on access to vulnerable populations throughout Darfur by the African Union-United Nations Hybrid Operation in Darfur and the humanitarian community, attacks by rebel groups, aerial bombardment by the Sudanese Armed Forces and the ongoing displacement of civilians. The Council expresses its deep condolences to the family of the peacekeeper killed on 5 April 2011 and urges the Operation and the Government of the Sudan to conduct a full and thorough investigation into the incident.

The Council reaffirms its support for the African Union-United Nations Hybrid Operation in Darfur, including the increasingly full implementation of its Chapter VII mandate to deliver its core tasks to protect civilians and assure humanitarian access, as defined in resolution 1769(2007) of 31 July 2007, and recalls the priority given to its efforts in support of the African Union-United Nations-led political process for Darfur. The Council demands that the Government of the Sudan and the armed movements cease hostilities and ensure full and unhindered access, by land and by air, for the Operation throughout the mission area and allow humanitarian workers to provide assistance to all populations in need. The Council notes the statement made by the Permanent Representative of the Sudan to the United Nations before the Council on 20 April 2011 that his Government would issue all outstanding 1,117 visas for Operation personnel, and urgently calls upon the Government of the Sudan to do so.

The Council reaffirms its support for the African Union-United Nations-led peace process for Darfur, hosted by Qatar, and the work of the Joint African Union-United Nations Chief Mediator for Darfur, Mr. Djibril Bassolé. The Council further reaffirms its support for the principles guiding the negotiations. The Council strongly urges all other rebel movements to join the peace process without further delay or preconditions. The Council urges the parties in Doha to make the necessary concessions to quickly reach a ceasefire and political agreement and looks forward to the outcome of the upcoming All Darfur Stakeholders Conference in Doha. The Council believes this conference should be fully representative of all of Darfur's populations and interest groups. The Council reiterates the importance of increased participation of women in the Sudanese peace processes.

The Council recognizes the potential complementary role that a Darfur-based political process could play to ensure the participation and support of the people of Darfur and better enable them to be involved in the implementation of the outcome of the Doha peace process. The Council is nonetheless concerned that important aspects of the enabling environment necessary for a Darfur-based political process are not in place, including (1) the civil and political rights of participants such that they can exercise their views without fear of retribution, (2) freedom of speech and assembly to permit open consultations, (3) freedom of movement of participants and the African Union-United Nations Hybrid Operation in Darfur, (4) proportional participation among Darfurians, (5) freedom from harassment, arbitrary arrest and intimidation, and (6) freedom from interference by the Government or armed movements. The Council calls upon the Government of the Sudan and the armed movements to contribute to the creation of such an enabling environment for a Darfur-based political process, working closely with the Operation as appropriate, and, in particular, calls upon the Government to fulfil its stated commitment to lift the state of emergency in Darfur.

The Council also calls upon the Government of the Sudan to release all political detainees, to allow free expression and to undertake effective efforts to ensure accountability for serious violations of human rights and international humanitarian law, by whomsoever perpetrated.

Extension of UNMIS. In his April report [S/2011/239], the Secretary-General said that at the request of the Government of Southern Sudan, the United Nations had commenced planning of a possible post-UNMIS presence in South Sudan. Meanwhile, in view of the situation, he recommended that the Security Council extend the UNMIS mandate through 9 July, when the CPA interim period would be completed.

SECURITY COUNCIL ACTION

On 27 April [meeting 6522], the Security Council unanimously adopted **resolution 1978(2011)**. The draft [S/2011/267] was submitted by the United States.

The Security Council,

Recalling all its previous resolutions and the statements by its President concerning the situation in the Sudan,

Considering the results of the referendum of Southern Sudan, announced on 7 February 2011 by the Southern Sudan Referendum Commission, and considering the request by the Government of Southern Sudan for a continued United Nations presence in South Sudan,

Determining that the situation in the region continues to constitute a threat to international peace and security,

1. *Decides* to extend until 9 July 2011 the mandate of the United Nations Mission in the Sudan as set out in resolution 1590(2005) of 24 March 2005;

2. *Announces its intent* to establish a mission to succeed the United Nations Mission in the Sudan;

3. *Requests* the Secretary-General to continue to consult with the parties to the Comprehensive Peace Agreement in this regard and to submit a report by 16 May 2011;

4. *Authorizes* the United Nations Mission in the Sudan to utilize its assets to prepare for the establishment of the above-mentioned successor mission;

5. *Decides* to remain actively seized of the matter.

Report of Secretary-General (May). Pursuant to Council resolution 1978(2011) (see p. 192), the Secretary-General on 17 May presented a special report [S/2011/314] assessing the outstanding provisions of CPA and recommending the establishment of a multidimensional operation, the United Nations Mission in South Sudan (UNMISS), also outlining its mandate, structure and components.

Although the National Congress Party and the Sudan People's Liberation Movement (SPLM) had ended the longest civil war in Africa through the implementation of the CPA, key issues—such as the settlement of the Abyei question, popular consultations on the future status of Southern Kordofan and Blue Nile States, and the redeployment of former SPLA troops in those two States—had yet to be resolved. With regard to the border, the main risk of conflict was related to the parties' mutual desire to control oil- and mineral-rich areas, as well as strategic locations on principal routes between the North and South. In addition to the five disputed areas—two along the Bahr el-Ghazal/Southern Darfur border and three near the western bank of the White Nile River—a range of local issues could exacerbate border tensions in other areas.

The dispute over the future status of the Abyei Area was the greatest challenge to CPA implementation. As at May, there was a high concentration of military forces from both sides in the region, where conflict between the Sudanese Armed Forces (SAF) and SPLA could easily escalate. While the Kadugli agreements had helped contain violence, no agreement had been reached on Abyei, even though the question had been addressed at the presidential level in negotiations facilitated by the AU High-level Implementation Panel.

Regarding post-CPA arrangements, the Government of the Sudan and SPLM/A, in December 2010, had agreed on a general political framework guiding the post-CPA political, economic and security relations of northern and southern Sudan. Although the framework was never formally signed, the parties decided to use the draft framework agreement as the reference document. The parties agreed to disengage their military forces 10 kilometres on both sides of the current borderline. They also settled the question of the dissolution of the Joint Integrated Units within 90 days of the official announcement of the referendum result, with the exception of those units deployed to Abyei, those securing the oil fields and those located in Blue Nile and Southern Kordofan States. That process was completed on 9 April. During the negotiations in April the parties discussed a Common Border Zone, which would facilitate the establishment of corridors for the safe movement of people and goods. They also discussed a mechanism to coordinate monitoring and verification of the implementation of the Zone, as well as third-party support to assist the border mechanism, but did not reach definite conclusions.

As for a UN peacekeeping operation in South Sudan, upon the request of that Government, a UN system assessment mission visited southern Sudan (16 February–31 March); and the Secretary-General's Policy Committee [YUN 2005, p. 1513] reviewed the mission's recommendations on 26 April. The main tasks of the new operations would include supporting the Government in peace consolidation, conflict prevention and protection of civilians, and assisting the authorities in establishing the rule of law and strengthening the security and justice sectors.

The Secretary-General urged the parties and the Security Council to consider a three-month technical rollover of UNMIS from 9 July to 9 October. During that period, UNMIS would start downsizing its presence in Khartoum and assist the parties in maintaining calm while seeking resolutions to the residual CPA and post-referendum issues. The Secretary-General intended to establish an advance team to set up the core capabilities of the new UN operation in South Sudan. In addition, the UN country team would immediately commence efforts to support the new State.

SECURITY COUNCIL ACTION

On 3 June [meeting 6544], following consultations among Security Council members, the President made statement **S/PRST/2011/12** on behalf of the Council:

> The Security Council expresses grave concern about the ongoing violence and rapidly deteriorating situation in Abyei since the Council addressed the issue in its press statement of 22 May 2011, in which the Council condemned the attack by Southern forces against a United Nations Mission in the Sudan convoy escorting Sudanese Armed Forces elements of Joint Integrated Units in Abyei on 19 May 2011, and also condemned the escalatory military operations being undertaken by the Sudanese Armed Forces, which have taken control of the area in and around Abyei town.
>
> The Council strongly condemns the Government of the Sudan's taking and continued maintenance of military control over the Abyei Area and the resulting displacement of tens of thousands of residents of Abyei. The Council calls upon the Sudanese Armed Forces to ensure an immediate halt to all looting, burning and illegal resettlement. The Council stresses that all those responsible for violations of international law, including humanitarian and human rights law, as well as those who ordered those acts, will be held accountable. The Council expresses grave

concern about the deteriorating humanitarian situation in the area and praises the efforts of the humanitarian community to deliver emergency assistance, including food, health care, shelter and water, to those affected by the conflict, despite continued insecurity in the region and despite severe limitations on access.

The Council condemns the fact that two of the three main supply routes from the North to the South have been blocked and that the Banton Bridge in Southern Abyei was destroyed by the Sudanese Armed Forces, which impedes needed trade and makes the return of civilians to Abyei more difficult. The Council calls for immediate measures to restore full access through all routes.

The Council calls upon all parties to respect humanitarian principles and allow all humanitarian personnel timely and unfettered access to vulnerable individuals and communities affected by the fighting. The Council further calls for conditions to be created that would allow the prompt and safe return of those displaced from their homes.

The Council strongly condemns all attacks against the Mission, including those of 19 and 24 May 2011, which are criminal acts against a United Nations mission and its personnel and which threaten to undermine the commitment of the parties to avoid a return to war.

The Council recalls the commitments made by Vice President Ali Osman Taha and First Vice President Salva Kiir that both parties shall remove any unconditional claims to Abyei in their draft national constitutions and urges the parties to avoid inflammatory rhetoric, especially from the leadership, which undermines the mutual commitment of the parties to resolve all remaining Comprehensive Peace Agreement and post-Agreement issues peacefully through negotiation. The Council again urges both parties to honour these commitments.

The Council expresses grave concern following the reports about the unusual, sudden influx of thousands of Misseriya into Abyei town and its environs that could force significant changes in the ethnic composition of the area. The Council condemns all unilateral actions meant to create facts on the ground that would prejudice the outcome of negotiations. The Council expresses its determination that the future status of Abyei shall be resolved by negotiations between the parties in a manner consistent with the Comprehensive Peace Agreement and not by the unilateral actions of either party.

The Council reiterates that the continued military operations of the Government of the Sudan and militia activities in Abyei constitute a serious violation of the Comprehensive Peace Agreement and the Kadugli agreements. The Council demands that the Government of the Sudan withdraw immediately from the Abyei Area. The Council further demands the immediate withdrawal of all military elements from Abyei. The Council demands that the Government of the Sudan and the Government of Southern Sudan cooperate fully with the Special Representative of the Secretary-General for the Sudan and Head of the United Nations Mission in the Sudan and the African Union High-Level Implementation Panel on the Sudan led by President Thabo Mbeki to establish immediately a viable security arrangement for Abyei, supported by the Mission, in which all Sudanese Armed Forces, Sudan People's Liberation Army and allied forces withdraw from the Abyei Area. The Council notes that the Mission remains ready to assist in the implementation of all relevant agreements reached by the parties. The Council underscores that failure by the Government of the Sudan to comply with and to fulfil the Comprehensive Peace Agreement jeopardizes the benefits that could flow from such compliance.

Given the ongoing insecurity in Abyei, the Council believes that the security and prosperity of both parties would benefit from a continuing United Nations-mandated presence in Abyei after 9 July 2011, as well as from United Nations assistance for the parties' management of their border after the independence of South Sudan. In this context, the Council urges the parties to reach agreement on a continuing United Nations-mandated presence.

The Council stresses that both parties will have much to gain if they show restraint and choose the path of dialogue, including ongoing high-level negotiations between the parties and negotiations under the auspices of the African Union High-level Implementation Panel and its Chairperson, President Thabo Mbeki, instead of resorting to violence or provocations.

The Council expresses deep concern about tensions in Blue Nile and Southern Kordofan States. The Council calls for discussions about post-Comprehensive Peace Agreement political and security arrangements for Blue Nile and Southern Kordofan States to resume immediately and for all parties to refrain from unilateral action pending the outcome of those negotiations. The Council stresses that Agreement structures intended to stabilize the security situation in Blue Nile and Southern Kordofan States, specifically the deployment of Joint Integrated Units, should continue until their expiration on 9 July 2011. The Council calls upon both parties to work to reduce tensions and promote calm in this sensitive region. The Council further underscores the need for the parties to respect the mandate of the Mission.

The Council underscores the responsibility of the parties to protect civilians, and to respect the Chapter VII mandate of the Mission for the protection of civilians under imminent threat of physical violence in Abyei. In this regard, the Council condemns in the strongest terms ongoing threats and intimidation against elements of the Mission. The Council expresses its strong ongoing support for the Mission, under the able leadership of the Special Representative of the Secretary-General, Mr. Haile Menkerios.

The Council will remain seized of this matter and will meet to review the implementation of the present statement in the coming days.

Communication. By a letter of 8 June [S/2011/350], South Africa transmitted to the Security Council a joint communiqué issued by the UN Security Council and the AU Peace and Security Council at their 21 May meeting in Addis Ababa, Ethiopia, in which they urged the parties to the CPA to reach an agreement on outstanding issues and post-CPA arrangements, under the auspices of the AU High-level Implementation Panel. In particular, they called on both parties to reach an agreement of the status of Abyei and, in that regard, they acknowledged the July 2009 ruling by the Permanent Court of Arbitration [YUN 2009, p. 232], which defined the borders of the Abyei Area.

Agreement between Sudan and SPLM. On 23 June [S/2011/384], the Secretary-General transmitted to the Council the Agreement between the Sudan and SPLM on Temporary Arrangements for the Administration and Security of the Abyei Area, signed in Addis Ababa on 20 June under the auspices of the AU High-level Implementation Panel. The Agreement provided for the redeployment of SAF and SPLA from the Abyei Area immediately after the deployment of the Interim Security Force for Abyei (ISFA), composed of Ethiopian troops. The Agreement respected the provisions of the Abyei Protocol to the CPA; established the Abyei Area Administration and the Abyei Joint Oversight Committee; and provided for ISFA functions, as well as security arrangements and the continuation of negotiations for the final status of Abyei. ISFA would deploy in the Abyei Area as soon as authorized by the United Nations.

Establishment of UNISFA. Following the 20 June Agreement between the Sudan and SPLM, the Security Council on 27 June established the United Nations Interim Security Force for Abyei (UNISFA).

SECURITY COUNCIL ACTION

On 27 June [meeting 6567], the Security Council unanimously adopted **resolution 1990(2011)**. The draft [S/2011/389] was submitted by Colombia, Gabon, Nigeria, South Africa and the United States.

The Security Council,

Recalling its previous resolutions and the statements by its President on the situation in the Sudan, and noting the priority it attaches to the implementation of the Comprehensive Peace Agreement,

Reaffirming its commitment to the principles of sovereignty and territorial integrity and to peace, stability and security throughout the region,

Reaffirming its previous resolutions 1674(2006) of 28 April 2006 and 1894(2009) of 11 November 2009 on the protection of civilians in armed conflict, its resolution 1882(2009) of 4 August 2009 on children and armed conflict, its resolution 1502(2003) of 26 August 2003 on the protection of humanitarian and United Nations personnel, and its resolutions 1325(2000) of 31 October 2000, 1820(2008) of 19 June 2008, 1888(2009) of 30 September 2009 and 1889(2009) of 5 October 2009 on women and peace and security,

Welcoming the Agreement between the Government of the Sudan and the Sudan People's Liberation Movement on Temporary Arrangements for the Administration and Security of the Abyei Area, reached on 20 June 2011 in Addis Ababa,

Commending the assistance provided to the parties by the African Union High-Level Implementation Panel on the Sudan and its Chairperson, President Thabo Mbeki, the Prime Minister of Ethiopia, Mr. Meles Zenawi, and the Special Representative of the Secretary-General for the Sudan, Mr. Haile Menkerios,

Noting the Government of the Sudan and the Sudan People's Liberation Movement's request for the assistance of the Government of Ethiopia with regard to this matter,

Noting also the readiness of the United Nations and the international community to assist the parties in establishing and implementing mutual security arrangements in support of the objectives of the Comprehensive Peace Agreement,

Bearing in mind the importance of coherence of United Nations assistance in the region,

Deeply concerned by the current situation in the Abyei Area, and by all acts of violence committed against civilians in violation of international humanitarian law and human rights law, including the killing and displacement of significant numbers of civilians,

Reaffirming the importance of full and urgent implementation of the Comprehensive Peace Agreement by both parties,

Calling upon all parties involved to provide humanitarian personnel with full and unimpeded access to civilians in need of assistance and all facilities necessary for their operations, in accordance with international humanitarian law,

Urging all parties to facilitate the rapid return of internally displaced persons,

Noting the intent of the parties to establish a special unit of the Abyei Police Service which shall deal with particular issues related to nomadic migration,

Welcoming and encouraging efforts by the United Nations to sensitize peacekeeping personnel in the prevention and control of HIV/AIDS and other communicable diseases in all of its peacekeeping operations,

Calling upon all parties to engage constructively in negotiations towards the final agreement on the status of Abyei,

Recognizing that the current situation in Abyei demands an urgent response and constitutes a threat to international peace and security,

1. *Decides* to establish, for a period of six months, the United Nations Interim Security Force for Abyei, taking into account the Agreement between the Government of the Sudan and the Sudan People's Liberation Movement on Temporary Arrangements for the Administration and Security of the Abyei Area, and further decides that the Force shall comprise a maximum of 4,200 military personnel, 50 police personnel and appropriate civilian support;

2. *Decides* that the Force shall have the following mandate, in addition to tasks set out in paragraph 3:

(*a*) Monitor and verify the redeployment of any Sudanese Armed Forces and the Sudan People's Liberation Army or its successor, from the Abyei Area as defined by the Permanent Court of Arbitration; henceforth, the Abyei Area shall be demilitarized from any forces other than the Force and the Abyei Police Service;

(*b*) Participate in relevant Abyei Area bodies as stipulated in the Agreement;

(*c*) Provide, in cooperation with other international partners in the mine action sector, demining assistance and technical advice;

(*d*) Facilitate the delivery of humanitarian aid and the free movement of humanitarian personnel in coordination with relevant Abyei Area bodies as defined by the Agreement;

(*e*) Strengthen the capacity of the Abyei Police Service by providing support, including the training of personnel, and coordinate with the Abyei Police Service on matters of law and order; and

(f) When necessary and in cooperation with the Abyei Police Service, provide security for oil infrastructure in the Abyei Area;

3. *Acting* under Chapter VII of the Charter of the United Nations, authorizes the Force, within its capabilities and its area of deployment, to take the actions necessary:

(a) To protect Force personnel, facilities, installations and equipment;

(b) To protect United Nations personnel, facilities, installations and equipment;

(c) To ensure the security and freedom of movement of United Nations personnel, humanitarian personnel and members of the Joint Military Observation Committee and Joint Military Observer Teams;

(d) Without prejudice to the responsibilities of the relevant authorities, to protect civilians in the Abyei Area under imminent threat of physical violence;

(e) To protect the Abyei Area from incursions by unauthorized elements, as defined in the Agreement; and

(f) To ensure security in the Abyei Area;

4. *Requests* that the Secretary-General and the Government of the Sudan, in consultation with the Government of Southern Sudan or its successor, conclude a status-of-forces agreement immediately after the adoption of the present resolution, taking into consideration General Assembly resolution 64/77 of 7 December 2009 on the safety and security of humanitarian personnel and protection of United Nations personnel, and, acting under Chapter VII of the Charter, decides that, until such an agreement is concluded, the status-of-forces agreement for the United Nations Mission in the Sudan shall apply mutatis mutandis in respect of the Force;

5. *Calls upon* all Member States to ensure the free, unhindered and expeditious movement to and from Abyei of all personnel, as well as equipment, provisions, supplies and other goods, including vehicles and spare parts, which are for the exclusive and official use of the Force;

6. *Underscores* the imperative of expeditious deployment of the Force, and urges the Secretary-General to take the steps necessary to ensure rapid and efficient implementation;

7. *Urges* the Government of the Sudan and the Government of Southern Sudan or its successor to fully cooperate with each other and provide full support to the Force, enabling it to fully implement the mandate;

8. *Stresses* that improved cooperation between the Government of the Sudan and the Government of Southern Sudan or its successor is also critical for peace, security and stability and the future relations between them;

9. *Calls upon* the Government of the Sudan and the Government of Southern Sudan or its successor urgently to fulfil their commitment under the Comprehensive Peace Agreement to resolve peacefully the final status of Abyei, and calls upon them to consider in good faith proposals that the African Union High-level Implementation Panel on the Sudan shall make to resolve this matter;

10. *Requests* the Secretary-General to ensure that effective human rights monitoring is carried out and the results included in his reports to the Security Council;

11. *Also requests* the Secretary-General to keep the Council regularly informed of the progress in implementing the Agreement and to report to the Council no later than thirty days after the adoption of the present resolution and every sixty days thereafter;

12. *Decides* to review the role of the Force in the implementation of the Agreement no later than three months after the adoption of the present resolution;

13. *Requests* the Secretary-General to take the necessary measures to ensure full compliance of the Force with the United Nations zero-tolerance policy on sexual exploitation and abuse and to keep the Council informed if cases of such conduct occur;

14. *Decides* to remain actively seized of the matter.

Further developments

On 28 June, the Sudan and SPLM signed a Framework Agreement on Political and Security Arrangements in Blue Nile and Southern Kordofan States. On 29 June, the parties signed an Agreement on Border Security and the Joint Political and Security Mechanism, reaffirming their commitment to the 7 December 2010 Agreement on the establishment of a Joint Political and Security Mechanism and to a Joint Position Paper on Border Security signed on 30 May 2011. The Agreement on Border Security provided for the establishment of a safe demilitarized border zone, pending the resolution of the status of the disputed areas and the final demarcation of the border, and requested UNISFA to provide protection for an international border monitoring verification mission.

Communications. On 5 July [S/2011/411], Ethiopia, as chair of the Intergovernmental Authority on Development (IGAD), transmitted the communiqué of the thirty-ninth extraordinary session of the IGAD Council of Ministers (Malabo, Equatorial Guinea, 28 June). The IGAD Council of Ministers welcomed the establishment of the Abyei Area Administration and called on the AU High-level Implementation Panel to continue with its engagement with the parties.

Independence of South Sudan and establishment of UNMISS. The Secretary-General reported [S/2011/678] that on 9 July, with the expiration of the interim period under the CPA, South Sudan was formally declared independent. President Omar Al-Bashir of the Sudan, the Secretary-General and the President of the General Assembly participated in the ceremony in Juba, during which the President of South Sudan, Salva Kiir, took the oath of office, promulgated the Transitional Constitution and declared a public amnesty for all militia groups. President Kiir highlighted the challenges that South Sudan faced in governance and political inclusiveness. President Al-Bashir pledged to work closely with President Kiir to resolve outstanding issues. With the independence of the country, and the end of the UNMIS mandate, the United Nations Mission in South Sudan (UNMISS) was established for an initial period of one year.

SECURITY COUNCIL ACTION

On 8 July [meeting 6576], the Security Council unanimously adopted **resolution 1996(2011)**. The draft [S/2011/416] was submitted by France, Gabon, Germany, Nigeria, Portugal, South Africa, the United Kingdom and the United States.

The Security Council,

Welcoming the establishment of the Republic of South Sudan on 9 July 2011 upon its proclamation as an independent State,

Reaffirming its strong commitment to the sovereignty, independence, territorial integrity and national unity of the Republic of South Sudan,

Recalling the statement by its President of 11 February 2011, in which it affirmed that national ownership and national responsibility are key to establishing sustainable peace and the primary responsibility of national authorities in identifying their priorities and strategies for post-conflict peacebuilding,

Stressing the need for a comprehensive and integrated approach to peace consolidation that strengthens coherence between political, security, development, human rights and rule of law activities and addresses the underlying causes of conflict, and underlining that security and development are closely interlinked and mutually reinforcing and key to attaining sustainable peace,

Deploring the persistence of conflict and violence and its effect on civilians, including the killing and displacement of significant numbers of civilians, and noting the importance of sustained cooperation and dialogue with civil society in the context of stabilizing the security situation and ensuring the protection of civilians,

Underscoring the need for coherent United Nations activities in the Republic of South Sudan, which requires clarity about roles and responsibilities and collaboration between the United Nations Mission in South Sudan and the United Nations country team, and noting the need for cooperation with other relevant actors in the region, including the African Union-United Nations Hybrid Operation in Darfur, the United Nations Interim Security Force for Abyei and the United Nations Organization Stabilization Mission in the Democratic Republic of the Congo,

Recalling previous statements on post-conflict peacebuilding, stressing the importance of institution-building as a critical component of peacebuilding, and emphasizing a more effective and coherent national and international response to enable countries emerging from conflict to deliver core government functions, including managing political disputes peacefully, and making use of existing national capacities in order to ensure national ownership of this process,

Emphasizing the vital role of the United Nations to support national authorities, in close consultation with international partners, to consolidate the peace and prevent a return to violence and therefore to develop an early strategy in support of national peacebuilding priorities, including establishment of core government functions, provision of basic services, establishment of the rule of law, respect for human rights, management of natural resources, development of the security sector, tackling youth unemployment and revitalization of the economy,

Recognizing the importance of supporting peacebuilding efforts in order to lay the foundation for sustainable development,

Underscoring the need for forging stronger and well-defined partnerships among the United Nations, development agencies, bilateral partners and other relevant actors, regional and subregional institutions and the international financial institutions, to implement national strategies aimed at effective institution-building, which are based on national ownership, the achievement of results and mutual accountability,

Recognizing the need for the Security Council to show flexibility in making necessary adjustments to the mission priorities, where appropriate, according to progress achieved, lessons learned or changing circumstances on the ground,

Recognizing also the need to broaden and deepen the pool of available civilian experts, especially women and experts from developing countries, to help to develop national capacity, and encouraging Member States, the United Nations and other partners to strengthen cooperation and coordination to ensure that relevant expertise is mobilized to support the peacebuilding needs of the Government of the Republic of South Sudan and the people of the Republic of South Sudan,

Recalling its resolutions 1612(2005) of 26 July 2005 and 1882(2009) of 4 August 2009 and the statements by its President of 29 April 2009 and 16 June 2010 on children and armed conflict, and taking note of the reports of the Secretary-General of 29 August 2007 and 10 February 2009 on children and armed conflict in the Sudan and the conclusions on children and armed conflict in the Sudan endorsed by the Security Council Working Group on Children and Armed Conflict,

Reaffirming its resolutions 1674(2006) of 28 April 2006 and 1894(2009) of 11 November 2009 on the protection of civilians in armed conflict and its resolution 1502(2003) of 26 August 2003 on the protection of humanitarian and United Nations personnel,

Reaffirming also its resolutions 1325(2000) of 31 October 2000, 1820(2008) of 19 June 2008, 1888(2009) of 30 September 2009, 1889(2009) of 5 October 2009 and 1960(2010) of 16 December 2010 on women and peace and security, and reiterating the need for the full, equal and effective participation of women at all stages of peace processes, given their vital role in the prevention and resolution of conflict and peacebuilding; reaffirming the key role women can play in re-establishing the fabric of recovering society, and stressing the need for their involvement in the development and implementation of post-conflict strategies in order to take into account their perspectives and needs,

Acknowledging the importance of drawing on best practices, past experience and lessons learned from other missions, especially by troop- and police-contributing countries, in line with ongoing United Nations peacekeeping reform initiatives, including the New Horizon document, the global field support strategy and the review of civilian capacity in the aftermath of conflict,

Bearing in mind the Agreement between the Government of the Sudan and the Sudan People's Liberation Movement on Temporary Arrangements for the Administration and Security of the Abyei Area of 20 June 2011, the Framework Agreement between the Government of the Sudan and the Sudan People's Liberation Movement (North) on Political and Security Arrangements in Blue Nile and Southern Kordofan States of 28 June 2011, and the Agreement between the Government of the Sudan and the Government of South Sudan on Border Security and the Joint Political and Security Mechanism of 29 June 2011,

Determining that the situation faced by South Sudan continues to constitute a threat to international peace and security in the region,

Acting under Chapter VII of the Charter of the United Nations,

1. *Decides* to establish as of 9 July 2011 the United Nations Mission in South Sudan for an initial period of one year with the intention to renew for further periods as may be required, also decides that the Mission shall consist of up to 7,000 military personnel, including military liaison officers and staff officers, up to 900 civilian police personnel, including, as appropriate, formed units, and an appropriate civilian component, including technical human rights investigation expertise; and further decides to review in three and six months whether the conditions on the ground could allow a reduction of military personnel to a level of 6,000;

2. *Welcomes* the appointment by the Secretary-General of his Special Representative for South Sudan, and requests the Secretary-General, through his Special Representative, to direct the operations of an integrated Mission, coordinate all activities of the United Nations system in the Republic of South Sudan, and support a coherent international approach to a stable peace in the Republic of South Sudan;

3. *Decides* that the mandate of the Mission shall be to consolidate peace and security and to help to establish the conditions for development in the Republic of South Sudan, with a view to strengthening the capacity of the Government of the Republic of South Sudan to govern effectively and democratically and establish good relations with its neighbours, and accordingly authorizes the Mission to perform the following tasks:

(*a*) Support for peace consolidation and thereby fostering longer-term State-building and economic development, by:
   (i) Providing good offices, advice and support to the Government of the Republic of South Sudan on political transition, governance and establishment of State authority, including the formulation of national policies in this regard;
   (ii) Promoting popular participation in political processes, including by advising and supporting the Government of the Republic of South Sudan on an inclusive constitutional process; the holding of elections in accordance with the constitution; promoting the establishment of an independent media; and ensuring the participation of women in decision-making forums;

(*b*) Support the Government of the Republic of South Sudan in exercising its responsibilities for conflict prevention, mitigation and resolution and protect civilians by:
   (i) Exercising good offices, confidence-building, and facilitation at the national, state and county levels within capabilities to anticipate, prevent, mitigate and resolve conflict;
   (ii) Establishment and implementation of a mission-wide early warning capacity, with an integrated approach to information-gathering, monitoring, verification, early warning and dissemination, and follow-up mechanisms;
   (iii) Monitoring, investigating, verifying and reporting regularly on human rights and potential threats against the civilian population as well as actual and potential violations of international humanitarian and human rights law, working as appropriate with the Office of the United Nations High Commissioner for Human Rights, bringing these to the attention of the authorities as necessary, and immediately reporting gross violations of human rights to the Security Council;
   (iv) Advising and assisting the Government of the Republic of South Sudan, including the military and police at the national and local levels as appropriate, in fulfilling its responsibility to protect civilians, in compliance with international humanitarian, human rights and refugee law;
   (v) Deterring violence, including through proactive deployment and patrols in areas at high risk of conflict, within its capabilities and in its areas of deployment, protecting civilians under imminent threat of physical violence, in particular when the Government of the Republic of South Sudan is not providing such security;
   (vi) Providing security for United Nations and humanitarian personnel, installations and equipment necessary for the implementation of mandated tasks, bearing in mind the importance of mission mobility, and contributing to the creation of security conditions conducive to safe, timely and unimpeded humanitarian assistance;

(*c*) Support the Government of the Republic of South Sudan, in accordance with the principles of national ownership, and in cooperation with the United Nations country team and other international partners, in developing its capacity to provide security, to establish the rule of law and to strengthen the security and justice sectors by:
   (i) Supporting the development of strategies for security sector reform, rule of law, and justice sector development, including human rights capacities and institutions;
   (ii) Supporting the Government of the Republic of South Sudan in developing and implementing a national disarmament, demobilization and reintegration strategy, in cooperation with international partners, with particular attention to the special needs of women and child combatants;
   (iii) Strengthening the capacity of the Republic of South Sudan Police Services through advice on policy, planning and legislative development, as well as training and mentoring in key areas;
   (iv) Supporting the Government of the Republic of South Sudan in developing a military justice system that is complementary to the civil justice system;
   (v) Facilitating a protective environment for children affected by armed conflict, through the implementation of a monitoring and reporting mechanism;
   (vi) Supporting the Government of the Republic of South Sudan in conducting demining activities within available resources and strengthening the capacity of the Republic of South Sudan Demining Authority to conduct mine action in accordance with the International Mine Action Standards;

4. *Authorizes* the Mission to use all means necessary, within the limits of its capacity and in the areas where its units are deployed, to carry out its protection mandate as set out in paragraphs 3 (*b*) (iv) to (vi);

5. *Requests* the Government of the Sudan and the Government of the Republic of South Sudan to propose by 20 July 2011 modalities for the implementation of the agreement on border monitoring of 29 June 2011, and, in case the parties fail to do so, requests the Mission to observe and report on any flow of personnel, arms and related materiel across the border with the Sudan;

6. *Demands* that the Government of the Republic of South Sudan and all relevant parties cooperate fully in the deployment, operations and monitoring, verification and reporting functions of the Mission, in particular by guaranteeing the safety, security and unrestricted freedom of movement of United Nations personnel, as well as of associated personnel throughout the territory of the Republic of South Sudan;

7. *Calls upon* all Member States to ensure the free, unhindered and expeditious movement to and from the Republic of South Sudan of all personnel, as well as equipment, provisions, supplies and other goods, including vehicles and spare parts, which are for the exclusive and official use of the Mission;

8. *Calls upon* all parties to allow, in accordance with relevant provisions of international law, the full, safe and unhindered access of relief personnel to all those in need and the delivery of humanitarian assistance, in particular to internally displaced persons and refugees;

9. *Demands* that all parties, in particular rebel militias and the Lord's Resistance Army, immediately cease all forms of violence and human rights abuses against the civilian population in South Sudan, in particular gender-based violence, including rape and other forms of sexual abuse, as well as all violations and abuses against children in violation of applicable international law, such as their recruitment and use, killing and maiming and abduction, with a view to specific and time-bound commitments to combat sexual violence in accordance with resolution 1960(2010) and violence and abuses against children;

10. *Calls upon* the Government of the Republic of South Sudan and the Sudan People's Liberation Army to renew the action plan (signed by the United Nations and the Sudan People's Liberation Army on 20 November 2009) to end the recruitment and use of child soldiers that expired in November 2010, and requests the Mission to advise and assist the Government in this regard; and further requests the Secretary-General to strengthen child protection in United Nations system activities in the Republic of South Sudan and ensure continued monitoring and reporting of the situation of children;

11. *Encourages* the Government of the Republic of South Sudan to ratify into law and implement key international human rights treaties and conventions, including those related to women and children, refugees and statelessness, and requests the Mission to advise and assist the Government in this regard;

12. *Calls upon* the Government of the Republic of South Sudan to take measures to improve women's participation in the outstanding issues of the Comprehensive Peace Agreement and post-independence arrangements and to enhance the engagement of South Sudanese women in public decision-making at all levels, including by promoting women's leadership, supporting women's organizations and countering negative societal attitudes about women's capacity to participate equally;

13. *Calls upon* the authorities of the Republic of South Sudan to combat impunity and to hold accountable all perpetrators of human rights and international humanitarian law violations, including those committed by illegal armed groups or elements of the Republic of South Sudan Security Forces;

14. *Calls upon* the Government of the Republic of South Sudan to end prolonged, arbitrary detention and to establish a safe, secure and humane prison system through the provision of advice and technical assistance, in cooperation with international partners, and requests the Mission to advise and assist the Government in this regard;

15. *Calls upon* the Mission to coordinate with the Government of the Republic of South Sudan and participate in regional coordination and information mechanisms to improve protection of civilians and support disarmament, demobilization and reintegration efforts in the light of the attacks by the Lord's Resistance Army in the Republic of South Sudan, and requests the Secretary-General to include in his trimesterly reports on the Mission a summary of co-operation and information-sharing between the Mission, the African Union-United Nations Hybrid Operation in Darfur, the United Nations Organization Stabilization Mission in the Democratic Republic of the Congo and regional and international partners in addressing the Lord's Resistance Army threats;

16. *Requests* that the Secretary-General transfer appropriate functions performed by the United Nations Mission in the Sudan to the United Nations Mission in South Sudan, together with appropriate staff and logistics necessary for achieving the new scope of functions to be performed, on the date when the United Nations Mission in South Sudan is established, and begin the orderly liquidation of the United Nations Mission in the Sudan;

17. *Authorizes* the Secretary-General to take the necessary steps in order to ensure inter-mission cooperation, and authorizes, within the overall troop ceiling set out in paragraph 1 above, appropriate transfers of troops from other missions, subject to the agreement of the troop-contributing countries and without prejudice to the performance of the mandates of these United Nations missions;

18. *Requests* the Special Representative of the Secretary-General for South Sudan and the United Nations Mission in South Sudan to work with the Government of the Republic of South Sudan, the United Nations country team and bilateral and multilateral partners, including the World Bank, and report back to the Council within four months on a plan for United Nations system support to specific peacebuilding tasks, especially security sector reform, police institutional development, rule of law and justice sector support, human rights capacity-building, early recovery, formulation of national policies related to key issues of State-building and development, and establishing the conditions for development, consistent with national priorities and with a view to contributing to the development of a common framework for monitoring progress in these areas;

19. *Requests* the Secretary-General to report to the Council on the expected timeline of the deployment of all Mission elements, including the status of consultations with troop-

and police-contributing countries and of the deployment of key enablers; and, stressing the importance of achievable and realistic targets against which the progress of the Mission can be measured, also requests the Secretary-General, following consultations with the Government of the Republic of South Sudan, to present benchmarks for the Mission to the Council within four months and to keep the Council regularly informed of progress every four months thereafter;

20. *Stresses* the need for the United Nations, international financial institutions and bilateral and multilateral partners to work closely with the Government of the Republic of South Sudan to ensure that international assistance is consistent with national priorities, including the South Sudan Development Plan, and can deliver prioritized support that reflects the specific peacebuilding needs and priorities of the Republic of South Sudan; and requests the Special Representative of the Secretary-General to represent the United Nations system in relevant international assistance mechanisms and processes;

21. *Encourages* the Secretary-General to explore ideas in the independent report of the Senior Advisory Group on civilian capacity in the aftermath of conflict that could be implemented in the Republic of South Sudan;

22. *Requests* the Secretary-General, in particular, to utilize to the greatest extent possible opportunities for co-location of appropriate Mission components with the Republic of South Sudan counterparts in the interest of building national capacity; and to seek opportunities to deliver early peace dividends by utilizing local procurement and otherwise enhancing, to the extent possible, the contribution of the Mission to the economy;

23. *Also requests* the Secretary-General to continue the measures necessary to ensure full compliance by the Mission with the United Nations zero-tolerance policy on sexual exploitation and abuse and to keep the Council fully informed, and urges troop-contributing countries to take appropriate preventive action, including predeployment awareness training, and other action to ensure full accountability in cases of such conduct involving their personnel;

24. *Reaffirms* the importance of appropriate gender expertise and training in missions mandated by the Council in accordance with resolutions 1325(2000) and 1820(2008), recalls the need to address violence against women and girls as a tool of warfare, looks forward to the appointment of women's protection advisers in accordance with resolutions 1888(2009), 1889(2009) and 1960(2010), requests the Secretary-General to establish monitoring, analysis and reporting arrangements on conflict-related sexual violence, including rape in situations of armed conflict and in post-conflict and other situations relevant to the implementation of resolution 1888(2009), as appropriate, and encourages the Mission as well as the Government of the Republic of South Sudan to actively address these issues;

25. *Requests* the Secretary-General to consider HIV-related needs of people living with, affected by and vulnerable to HIV, including women and girls, when fulfilling mandated tasks, and in this context encourages the incorporation, as appropriate, of HIV prevention, treatment, care and support, including voluntary and confidential counselling and testing programmes in the Mission;

26. *Requests* that the Secretary-General and the Government of the Republic of South Sudan conclude a status-of-forces agreement within thirty days of the adoption of the present resolution, taking into consideration General Assembly resolution 58/82 of 9 December 2003 on the scope of legal protection under the Convention on the Safety of United Nations and Associated Personnel, and decides that, pending the conclusion of such an agreement, the model status-of-forces agreement of 9 October 1990 shall apply provisionally;

27. *Decides* that the present resolution shall take effect on 9 July 2011;

28. *Decides also* to remain actively seized of the matter.

Withdrawal of UNMIS. On 31 May [S/2011/333], the Secretary-General transmitted to the Security Council a 27 May letter from the Sudan announcing the country's decision to terminate the presence of UNMIS in the Sudan as of 9 July.

The Council, on 11 July, decided to withdraw UNMIS, effective that day (see below).

SECURITY COUNCIL ACTION

On 11 July [meeting 6579], the Security Council unanimously adopted **resolution 1997(2011)**. The draft [S/2011/417] was prepared during prior consultations among Council members.

The Security Council,

Recalling its resolutions and the statements by its President concerning the Sudan, including resolutions 1590(2005) of 24 March 2005, 1627(2005) of 23 September 2005, 1663(2006) of 24 March 2006, 1706(2006) of 31 August 2006, 1709(2006) of 22 September 2006, 1714(2006) of 6 October 2006, 1755(2007) of 30 April 2007, 1812(2008) of 30 April 2008, 1870(2009) of 30 April 2009, 1919(2010) of 29 April 2010 and 1978(2011) of 27 April 2011,

Taking note of the letter dated 27 May 2011 from the Minister for Foreign Affairs of the Sudan to the Secretary-General, transmitted to the Security Council on 31 May 2011, informing the President of the Security Council of his Government's wish to terminate the United Nations Mission in the Sudan on 9 July 2011,

Reaffirming its commitment to the sovereignty, unity, territorial integrity and political independence of the Sudan and South Sudan and to the cause of peace in the region,

Emphasizing the need for the orderly withdrawal of the Mission following the termination of the mandate of the Mission on 9 July 2011,

Having examined the report of the Secretary-General of 17 May 2011,

1. *Decides* to withdraw the United Nations Mission in the Sudan effective 11 July 2011;

2. *Calls upon* the Secretary-General to complete the withdrawal of all uniformed and civilian Mission personnel, other than those required for the liquidation of the Mission, by 31 August 2011;

3. *Requests* that the Secretary-General transfer appropriate staff, equipment, supplies and other assets from the United Nations Mission in the Sudan to the United Nations Mission in South Sudan and the United Nations Interim Security Force for Abyei, together with appropriate staff and logistics necessary for achieving the new scope of functions to be performed;

4. *Requests* the Government of the Sudan to fully respect all provisions of the status-of-forces agreement of 28 December 2005 and, in particular, to guarantee unimpeded access by the United Nations to United Nations premises, which shall remain under the exclusive control and authority of the United Nations, to ensure full freedom of movement of the United Nations Mission in the Sudan, its members and its contractors as well as of their vehicles and aircraft, authorizing the redeployment within the Sudan and the unimpeded export by the United Nations of its equipment, supplies and other assets, and to grant exemptions from all taxes, fees, charges and other duties as provided for under the agreement and its amendment, until the final departure of all its military and civilian personnel from the Sudan;

5. *Underscores* the need for a smooth transition from the United Nations Mission in the Sudan to the United Nations Interim Security Force for Abyei and to the United Nations Mission in South Sudan;

6. *Requests* the Secretary-General to consult with the parties, the African Union High-level Implementation Panel on the Sudan and other partners and to present to the Security Council options for United Nations support to new security arrangements in Blue Nile and Southern Kordofan States in line with the Framework Agreement between the Government of the Sudan and the Sudan People's Liberation Movement (North) on Political and Security Arrangements in Blue Nile and Southern Kordofan States of 28 June 2011, and expresses its readiness to continue current United Nations operations in these states, with the consent of the parties, until those new security arrangements have been implemented;

7. *Decides* to remain actively seized of the matter.

Admission of South Sudan to UN membership

On 9 July [A/65/900-S/2011/418], the Secretary-General transmitted to the General Assembly and the Security Council the application of the Republic of South Sudan for admission to membership in the United Nations, contained in a letter of the same day from the President of South Sudan.

On 13 July [S/PV.6582], the Council, by **resolution 1999(2011)** (see p. 1353), recommended to the Assembly that the country be admitted to UN membership. At the same meeting, the Council President, by statement **S/PRST/2011/14** (ibid.), congratulated the country on that historic occasion.

On 14 July, the Assembly, by **resolution 65/308** (see p. 1354), admitted South Sudan to membership in the United Nations.

Further developments

Communication. By a letter of 14 July [S/2011/434], Ethiopia submitted the communiqué of the eighteenth extraordinary summit meeting of the IGAD Assembly of Heads of State and Government on the activities in the Sudan, Somalia and Eritrea (Addis Ababa, Ethiopia, 4 July). The Assembly welcomed the agreement signed on 20 June by the Sudan and South Sudan to guarantee stability in Abyei and other border areas; commended Ethiopia for offering troops; and mandated the IGAD Chairperson to support negotiations and the implementation of any agreements reached.

Report of Secretary-General (July). Pursuant to Security Council resolution 1990(2011) (see p. 195), the Secretary-General reported [S/2011/451] on progress in implementing the 20 June Agreement between the Sudan and SPLM on Temporary Arrangements for the Administration and Security of the Abyei Area. The status of that disputed area remained unresolved; as such, it was a major source of tension between the Sudan and SPLM and one of the greatest obstacles to CPA implementation and stability. In May, an outbreak of violence culminated in SAF taking control of Abyei town and the entire area north of the Kiir/Bahr el-Arab River, with the displacement of the local population. SPLA remained in control of the area south of the river. On 21 May, following the takeover of Abyei town, the Sudan unilaterally dissolved the Abyei Administration. As a result, little progress was made on the core aspects of the Abyei Protocol to the CPA, following the rejection of the conclusions of the Abyei Boundaries Commission by the National Congress Party, the rejection of the Permanent Court of Arbitration ruling by the Misseriya communities and the incomplete implementation of the wealth-sharing provisions. The referendum on the future of Abyei also stalled as a result of disputes over the criteria for participation and the border.

The Council, by resolution 1990(2011), authorized the deployment of UNISFA, composed of Ethiopian troops, to monitor and verify the withdrawal of all armed forces from Abyei. As of 25 July, 453 troops had arrived in the Abyei Area, located in Abyei town and Diffra. An advance force headquarters was functional, logistics support was in place and the induction of troops was progressing. The deployment, however, was encountering a number of challenges, such as insufficient accommodation for troops. The Secretary-General stressed that the agreements of 20 and 29 June, as well as the role of the United Nations in Abyei, were to be understood as part of a temporary solution to the situation. The presence of an international force in Abyei must enable and not delay negotiations on a permanent solution to the area's status, in accordance with the CPA and the principles of the Permanent Court of Arbitration.

Appointment of Special Envoy. By a letter of 27 July [S/2011/474], the Secretary-General informed the Security Council of his intention to appoint Haile Menkerios (South Africa) as his Special Envoy for the Sudan and South Sudan, as at 1 August. Mr. Menkerios had served as the Secretary-General's Special Representative for the Sudan since 1 March 2010. In his new capacity he would continue to assist the parties to reach a settlement on residual CPA and post-secession issues. On 29 July [S/2011/475], the Council took note of that intention.

Security Council statement. By a 3 August press statement [SC/10353], the Council expressed its sadness at the deaths on 2 August of four UNISFA peacekeepers from Ethiopia caused by a landmine explosion.

Communications. By a letter of 5 August [S/2011/510], the Secretary-General transmitted to the Security Council the Agreement on the Border Monitoring Support Mission between the Sudan and South Sudan, signed on 30 July, and expressed his intention to request UNISFA to undertake a reconnaissance mission along the border between the two countries. On 9 August [S/2011/511], the Council took note of that intention.

From 17 August through 2 September, the Sudan submitted several letters to the Security Council on the situation in Southern Kordofan. On 17 August [S/2011/522], the Sudan transmitted its comments on the periodic report of the United Nations High Commissioner for Human Rights, rejecting the method adopted to collect and formulate information concerning the events in Southern Kordofan. On the same day [S/2011/524], the Sudan informed the Council of the establishment on 16 August of a national committee to assess the human rights situation in the wake of incidents triggered by SPLA after the failure of their candidate to win the post of state governor in May. On 22 August [S/2011/530], the Council was informed that Ethiopia's Prime Minister, Meles Zenawi, in a mediation effort, had met in Khartoum the previous day with Sudanese President Al-Bashir and an SPLA/Northern Sector leader to find a peaceful settlement. On the same day [S/2011/531], the Sudan informed the Council that Sudanese authorities had begun, in coordination with the Office for the Coordination of Humanitarian Affairs and UN agencies, to channel relief materials to the people in Southern Kordofan. On 25 August [S/2011/539], the Sudan informed the Council that President Al-Bashir had declared a unilateral two-week ceasefire as a goodwill gesture. On 29 August [S/2011/551], the Sudan transmitted a complaint regarding the continuous violations by South Sudan and the SPLM/Northern Sector of the provisions of the CPA, including military activities. On 1 September [S/2011/553], the Sudan appealed to the Council to use its good offices to urge SPLMA to respect the ceasefire and begin direct negotiations with the Sudan for a final settlement concerning Southern Kordofan.

By letters sent on 2, 4 and 12 September, respectively [S/2011/557, S/2011/558, S/2011/565], the Sudan said that military attacks by SPLMA had taken place in Blue Nile State.

Abyei Joint Oversight Committee. By a letter of 19 September [S/2011/593], the Secretary-General transmitted to the Security Council an agreement reached by the Sudan and South Sudan during the first meeting of the Abyei Joint Oversight Committee (Addis Ababa, 7–8 September), convened by the AU High-level Implementation Panel.

Report of Secretary-General (September). Pursuant to Council resolution 1990(2011), the Secretary-General on 29 September reported [S/2011/603] on the situation in Abyei. Under the terms of the 20 June Agreement on temporary arrangements for the administration and security of Abyei, all armed forces were to withdraw from the area and UNISFA was to provide the sole military presence. At the first meeting of the Abyei Joint Oversight Committee, the parties agreed that the withdrawal of the armed forces and SPLA would begin on 11 September and conclude by 30 September. As of 23 September, however, UNISFA had not witnessed any withdrawal: Sudanese troops remained in the area north of the Kiir/Bahr el-Arab River, including Abyei town, and SPLA in the area south of the river. The Secretary-General underlined that the stabilization of the security situation depended on that withdrawal, which was necessary for the return of the displaced population. Moreover, the parties had yet to agree on the chairmanship of the Abyei Area Administration, which was preventing the establishment of that body. As a result, there was no formal civilian authority in the area.

As at 20 September, 1,798 military personnel had been deployed to UNISFA, with operating bases in Abyei town, Agok and Diffra. The Force headquarters was functional, a mission start-up team was in place and the occupation of four additional bases was being planned. UNISFA was to take over the UN logistics base at Kadugli. Since 23 August, UNISFA had been patrolling Abyei and other towns, as well as the main routes. The Mission had also undertaken demining operations, pending the deployment of the United Nations Mine Action Service. The initial deployment of UNISFA took place despite numerous obstacles, including heavy rains, which washed away the land route between Kadugli and Abyei, and delays in the issuance of flight authorizations and visas. To enhance cooperation and address deployment issues, a quadripartite consultative mechanism for UNISFA was established between the United Nations, Ethiopia, the Sudan and South Sudan; its first meeting was held on 26 September in New York.

On 30 July, the Sudan and South Sudan signed an agreement on a border monitoring support mission, recommitting themselves to the establishment of a joint border monitoring mechanism and envisaging a key role for UNISFA. In August, the Head of UNISFA, Lieutenant General Tadesse Werede Tesfay, conducted a reconnaissance mission of the border with representatives of the Sudan and South Sudan to define the possible structure and modalities of the border monitoring support mission. The results were discussed during a meeting of the Joint Political and Security Mechanism on 18 September, chaired by President Thabo Mbeki. Further to the outcome of the meeting, the Secretary-General proposed that the mandate of UNISFA be adjusted to incorporate, within the authorized troop strength of 4,200, additional tasks, such as assisting in ensuring the observance along the border of the security commitments agreed by the parties; supporting the operational activities of the parties along the safe demilitarized border zone; and coordinating monitoring and verification of the implementation of the Joint Position Paper on Border Security of 30 May. To accomplish those tasks, UNISFA would be reconfigured to comprise a dedicated capacity for the border mechanism, including 297 force protection personnel, 90 military observers and 146 enabling elements. The proposal was predicated on the cooperation of the Sudan and South Sudan in ensuring the freedom of movement of UNISFA, given that the border was approximately 2,100 kilometres long and had very limited road infrastructure, which became impassable during the rainy season.

Communications. On 10 October [S/2011/626], the Sudan transmitted to the Council the final communiqué of the visit of the President of South Sudan to Khartoum (8–9 October). The communiqué included the basic principles that the two parties had agreed on in order to build relations of good-neighbourliness. It also stipulated that the two parties would settle the pending issues and any future issues through peaceful means. With respect to interim economic and financial arrangements, including oil, it was agreed that joint committees would take action if the parties failed to make progress. Regarding Abyei, the parties agreed on the full implementation of the temporary arrangements until a final settlement was concluded.

On the same day [S/2011/628], the Secretary-General, referring to the additional tasks of UNISFA mentioned in his report of 29 September, informed the Security Council that a preliminary assessment showed costs of approximately $35.6 million for the first year of operations for support to the border mechanism. Should the Council approve the proposed amendment of the mandate, a request for additional funding would be presented to the General Assembly.

Report of Secretary-General (2 November). Pursuant to Security Council resolution 1996(2011) (see p. 197), the Secretary-General on 2 November [S/2011/678] provided an assessment of the situation in South Sudan and an update on the activities of UNMISS since its establishment on 8 July.

Both the Government of South Sudan and UNMISS were in a start-up phase, and consultations had just begun between the Mission and the Government. More than 2,000 international and national civilian staff, 203 UN military observers, 64 staff officers and 378 UN police had been transferred by 31 July from the United Nations Mission in the Sudan to UNMISS.

On 10 July, President Kiir issued a decree reappointing almost all incumbent cabinet members as caretaker ministers. The Vice-President of the former Southern Sudan, Riek Machar, was sworn in as Vice-President of South Sudan on 11 July.

On 18 July, the Government introduced its new currency, the South Sudanese pound, and stopped the circulation of the Sudanese pound on 1 September. The Bank of South Sudan converted approximately 1.77 billion Sudanese pounds in circulation in South Sudan to South Sudanese pounds at a one-to-one rate of exchange.

On 1 August, the President issued decrees appointing the 332-member National Legislative Assembly and a new entity, the 50-member Council of States. The Assembly comprised the members of the former Southern Sudan Legislative Assembly, together with 96 former members of the National Assembly of the Sudan elected from Southern constituencies and 66 new members appointed by the President. While the Assembly remained composed predominantly of members of SPLM, 10 per cent of the seats were distributed among five opposition parties.

On 8 August, the President addressed the joint inaugural session of the Assembly and the Council, highlighting five priorities: education, health care, infrastructure development, the rule of law and the transformation of SPLA. He announced specific objectives for each, to be attained within 100 days, and expressed his commitment to achieving critical legislation for transparency and accountability, also within 100 days. The Nationality Act, defining who was a citizen of South Sudan, was adopted. Thanks to UNMISS good offices, the Government engaged in an inclusive consultative process with all stakeholders, and each draft law was presented to political parties for discussion before its submission.

Also on 8 August, as requested by Council resolution 1996(2011), UNMISS and South Sudan signed a status-of-forces agreement guaranteeing the Mission's freedom of movement throughout the country without requiring additional clearance. UNMISS had been sharing the monthly military patrol programme with SPLA.

On 26 August, the President issued decrees appointing a Government of 29 ministers and 27 deputy ministers. Prior to that, he had issued decrees appointing a new Chief Justice of the Supreme Court and a new Governor of the Central Bank. With few exceptions, the major political stakeholders in the previous Government held positions in the new Cabinet. While the Cabinet remained composed predominantly of SPLM members, five other political parties were also represented.

Intercommunal conflict continued in Jonglei State, with a significant impact on the civilian populations. Following repeated clashes between the Lou Nuer and Murle communities, UNMISS conducted daily air patrols, deployed a military presence, intensified air reconnaissance and sent assessment missions. In August, the Government launched civilian disarmament operations in Lakes, Unity and Warrap States.

On the security front, the Government sought to neutralize internal security threats through the integration of militia groups into SPLA, alongside efforts aimed at political reconciliation. Militia groups outside that process and intercommunal violence, however, remained sources of insecurity, especially in Jonglei State. With regard to bilateral relations with the Sudan, lack of progress characterized the negotiations on outstanding CPA and post-independence issues, in particular on financial arrangements, Abyei and border demarcation. Presidents Al-Bashir and Kiir recommitted to working together to solve those questions at an 8 October meeting in Khartoum. The Secretary-General noted that while most of the threats posed to security and stability in South Sudan were internal, the lack of stabilization of its relations with the Sudan weighed heavily on the new Government, particularly amid the intensifying conflict in the border regions.

As at 22 September, the strength of the UNMISS military component stood at 5,329, out of the 7,000 troops authorized. During the reporting period, the Mission cleared 293,411 square metres of land in 12 communities; destroyed 10 anti-personnel mines, 12 anti-tank mines, 590 items of small arms ammunition and 2,465 items of unexploded ordnance; and opened 121 kilometres of road. UNMISS also initiated prevention and deterrence operations in Jonglei State and support to the reconciliation efforts of traditional and Government leaders.

The Secretary-General underlined that the transition of South Sudan from decades of war to sustainable peace presented huge challenges and came with high expectations within and outside the country. A priority was to develop governance institutions based on the principles of political inclusiveness and transparency, towards which the Government and the President had taken steps. The security situation remained a concern, particularly in Jonglei and Upper Nile States, where conflict had brought significant humanitarian consequences. It was the Government's primary responsibility to protect civilians, plan for long-term stability, address the root causes of conflicts and provide adequate resources to extend its authority to the most remote and conflict-affected areas.

Communications. On 4 November [S/2011/691], the Sudan informed the Security Council that South Sudan was supporting the insurgency in Blue Nile State, and that a large number of rebels who had fled from that state had been hosted in South Sudan. On 14 November [S/2011/714], the Sudan stated that South Sudan had hosted two meetings of four rebel factions that had formed, under the sponsorship of South Sudan, the Sudanese Revolutionary Front, which had the aim of overthrowing the Khartoum Government. On 11 November [S/2011/708] and 15 November [S/2011/718], South Sudan rejected all such claims as false and stated that the Khartoum Government had carried out bombings in Upper Nile and Unity States.

Security Council statement. By a press statement of 4 November [SC/10436], the Council called on SAF and SPLA to redeploy their forces from the Abyei Area and finalize the establishment of the Abyei Area Administration.

Report of Secretary-General (27 November). Pursuant to Security Council resolution 1990(2011), the Secretary-General on 27 November reported [S/2011/741] on the situation in Abyei. The area remained calm but unpredictable, owing to the presence of the armed forces and police of the Sudan and South Sudan in the areas north and south of the Kiir/Bahr el-Arab River, respectively, in violation of the provision of the 20 June Agreement to withdraw all armed forces. The Sudan linked its withdrawal to other provisions of the Agreement, including the establishment of the Abyei Area Administration, while South Sudan maintained that it would withdraw at the same time as the Sudan. Little progress was achieved in establishing the Abyei Area Administration. Under the Agreement, the Administration was to be led by a Chief Administrator nominated by South Sudan and agreed to by the Sudan, and a Deputy Chief Administrator nominated by the Sudan and agreed to by South Sudan. The Chair of the Legislative Council would be nominated by the Sudan. Progress towards establishing those bodies, however, had been delayed due to reservations by South Sudan in relation to the nominations by the Sudan.

With the onset of the dry season, road conditions improved, enhancing the presence of UNISFA. The Mission conducted regular air and ground patrols and established temporary bases in critical areas to improve its monitoring capabilities. Operating bases were established in Abyei and other towns. UNISFA also regularly liaised with local communities. The construction of a new bridge by Ethiopian engineers—which was completed on 28 October and replaced the Banton bridge destroyed by the Sudan during the conflict in May—provided an important crossing point between Abyei town and Agok and bettered UNISFA access to the entire area of operations. The annual Misseriya migration southwards through the Abyei Area began during the reporting period. On 1 November, Misseriya elements with approximately 2,000 head of cattle reached Goli, 25 kilometres north of Abyei town. The presence of armed elements among the migrating population was a cause for concern. UNISFA provided assistance for a safe migration and engaged with the Misseriya leaders to stress that armed elements should not enter Abyei.

As at 14 November, UNISFA had recovered and disposed of 100 unexploded ordnance and mines. Neither the Sudan nor South Sudan, however, had provided maps of mine locations.

During the reporting period, a second battalion joined UNISFA. The Mission, however, continued to face delays in the issuance of visas and in the deployment of its civilian personnel from Khartoum. The Sudan had not formalized the transfer of the Kadugli logistics base from UNMIS to UNISFA.

The Secretary-General was encouraged by the deployment of two thirds of UNISFA authorized troops, as well as by the Mission's efforts to mitigate tensions between the Ngok Dinka and the Misseriya communities. He was concerned, however, that the Sudan and South Sudan had not lived up to their commitments under the 20 June Agreement. He called on them to withdraw their forces from the Abyei Area and to provide full cooperation to the AU High-level Implementation Panel towards the implementation of the Agreement. He also urged them to work with the Panel and his Special Envoy to solve the outstanding issues. The Secretary-General recommended that the Council renew the Mission's mandate for a six-month period.

SECURITY COUNCIL ACTION

On 14 December [meeting 6683], the Security Council unanimously adopted **resolution 2024(2011)**. The draft [S/2011/770] was submitted by France, the United Kingdom and the United States.

The Security Council,

Recalling its previous resolutions and the statements by its President on the situation in the Sudan and South Sudan, including resolution 1990(2011) of 27 June 2011, by which the Security Council established the United Nations Interim Security Force for Abyei,

Reaffirming its commitment to the principles of sovereignty and territorial integrity and to peace, stability and security throughout the region,

Commending the assistance provided to the parties by the African Union High-level Implementation Panel and its Chairperson, President Thabo Mbeki, the Prime Minister of Ethiopia, Mr. Meles Zenawi, the Special Envoy of the Secretary-General for the Sudan and South Sudan, Mr. Haile Menkerios, and the Head of Mission for the United Nations Interim Security Force for Abyei, Lieutenant General Tadesse Werede Tesfay,

Welcoming the Agreement between the Government of the Sudan and the Government of Southern Sudan on Border Security and the Joint Political and Security Mechanism of 29 June 2011, taking note of the commitment in paragraph 2 to create a Safe Demilitarized Border Zone, and further taking note of the request for assistance from the United Nations to provide external support for monitoring and verification in the Safe Demilitarized Border Zone,

Welcoming also the Agreement on the Border Monitoring Support Mission between the Government of the Sudan and the Government of South Sudan of 30 July 2011, which elaborates on the establishment of the Joint Border Verification and Monitoring Mechanism with an area of responsibility corresponding to the Safe Demilitarized Border Zone, and the Joint Political and Security Mechanism, and taking note of the request by the parties for the assistance of the United Nations to support the operational activities of the Joint Border Verification and Monitoring Mechanism,

Underlining the importance of building mutual trust, confidence and an environment which encourages long-term stability and economic development,

Recognizing the urgent need for the Sudan and South Sudan to commence the process of border normalization, and recognizing further that the situation along the border between the Sudan and South Sudan constitutes a threat to international peace and security,

1. *Decides* that, in addition to the tasks set out in paragraph 2 of resolution 1990(2011), the mandate of the United Nations Interim Security Force for Abyei shall include the following additional tasks in support of the Joint Border Verification and Monitoring Mechanism; these additional tasks shall be carried out by the Force within its authorized capabilities and within an operational area expanded to include the Safe Demilitarized Border Zone, the Joint Border Verification and Monitoring Mechanism headquarters, sector headquarters and team sites:

(*a*) Assist the parties in ensuring the observance within the Safe Demilitarized Border Zone of the security commitments agreed upon by them in the above-mentioned Agreement on Border Security and the Joint Political and Security Mechanism of 29 June 2011 and Agreement on the Border Monitoring Support Mission of 30 July 2011;

(*b*) Support the operational activities of the Joint Border Verification and Monitoring Mechanism, including its sectors and teams, in undertaking verifications, investigations, monitoring, arbitrations, liaison coordinating, reporting, information exchange and patrols, and by providing security, as appropriate;

(*c*) Assist and advise the Joint Border Verification and Monitoring Mechanism in its overall coordination of planning monitoring and verification of the implementation of the Joint Position Paper on Border Security of 30 May 2011;

(*d*) Assist the Joint Border Verification and Monitoring Mechanism to maintain the necessary chart, geographical and mapping references, which shall be used for the purpose of monitoring the implementation of paragraph 2 of the Agreement on Border Security and the Joint Political and Security Mechanism of 29 June 2011;

(*e*) Facilitate liaison between the parties;

(*f*) Support the parties, when requested, in developing effective bilateral management mechanisms along the border;

(*g*) Assist in building mutual trust;

2. *Requests* the Governments of South Sudan and the Sudan to implement fully their commitments under the above-referenced Agreements of 29 June and 30 July 2011;

3. *Calls upon* all Member States, in particular the Sudan and South Sudan, to ensure the free, unhindered and expeditious movement to and from Abyei and throughout the Safe Demilitarized Border Zone of all personnel, as well as equipment, provisions, supplies and other goods, including vehicles, aircraft and spare parts, which are for the exclusive and official use of the Force;

4. *Urges* the Government of the Sudan and the Government of South Sudan to cooperate fully with each other and to provide full support to the Force, enabling it to implement fully its mandate;

5. *Requests* the Secretary-General to keep the Security Council informed of progress in implementing the additional tasks listed in paragraph 1 of the present resolution in his regular reports to the Council on the implementation of the mandate of the Force, to bring to the Council's immediate attention any serious violations of the above-referenced agreements, and to look for and implement ways to strengthen inter-mission cooperation within the region;

6. *Decides* to remain seized of the matter.

On 22 December [meeting 6699], the Security Council unanimously adopted **resolution 2032(2011)**. The draft [S/2011/794] was submitted by the United States.

The Security Council,

Recalling its previous resolutions and the statements by its President on the situation in the Sudan and South Sudan, in particular resolutions 1990(2011) of 27 June 2011 and 2024(2011) of 14 December 2011,

Reaffirming its commitment to the principles of sovereignty and territorial integrity and to peace, stability and security throughout the region,

Affirming the priority it attaches to the full and urgent implementation of all outstanding issues from the Comprehensive Peace Agreement of 9 January 2005,

Reaffirming its previous resolutions 1674(2006) of 28 April 2006 and 1894(2009) of 11 November 2009 on the protection of civilians in armed conflict, its resolutions 1612(2005) of 26 July 2005, 1882(2009) of 4 August 2009 and 1998(2011) of 12 July 2011 on children and armed conflict, its resolution 1502(2003) of 26 August 2003 on the protection of humanitarian and United Nations personnel and its resolutions 1325(2000) of 31 October 2000, 1820(2008) of 19 June 2008, 1888(2009) of 30 September 2009 and 1889(2009) of 5 October 2009 on women and peace and security,

Recalling the commitments made by the Government of the Sudan and the Government of South Sudan in the Agreement between the Government of the Sudan and the Sudan People's Liberation Movement on Temporary Arrangements for the Administration and Security of the Abyei Area of 20 June 2011, the Agreement between the Government of the Sudan and the Government of Southern Sudan on Border Security and the Joint Political and Security Mechanism of 29 June 2011 and the Agreement on the Border Monitoring Support Mission between the Government of the Sudan and the Government of South Sudan of 30 July 2011,

Welcoming the meeting of the Presidents of the Sudan and South Sudan of 9 October 2011, and the intentions they expressed to resolve their disputes by peaceful means,

Stressing that both countries will have much to gain if they show restraint and choose the path of dialogue instead of resorting to violence or provocations,

Commending the continued assistance provided to the parties by the African Union High-level Implementation Panel and its Chairperson, President Thabo Mbeki, the Prime Minister of Ethiopia, Mr. Meles Zenawi, the Special Envoy of the Secretary-General for the Sudan and South Sudan, Mr. Haile Menkerios, and the Head of Mission for the United Nations Interim Security Force for Abyei, Lieutenant General Tadesse Werede Tesfay,

Noting the continued readiness of the United Nations and the international community to assist the parties in establishing and implementing mutual security arrangements in support of the objectives of the Comprehensive Peace Agreement,

Commending the rapid deployment of the Force to the Abyei Area and the efforts of the United Nations and the Government of Ethiopia in that regard,

Urging the Government of the Sudan and the Government of South Sudan rapidly to conclude negotiations with the United Nations on a status-of-forces agreement,

Bearing in mind the importance of coherence of United Nations assistance in the region,

Welcoming and encouraging efforts by the United Nations to sensitize peacekeeping personnel in the prevention and control of HIV/AIDS and other communicable diseases in all of its peacekeeping operations,

Deeply concerned by all acts of violence committed in the Abyei Area against civilians in violation of international humanitarian law and human rights law, including the killing and displacement of significant numbers of civilians,

Stressing the need for effective human rights monitoring,

Welcoming the meeting of the Abyei Joint Oversight Committee held on 13 December 2011, at which the Committee reaffirmed the urgency of facilitating the delivery of humanitarian assistance to all affected communities in the Abyei Area,

Deeply concerned by the continued presence of military and police personnel from the Sudan and South Sudan in the Abyei Area, in violation of the Agreement of 20 June 2011, which poses a threat to the safe migration of Misseriya nomads and the return of Ngok Dinka refugees to their homes and prevents the Force from implementing fully its mandate,

Concerned by delays in the establishment of the Abyei Area Administration,

Noting the lack of progress in establishing the Abyei Police Service, including a special unit to deal with particular issues related to nomadic migration,

Concerned by delays in the clearance of landmines in the Abyei Area, which hinders the safe return of internally displaced persons to their homes,

Expressing its determination that the future status of Abyei shall be resolved by negotiations between the parties in a manner consistent with the Comprehensive Peace Agreement and not by the unilateral actions of either party, and calling upon all parties to engage constructively in negotiations towards the final agreement on the status of Abyei,

Deeply concerned by the reported build-up of armed forces of the Sudan and South Sudan near their mutual border and inflammatory rhetoric from both sides, which increases the risk of direct confrontation between them,

Recognizing that the current situation in Abyei and along the border between the Sudan and South Sudan constitutes a threat to international peace and security,

1. *Decides* to extend, for a period of five months, the mandate of the United Nations Interim Security Force for Abyei as set out in paragraph 2 of resolution 1990(2011) and modified by resolution 2024(2011), and, acting under Chapter VII of the Charter of the United Nations, including the tasks set out in paragraph 3 of resolution 1990(2011);

2. *Recognizes* that the ability of the Force to carry out effectively its mandate will depend on the fulfilment by the Governments of the Sudan and South Sudan of the commitments agreed between the two parties and with the United Nations;

3. *Demands* that the Governments of the Sudan and South Sudan redeploy all remaining military and police personnel from the Abyei Area immediately and without preconditions, and urgently finalize the establishment of the Abyei Area Administration and the Abyei Police Service, in accordance with their commitments in the Agreement on Temporary Arrangements for the Administration and Security of the Abyei Area of 20 June 2011;

4. *Urges* the Government of the Sudan and the Government of South Sudan to make use of the Joint Political and Security Mechanism to resolve outstanding issues related to the finalization of the Safe Demilitarized Border Zone, the resolution of disputed border areas, border demarcation and the mapping of the border zone;

5. *Calls upon* all Member States, in particular the Sudan and South Sudan, to ensure the free, unhindered and expeditious movement to and from Abyei and throughout the Safe Demilitarized Border Zone of all personnel, as well as equipment, provisions, supplies and other goods, including vehicles, aircraft and spare parts, which are for the exclusive and official use of the Force;

6. *Urges* the Government of the Sudan and the Government of South Sudan to cooperate fully with each other and to provide full support to the Force, enabling it to fully implement the mandate;

7. *Requests* the Government of the Sudan and the Government of South Sudan to facilitate the deployment of the United Nations Mine Action Service as well as the identification and clearance of mines in the Abyei Area;

8. *Calls upon* the Government of the Sudan and the Government of South Sudan urgently to fulfil their commitment under the Comprehensive Peace Agreement of 9 January 2005 to resolve peacefully the final status of Abyei, and calls upon them to consider in good faith proposals that the African Union High-level Implementation Panel shall make to resolve this matter;

9. *Urges* all parties involved to provide humanitarian personnel with full, safe and unhindered access to civilians in need of assistance and all facilities necessary for their operations, in accordance with applicable international humanitarian law;

10. *Requests* the Secretary-General to ensure that effective human rights monitoring is carried out and the results included in his reports to the Security Council, and calls upon the Government of the Sudan and the Government of South Sudan to extend their full cooperation to the Secretary-General to this end;

11. *Also requests* the Secretary-General to take the measures necessary to ensure full compliance of the Force with the United Nations zero-tolerance policy on sexual exploitation and abuse and to keep the Council informed if cases of such conduct occur;

12. *Stresses* that improved cooperation between the Government of the Sudan and the Government of South Sudan is also critical for peace, security and stability and future relations between them;

13. *Requests* the Secretary-General to continue to inform the Council of progress in implementing the mandate of the Force at sixty-day intervals and continue to bring to the Council's immediate attention any serious violations of the above-referenced agreements, and to look for and implement ways to strengthen inter-mission cooperation within the region;

14. *Decides* to remain actively seized of the matter.

Communications. On 8 December [S/201/763], South Sudan informed the Security Council that the Sudan had violated the territorial integrity of South Sudan on several occasions, including on 3 December, when it attacked and occupied the town of Jaw in Unity State.

On 23 December [S/2011/816], the Secretary-General transmitted to the Council a 9 December letter from the Chairperson of the AU Commission requesting the circulation of an AU Peace and Security Council communiqué of 30 November and of a report on the activities of the AU High-level Implementation Panel.

By a 29 December letter [S/2011/810], the Sudan informed the Council that, following clashes between the forces of the Justice and Equality Movement (JEM) and SAF at the border between North Kordofan and Darfur, during which the JEM leader, Khalil Ibrahim Muhammad, was killed, some 350 JEM members crossed into South Sudan. The Sudan expected South Sudan to disarm and extradite wanted individuals to the Sudan.

Year-end developments. In a subsequent report on South Sudan [S/2012/140], the Secretary-General noted that as critical pieces of legislation were adopted or initiated, the Government had taken further steps towards establishing national institutions, meeting key transitional political milestones and combating corruption. In November, the President issued a decree appointing the South Sudan Anti-Corruption Commission. The Public Financial Management and Accountability Bill was adopted in November, the Conduct of Business Regulations Bill was adopted in December. In accordance with a presidential decree issued on 9 December, the Anti-Corruption Commission requested senior Government officials to declare their income, assets and liabilities and confirm their abstention from involvement in private businesses by 31 March 2012. Officials who failed to abide by the decree would be required to resign. On 22 December, the Government established a committee with external independent experts to investigate an alleged grains scandal. The case was reported to involve up to $1 billion worth of contracts between the Ministry of Finance and companies that were to distribute grains to states affected by food shortages in 2008. The grains were intended to be sold at a low price and the collected monies remitted to the Ministry. Some companies, however, failed to deliver the grains, and it was alleged that not all of the money from the sold grains was remitted.

On 27 September, the Bank of South Sudan introduced an exchange target rate of 2.95 South Sudanese pounds to 1 United States dollar in an effort to stabilize the currency. The volatility in the exchange rate induced currency speculation, which, together with commodity shortages, contributed to increased inflation.

New embassies opened in Juba, bringing the number of foreign diplomatic missions to 18. The Diplomatic and Consular Act was adopted on 14 December to expedite the deployment of South Sudanese diplomats. South Sudan also joined a number of international organizations, including IGAD on 25 November, and the International Conference on the Great Lakes Region on 16 December.

As to the security situation, intercommunal violence escalated in Jonglei State in December, resulting in casualties, displacement of civilians and challenges to civil authorities. Warrap, Unity and Lakes States witnessed a resurgence of intercommunal violence. While rebel militia groups remained a security threat, their activities were limited during the reporting period. On 20 December, the Government announced that militia leader George Athor had been killed by SPLA, following which the activities of his South Sudan Democratic Movement/Army significantly declined. South Sudan Liberation Army activity in Unity State also remained limited. The peace process initiated in late August to reconcile the Lou Nuer and Murle communities collapsed in early December. Following attacks, allegedly by Murle, UNMISS on 8 December received reports of Lou Nuer youth mobilizing for a large assault. An UNMISS patrol on 23 December identified a column of approximately 2,000 armed Lou Nuer youth moving south through Murle territory, looting and burning villages along the way. By 26 December, UNMISS early warning alerts to tens of thousands of civilians, and pre-emptive positioning in key centres, ensured that virtually all of the population of a targeted town left before attackers arrived. UNMISS positions were reinforced with additional troops and 31 vulnerable civilians were evacuated to safety by Mission personnel. On 31 December, part of the Lou Nuer group entered another targeted town, but SPLA and UNMISS defensive positions halted their advance.

At year's end, the UNMISS civilian component had 770 international staff, 1,386 national staff and 232 UN Volunteers. Four infantry battalions were deployed in three areas of responsibility. The Mission maintained 15 operating bases, providing a permanent presence in all states except Warrap. UNMISS conducted tasks including patrolling, deterrence through forward deployment, protection of civilians, protection of humanitarian convoys, assessment and reconnaissance, in addition to static force protection in all operating bases. Security developments countrywide forced the Mission to maintain an even higher operational status. The need to maintain deployments in Jonglei State for an extended duration increased the burden on the Mission's strained troop levels and logistical resources. The Secretary-General urged Jonglei community leaders to call for an end to hate messages and the Government to bring to justice those responsible for inciting violence through hate rhetoric. UNMISS began preparations for a large-scale turnover of its contingents, including the insertion of 2,700 new troops from Cambodia, Mongolia, Nepal and Rwanda; the rotation of approximately 1,800 Indian troops; and the repatriation of almost 1,200 troops to Bangladesh. UN police were stationed in all 10 state capitals and in 23 counties. Police operations focused on capacity-building for the South Sudan police, in collaboration with UNDP. UN police and UNDP supported a programme of screening and registering all South Sudan police officers and correction officers in the prison services across all 10 states. In support of South Sudan police deployments, UNDP completed the construction of 54 new police stations and posts across the 10 states.

The Secretary-General appealed to Member States to make available military utility helicopters to enhance UNMISS mobility and access to vulnerable populations. He expressed concern for the deteriorating relations between South Sudan and the Sudan.

In a subsequent report on Abyei [S/2012/68], the Secretary-General said that the security situation remained volatile, owing to the continued presence of security forces, the migration of Misseriya nomads and the return of displaced Ngok Dinka. The Head of UNISFA engaged with SAF and SPLA to secure their commitment to refrain from any hostile action that might disrupt the return of Ngok Dinka and the migration of Misseriya nomads. While no intercommunal conflict was reported, UNISFA continued to conduct patrols throughout the area, focusing on zones that were receiving both returnees and nomads.

On the political front, the establishment of the Abyei Area Administration was hampered by differences between the Sudan and South Sudan. At the second meeting of the Abyei Joint Oversight Committee (12 and 13 December), the parties agreed to allow the unhindered access of humanitarian agencies to all Abyei communities in need of assistance. During the first meeting of the Joint Political and Security Mechanism on 17 September, the parties agreed to establish border crossings and recommitted themselves to implementing the security agreements, pending the creation of a reference map of the safe demilitarized border zone. The parties had yet to agree to the map proposed by the AU High-level Implementation Panel, thus precluding the holding of another meeting of the Mechanism. The fundamental issues between the parties remained the proposal for a timeline for demarcation and the use of arbitration as a way to resolve disputes over contested areas. In addition, no clear agreement was reached regarding the demarcation of the undisputed part of the border (80 per cent) or the delineation and demarcation of the disputed part (20 per cent). In the meantime, UNISFA was making the arrangements necessary to prepare for the additional tasks that it was mandated to carry out by Council resolution 2024(2011). No discussion took place on the final status of Abyei. Both Presidents Al-Bashir and Kiir had asked the AU High-level Implementation Panel to propose a final status arrangement, as the parties had been unable to reach a compromise. The Panel, however, focused its efforts on the full implementation of the Agreement, not on other proposals.

By the end of the year, the third wave of Ethiopian troop deployment had taken place, bringing the deployment of authorized UNISFA troops near completion. Most UNISFA forces would remain accommodated in tents until the Sudan granted visas to UN engineering specialists selected to carry out construction work. Meanwhile, a contractor was hired to build the camps using hardwall accommodations received from liquidating UNMIS. Repairs commenced on priority roads in the area of operations linking villages and humanitarian lines of communications. In November, UNISFA inherited from UNMIS the Kadugli logistic base, its infrastructure and equipment.

The Secretary-General noted that, for the successful implementation of the Mission's revised mandate, it was essential that the two parties extend their fullest cooperation, especially by reaching an agreement on the maps and geographical references for the safe demilitarized border zone. Similarly, the Sudan should expedite the issuance of visas for UN personnel assigned to UNISFA to perform tasks that were critical for the functioning of the Mission.

Children and armed conflict

Report of Secretary-General. Pursuant to Security Council resolution 1612(2005) [YUN 2005, p. 863], the Secretary-General in July submitted his fourth report on children and armed conflict in the Sudan [S/2011/413], covering the period from January 2009 to February 2011. According to the report, some progress was reported in the signing of action plans with State and non-State actors and in the release of children. The report showed the continued presence of children in the armed forces, its associated groups, the police forces, SPLA, and several armed groups in Darfur. Of particular concern were the killing and maiming of children and sexual violence against children.

SPLA recruited 328 boys during the reporting period, representing an increase in the recruitment of children by that group compared with the previous reporting period (1 August 2007–30 December 2008) [YUN 2009, p. 246], although a larger number of children were also released. Most recruitment cases were recorded in states of the South. In January and February 2011 alone, 20 boys were seen in SPLA convoys protecting high-ranking SPLA officials, wearing SPLA uniforms and/or in possession of weapons. Four cases of children serving with the Southern Sudan police were registered, although the actual number was estimated to be higher, given the large-scale police recruitment campaign during the run-up to the referendum.

The recruitment and use of children by SPLA was also verified in the so-called "three areas" (Abyei, Southern Kordofan, Blue Nile). Since early 2011, children were repeatedly observed in Misseriya and Dinka Ngok armed groups, particularly in villages north and east of Abyei town. There was an increase in the number of reported cases of sexual violence against and rape of girls by SPLA: between 28 February and 3 March 2010, 10 girls had been sexually assaulted and/or raped by SPLA soldiers during armed clashes in Warrap State.

The United Nations-Government Coordination Mechanism for Children and Armed Conflict in the Sudan, established in 2008, allowed informal exchanges between the Government and the UN country task force for the monitoring and reporting of grave violations against children. On 20 November 2009, the Secretary-General's Special Representative for Children and Armed Conflict witnessed the signing of the SPLA action plan to end the recruitment of child soldiers. The action plan set up modalities for the release of children associated with SPLA, as well as awareness-raising and capacity-building activities. Following advocacy by UNMIS, SPLA committed to cooperating with the United Nations, in particular in the "three areas". In February 2011, SPLA agreed to continue verification activities with the United Nations and the Southern Sudan Disarmament, Demobilization and Reintegration Commission, pending an official extension of the action plan. Key aspects of the plan, however, remained to be implemented.

The Secretary-General noted that adoption of the Federal Child Act, the Sudan Armed Forces Act and the Southern Sudan's Child Act, as well as the establishment of a child rights unit in the armed forces and SPLA, would contribute to a protective environment for children affected by armed conflict. He called on the Sudan and Southern Sudan to commit to disseminating and implementing child protection legislation; to ensure that sufficient resources were dedicated to mainstreaming child protection in their security forces; and to guarantee that child protection was taken into account during military operations. He urged SPLA to fully implement the 2009 action plan, and the Sudan to accelerate its dialogue with the United Nations with a view to developing a concrete time-bound plan. He urged the Sudan to ensure unimpeded access for humanitarian assistance to children, and to end impunity of rape and sexual violence against children through rigorous investigation and prosecution. Meanwhile, the United Nations would reach out to armed groups to elicit commitments on action plans to end the recruitment and use of children.

Working group. After examining the Secretary-General's report, the Working Group on Children and Armed Conflict, on 30 September, submitted its conclusions on children and armed conflict in the Sudan [S/AC.51/2012/1]. The Working Group urged the Government to ensure the long-term reintegration of children formerly associated with armed groups. It urged all parties to ensure the protection of children in Southern Kordofan and Blue Nile States and in the Abyei Area.

In a public statement by its Chair, the Working Group urged all parties to halt the recruitment and use of children, and encouraged the United Nations to reach out to all parties, particularly those not engaged with the Organization. The Group recommended that the Security Council President address a letter to the Sudan encouraging it to uphold its commitment to the implementation and enforcement of child protection legislation, and that the Secretary-General submit two separate reports for the Sudan and South Sudan following the independence of South Sudan.

At the same meeting, the Working Group submitted its conclusions on children and armed conflict in South Sudan [S/AC.51/2012/2]. The Working Group urged all parties in the Abyei Area to ensure the protection of children and condemned actions by the Lord's Resistance Army in South Sudan. Concern was expressed over the growing trend of inter-ethnic clashes leading to the abduction of, sexual violence against and killing and maiming of children, particularly in Jonglei.

In a public statement, the Chair of the Working Group welcomed the adoption of the Child Act of South Sudan. It encouraged the Government to consider ratifying the Convention on the Rights of the Child and its Optional Protocol on the involvement of children in armed conflict, and urged it to ensure the protection of schools and to prioritize long-term reintegration and rehabilitation for children affected by armed conflict. The Working Group requested the Secretary-General to ensure the strengthening of the monitoring and reporting mechanism on children and armed conflict in South Sudan, and to ensure that UNMISS carried out its protection mandate where children were vulnerable.

UNMIS

The United Nations Mission in the Sudan (UNMIS) was established by Security Council resolution 1590(2005) [YUN 2005, p. 304] to support implementation of the Comprehensive Peace Agreement (CPA); facilitate and coordinate the voluntary return of refugees and internally displaced persons (IDPs); assist with demining; and protect and promote human rights.

With the establishment of South Sudan as an independent country on 9 July, and the consequent end of the interim period set up by the Government of the Sudan and the Sudan People's Liberation Movement (SPLM) under the CPA, the mandate of UNMIS ended on that day.

OIOS report. In a February report [A/65/752], the Office of Internal Oversight Services (OIOS) evaluated UNMIS performance and achievements. OIOS concluded that, even though the objective of the CPA—to make unity attractive—had not been met, UNMIS support to the implementation of the Agreement had contributed to the holding of the ceasefire between the north and south of the Sudan. Most of the governmental bodies and laws stipulated in the Agreement and a wealth-sharing arrangement had come into existence. The Mission's focus on Darfur during its first years of deployment, however, had meant that the CPA did not receive the required attention. Integration between UNMIS and the UN country team had been weak, especially in the areas of disarmament, demobilization and reintegration and elections. The challenges faced by the Mission with respect to the protection of civilians had affected its credibility.

OIOS recommended ensuring a more effective partnership between the Mission and the UN country team; making more use of the logistics bases at Brindisi, Italy, and Entebbe, Uganda, for the creation of a new peacekeeping operation rather than tasking existing missions to assist with start-up; providing more security information and analysis to the UN country team and non-governmental organizations; reporting more comprehensively on human rights violations; finalizing a contingency plan for the post-referendum period; developing exit strategies for peacekeeping missions; and implementing the comprehensive strategy on the protection of civilians.

Financing

In a performance report on the budget of UNMIS for the period from 1 July 2009 to 30 June 2010 [A/65/630 & Corr.1], the Secretary-General reported expenditure of $932,452,000 gross ($907,532,200 net) against an appropriation of $958,350,200 gross ($936,133,000 net). He requested that the General Assembly decide on the treatment of the unencumbered balance of $25,898,200 and on the treatment of other income amounting to $26,153,900. ACABQ, in April [A/65/743/Add.10], recommended that the unencumbered balance, as well as other income/adjustments, be credited to Member States.

In February [A/65/731], the Secretary-General submitted budget estimates for UNMIS for the period from 1 July 2011 to 30 June 2012, totalling $947,076,900 gross ($919,645,300 net). The budget provided for the deployment of 525 military observers, 9,450 military contingent personnel, 715 UN police officers, 997 international staff, 3,120 national staff, 353 UN Volunteers, 40 Government-provided personnel and 19 temporary positions. Taking into account Security Council resolution 1978(2011) (see p. 192), ACABQ, in April [A/65/743/Add.10], recommended appropriations of $473,538,450 for the maintenance of UNMIS for the six-month period from 1 July 2011 to 31 December 2011. In that connection, the Secretary-General should submit a revised budget proposal.

GENERAL ASSEMBLY ACTION

On 30 June [meeting 106], the General Assembly, on the recommendation of the Fifth Committee [A/65/656/Add.1], adopted **resolution 65/257 B** without vote [agenda item 157].

Financing of the United Nations Mission in the Sudan

The General Assembly,

Having considered the reports of the Secretary-General on the financing of the United Nations Mission in the Sudan and the related report of the Advisory Committee on Administrative and Budgetary Questions,

Recalling Security Council resolution 1590(2005) of 24 March 2005, by which the Council established the United Nations Mission in the Sudan for an initial period of six months as from 24 March 2005, and the subsequent resolutions by which the Council extended the mandate of the Mission, the latest of which was resolution 1978(2011) of 27 April 2011, by which the Council extended the mandate of the Mission until 9 July 2011,

Recalling also Security Council resolution 1990(2011) of 27 June 2011, by which the Council established the United Nations Interim Security Force for Abyei for an initial period of six months from 27 June 2011,

Recalling further its resolution 59/292 of 21 April 2005 on the financing of the Mission and its subsequent resolutions thereon, the latest of which was resolution 65/257 A of 24 December 2010,

Recalling its resolution 58/315 of 1 July 2004,

Reaffirming the general principles underlying the financing of United Nations peacekeeping operations, as stated in General Assembly resolutions 1874(S-IV) of 27 June 1963, 3101(XXVIII) of 11 December 1973 and 55/235 of 23 December 2000,

Noting with appreciation that voluntary contributions have been made to the Trust Fund in Support of the Peace Process in the Sudan,

Mindful of the fact that it is essential to provide the Mission with the financial resources necessary to enable it to fulfil its responsibilities under the relevant resolutions of the Security Council,

1. *Requests* the Secretary-General to entrust the Head of Mission with the task of formulating future budget proposals in full accordance with the provisions of General Assembly resolutions 59/296 of 22 June 2005, 60/266 of 30 June 2006, 61/276 of 29 June 2007, 64/269 of 24 June 2010 and 65/289 of 30 June 2011, as well as other relevant resolutions;

2. *Takes note* of the status of contributions to the United Nations Mission in the Sudan as at 30 April 2011, including the contributions outstanding in the amount of 133.1 million United States dollars, representing some 2 per cent of the total assessed contributions, notes with concern that only forty-seven Member States have paid their assessed contributions in full, and urges all other Member States, in particular those in arrears, to ensure payment of their outstanding assessed contributions;

3. *Expresses its appreciation* to those Member States which have paid their assessed contributions in full, and urges all other Member States to make every possible effort to ensure payment of their assessed contributions to the Mission in full;

4. *Expresses concern* at the financial situation with regard to peacekeeping activities, in particular as regards the reimbursements to troop contributors that bear additional burdens owing to overdue payments by Member States of their assessments;

5. *Also expresses concern* at the delay experienced by the Secretary-General in deploying and providing adequate resources to some recent peacekeeping missions, in particular those in Africa;

6. *Emphasizes* that all future and existing peacekeeping missions shall be given equal and non-discriminatory treatment in respect of financial and administrative arrangements;

7. *Also emphasizes* that all peacekeeping missions shall be provided with adequate resources for the effective and efficient discharge of their respective mandates;

8. *Requests* the Secretary-General to ensure that proposed peacekeeping budgets are based on the relevant legislative mandates;

9. *Endorses* the conclusions and recommendations contained in the report of the Advisory Committee on Administrative and Budgetary Questions, subject to the provisions of the present resolution, and requests the Secretary-General to ensure their full implementation;

10. *Reaffirms* section XX of resolution 61/276, and encourages the Secretary-General, where feasible, to enhance regional and inter-mission cooperation with a view to achieving greater synergies in the use of the resources of the Organization and the implementation of mandates of the

missions, while bearing in mind that individual missions are responsible for the preparation and implementation of their own budgets and for controlling their own assets and logistical operations;

11. *Requests* the Secretary-General to ensure that future budget submissions contain sufficient information, explanation and justification of the proposed resource requirements relating to operational costs in order to allow Member States to take well-informed decisions;

12. *Also requests* the Secretary-General to ensure the full implementation of the relevant provisions of its resolutions 59/296, 60/266, 61/276, 64/269 and 65/289;

13. *Further requests* the Secretary-General to take all action necessary to ensure that the Mission is administered with a maximum of efficiency and economy;

14. *Authorizes* the Secretary-General to draw upon the resources approved for the Mission in entering into commitments for the period from 1 July to 31 December 2011 for the United Nations Interim Security Force for Abyei and any further missions established by the Security Council before 31 December 2011 in support of the implementation of the Comprehensive Peace Agreement;

15. *Notes* the intention of the Security Council, as stated in its resolution 1978(2011), to establish a successor mission to the United Nations Mission in the Sudan, and authorizes the Secretary-General to draw upon the resources approved for the Mission in entering into commitments for a successor mission for the period from 1 July to 31 December 2011;

16. *Also notes* that the overall level of appropriation has been adjusted in accordance with the terms of resolution 65/289;

Financial performance report for the period from 1 July 2009 to 30 June 2010

17. *Takes note* of the report of the Secretary-General on the financial performance of the Mission for the period from 1 July 2009 to 30 June 2010;

Budget estimates for the period from 1 July 2011 to 30 June 2012

18. *Decides* to appropriate to the Special Account for the United Nations Mission in the Sudan the amount of 513,330,150 dollars for the period from 1 July to 31 December 2011, inclusive of 482,460,550 dollars for the maintenance of the Mission, 26,158,400 dollars for the support account for peacekeeping operations and 4,711,200 dollars for the United Nations Logistics Base at Brindisi, Italy;

Financing of the appropriation

19. *Also decides* to apportion among Member States the amount of 24,838,556 dollars for the period from 1 to 9 July 2011, in accordance with the levels updated in General Assembly resolution 64/249 of 24 December 2009 and taking into account the scale of assessments for 2011, as set out in its resolution 64/248 of 24 December 2009;

20. *Further decides* that, in accordance with the provisions of its resolution 973(X) of 15 December 1955, there shall be set off against the apportionment among Member States, as provided for in paragraph 19 above, their respective share in the Tax Equalization Fund of 794,816 dollars, comprising the estimated staff assessment income of 663,668 dollars approved for the Mission, the prorated share of 107,201 dollars of the estimated staff assessment income approved for the support account and the prorated share of 23,947 dollars of the estimated staff assessment income approved for the United Nations Logistics Base;

21. *Decides* to apportion among Member States the amount of 488,491,594 dollars for the period from 10 July to 31 December 2011, for the administrative liquidation of the Mission, the United Nations Interim Security Force for Abyei, a successor mission to the United Nations Mission in the Sudan as stated in Security Council resolution 1978(2011) and any further missions established by the Council before 31 December 2011 in support of the implementation of the Comprehensive Peace Agreement, in accordance with the levels updated in General Assembly resolution 64/249, and taking into account the scale of assessments for 2011, as set out in Assembly resolution 64/248;

22. *Also decides* that, in accordance with the provisions of its resolution 973(X), there shall be set off against the apportionment among Member States, as provided for in paragraph 21 above, their respective share in the Tax Equalization Fund of 15,631,384 dollars, comprising the estimated staff assessment income of 13,052,132 dollars approved for the Mission, the prorated share of 2,108,299 dollars of the estimated staff assessment income approved for the support account and the prorated share of 470,953 dollars of the estimated staff assessment income approved for the United Nations Logistics Base;

23. *Further decides* that, for Member States that have fulfilled their financial obligations to the Mission, there shall be set off against the apportionment, as provided for in paragraph 19 above, their respective share of the unencumbered balance and other income in the total amount of 52,052,100 dollars in respect of the financial period ended 30 June 2010, in accordance with the levels updated in General Assembly resolution 64/249, and taking into account the scale of assessments for 2010, as set out in Assembly resolution 64/248;

24. *Decides* that, for Member States that have not fulfilled their financial obligations to the Mission, there shall be set off against their outstanding obligations their respective share of the unencumbered balance and other income in the total amount of 52,052,100 dollars in respect of the financial period ended 30 June 2010, in accordance with the scheme set out in paragraph 23 above;

25. *Also decides* that the increase of 2,702,700 dollars in the estimated staff assessment income in respect of the financial period ended 30 June 2010 shall be added to the credits from the amount of 52,052,100 dollars referred to in paragraphs 23 and 24 above;

26. *Emphasizes* that no peacekeeping mission shall be financed by borrowing funds from other active peacekeeping missions;

27. *Encourages* the Secretary-General to continue to take additional measures to ensure the safety and security of all personnel participating in the Mission under the auspices of the United Nations, bearing in mind paragraphs 5 and 6 of Security Council resolution 1502(2003) of 26 August 2003;

28. *Invites* voluntary contributions to the Mission in cash and in the form of services and supplies acceptable to the Secretary-General, to be administered, as appropriate,

in accordance with the procedure and practices established by the General Assembly;

29. *Decides* to include in the provisional agenda of its sixty-sixth session the item entitled "Financing of the United Nations Mission in the Sudan".

Revised budget

In October, the Secretary-General presented the revised budgetary requirements for the period 1 July 2011 to 30 June 2012 [A/66/519], amounting to $137,532,000 gross (134,054,300 net). The Secretary-General requested the General Assembly to reduce the appropriation of $482,460,550 approved by Assembly resolution 65/257 B (see p. 211) by $344,928,550 to the amount of $137,532,000. In November [A/66/575], ACABQ recommended approval of the proposed revised estimates.

GENERAL ASSEMBLY ACTION

On 24 December [meeting 93], the General Assembly, on the recommendation of the Fifth Committee [A/66/635], adopted **resolution 66/244** without vote [agenda item 162].

Financing of the United Nations Mission in the Sudan

The General Assembly,

Having considered the report of the Secretary-General on the financing of the United Nations Mission in the Sudan and the related report of the Advisory Committee on Administrative and Budgetary Questions,

Recalling Security Council resolution 1997(2011) of 11 July 2011, by which the Council decided to withdraw the United Nations Mission in the Sudan effective 11 July 2011 and called upon the Secretary-General to complete the withdrawal of all uniformed and civilian Mission personnel, other than those required for the liquidation of the Mission, by 31 August 2011,

Recalling also its resolution 59/292 of 21 April 2005 on the financing of the United Nations Mission in the Sudan and its subsequent resolutions thereon, the latest of which was resolution 65/257 B of 30 June 2011, in which the General Assembly authorized the Secretary-General to draw upon the resources approved for the Mission in entering into commitments for the period from 1 July to 31 December 2011 for the United Nations Interim Security Force for Abyei and any further missions established by the Security Council before 31 December 2011 in support of the implementation of the Comprehensive Peace Agreement, noted the intention of the Council, as stated in its resolution 1978(2011), to establish a successor mission to the United Nations Mission in the Sudan, and also authorized the Secretary-General to draw upon the resources approved for the Mission in entering into commitments for a successor mission for the period from 1 July to 31 December 2011,

1. *Endorses* the conclusions and recommendations contained in the report of the Advisory Committee on Administrative and Budgetary Questions, and requests the Secretary-General to ensure their full implementation;

2. *Takes note* of the status of contributions to the United Nations Mission in the Sudan as at 19 December 2011, including the contributions outstanding, representing some 3 per cent of the total assessed contributions, notes with concern that only fifty-five Member States have paid their assessed contributions in full, and urges all other Member States, in particular those in arrears, to ensure payment of their outstanding assessed contributions;

3. *Expresses its appreciation* to those Member States which have paid their assessed contributions in full, and urges all other Member States to make every possible effort to ensure payment of their assessed contributions to the Mission in full;

4. *Requests* the Secretary-General to provide detailed information on the administration of the termination indemnity in the context of the performance report for the Mission;

Budget estimates for the period from 1 July 2011 to 30 June 2012

5. *Decides* to reduce the appropriation of 482,460,550 United States dollars approved for the maintenance of the Mission for the period from 1 July to 31 December 2011 under the terms of its resolution 65/257 B by the amount of 344,928,550 dollars, to 137,532,000 dollars for the withdrawal and administrative liquidation of the Mission for the period from 1 July 2011 to 30 June 2012;

Financing of the appropriation

6. *Also decides* to apply to the Special Account for the United Nations Mission in the Sudan the total amount of 137,532,000 dollars from the amount of 482,460,550 dollars previously apportioned under the terms of its resolution 65/257 B for the Mission, the United Nations Interim Security Force for Abyei and the United Nations Mission in South Sudan in accordance with the levels updated in General Assembly resolution 64/249 of 24 December 2009, taking into account the scale of assessments for 2011, as set out in its resolution 64/248 of 24 December 2009;

7. *Further decides* to reduce by 10,238,100 dollars the amount of the estimated staff assessment income approved for the maintenance of the United Nations Mission in the Sudan for the period from 1 July to 31 December 2011 under the terms of its resolution 65/257 B from 13,715,800 dollars to 3,477,700 dollars;

8. *Takes note* of the remaining balance of the estimated staff assessment income in the amount of 10,238,100 dollars;

9. *Decides* to keep under review during its sixty-sixth session the item entitled "Financing of the United Nations Mission in the Sudan".

On 24 December, by **decision 66/557**, the General Assembly decided that the agenda item on the financing of UNMIS would remain for consideration during its resumed sixty-sixth (2012) session.

UNMISS

With the establishment of South Sudan as an independent country on 9 July, and the consequent end of the interim period set up by the Government of the Sudan and SPLM under the CPA, the mandate of the United Nations Mission in the Sudan (UNMIS) ended on that day. On 8 July, by resolution 1996(2011) (see p. 197), the Security Council established a successor mission, the United Nations Mission in South Sudan (UNMISS), for an initial period of one year. The UNMISS mandate was to consolidate peace and security and help establish conditions for development in South Sudan, with a view to strengthening the capacity of the Government to rule effectively and democratically and establish good relations with its neighbours.

Appointments. By a 13 June letter [S/2011/361], the Secretary-General informed the Security Council of his intention to appoint Hilde Frafjord Johnson (Norway) as his Special Representative for South Sudan and Head of UNMISS. The Council took note of that intention on 15 June [S/2011/362].

Financing

In October, the Secretary-General submitted a budget for UNMISS for the period from 1 July 2011 to 30 June 2012 [A/66/532] in the amount of $738,266,500 gross ($727,964,500 net). The budget provided for the deployment of 166 military observers, 6,834 military contingent personnel, 900 UN police officers, 957 international staff, 1,590 national staff, 506 UN Volunteers, 81 Government-provided personnel and 500 temporary positions. The Secretary-General recommended that the General Assembly establish a special account for the Mission; apply to that account $277,915,150 from the amount of $482,460,550 previously assessed, by resolution 65/257 B (see p. 211), for UNMIS, UNISFA and UNMISS; and assess an amount of $460,351,350 for the period from 9 July 2011 to 30 June 2012.

In December [A/66/592], ACABQ recommended approving those proposals.

GENERAL ASSEMBLY ACTION

On 24 December [meeting 93], the General Assembly, on the recommendation of the Fifth Committee [A/66/634], adopted **resolution 66/243 A** without vote [agenda item 161].

Financing of the United Nations Mission in South Sudan

The General Assembly,

Having considered the report of the Secretary-General on the financing of the United Nations Mission in South Sudan and the related report of the Advisory Committee on Administrative and Budgetary Questions,

Recalling Security Council resolution 1978(2011) of 27 April 2011, by which the Council announced its intent to establish a mission to succeed the United Nations Mission in the Sudan,

Recalling also Security Council resolution 1996(2011) of 8 July 2011, by which the Council established as of 9 July 2011 the United Nations Mission in South Sudan for an initial period of one year with the intention to renew for further periods as might be required,

Recalling further its resolution 65/257 B of 30 June 2011, in which it authorized the Secretary-General to draw upon the resources approved for the United Nations Mission in the Sudan in entering into commitments for the period from 1 July to 31 December 2011 for the United Nations Interim Security Force for Abyei and any further missions established by the Security Council before 31 December 2011 in support of the implementation of the Comprehensive Peace Agreement, noted the intention of the Security Council, as stated in its resolution 1978(2011), to establish a successor mission to the United Nations Mission in the Sudan, and also authorized the Secretary-General to draw upon the resources approved for the Mission in entering into commitments for a successor mission for the period from 1 July to 31 December 2011,

Reaffirming the general principles underlying the financing of United Nations peacekeeping operations, as stated in General Assembly resolutions 1874(S-IV) of 27 June 1963, 3101(XXVIII) of 11 December 1973 and 55/235 of 23 December 2000,

Mindful of the fact that it is essential to provide the United Nations Mission in South Sudan with the financial resources necessary to enable it to fulfil its responsibilities under the relevant resolution of the Security Council,

1. *Requests* the Secretary-General to entrust the Head of Mission with the task of formulating future budget proposals in full accordance with the provisions of General Assembly resolutions 59/296 of 22 June 2005, 60/266 of 30 June 2006, 61/276 of 29 June 2007, 64/269 of 24 June 2010 and 65/289 of 30 June 2011, as well as other relevant resolutions;

2. *Expresses concern* at the financial situation with regard to peacekeeping activities, in particular as regards the reimbursements to troop contributors that bear additional burdens owing to overdue payments by Member States of their assessments;

3. *Emphasizes* that all future and existing peacekeeping missions shall be given equal and non-discriminatory treatment in respect of financial and administrative arrangements;

4. *Also emphasizes* that all peacekeeping missions shall be provided with adequate resources for the effective and efficient discharge of their respective mandates;

5. *Requests* the Secretary-General to ensure that proposed peacekeeping budgets are based on the relevant legislative mandates;

6. *Endorses* the conclusions and recommendations contained in the report of the Advisory Committee on Administrative and Budgetary Questions, and requests the Secretary-General to ensure their full implementation;

7. *Notes* the application of the standardized funding model in the budget formulation, and in this regard requests the Secretary-General to present analyses and lessons learned from its first application in the context of the performance report for the United Nations Mission in South Sudan;

8. *Requests* the Secretary-General to ensure the full implementation of the relevant provisions of its resolutions 59/296, 60/266, 61/276, 64/269 and 65/289;

9. *Also requests* the Secretary-General to take all action necessary to ensure that the Mission is administered with a maximum of efficiency and economy;

**Budget estimates for the period
from 1 July 2011 to 30 June 2012**

10. *Authorizes* the Secretary-General to establish a special account for the Mission for the purpose of accounting for the income received and expenditure incurred in respect of the Mission;

11. *Decides* to appropriate to the Special Account for the United Nations Mission in South Sudan the amount of 722,129,600 United States dollars for the period from 1 July 2011 to 30 June 2012 for the maintenance of the Mission;

Financing of the appropriation

12. *Also decides* to apply to the Special Account the total amount of 277,915,150 dollars from the amount of 482,460,550 dollars previously apportioned under the terms of its resolution 65/257 B for the United Nations Mission in the Sudan, the United Nations Interim Security Force for Abyei and the United Nations Mission in South Sudan, in accordance with the levels updated in General Assembly resolution 64/249 of 24 December 2009, taking into account the scale of assessments for 2011, as set out in its resolution 64/248 of 24 December 2009;

13. *Further decides* to apply to the Special Account the amount of 8,874,300 dollars, representing the respective share of Member States in the Tax Equalization Fund of the balance of the estimated staff assessment income approved for the United Nations Mission in the Sudan and already set off against the apportionment among Member States under the terms of resolution 65/257 B and in accordance with the provisions of its resolution 973(X) of 15 December 1955;

14. *Decides* to apportion among Member States the amount of 444,214,450 dollars for the period from 9 July 2011 to 30 June 2012, in accordance with the levels updated in General Assembly resolution 64/249, taking into account the scale of assessments for 2011 and 2012, as set out in resolution 64/248;

15. *Also decides* that, in accordance with the provisions of its resolution 973(X), there shall be set off against the apportionment among Member States, as provided for in paragraph 14 above, their respective share in the Tax Equalization Fund of 1,202,520 dollars, representing the balance of the estimated staff assessment income of 10,076,820 dollars approved for the Mission;

16. *Emphasizes* that no peacekeeping mission shall be financed by borrowing funds from other active peacekeeping missions;

17. *Encourages* the Secretary-General to continue to take additional measures to ensure the safety and security of all personnel participating in the Mission under the auspices of the United Nations, bearing in mind paragraphs 5 and 6 of Security Council resolution 1502(2003) of 26 August 2003;

18. *Invites* voluntary contributions to the Mission in cash and in the form of services and supplies acceptable to the Secretary-General, to be administered, as appropriate, in accordance with the procedure and practices established by the General Assembly;

19. *Decides* to keep under review during its sixty-sixth session the item entitled "Financing of the United Nations Mission in South Sudan".

On 24 December, the General Assembly decided that the agenda item on the financing of UNMISS would remain for consideration during its resumed sixty-sixth (2012) session (**decision 66/557**).

UNISFA

The Security Council, by resolution 1990(2011) of 27 June (see p. 195), established the United Nations Interim Security Force for Abyei (UNISFA) for six months, following the violence, escalating tensions and population displacement in the Abyei region, as Southern Sudan was preparing to declare its independence. The Abyei region, straddling northern and southern Sudan, had been claimed by both sides. The operation answered the call for swift Council action in the wake of the 20 June Agreement between the Sudanese Government and SPLM to withdraw their respective forces and allow Ethiopian peacekeepers in Abyei. Under the agreement, the two sides concurred on the need for a third party to monitor the border between the north and south. UNISFA was tasked with monitoring the border and facilitating the delivery of humanitarian aid, and was authorized to use force in protecting civilians and humanitarian workers. On 22 December, by resolution 2032(2011) (see p. 206), the Council extended the Mission's mandate by five months.

Appointments. By a letter of 22 July [S/2011/461], the Secretary-General informed the Security Council of his intention to appoint Lieutenant General Tadesse Werede Tesfay (Ethiopia) as Head of Mission and UNISFA Force Commander. The Council took note of the Secretary-General's intention on 26 July [S/2011/462].

Financing

In October, the Secretary-General submitted the budget for UNISFA for the period from 1 July 2011 to 30 June 2012 [A/66/526] in the amount of $180,691,900 gross ($179,328,100 net). The budget provided for the deployment of 135 military observers, 4,065 military contingent personnel, 50 police officers, 97 international staff, 60 national staff and 20 UN Volunteers. The Secretary-General recommended that the General Assembly establish a special account for UNISFA; apply to that account $67,013,400 from the amount of $482,460,550 previously assessed for UNMIS, UNISFA and UNMISS; and assess an additional amount of $21,389,626 for the maintenance of UNISFA for the period from 1 July to 27 December 2011 and $92,288,874 for the period from 28 December 2011 to 30 June 2012, should the Security Council decide to continue the mandate of the Mission.

ACABQ, in November [A/66/576], recommended reducing the proposed requirement by $20,635,900 and appropriating $160,056,000 for the maintenance of UNISFA. Further, ACABQ recommended assessing an additional amount of $11,293,568 for the maintenance of the Mission for the period from 1 July to 27 December 2011 and $81,749,032 for the period from 28 December 2011 to 30 June 2012, should the Council decide to continue the mandate of UNISFA. ACABQ endorsed the other recommendations of the Secretary-General.

GENERAL ASSEMBLY ACTION

On 24 December [meeting 93], the General Assembly, on the recommendation of the Fifth Committee [A/66/632], adopted **resolution 66/241 A** without vote [agenda item 147].

Financing of the United Nations Interim Security Force for Abyei

The General Assembly,

Having considered the report of the Secretary-General on the financing of the United Nations Interim Security Force for Abyei and the related report of the Advisory Committee on Administrative and Budgetary Questions,

Recalling Security Council resolution 1990(2011) of 27 June 2011, by which the Council established the United Nations Interim Security Force for Abyei for a period of six months,

Recalling also its resolution 65/257 B of 30 June 2011, in which it authorized the Secretary-General to draw upon the resources approved for the United Nations Mission in the Sudan in entering into commitments for the period from 1 July to 31 December 2011 for the United Nations Interim Security Force for Abyei and any further missions established by the Security Council before 31 December 2011 in support of the implementation of the Comprehensive Peace Agreement,

Reaffirming the general principles underlying the financing of United Nations peacekeeping operations, as stated in General Assembly resolutions 1874(S-IV) of 27 June 1963, 3101(XXVIII) of 11 December 1973 and 55/235 of 23 December 2000,

Mindful of the fact that it is essential to provide the Force with the necessary financial resources to enable it to fulfil its responsibilities under the relevant resolution of the Security Council,

1. *Requests* the Secretary-General to entrust the Head of Mission with the task of formulating future budget proposals in full accordance with the provisions of General Assembly resolutions 59/296 of 22 June 2005, 60/266 of 30 June 2006, 61/276 of 29 June 2007, 64/269 of 24 June 2010 and 65/289 of 30 June 2011, as well as other relevant resolutions;

2. *Expresses concern* at the financial situation with regard to peacekeeping activities, in particular as regards the reimbursements to troop contributors that bear additional burdens owing to overdue payments by Member States of their assessments;

3. *Emphasizes* that all future and existing peacekeeping missions shall be given equal and non-discriminatory treatment in respect of financial and administrative arrangements;

4. *Also emphasizes* that all peacekeeping missions shall be provided with adequate resources for the effective and efficient discharge of their respective mandates;

5. *Requests* the Secretary-General to ensure that proposed peacekeeping budgets are based on the relevant legislative mandates;

6. *Endorses* the conclusions and recommendations contained in the report of the Advisory Committee on Administrative and Budgetary Questions, subject to the provisions of the present resolution, and requests the Secretary-General to ensure their full implementation;

7. *Requests* the Secretary-General to ensure the full implementation of the relevant provisions of its resolutions 59/296, 60/266, 61/276, 64/269 and 65/289;

8. *Also requests* the Secretary-General to take all action necessary to ensure that the Force is administered with a maximum of efficiency and economy;

Budget estimates for the period from 1 July 2011 to 30 June 2012

9. *Authorizes* the Secretary-General to establish a special account for the Force for the purpose of accounting for the income received and expenditure incurred in respect of the Force;

10. *Decides* to appropriate to the Special Account for the United Nations Interim Security Force for Abyei the amount of 175,500,000 United States dollars for the period from 1 July 2011 to 30 June 2012 for the maintenance of the Force;

Financing of the appropriation

11. *Also decides* to apply to the Special Account the total amount of 67,013,400 dollars from the amount of 482,460,550 dollars previously apportioned under the terms of its resolution 65/257 B for the United Nations Mission in the Sudan, the United Nations Interim Security Force for Abyei and the United Nations Mission in South Sudan, in accordance with the levels updated in General Assembly resolution 64/249 of 24 December 2009, taking into account the scale of assessments for 2011, as set out in its resolution 64/248 of 24 December 2009;

12. *Further decides* to apply to the Special Account the amount of 1,363,800 dollars, representing the respective share of Member States in the Tax Equalization Fund of the balance of the estimated staff assessment income approved for the Force and already set off against the apportionment among Member States under the terms of resolution 65/257 B and in accordance with the provisions of its resolution 973(X) of 15 December 1955;

13. *Decides* to apportion among Member States the amount of 18,849,503 dollars for the period from 1 July to 27 December 2011, in accordance with the levels updated in General Assembly resolution 64/249, taking into account the scale of assessments for 2011, as set out in resolution 64/248;

14. *Also decides* to apportion among Member States the amount of 89,637,097 dollars for the period from 28 December 2011 to 30 June 2012, at a monthly rate of 14,625,000 dollars, in accordance with the levels updated in General Assembly resolution 64/249, taking into account the scale of assessments for 2011 and 2012, as set out in resolution 64/248, subject to a decision of the Security Council to extend the mandate of the Force;

15. *Emphasizes* that no peacekeeping mission shall be financed by borrowing funds from other active peacekeeping missions;

16. *Encourages* the Secretary-General to continue to take additional measures to ensure the safety and security of all personnel participating in the Force under the auspices of the United Nations, bearing in mind paragraphs 5 and 6 of Security Council resolution 1502(2003) of 26 August 2003;

17. *Invites* voluntary contributions to the Force in cash and in the form of services and supplies acceptable to the Secretary-General, to be administered, as appropriate, in accordance with the procedure and practices established by the General Assembly;

18. *Decides* to keep under review during its sixty-sixth session the item entitled "Financing of the United Nations Interim Security Force for Abyei".

On 24 December, by **decision 66/557**, the General Assembly decided that the agenda item on the financing of unisfa would remain for consideration during its resumed sixty-sixth (2012) session.

Darfur

The situation in Darfur remained precarious in 2011. Some progress was made towards a negotiated resolution to the conflict and the launch of a Darfur-based political process. At the negotiations in Doha, Qatar, the parties—the Sudan, the Liberation and Justice Movement (ljm) and the Justice and Equality Movement (jem)—discussed a draft text submitted by the African Union-United Nations Joint Mediation. At the All Darfur Stakeholders Conference, held in Doha in May, the parties agreed that the Doha draft document would form the basis for reaching a permanent ceasefire, a peace settlement, and sustainable peace and stability. On 14 July, the Sudan and ljm signed the Agreement on the adoption of the Doha Document for Peace in Darfur, pledging to implement the Doha Document and calling on other armed movements to sign it. On 16 July, the Sudan and ljm signed the Protocol on the Political Participation of the Liberation and Justice Movement and Integration of Its Forces. The Protocol provided for the allocation of political appointments to ljm, including positions in the Darfur Regional Authority, as well as for the integration of ljm fighters into the Sudanese Armed Forces (saf). On 23 October, the chair of ljm, Eltigani Seisi, was sworn in by the President of the Sudan as Chair of the Darfur Regional Authority. The African Union-United Nations Hybrid Operation in Darfur (unamid) continued to protect civilians, support the delivery of humanitarian assistance and further the peace process. The Security Council, on 29 July, extended the Mission's mandate until 31 July 2012.

Political and security developments

Communication. By a 5 January letter [S/2011/17], the Sudan transmitted to the Security Council a concept paper on its position on the Darfur peace talks in Doha. The Sudan stated that it had not definitively withdrawn from the Doha mediation process. It had recalled its delegation on 31 December 2010, however, deeming that two years of negotiations were sufficient to prepare a draft peace document. The Sudan stood ready to receive that draft and discuss it within the au-UN Joint Mediation.

Report of Secretary-General (January). Pursuant to Security Council resolution 1935(2010) [YUN 2010, p. 262], the Secretary-General submitted a 28 January report on the African Union-United Nations Hybrid Operation in Darfur (unamid) [S/2011/22]. Progress had been achieved in the peace negotiations in Doha [YUN 2010, p. 266]. The Joint Mediation and the Joint au-UN Chief Mediator for Darfur, Djibril Bassolé, worked directly with the parties to reconcile the outstanding differences. The main points of disagreement were related to the powers of a regional authority to implement the peace agreement in Darfur, a vice-presidency post for Darfur, as well as issues related to security arrangements, power-sharing and compensation. On 6 January, the Arab-African Ministerial Committee and the Joint Mediation held a meeting in Doha under the auspices of Qatar. Participants expressed concern at the humanitarian and security situation in Darfur, noted progress in the negotiations between the Government and ljm and the presence of jem in Doha, and renewed their support for the peace process.

The Secretary-General condemned continued attacks on unamid and humanitarian personnel. He called on the Sudan to ensure law and order in Darfur and bring to justice those accountable for attacks, kidnapping and banditry targeting unamid and humanitarian personnel. He welcomed the return to their families of unamid and World Food Programme personnel who had been held hostage between October 2010 and January 2011. He noted that unamid had made strides in its deployment, but had experienced difficulties in obtaining visas for its staff.

Communications. On 11 March [S/2011/128], the Sudan transmitted to the Security Council a position paper regarding the referendum on the administrative status of Darfur. On 6 April [S/2011/232], the Sudan transmitted the outcome of the second working-level meeting of the Tripartite Mechanism (Khartoum, 31 March), comprising the Sudan, the United Nations and the au, during which an agreement had been reached regarding the issuance of visas for crucial military, police and civilian personnel. On 7 April [S/2011/233], the Sudan transmitted clarification points regarding the referendum on the administrative status of Darfur, to be conducted on 29 March in accordance with the 2006 Darfur Peace Agreement [YUN 2006, p. 274].

Reports of Secretary-General (April). On 14 April [S/2011/244], pursuant to Security Council resolution 1935(2010), the Secretary-General reported on progress made towards implementing the UNAMID mandate. The report, which covered the period from 1 January to 31 March 2011, also addressed the progress made against benchmarks contained in his November 2009 report [YUN 2009, p. 257].

At the political level, some progress was made towards a negotiated resolution to the conflict and the launch of the Darfur political process. The AU-UN Joint Mediation continued consultations with the Government, armed movements and other Darfur stakeholders. On 29 January, the leaders of LJM and JEM issued a joint statement reaffirming their commitment to the Doha negotiations and to working together towards a settlement to the conflict. The delegation of the Government, which left the Doha negotiations on 31 December 2010, returned to the talks. At a meeting of the Joint Chief Mediator with the leader of JEM, Khalil Ibrahim (Tripoli, Libya, 15 February), the latter confirmed that JEM was prepared to collaborate with LJM in negotiating with the Government. On 17 February, the Joint Chief Mediator and the Minister of State for Foreign Affairs of Qatar held separate meetings with representatives of the Government, LJM and JEM. It was agreed that the Mediator would provide the parties with draft texts on each of the issues under negotiation, which would serve as a framework for a final comprehensive agreement. Subsequently, JEM agreed to enter into direct talks with the Government. On 22 February, the Joint Mediation presented draft texts covering four areas on which there was broad agreement: wealth-sharing; compensation and the return of IDPs and refugees; justice and reconciliation; and human rights and fundamental freedoms. The Joint Mediation subsequently received the parties' positions on those drafts, without substantive disagreements.

On the administrative status of Darfur, the Government announced that it had decided to hold a referendum before 9 July, the day Southern Sudan was scheduled to secede, in accordance with article 55 of the Darfur Peace Agreement. On 7 March, the Government indicated that it had decided to create two new states in Darfur: a central state with Zalingei, currently in West Darfur, as its capital; and a state in the south-east with El Daein, currently in South Darfur, as its capital. After negative reactions to those announcements—perceived as unilateral—from LJM and JEM, as well as other armed movements, political parties and civil society, the Government on 14 March issued a statement specifying that all issues, including the administrative status of Darfur, remained open for negotiation and that all provisions of an agreement reached in Doha would be implemented.

In a retreat for special envoys and international actors convened by UNAMID (Nyala, 18 February), it was agreed that the Darfur political process should take place in an environment that would ensure freedom of speech and freedom of movement for participants, proportional participation among Darfurians, and freedom from interference by the Government or armed movements.

Concerning the security situation, fighting between the Government and movement forces continued to be a major source of insecurity in parts of Darfur. The incidence of intercommunal conflict remained low, as did attacks on UNAMID. Relations between the Government and the Sudan Liberation Army (SLA)-Minni Minawi faction remained strained. In January, SAF clashed with JEM forces, as well as with SLA-Abdul Wahid forces in Western Darfur. In February, the armed forces bombed several villages in northern Darfur.

Regarding the Mission's benchmarks set out in the Secretary-General's report of 16 November 2009, some progress had been made against the first benchmark—achieving a comprehensive political solution to the conflict through the implementation of the Darfur Peace Agreement or subsequent agreement—as broad consensus was reached between the Government, LJM and JEM on elements of a comprehensive peace settlement. Progress against the second benchmark—restoring a stable and secure environment throughout Darfur—was mixed. While no new ceasefires were reached and fighting between Government and movement forces continued, the incidence of intercommunal fighting remained low. Progress against the third benchmark—enhancing the rule of law, governance and human rights protection, and the provision of assistance to effective State institutions—was limited. The fourth benchmark—stabilizing the humanitarian situation and facilitating humanitarian access to populations in need—saw neither major advancement nor regression. UNAMID and humanitarian workers were able to access most areas affected by fighting, as well as parts of Jebel Marra.

The Mission was facing difficulties in recruiting and retaining qualified civilian staff, owing to the harsh living conditions and unpredictable security situation. The Mission's military staff conducted 5,189 routine patrols, 484 humanitarian escorts, 1,774 night patrols, 954 short-range patrols, 685 long-range patrols, and 1,533 logistic and administrative patrols. On average, 150 military patrols were conducted daily. UNAMID police conducted 11,764 patrols. The readiness of military contingents was gradually improving, as contributors deployed additional vehicles. At the tenth meeting of the Tripartite Mechanism (Addis Ababa, 3 February), it was agreed that tripartite arrangements would be restructured and that meetings would be held at technical and strategic levels to review operational and political issues, respectively. The Mission was experiencing considerable delays in the issuance of visas. UNAMID destroyed over 200 ordnance items and delivered risk awareness training to approximately 28,000 civilians. The Darfur Security Arrangements Implementation Commission [YUN 2006, p. 275], established under the Darfur Peace Agreement, began the voluntary disarmament of some 2,000 members of SLA-Mustafa Terab, a breakaway faction of SLA-Minni Minawi. In February, the Commission processed 485 members of that faction in El Fasher and Nyala. The exercise was observed by UNAMID. Of the 96 sites identified by the Mission for drilling to access water, 24 were in use and the water was being shared with local communities.

Pursuant to Security Council presidential statement S/PRST/2011/3 (see p. 190), the Secretary-General on 15 April submitted a report [S/2011/252] on the implementation of the Darfur political process, which focused on the creation of an enabling environment for that process and its sequencing vis-à-vis the Doha negotiations. The process was envisaged as a forum to enable the engagement of the people of Darfur in the procedures necessary to resolve the political conflict. It was expected to enhance popular support for the outcomes of the Doha negotiations and enable the people of Darfur to participate in their implementation. In an 8 April communiqué, the AU Peace and Security Council stated that the process should be implemented concurrently with and as a complement to the Doha negotiations. There was disagreement, however, on whether the processes should be held sequentially or concurrently. A Darfur political process secretariat had been established at UNAMID headquarters to oversee implementation; it reported to the Joint Special Representative and the Chair of the AU High-level Implementation Panel. Darfur political process subunits were being established in El Fasher, Nyala, El Geneina and Zalengei. Participants in the process would include representatives of women, native administrations, IDPs, civil society and youth. While there was an opportunity for the armed movements to participate, JEM, SLA-Minni Minawi and SLA-Abdul Wahid expressed reservations, alleging that the process and its outcome would be influenced by the Government. LJM expressed support for the process, but only after the conclusion of the Doha negotiations and a signed agreement.

As for the Doha negotiations, the parties—the Government, JEM and LJM—were discussing the draft texts submitted by the Joint Mediation that would serve as a framework for a final comprehensive agreement. The Joint Chief Mediator intended to hold an All Darfur Stakeholders Conference to discuss and jointly endorse the text of a peace agreement/framework. In the meantime, JEM and LJM had expressed their intent to work together towards reaching a comprehensive settlement of the conflict. JEM also indicated that it had reached out to the SLA-Abdul Wahid and SLA-Minni Minawi factions to join the process. When the Joint Special Representative met Abdul Wahid on 21 March, however, he stated that he would not join the negotiations in Doha.

As for the establishment of an enabling environment, the Government agreed with the Joint Special Representative and the AU High-level Implementation Panel that such an environment was necessary to guarantee the credibility of the political process. At his meeting with the Joint Special Representative on 21 March, the President of the Sudan confirmed that his Government intended to abolish the emergency laws in Darfur in order to facilitate the political process and other political efforts.

The Secretary-General noted that the military situation in Darfur undermined confidence in the Government and contributed to scepticism among the population about its willingness to establish an enabling environment for the political process. He therefore called on the Government and the armed movements to halt hostilities. He called on the armed movements to place their trust in the United Nations and the AU to mediate a comprehensive agreement in Doha and to work towards putting in place the enabling conditions for the political process. He further called on Abdul Wahid to join the process and on Minni Minawi to reconcile with the Government.

Communication. On 1 June [S/2011/335], Qatar transmitted to the Secretary-General the Statement by the Joint Mediation regarding the All Darfur Stakeholders Conference (Doha, 27–31 May). The Conference endorsed the Doha draft document as a basis for concluding a permanent ceasefire, a comprehensive peaceful settlement including all parties, and sustainable peace and stability. It also endorsed the formation of a Darfur Implementation Follow-up Commission, chaired by Qatar and composed of international partners. The Commission would work with the United Nations and the AU to assist the parties in concluding and implementing a comprehensive peace settlement.

Report of Secretary-General (July). Pursuant to Security Council resolution 1935(2010), the Secretary-General on 8 July submitted a report [S/2011/422] on UNAMID, which covered the period from 1 April to 30 June. On 27 April, the Joint Mediation team presented a draft peace agreement to the Government, LJM and JEM. The draft was based on points of agreement discussed with the parties, as well as proposals from the team on points of divergence, such as the administrative status of Darfur. The Government and LJM subsequently expressed their support for the draft, while JEM sought further negotiations with the Government, which broke down on 3 May due to a disagreement over the scope and procedures of the negotiation process.

The All Darfur Stakeholders Conference brought together approximately 500 participants from the parties to the conflict, political parties, civil society and the Darfurian diaspora. The draft text of the agreement was not circulated. Stakeholders were presented, however, with the key elements contained in the draft as the basis for their discussions. At the closing ceremony, participants endorsed a communiqué that provided for the Doha draft document to form the basis for reaching a permanent ceasefire, a comprehensive and inclusive peace settlement, and sustainable peace and stability. On 14 June, JEM questioned the inclusiveness of the Conference but asserted its willingness to continue to negotiate. SLA-Abdul Wahid and SLA-Minni Minawi did not participate in the Conference, nor did they pronounce themselves on its outcome. In the meantime, UNAMID, in conjunction with the AU High-Level Implementation Panel, continued to plan for the Darfur political process, and the Government reiterated its commitment to suspend the emergency laws in Darfur.

The National Electoral Commission commenced preparations for a referendum on the status of Darfur and, on 12 April, requested technical assistance from UNAMID and UNMIS. The issue remained a part of the negotiations between the Government and LJM, and on 26 June, the parties agreed that the referendum would be held one year after the signing of an agreement. On 5 May, the Council of Ministers passed legislation on the creation of two additional states in Darfur (see p. 218). Several movements, including SLA-Abdul Wahid, SLA-Minni Minawi, opposition parties and some sectors of civil society complained to UNAMID that the creation of two additional states would exacerbate divisions between ethnic groups.

Armed movements formed several new alliances in the reporting period. On 14 May, SLA-Abdul Wahid and SLA-Minni Minawi issued a Declaration of Alliance in which they announced their agreement to work together. Similarly, on 8 May, an alliance between SLA-Abdul Wahid and the SLA-Juba faction was announced, and on 20 May, the SLA-Abdul Wahid and the SLA-Mother faction announced that they had reunited under the leadership of Abdul Wahid. On 18 May, a breakaway faction of LJM signed an agreement with JEM, and on 25 May, the same faction entered into an alliance with SLA-Minni Minawi.

On 5 August, an attack against a UNAMID patrol resulted in the death of a Sierra Leonean peacekeeper and serious injury to another. The Security Council condemned the attack on 8 August [SC/10355].

At the Darfur International Conference: Water for Sustainable Peace (Khartoum, 27–28 June), co-chaired by the Government, UNAMID and the UN country team, participants sought to create an integrated framework for water management in Darfur. Addressing water issues would contribute to sustainable peace, as access to water was one of the root causes of the conflict in Darfur.

The Secretary-General observed that the Darfur peace process had reached a critical juncture. Negotiations between the Government and LJM appeared to be nearing a conclusion. The All Darfur Stakeholders Conference discussions and the draft agreement between the Government and LJM represented the basis for advancing the peace process. SLA-Abdul Wahid and SLA-Minni Minawi, however, continued to pursue their objectives through military means, and negotiations between the Government and JEM seemed to be stalled. The Secretary-General urged the international community to present a unified message to all parties to cease hostilities and enter into negotiations. He urged the Government to deliver on its commitment to lift the emergency laws in Darfur. The Secretary-General noted that, despite the restrictions on the movements of UNAMID and humanitarian organizations, the Mission had made strides in implementing its protection of civilians mandate. He therefore recommended a one-year extension of UNAMID.

Communications. On 24 July [A/65/914-S/2011/449], Qatar transmitted to the Secretary-General the Agreement between the Sudan and the Liberation and Justice Movement for the Adoption of the Doha Document for Peace in Darfur, signed on 14 July.

On 27 July [S/2001/466] the Secretary-General forwarded to the Security Council an AU letter transmitting the communiqué of the 286th meeting of the AU Peace and Security Council (Addis Ababa, 19 July), by which it renewed the mandate of UNAMID until 31 July 2012 and urged the Security Council to take a similar action.

SECURITY COUNCIL ACTION

On 29 July [meeting 6597], the Security Council unanimously adopted **resolution 2003(2011)**. The draft [S/2011/471] was submitted by the United Kingdom.

The Security Council,

Reaffirming all its previous resolutions and the statements by its President concerning the situation in the Sudan, and underlining the importance of full compliance with them,

Reaffirming also its strong commitment to the sovereignty, unity, independence and territorial integrity of the Sudan and its determination to work with the Government of the Sudan, in full respect of its sovereignty, to assist in tackling the various challenges in the Sudan,

Recalling its previous resolutions 1674(2006) of 28 April 2006 and 1894(2009) of 11 November 2009 on the protection of civilians in armed conflict, in which it reaffirms, inter alia, the relevant provisions of the 2005 World Summit Outcome, its resolutions 1612(2005) of 26 July 2005, 1882(2009) of 4 August 2009 and 1998(2011) of 12 July 2011 on children and armed conflict, its resolution 1502(2003) of 26 August 2003 on the protection of humanitarian and United Nations personnel and its resolution 1325(2000) of 31 October 2000 and associated resolutions on women and peace and security and children and armed conflict,

Recalling also its resolutions reaffirming that there can be no peace without justice, and recalling the importance that the Security Council attaches to ending impunity and to ensuring justice for crimes committed in Darfur,

Bearing in mind the Convention relating to the Status of Refugees of 28 July 1951 and the Protocol thereto, of 31 January 1967, along with the Organization of African Unity Convention governing the specific aspects of refugee problems in Africa of 10 September 1969, as well as the African Union Convention for the Protection and Assistance of Internally Displaced Persons in Africa of 23 October 2009,

Recalling the report of the Secretary-General of 10 February 2009 on children and armed conflict in the Sudan, including his recommendations, recalling the conclusions on children and armed conflict in the Sudan endorsed by the Security Council Working Group on Children and Armed Conflict, and recalling the report of the Secretary-General of 5 July 2011 on children and armed conflict in the Sudan,

Expressing its strong commitment and determination to support the African Union-United Nations Darfur peace process hosted by Qatar, deploring the fact that some groups continue to refuse to join this process, and strongly urging them to do so without further delay or preconditions,

Welcoming the outcome of the All Darfur Stakeholders Conference, held in Doha from 27 to 31 May 2011, and the signing on 14 July 2011 of the Agreement between the Government of the Sudan and the Liberation and Justice Movement for the Adoption of the Doha Document for Peace in Darfur as an important step forward in the peace process and as a basis for consultations on an impartial Darfur-based political process held in the necessary enabling environment, and calling upon the Government of the Sudan and all the armed movements to make every effort to reach a comprehensive peace settlement on the basis of the Doha Document for Peace in Darfur, and to agree on a permanent ceasefire without delay,

Welcoming also the establishment of the Implementation Follow-up Commission, chaired by Qatar and the continued engagement of Qatar with the African Union and the United Nations to support an internationally facilitated Darfur peace process, including the Government of the Sudan and all the armed movements, and encouraging the African Union and the United Nations actively to pursue their efforts,

Underlining, without prejudice to the primary responsibility of the Security Council for the maintenance of international peace and security, the importance of the partnership between the United Nations and the African Union, consistent with Chapter VIII of the Charter of the United Nations, with regard to the maintenance of peace and security in Africa, particularly in the Sudan, and welcoming, in particular, the efforts of the African Union High-level Implementation Panel on the Sudan under the leadership of President Thabo Mbeki, working in cooperation with the African Union-United Nations Hybrid Operation in Darfur, to address in a comprehensive and inclusive manner the challenges of peace, justice and reconciliation in Darfur,

Welcoming the report of the Secretary-General of 8 July 2011 on the African Union-United Nations Hybrid Operation in Darfur,

Stressing the need for the Council to pursue a rigorous, strategic approach to peacekeeping deployments, with a view to enhancing the effectiveness of peacekeeping missions, welcoming and further encouraging the increasingly full implementation by the African Union-United Nations Hybrid Operation in Darfur of its Chapter VII mandate, and underlining in this regard the importance of addressing the requirement for the Operation to be able to deter threats to the implementation of its mandate and the safety and security of its peacekeeping personnel in accordance with the Charter,

Expressing its deep concern at the deteriorating security situation in some parts of Darfur, including ceasefire violations, attacks by rebel groups, aerial bombardment by the Government of the Sudan, inter-tribal fighting, attacks on humanitarian personnel and peacekeepers, which have restricted humanitarian access to conflict areas where vulnerable civilian populations reside, as contained in the report of the Secretary-General of 8 July 2011, and the displacement of tens of thousands of civilians, and calling upon all parties to cease hostilities, including all acts of violence committed against civilians, and urgently facilitate unhindered humanitarian access,

Expressing its concern at the return to hostilities between the Government of the Sudan and the Sudan Liberation Army, Minni Minawi faction, and the ongoing hostilities between the Government of the Sudan and the Sudan Liberation Army, Abdul Wahid faction and the Justice and Equality Movement, and reiterating that there can be no military solution to the conflict in Darfur and that an inclusive political settlement is essential to re-establishing peace,

Reiterating its condemnation of all violations of international human rights and humanitarian law in Darfur and in relation to Darfur, calling upon all parties to comply with their obligations under international human rights and humanitarian law, emphasizing the need to bring to justice the perpetrators of such crimes, and urging the Government of the Sudan to comply with its obligations in this respect,

Reaffirming its concern over the negative effect of the ongoing violence in Darfur on the stability of the Sudan as a whole as well as the region, welcoming improved relations between the Sudan and Chad, as well as the deployment of a joint force, including forces from the Central African Republic under a joint command along the border, and encouraging the Sudan, Chad and the Central African Republic to continue to cooperate in order to achieve peace and stability in Darfur and the wider region,

Expressing its concern about alleged links between armed movements in Darfur and groups outside Darfur,

Determining that the situation in the Sudan constitutes a threat to international peace and security,

1. *Decides* to extend the mandate of the African Union-United Nations Hybrid Operation in Darfur as set out in resolution 1769(2007) of 31 July 2007 for a further twelve months, until 31 July 2012;

2. *Welcomes* the intention of the Secretary-General to review, in consultation with the African Union, the uniformed personnel required for the African Union-United Nations Hybrid Operation in Darfur to ensure the most efficient and effective implementation of the mandate of the Operation, and requests the Secretary-General to report on this issue within the framework set out in paragraph 13 below and no later than one hundred and eighty days from the adoption of the present resolution;

3. *Underlines* the need for the African Union-United Nations Hybrid Operation in Darfur to make full use of its mandate and capabilities, giving priority in decisions about the use of available capacity and resources to (*a*) the protection of civilians across Darfur, including through proactive deployment and patrols in areas at high risk of conflict, securing internally displaced persons camps and adjacent areas, and implementation of a mission-wide early warning strategy and capacity, and (*b*) ensuring safe, timely and unhindered humanitarian access and the safety and security of humanitarian personnel and humanitarian activities, so as to facilitate the unimpeded delivery of humanitarian assistance throughout Darfur; and requests the Operation to maximize the use of its capabilities, in cooperation with the United Nations country team and other international and non-governmental actors, in the implementation of its mission-wide comprehensive strategy for the achievement of these objectives;

4. *Reaffirms* the importance of promoting the African Union-United Nations-led peace and political process for Darfur, welcomes the priority given to the continuing efforts of the African Union-United Nations Hybrid Operation in Darfur to support and complement this work in accordance with paragraphs 6, 7 and 8 below, and welcomes the efforts of the African Union High-level Implementation Panel on the Sudan in this regard;

5. *Emphasizes* the Chapter VII mandate of the African Union-United Nations Hybrid Operation in Darfur, as defined in resolution 1769(2007), to deliver its core tasks to protect civilians without prejudice to the primary responsibility of the Government of the Sudan and to ensure the freedom of movement and security of the Operation's own personnel and humanitarian workers;

6. *Demands* that all parties to the conflict, including all armed movements, engage immediately and without preconditions to make every effort to reach a permanent ceasefire and a comprehensive peace settlement on the basis of the Doha Document for Peace in Darfur, in order to bring a stable and durable peace to the region;

7. *Recognizes*, in this context, the potential complementary role of a Darfur-based political process led by the African Union and the United Nations, calls upon the Government of the Sudan and the armed movements to contribute to the creation of the enabling environment necessary for a Darfur-based political process that allows the systematic and sustained engagement of all Darfurian stakeholders in constructive and open dialogue, and notes that, despite some positive developments in the peace process, important elements of the enabling environment necessary for a Darfur-based political process, including but not limited to respect for the civil and political rights of participants, such that they can exercise their views without fear of retribution, freedom of speech and assembly to permit open consultations, freedom of movement of participants and the African Union-United Nations Hybrid Operation in Darfur, proportional participation among Darfurians, freedom from harassment, arbitrary arrest and intimidation, and freedom from interference by the Government or the armed movements, are not yet in place;

8. *Requests* the Secretary-General to include in his regular reports referred to in paragraph 13 below assessments of the elements set out in paragraph 7 above to enable the Security Council, taking into account the views of the African Union, to determine the further engagement of the African Union-United Nations Hybrid Operation in Darfur in support of the Darfur-based political process;

9. *Welcomes* the intention of the Secretary-General to develop a road map for the Darfur peace process, and requests the Secretary-General, in this regard, to work in close consultation with the African Union, also consulting, as appropriate, all Sudanese stakeholders and the Implementation Follow-up Commission, and taking into account paragraphs 6, 7 and 8 above, and requests the Secretary-General to report to the Council on the road map in his next ninety-day report;

10. *Commends* the contribution of troop- and police-contributing countries and donors to the African Union-United Nations Hybrid Operation in Darfur, strongly condemns all attacks on the Operation, underlines that any attack or threat of attack on the Operation is unacceptable, demands that there be no recurrence of such attacks, stresses the need to enhance the safety and security of Operation personnel, as well as the need to put an end to impunity for those who attack peacekeepers, and in this regard urges the Government of the Sudan to do its utmost to bring the perpetrators of any such crimes to justice;

11. *Also commends* the credible work of the Tripartite Mechanism but expresses deep concern at continuing restrictions placed upon the movement and operations of the African Union-United Nations Hybrid Operation in Darfur, particularly to areas of recent conflict; calls upon all parties in Darfur to remove all obstacles to the full and proper discharge by the Operation of its mandate, including by ensuring its security and freedom of movement; and in this regard demands that the Government of the Sudan comply with the status-of-forces agreement fully and without delay, particularly regarding flight and equipment clearances, the removal of all obstacles to the use of aerial assets of the Operation and the timely provision of visas for Operation personnel; deplores the continued delays in the provision of such visas, which threaten seriously to undermine the ability of the Operation to implement its mandate, and urges the Government of the Sudan to deliver on its welcome commitment to clear the backlog of visa applications; and expresses deep concern that national staff members of the Operation were detained by the Government of the Sudan in violation of the status-of-forces agreement, and demands that the Government respect the

rights of Operation personnel under the status-of-forces agreement;

12. *Demands* that the African Union-United Nations Hybrid Operation in Darfur be given a licence for its own radio transmitter, in line with the provisions of the status-of-forces agreement, so that it can communicate freely with all Darfurian stakeholders;

13. *Requests* the Secretary-General to continue reporting to the Council every ninety days on progress made towards implementing across Darfur the mandate of the African Union-United Nations Hybrid Operation in Darfur, including on progress towards and obstacles to the implementation of the strategy referred to in paragraph 3 above, also including an assessment of progress against the benchmarks and indicators set out in annex II to the report of the Secretary-General of 16 November 2009 as well as on progress in the security and humanitarian situation, including in the internally displaced persons sites and refugee camps, human rights, violations of international humanitarian and human rights law, and early recovery and compliance by all parties with their international obligations;

14. *Demands* that all parties to the conflict in Darfur immediately end violence and attacks on civilians, peacekeepers and humanitarian personnel, and comply with their obligations under international human rights and humanitarian law; affirms in this context the Council's condemnation of serious violations of international humanitarian law and human rights law; calls for an immediate cessation of hostilities and for all parties to commit themselves to a sustained and permanent ceasefire; requests the Secretary-General to consult with relevant parties with a view to developing a more effective ceasefire monitoring mechanism; and underlines the need for the African Union-United Nations Hybrid Operation in Darfur to report on major instances of violence which undermines the full and constructive efforts of the parties towards peace;

15. *Expresses its serious concern* at the deterioration of the humanitarian situation in some parts of Darfur, the continued threats to humanitarian organizations and the restricted humanitarian access in Darfur resulting from increased insecurity, attacks against humanitarian workers and denial of access by the parties to the conflict, calls for the full implementation of the joint communiqué between the Government of the Sudan and the United Nations on facilitation of humanitarian activities in Darfur, including regarding the timely issuance of visas and travel permits for humanitarian organizations, demands that the Government of the Sudan, all militias, armed groups and all other stakeholders ensure the full, safe and unhindered access of humanitarian organizations and relief personnel and the delivery of humanitarian assistance to populations in need, and underscores the importance of upholding the principles of neutrality, impartiality and independence in the provision of humanitarian assistance;

16. *Condemns* human rights violations in and relating to Darfur, including arbitrary arrests and detentions, expresses deep concern about the situation of all those so detained, including civil society members and internally displaced persons, and emphasizes the importance of ensuring the ability of the African Union-United Nations Hybrid Operation in Darfur, within its current mandate, and of other relevant organizations to monitor such cases; calls upon the Government of the Sudan fully to respect its obligations, including by fulfilling its commitment to lift the state of emergency in Darfur, releasing all political prisoners, allowing free expression and undertaking effective efforts to ensure accountability for serious violations of international human rights and humanitarian law, by whomsoever perpetrated, and emphasizes the importance of the Operation acting to promote human rights, to bring abuses to the attention of the authorities and to report gross violations to the Council;

17. *Notes* that conflict in one area of the Sudan affects other areas of the Sudan and the wider region; and urges close coordination among United Nations missions in the region, including the African Union-United Nations Hybrid Operation in Darfur, the United Nations Interim Security Force for Abyei and the United Nations Mission in South Sudan, and requests the Secretary-General to ensure effective inter-mission cooperation;

18. *Stresses* the importance of achieving dignified and durable solutions for refugees and internally displaced persons and of ensuring their full participation in the planning and management of these solutions, demands that all parties to the conflict in Darfur create the conditions conducive to allowing the voluntary, safe, dignified and sustainable return of refugees and internally displaced persons or their local integration, notes potentially encouraging reports of some voluntary returns of internally displaced persons to their villages and places of origin, as indicated in the report of the Secretary-General of 8 July 2011, stresses the importance of the Joint Verification Mechanism in verifying the voluntariness of returns, and expresses its deep concern over some bureaucratic obstacles that undermine its effectiveness and independence;

19. *Notes* that security and freedom of movement will greatly facilitate early recovery initiatives and a return to normalcy in Darfur; stresses the importance of early recovery efforts in Darfur when such interventions are suitable, and in this respect encourages the African Union-United Nations Hybrid Operation in Darfur, within its current mandate, to facilitate the work of the United Nations country team and expert agencies on early recovery and reconstruction in Darfur, inter alia, through the provision of area security; and calls upon all parties to provide unhindered access and upon the Government of the Sudan to lift all access restrictions, to work to resolve the root causes of the Darfur crisis and to increase investment in early recovery activity;

20. *Commends* the outcome of the Darfur International Conference on Water, held in Khartoum on 27 and 28 June 2011, as a step towards sustainable peace, and calls upon the African Union-United Nations Hybrid Operation in Darfur, where consistent with its mandate, and all other United Nations agencies, in particular the United Nations Children's Fund, the United Nations Development Programme and the United Nations Environment Programme, as well as international actors and donors to meet their commitments made at that conference;

21. *Expresses its deep concern* over the persistent localized conflicts and violence and their effect on civilians, but in this context notes a reduction in inter-tribal clashes and calls upon all parties to put an end to such clashes and to pursue reconciliation; expresses its deep concern over the proliferation of arms, in particular small arms and light weapons, and in this regard requests the African Union-

United Nations Hybrid Operation in Darfur to continue to support local conflict resolution mechanisms, to monitor whether any arms or related material are present in Darfur in accordance with its mandate as set out in paragraph 9 of resolution 1769(2007), and in this context to continue to cooperate with the Panel of Experts on the Sudan established by resolution 1591(2005) of 29 March 2005 in order to facilitate its work;

22. *Demands* that the parties to the conflict immediately take appropriate measures to protect civilians, including women and children, from all forms of sexual violence, in line with resolution 1820(2008) of 19 June 2008, and requests the African Union-United Nations Hybrid Operation in Darfur to report on sexual and gender-based violence, as well as to assess progress towards the elimination of sexual and gender-based violence, and further emphasizes the need to include protection for women and children from sexual violence and gender-based violence, as part of the mission-wide protection of civilians strategy identified in paragraph 3 above, and requests the Secretary-General to ensure that the relevant provisions of resolutions 1325(2000) of 31 October 2000, 1820(2008), 1888(2009) of 30 September 2009, 1889(2009) of 5 October 2009 and 1960(2010) of 16 December 2010 are implemented by the Operation, including the participation of women through the appointment of women's protection advisers, and to include information on this in his reporting to the Council;

23. *Requests* the Secretary-General to ensure (*a*) continued monitoring and reporting, as part of the reports referred to in paragraph 13 above, of the situation of children, and (*b*) continued dialogue with the parties to the conflict towards the preparation of time-bound action plans to end the recruitment and use of child soldiers and other violations of international humanitarian law and human rights law against children;

24. *Also requests* the Secretary-General periodically to review and update the concept of operations and rules of engagement of the African Union-United Nations Hybrid Operation in Darfur in line with the mandate of the Operation under relevant Council resolutions and to report, as part of the reports referred to in paragraph 13 above, on this to the Council and troop-contributing countries;

25. *Decides* to remain seized of the matter.

Report of Secretary-General (October). Pursuant to resolution 2003(2011) (see p. 220), the Secretary-General submitted a 12 October report [S/2011/643] on UNAMID covering the period from 1 July to 30 September. The Government and LJM signed the Agreement on the Adoption of the Doha Document for Peace in Darfur on 14 July (ibid.). The Document contained provisions that comprehensively addressed the causes of the conflict. Signatories pledged to implement the Document and called upon other armed movements to sign it. The Sudan set a time limit of three months for the parties to do so.

Following additional negotiations, the Sudan and LJM on 16 July signed the Protocol on the Political Participation of the Liberation and Justice Movement and Integration of Its Forces. The Protocol provided for the allocation of political appointments to LJM, including positions in the Darfur Regional Authority and one state governorship, as well as the integration of LJM fighters in SAF. The inaugural meeting of the Ceasefire Commission—provided for in the Agreement on the Adoption of the Doha Document—was held in El Fasher on 22 August under the chairmanship of UNAMID. In meetings with UNAMID, the Governors of the three Darfur states—North Darfur, South Darfur and West Darfur—expressed their support for the implementation of the Document. In addition, the state governments entered into several local agreements with breakaway opposition movements.

In a 7 September meeting in Khartoum, the Government and LJM agreed on the creation of joint technical committees to assist with the implementation of the Doha Document provisions relating to the release of political prisoners and the establishment of the Darfur Regional Authority. On 11 September, Qatar convened the inaugural meeting of the Implementation Follow-up Commission in Doha. In other important steps towards the implementation of the Doha Document, the Sudan established the Darfur Peace Follow-up Office and appointed Darfurians to the posts of Second Vice-President of the Sudan and Head of the Darfur Regional Authority.

The UN Secretariat, the AU Commission, Sudanese stakeholders and members of the Implementation Follow-up Commission had been developing a new road map for the Darfur peace process. It became evident, however, that additional consultations were needed to develop a road map that enjoyed broad-based support. A retreat of special envoys was scheduled in El Geneina on 19 October for that purpose.

On 7 August, SLA-Abdul Wahid, SLA-Minni Minawi and the Sudanese People's Liberation Movement-North signed an alliance agreement in South Kordofan, calling for a State that accommodated the cultural, religious and ethnic diversity of the people of the Sudan. The movements also agreed to work towards unifying Sudanese political forces to overthrow the National Congress Party-led Government—a development that might cause a re-escalation of the conflict.

The security situation remained volatile, despite the decrease of direct clashes between government forces and armed movements. On 17 July, SAF conducted air operations in South Darfur, and UNAMID confirmed that 10 bombs had been dropped. Other clashes occurred in West Darfur; UNAMID, however, was unable to confirm casualties, owing to movement restrictions.

UNAMID continued to collaborate with specialized agencies in protecting civilians. Recorded protection incidents decreased from an average of 10 per day in

2010 to 6 per day since 1 January 2011. In addition, UNAMID worked with UNHCR to provide security and assistance to IDPs and returnees by patrolling IDP camps, returnee villages and humanitarian convoys delivering assistance to returnees. The relative stability of West Darfur contributed to the return of Sudanese refugees from Chad.

The Mission's personnel had drilled five additional water boreholes, bringing the number of wells completed since the deployment of UNAMID to 41. UNAMID located and destroyed over 434 unexploded ordnance items, assessed 54 kilometres of road and delivered risk-awareness training to 73,287 beneficiaries. In July, UNAMID assisted the Sudan Disarmament, Demobilization and Reintegration Commission in demobilizing 188 ex-combatants in North Darfur. At the eleventh meeting of the Tripartite Coordination Mechanism (New York, 24 September), participants welcomed efforts undertaken to address restrictions of movement in Darfur.

The Secretary-General urged the signatories of the Agreement on the Adoption of the Doha Document to implement the ceasefire and security arrangements, as well as all other aspects of the Agreement.

Report of Secretary-General (December). Pursuant to Council resolution 2003(2011), the Secretary-General on 30 December issued a report [S/2011/814] on UNAMID covering developments from 1 October to the end of December. The parties signatory to the Document for Peace in Darfur took a number of steps towards its implementation. On 22 October, the chair of LJM, Eltigani Seisi, travelled to the Sudan to consult with the Government and local stakeholders. In a statement issued on the same day, the Government indicated that Mr. Seisi's return to the Sudan marked the beginning of the implementation phase of the Doha Document.

On 23 October, Mr. Seisi was sworn in by the President of the Sudan as Chair of the Darfur Regional Authority, the body responsible for overseeing the implementation of the Doha Document. From 24 to 29 October, Mr. Seisi travelled to different locations in Darfur to meet with Government and local stakeholders. His interlocutors expressed mixed views about the readiness of the parties to implement the Document, noting, among other things, the absence of support for the Document by non-signatory movements.

Since 12 October, the Ceasefire Commission had met four times in El Fasher under the chairmanship of the UNAMID Force commander, during which the parties—the Government and LJM—submitted information on the disposition and locations of their forces and agreed to verification procedures. Verification had not begun, however, as LJM had not yet nominated its representatives for the ceasefire team. The verification exercise was a prerequisite for the provision of non-military logistical support; disarmament, demobilization and reintegration; and the integration of LJM combatants into the armed forces. The Government had submitted its information on the disposition of its forces to the Joint Chief Mediator on the day it signed the Document, but as at 13 October, LJM had not yet done so. The inaugural meeting of the Joint Commission, established under the Doha Document to monitor the implementation of the ceasefire arrangements and arbitrate on issues referred to it by the Ceasefire Commission, was held in Khartoum on 18 December. Participants received a briefing on the activities of the Ceasefire Commission, adopted rules of procedure and deliberated on outstanding issues, including the status of LJM fighters located outside the Sudan, LJM political prisoners and the verification of forces. The inauguration of the Darfur Regional Authority, which should have occurred within 30 days of the signing of the Doha Document, had not taken place. The Government informed UNAMID that the delay was due to the inability of LJM to agree on a structure for the body. UNAMID was providing advice to LJM on the organizational structure of the Authority.

The parties, in mid-October, began to disseminate information about the Doha Document to civil society groups. The AU-UN Joint Special Representative for Darfur and Joint Chief Mediator ad interim, Ibrahim Gambari, appointed in June, hosted a retreat for special envoys (El Geneina, 19–20 October) to promote a shared understanding of the situation in Darfur and the way ahead. Representatives of the AU Commission, the AU High-level Implementation Panel, Canada, China, the European Union, France, Germany, Japan, the Russian Federation, South Africa, Sweden, the United Kingdom and the United States attended the retreat. In the outcome statement, participants urged the signatories to the Doha Document to remain committed to its implementation and called on non-signatories to pursue a negotiated solution to the conflict.

The Joint Special Representative and Joint Chief Mediator ad interim encouraged the Government and non-signatory movements to resume negotiations. The Government expressed its willingness to do so only after the movements had renounced their call for a Government change "by all possible means," and only on the sections of the Doha Document related to political appointments and security arrangements. JEM was willing to resume negotiations provided that all aspects of the Document were open for discussion. In that connection, JEM had produced a "counter-draft" of the Document containing significant amendments. SLA-Minni Minawi and SLA-Abdul Wahid had rejected the use of the Document as the basis for negotiations. On 2 November, the JEM lead negotiator declared in Doha that he and other former JEM members had formed a breakaway faction and were ready to enter into talks with the Government using the Doha Document as the basis for negotiations. As at 19 December, the talks had not begun. On 11 November, the JEM-Khalil Ibrahim faction joined the Sudanese Revolutionary Front, established on 7 August by the Sudan People's Liberation Movement-North, SLA-Minni Minawi and SLA-Abdul Wahid. Two of the alliance's objectives were to overthrow the National Congress Party-led Government and establish a six-year transitional government. On 25 December, senior JEM-Khalil Ibrahim personnel confirmed to UNAMID that the movement's leader, Khalil Ibrahim, had been killed in a military engagement while moving from Northern Darfur to North Kordofan.

The situation regarding the enabling environment for a Darfur political process remained unchanged. UNAMID began to assess the views of Darfurian stakeholders on the role of internal dialogue in the peace process, which would be taken into account when developing a revised plan for internal dialogue. The Secretary-General intended to submit the road map for the Darfur peace process to the Security Council once consultations between the United Nations and the AU were finalized.

Incidents of fighting remained relatively few. The security situation for IDPs and vulnerable groups, however, as well as for humanitarian and UN personnel, remained of concern. In response to the tensions between farmers and pastoralists, UNAMID increased its engagement with the native administration and local government authorities, and provided support for reconciliation mechanisms. Between 1 October and 12 December, UNAMID carried out 19,644 military and police patrols, during which the Mission's movements by land were restricted on 31 occasions. Two attacks against UNAMID took place, on 10 October and 6 November, respectively, during which four peacekeepers were killed and many others were wounded. The Security Council condemned those attacks [SC/10407, SC/10439].

Regarding protection of civilians, UNAMID began to deploy civilian staff to team sites in rural areas. The staff would monitor and report on protection issues, provide expert assistance to military and police personnel and work with local authorities and humanitarian organizations.

As at 13 December, the size of UNAMID civilian personnel stood at 4,489, representing 85 per cent of the approved strength; military personnel stood at 17,906, representing 91.5 per cent of the authorized strength; and police personnel stood at 2,755, representing 73 per cent of the authorized strength. During the reporting period, UNAMID military personnel conducted 10,501 patrols and UNAMID police conducted 9,143 patrols. Since the Secretary-General's previous report, seven additional water boreholes had been drilled, bringing to 48 the number of wells completed since the deployment of UNAMID.

The Secretary-General observed that while some progress related to appointments and the Ceasefire Commission had been made, it was imperative to take concrete measures related to the needs of the people of Darfur. In that regard, he called on the signatory parties to the Agreement to establish the Darfur Regional Authority without delay. He called on non-signatory movements and the Government to recommit to discussing all issues at the negotiating table without preconditions. Further, he called on the Government to ensure that the human rights of the people of Darfur were protected. He expressed concern about the security of humanitarian and UNAMID personnel, expressed relief for the release of an aid worker kidnapped in Nyala on 14 August, and called for judicial accountability of those responsible of attacks on peacekeepers. UNAMID lost four of its personnel during the reporting period and 34 since the establishment of the Mission on 1 January 2008.

Activities of ICC Prosecutor

The Prosecutor of the International Criminal Court (ICC), Luis Moreno-Ocampo, reported to the Security Council in June and December on the activities undertaken by his Office with regard to Darfur.

Communications. On 12 April [S/2011/236], the Secretary-General conveyed to the Security Council a communication of 11 March from the ICC Registrar transmitting the "Decision on the Confirmation of Charges", issued by Pre-Trial Chamber I of the Court on 7 March in the case of *The Prosecutor v. Abdallah Banda Abakaer and Saleh Mohammed Jerbo Jamus*. The Chamber confirmed the charges of war crimes against the two JEM commanders and committed them to trial in relation to the killing of 12 peacekeepers of the AU Mission in the Sudan (AMIS) in Haskanita, South Darfur, in 2007 [YUN 2007, p. 255].

On 17 May [S/2011/318], the Secretary-General transmitted to the Council a notification of 12 May from the ICC Registrar informing the Council and the States parties to the Rome Statute [YUN 1998, p. 1209] about President Omar Al-Bashir's visit to Djibouti on 8 May, despite the ICC warrants of arrest against him and Djibouti's obligation, as a State party, to cooperate with the Court in relation to the enforcement of warrants of arrest.

Briefings by ICC Prosecutor. Briefing the Security Council on 8 June [S/PV.6548], the ICC Prosecutor said that rebel commanders Abdallah Banda and Saleh Jerbo had led 1,000 troops to carry out an attack against AMIS, in 2007, killing 12 peacekeepers, injuring eight, destroying that Mission's camp and looting vehicles, fuel and money. As a result, millions of civilians who were under the peacekeepers' protection were affected. On 7 March, the Pre-Trial Chamber confirmed the charges for war crimes against the two commanders. On 16 May, the prosecution and the defence jointly agreed that the defence would contest only three issues during the trial: whether the 2007 attack on the Haskanita base was unlawful; whether the accused were aware of the unlawful nature of the attack; and whether AMIS could be considered a peacekeeping mission in accordance with the UN Charter. As at 8 June, the dates of the hearing had not been scheduled.

The arrest warrants against President Al-Bashir documented a genocidal policy, implemented since 2003, against three ethnic groups: the Fur, Massalit and Zaghawa, who currently lived mainly in IDP or refugee camps. The Court documented that the crimes in Darfur were the consequence of a strategic decision undertaken by the highest authorities of the Sudan. The Prosecutor said that President Al-Bashir did not stop the commission of the genocide, and was blocking the dissemination of information about the fate of the displaced. He and his supporters denied the crimes and diverted attention by publicizing ceasefires that were violated as soon as they were announced. At the same time, he threatened the international community with retaliation—such as the expulsion of humanitarian organizations in March 2009—and turned public knowledge of his crimes into a negotiating tool, asking for rewards for not committing new genocides. The extermination of any tribe deemed disloyal to the regime was a policy calculated to ensure that the armed forces and associated militia would continue with the same modus operandi. It was the Council's responsibility to use the information exposed by ICC to stop the crimes in Darfur and protect the civilians there.

Briefing the Security Council on 15 December [S/PV.6688], the Prosecutor said that three investigations were conducted on the Darfur situation. In the first case, the Court investigated attacks by Sudanese forces against civilians from 2003 to 2005, which caused the displacement of 4 million people to a hostile environment. The evidence showed that SAF bombed villages in Darfur and surrounded them; ground troops then moved in to kill, rape and pillage civilians in their homes. It also showed the key role played by Ahmad Harun as the Government's coordinator of the Sudan forces, and by militia/Janjaweed leader Ali Kushayb as the ground commander of some of the attacks. In addition to the 2007 arrest warrants against both individuals for war crimes and crimes against humanity, a few days prior to the briefing, the Office of the Prosecutor had requested an additional warrant of arrest for Abdelrahim Mohamed Hussein, currently Minister of Defence. Mr. Hussein had played a central role in coordinating the crimes, including in recruiting, mobilizing and deploying the militia/Janjaweed as part of Government forces, with the knowledge that those forces would commit crimes.

In the second case, evidence showed the responsibility of President Al-Bashir in launching attacks against villages and instructing his forces to take no prisoners or wounded. The President denied assistance to entire groups forced out of their homes to inhospitable areas. He ordered a different type of attack against IDPs or refugees in camps through rape and hunger, and appointed Ahmad Harun Minister of State for Humanitarian Affairs to be in charge of the victims he had displaced. Mr. Harun obstructed humanitarian efforts. Two arrest warrants were issued against President Al-Bashir, in 2009 for war crimes and crimes against humanity, including the crimes of extermination and rape, and in 2010 for three counts of genocide. In 2009, after the issuance of the first warrant, to avoid isolation, President Al-Bashir campaigned at the AU and elsewhere for political support, which he finally attained from Libya, Malawi and Chad.

The third case was against the commanders of the rebel groups responsible for the attacks on AMIS in 2007. The trial was to start in 2012. The individuals involved in the three cases were identified as responsible for the most serious crimes committed in Darfur over the previous six years. The Court was evaluating the responsibility of Mr. Abu Garda, the leader of the 2007 rebel attack, against whom charges had not been confirmed.

Following the Prosecutor's statement, the Sudan replied that numerous statements made by UN officials, including from DPKO, refuted the Prosecutor's findings and stated that the ICC had no competence in the Sudan, as the country was not a party to the Rome Statute. The Prosecutor had ignored the most important historic event in Darfur, namely, the signing of the Doha Document.

Sanctions

The Security Council, by resolution 1556(2004) [YUN 2004, p. 240], imposed an arms embargo on all non-governmental entities and individuals, including the Janjaweed militias, operating in Darfur, in response to the human rights abuses and deteriorating humanitarian situation in the region. By resolution 1591(2005) [YUN 2005, p. 319], the Council imposed a travel ban and assets freeze, and established a Committee to oversee implementation of the sanctions against individuals to be designated by that Committee. As requested in that resolution, the Secretary-General in 2005 established a Panel of Experts [ibid., p. 322], which was mandated to assist the Committee in monitoring implementation of the arms embargo and sanctions; make recommendations to the

Committee on possible Council action; and provide information on individuals who impeded the peace process, committed violations of international law, or were responsible for offensive military overflight. By resolution 1945(2010) [YUN 2010, p. 270], the Council strengthened the arms embargo and clarified the exceptions to that measure.

Communications. From April through July, Japan [S/AC.47/2011/1], the United States [S/AC.47/2011/2] and Colombia [S/AC.47/2011/3], respectively, submitted to the Security Council Committee established pursuant to resolution 1591(2005) their reports on the implementation of sanctions imposed by Council resolutions 1556(2004), 1591(2005) and 1945(2010).

Appointments. By letters of 19 January [S/2011/27], 7 February [S/2011/60] and 24 February [S/2011/96] to the Security Council, the Secretary-General appointed five new specialists—dealing with aviation, international humanitarian law, finance, regional issues and arms—to serve on the Panel of Experts. Following the resignation of four of the experts and the expiration of contract of the fifth, the Secretary-General, by letters of 3 October [S/2011/613, S/2011/614] and 24 October [S/2011/658], informed the Council that he had appointed five new experts.

Report of Panel of Experts. In response to resolution 1891(2009) [YUN 2009, p. 263], the Chairman of the Security Council Committee, on 8 March, transmitted to the Council the final report [S/2011/111], dated 20 September 2010, of the Panel of Experts.

According to the report, the security situation in Darfur remained precarious, despite claims by the Government of improvements over previous years. Armed clashes took place between Government and rebel forces, as well as between and within rebel groups, resulting in the death and displacement of thousands of civilians. Insecurity was further aggravated by armed violence committed by non-governmental actors. The arms embargo, which was intended to limit the ability of belligerents to engage in armed violence, remained without any discernible impact; ammunition, in particular, continued to enter Darfur. Ammunition transferred to Darfur after the embargo was imposed in 2005 had reached various belligerents and non-belligerents responsible for the insecurity in Darfur. The Government categorically rejected the notion that it had violated the arms embargo, even though it confirmed having repatriated armed personnel to Darfur since 2005 and having transferred 12,000 armed police personnel to Darfur in recent years. The Government also reaffirmed that, in its understanding, the arms embargo only pertained to military materiel transferred to SAF in Darfur for the purpose of engaging armed rebel groups. It excluded the supply of arms and ammunition to other Government actors, such as the Central Reserve Police, from the scope of the embargo. According to the Government, military aviation assets used for purposes other than engaging rebel groups in Darfur were also exempt from the embargo. The Government thereby justified the temporary presence of a new type of fighter jet in Darfur. Furthermore, the Government did not deny the bombing of rebel positions in the first half of 2010, but it rejected, as anti-Government propaganda, reports of killings of civilians.

The Panel of Experts could not document any concrete action by the Government to implement the travel and financial sanctions imposed by the Security Council on four individuals. Rather, the Government disagreed with the designation of two of them, who, it argued, were unjustly subjected to the measures.

SECURITY COUNCIL ACTION

On 17 May [meeting 6537], the Security Council unanimously adopted **resolution 1982(2011)**. The draft [S/2011/305] was submitted by the United States.

The Security Council,

Recalling its previous resolutions and the statements by its President concerning the Sudan,

Recalling also the interim report of 30 March 2011 of the Panel of Experts on the Sudan appointed by the Secretary-General pursuant to paragraph 3 (*b*) of resolution 1591(2005) of 29 March 2005, whose mandate was extended by subsequent resolutions,

Determining that the situation in the Sudan continues to constitute a threat to international peace and security in the region,

Acting under Chapter VII of the Charter of the United Nations,

1. *Reaffirms* the importance of the measures set out in previous resolutions, including resolution 1945(2010) of 14 October 2010;

2. *Decides* to extend until 19 February 2012 the mandate of the Panel of Experts on the Sudan originally appointed pursuant to resolution 1591(2005), previously extended by resolutions 1651(2005) of 21 December 2005, 1665(2006) of 29 March 2006, 1713(2006) of 29 September 2006, 1779(2007) of 28 September 2007, 1841(2008) of 15 October 2008, 1891(2009) of 13 October 2009 and 1945(2010), and requests the Secretary-General to take the necessary administrative measures as expeditiously as possible;

3. *Requests* the Panel of Experts to provide a final report no later than thirty days prior to the termination of its mandate to the Security Council, with findings and recommendations;

4. *Decides* to remain actively seized of the matter.

Security Council Committee. The Chairman of the Committee transmitted to the Council a report summarizing the Committee's activities in 2011 [S/2012/18]. The Committee held five informal consultations: on 23 February, 11 April, 28 June, 22 July and 10 November. The Committee received three reports of Member States on actions taken to implement measures imposed by resolutions 1591(2005) and 1556(2004). In January, it received a proposal for designating an individual as subject to the travel ban and assets freeze; the proposal was on technical hold.

During its April consultations, the Committee heard a presentation by the Panel of Experts through videoconference from Addis Ababa of its interim report. The presentation focused on how the delay in access to the Sudan due to a lack of visas was affecting the Panel's work. During its consultations in June, the Committee heard a midterm briefing by the Panel. The Panel had spent nearly seven weeks in the Sudan since its arrival there on 2 May and had determined that some of the ammunition cartridges observed during its field visits appeared to have been manufactured after the imposition of the arms embargo, thereby indicating violations of that sanction. The Panel reported that the Sudan had not implemented the assets freeze in relation to the four designated individuals. During its July consultations, the Committee met with the AU-UN Joint Special Representative for Darfur, Ibrahim Gambari, who briefed the Committee on, among other topics, the logistical support provided by UNAMID to the Panel. It stressed the importance of providing adequate resources to the Mission in order to enhance its arms embargo monitoring capacity. On 9 August, the Panel of Experts reported that they had been granted visas relatively quickly but remained grounded in Khartoum owing to the lack of permits to enter Darfur. The permits were issued almost one month later. In its consultations in November, the Committee met with a newly reconstituted Panel via videoconference from Addis Ababa. Committee members highlighted the areas on which the Panel should focus, and were informed that for its third trip to the Sudan, the Panel members were granted visas and permits to enter Darfur.

During the reporting period, the Committee transmitted to the Security Council four reports, each covering a 90-day period and describing the Committee's activities since the Chairman's latest briefing to the Council. The Committee had not received any requests either to remove the names of individuals on the consolidated list of persons subject to the travel ban and assets freeze or to grant exemptions to the targeted sanctions.

Children and armed conflict

The Secretary-General's fourth report [S/2011/413] on children and armed conflict in the Sudan, covering the period from January 2009 to February 2011, showed the continued presence of children in several armed groups in Darfur. Of particular concern were the killing and maiming of children, and sexual violence against children. The report emphasized the priority of combating impunity for all grave violations and outlined response efforts undertaken by national and international actors to address those violations. Reporting on violations was hampered by insecurity and lack of access to non-government-controlled areas, as well as by government restrictions. During the reporting period, 501 children, including 6 girls, were verified as being associated with at least 10 armed forces and armed groups in Darfur. The decrease might be due in part to advocacy with the armed forces and groups to raise awareness, resulting in commitments to end the recruitment and use of child soldiers. Since 2009, armed groups registered more than 1,000 children for reintegration with the Northern Sudan Disarmament, Demobilization and Reintegration Commission. Cases of the re-recruitment of children were also reported. From February 2009 to February 2011, the North Sudan DDR Commission, with the support of the United Nations, registered 1,041 former child soldiers in Darfur. A verification exercise resulted in the removal of 97 individuals from that list in Western Darfur, and confirmed 860 children as eligible for reintegration programmes. In January 2011, SLA-Free Will and SLA-Abu Gasim jointly presented a list of 84 children in Northern Darfur to the Commission as part of the implementation of their action plans to end the recruitment and use of children in armed conflict.

During the reporting period, 27 children were killed and 36 others maimed in Darfur. The exact number of child casualties resulting from Government aerial attacks, ground fighting between armed groups or ethnic clashes, however, was unknown. Most cases were attributed to pro-Government militias and Government forces, but actual responsibility was difficult to establish.

Twelve children were killed and 26 were maimed in incidents related to mine and unexploded ordnance in 2009, while in 2010, 6 children were killed and 14 were maimed. All victims were boys. During the reporting period, the United Nations received 52 allegations of sexual violence, of which 49 were verified and reported to the Sudanese police. The UN country task force for the monitoring and reporting of grave violations against children met on different occasions with Government and armed forces officials to discuss the preparation of an action plan to end the associations of children with the armed forces. A child rights unit was established within the armed forces to train officers on international standards relating to child rights and child protection. In March 2009, following an agreement between the North Sudan Disarmament, Demobilization and Reintegration Commission and the Transitional Darfur Regional Authority on an operational plan for DDR of children in Darfur, the six armed groups that had signed the Darfur Peace Agreement submitted the names of nearly 2,000 children for participation in the Darfur reintegration programme. UNAMID police created a special unit on rape to strengthen responses to sexual violence in Darfur.

UNAMID

The African Union-United Nations Hybrid Operation in Darfur was established in 2007 by Council resolution 1769(2007) [YUN 2007, p. 251] as the first AU-UN hybrid peacekeeping mission, replacing the AU Mission in the Sudan (AMIS). Its core mandate was the protection of civilians. Other tasks included contributing to security for humanitarian assistance, monitoring and verifying implementation of agreements, assisting the political process, promoting human rights and the rule of law, and monitoring and reporting on the situation along the borders with Chad and the Central African Republic.

By resolution 2003(2011) of 29 July (see p. 220), the Security Council extended the mandate of UNAMID to 31 July 2012.

As at 13 December, the strength of UNAMID military personnel stood at 17,906, representing 91.5 per cent of the authorized strength of 19,555; the Mission's civilian staff stood at 4,489, representing 85 per cent of the approved strength of 5,285; and UNAMID police stood at 2,755, representing 73 per cent of the authorized strength of 3,772.

Financing

In his performance report on the UNAMID budget for the period from 1 July 2009 to 30 June 2010 [A/65/631], the Secretary-General reported an expenditure of $1,547,855,300 gross ($1,520,571,300 net) against an apportionment of $1,598,942,200 gross ($1,573,881,900 net). The Secretary-General recommended that the General Assembly decide on the treatment of the unencumbered balance of $51,086,900 and of other income/adjustments amounting to $124,887,200 from interest income ($13,046,900), other/miscellaneous income ($6,282,900), and cancellation of prior-period obligations ($105,557,400). In April [A/65/743/Add.13], ACABQ recommended that the unencumbered balance, as well as other income/adjustments, be credited to Member States.

In February, the Secretary-General submitted budget proposals for the period from 1 July 2011 to 30 June 2012 [A/65/740], amounting to $1,708,748,400 gross (1,680,586,600 net). The budget provided for the deployment of 260 military observers, 19,295 military contingent personnel, 3,772 UN police officers, 2,660 formed police unit personnel, 1,289 international staff, 3,381 national staff, 616 UN Volunteers and 6 Government-provided personnel. In April [A/65/743/Add.13], ACABQ recommended a reduction of $14,141,400, which would bring the amount to $1,694,607,000.

GENERAL ASSEMBLY ACTION

On 30 June [meeting 106], the General Assembly, on the recommendation of the Fifth Committee [A/65/888], adopted **resolution 65/305** without vote [agenda item 159].

Financing of the African Union-United Nations Hybrid Operation in Darfur

The General Assembly,

Having considered the reports of the Secretary-General on the financing of the African Union-United Nations Hybrid Operation in Darfur and the related report of the Advisory Committee on Administrative and Budgetary Questions,

Recalling Security Council resolution 1769(2007) of 31 July 2007, by which the Council established the African Union-United Nations Hybrid Operation in Darfur for an initial period of twelve months from 31 July 2007, and the subsequent resolutions by which the Council extended the mandate of the Operation, the latest of which was resolution 1935(2010) of 30 July 2010, by which the Council extended the mandate of the Operation until 31 July 2011,

Recalling also its resolution 62/232 A of 22 December 2007 on the financing of the Operation and its subsequent resolutions thereon, the latest of which was resolution 64/285 of 24 June 2010,

Reaffirming the general principles underlying the financing of United Nations peacekeeping operations, as stated in its resolutions 1874(S-IV) of 27 June 1963, 3101(XXVIII) of 11 December 1973 and 55/235 of 23 December 2000,

Mindful of the fact that it is essential to provide the Operation with the necessary financial resources to enable it to fulfil its responsibilities under the relevant resolutions of the Security Council,

Noting the hybrid nature of the Operation, and in that regard stressing the importance of ensuring full coordination of efforts between the African Union and the United Nations at the strategic level, unity of command at the operational level and clear delegation of authority and accountability lines,

1. *Requests* the Secretary-General to entrust the Head of Mission with the task of formulating future budget proposals in full accordance with the provisions of General Assembly resolutions 59/296 of 22 June 2005, 60/266 of 30 June 2006, 61/276 of 29 June 2007, 64/269 of 24 June 2010 and 65/289 of 30 June 2011, as well as other relevant resolutions;

2. *Takes note* of the status of contributions to the African Union-United Nations Hybrid Operation in Darfur as at 30 April 2011, including the contributions outstanding in the amount of 262.5 million United States dollars, representing some 4 per cent of the total assessed contributions, notes with concern that only seventy-nine Member States have paid their assessed contributions in full, and urges all other Member States, in particular those in arrears, to ensure payment of their outstanding assessed contributions;

3. *Expresses its appreciation* to those Member States which have paid their assessed contributions in full, and urges all other Member States to make every possible effort to ensure payment of their assessed contributions to the Operation in full;

4. *Expresses concern* at the financial situation with regard to peacekeeping activities, in particular as regards the reimbursements to troop contributors that bear additional burdens owing to overdue payments by Member States of their assessments;

5. *Also expresses concern* at the delay experienced by the Secretary-General in deploying and providing adequate resources to some recent peacekeeping missions, in particular those in Africa;

6. *Emphasizes* that all future and existing peacekeeping missions shall be given equal and non-discriminatory treatment in respect of financial and administrative arrangements;

7. *Also emphasizes* that all peacekeeping missions shall be provided with adequate resources for the effective and efficient discharge of their respective mandates;

8. *Requests* the Secretary-General to ensure that proposed peacekeeping budgets are based on the relevant legislative mandates;

9. *Endorses* the conclusions and recommendations contained in the report of the Advisory Committee on Administrative and Budgetary Questions, subject to the provisions of the present resolution, and requests the Secretary-General to ensure their full implementation;

10. *Requests* the Secretary-General to take steps to ensure that all personnel adhere fully to the security procedures in place;

11. *Reaffirms* section XX of resolution 61/276, and encourages the Secretary-General, where feasible, to enhance regional and inter-mission cooperation with a view to achieving greater synergies in the use of the resources of the Organization and the implementation of the mandates of the missions, while bearing in mind that individual missions are responsible for the preparation and implementation of their own budgets and for controlling their own assets and logistical operations;

12. *Requests* the Secretary-General to ensure the full implementation of the relevant provisions of resolutions 59/296, 60/266, 61/276, 64/269 and 65/289;

13. *Also requests* the Secretary-General to take all action necessary to ensure that the Operation is administered with a maximum of efficiency and economy;

14. *Further requests* the Secretary-General to ensure that future budget submissions contain sufficient information, explanation and justification of the proposed resource requirements relating to operational costs in order to allow Member States to take well-informed decisions;

15. *Stresses* the importance of strengthened accountability in the Organization and of ensuring greater accountability of the Secretary-General to Member States, inter alia, for the effective and efficient implementation of legislative mandates on procurement and the related use of financial and human resources, as well as the provision of necessary information on procurement-related matters to enable Member States to make well-informed decisions;

16. *Requests* the Secretary-General to ensure that all procurement projects for the Organization are in full compliance with relevant resolutions;

17. *Decides* not to abolish the child protection posts, requests the Secretary-General to make every effort to fill them, and also requests the Secretary-General to identify an equivalent number of posts at the same level that have been vacant for more than one year to offset the financial impact of retaining the child protection posts, without affecting operational requirements or mandate implementation, and to report thereon in the context of the performance report;

18. *Notes* that the overall level of appropriation has been adjusted in accordance with the terms of resolution 65/289;

Financial performance report for the period from 1 July 2009 to 30 June 2010

19. *Takes note* of the report of the Secretary-General on the financial performance of the Operation for the period from 1 July 2009 to 30 June 2010;

Budget estimates for the period from 1 July 2011 to 30 June 2012

20. *Decides* to appropriate to the Special Account for the African Union-United Nations Hybrid Operation in Darfur the amount of 1,797,327,600 dollars for the period from 1 July 2011 to 30 June 2012, inclusive of 1,689,305,500 dollars for the maintenance of the Operation, 91,536,100 dollars for the support account for peacekeeping operations and 16,486,000 dollars for the United Nations Logistics Base at Brindisi, Italy;

Financing of the appropriation

21. *Also decides* to apportion among Member States the amount of 149,777,300 dollars for the period from 1 to 31 July 2011, in accordance with the levels updated in General Assembly resolution 64/249 of 24 December 2009, and taking into account the scale of assessments for 2011, as set out in Assembly resolution 64/248 of 24 December 2009;

22. *Further decides* that, in accordance with the provisions of its resolution 973(X) of 15 December 1955, there shall be set off against the apportionment among Member States, as provided for in paragraph 21 above, their respective share in the Tax Equalization Fund of 3,137,200 dollars, comprising the estimated staff assessment income of 2,346,816 dollars approved for the Operation, the prorated share of 646,050 dollars of the estimated staff assessment income approved for the support account and the prorated share of 144,334 dollars of the estimated staff assessment income approved for the United Nations Logistics Base;

23. *Decides* to apportion among Member States the amount of 1,647,550,300 dollars for the period from 1 August 2011 to 30 June 2012, at a monthly rate of 149,777,300 dollars, in accordance with the levels updated in resolution 64/249, and taking into account the scale of assessments for 2011 and 2012, as set out in resolution 64/248, subject to a decision of the Security Council to extend the mandate of the Operation;

24. *Also decides* that, in accordance with the provisions of resolution 973(X), there shall be set off against the apportionment among Member States, as provided for in paragraph 23 above, their respective share in the Tax Equalization Fund of 34,509,200 dollars, comprising the estimated staff assessment income of 25,814,984 dollars approved for the Operation, the prorated share of 7,106,550 dollars of the estimated staff assessment income approved for the support account and the prorated share of 1,587,666 dollars of the estimated staff assessment income approved for the United Nations Logistics Base;

25. *Further decides* that, for Member States that have fulfilled their financial obligations to the Operation, there

shall be set off against their apportionment, as provided for in paragraph 21 above, their respective share of the unencumbered balance and other income in the total amount of 175,974,100 dollars in respect of the financial period ended 30 June 2010, in accordance with the levels updated in resolution 64/249, and taking into account the scale of assessments for 2010, as set out in resolution 64/248;

26. *Decides* that, for Member States that have not fulfilled their financial obligations to the Operation, there shall be set off against their outstanding obligations their respective share of the unencumbered balance and other income in the total amount of 175,974,100 dollars in respect of the financial period ended 30 June 2010, in accordance with the scheme set out in paragraph 25 above;

27. *Also decides* that the increase of 2,223,700 dollars in the estimated staff assessment income in respect of the financial period ended 30 June 2010 shall be added to the credits from the amount of 175,974,100 dollars referred to in paragraphs 25 and 26 above;

28. *Emphasizes* that no peacekeeping mission shall be financed by borrowing funds from other active peacekeeping missions;

29. *Encourages* the Secretary-General to continue to take additional measures to ensure the safety and security of all personnel participating in the Operation under the auspices of the United Nations, bearing in mind paragraphs 5 and 6 of Security Council resolution 1502(2003) of 26 August 2003;

30. *Invites* voluntary contributions to the Operation in cash and in the form of services and supplies acceptable to the Secretary-General, to be administered, as appropriate, in accordance with the procedure and practices established by the General Assembly;

31. *Decides* to include in the provisional agenda of its sixty-sixth session the item entitled "Financing of the African Union-United Nations Hybrid Operation in Darfur".

On 24 December, by **decision 66/557**, the General Assembly decided that the agenda item on the financing of unamid would remain for consideration during its resumed sixty-sixth (2012) session.

Chad–Sudan

In 2011, relations between the Sudan and Chad were cordial, contributing to the security and stability in the region, particularly in Western Darfur. The two countries continued to cooperate through a joint border security force [YUN 2010, p. 275], which had been deployed since April 2010 and had increased to 5,000 personnel. On 16 March, both Governments extended the mandate of the joint force until September. On 5 May, the headquarters of the Chad-Sudan Joint Border Patrol Force was transferred from Abéché, Chad, to El Geneina, West Darfur, the Sudan, as provided for in the Dakar Agreement [YUN 2008, p. 268]. On 23 May, a tripartite summit in Khartoum involving the Sudan, Chad and the Central African Republic (car) led to the signing of the Khartoum Declaration, under which the parties committed to establishing a triple joint force to monitor their borders.

Pursuant to Security Council presidential statement S/PRST/2010/29 [YUN 2010, p. 168], the Secretary-General submitted an April report [S/2011/278] on the protection of civilians in Chad following the withdrawal of the United Nations Mission in the Central African Republic and Chad (minurcat) on 31 December 2010 [YUN 2010, p. 169]. The report, covering the period from 1 December 2010 to 30 April 2011, assessed the steps that Chad, the United Nations and the humanitarian community had taken to address protection concerns.

Regarding security, the majority of combatants—an estimated 16,000—from Chadian opposition armed groups had returned to Chad from neighbouring countries. No armed clashes took place between those returnees and the Chadian security forces, despite the fact that the former had not demobilized. Remnants of Chadian opposition armed groups, however, remained present outside Chadian territory, in the Sudan and in the north-east of the car. The withdrawal of minurcat did not adversely affect the security situation in eastern Chad. Patrols and escorts by the Détachement intégré de sécurité (dis) [YUN 2008, p. 159] and the deployment of the joint border force improved security in the area. Dis took charge of security in and around refugee and idp camps and of humanitarian operations, while the joint border force secured the border area. A number of the root causes of conflict in Chad, however, such as competition over scarce resources, poor governance and insufficient respect for human rights remained, and the population continued to face the threat of violence.

On the political front, on 11 January, Chad celebrated its fiftieth year of independence. Animosity among the main political factions had declined and most political parties participated in the legislative elections of 13 February, in accordance with the political agreement signed on 13 August 2007 [YUN 2007, p. 155]. The elections were carried out peacefully and the Constitutional Council published the final results, according to which 113 seats out of 188 were won by the ruling party, the Mouvement patriotique du salut. The Constitutional Council, however, subsequently annulled the results of the vote in three districts, representing 13 seats, after finding serious irregularities.

Despite the improvement in the security situation, humanitarian needs remained immense: 2.5 million people required humanitarian assistance and 131,000 people were internally displaced. The population faced daily threats of banditry carried out by armed actors. With the departure of minurcat, the capacity of the United Nations to monitor and report attacks against civilians was severely reduced.

On 28 January, in N'Djamena, Chad and the Sudan signed a memorandum of understanding on cooperation in relation to Sudanese refugees, which set out a framework for repatriation. In January, the programme for resettling Sudanese refugees from Chad to third countries was temporarily suspended, due to the Sudan's concern that the programme might have a negative impact on the prospect of refugees returning to the Sudan.

In resolution 1923(2010) [YUN 2010, p. 159], the Security Council had taken note of the commitment of Chad, in view of the withdrawal of MINURCAT, to assume full responsibility for the security and protection of the population in eastern Chad and, in so doing, to achieve specific benchmarks related to the protection of civilians. Chad made progress in meeting those benchmarks, namely, the voluntary return and resettlement in secure conditions of IDPs, the demilitarization of refugee and IDP camps, and improved security for refugees, IDPs, civilians and humanitarian workers. The Secretary-General noted that the benchmarks should remain the measure by which progress on the protection of civilians was assessed.

Children and armed conflict

Report of Secretary-General. In February, the Secretary-General submitted his third report [S/2011/64] on the situation of children and armed conflict in Chad, covering the period from July 2008 to December 2010. The report concluded that recruitment and use of children by armed forces and groups was an ongoing phenomenon. It also noted, however, a large number of cases of children who returned or were released from various armed groups. Children continued to be targets of sexual and gender-based violence, and there remained a considerable danger of mines and other explosive remnants of war. The United Nations and other humanitarian organizations sought to address violations against children, and the Government made efforts to address the issue of recruitment and use of children. Those efforts culminated in a regional conference (N'Djamena, 7–9 June 2010) to end the recruitment and use of children. The conference brought together representatives of Cameroon, the Central African Republic, Chad, Niger, Nigeria and the Sudan. Chad hosted the first meeting (N'Djamena, 2–3 August 2010) of the monitoring committee to follow up on the N'Djamena Declaration, which was adopted at the conference. The Central African Republic hosted the second meeting (Bangui, 26–27 October 2010). The report contained recommendations aimed at securing strengthened action for the protection of children in Chad.

Working Group. The Security Council Working Group on Children and Armed Conflict examined the Secretary-General's report at its twenty-ninth meeting on 25 February [S/AC.51/2011/4]. The Chair of the Working Group, in a statement, urged all parties to the conflict, including those armed groups not engaged in the peace process, to halt the recruitment and use of children and to release all children remaining within their ranks.

Somalia

In 2011, the peace process in Somalia was at a critical juncture. At the beginning of the year, the Transitional Federal Government and its allies, with the support of the African Union Mission in Somalia (AMISOM), launched a major offensive in the capital, Mogadishu, and in areas of southern and central Somalia, gaining ground against the Islamist militant organization Al-Shabaab. An offensive by Ahlu Sunnah Wal Jama'a and other groups allied with the Government against Al-Shabaab focused on the Ethiopia-Kenya-Somalia border. Al-Shabaab continued to receive arms and ammunition through southern Somali ports and acquired financial resources from extortion, illegal exports and taxation. In February, it carried out two attacks in Mogadishu, which resulted in several casualties, including civilians. The Security Council in March reaffirmed its support for the Djibouti Agreement as the basis for the resolution of the conflict and urged the transitional federal institutions to broaden and consolidate the reconciliation process, complete the outstanding transitional tasks and prioritize the completion of the constitution and the delivery of basic services to the population. On 9 June, the President, Sheikh Sharif Sheikh Ahmed, and the Speaker of the Transitional Federal Parliament, Sharif Hassan Sheikh Adan, ended a political stalemate between the executive and the legislature by signing the Kampala Accord, which deferred elections for one year and provided for the establishment of a road map on ending the transition. The road map was adopted on 6 September in Mogadishu at a Consultative Meeting on Ending the Transition in Somalia, facilitated by the United Nations Political Office for Somalia (UNPOS) and attended by high-level representatives of the Transitional Federal Institutions, the regional states of Puntland, Galmudug and Ahlu Sunna Wal Jama'a, and most international partners. The document set out priority tasks to be completed by 20 August 2012 in the areas of security, constitutional reform and elections, outreach and reconciliation, and good governance.

The humanitarian situation worsened during the year: the drought left over 2 million Somalis in need of humanitarian assistance and resulted in higher flows of refugees to neighbouring countries. Pirate attacks off the coast of Somalia remained a challenge.

Political and security developments

Security Council consideration (January). On 14 January [S/PV.6467], the Council received briefings by the Secretary-General's Special Representative for Somalia, Augustine Mahiga, and the Prime Minister of Somalia, Mohamed Abdullahi Mohamed. The Special Representative stressed the importance of a stable Government and the need for cutting off supply channels for extremist groups.

Security Council consideration (March). On 10 March [S/PV.6494], the Security Council held an open debate on a comprehensive strategy for realizing peace and security in Somalia. It had before it a concept note submitted by China [S/2011/114]. Addressing the Council, the Secretary-General noted that the military gains of the Transitional Federal Government and AMISOM were fragile and violence continued to rage. In recent fighting, AMISOM peacekeepers from Burundi and Uganda had lost their lives, as had numerous civilians. AMISOM would be more effective if it had more resources, including helicopters and support for intelligence, surveillance and reconnaissance. The Secretary-General encouraged States to support the Mission so that it might reach its full authorized strength of 12,000. That would allow the Government to increase the space under its control, foster links between the Government and its citizens, and promote dialogue and reconciliation. It would also make it possible for the United Nations to expand its presence in Somalia. Prime Minister Mohamed said that his Government had been promoting good governance through accountability and transparency in financial management. He emphasized the need to deploy the additional 4,000 AU troops approved by the Council in resolution 1964(2010) [YUN 2010, p. 282].

SECURITY COUNCIL ACTION

On 10 March [meeting 6494], following consultations among Security Council members, the President made statement **S/PRST/2011/6** on behalf of the Council:

> The Security Council stresses the need for a comprehensive strategy to encourage the establishment of peace and stability in Somalia through the collaborative efforts of all stakeholders in the fields of the political process, security sector-building, humanitarian relief, protection of civilians, human rights, socio-economic development, counter-terrorism and combating piracy. The Council reiterates its grave concern at the continued instability in Somalia which has led to a multitude of problems, including terrorism, acts of piracy and armed robbery at sea off the coast of Somalia and a dire humanitarian situation.
>
> The Council reaffirms its support for the Djibouti Agreement as the basis for the resolution of the conflict in Somalia. It urges the transitional federal institutions to broaden and consolidate the reconciliation process, intensify efforts to complete the outstanding transitional tasks and prioritize the timely completion of the constitution and the delivery of basic services to the population, paving the ground for a better future for Somalis, including their economic and social development and the realization of their human rights.
>
> The Council welcomes the work of Mr. Augustine P. Mahiga, Special Representative of the Secretary-General for Somalia, to support the Somali people in reaching agreement on post-transitional arrangements in consultation with the international community. It strongly urges the transitional federal institutions to engage in this process in a more constructive, open and transparent manner that promotes broader political dialogue and participation in line with the spirit of the Djibouti Agreement. The Council requests the Secretary-General to assess, in his regular reports delivered to the Council before the end of the transitional period, the respect for these principles. These principles are essential for future cooperation between the international community and the transitional federal institutions. The Council notes that the transitional period will end in August 2011. The Council regrets the decision by the Transitional Federal Parliament to extend its mandate unilaterally and without carrying out necessary reforms and urges the transitional federal institutions to refrain from any further unilateral action.
>
> The Council expresses its strong support for the work of the Special Representative, Mr. Mahiga, welcomes his efforts and those of the United Nations, and calls for an increased United Nations presence and increased coherence of United Nations activities in Somalia.
>
> The Council affirms the importance of the development of government institutions and the strengthening of civilian capacity-building across Somalia, including ensuring the participation of women in public life, the prevention and resolution of conflict, peacebuilding and socio-economic reconstruction. The Council urges the international community to mobilize additional support to the Transitional Federal Government, and local and regional administrations in this regard.
>
> The Council expresses its serious concern about the worsening humanitarian situation in Somalia and the impact of the current drought, which have left over 2 million Somalis in urgent need of humanitarian assistance and have resulted in significantly higher flows of refugees to neighbouring countries. The Council also expresses its concern at the continuing decline in humanitarian funding for Somalia. The Council commends the work of humanitarian aid workers and urges all Member States to contribute to current and future consolidated humanitarian appeals.
>
> The Council strongly condemns the targeting and obstruction of the delivery of humanitarian aid by Al-Shabaab and other armed groups in Somalia and demands that all parties ensure full, safe and unhindered access for the timely delivery of humanitarian aid.
>
> The Council emphasizes the importance of strengthening the Somali security forces, including the development of effective command and control. While emphasizing that the Somalis hold the primary responsibility for achieving political stability, security and the rule of law, the Council urges Member States and regional and international organizations to contribute generously and promptly to the United Nations trust fund for the Somali security institutions and to provide assistance to the Somali security forces.

The Council recognizes the progress made by the African Union Mission in Somalia and the Somali National Security Forces in consolidating security and stability in Mogadishu. The Council deeply regrets the loss of life in the recent fighting and recognizes the significant sacrifices made by the Mission and the Somali National Security Forces. The Council expresses its sincere gratitude to the Governments of Burundi and Uganda for their commitment to the Mission, and expresses its condolences to them and to the Transitional Federal Government and the Somali people.

The Council condemns all attacks, including terrorist attacks on the Transitional Federal Government, the African Union Mission in Somalia and the civilian population by armed opposition groups and foreign fighters, particularly Al-Shabaab.

The Council stresses the importance of predictable, reliable and timely resources for the African Union Mission in Somalia in order for it to better fulfil its mandate. The Council calls upon the international community to make contributions urgently and without caveats to the United Nations trust fund for the Mission or directly in support of the Mission. It notes the recommendations on Somalia made by the Peace and Security Council of the African Union on 15 October 2010 and underlines its intention to keep the situation under review. It encourages the full deployment of 4,000 additional Mission troops as authorized by the Security Council in its resolution 1964(2010) as soon as possible.

The Security Council stresses the responsibility of all parties and armed groups in Somalia to comply with their obligations to protect the civilian population from the effects of hostilities, in particular by avoiding any indiscriminate or excessive use of force. The Council expresses deep concern about the continuing violations and abuses committed against children in Somalia by parties to the conflict and urges the immediate implementation of all conclusions of its Working Group on Children and Armed Conflict on Somalia.

The Council remains gravely concerned about the threat posed by piracy and armed robbery off the coast of Somalia, especially by the extended range of the piracy threat into the western Indian Ocean, the increase in pirate capacities and the increasing violence employed by the pirates. The Council condemns in the strongest terms such violence, including hostage-taking, murder and other acts of violence against individuals. The Council recognizes that the ongoing instability in Somalia contributes to the problem of piracy and armed robbery and stresses the need for a comprehensive response to tackle piracy and its underlying causes.

The Council calls upon all Member States, in particular those in the region, to refrain from any action in contravention of the Somalia and Eritrea arms embargoes and to take all necessary steps to hold violators accountable, and affirms the importance of enhancing the monitoring of the Somalia and Eritrea arms embargoes through persistent and vigilant investigation into the violations, bearing in mind that strict enforcement of the arms embargos will improve the overall security situation in the region.

The Council welcomes the endeavours of the African Union, the Intergovernmental Authority on Development and other regional organizations to promote peace and stability in Somalia and reiterates its full support to the African Union Mission in Somalia and its troop- and police-contributing countries, especially Burundi and Uganda

Report of Secretary-General (April). Pursuant to Security Council presidential statements S/PRST/2001/30 [YUN 2001, p. 210] and S/PRST/2011/6 and various Council resolutions, the Secretary-General, in April [S/2011/277], reported on major developments in Somalia since his December 2010 report [YUN 2010, p. 285].

At the beginning of 2011, the Transitional Federal Government and its allies, with the support of AMISOM, launched a major offensive in Mogadishu and areas of southern and central Somalia, gaining ground against Al-Shabaab. The offensive by Ahlu Sunnah Wal Jama'a and other groups allied with the Government against Al-Shabaab focused on the Ethiopia-Kenya-Somalia border. Al-Shabaab continued to receive arms and ammunition through southern Somali ports and acquired financial resources from extortion, illegal exports and taxation. In February, it carried out two attacks resulting in several casualties, including civilians.

On the political front, the Government in January set out a ministerial action plan and a work programme for the first 100 days of its term. As recommended on 30 January by the Assembly of Heads of State of the Intergovernmental Authority on Development (IGAD), the Transitional Federal Parliament on 4 February extended its term for three years. In March, the Council of Ministers announced its intention to extend itself until August 2012. The Parliament's decision prompted a negative reaction from various parts, as it was considered unilateral.

On 20 January, the Joint Security Committee [YUN 2008, p. 281], established by the Djibouti Agreement, met in Djibouti and agreed on priorities for security sector development during the transitional period. The Committee recommended a revision of the National Security and Stabilization Plan, which was to be adopted six months later. At a high-level meeting on Somalia (Addis Ababa, 31 January) organized by the UN Secretary-General and the Chairperson of the AU Commission, participants called for cohesion among the transitional federal institutions, broader political outreach by the Government, increased international assistance, coordinated support to the Government and the strengthening of AMISOM. On 23 February, AMISOM, IGAD and the United Nations Political Office for Somalia (UNPOS) signed a joint regional strategy to enhance coordination between the three institutions, as well as with the international community.

In March, President Sharif dismissed the heads of the army, police, intelligence and prison services, accusing them of being corrupt. New heads were appointed on 29 March. On 4 April, Prime Minister

Mohamed addressed a letter to the Secretary-General concerning the UN presence in Somalia and urging UN offices, agencies and funds to relocate to Somalia within 90 days to help support the Government. As at April, 850 UN staff were stationed in the country, in the capital as well as in Somaliland and Puntland. Meanwhile, the establishment of a UN "light footprint" in Mogadishu [YUN 2010, p. 281] continued to progress. The Secretary-General's Special Representative led discussions with the transitional federal institutions, regional stakeholders and international partners on arrangements to complete the transition. He convened a consultative meeting (Nairobi, 12–13 April), which was attended by representatives of the Transitional Federal Parliament, Puntland, Ahlu Sunnah Wal Jama'a and the international community.

Burundi and Uganda reaffirmed their commitment to deploy the additional 4,000 troops requested by the Security Council to increase the AMISOM force strength from 8,000 to 12,000. As a first step, Burundi deployed an additional 1,000 troops in the first week of March, bringing the AMISOM strength to about 9,000.

UNPOS continued to support the draft of a new constitution through consultations with the transitional federal institutions, IGAD, the AU and international partners, focusing on priority and divisive issues. The consultations resulted in a political road map elaborating the steps of the various components of the process.

The Secretary-General urged the Government to deliver on the political and development tracks and stabilize security in areas recovered from Al-Shabaab. He called on all parties to ensure the protection of civilians and unrestricted delivery of humanitarian assistance. The Secretary-General condemned Al-Shabaab's deliberate use of civilians as shields and the launching of attacks from populated areas. He also called on Member States to contribute to the United Nations trust fund in support of AMISOM.

SECURITY COUNCIL ACTION

On 11 May [meeting 6532], following consultations among Security Council members, the President made statement **S/PRST/2011/10** on behalf of the Council:

> The Security Council reiterates its grave concern at the continued instability in Somalia which has led to a multitude of problems, including terrorism, acts of piracy and armed robbery at sea off the coast of Somalia, hostage-taking and a dire humanitarian situation, and reiterates the need for a comprehensive strategy to encourage the establishment of peace and stability in Somalia through the collaborative efforts of all stakeholders.
>
> The Council reiterates its respect for the sovereignty, territorial integrity, political independence and unity of Somalia. It reaffirms its support for the Djibouti Agreement and peace process as the basis for the resolution of the conflict in Somalia. It reiterates the importance of political outreach and reconciliation in Somalia, and stresses the importance of broad-based, representative institutions reached through a political process ultimately inclusive of all.
>
> The Council expresses its support for the work of Mr. Augustine P. Mahiga, Special Representative of the Secretary-General for Somalia, the United Nations and the African Union to promote peace and reconciliation in Somalia.
>
> The Council notes that the transitional period will end in August 2011. It commends the work of the Special Representative to facilitate the consultative process among Somalis in their efforts to reach an agreement on post-transitional arrangements, in consultation with the international community and within the framework of the Djibouti Agreement. In this regard, it welcomes the high-level consultative meeting held in Nairobi on 12 and 13 April 2011. The Council welcomes the participation of a wide range of Somali stakeholders and partners. It deeply regrets the failure of the Transitional Federal Government to participate in this consultative meeting and urges the Transitional Federal Government to engage fully, constructively and without further delay in the consultative process facilitated by the Special Representative, and to support his efforts to move the peace process forward.
>
> The Council welcomes the upcoming consultative meeting to be held in Mogadishu, which will further the debate generated at the high-level consultative meeting held in Nairobi. The Council urges all Somali stakeholders to participate in this meeting and play a role in finalizing arrangements for ending the transition in August 2011. It calls upon the international community, the United Nations and international organizations to fully support this meeting.
>
> The Council reiterates the primary responsibility of Somalis to achieve peace, security and reconciliation in Somalia. It regrets the decisions taken by the transitional federal institutions to extend their mandates unilaterally and urges them to refrain from further unilateral action. The Council urges the transitional federal institutions to focus on implementing reforms to build their legitimacy, representativeness and credibility, and to reach agreement as soon as possible on the holding of elections for the positions of President and Speaker of Parliament, without which there can be no extension.
>
> The Council expresses concern at the discord between the transitional federal institutions and its impact on the political process and the security situation. It calls upon the transitional federal institutions to ensure cohesion, unity and focus on the completion of the transitional tasks set out in the Djibouti Agreement and the Transitional Federal Charter. It stresses the importance of cooperation and collective leadership by the President and the Speaker.
>
> The Council notes with concern that many core transitional tasks remain outstanding and urges the transitional federal institutions to demonstrate tangible results on the completion of these tasks before the end of the transition, prioritizing progress on reconciliation, the constitution and facilitating the delivery of basic services. It notes its inten-

tion to keep the situation under review, and notes that its future support to the transitional federal institutions will be contingent upon the delivery of tangible results.

The Council strongly commends the progress made by the African Union Mission in Somalia and the Somali security forces in consolidating security and stability in Mogadishu and recognizes the significant sacrifices made by these forces. It calls upon the Transitional Federal Government to take advantage of these tactical gains by demonstrating progress on facilitating the delivery of basic services, the integration of military objectives into a clear political strategy in line with the Djibouti Agreement, and all the other benchmarks spelled out in paragraph 3 of resolution 1964(2010). It calls for an increased United Nations presence in Mogadishu and other parts of Somalia, and calls upon the United Nations to work in a coordinated manner.

The Council reiterates its full support to the African Union Mission in Somalia and expresses its continued appreciation for the commitment of troops by the Governments of Burundi and Uganda. It stresses the importance of predictable, reliable and timely resources for the Mission in order for it to better fulfil its mandate. The Council calls upon the international community to make contributions urgently to the Mission, without caveats. It notes the recommendations on Somalia made by the Peace and Security Council of the African Union on 15 October 2010 and underlines its intention to keep the situation under review.

The Security Council calls upon all States, particularly those in the region, to fully implement the Somalia and Eritrea arms embargoes. The Council condemns attacks, including terrorist attacks, on the Transitional Federal Government, the African Union Mission in Somalia and the civilian population by armed opposition groups and foreign fighters, particularly Al-Shabaab. It calls upon all opposition groups to lay down their arms and join the peace process.

Kampala Accord

As reported by the Secretary-General [S/2011/549], the Kampala Accord, signed on 9 June, dealt with the controversy between President Sharif and the Speaker of the Transitional Federal Parliament, Sharif Hassan, over the date for the elections for the Presidency, the Speaker and the Speaker's deputies. The Speaker maintained that the elections should be held before the end of the transition, on 20 August, while the President preferred that elections be postponed for a year. Following a Security Council mission to the region in May and a meeting (Kampala, Uganda, 2–3 June) of the International Contact Group on Somalia [YUN 2006, p. 307], the Special Representative for Somalia and the President of Uganda, Yoweri Museveni, brought the President and the Speaker together. The negotiations resulted in the Kampala Accord, in which both sides agreed to defer the elections for 12 months from August 2011. The Accord also provided for the resignation of Prime Minister Mohamed within 30 days, the appointment and endorsement by Parliament of a new Prime Minister and Cabinet, and an undertaking by the Government and the Parliament to work together with the international community to establish a road map with benchmarks, timelines and compliance mechanisms for implementing priority tasks. It also provided for the Heads of State and Government of IGAD and the East African Community to monitor compliance with the road map, with the participation of the United Nations and the AU.

SECURITY COUNCIL ACTION

On 24 June [meeting 6564], following consultations among Security Council members, the President made statement **S/PRST/2011/13** on behalf of the Council:

> The Security Council reiterates its respect for the sovereignty, territorial integrity, political independence and unity of Somalia. It reaffirms its support for the Djibouti Agreement and peace process as the basis for the resolution of the conflict in Somalia. It also reiterates the need for a comprehensive strategy to encourage the establishment of peace and stability in Somalia through the collaborative efforts of all stakeholders.
>
> The Council welcomes the signing of the Kampala Accord on 9 June 2011, and commends the leadership shown by President Museveni and the Special Representative of the Secretary-General for Somalia, Mr. Augustine P. Mahiga, in facilitating this agreement.
>
> The Council calls upon the signatories to the Kampala Accord to honour their obligations. It takes note of the appointment of the new Prime Minister of the Transitional Federal Government and looks forward to the prompt appointment of a new Cabinet. It calls upon the signatories to ensure cohesion, unity and focus on the completion of the transitional tasks set out in the Djibouti Agreement and the Transitional Federal Charter. It calls upon the transitional federal institutions to build broad-based representative institutions through a political process ultimately inclusive of all, taking into account the need to ensure the participation of women in public life.
>
> In this regard, and recalling the Council's meetings with Somali parties in Nairobi on 25 May 2011, the Council calls upon the transitional federal institutions to consult widely with other Somali groups, including local and regional administrations, and to work closely with the countries of the region, regional organizations and the wider international community. It welcomes the upcoming consultative meeting, with the participation of the transitional federal institutions and all Somali stakeholders, which should agree on a road map of key tasks and priorities to be delivered over the next 12 months, with clear timelines and benchmarks, to be implemented by the transitional federal institutions. The Council notes that future support to the transitional federal institutions will be contingent upon completion of these key tasks. The Council urges all Somali stakeholders to participate constructively and responsibly in this meeting.
>
> The Council reiterates the primary responsibility of Somalis to achieve peace, security and reconciliation

in Somalia. It recalls that targeted measures can be imposed on those that engage in or provide support for acts that threaten the peace, security or stability of Somalia, including acts that threaten the Djibouti Agreement or the political process or threaten the transitional federal institutions or the African Union Mission in Somalia by force, violate the arms embargo or obstruct the delivery of or access to humanitarian assistance in Somalia.

The Council commends the progress made by the African Union Mission in Somalia and the Somali security forces in consolidating security and stability in Mogadishu, and recognizes the significant sacrifices made by these forces.

Communications. On 5 July [S/2011/411], Ethiopia, as chair of IGAD, transmitted the communiqué of the thirty-ninth extraordinary session of the IGAD Council of Ministers (Malabo, Equatorial Guinea, 28 June), held to consider the security and political situation in Somalia, among other topics. The IGAD Council of Ministers welcomed the signing of the Kampala Accord and the appointment of a new Prime Minister. It urged IGAD member States to provide greater support to the Transitional Federal Government and Ahlu Sunna Wal Jama'a forces in order to enable them to gain control of more areas.

On 14 July [S/2011/434], Ethiopia submitted the communiqué of the eighteenth extraordinary summit meeting of the IGAD Assembly of Heads of State and Government on the activities in Eritrea, Somalia and the Sudan (Addis Ababa, 4 July). The Assembly welcomed the signing of the Kampala Accord, urged all parties to work towards its full implementation, and called on the AU, the United Nations and the international community working on Somalia to relocate to Mogadishu.

Report of Secretary-General (August). In August [S/2011/549], the Secretary-General reported on major developments in Somalia between 28 April and 15 August. Following the signature of the Kampala Accord, the former Planning Minister, Abdiweli Mohamed Ali, was endorsed by Parliament on 28 June as the new Prime Minister. On 11 July, the Parliament voted in favour of the Accord. On 20 July, the Prime Minister appointed a Cabinet of 18 ministers, which was approved by the Parliament on 23 July and sworn in on 28 July. Following months of intense military operations, Al-Shabaab on 6 August withdrew from positions it had held in Mogadishu for nearly two years, thus giving the Government the opportunity to extend its area of control over the entire capital and enhance its legitimacy by delivering services to the residents. The Al-Shabaab withdrawal compelled AMISOM and Government troops to become overextended. Groups loosely allied with the Government fought Al-Shabaab in southern Somalia, where the group continued to maintain a significant presence.

With the end of the transitional period approaching, Somalia witnessed a proliferation of entities claiming to be regional administrations, some with claims over the same areas. UNPOS encouraged those administrations to adopt a united approach and to cooperate with the transitional federal institutions.

The establishment of the "light footprint" in Mogadishu progressed. UNPOS deployed 41 of its staff in different areas of the country. In June and July, UNPOS facilitated the work of a preparatory committee for the consultative meeting on ending the transition, comprising representatives of the Government, the Parliament, Puntland and Galmudug. The Under-Secretary-General for Political Affairs visited the region on 20 and 21 July and met with the UN country team, UNPOS, AMISOM and the leaders of the transitional federal institutions to discuss the political and security situation, as well as the humanitarian crisis. In line with the joint regional strategy signed on 23 February, the Secretary-General's Special Representative worked closely with IGAD and AMISOM and co-chaired a monthly principals' working group on Somalia. UNPOS continued to train the police and developed a security sector development strategy for 2011–2013. The eighth Joint Security Committee meeting (Entebbe, Uganda, 23 June) was followed by the third meeting of Somali religious leaders and traditional elders (Entebbe, 24–26 June), which proposed the establishment, in southern central Somalia, of a permanent structure composed of traditional elders and clan leaders. AMISOM explosive ordnance disposal teams destroyed 972 items of unexploded ordnance in Mogadishu, bringing the number of items destroyed since 2009 to 6,761. The United Nations Support Office for the African Union Mission in Somalia continued to provide logistical support to AMISOM.

The negotiations initiated by the Somaliland President between conflicting clans in the Sool region resulted, in June, in a reconciliation conference, which led to an agreement covering prisoner release, illegal land-grabbing and the digging of boreholes.

The Secretary-General appealed to Member States to provide support for the deployment of additional resources to AMISOM. Recognizing that significant gaps remained in the UN support package to AMISOM, he recommended enhancing the package so that the Mission could count on predictable and sustainable funds. He urged the Transitional Federal Government to improve command and control over its military and to ensure that its arms and equipment did not fall into the hands of armed opposition groups. It was essential, he noted, to seize the opportunities created by the Kampala Accord, the political road map and the withdrawal of Al-Shabaab from Mogadishu; to preserve the gains on the security and political fronts; to assist the Government in consolidating its authority over the capital; and to engage in a national reconciliation process. Echoing a similar recommendation made in August by the AU, the Secretary-General recommended the creation, as part of AMISOM and under its command, of a guard force to facilitate the deployment of civilian staff and provide protection for the AU and the United Nations in Mogadishu.

Communications. On 13 September [S/2011/586], the Secretary-General submitted to the Security Council a letter from the Chairperson of the AU Commission concerning the meeting held on the same day by the AU Peace and Security Council on the situation in Somalia.

On 21 September [S/2011/591], the Secretary-General provided the Council with more information about the inclusion of additional support requirements for AMISOM troops into the UN support package, and the proposed AMISOM guard force.

The Council, on 29 September [S/2011/602], informed the Secretary-General that it had extended the additional requirements concerning the logistical support package. The establishment of a guard force would be addressed in the context of the renewal of resolution 1964(2010).

SECURITY COUNCIL ACTION

On 30 September [meeting 6626], the Security Council unanimously adopted **resolution 2010(2011)**. The draft [S/2011/595] was submitted by France, Germany, Nigeria, Portugal and the United Kingdom.

The Security Council,

Recalling all its previous resolutions and the statements by its President concerning the situation in Somalia, the protection of civilians in armed conflict, women and peace and security, and children and armed conflict,

Reaffirming its respect for the sovereignty, territorial integrity, political independence and unity of Somalia,

Reiterating its commitment to a comprehensive and lasting settlement of the situation in Somalia,

Reiterating its full support for the Djibouti peace process and the Transitional Federal Charter, which provide the framework for reaching a lasting political solution in Somalia, recognizing the need to promote reconciliation and dialogue among the Somali population, and stressing the importance of broad-based and representative institutions reached through a political process ultimately inclusive of all,

Reaffirming its support for the Transitional Federal Government in its role as part of the Djibouti peace process, stressing the primary responsibility of the transitional federal institutions to work in a cohesive and united manner and to intensify their efforts to complete the transitional tasks set out in the Djibouti Agreement and the Transitional Federal Charter, and calling upon the transitional federal institutions to coordinate closely with other Somali groups, including local and regional administrations,

Reiterating its emphasis on the need for a comprehensive strategy to encourage the establishment of peace and security in Somalia through the collaborative effort of all stakeholders,

Commending the Special Representative of the Secretary-General for Somalia, Mr. Augustine P. Mahiga, as well as the Special Representative of the Chairperson of the African Union Commission for Somalia, Mr. Boubacar Gaoussou Diarra, and reaffirming its strong support for their efforts,

Welcoming the work of former President Jerry Rawlings as the African Union High Representative for Somalia,

Recalling the signing of the Kampala Accord on 9 June 2011, noting the decision to defer elections of the President and the Speaker and his deputies for twelve months until 20 August 2012 under the terms of the Accord, and strongly urging the signatories to honour their obligations,

Welcoming the agreement of a road map, facilitated by the Special Representative of the Secretary-General, Mr. Mahiga, at the consultative meeting held in Mogadishu from 4 to 6 September 2011, that sets out key tasks and priorities to be delivered by the transitional federal institutions over the next twelve months, with clear timelines, benchmarks and compliance mechanisms, urging the transitional federal institutions, as holding the primary responsibility for implementing the road map, and the other signatories, to adhere to their commitments in the road map, and noting that future support for the transitional federal institutions will be contingent upon completion of these tasks,

Recognizing that peace and stability in Somalia depend on reconciliation and effective governance across the whole of Somalia, and urging all Somali parties to renounce violence and to work together to build peace and stability,

Urging the transitional federal institutions to increase their transparency and combat corruption to increase their legitimacy and credibility, and to enable continued support from the international community,

Expressing grave concern at the dire and worsening humanitarian situation in Somalia and the impact of the drought and famine on the people of Somalia, in particular women and children, calling upon all parties, in accordance with international humanitarian law, to allow for safe and unhindered access to humanitarian agencies at this critical time, and underscoring the importance of upholding the principles of neutrality, impartiality, humanity and independence in the provision of humanitarian assistance,

Strongly condemning the targeting, obstruction or prevention of the delivery of humanitarian aid in Somalia by any parties, especially armed groups, and deploring any attacks on humanitarian personnel,

Expressing serious concern that the United Nations consolidated appeal for Somalia is not fully funded, stressing the need for urgent mobilization of resources to those in need, and calling upon all Member States to contribute to current and future consolidated humanitarian appeals,

Commending the contribution of the African Union Mission in Somalia to lasting peace and stability in Somalia, recognizing the significant sacrifices made by these forces, expressing its appreciation for the continued commitment of troops and equipment to the Mission by the Governments of Uganda and Burundi, and calling upon other States members of the African Union to consider contributing troops to the Mission,

Reiterating its serious concern at the continued fighting in Somalia and its impact on the civilian population, condemning all attacks, including terrorist attacks on the Transitional Federal Government, the Mission and the civilian population by armed opposition groups and foreign fighters, particularly Al-Shabaab, and stressing the terrorist threat that Somali armed opposition groups and foreign fighters, particularly Al-Shabaab, constitute for Somalia and for the international community,

Welcoming recent improvements in the security situation in Mogadishu, commending the efforts of the Mission and the Somali security forces, encouraging them to consolidate these gains, and urging the transitional federal institutions to capitalize upon the improved security situation by promptly facilitating agreement on and the implementation of a stabilization plan for Mogadishu and by facilitating the delivery of basic services and providing good governance to all of its citizens,

Calling upon the Transitional Federal Government to remain united and redouble its efforts to complete the priority tasks and goals agreed on in the road map paving the ground for a better future for Somalis, including their economic and social development and the realization of their human rights, while recognizing the need for the cooperation and support of the international community to the Transitional Federal Government and local and regional administrations in this regard,

Reaffirming the importance of the re-establishment, training, equipping and retention of Somali security forces, which is vital for the long-term stability and security of Somalia, expressing its support for the ongoing European Union Training Mission for Somalia, emphasizing the importance of coordinated, timely and sustained support from the international community, and encouraging the Somali security forces to demonstrate their effectiveness by working with the African Union Mission in Somalia to consolidate security throughout Mogadishu,

Commending Member States and organizations which have made contributions in support of the Mission and Somalia, encouraging the international community to mobilize additional funding as appropriate, recognizing the importance of timely and predictable funding, and stressing the need for effective coordination among donors, the United Nations and the African Union,

Recalling its resolutions 1950(2010) of 23 November 2010 and 1976(2011) of 11 April 2011, expressing its grave concern at the threat posed by piracy and armed robbery at sea off the coast of Somalia, recognizing that the ongoing instability in Somalia contributes to the problem of piracy and armed robbery at sea off the coast of Somalia, and hostage-taking, stressing the need for a comprehensive response to tackle piracy, including the need to investigate and prosecute those who illicitly finance, plan, organize or unlawfully profit from pirate attacks, and its underlying causes by the international community and the transitional federal institutions, and welcoming the efforts of the Contact Group on Piracy off the Coast of Somalia, States and international and regional organizations,

Welcoming the report of the Secretary-General of 30 August 2011 and the recommendations contained therein for continued action on the political, security and recovery tracks by the transitional federal institutions with the support of the international community,

Determining that the situation in Somalia continues to constitute a threat to international peace and security in the region,

Acting under Chapter VII of the Charter of the United Nations,

1. *Decides* to authorize the States members of the African Union to maintain the deployment until 31 October 2012 of the African Union Mission in Somalia, which shall be authorized to take all measures necessary to carry out its existing mandate, as set out in paragraph 9 of resolution 1772(2007) of 20 August 2007, and requests the African Union to urgently increase its force strength to its mandated level of 12,000 uniformed personnel, thereby enhancing its ability to carry out its mandate;

2. *Calls upon* the transitional federal institutions to abide by the terms of the road map of key tasks and priorities to be delivered by the transitional federal institutions over the next twelve months, with clear timelines, benchmarks and compliance mechanisms, notes that the future support of the Security Council to the transitional federal institutions will be contingent upon the completion of these tasks, and requests the Secretary-General to provide an update on progress made by the transitional federal institutions against the road map in his reports to the Council;

3. *Notes* the recommendations on Somalia made by the Peace and Security Council of the African Union on 13 September 2011, and underlines its intention to keep the situation on the ground under review and to take into account in its future decisions on the Mission progress by the transitional federal institutions in completing the key tasks as set out in the road map referred to in paragraph 2 above;

4. *Welcomes* the steps taken by the United Nations Political Office for Somalia and other United Nations offices and agencies, including the United Nations Support Office for the African Union Mission in Somalia, to increase the presence of the United Nations organizations and their staff in Somalia as an important element of the effective fulfilment of their mandate, and urges the establishment of a more permanent and increasing presence by the United Nations in Somalia, in particular in Mogadishu, consistent with the security conditions, as outlined in the reports of the Secretary-General of 16 April 2009 and 9 September 2010;

5. *Recalling* the report of 13 September 2011 of the Chairperson of the African Union Commission and the report of the Secretary-General of 30 August 2011, agrees that an increase in United Nations organizations and their staff and other official international visitors in Mogadishu is placing additional pressure on the Mission to provide security, escort and protection services, encourages the United Nations to work with the African Union to develop a guard force of an appropriate size, within the mandated troop levels of the Mission, to provide security, escort and protection services to personnel from the international community, including the United Nations, and expresses its intention to review and consider thoroughly the possible need to adjust the mandated troop levels of the Mission when it reaches its current mandated level of 12,000 troops;

6. *Requests* the Secretary-General to continue to provide technical and expert advice to the African Union in the planning and deployment of the Mission, through the United Nations Office to the African Union, including on the concept of operations of the Mission;

7. *Welcomes* the progress made by the Mission in reducing civilian casualties during its operations, and urges the Mission to continue to undertake its efforts to prevent

civilian casualties and to develop an effective approach to the protection of civilians as requested by the Peace and Security Council;

8. *Requests* the Mission to continue to assist the Transitional Federal Government in the development of the Somali Police Force and the National Security Force, in particular the implementation of an effective chain of command and control of the Somali security forces, and to assist the integration of Somali units trained by other Member States or organizations inside and outside Somalia;

9. *Notes* the important role that an effective police presence can play in the stabilization of Mogadishu, stresses the need to continue to develop an effective Somali police force, and welcomes the desire of the African Union to develop a police component within the Mission;

10. *Requests* the Secretary-General to continue to provide a logistical support package for the Mission, called for in resolution 1863(2009) of 16 January 2009, for a maximum of 12,000 uniformed Mission personnel, including the guard force referred to in paragraph 5 above, comprising equipment and services, including public information support, but not including the transfer of funds, as described in the letter dated 30 January 2009 from the Secretary-General to the President of the Security Council, until 31 October 2012, ensuring the accountability and transparency of expenditure of United Nations funds as set out in paragraph 6 of resolution 1910(2010) of 28 January 2010;

11. *Decides*, on an exceptional basis and owing to the unique character of the Mission, to extend the logistical support package for the Mission for a maximum of 12,000 troops as described in the exchange of letters between the Secretary-General and the President of the Security Council of 21 and 29 September 2011 while continuing to ensure maximum efficiency and engagement of relevant bilateral support;

12. *Considers* that counter-improvised explosive device and explosive ordnance disposal activities, as described in the letter dated 30 January 2009 from the Secretary-General to the President of the Security Council, may be provided through the logistical support package, while continuing to ensure maximum efficiency and engagement of relevant bilateral support;

13. *Recalls* its statement of intent regarding the establishment of a United Nations peacekeeping operation, as expressed in resolution 1863(2009), notes that any decision to deploy such an operation would take into account, inter alia, the conditions set out in the reports of the Secretary-General of 16 April 2009 and 30 December 2010, and requests the Secretary-General to take the steps identified in paragraphs 82 to 86 of his report of 16 April 2009, subject to the conditions in this report;

14. *Reiterates its call* to Member States and regional and international organizations to support the Mission through the provision of equipment, technical assistance and funding without caveats to the United Nations trust fund for the African Union Mission in Somalia, or to make direct bilateral donations in support of the Mission, including for the urgent need for the reimbursement of contingent-owned equipment, and for the provision of compassionate flights for Mission troops, and encourages donors to work closely with the United Nations and the African Union in order to ensure that the appropriate funds and equipment are promptly provided;

15. *Emphasizes* that, in order to ensure Somalia's long-term security, effective development of Somali security forces is needed, and reiterates its call to Member States and regional and international organizations to contribute generously and promptly to the United Nations trust fund for the Somali security institutions and to offer assistance to the Somali security forces, including through training, technical assistance and equipment in coordination with the Mission, consistent with paragraphs 11 (*b*) and 12 of resolution 1772(2007);

16. *Requests* the Secretary-General to continue to assist the Transitional Federal Government in developing the transitional security institutions, including the Somali Police Force and the National Security Force, and to continue to support the Transitional Federal Government in developing a Somali-owned national security strategy which reflects respect for the rule of law and the protection of human rights, as well as the legal and policy framework for the operation of its security forces, including governance, vetting and oversight mechanisms;

17. *Reaffirms* that the measures imposed by paragraph 5 of resolution 733(1992) of 23 January 1992 and further elaborated upon in paragraphs 1 and 2 of resolution 1425(2002) of 22 July 2002 shall not apply to supplies and technical assistance provided in accordance with paragraphs 11 (*b*) and 12 of resolution 1772(2007) to the Transitional Federal Government for the purposes of the development of its security sector institutions, consistent with the Djibouti peace process and subject to the notification procedure set out in paragraph 12 of resolution 1772(2007);

18. *Reiterates its call upon* all Somali parties to support the Djibouti Agreement, and calls for the end of all hostilities, acts of armed confrontation and efforts to undermine stability in Somalia and the Transitional Federal Government;

19. *Requests* the Secretary-General, through his Special Representative for Somalia, to continue to extend his good offices to facilitate reconciliation among all Somalis and the peace process in general, with the support of the international community, including, as appropriate, support to reconciliation and peace efforts at the local level;

20. *Notes* the important role that regional administrations and civil society can play in the political process, and encourages intensified dialogue and political outreach with these groups by the transitional federal institutions;

21. *Encourages* the international community to provide, as part of the continuing support to Somalia, further support to peacebuilding, capacity-building and good governance efforts in areas of relative stability within Somalia, including, but not limited to, Somaliland and Puntland;

22. *Condemns* all attacks against civilians in Somalia, calls for the immediate cessation of all acts of violence, including sexual and gender-based violence, or abuses committed against civilians, including women and children, and humanitarian personnel in violation of international humanitarian law and human rights law, and stresses the responsibility of all parties in Somalia to comply with their obligations to protect the civilian population from the effects of hostilities, in particular by avoiding any indiscriminate attacks or excessive use of force;

23. *Expresses serious concern* about the reports of continuing human rights violations in Somalia, and stresses

the importance of investigating these alleged human rights violations and bringing those responsible to justice;

24. *Recalls* the conclusions on children and armed conflict in Somalia endorsed by the Security Council Working Group on Children and Armed Conflict, calls upon all parties to end grave violations and abuses committed against children in Somalia, urges the Transitional Federal Government to develop and implement a concrete time-bound action plan to halt the recruitment and use of children, requests the Secretary-General to continue his dialogue with the Transitional Federal Government in this regard, and reiterates its request to the Secretary-General to strengthen the child protection component of the United Nations Political Office for Somalia and to ensure continued monitoring and reporting of the situation of children in Somalia;

25. *Expresses serious concern* about increasing reports of conflict-related sexual violence in Somalia, calls upon all parties to cease such violations and abuses, and requests the Secretary-General to implement the relevant provisions of resolutions 1325(2000) of 31 October 2000, 1820(2008) of 19 June 2008, 1888(2009) of 30 September 2009, 1889(2009) of 5 October 2009 and 1960(2010) of 16 December 2010, including the strengthening of the women's protection component of the United Nations Political Office for Somalia;

26. *Demands* that all parties and armed groups take appropriate steps to ensure the safety and security of humanitarian personnel and supplies, and further demands that all parties ensure full, safe and unhindered access for the timely delivery of humanitarian aid to persons in need of assistance across Somalia;

27. *Requests* the Secretary-General, through his Special Representative for Somalia and the United Nations Political Office for Somalia, to redouble efforts to coordinate effectively and develop an integrated approach to all activities of the United Nations system in Somalia, to provide good offices and political support for the efforts to establish lasting peace and stability in Somalia, and to mobilize resources and support from the international community for both the immediate recovery and the long-term economic development of Somalia taking into account the recommendations contained in his report of 31 December 2009, and stresses the importance that the United Nations Political Office for Somalia and other United Nations offices and agencies work transparently and coordinate with the international community;

28. *Requests* the strengthening of cooperation among the Intergovernmental Authority on Development, the African Union and the United Nations to allow for an appropriate division of responsibilities in Somalia in an effort to reduce duplication of effort and ensure proper utilization of resources, and to include updates on this topic in the regular reports of the Secretary-General on Somalia;

29. *Requests* the Secretary-General to report on all aspects of the present resolution every four months, and expresses its intention to review the situation, as part of his reporting obligations, as specified in the statement by its President of 31 October 2001 and its resolutions 1863(2009), 1872(2009) of 26 May 2009, 1910(2010) and 1964(2010) of 22 December 2010;

30. *Decides* to remain actively seized of the matter.

Security Council statement. On 4 October [SC/10402], the Security Council condemned the attack that occurred on that day in Mogadishu, which resulted in the death of 170 people.

Communication. On 17 October [S/2011/646], Kenya informed the Security Council that the country, in direct consultations and liaison with the Transitional Federal Government, after several attacks on Kenyan territory by Al-Shabaab, had decided to undertake remedial and pre-emptive action.

Report of Secretary-General (December). On 9 December, the Secretary-General reported [S/2011/759] on major developments between 30 August and 30 November. That period was dominated by the adoption by the transitional federal institutions of a comprehensive road map for ending the transition, in accordance with the June Kampala Accord. The road map set out priority tasks to be completed by 20 August 2012 in the areas of security, constitutional reform and elections, outreach and reconciliation, and good governance. It was adopted at a consultative meeting (Mogadishu, 4–6 September) chaired by the Secretary-General's Special Representative. Attendees included the President, Speaker and Prime Minister of Somalia, the Presidents of Puntland and Galmudug, and representatives of Ahlu Sunnah Wal Jama'a. On 15 October, Kenya launched "Operation Defend the Nation" into Somali territory. The operation followed a series of kidnappings of foreigners, including aid workers in Kenya, which the country attributed to Al-Shabaab. On 31 October, Kenya and the Transitional Federal Government issued a joint communiqué clarifying that the Kenyan security operation inside Somalia was based on the right to self-defence under Article 51 of the UN Charter. The communiqué stated that the threat must be fought jointly by the two nations with the support of the international community.

The Secretary-General's Special Representative used his good offices to back the transitional federal institutions in implementing the road map. Meanwhile, UNPOS worked with the Government to address the emergence of regional administrations, especially those in south-central Somalia. On 23 September, on the margins of the General Assembly, the Secretary-General convened a mini-summit on Somalia to mobilize international support. The International Contact Group on Somalia held its twentieth meeting (Copenhagen, Denmark, 29–30 September), in which all signatories to the road map participated.

The Secretary-General noted that, in implementing the road map, a number of agreed deadlines had been missed. The compliance mechanisms envisaged in the road map had yet to meet. A technical committee, however, comprising representatives of the transitional federal institutions, the regions and the international community, had met twice and agreed that progress would be tracked through four subcommittees—on a draft constitution, reconciliation, parliamentary reform and good governance—while the Joint Security Committee would be responsible for security.

The Joint Security Committee held a two-day meeting (Mogadishu, 27–28 October) chaired by the Secretary-General's Special Representative and the Prime Minister, with representation from Puntland, Galmudug and Ahlu Sunnah Wal Jama'a. The Committee agreed on the need for the equitable sharing of resources across the security sector. On 26 October, the Council of Ministers approved a draft national security and stabilization plan, which was then referred to the Parliament for adoption. Progress was made in establishing the technical bodies required to finalize a new constitution, although major substantive issues, such as the borders of the country, the role of sharia, the nature of the State (federal or unitary) and the system of Government (presidential or parliamentary) had yet to be resolved. On 23 September, the Government appointed a nine-member committee of experts who would work together with the Independent Federal Constitution Commission to finalize the constitution and carry out public consultation.

Regarding security, the Government and its allied forces made continued gains against Al-Shabaab. Groups and entities loosely allied with the Government expanded their presence in two southern regions, following the start of the Kenyan operation on 15 October. Multiple killings and attacks took place in Puntland.

Efforts towards reaching the Mission's mandated troop capacity of 12,000 brought the strength of AMISOM to approximately 9,800 by late November. On 2 December, following meetings of the Chiefs of Defence Staff of AMISOM and the AU Peace and Security Council, the latter issued a communiqué requesting Kenya to consider integrating its forces into AMISOM, and welcoming the decision of Ethiopia to support the AMISOM-Transitional Federal Government-Kenya operation.

The international community continued its support for the building of security institutions. At the end of November, the Somali national security force numbered some 10,300 troops within Mogadishu. The strength of the police force, trained with international assistance, stood at 5,370. The police's response to calls relating to explosive threats indicated its increased ability to take action in areas where AMISOM could not. As at 30 November, 104 judges and prosecutors in Mogadishu, Somaliland and Puntland were enrolled in training courses supported by UNDP.

The Secretary-General observed that while there had been a generous response to the humanitarian emergencies, the resources available to the United Nations and AMISOM were not commensurate with the challenges or the mandates given. Somalia needed sustained help in order to implement the road map, and the Mission remained underequipped and underfunded. The Secretary-General welcomed the approval of the national security and stabilization plan by the Council of Ministers. He remained concerned about Al-Shabaab's ban on several UN agencies and non-governmental organizations operating in areas under its control, as well as about the impact that ongoing fighting was having on civilians.

Visit to Somalia. The Secretary-General, together with the General Assembly President, visited Mogadishu on 9 December, asking the leadership to implement the road map, stressing that the transition had to end in August 2012 and urging the leadership to accelerate constitutional and parliamentary reforms.

Year-end developments. In a further report [S/2012/74], the Secretary-General said that at the first Somali National Consultative Constitutional Conference (Garowe, Puntland, Somalia, 21–23 December), the leaders of the transitional federal institutions, Puntland, Galmudug and Ahlu Sunnah Wal Jama'a agreed on an approach for ending the transition. The "Garowe Principles" provided for the adoption of the provisional constitution by a Constituent Assembly to be nominated by all road map signatories and civil society, and for the creation of a bicameral federal legislature, comprising a lower house of 225 representatives, and an upper house comprising representatives of federal States and regional administrations. Outside Mogadishu, the combined operations of Kenyan military and Ethiopian troops working with forces allied with the Government gained ground, including by taking Beledweyne on 31 December.

Extension of UNPOS. The Secretary-General in a 29 December letter [S/2011/802], informed the Security Council of the work of UNPOS, the mandate of which would expire on 31 December. He also outlined the tasks that the Office would carry out during the 2012–2013 biennium. The Security Council took note of that letter on 30 December [S/2011/803].

Piracy

Although successful pirate attacks off the coast of Somalia declined from 55 in 2010 to 33 in 2011, attempted attacks in the high-risk area increased from 174 in 2010 to 287 in 2011. To counter piracy, the Secretary-General's Special Adviser on Legal Issues related to Piracy off the Coast of Somalia in January recommended establishing two specialized courts in Somaliland and Puntland and an additional Somali court outside of the country. The Contact Group on Piracy off the Coast of Somalia met in New York in March, July and November. The Secretary-General warned that piracy off the coast of Somalia had become an entrenched criminal enterprise with a growing geographical area of operations, larger scale attacks, increased levels of violence and higher ransoms.

Report of Special Adviser. In January, Jack Lang (France), the Special Adviser to the Secretary-General on Legal Issues related to Piracy off the Coast of Somalia, appointed in 2010 [YUN 2010, p. 290], submitted his report [S/2011/30] to the Security Council. He noted that piracy was undergoing "industrialization"; new professions (intermediaries, negotiators and interpreters) and activities (money-laundering, trafficking of weapons and migrants) linked to the phenomenon were emerging or prospering, making the Somali population increasingly dependent on piracy. That had been accompanied by intensified violence, as well as by the geographical expansion of the attacks in the Indian Ocean. Nearly 1,900 people and 105 vessels had been taken in two years. From an economic standpoint, piracy had a negative impact on the major economic sectors of the region, notably tourism and fishery, and had resulted in higher prices and lower security in the delivery of energy supplies. Piracy was one of the main obstacles to the delivery of food aid, the lifeline for more than 2 million Somalis or about 27 per cent of the population. It had a negative impact on international trade: some 23,000 ships and 30 per cent of the world's oil supply transited the area every year. Since the area had been classified as a war zone, insurance premiums were increasing drastically.

As at May 2010, 9 out of 10 captured pirates had not been prosecuted. The practice of releasing pirates after destroying their boats and weapons had become the rule. The Special Adviser recommended measures to lift the legal obstacles to prosecuting pirates and imprisoning them, such as incorporating the crime of piracy into domestic legislation. The Somali criminal code made no provision for the offence of piracy. A bill criminalizing piracy and intended for application throughout the Somali territory had been developed under the aegis of the United Nations Office on Drugs and Crime. Although that bill had been adopted by the Parliament of Puntland in December 2010 and the government of Somaliland had agreed to submit it to its Parliament, it had yet to be adopted by the Parliament of Mogadishu. In most of the States in which prosecutions had been initiated, the legal system required testimony in person. That requirement was a major obstacle to a swift trial. A solution would be to allow testimony by videoconferencing, which would require amending the code of criminal procedure of prosecuting States. Another obstacle to prosecuting pirates was the lack of correctional facilities in the States of the region.

The Special Adviser recommended a comprehensive, multidimensional plan targeting Puntland—the epicentre of piracy—and Somaliland comprising three components: economic, security and jurisdictional/correctional. That plan would rely on the will of regional authorities. In return for international development assistance, those authorities would take action to apprehend those behind acts of piracy, restore the rule of law in areas harbouring pirates and monitor the coasts, starting with the major pirate bases. The economic component was aimed at developing activities that could not prosper in an environment of piracy, safeguarding the sovereignty of the authorities over their territory and regulating activities to ensure that their development did not spark an increase in piracy. Priority sectors included port and fishery operations, livestock exports, telecommunications, alternative energy and the banking sector. The security component would help to build the capacity of authorities. Police units should be re-established in areas of lawlessness and a land-based coastguard support function should be developed. It was also necessary to strike at the source of piracy networks by going after the persons behind them, who had been identified but who had taken refuge in areas where they were protected. To that end, the forensic capacities of States in the region had to be enhanced, evidence had to be made more readily admissible in court and sanctions must be imposed on the masterminds. With respect to the jurisdictional/correctional component, the report recommended establishing a court system comprising a specialized court in Puntland, a specialized court in Somaliland and a specialized extraterritorial Somali court that could be temporarily located in Arusha, United Republic of Tanzania. The specialized court in Puntland and the extraterritorial Somali court were priorities, given the possibility of granting them universal jurisdiction. The correctional capacities of Puntland and Somaliland would be strengthened by the immediate construction of two prisons, one in each area, each with the capacity to hold 500 prisoners and with protected status to allow for international monitoring. A third prison would be built soon afterwards. The three-year funding needs for the legal and jurisdictional/correctional components would be at least $25 million, while the cost of maritime piracy was estimated at $7 to $12 billion.

Communication. On 28 February [S/2011/107 & Corr.1], Somalia informed the Security Council that vessels of the North Atlantic Treaty Organization (NATO) Standing Naval Maritime Groups were permitted to enter the territorial or internal waters of Somalia for anti-piracy functions.

SECURITY COUNCIL ACTION

On 11 April [meeting 6512], the Security Council unanimously adopted **resolution 1976(2011)**. The draft [S/2011/228] was submitted by 12 Member States.

The Security Council,

Recalling its previous resolutions concerning the situation in Somalia, especially resolutions 1918(2010) of 27 April 2010 and 1950(2010) of 23 November 2010,

Continuing to be gravely concerned by the growing threat that piracy and armed robbery at sea against vessels pose to the situation in Somalia and other States in the region, as well as to international navigation, the safety of commercial maritime routes and the safety of seafarers and other persons, and also gravely concerned by the increased level of violence employed by pirates and persons involved in armed robbery at sea off the coast of Somalia,

Strongly condemning the growing practice of hostage-taking by pirates operating off the coast of Somalia, expressing serious concern at the inhuman conditions that hostages face in captivity, recognizing the adverse impact on their families, calling for the immediate release of all hostages, and noting the importance of cooperation between Member States on the issue of hostage-taking,

Emphasizing the importance of finding a comprehensive solution to the problem of piracy and armed robbery at sea off the coast of Somalia,

Stressing the need to build Somalia's potential for sustainable economic growth as a means to tackle the underlying causes of piracy, including poverty, thus contributing to a durable eradication of piracy and armed robbery at sea off the coast of Somalia and illegal activities connected therewith,

Reaffirming its respect for the sovereignty, territorial integrity, political independence and unity of Somalia, including Somalia's rights with respect to offshore natural resources, including fisheries, in accordance with international law, recalling the importance of preventing, in accordance with international law, illegal fishing and illegal dumping, including of toxic substances, and stressing the need to investigate allegations of such illegal fishing and dumping,

Being concerned, at the same time, that allegations of illegal fishing and dumping of toxic waste in Somali waters have been used by pirates in an attempt to justify their criminal activities,

Reaffirming that international law, as reflected in the United Nations Convention on the Law of the Sea of 10 December 1982, in particular articles 100, 101 and 105 thereof, sets out the legal framework applicable to combating piracy and armed robbery at sea, as well as other ocean activities,

Reaffirming also that the provisions of the present resolution apply only with respect to the situation in Somalia and do not affect the rights and obligations or responsibilities of Member States under international law,

Reiterating its call upon States and regional organizations that have the capacity to do so to take part in the fight against piracy and armed robbery at sea off the coast of Somalia, in particular, consistent with resolution 1950(2010) and applicable international law, including human rights law, by deploying naval vessels, arms and military aircraft and through seizures and disposition of boats, vessels, arms and other related equipment used in the commission of piracy and armed robbery at sea off the coast of Somalia, or for which there are reasonable grounds for suspecting such use,

Underlining the importance of enhancing ongoing work to address the problems caused by the limited capacity of the judicial systems of Somalia and other States in the region to effectively prosecute suspected pirates,

Noting with appreciation the assistance being provided by the United Nations, including the United Nations Office on Drugs and Crime, and other international organizations and donors, in coordination with the Contact Group on Piracy off the Coast of Somalia, to enhance the capacity of the judicial and corrections systems in Somalia, Kenya, Seychelles and other States in the region to prosecute suspected, and imprison convicted, pirates consistent with applicable international human rights law,

Commending those States that have amended their domestic law in order to criminalize piracy and facilitate the prosecution of suspected pirates in their national courts consistent with applicable international law, including human rights law, and stressing the need for States to continue their efforts in this regard,

Noting with concern, at the same time, that the domestic law of a number of States lacks provisions criminalizing piracy and/or procedural provisions for effective criminal prosecution of suspected pirates,

Further expressing concern over a large number of persons suspected of piracy having to be released without facing justice, reaffirming that the failure to prosecute persons responsible for acts of piracy and armed robbery at sea off the coast of Somalia undermines anti-piracy efforts of the international community, and being determined to create conditions to ensure that pirates are held accountable,

Recognizing the urgent need to take decisive further steps to boost anti-piracy efforts,

Expressing its gratitude for the work done by the Special Adviser to the Secretary-General on Legal Issues related to Piracy off the Coast of Somalia, Mr. Jack Lang, in order to explore new solutions to counter more effectively piracy and armed robbery at sea off the coast of Somalia, including by more effective prosecution of suspected, and imprisonment of convicted, pirates, and taking note with appreciation of the conclusions and proposals set forth in the report of the Special Adviser to the Security Council,

Determining that the incidents of piracy and armed robbery at sea off the coast of Somalia exacerbate the situation in Somalia, which continues to constitute a threat to international peace and security in the region,

1. *Welcomes* the report of the Special Adviser to the Secretary-General on Legal Issues related to Piracy off the Coast of Somalia;

2. *Recognizes* that the ongoing instability in Somalia is one of the underlying causes of the problem of piracy and contributes to the problem of piracy and armed robbery at sea off the coast of Somalia, and stresses the need for a comprehensive response to tackle piracy and its underlying causes by the international community;

3. *Calls upon* States to cooperate, as appropriate, on the issue of hostage-taking;

4. *Requests* States, the United Nations Office on Drugs and Crime, the United Nations Development Programme, the United Nations Political Office for Somalia and regional organizations to assist the Transitional Federal Government and regional authorities in Somalia in establishing a system of governance, rule of law and police control in

lawless areas where land-based activities related to piracy are taking place, and also requests the Transitional Federal Government and regional authorities in Somalia to increase their own efforts in this regard;

5. *Requests* States and regional organizations to support sustainable economic growth in Somalia. thus contributing to a durable eradication of piracy and armed robbery at sea off the coast of Somalia, as well as other illegal activities connected therewith, in particular in priority areas recommended by the Istanbul conference on piracy in Somalia, held from 21 to 23 May 2010;

6. *Invites* States and regional organizations to continue their support and assistance to Somalia in its efforts to develop national fisheries and port activities in line with the Regional Plan of Action for Maritime Security in Eastern and Southern Africa and the Indian Ocean, and in this regard emphasizes the importance of the earliest possible delimitation of Somalia's maritime spaces in accordance with the United Nations Convention on the Law of the Sea;

7. *Recalls* the sixth and seventh preambular paragraphs of the present resolution and paragraph 2 of resolution 1950(2010), and requests the Secretary-General to report within six months on the protection of Somali natural resources and waters, and on alleged illegal fishing and illegal dumping, including of toxic substances, off the coast of Somalia, taking into account the studies on this matter previously conducted by the United Nations Environment Programme and other competent agencies and organizations, and expresses its readiness to keep the matter under review;

8. *Urges* States, individually or within the framework of competent international organizations, to positively consider investigating allegations of illegal fishing and illegal dumping, including of toxic substances, with a view to prosecuting such offences when committed by persons under their jurisdiction;

9. *Calls upon* States and regional organizations cooperating with the Transitional Federal Government in the fight against piracy off the coast of Somalia to further increase their coordination to effectively deter, prevent and respond to pirate attacks, including through the Contact Group on Piracy off the Coast of Somalia;

10. *Encourages* States and regional organizations co-operating with the Transitional Federal Government to assist Somalia in strengthening its coastguard capacity, in particular by supporting the development of land-based coastal monitoring and increasing their cooperation with the Somali regional authorities in this regard, as appropriate, after having any necessary approval from the Security Council Committee pursuant to resolutions 751(1992) and 1907(2009);

11. *Calls upon* States, regional organizations, the United Nations, the International Maritime Organization and other appropriate partners to provide all necessary technical and financial support for the implementation of the Code of Conduct concerning the Repression of Piracy and Armed Robbery against Ships in the Western Indian Ocean and the Gulf of Aden (Djibouti Code of Conduct), the Regional Plan of Action for Maritime Security in Eastern and Southern Africa and the Indian Ocean, agreed by ministers in Mauritius on 7 October 2010, and the regional needs assessment report of the Contact Group on Piracy off the Coast of Somalia, recognizing the political will expressed by regional countries in these documents to combat piracy by all means possible, including through prosecution and imprisonment;

12. *Commends* the efforts of the shipping industry, in cooperation with the Contact Group on Piracy off the Coast of Somalia and the International Maritime Organization, in developing and disseminating the updated version of the Best Management Practices to Deter Piracy off the Coast of Somalia and in the Arabian Sea Area, and emphasizes the critical importance for the shipping industry of applying the best practices recommended therein;

13. *Urges* all States, including States in the region, to criminalize piracy under their domestic law, emphasizing the importance of criminalizing incitement, facilitation, conspiracy and attempts to commit acts of piracy;

14. *Recognizes* that piracy is a crime subject to universal jurisdiction, and in that regard reiterates its call upon States to favourably consider the prosecution of suspected, and imprisonment of convicted, pirates apprehended off the coast of Somalia, consistent with applicable international human rights law;

15. *Underlines* the need to investigate and prosecute those who illicitly finance, plan, organize or unlawfully profit from pirate attacks off the coast of Somalia, recognizing that individuals and entities who incite or intentionally facilitate an act of piracy are themselves engaging in piracy as defined under international law, and expresses its intention to keep under review the possibility of applying targeted sanctions against such individuals and entities if they meet the listing criteria set out in paragraph 8 of resolution 1844(2008) of 20 November 2008;

16. *Invites* States, individually or in cooperation with regional organizations, the United Nations Office on Drugs and Crime and the International Criminal Police Organization (INTERPOL), to examine their domestic legal frameworks for detention at sea of suspected pirates to ensure that their laws provide reasonable procedures, consistent with applicable international human rights law, and also invites States to examine domestic procedures for the preservation of evidence that may be used in criminal proceedings to ensure the admissibility of such evidence, and encourages the Contact Group on Piracy off the Coast of Somalia to contribute to this work;

17. *Invites* States and regional organizations, individually or in cooperation with, among others, the United Nations Office on Drugs and Crime and INTERPOL, to assist Somalia and other States of the region in strengthening their counter-piracy law enforcement capacities, including implementation of anti-money-laundering laws, establishment of financial investigation units and strengthening of forensic capacities, as tools against international criminal networks involved in piracy, and stresses in this context the need to support the investigation and prosecution of those who illicitly finance, plan, organize or unlawfully profit from pirate attacks off the coast of Somalia;

18. *Underlines* the importance of continuing to enhance the collection, preservation and transmission to competent authorities of evidence of acts of piracy and armed robbery at sea off the coast of Somalia, and welcomes further work of the International Maritime Organization, INTERPOL and industry groups to assist in providing guidance to seafarers on the preservation of crime scenes following acts of piracy, noting the importance for the successful

prosecution of acts of piracy of enabling seafarers to give evidence in criminal proceedings;

19. *Urges* States and international organizations to share evidence and information for anti-piracy law enforcement purposes with a view to ensuring effective prosecution of suspected, and imprisonment of convicted, pirates;

20. *Requests* States, the United Nations Office on Drugs and Crime and regional organizations to consider, consistent with applicable rules of international human rights law, measures aimed at facilitating the transfer of suspected pirates for trial, and convicted pirates for imprisonment, including through relevant transfer agreements or arrangements, and commends the efforts to date of the Contact Group on Piracy off the Coast of Somalia in this regard;

21. *Welcomes* the readiness of the national and regional administrations of Somalia to cooperate with each other and with States that have prosecuted suspected pirates with a view to enabling convicted pirates to be repatriated back to Somalia under suitable prisoner transfer arrangements, consistent with applicable international law, including international human rights law, recognizes in this regard the discussions between the Government of Seychelles and the national and regional administrations of Somalia, which resulted in an agreement in principle on a legal framework for the transfer of convicted pirates to Somalia after their prosecution and conviction in Seychelles, and encourages States to continue their efforts in this regard;

22. *Urges* States, the United Nations Office on Drugs and Crime, based on support from donors, and regional organizations to consolidate international assistance to increase prison capacity in Somalia, including by constructing in the short term additional prisons in Puntland and Somaliland, and requests the Office to continue to provide training for prison staff in accordance with relevant international human rights standards and to continue to provide monitoring of compliance with such standards;

23. *Requests* the Transitional Federal Government, with the assistance of the United Nations Office on Drugs and Crime, to elaborate and adopt a complete set of counter-piracy laws, and in this regard welcomes the positive steps made in Puntland and the progress being made in Somaliland;

24. *Emphasizes* the need to ensure effective coordination of anti-piracy efforts, and in that regard requests the Secretary-General to strengthen the United Nations Political Office for Somalia as the United Nations focal point for counter-piracy, including the Kampala process;

25. *Supports* the ongoing efforts of regional States in the development of anti-piracy courts or chambers in the region, welcomes support by States and international organizations, in consultation with the Contact Group on Piracy off the Coast of Somalia, to such efforts, and requests the Secretary-General to take appropriate measures to assist States and international organizations in such activities;

26. *Decides* to urgently consider the establishment of specialized Somali courts to try suspected pirates both in Somalia and in the region, including an extraterritorial Somali specialized anti-piracy court, as referred to in the recommendations contained in the report of the Special Adviser to the Secretary-General on Legal Issues related to Piracy off the Coast of Somalia, consistent with applicable human rights law, requests the Secretary-General to report within two months on the modalities of such prosecution mechanisms, including on the participation of international personnel and on other international support and assistance, taking into account the work of the Contact Group on Piracy off the Coast of Somalia and in consultation with concerned regional States, and expresses its intention to take further decisions on this matter;

27. *Urges* both State and non-State actors affected by piracy, most notably the international shipping community, to provide support for the above-mentioned judicial and detention-related projects through the Trust Fund to Support Initiatives of States Countering Piracy off the Coast of Somalia;

28. *Decides* to remain seized of the matter.

Report of the Secretary-General (June). Pursuant to Council resolution 1976(2011) (see p. 244), the Secretary-General submitted a 15 June report [S/2011/360] on the modalities for the establishment of specialized Somali anti-piracy courts. With respect to the establishment of such courts in Somalia, piracy trials were being conducted by courts in Somaliland and Puntland and, with assistance from the United Nations, those trials were expected to reach international standards in around three years. That time frame would open the way for naval States to enter into arrangements with Somali authorities for the transfer of piracy suspects. It remained necessary for Somali law to be revised to provide a sound criminal and procedural basis for such prosecutions. Construction, refurbishment and training would result in increased prison spaces in line with international standards in Somaliland and Puntland in around two years.

The Transitional Federal Government and Somali regional authorities were opposed to the establishment of any Somali court outside of Somalia. Of the countries consulted as potential host States—Djibouti, Kenya, Mauritius, Seychelles and Tanzania—Tanzania had expressed its readiness to accommodate the court within the premises of the International Criminal Tribunal for Rwanda (ICTR) in Arusha. That solution, however, raised security concerns, as hosting the anti-piracy court would increase the security risks to ICTR, and potentially to the United Nations.

A key question would be whether the extraterritorial court should have jurisdiction to prosecute large numbers of low-level perpetrators of acts of piracy, a more limited number of financiers and planners of piracy, or both. Meanwhile, information-sharing and the investigation and prosecution of the financiers and planners of piracy would be a strategically effective and cost-effective means of supplementing current prosecution efforts.

SECURITY COUNCIL ACTION

On 24 October [meeting 6635], the Security Council unanimously adopted **resolution 2015(2011)**. The draft [S/2011/650] was submitted by 16 Member States.

The Security Council,

Recalling its previous resolutions concerning the situation in Somalia, especially resolutions 1918(2010) of 27 April 2010 and 1976(2011) of 11 April 2011,

Continuing to be gravely concerned by the growing threat that piracy and armed robbery at sea against vessels off the coast of Somalia pose to the situation in Somalia, States in the region and other States, as well as to international navigation, the safety of commercial maritime routes and the safety of seafarers and other persons, and also gravely concerned by the increased level of violence employed by pirates and persons involved in armed robbery at sea off the coast of Somalia,

Emphasizing the importance of finding a comprehensive solution to the problem of piracy and armed robbery at sea off the coast of Somalia,

Stressing the need to build Somalia's potential for sustainable economic growth as a means to tackle the underlying causes of piracy, including poverty, thus contributing to a durable eradication of piracy and armed robbery at sea off the coast of Somalia and illegal activities connected therewith,

Reaffirming its respect for the sovereignty, territorial integrity, political independence and unity of Somalia,

Reaffirming that international law, as reflected in the United Nations Convention on the Law of the Sea of 10 December 1982, in particular articles 100, 101 and 105 thereof, sets out the legal framework applicable to combating piracy and armed robbery at sea, as well as other ocean activities,

Reaffirming also that the provisions of the present resolution apply only with respect to the situation in Somalia and do not affect the rights and obligations or responsibilities of Member States under international law,

Bearing in mind the Code of Conduct concerning the Repression of Piracy and Armed Robbery against Ships in the Western Indian Ocean and the Gulf of Aden (Djibouti Code of Conduct), and recognizing the commitment of signatory States to review their national legislation with a view to ensuring that national laws to criminalize piracy and armed robbery against ships, and adequate guidelines for the exercise of jurisdiction, the conduct of investigations and prosecutions of alleged offenders, are in place,

Commending those States that have amended their domestic law in order to criminalize piracy and facilitate the prosecution of suspected pirates in their national courts consistent with applicable international law, including human rights law, and stressing the need for States to continue their efforts in this regard,

Noting with concern, at the same time, that the domestic law of a number of States lacks provisions criminalizing piracy and/or procedural provisions for effective criminal prosecution of suspected pirates,

Reaffirming the importance of national prosecution of suspected pirates for combating piracy off the coast of Somalia,

Strongly condemning the continuing practice of hostage-taking by suspected pirates operating off the coast of Somalia, expressing serious concern at the inhuman conditions that hostages face in captivity, recognizing the adverse impact on their families, calling for the immediate release of all hostages, and noting the importance of cooperation between Member States on the issue of hostage-taking and the need for the prosecution of suspected pirates for taking hostages,

Recognizing that, despite the efforts to date by States to prosecute suspected pirates at the national level, the ongoing work in this regard is still insufficient and that more must be done to ensure that suspected pirates are effectively brought to justice,

Reiterating its concern over a large number of persons suspected of piracy having to be released without facing justice, reaffirming that the failure to prosecute persons responsible for acts of piracy and armed robbery at sea off the coast of Somalia undermines anti-piracy efforts of the international community, and being determined to create conditions to ensure that pirates are held accountable,

Noting with interest the conclusion in the report of the Secretary-General on the modalities for the establishment of specialized Somali anti-piracy courts that, assuming that sufficient international assistance is provided, piracy trials being conducted by courts in Somaliland and Puntland are expected to reach international standards in about three years, and expressing its hope, consistent with the mentioned report of the Secretary-General, that this timeline will be accelerated if suitable experts, including those from the Somali diaspora, can be identified and recruited,

Welcoming the consultations between the United Nations and regional States, including Seychelles, Mauritius and the United Republic of Tanzania, and the willingness expressed by the United Republic of Tanzania to assist the international community, under the right conditions, to prosecute suspected pirates in its territory,

Determining that the incidents of piracy and armed robbery at sea off the coast of Somalia exacerbate the situation in Somalia, which continues to constitute a threat to international peace and security in the region,

1. *Reaffirms* that the ultimate goal of enhancing Somali responsibility and active involvement in efforts to prosecute suspected pirates, as emphasized by the Special Adviser to the Secretary-General on Legal Issues related to Piracy off the Coast of Somalia in his report transmitted to the Security Council on 19 January 2011, remains highly relevant in the overall context of fighting piracy;

2. *Recognizes* the primary role of the Transitional Federal Government and the relevant Somali regional authorities in eradicating piracy off the coast of Somalia;

3. *Welcomes* in this regard the fact that the Somalia end-of-transition road map of 6 September 2011 includes developing counter-piracy policy and legislation in conjunction with regional entities as a key task of the transitional federal institutions, and notes that the Security Council has made its future support to the transitional federal institutions contingent upon the completion of the tasks contained in the road map;

4. *Takes note with appreciation* of the report of the Secretary-General on the modalities for the establishment of specialized Somali anti-piracy courts prepared pursuant to paragraph 26 of resolution 1976(2011);

5. *Reiterates its call upon* all States, and in particular flag, port and coastal States, States of the nationality of victims as well as of perpetrators of piracy and armed robbery, and other States with relevant jurisdiction under international law and national legislation, to cooperate in determining jurisdiction and in the investigation and prosecution of all persons responsible for acts of piracy and

armed robbery off the coast of Somalia, including anyone who incites or facilitates an act of piracy, consistent with applicable international law, including human rights law;

6. *Calls upon* States to cooperate also, as appropriate, on the prosecution of suspected pirates for taking hostages;

7. *Reiterates its request*, as a matter of urgency, to the Transitional Federal Government and relevant Somali regional authorities to elaborate, with the assistance of the United Nations Office on Drugs and Crime and the United Nations Development Programme, and adopt a complete set of counter-piracy laws, including laws to prosecute those who illicitly finance, plan, organize, facilitate or profit from pirate attacks, with a view to ensuring the effective prosecution of suspected pirates and those associated with piracy attacks in Somalia, the post-conviction transfer of pirates prosecuted elsewhere to Somalia and the imprisonment of convicted pirates in Somalia, as soon as possible, and strongly urges the Transitional Federal Government and regional authorities of Somalia to expeditiously address any other existing obstacles that impede progress in this regard, and requests the Transitional Federal Government and relevant regional authorities of Somalia to provide a report to the Council by 31 December 2011 on action taken in each of the areas above;

8. *Calls upon* the United Nations Office on Drugs and Crime, the United Nations Development Programme and other international partners to further their efforts to support the development of domestic legislation, agreements and mechanisms that would allow the effective prosecution of suspected pirates and the transfer and imprisonment of convicted pirates;

9. *Strongly urges* States that have not already done so to criminalize piracy under their domestic law, and reiterates its call upon States to favourably consider the prosecution of suspected, and imprisonment of convicted, pirates apprehended off the coast of Somalia, consistent with applicable international law, including international human rights law;

10. *Urges* States and international organizations to share evidence and information for anti-piracy law enforcement purposes with a view to ensuring effective prosecution of suspected, and imprisonment of convicted, pirates;

11. *Calls upon* all Member States to report, no later than 31 December 2011, to the Secretary-General on measures they have taken to criminalize piracy under their domestic law and to prosecute and support the prosecution of individuals suspected of piracy off the coast of Somalia and the imprisonment of convicted pirates, and requests the Secretary-General to compile this information and to circulate this compilation as a document of the Council;

12. *Commends* the ongoing work of the United Nations Office on Drugs and Crime and the United Nations Development Programme, as described in the report of the Secretary-General, in supporting counter-piracy trials and increased prison capacity in Somalia, consistent with the recommendation of the Special Adviser to the Secretary-General on Legal Issues related to Piracy off the Coast of Somalia;

13. *Reaffirms* that the efforts to promote effective judicial mechanisms to prosecute suspected pirates should be continued and intensified;

14. *Welcomes* the undertaking of the Secretary-General, in connection with his report, to further proactively assist, at the request of the Council, in the taking of appropriate next steps aimed at further enhancing counter-piracy prosecution efforts;

15. *Requests* States and regional organizations to consider possible ways to seek and allow for the effective contribution of the Somali diaspora to anti-piracy efforts, in particular in the area of prosecution, as advised in the report of the Secretary-General;

16. *Decides* to continue its consideration, as a matter of urgency, without prejudice to any further steps to ensure that pirates are held accountable, of the establishment of specialized anti-piracy courts in Somalia and other States in the region with substantial international participation and/or support, and requests that the Secretary-General, in conjunction with the United Nations Office on Drugs and Crime and the United Nations Development Programme, further consult with Somalia and regional States willing to establish such anti-piracy courts on the kind of international assistance, including the provision of international personnel, that would be required to help to make such courts operational; the procedural arrangements required for the transfer of apprehended pirates and related evidence; the projected case capacity of such courts; and the projected timeline and costs for such courts, and to provide to the Council in the light of such consultations within ninety days detailed implementation proposals for the establishment of such courts, as appropriate;

17. *Underlines* the importance for such courts to have jurisdiction to be exercised over not only suspects captured at sea, but also anyone who incites or intentionally facilitates piracy operations, including key figures of criminal networks involved in piracy who illicitly plan, organize, facilitate or finance and profit from such attacks;

18. *Recognizes* that any increase in prosecution capacity must necessarily be accompanied by a related increase in prison capacity, and calls upon both Somali authorities, the United Nations Office on Drugs and Crime, the United Nations Development Programme and other international partners to support the construction and responsible operation of prisons in Somalia in accordance with international law;

19. *Calls upon* Member States, regional organizations and other appropriate partners to support efforts to establish specialized anti-piracy courts in the region by making or facilitating arrangements for the provision of international experts, including those from the Somali diaspora, through secondment or otherwise, and to otherwise support the work of the United Nations Office on Drugs and Crime, the United Nations Development Programme or others in this regard through contributions to the Trust Fund to Support Initiatives of States Countering Piracy off the Coast of Somalia;

20. *Decides* to remain seized of the matter.

Reports of Secretary-General (October). On 25 October, pursuant to Council resolution 1950(2010) [YUN 2010, p. 291], the Secretary-General reported [S/2011/662] on piracy and armed robbery off the coast of Somalia. The report was based on information received as at 3 October and examined activities undertaken by Member States, regional organizations, the United Nations and its partners.

The International Maritime Organization (IMO) indicated that, in the first nine months of 2011, 185 attacks against ships off the coast of Somalia had taken place, resulting in the hijacking of 28 ships. As at early October, 316 people and 15 vessels were being held hostage, mainly in Puntland and Galmudug. When compared with the previous year, those figures showed a decrease of piracy, achieved through a combination of actions by naval forces and self-protection measures. The international naval presence had warded off 75 per cent of attacks and had allowed the delivery of humanitarian assistance. Due to the monsoon period, the incidence of attacks was reduced in the Somali Basin and western Indian Ocean, but increased closer to the Omani coast. The geographic spread of pirate activities put increased strain on scarce naval forces. The Contact Group on Piracy off the Coast of Somalia [YUN 2009, p. 286] continued to play a key role in countering piracy. One of its key proposals had been the tracking of financial flows of masterminds of piracy. Despite those efforts, however, Somali pirates were expanding their operations, and there were reports of linkages between Al-Shabaab and pirate groups. The fight against piracy could be won only through an integrated strategy that tackled deterrence, security and the rule of law, and development. Counter-piracy efforts should be a more integral element of the Somalia peace process. In that regard, the segments related to counter-piracy of the road map adopted in September were a step in the right direction. The Trust Fund to Support Initiatives of States Countering Piracy off the Coast of Somalia [YUN 2010, p. 287] supported projects ranging from renovating overcrowded prisons to building up capacity to prosecute and incarcerate convicted pirates. While the elimination of piracy was a central goal, it would be important to lay out interim priorities. One such priority would be to complement maritime security operations with more efforts inshore, in the zone between the coast and international waters.

Pursuant to Security Council resolution 1976(2011) (see p. 244), the Secretary-General, on 25 October [S/2011/661], reported on the protection of Somali natural resources and waters. Allegations of illegal fishing and toxic waste dumping, as well as their links to piracy, required further investigation. The road map adopted in September contained important measures to be taken by the Transitional Federal Government to address potential illegal, unreported and unregulated fishing. One such measure was to declare an exclusive economic zone off the Somali coast in accordance with the United Nations Convention on the Law of the Sea [YUN 1982, p. 181]. It was equally important to address the conditions that enabled illegal charcoal trading, controlled by Al-Shabaab, which had put livelihoods at risk through the depletion of the primary forest cover in southern Somalia, thus exacerbating the humanitarian crisis. The United Nations, together with the au and amisom, was working to support the Government to reform its security sector and build up an adequate police force. The limited capacity of the Government to implement the international agreements on resource management and environmental protection needed to be expanded. The Secretary-General urged Member States to investigate allegations of illegal fishing and illegal dumping, including of toxic substances, with a view to prosecuting such offences when committed by persons or entities under their jurisdiction.

The United Nations would assist the Government and regional authorities in establishing marine protected areas, as well as in helping to devise conservation and management measures. Member States needed to strengthen efforts to prevent illegal, unreported and unregulated fishing. The challenges to Somalia's natural resources had to be addressed simultaneously at the local, regional and national levels. The Government, together with the Parliament, should work collaboratively with the regional authorities of Puntland, Somaliland and Galmudug to meet those challenges.

SECURITY COUNCIL ACTION

On 22 November [meeting 6663], the Security Council unanimously adopted **resolution 2020(2011)**. The draft [S/2011/725] was submitted by France, Germany, India, Norway, the Russian Federation, the United Kingdom and the United States.

The Security Council,

Recalling its previous resolutions concerning the situation in Somalia, especially resolutions 1814(2008) of 15 May 2008, 1816(2008) of 2 June 2008, 1838(2008) of 7 October 2008, 1844(2008) of 20 November 2008, 1846(2008) of 2 December 2008, 1851(2008) of 16 December 2008, 1897(2009) of 30 November 2009, 1918(2010) of 27 April 2010, 1950(2010) of 23 November 2010, 1976(2011) of 11 April 2011 and 2015(2011) of 24 October 2011, as well as the statement by its President of 25 August 2010,

Continuing to be gravely concerned by the ongoing threat that piracy and armed robbery at sea against vessels pose to the prompt, safe and effective delivery of humanitarian aid to Somalia and the region, to the safety of seafarers and other persons, to international navigation and the safety of commercial maritime routes and to other vulnerable ships, including fishing activities in conformity with international law, and also gravely concerned by the extended range of the piracy threat into the western Indian Ocean and adjacent sea areas and the increase in pirate capacities,

Expressing its concern about the reported involvement of children in piracy off the coast of Somalia,

Recognizing that the ongoing instability in Somalia contributes to the problem of piracy and armed robbery at sea off the coast of Somalia, and stressing the need for a comprehensive response by the international community to repress piracy and armed robbery at sea and tackle its underlying causes,

Recognizing also the need to investigate and prosecute not only suspects captured at sea, but also anyone who incites or intentionally facilitates piracy operations, including key figures of criminal networks involved in piracy who illicitly plan, organize, facilitate or finance and profit from such attacks, and reiterating its concern over a large number of persons suspected of piracy having to be released without facing justice, reaffirming that the failure to prosecute persons responsible for acts of piracy and armed robbery at sea off the coast of Somalia undermines anti-piracy efforts of the international community, and being determined to create conditions to ensure that pirates are held accountable,

Reaffirming its respect for the sovereignty, territorial integrity, political independence and unity of Somalia, including Somalia's rights with respect to offshore natural resources, including fisheries, in accordance with international law, recalling the importance of preventing, in accordance with international law, illegal fishing and illegal dumping, including of toxic substances, stressing the need to investigate allegations of such illegal fishing and dumping, and taking note with appreciation in this respect of the report of the Secretary-General on the protection of Somali natural resources and waters prepared pursuant to paragraph 7 of Security Council resolution 1976(2011),

Further reaffirming that international law, as reflected in the United Nations Convention on the Law of the Sea of 10 December 1982, sets out the legal framework applicable to combating piracy and armed robbery at sea, as well as other ocean activities,

Again taking into account the crisis situation in Somalia and the limited capacity of the Transitional Federal Government to interdict or, upon interdiction, to prosecute pirates or to patrol or secure the waters off the coast of Somalia, including the international sea lanes and Somalia's territorial waters,

Noting the several requests of the Transitional Federal Government for international assistance to counter piracy off the coast of Somalia, including the letter dated 10 November 2011 from the Permanent Representative of Somalia to the United Nations expressing the appreciation of the Transitional Federal Government to the Security Council for its assistance, expressing the willingness of the Transitional Federal Government to consider working with other States and regional organizations to combat piracy and armed robbery at sea off the coast of Somalia, and requesting that the provisions of resolution 1897(2009) be renewed for an additional twelve months,

Commending the efforts of the European Union operation Atalanta, the North Atlantic Treaty Organization operations Allied Protector and Ocean Shield, the Combined Maritime Forces' Combined Task Force 151 and other States acting in a national capacity in cooperation with the Transitional Federal Government and each other to suppress piracy and to protect vulnerable ships transiting through the waters off the coast of Somalia, and welcoming the efforts of individual countries, including China, India, Iran (Islamic Republic of), Japan, Malaysia, the Republic of Korea, the Russian Federation, Saudi Arabia and Yemen, which have deployed ships and/or aircraft in the region, as stated in the report of the Secretary-General,

Welcoming the capacity-building efforts in the region made by the International Maritime Organization Code of Conduct concerning the Repression of Piracy and Armed Robbery against Ships in the Western Indian Ocean and the Gulf of Aden (Djibouti Code of Conduct), the Djibouti Code Trust Fund and the Trust Fund to Support Initiatives of States Countering Piracy off the Coast of Somalia, and recognizing the need for all engaged international and regional organizations to cooperate fully,

Noting with appreciation the efforts made by the International Maritime Organization and the shipping industry to develop and update guidance, best management practices and recommendations to assist ships to prevent and suppress piracy attacks off the coast of Somalia, including in the Gulf of Aden and the Indian Ocean area, and recognizing the work of the International Maritime Organization and the Contact Group on Piracy off the Coast of Somalia on privately contracted armed security personnel on board ships in high-risk areas,

Noting with concern that the continuing limited capacity and domestic legislation to facilitate the custody and prosecution of suspected pirates after their capture has hindered more robust international action against the pirates off the coast of Somalia, and in some cases has led to pirates being released without facing justice, regardless of whether there is sufficient evidence to support prosecution, and reiterating that, consistent with the provisions of the United Nations Convention on the Law of the Sea concerning the repression of piracy, the Convention for the Suppression of Unlawful Acts against the Safety of Maritime Navigation of 10 March 1988 provides for parties to create criminal offences, establish jurisdiction and accept delivery of persons responsible for or suspected of seizing or exercising control over a ship by force or threat thereof or any other form of intimidation,

Underlining the importance of continuing to enhance the collection, preservation and transmission to competent authorities of evidence of acts of piracy and armed robbery at sea off the coast of Somalia, and welcoming the ongoing work of the International Maritime Organization, the International Criminal Police Organization (INTERPOL) and industry groups to develop guidance to seafarers on the preservation of crime scenes following acts of piracy, and noting the importance for the successful prosecution of acts of piracy of enabling seafarers to give evidence in criminal proceedings,

Noting the consensus at the ninth plenary session of the Contact Group on Piracy off the Coast of Somalia on 14 July 2011 to establish a formal Working Group 5 on illicit financial flows linked to piracy off the coast of Somalia,

Recognizing that pirates are turning increasingly to kidnapping and hostage-taking and that these activities help to generate funding to purchase weapons, gain recruits and continue their operational activities, thereby jeopardizing the safety and security of innocent civilians and restricting the flow of free commerce,

Reaffirming international condemnation of acts of kidnapping and hostage-taking, including acts condemned in the International Convention against the Taking of Hostages, and strongly condemning the continuing practice of hostage-taking by suspected pirates operating off the coast of Somalia, expressing serious concern at the inhuman conditions that hostages face in captivity, recognizing the adverse impact on their families, calling for the immediate release of all hostages, and noting the importance of cooperation between Member States on the issue of hostage-taking and the need for the prosecution of suspected pirates for taking hostages,

Commending the efforts of Kenya and Seychelles to prosecute suspected pirates in their national courts, welcoming the engagement of Mauritius and the United Republic of Tanzania, and noting with appreciation the assistance being provided by the United Nations Office on Drugs and Crime, the Trust Fund to Support Initiatives of States Countering Piracy off the Coast of Somalia and other international organizations and donors, in coordination with the Contact Group on Piracy off the Coast of Somalia, to support Kenya, Seychelles, Somalia and other States in the region, including Yemen, to take steps to prosecute, or incarcerate in a third State after prosecution elsewhere, pirates, including facilitators and financiers ashore, consistent with applicable international human rights law, and emphasizing the need for States and international organizations to further enhance international efforts in this regard,

Welcoming the readiness of the national and regional administrations of Somalia to cooperate with each other and with States that have prosecuted suspected pirates with a view to enabling convicted pirates to be repatriated back to Somalia under suitable prisoner transfer arrangements, consistent with applicable international law, including international human rights law,

Welcoming also the report of the Secretary-General, as requested in resolution 1950(2010), on the implementation of that resolution and on the situation with respect to piracy and armed robbery at sea off the coast of Somalia,

Taking note with appreciation of the report of the Secretary-General on the modalities for the establishment of specialized Somali anti-piracy courts prepared pursuant to paragraph 26 of resolution 1976(2011), and the ongoing efforts within the Contact Group on Piracy off the Coast of Somalia and the United Nations Secretariat to explore possible additional mechanisms to effectively prosecute persons suspected of piracy and armed robbery at sea off the coast of Somalia, including those ashore who incite or intentionally facilitate acts of piracy,

Stressing the need for States to consider possible methods to assist the seafarers who are victims of pirates, and welcoming in this regard the ongoing work within the Contact Group on Piracy off the Coast of Somalia and the International Maritime Organization on developing guidelines for the care of seafarers and other persons who have been subjected to acts of piracy,

Noting with appreciation the ongoing efforts of the United Nations Office on Drugs and Crime and the United Nations Development Programme to support efforts to enhance the capacity of the corrections system in Somalia, including regional authorities, notably with the support of the Trust Fund to Support Initiatives of States Countering Piracy off the Coast of Somalia, to incarcerate convicted pirates consistent with applicable international human rights law,

Bearing in mind the Djibouti Code of Conduct, and recognizing the efforts of signatory States to develop the appropriate regulatory and legislative frameworks to combat piracy, enhance their capacity to patrol the waters of the region, interdict suspect vessels and prosecute suspected pirates,

Emphasizing that peace and stability within Somalia, the strengthening of State institutions, economic and social development and respect for human rights and the rule of law are necessary to create the conditions for a durable eradication of piracy and armed robbery at sea off the coast of Somalia, and further emphasizing that Somalia's long-term security rests with the effective development by the Transitional Federal Government of the National Security Force, including the Somali Police Force, within the framework of the Djibouti Agreement and in line with a national security strategy,

Welcoming in this regard the fact that the road map to end the transition in Somalia, of 6 September 2011, calls for the Transitional Federal Government to develop counter-piracy policy and legislation in conjunction with regional entities, and the declaration of an exclusive economic zone, as key tasks of the transitional federal institutions, and notes that the Security Council has made its future support to the transitional federal institutions contingent upon the completion of the tasks contained in the road map,

Determining that the incidents of piracy and armed robbery at sea off the coast of Somalia exacerbate the situation in Somalia, which continues to constitute a threat to international peace and security in the region,

Acting under Chapter VII of the Charter of the United Nations,

1. *Reiterates* that it condemns and deplores all acts of piracy and armed robbery against vessels in the waters off the coast of Somalia;

2. *Recognizes* that the ongoing instability in Somalia is one of the underlying causes of the problem of piracy and contributes to the problem of piracy and armed robbery at sea off the coast of Somalia;

3. *Stresses* the need for a comprehensive response to repress piracy and tackle its underlying causes by the international community;

4. *Recognizes* the need to investigate and prosecute not only suspects captured at sea, but also anyone who incites or intentionally facilitates piracy operations, including key figures of criminal networks involved in piracy who illicitly plan, organize, facilitate or finance and profit from such attacks;

5. *Calls upon* States to cooperate also, as appropriate, on the issue of hostage-taking, and the prosecution of suspected pirates for taking hostages;

6. *Notes again with concern* the findings contained in the report of the Monitoring Group on Somalia of 20 November 2008 that escalating ransom payments and the lack of enforcement of the arms embargo established by resolution 733(1992) of 23 January 1992 are fuelling the growth of piracy off the coast of Somalia, and calls upon all States to cooperate fully with the Monitoring Group on Somalia and Eritrea, including on information-sharing regarding possible arms embargo violations;

7. *Renews its call upon* States and regional organizations that have the capacity to do so to take part in the fight against piracy and armed robbery at sea off the coast of Somalia, in particular, consistent with the present resolution and international law, by deploying naval vessels, arms and military aircraft and through seizures and disposition of boats, vessels, arms and other related equipment used in the commission of piracy and armed robbery at sea off the coast of Somalia, or for which there are reasonable grounds for suspecting such use;

8. *Commends* the work of the Contact Group on Piracy off the Coast of Somalia to facilitate coordination in order to deter acts of piracy and armed robbery at sea off the coast of Somalia, in cooperation with the International Maritime

Organization, flag States and the Transitional Federal Government, and urges States and international organizations to continue to support these efforts;

9. *Encourages* Member States to continue to cooperate with the Transitional Federal Government in the fight against piracy and armed robbery at sea, notes the primary role of the Transitional Federal Government in the fight against piracy and armed robbery at sea off the coast of Somalia, and decides to renew for a further period of twelve months from the date of the present resolution, the authorizations as set out in paragraph 10 of resolution 1846(2008) and paragraph 6 of resolution 1851(2008), as renewed by paragraph 7 of resolution 1897(2009) and paragraph 7 of resolution 1950(2010), granted to States and regional organizations cooperating with the Transitional Federal Government in the fight against piracy and armed robbery at sea off the coast of Somalia, for which advance notification has been provided by the Transitional Federal Government to the Secretary-General;

10. *Affirms* that the authorizations renewed in the present resolution apply only with respect to the situation in Somalia and shall not affect the rights or obligations or responsibilities of Member States under international law, including any rights or obligations, under the United Nations Convention on the Law of the Sea, with respect to any other situation, and underscores, in particular, that the present resolution shall not be considered as establishing customary international law; and affirms further that such authorizations have been renewed only following the receipt of the letter dated 10 November 2011 conveying the consent of the Transitional Federal Government;

11. *Also affirms* that the measures imposed by paragraph 5 of resolution 733(1992) and further elaborated upon in paragraphs 1 and 2 of resolution 1425(2002) of 22 July 2002 do not apply to weapons and military equipment destined for the sole use of Member States and regional organizations taking measures in accordance with paragraph 9 above or to supplies of technical assistance to Somalia solely for the purposes set out in paragraph 6 of resolution 1950(2010) which have been exempted from those measures in accordance with the procedure set out in paragraphs 11 (*b*) and 12 of resolution 1772(2007) of 20 August 2007;

12. *Requests* that cooperating States take appropriate steps to ensure that the activities they undertake pursuant to the authorizations in paragraph 9 above do not have the practical effect of denying or impairing the right of innocent passage to the ships of any third State;

13. *Calls upon* Member States to assist Somalia, at the request of the Transitional Federal Government and with notification to the Secretary-General, to strengthen capacity in Somalia, including regional authorities, to bring to justice those who are using Somali territory to plan, facilitate or undertake criminal acts of piracy and armed robbery at sea, and stresses that any measures taken pursuant to the present paragraph shall be consistent with applicable international human rights law;

14. *Calls upon* all States, in particular flag, port and coastal States, States of the nationality of victims and perpetrators of piracy and armed robbery and other States with relevant jurisdiction under international law and national legislation to cooperate in determining jurisdiction and in the investigation and prosecution of all persons responsible for acts of piracy and armed robbery off the coast of Somalia, including anyone who incites or facilitates an act of piracy, consistent with applicable international law, including international human rights law, to ensure that all pirates handed over to judicial authorities are subject to a judicial process, and to render assistance by, among other actions, providing disposition and logistics assistance with respect to persons under their jurisdiction and control, such as victims and witnesses and persons detained as a result of operations conducted under the present resolution;

15. *Also calls upon* all States to criminalize piracy under their domestic law and to favourably consider the prosecution of suspected, and imprisonment of convicted, pirates apprehended off the coast of Somalia, and their facilitators and financiers ashore, consistent with applicable international law, including international human rights law;

16. *Reiterates* its decision to continue its consideration, as a matter of urgency, of the establishment of specialized anti-piracy courts in Somalia and other States in the region with substantial international participation and/or support, as set forth in resolution 2015(2011), and the importance of such courts having jurisdiction over not only suspects captured at sea, but also anyone who incites or intentionally facilitates piracy operations, including key figures of criminal networks involved in piracy who illicitly plan, organize, facilitate or finance and profit from such attacks, emphasizes the need for strengthened cooperation of States and regional and international organizations in holding such individuals accountable, and encourages the Contact Group on Piracy off the Coast of Somalia to continue its discussions in this regard;

17. *Urges* all States to take appropriate actions under their existing domestic law to prevent the illicit financing of acts of piracy and the laundering of its proceeds;

18. *Urges* States, in cooperation with INTERPOL and the European Police Office (Europol), to further investigate international criminal networks involved in piracy off the coast of Somalia, including those responsible for illicit financing and facilitation;

19. *Commends* INTERPOL for the creation of a global piracy database designed to consolidate information about piracy off the coast of Somalia and facilitate the development of actionable analysis for law enforcement, and urges all States to share such information with INTERPOL for use in the database, through appropriate channels;

20. *Stresses*, in this context, the need to support the investigation and prosecution of those who illicitly finance, plan, organize or unlawfully profit from pirate attacks off the coast of Somalia;

21. *Urges* States and international organizations to share evidence and information for anti-piracy law enforcement purposes with a view to ensuring effective prosecution of suspected, and imprisonment of convicted, pirates;

22. *Commends* the establishment of the Trust Fund to Support Initiatives of States Countering Piracy off the Coast of Somalia and the International Maritime Organization Djibouti Code Trust Fund, and urges both State and non-State actors affected by piracy, most notably the international shipping community, to contribute to them;

23. *Urges* States parties to the United Nations Convention on the Law of the Sea and the Convention for the Sup-

pression of Unlawful Acts against the Safety of Maritime Navigation to implement fully their relevant obligations under these Conventions and customary international law and to cooperate with the United Nations Office on Drugs and Crime, the International Maritime Organization, other States and other international organizations to build judicial capacity for the successful prosecution of persons suspected of piracy and armed robbery at sea off the coast of Somalia;

24. *Urges* States individually or within the framework of competent international organizations to positively consider investigating allegations of illegal fishing and illegal dumping, including of toxic substances, with a view to prosecuting such offences when committed by persons under their jurisdiction; and takes note of the intention of the Secretary-General to include updates on these issues in his future reports relating to piracy off the coast of Somalia;

25. *Welcomes* the recommendations and guidance of the International Maritime Organization on preventing and suppressing piracy and armed robbery against ships, underlines the importance of implementation of such recommendations and guidance by all stakeholders, including the shipping industry, urges States, in collaboration with the shipping and insurance industries, and the International Maritime Organization to continue to develop and implement avoidance, evasion and defensive best practices and advisories to take when under attack or when sailing in the waters off the coast of Somalia, and further urges States to make their citizens and vessels available for forensic investigation, as appropriate, at the first port of call immediately following an act or attempted act of piracy or armed robbery at sea or release from captivity;

26. *Invites* the International Maritime Organization to continue its contributions to the prevention and suppression of acts of piracy and armed robbery against ships in coordination, in particular, with the United Nations Office on Drugs and Crime, the World Food Programme, the shipping industry and all other parties concerned, and recognizes the role of the International Maritime Organization concerning privately contracted armed security personnel on board ships in high-risk areas;

27. *Notes* the importance of securing the safe delivery of World Food Programme assistance by sea, and welcomes the ongoing work of the World Food Programme, the European Union operation Atalanta and flag States with regard to vessel protection detachments on World Food Programme vessels;

28. *Requests* States and regional organizations cooperating with the Transitional Federal Government to inform the Security Council and the Secretary-General in nine months of the progress of actions undertaken in the exercise of the authorizations provided in paragraph 9 above, and further requests all States contributing through the Contact Group on Piracy off the Coast of Somalia to the fight against piracy off the coast of Somalia, including Somalia and other States in the region, to report by the same deadline on their efforts to establish jurisdiction and cooperation in the investigation and prosecution of piracy;

29. *Requests* the Secretary-General to report to the Security Council within eleven months of the adoption of the present resolution on the implementation of the present resolution and on the situation with respect to piracy and armed robbery at sea off the coast of Somalia;

30. *Expresses its intention* to review the situation and to consider, as appropriate, renewing the authorizations provided in paragraph 9 above for additional periods upon the request of the Transitional Federal Government;

31. *Decides* to remain seized of the matter.

Children and armed conflict

At its twenty-ninth meeting, on 25 February 2011, the Security Council Working Group on Children and Armed Conflict adopted its conclusions on children and armed conflict in Somalia [YUN 2010, p. 296]. On 7 April [S/2011/230], the Council transmitted to the Secretary-General a letter of 21 March from the Chairman of the Working Group based on those conclusions. The Group's Chairman requested the Secretary-General to strengthen monitoring and reporting of the situation of children, to support the Transitional Federal Government in preparing a time-bound action plan to end the recruitment and use of child soldiers, and to conduct a dialogue with all other stakeholders.

Sanctions

By resolution 733(1992) [YUN 1992, p. 199], the Security Council imposed a general and complete arms embargo on Somalia, and by resolution 751(1992) [ibid., p. 202], established a Committee to oversee the embargo, expanding its mandate by resolution 1907(2009) [YUN 2009, p. 299]. Subsequently, the Council outlined certain exemptions to the embargo and further elaborated the scope of the measures. Following the adoption of resolution 1907(2009), which imposed a sanctions regime on Eritrea and expanded the Committee's mandate, the Committee in 2010 changed its name to the "Security Council Committee pursuant to resolutions 751(1992) and 1907(2009) concerning Somalia and Eritrea".

The Council in 2002, by resolution 1425(2002) [YUN 2002, p. 206], established a Panel of Experts on Somalia to generate information on violations of the arms embargo with a view to strengthening it. The Panel of Experts was succeeded by the Monitoring Group on Somalia established pursuant to resolution 1519(2003) [YUN 2003, p. 254] to focus on arms embargo violations. Subsequent resolutions extended and expanded the mandate of the Monitoring Group. After the adoption of resolution 1907(2009) the Monitoring Group changed its name to the "Monitoring Group on Somalia and Eritrea".

By resolution 1916(2010) [YUN 2010, p. 298], the Council decided that the assets freeze that it had imposed by paragraph 3 of resolution 1844(2008) [YUN 2008, p. 297] should not apply to the payment of funds, other financial assets or economic resources necessary to ensure the timely delivery of humanitarian assistance in Somalia. By the same resolution, the Council requested the Resident and Humanitarian Coordinator for Somalia to report to the Council every 120 days on any impediments to the delivery of humanitarian assistance. In resolution 1972(2011) (see below), the Council renewed that exemption for 16 months and asked the Humanitarian Coordinator to report to the Council by 15 November.

Report of Humanitarian Coordinator (March). In accordance with resolution 1916(2010), the Chairman of the Security Council Committee pursuant to resolutions 751(1992) and 1907(2009) concerning Somalia and Eritrea, on 11 March, transmitted to the Council the third report [S/2011/125] of the United Nations Resident and Humanitarian Coordinator for Somalia, covering the period from November 2010 to March 2011. The report focused on the regions of Somalia under the control of Al-Shabaab, outlining the constraints to humanitarian access, as well as on the mitigation measures put in place to address politicization, misuse and misappropriation of aid. In mid-December, drought began in most parts of Somalia, affecting children in particular. More than 400 schools serving nearly 55,000 pupils countrywide were closed because families were forced to move as water sources dried up. Non-State armed actors continued to impose conditions on the humanitarian organizations operating in drought-affected regions and were responsible for a number of incidents against humanitarian staff, assets and facilities. In December 2010 and January 2011 alone, 14 security incidents affected humanitarian organizations, which resulted in delays in the delivery of assistance. Armed violence between the Federal Government, amisom and Al-Shabaab continued. The number of deaths was unknown. Approximately 93,000 people were internally displaced, with most of those displacements occurring in Mogadishu. The number of people in need of humanitarian assistance or livelihood support increased by 20 per cent, from 2 million to 2.4 million, corresponding to 32 per cent of the population. Somalia had one of the highest malnutrition rates in the world. Acute childhood malnutrition increased from 15 to 20 per cent during the reporting period. Approximately 75 per cent of those affected (around 241,000 children) lived in southern Somalia. Humanitarian operations continued but were heavily affected by the conduct of all parties to the conflict. Most of those requiring assistance resided in areas under the control of non-State armed actors. Risk mitigation measures, such as the independent auditing of projects funded by the Common Humanitarian Fund, risk management training programmes and the development of a contractor information management system, had improved dramatically. As a result, there was greater confidence that humanitarian assistance was reaching the intended beneficiaries.

SECURITY COUNCIL ACTION

On 17 March [meeting 6496], the Security Council unanimously adopted **resolution 1972(2011)**. The draft [S/2011/140] was submitted by the United Kingdom.

The Security Council,

Reaffirming all its previous resolutions and the statements by its President concerning the situation in Somalia, in particular resolution 733(1992) of 23 January 1992, which established an embargo on all deliveries of weapons and military equipment to Somalia (hereinafter referred to as "the Somalia arms embargo"), as elaborated upon and amended in subsequent relevant resolutions, as well as resolutions 1844(2008) of 20 November 2008 and 1916(2010) of 19 March 2010,

Reaffirming its respect for the sovereignty, territorial integrity, political independence and unity of Somalia,

Condemning flows of weapons, ammunition supplies, and financial and technical assistance related to such supplies, to and through Somalia in violation of the Somalia arms embargo as a serious threat to peace and stability in Somalia,

Reiterating its insistence that all States, in particular those in the region, should refrain from any action in contravention of the Somalia arms embargo and take all necessary steps to hold violators accountable,

Calling upon all States to effectively implement the targeted measures imposed in resolution 1844(2008),

Underscoring the importance of upholding the principles of neutrality, impartiality, humanity and independence in the provision of humanitarian assistance,

Noting the reviews conducted by the Security Council on the effects of the measures set out in paragraph 5 of resolution 1916(2010), and taking note of the reports of the United Nations Resident and Humanitarian Coordinator for Somalia transmitted on 12 July and 23 November 2010 and 11 March 2011,

Determining that the situation in Somalia continues to constitute a threat to international peace and security in the region,

Acting under Chapter VII of the Charter of the United Nations,

1. *Stresses* the obligation of all States to comply fully with the measures imposed by resolution 733(1992) as elaborated upon and amended in subsequent relevant resolutions, and the measures imposed by resolution 1844(2008);

2. *Reaffirms* the obligation on all parties to promote and ensure compliance with international humanitarian law in Somalia;

3. *Underscores* the importance of humanitarian aid operations, condemns any politicization of humanitarian assistance, or misuse or misappropriation, and calls upon Member States and the United Nations to take all feasible steps to mitigate the aforementioned practices in Somalia;

4. *Decides* that, for a period of sixteen months from the date of the present resolution, and without prejudice to humanitarian assistance programmes conducted elsewhere, the obligations imposed on Member States in paragraph 3 of resolution 1844(2008) shall not apply to the payment of funds, other financial assets or economic resources necessary to ensure the timely delivery of urgently needed humanitarian assistance in Somalia by the United Nations, its special-

ized agencies or programmes, humanitarian organizations having observer status in the General Assembly that provide humanitarian assistance, or their implementing partners;

5. *Requests* the Emergency Relief Coordinator to report to the Security Council by 15 November 2011 and again by 15 July 2012 on the implementation of paragraphs 3 and 4 above and on any impediments to the delivery of humanitarian assistance in Somalia, and requests relevant United Nations agencies and humanitarian organizations having observer status in the General Assembly that provide humanitarian assistance to assist the United Nations Resident and Humanitarian Coordinator for Somalia in the preparation of such reports by providing information relevant to paragraphs 3 and 4 above;

6. *Decides* to remain actively seized of the matter.

Report of Monitoring Group. On 18 July [S/2011/433], the Chairman of the Security Council Committee pursuant to resolutions 751(1992) and 1907(2009) concerning Somalia and Eritrea transmitted to the Council the report of the Monitoring Group on Somalia and Eritrea. According to the report, more than half of Somali territory, including Somaliland, Puntland, Gaalmudug and Himan iyo Heeb, was controlled by responsible, comparatively stable authorities that had demonstrated, to varying degrees, their capacity to provide relative peace and security to their populations. In Somaliland, the authorities maintained security and stability, kept their coastline pirate-free and, in June 2010, consolidated their nascent democratic institutions with a presidential election. In Puntland, the administration also maintained relative peace and stability, although targeted killings were on the rise in major towns, and made gains against piracy. Those authorities, however, faced growing threats in the disputed regions of Sool and Sanaag, where local militia had merged with Al-Shabaab. Much of Galguduud region was controlled by anti-Al-Shabaab militias loosely unified under the umbrella of Ahlu Sunna wal Jama'a, but lacked a functional authority. Other southern anti-Al-Shabaab militias appeared to be proxies for neighbouring States rather than emergent local authorities, and it was unclear to what extent they might be able to deliver lasting peace and security.

The Transitional Federal Government had left much of the country to Al-Shabaab, which controlled the greater part of Somali territory between the Kenyan border and southern parts of Mudug and Galguduud regions. In Mogadishu, AMISOM, together with pro-Government militias, made some gains against Al-Shabaab. In the absence of a coherent Government security sector, the most effective allies of AMISOM were clan-based militias with loyalties to individual commanders and who looked to the AU rather than the Government for leadership and support. The intense fighting, combined with the drought and Al-Shabaab restrictions on access for humanitarian organizations, triggered an acute humanitarian crisis, including an exodus of refugees into neighbouring countries. The principal impediments to security and stabilization in southern Somalia were the Government leadership's lack of vision or cohesion, its corruption and its failure to advance the political process. Also damaging was the Government's resistance to engagement with local political and military forces elsewhere in the country. Instead, attempts by the Government's leadership to monopolize power and resources had aggravated frictions within the transitional federal institutions, obstructed the transitional process and crippled the war against Al-Shabaab.

The response of Al-Shabaab to military setbacks in Mogadishu, the central regions and the Juba Valley was to expand its control over the southern Somali economy. Given its lack of popular support, political fractiousness and military limitations, Al-Shabaab's greatest asset was its economic strength. The Monitoring Group estimated that Al-Shabaab generated between $70 and $100 million per year in revenue from taxation and extortion in areas under its control, notably the export of charcoal and cross-border contraband into Kenya. Given the corrupt and predatory practices of the Government, many Somali businessmen found Al-Shabaab to be better for business, and from a purely commercial perspective had little interest in seeing the group displaced by the Government.

Eritrean involvement in Somalia represented a small but troubling part of the overall equation. Asmara's continuing relationship with Al-Shabaab appeared designed to legitimize and embolden the group rather than to curb its extremist orientation or encourage its participation in a political process.

A growing concern was the increased use of private maritime security companies for armed protection on commercial and private vessels. There was near-total opacity with respect to the operations of more than 78 per cent of those companies, suggesting the need for a comprehensive and robust regulatory framework. The Monitoring Group believed that at least two such companies had violated the arms embargo by engaging in unauthorized training and equipping of Somali militias—one with the intention of trafficking in arms and narcotic drugs.

SECURITY COUNCIL ACTION

On 29 July [meeting 6596], the Security Council unanimously adopted **resolution 2002(2011)**. The draft [S/2011/470] was submitted by France, Gabon, Germany and the United Kingdom.

The Security Council,

Reaffirming its previous resolutions and the statements by its President concerning the situation in Somalia and concerning Eritrea, in particular resolution 733(1992) of 23 January 1992, which established an embargo on all deliveries of weapons and military equipment to Somalia (hereinafter referred to as "the Somalia arms embargo"), and resolutions

1519(2003) of 16 December 2003, 1558(2004) of 17 August 2004, 1587(2005) of 15 March 2005, 1630(2005) of 14 October 2005, 1676(2006) of 10 May 2006, 1724(2006) of 29 November 2006, 1744(2007) of 20 February 2007, 1766(2007) of 23 July 2007, 1772(2007) of 20 August 2007, 1801(2008) of 20 February 2008, 1811(2008) of 29 April 2008, 1844(2008) of 20 November 2008, 1853(2008) of 19 December 2008, 1862(2009) of 14 January 2009, 1907(2009) of 23 December 2009, 1916(2010) of 19 March 2010 and 1972(2011) of 17 March 2011,

Recalling that, as set out in its resolutions 1744(2007) and 1772(2007), the arms embargo on Somalia does not apply to (*a*) weapons and military equipment, technical training and assistance intended solely for the support of or use by the African Union Mission in Somalia, and (*b*) supplies and technical assistance by States intended solely for the purpose of helping to develop security sector institutions, consistent with the political process set out in those resolutions and in the absence of a negative decision by the Security Council Committee established pursuant to resolution 751(1992), the mandate of which was expanded pursuant to resolution 1907(2009) (hereinafter referred to as "the Committee"), within five working days of receiving an advance notification of such supplies or assistance on a case-by-case basis,

Recalling also its resolutions 1612(2005) of 26 July 2005, 1882(2009) of 4 August 2009 and 1998(2011) of 12 July 2011 on children and armed conflict, resolutions 1325(2000) of 31 October 2000, 1820(2008) of 19 June 2008, 1888(2009) of 30 September 2009, 1889(2009) of 5 October 2009 and 1960(2010) of 16 December 2010 on women and peace and security, and resolutions 1265(1999) of 17 September 1999, 1296(2000) of 19 April 2000, 1325(2000), 1612(2005), 1674(2006) of 28 April 2006, 1738(2006) of 23 December 2006, 1820(2008), 1882(2009), 1888(2009) and 1889(2009) on the protection of civilians in armed conflict,

Reaffirming its respect for the sovereignty, territorial integrity, political independence and unity of Somalia, Djibouti and Eritrea respectively,

Reaffirming that the Djibouti peace agreement and the peace process represent the basis for a resolution of the conflict in Somalia, reiterating its commitment to a comprehensive and lasting settlement of the situation in Somalia based on the Transitional Federal Charter, and reiterating the urgent need for all Somali leaders to take tangible steps to continue political dialogue,

Taking note of the report of the Monitoring Group on Somalia and Eritrea, submitted on 18 July 2011 pursuant to paragraph 6 (*k*) of resolution 1916(2010), and the observations and recommendations contained therein,

Condemning flows of weapons and ammunition supplies to and through Somalia and Eritrea in violation of the Somalia arms embargo and the Eritrea arms embargo established pursuant to resolution 1907(2009) (hereinafter referred to as "the Eritrea arms embargo") as a serious threat to peace and stability in the region,

Calling upon all Member States, in particular those in the region, to refrain from any action in contravention of the Somalia and Eritrea arms embargoes and to take all necessary steps to hold violators accountable,

Reaffirming the importance of enhancing the monitoring of the Somalia and Eritrea arms embargoes through persistent and vigilant investigation into the violations, bearing in mind that strict enforcement of the arms embargoes will improve the overall security situation in the region,

Expressing its concern at acts of intimidation against the Monitoring Group and interference with the work of the Monitoring Group,

Reiterating its serious concern about the worsening humanitarian situation in Somalia and the impact of the current drought and famine, strongly condemning the targeting and obstruction of the delivery of humanitarian aid by armed groups in Somalia, which has prevented the delivery of such aid in some areas, and deploring the repeated attacks on humanitarian personnel,

Reiterating its condemnation in the strongest terms of all acts of violence, abuses and violations, including sexual and gender-based violence, committed against civilians, including children, in violation of applicable international law, stressing that the perpetrators must be brought to justice, recalling all its relevant resolutions on women and peace and security, on children and armed conflict and on the protection of civilians in armed conflict, and considering, therefore, that the existing designation criteria for targeted measures under resolution 1844(2008) need to be reaffirmed and further strengthened,

Reaffirming the need for both the transitional federal institutions and donors to be mutually accountable and transparent in the allocation of financial resources,

Calling for the end of the misappropriation of financial funds, which undermines the ability of local authorities to deliver services in Somalia,

Determining that the situation in Somalia, Eritrea's actions undermining peace and reconciliation in Somalia, as well as the dispute between Djibouti and Eritrea continue to constitute a threat to international peace and security in the region,

Acting under Chapter VII of the Charter of the United Nations,

1. *Decides* that the measures in paragraphs 1, 3 and 7 of resolution 1844(2008) shall apply to individuals, and that the provisions of paragraphs 3 and 7 of that resolution shall apply to entities, designated by the Committee:

(*a*) As engaging in or providing support for acts that threaten the peace, security or stability of Somalia, including acts that threaten the Djibouti Agreement of 19 August 2008 or the political process, or threaten the transitional federal institutions or the African Union Mission in Somalia by force;

(*b*) As having acted in violation of the general and complete arms embargo reaffirmed in paragraph 6 of resolution 1844(2008);

(*c*) As obstructing the delivery of humanitarian assistance to Somalia, or access to or distribution of humanitarian assistance in Somalia;

(*d*) As being political or military leaders recruiting or using children in armed conflicts in Somalia in violation of applicable international law;

(*e*) As being responsible for violations of applicable international law in Somalia involving the targeting of civilians, including children and women, in situations of armed conflict, including killing and maiming, sexual and gender-based violence, attacks on schools and hospitals and abduction and forced displacement;

2. *Considers* that acts under paragraph 1 (*a*) above may include, but are not limited to, the misappropriation

of financial resources, which undermines the ability of the transitional federal institutions to fulfil their obligations in delivering services within the framework of the Djibouti Agreement;

3. *Considers also* that all non-local commerce via Al-Shabaab-controlled ports, that constitutes financial support for a designated entity, poses a threat to the peace, stability and security of Somalia, and thereby individuals and entities engaged in such commerce may be designated by the Committee and made subject to the targeted measures established by resolution 1844(2008);

4. *Calls upon* the Transitional Federal Government to consider banning all trade by large merchant vessels with Al-Shabaab-controlled ports;

5. *Demands* that all parties ensure full, safe and unhindered access for the timely delivery of humanitarian aid to persons in need of assistance across Somalia, underlines its grave concern at the worsening humanitarian situation in Somalia, urges all parties and armed groups to take appropriate steps to ensure the safety and security of humanitarian personnel and supplies, and expresses its readiness to apply targeted sanctions against such individuals and entities if they meet the listing criteria set out in paragraph 1 (*c*) above;

6. *Decides* to extend the mandate of the Monitoring Group referred to in paragraph 3 of resolution 1558(2004), which was extended by paragraph 6 of resolution 1916(2010), and requests the Secretary-General to take the necessary administrative measures as expeditiously as possible to re-establish the Monitoring Group on Somalia and Eritrea for a period of twelve months from the date of the present resolution, consisting of eight experts, drawing, as appropriate, on the expertise of the members of the Monitoring Group established pursuant to resolution 1916(2010), and consistent with resolution 1907(2009), in order to fulfil its expanded mandate, this mandate being as follows:

(*a*) To assist the Committee in monitoring the implementation of the measures imposed in paragraphs 1, 3 and 7 of resolution 1844(2008), including by reporting any information on violations, and to include in its reports to the Committee any information relevant to the potential designation of the individuals and entities described in paragraph 1 above;

(*b*) To assist the Committee in compiling narrative summaries, referred to in paragraph 14 of resolution 1844(2008), of individuals and entities designated pursuant to paragraph 1 above;

(*c*) To investigate any seaport operations in Somalia that may generate revenue for Al-Shabaab, an entity designated by the Committee for meeting the listing criteria in resolution 1844(2008);

(*d*) To continue the tasks outlined in paragraphs 3 (*a*) to (*c*) of resolution 1587(2005), paragraphs 23 (*a*) to (*c*) of resolution 1844(2008) and paragraphs 19 (*a*) to (*d*) of resolution 1907(2009);

(*e*) To investigate, in coordination with relevant international agencies, all activities, including in the financial, maritime and other sectors, which generate revenues used to commit violations of the Somalia and Eritrea arms embargoes;

(*f*) To investigate any means of transport, routes, seaports, airports and other facilities used in connection with violations of the Somalia and Eritrea arms embargoes;

(*g*) To continue refining and updating information on the draft list of those individuals and entities that engage in acts described in paragraph 1 above, inside and outside Somalia, and their active supporters, for possible future measures by the Security Council, and to present such information to the Committee as and when the Committee deems appropriate;

(*h*) To compile a draft list of those individuals and entities that engage in acts described in paragraphs 15 (*a*) to (*e*) of resolution 1907(2009), inside and outside Eritrea, and their active supporters, for possible future measures by the Council, and to present such information to the Committee as and when the Committee deems appropriate;

(*i*) To continue making recommendations based on its investigations, on the previous reports of the Panel of Experts appointed pursuant to resolutions 1425(2002) of 22 July 2002 and 1474(2003) of 8 April 2003, and on the previous reports of the Monitoring Group appointed pursuant to resolutions 1519(2003), 1558(2004), 1587(2005), 1630(2005), 1676(2006), 1724(2006), 1766(2007), 1811(2008), 1853(2008) and 1916(2010);

(*j*) To work closely with the Committee on specific recommendations for additional measures to improve overall compliance with the Somalia and Eritrea arms embargoes, as well as the measures imposed in paragraphs 1, 3 and 7 of resolution 1844(2008) and paragraphs 5, 6, 8, 10, 12 and 13 of resolution 1907(2009) concerning Eritrea;

(*k*) To assist in identifying areas where the capacities of States in the region can be strengthened to facilitate the implementation of the Somalia and Eritrea arms embargoes, as well as the measures imposed in paragraphs 1, 3 and 7 of resolution 1844(2008) and paragraphs 5, 6, 8, 10, 12 and 13 of resolution 1907(2009) concerning Eritrea;

(*l*) To provide to the Council, through the Committee, a midterm briefing within six months of its establishment, and to submit progress reports to the Committee on a monthly basis;

(*m*) To submit, for consideration by the Council, through the Committee, two final reports, one focusing on Somalia, the other on Eritrea, covering all the tasks set out above, no later than fifteen days prior to the termination of the mandate of the Monitoring Group;

7. *Requests* the Secretary-General to make the necessary financial arrangements to support the work of the Monitoring Group;

8. *Requests* the Committee, in accordance with its mandate and in consultation with the Monitoring Group and other relevant United Nations entities, to consider the recommendations contained in the reports of the Monitoring Group and to recommend to the Council ways to improve implementation of and compliance with the Somalia and Eritrea arms embargoes as well as implementation of the targeted measures imposed by paragraphs 1, 3 and 7 of resolution 1844(2008) and paragraphs 5, 6, 8, 10, 12 and 13 of resolution 1907(2009), in response to continuing violations;

9. *Decides* that, for a period of twelve months from the date of the present resolution, and without prejudice to humanitarian assistance programmes conducted elsewhere, the obligations placed on Member States in paragraph 3 of resolution 1844(2008) shall not apply to the payment of funds, other financial assets or economic resources necessary to ensure the timely delivery of urgently needed humanitarian assistance in Somalia by the United Nations, its specialized agencies or programmes, humanita-

rian organizations having observer status in the General Assembly that provide humanitarian assistance, and their implementing partners, including bilaterally or multilaterally funded non-governmental organizations participating in the United Nations Consolidated Appeal for Somalia;

10. *Urges* all parties and all States, including Eritrea, other States in the region, and the Transitional Federal Government, as well as international, regional and subregional organizations, to ensure cooperation with the Monitoring Group, and ensure the safety of the members of the Monitoring Group and unhindered access, in particular to persons, documents and sites that the Monitoring Group deems relevant to the execution of its mandate;

11. *Decides* to remain actively seized of the matter.

Appointments. In accordance with Council resolution 2002(2011) (see p. 256), the Secretary-General, by letters of 24 August [S/2011/536], 8 September [S/2011/560] and 15 November [S/2011/720], informed the Council that he had re-established the Monitoring Group on Somalia and Eritrea and appointed four experts for the Somalia component, three for the Eritrea component and a group coordinator.

Report of Humanitarian Coordinator (November). In accordance with Council resolution 1972(2011), the Chairman of the Security Council Committee concerning Somalia and Eritrea in November transmitted the fourth report [S/2011/694] of the United Nations Resident and Humanitarian Coordinator for Somalia, covering the period from April to November. During that period, the security environment varied by region, with the north and north-east areas being generally stable and south and central Somalia, including Mogadishu, volatile. On 16 October, Kenyan forces entered Somalia to curtail the operation of Al-Shabaab, which had become a threat to Kenya's security and economy. Central and southern Somalia remained the epicentre of the drought and famine crisis. While access to populations in need remained difficult, it was possible to deliver humanitarian assistance to most regions of the country.

The humanitarian situation was complex, as the areas most in need of assistance, primarily in the south, were under the control of non-State groups. Insecurity, however, also remained high in areas under the control of pro-Government groups, undermining humanitarian access. Until the second quarter of the year, conflict was the main reason for displacement. From June onward, drought and famine became the major reason for displacement. In July, over 55,000 internal displacements were recorded. Mogadishu received an average of 1,000 arrivals a day in July and August. Others fled to neighbouring countries: some 294,000 Somalis became refugees during the reporting period. By September, the lack of rain and the consequent drought led to famine in most part of the south, increasing the number of people at risk of dying to around 750,000. Due to the famine and the prolonged conflict, the number of people in need of humanitarian assistance increased from 2.4 million in March to 4 million in September. The number of malnourished children grew from 390,000 to 450,000. During the reporting period, approximately 900 national and international UN staff were based in Somalia and new humanitarian actors started to operate in the country. Since July, the number of beneficiaries receiving food assistance had tripled, from 770,000 to 2.2 million people, 77 per cent of whom were located in the south. Health partners distributed 79,000 insecticide-treated nets to 39,500 households. Over 755,000 children under the age of 15 were vaccinated against measles in Mogadishu and some 13,000 households in the south received cash transfers and/or food vouchers.

As requested in resolution 1972(2011), several steps were taken to mitigate the politicization, the misuse and the misappropriation of humanitarian assistance. The UN country team established a Risk Management Unit to facilitate assistance while mitigating risks associated with its delivery. Additional risk management training was provided to UN employees, to key implementing partners and donors and to employees of the Transitional Federal Government. The Common Humanitarian Fund continued to receive the support of donors, which reflected their confidence in the Fund's accountability: since the beginning of 2011, $73 million had been allocated; 72 per cent of that amount was committed to projects in central and southern Somalia.

Security Council Committee. The Security Council Committee pursuant to resolutions 751(1992) and 1907(2009) concerning Somalia and Eritrea reported on its activities in 2011 [S/2012/7]. During that period, the Committee met nine times in informal consultations. It approved 10 requests for exemptions to the arms embargo for non-lethal military equipment pursuant to resolution 1356(2001) [YUN 2001, p. 212] and 7 requests for exemptions to the arms embargo pursuant to resolution 1772(2007) [YUN 2007, p. 276]. On 28 July, the Committee added two individuals to the list of individuals and entities subject to the travel ban, assets freeze and targeted arms embargo.

United Nations Political Office for Somalia

The United Nations Political Office for Somalia (UNPOS) was established in 1995 [YUN 1995, p. 400] to assist the Secretary-General in advancing the cause of peace and reconciliation through dialogue among the Somali parties. Subsequently, UNPOS focused on the mediation of agreements between the transitional federal institutions and the factions previously opposed to them, in parallel to strengthening the transitional federal institutions in the area of security, justice, media and gender. The mandate of UNPOS included facilitating national reconciliation, good governance and the rule of law; assisting in the re-establishment of Somali security forces, including the military and police; supporting the Transitional Federal Government in developing a security strategy; overseeing the implementation of initiatives to counter piracy; and mobilizing international resources for long-term economic development.

In 2011, UNPOS led the United Nations Strategic Policy Group, which set policy guidance on political, security, development and humanitarian activities. It led the Joint Security Committee, which coordinated all security sector activities between the Government, the United Nations, AMISOM, IGAD, the East African Standby Force and donor countries. It headed the Nairobi Cluster on Piracy, through which it provided a political lead and ensured the coordination of efforts among UN agencies and the international community. The UNPOS Human Rights Unit worked closely with AMISOM and UN agencies on protection of civilians, children associated with armed forces and groups, and rule-of-law issues. The Office chaired the International Contact Group on Somalia, a political group bringing together more than 40 countries and regional organizations.

Augustine P. Mahiga (Tanzania) continued to serve as the Secretary-General's Special Representative for Somalia and Head of UNPOS.

Financing

In October [A/66/354/Add.3], the Secretary-General proposed resource requirements for UNPOS totalling $17,803,800 gross ($17,404,500 net) for 2012, as compared with approved resources of $16,345,000 for 2011.

In December [A/66/7/Add.12], ACABQ recommended that the proposed requirement of $17,404,500 be reduced by $235,600.

The General Assembly, by section IX of **resolution 66/247** of 24 December (see p. 1393), endorsed the recommendations of the Advisory Committee.

African Union Mission in Somalia

The African Union Mission in Somalia (AMISOM) was authorized in 2007 [YUN 2007, p. 268] by the AU Peace and Security Council to support the transitional federal institutions in their efforts to stabilize the country, facilitate the provision of humanitarian assistance, and create conditions conducive to stabilization, reconstruction and development. By resolution 1744(2007) [ibid., p. 269], the Security Council approved the Mission's mandate, which was renewed every six months. By resolution 2010(2011) (see p. 239), the Council authorized AU member States to maintain the deployment of the Mission until 31 October 2012, requested the AU to increase its force to its mandated level of 12,000 uniformed personnel and extended the logistical support to the Mission accordingly.

According to the Secretary-General [A/65/809], the continued deployment of AMISOM in Mogadishu to support the Transitional Federal Government remained critical to helping secure the capital while accountable Somali institutions were re-established. The Mission, however, needed both the UN logistical support and donor assistance in order to achieve its mandated strength of 12,000 troops and 270 civilian police. AMISOM operated in an environment with high levels of violence, which had profound effects on the operations of the United Nations Support Office for AMISOM—the Mission's main external support organization.

Financing

The Secretary-General's performance report on the financing of support for AMISOM for the period from 1 July 2009 to 30 June 2010 [A/65/619] detailed expenditures of $164,278,800 gross ($162,353,500 net) against an apportionment of $213,580,000 gross ($211,221,300 net).

In April [A/65/809], the Secretary-General submitted a budget for the financing of support to AMISOM for the period from 1 July 2011 to 30 June 2012 in the amount of $303,911,900 gross ($300,444,200 net). The budget provided for the deployment of 179 international staff and 126 national staff in support of an authorized strength of 12,000 AMISOM military contingent personnel and 270 AU police officers.

In April [A/65/743/Add.16], ACABQ recommended a reduction of $4,984,900, bringing the amount to $298,927,000 gross.

GENERAL ASSEMBLY ACTION

On 30 June [meeting 106], the General Assembly, on the recommendation of the Fifth Committee [A/65/889], adopted **resolution 65/306** without vote [agenda item 160].

Financing of support of the African Union Mission in Somalia

The General Assembly,

Having considered the reports of the Secretary-General on the financing of support of the African Union Mission in Somalia and the related report of the Advisory Committee on Administrative and Budgetary Questions,

Recalling Security Council resolution 1863(2009) of 16 January 2009, by which the Council expressed its intent to establish a United Nations peacekeeping operation in Somalia as a follow-on force to the African Union Mission in Somalia, subject to its further decision by 1 June 2009, and requested the Secretary-General, in order for the forces of the Mission to be incorporated into a United Nations peacekeeping operation, to provide a United Nations logistical support package to the Mission, including equipment and services,

Recalling also Security Council resolution 1964(2010) of 22 December 2010, by which the Council requested the Secretary-General to continue to provide a logistical support package to the African Union Mission in Somalia until 30 September 2011,

Recalling further its resolution 64/287 of 24 June 2010 on the financing of support to the African Union Mission in Somalia,

Reaffirming the general principles underlying the financing of United Nations peacekeeping operations, as stated in General Assembly resolutions 1874(S-IV) of 27 June 1963, 3101(XXVIII) of 11 December 1973 and 55/235 of 23 December 2000,

Noting with appreciation that voluntary contributions have been made to the United Nations Trust Fund established to support the African Union Mission in Somalia,

1. *Endorses* the conclusions and recommendations contained in the report of the Advisory Committee on Administrative and Budgetary Questions, subject to the provisions of the present resolution, and requests the Secretary-General to ensure their full implementation;

2. *Requests* the Secretary-General to take appropriate measures to ensure effectiveness, efficiency and transparency with regard to the use of United Nations resources, bearing in mind the specific nature of the support package;

3. *Stresses* the importance of strict adherence to the existing United Nations procurement rules and regulations;

4. *Notes* that the overall level of appropriation has been adjusted in accordance with the terms of General Assembly resolution 65/289 of 30 June 2011;

Financial performance report for the period from 1 July 2009 to 30 June 2010

5. *Takes note* of the report of the Secretary-General on the financial performance of the support of the African Union Mission in Somalia for the period from 1 July 2009 to 30 June 2010;

Budget estimates for the period from 1 July 2011 to 30 June 2012

6. *Decides* to appropriate to the Special Account for the support provided to the African Union Mission in Somalia the amount of 309,690,900 United States dollars for the period from 1 July 2011 to 30 June 2012, inclusive of the amount of 291,092,700 dollars for the maintenance of the entity, 15,759,800 dollars for the support account for peacekeeping operations and 2,838,400 dollars for the United Nations Logistics Base at Brindisi, Italy;

Financing of the appropriation

7. *Also decides* to apportion among Member States the amount of 77,422,725 dollars for the period from 1 July to 30 September 2011, in accordance with the levels updated in General Assembly resolution 64/249 of 24 December 2009, and taking into account the scale of assessments for 2011, as set out in Assembly resolution 64/248 of 24 December 2009;

8. *Further decides* that, in accordance with the provisions of its resolution 973(X) of 15 December 1955, there shall be set off against the apportionment among Member States, as provided for in paragraph 7 above, their respective share in the Tax Equalization Fund of 1,255,950 dollars, comprising the estimated staff assessment income of 847,700 dollars approved for the entity, the prorated share of 333,700 dollars of the estimated staff assessment income approved for the support account and the prorated share of 74,550 dollars of the estimated staff assessment income approved for the United Nations Logistics Base;

9. *Decides* to apportion among Member States the amount of 232,268,175 dollars for the period from 1 October 2011 to 30 June 2012 at a monthly rate of 25,807,575 dollars, in accordance with the levels updated in resolution 64/249 and taking into account the scale of assessments for 2011 and 2012, as set out in resolution 64/248, subject to a decision of the Security Council to extend the mandate;

10. *Also decides* that, in accordance with the provisions of resolution 973(X), there shall be set off against the apportionment among Member States, as provided for in paragraph 9 above, their respective share in the Tax Equalization Fund of 3,767,850 dollars, comprising the estimated staff assessment income of 2,543,100 dollars approved for the entity, the prorated share of 1,001,100 dollars of the estimated staff assessment income approved for the support account and the prorated share of 223,650 dollars of the estimated staff assessment income approved for the United Nations Logistics Base;

11. *Further decides* that, for Member States that have fulfilled their financial obligations to the entity, there shall be set off against their apportionment, as provided for in paragraph 7 above, their respective share of the unencumbered balance and other income in the total amount of 54,457,900 dollars in respect of the financial period ended 30 June 2010, in accordance with the levels updated by the General Assembly in resolution 64/249, taking into account the scale of assessments for 2010, as set out in resolution 64/248;

12. *Decides* that, for Member States that have not fulfilled their financial obligations to the entity, there shall be set off against their outstanding obligations their respective share of the unencumbered balance and other income in the total amount of 54,457,900 dollars in respect of the financial period ended 30 June 2010, in accordance with the scheme set out in paragraph 11 above;

13. *Also decides* that the decrease of 433,400 dollars in the estimated staff assessment income in respect of the financial period ended 30 June 2010 shall be set off against the credits from the amount of 54,457,900 dollars referred to in paragraphs 11 and 12 above;

14. *Invites* voluntary contributions to the United Nations Trust Fund established to support the African Union Mission in Somalia;

15. *Decides* to include in the provisional agenda of its sixty-sixth session the item entitled "Financing of the activities arising from Security Council resolution 1863(2009)".

The General Assembly, on 24 December, decided that the agenda item on financing of the activities arising from Security Council resolution 1863(2009) would remain for consideration during its resumed sixty-sixth (2012) session (**decision 66/557**).

Eritrea

Eritrea achieved independence from Ethiopia in 1993, following a 30-year war for independence and a subsequent referendum. Since then, Eritrea's relations with its neighbours had been turbulent. In the process of defining the new State's borders, the country clashed with Ethiopia, Yemen and Djibouti and maintained a complex relationship with the Sudan. In December 2009, invoking Eritrea's alleged support for Somali armed opposition groups and its border conflict with Djibouti, the Security Council imposed a sanctions regime on Eritrea, including a general and complete arms embargo, as well as a travel ban and an asset freeze on individuals and entities. In 2011, by resolution 2023(2011) (see p. 263), the Council expanded the restrictive measures regarding Eritrea in the area of "diaspora taxes", the Eritrean mining sector and financial services.

Sanctions

Report of Monitoring Group. On 18 July [S/2011/433], the Chairman of the Security Council Committee pursuant to resolutions 751(1992) [YUN 1992, p. 202] and 1907(2009) [YUN 2009, p. 299] concerning Somalia and Eritrea transmitted to the Council the report of the Monitoring Group on Somalia and Eritrea. According to the report, Eritrean involvement in Somalia continued in 2011. Asmara's relationship with Al-Shabaab appeared designed to legitimize and embolden the group rather than to curb its extremist orientation or encourage its participation in a political process. Eritrean involvement in Somalia reflected a broader pattern of intelligence and special operations activity, including training, financial and logistical support to armed opposition groups in Djibouti, Ethiopia, the Sudan and possibly Uganda, in violation of Security Council resolution 1907(2009). Eritrea's support for such groups could only be understood in the context of its unresolved border dispute with Ethiopia. It was also symptomatic of the systematic subversion of the Government of Eritrea by a small number of political, military and intelligence officials, who chose to conduct the affairs of state via informal and often illicit mechanisms, including people smuggling, arms trafficking, money-laundering and extortion. Such irregular financial practices and the imposition of a "diaspora tax" on Eritreans and foreign nationals of Eritrean origin living abroad explained how a country as poor as Eritrea managed to support armed opposition groups across the region. From 2011 onwards, however, Eritrea's emerging mining sector—especially gold mining—was likely to become the country's principal source of hard currency.

The Group investigated a variety of Eritrean activities in support of armed groups throughout the region and identified four categories of such activities: support to Somali armed opposition groups in violation of resolutions 1844(2008) [YUN 2008, p. 297] and 1907(2009); support to Ethiopian armed opposition groups via Somalia, in violation of resolutions 1844(2008) and 1907(2009); support to non-Somali armed groups engaged in acts of destabilization or terrorism in violation of resolution 1907(2009); and operations using proxy forces that fell under direct Eritrean command and control, falsely flagged as domestic opposition groups, in violation of resolution 1907(2009).

It was the Monitoring Group's assessment that the Eritrean leadership committed multiple violations of Security Council resolutions 1844(2008) and 1907(2009). In January, Eritrea organized and directed a failed plot to disrupt the AU summit in Addis Ababa by bombing civilian and governmental targets. The Eritrean intelligence apparatus responsible for the AU summit plot was also active in Kenya, Somalia, the Sudan and Uganda.

Regarding the border dispute between Djibouti and Eritrea [YUN 2008, p. 315], the Monitoring Group reported that, although a formal ceasefire had been announced on 9 June 2010 under the auspices of Qatar [YUN 2010, p. 304], Eritrea continued to provide support for a splinter group of the Front pour la restauration de l'unité et de la démocratie. The group was active in the north of Djibouti, where it conducted military operations with the aim of harassing Djiboutian forces but also, according to Djiboutian officials, engaged in banditry and extortion to sustain itself.

Both Eritrea and Ethiopia hosted opposition forces from the other. Citing national security reasons, Eritrea refused to answer the Monitoring Group's questions relating to support for Ethiopian armed opposition groups. The Group received credible information of Eritrean support for seven Ethiopian groups; for two of the groups—the Ogaden National Liberation Front (ONLF) and the Oromo Liberation Front (OLF)—the Monitoring Group also independently verified the allegations. OLF was to execute the operation to disrupt the AU summit in Addis Ababa.

Eritrea sought to open a "second front" against Ethiopia in Somalia by providing assistance to a militia faction, and, through it, to Ethiopian armed opposition groups, including ONLF and OLF. Eritrea consistently denied having interfered in the internal affairs of Somalia. Nevertheless, the Monitoring Group believed that Eritrea retained linkages to Somali armed groups. The Monitoring Group had obtained documentary evidence of Eritrean payments to a number of individuals with links to Al-Shabaab.

The Monitoring Group concluded that, while in the past Eritrean support to foreign armed opposition groups had been limited to conventional military operations, the plot to disrupt the AU summit in Addis Ababa represented a shift in tactics. Such actions could not be justified in the context of Eritrea's bilateral dispute with Ethiopia. The Monitoring Group therefore recommended ways and means to curtail the capability of the Eritrean external operations directorate to conduct future operations of that nature.

Appointments. On 24 August [S/2011/536], the Secretary-General informed the Security Council that, in accordance with Council resolution 2002(2011) (see p. 256), he had re-established the eight-member Monitoring Group on Somalia and Eritrea, appointing three experts for the Eritrea component.

Security Council Committee. The Security Council Committee pursuant to resolutions 751(1992) and 1907(2009) concerning Somalia and Eritrea reported [S/2012/7] on its activities in 2011 (see p. 259). During informal consultations on 22 July, the Committee received a briefing by a delegation from Eritrea on the Monitoring Group's findings pertaining to the country. The delegation announced that it would submit a comprehensive response to the Group's report, which it did on 20 October.

Communications. From March through December, Eritrea submitted a series of letters [S/2011/181, S/2011/623, S/2011/652, S/2011/663, S/2011/672, S/2011/681, S/2011/729, S/2011/753] to the Security Council. On 20 October [S/2011/652], Eritrea responded to the report of the Monitoring Group on Somalia and Eritrea (see above), stating that the report was encumbered by seemingly serious allegations without conclusive evidence of any Eritrean violations in regards to Somalia and Djibouti, as well as the arms embargo on Eritrea. By a letter of 25 October [S/2011/663], Eritrea's President, Isaias Afwerki, requested to address the Security Council in the light of the ongoing negotiations on the adoption of additional economic and financial measures on Eritrea. By a letter of 3 December [S/2011/753], Eritrea complained about the short notice given to President Afwerki to address the Council. Other letters [S/2011/623, S/2011/672, S/2011/681, S/2011/729] referred to the draft resolution on Eritrea.

On 5 July [S/2011/411] and 14 July [S/2011/434], Ethiopia, in its capacity as chair of the Intergovernmental Authority on Development (IGAD), transmitted the communiqué of the thirty-ninth extraordinary session of the IGAD Council of Ministers (Malabo, Equatorial Guinea, 28 June) and the communiqué of the eighteenth Extraordinary Summit Meeting of the IGAD Assembly of Heads of State and Government on the activities in the Sudan, Somalia and Eritrea (Addis Ababa, Ethiopia, 4 July). Both extraordinary sessions were held to consider the security and political situation in Somalia and the Sudan, as well as Eritrea's activities in the region. In both communiqués, IGAD condemned Eritrea's activities, which contributed to the destabilization the region, and called on the AU and the Security Council to fully implement the existing sanctions and impose additional sanctions on the Eritrean regime.

On 6 October, Djibouti transmitted a letter [S/2011/617] to the Secretary-General relating to two Djiboutian prisoners of war who had escaped from a prison in Eritrea, had reached the Sudan and had been repatriated to Djibouti. Eritrea denied that there were any Djiboutian prisoners of war. Djibouti maintained that there were 19 such prisoners.

SECURITY COUNCIL ACTION

On 5 December [meeting 6674], the Security Council adopted **resolution 2023(2011)** by vote (13-0-2). The draft [S/2011/744] was submitted by Gabon and Nigeria.

The Security Council,

Recalling its previous resolutions and the statements by its President concerning the situation in Somalia and the border dispute between Djibouti and Eritrea, in particular resolutions 751(1992) of 24 April 1992, 1844(2008) of 20 November 2008, 1862(2009) of 14 January 2009, 1907(2009) of 23 December 2009, 1916(2010) of 19 March 2010, 1998(2011) of 12 July 2011 and 2002(2011) of 29 July 2011 and the statements of 12 June 2008 and 15 May and 9 July 2009,

Reaffirming its respect for the sovereignty, territorial integrity and political independence and unity of Somalia, Djibouti and Eritrea, respectively, as well as of all other States of the region,

Reiterating its full support for the Djibouti peace process and the Transitional Federal Charter, which provide the framework for reaching a lasting political solution in Somalia, and welcoming the Kampala Accord of 9 June 2011 and the road map agreed on 6 September 2011,

Calling upon all States in the region to peacefully resolve their disputes and normalize their relations in order to lay the foundation for durable peace and lasting security in the Horn of Africa, and encouraging these States to provide the necessary cooperation to the African Union in its efforts to resolve these disputes,

Reiterating its grave concern about the border dispute between Eritrea and Djibouti and the importance of resolving it, calling upon Eritrea to pursue with Djibouti in good faith the scrupulous implementation of the agreement of 6 June 2010, concluded under the auspices of Qatar, in order to resolve their border dispute and consolidate the normalization of their relations, and welcoming the mediation efforts of Qatar and the continued engagement of regional actors, the African Union and the United Nations,

Taking note of the letter dated 6 October 2011 from the Permanent Representative of Djibouti to the United Nations addressed to the Secretary-General, in which the Secretary-General was informed of the escape of two Djiboutian prisoners of war from an Eritrean prison, while noting that the Government of Eritrea has to this date denied detaining any Djiboutian prisoners of war,

Expressing grave concern at the findings of the Monitoring Group on Somalia and Eritrea, in its report transmitted on 18 July 2011, that Eritrea has continued to provide political, financial, training and logistical support to armed opposition groups, including Al-Shabaab, engaged in undermining peace, security and stability in Somalia and the region,

Condemning the planned terrorist attack of January 2011 to disrupt the African Union summit in Addis Ababa, as expressed in the findings of the report of the Monitoring Group,

Taking note of the decision of the Assembly of Heads of State and Government of the African Union, held in January 2010, and the communiqué of the meeting of the African Union Peace and Security Council held on 8 January 2010 welcoming the adoption by the United Nations Security Council on 23 December 2009 of resolution 1907(2009), which imposes sanctions on Eritrea for, among other things, providing political, financial and logistical support to armed groups engaged in undermining peace and reconciliation in Somalia and regional stability; stressing the need to pursue vigorously the effective implementation of resolution 1907(2009), and expressing its intention to apply targeted sanctions against individuals and entities if they meet the listing criteria set out in paragraph 15 of resolution 1907(2009) and paragraph 8 of resolution 1844(2008),

Taking note also of the decision of the Assembly of the Heads of State and Government of the Intergovernmental Authority on Development at its eighteenth extraordinary summit meeting calling upon the Security Council to take measures to ensure that Eritrea desists from its destabilization activities in the Horn of Africa,

Taking note further of the letter dated 20 October 2011 from the Permanent Representative of Eritrea to the United Nations addressed to the President of the Security Council containing a document responding to the report of the Monitoring Group,

Strongly condemning any acts by Eritrea that undermine peace, security and stability in the region, and calling upon all Member States to comply fully with the terms of the arms embargo imposed by paragraph 5 of resolution 733(1992) of 23 January 1992, as elaborated on and amended by subsequent resolutions,

Determining that the failure of Eritrea to fully comply with resolutions 1844(2008), 1862(2009) and 1907(2009) and its actions undermining peace and reconciliation in Somalia and the Horn of Africa region as well as the dispute between Djibouti and Eritrea constitute a threat to international peace and security,

Mindful of its primary responsibility under the Charter of the United Nations for the maintenance of international peace and security,

Acting under Chapter VII of the Charter,

1. *Condemns* the violations by Eritrea of Security Council resolutions 1844(2008), 1862(2009) and 1907(2009) by providing continued support to armed opposition groups, including Al-Shabaab, engaged in undermining peace and reconciliation in Somalia and the region;

2. *Supports* the call by the African Union for Eritrea to resolve its border disputes with its neighbours and calls upon the parties to peacefully resolve their disputes, normalize their relations and promote durable peace and lasting security in the Horn of Africa, and encourages the parties to provide the necessary cooperation to the African Union in its efforts to resolve these disputes;

3. *Reiterates* that all Member States, including Eritrea, shall comply fully with the terms of the arms embargo imposed by paragraph 5 of resolution 733(1992), as elaborated on and amended by subsequent resolutions;

4. *Reiterates also* that Eritrea shall fully comply with resolution 1907(2009) without any further delay, and stresses the obligation of all States to comply with the measures imposed by resolution 1907(2009);

5. *Notes* the withdrawal by Eritrea of its forces following the stationing of Qatari observers in the disputed areas along the border with Djibouti, calls upon Eritrea to engage constructively with Djibouti to resolve the border dispute, and reaffirms its intention to take further targeted measures against those who obstruct the implementation of resolution 1862(2009);

6. *Demands* that Eritrea make available information pertaining to Djiboutian combatants missing in action since the clashes of 10 to 12 June 2008 so that those concerned may ascertain the presence and condition of Djiboutian prisoners of war;

7. *Demands also* that Eritrea cease all direct or indirect efforts to destabilize States, including through financial, military, intelligence and non-military assistance, such as the provision of training centres, camps and other similar facilities for armed groups, passports, living expenses or travel facilitation;

8. *Calls upon* all States, in particular States of the region, in order to ensure strict implementation of the arms embargo established by paragraphs 5 and 6 of resolution 1907(2009), to inspect in their territory, including seaports and airports, in accordance with national authorities and legislation and consistent with international law, all cargo bound to or from Eritrea, if the State concerned has information that provides reasonable grounds to believe that the cargo contains items, the supply, sale, transfer or export of which is prohibited by paragraphs 5 or 6 of resolution 1907(2009), and recalls the obligations contained in paragraphs 8 and 9 of resolution 1907(2009) with respect to the discovery of items prohibited by paragraphs 5 or 6 of resolution 1907(2009) and paragraph 5 of resolution 733(1992) as elaborated on and amended by subsequent resolutions;

9. *Expresses its intention* to apply targeted sanctions against individuals and entities if they meet the listing criteria set out in paragraph 15 of resolution 1907(2009) and paragraph 1 of resolution 2002(2011), and requests the Security Council Committee pursuant to resolutions 751(1992) and 1907(2009) to review, as a matter of urgency, listing proposals from Member States;

10. *Condemns* the use of the "diaspora tax" on the Eritrean diaspora by the Government of Eritrea to destabilize the Horn of Africa region or violate relevant resolutions, including resolutions 1844(2008), 1862(2009) and 1907(2009), including for purposes such as procuring arms and related materiel for transfer to armed opposition groups or providing any services or financial transfers provided directly or indirectly to such groups, as outlined in the findings of the Monitoring Group on Somalia and Eritrea in its report of 18 July 2011, and decides that Eritrea shall cease these practices;

11. *Decides* that Eritrea shall cease using extortion, threats of violence, fraud and other illicit means to collect taxes outside of Eritrea from its nationals or other individuals of Eritrean descent, decides further that States shall take appropriate measures to hold accountable, consistent with international law, those individuals on their territory who are acting, officially or unofficially, on behalf of the Government of Eritrea or the People's Front for Democracy and Justice contrary to the prohibitions imposed in the present paragraph and the laws of the States concerned, and calls

upon States to take such action as may be appropriate consistent with their domestic law and relevant international instruments, including the Vienna Convention on Diplomatic Relations of 1961 and the Vienna Convention on Consular Relations of 1963, to prevent such individuals from facilitating further violations;

12. *Expresses concern* at the potential use of the Eritrean mining sector as a financial source to destabilize the Horn of Africa region, as outlined in the final report of the Monitoring Group, and calls upon Eritrea to show transparency in its public finances, including through cooperation with the Monitoring Group, in order to demonstrate that the proceeds of these mining activities are not being used to violate relevant resolutions, including resolutions 1844(2008), 1862(2009), 1907(2009) and the present resolution;

13. *Decides* that States, in order to prevent funds derived from the mining sector of Eritrea contributing to violations of resolutions 1844(2008), 1862(2009), 1907(2009) or the present resolution, shall take appropriate measures to promote the exercise of vigilance by their nationals, persons subject to their jurisdiction and firms incorporated in their territory or subject to their jurisdiction that are doing business in this sector in Eritrea, including through the issuance of due diligence guidelines, and requests in this regard the Committee, with the assistance of the Monitoring Group, to draft guidelines for the optional use of Member States;

14. *Urges* all States to introduce due diligence guidelines to prevent the provision of financial services, including insurance or reinsurance, or the transfer to, through or from their territory, or to or by their nationals or entities organized under their laws (including branches abroad), or persons or financial institutions in their territory, of any financial or other assets or resources if such services, assets or resources, including new investment in the extractives sector, would contribute to violation by Eritrea of relevant resolutions, including resolutions 1844(2008), 1862(2009), 1907(2009) and the present resolution;

15. *Calls upon* all States to report to the Council within one hundred and twenty days on steps taken to implement the provisions of the present resolution;

16. *Decides* to further expand the mandate of the Monitoring Group re-established by resolution 2002(2011), to monitor and report on the implementation of the measures imposed in the present resolution and undertake the tasks outlined below:

(*a*) Assist the Committee in monitoring the implementation of the measures imposed in paragraphs 10 to 14 above, including by reporting any information on violations;

(*b*) Consider any information relevant to paragraph 6 above that should be brought to the attention of the Committee;

17. *Urges* all States, relevant United Nations bodies and other interested parties to cooperate fully with the Committee and the Monitoring Group, including by supplying any information at their disposal on the implementation of the measures decided in resolutions 1844(2008), 1907(2009) and the present resolution, in particular incidents of non-compliance;

18. *Affirms* that it shall keep the actions of Eritrea under continuous review and that it shall be prepared to adjust the measures, including through their strengthening, modification or lifting, in the light of compliance by Eritrea with the provisions of resolutions 1844(2008), 1862(2009), 1907(2009) and the present resolution;

19. *Requests* the Secretary-General to report within one hundred and eighty days on compliance by Eritrea with the provisions of resolutions 1844(2008), 1862(2009), 1907(2009) and the present resolution;

20. *Decides* to remain seized of the matter.

VOTE ON RESOLUTION 2023(2011):

In favour: Bosnia and Herzegovina, Brazil, Colombia, France, Gabon, Germany, India, Lebanon, Nigeria, Portugal, South Africa, United Kingdom, United States.
Against: None.
Abstaining: China, Russian Federation.

Communication. By a letter of 20 December [S/2011/792] to the Security Council, Eritrea responded to the adoption of resolution 2023(2011), highlighting the negative consequences of the expanded sanctions imposed on the country. The letter also analysed topics such as Eritrea's sovereignty, alleged support to armed opposition groups, the arms embargo, the "diaspora tax" and the expanded mandate of the Monitoring Group.

Eritrea–Ethiopia

UNMEE

In June 2000, after two years of fighting in a border dispute, Ethiopia and Eritrea signed a cessation of hostilities agreement. In July of that year, by resolution 1312(2000) [YUN 2000, p. 174], the Security Council established the United Nations Mission in Ethiopia and Eritrea (unmee) to maintain liaison with the parties and establish a mechanism for verifying the ceasefire. In September 2000, the Council, by resolution 1320(2000) [ibid., p. 176], authorized unmee to monitor the cessation of hostilities and to help ensure the observance of security commitments. On 30 July 2008, by resolution 1827(2008) [YUN 2008, p. 310], the Council terminated the unmee mandate, effective 31 July 2008. In December 2010, the Secretary-General issued a report [YUN 2010, p. 308] providing information on the final disposition of the Mission's assets.

ACABQ report. In February [A/65/748], acabq considered the Secretary-General's 2010 report. The General Assembly had approved donations of assets to Ethiopia and Eritrea and to the au in support of amisom. Acabq noted that, unlike the donations to Ethiopia and the au, the donation to Eritrea had not been accepted. The Advisory Committee recommended that lessons learned from the liquidation of unmee be documented and taken into account in other liquidating missions.

GENERAL ASSEMBLY ACTION

On 30 June [meeting 106], the General Assembly, on the recommendation of the Fifth Committee [A/65/878], adopted **resolution 65/298** without vote [agenda item 151].

Financing of the United Nations Mission in Ethiopia and Eritrea

The General Assembly,

Having considered the report of the Secretary-General on the financing of the United Nations Mission in Ethiopia and Eritrea and the related report of the Advisory Committee on Administrative and Budgetary Questions,

Recalling Security Council resolution 1312(2000) of 31 July 2000, by which the Council established the United Nations Mission in Ethiopia and Eritrea, and the subsequent resolutions by which the Council extended the mandate of the Mission, the last of which was resolution 1798(2008) of 30 January 2008, by which the Council extended the mandate of the Mission until 31 July 2008,

Recalling also Security Council resolution 1827(2008) of 30 July 2008, by which the Council terminated the mandate of the Mission effective on 31 July 2008,

Recalling further its resolution 55/237 of 23 December 2000 on the financing of the Mission and its subsequent resolutions and decisions thereon, the latest of which was resolution 64/277 of 24 June 2010,

Reaffirming the general principles underlying the financing of United Nations peacekeeping operations, as stated in General Assembly resolutions 1874(S-IV) of 27 June 1963, 3101(XXVIII) of 11 December 1973 and 55/235 of 23 December 2000,

Noting with appreciation that voluntary contributions have been made to the Mission,

1. *Takes note* of the status of contributions to the United Nations Mission in Ethiopia and Eritrea as at 30 April 2011, including the credits in the amount of 2.5 million United States dollars;

2. *Endorses* the conclusions and recommendations contained in the report of the Advisory Committee on Administrative and Budgetary Questions, and requests the Secretary-General to ensure their full implementation;

Disposition of assets of the United Nations Mission in Ethiopia and Eritrea

3. *Takes note* of the report of the Secretary-General on the final disposition of the assets of the Mission;

4. *Encourages* Member States that are owed credits for the closed peacekeeping mission accounts to apply those credits to any accounts where the Member State concerned has outstanding assessed contributions;

5. *Decides* to include in the provisional agenda of its sixty-sixth session the item entitled "Financing of the United Nations Mission in Ethiopia and Eritrea".

The General Assembly, on 24 December, decided that the agenda item on the financing of UNMEE would remain for consideration during its resumed sixty-sixth (2012) session (**decision 66/557**).

North Africa

Libyan Arab Jamahiriya

In 2011, an internal crisis in the Libyan Arab Jamahiriya escalated into a civil conflict. On 15 February, the Government met a peaceful protest, held by families calling for the release of a lawyer who was representing their claims in respect of the 1996 Abu Salim prison massacre, with lethal repression. Subsequently, civilians across Libya took up arms against the Government.

The international community, including the United Nations, the AU, the EU and the League of Arab States, launched several diplomatic initiatives to end the crisis. On 26 February, the Security Council referred the situation in Libya to the Prosecutor of the International Criminal Court (ICC); imposed an arms embargo, a travel ban and asset freeze on Libya's leader, Colonel Muammar Qadhafi, and members of his circle; and established a sanctions committee to monitor implementation of the sanctions. On 1 March, the General Assembly suspended Libya's membership in the Human Rights Council. On 17 March, the Security Council demanded an immediate ceasefire and an end to violence against civilians; authorized Member States to take all necessary measures to protect civilians; established a no-fly zone in the airspace of Libya to help protect civilians; established a ban on all flights from, to and over Libya; and requested the Secretary-General to create a panel of experts to help oversee the sanctions. On 19 March, United States and European forces launched an air strike campaign to establish a no-fly zone over the country and protect civilians. Meanwhile, the Secretary-General's Special Envoy for Libya carried out mediation efforts and sought to establish a ceasefire.

After months of intense fighting between Colonel Qadhafi loyalists and opposition forces, the latter, on 20 October, took the city of Sirte and Colonel Qadhafi was killed. On 23 October, the National Transitional Council—the political leadership of the anti-Qadhafi movement—declared Libya fully liberated and took charge of the country, representing Libya both at the United Nations and in other international settings. The United Nations Support Mission in Libya (UNSMIL), established by the Council in September, sought to support the country's authorities in their post-conflict efforts.

Political and security developments

Communication. On 21 February [S/2011/102], Libya requested an urgent meeting of the Security Council to discuss the grave situation in the country and take appropriate action.

Security Council consideration (February). On 22 February [S/PV.6486], the Under-Secretary-General for Political Affairs, B. Lynn Pascoe, briefed the Security Council on the situation in Libya. On the same day, by a press statement [SC/10180], the Council condemned the violence and use of force against civilians, stated that it deplored the repression against peaceful demonstrators, and expressed regret at the deaths of hundreds of civilians. The Council called on the Government to meet its responsibility to protect its population.

Briefing the Council on 25 February [S/PV.6490], the Secretary-General stated that estimates indicated that more than 1,000 people had been killed in Libya since the outbreak of the violence. The eastern part of the country was reported to be under the control of opposition elements. There were daily clashes in at least three cities near Tripoli. In the capital, people could not leave their houses for fear of being shot by Government forces or militias. The press, human rights groups and civilians reported indiscriminate killings, arbitrary arrests, the shooting of peaceful demonstrators, the detention and torture of opposition representatives and the use of foreign mercenaries. The Secretary-General noted that the first obligation of the international community was to do everything possible to ensure the immediate protection of civilians at risk. He underscored the statement of the High Commissioner for Human Rights, who, on 25 February, reminded Member States that, when a State failed to protect its population from serious international crimes, the international community had the responsibility to step in. UNHCR staff reported that, since 22 February, some 22,000 people had fled Libya through Tunisia and 15,000 through Egypt. Many leaders and international organizations, such as the League of Arab States (LAS), the AU and the EU, made strong statements calling for an immediate end to the violence and condemning what appeared to be gross human rights violations. The challenge for the international community was how to provide real protection and halt the violence.

Human Rights Council action. On 25 February, at its special session on Libya, the Human Rights Council, by resolution S-15/1 (see p. 604), decided to dispatch an international commission of inquiry to investigate alleged violations of international human rights law in Libya; establish the circumstances of such violations and of the crimes perpetrated; and, where possible, identify those responsible. The Council recommended that the General Assembly consider applying the measures foreseen in paragraph 8 of Assembly resolution 60/251 [YUN 2006, p. 757], which provided for the suspension of a country's right of membership in the Council because of gross and systematic violations of human rights.

SECURITY COUNCIL ACTION

On 26 February [meeting 6491], the Security Council unanimously adopted **resolution 1970(2011)**. The draft [S/2011/95] was submitted by 11 Member States.

The Security Council,

Expressing grave concern at the situation in the Libyan Arab Jamahiriya, and condemning the violence and use of force against civilians,

Deploring the gross and systematic violation of human rights, including the repression of peaceful demonstrators, expressing deep concern at the deaths of civilians, and rejecting unequivocally the incitement to hostility and violence against the civilian population made from the highest level of the Libyan Government,

Welcoming the condemnation by the League of Arab States, the African Union and the Secretary General of the Organization of the Islamic Conference of the serious violations of human rights and international humanitarian law that are being committed in the Libyan Arab Jamahiriya,

Taking note of the letter dated 26 February 2011 from the Permanent Representative of the Libyan Arab Jamahiriya to the United Nations addressed to the President of the Security Council,

Welcoming Human Rights Council resolution S-15/1 of 25 February 2011, including the decision to urgently dispatch an independent international commission of inquiry to investigate all alleged violations of international human rights law in the Libyan Arab Jamahiriya, to establish the facts and circumstances of such violations and of the crimes perpetrated and, where possible, to identify those responsible,

Considering that the widespread and systematic attacks currently taking place in the Libyan Arab Jamahiriya against the civilian population may amount to crimes against humanity,

Expressing concern at the plight of refugees forced to flee the violence in the Libyan Arab Jamahiriya,

Expressing concern also at the reports of shortages of medical supplies to treat the wounded,

Recalling the responsibility of the Libyan authorities to protect the Libyan population,

Underlining the need to respect the freedoms of peaceful assembly and of expression, including freedom of the media,

Stressing the need to hold to account those responsible for attacks, including by forces under their control, on civilians,

Recalling article 16 of the Rome Statute of the International Criminal Court, under which no investigation or prosecution may be commenced or proceeded with by the Court for a period of twelve months after a Security Council request to that effect,

Expressing concern for the safety of foreign nationals and their rights in the Libyan Arab Jamahiriya,

Reaffirming its strong commitment to the sovereignty, independence, territorial integrity and national unity of the Libyan Arab Jamahiriya,

Mindful of its primary responsibility for the maintenance of international peace and security under the Charter of the United Nations,

Acting under Chapter VII of the Charter, and taking measures under its Article 41,

1. *Demands* an immediate end to the violence, and calls for steps to fulfil the legitimate demands of the population;

2. *Urges* the Libyan authorities:

(*a*) To act with the utmost restraint, respect human rights and international humanitarian law, and allow immediate access for international human rights monitors;

(*b*) To ensure the safety of all foreign nationals and their assets and facilitate the departure of those wishing to leave the country;

(c) To ensure the safe passage of humanitarian and medical supplies, and humanitarian agencies and workers, into the country; and

(d) To immediately lift restrictions on all forms of media;

3. *Requests* all Member States, to the extent possible, to cooperate in the evacuation of those foreign nationals wishing to leave the country;

Referral to the International Criminal Court

4. *Decides* to refer the situation in the Libyan Arab Jamahiriya since 15 February 2011 to the Prosecutor of the International Criminal Court;

5. *Decides also* that the Libyan authorities shall cooperate fully with and provide any necessary assistance to the International Criminal Court and the Prosecutor pursuant to the present resolution and, while recognizing that States not party to the Rome Statute of the Court have no obligation under the Rome Statute, urges all States and concerned regional and other international organizations to cooperate fully with the Court and the Prosecutor;

6. *Decides further* that nationals, current or former officials or personnel from a State outside the Libyan Arab Jamahiriya which is not a party to the Rome Statute shall be subject to the exclusive jurisdiction of that State for all alleged acts or omissions arising out of or related to operations in the Libyan Arab Jamahiriya established or authorized by the Security Council, unless such exclusive jurisdiction has been expressly waived by the State;

7. *Invites* the Prosecutor to address the Council within two months of the adoption of the present resolution and every six months thereafter on actions taken pursuant to the present resolution;

8. *Recognizes* that none of the expenses incurred in connection with the referral, including expenses related to investigations or prosecutions in connection with that referral, shall be borne by the United Nations and that such costs shall be borne by the parties to the Rome Statute and those States that wish to contribute voluntarily;

Arms embargo

9. *Decides* that all Member States shall immediately take the measures necessary to prevent the direct or indirect supply, sale or transfer to the Libyan Arab Jamahiriya, from or through their territories or by their nationals, or using their flag vessels or aircraft, of arms and related materiel of all types, including weapons and ammunition, military vehicles and equipment, paramilitary equipment, and spare parts for the aforementioned, and technical assistance, training, and financial or other assistance, related to military activities or the provision, maintenance or use of any arms and related materiel, including the provision of armed mercenary personnel, whether or not originating in their territories, and decides further that this measure shall not apply to:

(a) Supplies of non-lethal military equipment intended solely for humanitarian or protective use, and related technical assistance or training, as approved in advance by the Security Council Committee established pursuant to paragraph 24 below;

(b) Protective clothing, including flak jackets and military helmets, temporarily exported to the Libyan Arab Jamahiriya by United Nations personnel, representatives of the media and humanitarian and development workers and associated personnel, for their personal use only; or

(c) Other sales or supply of arms and related materiel, or provision of assistance or personnel, as approved in advance by the Committee;

10. *Decides also* that the Libyan Arab Jamahiriya shall cease the export of all arms and related materiel and that all Member States shall prohibit the procurement of such items from the Libyan Arab Jamahiriya by their nationals, or using their flagged vessels or aircraft, and whether or not originating in the territory of the Libyan Arab Jamahiriya;

11. *Calls upon* all States, in particular States neighbouring the Libyan Arab Jamahiriya, to inspect, in accordance with their national authorities and legislation and consistent with international law, in particular the law of the sea and relevant international civil aviation agreements, all cargo to and from the Libyan Arab Jamahiriya, in their territory, including seaports and airports, if the State concerned has information that provides reasonable grounds to believe that the cargo contains items, the supply, sale, transfer or export of which is prohibited by paragraphs 9 or 10 of the present resolution for the purpose of ensuring strict implementation of those provisions;

12. *Decides* to authorize all Member States to, and that all Member States shall, upon discovery of items prohibited by paragraphs 9 or 10 of the present resolution, seize and dispose (such as through destruction, rendering inoperable, storage or transferring to a State other than the originating or destination States for disposal) items, the supply, sale, transfer or export of which is prohibited by paragraphs 9 or 10 of the present resolution, and decides further that all Member States shall cooperate in such efforts;

13. *Requires* any Member State, when it undertakes an inspection pursuant to paragraph 11 above, to submit promptly an initial written report to the Committee containing, in particular, an explanation of the grounds for the inspections, the results of such inspections, and whether or not cooperation was provided, and, if prohibited items for transfer are found, further requires such Member States to submit to the Committee, at a later stage, a subsequent written report containing relevant details on the inspection, seizure and disposal, and relevant details of the transfer, including a description of the items, their origin and intended destination, if this information is not in the initial report;

14. *Encourages* Member States to take steps to strongly discourage their nationals from travelling to the Libyan Arab Jamahiriya to participate in activities on behalf of the Libyan authorities that could reasonably contribute to the violation of human rights;

Travel ban

15. *Decides* that all Member States shall take the measures necessary to prevent the entry into or transit through their territories of individuals listed in annex I to the present resolution or designated by the Committee established pursuant to paragraph 24 below, provided that nothing in the present paragraph shall oblige a State to refuse its own nationals entry into its territory;

16. *Decides also* that the measures imposed by paragraph 15 above shall not apply:

(a) Where the Committee determines on a case-by-case basis that such travel is justified on the grounds of humanitarian need, including religious obligation;

(b) Where entry or transit is necessary for the fulfilment of a judicial process;

(c) Where the Committee determines on a case-by-case basis that an exemption would further the objectives of peace and national reconciliation in the Libyan Arab Jamahiriya and stability in the region; or

(d) Where a State determines on a case-by-case basis that such entry or transit is required to advance peace and stability in the Libyan Arab Jamahiriya and the State subsequently notifies the Committee within forty-eight hours of making such a determination;

Asset freeze

17. *Decides further* that all Member States shall freeze without delay all funds, other financial assets and economic resources which are on their territories, which are owned or controlled, directly or indirectly, by the individuals or entities listed in annex II to the present resolution or designated by the Committee established pursuant to paragraph 24 below, or by individuals or entities acting on their behalf or at their direction, or by entities owned or controlled by them, and decides further that all Member States shall ensure that any funds, financial assets or economic resources are prevented from being made available by their nationals or by any individuals or entities within their territories, to or for the benefit of the individuals or entities listed in annex II to the present resolution or individuals designated by the Committee;

18. *Expresses its intention* to ensure that assets frozen pursuant to paragraph 17 above shall at a later stage be made available to and for the benefit of the people of the Libyan Arab Jamahiriya;

19. *Decides* that the measures imposed by paragraph 17 above do not apply to funds, other financial assets or economic resources that have been determined by relevant Member States:

(a) To be necessary for basic expenses, including payment for foodstuffs, rent or mortgage, medicines and medical treatment, taxes, insurance premiums and public utility charges or exclusively for payment of reasonable professional fees and reimbursement of incurred expenses associated with the provision of legal services in accordance with national laws, or fees or service charges, in accordance with national laws, for routine holding or maintenance of frozen funds, other financial assets and economic resources, after notification by the relevant State to the Committee of the intention to authorize, where appropriate, access to such funds, other financial assets or economic resources and in the absence of a negative decision by the Committee within five working days of such notification;

(b) To be necessary for extraordinary expenses, provided that such determination has been notified by the relevant State or Member States to the Committee and has been approved by the Committee; or

(c) To be the subject of a judicial, administrative or arbitral lien or judgment, in which case the funds, other financial assets and economic resources may be used to satisfy that lien or judgment, provided that the lien or judgment was entered into prior to the date of the present resolution, is not for the benefit of a person or entity designated pursuant to paragraph 17 above, and has been notified by the relevant State or Member States to the Committee;

20. *Decides also* that Member States may permit the addition to the accounts frozen pursuant to the provisions of paragraph 17 above of interest or other earnings due on those accounts or payments due under contracts, agreements or obligations that arose prior to the date on which those accounts became subject to the provisions of the present resolution, provided that any such interest, other earnings and payments continue to be subject to these provisions and are frozen;

21. *Decides further* that the measures in paragraph 17 above shall not prevent a designated person or entity from making payment due under a contract entered into prior to the listing of such a person or entity, provided that the relevant States have determined that the payment is not directly or indirectly received by a person or entity designated pursuant to paragraph 17 above, and after notification by the relevant States to the Committee of the intention to make or receive such payments or to authorize, where appropriate, the unfreezing of funds, other financial assets or economic resources for this purpose, ten working days prior to such authorization;

Designation criteria

22. *Decides* that the measures contained in paragraphs 15 and 17 above shall apply to the individuals and entities designated by the Committee, pursuant to paragraphs 24 (b) and (c) below respectively:

(a) Involved in or complicit in ordering, controlling or otherwise directing, the commission of serious human rights abuses against persons in the Libyan Arab Jamahiriya, including by being involved in or complicit in planning, commanding, ordering or conducting attacks, in violation of international law, including aerial bombardments, on civilian populations and facilities; or

(b) Acting for or on behalf of or at the direction of individuals or entities identified in subparagraph (a);

23. *Strongly encourages* Member States to submit to the Committee names of individuals who meet the criteria set out in paragraph 22 above;

New sanctions committee

24. *Decides* to establish, in accordance with rule 28 of its provisional rules of procedure, a Committee of the Security Council consisting of all the members of the Council (hereinafter "the Committee"), to undertake the following tasks:

(a) To monitor implementation of the measures imposed in paragraphs 9, 10, 15 and 17 above;

(b) To designate those individuals subject to the measures imposed by paragraph 15 above and to consider requests for exemptions in accordance with paragraph 16 above;

(c) To designate those individuals subject to the measures imposed by paragraph 17 above and to consider requests for exemptions in accordance with paragraphs 19 and 20 above;

(d) To establish such guidelines as may be necessary to facilitate the implementation of the measures imposed above;

(e) To report within thirty days to the Council on its work for the first report and thereafter to report as deemed necessary by the Committee;

(f) To encourage a dialogue between the Committee and interested Member States, in particular those in the region, including by inviting representatives of such States to meet with the Committee to discuss implementation of the measures;

(*g*) To seek from all States whatever information it may consider useful regarding the actions taken by them to implement effectively the measures imposed above;

(*h*) To examine and take appropriate action on information regarding alleged violations or non-compliance with the measures contained in the present resolution;

25. *Calls upon* all Member States to report to the Committee within one hundred and twenty days of the adoption of the present resolution on the steps they have taken with a view to implementing effectively paragraphs 9, 10, 15 and 17 above;

Humanitarian assistance

26. *Also calls upon* all Member States, working together and acting in cooperation with the Secretary-General, to facilitate and support the return of humanitarian agencies and make available humanitarian and related assistance in the Libyan Arab Jamahiriya, and requests the States concerned to keep the Council regularly informed of the progress of actions undertaken pursuant to the present paragraph, and expresses its readiness to consider taking additional appropriate measures, as necessary, to achieve this;

Commitment to review

27. *Affirms* that it shall keep the actions of the Libyan authorities under continuous review and that it shall be prepared to review the appropriateness of the measures contained in the present resolution, including the strengthening, modification, suspension or lifting of the measures, as may be needed at any time in the light of the Libyan authorities' compliance with relevant provisions of the present resolution;

28. *Decides* to remain actively seized of the matter.

Annex I

Travel ban

1. Al-Baghdadi, Dr. Abdulqader Mohammed
Passport number: B010574. Date of birth: 01/07/1950.
Head of the Liaison Office of the Revolutionary Committees. Revolutionary Committees involved in violence against demonstrators.

2. Dibri, Abdulqader Yusef
Date of birth: 1946. Place of birth: Houn, Libya.
Head of Muammar Qadhafi's personal security. Responsibility for regime security. History of directing violence against dissidents.

3. Dorda, Abu Zayd Umar
Director, External Security Organisation. Regime loyalist. Head of external intelligence agency.

4. Jabir, Major General Abu Bakr Yunis
Date of birth: 1952. Place of birth: Jalo, Libya.
Defence Minister. Overall responsibility for actions of armed forces.

5. Matuq, Matuq Mohammed
Date of birth: 1956. Place of birth: Khoms, Libya.
Secretary for Utilities. Senior member of regime. Involvement with Revolutionary Committees. Past history of involvement in suppression of dissent and violence.

6. Qadhaf Al-dam, Sayyid Mohammed
Date of birth: 1948. Place of birth: Sirte, Libya.
Cousin of Muammar Qadhafi. In the 1980s, Sayyid was involved in the dissident assassination campaign and allegedly responsible for several deaths in Europe. He is also thought to have been involved in arms procurement.

7. Qadhafi, Aisha Muammar
Date of birth: 1978. Place of birth: Tripoli, Libya.
Daughter of Muammar Qadhafi. Closeness of association with regime.

8. Qadhafi, Hannibal Muammar
Passport number: B/002210. Date of birth: 20/09/1975. Place of birth: Tripoli, Libya.
Son of Muammar Qadhafi. Closeness of association with regime.

9. Qadhafi, Khamis Muammar
Date of birth: 1978. Place of birth: Tripoli, Libya.
Son of Muammar Qadhafi. Closeness of association with regime. Command of military units involved in repression of demonstrations.

10. Qadhafi, Mohammed Muammar
Date of birth: 1970. Place of birth: Tripoli, Libya.
Son of Muammar Qadhafi. Closeness of association with regime.

11. Qadhafi, Muammar Mohammed Abu Minyar
Date of birth: 1942. Place of birth: Sirte, Libya.
Leader of the Revolution, Supreme Commander of Armed Forces. Responsibility for ordering repression of demonstrations, human rights abuses.

12. Qadhafi, Mutassim
Date of birth: 1976. Place of birth: Tripoli, Libya.
National Security Adviser. Son of Muammar Qadhafi. Closeness of association with regime.

13. Qadhafi, Saadi
Passport number: 014797. Date of birth: 25/05/1973. Place of birth: Tripoli, Libya.
Commander Special Forces. Son of Muammar Qadhafi. Closeness of association with regime. Command of military units involved in repression of demonstrations.

14. Qadhafi, Saif al-Arab
Date of birth: 1982. Place of birth: Tripoli, Libya.
Son of Muammar Qadhafi. Closeness of association with regime.

15. Qadhafi, Saif al-Islam
Passport number: B014995. Date of birth: 25/06/1972. Place of birth: Tripoli, Libya.
Director, Qadhafi Foundation. Son of Muammar Qadhafi. Closeness of association with regime. Inflammatory public statements encouraging violence against demonstrators.

16. Al-Senussi, Colonel Abdullah
Date of birth: 1949. Place of birth: Sudan.
Director Military Intelligence. Military Intelligence involvement in suppression of demonstrations. Past history includes suspicion of involvement in Abu Selim prison massacre. Convicted in absentia for bombing of UTA flight. Brother-in-law of Muammar Qadhafi.

Annex II

Asset freeze

1. Qadhafi, Aisha Muammar

Date of birth: 1978. Place of birth: Tripoli, Libya.
Daughter of Muammar Qadhafi. Closeness of association with regime.

2. Qadhafi, Hannibal Muammar
Passport number: B/002210. Date of birth: 20/09/1975. Place of birth: Tripoli, Libya.
Son of Muammar Qadhafi. Closeness of association with regime.

3. Qadhafi, Khamis Muammar
Date of birth: 1978. Place of birth: Tripoli, Libya.
Son of Muammar Qadhafi. Closeness of association with regime. Command of military units involved in repression of demonstrations.

4. Qadhafi, Muammar Mohammed Abu Minyar
Date of birth: 1942. Place of birth: Sirte, Libya.
Leader of the Revolution, Supreme Commander of Armed Forces. Responsibility for ordering repression of demonstrations, human rights abuses.

5. Qadhafi, Mutassim
Date of birth: 1976. Place of birth: Tripoli, Libya.
National Security Adviser. Son of Muammar Qadhafi. Closeness of association with regime.

6. Qadhafi, Saif al-Islam
Passport number: B014995. Date of birth: 25/06/1972. Place of birth: Tripoli, Libya.
Director, Qadhafi Foundation. Son of Muammar Qadhafi. Closeness of association with regime. Inflammatory public statements encouraging violence against demonstrators.

Communication. On 28 February [A/65/766-S/2011/103], the Russian Federation transmitted to the Secretary-General the Joint Russia-European Union Statement of 24 February on the Situation in North Africa and the Middle East. Therein Russia and the EU expressed support for the statements made by the LAS Council and the Security Council and condemned the use of military force to break up peaceful demonstrations, as well as any other manifestations of violence. In particular, they condemned the violence and the use of force against civilians in Libya.

Suspension of Libya's membership in Human Rights Council. On 1 March, by **resolution 65/265** (see p. 605), the General Assembly suspended Libya's right of membership in the Human Rights Council.

Appointment of Special Envoy. On 10 March [S/2011/126], the Secretary-General informed the Security Council of his decision to appoint Abdel-Elah Mohamed Al-Khatib (Jordan) as his Special Envoy to Libya. The Council took note that decision on 11 March [S/2011/127].

Communications. On 14 March [S/2011/133], Hungary, at the request of the EU, transmitted to the Secretary-General the declaration adopted by the extraordinary session of the European Council (Brussels, Belgium, 11 March). The session discussed developments in Libya and the neighbouring region and the political direction for future EU action.

On 14 March [S/2011/137], LAS transmitted to the Security Council resolution 7360, adopted by the LAS Council at its extraordinary ministerial session (Cairo, Egypt, 12 March), which called on the Security Council to impose a no-fly zone on Libyan military aviation and to take measures to protect civilians.

By a note of 16 March [S/2011/141], the Security Council President stated that, following consultations among Council members, it had been agreed that issues pertaining to Libya would, as from 16 March, be considered under the agenda item entitled "The situation in Libya". That item would include those issues previously considered under "Peace and security in Africa".

SECURITY COUNCIL ACTION

On 17 March [meeting 6498], the Security Council adopted **resolution 1973(2011)** by vote (10-0-5). The draft [S/2011/142] was submitted by France, Lebanon, the United Kingdom and the United States.

The Security Council,

Recalling its resolution 1970(2011) of 26 February 2011,

Deploring the failure of the Libyan authorities to comply with resolution 1970(2011),

Expressing grave concern at the deteriorating situation, the escalation of violence and the heavy civilian casualties,

Reiterating the responsibility of the Libyan authorities to protect the Libyan population, and reaffirming that parties to armed conflicts bear the primary responsibility to take all feasible steps to ensure the protection of civilians,

Condemning the gross and systematic violation of human rights, including arbitrary detentions, enforced disappearances, torture and summary executions,

Condemning also acts of violence and intimidation committed by the Libyan authorities against journalists, media professionals and associated personnel, and urging these authorities to comply with their obligations under international humanitarian law as outlined in resolution 1738(2006) of 23 December 2006,

Considering that the widespread and systematic attacks currently taking place in the Libyan Arab Jamahiriya against the civilian population may amount to crimes against humanity,

Recalling paragraph 26 of resolution 1970(2011), in which the Security Council expressed its readiness to consider taking additional appropriate measures, as necessary, to facilitate and support the return of humanitarian agencies and make available humanitarian and related assistance in the Libyan Arab Jamahiriya,

Expressing its determination to ensure the protection of civilians and civilian populated areas and the rapid and unimpeded passage of humanitarian assistance and the safety of humanitarian personnel,

Recalling the condemnation by the League of Arab States, the African Union and the Secretary General of the Organization of the Islamic Conference of the serious violations of human rights and international humanitarian law that have been and are being committed in the Libyan Arab Jamahiriya,

Taking note of the final communiqué of the Organization of the Islamic Conference of 8 March 2011 and the communiqué of the Peace and Security Council of the African Union of 10 March 2011, by which it established the Ad Hoc High-level Committee on Libya,

Taking note also of the decision of the Council of the League of Arab States of 12 March 2011 to call for the imposition of a no-fly zone on Libyan military aviation and establishment of safe areas in places exposed to shelling as a precautionary measure that allows the protection of the Libyan people and foreign nationals residing in the Libyan Arab Jamahiriya,

Taking note further of the Secretary-General's call on 16 March 2011 for an immediate ceasefire,

Recalling its decision to refer the situation in the Libyan Arab Jamahiriya since 15 February 2011 to the Prosecutor of the International Criminal Court, and stressing that those responsible for or complicit in attacks targeting the civilian population, including aerial and naval attacks, must be held to account,

Reiterating its concern at the plight of refugees and foreign workers forced to flee the violence in the Libyan Arab Jamahiriya, welcoming the response of neighbouring States, in particular Tunisia and Egypt, to address the needs of those refugees and foreign workers, and calling upon the international community to support those efforts,

Deploring the continuing use of mercenaries by the Libyan authorities,

Considering that the establishment of a ban on all flights in the airspace of the Libyan Arab Jamahiriya constitutes an important element for the protection of civilians as well as the safety of the delivery of humanitarian assistance and a decisive step for the cessation of hostilities in the Libyan Arab Jamahiriya,

Expressing concern for the safety of foreign nationals and their rights in the Libyan Arab Jamahiriya,

Welcoming the appointment by the Secretary-General of his Special Envoy to the Libyan Arab Jamahiriya, Mr. Abdel-Elah Mohamed Al-Khatib, and supporting his efforts to find a sustainable and peaceful solution to the crisis in the Libyan Arab Jamahiriya,

Reaffirming its strong commitment to the sovereignty, independence, territorial integrity and national unity of the Libyan Arab Jamahiriya,

Determining that the situation in the Libyan Arab Jamahiriya continues to constitute a threat to international peace and security,

Acting under Chapter VII of the Charter of the United Nations,

1. *Demands* the immediate establishment of a ceasefire and a complete end to violence and all attacks against, and abuses of, civilians;

2. *Stresses* the need to intensify efforts to find a solution to the crisis which responds to the legitimate demands of the Libyan people, and notes the decisions of the Secretary-General to send his Special Envoy to the Libyan Arab Jamahiriya and of the Peace and Security Council of the African Union to send its Ad Hoc High-level Committee on Libya to the Libyan Arab Jamahiriya with the aim of facilitating dialogue to lead to the political reforms necessary to find a peaceful and sustainable solution;

3. *Demands* that the Libyan authorities comply with their obligations under international law, including international humanitarian law, human rights and refugee law, and take all measures to protect civilians and meet their basic needs and to ensure the rapid and unimpeded passage of humanitarian assistance;

Protection of civilians

4. *Authorizes* Member States that have notified the Secretary-General, acting nationally or through regional organizations or arrangements, and acting in cooperation with the Secretary-General, to take all necessary measures, notwithstanding paragraph 9 of resolution 1970(2011), to protect civilians and civilian populated areas under threat of attack in the Libyan Arab Jamahiriya, including Benghazi, while excluding a foreign occupation force of any form on any part of Libyan territory, and requests the Member States concerned to inform the Secretary-General immediately of the measures they take pursuant to the authorization conferred by the present paragraph which shall be immediately reported to the Security Council;

5. *Recognizes* the important role of the League of Arab States in matters relating to the maintenance of international peace and security in the region, and, bearing in mind Chapter VIII of the Charter of the United Nations, requests the States members of the League of Arab States to cooperate with other Member States in the implementation of paragraph 4 above;

No-fly zone

6. *Decides* to establish a ban on all flights in the airspace of the Libyan Arab Jamahiriya in order to help to protect civilians;

7. *Decides also* that the ban imposed by paragraph 6 above shall not apply to flights whose sole purpose is humanitarian, such as delivering or facilitating the delivery of assistance, including medical supplies, food, humanitarian workers and related assistance, or evacuating foreign nationals from the Libyan Arab Jamahiriya, nor shall it apply to flights authorized by paragraphs 4 or 8, nor to other flights which are deemed necessary by States acting under the authorization conferred in paragraph 8 below to be for the benefit of the Libyan people, and that these flights shall be coordinated with any mechanism established under paragraph 8;

8. *Authorizes* Member States that have notified the Secretary-General of the United Nations and the Secretary General of the League of Arab States, acting nationally or through regional organizations or arrangements, to take all measures necessary to enforce compliance with the ban on flights imposed by paragraph 6 above, as necessary, and requests the States concerned, in cooperation with the League of Arab States, to coordinate closely with the Secretary-General of the United Nations on the measures they are taking to implement this ban, including by establishing an appropriate mechanism for implementing the provisions of paragraphs 6 and 7 above;

9. *Calls upon* all Member States, acting nationally or through regional organizations or arrangements, to provide assistance, including any necessary overflight approvals, for

the purposes of implementing paragraphs 4, 6, 7 and 8 above;

10. *Requests* the Member States concerned to coordinate closely with each other and with the Secretary-General of the United Nations on the measures they are taking to implement paragraphs 4, 6, 7 and 8 above, including practical measures for the monitoring and approval of authorized humanitarian or evacuation flights;

11. *Decides* that the Member States concerned shall inform the Secretary-General of the United Nations and the Secretary General of the League of Arab States immediately of measures taken in exercise of the authority conferred by paragraph 8 above, including to supply a concept of operations;

12. *Requests* the Secretary-General of the United Nations to inform the Security Council immediately of any actions taken by the Member States concerned in exercise of the authority conferred by paragraph 8 above and to report to the Council within seven days and every month thereafter on the implementation of the present resolution, including information on any violations of the flight ban imposed by paragraph 6 above;

Enforcement of the arms embargo

13. *Decides* that paragraph 11 of resolution 1970(2011) shall be replaced by the following paragraph: "Calls upon all Member States, in particular States of the region, acting nationally or through regional organizations or arrangements, in order to ensure strict implementation of the arms embargo established by paragraphs 9 and 10 of resolution 1970(2011), to inspect in their territory, including seaports and airports, and on the high seas, vessels and aircraft bound to or from the Libyan Arab Jamahiriya, if the State concerned has information that provides reasonable grounds to believe that the cargo contains items, the supply, sale, transfer or export of which is prohibited by paragraphs 9 or 10 of resolution 1970(2011) as modified by the present resolution, including the provision of armed mercenary personnel, calls upon all flag States of such vessels and aircraft to cooperate with such inspections, and authorizes Member States to use all measures commensurate to the specific circumstances to carry out such inspections";

14. *Requests* Member States which are taking action under paragraph 13 above on the high seas to coordinate closely with each other and with the Secretary-General, and further requests the States concerned to inform the Secretary-General and the Security Council Committee established pursuant to paragraph 24 of resolution 1970(2011) ("the Committee") immediately of measures taken in exercise of the authority conferred by paragraph 13 above;

15. *Requires* any Member State, whether acting nationally or through regional organizations or arrangements, when it undertakes an inspection pursuant to paragraph 13 above, to submit promptly an initial written report to the Committee containing, in particular, an explanation of the grounds for the inspection, the results of such inspection, and whether or not cooperation was provided, and, if prohibited items for transfer are found, further requires such Member States to submit to the Committee, at a later stage, a subsequent written report containing relevant details on the inspection, seizure and disposal, and relevant details of the transfer, including a description of the items, their origin and their intended destination, if this information is not in the initial report;

16. *Deplores* the continuing flows of mercenaries into the Libyan Arab Jamahiriya, and calls upon all Member States to comply strictly with their obligations under paragraph 9 of resolution 1970(2011) to prevent the provision of armed mercenary personnel to the Libyan Arab Jamahiriya;

Ban on flights

17. *Decides* that all States shall deny permission to any aircraft registered in the Libyan Arab Jamahiriya or owned or operated by Libyan nationals or companies to take off from, land in or overfly their territory unless the particular flight has been approved in advance by the Committee, or in the case of an emergency landing;

18. *Decides also* that all States shall deny permission to any aircraft to take off from, land in or overfly their territory, if they have information that provides reasonable grounds to believe that the aircraft contains items, the supply, sale, transfer or export of which is prohibited by paragraphs 9 and 10 of resolution 1970(2011) as modified by the present resolution, including the provision of armed mercenary personnel, except in the case of an emergency landing;

Asset freeze

19. *Decides further* that the asset freeze imposed by paragraphs 17, 19, 20 and 21 of resolution 1970(2011) shall apply to all funds, other financial assets and economic resources which are on their territories, which are owned or controlled, directly or indirectly, by the Libyan authorities, as designated by the Committee, or by individuals or entities acting on their behalf or at their direction, or by entities owned or controlled by them, as designated by the Committee, and decides further that all States shall ensure that any funds, financial assets or economic resources are prevented from being made available by their nationals or by any individuals or entities within their territories to or for the benefit of the Libyan authorities, as designated by the Committee, or individuals or entities acting on their behalf or at their direction, or entities owned or controlled by them, as designated by the Committee, and directs the Committee to designate such Libyan authorities, individuals or entities within thirty days of the date of the adoption of the present resolution and as appropriate thereafter;

20. *Affirms its determination* to ensure that assets frozen pursuant to paragraph 17 of resolution 1970(2011) shall, at a later stage, as soon as possible be made available to and for the benefit of the people of the Libyan Arab Jamahiriya;

21. *Decides* that all States shall require their nationals, persons subject to their jurisdiction and firms incorporated in their territory or subject to their jurisdiction to exercise vigilance when doing business with entities incorporated in the Libyan Arab Jamahiriya or subject to its jurisdiction, and any individuals or entities acting on their behalf or at their direction, and entities owned or controlled by them, if the States have information that provides reasonable grounds to believe that such business could contribute to violence and the use of force against civilians;

Designations

22. *Decides also* that the individuals listed in annex I shall be subject to the travel restrictions imposed in paragraphs 15 and 16 of resolution 1970(2011), and decides further that the individuals and entities listed in annex II shall be subject to the asset freeze imposed in paragraphs 17, 19, 20 and 21 of resolution 1970(2011);

23. *Decides further* that the measures specified in paragraphs 15, 16, 17, 19, 20 and 21 of resolution 1970(2011) shall apply also to individuals and entities determined by the Council or the Committee to have violated the provisions of resolution 1970(2011), particularly paragraphs 9 and 10 thereof, or to have assisted others in doing so;

Panel of Experts

24. *Requests* the Secretary-General to create for an initial period of one year, in consultation with the Committee, a group of up to eight experts ("Panel of Experts"), under the direction of the Committee, to carry out the following tasks:

(*a*) Assist the Committee in carrying out its mandate as specified in paragraph 24 of resolution 1970(2011) and the present resolution;

(*b*) Gather, examine and analyse information from States, relevant United Nations bodies, regional organizations and other interested parties regarding the implementation of the measures decided in resolution 1970(2011) and the present resolution, in particular incidents of non-compliance;

(*c*) Make recommendations on actions that the Council, or the Committee or State, may consider to improve implementation of the relevant measures;

(*d*) Provide to the Council an interim report on its work no later than ninety days after the appointment of the Panel of Experts, and a final report to the Council no later than thirty days prior to the termination of its mandate, with its findings and recommendations;

25. *Urges* all States, relevant United Nations bodies and other interested parties to cooperate fully with the Committee and the Panel of Experts, in particular by supplying any information at their disposal on the implementation of the measures decided in resolution 1970(2011) and the present resolution, in particular incidents of non-compliance;

26. *Decides* that the mandate of the Committee as set out in paragraph 24 of resolution 1970(2011) shall also apply to the measures decided in the present resolution;

27. *Decides also* that all States, including the Libyan Arab Jamahiriya, shall take the measures necessary to ensure that no claim shall lie at the instance of the Libyan authorities, or of any person or body in the Libyan Arab Jamahiriya, or of any person claiming through or for the benefit of any such person or body, in connection with any contract or other transaction where its performance was affected by reason of the measures taken by the Council in resolution 1970(2011), the present resolution and related resolutions;

28. *Reaffirms its intention* to keep the actions of the Libyan authorities under continuous review, and underlines its readiness to review at any time the measures imposed by the present resolution and resolution 1970(2011), including by strengthening, suspending or lifting those measures, as appropriate, based on compliance by the Libyan authorities with the present resolution and resolution 1970(2011);

29. *Decides* to remain actively seized of the matter.

Libya: Designations pursuant to Security Council resolution 1973(2011)

Number	Name	Justification	Identifiers
Annex I: Travel ban			
1	QUREN SALIH QUREN AL QADHAFI	Libyan Ambassador to Chad. Has left Chad for Sabha. Involved directly in recruiting and coordinating mercenaries for the regime.	
2	Colonel AMID HUSAIN AL KUNI	Governor of Ghat (South Libya). Directly involved in recruiting mercenaries.	
Annex II: Asset freeze			
1	Dorda, Abu Zayd Umar	Position: Director, External Security Organisation	
2	Jabir, Major General Abu Bakr Yunis	Position: Defence Minister	**Title:** Major General **DOB:**-/-/1952. **POB:** Jalo, Libya
3	Matuq, Matuq Mohammed	Position: Secretary for Utilities	**DOB:**-/-/1956. **POB:** Khoms, Libya
4	Qadhafi, Mohammed Muammar	Son of Muammar Qadhafi. Closeness of association with regime	**DOB:**-/-/1970. **POB:** Tripoli, Libya
5	Qadhafi, Saadi	Commander Special Forces. Son of Muammar Qadhafi. Closeness of association with regime. Command of military units involved in repression of demonstrations	**DOB:** 25/05/1973. **POB:** Tripoli, Libya
6	Qadhafi, Saif al-Arab	Son of Muammar Qadhafi. Closeness of association with regime	**DOB:**-/-/1982. **POB:** Tripoli, Libya
7	Al-Senussi, Colonel Abdullah	Position: Director Military Intelligence	**Title:** Colonel **DOB:**-/-/1949. **POB:** Sudan
Entities			
1	Central Bank of Libya	Under control of Muammar Qadhafi and his family, and potential source of funding for his regime.	
2	Libyan Investment Authority	Under control of Muammar Qadhafi and his family, and potential source of funding for his regime.	**a.k.a.:** Libyan Arab Foreign Investment Company (LAFICO) **Address:** 1 Fateh Tower Office, No. 99 22nd Floor, Borgaida Street, Tripoli, Libya, 1103
3	Libyan Foreign Bank	Under control of Muammar Qadhafi and his family, and a potential source of funding for his regime.	
4	Libyan Africa Investment Portfolio	Under control of Muammar Qadhafi and his family, and potential source of funding for his regime.	**Address:** Jamahiriya Street, LAP Building, PO Box 91330, Tripoli, Libya
5	Libyan National Oil Corporation	Under control of Muammar Qadhafi and his family, and potential source of funding for his regime.	**Address:** Bashir Saadwi Street, Tripoli, Tarabulus, Libya

VOTE ON RESOLUTION 1973(2011):

In favour: Bosnia and Herzegovina, Colombia, France, Gabon, Lebanon, Nigeria, Portugal, South Africa, United Kingdom, United States.

Against: None.

Abstaining: Brazil, China, Germany, India, Russian Federation.

Communications. In response to Council resolution 1973(2011) (see p. 271), several Member States between 18 and 30 March sent letters and notes to the Secretary-General or identical letters to the Secretary-General and the Council President to inform them of the measures they intended to take or had taken in implementing that resolution: the United Kingdom [S/2011/149, S/2011/157, S/2011/177], France [S/2011/150, S/2011/155, S/2011/175, S/2011/212], the United States [S/2011/152, S/2011/156], Denmark [S/2011/153], Canada [S/2011/154, S/2011/191], Italy [S/2011/158, S/2011/185],

Qatar [S/2011/163, S/2011/195], Ukraine [S/2011/164, S/2011/165], Belgium [S/2011/166], Norway [S/2011/167, S/2011/193], Spain [S/2011/168, S/2011/197], the United Arab Emirates [S/2011/169, S/2011/192], Senegal [S/2011/172], Kuwait [S/2011/184], the Syrian Arab Republic [S/2011/186] and the Netherlands [S/2011/196].

On 18 March [S/2011/151], the Security Council transmitted to the Secretary-General a communication from the AU regarding the visit of the AU Ad Hoc High-level Committee on Libya to Tripoli and Benghazi.

On 31 March [S/2011/222], in accordance with Council resolutions 1970(2011) and 1973(2011), Spain informed the Secretary-General of the humanitarian assistance it provided to civilians and persons displaced by the conflict.

On 19 March, in identical letters addressed to the Secretary-General and the Security Council [A/65/792-S/2011/159], Lebanon transmitted a complaint against the Libyan regime following the attack on the Lebanese Embassy in Tripoli on 18 March.

Between 19 and 24 March, Libya addressed four letters to the Security Council. On 19 March [S/2011/160], the Libyan authorities affirmed their commitment to an immediate ceasefire and the deployment of international monitors to oversee it. Also on 19 March [S/2011/161], Libya argued that the ban imposed on Libyan airspace had paved the way for military aggression. France and the United States had bombarded civilian sites, in violation of international law, and Libya called on the Council to hold an emergency meeting to halt the aggression. On 24 March [S/2011/178], Libya called for urgent action to halt the military operations against the country. Also on 24 March [S/2011/179], Libya requested to use the assets in frozen accounts for basic expenses, including food and medicines.

Security Council consideration (March). On 24 March, the Secretary-General briefed the Security Council on the situation in Libya [S/PV.6505]. He recalled that at the summit convened by French President Nicolas Sarkozy (Paris, 19 March), the international community had called for an immediate ceasefire and agreed to undertake the necessary measures to stop the campaign of violence by the Libyan regime against its own people. Those issues had dominated the Secretary-General's recent travels, during which the authorities of Egypt and Tunisia had expressed concern about their nationals in Libya and the burden of caring for refugees at their borders.

Regarding the implementation of resolutions 1970(2011) and 1973(2011), the Secretary-General said that military strikes by United States and European forces had started on 19 March to establish a no-fly zone over Libya, and were ongoing. Libyan authorities claimed that they had instituted a ceasefire, but there was no evidence that that was the case. To the contrary, battles continued in three Libyan cities.

Since the beginning of the crisis, the United Nations had engaged in strong diplomatic efforts, including the visit to Tripoli on 13 March by the Secretary-General's Special Envoy to Libya and the United Nations Humanitarian Coordinator, where they met with the Foreign Minister and other officials. On 21 March, the Special Envoy met in Tobruk with the leaders of the Libyan armed opposition, including the Chairman of the National Transitional Council (NTC). On 23 March, the Secretary-General, in an informal meeting with the AU Commission Chairman, discussed how the United Nations and the AU could work together to resolve the crisis.

More than 335,658 people had fled Libya since the beginning of the crisis. Some 9,000 remained stranded along Libya's borders with Tunisia and Egypt. As at 21 March, the International Organization for Migration (IOM) and UNHCR had helped more than 60,000 people leave the country.

Communications. On 29 March [S/2011/203], the Secretary-General forwarded to the Security Council communications from the North Atlantic Treaty Organization (NATO), conveying notifications related to NATO activities pursuant to Council resolution 1973(2011).

On 29 March [S/2011/204], the United Kingdom informed the Council of a conference on Libya held on the same day in London, in which leaders from the United Nations, LAS, the AU, the Organization of the Islamic Conference (OIC), the EU and NATO discussed the situation in the country. Participants agreed that the Qadhafi regime had lost its legitimacy and that Libyans had to be free to determine their own future.

In identical letters of 29 March [A/65/803-S/2011/209] to the Secretary-General and the Security Council, the Russian Federation transmitted a Declaration by the State Duma on the situation in Libya. The State Duma argued that resolution 1973(2011) did not set clear limits on the use of military force and expressed concern at the extent and forms of military force used against Libya.

On 31 March [S/2011/214], Cambodia, Cuba, Equatorial Guinea, Nicaragua, Saint Vincent and the Grenadines and Venezuela transmitted to the Security Council a letter of 28 March, signed by them and by Antigua and Barbuda, Bolivia, Dominica, Ecuador, Indonesia, Mali, Namibia and Viet Nam, requesting the Council to take urgent measures leading to an immediate ceasefire and a peaceful solution reflecting the will of the Libyan people.

In response to Council resolution 1973(2011), between 1 and 26 April, Italy [S/2011/216, S/2011/270], Sweden [S/2011/217, S/2011/262], Jordan [S/2011/238], the United Kingdom [S/2011/269] and France [S/2011/274] notified the Secretary-General of the measures they had taken or intended to take to implement the resolution.

Security Council consideration (April). On 4 April [S/PV.6509], the Secretary-General's Special Envoy to Libya briefed the Council on developments since the Secretary-General's 24 March briefing. Despite the effectiveness of the efforts made by coalition members to implement a no-fly zone and to protect civilians, fighting continued between the ground forces of the armed opposition and Colonel Qadhafi's loyalists. On 31 March, Colonel Qadhafi's ground forces recaptured a strategic oil town, Ras Lanouf, and moved very close to another major eastern city, Brega, nearly reversing the advances made by opposition fighters since the international air strikes began 19 March. Also on 31 March, one of the most senior officials of the regime, Foreign Affairs Minister Musa Kousa, flew to London and declared that he could no longer serve as a representative of the Libyan Government.

On 31 March, the Special Envoy undertook his second mission to Libya, starting with a one-day visit to Tripoli, where he met with Government officials and reiterated the international community's demand for the full implementation of Council resolutions 1970(2011) and 1973(2011). The Libyan authorities expressed their willingness to accept a ceasefire under the supervision of impartial observers if the NTC did the same. On 1 April, the Special Envoy met in Benghazi with the Chairman and members of the NTC. They set out their vision of a democratic Libya, their initial priority being to restore constitutional legitimacy through a referendum. While they were willing to implement a ceasefire, that alone would not be sufficient to end the conflict. They indicated that the aim of the people's uprising was to see the departure of Colonel Qadhafi.

On the regional front, on 25 March, a ruling of the African Court on Human and Peoples' Rights called upon the Libyan Government to refrain from any actions that would result in the loss of life or violation of the physical integrity of persons, and requested that the Government report to it within 15 days on actions taken to comply with that ruling.

Information about the humanitarian situation remained limited, due to lack of access to different parts of the country. Overall, humanitarian conditions, especially in areas where fighting was taking place, remained serious, particularly regarding medical and protection needs.

Contact Group on Libya. On 14 April [S/2011/246], Qatar and the United Kingdom, the Chairs of the first meeting of the Contact Group on Libya (Doha, Qatar, 13 April), transmitted to the Security Council the statement issued by the Chairs. The Contact Group was intended to serve as major point of contact with the Libyan people, coordinate international policy and be a forum for discussion of post-conflict humanitarian support. The meeting was attended by representatives of 21 countries, the United Nations, LAS, NATO, the EU, OIC and the Cooperation Council for the Arab States of the Gulf. Participants welcomed the NATO leadership of military operations, underlined that a political solution would be the only way to bring lasting peace, and reaffirmed their commitment to the sovereignty and territorial integrity of Libya. They expressed their belief that the continuation of the Qadhafi regime would threaten any resolution of the crisis, as it had lost all legitimacy, and that an inclusive political process should empower the Libyan people to determine their own future. The Group acknowledged that the NTC was a legitimate interlocutor that represented the aspirations of the Libyan people.

Security Council consideration (May). Briefing the Council on 3 May [S/PV.6527], the Special Envoy to Libya said that intense fighting had expanded into the south and west of the country and, on one occasion, had spilled over into the Tunisian city of Dehiba, when pro-Qadhafi and opposition forces had attempted to control the key border post on either side of the Libyan-Tunisian frontier. The Tunisian army had strengthened its positions on the southern border with Libya. Thousands of ethnic Berbers had fled from Libya into Tunisia. Fighting had also intensified in the western city of Misrata, Libya's third-largest city.

On 17 April, the Special Envoy and the Under-Secretary-General for Humanitarian Affairs, Valerie Amos, visited Tripoli, where they met with senior Government officials. The Government signed a humanitarian agreement with the United Nations to allow international humanitarian access to all conflict-affected areas. On 25 April, the Special Envoy attended the meeting of the AU Ad Hoc High-level Committee on Libya, whose position was that the parties should negotiate and that the AU should play, in cooperation with the United Nations, a major role in monitoring a ceasefire mechanism. On 29 April, the Special Envoy met with the NTC in Benghazi. On 30 April, he received a message from Colonel Qadhafi, reporting that NATO had bombed his family's home, killing his son and some of his grandchildren, while he and his wife had survived the attack. Colonel Qadhafi called on the international community to act, saying that the situation was no longer tolerable. The UN premises in Tripoli were ransacked later that night and the UN humanitarian mission in Tripoli had to leave, due to the security situation.

Sea mines were discovered offshore of Misrata on 30 April. Reports indicated that Government forces were bombarding the port area and other parts of that city. A ship belonging to IOM was prevented from docking. IOM was able, however, to evacuate 12,000 people from the city, mostly third-country nationals.

While both parties informed the Special Envoy that they were ready to implement a ceasefire, for the Libyan authorities that meant an end to NATO military action. The NTC, on the other hand, indicated that a ceasefire would not be sufficient to end the conflict if it was not directly linked to the departure of Colonel Qadhafi and his family.

Briefing the Council on 31 May [S/PV.6541], the Under-Secretary-General for Political Affairs said that fighting between the Government and opposition forces continued, the NATO operation had intensified and defections from the regime seemed to be on the rise. Opposition forces had gained control of Misrata and reportedly pushed government troops westward, but fighting on the outskirts of Misrata continued and the city was only accessible by sea. Government forces intensified their campaign to take strategic positions in the western Nafusa mountains, close to the border with Tunisia. Tensions between refugees and local residents along the border escalated. Unrest at Choucha camp in Tunisia on 23 and 24 May resulted in the deaths of four camp residents and the injury of 19 others. On 27 May, two thirds of the camp was looted or burned. Approximately 3,000 refugees, mainly from Côte d'Ivoire, Eritrea and Somalia, lived in the camp.

According to the NTC, 6,000 families in Benghazi district required assistance. Fuel shortages were reported both there and in Tripoli. The Government requested the United Nations to intervene to allow shipments of gasoline to enter the country so that basic services could continue. Over 13,700 people had been evacuated from Misrata. On 21 and 22 May, IOM delivered additional food supplies.

The United Nations established its presence in Benghazi and Tobruk. UN staff in Tripoli had to relocate on 2 May, but after discussions with the Government on security, a UN humanitarian team returned on 29 May.

The parties remained far apart on even beginning negotiations. The Secretary-General, his Special Envoy to Libya, the AU and other stakeholders made every effort to narrow the differences. On 25 May, the Secretary-General attended the extraordinary session of the AU Assembly, which was mainly devoted to the Libyan crisis. At the G8 summit (Deauville, France, 26–27 May), the Secretary-General called for increased humanitarian assistance for the affected populations in Libya and in neighbouring countries.

The Special Envoy was working to narrow the differences between the two parties so as to get indirect talks under way. He presented his proposals to Government officials in Tripoli on 15 May and to the NTC representatives in Doha on 24 May. The proposals revolved around the need to end hostilities, agree on a transitional arrangement, provide safe humanitarian access, and fully implement Security Council resolutions 1970(2011) and 1973(2011).

The Secretary-General had initiated a regional and international partnership on Libya by co-chairing on 14 April a meeting with the AU, the EU, LAS and OIC. The Under-Secretary-General for Political Affairs chaired a similar meeting on 5 May in Rome. Another meeting took place on 30 May in Cairo, chaired by the outgoing LAS Secretary-General and attended by the Special Envoy to Libya. It focused on coordinating positions to end the conflict.

The Special Envoy had received more than 20 letters and documents from the Government and the NTC stating their positions. The Government called on the United Nations to assist in finding measures to stop the bombing of civilians, and stated that it continued to comply with resolutions 1970(2011) and 1973(2011), allowing the passage of ships carrying humanitarian aid.

The Under-Secretary-General concluded that three points were critical: the protection of civilians in areas where the fighting was taking place; the engagement of the parties in direct negotiations; and contingency plans for post-conflict peacebuilding.

Communications. In response to Security Council resolutions 1970(2011) and 1973(2011), between 5 and 31 May, the Secretary-General received communications from the United Kingdom [S/2011/287], Egypt [S/2011/288], the former Yugoslav Republic of Macedonia [S/2011/294], Qatar [S/2011/321], Kuwait [S/2011/306] and Greece [S/2011/334], notifying him of the measures they had taken to implement those resolutions.

On 16 May [S/2011/307], the Secretary-General transmitted to the Security Council a communication dated 29 April from the Chairperson of the AU Commission, containing the communiqué on the situation in Libya adopted by the AU Peace and Security Council at its 275th meeting (Addis Ababa, 26 April).

On 31 May [S/2011/346], Qatar sent a letter to the Secretary-General regarding the exportation of oil extracted from the areas under control of the NTC. Qatar had recognized the NTC as the sole legitimate representative of the Libyan people and could, therefore, buy such oil or act as an intermediary in its sale.

On 1 June [S/2011/336], Jordan transmitted to the Secretary-General a request to secure overflight clearance in Libya and permission to land in Benghazi for a Jordanian aircraft carrying humanitarian aid.

On 2 June [S/2011/337], the AU transmitted to the Security Council the "Declaration on the state of peace and security in Africa" and the "Decision on the peaceful resolution of the Libyan crisis", adopted by the AU Assembly at its extraordinary session (Addis Ababa, 25 May).

On 8 June [S/2011/350], South Africa transmitted to the Security Council a joint communiqué adopted by the members of the UN Security Council and the AU Peace and Security Council at their fifth consultative meeting (Addis Ababa, 21 May).

Turkey [S/2011/349], on 8 June, and the United States [S/2011/372], on 16 June, informed the Secretary-General of activities to implement Council resolutions 1970(2011) and 1973(2011).

Security Council consideration (June). On 15 June [S/PV.6555], Mauritania's Minister for Foreign Affairs and Cooperation, Hamady Ould Hamady, briefed the Council on behalf of the AU Ad Hoc High-level Committee on Libya. The briefing was held in response to the request contained in the AU Assembly "Decision on the peaceful resolution of the Libyan crisis" of 25 May and focused on the actions that the AU had taken since the beginning of the crisis.

Briefing the Council on 27 June [S/PV.6566], the Under-Secretary-General for Political Affairs said that while there was no detailed understanding of the military situation on the ground, press reports pointed to heavy fighting some 50 miles from Tripoli, shelling by regime forces in Misrata and NATO air strikes in Tripoli.

At the second high-level meeting of regional organizations (Cairo, 18 June), the representatives of the AU, EU, LAS and OIC, as well as the Secretary-General (via videoconference) and his Special Envoy to Libya, exchanged views on ways to end the conflict. The Special Envoy was in close contact with both parties. On 7 and 8 June, he met with government officials in Tripoli and with NTC representatives in Benghazi and discussed their respective views on a transition process. The authorities in Tripoli emphasized the centrality of the United Nations in dealing with the crisis. In Benghazi, the Special Envoy stressed to the NTC the importance of engaging in a dialogue that would lead to a political solution.

The Under-Secretary-General informed the Council that the ICC had issued arrest warrants for Colonel Muammar Qadhafi, his son, Saif al-Islam Qadhafi, and military intelligence chief Abdullah Al-Senussi on charges of crimes against humanity.

With regard to the humanitarian situation, as at 23 June, over 1.1 million people had crossed the borders into Algeria, Chad, Egypt, the Niger, the Sudan and Tunisia. An estimated 3,000 individuals remained stranded at border points in Egypt, the Niger and Tunisia. Since 29 May, the UN humanitarian agencies had been able to access Tripoli and key towns of the Nafusa mountains, as well as opposition-controlled areas.

Several of Libya's neighbouring countries had raised concerns about the impact of the crisis. The loss of remittances from migrant workers and reports of flows of arms from Libya to the Sahel could further complicate the fragile situation in the region. For instance, more than 70,500 Chadians and 82,000 people from Niger had returned to their countries.

Communications. France [S/2011/402], on 30 June, and Qatar [S/2011/450], on 22 July, notified the Secretary-General of measures they had taken under resolution 1973(2011).

On 22 July [S/2011/455], the Secretary-General transmitted to the Security Council a communication dated 7 July from the Chair of the AU Commission regarding the decision on the situation in Libya adopted by the seventeenth ordinary session of the AU Assembly of Heads of State and Government (Malabo, Equatorial Guinea, 30 June–1 July). Also attached was a document containing proposals for a framework agreement on a political solution to the crisis, as presented by the AU Ad Hoc High-level Committee on Libya and endorsed by the AU Assembly.

Security Council consideration (July). On 28 July [S/PV.6595], the Under-Secretary-General for Political Affairs informed the Security Council that, as the fighting continued for the fifth month, there had been some marginal gains by the opposition forces but no dramatic changes in the overall situation. Opposition forces attempted to advance towards Tripoli, while Government forces targeted strategic areas under opposition control. NATO operations continued, primarily against sites around Tripoli. The Under-Secretary-General reiterated that a ceasefire tied to transitional arrangements addressing the aspirations of the Libyan people was the only sustainable political solution. From the outset, the United Nations had worked closely with the parties in Libya, with regional organizations and with the international community. It remained critical that the international community spoke with one voice.

The Special Envoy to Libya had submitted a proposal on how to end the conflict, and both sides had expressed their readiness to study and discuss it further. The proposal was designed to simultaneously establish a ceasefire and create an institutional mechanism for managing the transition. On 25 July, the Special Envoy travelled to Benghazi to continue those discussions. During his meeting with the NTC, its members insisted that they could not engage in talks for the establishment of a new transitional entity while the regime in Tripoli was in place. They emphasized that meeting the legitimate aspirations of the Libyan people had to be the aim of the negotiations, and that included the departure of Colonel Qadhafi. On 26 July, the Special Envoy travelled to Tripoli for talks with Libyan Prime Minister Al Baghdadi Ali Al-Mahmoudi, who reiterated the Government's position, namely, that it was not ready to engage in a political process that implied the stepping down of Colonel Qadhafi.

The Contact Group on Libya held its fourth meeting (Istanbul, Turkey, 15 July). The Chairperson's final statement recognized the NTC as the legitimate governing authority until the establishment of an interim authority. The AU Ad Hoc High-level Committee on Libya convened a technical meeting (Addis Ababa, 18 July), to which both the NTC and the Government were invited. The Government sent a delegation, while the NTC did not participate.

The Under-Secretary-General reported that the number of people who had left Libya and had not returned since the start of the conflict was estimated at over 630,000, including some 100,000 Libyans. Another 200,000 Libyans had been internally displaced. The number of people stranded at border points in Egypt, Tunisia and the Niger had been reduced to about 2,600, mostly third-country nationals, some of whom were asylum seekers who could not return to their homes. Additionally, around 22,000 people, mostly African migrants, had arrived by boat in Italy and Malta from Libya. At least 1,400 people had died during those journeys or were missing.

The Government had repeatedly complained about the shortage of medical supplies, vaccines and equipment. In addition, major fuel shortages were reported in Tripoli. Humanitarian aid and fuel were arriving regularly in opposition-controlled areas, although some shortages occurred there too. Both the Government and the NTC had requested the use of frozen assets to meet humanitarian needs.

The Special Adviser on post-conflict planning in Libya, Ian Martin, appointed by the Secretary-General on 26 April, continued preparatory work within the United Nations and with key partners on ways to proceed once the conflict was resolved. Early contingency planning was being undertaken by DPKO for possible UN military and police roles following a ceasefire.

Since the adoption of resolution 1973(2011), the Secretary-General had received 43 communications from more than 20 Member States and regional organizations informing him of action taken in implementing that resolution. In addition, NATO had submitted its third and fourth monthly reports, dated 27 June and 20 July, respectively.

Communications. On 26 August, Venezuela transmitted identical letters, to the Secretary-General [A/65/936] and to the Security Council [S/2011/544], concerning the attack by the NTC on the Venezuelan embassy in Tripoli on 23 August. Venezuela confirmed that it recognized only the Government of Muammar Qadhafi.

Change of Government

Security Council consideration (August). Briefing the Council on 30 August [S/PV.6606], the Secretary-General said that members of the Qadhafi family had sought asylum in Algeria. The NTC appeared to be largely in control of Tripoli and other cities, while fighting continued in some parts of the country. The Secretary-General had spoken on several occasions with the NTC Chairman, Mustafa Abdel Jalil, and with many world leaders, discussing the role of the United Nations in Libya in the months ahead, including in such areas as election assistance, transitional justice and policing, as well as humanitarian needs.

On 26 August, the Secretary-General held a videoconference with the heads of LAS, OIC, the AU and the EU, all of whom agreed that the international community had to come together with a well-coordinated programme of action led by the United Nations. Following that meeting, the LAS Council held an extraordinary ministerial session (Cairo, 27 August) and agreed that the NTC should fill the seat of Libya in LAS meetings. Participants called on the United Nations to allow the NTC to do the same. The Deputy Secretary-General attended the AU Peace and Security Council meeting (Addis Ababa, 26 August), where African leaders stressed the need for national reconciliation and underscored the AU commitment to working with all Libyan stakeholders.

The Secretary-General observed that signs of progress could be seen in Libya: hospitals were reopening; the World Food Programme had sent a large humanitarian convoy from Tunisia, carrying water, medical supplies and blood; the World Health Organization was sending medical supplies; and Tripoli's seaport was open and functioning. Water supplies, however, were short. It was also important that the sanctions committee established by resolution 1970(2011) acted to release $1.5 billion in frozen Libyan assets for humanitarian assistance. The first allocation of those assets—$110 million—had just been made.

The Secretary-General underscored the importance of deploying UN personnel on the ground as quickly as possible, under a robust Security Council mandate. To that purpose, his Special Adviser had been consulting daily with the NTC and other Libyan stakeholders. All efforts were based on three principles: national ownership, rapid response and delivery, and effective coordination.

Change of country name. Following the adoption by the General Assembly of **resolution 66/1 A** (see p. 1357) on the credentials of representatives to the Assembly, Libya notified the United Nations of a 3 August Declaration by the NTC changing the official name of the Libyan Arab Jamahiriya to "Libya" and changing Libya's national flag.

Communication. On 12 September [A/65/943-S/2011/571], Venezuela transmitted to the Secretary-General the Special Statement of the Ministers for Foreign Affairs of the Bolivarian Alliance for the

Peoples of Our America-People's Trade Agreement on the situation in Libya and Syria, adopted in Caracas, Venezuela, on 9 September.

Establishment of UNSMIL. In a 7 September letter [S/2011/542] to the Security Council, the Secretary-General proposed the establishment of an integrated United Nations Support Mission in Libya (UNSMIL) for an initial period of three months. The Mission would be headed by a Special Representative, and its mandate would include assistance and support to national efforts to restore public security, undertake inclusive political dialogue, extend State authority and protect human rights.

On 15 September [S/2011/578], the Secretary-General transmitted to the Council a letter dated 14 September from the Prime Minister of the National Transitional Council of Libya, Mahmoud Jibril, seeking the assistance of the United Nations in stabilizing and rebuilding the country.

SECURITY COUNCIL ACTION

On 16 September [meeting 6620], the Security Council unanimously adopted **resolution 2009(2011)**. The draft [S/2011/580] was submitted by Bosnia and Herzegovina, Colombia, France, Gabon, Germany, Lebanon, Portugal, the United Kingdom and the United States.

The Security Council,

Reaffirming its strong commitment to the sovereignty, independence, territorial integrity and national unity of Libya,

Reaffirming its previous resolutions 1674(2006) of 28 April 2006 and 1894(2009) of 11 November 2009 on the protection of civilians in armed conflict, resolutions 1612(2005) of 26 July 2005, 1882(2009) of 4 August 2009 and 1998(2011) of 12 July 2011 on children and armed conflict, and resolutions 1325(2000) of 31 October 2000, 1820(2008) of 19 June 2008, 1888(2009) of 30 September 2009, 1889(2009) of 5 October 2009 and 1960(2010) of 16 December 2010 on women and peace and security,

Recalling its decision to refer the situation in Libya to the Prosecutor of the International Criminal Court, and the importance of cooperation for ensuring that those responsible for violations of human rights and international humanitarian law or complicit in attacks targeting the civilian population are held accountable,

Strongly condemning all violations of applicable human rights and international humanitarian law, including violations that involve unlawful killings, other uses of violence against civilians, or arbitrary arrests and detentions, in particular of African migrants and members of minority communities,

Also strongly condemning sexual violence, particularly against women and girls, and the recruitment and use of children in situations of armed conflict in contravention of applicable international law,

Considering that the voluntary and sustainable return of refugees and internally displaced persons will be a critical factor for the consolidation of peace in Libya,

Stressing that national ownership and national responsibility are key to establishing sustainable peace and the primary responsibility of national authorities in identifying their priorities and strategies for post-conflict peacebuilding,

Recalling the letter dated 7 September 2011 from the Secretary-General to the President of the Security Council, and welcoming his intention to dispatch, at the request of the Libyan authorities, an initial deployment of personnel, to be led by a Special Representative of the Secretary-General for Libya,

Taking note of the letter dated 14 September 2011 from Mr. Mahmoud Jibril, Prime Minister of the National Transitional Council of Libya, to the Secretary-General,

Expressing its gratitude to the Special Envoy of the Secretary-General to Libya, Mr. Abdel-Elah Mohamed Al-Khatib, for his efforts to find a sustainable and peaceful solution in Libya,

Reaffirming that the United Nations should lead the effort of the international community in supporting the Libyan-led transition and rebuilding process aimed at establishing a democratic, independent and united Libya, welcoming the contributions in this regard of the Secretary-General's high-level meeting of regional organizations of 26 August 2011 and the Paris Conference on Libya, of 1 September 2011, and welcoming also the efforts of the African Union, the League of Arab States, the European Union and the Organization of Islamic Cooperation,

Expressing its concern at the proliferation of arms in Libya and its potential impact on regional peace and security,

Recalling its resolutions 1970(2011) of 26 February 2011 and 1973(2011) of 17 March 2011,

Recalling its determination to ensure that assets frozen pursuant to resolutions 1970(2011) and 1973(2011) shall, as soon as possible, be made available to and for the benefit of the people of Libya, welcoming steps taken by the Security Council Committee established pursuant to resolution 1970(2011) and Member States in this regard, and underscoring the importance of making these assets available in a transparent and responsible manner in conformity with the needs and wishes of the Libyan people,

Mindful of its primary responsibility for the maintenance of international peace and security under the Charter of the United Nations,

Acting under Chapter VII of the Charter, and taking measures under its Article 41,

1. *Takes note* of the developments in Libya, welcomes the improved situation there, and looks forward to stability in Libya;

2. *Looks forward* to the establishment of an inclusive, representative transitional Government of Libya, and emphasizes the need for the transitional period to be underpinned by a commitment to democracy, good governance, the rule of law and respect for human rights;

3. *Emphasizes* the importance of promoting the equal and full participation of women and minority communities in the discussions related to the political process in the post-conflict phase;

4. *Welcomes* the statements of the National Transitional Council appealing for unity, national reconciliation and justice, and its call for Libyans of all beliefs and

backgrounds to refrain from reprisals, including arbitrary detentions;

5. *Encourages* the National Transitional Council to implement its plans:

(*a*) To protect Libya's population, restore government services and allocate Libya's funds openly and transparently;

(*b*) To prevent further abuses and violations of human rights and international humanitarian law and to put an end to impunity;

(*c*) To ensure a consultative, inclusive political process with a view to agreement on a constitution and the holding of free and fair elections;

(*d*) To ensure the safety of foreign nationals in Libya, particularly those who have been threatened, mistreated and/or detained; and

(*e*) To prevent the proliferation of man-portable surface-to-air missiles, small arms and light weapons, and meet Libya's arms control and non-proliferation obligations under international law;

6. *Notes* the calls by the National Transitional Council to avoid acts of reprisals, including against migrant workers;

7. *Calls upon* the Libyan authorities to promote and protect human rights, including those of people belonging to vulnerable groups, and to comply with their obligations under international law, including international humanitarian law and human rights law, and calls for those responsible for violations, including sexual violence, to be held accountable in accordance with international standards;

8. *Strongly urges* the Libyan authorities to ensure the protection of diplomatic personnel and premises in accordance with the Vienna Convention on Diplomatic Relations of 1961;

9. *Expresses its resolve* to assist the people of Libya to achieve these goals, and urges all Member States to assist the people of Libya, as appropriate;

10. *Urges* all Member States to cooperate closely with the Libyan authorities in their efforts to end impunity, in accordance with the international obligations of Libya;

11. *Calls upon* the Libyan authorities to comply with the international obligations of Libya, including obligations set forth in the Charter of the United Nations, in accordance with international law, and further calls upon the Libyan authorities to honour extant contracts and obligations, in accordance with the present resolution and other relevant resolutions, and the law applicable to such contracts and obligations;

United Nations mandate

12. *Decides* to establish a United Nations Support Mission in Libya, under the leadership of a Special Representative of the Secretary-General for Libya, for an initial period of three months, and decides further that the mandate of the Mission shall be to assist and support Libyan national efforts:

(*a*) To restore public security and order and promote the rule of law;

(*b*) To undertake inclusive political dialogue, promote national reconciliation and embark upon the constitution-making and electoral process;

(*c*) To extend State authority, including through strengthening emerging accountable institutions and the restoration of public services;

(*d*) To promote and protect human rights, particularly for those belonging to vulnerable groups, and support transitional justice;

(*e*) To take the immediate steps required to initiate economic recovery; and

(*f*) To coordinate support that may be requested from other multilateral and bilateral actors, as appropriate;

Arms embargo

13. *Decides* that the measure imposed by paragraph 9 of resolution 1970(2011) shall also not apply to the supply, sale or transfer to Libya of:

(*a*) Arms and related materiel of all types, including technical assistance, training and financial and other assistance, intended solely for security or disarmament assistance to the Libyan authorities and notified to the Security Council Committee established pursuant to resolution 1970(2011) in advance and in the absence of a negative decision by the Committee within five working days of such a notification;

(*b*) Small arms, light weapons and related materiel, temporarily exported to Libya for the sole use of United Nations personnel, representatives of the media and humanitarian and development workers and associated personnel, notified to the Committee in advance and in the absence of a negative decision by the Committee within five working days of such a notification;

Asset freeze

14. *Decides* that the Libyan National Oil Corporation and Zueitina Oil Company shall no longer be subject to the asset freeze and other measures imposed in paragraphs 17, 19, 20 and 21 of resolution 1970(2011) and paragraph 19 of resolution 1973(2011);

15. *Decides also* to modify the measures imposed in paragraphs 17, 19, 20 and 21 of resolution 1970(2011) and paragraph 19 of resolution 1973(2011) with respect to the Central Bank of Libya, the Libyan Arab Foreign Bank, the Libyan Investment Authority and the Libyan Africa Investment Portfolio as follows:

(*a*) Funds, other financial assets and economic resources outside of Libya of the entities mentioned above in the present paragraph that are frozen as of the date of the present resolution pursuant to measures imposed in paragraph 17 of resolution 1970(2011) or paragraph 19 of resolution 1973(2011) shall remain frozen by States unless subject to an exemption as set out in paragraphs 19, 20 or 21 of that resolution or paragraph 16 below;

(*b*) Except as provided in (*a*), the Central Bank of Libya, the Libyan Arab Foreign Bank, the Libyan Investment Authority and the Libyan Africa Investment Portfolio shall otherwise no longer be subject to the measures imposed in paragraph 17 of resolution 1970(2011), including that States are no longer required to ensure that any funds, financial assets or economic resources are prevented from being made available by their nationals or by any individuals or entities within their territories to or for the benefit of these entities;

16. *Decides further* that, in addition to the provisions of paragraph 19 of resolution 1970(2011), the measures imposed by paragraph 17 of that resolution, as modified

by paragraph 15 above and paragraph 19 of resolution 1973(2011), do not apply to funds, other financial assets or economic resources of the Central Bank of Libya, the Libyan Arab Foreign Bank, the Libyan Investment Authority and the Libyan Africa Investment Portfolio, provided that:

(a) A Member State has provided notice to the Committee of its intent to authorize access to funds, other financial assets or economic resources, for one or more of the following purposes and in the absence of a negative decision by the Committee within five working days of such a notification:
  (i) Humanitarian needs;
  (ii) Fuel, electricity and water for strictly civilian uses;
  (iii) Resuming Libyan production and sale of hydrocarbons;
  (iv) Establishing, operating or strengthening institutions of civilian government and civilian public infrastructure; or
  (v) Facilitating the resumption of banking sector operations, including to support or facilitate international trade with Libya;

(b) A Member State has notified the Committee that those funds, other financial assets or economic resources shall not be made available to or for the benefit of the individuals subject to the measures imposed in paragraph 17 of resolution 1970(2011) or paragraph 19 of resolution 1973(2011);

(c) The Member State has consulted in advance with the Libyan authorities about the use of such funds, other financial assets or economic resources; and

(d) The Member State has shared with the Libyan authorities the notification submitted pursuant to the present paragraph and the Libyan authorities have not objected within five working days to the release of such funds, other financial assets or economic resources;

17. *Calls upon* States to exercise vigilance when acting pursuant to paragraph 16 above and to give due consideration to the use of international financial mechanisms to promote transparency and prevent misappropriation, in the light of the challenges that yet remain for the Libyan authorities;

18. *Requests* the International Monetary Fund and the World Bank to work with the Libyan authorities on an assessment of Libya's public financial management framework, which would recommend steps to be taken by Libya to ensure a system of transparency and accountability with respect to the funds held by Libyan governmental institutions, including the Libyan Investment Authority, the Libyan National Oil Corporation, the Libyan Arab Foreign Bank, the Libyan Africa Investment Portfolio and the Central Bank of Libya, and further requests that the Committee be informed of the results of that assessment;

19. *Directs* the Committee, in consultation with the Libyan authorities, to review continuously the remaining measures imposed by resolutions 1970(2011) and 1973(2011) with respect to the Central Bank of Libya, the Libyan Arab Foreign Bank, the Libyan Investment Authority and the Libyan Africa Investment Portfolio, and decides that the Committee shall, in consultation with the Libyan authorities, lift the designation of these entities as soon as is practical to ensure that the assets are made available to and for the benefit of the people of Libya;

No-fly zone and ban on flights

20. *Takes note* of the improved situation in Libya, emphasizes its intention to keep the measures imposed by paragraphs 6 to 12 of resolution 1973(2011) under continuous review, and underlines its readiness, as appropriate and when circumstances permit, to lift those measures and to terminate the authorization given to Member States in paragraph 4 of resolution 1973(2011), in consultation with the Libyan authorities;

21. *Decides* that the measures in paragraph 17 of resolution 1973(2011) shall cease to have effect from the date of the present resolution;

Cooperation and reporting

22. *Requests* the Secretary-General to report on the implementation of the present resolution in fourteen days from its adoption, and every month thereafter, or more frequently as he sees fit;

23. *Decides* to remain actively seized of the matter.

Appointments. On 16 September [S/2011/587], the Secretary-General informed the Council of his intention to appoint Ian Martin (United Kingdom) as his Special Representative and Head of UNSMIL and Georg Charpentier (Finland) as his Deputy Special Representative and Resident Coordinator ad interim. The Council took note of his intention on 19 September [S/2011/588].

Security Council consideration (September). Briefing the Council on 26 September [S/PV.6622], the Under-Secretary-General for Political Affairs said that the Secretary-General's Special Representative, Ian Martin, had returned to Tripoli, where UNSMIL was being established. Fighting, however, continued in Sirte, Bani Walid and a few other pockets of resistance; NATO continued its military operations in Sirte. The humanitarian country team was working with the authorities to provide support in conflict areas. The NTC leadership was attempting to restore security; however, reports had shown that the situation in some parts of the country remained fragile. The main challenges faced by the NTC were the establishment of an inclusive interim Government that reflected the diversity of the Libyan society; the control of large stocks of sophisticated arms, including ground-to-air missiles and chemical weapons; the securing of mass grave sites that might help clarify the fate of many disappeared persons; and the welfare of African migrants and third-country nationals.

On 20 September, on the margins of the General Assembly, the Secretary-General convened a high-level meeting on Libya, at which participants officially welcomed the NTC as the legitimate delegation representing the Libyan people at the United Nations.

With regard to UNSMIL, essential personnel were already deployed in Tripoli and Benghazi. On the humanitarian front, approximately 60,000 new displacements of Libyans had been recorded since mid-August, as fighting intensified around Sirte and Bani Walid.

Addressing the Council, the Chairman of the NTC Executive Office, Mahmoud Jibril, said that the legitimacy of the NTC would depend on its capacity to meet the basic needs of citizens. He called on the Council to lift the assets freeze so that the Libyan people could begin the reconstruction process.

Communications. By a 25 October letter to the Council [S/2011/660], Libya announced the full liberation of the country from the Qadhafi regime. The city of Sirte had been taken and Colonel Qadhafi had died on 20 October after suffering serious injuries during the clash between his loyalists and the revolutionaries. The danger that justified a no-fly zone over Libya no longer existed, and the new authorities were able to protect civilians without outside assistance. Libya, therefore, requested the Council to terminate by 31 October the authorization provided under Council resolution 1973(2011) relating to the imposition of a no-fly zone and the protection of civilians.

In a 26 October letter to the Secretary-General [A/C.3/66/3], Venezuela condemned the "barbaric policies" pursued by NATO and its allies in Libya.

Security Council consideration (October). Briefing the Council on 26 October [S/PV.6639], the Secretary-General's Special Representative for Libya said that on 23 October he had represented the Secretary-General at Libya's Declaration of Liberation in Benghazi, the city where the popular movement had begun on 17 February. A peaceful movement, sparked by the demand of families to know the fate of their loved ones who had disappeared in a prison massacre, was met with lethal repression, and civilians across Libya took up arms in a revolution to end decades of denial of political freedoms, human rights violations, corruption and social inequality. The security situation, however, was still volatile in parts of the south, with tensions related to a mix of ethnic and political loyalties. In the final weeks of the conflict, the Secretary-General had called on the remaining supporters of the former regime to cease fighting. In Sirte, Bani Walid and Sabha, however, they had not done so, thus increasing the final death toll.

The Special Representative said that Muammar and Motassim Qadhafi were mistreated and killed in circumstances that required investigation. There were other disturbing reports that killings amounting to war crimes had been committed on both sides in the final battle for Sirte. Such killings had taken place contrary to the orders of the NTC, which had announced an investigation. Those killings were also within the scope of the International Commission of Inquiry mandated by the Human Rights Council. Meanwhile, the whereabouts of the other two persons indicted by the ICC, Saif al-Islam Qadhafi and Abdullah Al-Senussi, remained uncertain.

The NTC had committed to establishing, within 30 days from the Declaration of Liberation, an interim Government with an inclusive administration; to adopting electoral legislation within 90 days; and to holding elections within 240 days to give legitimacy to a new Government. UNSMIL had been engaging with NTC members on the electoral process.

With regard to security, the issue at the top of the agenda for the NTC and the forthcoming Government was the removal of heavy weaponry from city centres, to be followed by the collection of light arms. UNSMIL was facilitating coordination among the authorities, international organizations—including the Organization for the Prohibition of Chemical Weapons (OPCW) and the International Atomic Energy Agency (IAEA)—and Member States offering assistance. The Special Representative noted that under the Qadhafi regime, Libya had accumulated the largest known stockpile of shoulder-fired anti-aircraft missiles, known as man-portable air defence systems (MANPADs), of any non-MANPADs-producing country. Thousands were destroyed during NATO operations. Large numbers of MANPADs, munitions and mines, however, had been looted. In addition, the prevalence of newly laid mines was a reason for concern. In Tripoli, many stockpiles were suspected to have been hidden in residential areas by Qadhafi forces to conceal them from airstrikes, and most of them remained unsecured. The flow of weapons was also a source of concern for Libya's neighbours. Another priority was the beginning of a national reconciliation process and a coherent approach, led by the NTC, to human rights and transitional justice issues.

SECURITY COUNCIL ACTION

On 27 October [meeting 6640], the Security Council unanimously adopted **resolution 2016(2011)**. The draft [S/2011/669] was submitted by Bosnia and Herzegovina, France, Germany, Lebanon, Nigeria, Portugal, the Russian Federation, the United Kingdom and the United States.

The Security Council,

Recalling its resolutions 1970(2011) of 26 February 2011, 1973(2011) of 17 March 2011 and 2009(2011) of 16 September 2011,

Reaffirming its strong commitment to the sovereignty, independence, territorial integrity and national unity of Libya,

Taking note of the National Transitional Council's "Declaration of Liberation" of 23 October 2011 in Libya,

Looking forward to a future for Libya based on national reconciliation, justice, respect for human rights and the rule of law,

Reiterating the importance of promoting the full and effective participation of members of all social and ethnic groups, including the equal participation of women and minority communities in the discussions related to the post-conflict phase,

Recalling its decision to refer the situation in Libya to the Prosecutor of the International Criminal Court, and the importance of cooperation for ensuring that those responsible for violations of human rights and international humanitarian law or complicit in attacks targeting the civilian population are held accountable,

Reiterating that the voluntary and sustainable return of refugees and internally displaced persons will be an important factor for the consolidation of peace in Libya,

Expressing its concern at the proliferation of arms in Libya and its potential impact on regional peace and security, and also expressing its intention expeditiously to address that issue further,

Expressing grave concern about continuing reports of reprisals, arbitrary detentions, wrongful imprisonment and extrajudicial executions in Libya,

Reiterating its call to the Libyan authorities to promote and protect human rights and fundamental freedoms, including those of people belonging to vulnerable groups, and to comply with their obligations under international law, including international humanitarian law and human rights law, and urging respect for the human rights of all people in Libya, including former officials and detainees, during and after the transitional period,

Recalling its decisions in resolution 2009(2011):

(*a*) To modify the provisions of the arms embargo imposed by paragraph 9 of resolution 1970(2011) to provide for additional exemptions,

(*b*) To terminate the asset freeze imposed by paragraphs 17, 19, 20 and 21 of resolution 1970(2011) and paragraph 19 of resolution 1973(2011) with respect to the Libyan National Oil Corporation and Zueitina Oil Company, and to modify the asset freeze imposed by paragraphs 17, 19, 20 and 21 of resolution 1970(2011) and paragraph 19 of resolution 1973(2011) with respect to the Central Bank of Libya, the Libyan Arab Foreign Bank, the Libyan Investment Authority and the Libyan Africa Investment Portfolio, and

(*c*) To cease the measures imposed by paragraph 17 of resolution 1973(2011),

Recalling also its intention to keep the measures imposed by paragraphs 6 to 12 of resolution 1973(2011) under continuous review and to lift, as appropriate and when circumstances permit, those measures and to terminate the authorization given to Member States in paragraph 4 of resolution 1973(2011), in consultation with the Libyan authorities,

Mindful of its primary responsibility for the maintenance of international peace and security under the Charter of the United Nations,

Acting under Chapter VII of the Charter,

1. *Welcomes* the positive developments in Libya which will improve the prospects for a democratic, peaceful and prosperous future there;

2. *Looks forward* to the swift establishment of an inclusive, representative transitional Government of Libya, and reiterates the need for the transitional period to be underpinned by a commitment to democracy, good governance, the rule of law, national reconciliation and respect for the human rights and fundamental freedoms of all people in Libya;

3. *Strongly urges* the Libyan authorities to refrain from reprisals, including arbitrary detentions, calls upon the Libyan authorities to take all steps necessary to prevent reprisals, wrongful imprisonment and extrajudicial executions, and underscores the responsibility of the Libyan authorities for the protection of Libya's population, including foreign nationals and African migrants;

4. *Urges* all Member States to cooperate closely with the Libyan authorities in their efforts to end impunity for violations of international human rights and international humanitarian law;

Protection of civilians

5. *Decides* that the provisions of paragraphs 4 and 5 of resolution 1973(2011) shall be terminated from 23.59 hours Libyan local time on 31 October 2011;

No-fly zone

6. *Decides* that the provisions of paragraphs 6 to 12 of resolution 1973(2011) shall be terminated from 23.59 hours Libyan local time on 31 October 2011;

7. *Decides also* to remain actively seized of the matter.

Security Council consideration. On 31 October [S/PV.6644], the Security Council addressed the proliferation of arms in Libya, in particular portable surface-to-air missiles.

SECURITY COUNCIL ACTION

On 31 October [meeting 6644], the Security Council unanimously adopted **resolution 2017(2011)**. The draft [S/2011/670] was submitted by France, Nigeria, Portugal, the Russian Federation, the United Kingdom and the United States.

The Security Council,

Recalling its previous resolutions 1373(2001) of 28 September 2001, 1526(2004) of 30 January 2004, 1540(2004) of 28 April 2004, 1970(2011) of 26 February 2011, 1973(2011) of 17 March 2011, 1977(2011) of 20 April 2011, 1989(2011) of 17 June 2011, 2009(2011) of 16 September 2011 and 2016(2011) of 27 October 2011, and the statements by its President of 17 February 2005 and 19 March 2010,

Reaffirming its strong commitment to the sovereignty, independence, territorial integrity and national unity of Libya,

Stressing that national ownership and national responsibility are key to establishing sustainable peace in Libya,

Stressing also the importance of the United Nations Support Mission in Libya, in accordance with its mandate under resolution 2009(2011), assisting and supporting Libyan national efforts, inter alia, to restore public security and order,

Recalling that, pursuant to paragraph 10 of resolution 1970(2011), Member States are obliged to prohibit the procurement of all arms and related materiel from Libya by their nationals, or using their flagged vessels or aircraft, and whether or not originating in the territory of Libya,

Expressing its concern at the proliferation of all arms and related materiel of all types, in particular man-portable surface-to-air missiles, from Libya in the region and its potential impact on regional and international peace and security,

Underlining the risk of destabilization posed by the dissemination in the Sahel region of illicit small arms and light weapons, and recalling in that regard the report of the Secretary-General on the activities of the United Nations Office for West Africa, which, inter alia, calls for strengthened cooperation in the Sahel area, as well as the work of the United Nations Regional Office for Central Africa,

Recognizing the urgent need for additional efforts to be made at the national, regional and international levels, in order to prevent the proliferation of all arms and related materiel of all types, in particular man-portable surface-to-air missiles, in the region,

Recognizing also the urgent need to secure and destroy chemical weapons stockpiles in Libya, in accordance with its international obligations,

Emphasizing that the proliferation of all arms and related materiel of all types, in particular man-portable surface-to-air missiles, in the region could fuel terrorist activities, including those of Al-Qaida in the Islamic Maghreb,

Reaffirming, in that regard, that terrorism constitutes one of the most serious threats to international peace and security,

Reiterating the obligation of Member States to cooperate in order to prevent the movement of terrorist groups and the proliferation of arms in support of terrorist activities, inter alia, through effective border control,

Mindful of its primary responsibility for the maintenance of international peace and security,

1. *Calls upon* the Libyan authorities to take all steps necessary to prevent the proliferation of all arms and related materiel of all types, in particular man-portable surface-to-air missiles, to ensure their proper custody, as well as to meet Libya's arms control, disarmament and non-proliferation obligations under international law, through the full implementation of their plans in this regard;

2. *Also calls upon* the Libyan authorities to continue their close coordination with the Organization for the Prohibition of Chemical Weapons, with the aim of destroying their stockpiles of chemical weapons, in accordance with their international obligations;

3. *Calls upon* States in the region to consider appropriate measures to prevent the proliferation of all arms and related materiel of all types, in particular man-portable surface-to-air missiles, in the region;

4. *Calls upon* Member States and international and regional organizations and entities, including relevant United Nations bodies, to provide the necessary assistance to the Libyan authorities and States in the region in order to achieve this goal;

5. *Requests* the Security Council Committee established pursuant to resolution 1970(2011), with assistance from its Panel of Experts, in cooperation with the Counter-Terrorism Committee Executive Directorate, working with other relevant United Nations bodies, including the International Civil Aviation Organization, and in consultation with international and regional organizations and entities, to assess the threats and challenges, in particular related to terrorism, posed by the proliferation of all arms and related materiel of all types, in particular man-portable surface-to-air missiles, from Libya in the region, and to submit a report to the Council on proposals to counter this threat and to prevent the proliferation of arms and related materiel, including, inter alia, measures to secure these arms and related materiel, to ensure that stockpiles are managed safely and securely, to strengthen border control and to enhance transport security;

6. *Requests* the Secretary-General to include in his reports to the Council pursuant to resolution 2009(2011) updates on the implementation of the present resolution;

7. *Decides* to remain seized of the matter.

General Assembly action. By **resolution 66/11** of 18 November (see p. 606), the General Assembly restored the rights of membership of Libya in the Human Rights Council.

Report of Secretary-General (November). Pursuant to Council resolution 2001(2011), the Secretary-General on 22 November submitted a report [S/2011/727] on UNSMIL.

On 31 October, the NTC, having relocated to Tripoli, announced the appointment of Abdurrahim el-Keib as the country's new interim Prime Minister. Mr. El-Keib was selected through a transparent voting process. A major challenge facing the NTC was the consolidation of security, particularly in Tripoli, where there were a large number of armed revolutionary "brigades". Clashes among rival brigades resulted in the deaths of several fighters. To address those challenges, the new authorities brought the responsibility for the security situation in Tripoli under the umbrella of a Supreme Security Committee comprising three NTC members.

On 3 November, an OPCW team carried out an inspection at the Ruwagha depot, in the south-east of the country, the first since February. The team confirmed that the depot had stockpiles of sulphur mustard and other chemical agents, and took measures to ensure the integrity of the stockpiles until destruction operations could resume. Two previously undeclared sites were identified and secured by Libyan counterparts, who notified OPCW on 1 November.

Concerning the deployment of UNSMIL, as at 31 October, 43 international staff members, including the Deputy Special Representative and experts in priority areas, had been deployed to Libya—40 in Tripoli and 3 in Benghazi. The UN country team was gradually resuming its operations.

The Secretary-General and the General Assembly President visited Libya on 2 November and met with the NTC Chairman and the Prime Minister to reaffirm the key role of the United Nations in supporting national efforts in the post-conflict phase.

The Secretary-General noted that the challenge of national reconciliation was of overwhelming importance. However deep the anger at the war crimes committed by the former regime was, the NTC had to continue its calls to avoid acts of revenge and had to investigate abuses by its own fighters.

The prolongation of the conflict had delayed the formation of an interim Government and other essential developments. The Secretary-General therefore recommended a three-month extension of UNSMIL.

Security Council consideration (November). On 28 November [S/PV.6669], the Secretary-General's Special Representative for Libya informed the Security Council that, on 22 November, the NTC had approved the interim Government formed by Prime

Minister el-Keib. On 24 November, the new Government's ministers were sworn in and the Special Representative met with the Prime Minister to discuss the priorities for his Government and for the support of the United Nations.

In the area of security, the new Minister of Defence had been tasked with shaping a new army and integrating regular military and civilian brigades, and managing tensions among them. The brigades remained the providers of public security, notwithstanding the growing deployment of police. Undisciplined elements of those brigades, however, could threaten public security, as incidents around Tripoli had shown.

The other main aspect of the security situation was the presence and proliferation of conventional and non-conventional weapons in Libya and in neighbouring countries. In Libya the Minister of Defence had, with the support of bilateral partners, identified, secured, stored and disabled those weapons. It was difficult, however, to make assumptions about the number of MANPADS circulating in Libya or in neighbouring countries. As far as chemical weapons and nuclear materials were concerned, the picture was more encouraging. The UN-led Joint Mine Action Coordination Team was clearing areas and promoting risk education for affected population. There was, however, an urgent need to expand those activities.

The Special Representative underscored Libya's need for liquid funds, specifying that asset-holding countries were striving to overcome the technical requirements necessary for funds to flow.

Progress had been made concerning election preparations. On 20 November, the NTC appointed an eight-member committee to study requirements for the election process, work with international organizations and prepare the appointment of a chairperson and members of an electoral commission and its budget.

The Special Representative noted that the Secretary-General had recommended a three-month extension of UNSMIL because it would not have been appropriate to make recommendations for a 12-month period before the Government was in place.

SECURITY COUNCIL ACTION

On 2 December [meeting 6673], the Security Council unanimously adopted **resolution 2022(2011)**. The draft [S/2011/752] was submitted by France, Germany, Lebanon, Portugal, the United Kingdom and the United States.

The Security Council,

Recalling its resolutions 1970(2011) of 26 February 2011, 1973(2011) of 17 March 2011, 2009(2011) of 16 September 2011, 2016(2011) of 27 October 2011 and 2017(2011) of 31 October 2011,

Reaffirming its strong commitment to the sovereignty, independence, territorial integrity and national unity of Libya,

Recalling its decision to establish the United Nations Support Mission in Libya for an initial period of three months until 16 December 2011 to assist and support Libyan national efforts in the post-conflict phase,

Welcoming the establishment of the transitional Government of Libya on 22 November 2011, and stressing its key role in creating the conditions conducive to the full implementation of the mandate of the Mission,

Welcoming also the engagement of the Secretary-General and the President of the General Assembly, including through their recent visit to Libya, which affirmed the key role of the United Nations in supporting Libyan national efforts in the post-conflict phase,

Looking forward to an assessment of needs by the Mission and the transitional Government of Libya by 16 March 2012, cooperating with all relevant international partners, including the international financial institutions, with a view to continuing the work of the United Nations in coordinating international support to the transitional Government of Libya on the basis of its needs,

Stressing the importance of the continued support by the United Nations, including the Mission, to the transitional Government of Libya in addressing immediate priorities as set out in paragraph 12 of resolution 2009(2011),

Taking note of the report of the Secretary-General on the Mission, including the recommendation for a three-month extension of the mandate of the Mission,

1. *Decides* to extend the mandate of the United Nations Support Mission in Libya established pursuant to paragraph 12 of resolution 2009(2011) until 16 March 2012, and looks forward to the report of the Secretary-General, including recommendations on the next phase of support by the Mission to Libya;

2. *Decides also* that the mandate of the Mission shall, in addition, include, in coordination and consultation with the transitional Government of Libya, assisting and supporting Libyan national efforts to address the threats of proliferation of all arms and related materiel of all types, in particular man-portable surface-to-air missiles, taking into account, among other things, the report referred to in paragraph 5 of resolution 2017(2011);

3. *Decides further* to remain actively seized of the matter.

Communication. On 7 December [A/66/594-S/2011/758], the Russian Federation conveyed to the Secretary-General the outcome of a meeting on the Middle East and North Africa (Moscow, 24 November) attended by the Deputy Ministers for Foreign Affairs of Brazil, China, India, Russia and South Africa.

Report of assessment mission. The Secretary-General transmitted to the Security Council the report [S/2012/42] of the UN inter-agency assessment mission (7–23 December) on the impact of the Libyan crisis in the Sahel region. Through the years, as a result of its oil wealth, Libya had become a magnet for many impoverished sub-Saharan Africans. Following the crisis in Libya, millions of economic migrants from Chad,

Mali, Mauritania, the Niger and other countries were forced to flee. Overnight, the Governments of the region had to contend with the impact of the crisis on an already challenging humanitarian, development and security situation. That included the influx of returnees, the smuggling of weapons from the Libyan stockpiles, terrorist activities, youth unemployment, drug and human trafficking and a surge in criminality. The region also faced an impending food and nutrition crisis.

The impact of the Libyan crisis on Sahelian countries had differed depending on the geographic location and on the political and economic agreements with the Qadhafi regime. While the mission had noted the determination of the Governments of the region to address the different challenges, in particular the threat posed by Al-Qaida in the Islamic Maghreb, Boko Haram and other criminal groups, and the proliferation of weapons, it had concluded that most countries lacked the means to adequately do so. It therefore recommended that any strategy to mitigate the impact of the Libyan crisis take into account the root causes of the problems in the region by supporting capacity-building for Government initiatives to address the immediate crises; strengthening regional mechanisms for border control; mobilizing international support; and creating an overarching mechanism that would bring the affected countries together to find coordinated solutions.

Security Council consideration (December). Briefing the Council on 22 December [S/PV.6698], the Secretary-General's Special Representative for Libya said that on 19 December, a first coordination meeting on border security and management brought the Ministries of Defence, Interior and Foreign Affairs together with Member States and organizations that had offered assistance. The meeting highlighted the need to strengthen both security and civilian management capacities at Libya's land and maritime borders in order to tackle issues such as drug and weapons trafficking and illegal immigration. The creation of the National Agency for the Security of Borders and Strategic Installations under the Ministry of Defence was a welcome development. UNSMIL was requested to convene regular coordination meetings on support to the police and on border security and management. UNSMIL also agreed with the Ministry of Defence to establish a task force on MANPADS to facilitate a country-wide mapping of weapons and storage sites and to coordinate the identification, collection and disabling efforts of all partners involved. UNSMIL, with the United Nations Mine Action Service (UNMAS), was also working with the Ministry of Defence on developing a programme for the registration of weapons held by the revolutionary brigades. In early December, the United States Government signed an agreement with the Ministry of Defence for the inventory of all weapons and ammunition storage areas in Libya and the destruction of conventional weapons, the implementation of which was coordinated with UNMAS through the task force.

On 28 November, the authorities submitted to OPCW a detailed declaration of chemical materials and weapons found at two previously undeclared sites. On 9 December, IAEA completed its visit to Libya, during which its representatives inspected a nuclear facility in Tripoli and the yellowcake storage facilities in Sabha. Mine action partners had 26 clearance teams on the ground. UNSMIL monitored the situation of detainees; efforts were under way to transfer detention centres from the control of the brigades to the control of the judicial police.

On 10 December, the NTC organized a national conference on reconciliation. While humanitarian operations would come to a close at the end of the year, the United Nations would continue to support the national authorities in assisting internally displaced Libyans.

Activities of ICC Prosecutor

The Prosecutor of the International Criminal Court (ICC), Luis Moreno-Ocampo, briefed the Security Council in May and November on the activities undertaken by his Office with regard to Libya.

Briefing the Council on 4 May [S/PV.6528], the ICC Prosecutor said that, following the Council referral on 26 February of the situation in Libya to the ICC, the Court opened an investigation on 3 March. As of 26 April, it had conducted 15 missions to 10 States and 45 interviews with individuals with direct knowledge of the crimes committed, and collected and reviewed more than 569 documents, including videos and pictures. The Office had taken no statement inside Libya in order to protect witnesses.

The evidence collected by the Office of the Prosecutor confirmed that widespread and systematic attacks against the civilian population, including murder and persecution as crimes against humanity, continued to be committed. Since the beginning of the armed conflict, information on the alleged commission of war crimes had also emerged.

In reference to the crimes against humanity, evidence showed that security forces systematically shot at peaceful protesters, following the same modus operandi in multiple locations. The evidence showed that Libyan security forces hired and brought into Libya mercenaries as early as January, in preparation for possible demonstrations in the country, following the popular uprising in Egypt and Tunisia. On 17 February, thousands of peaceful demonstrators congregated in the square around the High Court of Benghazi. Security forces entered the square and reportedly fired live ammunition into the crowd. The efforts to cover up the crimes made it difficult to ascertain the precise number of victims, but there was credible information suggesting that, as the result of such shootings, 500 to 700 persons had died in February alone.

In addition to such incidents, information collected by the Office showed that civilians in Tripoli and other areas under the control of the regime were subject to different forms of persecution, such as systematic arrests, torture, killings and enforced disappearances. The victims were civilians who had participated in demonstrations, were considered disloyal to the regime, or had talked to international media. Further, citizens of Egypt and Tunisia were arrested and expelled en masse because of their perceived association with the popular uprising.

The Prosecutor expressed his intention to present a case before the ICC Pre-Trial Chamber and to request the judges to issue arrest warrants against three individuals who appeared to bear the greatest responsibility for crimes against humanity committed since 15 February. The NTC committed itself to implementing any arrest warrant.

In his 2 November briefing [S/PV.6647], the Prosecutor said that on 16 May, his Office had requested arrest warrants against three individuals. After evaluating the evidence, on 27 June the Judges of Pre-Trial Chamber I issued arrest warrants for Muammar Qadhafi, Saif al-Islam Qadhafi and Abdullah Al-Senussi for murder and persecution as crimes against humanity under the Rome Statute. Muammar Qadhafi died on 20 October, and the ICC Registry was seeking to obtain official documents from the Government to certify his death. The Office was galvanizing efforts to ensure that the other two indictees faced justice.

The Prosecutor observed that there were allegations of crimes committed by NATO and NTC forces, as well as additional crimes committed by Qadhafi forces. His Office would examine those allegations, taking into consideration, however, that the new Libyan authorities were preparing a strategy to address them. In accordance with the Rome Statute, the ICC should not intervene if there were genuine national proceedings under way.

Sanctions

By its resolution 1970(2011) (see p. 267), the Security Council imposed on Libya an arms embargo, as well as a travel ban and an asset freeze against individuals listed in two annexes. By its resolution 1973(2011) (see p. 271), the Council strengthened the enforcement of the arms embargo and expanded the scope of the asset freeze to include the exercise of vigilance when doing business with Libyan entities, if States had grounds to believe that such business could contribute to violence and use of force against civilians. The resolution listed additional individuals subject to the asset freeze and the travel ban, and established a Panel of Experts (see below). Resolution 2009(2011) (see p. 280) introduced exceptions to the arms embargo and removed two listed entities subject to the asset freeze, while allowing the four remaining entities to be subjected to a partial asset freeze.

Security Council Committee. The Security Council Committee pursuant to resolution 1970(2011) concerning Libya was established on 26 February to oversee the sanctions measures and to undertake the tasks set out in that resolution. The Chair of the Committee transmitted to the Security Council the report of the Committee's activities between 26 February and 31 December [S/2012/32]. In 2011, the Committee held one formal meeting and six informal consultations. On 24 June, the Committee listed two additional individuals subject to the travel ban and asset freeze and one additional entity subject to the asset freeze. On 16 December, pursuant to a request received from the Libyan authorities, the Committee removed the names of two entities from its list of individuals and entities subject to the travel ban and/or asset freeze. As at 31 December, 5 individuals were subject to the travel ban, 15 individuals were subject to both the travel ban and the asset freeze, and 2 entities were subject to a partial asset freeze.

The most noteworthy development was the delisting of the Central Bank of Libya and the Libyan Foreign Bank, on 16 December, upon the request of the Libyan authorities. The Committee received 23 reports of inspections of cargo, 22 from NATO and 1 from a Member State.

The Committee received reports from 54 Member States, listed in an annex to the report, on the steps they had taken to implement the paragraphs of resolution 1970(2011) related to the arms embargo, travel ban and asset freeze. It received over 160 notifications of exemption, most of which were approved, including 17 requests for exemptions related to the arms embargo and 83 related to the asset freeze. The notifications and exemption requests amounted to at least $18 billion that were unfrozen through the Committee.

Appointments. On 10 May [S/2011/293], 16 May [S/2011/313], and 21 June [S/2011/377], the Secretary-General informed the Security Council, as requested in resolution 1973(2011), that he had appointed the eight members of the Panel of Experts.

Panel of Experts. The mandate of the Panel of Experts included assisting the Committee in carrying out its mandate; addressing information from States, UN bodies and other parties regarding the implementation of the measures decided in resolutions 1970(2011) and 1973(2011), in particular incidents of non-compliance; and recommending action to improve implementation of those measures. The Panel submitted to the Committee an interim report dated 10 August and a progress report dated 8 September. In its interim report, the Panel included 11 recommendations, of which 6 related to the arms embargo, 4 related to the asset freeze and 1 related to a procedural matter concerning communication with the Committee. In its progress report, the Panel included one recommendation relating to the asset freeze.

Financing

On 11 May [A/65/328/Add.7], the Secretary-General submitted resource requirements for the Panel of Experts on Libya for the period from 1 April to 31 December 2011 amounting to $2,156,900 gross ($2,126,800 net).

On 20 May [A/65/602/Add.2], ACABQ clarified that, upon enquiry, the Committee had been informed that the Panel would become operational on 1 June. Thus, ACABQ recommended approval of revised requirements for the period from 1 June to 31 December, amounting to $1,693,500 gross ($1,670,400 net).

By **resolution 65/288** of 30 June (see p. 1381), the General Assembly approved the budget of the Panel of Experts for the period from 1 June to 31 December in the amount of $1,693,500 gross ($1,670,400 net).

UNSMIL

The United Nations Support Mission in Libya (UNSMIL) was established on 16 September by Security Council resolution 2009(2011) (see p. 280), at the request of the Libyan authorities, to support the country's transitional authorities in their post-conflict efforts.

UNSMIL was established for an initial three-month period ending 16 December 2011. The Mission was mandated to assist national efforts to restore public security and promote the rule of law; undertake inclusive political dialogue, promote national reconciliation and embark upon the constitution-making and electoral processes; extend State authority; promote and protect human rights and support transitional justice; initiate economic recovery; and coordinate support.

By resolution 2022(2011) (see p. 286), the Security Council expanded the Mission's mandate, to include assisting Libyan efforts to address the proliferation of arms and related material. It also extended the Mission's mandate until 16 March 2012.

Ian Martin (United Kingdom), appointed on 16 September [S/2011/587], served as the Secretary-General's Special Representative and Head of UNSMIL.

Financing

On 2 November [A/66/354 & Corr.1], the Secretary-General submitted resource requirements for 2012 for 30 special political missions authorized by the General Assembly and/or the Security Council. The total requirements for UNSMIL amounted to $36,145,200 gross ($32,575,800 net). An allotment of $9,961,500 had been provided for the Mission's initial three-months period ending on 16 December 2011, in accordance with Council resolution 2009(2011). The Secretary-General's report of 15 November [A/66/354/Add.6] confirmed those requirements.

ACABQ, in December [A/66/7/Add.13], observed that conditions on the ground were evolving, and it would be premature to adopt a one-year budget. The Committee suggested that the Secretary-General submit a revised budget following a decision of the Council based on the Secretary-General's proposal. Taking into account the pattern of expenditure of the Mission in 2011, ACABQ recommended that the General Assembly authorize the Secretary-General to enter into commitments in an amount not exceeding $16 million to cover the Mission's operational requirements for the period from 1 January to 30 June 2012, and that resources required beyond 15 March 2012 be made available subject to the extension of the Mission's mandate.

On 24 December, in section IX of **resolution 66/247** (see p. 1393), the Assembly authorized the Secretary-General to enter into commitments in an amount not to exceed $16 million.

Western Sahara

In 2011, as the Organization marked the twentieth anniversary of the United Nations Mission for the Referendum in Western Sahara (MINURSO) and the successful maintenance of the ceasefire between Morocco and the Frente Popular para la Liberacíon de Saguía el-Hamra y de Río de Oro (Frente Polisario), the situation of Western Sahara remained unresolved and negotiations towards a peace agreement continued. MINURSO encountered increasing challenges to its role and activities. While remaining a constituting element of the Mission's mandate, all activities in preparation of a referendum on self-determination had been suspended due to disagreements between the parties. Fundamental activities such as the monitoring and reporting of developments were hindered, owing to the restrictions on MINURSO freedom of movement inside the Territory.

Under a plan presented in 2007 by Frente Polisario [YUN 2007, p. 296], the Territory's final status should be decided in a referendum on self-determination that included independence as an option. Morocco, in turn, had presented a plan for autonomy [ibid., p. 297]. In 2011, the parties met at regular intervals; reaffirmed their commitment to the negotiating process; agreed to continue discussing specific subjects of mutual interest, such as natural resources and demining; and took steps on confidence-building measures. On the core issues concerning the future status of Western Sahara and the means by which the self-determination of the people of the Territory was to occur, however, no progress was registered.

Political and security developments

Report of Secretary-General (April). Pursuant to Security Council resolution 1920(2010) [YUN 2010, p. 310], the Secretary-General in April submitted a report [S/2011/249] covering developments in Western Sahara since his 2010 report [ibid., p. 309]. Following the protests in 2010 at the Gdim Izik encampment [ibid., p. 311], the general situation remained tense, particularly between the Saharan population and Moroccan forces.

In January, Morocco claimed that it had dismantled a 27-member terrorist ring 35 kilometres west of the berm—the buffer strip stretching along the entire length of the disputed territory and separating the Moroccan-administered portion (west) from the area controlled by the Frente Polisario (east). Morocco alleged that foreign elements from Al-Qaida in the Maghreb might have infiltrated Western Sahara. Minurso could not corroborate that information. On 26 February, in Dakhla, on the eve of the thirty-fifth anniversary of the "Sahrawi Arab Democratic Republic", unrest between Saharan protesters and Moroccan civilians led to the injury of several people and the destruction of property.

The popular movements in the Arab world seeking political and socioeconomic reforms encouraged protests in Morocco and within the Saharan refugee camps in Tindouf, Algeria. Against that backdrop, the King of Morocco, Mohamed VI, declared that the country would conduct a substantial revision of the Constitution to confirm a process of regionalization and democratization, and would submit such revision to a referendum, including in Western Sahara. The King declared that Western Sahara would be the first "region" to benefit from such reforms.

On the political front, the fifth (Manhasset, United States, 21–23 January) and sixth (Mellieha, Malta, 7–9 March) rounds of informal talks took place, mediated by the Secretary-General's Personal Envoy for Western Sahara, Christopher Ross, and attended by the neighbouring States (Algeria, Mauritania). The parties agreed to hold a seventh round of informal talks and to hold further rounds regularly until enough progress was made to convene a round of formal negotiations.

Family visits by air for Sahrawi refugees in the camps near Tindouf and their families in Western Sahara were resumed on 7 January. Since then, eight round trips had been conducted, enabling 894 persons to travel or receive relatives on both sides.

As at 15 March, the military component of minurso stood at 231 personnel. From 1 April 2010 to 15 March 2011, minurso performed 8,168 ground patrols and 710 aerial patrols, monitoring units of the Royal Moroccan Army and the military forces of the Frente Polisario and monitoring adherence to the military agreements. While minurso continued to maintain good relations with the Royal Moroccan Army and Frente Polisario, both sides abstained from dealing directly with each other, communicating only through minurso. The Mission recorded 126 violations of Military Agreement No. 1 [YUN 1998, p. 194] by the Royal Moroccan Army and 12 by Frente Polisario. Those violations did not constitute a threat to regional security; they did, however, indicate an erosion in the standing of the agreement, which regulated the activities related to the monitoring of the ceasefire. The violations also showed a decline in the parties' relationship with minurso as military observer. During the reporting period, restrictions on the freedom of movement of minurso observers by both parties increased significantly.

The Secretary-General suggested that the Security Council recommend to the parties the following initiatives: to deepen their examination of each other's proposals and seek common ground on the points of convergence; to devote additional energy to discussing governance issues; and to include respected representatives of Western Sahara in the discussion of issues related to its final status and the exercise of self-determination. The Secretary-General considered the presence of minurso in the Territory relevant as a guarantor for the stability of the ceasefire, and recommended extending the Mission's mandate until 30 April 2012.

Communication. In a letter of 28 March [S/2011/207], Morocco informed the Security Council of the establishment of a National Human Rights Council, the transformation of the Ombudsman into a "mediator institution" between citizens and administrations, and the creation of an interministerial delegation in charge of human rights.

SECURITY COUNCIL ACTION

On 27 April [meeting 6523], the Security Council unanimously adopted **resolution 1979(2011)**. The draft [S/2011/268] was submitted by France, the Russian Federation, Spain, the United Kingdom and the United States.

The Security Council,

Recalling and reaffirming all its previous resolutions on Western Sahara,

Reaffirming its strong support for the efforts of the Secretary-General and his Personal Envoy for Western Sahara to implement resolutions 1754(2007) of 30 April 2007, 1783(2007) of 31 October 2007, 1813(2008) of 30 April 2008, 1871(2009) of 30 April 2009 and 1920(2010) of 30 April 2010,

Reaffirming its commitment to assist the parties to achieve a just, lasting and mutually acceptable political solution which will provide for the self-determination of the people of Western Sahara in the context of arrangements consistent with the principles and purposes of the Charter of the United Nations, and noting the role and responsibilities of the parties in this respect,

Reiterating its call upon the parties and States of the region to cooperate more fully with the United Nations and with each other and to strengthen their involvement to end the current impasse and to achieve progress towards a political solution,

Welcoming the efforts of the Secretary-General to keep all peacekeeping operations, including the United Nations Mission for the Referendum in Western Sahara, under close review, and reiterating the need for the Security Council to pursue a rigorous, strategic approach to peacekeeping deployments,

Expressing serious concern about the increase in violations of existing agreements, and calling upon the parties to respect their relevant obligations,

Taking note of the proposal presented by Morocco to the Secretary-General on 11 April 2007 and welcoming serious and credible Moroccan efforts to move the process forward towards resolution, and taking note also of the proposal presented by the Frente Popular para la Liberación de Saguía el-Hamra y de Río de Oro to the Secretary-General on 10 April 2007,

Inviting, in this context, the parties to demonstrate further political will towards a solution, including by expanding upon their discussion of each other's proposals,

Taking note of the four rounds of negotiations held under the auspices of the Secretary-General, and the continued rounds of informal talks held in Manhasset, United States of America, and in Mellieha, Malta, and welcoming the progress made by the parties to enter into direct negotiations,

Welcoming the agreement by the parties to explore innovative negotiating approaches and discrete subjects,

Stressing the importance of improving the human rights situation in Western Sahara and the Tindouf camps, and encouraging the parties to work with the international community to develop and implement independent and credible measures to ensure full respect for human rights, bearing in mind their relevant obligations under international law,

Welcoming the establishment of the National Council on Human Rights in Morocco and the proposed component regarding Western Sahara, and the commitment of Morocco to ensure unqualified and unimpeded access to all special procedures of the United Nations Human Rights Council,

Welcoming also the implementation of the enhanced refugee protection programme developed by the Office of the United Nations High Commissioner for Refugees in coordination with the Frente Popular para la Liberación de Saguía el-Hamra y de Río de Oro, which will include human rights training and awareness initiatives,

Requesting the Office of the High Commissioner to maintain its consideration of a refugee registration in the Tindouf refugee camps,

Welcoming the agreement of the parties expressed in the communiqué of the Personal Envoy of the Secretary-General of 18 March 2008, looking forward to the inauguration of family visits by land and the continuation of the existing programme by air, and encouraging the parties to cooperate with the United Nations High Commissioner for Refugees in implementing their agreement,

Welcoming also the commitment of the parties to continue the process of negotiations through the United Nations-sponsored talks,

Recognizing that the consolidation of the status quo is not acceptable in the long term, and noting further that progress in the negotiations is essential in order to improve the quality of life of the people of Western Sahara in all its aspects,

Affirming its support for the Personal Envoy of the Secretary-General, Mr. Christopher Ross, and his work in facilitating negotiations between the parties, and welcoming his ongoing consultations with the parties and neighbouring States,

Also affirming its support for the Special Representative of the Secretary-General for Western Sahara and Head of the United Nations Mission for the Referendum in Western Sahara, Mr. Hany Abdel-Aziz,

Having considered the report of the Secretary-General of 1 April 2011,

1. *Reaffirms* the need for full respect of the military agreements reached with the United Nations Mission for the Referendum in Western Sahara with regard to the ceasefire, and calls upon the parties to adhere fully to those agreements;

2. *Calls upon* all parties to cooperate fully with the operations of the Mission and to ensure the security of, as well as unhindered and immediate access for, the United Nations and associated personnel in carrying out their mandate, in conformity with existing agreements;

3. *Welcomes* the commitment of the parties to continue the process of holding small, informal talks in preparation for a fifth round of negotiations, and recalls its endorsement of the recommendation in the report of the Secretary-General of 14 April 2008 that realism and a spirit of compromise by the parties are essential to achieve progress in negotiations;

4. *Calls upon* the parties to continue to show political will and to work in an atmosphere propitious for dialogue in order to enter into a more intensive and substantive phase of negotiations, thus ensuring the implementation of resolutions 1754(2007), 1783(2007), 1813(2008), 1871(2009) and 1920(2010) and the success of negotiations, inter alia, by devoting attention to the ideas set out in paragraph 120 of the report of the Secretary-General of 1 April 2011;

5. *Affirms its strong support* for the commitment of the Secretary-General and his Personal Envoy towards a solution to the question of Western Sahara in this context, and welcomes the intensified pace of meetings and contacts;

6. *Calls upon* the parties to continue negotiations under the auspices of the Secretary-General without preconditions and in good faith, taking into account the efforts made since 2006 and subsequent developments, with a view to achieving a just, lasting and mutually acceptable political solution which will provide for the self-determination of the people of Western Sahara in the context of arrangements consistent with the principles and purposes of the Charter of the United Nations, and notes the role and responsibilities of the parties in this respect;

7. *Invites* Member States to lend appropriate assistance to these talks;

8. *Requests* the Secretary-General to keep the Security Council informed on a regular basis, and at least twice a year, of the status and progress of these negotiations under

his auspices, and expresses its intention to meet to receive and discuss his report;

9. *Also requests* the Secretary-General to provide a report on the situation in Western Sahara well before the end of the mandate period;

10. *Welcomes* the commitment of the parties and the neighbouring States to hold periodic meetings with the Office of the United Nations High Commissioner for Refugees to review and, where possible, expand confidence-building measures;

11. *Urges* Member States to provide voluntary contributions to fund confidence-building measures that allow for increased contact between separated family members, especially family visits, as well as other confidence-building measures that may be agreed upon between the parties;

12. *Requests* the Secretary-General to examine in his next report the existing challenges to the operations of the Mission, reflecting on the situation on the ground;

13. *Decides* to extend the mandate of the Mission until 30 April 2012;

14. *Requests* the Secretary-General to continue to take the measures necessary to ensure full compliance in the Mission with the United Nations zero-tolerance policy on sexual exploitation and abuse and to keep the Council informed, and urges troop-contributing countries to take appropriate preventive action, including predeployment awareness training, and other action to ensure full accountability in cases of such conduct involving their personnel;

15. *Decides* to remain seized of the matter.

Report of Secretary-General (August). Pursuant to General Assembly resolution 65/112 [YUN 2010, p. 312], the Secretary-General in August submitted a report [A/66/260] on the question of Western Sahara, covering the period from 1 July 2010 to 30 June 2011.

The seventh round of informal talks (Manhasset, 5–7 June) sought to review and exchange views on the guidance provided in Council resolution 1979(2011) (see above) and to encourage the parties to deepen their discussion of their respective proposals. At the end of the meeting, while it was clear that neither party was prepared to accept the proposal of the other, both sides engaged in exchanges on a mechanism for self-determination for the Sahrawi people. They also discussed demining and asked for UN assistance in proposing a framework for future exchanges on natural resources. Regarding confidence-building measures, the parties and the neighbouring States reiterated their support for the implementation of family visits by road. The parties agreed to hold another round of informal talks in July.

Further developments. In a later report [S/2012/197], the Secretary-General said that, since April, peaceful demonstrations of Western Saharans were held periodically in Laayoune and other major towns, seeking self-determination for the Territory, the release of political prisoners, and employment and social welfare benefits. Deadly violence, however, erupted in the coastal city of Dakhla on 25 September. The parties gave conflicting accounts of the events. Frente Polisario contended that one Western Saharan had been killed and more than 100 others arrested when Moroccan civilians, backed by Moroccan security forces, attacked a peaceful Western Saharan demonstration. Morocco stated that seven people, including two police officers, and three civilians who had been run over by a vehicle driven by known criminals, had been killed in the clashes. The Secretary-General's Special Representative for Western Sahara, Hany Abdel-Aziz, visited Dakhla in September. In November, MINURSO deployed a political affairs officer to the area to assess the situation after the incident.

King Mohammed VI appointed a consultative commission to draft a new constitution for Morocco, which was endorsed by a public referendum on 1 July. The text contained provisions related to the "regionalization" of the provinces, including Western Sahara, and to the Moroccan autonomy plan for Western Sahara. On two occasions, the King reiterated Morocco's readiness to achieve a solution to the conflict within the framework of the Kingdom's territorial integrity.

Frente Polisario held its thirteenth General Peoples' Congress in December. Frente Polisario leaders maintained the requirement for a referendum on self-determination and independence for Western Sahara throughout the proceedings. Participants, particularly the younger generation, called for the adoption of further reforms, including new approaches to change the status quo.

The parties held an eighth round of informal talks (Manhasset, 19–21 July) to re-examine their respective proposals and to discuss innovative approaches and discrete subjects previously agreed. The parties maintained their respective positions; they agreed, however, on holding an expert-level meeting in Geneva on natural resources and to begin building a common database of natural resources. A new round of informal talks was scheduled for March 2012.

The Secretary-General's Personal Envoy visited the capitals of the member States of the Group of Friends of Western Sahara: Washington, D.C. in October, Madrid, Paris and Moscow in November and London in December, holding bilateral meetings with the parties and the neighbouring States. In particular, the Personal Envoy sought support for two ideas that might help the parties overcome their inability to move beyond their mutually exclusive positions: consultations with a cross-section of Western Saharans and consultations with a group of respected Maghreb representatives on Western Sahara. While the members of the Group of Friends expressed broad support for the two initiatives, both Morocco and Frente Polisario subsequently expressed reservations.

The Personal Envoy co-chaired an expert-level meeting of the parties (Geneva, November) on natural resources in Western Sahara. The discussion was to be merely technical. The parties, however, engaged in mutual accusations of a political nature, resulting in limited technical exchanges.

GENERAL ASSEMBLY ACTION

On 9 December [meeting 81], the General Assembly, on the recommendation of the Fourth (Special Political and Decolonization) Committee [A/66/434], adopted **resolution 66/86** without vote [agenda item 60].

Question of Western Sahara

The General Assembly,

Having considered in depth the question of Western Sahara,

Reaffirming the inalienable right of all peoples to self-determination and independence, in accordance with the principles set forth in the Charter of the United Nations and General Assembly resolution 1514(XV) of 14 December 1960 containing the Declaration on the Granting of Independence to Colonial Countries and Peoples,

Recognizing that all available options for self-determination of the Territories are valid as long as they are in accordance with the freely expressed wishes of the people concerned and in conformity with the clearly defined principles contained in General Assembly resolutions 1514(XV) of 14 December 1960 and 1541(XV) of 15 December 1960 and other resolutions of the Assembly,

Recalling its resolution 65/112 of 10 December 2010,

Recalling also all resolutions of the General Assembly and the Security Council on the question of Western Sahara,

Recalling further Security Council resolutions 658(1990) of 27 June 1990, 690(1991) of 29 April 1991, 1359(2001) of 29 June 2001, 1429(2002) of 30 July 2002, 1495(2003) of 31 July 2003, 1541(2004) of 29 April 2004, 1570(2004) of 28 October 2004, 1598(2005) of 28 April 2005, 1634(2005) of 28 October 2005, 1675(2006) of 28 April 2006 and 1720(2006) of 31 October 2006,

Underlining the adoption of Security Council resolutions 1754(2007) on 30 April 2007, 1783(2007) on 31 October 2007, 1813(2008) on 30 April 2008, 1871(2009) on 30 April 2009, 1920(2010) on 30 April 2010 and 1979(2011) on 27 April 2011,

Expressing its satisfaction that the parties met on 18 and 19 June 2007, on 10 and 11 August 2007, from 7 to 9 January 2008 and from 16 to 18 March 2008 under the auspices of the Personal Envoy of the Secretary-General for Western Sahara and in the presence of the neighbouring countries and that they have agreed to continue the negotiations,

Also expressing its satisfaction at the holding of eight informal meetings convened by the Personal Envoy of the Secretary-General on 9 and 10 August 2009 in Dürnstein, Austria, on 10 and 11 February 2010 in Westchester County, New York, United States of America, from 7 to 10 November 2010, from 16 to 18 December 2010 and from 21 to 23 January 2011, all on Long Island, New York, from 7 to 9 March 2011 in Mellieha, Malta, and from 5 to 7 June 2011 and from 19 to 21 July 2011, both on Long Island, to prepare for the fifth round of negotiations,

Calling upon all the parties and the States of the region to cooperate fully with the Secretary-General and his Personal Envoy and with each other,

Reaffirming the responsibility of the United Nations towards the people of Western Sahara,

Welcoming, in this regard, the efforts of the Secretary-General and his Personal Envoy in search of a mutually acceptable political solution to the dispute, which will provide for the self-determination of the people of Western Sahara,

Having examined the relevant chapter of the report of the Special Committee on the Situation with regard to the Implementation of the Declaration on the Granting of Independence to Colonial Countries and Peoples for 2011,

Having also examined the report of the Secretary-General on the question of Western Sahara,

1. *Takes note* of the report of the Secretary-General;
2. *Supports* the process of negotiations initiated by Security Council resolution 1754(2007) and further sustained by Council resolutions 1783(2007), 1813(2008), 1871(2009), 1920(2010) and 1979(2011) with a view to achieving a just, lasting and mutually acceptable political solution, which will provide for the self-determination of the people of Western Sahara, and commends the efforts undertaken by the Secretary-General and his Personal Envoy in this respect;
3. *Welcomes* the commitment of the parties to continue to show political will and work in an atmosphere propitious for dialogue, in order to enter into a more intensive phase of negotiations, in good faith and without preconditions, taking note of efforts and developments since 2006, thus ensuring implementation of Security Council resolutions 1754(2007), 1783(2007), 1813(2008), 1871(2009), 1920(2010) and 1979(2011) and the success of negotiations;
4. *Also welcomes* the ongoing negotiations between the parties held on 18 and 19 June 2007, on 10 and 11 August 2007, from 7 to 9 January 2008 and from 16 to 18 March 2008 in the presence of the neighbouring countries and under the auspices of the United Nations;
5. *Calls upon* the parties to cooperate with the International Committee of the Red Cross, and calls upon them to abide by their obligations under international humanitarian law;
6. *Requests* the Special Committee on the Situation with regard to the Implementation of the Declaration on the Granting of Independence to Colonial Countries and Peoples to continue to consider the situation in Western Sahara and to report thereon to the General Assembly at its sixty-seventh session;
7. *Invites* the Secretary-General to submit to the General Assembly at its sixty-seventh session a report on the implementation of the present resolution.

MINURSO

The United Nations Mission for the Referendum in Western Sahara (MINURSO) was established by Security Council resolution 690(1991) [YUN 1991, p. 794] in accordance with settlement proposals accepted on 30 August 1988 by Morocco and Frente Polisario. The implementation plan, as approved by the Council, provided for a transitional period for the preparation of a referendum in which the people of Western Sahara would choose between independence and integration with Morocco.

MINURSO continued to monitor compliance with the formal ceasefire between Frente Polisario and Morocco. Military Agreement No. 1, which MINURSO had signed separately with the parties [YUN 1998, p. 194], remained the basic legal instrument governing the ceasefire monitoring of the disputed Territory. The Mission's military observers carried out monitoring through a combination of ground and air patrols and observation posts, and through inspections of larger-than-company-size military units. Bilateral Military Agreements Nos. 2 and 3 [YUN 1999, pp. 179–180], committing both parties to cooperating with MINURSO in the exchange of mine-related information, marking of mined areas and destruction of mines and unexploded ordnance, remained in force. The Mission also provided support to assistance programmes to address the plight of displaced and separated Sahrawi families.

MINURSO continued to be headed by Hany Abdel-Aziz (Egypt), the Special Representative of the Secretary-General for Western Sahara.

Appointments. By a letter of 22 July [S/2011/459], the Secretary-General informed the Security Council of his intention to appoint Major General Abdul Hafiz (Bangladesh) as Force Commander of MINURSO, replacing Major General Jingmin Zhao (China), who had completed his assignment on 10 April. The Council took note of his intention on 26 July [S/2011/460].

Financing

The Secretary-General's performance report on the budget of MINURSO for the period from 1 July 2009 to 30 June 2010 [A/65/665] reported an expenditure of $51,936,200 gross ($49,608,600 net) against an apportionment of $53,527,600 gross ($51,338,900 net).

In February [A/65/720 & Corr.1], the Secretary-General submitted the budget for the period from 1 July 2011 to 30 June 2012, in the amount of $61,429,700 gross ($58,668,400 net), exclusive of budgeted voluntary contributions in kind in the amount of $1,769,900. The budget provided for the deployment of 203 military observers, 27 military contingent personnel, 6 UN police officers, 102 international staff, 172 national staff, 20 United Nations Volunteers, and 10 Government-provided personnel.

In March [A/65/743/Add.5], ACABQ recommended that, for the period from 1 July 2009 to 30 June 2010, the unencumbered balance of $1,591,400, as well as other income/adjustments for $795,300, be credited to Member States. With regard to the 2011–2012 budget, the Committee recommended approval of the Secretary-General's proposal.

GENERAL ASSEMBLY ACTION

On 30 June [meeting 106], the General Assembly, on the recommendation of the Fifth Committee [A/65/887] adopted **resolution 65/304** without vote [agenda item 158].

Financing of the United Nations Mission for the Referendum in Western Sahara

The General Assembly,

Having considered the reports of the Secretary-General on the financing of the United Nations Mission for the Referendum in Western Sahara and the related report of the Advisory Committee on Administrative and Budgetary Questions,

Recalling Security Council resolution 690(1991) of 29 April 1991, by which the Council established the United Nations Mission for the Referendum in Western Sahara, and the subsequent resolutions by which the Council extended the mandate of the Mission, the latest of which was resolution 1979(2011) of 27 April 2011, by which the Council extended the mandate of the Mission until 30 April 2012,

Recalling also its resolution 45/266 of 17 May 1991 on the financing of the Mission and its subsequent resolutions and decisions thereon, the latest of which was resolution 64/284 of 24 June 2010,

Reaffirming the general principles underlying the financing of United Nations peacekeeping operations, as stated in General Assembly resolutions 1874(S-IV) of 27 June 1963, 3101(XXVIII) of 11 December 1973 and 55/235 of 23 December 2000,

Noting with appreciation that voluntary contributions have been made to the Mission,

Mindful of the fact that it is essential to provide the Mission with the financial resources necessary to enable it to fulfil its responsibilities under the relevant resolutions of the Security Council,

1. *Requests* the Secretary-General to entrust the Head of Mission with the task of formulating future budget proposals in full accordance with the provisions of General Assembly resolutions 59/296 of 22 June 2005, 60/266 of 30 June 2006, 61/276 of 29 June 2007, 64/269 of 24 June 2010 and 65/289 of 30 June 2011, as well as other relevant resolutions;

2. *Takes note* of the status of contributions to the United Nations Mission for the Referendum in Western Sahara as at 30 April 2011, including the contributions outstanding in the amount of 44.3 million United States dollars, representing some 5 per cent of the total assessed contributions, notes with concern that only ninety-seven Member States have paid their assessed contributions in full, and urges all other Member States, in particular those in arrears, to ensure payment of their outstanding assessed contributions;

3. *Expresses its appreciation* to those Member States which have paid their assessed contributions in full, and urges all other Member States to make every possible effort to ensure payment of their assessed contributions to the Mission in full;

4. *Expresses concern* at the financial situation with regard to peacekeeping activities, in particular as regards the reimbursements to troop contributors that bear ad-

ditional burdens owing to overdue payments by Member States of their assessments;

5. *Also expresses concern* at the delay experienced by the Secretary-General in deploying and providing adequate resources to some recent peacekeeping missions, in particular those in Africa;

6. *Emphasizes* that all future and existing peacekeeping missions shall be given equal and non-discriminatory treatment in respect of financial and administrative arrangements;

7. *Also emphasizes* that all peacekeeping missions shall be provided with adequate resources for the effective and efficient discharge of their respective mandates;

8. *Requests* the Secretary-General to ensure that proposed peacekeeping budgets are based on the relevant legislative mandates;

9. *Endorses* the conclusions and recommendations contained in the report of the Advisory Committee on Administrative and Budgetary Questions, subject to the provisions of the present resolution, and requests the Secretary-General to ensure their full implementation;

10. *Notes* the consistent underutilization of the budget for flight hours, and encourages the Secretary-General to take this trend into account in future budget submissions;

11. *Welcomes* the initiative to implement two quick-impact projects as part of the effort to enhance relations with the local population, and encourages the timely implementation of the projects;

12. *Requests* the Secretary-General to ensure the full implementation of the relevant provisions of its resolutions 59/296, 60/266, 61/276, 64/269 and 65/289;

13. *Also requests* the Secretary-General to take all necessary action to ensure that the Mission is administered with a maximum of efficiency and economy;

14. *Notes* that the overall level of appropriation has been adjusted in accordance with the terms of resolution 65/289;

Financial performance report for the period from 1 July 2009 to 30 June 2010

15. *Takes note* of the report of the Secretary-General on the financial performance of the Mission for the period from 1 July 2009 to 30 June 2010;

Budget estimates for the period from 1 July 2011 to 30 June 2012

16. *Decides* to appropriate to the Special Account for the United Nations Mission for the Referendum in Western Sahara the amount of 65,398,400 dollars for the period from 1 July 2011 to 30 June 2012, inclusive of 61,449,400 dollars for the maintenance of the Mission, 3,346,300 dollars for the support account for peacekeeping operations and 602,700 dollars for the United Nations Logistics Base at Brindisi, Italy;

Financing of the appropriation

17. *Also decides* to apportion among Member States the amount of 54,498,667 dollars for the period from 1 July 2011 to 30 April 2012, in accordance with the levels updated in General Assembly resolution 64/249 of 24 December 2009, and taking into account the scale of assessments for 2011 and 2012, as set out in Assembly resolution 64/248 of 24 December 2009;

18. *Further decides* that, in accordance with the provisions of its resolution 973(X) of 15 December 1955, there shall be set off against the apportionment among Member States, as provided for in paragraph 17 above, their respective share in the Tax Equalization Fund of 2,590,083 dollars, comprising the estimated staff assessment income of 2,301,083 dollars approved for the Mission, the prorated share of 236,250 dollars of the estimated staff assessment income approved for the support account and the prorated share of 52,750 dollars of the estimated staff assessment income approved for the United Nations Logistics Base;

19. *Decides* to apportion among Member States the amount of 10,899,733 dollars for the period from 1 May to 30 June 2012, at a monthly rate of 5,449,866 dollars, in accordance with the levels updated in resolution 64/249, and taking into account the scale of assessments for 2012, as set out in resolution 64/248, subject to a decision of the Security Council to extend the mandate of the Mission;

20. *Also decides* that, in accordance with the provisions of resolution 973(X), there shall be set off against the apportionment among Member States, as provided for in paragraph 19 above, their respective share in the Tax Equalization Fund of 518,017 dollars, comprising the estimated staff assessment income of 460,217 dollars approved for the Mission, the prorated share of 47,250 dollars of the estimated staff assessment income approved for the support account and the prorated share of 10,550 dollars of the estimated staff assessment income approved for the United Nations Logistics Base;

21. *Further decides* that, for Member States that have fulfilled their financial obligations to the Mission, there shall be set off against their apportionment, as provided for in paragraph 17 above, their respective share of the unencumbered balance and other income in the total amount of 2,386,700 dollars in respect of the financial period ended 30 June 2010, in accordance with the levels updated in resolution 64/249, and taking into account the scale of assessments for 2010, as set out in resolution 64/248;

22. *Decides* that, for Member States that have not fulfilled their financial obligations to the Mission, there shall be set off against their outstanding obligations their respective share of the unencumbered balance and other income in the total amount of 2,386,700 dollars in respect of the financial period ended 30 June 2010, in accordance with the scheme set out in paragraph 21 above;

23. *Also decides* that the increase of 138,900 dollars in the estimated staff assessment income in respect of the financial period ended 30 June 2010 shall be added to the credits from the amount of 2,386,700 dollars referred to in paragraphs 21 and 22 above;

24. *Emphasizes* that no peacekeeping mission shall be financed by borrowing funds from other active peacekeeping missions;

25. *Encourages* the Secretary-General to continue to take additional measures to ensure the safety and security of all personnel participating in the Mission under the auspices of the United Nations, bearing in mind paragraphs 5 and 6 of Security Council resolution 1502(2003) of 26 August 2003;

26. *Invites* voluntary contributions to the Mission in cash and in the form of services and supplies acceptable to

the Secretary-General, to be administered, as appropriate, in accordance with the procedure and practices established by the General Assembly;

27. *Decides* to include in the provisional agenda of its sixty-sixth session the item entitled "Financing of the United Nations Mission for the Referendum in Western Sahara".

The General Assembly, on 24 December, decided that the agenda item on the financing of minurso would remain for consideration during its resumed sixty-sixth (2012) session (**decision 66/557**).

Other issues

Egypt and Tunisia

In 2011, the Secretary-General followed closely developments in the region that spread from Tunisia (see p. 761) to other countries. In a statement of 18 January [SG/SM/13355], he renewed his concern about the growing violence in Tunisia and called for efforts to restore peace and stability, appealing for broad-based consultations to establish an inclusive interim Government, leading to the holding of credible elections.

On 11 February [SG/SM/13400], in the wake of Egyptian President Hosni Mubarak's resignation, the Secretary-General said that he respected what must have been a difficult decision, taken in the wider interests of the Egyptian people. He called for a peaceful transition that included free and fair elections leading to the establishment of civilian rule, and urged the interim authorities to chart a path forward with the participation of all stakeholders.

On 23 October [SG/SM/13898], the Secretary-General congratulated the people and the interim authorities of Tunisia for holding a historic Constituent Assembly election on 23 October in a peaceful and orderly manner. He commended the Independent High Authority for the Elections for its role in ensuring a transparent electoral process. At the request of the authorities, the United Nations provided technical electoral assistance.

On 21 November [SG/SM/13960], the Secretary-General expressed concern about violence in Egypt, particularly in Cairo. Deploring the loss of life and the many injuries, he called on the transitional authorities to guarantee the protection of the right to peaceful protest. He urged restraint by all parties to enable a peaceful and inclusive electoral process.

On 29 November [SG/SM/13980], the Secretary-General commended the population and authorities of Egypt for the enthusiastic participation in a first stage of the electoral process and for the generally calm and orderly manner in which voting had taken place.

On 18 December [SG/SM/14029], the Secretary-General expressed concern at the resurgence of violence in Cairo, which had led to civilian deaths and hundreds of injuries. He expressed alarm at the excessive use of force employed by the security forces against protestors, and called for the transitional authorities to act with restraint and uphold the right to peaceful protest.

Mauritius–United Kingdom

By a 26 September letter [A/66/501], the United Kingdom transmitted to the General Assembly a statement in exercise of the right of reply to the remarks made by the Prime Minister of Mauritius on 24 September [A/66/PV.22]. The United Kingdom maintained that the British Indian Ocean Territory was British and did not recognize the sovereignty claim of the Mauritian Government. The British Government, however, recognized Mauritius as the only State that had a right to assert a claim of sovereignty when the United Kingdom relinquished its own sovereignty, once the Territory was no longer required for defence purposes.

Chapter III

Americas

During 2011, the United Nations continued to advance the cause of lasting peace, human rights, good governance and the rule of law in the Americas.

In Haiti, the humanitarian situation remained fragile following the devastating earthquake of 2010, with 800,000 people still living in camps. Furthermore, the lack of adequate water, sanitation and health-care infrastructure had allowed a cholera outbreak to spread. Nevertheless, Haiti held successful presidential elections: on 20 March, Michel Joseph Martelly won the popular vote in the second round and became the country's president. The United Nations Stabilization Mission in Haiti (minustah) coordinated the international support to the electoral process, including assisting in setting up 1,500 registration centres for displaced voters, inspecting all 1,483 voting centres and identifying new locations to replace those that had been damaged or destroyed. The Secretary-General in August recommended a partial drawdown of minustah by mid-2012, leading to the Security Council's decision in October to reduce the force's strength to pre-earthquake levels. The Council extended the mandate of minustah until October 2012.

In Guatemala, the International Commission against Impunity continued to implement its mandate. In November, the Secretary-General provided the General Assembly with an update on the activities of the Commission and the role of the United Nations in implementing its mandate.

Regarding the border disputes between Costa Rica and Nicaragua, the International Court of Justice (icj) in March requested the parties to refrain from sending to or maintaining in the disputed territory, any personnel, whether civilian police or security. Nicaragua in December filed suit against Costa Rica at the icj, citing violations of its sovereignty and major environmental damage to its territory due to Costa Rica's construction of a road along the banks of the San Juan River.

The General Assembly in October again called on States to refrain from promulgating laws and measures such as the embargo against Cuba by the United States.

Central America

In 2011, Central America further consolidated peace and built democratic and equitable societies on the foundation developed in years of successful UN peacemaking efforts. The Organization continued to assist the region through development programmes and other means.

On 24 December, the Assembly decided that the item on the situation in Central America: progress in fashioning a region of peace, freedom, democracy and development, would remain for consideration during its resumed sixty-sixth (2012) session (**decision 66/557**).

Guatemala

International Commission against Impunity

In 2011, the International Commission against Impunity in Guatemala (cicig), established in 2007 [YUN 2007, p. 318] with the concurrent entry into force of the 2006 agreement between the country and the United Nations [YUN 2006, p. 870], continued to implement its mandate. Under the terms of the agreement, which set up the Commission as an independent, non-UN organ, the main cicig objective was to assist, strengthen and support State institutions responsible for investigating and prosecuting crimes allegedly committed by illegal security forces and clandestine security organizations, and other criminal conduct related to those entities.

Report of Secretary-General. In accordance with General Assembly resolution 65/181 [YUN 2010, p. 318], the Secretary-General in November [A/66/567] updated the Assembly on the work of cicig. On 13 January, following an exchange of letters between Guatemalan authorities and the Secretariat, the mandate of the Commission was extended for an additional two years until 3 September 2013.

From September 2010 to August 2011, the Commission received 201 complaints and carried out 62 investigations, acting as complementary prosecutor in 20 of them. The Commission had established a productive working relationship with the Office of the Public Prosecutor—its principal national counterpart—and with the Ministry of the Interior. The relationship between the Commission and the judiciary, however, experienced some difficulties, with the Commission alleging irregular conduct on the part of certain judges, including decisions that had the effect of promoting impunity, which had not been addressed adequately by the judiciary. In accordance with its 2011–2013 strategic plan, the Commission was placing a priority on its investigations and prosecutions, as well as on institutional strengthening activities, with a view to enhancing national capacities to fight impunity.

Together with the United Nations Children's Fund, the Commission supported the creation of a section to investigate trafficking in persons, femicide and violence against women. It further continued to promote institutional and legal reforms intended to strengthen Guatemalan institutions in the fight against crime and impunity. The legislature, however, made slow progress in the approval of the legislative proposals formulated by the Commission. As for the prosecution of major crimes, recent reforms and improvements suggested that the Commission was making a positive contribution to the strengthening of national institutions.

The Commission had an annual budget of $20 million. Due to reductions in the contributions from donors, it had been obliged to prepare a revised $15.4 million budget, which necessitated a cut in both personnel and activities. The Secretary-General urged Member States to continue their support for the Commission.

Honduras

Communications. In a letter [A/65/849] dated 23 May, Nicaragua transmitted to the Secretary-General a statement of the Presidents of Guatemala, El Salvador, Honduras and Nicaragua, adopted at a meeting (Managua, Honduras, 22 May) regarding the situation in Honduras. In the light of the Agreement for National Reconciliation and Consolidation of the Democratic System in the Republic of Honduras, signed in Cartagena de Indias, Colombia, on 22 May, the Presidents expressed support for the Agreement promoted by the Presidents of Venezuela and Colombia, which paved the way for the readmission of Honduras to the Organization of American States (oas) subsequent to its withdrawal during the democracy breakdown of 2009 [YUN 2009, p. 316], and its full participation in the Central American Integration System. They requested the countries of the Americas to support that decision, with a view to the early admission of Honduras to the oas and all international forums. The President of Nicaragua directed the immediate and full restoration and normalization of Nicaragua's relations with Honduras.

On 15 July [A/65/908], Honduras transmitted to the Secretary-General and the General Assembly the oas Resolution on "Participation of Honduras in the Organization of American States", adopted on 1 June, by which Honduras returned to that organization as a full member.

Nicaragua–Costa Rica

By a letter of 13 April [S/2011/243], the Secretary-General transmitted to the Security Council the texts on the Order of the International Court of Justice, made on 8 March, following an application filed by Costa Rica on 18 November 2010 [YUN 2010, p. 319]. The Order of the Court indicated provisional measures in the case concerning *Certain Activities carried out by Nicaragua in the Border Area (Costa Rica v. Nicaragua)*. It requested each party to refrain from sending to, or maintaining in the disputed territory, any personnel, whether civilian, police or security. The Court held that Costa Rica might dispatch personnel charged with the protection of the environment to the disputed territory on the condition that Costa Rica consult with the secretariat of the Ramsar Convention on Wetlands in regard to those actions, and give Nicaragua prior notice of them. The Court also called on the parties to refrain from any action that might aggravate or extend the dispute before the Court or make it more difficult to resolve, and to inform the Court as to their compliance with the provisional measures (see p. 1237).

On 22 December 2011, Nicaragua submitted a case to the Court against Costa Rica concerning the *Construction of a Road in Costa Rica along the San Juan River*, with regard to violations of Nicaraguan sovereignty and environmental damages to its territory. Nicaragua contended that Costa Rica was carrying out major construction work along most of the border area between the two countries with grave environmental consequences (see p. 1239).

Haiti

After a wrenching electoral process that lasted until April, the first peaceful transition from one democratically elected president to another in Haiti took place when Michel Joseph Martelly was sworn in as René Garcia Préval's successor on 14 May. A nearly five-month political crisis ensued, however, over the appointment of a Government. It was an early sign of the difficulties ahead for the new administration to build consensus in a divided Parliament on national priorities such as reconstruction, rule of law, security sector reform, elections and constitutional reforms. Against that volatile backdrop, a spreading cholera epidemic added new challenges to recovery efforts.

The United Nations Stabilization Mission in Haiti (minustah) [YUN 2004, p. 294] assisted the Government and the national police to assume responsibility for security in the country. It sought to facilitate a political agreement between the executive and legislative branches on a concrete agenda in critical areas. It also focused on building national capacity to maintain the rule of law, protect human rights and organize elections.

Political and security developments

Security Council action. The Security Council, by a press statement of 13 January [SC/10150], commemorated the one-year anniversary of the devastating earthquake that struck Haiti on 12 January 2010. The Council reaffirmed its support for Haiti and called for the swift disbursement of the remaining pledges to further the country's recovery.

Security Council consideration. On 20 January [S/PV.6471], the Under-Secretary-General for Peacekeeping Operations, Alain Le Roy, and the Under-Secretary-General for Humanitarian Affairs and Emergency Relief Coordinator, Valerie Amos, briefed the Council on the situation in Haiti. Mr. Le Roy reported that the overall security situation remained calm but fragile, given the ongoing electoral dispute. Ms. Amos said that 800,000 people remained in camps, and the lack of adequate water, sanitation and health-care infrastructure had allowed a cholera outbreak in October 2010 to spread [YUN 2010, p. 327]. The disease had affected almost 200,000 people, and more than 3,700 had died.

Report of Secretary-General. In accordance with Security Council resolution 1944(2010) [YUN 2010, p. 324], the Secretary-General in March submitted a report [S/2011/183] reviewing major developments since his previous report [YUN 2010, p. 328]. Following the first round of elections on 28 November 2010, marred by intimidation and fraud, many of the major cities, including Port-au-Prince, had experienced violence and civil unrest after the preliminary announcement of the results. The Organization of American States (OAS), responding to a request of President Préval, sent a team of technical experts to assist in the electoral verification process and the legal challenges to the preliminary results. The OAS mission began its work on 31 December and issued its report on 13 January 2011. The mission recommended the exclusion of certain *procès verbaux*, or tally sheets, leading to the placement of Michel Martelly of the Repons Peyizan party as second-ranking candidate, instead of Jude Célestin of the Inite ruling party, although the estimated difference between them was small, with some 3,000 votes separating the two. The Provisional Electoral Council accepted those findings and officially confirmed Mirlande Manigat (Rassemblement des démocrates nationaux progressistes) and Mr. Martelly as the first- and second-place winners of the first round. During the second round of elections on 20 March, which experienced only minor irregularities, election-related violence was limited to the regions. In most cases, MINUSTAH personnel were able to restore order, allowing voting to proceed.

With regard to the security situation, the public perception that MINUSTAH peacekeepers deployed in the Centre Department had possibly introduced cholera, negatively affected the image of the Mission and led to localized violent episodes of unrest, particularly against UN vehicles and premises. Despite difficulties in data collection and the underreporting of crimes, statistics compiled by MINUSTAH indicated a steady increase in serious crime, including murder, from 2009 to 2010. Rape and kidnapping were of great concern. Furthermore, gang activities grew in impoverished areas of Port-au-Prince, and crime, including sexual and gender-based violence, increased in the camps for internally displaced persons. While the operational performance of the national police had generally improved since the earthquake, the association of some officers with organized crime, including drug trafficking, kidnapping and armed robbery, remained a concern.

The Secretary-General concluded that Haiti had the chance to make a fresh start under a new Administration. A new leadership must try to heal the wounds of a deeply polarized society and provide jobs, education and services. The United Nations would work with the new Government and all sections of society to enhance the rule of law and to ensure that the population enjoy its fundamental rights.

Security Council consideration. The Council on 6 April held a high-level open debate on Haiti [S/PV.6510], chaired by the President of Colombia, Juan Manuel Santos Calderón. The Council had before it a concept paper by Colombia [S/2011/218] and the report of the Secretary-General (see above).

President Calderón stressed that the international community had a moral duty to assist in rebuilding the country, physically and institutionally. It should do so in a coordinated manner, seeking concrete and long-term achievements and leaving aside the chaos of well-intentioned but short-term cooperation without lasting outcomes. Haitian President Préval called on his country's newly elected leaders to govern in a spirit of peace, openness, inclusion, dialogue and respect for the rights of association and expression, and on the opposition to adopt a positive, cooperative attitude, even in their role as Government critic. The Secretary-General, pointing to Haiti's dysfunctional judicial system, overcrowded prisons, unreliable property records and non-transparent public expenditures, stressed the importance of rule-of-law reform. He further asked for additional financial support and large-scale investments in Haiti's water and sanitation system to prevent another cholera outbreak. The United Nations Special Envoy for Haiti, former United States President William J. Clinton, recommended long-term capacity-building of the Government, increased funding for education programmes, improvement of the housing situation, enhanced debris management, and the registration of all NGO projects with the Interim Haiti Recovery Commission. More than 30 representatives of Member States and the European Union participated in the debate, as well as the Secretary-General of the OAS, the President of the Inter-American Development Bank and the Special Representative of the Caribbean Community (CARICOM) for Haiti.

SECURITY COUNCIL ACTION

On 6 April [meeting 6510], following consultations among Security Council members, the President made statement **S/PRST/2011/7** on behalf of the Council:

> The Security Council reaffirms its strong commitment to the sovereignty, independence, territorial integrity and unity of Haiti, and emphasizes that the Government and people of Haiti bear the primary responsibility for the attainment of peace and stability and for the recovery efforts in Haiti. The Council acknowledges the contribution that the international community is making to support the stabilization process in Haiti, including the strengthening of its legislative, judicial and executive institutions.
>
> The Council recognizes the interconnected nature of the challenges in Haiti, and reaffirms that sustainable progress on security, institutional capacity-building, including rule of law, as well as consolidation of national government structures, democracy, promotion and protection of human rights and development, is mutually reinforcing. The Council appreciates the efforts made by the Government of Haiti and the international community to address these challenges.
>
> The Council welcomes the ongoing electoral process in Haiti and stresses the importance of its completion in a peaceful, credible and legitimate way, which will contribute to the consolidation of democracy, allow for the completion of constitutional reform and provide a strong basis for the continuing reconstruction efforts. The Council recognizes the important contribution of the United Nations Stabilization Mission in Haiti and the Organization of American States and other international, regional and subregional organizations in supporting the political process.
>
> The Council underlines that security and development are closely interlinked and mutually reinforcing, and reiterates the need for security to be accompanied by social and economic development. In this context, the Council acknowledges that rapid and tangible progress in the recovery and reconstruction of Haiti is fundamental to achieving lasting stability.
>
> The Council recognizes the various challenges in Haiti and stresses the fundamental role of the Mission in supporting the Haitian authorities in the creation of a secure and stable environment conducive to economic recovery, including by implementing labour-intensive projects, and the provision of basic services in Haiti.
>
> The Council expresses its concern about the situation of vulnerable groups, including internally displaced persons and children as victims of trafficking, and the increase of sexual and gender-based violence. In this regard, the Council encourages the Mission and the United Nations country team to continue assisting the Government of Haiti in providing adequate protection to the civilian population, with particular attention to the needs of internally displaced persons and other vulnerable groups, especially women and children.
>
> The Council stresses that there can be no genuine stability or sustainable development in Haiti without strengthening its democratic institutions. In this regard, the Council emphasizes the importance of promoting the rule of law in strengthening the Haitian institutions. The Council further reaffirms the responsibility of the Mission in supporting the Haitian State in the fields of rule of law, good governance, extension of State authority and the promotion and protection of human rights, in accordance with its mandate.
>
> The Council stresses the crucial importance of strengthening the Haitian National Police to ensure its ability to maintain law and order and to tackle violent crime, particularly sexual and gender-based violence, as well as gang violence and transnational organized crime. In this regard, the Council welcomes the continued support of the United Nations and the international community to the Haitian authorities and calls for continued support by the Mission in the vetting, mentoring and training of the Haitian National Police and corrections personnel and the intensification of cooperation to face this challenge, including assistance in counter-narcotics efforts and training in human rights.
>
> The Council recognizes Haiti's long-term recovery challenge and calls upon the international community to continue to support the Haitian authorities in order to ensure that the most vulnerable segments of the population have access to basic social services and justice.
>
> The Council acknowledges the efforts of the donor community and calls upon it to fulfil without delay all pledges, including those made at the International Donors' Conference entitled "Towards a New Future for Haiti", held in New York on 31 March 2010. The Council welcomes the work of the Interim Haiti Recovery Commission in focusing donor efforts on the top priority areas for recovery, and encourages all reconstruction donors and non-governmental and international organizations to continue to channel their efforts through the Commission.
>
> The Council reiterates the need for Member States and other stakeholders to continue to support the Haitian authorities in strengthening Haiti's core governance structures, implementing the Government of Haiti's Action Plan for National Recovery and Development of Haiti as an efficient and coherent framework.
>
> While acknowledging the willingness of the international community to continue to partner with the Government of Haiti in establishing future long-term security and development strategies that are mindful of a cohesive framework, the Council stresses the importance of consistent coordination and joint efforts among the Government of Haiti, the United Nations, the Interim Haiti Recovery Commission and other stakeholders with a view to producing sustainable results.
>
> The Council welcomes the willingness of regional and subregional organizations to contribute to the ongoing pro-

cess of stabilization, reconstruction and further consolidation of democracy in Haiti. In this respect, the Council calls upon the Mission to continue to work closely with such organizations, as well as international financial institutions and other stakeholders, among them the Organization of American States, the European Union, the Caribbean Community, the Union of South American Nations and the Inter-American Development Bank.

The Council expresses its appreciation to the Member States which support the recovery and stabilization process in Haiti, including the troop- and police-contributing countries of the Mission. The Council expresses its gratitude to the United Nations Special Envoy for Haiti, Mr. William J. Clinton, former President of the United States of America, the Special Representative of the Secretary-General for Haiti, Mr. Edmond Mulet, and the personnel of the Mission for their dedication and personal involvement in the ongoing stabilization and recovery efforts in Haiti in accordance with their respective mandates and in strong coordination with all United Nations entities and Member States.

Panel of experts on cholera outbreak

The independent panel of experts on the cholera outbreak in Haiti in October 2010 [YUN 2010, p. 327], appointed by the Secretary-General in January, completed its work on 4 May and presented its final report. The panel concluded that the outbreak had been caused by a confluence of circumstances, including the contamination of the Meye Tributary System of the Artibonite River with a pathogenic strain of the current South Asian-type *Vibrio cholerae bacterium*, poor water and sanitation conditions, and the widespread use of river water for washing, bathing, drinking and recreation, and that it was not the fault of—or due to deliberate action by—a group or individual. The Secretary-General subsequently convened a senior-level integrated task force to ensure follow-up to the panel's recommendations to the United Nations, the Government of Haiti and the international comunity to help privent the future introduction and spread of cholera.

Further developments

Ad Hoc Advisory Group. The Ad Hoc Advisory Group on Haiti, mandated by Economic and Social Council decision 2004/322 [YUN 2004, p. 939] to follow and advise on the long-term development of the country, in July submitted a report [E/2011/133] based principally on the findings of the Group's visit to Haiti (15–18 June) (see p. 899).

On 28 July (**decision 2011/268**), the Economic and Social Council requested the Advisory Group to report on its activities in support of the recovery, reconstruction and development of Haiti to the Council's substantive session of 2012.

Report of Secretary-General. In August [S/2011/540], the Secretary-General reported that—for the first time in its history—Haiti had experienced a peaceful transfer of power from one democratically elected president to another from the opposition. Following his victory in the second-round presidential run-off, which was held on 20 March, Michel Martelly was sworn in as René Préval's successor on 14 May. The political stalemate between the President and Parliament, however, risked undermining political progress and exacerbating the security situation, and posed a major obstacle to the attainment of the mandated objectives of MINUSTAH. The appeal board of the Provisional Electoral Council overturned the results for 17 seats in the lower house and 2 in the Senate. The overwhelming majority of those decisions favoured the former governing party, Inite, raising concern among national and international observers, whereupon the joint electoral observation mission of the OAS and CARICOM examined those cases. In 15 cases the results were upheld, following the recommendation of the OAS-CARICOM mission, and new results were published on 18 June. The executive branch subsequently halted the publication of the results in the four remaining cases.

The overall security situation remained relatively calm, albeit fragile, with sporadic instances of civil unrest throughout the country linked to the electoral process. Since the earthquake, there had been an increase in all major crime categories, as well as in minor categories such as theft, robbery and assault. While the incidence of violent demonstrations had decreased significantly, the risk of civil unrest remained high. MINUSTAH military and police personnel continued to play a vital role in maintaining overall security and stability, particularly during the unpredictable post-electoral period. Although the performance of the national police was slowly improving, the institution was not in a position to assume full responsibility for the provision of internal security.

As of June, there were approximately 634,000 internally displaced persons living at 1,001 sites. The construction of at least 73,000 transitional shelters had been completed. Since early 2011, humanitarian partners had distributed 117,200 tents, 1,185,052 tarpaulins and 2.5 million relief items such as blankets, mats and kitchen sets.

After an initial peak in November 2010, the cholera epidemic reached a second peak in late May/early June 2011 as a result of heavy rains, causing more than 5,500 deaths and over 360,000 cumulative cases by the end of May. The humanitarian community, including the United Nations Children's Fund (UNICEF) and the World Health Organisation (WHO) as well as the Pan American Health Organization, and MINUSTAH continued to support the national response to the outbreak. As of July, there were 34 cholera treatment centres, 189 treatment units and 858 oral rehydration points throughout the country. Following the surge in the strength of MINUSTAH to address the aftermath of the earthquake [YUN 2010, p. 320], the Secretary-General deemed that a partial drawdown of the Mission's surge capabilities would be unlikely to undermine the progress made on the security front and would not affect the ability of MINUSTAH to carry out its functions. He therefore recommended that the Security Council reduce the Mission's authorized military strength by 1,600 personnel, and the authorized police strength by approximately 1,150 formed police unit officers. He also recommended extending the mandate of the Mission until 15 October 2012.

Security Council consideration. On 16 September [S/PV.6618], the Head of MINUSTAH, Mariano Fernández Amunátegui, briefed the Council on the situation in Haiti. He underlined the importance of political will and cooperation to enable the country to take on the full weight of security and self-governance, including the rule of law, and stressed the need for the appointment of a Prime Minister. Some 634,000 people remained displaced, funding for reconstruction had slowed, and high food and fuel prices, as well as the continuing cholera epidemic, continued to have an impact on the population.

SECURITY COUNCIL ACTION

On 14 October [meeting 6631], the Security Council unanimously adopted **resolution 2012(2011)**. The draft [S/2011/637] was submitted by 11 Member States.

The Security Council,

Reaffirming its previous resolutions on Haiti, in particular resolutions 1542(2004) of 30 April 2004, 1576(2004) of 29 November 2004, 1608(2005) of 22 June 2005, 1658(2006) of 14 February 2006, 1702(2006) of 15 August 2006, 1743(2007) of 15 February 2007, 1780(2007) of 15 October 2007, 1840(2008) of 14 October 2008, 1892(2009) of 13 October 2009, 1908(2010) of 19 January 2010, 1927(2010) of 4 June 2010 and 1944(2010) of 14 October 2010,

Reaffirming its strong commitment to the sovereignty, independence, territorial integrity and unity of Haiti,

Recognizing that Haiti has made considerable strides since the tragic earthquake of 12 January 2010, in particular that, for the first time in its history, Haiti has experienced a peaceful transfer of power between one democratically elected president and another from the opposition,

Recognizing also, as has the Government of Haiti, that the overall security situation, while fragile, has improved since the adoption of resolutions 1908(2010), 1927(2010) and 1944(2010), allowing a partial drawdown of the military and police capabilities of the United Nations Stabilization Mission in Haiti as the first step to ending the temporary surge capacities decided by the Security Council after the earthquake, while continuing to adapt the strength of the Mission without undermining the security and stability of Haiti, and recognizing the importance of condition-based and security-related decisions about the future of the Mission,

Welcoming the appointment of a Prime Minister and a Supreme Court President, and calling upon all the relevant political actors in Haiti, in particular the executive and legislative branches, to engage in an effective dialogue towards a political agreement that would consolidate a concrete forward agenda for progress in key areas, such as Haiti's security, budget, recovery and development priorities, elections and electoral reform, including the participation of women in the electoral processes and the completion of constitutional reform,

Acknowledging that Haiti continues to face significant humanitarian challenges, with more than 600,000 internally displaced persons still dependent on assistance for their basic survival, an ongoing cholera epidemic and an extreme vulnerability to natural disasters,

Emphasizing that progress in the recovery and reconstruction of Haiti, as well as in Haiti's social and economic development, including through effective international development assistance and increased Haitian institutional capacity to benefit from this assistance, is crucial to achieving lasting and sustainable stability, and reiterating the need for security to be accompanied by social and economic development,

Stressing the leading role of the Government of Haiti in the post-disaster recovery and reconstruction process, including risk reduction and preparedness efforts, and underlining the necessity for increased coordination and complementary efforts among all United Nations actors and other relevant stakeholders in assisting the Government in this regard, as well as in the overall support to Haiti's social and economic development,

Recognizing the work done so far by the Interim Haiti Recovery Commission, to which the United Nations continues to provide coherent policy advice and technical support, and also by the Haiti Reconstruction Fund, which both play a central role in the medium- and long-term reconstruction efforts in Haiti,

Commending the wide range of recovery efforts undertaken by the United Nations system in Haiti, especially the United Nations-supported housing and debris removal programmes and the successful use of military engineering units of the Mission to address urgent needs in the immediate aftermath of the 12 January 2010 earthquake, emphasizing the importance of increasing the participation of Haitian authorities and international and civilian actors in these tasks,

Urging donors to fulfil without delay the pledges made at the International Donors' Conference entitled "Towards a New Future for Haiti", held in New York on 31 March 2010, in order to continue producing tangible and visible reconstruction dividends, and underlining national responsibility to provide clear guidance and priorities,

Emphasizing the role of regional organizations in the ongoing process of stabilization and reconstruction of Haiti, and calling upon the Mission to continue to work closely with regional and subregional organizations, international financial institutions and other stakeholders, in particular the Organization of American States and the Caribbean Community,

Recognizing the interconnected nature of the challenges in Haiti, reaffirming that sustainable progress on security, the rule of law and institutional reform, national reconciliation and development is mutually reinforcing, and welcoming the continuing efforts of the Government of Haiti and the international community to address these challenges,

Expressing its concern that criminal gangs remain a threat to the stability of Haiti,

Recognizing that the overall security situation has improved, but further expressing its concern that trends since the earthquake reveal an increase in all major categories of crime, including murder, rape and kidnapping, in Port-au-Prince and the West Department,

Acknowledging that sexual and gender-based violence remains a serious concern, particularly in marginalized districts of Port-au-Prince, camps for internally displaced persons and remote areas of the country,

Welcoming the efforts of the Haitian National Police to increase patrolling and enhance its presence and direct engagement with the population, which may have contributed to an increase in the reporting of crimes,

Recognizing that strengthening national human rights institutions and respect for human rights, due process, combating criminality and sexual and gender-based violence, and putting an end to impunity are essential to ensuring the rule of law and security in Haiti,

Recognizing also the critical role of the Mission in ensuring stability and security in Haiti and recognizing further the complementary roles that the Mission and the United Nations country team have fulfilled to date in assisting Haiti in its recovery efforts, reaffirming the authority of the Special Representative of the Secretary-General for Haiti in the coordination and conduct of all activities of United Nations agencies, funds and programmes in Haiti, and stressing the importance of the Special Representative ensuring further coordination between the Mission and the United Nations country team in connection with the aspects of their respective mandates that are correlated, with special attention to the strengthening of Haitian institutional capabilities, including in the areas of reconstruction and development,

Commending the Mission for continuing to assist the Government of Haiti to ensure a secure and stable environment, expressing its gratitude to the personnel of the Mission and to their countries, and paying tribute to those injured or killed in the line of duty,

Welcoming the commitment by the Government of Haiti to strengthen the rule of law, and calling upon the Government, in coordination with the international community, to continue to advance security sector reform, including, in particular, the development and implementation of the next five-year Haitian National Police development plan, which will take effect after December 2011, underscoring the need for the Government, with the assistance of the international community, as requested, to take steps to ensure that the Haitian National Police meets the benchmarks for reform contained in the plan, and encouraging the Government, with the support of the Mission, to regularly inform the Haitian people of progress towards these benchmarks,

Underscoring the importance of the Haitian National Police being adequately funded, and encouraging the Government of Haiti to take advantage of the support being provided by the international community to guarantee the provision of adequate security for the Haitian people,

Underlining the need to further strengthen the Haitian judicial and correctional systems, in order to support a more integrated and cohesive Haitian security sector, welcoming the improvements in the judiciary towards the availability of adequate human and material capabilities, and acknowledging that the attendant human rights concerns that still remain in the correctional system, such as prolonged pretrial detentions, prison overcrowding and access to health care services, are significant challenges to sustainable administrative reforms,

Welcoming the efforts of the former President of the United States of America, Mr. William J. Clinton, as the United Nations Special Envoy for Haiti, to enhance the United Nations recovery response, in both humanitarian and development operations as well as tracking aid pledges and disbursement of funds, liaising with the Interim Haiti Recovery Commission and the international financial institutions, and working to ensure coherence across United Nations operations in Haiti, and noting the importance of regular reporting on these activities,

Stressing the importance of a strong coordination among the Office of the Special Envoy and other United Nations entities and Member States, and stressing the need for coordination among all international actors on the ground,

Underlining the need for the implementation of highly effective and visible labour-intensive projects that help to create jobs and deliver basic social services,

Welcoming the report of the Secretary-General of 25 August 2011,

Determining that the situation in Haiti continues to constitute a threat to international peace and security in the region, despite the progress achieved thus far,

Acting under Chapter VII of the Charter of the United Nations, as described in section I of paragraph 7 of resolution 1542(2004),

1. *Decides* to extend the mandate of the United Nations Stabilization Mission in Haiti, as contained in resolutions 1542(2004), 1608(2005), 1702(2006), 1743(2007), 1780(2007), 1840(2008), 1892(2009), 1908(2010), 1927(2010) and 1944(2010), until 15 October 2012, with the intention of further renewal;

2. *Also decides* that the overall force levels of the Mission will consist of up to 7,340 troops of all ranks and a police component of up to 3,241 personnel, consistent with paragraph 50 of the report of the Secretary-General;

3. *Affirms* that future adjustments to the force configuration should be based on the overall security situation on the ground, taking into account the impact of social and political realities on the stability and security of Haiti, the increasing development of Haitian State capabilities, including the ongoing strengthening of the Haitian National Police, and the national authorities' increasing exercise of the Haitian State's responsibility for the maintenance of stability and security in the country;

4. *Recognizes* the ownership and primary responsibility of the Government and the people of Haiti over all aspects of the country's stabilization, welcomes the steps taken by the Mission to provide logistical and technical expertise, within available means, to assist the Government of Haiti, as requested, to continue operations to build the capacity of its rule of law institutions at the national and local levels and to speed up the implementation of the Government's

resettlement strategy for displaced persons, in the knowledge that such measures are temporary and will be phased out as Haitian capacity grows, and calls upon the Mission to proceed swiftly with activities in this regard as recommended by the Secretary-General;

5. *Welcomes* the efforts of the Government of Haiti to build institutional capacity in security and the rule of law at all levels, including through decentralization efforts, and calls upon the Mission, consistent with its mandate, and other relevant actors to continue to provide support to strengthen self-sustaining security sector State institutions, especially outside Port-au-Prince, with a view to further enhancing the ability of the Government to extend State authority throughout Haiti, ensure greater countrywide presence of the State, and promote good governance at local levels;

6. *Recognizes* that, following the holding of presidential and legislative elections, a stable political and institutional environment is crucial for stability and the progress of recovery and reconstruction efforts, reaffirms its call upon the Mission to support the political process under way in Haiti, including through the offices of the Special Representative of the Secretary-General for Haiti, and encourages the Mission to continue its support for the upcoming partial legislative and local elections and to coordinate international electoral assistance to Haiti in cooperation with other international stakeholders, including the Organization of American States and the Caribbean Community;

7. *Welcomes* ongoing efforts by the Mission to increase coordination with the Haitian National Police and to strengthen the capacity of the National Police in order for the National Police to take full responsibility for Haiti's security needs, including border management and security efforts in order to assess threats and deter illicit activities, and calls upon Haiti's international and regional partners to intensify their assistance to the Government of Haiti in this regard, as requested;

8. *Encourages* the Haitian authorities to take full advantage of that support, notably in enhancing Haitian National Police capacity, modernizing key legislation and in the implementation of the national justice reform plan, to take the necessary steps, including nominations, that will allow superior judicial institutions to function adequately, and to address the issue of prolonged pretrial detentions and prison overcrowding, with special regard to women and children;

9. *Calls upon* the Government of Haiti, with the support of the Mission, to prioritize the development and implementation of the next five-year Haitian National Police development plan, which will succeed the current reform plan upon its expiration in December 2011, and requests the Mission, with additional support, as appropriate and within existing resources, from locally employed interpreters to continue to support vetting, mentoring and training of the police and corrections personnel and strengthening the institutional and operational capacities of the correctional services, as well as to continue to provide technical guidance to donor-funded projects, as requested, for the rehabilitation and construction of police and correctional facilities;

10. *Welcomes* the resumption of training and promotions of recruits for the Haitian National Police, stresses the necessity of accountability and a robust vetting process, and underscores the vital importance of maintaining and increasing the support of the international community for capacity-building of the National Police, particularly through enhanced mentoring and training of specialized units;

11. *Encourages* the Mission, in cooperation with the appropriate international actors, to assist the Government of Haiti in tackling the risk of a resurgence in gang violence, organized crime, drug trafficking and trafficking in children;

12. *Calls upon* all donors and international and non-governmental organizations to coordinate their efforts and to work closely with the Interim Haiti Recovery Commission, or its successor institution, in order to strengthen the capacity of the Government of Haiti to fulfil the Action Plan for National Recovery and Development of Haiti;

13. *Requests* the United Nations country team, and calls upon all actors, to complement security and development operations undertaken by the Government of Haiti with the support of the Mission with activities aimed at effectively improving the living conditions of the concerned populations, in particular women and children;

14. *Requests* the Mission to continue to implement quick-impact projects that further enhance the trust of the Haitian population towards the Mission;

15. *Encourages* the Mission to continue assisting the Government of Haiti in providing adequate protection to the civilian population, with particular attention to the needs of internally displaced persons and other vulnerable groups, especially women and children, including through joint community policing in the camps, along with strengthened mechanisms to address sexual and gender-based violence, and recalls Security Council resolution 1894(2009) of 11 November 2009 and requests the Secretary-General to develop, in close consultation with the Government of Haiti, troop- and police-contributing countries and other relevant actors, a comprehensive plan for the protection of civilians;

16. *Strongly condemns* the grave violations against children affected by armed violence, as well as widespread rape and other sexual abuse of women and girls, and calls upon the Government of Haiti, with the support of the Mission and the United Nations country team, to continue to promote and protect the rights of women and children as set out in Council resolutions 1325(2000) of 31 October 2000, 1612(2005) of 26 July 2005, 1820(2008) of 19 June 2008, 1882(2009) of 4 August 2009, 1888(2009) of 30 September 2009 and 1889(2009) of 5 October 2009;

17. *Requests* the Secretary-General to continue to take the measures necessary to ensure full compliance of all Mission personnel with the United Nations zero-tolerance policy on sexual exploitation and abuse, and to keep the Council informed, and urges troop- and police-contributing countries to ensure that acts involving their personnel are properly investigated and punished;

18. *Reaffirms* the human rights mandate of the Mission, recognizes that respect for human rights, in particular attention to individual accountability for grave violations under past governments, is essential to the stability of Haiti, urges the Government of Haiti to ensure the respect and protection of human rights by the Haitian National Police and the judiciary, and calls upon the Mission to provide monitoring and support in this regard;

19. *Welcomes* the important work done by the Mission in support of urgent needs in Haiti, encourages the Mission, within its mandate, to continue to make full use of existing means and capabilities, including its engineers, with a view to further enhancing stability in the country, requests the Mission to develop its longer-term planning, and further requests the Secretary-General to include in his next report an indication of the Mission's plans to encourage greater Haitian ownership of reconstruction activity in Haiti;

20. *Requests* the Mission to continue to pursue its expanded community violence reduction approach, adapting the programme to the changing requirements of the post-earthquake Haitian context with a particular focus on the displaced and those living in violence-affected neighbourhoods;

21. *Also requests* the Mission to continue to support the Haitian authorities in their efforts to control the flow of small arms, including labour-intensive projects, the development of a weapons registry, the revision of current laws on importation and possession of arms, reform of the weapons permit system and the development and implementation of a national community policing doctrine;

22. *Underscores* the importance of planning documents for the military and police components of the Mission, such as the concept of operations and rules of engagement, being regularly updated, as appropriate, and in line with the provisions of all its relevant resolutions, and requests the Secretary-General to report on them to the Council and troop- and police-contributing countries;

23. *Requests* the Secretary-General to report to the Council on the implementation of the mandate of the Mission, semi-annually and no later than forty-five days prior to its expiration;

24. *Also requests* the Secretary-General to include in his reports a comprehensive assessment of threats to security in Haiti and give particular attention to the protective environment for all, in particular women and children, and progress in the sustainable resettlement of displaced persons, and to propose, as appropriate, options to reconfigure the composition of the Mission;

25. *Decides* to remain seized of the matter.

Year-end developments. In a later report [S/2012/128 & Corr.1], the Secretary-General said that on 16 September, four months into the term of President Martelly, the Chamber of Deputies unanimously voted to ratify his third nominee for Prime Minister, Garry Conille. The Senate ratified President Martelly's choice shortly thereafter, following intense debate and negotiation over the composition of the Cabinet. Mr. Conille and his Cabinet, which included several confidants of President Martelly, were sworn in on 18 October.

Political controversies contributed to a strained relationship between the executive and legislative branches. One concerned the arrest, in October, despite his parliamentary immunity, of Deputy Arnel Bélizaire (West Department), which in November led to the resignation, under intense parliamentary pressure, of the Minister of Justice, Josué Pierre-Louis.

In line with his campaign promise to re-establish the Haitian army, President Martelly on 16 September unveiled a preliminary plan outlining the mission and strength of the new army, and established a civil commission reviewing the reinstatement of the armed forces by presidential decree in December. On 21 December, on the occasion of a visit to Haiti by the Club de Madrid, the President further announced his intention to advance in the process of publishing the constitutional amendments.

The overall security situation remained relatively stable, albeit fragile, owing to sporadic instances of civil unrest linked primarily to political uncertainty and socioeconomic grievances. The incidence of politically motivated violence diminished significantly. There was no significant change in the incidence of crimes such as murder, rape and kidnapping compared with the previous reporting period. MINUSTAH military and police personnel continued to play a vital role in maintaining overall security and stability.

General Assembly action. On 24 December, the Assembly decided that the item on the situation of democracy and human rights in Haiti would remain for consideration during its resumed sixty-sixth (2012) session (**decision 66/557**).

MINUSTAH

In 2011, the United Nations Stabilization Mission in Haiti (MINUSTAH), established by Security Council resolution 1542(2004) [YUN 2004, p. 294], maintained its focus on ensuring a secure and stable environment, supporting the electoral process and reform of rule-of-law structures, strengthening State institutions, providing humanitarian and development assistance, and protecting and promoting human rights. MINUSTAH was based in Port-au-Prince. By resolution 2012(2011), the Council extended MINUSTAH's mandate until 15 October 2012.

Appointments. On 23 March [S/2011/187], the Secretary-General informed the Security Council of his intention to appoint Major General Luiz Eduardo Ramos Pereira (Brazil) as Force Commander of the Mission, replacing Major General Luiz Guilherme Paul Cruz (Brazil), who completed his assignment on 31 March. The Council took note of the appointment on 25 March [S/2011/188].

On 12 May [S/2011/301], the Secretary-General informed the Council of his intention to appoint Mariano Fernández (Chile) as his Special Representative and Head of MINUSTAH, replacing Edmond Mulet (Guatemala), who would complete his assignment on 31 May. The Council took note of that intention on 13 May [S/2011/302].

Activities

During 2011, the Secretary-General reported to the Security Council on MINUSTAH activities and developments in Haiti for the periods from 1 September 2010 to 20 March 2011 [S/2011/183] and from 24 March to 31 August [S/2011/540]. A later report [S/2012/128 & Corr.1] covered activities for the remainder of the year. In addition to political and security aspects, the reports summarized MINUSTAH activities dealing with electoral support, military and police, protection of vulnerable groups, community violence reduction, support for State institutions, rule of law, justice, corrections, human rights, gender, child protection, HIV/AIDS, quick-impact projects, the conduct and discipline of UN personnel, public information and outreach, and mission support.

Financing

In February [A/65/703 & Corr.1], the Secretary-General submitted the performance report on the budget of MINUSTAH for the period from 1 July 2009 to 30 June 2010, which showed expenditures of $713,740,600 against an appropriation of $732,393,000, leaving an unencumbered balance of $18,652,400 and other income and adjustments in the amount of $8,103,100. The Advisory Committee on Administrative and Budgetary Questions (ACABQ) [A/65/743/Add.15] recommended that the unencumbered balance as well as other income and adjustments be credited to Member States.

In March, the Secretary-General submitted a report [A/65/776] presenting the proposed budget for MINUSTAH for the period from 1 July 2011 to 30 June 2012, which amounted to $810,305,000. The budget provided for the deployment of 8,940 military contingent personnel, 1,451 UN police officers, 2,940 formed police personnel, 668 international staff, 1,532 national staff and 277 United Nations Volunteers, including temporary positions. ACABQ [A/65/743/Add.15] recommended that the General Assembly appropriate an amount of $793,305,000. It further recommended that the amount of $230,314,400 be assessed for the period from 1 July to 15 October 2011 and that the amount of $562,990,600 be assessed for the period from 16 October 2011 to 30 June 2012 at a monthly rate of $66,108,750, should the Security Council decide to extend the Mission's mandate.

GENERAL ASSEMBLY ACTION

On 30 June [meeting 106], the General Assembly, on the recommendation of the Fifth (Administrative and Budgetary) Committee [A/65/655/Add.1], adopted **resolution 65/256 B** without vote [agenda item 153].

B

Financing of the United Nations Stabilization Mission in Haiti

The General Assembly,

Having considered the reports of the Secretary-General on the financing of the United Nations Stabilization Mission in Haiti and the related report of the Advisory Committee on Administrative and Budgetary Questions,

Recalling Security Council resolution 1529(2004) of 29 February 2004, by which the Council declared its readiness to establish a United Nations stabilization force to support continuation of a peaceful and constitutional political process and the maintenance of a secure and stable environment in Haiti,

Recalling also Security Council resolution 1542(2004) of 30 April 2004, by which the Council decided to establish the United Nations Stabilization Mission in Haiti for an initial period of six months, and the subsequent resolutions by which the Council extended the mandate of the Mission, the latest of which was resolution 1944(2010) of 14 October 2010, by which the Council decided to extend the mandate of the Mission until 15 October 2011 and to maintain the current overall force levels, which consist of a military component of up to 8,940 troops of all ranks and of a police component of up to 4,391 police,

Recalling further its resolution 58/315 of 1 July 2004,

Recalling its resolution 58/311 of 18 June 2004 on the financing of the Mission and its subsequent resolutions thereon, the latest of which was resolution 65/256 A of 24 December 2010,

Reaffirming the general principles underlying the financing of United Nations peacekeeping operations, as stated in General Assembly resolutions 1874(S-IV) of 27 June 1963, 3101(XXVIII) of 11 December 1973 and 55/235 of 23 December 2000,

Mindful of the fact that it is essential to provide the Mission with the financial resources necessary to enable it to fulfil its responsibilities under the relevant resolutions of the Security Council,

1. *Requests* the Secretary-General to entrust the Head of Mission with the task of formulating future budget proposals in full accordance with the provisions of General Assembly resolutions 59/296 of 22 June 2005, 60/266 of 30 June 2006, 61/276 of 29 June 2007, 64/269 of 24 June 2010 and 65/289 of 30 June 2011, as well as other relevant resolutions;

2. *Takes note* of the status of contributions to the United Nations Stabilization Mission in Haiti as at 30 April 2011, including the contributions outstanding in the amount of 129.8 million United States dollars, representing some 4 per cent of the total assessed contributions, notes with concern that only forty-six Member States have paid their assessed contributions in full, and urges all other Member States, in particular those in arrears, to ensure payment of their outstanding assessed contributions;

3. *Expresses its appreciation* to those Member States which have paid their assessed contributions in full, and urges all other Member States to make every possible effort to ensure payment of their assessed contributions to the Mission in full;

4. *Expresses concern* at the financial situation with regard to peacekeeping activities, in particular as regards the reimbursements to troop contributors that bear additional burdens owing to overdue payments by Member States of their assessments;

5. *Also expresses concern* at the delay experienced by the Secretary-General in deploying and providing adequate resources to some recent peacekeeping missions, in particular those in Africa;

6. *Emphasizes* that all future and existing peacekeeping missions shall be given equal and non-discriminatory treatment in respect of financial and administrative arrangements;

7. *Also emphasizes* that all peacekeeping missions shall be provided with adequate resources for the effective and efficient discharge of their respective mandates;

8. *Requests* the Secretary-General to ensure that proposed peacekeeping budgets are based on the relevant legislative mandates;

9. *Endorses* the conclusions and recommendations contained in the report of the Advisory Committee on Administrative and Budgetary Questions, subject to the provisions of the present resolution, and requests the Secretary-General to ensure their full implementation;

10. *Affirms* that qualified candidates who are of Haitian origin and are holders of other nationalities are eligible to apply for international posts in the Mission, in compliance with the relevant United Nations legislative mandates and guidelines on recruitment and selection;

11. *Expresses deep concern* over the continuing high vacancy rate in the Mission, especially in the National temporary positions, and its negative impact on the work of the Mission;

12. *Requests* the Secretary-General to keep under review the Mission requirements for the "tiger team";

13. *Regrets* that the share of procurement activities awarded to local vendors has substantially decreased during the current financial year, and reiterates its request to the Secretary-General to ensure that the Mission increases procurement opportunities for local vendors;

14. *Recalls* paragraph 41 of the report of the Advisory Committee, and requests the Secretary-General to ensure the efficient, expeditious and full implementation of the total amount allocated to quick-impact projects for the period from 1 July 2011 to 30 June 2012 in order, inter alia, to contribute to the recovery effort and foster better relations with the local communities;

15. *Requests* the Secretary-General, in submitting his next budget proposal for the Mission, to fully review current needs assessments on the ground regarding quick-impact projects, taking into account the related guidelines of the Department of Peacekeeping Operations of the Secretariat on quick-impact projects;

16. *Recalls* paragraph 7 of section III of resolution 64/269;

17. *Reaffirms* the important role of the expanded community violence reduction approach in the post-earthquake context, in particular in assisting the displaced people and those living in violence-affected neighbourhoods;

18. *Requests* the Secretary-General to strengthen coordination among the Mission, the United Nations country team and other United Nations entities, including in addressing the root causes of unexpected emergencies, such as the situation resulting from the cholera outbreak;

19. *Also requests* the Secretary-General to intensify his efforts to put into effect measures to mitigate the environmental impact of the Mission on Haiti;

20. *Further requests* the Secretary-General to ensure the full implementation of the relevant provisions of resolutions 59/296, 60/266, 61/276, 64/269 and 65/289;

21. *Requests* the Secretary-General to take all action necessary to ensure that the Mission is administered with a maximum of efficiency and economy;

22. *Notes* that the overall level of appropriation has been adjusted in accordance with the terms of resolution 65/289;

Financial performance report for the period from 1 July 2009 to 30 June 2010

23. *Takes note* of the report of the Secretary-General on the financial performance of the Mission for the period from 1 July 2009 to 30 June 2010;

Budget estimates for the period from 1 July 2011 to 30 June 2012

24. *Decides* to appropriate to the Special Account for the United Nations Stabilization Mission in Haiti the amount of 844,258,700 dollars for the period from 1 July 2011 to 30 June 2012, inclusive of 793,517,100 dollars for the maintenance of the Mission, 42,997,600 dollars for the support account for peacekeeping operations and 7,744,000 dollars for the United Nations Logistics Base at Brindisi, Italy;

Financing of the appropriation

25. *Also decides* to apportion among Member States the amount of 246,242,100 dollars for the period from 1 July to 15 October 2011, in accordance with the levels updated in General Assembly resolution 64/249 of 24 December 2009, and taking into account the scale of assessments for 2011, as set out in Assembly resolution 64/248 of 24 December 2009;

26. *Further decides* that, in accordance with the provisions of its resolution 973(X) of 15 December 1955, there shall be set off against the apportionment among Member States, as provided for in paragraph 25 above, their respective share in the Tax Equalization Fund of 6,569,900 dollars, comprising the estimated staff assessment income of 5,270,400 dollars approved for the Mission, the prorated share of 1,062,200 dollars of the estimated staff assessment income approved for the support account and the prorated share of 237,300 dollars of the estimated staff assessment income approved for the United Nations Logistics Base;

27. *Decides* to apportion among Member States the amount of 598,016,600 dollars for the period from 16 October 2011 to 30 June 2012 at a monthly rate of 70,354,892 dollars, in accordance with the levels updated in its resolution 64/249, and taking into account the scale of assessments for 2011 and 2012, as set out in its resolution 64/248, subject to a decision of the Security Council to extend the mandate of the Mission;

28. *Also decides* that, in accordance with the provisions of its resolution 973(X), there shall be set off against the apportionment among Member States, as provided for

in paragraph 27 above, their respective share in the Tax Equalization Fund of 15,955,400 dollars, comprising the estimated staff assessment income of 12,799,600 dollars approved for the Mission, the prorated share of 2,579,500 dollars of the estimated staff assessment income approved for the support account and the prorated share of 576,300 dollars of the estimated staff assessment income approved for the United Nations Logistics Base;

29. *Further decides* that, for Member States that have fulfilled their financial obligations to the Mission, there shall be set off against the apportionment, as provided for in paragraph 25 above, their respective share of the unencumbered balance and other income in the total amount of 26,755,500 dollars in respect of the financial period ended 30 June 2010, in accordance with the levels updated in its resolution 64/249, and taking into account the scale of assessments for 2010, as set out in its resolution 64/248;

30. *Decides* that, for Member States that have not fulfilled their financial obligations to the Mission, there shall be set off against their outstanding obligations their respective share of the unencumbered balance and other income in the total amount of 26,755,500 dollars in respect of the financial period ended 30 June 2010, in accordance with the scheme set out in paragraph 29 above;

31. *Also decides* that the increase in the estimated staff assessment income of 85,500 dollars in respect of the financial period ended 30 June 2010 shall be added to the credits from the amount of 26,755,500 dollars referred to in paragraphs 29 and 30 above;

32. *Emphasizes* that no peacekeeping mission shall be financed by borrowing funds from other active peacekeeping missions;

33. *Encourages* the Secretary-General to continue to take additional measures to ensure the safety and security of all personnel participating in the Mission under the auspices of the United Nations, bearing in mind paragraphs 5 and 6 of Security Council resolution 1502(2003) of 26 August 2003;

34. *Invites* voluntary contributions to the Mission in cash and in the form of services and supplies acceptable to the Secretary-General, to be administered, as appropriate, in accordance with the procedure and practices established by the General Assembly;

35. *Decides* to include in the provisional agenda of its sixty-sixth session the item entitled "Financing of the United Nations Stabilization Mission in Haiti".

On 24 December, the Assembly decided that the agenda item on the financing of MINUSTAH would remain for consideration during its resumed sixty-sixth (2012) session (**decision 66/557**).

Other issues

Cuba–United States

In response to General Assembly resolution 65/6 [YUN 2010, p. 334], the Secretary-General in August submitted a report [A/66/114] on information received as at 11 July from 141 States, the European Union and 26 UN bodies and specialized agencies on the implementation of that resolution. The resolution called on States to refrain from the unilateral application of economic and trade measures against other States, and urged them to repeal or invalidate such measures.

Communications. On 18 February, Cuba transmitted a letter [A/65/750] to the Secretary-General with regard to United Nations Development Programme funds, amounting to $3 million and intended for health projects in Cuba, which had been frozen by the Office of Foreign Assets Control of the United States Department of the Treasury. In a letter of 25 August [A/65/935], Cuba transmitted a statement in reference to the inclusion of the country in the list of alleged "State sponsors of international terrorism" by the United States Department of State. On 27 October [A/66/534], Cuba transmitted the Final Declaration of the Eighth Forum of Cuban Civil Society against the Embargo, adopted in Havana on 19 October.

GENERAL ASSEMBLY ACTION

On 25 October [meeting 41], the General Assembly adopted **resolution 66/6** [draft: A/66/L.4] by recorded vote (186-2-3) [agenda item 41].

Necessity of ending the economic, commercial and financial embargo imposed by the United States of America against Cuba

The General Assembly,

Determined to encourage strict compliance with the purposes and principles enshrined in the Charter of the United Nations,

Reaffirming, among other principles, the sovereign equality of States, non-intervention and non-interference in their internal affairs and freedom of international trade and navigation, which are also enshrined in many international legal instruments,

Recalling the statements of the Heads of State or Government at the Ibero-American Summits concerning the need to eliminate the unilateral application of economic and trade measures by one State against another that affect the free flow of international trade,

Concerned about the continued promulgation and application by Member States of laws and regulations, such as that promulgated on 12 March 1996 known as "the Helms-Burton Act", the extraterritorial effects of which affect the sovereignty of other States, the legitimate interests of entities or persons under their jurisdiction and the freedom of trade and navigation,

Taking note of declarations and resolutions of different intergovernmental forums, bodies and Governments that express the rejection by the international community and public opinion of the promulgation and application of measures of the kind referred to above,

Recalling its resolutions 47/19 of 24 November 1992, 48/16 of 3 November 1993, 49/9 of 26 October 1994, 50/10 of 2 November 1995, 51/17 of 12 November 1996, 52/10 of 5 November 1997, 53/4 of 14 October 1998, 54/21 of 9 November 1999, 55/20 of 9 November 2000, 56/9 of 27 November 2001, 57/11 of 12 November 2002, 58/7 of 4 November 2003, 59/11 of 28 October 2004, 60/12 of 8 November 2005, 61/11 of 8 November 2006, 62/3 of 30 October 2007, 63/7 of 29 October 2008, 64/6 of 28 October 2009 and 65/6 of 26 October 2010,

Concerned that, since the adoption of its resolutions 47/19, 48/16, 49/9, 50/10, 51/17, 52/10, 53/4, 54/21, 55/20, 56/9, 57/11, 58/7, 59/11, 60/12, 61/11, 62/3, 63/7, 64/6 and 65/6, further measures of that nature aimed at strengthening and extending the economic, commercial and financial embargo against Cuba continue to be promulgated and applied, and concerned also about the adverse effects of such measures on the Cuban people and on Cuban nationals living in other countries,

1. *Takes note* of the report of the Secretary-General on the implementation of resolution 65/6;

2. *Reiterates its call upon* all States to refrain from promulgating and applying laws and measures of the kind referred to in the preamble to the present resolution, in conformity with their obligations under the Charter of the United Nations and international law, which, inter alia, reaffirm the freedom of trade and navigation;

3. *Once again urges* States that have and continue to apply such laws and measures to take the necessary steps to repeal or invalidate them as soon as possible in accordance with their legal regime;

4. *Requests* the Secretary-General, in consultation with the appropriate organs and agencies of the United Nations system, to prepare a report on the implementation of the present resolution in the light of the purposes and principles of the Charter and international law and to submit it to the General Assembly at its sixty-seventh session;

5. *Decides* to include in the provisional agenda of its sixty-seventh session the item entitled "Necessity of ending the economic, commercial and financial embargo imposed by the United States of America against Cuba".

RECORDED VOTE ON RESOLUTION 66/6:

In favour: Afghanistan, Albania, Algeria, Andorra, Angola, Antigua and Barbuda, Argentina, Armenia, Australia, Austria, Azerbaijan, Bahamas, Bahrain, Bangladesh, Barbados, Belarus, Belgium, Belize, Benin, Bhutan, Bolivia, Bosnia and Herzegovina, Botswana, Brazil, Brunei Darussalam, Bulgaria, Burkina Faso, Burundi, Cambodia, Cameroon, Canada, Cape Verde, Central African Republic, Chad, Chile, China, Colombia, Comoros, Congo, Costa Rica, Côte d'Ivoire, Croatia, Cuba, Cyprus, Czech Republic, Democratic People's Republic of Korea, Democratic Republic of the Congo, Denmark, Djibouti, Dominica, Dominican Republic, Ecuador, Egypt, El Salvador, Equatorial Guinea, Eritrea, Estonia, Ethiopia, Fiji, Finland, France, Gabon, Gambia, Georgia, Germany, Ghana, Greece, Grenada, Guatemala, Guinea, Guinea-Bissau, Guyana, Haiti, Honduras, Hungary, Iceland, India, Indonesia, Iran, Iraq, Ireland, Italy, Jamaica, Japan, Jordan, Kazakhstan, Kenya, Kiribati, Kuwait, Kyrgyzstan, Lao People's Democratic Republic, Latvia, Lebanon, Lesotho, Liberia, Liechtenstein, Lithuania, Luxembourg, Madagascar, Malawi, Malaysia, Maldives, Mali, Malta, Mauritania, Mauritius, Mexico, Monaco, Mongolia, Montenegro, Morocco, Mozambique, Myanmar, Namibia, Nauru, Nepal, Netherlands, New Zealand, Nicaragua, Niger, Nigeria, Norway, Oman, Pakistan, Panama, Papua New Guinea, Paraguay, Peru, Philippines, Poland, Portugal, Qatar, Republic of Korea, Republic of Moldova, Romania, Russian Federation, Rwanda, Saint Kitts and Nevis, Saint Lucia, Saint Vincent and the Grenadines, Samoa, San Marino, Sao Tome and Principe, Saudi Arabia, Senegal, Serbia, Seychelles, Sierra Leone, Singapore, Slovakia, Slovenia, Solomon Islands, Somalia, South Africa, South Sudan, Spain, Sri Lanka, Sudan, Suriname, Swaziland, Switzerland, Syrian Arab Republic, Tajikistan, Thailand, the former Yugoslav Republic of Macedonia, Timor-Leste, Togo, Tonga, Trinidad and Tobago, Tunisia, Turkey, Turkmenistan, Tuvalu, Uganda, Ukraine, United Arab Emirates, United Kingdom, United Republic of Tanzania, Uruguay, Uzbekistan, Vanuatu, Venezuela, Viet Nam, Yemen, Zambia, Zimbabwe.

Against: Israel, United States.

Abstaining: Marshall Islands, Micronesia, Palau.

Chapter IV

Asia and the Pacific

The United Nations, in 2011, continued its efforts to address political and security challenges in Asia and the Pacific in order to restore peace and stability and to promote economic and social development in the region.

In Afghanistan, the phased transition of security responsibility from the International Security Assistance Force (ISAF), a multinational force led by the North Atlantic Treaty Organization, to the Afghan National Security Forces began in July. The Security Council welcomed the start of the process to transfer responsibility to the Afghan Government country-wide by the end of 2014 and extended its authorization of ISAF until October 2012. The United Nations Assistance Mission in Afghanistan (UNAMA) continued to foster political dialogue, coordinate international humanitarian and development activities, and assist the Government in institution-building. In March, the Council extended the mandate of UNAMA by another year. While the assassination of former Afghan President Burhanuddin Rabbani on 20 September 2011 had adverse political and security implications, progress was achieved later in the year at the Istanbul Conference for Afghanistan held in November and the Bonn Conference in December. In other developments, the Council separated the Al-Qaida and Taliban sanctions regime to strengthen the effectiveness of targeted sanctions against Al-Qaida and its affiliates.

Iraq continued to make progress in consolidating its young democracy, strengthening the rule of law, developing its institutions and addressing economic and social challenges. The Secretary-General's Special Representative for Iraq and Head of the United Nations Assistance Mission for Iraq (UNAMI) continued to engage political figures and parties in order to advance negotiations on outstanding issues related to the Government formation process and to facilitate political dialogue on Iraq's disputed territories. The Council extended the UNAMI mandate until July 2012. At the end of the year, although tensions had risen between the main political blocs in the country, the withdrawal of United States military forces from the country marked another milestone in Iraq's progress. On 27 December, all major political blocs consented to the convening of a national conference.

The overall situation in Timor-Leste remained generally calm, with further progress towards the consolidation of peace, stability and development. Political parties intensified their activities in preparation for the 2012 presidential and parliamentary elections. In February 2011, the Council extended the mandate of the United Nations Integrated Mission in Timor-Leste (UNMIT) for one year and requested UNMIT to support preparations for the elections. On 27 March, the Polícia Nacional de Timor-Leste resumed responsibility for all police operations in the country.

The Security Council Committee established to oversee the implementation of sanctions measures against the Democratic People's Republic of Korea continued its work. In June, the Council extended the mandate of the Panel of Experts, which carried out certain tasks under the Committee's direction, until 12 June 2012.

The United Nations continued to address Iran's nuclear programme and the sanctions imposed by the Council in that regard. The International Atomic Energy Agency (IAEA) reported that Iran had not implemented the Additional Protocol to Iran's Safeguards Agreement or the relevant resolutions of the Council and the IAEA Board of Governors, nor had it permitted the Agency to confirm that all nuclear material in Iran was being used in peaceful activities. In June, the Council extended for another year the mandate of the Panel of Experts established to assist the Sanctions Committee.

The mandate of the United Nations Mission in Nepal (UNMIN) ended on 15 January. In a 14 January presidential statement, the Council reaffirmed its support for the peace process and called on the Nepalese caretaker Government and all political parties to continue to fulfil the commitments they had made in the 2006 Comprehensive Peace Agreement.

During the year, the Council expressed concern about the deteriorating security and humanitarian situation in Yemen and welcomed the mediation efforts of the Secretary-General, through his Special Adviser, and of the Gulf Cooperation Council (GCC). On 21 October, the Council adopted a resolution demanding all sides to reject the use of violence to achieve political goals, and calling for all parties to sign and implement the GCC initiative for an inclusive, orderly and Yemeni-led process of political transition.

Afghanistan

In 2011, the international community continued to assist the Government of Afghanistan to lay the foundations for peace and stability and the restoration of economic and social development through the United Nations Assistance Mission in Afghanistan (UNAMA), under the direction of the Special Representative of the Secretary-General and Head of Mission, and the International Security Assistance Force (ISAF), led by the North Atlantic Treaty Organization (NATO).

The Secretary-General submitted four progress reports to the General Assembly and the Security Council, in March [A/65/783-S/2011/120], June [A/65/873-S/2011/381], September [A/66/369-S/2011/590] and December [A/66/604-S/2011/772], on the situation in Afghanistan and on UNAMA activities as well as a later report including information relating to 2011 [A/66/728-S/2012/133]. The Secretary-General also submitted to the Council a February report [S/2011/55] on children and armed conflict in Afghanistan.

The NATO Secretary-General, through the UN Secretary-General, reported to the Council on ISAF activities [S/2011/124, S/2011/364, S/2011/562, S/2011/760, S/2012/150]. The Council, by resolution 1974(2011) of 22 March, extended the mandate of UNAMA until 23 March 2012. By resolution 2011(2011) of 12 October, it extended the authorization of ISAF until 13 October 2012.

Staffan de Mistura (Sweden) completed his assignment as the Special Representative of the Secretary-General for Afghanistan on 31 December. In November, the Council took note of the Secretary-General's intention to appoint Ján Kubriš (Slovakia) to replace Mr. de Mistura.

Political and security developments

Report of Secretary-General (March). In his March report on the situation in Afghanistan [A/65/783-S/2011/120], the Secretary-General said that the inauguration of the National Assembly by President Hamid Karzai took place on 26 January after a series of meetings between the President, elected members of parliament and unsuccessful candidates, during which the UN Special Representative extended his good offices. The inauguration ceremony brought together the newly elected Lower House (Wolesi Jirga) and Upper House (Meshrano Jirga) in a joint session. On 27 January, the new Meshrano Jirga Speaker was named and the leadership of the Wolesi Jirga was elected on 27 February. On 19 February, President Karzai presented the list of 34 presidential appointees to the Meshrano Jirga.

The security situation continued to deteriorate, with 1,664 incidents in January, compared to a monthly average of 1,620 in 2010 and 960 in 2009. Armed clashes and the use of improvised explosive devices constituted the majority of incidents. The southern city of Kandahar and its surrounding areas remained the focus of attacks, including abductions and assassinations. The Afghan National Security Forces and international military forces intensified their operations. Pro-Government forces reportedly inflicted losses on mid-level commanders of networks of anti-Government elements. As a result of the increased tempo of security operations in northern and western provinces, an increasing number of anti-Government elements were seeking to join local reintegration programmes. As a reaction, insurgents were increasingly attacking those who chose to reconcile and reintegrate with the Government.

On implementation of the Kabul process, which was developed at the 2010 International Conference on Afghanistan (Kabul Conference) [YUN 2010, p. 347], six national priority programmes were elaborated and consultations were initiated with donors. Two priority programmes (on public financial management and economic reform and on the Afghan Peace and Reintegration Programme) were endorsed and their implementation had begun.

International development partners expressed concern at the continued absence of an International Monetary Fund (IMF) country programme, the establishment of which was dependent on agreement between the Government and IMF on how to deal with the Kabul Bank, which had been declared bankrupt. The Secretary-General stated that, without an IMF programme, it would be difficult for international partners to meet the Kabul Conference commitment to direct funds through the Government's budget.

The Secretary-General said that two immediate challenges had to be overcome in the transition process that would lead to Afghan institutions taking over full responsibility from NATO for security across the country: tension between the executive, legislative and judiciary branches over the status of parliament; and the impasse over the Kabul Bank. He warned that if the tension over the status of parliament continued, or led to an entrenched political crisis, it would be detrimental to the credibility, effectiveness and inclusiveness that was necessary for the Government to lead the transition process. He acknowledged that flaws in the election process had created a parliament where the Pashtun population in some areas was underrepresented compared to the previous parliament; the problem needed to be addressed, but the manner in which it was addressed would have consequences for the transition process and the future stability of Afghanistan. He said his Special Representative had been working closely with all parties to find an appropriate solution, while underscoring that any solution should not be achieved at the expense of the electoral institutions, the constitutional separation of powers, the confidence of the international community, or indeed that of the Afghan people.

The delay in resolving the issue of the Kabul Bank had implications for the prospect of international partners aligning assistance with Afghanistan's national priority programmes; it had weakened confidence in the country's financial system and prevented an agreement on a new IMF country programme. He reaffirmed the three key principles of the UN approach to the Kabul process and transition: the transition had to be Afghan-owned, be planned and implemented in a sustainable manner, and ensure the protection and promotion of the rights of all Afghans. The United Nations was committed to continuing to support the Kabul process, through a constructive, comprehensive, transparent, practically focused and complementary partnership with all stakeholders. The Secretary-General recommended that the UNAMA mandate be renewed for an additional 12 months.

Security Council consideration (March). On 17 March [S/PV.6497], the Security Council discussed the situation in Afghanistan. The Special Representative and Head of UNAMA stated that the primary focus in the near future would be on the planned transition to Afghan forces of responsibility for security; he confirmed that the United Nations would continue to support the country after the transition. Afghanistan introduced its Government's 4 March request [S/2011/118] for the renewal of the UNAMA mandate and for a comprehensive review of the mandate. Council members expressed concern about the security situation, particularly with regard to the protection of civilians, underlined the importance of a transition to full Afghan responsibility and ownership, and reiterated the support of the international community in ensuring the success of that process.

On 22 March, the Council adopted resolution 1974(2011) (see below), by which it extended the UNAMA mandate until 23 March 2012 and requested the Secretary-General to conduct a comprehensive review of UNAMA activities and of UN support in Afghanistan by the end of 2011.

Communications. In a 28 January letter [A/65/726-S/2011/68], Afghanistan and the Russian Federation transmitted to the Secretary-General the Joint Declaration by the Russian and Afghan Presidents following the Russian-Afghan summit talks (Moscow, 20–21 January). The Presidents stressed the importance of developing mutually beneficial economic cooperation between the two countries.

On 17 February [A/65/763-S/2011/100], Belarus, as chair of the Collective Security Treaty Organization (CSTO), transmitted to the Secretary-General the statement by the Heads of States members of CSTO on the threat of narcotic drugs emanating from Afghanistan.

On 25 February [S/2011/110], the Russian Federation and the United Kingdom transmitted to the Security Council a 15 February joint press statement by the Secretary of State for Foreign and Commonwealth Affairs of the United Kingdom and the Minister for Foreign Affairs of the Russian Federation on Afghanistan, in which the Ministers stressed that they would work together through the NATO-Russian Council to support the Afghan Government throughout the transition process.

SECURITY COUNCIL ACTION

On 22 March [meeting 6500], the Security Council unanimously adopted **resolution 1974(2011)**. The draft [S/2011/147] was submitted by Germany.

The Security Council,
Recalling its previous resolutions on Afghanistan, in particular resolution 1917(2010) of 22 March 2010, in which it extended until 23 March 2011 the mandate of the United Nations Assistance Mission in Afghanistan as established by resolution 1662(2006) of 23 March 2006, and recalling also the report of the Security Council mission to Afghanistan from 21 to 24 June 2010,

Reaffirming its strong commitment to the sovereignty, independence, territorial integrity and national unity of Afghanistan,

Stressing the importance of a comprehensive approach to address the situation in Afghanistan, and recognizing that there is no purely military solution to ensure the stability of Afghanistan,

Reaffirming its continued support for the Government and people of Afghanistan as they rebuild their country, strengthen the foundations of sustainable peace and constitutional democracy and assume their rightful place in the community of nations,

Welcoming the results of the Kabul International Conference on Afghanistan, held on 20 July 2010, which constituted a milestone in the Kabul Process towards accelerated Afghan leadership and ownership, strengthened international partnership and regional cooperation, improved Afghan governance, enhanced capabilities of Afghan security forces, economic growth and better protection for the rights of all Afghan citizens, including women, and welcoming specifically the commitments made by the Government of Afghanistan, including the development of a framework, timelines and benchmarks for the new national priority programmes, progress towards transition to an Afghan security lead, improvement of governance and tackling of corruption,

Reaffirming the commitments made at the London Conference on Afghanistan, held on 28 January 2010, which set a clear agenda and agreed priorities for the way ahead on Afghanistan, underpinned by a comprehensive strategy to be taken forward by the Government of Afghanistan with the support of the region and the international community and with a central and impartial coordinating role for the United Nations,

Looking forward to the international conference on Afghanistan to be held in Bonn, Germany, in December 2011, under the leadership of the Government of Afghanistan,

Reaffirming in this context its support for the implementation, under the ownership of the Afghan people, of the commitments set out in the London and Kabul Conference communiqués, of the Afghanistan National Development Strategy and of the National Drug Control Strategy, recognizing the threat posed by illicit drug production, trade and trafficking to international peace and stability in different regions of the world and the important role played by the United Nations Office on Drugs and Crime in this regard, and noting that sustained and coordinated efforts by all relevant actors are required to consolidate progress made towards their implementation and to overcome continuing challenges,

Stressing the central and impartial role that the United Nations continues to play in promoting peace and stability in Afghanistan by leading the efforts of the international community, including, jointly with the Government of Afghanistan, the coordination and monitoring of efforts in implementing the Kabul Process through the Joint Coordination and Monitoring Board in support of the priorities set up by the Government, and expressing its appreciation and strong support for the ongoing efforts of the Secretary-General, his Special Representative for Afghanistan and, in particular, the women and men of the Mission who are serving in difficult conditions to help the people of Afghanistan,

Recalling the conclusions of the Consultative Peace Jirga, and welcoming the establishment of the High Peace Council and its outreach efforts both within and outside Afghanistan,

Recognizing the courage and dedication of millions of women and men who exercised their right to vote, in the face of serious security threats, in the 2010 legislative elections, recognizing also the Afghan leadership in the elections, including the work of the Independent Electoral Commission and the Electoral Complaints Commission, welcoming the inauguration of a new Wolesi Jirga, recalling the Government of Afghanistan's commitments at the Kabul Conference to long-term electoral reform, and stressing the need for completing electoral reforms in order to ensure that future elections will be transparent, credible and democratic, and reaffirming that Afghanistan's peaceful future lies in the building of a stable, secure, economically self-sufficient State, free of terrorism and narcotics and based on strengthened democratic institutions, respect for the separation of powers, reinforced constitutional checks and balances and the guarantee and enforcement of citizens' rights and obligations,

Welcoming the contribution of the International Contact Group on Afghanistan to the United Nations efforts in coordinating and broadening international support for Afghanistan, in particular the outcome of the last meeting of the International Contact Group, hosted by the Organization of the Islamic Conference in Jeddah, Saudi Arabia, on 3 March 2011, which demonstrated the increasing support of regional and other countries for peace, stability and development in Afghanistan,

Stressing the crucial importance of advancing regional cooperation as an effective means to promote security, stability and economic and social development in Afghanistan, recalling the importance of the Kabul Declaration on Good-neighbourly Relations of 22 December 2002, welcoming in this regard the continued commitment of the international community to support stability and development in Afghanistan, noting international and regional initiatives, such as the Istanbul "Heart of Asia" summit, the quadrilateral summit of Afghanistan, Pakistan, Tajikistan and the Russian Federation, as well as initiatives by the Shanghai Cooperation Organization, and looking forward to the Fifth Regional Economic Cooperation Conference on Afghanistan, to be held in Tajikistan in the fall of 2011,

Welcoming the efforts of countries that are increasing their civilian and humanitarian efforts to assist the Government and the people of Afghanistan, and encouraging the international community to further enhance its contributions in a coordinated manner with the Afghan authorities and the Mission,

Welcoming also the agreement, reached at the North Atlantic Treaty Organization summit, held in Lisbon on 19 and 20 November 2010, between the Government of Afghanistan and countries contributing to the International Security Assistance Force to gradually transfer lead security responsibility in Afghanistan to the Afghan National Security Forces country-wide by the end of 2014, taking note of the declaration by the North Atlantic Treaty Organization and the Government of Afghanistan on an enduring partnership, signed at Lisbon on 20 November 2010, acknowledging the joint efforts under the Inteqal (transition) process, welcoming the progress made so far in preparing the transition of a first tranche of provinces and municipal areas, and looking forward to the continued implementation of the transition process,

Recognizing once again the interconnected nature of the challenges in Afghanistan, reaffirming that sustainable progress on security, governance, human rights, the rule of law and development, as well as the cross-cutting issues of anti-corruption, counter-narcotics and transparency, is mutually reinforcing, and welcoming the continuing efforts of the Government of Afghanistan and the international community to address these challenges through a comprehensive approach,

Stressing the importance of a comprehensive approach in addressing the challenges in Afghanistan to a successful transition to Afghan security leadership beginning in early 2011, recognizing that security gains must be supported by progress in Afghan governance and development capacity, noting in this context the synergies in the objectives of the Mission and of the International Security Assistance Force as also noted in resolution 1943(2010) of 13 October 2010, and stressing the need for strengthened cooperation, coordination and mutual support, taking due account of their respective designated responsibilities,

Reiterating the need for all United Nations agencies, funds and programmes, through the country team mechanism and a "One United Nations" approach and under the guidance of the Special Representative of the Secretary-General for Afghanistan, to increase efforts to achieve greater coherence, coordination, efficiency and full alignment with the national priority programmes identified by the Government of Afghanistan,

Stressing the need to further improve the reach, quality and quantity of humanitarian aid, ensuring efficient, effective and timely coordination and delivery of humanitarian assistance, including through enhanced coordination among the United Nations agencies, funds and programmes under the authority of the Special Representative and between the United Nations and other donors, especially where it is most needed, emphasizing in this regard the need for all, within the framework of humanitarian assistance, of upholding and respecting the humanitarian principles of humanity, neutrality, impartiality and independence,

Reiterating its concern about the security situation in Afghanistan, in particular the ongoing violent and terrorist activities by the Taliban, Al-Qaida, other violent extremist groups, illegal armed groups, criminals and those involved in the production of or trafficking or trade in illicit drugs, and the strong links between terrorism activities and illicit drugs, resulting in threats to the local population, including children, national security forces and international military and civilian personnel,

Recognizing the continuously alarming threats posed by the Taliban, Al-Qaida, other violent extremist groups and illegal armed groups as well as the challenges related to the efforts to address such threats, and expressing its serious concern over the harmful consequences of violent and terrorist activities by the Taliban, Al-Qaida, other violent extremist groups and illegal armed groups on the capacity of the Government of Afghanistan to guarantee the rule of law, to provide security and basic services to the Afghan people and to ensure the improvement and protection of their human rights and fundamental freedoms,

Recalling its resolutions 1674(2006) of 28 April 2006, 1738(2006) of 23 December 2006 and 1894(2009) of 11 November 2009 on the protection of civilians in armed conflict, expressing its serious concern about the increased high number of civilian casualties in Afghanistan, in particular casualties among women and children, the large majority of which are caused by the Taliban, Al-Qaida, other violent extremist groups and illegal armed groups, reaffirming that all parties to armed conflict must take all feasible steps to ensure the protection of affected civilians, calling for all parties to comply with their obligations under international humanitarian and human rights law and for all appropriate measures to be taken to ensure the protection of civilians, and recognizing the importance of the ongoing monitoring of and reporting to the Security Council, including by the International Security Assistance Force, on the situation of civilians and, in particular, civilian casualties, taking note of the progress made by Afghan and international forces in minimizing civilian casualties,

Expressing its concern about the serious threat that antipersonnel mines, remnants of war and improvised explosive devices pose to the civilian population, and stressing the need to refrain from the use of weapons and devices prohibited by international law,

Supporting the Government of Afghanistan's continued ban of ammonium nitrate fertilizer, and urging prompt action to implement regulations for the control of all explosive materials and precursor chemicals, thereby reducing the ability of insurgents to use them for improvised explosive devices,

Recalling the declaration addressed to the International Narcotics Control Board by the Government of Afghanistan that there is no legal use for acetic anhydride in Afghanistan for the time being and that producing and exporting countries should abstain from authorizing the export of this substance to Afghanistan without a request from the Government of Afghanistan, and encouraging, pursuant to resolution 1817(2008) of 11 June 2008, Member States to increase their cooperation with the Board, notably by complying fully with the provisions of article 12 of the United Nations Convention against Illicit Traffic in Narcotic Drugs and Psychotropic Substances, of 1988,

Recalling its resolutions 1265(1999) of 17 September 1999, 1296(2000) of 19 April 2000, 1674(2006), 1738(2006) and 1894(2009) on the protection of civilians in armed conflict, its resolutions 1325(2000) of 31 October 2000, 1820(2008) of 19 June 2008, 1888(2009) of 30 September 2009, 1889(2009) of 5 October 2009 and 1960(2010) of 16 December 2010 on women and peace and security and its resolutions 1612(2005) of 26 July 2005 and 1882(2009) of 4 August 2009 on children and armed conflict, and taking note of the report of the Secretary-General on children and armed conflict in Afghanistan,

1. *Welcomes* the report of the Secretary-General of 9 March 2011;

2. *Expresses its appreciation* for the United Nations long-term commitment to work with the Government and people of Afghanistan, and reiterates its full support for the work of the United Nations Assistance Mission in Afghanistan and the Special Representative of the Secretary-General for Afghanistan;

3. *Decides* to extend until 23 March 2012 the mandate of the Mission, as defined in its resolutions 1662(2006), 1746(2007) of 23 March 2007, 1806(2008) of 20 March 2008, 1868(2009) and 1917(2010) and in paragraphs 4 to 6 below;

4. *Calls upon* the United Nations, with the support of the international community, to support the Government of Afghanistan's national priority programmes covering the issues of security, governance, justice and economic and social development and to support the full implementation of mutual commitments made on these issues at the Kabul and London Conferences, as well as on continuing implementation of the National Drug Control Strategy, and requests that the Mission assist the Government on its way towards Afghan leadership, as defined by the Kabul Process;

5. *Decides* that the Mission and the Special Representative, within their mandate and guided by the principle of reinforcing Afghan sovereignty, ownership and leadership, shall continue to lead the international civilian efforts, in accordance with the London and Kabul Conference communiqués, and with a particular focus on the priorities laid down below:

(*a*) Promote, as co-chair of the Joint Coordination and Monitoring Board, more coherent support by the international community to the development and governance priorities of the Government of Afghanistan, including through support for the ongoing development of the new national priority programmes, mobilization of resources, coordination of international donors and organizations, and direction of the contributions of United Nations agencies, funds and programmes, in particular for counternarcotics, reconstruction and development activities; at the same time, support efforts to increase the proportion of development aid delivered through the Government, and support efforts to increase the transparency and effectiveness of the Government's use of such resources;

(*b*) Strengthen cooperation with the International Security Assistance Force and the Senior Civilian Representative of the North Atlantic Treaty Organization at all levels and throughout the country in support of the transition to Afghan leadership agreed to at the Kabul and London Conferences and the Lisbon summit, in a sustainable manner to ensure the protection and promotion of the rights of all Afghans, in accordance with their existing mandates, in order to improve civil-military coordination, to facilitate the timely exchange of information and to ensure coherence between the activities of national and international security forces and of civilian actors in support of an Afghan-led development and stabilization process, including through engagement with provincial reconstruction teams and engagement with non-governmental organizations, in particular through participation in the Joint Afghan-North Atlantic Treaty Organization Inteqal Board as an observer;

(c) Provide outreach as well as good offices to support, if requested by the Government of Afghanistan, the Afghan-led process of peace and reconciliation, including through the implementation of the Afghan Peace and Reintegration Programme and proposing and supporting confidence-building measures within the framework of the Afghan Constitution and with full respect for the implementation of measures and application of the procedures introduced by the Security Council in its resolutions 1267(1999) of 15 October 1999, 1822(2008) of 30 June 2008 and 1904(2009) of 17 December 2009 as well as other relevant resolutions of the Council;

(d) Support, at the request of the Afghan authorities, the organization of future Afghan elections, as well as supporting work on the sustainability and integrity of the electoral process, as agreed at the London and Kabul Conferences, and provide capacity-building and technical assistance to the Afghan institutions involved in this process;

6. *Reaffirms* that the Mission and the Special Representative shall continue to lead international civilian efforts in the following priority areas:

(a) Support regional cooperation to work towards a stable and prosperous Afghanistan, building on the achievements made;

(b) Through a strengthened Mission presence, promote, in support of the efforts of the Government of Afghanistan, the implementation of the Kabul Process throughout the country, including through enhanced cooperation with the United Nations Office on Drugs and Crime, and facilitate inclusion in and understanding of the policies of the Government;

(c) Support the efforts of the Government of Afghanistan to improve governance and the rule of law, including transitional justice, budget execution and the fight against corruption, throughout the country in accordance with the Kabul Process, with a view to helping to bring the benefits of peace and the delivery of services in a timely and sustainable manner;

(d) Continue, with the support of the Office of the United Nations High Commissioner for Human Rights, to cooperate with the Afghan Independent Human Rights Commission, to cooperate also with the Government of Afghanistan and relevant international and local non-governmental organizations to monitor the situation of civilians, to coordinate efforts to ensure their protection, to promote accountability and to assist in the full implementation of the fundamental freedoms and human rights provisions of the Afghan Constitution and international treaties to which Afghanistan is a State party, in particular those regarding the full enjoyment by women of their human rights;

(e) Coordinate and facilitate the delivery of humanitarian assistance, in support of the Government of Afghanistan and in accordance with humanitarian principles, with a view to building the capacity of the Government so it can assume the central and coordinating role in the future, including by providing effective support to national and local authorities in assisting and protecting internally displaced persons and to creating conditions conducive to the voluntary, safe, dignified and sustainable return of refugees and internally displaced persons;

7. *Calls upon* all Afghan and international parties to coordinate with the Mission in the implementation of its mandate and in efforts to promote the security and freedom of movement of United Nations and associated personnel throughout the country;

8. *Reiterates* the need to ensure the security of United Nations staff and its support for the measures already taken by the Secretary-General in this regard;

9. *Stresses* the importance of a strong presence of the Mission and United Nations agencies, funds and programmes in the provinces, encourages the Secretary-General to continue his current efforts to take the measures necessary to address the security issues associated with their presence, and strongly supports the authority of the Special Representative in the coordination of all activities of United Nations agencies, funds and programmes in Afghanistan;

10. *Underscores* the importance of a sustainable democratic development in Afghanistan, with all Afghan institutions acting within their clearly defined areas of competence, in accordance with the relevant laws and the Afghan Constitution, welcomes in this regard the commitment of the Government of Afghanistan to work closely with the United Nations to build on the lessons learned from the 2009 and 2010 elections to deliver further improvements to the electoral process, including addressing the sustainability of the electoral process, and, taking into account the commitments made at the London and Kabul Conferences, reaffirms the leading role of the Mission in supporting, at the request of the Government, the realization of these commitments, and requests that, upon the request of the Government, the Mission provide technical assistance to the relevant Afghan institutions to support constructive electoral reforms; and further calls upon members of the international community to provide assistance, as appropriate;

11. *Welcomes* the renewed efforts of the Government of Afghanistan, including through the national Consultative Peace Jirga, held from 2 to 4 June 2010, the establishment of the High Peace Council and the implementation of the Afghan Peace and Reintegration Programme, to promote dialogue with those elements in opposition to the Government who are ready to renounce violence, break ties with Al-Qaida and other terrorist organizations, denounce terrorism and accept the Afghan Constitution, particularly as it relates to gender and human rights issues, and encourages the Government of Afghanistan to make use of the good offices of the Mission to support this process, as appropriate, in full respect of the implementation of measures and procedures introduced by the Security Council in resolutions 1267(1999), 1822(2008) and 1904(2009) as well as other relevant resolutions of the Council, also welcomes the measures taken by the Government, encourages it to

continue to increase the participation of women, minorities and civil society in outreach and consultation processes, and recalls that women can play a vital role in the peace process, as recognized in Council resolution 1325(2000) and related resolutions;

12. *Stresses* the role of the Mission in supporting the process of peace and reconciliation, including the Afghan Peace and Reintegration Programme, as mandated in the present resolution, and encourages the international community to assist the efforts of the Government of Afghanistan in this regard, including through continued support to the Peace and Reintegration Trust Fund, and in this context notes the conference on reintegration to be hosted by the Government of Afghanistan in Kabul in the spring of 2011;

13. *Welcomes* ongoing efforts by the Government of Afghanistan, its neighbouring and regional partners and international organizations, including the Organization of the Islamic Conference, to foster trust and cooperation with each other, as well as recent cooperation initiatives developed by the countries concerned and regional organizations, including the Fifth Trilateral Summit of Afghanistan, Pakistan and Turkey, held in Istanbul, Turkey, on 24 December 2010, and the results of the latest Istanbul Conference, of 3 November 2010, notes the proposed Afghanistan regional conference to be organized by Turkey, and looks forward to the Fifth Regional Economic Cooperation Conference on Afghanistan, to be held in Tajikistan in the fall of 2011, further welcomes the reaffirmation in the Kabul Conference communiqué of the principles set out in the Kabul Declaration on Good-neighbourly Relations of 22 December 2002, and stresses the importance of increasing cooperation between Afghanistan and its partners against the Taliban, Al-Qaida, other violent extremist groups and illegal armed groups, in promoting peace and prosperity in Afghanistan and in fostering cooperation in the economic and development sectors as a means to achieve the full integration of Afghanistan into regional dynamics and the global economy;

14. *Reaffirms* the central role played by the Joint Coordination and Monitoring Board in coordinating, facilitating and monitoring the implementation of the Afghanistan National Development Strategy and the national priority programmes, and calls upon all relevant actors to enhance their cooperation with the Board in this regard with a view to further improving its efficiency;

15. *Calls upon* international donors and organizations and the Government of Afghanistan to adhere to their commitments made at the Kabul Conference and previous international conferences, and reiterates the importance of further efforts in improving aid coordination and effectiveness, including by ensuring transparency, combating corruption and enhancing the capacity of the Government to coordinate aid;

16. *Calls upon* the Government of Afghanistan, with the assistance of the international community, including the International Security Assistance Force and the Operation Enduring Freedom coalition, in accordance with their respective designated responsibilities as they evolve, to continue to address the threat to the security and stability of Afghanistan posed by the Taliban, Al-Qaida, other violent extremist groups, illegal armed groups, criminals and those involved in the production of or trafficking or trade in illicit drugs;

17. *Condemns in the strongest terms* all attacks, including improvised explosive device attacks, suicide attacks, assassinations and abductions, targeting civilians and Afghan and international forces and their deleterious effect on the stabilization, reconstruction and development efforts in Afghanistan, and condemns further the use by the Taliban and other extremist groups of civilians as human shields;

18. *Condemns* attacks against humanitarian workers, emphasizing that the attacks impede efforts to aid the people of Afghanistan, and underlines the need for all parties to ensure safe and unhindered access of all humanitarian actors, including United Nations staff and associated personnel, and to comply fully with applicable international humanitarian law;

19. *Welcomes* the achievements to date in the implementation of the Mine Action Programme for Afghanistan, and encourages the Government of Afghanistan, with the support of the United Nations and all the relevant actors, to continue its efforts towards the removal of anti-personnel landmines, anti-tank landmines and explosive remnants of war in order to reduce the threats posed to human life and peace and security in the country; and expresses the need to provide assistance for the care, rehabilitation and economic and social reintegration of victims, including persons with disabilities;

20. *Recognizes* the progress made by the International Security Assistance Force and other international forces in minimizing the risk of civilian casualties, as described in the report of the Mission of 9 March 2011 on the protection of civilians in armed conflict, and calls upon them to continue to make robust efforts in this regard, notably by the continuous review of tactics and procedures and the conduct of after-action reviews and investigations in cooperation with the Government of Afghanistan in cases where civilian casualties have occurred and when the Government finds these joint investigations appropriate;

21. *Emphasizes* the importance of ensuring access for relevant organizations, as applicable, to all prisons and places of detention in Afghanistan, and calls for full respect for relevant international law, including humanitarian law and human rights law;

22. *Expresses its strong concern* about the recruitment and use of children by Taliban forces in Afghanistan as well as the killing and maiming of children as a result of the conflict, reiterates its strong condemnation of the recruitment and use of child soldiers in violation of applicable international law and all other violations and abuses committed against children in situations of armed conflict, in particular attacks against schools and education and health-care facilities, and the use of children in suicide attacks, calls for those responsible to be brought to justice, stresses the importance of implementing resolutions 1612(2005) and 1882(2009) in this context, and requests the Secretary-General to continue to strengthen the child protection component of the Mission, in particular through the appointment of child protection advisers;

23. *Welcomes* the recent signing of a comprehensive, time-bound and verifiable action plan by the Government of Afghanistan and the United Nations to halt the use and recruitment of children into the Afghan National Security Forces;

24. *Reiterates* the importance of increasing, within a comprehensive framework, the functionality, professionalism and accountability of the Afghan security sector through appropriate vetting procedures, training, mentoring, equipping and empowerment efforts, for both women and men, in order to accelerate progress towards the goal of self-sufficient and ethnically balanced Afghan security forces providing security and ensuring the rule of law throughout the country;

25. *Welcomes*, in this context, the continued progress in the development of the Afghan National Army and its improved ability to plan and undertake operations, and encourages sustained training efforts, including through the contribution of trainers, resources and operational mentoring and liaison teams through the North Atlantic Treaty Organization Training Mission–Afghanistan, and advice in developing a sustainable defence planning process as well as assistance in defence reform initiatives;

26. *Takes note* of the ongoing efforts of the Afghan authorities to enhance the capabilities of the Afghan National Police, calls for further efforts towards that goal, and stresses the importance, in this context, of international assistance through financial support and the provision of trainers and mentors, including the contribution of the North Atlantic Treaty Organization Training Mission–Afghanistan, the European Gendarmerie Force contribution to this mission and the European Union through the European Union Police Mission in Afghanistan;

27. *Welcomes* the progress in the implementation by the Government of Afghanistan of the programme of disbandment of illegal armed groups and its integration with the Afghan Peace and Reintegration Programme, and calls for accelerated and harmonized efforts for further progress, with support from the international community;

28. *Takes note* of the recent progress in addressing, and the drop in, opium production, remains concerned at the serious harm that opium cultivation, production and trafficking and consumption continue to cause to the security, development and governance of Afghanistan as well as to the region and internationally, calls upon the Government of Afghanistan, with the assistance of the international community, to accelerate the implementation of the National Drug Control Strategy, including through alternative livelihood programmes, and to mainstream counter-narcotics throughout national programmes, and encourages additional international support for the four priorities identified in the Strategy; and commends the support provided by the United Nations Office on Drugs and Crime to the Triangular Initiative and the Central Asian Regional Information and Coordination Centre within the framework of the Paris Pact initiative and the Rainbow Strategy, as well as the contribution of the Domodedovo Police Academy of the Russian Federation;

29. *Calls upon* States to strengthen international and regional cooperation to counter the threat to the international community posed by the production, trafficking and consumption of illicit drugs originating in Afghanistan, in accordance with the principle of common and shared responsibility in addressing the drug problem of Afghanistan, including by strengthening the law enforcement capacity and cooperation against the trafficking in illicit drugs and precursor chemicals and money-laundering and corruption linked to such trafficking, notes the proposed Third Ministerial Conference on Drug Trafficking Routes from Afghanistan, to be held in 2011 within the framework of the Paris Pact initiative and its "Paris-Moscow" process, and in this regard calls for full implementation of Council resolution 1817(2008);

30. *Calls for* the continuation of the Paris Pact initiative in countering the production, trafficking and consumption of opium and heroin from Afghanistan and the elimination of poppy crops and drug laboratories and stores as well as the interception of drug convoys, underlines the importance of border management cooperation, and welcomes the intensified cooperation of the relevant United Nations institutions with the Organization for Security and Cooperation in Europe and the Collective Security Treaty Organization in this regard;

31. *Reiterates* the importance of the full, sequenced, timely and coordinated implementation of the National Priority Programme on Law and Justice for All, by all the relevant Afghan institutions and other actors, in view of accelerating the establishment of a fair and transparent justice system, eliminating impunity and contributing to the affirmation of the rule of law throughout the country;

32. *Stresses*, in this context, the importance of further progress in the reconstruction and reform of the prison sector in Afghanistan, in order to improve respect for the rule of law and human rights therein;

33. *Notes with strong concern* the effects of widespread corruption on security, good governance, counter-narcotics efforts and economic development, and urges the Government of Afghanistan, with the assistance of the international community, to vigorously lead the fight against corruption and to enhance its efforts to establish a more effective, accountable and transparent administration;

34. *Encourages* all Afghan institutions, including the executive and legislative branches, to work in a spirit of cooperation, calls upon the Government of Afghanistan to pursue continued legislative and public administration reform in order to ensure good governance, with full representation of all Afghan women and men, and accountability at both the national and the subnational levels, and stresses the need for further international efforts to provide technical assistance in this area;

35. *Calls for* full respect for human rights and fundamental freedoms and international humanitarian law throughout Afghanistan, welcomes the growth in Afghan free media, but notes with concern the continued restrictions on freedom of the media and attacks against journalists, commends the Afghan Independent Human Rights Commission for its courageous efforts to monitor respect for human rights in Afghanistan as well as to foster and protect those rights and to promote the emergence of a pluralistic civil society, and stresses the importance of full cooperation with the Commission by all relevant actors; and supports broad engagement across government agencies and civil society for the realization of the mutual commitments made, including the commitment to provide sufficient government financing for the Commission;

36. *Recognizes* that, despite progress achieved on gender equality, enhanced efforts are necessary to secure the rights of women and girls, strongly condemns continuing forms of discrimination and violence against women and girls, in particular violence aimed at preventing girls from attending school, and stresses the importance of implementing reso-

lutions 1325(2000), 1820(2008), 1888(2009), 1889(2009) and 1960(2010) and of ensuring that women fleeing domestic violence are able to find safe and secure refuge;

37. *Welcomes* the commitment by the Government of Afghanistan to strengthen the participation of women in all Afghan governance institutions, including elected and appointed bodies and the civil service, supports efforts to accelerate implementation of the National Action Plan for the Women of Afghanistan, to integrate its benchmarks into the national priority programmes and to develop a strategy to implement the Law on the Elimination of Violence Against Women, including services to victims, recalls that the promotion and protection of women's rights are an integral part of peace, reintegration and reconciliation, and requests the Secretary-General to continue to include in his reports to the Security Council relevant information on the process of integration of women into the political, economic and social life of Afghanistan;

38. *Also welcomes* the cooperation of the Government of Afghanistan and the Mission with the Security Council Committee established pursuant to resolution 1267(1999) in the implementation of resolution 1904(2009), including by providing relevant information for updating the Consolidated List and by identifying individuals and entities participating in the financing or support of acts or activities of Al-Qaida and the Taliban using proceeds derived from illicit cultivation and production of and trafficking in narcotic drugs and their precursors, and encourages the continuation of such cooperation;

39. *Calls for* the strengthening of the process of regional economic cooperation, including measures to facilitate regional trade, to increase foreign investments and to develop infrastructure, noting Afghanistan's historical role as a land bridge in Asia;

40. *Recognizes* the importance of the voluntary, safe, orderly return and sustainable reintegration of the remaining Afghan refugees for the stability of the country and the region, and calls for continued and enhanced international assistance in this regard;

41. *Affirms* the importance of the voluntary, safe, orderly return and sustainable reintegration of internally displaced persons;

42. *Requests* that the Secretary-General report to the Council every three months on developments in Afghanistan and include in his reports an evaluation of progress made against the benchmarks for measuring and tracking progress in the implementation of the mandate of the Mission and priorities as set out in the present resolution;

43. *Also requests* that the Secretary-General conduct a comprehensive review of the mandated activities of the Mission and the United Nations support in Afghanistan, including the Mission presence throughout the country, in consultation with the Government of Afghanistan and relevant international stakeholders, by the end of 2011, with the aim of strengthening national ownership and leadership consistent with the Kabul Process, taking into account the evolving nature of the presence of the international community and the role of the International Security Assistance Force, and including first experiences with the Transition (Inteqal), with a view to informing the review by the Council of the mandate of the Mission in March 2012; and calls upon all actors concerned to cooperate with the Mission in this process;

44. *Decides* to remain actively seized of the matter.

Attack against UN centre. On 1 April, a demonstration against the burning of the Koran in the United States turned violent and protestors ransacked the UNAMA compound in Mazar-e-Sharif. Three UNAMA international staff and four international guards were killed. The Secretary-General's Chef de Cabinet and the Under-Secretary-General for Safety and Security travelled to Afghanistan to meet with staff members and to discuss the incident with Afghan authorities. The Security Council condemned the attack and called on the Government of Afghanistan to bring those responsible to justice and take all possible steps to protect UN personnel and premises [SC/10216].

Report of Secretary-General (June). In a June report [A/65/873-S/2011/381], the Secretary-General said that the period covered by his report overlapped with the beginning of the implementation of the transition towards greater Afghan leadership and ownership, which was taking place amidst lingering internal and external tensions and against the backdrop of intensified military operations and the resumption of fierce seasonal anti-Government attacks; the civilian population was bearing the brunt of the unrest. Against that background, UNAMA continued to align its strategic priorities with its renewed mandate, in line with the needs and aspirations of the Afghan people, and in support of Government-led initiatives. Political conflict within the newly elected Lower House of the National Assembly (Wolesi Jirga) continued. A recount of ballots was completed on 27 April, but the results had not been disclosed. The National Assembly completed the selection of the administrative boards of both the Lower House and Upper House (Meshrano Jirga), which were broadly representative regionally and ethnically, although lacking female participation. Efforts to strengthen political outreach activities continued. The High Peace Council, which was mandated in 2010 by President Karzai to promote peace and national unity [YUN 2010, p. 356] and was accompanied and supported logistically by UNAMA, visited the provinces of Badghis, Helmand, Kandahar, Khost and Uruzgan to discuss reconciliation and reintegration with provincial authorities, elders, reconcilees and other stakeholders. In consultation with the High Peace Council, the Special Representative and UNAMA engaged provincial council representatives, religious and community leaders, civil society, youth, women's groups and emerging political groups to discuss peace and reconciliation and ways to engage opposition groups and begin an inclusive dialogue with all segments of the Afghan population. Meanwhile, the UNAMA Salaam Support Group continued to promote confidence-building measures through advocacy on access to basic services, including compliance with international humanitarian law by all parties to the conflict. Progress was reported on the reintegration of insurgents. In March and April, two reintegration events involving Taliban members occurred in Kandahar, representing a significant development in a region that had seen limited progress. According to the United Nations Development Programme, by the end of May, the number of individuals who joined the Afghanistan Peace and Reintregation Programme reached 1,809 throughout 17 provinces.

Security for the United Nations in Afghanistan had become increasingly challenging; the number of security incidents was 51 per cent higher than in the same period in 2010. Following the 1 April UNAMA compound attack, additional measures were taken to accelerate the process of reinforcement of UNAMA offices and residences. The Afghan National Security Forces and ISAF intensified and diversified their operations and continued to clear areas of insurgents, who were conducting asymmetric attacks against Afghan security officials, particularly high-profile police commanders. Thousands of demonstrators in several locations protested ISAF activities, including night searches and alleged harassment and detention of religious figures, and expressed general frustration with the international community in Afghanistan. The level of civil unrest marked a departure from the previous sporadic demonstrations against the international civil and military presence and raised serious concern.

The process of transition towards Afghan security responsibility, as approved and formally initiated at the NATO Summit (Lisbon, Portugal, 19–20 November 2010) [YUN 2010, p. 356], moved forward with the 22 March announcement by President Karzai of the first areas identified for transition starting in July. ISAF undertook a two-stage planning process for transition in coordination with the Afghan Transition Coordination Commission. As an observer of the process, UNAMA engaged with Government and ISAF interlocutors with a view to avoiding parallel processes that might be counterproductive for the development of Afghan institutions and mitigating any detrimental shift of resources to transition areas away from non-transition areas. The Mission continued to facilitate dialogue among development partners, and between those partners and ISAF, to ensure that development perspectives were taken into account in transition design and planning.

The Secretary-General observed that the Security Council's decision (resolution 1989(2011)) (see p. 341) to separate the Al-Qaida and Taliban sanctions regime established by resolution 1267(1999) [YUN 1999, p. 265], was a positive development in support of Afghan-led reconciliation efforts. He urged the Government and the international community to continue to give due consideration to the tools offered by the sanctions regime. Further confidence-building measures by all sides could help lay the foundations for a political process.

Security Council consideration (July). On 6 July [S/PV.6574], the Council focused on the transition towards Afghan security responsibility, which, according to the Special Representative of the Secretary-General and Head of UNAMA, was on track. UNAMA, on the basis of its mandate, was prepared to facilitate the social, economic and human rights aspects of the transition. Afghanistan said that the transition was a carefully formulated strategy for a gradual transfer of security responsibilities to Afghan authorities and a drawdown of international forces.

Report of Secretary-General (September). In a September report [A/66/369-S/2011/590], the Secretary-General said that, since the inauguration of the National Assembly in January, UNAMA had urged the different branches of Government to work together for a solution to the post-electoral deadlock. On 23 June, a Special Court created by the Supreme Court ordered 62 changes to the composition of the 249-member Wolesi Jirga. On 10 August, President Karzai issued a decree instructing the Independent Electoral Commission to finalize the matter without delay. The Commission re-examined the 62 cases highlighted by the Special Court and, on 21 August, announced nine changes to the membership of the Wolesi Jirga. On 3 September, eight of the nine individuals were sworn in, and the ninth candidate was sworn in on 10 September.

The reporting period witnessed considerable political volatility and disconcerting levels of insecurity for the Afghan people amid a process of transition to Afghan leadership and responsibility for security. As at the end of August, the average monthly number of incidents for 2011 was 2,108, up 39 per cent compared with the same period in 2010. Insurgents continued to launch complex suicide attacks in urban centres, including attacks on the InterContinental Hotel in Kabul on 28 June, on the British Council in Kabul on 19 August and in the vicinity of the United States Embassy in Kabul on 13 September. The focus of suicide attacks was no longer southern Afghanistan; the central region accounted for 21 per cent of such attacks. Targeted assassinations of high-ranking Government officials, members of the security forces and influential local political and religious leaders continued; there were 54 such incidents in July and 72 in August, which killed 89 and 93 individuals, respectively. On 17 July, the formal process of transition of responsibility for security to the Afghan National Security Forces started in Bamyan, Kabul (except in Sarobi district), Panjsher, the municipalities and corresponding districts of Herat, Mazar-e-Sharif, Mehtarlam and Lashkar Gah. Those areas continued to face a resilient insurgency that was attempting to challenge the capacity of Afghan forces to maintain security. The Secretary-General observed that, for the transition to be successful, it was important that the

Afghan National Security Forces continued to demonstrate enhanced independent capability and professionalism to assume an increasing level of responsibility and accountability. The formal agreement to increase the size of the Forces was a positive development. UNAMA continued to monitor and provide advice both to the Government and ISAF on community-based security initiatives, including the Police-e-Mahali (Afghan Local Police), given the possible fallout linked to issues of impunity, command and control, vetting and the risk of ethnically or politically biased militias re-emerging.

Assassination of former Afghan President. On 21 September [SC/10391], the Security Council condemned the 20 September terrorist attack that had caused the death of Burhanuddin Rabbani, Chair of the Afghan High Peace Council and former President of Afghanistan.

Security Council consideration (September). During the 29 September Council debate [S/PV.6625], the Special Representative of the Secretary-General called for more efforts to protect civilians. The Minister for Foreign Affairs of Afghanistan, Zalmai Rassoul, stressed that the reconciliation process would continue despite the loss of the Afghan High Peace Council Chair, adding that regional and international support was needed if the process was to succeed. Council members expressed support for UNAMA and underlined the importance of continuing the reconciliation process, as well as the successful transition to full Afghan responsibility and ownership.

GENERAL ASSEMBLY ACTION

On 21 November [meeting 62], the General Assembly adopted **resolution 66/13** [draft: A/66/L.10 & Add.1] without vote [agenda item 38].

The situation in Afghanistan

The General Assembly,

Recalling its resolution 65/8 of 4 November 2010 and all its previous relevant resolutions,

Recalling also all relevant Security Council resolutions and statements by the President of the Council on the situation in Afghanistan, in particular resolutions 1974(2011) of 22 March 2011 and 2011(2011) of 12 October 2011,

Reaffirming its strong commitment to the sovereignty, independence, territorial integrity and national unity of Afghanistan, and respecting its multicultural, multi-ethnic and historical heritage,

Recognizing once again the interconnected nature of the challenges in Afghanistan, reaffirming that sustainable progress on security, governance, human rights, the rule of law and development, as well as on the cross-cutting theme of counter-narcotics, is mutually reinforcing, and welcoming the continuing efforts of the Government of Afghanistan and the international community to address these challenges in a coherent manner,

Recalling the long-term commitment of the international community to Afghanistan, including the mutual commitments made at the London and Kabul Conferences, held on 28 January and 20 July 2010, respectively, looking forward to the upcoming comprehensive review by the Secretary-General, in consultation with the Government of Afghanistan and relevant international stakeholders, of the mandated activities of the United Nations Assistance Mission in Afghanistan and of United Nations support in Afghanistan, with the aim of strengthening national ownership and leadership consistent with the Kabul process, and taking into account the evolving nature of the presence of the international community,

Looking forward to the International Afghanistan Conference on Afghanistan and the International Community: From Transition to the Transformation Decade, to be held in Bonn, Germany, on 5 December 2011, chaired by the Government of Afghanistan, at which civil aspects of transition, the long-term commitment of the international community in Afghanistan within the region and the support of the political process will be further defined,

Supporting increased regional efforts towards the continued implementation of previous declarations of good-neighbourly relations, welcoming the Conference on Security and Cooperation in the Heart of Asia, held in Istanbul, Turkey, on 2 November 2011, at which Afghanistan and its regional partners, with the support of the international community, affirmed their commitment to promoting regional security and cooperation through confidence-building measures, and looking forward to the first follow-up to the Istanbul Conference for Afghanistan, scheduled to convene at the ministerial level in Kabul in June 2012,

Noting regional initiatives, such as those being implemented within the framework of the Shanghai Cooperation Organization, the Collective Security Treaty Organization, the European Union, the Organization for Security and Cooperation in Europe, the South Asian Association for Regional Cooperation, the Economic Cooperation Organization and other relevant initiatives aimed at increased regional economic cooperation with Afghanistan, such as the Regional Economic Cooperation Conference on Afghanistan and the Central Asian Regional Economic Cooperation Programme, and noting also the ministerial meeting to enhance trade connectivity along historical trade routes, held in New York on 22 September 2011,

Underlining the significance of the agreement reached between the Government of Afghanistan and countries contributing to the International Security Assistance Force, at the North Atlantic Treaty Organization summit, held in Lisbon on 19 and 20 November 2010, to gradually transfer lead security responsibility in Afghanistan to the Government of Afghanistan country-wide by the end of 2014, welcoming the ongoing implementation of the transition, looking forward to its phased extension to the rest of the country, underlining the continuing role of the Assistance Force in support of the Government of Afghanistan and in promoting a responsible transition and the importance of the enhancement of the operational capabilities of the Afghan National Security Forces, stressing the long-term commitment, beyond 2014, of the international community to support the further development, including training, and professionalization of the Afghan National Security Forces and their capacity to counter continued threats to Afghanistan's security, with a view to establishing lasting peace, security and stability, and noting that these issues will be discussed at the North Atlantic Treaty Organization summit in Chicago, United States of America, in 2012,

Reiterating the urgent need to tackle the challenges in Afghanistan, in particular the ongoing violent criminal and terrorist activities by the Taliban, Al-Qaida and other violent and extremist groups and criminals, including those involved in the narcotics trade, and the development of Government of Afghanistan institutions, including at the subnational level, the strengthening of the rule of law and democratic processes, the fight against corruption, the acceleration of justice sector reform, the promotion of national reconciliation, without prejudice to the fulfilment of the measures introduced by the Security Council in its resolutions 1267(1999) of 15 October 1999 and 1988(2011) and 1989(2011) of 17 June 2011 and other relevant resolutions, an Afghan-led transitional justice process, the safe and voluntary return of Afghan refugees and internally displaced persons in an orderly and dignified manner, the promotion and protection of human rights and the advancement of economic and social development,

Deeply concerned about the continued high level of violence in Afghanistan, condemning in the strongest terms all violent attacks, and recognizing in that regard the continuously alarming threats posed by the Taliban, Al-Qaida and other violent and extremist groups, as well as the challenges related to the efforts to address such threats,

Expressing its serious concern about the high number of civilian casualties, recalling that the Taliban, Al-Qaida and other violent and extremist groups are responsible for the significant majority of the civilian casualties in Afghanistan, and calling for compliance with international humanitarian and human rights law and for all appropriate measures to be taken to ensure the protection of civilians,

Recognizing further progress made by the Assistance Force, authorized by the Security Council, and other international forces in ensuring the protection of the civilian population and in minimizing civilian casualties, and calling upon them to continue to make enhanced efforts in this regard, notably through the continuous review of tactics and procedures and the conduct of after-action reviews and investigations in cooperation with the Government of Afghanistan in cases where civilian casualties have occurred and when the Government finds these joint investigations appropriate,

Noting the importance of the national Government being inclusive and representative of the ethnic diversity of the country and ensuring also the full and equal participation of women,

1. *Emphasizes* the central and impartial role of the United Nations in promoting peace and stability in Afghanistan, expresses its appreciation and strong support for all efforts of the Secretary-General and his Special Representative in this regard, expresses its appreciation also for the work of the United Nations Assistance Mission in Afghanistan in accordance with Security Council resolution 1974(2011), stresses the leading role of the Assistance Mission in Afghanistan in seeking to further improve the coherence and coordination of international civilian efforts, guided by the principle of reinforcing Afghan ownership and leadership, and in this regard looks forward to the results of the upcoming comprehensive review of the mandated activities of the Assistance Mission and of United Nations support in Afghanistan, as mandated by the Council in resolution 1974(2011);

2. *Welcomes* the reports of the Secretary-General and the recommendations contained therein;

3. *Pledges its continued support* to the Government and people of Afghanistan, as they rebuild a stable, secure, economically self-sufficient State, free of terrorism and narcotics, and strengthen the foundations of a constitutional democracy, as a responsible member of the international community;

4. *Appreciates* the renewed commitment by the Government of Afghanistan to the Afghan people and the renewed commitment by the international community to Afghanistan expressed in the communiqués of the London and Kabul Conferences, reiterates in this regard its appreciation for the Afghanistan National Development Strategy, underlines the need for continued development and implementation, including costing plans, of the national priority programmes, and looks forward to the presentation of the remaining national priority programmes;

5. *Welcomes* further efforts by the Government of Afghanistan to achieve the Millennium Development Goals, and acknowledges, to that effect, the important work being done through the interministerial coordination mechanism and its role in prioritizing and implementing the National Development Strategy and the national priority programmes;

6. *Encourages* all partners to support constructively the Kabul process, building upon a deep and broad international partnership towards further increased Afghan responsibility and ownership in security, governance and development, aiming at a secure, prosperous and democratic Afghanistan, focusing on strengthening the constitutional checks and balances that guarantee citizen rights and obligations, and implementing structural reform to enable an accountable and effective Government to deliver concrete progress to its people;

7. *Supports* the continuing and growing ownership of reconstruction and development efforts by the Government of Afghanistan, and emphasizes the crucial need to achieve ownership and accountability in all fields of governance and to improve institutional capabilities, including at the subnational level, in order to use aid more effectively;

Security and transition

8. *Reiterates once again its serious concern* about the security situation in Afghanistan, stresses the need to continue to address the threat to the security and stability of Afghanistan caused by the ongoing violent and terrorist activity by the Taliban, Al-Qaida and other violent and extremist groups and criminals, including those involved in the narcotics trade, and reiterates in this regard its call for the full implementation of measures and application of procedures introduced in relevant Security Council resolutions, in particular resolutions 1267(1999), 1988(2011) and 1989(2011);

9. *Condemns in the strongest terms* all acts of violence and intimidation and attacks, including improvised explosive device attacks, suicide attacks, assassinations, including of public figures, abductions, the indiscriminate targeting of civilians, attacks against humanitarian workers and the targeting of Afghan and international forces, and their deleterious effect on the stabilization, reconstruction and

development efforts in Afghanistan, and condemns further the use, by the Taliban, Al-Qaida and other violent and extremist groups, of civilians as human shields;

10. *Stresses* the need for the Government of Afghanistan and the international community to continue to work closely together in countering these acts, which are threatening peace and stability in Afghanistan and the democratic process, the achievements and continued implementation of the Afghanistan reconstruction and development process as well as humanitarian aid measures, and calls upon all Member States to deny those groups any form of sanctuary or financial, material and political support;

11. *Expresses deep regret* at the resulting loss of life and physical harm inflicted upon Afghan civilians and civilians of other nationalities, including the personnel of Afghan and international agencies and all other humanitarian workers and the diplomatic corps, the Assistance Mission, as well as upon the personnel of the Afghan National Security Forces, the International Security Assistance Force and the Operation Enduring Freedom coalition, and pays homage to all those who have lost their lives;

12. *Stresses* the importance of the provision of sufficient security, calls upon the Government of Afghanistan, with the assistance of the international community, to continue to address the threat to the security and stability of Afghanistan, and commends the Afghan National Security Forces and their international partners for their efforts in this regard;

13. *Notes* that the responsibility for providing security and law and order throughout the country resides with the Government of Afghanistan, supported by the international community, and underlines the importance of further extending central government authority, including the strengthening of the presence of Afghan security forces, to all provinces of Afghanistan, consistent with the goal of transition;

14. *Expresses its support* for the objective of the Government of Afghanistan, as endorsed by the Joint Coordination and Monitoring Board, to ensure that the Afghan National Security Forces have the necessary strength and operational capability to take over the lead security responsibility from the Assistance Force in all provinces by the end of 2014, and calls upon the international community to provide the support necessary to increase security, as well as to provide continued support by training, equipping and contributing to the financing of the Afghan National Security Forces to take on the task of securing their country;

15. *Welcomes* the start of the transition process for lead security responsibility in July 2011, as agreed upon by the Government of Afghanistan and the countries taking part in the Assistance Force, commends the continuing progress that has been made in this regard, looks forward to the further stages in the transition, also welcomes the commitment of Afghanistan's international partners to support the Government in creating the conditions necessary to allow for transition and to continue to support the transition process to enable it to advance to the point at which the Afghan National Security Forces are fully capable of meeting the security needs of the country, including public order, law enforcement, the security of Afghanistan's borders and preservation of the constitutional rights of Afghan citizens, and calls upon Member States to continue to support the transition process with the necessary continued financial and technical support;

16. *Also welcomes*, in this regard, the presence of the Assistance Force and the Operation Enduring Freedom coalition, expresses its appreciation for the support they have provided to the Afghan National Army, as well as for the assistance provided to the Afghan National Police by international partners, in particular by the North Atlantic Treaty Organization through its training mission in Afghanistan and by the European Gendarmerie Force contribution to that mission, acknowledges the continued deployment of the European Union Police Mission in Afghanistan as well as other bilateral training programmes, and, in light of the transition process, encourages further coordination where appropriate;

17. *Further welcomes* the commitment of the Government of Afghanistan, with a view to ensuring stability and providing conditions for the effective rule of law, to continue the implementation of the Afghan National Police Strategy and the National Police Plan underpinning it, to build a strong, professional police force, with a focus on the ongoing institutional and administrative reforms of the Ministry of the Interior, including the implementation of its anti-corruption action plan, and leadership development, as well as to progressively enhance the quality and increase the strength of the Afghan National Police, with the necessary continued financial and technical support by the international community;

18. *Calls upon* Member States to continue contributing personnel, equipment and other resources to the Assistance Force and to adequately support the evolution of the provincial reconstruction teams in close coordination with the Government of Afghanistan and the Assistance Mission;

19. *Notes*, in the context of the comprehensive approach and the ongoing transition process, the continued importance of the synergies in the objectives of the Assistance Mission and the Assistance Force, and emphasizes, in particular, the continued need to maintain, strengthen and review civil-military relations among international actors, as appropriate, at all levels in order to ensure complementarity of action based on the different mandates and comparative advantages of the humanitarian, development, law enforcement and military actors present in Afghanistan;

20. *Urges* the Afghan authorities, with the support of the international community, to take all possible steps to ensure the safety, security and free movement of all United Nations, development and humanitarian personnel and their full, safe and unhindered access to all affected populations, and to protect the property of the United Nations and of development or humanitarian organizations, and notes the efforts made in regulating private security contractors operating in Afghanistan;

21. *Also urges* the Afghan authorities to make every effort, in accordance with General Assembly resolution 60/123 of 15 December 2005 on the safety and security of humanitarian personnel and protection of United Nations personnel, to bring to justice the perpetrators of attacks;

22. *Stresses* the importance of advancing the full implementation of the programme of disbandment of illegal armed groups throughout the country, under Afghan ownership, while ensuring coordination and coherence with other relevant efforts, including security sector reform, community development, counter-narcotics, district-level development and Afghan-led initiatives to ensure that entities and individuals do not illegally participate in the political process, in particular in future elections, in accordance with adopted laws and regulations in Afghanistan;

23. *Expresses its appreciation* for the progress achieved by the Government of Afghanistan in the programme of disbandment of illegal armed groups and its integration into the Afghan Peace and Reintegration Programme, welcomes the continued commitment of the Government to work actively at the national, provincial and local levels to advance this commitment, stresses the importance of all efforts to create sufficient legal income-earning opportunities, and calls for continued international support for these efforts;

24. *Remains deeply concerned* about the persisting problem of anti-personnel landmines and explosive remnants of war, which constitute a great danger to the population and a major obstacle to the resumption of economic activities and to recovery and reconstruction efforts;

25. *Welcomes* the progress achieved through the Mine Action Programme for Afghanistan, supports the Government of Afghanistan in its efforts to meet its responsibilities under the Convention on the Prohibition of the Use, Stockpiling, Production and Transfer of Anti-personnel Mines and on Their Destruction, to cooperate fully with the Mine Action Programme coordinated by the United Nations and to eliminate all known or new stocks of anti-personnel landmines, and acknowledges the need for continued assistance from the international community in this regard;

26. *Notes* the ratification by Afghanistan of the Convention on Cluster Munitions;

Peace, reconciliation and reintegration

27. *Welcomes* the adoption of Security Council resolutions 1988(2011) and 1989(2011) succeeding resolutions 1267(1999), and 1904(2009) of 17 December 2009, welcomes also the establishment of the 1988 Committee and the measures in resolution 1988(2011) with respect to individuals, groups, undertakings and entities associated with the Taliban in constituting a threat to the peace, stability and security of Afghanistan, calls for the full implementation of measures and application of procedures introduced in the relevant Council resolutions, in particular resolutions 1267(1999) and 1988(2011), and calls for consultations, as appropriate, with the Government of Afghanistan as stipulated in resolution 1988(2011);

28. *Expresses its support* for the Government of Afghanistan-led comprehensive process of peace and reconciliation, as recommended by the national Consultative Peace Jirga in June 2010, commends the renewed efforts of the Afghan Government, including the efforts of the High Peace Council and the ongoing implementation of the Afghan Peace and Reintegration Programme with the aim of promoting an inclusive dialogue between all Afghan groups, including those elements in opposition to the Government who are prepared to renounce violence, denounce terrorism, break ties with Al-Qaida and other terrorist organizations and abide by the Afghan Constitution, and expresses its support for calls upon those concerned to engage in dialogue with the goal of meeting these conditions and reconcile and reintegrate, without prejudice to the implementation of measures and application of procedures introduced by the Security Council in its resolutions 1267(1999), 1988(2011), 1989(2011) and all other relevant resolutions in this regard;

29. *Strongly condemns* the assassination of Professor Burhanuddin Rabbani, Chairman of the High Peace Council, emphasizes the importance of all States with relevant information extending to the Afghan authorities the assistance they may need and all relevant information they may possess pertaining to this terrorist attack, stresses the need for calm and solidarity in Afghanistan at this time and for all parties to reduce tensions, and expresses its firm commitment to support the Government of Afghanistan in its efforts to advance the peace and reconciliation process, in line with the Kabul communiqué and within the framework of the Afghan Constitution and application of the procedures introduced by the Security Council in its resolutions 1267(1999) and 1988(2011) as well as other relevant resolutions of the Council;

30. *Calls upon* all relevant States and international organizations to remain engaged in the Afghan-led peace process, and recognizes the impact terrorist attacks have on the Afghan people and risk having on future prospects for a peace settlement;

31. *Underlines* the fact that reconciliation efforts should enjoy the support of all Afghans, including civil society, minorities and women's groups;

32. *Calls upon* the Government of Afghanistan to ensure that the Afghan Peace and Reintegration Programme is implemented in an inclusive manner consistent with the Afghan Constitution and the international legal obligations of Afghanistan, while upholding the human rights of all Afghans and countering impunity;

33. *Welcomes* the establishment of the Peace and Reintegration Trust Fund, recalls the respective commitments made at the London and Kabul Conferences, and stresses the importance of continued contributions by the international community to the Trust Fund;

34. *Recognizes* the ongoing progress in the reconciliation with the Government of Afghanistan of those Taliban individuals who have rejected the terrorist ideology of Al-Qaida and its followers, abide by the Constitution and support a peaceful resolution to the continuing conflict in Afghanistan, calls upon the Taliban to accept the offer put forward by President Hamid Karzai to renounce violence, sever ties with terrorist groups, abide by the Constitution and join the peace and reconciliation process, and recognizes also that, notwithstanding the evolution of the situation in Afghanistan and progress in reconciliation, security remains a serious challenge in Afghanistan and the region;

35. *Also recognizes* the increased number of reintegrees who have joined the Afghan Peace and Reintegration Programme, welcomes the results of the review conference of the Programme held in May 2011 and recent efforts to ensure its implementation, encourages further efforts to address remaining operational challenges, including through an appropriate vetting mechanism and by ensuring this work is linked to wider efforts to address conflict and grievance resolution at the local level, and further encourages the international community to support this Afghan-led effort;

Governance, rule of law and human rights

36. *Emphasizes* that good governance, the rule of law and human rights form the foundation for the achievement of a stable and prosperous Afghanistan, and notes the importance of building the capacity of the Government of Afghanistan to promote and protect human rights, the rule of law and governance in an accountable and effective manner;

A. Democracy

37. *Recognizes* the importance of holding free, fair, transparent, credible, secure and inclusive elections as crucial steps towards consolidating democracy for all Afghans, stresses the responsibility of the Afghan authorities in this regard, also stresses the need for the timely and orderly preparation of elections, calls upon the international community to continue to provide financial and technical assistance, stresses the leading role of the Assistance Mission in coordinating these efforts, and calls upon the international community to support the Government of Afghanistan and the relevant Afghan institutions;

38. *Welcomes* the settlement of the institutional impasse after the decision to leave the Independent Electoral Commission with the final authority in electoral questions, reiterates the commitment of the Afghan Government in the Kabul communiqué to address long-term electoral reform, based on lessons learned in previous elections, including the 2010 parliamentary elections, and reaffirms that Afghanistan's peaceful future lies in strengthened and transparent democratic institutions, respect for the separation of powers, reinforced constitutional checks and balances and the guarantee and enforcement of citizens' rights and obligations;

B. Justice

39. *Also welcomes* the steps taken by the Government of Afghanistan on justice sector reform and the commitment to improving access to the delivery of justice throughout Afghanistan made by the Government of Afghanistan at the Kabul Conference, stresses the need for further accelerated progress towards the establishment of a fair, transparent and effective justice system, in particular by implementing the National Justice Programme, the National Justice Strategy and the forthcoming National Priority Programme on Law and Justice for All in a timely manner and by providing security and ensuring the rule of law throughout the country, and urges the international community to continue to support the efforts of the Government in these areas in a coordinated manner;

40. *Acknowledges* the progress made by the Government of Afghanistan and the international community in devoting adequate resources to the reconstruction and reform of the prison sector in order to improve respect for the rule of law and human rights therein, while reducing physical and mental health risks to inmates;

41. *Encourages* further efforts by the Government of Afghanistan, with the support of the Assistance Mission, the international community and other partners, including the Afghan Independent Human Rights Commission, in protecting and preventing abuses of the human rights of those detained in all Afghan prisons and detention facilities, consistent with the Afghan Constitution, Afghan laws and international obligations, and in ensuring respect for human rights and the rule of law within Afghanistan, welcomes the cooperation of the Government of Afghanistan, as well as the efforts of the international community to provide support in this regard, takes note of the recommendations contained in the report of the Assistance Mission of 10 October 2011, and reiterates the importance of following the appropriate legal procedures in order to ensure justice;

42. *Emphasizes* the importance of ensuring access for relevant organizations to all prisons in Afghanistan, and calls for full respect for relevant international law, including humanitarian law and human rights law, where applicable, including with regard to minors, if detained;

C. Public administration

43. *Urges* the Government of Afghanistan to continue to effectively reform the public administration sector in order to implement the rule of law and to ensure good governance and accountability, in accordance with the Kabul process, at both the national and subnational levels, with the support of the international community, welcomes the efforts of the Government and commitments made at the Kabul Conference in this regard, stresses the importance of transparent appointment and promotion procedures for civil servants, and continues to encourage the Government to make active use of the Senior Appointments Panel;

44. *Encourages* the international community, including all donor nations as well as international institutions and organizations, governmental and non-governmental, to assist the Government of Afghanistan in making capacity-building and human resources development a cross-cutting priority and to align, in a coordinated manner, with efforts by the Government, including the work of the Independent Administrative Reform and Civil Service Commission, to build administrative capacity at the national and subnational levels;

45. *Reiterates* the importance of institution-building in complementing and contributing to the development of an economy characterized by sound macroeconomic policies, the development of a financial sector that provides services, inter alia, to microenterprises, small and medium-sized enterprises and households, transparent business regulations and accountability, and emphasizes the connection between generating economic growth, including through infrastructural projects, and the creation of job opportunities in Afghanistan;

46. *Recalls* the ratification by Afghanistan of the United Nations Convention against Corruption, reiterates its appreciation for the anti-corruption commitments made by the Government of Afghanistan at the London and Kabul Conferences, calls for further action by the Government to fulfil those commitments in order to establish a more effective, accountable and transparent administration at the national, provincial and local levels of Government, welcomes continued international support to that end, and notes with deep concern the effects of corruption with regard to security, good governance, the combating of the narcotics industry and economic development;

47. *Welcomes* the principles of effective partnership set out in the communiqué of the Kabul Conference, in this context calls for the full implementation of the commitments made at the London Conference and reaffirmed at the Kabul Conference to align and channel increasing international resources through the budget of the Government of Afghanistan and in greater alignment with Afghan priorities, encourages all partners to work with the Government to implement the "Operational guide: criteria for effective off-budget development finance", to improve procurement procedures and due diligence in international contracting procedures and to promote Afghan parliamentary oversight of expenditures and development program-

ming, and recalls that progress in this area requires that the necessary reforms of the public financial management systems be achieved, corruption be reduced, budget execution be improved and revenue collection be increased;

48. *Underlines* the importance of the recent agreement of the Government of Afghanistan with the International Monetary Fund on a three-year arrangement reaffirming the commitment to successful cooperation based on effective and transparent economic reforms;

49. *Welcomes* the Subnational Governance Policy, underscores the importance of more visible, accountable and capable subnational institutions and actors in reducing the political space for insurgents, emphasizes the importance of the Kabul process being accompanied by the implementation of national programmes at the subnational level, encourages the capacity-building and empowerment of local institutions in a phased and fiscally sustainable manner, and calls for the predictable and regular allocation of more resources to provincial authorities, including continued vital support from the Assistance Mission and the international community;

50. *Urges* the Government of Afghanistan to address, with the assistance of the international community, the question of claims for land property through a comprehensive land titling programme, including formal registration of all property and improved security of property rights, and welcomes the steps already taken by the Government in this regard;

D. Human rights

51. *Recalls* the constitutional guarantee of respect for human rights and fundamental freedoms for all Afghans as a significant political achievement, calls for full respect for the human rights and fundamental freedoms of all, without discrimination of any kind, and stresses the need to fully implement the human rights provisions of the Afghan Constitution, in accordance with obligations under applicable international law, including those regarding the full enjoyment by women and children of their human rights;

52. *Acknowledges and encourages* the efforts made by the Government of Afghanistan in promoting respect for human rights, and expresses its concern at the harmful consequences of violent and terrorist activities by the Taliban, Al-Qaida and other violent and extremist groups and criminals for the enjoyment of human rights and for the capacity of the Government of Afghanistan to ensure human rights and fundamental freedoms for all Afghans, notes with concern reports of continued violations of human rights and of international humanitarian law, including violent or discriminatory practices, violations committed against persons belonging to ethnic and religious minorities, as well as against women and children, in particular girls, stresses the need to promote tolerance and religious freedom as guaranteed by the Afghan Constitution, emphasizes the necessity of investigating allegations of current and past violations, and stresses the importance of facilitating the provision of efficient and effective remedies to the victims and of bringing the perpetrators to justice in accordance with national and international law;

53. *Commends* the Government of Afghanistan for its active participation in the universal periodic review process, calls for continued active participation of Afghan civil society in this process, and encourages the timely implementation of the recommendations addressed in the relevant report;

54. *Stresses* the need to ensure respect for the right to freedom of expression and the right to freedom of thought, conscience or belief as enshrined in the Afghan Constitution, in this regard calls for full implementation of the mass media law, while noting with concern the continuing intimidation and violence targeting Afghan journalists and challenges to the independence of the media, condemns cases of the abduction and even killing of journalists by terrorist as well as extremist and criminal groups, and urges that harassment and attacks on journalists be investigated by Afghan authorities and that those responsible be brought to justice;

55. *Reiterates* the important role of the Afghan Independent Human Rights Commission in the promotion and protection of human rights and fundamental freedoms, stresses the need to guarantee its constitutional status and implement its mandate, focusing on communities across Afghanistan, so as to foster a more informed public and increase Government accountability, welcomes the decision of the Government of Afghanistan to take full responsibility for the core funding of the Commission, urges the Commission to cooperate closely with Afghan civil society, and calls upon the international community for continued support in this regard;

56. *Recalls* Security Council resolutions 1674(2006) of 28 April 2006, 1738(2006) of 23 December 2006, 1894(2009) of 11 November 2009 and the mid-year report of July 2011 on the protection of civilians in armed conflict, prepared by the Assistance Mission, expresses its serious concern at the high number of civilian casualties, including women and children, and its impact on local communities, notes that the Taliban, Al-Qaida and other violent and extremist groups remain responsible for the significant majority of civilian casualties, reiterates its call for all feasible steps to be taken to ensure the protection of civilians, and calls for additional appropriate steps in this regard and for full compliance with international humanitarian and human rights law;

57. *Also recalls* Security Council resolutions 1325(2000) of 31 October 2000, 1820(2008) of 19 June 2008, 1888(2009) of 30 September 2009, 1889(2009) of 5 October 2009 and 1960(2010) of 16 December 2010 on women and peace and security, and reiterates the importance of upholding international obligations for the advancement of women's rights as enshrined in the Afghan Constitution;

58. *Commends* the efforts of the Government of Afghanistan to mainstream gender issues, including into the national priority programmes, and to protect and promote the equal rights of women and men as guaranteed, inter alia, by virtue of its ratification of the Convention on the Elimination of All Forms of Discrimination against Women, and by the Afghan Constitution and the implementation of the National Action Plan for Women, reiterates the continued importance of the full and equal participation of women in all spheres of Afghan life, and of equality before the law and equal access to legal counsel without discrimination of any kind, and stresses the need for continued progress on gender issues in accordance with the obligations of Afghanistan under international law;

59. *Strongly condemns* incidents of discrimination and violence against women and girls, in particular if directed against women activists and women prominent in public

life, wherever they occur in Afghanistan, including killings, maiming and "honour killings" in certain parts of the country;

60. *Reiterates its appreciation* for the Elimination of Violence against Women Special Fund of the United Nations Entity for Gender Equality and the Empowerment of Women (UN-Women) as well as for its Urgent Response Fund, which continues to address targeted violence against women and women's rights defenders in Afghanistan, and stresses the need for continued financial contributions by the international community to those funds;

61. *Welcomes* the achievements and efforts of the Government of Afghanistan in countering discrimination, urges the Government to actively involve all elements of Afghan society, in particular women, in the development and implementation of relief, rehabilitation, recovery and reconstruction programmes, as well as in national priority programmes, and accurately track the progress of the full integration of women into political, economic and social life, stresses the need for continued progress on gender equality, in accordance with its obligations under international law and in the empowerment of women in Afghan politics and public administration, including in leadership positions and at the subnational level, also stresses the need to facilitate the access of women to employment and to ensure female literacy and training, and calls upon the international community to continue to provide support in this regard;

62. *Stresses* the need to ensure respect for the human rights and fundamental freedoms of children in Afghanistan, and recalls the need for the full implementation of the Convention on the Rights of the Child and the two Optional Protocols thereto by all States parties, as well as of Security Council resolutions 1612(2005) of 26 July 2005, 1882(2009) of 4 August 2009 and 1998(2011) of 12 July 2011 on children and armed conflict;

63. *Expresses its concern*, in this regard, about the ongoing recruitment and use of children by illegal armed and terrorist groups in Afghanistan, stresses the importance of ending the use of children contrary to international law, expresses appreciation for the progress achieved by and the firm commitment of the Government of Afghanistan in this regard, including its strong condemnation of any exploitation of children, as indicated by the establishment of the Inter-ministerial Steering Committee for the Protection of the Rights of Children, the appointment of a focal point on child protection and the signing by the Government of Afghanistan, in January 2011, of an action plan, including the annexes thereto, on children associated with national security forces in Afghanistan, and calls for the full implementation of the provisions of the action plan, in close cooperation with the Assistance Mission;

64. *Recognizes* the special needs of girls, strongly condemns terrorist attacks as well as threats of attacks on educational facilities, especially on those for Afghan girls, and/or hospitals and protected persons in relation to them in Afghanistan, in contravention of applicable international law, and expresses deep concern about the high number of school closures as a result of terrorist attacks or threats of attacks;

65. *Welcomes* the adoption by the Government of Afghanistan of the National Plan of Action on Combating Child Trafficking, also welcomes initiatives to pass legislation on human trafficking, guided by the Protocol to Prevent, Suppress and Punish Trafficking in Persons, Especially Women and Children, supplementing the United Nations Convention against Transnational Organized Crime, and stresses the importance of considering becoming a party to the Protocol;

Social and economic development

66. *Urgently appeals* to all States, the United Nations system and international and non-governmental organizations, including the international and regional financial institutions, to continue to provide, in close coordination with the Government of Afghanistan and in accordance with Afghan priorities and the National Development Strategy, all possible and necessary humanitarian, recovery, reconstruction, development, financial, educational, technical and material assistance for Afghanistan, and recalls in this regard the leading role of the Assistance Mission in seeking to further improve the coherence and coordination of international efforts;

67. *Stresses* the need for a continued strong international commitment to humanitarian assistance and for programmes, under the ownership of the Government of Afghanistan, of recovery, rehabilitation, reconstruction and development, while expressing its appreciation to the United Nations system and to all States and international and non-governmental organizations whose international and local staff continue to respond positively to the humanitarian, transition and development needs of Afghanistan despite security concerns and difficulties of access in certain areas;

68. *Expresses its appreciation* for the humanitarian and development assistance work of the international community in the reconstruction and development of Afghanistan, recognizes the necessity for further improvement in the living conditions of the Afghan people, and emphasizes the need to strengthen and support the development of the capacity of the Government of Afghanistan to deliver basic social services, in particular education and public health services, and to promote development;

69. *Urges* the Government of Afghanistan to enhance efforts to reform key service delivery sectors, such as energy and drinking water supply, as preconditions for progress in social and economic development, commends the Government for its efforts to date to reach fiscal sustainability, notes the challenges ahead, and urges continued commitment to revenue generation;

70. *Expresses its appreciation* for the work of the provincial reconstruction teams as they work within the provincial context to support national priorities to build the capacities of local institutions;

71. *Encourages* the international community and the corporate sector to support the Afghan economy as a measure for long-term stability and to explore possibilities for increased trade and investments and enhanced local procurements, and further encourages the Government of Afghanistan to continue to promote an economic environment favourable for private-sector investments at both the national and subnational levels;

72. *Urgently encourages* all States as well as intergovernmental and non-governmental organizations to expand agricultural cooperation with Afghanistan, within the National Agricultural Development Framework and in line with the National Development Strategy, with a view to helping to eradicate poverty and ensure social and economic development, including in rural communities;

73. *Reiterates* the necessity of providing Afghan children, especially Afghan girls, with educational and health facilities in all parts of the country, welcomes the progress achieved in the sector of public education, recalls the National Education Strategic Plan as a promising basis for further achievements, encourages the Government of Afghanistan, with the assistance of the international community, to expand those facilities, train professional staff and promote full and equal access to them by all members of Afghan society, including in remote areas, and reiterates further the need to provide vocational training for adolescents;

74. *Commends* the relief efforts by the Government of Afghanistan and donors, but continues to express its concern at the overall humanitarian situation, stresses the continued need for food assistance, and calls for continued international support for and the early fulfilment, before the approaching winter, of the funding targets of the Afghanistan Humanitarian Action Plan;

75. *Recognizes* that underdevelopment and lack of capacity increase the vulnerability of Afghanistan to natural disasters and to harsh climate conditions, and urges in this regard the Government of Afghanistan, with the support of the international community, to increase its efforts aimed at strengthening disaster risk reduction at the national and subnational levels and at modernizing the agricultural sector and strengthening its agricultural production, thereby reducing the vulnerability of Afghanistan to adverse external conditions such as drought, flooding and other natural disasters;

76. *Expresses its appreciation* to those Governments that continue to host Afghan refugees, in particular Pakistan and the Islamic Republic of Iran, acknowledging the huge burden they have so far shouldered in this regard, and asks for continued generous support by the international community, with a view to facilitating their voluntary, safe, dignified and sustainable return, rehabilitation and reintegration;

77. *Reiterates* to host countries and the international community the obligations under international refugee law with respect to the protection of refugees, the principle of voluntary return and the right to seek asylum and to ensure full, safe and unhindered access for humanitarian relief agencies in order to provide protection and assistance to the refugees, and calls upon countries to continue to accept an appropriate number of Afghan refugees for resettlement, as a manifestation of their shared responsibility and solidarity;

78. *Welcomes* the continued return of Afghan refugees and internally displaced persons, in a voluntary, safe, dignified and sustainable manner, while noting with concern that conditions in parts of Afghanistan are not yet conducive to a safe and sustainable return to some places of origin;

79. *Urges* the Government of Afghanistan, acting with the support of the international community, to continue to strengthen its efforts to create the conditions for sustainable return by continuing to strengthen its absorption capacity for the full rehabilitation and reintegration of the remaining Afghan refugees and internally displaced persons;

80. *Notes*, in this regard, the continued constructive work between the countries of the region, as well as the tripartite agreements between the Office of the United Nations High Commissioner for Refugees, the Government of Afghanistan and the Governments of countries hosting refugees from Afghanistan, in particular Pakistan and the Islamic Republic of Iran;

Regional cooperation

81. *Stresses* the crucial role of advancing constructive regional cooperation in promoting peace, security, stability and economic and social development in Afghanistan, encourages further improved relations and enhanced engagement between Afghanistan and its neighbours, and calls for further efforts in this regard, including by regional organizations;

82. *Commends* the continuing efforts of the signatories of the Kabul Declaration on Good-neighbourly Relations of 22 December 2002 to implement their commitments under the Declaration, calls upon all other States to respect and support the implementation of those provisions, and welcomes the reaffirmation, in the Kabul Conference communiqué, of the principles set out in the Declaration;

83. *Welcomes and encourages* further efforts by the Government of Afghanistan and its neighbouring partners to foster trust and cooperation with each other, and looks forward, where appropriate, to increasing cooperation between Afghanistan, all its neighbouring and regional partners and regional organizations against the Taliban, Al-Qaida and other extremist and criminal groups and in promoting peace and prosperity in Afghanistan, in the region and beyond;

84. *Welcomes*, in this regard, the increased efforts by the Government of Afghanistan, its neighbouring and regional partners and international organizations to foster trust and cooperation with each other, as well as recent cooperation initiatives developed by the countries concerned and regional organizations, including the trilateral summits of Afghanistan, Pakistan and Turkey; Afghanistan, the Islamic Republic of Iran and Pakistan; Pakistan, Afghanistan and the United States of America; and Afghanistan, Pakistan and the United Arab Emirates; and the quadrilateral summits of Afghanistan, Pakistan, Tajikistan and the Russian Federation, as well as those of the Tripartite Commission, comprising Afghanistan, Pakistan and the Assistance Force, and the European Union, the Organization of Islamic Cooperation, the Organization for Security and Cooperation in Europe, the South Asian Association for Regional Cooperation and the Shanghai Cooperation Organization;

85. *Also welcomes* the Conference on Security and Cooperation in the Heart of Asia, and encourages Afghanistan and its regional partners to actively endeavour to implement confidence-building measures within the framework set out in the Istanbul Process on Regional Security and Cooperation for a Secure and Stable Afghanistan, adopted on 2 November 2011;

86. *Expresses its appreciation* for all efforts to increase regional economic cooperation aimed at promoting economic cooperation between Afghanistan, regional neighbours, international partners and financial institutions, recognizes, inter alia, the important role of the Regional Economic Cooperation Conference on Afghanistan, the Economic Cooperation Organization, the Central Asian Regional Economic Cooperation Programme, the South Asian Association for Regional Cooperation, as well as the Shanghai Cooperation Organization, the European Union and the Organization for Security and Cooperation in Europe in promoting the development of Afghanistan, and looks forward to the Fifth Regional Economic Cooperation Conference on Afghanistan, to be held in Tajikistan on 26 and 27 March 2012;

87. *Welcomes and urges* further efforts to strengthen the process of regional economic cooperation, including measures to facilitate regional trade and transit, including through regional and bilateral transit trade agreements, expanded consular visa cooperation and facilitation of business travel, to expand trade, to increase foreign investments and to develop infrastructure, including infrastructural connectivity, energy supply, transport and integrated border management, with a view to promoting sustainable economic growth and the creation of jobs in Afghanistan, noting the historic role of Afghanistan as a land bridge in Asia;

88. *Encourages* the Group of Eight countries to continue to stimulate and support cooperation between Afghanistan and its neighbours through mutual consultation and agreement, including on development projects in areas such as infrastructural connectivity, border management and economic development, and in this regard looks forward to the creation of the Afghan rail authority announced at the regional rail conference in Paris on 4 and 5 July 2011;

Counter-narcotics

89. *Welcomes* the efforts of the Government of Afghanistan in fighting drug production in Afghanistan, takes note of the report of the United Nations Office on Drugs and Crime, the *Afghanistan Opium Survey 2011*, released in December 2011, reiterates its deep concern about the increase in the cultivation and production of illicit narcotic drugs in Afghanistan, mainly concentrated in areas where the Taliban, Al-Qaida and other violent and extremist groups and criminals are particularly active, as well as the ongoing drug trafficking, and, based on the principle of common and shared responsibility, stresses the need for strengthened joint, more coordinated and resolute efforts by the Government of Afghanistan, supported by the international and regional actors as well as the Assistance Force, within their designated responsibilities, to fight this menace;

90. *Stresses* the importance of a comprehensive and balanced approach in addressing the drug problem of Afghanistan, which, to be effective, must be integrated into the wider context of efforts carried out in the areas of security, governance, the rule of law and human rights, and economic and social development;

91. *Also stresses*, in this regard, that the development of alternative livelihood programmes is of key importance in the success of the counter-narcotics efforts in Afghanistan and that sustainable strategies require international cooperation, and urges the Government of Afghanistan, assisted by the international community, to promote the development of sustainable livelihoods in the formal production sector, as well as in other sectors, and to improve access to reasonable and sustainable credit and financing in rural areas, thus improving substantially the lives, health and security of the people, particularly in rural areas;

92. *Notes with great concern* the strong nexus between the drug trade and terrorist activities by the Taliban, Al-Qaida and other violent and extremist groups and criminal groups, which pose a serious threat to security, the rule of law and development in Afghanistan, and stresses the importance of the full implementation of all relevant Security Council resolutions in this regard, including resolutions 1735(2006) of 22 December 2006 and 1822(2008) of 30 June 2008;

93. *Calls upon* all Member States, in this regard, to further intensify their efforts to reduce the demand for drugs in their respective countries and globally in order to contribute to the sustainability of the elimination of illicit cultivation in Afghanistan;

94. *Stresses* the need to prevent trafficking in and diversion of chemical precursors used in the illicit manufacturing of drugs in Afghanistan, and calls for the full implementation of Security Council resolution 1817(2008) of 11 June 2008 in this regard;

95. *Supports* the fight against the illicit trafficking in drugs from and precursors to Afghanistan and neighbouring States and countries along trafficking routes, including increased cooperation among them in strengthening antinarcotic controls and the monitoring of the international trade in chemical precursors, and underlines the importance of technical assistance and support to the most affected transit States to support their capacities in this regard;

96. *Urges* the Government of Afghanistan, supported by the international community, to work to mainstream counter-narcotics throughout all the national programmes and to ensure that counter-narcotics is a fundamental part of the comprehensive approach, as well as to increase its efforts against opium cultivation and drug trafficking in accordance with the balanced eight-pillar plan of the updated Afghan National Drug Control Strategy;

97. *Commends* the efforts of the Government of Afghanistan in this regard, as well as the efforts to update and carry out the National Drug Control Strategy, including the Prioritized Implementation Plan and benchmarks, urges the Government and the international community to take decisive action, in particular to stop the processing of and trade in drugs, by pursuing the concrete steps set out in the Strategy and through initiatives such as the Good Performers Initiative established to provide incentives for governors to reduce cultivation in their provinces, and encourages the Afghan authorities to work at the provincial level on elaborating counter-narcotics implementation plans;

98. *Calls upon* the international community to continue to assist the Government of Afghanistan in implementing its National Drug Control Strategy, aimed at eliminating the cultivation, production, trafficking in and consumption of illicit drugs, including through increased support for Afghan law enforcement and criminal justice agencies, agricultural and rural development for the creation of alternative livelihoods for farmers, demand reduction, the elimination of illicit crops, increased public awareness and the building of the capacity of drug control institutions and care and treatment centres for drug addicts, and reiterates its call upon the international community to channel counter-narcotics funding through the Government to the extent possible;

99. *Recalls* the need to strengthen international and regional cooperation with Afghanistan in its sustained efforts to address drug production and trafficking, recognizes the threat posed by illicit drug production, trade and trafficking to international peace and stability in the region and beyond, also recognizes the progress achieved by relevant initiatives within the framework of the Paris Pact initiative of the United Nations Office on Drugs and Crime, stresses the importance of further progress in the implementation of these initiatives, and welcomes the upcoming ministerial meeting of the Paris Pact initiative to be held in Vienna,

in continuation of the "Paris-Moscow" process, as well as the intent of the Government of Afghanistan to strengthen international and regional cooperation in this regard;

100. *Pays homage* to all those who have innocently lost their lives in the fight against drug traffickers, in particular members of the security forces of Afghanistan and its neighbours;

101. *Welcomes* initiatives to enhance border management cooperation between Afghanistan and its neighbours in ensuring comprehensive measures for drug control, including the financial dimension, emphasizes the importance of pursuing such cooperation, especially through bilateral arrangements and those launched by the Collective Security Treaty Organization, the Conference on Interaction and Confidence-building Measures in Asia, the Economic Cooperation Organization, the Shanghai Cooperation Organization, the Central Asian Anti-Drug Quartet and others, and welcomes the intention of the Government of Afghanistan to strengthen international and regional cooperation with relevant partners in the field of border control;

102. *Stresses* the importance of further, effective cooperative support by relevant international and regional actors, including the United Nations and the Assistance Force, within its designated responsibilities, to Afghan-led sustained efforts to address the threat posed by the illicit production of and trafficking in drugs, welcomes in this regard the regional programme on Afghanistan and neighbouring countries of the United Nations Office on Drugs and Crime, and encourages the respective countries to continue to participate;

103. *Acknowledges* the regional activities carried out by Afghanistan, the Islamic Republic of Iran and Pakistan within the framework of their triangular initiative to counter narcotics, and welcomes the next ministerial meetings to be held in Kabul and Tehran, consecutively;

Coordination

104. *Expresses its appreciation* for the work of the Assistance Mission as mandated by the Security Council in its resolution 1974(2011), and stresses the continued importance of the central and impartial coordinating role of the United Nations in promoting a more coherent international engagement;

105. *Welcomes* the presence of the Assistance Mission in the provinces, which ensures that the United Nations can fulfil its essential coordinating and support role, as requested by the Government of Afghanistan, security conditions permitting;

106. *Stresses* the need to ensure that the Assistance Mission is adequately resourced and protected by the Afghan authorities, with international support, as appropriate, to fulfil its mandate;

107. *Acknowledges* the central role played by the Joint Coordination and Monitoring Board, stresses that the role of the Board is to support Afghanistan by, inter alia, monitoring and supporting the Kabul process and coordinating international assistance and reconstruction programmes, and welcomes further efforts to provide appropriate guidance and promote a more coherent international engagement;

108. *Expresses its appreciation for and emphasizes the importance* of the continued and long-term commitment of the international community to supporting the stability and development of Afghanistan, and recalls the additional international support as pledged;

109. *Requests* the Secretary-General to report to the General Assembly every three months on developments in Afghanistan, as well as on the progress made in the implementation of the present resolution;

110. *Decides* to include in the provisional agenda of its sixty-seventh session the item entitled "The situation in Afghanistan".

Terrorist attacks. In a 31 October press statement [SC/10432], the Security Council condemned the terrorist attack against the guest house of the Office of the United Nations High Commissioner for Refugees (UNHCR) in Kandahar, which resulted in the deaths and injury of UN staff and of Afghan police officers who were protecting them.

On 8 December [SC/10474], the Council condemned the 6 December terrorist attacks in Kabul and Mazar-e-Sharif, which resulted in numerous deaths.

Istanbul Conference. The Istanbul Conference for Afghanistan: Security and Cooperation in the Heart of Asia (Istanbul, Turkey, 2 November) [A/66/601-S/2011/767], co-chaired by Afghanistan and Turkey and facilitated by UNAMA, aimed to strengthen dialogue and cooperation with neighbouring countries. The Istanbul Process on Regional Security and Cooperation for a Secure and Stable Afghanistan was adopted by the 13 participating countries—neighbours, near neighbours and countries in the region—and welcomed and supported by 22 other countries, institutions and organizations. It reaffirmed general principles of regional cooperation and included a list of confidence-building measures for consideration by the countries of the region.

Report of Secretary-General (December). In a December report [A/66/604-S/2011/772], the Secretary-General stated that the 20 September assassination of the head of the High Peace Council and former President of Afghanistan, Burhanuddin Rabbani, by a suicide bomber had significant political and security implications. Mr. Rabbani's death had intensified internal political manoeuvring and weakened trust between factions and ethnic groups. It was critical for Afghanistan, with the support of its partners and the United Nations on the ground, to make a concerted effort to forge a national consensus on key issues by involving civil society in a broad-based dialogue aimed at advancing the peace process and reinforcing the country's institutions; sustaining the momentum of the regional process agreed to at the Istanbul Conference in November (see above); ensuring a unified, predictable, transparent and well-resourced economic and development agenda, through an invigorated Kabul Process; and buttressing its key partnerships for the long term, beyond 2014. A proper investigation of Mr. Rabbani's assassination would help restore confidence and prevent any further loss of momentum towards Afghan-led reconciliation. At a traditional Loya Jirga (Kabul, 16–19 November), the mandate of the High Peace Council was reaffirmed and the Government was asked to appoint a new Chair. The gathering also advocated negotiations only with known and legitimate representatives of the insurgency and noted that sincere cooperation by Pakistan was needed for a peace process to succeed. The National Assembly had again become active, with a quorum reached in the Wolesi Jirga on 8 October, concluding a year-long, post-electoral disagreement.

In line with seasonal trends, security-related events declined compared to the previous three-month period. The most significant event directly impacting UN staff was a complex attack carried out in Kandahar on 31 October, in which three UN national staff members were killed and two were injured at the UNHCR compound. The operational environment for humanitarian and development work remained volatile, and UN national staff and staff working for non-governmental organizations continued to suffer sporadic intimidation from insurgent and criminal elements. UNAMA continued to monitor and provide advice on community-based security initiatives, including the Afghan Local Police, the Critical Infrastructure Protection Programme and other local defence initiatives, which continued to grow.

On 14 November, the IMF Executive Board and the Government successfully concluded negotiations on a three-year IMF programme for Afghanistan. The Government firmly committed itself to an aggressive programme of efficiency and reform with a focus on increasing domestic revenue collection, strengthening the financial sector and implementing a progressive pro-poor taxation regime.

Bonn Conference. By a 6 December letter [A/66/597-S/2011/762], Afghanistan and Germany forwarded to the Secretary-General the conference conclusions of the International Afghanistan Conference entitled "Afghanistan and the International Community: From Transition to the Transformation Decade" (Bonn, Germany, 5 December). The Conference reaffirmed the long-term commitment of the international community to support of Afghanistan beyond 2014. Shifting strategy from stabilization to long-term development cooperation, participants recommitted themselves to aligning assistance with Government priorities and to improving the efficiency of aid resources, including through the channelling of a growing share of aid through the Government budget.

Security Council consideration (December). On 19 December [S/PV.6690], the Security Council considered the Secretary-General's report (see above). The UN Under-Secretary-General for Peacekeeping Operations, Hervé Ladsous, said that the Organization was committed to supporting the Government of Afghanistan and its people for the long term. He noted the large-scale attacks of past weeks and the still-volatile security situation, which was affecting the work of UNAMA. The Deputy Minister for Foreign Affairs of Afghanistan said that it had been a year of milestones, but achievements had come at a price and terrorism remained a threat. The Special Representative, Staffan de Mistura, delivered his final briefing. His replacement, Ján Kubiš, was introduced to the Council.

SECURITY COUNCIL ACTION

On 19 December [meeting 6690], following consultations among Council members, the President made statement **S/PRST/2011/22** on behalf of the Council:

The Security Council welcomes the International Afghanistan Conference on Afghanistan and the International Community: From Transition to the Transformation Decade, held in Bonn, Germany, on 5 December 2011 and its conference conclusions.

The Council welcomes also the declaration in Bonn that the process of transition, to be completed by the end of 2014, should be followed by a decade of transformation (2015–2024) in which Afghanistan consolidates its sovereignty by strengthening a fully functioning, sustainable State in the service of its people.

The Council welcomes, furthermore, against this background, the strategic consensus between Afghanistan and the international community on a renewed and enduring partnership for this transformation decade which entails firm mutual commitments.

The Council notes that the process of transition entails the assumption of the leadership responsibility by the Government of Afghanistan.

The Council commends the outcome of the Conference on Security and Cooperation in the Heart of Asia, held in Istanbul, Turkey, on 2 November 2011.

The Council underlines the crucial role of the United Nations in Afghanistan, expresses its gratitude for Mr. Staffan de Mistura's outstanding contribution to the work of the United Nations Assistance Mission in Afghanistan, and looks forward to working with the incoming Special Representative of the Secretary-General for Afghanistan, Mr. Ján Kubiš.

The Council welcomes the intention of the Government of Japan to host a ministerial conference in Tokyo in July 2012.

Further developments

In a later report [A/66/728-S/2012/133], the Secretary-General stated that following the 5 December Bonn Conference (see above), the political debate in Afghanistan had been dominated by the possible establishment of a Taliban office to facilitate dialogue and its location, potentially in Qatar. On 15 December, it was agreed at a meeting between President Karzai and prominent national figures that a practical mechanism to engage the armed opposition was required; it was also emphasized that any peace process must be led and owned by the Afghans. Participants backed proposals to establish a Taliban office, but indicated a preference that it be located in Afghanistan, Saudi Arabia or Turkey. On 20 December, the Government circulated to diplomatic missions an 11-point statement setting out its conditions for such interaction and emphasizing that the gains of the preceding 10 years should not be lost. On 19 December, five members of the Independent Election Commission were sworn in.

In December, the Management Committee for the Afghanistan Reconstruction Trust Fund approved the first instalment of $100 million (total $350 million) for the implementation of the five-year capacity-building for results programme.

UNAMA

The United Nations Assistance Mission in Afghanistan (unama) was established by Security Council resolution 1401(2002) [YUN 2002, p. 264] to promote, among other things, national reconciliation and the responsibilities entrusted to the United Nations under the 2001 Bonn Agreement [YUN 2001, p. 263]. It comprised the Office of the Special Representative, two substantive pillars—one political and one on relief, recovery and reconstruction—and an administrative component. Unama was headquartered in Kabul, with regional offices in Bamyan, Gardez, Herat, Jalalabad, Kabul, Kandahar, Kunduz and Mazar-e-Sharif and provincial offices in Badakhshan, Badghis, Baghlan, Daikundi, Farah, Faryab, Ghor, Khost, Kunar, Nimroz, Sari Pul, Sheberghan, Taluqan, Uruzgan and Zabul. By resolution 1974(2011) (see p. 312), the Council extended the unama mandate until 23 March 2012.

Appointment of Special Representative. On 22 November [S/2011/733], the Secretary-General informed the Security Council of his intention to appoint Ján Kubiš (Slovakia) as his Special Representative for Afghanistan and Head of unama, effective January 2012, to replace Staffan de Mistura (Sweden), who would complete his assignment on 31 December 2011. On 23 November [S/2011/734], the Council took note of the intention.

Financing

In November [A/66/354/Add.4], the Secretary-General submitted to the General Assembly the proposed resource requirements for unama for 2012, totalling $241,533,500 net ($259,451,700 gross). In December [A/66/7/Add.12], the Advisory Committee on Administrative and Budgetary Questions recommended approval of those figures.

On 24 December, the Assembly, in section IX of **resolution 66/247** (see p. 1393), approved the unama budget for the 2012–2013 biennium.

International Security Assistance Force

The International Security Assistance Force (isaf), a multinational force established by Security Council resolution 1386(2001) [YUN 2001, p. 267], was mandated, among other things, to assist the Government of Afghanistan in the maintenance of security in Kabul and its surrounding areas. By Council resolution 1510(2003) [YUN 2003, p. 310], the isaf mandate was expanded to include the maintenance of security outside Kabul and its environs.

During 2011, the Secretary-General transmitted to the Council, in accordance with resolutions 1386(2001) and 1943(2010) [YUN 2010, p. 358], reports from isaf on its activities for the periods from 1 November 2010 to 31 January 2011 [S/2011/124], 1 February to 30 April [S/2011/364], 1 May to 31 July [S/2011/562] and 1 August to 31 October [S/2011/760]. Activities from 1 November 2011 to 31 January 2012 were covered in a later report [S/2012/150].

For the periods covered by the reports, isaf suffered 8,182 casualties, including 597 killed in action, 6,787 wounded in action and 77 non-battle-related deaths. As at 18 October, total isaf strength stood at 130,638 personnel provided by all 28 nato members and 21 non-nato countries.

One of the main tasks of isaf was the further professionalization of the Afghan National Security Forces as they prepared to assume the security lead and the transition process in 2014. The Forces remained on track in terms of both size and quality to reach the October 2012 growth target of 352,000. With isaf support and advice, the Afghan National Security Forces were becoming increasingly capable in general and were improving their ability to conduct autonomous operations: in 2011, they added 57,000 soldiers and police to their numbers. Almost 40 per cent of conventional and special forces operations were led by Afghan forces, and approximately 90 per cent of the operations were partnered with isaf. Transition to Afghan National Security Forces-led security commenced on 22 July.

The protection of the Afghan population remained the highest priority for isaf. Among several initiatives, isaf dedicated special attention to the understanding and prevention of events that could result in civilian casualties. New tactical directives were issued, and the entire isaf force received retraining based on them. The first quarterly civilian casualties mitigation conference was held on 28 June; the objective was to establish a direct dialogue with the Afghan population's representatives to address people's concerns and explain isaf activities. Isaf also established the civilian casualties mitigation working group to examine policies and procedures. In the last months of 2011, isaf actions were attributed to only 6 per cent of all civilian casualty-related incidents, which was representative of the continued decreasing trend when compared to previous reports. December 2011 represented the lowest monthly number of ISAF-caused civilian casualties since accurate record-keeping began in January 2009.

ISAF continued to support Government counter-narcotics programmes and operations in order to disrupt, neutralize and influence the narcotics industry and its funding of the insurgency. ISAF assisted the Afghan security forces in seizing a record amount of narcotics and precursor chemicals in 2011, especially morphine, well in excess of the total seized in 2010. As a result of those successful operations, however, opium prices reached a near-record high in 2011, which drove farmers to plant poppies in large numbers in more remote areas with limited security. The reports also described ISAF support to Afghan-led governance efforts in areas of transition, reintegration, counter-corruption and rule of law improvement, as well as ISAF support to the development efforts of the Government.

SECURITY COUNCIL ACTION

On 12 October [meeting 6629], the Security Council unanimously adopted **resolution 2011(2011)**. The draft [S/2011/630] was submitted by Germany.

The Security Council,

Reaffirming its previous resolutions on Afghanistan, in particular its resolutions 1386(2001) of 20 December 2001, 1510(2003) of 13 October 2003, 1943(2010) of 13 October 2010 and 1974(2011) of 22 March 2011,

Reaffirming also its resolutions 1267(1999) of 15 October 1999, 1368(2001) of 12 September 2001, 1373(2001) of 28 September 2001, 1822(2008) of 30 June 2008, 1904(2009) of 17 December 2009 and 1988(2011) and 1989(2011) of 17 June 2011, and reiterating its support for international efforts to root out terrorism in accordance with the Charter of the United Nations,

Recalling its resolutions 1265(1999) of 17 September 1999, 1296(2000) of 19 April 2000, 1674(2006) of 28 April 2006, 1738(2006) of 23 December 2006 and 1894(2009) of 11 November 2009 on the protection of civilians in armed conflict, its resolutions 1325(2000) of 31 October 2000, 1820(2008) of 19 June 2008, 1888(2009) of 30 September 2009, 1889(2009) of 5 October 2009 and 1960(2010) of 16 December 2010 on women and peace and security, and its resolutions 1612(2005) of 26 July 2005, 1882(2009) of 4 August 2009 and 1998(2011) of 12 July 2011 on children and armed conflict, and noting as well the report of the Secretary-General on children and armed conflict in Afghanistan and the subsequent conclusions of its Working Group on Children and Armed Conflict,

Reaffirming its strong commitment to the sovereignty, independence, territorial integrity and national unity of Afghanistan,

Recognizing that the responsibility for providing security and law and order throughout the country resides with the Afghan authorities, stressing the role of the International Security Assistance Force in assisting the Government of Afghanistan to improve the security situation and build its own security capabilities, and welcoming the cooperation of the Government with the Force,

Welcoming the communiqués of the London Conference on Afghanistan, held on 28 January 2010, and the Kabul International Conference on Afghanistan, held on 20 July 2010, which set a clear agenda and agreed priorities for the way ahead on Afghanistan, and underlining the pivotal importance of strengthening Afghan ownership and leadership, consistent with the Kabul Process, in all fields of governance,

Recognizing once again the interconnected nature of the challenges in Afghanistan, reaffirming that sustainable progress on security, governance, human rights, the rule of law and development, as well as the cross-cutting issues of counter-narcotics, anti-corruption and accountability, is mutually reinforcing and that governance and development programmes prioritized for implementation in transition should be consistent with the goals set forth in the Kabul Process and the national priority programmes, and welcoming the continuing efforts of the Government of Afghanistan and the international community to address these challenges through a comprehensive approach,

Stressing, in this context, the need for further efforts by the Government of Afghanistan to fight corruption, promote transparency and increase its accountability, in line with the commitment of the Government to strengthen measures to combat corruption after the London and Kabul Conferences,

Underlining the significance of the agreement reached between the Government of Afghanistan and countries contributing to the International Security Assistance Force at the North Atlantic Treaty Organization summit held in Lisbon on 19 and 20 November 2010 to gradually transfer lead security responsibility in Afghanistan to the Government country-wide by the end of 2014, welcoming the ongoing implementation of the first phase of transition and looking forward to the phased extension of the process to the rest of the country, underlining the continuing role of the Force, in support of the Government, in promoting a responsible transition and the importance of the enhancement of the capabilities of the Afghan National Security Forces, stressing the long-term commitment, beyond 2014, of the international community to support the further development, including training, and professionalization of the Afghan National Security Forces and their capacity to counter continued threats to Afghanistan's security, with a view to lasting peace, security and stability, and noting that these issues will be discussed at the forthcoming North Atlantic Treaty Organization summit in Chicago, United States of America,

Welcoming the long-term commitments undertaken by Afghanistan's international partners, including the North Atlantic Treaty Organization and the European Union, neighbouring States and regional partners to continue supporting Afghanistan beyond transition, stressing the importance of their complementary nature, including with future bilateral partnerships decided upon by the Government of Afghanistan,

Looking forward to the International Afghanistan Conference on Afghanistan and the International Community: From Transition to the Transformation Decade, to be held in Bonn, Germany, on 5 December 2011, at which civil aspects of transition, the long-term commitment of the international community in Afghanistan within the region and the support of the political process will be further defined,

Also looking forward to the Conference on Security and Cooperation in the Heart of Asia, which will be held in Istanbul, Turkey, on 2 November 2011,

Noting regional initiatives, such as those being implemented within the framework of the Shanghai Cooperation Organization, the Collective Security Treaty Organization, the European Union, the Organization for Security and Cooperation in Europe, the South Asian Association for Regional Cooperation and other relevant initiatives aimed at increased regional economic cooperation with Afghanistan, such as the vision of the New Silk Road, and looking forward to the Fifth Regional Economic Cooperation Conference on Afghanistan, to be held in Tajikistan on 26 and 27 March 2012,

Stressing the central and impartial role that the United Nations continues to play in promoting peace and stability in Afghanistan by leading the efforts of the international community, noting in this context the synergies in the objectives of the United Nations Assistance Mission in Afghanistan and of the International Security Assistance Force, and, as transition moves forward, stressing the need for strengthened cooperation, coordination and mutual support, taking due account of their respective designated responsibilities and the evolving nature of the presence of the international community,

Expressing its serious concern about the security situation in Afghanistan, in particular the ongoing violent and terrorist activities by the Taliban, Al-Qaida, other illegal armed groups and criminals, including those involved in the narcotics trade, as described in the reports of the Secretary-General since the adoption of resolution 1943(2010), and the strong links between terrorism activities and illicit drugs, resulting in threats to the local population, including children, as well as to the national security forces and international military and civilian personnel,

Welcoming the efforts of the Government of Afghanistan to update and improve the National Drug Control Strategy, with a particular emphasis on a partnership approach to ensure joint, effective implementation and coordination, encouraging the International Security Assistance Force to further effectively support, within its designated responsibilities, Afghan-led sustained efforts to address drug production and trafficking, in cooperation with relevant international and regional actors, and recognizing the threat posed by illicit drug production, trade and trafficking to international peace and stability in different regions of the world, and the important role played by the United Nations Office on Drugs and Crime in this regard,

Expressing its concern over the harmful consequences of violent and terrorist activities by the Taliban, Al-Qaida and other violent and extremist groups on the capacity of the Government of Afghanistan to guarantee the rule of law, to provide security and basic services to the Afghan people and to ensure the full enjoyment of their human rights and fundamental freedoms,

Reiterating its support for the continuing endeavours of the Government of Afghanistan, with the assistance of the international community, including the International Security Assistance Force and the Operation Enduring Freedom coalition, to improve the security situation and to continue to address the threat posed by the Taliban, Al-Qaida and other violent and extremist groups, and stressing in this context the need for sustained international efforts, including those of the Force and the coalition,

Condemning in the strongest terms all attacks, including improvised explosive device attacks, suicide attacks, assassinations and abductions, indiscriminate targeting of civilians, attacks against humanitarian workers and targeting of Afghan and international forces, and their deleterious effect on the stabilization, reconstruction and development efforts in Afghanistan, and condemning further the use by the Taliban, Al-Qaida and other violent and extremist groups of civilians as human shields,

Condemning in particular the recent terrorist attacks against the InterContinental Hotel, the British Council building, the International Security Assistance Force headquarters and the Embassy of the United States of America in Kabul, and deploring the loss of life in these attacks, including of Afghan civilians, police and security forces,

Welcoming the achievements of the Government of Afghanistan in banning ammonium nitrate fertilizer, and urging continued action to implement regulations for the control of all explosive materials and precursor chemicals, thereby reducing the ability of insurgents to use them for improvised explosive devices,

Noting the ratification by Afghanistan of the Convention on Cluster Munitions,

Recognizing the continuing threats posed by the Taliban, Al-Qaida and other violent and extremist groups, as well as the challenges related to the efforts to address such threats,

Expressing its serious concern about the increased high number of civilian casualties in Afghanistan, in particular casualties among women and children, the increasingly large majority of which are caused by the Taliban, Al-Qaida and other violent and extremist groups, reaffirming that all parties to armed conflict must take all feasible steps to ensure the protection of affected civilians, especially women, children and displaced persons, calling for all parties to comply with their obligations under international humanitarian and human rights law and for all appropriate measures to be taken to ensure the protection of civilians, recognizing the importance of the ongoing monitoring of and reporting to the Security Council, including by the International Security Assistance Force, on the situation of civilians and, in particular, civilian casualties, and noting in this regard the work of the Force's Civilian Casualty Tracking Cell,

Taking note of the further progress made by the International Security Assistance Force and other international forces in minimizing civilian casualties, as recognized in the 2011 midyear report of the United Nations Assistance Mission in Afghanistan on the protection of civilians in armed conflict, urging the International Security Assistance Force and other international forces to continue to undertake enhanced efforts to prevent civilian casualties, including the increased focus on protecting the Afghan population as a central element of the mission, and noting the importance of conducting continuous reviews of tactics and procedures and after-action reviews and investigations in cooperation with the Government of Afghanistan in cases where civilian casualties have occurred and when the Government finds these joint investigations appropriate,

Expressing its strong concern about the recruitment and use of children by Taliban forces in Afghanistan as well as the killing and maiming of children as a result of the conflict, supporting the decree by the Minister of the Interior of 6 July 2011 reaffirming the commitment of the Government of Afghanistan to preventing violations of the rights of the child, welcoming the establishment of the Inter-Ministerial Steering Committee for the Protection of the Rights of Children and the subsequent signing by the Government of an action plan, and the annexes thereto, on children associated with national security forces in Afghanistan, and calling for the full implementation of the provisions of the action plan, in close cooperation with the United Nations Assistance Mission in Afghanistan,

Acknowledging the progress made and the challenges remaining in security sector reform and governance, welcoming the support and assistance extended to the Afghan National Police by the international partners in this regard, in particular the continued commitment of the North Atlantic Treaty Organization Training Mission–Afghanistan, the European Gendarmerie Force contribution to this mission and assistance extended to the Afghan National Police, including through the European Union Police Mission in Afghanistan and, in the context of transition, welcoming the increased capacities and capabilities of the Afghan National Security Forces, stressing the need for Afghanistan, together with international donors, to further strengthen the Afghan National Army and the Afghan National Police, and urging, inter alia, continued professional training measures to ensure Afghan capability to assume, in a sustainable manner, increasing responsibilities and leadership of security operations and maintain public order, law enforcement, the security of Afghanistan's borders and the preservation of the constitutional rights of Afghan citizens, as well as to increase its efforts in the disbandment of illegal armed groups and counter-narcotics, as outlined in the London Conference and Kabul Conference communiqués,

Stressing, in this context, the importance of further progress by the Government of Afghanistan in ending impunity and strengthening judicial institutions, in the reconstruction and reform of the prison sector, and the rule of law and respect for human rights within Afghanistan, including for women and girls, and, in particular, women's rights under the Constitution to fully participate in the political, economic and social spheres of Afghan life,

Reiterating its call upon all Afghan parties and groups to engage constructively in peaceful political dialogue within the framework of the Afghan Constitution, to work together with international donors for the socioeconomic development of the country and to avoid resorting to violence, including through the use of illegal armed groups, supporting the aims of the High Peace Council,

Strongly condemning the assassination of Professor Burhanuddin Rabbani, Chairman of the High Peace Council, emphasizing the importance of all States with relevant information extending to the Afghan authorities the assistance they may need and all relevant information they may possess pertaining to this terrorist attack, stressing the need for calm and solidarity in Afghanistan at this time and for all parties to reduce tensions, and reiterating its firm commitment to support the Government of Afghanistan in its efforts to advance the peace and reconciliation process, in line with the Kabul Conference communiqué and within the framework of the Afghan Constitution and application of the procedures introduced by the Security Council in its resolution 1988(2011) as well as other relevant resolutions of the Council,

Stressing the importance of a comprehensive political process in Afghanistan to support reconciliation for all those who are prepared to meet the conditions for reconciliation in the Kabul Conference communiqué supported by the Government of Afghanistan and the international community, with full respect for the implementation of measures and application of the procedures introduced by the Council in its resolutions 1267(1999) and 1988(2011) as well as other relevant resolutions of the Council, calling upon all relevant States to remain engaged in the peace process, and recognizing the impact terrorist attacks have on the Afghan people and risk having on future prospects for a peace settlement,

Recognizing that an increased number of Taliban have reconciled with the Government of Afghanistan, have rejected the terrorist ideology of Al-Qaida and its followers and support a peaceful resolution to the continuing conflict in Afghanistan, recognizing also that notwithstanding the evolution of the situation in Afghanistan and progress in reconciliation, security remains a serious challenge in Afghanistan and the region,

Recognizing also the increased number of reintegrees who have joined the Afghan Peace and Reintegration Programme, welcoming the results of the review conference of the Programme held in May 2011 and recent efforts to ensure its implementation, encouraging further efforts to address remaining operational challenges, including through an appropriate vetting mechanism, and further encouraging the international community to support this Afghan-led effort,

Welcoming the settlement of the institutional impasse after the decision to leave the Independent Electoral Commission with the final authority in electoral questions, reiterating the commitment of the Government of Afghanistan in the Kabul Conference communiqué to address long-term electoral reform, based on lessons learned in previous elections, including the 2010 parliamentary elections, and reaffirming that Afghanistan's peaceful future lies in the building of a stable, secure, economically self-sufficient State, free of terrorism and narcotics, based on strengthened democratic institutions, respect for the separation of powers, reinforced constitutional checks and balances and the guarantee and enforcement of citizens' rights and obligations,

Recognizing the importance of the contribution of neighbouring and regional partners as well as regional organizations, including the European Union, the Organization for Security and Cooperation in Europe, the Shanghai Cooperation Organization, the Collective Security Treaty Organization and the South Asian Association for Regional Cooperation, to the stabilization of Afghanistan, stressing the crucial importance of advancing regional cooperation as an effective means to promote security, governance and development in Afghanistan, and welcoming and supporting increased regional efforts towards the continued implementation of previous declarations of good-neighbourly relations,

Welcoming the efforts of the international community carried out to strengthen the coherence of military and civilian actions, including those within the framework of the International Security Assistance Force,

Welcoming also the continued coordination between the International Security Assistance Force and the Operation Enduring Freedom coalition, and in-theatre cooperation established between the Force and the European Union presence in Afghanistan,

Expressing its appreciation for the leadership provided by the North Atlantic Treaty Organization and for the contributions of many nations to the International Security Assistance Force and to the Operation Enduring Freedom coalition, which operates within the framework of the counter-terrorism operations in Afghanistan and in accordance with the applicable rules of international law,

Determining that the situation in Afghanistan still constitutes a threat to international peace and security,

Determined to ensure the full implementation of the mandate of the International Security Assistance Force, in coordination with the Government of Afghanistan,

Acting, for these reasons, under Chapter VII of the Charter,

1. *Decides* to extend the authorization of the International Security Assistance Force, as defined in resolutions 1386(2001) and 1510(2003), for a period of twelve months, until 13 October 2012;

2. *Authorizes* the Member States participating in the International Security Assistance Force to take all necessary measures to fulfil its mandate;

3. *Recognizes* the need for the International Security Assistance Force to meet all its operational requirements, welcomes the agreement between the Government of Afghanistan and countries contributing to the Force to gradually transfer lead security responsibility in Afghanistan to the Government country-wide by the end of 2014, and the start of the transition process in July 2011, and calls upon Member States to contribute personnel, equipment and other resources to the Force and to continue to pursue their efforts to support security and stability in Afghanistan;

4. *Welcomes* the Enduring Partnership Declaration agreed by the North Atlantic Treaty Organization and the Government of Afghanistan at the Lisbon summit in November 2010 and, in particular, the intention expressed therein to provide, within the framework of the Enduring Partnership, sustained practical support aimed at improving and sustaining Afghanistan's capacity and capability to tackle continued threats to its security, stability and integrity, and to contribute to the security of the region through the stabilization of the situation in Afghanistan;

5. *Stresses* the importance of increasing, within a comprehensive framework, the functionality, professionalism and accountability of the Afghan security sector, encourages the International Security Assistance Force and other partners to sustain their efforts, as resources permit, to train, mentor and empower the Afghan National Security Forces in order to accelerate progress towards the goal of self-sufficient, sustainable, accountable and ethnically balanced Afghan security forces providing security and ensuring the rule of law throughout the country, welcomes the increasing leadership role played by the Afghan authorities in security responsibilities throughout the country, and stresses the importance of supporting the planned expansion of the Afghan National Army and the Afghan National Police;

6. *Calls upon* the International Security Assistance Force and the Senior Civilian Representative of the North Atlantic Treaty Organization to continue to work in close consultation with the Government of Afghanistan and the Special Representative of the Secretary-General for Afghanistan in accordance with Security Council resolution 1974(2011), as well as with the Operation Enduring Freedom coalition, in the implementation of the mandate of the Force;

7. *Requests* the leadership of the International Security Assistance Force to keep the Council regularly informed, through the Secretary-General, on the implementation of its mandate, including through the timely provision of quarterly reports;

8. *Decides* to remain actively seized of the matter.

Children and armed conflict

Report of Secretary-General (February). In accordance with Security Council resolution 1612(2005) [YUN 2005, p. 863], the Secretary-General, in February, submitted his second country report [S/2011/55] on children and armed conflict in Afghanistan, covering the period from 1 September 2008 to 30 August 2010. He stated that 2010 was the most volatile year in security terms since the fall of the Taliban in 2001. During the reporting period, 1,795 children were injured or killed because of conflict-related violence, although the figures were assumed to be underreported as access to conflict-affected areas remained difficult. Children continued to be casualties of suicide attacks, improvised explosive devices and rocket attacks by armed groups, including the Taliban. They were also victims of air strikes and night searches by pro-Government forces. In addition, 568 children were injured or killed as a result of landmines and other explosive remnants of war.

Sexual violence in Afghanistan, including against children, was pervasive and mostly underreported. Isolated reports were received of sexual violence committed against children by members of the Afghan National Security Forces. Moreover, there continued to be reports of children, especially boys, being sexually abused and exploited by armed groups, including through the practice of *baccha baazi* (dancing boys). Child sexual abuse, against both girls and boys, was not clearly defined as a crime in Afghan law and perpetrators of such violations were rarely held accountable. A total of 77 cases of abducted children, both boys and girls, were reported to the Country Task Force for Monitoring and Reporting during the reporting period. There were a variety of reasons for abduction by armed groups, including retaliation, recruitment, ransom, and to pressure an exchange or release of certain individuals detained by the authorities. Attacks on schools and hospitals, including damage to schools, killing and injury of students and education personnel, threats and intimidation, and forced school closures, also increased. Most incidents were perpetrated by armed opposition groups, but also by communal and traditional elements opposed to girls' education. The recruitment and use of children by parties to the conflict was observed throughout the country. While many cases reported by the media and other sources could not be confirmed owing to access and security considerations, the Country Task Force for Monitoring and Reporting verified 26 out of 47 reported incidents that provided evidence that children were recruited by armed groups as well as by Afghan National Security Forces, including the Afghan National Police. Cases of children who carried out suicide attacks or who were used to plant explosives were reported. Children continued to be detained for alleged association with armed groups in international military forces detention facilities in contravention of international law.

The Secretary-General's Special Representative for Children and Armed Conflict, Radhika Coomaraswamy (Sri Lanka), visited Afghanistan from 20 to 26 February 2010 to follow up on the 2009 conclusions of the Security Council Working Group on Children and Armed Conflict [YUN 2009, p. 351]. She noted the political will expressed by the Government to protect children and to heed the conclusions. She also noted the productive engagement of the ISAF/United States Forces Joint Commander and the NATO Senior Civilian Representative on protection of children in conflict through continued review of tactics and procedures, and post-incident investigations.

The Secretary-General acknowledged that progress had been made since the previous reporting period, especially in terms of dialogue with the Government on the protection of children. He welcomed the Government's commitment to signing an Action Plan against recruitment and use of children in the Afghan National Security Forces, with annexes on sexual violence against children and the killing and maiming of children. A number of initiatives had taken place to address the violations and abuses committed against children affected by conflict in Afghanistan, including: legal aid for children, including for children—supported by the United Nations Children's Fund—detained on charges of alleged association with armed groups; negotiations by relevant organizations with the Government, armed opposition groups and community elders to facilitate health-care access and delivery; negotiation towards community-based protection of schools; and support to schools. The report concluded with recommendations to national and international actors to strengthen the protection of war-affected children in Afghanistan.

Working Group conclusions. Having examined the Secretary-General's second country report (see above) on 25 February, the Security Council Working Group on Children and Armed Conflict in May submitted its conclusions on children and armed conflict in Afghanistan [S/AC.51/2011/3], including its recommendations. On 2 June, the Security Council President transmitted to the Secretary-General a letter [S/2011/339] from the Chairman of the Working Group based on its conclusions.

Sanctions

UN sanctions-related activities were guided by the measures adopted by Security Council resolution 1904(2009) [YUN 2009, p. 355] and previous resolutions against Osama bin Laden, Al-Qaida, the Taliban, their associates and associated entities, which further refined the financial measures, travel ban and arms embargo imposed on those persons identified in the consolidated list created in accordance with resolution 1267(1999) [YUN 1999, p. 265]. The Al-Qaida and Taliban Sanctions Committee, established by resolution 1267(1999), oversaw the implementation of those measures.

On 2 May [SG/SM/13535], the Secretary-General said that the death of Osama bin Laden marked a watershed moment in the global fight against terrorism. On the same date, by presidential statement **S/PRST/2011/9** (see p. 52), the Council welcomed the news that bin Laden would never again be able to perpetrate acts of terrorism.

Separation of Al-Qaida and Taliban sanctions regime

On 17 June, the Security Council adopted resolution 1989(2011) (see p. 341), which changed the scope of the Committee's mandate, focusing it exclusively on Al-Qaida and associated individuals and entities. In the light of the change, the Council, on 30 June, changed the name of the Committee to "Security Council Committee pursuant to resolutions 1267(1999) and 1989(2011) concerning Al-Qaida and associated individuals and entities" (Al-Qaida Sanctions Committee).

In its resolutions 1988(2011) (see p. 337) and 1989(2011), the Council also decided to separate the former Al-Qaida/Taliban "Consolidated List" into two lists. The Al-Qaida Sanctions List, therefore, included only the names of "those individuals, groups, undertakings and entities associated with Al-Qaida". The names of Taliban individuals, formerly included on the Consolidated List, were transferred to the sanctions regime established pursuant to resolution 1988(2011).

In 2011, Peter Wittig (Germany) was the Chairman of both Committees, which were assisted by an Analytical Support and Sanctions Monitoring Team established by Council resolution 1526(2004) [YUN 2004, p. 332] and extended by resolution 1989(2011).

The Office of the Ombudsperson, established by Council resolution 1904(2009) [YUN 2009, p. 355] to assist the Al-Qaida and Taliban Sanctions Committee in considering requests for delisting and in addressing the right of a listed individual to a review of the listing by an independent mechanism, had its mandate extended by Council resolution 1989(2011) to assist the newly established Al-Qaida Sanctions Committee. On 30 June [S/2011/404], the Secretary-General informed the Council that he had reappointed Kimberly Prost (Canada) to serve as Ombudsperson until 31 December 2012.

SECURITY COUNCIL ACTION

On 17 June 2011 [meeting 6557], the Security Council unanimously adopted **resolution 1988(2011)**. The draft [S/2011/368] was submitted by France, Germany, Portugal, the United Kingdom and the United States.

The Security Council,

Recalling its previous resolutions on international terrorism and the threat it poses to Afghanistan, in particular resolutions 1267(1999) of 15 October 1999, 1333(2000) of 19 December 2000, 1363(2001) of 30 July 2001, 1373(2001) of 28 September 2001, 1390(2002) of 16 January 2002, 1452(2002) of 20 December 2002, 1455(2003) of 17 January 2003, 1526(2004) of 30 January 2004, 1566(2004) of 8 October 2004, 1617(2005) of 29 July 2005, 1624(2005) of 14 September 2005, 1699(2006) of 8 August 2006, 1730(2006) of 19 December 2006, 1735(2006) of 22 December 2006, 1822(2008) of 30 June 2008 and 1904(2009) of 17 December 2009, and the relevant statements by its President,

Recalling also its previous resolutions in which it extended until 23 March 2012 the mandate of the United Nations Assistance Mission in Afghanistan as established by resolution 1974(2011) of 22 March 2011,

Reaffirming that the situation in Afghanistan still constitutes a threat to international peace and security, and expressing its strong concern about the security situation in Afghanistan, in particular the ongoing violent and terrorist activities by the Taliban, Al-Qaida, illegal armed groups, criminals and those involved in the narcotics trade, and the strong links between terrorism activities and illicit drugs, resulting in threats to the local population, including children, national security forces and international military and civilian personnel,

Reaffirming its strong commitment to the sovereignty, independence, territorial integrity and national unity of Afghanistan,

Stressing the importance of a comprehensive political process in Afghanistan to support reconciliation among all Afghans, and recognizing that there is no purely military solution that will ensure the stability of Afghanistan,

Recalling the Government of Afghanistan's strong desire to seek national reconciliation, as set forth in the Bonn Agreement of 5 December 2001, at the London Conference on Afghanistan, held on 28 January 2010, and at the Kabul International Conference on Afghanistan, held on 20 July 2010,

Recognizing that the security situation in Afghanistan has evolved and that some members of the Taliban have reconciled with the Government of Afghanistan, have rejected the terrorist ideology of Al-Qaida and its followers and support a peaceful resolution to the continuing conflict in Afghanistan,

Recognizing also that, notwithstanding the evolution of the situation in Afghanistan and progress in reconciliation, the situation in Afghanistan remains a threat to international peace and security, and reaffirming the need to combat this threat by all means, in accordance with the Charter of the United Nations and international law, including applicable human rights, refugee and humanitarian law, stressing in this regard the important role that the United Nations plays in this effort,

Recalling that the conditions for reconciliation, open to all Afghans, set forth in the Kabul communiqué of 20 July 2010, supported by the Government of Afghanistan and the international community, include the renunciation of violence, no links to international terrorist organizations, and respect for the Afghan Constitution, including the rights of women and persons belonging to minorities,

Stressing the importance of all individuals, groups, undertakings and entities participating, by any means, in the financing or support of acts or activities of those previously designated as the Taliban, as well as those individuals, groups, undertakings and entities associated with the Taliban in constituting a threat to the peace, stability and security of Afghanistan, accepting the Government of Afghanistan's offer of reconciliation,

Taking note of the request by the Government of Afghanistan that the Security Council support national reconciliation by removing Afghan names from the United Nations sanctions lists for those who respect the conditions for reconciliation and, therefore, have ceased to engage in or support activities that threaten the peace, stability and security of Afghanistan,

Welcoming the results of the Consultative Peace Jirga, held from 2 to 4 June 2010, in which 1,600 Afghan delegates, representing a broad cross-section of all Afghan ethnic and religious groups, government officials, religious scholars, tribal leaders, civil society and Afghan refugees residing in the Islamic Republic of Iran and Pakistan, discussed an end to insecurity and developed a plan for lasting peace in the country,

Welcoming also the establishment of the High Peace Council and its outreach efforts, both within and outside Afghanistan,

Stressing the central and impartial role that the United Nations continues to play in promoting peace, stability and security in Afghanistan, and expressing its appreciation and strong support for the ongoing efforts of the Secretary-General, his Special Representative for Afghanistan and the Mission's Salaam Support Group to assist the peace and reconciliation efforts of the High Peace Council,

Reiterating its support for the fight against the illicit production of and trafficking in drugs from, and chemical precursors to, Afghanistan, in neighbouring countries, countries on trafficking routes, drug destination countries and precursor-producing countries,

Expressing concern at the increase in incidents of kidnapping and hostage-taking with the aim of raising funds or gaining political concessions, and expressing the need for this issue to be addressed,

Reiterating the need to ensure that the present sanctions regime contributes effectively to ongoing efforts to combat the insurgency and support the work of the Government of Afghanistan to advance reconciliation in order to bring about peace, stability and security in Afghanistan, and considering the deliberations of the Security Council Committee established pursuant to resolution 1267(1999) on the recommendation of its Analytical Support and Sanctions

Monitoring Team, in its eleventh report to the Committee, that Member States treat listed Taliban and listed individuals and entities of Al-Qaida and its affiliates differently in promoting peace and stability in Afghanistan,

Reaffirming international support for Afghan-led reconciliation efforts, and expressing its intention to give due regard to lifting sanctions on those who reconcile,

Acting under Chapter VII of the Charter,

Measures

1. *Decides* that all States shall take the following measures with respect to individuals and entities designated prior to this date as the Taliban, and other individuals, groups, undertakings and entities associated with them, as specified in section A ("Individuals associated with the Taliban") and section B ("Entities and other groups and undertakings associated with the Taliban") of the Consolidated List of the Committee, established pursuant to resolutions 1267(1999) and 1333(2000) as of the date of adoption of the present resolution, as well as other individuals, groups, undertakings and entities associated with the Taliban in constituting a threat to the peace, stability and security of Afghanistan as designated by the Committee established pursuant to paragraph 30 below (hereinafter known as "the List"):

(*a*) Freeze without delay the funds and other financial assets or economic resources of those individuals, groups, undertakings and entities, including funds derived from property owned or controlled, directly or indirectly, by them or by persons acting on their behalf or at their direction, and ensure that neither these nor any other funds, financial assets or economic resources are made available, directly or indirectly, for the benefit of such persons by their nationals or by persons within their territories;

(*b*) Prevent the entry into or transit through their territories of those individuals, provided that nothing in the present paragraph shall oblige any State to deny entry into or require the departure from its territories of its own nationals and that the present paragraph shall not apply where entry or transit is necessary for the fulfilment of a judicial process, or the Committee determines on a case-by-case basis only that entry or transit is justified, including where this directly relates to supporting efforts by the Government of Afghanistan to promote reconciliation;

(*c*) Prevent the direct or indirect supply, sale or transfer to those individuals, groups, undertakings and entities, from their territories or by their nationals outside their territories, or using their flag vessels or aircraft, of arms and related materiel of all types, including weapons and ammunition, military vehicles and equipment, paramilitary equipment, and spare parts for the aforementioned, and technical advice, assistance or training related to military activities;

2. *Decides also* that those previously designated as the Taliban, and other individuals, groups, undertakings and entities associated with them, whose names were inscribed in section A ("Individuals associated with the Taliban") and section B ("Entities and other groups and undertakings associated with the Taliban") of the Consolidated List maintained by the Security Council Committee established pursuant to resolution 1267(1999) concerning Al-Qaida and the Taliban and associated individuals and entities on the date of adoption of the present resolution shall no longer be a part of the Consolidated List, but shall henceforth be on the List described in paragraph 1 above, and decides further that all States shall take the measures set forth in paragraph 1 above against those listed individuals, groups, undertakings and entities;

3. *Decides further* that the acts or activities indicating that an individual, group, undertaking or entity is eligible for designation under paragraph 1 above include:

(*a*) Participating in the financing, planning, facilitating, preparing or perpetrating of acts or activities by, in conjunction with, under the name of, on behalf of, or in support of;

(*b*) Supplying, selling or transferring arms and related materiel to;

(*c*) Recruiting for; or

(*d*) Otherwise supporting acts or activities of those designated and other individuals, groups, undertakings and entities associated with the Taliban in constituting a threat to the peace, stability and security of Afghanistan;

4. *Affirms* that any undertaking or entity owned or controlled, directly or indirectly by, or otherwise supporting, such an individual, group, undertaking or entity on the List shall be eligible for designation;

5. *Notes* that such means of financing or support include but are not limited to the use of proceeds derived from illicit cultivation and production of and trafficking in narcotic drugs and their precursors originating in and transiting through Afghanistan;

6. *Confirms* that the requirements in paragraph 1 (*a*) above apply to financial and economic resources of every kind, including but not limited to those used for the provision of Internet hosting or related services, used for the support of the Taliban on the List, and other individuals, groups, undertakings and entities associated with them, as well as other individuals, groups, undertakings and entities associated with the Taliban in constituting a threat to the peace, stability and security of Afghanistan and other individuals, groups, undertakings or entities associated with them;

7. *Confirms also* that the requirements in paragraph 1 (*a*) above shall also apply to the payment of ransoms to individuals, groups, undertakings or entities on the List;

8. *Decides* that Member States may permit the addition to accounts frozen pursuant to the provisions of paragraph 1 above of any payment in favour of listed individuals, groups, undertakings or entities, provided that any such payments continue to be subject to the provisions in paragraph 1 above and are frozen;

9. *Decides also* that all Member States may make use of the provisions set out in paragraphs 1 and 2 of resolution 1452(2002), as amended by resolution 1735(2006), regarding available exemptions with regard to the measures in paragraph 1 (*a*) above, and encourages their use by Member States;

Listing

10. *Encourages* all Member States to submit to the Committee established pursuant to paragraph 30 below ("the Committee") for inclusion on the List names of individuals, groups, undertakings and entities participating, by any means, in the financing or support of acts or activities described in paragraph 3 above;

11. *Decides* that, when proposing names to the Committee for inclusion on the List, Member States shall provide the Committee with as much relevant information

as possible on the proposed name, in particular sufficient identifying information to allow for the accurate and positive identification of individuals, groups, undertakings and entities, and to the extent possible, the information required by the International Criminal Police Organization (INTERPOL) to issue a Special Notice;

12. *Decides also* that, when proposing names to the Committee for inclusion on the List, Member States shall also provide a detailed statement of case, and that the statement of case shall be releasable, upon request, except for the parts that a Member State identifies as being confidential to the Committee, and may be used to develop the narrative summary of reasons for listing described in paragraph 13 below;

13. *Directs* the Committee, with the assistance of the Analytical Support and Sanctions Monitoring Team and in coordination with the relevant designating States, to make accessible on the Committee website, at the same time that a name is added to the List, a narrative summary of reasons for listing for the corresponding entry;

14. *Calls upon* all members of the Committee and the Monitoring Team to share with the Committee any information they may have available regarding a listing request from a Member State so that this information may help to inform the decision of the Committee on designation and provide additional material for the narrative summary of reasons for listing described in paragraph 13 above;

15. *Requests* the Secretariat to publish on the Committee website all relevant publicly releasable information, including the narrative summary of reasons for listing, immediately after a name is added to the List, and highlights the importance of making the narrative summary of reasons for listing available in all official languages of the United Nations in a timely manner;

16. *Calls upon* Member States, when considering the proposal of a new designation, to consult with the Government of Afghanistan on the designation prior to submission to the Committee, where appropriate, and encourages all Member States considering the proposal of a new designation to seek advice from the United Nations Assistance Mission in Afghanistan, where appropriate;

17. *Decides* that the Committee shall, after publication but within three working days after a name is added to the List, notify the Government of Afghanistan, the Permanent Mission of Afghanistan and the Permanent Mission of the State(s) where the individual or entity is believed to be located and, in the case of non-Afghan individuals or entities, the State(s) of which the person is believed to be a national;

De-listing

18. *Directs* the Committee to remove expeditiously on a case-by-case basis individuals and entities that no longer meet the listing criteria outlined in paragraph 3 above, and requests that the Committee give due regard to requests for removal of individuals who meet the reconciliation conditions agreed to by the Government of Afghanistan and the international community, which include the renunciation of violence, no links to international terrorist organizations, including Al-Qaida, or any cell, affiliate, splinter group or derivative thereof, and respect for the Afghan Constitution, including the rights of women and persons belonging to minorities;

19. *Calls upon* Member States to coordinate their de-listing requests, as appropriate, with the Government of Afghanistan to ensure coordination with the peace and reconciliation efforts of the Government;

20. *Decides* that individuals and entities seeking removal from the List without the sponsorship of a Member State are eligible to submit such requests to the Focal Point mechanism established in resolution 1730(2006);

21. *Encourages* the Mission to support and facilitate cooperation between the Government of Afghanistan and the Committee to ensure that the Committee has sufficient information to consider de-listing requests, and directs the Committee established pursuant to paragraph 30 of the present resolution to consider de-listing requests in accordance with the following principles, where relevant:

(*a*) De-listing requests concerning reconciled individuals should, if possible, include a communication from the High Peace Council through the Government of Afghanistan confirming the reconciled status of the individual according to the reconciliation guidelines, or, in the case of individuals reconciled under the Strengthening Peace Programme, documentation attesting to their reconciliation under the previous programme, as well as current address and contact information;

(*b*) De-listing requests concerning individuals who formerly held positions in the Taliban regime prior to 2002 who no longer meet the listing criteria outlined in paragraph 3 of the present resolution should, if possible, include a communication from the Government of Afghanistan confirming that the individual is not an active supporter of, or participant in, acts that threaten the peace, stability and security of Afghanistan, as well as current address and contact information;

(*c*) De-listing requests for reportedly deceased individuals should include an official statement of death from the State of nationality, residence or other relevant State;

22. *Requests* all Member States, but particularly the Government of Afghanistan, to inform the Committee if they become aware of any information indicating that an individual, group, undertaking or entity that has been de-listed should be considered for designation under paragraph 1 of the present resolution, and further requests that the Government provide to the Committee an annual report on the status of reportedly reconciled individuals who have been de-listed by the Committee in the previous year;

23. *Directs* the Committee to consider expeditiously any information indicating that a de-listed individual has returned to activities set forth in paragraph 3 of the present resolution, including by engaging in acts inconsistent with the reconciliation conditions outlined in paragraph 18 of the present resolution, and requests the Government of Afghanistan or other Member States, where appropriate, to submit a request to add that individual's name back on the List;

24. *Decides* that the Secretariat shall, as soon as possible after the Committee has made a decision to remove a name from the List, transmit the decision to the Government of Afghanistan and the Permanent Mission of Afghanistan for notification, and the Secretariat should also, as soon as possible, notify the Permanent Mission of the State(s) in which the individual or entity is believed to be located and, in the case of non-Afghan individuals or entities, the State(s) of nationality, and decides further that States receiving such notification shall take measures, in accordance with domestic laws and practices, to notify or inform the concerned individual or entity of the de-listing in a timely manner;

Review and maintenance of the List

25. *Recognizes* that the ongoing conflict in Afghanistan, and the urgency that the Government of Afghanistan and the international community attach to a peaceful political solution to the conflict, requires timely and expeditious modifications to the List, including the addition and removal of individuals and entities, urges the Committee to decide on de-listing requests in a timely manner, requests the Committee to review each entry on the List on a regular basis, including, as appropriate, by means of reviews of individuals considered to be reconciled, individuals whose entries lack identifiers, individuals reportedly deceased, and entities reported or confirmed to have ceased to exist, directs the Committee to establish guidelines for such reviews accordingly, and requests the Monitoring Team to circulate to the Committee every six months:

(a) A list of individuals on the List whom the Government of Afghanistan considers to be reconciled along with relevant documentation as outlined in paragraph 21 (a) above;

(b) A list of individuals and entities on the List whose entries lack identifiers necessary to ensure effective implementation of the measures imposed upon them; and

(c) A list of individuals on the List who are reportedly deceased and entities that are reported or confirmed to have ceased to exist, along with the documentation requirements outlined in paragraph 21 (c) above;

26. *Urges* the Committee to ensure that there are fair and clear procedures for the conduct of its work, and directs the Committee to establish guidelines accordingly, as soon as possible, in particular with respect to paragraphs 9, 10, 11, 12, 17, 20, 21, 24, 25 and 27 of the present resolution;

27. *Encourages* Member States and relevant international organizations to send representatives to meet with the Committee to share information and discuss any relevant issues, and welcomes periodic briefings from the Government of Afghanistan on the impact of targeted sanctions on deterring threats to the peace, stability and security of Afghanistan and supporting Afghan-led reconciliation;

Cooperation with the Government of Afghanistan

28. *Encourages* continued cooperation between the Committee, the Government of Afghanistan and the Mission, including by identifying and providing detailed information regarding individuals and entities participating in the financing or support of acts or activities set forth in paragraph 3 of the present resolution, and by inviting representatives of the Mission to address the Committee;

29. *Welcomes* the Government of Afghanistan's desire to assist the Committee in the coordination of listing and de-listing requests and in the submission of all relevant information to the Committee;

New sanctions committee

30. *Decides* to establish, in accordance with rule 28 of its provisional rules of procedure, a Committee of the Security Council consisting of all the members of the Council ("the Committee"), to undertake the following tasks:

(a) To consider listing requests, de-listing requests and proposed updates to the existing information relevant to the List referred to in paragraph 1 above;

(b) To consider listing requests, de-listing requests and proposed updates to the existing information relevant to section A ("Individuals associated with the Taliban") and section B ("Entities and other groups and undertakings associated with the Taliban") of the Consolidated List that were pending before the Committee established pursuant to resolution 1267(1999) concerning Al-Qaida and the Taliban and associated individuals and entities as of the date of adoption of the present resolution;

(c) To update regularly the List referred to in paragraph 1 above;

(d) To make accessible on the Committee website narrative summaries of reasons for listing for all entries on the List;

(e) To review the names on the List;

(f) To make periodic reports to the Council on information submitted to the Committee regarding the implementation of the present resolution, including regarding non-compliance with the measures imposed by the resolution;

(g) To ensure that fair and clear procedures exist for placing individuals and entities on the List and for removing them as well as for granting humanitarian exemptions;

(h) To examine the reports presented by the Monitoring Team;

(i) To monitor implementation of the measures imposed in paragraph 1 above;

(j) To consider requests for exemptions in accordance with paragraphs 1 and 9 above;

(k) To establish such guidelines as may be necessary to facilitate the implementation of the measures imposed above;

(l) To encourage a dialogue between the Committee and interested Member States, in particular those in the region, including by inviting representatives of such States to meet with the Committee to discuss implementation of the measures;

(m) To seek from all States whatever information it may consider useful regarding the actions taken by them to implement effectively the measures imposed above;

(n) To examine and take appropriate action on information regarding alleged violations or non-compliance with the measures contained in the present resolution;

(o) To facilitate, through the Monitoring Team and specialized United Nations agencies, assistance in capacity-building for enhancing implementation of the measures, upon request by Member States; and

(p) To cooperate with other relevant Security Council sanctions committees, in particular the Committee established pursuant to resolution 1267(1999);

Monitoring Team

31. *Decides also*, in order to assist the Committee in fulfilling its mandate, that the Monitoring Team of the Committee established pursuant to resolution 1267(1999), established pursuant to paragraph 7 of resolution 1526(2004), shall also support the Committee for a period of eighteen months, with the mandate set forth in the annex to the present resolution, and requests the Secretary-General to make any necessary arrangements to this effect;

Coordination and outreach

32. *Recognizes* the need to maintain contact with relevant Security Council committees, international organizations and expert groups, including the Committee established pursuant to resolution 1267(1999), the Committee established pursuant to resolution 1373(2001) concerning

counter-terrorism (the Counter-Terrorism Committee), the United Nations Office on Drugs and Crime, the Counter-Terrorism Committee Executive Directorate and the Committee established pursuant to resolution 1540(2004), particularly given the continuing presence and negative influence on the Afghan conflict of Al-Qaida and any cell, affiliate, splinter group or derivative thereof;

33. *Encourages* the Mission to provide assistance to the High Peace Council, at its request, to encourage listed individuals to reconcile;

Reviews

34. *Decides* to review the implementation of the measures outlined in the present resolution in eighteen months and make adjustments, as necessary, to support peace and stability in Afghanistan;

35. *Decides also* to remain actively seized of the matter.

ANNEX

In accordance with paragraph 31 of this resolution, the Monitoring Team shall operate under the direction of the Committee and shall have the following responsibilities:

(*a*) To submit, in writing, two comprehensive, independent reports to the Committee, the first by 31 March 2012 and the second by 31 October 2012, on implementation by Member States of the measures referred to in paragraph 1 of this resolution, including specific recommendations for improved implementation of the measures and possible new measures;

(*b*) To assist the Committee in regularly reviewing names on the List, including by undertaking travel and contact with Member States, with a view to developing the Committee's record of the facts and circumstances relating to a listing;

(*c*) To assist the Committee in following up on requests to Member States for information, including with respect to implementation of the measures referred to in paragraph 1 of this resolution;

(*d*) To submit a comprehensive programme of work to the Committee for its review and approval, as necessary, in which the Monitoring Team should detail the activities envisaged in order to fulfil its responsibilities, including proposed travel;

(*e*) To assist the Committee with its analysis of non-compliance with the measures referred to in paragraph 1 of this resolution by collating information collected from Member States and submitting case studies, both on its own initiative and upon the Committee's request, to the Committee for its review;

(*f*) To present to the Committee recommendations which could be used by Member States to assist them with the implementation of the measures referred to in paragraph 1 of this resolution and in preparing proposed additions to the List;

(*g*) To assist the Committee in its consideration of proposals for listing, including by compiling and circulating to the Committee information relevant to the proposed listing and preparing a draft narrative summary, referred to in paragraph 13 of this resolution;

(*h*) To bring to the attention of the Committee new or noteworthy circumstances that may warrant a de-listing, such as publicly reported information on a deceased individual;

(*i*) To consult with Member States in advance of travel to selected Member States, based on its programme of work as approved by the Committee;

(*j*) To encourage Member States to submit names and additional identifying information for inclusion on the List, as instructed by the Committee;

(*k*) To present to the Committee additional identifying and other information to assist the Committee in its efforts to keep the List as updated and accurate as possible;

(*l*) To collate, assess, monitor and report on and make recommendations regarding implementation of the measures, to pursue case studies, as appropriate, and to explore in depth any other relevant issues as directed by the Committee;

(*m*) To consult with Member States and other relevant organizations and bodies, including the United Nations Assistance Mission in Afghanistan, and engage in regular dialogue with representatives in New York and in capitals, taking into account their comments, especially regarding any issues that might be contained in the reports of the Monitoring Team referred to in paragraph (*a*) of this annex;

(*n*) To consult with Member States' intelligence and security services, including through regional forums, in order to facilitate the sharing of information and to strengthen enforcement of the measures;

(*o*) To consult with relevant representatives of the private sector, including financial institutions, to learn about the practical implementation of the assets freeze and to develop recommendations for the strengthening of that measure;

(*p*) To work with relevant international and regional organizations in order to promote awareness of, and compliance with, the measures;

(*q*) To work with INTERPOL and Member States to obtain photographs of listed individuals for possible inclusion in INTERPOL Special Notices;

(*r*) To assist other subsidiary bodies of the Security Council, and their expert panels, upon request, with enhancing their cooperation with INTERPOL, referred to in resolution 1699(2006);

(*s*) To assist the Committee in facilitating assistance in capacity-building for enhancing implementation of the measures, upon request by Member States;

(*t*) To report to the Committee, on a regular basis or when the Committee so requests, through oral and/or written briefings on the work of the Monitoring Team, including its visits to Member States and its activities;

(*u*) To submit to the Committee within ninety days a written report and recommendations on linkages between those individuals, groups, undertakings and entities eligible for designation under paragraph 1 of this resolution and Al-Qaida, with a particular focus on entries that appear on both the Al-Qaida Sanctions List and the List referred to in paragraph 1 of this resolution, and thereafter submit such a report and recommendations periodically; and

(*v*) Any other responsibility identified by the Committee.

Also on 17 June [meeting 6557], the Security Council unanimously adopted **resolution 1989(2011)**. The draft [S/2011/369] was submitted by France, Germany, the United Kingdom and the United States.

The Security Council,

Recalling its resolutions 1267(1999) of 15 October 1999, 1333(2000) of 19 December 2000, 1363(2001) of 30 July 2001, 1373(2001) of 28 September 2001, 1390(2002) of 16 January 2002, 1452(2002) of 20 December 2002, 1455(2003) of 17 January 2003, 1526(2004) of 30 January 2004, 1566(2004) of 8 October 2004, 1617(2005) of 29 July 2005, 1624(2005) of 14 September 2005, 1699(2006) of 8 August 2006, 1730(2006) of 19 December 2006, 1735(2006) of 22 December 2006, 1822(2008) of 30 June 2008, 1904(2009) of 17 December 2009 and 1988(2011) of 17 June 2011, and the relevant statements by its President,

Reaffirming that terrorism in all its forms and manifestations constitutes one of the most serious threats to peace and security and that any acts of terrorism are criminal and unjustifiable regardless of their motivations, whenever and by whomsoever committed, and reiterating its unequivocal condemnation of Al-Qaida and other individuals, groups, undertakings and entities associated with it, for ongoing and multiple criminal terrorist acts aimed at causing the deaths of innocent civilians and other victims and the destruction of property and greatly undermining stability,

Reaffirming also that terrorism cannot and should not be associated with any religion, nationality or civilization,

Recalling the statement by the President of the Security Council of 2 May 2011, which notes that Osama bin Laden will no longer be able to perpetrate acts of terrorism,

Reaffirming the need to combat by all means, in accordance with the Charter of the United Nations and international law, including applicable international human rights, refugee and humanitarian law, threats to international peace and security caused by terrorist acts, stressing in this regard the important role that the United Nations plays in leading and coordinating this effort,

Expressing concern at the increase in incidents of kidnapping and hostage-taking by terrorist groups with the aim of raising funds or gaining political concessions, and expressing the need for this issue to be addressed,

Stressing that terrorism can only be defeated by a sustained and comprehensive approach involving the active participation and collaboration of all States and international and regional organizations to impede, impair, isolate and incapacitate the terrorist threat,

Emphasizing that sanctions are an important tool under the Charter in the maintenance and restoration of international peace and security, and stressing in this regard the need for robust implementation of the measures in paragraph 1 of the present resolution as a significant tool in combating terrorist activity,

Urging all Member States to participate actively in maintaining and updating the list created pursuant to resolutions 1267(1999) and 1333(2000) ("the Consolidated List") by contributing additional information pertinent to current listings, by submitting de-listing requests when appropriate, and by identifying and nominating for listing additional individuals, groups, undertakings and entities which should be subject to the measures referred to in paragraph 1 of the present resolution,

Reminding the Security Council Committee established pursuant to resolution 1267(1999) ("the Committee") to remove expeditiously and on a case-by-case basis individuals and entities that no longer meet the criteria for listing outlined in the present resolution,

Recognizing the challenges, both legal and otherwise, to the measures implemented by Member States under paragraph 1 of the present resolution, welcoming improvements to the procedures of the Committee and the quality of the Consolidated List, and expressing its intention to continue efforts to ensure that procedures are fair and clear,

Welcoming in particular the successful completion of the review of all names on the Consolidated List pursuant to paragraph 25 of resolution 1822(2008) and the significant progress made to enhance the integrity of the Consolidated List,

Welcoming the establishment of the Office of the Ombudsperson pursuant to resolution 1904(2009) and the role it has performed since its establishment, noting the important role of the Ombudsperson in improving fairness and transparency, recalling the firm commitment of the Council to ensuring that the Office is able to continue to carry out its role effectively, in accordance with its mandate, and recalling also the statement by the President of the Council of 28 February 2011,

Reiterating that the measures referred to in paragraph 1 of the present resolution are preventative in nature and are not reliant upon criminal standards set out under national law,

Welcoming the second review in September 2010 by the General Assembly of the United Nations Global Counter-Terrorism Strategy of 8 September 2006 and the creation of the Counter-Terrorism Implementation Task Force to ensure overall coordination and coherence in the counter-terrorism efforts of the United Nations system,

Welcoming also the continuing cooperation between the Committee and the International Criminal Police Organization (INTERPOL), the United Nations Office on Drugs and Crime, in particular on technical assistance and capacity-building, and all other United Nations bodies, and encouraging further engagement with the Counter-Terrorism Implementation Task Force to ensure overall coordination and coherence in the counter-terrorism efforts of the United Nations system,

Recognizing the need to take measures to prevent and suppress the financing of terrorism and terrorist organizations, including from the proceeds of organized crime, inter alia, the illicit production of and trafficking in drugs and their chemical precursors, and the importance of continued international cooperation with that aim,

Noting with concern the continued threat to international peace and security posed by Al-Qaida and other individuals, groups, undertakings and entities associated with it, reaffirming its resolve to address all aspects of that threat, and considering the deliberations of the Committee on the recommendation of its Analytical Support and Sanctions Monitoring Team, in its eleventh report to the Committee, that Member States treat listed Taliban and listed individuals and entities of Al-Qaida and its affiliates differently,

Noting that, in some instances, certain individuals, groups, undertakings and entities that meet the criteria for listing set forth in paragraph 3 of resolution 1988(2011) may also meet the criteria for listing set forth in paragraph 4 of the present resolution,

Acting under Chapter VII of the Charter,

Measures

1. *Decides* that all States shall take the following measures, as previously imposed by paragraph 8 (*c*) of resolution 1333(2000) and paragraphs 1 and 2 of resolution 1390(2002), with respect to Al-Qaida and other individuals, groups, undertakings and entities associated with it, including those referred to in section C ("Individuals associated with Al-Qaida") and section D ("Entities and other groups and undertakings associated with Al-Qaida") of the Consolidated List established pursuant to resolutions 1267(1999) and 1333(2000), as well as those designated after the date of adoption of the present resolution, which shall henceforth be known as "the Al-Qaida Sanctions List":

(*a*) Freeze without delay the funds and other financial assets or economic resources of those individuals, groups, undertakings and entities, including funds derived from property owned or controlled, directly or indirectly, by them or by persons acting on their behalf or at their direction, and ensure that neither these nor any other funds, financial assets or economic resources are made available, directly or indirectly, for the benefit of such persons, by their nationals or by persons within their territories;

(*b*) Prevent the entry into or transit through their territories of those individuals, provided that nothing in the present paragraph shall oblige any State to deny entry into or require the departure from its territories of its own nationals and that the present paragraph shall not apply where entry or transit is necessary for the fulfilment of a judicial process or the Committee determines on a case-by-case basis only that entry or transit is justified;

(*c*) Prevent the direct or indirect supply, sale or transfer to those individuals, groups, undertakings and entities, from their territories or by their nationals outside their territories, or using their flag vessels or aircraft, of arms and related materiel of all types, including weapons and ammunition, military vehicles and equipment, paramilitary equipment, and spare parts for the aforementioned, and technical advice, assistance or training related to military activities;

2. *Notes* that, pursuant to resolution 1988(2011), the Taliban and other individuals, groups, undertakings and entities associated with them, as previously included in section A ("Individuals associated with the Taliban) and section B ("Entities and other groups and undertakings associated with the Taliban") of the Consolidated List established pursuant to resolutions 1267(1999) and 1333(2000) are not governed by the present resolution, and decides that henceforth the Al-Qaida Sanctions List shall include only the names of those individuals, groups, undertakings and entities associated with Al-Qaida;

3. *Directs* the Committee to transmit to the Security Council Committee established pursuant to resolution 1988(2011) all listing submissions, de-listing requests and proposed updates to the existing information relevant to section A ("Individuals associated with the Taliban") and section B ("Entities and other groups and undertakings associated with the Taliban") of the Consolidated List that were pending before the Committee as of the date of adoption of the present resolution, so that the Committee established pursuant to resolution 1988(2011) can consider those matters in accordance with resolution 1988(2011);

4. *Reaffirms* that acts or activities indicating that an individual, group, undertaking or entity is associated with Al-Qaida include:

(*a*) Participating in the financing, planning, facilitating, preparing or perpetrating of acts or activities by, in conjunction with, under the name of, on behalf of, or in support of;

(*b*) Supplying, selling or transferring arms and related materiel to;

(*c*) Recruiting for; or otherwise supporting acts or activities of Al-Qaida or any cell, affiliate, splinter group or derivative thereof;

5. *Also reaffirms* that any undertaking or entity owned or controlled, directly or indirectly, by, or otherwise supporting, such an individual, group, undertaking or entity associated with Al-Qaida shall be eligible for designation;

6. *Confirms* that the requirements in paragraph 1 (*a*) above apply to financial and economic resources of every kind, including but not limited to those used for the provision of Internet hosting or related services, used for the support of Al-Qaida and other individuals, groups, undertakings or entities associated with it;

7. *Notes* that such means of financing or support include but are not limited to the use of proceeds derived from crime, including the illicit cultivation and production of and trafficking in narcotic drugs and their precursors;

8. *Confirms* that the requirements in paragraph 1 (*a*) above shall also apply to the payment of ransoms to individuals, groups, undertakings or entities on the Al-Qaida Sanctions List;

9. *Decides* that Member States may permit the addition to accounts frozen pursuant to the provisions of paragraph 1 above of any payment in favour of listed individuals, groups, undertakings or entities, provided that any such payments continue to be subject to the provisions in paragraph 1 above and are frozen;

10. *Encourages* Member States to make use of the provisions regarding available exemptions to the measures in paragraph 1 (*a*) above, set out in paragraphs 1 and 2 of resolution 1452(2002), as amended by resolution 1735(2006), and directs the Committee to review the procedures for exemptions as set out in the Committee guidelines to facilitate their use by Member States and to continue to ensure that exemptions are granted expeditiously and transparently;

11. *Directs* the Committee to cooperate with other relevant Security Council sanctions committees, in particular the Committee established pursuant to resolution 1988(2011);

Listing

12. *Encourages* all Member States to submit to the Committee for inclusion on the Al-Qaida Sanctions List names of individuals, groups, undertakings and entities participating, by any means, in the financing or support of acts or activities of Al-Qaida and other individuals, groups, undertakings and entities associated with it, as described in paragraph 2 of resolution 1617(2005) and reaffirmed in paragraph 4 above;

13. *Reaffirms* that, when proposing names to the Committee for inclusion on the Al-Qaida Sanctions List, Member States shall act in accordance with paragraph 5 of resolution 1735(2006) and paragraph 12 of resolution 1822(2008) and provide a detailed statement of case, and decides further that the statement of case shall be releasable, upon request, except for the parts that a Member State

identifies as being confidential to the Committee, and may be used to develop the narrative summary of reasons for listing described in paragraph 16 below;

14. *Decides* that Member States proposing a new designation, as well as Member States that have proposed names for inclusion on the Al-Qaida Sanctions List before the adoption of the present resolution, shall specify whether the Committee, or the Ombudsperson, or the Secretariat or the Analytical Support and Sanctions Monitoring Team on behalf of the Committee, may make known the status of the Member State as a designating State; and strongly encourages designating States to respond positively to such a request;

15. *Decides also* that Member States, when proposing names to the Committee for inclusion on the Al-Qaida Sanctions List shall use the standard form for listing, and provide the Committee with as much relevant information as possible on the proposed name, in particular sufficient identifying information to allow for the accurate and positive identification of individuals, groups, undertakings and entities, and to the extent possible, the information required by INTERPOL to issue a Special Notice, and directs the Committee to update, as necessary, the standard form for listing in accordance with the provisions of the present resolution; and further directs the Monitoring Team to report to the Committee on further steps that could be taken to improve identifying information;

16. *Welcomes* efforts by the Committee, with the assistance of the Monitoring Team and in coordination with the relevant designating States, to make accessible on the Committee website, at the same time that a name is added to the Al-Qaida Sanctions List, a narrative summary of reasons for listing for the corresponding entry, and directs the Committee, with the assistance of the Monitoring Team and in coordination with the relevant designating States, to continue its efforts to make accessible on the Committee website narrative summaries of reasons for all listings;

17. *Encourages* Member States and relevant international organizations and bodies to inform the Committee of any relevant court decisions and proceedings so that the Committee can consider them when it reviews a corresponding listing or updates a narrative summary of reasons for listing;

18. *Calls upon* all members of the Committee and the Monitoring Team to share with the Committee any information they may have available regarding a listing request from a Member State so that this information may help to inform the decision of the Committee on designation and provide additional material for the narrative summary of reasons for listing described in paragraph 16 above;

19. *Reaffirms* that the Secretariat shall, after publication but within three working days after a name is added to the Al-Qaida Sanctions List, notify the permanent mission of the country or countries where the individual or entity is believed to be located and, in the case of individuals, the country of which the person is a national (to the extent this information is known), in accordance with paragraph 10 of resolution 1735(2006), requests the Secretariat to publish on the Committee website all relevant publicly releasable information, including the narrative summary of reasons for listing, immediately after a name is added to the Al-Qaida Sanctions List, and highlights the importance of making the narrative summary of reasons for listing available in all official languages of the United Nations in a timely manner;

20. *Also reaffirms* the provisions in paragraph 17 of resolution 1822(2008) regarding the requirement that Member States take all possible measures, in accordance with their domestic laws and practices, to notify or inform in a timely manner the listed individual or entity of the designation and to include with this notification the narrative summary of reasons for listing, a description of the effects of designation, as provided in the relevant resolutions, the procedures of the Committee for considering de-listing requests, including the possibility of submitting such a request to the Ombudsperson in accordance with paragraph 21 and annex II to the present resolution, and the provisions of resolution 1452(2002) regarding available exemptions;

De-listing/Ombudsperson

21. *Decides* to extend the mandate of the Office of the Ombudsperson, established by resolution 1904(2009), as reflected in the procedures outlined in annex II to the present resolution, for a period of eighteen months from the date of adoption of the present resolution, decides that the Ombudsperson shall continue to receive requests from individuals, groups, undertakings or entities seeking to be removed from the Al-Qaida Sanctions List in an independent and impartial manner and shall neither seek nor receive instructions from any Government, and decides that the Ombudsperson shall present to the Committee observations and a recommendation on the de-listing of those individuals, groups, undertakings or entities that have requested removal from the Al-Qaida Sanctions List through the Office of the Ombudsperson, either a recommendation to retain the listing or a recommendation that the Committee consider de-listing;

22. *Decides also* that the requirement for States to take the measures described in paragraph 1 of the present resolution shall remain in place with respect to that individual, group, undertaking or entity where the Ombudsperson recommends retaining the listing in the comprehensive report of the Ombudsperson on a de-listing request pursuant to annex II to the present resolution;

23. *Decides further* that the requirement for States to take the measures described in paragraph 1 of the present resolution shall terminate with respect to that individual, group, undertaking or entity sixty days after the Committee completes consideration of a comprehensive report of the Ombudsperson, in accordance with annex II to the present resolution, including paragraph 6 (*h*) thereof, where the Ombudsperson recommends that the Committee consider de-listing, unless the Committee decides by consensus before the end of that sixty-day period that the requirement shall remain in place with respect to that individual, group, undertaking or entity; provided that, in cases where consensus does not exist, the Chair shall, on the request of a Committee member, submit the question of whether to de-list that individual, group, undertaking or entity to the Security Council for a decision within a period of sixty days; and provided further that, in the event of such a request, the requirement for States to take the measures described in paragraph 1 of the present resolution shall remain in force for that period with respect to that individual,

group, undertaking or entity until the question is decided by the Council;

24. *Requests* the Secretary-General to strengthen the capacity of the Office of the Ombudsperson to ensure its continued ability to carry out its mandate in an effective and timely manner;

25. *Strongly urges* Member States to provide all relevant information to the Ombudsperson, including providing any relevant confidential information, where appropriate, and confirms that the Ombudsperson must comply with any confidentiality restrictions that are placed on such information by Member States providing it;

26. *Requests* that Member States and relevant international organizations and bodies encourage individuals and entities that are considering challenging or are already in the process of challenging their listing through national and regional courts to seek removal from the Al-Qaida Sanctions List by submitting de-listing petitions to the Office of the Ombudsperson;

27. *Decides* that, when the designating State submits a de-listing request, the requirement for States to take the measures described in paragraph 1 of the present resolution shall terminate with respect to that individual, group, undertaking or entity after sixty days unless the Committee decides by consensus before the end of that sixty-day period that the measures shall remain in place with respect to that individual, group, undertaking or entity; provided that, in cases where consensus does not exist, the Chair shall, on the request of a Committee member, submit the question of whether to de-list that individual, group, undertaking or entity to the Security Council for a decision within a period of sixty days; and provided further that, in the event of such a request, the requirement for States to take the measures described in paragraph 1 of the present resolution shall remain in force for that period with respect to that individual, group, undertaking or entity until the question is decided by the Council;

28. *Decides also* that, for purposes of submitting a de-listing request in paragraph 27 above, consensus must exist between or among all designating States in cases where there are multiple designating States; and decides further that co-sponsors of listing requests shall not be considered designating States for purposes of paragraph 27 above;

29. *Strongly urges* designating States to allow the Ombudsperson to reveal their identities as designating States to those listed individuals and entities that have submitted de-listing petitions to the Ombudsperson;

30. *Directs* the Committee to continue to work, in accordance with its guidelines, to consider de-listing requests of Member States for the removal from the Al-Qaida Sanctions List of individuals, groups, undertakings and entities that are alleged to no longer meet the criteria established in the relevant resolutions, and set out in paragraph 4 of the present resolution, which shall be placed on the agenda of the Committee upon request of a member of the Committee, and encourages Member States to provide reasons for submitting their de-listing requests;

31. *Encourages* States to submit de-listing requests for individuals that are officially confirmed to be dead, particularly where no assets are identified, and for entities reported or confirmed to have ceased to exist, while at the same time taking all reasonable measures to ensure that the assets that had belonged to these individuals or entities have not been or will not be transferred or distributed to other individuals, groups, undertakings and entities on the Al-Qaida Sanctions List;

32. *Encourages* Member States, when unfreezing the assets of a deceased individual or an entity that is reported or confirmed to have ceased to exist as a result of a de-listing, to recall the obligations set forth in resolution 1373(2001) and, in particular, to prevent unfrozen assets from being used for terrorist purposes;

33. *Calls upon* the Committee, when considering de-listing requests, to give due consideration to the opinions of the designating State(s), State(s) of residence, nationality, location or incorporation, and other relevant States as determined by the Committee, directs Committee members to provide their reasons for objecting to de-listing requests at the time the request is objected to, and calls upon the Committee to share its reasons with relevant Member States and national and regional courts and bodies, where appropriate;

34. *Encourages* all Member States, including designating States and States of residence and nationality, to provide all information to the Committee relevant to the review by the Committee of de-listing petitions, and to meet with the Committee, if requested, to convey their views on de-listing requests, and further encourages the Committee, where appropriate, to meet with representatives of national or regional organizations and bodies that have relevant information on de-listing petitions;

35. *Confirms* that the Secretariat shall, within three days after a name is removed from the Al-Qaida Sanctions List, notify the permanent mission of the State(s) of residence, nationality, location or incorporation (to the extent this information is known), and decides that States receiving such notification shall take measures, in accordance with their domestic laws and practices, to notify or inform the concerned individual or entity of the de-listing in a timely manner;

Review and maintenance of the Al-Qaida Sanctions List

36. *Encourages* all Member States, in particular designating States and States of residence or nationality, to submit to the Committee additional identifying and other information, along with supporting documentation, on listed individuals, groups, undertakings and entities, including updates on the operating status of listed entities, groups and undertakings, the movement, incarceration or death of listed individuals and other significant events, as such information becomes available;

37. *Requests* the Monitoring Team to circulate to the Committee every six months a list of individuals and entities on the Al-Qaida Sanctions List whose entries lack identifiers necessary to ensure effective implementation of the measures imposed upon them, and directs the Committee to review these listings to decide whether they remain appropriate;

38. *Reaffirms* that the Monitoring Team should circulate to the Committee every six months a list of individuals on the Al-Qaida Sanctions List who are reportedly deceased, along with an assessment of relevant information, such as the certification of death, and to the extent possible, the status and location of frozen assets and the names of any individuals or entities that would be in a position to receive any unfrozen assets, directs the Committee to review these listings to decide whether they remain appropriate, and calls upon the Committee to remove listings of

deceased individuals, where credible information regarding death is available;

39. *Also reaffirms* that the Monitoring Team should circulate to the Committee every six months a list of entities on the Al-Qaida Sanctions List that are reported or confirmed to have ceased to exist, along with an assessment of any relevant information, directs the Committee to review these listings to decide whether they remain appropriate, and calls upon the Committee to remove such listings where credible information is available;

40. *Directs* the Committee, in the light of the completion of the review described in paragraph 25 of resolution 1822(2008), to conduct an annual review of all names on the Al-Qaida Sanctions List that have not been reviewed in three or more years ("the triennial review"), in which the relevant names are circulated to the designating States and States of residence, nationality, location or incorporation, where known, pursuant to the procedures set forth in the Committee guidelines, to ensure that the Al-Qaida Sanctions List is as updated and accurate as possible by identifying listings that no longer remain appropriate and confirming listings that remain appropriate, and notes that the consideration by the Committee of a de-listing request after the date of adoption of the present resolution, pursuant to the procedures set out in annex II to the present resolution, should be considered equivalent to a review conducted pursuant to paragraph 26 of resolution 1822(2008);

Measures—implementation

41. *Reiterates* the importance of all States identifying, and if necessary introducing, adequate procedures to implement fully all aspects of the measures described in paragraph 1 above; and, recalling paragraph 7 of resolution 1617(2005), strongly urges all Member States to implement the comprehensive international standards embodied in the Forty Recommendations on Money Laundering and the nine Special Recommendations on Terrorist Financing of the Financial Action Task Force, and encourages Member States to utilize the guidance provided in Special Recommendation III for effective implementation of targeted counter-terrorism sanctions;

42. *Directs* the Committee to continue to ensure that fair and clear procedures exist for placing individuals and entities on the Al-Qaida Sanctions List and for removing them as well as for granting exemptions as per resolution 1452(2002), and directs the Committee to keep its guidelines under active review in support of these objectives;

43. *Also directs* the Committee, as a matter of priority, to review its guidelines with respect to the provisions of the present resolution, in particular paragraphs 10, 12, 14, 15, 17, 21, 23, 27, 28, 30, 33, 37 and 40;

44. *Encourages* Member States, including through their permanent missions, and relevant international organizations to meet with the Committee for in-depth discussion on any relevant issues;

45. *Requests* the Committee to report to the Council on its findings regarding implementation efforts by Member States, and to identify and recommend steps necessary to improve implementation;

46. *Directs* the Committee to identify possible cases of non-compliance with the measures pursuant to paragraph 1 above and to determine the appropriate course of action on each case, and requests the Chair of the Committee, in periodic reports to the Council pursuant to paragraph 55 below, to provide progress reports on the work of the Committee on this issue;

47. *Urges* all Member States, in their implementation of the measures set out in paragraph 1 above, to ensure that fraudulent, counterfeit, stolen and lost passports and other travel documents are invalidated and removed from circulation, in accordance with domestic laws and practices, as soon as possible, and to share information on those documents with other Member States through the INTERPOL database;

48. *Encourages* Member States to share with the private sector, in accordance with their domestic laws and practices, information in their national databases related to fraudulent, counterfeit, stolen and lost identity or travel documents pertaining to their own jurisdictions and, if a listed party is found to be using a false identity, including to secure credit or fraudulent travel documents, to provide the Committee with information in this regard;

49. *Confirms* that no matter should be left pending before the Committee for a period longer than six months, unless the Committee determines on a case-by-case basis that extraordinary circumstances require additional time for consideration, in accordance with the Committee guidelines;

50. *Encourages* designating States to inform the Monitoring Team whether a national court or other legal authority has reviewed an individual's case and whether any judicial proceedings have begun, and to include any other relevant information when it submits its standard form for listing;

51. *Requests* the Committee to facilitate, through the Monitoring Team or specialized United Nations agencies, assistance on capacity-building for enhancing implementation of the measures, upon request by Member States;

Coordination and outreach

52. *Reiterates* the need to enhance ongoing cooperation between the Committee, the Security Council Committee established pursuant to resolution 1373(2001) concerning counter-terrorism (the Counter-Terrorism Committee) and the Security Council Committee established pursuant to resolution 1540(2004), as well as their respective groups of experts, including through, as appropriate, enhanced information-sharing, and coordination on visits to countries within their respective mandates, on facilitating and monitoring technical assistance, on relations with international and regional organizations and agencies and on other issues of relevance to all three Committees, expresses its intention to provide guidance to the Committees on areas of common interest in order better to coordinate their efforts and facilitate such cooperation, and requests the Secretary-General to make the necessary arrangements for the groups of experts to be co-located as soon as possible;

53. *Encourages* the Monitoring Team and the United Nations Office on Drugs and Crime to continue their joint activities, in cooperation with the Counter-Terrorism Committee Executive Directorate and the experts of the Committee established pursuant to resolution 1540(2004), to assist Member States in their efforts to comply with their obligations under the relevant resolutions, including by organizing regional and subregional workshops;

54. *Requests* the Committee to consider, where and when appropriate, visits to selected countries by the Chair and/or members of the Committee to enhance the full and effective implementation of the measures referred to in paragraph 1 above, with a view to encouraging States to comply fully with the present resolution and resolutions 1267(1999), 1333(2000), 1390(2002), 1455(2003), 1526(2004), 1617(2005), 1735(2006), 1822(2008) and 1904(2009);

55. *Also requests* the Committee to report orally, through its Chair, at least every one hundred and eighty days to the Council on the state of the overall work of the Committee and the Monitoring Team and, as appropriate, in conjunction with the reports by the Chairs of the Counter-Terrorism Committee and the Committee established pursuant to resolution 1540(2004), and further requests the Chair to hold periodic briefings for all interested Member States;

Monitoring Team

56. *Decides*, in order to assist the Committee in fulfilling its mandate, as well as to support the Ombudsperson, to extend the mandate of the current New York-based Monitoring Team and its members, established pursuant to paragraph 7 of resolution 1526(2004), for a further period of eighteen months, under the direction of the Committee, with the responsibilities outlined in annex I to the present resolution, and requests the Secretary-General to make the necessary arrangements to this effect;

57. *Directs* the Monitoring Team to review the procedures of the Committee for granting exemptions pursuant to resolution 1452(2002) and to provide recommendations on how the Committee can improve the process for granting such exemptions;

58. *Also directs* the Monitoring Team to keep the Committee informed of instances of non-compliance with the measures imposed in the present resolution, and further directs the Monitoring Team to provide recommendations to the Committee on actions taken to respond to non-compliance;

Reviews

59. *Decides* to review the measures described in paragraph 1 above with a view to their possible further strengthening in eighteen months, or sooner if necessary;

60. *Decides also* to remain actively seized of the matter.

ANNEX I

In accordance with paragraph 56 of this resolution, the Monitoring Team shall operate under the direction of the Committee and shall have the following responsibilities:

(*a*) To submit, in writing, two comprehensive, independent reports to the Committee, the first by 31 March 2012 and the second by 31 October 2012, on implementation by Member States of the measures referred to in paragraph 1 of this resolution, including specific recommendations for improved implementation of the measures and possible new measures;

(*b*) To assist the Ombudsperson in carrying out his or her mandate as specified in annex II to this resolution;

(*c*) To assist the Committee in regularly reviewing names on the Al-Qaida Sanctions List, including by undertaking travel and contact with Member States, with a view to developing the Committee's record of the facts and circumstances relating to a listing;

(*d*) To analyse reports submitted pursuant to paragraph 6 of resolution 1455(2003), the checklists submitted pursuant to paragraph 10 of resolution 1617(2005) and other information submitted by Member States to the Committee, as instructed by the Committee;

(*e*) To assist the Committee in following up on requests to Member States for information, including with respect to implementation of the measures referred to in paragraph 1 of this resolution;

(*f*) To submit a comprehensive programme of work to the Committee for its review and approval, as necessary, in which the Monitoring Team should detail the activities envisaged in order to fulfil its responsibilities, including proposed travel, based on close coordination with the Counter-Terrorism Committee Executive Directorate and the group of experts of the Committee established pursuant to resolution 1540(2004) to avoid duplication and reinforce synergies;

(*g*) To work closely and share information with the Counter-Terrorism Committee Executive Directorate and the group of experts of the Committee established pursuant to resolution 1540(2004) to identify areas of convergence and overlap and to help to facilitate concrete coordination, including in the area of reporting, among the three Committees;

(*h*) To participate actively in and support all relevant activities under the United Nations Global Counter-Terrorism Strategy, including within the Counter-Terrorism Implementation Task Force established to ensure overall coordination and coherence in the counter-terrorism efforts of the United Nations system, in particular through its relevant working groups;

(*i*) To assist the Committee with its analysis of non-compliance with the measures referred to in paragraph 1 of this resolution by collating information collected from Member States and submitting case studies, both on its own initiative and upon the Committee's request, to the Committee for its review;

(*j*) To present to the Committee recommendations which could be used by Member States to assist them with the implementation of the measures referred to in paragraph 1 of this resolution and in preparing proposed additions to the Al-Qaida Sanctions List;

(*k*) To assist the Committee in its consideration of proposals for listing, including by compiling and circulating to the Committee information relevant to the proposed listing, and preparing a draft narrative summary, referred to in paragraph 16 of this resolution;

(*l*) To bring to the attention of the Committee new or noteworthy circumstances that may warrant a de-listing, such as publicly reported information on a deceased individual;

(*m*) To consult with Member States in advance of travel to selected Member States, based on its programme of work as approved by the Committee;

(*n*) To coordinate and cooperate with the national counter-terrorism focal point or similar coordinating body in the country of the visit, where appropriate;

(*o*) To encourage Member States to submit names and additional identifying information for inclusion on the Al-Qaida Sanctions List, as instructed by the Committee;

(*p*) To present to the Committee additional identifying and other information to assist the Committee in its efforts to keep the Al-Qaida Sanctions List as updated and accurate as possible;

(*q*) To study and report to the Committee on the changing nature of the threat of Al-Qaida and the best measures to confront it, including by developing a dialogue with relevant scholars and academic bodies, in consultation with the Committee;

(*r*) To collate, assess, monitor and report on and make recommendations regarding implementation of the measures, including implementation of the measure in paragraph 1 (*a*) of this resolution as it pertains to preventing the criminal misuse of the Internet by Al-Qaida and other individuals, groups, undertakings and entities associated with it; to pursue case studies, as appropriate; and to explore in depth any other relevant issues as directed by the Committee;

(*s*) To consult with Member States and other relevant organizations, including through regular dialogue with representatives in New York and in capitals, taking into account their comments, especially regarding any issues that might be contained in the reports of the Monitoring Team referred to in paragraph (*a*) of this annex;

(*t*) To consult with Member States' intelligence and security services, including through regional forums, in order to facilitate the sharing of information and to strengthen enforcement of the measures;

(*u*) To consult with relevant representatives of the private sector, including financial institutions, to learn about the practical implementation of the assets freeze and to develop recommendations for the strengthening of that measure;

(*v*) To work with relevant international and regional organizations in order to promote awareness of, and compliance with, the measures;

(*w*) To assist the Committee in facilitating assistance on capacity-building for enhancing implementation of the measures, upon request by Member States;

(*x*) To work with INTERPOL and Member States to obtain photographs of listed individuals for possible inclusion in INTERPOL Special Notices;

(*y*) To assist other subsidiary bodies of the Security Council, and their expert panels, upon request, with enhancing their cooperation with INTERPOL, referred to in resolution 1699(2006);

(*z*) To report to the Committee, on a regular basis or when the Committee so requests, through oral and/or written briefings on the work of the Monitoring Team, including its visits to Member States and its activities;

(*aa*) To submit to the Committee within ninety days a written report and recommendations on linkages between Al-Qaida and those individuals, groups, undertakings or entities eligible for designation under paragraph 1 of resolution 1988(2011), with a particular focus on entries that appear on both the Al-Qaida Sanctions List and the 1988 List, and thereafter to submit such a report and recommendations periodically; and

(*bb*) Any other responsibility identified by the Committee.

Annex II

In accordance with paragraph 21 of this resolution, the Office of the Ombudsperson shall be authorized to carry out the following tasks upon receipt of a de-listing request submitted by, or on behalf of, an individual, group, undertaking or entity on the Al-Qaida Sanctions List or by the legal representative or estate of such individual, group, undertaking or entity ("the petitioner").

The Security Council recalls that Member States are not permitted to submit de-listing petitions on behalf of an individual, group, undertaking or entity to the Office of the Ombudsperson.

Information-gathering (four months)

1. Upon receipt of a de-listing request, the Ombudsperson shall:

(*a*) Acknowledge to the petitioner the receipt of the de-listing request;

(*b*) Inform the petitioner of the general procedure for processing de-listing requests;

(*c*) Answer specific questions from the petitioner about Committee procedures;

(*d*) Inform the petitioner in case the petition fails to properly address the original designation criteria, as set forth in paragraph 4 of this resolution, and return it to the petitioner for his or her consideration; and

(*e*) Verify if the request is a new request or a repeated request and, if it is a repeated request to the Ombudsperson and it does not contain any additional information, return it to the petitioner for his or her consideration.

2. For de-listing petitions not returned to the petitioner, the Ombudsperson shall immediately forward the de-listing request to the members of the Committee, designating State(s), State(s) of residence and nationality or incorporation, relevant United Nations bodies and any other States deemed relevant by the Ombudsperson. The Ombudsperson shall ask these States or relevant United Nations bodies to provide, within four months, any appropriate additional information relevant to the de-listing request. The Ombudsperson may engage in dialogue with these States to determine:

(*a*) The opinions of these States on whether the de-listing request should be granted; and

(*b*) Information, questions or requests for clarifications that these States would like to be communicated to the petitioner regarding the de-listing request, including any information or steps that might be taken by a petitioner to clarify the de-listing request.

3. The Ombudsperson shall also immediately forward the de-listing request to the Monitoring Team, which shall provide to the Ombudsperson, within four months:

(*a*) All information available to the Monitoring Team that is relevant to the de-listing request, including court decisions and proceedings, news reports and information that States or relevant international organizations have previously shared with the Committee or the Monitoring Team;

(*b*) Fact-based assessments of the information provided by the petitioner that is relevant to the de-listing request; and

(*c*) Questions or requests for clarifications that the Monitoring Team would like asked of the petitioner regarding the de-listing request.

4. At the end of this four-month period of information-gathering, the Ombudsperson shall present a written update to the Committee on progress to date, including details regarding which States have supplied information. The Ombudsperson may extend this period once for up to two months if he or she assesses that more time is required for information-gathering, giving due consideration to requests by Member States for additional time to provide information.

Dialogue (two months)

5. Upon completion of the information-gathering period, the Ombudsperson shall facilitate a two-month period of engagement, which may include dialogue with the petitioner. Giving due consideration to requests for additional time, the Ombudsperson may extend this period once for up to two months if he or she assesses that more time is required for engagement and the drafting of the comprehensive report described in paragraph 7 below. The Ombudsperson may shorten this time period if he or she assesses that less time is required.

6. During this period of engagement, the Ombudsperson:

(*a*) May ask the petitioner questions or request additional information or clarifications that may help the Committee's consideration of the request, including any questions or information requests received from relevant States, the Committee and the Monitoring Team;

(*b*) Should request from the petitioner a signed statement in which the petitioner declares that they have no ongoing association with Al-Qaida, or any cell, affiliate, splinter group or derivative thereof, and undertakes not to associate with Al-Qaida in the future;

(*c*) Should meet with the petitioner, to the extent possible;

(*d*) Shall forward replies from the petitioner back to relevant States, the Committee and the Monitoring Team and follow up with the petitioner in connection with incomplete responses by the petitioner;

(*e*) Shall coordinate with States, the Committee and the Monitoring Team regarding any further inquiries of, or response to, the petitioner;

(*f*) During the information-gathering or dialogue phase, the Ombudsperson may share with relevant States information provided by a State, including that State's position on the de-listing request, if the State which provided the information consents;

(*g*) In the course of the information-gathering and dialogue phases and in the preparation of the report, the Ombudsperson shall not disclose any information shared by a State on a confidential basis, without the express written consent of that State; and

(*h*) During the dialogue phase, the Ombudsperson shall give serious consideration to the opinions of designating States, as well as other Member States that come forward with relevant information, in particular those Member States most affected by acts or associations that led to the original designation.

7. Upon completion of the period of engagement described above, the Ombudsperson, with the help of the Monitoring Team, shall draft and circulate to the Committee a comprehensive report that will exclusively:

(*a*) Summarize and, as appropriate, specify the sources of, all information available to the Ombudsperson that is relevant to the de-listing request. The report shall respect confidential elements of Member States' communications with the Ombudsperson;

(*b*) Describe the activities of the Ombudsperson with respect to this de-listing request, including dialogue with the petitioner; and

(*c*) Based on an analysis of all the information available to the Ombudsperson and the recommendation of the Ombudsperson, lay out for the Committee the principal arguments concerning the de-listing request.

Committee discussion

8. After the Committee has had fifteen days to review the comprehensive report in all official languages of the United Nations, the Chair of the Committee shall place the de-listing request on the agenda of the Committee for consideration.

9. When the Committee considers the de-listing request, the Ombudsperson, aided by the Monitoring Team, as appropriate, shall present the comprehensive report in person and answer Committee members' questions regarding the request.

10. Committee consideration of the comprehensive report shall be completed no later than thirty days from the date the comprehensive report is submitted to the Committee for its review.

11. In cases where the Ombudsperson recommends retaining the listing, the requirement for States to take the measures in paragraph 1 of this resolution shall remain in place with respect to that individual, group, undertaking or entity, unless a Committee member submits a de-listing request, which the Committee shall consider under its normal consensus procedures.

12. In cases where the Ombudsperson recommends that the Committee consider de-listing, the requirement for States to take the measures described in paragraph 1 of this resolution shall terminate with respect to that individual, group, undertaking or entity sixty days after the Committee completes consideration of a comprehensive report of the Ombudsperson, in accordance with this annex, including paragraph 6 (*h*), unless the Committee decides by consensus before the end of that sixty-day period that the requirement shall remain in place with respect to that individual, group, undertaking or entity; provided that, in cases where consensus does not exist, the Chair shall, on the request of a Committee member, submit the question of whether to de-list that individual, group, undertaking or entity to the Security Council for a decision within a period of sixty days; and provided further that, in the event of such a request, the requirement for States to take the measures described in paragraph 1 of this resolution shall remain in force for that period with respect to that individual, group, undertaking or entity until the question is decided by the Council.

13. If the Committee decides to reject the de-listing request, then the Committee shall convey to the Ombudsperson its decision, setting out its reasons, and including any further relevant information about the decision of the Committee, and an updated narrative summary of reasons for listing.

14. After the Committee has informed the Ombudsperson that the Committee has rejected a de-listing request, then the Ombudsperson shall send to the petitioner, with an advance copy sent to the Committee, within fifteen days, a letter that:

(*a*) Communicates the decision of the Committee for continued listing;

(*b*) Describes, to the extent possible and drawing upon the comprehensive report of the Ombudsperson, the process and the publicly releasable factual information gathered by the Ombudsperson; and

(*c*) Forwards from the Committee all information about the decision provided to the Ombudsperson pursuant to paragraph 13 above.

15. In all communications with the petitioner, the Ombudsperson shall respect the confidentiality of Committee deliberations and confidential communications between the Ombudsperson and Member States.

Other tasks of the Office of the Ombudsperson

16. In addition to the tasks specified above, the Ombudsperson shall:

(a) Distribute publicly releasable information about Committee procedures, including Committee guidelines, fact sheets and other documents prepared by the Committee;

(b) Where their address is known, notify individuals or entities about the status of their listing, after the Secretariat has officially notified the permanent mission of the State or States, pursuant to paragraph 19 of this resolution; and

(c) Submit biannual reports summarizing the activities of the Ombudsperson to the Security Council.

Activities of sanctions committees

Al-Qaida Sanctions Committee

The Security Council Committee established in accordance with resolutions 1267(1999) [YUN 1999, p. 265] and 1989(2011) (see p. 341) concerning Al-Qaida and associated individuals and entities (Al-Qaida Sanctions Committee) was mandated to oversee the implementation of sanctions measures, consisting of an assets freeze, travel ban and arms embargo against individuals or entities belonging to or associated with Al-Qaida. Following the adoption of resolution 1989(2011), the Council changed the scope of the Committee's 1999 mandate, focusing it exclusively on Al-Qaida and associated individuals and entities, and changing the name of the Committee to "Security Council Committee pursuant to resolutions 1267(1999) and 1989(2011) concerning Al-Qaida and associated individuals and entities".

In a report covering the 2011 activities of the Al-Qaida Sanctions Committee [S/2012/305], information was provided on, among other things: maintenance and dissemination of the Al-Qaida Sanctions List; exemptions to the sanctions measures; the Committee's website; and implementation of the sanctions measures.

Office of Ombudsperson. The Office of the Ombudsperson was established by the Security Council in resolution 1904(2009) [YUN 2009, p. 355] for an initial period of 18 months to assist the Al-Qaida and Taliban Sanctions Committee in its consideration of de-listing requests. In June 2011, by the adoption of resolutions 1988(2011) and 1989(2011), the Council separated the Al-Qaida and Taliban sanctions regimes and decided that the individuals and entities associated with Al-Qaida on the list established pursuant to resolutions 1267(1999) and 1333(2000) (the Consolidated List) would be referred to as the Al-Qaida Sanctions List, which would fall under the purview of the Al-Qaida Sanctions Committee. The list of individuals and entities associated with the Taliban would fall under the purview of a separate committee, the Security Council Committee established pursuant to resolution 1988(2011) (see p. 337). In accordance with Council resolution 1989(2011), the scope of the mandate of the Ombudsperson extended only to the Al-Qaida Sanctions List. By that same resolution, the mandate of the Office of the Ombudsperson was extended by a further 18 months, until December 2012.

Report of Ombudsperson (January). In accordance with resolution 1904(2009) [YUN 2009, p. 355], the Ombudsperson submitted her first report [S/2011/29], in which she summarized the Office's activities in its first six months of operation, between 14 July 2010 and 15 January 2011. As at 15 January, seven requests for de-listing from the Consolidated List of the Al-Qaida and Taliban Sanctions Committee were submitted to the Ombudsperson. Six of them were accepted and were at various stages of the process. A description of the status of the cases was annexed to the report.

SECURITY COUNCIL ACTION

On 28 February [meeting 6492], following consultations among Security Council members, the President made statement **S/PRST/2011/5** on behalf of the Council:

> The Security Council underlines that terrorism constitutes one of the most serious threats to international peace and security, the enjoyment of human rights and the social and economic development of all Member States and undermines global stability and prosperity, and emphasizes the importance of the Al-Qaida and Taliban sanctions regime as an essential tool in combating the threat posed by terrorist activity.
>
> The Council recalls its primary responsibility for the maintenance of international peace and security under the Charter of the United Nations and further recalls Article 103 of the Charter.
>
> The Council stresses the need for full implementation of all its resolutions and the statements by its President on terrorism, including resolution 1904(2009).
>
> The Council recalls the establishment of the Office of the Ombudsperson pursuant to resolution 1904(2009) to assist in considering de-listing requests submitted by, or on behalf of, an individual, group, undertaking or entity on the list created pursuant to resolutions 1267(1999) and 1333(2000) ("the Consolidated List"), underlines its commitment to ensuring that the Office is able to continue to carry out its role effectively, in accordance with its mandate, and in this regard undertakes to renew the mandate of the Office in June 2011.
>
> The Council welcomes the first report of the Ombudsperson submitted pursuant to annex II to resolution 1904(2009) and the work of the Ombudsperson to date.
>
> The Council takes note of the observations in the report, to which it will respond in the context of the renewal of the mandate of the Ombudsperson in June

2011 in order to ensure that any necessary improvements to the Ombudsperson procedure are implemented.

The Council underlines the improvements to the procedures of the Security Council Committee established pursuant to resolution 1267(1999) ("the Committee") and to the Consolidated List, and the seriousness with which the Committee undertakes its mandate to carry out regular and in-depth reviews of entries on the Consolidated List, and expresses its intention to continue efforts to ensure that procedures are fair and clear.

The Council underlines the important role of the Ombudsperson in ensuring fair and clear procedures for individuals designated pursuant to resolution 1267(1999) and encourages individuals seeking de-listing from the Consolidated List to pursue their case through the Ombudsperson.

The Council welcomes the observation by the Ombudsperson that States have been cooperative in responding to requests and providing information in the cases and looks forward to continued cooperation by Member States with the Office of the Ombudsperson.

Report of Ombudsperson (July). In her second report [S/2011/447], covering the period between 21 January and 21 July, the Ombudsperson stated that, as at 21 July, 14 requests for de-listing from the Al-Qaida Sanctions Committee List had been submitted. All of them were accepted and were at various stages of the process. Comprehensive reports, two of which included recommendations, had been circulated to the Committee in six cases. The Ombudsperson had formally presented the comprehensive reports to the Committee in three cases. Two of the cases resulted in de-listing and the third case remained under consideration. A description of the status of all cases was contained in an annex to the report.

In a later report [S/2012/49] covering activities from 21 July 2011 until 20 January 2012, the Ombudsperson provided an update on the de-listing cases.

Security Council Committee established pursuant to resolution 1988(2011)

By resolution 1988(2011) of 17 June (see p. 337), the Security Council established a new sanctions regime and requested States to take measures in connection with any individuals, groups, undertakings and entities associated with the Taliban in constituting a threat to the peace, stability and security of Afghanistan as designated by the Committee on the List established pursuant to resolution 1988(2011).

The Chairman of the Security Council Committee established pursuant to resolution 1988(2011) submitted to the Council the Committee's report [S/2012/543] on its activities from 17 June to 31 December 2011. During the reporting period, the Committee removed the names of 15 individuals from the 1988(2011) Sanctions List and added the names of 4 individuals.

Monitoring Team

In April, the Chair of the Security Council Committee concerning Al-Qaida and the Taliban and associated individuals and entities transmitted to the Council the eleventh report of the Analytical Support and Sanctions Monitoring Team [S/2011/245] in accordance with Council resolution 1904(2009) [YUN 2009, p. 355].

On 21 November [S/2011/728], the Chair transmitted to the Council the Committee's position on the recommendations contained in the Monitoring Team's eleventh report.

On 20 December, the Chair of the Al-Qaida Sanctions Committee transmitted to the Council a report of the Monitoring Team [S/2011/790] on past and existing links between Al-Qaida and the Taliban.

Expert members. On 30 June [S/2011/403], the Secretary-General informed the Council that he had reappointed seven experts of the Monitoring Team to serve until 31 December 2012. On 20 December [S/2011/789], he informed the Council that he had appointed a replacement of a Monitoring Team expert until 31 December 2012.

Iraq

In 2011, the United Nations, through the Special Representative of the Secretary-General for Iraq and the United Nations Assistance Mission for Iraq (UNAMI), continued to assist the country in its transition to democratic governance and in promoting reconstruction and reconciliation. During the year, political tensions intensified as Iraqi leaders faced difficulties in implementing the November 2010 power-sharing agreements that led to the formation of the new Government. In addition, several protests over the provision of basic services, the lack of employment opportunities and corruption resulted in violence. As the scheduled drawdown of United States Forces in Iraq continued, the Iraqi security forces were being deployed throughout the country; but given their limited air and ground assets, they faced challenges in securing all areas of the country. The overall security situation remained tense and targeted attacks against civilians, Government officials and security personnel continued. On 28 July, the Security Council extended the UNAMI mandate until 31 July 2012. At the end of the year, the United States Forces completed their planned withdrawal from the country.

In August, the Secretary-General informed the Council of his intention to name Martin Kobler (Germany) as his Special Representative and Head of UNAMI, succeeding Ad Melkert (Netherlands).

Political and security developments

Report of Secretary-General (March). In a March report on UNAMI activities [S/2011/213], submitted in response to Security Council resolution 1936(2010) [YUN 2010, p. 366] and covering developments since his November 2010 report [ibid., p. 367], the Secretary-General said that the formation of the new Government on 21 December [ibid., p. 370] brought to an end the nine-month political stalemate that followed the national elections held on 7 March [ibid., p. 364] and should enable Iraqi leaders to begin to tackle major political, social and economic challenges. Several aspects of the 11 November 2010 power-sharing agreement [ibid., p. 367] had yet to be addressed, however, including the appointment of the Minister of Planning and heads of three key security-related ministries. Since late February 2011, a number of protests had occurred across Iraq over the provision of basic services, the lack of employment opportunities and alleged corruption of officials, with several violent demonstrations resulting in an estimated 20 people killed and 116 injured. On 27 February, Prime Minister Nouri al-Maliki issued a statement requiring Government ministries to take urgent steps over a period of 100 days to improve living conditions and access to essential services.

Clashes also occurred between security forces and protesters in the Sulemaniyah area of the Kurdistan region, and the political and security situation in the disputed internal boundaries remained of particular concern. On the night of 25 to 26 February, approximately 5,000 Peshmerga troops entered the Kirkuk governorate from the Kurdistan region, passing through the combined security mechanism of the Iraqi Army and the Peshmerga forces, which was intended to prevent tensions on the ground. Those developments, together with the planned drawdown of the United States military, underscored the need to review the combined security mechanism through a comprehensive dialogue that addressed the root causes of tensions in northern Iraq.

The Secretary-General's Special Representative continued to engage political figures and parties in an effort to facilitate negotiations on outstanding issues related to the Government formation process and to initiate political dialogue on Iraq's disputed territories. After the formation of the new Government, the Special Representative held consultations with representatives of the Government of Iraq and of the Kurdistan Regional Government (KRG) on the possibility of establishing a successor arrangement to the high-level task force for advancing dialogue on issues related to disputed internal boundaries and the status of Kirkuk. In addition, UNAMI was preparing an integrated economic package aimed at vulnerable populations in the disputed territories and was working on confidence-building measures previously agreed upon by the task force in the areas of property claims and restitution, detainees and the educational curriculum and language rights.

Among other activities, UNAMI continued to support the Iraqi Independent High Electoral Commission in maintaining operational readiness. On 31 January, on behalf of the Iraq Partners Forum, the Special Representative submitted to Prime Minister al-Maliki the "Iraq Briefing Book", which outlined policy recommendations in areas such as private sector development, the provision of essential services, human rights and governance reform. UNAMI and the UN country team also held discussions with Government officials to assess how the United Nations Development Assistance Framework (UNDAF) process could help mitigate the factors that had sparked the civil unrest, including high unemployment, especially among the young, the lack of essential services and corruption. Five UNDAF priority working groups had been formed (governance and human rights; inclusive economic growth; environmental management; quality essential services; and investing in human capital) and the Iraq UNDAF multi-donor trust fund had been launched. As at January 2011, the Iraq UNDAF was 27.26 per cent funded. Of the $1.9 billion requested for the 2011–2014 period, $518.431 million was available.

The security environment remained volatile, with persistent and unpredictable changes in the situation. Over 3,000 security incidents took place during the reporting period, which resulted in at least 950 civilian deaths. The continued targeting of Iraq's Christian community, as a result of which hundreds of families had been displaced to Erbil from Baghdad and Mosul, was a source of concern. The Secretary-General renewed his call on the Government to do its utmost to protect all communities that continued to be targeted for their religious beliefs. Expressing concern over the use of force by Iraq's security forces in handling some protests, as well as reports of arbitrary arrests, detention and torture, and the ill-treatment of media personnel covering those events, he also called on the Government to conduct an independent investigation into the alleged violations and to ensure a measured approach that exercised maximum restraint in dealing with future protests.

While commending Iraq's political leaders for their commitment to dialogue and consensus building, the Secretary-General stated that further steps should be taken to complete the Government formation process, including appointments to key security posts. He called for the establishment of the National Council for Strategic Policies, as agreed in the power-sharing accord. Recent demonstrations and the ensuing violence showed that Iraq was not immune to the wave of civil unrest affecting the region, and underscored the need to address the poor state of public services, high unemployment rates and the perceived failure to tackle corruption.

Security Council consideration (April). On 8 April [S/PV.6511], the Special Representative of the Secretary-General and Head of unami, Ad Melkert, expressed the hope that the appointment that week of the Minister of Planning would contribute to fostering progress on the social and economic front. While developments in Iraq were no longer at the forefront of international media coverage, Iraq's stability was under pressure. Particularly as the United States Forces prepared to leave, Iraq should not be forgotten and the international community should stand ready to continue its support.

Report of Secretary-General (July). In a July report on unami operations [S/2011/435], the Secretary-General said that demonstrations continued in Iraq with protesters calling primarily for job creation, an improvement in the delivery of essential services and an end to corruption. On 8 April and 25 May, the Sadrists organized a large demonstration in Baghdad and demanded that United States Forces leave Iraq by the end of 2011. Since February, in response to public protests, the Government had been working to fulfil its pledge to improve the socioeconomic situation. On 14 June, the Prime Minister addressed the nation on the progress made by his Government. A further effort to accelerate policy decisions and implementation over the next three months had been agreed upon. There were continuing disagreements among the main political blocs regarding who should head the country's top three security ministries.

On 31 March, Kurdish Peshmerga troops that had been deployed around the city of Kirkuk since 25 February withdrew and returned to the Kurdistan region. The incident served as a reminder of the challenges that remained as the United States Forces in Iraq drew down and the combined security mechanism came to an end. The United States Forces continued their planned withdrawal from the country with the intention of completing their departure by 31 December.

The standing consultative mechanism, an initiative launched in March under unami auspices that brought together representatives of key political blocs to discuss outstanding issues related to disputed internal territories, including Kirkuk, met several times during the reporting period. On 26 May, the mechanism focused on the future of the combined security mechanism, including a possible liaison role for unami under its mandate. On 16 June, a meeting was held that brought together for the first time all members of the Council of Representatives from Kirkuk in order to discuss issues related to power-sharing and the prospects of holding provincial council elections in Kirkuk. From 10 to 14 June, the UN Under-Secretary-General for Political Affairs, B. Lynn Pascoe, visited Iraq and met with senior Government officials. He reiterated the commitment of the United Nations to continue assisting Iraq and discussed ways in which the Organization could focus its efforts to best respond to the needs of the Iraqi people. He emphasized the readiness of unami to provide further assistance in identifying mutually agreeable solutions to pending issues related to the disputed internal territories. He also stressed the commitment of the UN country team to provide technical advice and expertise in addressing development, human rights and humanitarian challenges.

The security environment remained challenging, with attacks taking place against Iraqi security forces and in a mosque and a hospital. There were also increased levels of indirect-fire attacks against the bases of the United States Forces and against Baghdad International Airport and the International Zone in Baghdad. On 15 May, 11 rockets struck the International Zone, followed by four rockets on 9 June. Those incidents, together with ongoing bomb attacks by armed opposition groups, underlined the continuing threat UN operations faced. Unami was working on the transition of security support from the United States Forces to the Iraqi security forces and was taking steps to put in place the necessary logistical arrangements to substitute the support of the United States Forces. Unami was also continuing preparations to ensure that it was able to sustain a presence in Kirkuk and Basra.

Almost seven months after the Council of Representatives approved the new Iraqi Government, and 16 months after the historic parliamentary elections of March 2010 [YUN 2010, p. 364], the Government formation process still faced outstanding issues, particularly regarding appointments to key security posts. The Secretary-General called on political leaders to put aside their differences and move swiftly to agree on the way forward. In the light of the demonstrations in many parts of Iraq calling for better social services, job creation and an end to corruption, the UN country team would continue to expand its presence and to provide support through the priorities identified in the undaf and the National Development Plan 2010–2014. Although the status of Kirkuk and other disputed internal territories remained divisive issues, the Secretary-General was encouraged by recent efforts by key Iraqi stakeholders to find common ground. He encouraged the Iraqi Government and the Kurdistan Regional Government to continue to use the standing consultative mechanism to find mutually acceptable solutions that served the interests of national reconciliation and long-term stability, and indicated that the

United Nations stood ready to assist in that process upon the Government's request.

Communication. In a 27 July note [S/2011/464] to the Secretary-General, Iraq expressed its wish that the UNAMI mandate be extended for a further period of 12 months.

SECURITY COUNCIL ACTION

On 28 July [meeting 6594], the Security Council unanimously adopted **resolution 2001(2011)**. The draft [S/2011/465] was submitted by the United States.

The Security Council,

Recalling all its previous relevant resolutions on Iraq, in particular resolutions 1500(2003) of 14 August 2003, 1546(2004) of 8 June 2004, 1557(2004) of 12 August 2004, 1619(2005) of 11 August 2005, 1700(2006) of 10 August 2006, 1770(2007) of 10 August 2007, 1830(2008) of 7 August 2008, 1883(2009) of 7 August 2009 and 1936(2010) of 5 August 2010,

Reaffirming the independence, sovereignty, unity and territorial integrity of Iraq,

Emphasizing the importance of the stability and security of Iraq for the people of Iraq, the region and the international community,

Encouraging the Government of Iraq to continue strengthening democracy and the rule of law, improving security and public order and combating terrorism and sectarian violence across the country, and reiterating its support for the people and Government of Iraq in their efforts to build a secure, stable, federal, united and democratic nation, based on the rule of law and respect for human rights,

Welcoming improvements in the security situation in Iraq achieved through concerted political and security efforts, and stressing that challenges to security in Iraq still exist and that improvements need to be sustained through meaningful political dialogue and national unity,

Underscoring the need for all communities in Iraq to participate in the political process and an inclusive political dialogue, to refrain from statements and actions which could aggravate tensions, to reach a comprehensive solution on the distribution of resources, and to ensure stability and develop a just and fair solution for the nation's disputed internal boundaries and work towards national unity,

Reaffirming the importance of the United Nations, in particular the United Nations Assistance Mission for Iraq, in advising, supporting and assisting the people and Government of Iraq to strengthen democratic institutions, advance inclusive political dialogue and national reconciliation, facilitate regional dialogue, develop processes acceptable to the Government of Iraq to resolve disputed internal boundaries, aid vulnerable groups, including refugees and internally displaced persons, strengthen gender equality, promote the protection of human rights, and promote judicial and legal reform, and emphasizing the importance of the United Nations, in particular the Mission, prioritizing advice, support and assistance to the people and Government of Iraq to achieve these goals,

Urging the Government of Iraq to continue to promote and protect human rights and also to consider additional steps to support the Independent High Commission for Human Rights,

Recognizing the efforts of the Government of Iraq in the promotion and protection of the human rights of women, reaffirming its resolutions 1325(2000) of 31 October 2000, 1820(2008) of 19 June 2008, 1888(2009) of 30 September 2009, 1889(2009) of 5 October 2009 and 1960(2010) of 16 December 2010 on women and peace and security, and reiterating the need for the full, equal and effective participation of women, reaffirming the key role that women can play in re-establishing the fabric of society, and stressing the need for their involvement in the development of national strategies in order to take into account their perspectives,

Expressing the importance of addressing humanitarian issues confronting the Iraqi people, and stressing the need to continue to form a coordinated response and to provide adequate resources to address these issues,

Underscoring the sovereignty of the Government of Iraq, reaffirming that all parties should continue to take all feasible steps and to develop modalities to ensure the protection of affected civilians, including children, women and members of religious and ethnic minority groups, and should create conditions conducive to the voluntary, safe, dignified and sustainable return of refugees and internally displaced persons or local integration of internally displaced persons, welcoming commitments and encouraging continued efforts of the Government for the relief of internally displaced persons, refugees and returnees, and noting the important role of the Office of the United Nations High Commissioner for Refugees, based on its mandate, in providing continued advice and support to the Government, in coordination with the Mission, on these issues,

Urging all those concerned, as set forth in international humanitarian law, including the Geneva Conventions of 1949 and the Regulations annexed to the Hague Convention IV of 1907, to allow full unimpeded access by humanitarian personnel to all people in need of assistance and to make available, as far as possible, all facilities necessary for their operations, and to promote the safety, security and freedom of movement of humanitarian personnel and United Nations and associated personnel and their assets,

Welcoming the important progress that Iraq has made towards regaining the international standing it held prior to the adoption of resolution 661(1990) on 6 August 1990, calling upon the Government of Iraq to continue ongoing cooperation with the Government of Kuwait to address outstanding issues and to meet its outstanding obligations under the relevant Chapter VII Security Council resolutions pertaining to the situation between Iraq and Kuwait, and underscoring the importance of ratification of the Additional Protocol to its comprehensive safeguards agreement,

Expressing its deep gratitude to all the United Nations staff in Iraq for their courageous and tireless efforts,

1. *Decides* to extend the mandate of the United Nations Assistance Mission for Iraq for a period of twelve months;

2. *Decides also* that the Special Representative of the Secretary-General for Iraq and the Mission, at the request of the Government of Iraq, and taking into account the letter dated 27 July 2011 from the Minister for Foreign Affairs of Iraq to the Secretary-General, shall continue to pursue their mandate as stipulated in resolution 1936(2010);

3. *Recognizes* that security of United Nations personnel is essential for the Mission to carry out its work for the benefit of the people of Iraq, and calls upon the Government of Iraq

and other Member States to continue to provide security and logistical support to the United Nations presence in Iraq;

4. *Welcomes* the contributions of Member States in providing the Mission with the financial, logistical and security resources and support that it needs to fulfil its mission, and calls upon Member States to continue to provide the Mission with sufficient resources and support;

5. *Expresses its intention* to review the mandate of the Mission in twelve months or sooner, if requested by the Government of Iraq;

6. *Requests* the Secretary-General to report to the Security Council every four months on the progress made towards the fulfilment of all responsibilities of the Mission;

7. *Decides* to remain seized of the matter.

Appointment of Special Representative. On 4 August [S/2011/502], the Secretary-General informed the Security Council of his intention to appoint Martin Kobler (Germany) as his Special Representative and Head of UNAMI to succeed Ad Melkert (Netherlands). On 8 August [S/2011/503], the Council took note of the appointment.

Report of Secretary-General (November). In response to resolution 2001(2011) (see p. 354), the Secretary-General submitted a November report [S/2011/736] in which he stated that Iraqi political leaders continued to discuss the implementation of power-sharing agreements reached in November 2010 [YUN 2010, p. 367] that led to the formation of the current Government. Despite considerable efforts to form a national partnership Government, a number of issues remained, particularly with regard to who would head the country's main security ministries. He urged political leaders to come to an understanding on implementing their past agreements so that the country could move forward and focus on addressing other pressing challenges.

Following the withdrawal of the United States Forces in Iraq from Diyala governorate on 15 August, an additional brigade of Kurdish Peshmerga forces was deployed to the area. The arrival of those forces, which were normally supervised jointly by the Iraqi security forces, Kurdish troops and the United States Forces in Iraq, resulted in some tension. Arrangements for the combined security mechanism in the disputed internal territories of Iraq after the withdrawal of the United States Forces remained to be defined.

The decision by the Salah ad-Din Provincial Council to initiate the process to declare itself an autonomous region, followed by similar calls in several other governorates, and an incident in Khanaqin, where residents protested against the Prime Minister's request for the KRG flag to be removed from the District's administrative buildings, underscored the need for greater understanding and cooperation between the Government of Iraq, KRG and the provincial councils. The Secretary-General urged the Government and KRG to focus on resolving outstanding issues between them, particularly with respect to the pending oil and gas law and the disputed territories. UNAMI continued its efforts to promote political dialogue, primarily through the standing consultative mechanism. In the light of the planned departure of the United States Forces, the Secretary-General urged the Government and KRG to define the future of the combined security mechanism in the disputed internal territories. He also welcomed the start of the process to appoint a new Board of Commissioners of the Independent High Electoral Commission to ensure a smooth transition once the tenure of the existing Board expired in May 2012; encouraged transparency in the selection of the new Commissioners; and reiterated the readiness of the United Nations to extend technical advice and support in that regard.

The Secretary-General remained concerned by reports of continued human rights violations, particularly the pattern of violence. He encouraged the Government and KRG to finalize action plans on human rights and called on the Government to investigate allegations of violations. During the reporting period, targeted attacks against civilians, Government officials and security personnel continued. By some estimates, more than 10 Iraqis were killed or injured, on average, each day. On 15 July, two car bombs reportedly killed at least eight people and injured at least 35 more in Karbala. On 25 September, attacks against Government buildings in Karbala governorate resulted in the deaths of dozens of civilians and the injury of many others. Attacks continued to be perpetrated against civilians because of their religious and ethnic affiliations, and against minorities. On 15 August, a car bomb in a market in Al-Kut killed more than 60 people, including 16 children.

The situation in Camp Ashraf (a refugee camp for exiled Iranians) remained worrisome, and there was a need to find a peaceful and durable solution, given the short time remaining before the Government's announced closure date of 31 December. The Secretary-General appealed to the Government to give the Office of the UN High Commissioner for Refugees the time and space it needed to interview and register camp residents for resettlement. He also hoped that the Government would be willing to show some flexibility on the timing of the camp's closure pending tangible progress in the relocation of residents outside Iraq before the end of the year.

On regional issues, the Secretary-General condemned the continuing terrorist attacks by the Kurdistan Workers Party and the Party of Free Life of Kurdistan against Iraq's neighbours, including Turkey and Iran, and urged Iraq and affected countries to continue to engage in a constructive dialogue in order to find a peaceful solution to that challenge.

Year-end developments. In a later report [S/2012/185], the Secretary-General stated that tensions had risen between the main political blocs in Iraq. Al-Iraqiya suspended its participation in plenary sessions of the Council of Representatives on 17 December, calling for national dialogue and full implementation of the November 2010 agreement on power-sharing [YUN 2010, p. 367]. Political tensions between the State of Law Coalition and Al-Iraqiya escalated further when the Higher Judicial Council issued an arrest warrant for Vice-President Tariq al-Hashimi, a senior member of Al-Iraqiya, on 19 December on charges related to terrorism. On 27 December, President Jalal Talabani and the Speaker of the Council of Representatives agreed to convene a national conference of all political blocs, to which all major parties consented. The Secretary-General urged all concerned to redouble their efforts to make that conference a success and ensure that it was held in a spirit of inclusiveness, compromise and partnership, within the framework of the Constitution. He pledged UNAMI's support for such an initiative.

In order to prevent violence that could have resulted from the forcible closure of Camp New Iraq (formerly Camp Ashraf) by the Government, UNAMI signed a memorandum of understanding with the Government on 25 December providing for the relocation of the residents of Camp New Iraq to a temporary transit location, Camp Hurriya (formerly Camp Liberty), near Baghdad International Airport. On 21 December, in response to the Secretary-General's request, Prime Minister al-Maliki extended the deadline for the closure of Camp New Iraq from 31 December to 30 April 2012.

In accordance with the 2008 status-of-forces agreement between the Governments of Iraq and the United States [YUN 2008, p. 389], United States forces completed their withdrawal from Iraq on 18 December. Earlier, on 11 and 12 December, Prime Minister Al-Maliki visited the United States and met with President Barack Obama to discuss bilateral relations. Both reiterated their commitment to the 2008 Strategic Framework Agreement between the two Governments.

UNAMI

The United Nations Assistance Mission for Iraq (UNAMI), established by Security Council resolution 1500(2003) [YUN 2003, p. 346], continued to support the Secretary-General in fulfilling his mandate under Council resolution 1483(2003) [ibid., p. 338], as extended by resolution 1546(2004) [YUN 2004, p. 348]. The Secretary-General's Special Representative and Head of UNAMI and his substantive, security and administrative support staff were based in Baghdad, with regional offices in Basra, Erbil and Kirkuk.

Financing

In a November report [A/66/354/Add.5 & Corr.1], the Secretary-General submitted to the General Assembly the proposed resource requirements for UNAMI for 2012, totalling $172,790,400 net ($184,698,700 gross). In December ACABQ [A/66/7/Add.12], recommended that the Assembly approve the requested resources, subject to its observations and recommendations.

On 24 December, in section IX of **resolution 66/247** (see p. 1393), the Assembly approved the budgets for the 29 special political missions, including UNAMI, totalling $583,383,800.

Post-Development Fund mechanism

The International Advisory and Monitoring Board (IAMB) for Iraq, established by Security Council resolution 1483(2003) [YUN 2003, p. 338] to ensure that the Development Fund for Iraq was used in a transparent manner for the benefit of the Iraqi people and that Iraqi export sales of petroleum products were consistent with international market best practices, concluded its work on 30 June, in accordance with Council resolution 1956(2010) [YUN 2010, p. 371]. The period from January 1 to June 30 was transitional in nature, with IAMB focusing on transitioning to the successor body. The Governing Council of the United Nations Compensation Commission took up the task of monitoring the developments following the expiration of the IAMB mandate on 30 June 2011 and the transfer of the oversight of the control, reporting and use of Iraqi oil export revenues to the Iraqi Committee of Financial Experts, established in 2006 by the Council of Ministers [YUN 2007, p. 353].

In February [A/65/328/Add.6], the Secretary-General proposed requirements for the United Nations Representative on the International Advisory and Monitoring Board of the Development Fund for Iraq, for the period from 1 January to 30 June, totalling $24,600 net ($24,600 gross), which ACABQ endorsed in March [A/65/602/Add.1].

On 4 April, the General Assembly, in section II of **resolution 65/268** (see p. 1378), approved those amounts.

Iraq progress report. In a 29 April letter [S/2011/290] to the Security Council, Iraq forwarded a report from its Government on progress towards the transition to a post-Development Fund for Iraq mechanism in accordance with Council resolution 1956(2010) [YUN 2010, p. 371]. Iraq confirmed that it would continue to use the same mechanism established by resolution 1483(2003) or the transfer of 5 per cent of the proceeds from all export sales of petroleum, petroleum products and natural gas from Iraq to the Compensation Fund because it considered the mechanism to be transparent and because it would ensure that Iraq would be able to continue to meet its obligations as provided for in paragraph 21 of resolution 1483(2003). Iraq would consult the UN Secretariat on in-kind payments of export sales of petroleum, petroleum products and natural gas from Iraq, with a view to finding a transparent mechanism to ensure that the equivalent of 5 per cent of such transactions was deposited into the Compensation Fund pursuant to paragraph 3 of resolution 1956(2010).

Report of Secretary-General. In response to Security Council resolution 1956(2010), the Secretary-General, in December, submitted his first report [S/2011/795] on the United Nations Compensation Fund, which assessed performance following the 30 June transition to a post-Development Fund mechanism. With regard to the issue of arrangements for ensuring that payments were made to the Compensation Fund, the Governing Council of the Compensation Commission noted with satisfaction that since the transfer of the oversight function to the Government of Iraq, there had been no change in the mechanism and that payments continued to be transferred to the Compensation Fund through the Federal Reserve Bank of New York. Prior to the transfer of the oversight function from IAMB to the Committee of Financial Experts, the average monthly income to the Compensation Fund for the first half of 2011 was $319.3 million. The average monthly income for the five months following the transfer was $341 million, with $1.3 billion transferred in the quarter following the transition and approximately $1 billion expected in the final quarter of 2011. Since the transition, the Compensation Commission had made two payments to Kuwait of more than $1 billion each; the first was made on 28 July and the second on 27 October. While all the indicators were positive and suggested that the Government of Iraq was compliant with its obligations under paragraph 21 of resolution 1483(2003), only after an audit of the successor account to the Development Fund for Iraq would it be possible to confirm that conclusion. In that regard, it was noted that the Committee of Financial Experts had appointed the firm of Ernst & Young to conduct the 2011 audit of the Development Fund for Iraq and its successor account.

Security Council Committee established by resolution 1518(2003)

The Chairman of the Security Council Committee established by resolution 1518(2003) [YUN 2003, p. 362] submitted to the Council the Committee's annual report for 2011 [S/2011/806]. The Committee was established to continue to identify, in accordance with paragraphs 19 and 23 of resolution 1483(2003) [YUN 2003, p. 338], individuals and entities associated with the former Iraqi regime whose funds, other financial assets and economic resources should be frozen and transferred to the Development Fund for Iraq. At year's end, the Committee's list of individuals contained 86 names; its list of entities contained 208 names.

The Committee noted that the de-listing of three individuals in 2011 had brought to a conclusion one of two separate matters that had been pending before the Committee since 2007. The Committee received two communications on 23 June from Iraq proposing the addition of eight names to the list of individuals established pursuant to Security Council resolution 1483(2003) and the amendment of the entries for two names already included in the same list. That request remained pending before the Committee at the end of the year.

Non-proliferation and disarmament obligations

In response to Security Council resolution 1957(2010) [YUN 2010, p. 374], the Secretary-General submitted an October report [S/2011/607] on progress made by Iraq on its commitment to ratify the Additional Protocol to the Comprehensive Safeguards Agreement, concluded in the context of the 1968 Treaty on the Non-Proliferation of Nuclear Weapons, adopted by the General Assembly in resolution 2373(XXII) [YUN 1968, p. 17], and meet its obligations under the 1992 Convention on the Prohibition of the Development, Production, Stockpiling and Use of Chemical Weapons and on Their Destruction [YUN 1992, p. 65]. Information was provided by the International Atomic Energy Agency (IAEA) and the Organization for the Prohibition of Chemical Weapons (OPCW). IAEA stated that, as at 5 September, the Additional Protocol to the Comprehensive Safeguards Agreement had not entered into force in Iraq, but since 17 February 2010, it had continued to be implemented provisionally pending its entry into force. On 30 September 2011, OPCW reported that Iraq had acceded to the Chemical Weapons Convention on 13 January 2009 [YUN 2009, p. 542] and that on 12 February 2009 the Convention had entered into force. On 12 February 2009, Iraq had notified OPCW that it had designated the Iraq National Monitoring Directorate to serve as the national focal point for liaison with OPCW. Iraq had also submitted declarations under the various provisions of the Convention towards fulfilling its obligations. In that regard, it noted that OPCW had carried out the initial technical inspection of various former production and storage facilities from 1 to 4 May 2011.

Children and armed conflict

In accordance with Security Council resolutions 1612(2005) [YUN 2005, p. 863] and 1882(2009) [YUN 2009, p. 740], in June, the Secretary-General submitted the first report [S/2011/366] on children and armed conflict in Iraq to be presented to the Council and its Working Group on Children and Armed Conflict, covering the period from January 2008 to December 2010. The report highlighted trends and patterns of grave violations against children in the context of the continuing conflict in Iraq, such as the recruitment and use of children, including the use of children as suicide bombers; the killing and maiming of children; rape or other grave sexual violence against children; abduction; attacks on schools and hospitals; and denial of humanitarian access. The report identified parties to the conflict responsible for those violations. The Secretary-General noted that access to affected populations and children for monitoring and verification purposes was not consistent.

The delay in forming the new Government after the March 2010 elections [YUN 2010, p. 364] resulted in the absence of formal dialogue on children affected by armed conflict between the United Nations and the Government. On 13 January 2011, the Secretary-General's Special Representative and the Representative of the United Nations Children's Fund (UNICEF) met with the Minister for Foreign Affairs to initiate discussions on the Council resolution 1612(2005) process regarding the implementation of the monitoring and reporting mechanism. The Minister agreed to appoint a high-level representative to liaise with the country task force on monitoring and reporting and welcomed the implementation of the mechanism in the framework of Council resolutions 1612(2005) and 1882(2009). In addition, the Government established an intergovernmental committee on Council resolution 1612(2005) in April.

The Secretary-General urged the Iraqi security forces and United States Forces in Iraq to ensure that their rules of engagement included special protection measures for children and were implemented fully; recommended that the Ministry of Defence develop appropriate age verification procedures with respect to the Awakening Councils (a Sunni movement providing security under the control of the Iraqi Ministry of Defence), and that it take appropriate measures to improve the protection of children through a final screening of all remaining Awakening Council members in coordination with child-protection partners; encouraged the Iraqi security forces to work closely with UNAMI child protection to devise a training regime for the Iraqi security forces on grave child rights violations and to devise an "alert system" to regularly apprise the country task force on monitoring and reporting of possible grave rights violations in real time; requested the Government to conduct investigations and prosecutions of the crime of recruitment and use of children, to grant the United Nations and human rights monitoring bodies full access to detention facilities, including all those housing children at any stage of the judicial process, and to work with UNAMI and UNICEF to develop ways to prevent prolonged detention and identify alternatives for those children; encouraged the Government to cooperate with the country task force on monitoring and reporting with a view to halting grave violations of children's rights, as stipulated by the Council in resolutions 1612(2005) and 1882(2009); and called on the country task force to share information, make recommendations and provide assistance to the Iraq intergovernmental committee on Council resolution 1612(2005).

Report of Working Group. The Security Council Working Group on Children and Armed Conflict, established by resolution 1612(2005) [YUN 2005, p. 863], having considered the Secretary-General's report on 22 June, issued its conclusions and recommendations on children and armed conflict in Iraq in October [S/AC.51/2011/6]. The Working Group encouraged the Government to follow up on commitments made to adopt additional measures to criminalize the recruitment and use of children in armed conflict by armed groups, and underlined the importance of granting the United Nations and other humanitarian organizations access to children held in detention facilities. It agreed to address a message, through public statements by the Chair of the Working Group, to the armed groups mentioned in the Secretary-General's report, urging them to halt violations and abuses against children and to release all children remaining within their ranks. It would also address a message to civil and religious leaders urging them to publicly condemn the use of children, especially as suicide bombers.

Communication. On 8 November, the Security Council transmitted to the Secretary-General a letter [S/2011/697] from the Working Group's Chairman, requesting that the Secretary-General, through UNAMI and UNICEF, devise ways to ensure the proper deployment and outreach of child protection actors throughout Iraq. It also requested the Secretary-General to direct the country task force on monitoring and reporting in Iraq to exchange information with, make recommendations and provide necessary assistance to the intergovernmental committee on Council resolution 1612(2005) established by the Government of Iraq.

Oil-for-food programme

Under the UN oil-for-food programme, established by Security Council resolution 986(1995) [YUN 1995, p. 475], Iraq had been authorized to sell petroleum and petroleum products to finance humanitarian assistance, thereby alleviating the adverse consequences of the sanctions imposed by the Council. The programme was phased out in November 2003 [YUN 2003, p. 362].

On 12 September, by **decision 65/555**, the General Assembly deferred consideration of the agenda item "Follow-up to the recommendations on administrative management and internal oversight of the Independent Inquiry Committee into the UN Oil-for-Food Programme" to its sixty-sixth (2011) session. On 24 December (**decision 66/557**), the Assembly decided that the item would remain for consideration at its resumed sixty-sixth (2012) session.

UN Iraq account

Following the termination of all activities under the UN oil-for-food programme [YUN 2003, p. 362], the United Nations retained responsibility for the administration and execution of letters of credit issued under the programme by the bank holding the UN Iraq Account, Banque Nationale de Paris Paribas, for purchasing humanitarian supplies for the south/centre of Iraq, until such letters were executed or expired, in accordance with Security Council resolution 1483(2003) [ibid., p. 338]. At that stage, some 3,009 prioritized contracts, with associated letters of credit valued at approximately $8 billion, were considered essential for the reconstruction and/or humanitarian needs of the Iraqi people.

The Secretary-General informed the Council in December 2010 [YUN 2010, p. 375] that all 43 of the outstanding letters of credit, worth approximately $101 million, had expired according to their terms, and six could not be paid due to the inability to locate the beneficiaries or the beneficiaries not providing the documentation required by the relevant letter of credit. By resolution 1958(2010) of 24 December [ibid., p. 376], the Council requested the Secretary-General to take actions to terminate all residual activities under the oil-for-food programme, including establishing an escrow account retaining $20 million for the Organization's expenses terminating those activities and $131 million for providing indemnification to the United Nations, its representatives, agents and independent contractors until 31 December 2016.

As at 31 December 2010, the remaining 43 outstanding letters of credit were cancelled; a new escrow account in the amount of $151 million was established; and an amount of $656 million was transferred from the UN escrow (Iraq) accounts to the Development Fund for Iraq (DFI), bringing the total amount transferred to DFI from 2003 to 2010 to $11.1 billion. The remaining balances were transferred to DFI on 6 June 2011.

Reports of Board of Auditors. In July, the Secretary-General transmitted to the Security Council the report [S/2011/479] of the Board of Auditors on the United Nations escrow (Iraq) accounts for the year ended 31 December 2010, reflecting the transactions covering the seventh year of the phase-down operations following the termination of the oil-for-food programme in November 2003.

Income for the year totalled $3.7 million, while expenditures amounted to $46.9 million, resulting in a shortfall of income over expenditure of $43.2 million. As at 31 December 2010, total assets amounted to $5 million, while liabilities amounted to $316,000 and reserves and fund balances were reduced to $4.7 million.

As at 31 December 2010, the escrow (Iraq) accounts were still under liquidation. The major factors affecting the full closure of the accounts were a delay in the disposal of non-expendable property and the non-settlement of small accounts receivable and payable balances. The Board recommended that measures be taken to dispose of the remaining non-expendable property; settle the outstanding accounts payable and receivable; and transfer all remaining unencumbered funds in the escrow accounts to DFI in accordance with relevant Council resolutions. Subsequently, the Board was informed that the receivable and payable balances had been cleared up and the remainder had been transferred to DFI on 6 June 2011. The disposal of the non-expendable property had also been completed, except for that held by one agency.

In July, the Secretary-General transmitted to the Council the report [S/2011/480] of the Board of Auditors on the audit of the United Nations escrow account established by Council resolution 1958(2010) for the period from 15 to 31 December 2010. In accordance with resolution 1958(2010), the sum of $151 million was transferred from the United Nations escrow (Iraq) accounts to a new escrow account, comprising $20 million in the administration fund and $131 million in the indemnification reserve fund. As at 31 December 2010, total income (from interest) amounted to $6,000, while no expenditure was incurred; the cash balance was $151 million. As requested in resolution 1958(2010), the Secretary-General terminated all residual activities under the oil-for-food programme. As a result, the remaining 43 outstanding letters of credit with an aggregate value of $101 million were cancelled as at 31 December 2010. The claims of the 43 letters of credit, however, were not disclosed as contingent liabilities in the notes to the financial statements. The Board was of the view that there should have been consistency of accounting treatment for cancelled letters of credit for which claims still existed. Measures were subsequently taken to address the findings noted during the audit, and corresponding changes were reflected in the revised financial statements.

Iraq-Kuwait

POWs, Kuwaiti property and missing persons

In response to Security Council resolution 1284(1999) [YUN 1999, p. 230], the Secretary-General reported in 2011 on Iraq's compliance with its obligations regarding the issue of missing Kuwaiti and third-country nationals and the repatriation of Kuwaiti property seized by Iraq during its occupation of Kuwait as of August 1990 [YUN 1990, p. 189]. The High-level Coordinator for compliance by Iraq with its obligations regarding the return of Kuwaiti nationals and property, Gennady Tarasov (Russian Federation) briefed the Council in June and December.

Report of Secretary-General (June). In his June report [S/2011/373], the Secretary-General stated that the adoption of Council resolutions 1956(2010) [YUN 2010, p. 371], 1957(2010) [ibid., p. 374] and 1958(2010) [ibid., p. 376] lifted several major Chapter VII mandates on Iraq. Thus, Iraq's remaining obligations to Kuwait mainly concerned the files of missing persons and property. During the first half of 2011, the High-level Coordinator focused his activities on building confidence and cooperation between Kuwait and Iraq with a view to strengthening their practical engagement in the search for missing persons and property and encouraging them to achieve visible and significant progress towards the implementation of the objectives of Council resolution 1284(1999). A high-level Iraqi-Kuwaiti exchange of visits provided a positive environment for the Co-ordinator's contacts with the representatives of the two countries, as well as with the other members of the Tripartite Commission [YUN 2001, p. 293], composed of representatives of Iraq, Kuwait and the 1990–1991 coalition (France, Saudi Arabia, United Kingdom, United States) and its Technical Subcommittee, which remained the primary body for dealing with the issue of persons unaccounted for from the 1990–1991 Gulf War. A priority was to assist and facilitate the setting up of an effective mechanism within the framework of the Technical Subcommittee to conduct regular exploratory missions to sites on Iraqi territory where Kuwaiti and third-country victims might have been buried. On 22 and 23 May, the High-level Coordinator met with Iraq's Minister for Human Rights, who noted that the 18 May high-level consultative meeting of the Tripartite Commission had, for the first time in many years, demonstrated the determination of all participants to attain speedy progress. Kuwait had provided a grant of $974,000 to help build Iraq's capacity in mass-grave excavations and identification of missing persons. He reiterated that Iraq would cooperate with the efforts of the Coordinator to achieve his mandate. The Secretary-General expressed concern at the lack of progress in the search for the Kuwaiti national archives, and the Coordinator urged Iraq to set up an official body to exert credible efforts to find them. The Secretary-General concluded that the emerging pattern of joint exploratory/excavation missions in the framework of the Technical Subcommittee was a promising approach for expediting practical progress on the ground. He warned that the task of discovering the fate of missing Kuwaiti and third-country nationals should not be influenced by political factors and considerations. Since the organizational and logistical aspects of the search for the missing persons appeared to be in place, the goal of finding and identifying the victims and finally closing their cases was an imperative. He recommended that the Council extend the financing of the High-level Coordinator's mandate until December 2011.

Annexed to the report was an 18 April letter from the Acting Chairman of the Kuwaiti National Committee for Missing Persons and Prisoner of War Affairs, which summarized information on Kuwaiti and third-country nationals whose remains were found in Iraq in 2003 and 2004.

Security Council press statement. On 22 June [SC/10289], following a briefing from the High-level Coordinator, Council members supported the Secretary-General's recommendation to extend the financing of the activities of the High-level Coordinator, noted the limited progress made in clarifying the fate of the Kuwaiti national archives, and urged Iraq to establish an effective national body to lead and coordinate efforts with regard to the Kuwaiti national archives and property, and report the results to the United Nations.

Report of Secretary-General (December). In a December report [S/2011/754], the Secretary-General said that the High-level Coordinator was actively engaged with both Iraq and Kuwait to assist them in building mutual trust and confidence with a view to intensifying the search for missing persons. His priority was to facilitate, within the framework of the Technical Subcommittee and under the aegis of the International Committee of the Red Cross, the sending of joint exploratory missions to sites on Iraqi territory where Kuwaiti and third-country persons might have been buried. Three such missions had been conducted. Although no human remains had been discovered, the missions represented a promising format for further work on the ground and had the potential to become an effective functional mechanism to probe the fate of missing persons. In November, the High-level Coordinator, on the sidelines of the Tripartite Commission meeting in Geneva, met the Minister of Human Rights of Iraq, Mohammed S. Al-Sudaney, as well as the Kuwaiti delegation. Minister Al-Sudaney outlined

Iraqi efforts to gather information and expand the database on potential sites containing mass graves. He also noted that his Ministry had prepared a plan of action for 2012 that accorded priority to more investigations at Khamisiyah, Ramadi and Hilla in Iraq. The Minister indicated that Iraq had received the equipment purchased with the $974,000 Kuwaiti grant for the excavation of mass graves and the identification of missing persons. Following the November Tripartite Commission meeting, the members of the Commission decided to step up the information-gathering process on the possible burial sites and agreed to work out a plan of action in both Iraq and Kuwait for 2012. In a related development, 32 sets of remains of Iraqi military personnel, discovered earlier in the year by a Technical Subcommittee mission in Kuwait, were handed over to the Iraqi authorities in July. A similar mission went to northern Kuwait at the end of November. Thus, the Technical Subcommittee had become "a two-way street", dealing with missing persons from both countries. The Secretary-General stated that while three exploratory missions carried out inside Iraq had not uncovered any remains of missing persons, their efforts had established confidence that serious engagement was under way. He recommended that the Security Council extend the financing of the Coordinator's mandate until 30 June 2012.

Security Council press statement. On 15 December, the Council was briefed by the High-level Coordinator. In a statement to the press [SC/10490], Council members welcomed the continued cooperation by Iraq and Kuwait and their high-level commitments to full implementation of all Iraqi obligations under the relevant Council resolutions. They also stressed the need for Iraq to build on steps already taken to fully meet those commitments.

Communications. On 21 June [S/2011/382], Iraq transmitted to the Council its position on the Secretary-General's June report (see p. 360). It objected to the extension of the High-level Coordinator's mandate, stating that national committees existed that were responsible for the issues of property, archives and missing Kuwaitis, and that the Tripartite Commission and its Technical Subcommittee also dealt with the issue of missing Kuwaitis.

On 13 July [S/2011/428], Kuwait transmitted a letter from its Deputy Prime Minister and Minister for Foreign Affairs concerning developments regarding Iraq's outstanding obligations on issues regarding prisoners and the return of property and the national archives; maintenance of border markers; and compensation. It welcomed the Council's 22 June press statement [SC/10289] (see p. 360) and expressed its support for the continuation of the mandate of the High-level Coordinator in order to ensure the implementation of Council resolution 1284(1999).

On 6 September [S/2011/568], Iraq transmitted a letter from its Minister for Foreign Affairs to the Secretary-General regarding the Council's 22 June press statement. The Minister pledged full Iraqi cooperation in that regard and stated that Iraq did not see the need to extend the High-level Coordinator's mandate beyond 31 December 2011, since existing international and Iraqi national bodies could work effectively for the benefit of Iraq and Kuwait.

On 15 November [S/2011/721], the Permanent Representative of Iraq stated that his Government had implemented the recommendations contained in the Secretary-General's June report and that the Iraqi authorities had approved the establishment of a committee to coordinate efforts relating to the Kuwaiti national archives. He also reported that 136 microfilm cassettes that included the archive of the official newspaper *Kuwait Today* had been handed over by an Iraqi citizen and that the Kuwaiti Embassy in Baghdad had been informed.

Financing of High-level Coordinator. In a 14 February letter [S/2011/98] to the Security Council, the Secretary-General said that the 2010 mandated activities for the High-level Coordinator had led to expenditures of $271,903. Those funds were provided through transfers from the Iraq escrow account. A further allocation of $239,750 would be necessary to finance the activities of the High-level Coordinator and his staff until 30 June 2011. Should the Council agree, those funds would be transferred within the escrow account and made available to the UN Department of Political Affairs. On 3 March [S/2011/99], the Council informed the Secretary-General of its concurrence with the proposal.

On 26 July [S/2011/477], the Secretary-General informed the Council that expenditures for the activities of the High-level Coordinator amounted to $168,405 from 1 January to 30 June 2011. It would be necessary to allocate resources of $214,600 to support those activities until 31 December. The Council approved that amount on 29 July [S/2011/478].

UN Compensation Commission and Fund

The United Nations Compensation Commission, established in 1991 [YUN 1991, p. 195] for the resolution and payment of claims against Iraq for losses and damages resulting from its 1990 invasion and occupation of Kuwait [YUN 1990, p. 189], continued in 2011 to expedite the settlement of claims through the United Nations Compensation Fund, which was established at the same time as the Commission. Under Security Council resolution 1483(2003) [YUN 2003, p. 338], the Fund received 5 per cent of the proceeds generated by export sales of Iraqi petroleum, petroleum products and natural gas.

During 2011, the Commission paid out $680 million to Kuwait on 27 January for distribution to nine claimants; $880 million on 28 April to nine claimants; $1,059 million on 28 July to nine claimants; and $1,038.4 million on 27 October to eight claimants. As at 27 October, the Compensation Commission had made available $34.3 billion to over 100 Governments and international organizations for distribution to 1.5 million successful claimants in all categories.

Governing Council. The Commission's Governing Council held two sessions in Geneva in 2011—the seventy-first (5–7 April) [S/2011/284] and the seventy-second (11–13 October) [S/2011/639]—at which it considered reports on the activities of the Commission; the consultations between Iraq and Kuwait under the auspices of the Commission regarding the unpaid balance owed to Kuwait; the arrangements for ensuring that payments were made to the Compensation Fund; the Follow-up Programme for Environmental Awards; and in-kind transactions. Having considered the progress made by the participating Governments under the Follow-up Programme, which monitored the implementation of approximately $4.3 billion of environmental remediation and restoration projects being undertaken by the Governments of Iran, Jordan, Kuwait and Saudi Arabia, the Governing Council adopted decision 269 [S/AC.26/Dec.269(2011)] concerning the fulfilment of the Follow-up Programme. That decision provided that the mandate of the Programme would be fulfilled when the participating Governments established structural systems and controls and provided adequate assurances for their maintenance and for the use of the award funds for the completion of the projects and a determination to that effect by the Governing Council.

On 24 December, the General Assembly decided that the item on the "Consequences of the Iraqi occupation of and aggression against Kuwait" would remain for consideration during its resumed sixty-sixth (2012) session (**decision 66/557**).

Communication. In a 27 December letter [S/2011/800], the Iraqi Foreign Minister requested the Security Council to allow Iraq access to the complete archives of requests for compensation submitted to the Commission.

Timor-Leste

During 2011, the United Nations Integrated Mission in Timor-Leste (UNMIT), established by Security Council resolution 1704(2006) [YUN 2006, p. 422], continued to carry out its mandate to assist the Government in consolidating stability, enhancing democratic governance and facilitating political dialogue. It also provided support to the national police; helped strengthen the country's human rights capacity; and cooperated with UN bodies and their partners in peacebuilding and capacity-building. In February, the Council extended the UNMIT mandate until 26 February 2012.

Political and security developments

Report of Secretary-General (January). Pursuant to Security Council resolution 1912(2010) [YUN 2010, p. 379], the Secretary-General submitted a January report [S/2011/32] on developments in Timor-Leste and on the activities of UNMIT for the period from 21 September 2010 to 7 January 2011. The overall situation in the country was calm with general trends showing progress towards long-term peace, stability and development. On 3 January, the Secretary of State for the Council of Ministers issued a press release stressing that the Government would mobilize resources to ensure peace, growth and a prosperous Timor-Leste for all future generations. The security environment remained stable, with no major incidents of public disorder or spikes in reported crime, including in districts where the national police had resumed primary policing responsibilities. There was a planned reduction in UNMIT police strength during the reporting period, with 1,480 officers (including 76 women) deployed as at 7 January, 523 of whom were in the formed police units. Of those, 326 officers were deployed in Dili and 197 in other districts. While UNMIT police continued to perform the mandated task of interim law enforcement, they increasingly focused their efforts on supporting the training, capacity-building and institutional development of the national police. Close liaison with the international security forces also continued. Noting the progress achieved in the resumption of primary policing responsibilities by the national police, the Secretary-General concluded that completion in all the districts and units was likely in the coming months, marking the beginning of the reconstitution phase at which time UNMIT would hand over to the national police responsibility for the conduct and the command and control of all police operations in Timor-Leste. Following the handover, there would be a continuing need for an UNMIT police presence to support the further institutional development and capacity-building of the national police, as well as to provide operational support, particularly during the 2012 presidential and parliamentary elections. He recommended an extension of the UNMIT mandate for a period of 12 months, with the same composition and authorized levels of personnel, while continuing the gradual decrease of police personnel as outlined in the report.

On 24 February, by resolution 1969(2011) (see below), the Council extended the mandate of UNMIT for one year. After successful elections, the Mission would be expected to be drawn down towards the end of 2012. The Council requested UNMIT to support the preparation of parliamentary and presidential elections planned for 2012.

SECURITY COUNCIL ACTION

On 24 February [meeting 6487], the Security Council unanimously adopted **resolution 1969(2011)**. The draft [S/2011/86] was submitted by 20 countries.

The Security Council,

Reaffirming all its previous resolutions and the statements by its President on the situation in Timor-Leste, in particular resolutions 1599(2005) of 28 April 2005, 1677(2006) of 12 May 2006, 1690(2006) of 20 June 2006, 1703(2006) of 18 August 2006, 1704(2006) of 25 August 2006, 1745(2007) of 22 February 2007, 1802(2008) of 25 February 2008, 1867(2009) of 26 February 2009 and 1912(2010) of 26 February 2010,

Welcoming the report of the Secretary-General of 25 January 2011,

Reaffirming its full commitment to the sovereignty, independence, territorial integrity and national unity of Timor-Leste and the promotion of long-term stability in the country,

Taking note of the general stability through further improvements in the political and security situation, and welcoming the strong commitment of the leadership and other stakeholders in Timor-Leste to fostering national dialogue and peaceful and inclusive participation in democratic processes and their ongoing efforts to promote continued peace, stability and unity,

Welcoming the efforts of the Government of Timor-Leste to promote cooperation and dialogue between local and national authorities, including through consultations on the Government's development plans for 2011, held from 27 to 29 December 2010, and encouraging further efforts in this regard,

Welcoming also the efforts of the political leadership of Timor-Leste to create opportunities for all political parties to make contributions to issues of national interest, as exemplified by the concluding conference of the National Consensus Dialogue on Truth, Justice and Reconciliation, held from 21 to 23 October 2010,

Reaffirming the need for respect for the independence of the judiciary, stressing the need to act against impunity, while noting the continuing serious resource constraints of the judicial system, and encouraging the leadership of Timor-Leste to continue to increase its efforts to establish accountability for serious criminal offences, including those committed during the 2006 crisis, as recommended by the Independent Special Commission of Inquiry for Timor-Leste,

Welcoming the commencement on 21 September 2010 of deliberations by the National Parliament of Timor-Leste on the draft laws on reparations and on the establishment of follow-on institutions to the Commission for Reception, Truth and Reconciliation and the Commission for Truth and Friendship, pursuant to the resolution of the National Parliament adopted on 14 December 2009, and encouraging further progress in finalizing this legislation,

Welcoming also the progress made in strengthening capacities in the justice and corrections sectors, which has resulted in enhanced access to justice, reductions in pending criminal prosecution cases and improved prison infrastructure, as well as the enactment of important legislation, such as the Criminal Code and the Law against Domestic Violence,

Recognizing the steps taken by the Government of Timor-Leste to further strengthen the institutional capacities and effectiveness of the Anti-Corruption Commission and the Civil Service Commission and to consolidate broad support for anti-corruption measures, and emphasizing the importance of effective laws, institutions, mechanisms and norms relating to the transparency, accountability and efficiency of public administration for the long-term stability and development of the country,

Welcoming the commencement of a jointly owned transition planning and implementation mechanism, including the first meeting of the High-Level Committee on Transition and agreement on the establishment of seven joint technical working groups, and stressing the importance of this process proceeding in a manner that supports national priorities and concerns,

Welcoming also the further progress towards the full resumption of primary policing responsibilities by the National Police of Timor-Leste,

Reaffirming the need to implement fully the "Arrangement on the Restoration and Maintenance of Public Security in Timor-Leste and on Assistance to the Reform, Restructuring and Rebuilding of the Timorese National Police and the Ministry of the Interior", concluded between the Government of Timor-Leste and the United Nations Integrated Mission in Timor-Leste on 1 December 2006, and expressing concern that the Government has certified 52 National Police officers who face serious disciplinary and criminal charges,

Noting the continuing need for support to the further institutional development and capacity-building of the National Police of Timor-Leste, particularly through the transfer of skills to address existing demands, following its resumption of policing responsibilities in all districts and units,

Expressing its full support for the role of the international security forces in assisting the Government of Timor-Leste and the Mission in the maintenance of law and stability, in response to the requests of the Government,

Welcoming the progress of the Government of Timor-Leste in achieving strong economic growth and socioeconomic development, including reductions in the percentage of the population living in poverty and the improvement of human development indicators, while acknowledging the challenges that remain in achieving inclusive and sustainable growth, particularly through the promotion of rural development, the private sector and employment generation, especially for the youth, and by regulating land and property titles and ownership,

Welcoming also the commitment and action of the Government of Timor-Leste to promote the objectives of Security Council resolution 1325(2000) of 31 October 2000, including measures taken to protect women and girls from gender-based violence, especially those measures relating to the implementation of the new Law against Domestic Violence, and the work of the Vulnerable Persons Units of the National Police of Timor-Leste, and other measures relating to the situation of women and girls,

Noting the efforts of the Government of Timor-Leste to finalize the National Strategic Development Plan covering the period from 2011 to 2030, and stressing the need to continue such efforts,

Recalling that, while Timor-Leste has seen progress in many aspects of its political, economic and social development, as well as in human resources development and institution-building, the country still faces many challenges in areas related to the underlying factors of the 2006 crisis and needs the continued assistance of bilateral and multilateral partners in order to fully realize its potential for equitable and sustainable growth,

Acknowledging the contribution that Timor-Leste has made in demonstrating the critical importance of institution-building in post-conflict peacebuilding,

Stressing the importance for Timor-Leste's long-term stability of ensuring a peaceful, credible and transparent electoral process in 2012,

Stressing also the importance of promoting a continued understanding of, and respect for, the checks and balances among the core institutions of State,

Welcoming the continued efforts of the Government of Timor-Leste in providing for the full reintegration of internally displaced persons into their communities and into the Timorese society,

Recognizing the important role that the Mission continues to play in promoting peace, stability and development in Timor-Leste, and expressing its appreciation for the efforts of the Mission and the United Nations country team, under the leadership of the Special Representative of the Secretary-General for Timor-Leste,

1. *Decides* to extend the mandate of the United Nations Integrated Mission in Timor-Leste until 26 February 2012 at the current authorized levels;

2. *Urges* all parties in Timor-Leste, in particular political leaders, to continue to work together and engage in political dialogue and to consolidate peace, democracy, the rule of law, sustainable social and economic development, the promotion of protection of human rights and the advancement of national reconciliation in the country, and reaffirms its full support for the continued efforts of the Special Representative of the Secretary-General for Timor-Leste aimed at addressing critical political and security-related issues facing the country, including enhancing a culture of democratic governance, through inclusive and collaborative processes;

3. *Requests* the Mission to extend the necessary support, within its current mandate, for the preparation of the parliamentary and presidential elections of 2012, as requested by the Government of Timor-Leste and in accordance with the recommendations of the planned electoral assessment mission, and encourages the international community to assist in this process;

4. *Reaffirms* the importance that the Government of Timor-Leste continues the review and reform of the security sector in Timor-Leste, in particular the need to delineate roles and responsibilities between the Falintil-Forças de Defesa de Timor-Leste and the National Police of Timor-Leste, to strengthen legal frameworks and to enhance civilian oversight and accountability mechanisms of both security institutions, and requests the Mission to continue to support the Government, as requested, in its efforts in the country;

5. *Emphasizes* the importance of taking all measures necessary to ensure the credibility and integrity of the National Police of Timor-Leste, including resolving any outstanding disciplinary and criminal charges faced by National Police officers;

6. *Encourages* further efforts to complete the resumption of primary policing responsibilities by the National Police of Timor-Leste in all districts and units, on the basis of the criteria mutually agreed upon by the Government of Timor-Leste and the Mission, including through jointly agreed measures to enhance the institutional capacity of the National Police in the remaining districts and units;

7. *Endorses* the reconfiguration of the Mission police component to take account of the changing nature of its role and function in Timor-Leste and the plan for its drawdown, in accordance with the wishes of the Government of Timor-Leste, conditions on the ground and following the successful completion of the 2012 electoral process, as recommended in paragraph 61 of the report of the Secretary-General;

8. *Requests* the Mission to continue to provide interim law enforcement and to ensure the maintenance of public security in those districts and units in which the National Police of Timor-Leste has yet to resume primary policing responsibilities and, following the resumption of primary policing responsibilities by the National Police, to provide operational support to the National Police, within its current mandate, as mutually agreed between the Government of Timor-Leste and the Mission;

9. *Also requests* the Mission to support the further institutional development and capacity-building of the National Police of Timor-Leste following its resumption of primary policing responsibilities in all districts and units, including through the prompt deployment of the 19 additional civilian experts within its police component as referred to in the report of the Secretary-General, expresses its support for the work of the joint working group of the National Police and the Mission police in developing a plan for further capacity-building support for the National Police focusing on the five major areas for its further development identified in the Strategic Development Plan for the National Police for 2011–2012, and emphasizes the significant role to be played in this by other bilateral and multilateral partners and the importance of promoting Timorese leadership;

10. *Underscores* the need for the concept of operations and rules of engagement to be regularly updated as necessary and to be fully in line with the provisions of the present resolution;

11. *Reaffirms* the importance of ongoing efforts to achieve accountability and justice, expresses its support for the work of the Mission in assisting the Government of Timor-Leste in this regard, within its mandate, as well as for the initiatives to strengthen the Office of the Provedor for Human Rights and Justice, and underlines the importance of the implementation by the Government of the recommendations contained in the report of the Independent Special Commission of Inquiry for Timor-Leste of 2 October 2006, including paragraphs 225 to 228 thereof;

12. *Underlines* the importance of a coordinated approach to the justice sector reform, taking into account the recommendations of the independent comprehensive

needs assessment and through the implementation of the Government of Timor-Leste's Justice Sector Strategic Plan, and the ongoing need to increase Timorese ownership and strengthen national capacity in judicial line functions, including the training and specialization of national lawyers and judges, and emphasizes the need for sustained support of the international community in capacity-building and strengthening of institutions in this sector, building on the recent positive developments, including the drafting and enactment of important legislation, such as the Criminal Code and the Law against Domestic Violence;

13. *Requests* the Mission to continue its efforts, adjusting them as necessary to enhance the effectiveness of the judiciary, in assisting the Government of Timor-Leste in carrying out the proceedings recommended by the Commission of Inquiry;

14. *Calls upon* the Mission to continue to support the Government of Timor-Leste in its efforts to coordinate donor cooperation in areas of institutional capacity-building;

15. *Recognizes* the importance of the development plans devised by the Government of Timor-Leste, especially the attention paid to infrastructure, rural development and human resources capacity development, and in this regard calls upon the Mission to continue to cooperate and coordinate with the United Nations agencies, funds and programmes, as well as all relevant partners, to support the Government and relevant institutions in designing poverty reduction, education improvement, promotion of sustainable livelihood and economic growth policies;

16. *Encourages* the Government of Timor-Leste to strengthen peacebuilding perspectives in such areas as employment and empowerment, especially focusing on rural areas and youth, as well as local socio-economic development, in particular in the agricultural sector;

17. *Requests* the Mission to fully take into account gender considerations as set out in Security Council resolutions 1325(2000), 1820(2008) of 19 June 2008, 1888(2009) of 30 September 2009 and 1889(2009) of 5 October 2009 as a cross-cutting issue throughout its mandate, stressing the importance of strengthening the responsiveness of the security sector to the specific needs of women, and reaffirms Council resolutions 1674(2006) of 28 April 2006 and 1894(2009) of 11 November 2009 on the protection of civilians and resolution 1502(2003) of 26 August 2003 on the protection of humanitarian and United Nations personnel;

18. *Requests* the Secretary-General to continue to take the measures necessary to ensure full compliance by the Mission with the United Nations zero-tolerance policy on sexual exploitation and abuse and to keep the Council informed, and urges those countries contributing troops and police to take appropriate preventive action and to ensure full accountability in cases of such conduct involving their personnel;

19. *Also requests* the Secretary-General to keep the Council regularly informed of the developments on the ground and to submit to the Council, no later than 15 October 2011 and 26 January 2012, reports that include an update regarding the High-Level Committee on Transition and progress concerning the critical tasks that will need to be accomplished post-election, and on planning concerning the United Nations presence in Timor-Leste beyond the 2012 elections;

20. *Reaffirms* the importance of the medium-term strategy and benchmarks for measuring and tracking progress in Timor-Leste and assessing the level and form of United Nations support and cooperation with the Government of Timor-Leste while keeping the benchmarks under active review, and underlines the importance of ownership of the strategy by the leaders and people of Timor-Leste in this process;

21. *Encourages* the Government of Timor-Leste, the Mission, the United Nations country team and other relevant stakeholders, including within the framework of the High-Level Committee on Transition, to continue to intensify the ongoing discussion on the strategy and modalities for the transition and preparation for future changes to the nature and scope of the United Nations presence on the ground post-Mission;

22. *Decides* to remain seized of the matter.

Report of Secretary-General (October). In response to Security Council resolution 1969(2011) (see p. 363), the Secretary-General submitted an October report [S/2011/641] on developments in Timor-Leste and the activities of UNMIT for the period from 8 January to 20 September. The overall situation remained generally calm, with continued progress towards the consolidation of peace, stability and development. Political parties intensified their internal organizational activities in preparation for the 2012 presidential and parliamentary elections. The Congresso Nacional da Reconstrução de Timor-Leste (CNRT), the largest party in the Alliance for a Parliamentary Majority Government, held its second national congress from 29 April to 2 May 2011. The Prime Minister, Kay Rala Xanana Gusmão, and Dionisio Babo Soares were re-elected CNRT President and Secretary-General, respectively. President José Ramos-Horta continued his efforts to foster national unity and stability by means of public messages and the organization of high-profile events, including the second "Dili–City of Peace" marathon in June and the third "Tour de Timor" bicycle race in September.

On 27 March, the national police—the Polícia Nacional de Timor-Leste (PNTL)—resumed responsibility for the conduct, command and control of all police operations in the country. The resumption did not detrimentally affect the continuing low crime rate. UNMIT police continued to provide operational support to PNTL in such areas as close protection, joint patrols and border policing. A number of incidents involving martial arts and youth groups occurred, as well as some friction between PNTL and members of the defence forces—the Falintil-Forças de Defesa de Timor-Leste. Given the generally calm security situation and positive political climate, UNMIT, jointly with the Government, was proceeding with the transition process on the assumption that the overall situation would remain stable and peaceful, allowing for continued planning for the Mission's departure by the end of 2012. The joint transition plan set out four possible models for UN engagement after the withdrawal of UNMIT, three of them based on experience gained in other countries and one suggested by the Government, subject to a strategic assessment and noting that any option would need to be discussed with the Government that would be formed following the 2012 elections. The Secretary-General stated that the upcoming electoral period, with likely active campaigning and intense political competition, could pose a test for PNTL, which continued to face logistical constraints. It would therefore be particularly important to ensure that PNTL had the ability to respond to potential security challenges during the electoral period and beyond. The UNMIT police would stand ready to provide operational support to PNTL during that crucial period.

Year-end developments. In a later report [S/2012/43], the Secretary-General said that the overall situation in Timor-Leste remained calm. Political parties continued their preparations for the 2012 presidential and parliamentary elections, with several parties holding national congresses. Party leaders continued to call for security and stability during the electoral period. In a speech on 28 November, the thirty-sixth anniversary of the Timor-Leste Declaration of Independence, President Ramos-Horta commended all Timorese for contributing to a positive atmosphere of peace and hope. Despite the general calm, a number of violent incidents involving martial arts groups occurred, including a fight between two rival martial arts groups in Dili on 19 December that resulted in one person's death. In response to that and other incidents, the Council of Ministers adopted a 22 December resolution prohibiting and criminalizing certain activities of martial arts groups for one year and also banning certain gambling activities for an indefinite period. The Secretary-General stated that, to ensure continued stability, it was critical to intensify efforts to further strengthen the institutional development of PNTL, particularly in the areas of criminal investigations, community policing and internal accountability. He encouraged Member States, as well as bilateral and multilateral partners, to engage with the Government and UNMIT to ensure continued support in those areas, and reiterated his appeal to all countries concerned to approve requests for the extension of deployment of police officers serving in key UNMIT positions.

On the preparations for the 2012 presidential and parliamentary elections, the Secretary-General said that steady progress had been made, as reflected by the approval of subsidiary electoral legislation by the National Electoral Commission, the successful conduct of voter registration and ongoing efforts by the electoral management bodies to increase the participation of women and youth in the electoral process. The Special Representative would continue to play her good offices role vis-à-vis all parties to ensure a peaceful and credible political process. The Secretary-General noted that the upcoming elections could reignite localized tensions among individuals and groups, including martial arts groups, and pose a test for PNTL's ability to respond to security challenges. UNMIT police would stand ready to provide operational support to PNTL during the electoral period and, if requested, beyond.

UNAMET

The United Nations Mission in East Timor (UNAMET) was established by Security Council resolution 1246(1999) [YUN 1999, p. 283] to conduct the 1999 popular consultation to ascertain the East Timorese people's will on the future status of East Timor [ibid., p. 288]; its mandate ended on 30 November 1999, in accordance with resolution 1262(1999) [ibid., p. 287].

On 12 September, by **decision 65/556**, the General Assembly deferred consideration of UNAMET financing until its sixty-sixth (2011) session. On 24 December, it decided that the item would remain for consideration during its resumed sixty-sixth (2012) session (**decision 66/557**).

UNMIT

The United Nations Integrated Mission in Timor-Leste (UNMIT) was established by Security Council resolution 1704(2006) [YUN 2006, p. 422] to support the Government in consolidating stability, enhancing a culture of democratic governance and facilitating political dialogue; ensure the maintenance of public security; assist the Government in reviewing the role and needs of the security sector; strengthen capacity for promoting human rights, justice and reconciliation; and assist in implementing the Secretary-General's recommendations on justice and reconciliation. The mission continued to be headed by Ameerah Haq (Bangladesh), who served as the Secretary-General's Special Representative for Timor-Leste.

Financing

In June, the General Assembly had before it the performance report on the UNMIT budget from 1 July 2009 to 30 June 2010 [A/65/687], with expenditures amounting to $191,118,800 against an apportionment of $205,939,400, resulting in an unencumbered balance of $14,820,600. The Assembly also had before it the proposed UNMIT budget for 1 July 2011 to 30 June 2012 [A/65/746] in the amount of $196,744,800, and the related comments and recommendations of the ACABQ [A/65/743/Add.6].

GENERAL ASSEMBLY ACTION

On 30 June [meeting 106], the General Assembly, on the recommendation of the Fifth (Administrative and Budgetary) Committee [A/65/883], adopted **resolution 65/297** without vote [agenda item 150].

Financing of the United Nations Integrated Mission in Timor-Leste

The General Assembly,

Having considered the reports of the Secretary-General on the financing of the United Nations Integrated Mission in Timor-Leste and the related report of the Advisory Committee on Administrative and Budgetary Questions,

Recalling Security Council resolution 1704(2006) of 25 August 2006, by which the Council decided to establish a follow-on mission in Timor-Leste, the United Nations Integrated Mission in Timor-Leste, for an initial period of six months, with the intention to renew it for further periods, and the subsequent resolutions by which the Council extended the mandate of the Mission, the latest of which was resolution 1969(2011) of 24 February 2011, by which the Council extended the mandate of the Mission until 26 February 2012,

Recalling also its resolutions 61/249 A of 22 December 2006 and 61/249 B of 2 April 2007 on the financing of the Mission and its subsequent resolutions thereon, the latest of which was resolution 64/276 of 24 June 2010,

Reaffirming the general principles underlying the financing of United Nations peacekeeping operations, as stated in General Assembly resolutions 1874(S-IV) of 27 June 1963, 3101(XXVIII) of 11 December 1973 and 55/235 of 23 December 2000,

Mindful of the fact that it is essential to provide the Mission with the financial resources necessary to enable it to fulfil its responsibilities under the relevant resolutions of the Security Council,

1. *Requests* the Secretary-General to entrust the Head of Mission with the task of formulating future budget proposals in full accordance with the provisions of General Assembly resolutions 59/296 of 22 June 2005, 60/266 of 30 June 2006, 61/276 of 29 June 2007, 64/269 of 24 June 2010 and 65/289 of 30 June 2011, as well as other relevant resolutions;

2. *Takes note* of the status of contributions to the United Nations Integrated Mission in Timor-Leste as at 30 April 2011, including the contributions outstanding in the amount of 56.1 million United States dollars, representing some 6.3 per cent of the total assessed contributions, notes with concern that only forty-two Member States have paid their assessed contributions in full, and urges all other Member States, in particular those in arrears, to ensure payment of their outstanding assessed contributions;

3. *Expresses its appreciation* to those Member States which have paid their assessed contributions in full, and urges all other Member States to make every possible effort to ensure payment of their assessed contributions to the Mission in full;

4. *Expresses concern* at the financial situation with regard to peacekeeping activities, in particular as regards the reimbursements to troop contributors that bear additional burdens owing to overdue payments by Member States of their assessments;

5. *Also expresses concern* at the delay experienced by the Secretary-General in deploying and providing adequate resources to some recent peacekeeping missions, in particular those in Africa;

6. *Emphasizes* that all future and existing peacekeeping missions shall be given equal and non-discriminatory treatment in respect of financial and administrative arrangements;

7. *Also emphasizes* that all peacekeeping missions shall be provided with adequate resources for the effective and efficient discharge of their respective mandates;

8. *Requests* the Secretary-General to ensure that proposed peacekeeping budgets are based on the relevant legislative mandates;

9. *Endorses* the conclusions and recommendations contained in the report of the Advisory Committee on Administrative and Budgetary Questions, subject to the provisions of the present resolution, and requests the Secretary-General to ensure their full implementation;

10. *Requests* the Secretary-General to ensure the full implementation of the relevant provisions of its resolutions 59/296, 60/266, 61/276, 64/269 and 65/289;

11. *Also requests* the Secretary-General to take all action necessary to ensure that the Mission is administered with a maximum of efficiency and economy;

12. *Notes* that the overall level of appropriation has been adjusted in accordance with the terms of resolution 65/289;

Financial performance report for the period from 1 July 2009 to 30 June 2010

13. *Takes note* of the report of the Secretary-General on the financial performance of the Mission for the period from 1 July 2009 to 30 June 2010;

Budget estimates for the period from 1 July 2011 to 30 June 2012

14. *Decides* to appropriate to the Special Account for the United Nations Integrated Mission in Timor-Leste the amount of 208,603,700 dollars for the period from 1 July 2011 to 30 June 2012, inclusive of 196,077,500 dollars for the maintenance of the Mission, 10,614,500 dollars for the support account for peacekeeping operations and 1,911,700 dollars for the United Nations Logistics Base at Brindisi, Italy;

Financing of the appropriation

15. *Also decides* to apportion among Member States the amount of 137,270,825 dollars for the period from 1 July 2011 to 26 February 2012, in accordance with the levels updated in General Assembly resolution 64/249 of 24 December 2009, and taking into account the scale of assessments for 2011 and 2012, as set out in Assembly resolution 64/248 of 24 December 2009;

16. *Further decides* that, in accordance with the provisions of its resolution 973(X) of 15 December 1955, there shall be set off against the apportionment among Member States, as provided for in paragraph 15 above, their respective share in the Tax Equalization Fund of 6,760,632 dollars, comprising the estimated staff assessment income of 6,036,914 dollars approved for the Mission, the prorated share of 591,583 dollars of the estimated staff assessment income approved for the support account and the prorated share of 132,135 dollars of the estimated staff assessment income approved for the United Nations Logistics Base;

17. *Decides* to apportion among Member States the amount of 71,332,875 dollars for the period from 27 February to 30 June 2012 at a monthly rate of 17,383,641 dollars, in accordance with the levels updated in General Assembly resolution 64/249, and taking into account the scale of assessments for 2012, as set out in Assembly resolution 64/248, subject to a decision of the Security Council to extend the mandate of the Mission;

18. *Also decides* that, in accordance with the provisions of its resolution 973(X), there shall be set off against the apportionment among Member States, as provided for in paragraph 17 above, their respective share in the Tax Equalization Fund of 3,513,168 dollars, comprising the estimated staff assessment income of 3,137,086 dollars approved for the Mission, the prorated share of 307,417 dollars of the estimated staff assessment income approved for the support account and the prorated share of 68,665 dollars of the estimated staff assessment income approved for the United Nations Logistics Base;

19. *Further decides* that, for Member States that have fulfilled their financial obligations to the Mission, there shall be set off against the apportionment, as provided for in paragraph 15 above, their respective share of the unencumbered balance and other income in the total amount of 17,795,500 dollars in respect of the financial period ended 30 June 2010, in accordance with the levels updated in General Assembly resolution 64/249, and taking into account the scale of assessments for 2010, as set out in Assembly resolution 64/248;

20. *Decides* that, for Member States that have not fulfilled their financial obligations to the Mission, there shall be set off against their outstanding obligations their respective share of the unencumbered balance and other income in the total amount of 17,795,500 dollars in respect of the financial period ended 30 June 2010, in accordance with the scheme set out in paragraph 19 above;

21. *Also decides* that the increase of 947,800 dollars in the estimated staff assessment income in respect of the financial period ended 30 June 2010 shall be added to the credits from the amount of 17,795,500 dollars referred to in paragraphs 19 and 20 above;

22. *Emphasizes* that no peacekeeping mission shall be financed by borrowing funds from other active peacekeeping missions;

23. *Encourages* the Secretary-General to continue to take additional measures to ensure the safety and security of all personnel participating in the Mission under the auspices of the United Nations, bearing in mind paragraphs 5 and 6 of Security Council resolution 1502(2003) of 26 August 2003;

24. *Invites* voluntary contributions to the Mission in cash and in the form of services and supplies acceptable to the Secretary-General, to be administered, as appropriate, in accordance with the procedure and practices established by the General Assembly;

25. *Decides* to include in the provisional agenda of its sixty-sixth session the item entitled "Financing of the United Nations Integrated Mission in Timor-Leste".

On 24 December, the General Assembly decided that the agenda item on the financing of UNMIT would remain for consideration during its resumed sixty-sixth (2012) session (**decision 66/557**).

Democratic People's Republic of Korea

In 2011, the United Nations continued to address the non-proliferation of nuclear weapons in the Democratic People's Republic of Korea (DPRK) and related issues.

Non-proliferation

The mandate of the Security Council Committee established by resolution 1718(2006) [YUN 2006, p. 444] on the DPRK was to oversee the implementation of the sanctions measures in that resolution, which included an arms embargo; a nuclear, ballistic missiles and other weapons of mass destruction programmes-related embargo; and a travel ban and/or an assets freeze on designated persons and entities. By resolution 1874(2009) [YUN 2009, p. 384], the Council established a Panel of Experts to carry out certain tasks under the direction of the Committee. By resolution 1985(2011) (see below), the Council extended the Panel's mandate until 12 June 2012.

The Sanctions Committee held one formal meeting and six sessions of informal consultations in 2011. During the formal meeting on 12 September, the Ambassador of the Russian Federation to the DPRK briefed the Committee on the difficulties faced by some diplomatic missions in the DPRK in the context of paragraph 21 of resolution 1874(2009).

SECURITY COUNCIL ACTION

On 10 June [meeting 6553], the Security Council unanimously adopted **resolution 1985(2011)**. The draft [S/2011/354] was submitted by the United States.

The Security Council,

Recalling its previous relevant resolutions, including resolutions 825(1993) of 11 May 1993, 1540(2004) of 28 April 2004, 1695(2006) of 15 July 2006, 1718(2006) of 14 October 2006, 1874(2009) of 12 June 2009, 1887(2009) of 24 September 2009 and 1928(2010) of 7 June 2010, as well as the statements by its President of 6 October 2006 and 13 April 2009,

Recalling also the creation, pursuant to paragraph 26 of resolution 1874(2009), of the Panel of Experts on the Democratic People's Republic of Korea, under the direction of the Security Council Committee established pursuant to resolution 1718(2006), to carry out the tasks provided for in that paragraph,

Recalling further the interim report of 12 November 2010 of the Panel of Experts appointed by the Secretary-General pursuant to paragraph 26 of resolution 1874(2009), and the final report of the Panel, of 12 May 2011,

Recalling the methodological standards for reports of sanctions monitoring mechanisms contained in the report of the Informal Working Group of the Security Council on General Issues of Sanctions,

Noting, in that regard, the importance of credible, fact-based, independent assessments, analysis and recommendations, in accordance with the mandate of the Panel of Experts,

Determining that the proliferation of nuclear, chemical and biological weapons, as well as their means of delivery, continues to constitute a threat to international peace and security,

Acting under Article 41 of Chapter VII of the Charter of the United Nations,

1. *Decides* to extend until 12 June 2012 the mandate of the Panel of Experts on the Democratic People's Republic of Korea, as specified in paragraph 26 of resolution 1874(2009), and requests the Secretary-General to take the necessary administrative measures to this effect;

2. *Requests* the Panel of Experts to provide to the Security Council Committee established pursuant to resolution 1718(2006), no later than 12 November 2011, a midterm report on its work, and requests that, after a discussion with the Committee, the Panel submit to the Council its midterm report by 12 December 2011, and also requests a final report to the Committee, no later than thirty days prior to the termination of the mandate of the Panel, with its findings and recommendations, and further requests that, after a discussion with the Committee, the Panel submit to the Council its final report upon termination of the mandate of the Panel;

3. *Also requests* the Panel of Experts to provide to the Committee a planned programme of work no later than thirty days after the appointment of the Panel, encourages the Committee to engage in regular discussions about this programme of work, and further requests the Panel to provide to the Committee any updates to this programme of work;

4. *Urges* all States, relevant United Nations bodies and other interested parties to cooperate fully with the Committee and with the Panel of Experts, in particular by supplying any information at their disposal on the implementation of the measures imposed by resolutions 1718(2006) and 1874(2009);

5. *Decides* to remain actively seized of the matter.

Panel of experts. Pursuant to Security Council resolution 1985(2011) (see p. 368) the Secretary-General in June informed the Council [S/2011/391] that he had renewed the mandate of the Panel's seven experts. In August [S/2011/533], he informed the Council of the replacement of two experts.

Sanctions Committee report. Reporting to the Security Council on the activities of the Sanctions Committee in 2011 [S/2012/17], the Committee Chairman said that during the reporting period, 14 Member States reported to the Committee on the steps they had taken to implement provisions of resolutions 1718(2006) and 1874(2009), including financial measures set out in resolution 1874(2009). The Committee approved two Implementation Assistance Notices, one on 21 January to assist Member States in preparing and submitting the requested reports and another on 5 December regarding the ban on the supply, sale or transfer of luxury goods referred to in resolutions 1718(2006) and 1874(2009). The Committee received three new reports of alleged violations, as well as information on two previously reported cases of alleged violations. In one of the cases, the Committee replied to the Member State in a note verbale. All of the reported cases were being investigated with the support and technical expertise of the Committee's Panel of Experts. A list of the reports of Member States, excluding those which had requested confidentiality, was annexed to the report.

Other issues

Republic of Korea naval ship sinking (2010)

The Security Council, in presidential statement S/PRST/2010/13 [YUN 2010, p. 387], in view of the findings of the Joint Civilian-Military Investigation Group, which concluded that the DPRK was responsible for the 2010 sinking of a Republic of Korea naval ship, the *Cheonan*, condemned the attack and called for full adherence to the 1953 Korean Armistice Agreement [YUN 1953, p. 136].

Communication. On 11 March, the DPRK transmitted a letter [S/2011/129] containing a 23 February announcement by the DPRK Inspection Group of the National Defence Commission regarding the Yonphyong Island shelling and the *Cheonan* case.

Iran

In 2011, the United Nations continued to address Iran's nuclear programme and the sanctions imposed by the Security Council in resolution 1737(2006) [YUN 2006, p. 436] and reinforced by resolutions 1747(2007) [YUN 2007, p. 374], 1803(2008) [YUN 2008, p. 409], 1835(2008) [ibid., p. 414] and 1929(2010) [YUN 2010, p. 396]. The Committee established pursuant to resolution 1737(2006) continued to oversee the implementation of the sanctions regime. On 9 June, by resolution 1984(2011) (see p. 370), the Council extended until 9 June 2012 the mandate of the Panel of Experts established pursuant to resolution 1929(2010) to assist the Sanctions Committee in carrying out its mandate.

During the year the International Atomic Energy Agency (IAEA) reported that Iran had not implemented the Additional Protocol to Iran's Safeguards Agreement or the relevant resolutions of the Council and the IAEA Board of Governors. It had also failed to permit the Agency to confirm that all nuclear material in Iran was being used in peaceful activities. Iran maintained that its nuclear programme was for peaceful purposes.

Non-proliferation

IAEA reports

During 2011, the Security Council had before it five reports by the IAEA Director General on Iran's implementation of the 1974 Non-Proliferation Treaty (NPT) Safeguards Agreement between Iran and IAEA and relevant Council resolutions. Each report stated that the Agency had continued activities to verify the non-diversion of declared nuclear material and elaborated on that process, including cooperation issues and difficulties encountered.

IAEA reports (February and May). In February [GOV/2011/7], the IAEA Director General reported on developments since his November 2010 report [YUN 2010, p. 405], focusing on areas where Iran had not fully implemented its binding obligations. With regard to reprocessing activities, IAEA carried out an inspection and design information verification at the Tehran Research Reactor on 5 February, and at the Molybdenum, Iodine and Xenon Radioisotope Production Facility on 6 February. It could confirm that there were no ongoing reprocessing-related activities in Iran only with respect to those two facilities, and the other facilities to which the Agency had access. Attached to the report was an overview of the implementation of Iran's NPT Safeguards Agreement and relevant provisions of Council resolutions on Iran.

In response to Council resolution 1929(2010) [YUN 2010, p. 396], the Council President, by a 24 May note [S/2011/327], circulated the Director General's May report [GOV/2011/29] on Iran's implementation of the NPT Safeguards Agreement and relevant provisions of Council resolutions. The Director General stated that, on 6 May, he had sent a letter to the Vice President of Iran and Head of the Atomic Energy Organization of Iran reiterating IAEA concerns about the existence of possible military dimensions to Iran's nuclear programme; requesting that Iran provide prompt access to relevant locations, equipment, documentation and persons; and noting that, with Iran's substantive and proactive engagement, the Agency would be able to make progress in its verification of the correctness and completeness of Iran's declarations.

Security Council consideration. On 22 March [S/PV.6502] and 23 June [S/PV.6563], the Sanctions Committee Chair briefed the Council on the implementation of sanctions against Iran, stating that the Committee had received information concerning sanctions violations and had examined and followed up on those cases. On 22 March, the Chair noted that the Committee, in the light of the recommendations in the midterm report of the Panel of Experts, had agreed to consider disseminating additional optional guidance on submitting implementation reports and to periodically organize open briefings. The Panel submitted its final report to the Council on 7 May. On 23 June, the Chair informed the Council that the Committee had discussed the Panel's recommendations and that it would continue to consider actions to implement some of the recommendations. The Committee had requested the Panel to draft a series of implementation assistance notices based on five thematic areas of its recommendations. On 9 June, by resolution 1984(2011) (see below), the Council extended the mandate of the Panel of Experts until 9 June 2012.

SECURITY COUNCIL ACTION

On 9 June [meeting 6552], the Security Council adopted **resolution 1984(2011)** by vote (14-0-1). The draft [S/2011/348] was submitted by France, Germany, the United Kingdom and the United States.

The Security Council,

Recalling its previous relevant resolutions, including resolutions 1696(2006) of 31 July 2006, 1737(2006) of 23 December 2006, 1747(2007) of 24 March 2007, 1803(2008) of 3 March 2008, 1835(2008) of 27 September 2008, 1887(2009) of 24 September 2009 and 1929(2010) of 9 June 2010, as well as the statement by its President of 29 March 2006, and reaffirming their provisions,

Recalling also the creation, pursuant to paragraph 29 of resolution 1929(2010), of the Panel of Experts on the Islamic Republic of Iran, under the direction of the Security Council Committee established pursuant to resolution 1737(2006), to carry out the tasks provided for in that paragraph,

Recalling further the interim report of 4 February 2011 of the Panel of Experts appointed by the Secretary-General pursuant to paragraph 29 of resolution 1929(2010), and final report of the Panel, of 7 May 2011,

Recalling the methodological standards for reports of sanctions monitoring mechanisms contained in the report of the Informal Working Group of the Security Council on General Issues of Sanctions,

Noting, in that regard, the importance of credible, fact-based, independent assessments, analysis and recommendations, in accordance with the mandate of the Panel of Experts,

Determining that the proliferation of weapons of mass destruction, as well as their means of delivery, continues to constitute a threat to international peace and security,

Acting under Article 41 of Chapter VII of the Charter of the United Nations,

1. *Decides* to extend until 9 June 2012 the mandate of the Panel of Experts on the Islamic Republic of Iran, as specified in paragraph 29 of resolution 1929(2010), and requests the Secretary-General to take the necessary administrative measures to this effect;

2. *Requests* the Panel of Experts to provide to the Security Council Committee established pursuant to resolution 1737(2006), no later than 9 November 2011, a midterm report on its work, and requests that, after a discussion with the Committee, the Panel submit to the Council its midterm report by 9 December 2011, and also requests a final report to the Committee, no later than thirty days prior to the termination of the mandate of the Panel, with its findings and recommendations, and further requests that, after a discussion with the Committee, the Panel submit to the Council its final report upon termination of the mandate of the Panel;

3. *Also requests* the Panel of Experts to provide to the Committee a planned programme of work no later than thirty days after the appointment of the Panel, encourages the Committee to engage in regular discussions about this programme of work, and further requests the Panel to provide to the Committee any updates to this programme of work;

4. *Urges* all States, relevant United Nations bodies and other interested parties to cooperate fully with the Committee and with the Panel of Experts, in particular by sup-

plying any information at their disposal on the implementation of the measures imposed by resolutions 1737(2006), 1747(2007), 1803(2008) and 1929(2010);

5. *Decides* to remain actively seized of the matter.

VOTE ON RESOLUTION 1984(2011):

In favour: Bosnia and Herzegovina, Brazil, China, Colombia, France, Gabon, Germany, India, Nigeria, Portugal, Russian Federation, South Africa, United Kingdom, United States.

Against: None.

Abstaining: Lebanon.

IAEA reports (September and November). By a 2 September note [S/2011/555], the Council President circulated the IAEA Director General's September report on the application of safeguards in Iran [GOV/2011/54]. The Director General stated that he had held meetings (Vienna, 21 June and 12 July) with Dr. Fereydoun Abbasi, the Vice President of Iran and Head of the Atomic Energy Organization of Iran, and Dr. Ali Akbar Salehi, the Iranian Minister for Foreign Affairs, respectively. In response to an invitation from Iran, the IAEA Deputy Director General for Safeguards went to Iran in August and visited the Bushehr Nuclear Power Plant, the enrichment plants at Natanz and Fordow, the IR-40 Reactor and Heavy Water Production Plant at Arak, and the conversion and fuel fabrication facilities at Esfahan. Iran also provided access to an installation where research and development on advanced centrifuges was taking place. During his visit, the Deputy Director General also held meetings with Dr. Abbasi.

In a 26 May letter to the Director General, Dr. Abbasi explained Iran's position on the issue of possible military dimensions to Iran's nuclear programme. The Director General, in a 3 June response, reminded Iran that it should fully implement all of its obligations in order to establish international confidence in the exclusively peaceful nature of its nuclear programme.

In an 8 November report [GOV/2011/65], the Director General stated that he met Dr. Abbasi on 19 September in Vienna and discussed issues related to the implementation of Iran's Safeguards Agreement and other relevant obligations. In a 30 September letter, IAEA reiterated its invitation to Iran to re-engage with it on the outstanding issues related to possible military dimensions to Iran's nuclear programme and the actions required of Iran to resolve those issues. On 30 October, Dr. Abbasi referred to his previous discussions with the Director General and expressed the will of Iran to remove ambiguities, if any, suggesting that the IAEA Deputy Director General should visit Iran for discussions. In his reply of 2 November, the Director General indicated his readiness to send the Deputy Director General to discuss the issues identified in his forthcoming report to the IAEA Board of Governors. The report contained an annex setting out in more detail the basis for IAEA concerns about possible military dimensions to Iran's nuclear programme.

Year-end developments. A later IAEA report [GOV/2012/9], covering developments from 9 November to the end of 2011 indicated that the IAEA Board of Governors adopted resolution GOV/2011/69 (18 November 2011) stressing that it was essential for Iran and IAEA to intensify their dialogue aimed at the resolution of all outstanding substantive issues, including access to all relevant information, documentation, sites, material and personnel in Iran. The Board called on Iran to engage seriously and without preconditions in talks aimed at restoring international confidence in the exclusively peaceful nature of Iran's nuclear programme.

Security Council Committee

The Security Council Committee established pursuant to resolution 1737(2006) [YUN 2006, p. 436] continued to monitor the implementation of the embargo relating to Iran on proliferation-sensitive nuclear activities and the development of nuclear weapon delivery systems; the ban on the export and procurement of any arms and related materiel from Iran; financial and business restrictions; and an assets freeze and a travel ban on designated individuals and entities. Those sanctions were renewed by resolutions 1747(2007) [YUN 2007, p. 374], 1803(2008) [YUN 2008, p. 409] and 1929(2010) [YUN 2010, p. 396].

The Committee was assisted by the Panel of Experts created by resolution 1929(2010) to carry out, under the direction of the Committee, the tasks provided for in the resolution. By resolution 1984(2011) (see p. 370), the Council extended the Panel's mandate until 9 June 2012. The Panel consisted of eight members, who were reappointed by the Secretary-General on 30 June [S/2011/405].

Security Council Committee report. In a report to the Security Council on the activities of the Committee in 2011 [S/2012/192], the Committee Chair stated that the guidelines of the Committee for the conduct of its work went through a substantial revision and new guidelines were approved on 19 August. The Committee met four times in informal consultations (4 March, 8 June, 16 June, 7 December). The Committee received 96 implementation reports from Member States under resolution 1737(2006), 83 reports under resolution 1747(2007), 77 reports under resolution 1803(2008) and 77 reports under resolution 1929(2010). During the year, the Committee received six notifications of reported violations of Council measures relating to Iran. In response, the Committee dispatched letters to most reporting States expressing its appreciation for the information provided and urging them to continue to cooperate closely with the Committee and the Panel of Experts in their investigation of the cases.

In accordance with its mandate, the Panel of Experts carried out inspections of five of the six reported cases with the consent and cooperation of the reporting States. As required by its mandate, the Panel provided its findings and recommendations in separate reports to the Committee. During the year the Panel submitted midterm (4 February) and final (7 May) reports pursuant to Council resolution 1929(2010) and an interim report (9 November) in accordance with resolution 1984(2011). It also provided to the Committee quarterly assessments of Member States' implementation reports in accordance with paragraph 31 of resolution 1929(2010).

Communications. In a 24 June letter [A/65/876] to the Secretary-General, Iran stated that the declaration by the United States of new unilateral sanctions against some Iranian companies and individuals had the objective of depriving the Iranian people of their most basic human rights. In an 8 September letter [S/2011/563] to the Security Council, Iran expressed its deep concern over and strong condemnation of remarks by the President of France about Iran's nuclear activities.

Nepal

The United Nations Mission in Nepal (UNMIN), a special political mission in support of the peace process in Nepal, was established in 2007 by Security Council resolution 1740(2007) [YUN 2007, p. 385] to help implement the 2006 Comprehensive Peace Agreement [YUN 2006, p. 449] by monitoring the management of arms and armed personnel of the Nepal Army and the Maoist Army and by providing technical support for the election of a Constituent Assembly. By resolution 1939(2010) [YUN 2010, p. 393], the Council decided that UNMIN's mandate would terminate on 15 January 2011.

In a 14 January presidential statement, the Council reaffirmed its support for the peace process and called on the Nepalese caretaker Government and all political parties to redouble their efforts to continue to fulfil the commitments they had made in the Comprehensive Peace Agreement. The mandate of UNMIN ended on 15 January 2011.

Political and security developments

Security Council consideration. On 5 January [S/PV.6465], the Security Council discussed the Secretary-General's 2010 report [YUN 2010, p. 394] on the request of Nepal for UN assistance in support of its peace process. The Representative of the Secretary-General and Head of UNMIN, Karin Landgren (Sweden), informed the Council that, although the peace process was incomplete, UNMIN had performed its mandated tasks and contributed significantly to Nepal's political gains. Nepal expressed appreciation for the Mission's contributions to consolidating peace, stressing that the Government was working hard towards the same end.

UNMIN termination

Communication. On 5 January [S/2011/1], the Secretary-General transmitted to the Security Council three letters from Nepal. One of those, from the office of the caretaker Government, dated 31 December 2010, provided information on how, from its point of view, issues relating to the monitoring of arms and armies and dispute-resolution mechanisms should be handled after the withdrawal of UNMIN on 15 January 2011. It also requested the transfer of essential documents and equipment used by UNMIN to either the Special Committee representing all the major political parties or a designated mechanism. The two letters, from the Chairman of the Unified Communist Party of Nepal (Maoist), Pushpa Kamal Dahal Prachanda, dated 30 December 2010 and 4 January 2011, respectively, requested the extension of UNMIN tenure or the setting up of a UN political office to follow up the peace process; and raised objections to all the key elements contained in the 31 December 2010 letter from the Nepal caretaker Government.

SECURITY COUNCIL ACTION

On 14 January [meeting 6466], following consultations among Security Council members, the President made statement **S/PRST/2011/1** on behalf of the Council:

As the United Nations Mission in Nepal completes its preparations for its departure on 15 January 2011, the Security Council expresses its appreciation and thanks to the Representative of the Secretary-General in Nepal, Ms. Karin Landgren, and the Mission team for their efforts in assisting the people of Nepal as they work to complete the peace process.

The Council reaffirms its support for the peace process and calls upon the caretaker Government of Nepal and all political parties to redouble their efforts, to continue to work together in the spirit of consensus to fulfil the commitments that they made in the Comprehensive Peace Agreement and other agreements, and to resolve expeditiously the outstanding issues of the peace process. The Council encourages Nepal to complete its new constitution within the foreseen time frame to help it to build a better, more equitable and democratic future for its people.

The Council welcomes the ongoing engagement of the Secretary-General and United Nations bodies as they continue to be supportive of the peace process and the people of Nepal.

The Council will continue to be supportive of the peace process in Nepal.

Yemen

Political and security developments

In 2011, the United Nations addressed the deteriorating security and humanitarian situation in Yemen amid the country's process of political transition in a context of civil unrest.

In a 24 June press statement [SC/10296], the Security Council expressed concern about the deteriorating security and humanitarian situation in Yemen and welcomed the ongoing mediation efforts of the Gulf Cooperation Council (GCC).

On 9 August, the Secretary-General's Special Adviser on Yemen, Jamal Benomar (Morocco), briefed the Council on his visit to the country in July. He said that he had facilitated the first direct face-to-face meeting among the Yemeni parties on resolving the crisis facing the country. The parties had agreed to work on the GCC initiative and effect a political transition aimed at restoring security.

In a 9 August press statement [SC/10357], the Council urged all sides to reject violence and show maximum restraint. It called on the Yemeni parties to move forward an inclusive, orderly and Yemeni-led process of political transition and welcomed the efforts of the Secretary-General, through his Special Adviser, and those of GCC. In a 24 September press statement [SC/10394], the Council expressed concern at the continued deterioration of the economic, humanitarian and security situation, including the threat from Al-Qaida.

On 11 October, the Council was briefed by the Special Adviser, who described developments in Yemen, including a consensus reached by the parties to endorse the Vice-President, Abd Rabbuh Mansur Hadi, who was steering the transition to succeed President Ali Abdullah Saleh. He acknowledged the continued relevance of the GCC initiative in the search for peace but pointed out that President Saleh's refusal to endorse the GCC initiative in line with the agreements reached in July remained an impediment to a political solution.

On 21 October, the Council adopted resolution 2014(2011) (see below), in which it condemned the continued human rights violations by the Yemeni authorities, such as the excessive use of force against peaceful protestors, as well as the use of force and human rights abuses by other actors; demanded all sides to reject the use of violence to achieve political goals; and called for all parties to sign and implement the GCC initiative for an inclusive, orderly and Yemeni-led process of political transition.

SECURITY COUNCIL ACTION

On 21 October [meeting 6634], the Security Council unanimously adopted **resolution 2014(2011)**. The draft [S/2011/651] was submitted by France, Germany, Portugal, the United Kingdom and the United States.

The Security Council,

Recalling its statements to the press of 24 June, 9 August and 24 September 2011,

Expressing grave concern at the situation in Yemen,

Reaffirming its strong commitment to the unity, sovereignty, independence and territorial integrity of Yemen,

Welcoming the statement of the Secretary-General of 23 September 2011 urging all sides to engage in a constructive manner to achieve a peaceful resolution to the current crisis,

Welcoming also the engagement of the Gulf Cooperation Council, and reaffirming the support of the Security Council for the efforts of the Gulf Cooperation Council to resolve the political crisis in Yemen,

Welcoming further the continuing efforts of the good offices of the Secretary-General, including the visits to Yemen by the Special Adviser to the Secretary-General on Yemen,

Taking note of the Human Rights Council resolution on Yemen, and underlining the need for a comprehensive, independent and impartial investigation consistent with international standards into alleged human rights abuses and violations, with a view to avoiding impunity and ensuring full accountability, and noting in this regard the concerns expressed by the United Nations High Commissioner for Human Rights,

Welcoming the statement of 23 September 2011 by the Ministerial Council of the Gulf Cooperation Council, in which it called for the immediate signing by President Saleh and implementation of the Gulf Cooperation Council initiative, condemned the use of force against unarmed demonstrators and called for restraint, a commitment to a full and immediate ceasefire and the formation of a commission to investigate the events that led to the killing of innocent Yemeni people,

Expressing serious concern at the worsening security situation, including armed conflict, the deteriorating economic and humanitarian situation due to the lack of progress on a political settlement, and the potential for the further escalation of violence,

Reaffirming its resolutions 1325(2000) of 31 October 2000, 1820(2008) of 19 June 2008, 1888(2009) of 30 September 2009, 1889(2009) of 5 October 2009 and 1960(2010) of 16 December 2010 on women and peace and security, and reiterating the need for the full, equal and effective participation of women at all stages of peace processes, given their vital role in the prevention and resolution of conflict and peacebuilding, reaffirming the key role that women play in re-establishing the fabric of society, and stressing the need for their involvement in conflict resolution in order to take into account their perspective and needs,

Expressing serious concern about the increasing number of internally displaced persons and refugees in Yemen, the alarming levels of malnutrition caused by drought and soaring fuel and food prices, the increasing interruption of basic supplies and social services and increasingly difficult access to safe water and health care,

Expressing serious concern also at the increased threat from Al-Qaida in the Arabian Peninsula and the risk of new terror attacks in parts of Yemen, and reaffirming that terrorism in all its forms and manifestations constitutes one of the most serious threats to international peace and security and that any acts of terrorism are criminal and unjustifiable regardless of their motivations,

Condemning all terrorist and other attacks against civilians and against the authorities, including those aimed at jeopardizing the political process in Yemen, such as the attack on the presidential compound in Sana'a on 3 June 2011,

Recalling the primary responsibility of the Government of Yemen to protect its population,

Stressing that the best solution to the current crisis in Yemen is through an inclusive and Yemeni-led political process of transition that meets the legitimate demands and aspirations of the Yemeni people for change,

Reaffirming its support for the presidential decree of 12 September 2011, which is designed to find a political agreement acceptable to all parties and to ensure a peaceful and democratic transition of power, including the holding of early presidential elections,

Stressing the importance of the stability and security of Yemen, particularly regarding overall international counter-terrorism efforts,

Mindful of its primary responsibility for the maintenance of international peace and security under the Charter of the United Nations, and emphasizing the threats to regional security and stability posed by the deterioration of the situation in Yemen in the absence of a lasting political settlement,

1. *Expresses profound regret* at the hundreds of deaths, mainly of civilians, including women and children;

2. *Strongly condemns* the continued human rights violations by the Yemeni authorities, such as the excessive use of force against peaceful protestors as well as the acts of violence, use of force and human rights abuses perpetrated by other actors, and stresses that all those responsible for violence, human rights violations and abuses should be held accountable;

3. *Demands* that all sides immediately reject the use of violence to achieve political goals;

4. *Reaffirms* its view that the signature and implementation as soon as possible of a settlement agreement on the basis of the Gulf Cooperation Council initiative is essential for an inclusive, orderly and Yemeni-led process of political transition, notes the signing of the Gulf Cooperation Council initiative by some opposition parties and the General People's Congress, calls upon all parties in Yemen to commit themselves to implementation of a political settlement based upon this initiative, notes the commitment by the President of Yemen to immediately sign the Gulf Cooperation Council initiative and encourages him, or those authorized to act on his behalf, to do so and to implement a political settlement based upon it, and calls for this commitment to be translated into action, in order to achieve a peaceful political transition of power, as stated in the Gulf Cooperation Council initiative and the presidential decree of 12 September 2011, without further delay;

5. *Demands* that the Yemeni authorities immediately ensure that their actions comply with obligations under applicable international humanitarian and human rights law, allow the people of Yemen to exercise their human rights and fundamental freedoms, including their rights of peaceful assembly, to demand redress for their grievances and to freedom of expression, including for members of the media, and take action to end attacks against civilians and civilian targets by security forces;

6. *Calls upon* all parties concerned to ensure the protection of women and children and to improve the participation of women in conflict resolution, and encourages all parties to facilitate the equal and full participation of women at decision-making levels;

7. *Urges* all opposition groups to commit to playing a full and constructive part in the agreement and implementation of a political settlement on the basis of the Gulf Cooperation Council initiative, and demands that all opposition groups refrain from violence and cease the use of force to achieve political aims;

8. *Demands* that all armed groups remove all weapons from areas of peaceful demonstration, refrain from violence and provocation and refrain from the recruitment of children, and urges all parties not to target vital infrastructure;

9. *Expresses* its concern over the presence of Al-Qaida in the Arabian Peninsula and its determination to address this threat in accordance with the Charter of the United Nations and international law, including applicable human rights, refugee and humanitarian law;

10. *Encourages* the international community to provide humanitarian assistance to Yemen, and in this regard requests all parties in Yemen to facilitate the work of the United Nations agencies and other relevant organizations and ensure full, safe and unhindered access for the timely delivery of humanitarian aid to persons in need across Yemen;

11. *Requests* the Secretary-General to continue his good offices, including through visits by his Special Adviser on Yemen, and to continue to urge all Yemeni stakeholders to implement the provisions of the present resolution and encourage all States and regional organizations to contribute to this objective;

12. *Also requests* the Secretary-General to report on the implementation of the present resolution within thirty days of its adoption and every sixty days thereafter;

13. *Decides* to remain actively seized of the matter.

Further developments

On 28 November, the Special Adviser informed the Security Council of developments leading up to the signing in Riyadh on 23 November of the GCC initiative by President Saleh, and of the implementation mechanism by the parties. Also on 28 November [SC/10460], the Council welcomed the 23 November agreement by the Yemeni parties, based on the GCC initiative, and urged the parties to reject violence, to refrain from any further provocations and to fully implement **resolution 2014(2011)**.

On 21 December, the Special Adviser briefed the Council on the outcome of his trip to Yemen from 8 to 17 December, during which he had met with the President and Vice-President and other political actors, as well as protestors in Sana'a and Taiz, southern movements in Aden and Huthi leaders in Saada. He underlined that progress had been achieved in fulfilling the GCC initiative, but the situation remained highly fragile.

In a 22 December press statement [SC/10504], the Council welcomed the progress made in implementing the political transition, on the basis of the GCC initiative, as well as the implementation mechanism, which was resulting in a peaceful transition of power.

(See also PART TWO, Chapter III).

Other issues

India–Pakistan

The United Nations Military Observer Group in India and Pakistan (UNMOGIP) continued in 2011 to monitor the situation in Jammu and Kashmir.

By a 14 July letter [S/2011/431], the Secretary-General proposed to the Security Council that Thailand be added to the list of contributors to UNMOGIP, as Italy had notified the Secretariat in March of its intention to reduce its contribution of military observers starting in the second half of 2011. The Council took note of his proposal on 18 July [S/2011/432].

Pakistan

By a 27 November letter [S/2011/740], Pakistan forwarded to the Secretary-General a statement by the Defence Committee of the Cabinet of Pakistan on the North Atlantic Treaty Organization/International Security Assistance Force (NATO/ISAF) aircraft attack on Pakistani border posts on 26 November, which killed 24 officers and soldiers of the Pakistan Army and injured 13 personnel. It condemned the attack, stating it constituted a breach of sovereignty, violated international law and had gravely dented the fundamental basis of Pakistan's cooperation with NATO/ISAF against militancy and terror.

Sri Lanka

Children and armed conflict

In response to Security Council resolutions 1612(2005) [YUN 2005, p. 863] and 1882(2009) [YUN 2009, p. 739], the Secretary-General, in December, submitted his fourth report on children and armed conflict in Sri Lanka [S/2011/793], covering the period from 1 February 2009 to 30 June 2011. The report provided information on progress made by the national authorities before and since the declaration by the Government that the conflict in Sri Lanka had ended in May 2009. In particular, it highlighted the progress achieved in separating children from Tamil Makkal Viduthalai Pulikal (TMVP) and Liberation Tigers of Tamil Eelam (LTTE) and reintegrating them into society. It detailed the Government's efforts, with UN support, to trace children who were separated from their parents in the final stages of the conflict and addressed the need to further such efforts.

The report also discussed a number of concerns, the primary of which were the need to establish accountability for the recruitment and use of children by remnants of TMVP and to locate missing children. The report contained a series of recommendations on strengthening the commendable efforts undertaken by the Government on behalf of children formerly associated with TMVP and LTTE. It also encouraged the Government to investigate violations and to continue to address outstanding protection issues with regard to children affected by the conflict.

Thailand–Cambodia

In a 5 February letter [S/2011/56] to the Security Council, Cambodia transmitted a letter from its Deputy Prime Minister and Minister for Foreign Affairs concerning aggression against Cambodia by Thailand and the explosive situation at the border between the two countries. In a response of the same date [S/2011/57], Thailand provided information on the recent incidents between the two countries. On 6 February [S/2011/58], Cambodia transmitted a letter from Prime Minister Hun Sen that detailed the worsening situation at the border with Thailand and requested an urgent meeting of the Council to address Thailand's aggression. On 7 February [S/2011/59], Thailand reaffirmed its position, providing information on further developments relating to the border incidents.

On 14 February, following armed clashes, the Council, in the presence of the Deputy Prime Minister and Minister for Foreign Affairs of Cambodia, Hor Namhong, and the Minister for Foreign Affairs of Thailand, Kasit Piromya, expressed its concern about the situation between Cambodia and Thailand and the dispute around the temple site of Preah Vihear. In a press statement [SC/10174], the Council called on both sides to display maximum restraint and to resolve the situation peacefully and through dialogue. It expressed support for the efforts of the Association of Southeast Asian Nations (ASEAN) in the matter.

On 22 April [S/2011/264], Cambodia forwarded to the Council a letter from its Deputy Prime Minister on armed attacks that day by Thailand against Cambodia in the area of Ta Mone and Ta Krabey

Temples located inside Cambodian territory. On the same date [S/2011/265], Thailand transmitted a statement by its Foreign Ministry regarding unprovoked armed attacks by Cambodian troops on Thai territory in the area of Ta Kwai Temple and along the Thai-Cambodian border near Tamuen Temples in Surin Province on 22 April.

On 17 May, after new incidents along the border, the Council discussed the situation, including the efforts by the Chair of asean to resolve the issue.

In a 24 May letter [S/2011/328], Cambodia described efforts within asean with regard to the deployment of an Indonesian observers team to the affected areas of the Cambodia-Thailand border. It accused Thailand of failing to give a positive reply to the asean initiative. Thailand, on 3 June [S/2011/338], responded that Cambodia's account of the asean efforts was incomplete and misleading.

In an 18 July letter [S/2011/446] to the Security Council, Cambodia forwarded the summary of the Order of 18 July of the International Court of Justice (icj) regarding Cambodia's request for the indication of provisional measures pending the Court's ruling on the request for interpretation of the Judgment of 15 June 1962 in the case concerning the Temple of Preah Vihear [YUN 1962, p. 467]. Icj found that both Parties should immediately withdraw their military personnel from the provisional demilitarized zone defined by it, and refrain from any military presence within that zone and from any armed activity directed at that zone (see p. 1238).

United Arab Emirates–Iran

The Greater Tunb, Lesser Tunb and Abu Musa

On 15 February [S/2011/82], the United Arab Emirates requested the Security Council to retain on its agenda for 2011 the item "Letter dated 3 December 1971 from the Permanent Representatives of Algeria, Iraq, the Libyan Arab Republic and the People's Democratic Republic of Yemen to the United Nations addressed to the President of the Security Council" [YUN 1971, p. 209] concerning Iran's occupation of the Greater Tunb, the Lesser Tunb and Abu Musa—three islands belonging to the United Arab Emirates—until such time as the dispute was resolved by peaceful means through direct negotiations or through icj.

The League of Arab States (las), in a 9 March letter [S/2011/122], transmitted resolution 7310, adopted by the las Council (Cairo, Egypt, 2 March) concerning the occupation by Iran of the three islands. It stressed the importance of the matter remaining on the Security Council's agenda until Iran terminated its occupation and the United Arab Emirates restored its complete sovereignty over the islands.

Chapter V

Europe and the Mediterranean

The restoration of peace and stability in the post-conflict countries in Europe and the Mediterranean region advanced in 2011, as efforts to re-establish their institutions and social and economic infrastructure continued. A number of issues remained unresolved.

The international community, led by the European Union (EU), continued to assist Bosnia and Herzegovina in moving along the path towards closer EU integration. Progress towards integration stagnated, however, as contentious political discourse slowed the country's institution-building efforts. By year's end, a return to political cooperation allowed for some advancement, such as the six-party agreement on Government formation, the passage of the annual State budget and improved relations among the main political parties.

The situation in northern Kosovo remained unstable, and tensions carried on into 2011 from the aftermath of the 2010 International Court of Justice advisory opinion on Kosovo's declaration of independence. A February presidential election ended controversially, resulting in a constitutional review and reformation of Kosovo's electoral system. In July, violence broke out and continued throughout the remainder of the year between Kosovo authorities and northern Kosovo Serbs.

Although the United Nations continued to support the negotiation process to find a solution to the dispute between Greece and the former Yugoslav Republic of Macedonia regarding the name of the latter country, the issue remained unresolved at year's end.

The Georgian-Abkhaz peace process continued to be affected by the August 2008 war in South Ossetia and its aftermath, as well as by Georgian-Russian relations. International discussions under the co-chairmanship of the EU, the Organization for Security and Cooperation in Europe and the United Nations to address security, stability and humanitarian issues in Georgia continued to be held throughout the year. On 29 June, the General Assembly adopted a resolution on the status of internally displaced persons (IDPs) and refugees from Abkhazia, Georgia, and the Tskhinvali region/South Ossetia, Georgia, in which it called on all participants in the international discussions to ensure respect for human rights and create favourable security conditions conducive to the voluntary, safe, dignified and unhindered return of all IDPs and refugees to their places of origin.

No progress was made towards the settlement of the conflict between Armenia and Azerbaijan over the occupied Nagorny Karabakh region of Azerbaijan.

The United Nations continued efforts through the Secretary-General's good offices to help resolve the Cyprus problem. United Nations-sponsored peace talks continued in 2011 and increased international focus on reaching a lasting solution in Cyprus. The United Nations Peacekeeping Force in Cyprus continued to cooperate with the two communities, to facilitate projects benefiting Greek and Turkish Cypriots in the buffer zone and to help restore normal conditions and humanitarian functions in the island.

Bosnia and Herzegovina

In 2011, the international community continued to assist the two entities comprising the Republic of Bosnia and Herzegovina—the Federation of Bosnia and Herzegovina (where mainly Bosnian Muslims (Bosniacs) and Bosnian Croats resided) and the Republika Srpska (where mostly Bosnian Serbs resided)—in implementing the 1995 General Framework Agreement for Peace in Bosnia and Herzegovina and the annexes thereto (the Peace Agreement) [YUN 1995, pp. 544 & 551]. Since the conclusion and withdrawal of the United Nations Mission in Bosnia and Herzegovina (UNMIBH) in December 2002 [YUN 2002, p. 359], those efforts had been led by the European Union (EU) and accomplished through the activities of the Office of the High Representative for the Implementation of the Peace Agreement on Bosnia and Herzegovina (OHR), responsible for the Agreement's civilian aspects [YUN 1996, p. 293]; the European Union Police Mission in Bosnia and Herzegovina (EUPM), responsible for helping to develop sustainable policing arrangements, which was launched in 2003 [YUN 2003, p. 409] to ensure follow-on to UNMIBH; and the European Union Force (EUFOR) mission, responsible for the Agreement's military aspects, which were transferred to it by the North Atlantic Treaty Organization (NATO) in 2004 [YUN 2004, p. 401]. The Peace Implementation Council (PIC) and its Steering Board continued to monitor and facilitate the Agreement's implementation.

The High Representative for Bosnia and Herzegovina reported on progress made in the implementation process and related political developments during the year in the context of his mission implementation plan, which set out a number of core tasks to be accomplished [YUN 2003, p. 401].

The year 2011 proved to be challenging for Bosnia and Herzegovina's implementation of the Peace Agreement. On 1 September, the High Representative formally turned over his duties as European Union Special Representative to Peter Sørensen (Denmark), thus welcoming a stronger EU presence in Bosnia and Herzegovina in guiding the reform process in relation to the country's accession to EU. The year ended with a return to political dialogue by the leaders of the main political parties; however, little progress was achieved in addressing key reforms required for further advancement towards EU and NATO integration. Nationalistic and divisive rhetoric disputing the sovereignty and constitutional order of Bosnia and Herzegovina that increased following the October 2010 general elections [YUN 2010, p. 411] had continued into 2011. As a result, there was no concrete progress in delivering the reforms required for the closure of OHR.

The Security Council, by resolution 2019(2011), extended the mandate of EUFOR for a further 12-month period (see p. 380).

Implementation of Peace Agreement

Civilian aspects

The civilian aspects of the 1995 Peace Agreement [YUN 1995, pp. 544 & 551] entailed a broad range of activities, including the provision of humanitarian aid and resources for infrastructure rehabilitation, the establishment of political and constitutional institutions, the promotion of respect for human rights and the holding of free and fair elections. The High Representative for the Implementation of the Peace Agreement, who chaired the PIC Steering Board and other key implementation bodies, was the final authority with regard to implementing the civilian aspects of the Peace Agreement [YUN 1996, p. 293].

Office of High Representative

The High Representative for Bosnia and Herzegovina, Valentin Inzko (Austria), reported to the Security Council, through the Secretary-General, on the peace implementation process for the periods 16 October 2010 to 20 April 2011 [S/2011/283], 21 April to 15 October [S/2011/682] and 16 October 2011 to 20 April 2012 [S/2012/307] (see pp. 378–379). The Council considered the reports on 9 May [S/PV.6529] and 15 November [S/PV.6659].

OHR–EUSR transition. On 1 September, the High Representative turned over his duties as European Union Special Representative (EUSR) to Peter Sørensen (Denmark), who had been appointed in July by the EU as the new head of the EU delegation and the new EUSR in Bosnia and Herzegovina. That allowed the High Representative to focus his efforts solely on the implementation of the civilian aspects of the Peace Agreement by carrying out duties mandated in annex 10 of the Peace Agreement [YUN 1996, p. 293]. OHR and EUSR worked together to support Bosnia and Herzegovina's European integration process. Following the departure of 26 staff members to the Office of the EUSR in August, OHR continued to cut overhead costs.

Political situation and other developments

The High Representative, briefing the Security Council on 9 May [S/PV.6529], presented his thirty-ninth report [S/2011/283], which described the most serious and direct challenges to the Peace Agreement since it was signed 15 years earlier. On 13 April, the Republika Srpska National Assembly (RSNA) adopted a set of conclusions rejecting the authority and the competences of State-level judicial institutions as well as challenging the role of the High Representative and his powers and in particular the laws enacted by the High Representative. The conclusions undermined the entire constitutional system of division of responsibilities between the State and the entities as established by annex 4 of the Peace Agreement, as well as the Constitution of Bosnia and Herzegovina. The Republika Srpska authorities also adopted a decision on a referendum on the Bosnia and Herzegovina judicial institutions, the legislation creating them, and the powers of the High Representative. The holding of a referendum on the High Representative's powers and Bosnia and Herzegovina legislation were in breach of the Bosnia and Herzegovina Constitutional Framework and the country's international obligations.

Briefing the Security Council on 15 November [S/PV.6659], the High Representative presented his fortieth report [S/2011/682]. The report stated that Bosnia and Herzegovina continued to struggle with political stagnation in reforms. The political environment was marked by immobility, due in large part to the inability of the six largest political parties to form a State-level Government. Opposition from the entities—in particular the Republika Srpska—continued to prevent the adoption of an adequate State-level budget for 2011. Consequently, State institutions had operated under restricted temporary financing since the beginning of the year, which had limited their capacity as well as their ability to meet their obligations.

Under strong international pressure, RSNA voted on 1 June to repeal its decision of 13 April to hold a referendum. Despite the withdrawal of the planned referendum and the promise to review the conclusions, those conclusions remained in force and appeared to be shaping the policies of the Republika Srpska authorities. For example, in June the National Assembly appointed a judge from Republika Srpska to the Bosnia and Herzegovina Constitutional Court without prior consultation with that body, as the rules of the Court required. That move seemed to reflect the Republika Srpska policy—as contained in the conclusions of 13 April—to dispute the rules of the Constitutional Court. RSNA continued its legal and political actions and sharp rhetoric that had challenged the country's State-level institutions, competencies and laws, as well as the authority of OHR under the Peace Agreement, and relevant resolutions of the Security Council. Owing to the continuing stalemate over Government formation following the elections of 3 October 2010, the old Council of Ministers continued in a caretaker capacity.

Some Federation politicians had also used unwelcome rhetoric; party leaders continued to press for a third entity with a Croat majority and revived the Croat National Council. The two leading Croat parties continued to question the legality and legitimacy of the incumbent Federation Government, demanding that it be reshuffled to include them, as the "sole legitimate representatives of the Croat people". Some Bosniak political leaders escalated their rhetoric in response to statements by the Republika Srpska leadership and warned of possible conflict were there to be an attempt to divide the country. Nevertheless, in September, the leaders of the six parties began to engage in serious negotiations on Government formation and the adoption of reforms towards EU and NATO membership.

At meetings at the level of political directors in March, July and December, the PIC Steering Board expressed its concern over the political situation in the country, the failure to appoint a State government and the failure to address the remaining objectives and conditions for the closure of OHR.

Backsliding occurred on some of the outstanding items among the five objectives and two conditions necessary for the closure of OHR during the year. To prevent Republika Srpska from disposing of State property prior to the resolution of planned legal challenges before the Bosnia and Herzegovina Constitutional Court, on 5 January the High Representative issued an Order suspending the application of the Republika Srpska State Property Law until a final decision of the Constitutional Court on that Law entered into force, during which any change of ownership rights over State property in the territory of Republika Srpska was prohibited. On 6 January, the Republika Srpska State Property Law was challenged at the Constitutional Court.

Concerning the Brcko District, neither the Brcko District Supervisor nor the High Representative was able to conclude that all obligations under the Brcko Final Award had been fulfilled [YUN 1997, p. 307]. Republika Srpska authorities sent ambiguous signals regarding various commitments under the Brcko Final Award, including the question of the territorial boundaries of the Brcko District. OHR continued to seek a dialogue with Republika Srpska officials to resolve outstanding issues related to the territorial and other obligations stemming from the Final Award and other legal acts. The Republika Srpska authorities declined to provide assurances that they would fully honour annex 2 and all aspects of the Brcko Final Award. The Federation provided such assurances early in 2011. Some other entity obligations to the Brcko District had also not been fully met, including resolution of the issue of entity citizenship and voting rights for residents of the District. Given the District's strategic position, any future disagreement over implementation of the Final Award would potentially have negative consequences for the stability of the Brcko District and Bosnia and Herzegovina. OHR continued to take steps to ensure that both entities fully complied with their commitments under the Final Award.

With regard to cooperation of Bosnia and Herzegovina with the International Tribunal for the Former Yugoslavia, the report stated that, with the arrest on 26 May of Ratko Mladic—the last remaining fugitive accused of crimes related to the Bosnian war and who had been a fugitive since his indictment on 25 July 1995 [YUN 1995, p. 1314]—the High Representative lifted all remaining bans on officials related to non-cooperation with the Tribunal on 10 June. During the year, the cooperation of Bosnia and Herzegovina with the Tribunal remained satisfactory, although local institutions showed a less-than-dedicated approach to ensuring that individuals responsible for war crimes served their sentences, as shown in past cases of prisoner escape from the territory of Bosnia and Herzegovina.

In a later report [S/2012/307], the High Representative stated that despite the setbacks, the country ended 2011 with politicians engaging in political dialogue and reaching agreements necessary for progress to be made. On 28 December, after nearly 15 months of stalemate following the October 2010 elections, the leaders of the six main political parties reached a broad agreement that included forming the Council of Ministers. The 28 December agreement included a commitment to adopt a budget for 2011 and two key EU-related pieces of legislation—the State Aid Law and the Census Law.

Other topics covered in the High Representative's report included Mostar, defence and intelligence reform.

Judicial reform

The implementation of the National Justice Sector Reform Strategy for 2008–2012 [YUN 2008, p. 430] suffered from a lack of political will. The enforcement of the action plan for the implementation of the Strategy was monitored by civil society, which frequently reported on a lack of dedication at the political level.

Implementation of the War Crimes Prosecution Strategy remained slow; however, a database had been established, and categorization and determination at which level—State or entity—war crimes cases should be investigated and/or tried was under way. In November the Prosecutor's Office fulfilled one of the basic obligations of the Strategy, pending since 2009, by delivering data on all war crimes cases that the Prosecutor's Office had taken since 1 March 2003 to the Court, which would decide on the transfer of less complex cases to entity courts pursuant to territorial jurisdiction.

Economic reform

In line with the 28 December agreement (see p. 379), the Council of Ministers, on 31 December, adopted a budget for 2011, as well as a decision on temporary financing for 2012. As a result, the country could resume servicing its international financial obligations and financing State institutions. Nevertheless, the 2011 budget was not adopted in line with annex 4 to the Peace Agreement (the Constitution of Bosnia and Herzegovina) [YUN 1995, p. 544], which required that the Council of Ministers recommend a budget to the Presidency, which then proposed it to the Parliamentary Assembly, where it could be adopted. That left both the 2011 State budget and the temporary financing for 2012 open to challenges before the Constitutional Court.

Public administration reform

Limited progress was made in public administration reform. Numerous senior civil service appointments remained long overdue at the State level. The Office of the Public Administration Reform Coordinator reported to the Council of Ministers that the Public Administration Reform Strategy and its action plans had been revised and the implementation rate was approximately 50 per cent. Despite the 2010 rulings [YUN 2010, p. 412] of the Constitutional Court that certain articles of the Federation Law on Ministries and the entity's Law on Civil Service were not in compliance with the Federation Constitution, the Law on Civil Service had yet to be harmonized with the Constitutional Court Decision.

Media development

Political influence over public media—especially television—in both entities continued to be problematic. In addition, there was no progress in implementing the public broadcasting legislation adopted in 2005 [YUN 2005, p. 462]. During the year, officials from Republika Srpska called for the abolishment of the Bosnia and Herzegovina public broadcaster, while party leaders from the Federation called for a parliamentary review of the Public Broadcasting Service and for amendments to the Law on Communications that would make the Parliamentary Assembly directly responsible for appointing the media regulator. The three public broadcasters constituting the country's media system continued to disagree on the system's organization, thereby delaying the establishment of the Public Broadcasting Corporation, crucial for developments such as the transition to digital broadcasting. In addition, the Parliamentary Assembly had not appointed new governors for the Public Broadcasting System. The Communications Regulatory Agency was functioning with an acting Director-General and a Council whose mandate had expired, affecting the Agency's credibility and its operations.

From January to September, attacks against the media increased 30 per cent compared to the same period in 2010. The Free Media Helpline, a service operating within the Bosnia and Herzegovina Union of Journalists, registered 42 cases of threats and pressures, physical attacks, denial of information, mobbing, and one case of a death threat.

Return of refugees and displaced persons

A United Nations High Commissioner for Refugees envoy, appointed early in 2011 to work on the protracted displacement situation in the Western Balkans, visited Bosnia and Herzegovina numerous times in 2011 to support the Governments in devising a regional programme for durable solutions for the most vulnerable. Bosnia and Herzegovina played an important role in that process, with the Ministry for Human Rights and Refugees serving as the regional coordinator. In November, the Ministers for Foreign Affairs of Bosnia and Herzegovina, Croatia, Montenegro and Serbia signed a joint declaration committing their Governments to cooperate to end the displacement of refugees, returnees and internally displaced persons, and enable them to live as equal citizens.

SECURITY COUNCIL ACTION

On 16 November [meeting 6661], the Security Council unanimously adopted **resolution 2019(2011)**. The draft [S/2011/713] was submitted by France, Germany, Italy, Nigeria, Portugal, the Russian Federation, Spain, the United Kingdom and the United States.

The Security Council,
Recalling all its previous relevant resolutions concerning the conflicts in the former Yugoslavia and the relevant statements by its President, including resolutions 1031(1995) of 15 December 1995, 1088(1996) of 12 December 1996,

1423(2002) of 12 July 2002, 1491(2003) of 11 July 2003, 1551(2004) of 9 July 2004, 1575(2004) of 22 November 2004, 1639(2005) of 21 November 2005, 1722(2006) of 21 November 2006, 1764(2007) of 29 June 2007, 1785(2007) of 21 November 2007, 1845(2008) of 20 November 2008, 1869(2009) of 25 March 2009, 1895(2009) of 18 November 2009 and 1948(2010) of 18 November 2010,

Reaffirming its commitment to the political settlement of the conflicts in the former Yugoslavia, preserving the sovereignty and territorial integrity of all States there within their internationally recognized borders,

Emphasizing its full support for the continued role in Bosnia and Herzegovina of the High Representative for Bosnia and Herzegovina,

Underlining its commitment to support the implementation of the General Framework Agreement for Peace in Bosnia and Herzegovina and the annexes thereto (collectively the "Peace Agreement"), as well as the relevant decisions of the Peace Implementation Council,

Recalling all the agreements concerning the status of forces referred to in appendix B to annex 1-A of the Peace Agreement, and reminding the parties of their obligation to continue to comply therewith,

Recalling also the provisions of its resolution 1551(2004) concerning the provisional application of the status-of-forces agreements contained in appendix B to annex 1-A of the Peace Agreement,

Emphasizing its appreciation to the High Representative, the Commander and personnel of the multinational stabilization force (the European Union Force-Althea), the Senior Military Representative and personnel of the North Atlantic Treaty Organization Headquarters Sarajevo, the Organization for Security and Cooperation in Europe, the European Union and the personnel of other international organizations and agencies in Bosnia and Herzegovina for their contributions to the implementation of the Peace Agreement,

Welcoming the adoption by the authorities of Bosnia and Herzegovina of a revised strategy for the implementation of annex 7 of the Peace Agreement, focused on the strategy for the return of refugees, and emphasizing that a comprehensive and coordinated return of refugees and displaced persons throughout the region continues to be crucial to lasting peace,

Recalling the declarations of the ministerial meetings of the Peace Implementation Council,

Recognizing that full implementation of the Peace Agreement is not yet complete, while paying tribute to the achievements of the authorities at State and entity level in Bosnia and Herzegovina and of the international community in the sixteen years since the signing of the Peace Agreement,

Noting that the overall security situation in Bosnia and Herzegovina has been calm and stable for several years,

Emphasizing the importance of Bosnia and Herzegovina's progress towards Euro-Atlantic integration on the basis of the Peace Agreement, while recognizing the importance of Bosnia and Herzegovina's transition to a functional, reform-oriented, modern and democratic European country,

Taking note of the reports of the High Representative, including his latest report, of 2 November 2011,

Determined to promote the peaceful resolution of the conflicts in accordance with the purposes and principles of the Charter of the United Nations,

Recalling the relevant principles contained in the Convention on the Safety of United Nations and Associated Personnel of 9 December 1994 and the statement by its President of 9 February 2000,

Welcoming and encouraging efforts by the United Nations to sensitize peacekeeping personnel in the prevention and control of HIV/AIDS and other communicable diseases in all its peacekeeping operations,

Welcoming the decision taken by the Ministers for Foreign Affairs of the European Union on 25 January 2010 to start providing non-executive capacity-building and training support, within the framework of the European Union Force-Althea,

Welcoming also the conclusions of the Ministers for Foreign Affairs of the European Union on 10 October 2011, which confirmed the commitment of the European Union at this stage to a continuing executive mandate for a reconfigured European Union Force-Althea to support Bosnia and Herzegovina's efforts to maintain the safe and secure environment and the authorities' deterrence capacity, under a renewed United Nations mandate, while focusing its main efforts on the provision of non-executive capacity-building and training support in order to contribute to strengthening local ownership and capacity,

Recalling the letters between the European Union and the North Atlantic Treaty Organization sent to the Security Council on 19 November 2004 on how those organizations will cooperate together in Bosnia and Herzegovina, in which both organizations recognize that the European Union Force-Althea will have the main peace stabilization role under the military aspects of the Peace Agreement,

Recalling also the confirmation by the Presidency of Bosnia and Herzegovina, on behalf of Bosnia and Herzegovina, including its constituent entities, of the arrangements for the European Union Force-Althea and the North Atlantic Treaty Organization Headquarters presence,

Welcoming the increased engagement and reinforced role of the European Union in Bosnia and Herzegovina and the continued engagement of the North Atlantic Treaty Organization,

Reiterating once again its calls upon the authorities in Bosnia and Herzegovina to implement in full their undertakings, as also confirmed in the declaration by the Steering Board of the Peace Implementation Council of 7 July 2011, and recognizing, in particular, the need to find a solution on State and defence property,

Calling upon the political leaders, following the elections of 3 October 2010, to fulfil their democratic responsibility and form a new Council of Ministers of Bosnia and Herzegovina which will address with urgency important policies and priorities,

Calling upon all Bosnia and Herzegovina's political leaders to refrain from divisive rhetoric and to make further concrete and tangible progress towards European Union integration,

Determining that the situation in the region continues to constitute a threat to international peace and security,

Acting under Chapter VII of the Charter,

1. *Reaffirms once again its support* for the General Framework Agreement for Peace in Bosnia and Herzegovina and the annexes thereto (collectively the "Peace Agreement"), as well as for the Dayton Agreement on Implementing the Federation of Bosnia and Herzegovina

of 10 November 1995, and calls upon the parties to comply strictly with their obligations under the Agreements;

2. *Reiterates* that the primary responsibility for the further successful implementation of the Peace Agreement lies with the authorities in Bosnia and Herzegovina themselves and that the continued willingness of the international community and major donors to assume the political, military and economic burden of implementation and reconstruction efforts will be determined by the compliance and active participation by all the authorities in Bosnia and Herzegovina in implementing the Peace Agreement and rebuilding a civil society, in particular in full cooperation with the International Tribunal for the Prosecution of Persons Responsible for Serious Violations of International Humanitarian Law Committed in the Territory of the Former Yugoslavia since 1991, in strengthening joint institutions, which foster the building of a fully functioning self-sustaining State able to integrate itself into the European structures, and in facilitating returns of refugees and displaced persons;

3. *Reminds* the parties once again that, in accordance with the Peace Agreement, they have committed themselves to cooperate fully with all entities involved in the implementation of this peace settlement, as described in the Peace Agreement, or which are otherwise authorized by the Security Council, including the International Tribunal for the Former Yugoslavia, as it carries out its responsibilities for dispensing justice impartially, and underlines that full cooperation by States and entities with the Tribunal includes, inter alia, the surrender for trial or apprehension of all persons indicted by the Tribunal and the provision of information to assist in Tribunal investigations;

4. *Emphasizes its full support* for the role of the High Representative for Bosnia and Herzegovina in monitoring the implementation of the Peace Agreement and giving guidance to and coordinating the activities of the civilian organizations and agencies involved in assisting the parties to implement the Peace Agreement, and reaffirms that, under annex 10 of the Peace Agreement, the High Representative is the final authority in theatre regarding the interpretation of civilian implementation of the Peace Agreement and that, in case of dispute, he may give his interpretation and make recommendations, and make binding decisions as he judges necessary on issues as elaborated by the Peace Implementation Council in Bonn, Germany, on 9 and 10 December 1997;

5. *Expresses its support* for the declarations of the ministerial meetings of the Peace Implementation Council;

6. *Reaffirms* its intention to keep implementation of the Peace Agreement and the situation in Bosnia and Herzegovina under close review, taking into account the reports submitted pursuant to paragraphs 18 and 21 below, and any recommendations those reports might include, and its readiness to consider the imposition of measures if any party fails significantly to meet its obligations under the Peace Agreement;

7. *Recalls* the support of the authorities of Bosnia and Herzegovina for the European Union Force-Althea and the continued North Atlantic Treaty Organization presence and their confirmation that both are the legal successors to the Stabilization Force for the fulfilment of their missions for the purposes of the Peace Agreement, its annexes and appendices and relevant Security Council resolutions and can take such actions as are required, including the use of force, to ensure compliance with annexes 1-A and 2 of the Peace Agreement and relevant Council resolutions;

8. *Pays tribute* to those Member States which participated in the multinational stabilization force (the European Union Force-Althea), and in the continued North Atlantic Treaty Organization presence, established in accordance with its resolution 1575(2004) and extended by its resolutions 1639(2005), 1722(2006), 1785(2007), 1845(2008), 1895(2009) and 1948(2010), and welcomes their willingness to assist the parties to the Peace Agreement by continuing to deploy a multinational stabilization force (the European Union Force-Althea) and by maintaining a continued North Atlantic Treaty Organization presence;

9. *Welcomes* the intention of the European Union to maintain a European Union military operation (the European Union Force-Althea) in Bosnia and Herzegovina from November 2011;

10. *Authorizes* the Member States acting through or in cooperation with the European Union to establish for a further period of twelve months, starting from the date of the adoption of the present resolution, a multinational stabilization force (the European Union Force-Althea) as a legal successor to the Stabilization Force under unified command and control, which will fulfil its missions in relation to the implementation of annexes 1-A and 2 of the Peace Agreement in cooperation with the North Atlantic Treaty Organization Headquarters presence in accordance with the arrangements agreed between the North Atlantic Treaty Organization and the European Union as communicated to the Security Council in their letters of 19 November 2004, which recognize that the European Union Force-Althea will have the main peace stabilization role under the military aspects of the Peace Agreement;

11. *Welcomes* the decision of the North Atlantic Treaty Organization to continue to maintain a presence in Bosnia and Herzegovina in the form of a North Atlantic Treaty Organization Headquarters in order to continue to assist in implementing the Peace Agreement in conjunction with the European Union Force-Althea, and authorizes the Member States acting through or in cooperation with the North Atlantic Treaty Organization to continue to maintain a North Atlantic Treaty Organization Headquarters as a legal successor to the Stabilization Force under unified command and control, which will fulfil its missions in relation to the implementation of annexes 1-A and 2 of the Peace Agreement in cooperation with the European Union Force-Althea in accordance with the arrangements agreed between the North Atlantic Treaty Organization and the European Union as communicated to the Security Council in their letters of 19 November 2004, which recognize that the European Union Force-Althea will have the main peace stabilization role under the military aspects of the Peace Agreement;

12. *Reaffirms* that the Peace Agreement and the provisions of its previous relevant resolutions shall apply to and in respect of both the European Union Force-Althea and the North Atlantic Treaty Organization presence as they have applied to and in respect of the Stabilization Force and that, therefore, references in the Peace Agreement, in particular in annex 1-A and the appendices thereto, and in relevant resolutions to the Implementation Force and/or the Stabilization Force, the North Atlantic Treaty Organization and the North Atlantic Council shall be read

as applying, as appropriate, to the North Atlantic Treaty Organization presence, the European Union Force-Althea, the European Union and the Political and Security Committee and Council of the European Union respectively;

13. *Expresses its intention* to consider the terms of further authorization as necessary in the light of developments in the implementation of the Peace Agreement and the situation in Bosnia and Herzegovina;

14. *Authorizes* the Member States acting under paragraphs 10 and 11 above to take all measures necessary to effect the implementation of and to ensure compliance with annexes 1-A and 2 of the Peace Agreement, and stresses that the parties shall continue to be held equally responsible for the compliance with those annexes and shall be equally subject to such enforcement action by the European Union Force-Althea and the North Atlantic Treaty Organization presence as may be necessary to ensure the implementation of those annexes and the protection of the European Union Force-Althea and the North Atlantic Treaty Organization presence;

15. *Authorizes* Member States to take all necessary measures, at the request of either the European Union Force-Althea or the North Atlantic Treaty Organization Headquarters, in defence of the European Union Force-Althea or the North Atlantic Treaty Organization presence respectively, and to assist both organizations in carrying out their missions, and recognizes the right of both the European Union Force-Althea and the North Atlantic Treaty Organization presence to take all measures necessary to defend themselves from attack or threat of attack;

16. *Authorizes* the Member States acting under paragraphs 10 and 11 above, in accordance with annex 1-A of the Peace Agreement, to take all measures necessary to ensure compliance with the rules and procedures governing command and control of airspace over Bosnia and Herzegovina with respect to all civilian and military air traffic;

17. *Demands* that the parties respect the security and freedom of movement of the European Union Force-Althea, the North Atlantic Treaty Organization presence and other international personnel;

18. *Requests* the Member States acting through or in cooperation with the European Union and the Member States acting through or in cooperation with the North Atlantic Treaty Organization to report to the Security Council on the activity of the European Union Force-Althea and the North Atlantic Treaty Organization Headquarters presence respectively, through the appropriate channels and at least at three-monthly intervals;

19. *Invites* all States, in particular those in the region, to continue to provide appropriate support and facilities, including transit facilities, for the Member States acting under paragraphs 10 and 11 above;

20. *Reiterates its appreciation* for the deployment by the European Union of its Police Mission to Bosnia and Herzegovina since 1 January 2003;

21. *Requests* the Secretary-General to continue to submit to the Security Council reports of the High Representative, in accordance with annex 10 of the Peace Agreement and the conclusions of the Peace Implementation Conference held in London on 4 and 5 December 1996, and later Peace Implementation Conferences, on the implementation of the Peace Agreement and, in particular, on compliance by the parties with their commitments under the Agreement;

22. *Decides* to remain seized of the matter.

Military and police aspects

EUFOR

The European Union Force (EUFOR) mission in Bosnia and Herzegovina executed the military aspects of the Peace Agreement as specified in annexes 1-A and 2, which were transferred to it by NATO in 2004 [YUN 2004, p. 401]. Its 2011 activities were described in four reports, covering the periods from 1 September 2010 to 28 February 2011 [S/2012/138], 1 March to 31 May 2011 [S/2011/717], 1 June to 31 August [S/2012/138], and 1 September to 30 November 2011 [S/2012/138], submitted by the EU High Representative for Foreign Affairs and Security Policy in accordance with various Security Council resolutions.

As at November 2011, the force of some 1,200 EUFOR troops was concentrated in Sarajevo, with liaison and observation teams deployed throughout Bosnia and Herzegovina. EUFOR continued to implement its key military tasks of supporting the country's efforts to maintain a safe and secure environment and providing capacity-building and training support to the armed forces of Bosnia and Herzegovina. It also continued to support and advise the EU Special Representative, the European Union Police Mission and other international community actors in Bosnia and Herzegovina, on various issues including counter-terrorism and the fight against organized crime. EUFOR continued monitoring activities related to ammunition and weapons storage sites, the civilian and military movement of weapons and military equipment, the disposal of surplus weapons and ammunition, and defence industry factories.

EUPM

The European Union Police Mission (EUPM), which was established as part of a broader rule-of-law approach and welcomed by the Security Council in presidential statement S/PRST/2002/33 [YUN 2002, p. 363], became operational on 1 January 2003. In 2011, EUPM continued to support the development of the county's law enforcement agencies in the fight against organized crime and corruption, promoting cooperation between police and prosecutors and between police and the prison structure, and enhancing accountability within police bodies. It also continued to work on the harmonization of the legal framework for police officers and police bodies and to support further implementation of the police reform laws of April 2008 [YUN 2008, p. 434] through its mentoring of the Directorate for Police Coordination. All bodies and agencies foreseen by the 2008 police reform laws had been established and possessed the necessary conditions to begin to function.

In December, the EU Council extended the Mission's mandate until 30 June 2012 to prepare for the transition from the Mission to EU pre-accession assistance and a strengthened EU Special Representative in Bosnia and Herzegovina.

Kosovo

In 2011, the United Nations Interim Administration Mission in Kosovo (UNMIK) continued to fulfil its mandate based on Security Council resolution 1244(1999) [YUN 1999, p. 353] and the reconfigured functions outlined in the Secretary-General's June and November 2008 reports [YUN 2008, pp. 438 & 441], following Kosovo's declaration of independence in February 2008 [ibid., p. 437], the entry into force of the Kosovo Constitution on 15 June [ibid., p. 439] and the deployment of the European Union Rule of Law Mission in Kosovo (EULEX) throughout Kosovo in December of that year [ibid., p. 442]. Serbia condemned Kosovo's declaration of independence and maintained that action by Kosovo's Provisional Institutions violated resolution 1244(1999), which reaffirmed Serbia's sovereignty and territorial integrity, including Kosovo and Metohija. The position of the United Nations on the status of Kosovo was of status neutrality.

Political and security developments

Reports of Secretary-General. The Secretary-General reported on the implementation of the mandate of UNMIK covering the periods from 19 October 2010 to 15 January 2011 [S/2011/43], 16 January to 15 April [S/2011/281], 16 April to 15 July [S/2011/514], 16 July to 15 October [S/2011/675] and 16 October 2011 to 15 January 2012 [S/2012/72].

In 2011, UNMIK continued to engage with all communities, as well as with Belgrade and Pristina and international actors, in furthering peace and stability in Kosovo and the region. The Special Representative of the Secretary-General continued to cultivate good faith relations with all sides to encourage dialogue and bridge differences. He maintained close cooperation with EULEX, which had been established within the status-neutral framework of the United Nations. UNMIK efforts were complemented by the humanitarian and development activities of the UN agencies, funds and programmes.

The 12 December 2010 Assembly elections ended controversially [YUN 2010, p. 417], with recounts and revotes being held in municipalities across Kosovo in January 2011. On 10 January, the Central Elections Commission (CEC) announced the preliminary results Kosovo-wide; however, on 12 January the European Network of Election Monitoring Organizations announced that a high number of irregularities during the Kosovo Assembly elections affected the trust in the democratic process. On 7 February, CEC declared the official final results of the Assembly elections, which sparked political turmoil due to the formation of a coalition government between rival parties. On 21 February, the Assembly convened a constitutive session in which deputies elected the new Assembly Presidency and Speaker of the Assembly. The following day, the Assembly elected Behgjet Pacolli as the President of Kosovo. On 1 March, a political crisis emerged after opposition members of the Assembly challenged the legality of the presidential election process. On 30 March, a court ruling found that the election procedure had violated the Constitution due to the absence of a second candidate and because the necessary quorum had not been met. On 6 April, following intensive talks and diplomatic mediation, a consensus was reached among the coalition parties to amend presidential election procedures and the electoral system. Atifete Jahjaga was chosen to serve as interim President until autumn 2012.

Having overcome the electoral crisis, the authorities focused their attention on ensuring institutional stability. Early in May, the ad hoc Assembly Committee on the reform of electoral law, composed of representatives from all Assembly caucuses, commenced its work. The Assembly Committee prepared a proposal introducing multiple electoral districts and a majority system for the legislative elections. Debate on the reform began, and once the Committee reached agreement on the changes, a two-thirds majority of the Assembly would be required for adoption.

Engagement and dialogue between Kosovo and Serbia continued in 2011. Serbian Government officials, including the Principal Deputy Prime Minister and Minister of the Interior, Ivica Dačić, suggested that "territorial adjustments" might be brought to the table in order to reach a final settlement for Kosovo. The suggestion resulted in sharp retorts from Pristina and Washington. Kosovo authorities argued that the only way to resolve ethnic problems in Kosovo, and in the Western Balkans, was through full implementation of the Ahtisaari plan [YUN 2007, pp. 398 & 399] and European integration. Kosovo Serb political groups also opposed the idea of territorial adjustments, regardless of whether they lived north or south of the Ibër/Ibar River and regardless of their orientation towards Belgrade or Pristina. Those living south of the River feared that territorial adjustments would leave them unprotected, while the northern Kosovo Serbs argued that they were against the Serbian national interest and prohibited by the Serbian Constitution, as they implied recognition of Kosovo's independence. In contrast, the head of the Kosovo Albanian opposition group Vetëvendosje, Albin Kurti, pledged to work towards the union of Kosovo with Albania.

On 12 May, the head of the Belgrade delegation in the dialogue with Pristina, Borislav Stefanović, travelled to Pristina and met with the Deputy Prime Minister and Justice Minister, Hajredin Kuçi; the head of the Pristina delegation in the dialogue, Deputy Prime Minister Edita Tahiri; the United States Ambassador; and the interim EU Special Representative. The visit sparked protests by some 200 supporters of Vetëvendosje, which turned violent and resulted in injuries to several people, including police officers, and damage to some vehicles. The Kosovo authorities condemned the protest.

The process of dialogue, welcomed by the General Assembly in resolution 64/298 [YUN 2010, p. 1287] and facilitated by the EU, continued. The fourth and fifth rounds of meetings were held in Brussels on 17 and 18 May and on 2 July. The Political Director of the Serbian Ministry of Foreign Affairs and the Deputy Prime Minister of Kosovo continued to lead their respective delegations in the talks. The fourth round of discussions focused on civil registry, cadastral records, freedom of movement, telecommunications and energy issues. The fifth meeting brought concrete results. On civil registry, the parties agreed that a joint committee chaired by EULEX would continue identifying gaps in missing civil registry books, allowing greater legal certainty for people living in Kosovo as well as facilitating the resolution of related issues in court. The agreement on freedom of movement would enable people to cross the administrative boundary line using their identity cards or driving licences. The parties also agreed, in principle, on the acceptance of university and school diplomas, which was expected to be implemented through the certification by a mutually agreed international body or a third-party academic institution.

During the year, the security situation remained relatively calm. In July, however, following the cancellation of the 20 July EU-facilitated dialogue session, Kosovo authorities imposed an embargo on imports from Serbia as a reciprocal measure in response to the treatment by Serbia of goods originating in Kosovo. On 25 July, Kosovo authorities attempted to deploy Kosovo Police Regional Operations Special Units (ROSU) to the two authorized boundary/border crossings in northern Kosovo, Gate 1 (Jarinjë/Jarinje) and Gate 31 (Bërnjak/Brnjak). Those actions were not coordinated with the international presences or the communities on the ground. In reaction to the actions of Pristina, local Kosovo Serbs, who continued to reject the authority of the Kosovo institutions, erected roadblocks along the routes leading to the two gates, effectively blocking ROSU movements. The Kosovo Force (KFOR) intervened to facilitate the withdrawal of the Units from northern Kosovo, but a gunfight erupted during the ROSU movement, resulting in the death of a ROSU officer near Zubin Potok on 26 July. A EULEX investigation into the killing led to the issuance of arrest warrants for six individuals.

On 27 July, while Serb demonstrators gathered at the crossing point, some individuals set fire to the Customs facilities at Gate 1. Members of the Serb community also established roadblocks on all major roads in northern Kosovo, insisting that they would maintain them until Gates 1 and 31 were returned to the status quo before 25 July, when EULEX was in charge of the gates. In response to the violence, KFOR temporarily closed the two gates and declared them "military restricted areas". On 5 August, the KFOR Commander mediated an 11-point "common understanding" between Belgrade and Pristina, which opened the way for the lessening of tensions, despite different interpretations by the two sides. The understanding, which involved KFOR remaining in control of the gates until the resumption of the EU-facilitated dialogue and with a deadline of 15 September, led to a gradual—although not full—de-escalation of tensions in northern Kosovo and the removal of almost all roadblocks.

At the dialogue session held in Brussels on 2 September, Serbia agreed to recognize the Kosovo Customs stamps, thereby enabling the resumption of mutual trade flows. On 16 September, EULEX assumed control of both gates and ensured the presence of one Kosovo Customs officer, in an observer capacity, and two Kosovo border police officers at each. Nevertheless, the Kosovo Serbs in the north reinforced their roadblocks at Gates 1 and 31 and erected additional roadblocks along other routes in order to protest the deployment of Kosovo Customs officers at the gates, and what the protestors alleged was the non-status-neutral stance of KFOR and EULEX. While the northern gates remained effectively closed by the roadblocks, multiple bypass and alternate routes were used by local Kosovo Serbs circumventing the two crossings authorized by UNMIK in 2001.

On 27 September, protesters at Gate 1 attempted to remove barbed wire laid by KFOR to protect a EULEX vehicle checkpoint at a bypass road used by the Kosovo Serbs. KFOR responded with tear gas and rubber bullets. KFOR reported that in the ensuing melee, the protestors hurled pipe bombs at the soldiers and, when a protester attempted to seize a KFOR soldier's weapon, a second soldier used live ammunition and shot the assailant in the leg. Nine KFOR soldiers incurred injuries. According to the manager of the hospital in northern Mitrovica, seven patients were admitted with gunshot injuries incurred in the clash, while 19 protesters who sustained minor injuries caused by rubber bullets were treated in local health facilities and 92 people were reportedly treated for exposure to tear gas.

On 30 September, the Secretary-General received a letter [S/2011/604] from Serbia requesting an urgent investigation by the United Nations "to establish all relevant facts in connection with the use of armed force against civilians on 27 September", which he transmitted to the Security Council. The Secretary-General of the North Atlantic Treaty Organization (NATO) declared that KFOR had acted in conformity with its mandate and that no special investigation was warranted.

Those events contributed to a deterioration in the security situation in northern Kosovo, a polarization of positions and a widening of the gap between the communities in northern Kosovo and the institutions in Pristina. UNMIK continued to act as an impartial mediator and was perceived as such by all stakeholders. UNMIK engaged all parties, urging them to exercise restraint and emphasizing the need for dialogue in order to find sustainable solutions to disputes and long-standing issues related to northern Kosovo. The Acting Special Representative of the Secretary-General, Farid Zarif (Afghanistan), urged all parties to prevent any further violence. He also encouraged EULEX and KFOR to engage with the northern Kosovo Serbs to increase coordination and information-sharing and build confidence in the communities. As a result, weekly coordination meetings were initiated, including with northern Kosovo Serb representatives, KFOR, EULEX, OSCE and UNMIK.

The Security Council considered the Secretary-General's reports [S/2011/43, S/2011/281, S/2011/514, S/2011/675] on 16 February [S/PV.6483], 12 May [S/PV.6534], 30 August [S/PV.6604] and 29 November [S/PV.6670], respectively.

Year-end developments. In a later report [S/2012/72], the Secretary-General reported that tensions in northern Kosovo remained high, significantly impacting the dialogue between Pristina and Belgrade facilitated by EU, as well as the discussions on the European perspective of the region. On 9 December, the EU Council postponed its decision on Serbia's EU candidate status until March 2012. Kosovo was discussed on 5 December, with the Council envisaging in its conclusions the opening of a dialogue on visa liberalization and access to some additional EU programmes.

The EU-facilitated dialogue resumed at the end of November, following a three-month hiatus. The seventh and eighth rounds of the dialogue were held in Brussels on 21 and 22 November and from 30 November to 2 December. An agreement was reached on the application of the EU concept of the integrated management of crossing points. In addition, at the beginning of December the first original civil registry book from the municipality of Lipjan was copied and certified by EULEX in an operational follow-up to the agreement reached in early July, and was subsequently handed over from Belgrade to Pristina through EULEX on 6 December. On 26 December, implementation began of the 2 July understanding on freedom of movement, allowing residents of Kosovo and of Serbia to travel in and through their respective areas of control with accepted identity documents. Following agreement in principle on the acceptance of university diplomas, reached on 2 July, the parties agreed on 22 November that the European University Association would verify and certify diplomas issued by universities of each party for use by the other in the context of further education and public employment.

In November and December, violent clashes between northern Kosovo Serbs and KFOR resulted in interventions from UNMIK and EULEX, as well as officials from Pristina and Belgrade and the international community. UNMIK interventions on the ground proved to be a significant contribution to the restoration of freedom of movement for KFOR throughout northern Kosovo. In contrast, freedom of movement for EULEX was severely hampered by northern Kosovo Serbs, who allowed passage by EULEX only on a case-by-case basis. Towards the end of the year, a compromise arrangement allowing for EULEX movement, advocated by the UN Special Representative, was successfully applied in several instances. Despite efforts to de-escalate tensions, at year's end, the situation remained volatile.

EULEX

The European Union Rule of Law Mission in Kosovo (EULEX), established to undertake an enhanced operational role in the rule-of-law area, with a focus on policing, justice and customs, became fully operational in April 2009 [YUN 2009, p. 412]. It operated under the overall authority and within the status-neutral framework of the United Nations and submitted reports to it on a regular basis.

The EU High Representative for Foreign Affairs and Security Policy reported that in 2011 EULEX continued to work with the Kosovo rule-of-law authorities on targeted monitoring, mentoring and advising activities. The Kosovo police achieved success in assuming more tasks and undergoing organizational restructuring, while the Kosovo Customs maintained a good level of performance and continued to modernize its procedures with EULEX assistance. On 19 September, the EU-compatible Border Management System began operating throughout Kosovo, marking the culmination of cooperative efforts between EULEX, the European Commission and Kosovo border police to modernize border controls and improve safety and security at Kosovo's entry points.

EULEX carried out investigations and prosecutions in cases involving war crimes, with indictments and verdicts delivered in the trials of several high-profile suspects. The so-called "Geci" trial, which began in March under the direction of the Mitrovicë/Mitrovica District Court, ended on 29 July with a panel of EULEX and local judges pronouncing the defendants guilty and handing down prison terms of 6 to 15 years. EULEX also pursued the investigation of the former Minister of Transport and Telecommunications, Fatmir Limaj, together with nine other former Kosovo Liberation Army members arrested in March. On 25 July, EULEX prosecutors in the Special Prosecution Office of Kosovo filed an indictment against the group, with a EULEX judge from the Pristina District Court confirming the indictment on 26 August and sending the case to trial, which began on 11 November. Following inquiries by the Mission as to the immunity from arrest of Kosovo Assembly members, the government referred the issue to the Kosovo Constitutional Court, which ruled on 20 September that neither members of parliament, nor the Prime Minister or other ministers were immune from criminal prosecution for actions taken outside the scope of their duties, and that they could be arrested or detained. The decision made it possible for EULEX to pursue the case without having to deal with an immunity claim. On 23 November, a mixed panel of EULEX judges and a Kosovo judge rendered a verdict in the so-called "Bllaca" case against Fahredin Gashi et al., finding the defendant guilty of war crimes and sentencing him to 18 years in prison. The case was led by a EULEX prosecutor from the Kosovo Special Prosecution Office.

The reports to the UN Secretary-General of the EU High Representative for Foreign Affairs and Security Policy on EULEX activities in 2011 were annexed to the Secretary-General's reports to the Security Council on UNMIK [S/2011/43, S/2011/281, S/2011/514, S/2011/675, S/2012/72].

UNMIK

The United Nations Interim Administration Mission in Kosovo (UNMIK), established in 1999 [YUN 1999, p. 357] to facilitate a political process to determine Kosovo's political future, comprised five components: interim administration; institution-building; economic reconstruction; humanitarian affairs; and police and justice. Following Kosovo's declaration of independence in 2008 [YUN 2008, p. 437] and the deployment of EULEX in 2009 [YUN 2009, p. 412], the profile and size of UNMIK was reconfigured. The Mission's strategic goal remained the promotion of security, stability and respect for human rights in Kosovo and in the region through engagement with all communities in Kosovo, with the leadership in Belgrade and Pristina, and with regional and international actors.

Appointment of Special Representative. UNMIK was headed by the Special Representative of the Secretary-General, Lamberto Zannier (Italy) until 30 June. On 7 October [S/2011/631], the Secretary-General informed the Security Council of his intention to appoint Farid Zarif (Afghanistan) as his Special Representative for Kosovo and Head of UNMIK. The Council took note of that intention on 11 October [S/2011/632].

Financing

In June, the General Assembly considered the performance report on the UNMIK budget for the period from 1 July 2009 to 30 June 2010 [A/65/621], the proposed budget for 1 July 2011 to 30 June 2012 [A/65/711] and the related report of the Advisory Committee on Administrative and Budgetary Questions (ACABQ) [A/65/743/Add.4].

GENERAL ASSEMBLY ACTION

On 30 June [meeting 106], the General Assembly, on the recommendation of the Fifth (Administrative and Budgetary) Committee [A/65/884], adopted **resolution 65/300** without vote [agenda item 154].

Financing of the United Nations Interim Administration Mission in Kosovo

The General Assembly,

Having considered the reports of the Secretary-General on the financing of the United Nations Interim Administration Mission in Kosovo and the related report of the Advisory Committee on Administrative and Budgetary Questions,

Recalling Security Council resolution 1244(1999) of 10 June 1999 regarding the establishment of the United Nations Interim Administration Mission in Kosovo,

Recalling also its resolution 53/241 of 28 July 1999 on the financing of the Mission and its subsequent resolutions thereon, the latest of which was resolution 64/279 of 24 June 2010,

Acknowledging the complexity of the Mission,

Reaffirming the general principles underlying the financing of United Nations peacekeeping operations, as stated in General Assembly resolutions 1874(S-IV) of 27 June 1963, 3101(XXVIII) of 11 December 1973 and 55/235 of 23 December 2000,

Mindful of the fact that it is essential to provide the Mission with the financial resources necessary to enable it to fulfil its responsibilities under the relevant resolution of the Security Council,

Mindful also of the need to ensure coordination and cooperation with the European Union Rule of Law Mission in Kosovo,

1. *Requests* the Secretary-General to entrust the Head of Mission with the task of formulating future budget proposals in full accordance with the provisions of General Assembly resolutions 59/296 of 22 June 2005, 60/266 of 30 June 2006, 61/276 of 29 June 2007, 64/269 of 24 June 2010 and 65/289 of 30 June 2011, as well as other relevant resolutions;

2. *Takes note* of the status of contributions to the United Nations Interim Administration Mission in Kosovo as at

30 April 2011, including the contributions outstanding in the amount of 38.2 million United States dollars, representing some 1 per cent of the total assessed contributions, notes with concern that only one hundred and one Member States have paid their assessed contributions in full, and urges all other Member States, in particular those in arrears, to ensure payment of their outstanding assessed contributions;

3. *Expresses its appreciation* to those Member States which have paid their assessed contributions in full, and urges all other Member States to make every possible effort to ensure payment of their assessed contributions to the Mission in full;

4. *Expresses concern* at the financial situation with regard to peacekeeping activities, in particular as regards the reimbursements to troop contributors that bear additional burdens owing to overdue payments by Member States of their assessments;

5. *Also expresses concern* at the delay experienced by the Secretary-General in deploying and providing adequate resources to some recent peacekeeping missions, in particular those in Africa;

6. *Emphasizes* that all future and existing peacekeeping missions shall be given equal and non-discriminatory treatment in respect of financial and administrative arrangements;

7. *Also emphasizes* that all peacekeeping missions shall be provided with adequate resources for the effective and efficient discharge of their respective mandates;

8. *Requests* the Secretary-General to ensure that proposed peacekeeping budgets are based on the relevant legislative mandates;

9. *Endorses* the conclusions and recommendations contained in the report of the Advisory Committee on Administrative and Budgetary Questions, subject to the provisions of the present resolution, and requests the Secretary-General to ensure their full implementation;

10. *Takes note* of paragraph 29 of the report of the Advisory Committee on Administrative and Budgetary Questions, decides that the two posts of Forensic Anthropologist Officer and Legal Officer in the Rule of Law Liaison Office should not be converted to National Officer posts and also decides to establish the Reporting Officer post in the Office for Community Support and Facilitation as an international P-2 post;

11. *Requests* the Secretary-General to ensure the full implementation of the relevant provisions of resolutions 59/296, 60/266, 61/276, 64/269 and 65/289;

12. *Also requests* the Secretary-General to take all action necessary to ensure that the Mission is administered with a maximum of efficiency and economy;

Financial performance report for the period from 1 July 2009 to 30 June 2010

13. *Takes note* of the report of the Secretary-General on the financial performance of the Mission for the period from 1 July 2009 to 30 June 2010;

Budget estimates for the period from 1 July 2011 to 30 June 2012

14. *Decides* to appropriate to the Special Account for the United Nations Interim Administration Mission in Kosovo the amount of 47,802,200 dollars for the period from 1 July 2011 to 30 June 2012, inclusive of 44,914,800 dollars for the maintenance of the Mission, 2,446,700 dollars for the support account for peacekeeping operations and 440,700 dollars for the United Nations Logistics Base, Brindisi, Italy;

Financing of the appropriation

15. *Also decides* to apportion among Member States the amount of 47,802,200 dollars, in accordance with the levels updated in General Assembly resolution 64/249 of 24 December 2009, and taking into account the scale of assessments for 2011 and 2012, as set out in Assembly resolution 64/248 of 24 December 2009;

16. *Further decides* that, in accordance with the provisions of its resolution 973(X) of 15 December 1955, there shall be set off against the apportionment among Member States, as provided for in paragraph 15 above, their respective share in the Tax Equalization Fund in the amount of 4,634,800 dollars, comprising the estimated staff assessment income of 4,381,300 dollars approved for the Mission, the prorated share of 207,200 dollars of the estimated staff assessment income approved for the support account and the prorated share of 46,300 dollars of the estimated staff assessment income approved for the United Nations Logistics Base;

17. *Decides* that, for Member States that have fulfilled their financial obligations to the Mission, there shall be set off against the apportionment, as provided for in paragraph 15 above, their respective share of the unencumbered balance and other income in the total amount of 8,297,100 dollars in respect of the financial period ended 30 June 2010, in accordance with the levels updated in General Assembly resolution 64/249, and taking into account the scale of assessments for 2010, as set out in Assembly resolution 64/248;

18. *Also decides* that, for Member States that have not fulfilled their financial obligations to the Mission, there shall be set off against their outstanding obligations their respective share of the unencumbered balance and other income in the total amount of 8,297,100 dollars in respect of the financial period ended 30 June 2010, in accordance with the scheme set out in paragraph 17 above;

19. *Further decides* that the increase of 1,054,300 dollars in the estimated staff assessment income in respect of the financial period ended 30 June 2010 shall be added to the credits from the amount of 8,297,100 dollars referred to in paragraphs 17 and 18 above;

20. *Emphasizes* that no peacekeeping mission shall be financed by borrowing funds from other active peacekeeping missions;

21. *Encourages* the Secretary-General to continue to take additional measures to ensure the safety and security of all personnel participating in the Mission under the auspices of the United Nations, bearing in mind paragraphs 5 and 6 of Security Council resolution 1502(2003) of 26 August 2003;

22. *Invites* voluntary contributions to the Mission in cash and in the form of services and supplies acceptable to the Secretary-General, to be administered, as appropriate, in accordance with the procedure and practices established by the General Assembly;

23. *Decides* to include in the provisional agenda of its sixty-sixth session the item entitled "Financing of the United Nations Interim Administration Mission in Kosovo".

On 24 December, by **decision 66/557**, the General Assembly decided that the agenda item on the financing of UNMIK would remain for consideration during its resumed sixty-sixth (2012) session.

KFOR

In accordance with resolution 1244(1999) [YUN 1999, p. 353], the Secretary-General transmitted to the Security Council reports on the activities during 2011 of the Kosovo Force (KFOR) covering the periods from 1 January to 31 March [S/2011/363], 1 April to 30 June [S/2011/548], 1 July to 30 September [S/2012/120] and 1 October to 31 December [S/2012/169]. As at 31 December, the total number of KFOR troops in theatre was 5,700. That included an Operational Reserve Force battalion, which was deployed in theatre in the aftermath of the events of July in the northern part of Kosovo (see p. 385).

During the year, KFOR, in close coordination with EULEX and the Kosovo Police, worked towards guaranteeing a safe and secure environment and freedom of movement for all citizens in Kosovo. The situation in northern Kosovo remained volatile. Several roadblocks continued to hamper the freedom of movement of the local population, as well as of KFOR and of EULEX, although overall freedom of movement improved by the end of the year. KFOR monitored the security situation on the ground and maintained its deterrent posture.

Communications. During the year, Serbia addressed letters to the Security Council or the Secretary-General dealing with the situation in northern Kosovo [S/2011/256, S/2011/456, S/2011/482, S/2011/574, S/2011/575, S/2011/604].

The former Yugoslav Republic of Macedonia

Relations with Greece

In 2011, the United Nations continued to support the negotiation process to find a solution to the dispute between Greece and the former Yugoslav Republic of Macedonia (FYROM) regarding the name of the latter. The 1995 Interim Accord on the normalization of relations between FYROM and Greece [YUN 1995, p. 599] detailed the difference between the two countries on the name issue. During the year, the countries exchanged views in the context of article 5 of the Accord, which provided for the continuation of negotiations with a view to reaching agreement on their differences, as described in Security Council resolutions 817(1993) [YUN 1993, p. 208] and 845(1993) [ibid., p. 209]. The Personal Envoy of the Secretary-General for the Greece-FYROM talks, Matthew Nimetz, continued to hold informal meetings with the parties. The issue remained unresolved at year's end.

Communication. In a 15 February letter [A/65/735-S/2011/76] to the Secretary-General, FYROM discussed the ongoing naming dispute.

Georgia

In 2011, international efforts continued to advance the Georgian-Abkhaz peace process, based on the 2001 Basic Principles for the Distribution of Competences between Tbilisi (Georgia's Government) and Sukhumi (the Abkhaz leadership) [YUN 2001, p. 386]. That document was intended to serve as a framework for negotiations on the status of Abkhazia as a sovereign entity within the State of Georgia. Following the non-extension of the mandate of the United Nations Observer Mission in Georgia in June 2009 [YUN 2009, p. 418], the United Nations continued to support the Geneva international discussions on security and stability and the return of internally displaced persons (IDPs) and refugees.

Geneva talks. In accordance with the 12 August 2008 six-point ceasefire plan between Georgia and the Russian Federation [YUN 2008, p. 456] and the 8 September 2008 provisions for implementing the ceasefire plan [ibid., p. 457], international discussions under the co-chairmanship of the European Union (EU), the United Nations and the Organization for Security and Cooperation in Europe (OSCE) to address security and stability and humanitarian issues in Georgia continued to be held throughout 2011. At the fifteenth (4 March), sixteenth (7 June), seventeenth (4 October) and eighteenth (14 December) sessions, participants met in two parallel working groups.

Working Group I discussed the security situation and concerns regarding detentions, procedures for crossings and other developments on the ground, including reports of military-related activities. It also continued discussions on the key issues of non-use of force and international security arrangements. Working Group II addressed the rights of IDPs, including their right of return and the humanitarian needs of all affected populations. The discussions focused on finding consensus on a framework document affirming the principles governing the treatment of IDPs, the need for humanitarian access and the importance of finding durable solutions to displacement, including voluntary return in safety and dignity. It also discussed possible humanitarian measures to meet the needs of IDPs, including access to gas supply and to potable and irrigation water.

The Geneva discussions remained the only forum for stakeholders to address the issues identified in resolution 65/287 on IDPs and refugees (see p. 390).

By **resolution 65/288** of 30 June, the General Assembly approved the budget for the United Nations Representative to the Geneva International Discussions for the period from 1 May to 31 December in the amount of $1,590,600 gross (see p. 1381).

IDPs and refugees. In response to General Assembly resolution 64/296 [YUN 2010, p. 421] and 65/287 (see below), the Secretary-General submitted reports on the status of IDPs and refugees from Abkhazia and the Tskhinvali region/South Ossetia, covering the periods from 1 June 2010 to 30 March 2011 [A/65/846] and from 1 April 2011 to 30 March 2012 [A/66/813]. The reports focused on the right of return of all refugees and IDPs and their descendants; prohibition of forced demographic changes; humanitarian access; the importance of preserving the property rights of refugees and IDPs; and the development of a timetable to ensure the prompt voluntary return of all refugees and IDPs to their homes. According to the Georgian Ministry for Internally Displaced Persons from the Occupied Territories, Accommodation and Refugees, as at 31 December 2010 there were 256,528 registered IDPs, representing an increase over the 249,365 persons registered in 2009, which was mainly attributable to the children born to internally displaced families and late registrations.

GENERAL ASSEMBLY ACTION

On 29 June [meeting 105], the General Assembly adopted **resolution 65/287** [draft: A/65/L.74] by recorded vote (57-13-74) [agenda item 34].

Status of internally displaced persons and refugees from Abkhazia, Georgia, and the Tskhinvali region/South Ossetia, Georgia

The General Assembly,

Recalling all its relevant resolutions on the protection of and assistance to internally displaced persons, including its resolutions 62/153 of 18 December 2007, 62/249 of 15 May 2008, 63/307 of 9 September 2009, 64/162 of 18 December 2009 and 64/296 of 7 September 2010,

Recalling also all relevant Security Council resolutions on Georgia relating to the need for all parties to work towards a comprehensive peace and the return of internally displaced persons and refugees to their places of origin, and stressing the importance of their full and timely implementation,

Recognizing the Guiding Principles on Internal Displacement as the key international framework for the protection of internally displaced persons,

Concerned by forced demographic changes resulting from the conflicts in Georgia,

Concerned also by the humanitarian situation caused by armed conflict in August 2008, which resulted in the further forced displacement of civilians,

Mindful of the urgent need to find a solution to the problems related to forced displacement in Georgia,

Underlining the importance of the discussions that commenced in Geneva on 15 October 2008 and of continuing to address the issue of the voluntary, safe, dignified and unhindered return of internally displaced persons and refugees on the basis of internationally recognized principles and conflict-settlement practices,

Taking note of the report of the Secretary-General concerning the implementation of resolution 64/296,

1. *Recognizes* the right of return of all internally displaced persons and refugees and their descendants, regardless of ethnicity, to their homes throughout Georgia, including in Abkhazia and South Ossetia;
2. *Stresses* the need to respect the property rights of all internally displaced persons and refugees affected by the conflicts in Georgia and to refrain from obtaining property in violation of those rights;
3. *Reaffirms* the unacceptability of forced demographic changes;
4. *Underlines* the urgent need for unimpeded access for humanitarian activities to all internally displaced persons, refugees and other persons residing in all conflict-affected areas throughout Georgia;
5. *Calls upon* all participants in the Geneva discussions to intensify their efforts to establish a durable peace, to commit to enhanced confidence-building measures and to take immediate steps to ensure respect for human rights and create favourable security conditions conducive to the voluntary, safe, dignified and unhindered return of all internally displaced persons and refugees to their places of origin;
6. *Underlines* the need for the development of a timetable to ensure the voluntary, safe, dignified and unhindered return of all internally displaced persons and refugees affected by the conflicts in Georgia to their homes;
7. *Requests* the Secretary-General to submit to the General Assembly at its sixty-sixth session a comprehensive report on the implementation of the present resolution;
8. *Decides* to include in the provisional agenda of its sixty-sixth session the item entitled "Protracted conflicts in the GUAM area and their implications for international peace, security and development".

RECORDED VOTE ON RESOLUTION 65/287:

In favour: Albania, Andorra, Antigua and Barbuda, Australia, Austria, Azerbaijan, Belgium, Bosnia and Herzegovina, Bulgaria, Canada, Congo, Costa Rica, Croatia, Czech Republic, Denmark, Estonia, Finland, France, Georgia, Germany, Greece, Guinea-Bissau, Honduras, Hungary, Iceland, Ireland, Italy, Japan, Latvia, Liechtenstein, Lithuania, Luxembourg, Malawi, Maldives, Malta, Marshall Islands, Micronesia, Monaco, Montenegro, Netherlands, New Zealand, Norway, Poland, Portugal, Republic of Moldova, Romania, Saint Lucia, Saint Vincent and the Grenadines, San Marino, Slovakia, Slovenia, Spain, Sweden, Tuvalu, United Kingdom, United States, Vanuatu.

Against: Armenia, Cuba, Democratic People's Republic of Korea, Lao People's Democratic Republic, Myanmar, Nicaragua, Russian Federation, Serbia, Sri Lanka, Sudan, Syrian Arab Republic, Venezuela, Viet Nam.

Abstaining: Argentina, Bahamas, Bahrain, Bangladesh, Barbados, Bhutan, Bolivia, Brazil, Brunei Darussalam, Burkina Faso, Burundi, Cameroon, Chile, China, Colombia, Cyprus, Djibouti, Dominican Republic, Ecuador, Egypt, Gabon, Gambia, Grenada, Guatemala, Guinea, Guyana, Haiti, India, Indonesia, Israel, Jamaica, Jordan, Kazakhstan, Kenya, Kuwait, Kyrgyzstan, Lebanon, Madagascar, Malaysia, Mali, Mauritius, Mexico, Mongolia, Morocco, Nepal, Oman, Pakistan, Panama, Papua New Guinea, Paraguay, Peru, Philippines, Qatar, Republic of Korea, Samoa, Saudi Arabia, Senegal, Singapore, Solomon Islands, Somalia, Switzerland, Tajikistan, Thailand, the former Yugoslav Republic of Macedonia, Timor-Leste, Togo, Tonga, Trinidad and Tobago, Tunisia, Turkey, United Republic of Tanzania, Uruguay, Yemen, Zambia.

Chapter V: Europe and the Mediterranean

Appointment of Special Representative. On 2 May [S/2011/279], the Security Council took note of the Secretary-General's intention [YUN 2010, p. 422] to appoint Antti Turunen (Finland) as the UN representative in support of the Joint Incident Prevention and Response Mechanism and the international discussions in Geneva on security and stability and the return of IDPs and refugees.

Communications. Throughout 2011, Georgia submitted identical letters to the Secretary-General and the Security Council pertaining to issues with Abkhazia, the Tskhinvali region/South Ossetia and the Russian Federation. The letters addressed the Geneva discussions [A/65/769-S/2011/109, A/65/778-S/2011/123, A/66/504-S/2011/625, A/66/618-S/2011/778]; Russia's political and economic recognition of Abkhazia and the Tskhinvali region/South Ossetia [A/65/694-S/2011/28, A/65/745-S/2011/81, A/65/795-S/2011/171, A/65/831-S/2011/275, A/65/858-S/2011/342, A/65/917-S/2011/481, A/65/938-S/2011/550, A/66/530-S/2011/666, A/66/547-S/2011/699, A/66/554-S/2011/712, A/66/588-S/2011/766]; Russian use of military bases in Abkhazia and the Tskhinvali region/South Ossetia [A/65/699-S/2011/36, A/65/930-S/2011/517, A/66/387-S/2011/596, A/66/538-S/2011/688]; the 1 April decision of the International Court of Justice in the proceeding Georgia v. Russian Federation [A/65/804-S/2011/220] (see p. 1232); the third anniversary of the 2008 conflict [A/65/927-S/2011/505]; and airspace violations [A/65/941-S/2011/564]; as well as random acts of violence [A/65/845-S/2011/323, A/65/870-S/2011/374], terrorism [A/65/867-S/2011/356] and kidnapping [A/65/871-S/2011/376].

On 24 January [S/2011/33], Russia submitted a letter to the Security Council on the Georgian-Abkhaz conflict enclosing a letter to the Secretary-General by the President of the "Republic of Abkhazia" (annex I) and a statement by the President of the "Republic of South Ossetia" (annex II).

On 17 June [A/65/869-S/2011/386], Russia transmitted a letter to the Security Council and the Secretary-General summarizing the outcome of the sixteenth Geneva discussions held on 7 June.

UNOMIG

The United Nations Observer Mission in Georgia (UNOMIG) was established by Security Council resolution 858(1993) [YUN 1993, p. 509]. It monitored compliance with the 1994 Moscow Agreement [YUN 1994, p. 583] and fulfilled other tasks as mandated by Council resolution 937(1994) [ibid., p. 584] and subsequent resolutions. It later also carried out functions under the 12 August 2008 six-point ceasefire agreement [YUN 2008, p. 456] and 8 September implementing measures [ibid., p. 457]. In June 2009, Council members were unable to agree on the future activities of a UN stabilization mission, and the UNOMIG mandate was terminated effective 16 June 2009 [YUN 2009, p. 418].

Financing

In June, the General Assembly had before it the Secretary-General's performance report on the UNOMIG budget for the period from 1 July 2009 to 30 June 2010 [A/65/681] and the related ACABQ report [A/65/743/Add.1].

GENERAL ASSEMBLY ACTION

On 30 June [meeting 106], the General Assembly, on the recommendation of the Fifth Committee [A/65/879], adopted **resolution 65/299** without vote [agenda item 152].

Financing of the United Nations Observer Mission in Georgia

The General Assembly,

Having considered the report of the Secretary-General on the financial performance of the United Nations Observer Mission in Georgia for the period from 1 July 2009 to 30 June 2010 and the related report of the Advisory Committee on Administrative and Budgetary Questions,

Recalling Security Council resolution 854(1993) of 6 August 1993, by which the Council approved the deployment of an advance team of up to ten United Nations military observers for a period of three months and the incorporation of the advance team into a United Nations observer mission if such a mission was formally established by the Council,

Recalling also Security Council resolution 858(1993) of 24 August 1993, by which the Council established the United Nations Observer Mission in Georgia, and the subsequent resolutions by which the Council extended the mandate of the Observer Mission, the last of which was resolution 1866(2009) of 13 February 2009,

Recalling further its decision 48/475 A of 23 December 1993 on the financing of the Observer Mission and its subsequent resolutions and decisions thereon, the latest of which was resolution 64/234 of 22 December 2009,

Reaffirming the general principles underlying the financing of United Nations peacekeeping operations, as stated in General Assembly resolutions 1874(S-IV) of 27 June 1963, 3101(XXVIII) of 11 December 1973 and 55/235 of 23 December 2000,

1. *Takes note* of the status of contributions to the United Nations Observer Mission in Georgia as at 30 April 2011, including the contributions outstanding in the amount of 4.9 million United States dollars, representing some 1 per cent of the total assessed contributions, notes with concern that only one hundred and twenty-seven Member States have paid their assessed contributions in full, and urges all other Member States, in particular those in arrears, to ensure payment of their outstanding assessed contributions;

2. *Expresses its appreciation* to those Member States which have paid their assessed contributions in full, and urges all other Member States to make every possible effort

to ensure payment of their assessed contributions to the Observer Mission in full;

3. *Endorses* the conclusions and recommendations contained in the report of the Advisory Committee on Administrative and Budgetary Questions, and requests the Secretary-General to ensure their full implementation;

Financial performance report for the period from 1 July 2009 to 30 June 2010

4. *Takes note* of the report of the Secretary-General on the financial performance of the Observer Mission for the period from 1 July 2009 to 30 June 2010;

5. *Decides* that Member States that have fulfilled their financial obligations to the Observer Mission shall be credited with their respective share of the unencumbered balance and other income in the amount of 1,806,800 dollars in respect of the financial period ended 30 June 2010, in accordance with the levels updated in General Assembly resolution 64/249 of 24 December 2009, and taking into account the scale of assessments for 2010, as set out in Assembly resolution 64/248 of 24 December 2009;

6. *Also decides* that, for Member States that have not fulfilled their financial obligations to the Observer Mission, their respective share of the unencumbered balance and other income in the amount of 1,806,800 dollars in respect of the financial period ended 30 June 2010 shall be set off against their outstanding obligations, in accordance with the scheme set out in paragraph 5 above;

7. *Further decides* that the increase of 157,600 dollars in the estimated staff assessment income in respect of the financial period ended 30 June 2010 shall be added to the credits from the amount of 1,806,800 dollars referred to in paragraphs 5 and 6 above;

8. *Decides* to include in the provisional agenda of its sixty-sixth session the item entitled "Financing of the United Nations Observer Mission in Georgia".

On 24 December, by **decision 66/557**, the General Assembly decided that the agenda item on the financing of UNOMIG would remain for consideration during its resumed sixty-sixth (2012) session.

Armenia and Azerbaijan

In 2011, Armenia and Azerbaijan maintained their positions with regard to the Nagorny Karabakh region of Azerbaijan. The conflict, which began in 1992 [YUN 1992, p. 388], was followed by a ceasefire agreement in May 1994 [YUN 1994, p. 577]. Both sides addressed communications regarding the conflict to the Secretary-General. The Organization for Security and Cooperation in Europe (OSCE) Minsk Group (France, Russian Federation, United States) continued to mediate the dispute between the two countries.

Communications. In letters dated 4 February [A/65/723-S/2011/62], 11 March [A/65/780-S/2011/132], 4 April [A/65/808-S/2011/226], 15 April [A/65/821-S/2011/251], 20 May [A/65/847-S/2011/325], 20 June [A/65/872-S/2011/379], 14 July [A/65/906-S/2011/429], 25 July [A/65/915-S/2011/457], 3 August [A/65/921-S/2011/492], 9 September [A/65/942-S/2011/573], 25 October [A/66/528-S/2011/668] and 29 December [A/66/651-S/2011/809], Azerbaijan drew the Secretary-General's attention to violations of the ceasefire by the military forces of Armenia during the year.

On 29 March [A/65/801-S/2011/208], Azerbaijan transmitted to the Secretary-General a communication regarding a field assessment mission to the occupied territories of Azerbaijan conducted by the Co-Chairs of the OSCE Minsk Group. Azerbaijan stated that the mission report revealed a continuation of the policy of illegal settlement by ethnic Armenians in the occupied territories of Azerbaijan. Armenia responded in a letter to the Secretary-General dated 7 April [A/65/813-S/2011/234] that Azerbaijan misinterpreted the report in order to justify its militaristic rhetoric.

In a letter of 15 September [A/66/366-S/2011/584], Azerbaijan drew the Secretary-General's attention to the so-called "parliamentary elections" to be held on 18 September in occupied Nagorny Karabakh. On 4 October [A/66/499-S/2011/621], Armenia responded that the elections were a display of the right to vote for the population of Nagorny Karabakh. In an additional letter dated 5 October [A/66/500-S/2011/622], Armenia transmitted a statement from the Ministry of Foreign Affairs of the Nagorny Karabakh Republic that expressed satisfaction with the 18 September elections, calling them a successful manifestation of the democratic process positively assessed by international observers.

Armenia reported on violations of the ceasefire by the armed forces of Azerbaijan in letters dated 22 February [A/65/749-S/2011/87], 9 April [A/65/816-S/2011/237], 29 April [A/65/833-S/2011/285], 28 May [A/65/848-S/2011/326], 1 July [A/65/898-S/2011/412], 8 July [A/65/899-S/2011/423], 4 August [A/65/924-S/2011/495], 16 August [A/65/932-S/2011/519], 10 November [A/66/552-S/2011/706] and 13 December [A/66/607-S/2011/774].

By **decision 65/552** of 12 September, the General Assembly deferred consideration of the item on the situation in the occupied territories of Azerbaijan and included it in the draft agenda of its sixty-sixth (2012) session.

Cyprus

The United Nations continued its sponsorship of the peace talks in Cyprus. The Secretary-General's Special Adviser on Cyprus, with support from his Special Representative, assisted the Greek Cypriot and Turkish Cypriot leaders in implementing the

8 July 2006 Set of Principles and Decision [YUN 2006, p. 487], which included commitment to the unification of Cyprus based on a bizonal, bicommunal federation and political equality, and an agreement to meet regularly on issues affecting the day-to-day life of the Cypriot people. In 2011, discussions centred on key outstanding issues: governance and power-sharing, property and citizenship. The leaders made progress on those areas and reached further convergence on a number of other issues.

The two sides continued to withhold access to the four remaining mined areas in the buffer zone. No agreements were made to extend demining operations to areas outside the buffer zone, and demining in Cyprus ceased in January.

The United Nations Peacekeeping Force in Cyprus (UNFICYP) continued to assist in the restoration of normal conditions and in humanitarian functions. The Security Council twice extended the UNFICYP mandate, the second time until 19 July 2012.

Political and security developments

Good offices mission

During the year, the Special Adviser on Cyprus continued to facilitate the negotiations aimed at reaching a comprehensive settlement that would safeguard the fundamental and legitimate rights and interests of Greek Cypriots and Turkish Cypriots. He was supported by the Secretary-General's Special Representative and Head of UNFICYP, who served as his deputy on issues relating to the good offices of the Secretary-General. The Secretary-General described UN mediation efforts during 2011 in reports to the Security Council of 4 March [S/2011/112] and 8 August [S/2011/498], as well as in a later report [S/2012/149].

The Secretary-General met with the Greek Cypriot leader, Demetris Christofias, and the Turkish Cypriot leader, Derviş Eroğlu, on 26 January and 7 July in Geneva, and on 30 and 31 October in New York. On 7 July, while expressing his disappointment in the lack of progress, the Secretary-General was able to identify with the two leaders some of the stumbling blocks that had stood in the way of reaching a comprehensive settlement. The parties agreed on the need to accelerate the pace of the talks and accepted the Secretary-General's recommendation to engage in negotiations for two full days each week. They also agreed that, without prejudice to the central principle of a Cypriot-owned and Cypriot-led process, there would be enhanced UN involvement.

In response to the Secretary-General's request to move forward in the remaining areas of divergence on governance and power-sharing, both sides presented a number of bridging proposals. Discussions on European Union (EU) matters reached convergence on certain issues related to the representation of Cyprus in Brussels and decision-making in EU bodies. The primary remaining divergence related to the incorporation of a settlement into EU law. Discussions on economic matters addressed progress made on core issues. An agreement was made on the use of both population and consumption as criteria for calculating how, for a certain transitional period, the north's relative economic disadvantage should be addressed. Less progress was made on property, territory, and security and guarantees.

In March, the sides began discussing the internal aspects of security. The discussions focused on policing and law enforcement arrangements in a united Cyprus at both the federal level and that of the federated units or constituent States. The sides came close to agreement on the details of that issue, although several important outstanding aspects remained to be resolved.

On property, the Secretary-General reported that both sides made use of the international technical experts whose services he offered when he met with the leaders in Geneva in January. That had enabled each side to explore a range of technical issues and to further develop proposals. The Secretary-General noted, however, that there remained fundamental disagreement on the issue of conditions for restitution and the mode for exchange.

Discussions on governance, which focused on the capacity to conclude international treaties and the procedure for doing so and the federal-level decision-making procedure with regard to foreign affairs, led to convergence on the principle of representation abroad. The sides reached agreement on international treaties binding on the united Cyprus. As a result, the Subcommittee on International Treaties resumed its work. The technical committees, established in 2008 [YUN 2008, p. 464], continued to meet on the implementation of confidence-building measures to improve the daily lives of Cypriots. Three of the seven technical committees, which had been dormant since July 2008, had resumed their work. The Secretary-General reported that, at the October meetings, the two sides moved closer on core issues relating to governance and power-sharing, citizenship, property and territory. Moreover, the sides engaged in a paring-down process that resulted in focusing on what both sides termed as the "core core" issues: the election of the executive, the number of persons who would become citizens of a united Cyprus and the basic design of a property regime.

Communications. Throughout 2011, the Secretary-General received letters from the Government of Cyprus and from Turkish Cypriot authorities containing charges and counter-charges, protests and accusations, and explanations of positions. Letters from the "Turkish Republic of Northern Cyprus" were transmitted by Turkey. In communications dated between 15 March and 5 December, Cyprus reported violations of international air traffic regulations and the national airspace of Cyprus by Turkish military aircraft [A/65/786-S/2011/145, A/65/901-S/2011/424, A/65/923-S/2011/493, A/66/585-S/2011/755]. The "Turkish Republic of Northern Cyprus" refuted the allegations, stating that the flights mentioned took place within the sovereign airspace of the "Turkish Republic of Northern Cyprus" [A/65/688-S/2011/12, A/65/806-S/2011/235, A/65/913-S/2011/448].

On 20 January, Cyprus transmitted a letter to the Secretary-General [A/65/695-S/2011/31] regarding the signing of the Agreement on Delimitation of the Exclusive Economic Zone, which was co-signed by Cyprus and Israel. Cyprus stated that the international agreements it had signed aimed at promoting its economic interests and benefiting the people of Cyprus as a whole. Turkey responded on 25 January [A/65/702-S/2011/46] that the "Government of the Republic of Cyprus" had no legal or moral right or the jurisdiction to represent or act on behalf of the whole island.

In a letter dated 27 April [A/65/829-S/2011/276], Turkey drew attention to the seventh anniversary of the referendums on the UN Comprehensive Settlement Plan of 2004 [YUN 2004, p. 438], stressing the need for a mutually acceptable settlement agreement.

Responding to the announcement of the start of Greek Cypriot drilling for underwater natural resource exploration, planned to begin in October, Turkey stated on 15 August [A/65/933-S/2011/523] that the Greek Cypriot Administration had no legal rights to drill for underwater natural resources on the southern side of the island or enter into international agreements concerning maritime jurisdiction areas or economic zones. In a letter dated 16 August [A/65/934-S/2011/526], Turkey transmitted a press release regarding the Greek Cypriot Administration's gas exploration activities in the Eastern Mediterranean.

On 24 December, the General Assembly decided that the agenda item on the question of Cyprus would remain for consideration at its resumed sixty-sixth (2012) session (**decision 66/557**).

UNFICYP

The United Nations Peacekeeping Force in Cyprus (UNFICYP), established in 1964 [YUN 1964, p. 165], continued in 2011 to monitor the ceasefire lines between the Turkish and Turkish Cypriot forces on the northern side of the island and the Cypriot National Guard on the southern side; maintain the military status quo and prevent recurrence of fighting; and undertake humanitarian and economic activities.

Lisa Buttenheim (United States) continued to be the Secretary-General's Special Representative for Cyprus and Head of UNFICYP.

On 10 January [S/2011/13], the Secretary-General informed the Security Council of his intention to appoint Major General Chao Liu (China) as the Force Commander of UNFICYP, replacing Rear Admiral Mario Sánchez Debernardi (Peru). The Council took note of the intention on 12 January [S/2011/14]. During 2011, Alexander Downer (Australia) continued as the Secretary-General's Special Adviser on Cyprus.

As at 31 October, UNFICYP comprised 860 troops and 69 civilian police.

The Secretary-General submitted two reports covering UNFICYP activities for the periods from 21 November 2010 to 20 May 2011 [S/2011/332] and 21 May to 20 November [S/2011/746 & Corr.1].

Activities

Report of Secretary-General (May). In his May report [S/2011/332], the Secretary-General stated that the situation in the buffer zone remained stable. The opposing forces continued occasionally to employ low-level measures that provoked reaction from the other side, mostly in areas around Nicosia.

The Cyprus National Guard had worked with UNFICYP on assessing military confidence-building measures that UNFICYP had proposed, such as the unmanning or closing of observation posts where opposing troops were in close proximity. No concrete steps had been taken by the Turkish forces/Turkish Cypriot security forces in that regard.

The two sides continued to withhold access to the four remaining mined areas in the buffer zone, one under the control of the Turkish forces and three under the control of the Cyprus National Guard. No agreements were made to extend demining operations to areas outside the buffer zone, and demining in Cyprus ceased in January. The Secretary-General's Special Representative wrote to the Greek Cypriot and Turkish Cypriot leaders reiterating the position of the Security Council, and urged the parties to agree to extend the operation beyond the buffer zone. The parties made no progress, however, in releasing the remaining minefields for clearance.

Cypriots from both sides continued to seek assistance from UNFICYP in addressing day-to-day issues arising from the division of the island, including in relation to economic, social and educational matters and commemorative, religious and socio-cultural gatherings. The Force facilitated the implementation of a variety of bicommunal projects by the United Nations Development Programme by allowing access to certain sensitive areas of the buffer zone. In the old town of Nicosia, UNFICYP supported an

EU-funded project led by the two Nicosia municipalities on the stabilization of buildings at the Ledra Street/Lokmaçı crossing. UNFICYP facilitated four meetings of the Committee on Crossings and several site visits to different locations in the buffer zone.

UNFICYP facilitated more than 100 bicommunal events with the participation of 6,300 people from both communities. The Force also continued to deliver weekly humanitarian assistance to 356 Greek Cypriots and 126 Maronites in the north and to facilitate solutions for their medical and health-care needs.

Supported by UNFICYP, the Technical Committee on Cultural Heritage and its advisory board continued to plan for the preservation, protection and restoration of immovable cultural heritage throughout the island.

As UNFICYP continued to play an essential role on the island, including in support of the good offices mission, the Secretary-General recommended that the Security Council extend the Force's mandate until 15 December 2011.

SECURITY COUNCIL ACTION

On 13 June [meeting 6554], the Security Council unanimously adopted **resolution 1986(2011)**. The draft [S/2011/355] was submitted by China, France, the Russian Federation, the United Kingdom and the United States.

The Security Council,

Welcoming the report of the Secretary-General of 31 May 2011 on the United Nations operation in Cyprus and his report of 4 March 2011 on his mission of good offices in Cyprus,

Noting that the Government of Cyprus has agreed that, in view of the prevailing conditions on the island, it is necessary to keep the United Nations Peacekeeping Force in Cyprus beyond 15 June 2011,

Echoing the Secretary-General's firm belief that the responsibility for finding a solution lies first and foremost with the Cypriots themselves, and reaffirming the primary role of the United Nations in assisting the parties to bring the Cyprus conflict and division of the island to a comprehensive and durable settlement,

Welcoming the progress made so far in the fully fledged negotiations, and the leaders' joint statements, including those of 23 May and 1 July 2008,

Expressing concern at the continued slow pace of progress, stressing that the status quo is unsustainable, and strongly urging the leaders to increase the momentum of the negotiations, particularly on the core issues, to reach an enduring, comprehensive and just settlement based on a bicommunal, bizonal federation with political equality, as set out in the relevant Security Council resolutions,

Emphasizing the importance that the international community attaches to all parties engaging fully, flexibly and constructively in the negotiations, echoing the view of the Secretary-General that a solution is well within reach, and looking forward to decisive progress in the near future, including leading up to the Secretary-General's meeting with the leaders in July 2011, building on the progress made to date,

Welcoming the efforts of the Secretary-General to stimulate progress during his meeting with the two leaders on 26 January 2011 and his intention to meet with the two leaders in July 2011, and noting his intention to submit to the Council in July 2011 an updated assessment on the state of the process,

Noting the need to advance the consideration of and discussions on military confidence-building measures, and calling for renewed efforts to implement all remaining confidence-building measures and for agreement on and implementation of further steps to build trust between the communities,

Reaffirming the importance of continued crossings of the Green Line by Cypriots, and encouraging the opening by mutual agreement of other crossing points,

Convinced of the many important benefits for all Cypriots that would flow from a comprehensive and durable Cyprus settlement, urging the two sides and their leaders to foster positive public rhetoric, and encouraging them clearly to explain the benefits of the settlement, as well as the need for increased flexibility and compromise in order to secure it, to both communities well in advance of any eventual referendums,

Considering that undermining the credibility of the United Nations undermines the peace process itself,

Highlighting the supportive role that the international community will continue to play in helping the Greek Cypriot and Turkish Cypriot leaders to exploit fully the current opportunity,

Taking note of the assessment of the Secretary-General that the security situation on the island and along the Green Line remains stable, and urging all sides to avoid any action which could lead to an increase in tension, undermine the progress achieved so far or damage the goodwill on the island,

Recalling the Secretary-General's firm belief that the situation in the buffer zone would be improved if both sides accepted the 1989 aide-memoire used by the United Nations,

Noting with regret that the sides are withholding access to the remaining minefields in the buffer zone and that demining in Cyprus has ceased as a result, noting the continued danger posed by mines in Cyprus, and urging rapid agreement on facilitating the recommencement of demining operations and clearance of the remaining minefields,

Welcoming the progress and continuation of the important activities of the Committee on Missing Persons in Cyprus, and trusting that this process will promote reconciliation between the communities,

Agreeing that active participation of civil society groups is essential to the political process and can contribute to making any future settlement sustainable, welcoming all efforts to promote bicommunal contacts and events, including on the part of all United Nations bodies on the island, and urging the two sides to promote the active engagement of civil society and the encouragement of cooperation between economic and commercial bodies and to remove all obstacles to such contacts,

Stressing the need for the Council to pursue a rigorous, strategic approach to peacekeeping deployments,

Welcoming the intention of the Secretary-General to keep all peacekeeping operations, including those of the Force, under close review, and noting the importance of contingency planning in relation to the settlement, including recommendations, as appropriate, for further adjustments to the mandate, force levels and concept of operations of the Force, taking into account developments on the ground and the views of the parties,

Welcoming also the continued efforts of Mr. Alexander Downer as the Special Adviser to the Secretary-General on Cyprus with a mandate to assist the parties in the conduct of fully fledged negotiations aimed at reaching a comprehensive settlement, and the efforts of Ms. Lisa Buttenheim as the Special Representative of the Secretary-General in Cyprus,

Echoing the Secretary-General's gratitude to the Government of Cyprus and the Government of Greece for their voluntary contributions to the funding of the Force and his request for further voluntary contributions from other countries and organizations, and expressing its appreciation to Member States that contribute personnel to the Force,

Welcoming and encouraging efforts by the United Nations to sensitize peacekeeping personnel in the prevention and control of HIV/AIDS and other communicable diseases in all its peacekeeping operations,

1. *Welcomes* the progress made so far in the fully fledged negotiations and the prospect of further progress in the near future towards a comprehensive and durable settlement that this has created;

2. *Takes note* of the report of the Secretary-General;

3. *Recalls* Security Council resolution 1953(2010) of 14 December 2010, and calls upon the two leaders:

(*a*) To intensify the momentum of negotiations, engage in the process in a constructive and open manner and work on reaching convergences on the remaining core issues in preparation for their meeting with the Secretary-General in July 2011;

(*b*) To improve the public atmosphere in which the negotiations are proceeding, including by focusing public messages on convergences and the way ahead and delivering more constructive and harmonized messages;

(*c*) To increase the participation of civil society in the process, as appropriate;

4. *Urges* the implementation of confidence-building measures, and looks forward to agreement on and implementation of further such steps, including military confidence-building measures and the opening of other crossing points;

5. *Urges* all parties to be more forthcoming in accommodating the exhumation requirements of the Committee for Missing Persons in Cyprus throughout the island, including in military areas in the north;

6. *Reaffirms* all its relevant resolutions on Cyprus, in particular resolution 1251(1999) of 29 June 1999 and subsequent resolutions;

7. *Expresses its full support* for the United Nations Peacekeeping Force in Cyprus, and decides to extend its mandate for a further period ending 15 December 2011;

8. *Calls upon* both sides to continue to engage, as a matter of urgency and while respecting the mandate of the Force, in consultations with the Force on the demarcation of the buffer zone and on the United Nations 1989 aide-memoire, with a view to reaching early agreement on outstanding issues;

9. *Calls upon* the Turkish Cypriot side and Turkish forces to restore in Strovilia the military status quo which existed there prior to 30 June 2000;

10. *Calls upon* both sides to allow access to deminers and to facilitate the removal of the remaining mines in Cyprus within the buffer zone, and urges both sides to extend demining operations outside the buffer zone;

11. *Requests* the Secretary-General to submit a report on the implementation of the present resolution, including on contingency planning in relation to the settlement, by 1 December 2011 and to keep the Council updated on events as necessary;

12. *Welcomes* the efforts being undertaken by the Force to implement the Secretary-General's zero-tolerance policy on sexual exploitation and abuse and to ensure full compliance of its personnel with the United Nations code of conduct, requests the Secretary-General to continue to take all necessary action in this regard and to keep the Council informed, and urges troop-contributing countries to take appropriate preventive action, including conducting predeployment awareness training, and to take disciplinary action and other action to ensure full accountability in cases of such conduct involving their personnel;

13. *Decides* to remain seized of the matter.

Report of Secretary-General (November). In his November report [S/2011/746 & Corr.1], the Secretary-General said that the situation in the buffer zone remained stable and the overall number of military violations committed by the opposing forces had decreased. The relationship between UNFICYP and the opposing forces continued to be good. For the fourth successive year, both the Cyprus National Guard and the Turkish forces announced the cancellation of their major annual exercises, which was a welcome development. Discussions on military confidence-building measures had been initiated by UNFICYP but had not had the support and cooperation of the opposing forces. Also, restrictions on the movement of locally employed UN civilian personnel continued. Positions established, in violation of the status quo, by the opposing forces in the Dherinia area had remained unchanged, and civilians continued to challenge UNFICYP authority within the buffer zone, in particular through unauthorized farming and hunting activities.

The two sides continued to withhold access to the four remaining mined areas in the buffer zone. No agreements were made to extend demining operations and the mine clearance operation remained suspended.

Cypriots from both sides continued to seek assistance from UNFICYP in addressing day-to-day issues arising from the division of the island, including in relation to economic, social and educational matters and commemorative, religious and socio-cultural gatherings. In the south, UNFICYP continued to assist local authorities and community representatives in their efforts to provide welfare services for the Turkish Cypriots in need. The Force also assisted in addressing the legal and humanitarian issues in connection with the imprisonment of nine Turkish Cypriots in the south and six Greek Cypriots in the north and temporary arrests of individuals on both sides, as well as defusing the tensions which arose during the annual Turkish Cypriot pilgrimage to Hala Sultan Tekke in Larnaca in August. In addition, UNFICYP facilitated 20 religious and commemorative events, involving some 6,000 individuals, which were held in or required crossing of the buffer zone; 80 bicommunal events to foster cooperation and reconciliation, with the participation of 3,000 people from both communities; and three meetings of the Committee on Crossings.

The Committee on Missing Persons continued to carry out its bicommunal project on the exhumation, identification and return of remains of missing persons. As at November, the Committee's bicommunal teams of archaeologists had exhumed the remains of more than 800 individuals on both sides of the island. The remains of nearly 500 persons had undergone examination at the Committee's anthropological laboratory in the United Nations Protected Area in Nicosia. The remains of over 300 individuals had been returned to their respective families.

The Secretary-General recommended that the Security-Council extend the Force's mandate until 15 June 2012.

SECURITY COUNCIL ACTION

On 14 December [meeting 6685], the Security Council unanimously adopted **resolution 2026(2011)**. The draft [S/2011/771] was submitted by China, France, the Russian Federation, the United Kingdom and the United States.

The Security Council,

Welcoming the report of the Secretary-General of 30 November 2011 on the United Nations operation in Cyprus,

Noting that the Government of Cyprus has agreed that, in view of the prevailing conditions on the island, it is necessary to keep the United Nations Peacekeeping Force in Cyprus beyond 15 December 2011,

Echoing the Secretary-General's firm belief that the responsibility for finding a solution lies first and foremost with the Cypriots themselves, and reaffirming the primary role of the United Nations in assisting the parties to bring the Cyprus conflict and division of the island to a comprehensive and durable settlement,

Welcoming the progress made so far in the fully fledged negotiations, and the leaders' joint statements, including those of 23 May and 1 July 2008,

Welcoming also the move towards a more intensive phase of negotiations, stressing that the status quo is unsustainable, and strongly urging the leaders to increase the momentum of the negotiations, particularly on the core issues, to reach an enduring, comprehensive and just settlement based on a bicommunal, bizonal federation with political equality, as set out in the relevant Security Council resolutions,

Emphasizing the importance that the international community attaches to all parties engaging fully, flexibly and constructively in the negotiations, echoing the Secretary-General's view that a comprehensive settlement can be achieved, looking forward to decisive progress in the near future, leading up to the Secretary-General's meeting with the leaders in January 2012, and echoing the Secretary-General's expectation that "all internal aspects of a settlement will have been resolved by then so that we can move to a multilateral conference shortly thereafter" with the consent of the two sides,

Welcoming the efforts of the Secretary-General to stimulate progress during his meeting with the two leaders on 30 and 31 October 2011 and his intention to meet with the two leaders in January 2012, and noting his intention to submit to the Council in January 2012 an updated assessment on the state of the process,

Noting the need to advance the consideration of and discussions on military confidence-building measures, and calling for renewed efforts to implement all remaining confidence-building measures and for agreement on and implementation of further steps to build trust between the communities,

Reaffirming the importance of continued crossings of the Green Line by Cypriots, and encouraging the opening by mutual agreement of other crossing points,

Convinced of the many important benefits for all Cypriots that would flow from a comprehensive and durable Cyprus settlement, urging the two sides and their leaders to foster positive public rhetoric, and encouraging them clearly to explain the benefits of the settlement, as well as the need for increased flexibility and compromise in order to secure it, to both communities well in advance of any eventual referendums,

Considering that undermining the credibility of the United Nations undermines the peace process itself,

Highlighting the importance of the supporting role of the international community, and in particular that of the parties concerned, in taking practical steps towards helping the Greek Cypriot and Turkish Cypriot leaders to exploit fully the current opportunity,

Taking note of the assessment of the Secretary-General that the security situation on the island and along the Green Line remains stable, and urging all sides to avoid any action which could lead to an increase in tension, undermine the progress achieved so far or damage the goodwill on the island,

Recalling the Secretary-General's firm belief that the situation in the buffer zone would be improved if both sides accepted the 1989 aide-memoire used by the United Nations,

Noting with regret that the sides are withholding access to the remaining minefields in the buffer zone and that demining in Cyprus has ceased as a result, noting the continued danger posed by mines in Cyprus, and urging rapid agreement on facilitating the recommencement of demining operations and clearance of the remaining minefields,

Highlighting the importance of the activities of the Committee on Missing Persons in Cyprus, urging the opening up of access to all areas to allow the Committee to carry out its work, and trusting that this process will promote reconciliation between the communities,

Agreeing that active participation of civil society groups, including women's groups, is essential to the political process and can contribute to making any future settlement sustainable, recalling that women play an important role in peace processes, welcoming all efforts to promote bicommunal contacts and events, including on the part of all United Nations bodies on the island, and urging the two sides to promote the active engagement of civil society and the encouragement of cooperation between economic and commercial bodies and to remove all obstacles to such contacts,

Stressing the need for the Council to pursue a rigorous, strategic approach to peacekeeping deployments,

Welcoming the intention of the Secretary-General to keep all peacekeeping operations, including those of the Force, under close review, and noting the importance of contingency planning in relation to the settlement, including recommendations, as appropriate, for further adjustments to the mandate, force levels and other resources and concept of operations of the Force, taking into account developments on the ground and the views of the parties,

Welcoming also the continued efforts of Mr. Alexander Downer as the Special Adviser to the Secretary-General on Cyprus with a mandate to assist the parties in the conduct of fully fledged negotiations aimed at reaching a comprehensive settlement, and the efforts of Ms. Lisa Buttenheim as the Special Representative of the Secretary-General in Cyprus,

Echoing the Secretary-General's gratitude to the Government of Cyprus and the Government of Greece for their voluntary contributions to the funding of the Force and his request for further voluntary contributions from other countries and organizations, and expressing its appreciation to Member States that contribute personnel to the Force,

Welcoming and encouraging efforts by the United Nations to sensitize peacekeeping personnel in the prevention and control of HIV/AIDS and other communicable diseases in all its peacekeeping operations,

1. *Welcomes* the encouraging progress made so far in the fully fledged negotiations and the prospect of further decisive progress in the coming months towards a comprehensive and durable settlement that this has created;

2. *Takes note* of the report of the Secretary-General of 8 August 2011;

3. *Recalls* Security Council resolution 1986(2011) of 13 June 2011, and calls upon the two leaders:

(a) To intensify the momentum of negotiations, engage in the process in a constructive and open manner and work on reaching convergences on the remaining core issues in preparation for their meeting with the Secretary-General in January 2012 and for further work in the following months towards a settlement;

(b) To improve the public atmosphere in which the negotiations are proceeding, including by focusing public messages on convergences and the way ahead and delivering more constructive and harmonized messages;

(c) To increase the participation of civil society in the process, as appropriate;

4. *Urges* the implementation of confidence-building measures, and looks forward to agreement on and implementation of further such steps, including military confidence-building measures and the opening of other crossing points;

5. *Urges* all parties to be more forthcoming in accommodating the exhumation requirements of the Committee on Missing Persons in Cyprus throughout the island, including in military areas in the north;

6. *Reaffirms* all its relevant resolutions on Cyprus, in particular resolution 1251(1999) of 29 June 1999 and subsequent resolutions;

7. *Expresses its full support* for the United Nations Peacekeeping Force in Cyprus, and decides to extend its mandate for a further period ending 19 July 2012;

8. *Calls upon* both sides to continue to engage, as a matter of urgency and while respecting the mandate of the Force, in consultations with the Force on the demarcation of the buffer zone and on the United Nations 1989 aide-memoire, with a view to reaching early agreement on outstanding issues;

9. *Calls upon* the Turkish Cypriot side and Turkish forces to restore in Strovilia the military status quo which existed there prior to 30 June 2000;

10. *Calls upon* both sides to allow access to deminers and to facilitate the removal of the remaining mines in Cyprus within the buffer zone, and urges both sides to extend demining operations outside the buffer zone;

11. *Requests* the Secretary-General to submit a report on the implementation of the present resolution, including on contingency planning in relation to the settlement, by 1 July 2012 and to keep the Council updated on events as necessary;

12. *Welcomes* the efforts being undertaken by the Force to implement the Secretary-General's zero-tolerance policy on sexual exploitation and abuse and to ensure full compliance of its personnel with the United Nations code of conduct, requests the Secretary-General to continue to take all necessary action in this regard and to keep the Council informed, and urges troop-contributing countries to take appropriate preventive action, including conducting predeployment awareness training, and to take disciplinary action and other action to ensure full accountability in cases of such conduct involving their personnel;

13. *Decides* to remain seized of the matter.

Financing

In June, the General Assembly considered the Secretary-General's report on UNFICYP financial performance for the period from 1 July 2009 to 30 June 2010 [A/65/625], the proposed UNFICYP budget for the period from 1 July 2011 to 30 June 2012 [A/65/706] and the related ACABQ report [A/65/743/Add.2].

GENERAL ASSEMBLY ACTION

On 30 June [meeting 106], the General Assembly, on the recommendation of the Fifth Committee [A/65/882], adopted **resolution 65/295** without vote [agenda item 146].

Financing of the United Nations Peacekeeping Force in Cyprus

The General Assembly,

Having considered the reports of the Secretary-General on the financing of the United Nations Peacekeeping Force in Cyprus and the related report of the Advisory Committee on Administrative and Budgetary Questions,

Recalling Security Council resolution 186(1964) of 4 March 1964, regarding the establishment of the United

Nations Peacekeeping Force in Cyprus, and the subsequent resolutions by which the Council extended the mandate of the Force, the latest of which was resolution 1986(2011) of 13 June 2011, by which the Council extended the mandate of the Force until 15 December 2011,

Recalling also its resolution 47/236 of 14 September 1993 on the financing of the Force and its subsequent resolutions and decisions thereon, the latest of which was resolution 64/274 of 24 June 2010,

Reaffirming the general principles underlying the financing of United Nations peacekeeping operations, as stated in General Assembly resolutions 1874(S-IV) of 27 June 1963, 3101(XXVIII) of 11 December 1973 and 55/235 of 23 December 2000,

Noting with appreciation that voluntary contributions have been made to the Force by certain Governments,

Noting that voluntary contributions were insufficient to cover all the costs of the Force, including those incurred by troop-contributing Governments prior to 16 June 1993, and regretting the absence of an adequate response to appeals for voluntary contributions, including that contained in the letter dated 17 May 1994 from the Secretary-General to all Member States,

Mindful of the fact that it is essential to provide the Force with the financial resources necessary to enable it to fulfil its responsibilities under the relevant resolutions of the Security Council,

1. *Requests* the Secretary-General to entrust the Head of Mission with the task of formulating future budget proposals in full accordance with the provisions of General Assembly resolutions 59/296 of 22 June 2005, 60/266 of 30 June 2006, 61/276 of 29 June 2007, 64/269 of 24 June 2010 and 65/289 of 30 June 2011, as well as other relevant resolutions;

2. *Takes note* of the status of contributions to the United Nations Peacekeeping Force in Cyprus as at 30 April 2011, including the contributions outstanding in the amount of 17.9 million United States dollars, representing some 4 per cent of the total assessed contributions, notes with concern that only forty-seven Member States have paid their assessed contributions in full, and urges all other Member States, in particular those in arrears, to ensure payment of their outstanding assessed contributions;

3. *Expresses its appreciation* to those Member States which have paid their assessed contributions in full, and urges all other Member States to make every possible effort to ensure payment of their assessed contributions to the Force in full;

4. *Expresses concern* at the delay experienced by the Secretary-General in deploying and providing adequate resources to some recent peacekeeping missions, in particular those in Africa;

5. *Emphasizes* that all future and existing peacekeeping missions shall be given equal and non-discriminatory treatment in respect of financial and administrative arrangements;

6. *Also emphasizes* that all peacekeeping missions shall be provided with adequate resources for the effective and efficient discharge of their respective mandates;

7. *Requests* the Secretary-General to ensure that proposed peacekeeping budgets are based on the relevant legislative mandates;

8. *Endorses* the conclusions and recommendations contained in the report of the Advisory Committee on Administrative and Budgetary Questions, subject to the provisions of the present resolution, and requests the Secretary-General to ensure their full implementation;

9. *Notes* the progress that has been made thus far by the host Government and the Force with respect to the renovation of the accommodations for military contingent personnel, as well as other personnel of the Force, and requests the Secretary-General to continue to make every effort, in coordination with the host Government, to ensure that the renovations are completed as scheduled, without any further delays, and to report thereon in the context of the next budget submission;

10. *Requests* the Secretary-General to ensure the full implementation of the relevant provisions of resolutions 59/296, 60/266, 61/276, 64/269 and 65/289;

11. *Also requests* the Secretary-General to take all action necessary to ensure that the Force is administered with a maximum of efficiency and economy;

12. *Further requests* the Secretary-General to ensure accurate planning of flight hours, in order to avoid underexpenditure due to the lower number of actual flight hours compared to the planned hours;

13. *Notes* that the overall level of appropriation has been adjusted in accordance with the terms of resolution 65/289;

Financial performance report for the period from 1 July 2009 to 30 June 2010

14. *Takes note* of the report of the Secretary-General on the financial performance of the Force for the period from 1 July 2009 to 30 June 2010;

Budget estimates for the period from 1 July 2011 to 30 June 2012

15. *Decides* to appropriate to the Special Account for the United Nations Peacekeeping Force in Cyprus the amount of 60,121,200 dollars for the period from 1 July 2011 to 30 June 2012, inclusive of 56,512,000 dollars for the maintenance of the Force, 3,058,400 dollars for the support account for peacekeeping operations and 550,800 dollars for the United Nations Logistics Base, at Brindisi, Italy;

Financing of the appropriation

16. *Notes with appreciation* that a one-third share of the net appropriation, equivalent to 19,114,267 dollars, will be funded through voluntary contributions from the Government of Cyprus and the amount of 6.5 million dollars from the Government of Greece;

17. *Decides* to apportion among Member States the amount of 34,506,933 dollars at a monthly rate of 2,875,578 dollars, in accordance with the levels updated in General Assembly resolution 64/249 of 24 December 2009, and taking into account the scale of assessments for 2011 and 2012, as set out in Assembly resolution 64/248 of 24 December 2009, subject to a decision of the Security Council to extend the mandate of the Force;

18. *Also decides* that, in accordance with the provisions of its resolution 973(X) of 15 December 1955, there shall be set off against the apportionment among Member States, as provided for in paragraph 17 above, their respective share in the Tax Equalization Fund of 2,721,000 dollars, comprising the estimated staff assessment income of 2,404,200 dollars approved for the Force, the prorated share of 259,000

dollars of the estimated staff assessment income approved for the support account and the prorated share of 57,800 dollars of the estimated staff assessment income approved for the United Nations Logistics Base;

19. *Further decides* that, for Member States that have fulfilled their financial obligations to the Force, there shall be set off against the apportionment, as provided for in paragraph 17 above, their respective share of the unencumbered balance and other income in the amount of 1,361,709 dollars in respect of the financial period ended 30 June 2010, in accordance with the levels updated in General Assembly resolution 64/249, and taking into account the scale of assessments for 2010, as set out in Assembly resolution 64/248;

20. *Decides* that, for Member States that have not fulfilled their financial obligations to the Force, there shall be set off against their outstanding obligations their respective share of the unencumbered balance and other income in the amount of 1,361,709 dollars in respect of the financial period ended 30 June 2010, in accordance with the scheme set out in paragraph 19 above;

21. *Also decides* that the increase of 255,600 dollars in the estimated staff assessment income in respect of the financial period ended 30 June 2010 shall be added to the credits from the amount of 1,361,709 dollars referred to in paragraphs 19 and 20 above;

22. *Further decides*, taking into account its voluntary contribution for the financial period ended 30 June 2010, that one third of the unencumbered balance and other income in the amount of 828,604 dollars in respect of the financial period ended 30 June 2010 shall be returned to the Government of Cyprus;

23. *Decides*, taking into account its voluntary contribution for the financial period ended 30 June 2010, that the prorated share of other income in the amount of 297,987 dollars in respect of the financial period ended 30 June 2010 shall be returned to the Government of Greece;

24. *Also decides* to continue to maintain as separate the account established for the Force for the period prior to 16 June 1993, invites Member States to make voluntary contributions to that account, and requests the Secretary-General to continue his efforts in appealing for voluntary contributions to the account;

25. *Emphasizes* that no peacekeeping mission shall be financed by borrowing funds from other active peacekeeping missions;

26. *Encourages* the Secretary-General to continue to take additional measures to ensure the safety and security of all personnel participating in the Force under the auspices of the United Nations, bearing in mind paragraphs 5 and 6 of Security Council resolution 1502(2003) of 26 August 2003;

27. *Invites* voluntary contributions to the Force in cash and in the form of services and supplies acceptable to the Secretary-General, to be administered, as appropriate, in accordance with the procedure and practices established by the General Assembly;

28. *Decides* to include in the provisional agenda of its sixty-sixth session the item entitled "Financing of the United Nations Peacekeeping Force in Cyprus".

On 24 December, the General Assembly decided that the agenda item on UNFICYP financing would remain for consideration at its resumed sixty-sixth (2012) session (**decision 66/557**).

Other issues

Strengthening of security and cooperation in the Mediterranean

In response to General Assembly resolution 65/90 [YUN 2010, p. 431], the Secretary-General submitted a July report [A/66/122] containing replies received from Iraq, Jordan, Lebanon, the Netherlands and Spain to his 11 April note requesting the views of States on ways to strengthen security and cooperation in the Mediterranean region.

GENERAL ASSEMBLY ACTION

On 2 December [meeting 71], the General Assembly, on the recommendation of the First (Disarmament and International Security) Committee [A/66/417], adopted **resolution 66/63** without vote [agenda item 103].

Strengthening of security and cooperation in the Mediterranean region

The General Assembly,

Recalling its previous resolutions on the subject, including resolution 65/90 of 8 December 2010,

Reaffirming the primary role of the Mediterranean countries in strengthening and promoting peace, security and cooperation in the Mediterranean region,

Welcoming the efforts deployed by the Euro-Mediterranean countries to strengthen their cooperation in combating terrorism, in particular through the adoption of the Euro-Mediterranean Code of Conduct on Countering Terrorism by the Euro-Mediterranean Summit, held in Barcelona, Spain, on 27 and 28 November 2005,

Bearing in mind all the previous declarations and commitments, as well as all the initiatives taken by the riparian countries at the recent summits, ministerial meetings and various forums concerning the question of the Mediterranean region,

Recalling, in this regard, the adoption on 13 July 2008 of the Joint Declaration of the Paris Summit for the Mediterranean, which launched a reinforced partnership, named the "Barcelona Process: Union for the Mediterranean", and the common political will to revive efforts to transform the Mediterranean into an area of peace, democracy, cooperation and prosperity,

Welcoming the entry into force of the African Nuclear-Weapon-Free Zone Treaty (Treaty of Pelindaba) as a contribution to the strengthening of peace and security both regionally and internationally,

Recognizing the indivisible character of security in the Mediterranean and that the enhancement of cooperation among Mediterranean countries with a view to promoting the economic and social development of all peoples of the region will contribute significantly to stability, peace and security in the region,

Recognizing also the efforts made so far and the determination of the Mediterranean countries to intensify the process of dialogue and consultations with a view to resolving the problems existing in the Mediterranean region and to eliminating the causes of tension and the consequent threat to peace and security, as well as their growing awareness of the need for further joint efforts to strengthen economic, social, cultural and environmental cooperation in the region,

Recognizing further that prospects for closer Euro-Mediterranean cooperation in all spheres can be enhanced by positive developments worldwide, in particular in Europe, in the Maghreb and in the Middle East,

Reaffirming the responsibility of all States to contribute to the stability and prosperity of the Mediterranean region and their commitment to respecting the purposes and principles of the Charter of the United Nations as well as the provisions of the Declaration on Principles of International Law concerning Friendly Relations and Cooperation among States in accordance with the Charter of the United Nations,

Noting the peace negotiations in the Middle East, which should be of a comprehensive nature and represent an appropriate framework for the peaceful settlement of contentious issues in the region,

Expressing its concern at the persistent tension and continuing military activities in parts of the Mediterranean that hinder efforts to strengthen security and cooperation in the region,

Taking note of the report of the Secretary-General,

1. *Reaffirms* that security in the Mediterranean is closely linked to European security as well as to international peace and security;

2. *Expresses its satisfaction* at the continuing efforts by Mediterranean countries to contribute actively to the elimination of all causes of tension in the region and to the promotion of just and lasting solutions to the persistent problems of the region through peaceful means, thus ensuring the withdrawal of foreign forces of occupation and respecting the sovereignty, independence and territorial integrity of all countries of the Mediterranean and the right of peoples to self-determination, and therefore calls for full adherence to the principles of non-interference, non-intervention, non-use of force or threat of use of force and the inadmissibility of the acquisition of territory by force, in accordance with the Charter and the relevant resolutions of the United Nations;

3. *Commends* the Mediterranean countries for their efforts in meeting common challenges through coordinated overall responses, based on a spirit of multilateral partnership, towards the general objective of turning the Mediterranean basin into an area of dialogue, exchanges and cooperation, guaranteeing peace, stability and prosperity, encourages them to strengthen such efforts through, inter alia, a lasting multilateral and action-oriented cooperative dialogue among States of the region, and recognizes the role of the United Nations in promoting regional and international peace and security;

4. *Recognizes* that the elimination of the economic and social disparities in levels of development and other obstacles, as well as respect and greater understanding among cultures in the Mediterranean area, will contribute to enhancing peace, security and cooperation among Mediterranean countries through the existing forums;

5. *Calls upon* all States of the Mediterranean region that have not yet done so to adhere to all the multilaterally negotiated legal instruments related to the field of disarmament and non-proliferation, thus creating the conditions necessary for strengthening peace and cooperation in the region;

6. *Encourages* all States of the region to favour the conditions necessary for strengthening the confidence-building measures among them by promoting genuine openness and transparency on all military matters, by participating, inter alia, in the United Nations system for the standardized reporting of military expenditures and by providing accurate data and information to the United Nations Register of Conventional Arms;

7. *Encourages* the Mediterranean countries to strengthen further their cooperation in combating terrorism in all its forms and manifestations, including the possible resort by terrorists to weapons of mass destruction, taking into account the relevant resolutions of the United Nations, and in combating international crime and illicit arms transfers and illicit drug production, consumption and trafficking, which pose a serious threat to peace, security and stability in the region and therefore to the improvement of the current political, economic and social situation and which jeopardize friendly relations among States, hinder the development of international cooperation and result in the destruction of human rights, fundamental freedoms and the democratic basis of pluralistic society;

8. *Requests* the Secretary-General to submit a report on means to strengthen security and cooperation in the Mediterranean region;

9. *Decides* to include in the provisional agenda of its sixty-seventh session the item entitled "Strengthening of security and cooperation in the Mediterranean region".

Organization for Democracy and Economic Development

The Organization for Democracy and Economic Development-GUAM (Georgia, Ukraine, Azerbaijan, Republic of Moldova), a regional cooperation organization established by the 2006 Kyiv Declaration [YUN 2006, p. 486], was headquartered in Kyiv, Ukraine. On the issue of conflict settlement, GUAM emphasized respect for sovereignty, territorial integrity and the inviolability of the internationally recognized borders of its member States.

On 24 December, the General Assembly decided that the agenda item on the protracted conflicts in the GUAM area and their implications for international peace, security and development would remain for consideration at its resumed sixty-sixth (2012) session (**decision 66/557**).

Chapter VI

Middle East

In 2011, the United Nations worked to restart talks between the Israelis and the Palestinians with a view to reaching a final settlement under which two States—Israel and Palestine—would exist side by side in peace. The peace effort remained stalled, however, due to several factors, including Israel's continued blockade of Gaza on both land and sea; indiscriminate rocket and mortar fire directed against Israel by Hamas, the ruling political party in Gaza, followed by retaliatory Israeli airstrikes in the Occupied Palestinian Territory; renewed Israeli settlement building and settler violence; and the confiscation of land and destruction of Palestinian property by Israelis in the West Bank. The United Nations considered Palestinian Authority (pa) functions in several areas to be sufficient for a viable State government. The two main political parties of Palestine—Fatah and Hamas—signed a unity agreement to work together in bringing a unified Palestinian State to fruition, but ultimately could not agree on several concessions.

On 23 September, Palestine applied for United Nations membership. The Organization took no action with regard to Palestine's application, but the United Nations Educational, Scientific and Cultural Organization granted Palestine full membership in October. Consequently, the United States and Israel cut certain sectors of aid to Palestine.

The Quartet—a coordinating mechanism for international peace efforts, comprising the European Union, the Russian Federation, the United States and the United Nations—met several times over the year. On 23 September, it proposed a timed framework to restart the peace talks between the Palestinians and the Israelis. The plan included an agreed agenda and method of procedure; comprehensive proposals on territory and security; and a donors' conference to appeal for sustained support to the Palestinians' State-building actions.

On 18 October, Hamas released Israeli Sergeant Gilad Shalit, who had been held in Gaza without international access since 2006, in exchange for 477 Palestinian prisoners—many of whom had been jailed for involvement in attacks on Israelis. The Secretary-General called Shalit's release and the freeing of Palestinian prisoners a humanitarian breakthrough.

The Security Council held 19 meetings throughout the year on the situation in the Middle East, including the Palestinian question. The panel investigating the May 2010 flotilla incident submitted to the Council a final report, which questioned the true objectives of the flotilla organizers and acknowledged the threat to Israel's security from militant groups in Gaza. The decision of the Israel Defense Forces to board the vessels far from the blockade zone, however, was deemed excessive, as was its mistreatment of passengers before they were deported.

The United Nations Relief and Works Agency for Palestine Refugees in the Near East faced further challenges due to the displacement of people as a result of the political and social unrest that occurred in parts of the Middle East and North Africa. The Agency addressed the needs of refugees across the region, including Syrian refugees in Lebanon, who had fled Government suppression of popular uprisings, but budget shortfalls prevented it from meeting the increased demand for its services.

In Lebanon, the Government of National Unity collapsed in January. The absence of political authority in the months that followed led to institutional paralysis and a deterioration of security conditions. In June, the Prime Minister-Designate announced the formation of a new Government, which won a vote of confidence in July. The Special Tribunal established to investigate and prosecute the perpetrators of the 2005 assassination of former Lebanese Prime Minister Rafiq Hariri indicted four suspects in the attack and ruled in favour of a trial in absentia. In August, the mandate of United Nations Interim Force in Lebanon (unifil) was renewed for one year. Unifil withstood three direct terrorist attacks in 2011.

Anti-Government demonstrations in the Syrian Arab Republic began in March and increased steadily in geographic scope and size. Dissidents called for the downfall of the regime, echoing slogans heard across the region. The Syrian authorities reacted with a mix of reform measures and progressively more violent repression, which the Secretary-General condemned. In an August presidential statement, the Security Council also condemned violations of human rights and the use of force against civilians by the Syrian authorities; it called for an end to violence and urged all sides to act with restraint and refrain from reprisals. The Secretary-General also urged President Bashar Al-Assad to end the military campaign against the Syrian people and to engage in meaningful reform. Syrian security forces, however, continued to clash with protesters. The resulting death toll eventually surpassed 3,000 people on both sides.

The mandate of the United Nations Disengagement Observer Force (UNDOF) in the Golan Heights was renewed twice in 2011. The United Nations Truce Supervision Organization continued to assist UNIFIL and UNDOF by providing unarmed military observers to supervise armistice agreements, ceasefires and related tasks.

Peace process

Diplomatic efforts

In 2011, the United Nations worked to create conditions conducive to a resumption of talks between Israel and the Palestinian Authority (PA), to be followed by formal negotiations on a two-State solution. The PA, led by President Mahmoud Abbas, pursued a vigorous agenda of State-building and closely consulted with Egypt to forge a coalition agreement among its political factions, including Fatah and Hamas, which controlled Gaza. The accord failed to achieve a plan for a cohesive government, thus preventing national elections and weakening Israel's confidence in the process. Nevertheless, Palestine submitted its application for UN membership in September. In October, the United Nations Educational, Scientific and Cultural Organization (UNESCO) granted Palestine full membership. Consequently, the United States and Israel cut certain sectors of aid to Palestine. Ultimately, continued rocket and mortar fire emanating from militants in Gaza, the naval and land blockade imposed by Israel, increased settler violence in the West Bank and other incidents reduced the prospects for peace. At year's end, the parties stood further away from a solution, despite significant efforts by the Quartet—a coordinating mechanism for international peace efforts, comprising the Russian Federation, the United States, the European Union (EU) and the United Nations—and the Arab Peace Initiative [YUN 2002, p. 419]. Although the Palestinian economy experienced an increase in gross domestic product, it continued to rely heavily on aid and the illegal "tunnel economy".

The Security Council discussed the situation in the Middle East, some also including the Palestinian question, at meetings held on 19 January [S/PV.6470], 18 February [S/PV.6484], 24 February [S/PV.6488], 22 March [S/PV.6501], 21 April [S/PV.6520], 27 April [S/PV.6524], 19 May [S/PV.6540], 23 June [S/PV.6562], 30 June [S/PV.6572], 26 July [S/PV.6590], 3 August [S/PV.6598], 25 August [S/PV.6602], 30 August [S/PV.6605], 27 September [S/PV.6623], 4 October [S/PV.6627], 24 October [S/PV.6636], 21 November [S/PV.6662], 20 December [S/PV.6692] and 21 December [S/PV.6693].

Five communications dealing with Council meeting participation were issued during the year: 17 January [S/2011/23], 18 February [S/2011/79], 18 April [S/2011/259], 21 July [S/2011/444] and 20 October [S/2011/653].

Occupied Palestinian Territory

Political and security developments

Communications. On 7 January [A/ES-10/508-S/2011/6], the PA, in identical letters addressed to the Secretary-General and the Security Council President, expressed concern over the killings of three Palestinian civilians by Israeli forces in the Occupied Palestinian Territory: a 35-year-old woman died after inhaling tear gas during a peaceful demonstration on 1 January; a 25-year-old man was killed at a military checkpoint in the West Bank on 2 January; and a 66-year-old man was killed in a raid against a home on 7 January.

In a 13 January letter [A/65/692-S/2011/51], Guyana informed the Secretary-General that it formally recognized the State of Palestine.

Security Council consideration. On 19 January [S/PV.6470], the Under-Secretary-General for Political Affairs, B. Lynn Pascoe, briefed the Council on the situation in the Middle East. He reported that the Israeli-Palestinian negotiations remained at a deadlock. The Office of the Secretary-General supported the efforts of the United States to engage in substantive parallel talks with the parties. The United States Special Envoy to the Middle East, George Mitchell, visited the region in December 2010, and Israeli and Palestinian negotiators held separate consultations with the United States in Washington, D.C., in January 2011. The continued Israeli search operations in the West Bank undermined the PA, however, in opposition to the strategic goal. All parties needed to refrain from targeting or endangering civilians and cease acts of violence.

Communication. On 1 February [S/2011/49], Israel, in identical letters addressed to the Secretary-General and the Security Council President, brought to their attention a 31 January incident in which three long-range rockets launched from Gaza exploded in southern Israel near the cities of Netivot and Ofakim, and in the area of Eshkol. In response to the attacks, Israel would exercise its right to self-defence and take all necessary measures to protect its citizens.

Quartet meeting. On 5 February [SG/2168], the Quartet—including the Secretary-General, Russian Foreign Minister Sergey Lavrov, United States Secretary of State Hillary Rodham Clinton, United States Special Envoy George Mitchell, EU High Representative for Foreign Affairs and Security Policy Catherine Ashton and Quartet Representative Tony Blair—urged Palestine and Israel to overcome obstacles in their own countries to bring about renewed talks. It reaffirmed that negotiations should lead to an outcome that ended the occupation that began in 1967 and resolved all permanent status issues to achieve a two-State solution. The Quartet reiterated its support for concluding the negotiations by September. It would seek to meet separately with Israeli and Palestinian negotiators in Brussels, Belgium, as well as with representatives of the Arab Peace Initiative Committee, and would consider their views on how to resume negotiations on all core issues, including borders and security. The Quartet considered the implications on the Arab-Israeli peace process of the recent developments in Egypt and elsewhere in the region, and agreed to discuss the issue further in upcoming meetings.

The Quartet encouraged the full implementation of the package of measures announced by Israeli Prime Minister Benjamin Netanyahu and Mr. Blair for the West Bank and Gaza. It regretted the discontinuation of Israel's 10-month moratorium on settlement activity. It reaffirmed that unilateral actions by either party could not prejudge the outcome of negotiations and would not be recognized by the international community. The Quartet condemned rocket fire from Gaza and stressed the need for calm and security for both peoples. It believed that further delay in the resumption of talks was detrimental to prospects for regional peace and security.

Communications. On 9 February [S/2011/65], Israel, in identical letters addressed to the Secretary-General and the Security Council President, detailed an attack from Gaza on 8 February, in which four mortars struck the area of Sha'ar Hanegev in southern Israel.

On 23 February [S/2011/90], Israel, in identical letters to the Secretary-General and the Council President, stated that earlier that day a Grad-type rocket had been launched towards Be'er Sheva, the largest city in southern Israel. The rocket exploded in the backyard of a house and wounded 10 civilians. The attack followed the launching of three mortars towards a kibbutz in the Sha'ar Hanegev Regional Council and the detonation of an explosive aimed at Israel Defense Forces (IDF) personnel performing routine activity near the security fence in northern Gaza.

Security Council consideration. On 24 February [S/PV.6488], the Special Coordinator for the Middle East Peace Process and Personal Representative of the Secretary-General, Robert Serry, briefed the Council. He said that shifting regional dynamics added uncertainty to the Middle East peace process; progress towards a negotiated solution would contribute to stabilizing the region. There was low confidence and trust among the parties involved in the peace talks, however, as well as in international efforts to help them overcome their differences.

Israel continued to build 2,000 units in the West Bank after the moratorium expired on 26 September 2010. The Special Coordinator said that Israel needed to adhere to the call of the international community, the provisions of international law and the road map to a permanent two-State solution [YUN 2003, p. 464] by freezing all settlement activity, including in East Jerusalem.

The PA advanced its State-building agenda; its established institutions represented the basis of a "State-in-waiting". On 4 February, Prime Minister Netanyahu and Quartet Representative Blair agreed on a package of measures designed to help improve Palestinian livelihoods and support economic growth in the West Bank and Gaza; it was imperative that the measures be implemented in full. On 14 February, Palestinian Prime Minister Salam Fayyad submitted his Government's resignation, and President Abbas tasked him with forming a new Government. The Special Coordinator noted the Prime Minister's suggestion to form a Government of national unity based on non-violence as a first step towards advancing reconciliation between Palestinian factions. It was critical that the donor community support the PA and the reform agenda, even though the PA had halved its dependence on budgetary assistance since 2008.

Communications. On 24 February [A/65/766-S/2011/103], the Russian Federation and the EU issued a joint statement on the situation in North Africa and the Middle East. They stressed that current upheavals in the region should not be used as a pretext for maintaining an impasse in efforts to establish peace in the Middle East; on the contrary, such efforts should be intensified. The achievement of a just settlement of the Arab-Israeli conflict was an important component of efforts aimed at stabilization and sustainable development of the region as a whole. Russia and the EU would seek, at the next Quartet ministerial meeting, the adoption of effective decisions encouraging the resumption of Palestinian-Israeli dialogue to open the way to a comprehensive settlement. They reaffirmed their support for efforts to re-establish Palestinian unity on the basis of principles enshrined in the Arab Peace Initiative.

On 12 March [S/2011/136], Israel transmitted identical letters to the Secretary-General and the Council President expressing concern over the killing of a family of five, including two young children and a baby, in the Israeli community of Itamar by terrorists on 11 March. Israel expected the PA to cooperate with Israel in apprehending those responsible for the attack and take action to prevent such crimes from occurring in the future.

Quartet statement. On 14 March [SG/2172], the Quartet condemned the murder that day of an Israeli family of five, including three small children, in the West Bank. It welcomed President Abbas' condemnation of the killings and called for those responsible to be brought to justice.

Communications. On 18 March [S/2011/148], Israel, in identical letters addressed to the Secretary-General and the Security Council President, stated that on 15 March, approximately 40 tons of weaponry were found aboard the cargo vessel *Victoria*, sailing to Egypt from the port of Mersin, Turkey, flying the flag of Liberia. Among the ship's cargo were three containers carrying advanced C-704 anti-ship missiles and their launchers, radar and fire control systems, mortar shells and munitions originating from Iran. The attempt to transfer weaponry from Iran to terrorist organizations in Gaza constituted a violation of several Council resolutions, including resolutions 1373(2001) [YUN 2001, p. 61], 1747(2007) [YUN 2007, p. 374] and 1860(2009) [YUN 2009, p. 434].

On 19 March [S/2011/162], Israel, in identical letters to the Secretary-General and the Council President, stated that approximately 50 mortars were fired from Gaza into southern Israel that day. The attacks, for which Hamas claimed responsibility, represented an unprecedented increase in projectile fire emanating from Gaza since the end of Israel's Operation Cast Lead in 2009 [YUN 2009, p. 434].

Security Council consideration. On 22 March [S/PV.6501], the Assistant Secretary-General for Political Affairs, Oscar Fernandez-Taranco, briefed the Council on the situation in the Middle East. Violent incidents and tensions had increased since February, and there was a lack of results in efforts to restart the Israeli-Palestinian negotiations. As agreed on 5 February (see p. 403), Quartet envoys had met separately with Palestinian and Israeli negotiators, and were considering the views of the parties on renewing talks on all core issues, including borders and security.

Israel deployed forces in several areas throughout the West Bank to detain the perpetrators of the 11 March murder of an Israeli family in Itamar (see p. 404) and to contain attempts by Israeli settlers to attack Palestinians and their property in reprisal. The Office for the Coordination of Humanitarian Affairs recorded 8 incidents that resulted in injuries to Palestinians and 23 that caused damage to their property. Israeli forces reinstated the Hawwara checkpoint near Nablus and conducted 320 search operations in the West Bank.

On 7 March, Israel announced its intention to demolish all illegal West Bank outposts built on private Palestinian land by the end of 2011. The declaration failed to address the existence of more than 100 other West Bank outposts constructed in violation of international law and Israel's own regulations on settlement building. On 12 March, Israel approved the construction of about 400 housing units in the West Bank as a reaction to the Itamar murders.

On 15 March, demonstrations involving more than 100,000 people calling for an end to the Israeli occupation and the Palestinian political divide took place in most major West Bank cities and in Gaza. Hamas security forces quashed the protests, and the following day suppressed a student gathering, causing several injuries. On 19 March, Hamas forces stormed the bureaux of several international news agencies, attacking journalists, confiscating tapes and destroying equipment.

Despite difficulties, preparations for municipal elections continued. The Palestinian Central Elections Committee organized voter registration in the West Bank from 9 to 15 March, although it could not open offices in Gaza due to Hamas control. President Abbas on 8 March confirmed that local elections scheduled for 9 July would take place on time, but presidential and legislative elections would not be held unless the West Bank and Gaza participated simultaneously.

Communications. On 23 March [S/2011/176], in identical letters to the Secretary-General and the Council President, Israel stated that a bomb planted by terrorists exploded at a bus stop outside the International Convention Centre in Jerusalem, killing one woman and injuring more than 40 people. In the previous week, Israel had been the target of 63 mortar shells and four rockets launched from Gaza, for which it held Hamas responsible.

On 7 April [S/2011/227], Israel stated that a school bus travelling near Kibbutz Sa'ad in southern Israel was struck and destroyed by a Kornet anti-tank missile fired from Gaza. Two civilians were wounded during the attack: a 16-year-old boy and the bus driver. The strike was part of a barrage of some 45 mortars and Qassam rockets fired from Gaza into communities in southern Israel. On 10 April [S/2011/231], Israel said that since the 7 April incident, terrorist organizations in Gaza had fired approximately 131 projectiles, including 12 Grad missiles, 70 Qassam rockets and 49 mortars, at communities in southern Israel.

On 8 April [A/ES-10/516-S/2011/229], Palestine, in identical letters addressed to the Secretary-General and the Security Council President, stated that a series of Israeli air strikes and artillery fire against Gaza had killed 13 Palestinians and injured a number of others over the previous 24 hours. The Palestinian leadership appealed to the international community to call on Israel to cease its attacks against Gaza.

Security Council consideration. The Under-Secretary-General for Political Affairs, briefing the Security Council on 21 April [S/PV.6520], said that both parties in the Israeli-Palestinian peace process should be concerned that the political track was falling behind the significant progress made by the PA in its State-building agenda. The United Nations made clear in its 13 April report to the Ad Hoc Liaison Committee for the Coordination of the International Assistance to Palestinians that in the six areas in which it was most engaged with the PA, governmental functions were sufficient for a viable State. The six areas comprised governance, rule of law and human rights; livelihoods and productive sectors; education and culture; health; social protection; and infrastructure and water. The World Bank and the International Monetary Fund also reported strong progress in institution-building. Those achievements, however, remained limited to certain areas of the Occupied Palestinian Territory and did not apply to East Jerusalem, Area C or Gaza.

During the reporting period, Gaza and Israel had witnessed the highest levels of violence since the end of Operation Cast Lead [YUN 2009, p. 434]. The United Nations was alarmed over Hamas' actions to escalate violence, which endangered civilians on both sides and risked a deeper confrontation with Israel. The Secretary-General condemned the firing of rockets from Gaza and called for its cessation. He reiterated his calls for maximum restraint by Israel, and stated that Israel's closure of the Kerem Shalom crossing point to Gaza illustrated the detrimental effects of the violence on the humanitarian situation. Two suspects from the Palestinian village of Awarta were arrested for allegedly perpetrating the murder of the Israeli family in Itamar on 11 March, and a number of others were arrested as alleged accomplices.

Communications. On 2 May [A/ES-10/517-S/2011/280], Palestine submitted identical letters to the Secretary-General and the Council President, stating that on 1 May, the Israeli Minister of Finance declared the suspension of the transfer of taxes collected by Israel on behalf of the PA. Israeli officials claimed that the measure was taken in response to the announcement of an agreement regarding Palestinian unity and reconciliation. Palestine said that the suspension of tax revenues and other levies owed to the PA constituted an act of piracy and would have detrimental consequences for the Palestinian civilian population.

On 16 May [A/ES-10/519-S/2011/308], Palestine informed the Secretary-General and the Council that on 15 May, thousands of Palestinian civilians in the Occupied Palestinian Territory and elsewhere in the region participated in peaceful demonstrations on the anniversary of Al-Nakba, the dispossession and uprooting of more than 750,000 Palestinians from their homes and land in 1948, calling for an end to the Israeli occupation of Palestinian land. Israeli security forces responded to demonstrations in the Occupied Palestinian Territory, the southern Lebanese town of Maroun al-Ras (see p. 459) and the town of Majdal Shams in the occupied Syrian Golan (see p. 474) with excessive force, firing tear gas, rubber bullets, stun grenades and live ammunition at unarmed protesters. At least 17 civilians were killed, including children, and more than 300 were wounded, the majority of whom were Palestine refugees. At the same time, Israel carried out air raids in the Beit Hanoun area of Gaza.

On 19 May [S/2011/322], Israel, in identical letters to the Secretary-General and the Security Council President, stated that on 16 May a Malaysian-owned ship, *MV Finch*, sailing under the Moldovan flag, challenged Israel's naval blockade of Gaza. The action was sponsored by the Perdana Global Peace Foundation (PGPF), an organization that had made previous attempts to violate the blockade, including participation in the 2010 flotilla incident [YUN 2010, p. 439]. According to PGPF, the ship was carrying 12 people and 7.5 kilometres of sewerage pipe, which were to be delivered to Gaza. IDF rerouted the vessel to the Port of El Arish in Egypt. Israel said that the attempt to violate the blockade was designed to serve a political agenda, not to advance a humanitarian goal.

Security Council consideration. On 19 May [S/PV.6540], the Special Coordinator for the Middle East Peace Process and Personal Representative of the Secretary-General briefed the Council on two significant events: the conclusion in April, under Egyptian auspices, of a reconciliation accord between Palestinian factions; and clashes in May between Israeli security forces and Palestinians in Lebanon, Syria and the Occupied Palestinian Territory during the largest demonstration of Palestinians in many years. In the absence of negotiations and amid continued Israeli settlement expansion, the PA was preparing to approach the United Nations in September to seek recognition of a Palestinian State. Egypt and the United Nations had assisted in securing relative calm between Israel and Gaza, and security cooperation and performance had been sustained in the West Bank.

An accord unifying the factions of Palestinian leadership was signed by Fatah, Hamas and other groups on 4 May in Cairo. Under the accord, the Prime Minister and other cabinet ministers would agree to a Government of national technocrats. The Government would prepare for simultaneous elections for the Palestinian Legislative Council, the presidency and the Palestinian National Council, organized and overseen by reformed electoral institutions. During the transitional period, the Government would re-unify Palestinian institutions and follow up on Gaza reconstruction. President Abbas had reiterated his commitment to the platform of the Palestine Liberation Organization (PLO), which had accepted resolutions 242(1967) [YUN 1967, p. 257] and 338(1973) [YUN 1973, p. 213], recognized Israel's right to exist in peace and security and renounced violence and terrorism. The accord also envisaged the reform of Palestinian security forces on a national and professional basis, as well as the establishment of a security committee, with the participation of Egypt.

Some statements made by Hamas suggested that the faction was ready, within the framework of the accord, to submit to national decisions on issues on which it maintained extreme positions. Other statements called on the PLO to renounce its recognition of Israel and stressed that the movement's sole programme was resistance. Nevertheless, the reunification of Gaza and the West Bank remained a vital goal for all interested in peace. The Secretary-General called on all Governments concerned to discourage flotillas bound for Gaza, which could escalate the situation.

Quartet statement. On 20 May [SG/2174], the Quartet expressed its support for the vision of Israeli-Palestinian peace outlined by United States President Barack Obama on 19 May, in which negotiations would result in two States with permanent borders based on the 1967 lines with mutually agreed swaps. Security arrangements should be robust enough to prevent a resurgence of terrorism; stop the infiltration of weapons and provide border security; and allow a phased withdrawal of Israeli military forces coordinated with the assumption of Palestinian security responsibility in a sovereign, non-militarized State. The Quartet agreed that moving forward on the basis of territory and security provided a foundation for Israelis and Palestinians to reach a final resolution of the conflict.

Communications. In an 8 June letter to the Secretary-General [S/2011/357], Malaysia, responding to Israel's 19 May letter (see p. 406), stated that PGPF had organized a humanitarian mission to deliver pipes to help restore the sewerage system in Gaza. The vessel carrying the supplies, registered as *MV Finch*, was attacked by IDF when it reached Palestinian territorial waters on 16 May.

On 6 June [A/ES-10/521-S/2011/343], Palestine, in identical letters to the Secretary-General and the Council President, stated that on 5 June Palestinian civilians in the Occupied Palestinian Territory protesting the Israeli occupation were fired at with tear gas, sound bombs and rubber bullets as they approached a military checkpoint in the Qalandiya area between Ramallah and Jerusalem. It was reported that at least 120 civilians were injured. In the occupied Syrian Golan, Israeli forces killed 23 unarmed Palestinian civilians and injured dozens more in a confrontation during a protest near the town of Majdal Shams (see p. 474). The demonstrations marked the forty-fourth year of Israel's military occupation of the Territory, including East Jerusalem.

On 21 June [S/2011/378], Israel, in identical letters to the Secretary-General and the Council President, stated that a group of non-governmental organizations (NGOs) was planning to challenge Israel's naval blockade of Gaza with a flotilla of ships. Reports indicated that the ships were to set sail from several ports in Europe and elsewhere, and would arrive in the vicinity of Gaza around 25 or 26 June.

Security Council consideration. On 23 June [S/PV.6562], the Under-Secretary-General for Political Affairs, briefing the Security Council on the situation in the Middle East, said that the Israeli-Palestinian political process remained at a dangerous standstill; the resumption of meaningful negotiations had become urgent. Fatah and Hamas continued to meet under Egyptian auspices to discuss implementation of the 4 May reconciliation accord, but the parties had not reached consensus on the composition of the proposed Government.

Quartet statement. On 5 July [SG/2175], the Quartet expressed its concern about the unsustainable conditions facing the civilian population in Gaza, but also noted that, over the previous year, there had been a marked increase in international project activity, as well as the facilitation of some exports. The Quartet commended Israel's recent approval of materials for the construction of new homes and schools by the United Nations Relief and Works Agency for Palestine Refugees in the Near East, but more needed to be done to increase the flow of people and goods to and from Gaza, including a liberalization of the market in aggregate, steel bar and cement. The Quartet recognized that Israel had legitimate security concerns, and was committed to working with Israel, Egypt and the international community to prevent the illicit trafficking of arms and ammunition into Gaza. The Quartet urged those wishing to deliver goods to the people of Gaza to do so through established land channels to allow for the inspection of cargo. It called on all Governments concerned to discourage humanitarian flotillas, which risked the safety of their participants and carried the potential for incitement. The Quartet also called for an end to the five-year detention of Israeli Staff Sergeant Gilad Shalit, who had been taken prisoner in 2006 [YUN 2006, p. 510].

Communications. On 14 July [S/2011/430], Israel, in identical letters to the Secretary-General and the Security Council President, stated that, since 16 June, terrorists in Gaza had launched more than 15 rockets and mortars into southern Israel, including six attacks in the previous five days. Israel held Hamas responsible for the attacks.

On 19 July [A/ES-10/524-S/2011/439], Palestine, in identical letters addressed to the Secretary-General and the Council President, stated that Israel continued to use excessive and lethal force against Palestinian civilians, including air strikes on Gaza, causing civilian casualties, as well as the destruction of Palestinian homes and natural resources. Palestine expressed concern over the seizure by the Israeli military of a French civilian boat, the *Dignité-al Karama*, which was sailing to Gaza to deliver humanitarian aid to more than 1.5 million Palestinians. Israel had also attacked eight Palestinian fishing boats, as well as an international boat that monitored Gaza's coastline. It had increased military raids in the West Bank, including a raid on a summer camp for children.

On 20 July [A/ES-10/525-S/2011/445], Palestine, in identical letters to the Secretary-General and the Security Council President, said that the plight of Palestinian prisoners in Israel continued to deteriorate. More than 6,000 Palestinian civilians, including at least 245 children and 37 women, as well as 19 elected officials, were imprisoned or arbitrarily detained by Israel. The overwhelming majority of the Palestinian prisoners and detainees were routinely subjected to psychological and physical mistreatment, unsanitary and unhygienic conditions, inadequate health care, forced interrogations, denial of due process, solitary confinement and, in many cases, torture. Thousands of Palestinian prisoners and detainees had been transferred to prisons outside the Occupied Palestinian Territory in direct contravention of the Fourth Geneva Convention.

Security Council consideration. The Special Coordinator for the Middle East Peace Process and Personal Representative of the Secretary-General, briefing the Security Council on 26 July [S/PV.6590], reported that both President Abbas and Prime Minister Netanyahu had reiterated their desire to resume peace negotiations. Real security and economic gains had been made, benefiting both peoples. Better governance, increased investment, improvements in movement and access, and donor engagement strengthened the West Bank's economy in a difficult global environment. The training and deployment of thousands of Palestinian security officers and intensified security coordination had dismantled terrorist cells and combated extremist incitement. The agenda, however, would soon reach its limits without more political and physical space, which required Israel to roll back occupation measures, as well as continued donor support. Issues related to settler violence, movement and access limitations, and the route of the barrier wall continued to cause friction between the parties. Civil society groups and political figures called for intensified peaceful protests against the status quo and for the realization of the Palestinian right of self-determination.

The United Nations and the Quartet urged Israel to allow building materials into Gaza for use by its private sector. The illegal tunnel trade in such materials empowered those who controlled smuggling at the expense of the legitimate commercial sector. Israel should also enable exports to foreign countries and the West Bank. The freer movement of people to and from Gaza was vital if Gazans were to enjoy basic rights, normal interaction with the outside world and human dignity.

The Special Coordinator said that the longer reconciliation was delayed between Palestinian factions, the more hostile developments would push the West Bank and Gaza further apart, with grave consequences for prospects for a viable Palestinian State. In Gaza, Hamas authorities sought to audit international NGOs with on-site inspections. The United Nations urged full respect for the free and independent exercise of those organizations' functions, as well as the work of UN agencies. On 25 June, a bomb was detonated in Gaza near the compound of the Office of the United Nations Special Coordinator in the Occupied Territories.

Communications. In identical letters of 8 August [A/ES-10/526-S/2011/500] addressed to the Secretary-General and the Security Council President, Palestine stated that, during the month of Ramadan, Israel had employed indiscriminate and disproportionate force, causing death and injury to civilians. In a 1 August incident, Israeli forces raided the Qalandiya refugee camp in the West Bank, killing two young men. Scores of Palestinian civilians were also injured and many were illegally detained. Over the previous week, Israel had launched multiple air strikes against Gaza, including one that targeted a group of fishermen on the shores of Rafah.

On 9 August [S/2011/504], Israel, in identical letters addressed to the Secretary-General and the Council President, stated that since 14 July terrorists in Gaza had launched 16 rockets and 6 mortars into southern Israel, targeting areas with large civilian populations.

Quartet statement. On 16 August [SG/2176], the Quartet expressed concern over Israel's announcement to advance planning for new housing units in Ariel and East Jerusalem, and reiterated its position on that issue from its statement of 12 March 2010 [YUN 2010, p. 438]. Unilateral action by either party could not prejudge the outcome of negotiations and would not be recognized by the international community. Ultimately, responsibility rested with Israeli and Palestinian leaders to avoid actions by their Governments that undermined the goals all parties sought to achieve.

Communications. On 17 August [S/2011/520], Israel, in identical letters addressed to the Secretary-General and the Security Council President, drew attention to the escalation of rocket and mortar fire from Gaza targeting Israel. Since 9 August, one rocket and some six mortars had been fired into southern Israel. In the previous month, some 29 rockets and mortars had landed in Israeli communities, and all areas of southern Israel faced the threat of attack.

On 19 August [A/ES-10/529-S/2011/528], Palestine, in identical letters to the Secretary-General and the Council President, stated that a series of Israeli military air strikes against Gaza launched on 18 August resulted in the death 10 Palestinians, including two children. More than 20 Palestinian civilians, mainly children and women, were injured.

On 22 August [A/ES-10/530-S/2011/529], Palestine said that the Israeli military attacks against Gaza over the previous two days had raised the death toll among Palestinian civilians to 15 people since the latest attacks began on 18 August; more than 40 people were wounded. Many of the injured sustained severe burns and the loss of limbs. The attacks damaged essential infrastructure, as well as the office of the Organization of Islamic Cooperation, which had been coordinating and delivering humanitarian aid to the civilian population. Israeli forces raided Hebron and the surrounding area in the West Bank, arresting more than 60 people, including a member of the Palestinian Legislative Council.

Also on 22 August [S/2011/532], Israel, in identical letters addressed to the Secretary-General and the Council President, stated that terrorists from Gaza infiltrated southern Israel from the Sinai Peninsula in Egypt and attacked two public buses and two cars with firearms and explosives on 18 August, killing six civilians and injuring 15 others. When Israeli police arrived, the terrorists opened fire, killing an officer and an IDF soldier, and injuring four members of the Israeli security forces. Since that date, Israel had been subjected to the most severe escalation of rocket and mortar fire from Gaza since the end of Operation Cast Lead [YUN 2009, p. 434], with more than 100 rockets and dozens of mortars fired at major Israeli cities and towns.

Quartet statement. On 22 August [SG/2177], the Quartet condemned the 18 August attacks in southern Israel and all acts of terrorism. It reiterated its concern about the unsustainable situation in Gaza, as well as the risk of its escalation, and called for restraint from all sides. The Quartet also expressed concern about the security situation in the Sinai Peninsula. Recent commitments by Egypt to address the situation were important, and the Quartet encouraged the Government to find a lasting resolution.

Security Council consideration. On 25 August [S/PV.6602], the Under-Secretary-General for Political Affairs briefed the Council on the situation in the Middle East. He said that the deadlines set the previous year for resolving permanent status issues and completing the Palestinian State-building agenda had arrived. The political deadlock persisted, however, and significant differences remained between the parties regarding the terms framing negotiations.

The Special Coordinator visited Cairo on 21 August and worked with Egypt to restore the fragile calm that had prevailed since April. Without a political breakthrough—and with Israeli settlement activity continuing—the PLO Executive Committee announced, on 28 July, its support for the Palestinian leadership's intention to approach the General Assembly and the Security Council to request Palestinian statehood. On 4 August, the Arab Peace Initiative Committee announced the Arab League's plan to call on UN Member States to recognize a Palestinian State within the 1967 lines, with East Jerusalem as its capital, and to submit an application for full UN membership. Although the United Nations had assessed that the PA State-building agenda had laid the foundations of a Palestinian State, those achievements had to be consolidated and bolstered by genuine political prospects for statehood achieved through substantive negotiations. The PA also needed to have the financial means to sustain its State-building and reform agenda; it required $250 million in additional commitments to meet its obligations. Fatah and Hamas representatives continued to meet on the implementation of the reconciliation accord. On 22 August, President Abbas postponed local elections—originally scheduled for 22 October—without setting a new date, stating that conditions should first be in place for the election commission to work in all of the territory.

Restrictions remained on access for prayers at the Al-Aqsa mosque during the month of Ramadan. Israeli authorities initially eased access to East Jerusalem for West Bank Palestinians, allowing about 117,000 Palestinians to enter the city on the second Friday of Ramadan, but restrictions were later tightened again. On 17 August, Israel extended the closure of Orient House and the Chamber of Commerce in East Jerusalem to enforce its ongoing ban on Palestinian Government institutions in the city. Such actions ran contrary to Israel's obligations under the road map.

Communications. On 26 August [A/ES-10/531-S/2011/541], Palestine, in identical letters to the Secretary-General and the Security Council President, stated that air strikes carried out by Israel against civilian areas in Gaza resulted in 11 Palestinian civilians killed and more than 30 people injured.

On 29 August [A/65/939-S/2011/543], Saint Vincent and the Grenadines informed the Secretary-General that it had decided to formally recognize the State of Palestine.

In a 17 September letter addressed to the Secretary-General [A/66/395-S/2011/611], the President of Venezuela, Hugo Chávez Frías, confirmed Venezuela's full support for the recognition of the Palestinian State and Palestine's right to become a free, sovereign and independent country.

Application of Palestine to United Nations membership. On 23 September [A/66/371-S/2011/592], the Secretary-General circulated the application of Palestine for admission to membership in the United Nations, contained in a letter from President Abbas received that day. President Abbas said that the application was submitted based on the Palestinian people's natural, legal and historic rights, and based on General Assembly resolution 181(II) [YUN 1947–48, p. 247] as well as the Declaration of Independence of the State of Palestine of 15 November 1988 and its acknowledgement by the Assembly in resolution 43/177 [YUN 1988, p. 208]. Palestine affirmed its commitment to the achievement of a just, lasting and comprehensive solution of the Israeli-Palestinian conflict based on the vision of two States living side by side in peace and security. Appended to the letter was a declaration, made pursuant to the rules of procedure of the Security Council and the General Assembly, in which President Abbas stated that the State of Palestine was a peace-loving nation, that it accepted the obligations contained in the Charter of the United Nations and undertook to fulfil them. Annexed to the Secretary-General's note was a separate letter dated 23 September from President Abbas to the Secretary-General that provided background information on Palestine's application.

The General Assembly took note of Palestine's application to UN membership in resolutions 66/14 (see p. 435) and 66/17 (see p. 414) of 30 November, and in resolution 66/76 of 9 December (see p. 426). The United Nations, however, took no further action on the matter in 2011.

Quartet meeting. The Quartet—including the Secretary-General, the Russian Foreign Minister, the United States Secretary of State, the EU High Representative for Foreign Affairs and Security Policy and Quartet Representative Tony Blair—met in New York on 23 September [SG/2178] and noted the application for membership for a State of Palestine in the United Nations, which was before the Security Council. It reiterated its appeal to the parties to resume direct, bilateral Israeli-Palestinian negotiations without delay or preconditions. To that end, the Quartet proposed that within one month a preparatory meeting be held between the parties to agree on an agenda and a method of proceeding in the negotiation. At the meeting, both sides would commit to the objective that any negotiation would reach an agreement within a time frame agreed to by the parties but not lasting longer than the end of 2012. The Quartet expected the parties to come forward with comprehensive proposals on territory and security within three months, and achieve substantial progress on the proposals within six months. A donors' conference would be held, during which the international community would give sustained support to PA Statebuilding actions developed by Prime Minister Fayyad under the leadership of President Abbas. The Quartet would identify additional steps to support Palestinian statehood and secure greater independence and sovereignty for the PA over its affairs. It called on the parties to refrain from provocative actions.

Security Council consideration. The Under-Secretary-General for Political Affairs, briefing the Security Council on 27 September [S/PV.6623], said that efforts to build robust institutions and revive the Palestinian economy had resulted in security and economic improvements. Incidents of Israeli settler violence increased, including, on 5 September, an arson attack on a mosque—the fifth such attack in the previous two months.

Communications. On 30 September [A/ES-10/533-S/2011/606], Palestine, in identical letters to the Secretary-General and the Security Council President, highlighted recent violations and crimes committed by Israel against the Palestinians, including punitive and humiliating measures, such as solitary confinement, unhygienic conditions and physical and mental abuse, inflicted on thousands of imprisoned Palestinians; daily military raids and arrests; the arrest and detention of Ahmad Attoun, a Palestinian elected official from East Jerusalem; and the continued Israeli demolition of Palestinian homes and properties.

On 10 October [A/ES-10/534-S/2011/629], Palestine informed the Secretary-General and the Council President that the situation of Palestinian political prisoners and detainees illegally held by Israel continued to deteriorate. On 27 September, Palestinians held in Israeli prisons and detention centres began a hunger strike to protest oppressive measures by Israel that threatened their lives and deprived them of their basic human rights. The situation of Palestinian prisoners worsened after Prime Minister Netanyahu announced plans to "toughen" conditions on the more than 6,000 Palestinian civilians, including at least 280 children and 38 women, as well as 22 elected officials imprisoned or arbitrarily detained. Acts of violence, lawlessness and terror perpetrated by Israeli settlers against Palestinian civilians and their properties in the Occupied Palestinian Territory included the killing of one person and the injuring of two others in a hit-and-run accident; the burning and desecration of mosques; the uprooting, burning and destruction of more than 3,000 olive trees and grapevines; the burning of agricultural land in response to weekly peaceful protests against the construction of the wall; and the flooding of agricultural land with sewage from settlements. Such violations took place in full view of the Israeli forces, which continued to protect settlers.

Security Council consideration. On 24 October [S/PV.6636], the Under-Secretary-General for Political Affairs informed the Security Council that on 18 October, Israel and Hamas implemented the first stage of a prisoner exchange agreement. Hamas released Israeli Sergeant Gilad Shalit, who had been held in Gaza without international access since 2006 [YUN 2006, p. 510], in exchange for 477 Palestinian prisoners —many of whom had been jailed for involvement in attacks on Israelis. Palestinian prisoners suspended the hunger strike the day before the prisoner transfer, following the reported agreement to end solitary confinement.

Settler attacks on Palestinians resulted in one death and 19 injuries. On 3 October, a mosque was set on fire in the village of Tuba Zangaria in Israel. Subsequently, Muslim, Christian and Jewish holy sites were desecrated in several towns in Israel.

Communications. In identical letters of 27 October [S/2011/671], addressed to the Secretary-General and the Security Council President, Israel stated that on 26 October, terrorists in Gaza fired a modified Katyusha rocket into Israel that exploded in the vicinity of Ashdod. On 29 October [S/2011/674], Israel said that major cities were bombarded that day with dozens of rockets and mortars launched from Gaza. The attacks killed one Israeli civilian and injured a number of others. The increasing sophistication of the rockets used in such attacks was a direct result of the smuggling of advanced weapons from Iran and other parties into the area.

On 1 November [A/ES-10/537-S/2011/676], Palestine, in identical letters addressed to the Secretary-General and the Security Council President, expressed its concern about the military escalation by Israel against Gaza. Over the previous four days, Israeli air strikes killed at least 11 Palestinians and injured scores of others. Palestine also noted the repeated calls by senior Israeli Government officials, including Foreign Minister Avigdor Lieberman, for a full-scale ground invasion of Gaza, in addition to repeated hostile declarations against the Palestinian people and their leadership.

On 2 November [S/2011/679], Israel, in identical letters to the Secretary-General and the Council President, stated that two boats were headed in the direction of Gaza with the stated intention of violating Israel's naval blockade of the area. Reports indicated that they set sail from a port in Turkey. Launched under the false pretext of providing humanitarian assistance, the flotilla was a provocation clearly designed to serve an extremist political agenda. Israel was not interested in confrontation, but was determined to enforce the naval blockade of Gaza.

In a 4 November letter addressed to the Secretary-General and the Council President [S/2011/690], Turkey stated that the boats headed to Gaza had no connection with Turkey.

On 9 November [S/2011/700], Israel, in identical letters to the Secretary-General and the Council President, stated that on 6 November, two rockets fell on Kibbutz Zikim, injuring a man. The attacks followed a significant escalation of rocket fire over the previous two weeks, during which more than 60 rockets, missiles and mortars were launched into the major cities and communities of southern Israel. There was no question that Hamas and the other terrorists in Gaza who carried out the attacks were targeting Israeli civilians.

In an 11 November letter to the Security Council President [S/2011/709], Iran, referring to Israel's letters of 27 and 29 October (see above), rejected allegations concerning the smuggling of advanced weapons into Gaza; the allegations were based on false and misleading information.

On 15 November [S/2011/719], Israel, in identical letters to the Secretary-General and the Council President, stated that two long-range rockets were fired that day from Gaza into a kibbutz in southern Israel in the area of Sha'ar Hanegev. One rocket destroyed a farm building, exploding in close proximity to a kindergarten classroom.

Security Council consideration. On 21 November [S/PV.6662], the Special Coordinator for the Middle East Peace Process and Personal Representative of the Secretary-General briefed the Council on the situation in the Middle East. He stated that the Quartet Representative and Quartet envoys met separately with Israeli and Palestinian representatives in Jerusalem on 26 October and 14 November within the framework of the 23 September Quartet statement. Nevertheless, direct negotiations without preconditions, in which the parties would be expected to table territorial and security proposals within 90 days, were not taking place. Provocations continued to damage confidence and made the resumption of direct negotiations difficult. King Abdullah II of Jordan visited Ramallah on 21 November to hold consultations with President Abbas, underscoring his concern at the situation, as well as his support for the PA and the creation of a Palestinian State.

On 1 November, Israel announced the accelerated construction of settlement housing units in occupied East Jerusalem following a 31 October UNESCO General Conference vote to admit Palestine as a member of the organization. On 2 November [SG/SM/13918], the Secretary-General criticized Israeli settlement activity, which ran contrary to international law and the road map [YUN 2003, p. 464], and prejudiced final status negotiations. Israel also reacted to the UNESCO outcome by freezing the transfer of value-added tax and customs revenues it collected on behalf of the PA pursuant to the 1994 Paris Protocol on Economic Relations. Those funds amounted to approximately $100 million per month—two-thirds of PA annual revenues. The action threatened the State-building gains made by the PA, including the increased good governance and the development of the security forces that upheld law and order in the West Bank. The United States also decided to partially withhold the assistance funds that it had been providing to the PA. In addition to halting its settlement obligations, Israel needed to heed the calls of the Secretary-General and other international leaders to unfreeze transfers to the PA, in accordance with existing agreements. Donors also were urged to unblock their funding to the PA.

During a speech that marked the seventh anniversary of President Yasser Arafat's death in 2004 [YUN 2004, p. 471], President Abbas firmly rejected violence, but called for the widest possible Palestinian non-violent resistance. Nevertheless, violent incidents continued. Citing security concerns, IDF conducted 218 operations, during which 44 Palestinians were injured, including 3 children, and 113 were arrested. Between 29 and 31 October, dozens of Grad and homemade rockets, as well as mortars, landed in Israel. Israel conducted air strikes in Gaza, targeting mainly Islamic Jihad militants. Diplomatic efforts led by Egypt helped to restore relative calm on 1 November. Islamic Jihad released footage purporting to show its possession of sophisticated mobile rocket launchers smuggled into Gaza, highlighting the need for more effective steps to prevent the illicit trafficking of arms and ammunition. A 14 November Israeli airstrike injured a French consular official in Gaza, as well as his daughter and pregnant wife. The United Nations reiterated the Secretary-General's call for Israel to exercise maximum restraint and minimize the risk to civilians.

In a positive development, Israel, on 8 November, granted four new sets of approvals for construction projects in Gaza, valued at approximately $5.5 million, to be carried out by the United Nations Development Programme, the International Committee of the Red Cross, Sweden and the United States Agency for International Development.

Communications. On 29 November [S/2011/742], Israel, in identical letters to the Secretary-General and the Security Council President, stated that on 25 November, a rocket fired from Gaza exploded in the immediate vicinity of Kibbutz Nachal Oz. Over the previous two months, terrorists in Gaza had launched more than 70 rockets and mortars into the major cities, towns and communities of southern Israel, deliberately targeting civilians.

On 12 December [A/ES-10/542-S/2011/768], Palestine, in identical letters to the Secretary-General and the Council President, stated that Israel was escalating military assaults and human rights violations against the Palestinian people. On 9 December, a missile launched by an Israeli warplane into a civilian area in north-west Gaza City caused the collapse of a family home, killing two people and injuring 12 others. On the same date, Israeli forces in a village north of Ramallah fired tear gas canisters at protesters at close range; one of the protesters was struck by a canister and died of his wounds the following day. Mourners at the funeral were also struck with tear gas canisters fired by IDF; six were arrested, including four Israelis and two international activists. Earlier in the week, at least 300 Israeli soldiers in armoured vehicles stormed two villages near Ramallah, raiding homes and mosques.

Security Council consideration. On 20 December [S/PV.6692], the Assistant Secretary-General for Political Affairs informed the Security Council that credible progress in the search for peace between Israel and the Palestinians had become urgent, but remained elusive because of tensions on the ground, deep mistrust between the parties and volatile regional dynamics. In December, four mosques were set on fire or otherwise desecrated; Israeli extremists stormed an IDF base and blocked roads in the West Bank; and Israeli settlement activity and the demolition of Palestinian structures continued. Palestinian forces maintained close cooperation with Israeli security forces, which led to the arrest of a number of suspected perpetrators of violence against Palestinians and their property.

On 30 November, Israel decided to renew the transfer of tax and customs revenues owed to the PA, which had been withheld after the 31 October UNESCO vote. The Palestinian flag was raised at UNESCO headquarters on 13 December, but the PA had not taken further steps towards membership in other UN bodies or specialized agencies. On 14 December, Quartet envoys and Quartet Representative Blair held a third round of separate meetings with the Israeli and Palestinian negotiators to help the parties resume direct talks.

The United Nations was concerned about the de facto authorities' intent to tax the Bank of Palestine and the Palestine Islamic Bank, as well as the enforcement of the subsequent travel ban on senior bank staff. The regular functioning of the banking sector remained vital to the Gaza economy. The United Nations also relied on those institutions' financial services for its operations in Gaza. A series of meetings among the Palestinian factions began in Cairo to advance Palestinian reconciliation.

Panel of Inquiry on 2010 flotilla incident

In September, the Secretary-General submitted to the Security Council the report of the Panel of Inquiry on the 31 May 2010 flotilla incident, established in August 2010 [YUN 2010, p. 441] following the incident, in which IDF boarded a six-ship convoy carrying humanitarian aid bound for Gaza, resulting in the deaths of nine passengers and the wounding of many others [ibid., p. 439]. The Panel examined and identified the facts, circumstances and context of the incident, and recommended ways of avoiding similar incidents in the future. In doing so, it neither acted as a court nor adjudicated legal findings.

The Panel found that Israel faced a real threat to its security from militant groups in Gaza, and the naval blockade was imposed as a legitimate security measure to prevent weapons from entering Gaza by sea. The flotilla acted recklessly in attempting to breach the blockade, but most of the flotilla participants did not have violent intentions. Nevertheless, serious questions about the conduct, true nature and objectives of the flotilla organizers existed, and the flotilla's actions needlessly carried the potential for escalation. Turkey and Israel attempted to ensure that events did not endanger lives or international peace and security. Turkish officials approached the flotilla organizers to persuade them to change course if necessary and avoid an encounter with Israeli forces. More could have been done, however, to warn the flotilla participants of the risks involved and to dissuade them from their actions. Israel's decision to board the vessels with such substantial force at a great distance from the blockade zone and with no final warning was excessive and unreasonable; non-violent options should have been used first, and the operation should have been reassessed when resistance became apparent. IDF personnel faced significant, organized and violent resistance from a group of passengers when they boarded the *Mavi Marmara*, which required them to fight for their own protection. The loss of life and injuries that resulted from the takeover of the vessel was unacceptable, however, and no satisfactory explanation for the deaths was provided by Israel. Forensic evidence showing that most of the deceased were shot multiple times, including in the back or at close range, was not adequately explained in the material presented by Israel. Israeli authorities mistreated passengers until they were deported. The mistreatment included physical harassment and intimidation, unjustified confiscation of belongings and the denial of consular assistance.

The Panel recommended that Israel should keep the naval blockade under regular review, bearing in mind its consequences and the fundamental importance of the freedom of navigation on the Mediterranean. It should continue to ease its restrictions on movement of goods and persons to and from Gaza with a view to lifting its closure in order to alleviate the unsustainable humanitarian and economic situation of the civilian population. Humanitarian missions wishing to assist the Gaza population should do so through established procedures and use the designated land crossings in consultation with Israel and the PA. Israel should issue a statement of regret and offer payment for the benefit of the deceased and injured victims and their families. Turkey and Israel should resume full diplomatic relations in the interests of stability in the Middle East and international peace and security.

Peaceful settlement of the question of Palestine

In a September report [A/66/367-S/2011/585], submitted in accordance with General Assembly resolution 65/16 [YUN 2010, p. 446] and covering the period from September 2010 through August 2011, the Secretary-General presented his observations on the state of the Israeli-Palestinian conflict and on international efforts to move the peace process forward. The Security Council considered the situation in Palestine every month under the agenda item "The situation in the Middle East, including the question of Palestine".

In an 11 May note, the Secretary-General sought the positions of Egypt, Israel, Jordan, Lebanon and the Syrian Arab Republic, as well as the PLO, regarding steps they had taken to implement resolution 65/16. The Secretary-General received replies from Israel and the PLO.

Israel, in a 5 July note, stated that it had voted against the resolution. Although it made significant efforts in 2011 to renew peace negotiations with the PA and foster economic growth and development, Palestinian terrorism continued and the nature of terrorist attacks escalated. During the first five months of the year, 278 attacks were carried out in or emanated from the West Bank, resulting in the deaths of 11 Israeli citizens; 163 terrorist attacks emanated from Gaza. The PA continued its campaign of incitement designed to legitimize terrorism. Hamas, with Iran's support, continued to stockpile weapons of increasing lethality and range. Despite the campaign of violence and incitement, Israel continued to facilitate the entry of large quantities of humanitarian supplies and other products into Gaza, and to ease security-related restrictions in the West Bank. Israel also repeatedly extended an open invitation to restart peace talks with the Palestinians with no preconditions.

In a 27 June note, Palestine said that resolution 65/16 was central to justly and peacefully resolve the question of its future. A strong international consensus existed in support of an independent, viable and contiguous State of Palestine. The pretexts used by Israel to justify its illegal settlement campaign constituted arbitrary preconditions imposed to exact further political gains. Israel's disrespect for the agreed principles of the negotiation process left the Palestinian side without a partner for peace. The Palestinian leadership continued—with significant international support—to develop and strengthen Palestine's institutions in preparation for the State's independence. The leadership also promoted reconciliation and unity among the Palestinian political factions.

The Secretary-General observed that efforts to achieve the peaceful settlement of the question of Palestine made little progress during the reporting period, and confidence between the parties in the political process reached a new low. As settlement activity continued, the PA, with the support of the Arab Peace Initiative Committee, confirmed its intention to approach the General Assembly to call on Member States to recognize a Palestinian State, and to apply for full membership in the United Nations. Israel expressed its strong opposition to such action.

Settler violence against Palestinians in the West Bank increased during the reporting period, including 366 attacks, which resulted in the deaths of three Palestinians and the injury of 182. Four Muslim holy sites were desecrated, and arsonists set two mosques on fire. Palestinians attacked settlers on 63 occasions, killing six Israelis and wounding 27. Fourteen Palestinians, including three militants, were killed by IDF, and 1,398 were wounded.

The Secretary-General reported an escalation of tension between Gaza and Israel during the reporting period. Palestinian militants fired 961 rockets and mortar shells, killing two Israeli civilians and injuring 36; one member of the Israeli military was killed and two were injured. IDF conducted 224 air strikes and 122 incursions, killing 43 Palestinian civilians and injuring 350; 70 militants were also killed and 70 were injured. The United Nations expressed concern over the intensification of fighting by Hamas and other militant groups, and called for maximum restraint on the part of Israel. It engaged with Israel and within the Quartet to promote reconstruction in Gaza, further liberalize imports, particularly construction materials, and allow exports. The United Nations called for the free movement of people and a full reopening of land crossings. It put forward programming aimed at revitalizing the private sector and rehabilitating public health infrastructure. By the end of August, Israel had approved $265 million in UN reconstruction projects.

GENERAL ASSEMBLY ACTION

On 30 November [meeting 69], the General Assembly adopted **resolution 66/17** [draft: A/66/L.18 & Add.1] by recorded vote (167-7-4) [agenda item 37].

Peaceful settlement of the question of Palestine

The General Assembly,

Recalling its relevant resolutions, including those adopted at its tenth emergency special session,

Recalling also its resolution 58/292 of 6 May 2004,

Recalling further relevant Security Council resolutions, including resolutions 242(1967) of 22 November 1967, 338(1973) of 22 October 1973, 1397(2002) of 12 March 2002, 1515(2003) of 19 November 2003, 1544(2004) of 19 May 2004 and 1850(2008) of 16 December 2008,

Recalling the affirmation by the Security Council of the vision of a region where two States, Israel and Palestine, live side by side within secure and recognized borders,

Noting with concern that it has been more than sixty years since the adoption of its resolution 181(II) of 29 November 1947 and forty-four years since the occupation of Palestinian territory, including East Jerusalem, in 1967,

Having considered the report of the Secretary-General submitted pursuant to the request made in its resolution 65/16 of 30 November 2010,

Reaffirming the permanent responsibility of the United Nations with regard to the question of Palestine until the question is resolved in all its aspects in accordance with international law and relevant resolutions,

Recalling the advisory opinion rendered on 9 July 2004 by the International Court of Justice on the *Legal Consequences of the Construction of a Wall in the Occupied Palestinian Territory*, and recalling also its resolutions ES-10/15 of 20 July 2004 and ES-10/17 of 15 December 2006,

Convinced that achieving a just, lasting and comprehensive settlement of the question of Palestine, the core of the Arab-Israeli conflict, is imperative for the attainment of comprehensive and lasting peace and stability in the Middle East,

Stressing that the principle of equal rights and self-determination of peoples is among the purposes and principles enshrined in the Charter of the United Nations,

Reaffirming the principle of the inadmissibility of the acquisition of territory by war,

Recalling its resolution 2625(XXV) of 24 October 1970,

Reaffirming the illegality of the Israeli settlements in the Palestinian territory occupied since 1967, including East Jerusalem,

Stressing the extremely detrimental impact of Israeli settlement policies, decisions and activities in the Occupied Palestinian Territory, including East Jerusalem, on efforts to resume and advance the peace process and to achieve peace in the Middle East,

Reaffirming the illegality of Israeli actions aimed at changing the status of Jerusalem, including settlement construction and expansion, home demolitions, evictions of Palestinian residents, excavations in and around religious and historic sites, and all other unilateral measures aimed at altering the character, status and demographic composition of the city and of the Territory as a whole,

Reaffirming also that the construction by Israel, the occupying Power, of a wall in the Occupied Palestinian Territory, including in and around East Jerusalem, and its associated regime are contrary to international law,

Expressing deep concern about the continuing Israeli policy of closures and severe restrictions on the movement of persons and goods, including medical and humanitarian, via the imposition of prolonged closures and severe economic and movement restrictions that in effect amount to a blockade, as well as of checkpoints and a permit regime throughout the Occupied Palestinian Territory, including East Jerusalem, and the consequent negative impact on the contiguity of the Territory and the serious socioeconomic and humanitarian situation of the Palestinian people, which is critical in the Gaza Strip, and on the efforts aimed at rehabilitating and developing the damaged Palestinian economy, while taking note of recent developments regarding the situation of access to the Gaza Strip,

Recalling the mutual recognition between the Government of the State of Israel and the Palestine Liberation

Organization, the representative of the Palestinian people, and the need for full compliance with the agreements concluded between the two sides,

Recalling also the endorsement by the Security Council, in resolution 1515(2003), of the Quartet road map to a permanent two-State solution to the Israeli-Palestinian conflict and the call in Council resolution 1850(2008) for the parties to fulfil their obligations under the road map and to refrain from any steps that could undermine confidence or prejudice the outcome of negotiations, and recalling further in this regard the relevant Quartet statements, including that of 23 September 2011,

Noting the Israeli withdrawal in 2005 from the Gaza Strip and parts of the northern West Bank and the dismantlement of the settlements therein as a step towards the implementation of the road map, and stressing in this regard the road-map obligation upon Israel to freeze settlement activity, including so-called "natural growth", and to dismantle all settlement outposts erected since March 2001,

Recalling the Arab Peace Initiative adopted by the Council of the League of Arab States at its fourteenth session, held in Beirut on 27 and 28 March 2002,

Expressing support for the agreed principles for bilateral negotiations, as affirmed by the parties in the Israeli-Palestinian Joint Understanding reached at the international conference held in Annapolis, United States of America, on 27 November 2007, aimed at concluding a peace treaty resolving all outstanding issues, including all core issues, without exception, for the achievement of a just, lasting and peaceful settlement of the Israeli-Palestinian conflict and ultimately of the Arab-Israeli conflict as a whole for the realization of a comprehensive peace in the Middle East,

Reiterating support for the convening of an international conference in Moscow, as envisioned by the Security Council in resolution 1850(2008) and the Quartet statement of 23 September 2011, for the advancement and acceleration of a resumed peace process,

Noting the important contribution to the peace process of the United Nations Special Coordinator for the Middle East Peace Process and Personal Representative of the Secretary-General to the Palestine Liberation Organization and the Palestinian Authority, including within the framework of the activities of the Quartet,

Noting also the continuing efforts of the Quartet's Special Representative towards the resumption of the peace process, in particular the efforts to strengthen Palestinian institutions, promote Palestinian economic development and mobilize donor support,

Welcoming the meeting of the Ad Hoc Liaison Committee for the Coordination of the International Assistance to Palestinians, under the chairmanship of Norway, at United Nations Headquarters on 18 September 2011, at which, based on relevant reports by the United Nations, the World Bank and the International Monetary Fund, the donor countries reconfirmed the assessment that the institutions of the Palestinian Authority are above the threshold of a functioning State in the key sectors studied and reaffirmed the necessity of continued donor support for the Palestinian Authority,

Recognizing the efforts being undertaken by the Palestinian Authority, with international support, to rebuild, reform and strengthen its damaged institutions, emphasizing the need to preserve and further develop Palestinian institutions and infrastructure and commending, in this regard, the implementation of the Palestinian Authority's August 2009 plan for constructing the institutions of an independent Palestinian State within a twenty-four-month period, and the significant achievements made, as confirmed by international institutions, including the World Bank, the International Monetary Fund and the United Nations, in their reports to the meeting of the Ad Hoc Liaison Committee on 13 April 2011,

Welcoming the continued efforts and tangible progress made in the security sector by the Palestinian Authority, calling upon the parties to continue cooperation that benefits both Palestinians and Israelis, in particular by promoting security and building confidence, and expressing the hope that such progress will be extended to all major population centres,

Reiterating its concern over the negative developments that have continued to occur in the Occupied Palestinian Territory, including East Jerusalem, including the large number of deaths and injuries, mostly among Palestinian civilians, the construction and expansion of settlements and the wall, acts of violence, vandalism and brutality committed against Palestinian civilians by Israeli settlers in the West Bank, the widespread destruction of public and private Palestinian property and infrastructure, the internal displacement of civilians and the serious deterioration of the socioeconomic and humanitarian conditions of the Palestinian people,

Expressing grave concern, in particular, over the crisis in the Gaza Strip as a result of the continuing prolonged Israeli closures and severe economic and movement restrictions that in effect amount to a blockade and the military operations in the Gaza Strip between December 2008 and January 2009, which caused extensive loss of life and injury, particularly among Palestinian civilians, including children and women, widespread damage and destruction to Palestinian homes, properties, vital infrastructure, public institutions, including hospitals and schools, and United Nations facilities, and internal displacement of civilians,

Stressing the need for the full implementation by all parties of Security Council resolution 1860(2009) of 8 January 2009 and General Assembly resolution ES-10/18 of 16 January 2009,

Expressing concern over continuing military actions in the Occupied Palestinian Territory, including raids and arrest campaigns, and over the continued imposition of hundreds of checkpoints and obstacles to movement in and around Palestinian population centres by the Israeli occupying forces, and emphasizing in this regard the need for the implementation by both sides of the Sharm el-Sheikh understandings,

Emphasizing the importance of the safety, protection and well-being of all civilians in the whole Middle East region, and condemning all acts of violence and terror against civilians on both sides,

Expressing the hope for speedy progress towards Palestinian reconciliation for the restoration of Palestinian unity, under the leadership of the President of the Palestinian Authority, Mahmoud Abbas, and consistent with Palestine

Liberation Organization commitments, and of the situation in the Gaza Strip to that which existed prior to June 2007, and calling for the continuation of the serious efforts being exerted by Egypt, the League of Arab States and other concerned parties towards the achievement of this aim,

Stressing the urgent need for sustained and active international involvement, including by the Quartet, to support both parties in resuming, advancing and accelerating the peace process negotiations for the achievement of a just, lasting and comprehensive peace settlement, on the basis of United Nations resolutions, the road map and the Arab Peace Initiative,

Noting the Quartet's determination in the recent period to support the parties throughout the negotiations, which can be completed and resolve all final status issues within one year, and in the implementation of an agreement between the two sides that ends the occupation which began in 1967 and results in the independence of a democratic, contiguous and viable Palestinian State living side by side in peace and security with Israel and its other neighbours,

Taking note of the application of Palestine for admission to membership in the United Nations, submitted on 23 September 2011,

Acknowledging the efforts being undertaken by civil society to promote a peaceful settlement of the question of Palestine,

Recalling the findings by the International Court of Justice, in its advisory opinion, including on the urgent necessity for the United Nations as a whole to redouble its efforts to bring the Israeli-Palestinian conflict, which continues to pose a threat to international peace and security, to a speedy conclusion, thereby establishing a just and lasting peace in the region,

Affirming once again the right of all States in the region to live in peace within secure and internationally recognized borders,

1. *Reaffirms* the necessity of achieving a peaceful settlement of the question of Palestine, the core of the Arab-Israeli conflict, in all its aspects, and of intensifying all efforts towards that end, and stresses in this regard the urgency of salvaging the prospects for realizing the two-State solution of Israel and Palestine, living side by side in peace and security within recognized borders, based on the pre-1967 borders;

2. *Also reaffirms* its full support for the Middle East peace process, based on the relevant United Nations resolutions, the terms of reference of the Madrid Conference, including the principle of land for peace, the Arab Peace Initiative adopted by the Council of the League of Arab States at its fourteenth session, and the Quartet road map to a permanent two-State solution to the Israeli-Palestinian conflict, and for the existing agreements between the Israeli and Palestinian sides, stresses the necessity for the establishment of a comprehensive, just and lasting peace in the Middle East, and welcomes in this regard the ongoing efforts of the Quartet and of the League of Arab States;

3. *Encourages* continued serious regional and international efforts to follow up and promote the Arab Peace Initiative, including by the Ministerial Committee formed at the Riyadh summit in March 2007;

4. *Urges* the parties to undertake, with the support of the Quartet and the international community, immediate and concrete steps in follow-up to the Israeli-Palestinian Joint Understanding reached at the international conference held in Annapolis, including through the resumption of active and serious bilateral negotiations;

5. *Encourages*, in this regard, the convening of an international conference in Moscow, as envisioned by the Security Council in resolution 1850(2008), for the advancement and acceleration of a resumed peace process;

6. *Calls upon* both parties to act on the basis of international law and their previous agreements and obligations, in particular adherence to the road map, irrespective of reciprocity, in order to create the conditions necessary for the resumption and accelerated advancement of negotiations in the near term;

7. *Calls upon* the parties themselves, with the support of the Quartet and other interested parties, to exert all efforts necessary to halt the deterioration of the situation and to reverse all unilateral and unlawful measures taken on the ground since 28 September 2000;

8. *Calls upon* the parties to observe calm and restraint and to refrain from provocative actions and inflammatory rhetoric, especially in areas of religious and cultural sensitivity;

9. *Underscores* the need for the parties to take confidence-building measures aimed at improving the situation on the ground, promoting stability and fostering the peace process, including the need for the further release of prisoners following the exchange of prisoners in October 2011;

10. *Stresses* the need for the removal of checkpoints and other obstructions to the movement of persons and goods throughout the Occupied Palestinian Territory, including East Jerusalem, and the need for respect and preservation of the territorial unity, contiguity and integrity of all of the Occupied Palestinian Territory, including East Jerusalem;

11. *Also stresses* the need for an immediate and complete cessation of all acts of violence, including military attacks, destruction and acts of terror;

12. *Reiterates its demand* for the full implementation of Security Council resolution 1860(2009);

13. *Reiterates* the need for the full implementation by both parties of the Agreement on Movement and Access and of the Agreed Principles for the Rafah Crossing, of 15 November 2005, and the need, specifically, to allow for the sustained opening of all crossings into and out of the Gaza Strip for humanitarian supplies, movement and access, as well as for commercial flows and all necessary construction materials, which are essential for alleviating the humanitarian crisis, improving the living conditions of the Palestinian people and promoting the recovery of the Palestinian economy;

14. *Stresses*, in this regard, the urgent necessity for the advancement of reconstruction in the Gaza Strip, including through the completion of numerous suspended projects managed by the United Nations and the accelerated implementation of United Nations-led civilian reconstruction activities;

15. *Calls upon* Israel, the occupying Power, to comply strictly with its obligations under international law, including international humanitarian law, and to cease all of its measures that are contrary to international law and unilateral actions in the Occupied Palestinian Terri-

tory, including East Jerusalem, that are aimed at altering the character, status and demographic composition of the Territory, including via the confiscation and de facto annexation of land, and thus at prejudging the final outcome of peace negotiations;

16. *Reiterates its demand* for the complete cessation of all Israeli settlement activities in the Occupied Palestinian Territory, including East Jerusalem, and in the occupied Syrian Golan, and calls for the full implementation of the relevant Security Council resolutions;

17. *Stresses*, in this regard, the need for Israel forthwith to abide by its road-map obligation to freeze all settlement activity, including so-called "natural growth", and to dismantle settlement outposts erected since March 2001;

18. *Calls for* the cessation of all provocations, including by Israeli settlers, in East Jerusalem, including in and around religious sites;

19. *Demands*, accordingly, that Israel, the occupying Power, comply with its legal obligations under international law, as mentioned in the advisory opinion rendered on 9 July 2004 by the International Court of Justice and as demanded in General Assembly resolutions ES-10/13 of 21 October 2003 and ES-10/15, and, inter alia, that it immediately cease its construction of the wall in the Occupied Palestinian Territory, including East Jerusalem, and calls upon all States Members of the United Nations to comply with their legal obligations, as mentioned in the advisory opinion;

20. *Reaffirms its commitment*, in accordance with international law, to the two-State solution of Israel and Palestine, living side by side in peace and security within recognized borders, based on the pre-1967 borders;

21. *Stresses* the need for:

(*a*) The withdrawal of Israel from the Palestinian territory occupied since 1967, including East Jerusalem;

(*b*) The realization of the inalienable rights of the Palestinian people, primarily the right to self-determination and the right to their independent State;

22. *Also stresses* the need for a just resolution of the problem of Palestine refugees in conformity with its resolution 194(III) of 11 December 1948;

23. *Calls upon* the parties to resume and accelerate direct peace negotiations towards the conclusion of a final peaceful settlement on the basis of relevant United Nations resolutions, especially of the Security Council, the terms of reference of the Madrid Conference, the road map and the Arab Peace Initiative;

24. *Urges* Member States to expedite the provision of economic, humanitarian and technical assistance to the Palestinian people and the Palestinian Authority during this critical period in order to help to alleviate the serious humanitarian situation in the Occupied Palestinian Territory, including East Jerusalem, which is critical in the Gaza Strip, to rehabilitate the Palestinian economy and infrastructure and to support the development and strengthening of Palestinian institutions and Palestinian Statebuilding efforts in preparation for independence;

25. *Requests* the Secretary-General to continue his efforts with the parties concerned, and in consultation with the Security Council, towards the attainment of a peaceful settlement of the question of Palestine and the promotion of peace in the region and to submit to the General Assembly at its sixty-seventh session a report on these efforts and on developments on this matter.

RECORDED VOTE ON RESOLUTION 66/17:

In favour: Afghanistan, Albania, Algeria, Andorra, Antigua and Barbuda, Argentina, Armenia, Austria, Azerbaijan, Bahamas, Bahrain, Bangladesh, Barbados, Belarus, Belgium, Belize, Benin, Bhutan, Bolivia, Bosnia and Herzegovina, Botswana, Brazil, Brunei Darussalam, Bulgaria, Burkina Faso, Cambodia, Cape Verde, Chad, Chile, China, Colombia, Comoros, Congo, Costa Rica, Cuba, Cyprus, Czech Republic, Democratic People's Republic of Korea, Denmark, Djibouti, Dominican Republic, Ecuador, Egypt, El Salvador, Equatorial Guinea, Eritrea, Estonia, Ethiopia, Fiji, Finland, France, Gabon, Gambia, Georgia, Germany, Ghana, Greece, Grenada, Guatemala, Guinea, Guinea-Bissau, Guyana, Haiti, Hungary, Iceland, India, Indonesia, Iran, Iraq, Ireland, Italy, Jamaica, Japan, Jordan, Kazakhstan, Kenya, Kuwait, Kyrgyzstan, Lao People's Democratic Republic, Latvia, Lebanon, Lesotho, Liberia, Libya, Liechtenstein, Lithuania, Luxembourg, Malaysia, Maldives, Mali, Malta, Mauritania, Mauritius, Mexico, Monaco, Mongolia, Montenegro, Morocco, Mozambique, Myanmar, Namibia, Nepal, Netherlands, New Zealand, Nicaragua, Nigeria, Norway, Oman, Pakistan, Panama, Papua New Guinea, Paraguay, Peru, Philippines, Poland, Portugal, Qatar, Republic of Korea, Republic of Moldova, Romania, Russian Federation, Saint Kitts and Nevis, Saint Lucia, Saint Vincent and the Grenadines, Samoa, San Marino, Sao Tome and Principe, Saudi Arabia, Senegal, Serbia, Sierra Leone, Singapore, Slovakia, Slovenia, Solomon Islands, Somalia, South Africa, Spain, Sri Lanka, Sudan, Suriname, Swaziland, Sweden, Switzerland, Syrian Arab Republic, Tajikistan, Thailand, the former Yugoslav Republic of Macedonia, Timor-Leste, Togo, Trinidad and Tobago, Tunisia, Turkey, Turkmenistan, Uganda, Ukraine, United Arab Emirates, United Kingdom, United Republic of Tanzania, Uruguay, Uzbekistan, Vanuatu, Venezuela, Viet Nam, Yemen, Zambia, Zimbabwe.

Against: Canada, Israel, Marshall Islands, Micronesia, Nauru, Palau, United States.

Abstaining: Australia, Cameroon, Côte d'Ivoire, Tonga.

In **resolution 66/146** of 19 December (see p. 681), the Assembly reaffirmed the right of the Palestinian people to self-determination, including their right to an independent State of Palestine. By **decision 66/557** of 24 December, the Assembly decided that the items on the situation in the Middle East and the question of Palestine would remain for consideration during its resumed sixty-sixth (2012) session.

Israeli settlements

The issue of Israeli settlements in the West Bank, including in East Jerusalem, remained central to the question of the Occupied Palestinian Territory and the peace negotiations. The road map [YUN 2003, p. 464] and the Joint Understanding [YUN 2007, p. 446] reached at the 2007 Annapolis Conference [ibid., p. 445] committed Israel to dismantle all settlement outposts erected since 2001 and, consistent with the 2001 report of the Sharm el-Sheikh Fact-Finding Committee (Mitchell Report) [YUN 2001, p. 409], to freeze all settlement activity, including "natural growth".

Communications. In a series of letters issued throughout the year, Palestine brought to the attention of the Secretary-General and the Security Council the ongoing construction and expansion of Israeli settlements in the Occupied Palestinian Territory, especially in and around East Jerusalem, as well as other Israeli activities that adversely affected Palestinian civilians living in the Territory [A/ES-10/509-S/2011/9, A/ES-10/510-S/2011/42, A/ES-10/511-S/2011/80, A/ES-10/512-S/2011/113, A/ES-10/513-S/2011/144, A/ES-10/514-S/2011/173, A/ES-10/515-S/2011/224, A/ES-10/518-S/2011/304, A/ES-10/520-S/2011/331, A/ES-10/523-S/2011/414, A/65/929-S/2011/513, A/ES-10/527-S/2011/515, A/ES-10/528-S/2011/521, A/ES-10/532-S/2011/597, A/ES-10/535-S/2011/645, A/ES-10/536-S/2011/665, A/ES-10/538-S/2011/680, A/ES-10/539-S/2011/724, A/ES-10/540-S/2011/761, A/ES-10/541-S/2011/765, A/ES-10/543-S/2011/783]. Israeli violations against Palestinians included the killing and wounding of Palestinian civilians by Israeli forces and settlers; the demolition of Palestinian homes and structures; the continued blockade of, and airstrikes targeting, Gaza; the deportation of Palestinian civilians; the destruction of the Ma'man Allah Cemetery in Jerusalem; and the continued construction of the separation wall [YUN 2004, p. 452].

The Special Rapporteur on the situation of human rights in the Palestinian territories occupied since 1967 [A/66/358] (see p. 783) also addressed the issue of Israeli settlements and their impact on the enjoyment of human rights by the Palestinians.

Report of Secretary-General. In response to General Assembly resolution 65/104 [YUN 2010, p. 451], the Secretary-General submitted a September report [A/66/364], prepared by the Office of the United Nations High Commissioner for Human Rights (OHCHR), covering the period from September 2010 to July 2011. The report addressed the continuation of Israeli settlement construction in the occupied Arab territories and its impact on the human rights of the residents, including violence by Israeli settlers against Palestinians and their property, and the lack of accountability for such violence. Under phase I of the road map, Israel had committed to freezing all settlement activity from March 2001. The agreement was consistent with the recommendation contained in the Mitchell Report, which stated that Israel should cease all settlement activity, including the "natural growth" of existing settlements [YUN 2009, p. 444].

Settlement activities resumed when Israel's 10-month moratorium on the building of new settlements in the West Bank [YUN 2010, p. 450] expired in September 2010. The most recent figures indicated that 296,586 settlers lived in at least 123 settlements and 100 "outposts"—settlements not authorized by Israel—in the West Bank, not including East Jerusalem. Nearly 192,000 Israeli settlers occupied 50,000 units in at least 12 settlements in East Jerusalem, which brought the total number of settlers living in the Occupied Palestinian Territory to almost half a million. As settlements expanded, Israel continued to restrict land allocation and planning for Palestinian construction, which resulted in the lack of building permits for Palestinians and the constant risk of eviction and demolition. The Human Rights Committee concluded that the planning systems in the West Bank, particularly in Area C and in East Jerusalem, were discriminatory and disproportionately favoured the Israeli population.

The demolition of Palestinian structures increased sharply during the reporting period. Between August 2010 and June 2011, Israeli authorities demolished 149 residences in Area C of the West Bank, displacing 820 people; another 23 residences were demolished in East Jerusalem, displacing 117 people. The Office for the Coordination of Humanitarian Affairs (OCHA) reported that, in the first half of 2011, 342 Palestinian-owned structures, including 125 residential buildings and 20 rainwater cisterns, were demolished; 656 people lost their homes. More than 3,000 demolition orders remained outstanding, including 18 targeting schools. Impunity for settlers that perpetrated violent attacks also continued. IDF not only failed to protect Palestinians, but instances of direct IDF involvement in violence against Palestinians had been documented. Some victims of settler violence attempted to file complaints with the Israeli police—the body responsible for investigating the incidents—but to do so, they usually had to enter Israeli settlements, which required special permits. When violence was committed or was suspected to have been committed by Palestinians against Israeli settlers, however, Israeli authorities often mobilized considerable resources to apprehend the perpetrators. OCHA reported that between September 2010 and June 2011, Israeli forces carried out 3,791 search-and-arrest operations and arrested 2,760 Palestinians.

The Secretary-General recommended that Israel freeze all settlement activities in the West Bank, including occupied East Jerusalem, and dismantle all "outposts". Israel should end its discriminatory policies and practices against Palestinians, in particular those that violated Palestinians' right to adequate housing. It should prevent attacks by Israeli settlers against Palestinian civilians and their property in the West Bank, including East Jerusalem. Israel should ensure that allegations concerning criminal acts committed by settlers or IDF were subject to independent, impartial and prompt investigations, and that all persons were equal before the law.

GENERAL ASSEMBLY ACTION

On 9 December [meeting 81], the General Assembly, on the recommendation of the Fourth (Special Political and Decolonization) Committee [A/66/427], adopted **resolution 66/78** by recorded vote (162-7-4) [agenda item 53].

Israeli settlements in the Occupied Palestinian Territory, including East Jerusalem, and the occupied Syrian Golan

The General Assembly,

Guided by the principles of the Charter of the United Nations, and affirming the inadmissibility of the acquisition of territory by force,

Recalling its relevant resolutions, including resolution 65/104 of 10 December 2010, as well as those resolutions adopted at its tenth emergency special session,

Recalling also the relevant resolutions of the Security Council, including resolutions 242(1967) of 22 November 1967, 446(1979) of 22 March 1979, 465(1980) of 1 March 1980, 476(1980) of 30 June 1980, 478(1980) of 20 August 1980, 497(1981) of 17 December 1981 and 904(1994) of 18 March 1994,

Reaffirming the applicability of the Geneva Convention relative to the Protection of Civilian Persons in Time of War, of 12 August 1949, to the Occupied Palestinian Territory, including East Jerusalem, and to the occupied Syrian Golan,

Affirming that the transfer by the occupying Power of parts of its own civilian population into the territory it occupies constitutes a breach of the Fourth Geneva Convention and relevant provisions of customary law, including those codified in Additional Protocol I to the four Geneva Conventions,

Recalling the advisory opinion rendered on 9 July 2004 by the International Court of Justice on the *Legal Consequences of the Construction of a Wall in the Occupied Palestinian Territory*, and recalling also General Assembly resolutions ES-10/15 of 20 July 2004 and ES-10/17 of 15 December 2006,

Noting that the International Court of Justice concluded that "the Israeli settlements in the Occupied Palestinian Territory (including East Jerusalem) have been established in breach of international law",

Taking note of the recent report of the Special Rapporteur of the Human Rights Council on the situation of human rights in the Palestinian territories occupied since 1967,

Recalling the Declaration of Principles on Interim Self-Government Arrangements of 13 September 1993 and the subsequent implementation agreements between the Palestinian and Israeli sides,

Recalling also the Quartet road map to a permanent two-State solution to the Israeli-Palestinian conflict, and emphasizing specifically its call for a freeze on all settlement activity, including so-called "natural growth", and the dismantlement of all settlement outposts erected since March 2001, and the need for Israel to uphold its obligations and commitments in this regard,

Aware that Israeli settlement activities involve, inter alia, the transfer of nationals of the occupying Power into the occupied territories, the confiscation of land, the displacement of Palestinian families, the exploitation of natural resources and other actions against the Palestinian civilian population and the civilian population in the occupied Syrian Golan that are contrary to international law,

Bearing in mind the extremely detrimental impact of Israeli settlement policies, decisions and activities on the efforts to resume and advance the peace process, on the credibility of the peace process, and on the prospects for the achievement of peace in the Middle East in accordance with the two-State solution of Israel and Palestine, living side by side in peace and security within recognized borders, on the basis of the pre-1967 borders,

Expressing grave concern about the continuation by Israel, the occupying Power, of settlement activities in the Occupied Palestinian Territory, including East Jerusalem, in violation of international humanitarian law, relevant United Nations resolutions, the agreements reached between the parties and obligations under the Quartet road map, and in defiance of the calls by the international community to cease all settlement activities,

Expressing grave concern in particular about Israel's construction and expansion of settlements in and around occupied East Jerusalem, including its so-called E-1 plan that aims to connect its illegal settlements around and further isolate occupied East Jerusalem, the continuing demolition of Palestinian homes and eviction of Palestinian families from the city, the revocation of Palestinian residency rights in the city, and ongoing settlement activities in the Jordan Valley,

Expressing grave concern about the continuing unlawful construction by Israel of the wall inside the Occupied Palestinian Territory, including in and around East Jerusalem, and expressing its concern in particular about the route of the wall in departure from the Armistice Line of 1949, which is causing humanitarian hardship and a serious decline of socioeconomic conditions for the Palestinian people, is fragmenting the territorial contiguity of the Territory and undermining its viability, and could prejudge future negotiations and make the two-State solution physically impossible to implement,

Deeply concerned that the wall's route has been traced in such a way as to include the great majority of the Israeli settlements in the Occupied Palestinian Territory, including East Jerusalem,

Deploring settlement activities in the Occupied Palestinian Territory, including East Jerusalem, and in the occupied Syrian Golan and any activities involving the confiscation of land, the disruption of the livelihood of protected persons and the de facto annexation of land,

Recalling the need to end all acts of violence, including acts of terror, provocation, incitement and destruction,

Gravely concerned about the rising incidents of violence, harassment, provocation and incitement by illegal armed Israeli settlers in the Occupied Palestinian Territory, including East Jerusalem, against Palestinian civilians, including children, and their properties, including historic and religious sites, and agricultural lands,

Noting the Israeli withdrawal from within the Gaza Strip and parts of the northern West Bank and the importance of the dismantlement of the settlements therein as a step towards the implementation of the road map, and calling, in this regard, for respect of the road map obligation upon Israel to freeze settlement activity, including so-called "natural growth", and to dismantle all settlement outposts erected since March 2001,

Taking note of the relevant reports of the Secretary-General,

Taking note also of the special meeting of the Security Council convened on 26 September 2008, as well as of the meeting of the Council of 18 February 2011,

1. *Reaffirms* that the Israeli settlements in the Palestinian territory, including East Jerusalem, and in the occupied Syrian Golan are illegal and an obstacle to peace and economic and social development;

2. *Calls upon* Israel to accept the de jure applicability of the Geneva Convention relative to the Protection of Civilian Persons in Time of War, of 12 August 1949, to the Occupied Palestinian Territory, including East Jerusalem, and to the occupied Syrian Golan and to abide scrupulously by the provisions of the Convention, in particular article 49;

3. *Also calls upon* Israel, the occupying Power, to comply strictly with its obligations under international law, including international humanitarian law, with respect to the alteration of the character, status and demographic composition of the Occupied Palestinian Territory, including East Jerusalem;

4. *Reiterates its demand* for the immediate and complete cessation of all Israeli settlement activities in all of the Occupied Palestinian Territory, including East Jerusalem, and in the occupied Syrian Golan, and calls, in this regard, for the full implementation of all the relevant resolutions of the Security Council, including, inter alia, resolutions 446(1979) of 22 March 1979, 452(1979) of 20 July 1979, 465(1980) of 1 March 1980, 476(1980) of 30 June 1980 and 1515(2003) of 19 November 2003;

5. *Demands* that Israel, the occupying Power, comply with its legal obligations, as mentioned in the advisory opinion rendered on 9 July 2004 by the International Court of Justice;

6. *Reiterates its call* for the prevention of all acts of violence and harassment by Israeli settlers, especially against Palestinian civilians and their properties, including historic and religious sites, and agricultural lands, and stresses the need for the implementation of Security Council resolution 904(1994), in which the Council called upon Israel, the occupying Power, to continue to take and implement measures, including confiscation of arms, aimed at preventing illegal acts of violence by Israeli settlers, and called for measures to be taken to guarantee the safety and protection of the Palestinian civilians in the occupied territory;

7. *Requests* the Secretary-General to report to the General Assembly at its sixty-seventh session on the implementation of the present resolution.

RECORDED VOTE ON RESOLUTION 66/78:

In favour: Afghanistan, Albania, Algeria, Andorra, Angola, Antigua and Barbuda, Argentina, Armenia, Australia, Austria, Azerbaijan, Bahamas, Bahrain, Bangladesh, Barbados, Belarus, Belgium, Belize, Benin, Bhutan, Bolivia, Bosnia and Herzegovina, Botswana, Brazil, Brunei Darussalam, Bulgaria, Burkina Faso, Burundi, Cambodia, Cape Verde, Chad, Chile, China, Colombia, Congo, Costa Rica, Croatia, Cuba, Cyprus, Czech Republic, Democratic People's Republic of Korea, Denmark, Djibouti, Dominican Republic, Ecuador, Egypt, El Salvador, Eritrea, Estonia, Ethiopia, Fiji, Finland, France, Germany, Ghana, Greece, Grenada, Guatemala, Guinea, Guinea-Bissau, Guyana, Haiti, Honduras, Hungary, Iceland, India, Indonesia, Iran, Iraq, Ireland, Italy, Jamaica, Japan, Jordan, Kazakhstan, Kenya, Kuwait, Kyrgyzstan, Lao People's Democratic Republic, Latvia, Lebanon, Lesotho, Liberia, Libya, Liechtenstein, Lithuania, Luxembourg, Madagascar, Malawi, Malaysia, Maldives, Mali, Malta, Mauritania, Mauritius, Mexico, Monaco, Mongolia, Montenegro, Morocco, Mozambique, Namibia, Nepal, Netherlands, New Zealand, Nicaragua, Norway, Oman, Pakistan, Papua New Guinea, Paraguay, Peru, Philippines, Poland, Portugal, Qatar, Republic of Korea, Republic of Moldova, Romania, Russian Federation, Saint Lucia, Saint Vincent and the Grenadines, Samoa, San Marino, Saudi Arabia, Senegal, Serbia, Sierra Leone, Singapore, Slovakia, Slovenia, Solomon Islands, Somalia, South Africa, Spain, Sri Lanka, Sudan, Swaziland, Sweden, Switzerland, Syrian Arab Republic, Tajikistan, Thailand, the former Yugoslav Republic of Macedonia, Timor-Leste, Togo, Trinidad and Tobago, Tunisia, Turkey, Turkmenistan, Tuvalu, Uganda, Ukraine, United Arab Emirates, United Kingdom, Uruguay, Uzbekistan, Venezuela, Viet Nam, Yemen, Zambia, Zimbabwe.

Against: Canada, Israel, Marshall Islands, Micronesia, Nauru, Palau, United States.

Abstaining: Cameroon, Côte d'Ivoire, Panama, Vanuatu.

Jerusalem

Report of Secretary-General. On 6 September [A/66/338], the Secretary-General reported that as at 31 August, one Member State (Syrian Arab Republic), had replied to his request for information on steps taken or envisaged to implement General Assembly resolution 65/17 [YUN 2010, p. 452] on Jerusalem. Resolution 65/17 stressed that a comprehensive, just and lasting solution to the question of Jerusalem should take into account the legitimate concerns of both the Palestinian and Israeli sides and include internationally guaranteed provisions to ensure the freedom of religion and of conscience of its residents, as well as permanent, free and unhindered access to the holy places by the people of all religions and nationalities.

GENERAL ASSEMBLY ACTION

On 30 November [meeting 69], the General Assembly adopted **resolution 66/18** [draft: A/66/L.19 & Add.1] by recorded vote (164-7-5) [agenda item 36].

Jerusalem

The General Assembly,

Recalling its resolution 181(II) of 29 November 1947, in particular its provisions regarding the City of Jerusalem,

Recalling also its resolution 36/120 E of 10 December 1981 and all its subsequent relevant resolutions, including resolution 56/31 of 3 December 2001, in which it, inter alia, determined that all legislative and administrative measures and actions taken by Israel, the occupying Power, which have altered or purported to alter the character and status of the Holy City of Jerusalem, in particular the so-called "Basic Law" on Jerusalem and the proclamation of Jerusalem as the capital of Israel, were null and void and must be rescinded forthwith,

Recalling further the Security Council resolutions relevant to Jerusalem, including resolution 478(1980) of 20 August 1980, in which the Council, inter alia, decided not to recognize the "Basic Law" on Jerusalem,

Recalling the advisory opinion rendered on 9 July 2004 by the International Court of Justice on the *Legal Consequences of the Construction of a Wall in the Occupied Palestinian Territory*, and recalling its resolution ES-10/15 of 20 July 2004,

Expressing its grave concern about any action taken by any body, governmental or non-governmental, in violation of the above-mentioned resolutions,

Expressing its grave concern also, in particular, about the continuation by Israel, the occupying Power, of illegal settlement activities, including the so-called E-1 plan, its construction of the wall in and around East Jerusalem, its restrictions on access to and residence in East Jerusalem and the further isolation of the city from the rest of the Occupied Palestinian Territory, which are having a detrimental effect on the lives of Palestinians and could prejudge a final status agreement on Jerusalem,

Expressing its grave concern further about the continuing Israeli demolition of Palestinian homes, the revocation of residency rights and the eviction and displacement of numerous Palestinian families from East Jerusalem neighbourhoods, as well as other acts of provocation and incitement, including by Israeli settlers, in the city,

Expressing its concern about the Israeli excavations undertaken in the Old City of Jerusalem, including in and around religious sites,

Reaffirming that the international community, through the United Nations, has a legitimate interest in the question of the City of Jerusalem and in the protection of the unique spiritual, religious and cultural dimensions of the city, as foreseen in relevant United Nations resolutions on this matter,

Having considered the report of the Secretary-General on the situation in the Middle East,

1. *Reiterates its determination* that any actions taken by Israel, the occupying Power, to impose its laws, jurisdiction and administration on the Holy City of Jerusalem are illegal and therefore null and void and have no validity whatsoever, and calls upon Israel to immediately cease all such illegal and unilateral measures;

2. *Stresses* that a comprehensive, just and lasting solution to the question of the City of Jerusalem should take into account the legitimate concerns of both the Palestinian and Israeli sides and should include internationally guaranteed provisions to ensure the freedom of religion and of conscience of its inhabitants, as well as permanent, free and unhindered access to the holy places by the people of all religions and nationalities;

3. *Requests* the Secretary-General to report to the General Assembly at its sixty-seventh session on the implementation of the present resolution.

RECORDED VOTE ON RESOLUTION 66/18:

In favour: Afghanistan, Albania, Algeria, Andorra, Antigua and Barbuda, Argentina, Armenia, Australia, Austria, Azerbaijan, Bahamas, Bahrain, Bangladesh, Barbados, Belarus, Belgium, Belize, Benin, Bhutan, Bolivia, Bosnia and Herzegovina, Botswana, Brazil, Brunei Darussalam, Bulgaria, Cambodia, Cape Verde, Chad, Chile, China, Colombia, Comoros, Congo, Costa Rica, Côte d'Ivoire, Cuba, Cyprus, Czech Republic, Democratic People's Republic of Korea, Denmark, Djibouti, Dominican Republic, Ecuador, Egypt, El Salvador, Eritrea, Estonia, Ethiopia, Fiji, Finland, France, Gambia, Georgia, Germany, Ghana, Greece, Grenada, Guatemala, Guinea, Guinea-Bissau, Guyana, Honduras, Hungary, Iceland, India, Indonesia, Iran, Iraq, Ireland, Italy, Jamaica, Japan, Jordan, Kazakhstan, Kenya, Kuwait, Kyrgyzstan, Lao People's Democratic Republic, Latvia, Lebanon, Lesotho, Liberia, Libya, Liechtenstein, Lithuania, Luxembourg, Malaysia, Maldives, Mali, Malta, Mauritania, Mauritius, Mexico, Monaco, Mongolia, Montenegro, Morocco, Mozambique, Myanmar, Namibia, Nepal, Netherlands, New Zealand, Nicaragua, Nigeria, Norway, Oman, Pakistan, Papua New Guinea, Paraguay, Peru, Philippines, Poland, Portugal, Qatar, Republic of Korea, Republic of Moldova, Romania, Russian Federation, Saint Kitts and Nevis, Saint Lucia, Saint Vincent and the Grenadines, Samoa, San Marino, Sao Tome and Principe, Saudi Arabia, Senegal, Serbia, Singapore, Slovakia, Slovenia, Solomon Islands, Somalia, South Africa, Spain, Sri Lanka, Sudan, Suriname, Swaziland, Sweden, Switzerland, Syrian Arab Republic, Tajikistan, Thailand, the former Yugoslav Republic of Macedonia, Timor-Leste, Togo, Trinidad and Tobago, Tunisia, Turkey, Turkmenistan, Uganda, Ukraine, United Arab Emirates, United Kingdom, United Republic of Tanzania, Uruguay, Uzbekistan, Vanuatu, Venezuela, Viet Nam, Yemen, Zambia, Zimbabwe.

Against: Canada, Israel, Marshall Islands, Micronesia, Nauru, Palau, United States.

Abstaining: Cameroon, Equatorial Guinea, Haiti, Panama, Tonga.

Other matters

Israeli practices affecting human rights of Palestinian people

Report of Special Committee. By a 22 September note [A/66/370], the Secretary-General submitted the forty-third report of the Special Committee to Investigate Israeli Practices Affecting the Human Rights of the Palestinian People and Other Arabs of the Occupied Territories (Special Committee on Israeli Practices), established by General Assembly resolution 2443(XXIII) [YUN 1968, p. 555]. The report, submitted in response to Assembly resolution 65/102 [YUN 2010, p. 458], described the activities of the Special Committee as well as the situation of human rights in the territories considered by the Committee to be occupied by Israel: the Syrian Golan (see also p. 471) and the Occupied Palestinian Territory of the West Bank, including East Jerusalem, and the Gaza Strip. The report reflected information gathered during the Special Committee's first-ever visit to the Occupied Palestinian Territory, specifically Gaza, after crossing Egypt's border with the territory. Meetings were held in Gaza from 21 to 25 July, during which the Special Committee met with 24 witnesses. The Committee also convened meetings in Jordan (26–28 July). It was unable to convene meetings in the Syrian Arab Republic due to the unrest that took place there during the reporting period, but engaged with interlocutors in the occupied Syrian Golan by way of teleconferences. Owing to the continuing practice of non-recognition of and non-cooperation with the Special Committee by Israel, the Committee was unable to directly access all of the occupied territories within its mandate or consult with Israeli authorities.

The Special Committee observed that Israel's blockade of Gaza, which had been in place for more than four years, punished the civilian population. The blockade neither undermined support for the de facto authorities in Gaza, nor enhanced Israel's security. Israeli-enforced restrictions on freedom of movement within Gaza—in particular their impacts on the agricultural and fishing industries—and Israel's regulations on the importation of materials necessary to reconstruct or build houses, schools and other infrastructure destroyed by Israel during the 2008–2009 Gaza conflict [YUN 2009, p. 434] were among the most urgent concerns that emerged during the Special Committee's meetings in Gaza. Gaza's private-sector economy had nearly come to a halt: 90 per cent of factories in Gaza had closed due to the lack of access to raw materials; 90,000 Gazans had lost their jobs in Israel owing to the blockade; and real wages for those who did have jobs decreased by 30 per cent. It was widely acknowledged that a significant amount of goods, including building supplies and medicines, entered Gaza through underground tunnels, and their provenance and quality were unregulated. Some smuggled materials were found to be carcinogenic. In that context, concern was expressed regarding the trustworthiness of smuggled medicines.

The Special Committee called on Israel to take immediate action to reverse indicators of poor children's health in Gaza and to desist from its policies and practices that denied thousands of children their right to education. Israel was urged to consider the potential consequences for the children of Gaza being raised in an environment characterized by deprivation and lack of opportunities.

The Special Committee expressed concern over Israel's continued detainment of thousands of Palestinians—many for extended periods of time—under conditions that appeared to violate international law. It was also alarmed by allegations concerning the treatment of detained children, and noted that such treatment would amount to torture or cruel, inhuman or degrading treatment or punishment. The Committee called on Israel to bring its policies and practices concerning the arrest, detention and sentencing of minors and other Palestinians in line with international laws and standards.

The Special Committee expressed alarm concerning allegations that Israel enforced restrictions of movement within certain areas of Gaza, including its fishing areas, and the implementation of a so-called "buffer zone" in Palestinian territory adjacent to Israel through the use of live fire. The Committee reiterated its call for Israel to lift its illegal siege of Gaza and ensure a consistent and sufficient supply of food, medicines and other basic supplies and services, in line with Security Council resolution 1860(2009) [YUN 2009, p. 434]. Israel also needed to clarify the restrictions it intended to administer on the freedom of movement within Gaza and should not enforce restrictions through the use of live weapons fire.

Regarding the West Bank, the Special Committee expressed dismay that many of Israel's policies and practices, including the confiscation of Palestinian land, demolition of Palestinian homes, displacement of Palestinian civilians and expansion of Israeli settlements, continued to take place on a widespread and systematic basis. It called on Israel to desist from confiscating land in the West Bank and return it to its rightful owners; and cease the demolition of homes and provide reparation to those whose homes had been demolished. The Committee also stressed the need for Israel to cease building settlements in the Occupied Palestinian Territory and to dismantle all those previously built. It called on Israel to end violence against Palestinians by Israeli settlers, and to ensure access to water for Syrians in the occupied Golan on terms equal to those available to Israeli settlers.

Report of Secretary-General. In response to General Assembly resolution 65/105 [YUN 2010, p. 455], the Secretary-General submitted a September report [A/66/356] on Israeli practices affecting the human rights of the Palestinian people in the Occupied Palestinian Territory, including East Jerusalem, covering the period from 20 August 2010 to 30 June 2011. The information contained in the report was based on data gathered by OHCHR and other UN entities in the Occupied Palestinian Territory, as well as information obtained from Israeli and Palestinian sources, NGOs, human rights defenders and the media. The report examined themes identified in resolution 65/105, including the right to life and security, particularly the killing and injury of civilians; displacement and other practices affecting the demographic composition of the Occupied Palestinian Territory; the firing of rockets and mortars against Israeli civilian areas; restrictions on the freedom of movement and goods; and arrests and detention.

The majority of casualties related to armed conflict occurred in Gaza. The most intense escalation of incidents since the end of Gaza conflict in 2009 [YUN 2009, p. 434] occurred in April, when IDF attacks on targets in Gaza resulted in the death of 23 Palestinians, including nine civilians. The killing of non-combatants raised questions regarding IDF respect for the basic provisions of international law when carrying out an offensive. The Secretary-General recommended that Israel ensure that any IDF attack respected the principles of conduct of hostilities, namely distinction, proportionality and precautions. Field commanders should evaluate the timing of attacks and the military advantage expected to be gained from responding immediately to the launch of rockets or mortars when appropriate means were not available to mitigate the risk to civilians.

During the reporting period, Palestinian armed groups fired 325 rockets and 389 mortar shells at Israel. In April, a missile attack resulted in the death of a 16-year-old Israeli boy. The launching of such weapons ran contrary to international humanitarian law, which prohibited random attacks, the targeting of civilians, the use of inherently indiscriminate arms and acts aimed at spreading terror in the general population. Palestinian armed groups needed to comply with international law and cease such indiscriminate attacks.

Excessive use of violent measures in policing operations by Israeli security forces in the West Bank continued. Unarmed civilians were injured or killed at checkpoints during routine patrols or arrest operations. In three OHCHR-documented cases, 13 fishermen were arrested and their boats confiscated, although they had not travelled beyond the three-nautical-mile buffer zone and posed no threat to Israeli naval forces. OHCHR also recorded 26 cases in which IDF shot and injured Palestinians who were collecting rubble and scrap metal within a distance of between 200 and 1,000 metres from the Green Line. The Secretary-General recommended that Israel prevent further incidents of excessive use of force.

Israel continued its policy of revoking the permanent residency status of Palestinians residing in East Jerusalem if they lived outside Israel or East Jerusalem for seven years, or obtained permanent residency in another country. The requirement of "loyalty to the State of Israel" for East Jerusalem residents to maintain their residency was analogous to compelling residents to swear "allegiance to the hostile power", which violated the Hague Regulations. Israel had to end its policies resulting in the forcible transfer of civilians in the Occupied Palestinian Territory and should desist from revoking the residency status of those living in East Jerusalem.

OCHA reported a sharp rise in the number of demolitions of homes and other buildings in the first half of 2011. The 1949 Geneva Convention relative to the Protection of Civilian Persons in Time of War (Fourth Geneva Convention) prohibited the destruction of homes in the occupied territory except when rendered absolutely necessary by military operations; no such operations had taken place in the West Bank for years. The Secretary-General stated that Israel should cease the demolition of houses and other structures in the Occupied Palestinian Territory and modify planning and zoning rules to ensure adequate housing for the Palestinian residents of Area C and East Jerusalem. He recommended that Israel comply with the 2004 advisory opinion of the International Court of Justice concerning the construction of the wall [YUN 2004, p. 1273], in particular by halting construction of the barrier and dismantling or rerouting the constructed section to the Green Line.

According to NGO sources, approximately 5,500 Palestinians were held in Israeli detention as at June. The vast majority was held in prisons and detention centres outside the occupied territory, in violation of the Fourth Geneva Convention. The frequent and extensive use of administrative detention by Israel also infringed on the right to a fair trial. Taking into account the observations of the Human Rights Committee, the Secretary-General recommended that Israel conduct an independent review of its administrative detention policy with a view to terminating it and removing its derogation regarding article 9 of the International Covenant on Civil and Political Rights [YUN 1966, p. 423].

Report of Special Rapporteur. By a 13 September note [A/66/358], the Secretary-General transmitted to the General Assembly the report of the Special Rapporteur, Richard Falk, on the situation of human rights in the Palestinian territories occupied since 1967 (see p. 783).

(For information on the right of the Palestinian people to self-determination, see p. 681, and on the human rights situation in the territories occupied by Israel, see p. 782).

UN Register of Damage. On 27 June, in accordance with General Assembly resolution ES-10/17 [YUN 2006, p. 529], the Secretary-General submitted to the Assembly a progress report of the Board of the United Nations Register of Damage Caused by the Construction of the Wall in the Occupied Palestinian Territory [A/ES-10/522] covering the period from 19 June 2010 to 10 June 2011. During that period, the Board held four meetings in Vienna to review 1,426 claim forms that had been translated and processed by the office staff, and included in the Register most of the losses set out in those forms. As at 10 June, the Board had reviewed 3,255 claim forms; it included in the Register most of the losses set out in 2,977 forms.

Israel continued to consider that any claims related to damage caused by the building of the wall should be addressed through the existing Israeli mechanism. The Register, however, maintained constructive contacts with relevant Israeli authorities and did not experience any difficulties with access, freedom of movement, security, delivery of needed materials or issuance of required visas.

GENERAL ASSEMBLY ACTION

On 9 December [meeting 81], the General Assembly, on the recommendation of the Fourth Committee [A/66/427], adopted **resolution 66/79** by recorded vote (159-9-4) [agenda item 53].

Israeli practices affecting the human rights of the Palestinian people in the Occupied Palestinian Territory, including East Jerusalem

The General Assembly,

Recalling the Universal Declaration of Human Rights,

Recalling also the International Covenant on Civil and Political Rights, the International Covenant on Economic, Social and Cultural Rights and the Convention on the Rights of the Child, and affirming that these human rights instruments must be respected in the Occupied Palestinian Territory, including East Jerusalem,

Reaffirming its relevant resolutions, including resolution 65/105 of 10 December 2010 as well as those adopted at its tenth emergency special session,

Recalling the relevant resolutions of the Human Rights Council,

Recalling also the relevant resolutions of the Security Council, and stressing the need for their implementation,

Having considered the report of the Special Committee to Investigate Israeli Practices Affecting the Human Rights of the Palestinian People and Other Arabs of the Occupied Territories and the report of the Secretary-General,

Taking note of the recent reports of the Special Rapporteur of the Human Rights Council on the situation of human rights in the Palestinian territories occupied since 1967, as well as of other relevant recent reports of the Human Rights Council,

Aware of the responsibility of the international community to promote human rights and ensure respect for international law, and recalling, in this regard, its resolution 2625(XXV) of 24 October 1970,

Recalling the advisory opinion rendered on 9 July 2004 by the International Court of Justice, and recalling also General Assembly resolutions ES-10/15 of 20 July 2004 and ES-10/17 of 15 December 2006,

Noting in particular the Court's reply, including that the construction of the wall being built by Israel, the occupying Power, in the Occupied Palestinian Territory, including in and around East Jerusalem, and its associated regime are contrary to international law,

Reaffirming the principle of the inadmissibility of the acquisition of territory by force,

Reaffirming also the applicability of the Geneva Convention relative to the Protection of Civilian Persons in Time of War, of 12 August 1949, to the Occupied Palestinian Territory, including East Jerusalem, and other Arab territories occupied by Israel since 1967,

Reaffirming further the obligation of the States parties to the Fourth Geneva Convention under articles 146, 147 and 148 with regard to penal sanctions, grave breaches and responsibilities of the High Contracting Parties,

Reaffirming that all States have the right and the duty to take actions in conformity with international law and international humanitarian law to counter deadly acts of violence against their civilian population in order to protect the lives of their citizens,

Stressing the need for full compliance with the Israeli-Palestinian agreements reached within the context of the Middle East peace process, including the Sharm el-Sheikh understandings, and the implementation of the Quartet road map to a permanent two-State solution to the Israeli-Palestinian conflict,

Stressing also the need for the full implementation of the Agreement on Movement and Access and the Agreed Principles for the Rafah Crossing, both of 15 November 2005, to allow for the freedom of movement of the Palestinian civilian population within and into and out of the Gaza Strip,

Expressing grave concern about the continuing systematic violation of the human rights of the Palestinian people by Israel, the occupying Power, including that arising from the excessive use of force and military operations causing death and injury to Palestinian civilians, including children, women and non-violent, peaceful demonstrators; the use of collective punishment; the closure of areas; the confiscation of land; the establishment and expansion of settlements; the construction of a wall in the Occupied Palestinian Territory in departure from the Armistice Line of 1949; the destruction of property and infrastructure; and all other actions by it designed to change the legal status, geographical nature and demographic composition of the Occupied Palestinian Territory, including East Jerusalem,

Gravely concerned in particular about the critical humanitarian and security situation in the Gaza Strip, including that resulting from the prolonged closures and severe economic and movement restrictions that in effect amount to a blockade and the military operations between December 2008 and January 2009, which caused extensive loss of life and injury, particularly among Palestinian civilians, including children and women, widespread destruction and damage to Palestinian homes, properties, vital infrastructure and public institutions, including hospitals, schools and United Nations facilities and the internal displacement of civilians, as well as about the firing of rockets into Israel,

Stressing the need for the full implementation by all parties of Security Council resolution 1860(2009) of 8 January 2009 and General Assembly resolution ES-10/18 of 16 January 2009,

Gravely concerned by reports regarding serious human rights violations and grave breaches of international humanitarian law committed during the military operations in the Gaza Strip between December 2008 and January 2009, including the findings in the summary by the Secretary-General of the report of the Board of Inquiry and in the report of the United Nations Fact-finding Mission on the Gaza Conflict, and reiterating the necessity for serious follow-up by all parties of the recommendations addressed to them towards ensuring accountability and justice,

Expressing deep concern about the short- and long-term detrimental impact of such widespread destruction and the continued impeding of the reconstruction process by Israel, the occupying Power, on the human rights situation and on the socioeconomic and humanitarian conditions of the Palestinian civilian population,

Also expressing deep concern about the Israeli policy of closures and the imposition of severe restrictions, checkpoints, several of which have been transformed into structures akin to permanent border crossings, and a permit regime, all of which obstruct the freedom of movement of persons and goods, including medical and humanitarian goods, throughout the Occupied Palestinian Territory, including East Jerusalem, and impair the Territory's contiguity, and about the consequent violation of the human rights of the Palestinian people and the negative impact on their socioeconomic situation and the efforts aimed at rehabilitating and developing the Palestinian economy, which remains that of a humanitarian crisis in the Gaza Strip, while taking note of recent developments with regard to the situation of access there,

Further expressing deep concern that thousands of Palestinians, including many children and women, continue to be held in Israeli prisons or detention centres under harsh conditions, including, inter alia, unhygienic conditions, solitary confinement, lack of proper medical care, denial of family visits and denial of due process, that impair their well-being, and expressing deep concern also about the ill-treatment and harassment of any Palestinian prisoners and all reports of torture,

Expressing concern about the possible consequences of the enactment by Israel, the occupying Power, of military orders regarding the detention, imprisonment and deportation of Palestinian civilians from the Occupied Palestinian Territory, including East Jerusalem, and recalling, in this regard, the prohibition under international humanitarian law of the deportation of civilians from occupied territories,

Convinced of the need for an international presence to monitor the situation, to contribute to ending the violence and protecting the Palestinian civilian population and to help the parties implement the agreements reached, and, in this regard, recalling the positive contribution of the Temporary International Presence in Hebron,

Taking note of the continued efforts and tangible progress made in the security sector by the Palestinian Authority, calling upon the parties to continue cooperation that benefits both Palestinians and Israelis, in particular by promoting security and building confidence, and expressing the hope that such progress will be extended to all major population centres,

Emphasizing the right of all people in the region to the enjoyment of human rights as enshrined in the international human rights covenants,

1. *Reiterates* that all measures and actions taken by Israel, the occupying Power, in the Occupied Palestinian Territory, including East Jerusalem, in violation of the relevant provisions of the Geneva Convention relative to the Protection of Civilian Persons in Time of War, of 12 August 1949, and contrary to the relevant resolutions of the Security Council, are illegal and have no validity;

2. *Demands* that Israel, the occupying Power, cease all practices and actions that violate the human rights of the Palestinian people, including the killing and injury of civilians, the arbitrary detention and imprisonment of civilians and the destruction and confiscation of civilian property, and that it fully respect human rights law and comply with its legal obligations in this regard;

3. *Also demands* that Israel, the occupying Power, comply fully with the provisions of the Fourth Geneva Convention of 1949 and cease immediately all measures and actions taken in violation and in breach of the Convention;

4. *Further demands* that Israel, the occupying Power, cease all of its settlement activities, the construction of the wall and any other measures aimed at altering the character, status and demographic composition of the Occupied Palestinian Territory, including in and around East Jerusalem, all of which, inter alia, gravely and detrimentally impact the human rights of the Palestinian people and the prospects for a peaceful settlement;

5. *Condemns* all acts of violence, including all acts of terror, provocation, incitement and destruction, especially the excessive use of force by the Israeli occupying forces against Palestinian civilians, particularly in the Gaza Strip, which have caused extensive loss of life and vast numbers of injuries, including among children, massive damage and destruction to homes, properties, vital infrastructure and public institutions, including hospitals, schools and United Nations facilities, and agricultural lands, and internal displacement of civilians;

6. *Expresses grave concern* at the firing of rockets against Israeli civilian areas resulting in loss of life and injury;

7. *Reiterates its demand* for the full implementation of Security Council resolution 1860(2009);

8. *Demands* that Israel, the occupying Power, comply with its legal obligations under international law, as mentioned in the advisory opinion rendered on 9 July 2004 by the International Court of Justice and as demanded in General Assembly resolutions ES-10/15 of 20 July 2004 and ES-10/13 of 21 October 2003, and that it immediately cease the construction of the wall in the Occupied Palestinian Territory, including in and around East Jerusalem, dismantle forthwith the structure situated therein, repeal or render ineffective all legislative and regulatory acts relating thereto, and make reparation for all damage caused by the construction of the wall, which has gravely impacted the human rights and the socioeconomic living conditions of the Palestinian people;

9. *Reiterates* the need for respect for the territorial unity, contiguity and integrity of all of the Occupied Palestinian Territory and for guarantees of the freedom of movement of persons and goods within the Palestinian territory, including movement into and from East Jerusalem, into and from the Gaza Strip, between the West Bank and Gaza Strip, and to and from the outside world;

10. *Calls upon* Israel, the occupying Power, to cease its imposition of prolonged closures and economic and movement restrictions, including those amounting to a blockade on the Gaza Strip, and, in this regard, to fully implement the Agreement on Movement and Access and the Agreed Principles for the Rafah Crossing, both of 15 November 2005, in order to allow for the sustained and regular movement of persons and goods and for the acceleration of long overdue reconstruction in the Gaza Strip;

11. *Urges* Member States to continue to provide emergency assistance to the Palestinian people to alleviate the financial crisis and the dire socioeconomic and humanitarian situation, particularly in the Gaza Strip;

12. *Emphasizes* the need to preserve and develop the Palestinian institutions and infrastructure for the provision of vital public services to the Palestinian civilian population

and the promotion of human rights, including civil, political, economic, social and cultural rights;

13. *Requests* the Secretary-General to report to the General Assembly at its sixty-seventh session on the implementation of the present resolution.

RECORDED VOTE ON RESOLUTION 66/79:

In favour: Afghanistan, Albania, Algeria, Andorra, Angola, Antigua and Barbuda, Argentina, Armenia, Austria, Azerbaijan, Bahamas, Bahrain, Bangladesh, Barbados, Belarus, Belgium, Belize, Benin, Bhutan, Bolivia, Bosnia and Herzegovina, Botswana, Brazil, Brunei Darussalam, Bulgaria, Burundi, Cambodia, Cape Verde, Chad, Chile, China, Colombia, Congo, Costa Rica, Croatia, Cuba, Cyprus, Czech Republic, Democratic People's Republic of Korea, Denmark, Djibouti, Dominican Republic, Ecuador, Egypt, Eritrea, Estonia, Ethiopia, Fiji, Finland, France, Germany, Ghana, Greece, Grenada, Guatemala, Guinea, Guinea-Bissau, Guyana, Haiti, Honduras, Hungary, Iceland, India, Indonesia, Iran, Iraq, Ireland, Italy, Jamaica, Japan, Jordan, Kazakhstan, Kenya, Kuwait, Kyrgyzstan, Lao People's Democratic Republic, Latvia, Lebanon, Lesotho, Liberia, Libya, Liechtenstein, Lithuania, Luxembourg, Madagascar, Malawi, Malaysia, Maldives, Mali, Malta, Mauritania, Mauritius, Mexico, Monaco, Mongolia, Montenegro, Morocco, Mozambique, Namibia, Nepal, Netherlands, New Zealand, Nicaragua, Norway, Oman, Pakistan, Papua New Guinea, Paraguay, Peru, Philippines, Poland, Portugal, Qatar, Republic of Korea, Republic of Moldova, Romania, Russian Federation, Saint Lucia, Saint Vincent and the Grenadines, Samoa, San Marino, Saudi Arabia, Senegal, Serbia, Sierra Leone, Singapore, Slovakia, Slovenia, Solomon Islands, Somalia, South Africa, Spain, Sri Lanka, Sudan, Swaziland, Sweden, Switzerland, Syrian Arab Republic, Tajikistan, Thailand, the former Yugoslav Republic of Macedonia, Timor-Leste, Togo, Trinidad and Tobago, Tunisia, Turkey, Turkmenistan, Tuvalu, Uganda, Ukraine, United Arab Emirates, United Kingdom, Uruguay, Uzbekistan, Venezuela, Viet Nam, Yemen, Zambia, Zimbabwe.

Against: Australia, Canada, Israel, Marshall Islands, Micronesia, Nauru, Palau, Panama, United States.

Abstaining: Cameroon, Côte d'Ivoire, El Salvador, Vanuatu.

Work of Special Committee

In response to General Assembly resolution 65/102 [YUN 2010, p. 458], the Secretary-General issued a September report on the work of the Special Committee [A/66/373]. The Special Committee made its first trip to the Occupied Palestinian Territory—specifically to Gaza—by crossing Egypt's border with the territory. Various UN agencies, especially OHCHR, as well as the offices of the resident coordinators in Egypt and Jordan, provided support to the Special Committee during the implementation of its mandate. The Special Committee collected testimony from 53 victims, witnesses and human rights organizations during its mission.

The News and Media Division of the UN Department of Public Information ensured the wide dissemination of information about the Special Committee's work. The Committee's meetings and statements were covered by eight press releases in English and French. The English and French platforms of the UN News Centre posted 14 stories about the work of the Special Committee throughout the year and circulated them through a subscriber base of tens of thousands of readers. UN Radio provided regular segments and feature stories in eight languages—Kiswahili and Portuguese, in addition to the six UN official languages—on the work and events associated with the Special Committee, as well as related issues, such as Israeli settlement activity, the demolition of Palestinian homes and the Israeli blockade of the Gaza Strip. The UN Webcast provided coverage of 65 open UN meetings, briefings and events related to the Palestinian question. The UN Television Section produced two videos on women's issues in the Occupied Palestinian Territory.

GENERAL ASSEMBLY ACTION

On 9 December [meeting 81], the General Assembly, on the recommendation of the Fourth Committee [A/66/427], adopted **resolution 66/76** by recorded vote (86-9-75) [agenda item 53].

Work of the Special Committee to Investigate Israeli Practices Affecting the Human Rights of the Palestinian People and Other Arabs of the Occupied Territories

The General Assembly,

Guided by the purposes and principles of the Charter of the United Nations,

Guided also by international humanitarian law, in particular the Geneva Convention relative to the Protection of Civilian Persons in Time of War of 12 August 1949, as well as international standards of human rights, in particular the Universal Declaration of Human Rights and the International Covenants on Human Rights,

Recalling its relevant resolutions, including resolutions 2443(XXIII) of 19 December 1968 and 65/102 of 10 December 2010, and the relevant resolutions of the Commission on Human Rights and the Human Rights Council, including resolution S-12/1, adopted by the Council at its twelfth special session on 16 October 2009,

Recalling also the relevant resolutions of the Security Council,

Taking into account the advisory opinion rendered on 9 July 2004 by the International Court of Justice on the *Legal Consequences of the Construction of a Wall in the Occupied Palestinian Territory*, and recalling, in this regard, General Assembly resolution ES-10/15 of 20 July 2004,

Recalling its resolution 58/292 of 6 May 2004,

Convinced that occupation itself represents a gross and grave violation of human rights,

Gravely concerned about the continuing detrimental impact of ongoing unlawful Israeli practices and measures in the Occupied Palestinian Territory, including East Jerusalem, including the excessive use of force by the Israeli occupying forces against Palestinian civilians, resulting in the death and injury of civilians, the widespread destruction of property and vital infrastructure, ongoing settlement activities and construction of the wall, the internal displacement of civilians, the imposition of collective punishment measures, particularly against the civilian population in the Gaza Strip, and the detention and imprisonment of thousands of Palestinians,

Gravely concerned in particular by reports regarding serious human rights violations and grave breaches of international humanitarian law committed during the military operations in the Gaza Strip between December 2008 and January 2009, including the findings in the summary by the Secretary-General of the report of the Board of Inquiry and in the report of the United Nations Fact-Finding Mission on the Gaza Conflict, and stressing the necessity for serious follow-up by all parties to the recommendations addressed to them towards ensuring accountability and justice,

Having considered the report of the Special Committee to Investigate Israeli Practices Affecting the Human Rights of the Palestinian People and Other Arabs of the Occupied Territories and the relevant reports of the Secretary-General,

Recalling the Declaration of Principles on Interim Self-Government Arrangements of 13 September 1993 and the subsequent implementation agreements between the Palestinian and Israeli sides,

Stressing the urgency of bringing a complete end to the Israeli occupation that began in 1967 and thus an end to the violation of the human rights of the Palestinian people, and of allowing for the realization of their inalienable human rights, including their right to self-determination and their independent State,

Taking note of the application of Palestine for admission to membership in the United Nations, submitted on 23 September 2011,

1. *Commends* the Special Committee to Investigate Israeli Practices Affecting the Human Rights of the Palestinian People and Other Arabs of the Occupied Territories for its efforts in performing the tasks assigned to it by the General Assembly and for its impartiality;

2. *Reiterates its demand* that Israel, the occupying Power, cooperate, in accordance with its obligations as a State Member of the United Nations, with the Special Committee in implementing its mandate;

3. *Deplores* those policies and practices of Israel that violate the human rights of the Palestinian people and other Arabs of the occupied territories, as reflected in the report of the Special Committee covering the reporting period;

4. *Expresses grave concern* about the critical situation in the Occupied Palestinian Territory, including East Jerusalem, particularly in the Gaza Strip, as a result of unlawful Israeli practices and measures, and especially condemns and calls for the immediate cessation of all illegal Israeli settlement activities and the construction of the wall, as well as the excessive and indiscriminate use of force against the civilian population, the destruction and confiscation of properties, measures of collective punishment, and the detention and imprisonment of thousands of civilians;

5. *Requests* the Special Committee, pending complete termination of the Israeli occupation, to continue to investigate Israeli policies and practices in the Occupied Palestinian Territory, including East Jerusalem, and other Arab territories occupied by Israel since 1967, especially Israeli violations of the Geneva Convention relative to the Protection of Civilian Persons in Time of War of 12 August 1949, and to consult, as appropriate, with the International Committee of the Red Cross according to its regulations in order to ensure that the welfare and human rights of the peoples of the occupied territories are safeguarded and to report to the Secretary-General as soon as possible and whenever the need arises thereafter;

6. *Also requests* the Special Committee to submit regularly to the Secretary-General periodic reports on the current situation in the Occupied Palestinian Territory, including East Jerusalem;

7. *Further requests* the Special Committee to continue to investigate the treatment and status of the thousands of prisoners and detainees, including children and women, in Israeli prisons and detention centres in the Occupied Palestinian Territory, including East Jerusalem, and other Arab territories occupied by Israel since 1967;

8. *Requests* the Secretary-General:

(*a*) To provide the Special Committee with all necessary facilities, including those required for its visits to the occupied territories, so that it may investigate the Israeli policies and practices referred to in the present resolution;

(*b*) To continue to make available such staff as may be necessary to assist the Special Committee in the performance of its tasks;

(*c*) To circulate regularly to Member States the periodic reports mentioned in paragraph 6 above;

(*d*) To ensure the widest circulation of the reports of the Special Committee and of information regarding its activities and findings, by all means available, through the Department of Public Information of the Secretariat and, where necessary, to reprint those reports of the Special Committee that are no longer available;

(*e*) To report to the General Assembly at its sixty-seventh session on the tasks entrusted to him in the present resolution;

9. *Decides* to include in the provisional agenda of its sixty-seventh session the item entitled "Report of the Special Committee to Investigate Israeli Practices Affecting the Human Rights of the Palestinian People and Other Arabs of the Occupied Territories".

RECORDED VOTE ON RESOLUTION 66/76:

In favour: Afghanistan, Algeria, Antigua and Barbuda, Armenia, Azerbaijan, Bahrain, Bangladesh, Barbados, Belarus, Belize, Bhutan, Bolivia, Brazil, Brunei Darussalam, Cambodia, Chile, China, Congo, Cuba, Democratic People's Republic of Korea, Djibouti, Dominican Republic, Ecuador, Egypt, Ghana, Grenada, Guinea, Guinea-Bissau, Guyana, India, Indonesia, Iran, Iraq, Jamaica, Jordan, Kazakhstan, Kenya, Kuwait, Kyrgyzstan, Lao People's Democratic Republic, Lebanon, Lesotho, Liberia, Libya, Malawi, Malaysia, Maldives, Mali, Mauritania, Mauritius, Morocco, Mozambique, Namibia, Nepal, Nicaragua, Oman, Pakistan, Qatar, Saint Lucia, Saint Vincent and the Grenadines, Saudi Arabia, Senegal, Sierra Leone, Singapore, Solomon Islands, Somalia, South Africa, Sri Lanka, Sudan, Swaziland, Syrian Arab Republic, Tajikistan, Togo, Trinidad and Tobago, Tunisia, Turkey, Turkmenistan, Tuvalu, Uganda, United Arab Emirates, Uzbekistan, Venezuela, Viet Nam, Yemen, Zambia, Zimbabwe.

Against: Australia, Canada, Israel, Marshall Islands, Micronesia, Nauru, Palau, Panama, United States.

Abstaining: Albania, Andorra, Angola, Argentina, Austria, Bahamas, Belgium, Benin, Bosnia and Herzegovina, Botswana, Bulgaria, Burkina Faso, Burundi, Cameroon, Colombia, Costa Rica, Côte d'Ivoire, Croatia, Cyprus, Czech Republic, Denmark, El Salvador, Estonia, Ethiopia, Fiji, Finland, France, Germany, Greece, Guatemala, Haiti, Honduras, Hungary, Iceland, Ireland, Italy, Japan, Latvia, Liechtenstein, Lithuania, Luxembourg, Malta, Mexico, Monaco, Mongolia, Montenegro, Netherlands, New Zealand, Norway, Papua New Guinea, Paraguay, Peru, Philippines, Poland, Portugal, Republic of Korea, Republic of Moldova, Romania, Russian Federation, Samoa, San Marino, Serbia, Slovakia, Slovenia, Spain, Sweden, Switzerland, Thailand, the former Yugoslav Republic of Macedonia, Timor-Leste, Tonga, Ukraine, United Kingdom, Uruguay, Vanuatu.

Economic and social situation

A May report [A/66/78-E/2011/13] on the economic and social repercussions of the Israeli occupation on the living conditions of the Palestinian people in the Occupied Palestinian Territory, including East Jerusalem, and of the Arab population in the occupied Syrian Golan was prepared by the Economic and Social Commission for Western Asia, in accordance with Economic and Social Council resolution 2010/31 [YUN 2010, p. 460] and General Assembly resolution 65/179 [ibid., p. 463].

The report stated that Israeli settlements, their infrastructure and the territory zoned for their expansion were the largest factors shaping the system of access restrictions applied to the Palestinian population in the West Bank. Palestinian land and structures were at risk of confiscation for Israeli purposes, such as construction of the wall and the roads serving its settlements. In some areas, Israeli settlers unilaterally established and enforced the restricted areas, and in others the Israeli military erected fences around settlements and declared them special security zones.

The blockade imposed by Israel on the Gaza Strip following the forceful takeover of Gaza by Hamas in June 2007 [YUN 2007, p. 441] remained in effect, and movement in and out of Gaza remained difficult for its population; a limited number of people who required urgent medical care and those accompanying them could enter Israel with permits. The December 2010 announcement by Israeli authorities of an easing of export restrictions remained mostly unimplemented. Palestinians had limited access to surface water resources, such as the Jordan River, and Israel extracted 80 per cent of the estimated potential of the aquifers under the West Bank. Israel also overdrew more than half of the potential water by means of deep wells without regular consultation with the PA. Such action led to a drop in water tables and the continued drying up of Palestinian wells.

In the occupied Syrian Golan, the Israeli control and the closed crossing into the Syrian Arab Republic created obstacles to economic development and the normalization of the social fabric. Syrian citizens who wished to maintain their Syrian Arab identity faced restricted prospects of earning a living.

ECONOMIC AND SOCIAL COUNCIL ACTION

On 28 July [meeting 49], the Economic and Social Council adopted **resolution 2011/41** [draft: E/2011/L.47] by roll-call vote (43-3-3) [agenda item 11].

Economic and social repercussions of the Israeli occupation on the living conditions of the Palestinian people in the Occupied Palestinian Territory, including East Jerusalem, and the Arab population in the occupied Syrian Golan

The Economic and Social Council,

Recalling General Assembly resolution 65/179 of 20 December 2010,

Recalling also its resolution 2010/31 of 23 July 2010,

Guided by the principles of the Charter of the United Nations affirming the inadmissibility of the acquisition of territory by force, and recalling relevant Security Council resolutions, including resolutions 242(1967) of 22 November 1967, 252(1968) of 21 May 1968, 338(1973) of 22 October 1973, 465(1980) of 1 March 1980 and 497(1981) of 17 December 1981,

Recalling the resolutions of the tenth emergency special session of the General Assembly, including resolutions ES-10/13 of 21 October 2003, ES-10/14 of 8 December 2003, ES-10/15 of 20 July 2004 and ES-10/17 of 15 December 2006,

Reaffirming the applicability of the Geneva Convention relative to the Protection of Civilian Persons in Time of War, of 12 August 1949, to the Occupied Palestinian Territory, including East Jerusalem, and other Arab territories occupied by Israel since 1967,

Recalling the International Covenant on Civil and Political Rights, the International Covenant on Economic, Social and Cultural Rights and the Convention on the Rights of the Child, and reaffirming that these human rights instruments must be respected in the Occupied Palestinian Territory, including East Jerusalem, as well as in the occupied Syrian Golan,

Stressing the importance of the revival and acceleration of serious and credible negotiations within the Middle East peace process on the basis of Security Council resolutions 242(1967), 338(1973), 425(1978) of 19 March 1978, 1397(2002) of 12 March 2002, 1515(2003) of 19 November 2003, 1544(2004) of 19 May 2004 and 1850(2008) of 16 December 2008, the principle of land for peace, the Arab Peace Initiative and the Quartet road map, as well as compliance with the agreements reached between the Government of Israel and the Palestine Liberation Organization, the representative of the Palestinian people,

Reaffirming the principle of the permanent sovereignty of peoples under foreign occupation over their natural resources, and expressing concern in that regard about the exploitation of natural resources by Israel, the occupying Power, in the Occupied Palestinian Territory, including East Jerusalem, and in the occupied Syrian Golan,

Convinced that the Israeli occupation has gravely impeded the efforts to achieve sustainable development and a sound economic environment in the Occupied Palestinian Territory, including East Jerusalem, and in the occupied Syrian Golan, and expressing grave concern about the consequent deterioration of economic and living conditions,

Commending, in that regard, the efforts of the Palestinian Authority to improve the economic and social situation in the Occupied Palestinian Territory, especially in the areas of governance, the rule of law and human rights, livelihoods and productive sectors, education and culture, health, social protection, infrastructure and water,

Gravely concerned, in that regard, about the accelerated construction of settlements and implementation of other related measures by Israel in the Occupied Palestinian Territory, particularly in and around occupied East Jerusalem, as well as in the occupied Syrian Golan, in violation of international humanitarian law and relevant United Nations resolutions,

Expressing deep concern about the rising incidence of violence, harassment, provocation and incitement by illegal armed Israeli settlers in the Occupied Palestinian Territory, including East Jerusalem, against Palestinian civilians, including children, and their properties, including historic and religious sites, and agricultural lands,

Gravely concerned by the serious repercussions on the economic and social conditions of the Palestinian people caused by Israel's construction of the wall and its associated regime inside the Occupied Palestinian Territory, including in and around East Jerusalem, and the resulting violation of their economic and social rights, including the right to work, to health, to education, to property, to an adequate standard of living and to freedom of access and movement,

Recalling, in that regard, the advisory opinion rendered on 9 July 2004 by the International Court of Justice on the *Legal Consequences of the Construction of a Wall in the Occupied Palestinian Territory* and General Assembly resolution ES-10/15, and stressing the need to comply with the obligations mentioned therein,

Expressing grave concern at the extensive destruction by Israel, the occupying Power, of properties, including the increased demolition of homes, economic institutions, agricultural lands and orchards, in the Occupied Palestinian Territory, including East Jerusalem, in particular in connection with its construction of the wall, contrary to international law, in the Occupied Palestinian Territory, including in and around East Jerusalem,

Expressing grave concern also over the continuing and intensifying policy of home demolitions, evictions and revocation of residency rights, which have caused the further displacement of the Palestinian population in and around occupied East Jerusalem, as well as measures to further isolate the city from its natural Palestinian environs, including through the accelerated construction of settlements, the construction of the wall, the confiscation of land and the continued imposition of checkpoints, which have seriously exacerbated the already critical socio-economic situation being faced by the Palestinian population,

Expressing grave concern further about Israeli military operations and the continuing Israeli policy of closures and severe restrictions on the movement of persons and goods, including humanitarian personnel and food, medical, fuel, construction material and other essential supplies, via the imposition of crossing closures, checkpoints and a permit regime throughout the Occupied Palestinian Territory, including East Jerusalem, and the consequent negative impact on the socio-economic situation of the Palestinian people, in particular the Palestinian refugee population, which remains that of a humanitarian crisis,

Taking note of recent developments regarding the situation of access to the Gaza Strip, although grave hardships continue to prevail as a result of the prolonged Israeli closures and severe economic and movement restrictions that in effect amount to a blockade, and calling in that regard for the full implementation of Security Council resolution 1860(2009) of 8 January 2009 with a view to ensuring the full opening of the border crossings for the sustained and regular movement of persons and goods, including humanitarian aid, commercial flows and construction materials,

Deploring the heavy casualties among civilians, including hundreds of children and women, the internal displacement of thousands of civilians and widespread damage to homes, vital civilian infrastructure, hospitals, schools, food supply installations, economic, industrial and agricultural properties and several United Nations facilities in the Gaza Strip, which have a grave impact on the provision of vital health and social services to Palestinian women and their families and on their socio-economic living conditions, all caused by the military operations in December 2008 and January 2009,

Recalling, in that regard, the relevant United Nations reports, including those of the Economic and Social Council, the Economic and Social Commission for Western Asia and the Human Rights Council,

Expressing deep concern about the short- and long-term detrimental impact of such widespread destruction and the hampering of the reconstruction process by Israel, the occupying Power, on the socio-economic and humanitarian conditions of the Palestinian civilian population in the Gaza Strip, and calling in that regard for the immediate acceleration of the reconstruction process in the Gaza Strip with the assistance of the donor countries, including the disbursement of funds pledged at the International Conference in Support of the Palestinian Economy for the Reconstruction of Gaza, held in Sharm el-Sheikh, Egypt, on 2 March 2009,

Gravely concerned at various reports of the United Nations and specialized agencies regarding the substantial aid dependency caused by prolonged border closures, inordinate rates of unemployment, widespread poverty and severe humanitarian hardships, including food insecurity and rising health-related problems, including high levels of malnutrition, among the Palestinian people, especially children, in the Occupied Palestinian Territory, including East Jerusalem,

Expressing grave concern at the deaths and injuries caused to civilians, including children, women and peaceful demonstrators, and emphasizing that the Palestinian civilian population must be protected in accordance with international humanitarian law,

Emphasizing the importance of the safety and well-being of all civilians, and calling for the cessation of all acts of violence, including all acts of terror, provocation, incitement and destruction, and all firing of rockets,

Expressing deep concern that thousands of Palestinians, including hundreds of children and women, continue to be held in Israeli prisons or detention centres under harsh conditions,

Conscious of the urgent need for the reconstruction and development of the economic and social infrastructure of the Occupied Palestinian Territory, including East Jerusalem, as well as the urgent need to address the humanitarian crisis facing the Palestinian people, including by ensuring the unimpeded provision of humanitarian assistance and the sustained and regular flow of persons and goods into and out of the Gaza Strip,

Commending the important work being done by the United Nations, the specialized agencies and the donor community in support of the economic and social development of the Palestinian people in line with their national development and State-building plan, which is to be completed by the end of August 2011, as well as the assistance being provided in the humanitarian field,

Recognizing the efforts being undertaken by the Palestinian Authority, with international support, to rebuild, reform and strengthen its damaged institutions and promote good governance, and emphasizing the need to preserve the Palestinian national institutions and infrastructure and to ameliorate economic and social conditions,

Welcoming in that regard, and calling upon the international community to continue its strong support for, the plan of the Palestinian Authority entitled "Palestine: Ending the Occupation, Establishing the State", for constructing the institutions of a Palestinian State by September 2011,

Stressing the importance of national unity among the Palestinian people, and emphasizing the need for the respect and preservation of the territorial integrity and unity of the Occupied Palestinian Territory, including East Jerusalem,

Calling upon both parties to fulfil their obligations under the road map in cooperation with the Quartet,

1. *Calls for* the full opening of the border crossings of the Gaza Strip, in line with Security Council resolution 1860(2009), to ensure humanitarian access as well as the sustained and regular flow of persons and goods and the lifting of all movement restrictions imposed on the Palestinian people, including those restrictions arising from ongoing Israeli military operations and the multilayered closures system, and for other urgent measures to be taken to alleviate the serious humanitarian situation in the Occupied Palestinian Territory, which is critical in the Gaza Strip, and calls for compliance by Israel, the occupying Power, with all of its legal obligations under international humanitarian law and United Nations resolutions in that regard;

2. *Stresses* the need to preserve the territorial contiguity, unity and integrity of the Occupied Palestinian Territory, including East Jerusalem, and to guarantee the freedom of movement of persons and goods throughout the Occupied Palestinian Territory, including East Jerusalem, as well as to and from the outside world;

3. *Also stresses* the need to preserve and develop Palestinian national institutions and infrastructure for the provision of vital public services to the Palestinian civilian population and to contribute to the promotion and protection of human rights, including economic and social rights;

4. *Demands* that Israel comply with the Protocol on Economic Relations between the Government of Israel and the Palestine Liberation Organization, signed in Paris on 29 April 1994;

5. *Calls upon* Israel to restore and replace civilian properties, vital infrastructure, agricultural lands and governmental institutions that have been damaged or destroyed as a result of its military operations in the Occupied Palestinian Territory;

6. *Reiterates* the call for the full implementation of the Agreement on Movement and Access of 15 November 2005, particularly the urgent and uninterrupted reopening of all crossings into the Gaza Strip, which is crucial to ensuring the passage of foodstuffs and essential supplies, including construction materials and adequate fuel supplies, as well as to ensuring the unhindered access of the United Nations and related agencies and regular commercial flows necessary for economic recovery to and within the Occupied Palestinian Territory;

7. *Calls upon* all parties to respect the rules of international humanitarian law and to refrain from violence against the civilian population, in accordance with the Geneva Convention relative to the Protection of Civilian Persons in Time of War, of 12 August 1949;

8. *Reaffirms* the inalienable right of the Palestinian people and the Arab population of the occupied Syrian Golan to all their natural and economic resources, and calls upon Israel, the occupying Power, not to exploit, endanger or cause loss or depletion of those resources;

9. *Calls upon* Israel, the occupying Power, to cease its destruction of homes and properties, economic institutions and agricultural lands and orchards in the Occupied Palestinian Territory, including East Jerusalem, as well as in the occupied Syrian Golan;

10. *Also calls upon* Israel, the occupying Power, to end immediately its exploitation of natural resources, including water and mining resources, and to cease the dumping of all kinds of waste materials in the Occupied Palestinian Territory, including East Jerusalem, and in the occupied Syrian Golan, which gravely threaten their natural resources, namely, the water, land and energy resources, and present a serious environmental hazard and health threat to the civilian populations, and also calls upon Israel, the occupying Power, to remove all obstacles that obstruct implementation of critical environmental projects, including the sewage treatment plants in the Gaza Strip;

11. *Reaffirms* that the construction and expansion of Israeli settlements and related infrastructure in the Occupied Palestinian Territory, including East Jerusalem, and the occupied Syrian Golan, are illegal and constitute a major obstacle to economic and social development and to the achievement of peace, and calls for the full cessation of all settlement and settlement-related activity, including full cessation of all measures aimed at altering the demographic composition, legal status and character of the occupied territories, including, in particular, in and around Occupied East Jerusalem, in compliance with relevant Security Council resolutions and international law, including the Geneva Convention relative to the Protection of Civilian Persons in Time of War;

12. *Also reaffirms* that the ongoing construction by Israel of the wall in the Occupied Palestinian Territory, including in and around East Jerusalem, is contrary to international law and is isolating East Jerusalem, fragmenting the West Bank and seriously debilitating the economic and social development of the Palestinian people, and calls in that regard for full compliance with the legal obliga-

tions mentioned in the 9 July 2004 advisory opinion of the International Court of Justice and in General Assembly resolution ES-10/15 and subsequent relevant resolutions;

13. *Calls upon* Israel to comply with the provisions of the Geneva Convention relative to the Protection of Civilian Persons in Time of War and to facilitate visits of the Syrian citizens of the occupied Syrian Golan whose family members reside in their mother homeland, the Syrian Arab Republic, via the Qunaitra entrance;

14. *Emphasizes* the importance of the work of United Nations organizations and agencies in the Occupied Palestinian Territory, including East Jerusalem, and of the United Nations Special Coordinator for the Middle East Peace Process and Personal Representative of the Secretary-General to the Palestine Liberation Organization and the Palestinian Authority;

15. *Reiterates* the importance of the revival and accelerated advancement of negotiations of the peace process on the basis of relevant United Nations resolutions, including Security Council resolutions 242(1967), 338(1973), 425(1978), 1397(2002), 1515(2003), 1544(2004) and 1850(2008), the Madrid Conference, the principle of land for peace, the Arab Peace Initiative and the Quartet road map, as well as compliance with the agreements reached between the Government of Israel and the Palestine Liberation Organization, the representative of the Palestinian people, in order to pave the way for the establishment of the independent Palestinian State and the achievement of a just, lasting and comprehensive peace settlement;

16. *Requests* the Secretary-General to submit to the General Assembly at its sixty-sixth session, through the Economic and Social Council, a report on the implementation of the present resolution and to continue to include in the report of the United Nations Special Coordinator an update on the living conditions of the Palestinian people, in collaboration with relevant United Nations agencies;

17. *Decides* to include the item entitled "Economic and social repercussions of the Israeli occupation on the living conditions of the Palestinian people in the Occupied Palestinian Territory, including East Jerusalem, and the Arab population in the occupied Syrian Golan" in the agenda of its substantive session of 2012.

ROLL-CALL VOTE ON RESOLUTION 2011/41:

In favour: Argentina, Bahamas, Bangladesh, Belgium, Chile, China, Ecuador, Egypt, Estonia, Finland, France, Germany, Ghana, Guatemala, Hungary, India, Iraq, Italy, Japan, Latvia, Malta, Mauritius, Mexico, Mongolia, Morocco, Namibia, Nicaragua, Norway, Pakistan, Peru, Philippines, Qatar, Republic of Korea, Russian Federation, Saudi Arabia, Senegal, Slovakia, Spain, Switzerland, Ukraine, United Kingdom, Venezuela, Zambia.

Against: Australia, Canada, United States.

Abstaining: Cameroon, Côte d'Ivoire, Rwanda.

GENERAL ASSEMBLY ACTION

On 22 December [meeting 91], the General Assembly, on the recommendation of the Second (Economic and Financial) Committee [A/66/449], adopted **resolution 66/225** by recorded vote (167-7-6) [agenda item 61].

Permanent sovereignty of the Palestinian people in the Occupied Palestinian Territory, including East Jerusalem, and of the Arab population in the occupied Syrian Golan over their natural resources

The General Assembly,

Recalling its resolution 65/179 of 20 December 2010, and taking note of Economic and Social Council resolution 2011/41 of 28 July 2011,

Recalling also its resolutions 58/292 of 6 May 2004 and 59/251 of 22 December 2004,

Reaffirming the principle of the permanent sovereignty of peoples under foreign occupation over their natural resources,

Guided by the principles of the Charter of the United Nations, affirming the inadmissibility of the acquisition of territory by force, and recalling relevant Security Council resolutions, including resolutions 242(1967) of 22 November 1967, 465(1980) of 1 March 1980 and 497(1981) of 17 December 1981,

Recalling its resolution 2625(XXV) of 24 October 1970,

Reaffirming the applicability of the Geneva Convention relative to the Protection of Civilian Persons in Time of War, of 12 August 1949, to the Occupied Palestinian Territory, including East Jerusalem, and other Arab territories occupied by Israel since 1967,

Recalling, in this regard, the International Covenant on Civil and Political Rights and the International Covenant on Economic, Social and Cultural Rights, and affirming that these human rights instruments must be respected in the Occupied Palestinian Territory, including East Jerusalem, as well as in the occupied Syrian Golan,

Recalling also the advisory opinion rendered on 9 July 2004 by the International Court of Justice on the *Legal Consequences of the Construction of a Wall in the Occupied Palestinian Territory*, and recalling further its resolutions ES-10/15 of 20 July 2004 and ES-10/17 of 15 December 2006,

Expressing its concern about the exploitation by Israel, the occupying Power, of the natural resources of the Occupied Palestinian Territory, including East Jerusalem, and other Arab territories occupied by Israel since 1967,

Expressing its grave concern about the extensive destruction by Israel, the occupying Power, of agricultural land and orchards in the Occupied Palestinian Territory, including the uprooting of a vast number of fruit-bearing trees and the destruction of farms and greenhouses, and the grave environmental and economic impact in this regard,

Expressing its concern about the widespread destruction caused by Israel, the occupying Power, to vital infrastructure, including water pipelines and sewage networks, in the Occupied Palestinian Territory, in particular in the Gaza Strip in the recent period, which, inter alia, pollutes the environment and negatively affects the water supply and other natural resources of the Palestinian people,

Taking note, in this regard, of the 2009 report by the United Nations Environment Programme regarding the grave environmental situation in the Gaza Strip, and stressing the need for follow-up to the recommendations contained therein,

Aware of the detrimental impact of the Israeli settlements on Palestinian and other Arab natural resources, especially as a result of the confiscation of land and the forced diversion of water resources, and of the dire socioeconomic consequences in this regard,

Aware also of the detrimental impact on Palestinian natural resources being caused by the unlawful construction of the wall by Israel, the occupying Power, in the Occupied Palestinian Territory, including in and around East Jerusalem, and of its grave effect as well on the economic and social conditions of the Palestinian people,

Reaffirming the need for the resumption and accelerated advancement of negotiations within the Middle East peace process, on the basis of Security Council resolutions 242(1967), 338(1973) of 22 October 1973, 425(1978) of 19 March 1978 and 1397(2002) of 12 March 2002, the principle of land for peace, the Arab Peace Initiative and the Quartet performance-based road map to a permanent two-State solution to the Israeli-Palestinian conflict, as endorsed by the Security Council in its resolution 1515(2003) of 19 November 2003 and supported by the Council in its resolution 1850(2008) of 16 December 2008, for the achievement of a final settlement on all tracks,

Noting the Israeli withdrawal from within the Gaza Strip and parts of the northern West Bank and the importance of the dismantlement of settlements therein in the context of the road map, and calling in this regard for respect of the road map obligation upon Israel to freeze settlement activity, including so-called "natural growth", and to dismantle all settlement outposts erected since March 2001,

Stressing the need for respect and preservation of the territorial unity, contiguity and integrity of all of the Occupied Palestinian Territory, including East Jerusalem,

Recalling the need to end all acts of violence, including acts of terror, provocation, incitement and destruction,

Taking note of the note by the Secretary-General transmitting the report prepared by the Economic and Social Commission for Western Asia on the economic and social repercussions of the Israeli occupation on the living conditions of the Palestinian people in the Occupied Palestinian Territory, including East Jerusalem, and of the Arab population in the occupied Syrian Golan,

1. *Reaffirms* the inalienable rights of the Palestinian people and of the population of the occupied Syrian Golan over their natural resources, including land, water and energy resources;

2. *Demands* that Israel, the occupying Power, cease the exploitation, damage, cause of loss or depletion, and endangerment of the natural resources in the Occupied Palestinian Territory, including East Jerusalem, and in the occupied Syrian Golan;

3. *Recognizes* the right of the Palestinian people to claim restitution as a result of any exploitation, damage, loss or depletion, or endangerment of their natural resources resulting from illegal measures taken by Israel, the occupying Power, in the Occupied Palestinian Territory, including East Jerusalem, and expresses the hope that this issue will be dealt with within the framework of the final status negotiations between the Palestinian and Israeli sides;

4. *Stresses* that the wall and settlements being constructed by Israel in the Occupied Palestinian Territory, including in and around East Jerusalem, are contrary to international law and are seriously depriving the Palestinian people of their natural resources, and calls in this regard for full compliance with the legal obligations affirmed in the 9 July 2004 advisory opinion of the International Court of Justice and in relevant United Nations resolutions, including General Assembly resolution ES-10/15;

5. *Calls upon* Israel, the occupying Power, to comply strictly with its obligations under international law, including international humanitarian law, with respect to the alteration of the character and status of the Occupied Palestinian Territory, including East Jerusalem;

6. *Also calls upon* Israel, the occupying Power, to cease all actions harming the environment, including the dumping of all kinds of waste materials in the Occupied Palestinian Territory, including East Jerusalem, and in the occupied Syrian Golan, which gravely threaten their natural resources, namely water and land resources, and which pose an environmental, sanitation and health threat to the civilian populations;

7. *Further calls upon* Israel to cease its destruction of vital infrastructure, including water pipelines and sewage networks, which, inter alia, has a negative impact on the natural resources of the Palestinian people;

8. *Requests* the Secretary-General to report to the General Assembly at its sixty-seventh session on the implementation of the present resolution, including with regard to the cumulative impact of the exploitation, damage and depletion by Israel of natural resources in the Occupied Palestinian Territory, including East Jerusalem, and in the occupied Syrian Golan, and decides to include in the provisional agenda of its sixty-seventh session the item entitled "Permanent sovereignty of the Palestinian people in the Occupied Palestinian Territory, including East Jerusalem, and of the Arab population in the occupied Syrian Golan over their natural resources".

RECORDED VOTE ON RESOLUTION 66/225:

In favour: Afghanistan, Albania, Algeria, Andorra, Angola, Antigua and Barbuda, Argentina, Armenia, Austria, Azerbaijan, Bahamas, Bahrain, Bangladesh, Barbados, Belarus, Belgium, Belize, Benin, Bhutan, Bolivia, Bosnia and Herzegovina, Botswana, Brazil, Brunei Darussalam, Bulgaria, Burkina Faso, Burundi, Cambodia, Cape Verde, Chad, Chile, China, Colombia, Comoros, Congo, Costa Rica, Croatia, Cuba, Cyprus, Czech Republic, Democratic People's Republic of Korea, Denmark, Djibouti, Dominica, Dominican Republic, Ecuador, Egypt, Eritrea, Estonia, Ethiopia, Fiji, Finland, France, Gabon, Georgia, Germany, Greece, Grenada, Guatemala, Guinea, Guinea-Bissau, Guyana, Haiti, Honduras, Hungary, Iceland, India, Indonesia, Iran, Iraq, Ireland, Italy, Jamaica, Japan, Jordan, Kazakhstan, Kenya, Kuwait, Kyrgyzstan, Lao People's Democratic Republic, Latvia, Lebanon, Lesotho, Liberia, Libya, Liechtenstein, Lithuania, Luxembourg, Madagascar, Malawi, Malaysia, Maldives, Mali, Malta, Mauritania, Mauritius, Mexico, Monaco, Mongolia, Montenegro, Morocco, Mozambique, Myanmar, Namibia, Nepal, Netherlands, New Zealand, Nicaragua, Niger, Nigeria, Norway, Oman, Pakistan, Papua New Guinea, Paraguay, Peru, Philippines, Poland, Portugal, Qatar, Republic of Korea, Republic of Moldova, Romania, Russian Federation, Saint Lucia, Saint Vincent and the Grenadines, San Marino, Saudi Arabia, Senegal, Serbia, Sierra Leone, Singapore, Slovakia, Slovenia, Solomon Islands, Somalia, South Africa, Spain, Sri Lanka, Sudan, Suriname, Swaziland, Sweden, Switzerland, Syrian Arab Republic, Tajikistan,

Thailand, the former Yugoslav Republic of Macedonia, Timor-Leste, Togo, Trinidad and Tobago, Tunisia, Turkey, Turkmenistan, Tuvalu, Uganda, Ukraine, United Arab Emirates, United Kingdom, United Republic of Tanzania, Uruguay, Uzbekistan, Venezuela, Viet Nam, Yemen, Zambia, Zimbabwe.

Against: Canada, Israel, Marshall Islands, Micronesia, Nauru, Palau, United States.

Abstaining: Australia, Cameroon, Côte d'Ivoire, El Salvador, Panama, Tonga.

Fourth Geneva Convention

The applicability of the 1949 Geneva Convention relative to the Protection of Civilian Persons in Time of War (Fourth Geneva Convention) to the Israeli-occupied territories was reaffirmed during the year by the General Assembly and several other UN bodies, including the Special Committee on Israeli Practices.

Report of Secretary-General. The Secretary-General, in a September report [A/66/362], informed the General Assembly that Israel had not replied to his June request for information on steps taken or envisaged to implement resolution 65/103 [YUN 2010, p. 464], which demanded that Israel accept the de jure applicability of the Fourth Geneva Convention to the Occupied Palestinian Territory, including East Jerusalem, and other Arab territories occupied since 1967, and that it comply with its provisions. The Secretary-General had also drawn the attention of the High Contracting Parties to the Convention to resolution 65/103, which called on them to ensure Israel's respect for the Convention's provisions. No Member States replied to his request for information on steps taken to implement the resolution.

GENERAL ASSEMBLY ACTION

On 9 December [meeting 81], the General Assembly, on the recommendation of the Fourth Committee [A/66/427], adopted **resolution 66/77** by recorded vote (164-7-2) [agenda item 53].

Applicability of the Geneva Convention relative to the Protection of Civilian Persons in Time of War, of 12 August 1949, to the Occupied Palestinian Territory, including East Jerusalem, and the other occupied Arab territories

The General Assembly,

Recalling its relevant resolutions, including resolution 65/103 of 10 December 2010,

Bearing in mind the relevant resolutions of the Security Council,

Recalling the Regulations annexed to The Hague Convention IV of 1907, the Geneva Convention relative to the Protection of Civilian Persons in Time of War, of 12 August 1949, and relevant provisions of customary law, including those codified in Additional Protocol I to the four Geneva Conventions,

Having considered the report of the Special Committee to Investigate Israeli Practices Affecting the Human Rights of the Palestinian People and Other Arabs of the Occupied Territories and the relevant reports of the Secretary-General,

Considering that the promotion of respect for the obligations arising from the Charter of the United Nations and other instruments and rules of international law is among the basic purposes and principles of the United Nations,

Recalling the advisory opinion rendered on 9 July 2004 by the International Court of Justice, and also recalling General Assembly resolution ES-10/15 of 20 July 2004,

Noting in particular the Court's reply, including that the Fourth Geneva Convention is applicable in the Occupied Palestinian Territory, including East Jerusalem, and that Israel is in breach of several of the provisions of the Convention,

Recalling the Conference of High Contracting Parties to the Fourth Geneva Convention on measures to enforce the Convention in the Occupied Palestinian Territory, including East Jerusalem, held on 15 July 1999, as well as the Declaration adopted by the reconvened Conference on 5 December 2001 and the need for the parties to follow up the implementation of the Declaration,

Welcoming and encouraging the initiatives by States parties to the Convention, both individually and collectively, according to article 1 common to the four Geneva Conventions, aimed at ensuring respect for the Convention, as well as the continuing efforts of the depositary State of the Geneva Conventions in this regard,

Stressing that Israel, the occupying Power, should comply strictly with its obligations under international law, including international humanitarian law,

1. *Reaffirms* that the Geneva Convention relative to the Protection of Civilian Persons in Time of War, of 12 August 1949, is applicable to the Occupied Palestinian Territory, including East Jerusalem, and other Arab territories occupied by Israel since 1967;

2. *Demands* that Israel accept the de jure applicability of the Convention in the Occupied Palestinian Territory, including East Jerusalem, and other Arab territories occupied by Israel since 1967, and that it comply scrupulously with the provisions of the Convention;

3. *Calls upon* all High Contracting Parties to the Convention, in accordance with article 1 common to the four Geneva Conventions and as mentioned in the advisory opinion of the International Court of Justice of 9 July 2004, to continue to exert all efforts to ensure respect for its provisions by Israel, the occupying Power, in the Occupied Palestinian Territory, including East Jerusalem, and other Arab territories occupied by Israel since 1967;

4. *Reiterates* the need for speedy implementation of the relevant recommendations contained in the resolutions adopted by the General Assembly, including at its tenth emergency special session and including resolution ES-10/15, with regard to ensuring respect by Israel, the occupying Power, for the provisions of the Convention;

5. *Requests* the Secretary-General to report to the General Assembly at its sixty-seventh session on the implementation of the present resolution.

RECORDED VOTE ON RESOLUTION 66/77:

In favour: Afghanistan, Albania, Algeria, Andorra, Angola, Antigua and Barbuda, Argentina, Armenia, Australia, Austria, Azerbaijan, Bahamas, Bahrain, Bangladesh, Barbados, Belarus, Belgium, Belize, Benin, Bhutan, Bolivia, Bosnia and Herzegovina, Botswana, Brazil, Brunei Darussalam, Bulgaria, Burkina Faso, Burundi, Cambodia, Cape Verde, Chad, Chile, China, Colombia, Congo, Costa Rica, Côte d'Ivoire, Croatia, Cuba, Cyprus, Czech Republic, Democratic People's Republic of Korea, Denmark, Djibouti, Dominican Republic, Ecuador, Egypt, El Salvador, Estonia, Ethiopia, Fiji, Finland, France, Germany, Ghana, Greece, Grenada, Guatemala, Guinea, Guinea-Bissau, Guyana, Haiti, Honduras, Hungary, Iceland, India, Indonesia, Iran, Iraq, Ireland, Italy, Jamaica, Japan, Jordan, Kazakhstan, Kenya, Kuwait, Kyrgyzstan, Lao People's Democratic Republic, Latvia, Lebanon, Lesotho, Liberia, Libya, Liechtenstein, Lithuania, Luxembourg, Madagascar, Malawi, Malaysia, Maldives, Mali, Malta, Mauritania, Mauritius, Mexico, Monaco, Mongolia, Montenegro, Morocco, Mozambique, Namibia, Nepal, Netherlands, New Zealand, Nicaragua, Norway, Oman, Pakistan, Panama, Papua New Guinea, Paraguay, Peru, Philippines, Poland, Portugal, Qatar, Republic of Korea, Republic of Moldova, Romania, Russian Federation, Saint Lucia, Saint Vincent and the Grenadines, Samoa, San Marino, Saudi Arabia, Senegal, Serbia, Sierra Leone, Singapore, Slovakia, Slovenia, Solomon Islands, Somalia, South Africa, Spain, Sri Lanka, Sudan, Swaziland, Sweden, Switzerland, Syrian Arab Republic, Tajikistan, Thailand, the former Yugoslav Republic of Macedonia, Timor-Leste, Togo, Tonga, Trinidad and Tobago, Tunisia, Turkey, Turkmenistan, Tuvalu, Uganda, Ukraine, United Arab Emirates, United Kingdom, Uruguay, Uzbekistan, Venezuela, Viet Nam, Yemen, Zambia, Zimbabwe.

Against: Canada, Israel, Marshall Islands, Micronesia, Nauru, Palau, United States.

Abstaining: Cameroon, Vanuatu.

Issues related to Palestine

General aspects

In 2011, the General Assembly, the Committee on the Exercise of the Inalienable Rights of the Palestinian People and other UN bodies addressed issues related to Palestine, and several UN programmes and agencies continued to provide assistance to the Palestinian people.

Committee on Palestinian Rights

As mandated by General Assembly resolution 65/13 [YUN 2010, p. 466], the Committee on the Exercise of the Inalienable Rights of the Palestinian People (Committee on Palestinian Rights) reviewed and reported on the Palestine question and made suggestions to the Assembly, the Security Council and the Secretary-General. The Committee continued to mobilize the international community in support of the Palestinian people, in cooperation with UN bodies, Governments, intergovernmental and civil society organizations and others. The Committee's report [A/66/35] covered the period from 7 October 2010 to 6 October 2011.

The peace process that began with the 1991 Madrid Peace Conference [YUN 1991, p. 221] remained deadlocked, while the broader region underwent dramatic changes. The September target date for the conclusion of an Israeli-Palestinian peace settlement passed without a breakthrough. The Committee emphasized that the status quo was unsustainable and called for a resumption of negotiations towards the two-State solution on the basis of relevant Security Council resolutions, the terms of reference of the Madrid Peace Conference, the road map [YUN 2003, p. 464] and the Arab Peace Initiative [YUN 2002, p. 419]. The Committee was opposed to all settlement activities by Israel, which harmed the peace process and contravened international law. The Committee called on the Quartet to translate the principles articulated by United States President Barack Obama on 19 May (see p. 407) into comprehensive final status parameters.

Progress towards the realization of the inalienable rights of the Palestinians required a dismantlement of the Israeli occupation and its associated regime of settlements, checkpoints, the separation wall, demolitions, land confiscations and expulsions, which had intensified, particularly in East Jerusalem and in Area C. The financial situation of the Palestinian Authority (PA) should be stabilized to enable it to sustain its State-building momentum; the Committee condemned any illegal seizure by Israel of PA revenues.

The Committee remained concerned by systematic violations of humanitarian and human rights law, which particularly affected women, children and prisoners. The Committee reiterated its call for an unconditional end to attacks against civilians, including rocket fire from Gaza and air strikes on populated areas in Gaza, settler violence and the shooting of unarmed protesters. Israel should lift the Gaza blockade in accordance with Council resolution 1860(2009) [YUN 2009, p. 434]. The Council and the High Contracting Parties to the Fourth Geneva Convention should guarantee the protection of civilians in all situations and ensure accountability for violations of international law.

The Committee continued to advance international awareness of the various aspects of the question of Palestine, the peaceful settlement of the question and the worldwide support for the rights of the Palestinian people through its programme of global meetings and conferences: United Nations International Meeting on the Question of Palestine (Vienna, 7–8 March); United Nations Latin American and Caribbean Meeting in Support of Israeli-Palestinian Peace (Montevideo, Uruguay, 29–30 March); United Nations Meeting of Civil Society in Support of Israeli-

Palestinian Peace (Montevideo, 31 March); United Nations Seminar on Assistance to the Palestinian People (Helsinki, Finland, 28–29 April); and United Nations International Meeting in Support of the Israeli-Palestinian Peace Process (Brussels, Belgium, 28–29 June).

GENERAL ASSEMBLY ACTION

On 30 November [meeting 69], the General Assembly adopted **resolution 66/14** [draft: A/66/L.15 & Add.1] by recorded vote (115-8-53) [agenda item 37].

Committee on the Exercise of the Inalienable Rights of the Palestinian People

The General Assembly,

Recalling its resolutions 181(II) of 29 November 1947, 194(III) of 11 December 1948, 3236(XXIX) of 22 November 1974, 3375(XXX) and 3376(XXX) of 10 November 1975, 31/20 of 24 November 1976 and all its subsequent relevant resolutions, including those adopted at its emergency special sessions and its resolution 65/13 of 30 November 2010,

Recalling also its resolution 58/292 of 6 May 2004,

Having considered the report of the Committee on the Exercise of the Inalienable Rights of the Palestinian People,

Recalling the mutual recognition between the Government of the State of Israel and the Palestine Liberation Organization, the representative of the Palestinian people, as well as the existing agreements between the two sides and the need for full compliance with those agreements,

Affirming its support for the Middle East peace process on the basis of the relevant United Nations resolutions, the terms of reference of the Madrid Conference, including the principle of land for peace, the Arab Peace Initiative adopted by the Council of the League of Arab States at its fourteenth session and the Quartet road map to a permanent two-State solution to the Israeli-Palestinian conflict, endorsed by the Security Council in resolution 1515(2003) of 19 November 2003,

Recalling the advisory opinion rendered on 9 July 2004 by the International Court of Justice on the *Legal Consequences of the Construction of a Wall in the Occupied Palestinian Territory*, and recalling also its resolutions ES-10/15 of 20 July 2004 and ES-10/17 of 15 December 2006,

Taking note of the application of Palestine for admission to membership in the United Nations, submitted on 23 September 2011,

Reaffirming that the United Nations has a permanent responsibility towards the question of Palestine until the question is resolved in all its aspects in a satisfactory manner in accordance with international legitimacy,

1. *Expresses its appreciation* to the Committee on the Exercise of the Inalienable Rights of the Palestinian People for its efforts in performing the tasks assigned to it by the General Assembly, and takes note of its annual report, including the conclusions and valuable recommendations contained in chapter VII thereof;

2. *Requests* the Committee to continue to exert all efforts to promote the realization of the inalienable rights of the Palestinian people, including their right to self-determination, to support the Middle East peace process for the achievement of the two-State solution on the basis of the pre-1967 borders and the just resolution of all final status issues and to mobilize international support for and assistance to the Palestinian people, and in this regard authorizes the Committee to make such adjustments in its approved programme of work as it may consider appropriate and necessary in the light of developments and to report thereon to the General Assembly at its sixty-seventh session and thereafter;

3. *Also requests* the Committee to continue to keep under review the situation relating to the question of Palestine and to report and make suggestions to the General Assembly, the Security Council or the Secretary-General, as appropriate;

4. *Further requests* the Committee to continue to extend its cooperation and support to Palestinian and other civil society organizations and to continue to involve additional civil society organizations and parliamentarians in its work in order to mobilize international solidarity and support for the Palestinian people, particularly during this critical period of political instability, humanitarian hardship and financial crisis, with the overall aim of promoting the achievement by the Palestinian people of its inalienable rights and a just, lasting and peaceful settlement of the question of Palestine, the core of the Arab-Israeli conflict, on the basis of the relevant United Nations resolutions, the terms of reference of the Madrid Conference, including the principle of land for peace, the Arab Peace Initiative and the Quartet road map;

5. *Requests* the United Nations Conciliation Commission for Palestine, established under General Assembly resolution 194(III), and other United Nations bodies associated with the question of Palestine to continue to cooperate fully with the Committee and to make available to it, at its request, the relevant information and documentation which they have at their disposal;

6. *Invites* all Governments and organizations to extend their cooperation to the Committee in the performance of its tasks;

7. *Requests* the Secretary-General to circulate the report of the Committee to all the competent bodies of the United Nations, and urges them to take the necessary action, as appropriate;

8. *Also requests* the Secretary-General to continue to provide the Committee with all the necessary facilities for the performance of its tasks.

RECORDED VOTE ON RESOLUTION 66/14:

In favour: Afghanistan, Algeria, Antigua and Barbuda, Argentina, Armenia, Azerbaijan, Bahamas, Bahrain, Bangladesh, Barbados, Belarus, Belize, Benin, Bhutan, Bolivia, Botswana, Brazil, Brunei Darussalam, Burkina Faso, Cambodia, Cape Verde, Chad, Chile, China, Comoros, Congo, Costa Rica, Côte d'Ivoire, Cuba, Cyprus, Democratic People's Republic of Korea, Djibouti, Dominican Republic, Ecuador, Egypt, El Salvador, Equatorial Guinea, Eritrea, Ethiopia, Fiji, Gabon, Gambia, Ghana, Grenada, Guinea, Guinea-Bissau, Guyana, Haiti, India, Indonesia, Iran, Iraq, Jamaica, Jordan, Kazakhstan, Kenya, Kuwait, Kyrgyzstan, Lao People's Democratic Republic, Lebanon, Lesotho, Liberia, Libya, Malaysia, Maldives, Mali, Malta, Mauritania, Mauritius, Mexico, Morocco, Mozambique, Myanmar, Namibia, Nepal, Nicaragua, Nigeria, Oman, Pakistan, Paraguay, Philippines, Qatar, Saint Kitts and Nevis, Saint Lucia, Saint Vincent and the Grenadines, Saudi Arabia, Senegal, Sierra

Leone, Singapore, Solomon Islands, Somalia, South Africa, Sri Lanka, Sudan, Suriname, Swaziland, Syrian Arab Republic, Tajikistan, Thailand, Togo, Trinidad and Tobago, Tunisia, Turkey, Turkmenistan, Uganda, United Arab Emirates, United Republic of Tanzania, Uruguay, Uzbekistan, Vanuatu, Venezuela, Viet Nam, Yemen, Zambia, Zimbabwe.

Against: Australia, Canada, Israel, Marshall Islands, Micronesia, Nauru, Palau, United States.

Abstaining: Albania, Andorra, Austria, Belgium, Bosnia and Herzegovina, Bulgaria, Cameroon, Colombia, Czech Republic, Denmark, Estonia, Finland, France, Georgia, Germany, Greece, Guatemala, Honduras, Hungary, Iceland, Ireland, Italy, Japan, Latvia, Liechtenstein, Lithuania, Luxembourg, Monaco, Montenegro, Netherlands, New Zealand, Norway, Panama, Papua New Guinea, Peru, Poland, Portugal, Republic of Korea, Republic of Moldova, Romania, Russian Federation, Samoa, San Marino, Serbia, Slovakia, Slovenia, Spain, Sweden, Switzerland, the former Yugoslav Republic of Macedonia, Tonga, Ukraine, United Kingdom.

Division for Palestinian Rights

The Division for Palestinian Rights in the UN Department of Political Affairs conducted research and monitoring activities and responded to requests for information and briefings on the question of Palestine, as mandated by General Assembly resolution 34/65 D [YUN 1979, p. 379]. The Division also prepared publications for dissemination, including reports on international meetings and conferences, under the guidance and auspices of the Committee on Palestinian Rights. It administered and continued to develop the United Nations Information System on the Question of Palestine and the "Question of Palestine" web portal. The Division also enhanced its annual training programme for PA staff. The Committee, in its annual report [A/66/35], requested the Division to continue its substantive and secretariat support, the programme of research, monitoring and publications, and other informational activities.

GENERAL ASSEMBLY ACTION

On 30 November [meeting 69], the General Assembly adopted **resolution 66/15** [draft: A/66/L.16 & Add.1] by recorded vote (114-9-54) [agenda item 37].

Division for Palestinian Rights of the Secretariat

The General Assembly,

Having considered the report of the Committee on the Exercise of the Inalienable Rights of the Palestinian People,

Taking note, in particular, of the action taken by the Committee on the Exercise of the Inalienable Rights of the Palestinian People and the Division for Palestinian Rights of the Secretariat in accordance with their mandates,

Recalling its resolution 32/40 B of 2 December 1977 and all its subsequent relevant resolutions, including its resolution 65/14 of 30 November 2010,

1. *Notes with appreciation* the action taken by the Secretary-General in compliance with its resolution 65/14;

2. *Considers* that, by providing substantive support to the Committee on the Exercise of the Inalienable Rights of the Palestinian People in the implementation of its mandate, the Division for Palestinian Rights of the Secretariat continues to make a most useful and constructive contribution to raising international awareness of the question of Palestine and of the urgency of a peaceful settlement of the question of Palestine in all its aspects on the basis of international law and United Nations resolutions and the efforts being exerted in this regard, and to generating international support for the rights of the Palestinian people;

3. *Requests* the Secretary-General to continue to provide the Division with the necessary resources and to ensure that it continues to carry out its programme of work as detailed in relevant earlier resolutions, in consultation with the Committee on the Exercise of the Inalienable Rights of the Palestinian People and under its guidance;

4. *Requests* the Division, in particular, to continue to monitor developments relevant to the question of Palestine, organize international meetings and conferences in various regions with the participation of all sectors of the international community, liaise and cooperate with civil society and parliamentarians, develop and expand the "Question of Palestine" website and the documents collection of the United Nations Information System on the Question of Palestine, prepare and widely disseminate publications and information materials on various aspects of the question of Palestine and develop and enhance the annual training programme for staff of the Palestinian Authority in contribution to Palestinian capacity-building efforts;

5. *Also requests* the Division, as part of the observance of the International Day of Solidarity with the Palestinian People on 29 November, to continue to organize, under the guidance of the Committee on the Exercise of the Inalienable Rights of the Palestinian People, an annual exhibit on Palestinian rights or a cultural event in cooperation with the Permanent Observer Mission of Palestine to the United Nations, and encourages Member States to continue to give the widest support and publicity to the observance of the Day of Solidarity;

6. *Requests* the Secretary-General to ensure the continued cooperation with the Division of the United Nations system entities with programme components addressing various aspects of the question of Palestine and the situation in the Occupied Palestinian Territory, including East Jerusalem;

7. *Invites* all Governments and organizations to extend their cooperation to the Division in the performance of its tasks.

RECORDED VOTE ON RESOLUTION 66/15:

In favour: Afghanistan, Algeria, Antigua and Barbuda, Argentina, Azerbaijan, Bahamas, Bahrain, Bangladesh, Barbados, Belarus, Belize, Benin, Bhutan, Bolivia, Botswana, Brazil, Brunei Darussalam, Burkina Faso, Cambodia, Cape Verde, Chad, Chile, China, Comoros, Congo, Costa Rica, Côte d'Ivoire, Cuba, Cyprus, Democratic People's Republic of Korea, Djibouti, Dominican Republic, Ecuador, Egypt, El Salvador, Equatorial Guinea, Eritrea, Ethiopia, Gabon, Gambia, Ghana, Grenada, Guinea, Guinea-Bissau, Guyana, Haiti, India, Indonesia, Iran, Iraq, Jamaica, Jordan, Kazakhstan, Kenya, Kuwait, Kyrgyzstan, Lao People's Democratic

Republic, Lebanon, Lesotho, Liberia, Libya, Malaysia, Maldives, Mali, Malta, Mauritania, Mauritius, Mexico, Morocco, Mozambique, Myanmar, Namibia, Nepal, Nicaragua, Nigeria, Oman, Pakistan, Paraguay, Philippines, Qatar, Saint Kitts and Nevis, Saint Lucia, Saint Vincent and the Grenadines, Sao Tome and Principe, Saudi Arabia, Senegal, Sierra Leone, Singapore, Solomon Islands, Somalia, South Africa, Sri Lanka, Sudan, Suriname, Swaziland, Syrian Arab Republic, Tajikistan, Thailand, Togo, Trinidad and Tobago, Tunisia, Turkey, Turkmenistan, Uganda, United Arab Emirates, United Republic of Tanzania, Uruguay, Uzbekistan, Vanuatu, Venezuela, Viet Nam, Yemen, Zambia, Zimbabwe.

Against: Australia, Canada, Israel, Marshall Islands, Micronesia, Nauru, New Zealand, Palau, United States.

Abstaining: Albania, Andorra, Armenia, Austria, Belgium, Bosnia and Herzegovina, Bulgaria, Cameroon, Colombia, Czech Republic, Denmark, Estonia, Fiji, Finland, France, Georgia, Germany, Greece, Guatemala, Honduras, Hungary, Iceland, Ireland, Italy, Japan, Latvia, Liechtenstein, Lithuania, Luxembourg, Monaco, Montenegro, Netherlands, Norway, Panama, Papua New Guinea, Peru, Poland, Portugal, Republic of Korea, Republic of Moldova, Romania, Russian Federation, Samoa, San Marino, Serbia, Slovakia, Slovenia, Spain, Sweden, Switzerland, the former Yugoslav Republic of Macedonia, Tonga, Ukraine, United Kingdom.

Special information programme

As requested by the General Assembly in resolution 65/15 [YUN 2010, p. 469], the UN Department of Public Information continued its special information programme on the question of Palestine, which included the organization of its annual training programme for Palestinian journalists and the International Media Seminar on Peace in the Middle East (Budapest, Hungary, 12–13 July). UN Radio provided regular coverage of issues and events connected to the question of Palestine in the six official UN languages, as well as Swahili and Portuguese. The UN News Centre published some 300 stories in English; 144 press releases were issued in English and French, including summaries of meetings and press conferences, in addition to statements by the Secretary-General and other UN officials.

GENERAL ASSEMBLY ACTION

On 30 November [meeting 69], the General Assembly adopted **resolution 66/16** [draft: A/66/L.17 & Add.1] by recorded vote (168-8-3) [agenda item 37].

Special information programme on the question of Palestine of the Department of Public Information of the Secretariat

The General Assembly,

Having considered the report of the Committee on the Exercise of the Inalienable Rights of the Palestinian People,

Taking note, in particular, of the information contained in chapter VI of that report,

Recalling its resolution 65/15 of 30 November 2010,

Convinced that the worldwide dissemination of accurate and comprehensive information and the role of civil society organizations and institutions remain of vital importance in heightening awareness of and support for the inalienable rights of the Palestinian people, including the right to self-determination and independence, and for the efforts to achieve a just, lasting and peaceful settlement of the question of Palestine,

Recalling the mutual recognition between the Government of the State of Israel and the Palestine Liberation Organization, the representative of the Palestinian people, as well as the existing agreements between the two sides,

Affirming its support for the Middle East peace process on the basis of the relevant United Nations resolutions, the terms of reference of the Madrid Conference, including the principle of land for peace, the Arab Peace Initiative adopted by the Council of the League of Arab States at its fourteenth session, and the Quartet road map to a permanent two-State solution to the Israeli-Palestinian conflict, endorsed by the Security Council in resolution 1515(2003) of 19 November 2003,

Recalling the advisory opinion rendered on 9 July 2004 by the International Court of Justice on the *Legal Consequences of the Construction of a Wall in the Occupied Palestinian Territory,*

Reaffirming that the United Nations has a permanent responsibility towards the question of Palestine until the question is resolved in all its aspects in a satisfactory manner in accordance with international legitimacy,

1. *Notes with appreciation* the action taken by the Department of Public Information of the Secretariat in compliance with resolution 65/15;

2. *Considers* that the special information programme on the question of Palestine of the Department is very useful in raising the awareness of the international community concerning the question of Palestine and the situation in the Middle East and that the programme is contributing effectively to an atmosphere conducive to dialogue and supportive of the peace process and should receive the necessary support for the fulfilment of its tasks;

3. *Requests* the Department, in full cooperation and coordination with the Committee on the Exercise of the Inalienable Rights of the Palestinian People, to continue, with the necessary flexibility as may be required by developments affecting the question of Palestine, its special information programme for 2011–2012, in particular:

(*a*) To disseminate information on all the activities of the United Nations system relating to the question of Palestine and the peace process, including reports on the work carried out by the relevant United Nations organizations, as well as on the efforts of the Secretary-General and his Special Envoy vis-à-vis the peace process;

(*b*) To continue to issue, update and modernize publications and audiovisual materials on the various aspects of the question of Palestine in all fields, including materials concerning the relevant recent developments in that regard, in particular the efforts to achieve a peaceful settlement of the question of Palestine;

(*c*) To expand its collection of audiovisual material on the question of Palestine, to continue the production and preservation of such material and to update, on a periodic basis, the public exhibit on the question of Palestine displayed in the General Assembly building as well as at United Nations headquarters in Geneva and Vienna;

(d) To organize and promote fact-finding news missions for journalists to the Occupied Palestinian Territory, including East Jerusalem, and Israel;

(e) To organize international, regional and national seminars or encounters for journalists aimed in particular at sensitizing public opinion to the question of Palestine and the peace process and at enhancing dialogue and understanding between Palestinians and Israelis for the promotion of a peaceful settlement to the Israeli-Palestinian conflict, including by fostering and encouraging the contribution of the media in support of peace between the two sides;

(f) To continue to provide assistance to the Palestinian people in the field of media development, in particular to strengthen the annual training programme for Palestinian broadcasters and journalists;

4. *Encourages* the Department to formulate ways for the media and representatives of civil society to engage in open and positive discussions to explore means for encouraging people-to-people dialogue and promoting peace and mutual understanding in the region.

RECORDED VOTE ON RESOLUTION 66/16:

In favour: Afghanistan, Albania, Algeria, Andorra, Antigua and Barbuda, Argentina, Armenia, Austria, Azerbaijan, Bahamas, Bahrain, Bangladesh, Barbados, Belarus, Belgium, Belize, Benin, Bhutan, Bolivia, Bosnia and Herzegovina, Botswana, Brazil, Brunei Darussalam, Bulgaria, Burkina Faso, Cambodia, Cape Verde, Chad, Chile, China, Colombia, Comoros, Congo, Costa Rica, Côte d'Ivoire, Cuba, Cyprus, Czech Republic, Democratic People's Republic of Korea, Denmark, Djibouti, Dominican Republic, Ecuador, Egypt, El Salvador, Equatorial Guinea, Eritrea, Estonia, Ethiopia, Fiji, Finland, France, Gabon, Gambia, Georgia, Germany, Ghana, Greece, Grenada, Guatemala, Guinea, Guinea-Bissau, Guyana, Haiti, Hungary, Iceland, India, Indonesia, Iran, Iraq, Ireland, Italy, Jamaica, Japan, Jordan, Kazakhstan, Kenya, Kuwait, Kyrgyzstan, Lao People's Democratic Republic, Latvia, Lebanon, Lesotho, Liberia, Libya, Liechtenstein, Lithuania, Luxembourg, Malaysia, Maldives, Mali, Malta, Mauritania, Mauritius, Mexico, Monaco, Mongolia, Montenegro, Morocco, Mozambique, Myanmar, Namibia, Nepal, Netherlands, New Zealand, Nicaragua, Nigeria, Norway, Oman, Pakistan, Panama, Papua New Guinea, Paraguay, Peru, Philippines, Poland, Portugal, Qatar, Republic of Korea, Republic of Moldova, Romania, Russian Federation, Saint Kitts and Nevis, Saint Lucia, Saint Vincent and the Grenadines, Samoa, San Marino, Sao Tome and Principe, Saudi Arabia, Senegal, Serbia, Sierra Leone, Singapore, Slovakia, Slovenia, Solomon Islands, Somalia, South Africa, Spain, Sri Lanka, Sudan, Suriname, Swaziland, Sweden, Switzerland, Syrian Arab Republic, Tajikistan, Thailand, the former Yugoslav Republic of Macedonia, Timor-Leste, Togo, Trinidad and Tobago, Tunisia, Turkey, Turkmenistan, Uganda, Ukraine, United Arab Emirates, United Kingdom, United Republic of Tanzania, Uruguay, Uzbekistan, Vanuatu, Venezuela, Viet Nam, Yemen, Zambia, Zimbabwe.

Against: Australia, Canada, Israel, Marshall Islands, Micronesia, Nauru, Palau, United States.

Abstaining: Cameroon, Honduras, Tonga.

Assistance to Palestinians

UN activities

In response to General Assembly resolution 65/134 [YUN 2010, p. 472], the Secretary-General submitted a report [A/66/80-E/2011/111] on assistance to the Palestinian people from May 2010 to April 2011. The report described the work of the United Nations, in cooperation with the PA, donors and civil society, to support the Palestinian population and institutions. It assessed the aid received by the Palestinian people, the needs still unmet and proposals for responding to such needs.

Key elements of Security Council resolution 1860(2009) [YUN 2009, p. 434] remained unfulfilled. Hamas retained de facto control of Gaza, and Israel continued its closure of the territory. The flow of construction materials entering Gaza through the tunnels between Gaza and Egypt was significantly higher than the amount entering through Israeli-controlled crossings. Additional strictures on land and sea access put in place by the Israel Defense Forces following Israel's Operation Cast Lead [YUN 2009, p. 434] denied Palestinians almost all access within 1,000 to 1,500 metres of the border. Inaccessibility to 35 per cent of Gaza's agricultural land and 85 per cent of the maritime space affected 178,000 people.

Israeli authorities continued to ease the movement of Palestinians between urban centres in the West Bank, excluding East Jerusalem. Approximately 500 closure obstacles were in place inside the West Bank, 50 fewer than at the beginning of the reporting period. The volume of people travelling through the Erez crossing point—the only passage for the movement of people between Gaza and the West Bank via Israel—rose slightly. Access and operational space for humanitarian agency staff remained restricted. Between May 2010 and March 2011, 512 reported incidents of delayed or denied access of UN staff at Israeli checkpoints resulted in a loss of approximately 344 working days.

Despite restrictions, the United Nations continued to coordinate and deliver humanitarian assistance, including food aid, to more than 1 million people; water and sanitation support to more than 1.5 million; and health and nutrition services to nearly 2.5 million. The United Nations Relief and Works Agency for Palestine Refugees in the Near East (UNRWA) provided free education to more than 260,000 students in 325 schools in Gaza and the West Bank and vocational training to 1,840 youth from the West Bank. The United Nations Children's Fund (UNICEF) supported a PA initiative focused on remedial learning programmes to around 20,000 children. The International Labour Organization (ILO) and UNRWA implemented a skills development programme targeting refugee shelter construction in Gaza. Ilo and the United Nations Development Programme promoted entrepreneurship and self-employment, and the United Nations Educational, Scientific and Cultural Organization provided technical assistance for the national teacher education strategy. The World Bank-funded Social Safety Net Reform Project merged with European Union-funded programmes to provide 63,000 poor households with cash transfers. The Food and Agriculture Organization of the United Nations supported the pa Ministry of Agriculture in devising a national strategy for Palestine's agricultural development sector. The United Nations enhanced pa efforts to collect revenue and accelerate customs clearance procedures. The United Nations Conference on Trade and Development (UNCTAD) (see also below) continued to support the modernization of Palestinian customs through training on automated systems.

Unicef, with the Ministry of Health, maintained high immunization coverage across the Occupied Palestinian Territory through procurement of the polio vaccine for the protection of 42,000 children and the provision of logistical support for acquiring other vaccines. The World Health Organization (who) helped fill gaps in pharmaceutical supplies in Gaza and contributed medical equipment, spare parts and technical assistance to maintain, repair and improve existing equipment.

The United Nations Population Fund (UNFPA) helped train 350 women from municipalities, health centres and non-governmental organizations on mental health, gender-based violence and human rights. It supported four community-based networks through which more than 35,000 vulnerable women benefited from 2,100 outreach sessions. UN-Women assisted the Mehwar Centre, which hosted and protected an average of 25 women per month, along with their children, from violence and honour killings. Unicef support included the finalization of a national strategy and action plan based on the amended Palestinian "Child Law" and advocating a non-violence policy in 93 schools in the West Bank and 20 schools in Gaza.

The Office of the High Commissioner for Human Rights, along with other UN agencies and civil society, participated in the revision of the Palestinian penal code, with the aim of ensuring that new legislation would be in accordance with international standards. The pa announced in 2011 that civilians would no longer be tried in military courts. The United Nations Office on Drugs and Crime developed general and specialized prison staff training, strengthened information management systems, created vocational programmes for inmates and worked to improve prison health.

The pa budgetary external financing requirement for 2011 was estimated at $1 billion, down more than 16 per cent from the previous year, reflecting the improved capacity of the pa to collect revenue. The 2011 Consolidated Appeals Process requested $576 million for critical humanitarian activities; as at 1 March, only 7 per cent of the requested funds had been received. A low response rate, against the backdrop of low financing in 2010, threatened the ability of UN agencies and their partners to provide critical assistance to the Palestinian people.

UNCTAD assistance to Palestinians

The UNCTAD Trade and Development Board, at its fifty-eighth session (Geneva, 12–23, 28 September) [TD/B/58/9], considered a secretariat report [TD/B/58/4] on assistance to the Palestinian people: developments in the economy of the Occupied Palestinian Territory. The report stated that although the Territory's economy grew by 9.3 per cent in 2010, that growth was driven by donor support and did not alter worsening long-term development prospects caused by the ongoing loss of Palestinian land and natural resources, isolation from global markets and fragmentation. A modest relaxation of the Israeli blockade of Gaza enabled an improvement in the economy, but restrictions on imported raw materials constrained private-sector recovery and thwarted public investment in infrastructure. Gaza's manufacturing output declined by 4 per cent in 2010. Agricultural output rose significantly, although 35 per cent of Gaza's agricultural land and 85 per cent of its maritime space remained inaccessible to farmers and fishermen. Despite growth in gross domestic product (GDP) in 2010, poverty and food insecurity remained high throughout the Occupied Palestinian Territory. Using the consumption-based definition of poverty, 26 per cent of Palestinians in the Territory lived in poverty in 2010. According to the World Food Programme, 50 per cent of Palestinian households in the Territory were affected by food insecurity. The unemployment rate remained at around 30 per cent; unemployment stood at 47 per cent in Gaza, compared with 20 per cent in the West Bank. Palestinian youth under 30 were particularly vulnerable, with unemployment at 43 per cent.

The restrictions imposed on the movement of goods to, from and within the West Bank and Gaza stifled the emergence of an export sector capable of contributing to economic development. Improvements in living standards could not be achieved without building a dynamic, high-value-added export sector. Israel absorbed about 90 per cent of Palestinian exports and was the source for approximately 80 per cent of imports. A significant portion of Palestinian imports from Israel were produced in a third country and re-exported to the Occupied Palestinian Territory. The World Bank estimated that such products, known as "indirect imports", accounted for about one third of goods officially reported as Palestinian imports from Israel. The cost to the Palestinian treasury of not receiving tax revenue on indirect imports was estimated at around $480 million per year, equivalent to more than 25 per cent of public revenue; it accounted for a 10 per cent loss in GDP and 30,000 jobs per year. A mechanism to distinguish bona fide Israeli imports from indirect imports should be explored.

The PA carried out strict fiscal reforms to control the budget deficit, improve budgetary discipline and sustainability, and lessen dependence on donor aid. The recurrent budget deficit, on a cash basis, fell to 15 per cent in 2010 from 24 per cent in 2009. The decrease resulted from a combination of spending controls, including the containment of public employment and wages, as well as enhanced revenue collection. Tax revenue grew by 57 per cent in 2010; total public revenue grew by 22 per cent to $1.9 billion, while expenditure was reduced by 4 per cent. Donors financed $1.3 billion of the PA budget shortfall, or 42 per cent of total spending, indicating persistent fiscal weakness. The goal of achieving a sustainable budget deficit would remain elusive unless Israel lifted all restrictions on movement and access, and Palestinians gained access to their natural resources. Israeli control over the tax and customs clearance revenue made fiscal planning difficult, undermined the PA ability to pay the private-sector agents who supplied it with goods and services, and threatened its capacity to pay the salaries of more than 150,000 public employees.

The viability of a future independent Palestinian State depended on reintegrating the economy of East Jerusalem within the broader national economy and allowing it to resume its historic, pivotal economic role. The rehabilitation and restructuring of the fragmented East Jerusalem economy required a significant national effort to reconnect it to the Palestinian territory through better integration of trade, labour and financial markets. Impediments in access to finance and credit faced by Palestinians and businesses in East Jerusalem reduced long-term investment prospects. Palestinian banks did not operate in the Jerusalem Municipality, and the few Israeli bank branches in East Jerusalem failed to cover Palestinians' basic needs.

The UNCTAD programme of technical assistance to the Palestinian people included activities in four areas: trade policies and strategies; trade facilitation and logistics; finance and development; and enterprise, investment and competition policy. Progress was made under the Programme to Modernize and Strengthen Institutional and Managerial Capacities of the Palestinian Authority Customs Administration, Phase III; the project included the training of 48 customs employees. As a result, Palestinian Customs was able to implement new procedures and interface more effectively with the Israeli customs system. UNCTAD implemented the Development Account project entitled "Promoting Subregional Growth-oriented Economic and Trade Policies towards Achieving the Millennium Development Goals in Arab Countries of West Africa and North Africa", which benefited the Occupied Palestinian Territory and four other countries. UNCTAD also introduced the United Nations Chief Executives Board Inter-Agency Cluster on Trade and Productive Capacity into the Occupied Palestinian Territory, which aimed to develop the Palestinian trade sectors within a flexible framework of humanitarian interventions.

GENERAL ASSEMBLY ACTION

On 15 December [meeting 86], the General Assembly adopted **resolution 66/118** [draft: A/66/L.27 & Add.1] without vote [agenda item 70 (*b*)].

Assistance to the Palestinian people

The General Assembly,

Recalling its resolution 65/134 of 15 December 2010, as well as its previous resolutions on the question,

Recalling also the signing of the Declaration of Principles on Interim Self-Government Arrangements in Washington, D.C., on 13 September 1993, by the Government of the State of Israel and the Palestine Liberation Organization, the representative of the Palestinian people, and the subsequent implementation agreements concluded by the two sides,

Recalling further all relevant international law, including humanitarian and human rights law, and, in particular, the International Covenant on Civil and Political Rights, the International Covenant on Economic, Social and Cultural Rights, the Convention on the Rights of the Child and the Convention on the Elimination of All Forms of Discrimination against Women,

Gravely concerned at the difficult living conditions and humanitarian situation affecting the Palestinian people, in particular women and children, throughout the occupied Palestinian territory,

Conscious of the urgent need for improvement in the economic and social infrastructure of the occupied territory,

Welcoming, in this context, the development of projects, notably on infrastructure, to revive the Palestinian economy and improve the living conditions of the Palestinian people, stressing the need to create the appropriate conditions to facilitate the implementation of these projects, and noting the contribution of partners in the region and of the international community,

Aware that development is difficult under occupation and is best promoted in circumstances of peace and stability,

Noting the great economic and social challenges facing the Palestinian people and their leadership,

Emphasizing the importance of the safety and well-being of all people, in particular women and children, in the whole Middle East region, the promotion of which is facilitated, inter alia, in a stable and secure environment,

Deeply concerned about the negative impact, including the health and psychological consequences, of violence on the present and future well-being of children in the region,

Conscious of the urgent necessity for international assistance to the Palestinian people, taking into account the Palestinian priorities,

Expressing grave concern about the humanitarian situation in Gaza, and underlining the importance of emergency and humanitarian assistance,

Welcoming the results of the Conference to Support Middle East Peace, convened in Washington, D.C., on 1 October 1993, the establishment of the Ad Hoc Liaison Committee for the Coordination of the International Assistance to Palestinians and the work being done by the World Bank as its secretariat and the establishment of the Consultative Group, as well as all follow-up meetings and international mechanisms established to provide assistance to the Palestinian people,

Underlining the importance of the International Conference in Support of the Palestinian Economy for the Reconstruction of Gaza, held in Sharm el-Sheikh, Egypt, on 2 March 2009, in addressing the immediate humanitarian situation in Gaza and in mobilizing donors to provide financial and political support for the Palestinian Authority in order to alleviate the socioeconomic and humanitarian situation being faced by the Palestinian people,

Recalling the International Donors Conference for the Palestinian State, held in Paris on 17 December 2007, the Berlin Conference in Support of Palestinian Civil Security and the Rule of Law, held on 24 June 2008, and the Palestine Investment Conferences, held in Bethlehem from 21 to 23 May 2008 and on 2 and 3 June 2010,

Welcoming the latest meetings of the Ad Hoc Liaison Committee for the Coordination of the International Assistance to Palestinians, held in New York on 21 September 2010 and on 18 September 2011,

Welcoming also the activities of the Joint Liaison Committee, which provides a forum in which economic policy and practical matters related to donor assistance are discussed with the Palestinian Authority,

Welcoming further the implementation of the Palestinian Reform and Development Plan 2008–2010 and the presentation of the Palestinian National Development Plan 2011–2013 on governance, economy, social development and infrastructure, and stressing the need for continued international support for the Palestinian State-building process, as outlined in the summary of the Chair of the meeting of the Ad Hoc Liaison Committee in 2011,

Stressing the need for the full engagement of the United Nations in the process of building Palestinian institutions and in providing broad assistance to the Palestinian people,

Welcoming recent steps to ease the restrictions on movement and access in the West Bank, while stressing the need for further steps to be taken in this regard, and recognizing that such steps would improve living conditions and the situation on the ground and could promote further Palestinian economic development,

Acknowledging the recent measures announced by Israel regarding access to the Gaza Strip, while calling for full implementation and complementary measures that address the need for a fundamental change in policy that allows for the sustained and regular opening of the border crossings for the movement of persons and goods, including for the reconstruction and economic recovery of Gaza,

Welcoming the action of the Special Representative of the Quartet, Tony Blair, charged with developing, with the Government of the Palestinian Authority, a multi-year agenda to strengthen institutions, promote economic development and mobilize international funds,

Stressing the urgency of reaching a durable solution to the crisis in Gaza through the full implementation of Security Council resolution 1860(2009) of 8 January 2009,

Stressing also the importance of the regular opening of the crossings for the movement of persons and goods, for both humanitarian and commercial flows,

Noting the active participation of the United Nations Special Coordinator for the Middle East Peace Process and Personal Representative of the Secretary-General to the Palestine Liberation Organization and the Palestinian Authority in the activities of the Special Envoys of the Quartet,

Welcoming the endorsement by the Security Council, in resolution 1515(2003) of 19 November 2003, of the performance-based road map to a permanent two-State solution to the Israeli-Palestinian conflict, and stressing the need for its implementation and compliance with its provisions,

Commending the efforts within the Quartet made by the United States of America, the European Union, the United Nations and the Russian Federation in pursuing vigorously a two-State solution, noting the commitment of the Quartet to remain actively involved and the need for strong international support to promote the peace process, and calling for the resumption and acceleration of negotiations between the Israeli and Palestinian sides towards a comprehensive resolution of the Arab-Israeli conflict, on the basis of relevant Security Council resolutions and the terms of reference of the Madrid Conference, in order to ensure a political solution, with two States—Israel and an independent, democratic, contiguous and viable Palestinian State—living side by side in peace and security,

Having considered the report of the Secretary-General,

Expressing grave concern about continuing violence against civilians,

1. *Takes note* of the report of the Secretary-General;

2. *Expresses its appreciation* to the Secretary-General for his rapid response and efforts regarding assistance to the Palestinian people;

3. *Also expresses its appreciation* to the Member States, United Nations bodies and intergovernmental, regional and non-governmental organizations that have provided and continue to provide assistance to the Palestinian people;

4. *Stresses* the importance of the work of the United Nations Special Coordinator for the Middle East Peace Process and Personal Representative of the Secretary-General to the Palestine Liberation Organization and the Palestinian Authority and of the steps taken under the auspices of the Secretary-General to ensure the achievement of a coordinated mechanism for United Nations activities throughout the occupied territories;

5. *Urges* Member States, international financial institutions of the United Nations system, intergovernmental and non-governmental organizations and regional and interregional organizations to extend, as rapidly and as generously as possible, economic and social assistance to the Palestinian people, in close cooperation with the Palestine

Liberation Organization and through official Palestinian institutions;

6. *Welcomes*, in this regard, the meetings of the Ad Hoc Liaison Committee for the Coordination of the International Assistance to Palestinians in September 2010 and September 2011, and the outcome of the International Conference in Support of the Palestinian Economy for the Reconstruction of Gaza, at which donors pledged approximately 4.5 billion United States dollars to support the needs of the Palestinian people;

7. *Recalls* the International Donors Conference for the Palestinian State, the Berlin Conference in Support of Palestinian Civil Security and the Rule of Law, and the Palestine Investment Conferences;

8. *Stresses* the importance of following up on the results of the International Conference in Support of the Palestinian Economy for the Reconstruction of Gaza;

9. *Calls upon* donors that have not yet converted their budget support pledges into disbursements to transfer funds as soon as possible, encourages all donors to increase their direct assistance to the Palestinian Authority in accordance with its government programme in order to enable it to build a viable and prosperous Palestinian State, underlines the need for equitable burden-sharing by donors in this effort, and encourages donors to consider aligning funding cycles with the Palestinian Authority's national budget cycle;

10. *Calls upon* relevant organizations and agencies of the United Nations system to intensify their assistance in response to the urgent needs of the Palestinian people in accordance with priorities set forth by the Palestinian side;

11. *Expresses its appreciation* for the work of the United Nations Relief and Works Agency for Palestine Refugees in the Near East, and recognizes the vital role of the Agency in providing humanitarian assistance to the Palestinian people, particularly in the Gaza Strip;

12. *Calls upon* the international community to provide urgently needed assistance and services in an effort to alleviate the difficult humanitarian situation being faced by Palestinian women, children and their families and to help in the reconstruction and development of relevant Palestinian institutions;

13. *Stresses* the role that all funding instruments, including the European Commission's Palestinian-European Mechanism for the Management of Socio-Economic Aid and the World Bank trust fund, have been playing in directly assisting the Palestinian people;

14. *Urges* Member States to open their markets to exports of Palestinian products on the most favourable terms, consistent with appropriate trading rules, and to implement fully existing trade and cooperation agreements;

15. *Calls upon* the international donor community to expedite the delivery of pledged assistance to the Palestinian people to meet their urgent needs;

16. *Stresses*, in this context, the importance of ensuring free humanitarian access to the Palestinian people and the free movement of persons and goods;

17. *Also stresses* the need for the full implementation by both parties of the Agreement on Movement and Access and of the Agreed Principles for the Rafah Crossing, of 15 November 2005, to allow for the freedom of movement of the Palestinian civilian population, as well as for imports and exports, within and into and out of the Gaza Strip;

18. *Further stresses* the need to ensure the safety and security of humanitarian personnel, premises, facilities, equipment, vehicles and supplies, as well as the need to ensure safe and unhindered access by humanitarian personnel and delivery of supplies and equipment, in order to allow such personnel to efficiently perform their task of assisting affected civilian populations;

19. *Urges* the international donor community, United Nations agencies and organizations and non-governmental organizations to extend to the Palestinian people, as rapidly as possible, emergency economic assistance and humanitarian assistance, particularly in the Gaza Strip, to counter the impact of the current crisis;

20. *Stresses* the need for the continued implementation of the Paris Protocol on Economic Relations of 29 April 1994, fifth annex to the Israeli-Palestinian Interim Agreement on the West Bank and the Gaza Strip, signed in Washington, D.C., on 28 September 1995, including with regard to the full, prompt and regular transfer of Palestinian indirect tax revenues;

21. *Requests* the Secretary-General to submit a report to the General Assembly at its sixty-seventh session, through the Economic and Social Council, on the implementation of the present resolution, containing:

(*a*) An assessment of the assistance actually received by the Palestinian people;

(*b*) An assessment of the needs still unmet and specific proposals for responding effectively to them;

22. *Decides* to include in the provisional agenda of its sixty-seventh session the sub-item entitled "Assistance to the Palestinian people".

UNRWA

The United Nations Relief and Works Agency for Palestine Refugees in the Near East (UNRWA) continued to provide education, health, relief and social services, and microfinance to the growing refugee population in the Gaza Strip, the West Bank, Jordan, Lebanon and the Syrian Arab Republic.

Reports of Commissioner-General. The UNRWA Commissioner-General, in his later report on the work of the Agency in 2011 [A/67/13], stated that Palestine in the five fields of UNRWA operation experienced varying political, economic and security conditions against the backdrop of incidents in the Middle East and North Africa. Refugees had to contend with the impact of the continuing global economic downturn and persistent funding shortfalls, which precluded UNRWA from meeting their basic needs.

In Gaza, poverty remained high, with 54 per cent of the population food insecure and more than 75 per cent—or 1 million Gazans—dependent on international aid. Although GDP grew approximately 23 per cent and unemployment dropped to 33 per cent in 2011, those gains were largely driven by the "tunnel economy"—trade conducted by means of the tunnels to Gaza—as opposed to production and trade. Following negotiations, Israel granted UNRWA the ability to import construction materials for a number of projects. Of the total construction project portfolio, projects worth $167 million were approved.

UNRWA maintained its crisis operations in the Occupied Palestinian Territory under an emergency appeal for $379 million, of which donors funded $153.7 million, or around 40 per cent. In Gaza, the Agency improved its targeting and programme responses and reduced its emergency food assistance caseload from 714,000 refugees in the first round of assistance to 690,000 in the third round. It provided school meals to approximately 213,000 children per month and short-term job opportunities for 31,972 refugees. UNRWA health centres received an additional 80,000 patient visits in 2011 as compared with 2010.

At the end of 2011, the registered Palestine refugee population in Gaza stood at 1,167,572, of whom 780,000 had received food assistance from UNRWA. Through the UNRWA cash-for-work scheme, 8,000 jobs were created on a short-term basis, injecting an estimated $28 million into the local economy and benefiting approximately 32,000 refugees directly. The reconstruction of Gaza was a priority, and efforts were made to accelerate the implementation of a $667 million rebuilding plan. UNRWA completed construction of three health centres, six schools and 33 housing units. Overall, ongoing projects injected $54 million into Gaza's economy and created the equivalent of 5,200 jobs. Thirty-eight projects awaited Israeli approval at year's end, including four fully funded housing projects and 32 schools.

In the West Bank, where the registered Palestinian refugee population numbered 727,471, UNRWA field management undertook a community engagement programme aimed at enhancing service delivery and improving refugee self-reliance, and a year-long process to improve the database of food-insecure and vulnerable refugees. It transferred community mental health in schools and clinics from the Agency's emergency funding process to its framework of core activities, and transferred shelter rebuilding into project funding.

The registered Palestine refugee population in Syria stood at 486,946. Since the outbreak of protests in Syria and the conflict that followed (see p. 468), living conditions for Palestine refugees in that country had deteriorated significantly. The devaluation of the Syrian pound negatively affected livelihoods, exacerbated by a rise in the cost of basic commodities and services and a contraction of the wage labour market. UNRWA installations were temporarily closed in Dera'a, Douma, Hama, Homs and Khan Dunoun. Under conditions of conflict, UNRWA expanded humanitarian aid, prioritizing livelihood support to the elderly, female-headed households and families with special needs. It implemented a cash assistance programme for 3,500 households. At the end of the year, 17,000 households needed urgent cash assistance, a significant escalation over the Agency's normal social safety net programme.

Living conditions for the 436,154 registered Palestine refugees in Lebanon remained abject; they suffered high unemployment and poverty rates. The unity Government of Prime Minister Saad Hariri fell in January, leading to five months of political uncertainty and delays on refugee issues. In June, Prime Minister Najib Mikati formed a new Government (see p. 455) and called for full funding of UNRWA operations and the rebuilding of the Nahr el-Bared camp. As part of the first completed phase of the camp's reconstruction, UNRWA delivered 369 new shelters to refugee families in September and completed three new school buildings. Funding shortfalls challenged progress, however, and prolonged hardship for the 27,000 refugees displaced from the camp since 2007. At year's end, pledges amounting to $15.2 million were received against an appeal for $18.5 million to meet the basic needs of the displaced refugees awaiting reconstruction of the camp. Pledges amounting to $165.7 million were received against an appeal for $348 million for the reconstruction of the camp.

Jordan hosted the largest population of Palestine refugees—1,979,580 at the end of the year. UNRWA continued to identify efficiencies and savings to address funding shortfalls, while implementing health and education reform strategies. At five health centres, the Agency introduced the e-health system, which aimed to digitize the health records of patients at all UNRWA clinics, and a new appointment system, which helped reduce clinic overcrowding and delays at peak times; the reforms benefited more than 250,000 patients per year.

Israeli authorities, raising security concerns, continued to inhibit the freedom of movement of UNRWA personnel in the Occupied Palestinian Territory. Restrictions included closures of the West Bank and the Gaza Strip; prohibition of local staff from travelling in UN vehicles across the Erez crossing between Israel and Gaza; cumbersome procedures for obtaining permits for local staff to enter Israel and East Jerusalem; and searches of UN vehicles unless an occupant held an identification card issued by the Israeli Ministry of Foreign Affairs. Movement constraints imposed by the Israeli Government on the West Bank resulted in the loss of 163 staff days. Transit charges imposed by the Israeli authorities on shipments entering Gaza forced UNRWA to pay $344,744 in 2011.

Contrary to the 1946 General Convention on Privileges and Immunities of the United Nations [YUN 1946–47, p. 100], Israeli military and security forces entered UNRWA premises on two occasions. On another occasion, Israeli forces threw a percussion grenade inside the yard of the UNRWA Hebron boys' school while class was in session. In six incidents, Palestinians threatened or attacked Agency staff, including one attack in which staff members were held at gunpoint. Twelve incidents of unauthorized entry into UNRWA installations also occurred, including two incidents of live fire. In Gaza, students at, or adjacent to, UNRWA schools sustained gunshot wounds from unknown sources in three instances, and Agency outposts were struck by missiles or hand grenades fired by unidentified Palestinian groups on two occasions.

The Commissioner-General submitted to the General Assembly the annual report [A/66/13 & Add.1] on the work of UNRWA for 2010 [YUN 2010, p. 474], which included comments on the report contained in a letter from the Chair of the UNRWA Advisory Commission dated 22 June 2011 [ibid., p. 475].

Advisory Commission. The UNRWA Advisory Commission, in its later comments on the Agency's report on 2011 activities [A/67/13], expressed concern about the volatile situation in Gaza and the loss of life there. The restrictions on access and the outbreaks of violence in Gaza disproportionately affected the refugees and contributed to the increased need for UNRWA services. Gaza reconstruction projects amounting to $167 million were approved, but UNRWA continued to face challenges in receiving the approvals for rebuilding refugee shelters. In Gaza and the West Bank, the separation barrier, closures and other movement restrictions, and the destruction of homes and farms, hindered economic development, as well as the Agency's ability to carry out its mandated tasks. The Commission called for the removal of all Israeli restraints regarding the movement on UNRWA staff and goods.

The Commission noted the decline in living conditions for Palestine refugees in Syria since March, especially those in close proximity to the areas experiencing violence, and expressed its concern about the safety of refugees. It was also concerned about the security of UNRWA staff in Lebanon and stressed the need to help refugees in that country expand their opportunities and improve their living conditions. The Commission urged the international donor community to mobilize resources to ensure proper service delivery to Palestine refugees.

Report of Conciliation Commission. In response to General Assembly resolution 65/98 [YUN 2010, p. 476], the United Nations Conciliation Commission for Palestine submitted, in August, its sixty-fifth report [A/66/296], covering the period from 1 September 2010 to 31 August 2011. The Commission, which was established by Assembly resolution 194(III) [YUN 1948-49, p. 203] to facilitate the repatriation, resettlement and economic and social rehabilitation of the refugees and payment of compensation, stated that it had nothing to report since the submission of its sixty-fourth report in 2010 [YUN 2010, p. 476].

GENERAL ASSEMBLY ACTION

On 9 December [meeting 81], the General Assembly, on the recommendation of the Fourth Committee [A/66/426], adopted **resolution 66/72** by recorded vote (160-1-8) [agenda item 52].

Assistance to Palestine refugees

The General Assembly,

Recalling its resolution 194(III) of 11 December 1948 and all its subsequent resolutions on the question, including resolution 65/98 of 10 December 2010,

Recalling also its resolution 302(IV) of 8 December 1949, by which, inter alia, it established the United Nations Relief and Works Agency for Palestine Refugees in the Near East,

Recalling further the relevant resolutions of the Security Council,

Aware of the fact that, for more than six decades, the Palestine refugees have suffered from the loss of their homes, lands and means of livelihood,

Affirming the imperative of resolving the problem of the Palestine refugees for the achievement of justice and for the achievement of lasting peace in the region,

Acknowledging the essential role that the United Nations Relief and Works Agency for Palestine Refugees in the Near East has played for over sixty years since its establishment in ameliorating the plight of the Palestine refugees through the provision of education, health, relief and social services and ongoing work in the areas of camp infrastructure, microfinance, protection and emergency assistance,

Taking note of the report of the Commissioner-General of the United Nations Relief and Works Agency for Palestine Refugees in the Near East covering the period from 1 January to 31 December 2010,

Aware of the continuing needs of the Palestine refugees throughout all the fields of operation, namely, Jordan, Lebanon, the Syrian Arab Republic and the Occupied Palestinian Territory,

Expressing grave concern at the especially difficult situation of the Palestine refugees under occupation, including with regard to their safety, well-being and socioeconomic living conditions,

Expressing grave concern in particular at the critical humanitarian situation and socioeconomic conditions of the Palestine refugees in the Gaza Strip, and underlining the importance of emergency and humanitarian assistance and urgent reconstruction efforts,

Noting the signing of the Declaration of Principles on Interim Self-Government Arrangements on 13 September 1993 by the Government of Israel and the Palestine Liberation Organization and the subsequent implementation agreements,

1. *Notes with regret* that repatriation or compensation of the refugees, as provided for in paragraph 11 of General Assembly resolution 194(III), has not yet been effected, and that, therefore, the situation of the Palestine refugees continues to be a matter of grave concern and the Palestine refugees continue to require assistance to meet basic health, education and living needs;

2. *Also notes with regret* that the United Nations Conciliation Commission for Palestine has been unable to find

a means of achieving progress in the implementation of paragraph 11 of General Assembly resolution 194(III), and reiterates its request to the Conciliation Commission to continue exerting efforts towards the implementation of that paragraph and to report to the Assembly on the efforts being exerted in this regard as appropriate, but no later than 1 September 2012;

3. *Affirms* the necessity for the continuation of the work of the United Nations Relief and Works Agency for Palestine Refugees in the Near East and the importance of its unimpeded operation and its provision of services for the well-being and human development of the Palestine refugees and for the stability of the region, pending the just resolution of the question of the Palestine refugees;

4. *Calls upon* all donors to continue to make the most generous efforts possible to meet the anticipated needs of the United Nations Relief and Works Agency for Palestine Refugees in the Near East, including with regard to increased expenditures arising from the serious socioeconomic and humanitarian situation and instability in the region, particularly in the Occupied Palestinian Territory, and those mentioned in recent emergency appeals;

5. *Commends* the United Nations Relief and Works Agency for Palestine Refugees in the Near East for its provision of vital assistance to the Palestine refugees and its role as a stabilizing factor in the region and the tireless efforts of the staff of the Agency in carrying out its mandate;

6. *Decides* to invite Luxembourg, in accordance with the criterion set forth in General Assembly decision 60/522 of 8 December 2005, to become a member of the Advisory Commission of the United Nations Relief and Works Agency for Palestine Refugees in the Near East.

RECORDED VOTE ON RESOLUTION 66/72:

In favour: Afghanistan, Albania, Algeria, Andorra, Angola, Antigua and Barbuda, Argentina, Armenia, Australia, Austria, Azerbaijan, Bahamas, Bahrain, Bangladesh, Barbados, Belarus, Belgium, Belize, Benin, Bhutan, Bolivia, Bosnia and Herzegovina, Botswana, Brazil, Brunei Darussalam, Bulgaria, Burkina Faso, Burundi, Cambodia, Cape Verde, Chile, China, Colombia, Costa Rica, Côte d'Ivoire, Croatia, Cuba, Cyprus, Czech Republic, Democratic People's Republic of Korea, Denmark, Djibouti, Dominican Republic, Ecuador, Egypt, El Salvador, Eritrea, Estonia, Ethiopia, Fiji, Finland, France, Germany, Ghana, Greece, Grenada, Guatemala, Guinea, Guyana, Haiti, Honduras, Hungary, Iceland, India, Indonesia, Iraq, Ireland, Italy, Jamaica, Japan, Kazakhstan, Kenya, Kuwait, Kyrgyzstan, Lao People's Democratic Republic, Latvia, Lebanon, Lesotho, Liberia, Libya, Liechtenstein, Lithuania, Luxembourg, Madagascar, Malawi, Malaysia, Maldives, Mali, Malta, Mauritania, Mauritius, Mexico, Monaco, Mongolia, Montenegro, Morocco, Mozambique, Namibia, Nepal, Netherlands, New Zealand, Nicaragua, Norway, Oman, Pakistan, Panama, Papua New Guinea, Paraguay, Peru, Philippines, Poland, Portugal, Qatar, Republic of Korea, Republic of Moldova, Romania, Russian Federation, Saint Lucia, Saint Vincent and the Grenadines, Samoa, San Marino, Saudi Arabia, Senegal, Serbia, Sierra Leone, Singapore, Slovakia, Slovenia, Solomon Islands, Somalia, South Africa, Spain, Sri Lanka, Sudan, Swaziland, Sweden, Switzerland, Syrian Arab Republic, Tajikistan, Thailand, the former Yugoslav Republic of Macedonia, Timor-Leste, Togo, Tonga, Trinidad and Tobago, Tunisia, Turkey, Turkmenistan, Tuvalu, Uganda, Ukraine, United Arab Emirates, United Kingdom, Uruguay, Uzbekistan, Venezuela, Viet Nam, Yemen, Zambia, Zimbabwe.

Against: Israel.

Abstaining: Cameroon, Canada, Marshall Islands, Micronesia, Nauru, Palau, United States, Vanuatu.

Also on 9 December [meeting 81], the General Assembly, on the recommendation of the Fourth Committee [A/66/426], adopted **resolution 66/74** by recorded vote (165-7-2) [agenda item 52].

Operations of the United Nations Relief and Works Agency for Palestine Refugees in the Near East

The General Assembly,

Recalling its resolutions 194(III) of 11 December 1948, 212(III) of 19 November 1948, 302(IV) of 8 December 1949 and all subsequent related resolutions, including its resolution 65/100 of 10 December 2010,

Recalling also the relevant resolutions of the Security Council,

Having considered the report of the Commissioner-General of the United Nations Relief and Works Agency for Palestine Refugees in the Near East covering the period from 1 January to 31 December 2010,

Taking note of the letter dated 22 June 2011 from the Chair of the Advisory Commission of the United Nations Relief and Works Agency for Palestine Refugees in the Near East to the Commissioner-General,

Deeply concerned about the critical financial situation of the Agency, caused in part by the structural underfunding of the Agency, as well as its rising expenditures resulting from the deterioration of the socioeconomic and humanitarian conditions and the instability in the region and their significant negative impact on the provision of necessary Agency services to the Palestine refugees, including its emergency-related and development programmes,

Recalling Articles 100, 104 and 105 of the Charter of the United Nations and the Convention on the Privileges and Immunities of the United Nations,

Recalling also the Convention on the Safety of United Nations and Associated Personnel,

Affirming the applicability of the Geneva Convention relative to the Protection of Civilian Persons in Time of War, of 12 August 1949, to the Palestinian territory occupied since 1967, including East Jerusalem,

Aware of the continuing needs of the Palestine refugees in all fields of operation, namely, Jordan, Lebanon, the Syrian Arab Republic and the Occupied Palestinian Territory,

Gravely concerned about the extremely difficult socioeconomic conditions being faced by the Palestine refugees in the Occupied Palestinian Territory, including East Jerusalem, particularly in the refugee camps in the Gaza Strip, as a result of the continuing prolonged Israeli closures, the construction of settlements and the wall, and the severe economic and movement restrictions that in effect amount to a blockade, which have deepened unemployment and poverty rates among the refugees,

Gravely concerned also about the continuing negative repercussions of the military operations in the Gaza Strip between December 2008 and January 2009, which caused extensive loss of life and injury, particularly among Palestinian civilians, including children and women; widespread destruction and damage to Palestinian homes, properties, vital infrastructure and public institutions, including hospitals, schools and United Nations facilities; and internal displacement of civilians, including refugees,

Commending the extraordinary efforts by the Agency to provide emergency relief, medical, food, shelter and other humanitarian assistance to needy and displaced families in the Gaza Strip,

Recalling, in this regard, its resolution ES-10/18 of 16 January 2009 and Security Council resolution 1860(2009) of 8 January 2009,

Expressing regret over the continued restrictions that impede the Agency's efforts to repair and rebuild thousands of damaged or destroyed refugee shelters, and calling upon Israel to ensure the unimpeded import of essential construction materials into the Gaza Strip, while taking note of recent developments regarding the situation of access there,

Expressing concern about the severe classroom shortage in the Gaza Strip and the consequent negative impact on the right to education of refugee children as a result of the constraints on the ability of the Agency to construct new schools due to Israel's ongoing restrictions impeding the entry of necessary construction materials into the Gaza Strip,

Stressing the urgent need for the advancement of reconstruction in the Gaza Strip, including through the completion of suspended projects managed by the Agency, and for the accelerated implementation of other urgent United Nations-led civilian reconstruction activities,

Urging the continuing disbursement of pledges made at the International Conference in Support of the Palestinian Economy for the Reconstruction of Gaza, held in Sharm el-Sheikh, Egypt, on 2 March 2009, to accelerate the reconstruction process,

Noting with appreciation the completion of the first phase of the project to rebuild the Nahr el-Bared refugee camp, commending the Government of Lebanon, donors, the Agency and other concerned parties for the important progress made and for the continuing efforts to assist affected and displaced refugees, and emphasizing the need for additional funding to complete the reconstruction of the camp and end the displacement of its twenty-seven thousand residents without delay,

Aware of the valuable work done by the Agency in providing protection to the Palestinian people, in particular Palestine refugees,

Deploring the endangerment of the safety of the Agency's staff and the damage and destruction caused to the facilities and properties of the Agency, including damage caused to the Agency's "Summer Games" recreational properties, during the reporting period,

Deploring also, in particular, the extensive damage and destruction of Agency facilities in the Gaza Strip caused during the military operations between December 2008 and January 2009, including schools where civilians were sheltered and the Agency's main compound and warehouse, as reported in the summary by the Secretary-General of the report of the Board of Inquiry and in the report of the United Nations Fact-finding Mission on the Gaza Conflict,

Deploring further, in this regard, the breaches of the inviolability of United Nations premises, the failure to accord the property and assets of the Organization immunity from any form of interference and the failure to protect United Nations personnel, premises and property,

Deploring the killing and injury of Agency staff members by the Israeli occupying forces in the Occupied Palestinian Territory since September 2000,

Deploring also the killing and wounding of refugee children in the Agency schools by the Israeli occupying forces during the military operations between December 2008 and January 2009,

Deeply concerned about the continuing imposition of restrictions on the freedom of movement and access of the Agency's staff, vehicles and goods, and the injury, harassment and intimidation of the Agency's staff, which undermine and obstruct the work of the Agency, including its ability to provide essential basic and emergency services,

Aware of the agreement between the Agency and the Government of Israel,

Taking note of the agreement reached on 24 June 1994, embodied in an exchange of letters between the Agency and the Palestine Liberation Organization,

1. *Reaffirms* that the effective functioning of the United Nations Relief and Works Agency for Palestine Refugees in the Near East remains essential in all fields of operation;

2. *Expresses its appreciation* to the Commissioner-General of the United Nations Relief and Works Agency for Palestine Refugees in the Near East, as well as to all of the staff of the Agency, for their tireless efforts and valuable work, particularly in the light of the difficult conditions and unstable circumstances faced during the past year;

3. *Expresses special commendation* to the Agency for the essential role that it has played for over sixty years since its establishment in providing vital services for the well-being, human development and protection of the Palestine refugees and the amelioration of their plight;

4. *Expresses its appreciation* for the important support provided by the host Governments to the Agency in the discharge of its duties;

5. *Also expresses its appreciation* to the Advisory Commission of the United Nations Relief and Works Agency for Palestine Refugees in the Near East, and requests it to continue its efforts and to keep the General Assembly informed of its activities;

6. *Takes note with appreciation* of the report of the Working Group on the Financing of the United Nations Relief and Works Agency for Palestine Refugees in the Near East and the efforts to assist in ensuring the financial security of the Agency, and requests the Secretary-General to provide the necessary services and assistance to the Working Group for the conduct of its work;

7. *Commends* the Agency's six-year Medium-Term Strategy, which commenced in January 2010, and the continuing efforts of the Commissioner-General to increase the budgetary transparency and efficiency of the Agency, as reflected in the Agency's programme budget for the biennium 2012–2013;

8. *Also commends* the Agency for sustaining its reform efforts, and urges it to continue to apply maximum efficiency procedures to reduce operational and administrative costs and to maximize the use of resources;

9. *Takes note with appreciation* of the report of the Secretary-General on the strengthening of the management capacity of the United Nations Relief and Works Agency for Palestine Refugees in the Near East, and further urges all Member States to carefully consider its proposal for support by the Secretary-General of the institutional strengthening of the Agency through the provision of financial resources from the regular budget of the United Nations;

10. *Endorses* the efforts of the Commissioner-General to continue to provide humanitarian assistance, as far as practicable, on an emergency basis, and as a temporary measure, to persons in the area who are internally displaced and in serious need of continued assistance as a result of recent crises in the Agency's fields of operation;

11. *Welcomes* the progress made thus far by the Agency in rebuilding the Nahr el-Bared refugee camp in northern Lebanon, and calls for the expeditious completion of its reconstruction, for the continued provision of relief assistance to those displaced following its destruction in 2007 and for the alleviation of their ongoing suffering through the fulfilment of pledges made at the International Donor Conference for the Recovery and Reconstruction of the Nahr el-Bared Palestine Refugee Camp and Conflict-affected Areas of Northern Lebanon, held in Vienna on 23 June 2008;

12. *Encourages* the Agency, in close cooperation with other relevant United Nations entities, to continue making progress in addressing the needs and rights of children, women and persons with disabilities in its operations in accordance with the Convention on the Rights of the Child, the Convention on the Elimination of All Forms of Discrimination against Women, and the Convention on the Rights of Persons with Disabilities, respectively;

13. *Commends*, in this regard, the Agency's "Summer Games" initiative providing recreational, cultural and educational activities for children in the Gaza Strip and, recognizing its positive contribution, calls for full support of the initiative;

14. *Expresses concern* about the relocation of the international staff of the Agency from its headquarters in Gaza City and the disruption of operations at the headquarters due to the deterioration and instability of the situation on the ground;

15. *Calls upon* Israel, the occupying Power, to comply fully with the provisions of the Geneva Convention relative to the Protection of Civilian Persons in Time of War, of 12 August 1949;

16. *Also calls upon* Israel to abide by Articles 100, 104 and 105 of the Charter of the United Nations and the Convention on the Privileges and Immunities of the United Nations in order to ensure the safety of the personnel of the Agency, the protection of its institutions and the safeguarding of the security of its facilities in the Occupied Palestinian Territory, including East Jerusalem;

17. *Urges* the Government of Israel to expeditiously reimburse the Agency for all transit charges incurred and other financial losses sustained as a result of delays and restrictions on movement and access imposed by Israel;

18. *Calls upon* Israel particularly to cease obstructing the movement and access of the staff, vehicles and supplies of the Agency and to cease the levying of taxes, extra fees and charges, which affect the Agency's operations detrimentally;

19. *Reiterates its call upon* Israel to fully lift the restrictions impeding the import of necessary construction materials and supplies for the reconstruction and repair of thousands of damaged or destroyed refugee shelters, and for the implementation of suspended civilian infrastructure projects in refugee camps in the Gaza Strip, while noting the commencement of several projects in this regard;

20. *Requests* the Commissioner-General to proceed with the issuance of identification cards for Palestine refugees and their descendants in the Occupied Palestinian Territory;

21. *Notes with appreciation* the progress made by the Agency in the modernization of its archives through the Palestine Refugee Records Project, including the completion of phase I, and encourages the Commissioner-General to finalize the remaining components of the Project as rapidly as possible and to report on the progress made to the General Assembly at its sixty-seventh session;

22. *Also notes with appreciation* the success of the Agency's microfinance programme, and calls upon the Agency, in close cooperation with the relevant agencies, to continue to contribute to the development of the economic and social stability of the Palestine refugees in all fields of operation;

23. *Reiterates its appeals* to all States, the specialized agencies and non-governmental organizations to continue and to augment the special allocations for grants and scholarships for higher education to Palestine refugees in addition to their contributions to the regular budget of the Agency and to contribute to the establishment of vocational training centres for Palestine refugees, and requests the Agency to act as the recipient and trustee for the special allocations for grants and scholarships;

24. *Urges* all States, the specialized agencies and non-governmental organizations to continue and to increase their contributions to the Agency in order to address the serious financial constraints and underfunding, especially with respect to the Agency's regular budget deficit, noting that financial shortfalls have been exacerbated by the current humanitarian situation on the ground that has resulted in rising expenditures, in particular with regard to emergency services, and to support the Agency's valuable and necessary work in assisting the Palestine refugees in all fields of operation.

RECORDED VOTE ON RESOLUTION 66/74:

In favour: Afghanistan, Albania, Algeria, Andorra, Angola, Antigua and Barbuda, Argentina, Armenia, Australia, Austria, Azerbaijan, Bahamas, Bahrain, Bangladesh, Barbados, Belarus, Belgium, Belize, Benin, Bhutan, Bolivia, Bosnia and Herzegovina, Botswana, Brazil, Brunei Darussalam, Bulgaria, Burkina Faso, Burundi, Cambodia, Cape Verde, Chad, Chile, China, Colombia, Congo, Costa Rica, Côte d'Ivoire, Croatia, Cuba, Cyprus, Czech Republic, Democratic People's Republic of Korea, Denmark, Djibouti, Dominican Republic, Ecuador, Egypt, El Salvador, Eritrea, Estonia, Ethiopia, Fiji, Finland, France, Germany, Ghana, Greece, Grenada, Guatemala, Guinea, Guinea-Bissau, Guyana, Haiti, Honduras, Hungary, Iceland, India, Indonesia, Iran, Iraq, Ireland, Italy, Jamaica,

Japan, Jordan, Kazakhstan, Kenya, Kuwait, Kyrgyzstan, Lao People's Democratic Republic, Latvia, Lebanon, Lesotho, Liberia, Libya, Liechtenstein, Lithuania, Luxembourg, Madagascar, Malawi, Malaysia, Maldives, Mali, Malta, Mauritania, Mauritius, Mexico, Monaco, Mongolia, Montenegro, Morocco, Mozambique, Namibia, Nepal, Netherlands, New Zealand, Nicaragua, Norway, Oman, Pakistan, Panama, Papua New Guinea, Paraguay, Peru, Philippines, Poland, Portugal, Qatar, Republic of Korea, Republic of Moldova, Romania, Russian Federation, Saint Lucia, Saint Vincent and the Grenadines, Samoa, San Marino, Saudi Arabia, Senegal, Serbia, Sierra Leone, Singapore, Slovakia, Slovenia, Solomon Islands, Somalia, South Africa, Spain, Sri Lanka, Sudan, Swaziland, Sweden, Switzerland, Syrian Arab Republic, Tajikistan, Thailand, the former Yugoslav Republic of Macedonia, Timor-Leste, Togo, Tonga, Trinidad and Tobago, Tunisia, Turkey, Turkmenistan, Tuvalu, Uganda, Ukraine, United Arab Emirates, United Kingdom, Uruguay, Uzbekistan, Venezuela, Viet Nam, Yemen, Zambia, Zimbabwe.

Against: Canada, Israel, Marshall Islands, Micronesia, Nauru, Palau, United States.

Abstaining: Cameroon, Vanuatu.

UNRWA financing

In 2011, UNRWA expended $989.8 million against its cash and in-kind General Fund amounting to $1,226.7 million for the 2010–2011 biennium, with operations, projects and appeals funded by donors. The largest type of expenditure amounted to $572.6 million under the unrestricted regular budget, accounting for 57.9 per cent of total expenditure. Restricted fund activities, emergency activities and other initiatives accounted for 3.9 per cent, 22.4 per cent and 14.9 per cent, respectively. Education remained the largest programme, accounting for $333.8 million (58 per cent) of the unrestricted regular budget expenditure, followed by health at $98.7 million (17 per cent), support services at $95.7 million (17 per cent), relief and social services at $37.8 million (7 per cent) and infrastructure at $6.6 million (1 per cent).

An addendum to the Commissioner-General's report on UNRWA work in 2010 [A/66/13/Add.1] provided information on the 2012–2013 programme budget, which amounted to $2,011.4 million.

Working Group. The Working Group on the Financing of UNRWA held three meetings in 2011, on 15 and 30 September and 6 October [A/66/520]. The Working Group stated that in December 2010, UNRWA reduced its programme requirements for 2011 by $53.2 million to $568 million. Against that reduced budget, the Agency expected a deficit of $47.6 million at the end of 2011, representing approximately one month's operating costs of $48 million. The Working Group noted with concern the exceptionally large funding gap anticipated for the UNRWA General Fund for 2011 and the 2012–2013 biennium. It reiterated that it was the responsibility of the international community to ensure that UNRWA services were maintained at an acceptable level and that funding kept pace with the changing needs and growth of the refugee population. The structural nature of the Agency's financial crisis, whereby its General Fund was underfunded year after year, led it to finance its annual deficit partly by spending its working capital, which was virtually depleted. The Working Group reiterated its concern that if adequate resources were not provided, the achievements of the comprehensive reform of the Agency's work could be risked and its capacity to implement its mandate jeopardized. It was also concerned by the lack of funding for UNRWA projects; in particular, it was alarmed by the lack of funding received for the reconstruction of the Nahr el-Bared camp in Lebanon, the Agency's largest project to date. It called on donors, including countries of the Middle East region, to support the reconstruction and relief operations until the camp was rebuilt.

UNRWA launched an appeal for $379.7 million in December 2010 to address the urgent needs of Palestine refugees in the Occupied Palestinian Territory. By September 2011, it had received pledges of only $145 million, which fell short of meeting the basic needs of the 1.9 million registered refugees, or approximately half of the total population of Gaza and the West Bank, whose living conditions continued to decline.

Management capacity

In response to General Assembly resolution 64/89 [YUN 2009, p. 469], the Secretary-General submitted a February report [A/65/705] on strengthening UNRWA management capacity. The report presented UNRWA financial needs in the context of its regional role; described the shortfalls in extrabudgetary funding, as manifested in the Agency's eroded working capital reserve; and highlighted efforts to strengthen its donor base.

UNRWA initiated programme cycle management and a reform of its human resource operations; modernized and streamlined working methods and structures; launched a strategic approach to resource mobilization aimed at strengthening the donor base and tapping into new sources of funds; and strengthened the relationship between its headquarters and the fields of operation. A plan for sustaining change, the next phase of the reform process, was introduced in 2010, representing the Agency's commitment to maintaining the momentum of reforms and ensuring a higher quality of services to refugees. UNRWA established a Department of External Relations and Communications as an initial step towards strengthening resource development and advocacy, and to broaden the Agency's global visibility. It needed to implement an enterprise resource planning system that would support compliance with International Public Sector Accounting Standards (IPSAS) and improve procurement data management. UNRWA was working towards IPSAS implementation by 2012.

The backlog of shelters that UNRWA had been unable to repair or rebuild due to lack of funds had risen to over 25,000, affecting some 150,000 persons. UNRWA staff provided the key means of programme delivery, but also accounted for the largest single cost element of the General Fund. Staff numbers had risen in line with the steady growth in the number of refugees and the need to improve the quality of UNRWA services. International and area staff members were threatened in all fields of operation. The Commissioner-General determined that the safeguarding of headquarters facilities and a small number of other exposed locations had to be ensured, and complementary measures were required to improve staff safety.

Donors had shown a high degree of solidarity with the Palestine refugees over the decades, but rarely—if ever—had the level of funding met the Agency's planned programme expenditure. Without sustained investment in the quality of services provided, much of the progress made by UNRWA in assisting the Palestine refugee population to meet the Millennium Development Goals [YUN 2000, p. 51] would be undermined and reversed. The management reform process begun in 2005 needed to be maintained and deepened to ensure that UNRWA was able to utilize donor resources efficiently and fulfil its mandate. Extrabudgetary contributions from traditional and non-traditional donors had to rise significantly over the following five years to enable the Commissioner-General to implement the Agency's medium-term strategy over the 2010–2015 period, thus providing refugees with improved basic services. The Assembly was requested to take note of the perilous cash-flow situation faced by UNRWA; ask the Secretary-General to propose increased funding from the regular budget on an incremental basis over the next four bienniums, starting with an extra $5 million for 2012–2013; and decide that the approval of such increases was subject to justification in the context of proposed programme budgets and consideration by the Assembly.

GENERAL ASSEMBLY ACTION

On 18 April [meeting 86], the General Assembly, on the recommendation of the Fourth Committee [A/65/422/Add.1], adopted **resolution 65/272** by recorded vote (123-1) [agenda item 51].

Report of the Secretary-General on the strengthening of the management capacity of the United Nations Relief and Works Agency for Palestine Refugees in the Near East

The General Assembly,

Recalling its resolution 302(IV) of 8 December 1949, by which it established the United Nations Relief and Works Agency for Palestine Refugees in the Near East, and all subsequent related resolutions, including its resolution 65/100 of 10 December 2010,

Having considered the report of the Commissioner-General of the United Nations Relief and Works Agency for Palestine Refugees in the Near East covering the period from 1 January to 31 December 2009,

Taking note with appreciation of the report of the Working Group on the Financing of the United Nations Relief and Works Agency for Palestine Refugees in the Near East and the efforts of the Working Group to assist in ensuring the financial security of the Agency,

Reiterating its deep concern about the critical financial situation of the Agency, caused in part by the structural underfunding of the Agency, as well as its rising expenditures resulting from the deterioration of the socioeconomic and humanitarian conditions in the region and their significant negative impact on the provision of necessary Agency services to the Palestine refugees, including its emergency-related and development programmes,

Reiterating that the effective functioning of the Agency remains essential in all fields of operation,

Recognizing the need to maintain and extend the Agency's management reform process in order to enable the Agency to effectively deliver services to the Palestine refugees, most efficiently utilize donor resources and reduce operational and administrative costs, and encouraging in this regard the Agency's efforts to sustain change,

Recalling its resolution 3331 B (XXIX) of 17 December 1974, in which it decided that expenses for salaries of international staff in the service of the Agency which would otherwise be a charge on voluntary contributions should be financed by the regular budget of the United Nations for the duration of the Agency's mandate,

Recalling also the recommendation of the Working Group at its extraordinary meeting in June 2009 that the General Assembly review, at its next session, the basis for its decision in resolution 3331 B (XXIX) to provide funding to the Agency for international posts so as to enable the Agency to meet contemporary demands from stakeholders and the Assembly itself,

Stressing the need to continue supporting the institutional strengthening of the Agency, including the need to reinforce the Agency's resource mobilization and advocacy capacities as well as the need for more predictable funding, through the provision of financial resources from the regular budget of the United Nations, in accordance with the requests made in its resolutions 64/89 of 10 December 2009 and 65/100 of 10 December 2010,

1. *Takes note with appreciation* of the report of the Secretary-General on the strengthening of the management capacity of the United Nations Relief and Works Agency for Palestine Refugees in the Near East;

2. *Takes note* of the grave financial situation faced by the Agency, including recurrent budgetary shortfalls due to underfunding and rising costs;

3. *Calls upon* the Agency to continue its management reform process in order to enhance its ability to raise and efficiently utilize resources, reduce operational and administrative costs, and implement change for more effective delivery of services to its beneficiaries;

4. *Requests* the Secretary-General to continue to support the institutional strengthening of the Agency through

the provision of financial resources from the regular budget of the United Nations;

5. *Stresses* that approval of funding for the biennium 2012–2013 and for future bienniums, taking into consideration the recommendations in the report of the Secretary-General, is subject to justification in the context of the proposed programme budget for the relevant bienniums and consideration thereof by the General Assembly;

6. *Reiterates its appeal* to all States, the specialized agencies and non-governmental organizations to continue and to increase their contributions to the Agency in order to address the serious financial constraints and underfunding, especially with respect to the deficit in the Agency's General Fund, and to support the Agency's valuable and necessary work in assisting the Palestine refugees in all fields of operation;

7. *Urges* the Commissioner-General to continue his efforts to sustain and increase the support of traditional donors and to enhance income from non-traditional donors, including through partnerships with public and private entities;

8. *Requests* the Secretary-General to report to the General Assembly at its sixty-seventh session on the progress made with regard to the implementation of the present resolution.

RECORDED VOTE ON RESOLUTION 65/272:

In favour: Afghanistan, Albania, Algeria, Andorra, Argentina, Australia, Austria, Azerbaijan, Bahrain, Bangladesh, Belarus, Belgium, Bosnia and Herzegovina, Botswana, Brazil, Brunei Darussalam, Bulgaria, Burkina Faso, Cambodia, Canada, Central African Republic, Chile, China, Colombia, Congo, Costa Rica, Croatia, Cuba, Cyprus, Czech Republic, Democratic People's Republic of Korea, Denmark, Djibouti, Dominican Republic, Ecuador, Egypt, El Salvador, Estonia, Finland, France, Gabon, Germany, Ghana, Greece, Guatemala, Guinea, Haiti, Honduras, Hungary, Iceland, India, Indonesia, Iran, Italy, Jamaica, Japan, Kazakhstan, Kuwait, Lao People's Democratic Republic, Latvia, Lebanon, Lesotho, Liberia, Liechtenstein, Lithuania, Luxembourg, Malaysia, Mali, Malta, Mauritius, Mexico, Monaco, Mongolia, Montenegro, Morocco, Myanmar, Namibia, Nepal, Netherlands, New Zealand, Nicaragua, Norway, Oman, Pakistan, Panama, Peru, Philippines, Poland, Portugal, Qatar, Republic of Moldova, Romania, Russian Federation, Saint Vincent and the Grenadines, San Marino, Saudi Arabia, Serbia, Singapore, Slovakia, Slovenia, South Africa, Sri Lanka, Sudan, Suriname, Sweden, Switzerland, Syrian Arab Republic, Tajikistan, Thailand, the former Yugoslav Republic of Macedonia, Trinidad and Tobago, Tunisia, Turkey, Ukraine, United Arab Emirates, United Kingdom, United Republic of Tanzania, Uruguay, Vanuatu, Venezuela, Viet Nam, Yemen, Zimbabwe.

Against: Israel.

Displaced persons

In August [A/66/222], the Secretary-General submitted, in response to General Assembly resolution 65/99 [YUN 2010, p. 480], a report on persons displaced as a result of the June 1967 and subsequent hostilities; the resolution called for the accelerated return of such persons to their homes in the territories occupied by Israel. The Secretary-General stated that, based on information obtained from the UNRWA Commissioner-General for the period from 1 July 2010 to 30 June 2011, 207 refugees registered with the Agency had returned to the West Bank and 158 to Gaza from places outside the Occupied Palestinian Territory. The number of displaced registered refugees known by UNRWA to have returned since June 1967 amounted to about 33,639. The Agency was unable to estimate the total number of displaced inhabitants who had returned. It kept records only of registered refugees, and the records might be incomplete, particularly with respect to the location of such refugees.

On 9 and 11 May, the Secretary-General sought information from Member States on action taken or envisaged to implement resolution 65/99. In an 8 July note, Israel stated that although it voted against resolution 65/99, as it had done on similar resolutions in the past, it reaffirmed its intention to continue facilitating UNRWA humanitarian services. Israel remained concerned, however, by the political motivation of the resolutions and the one-sided view they presented, which did not reflect the reality on the ground. It supported a consolidation of UNRWA resolutions, a removal of extraneous political language and an application, in the Palestinian context, of the standard principles guiding the United Nations with respect to the treatment of refugees.

GENERAL ASSEMBLY ACTION

On 9 December [meeting 81], the General Assembly, on the recommendation of the Fourth Committee [A/66/426], adopted **resolution 66/73** by recorded vote (163-7-3) [agenda item 52].

Persons displaced as a result of the June 1967 and subsequent hostilities

The General Assembly,

Recalling its resolutions 2252(ES-V) of 4 July 1967, 2341 B (XXII) of 19 December 1967 and all subsequent related resolutions,

Recalling also Security Council resolutions 237(1967) of 14 June 1967 and 259(1968) of 27 September 1968,

Taking note of the report of the Secretary-General submitted in pursuance of its resolution 65/99 of 10 December 2010,

Taking note also of the report of the Commissioner-General of the United Nations Relief and Works Agency for Palestine Refugees in the Near East covering the period from 1 January to 31 December 2010,

Concerned about the continuing human suffering resulting from the June 1967 and subsequent hostilities,

Taking note of the relevant provisions of the Declaration of Principles on Interim Self-Government Arrangements of 13 September 1993 with regard to the modalities for the admission of persons displaced in 1967, and concerned that the process agreed upon has not yet been effected,

1. *Reaffirms* the right of all persons displaced as a result of the June 1967 and subsequent hostilities to return to their homes or former places of residence in the territories occupied by Israel since 1967;

2. *Stresses* the necessity for an accelerated return of displaced persons, and calls for compliance with the mechanism agreed upon by the parties in article XII of the Declaration of Principles on Interim Self-Government Arrangements of 13 September 1993 on the return of displaced persons;

3. *Endorses*, in the meanwhile, the efforts of the Commissioner-General of the United Nations Relief and Works Agency for Palestine Refugees in the Near East to continue to provide humanitarian assistance, as far as practicable, on an emergency basis, and as a temporary measure, to persons in the area who are currently displaced and in serious need of continued assistance as a result of the June 1967 and subsequent hostilities;

4. *Strongly appeals* to all Governments and to organizations and individuals to contribute generously to the Agency and to the other intergovernmental and non-governmental organizations concerned for the above-mentioned purposes;

5. *Requests* the Secretary-General, after consulting with the Commissioner-General, to report to the General Assembly before its sixty-seventh session on the progress made with regard to the implementation of the present resolution.

RECORDED VOTE ON RESOLUTION 66/73:

In favour: Afghanistan, Albania, Algeria, Andorra, Angola, Antigua and Barbuda, Argentina, Armenia, Australia, Austria, Azerbaijan, Bahamas, Bahrain, Bangladesh, Barbados, Belarus, Belgium, Belize, Benin, Bhutan, Bolivia, Bosnia and Herzegovina, Botswana, Brazil, Brunei Darussalam, Bulgaria, Burkina Faso, Burundi, Cambodia, Cape Verde, Chile, China, Colombia, Congo, Costa Rica, Côte d'Ivoire, Croatia, Cuba, Cyprus, Czech Republic, Democratic People's Republic of Korea, Denmark, Djibouti, Dominican Republic, Ecuador, Egypt, El Salvador, Eritrea, Estonia, Ethiopia, Fiji, Finland, France, Germany, Ghana, Greece, Grenada, Guatemala, Guinea, Guinea-Bissau, Guyana, Haiti, Honduras, Hungary, Iceland, India, Indonesia, Iran, Iraq, Ireland, Italy, Jamaica, Japan, Jordan, Kazakhstan, Kenya, Kuwait, Kyrgyzstan, Lao People's Democratic Republic, Latvia, Lebanon, Lesotho, Liberia, Libya, Liechtenstein, Lithuania, Luxembourg, Madagascar, Malawi, Malaysia, Maldives, Mali, Malta, Mauritania, Mauritius, Mexico, Monaco, Mongolia, Montenegro, Morocco, Mozambique, Namibia, Nepal, Netherlands, New Zealand, Nicaragua, Norway, Oman, Pakistan, Papua New Guinea, Paraguay, Peru, Philippines, Poland, Portugal, Qatar, Republic of Korea, Republic of Moldova, Romania, Russian Federation, Saint Lucia, Saint Vincent and the Grenadines, Samoa, San Marino, Saudi Arabia, Senegal, Serbia, Sierra Leone, Singapore, Slovakia, Slovenia, Solomon Islands, Somalia, South Africa, Spain, Sri Lanka, Sudan, Swaziland, Sweden, Switzerland, Syrian Arab Republic, Tajikistan, Thailand, the former Yugoslav Republic of Macedonia, Timor-Leste, Togo, Tonga, Trinidad and Tobago, Tunisia, Turkey, Turkmenistan, Tuvalu, Uganda, Ukraine, United Arab Emirates, United Kingdom, Uruguay, Uzbekistan, Venezuela, Viet Nam, Yemen, Zambia, Zimbabwe.

Against: Canada, Israel, Marshall Islands, Micronesia, Nauru, Palau, United States.

Abstaining: Cameroon, Panama, Vanuatu.

Palestinian women

In a report to the 2011 session of the Commission on the Status of Women [E/CN.6/2011/6], submitted in accordance with Economic and Social Council resolution 2010/6 [YUN 2010, p. 482], the Secretary-General summarized the situation of Palestinian women and reviewed the UN assistance they received between 1 September 2009 and 30 September 2010 with regard to education and training; health; economic empowerment and livelihoods; violence against women; power and decision-making; and institutional arrangements.

The consequences of years of occupation and conflict between the Israelis and the Palestinians, as well as multiple political and economic crises, continued to be felt, particularly in Gaza, where Israel's Operation Cast Lead [YUN 2009, p. 434] had undermined social services, infrastructure and homes. At the end of 2009, the participation of women in the formal labour force in the Occupied Palestinian Territory was among the lowest levels globally: 15.2 per cent in the West Bank and 9.1 per cent in Gaza. Imposed movement restrictions and the lack of a means of transport constituted crucial barriers to employment, and many women—in particular middle-aged women and women with low levels of education—turned to a range of informal activities to earn money, including petty trading, agriculture and livestock production. High unemployment levels among women led to significant levels of food insecurity. Unrwa offered short-term opportunities through its emergency job-creation programme, in which 35 per cent of all beneficiaries were women. The Agency's Microfinance and Microenterprise Department in Gaza disbursed 1,126 business loans to female entrepreneurs and gave 12 women grants to create income-generating projects. Although the quality of education available to women in the Occupied Palestinian Territory varied, access to and participation in education was increasing. During the 2009/10 academic year, girls represented 47.9 per cent of the total student population in schools run by unrwa in the Gaza Strip and 57.5 per cent in the West Bank. Illiteracy remained a serious obstacle hindering women's economic and political empowerment; 75.6 per cent of all illiterate adults were women. UN entities implemented initiatives to improve the access of women and girls to education, training and recreational activities. Through the unrwa Department of Education, 533 female students benefited from technical and vocational training at the Ramallah Women Training Centre, and 357 benefited in Gaza. The United Nations Development Fund for Women—later a part of UN-Women—provided 100 girls and women in the Jordan Valley with literacy classes, computer training and English language courses. UNICEF offered educational and recreational activities to more than 20,000 young women.

Concerns persisted regarding Palestinian women's maternal and child health due to mobility constraints and insufficient infrastructure. Food insecurity contributed to micronutrient deficiency and high levels of anaemia in infants and pregnant women. Post-traumatic stress and other psychological and behavioural disorders were an emerging health priority. Around 30 per cent of children screened at UNRWA schools reportedly suffered from mental health problems. Poverty and movement constraints left women unable to care for their children and relatives, which led to mental health problems, including anxiety and depression.

Palestinian women continued to be exposed to violence related to the Israeli occupation and factional tensions, as well as domestic violence, so-called "honour killings" and trafficking. Women and girls were reluctant to come forward to human rights organizations, the police and courts due to the lack of awareness of assistance mechanisms to help them, as well as the stigma attached to reporting abuse. The Palestinian Basic Law—the main statute underlying essential rights—established that Palestinians had equality without distinction based on sex, but gender-based discrimination persisted in a range of legal areas, including the penal code. A draft national strategy to combat violence against women promoted a legal structure and institutional mechanisms to protect women from violence, as well as improved social protection and health services for women victims of violence.

Palestinian women participated in both formal and informal realms of political life. In 2009, they represented 20 per cent of PA ministers. With the factional split and the freeze of the Palestinian Legislative Council in 2006 [YUN 2007, p. 462], however, efforts to promote women's active political participation, including in peacebuilding and negotiation, drastically decreased. They were often excluded from strategic meetings and decision-making processes, the internal reconciliation process and permanent status negotiations.

UNRWA served as the main comprehensive healthcare provider for Palestine refugees, focusing on primary health care and prevention; other UN entities supported access to reproductive health services. WHO expanded a pilot project aimed at improving the quality of maternal and newborn health from two hospitals to eight in Gaza. The initiative increased a mother's stay after childbirth from one hour to up to six hours, allowed for medical checkups on mothers and newborns, encouraged breastfeeding and offered basic health education. UNICEF delivered micronutrient supplements to more than 50,000 pregnant women and 55,000 children. UNRWA delivered food aid to 7,838 pregnant women and nursing mothers, and family planning services were provided to 23,141 clients. UNFPA supported clinical and psychosocial services to 30,000 women in the most underprivileged areas of the West Bank and Gaza through four local women's health centres.

The Secretary-General concluded that despite improvements in education for women, there was little positive evidence of their social, economic and legal empowerment. The recent easing of movement restrictions should be continued. All parties needed to ensure women's participation in conflict resolution and peacebuilding initiatives, including permanent status negotiations. UN entities should support the Palestinian Development Plan for 2011–2013, including its cross-sectoral national gender strategy. Stereotypical attitudes and practices that affected educational and training choices needed to be addressed, including through the revision of school curricula. UN partners should systematically address the bottlenecks preventing women's economic advancement, including the lack of access to productive resources and opportunities; limited connection to the transportation of goods; and lack of capacity for advancement resulting from insufficient education and training opportunities. In addition to ending impunity and punishing perpetrators of violence against women, legal frameworks should mandate support for victims and survivors, prevention measures and training for officials. Palestinian authorities and UN entities should collaborate to provide services for female survivors of violence, and the legal framework needed to be harmonized with the 1979 Convention on the Elimination of All Forms of Discrimination against Women [YUN 1979, p. 895].

ECONOMIC AND SOCIAL COUNCIL ACTION

On 26 July 2011 [meeting 44], the Economic and Social Council, on the recommendation of the Commission on the Status of Women [E/2011/27], adopted **resolution 2011/18** by roll-call vote (24-2-21) [agenda item 14 (a)].

Situation of and assistance to Palestinian women

The Economic and Social Council,

Having considered with appreciation the report of the Secretary-General,

Recalling the Nairobi Forward-looking Strategies for the Advancement of Women, in particular paragraph 260 concerning Palestinian women and children, the Beijing Platform for Action adopted at the Fourth World Conference on Women and the outcome documents of the twenty-third special session of the General Assembly entitled "Women 2000: gender equality, development and peace for the twenty-first century",

Recalling also its resolution 2010/6 of 20 July 2010 and other relevant United Nations resolutions, including General Assembly resolution 57/337 of 3 July 2003 on the prevention of armed conflict and Security Council resolution 1325(2000) of 31 October 2000 on women and peace and security,

Recalling further the Declaration on the Elimination of Violence against Women as it concerns the protection of civilian populations,

Recalling the International Covenant on Civil and Political Rights, the International Covenant on Economic, Social and Cultural Rights and the Convention on the Rights of the Child, and reaffirming that these human rights instruments must be respected in the Occupied Palestinian Territory, including East Jerusalem,

Expressing deep concern about the grave situation of Palestinian women in the Occupied Palestinian Territory, including East Jerusalem, resulting from the severe impact of the ongoing illegal Israeli occupation and all of its manifestations,

Expressing grave concern about the increased difficulties being faced by Palestinian women and girls living under Israeli occupation, including the continuation of home demolitions, evictions of Palestinians and arbitrary detention and imprisonment, as well as high rates of poverty, unemployment, food insecurity, inadequate water supply, incidents of domestic violence, and declining health, education and living standards, including the rising incidence of trauma and the decline in their psychological well-being, and expressing grave concern also about the dire humanitarian crisis and insecurity and instability on the ground in the Occupied Palestinian Territory, in particular in the Gaza Strip,

Deploring the dire economic and social conditions of Palestinian women and girls in the Occupied Palestinian Territory, including East Jerusalem, and the systematic violation of their human rights resulting from the severe impact of ongoing illegal Israeli practices, including the construction and expansion of settlements and the wall, which continue to constitute a major obstacle to peace on the basis of the two-State solution, and the continued imposition of closures and restrictions on the movement of persons and goods, which have detrimentally affected their right to health care, including access of pregnant women to health services for antenatal care and safe delivery, education, employment, development and freedom of movement,

Gravely concerned, in particular, about the critical socio-economic and humanitarian situation in the Gaza Strip, including that resulting from the Israeli military operations and the imposition of a blockade consisting of the prolonged closure of border crossings and severe restrictions on the movement of persons and goods, as well as the continued impeding of the reconstruction process by Israel, the occupying Power, which has detrimentally affected every aspect of the lives of the civilian population, especially women and children, in the Gaza Strip,

Stressing the importance of providing assistance, especially emergency assistance, to alleviate the dire socioeconomic and humanitarian situation being faced by Palestinian women and their families,

Emphasizing the importance of increasing the role of women in peacebuilding and decision-making with regard to conflict prevention and the peaceful resolution of conflicts as part of efforts to ensure the safety and well-being of all women in the region, and stressing the importance of their equal participation and involvement in all efforts for the achievement, maintenance and promotion of peace and security,

1. *Reaffirms* that the Israeli occupation remains the major obstacle for Palestinian women with regard to their advancement, self-reliance and integration into the development of their society, and stresses the importance of efforts to increase their role in decision-making with regard to conflict prevention and resolution and to ensure their equal participation and involvement in all efforts for the achievement, maintenance and promotion of peace and security;

2. *Calls upon*, in this regard, the international community to continue to provide urgently needed assistance, especially emergency assistance, and services in an effort to alleviate the dire humanitarian crisis being faced by Palestinian women and their families and to help in the reconstruction of relevant Palestinian institutions, with the integration of a gender perspective into all of its international assistance programmes, and affirms its support for the plan of August 2009 of the Palestinian Authority for constructing the institutions of an independent Palestinian State;

3. *Demands* that Israel, the occupying Power, comply fully with the provisions and principles of the Universal Declaration of Human Rights, the Regulations annexed to the Hague Convention IV of 1907, the Geneva Convention relative to the Protection of Civilian Persons in Time of War, of 12 August 1949, and all other relevant rules, principles and instruments of international law, including the International Covenants on Human Rights, in order to protect the rights of Palestinian women and their families;

4. *Urges* the international community to continue to give special attention to the promotion and protection of the human rights of Palestinian women and girls and to intensify its measures to improve the difficult conditions being faced by Palestinian women and their families living under Israeli occupation;

5. *Calls upon* Israel to facilitate the return of all refugees and displaced Palestinian women and children to their homes and properties, in compliance with the relevant United Nations resolutions;

6. *Requests* the Commission on the Status of Women to continue to monitor and take action with regard to the implementation of the Nairobi Forward-looking Strategies for the Advancement of Women, in particular paragraph 260 concerning Palestinian women and children, the Beijing Platform for Action and the outcome documents of the twenty-third special session of the General Assembly entitled "Women 2000: gender equality, development and peace for the twenty-first century";

7. *Requests* the Secretary-General to continue to review the situation, to assist Palestinian women by all available means, including those set out in his report, and to submit to the Commission on the Status of Women at its fifty-sixth session a report, including information provided by the Economic and Social Commission for Western Asia, on the progress made in the implementation of the present resolution.

ROLL-CALL VOTE ON RESOLUTION 2011/18:

In favour: Argentina, Bahamas, Chile, China, Ecuador, Egypt, Ghana, Guatemala, India, Iraq, Mauritius, Mexico, Morocco, Namibia, Nicaragua, Pakistan, Peru, Philippines, Qatar, Russian Federation, Saudi Arabia, Senegal, Venezuela, Zambia.

Against: Canada, United States.

Abstaining: Australia, Belgium, Cameroon, Côte d'Ivoire, Estonia, Finland, France, Germany, Hungary, Italy, Japan, Latvia, Malta, Norway, Republic of Korea, Rwanda, Slovakia, Spain, Switzerland, Ukraine, United Kingdom.

Property rights

In response to General Assembly resolution 65/101 [YUN 2010, p. 484], the Secretary-General submitted an August report [A/66/318] on Palestine refugees' properties and their revenues. Denmark and Israel had replied to his request for information from Member States on action taken or envisaged in relation to the implementation of resolutions 65/98, 65/99, 65/100 [YUN 2010, pp. 476, 480 & 477] and 65/101.

In a 2 June note, Denmark stated that, as part of its continuous support to UNRWA, it expected to contribute in 2011 an amount similar to its 2010 core contribution of 70 million Danish Kroner (DKr). It had given an additional DKr 5 million for the relief and recovery of the Nahr el-Bared camp in Lebanon in 2010. Regarding resolution 65/101, which urged States to provide the Secretary-General with information concerning Arab property, assets and property rights in Israel, Denmark reported on the overall political and developmental situation in the Occupied Palestinian Territory. It also monitored those issues through its support of human rights organizations in the field.

Israel, in its 8 July reply, reiterated its support for the humanitarian activities of UNRWA; it would continue to facilitate the extension of the Agency's humanitarian services to its beneficiaries. Despite a threat to its security, Israel had fostered conditions for Palestinian economic development and cooperation, including by liberalizing the system by which civilian goods entered Gaza and easing restrictions in the West Bank. Israel favoured the application, in the Palestinian context, of the standard principles guiding the United Nations with respect to the treatment of refugees. Specifically, the UNRWA mandate should define entitlement to its services in a manner consistent with the standard UN policy on refugees, and should include promotion of the UN goals of resettlement and local integration of refugees.

GENERAL ASSEMBLY ACTION

On 9 December [meeting 81], the General Assembly, on the recommendation of the Fourth Committee [A/66/426], adopted **resolution 66/75** by recorded vote (165-7-2) [agenda item 52].

Palestine refugees' properties and their revenues

The General Assembly,

Recalling its resolutions 194(III) of 11 December 1948 and 36/146 C of 16 December 1981 and all its subsequent resolutions on the question,

Taking note of the report of the Secretary-General submitted pursuant to its resolution 65/101 of 10 December 2010, as well as that of the United Nations Conciliation Commission for Palestine for the period from 1 September 2010 to 31 August 2011,

Recalling that the Universal Declaration of Human Rights and the principles of international law uphold the principle that no one shall be arbitrarily deprived of his or her property,

Recalling in particular its resolution 394(V) of 14 December 1950, in which it directed the Conciliation Commission, in consultation with the parties concerned, to prescribe measures for the protection of the rights, property and interests of the Palestine refugees,

Noting the completion of the programme of identification and evaluation of Arab property, as announced by the Conciliation Commission in its twenty-second progress report, and the fact that the Land Office had a schedule of Arab owners and a file of documents defining the location, area and other particulars of Arab property,

Expressing its appreciation for the preservation and modernization of the existing records, including the land records, of the Conciliation Commission, and stressing the importance of such records for a just resolution of the plight of the Palestine refugees in conformity with resolution 194(III),

Recalling that, in the framework of the Middle East peace process, the Palestine Liberation Organization and the Government of Israel agreed, in the Declaration of Principles on Interim Self-Government Arrangements of 13 September 1993, to commence negotiations on permanent status issues, including the important issue of the refugees,

1. *Reaffirms* that the Palestine refugees are entitled to their property and to the income derived therefrom, in conformity with the principles of equity and justice;

2. *Requests* the Secretary-General to take all appropriate steps, in consultation with the United Nations Conciliation Commission for Palestine, for the protection of Arab property, assets and property rights in Israel;

3. *Calls once again upon* Israel to render all facilities and assistance to the Secretary-General in the implementation of the present resolution;

4. *Calls upon* all the parties concerned to provide the Secretary-General with any pertinent information in their possession concerning Arab property, assets and property rights in Israel that would assist him in the implementation of the present resolution;

5. *Urges* the Palestinian and Israeli sides, as agreed between them, to deal with the important issue of Palestine refugees' properties and their revenues within the framework of the final status negotiations of the Middle East peace process;

6. *Requests* the Secretary-General to report to the General Assembly at its sixty-seventh session on the implementation of the present resolution.

RECORDED VOTE ON RESOLUTION 66/75:

In favour: Afghanistan, Albania, Algeria, Andorra, Angola, Antigua and Barbuda, Argentina, Armenia, Australia, Austria, Azerbaijan, Bahamas, Bahrain, Bangladesh, Barbados, Belarus, Belgium, Belize, Benin, Bhutan, Bolivia, Bosnia and Herzegovina, Botswana, Brazil, Brunei Darussalam, Bulgaria, Burkina Faso, Burundi, Cambodia, Cape Verde, Chad, Chile, China, Colombia, Congo, Costa Rica, Côte d'Ivoire, Croatia, Cuba, Cyprus, Czech Republic, Democratic People's Republic of Korea, Denmark, Djibouti, Dominican Republic, Ecuador, Egypt, El Salvador, Eritrea, Estonia, Ethiopia, Fiji, Finland, France, Germany, Ghana, Greece, Grenada, Guatemala, Guinea, Guinea-Bissau, Guyana, Haiti, Honduras, Hungary, Iceland, India, Indonesia, Iran, Iraq, Ireland, Italy, Jamaica, Japan, Jordan, Kazakhstan, Kenya, Kuwait, Kyrgyzstan, Lao People's Democratic Republic, Latvia, Lebanon, Lesotho, Liberia, Libya, Liechtenstein, Lithuania, Luxembourg, Madagascar, Malawi, Malaysia, Maldives, Mali, Malta, Mauritania, Mauritius, Mexico, Monaco, Mongolia, Montenegro, Morocco, Mozambique, Namibia, Nepal, Netherlands, New Zealand, Nicaragua, Norway, Oman, Pakistan, Panama, Papua New Guinea, Paraguay, Peru, Philippines, Poland, Portugal, Qatar, Republic of Korea, Republic of Moldova, Romania, Russian Federation, Saint Lucia, Saint Vincent and the Grenadines, Samoa, San Marino, Saudi Arabia, Senegal, Serbia, Sierra Leone, Singapore, Slovakia, Slovenia, Solomon Islands, Somalia, South Africa, Spain, Sri Lanka, Sudan, Swaziland, Sweden, Switzerland, Syrian Arab Republic, Tajikistan, Thailand, the former Yugoslav Republic of Macedonia, Timor-Leste, Togo, Tonga, Trinidad and Tobago, Tunisia, Turkey, Turkmenistan, Tuvalu, Uganda, Ukraine, United Arab Emirates, United Kingdom, Uruguay, Uzbekistan, Venezuela, Viet Nam, Yemen, Zambia, Zimbabwe.

Against: Canada, Israel, Marshall Islands, Micronesia, Nauru, Palau, United States.

Abstaining: Cameroon, Vanuatu.

Lebanon

Political tension in Lebanon increased markedly during 2011, fuelled by speculation and public pronouncements concerning the proceedings of the Special Tribunal for Lebanon, the collapse of the Government, ongoing tensions with Israel and the increase of Palestinian and Syrian refugees.

Unrest in the Syrian Arab Republic (see p. 468) affected Lebanon in mid-May through the influx of an estimated 4,000 persons fleeing violence in Syrian border towns. Israel and Lebanon made some progress in marking the Blue Line divisions between the countries, but the Syrian border remained amorphous due to the presence of paramilitary groups and disagreement among the parties. Hizbullah, the country's largest and most heavily armed paramilitary group, asserted its intention to stockpile weapons to defend the country against Israel, while Israel protested the continued harbouring of Hizbullah in Lebanon. Demonstrations along the Blue Line took place throughout the year and escalated to deadly ends in one major incident, resulting in several deaths and many wounded. The aiming and discharge of weapons among the Lebanese Armed Forces and the Israel Defense Forces occurred in many instances, but were mitigated by the United Nations Interim Force in Lebanon (UNIFIL). The Security Council renewed UNIFIL's mandate for another year and encouraged the resumption of the Lebanese National Dialogue to resolve all border issues, thus affirming Lebanon as a sovereign and unified State.

Political and security developments

The Secretary-General, reporting on political developments in Lebanon in April [S/2011/258], stated that one minister from President Michel Sleiman's bloc and 10 ministers from the opposition resigned from the Cabinet on 12 January, forcing the collapse of the Government of National Unity. The following day, President Sleiman requested that the Government continue to function in a caretaker capacity. On 25 January, President Sleiman requested Prime Minister-Designate Najib Mikati to form a new Government. The absence of political authority in the months that followed generated institutional paralysis and a deterioration of security conditions in the country. Political polarization deepened and Lebanon grew increasingly susceptible to the regional political tumult. Developments in neighbouring Syria deepened political and sectarian divisions. The divide between the two major political blocs—the 8 March and 14 March Alliances—increasingly revolved around the question of Syria, and demonstrations both in favour and against the Syrian regime took place in several Lebanese cities.

In October [S/2011/648], the Secretary-General reported that on 13 June, then Prime Minister-Designate Mikati announced the formation of a new Government, which won a vote of confidence on 7 July.

Security Council consideration. The Security Council considered the situation in Lebanon, UNIFIL and the implementation of Security Council resolutions 1559(2004) [YUN 2004, p. 506] and 1701(2006) [YUN 2006, p. 583] in meetings held throughout the year.

On 23 June [S/PV.6562] the Under-Secretary-General for Political Affairs, B. Lynn Pascoe, briefing the Council on the situation in Lebanon, said that the Secretary-General expected the new Government to reiterate its commitment to the implementation of resolution 1701(2006) and Lebanon's international obligations. The United Nations continued to monitor developments along Lebanon's northern border. The influx of Syrian nationals into Lebanon, which reached an estimated 4,000 persons in mid-May, had virtually stopped, a development attributable to Syria's placement of additional security measures along the border. The United Nations coordinated closely with Lebanon on the provision of assistance to the displaced, as well as on matters of protection and the determination of their status.

The Under-Secretary-General, speaking before the Council on 25 August [S/PV.6602], stated that on 3 and 4 August, the Lebanese Parliament held its first session since the formation of the Government on 7 July; it adopted a law that defined the maritime zones under Lebanon's sovereignty. The President of the Palestinian Authority (PA), Mahmoud Abbas, visited Lebanon from 16 to 19 August; he inaugurated a new Palestinian embassy in Beirut, marking the upgrade of the diplomatic representation of the Palestine Liberation Organization in Lebanon and Palestine's efforts to seek Lebanon's support for recognition as a State at the United Nations in September.

On 21 November [S/PV.6662], the Special Coordinator for the Middle East Peace Process and Personal Representative of the Secretary-General, Robert Serry, reported to the Council that developments in Syria continued to stoke political tension in Lebanon. Lebanon's 12 November vote against the League of Arab States proposal to suspend Syrian membership became a divisive issue between the coalition in power and the opposition. The situation along Lebanon's border with Syria also remained a concern. The Syrian army planted landmines on its side of the border in areas most commonly used as illegal crossing points into Lebanon.

On 24 October [S/PV.6636], the Under-Secretary-General for Political Affairs told the Council that on several occasions in October, the Syrian army opened fire across the border, carried out incursions into Lebanon and raided houses to capture fleeing nationals and army deserters. On 6 October, Syrian troops killed a Syrian national on Lebanese soil.

In **resolution 66/192** of 22 December (see p. 991), the General Assembly requested Israel to assume responsibility for compensation to Lebanon and other countries affected by the oil slick on Lebanese and Syrian shores caused by military action in 2006 [YUN 2006, p. 1215].

Communications. In communications received throughout the year, Lebanon reported on Israeli acts of aggression by air, land and sea, as well as violations of the Blue Line and, consequently, of Lebanese sovereignty and territorial integrity [A/65/709-S/2011/48, S/2011/52, A/65/722-S/2011/61, A/65/729-S/2011/71, A/65/754-S/2011/83, A/65/771-S/2011/115, A/65/785-S/2011/139, A/65/805-S/2011/174, A/65/798-S/2011/198, A/65/799-S/2011/199, A/65/860-S/2011/358, A/65/892-S/2011/426, A/65/922-S/2011/490, A/66/363-S/2011/581, A/66/390-S/2011/605, A/66/508-S/2011/608, A/66/494-S/2011/624, A/66/498-S/2011/620, A/66/515-S/2011/657, A/66/535-S/2011/677, A/66/589-S/2011/756, A/66/595-S/2011/776, A/66/622-S/2011/791, A/66/650-S/2011/801].

Implementation of resolution 1559(2004)

The Secretary-General submitted his thirteenth and fourteenth semi-annual reports on the implementation of Security Council resolution 1559(2004) [YUN 2004, p. 506], which called for strict respect of the sovereignty, territorial integrity, unity and political independence of Lebanon under the sole and exclusive authority of the Government; the withdrawal of all remaining foreign forces from Lebanon; and the disbanding and disarmament of all Lebanese and non-Lebanese militias.

Report of Secretary-General (April). In April [S/2011/258], the Secretary-General, in his thirteenth semi-annual report, stated that, owing to the political crisis and institutional paralysis in Lebanon, there had been no progress towards the implementation of the remaining provisions of resolution1559(2004) since his twelfth report in 2010 [YUN 2010, p. 486]. The Secretary-General was concerned by the increased tension in the country generated, inter alia, by speculation over the proceedings of the Special Tribunal for Lebanon (see p. 466). He urged political leaders to transcend sectarian and individual interests and promote the interests of the State. Resolution 1559(2004) and other Council resolutions pertaining to Lebanon remained the best guarantee for the country's long-term prosperity and stability as a democratic State.

Armed groups defying State control were incompatible with the objective of strengthening Lebanon's sovereignty and political independence, the protection of the country's unique pluralistic system and the rights of Lebanese citizens. The Secretary-General condemned the use of illegal weapons in Lebanon and appealed to parties within and outside the country to cease efforts to transfer and acquire weapons and to build paramilitary capacities outside the State's authority. Foreign financial and material support for Lebanon should be channelled transparently through the Government. He called on the leaders of Hizbullah to complete the group's transformation into a solely Lebanese political party and to disarm in a manner consistent with the 1989 Taif Agreement [YUN 1989, p. 203] and resolution 1559(2004); regional States were called on to assist in that transformation. The Secretary-General called on Lebanese leaders to reconvene, under the auspices of President Sleiman, the National Dialogue, the main mandate of which was to develop a national defence strategy that would address the issue of weapons outside State control.

There had been no progress regarding the dismantling of Palestinian military bases outside refugee camps. Paramilitary infrastructures of the Popular Front for the Liberation of Palestine-General Command (PFLP-GC) and Fatah al-Intifada remained beyond State authority. The bases, most of which straddled the Lebanon-Syria border, undermined Lebanese sovereignty and challenged the country's ability to manage its borders.

More needed to be done to improve the dismal living conditions of Palestine refugees in Lebanon, without prejudice to an overall resolution of the refugee questions within the framework of a comprehensive peace agreement. The Secretary-General called on the Government to alleviate the situation in refugee camps, and on Member States to offer assistance to consolidate political dialogue and security in the camps. The Secretary-General urged the international community to continue to equip and train the Lebanese Armed Forces (LAF). He urged Lebanon's neighbours to support the sovereignty and political independence of the country, and called on all parties to abide by resolutions 1559(2004), 1680(2006) [YUN 2006, p. 571] and 1701(2006) [YUN 2006, p. 583].

Communication. On 5 May [S/2011/286], Syria, in identical letters addressed to the Secretary-General and the Security Council President, said that references made in the Secretary-General's thirteenth semi-annual report on the implementation of resolution 1559(2004) (see above) were an explicit acknowledgement that Syria had fulfilled all obligations incumbent on it under the resolution. Syria did not accept references made in the report to the delineation of the Syrian-Lebanese border, which was a bilateral matter. It said that the real obstacle to the final delineation of the border was Israel's continued aggression and its occupation of the Syrian Golan and the Shab'a Farms. The Palestinian presence in Lebanon was governed by Lebanese-Palestinian agreements that did not concern Syria. The Palestinian positions located along the Syrian-Lebanese border that were noted in the report lay within Lebanese territory; therefore, Syria would not intervene in the matter.

Report of Secretary-General (October). In October, the Secretary-General submitted his fourteenth semi-annual report [S/2011/648] on the implementation of resolution 1559(2004).

He stated that the 68 Members of Parliament who voted in favour of the new Government in July represented the new majority, composed, inter alia, of Hizbullah, the Amal movement, the Free Patriotic Movement and others. Sixty Members of Parliament of the 14 March Alliance boycotted the vote to protest what they termed a coup by Hizbullah to reverse the results of the 2009 parliamentary elections [YUN 2009, p. 476]. In their opinion, Hizbullah and Syria had imposed the new Government on the country.

The Secretary-General reported that implementation of resolution 1559(2004) had not progressed over the previous six months. He condemned the possession and use of illegal weapons in Lebanon, in particular in populated areas. Hizbullah's arsenal of weapons posed a key challenge to the safety of Lebanese civilians and to the Government monopoly on the legitimate use of force. The issue had become even more urgent against the backdrop of the ongoing political upheavals across the region. The absence of progress on the disarming and disbanding of militias placed Lebanon in violation of its international obligations. Lebanon had to revitalize efforts to address the challenge posed by the continued presence of arms outside the authority of the State, and the Secretary-General called on President Sleiman and Prime Minister Mikati to take action in that regard. He encouraged the President and the Government to implement past decisions taken by the National Dialogue, including the dismantling of Palestinian military bases maintained outside the refugee camps by the Damascus-headquartered PFLP-GC and Fatah al-Intifada. Mindful that the two militias maintained close regional ties, the Secretary-General renewed his call on Syria to assist in the process.

The Secretary-General, recalling that two thirds of Palestinian refugees in Lebanon lived in dire poverty, called on the Government to implement amendments to the Labour Code and Social Security Law, adopted in 2010, to improve the employment prospects of refugees.

The political crisis in Syria (see p. 468) further hindered progress towards the delineation and the demarcation of the border between that country and Lebanon; the Secretary-General urged the two countries to move forward on the issue. He also urged Lebanon to implement a comprehensive border management strategy, which would enable better control of the country's international borders and prevent illegal arms transfers. The Secretary-General called on Syria to cease the violent incursions and raids into Lebanese towns and villages by Syrian security forces that resulted in death and injury, and to respect the sovereignty and territorial integrity of Lebanon, in accordance with resolution 1559(2004). Such incursions and the crisis in Syria carried the potential of igniting further tensions inside Lebanon and beyond.

Security incidents during the reporting period highlighted the need for Lebanese security forces to do more to prevent and respond to violence. Increased support for LAF and the Internal Security Forces remained critical. The Secretary-General deplored the continued Israeli violations of Lebanon's sovereignty and territorial integrity. He called on Israel to withdraw its forces from the northern part of the village of Ghajar and an adjacent area north of the Blue Line, and to cease its overflights of Lebanese airspace.

Communication. On 26 October [S/2011/667], Syria, in identical letters addressed to the Secretary-General and the Security Council President, presented its position on the Secretary-General's fourteenth semi-annual report (see above). It stated that the claim that the new Lebanese Government was imposed by Syria constituted blatant interference in the internal affairs of Lebanon; any change in government was part of the democratic process in that country. Furthermore, the introduction of references to Syria or its internal situation into the reports of the Secretary-General on implementation of resolution 1559(2004) was not acceptable because such matters did not fall within the mandate of his representative. Allegations of incidents of violence, cross-border gunfire or Syrian infiltration into Lebanon had been disproven.

Implementation of resolution 1701(2006) and UNIFIL activities

Security Council resolution 1701(2006) [YUN 2006, p. 583], which was approved by both the Lebanese and the Israeli Governments, brought about a ceasefire, effective 14 August 2006, between Israel and Hizbullah after a month-long conflict that caused hundreds of civilian deaths and major infrastructure damage throughout Lebanon. By the same resolution, the Council expanded the mandate of the United Nations Interim Force in Lebanon (UNIFIL) to undertake substantial new tasks, in addition to those mandated under resolutions 425(1978) [YUN 1978, p. 312] and 426(1978) [ibid.], and authorized an increase in the Force strength from 2,000 to a maximum of 15,000 troops. The Secretary-General updated the Council on the implementation of resolution 1701(2006) in three periodic reports during the year.

UNIFIL was established by Council resolution 425(1978), following Israel's invasion of Lebanon [YUN 1978, p. 296]. The Force was originally entrusted with confirming the withdrawal of Israeli forces, restoring international peace and security, and assisting Lebanon in regaining authority in southern Lebanon. Following a second invasion in 1982 [YUN 1982, p. 428], the Council, in resolution 511(1982) [ibid., p. 450], authorized the Force to carry out the additional task of providing protection and humanitarian assistance to the local population. Following the withdrawal of Israeli forces from Lebanon in 2000 [YUN 2000, p. 465], UNIFIL was reinforced in order to monitor those territories previously occupied by Israel, to prevent the recurrence of fighting and to create conditions for the restoration of Lebanese authority in the area.

Communications. On 26 January [A/65/708-S/2011/47], Lebanon, in identical letters addressed to the Secretary-General and the Security Council President, presented its position with respect to the comprehensive assessment that would be presented by the Secretary-General in his forthcoming report on the implementation of Security Council resolution 1701(2006) (see below). Lebanon believed that Israel had failed to honour its obligation to implement resolution 1701(2006) or to withdraw from all occupied Lebanese territory. Since the Secretary-General's previous report [YUN 2010, p. 490], Israel had committed 298 air, 24 sea and 149 land violations of Lebanese sovereignty. Networks of spies recruited by Israel constituted an attack on Lebanon's sovereignty. On 3 December 2010, Israeli forces detonated by remote control listening devices they had planted in Lebanese territory at Wadi Qaysiyah following the discovery of those devices by Lebanese workers; the detonation caused multiple injuries to two individuals. LAF also discovered and dismantled two other electronic devices planted by Israeli forces in Lebanese territory. Lebanon said that maps it received from Israel relating to cluster bombs Israel had dropped on populated areas were incomplete and imprecise. The bombs caused the death or injury of more than 400 persons. Lebanon demanded that information should be deposited regarding the dates on which cluster bombs were dropped, together with the quantity and types of bombs. The Israeli army continued to use launches to conduct illegal patrols inside Lebanese territorial waters close to the so-called "line of buoys", which Israel claimed approximated the southern border of Lebanese territorial waters. Israel's claims that weapons were stockpiled and military installations established in densely populated civilian areas in southern Lebanon were not true.

Lebanon stressed the importance of strengthening international assistance in building the capacities of the Lebanese Army and security forces and preparing them to defend Lebanese sovereignty and protect the Lebanese people. It decided to deploy two additional battalions south of the Litani River to further demonstrate its commitment to the implementation of resolution 1701(2006).

On 24 February [S/2011/93], Israel informed the Council of its concerns on key issues related to the implementation of resolution 1701(2006). Israel witnessed a lack of progress in enforcing the arms embargo in Lebanon, a key element of resolution 1701(2006) that sought to deny Hizbullah and other terrorist groups the means to build and reconstitute their illegal arsenals. Hizbullah possessed more than 55,000 missiles and rockets and continued to focus on acquiring more advanced weaponry. The accumulation of weapons was accomplished through joint and coordinated illegal arms transfers facilitated by the Syrian authorities across the Syrian-Lebanese border. No meaningful action had been taken by the relevant parties to combat illegal weapons transfers. Hizbullah continued to deploy weapons throughout the civilian villages of southern Lebanon, adjacent to schools, hospitals, houses of worship and residential buildings.

Report of Secretary-General (February). On 28 February, the Secretary-General submitted his fifteenth report [S/2011/91] on the implementation of Security Council resolution 1701(2006). He said that the paralysis of the Lebanese Government during most of the reporting period prevented progress in implementing some of the country's key obligations under the resolution. Nevertheless, relative stability and calm prevailed in the UNIFIL area of operations, and the cessation of hostilities between Israel and Lebanon, established in 2006, continued to hold. On 17 November 2010, Israel accepted, in principle, the UN proposal for a withdrawal of the Israel Defense Forces (IDF) from the northern part of Ghajar and the redeployment of IDF south of the Blue Line. The marking of the Blue Line, which required the clearance of minefields and the disposal of unexploded ordnance, continued slowly within the previously agreed five sectors, comprising 38 kilometres; 87 markers were in place out of an estimated 171. UNIFIL deminers cleared access to an additional 134 points to be marked. Following a special tripartite meeting dedicated to the visible marking of the Blue Line on 18 August, both parties signalled their readiness to accelerate the process, but a lack of flexibility in finding practical solutions to contentious points resulted in delays.

UNIFIL completed its investigation into the 3 September 2010 explosion that occurred at a house in Shahabiye (Sector West) [YUN 2010, p. 492] but, owing to possible evidence tampering, it could not determine the cause of the explosion or whether the house had been used for activities in contravention of resolution 1701(2006). Israeli officials questioned the UNIFIL conclusions regarding the investigation. The LAF report, shared with UNIFIL, stated that no evidence of bomb fragmentation or explosive material residue existed at the site.

LAF informed UNIFIL that, during excavations carried out by Lebanese workers in the vicinity of Majdal Silim (Sector West) on 3 December 2010, an explosion occurred resulting in the injury of two civilians (see p. 458). The following day, UNIFIL and LAF found what appeared to be the remains of a buried electronic device. UNIFIL launched an investigation but, despite repeated requests, it was shown neither the reports citing the testimonies of the two injured persons nor the remnants of an alleged Israeli sensor. IDF informed UNIFIL that it did not have any related information and could neither confirm nor deny Lebanon's claim.

With few exceptions, UNIFIL generally enjoyed freedom of movement throughout its area of operations, carrying out approximately 10,000 patrols each month. As called for in Security Council resolutions, UNIFIL and LAF expanded their coordinated activities and cooperation.

Lebanon did not report any breach of the arms embargo imposed by resolution 1701(2006). Israel maintained that Hizbullah continued to build up its military presence and capacity, including within the UNIFIL area of operations. It also charged that Hizbullah kept military units in populated areas in southern Lebanon, and that unauthorized weapons were transferred into Lebanon through UNIFIL-controlled sectors. The United Nations took seriously Israeli allegations that Hizbullah was building its armaments supply but was not in a position to verify such information independently.

There was no progress on the delineation and demarcation of the border between Lebanon and Syria or on the issue of the Shab'a Farms area. In a 4 January letter to the Secretary-General, the Minister for Foreign Affairs of Lebanon raised the issue of the maritime delimitation of the southern boundaries of Lebanon's exclusive economic zone and Lebanon's right to exploit the resources it contained. In his 7 February response to the caretaker Minister for Foreign Affairs, the Secretary-General recalled that, according to the law of the sea, boundaries should be delimited by agreements based on international law; the United Nations did not become involved unless mandated by competent UN organs or requested by all parties concerned to do so. With the agreement of the parties, the Secretariat stood ready to provide assistance in the matter and to pursue appropriate avenues to ensure that the exploration and exploitation of resources in maritime zones did not become a new source of friction or conflict between Lebanon and Israel.

Communications. On 15 May [A/65/841-S/2011/312], Lebanon, in identical letters to the Secretary-General and the Security Council President, reported that despite heightened measures taken by the Lebanese army in relation to the commemoration of the Nakbah that day in the town of Maroun al-Ras in southern Lebanon, Israeli forces fired at a group of unarmed civilians gathered there, killing 10 persons and wounding 112 others, some critically.

On 16 May [S/2011/309], Israel, in identical letters addressed to the Secretary-General and the Council President concerning the 15 May incident, stated that hundreds of individuals near the village of Maroun al-Ras sought to breach the Blue Line and enter Israel using violent means, including by throwing large objects. IDF operated with maximum restraint in confronting the significant threat of violence. Responsibility for any harm caused to the individuals involved in the demonstrations lay with Lebanon, which was tasked with preventing any infiltration of the Blue Line or incitements in its vicinity.

On 22 June [A/65/874-S/2011/400], Lebanon, in identical letters to the Secretary-General and the Council President, presented a paper expressing its position with respect to the Secretary-General's forthcoming report (see p. 460). Lebanon stated that, since the Secretary-General's fifteenth report (see above),

Israel had committed 336 air, 149 land and 60 sea violations of Lebanese sovereignty.

Report of Secretary-General (July). In July [S/2011/406], the Secretary-General submitted his sixteenth report on the implementation of resolution 1701(2006). The security arrangements put in place by the resolution were tested by a number of incidents since his previous report. The most deadly incident in the Blue Line area since the adoption of the resolution occurred on 15 May, when IDF, after firing initial warning shots, opened live fire against Palestinian demonstrators in the area of Maroun al-Ras in southern Lebanon. UNIFIL estimated that around 8,000 to 10,000 people, mostly Palestinian, participated in the demonstration organized by Palestinian and Lebanese groups, among them Hizbullah. While the majority of demonstrators commemorated the day peacefully, around 1,000 protesters crossed through a minefield and moved towards the Blue Line and the Israeli technical fence. Using cordons and firing in the air, LAF stopped a first attempt by a smaller group to reach the fence but was not able to prevent the second attempt. At the technical fence, demonstrators unearthed 23 anti-tank mines, threw stones and two petrol bombs across the fence, and attempted to climb it and bring it down. Following a verbal warning and firing into the air, IDF directed live fire at the protesters. LAF informed UNIFIL that seven people were killed and 111 were injured. Preliminary findings of a UNIFIL investigation indicated that the demonstrators carried out a provocative and violent act that constituted a violation of resolution 1701(2006). The number of LAF troops and the available equipment proved insufficient for the expected turnout at the event and the envisaged risks. Other than firing initial warning shots, IDF did not use conventional crowd control methods. The firing of live ammunition by IDF across the Blue Line, which resulted in the loss of civilian life and a significant number of casualties, constituted a violation of resolution 1701(2006) and was not commensurate with the threat to Israeli soldiers. With the exception of a request for UNIFIL to carry out helicopter patrols to monitor the situation from the air, LAF did not ask for UNIFIL assistance. IDF called on UNIFIL to intervene on the ground once the demonstrators reached the technical fence, but LAF insisted that UNIFIL stay away from the demonstrators to avoid additional friction. The Secretary-General called on the Lebanese authorities and LAF to prevent incidents on the Blue Line originating from Lebanon; on IDF to refrain from responding to such situations with live fire, except when required in immediate self-defence; and on both parties to work with UNIFIL to mitigate the risk of further violence.

Hizbullah acknowledged that it maintained a substantial arsenal separate from that of the Lebanese State for defensive purposes against Israel. The Secretary-General of Hizbullah, Hassan Nasrallah, stated publicly that his party would continue to train, exercise and arm itself to protect Lebanon and its natural resources against "potential Israeli attacks".

The situation in Lebanon was influenced by developments taking place in the region. The unrest in Syria since mid-March (see p. 468) had affected Lebanon most visibly in mid-May through the influx of an estimated 4,000 persons fleeing violence in Syrian border towns. Lebanon's northern border with Syria was managed by the Common Border Force, which comprised around 700 staff from Lebanon's security agencies. LAF deployed approximately 220 troops to support the Force in response to the large number of people crossing the border. By early June, many of the displaced had returned to Syria. At a 14 April meeting chaired by the Special Coordinator, donor countries reiterated the need for a national strategy for border management.

On 27 May, UNIFIL withstood a terrorist attack when an explosion caused by a remotely controlled roadside bomb hit a UNIFIL logistics convoy as it passed on the main coastal highway connecting Beirut to southern Lebanon—the main UNIFIL supply route. The attack injured six Italian peacekeepers, two seriously, in addition to causing minor injuries to two Lebanese civilians. The incident was the fourth attack against UNIFIL since the adoption of resolution 1701(2006) and the first in more than three years. As was the case in the previous instances, no one claimed responsibility for the attack. The Secretary-General condemned the attack and called on the Lebanese authorities to bring the perpetrators to justice. UNIFIL observed proceedings in the Lebanese military court against individuals accused of forming armed groups to carry out attacks against it. On 7 March, the court handed out nine sentences for possession of explosives and planning and conducting terrorist attacks against LAF and UNIFIL.

Despite the events of 15 and 27 May, the Secretary-General observed that relative stability and calm prevailed in the UNIFIL area of operations. Nevertheless, without progress in the full implementation of resolution 1701(2006), the situation along the Blue Line would remain fragile. He called on both parties to embrace the new strategic environment that UNIFIL had established in cooperation with LAF, and take the necessary steps to reach a permanent ceasefire.

Communications. On 1 August [S/2011/483], Israel, in identical letters addressed to the Secretary-General and the Security Council President, stated that, on that day, an LAF soldier opened fire on IDF soldiers situated south of the Blue Line. IDF responded in self-defence only after it was fired upon, acting with maximum restraint.

On 3 August [A/65/925-S/2011/487], Lebanon submitted a complaint against Israeli forces concerning the 1 August incident. It stated that an Israeli patrol comprising eight troops carrying a video camera crossed the Wazzani River (Blue Line) and penetrated some 15 metres into Lebanese territory. LAF responded by firing warning shots inside Lebanese territory, but not towards the Israeli patrol. After crossing back to the river's east bank and withdrawing behind the technical fence, IDF opened fire for 10 minutes using small and medium weapons and grenade launchers against Lebanese troops. An LAF soldier was slightly injured by Israeli gunfire.

Renewal of UNIFIL mandate. On 5 August [S/2011/488], the Secretary-General requested the Security Council to consider the renewal of the mandate of UNIFIL for one year, as also requested by the Minister for Foreign Affairs and Emigrants of Lebanon in a 22 July letter. UNIFIL continued to play a crucial role in ensuring peace and stability in southern Lebanon, as well as full respect for the Blue Line by both parties. In accordance with its mandate, UNIFIL monitored the cessation of hostilities and assisted LAF in taking steps towards the establishment of an area between the Blue Line and the Litani River free of any unauthorized armed personnel, assets and weapons.

The UNIFIL liaison and coordination arrangements with the parties, including the tripartite mechanism, facilitated constructive and pragmatic measures and served to build trust. After a long impasse in the process of visibly marking the Blue Line, the parties responded positively to the most recent UNIFIL initiative to proceed with the marking of non-contentious points. The parties also agreed to discuss maritime security issues through the tripartite mechanism. UNIFIL, following intensive engagement with both parties, finalized its proposal regarding security arrangements to facilitate the withdrawal of IDF from northern Ghajar. The long-term objective of UNIFIL was to gradually transfer its responsibilities on land and at sea to LAF and have it assume security control over the UNIFIL area of operations and Lebanese territorial waters, in line with resolution 1701(2006).

As at 15 July, the number of UNIFIL military personnel stood at 12,091, including 11,135 ground troops deployed in two sectors and 616 personnel serving in the Maritime Task Force. The UNIFIL civilian component numbered 354 international and 658 national staff.

Communication. In identical letters of 25 August addressed to the Secretary-General and the Security Council President [S/2011/537], Israel reiterated its support for UNIFIL. Nevertheless, several factors continued to exist in southern Lebanon in violation of Council resolutions 1559(2004) [YUN 2004, p. 506], 1680(2006) [YUN 2006, p. 571] and 1701(2006).

Israel reiterated its concerns regarding three core issues. First, Hizbullah's armed entrenchment and extensive military build-up in southern Lebanon placed a large portion of Israel's population under grave threat. The second issue related to Hizbullah's intentionally embedding its military infrastructure within civilian populated areas. The third concern was Hizbullah's attempt to obstruct UNIFIL by using so-called civilians to act against the Force and disrupt its freedom of movement.

SECURITY COUNCIL ACTION

On 30 August [meeting 6605], the Security Council unanimously adopted **resolution 2004(2011)**. The draft [S/2011/545] was submitted by France, Germany, Italy, Spain and the United States.

The Security Council,

Recalling all its previous resolutions on Lebanon, in particular resolutions 425(1978) and 426(1978) of 19 March 1978, 1559(2004) of 2 September 2004, 1680(2006) of 17 May 2006, 1701(2006) of 11 August 2006, 1773(2007) of 24 August 2007, 1832(2008) of 27 August 2008, 1884(2009) of 27 August 2009 and 1937(2010) of 30 August 2010, as well as the statements by its President on the situation in Lebanon,

Responding to the request of the Government of Lebanon to extend the mandate of the United Nations Interim Force in Lebanon for a new period of one year, without amendment, presented in the letter dated 22 July 2011 from the Minister for Foreign Affairs and Emigrants of Lebanon to the Secretary-General, and welcoming the letter dated 5 August 2011 from the Secretary-General to the President of the Security Council recommending this extension,

Reiterating its strong support for the territorial integrity, sovereignty and political independence of Lebanon,

Reaffirming its commitment to the full implementation of all provisions of resolution 1701(2006), and aware of its responsibilities to help to secure a permanent ceasefire and a long-term solution as envisioned in the resolution,

Calling upon all parties concerned to strengthen their efforts to fully implement all provisions of resolution 1701(2006) without delay,

Expressing deep concern at all violations in connection with resolution 1701(2006), in particular the latest grave violations of 15 May and 1 August 2011, and looking forward to the rapid finalization of the investigation by the Force with a view to preventing such incidents in the future,

Commending the Lebanese Armed Forces and the Force on steps taken to prevent an escalation of violence during protests on 5 June 2011,

Emphasizing the importance of full compliance with the prohibition on sales and supply of arms and related materiel established by resolution 1701(2006),

Recalling the utmost importance that all parties concerned respect the Blue Line in its entirety, and encouraging the parties to accelerate their efforts in coordination with the Force to visibly mark the Blue Line in its entirety,

Condemning in the strongest terms the terrorist attacks against peacekeepers of the Force on 27 May and 26 July

2011, as well as all attempts to threaten the security and stability of Lebanon, reaffirming its determination to ensure that no such acts of intimidation will prevent the Force from implementing its mandate in accordance with resolution 1701(2006), and welcoming the investigation launched by Lebanon and its commitment to bring to justice the perpetrators of these attacks and to protect the movements of the Force, as stated by the Lebanese Higher Defence Council on 12 August 2011,

Recalling the relevant principles contained in the Convention on the Safety of United Nations and Associated Personnel,

Commending the active role and dedication of the personnel of the Force, expressing its strong appreciation to Member States that contribute to the Force, and underlining the necessity that the Force have at its disposal all means and equipment necessary to carry out its mandate,

Recalling the request of the Government of Lebanon to deploy an international force to assist it to exercise its authority throughout the territory, and reaffirming the authority of the Force to take all necessary action, in areas of operations of its forces and as it deems within its capabilities, to ensure that its area of operations is not utilized for hostile activities of any kind and to resist attempts by forceful means to prevent it from discharging its mandate,

Welcoming the efforts of the Secretary-General to keep all peacekeeping operations, including the Force, under close review, and stressing the need for the Security Council to pursue a rigorous, strategic approach to peacekeeping deployments,

Calling upon Member States to assist the Lebanese Armed Forces as needed to enable them to perform their duties in line with resolution 1701(2006),

Determining that the situation in Lebanon continues to constitute a threat to international peace and security,

1. *Decides* to extend the present mandate of the United Nations Interim Force in Lebanon until 31 August 2012;

2. *Commends* the positive role of the Force, whose deployment together with the Lebanese Armed Forces has helped to establish a new strategic environment in southern Lebanon, welcomes the expansion of coordinated activities between the Force and the Lebanese Armed Forces, and calls for further enhancement of this cooperation;

3. *Welcomes*, in this regard, the engagement of the Force and the Lebanese Armed Forces in the strategic dialogue, which aims at carrying out analysis of ground forces and maritime assets and setting a series of benchmarks reflecting the correlation between the capacities and responsibilities of the Force vis-à-vis those of the Lebanese Armed Forces, with a view to identifying Lebanese Armed Forces requirements for implementing tasks mandated in resolution 1701(2006), calls for an acceleration of its pace, and requests in this regard the Secretary-General to conduct, before the end of the year, a strategic review of the Force in an effort to ensure, along with peacekeeping good practice, that the Force is configured most appropriately to fulfil its mandated tasks;

4. *Strongly calls upon* all parties concerned to respect the cessation of hostilities, to prevent any violation of the Blue Line and to respect it in its entirety and to cooperate fully with the United Nations and the Force;

5. *Condemns in the strongest terms* all terrorist attacks against the Force, and urges all parties to abide scrupulously by their obligation to respect the safety of the Force and other United Nations personnel and to ensure that the freedom of movement of the Force is fully respected and unimpeded, in conformity with its mandate and its rules of engagement, including by avoiding any course of action which endangers United Nations personnel, and in this regard calls for further cooperation between the Force and the Lebanese Armed Forces, in particular regarding coordinated and adjacent patrols, and for the rapid finalization of the investigation launched by Lebanon regarding the attacks of 27 May and 26 July 2011 in order to bring to justice the perpetrators of those attacks;

6. *Urges* all parties to cooperate fully with the Security Council and the Secretary-General to make tangible progress towards a permanent ceasefire and a long-term solution as envisioned in resolution 1701(2006), and emphasizes that more work remains to be done by the parties to advance the full implementation of resolution 1701(2006);

7. *Urges* the Government of Israel to expedite the withdrawal of its army from northern Ghajar without further delay in coordination with the Force, which has actively engaged Israel and Lebanon to facilitate such a withdrawal;

8. *Reaffirms its call upon* all States to fully support and respect the establishment between the Blue Line and the Litani River of an area free of any armed personnel, assets and weapons other than those of the Government of Lebanon and the Force;

9. *Welcomes* the efforts being undertaken by the Force to implement the Secretary-General's zero-tolerance policy on sexual exploitation and abuse and to ensure full compliance of its personnel with the United Nations code of conduct, requests the Secretary-General to continue to take all necessary action in this regard and to keep the Council informed, and urges troop-contributing countries to take preventive and disciplinary action to ensure that such acts are properly investigated and punished in cases involving their personnel;

10. *Requests* the Secretary-General to continue to report to the Council on the implementation of resolution 1701(2006) every four months, or at any time as he deems appropriate;

11. *Stresses* the importance of, and the need to achieve, a comprehensive, just and lasting peace in the Middle East, based on all its relevant resolutions, including resolutions 242(1967) of 22 November 1967, 338(1973) of 22 October 1973, 1515(2003) of 19 November 2003 and 1850(2008) of 16 December 2008;

12. *Decides* to remain actively seized of the matter.

Communications. On 9 November, Lebanon, in letters addressed to the Secretary-General [A/66/580] and the Security Council President [S/2011/711], presented its position with respect to the Secretary-General's forthcoming report on the implementation of Council resolution 1701(2006) (see p. 463). It stated that the Israeli army had committed 495 air, 107 land and 204 sea violations of Lebanese sovereignty since the Secretary-General's previous report. Israel had committed some 9,168 violations since the adoption of resolution 1701(2006).

Report of Secretary-General (November). On 14 November, the Secretary-General submitted his seventeenth report [S/2011/715] on the implementation of resolution 1701(2006). In its ministerial statement, the new Government of Lebanon expressed its commitment to the full implementation of the resolution. In keeping with that commitment, Prime Minister Mikati visited southern Lebanon and UNIFIL headquarters a few days after the Government was sworn in.

UNIFIL investigated the 1 August incident in which IDF and LAF exchanged fire along the Wazzani River (see p. 461). LAF said that it had fired warning shots to counter an intrusion into Lebanese territory and subsequently came under fire when IDF soldiers returned to the eastern side of the river. IDF maintained that its soldiers had not crossed the river or the Blue Line; rather, they came under fire from a Lebanese soldier as they completed their ascent of a hill towards the technical fence and returned fire. UNIFIL concluded that both parties breached the cessation of hostilities, which constituted a violation of resolution 1701(2006), but was unable to determine whether a ground violation of the Blue Line had occurred. Following the incident, UNIFIL increased the number of its patrols in the area.

UNIFIL generally enjoyed freedom of movement throughout its area of operations, conducting approximately 9,000 to 10,000 patrols each month. A small number of patrols were subject to freedom of movement restrictions, in which members of the local population threw stones and took UN equipment. A few cases included physical assault against UNIFIL personnel. Despite those incidents, the attitude of the local population towards UNIFIL remained generally positive. The Secretary-General called on the Lebanese authorities to take action against the perpetrators of incidents that impeded the freedom of movement of UNIFIL.

On 19 July, LAF informed UNIFIL that it approved the arrangements as a first phase in a process leading to Lebanon's full control over the northern part of Ghajar village and an adjacent area of land north of the Blue Line. IDF informed UNIFIL that the arrangements would require Israel's approval. The United Nations did not receive any response from the Government of Israel.

After an almost year-long hiatus in visibly marking the Blue Line, the parties responded positively to the UNIFIL initiative to proceed with the delineation of non-contentious points along the entire Line. UNIFIL identified 135 such points, which were being measured and marked. As at 31 October, UNIFIL demineers had cleared access to 176 points to be marked. Of those points, 135 were measured, 106 Blue Line markers were constructed and 97 markers were verified by both parties.

On 5 and 6 August, following an assassination attempt against the military commander of Fatah in Lebanon, heavy clashes between armed factions erupted in the Palestinian refugee camp of Ain el-Hilweh. A ceasefire was agreed on after hours of fighting that left a number of people injured. On 12 September, as a result of a personal dispute, fierce clashes involving the use of heavy weapons took place between Hizbullah militants and armed Palestinians on the outskirts of the Burj al-Barajneh refugee camp in Beirut, leaving several people injured. PA President Mahmoud Abbas visited Lebanon from 16 to 19 August and stressed that Palestine refugees in Lebanon had to abide by Lebanon's domestic laws.

LAF informed the United Nations that the deterioration of the security situation in Syria had prompted it to adopt increased border control measures in order to prevent the entry of arms and military personnel into Lebanon. LAF did not report incidents of arms smuggling from Syria to Lebanon, but other officials publicly stated that arms and fuel transfers across the border took place in both directions. As at late October, more than 3,100 Syrian nationals who fled the violence were jointly registered with Lebanon's High Relief Commission and the Office of the United Nations High Commissioner for Refugees (UNHCR). A number of cross-border incidents took place over the reporting period. The Syrian army shot across the border into Lebanese territory, targeting individuals who attempted to flee Syria, resulting in at least one death. It also conducted incursions into Lebanon across the eastern and the northern borders; some of the incursions extended 3 kilometres into Lebanese territory. LAF and Government officials consulted by the United Nations noted that the incidents took place in areas where the border was not delineated or demarcated. President Sleiman instructed LAF to establish contacts with the Syrian army with respect to the incursions in order to maintain respect for Lebanon's sovereignty.

The Secretary-General urged the new Government of Lebanon to strengthen its efforts to control the country's borders, including by adopting the comprehensive border management strategy to which the previous Government had committed in 2010. He also urged Syria to cooperate with Lebanon to achieve the delineation and demarcation of the border between them. The Secretary-General deplored the violent incursions into Lebanese towns and villages by Syrian security forces that resulted in death and injury, and called on Syria to cease such incursions and respect Lebanon's sovereignty and territorial integrity.

On 26 July, UNIFIL suffered its second direct terrorist attack within two months, when an explosion caused by a roadside bomb hit a UNIFIL logistics convoy south of the town of Saida; six UNIFIL peacekeepers serving with the French contingent were injured.

The Lebanese authorities informed UNIFIL that they were following leads in the investigations into the two attacks against UNIFIL along the main coastal highway, but no arrests had been made. The attack demonstrated the persistence of the terrorist threat against UNIFIL, especially along its main supply route outside its area of operations. In response, LAF reinforced its presence in key locations along the main UNIFIL supply route and accompanied all convoys north of the Litani River. The Secretary-General reiterated his condemnation of the attack.

Communications. On 25 November [S/2011/735], Syria, in identical letters to the Secretary-General and the Council President, stated its position with respect to the Secretary-General's seventeenth report (see above) on the implementation of resolution 1701(2006). Syria reasserted its commitment to providing all possible support and assistance to consolidate the authority and sovereignty of Lebanon over all Lebanese territory. It reiterated that it was unacceptable to discuss Syria or its internal situation in the reports of the Secretary-General on the implementation of resolution 1701(2006) because such matters were not part of the mandate of the Secretary-General's representative.

On 29 November [S/2011/743], Israel, in identical letters to the Secretary-General and the Council President, stated that a terrorist attack on Israel was launched from Lebanon earlier that day. Four rockets were fired into northern Israel, exploding in the heart of Western Galilee, a densely populated area. The rockets caused damage to numerous civilian buildings. Israel held the Government of Lebanon and LAF responsible for the attack, and expected them to take all necessary measures to prevent further acts of terrorism. The attack was a direct result of transfers of arms from Iran and Syria, which flowed unimpeded across the Syrian-Lebanese border.

On 13 December [S/2011/773], Iran, in a letter addressed to the Security Council President, categorically rejected the allegations made in Israel's 29 November letter (see above) concerning so-called "transfers of arms from Iran" into Lebanon. Iran's support for the resistance and Hizbullah was of a moral, humanitarian and political nature.

Security Council consideration. On 20 December [S/PV.6692], the Assistant Secretary-General for Political Affairs, briefing the Security Council on the situation in the Middle East, said that on 9 December, a roadside explosive device targeting a UNIFIL patrol was detonated in the suburbs of Tyre, injuring five peacekeepers and two Lebanese civilians. The Secretary-General and the Council condemned the attack, which was the third directed against UNIFIL in 2011 and the first in the UNIFIL area of operations since 2007. On 11 December, a rocket was fired from the general area of Qaissiyeh valley towards Israel; it hit a private home in the Lebanese village of Houla, a few kilometres from the Blue Line, causing serious injuries to a woman inside the house. On 19 December, four rockets that were ready to be launched were found by LAF in the UNIFIL area of operation. The Secretary-General condemned the rocket attacks. LAF and UNIFIL stepped up their individual and joint operations to prevent similar incidents.

UNIFIL financing

The General Assembly had before it the Secretary-General's performance report on the UNIFIL budget for the period from 1 July 2009 to 30 June 2010 [A/65/608 & Corr.1]. Expenditures amounted to $542,110,800 out of an appropriation of $589,799,200, leaving an unencumbered balance of $47,688,400. In February [A/65/756], the Secretary-General submitted the UNIFIL budget for the period from 1 July 2011 to 30 June 2012, amounting to $542,785,700. The budget provided for 15,000 military contingent personnel, 375 international staff and 726 national staff.

In April [A/65/743/Add.9], the Advisory Committee on Administrative and Budgetary Questions recommended that the unencumbered balance of $47,688,400, as well as other income and adjustments in the amount of $15,263,100 for the period ended 30 June 2010, be credited to Member States. It also recommended that the Assembly appropriate $542,652,500 for the maintenance of UNIFIL for the period from 1 July 2011 to 30 June 2012.

GENERAL ASSEMBLY ACTION

On 30 June [meeting 106], the General Assembly, on the recommendation of the Fifth (Administrative and Budgetary) Committee [A/65/880], adopted **resolution 65/303** by recorded vote (117-3-1) [agenda item 156 (*b*)].

**Financing of the United Nations
Interim Force in Lebanon**

The General Assembly,

Having considered the reports of the Secretary-General on the financing of the United Nations Interim Force in Lebanon and the related report of the Advisory Committee on Administrative and Budgetary Questions,

Recalling Security Council resolution 425(1978) of 19 March 1978 regarding the establishment of the United Nations Interim Force in Lebanon and the subsequent resolutions by which the Council extended the mandate of the Force, the latest of which was resolution 1937(2010) of 30 August 2010, by which the Council extended the mandate of the Force until 31 August 2011,

Recalling also its resolution S-8/2 of 21 April 1978 on the financing of the Force and its subsequent resolutions thereon, the latest of which was resolution 64/282 of 24 June 2010,

Reaffirming its resolutions 51/233 of 13 June 1997, 52/237 of 26 June 1998, 53/227 of 8 June 1999, 54/267 of 15 June 2000, 55/180 A of 19 December 2000, 55/180 B of

14 June 2001, 56/214 A of 21 December 2001, 56/214 B of 27 June 2002, 57/325 of 18 June 2003, 58/307 of 18 June 2004, 59/307 of 22 June 2005, 60/278 of 30 June 2006, 61/250 A of 22 December 2006, 61/250 B of 2 April 2007, 61/250 C of 29 June 2007, 62/265 of 20 June 2008, 63/298 of 30 June 2009 and 64/282 of 24 June 2010,

Reaffirming also the general principles underlying the financing of United Nations peacekeeping operations, as stated in General Assembly resolutions 1874(S-IV) of 27 June 1963, 3101(XXVIII) of 11 December 1973 and 55/235 of 23 December 2000,

Noting with appreciation that voluntary contributions have been made to the Force,

Mindful of the fact that it is essential to provide the Force with the financial resources necessary to enable it to fulfil its responsibilities under the relevant resolutions of the Security Council,

1. *Requests* the Secretary-General to entrust the Head of Mission with the task of formulating future budget proposals in full accordance with the provisions of General Assembly resolutions 59/296 of 22 June 2005, 60/266 of 30 June 2006, 61/276 of 29 June 2007, 64/269 of 24 June 2010 and 65/289 of 30 June 2011, as well as other relevant resolutions;

2. *Takes note* of the status of contributions to the United Nations Interim Force in Lebanon as at 30 April 2011, including the contributions outstanding in the amount of 59.5 million United States dollars, representing some 1 per cent of the total assessed contributions, notes with concern that only ninety-one Member States have paid their assessed contributions in full, and urges all other Member States, in particular those in arrears, to ensure payment of their outstanding assessed contributions;

3. *Expresses its appreciation* to those Member States which have paid their assessed contributions in full, and urges all other Member States to make every possible effort to ensure payment of their assessed contributions to the Force in full;

4. *Expresses deep concern* that Israel did not comply with resolutions 51/233, 52/237, 53/227, 54/267, 55/180 A, 55/180 B, 56/214 A, 56/214 B, 57/325, 58/307, 59/307, 60/278, 61/250 A, 61/250 B, 61/250 C, 62/265, 63/298 and 64/282;

5. *Stresses once again* that Israel should strictly abide by resolutions 51/233, 52/237, 53/227, 54/267, 55/180 A, 55/180 B, 56/214 A, 56/214 B, 57/325, 58/307, 59/307, 60/278, 61/250 A, 61/250 B, 61/250 C, 62/265, 63/298 and 64/282;

6. *Expresses concern* at the financial situation with regard to peacekeeping activities, in particular as regards the reimbursements to troop contributors that bear additional burdens owing to overdue payments by Member States of their assessments;

7. *Also expresses concern* at the delay experienced by the Secretary-General in deploying and providing adequate resources to some recent peacekeeping missions, in particular those in Africa;

8. *Emphasizes* that all future and existing peacekeeping missions shall be given equal and non-discriminatory treatment in respect of financial and administrative arrangements;

9. *Also emphasizes* that all peacekeeping missions shall be provided with adequate resources for the effective and efficient discharge of their respective mandates;

10. *Requests* the Secretary-General to ensure that proposed peacekeeping budgets are based on the relevant legislative mandates;

11. *Endorses* the conclusions and recommendations contained in the report of the Advisory Committee on Administrative and Budgetary Questions, subject to the provisions of the present resolution, and requests the Secretary-General to ensure their full implementation;

12. *Notes* that the overall level of appropriation has been adjusted in accordance with the terms of resolution 65/289;

13. *Requests* the Secretary-General to ensure the full implementation of the relevant provisions of resolutions 59/296, 60/266, 61/276, 64/269 and 65/289;

14. *Also requests* the Secretary-General to take all action necessary to ensure that the Force is administered with a maximum of efficiency and economy;

15. *Reiterates its request* to the Secretary-General to take the measures necessary to ensure the full implementation of paragraph 8 of resolution 51/233, paragraph 5 of resolution 52/237, paragraph 11 of resolution 53/227, paragraph 14 of resolution 54/267, paragraph 14 of resolution 55/180 A, paragraph 15 of resolution 55/180 B, paragraph 13 of resolution 56/214 A, paragraph 13 of resolution 56/214 B, paragraph 14 of resolution 57/325, paragraph 13 of resolution 58/307, paragraph 13 of resolution 59/307, paragraph 17 of resolution 60/278, paragraph 21 of resolution 61/250 A, paragraph 20 of resolution 61/250 B, paragraph 20 of resolution 61/250 C, paragraph 21 of resolution 62/265, paragraph 19 of resolution 63/298 and paragraph 18 of resolution 64/282, stresses once again that Israel shall pay the amount of 1,117,005 dollars resulting from the incident at Qana on 18 April 1996, and requests the Secretary-General to report on this matter to the General Assembly at its sixty-sixth session;

Financial performance report for the period from 1 July 2009 to 30 June 2010

16. *Takes note* of the report of the Secretary-General on the financial performance of the Force for the period from 1 July 2009 to 30 June 2010;

Budget estimates for the period from 1 July 2011 to 30 June 2012

17. *Decides* to appropriate to the Special Account for the United Nations Interim Force in Lebanon the amount of 580,331,600 dollars for the period from 1 July 2011 to 30 June 2012, inclusive of 545,470,600 dollars for the maintenance of the Force, 29,540,600 dollars for the support account for peacekeeping operations and 5,320,400 dollars for the United Nations Logistics Base at Brindisi, Italy;

Financing of the appropriation

18. *Also decides* to apportion among Member States the amount of 96,721,900 dollars for the period from 1 July to 31 August 2011, in accordance with the levels updated in General Assembly resolution 64/249 of 24 December 2009, and taking into account the scale of assessments for 2011, as set out in Assembly resolution 64/248 of 24 December 2009;

19. *Further decides* that, in accordance with the provisions of its resolution 973(X) of 15 December 1955, there shall be set off against the apportionment among Member States, as provided for in paragraph 18 above, their respective share in the Tax Equalization Fund in the amount of 2,558,100 dollars, comprising the estimated staff assessment income of 2,047,900 dollars approved for the Force, the prorated share of 417,000 dollars of the estimated staff assessment income approved for the support account and the prorated share of 93,200 dollars of the estimated staff assessment income approved for the United Nations Logistics Base;

20. *Decides* to apportion among Member States the amount of 483,609,700 dollars for the period from 1 September 2011 to 30 June 2012 at a monthly rate of 48,360,967 dollars, in accordance with the levels updated in resolution 64/249, and taking into account the scale of assessments for 2011 and 2012, as set out in resolution 64/248, subject to a decision of the Security Council to extend the mandate of the Force;

21. *Also decides* that, in accordance with the provisions of its resolution 973(X), there shall be set off against the apportionment among Member States, as provided for in paragraph 20 above, their respective share in the Tax Equalization Fund of 12,790,300 dollars, comprising the estimated staff assessment income of 10,239,500 dollars approved for the Force, the prorated share of 2,085,000 dollars of the estimated staff assessment income approved for the support account and the prorated share of 465,800 dollars of the estimated staff assessment income approved for the United Nations Logistics Base;

22. *Further decides* that, for Member States that have fulfilled their financial obligations to the Force, there shall be set off against the apportionment, as provided for in paragraph 18 above, their respective share of the unencumbered balance and other income in the total amount of 62,951,500 dollars in respect of the financial period ended 30 June 2010, in accordance with the levels updated in resolution 64/249, and taking into account the scale of assessments for 2010, as set out in resolution 64/248;

23. *Decides* that, for Member States that have not fulfilled their financial obligations to the Force, there shall be set off against their outstanding obligations their respective share of the unencumbered balance and other income in the total amount of 62,951,500 dollars in respect of the financial period ended 30 June 2010, in accordance with the scheme set out in paragraph 22 above;

24. *Also decides* that the increase of 1,081,300 dollars in the estimated staff assessment income in respect of the financial period ended 30 June 2010 shall be added to the credits from the amount of 62,951,500 dollars referred to in paragraphs 22 and 23 above;

25. *Emphasizes* that no peacekeeping mission shall be financed by borrowing funds from other active peacekeeping missions;

26. *Encourages* the Secretary-General to continue to take additional measures to ensure the safety and security of all personnel participating in the Force under the auspices of the United Nations, bearing in mind paragraphs 5 and 6 of Security Council resolution 1502(2003) of 26 August 2003;

27. *Invites* voluntary contributions to the Force in cash and in the form of services and supplies acceptable to the Secretary-General, to be administered, as appropriate, in accordance with the procedure and practices established by the General Assembly;

28. *Decides* to include in the provisional agenda of its sixty-sixth session, under the item entitled "Financing of the United Nations peacekeeping forces in the Middle East", the sub-item entitled "United Nations Interim Force in Lebanon".

RECORDED VOTE ON RESOLUTION 65/303:

In favour: Albania, Algeria, Antigua and Barbuda, Argentina, Armenia, Australia, Austria, Bahrain, Bangladesh, Barbados, Belarus, Belgium, Belize, Bosnia and Herzegovina, Brazil, Brunei Darussalam, Bulgaria, Burkina Faso, Cambodia, Cameroon, Chile, China, Colombia, Congo, Costa Rica, Côte d'Ivoire, Croatia, Cuba, Cyprus, Czech Republic, Democratic People's Republic of Korea, Denmark, Djibouti, Dominican Republic, Ecuador, Egypt, El Salvador, Eritrea, Estonia, Finland, France, Georgia, Germany, Greece, Guatemala, Guyana, Haiti, Honduras, Hungary, Iceland, India, Indonesia, Iran, Iraq, Ireland, Italy, Japan, Jordan, Kuwait, Lao People's Democratic Republic, Lebanon, Liechtenstein, Lithuania, Luxembourg, Madagascar, Malaysia, Maldives, Malta, Mauritania, Mauritius, Mexico, Monaco, Mongolia, Montenegro, Morocco, Myanmar, Namibia, Nepal, Netherlands, New Zealand, Norway, Oman, Pakistan, Panama, Peru, Philippines, Poland, Portugal, Qatar, Republic of Moldova, Romania, Russian Federation, Saudi Arabia, Senegal, Serbia, Singapore, Slovakia, Slovenia, South Africa, Spain, Sudan, Suriname, Sweden, Switzerland, Syrian Arab Republic, Thailand, the former Yugoslav Republic of Macedonia, Timor-Leste, Trinidad and Tobago, Ukraine, United Arab Emirates, United Kingdom, United Republic of Tanzania, Venezuela, Viet Nam, Yemen, Zimbabwe.

Against: Canada, Israel, United States.

Abstaining: Tuvalu.

On 24 December (**decision 66/557**), the Assembly decided that the agenda item on the financing of UNIFIL would remain for consideration during its resumed sixty-sixth (2012) session.

Special Tribunal for Lebanon

The Special Tribunal for Lebanon was established in 2007 [YUN 2007, p. 505] to investigate and prosecute the perpetrators of the terrorist bombing in Beirut on 14 February 2005 [YUN 2005, p. 551] that resulted in the death of former Lebanese Prime Minister Rafiq Hariri and 21 others. It succeeded the United Nations International Independent Investigation Commission, which was established by Security Council resolution 1595(2005) [ibid., p. 553]. The Tribunal consisted of the Chambers, the Registry, the Office of the Prosecutor and the Defence Office.

In 2011, the Chambers continued to deal with the application for access to investigative material filed in 2010 by Jamil El Sayed [YUN 2010, p. 496], one of four generals detained by Lebanon in connection with the Hariri attack but released on 29 April 2009 due to a lack of a sufficient evidentiary basis for his detention [YUN 2009, p. 488]. A hearing on the merits was held on 14 January.

The Tribunal, in its third annual report, covering the period from 1 March 2011 to 29 February 2012 [S/2012/205], stated that on 12 May 2011, the Pre-Trial Judge ordered the Prosecutor to release documents to Mr. El Sayed. On 19 July, the Appeals Chamber confirmed that Mr. El Sayed had an enforceable right, subject to limitations, to obtain documents from the Prosecutor relating to his detention in Lebanon. On 7 October, the Appeals Chamber held that the statements of certain witnesses had to be provided by the Prosecution to Mr. El Sayed, and returned the matter to the Pre-Trial Judge for further consideration. The Pre-Trial Judge subsequently issued orders giving effect to the decision of the Appeals Chamber.

On 17 January, the Prosecutor filed with the Pre-Trial Judge a confidential indictment that was subsequently amended on 11 March, 6 May and 10 June. On 28 June, the Pre-Trial Judge confirmed the indictment against Salim Jamil Ayyash, Mustafa Amine Badreddine, Hussein Hassan Oneissi and Assad Hassan Sabra for conspiracy to commit a terrorist attack and other crimes, including intentional homicide. On 30 June, the indictment and accompanying arrest warrants were transmitted to the Lebanese authorities. On 8 July, the Pre-Trial Judge issued international arrest warrants for the four accused. Initially, the indictment remained confidential in order to facilitate the search for and apprehension of the accused. Following a request by the Prosecutor, however, the Pre-Trial Judge partially lifted the confidentiality of the indictment on 28 July. On 16 August, the Pre-Trial Judge unsealed the indictment and his decision confirming it. On 18 August, the President of the Special Tribunal, Judge Antonio Cassese (Italy), ordered that service of the indictment be effected by alternative means, including public advertisement. He emphasized Lebanon's obligation to search for, serve the indictment on, and detain and transfer to The Hague each of the accused within its territory. Lebanese authorities were unsuccessful in their attempts to apprehend the accused.

On 8 September, President Cassese convened the Trial Chamber for the first time. On 17 October, the Pre-Trial Judge issued an order seizing the Trial Chamber of the question of whether to initiate proceedings in absentia in the *Ayyash et al.* case. On 11 November, the Trial Chamber received oral arguments from the Office of the Prosecutor, the Defence Office and the Victims' Participation Unit. The Prosecution submitted that initiating proceedings in absentia would be premature and that the Lebanese authorities should do more to locate and arrest the accused. The Defence Office submitted that the Trial Chamber should consider withdrawing the arrest warrants and notifying the accused of the possibility of appearing at the trial by videoconference. On 23 November, the Trial Chamber issued an interim decision, noting that it required further information from the Lebanese authorities before being able to rule whether the conditions for a trial in absentia had been met under the Rules of Procedure and Evidence.

On 30 June, the Pre-Trial Judge received from the Prosecutor a request to determine whether three attacks that took place against politicians Marwan Hamadeh on 1 October 2004, George Hawi on 21 June 2005 and Elias El-Murr on 12 July 2005 were connected to the attack of 14 February 2005. On 5 August 2011, the Prosecutor presented prima facie evidence that the three attacks were so connected. As a result of the decisions of the Pre-Trial Judge on jurisdiction over the connected attacks and subsequent deferral, the Office of the Prosecutor had exclusive jurisdiction to investigate and prosecute the attacks.

The approved budget for the Tribunal for 2011 amounted to $67.3 million.

Appointment of judges. In a 25 January letter [S/2011/38], the Secretary-General informed the Security Council President of his intention to appoint a panel to select a replacement for Judge Bert Swart (Netherlands), who was no longer able to perform his functions due to ill health. The UN Office of Legal Affairs had begun the process of identifying two judges of the selection panel. On 28 January [S/2011/39], the Council took note of the Secretary-General's intention and the information contained in his letter.

On 9 October, Judge Cassese stepped down from the Presidency on health grounds. On 10 October, the Appeals Chamber Judges unanimously elected Judge Sir David Baragwanath (New Zealand) as the Tribunal's second President. Judge Cassese died on 22 October.

In accordance with Security Council resolution 1757(2007) [YUN 2007, p. 506], the Secretary-General, in an 8 November letter [S/2011/702], informed the Council President of his intention to appoint a selection panel to choose a replacement for Judge Cassese. The selection panel also aimed to establish a roster of three to four suitable candidates for appointment as judges on short notice, should additional vacancies arise at the Special Tribunal. The UN Office of Legal Affairs commenced the process of identifying the two judges of the selection panel. On 10 November [S/2011/703], the Council took note of the Secretary-General's intention and the information contained in his letter.

Syrian Arab Republic

Following the wave of political and social unrest affecting some countries in North Africa, protests erupted in Syria in March 2011 and galvanized anti-Government sentiment in the form of continued demonstrations in every province of the country. Protesters initially demanded greater freedom and political and economic reforms, but later called for the downfall of the regime, echoing slogans heard elsewhere in the region. The Government reacted with considerable force to counter the uprisings; violent clashes between Government forces and protesters led to more than 3,000 deaths by October. The United Nations condemned Syria's suppression of the demonstrations, called for an end to human rights violations and recommended stringent measures should the Government not comply.

Political and security developments

Security Council consideration (April). On 27 April [S/PV.6524], the Under-Secretary-General for Political Affairs, B. Lynn Pascoe, briefed the Security Council on the situation in Syria based on reports from the Office for the Coordination of Humanitarian Affairs, the Office of the High Commissioner for Human Rights (OHCHR) and other UN entities. Anti-Government demonstrations began in mid-March, following the detention of 15 school children in Dar'a for writing anti-Government graffiti. The protests steadily increased in geographic scope and participation. Protesters initially demanded greater freedom and political and economic reforms, but increasingly called for the downfall of the regime, echoing slogans heard elsewhere in the region.

The Syrian authorities reacted with a mix of reform measures and increasingly violent repression, which the Secretary-General condemned. In a 30 March speech to Parliament, President Bashar al-Assad announced that the Government would undertake a series of political, social and economic initiatives to respond to the demands of the Syrian people, including an investigation into the killings committed during protests. A 7 April presidential decree granted citizenship to stateless Kurds residing in the north-east of Syria. On 15 April, the President pledged to release all protest-related detainees, with the exception of those accused of committing crimes "against the nation and the citizens". On 16 April, the President swore in a new Government, which he tasked with developing reforms, including the preparation of new laws on media and political parties. In a series of decrees issued on 21 April, he lifted the state of emergency, which had been in place since 1963; abolished the High Security Court; and recognized the right to peaceful protest, while strictly regulating it.

On 22 April, the largest demonstration to date took place across the country; protesters claimed that the reform measures were insufficient and came too late. Despite the promise of reform, the Government's crackdown intensified. Following the protest, the Syrian army started a major military operation against Dar'a and surrounding villages. Tanks and armed forces surrounded the towns of Duma and Al-Moadamyeh, near Damascus. There were reports that security forces opened fire on demonstrators in the cities of Djabla and Homs. Since mid-March, reliable reports and human rights groups estimated that more than 300 protesters had been killed by security forces and their supporters. OHCHR had also obtained information of wide-scale arrests of protesters, human rights defenders, lawyers, journalists and others. There were allegations of beatings and torture of people detained in connection with the protests, including children. Various reports, however, confirmed that the overwhelming majority of demonstrations were peaceful. In a few instances, protesters used force, resulting in the death of members of security forces.

The Secretary-General and the High Commissioner for Human Rights emphasized that all of the killings that took place during the demonstrations should be investigated, including the alleged killing of military and security officers. The Secretary-General issued statements on the situation on 18 March [SG/SM/13459], 23 March [SG/SM/13472], 2 April [SG/SM/13492] and 22 April [SG/SM/13521], and spoke with President Al-Assad. In his statements, the Secretary-General condemned the use of violence against peaceful demonstrators and called for an independent investigation into the killings. He conveyed the UN belief that the authorities should fulfil their obligations to protect civilians and respect international human rights, including the right to freedom of expression and peaceful assembly, as well as freedom of the press.

Addressing the Council, Syria stated that the goal of extremist groups perpetuating the violence in the country was the fall of the Government. The groups included armed criminals, and they continued to execute innocent citizens and members of the security forces, as well as attack Government facilities and law enforcement installations. Law enforcement authorities had exercised restraint to avoid killing civilians. It was natural, however, for the Syrian leadership to respond to terrorist actions and restore order to the country. The Government had taken action in response to legitimate popular demands. The President had met with delegations from every province to address citizen complaints directly.

Communication. On 9 June [S/2011/353], Syria, in a letter to the Secretary-General, stated that the demonstrations in most areas were no longer peaceful. Stockpiles of arms and ammunition had been discovered in several places, which confirmed that the problem had escalated to an onslaught on the security, stability and sovereignty of the country fomented from abroad. The resolutions against Syria promoted by certain members of international organizations constituted flagrant intervention in the country's internal affairs, and an attempt to destabilize it and control the destinies of its people at a time when Syria had declared its determination to carry out reforms and maintain independence and sovereignty. Annexed to the letter was a list of decrees, laws and decisions that had been issued by the Syrian leadership.

SECURITY COUNCIL ACTION

On 3 August [meeting 6598], following consultations among Security Council members, the President made statement **S/PRST/2011/16** on behalf of the Council:

> The Security Council expresses its grave concern at the deteriorating situation in the Syrian Arab Republic, and expresses profound regret at the death of many hundreds of people.
> The Council condemns the widespread violations of human rights and the use of force against civilians by the Syrian authorities.
> The Council calls for an immediate end to all violence and urges all sides to act with utmost restraint and to refrain from reprisals, including attacks against State institutions.
> The Council calls upon the Syrian authorities to fully respect human rights and to comply with their obligations under applicable international law. Those responsible for the violence should be held accountable.
> The Council notes the announced commitments by the Syrian authorities to reform and regrets the lack of progress in implementation, and calls upon the Government of the Syrian Arab Republic to implement its commitments.
> The Council reaffirms its strong commitment to the sovereignty, independence and territorial integrity of the Syrian Arab Republic. It stresses that the only solution to the current crisis in the Syrian Arab Republic is through an inclusive and Syrian-led political process, with the aim of effectively addressing the legitimate aspirations and concerns of the population, which will allow the full exercise of fundamental freedoms for the entire population, including freedom of expression and of peaceful assembly.
> The Council calls upon the Syrian authorities to alleviate the humanitarian situation in crisis areas by ceasing the use of force against affected towns, to allow expeditious and unhindered access for international humanitarian agencies and workers, and to cooperate fully with the Office of the United Nations High Commissioner for Human Rights.
> The Council requests the Secretary-General to update the Council on the situation in the Syrian Arab Republic within seven days.

Lebanon, speaking after the presidential statement, dissociated itself from it, as Lebanon believed that the statement did not help address the situation in Syria.

Communications. On 4 August [S/2011/499], Cuba, in a letter addressed to the Secretary-General, expressed concern at the Security Council's handling of the internal situation in Syria; the Western Powers were exerting pressure with a view to the adoption of resolutions condemning Syria's legitimate Government. Cuba rejected any attempt to undermine the independence, sovereignty and territorial integrity of Syria and reiterated its confidence in the Syrian people and Government to resolve their internal problems without foreign interference.

On 8 August [S/2011/501], Syria, in a letter to the Secretary-General, said that the Security Council, in its presidential statement (see above), based its position on information taken from only one side. The depiction of events in Syria contained numerous exaggerations. The number of casualties was similarly exaggerated, while the damage and human and material losses inflicted on Syria by armed gangs were deliberately ignored. The Syrian leadership believed that national dialogue was the best way to resolve the crisis. The difficulty of conducting that dialogue, due to the negativity of the opposition, would not divert Syria from moving along the path of reform, nor would Syria allow subversion and conspiracies to prevent the country from continuing towards its goal.

Security Council consideration (August). On 25 August [S/PV.6602], the Under-Secretary-General for Political Affairs informed the Council that the Secretary-General had repeatedly urged President Assad to end violence against the Syrian people and engage in meaningful reform. The President pledged to do so but did not uphold that commitment. The security forces continued to use excessive and lethal force against the protests, including in the provinces of Homs, Hamah, Dar'a, Idlib and Dayr Az Zawr, as well as in and around Damascus. Many civilians were killed and injured, and large-scale arbitrary arrests continued. Many world leaders, including those from the region, as well as the Secretary-General had urged President Assad to halt military operations.

Report of High Commissioner for Human Rights. In September [A/HRC/18/53], the High Commissioner for Human Rights submitted a report on the human rights situation in Syria (see p. 779). The report was prepared by OHCHR pursuant to Human Rights Council resolution S-16/1 (see p. 779), in which the Council, in the light of widespread anti-Government protests in the country and the grave deterioration of the human rights situation, requested the High Commissioner to dispatch a mission to Syria to investigate alleged violations of international human rights law and to establish the facts and circumstances of the crimes perpetrated.

Security Council consideration (September). On 27 September [S/PV.6623], the Under-Secretary-General for Political Affairs told the Security Council that the increase in Syrian nationals seeking refuge across the border with Lebanon reflected the escalating political and human rights crisis. The polarization continued to deepen between the Government, which appeared determined to pursue its policy of violent repression despite international and regional calls to change course, and a growing popular opposition protesting across the country. On 15 September, a coalition of Syrian opposition leaders announced the formation of a national council and released a national consensus charter affirming the peaceful, inclusive and non-sectarian character of the uprising. They also committed to the establishment of a modern State that would guarantee the rule of law and respect for human rights. On 12 September, the President of the Human Rights Council appointed three experts to form the international commission of inquiry mandated by the Council on 23 August (see p. 780). The United Nations underlined the importance of accountability for all human rights violations committed in Syria since March, and hoped that the Government would extend full cooperation to the commission.

Security Council consideration (October). On 24 October [S/PV.6636], the Under-Secretary-General for Political Affairs informed the Council that the crisis in Syria had led to the death of more than 3,000 people since March. The Secretary-General continued to call on the Syrian leadership to stop the killing and emphasized the need for the international community to act in a coherent manner to prevent further bloodshed. The League of Arab States (las) met on 16 October to discuss the situation in Syria; it called for dialogue and established a follow-up committee.

Communications. On 6 November [S/2011/692], Syria transmitted to the Secretary-General and the Security Council President a letter concerning the crisis in that country. Syria had agreed with the las ministerial committee on a plan of action to end the crisis. It called on those bearing arms to surrender their weapons and guaranteed their immediate release. On 4 November, however, the United States called on the armed individuals not to surrender their weapons. Syria considered that the United States, through its statement, had directly involved itself in the violent unrest in Syria. The statement reflected an attempt to thwart las in its effort to end the crisis.

On 12 November [S/2011/707], Syria transmitted to the Secretary-General, the Security Council President and the Chair of the Security Council Committee established pursuant to resolution 1373(2001) concerning counter-terrorism [YUN 2001, p. 61] a note on the findings of investigations conducted by the authorities regarding persons involved with arms smuggling from neighbouring countries; a list of names and nationalities of the persons involved in such activities and the types of weapons found in their possession; and a note on the communication technology used by the armed terrorist groups.

Security Council consideration (November). On 21 November [S/PV.6662], the Special Coordinator for the Middle East Peace Process and Personal Representative of the Secretary-General, Robert Serry, briefed the Council on the situation in Syria. Violent repression by the security forces escalated, and there were signs of an armed confrontation taking place in several areas of the country. Las intensified its efforts to stop the bloodshed and seek a political solution to the crisis, announcing on 2 November a work plan to which the Syrian Government agreed in principle. In the absence of full implementation by the authorities, however, the las Ministerial Council suspended Syria from participating in its meetings and activities, and considered imposing economic sanctions. The UN Secretary-General remained closely engaged with Arab partners and the las Secretary-General. The United Nations called for implementation of the Arab work plan.

The General Assembly, in **resolution 66/176** of 19 December (see p. 781), condemned the systematic human rights violations by Syrian authorities. It called on them to end such violations and implement the 2 November las Plan of Action (work plan).

Security Council consideration (December). On 20 December [S/PV.6692], the Assistant Secretary-General for Political Affairs, Oscar Fernandez-Taranco, informed the Council that instances of armed confrontation between Government forces and the opposition had increased. Las advanced its initiative to end the violence and promote a political solution. The United Nations was encouraged by the signing in Cairo on 19 December of a protocol to dispatch las monitors to Syria in support of a peaceful resolution of the crisis.

The United Nations continued to monitor the influx of displaced Syrian nationals into northern Lebanon. As at 16 December, the Office of the United Nations High Commissioner for Refugees and the Lebanese Government had registered 4,510 displaced persons, up from 3,581 the previous month; the increase was due largely to the recent registration of refugees who had crossed into Lebanon earlier. The number of wounded persons admitted to Lebanese health facilities as a result of fighting on the Syrian side of the border also increased. Turkey and Jordan hosted about 8,500 and 2,000 displaced Syrian nationals respectively. The United Nations coordinated closely with those Governments to provide assistance to displaced persons.

Communications. On 23 December [S/2011/797], Syria, in identical letters addressed to the Secretary-General and the President of the Security Council, stated that two terrorist attacks took place in Damascus that day. Two suicide bombers in two cars carrying more than 200 kilograms of explosives targeted two Government institutions located in heavily trafficked areas. More than 50 people were killed, including soldiers and civilians, and more than 200 were wounded. The strike provided clear indication that extremist terrorist groups, some linked to Al-Qaida, were involved in the planning and implementation of terrorist operations that targeted civilians, soldiers and State institutions.

On 27 December [S/2011/798], Syria transmitted to the Security Council three lists of members of the Syrian army and security forces, as well as the law enforcement forces, who had been killed by armed terrorist groups from 18 March to 24 November. Also on 27 December [S/2011/799], Syria transmitted to the Council a document providing statistics of the crimes of killing, kidnapping and theft that had taken place in the country between 15 March and 19 December. The document listed the number of civilian deaths at 2,131, deaths of military personnel at 913 and deaths of police personnel at 215. The number of abductions of civilians, military and police were listed at 666, 70 and 164, respectively.

On 30 December [S/2011/815], Syria transmitted to the Secretary-General and the Council President a list of the names of the 40 people who died as a result of the terrorist attacks of 23 December. It noted that 14 victims had not been identified.

The Syrian Golan

The Golan Heights in the Syrian Arab Republic, occupied by Israel since 1967, was effectively annexed when Israel extended its laws, jurisdiction and administration to the territory in 1981 [YUN 1981, p. 309]. In 2011, the General Assembly reiterated its demand that Israel withdraw from all the occupied Syrian Golan to the line of 4 June 1967, in implementation of the relevant Security Council resolutions, and that the two countries resume talks. The United Nations Disengagement Observer Force continued to supervise the ceasefire between Israel and Syria in the Golan Heights and to ensure the separation of militaries. The Force's mandate was extended twice during the year.

Communications. On 16 March [A/65/791-S/2011/146], Syria transmitted to the Secretary-General and Security Council President a 14 March letter concerning the 5 August 2010 arrest, on spurious charges, of two Syrian citizens, Majid al-Shair and his son, Fida al-Shair, by Israeli forces in the occupied Syrian Golan. On 17 February 2011, the Israeli District Court in Nazareth sentenced Majid al-Shair to a five-year prison term and his son to a three-year term.

Israel, in identical letters of 16 May to the Secretary-General and Council President [S/2011/310], stated that on 15 May, hundreds of people in Syria tore down the Alpha technical fence, in breach of the disengagement line between Israel and Syria. The infiltrators entered the village of Majdal Shams and conducted a violent demonstration against Israel Defense Forces (IDF). IDF acted with maximum restraint in confronting the threat of violence. Israel said that any harm caused to the people involved in the demonstrations lay with Syria, which was responsible for preventing infiltration of the disengagement line.

On 17 May [A/65/844-S/2011/315], Iran, in identical letters to the Secretary-General, the President of the General Assembly and the Council President, expressed its concerns regarding Israel's 15 May attack against demonstrators marking Nakba Day.

On 6 June [S/2011/344], Israel, in identical letters to the Secretary-General and the Council President, stated that on 5 June, hundreds of people tried to breach the disengagement line between Syria and Israel in a series of violent protests in the areas of Majdal Shams and Quneitra. Protesters threw Molotov cocktails and large objects at IDF members. IDF acted with maximum restraint in confronting the threat of violence and preventing any breach of the disengagement line. During the incident, IDF allowed members of the International Committee of the Red Cross to treat the wounded, but the protesters continued to act violently.

On 8 August [A/65/931-S/2011/518], Syria transmitted identical letters to the Secretary-General and the Council President containing a complaint against Israel, which had decided to build a separation wall in the occupied Syrian Golan, east of Majdal Shams.

Special Committee on Israeli Practices. The Special Committee to Investigate Israeli Practices Affecting the Human Rights of the Palestinian People and Other Arabs of the Occupied Territories, in its September report [A/66/370] (see also p. 421), stated that the situation in Syria prevented it from visiting the country during its mission to that region in July. It therefore engaged with witnesses and victims in the occupied Syrian Golan by way of teleconferences. Several concerns regarding Israel's compliance with its international legal obligations in relation to its occupation of the Syrian Golan were raised, and much of the testimony received was consistent with information obtained by the Committee in previous years.

Witnesses expressed frustration at the high prices they were forced to pay for water, which came from

Syrian territory. Israel's control of the water supply also resulted in diminished yields for Syrian farmers. During an unusually dry season in 2010, access to water was entirely cut off for Syrian farmers, and they reaped only 10 per cent of maximum agricultural production over the previous year. Israel continued to inhibit Syrian families from visiting their relatives outside the occupied Golan, and could maintain relationships only via telephone and the Internet, or through fences. Israel was building a 2-kilometre-long, 8-metre-high wall to cordon off the occupied Syrian Golan and consolidate Israel's annexation of Syrian territory. The border area around the occupied Golan remained heavily landmined.

The Special Committee called on Israel to ensure access to water for Syrians in the occupied Golan, including for agricultural purposes; to facilitate visits of Syrians in the occupied Golan with family members in other parts of Syrian territory; and to carry out a full, transparent investigation into the events of Nakba Day (15 May) (see p. 474) and Naksa Day (5 June) (see p. 474), with a view to explaining the many deaths and injuries of unarmed civilians.

Reports of Secretary-General. On 6 September [A/66/338], the Secretary-General reported that as at 31 August, one Member State (Syria) had replied to his request for information on steps taken or envisaged to implement General Assembly resolution 65/18 [YUN 2010, p. 498] on the Syrian Golan. The resolution demanded that Israel withdraw from all the occupied Syrian Golan to the line of 4 June 1967 in implementation of the relevant Security Council resolutions.

In response to resolution 65/106 [YUN 2010, p. 499], the Secretary-General submitted an October report [A/66/400] on the occupied Syrian Golan. He stated that no reply had been received in response to a note issued by OHCHR on his behalf and addressed to Israel requesting information on steps taken or envisaged concerning implementation of the resolution. Only Syria replied to a similar OHCHR note requesting information from Member States on the implementation of the resolution.

GENERAL ASSEMBLY ACTION

On 30 November [meeting 69], the General Assembly adopted **resolution 66/19** [draft: A/66/L.20 & Add.1] by recorded vote (119-7-53) [agenda item 36].

The Syrian Golan

The General Assembly,

Having considered the item entitled "The situation in the Middle East",

Taking note of the report of the Secretary-General on the situation in the Middle East,

Recalling Security Council resolution 497(1981) of 17 December 1981,

Reaffirming the fundamental principle of the inadmissibility of the acquisition of territory by force, in accordance with international law and the Charter of the United Nations,

Reaffirming once more the applicability of the Geneva Convention relative to the Protection of Civilian Persons in Time of War, of 12 August 1949, to the occupied Syrian Golan,

Deeply concerned that Israel has not withdrawn from the Syrian Golan, which has been under occupation since 1967, contrary to the relevant Security Council and General Assembly resolutions,

Stressing the illegality of the Israeli settlement construction and other activities in the occupied Syrian Golan since 1967,

Noting with satisfaction the convening in Madrid on 30 October 1991 of the Peace Conference on the Middle East, on the basis of Security Council resolutions 242(1967) of 22 November 1967, 338(1973) of 22 October 1973 and 425(1978) of 19 March 1978 and the formula of land for peace,

Expressing grave concern over the halt in the peace process on the Syrian track, and expressing the hope that peace talks will soon resume from the point they had reached,

1. *Declares* that Israel has failed so far to comply with Security Council resolution 497(1981);

2. *Also declares* that the Israeli decision of 14 December 1981 to impose its laws, jurisdiction and administration on the occupied Syrian Golan is null and void and has no validity whatsoever, as confirmed by the Security Council in its resolution 497(1981), and calls upon Israel to rescind it;

3. *Reaffirms its determination* that all relevant provisions of the Regulations annexed to the Hague Convention IV of 1907, and the Geneva Convention relative to the Protection of Civilian Persons in Time of War, continue to apply to the Syrian territory occupied by Israel since 1967, and calls upon the parties thereto to respect and ensure respect for their obligations under those instruments in all circumstances;

4. *Determines once more* that the continued occupation of the Syrian Golan and its de facto annexation constitute a stumbling block in the way of achieving a just, comprehensive and lasting peace in the region;

5. *Calls upon* Israel to resume the talks on the Syrian and Lebanese tracks and to respect the commitments and undertakings reached during the previous talks;

6. *Demands once more* that Israel withdraw from all the occupied Syrian Golan to the line of 4 June 1967 in implementation of the relevant Security Council resolutions;

7. *Calls upon* all the parties concerned, the co-sponsors of the peace process and the entire international community to exert all the necessary efforts to ensure the resumption of the peace process and its success by implementing Security Council resolutions 242(1967) and 338(1973);

8. *Requests* the Secretary-General to report to the General Assembly at its sixty-seventh session on the implementation of the present resolution.

RECORDED VOTE ON RESOLUTION 66/19:

In favour: Afghanistan, Algeria, Antigua and Barbuda, Argentina, Armenia, Azerbaijan, Bahamas, Bahrain, Bangladesh, Barbados, Belarus, Belize, Benin, Bhutan, Bolivia, Botswana,

Brazil, Brunei Darussalam, Burkina Faso, Cambodia, Cape Verde, Chad, Chile, China, Colombia, Comoros, Congo, Costa Rica, Cuba, Cyprus, Democratic People's Republic of Korea, Djibouti, Dominican Republic, Ecuador, Egypt, El Salvador, Eritrea, Ethiopia, Gambia, Ghana, Grenada, Guatemala, Guinea, Guinea-Bissau, Guyana, Honduras, India, Indonesia, Iran, Iraq, Jamaica, Jordan, Kazakhstan, Kenya, Kuwait, Kyrgyzstan, Lao People's Democratic Republic, Lebanon, Lesotho, Liberia, Libya, Madagascar, Malaysia, Maldives, Mali, Mauritania, Mauritius, Mexico, Mongolia, Morocco, Mozambique, Myanmar, Namibia, Nepal, Nicaragua, Nigeria, Oman, Pakistan, Papua New Guinea, Paraguay, Peru, Philippines, Qatar, Russian Federation, Saint Kitts and Nevis, Saint Lucia, Saint Vincent and the Grenadines, Sao Tome and Principe, Saudi Arabia, Senegal, Sierra Leone, Singapore, Solomon Islands, Somalia, South Africa, Sri Lanka, Sudan, Suriname, Swaziland, Syrian Arab Republic, Tajikistan, Thailand, Timor-Leste, Togo, Trinidad and Tobago, Tunisia, Turkey, Turkmenistan, Uganda, United Arab Emirates, United Republic of Tanzania, Uruguay, Uzbekistan, Vanuatu, Venezuela, Viet Nam, Yemen, Zambia, Zimbabwe.

Against: Canada, Israel, Marshall Islands, Micronesia, Nauru, Palau, United States.

Abstaining: Albania, Andorra, Australia, Austria, Belgium, Bosnia and Herzegovina, Bulgaria, Cameroon, Côte d'Ivoire, Czech Republic, Denmark, Equatorial Guinea, Estonia, Fiji, Finland, France, Georgia, Germany, Greece, Haiti, Hungary, Iceland, Ireland, Italy, Japan, Latvia, Liechtenstein, Lithuania, Luxembourg, Malta, Monaco, Montenegro, Netherlands, New Zealand, Norway, Panama, Poland, Portugal, Republic of Korea, Republic of Moldova, Romania, Samoa, San Marino, Serbia, Slovakia, Slovenia, Spain, Sweden, Switzerland, the former Yugoslav Republic of Macedonia, Tonga, Ukraine, United Kingdom.

On 9 December [meeting 81], the General Assembly, on the recommendation of the Fourth Committee [A/66/427], adopted **resolution 66/80** by recorded vote (162-1-11) [agenda item 53].

The occupied Syrian Golan

The General Assembly,

Having considered the report of the Special Committee to Investigate Israeli Practices Affecting the Human Rights of the Palestinian People and Other Arabs of the Occupied Territories,

Deeply concerned that the Syrian Golan, occupied since 1967, has been under continued Israeli military occupation,

Recalling Security Council resolution 497(1981) of 17 December 1981,

Recalling also its previous relevant resolutions, the most recent of which was resolution 65/106 of 10 December 2010,

Having considered the report of the Secretary-General submitted in pursuance of resolution 65/106,

Recalling its previous relevant resolutions in which, inter alia, it called upon Israel to put an end to its occupation of the Arab territories,

Reaffirming once more the illegality of the decision of 14 December 1981 taken by Israel to impose its laws, jurisdiction and administration on the occupied Syrian Golan, which has resulted in the effective annexation of that territory,

Reaffirming that the acquisition of territory by force is inadmissible under international law, including the Charter of the United Nations,

Reaffirming also the applicability of the Geneva Convention relative to the Protection of Civilian Persons in Time of War, of 12 August 1949, to the occupied Syrian Golan,

Bearing in mind Security Council resolution 237(1967) of 14 June 1967,

Welcoming the convening at Madrid of the Peace Conference on the Middle East on the basis of Security Council resolutions 242(1967) of 22 November 1967 and 338(1973) of 22 October 1973 aimed at the realization of a just, comprehensive and lasting peace, and expressing grave concern about the stalling of the peace process on all tracks,

1. *Calls upon* Israel, the occupying Power, to comply with the relevant resolutions on the occupied Syrian Golan, in particular Security Council resolution 497(1981), in which the Council, inter alia, decided that the Israeli decision to impose its laws, jurisdiction and administration on the occupied Syrian Golan was null and void and without international legal effect and demanded that Israel, the occupying Power, rescind forthwith its decision;

2. *Also calls upon* Israel to desist from changing the physical character, demographic composition, institutional structure and legal status of the occupied Syrian Golan and in particular to desist from the establishment of settlements;

3. *Determines* that all legislative and administrative measures and actions taken or to be taken by Israel, the occupying Power, that purport to alter the character and legal status of the occupied Syrian Golan are null and void, constitute a flagrant violation of international law and of the Geneva Convention relative to the Protection of Civilian Persons in Time of War, of 12 August 1949, and have no legal effect;

4. *Calls upon* Israel to desist from imposing Israeli citizenship and Israeli identity cards on the Syrian citizens in the occupied Syrian Golan, and from its repressive measures against the population of the occupied Syrian Golan;

5. *Deplores* the violations by Israel of the Geneva Convention relative to the Protection of Civilian Persons in Time of War, of 12 August 1949;

6. *Calls once again upon* Member States not to recognize any of the legislative or administrative measures and actions referred to above;

7. *Requests* the Secretary-General to report to the General Assembly at its sixty-seventh session on the implementation of the present resolution.

RECORDED VOTE ON RESOLUTION 66/80:

In favour: Afghanistan, Albania, Algeria, Andorra, Angola, Antigua and Barbuda, Argentina, Armenia, Australia, Austria, Azerbaijan, Bahamas, Bahrain, Bangladesh, Barbados, Belarus, Belgium, Belize, Benin, Bhutan, Bolivia, Bosnia and Herzegovina, Botswana, Brazil, Brunei Darussalam, Bulgaria, Burkina Faso, Burundi, Cambodia, Cape Verde, Chad, Chile, China, Colombia, Congo, Costa Rica, Croatia, Cuba, Cyprus, Czech Republic, Democratic People's Republic of Korea, Denmark, Djibouti, Dominica, Dominican Republic, Ecuador, Egypt, El Salvador, Eritrea, Estonia, Ethiopia, Fiji, Finland, France, Germany, Ghana, Greece, Grenada, Guatemala, Guinea, Guinea-Bissau, Guyana, Honduras, Hungary, Iceland, India, Indonesia, Iran, Iraq, Ireland, Italy, Jamaica, Japan, Jordan, Kazakhstan, Kenya, Kuwait, Kyrgyzstan, Lao People's Democratic Republic, Latvia, Lebanon, Lesotho, Liberia, Libya, Liechtenstein, Lithuania, Luxembourg, Madagascar, Malawi,

Malaysia, Maldives, Mali, Malta, Mauritania, Mauritius, Mexico, Monaco, Mongolia, Montenegro, Morocco, Mozambique, Namibia, Nepal, Netherlands, New Zealand, Nicaragua, Norway, Oman, Pakistan, Papua New Guinea, Paraguay, Peru, Philippines, Poland, Portugal, Qatar, Republic of Korea, Republic of Moldova, Romania, Russian Federation, Saint Lucia, Saint Vincent and the Grenadines, Samoa, San Marino, Saudi Arabia, Senegal, Serbia, Sierra Leone, Singapore, Slovakia, Slovenia, Solomon Islands, Somalia, South Africa, Spain, Sri Lanka, Sudan, Swaziland, Sweden, Switzerland, Syrian Arab Republic, Tajikistan, Thailand, the former Yugoslav Republic of Macedonia, Timor-Leste, Togo, Trinidad and Tobago, Tunisia, Turkey, Turkmenistan, Tuvalu, Uganda, Ukraine, United Arab Emirates, United Kingdom, Uruguay, Uzbekistan, Venezuela, Viet Nam, Yemen, Zambia, Zimbabwe.

Against: Israel.

Abstaining: Cameroon, Canada, Côte d'Ivoire, Haiti, Marshall Islands, Micronesia, Nauru, Palau, Tonga, United States, Vanuatu.

UNDOF

The mandate of the United Nations Disengagement Observer Force (UNDOF), established by Security Council resolution 350(1974) [YUN 1974, p. 205] to supervise the observance of the ceasefire between Israel and the Syrian Arab Republic in the Golan Heights and ensure the separation of their forces, was renewed twice in 2011, in June and December, each time for a six-month period.

UNDOF maintained an area of separation approximately 75 kilometres long and varying in width between 12.5 kilometres in the centre to less than 200 metres in the extreme south. The area of separation was inhabited and policed by the Syrian authorities, and no military forces other than UNDOF were permitted within it. As at 11 November, UNDOF comprised 1,043 troops from six Member States assisted by 76 military observers from the United Nations Truce Supervision Organization.

Reports of Secretary-General. The Secretary-General reported to the Security Council on UNDOF activities between 1 January and 30 June [S/2011/359] and 1 July and 31 December [S/2011/748]. In both reports, the Secretary-General stated that the ceasefire in the Israel-Syria sector was maintained and the UNDOF area of operation remained generally quiet. Anti-Government demonstrations, however, spread to several villages in the area of limitation on the Syrian side. UNDOF supervised the area of separation by means of fixed positions and patrols to ensure that Israeli and Syrian military forces were excluded from it.

UNDOF finalized its investigations into the events of 15 May (see below) and 5 June (see below), when demonstrations in the UNDOF area of operation commemorating the anniversaries of Nakba Day and Naksa Day, respectively, resulted in civilian casualties and jeopardized the ceasefire. On 15 May, approximately 4,000 civilians, mostly Palestinians, gathered at a location known as the "family shouting place" in the area of separation on the Bravo side of the UNDOF area of operation, opposite the village of Majdal Shams in the Israeli-occupied Golan (Alpha) side. The gathering was supervised by Syrian security forces and authorities, and IDF observed the demonstration from behind the technical fence. Approximately 300 of the demonstrators moved towards the Alpha side. IDF used tear gas and fired warning shots, followed by direct fire to disperse the crowds. Approximately 100 protesters entered Majdal Shams and demonstrated in the town centre. The majority of the civilians that had crossed the ceasefire line returned to the Syrian side. A total of 44 civilian casualties were reported.

On 5 June, demonstrators amassed opposite Majdal Shams. Protesters attempted to breach the ceasefire line. IDF used tear gas and smoke grenades to deter protesters and live fire to prevent them from crossing the ceasefire line. Up to 23 people were reported killed and many more were wounded.

The Secretary-General stated that he considered the continued presence of UNDOF in the area as essential. He recommended in June that the Security Council extend the Force's mandate until 31 December 2011 and in November until 30 June 2012 (see below).

Communication. On 20 June [S/2011/375], Syria, in identical letters addressed to the Secretary-General and the Security Council President, conveyed its position on the Secretary-General's report on UNDOF for the period from 1 January to 30 June (see above). It said that the reference made in the report to anti-Government demonstrations spreading to villages in the area of limitation constituted flagrant interference by the Secretariat in Syria's internal affairs. Syria also rejected the assertion that Syrian security forces and authorities supervised the gatherings in the area of separation.

SECURITY COUNCIL ACTION

On 30 June [meeting 6572], the Security Council unanimously adopted **resolution 1994(2011)**. The draft was prepared in consultations among Council members.

The Security Council,

Noting with concern that the situation in the Middle East is tense and is likely to remain so, unless and until a comprehensive settlement covering all aspects of the Middle East problem can be reached,

Having considered the report of the Secretary-General of 13 June 2011 on the United Nations Disengagement Observer Force, and reaffirming its resolution 1308(2000) of 17 July 2000,

Expressing grave concern at the serious events that occurred in the area of operations of the Force on 15 May and 5 June 2011 that put the long-held ceasefire in jeopardy,

1. *Calls upon* the parties concerned to implement immediately its resolution 338(1973) of 22 October 1973;
2. *Calls upon* all parties to cooperate fully with the operations of the United Nations Disengagement Observer Force and to ensure the security of as well as unhindered and immediate access for the United Nations personnel carrying out their mandate, in conformity with existing agreements;
3. *Recalls* the obligation on both parties to fully respect the terms of the disengagement of forces agreement of 31 May 1974, and calls upon the parties to exercise maximum restraint and prevent any breaches of the ceasefire and the area of separation;
4. *Welcomes* the efforts being undertaken by the Force to implement the Secretary-General's zero-tolerance policy on sexual exploitation and abuse and to ensure full compliance of its personnel with the United Nations code of conduct, requests the Secretary-General to continue to take all necessary action in this regard and to keep the Security Council informed, and urges troop-contributing countries to take preventive and disciplinary action to ensure that such acts are properly investigated and punished in cases involving their personnel;
5. *Decides* to renew the mandate of the Force for a period of six months, that is, until 31 December 2011;
6. *Requests* the Secretary-General to submit, at the end of this period, a report on developments in the situation and the measures taken to implement resolution 338(1973), including an assessment, with recommendations if any, of the operational capacity of the Force to ensure that it is most appropriately configured to fulfil its mandated tasks.

On 21 December [meeting 6693], the Security Council unanimously adopted **resolution 2028(2011)**. The draft [S/2011/779] was submitted by the Russian Federation and the United States.

The Security Council,

Noting with concern that the situation in the Middle East is tense and is likely to remain so, unless and until a comprehensive settlement covering all aspects of the Middle East problem can be reached,

Having considered the report of the Secretary-General of 30 November 2011 on the United Nations Disengagement Observer Force, and reaffirming its resolution 1308(2000) of 17 July 2000,

Expressing grave concern at the serious events that occurred in the area of operations of the Force on 15 May and 5 June 2011 that put the long-held ceasefire in jeopardy,

Noting that evolving conditions in the region could have an impact on the functioning of the Force,

1. *Calls upon* the parties concerned to implement immediately its resolution 338(1973) of 22 October 1973;
2. *Calls upon* all parties to cooperate fully with the operations of the United Nations Disengagement Observer Force and to ensure the security of as well as unhindered and immediate access for the United Nations personnel carrying out their mandate, in conformity with existing agreements;
3. *Recalls* the obligation on both parties to fully respect the terms of the disengagement of forces agreement of 31 May 1974, and calls upon the parties to exercise maximum restraint and prevent any breaches of the ceasefire and the area of separation;
4. *Welcomes* the efforts being undertaken by the Force to implement the Secretary-General's zero-tolerance policy on sexual exploitation and abuse and to ensure full compliance of its personnel with the United Nations code of conduct, requests the Secretary-General to continue to take all necessary action in this regard and to keep the Security Council informed, and urges troop-contributing countries to take preventive and disciplinary action to ensure that such acts are properly investigated and punished in cases involving their personnel;
5. *Welcomes* the Secretary-General's assessment of the operational capacity of the Force, and requests that he take steps to immediately implement the recommendations as outlined in paragraph 12 of his report;
6. *Decides* to renew the mandate of the Force for a period of six months, that is, until 30 June 2012;
7. *Requests* the Secretary-General to submit, at the end of this period, a report on developments in the situation and the measures taken to implement resolution 338(1973).

UNDOF financing

The General Assembly had before it the performance report of the Secretary-General on the UNDOF budget for the period from 1 July 2009 to 30 June 2010 [A/65/596], which showed expenditures amounting to $45,029,600 gross ($43,585,200 net) against an appropriation of $45,029,700 gross ($43,691,700 net); and the Secretary-General's report [A/65/710] on the UNDOF budget for the period from 1 July 2011 to 30 June 2012, which amounted to $49,561,700 gross ($48,035,000 net) and provided for the deployment of 1,047 military contingent personnel, 46 international staff and 110 national staff.

In a March report [A/65/743/Add.3], the Advisory Committee on Administrative and Budgetary Questions recommended to the Assembly an appropriation of $49,561,700 for the maintenance of UNDOF.

GENERAL ASSEMBLY ACTION

On 30 June [meeting 106], the General Assembly, on the recommendation of the Fifth Committee [A/65/886], adopted **resolution 65/302** without vote [agenda item 156 (*a*)].

Financing of the United Nations Disengagement Observer Force

The General Assembly,

Having considered the reports of the Secretary-General on the financing of the United Nations Disengagement Observer Force and the related report of the Advisory Committee on Administrative and Budgetary Questions,

Recalling Security Council resolution 350(1974) of 31 May 1974 regarding the establishment of the United Nations Disengagement Observer Force and the subsequent resolutions by which the Council extended the mandate of the Force, the latest of which was resolution 1994(2011) of 30 June 2011,

Recalling also its resolution 3211 B (XXIX) of 29 November 1974 on the financing of the United Nations Emergency Force and of the United Nations Disengagement Observer Force and its subsequent resolutions thereon, the latest of which was resolution 64/281 of 24 June 2010,

Reaffirming the general principles underlying the financing of United Nations peacekeeping operations, as stated in General Assembly resolutions 1874(S-IV) of 27 June 1963, 3101(XXVIII) of 11 December 1973 and 55/235 of 23 December 2000,

Mindful of the fact that it is essential to provide the Force with the financial resources necessary to enable it to fulfil its responsibilities under the relevant resolutions of the Security Council,

1. *Requests* the Secretary-General to entrust the Head of Mission with the task of formulating future budget proposals in full accordance with the provisions of General Assembly resolutions 59/296 of 22 June 2005, 60/266 of 30 June 2006, 61/276 of 29 June 2007, 64/269 of 24 June 2010 and 65/289 of 30 June 2011, as well as other relevant resolutions;

2. *Takes note* of the status of contributions to the United Nations Disengagement Observer Force as at 30 April 2011, including the contributions outstanding in the amount of 18.3 million United States dollars, representing some 1 per cent of the total assessed contributions, notes with concern that only forty-nine Member States have paid their assessed contributions in full, and urges all other Member States, in particular those in arrears, to ensure the payment of their outstanding assessed contributions;

3. *Expresses its appreciation* to those Member States which have paid their assessed contributions in full, and urges all other Member States to make every possible effort to ensure payment of their assessed contributions to the Force in full;

4. *Expresses concern* at the financial situation with regard to peacekeeping activities, in particular as regards the reimbursements to troop contributors that bear additional burdens owing to overdue payments by Member States of their assessments;

5. *Also expresses concern* at the delay experienced by the Secretary-General in deploying and providing adequate resources to some recent peacekeeping missions, in particular those in Africa;

6. *Emphasizes* that all future and existing peacekeeping missions shall be given equal and non-discriminatory treatment in respect of financial and administrative arrangements;

7. *Also emphasizes* that all peacekeeping missions shall be provided with adequate resources for the effective and efficient discharge of their respective mandates;

8. *Requests* the Secretary-General to ensure that proposed peacekeeping budgets are based on the relevant legislative mandates;

9. *Endorses* the conclusions and recommendations contained in the report of the Advisory Committee on Administrative and Budgetary Questions, subject to the provisions of the present resolution, and requests the Secretary-General to ensure their full implementation;

10. *Requests* the Secretary-General to ensure the full implementation of the relevant provisions of resolutions 59/296, 60/266, 61/276, 64/269 and 65/289;

11. *Also requests* the Secretary-General to take all action necessary to ensure that the Force is administered with a maximum of efficiency and economy;

12. *Notes* that the overall level of appropriation has been adjusted in accordance with the terms of resolution 65/289;

Financial performance report for the period from 1 July 2009 to 30 June 2010

13. *Takes note* of the report of the Secretary-General on the financial performance of the Force for the period from 1 July 2009 to 30 June 2010;

Budget estimates for the period from 1 July 2011 to 30 June 2012

14. *Decides* to appropriate to the Special Account for the United Nations Disengagement Observer Force the amount of 53,753,200 dollars for the period from 1 July 2011 to 30 June 2012, inclusive of 50,526,100 dollars for the maintenance of the Force, 2,734,600 dollars for the support account for peacekeeping operations and 492,500 dollars for the United Nations Logistics Base at Brindisi, Italy;

Financing of the appropriation

15. *Also decides* to apportion among Member States the amount of 53,753,200 dollars at a monthly rate of 4,479,434 dollars, in accordance with the levels updated in General Assembly resolution 64/249 of 24 December 2009, and taking into account the scale of assessments for 2011 and 2012, as set out in Assembly resolution 64/248 of 24 December 2009, subject to a decision of the Security Council to extend the mandate of the Force;

16. *Further decides* that, in accordance with the provisions of its resolution 973(X) of 15 December 1955, there shall be set off against the apportionment among Member States, as provided for in paragraph 15 above, their respective share in the Tax Equalization Fund of 1,810,000 dollars, comprising the estimated staff assessment income of 1,526,700 dollars approved for the Force, the prorated share of 231,600 dollars of the estimated staff assessment income approved for the support account and the prorated share of 51,700 dollars of the estimated staff assessment income approved for the United Nations Logistics Base;

17. *Decides* that, for Member States that have fulfilled their financial obligations to the Force, there shall be set off against the apportionment, as provided for in paragraph 15 above, their respective share of the unencumbered balance and other income in the amount of 852,500 dollars in respect of the financial period ended 30 June 2010, in accordance with the levels updated in General Assembly resolution 64/249, and taking into account the scale of assessments for 2010, as set out in Assembly resolution 64/248;

18. *Also decides* that, for Member States that have not fulfilled their financial obligations to the Force, there shall be set off against their outstanding obligations their respective share of the unencumbered balance and other income

in the amount of 852,500 dollars in respect of the financial period ended 30 June 2010, in accordance with the scheme set out in paragraph 17 above;

19. *Further decides* that the increase of 106,400 dollars in the estimated staff assessment income in respect of the financial period ended 30 June 2010 shall be added to the credits from the amount of 852,500 dollars referred to in paragraphs 17 and 18 above;

20. *Emphasizes* that no peacekeeping mission shall be financed by borrowing funds from other active peacekeeping missions;

21. *Encourages* the Secretary-General to continue to take additional measures to ensure the safety and security of all personnel participating in the Force under the auspices of the United Nations, bearing in mind paragraphs 5 and 6 of Security Council resolution 1502(2003) of 26 August 2003;

22. *Invites* voluntary contributions to the Force in cash and in the form of services and supplies acceptable to the Secretary-General, to be administered, as appropriate, in accordance with the procedure and practices established by the General Assembly;

23. *Decides* to include in the provisional agenda of its sixty-sixth session, under the item entitled "Financing of the United Nations peacekeeping forces in the Middle East", the sub-item entitled "United Nations Disengagement Observer Force".

On 24 December (**decision 66/557**), the Assembly decided that the agenda item on the financing of UNDOF would remain for consideration during its resumed sixty-sixth (2012) session.

UNTSO

In 2011, the United Nations Truce Supervision Organization (UNTSO), which was originally set up to monitor the ceasefire called for by Security Council resolution S/801 of 29 May 1948 [YUN 1947–48, p. 427] in the newly partitioned Palestine, continued its work. UNTSO unarmed military observers fulfilled evolving mandates—from supervising the four armistice agreements between Israel and its neighbours (Egypt, Jordan, Lebanon, Syrian Arab Republic) to monitoring other ceasefires, and performing other tasks. During the year, UNTSO worked with two remaining peacekeeping forces in the Middle East, the United Nations Disengagement Observer Force and the United Nations Interim Force in Lebanon.

UNTSO operated under a UN regular budget appropriation of $60.7 million for the 2010–2011 period.

Appointment of Head of Mission. In a 23 March letter [S/2011/189], the Secretary-General informed the Security Council of his intention to appoint Major General Juha Kilpia (Finland) as the Head of Mission and Chief of Staff of UNTSO. He would replace Major General Robert Mood (Norway), who completed his assignment in February. The Council took note of the Secretary-General's intention on 25 March [S/2011/190].

Chapter VII

Disarmament

The United Nations continued to work with Member States to advance effective international disarmament and non-proliferation norms in 2011. During the year, States parties to the Treaty on the Non-Proliferation of Nuclear Weapons (NPT) acted to implement the commitments made at the 2010 NPT Review Conference, while nuclear-weapon States, at their second Conference on Confidence Building Measures towards Nuclear Disarmament and Non-proliferation, reported their determination to work together in pursuit of nuclear disarmament, as well as other efforts called for in the 2010 NPT Review Conference action plan. Preparations were also under way for a conference in 2012 on the establishment of a Middle East zone free of weapons of mass destruction and their delivery systems.

Those developments were overshadowed by the continued lack of substantive progress in the Conference on Disarmament and the Disarmament Commission. In January, the Secretary-General suggested options for breaking the long-standing deadlock over the adoption of the Conference's programme of work. The General Assembly held an informal plenary meeting in July on revitalizing the work of the Conference and taking forward multilateral negotiations, and the Advisory Board on Disarmament Matters supported the option of establishing a high-level panel of eminent persons to address the issue. The Disarmament Commission was again unable to reach consensus on the key issues on its agenda: nuclear disarmament and non-proliferation, the adoption of a draft declaration of the 2010s as the fourth disarmament decade, and practical confidence-building measures in the field of conventional weapons.

Delegates attending the Seventh Conference on Facilitating the Entry into Force of the Comprehensive Nuclear-Test-Ban Treaty in September joined the Secretary-General in urging the nine countries whose ratifications were required for the Treaty's entry into force to act without further delay. There was no progress on a peaceful and negotiated denuclearization of the Korean peninsula through the six-party talks, and concern persisted with respect to the nuclear programme of Iran. Based on information available, the International Atomic Energy Agency assessed that it was very likely that the building destroyed at the Dair Alzour site in the Syrian Arab Republic was a nuclear reactor, which should have been declared to the Agency.

The issue of a fissile material cut-off treaty was discussed by the Conference on Disarmament. The discussion was intended to build confidence about such a treaty, generate momentum towards related negotiations, and build confidence among its member and observer States.

The Seventh Review Conference of the States Parties to the Bacteriological Weapons Convention, in December, declared its commitment to the purposes of the Convention and its determination to comply with its obligations. The sixteenth session of the Conference of States Parties to the Convention on the Prohibition of the Development, Production, Stockpiling and Use of Chemical Weapons and Their Destruction (CCW) established the International Support Network for Victims of Chemical Weapons. It also decided on components of an agreed framework to be implemented by States parties. Meanwhile, the Fourth Review Conference of the High Contracting Parties to CCW considered proposals for amendments to the Convention and its annexed Protocols, as well as for additional protocols. Preparations also continued for the convening of a Conference on an arms trade treaty in 2012.

UN machinery

Disarmament issues before the United Nations were considered mainly through the Security Council, the General Assembly and its First (Disarmament and International Security) Committee, the Disarmament Commission (a deliberative body) and the Conference on Disarmament (a multilateral negotiating forum which met in Geneva). The Organization also maintained efforts to engage civil society organizations concerned with disarmament issues.

The United Nations Office for Disarmament Affairs provided substantive and organizational support to UN bodies, fostered disarmament measures and disseminated impartial and up-to-date information.

Advancing the disarmament agenda

In his annual report on the work of the Organization [A/66/1], the Secretary-General noted that States parties had begun translating the commitments made at the 2010 Review Conference of the Parties to the

Treaty on the Non-Proliferation of Nuclear Weapons (NPT) [YUN 2010, p. 531] into agreed actions relating to nuclear disarmament, non-proliferation and the peaceful uses of nuclear energy. The Russian Federation and the United States brought into force the new Strategic Arms Reduction Treaty [ibid., p. 514] further limiting deployments of their strategic nuclear weapons. Nuclear-weapon States initiated dialogue on systematic and progressive efforts to accomplish the complete elimination of their nuclear arsenals, and preparations were under way for a conference in 2012 on the establishment of a Middle East zone free of weapons of mass destruction and their delivery systems. States and civil society continued to explore the requirements for achieving a world free of nuclear weapons, including by means of a universal and effectively verifiable nuclear weapons convention.

A source of great concern remained the lack of substantive progress made by the Conference on Disarmament. Further work was needed to implement the recommendations of the high-level meeting on revitalizing the Conference's work and taking forward multilateral disarmament negotiations [YUN 2010, p. 508]. No progress was made on a peaceful and negotiated denuclearization of the Korean peninsula through the six-party talks, and concern persisted with respect to the nuclear programme of Iran.

New issues emerged in the context of the nuclear accident at the Fukushima Daiichi nuclear power plant in Japan on 11 March. A UN system-wide study [SG/HLM/2011/1] on the implications of the Fukushima nuclear accident, launched by the Secretary-General, was to be presented to a high-level meeting on nuclear safety and security in September (see p. 587).

The Secretary-General attached importance to cooperation between the United Nations and regional organizations, as well as to the role of civil society organizations in regions affected by cross-border arms trafficking, unsecured weapons stockpiles and rising armed violence. The adoption of the Central African Convention for the Control of Small Arms and Light Weapons, Their Ammunition and All Parts and Components That Can Be Used for Their Manufacture, Repair and Assembly [YUN 2010, p. 118] represented an important contribution in that regard.

UN Office for Disarmament Affairs

The United Nations Office for Disarmament Affairs (UNODA) continued to provide for norm-setting in disarmament through the work of the General Assembly and its First Committee, the Disarmament Commission, the Conference on Disarmament and other bodies. It fostered disarmament measures, encouraged regional disarmament efforts, provided information on multilateral disarmament and reinforced the Organization's advocacy potential in disarmament and non-proliferation. The Office maintained regional centres for Africa, Asia and the Pacific, and Latin America and the Caribbean.

An important area of UNODA activities involved information dissemination, including raising public awareness of disarmament and non-proliferation issues, and maintaining close liaison with the United Nations Institute for Disarmament Research, other research and educational institutions, and non-governmental organizations (NGOs). In February, UNODA signed a memorandum of understanding with the International Action Network on Small Arms that included mainstreaming gender and diversity in the fields of arms control, disarmament, peace and security. The Office gave renewed attention to the participation of women in disarmament, non-proliferation and arms control decision-making at the international level, following the adoption of General Assembly resolution 65/69 on the subject [YUN 2010, p. 513].

During the year, UNODA issued its flagship publication, *The United Nations Disarmament Yearbook* [Sales No. E.11.IX.1], as well as the third edition of *Disarmament: A Basic Guide*.

Disarmament Commission

The United Nations Disarmament Commission, comprising all UN Member States, in 2011 was again unable to reach consensus on the key issues on its agenda. The Commission held eight plenary meetings (New York, 4–21 April) [A/66/42]. The main agenda items were recommendations for achieving nuclear disarmament and non-proliferation of nuclear weapons, addressed by the Commission's Working Group I (see below); elements of a draft declaration of the 2010s as the fourth disarmament decade, addressed by Working Group II; and practical confidence-building measures in the field of conventional weapons, addressed by Working Group III. Working Group I held seven meetings between 7 and 14 April, during which delegations made various proposals and exchanged views to bridge their respective positions, but were unable to achieve consensus. Working Group II, in seven meetings held between 6 and 14 April, completed a preliminary reading of the Chair's non-paper on the subject [YUN 2010, p. 507], which was subsequently revised. Working Group III held seven meetings from 15 to 20 April and discussed revised versions of the Chair's 2008 non-paper. On 21 April, the Commission adopted its report to the General Assembly.

GENERAL ASSEMBLY ACTION

On 2 December [meeting 71], the General Assembly, on the recommendation of the First (Disarmament and International Security) Committee [A/66/414], adopted **resolution 66/60** without vote [agenda item 100 (*b*)].

Report of the Disarmament Commission

The General Assembly,

Having considered the report of the Disarmament Commission,

Recalling its resolutions 47/54 A of 9 December 1992, 47/54 G of 8 April 1993, 48/77 A of 16 December 1993, 49/77 A of 15 December 1994, 50/72 D of 12 December 1995, 51/47 B of 10 December 1996, 52/40 B of 9 December 1997, 53/79 A of 4 December 1998, 54/56 A of 1 December 1999, 55/35 C of 20 November 2000, 56/26 A of 29 November 2001, 57/95 of 22 November 2002, 58/67 of 8 December 2003, 59/105 of 3 December 2004, 60/91 of 8 December 2005, 61/98 of 6 December 2006, 62/54 of 5 December 2007, 63/83 of 2 December 2008, 64/65 of 2 December 2009 and 65/86 of 8 December 2010,

Considering the role that the Disarmament Commission has been called upon to play and the contribution that it should make in examining and submitting recommendations on various problems in the field of disarmament and in promoting the implementation of the relevant decisions adopted by the General Assembly at its tenth special session,

1. *Takes note* of the report of the Disarmament Commission;

2. *Reaffirms* the validity of its decision 52/492 of 8 September 1998 concerning the efficient functioning of the Disarmament Commission;

3. *Recalls* its resolution 61/98, in which it adopted additional measures for improving the effectiveness of the Disarmament Commission's methods of work;

4. *Reaffirms* the mandate of the Disarmament Commission as the specialized, deliberative body within the United Nations multilateral disarmament machinery that allows for in-depth deliberations on specific disarmament issues, leading to the submission of concrete recommendations on those issues;

5. *Also reaffirms* the importance of further enhancing the dialogue and cooperation among the First Committee, the Disarmament Commission and the Conference on Disarmament;

6. *Requests* the Disarmament Commission to continue its work in accordance with its mandate, as set forth in paragraph 118 of the Final Document of the Tenth Special Session of the General Assembly, and with paragraph 3 of Assembly resolution 37/78 H of 9 December 1982, and to that end to make every effort to achieve specific recommendations on the items on its agenda, taking into account the adopted "Ways and means to enhance the functioning of the Disarmament Commission";

7. *Recommends* that the Disarmament Commission intensify consultations with a view to reaching agreement on the items on its agenda, in accordance with decision 52/492, before the start of its substantive session of 2012;

8. *Requests* the Disarmament Commission to meet for a period not exceeding three weeks during 2012, namely from 2 to 20 April, and to submit a substantive report to the General Assembly at its sixty-seventh session;

9. *Requests* the Secretary-General to transmit to the Disarmament Commission the annual report of the Conference on Disarmament, together with all the official records of the sixty-sixth session of the General Assembly relating to disarmament matters, and to render all assistance that the Commission may require for implementing the present resolution;

10. *Also requests* the Secretary-General to ensure full provision to the Disarmament Commission and its subsidiary bodies of interpretation and translation facilities in the official languages and to assign, as a matter of priority, all the necessary resources and services, including verbatim records, to that end;

11. *Decides* to include in the provisional agenda of its sixty-seventh session the sub-item entitled "Report of the Disarmament Commission".

Conference on Disarmament

The Conference on Disarmament, a multilateral negotiating body, held 45 formal and 10 informal plenary meetings in a three-part session (Geneva, 24 January–1 April, 16 May–1 July, and 2 August–16 September) [A/66/27]. The Conference agenda included seven items: the cessation of the nuclear arms race and nuclear disarmament; prevention of nuclear war (see p. 487); prevention of an arms race in outer space; effective international arrangements to assure non-nuclear States against the use or threat of use of nuclear weapons (see p. 492); new types of weapons of mass destruction and new systems of such weapons: radiological weapons (see p. 509); a comprehensive programme of disarmament (see p. 482); and transparency in armaments (see p. 533). The Conference did not reach a consensus on a programme of work for 2011.

Addressing the Conference on 26 January [CD/PV.1199], the Secretary-General reflected on its accomplishments as the world's single multilateral disarmament negotiating forum, its role and its function, and suggested options for breaking the long-standing deadlock and starting substantive work, including through the adoption by consensus of a programme of work. Numerous foreign ministers and heads of delegations also addressed the meeting, expressing support for the Conference and concern about the current situation, and setting out their national priorities for the work of the Conference. The Conference requested its current and incoming Presidents to conduct consultations during the intersessional period and make recommendations, and to keep the Conference informed of their consultations.

On 1 September, the Conference reported to the Secretary-General on the work done during the 2011 session on its agenda items [CD/1918]; and, on 15 September, adopted its report [CD/1926] for transmission to the General Assembly.

GENERAL ASSEMBLY ACTION

On 2 December [meeting 71], the General Assembly, on the recommendation of the First Committee [A/66/414], adopted **resolution 66/59** without vote [agenda item 100 (*a*)].

Report of the Conference on Disarmament

The General Assembly,

Having considered the report of the Conference on Disarmament,

Convinced that the Conference on Disarmament, as the sole multilateral disarmament negotiating forum of the international community, has the primary role in substantive negotiations on priority questions of disarmament,

Recognizing the addresses of the President of the General Assembly and the Secretary-General of the United Nations, as well as the addresses of Ministers for Foreign Affairs and other high-level officials in the Conference on Disarmament, as expressions of support for the endeavours of the Conference,

Recognizing also the need to conduct multilateral negotiations with the aim of reaching agreement on concrete issues, and considering that the present international climate should give additional impetus to multilateral negotiations,

Recalling, in this respect, that the Conference on Disarmament has a number of urgent and important issues for negotiation,

Noting the follow-up discussions to the high-level meeting on revitalizing the work of the Conference on Disarmament and taking forward multilateral negotiations, held on 24 September 2010 at the initiative of the Secretary-General, and acknowledging the continued support for the Conference expressed by high-level officials in 2011,

Noting with renewed concern that the Conference on Disarmament has been unable to commence its substantive work, including negotiations, for over a decade, as envisaged by the General Assembly in its resolution 65/85 of 8 December 2010, or to agree on a programme of work,

Welcoming the renewed overwhelming call for greater flexibility with respect to commencing the substantive work of the Conference on Disarmament without further delay, on the basis of a balanced and comprehensive programme of work,

Appreciating the continued cooperation among the States members of the Conference on Disarmament as well as the six successive Presidents of the Conference at its 2011 session,

Noting with appreciation the significant contributions made during the 2011 session to promote substantive discussions on issues on the agenda, as well as the discussions held on other issues that could also be relevant to the current international security environment,

Welcoming the enhanced engagement between civil society and the Conference on Disarmament at its 2011 session according to decisions taken by the Conference,

Stressing the urgent need for the Conference on Disarmament to commence its substantive work at the beginning of its 2012 session,

1. *Reaffirms* the role of the Conference on Disarmament as the sole multilateral disarmament negotiating forum of the international community;

2. *Calls upon* the Conference on Disarmament to further intensify consultations and explore possibilities with a view to adopting a balanced and comprehensive programme of work at the earliest possible date during its 2012 session, bearing in mind the decision on the programme of work adopted by the Conference on 29 May 2009;

3. *Expresses its appreciation* for the strong support expressed for the Conference on Disarmament during its 2011 session by Ministers for Foreign Affairs and other high-level officials, and takes into account their calls for greater flexibility with respect to commencing the substantive work of the Conference without further delay;

4. *Welcomes* the decision of the Conference on Disarmament to request the current President and the incoming President to conduct consultations during the intersessional period and, if possible, make recommendations, taking into account all relevant proposals, past, present and future, including those submitted as documents of the Conference, views presented and discussions held, and to endeavour to keep the membership of the Conference informed, as appropriate, of their consultations;

5. *Requests* all States members of the Conference on Disarmament to cooperate with the current President and successive Presidents in their efforts to guide the Conference to the early commencement of its substantive work, including negotiations, in its 2012 session;

6. *Recognizes* the importance of continuing consultations on the question of the expansion of the membership of the Conference on Disarmament;

7. *Requests* the Secretary-General to continue to ensure and strengthen, if needed, the provision to the Conference on Disarmament of all necessary administrative, substantive and conference support services;

8. *Requests* the Conference on Disarmament to submit to the General Assembly at its sixty-seventh session a report on its work;

9. *Decides* to include in the provisional agenda of its sixty-seventh session the sub-item entitled "Report of the Conference on Disarmament".

Follow-up to high-level meeting

The General Assembly held an informal plenary meeting (27–29 July) [A/65/PV.113] on the follow-up to the 2010 high-level meeting on revitalizing the work of the Conference on Disarmament and taking forward multilateral negotiations [YUN 2010, p. 508].

At the 2011 meeting of the Conference on Disarmament, at informal meetings held on 9, 14 and 30 June, members expressed their views on that high-level meeting. At a plenary meeting on 4 August, views were expressed on the debate in the Assembly meeting held from 27 to 29 July as a follow-up to its 2010 high-level plenary [CD/PV.1231]. The Secretary-General of the Conference on Disarmament and the UN Secretary-General's Personal Representative told the Conference that the Assembly's July meeting underscored the need to find a way out of the Conference's predicament. He said that the UN Secretary-General, in his address to the Assembly's meeting, had noted the different options identified by Member States for revitalizing the Conference, including the maintenance of the status quo, which risked rendering the Conference irrelevant and obsolete; adopting a new fundamental approach to the disarmament machinery, although no consensus existed on the convening of a fourth special session of the General Assembly on disarmament; and making incremental changes, which had their opponents as well. To address those differences, the Secretary-General was considering establishing a panel of eminent persons to address the different issues, further to the recommendations of the Advisory Board on Disarmament Matters (see p. 485). The Secretary-General of the Conference said that the Conference might resume its leading role as a multilateral disarmament forum, provided it was duly reformed. To that end, it was necessary to review its procedures, membership and agenda in the context of the international security environment.

GENERAL ASSEMBLY ACTION

On 2 December [meeting 71], the General Assembly, on the recommendation of the First Committee [A/66/420], adopted **resolution 66/66** without vote [agenda item 106].

Revitalizing the work of the Conference on Disarmament and taking forward multilateral disarmament negotiations

The General Assembly,

Recalling its resolution 65/93 of 8 December 2010,

Reaffirming the importance of disarmament in strengthening global security and promoting international stability,

Recognizing that the political will to advance the disarmament agenda has been strengthened in recent years and that the international political climate is conducive to the promotion of multilateral disarmament and moving towards the goal of a world without nuclear weapons,

Affirming the importance of multilateralism in negotiations in the area of disarmament and non-proliferation,

Mindful of the continuing importance of the Conference on Disarmament as the single multilateral disarmament negotiating forum, as stated during the first special session of the General Assembly devoted to disarmament,

Recalling the past achievements of the Conference on Disarmament in successfully negotiating arms control and disarmament instruments,

Reiterating its grave concern about the current status of the disarmament machinery, including the lack of substantive progress in the Conference on Disarmament for more than a decade, and stressing the need for greater efforts and flexibility to advance multilateral disarmament negotiations,

Welcoming the efforts by Member States to secure progress in multilateral disarmament and the support of the Secretary-General for such efforts, and recalling the high-level meeting on revitalizing the work of the Conference on Disarmament and taking forward multilateral disarmament negotiations, held in New York on 24 September 2010, and the follow-up plenary meeting of the General Assembly, held from 27 to 29 July 2011,

Noting with concern that, despite all efforts, the Conference on Disarmament has not been able to adopt and implement a programme of work during its 2011 session,

Recognizing the contribution of civil society in the area of disarmament, non-proliferation and arms control,

Mindful of the Charter of the United Nations, in particular Article 11 of Chapter IV concerning the functions and powers of the General Assembly in respect of disarmament,

1. *Welcomes* the opportunity provided by the high-level meeting on revitalizing the work of the Conference on Disarmament and taking forward multilateral disarmament negotiations, convened at the initiative of the Secretary-General in New York on 24 September 2010, and the follow-up plenary meeting of the General Assembly, held from 27 to 29 July 2011, to address the need to advance multilateral disarmament efforts;

2. *Expresses appreciation* for the support voiced for the urgent need to revitalize the work of multilateral disarmament bodies and to advance multilateral disarmament negotiations;

3. *Notes with appreciation* the continuing efforts and suggestions made by Member States and the Secretary-General with regard to revitalizing the multilateral disarmament machinery;

4. *Calls upon* States to intensify efforts aimed at creating an environment conducive to multilateral disarmament negotiations;

5. *Invites* States, in the appropriate forums, to explore, consider and consolidate options, proposals and elements for revitalization of the United Nations disarmament machinery as a whole, including the Conference on Disarmament;

6. *Urges* the Conference on Disarmament to adopt and implement a programme of work to enable it to resume substantive work on its agenda early in its 2012 session;

7. *Recognizes* the need to take stock, during the sixty-sixth session of the General Assembly, of all relevant efforts to take forward multilateral disarmament negotiations;

8. *Decides* to include in the provisional agenda of its sixty-seventh session the item entitled "Revitalizing the work of the Conference on Disarmament and taking forward multilateral disarmament negotiations", to review progress made in the implementation of the present resolution and, if necessary, to further explore options for taking forward multilateral disarmament negotiations.

Comprehensive programme of disarmament

The Conference on Disarmament discussed agenda item 6, "Comprehensive Programme of Disarmament", at two formal meetings (17 February, 17 March) and one informal meeting (25 May). Delegations reaffirmed or further elaborated their respective positions on the agenda item.

Multilateral disarmament agreements

As at 31 December, the following States had become parties to the multilateral arms regulation and disarmament agreements listed below (in chronological order, with the years in which they were signed or opened for signature).

Protocol for the Prohibition of the Use in War of Asphyxiating, Poisonous or Other Gases, and of Bacteriological Methods of Warfare (1925 Geneva Protocol): 137 parties

Antarctic Treaty (1959): 49 parties

Treaty Banning Nuclear Weapons Tests in the Atmosphere, in Outer Space and under Water (Partial Test Ban Treaty) (1963): 126 parties

Treaty on Principles Governing the Activities of States in the Exploration and Use of Outer Space, including the Moon and Other Celestial Bodies (Outer Space Treaty) (1967) [YUN 1966, p. 41, GA res. 2222(XXI), annex]: 100 parties

Treaty for the Prohibition of Nuclear Weapons in Latin America and the Caribbean (Treaty of Tlatelolco) (1967): 33 parties

Treaty on the Non-Proliferation of Nuclear Weapons (NPT) (1968) [YUN 1968, p. 17, GA res. 2373(XXII), annex]: 190 parties

Treaty on the Prohibition of the Emplacement of Nuclear Weapons and Other Weapons of Mass Destruction on the Sea-Bed and the Ocean Floor and in the Subsoil Thereof (Seabed Treaty) (1971) [YUN 1970, p. 18, GA res. 2660(XXV), annex]: 94 parties

Convention on the Prohibition of the Development, Production and Stockpiling of Bacteriological (Biological) and Toxin Weapons and on Their Destruction (BWC) (1972) [YUN 1971, p. 19, GA res. 2826(XXV), annex]: 163 parties

Convention on the Prohibition of Military or Any Other Hostile Use of Environmental Modification Techniques (1977) [YUN 1976, p. 45, GA res. 31/72, annex]: 76 parties

Agreement Governing the Activities of States on the Moon and Other Celestial Bodies (1979) [YUN 1979, p. 111, GA res. 34/68, annex]: 13 parties

Convention on Prohibitions or Restrictions on the Use of Certain Conventional Weapons Which May Be Deemed to Be Excessively Injurious or to Have Indiscriminate Effects (CCW) (1981): 114 parties

South Pacific Nuclear Free Zone Treaty (Rarotonga Treaty) (1985): 13 parties

Treaty on Conventional Armed Forces in Europe (CFE Treaty) (1990): 30 parties

Treaty on Open Skies (1992): 34 parties

Convention on the Prohibition of the Development, Production, Stockpiling and Use of Chemical Weapons and on Their Destruction (CWC) (1992): 188 parties

Southeast Asia Nuclear-Weapon-Free Zone Treaty (Bangkok Treaty) (1995): 10 parties

African Nuclear-Weapon-Free Zone Treaty (Pelindaba Treaty) (1996): 32 parties

Comprehensive Nuclear-Test-Ban Treaty (CTBT) (1996): 155 parties

Inter-American Convention against the Illicit Manufacturing of and Trafficking in Firearms, Ammunition, Explosives, and Other Related Materials (1997): 30 parties

Convention on the Prohibition of the Use, Stockpiling, Production and Transfer of Anti-personnel Mines and on Their Destruction (Mine-Ban Convention, formerly known as Ottawa Convention) (1997): 158 parties

Inter-American Convention on Transparency in Conventional Weapons Acquisitions (1999): 15 parties

Agreement on Adaptation of the CFE Treaty (1999): 3 parties

Treaty on a Nuclear-Weapon-Free Zone in Central Asia (CANWFZ Treaty) (2006): 5 parties

Convention on Cluster Munitions (2008): 67 Parties

Central African Convention for the Control of Small Arms and Light Weapons, their Ammunition and all Parts and Components that can be used for their Manufacture, Repair and Assembly (Kinshasa Convention) (2010): 11 signatories.

UN role in disarmament

Disarmament and development

In response to General Assembly resolution 65/52 [YUN 2010, p. 512], the Secretary-General in July [A/66/168] reported on trends to further strengthen the relationship between disarmament and development. The report contained information received from 10 countries (Cuba, Ecuador, Guatemala, Guyana, Lebanon, Mexico, Portugal, Qatar, Ukraine, Zambia) on measures to devote part of the resources made available by the implementation of disarmament and arms limitation agreements to economic and social development. As the Secretary-General noted, the Security Council held an open debate on the interdependence of security and development on 11 February [S/PV.6479]. In its resulting presidential statement **S/PRST/2011/4** (see p. 41), the Council observed that successful implementation of the many tasks that peacekeeping operations could be mandated to undertake in the areas of security sector reform, disarmament, demobilization and reintegration, rule of law and human rights required an understanding of the close interlinkage between security and development.

The Secretary-General's April report on small arms [S/2011/255] (see p. 524) drew attention to the interlinkage between armed violence and development. The significance of the nexus between disarmament and development was discussed during the debate on international assistance and capacity-building, at the Open-ended Meeting of Governmental Experts on the Implementation of the Programme of Action to Prevent, Combat and Eradicate the Illicit Trade in Small Arms and Light Weapons in All Its Aspects (New York, 9–13 May) (see p. 525). Special emphasis was placed on the need to improve the implementation capacity of States to enable them to trace illegal arms back to their point of diversion. Within the framework of the Geneva Declaration on Armed Violence and Development, the United Nations organized regional seminars in Nepal (16–18 March) and Nairobi (23–25 February) aimed at fostering discussions and experience-sharing at the regional level. The seminars also assessed the progress of implementation of armed violence reduction programmes and identified promising and innovative practices, as part of the preparations for the Second Ministerial Review Conference on the Geneva Declaration (Geneva, 31 October and 1 November) (see below).

Communication. In a 29 June letter addressed to the Secretary-General [A/65/896-S/2011/407], Egypt, in its capacity as Chair of the Coordinating Bureau of the Non-Aligned Movement, transmitted the outcome documents of the sixteenth Ministerial Conference of the Non-Aligned Movement (Bali, Indonesia, 23–27 May), which included a statement on the total elimination of nuclear weapons.

Ministerial Review Conference. As the Secretary-General later reported [A/67/176], the Second Ministerial Review Conference on the Geneva Declaration, hosted by Switzerland and the United Nations Development Programme, was held in Geneva on 31 October and 1 November. The Conference adopted an outcome document reaffirming the commitment of the signatory States to integrate armed violence reduction and prevention actions into development and security programmes, as well as to set clear priorities for the implementation of the Geneva Declaration by 2015.

GENERAL ASSEMBLY ACTION

On 2 December [meeting 71], the General Assembly, on the recommendation of the First Committee [A/66/412], adopted **resolution 66/30** without vote [agenda item 98 (*l*)].

Relationship between disarmament and development

The General Assembly,

Recalling that the Charter of the United Nations envisages the establishment and maintenance of international peace and security with the least diversion for armaments of the world's human and economic resources,

Recalling also the provisions of the Final Document of the Tenth Special Session of the General Assembly concerning the relationship between disarmament and development, as well as the adoption on 11 September 1987 of the Final Document of the International Conference on the Relationship between Disarmament and Development,

Recalling further its resolutions 49/75 J of 15 December 1994, 50/70 G of 12 December 1995, 51/45 D of 10 December 1996, 52/38 D of 9 December 1997, 53/77 K of 4 December 1998, 54/54 T of 1 December 1999, 55/33 L of 20 November 2000, 56/24 E of 29 November 2001, 57/65 of 22 November 2002, 59/78 of 3 December 2004, 60/61 of 8 December 2005, 61/64 of 6 December 2006, 62/48 of 5 December 2007, 63/52 of 2 December 2008, 64/32 of 2 December 2009 and 65/52 of 8 December 2010, and its decision 58/520 of 8 December 2003,

Bearing in mind the Final Document of the Twelfth Conference of Heads of State or Government of Non-Aligned Countries, held in Durban, South Africa, from 29 August to 3 September 1998, and the Final Document of the Thirteenth Ministerial Conference of the Movement of Non-Aligned Countries, held in Cartagena, Colombia, on 8 and 9 April 2000, as well as the Final Documents of the Fifteenth Summit Conference of Heads of State and Government of the Movement of Non-Aligned Countries, held in Sharm el-Sheikh, Egypt, from 11 to 16 July 2009, and of the Sixteenth Ministerial Conference and Commemorative Meeting of the Movement of Non-Aligned Countries, held in Bali, Indonesia, from 23 to 27 May 2011,

Mindful of the changes in international relations that have taken place since the adoption on 11 September 1987 of the Final Document of the International Conference on the Relationship between Disarmament and Development, including the development agenda that has emerged over the past decade,

Bearing in mind the new challenges for the international community in the fields of development, poverty eradication and the elimination of the diseases that afflict humanity,

Stressing the importance of the symbiotic relationship between disarmament and development and the important role of security in this connection, and concerned at increasing global military expenditure, which could otherwise be spent on development needs,

Recalling the report of the Group of Governmental Experts on the relationship between disarmament and development and its reappraisal of this significant issue in the current international context,

Bearing in mind the importance of following up on the implementation of the action programme adopted at the 1987 International Conference on the Relationship between Disarmament and Development,

1. *Stresses* the central role of the United Nations in the disarmament-development relationship, and requests the Secretary-General to strengthen further the role of the Organization in this field, in particular the high-level Steering Group on Disarmament and Development, in order to ensure continued and effective coordination and close cooperation between the relevant United Nations departments, agencies and sub-agencies;

2. *Requests* the Secretary-General to continue to take action, through appropriate organs and within available resources, for the implementation of the action programme adopted at the 1987 International Conference on the Relationship between Disarmament and Development;

3. *Urges* the international community to devote part of the resources made available by the implementation of disarmament and arms limitation agreements to economic and social development, with a view to reducing the ever-widening gap between developed and developing countries;

4. *Encourages* the international community to achieve the Millennium Development Goals and to make reference to the contribution that disarmament could provide in meeting them when it reviews its progress towards this purpose in 2012, as well as to make greater efforts to integrate disarmament, humanitarian and development activities;

5. *Encourages* the relevant regional and subregional organizations and institutions, non-governmental organizations and research institutes to incorporate issues related to the relationship between disarmament and development into their agendas and, in this regard, to take into account the report of the Group of Governmental Experts on the relationship between disarmament and development;

6. *Reiterates its invitation* to Member States to provide the Secretary-General with information regarding measures and efforts to devote part of the resources made available by the implementation of disarmament and arms limitation agreements to economic and social development, with a view to reducing the ever-widening gap between developed and developing countries;

7. *Requests* the Secretary-General to report to the General Assembly at its sixty-seventh session on the implementation of the present resolution, including the information provided by Member States pursuant to paragraph 6 above;

8. *Decides* to include in the provisional agenda of its sixty-seventh session the item entitled "Relationship between disarmament and development".

Advisory Board on Disarmament Matters

The Advisory Board on Disarmament Matters, which advised the Secretary-General and served as the Board of Trustees of the United Nations Institute for Disarmament Research (UNIDIR), held its fifty-fifth (New York, 23–25 February) and fifty-sixth (Geneva, 29 June–1 July) sessions. At both sessions, the Board focused on issues raised at the 2010 high-level meeting on revitalizing the work of the Conference on Disarmament [YUN 2010, p. 508], including the possible establishment of a high-level panel of eminent persons with special focus on its functioning. A report of the Secretary-General [A/66/125] summarized the Board's deliberations.

The Board noted that a number of delegations to the Conference on Disarmament were supportive of the establishment of such a panel, while some expressed reservations about its usefulness and questioned its ability to achieve any positive results. The Board also noted that the establishment of such a panel would have financial implications that would have to be clarified before its establishment. Should the Secretary-General consider that approach, most members agreed that the Board would concur, and support establishing the panel.

There was agreement that a fissile material cut-off treaty was a priority; a number of members underlined the importance of other core issues, including the peaceful uses of outer space and negative security assurances. The need to de-link negotiation of a fissile material cut-off treaty from the current technical problems of the Conference was also mentioned. It was stated that a cut-off treaty was an issue related to international security, which was quite different from some of the procedural problems faced by the Conference.

The Board recommended that the Secretary-General continue to encourage the Conference on Disarmament to achieve a breakthrough in the continuing impasse that would facilitate work on the core issues outlined in the Conference's 2009 decision [YUN 2009, p. 498]. Should a high-level panel of eminent persons be established, the Secretary-General should ask the panel to recommend ways to revitalize the entire UN disarmament machinery, especially the Conference. He should also consider establishing an institutional link between the Board and the proposed panel by inviting one or more current or former Board members to be part of that panel, taking into consideration the financial implications of its establishment; and continue to raise public awareness and encourage civil society groups and NGOs to offer their input on ways to overcome the prolonged stalemate at the Conference and move towards the ultimate goal of a world free of nuclear weapons.

In its capacity as the UNIDIR Board of Trustees, the Advisory Board adopted the Institute's 2011 programme and budget, and approved, for submission to the General Assembly, the report of the Institute's Director on its activities from August 2010 to July 2011, as well as the proposed programme of work and budget for 2012 and 2013. The Board reiterated that the UNIDIR subvention level should be increased in the 2012–2013 biennium, and urged the Secretary-General to secure an increase of the subvention in the UN regular budget.

Nuclear disarmament

In response to General Assembly resolutions 65/56 [YUN 2010, p. 520], 65/60 [ibid., p. 514] and 65/76 [ibid., p. 529], the Secretary-General submitted a July report [A/66/132 & Add.1], with a later addendum, on nuclear disarmament. He reported that some progress was achieved towards a world free of nuclear weapons, but consensus continued to elude the forums for the development of new international law relating to the elimination of nuclear weapons, including in the Conference on Disarmament and the Disarmament Commission. At the same time, some Governments and civil society organizations had initiated new efforts aimed at elaborating innovative solutions. Nuclear-weapon States continued to take steps to reduce their overall stockpiles of deployed nuclear warheads, increase transparency and accountability, and advance implementation of their nuclear disarmament commitments. The joint statement issued from the second Conference of Nuclear-Weapon States (Paris, 30 June–1 July) on confidence-building measures towards nuclear disarmament and non-proliferation conveyed the determination of those States to work together in pursuit of nuclear disarmament, as well as other efforts called for in the 2010 NPT Review Conference action plan [YUN 2010, p. 531]; described progress made towards the elaboration of an agreed glossary of definitions for key nuclear terms; and reported on the establishment of a working group dedicated to that task. The Conference also discussed political and technical challenges associated with verification in achieving further progress towards disarmament and ensuring non-proliferation, and pledged to continue the discussion at an expert-level meeting in London. It indicated that a third Conference would be held in the context of the first session of the Preparatory Committee for the 2015 NPT Review Conference.

On 5 February, the Treaty between the Russian Federation and the United States of America on Measures for the Further Reduction and Limitation of Strategic Offensive Arms [ibid., p. 514] entered into force. The Bilateral Consultative Commission established pursuant to the Treaty began work in March, and the parties initiated the regular release of public information pertaining to their aggregate holdings of nuclear warheads accountable under the Treaty. Despite those steps, the number of nuclear weapons in national arsenals remained in the thousands, including warheads maintained on high-alert status. Nuclear-weapon States continued to plan and implement major new programmes aimed at modernizing their nuclear arsenals, delivery systems and related research and development infrastructure, and to research, develop and deploy new nuclear weapons with new military capabilities. While the Comprehensive Nuclear-Test-Ban Treaty continued to lack the necessary ratifications for its entry into force, the recent ratification by one Member State was a welcome development.

The Conference on Disarmament, at its 2011 session, was unable to begin substantive work on the basis of an agreed programme of work, which gave rise to increasing concern regarding the status of the multilateral disarmament machinery and the relevance of the Conference, prompting some States to begin the consideration of alternative options. The Disarmament Commission, convening in April for the third part of its three-year cycle, was unable also to reach consensus on substantive matters pertaining to its three agenda items: recommendations for achieving the objective of nuclear disarmament and non-proliferation of nuclear weapons; elements of a draft declaration of the 2010s as the fourth disarmament decade; and practical confidence-building measures in the field of conventional weapons. The Secretary-General and the High Representative for Disarmament Affairs continued to promote nuclear disarmament and non-proliferation globally through direct interaction with Governments, civil society, civic leaders and parliamentarians, advocacy and other outreach activities.

Included in the report were replies from 11 Member States on measures that they had taken to implement resolution 65/76 concerning the follow-up to the advisory opinion of the International Court of Justice (see p. 498) on the *Legality of the Threat or Use of Nuclear Weapons*.

GENERAL ASSEMBLY ACTION

On 2 December [meeting 71], the General Assembly, on the recommendation of the First Committee [A/66/412], adopted **resolution 66/48** by recorded vote (117-49-13) [agenda item 98 (*r*)].

Reducing nuclear danger

The General Assembly,

Bearing in mind that the use of nuclear weapons poses the most serious threat to mankind and to the survival of civilization,

Reaffirming that any use or threat of use of nuclear weapons would constitute a violation of the Charter of the United Nations,

Convinced that the proliferation of nuclear weapons in all its aspects would seriously enhance the danger of nuclear war,

Convinced also that nuclear disarmament and the complete elimination of nuclear weapons are essential to remove the danger of nuclear war,

Considering that, until nuclear weapons cease to exist, it is imperative on the part of the nuclear-weapon States to adopt measures that assure non-nuclear-weapon States against the use or threat of use of nuclear weapons,

Considering also that the hair-trigger alert of nuclear weapons carries unacceptable risks of unintentional or accidental use of nuclear weapons, which would have catastrophic consequences for all mankind,

Emphasizing the need to adopt measures to avoid accidental, unauthorized or unexplained incidents arising from computer anomaly or other technical malfunctions,

Conscious that limited steps relating to de-alerting and de-targeting have been taken by the nuclear-weapon States and that further practical, realistic and mutually reinforcing steps are necessary to contribute to the improvement in the international climate for negotiations leading to the elimination of nuclear weapons,

Mindful that a diminishing role for nuclear weapons in the security policies of nuclear-weapon States would positively impact on international peace and security and improve the conditions for the further reduction and the elimination of nuclear weapons,

Reiterating the highest priority accorded to nuclear disarmament in the Final Document of the Tenth Special Session of the General Assembly and by the international community,

Recalling the advisory opinion of the International Court of Justice on the *Legality of the Threat or Use of Nuclear Weapons* that there exists an obligation for all States to pursue in good faith and bring to a conclusion negotiations leading to nuclear disarmament in all its aspects under strict and effective international control,

Recalling also the call in the United Nations Millennium Declaration to seek to eliminate the dangers posed by weapons of mass destruction and the resolve to strive for the elimination of weapons of mass destruction, particularly nuclear weapons, including the possibility of convening an international conference to identify ways of eliminating nuclear dangers,

1. *Calls for* a review of nuclear doctrines and, in this context, immediate and urgent steps to reduce the risks of unintentional and accidental use of nuclear weapons, including through de-alerting and de-targeting nuclear weapons;

2. *Requests* the five nuclear-weapon States to take measures towards the implementation of paragraph 1 above;

3. *Calls upon* Member States to take the necessary measures to prevent the proliferation of nuclear weapons in all its aspects and to promote nuclear disarmament, with the objective of eliminating nuclear weapons;

4. *Takes note* of the report of the Secretary-General submitted pursuant to paragraph 5 of its resolution 65/60 of 8 December 2010;

5. *Requests* the Secretary-General to intensify efforts and support initiatives that would contribute towards the full implementation of the seven recommendations identified in the report of the Advisory Board on Disarmament Matters that would significantly reduce the risk of nuclear war, and also to continue to encourage Member States to consider the convening of an international conference, as proposed in the United Nations Millennium Declaration, to identify ways of eliminating nuclear dangers, and to report thereon to the General Assembly at its sixty-seventh session;

6. *Decides* to include in the provisional agenda of its sixty-seventh session the item entitled "Reducing nuclear danger".

RECORDED VOTE ON RESOLUTION 66/48:

In favour: Afghanistan, Algeria, Angola, Antigua and Barbuda, Azerbaijan, Bahamas, Bahrain, Bangladesh, Barbados, Belize, Benin, Bhutan, Bolivia, Botswana, Brazil, Brunei Darussalam, Burkina Faso, Cambodia, Cameroon, Cape Verde, Chad, Chile, Colombia, Comoros, Congo, Costa Rica, Côte d'Ivoire, Cuba, Democratic People's Republic of Korea, Djibouti, Dominican Republic, Ecuador, Egypt, El Salvador, Eritrea, Ethiopia, Fiji, Ghana, Grenada, Guatemala, Guinea, Guinea-Bissau, Guyana, Haiti, Honduras, India, Indonesia, Iran, Iraq, Jamaica, Jordan, Kazakhstan, Kenya, Kuwait, Kyrgyzstan, Lao People's Democratic Republic, Lebanon, Lesotho, Liberia, Libya, Madagascar, Malaysia, Maldives, Mali, Mauritania, Mauritius, Mexico, Mongolia, Morocco, Mozambique, Myanmar, Namibia, Nepal, Nicaragua, Niger, Nigeria, Oman, Pakistan, Panama, Papua New Guinea, Paraguay, Peru, Philippines, Qatar, Saint Kitts and Nevis, Saint Lucia, Saint Vincent and the Grenadines, Samoa, Sao Tome and Principe, Saudi Arabia, Senegal, Seychelles, Sierra Leone, Singapore, Solomon Islands, South Africa, Sri Lanka, Sudan, Suriname, Swaziland, Syrian Arab Republic, Thailand, Togo, Tonga, Trinidad and Tobago, Tunisia, Turkmenistan, Uganda, United Arab Emirates, United Republic of Tanzania, Uruguay, Vanuatu, Venezuela, Viet Nam, Yemen, Zambia, Zimbabwe.

Against: Albania, Andorra, Australia, Austria, Belgium, Bosnia and Herzegovina, Bulgaria, Canada, Croatia, Cyprus, Czech Republic, Denmark, Estonia, Finland, France, Germany, Greece, Hungary, Iceland, Ireland, Israel, Italy, Latvia, Liechtenstein, Lithuania, Luxembourg, Malta, Micronesia, Monaco, Montenegro, Netherlands, New Zealand, Norway, Palau, Poland, Portugal, Republic of Moldova, Romania, San Marino, Slovakia, Slovenia, Spain, Sweden, Switzerland, the former Yugoslav Republic of Macedonia, Turkey, Ukraine, United Kingdom, United States.

Abstaining: Argentina, Armenia, Belarus, China, Georgia, Japan, Marshall Islands, Republic of Korea, Russian Federation, Serbia, Tajikistan, Timor-Leste, Uzbekistan.

Conference on Disarmament

The Conference on Disarmament discussed agenda items 1: "Cessation of the nuclear arms race and nuclear disarmament, and 2: "Prevention of nuclear war, including all related matters" in two plenary (1–3 February and 24 February–3 March) and two informal (29 March and 17–18 May) sessions [CD/1926]. Delegations reaffirmed or further elaborated their respective positions on those agenda items. Among the documents before the Conference were a joint press release transmitted by France, issued at the first meeting of the five permanent Security Council members in follow-up to the 2010 NPT Review Conference (Paris, 30 June–1 July) [CD/1914]; the 30 April Berlin statement on nuclear disarmament and non-proliferation issued by the Foreign Ministers of Australia, Canada, Chile, Germany, Japan, Mexico, the Netherlands, Poland, Turkey and the United Arab Emirates [CD/1908]; and a working paper on a Fissile Material Cut-off Treaty submitted by Bulgaria, Germany, Mexico, the Netherlands, Romania, Spain, Sweden and Turkey [CD/1910].

Communications. On 27 June, Colombia transmitted to the Secretary-General of the Conference on Disarmament a contribution on the state of the Conference and how to strengthen it [CD/1913]. On 29 June [A/65/896-S/2011/407], Egypt, as Chair of the Sixteenth Ministerial Conference of the Non-Aligned Movement, transmitted the Conference's outcome documents containing the statement on the total elimination of nuclear weapons.

GENERAL ASSEMBLY ACTION

On 2 December [meeting 71], the General Assembly, on the recommendation of the First Committee [A/66/412], adopted **resolution 66/51** by recorded vote (117-45-18) [agenda item 98 (*o*)].

Nuclear disarmament

The General Assembly,

Recalling its resolution 49/75 E of 15 December 1994 on a step-by-step reduction of the nuclear threat, and its resolutions 50/70 P of 12 December 1995, 51/45 O of 10 December 1996, 52/38 L of 9 December 1997, 53/77 X of 4 December 1998, 54/54 P of 1 December 1999, 55/33 T of 20 November 2000, 56/24 R of 29 November 2001, 57/79 of 22 November 2002, 58/56 of 8 December 2003, 59/77 of 3 December 2004, 60/70 of 8 December 2005, 61/78 of 6 December 2006, 62/42 of 5 December 2007, 63/46 of 2 December 2008, 64/53 of 2 December 2009 and 65/56 of 8 December 2010 on nuclear disarmament,

Reaffirming the commitment of the international community to the goal of the total elimination of nuclear weapons and the establishment of a nuclear-weapon-free world,

Bearing in mind that the Convention on the Prohibition of the Development, Production and Stockpiling of Bacteriological (Biological) and Toxin Weapons and on Their Destruction of 1972 and the Convention on the Prohibition of the Development, Production, Stockpiling and Use of Chemical Weapons and on Their Destruction of 1993 have already established legal regimes on the complete prohibition of biological and chemical weapons, respectively, and determined to achieve a nuclear weapons convention on the prohibition of the development, testing, production, stockpiling, loan, transfer, use and threat of use of nuclear weapons and on their destruction, and to conclude such an international convention at an early date,

Recognizing that there now exist conditions for the establishment of a world free of nuclear weapons, and stressing the need to take concrete practical steps towards achieving this goal,

Bearing in mind paragraph 50 of the Final Document of the Tenth Special Session of the General Assembly, the first special session devoted to disarmament, calling for the urgent negotiation of agreements for the cessation of the qualitative improvement and development of nuclear-weapon systems, and for a comprehensive and phased programme with agreed time frames, wherever feasible, for the progressive and balanced reduction of nuclear weapons and their means of delivery, leading to their ultimate and complete elimination at the earliest possible time,

Reaffirming the conviction of the States parties to the Treaty on the Non-Proliferation of Nuclear Weapons that the Treaty is a cornerstone of nuclear non-proliferation and nuclear disarmament, and the importance of the decision on strengthening the review process for the Treaty, the decision on principles and objectives for nuclear non-proliferation and disarmament, the decision on the extension of the Treaty and the resolution on the Middle East, adopted by the 1995 Review and Extension Conference of the Parties to the Treaty on the Non-Proliferation of Nuclear Weapons,

Stressing the importance of the thirteen steps for the systematic and progressive efforts to achieve the objective of nuclear disarmament leading to the total elimination of nuclear weapons, as agreed to by the States parties in the Final Document of the 2000 Review Conference of the Parties to the Treaty on the Non-Proliferation of Nuclear Weapons,

Recognizing the important work done at the 2010 Review Conference of the Parties to the Treaty on the Non-Proliferation of Nuclear Weapons, and affirming its action plan as an impetus to intensify work aimed at beginning negotiations for a nuclear weapons convention,

Reiterating the highest priority accorded to nuclear disarmament in the Final Document of the Tenth Special Session of the General Assembly and by the international community,

Reiterating its call for an early entry into force of the Comprehensive Nuclear-Test-Ban Treaty,

Taking note of the entry into force of the new strategic arms reduction treaty between the Russian Federation and the United States of America, in order to achieve further deep cuts in their strategic and tactical nuclear weapons, and stressing that such cuts should be irreversible, verifiable and transparent,

Recalling the entry into force of the Treaty on Strategic Offensive Reductions ("the Moscow Treaty") between the United States of America and the Russian Federation as a significant step towards reducing their deployed strategic nuclear weapons, while calling for further irreversible deep cuts in their nuclear arsenals,

Noting the positive statements by nuclear-weapon States of their intention to pursue actions in achieving a world free of nuclear weapons, while reaffirming the need for urgent concrete actions by nuclear-weapon States to achieve this goal within a specified framework of time, and urging them to take further measures for progress on nuclear disarmament,

Recognizing the complementarity of bilateral, plurilateral and multilateral negotiations on nuclear disarmament, and that bilateral negotiations can never replace multilateral negotiations in this respect,

Noting the support expressed in the Conference on Disarmament and in the General Assembly for the elaboration of an international convention to assure non-nuclear-weapon States against the use or threat of use of nuclear weapons, and the multilateral efforts in the Conference on Disarmament to reach agreement on such an international convention at an early date,

Recalling the advisory opinion of the International Court of Justice on the *Legality of the Threat or Use of Nuclear Weapons*, issued on 8 July 1996, and welcoming the unanimous reaffirmation by all Judges of the Court that there exists an obligation for all States to pursue in good faith and bring to a conclusion negotiations leading to nuclear disarmament in all its aspects under strict and effective international control,

Mindful of paragraph 102 of the Final Document of the Coordinating Bureau of the Non-Aligned Movement at its Ministerial Meeting, held in Havana from 27 to 30 April 2009,

Recalling paragraph 112 and other relevant recommendations in the Final Document of the Fifteenth Summit Conference of Heads of State and Government of the

Movement of Non-Aligned Countries, held in Sharm el-Sheikh, Egypt, from 11 to 16 July 2009, calling upon the Conference on Disarmament to establish, as soon as possible and as the highest priority, an ad hoc committee on nuclear disarmament and to commence negotiations on a phased programme for the complete elimination of nuclear weapons within a specified framework of time, including a nuclear weapons convention,

Noting the adoption of the programme of work for the 2009 session by the Conference on Disarmament on 29 May 2009, after years of stalemate, while regretting that the Conference has not been able to undertake substantive work on its agenda in 2011,

Reaffirming the importance and validity of the Conference on Disarmament as the sole multilateral negotiating forum on disarmament, and expressing the need to adopt and implement a balanced and comprehensive programme of work on the basis of its agenda and dealing with, inter alia, four core issues, in accordance with the rules of procedure, and by taking into consideration the security concerns of all States,

Reaffirming also the specific mandate conferred upon the Disarmament Commission by the General Assembly, in its decision 52/492 of 8 September 1998, to discuss the subject of nuclear disarmament as one of its main substantive agenda items,

Recalling the United Nations Millennium Declaration, in which Heads of State and Government resolved to strive for the elimination of weapons of mass destruction, in particular nuclear weapons, and to keep all options open for achieving this aim, including the possibility of convening an international conference to identify ways of eliminating nuclear dangers,

Recalling also the statement on the total elimination of nuclear weapons, adopted by the Sixteenth Ministerial Conference and Commemorative Meeting of the Movement of Non-Aligned Countries, held in Bali, Indonesia, from 23 to 27 May 2011, in which the Non-Aligned Movement reiterated its call for an international conference to identify ways and means of eliminating nuclear weapons, at the earliest possible date,

Reaffirming that, in accordance with the Charter of the United Nations, States should refrain from the use or threat of use of nuclear weapons in settling their disputes in international relations,

Seized of the danger of the use of weapons of mass destruction, particularly nuclear weapons, in terrorist acts and the urgent need for concerted international efforts to control and overcome it,

1. *Recognizes* that the time is now opportune for all the nuclear-weapon States to take effective disarmament measures to achieve the total elimination of these weapons at the earliest possible time;

2. *Reaffirms* that nuclear disarmament and nuclear non-proliferation are substantively interrelated and mutually reinforcing, that the two processes must go hand in hand and that there is a genuine need for a systematic and progressive process of nuclear disarmament;

3. *Welcomes and encourages* the efforts to establish new nuclear-weapon-free zones in different parts of the world, including the establishment of a Middle East zone free of nuclear weapons, on the basis of agreements or arrangements freely arrived at among the States of the regions concerned, which is an effective measure for limiting the further spread of nuclear weapons geographically and contributes to the cause of nuclear disarmament;

4. *Welcomes* the ongoing efforts between the States members of the Association of Southeast Asian Nations and the nuclear-weapon States, and encourages the nuclear-weapon States in their early signing of the Protocol to the Treaty on the South-East Asia Nuclear-Weapon-Free Zone;

5. *Recognizes* that there is a genuine need to diminish the role of nuclear weapons in strategic doctrines and security policies to minimize the risk that these weapons will ever be used and to facilitate the process of their total elimination;

6. *Urges* the nuclear-weapon States to stop immediately the qualitative improvement, development, production and stockpiling of nuclear warheads and their delivery systems;

7. *Also urges* the nuclear-weapon States, as an interim measure, to de-alert and deactivate immediately their nuclear weapons and to take other concrete measures to reduce further the operational status of their nuclear-weapon systems, while stressing that reductions in deployments and in operational status cannot substitute for irreversible cuts in, and the total elimination of, nuclear weapons;

8. *Reiterates its call upon* the nuclear-weapon States to undertake the step-by-step reduction of the nuclear threat and to carry out effective nuclear disarmament measures with a view to achieving the total elimination of these weapons within a specified framework of time;

9. *Calls upon* the nuclear-weapon States, pending the achievement of the total elimination of nuclear weapons, to agree on an internationally and legally binding instrument on a joint undertaking not to be the first to use nuclear weapons, and calls upon all States to conclude an internationally and legally binding instrument on security assurances of non-use and non-threat of use of nuclear weapons against non-nuclear-weapon States;

10. *Urges* the nuclear-weapon States to commence plurilateral negotiations among themselves at an appropriate stage on further deep reductions of nuclear weapons as an effective measure of nuclear disarmament;

11. *Underlines* the importance of applying the principles of transparency, irreversibility and verifiability to the process of nuclear disarmament and to nuclear and other related arms control and reduction measures;

12. *Also underlines* the importance of the unequivocal undertaking by the nuclear-weapon States, in the Final Document of the 2000 Review Conference of the Parties to the Treaty on the Non-Proliferation of Nuclear Weapons, to accomplish the total elimination of their nuclear arsenals leading to nuclear disarmament, to which all States parties are committed under article VI of the Treaty, and the reaffirmation by the States parties that the total elimination of nuclear weapons is the only absolute guarantee against the use or threat of use of nuclear weapons;

13. *Calls for* the full and effective implementation of the thirteen practical steps for nuclear disarmament contained in the Final Document of the 2000 Review Conference;

14. *Also calls for* the full implementation of the action plan as set out in the conclusions and recommendations for follow-on actions of the Final Document of the 2010 Review Conference of the Parties to the Treaty on the Non-

Proliferation of Nuclear Weapons, particularly the 22-point action plan on nuclear disarmament;

15. *Urges* the nuclear-weapon States to carry out further reductions of non-strategic nuclear weapons, based on unilateral initiatives and as an integral part of the nuclear arms reduction and disarmament process;

16. *Calls for* the immediate commencement of negotiations in the Conference on Disarmament on a non-discriminatory, multilateral and internationally and effectively verifiable treaty banning the production of fissile material for nuclear weapons or other nuclear explosive devices on the basis of the report of the Special Coordinator and the mandate contained therein;

17. *Urges* the Conference on Disarmament to commence as early as possible its substantive work during its 2012 session, on the basis of a comprehensive and balanced programme of work that takes into consideration all the real and existing priorities in the field of disarmament and arms control, including the immediate commencement of negotiations on such a treaty with a view to their conclusion within five years;

18. *Calls for* the conclusion of an international legal instrument or instruments on adequate and unconditional security assurances to non-nuclear-weapon States;

19. *Also calls for* the early entry into force and strict observance of the Comprehensive Nuclear-Test-Ban Treaty;

20. *Expresses its regret* that the Conference on Disarmament was unable to establish an ad hoc committee to deal with nuclear disarmament early in 2011, as called for by the General Assembly in its resolution 65/56;

21. *Reiterates its call upon* the Conference on Disarmament to establish, as soon as possible and as the highest priority, an ad hoc committee on nuclear disarmament early in 2012 and to commence negotiations on a phased programme of nuclear disarmament leading to the total elimination of nuclear weapons within a specified framework of time;

22. *Calls for* the convening of an international conference on nuclear disarmament in all its aspects at an early date to identify and deal with concrete measures of nuclear disarmament;

23. *Requests* the Secretary-General to submit to the General Assembly at its sixty-seventh session a report on the implementation of the present resolution;

24. *Decides* to include in the provisional agenda of its sixty-seventh session the item entitled "Nuclear disarmament".

RECORDED VOTE ON RESOLUTION 66/51:

In favour: Afghanistan, Algeria, Angola, Antigua and Barbuda, Argentina, Azerbaijan, Bahamas, Bahrain, Bangladesh, Barbados, Belize, Benin, Bhutan, Bolivia, Botswana, Brazil, Brunei Darussalam, Burkina Faso, Cambodia, Cameroon, Cape Verde, Chad, Chile, China, Colombia, Comoros, Congo, Costa Rica, Côte d'Ivoire, Cuba, Democratic People's Republic of Korea, Djibouti, Dominican Republic, Ecuador, Egypt, El Salvador, Eritrea, Ethiopia, Fiji, Ghana, Grenada, Guatemala, Guinea, Guinea-Bissau, Guyana, Haiti, Honduras, Indonesia, Iran, Iraq, Jamaica, Jordan, Kazakhstan, Kenya, Kuwait, Lao People's Democratic Republic, Lebanon, Lesotho, Liberia, Libya, Madagascar, Malawi, Malaysia, Maldives, Mali, Mauritania, Mexico, Mongolia, Morocco, Mozambique, Myanmar, Namibia, Nepal, Nicaragua, Niger, Nigeria, Oman, Panama, Papua New Guinea, Paraguay, Peru, Philippines, Qatar, Saint Kitts and Nevis, Saint Lucia, Saint Vincent and the Grenadines, Samoa, Sao Tome and Principe, Saudi Arabia, Senegal, Seychelles, Sierra Leone, Singapore, Solomon Islands, South Africa, Sri Lanka, Sudan, Suriname, Swaziland, Syrian Arab Republic, Thailand, Timor-Leste, Togo, Tonga, Trinidad and Tobago, Tunisia, Tuvalu, Uganda, United Arab Emirates, United Republic of Tanzania, Uruguay, Vanuatu, Venezuela, Viet Nam, Yemen, Zambia, Zimbabwe.

Against: Albania, Andorra, Australia, Belgium, Bosnia and Herzegovina, Bulgaria, Canada, Croatia, Cyprus, Czech Republic, Denmark, Estonia, Finland, France, Georgia, Germany, Greece, Hungary, Iceland, Israel, Italy, Latvia, Liechtenstein, Lithuania, Luxembourg, Micronesia, Monaco, Montenegro, Netherlands, Norway, Palau, Poland, Portugal, Republic of Moldova, Romania, San Marino, Slovakia, Slovenia, Spain, Switzerland, the former Yugoslav Republic of Macedonia, Turkey, Ukraine, United Kingdom, United States.

Abstaining: Armenia, Austria, Belarus, India, Ireland, Japan, Kyrgyzstan, Malta, Marshall Islands, Mauritius, New Zealand, Pakistan, Republic of Korea, Russian Federation, Serbia, Sweden, Tajikistan, Uzbekistan.

Fissile material

The issue of a fissile material cut-off treaty (FMCT) was discussed by the Conference on Disarmament in the context of its deliberations on the cessation of the nuclear arms race and nuclear disarmament and on the prevention of nuclear war, including all related matters.

Communications. The Conference had before it a 9 March communication from Australia [CD/1906] transmitting the Chair's report of the Australian-Japan experts side event on a fissile material cut-off treaty definitions (Geneva, 14–16 February), which addressed possible definitions in a future treaty banning the production of fissile material for nuclear weapons or other nuclear explosive devices. Attended by 45 member States of the Conference and 10 observer States, the Conference was intended to build confidence about FMCT and momentum towards related negotiations; inform and support the work of the Conference; and build confidence among its member and observer States. It did not represent a negotiation, nor a pre-negotiation, but an opportunity to exchange views.

Also before the Conference were a 23 May communication from Australia [CD/1909] transmitting the report of the Chair of the experts on a side event on FMCT verification (Geneva, 21–23 March); a 2 September communication from Japan [CD/1917] transmitting the Chair's report on a side event on the same subject (Geneva, 30 May and 1 June); a 12 September communication from Australia [CD/1919] transmitting "The 2011 Australia-Japan FMCT Experts Side Events: Chairs' Final Report"; a June working paper on FMCT [CD/1910] submitted by Bulgaria, Germany,

Mexico, the Netherlands, Romania, Spain, Sweden and Turkey, as a contribution to the discussion on its objectives and definitions with regard to the scope of such a treaty and its verification; and a press release transmitted by the United States regarding the P-5 consultations on FMCT [CD/1921].

GENERAL ASSEMBLY ACTION

On 2 December [meeting 71], the General Assembly, on the recommendation of the First Committee [A/66/412], adopted **resolution 66/44** by recorded vote (158-2-21) [agenda item 98 (*u*)].

Treaty banning the production of fissile material for nuclear weapons or other nuclear explosive devices

The General Assembly,

Recalling its resolutions 48/75 L of 16 December 1993, 53/77 I of 4 December 1998, 55/33 Y of 20 November 2000, 56/24 J of 29 November 2001, 57/80 of 22 November 2002, 58/57 of 8 December 2003, 59/81 of 3 December 2004, 64/29 of 2 December 2009 and 65/65 of 8 December 2010 on the subject of banning the production of fissile material for nuclear weapons or other nuclear explosive devices,

Recalling also document CD/1299 of 24 March 1995, in which all members of the Conference on Disarmament agreed on the mandate to negotiate a treaty banning the production of fissile material for nuclear weapons or other nuclear explosive devices and which would not preclude any delegation from raising for consideration, in negotiations, any issue noted therein,

Recalling further the support for the Conference on Disarmament expressed by the Security Council summit on nuclear disarmament and nuclear non-proliferation, held on 24 September 2009,

Convinced that a non-discriminatory, multilateral and internationally and effectively verifiable treaty banning the production of fissile material for nuclear weapons or other nuclear explosive devices would be a significant contribution to nuclear disarmament and non-proliferation,

Recognizing the importance of advancing all issues identified in decision CD/1864, adopted by consensus by the Conference on Disarmament on 29 May 2009,

Noting the determination of China, France, the Russian Federation, the United Kingdom of Great Britain and Northern Ireland and the United States of America at the meeting held in Paris on 30 June and 1 July 2011 to renew their efforts, with relevant parties, to achieve a treaty banning the production of fissile materials for nuclear weapons and other nuclear explosive devices at the earliest possible date in the Conference on Disarmament,

Expressing frustration with the years of stalemate in the Conference on Disarmament, which has prevented it from fulfilling its mandate as the world's single multilateral disarmament negotiating forum,

1. *Urges* the Conference on Disarmament to agree on and implement early in 2012 a comprehensive programme of work that includes the immediate commencement of negotiations on a treaty banning the production of fissile material for nuclear weapons or other nuclear explosive devices on the basis of document CD/1299 and the mandate contained therein;

2. *Resolves* to consider options for the negotiation of a treaty banning the production of fissile material for nuclear weapons or other nuclear explosive devices at its sixty-seventh session should the Conference on Disarmament fail to agree on and implement a comprehensive programme of work by the end of its 2012 session;

3. *Encourages* interested Member States, without prejudice to their national positions during future negotiations on such a treaty, to continue efforts, including within and on the margins of the Conference on Disarmament, in support of the commencement of negotiations, including through meetings involving scientific experts on various technical aspects of the treaty, drawing on available expertise from the International Atomic Energy Agency and other relevant bodies, as appropriate;

4. *Decides* to include in the provisional agenda of its sixty-seventh session the item entitled "Treaty banning the production of fissile material for nuclear weapons or other nuclear explosive devices".

RECORDED VOTE ON RESOLUTION 66/44:

In favour: Afghanistan, Albania, Andorra, Angola, Antigua and Barbuda, Argentina, Armenia, Australia, Austria, Azerbaijan, Bahamas, Bangladesh, Barbados, Belarus, Belgium, Belize, Benin, Bhutan, Bolivia, Bosnia and Herzegovina, Botswana, Brazil, Brunei Darussalam, Bulgaria, Burkina Faso, Cambodia, Cameroon, Canada, Cape Verde, Chad, Chile, China, Colombia, Congo, Costa Rica, Côte d'Ivoire, Croatia, Cuba, Cyprus, Czech Republic, Denmark, Dominican Republic, El Salvador, Eritrea, Estonia, Ethiopia, Fiji, Finland, France, Georgia, Germany, Ghana, Greece, Grenada, Guatemala, Guinea, Guinea-Bissau, Guyana, Haiti, Honduras, Hungary, Iceland, India, Ireland, Italy, Jamaica, Japan, Kazakhstan, Kenya, Kyrgyzstan, Lao People's Democratic Republic, Latvia, Lesotho, Liberia, Liechtenstein, Lithuania, Luxembourg, Madagascar, Malawi, Malaysia, Maldives, Mali, Malta, Marshall Islands, Mauritania, Mauritius, Mexico, Micronesia, Monaco, Mongolia, Montenegro, Morocco, Mozambique, Myanmar, Namibia, Nepal, Netherlands, New Zealand, Nicaragua, Niger, Nigeria, Norway, Palau, Panama, Papua New Guinea, Paraguay, Peru, Philippines, Poland, Portugal, Republic of Korea, Republic of Moldova, Romania, Russian Federation, Saint Kitts and Nevis, Saint Lucia, Saint Vincent and the Grenadines, Samoa, San Marino, Sao Tome and Principe, Senegal, Serbia, Seychelles, Sierra Leone, Singapore, Slovakia, Slovenia, Solomon Islands, South Africa, Spain, Sri Lanka, Suriname, Swaziland, Sweden, Switzerland, Tajikistan, Thailand, the former Yugoslav Republic of Macedonia, Timor-Leste, Togo, Tonga, Trinidad and Tobago, Turkey, Turkmenistan, Tuvalu, Uganda, Ukraine, United Arab Emirates, United Kingdom, United Republic of Tanzania, United States, Uruguay, Uzbekistan, Vanuatu, Venezuela, Viet Nam, Zambia, Zimbabwe.

Against: Democratic People's Republic of Korea, Pakistan.

Abstaining: Algeria, Bahrain, Comoros, Djibouti, Ecuador, Egypt, Indonesia, Iran, Iraq, Israel, Jordan, Kuwait, Lebanon, Libya, Oman, Qatar, Saudi Arabia, Sudan, Syrian Arab Republic, Tunisia, Yemen.

Security assurances

The Conference on Disarmament discussed agenda item 4: "Effective international arrangements to assure non-nuclear-weapon States against the use or threat of the use of nuclear weapons" (or "negative security assurances"), on 10 February and 10 March in formal sessions, and on 19 May in an informal session. The Conference had before it a working paper by Nigeria, submitted on behalf of member States of the Group of 21 (G-21) on negative security assurances [CD/1924].

The discussion reflected previously held divergent positions between those who wanted a legally binding framework to be negotiated in the Conference on Disarmament and others who wanted such assurances to be provided by all nuclear-weapon States through established nuclear-weapon-free zones. Members noted that statements made by the nuclear-weapon States on numerous occasions that they would not use or threaten to use nuclear weapons against non-nuclear-weapon States were insufficient, as such were unilateral, conditional and revocable. Some delegations maintained that the assurances given in relation to nuclear-weapon-free zones were inadequate, conditional and geographically limited. Nevertheless, the creation of such zones in Africa, South-East Asia, Central Asia and South America, as well as Mongolia's nuclear-weapon-free status, represented important forward-looking steps. It was also mentioned that granting negative security assurances would constitute a quid pro quo for States that renounced nuclear weapons, and hence such assurances would help combat proliferation. In that sense, granting legally binding assurances to non-nuclear-weapon States would be a confidence-building measure and a step towards the implementation by nuclear-weapon States of article VI of NPT, relating to nuclear disarmament.

GENERAL ASSEMBLY ACTION

On 2 December [meeting 71], the General Assembly, on the recommendation of the First Committee [A/66/409], adopted **resolution 66/26** by recorded vote (120-0-57) [agenda item 95].

Conclusion of effective international arrangements to assure non-nuclear-weapon States against the use or threat of use of nuclear weapons

The General Assembly,

Bearing in mind the need to allay the legitimate concern of the States of the world with regard to ensuring lasting security for their peoples,

Convinced that nuclear weapons pose the greatest threat to mankind and to the survival of civilization,

Noting that the renewed interest in nuclear disarmament should be translated into concrete actions for the achievement of general and complete disarmament under effective international control,

Convinced that nuclear disarmament and the complete elimination of nuclear weapons are essential to remove the danger of nuclear war,

Determined to abide strictly by the relevant provisions of the Charter of the United Nations on the non-use of force or threat of force,

Recognizing that the independence, territorial integrity and sovereignty of non-nuclear-weapon States need to be safeguarded against the use or threat of use of force, including the use or threat of use of nuclear weapons,

Considering that, until nuclear disarmament is achieved on a universal basis, it is imperative for the international community to develop effective measures and arrangements to ensure the security of non-nuclear-weapon States against the use or threat of use of nuclear weapons from any quarter,

Recognizing that effective measures and arrangements to assure non-nuclear-weapon States against the use or threat of use of nuclear weapons can contribute positively to the prevention of the spread of nuclear weapons,

Bearing in mind paragraph 59 of the Final Document of the Tenth Special Session of the General Assembly, the first special session devoted to disarmament, in which it urged the nuclear-weapon States to pursue efforts to conclude, as appropriate, effective arrangements to assure non-nuclear-weapon States against the use or threat of use of nuclear weapons, and desirous of promoting the implementation of the relevant provisions of the Final Document,

Recalling the relevant parts of the special report of the Committee on Disarmament submitted to the General Assembly at its twelfth special session, the second special session devoted to disarmament, and of the special report of the Conference on Disarmament submitted to the Assembly at its fifteenth special session, the third special session devoted to disarmament, as well as the report of the Conference on its 1992 session,

Recalling also paragraph 12 of the Declaration of the 1980s as the Second Disarmament Decade, contained in the annex to its resolution 35/46 of 3 December 1980, which states, inter alia, that all efforts should be exerted by the Committee on Disarmament urgently to negotiate with a view to reaching agreement on effective international arrangements to assure non-nuclear-weapon States against the use or threat of use of nuclear weapons,

Noting the in-depth negotiations undertaken in the Conference on Disarmament and its Ad Hoc Committee on Effective International Arrangements to Assure Non-Nuclear-Weapon States against the Use or Threat of Use of Nuclear Weapons, with a view to reaching agreement on this question,

Taking note of the proposals submitted under the item in the Conference on Disarmament, including the drafts of an international convention,

Taking note also of the relevant decision of the Thirteenth Conference of Heads of State or Government of Non-Aligned Countries, held at Kuala Lumpur on 24 and 25 February 2003, which was reiterated at the Fourteenth and Fifteenth Conferences of Heads of State or Government of Non-Aligned Countries, held at Havana and Sharm el-Sheikh, Egypt, on 15 and 16 September 2006, and 15 and 16 July 2009, respectively, as well as the relevant recommendations of the Organization of Islamic Cooperation,

Taking note further of the unilateral declarations made by all the nuclear-weapon States on their policies of non-use or non-threat of use of nuclear weapons against the non-nuclear-weapon States,

Noting the support expressed in the Conference on Disarmament and in the General Assembly for the elaboration of an international convention to assure non-nuclear-weapon States against the use or threat of use of nuclear weapons, as well as the difficulties pointed out in evolving a common approach acceptable to all,

Taking note of Security Council resolution 984(1995) of 11 April 1995 and the views expressed on it,

Recalling its relevant resolutions adopted in previous years, in particular resolutions 45/54 of 4 December 1990, 46/32 of 6 December 1991, 47/50 of 9 December 1992, 48/73 of 16 December 1993, 49/73 of 15 December 1994, 50/68 of 12 December 1995, 51/43 of 10 December 1996, 52/36 of 9 December 1997, 53/75 of 4 December 1998, 54/52 of 1 December 1999, 55/31 of 20 November 2000, 56/22 of 29 November 2001, 57/56 of 22 November 2002, 58/35 of 8 December 2003, 59/64 of 3 December 2004, 60/53 of 8 December 2005, 61/57 of 6 December 2006, 62/19 of 5 December 2007, 63/39 of 2 December 2008, 64/27 of 2 December 2009 and 65/43 of 8 December 2010,

1. *Reaffirms* the urgent need to reach an early agreement on effective international arrangements to assure non-nuclear-weapon States against the use or threat of use of nuclear weapons;

2. *Notes with satisfaction* that in the Conference on Disarmament there is no objection, in principle, to the idea of an international convention to assure non-nuclear-weapon States against the use or threat of use of nuclear weapons, although the difficulties with regard to evolving a common approach acceptable to all have also been pointed out;

3. *Appeals* to all States, especially the nuclear-weapon States, to work actively towards an early agreement on a common approach and, in particular, on a common formula that could be included in an international instrument of a legally binding character;

4. *Recommends* that further intensive efforts be devoted to the search for such a common approach or common formula and that the various alternative approaches, including, in particular, those considered in the Conference on Disarmament, be further explored in order to overcome the difficulties;

5. *Also recommends* that the Conference on Disarmament actively continue intensive negotiations with a view to reaching early agreement and concluding effective international agreements to assure the non-nuclear-weapon States against the use or threat of use of nuclear weapons, taking into account the widespread support for the conclusion of an international convention and giving consideration to any other proposals designed to secure the same objective;

6. *Decides* to include in the provisional agenda of its sixty-seventh session the item entitled "Conclusion of effective international arrangements to assure non-nuclear-weapon States against the use or threat of use of nuclear weapons".

RECORDED VOTE ON RESOLUTION 66/26:

In favour: Afghanistan, Algeria, Angola, Antigua and Barbuda, Azerbaijan, Bahamas, Bahrain, Bangladesh, Barbados, Belarus, Belize, Benin, Bhutan, Bolivia, Botswana, Brazil, Brunei Darussalam, Burkina Faso, Cambodia, Cameroon, Cape Verde, Chad, Chile, China, Colombia, Comoros, Congo, Costa Rica, Côte d'Ivoire, Cuba, Democratic People's Republic of Korea, Djibouti, Dominican Republic, Ecuador, Egypt, El Salvador, Ethiopia, Fiji, Ghana, Guatemala, Guinea, Guinea-Bissau, Guyana, Haiti, Honduras, India, Indonesia, Iran, Iraq, Jamaica, Japan, Jordan, Kazakhstan, Kenya, Kuwait, Kyrgyzstan, Lao People's Democratic Republic, Lebanon, Lesotho, Liberia, Libya, Madagascar, Malawi, Malaysia, Maldives, Mali, Mauritania, Mauritius, Mexico, Mongolia, Morocco, Mozambique, Myanmar, Namibia, Nepal, Nicaragua, Niger, Nigeria, Oman, Pakistan, Panama, Papua New Guinea, Paraguay, Peru, Philippines, Qatar, Saint Kitts and Nevis, Saint Lucia, Saint Vincent and the Grenadines, Samoa, Sao Tome and Principe, Saudi Arabia, Senegal, Seychelles, Sierra Leone, Singapore, Solomon Islands, Sri Lanka, Sudan, Suriname, Swaziland, Syrian Arab Republic, Tajikistan, Thailand, Timor-Leste, Togo, Tonga, Tunisia, Turkmenistan, Uganda, United Arab Emirates, United Republic of Tanzania, Uruguay, Uzbekistan, Vanuatu, Venezuela, Viet Nam, Yemen, Zambia, Zimbabwe.

Against: None.

Abstaining: Albania, Andorra, Argentina, Armenia, Australia, Austria, Belgium, Bosnia and Herzegovina, Bulgaria, Canada, Croatia, Cyprus, Czech Republic, Denmark, Estonia, Finland, France, Georgia, Germany, Greece, Hungary, Iceland, Ireland, Israel, Italy, Latvia, Liechtenstein, Lithuania, Luxembourg, Malta, Marshall Islands, Micronesia, Monaco, Montenegro, Netherlands, New Zealand, Norway, Palau, Poland, Portugal, Republic of Korea, Republic of Moldova, Romania, Russian Federation, San Marino, Serbia, Slovakia, Slovenia, South Africa, Spain, Sweden, the former Yugoslav Republic of Macedonia, Turkey, Tuvalu, Ukraine, United Kingdom, United States.

Comprehensive Nuclear-Test-Ban Treaty

Status

As at 31 December, 182 States had signed the 1996 Comprehensive Nuclear-Test-Ban Treaty (CTBT) adopted by General Assembly resolution 50/245 [YUN 1996, p. 454], and 155 States had ratified it. During the year, instruments of ratification were deposited by Ghana and Guinea. In accordance with article XIV, CTBT would enter into force 180 days after the 44 States possessing nuclear reactors listed in annex 2 of the Treaty had deposited their instruments of ratification. By year's end, 36 of those States had ratified the Treaty.

Report of Secretary-General. In July [A/66/155 & Add.1], responding to General Assembly resolution 65/91 [YUN 2010, p. 525], the Secretary-General reported in consultation with the Preparatory Commission for CTBT, on the efforts of States that had ratified the Treaty towards its universalization and possibilities for providing assistance on ratification procedures to States that requested it, covering the period June 2010–May 2011.

Conference on facilitating entry into force

The seventh Conference on Facilitating the Entry into Force of CTBT, convened by the Secretary-General in his capacity as CTBT depositary, took place in New York on 23 September [CTBT-Art.XIV/2011/6]. Over 160 countries committed themselves to promoting the Treaty's entry into force and joined the Secretary-General in urging the nine countries whose ratifications were required for the Treaty's entry into force (China, Democratic People's Republic of Korea, Egypt, India, Iran, Israel, Pakistan, United States) to act without further delay. A number of intergovernmental organizations, specialized agencies and related organizations as well as NGOs and the media were also present.

The Conference unanimously adopted a Final Declaration that called upon the remaining countries to sign and ratify the Treaty without delay. It outlined 10 practical measures for early entry into force and universalization of the Treaty, including various capacity-building and outreach activities; support for bilateral, regional and multilateral initiatives by interested States to promote the Treaty's entry into force and its universalization; and encouragement of cooperation with intergovernmental organizations and civil society to raise awareness of the Treaty.

GENERAL ASSEMBLY ACTION

On 2 December [meeting 71], the General Assembly, on the recommendation of the First Committee [A/66/418], adopted **resolution 66/64** by recorded vote (175-1-3) [agenda item 104].

Comprehensive Nuclear-Test-Ban Treaty

The General Assembly,

Reiterating that the cessation of nuclear-weapon test explosions or any other nuclear explosions constitutes an effective nuclear disarmament and non-proliferation measure, and convinced that this is a meaningful step in the realization of a systematic process for achieving nuclear disarmament,

Recalling that the Comprehensive Nuclear-Test-Ban Treaty, adopted by its resolution 50/245 of 10 September 1996, was opened for signature on 24 September 1996,

Stressing that a universal and effectively verifiable Treaty constitutes a fundamental instrument in the field of nuclear disarmament and non-proliferation and that, after more than fifteen years, its entry into force is more urgent than ever before,

Encouraged by the signing of the Treaty by one hundred and eighty-two States, including forty-one of the forty-four whose ratification is needed for its entry into force, and welcoming the ratification of the Treaty by one hundred and fifty-five States, including thirty-five of the forty-four whose ratification is needed for its entry into force, among which there are three nuclear-weapon States,

Recalling its resolution 65/91 of 8 December 2010,

Welcoming the adoption by consensus of the conclusions and recommendations for follow-on actions of the 2010 Review Conference of the Parties to the Treaty on the Non-Proliferation of Nuclear Weapons, which, inter alia, reaffirmed the vital importance of the entry into force of the Comprehensive Nuclear-Test-Ban Treaty as a core element of the international nuclear disarmament and non-proliferation regime and included specific actions to be taken in support of the entry into force of the Treaty,

Welcoming also the Joint Ministerial Statement on the Comprehensive Nuclear-Test-Ban Treaty, adopted at the ministerial meeting held in New York on 23 September 2010,

Recalling the Final Declaration adopted by the seventh Conference on Facilitating the Entry into Force of the Comprehensive Nuclear-Test-Ban Treaty, held in New York on 23 September 2011, convened pursuant to article XIV of the Treaty, and noting the improved prospects for ratification in several Annex 2 countries,

1. *Stresses* the vital importance and urgency of signature and ratification, without delay and without conditions, in order to achieve the earliest entry into force of the Comprehensive Nuclear-Test-Ban Treaty;

2. *Welcomes* the contributions by the States signatories to the work of the Preparatory Commission for the Comprehensive Nuclear-Test-Ban Treaty Organization, in particular its efforts to ensure that the verification regime of the Treaty will be capable of meeting the verification requirements of the Treaty upon its entry into force, in accordance with article IV of the Treaty;

3. *Underlines* the need to maintain momentum towards completion of all elements of the verification regime;

4. *Urges* all States not to carry out nuclear-weapon test explosions or any other nuclear explosions, to maintain their moratoriums in this regard and to refrain from acts that would defeat the object and purpose of the Treaty, while stressing that these measures do not have the same permanent and legally binding effect as the entry into force of the Treaty;

5. *Recalls* Security Council resolutions 1718(2006) of 14 October 2006 and 1874(2009) of 12 June 2009, emphasizes the importance of their implementation, and reaffirms its firm support for the Six-Party Talks;

6. *Urges* all States that have not yet signed the Treaty, in particular those whose ratification is needed for its entry into force, to sign and ratify it as soon as possible;

7. *Urges* all States that have signed but not yet ratified the Treaty, in particular those whose ratification is needed for its entry into force, to accelerate their ratification processes with a view to ensuring their earliest successful conclusion;

8. *Welcomes*, since its previous resolution on the subject, the ratification of the Treaty by Ghana and Guinea as a significant step towards the early entry into force of the Treaty;

9. *Also welcomes* the recent expressions by a number of the remaining States whose ratification is needed for the Treaty to enter into force of their intention to pursue and complete the ratification process;

10. *Urges* all States to remain seized of the issue at the highest political level and, where in a position to do so, to promote adherence to the Treaty through bilateral and joint outreach, seminars and other means;

11. *Requests* the Secretary-General, in consultation with the Preparatory Commission for the Comprehensive Nuclear-Test-Ban Treaty Organization, to prepare a report on the efforts of States that have ratified the Treaty towards its universalization and possibilities for providing assistance on ratification procedures to States that so request it, and to submit such a report to the General Assembly at its sixty-seventh session;

12. *Decides* to include in the provisional agenda of its sixty-seventh session the item entitled "Comprehensive Nuclear-Test-Ban Treaty".

RECORDED VOTE ON RESOLUTION 66/64:

In favour: Afghanistan, Albania, Algeria, Andorra, Angola, Antigua and Barbuda, Argentina, Armenia, Australia, Austria, Azerbaijan, Bahamas, Bahrain, Bangladesh, Barbados, Belarus, Belgium, Belize, Benin, Bhutan, Bolivia, Bosnia and Herzegovina, Botswana, Brazil, Brunei Darussalam, Bulgaria, Burkina Faso, Cambodia, Cameroon, Canada, Chad, Chile, China, Colombia, Comoros, Congo, Costa Rica, Côte d'Ivoire, Croatia, Cuba, Cyprus, Czech Republic, Denmark, Djibouti, Dominican Republic, Ecuador, Egypt, El Salvador, Eritrea, Estonia, Ethiopia, Fiji, Finland, France, Georgia, Germany, Ghana, Greece, Grenada, Guatemala, Guinea, Guinea-Bissau, Guyana, Haiti, Honduras, Hungary, Iceland, Indonesia, Iran, Iraq, Ireland, Israel, Italy, Jamaica, Japan, Jordan, Kazakhstan, Kenya, Kuwait, Kyrgyzstan, Lao People's Democratic Republic, Latvia, Lebanon, Lesotho, Liberia, Libya, Liechtenstein, Lithuania, Luxembourg, Madagascar, Malawi, Malaysia, Maldives, Mali, Malta, Marshall Islands, Mauritania, Mexico, Micronesia, Monaco, Mongolia, Montenegro, Morocco, Mozambique, Myanmar, Namibia, Nepal, Netherlands, New Zealand, Nicaragua, Niger, Nigeria, Norway, Oman, Pakistan, Palau, Panama, Papua New Guinea, Paraguay, Peru, Philippines, Poland, Portugal, Qatar, Republic of Korea, Republic of Moldova, Romania, Russian Federation, Saint Kitts and Nevis, Saint Lucia, Saint Vincent and the Grenadines, Samoa, San Marino, Sao Tome and Principe, Saudi Arabia, Senegal, Serbia, Seychelles, Sierra Leone, Singapore, Slovakia, Slovenia, Solomon Islands, South Africa, Spain, Sri Lanka, Sudan, Suriname, Swaziland, Sweden, Switzerland, Tajikistan, Thailand, the former Yugoslav Republic of Macedonia, Timor-Leste, Togo, Tonga, Trinidad and Tobago, Tunisia, Turkey, Turkmenistan, Tuvalu, Uganda, Ukraine, United Arab Emirates, United Kingdom, United Republic of Tanzania, United States, Uruguay, Uzbekistan, Venezuela, Viet Nam, Yemen, Zambia, Zimbabwe.

Against: Democratic People's Republic of Korea.

Abstaining: India, Mauritius, Syrian Arab Republic.

Also on 2 December [meeting 71], the Assembly, on the recommendation of the First Committee [A/66/412], adopted **resolution 66/40** by recorded vote (168-6-6) [agenda item 98 (*q*)].

Towards a nuclear-weapon-free world: accelerating the implementation of nuclear disarmament commitments

The General Assembly,

Recalling its resolution 65/59 of 8 December 2010,

Reiterating its grave concern at the danger to humanity posed by the possibility that nuclear weapons could be used, and recalling the expression of deep concern by the 2010 Review Conference of the Parties to the Treaty on the Non-Proliferation of Nuclear Weapons at the catastrophic humanitarian consequences of any use of nuclear weapons,

Reaffirming that nuclear disarmament and nuclear non-proliferation are mutually reinforcing processes requiring urgent irreversible progress on both fronts,

Recalling the decisions entitled "Strengthening the review process for the Treaty", "Principles and objectives for nuclear non-proliferation and disarmament" and "Extension of the Treaty on the Non-Proliferation of Nuclear Weapons" and the resolution on the Middle East, all of which were adopted at the 1995 Review and Extension Conference of the Parties to the Treaty on the Non-Proliferation of Nuclear Weapons, and the Final Document of the 2000 and the 2010 Review Conference of the Parties to the Treaty on the Non-Proliferation of Nuclear Weapons,

Recalling in particular the unequivocal undertaking by the nuclear-weapon States to accomplish the total elimination of their nuclear arsenals, leading to nuclear disarmament, in accordance with commitments made under article VI of the Treaty on the Non-Proliferation of Nuclear Weapons, and reaffirmed by the 2010 Review Conference,

Reaffirming the commitment of all States parties to the Treaty on the Non-Proliferation of Nuclear Weapons to apply the principles of irreversibility, verifiability and transparency in relation to the implementation of their treaty obligations,

Recognizing the continued vital importance of the entry into force of the Comprehensive Nuclear-Test-Ban Treaty to the advancement of nuclear disarmament and nuclear non-proliferation objectives, and welcoming the recent ratifications of the Treaty by Ghana and Guinea,

Reaffirming the conviction that the establishment of nuclear-weapon-free zones enhances global and regional peace and security, strengthens the nuclear non-proliferation regime and contributes towards realizing the objectives of nuclear disarmament,

Recalling that the 2010 Review Conference encouraged the establishment of further nuclear-weapon-free zones, on the basis of arrangements freely arrived at among the States of the region concerned, and expressing the hope that this will be followed by concerted international efforts to create such zones in areas where they do not currently exist, especially in the Middle East,

Noting with satisfaction the agreement at the 2010 Review Conference on practical steps to fully implement the 1995 resolution on the Middle East,

Recognizing positive developments in the context of nuclear-weapon-free zones, notably the ratification by the Russian Federation of Protocols I and II to the Treaty of Pelindaba, the submission by the United States of America to the United States Senate for advice and consent of the Protocols to the Treaty of Pelindaba and the Treaty of Rarotonga, the consultations between the Association of Southeast Asian Nations and nuclear-weapon States on the Protocol to the Treaty of Bangkok, and the holding of the second Conference of States Parties and Signatories to Treaties that Establish Nuclear-Weapon-Free Zones and Mongolia, in New York on 30 April 2010,

Welcoming the entry into force of the Treaty between the Russian Federation and the United States of America on Measures for the Further Reduction and Limitation of

Strategic Offensive Arms, while recalling the encouragement of the 2010 Review Conference to both States to continue discussions on follow-on measures in order to achieve deeper reductions in their nuclear arsenals,

Recalling that the 2010 Review Conference reaffirmed and recognized that the total elimination of nuclear weapons is the only absolute guarantee against the use or threat of use of nuclear weapons and the legitimate interest of non-nuclear-weapon States in receiving unequivocal and legally binding security assurances from nuclear-weapon States,

Deeply disappointed at the absence of progress towards multilateral negotiations on nuclear disarmament issues, including in the Conference on Disarmament, and underlining the importance of multilateralism in relation to nuclear disarmament, while recognizing the value also of bilateral and regional initiatives,

Mindful that the first meeting of the preparatory process for the 2015 Review Conference of the Parties to the Treaty on the Non-Proliferation of Nuclear Weapons, to take place in May 2012, will begin to lay the groundwork for monitoring the fulfilment by all States parties of their commitments in the 2010 Review Conference action plan, including those by the nuclear-weapon States to accelerate concrete progress on the steps leading to nuclear disarmament,

1. *Reiterates* that each article of the Treaty on the Non-Proliferation of Nuclear Weapons is binding on the States parties at all times and in all circumstances and that all States parties should be held fully accountable with respect to strict compliance with their obligations under the Treaty, and calls upon all States to comply fully with all decisions, resolutions and other commitments made at Review Conferences;

2. *Welcomes* the adoption by the 2010 Review Conference of the Parties to the Treaty on the Non-Proliferation of Nuclear Weapons of a substantive final document containing conclusions and recommendations for follow-on actions relating to nuclear disarmament, including concrete steps for the total elimination of nuclear weapons, nuclear non-proliferation, peaceful uses of nuclear energy and the Middle East, particularly implementation of the 1995 resolution on the Middle East;

3. *Also welcomes*, in particular, the resolve of the 2010 Review Conference to seek a safer world for all and to achieve the peace and security of a world without nuclear weapons, in accordance with the objectives of the Treaty on the Non-Proliferation of Nuclear Weapons;

4. *Further welcomes* the expression by the 2010 Review Conference of deep concern at the catastrophic humanitarian consequences of any use of nuclear weapons, and its reaffirmation of the need for all States at all times to comply with applicable international law, including international humanitarian law;

5. *Welcomes* the reaffirmation of the continued validity of the practical steps agreed to in the Final Document of the 2000 Review Conference of the Parties to the Treaty on the Non-Proliferation of Nuclear Weapons, including the specific reaffirmation of the unequivocal undertaking of the nuclear-weapon States to accomplish the total elimination of their nuclear arsenals leading to nuclear disarmament, to which all States parties are committed under article VI of the Treaty;

6. *Recalls* the commitment by the nuclear-weapon States to undertake further efforts to reduce and ultimately eliminate all types of nuclear weapons, deployed and non-deployed, including through unilateral, bilateral, regional and multilateral measures, underlines the recognition by the 2010 Review Conference of the legitimate interests of non-nuclear-weapon States in nuclear-weapon States constraining their development and qualitative improvement of nuclear weapons and ending their development of advanced new types of nuclear weapons, and calls upon the nuclear-weapon States to take steps in this regard;

7. *Encourages* further steps by all nuclear-weapon States, in accordance with the action plan on nuclear disarmament of the Final Document of the 2010 Review Conference, to ensure the irreversible removal of all fissile material designated by each nuclear-weapon State as no longer required for military purposes and to support the development of appropriate verification capabilities related to nuclear disarmament;

8. *Calls upon* all States parties to the Treaty on the Non-Proliferation of Nuclear Weapons to work towards the full implementation of the resolution on the Middle East adopted at the 1995 Review and Extension Conference of the Parties to the Treaty on the Non-Proliferation of Nuclear Weapons, recognizes the endorsement by the 2010 Review Conference of practical steps in a process leading to the full implementation of the 1995 resolution, including the convening of a conference in 2012, to be attended by all States of the region, on the establishment of a Middle East zone free of nuclear weapons and all other weapons of mass destruction, calls upon the Secretary-General and the co-sponsors of the 1995 resolution, in close consultation and cooperation with the States of the region, to undertake all necessary preparations for the convening of the 2012 conference, and in this regard welcomes the recent appointment of a facilitator and designation of a host Government;

9. *Continues to emphasize* the fundamental role of the Treaty on the Non-Proliferation of Nuclear Weapons in achieving nuclear disarmament and nuclear non-proliferation and calls upon all States parties to spare no effort to achieve the universality of the Treaty, and in this regard urges India, Israel and Pakistan to accede to the Treaty as non-nuclear-weapon States promptly and without conditions;

10. *Urges* the Democratic People's Republic of Korea to fulfil the commitments under the Six-Party Talks, including those in the September 2005 joint statement, to abandon all nuclear weapons and existing nuclear programmes and to return, at an early date, to the Treaty on the Non-Proliferation of Nuclear Weapons and to its adherence to the International Atomic Energy Agency safeguards agreement, with a view to achieving the denuclearization of the Korean Peninsula in a peaceful manner, and reaffirms its firm support for the Six-Party Talks;

11. *Encourages* all States to work together to overcome obstacles within the international disarmament machinery, including in the Conference on Disarmament, that are inhibiting efforts to advance the cause of nuclear disarmament in a multilateral context;

12. *Stresses*, while noting that the nuclear-weapon States met in Paris on 30 June and 1 July 2011 to consider progress on the commitments they made at the 2010

Review Conference, the importance of the fulfilment of the commitments made by the nuclear-weapon States at the 2010 Review Conference to accelerate concrete progress on the steps leading to nuclear disarmament contained in the Final Document of the 2000 Review Conference and of their prompt engagement to ensure substantial progress in advance of the 2015 Review Conference of the Parties to the Treaty on the Non-Proliferation of Nuclear Weapons;

13. *Recalls* that the commitment of the nuclear-weapon States to accelerate concrete progress on the steps leading to nuclear disarmament as envisaged in action 5 of the 2010 Review Conference action plan is:

(*a*) To rapidly move towards an overall reduction in the global stockpile of all types of nuclear weapons, as identified in action 3 of the action plan;

(*b*) To address the question of all nuclear weapons regardless of their type or their location as an integral part of the general nuclear disarmament process;

(*c*) To further diminish the role and significance of nuclear weapons in all military and security concepts, doctrines and policies;

(*d*) To discuss policies that could prevent the use of nuclear weapons and eventually lead to their elimination, lessen the danger of nuclear war and contribute to the non-proliferation and disarmament of nuclear weapons;

(*e*) To consider the legitimate interest of non-nuclear-weapon States in further reducing the operational status of nuclear-weapons systems in ways that promote international stability and security;

(*f*) To reduce the risk of accidental use of nuclear weapons;

(*g*) To further enhance transparency and mutual confidence;

14. *Calls upon* the nuclear-weapon States to implement these commitments in a manner that enables the States parties to monitor them regularly during each review cycle, and in this regard urges those States to report regularly on the implementation of the commitments;

15. *Welcomes* the announcements made by some nuclear-weapon States providing information about their nuclear arsenals, policies and disarmament efforts, urges those nuclear-weapon States that have not yet done so also to provide this information, and encourages the nuclear-weapon States to agree as soon as possible on a standard reporting format to facilitate this reporting;

16. *Calls upon* the nuclear-weapon States, in this regard and in reference to the outcome of the 2010 Review Conference, to regularly report on their efforts, including as part of any review of nuclear policies, to diminish the role and significance of nuclear weapons in all military and security concepts;

17. *Calls upon* all States parties to the Treaty on the Non-Proliferation of Nuclear Weapons to implement all elements of the 2010 Review Conference action plan in a faithful and timely manner so that progress across all of the pillars of the Treaty can be realized;

18. *Decides* to include in the provisional agenda of its sixty-seventh session the item entitled "Towards a nuclear-weapon-free world: accelerating the implementation of nuclear disarmament commitments" and to review the implementation of the present resolution at that session.

RECORDED VOTE ON RESOLUTION 66/40:

In favour: Afghanistan, Albania, Algeria, Andorra, Angola, Antigua and Barbuda, Argentina, Armenia, Australia, Austria, Azerbaijan, Bahamas, Bahrain, Bangladesh, Barbados, Belarus, Belgium, Belize, Benin, Bolivia, Bosnia and Herzegovina, Botswana, Brazil, Brunei Darussalam, Bulgaria, Burkina Faso, Cambodia, Cameroon, Canada, Cape Verde, Chad, Chile, Colombia, Comoros, Congo, Costa Rica, Côte d'Ivoire, Croatia, Cuba, Cyprus, Czech Republic, Denmark, Djibouti, Dominican Republic, Ecuador, Egypt, El Salvador, Eritrea, Estonia, Ethiopia, Fiji, Finland, Gabon, Georgia, Germany, Ghana, Grenada, Guatemala, Guinea, Guinea-Bissau, Guyana, Haiti, Honduras, Hungary, Iceland, Indonesia, Iran, Iraq, Ireland, Italy, Jamaica, Japan, Jordan, Kazakhstan, Kenya, Kuwait, Kyrgyzstan, Lao People's Democratic Republic, Latvia, Lebanon, Lesotho, Liberia, Libya, Liechtenstein, Lithuania, Luxembourg, Madagascar, Malawi, Malaysia, Maldives, Mali, Malta, Marshall Islands, Mauritania, Mauritius, Mexico, Mongolia, Montenegro, Morocco, Mozambique, Myanmar, Namibia, Nepal, Netherlands, New Zealand, Nicaragua, Niger, Nigeria, Norway, Oman, Panama, Papua New Guinea, Paraguay, Peru, Philippines, Poland, Portugal, Qatar, Republic of Korea, Republic of Moldova, Romania, Saint Kitts and Nevis, Saint Lucia, Saint Vincent and the Grenadines, Samoa, San Marino, Sao Tome and Principe, Saudi Arabia, Senegal, Serbia, Seychelles, Sierra Leone, Singapore, Slovakia, Slovenia, Solomon Islands, South Africa, Spain, Sri Lanka, Sudan, Suriname, Swaziland, Sweden, Switzerland, Syrian Arab Republic, Tajikistan, Thailand, the former Yugoslav Republic of Macedonia, Timor-Leste, Togo, Tonga, Trinidad and Tobago, Tunisia, Turkey, Turkmenistan, Tuvalu, Uganda, Ukraine, United Arab Emirates, United Republic of Tanzania, Uruguay, Uzbekistan, Vanuatu, Venezuela, Viet Nam, Yemen, Zambia, Zimbabwe.

Against: Democratic People's Republic of Korea, France, India, Israel, United Kingdom, United States.

Abstaining: Bhutan, China, Micronesia, Pakistan, Palau, Russian Federation.

Preparatory Commission for the CTBT Organization

In advance of the entry into force of the Comprehensive Nuclear-Test Ban Treaty and the establishment of the Commission for the Comprehensive Nuclear-Test-Ban Treaty Organization (CTBTO), a Preparatory Commission was established by the signatory States in 1996 [YUN 1996, p. 452]. In 2011, the Commission built on its efforts to promote the Treaty and expand the capabilities of its verification regime, and continued to develop the Treaty's verification regime. Further progress was made in expanding the coverage and data availability in all International Monitoring System (IMS) [YUN 1999, p. 472] technologies. The number of certified IMS stations and radionuclide laboratories reached 270, representing 80 per cent of the total foreseen by the Treaty. The Fukushima nuclear accident in Japan on 11 March presented an unexpected challenge for the Commission; and it responded by processing data collected from its IMS facilities into relevant products for States signatories and international organizations.

The Commission held its thirty-sixth (14–15 June) [CTBT/PC-36/2] and thirty-seventh (24 October) [CTBT/PC-37/2] sessions in Vienna to consider the reports of its working groups and to discuss organizational, budgetary and other matters.

Note by Secretary-General. In July [A/66/165], the Secretary-General transmitted to the General Assembly the report of the Executive Secretary of the Commission for 2010, pursuant to article IV, paragraph 1, of the Agreement to Regulate the Relationship between the United Nations and the Preparatory Commission for CTBTO, annexed to General Assembly resolution 54/280 [YUN 2000, p. 501].

Advisory opinion of the International Court of Justice

Pursuant to General Assembly resolution 65/76 [YUN 2010, p. 529] relating to the advisory opinion of the International Court of Justice that the threat of use of nuclear weapons was contrary to the UN Charter [YUN 1999, p. 461], the Secretary-General, in July [A/66/132 & Add.1], presented information from 11 Member States (Cuba, Guyana, Iraq, Jamaica, Japan, Kazakhstan, Lebanon, Mexico, Portugal, Turkmenistan, Venezuela) on measures they had taken to implement the resolution and towards nuclear disarmament.

GENERAL ASSEMBLY ACTION

On 2 December [meeting 71], the General Assembly, on the recommendation of the First Committee [A/66/412], adopted **resolution 66/46** by recorded vote (130-26-23) [agenda item 98 (*x*)].

Follow-up to the advisory opinion of the International Court of Justice on the *Legality of the Threat or Use of Nuclear Weapons*

The General Assembly,

Recalling its resolutions 49/75 K of 15 December 1994, 51/45 M of 10 December 1996, 52/38 O of 9 December 1997, 53/77 W of 4 December 1998, 54/54 Q of 1 December 1999, 55/33 X of 20 November 2000, 56/24 S of 29 November 2001, 57/85 of 22 November 2002, 58/46 of 8 December 2003, 59/83 of 3 December 2004, 60/76 of 8 December 2005, 61/83 of 6 December 2006, 62/39 of 5 December 2007, 63/49 of 2 December 2008, 64/55 of 2 December 2009 and 65/76 of 8 December 2010,

Convinced that the continuing existence of nuclear weapons poses a threat to humanity and all life on Earth, and recognizing that the only defence against a nuclear catastrophe is the total elimination of nuclear weapons and the certainty that they will never be produced again,

Reaffirming the commitment of the international community to the realization of the goal of a nuclear-weapon-free world through the total elimination of nuclear weapons,

Mindful of the solemn obligations of States parties, undertaken in article VI of the Treaty on the Non-Proliferation of Nuclear Weapons, particularly to pursue negotiations in good faith on effective measures relating to cessation of the nuclear arms race at an early date and to nuclear disarmament,

Recalling the principles and objectives for nuclear non-proliferation and disarmament adopted at the 1995 Review and Extension Conference of the Parties to the Treaty on the Non-Proliferation of Nuclear Weapons, the unequivocal commitment of nuclear-weapon States to accomplish the total elimination of their nuclear arsenals leading to nuclear disarmament, agreed at the 2000 Review Conference of the Parties to the Treaty on the Non-Proliferation of Nuclear Weapons, and the action points agreed at the 2010 Review Conference of the Parties to the Treaty on the Non-Proliferation of Nuclear Weapons as part of the conclusions and recommendations for follow-on actions on nuclear disarmament,

Sharing the deep concern at the catastrophic humanitarian consequences of any use of nuclear weapons, and in this context reaffirming the need for all States at all times to comply with applicable international law, including international humanitarian law,

Calling upon all nuclear-weapon States to undertake concrete disarmament efforts, and stressing that all States need to make special efforts to achieve and maintain a world without nuclear weapons,

Noting the five-point proposal for nuclear disarmament of the Secretary-General, in which he proposes, inter alia, the consideration of negotiations on a nuclear weapons convention or agreement on a framework of separate mutually reinforcing instruments, backed by a strong system of verification,

Recalling the adoption of the Comprehensive Nuclear-Test-Ban Treaty in its resolution 50/245 of 10 September 1996, and expressing its satisfaction at the increasing number of States that have signed and ratified the Treaty,

Recognizing with satisfaction that the Antarctic Treaty, the treaties of Tlatelolco, Rarotonga, Bangkok and Pelindaba and the Treaty on a Nuclear-Weapon-Free Zone in Central Asia, as well as Mongolia's nuclear-weapon-free status, are gradually freeing the entire southern hemisphere and adjacent areas covered by those treaties from nuclear weapons,

Recognizing the need for a multilaterally negotiated and legally binding instrument to assure non-nuclear-weapon States against the threat or use of nuclear weapons pending the total elimination of nuclear weapons,

Reaffirming the central role of the Conference on Disarmament as the sole multilateral disarmament negotiating forum,

Emphasizing the need for the Conference on Disarmament to commence negotiations on a phased programme for the complete elimination of nuclear weapons with a specified framework of time,

Stressing the urgent need for the nuclear-weapon States to accelerate concrete progress on the thirteen practical steps to implement article VI of the Treaty on the Non-Proliferation of Nuclear Weapons leading to nuclear disarmament, contained in the Final Document of the 2000 Review Conference,

Taking note of the Model Nuclear Weapons Convention that was submitted to the Secretary-General by Costa Rica and Malaysia in 2007 and circulated by the Secretary-General,

Desiring to achieve the objective of a legally binding prohibition of the development, production, testing, deployment, stockpiling, threat or use of nuclear weapons and their destruction under effective international control,

Recalling the advisory opinion of the International Court of Justice on the *Legality of the Threat or Use of Nuclear Weapons*, issued on 8 July 1996,

1. *Underlines once again* the unanimous conclusion of the International Court of Justice that there exists an obligation to pursue in good faith and bring to a conclusion negotiations leading to nuclear disarmament in all its aspects under strict and effective international control;

2. *Calls once again upon* all States immediately to fulfil that obligation by commencing multilateral negotiations leading to an early conclusion of a nuclear weapons convention prohibiting the development, production, testing, deployment, stockpiling, transfer, threat or use of nuclear weapons and providing for their elimination;

3. *Requests* all States to inform the Secretary-General of the efforts and measures they have taken with respect to the implementation of the present resolution and nuclear disarmament, and requests the Secretary-General to apprise the General Assembly of that information at its sixty-seventh session;

4. *Decides* to include in the provisional agenda of its sixty-seventh session the item entitled "Follow-up to the advisory opinion of the International Court of Justice on the *Legality of the Threat or Use of Nuclear Weapons*".

RECORDED VOTE ON RESOLUTION 66/46:

In favour: Afghanistan, Algeria, Angola, Antigua and Barbuda, Argentina, Austria, Azerbaijan, Bahamas, Bahrain, Bangladesh, Barbados, Belize, Benin, Bhutan, Bolivia, Bosnia and Herzegovina, Botswana, Brazil, Brunei Darussalam, Burkina Faso, Cambodia, Cape Verde, Chad, Chile, China, Colombia, Comoros, Congo, Costa Rica, Côte d'Ivoire, Cuba, Democratic People's Republic of Korea, Djibouti, Dominican Republic, Ecuador, Egypt, El Salvador, Eritrea, Ethiopia, Fiji, Ghana, Grenada, Guatemala, Guinea, Guinea-Bissau, Guyana, Haiti, Honduras, India, Indonesia, Iran, Iraq, Ireland, Jamaica, Jordan, Kazakhstan, Kenya, Kuwait, Lao People's Democratic Republic, Lebanon, Lesotho, Liberia, Libya, Madagascar, Malawi, Malaysia, Maldives, Mali, Malta, Mauritania, Mauritius, Mexico, Mongolia, Morocco, Mozambique, Myanmar, Namibia, Nepal, New Zealand, Nicaragua, Niger, Nigeria, Oman, Pakistan, Panama, Papua New Guinea, Paraguay, Peru, Philippines, Qatar, Saint Kitts and Nevis, Saint Lucia, Saint Vincent and the Grenadines, Samoa, San Marino, Sao Tome and Principe, Saudi Arabia, Senegal, Serbia, Seychelles, Sierra Leone, Singapore, Solomon Islands, South Africa, Sri Lanka, Sudan, Suriname, Swaziland, Sweden, Switzerland, Syrian Arab Republic, Thailand, Timor-Leste, Togo, Tonga, Trinidad and Tobago, Tunisia, Turkmenistan, Tuvalu, Uganda, Ukraine, United Arab Emirates, United Republic of Tanzania, Uruguay, Vanuatu, Venezuela, Viet Nam, Yemen, Zambia, Zimbabwe.

Against: Albania, Belgium, Bulgaria, Czech Republic, Denmark, Estonia, France, Germany, Greece, Hungary, Israel, Italy, Latvia, Lithuania, Luxembourg, Netherlands, Palau, Poland, Portugal, Russian Federation, Slovakia, Slovenia, Spain, Turkey, United Kingdom, United States.

Abstaining: Andorra, Armenia, Australia, Belarus, Canada, Croatia, Cyprus, Finland, Georgia, Iceland, Japan, Kyrgyzstan, Liechtenstein, Marshall Islands, Micronesia, Montenegro, Norway, Republic of Korea, Republic of Moldova, Romania, Tajikistan, the former Yugoslav Republic of Macedonia, Uzbekistan.

Prohibition of the use of nuclear weapons

In 2011, no progress was made on a convention on the prohibition of the use of nuclear weapons, as the Conference on Disarmament was unable to undertake negotiations on the subject as called for in General Assembly resolution 65/80 [YUN 2010, p. 530]. The Assembly reiterated its request to the Conference to commence negotiations.

GENERAL ASSEMBLY ACTION

On 2 December [meeting 71], the General Assembly, on the recommendation of the First Committee [A/66/413], adopted **resolution 66/57** by recorded vote (117-48-12) [agenda item 99 (*d*)].

Convention on the Prohibition of the Use of Nuclear Weapons

The General Assembly,

Convinced that the use of nuclear weapons poses the most serious threat to the survival of mankind,

Bearing in mind the advisory opinion of the International Court of Justice of 8 July 1996 on the *Legality of the Threat or Use of Nuclear Weapons*,

Convinced that a multilateral, universal and binding agreement prohibiting the use or threat of use of nuclear weapons would contribute to the elimination of the nuclear threat and to the climate for negotiations leading to the ultimate elimination of nuclear weapons, thereby strengthening international peace and security,

Conscious that some steps taken by the Russian Federation and the United States of America towards a reduction of their nuclear weapons and the improvement in the international climate can contribute towards the goal of the complete elimination of nuclear weapons,

Recalling that paragraph 58 of the Final Document of the Tenth Special Session of the General Assembly states that all States should actively participate in efforts to bring about conditions in international relations among States in which a code of peaceful conduct of nations in international affairs could be agreed upon and that would preclude the use or threat of use of nuclear weapons,

Reaffirming that any use of nuclear weapons would be a violation of the Charter of the United Nations and a crime against humanity, as declared in its resolutions 1653(XVI) of 24 November 1961, 33/71 B of 14 December 1978, 34/83 G of 11 December 1979, 35/152 D of 12 December 1980 and 36/92 I of 9 December 1981,

Determined to achieve an international convention prohibiting the development, production, stockpiling and use of nuclear weapons, leading to their ultimate destruction,

Stressing that an international convention on the prohibition of the use of nuclear weapons would be an important step in a phased programme towards the complete elimination of nuclear weapons, with a specified framework of time,

Noting with regret that the Conference on Disarmament, during its 2011 session, was unable to undertake negotiations on this subject as called for in General Assembly resolution 65/80 of 8 December 2010,

1. *Reiterates its request* to the Conference on Disarmament to commence negotiations in order to reach agreement on an international convention prohibiting the use or threat of use of nuclear weapons under any circumstances;

2. *Requests* the Conference on Disarmament to report to the General Assembly on the results of those negotiations.

RECORDED VOTE ON RESOLUTION 66/57:

In favour: Afghanistan, Algeria, Angola, Antigua and Barbuda, Argentina, Azerbaijan, Bahamas, Bahrain, Bangladesh, Barbados, Belize, Benin, Bhutan, Bolivia, Botswana, Brazil, Brunei Darussalam, Burkina Faso, Cambodia, Cameroon, Cape Verde, Chad, Chile, China, Colombia, Comoros, Congo, Costa Rica, Côte d'Ivoire, Cuba, Democratic People's Republic of Korea, Djibouti, Dominican Republic, Ecuador, Egypt, Eritrea, Ethiopia, Fiji, Ghana, Grenada, Guatemala, Guinea, Guinea-Bissau, Guyana, Haiti, Honduras, India, Indonesia, Iran, Iraq, Jamaica, Jordan, Kazakhstan, Kenya, Kuwait, Lao People's Democratic Republic, Lebanon, Lesotho, Liberia, Libya, Madagascar, Malawi, Malaysia, Maldives, Mali, Mauritania, Mauritius, Mexico, Mongolia, Morocco, Mozambique, Myanmar, Namibia, Nepal, Nicaragua, Niger, Nigeria, Oman, Pakistan, Panama, Papua New Guinea, Paraguay, Peru, Philippines, Qatar, Saint Kitts and Nevis, Saint Lucia, Saint Vincent and the Grenadines, Samoa, Sao Tome and Principe, Saudi Arabia, Senegal, Seychelles, Sierra Leone, Singapore, Solomon Islands, South Africa, Sri Lanka, Sudan, Suriname, Swaziland, Syrian Arab Republic, Thailand, Togo, Tonga, Trinidad and Tobago, Tunisia, Turkmenistan, Uganda, United Arab Emirates, United Republic of Tanzania, Uruguay, Venezuela, Viet Nam, Yemen, Zambia, Zimbabwe.

Against: Albania, Andorra, Australia, Austria, Belgium, Bosnia and Herzegovina, Bulgaria, Canada, Croatia, Cyprus, Czech Republic, Denmark, Estonia, Finland, France, Germany, Greece, Hungary, Iceland, Ireland, Israel, Italy, Latvia, Liechtenstein, Lithuania, Luxembourg, Malta, Micronesia, Monaco, Netherlands, New Zealand, Norway, Palau, Poland, Portugal, Republic of Moldova, Romania, San Marino, Slovakia, Slovenia, Spain, Sweden, Switzerland, the former Yugoslav Republic of Macedonia, Turkey, Ukraine, United Kingdom, United States.

Abstaining: Armenia, Belarus, El Salvador, Georgia, Japan, Kyrgyzstan, Marshall Islands, Republic of Korea, Russian Federation, Serbia, Tajikistan, Uzbekistan.

Non-proliferation

Non-proliferation treaty

Status

In 2011, the number of States parties to the Treaty on the Non-Proliferation of Nuclear Weapons (NPT) stood at 190. Regarded as the cornerstone of the global nuclear non-proliferation regime, the Treaty was adopted by the General Assembly in 1968 by resolution 2373(XXIII) [YUN 1968, p. 16], and entered into force in 1970. It was extended indefinitely in 1995 by Assembly resolution 50/70 [YUN 1995, p. 189].

Follow-up to 2010 review conference

During the year, States undertook additional actions to implement the commitments agreed to at the 2010 Review Conference of the Parties to the Treaty on the Non-Proliferation of Nuclear Weapons [YUN 2010, p. 531]. On 5 February, the Treaty between the Russian Federation and the United States of America on Measures for Further Reduction and Limitation of Strategic Offensive Arms [ibid., p. 505] entered into force. Nuclear-weapon States met (Paris, 30 June–1 July) to discuss the implementation of the action plan agreed to at the 2010 NPT Review Conference, with a view to elaborating a standard form for reporting information on their nuclear arsenals.

Other States continued to step up efforts to implement the commitments agreed to at the Conference and to advance the broader nuclear disarmament and non-proliferation agenda. The 10-nation Disarmament and Non-Proliferation Initiative continued its engagement, including at the ministerial level, to expedite NPT implementation. From February to July, Kazakhstan convened the Nuclear Discussion Forum in New York to engage in an in-depth discourse on nuclear non-proliferation, disarmament and security issues. Following the Secretary-General's 2008 five-point proposal for nuclear disarmament [YUN 2008, p. 565], a group of countries, led by Uruguay, continued to explore ways to elaborate a road map for the complete elimination of nuclear weapons, including by means of a universal legal instrument.

GENERAL ASSEMBLY ACTION

On 2 December [meeting 71], the General Assembly, on the recommendation of the First Committee [A/66/412], adopted **resolution 66/28** by recorded vote (118-52-6) [agenda item 98 (*b*)].

Follow-up to nuclear disarmament obligations agreed to at the 1995, 2000 and 2010 Review Conferences of the Parties to the Treaty on the Non-proliferation of Nuclear Weapons

The General Assembly,

Recalling its various resolutions in the field of nuclear disarmament, including its recent resolutions 64/31 of 2 December 2009 and 65/56, 65/76 and 65/80 of 8 December 2010,

Bearing in mind its resolution 2373(XXII) of 12 June 1968, the annex to which contains the Treaty on the Non-Proliferation of Nuclear Weapons,

Noting the provisions of article VIII, paragraph 3, of the Treaty regarding the convening of review conferences at five-year intervals,

Recalling its resolution 50/70 Q of 12 December 1995, in which the General Assembly noted that the States parties to the Treaty affirmed the need to continue to move with determination towards the full realization and effective implementation of the provisions of the Treaty, and accordingly adopted a set of principles and objectives,

Recalling also that, on 11 May 1995, the 1995 Review and Extension Conference of the Parties to the Treaty on the Non-Proliferation of Nuclear Weapons adopted three decisions on, respectively, strengthening the review process for the Treaty, principles and objectives for nuclear non-proliferation and disarmament, and extension of the Treaty,

Reaffirming the resolution on the Middle East adopted on 11 May 1995 by the 1995 Review and Extension Conference, in which the Conference reaffirmed the importance of the early realization of universal adherence to the Treaty and placement of nuclear facilities under full-scope International Atomic Energy Agency safeguards,

Reaffirming also its resolution 55/33 D of 20 November 2000, in which the General Assembly welcomed the adoption by consensus on 19 May 2000 of the Final Document of the 2000 Review Conference of the Parties to the Treaty on the Non-Proliferation of Nuclear Weapons, including, in particular, the documents entitled "Review of the operation of the Treaty, taking into account the decisions and the resolution adopted by the 1995 Review and Extension Conference" and "Improving the effectiveness of the strengthened review process for the Treaty",

Taking into consideration the unequivocal undertaking by the nuclear-weapon States, in the Final Document of the 2000 Review Conference, to accomplish the total elimination of their nuclear arsenals leading to nuclear disarmament, to which all States parties to the Treaty are committed under article VI of the Treaty,

Welcoming the adoption by the 2010 Review Conference of the Parties to the Treaty on the Non-Proliferation of Nuclear Weapons of a substantive Final Document containing conclusions and recommendations for follow-on actions relating to nuclear disarmament,

1. *Recalls* that the 2010 Review Conference of the Parties to the Treaty on the Non-Proliferation of Nuclear Weapons reaffirmed the continued validity of the practical steps agreed to in the Final Document of the 2000 Review Conference of the Parties to the Treaty on the Non-Proliferation of Nuclear Weapons;

2. *Determines* to pursue practical steps for systematic and progressive efforts to implement article VI of the Treaty on the Non-Proliferation of Nuclear Weapons and paragraphs 3 and 4 (*c*) of the decision on principles and objectives for nuclear non-proliferation and disarmament of the 1995 Review and Extension Conference of the Parties to the Treaty on the Non-Proliferation of Nuclear Weapons;

3. *Calls for* practical steps, as agreed to at the 2000 Review Conference of the Parties to the Treaty on the Non-Proliferation of Nuclear Weapons, to be taken by all nuclear-weapon States, which would lead to nuclear disarmament in a way that promotes international stability and, based on the principle of undiminished security for all:

(*a*) Further efforts to be made by the nuclear-weapon States to reduce their nuclear arsenals unilaterally;

(*b*) Increased transparency by the nuclear-weapon States with regard to nuclear weapons capabilities and the implementation of agreements pursuant to article VI of the Treaty and as a voluntary confidence-building measure to support further progress in nuclear disarmament;

(*c*) The further reduction of non-strategic nuclear weapons, based on unilateral initiatives and as an integral part of the nuclear arms reduction and disarmament process;

(*d*) Concrete agreed measures to reduce further the operational status of nuclear weapons systems;

(*e*) A diminishing role for nuclear weapons in security policies so as to minimize the risk that these weapons will ever be used and to facilitate the process of their total elimination;

(*f*) The engagement, as soon as appropriate, of all the nuclear-weapon States in the process leading to the total elimination of their nuclear weapons;

4. *Notes* that the 2000 and 2010 Review Conferences agreed that legally binding security assurances by the five nuclear-weapon States to the non-nuclear-weapon States parties to the Treaty strengthen the nuclear non-proliferation regime;

5. *Urges* the States parties to the Treaty to follow up on the implementation of the nuclear disarmament obligations under the Treaty agreed to at the 1995, 2000 and 2010 Review Conferences within the framework of review conferences and their preparatory committees;

6. *Decides* to include in the provisional agenda of its sixty-eighth session an item entitled "Follow-up to nuclear disarmament obligations agreed to at the 1995, 2000 and 2010 Review Conferences of the Parties to the Treaty on the Non-Proliferation of Nuclear Weapons".

RECORDED VOTE ON RESOLUTION 66/28:

In favour: Afghanistan, Algeria, Angola, Antigua and Barbuda, Argentina, Azerbaijan, Bahamas, Bahrain, Bangladesh, Barbados, Belarus, Belize, Benin, Bhutan, Bolivia, Botswana, Brazil, Brunei Darussalam, Burkina Faso, Cambodia, Cameroon, Cape Verde, Chad, Chile, Colombia, Comoros, Congo, Costa Rica, Côte d'Ivoire, Cuba, Democratic People's Republic of Korea, Djibouti, Dominican Republic, Ecuador, Egypt, El Salvador, Ethiopia, Fiji, Gabon, Ghana, Grenada, Guatemala, Guinea, Guinea-Bissau, Guyana, Haiti, Honduras, Indonesia, Iran, Iraq, Jamaica, Jordan, Kazakhstan, Kenya, Kuwait, Kyrgyzstan, Lao People's Democratic Republic, Lebanon, Lesotho, Liberia, Libya, Madagascar, Malawi, Malaysia, Maldives, Mali, Marshall Islands, Mauritania, Mauritius, Mexico, Mongolia, Morocco, Mozambique, Myanmar, Namibia, Nepal, Nicaragua, Niger, Nigeria, Oman, Papua New Guinea, Paraguay, Peru, Philippines, Qatar, Saint Kitts and Nevis, Saint Lucia, Saint Vincent and the Grenadines, Sao Tome and Principe, Saudi Arabia, Senegal, Seychelles, Sierra Leone, Singapore, Solomon Islands, South Africa, Sri Lanka, Sudan, Suriname, Swaziland, Syrian Arab Republic, Tajikistan, Thailand, Togo, Tunisia, Turkmenistan, Uganda, Ukraine, United Arab Emirates, United Republic of Tanzania, Uruguay, Uzbekistan, Vanuatu, Venezuela, Viet Nam, Yemen, Zambia, Zimbabwe.

Against: Albania, Andorra, Australia, Austria, Belgium, Bosnia and Herzegovina, Bulgaria, Canada, Croatia, Cyprus, Czech Republic, Denmark, Estonia, Finland, France, Germany, Greece, Hungary, Iceland, Ireland, Israel, Italy, Japan, Latvia, Liechtenstein, Lithuania, Luxembourg, Malta, Micronesia, Monaco, Montenegro, Netherlands, New Zealand, Norway, Palau, Panama, Poland, Portugal, Republic of Korea, Republic of Moldova, Romania, Russian Federation, San Marino, Serbia, Slovakia, Slovenia, Spain, Sweden, Switzerland, the former Yugoslav Republic of Macedonia, United Kingdom, United States.

Abstaining: Armenia, China, India, Pakistan, Samoa, Tonga.

Also on 2 December [meeting 71], the Assembly, on the recommendation of the First Committee [A/66/412], adopted **resolution 66/33** by recorded vote (175-0-3) [agenda item 98].

2015 Review Conference of the Parties to the Treaty on the Non-Proliferation of Nuclear Weapons and its Preparatory Committee

The General Assembly,

Recalling its resolution 2373(XXII) of 12 June 1968, the annex to which contains the Treaty on the Non-Proliferation of Nuclear Weapons,

Noting the provisions of article VIII, paragraph 3, of the Treaty regarding the convening of review conferences at five-year intervals,

Recalling the outcomes of the 1995 Review and Extension Conference of the Parties to the Treaty on the Non-Proliferation of Nuclear Weapons and of the 2000 Review Conference of the Parties to the Treaty,

Recalling also the decision of the 2000 Review Conference of the Parties to the Treaty on improving the effectiveness of the strengthened review process for the Treaty, which reaffirmed the provisions in the decision on strengthening the review process for the Treaty, adopted by the 1995 Review and Extension Conference of the Parties to the Treaty,

Noting the decision on strengthening the review process for the Treaty, in which it was agreed that review conferences should continue to be held every five years, and noting that, accordingly, the next review conference should be held in 2015,

Recalling the decision of the 2000 Review Conference that three sessions of the Preparatory Committee should be held in the years prior to the review conference,

Welcoming the successful outcome of the 2010 Review Conference of the Parties to the Treaty on the Non-Proliferation of Nuclear Weapons, held from 3 to 28 May 2010, and reaffirming the necessity of fully implementing the follow-on actions adopted at the Review Conference,

1. *Takes note* of the decision of the parties to the Treaty on the Non-Proliferation of Nuclear Weapons, following appropriate consultations, to hold the first session of the Preparatory Committee in Vienna from 30 April to 11 May 2012;

2. *Requests* the Secretary-General to render the necessary assistance and to provide such services, including summary records, as may be required for the 2015 Review Conference of the Parties to the Treaty on the Non-Proliferation of Nuclear Weapons and its Preparatory Committee.

RECORDED VOTE ON RESOLUTION 66/33:

In favour: Afghanistan, Albania, Algeria, Andorra, Angola, Antigua and Barbuda, Argentina, Armenia, Australia, Austria, Azerbaijan, Bahamas, Bahrain, Bangladesh, Barbados, Belarus, Belgium, Belize, Benin, Bhutan, Bolivia, Bosnia and Herzegovina, Botswana, Brazil, Brunei Darussalam, Bulgaria, Burkina Faso, Cambodia, Cameroon, Canada, Cape Verde, Chad, Chile, China, Colombia, Comoros, Congo, Costa Rica, Côte d'Ivoire, Croatia, Cuba, Cyprus, Czech Republic, Denmark, Djibouti, Dominican Republic, Ecuador, Egypt, El Salvador, Estonia, Ethiopia, Fiji, Finland, France, Gabon, Georgia, Germany, Ghana, Greece, Grenada, Guatemala, Guinea, Guinea-Bissau, Guyana, Haiti, Honduras, Hungary, Iceland, Indonesia, Iran, Iraq, Ireland, Italy, Jamaica, Japan, Jordan, Kazakhstan, Kenya, Kuwait, Kyrgyzstan, Lao People's Democratic Republic, Latvia, Lebanon, Lesotho, Liberia, Libya, Liechtenstein, Lithuania, Luxembourg, Madagascar, Malawi, Malaysia, Maldives, Mali, Malta, Marshall Islands, Mauritania, Mauritius, Mexico, Micronesia, Monaco, Mongolia, Montenegro, Morocco, Mozambique, Myanmar, Namibia, Nepal, Netherlands, New Zealand, Nicaragua, Niger, Nigeria, Norway, Oman, Palau, Panama, Papua New Guinea, Paraguay, Peru, Philippines, Poland, Portugal, Qatar, Republic of Korea, Republic of Moldova, Romania, Russian Federation, Saint Kitts and Nevis, Saint Lucia, Saint Vincent and the Grenadines, Samoa, San Marino, Sao Tome and Principe, Saudi Arabia, Senegal, Serbia, Seychelles, Sierra Leone, Singapore, Slovakia, Slovenia, Solomon Islands, South Africa, Spain, Sri Lanka, Sudan, Suriname, Swaziland, Sweden, Switzerland, Syrian Arab Republic, Tajikistan, Thailand, the former Yugoslav Republic of Macedonia, Timor-Leste, Togo, Tonga, Tunisia, Turkey, Turkmenistan, Uganda, Ukraine, United Arab Emirates, United Kingdom, United Republic of Tanzania, United States, Uruguay, Uzbekistan, Vanuatu, Venezuela, Viet Nam, Yemen, Zambia, Zimbabwe.

Against: None.

Abstaining: India, Israel, Pakistan.

Also on 2 December [meeting 71], the General Assembly, on the recommendation of the First Committee [A/66/412], adopted **resolution 66/45** by recorded vote (169-1-11) [agenda item 98 (*w*)].

United action towards the total elimination of nuclear weapons

The General Assembly,

Recalling the need for all States to take further practical steps and effective measures towards the total elimination of nuclear weapons, with a view to achieving a peaceful and secure world free of nuclear weapons, and in this regard confirming the determination of Member States to take united action,

Noting that the ultimate objective of the efforts of States in the disarmament process is general and complete disarmament under strict and effective international control,

Recalling its resolution 65/72 of 8 December 2010,

Expressing deep concern at the catastrophic humanitarian consequences of any use of nuclear weapons, and reaffirming the need for all States at all times to comply with applicable international law, including international humanitarian law, while convinced that every effort should be made to avoid nuclear war and nuclear terrorism,

Reaffirming that the enhancement of international peace and security and the promotion of nuclear disarmament are mutually reinforcing,

Reaffirming also that further advancement in nuclear disarmament will contribute to consolidating the international regime for nuclear non-proliferation, which is, inter alia, essential to international peace and security,

Reaffirming further the crucial importance of the Treaty on the Non-Proliferation of Nuclear Weapons as the cornerstone of the international nuclear non-proliferation regime and an essential foundation for the pursuit of the Treaty's three pillars, namely nuclear disarmament, nuclear non-proliferation and the peaceful uses of nuclear energy,

Recalling the decisions and the resolution of the 1995 Review and Extension Conference of the Parties to the Treaty on the Non-Proliferation of Nuclear Weapons and the Final Document of the 2000 and 2010 Review Conferences of the Parties to the Treaty on the Non-Proliferation of Nuclear Weapons,

Welcoming the successful outcome of the 2010 Review Conference of the Parties to the Treaty on the Non-Proliferation of Nuclear Weapons, held from 3 to 28 May 2010, in the year of the sixty-fifth anniversary of the atomic bombings in Hiroshima and Nagasaki, Japan, and reaffirming the necessity of fully implementing the action plan adopted at the Review Conference,

Noting the high-level meeting on revitalizing the work of the Conference on Disarmament and taking forward multilateral disarmament negotiations, convened by the Secretary-General on 24 September 2010, and the plenary meeting of the General Assembly to follow up on the high-level meeting, held from 27 to 29 July 2011,

Welcoming the entry into force on 5 February 2011 of the Treaty between the Russian Federation and the United States of America on Measures for the Further Reduction and Limitation of Strategic Offensive Arms,

Welcoming also the recent announcements on overall stockpiles of nuclear warheads by France, the United Kingdom of Great Britain and Northern Ireland and the United States of America, as well as the update of the Russian Federation on its nuclear arsenals, which further enhance transparency and increase mutual confidence,

Expressing deep concern regarding the growing dangers posed by the proliferation of weapons of mass destruction, inter alia, nuclear weapons, including that caused by proliferation networks,

Recognizing the importance of the objective of nuclear security, along with the shared goals of Member States of nuclear disarmament, nuclear non-proliferation and peaceful uses of nuclear energy, welcoming the Nuclear Security Summit, held on 12 and 13 April 2010, and looking forward to the Nuclear Security Summit to be held in Seoul in 2012,

Recognizing also the importance of the implementation of Security Council resolutions 1718(2006) of 14 October 2006 and 1874(2009) of 12 June 2009 urging the Democratic People's Republic of Korea to abandon all its nuclear weapons and existing nuclear programmes and immediately cease all related activities, expressing concern regarding the Democratic People's Republic of Korea's claimed uranium enrichment programme and light water reactor construction, and declaring that the Democratic People's Republic of Korea cannot have the status of a nuclear-weapon State under the Treaty on the Non-Proliferation of Nuclear Weapons under any circumstances,

1. *Reaffirms* the importance of all States parties to the Treaty on the Non-Proliferation of Nuclear Weapons complying with their obligations under all the articles of the Treaty;

2. *Also reaffirms* the vital importance of the universality of the Treaty on the Non-Proliferation of Nuclear Weapons, and calls upon all States not parties to the Treaty to accede as non-nuclear-weapon States to the Treaty promptly and without any conditions and, pending their accession to the Treaty, to adhere to its terms and take practical steps in support of the Treaty;

3. *Further reaffirms* the unequivocal undertaking by the nuclear-weapon States to accomplish the total elimination of their nuclear arsenals, leading to nuclear disarmament, to which all States parties to the Treaty on the Non-Proliferation of Nuclear Weapons are committed under article VI thereof;

4. *Calls upon* nuclear-weapon States to undertake further efforts to reduce and ultimately eliminate all types of nuclear weapons, deployed and non-deployed, including through unilateral, bilateral, regional and multilateral measures;

5. *Emphasizes* the importance of applying the principles of irreversibility, verifiability and transparency in relation to the process of nuclear disarmament and non-proliferation;

6. *Recognizes* that nuclear disarmament and achieving the peace and security of a world without nuclear weapons require openness and cooperation, affirms the importance of enhanced confidence through increased transparency and effective verification, emphasizes the importance of the commitment by the nuclear-weapon States at the 2010 Review Conference of the Parties to the Treaty on the Non-Proliferation of Nuclear Weapons to accelerate concrete progress on the steps leading to nuclear disarmament contained in the Final Document of the 2000 Review Conference of the Parties to the Treaty on the Non-Proliferation of Nuclear Weapons in a way that promotes international stability, peace and undiminished and increased security, and the call upon the nuclear-weapon States to report their undertakings in 2014 to the Preparatory Committee for the 2015 Review Conference of the Parties to the Treaty on the Non-Proliferation of Nuclear Weapons, and welcomes in this regard the convening in Paris on 30 June and 1 July 2011 of the first follow-up meeting to the 2010 Review Conference of the five nuclear-weapon States as a transparency and confidence-building measure among them;

7. *Welcomes* the ongoing implementation by the Russian Federation and the United States of America of the Treaty on Measures for the Further Reduction and Limitation of Strategic Offensive Arms, and encourages them to continue discussions on follow-on measures in order to achieve deeper reductions in their nuclear arsenals;

8. *Urges* all States that have not yet done so to sign and ratify the Comprehensive Nuclear-Test-Ban Treaty at the earliest opportunity, with a view to its early entry into force and universalization, stresses the importance of maintaining existing moratoriums on nuclear-weapon test explosions or any other nuclear explosions pending the entry into force of the Treaty, and reaffirms the importance of the continued development of the Treaty verification regime, which will be a significant contribution to providing assurance of compliance with the Treaty;

9. *Reiterates its call for* the immediate commencement of negotiations on a fissile material cut-off treaty and its early conclusion, regrets that negotiations have not yet started, and calls upon all nuclear-weapon States and States not parties to the Treaty on the Non-Proliferation of Nuclear Weapons to declare and maintain moratoriums on the production of fissile material for any nuclear weapons or other nuclear explosive devices pending the entry into force of the treaty;

10. *Calls upon* the nuclear-weapon States to take measures to further reduce the risk of an accidental or unau-

thorized launch of nuclear weapons in ways that promote international stability and security, while welcoming the measures already taken by several nuclear-weapon States in this regard;

11. *Also calls upon* the nuclear-weapon States to promptly engage with a view to further diminishing the role and significance of nuclear weapons in all military and security concepts, doctrines and policies;

12. *Recognizes* the legitimate interest of non-nuclear-weapon States in receiving unequivocal and legally binding security assurances from nuclear-weapon States which could strengthen the nuclear non-proliferation regime, recalls Security Council resolution 984(1995) of 11 April 1995, noting the unilateral statements by each of the nuclear-weapon States, and calls upon all nuclear-weapon States to fully respect their existing commitments with regard to security assurances;

13. *Encourages* the establishment of further nuclear-weapon-free zones, where appropriate, on the basis of arrangements freely arrived at among States of the region concerned and in accordance with the 1999 guidelines of the Disarmament Commission, and recognizes that, by signing and ratifying relevant protocols that contain negative security assurances, nuclear-weapon States would undertake individual legally binding commitments with respect to the status of such zones and not to use or threaten to use nuclear weapons against States parties to such treaties;

14. *Calls upon* all States to redouble their efforts to prevent and curb the proliferation of nuclear weapons and their means of delivery and to fully respect and comply with obligations undertaken to forswear nuclear weapons;

15. *Stresses* the importance of the universalization of the comprehensive safeguards agreements of the International Atomic Energy Agency to include States which have not yet adopted and implemented such an agreement, while also strongly reaffirming the follow-on action of the 2010 Review Conference encouraging all States which have not done so to conclude and bring into force as soon as possible the Model Protocol Additional to the Agreement(s) between State(s) and the International Atomic Energy Agency for the Application of Safeguards approved by the Board of Governors of the Agency on 15 May 1997, and the full implementation of relevant Security Council resolutions, including resolution 1540(2004) of 28 April 2004;

16. *Encourages* every effort to secure all vulnerable nuclear and radiological material, and calls upon all States to work cooperatively as an international community to advance nuclear security, while requesting and providing assistance, including in the field of capacity-building, as necessary;

17. *Encourages* all States to implement the recommendations contained in the report of the Secretary-General on the United Nations study on disarmament and non-proliferation education, in support of achieving a world without nuclear weapons, and to voluntarily share information on efforts they have been undertaking to that end;

18. *Commends and further encourages* the constructive role played by civil society in promoting nuclear non-proliferation and nuclear disarmament, and encourages all States to promote, in cooperation with civil society, disarmament and non-proliferation education which, inter alia, contributes to raising public awareness of the tragic consequences of the use of nuclear weapons and strengthens the momentum of international efforts to promote nuclear disarmament and non-proliferation;

19. *Decides* to include in the provisional agenda of its sixty-seventh session the item entitled "United action towards the total elimination of nuclear weapons".

RECORDED VOTE ON RESOLUTION 66/45:

In favour: Afghanistan, Albania, Algeria, Andorra, Angola, Antigua and Barbuda, Argentina, Armenia, Australia, Austria, Azerbaijan, Bahamas, Bahrain, Bangladesh, Barbados, Belarus, Belgium, Belize, Benin, Bhutan, Bolivia, Bosnia and Herzegovina, Botswana, Brunei Darussalam, Bulgaria, Burkina Faso, Cambodia, Cameroon, Canada, Cape Verde, Chad, Chile, Colombia, Comoros, Congo, Costa Rica, Côte d'Ivoire, Croatia, Cyprus, Czech Republic, Denmark, Djibouti, Dominican Republic, Egypt, El Salvador, Eritrea, Estonia, Ethiopia, Fiji, Finland, France, Gabon, Georgia, Germany, Ghana, Greece, Grenada, Guatemala, Guinea, Guinea-Bissau, Guyana, Haiti, Honduras, Hungary, Iceland, Indonesia, Iraq, Ireland, Italy, Jamaica, Japan, Jordan, Kazakhstan, Kenya, Kuwait, Kyrgyzstan, Lao People's Democratic Republic, Latvia, Lebanon, Lesotho, Liberia, Libya, Liechtenstein, Lithuania, Luxembourg, Madagascar, Malawi, Malaysia, Maldives, Mali, Malta, Marshall Islands, Mauritania, Mexico, Micronesia, Monaco, Mongolia, Montenegro, Morocco, Mozambique, Namibia, Nepal, Netherlands, New Zealand, Nicaragua, Niger, Nigeria, Norway, Oman, Palau, Panama, Papua New Guinea, Paraguay, Peru, Philippines, Poland, Portugal, Qatar, Republic of Korea, Republic of Moldova, Romania, Russian Federation, Saint Kitts and Nevis, Saint Lucia, Saint Vincent and the Grenadines, Samoa, San Marino, Sao Tome and Principe, Saudi Arabia, Senegal, Serbia, Seychelles, Sierra Leone, Singapore, Slovakia, Slovenia, Solomon Islands, Spain, Sri Lanka, Sudan, Suriname, Swaziland, Sweden, Switzerland, Tajikistan, Thailand, the former Yugoslav Republic of Macedonia, Timor-Leste, Togo, Tonga, Trinidad and Tobago, Tunisia, Turkey, Turkmenistan, Tuvalu, Uganda, Ukraine, United Arab Emirates, United Kingdom, United Republic of Tanzania, United States, Uruguay, Uzbekistan, Vanuatu, Venezuela, Viet Nam, Yemen, Zambia, Zimbabwe.

Against: Democratic People's Republic of Korea.

Abstaining: Brazil, China, Cuba, Ecuador, India, Iran, Israel, Mauritius, Myanmar, Pakistan, Syrian Arab Republic.

Also on 2 December [meeting 71], the General Assembly, on the recommendation of the First Committee [A/66/412], adopted **resolution 66/49** by recorded vote (161-0-18) [agenda item 98].

Compliance with non-proliferation, arms limitation and disarmament agreements and commitments

The General Assembly,

Recalling its resolution 63/59 of 2 December 2008 and other relevant resolutions on the question,

Recognizing the abiding concern of all Member States for ensuring respect for the rights and obligations arising from treaties to which they are parties and from other sources of international law,

Convinced that observance by Member States of the Charter of the United Nations and compliance with non-proliferation, arms limitation and disarmament agreements to which they are parties and with other agreed obligations are essential for regional and global peace, security and stability,

Stressing that failure by States parties to comply with such agreements and with other agreed obligations not only adversely affects the security of States parties but can also create security risks for other States relying on the constraints and commitments stipulated in those agreements,

Stressing also that the viability and effectiveness of non-proliferation, arms limitation and disarmament agreements and of other agreed obligations require that those agreements be fully complied with and enforced,

Concerned by non-compliance by some States with their respective obligations,

Noting that verification and compliance, and enforcement in a manner consistent with the Charter, are integrally related,

Recognizing the importance of and support for effective national, regional and international capacities for such verification, compliance and enforcement,

Recognizing also that full compliance by States with all their respective non-proliferation, arms limitation and disarmament agreements and with other agreed obligations they have undertaken contributes to efforts to prevent the development and proliferation, contrary to international obligations, of weapons of mass destruction, related technologies and means of delivery, as well as to efforts to deny non-State actors access to such capabilities,

1. *Underscores* the contribution that compliance with non-proliferation, arms limitation and disarmament agreements and with other agreed obligations makes to enhancing confidence and to strengthening international security and stability;

2. *Urges* all States to implement and to comply fully with their respective obligations;

3. *Welcomes* efforts by all States to pursue additional areas of cooperation, as appropriate, that can increase confidence in compliance with existing non-proliferation, arms limitation and disarmament agreements and commitments and reduce the possibility of misinterpretation and misunderstanding;

4. *Calls upon* all Member States to encourage and, for those States in a position to do so, to appropriately assist States which request assistance to increase their capacity to implement fully their obligations;

5. *Calls upon* Member States to support efforts aimed at the resolution of compliance questions by means consistent with such agreements and with international law;

6. *Welcomes* the role that the United Nations has played and continues to play in restoring the integrity of, and fostering negotiations on, certain arms limitation and disarmament and non-proliferation agreements and in the removal of threats to peace;

7. *Calls upon* all concerned States to take concerted action, in a manner consistent with relevant international law, to encourage, through bilateral and multilateral means, the compliance by all States with their respective non-proliferation, arms limitation and disarmament agreements and with other agreed obligations, and to hold those not in compliance with such agreements accountable for their non-compliance in a manner consistent with the Charter of the United Nations;

8. *Urges* those States not currently in compliance with their respective obligations and commitments to make the strategic decision to come back into compliance;

9. *Encourages* efforts by all States, the United Nations and other international organizations, pursuant to their respective mandates, to take action, consistent with the Charter, to prevent serious damage to international security and stability arising from non-compliance by States with their existing non-proliferation, arms limitation and disarmament obligations;

10. *Decides* to include in the provisional agenda of its sixty-ninth session an item entitled "Compliance with non-proliferation, arms limitation and disarmament agreements and commitments".

RECORDED VOTE ON RESOLUTION 66/49:

In favour: Afghanistan, Albania, Algeria, Andorra, Angola, Antigua and Barbuda, Argentina, Armenia, Australia, Austria, Azerbaijan, Bahamas, Bangladesh, Barbados, Belgium, Belize, Benin, Bhutan, Bosnia and Herzegovina, Botswana, Brazil, Brunei Darussalam, Bulgaria, Burkina Faso, Cambodia, Cameroon, Canada, Cape Verde, Chad, Chile, China, Colombia, Comoros, Congo, Costa Rica, Côte d'Ivoire, Croatia, Cyprus, Czech Republic, Denmark, Djibouti, Dominican Republic, El Salvador, Eritrea, Estonia, Ethiopia, Fiji, Finland, France, Gabon, Georgia, Germany, Ghana, Greece, Grenada, Guatemala, Guinea, Guinea-Bissau, Guyana, Haiti, Honduras, Hungary, Iceland, India, Indonesia, Iraq, Ireland, Israel, Italy, Jamaica, Japan, Jordan, Kazakhstan, Kenya, Kyrgyzstan, Latvia, Lesotho, Liberia, Libya, Liechtenstein, Lithuania, Luxembourg, Madagascar, Malawi, Malaysia, Maldives, Mali, Malta, Marshall Islands, Mauritania, Mauritius, Mexico, Micronesia, Monaco, Mongolia, Montenegro, Morocco, Mozambique, Myanmar, Namibia, Nepal, Netherlands, New Zealand, Niger, Nigeria, Norway, Palau, Panama, Papua New Guinea, Paraguay, Peru, Philippines, Poland, Portugal, Republic of Korea, Republic of Moldova, Romania, Russian Federation, Saint Kitts and Nevis, Saint Lucia, Saint Vincent and the Grenadines, Samoa, San Marino, Sao Tome and Principe, Senegal, Serbia, Seychelles, Sierra Leone, Singapore, Slovakia, Slovenia, Solomon Islands, South Africa, Spain, Sri Lanka, Suriname, Swaziland, Sweden, Switzerland, Tajikistan, Thailand, the former Yugoslav Republic of Macedonia, Timor-Leste, Togo, Tonga, Trinidad and Tobago, Tunisia, Turkey, Turkmenistan, Tuvalu, Uganda, Ukraine, United Arab Emirates, United Kingdom, United Republic of Tanzania, United States, Uruguay, Vanuatu, Viet Nam, Zambia, Zimbabwe.

Against: None.

Abstaining: Bahrain, Belarus, Bolivia, Cuba, Ecuador, Egypt, Iran, Kuwait, Lebanon, Nicaragua, Oman, Pakistan, Qatar, Saudi Arabia, Sudan, Syrian Arab Republic, Venezuela, Yemen.

Missiles

The Missile Technology Control Regime (MCTR), at its twenty-fifth plenary meeting (Buenos Aires, Argentina, 11–15 April), reviewed its efforts to prevent missile programmes and their proliferation. MCTR partners discussed the proliferation of weapons of mass destruction and their means of delivery. They reaffirmed the importance of addressing those challenges and the role of the MCTR in that regard. The MCTR guidelines and controls list constituted an international export control standard that was increasingly adhered to by MCTR non-members. Partners agreed to assist non-partner countries that supported the objectives and purposes of the Regime to contribute to missile non-proliferation. They also agreed to continue to assist interested countries in implementing the missile-related export controls mandated under Security Council resolution 1540(2004) [YUN 2004, p. 544], and to work with the Security Council Committee established pursuant to that resolution.

On 2 December, the General Assembly, by **decision 66/516**, decided to include in the provisional agenda of its sixty-seventh (2012) session the item entitled "Missiles".

Hague Code of Conduct

The 132 subscribing States to the Hague Code of Conduct against Ballistic Missile Proliferation (HCOC), adopted in 2002 [YUN 2002, p. 504], held their Tenth Regular Meeting (Vienna, 2–3 June). They discussed the strengthening of confidence-building measures, such as pre-launch notifications and annual declarations of ballistic missiles; space-launch vehicles; and the importance of outreach activities to foster the universalization of the Code and increase the number of subscribing States. They also reaffirmed the importance of HCOC as a confidence-building and transparency instrument in the framework of multilateral efforts against ballistic missile proliferation.

Non-proliferation of weapons of mass destruction

Security Council Committee on WMDs

Pursuant to resolution 1540(2004) [YUN 2004, p. 544], the Security Council set up a Committee to report on the implementation of that resolution, which dealt with the non-proliferation of weapons of mass destruction (WMDs). The Committee's mandate was extended to 25 April 2011 by resolutions 1673(2006) [YUN 2006, p. 635] and 1810(2008) [YUN 2008, p. 585]. By resolution 1977(2011) of 20 April (see below), the Council further extended the Committee's mandate for 10 years, until 25 April 2021.

On 26 January [S/2011/37], the Committee submitted its decision approving the extension of its ninth programme of work for the period from 1 February to 25 April 2011, and revising its current programme of work. It also decided to submit by 24 April a report on compliance with resolution 1540(2004).

SECURITY COUNCIL ACTION

On 20 April [meeting 6518], the Security Council unanimously adopted **resolution 1977(2011)**. The draft [S/2011/257] was submitted by Bosnia and Herzegovina, China, Colombia, France, Gabon, Germany, Lebanon, Nigeria, Portugal, the Russian Federation, South Africa, the United Kingdom and the United States.

The Security Council,

Reaffirming its resolutions 1540(2004) of 28 April 2004, 1673(2006) of 27 April 2006 and 1810(2008) of 25 April 2008,

Reaffirming also that the proliferation of nuclear, chemical and biological weapons, as well as their means of delivery, constitutes a threat to international peace and security,

Reaffirming further the need for all Member States to comply fully with their obligations and fulfil their commitments in relation to arms control, disarmament and the non-proliferation in all its aspects of all weapons of mass destruction and their means of delivery,

Reaffirming that prevention of the proliferation of nuclear, chemical and biological weapons should not hamper international cooperation in materials, equipment and technology for peaceful purposes, while goals of peaceful utilization should not be misused for proliferation purposes,

Remaining gravely concerned by the threat of terrorism and the risk that non-State actors may acquire, develop, traffic in or use nuclear, chemical and biological weapons and their means of delivery,

Reaffirming its resolve to take appropriate and effective actions against any threat to international peace and security caused by the proliferation of nuclear, chemical and biological weapons and their means of delivery, in conformity with its primary responsibilities, as provided for in the Charter of the United Nations,

Reaffirming its decision that none of the obligations in resolution 1540(2004) shall be interpreted so as to conflict with or alter the rights and obligations of States parties to the Treaty on the Non-Proliferation of Nuclear Weapons, the Convention on the Prohibition of the Development, Production, Stockpiling and Use of Chemical Weapons and on Their Destruction and the Convention on the Prohibition of the Development, Production and Stockpiling of Bacteriological (Biological) and Toxin Weapons and on Their Destruction or alter the responsibilities of the International Atomic Energy Agency or the Organization for the Prohibition of Chemical Weapons,

Noting that international cooperation between States, in accordance with international law, is required to counter the illicit trafficking by non-State actors in nuclear, chemical and biological weapons, their means of delivery and related materials,

Recognizing the need to enhance the coordination of efforts at the national, subregional, regional and international levels, as appropriate, in order to strengthen a global response to the serious challenge and threat to international peace and security posed by the proliferation of weapons of mass destruction and their means of delivery,

Emphasizing the need for States to take all appropriate national measures in accordance with their national authorities and legislation, and consistent with international law, to strengthen export controls, to control access to intangible transfers of technology and to information that could be used for weapons of mass destruction and their means of delivery, to prevent proliferation financing and shipments, and to secure sensitive materials,

Endorsing the work already carried out by the Security Council Committee established pursuant to resolution 1540(2004) (hereinafter "the 1540 Committee"), in accordance with its programmes of work, including the establishment of the working groups for facilitating the implementation of the programme of work,

Recognizing States' progress in implementing resolution 1540(2004), while noting that States have taken fewer measures in some of its areas,

Endorsing the valuable activities of the 1540 Committee with relevant international, regional and subregional organizations,

Taking note of international efforts towards full implementation of resolution 1540(2004), including on preventing the financing of proliferation-related activities, and taking into consideration the guidance of the framework of the Financial Action Task Force,

Noting that not all States have submitted to the 1540 Committee their national reports on implementation of resolution 1540(2004),

Noting also that the full implementation of resolution 1540(2004) by all States, including the adoption of national laws and measures to ensure implementation of these laws, is a long-term task that will require continuous efforts at the national, regional and international levels,

Recognizing, in that regard, the importance of dialogue between the 1540 Committee and Member States, and stressing that direct contact is an effective means of such dialogue,

Recognizing also that many States continue to require assistance in implementing resolution 1540(2004), emphasizing the importance of providing States, in response to their requests, with effective assistance that meets their needs, and welcoming the coordinating and facilitating role of the 1540 Committee in this regard,

Stressing, in that regard, the need for enhanced assistance and collaboration among States, between the 1540 Committee and States, and between the Committee and relevant international, regional and subregional organizations in assisting States to implement resolution 1540(2004),

Recognizing the importance of progress towards achieving the goals and objectives of the Nuclear Security Summit, held in Washington, D.C., on 12 and 13 April 2010, as a contribution to the effective implementation of resolution 1540(2004),

Calling upon States to work together urgently to prevent and suppress acts of nuclear terrorism, including through increased cooperation and full implementation of the relevant international conventions and through appropriate measures to reinforce the existing legal framework with a view to ensuring that those committing offences of nuclear terrorism are effectively held accountable,

Endorsing the 2009 comprehensive review of the status of implementation of resolution 1540(2004), and taking note of the findings and recommendations contained in its final document,

Acting under Chapter VII of the Charter,

1. *Reiterates* its decisions taken in, and the requirements of, resolution 1540(2004), and re-emphasizes the importance for all States to implement fully that resolution;

2. *Decides* to extend the mandate of the 1540 Committee for a period of ten years, until 25 April 2021;

3. *Decides also* that the 1540 Committee shall conduct a comprehensive review on the status of implementation of resolution 1540(2004), both after five years and prior to the renewal of its mandate, including, if necessary, recommendations on adjustments to the mandate, and that it shall submit to the Security Council a report on the conclusions of those reviews, and decides that, accordingly, the first review shall be held before December 2016;

4. *Again decides* that the 1540 Committee shall submit an annual programme of work to the Council before the end of May of each year, and decides that the next programme of work shall be prepared before 31 May 2011;

5. *Decides* to continue to provide the 1540 Committee with the assistance of experts, and to this end:

(*a*) Requests the Secretary-General to establish, in consultation with the 1540 Committee, a group of up to eight experts ("group of experts"), acting under the direction and purview of the Committee, composed of individuals with the appropriate experience and knowledge to provide the Committee with expertise, to assist the Committee in carrying out its mandate under resolutions 1540(2004), 1673(2006), 1810(2008) and the present resolution, including through facilitation of assistance to improve implementation of resolution 1540(2004);

(*b*) Requests, in that regard, the 1540 Committee to consider recommendations for the Committee and the group of experts on expertise requirements, broad geographical representation, working methods, modalities and structure, including consideration of the feasibility of a coordination and leadership position of the group of experts, and to present these recommendations to the Council no later than 31 August 2011;

Implementation

6. *Again calls upon* all States that have not yet submitted a first report on steps they have taken or intend to take to implement resolution 1540(2004) to submit such a report to the 1540 Committee without delay;

7. *Again encourages* all States that have submitted such reports to provide, when appropriate or upon the request of the 1540 Committee, additional information on their implementation of resolution 1540(2004), including, voluntarily, on States' effective practices;

8. *Encourages* all States to prepare, on a voluntary basis, national implementation action plans, with the assistance of the 1540 Committee as appropriate, mapping out their priorities and plans for implementing the key provisions of resolution 1540(2004) and to submit those plans to the Committee;

9. *Decides* that the 1540 Committee shall continue to intensify its efforts to promote the full implementation by all States of resolution 1540(2004), through its programme of work, which includes the compilation and general examination of information on the status of implementation by States of resolution 1540(2004) as well as efforts by States at outreach, dialogue, assistance and cooperation; and which addresses, in particular, all aspects of paragraphs 1 to 3 of that resolution, which encompasses (*a*) accountability, (*b*) physical protection, (*c*) border controls and law enforcement efforts, and (*d*) national export and trans-shipment controls, including controls on providing funds and services such as financing to such exports and trans-shipments; and includes, as necessary, specific priorities for its work, taking into account its annual review on the implementation of resolution 1540(2004), prepared with the assistance of the group of experts before the end of December of each year;

10. *Urges* the 1540 Committee to continue to engage actively with States and relevant international, regional and subregional organizations to promote the sharing of experience, lessons learned and effective practices in the areas covered by resolution 1540(2004), drawing, in particular,

on information provided by States as well as examples of successful assistance, and to liaise on the availability of programmes which might facilitate the implementation of resolution 1540(2004), while bearing in mind that customized assistance is useful for the effective implementation of resolution 1540(2004) at the national level;

11. *Encourages*, in that regard, the 1540 Committee, with the support of necessary relevant expertise, to actively engage in dialogue with States on the implementation of resolution 1540(2004), including through visits to States at their invitation;

12. *Requests* the 1540 Committee, with the support of the group of experts, to identify effective practices, templates and guidance with a view to developing a compilation, as well as to consider preparing a technical reference guide about resolution 1540(2004) to be used by States on a voluntary basis in implementing resolution 1540(2004), and in that regard encourages the Committee, at its discretion, to draw also on relevant expertise, including civil society and the private sector, with, as appropriate, their State's consent;

Assistance

13. *Encourages* States that have requests for assistance to convey them to the 1540 Committee, and encourages them to make use of the Committee's assistance template to that effect;

14. *Urges* States and relevant international, regional and subregional organizations to inform the 1540 Committee, as appropriate, of areas in which they are able to provide assistance; and calls upon States and such organizations, if they have not done so previously, to provide the Committee with a point of contact for assistance by 31 August 2011;

15. *Urges* the 1540 Committee to continue strengthening the role of the Committee in facilitating technical assistance for the implementation of resolution 1540(2004), in particular by engaging actively, with the support of the group of experts, in matching offers and requests for assistance, through such means as visits to States, at the invitation of the State concerned, assistance templates, action plans or other information submitted to the Committee;

16. *Supports* the continued efforts of the 1540 Committee to secure a coordinated and transparent assistance process that provides timely and ready availability of information for States seeking assistance and for States prepared to provide assistance;

17. *Encourages* meetings on assistance issues, with the participation of the 1540 Committee, between States prepared to offer assistance, States requesting assistance, other interested States and relevant international, regional and subregional organizations;

*Cooperation with international,
regional and subregional organizations*

18. *Calls upon* relevant international, regional and subregional organizations to designate and provide the 1540 Committee by 31 August 2011 with a point of contact or coordinator for the implementation of resolution 1540(2004), and encourages them to enhance cooperation and information-sharing with the Committee on technical assistance and all other issues of relevance for the implementation of resolution 1540(2004);

19. *Reiterates* the need to continue to enhance ongoing cooperation between the 1540 Committee, the Security Council Committee established pursuant to resolution 1267(1999) concerning Al-Qaida and the Taliban and associated individuals and entities and the Security Council Committee established pursuant to resolution 1373(2001) concerning counter-terrorism, including through, as appropriate, enhanced information-sharing, and coordination on visits to States, within their respective mandates, technical assistance and other issues of relevance to all three Committees; and expresses its intention to provide guidance to the Committees on areas of common interest in order to better coordinate their efforts;

Transparency and outreach

20. *Requests* the 1540 Committee to continue to institute transparency measures and activities, inter alia, by making the fullest possible use of the Committee website, and urges the Committee to conduct, with the participation of the group of experts, regular meetings open to all Member States on the activities of the Committee and the group of experts related to the aforementioned objectives;

21. *Also requests* the 1540 Committee to continue to organize and participate in outreach events on the implementation of resolution 1540(2004) at the international, regional, subregional and, as appropriate, national levels, and to promote the refinement of these outreach efforts to focus on specific thematic and regional issues related to implementation;

Administration and resources

22. *Recognizes* that the implementation of the mandate of the 1540 Committee requires sustained support and adequate resources, and to that end:

(*a*) Endorses the existing administrative and logistics support to the 1540 Committee from the Office for Disarmament Affairs of the Secretariat, and decides that the Committee should report to the Council by January 2012 on the possibility of strengthening this support, including through the strengthening of the regional capacity of the Office to support the implementation of the resolution at the regional, subregional and national levels;

(*b*) Calls upon the Secretariat to provide and maintain sufficient expertise to support activities of the 1540 Committee as outlined in the present resolution;

(*c*) Encourages States that are able to do so to provide resources to the Office of Disarmament Affairs to assist States in implementing their obligations under resolution 1540(2004) and to make available to the 1540 Committee "in-kind" contributions or cost-free training and expertise to help the group of experts to meet requests for assistance in a timely and effective manner;

(*d*) Invites the 1540 Committee to consider developing, in close cooperation with relevant international, regional and subregional organizations and other United Nations bodies, ways to utilize and maintain expertise, including, in particular, of former experts of the group, that could be made available for specific missions and assistance needs regarding the implementation of resolution 1540(2004);

(*e*) Urges the 1540 Committee to continue to encourage and take full advantage of voluntary financial contributions to assist States in identifying and addressing their needs for the implementation of resolution 1540(2004), and requests the Committee, at its discretion, to promote the efficient and effective use of the existing funding mechanisms within the United Nations system;

23. *Decides* to remain seized of the matter.

On 24 April [S/2011/266], the Committee informed the Council that it was continuing consideration of the report, and, taking into account Council resolution 1977(2011) (see above), it would submit the report to the Council by 24 May.

On 17 June [S/2011/380], the Committee submitted its tenth programme of work for the period from 1 June 2011 to 31 May 2012.

Committee report. In September [S/2011/579], the Committee on WMDs reported on its work to promote implementation of Council resolution 1520(2004). Since its last report [YUN 2008, p. 587], the Committee had facilitated and documented an upward trend in the progress made by States in implementing measures to prevent non-State actors from acquiring nuclear, chemical and biological weapons and their means of delivery. That work contributed to strengthened global non-proliferation and counter-terrorism regimes and to better preparation by States to prevent proliferation of such weapons to non-State actors. Some 140 States had adopted legislative measures to prohibit proliferation of nuclear, chemical and biological weapons, as compared to 65 States in 2006. The number of countries reporting national legal frameworks regarding the manufacture and production of nuclear materials rose from 32 in 2006 to 71 in 2009, and to more than 120 in 2011. The number of countries with legal frameworks prohibiting the manufacture, acquisition, stockpiling, development, transfer or use of biological weapons also increased significantly since 2008. Additionally, more countries reported provisions in their legal frameworks prohibiting the involvement of non-State actors in illicit activities related to chemical weapons.

The Committee continued to raise awareness of the importance of resolution 1540(2004) through its outreach and dialogue with Member States; its cooperation with international, regional and subregional organizations and other UN bodies; and its transparency with relation to the international community as a whole.

New types of WMDs

Conference on Disarmament. The issue of radiological weapons, which had been on the agenda of the Conference on Disarmament since 1979, was considered in plenary meetings on 17 February and 17 March, and in an informal plenary on 25 May, under agenda item 5, on "New types of weapons of mass destruction and new systems of such weapons; radiological weapons". Delegations reaffirmed or further elaborated their respective positions on the agenda item.

GENERAL ASSEMBLY ACTION

On 2 December [meeting 71], the General Assembly, on the recommendation of the First Committee [A/66/402], adopted **resolution 66/21** by recorded vote (168-1-1) [agenda item 88].

Prohibition of the development and manufacture of new types of weapons of mass destruction and new systems of such weapons: report of the Conference on Disarmament

The General Assembly,

Recalling its previous resolutions on the prohibition of the development and manufacture of new types of weapons of mass destruction and new systems of such weapons,

Recalling also its resolutions 51/37 of 10 December 1996, 54/44 of 1 December 1999, 57/50 of 22 November 2002, 60/46 of 8 December 2005 and 63/36 of 2 December 2008 relating to the prohibition of the development and manufacture of new types of weapons of mass destruction and new systems of such weapons,

Recalling further paragraph 77 of the Final Document of the Tenth Special Session of the General Assembly,

Determined to prevent the emergence of new types of weapons of mass destruction that have characteristics comparable in destructive effect to those of weapons of mass destruction identified in the definition of weapons of mass destruction adopted by the United Nations in 1948,

Noting with appreciation the discussions which have been held in the Conference on Disarmament under the item entitled "New types of weapons of mass destruction and new systems of such weapons; radiological weapons",

Noting the desirability of keeping the matter under review, as appropriate,

1. *Reaffirms* that effective measures should be taken to prevent the emergence of new types of weapons of mass destruction;

2. *Requests* the Conference on Disarmament, without prejudice to further overview of its agenda, to keep the matter under review, as appropriate, with a view to making, when necessary, recommendations on undertaking specific negotiations on identified types of such weapons;

3. *Calls upon* all States, immediately following any recommendations of the Conference on Disarmament, to give favourable consideration to those recommendations;

4. *Requests* the Secretary-General to transmit to the Conference on Disarmament all documents relating to the consideration of this item by the General Assembly at its sixty-sixth session;

5. *Requests* the Conference on Disarmament to report the results of any consideration of the matter in its annual reports to the General Assembly;

6. *Decides* to include in the provisional agenda of its sixty-ninth session the item entitled "Prohibition of the development and manufacture of new types of weapons of mass destruction and new systems of such weapons: report of the Conference on Disarmament".

RECORDED VOTE ON RESOLUTION 66/21:

In favour: Afghanistan, Albania, Algeria, Andorra, Angola, Antigua and Barbuda, Argentina, Australia, Austria, Azerbaijan, Bahamas, Bahrain, Bangladesh, Barbados, Belarus, Belgium, Belize, Benin, Bolivia, Bosnia and Herzegovina, Brazil, Brunei Darussalam, Bulgaria, Cambodia, Cameroon, Canada, Cape Verde, Chad, Chile, China, Colombia, Comoros, Congo, Costa Rica, Côte d'Ivoire, Croatia, Cuba, Cyprus, Czech Republic, Democratic People's Republic of Korea, Denmark, Djibouti, Dominican Republic, Ecuador, Egypt, El Salvador, Estonia, Ethiopia, Fiji, Finland, France, Georgia, Germany, Ghana, Greece, Guatemala, Guinea, Guinea-Bissau, Guyana, Haiti, Honduras, Hungary, Iceland, India, Indonesia, Iran, Iraq, Ireland, Italy, Jamaica, Japan, Jordan, Kazakhstan, Kenya, Kuwait, Kyrgyzstan, Lao People's Democratic Republic, Latvia, Lebanon, Lesotho, Liberia, Libya, Liechtenstein, Lithuania, Luxembourg, Madagascar, Malawi, Malaysia, Maldives, Mali, Malta, Marshall Islands, Mauritania, Mauritius, Mexico, Micronesia, Monaco, Mongolia, Montenegro, Morocco, Mozambique, Myanmar, Namibia, Nepal, Netherlands, New Zealand, Nicaragua, Niger, Nigeria, Norway, Oman, Pakistan, Palau, Panama, Papua New Guinea, Paraguay, Peru, Philippines, Poland, Portugal, Qatar, Republic of Korea, Republic of Moldova, Romania, Russian Federation, Saint Kitts and Nevis, Saint Lucia, Saint Vincent and the Grenadines, Samoa, San Marino, Sao Tome and Principe, Saudi Arabia, Senegal, Serbia, Seychelles, Sierra Leone, Singapore, Slovakia, Slovenia, Solomon Islands, South Africa, Spain, Sri Lanka, Sudan, Suriname, Swaziland, Sweden, Syrian Arab Republic, Tajikistan, Thailand, the former Yugoslav Republic of Macedonia, Togo, Tonga, Tunisia, Turkey, Turkmenistan, Ukraine, United Arab Emirates, United Kingdom, United Republic of Tanzania, Uruguay, Uzbekistan, Vanuatu, Venezuela, Viet Nam, Yemen, Zambia, Zimbabwe.

Against: United States.

Abstaining: Israel.

Terrorism and WMDs

The United Nations continued to promote international action against terrorism through collaborative efforts with Member States and regional and international organizations, and through the work of the Counter-Terrorism Committee (see p. 53) and the Al-Qaida and Taliban Sanctions Committee (see p. 336).

Report of Secretary-General. In response to General Assembly resolution 65/62 [YUN 2010, p. 535], the Secretary-General, in June [A/66/115 & Add.1], presented the views of 16 Member States and 15 international organizations, including UN agencies, on measures they had taken to prevent terrorists from acquiring WMDs, their means of delivery, and related materials and technologies.

IAEA report. The International Atomic Energy Agency (IAEA) Director-General, in a September report [GOV/2011/51-GC(55)/21] on nuclear security covering the period 1 July 2010–30 June 2011, stated that the Agency contributed to the work of the Counter Terrorism Implementation Task Force Working Group on Prevention and Responding to Weapons of Mass Destruction Attacks, particularly through its report on Interagency Coordination in the Event of a Nuclear or Radiological Terrorist Attack: Current Status, Future Prospects. It also cooperated with the Security Council 1540(2004) Committee (see p. 506) by sending experts to participate in a workshop on the resolution's implementation (Lima, Peru, 9–11 November 2010). The Agency further took part in the Global Initiative to Combat Nuclear Terrorism plenary meeting (Daejeon, Republic of Korea, 30 June). The number of States participating in the Agency's Illicit Trafficking Database Programme expanded to 112 participants as at 30 June. During the period in question, States reported 172 incidents of illicit trafficking. Fourteen of the incidents reported involved unauthorized possession and/or attempts to sell or smuggle nuclear material or radioactive sources; 32 involved the theft or loss of such materials, and in one third of those incidents, the material was not reported as recovered. The Agency conducted three nuclear security information management and coordination meetings designed to improve States' awareness of and participation in the Database programme, as well as to promote regional dialogue and the sharing of information and lessons learned related to combating illicit nuclear trafficking.

During the year, preparatory meetings were convened in Vienna (March), Seoul (June) and Helsinki (October) in advance of the 2012 second Nuclear Security Summit, which would focus on cooperative measures to combat the threat of nuclear terrorism, protection of nuclear materials and related facilities, and prevention of illicit trafficking of nuclear materials.

GENERAL ASSEMBLY ACTION

On 2 December [meeting 71], the General Assembly, on the recommendation of the First Committee [A/66/412], adopted **resolution 66/50** without vote [agenda item 98 (*s*)].

Measures to prevent terrorists from acquiring weapons of mass destruction

The General Assembly,

Recalling its resolution 65/62 of 8 December 2010,

Recognizing the determination of the international community to combat terrorism, as evidenced in relevant General Assembly and Security Council resolutions,

Deeply concerned by the growing risk of linkages between terrorism and weapons of mass destruction, and in particular by the fact that terrorists may seek to acquire weapons of mass destruction,

Cognizant of the steps taken by States to implement Security Council resolution 1540(2004) on the non-proliferation of weapons of mass destruction, adopted on 28 April 2004,

Recalling the entry into force on 7 July 2007 of the International Convention for the Suppression of Acts of Nuclear Terrorism,

Recalling also the adoption, by consensus, of amendments to strengthen the Convention on the Physical Protection of Nuclear Material by the International Atomic Energy Agency on 8 July 2005,

Noting the support expressed in the final document of the Fifteenth Summit Conference of Heads of State and Government of the Movement of Non-Aligned Countries, which was held in Sharm el-Sheikh, Egypt, from 11 to 16 July 2009, for measures to prevent terrorists from acquiring weapons of mass destruction,

Noting also that the Group of Eight, the European Union, the Regional Forum of the Association of Southeast Asian Nations and others have taken into account in their deliberations the dangers posed by the likely acquisition by terrorists of weapons of mass destruction and the need for international cooperation in combating it, and that the Global Initiative to Combat Nuclear Terrorism has been launched jointly by the Russian Federation and the United States of America,

Noting further the holding of the Nuclear Security Summit on 12 and 13 April 2010 in Washington, D.C.,

Noting the holding of the High-level Meeting on Nuclear Safety and Security, in New York on 22 September 2011,

Acknowledging the consideration of issues relating to terrorism and weapons of mass destruction by the Advisory Board on Disarmament Matters,

Taking note of the relevant resolutions adopted by the General Conference of the International Atomic Energy Agency at its fifty-fifth regular session,

Taking note also of the 2005 World Summit Outcome adopted at the high-level plenary meeting of the General Assembly in September 2005 and the adoption of the United Nations Global Counter-Terrorism Strategy on 8 September 2006,

Taking note further of the report of the Secretary-General submitted pursuant to paragraph 5 of resolution 65/62,

Mindful of the urgent need for addressing, within the United Nations framework and through international cooperation, this threat to humanity,

Emphasizing that progress is urgently needed in the area of disarmament and non-proliferation in order to maintain international peace and security and to contribute to global efforts against terrorism,

1. *Calls upon* all Member States to support international efforts to prevent terrorists from acquiring weapons of mass destruction and their means of delivery;

2. *Appeals* to all Member States to consider early accession to and ratification of the International Convention for the Suppression of Acts of Nuclear Terrorism;

3. *Urges* all Member States to take and strengthen national measures, as appropriate, to prevent terrorists from acquiring weapons of mass destruction, their means of delivery and materials and technologies related to their manufacture;

4. *Encourages* cooperation among and between Member States and relevant regional and international organizations for strengthening national capacities in this regard;

5. *Requests* the Secretary-General to compile a report on measures already taken by international organizations on issues relating to the linkage between the fight against terrorism and the proliferation of weapons of mass destruction and to seek the views of Member States on additional relevant measures, including national measures, for tackling the global threat posed by the acquisition by terrorists of weapons of mass destruction and to report to the General Assembly at its sixty-seventh session;

6. *Decides* to include in the provisional agenda of its sixty-seventh session the item entitled "Measures to prevent terrorists from acquiring weapons of mass destruction".

Multilateralism in disarmament and non-proliferation

In response to General Assembly resolution 65/54 [YUN 2010, p. 538], the Secretary-General, in June and September [A/66/111 & Add.1], presented replies received from Australia, Cuba, Lebanon, Mexico, Nicaragua, Panama, Qatar, Spain and Turkmenistan regarding their views on the promotion of multilateralism in the area of disarmament and non-proliferation.

GENERAL ASSEMBLY ACTION

On 2 December [meeting 71], the General Assembly, on the recommendation of the First Committee [A/66/412], adopted **resolution 66/32** by recorded vote (125-5-48) [agenda item 98 (*n*)].

Promotion of multilateralism in the area of disarmament and non-proliferation

The General Assembly,

Determined to foster strict respect for the purposes and principles enshrined in the Charter of the United Nations,

Recalling its resolution 56/24 T of 29 November 2001 on multilateral cooperation in the area of disarmament and non-proliferation and global efforts against terrorism and other relevant resolutions, as well as its resolutions 57/63 of 22 November 2002, 58/44 of 8 December 2003, 59/69 of 3 December 2004, 60/59 of 8 December 2005, 61/62 of 6 December 2006, 62/27 of 5 December 2007, 63/50 of 2 December 2008, 64/34 of 2 December 2009 and 65/54 of 8 December 2010 on the promotion of multilateralism in the area of disarmament and non-proliferation,

Recalling also the purpose of the United Nations to maintain international peace and security and, to that end, to take effective collective measures for the prevention and removal of threats to the peace and for the suppression of acts of aggression or other breaches of the peace, and to bring about by peaceful means, and in conformity with the principles of justice and international law, adjustment or settlement of international disputes or situations which might lead to a breach of the peace, as enshrined in the Charter,

Recalling further the United Nations Millennium Declaration, which states, inter alia, that the responsibility for managing worldwide economic and social development, as well as threats to international peace and security, must be shared among the nations of the world and should be exercised multilaterally and that, as the most universal and most representative organization in the world, the United Nations must play the central role,

Convinced that, in the globalization era and with the information revolution, arms regulation, non-proliferation and disarmament problems are more than ever the concern of all countries in the world, which are affected in one way or another by these problems and, therefore, should have the possibility to participate in the negotiations that arise to tackle them,

Bearing in mind the existence of a broad structure of disarmament and arms regulation agreements resulting from non-discriminatory and transparent multilateral negotiations with the participation of a large number of countries, regardless of their size and power,

Aware of the need to advance further in the field of arms regulation, non-proliferation and disarmament on the basis of universal, multilateral, non-discriminatory and transparent negotiations with the goal of reaching general and complete disarmament under strict international control,

Recognizing the complementarity of bilateral, plurilateral and multilateral negotiations on disarmament,

Recognizing also that the proliferation and development of weapons of mass destruction, including nuclear weapons, are among the most immediate threats to international peace and security which need to be dealt with, with the highest priority,

Considering that the multilateral disarmament agreements provide the mechanism for States parties to consult one another and to cooperate in solving any problems which may arise in relation to the objective of, or in the application of, the provisions of the agreements and that such consultations and cooperation may also be undertaken through appropriate international procedures within the framework of the United Nations and in accordance with the Charter,

Stressing that international cooperation, the peaceful settlement of disputes, dialogue and confidence-building measures would make an essential contribution to the creation of multilateral and bilateral friendly relations among peoples and nations,

Being concerned at the continuous erosion of multilateralism in the field of arms regulation, non-proliferation and disarmament, and recognizing that a resort to unilateral actions by Member States in resolving their security concerns would jeopardize international peace and security and undermine confidence in the international security system as well as the foundations of the United Nations itself,

Noting that the Fifteenth Summit Conference of Heads of State and Government of the Movement of Non-Aligned Countries, held in Sharm el-Sheikh, Egypt, from 11 to 16 July 2009, and the Sixteenth Ministerial Conference and Commemorative Meeting of the Movement of Non-Aligned Countries, held in Bali, Indonesia, from 23 to 27 May 2011, welcomed the adoption of resolutions 63/50 and 65/54, on the promotion of multilateralism in the area of disarmament and non-proliferation, and underlined the fact that multilateralism and multilaterally agreed solutions, in accordance with the Charter, provide the only sustainable method of addressing disarmament and international security issues,

Reaffirming the absolute validity of multilateral diplomacy in the field of disarmament and non-proliferation, and determined to promote multilateralism as an essential way to develop arms regulation and disarmament negotiations,

1. *Reaffirms* multilateralism as the core principle in negotiations in the area of disarmament and non-proliferation with a view to maintaining and strengthening universal norms and enlarging their scope;

2. *Also reaffirms* multilateralism as the core principle in resolving disarmament and non-proliferation concerns;

3. *Urges* the participation of all interested States in multilateral negotiations on arms regulation, non-proliferation and disarmament in a non-discriminatory and transparent manner;

4. *Underlines* the importance of preserving the existing agreements on arms regulation and disarmament, which constitute an expression of the results of international cooperation and multilateral negotiations in response to the challenges facing mankind;

5. *Calls once again upon* all Member States to renew and fulfil their individual and collective commitments to multilateral cooperation as an important means of pursuing and achieving their common objectives in the area of disarmament and non-proliferation;

6. *Requests* the States parties to the relevant instruments on weapons of mass destruction to consult and cooperate among themselves in resolving their concerns with regard to cases of non-compliance as well as on implementation, in accordance with the procedures defined in those instruments, and to refrain from resorting or threatening to resort to unilateral actions or directing unverified non-compliance accusations against one another to resolve their concerns;

7. *Takes note* of the report of the Secretary-General containing the replies of Member States on the promotion of multilateralism in the area of disarmament and non-proliferation, submitted pursuant to resolution 65/54;

8. *Requests* the Secretary-General to seek the views of Member States on the issue of the promotion of multilateralism in the area of disarmament and non-proliferation and to submit a report thereon to the General Assembly at its sixty-seventh session;

9. *Decides* to include in the provisional agenda of its sixty-seventh session the item entitled "Promotion of multilateralism in the area of disarmament and non-proliferation".

RECORDED VOTE ON RESOLUTION 66/32:

In favour: Afghanistan, Algeria, Angola, Antigua and Barbuda, Argentina, Azerbaijan, Bahamas, Bahrain, Bangladesh, Barbados, Belarus, Belize, Benin, Bhutan, Bolivia, Botswana, Brazil, Brunei Darussalam, Burkina Faso, Cambodia, Cameroon, Cape Verde, Chad, Chile, China, Colombia, Comoros, Congo, Costa Rica, Côte d'Ivoire, Cuba, Democratic People's Republic of Korea, Djibouti, Dominican Republic, Ecuador, Egypt, Ethiopia, Fiji, Gabon, Ghana, Grenada, Guatemala, Guinea, Guinea-Bissau, Guyana, Haiti, Honduras, Hungary, India, Indonesia, Iran, Iraq, Jamaica, Jordan, Kazakhstan, Kenya, Kuwait, Kyrgyzstan, Lao People's Democratic Republic, Lebanon, Lesotho, Liberia, Libya, Madagascar, Malawi, Malaysia, Maldives, Mali, Marshall Islands, Mauritania, Mauritius, Mexico, Mongolia, Morocco, Mozambique, Myanmar, Namibia, Nepal, Nicaragua, Niger, Nigeria, Oman, Pakistan, Panama, Papua New Guinea, Paraguay, Peru, Philippines, Qatar, Russian Federation, Saint Kitts and Nevis, Saint Lucia, Saint Vincent and the Grenadines, Sao Tome and Principe, Saudi Arabia, Senegal, Serbia, Seychelles, Sierra Leone, Singapore, Solomon Islands, Sri Lanka, Sudan, Suriname, Swaziland, Syrian Arab Republic, Tajikistan, Thailand, Timor-Leste, Togo, Tunisia, Turkmenistan, Tuvalu, Uganda, Ukraine, United Arab Emirates, United Republic of Tanzania, Uruguay, Uzbekistan, Vanuatu, Venezuela, Viet Nam, Yemen, Zambia, Zimbabwe.

Against: Israel, Micronesia, Palau, United Kingdom, United States.

Abstaining: Albania, Andorra, Armenia, Australia, Austria, Belgium, Bosnia and Herzegovina, Bulgaria, Canada, Croatia, Cyprus, Czech Republic, Denmark, El Salvador, Estonia, Finland, France, Georgia, Germany, Greece, Iceland, Ireland, Italy, Japan, Latvia, Liechtenstein, Lithuania, Luxembourg, Malta, Monaco, Montenegro, Netherlands, New Zealand, Norway, Poland, Portugal, Republic of Korea, Republic of Moldova, Romania, Samoa, San Marino, Slovakia, Slovenia, Spain, Sweden, Switzerland, the former Yugoslav Republic of Macedonia, Turkey.

IAEA safeguards

The verification programme of the International Atomic Energy Agency (IAEA) remained at the core of multilateral efforts to curb the proliferation of nuclear weapons. The Agency had an essential verification role under the NPT as well as other treaties, such as those establishing nuclear-weapon-free zones. Comprehensive safeguards agreements, concluded pursuant to the NPT, and the Model Additional Protocols to those agreements, which granted the Agency complementary verification authority, were approved by the IAEA Board of Governors in 1997 [YUN 1997, p. 486]; they remained the principal legal instruments strengthening the Agency's safeguards regime.

According to the IAEA 2011 annual report [GC(56)/2], safeguards were applied during the year for 178 States with safeguards agreements in force with the Agency. States for which both comprehensive safeguards agreements and additional protocols were in force numbered 109. For 58 of those States, the Agency concluded that all nuclear material remained in peaceful activities. For the remaining 51 States, the Agency was only able to conclude that declared nuclear material remained in peaceful nuclear activities, as it had not completed all the necessary evaluations under those States' respective additional protocols.

For 61 States with a comprehensive safeguards agreement in force but no additional protocol, the Agency was only able to draw the conclusion that declared nuclear material remained in peaceful nuclear activities. Safeguards were also implemented with regard to declared nuclear material in selected facilities in the five nuclear-weapon States with voluntary offer agreements. For those five States, the Agency concluded that nuclear material to which safeguards were applied in selected facilities remained in peaceful activities or had been withdrawn, as provided for in the agreements. The Secretariat could not draw any safeguards conclusions for 14 NPT non-nuclear-weapon States without safeguards agreements in force.

The General Assembly, in **resolution 66/7** of 2 November (see p. 964), took note of IAEA resolution GC(55)/DEC/11 on strengthening the effectiveness and improving the efficiency of the safeguards system and application of the Model Additional Protocol.

Democratic People's Republic of Korea

Throughout the year, the Democratic People's Republic of Korea (DPRK) continued to operate its uranium enrichment facility and to construct a light-water reactor at Yongbyon. On 17 December, the DPRK reportedly agreed to suspend its uranium enrichment programme in exchange for up to 240,000 tons of food aid, following two days of bilateral discussions in Beijing between the United States and the DPRK. According to news reports, as a "possible" precondition for the resumption of denuclearization talks, the DPRK agreed "to implement initial measures of denuclearization, including a suspension of its uranium enrichment programme". Due to the death on 17 December of the DPRK leader, Kim Jong-il, the implementation of the agreement was suspended. On 20 December, the IAEA Director General reaffirmed the Agency's readiness to redeploy inspectors to the Yongbyon nuclear site.

In September, the IAEA Director-General submitted to the IAEA Board of Governors and General Conference a report [GOV/2011/53-GC(55)/24] on the application of safeguards in the DPRK that provided a historical overview and update of developments of direct relevance to the Agency, along with information on the DPRK's nuclear programme. Since December 2002, the DPRK had not permitted the Agency to implement safeguards in the State; consequently, IAEA could not draw any safeguards conclusions regarding the country. The DPRK had also not implemented those measures that were binding upon it pursuant to Security Council resolutions 1718(2006) [YUN 2006, p. 444] and 1874(2009) [YUN 2009, p. 384].

IAEA General Conference. In a 22 September resolution [GC(55)/RES/13], the IAEA General Conference expressed concern regarding the DPRK's claimed uranium enrichment programme and light water reactor construction, and urged the country not to conduct any further nuclear tests and to comply with Security Council resolutions 1718(2006) and 1874(2009). It also called on the DPRK to comply with the NPT and to cooperate with the Agency in implementing its comprehensive safeguards.

(For more information on UN concern with the DPRK nuclear programme and related sanctions, see p. 368.)

Iran

During the year, the IAEA Director General submitted four reports to the Board of Governors [GOV/2011/7, GOV/2011/29, GOV/2011/54, GOV/2011/65] on the implementation of Iran's NPT safeguards agreement and relevant Security Council resolutions, including **resolution 1984(2011)** (see p. 370). While the Agency continued to verify the non-diversion of declared nuclear material at the nuclear facilities and locations outside the facilities declared by Iran under its comprehensive safeguards agreement, it was not able to provide credible assurance about the absence of undeclared nuclear material and activities in the country, and therefore to conclude that all nuclear material in that country was used in peaceful activities. Contrary to the relevant resolutions of the Board and the Security Council, Iran had not implemented the modified Code 3.1 of the Subsidiary Arrangements General Part to its comprehensive safeguards agreement, and had not suspended its enrichment-related activities or its heavy water-related activities and had not addressed the Agency's concerns about possible military dimensions to its nuclear programme.

IAEA Board of Governors. In a November resolution [GOV/2011/69], the Board stressed the need for Iran and IAEA to intensify their dialogue aimed at resolving all outstanding substantive issues, and expressed its continuing support for a diplomatic solution. It called on Iran to engage seriously and without preconditions in talks aimed at restoring international confidence in the exclusively peaceful nature of its nuclear programme, while respecting the legitimate right to the peaceful uses of nuclear energy consistent with the NPT.

(For more information on UN concern with Iran's nuclear programme and related sanctions, see p. 369.)

Middle East

Report of Director General. In a September report [GOV/2011/55-GC(55)/23] on the application of IAEA safeguards in the Middle East, the IAEA Director General noted that all States in the region except Israel were parties to the NPT and had undertaken to accept comprehensive Agency safeguards. A long-standing and fundamental difference of views between Israel and the other States of the region remained with regard to the application of comprehensive Agency safeguards to all nuclear activities. States in the region emphasized that there was no automatic sequence linking the application of comprehensive safeguards to all activities in the Middle East, or the establishment of a nuclear-weapon-free zone, to the prior conclusion of a peace settlement. Israel, however, took the view that Agency safeguards, as well as all other regional security issues, could not be addressed in isolation from the creation of stable regional security conditions and that those issues should be addressed in the framework of a regional security and arms control dialogue that could be resumed in the context of a multilateral peace process. The Director General undertook to continue consultations regarding the early application of comprehensive Agency safeguards on all nuclear activities in the region.

IAEA General Conference. In a resolution of 23 September [GC(55)/RES/14], the IAEA General Conference affirmed the need for all States in the region to accept the application of full-scope Agency safeguards to all nuclear activities as an important confidence-building measure towards enhancing peace and security in the establishment of a nuclear-weapon-free zone. It requested the Director General to continue consultations on the early application of full-scope Agency safeguards.

Report of Secretary-General. In October [A/66/153 (Part II)], responding to General Assembly resolution 65/88 [YUN 2010, p. 541], the Secretary-General reported that, apart from the IAEA resolution on the application of Agency safeguards in the Middle East (see above), he had not received any additional information since his 2009 report [ibid.].

GENERAL ASSEMBLY ACTION

On 2 December [meeting 71], the General Assembly, on the recommendation of the First Committee [A/66/415], adopted **resolution 66/61** by recorded vote (167-6-5) [agenda item 101].

The risk of nuclear proliferation in the Middle East

The General Assembly,

Bearing in mind its relevant resolutions,

Taking note of the relevant resolutions adopted by the General Conference of the International Atomic Energy Agency, the latest of which is resolution GC(55)/RES/14, adopted on 23 September 2011,

Cognizant that the proliferation of nuclear weapons in the region of the Middle East would pose a serious threat to international peace and security,

Mindful of the immediate need for placing all nuclear facilities in the region of the Middle East under full-scope safeguards of the Agency,

Recalling the decision on principles and objectives for nuclear non-proliferation and disarmament adopted by the 1995 Review and Extension Conference of the Parties to the Treaty on the Non-Proliferation of Nuclear Weapons on 11 May 1995, in which the Conference urged universal adherence to the Treaty as an urgent priority and called upon all States not yet parties to the Treaty to accede to it at the earliest date, particularly those States that operate unsafeguarded nuclear facilities,

Recognizing with satisfaction that, in the Final Document of the 2000 Review Conference of the Parties to the Treaty on the Non-Proliferation of Nuclear Weapons, the Conference undertook to make determined efforts towards the achievement of the goal of universality of the Treaty, called upon those remaining States not parties to the Treaty to accede to it, thereby accepting an international legally binding commitment not to acquire nuclear weapons or nuclear explosive devices and to accept Agency safeguards on all their nuclear activities, and underlined the necessity of universal adherence to the Treaty and of strict compliance by all parties with their obligations under the Treaty,

Recalling the resolution on the Middle East adopted by the 1995 Review and Extension Conference on 11 May 1995, in which the Conference noted with concern the continued existence in the Middle East of unsafeguarded nuclear facilities, reaffirmed the importance of the early realization of universal adherence to the Treaty and called upon all States in the Middle East that had not yet done so, without exception, to accede to the Treaty as soon as possible and to place all their nuclear facilities under full-scope Agency safeguards,

Noting with satisfaction that, in the Final Document of the 2010 Review Conference of the Parties to the Treaty on the Non-Proliferation of Nuclear Weapons, the Conference emphasized the importance of a process leading to full implementation of the 1995 resolution on the Middle East and decided, inter alia, that the Secretary-General of the United Nations and the co-sponsors of the 1995 resolution, in consultation with the States of the region, would convene a conference in 2012, to be attended by all States of the Middle East, on the establishment of a Middle East zone free of nuclear weapons and all other weapons of mass destruction, on the basis of arrangements freely arrived at by the States of the region and with the full support and engagement of the nuclear-weapon States,

Recalling that Israel remains the only State in the Middle East that has not yet become a party to the Treaty,

Concerned about the threats posed by the proliferation of nuclear weapons to the security and stability of the Middle East region,

Stressing the importance of taking confidence-building measures, in particular the establishment of a nuclear-weapon-free zone in the Middle East, in order to enhance peace and security in the region and to consolidate the global non-proliferation regime,

Emphasizing the need for all parties directly concerned to seriously consider taking the practical and urgent steps required for the implementation of the proposal to establish a nuclear-weapon-free zone in the region of the Middle East in accordance with the relevant resolutions of the General Assembly and, as a means of promoting this objective, inviting the countries concerned to adhere to the Treaty and, pending the establishment of the zone, to agree to place all their nuclear activities under Agency safeguards,

Noting that one hundred and eighty-two States have signed the Comprehensive Nuclear-Test-Ban Treaty, including a number of States in the region,

1. *Welcomes* the conclusions on the Middle East of the 2010 Review Conference of the Parties to the Treaty on the Non-Proliferation of Nuclear Weapons;

2. *Reaffirms* the importance of Israel's accession to the Treaty on the Non-Proliferation of Nuclear Weapons and placement of all its nuclear facilities under comprehensive International Atomic Energy Agency safeguards, in realizing the goal of universal adherence to the Treaty in the Middle East;

3. *Calls upon* that State to accede to the Treaty without further delay, not to develop, produce, test or otherwise acquire nuclear weapons, to renounce possession of nuclear weapons and to place all its unsafeguarded nuclear facilities under full-scope Agency safeguards as an important confidence-building measure among all States of the region and as a step towards enhancing peace and security;

4. *Requests* the Secretary-General to report to the General Assembly at its sixty-seventh session on the implementation of the present resolution;

5. *Decides* to include in the provisional agenda of its sixty-seventh session the item entitled "The risk of nuclear proliferation in the Middle East".

RECORDED VOTE ON RESOLUTION 66/61:

In favour: Afghanistan, Albania, Algeria, Andorra, Angola, Antigua and Barbuda, Argentina, Armenia, Austria, Azerbaijan, Bahamas, Bahrain, Bangladesh, Barbados, Belarus, Belgium, Belize, Benin, Bhutan, Bolivia, Bosnia and Herzegovina, Botswana, Brazil, Brunei Darussalam, Bulgaria, Burkina Faso, Cambodia, Cape Verde, Chad, Chile, China, Colombia, Comoros, Congo, Costa Rica, Côte d'Ivoire, Croatia, Cuba, Cyprus, Czech Republic, Democratic People's Republic of Korea, Denmark, Djibouti, Dominican Republic, Ecuador, Egypt, El Salvador, Eritrea, Estonia, Fiji, Finland, France, Gabon, Georgia, Germany, Ghana, Greece, Grenada, Guatemala, Guinea, Guinea-Bissau, Guyana, Haiti, Honduras, Hungary, Iceland, Indonesia, Iran, Iraq, Ireland, Italy, Jamaica, Japan, Jordan, Kazakhstan, Kenya, Kuwait, Kyrgyzstan, Lao People's Democratic Republic, Latvia, Lebanon, Lesotho, Liberia, Libya, Liechtenstein, Lithuania, Luxembourg, Madagascar, Malawi, Malaysia, Maldives, Malta, Mauritania, Mauritius, Mexico, Monaco, Mongolia, Montenegro, Morocco, Mozambique, Myanmar, Namibia, Nepal, Netherlands, New Zealand, Nicaragua, Nigeria, Norway, Oman, Pakistan, Papua New Guinea, Paraguay, Peru, Philippines, Poland, Portugal, Qatar, Republic of Korea, Republic of Moldova, Romania, Russian Federation, Saint Kitts and Nevis, Saint Lucia, Saint Vincent and the Grenadines, Samoa, San Marino, Sao Tome and Principe, Saudi Arabia, Senegal, Serbia, Seychelles, Sierra Leone, Singapore, Slovakia, Slovenia, Solomon Islands, South Africa, Spain, Sri Lanka, Sudan, Suriname, Swaziland, Sweden, Switzerland, Syrian Arab Republic, Tajikistan, Thailand, the former Yugoslav Republic of Macedonia, Timor-Leste, Togo, Trinidad and Tobago, Tunisia, Turkey, Turkmenistan, Tuvalu, Uganda, Ukraine, United Arab Emirates, United Kingdom, United Republic of Tanzania, Uruguay, Uzbekistan, Venezuela, Viet Nam, Yemen, Zambia, Zimbabwe.

Against: Canada, Israel, Marshall Islands, Micronesia, Palau, United States.

Abstaining: Australia, Cameroon, Ethiopia, India, Panama.

Syrian Arab Republic

During the year, the Director General submitted to the IAEA Board of Governors two reports [GOV/2011/30 & Corr.1, GOV/2011/8] on the implementation of the NPT safeguards agreement in the Syrian Arab Republic. The Director General stressed that Syria had not cooperated with the Agency since June 2008 in connection with the unresolved issues related to the Dair Alzour site [YUN 2008, p. 596] and three other locations allegedly functionally related to it. Based on information available, the Agency assessed that it was very likely that the building destroyed at the Dair Alzour site was a nuclear reactor, which should have been declared to the Agency. As for the three other locations, the Agency was unable to provide any assessment concerning their nature or operational status. The matter of a Miniature Neutron Source Reactor would be addressed in the routine implementation of safeguards.

IAEA Board of Governors. The IAEA Board of Governors, in a resolution of 9 June [GOV/2011/41], found that Syria's undeclared construction of a nuclear reactor at Dair Alzour and failure to provide design information for the facility were a breach of its NPT safeguards agreement, and constituted non-compliance with its obligations under its safeguards agreement with the Agency. It called on Syria to remedy its non-compliance and to respond to the Director General's requests for updated reporting and access so as to verify such reporting and resolve all outstanding questions. The Board decided to report Syria's non-compliance with its safeguards agreement to all members of the Agency and to the Security Council and General Assembly, and to provide to the Council all reports prepared by the Director General related to the issue.

On 21 June [S/2011/371], in response to the Board's resolution, the IAEA Director General transmitted to the Security Council that resolution as well as his report on the implementation of the NPT safeguards agreement in Syria.

Radioactive waste

As described in the IAEA 2011 annual report [GC(56)/2], the Agency, in November, and in collaboration with the Swedish Radiation Safety Authority, organized an international workshop in Stockholm on "High Level Radioactive Waste and Spent Fuel Management–Storage and Disposal". Workshop participants recommended that comprehensive strategies for high-level radioactive waste and spent fuel management be developed, with clearly defined endpoints, including disposal. The International Project on Demonstrating the Safety of Geological Disposal, finalized in May, focused on post-closure safety; a pilot study concluded that it was essential to develop an integrated safety case addressing both operational and post-closure safety. Participants requested that the work continue and a follow-up project be launched in 2012. The Agency convened a Ministerial Conference on Nuclear Safety (Vienna, 20–24 June) in response to the Fukushima Daiichi accident (see p. 964).

During the year, the International Project on Use of Safety Assessment in Planning and Implementation of Decommissioning of Facilities Using Radioactive Material, which began in 2008, was completed. Its main output consisted of recommendations on the use of decommissioning safety assessments in the planning and implementation of decommissioning, with an emphasis on a phased approach to the development of the safety assessment. The Agency continued to assist member States with decommissioning research reactors, including through technical reports and a guide on decommissioning policies and strategies. The Contact Expert Group for International Radioactive Waste Projects in the Russian Federation had as its priority the transfer of spent fuel from submarines in storage facilities at former naval bases to reprocessing plants; initial shipments from those bases were made during the year. Another priority was the management of legacy radioactive waste at former naval bases and the construction of a regional centre for conditioning and storage of radioactive waste.

GENERAL ASSEMBLY ACTION

On 2 December [meeting 71], the General Assembly, on the recommendation of the First Committee [A/66/412], adopted **resolution 66/52** without vote [agenda item 98 (*d*)].

Prohibition of the dumping of radioactive wastes

The General Assembly,

Bearing in mind resolutions CM/Res.1153(XLVIII) of 1988 and CM/Res.1225(L) of 1989, adopted by the Council of Ministers of the Organization of African Unity, concerning the dumping of nuclear and industrial wastes in Africa,

Welcoming resolution GC(XXXIV)/RES/530 establishing a Code of Practice on the International Transboundary Movement of Radioactive Waste, adopted on 21 September 1990 by the General Conference of the International Atomic Energy Agency at its thirty-fourth regular session,

Taking note of the commitment by the participants in the Summit on Nuclear Safety and Security, held in Moscow on 19 and 20 April 1996, to ban the dumping at sea of radioactive wastes,

Considering its resolution 2602 C (XXIV) of 16 December 1969, in which it requested the Conference of the Committee on Disarmament, inter alia, to consider effective methods of control against the use of radiological methods of warfare,

Aware of the potential hazards underlying any use of radioactive wastes that would constitute radiological warfare and its implications for regional and international security, in particular for the security of developing countries,

Recalling all its resolutions on the matter since its forty-third session in 1988, including its resolution 51/45 J of 10 December 1996,

Recalling also resolution GC(45)/RES/10 adopted by consensus on 21 September 2001 by the General Conference of the International Atomic Energy Agency at its forty-fifth regular session, in which States shipping radioactive materials are invited to provide, as appropriate, assurances to concerned States, upon their request, that the national regulations of the shipping State take into account the Agency's transport regulations and to provide them with relevant information relating to the shipment of such materials; the information provided should in no case be contradictory to the measures of physical security and safety,

Welcoming the adoption at Vienna, on 5 September 1997, of the Joint Convention on the Safety of Spent Fuel Management and on the Safety of Radioactive Waste Management, as recommended by the participants in the Summit on Nuclear Safety and Security,

Welcoming also the convening by the International Atomic Energy Agency of the Ministerial Conference on Nuclear Safety, held in Vienna from 20 to 24 June 2011, and its outcome, the Declaration of the International Atomic Energy Agency Ministerial Conference on Nuclear Safety, as well as the Action Plan on Nuclear Safety, endorsed by the General Conference of the Agency at its fifty-fifth regular session,

Noting the convening by the Secretary-General of the High-level Meeting on Nuclear Safety and Security, in New York on 22 September 2011,

Noting with satisfaction that the Joint Convention entered into force on 18 June 2001,

Noting that the first Review Meeting of the Contracting Parties to the Joint Convention on the Safety of Spent Fuel Management and on the Safety of Radioactive Waste Management was convened in Vienna from 3 to 14 November 2003,

Desirous of promoting the implementation of paragraph 76 of the Final Document of the Tenth Special Session of the General Assembly, the first special session devoted to disarmament,

1. *Takes note* of the part of the report of the Conference on Disarmament relating to radiological weapons;
2. *Also takes note* of the Declaration of the International Atomic Energy Agency Ministerial Conference on Nuclear Safety, the Action Plan on Nuclear Safety and the High-level Meeting on Nuclear Safety and Security, convened by the Secretary-General;
3. *Expresses grave concern* regarding any use of nuclear wastes that would constitute radiological warfare and have grave implications for the national security of all States;
4. *Calls upon* all States to take appropriate measures with a view to preventing any dumping of nuclear or radioactive wastes that would infringe upon the sovereignty of States;
5. *Requests* the Conference on Disarmament to take into account, in the negotiations for a convention on the prohibition of radiological weapons, radioactive wastes as part of the scope of such a convention;
6. *Also requests* the Conference on Disarmament to intensify efforts towards an early conclusion of such a convention and to include in its report to the General Assembly at its sixty-eighth session the progress recorded in the negotiations on this subject;
7. *Takes note* of resolution CM/Res.1356(LIV) of 1991, adopted by the Council of Ministers of the Organization of African Unity, on the Bamako Convention on the Ban on the Import of Hazardous Wastes into Africa and on the Control of Their Transboundary Movements within Africa;
8. *Expresses the hope* that the effective implementation of the International Atomic Energy Agency Code of Practice on the International Transboundary Movement of Radioactive Waste will enhance the protection of all States from the dumping of radioactive wastes on their territories;
9. *Appeals* to all Member States that have not yet taken the necessary steps to become party to the Joint Convention on the Safety of Spent Fuel Management and on the Safety of Radioactive Waste Management to do so as soon as possible;
10. *Decides* to include in the provisional agenda of its sixty-eighth session the item entitled "Prohibition of the dumping of radioactive wastes".

Nuclear-weapon-free zones

In 2011, nuclear-weapon-free zones (NWFZs), which represent regional approaches for strengthening global nuclear non-proliferation and disarmament norms and consolidating international efforts towards peace and security, comprised 84 million square kilometres of territory in terms of land area.

Africa

The African Nuclear-Weapon-Free Zone Treaty (Treaty of Pelindaba) [YUN 1995, p. 203], which entered into force in 2009 [YUN 2009, p. 533], had been ratified, as at 31 December, by 32 countries. Ghana ratified it during the year, leaving 18 of the 50 signatory States yet to ratify it. The African Nuclear-Weapon-Free Zone encompassed more than 30 million square kilometres, making it the largest of the five nuclear-weapon-free zones in the world.

GENERAL ASSEMBLY ACTION

On 2 December [meeting 71], the General Assembly, on the recommendation of the First Committee [A/66/404], adopted **resolution 66/23** without vote [agenda item 90].

African Nuclear-Weapon-Free Zone Treaty

The General Assembly,

Recalling its resolutions 51/53 of 10 December 1996 and 56/17 of 29 November 2001 and all its other relevant resolutions, as well as those of the Organization of African Unity and of the African Union,

Recalling also the signing of the African Nuclear-Weapon-Free Zone Treaty (Treaty of Pelindaba) in Cairo on 11 April 1996,

Recalling further the Cairo Declaration adopted on that occasion, which emphasized that nuclear-weapon-free zones, especially in regions of tension, such as the Middle East, enhance global and regional peace and security,

Recalling the statement made by the President of the Security Council on behalf of the members of the Council on 12 April 1996, affirming that the signature of the Treaty constituted an important contribution by the African countries to the maintenance of international peace and security,

Considering that the establishment of nuclear-weapon-free zones, especially in the Middle East, would enhance the security of Africa and the viability of the African nuclear-weapon-free zone,

1. *Recalls with satisfaction* the entry into force of the African Nuclear-Weapon-Free Zone Treaty (Treaty of Pelindaba) on 15 July 2009;
2. *Calls upon* African States that have not yet done so to sign and ratify the Treaty as soon as possible;
3. *Expresses its appreciation* to the nuclear-weapon States that have signed the Protocols to the Treaty that concern them, and calls upon those that have not yet ratified the Protocols that concern them to do so as soon as possible;
4. *Calls upon* the States contemplated in Protocol III to the Treaty that have not yet done so to take all necessary measures to ensure the speedy application of the Treaty to territories for which they are, de jure or de facto, internationally responsible and which lie within the limits of the geographical zone established in the Treaty;
5. *Calls upon* the African States parties to the Treaty on the Non-Proliferation of Nuclear Weapons that have not yet done so to conclude comprehensive safeguards agreements with the International Atomic Energy Agency pursuant to the Treaty, thereby satisfying the requirements of article 9 (*b*) of and annex II to the Treaty of Pelindaba, and to conclude additional protocols to their safeguards agreements on the basis of the Model Protocol approved by the Board of Governors of the Agency on 15 May 1997;
6. *Expresses its gratitude* to the Secretary-General of the United Nations, the Chair of the African Union Commission and the Director General of the International Atomic Energy Agency for the diligence with which they have rendered effective assistance to the signatories to the Treaty;
7. *Decides* to include in the provisional agenda of its sixty-seventh session the item entitled "African Nuclear-Weapon-Free Zone Treaty".

Asia

Central Asia

The Treaty on a Central Asian Nuclear-Weapon-Free Zone, which was signed in 2006 [YUN 2006, p. 644] by all five Central Asian States comprising the Zone (Kazakhstan, Kyrgyzstan, Tajikistan, Turkmenistan and Uzbekistan), entered into force in 2009 [YUN 2009, p. 534]. The Treaty required each State party to conclude an additional protocol with IAEA in addition to its comprehensive safeguards system. In November, the additional protocols of IAEA entered into force when Kyrgyzstan concluded the procedures for its adherence (following Uzbekistan in 1998, Tajikistan in 2004, Turkmenistan in 2006 and Kazakhstan in 2007).

South-East Asia

The 10 States parties to the Treaty on the South-East Asia Nuclear-Weapon-Free Zone (Bangkok Treaty), which opened for signature in 1995 [YUN 1995, p. 207] and entered into force in 1997 [YUN 1997, p. 495], continued to promote and strengthen implementation of the Treaty. During the year, consultations were renewed between the States parties to the Treaty and the five nuclear-weapon States towards enabling the nuclear-weapon States to sign the Protocol to the Treaty as soon as possible. Representatives of the Treaty's Executive Committee and the nuclear-weapon States met on 15 November in Bali, Indonesia, and concluded negotiations on outstanding issues related to the Treaty and its Protocol.

GENERAL ASSEMBLY ACTION

On 2 December [meeting 71], the General Assembly, on the recommendation of the First Committee [A/66/412], adopted **resolution 66/43** without vote [agenda item 98 (c)].

**Treaty on the South-East Asia
Nuclear-Weapon-Free Zone (Bangkok Treaty)**

The General Assembly,

Recalling its resolution 64/39 of 2 December 2009, entitled "Treaty on the South-East Asia Nuclear-Weapon-Free Zone (Bangkok Treaty)",

Welcoming the desire of the South-East Asian States to maintain peace and stability in the region in the spirit of peaceful coexistence and mutual understanding and cooperation,

Noting the entry into force of the Charter of the Association of Southeast Asian Nations on 15 December 2008, which states, inter alia, that one of the purposes of the Association is to preserve South-East Asia as a nuclear-weapon-free zone, free of all other weapons of mass destruction,

Noting also the convening of the second Conference of States Parties and Signatories of Treaties that Establish Nuclear-Weapon-Free Zones and Mongolia,

Reaffirming its conviction of the important role of nuclear-weapon-free zones, established, where appropriate, on the basis of arrangements freely arrived at among States of the region concerned and in accordance with the 1999 guidelines of the Disarmament Commission, in strengthening the nuclear non-proliferation regime, in contributing towards realizing the objectives of nuclear disarmament and in extending the areas of the world that are free of nuclear weapons, and, with particular reference to the responsibilities of the nuclear-weapon States, calling upon all States to seek a safer world for all and to achieve peace and security in a world without nuclear weapons in a way that promotes international stability and is based on the principle of undiminished security for all,

Convinced that the establishment of a South-East Asia Nuclear-Weapon-Free Zone, as an essential component of the Declaration on the Zone of Peace, Freedom and Neutrality, signed in Kuala Lumpur on 27 November 1971, will contribute towards strengthening the security of States within the Zone and towards enhancing international peace and security as a whole,

Noting the entry into force of the Treaty on the South-East Asia Nuclear-Weapon-Free Zone on 27 March 1997 and the tenth anniversary of its entry into force in 2007,

Welcoming the reaffirmation of South-East Asian States that the South-East Asia Nuclear-Weapon-Free Zone shall continue to play a pivotal role in the area of confidence-building measures, preventive diplomacy and the approaches to conflict resolution as enshrined in the Declaration of the Association of Southeast Asian Nations Concord II (Bali Concord II),

Reaffirming the inalienable right of all the parties to the Treaty on the South East Asia Nuclear-Weapon-Free Zone to develop research, production and use of nuclear energy for peaceful purposes without discrimination and in conformity with the Treaty on the Non-Proliferation of Nuclear Weapons,

Recognizing that by signing and ratifying the relevant protocols to the treaties establishing nuclear-weapon-free zones, nuclear-weapon States would undertake individual legally binding commitments to respect the status of such zones and not to use or threaten to use nuclear weapons against States parties to such treaties,

Recalling the applicable principles and rules of international law relating to the freedom of the high seas and the rights of innocent passage, archipelagic sea lanes passage or transit passage of ships and aircraft, particularly those of the United Nations Convention on the Law of the Sea,

1. *Welcomes* the commitment and efforts of the Commission for the Treaty on the South-East Asia Nuclear-Weapon-Free Zone to further enhance and strengthen the implementation of the Bangkok Treaty by implementing the Plan of Action for the period 2007–2012, adopted in Manila on 29 July 2007, and the recent decision of the Association of Southeast Asian Nations Political-Security Community Council, established under the Charter of the Association, to give priority to the implementation of the Plan of Action;

2. *Also welcomes* the resumption of direct consultations between the States parties to the Treaty on the South-East Asia Nuclear-Weapon-Free Zone and the five nuclear-weapon States, and encourages States parties to the Treaty to continue direct consultations with the five nuclear-

weapon States to resolve comprehensively, in accordance with the objectives and principles of the Treaty, existing outstanding issues on a number of provisions of the Treaty and the Protocol thereto;

3. *Encourages* nuclear-weapon States and States parties to the Treaty on the South-East Asia Nuclear-Weapon-Free Zone to work constructively with a view to ensuring the early accession of the nuclear weapon States to the Protocol to the Treaty;

4. *Underlines* the value of enhancing and implementing further ways and means of cooperation among the States parties to nuclear-weapon-free zone treaties and the protocols thereto;

5. *Decides* to include in the provisional agenda of its sixty-eighth session the item entitled "Treaty on the South-East Asia Nuclear-Weapon-Free Zone (Bangkok Treaty)".

Latin America and the Caribbean

The 33 States parties to the Treaty for the Prohibition of Nuclear Weapons in Latin America and the Caribbean (Treaty of Tlatelolco) [YUN 1967, p. 13] continued to consolidate the Treaty regime. The Treaty's Additional Protocol I, directed at States that were, de jure or de facto, responsible for territories within the Zone of Application of the Treaty, had been signed and ratified by France, the Netherlands, the United Kingdom and the United States. Additional Protocol II, directed at the nuclear-weapon States officially recognized by the international community, had been signed and ratified by China, France, the United Kingdom, the United States and the Soviet Union (now the Russian Federation).

Middle East

Report of Secretary-General. In response to General Assembly resolution 65/42 [YUN 2010, p. 547], the Secretary-General, in July [A/66/153 (Part I) & Add.1,2], reported on the establishment of a nuclear-weapon-free zone in the Middle East. He noted that recent political changes taking place throughout the region had not weakened the international consensus on the establishment of such a zone. In particular, States of the region that were party to the NPT continued to place importance on implementing the steps agreed to at the 2010 NPT Review Conference [YUN 2010, p. 531]. The Secretary-General initiated consultations with States of the region with a view to enacting the requisite steps, including the appointment of a facilitator and the designation of a host Government, for the convening of a conference in 2012 on the establishment of a Middle East zone free of nuclear weapons and all other weapons of mass destruction. The report included the views on the matter of 17 Member States—Australia, Austria, Burkina Faso, Cuba, Egypt, Estonia, Iran, Iraq, Ireland, Japan, Kazakhstan, Lebanon, Mexico, Portugal, Syria, Turkmenistan and Venezuela.

IAEA General Conference. On 23 September, the IAEA General Conference, adopted a resolution [GC(55)/RES/14] on the application of IAEA safeguards in the Middle East, by which it called on all States in the region to take measures, including confidence-building and verification measures, aimed at establishing a nuclear-weapon-free zone in the Middle East.

GENERAL ASSEMBLY ACTION

On 2 December [meeting 71], the General Assembly, on the recommendation of the First Committee [A/66/408], adopted **resolution 66/25** without vote [agenda item 94].

Establishment of a nuclear-weapon-free zone in the region of the Middle East

The General Assembly,

Recalling its resolutions 3263(XXIX) of 9 December 1974, 3474(XXX) of 11 December 1975, 31/71 of 10 December 1976, 32/82 of 12 December 1977, 33/64 of 14 December 1978, 34/77 of 11 December 1979, 35/147 of 12 December 1980, 36/87 A and B of 9 December 1981, 37/75 of 9 December 1982, 38/64 of 15 December 1983, 39/54 of 12 December 1984, 40/82 of 12 December 1985, 41/48 of 3 December 1986, 42/28 of 30 November 1987, 43/65 of 7 December 1988, 44/108 of 15 December 1989, 45/52 of 4 December 1990, 46/30 of 6 December 1991, 47/48 of 9 December 1992, 48/71 of 16 December 1993, 49/71 of 15 December 1994, 50/66 of 12 December 1995, 51/41 of 10 December 1996, 52/34 of 9 December 1997, 53/74 of 4 December 1998, 54/51 of 1 December 1999, 55/30 of 20 November 2000, 56/21 of 29 November 2001, 57/55 of 22 November 2002, 58/34 of 8 December 2003, 59/63 of 3 December 2004, 60/52 of 8 December 2005, 61/56 of 6 December 2006, 62/18 of 5 December 2007, 63/38 of 2 December 2008, 64/26 of 2 December 2009 and 65/42 of 8 December 2010 on the establishment of a nuclear-weapon-free zone in the region of the Middle East,

Recalling also the recommendations for the establishment of a nuclear-weapon-free zone in the region of the Middle East consistent with paragraphs 60 to 63, and in particular paragraph 63 (*d*), of the Final Document of the Tenth Special Session of the General Assembly,

Emphasizing the basic provisions of the above-mentioned resolutions, which call upon all parties directly concerned to consider taking the practical and urgent steps required for the implementation of the proposal to establish a nuclear-weapon-free zone in the region of the Middle East and, pending and during the establishment of such a zone, to declare solemnly that they will refrain, on a reciprocal basis, from producing, acquiring or in any other way possessing nuclear weapons and nuclear explosive devices and from permitting the stationing of nuclear weapons on their territory by any third party, to agree to place their nuclear facilities under International Atomic Energy Agency safeguards and to declare their support for the establishment of the zone and to deposit such declarations with the Security Council for consideration, as appropriate,

Reaffirming the inalienable right of all States to acquire and develop nuclear energy for peaceful purposes,

Emphasizing the need for appropriate measures on the question of the prohibition of military attacks on nuclear facilities,

Bearing in mind the consensus reached by the General Assembly since its thirty-fifth session that the establishment of a nuclear-weapon-free zone in the region of the Middle East would greatly enhance international peace and security,

Desirous of building on that consensus so that substantial progress can be made towards establishing a nuclear-weapon-free zone in the region of the Middle East,

Welcoming all initiatives leading to general and complete disarmament, including in the region of the Middle East, and in particular on the establishment therein of a zone free of weapons of mass destruction, including nuclear weapons,

Noting the peace negotiations in the Middle East, which should be of a comprehensive nature and represent an appropriate framework for the peaceful settlement of contentious issues in the region,

Recognizing the importance of credible regional security, including the establishment of a mutually verifiable nuclear-weapon-free zone,

Emphasizing the essential role of the United Nations in the establishment of a mutually verifiable nuclear-weapon-free zone,

Having examined the report of the Secretary-General on the implementation of resolution 65/42,

1. *Urges* all parties directly concerned seriously to consider taking the practical and urgent steps required for the implementation of the proposal to establish a nuclear-weapon-free zone in the region of the Middle East in accordance with the relevant resolutions of the General Assembly, and, as a means of promoting this objective, invites the countries concerned to adhere to the Treaty on the Non-Proliferation of Nuclear Weapons;

2. *Calls upon* all countries of the region that have not yet done so, pending the establishment of the zone, to agree to place all their nuclear activities under International Atomic Energy Agency safeguards;

3. *Takes note* of resolution GC(55)/RES/14, adopted on 23 September 2011 by the General Conference of the International Atomic Energy Agency at its fifty-fifth regular session, concerning the application of Agency safeguards in the Middle East;

4. *Notes* the importance of the ongoing bilateral Middle East peace negotiations and the activities of the multilateral Working Group on Arms Control and Regional Security in promoting mutual confidence and security in the Middle East, including the establishment of a nuclear-weapon-free zone;

5. *Invites* all countries of the region, pending the establishment of a nuclear-weapon-free zone in the region of the Middle East, to declare their support for establishing such a zone, consistent with paragraph 63 (*d*) of the Final Document of the Tenth Special Session of the General Assembly, and to deposit those declarations with the Security Council;

6. *Also invites* those countries, pending the establishment of the zone, not to develop, produce, test or otherwise acquire nuclear weapons or permit the stationing on their territories, or territories under their control, of nuclear weapons or nuclear explosive devices;

7. *Invites* the nuclear-weapon States and all other States to render their assistance in the establishment of the zone and at the same time to refrain from any action that runs counter to both the letter and the spirit of the present resolution;

8. *Takes note* of the report of the Secretary-General;

9. *Invites* all parties to consider the appropriate means that may contribute towards the goal of general and complete disarmament and the establishment of a zone free of weapons of mass destruction in the region of the Middle East;

10. *Requests* the Secretary-General to continue to pursue consultations with the States of the region and other concerned States, in accordance with paragraph 7 of resolution 46/30 and taking into account the evolving situation in the region, and to seek from those States their views on the measures outlined in chapters III and IV of the study annexed to the report of the Secretary-General of 10 October 1990 or other relevant measures, in order to move towards the establishment of a nuclear-weapon-free zone in the region of the Middle East;

11. *Also requests* the Secretary-General to submit to the General Assembly at its sixty-seventh session a report on the implementation of the present resolution;

12. *Decides* to include in the provisional agenda of its sixty-seventh session the item entitled "Establishment of a nuclear-weapon-free zone in the region of the Middle East".

South Pacific

As at 31 December, the number of States parties to the 1985 South Pacific Nuclear-Free Zone Treaty (Treaty of Rarotonga) [YUN 1985, p. 58] remained at 13. China and the Russian Federation had ratified Protocols 2 and 3, and France and the United Kingdom had ratified all three Protocols. Under Protocol 1, the States internationally responsible for territories situated within the zone would apply the relevant prohibitions of the Treaty to those territories; under Protocol 2, the five nuclear-weapon States would provide security assurances to parties or territories within the zone; and under Protocol 3, the five nuclear-weapon States would not carry out any nuclear tests in the zone.

Bacteriological (biological) and chemical weapons

In 2011, Member States continued to focus on strengthening the 1972 Convention on the Prohibition of the Development, Production and Stockpiling of Bacteriological (Biological) and Toxin Weapons and on Their Destruction (Biological Weapons Convention) (BWC) [YUN 1972, p. 5] and the Convention on the Prohibition of the Development, Production, Stockpiling and Use of Chemical Weapons and on Their Destruction (CWC) [YUN 1971. p. 19].

Bacteriological (biological) weapons

Bacteriological (biological) weapons convention

As at 31 December, 163 States had either ratified or acceded to the Convention on the Prohibition of the Development, Production and Stockpiling of Bacteriological (Biological) and Toxin Weapons and on Their Destruction (Biological Weapons Convention) (BWC). During the year, Burundi and Mozambique became parties.

Seventh Review Conference

Preparatory Committee

The Preparatory Committee for the Seventh Review Conference of the States Parties to BWC met from 13 to 15 April in Geneva [BWC/CONF.VII/PC/2]. The Committee decided that the Conference should be held in Geneva from 5 to 22 December, and recommended the provisional agenda of the Conference.

GENERAL ASSEMBLY ACTION

On 2 December [meeting 71], the General Assembly, on the recommendation of the First Committee [A/66/419], adopted **resolution 66/65** without vote [agenda item 105].

Convention on the Prohibition of the Development, Production and Stockpiling of Bacteriological (Biological) and Toxin Weapons and on Their Destruction

The General Assembly,

Recalling its previous resolutions relating to the complete and effective prohibition of bacteriological (biological) and toxin weapons and to their destruction,

Noting with satisfaction that there are one hundred and sixty-five States parties to the Convention on the Prohibition of the Development, Production and Stockpiling of Bacteriological (Biological) and Toxin Weapons and on Their Destruction, including all the permanent members of the Security Council,

Bearing in mind its call upon all States parties to the Convention to participate in the implementation of the recommendations of the review conferences of the parties to the Convention, including the exchange of information and data agreed to in the Final Declaration of the Third Review Conference of the Parties to the Convention on the Prohibition of the Development, Production and Stockpiling of Bacteriological (Biological) and Toxin Weapons and on Their Destruction, and to provide such information and data in conformity with standardized procedure to the Secretary-General on an annual basis and no later than 15 April,

Welcoming the reaffirmation made in the Final Declaration of the Fourth Review Conference that under all circumstances the use of bacteriological (biological) and toxin weapons and their development, production and stockpiling are effectively prohibited under article I of the Convention,

Recalling the decision reached at the Sixth Review Conference to hold four annual meetings of the States parties of one week's duration each year commencing in 2007, prior to the Seventh Review Conference, which is to be held no later than the end of 2011, and to hold a one-week meeting of experts to prepare for each meeting of the States parties,

1. *Notes with appreciation* that two additional States have acceded to the Convention on the Prohibition of the Development, Production and Stockpiling of Bacteriological (Biological) and Toxin Weapons and on Their Destruction, reaffirms its call upon all signatory States that have not yet ratified the Convention to do so without delay, and calls upon those States that have not signed the Convention to become parties thereto at the earliest possible date, thus contributing to the achievement of universal adherence to the Convention;

2. *Welcomes* the information and data provided to date, as well as the several measures to update the mechanism for the transmission of information in the framework of confidence-building measures agreed upon at the Sixth Review Conference of the States Parties to the Convention on the Prohibition of the Development, Production and Stockpiling of Bacteriological (Biological) and Toxin Weapons and on Their Destruction, and reiterates its call upon all States parties to the Convention to participate in the exchange of information and data agreed upon at the Third Review Conference;

3. *Recalls* the decisions on all provisions of the Convention reached at the Sixth Review Conference, and calls upon States parties to the Convention to participate in their implementation;

4. *Notes with appreciation* the work of the Implementation Support Unit within the Office for Disarmament Affairs of the Secretariat during the 2007–2010 intersessional process consistent with its mandate and in accordance with the decisions of the Sixth Review Conference;

5. *Welcomes* the successful holding of meetings as part of the 2007–2010 intersessional process, and in this context also welcomes the discussion aimed at the promotion of common understanding and effective action on topics agreed upon at the Sixth Review Conference;

6. *Notes* the success of the meeting of the Preparatory Committee for the Seventh Review Conference, held in Geneva from 13 to 15 April 2011, and welcomes the convening of the Seventh Review Conference in Geneva from 5 to 22 December 2011 pursuant to the decision of the Preparatory Committee;

7. *Recalls* that the Seventh Review Conference is mandated to consider issues identified in the review of the operation of the Convention as provided for in article XII thereof and any possible consensus follow-up action;

8. *Urges* all States parties to continue to work together to achieve a consensus outcome of the Seventh Review Conference which strengthens the Convention;

9. *Notes with appreciation* the events organized by some States parties for exchanges of views on the work of the Seventh Review Conference;

10. *Requests* the Secretary-General to continue to render the necessary assistance to the depositary Governments of the Convention, to provide such services as may be required for the implementation of the decisions and

recommendations of the review conferences and to render the necessary assistance and to provide such services as may be required for the Seventh Review Conference;

11. *Decides* to include in the provisional agenda of its sixty-seventh session the item entitled "Convention on the Prohibition of the Development, Production and Stockpiling of Bacteriological (Biological) and Toxin Weapons and on Their Destruction".

Conference

The Seventh Review Conference of the States Parties to BWC (Geneva, 5–22 December) [BWC/CONF.VII/7] reviewed the operation of the Convention, including new scientific and technological developments; progress made by States on the implementation of their obligations; and progress in the implementation of the decisions and recommendations of the Sixth Review Conference [YUN 2006, p. 651]. The Conference was attended by 103 States parties, as well as five States that had signed but not ratified the Convention and two States that were neither parties nor signatories, along with a number of UN agencies, international organizations and non-governmental organizations (NGOs).

On 22 December, the Conference adopted its Final Document [BWC/CONF.VII/7] containing a Declaration by which States parties stated their conviction that the Convention was essential for international peace and security; their commitment to the purposes of the Preamble and the provisions of the Convention; and their determination to comply with all obligations undertaken pursuant to the Convention and their recognition that States parties not in compliance with their obligations posed fundamental challenges to the Convention's viability, as would the use of bacteriological (biological) and toxin weapons by anyone at any time. The Conference reviewed the Convention's 15 articles, and reaffirmed the comprehensive scope of the Convention, as defined in article I. It noted that experimentation involving open air release of pathogens or toxins harmful to humans, animals and plants that had no justification for prophylactic, protective or other peaceful purposes was inconsistent with the undertakings contained in Article I. The Conference called for measures, including export controls, by States parties to ensure that direct and indirect transfers relevant to the Convention, to any recipient whatsoever, were authorized only when the intended use was for purposes not prohibited under the Convention. It encouraged States parties that had not yet done so, in accordance with the recommendation of the Sixth Review Conference, to designate a national focal point for coordinating national implementation of the Convention and communicating with other States parties and relevant international organizations. Noting the proposal by Iran at the Sixth Review Conference to amend Article I and the title of the Convention to include the prohibition of the use of biological weapons, the Conference reaffirmed that the provisions of that Article should in principle be implemented in such a way as not to affect the Convention's universality. The Conference decided to convene the Eighth Review Conference not later than 2016.

In other decisions and recommendations, the Conference established a database system to facilitate requests for and offers of exchange of assistance and cooperation among States parties and a sponsorship programme to be funded by voluntary contributions. Other decisions concerned topics to be addressed under standing agenda items, the reporting of confidence-building measures, meetings of States parties and experts, and the work of the Implementation Support Unit.

Chemical weapons
Chemical weapons convention

As at 31 December, the number of States that had either ratified or acceded to the Convention on the Prohibition of the Development, Production, Stockpiling and Use of Chemical Weapons and Their Destruction remained at 188. The number of signatories remained at 165. The Convention was adopted by the Conference on Disarmament in 1992 [YUN 1992, p. 65] and entered into force in 1997 [YUN 2007, p. 499].

Sixteenth Session of the Conference of States Parties

The sixteenth session of the Conference of States Parties (The Hague, 28 November–2 December) [C-16/5] was attended by 131 States parties, two signatory States attending as observers, international organizations, specialized agencies, other international bodies and 29 NGOs. The session had before it the report of the Organization for the Prohibition of Chemical Weapons on the implementation of the Convention in 2010 [YUN 2010, p. 552].

The Conference established the International Support Network for Victims of Chemical Weapons, to be financed through voluntary contributions. It decided to review progress and implementation of the action plan for the universality of the Convention at its eighteenth session, in particular the status of States not party whose non-adherence was a cause for concern. The Conference decided on components of an agreed framework to be implemented by States parties. The secretariat should report annually on progress in implementing the decision. The Director General of the Organization for the Prohibition of Chemical Weapons should report to the sixty-eighth session of the Executive Council on whether or not the final extended deadline of 29 April 2012 for the destruction of chemical weapons had been met, including information on quantities of weapons destroyed and that remained to be destroyed. The Conference also decided on measures to be implemented if the deadline had not been met. The Conference extended the deadline for the destruction of category 1 chemical weapons by the Libyan Arab Jamahiriya to 29 April 2012.

GENERAL ASSEMBLY ACTION

On 2 December [meeting 71], the General Assembly, on the recommendation of the First Committee [A/66/412], adopted **resolution 66/35** without vote [agenda item 98 (*p*)].

Implementation of the Convention on the Prohibition of the Development, Production, Stockpiling and Use of Chemical Weapons and on Their Destruction

The General Assembly,

Recalling its previous resolutions on the subject of chemical weapons, in particular resolution 65/57 of 8 December 2010, adopted without a vote, in which it noted with appreciation the ongoing work to achieve the objective and purpose of the Convention on the Prohibition of the Development, Production, Stockpiling and Use of Chemical Weapons and on Their Destruction,

Determined to achieve the effective prohibition of the development, production, acquisition, transfer, stockpiling and use of chemical weapons and their destruction,

Noting with satisfaction that, since the adoption of resolution 63/48 of 2 December 2008, four additional States have acceded to the Convention, bringing the total number of States parties to the Convention to one hundred and eighty-eight,

Reaffirming the importance of the outcome of the Second Special Session of the Conference of the States Parties to Review the Operation of the Chemical Weapons Convention (hereinafter "the Second Review Conference"), including the consensus final report, which addressed all aspects of the Convention and made important recommendations on its continued implementation,

Emphasizing that the Second Review Conference welcomed the fact that, eleven years after its entry into force, the Convention remained a unique multilateral agreement banning an entire category of weapons of mass destruction in a non-discriminatory and verifiable manner under strict and effective international control,

1. *Emphasizes* that the universality of the Convention on the Prohibition of the Development, Production, Stockpiling and Use of Chemical Weapons and on Their Destruction is fundamental to the achievement of its objective and purpose, acknowledges progress made in the implementation of the action plan for the universality of the Convention, and calls upon all States that have not yet done so to become parties to the Convention without delay;

2. *Underlines* the fact that implementation of the Convention makes a major contribution to international peace and security through the elimination of existing stockpiles of chemical weapons and the prohibition of the acquisition or use of chemical weapons, and provides for assistance and protection in the event of use, or threat of use, of chemical weapons and for international cooperation for peaceful purposes in the field of chemical activities;

3. *Stresses* the importance to the Convention that all possessors of chemical weapons, chemical weapons production facilities or chemical weapons development facilities, including previously declared possessor States, should be among the States parties to the Convention, and welcomes progress to that end;

4. *Reaffirms* the obligation of the States parties to the Convention to destroy chemical weapons and to destroy or convert chemical weapons production facilities within the time limits provided for by the Convention;

5. *Stresses* that the full and effective implementation of all provisions of the Convention, including those on national implementation (article VII) and assistance and protection (article X), constitutes an important contribution to the efforts of the United Nations in the global fight against terrorism in all its forms and manifestations;

6. *Notes* that the effective application of the verification system builds confidence in compliance with the Convention by States parties;

7. *Stresses* the importance of the Organization for the Prohibition of Chemical Weapons in verifying compliance with the provisions of the Convention as well as in promoting the timely and efficient accomplishment of all its objectives;

8. *Urges* all States parties to the Convention to meet in full and on time their obligations under the Convention and to support the Organization for the Prohibition of Chemical Weapons in its implementation activities;

9. *Welcomes* progress made in the national implementation of article VII obligations, commends the States parties and the Technical Secretariat for assisting other States parties, on request, with the implementation of the follow-up to the plan of action regarding article VII obligations, and urges States parties that have not fulfilled their obligations under article VII to do so without further delay, in accordance with their constitutional processes;

10. *Emphasizes* the continuing relevance and importance of the provisions of article X of the Convention, and welcomes the activities of the Organization for the Prohibition of Chemical Weapons in relation to assistance and protection against chemical weapons;

11. *Reaffirms* that the provisions of the Convention shall be implemented in a manner that avoids hampering the economic or technological development of States parties and international cooperation in the field of chemical activities for purposes not prohibited under the Convention, including the international exchange of scientific and technical information, and chemicals and equipment for the production, processing or use of chemicals for purposes not prohibited under the Convention;

12. *Emphasizes* the importance of article XI provisions relating to the economic and technological development of States parties, recalls that the full, effective and non-discriminatory implementation of those provisions contributes to universality, and also reaffirms the undertaking of the States parties to foster international cooperation for peaceful purposes in the field of chemical activities of the States parties and the importance of that cooperation and its contribution to the promotion of the Convention as a whole;

13. *Notes with appreciation* the ongoing work of the Organization for the Prohibition of Chemical Weapons to achieve the objective and purpose of the Convention, to ensure the full implementation of its provisions, including those for international verification of compliance with it, and to provide a forum for consultation and cooperation among States parties;

14. *Welcomes* the cooperation between the United Nations and the Organization for the Prohibition of Chemical Weapons within the framework of the Relationship Agreement between the United Nations and the Organization, in accordance with the provisions of the Convention;

15. *Decides* to include in the provisional agenda of its sixty-seventh session the item entitled "Implementation of the Convention on the Prohibition of the Development, Production, Stockpiling and Use of Chemical Weapons and on Their Destruction".

Organization for the Prohibition of Chemical Weapons

The Organization for the Prohibition of Chemical Weapons (opcw)—mandated to oversee the implementation of the cwc and to provide a forum for consultation—detailed in a report on its activities during 2011 [C-17/4] the three areas of work under the Convention: chemical disarmament; non-proliferation, assistance and protection; and international cooperation.

Opcw reported that as at 31 December, it had destroyed 51,505 metric tonnes, or 72 per cent of chemical weapons declared by the seven possessor States parties. It verified the destruction of some 6,429 metric tonnes of chemical weapons at chemical weapons destruction sites (Libya, Russian Federation, United States). At the end of the year, Libya had destroyed 54 per cent, the Russian Federation 60 per cent, and the United States 90 per cent of their respective declared stocks of Category 1 chemical weapons. Iraq had yet to commence its destruction operations. At the end of the review period, six chemical weapons production facilities (five in Iraq and one in the Russian Federation) remained to be certified as either destroyed or converted for purposes not prohibited under the Convention. Seven States parties reported new findings of old chemical weapons, while 25,974 chemical weapons abandoned by Japan on the territory of China were reported to have been destroyed.

Opcw carried out inspections at 209 chemical-industry facilities. In May, for the first time, it conducted chemical weapons-related on-site inspections in Iraq. The secretariat continued to promote universal adherence to the Convention, recognizing the complexities for the remaining eight States not party.

Conventional weapons

Towards an arms trade treaty

By resolution 64/48 [YUN 2009, p. 544], the General Assembly decided to convene in 2012 a Conference on the Arms Trade Treaty. The Preparatory Committee for the Conference held its second (New York, 28 February–4 March) [A/CONF.217/PC.II/L.2] and third (New York, 11–15 July) sessions in 2011. The latter had before it draft papers on implementation and final provisions of the proposed treaty [A/CONF.217/PC/III/1], transmitted by the Chairman of the Committee and based on the exchange of views at the Committee's first and second sessions.

Report of Secretary-General. In a July report, with later addenda [A/66/166 & Add.1,2], the Secretary-General transmitted the views of 19 Member States (Australia, Bangladesh, Bulgaria, Burkina Faso, China, Egypt, El Salvador, Germany, Guyana, Lebanon, Mexico, Netherlands, New Zealand, Norway, Panama, Portugal, Saudi Arabia, Switzerland, Turkmenistan) and the European Union on the proposed treaty elements and other issues relating to the Conference.

On 2 December (**decision 66/518**), the Assembly decided to hold the final session of the Preparatory Committee for the United Nations Conference on the Arms Trade Treaty in New York from 13 to 16 February 2012, to conclude its work and decide on procedural matters.

Small arms

In an April report on small arms [S/2011/255], submitted pursuant to Security Council Presidential statement S/PRST/2007/24 [YUN 2007, p. 570], the Secretary-General updated the Council on weapons trade and brokering, marking, record-keeping and tracing, stockpile management, armed violence and the use and misuse of small arms. The report gave special attention to the trade in ammunition, problems connected with storage and the importance of tracing ammunition found in conflict settings. According to the Secretary-General, in consideration of problems relating to the unregulated circulation of small arms, it was essential to focus on integrated policy approaches. Peacekeeping and peacebuilding activities and development assistance required planning for small arms control and armed violence reduction as a priority. In such contexts, it was vital that traditional arms control measures be integrated into interventions that targeted the demand for weapons and enhanced the ability of security providers and governance authorities to strengthen community security, manage conflict and mitigate violence. The Secretary-General concluded with a series of recommendations for strengthening coordination, particularly within the UN system, with regard to weapons tracing, record-keeping and marking, as well as securing ammunition stockpiles, integrating traditional arms control measures into conflict and post-conflict interventions, and increasing compliance by non-State armed groups.

UN Programme of Action on illicit trade in small arms

The Open-ended Meeting of Governmental Experts on the Implementation of the Programme of Action to Prevent, Combat and Eradicate the Illicit Trade in Small Arms and Light Weapons in All Its Aspects, adopted in 2001 [YUN 2001, p. 499], met in New York from 9 to 13 May [A/CONF.192/MGE/2011/1]. It considered challenges in implementing the International Instrument to Enable States to Identify and Trace, in a Timely and Reliable Manner, Illicit Small Arms and Light Weapons [YUN 2005, p. 621], including international cooperation and assistance. Discussions focused on weapons marking, record-keeping and cooperation in tracing, national frameworks, regional cooperation and international assistance and capacity-building. Participants recognized that weapons marking, record-keeping and tracing were mutually reinforcing activities that should be an integral part of national efforts to control small arms and light weapons. They also noted the enabling role that effective national frameworks, active regional and international cooperation, the provision of assistance and national capacity-building played in supporting implementation of the International Tracing Instrument and relevant provisions of the Programme of Action.

On 14 July [A/66/157], New Zealand transmitted to the Secretary-General the Chair's summary of key points of the discussion.

GENERAL ASSEMBLY ACTION

On 2 December [meeting 71], the General Assembly, on the recommendation of the First Committee [A/66/412], adopted **resolution 66/47** without vote [agenda item 98 (*t*)].

The illicit trade in small arms and light weapons in all its aspects

The General Assembly,

Recalling its resolution 65/64 of 8 December 2010, as well as all previous resolutions entitled "The illicit trade in small arms and light weapons in all its aspects", including resolution 56/24 V of 24 December 2001,

Emphasizing the importance of the continued and full implementation of the Programme of Action to Prevent, Combat and Eradicate the Illicit Trade in Small Arms and Light Weapons in All Its Aspects, adopted by the United Nations Conference on the Illicit Trade in Small Arms and Light Weapons in All Its Aspects,

Welcoming the tenth anniversary of the adoption of the Programme of Action, and recognizing its important contribution to international efforts on this matter,

Emphasizing the importance of the continued and full implementation of the International Instrument to Enable States to Identify and Trace, in a Timely and Reliable Manner, Illicit Small Arms and Light Weapons (the International Tracing Instrument),

Recalling the commitment of States to the Programme of Action as the main framework for measures within the activities of the international community to prevent, combat and eradicate the illicit trade in small arms and light weapons in all its aspects,

Underlining the need for States to enhance their efforts to build national capacity for the effective implementation of the Programme of Action and the International Tracing Instrument,

Welcoming the Open-ended Meeting of Governmental Experts on the Implementation of the Programme of Action to Prevent, Combat and Eradicate the Illicit Trade in Small Arms and Light Weapons in All Its Aspects, held in New York from 9 to 13 May 2011,

Welcoming also the early designation of Nigeria as the Chair of the second conference to review progress made in the implementation of the Programme of Action, to be held in 2012, and of its preparatory committee,

Stressing the importance of voluntary national reporting to follow up on the Programme of Action as a means of assessing overall implementation efforts, including implementation challenges and opportunities, and which could greatly facilitate the rendering of international cooperation and assistance to affected States,

Noting that tools developed by the Office for Disarmament Affairs of the Secretariat, including the Programme of Action Implementation Support System, and those developed by Member States could be used to assess progress made in the implementation of the Programme of Action,

Welcoming the coordinated efforts within the United Nations to implement the Programme of Action, including by developing the Programme of Action Implementation Support System, which forms an integrated clearing house for international cooperation and assistance for capacity-building in the area of small arms and light weapons,

Taking into account the importance of regional approaches to the implementation of the Programme of Action,

Noting with satisfaction regional and subregional efforts being undertaken in support of the implementation of the Programme of Action, and commending the progress that has already been made in this regard, including tackling both supply and demand factors that are relevant to addressing the illicit trade in small arms and light weapons,

Reiterating that illicit brokering in small arms and light weapons is a serious problem that the international community should address urgently,

Recognizing the efforts undertaken by non-governmental organizations in the provision of assistance to States for the implementation of the Programme of Action,

Taking note of the report of the Secretary-General, which includes an overview of the implementation of resolution 65/64,

1. *Underlines* the fact that the issue of the illicit trade in small arms and light weapons in all its aspects requires concerted efforts at the national, regional and international levels to prevent, combat and eradicate the illicit manufacture, transfer and circulation of small arms and light weapons, and that their uncontrolled spread in many regions of the world has a wide range of humanitarian and socioeconomic consequences and poses a serious threat to peace, reconciliation, safety, security, stability and sustainable development at the individual, local, national, regional and international levels;

2. *Encourages* all initiatives, including those of the United Nations, other international organizations, regional and subregional organizations, non-governmental organizations and civil society, for the successful implementation of the Programme of Action to Prevent, Combat and Eradicate the Illicit Trade in Small Arms and Light Weapons in All Its Aspects, and calls upon all Member States to contribute towards the continued implementation of the Programme of Action at the national, regional and global levels;

3. *Encourages* States to implement the recommendations contained in the report of the Group of Governmental Experts established pursuant to resolution 60/81 to consider further steps to enhance international cooperation in preventing, combating and eradicating illicit brokering in small arms and light weapons;

4. *Recalls* its endorsement of the report adopted at the fourth biennial meeting of States to consider the implementation of the Programme of Action, and encourages all States to implement, as appropriate, the measures highlighted in the section of the report entitled "The way forward";

5. *Endorses* the report adopted at the Open-ended Meeting of Governmental Experts on the Implementation of the Programme of Action to Prevent, Combat and Eradicate the Illicit Trade in Small Arms and Light Weapons in All Its Aspects, and takes note with appreciation of the Chair's summary of discussions, prepared under his own responsibility, reflecting his interpretation of the main points under discussion;

6. *Decides* that, pursuant to resolution 65/64, the second conference to review progress made in the implementation of the Programme of Action will be held in New York, from 27 August to 7 September 2012;

7. *Also decides* that the preparatory committee for the review conference will be convened in New York, from 19 to 23 March 2012;

8. *Encourages* all efforts to build national capacity for the effective implementation of the Programme of Action, including those highlighted in the report of the fourth biennial meeting of States, and, inter alia, through the strengthening of national coordination agencies or bodies and institutional infrastructure;

9. *Encourages* States to submit, on a voluntary basis, national reports on their implementation of the Programme of Action, notes that States will submit national reports on their implementation of the International Tracing Instrument, in advance of the convening of the preparatory committee but, to the extent possible, by the end of 2011, and encourages those States in a position to do so to use the reporting template made available by the Office for Disarmament Affairs and to include therein information, as appropriate, on progress made in the implementation of the measures highlighted in the reports of the third and fourth biennial meetings of States;

10. *Also encourages* States, on a voluntary basis, to make increasing use of their national reports as another tool for communicating assistance needs and information on the resources and mechanisms available to address such needs, and encourages States in a position to render such assistance to make use of these national reports;

11. *Encourages* States, relevant international and regional organizations and civil society with the capacity to do so to cooperate with and assist other States, upon request, in the preparation of comprehensive reports on their implementation of the Programme of Action;

12. *Calls upon* all States to implement the International Tracing Instrument by, inter alia, including in their national reports the name and contact information of the national points of contact and information on national marking practices used to indicate country of manufacture and/or country of import, as applicable;

13. *Recognizes* the urgent need to maintain and enhance national controls, in accordance with the Programme of Action, to prevent, combat and eradicate the illicit trade in small arms and light weapons, including their diversion to unauthorized recipients, taking into account, inter alia, their adverse humanitarian and socioeconomic consequences on the affected States;

14. *Invites* States, at the second review conference, to review progress made in the implementation of the Programme of Action, and, subject to the agenda of the conference to be agreed by the preparatory committee, encourages them to explore ways to strengthen its implementation, including consideration of the possibility of convening a further open-ended meeting of governmental experts;

15. *Encourages* States in a position to do so to provide financial assistance, through a voluntary sponsorship fund, that could be distributed, upon request, to States otherwise unable to participate in meetings on the Programme of Action;

16. *Encourages* interested States and relevant international and regional organizations in a position to do so to convene regional meetings to consider and advance the implementation of the Programme of Action, as well as the International Tracing Instrument, in preparation for the meetings on the Programme of Action;

17. *Emphasizes* the fact that initiatives by the international community with respect to international cooperation and assistance remain essential and complementary to national implementation efforts, as well as to those at the regional and global levels;

18. *Encourages* States to consider ways to enhance cooperation and assistance and to assess their effectiveness in order to ensure the implementation of the Programme of Action;

19. *Recognizes* the necessity for interested States to develop effective coordination mechanisms, where they do not exist, in order to match the needs of States with existing resources to enhance the implementation of the Programme of Action and to make international cooperation and assistance more effective, and in this regard encourages States to make use, as appropriate, of the Programme of Action Implementation Support System;

20. *Encourages* States to consider, among other mechanisms, the coherent identification of needs, priorities, national plans and programmes that may require international cooperation and assistance from States and regional and international organizations in a position to do so;

21. *Encourages* civil society and relevant organizations to strengthen their cooperation and work with States at the respective national and regional levels to achieve the implementation of the Programme of Action;

22. *Requests* the Secretary-General to report to the General Assembly at its sixty-seventh session on the implementation of the present resolution;

23. *Decides* to include in the provisional agenda of its sixty-seventh session the item entitled "The illicit trade in small arms and light weapons in all its aspects".

Assistance to States for curbing illicit small arms traffic

In July [A/66/177], the Secretary-General provided an overview of the activities undertaken by Member States, the UN system and other intergovernmental organizations regarding the implementation of General Assembly resolutions 65/50 [YUN 2010, p. 557] and 65/64 [ibid., p. 554] as well as the Programme of Action. He noted that during the reporting period, particular emphasis had been placed on strengthening the proper marking, record-keeping and tracing capacities of States as vital steps to hold accountable those who engaged in illicit transfers and the diversion of small arms. The coordination of small arms-related activities within the United Nations had been further strengthened. Given the use of the United Nations Register of Conventional Arms [YUN 1992, p. 75] for reporting small arms transfers, the stronger implementation of the Protocol against the Illicit Manufacturing of and Trafficking in Firearms, Their Parts and Components and Ammunition (Firearms Protocol) [YUN 2001, p. 1036], supplementing the United Nations Convention against Transnational Organized Crime [YUN 2000, p. 1048], the possible adoption of an arms trade treaty, and the forthcoming Review Conference on the Programme of Action, Member States had the opportunity to discuss further the relationship among those instruments in order to maximize their complementarity.

GENERAL ASSEMBLY ACTION

On 2 December [meeting 71], the General Assembly, on the recommendation of the First Committee [A/66/412], adopted **resolution 66/34** without vote [agenda item 98 (*k*)].

Assistance to States for curbing the illicit traffic in small arms and light weapons and collecting them

The General Assembly,

Recalling its resolution 65/50 of 8 December 2010 on assistance to States for curbing the illicit traffic in small arms and light weapons and collecting them,

Deeply concerned by the magnitude of human casualty and suffering, especially among children, caused by the illicit proliferation and use of small arms and light weapons,

Concerned by the negative impact that the illicit proliferation and use of those weapons continue to have on the efforts of States in the Sahelo-Saharan subregion in the areas of poverty eradication, sustainable development and the maintenance of peace, security and stability,

Bearing in mind the Bamako Declaration on an African Common Position on the Illicit Proliferation, Circulation and Trafficking of Small Arms and Light Weapons, adopted at Bamako on 1 December 2000,

Recalling the report of the Secretary-General entitled "In larger freedom: towards development, security and human rights for all", in which he emphasized that States must strive just as hard to eliminate the threat of illicit small arms and light weapons as they do to eliminate the threat of weapons of mass destruction,

Recalling also the International Instrument to Enable States to Identify and Trace, in a Timely and Reliable Manner, Illicit Small Arms and Light Weapons, adopted on 8 December 2005,

Recalling further the expression of support in the 2005 World Summit Outcome for the implementation of the Programme of Action to Prevent, Combat and Eradicate the Illicit Trade in Small Arms and Light Weapons in All Its Aspects,

Recalling the adoption, at the thirtieth ordinary summit of the Economic Community of West African States, held in Abuja in June 2006, of the Convention on Small Arms and Light Weapons, Their Ammunition and Other Related Materials, in replacement of the moratorium on the importation, exportation and manufacture of small arms and light weapons in West Africa,

Recalling also the entry into force of the Convention on Small Arms and Light Weapons, Their Ammunition and Other Related Materials on 29 September 2009,

Recalling further the decision taken by the Economic Community to establish a Small Arms Unit responsible for advocating appropriate policies and developing and implementing programmes, as well as the establishment of the Economic Community's Small Arms Control Programme, launched on 6 June 2006 in Bamako, in replacement of the Programme for Coordination and Assistance for Security and Development,

Taking note of the latest report of the Secretary-General on assistance to States for curbing the illicit traffic in small arms and light weapons and collecting them and the illicit trade in small arms and light weapons in all its aspects,

Recalling, in that regard, the decision of the European Union to significantly support the Economic Community in its efforts to combat the illicit proliferation of small arms and light weapons,

Recognizing the important role that civil society organizations play, by raising public awareness, in efforts to curb the illicit traffic in small arms and light weapons,

Recalling the report of the United Nations Conference to Review Progress Made in the Implementation of the Programme of Action to Prevent, Combat and Eradicate the Illicit Trade in Small Arms and Light Weapons in All Its Aspects, held in New York from 26 June to 7 July 2006,

1. *Commends* the United Nations and international, regional and other organizations for their assistance to States for curbing the illicit traffic in small arms and light weapons and collecting them;

2. *Encourages* the Secretary-General to pursue his efforts in the context of the implementation of General Assembly resolution 49/75 G of 15 December 1994 and the recommendations of the United Nations advisory missions aimed at curbing the illicit circulation of small arms and light weapons and collecting them in the affected States that so request, with the support of the United Nations Regional Centre for Peace and Disarmament in Africa and in close cooperation with the African Union;

3. *Encourages* the international community to support the implementation of the Economic Community of West

African States Convention on Small Arms and Light Weapons, Their Ammunition and Other Related Materials;

4. *Encourages* the countries of the Sahelo-Saharan subregion to facilitate the effective functioning of national commissions to combat the illicit proliferation of small arms and light weapons, and in that regard invites the international community to lend its support wherever possible;

5. *Encourages* the collaboration of civil society organizations and associations in the efforts of the national commissions to combat the illicit traffic in small arms and light weapons and in the implementation of the Programme of Action to Prevent, Combat and Eradicate the Illicit Trade in Small Arms and Light Weapons in All Its Aspects;

6. *Encourages* cooperation among State organs, international organizations and civil society in support of programmes and projects aimed at combating the illicit traffic in small arms and light weapons and collecting them;

7. *Calls upon* the international community to provide technical and financial support to strengthen the capacity of civil society organizations to take action to help to combat the illicit trade in small arms and light weapons;

8. *Invites* the Secretary-General and those States and organizations that are in a position to do so to continue to provide assistance to States for curbing the illicit traffic in small arms and light weapons and collecting them;

9. *Requests* the Secretary-General to continue to consider the matter and to report to the General Assembly at its sixty-seventh session on the implementation of the present resolution;

10. *Decides* to include in the provisional agenda of its sixty-seventh session the item entitled "Assistance to States for curbing the illicit traffic in small arms and light weapons and collecting them".

Stockpile management

In response to General Assembly resolution 61/72 [YUN 2006, p. 661], the Secretary-General in 2007 established a Group of Governmental Experts to consider further steps to enhance cooperation with regard to the issue of conventional ammunition stockpiles in surplus. In accordance with the recommendation in the Group's 2008 report on the issue [YUN 2008, p. 615], International Ammunition Technical Guidelines (IATG) were developed within the United Nations under the United Nations Safer Guard programme, drafted by an expert consultant, and reviewed by a technical review panel. From 5 to 8 September, the technical review panel held its third meeting in Rio de Janeiro, Brazil, and gave its final affirmation that the IATG technical content was complete, comprehensive and of the highest available standards.

GENERAL ASSEMBLY ACTION

On 2 December [meeting 71], the General Assembly, on the recommendation of the First Committee [A/66/412], adopted **resolution 66/42** without vote [agenda item 98 (*f*)].

Problems arising from the accumulation of conventional ammunition stockpiles in surplus

The General Assembly,

Mindful of contributing to the process initiated within the framework of the United Nations reform to make the Organization more effective in maintaining peace and security by giving it the resources and tools it needs for conflict prevention, peaceful resolution of disputes, peacekeeping, post-conflict peacebuilding and reconstruction,

Underlining the importance of a comprehensive and integrated approach to disarmament through the development of practical measures,

Taking note of the report of the Group of Experts on the problem of ammunition and explosives,

Recalling the recommendation contained in paragraph 27 of the report of the Open-ended Working Group to Negotiate an International Instrument to Enable States to Identify and Trace, in a Timely and Reliable Manner, Illicit Small Arms and Light Weapons, namely, to address the issue of small arms and light weapons ammunition in a comprehensive manner as part of a separate process conducted within the framework of the United Nations,

Noting with satisfaction the work and measures pursued at the regional and subregional levels with regard to the issue of conventional ammunition,

Recalling its decision 59/515 of 3 December 2004 and its resolutions 60/74 of 8 December 2005 and 61/72 of 6 December 2006, its resolution 63/61 of 2 December 2008, by which it welcomed the report of the Group of Governmental Experts established pursuant to resolution 61/72 to consider further steps to enhance cooperation with regard to the issue of conventional ammunition stockpiles in surplus, and its resolution 64/51 of 2 December 2009,

Taking note of the recommendations of the Group of Governmental Experts on developing technical guidelines for the stockpile management of conventional ammunition, which would be available for States on a voluntary basis, and on improving knowledge resource management on technical ammunition issues within the United Nations system, and taking note also of the subsequent establishment, within the Secretariat, of the "Safer Guard" knowledge resource management programme,

1. *Encourages* all interested States to assess, on a voluntary basis, whether, in conformity with their legitimate security needs, parts of their stockpiles of conventional ammunition should be considered to be in surplus, and recognizes that the security of such stockpiles must be taken into consideration and that appropriate controls with regard to the security and safety of stockpiles of conventional ammunition are indispensable at the national level in order to eliminate the risk of explosion, pollution or diversion;

2. *Appeals* to all interested States to determine the size and nature of their surplus stockpiles of conventional ammunition, whether they represent a security risk, their means of destruction, if appropriate, and whether external assistance is needed to eliminate this risk;

3. *Encourages* States in a position to do so to assist interested States within a bilateral framework or through international or regional organizations, on a voluntary and transparent basis, in elaborating and implementing programmes to eliminate surplus stockpiles or to improve their management;

4. *Encourages* all Member States to examine the possibility of developing and implementing, within a national, regional or subregional framework, measures to address accordingly the illicit trafficking related to the accumulation of such stockpiles;

5. *Takes note* of the replies submitted by Member States in response to the request of the Secretary-General for views regarding the risks arising from the accumulation of conventional ammunition stockpiles in surplus and regarding national ways of strengthening controls on conventional ammunition;

6. *Continues to encourage* States to implement the recommendations of the report of the Group of Governmental Experts established pursuant to resolution 61/72 to consider further steps to enhance cooperation with regard to the issue of conventional ammunition stockpiles in surplus;

7. *Welcomes* the completion of the International Ammunition Technical Guidelines and the establishment of the "Safer*Guard*" knowledge resource management programme for the stockpile management of conventional ammunition, developed by the Office for Disarmament Affairs of the Secretariat, with the full involvement of the Mine Action Service of the Department of Peacekeeping Operations of the Secretariat, in accordance with the recommendations of the report of the Group of Governmental Experts established pursuant to resolution 61/72;

8. *Encourages* States wishing to improve their national stockpile management capacity, prevent the growth of conventional ammunition surpluses and address wider risk mitigation to contact the "Safer*Guard*" programme, as well as potential national donors and regional organizations, as appropriate, with a view to developing cooperation, including, where relevant, technical expertise;

9. *Reiterates its decision* to address the issue of conventional ammunition stockpiles in surplus in a comprehensive manner;

10. *Decides* to include in the provisional agenda of its sixty-eighth session the item entitled "Problems arising from the accumulation of conventional ammunition stockpiles in surplus".

Convention on excessively injurious conventional weapons and Protocols

Status

As at 31 December, 114 States were parties to the 1980 Convention on Prohibitions or Restrictions on the Use of Certain Conventional Weapons Which May Be Deemed to Be Excessively Injurious or to Have Indiscriminate Effects (ccw) and its annexed Protocols on Non-Detectable Fragments (Protocol I) [YUN 1980, p. 76]; on Prohibitions or Restrictions on the Use of Mines, Booby Traps and Other Devices, as amended on 3 May 1996 (Protocol II) [ibid., p. 77]; and on Prohibitions or Restrictions on the Use of Incendiary Weapons (Protocol III) [ibid., p. 78].

Amended Protocol II, which entered into force in 1998 [YUN 1998, p. 844], had 98 parties, as Montenegro and Serbia became parties during the year. The 1995 Protocol on Blinding Laser Weapons (Protocol IV) [YUN 1995, p. 221], which took effect in 1998 [YUN 1998, p. 530], stood at 100 parties. The Protocol on Explosive Remnants of War (Protocol V), which was adopted in 2003 [YUN 2003, p. 566] and entered into force in 2006 [YUN 2006, p. 663], had 76 parties, as Argentina and Poland became parties during the year. The number of parties to the amendment to article I of the Convention, which entered into force in 2004 [YUN 2004, p. 563], stood at 75.

Group of Governmental Experts

The Group of Governmental Experts, established by the Second Review Conference of States Parties to ccw [YUN 2001, p. 504], held its first (21–25 February) [CCW/GGE/2011-I/4], second (28 March–1 April) [CCW/GGE/2011-II/4], and third (22–26 August) [CCW/GGE/2011-III/3] sessions in Geneva. States parties in 2009 [YUN 2009, p. 551] had mandated the Group to continue negotiations on a new protocol to the Convention that would address the humanitarian impact of cluster munitions, while striking a balance between military and humanitarian considerations, and to report to the next Meeting of the High Contracting Parties to the Convention. The Group continued consideration of the updated Chair's text of a draft protocol on cluster munitions [CCW/GGE/2011-III/1], and other past and current proposals [CCW/GGE/2011-III/WP.1/1 & Rev.1, CCW/GGE/2011-III/WP.2, CCW/GGE/2011-III/WP.3]. The Group did not reach a consensus, however, and noted that the text would be submitted for further consideration by the 2011 Fourth Review Conference of the Convention (see below).

Fourth Review Conference

The Fourth Review Conference of the High Contracting Parties to ccw (Geneva, 14–25 November) [CCW/CONF.IV/4 & Corr.1 & Add.1] reviewed the scope and operation of the Convention and its annexed Protocols, and considered proposals for amendments to them, as well as for additional protocols. The Conference adopted the Final Declaration of the Fourth Review Conference and five decisions. In the Declaration, the High Contracting Parties declared their commitment to respect and comply with the objectives and provisions of the Convention and its annexed Protocols, to implement them and to keep them under review to ensure that their provisions remained relevant to modern conflicts. They decided to convene an open-ended meeting of experts in 2012 to discuss further the implementation of international humanitarian law with regard to mines other than anti-personnel mines, and to report to the 2012 Meeting of the High Contracting Parties to the Convention. They also decided to commit to "An Accelerated

Plan of Action on Universalization of the Convention and its annexed Protocols" annexed to the Declaration; continue the Sponsorship Programme, which should explore options for promoting universalization and implementation of the Convention and its annexed Protocols; and enhance implementation of the Compliance Mechanism. The Conference decided on a calendar of meetings for 2012, and that the High Contracting Parties should review, in 2012, the ccw Implementation Support Unit's performance, staff and functioning.

Protocol V on Explosive Remnants of War

Meeting of Experts

The fifth meeting of Experts for Protocol V (Geneva, 6–8 April) focused on clearance, removal or destruction of explosive remnants of war and the article 4 generic electronic template [CCW/P.V/CONF/2011/3]; victim assistance [CCW/P.V/CONF/2011/8]; cooperation and assistance and requests for assistance [CCW/P.V/CONF/2011/4]; generic preventive measures [CCW/P.V/CONF/2011/6 & Rev.1]; national reporting [CCW/P.V/CONF/2011/5] and recording, retaining and submission [CCW/P.V/CONF/2011/7/Rev.2]; and the Web-based Information System.

Fifth Conference of
High Contracting Parties to Protocol V

States parties met for the Fifth Conference of High Contracting Parties to Protocol V (Geneva, 9–10 November) [CCW/P.V/CONF/2011/12 & Corr.1]. The Conference took note of the reports submitted by the coordinator, especially on generic preventive measures. It decided to continue the practice of addressing one specific technical issue directly related to the implementation of article 9 and part 3 of the Technical Annex of Protocol V, and invited all parties to share during the 2012 Meeting of Experts their national technical approaches and experience in that regard. They should indicate how the Guide for the Implementation of Part 3 of the Technical Annex [YUN 2010, p. 560] had contributed to the implementation of the Technical Annex. The Conference decided to develop a web page on generic preventive measures to facilitate access to declarations, presentations and current guidelines. It welcomed the establishment of the Web-based Information System for Protocol V, and requested the Implementation Support Unit to administer and supervise it and the UN Information and Communications Technology Service in Geneva to provide for the System's maintenance. It agreed to a text on Protocol V for submission to the Fourth Review Conference [CCW/P.V/CONF/2011/9] (see above). The Conference also decided that the Meeting of Experts should consider the issue of universalization of Protocol V.

Amended Protocol II on Mines, Booby-traps and Other devices

Meeting of Experts

The Amended Protocol II Meeting of Experts (Geneva, 4–5 April) reviewed the operation and status of the Protocol, and considered matters arising from States parties' reports and the development of technologies to protect civilians against the indiscriminate effects of mines, as well as the issue of improvised explosive devices (IEDs).

Annual Conference of
States Parties

The Thirteenth Annual Conference of the High Contracting parties to Amended Protocol II to the Convention on Mines, Booby-traps and Other Devices (Geneva, 11 November), in its Final Document [CCW/AP.II/CONF.13/6], recommended that the Secretary-General and the Conference president exercise their authority to achieve the goal of universality of the Protocol. The Conference decided that the Group of Experts should continue to review the operation and status of the Protocol and consider matters arising from the national annual reports, as well as the development of technologies to protect civilians against the indiscriminate effects of mines. It encouraged States parties and the Implementation Support Unit to intensify efforts to implement the Plan of Action to promote the Convention's universality [YUN 2006, p. 664], in particular through organizing more national and regional seminars aimed at promoting and explaining the Convention and Protocols. The Group of Experts should also analyse the implementation by States parties of their obligation to submit annual reports and study their content, focusing on the information submitted in Form B, "Mine clearance and rehabilitation programmes".

The Conference decided to continue information exchange on IEDs, IED incidents and their prevention, as well as their significance for the ccw framework, its norms and their implementation with respect to the IED threat; compile guidelines to address the diversion or illicit use of materials which could be used for IEDs; follow the International Ammunition Technical Guidelines process and exchange views with its technical review panel as a contribution to the review and implementation of the guidelines with the aim of enhancing IED prevention; and continue discussion on victim assistance.

GENERAL ASSEMBLY ACTION

On 2 December [meeting 71], the General Assembly, on the recommendation of the First Committee [A/66/416], adopted **resolution 66/62** without vote [agenda item 102].

Convention on Prohibitions or Restrictions on the Use of Certain Conventional Weapons Which May Be Deemed to Be Excessively Injurious or to Have Indiscriminate Effects

The General Assembly,

Recalling its resolution 65/89 of 8 December 2010,

Recalling with satisfaction the adoption and the entry into force of the Convention on Prohibitions or Restrictions on the Use of Certain Conventional Weapons Which May Be Deemed to Be Excessively Injurious or to Have Indiscriminate Effects and its amended article 1, the Protocol on Non-Detectable Fragments (Protocol I), the Protocol on Prohibitions or Restrictions on the Use of Mines, Booby Traps and Other Devices (Protocol II) and its amended version, the Protocol on Prohibitions or Restrictions on the Use of Incendiary Weapons (Protocol III), the Protocol on Blinding Laser Weapons (Protocol IV) and the Protocol on Explosive Remnants of War (Protocol V),

Welcoming the results of the Third Review Conference of the High Contracting Parties to the Convention on Prohibitions or Restrictions on the Use of Certain Conventional Weapons Which May Be Deemed to Be Excessively Injurious or to Have Indiscriminate Effects, held in Geneva from 7 to 17 November 2006,

Welcoming also the results of the 2010 Meeting of the High Contracting Parties to the Convention, held in Geneva on 25 and 26 November 2010,

Welcoming further the results of the Twelfth Annual Conference of the High Contracting Parties to Amended Protocol II, held in Geneva on 24 November 2010,

Welcoming the results of the Fourth Conference of the High Contracting Parties to Protocol V, held in Geneva on 22 and 23 November 2010,

Recalling the role played by the International Committee of the Red Cross in the elaboration of the Convention and the Protocols thereto, and welcoming the particular efforts of various international, non-governmental and other organizations in raising awareness of the humanitarian consequences of explosive remnants of war,

1. *Calls upon* all States that have not yet done so to take all measures to become parties, as soon as possible, to the Convention on Prohibitions or Restrictions on the Use of Certain Conventional Weapons Which May Be Deemed to Be Excessively Injurious or to Have Indiscriminate Effects and the Protocols thereto, as amended, with a view to achieving the widest possible adherence to these instruments at an early date and so as to ultimately achieve their universality;

2. *Calls upon* all States parties to the Convention that have not yet done so to express their consent to be bound by the Protocols to the Convention and the amendment extending the scope of the Convention and the Protocols thereto to include armed conflicts of a non-international character;

3. *Emphasizes* the importance of the universalization of the Protocol on Explosive Remnants of War (Protocol V);

4. *Welcomes* the additional ratifications and acceptances of or accessions to the Convention, as well as the consents to be bound by the Protocols thereto;

5. *Also welcomes* the adoption by the Third Review Conference of the High Contracting Parties to the Convention of a plan of action to promote universality of the Convention and the Protocols thereto, and expresses appreciation for the continued efforts of the Secretary-General, as depositary of the Convention and the Protocols thereto, the Chair of the Meeting of the High Contracting Parties to the Convention, the President of the Fourth Conference of the High Contracting Parties to Protocol V and the President of the Twelfth Annual Conference of the High Contracting Parties to Amended Protocol II, on behalf of the High Contracting Parties, to achieve the goal of universality;

6. *Recalls* the decision of the Third Review Conference of the High Contracting Parties to the Convention to establish a sponsorship programme within the framework of the Convention, and, with recognition of the value and importance of the programme, encourages States to contribute to the Sponsorship Programme;

7. *Welcomes* the decision of the 2010 Meeting of the High Contracting Parties to the Convention to convene the Fourth Review Conference of the High Contracting Parties to the Convention in Geneva from 14 to 25 November 2011;

8. *Acknowledges* the work of the Implementation Support Unit within the Geneva Branch of the Office for Disarmament Affairs of the Secretariat, which was established following a decision of the 2009 Meeting of the High Contracting Parties to the Convention;

9. *Welcomes* the commitment by States parties to continue to address the humanitarian problems caused by certain specific types of munitions in all their aspects, including cluster munitions, with a view to minimizing the humanitarian impact of these munitions;

10. *Also welcomes* the preparatory work for the Fourth Review Conference conducted by the Group of Governmental Experts of the High Contracting Parties to the Convention, acting under the overall responsibility of the President-designate, and notes that the issue of urgently addressing the humanitarian impact of cluster munitions, while striking a balance between military and humanitarian considerations, will be further addressed at the Fourth Review Conference in November 2011;

11. *Further welcomes* the commitment of States parties to the Protocol on Explosive Remnants of War (Protocol V) to the effective and efficient implementation of the Protocol and the implementation of the decisions of the First and Second Conferences of the High Contracting Parties to the Protocol establishing a comprehensive framework for the exchange of information and cooperation, and also welcomes the holding of the Meeting of Experts of the High Contracting Parties to the Protocol, in Geneva from 6 to 8 April 2011, as a mechanism for consultation and cooperation among the States parties;

12. *Notes* the decision of the Tenth Annual Conference of the High Contracting Parties to Amended Protocol II to establish an informal open-ended group of experts, and welcomes the holding of the third session of the Group of Experts of the High Contracting Parties to Amended Protocol II, in Geneva on 4 and 5 April 2011, to exchange national practices and experiences and to assess the implementation of the Protocol;

13. *Also notes* that, in conformity with article 8 of the Convention, conferences may be convened to examine amendments to the Convention or to any of the Protocols thereto, to examine additional protocols concerning other

categories of conventional weapons not covered by existing Protocols or to review the scope and application of the Convention and the Protocols thereto and to examine any proposed amendments or additional protocols;

14. *Requests* the Secretary-General to render the necessary assistance and to provide such services, including summary records, as may be required for the Fourth Review Conference of the High Contracting Parties to the Convention, to be held from 14 to 25 November 2011, and other annual conferences and expert meetings of the High Contracting Parties to Amended Protocol II and Protocol V, as well as for any continuation of the work after the meetings;

15. *Also requests* the Secretary-General, in his capacity as depositary of the Convention and the Protocols thereto, to continue to inform the General Assembly periodically, by electronic means, of ratifications and acceptances of and accessions to the Convention, its amended article 1 and the Protocols thereto;

16. *Decides* to include in the provisional agenda of its sixty-seventh session the item entitled "Convention on Prohibitions or Restrictions on the Use of Certain Conventional Weapons Which May Be Deemed to Be Excessively Injurious or to Have Indiscriminate Effects".

Cluster munitions

As at 31 December, there were 67 States parties to the Convention on Cluster Munitions, which was adopted in 2008 [YUN 2008, p. 623] and entered into force in 2010 [YUN 2010, p. 562]. During the year, Afghanistan, Botswana, Bulgaria, Cook Islands, Costa Rica, the Czech Republic, the Dominican Republic, El Salvador, Ghana, Grenada, Italy, Lithuania, Mozambique, the Netherlands, Portugal, Senegal, Swaziland, and Trinidad and Tobago became parties.

Anti-personnel mines

1997 Convention

As at 31 December, the number of States parties to the Convention on the Prohibition of the Use, Stockpiling, Production and Transfer of Anti-personnel Mines and on Their Destruction (Mine Ban Convention), which was adopted in 1997 [YUN 1997, p. 503] and entered into force in 1999 [YUN 1999, p. 498], increased to 158, with the ratification of South Sudan and Tuvalu.

Meeting of States parties

The Eleventh Meeting of the States Parties to the Mine Ban Convention (Phnom Penh, Cambodia, 28 November–2 December) [APLC/MSP.11/2011/8 & Corr.1] held 10 plenary sessions, attended by 82 States parties. Fourteen States non-parties, one State that had ratified the Convention but for which it had not entered into force, one signatory that had not ratified the Convention and a number of international and regional organizations and NGOs attended as observers.

The Meeting agreed to requests for extensions of deadlines for destruction of anti-personnel mines in mined areas under article 5 of the Convention by Algeria (until 1 April 2017), Chile (until 1 March 2020), the Congo (until 1 January 2013), the Democratic Republic of the Congo (until 1 January 2015) and Eritrea (until 1 February 2015). The Meeting, noting the need to develop a rational response to situations in which States parties that had never reported article 5 obligations discovered previously unknown mined areas, requested the President to prepare a constructive discussion on the matter in 2012, with a view to recommendations being submitted to the Twelfth (2012) Meeting of States Parties.

GENERAL ASSEMBLY ACTION

On 2 December [meeting 71], the General Assembly, on the recommendation of the First Committee [A/66/412], adopted **resolution 66/29** by recorded vote (162-0-18) [agenda item 98].

Implementation of the Convention on the Prohibition of the Use, Stockpiling, Production and Transfer of Anti-personnel Mines and on Their Destruction

The General Assembly,

Recalling its resolutions 54/54 B of 1 December 1999, 55/33 V of 20 November 2000, 56/24 M of 29 November 2001, 57/74 of 22 November 2002, 58/53 of 8 December 2003, 59/84 of 3 December 2004, 60/80 of 8 December 2005, 61/84 of 6 December 2006, 62/41 of 5 December 2007, 63/42 of 2 December 2008, 64/56 of 2 December 2009 and 65/48 of 8 December 2010,

Reaffirming its determination to put an end to the suffering and casualties caused by anti-personnel mines, which kill or injure thousands of people—women, girls, boys and men—every year, and which place people living in affected areas at risk and hinder the development of their communities,

Believing it necessary to do the utmost to contribute in an efficient and coordinated manner to facing the challenge of removing anti-personnel mines placed throughout the world and to assure their destruction,

Wishing to do the utmost in ensuring assistance for the care and rehabilitation, including the social and economic reintegration, of mine victims,

Noting with satisfaction the work undertaken to implement the Convention on the Prohibition of the Use, Stockpiling, Production and Transfer of Anti-personnel Mines and on Their Destruction and the substantial progress made towards addressing the global anti-personnel landmine problem,

Recalling the first to tenth meetings of the States parties to the Convention, held in Maputo (1999), Geneva (2000), Managua (2001), Geneva (2002), Bangkok (2003), Zagreb (2005), Geneva (2006), the Dead Sea (2007), Geneva (2008) and Geneva (2010) and the First Review Conference of the States Parties to the Convention, held in Nairobi (2004),

Recalling also the Second Review Conference of the States Parties to the Convention, held in Cartagena, Colombia, from 30 November to 4 December 2009, at which the international community reviewed the implementation of the Convention and the States parties adopted the Cartagena Declaration and the Cartagena Action Plan 2010–2014 to support enhanced implementation and promotion of the Convention,

Noting with satisfaction that additional States have ratified or acceded to the Convention, bringing the total number of States that have formally accepted the obligations of the Convention to one hundred and fifty-seven,

Emphasizing the desirability of attracting the adherence of all States to the Convention, and determined to work strenuously towards the promotion of its universalization and norms,

Noting with regret that anti-personnel mines continue to be used in some conflicts around the world, causing human suffering and impeding post-conflict development,

1. *Invites* all States that have not signed the Convention on the Prohibition of the Use, Stockpiling, Production and Transfer of Anti-personnel Mines and on Their Destruction to accede to it without delay;

2. *Urges* all States that have signed but have not ratified the Convention to ratify it without delay;

3. *Stresses* the importance of the full and effective implementation of and compliance with the Convention, including through the continued implementation of the Cartagena Action Plan 2010–2014;

4. *Urges* all States parties to provide the Secretary-General with complete and timely information as required under article 7 of the Convention in order to promote transparency and compliance with the Convention;

5. *Invites* all States that have not ratified the Convention or acceded to it to provide, on a voluntary basis, information to make global mine action efforts more effective;

6. *Renews its call upon* all States and other relevant parties to work together to promote, support and advance the care, rehabilitation and social and economic reintegration of mine victims, mine risk education programmes and the removal and destruction of anti-personnel mines placed or stockpiled throughout the world;

7. *Urges* all States to remain seized of the issue at the highest political level and, where in a position to do so, to promote adherence to the Convention through bilateral, subregional, regional and multilateral contacts, outreach, seminars and other means;

8. *Reiterates its invitation and encouragement* to all interested States, the United Nations, other relevant international organizations or institutions, regional organizations, the International Committee of the Red Cross and relevant non-governmental organizations to attend the Eleventh Meeting of the States Parties to the Convention, to be held in Phnom Penh from 28 November to 2 December 2011, and to participate in the future meeting programme of the Convention;

9. *Requests* the Secretary-General, in accordance with article 11, paragraph 2, of the Convention, to undertake the preparations necessary to convene the Twelfth Meeting of the States Parties to the Convention and, on behalf of the States parties and in accordance with article 11, paragraph 4, of the Convention, to invite States not parties to the Convention, as well as the United Nations, other relevant international organizations or institutions, regional organizations, the International Committee of the Red Cross and relevant non-governmental organizations, to attend the Twelfth Meeting of the States Parties and future meetings as observers;

10. *Decides* to remain seized of the matter.

RECORDED VOTE ON RESOLUTION 66/29:

In favour: Afghanistan, Albania, Algeria, Andorra, Angola, Antigua and Barbuda, Argentina, Armenia, Australia, Austria, Azerbaijan, Bahamas, Bahrain, Bangladesh, Barbados, Belarus, Belgium, Belize, Benin, Bhutan, Bolivia, Bosnia and Herzegovina, Botswana, Brazil, Brunei Darussalam, Bulgaria, Burkina Faso, Cambodia, Cameroon, Canada, Cape Verde, Chad, Chile, China, Colombia, Comoros, Congo, Costa Rica, Côte d'Ivoire, Croatia, Cyprus, Czech Republic, Denmark, Djibouti, Dominican Republic, Ecuador, El Salvador, Estonia, Ethiopia, Fiji, Finland, France, Gabon, Georgia, Germany, Ghana, Greece, Grenada, Guatemala, Guinea, Guinea-Bissau, Guyana, Haiti, Honduras, Hungary, Iceland, Indonesia, Iraq, Ireland, Italy, Jamaica, Japan, Jordan, Kazakhstan, Kenya, Kuwait, Kyrgyzstan, Lao People's Democratic Republic, Latvia, Lesotho, Liberia, Liechtenstein, Lithuania, Luxembourg, Madagascar, Malawi, Malaysia, Maldives, Mali, Malta, Marshall Islands, Mauritania, Mauritius, Mexico, Micronesia, Monaco, Mongolia, Montenegro, Morocco, Mozambique, Namibia, Netherlands, New Zealand, Nicaragua, Niger, Nigeria, Norway, Oman, Palau, Panama, Papua New Guinea, Paraguay, Peru, Philippines, Poland, Portugal, Qatar, Republic of Moldova, Romania, Saint Kitts and Nevis, Saint Lucia, Saint Vincent and the Grenadines, Samoa, San Marino, Sao Tome and Principe, Senegal, Serbia, Seychelles, Sierra Leone, Singapore, Slovakia, Slovenia, Solomon Islands, South Africa, Spain, Sri Lanka, Sudan, Suriname, Swaziland, Sweden, Switzerland, Tajikistan, Thailand, the former Yugoslav Republic of Macedonia, Timor-Leste, Togo, Tonga, Tunisia, Turkey, Turkmenistan, Tuvalu, Uganda, Ukraine, United Arab Emirates, United Kingdom, United Republic of Tanzania, Uruguay, Vanuatu, Venezuela, Yemen, Zambia, Zimbabwe.

Against: None.

Abstaining: Cuba, Democratic People's Republic of Korea, Egypt, India, Iran, Israel, Lebanon, Libya, Myanmar, Nepal, Pakistan, Republic of Korea, Russian Federation, Saudi Arabia, Syrian Arab Republic, United States, Uzbekistan, Viet Nam.

Practical disarmament

Disarmament Commission. The Disarmament Commission [A/66/42] included in its agenda the item "Practical confidence-building measures in the field of conventional weapons", but was unable to achieve a consensus on the matter.

Transparency

Eighty-six countries participated in the United Nations Register of Conventional Arms. Regional disparities remained a serious obstacle to achieving universal participation. Of the 86 reports received, 2 came from Africa, 19 from Asia and the Pacific, 16 from Latin America and the Caribbean, 21 from Eastern Europe and 28 from Western Europe and other States.

Conference on Disarmament. During the general debate of the Conference on Disarmament [A/66/27], delegations reaffirmed or further elaborated their respective positions on the issue. The Conference held two formal meetings (17 February and 17 March) and one informal meeting (25 May) on "Transparency in armaments".

UN Register of Conventional Arms

In response to General Assembly resolution 64/54 [YUN 2009, p. 556], the Secretary-General in July submitted the nineteenth annual report on the United Nations Register of Conventional Arms [A/66/127 & Corr.1,2 & Add.1], established in 1992 [YUN 1992, p. 75] to enhance transparency on arms transfers. The report presented information provided by 86 countries on the export and import of conventional arms, military holdings, procurement through national production and international transfers of small arms and light weapons for 2010.

GENERAL ASSEMBLY ACTION

On 2 December [meeting 71], the General Assembly, on the recommendation of the First Committee [A/66/412], adopted **resolution 66/39** by recorded vote (156-0-23) [agenda item 98 (*g*)].

Transparency in armaments

The General Assembly,

Recalling its resolutions 46/36 L of 9 December 1991, 47/52 L of 15 December 1992, 48/75 E of 16 December 1993, 49/75 C of 15 December 1994, 50/70 D of 12 December 1995, 51/45 H of 10 December 1996, 52/38 R of 9 December 1997, 53/77 V of 4 December 1998, 54/54 O of 1 December 1999, 55/33 U of 20 November 2000, 56/24 Q of 29 November 2001, 57/75 of 22 November 2002, 58/54 of 8 December 2003, 60/226 of 23 December 2005, 61/77 of 6 December 2006, 63/69 of 2 December 2008 and 64/54 of 2 December 2009, entitled "Transparency in armaments",

Continuing to take the view that an enhanced level of transparency in armaments contributes greatly to confidence-building and security among States and that the establishment of the United Nations Register of Conventional Arms constitutes an important step forward in the promotion of transparency in military matters,

Welcoming the consolidated reports of the Secretary-General on the Register, which include the returns of Member States for 2009 and 2010,

Welcoming also the response of Member States to the request contained in paragraphs 9 and 10 of resolution 46/36 L to provide data on their imports and exports of arms, as well as available background information regarding their military holdings, procurement through national production and relevant policies,

Welcoming further the inclusion by some Member States of their transfers of small arms and light weapons in their annual report to the Register as part of their additional background information,

Noting the focused discussions on transparency in armaments that took place in the Conference on Disarmament in 2010 and 2011,

Expressing its concern with respect to the reduction in reporting to the Register in the last two years,

Stressing that the continuing operation of the Register and its further development should be reviewed in order to secure a Register that is capable of attracting the widest possible participation,

1. *Reaffirms its determination* to ensure the effective operation of the United Nations Register of Conventional Arms, as provided for in paragraphs 7 to 10 of resolution 46/36 L;

2. *Calls upon* Member States, with a view to achieving universal participation, to provide the Secretary-General, by 31 May annually, with the requested data and information for the Register, including nil reports if appropriate, on the basis of resolutions 46/36 L and 47/52 L, the recommendations contained in paragraph 64 of the 1997 report of the Secretary-General on the continuing operation of the Register and its further development, the recommendations contained in paragraph 94 of the 2000 report of the Secretary-General and the appendices and annexes thereto, the recommendations contained in paragraphs 112 to 114 of the 2003 report of the Secretary-General, the recommendations contained in paragraphs 123 to 127 of the 2006 report of the Secretary-General and the recommendations contained in paragraphs 71 to 75 of the 2009 report of the Secretary-General;

3. *Invites* Member States in a position to do so, pending further development of the Register, to provide additional information on procurement through national production and military holdings and to make use of the "Remarks" column in the standardized reporting form to provide additional information such as types or models;

4. *Also invites* Member States in a position to do so to provide additional information on transfers of small arms and light weapons on the basis of the optional standardized reporting form, as adopted by the 2006 group of governmental experts, or by any other methods they deem appropriate;

5. *Reaffirms* its decision, with a view to further development of the Register, to keep the scope of and participation in the Register under review and, to that end:

(*a*) Recalls its request to Member States to provide the Secretary-General with their views on the continuing operation of the Register and its further development and on transparency measures related to weapons of mass destruction;

(*b*) Requests the Secretary-General, with the assistance of a group of governmental experts to be convened in 2012, within available resources, on the basis of equitable geographical representation, to prepare a report on the continuing operation of the Register and its further development, taking into account the work of the Conference on Disarmament, relevant deliberations within the United Nations, the views expressed by Member States and the reports of the Secretary-General on the continuing operation of the Register and its further development, with a view to taking a decision at its sixty-eighth session;

(*c*) Requests the Secretary-General to continue to assist Member States to build capacity to submit meaningful reports, including capacity to report on small arms and light weapons;

6. *Requests* the Secretary-General to implement the recommendations contained in his 2000, 2003, 2006 and 2009 reports on the continuing operation of the Register and its further development and to ensure that sufficient resources are made available for the Secretariat to operate and maintain the Register;

7. *Invites* the Conference on Disarmament to consider continuing its work undertaken in the field of transparency in armaments;

8. *Reiterates its call upon* all Member States to cooperate at the regional and subregional levels, taking fully into account the specific conditions prevailing in the region or subregion, with a view to enhancing and coordinating international efforts aimed at increased openness and transparency in armaments;

9. *Requests* the Secretary-General to report to the General Assembly at its sixty-eighth session on progress made in implementing the present resolution;

10. *Decides* to include in the provisional agenda of its sixty-eighth session the item entitled "Transparency in armaments".

RECORDED VOTE ON RESOLUTION 66/39:

In favour: Afghanistan, Albania, Andorra, Angola, Antigua and Barbuda, Argentina, Armenia, Australia, Austria, Azerbaijan, Bahamas, Bangladesh, Barbados, Belarus, Belgium, Belize, Benin, Bhutan, Bolivia, Bosnia and Herzegovina, Botswana, Brazil, Brunei Darussalam, Bulgaria, Burkina Faso, Cambodia, Cameroon, Canada, Cape Verde, Chad, Chile, China, Colombia, Congo, Costa Rica, Côte d'Ivoire, Croatia, Cyprus, Czech Republic, Denmark, Dominican Republic, Ecuador, El Salvador, Eritrea, Estonia, Ethiopia, Fiji, Finland, France, Gabon, Georgia, Germany, Ghana, Greece, Grenada, Guatemala, Guinea, Guinea-Bissau, Guyana, Haiti, Honduras, Hungary, Iceland, India, Indonesia, Ireland, Israel, Italy, Jamaica, Japan, Kazakhstan, Kenya, Kyrgyzstan, Lao People's Democratic Republic, Latvia, Lesotho, Liberia, Liechtenstein, Lithuania, Luxembourg, Madagascar, Malawi, Malaysia, Maldives, Mali, Malta, Marshall Islands, Mauritania, Mauritius, Mexico, Micronesia, Monaco, Mongolia, Montenegro, Mozambique, Namibia, Nepal, Netherlands, New Zealand, Nicaragua, Niger, Nigeria, Norway, Pakistan, Palau, Panama, Papua New Guinea, Paraguay, Peru, Philippines, Poland, Portugal, Republic of Korea, Republic of Moldova, Romania, Russian Federation, Saint Kitts and Nevis, Saint Lucia, Saint Vincent and the Grenadines, Samoa, San Marino, Sao Tome and Principe, Senegal, Serbia, Seychelles, Sierra Leone, Singapore, Slovakia, Slovenia, Solomon Islands, South Africa, Spain, Sri Lanka, Suriname, Swaziland, Sweden, Switzerland, Tajikistan, Thailand, the former Yugoslav Republic of Macedonia, Timor-Leste, Togo, Tonga, Trinidad and Tobago, Turkey, Turkmenistan, Tuvalu, Ukraine, United Kingdom, United States, Uruguay, Uzbekistan, Vanuatu, Venezuela, Zambia, Zimbabwe.

Against: None.

Abstaining: Algeria, Bahrain, Comoros, Cuba, Djibouti, Egypt, Iran, Iraq, Jordan, Kuwait, Lebanon, Libya, Morocco, Myanmar, Oman, Qatar, Saudi Arabia, Sudan, Syrian Arab Republic, Tunisia, United Arab Emirates, United Republic of Tanzania, Yemen.

Also on 2 December [meeting 71], the General Assembly, on the recommendation of the First Committee [A/66/412], adopted **resolution 66/41** without vote [agenda item 98].

National legislation on transfer of arms, military equipment and dual-use goods and technology

The General Assembly,

Recognizing that disarmament, arms control and non-proliferation are essential for the maintenance of international peace and security,

Recalling that effective national control of the transfer of arms, military equipment and dual-use goods and technology, including those transfers that could contribute to proliferation activities, is an important tool for achieving those objectives,

Recalling also that the States parties to the international disarmament and non-proliferation treaties have undertaken to facilitate the fullest possible exchange of materials, equipment and technological information for peaceful purposes, in accordance with the provisions of those treaties,

Considering that the exchange of national legislation, regulations and procedures on the transfer of arms, military equipment and dual-use goods and technology contributes to mutual understanding and confidence among Member States,

Convinced that such an exchange would be beneficial to Member States that are in the process of developing such legislation,

Welcoming the electronic database established by the Office for Disarmament Affairs of the Secretariat, in which all information exchanged pursuant to General Assembly resolutions 57/66 of 22 November 2002, 58/42 of 8 December 2003, 59/66 of 3 December 2004, 60/69 of 8 December 2005, 62/26 of 5 December 2007 and 64/40 of 2 December 2009, entitled "National legislation on transfer of arms, military equipment and dual-use goods and technology", can be consulted,

Reaffirming the inherent right of individual or collective self-defence in accordance with Article 51 of the Charter of the United Nations,

1. *Invites* Member States that are in a position to do so, without prejudice to the provisions contained in Security Council resolution 1540(2004) of 28 April 2004 and subsequent relevant Council resolutions, to enact or improve national legislation, regulations and procedures to exercise effective control over the transfer of arms, military equipment and dual-use goods and technology, while ensuring that such legislation, regulations and procedures are consistent with the obligations of States parties under international treaties;

2. *Encourages* Member States to provide, on a voluntary basis, information to the Secretary-General on their national legislation, regulations and procedures on the transfer of arms, military equipment and dual-use goods and technology, as well as the changes therein, and requests the Secretary-General to make that information accessible to Member States;

3. *Decides* to remain attentive to the matter.

Transparency of military expenditures

Group of Governmental Experts. In June [A/66/89 & Corr.1,2,3], the Secretary-General transmitted the report of the Group of Governmental Experts on the Operation and Further Development of the United Nations Standardized Instrument for Reporting Military Expenditures, established by General

Assembly resolution 35/142 B [YUN 1980, p. 88]. The Group reviewed the data and information submitted by Governments under the Standardized Instrument since its inception, as well as views and suggestions by Member States on ways to improve the operation of the standardized reporting system.

The Group concluded that transparency in military expenditures remained an essential element for building trust and confidence among States and, in conjunction with other measures undertaken at the global and regional levels, helped relieve international tensions. It underlined the necessity of using the standardized reporting form as a preferred method for reporting. It agreed on a common understanding of military expenditures and on modifications to the standardized and the simplified reporting forms, and developed a format for the "nil" report. All three formats were joined under a new title, "United Nations Report on Military Expenditures". States could choose the most appropriate reporting form and were encouraged to complement their national submissions with explanations and additional materials and documentation. The Group recommended including in the national report information on a national point of contact in order to facilitate communication between Member States and the Secretariat; that the Assembly establish a process for periodic review of the report to ensure its continued relevance and operation; and that the next review be scheduled in five years.

Report of Secretary-General. In response to Assembly resolution 64/22 [YUN 2009, p. 558], the Secretary-General presented, in June [A/66/117 & Add.1], reports from 51 Governments on their military expenditures for the latest fiscal year for which data were available.

The Office for Disarmament Affairs, in cooperation with the Stockholm International Peace Research Institute, published an occasional paper entitled *Promoting Further Openness and Transparency in Military Expenditures* [Sales No. E.10.IX.5] to facilitate the deliberations of the Group of Governmental Experts in their review of the operation of the Standardized Instrument for Reporting Military Expenditures, with a view to its further development.

GENERAL ASSEMBLY ACTION

On 2 December [meeting 71], the General Assembly, on the recommendation of the First Committee [A/66/401], adopted **resolution 66/20** without vote [agenda item 87 (*b*)].

Objective information on military matters, including transparency of military expenditures

The General Assembly,

Recalling its resolutions 53/72 of 4 December 1998, 54/43 of 1 December 1999, 56/14 of 29 November 2001, 58/28 of 8 December 2003, 60/44 of 8 December 2005, 62/13 of 5 December 2007 and 64/22 of 2 December 2009 on objective information on military matters, including transparency of military expenditures,

Recalling also its resolution 35/142 B of 12 December 1980, which introduced the United Nations system for the standardized reporting of military expenditures, its resolutions 48/62 of 16 December 1993, 49/66 of 15 December 1994, 51/38 of 10 December 1996 and 52/32 of 9 December 1997, calling upon all Member States to participate in it, and its resolution 47/54 B of 9 December 1992, endorsing the guidelines and recommendations for objective information on military matters and inviting Member States to provide the Secretary-General with relevant information regarding their implementation,

Noting that, since then, national reports on military expenditures and on the guidelines and recommendations for objective information on military matters have been submitted by a number of Member States belonging to different geographical regions,

Convinced that the improvement of international relations forms a sound basis for promoting further openness and transparency in all military matters,

Also convinced that transparency in military matters is an essential element for building a climate of trust and confidence between States worldwide and that a better flow of objective information on military matters can help to relieve international tension and is therefore an important contribution to conflict prevention,

Noting the role of the standardized reporting system, as instituted through its resolution 35/142 B, as an important instrument to enhance transparency in military matters,

Conscious that the value of the standardized reporting system would be enhanced by a broader participation of Member States,

Noting that a periodic review of the Standardized Instrument for Reporting Military Expenditures could facilitate its further development and maintain its continued relevance and operation, and recalling resolution 62/13, in which the General Assembly established the Group of Governmental Experts on the Operation and Further Development of the United Nations Standardized Instrument for Reporting Military Expenditures,

Recalling, in that regard, the report of the Secretary-General on ways and means to implement the guidelines and recommendations for objective information on military matters, including, in particular, on how to strengthen and broaden participation in the standardized reporting system,

Recalling also that the guidelines and recommendations for objective information on military matters recommended certain areas for further consideration, such as the improvement of the standardized reporting system,

Welcoming the report of the Group of Governmental Experts on further ways and means to implement the guidelines and recommendations for objective information on military matters, including, in particular, on how to strengthen and broaden participation in the standardized reporting system,

Noting the efforts of several regional organizations to promote transparency of military expenditures, including standardized annual exchanges of relevant information among their member States,

Emphasizing the continuing importance of the Standardized Instrument under the current political and economic circumstances,

Mindful of the provisions of the Charter of the United Nations, including its Article 26,

1. *Endorses* the report of the Group of Governmental Experts on the Operation and Further Development of the United Nations Standardized Instrument for Reporting Military Expenditures, the recommendations contained therein and the new title of the instrument, namely, the United Nations Report on Military Expenditures;

2. *Calls upon* Member States, with a view to achieving the broadest possible participation, to provide the Secretary-General, by 30 April annually, with reports on their military expenditures for the latest fiscal year for which data are available, using preferably and to the extent possible, one of the reporting forms, including a "nil" report if appropriate, on the basis of recommendations contained in paragraphs 68 to 71 of the report of the Group of Governmental Experts and annex II thereto, or as appropriate, any other format developed in the context of similar reporting on military expenditures to other international or regional organizations;

3. *Recommends* that, for the purpose of reporting by Member States of their national military expenditures in the framework of the Report on Military Expenditures, "military expenditures" be commonly understood to refer to all financial resources that a State spends on the uses and functions of its military forces and information on military expenditures represents an actual outlay in current prices and domestic currency;

4. *Also recommends* the guidelines and recommendations for objective information on military matters to all Member States for implementation, fully taking into account specific political, military and other conditions prevailing in a region, on the basis of initiatives and with the agreement of the States of the region concerned;

5. *Invites* Member States in a position to do so to supplement their reports, on a voluntary basis, with explanatory remarks regarding submitted data to explain or clarify the figures provided in the reporting forms, such as the total military expenditures as a share of gross domestic product, major changes from previous reports and any additional information reflecting their defence policy, military strategies and doctrines;

6. *Invites* Member States to provide, preferably with their annual report, their national points of contact, on the basis of annex II and paragraph 72 (*e*) of the report of the Group of Governmental Experts;

7. *Encourages* relevant international bodies and regional organizations to promote transparency of military expenditures and to enhance complementarities among reporting systems, taking into account the particular characteristics of each region, and to consider the possibility of an exchange of information with the United Nations;

8. *Takes note* of the annual reports of the Secretary-General;

9. *Requests* the Secretary-General, within available resources:

(*a*) To continue the practice of sending an annual note verbale to Member States requesting the submission of their Report on Military Expenditures;

(*b*) To circulate annually a note verbale to Member States detailing which reports on military expenditures were submitted and are available electronically on the website for military expenditures;

(*c*) To continue consultations with relevant international bodies, with a view to ascertaining requirements for adjusting the present instrument, with a view to encouraging wider participation, and to make recommendations, based on the outcome of those consultations and taking into account the views of Member States, on necessary changes to the content and structure of the standardized reporting system;

(*d*) To encourage relevant international bodies and organizations to promote transparency of military expenditures and to consult with those bodies and organizations with emphasis on examining possibilities for enhancing complementarities among international and regional reporting systems and for exchanging related information between those bodies and the United Nations;

(*e*) To continue to foster further cooperation with relevant regional organizations with a view to raising awareness of the Report on Military Expenditures and its role as a confidence-building measure;

(*f*) To encourage the United Nations regional centres for peace and disarmament in Africa, in Asia and the Pacific, and in Latin America and the Caribbean to assist Member States in their regions in enhancing their knowledge of the standardized reporting system;

(*g*) To promote international and regional/subregional symposiums and training seminars to explain the purpose of the standardized reporting system and to give relevant technical instructions;

(*h*) To report on experiences gained during such symposiums and training seminars;

(*i*) To provide, upon request, technical assistance to Member States lacking the capacity to report data, and to encourage Member States to voluntarily provide bilateral assistance to other Member States;

(*j*) To encourage the Office for Disarmament Affairs of the Secretariat, with the financial and technical support of interested States, as appropriate, to continue to improve the existing database on military expenditures with a view to making it more user-friendly and up-to-date technologically and to increasing its functionality;

10. *Encourages* Member States:

(*a*) To inform the Secretary-General about possible problems with the standardized reporting system and their reasons for not submitting the requested data;

(*b*) To continue to provide the Secretary-General with their views and suggestions on ways and means to improve the future functioning of and broaden participation in the standardized reporting system, including necessary changes to its content and structure;

11. *Recommends* the establishment of a process for periodic reviews, in order to ensure the continued relevance and operation of the Report on Military Expenditures and that another review of the continuing relevance and operation of the Report be conducted in five years;

12. *Decides* to include in the provisional agenda of its sixty-eighth session the item entitled "Objective information on military matters, including transparency of military expenditures".

Verification

On 2 December, the General Assembly took note of the report of the First Committee [A/66/405] on its consideration of the item entitled "Verification in all its aspects, including the role of the United Nations in the field of verification" (**decision 66/513**).

Other issues

Prevention of an arms race in outer space

Conference on Disarmament. The Conference on Disarmament discussed the prevention of an arms race in outer space in two formal meetings (8 February and 8 March) and one informal meeting (31 March) [CD/1926]. The Conference had before it the summary report on the tenth annual space security conference organized by the United Nations Institute for Disarmament Research in April [CD/1912] and a working paper by Nigeria on behalf of member States of the Group of 21 on the prevention of an arms race in outer space [CD/1925].

During the general debate [CD/PV.1203], delegations highlighted the growing global dependence on space technologies and the importance of keeping outer space safe for peaceful activities. They discussed the increase of space debris, the growing possibility of satellite collisions and the development of space-related weapon technology threatening outer space security. Many States expressed fear that the placement of weapons in outer space could deepen global insecurity, affecting all countries. Considering current international instruments insufficient to prevent an arms race in outer space, many delegations maintained that a specific international instrument was needed to strengthen or complement existing regimes.

GENERAL ASSEMBLY ACTION

On 2 December [meeting 71], the General Assembly, on the recommendation of the First Committee [A/66/410], adopted **resolution 66/27** by recorded vote (176-0-2) [agenda item 96].

Prevention of an arms race in outer space

The General Assembly,

Recognizing the common interest of all mankind in the exploration and use of outer space for peaceful purposes,

Reaffirming the will of all States that the exploration and use of outer space, including the Moon and other celestial bodies, shall be for peaceful purposes and shall be carried out for the benefit and in the interest of all countries, irrespective of their degree of economic or scientific development,

Reaffirming also the provisions of articles III and IV of the Treaty on Principles Governing the Activities of States in the Exploration and Use of Outer Space, including the Moon and Other Celestial Bodies,

Recalling the obligation of all States to observe the provisions of the Charter of the United Nations regarding the use or threat of use of force in their international relations, including in their space activities,

Reaffirming paragraph 80 of the Final Document of the Tenth Special Session of the General Assembly, in which it is stated that in order to prevent an arms race in outer space, further measures should be taken and appropriate international negotiations held in accordance with the spirit of the Treaty,

Recalling its previous resolutions on this issue, and taking note of the proposals submitted to the General Assembly at its tenth special session and at its regular sessions, and of the recommendations made to the competent organs of the United Nations and to the Conference on Disarmament,

Recognizing that prevention of an arms race in outer space would avert a grave danger for international peace and security,

Emphasizing the paramount importance of strict compliance with existing arms limitation and disarmament agreements relevant to outer space, including bilateral agreements, and with the existing legal regime concerning the use of outer space,

Considering that wide participation in the legal regime applicable to outer space could contribute to enhancing its effectiveness,

Noting that the Ad Hoc Committee on the Prevention of an Arms Race in Outer Space, taking into account its previous efforts since its establishment in 1985 and seeking to enhance its functioning in qualitative terms, continued the examination and identification of various issues, existing agreements and existing proposals, as well as future initiatives relevant to the prevention of an arms race in outer space, and that this contributed to a better understanding of a number of problems and to a clearer perception of the various positions,

Noting also that there were no objections in principle in the Conference on Disarmament to the re-establishment of the Ad Hoc Committee, subject to re-examination of the mandate contained in the decision of the Conference on Disarmament of 13 February 1992,

Emphasizing the mutually complementary nature of bilateral and multilateral efforts for the prevention of an arms race in outer space, and hoping that concrete results will emerge from those efforts as soon as possible,

Convinced that further measures should be examined in the search for effective and verifiable bilateral and multilateral agreements in order to prevent an arms race in outer space, including the weaponization of outer space,

Stressing that the growing use of outer space increases the need for greater transparency and better information on the part of the international community,

Recalling, in this context, its previous resolutions, in particular resolutions 45/55 B of 4 December 1990, 47/51 of 9 December 1992 and 48/74 A of 16 December 1993, in which, inter alia, it reaffirmed the importance of confidence-building measures as a means conducive to ensuring the attainment of the objective of the prevention of an arms race in outer space,

Conscious of the benefits of confidence- and security-building measures in the military field,

Recognizing that negotiations for the conclusion of an international agreement or agreements to prevent an arms race in outer space remain a priority task of the Conference on Disarmament and that the concrete proposals on confidence-building measures could form an integral part of such agreements,

Noting with satisfaction the constructive, structured and focused debate on the prevention of an arms race in outer space at the Conference on Disarmament in 2009, 2010 and 2011,

Taking note of the introduction by China and the Russian Federation at the Conference on Disarmament of the draft treaty on the prevention of the placement of weapons in outer space and of the threat or use of force against outer space objects,

Taking note also of the decision of the Conference on Disarmament to establish for its 2009 session a working group to discuss, substantially, without limitation, all issues related to the prevention of an arms race in outer space,

1. *Reaffirms* the importance and urgency of preventing an arms race in outer space and the readiness of all States to contribute to that common objective, in conformity with the provisions of the Treaty on Principles Governing the Activities of States in the Exploration and Use of Outer Space, including the Moon and Other Celestial Bodies;

2. *Reaffirms its recognition*, as stated in the report of the Ad Hoc Committee on the Prevention of an Arms Race in Outer Space, that the legal regime applicable to outer space does not in and of itself guarantee the prevention of an arms race in outer space, that the regime plays a significant role in the prevention of an arms race in that environment, that there is a need to consolidate and reinforce that regime and enhance its effectiveness and that it is important to comply strictly with existing agreements, both bilateral and multilateral;

3. *Emphasizes* the necessity of further measures with appropriate and effective provisions for verification to prevent an arms race in outer space;

4. *Calls upon* all States, in particular those with major space capabilities, to contribute actively to the objective of the peaceful use of outer space and of the prevention of an arms race in outer space and to refrain from actions contrary to that objective and to the relevant existing treaties in the interest of maintaining international peace and security and promoting international cooperation;

5. *Reiterates* that the Conference on Disarmament, as the sole multilateral disarmament negotiating forum, has the primary role in the negotiation of a multilateral agreement or agreements, as appropriate, on the prevention of an arms race in outer space in all its aspects;

6. *Invites* the Conference on Disarmament to establish a working group under its agenda item entitled "Prevention of an arms race in outer space" as early as possible during its 2012 session;

7. *Recognizes*, in this respect, the growing convergence of views on the elaboration of measures designed to strengthen transparency, confidence and security in the peaceful uses of outer space;

8. *Urges* States conducting activities in outer space, as well as States interested in conducting such activities, to keep the Conference on Disarmament informed of the progress of bilateral and multilateral negotiations on the matter, if any, so as to facilitate its work;

9. *Decides* to include in the provisional agenda of its sixty-seventh session the item entitled "Prevention of an arms race in outer space".

RECORDED VOTE ON RESOLUTION 66/27:

In favour: Afghanistan, Albania, Algeria, Andorra, Angola, Antigua and Barbuda, Argentina, Armenia, Australia, Austria, Azerbaijan, Bahamas, Bahrain, Bangladesh, Barbados, Belarus, Belgium, Belize, Benin, Bhutan, Bolivia, Bosnia and Herzegovina, Botswana, Brazil, Brunei Darussalam, Bulgaria, Burkina Faso, Cambodia, Cameroon, Canada, Cape Verde, Chad, Chile, China, Colombia, Comoros, Congo, Costa Rica, Côte d'Ivoire, Croatia, Cuba, Cyprus, Czech Republic, Democratic People's Republic of Korea, Denmark, Djibouti, Dominican Republic, Ecuador, Egypt, El Salvador, Estonia, Ethiopia, Fiji, Finland, France, Georgia, Germany, Ghana, Greece, Guatemala, Guinea, Guinea-Bissau, Guyana, Haiti, Honduras, Hungary, Iceland, India, Indonesia, Iran, Iraq, Ireland, Italy, Jamaica, Japan, Jordan, Kazakhstan, Kenya, Kuwait, Kyrgyzstan, Lao People's Democratic Republic, Latvia, Lebanon, Lesotho, Liberia, Libya, Liechtenstein, Lithuania, Luxembourg, Madagascar, Malawi, Malaysia, Maldives, Mali, Malta, Marshall Islands, Mauritania, Mauritius, Mexico, Micronesia, Monaco, Mongolia, Montenegro, Morocco, Mozambique, Myanmar, Namibia, Nepal, Netherlands, New Zealand, Nicaragua, Niger, Nigeria, Norway, Oman, Pakistan, Palau, Panama, Papua New Guinea, Paraguay, Peru, Philippines, Poland, Portugal, Qatar, Republic of Korea, Republic of Moldova, Romania, Russian Federation, Saint Kitts and Nevis, Saint Lucia, Saint Vincent and the Grenadines, Samoa, San Marino, Sao Tome and Principe, Saudi Arabia, Senegal, Serbia, Seychelles, Sierra Leone, Singapore, Slovakia, Slovenia, Solomon Islands, South Africa, Spain, Sri Lanka, Sudan, Suriname, Swaziland, Sweden, Switzerland, Syrian Arab Republic, Tajikistan, Thailand, the former Yugoslav Republic of Macedonia, Timor-Leste, Togo, Tonga, Tunisia, Turkey, Turkmenistan, Tuvalu, Uganda, Ukraine, United Arab Emirates, United Kingdom, United Republic of Tanzania, Uruguay, Uzbekistan, Vanuatu, Venezuela, Viet Nam, Yemen, Zambia, Zimbabwe.

Against: None.

Abstaining: Israel, United States.

On the same date, the Assembly decided to include in the provisional agenda of its sixty-eighth (2013) session the item entitled "Transparency and confidence-building in outer space activities" (**decision 66/517**).

Observance of environmental norms

In July [A/66/97 & Add.1], responding to General Assembly resolution 65/53 [YUN 2010, p. 569], the Secretary-General transmitted to the Assembly information received from Cuba, Ecuador, Lebanon, Panama, Portugal, Qatar and Ukraine on measures that they had adopted to promote the observance of environmental norms in the drafting and implementation of agreements on disarmament and arms control.

GENERAL ASSEMBLY ACTION

On 2 December [meeting 71], the General Assembly, on the recommendation of the First Committee [A/66/412], adopted **resolution 66/31** without vote [agenda item 98 (*m*)].

Observance of environmental norms in the drafting and implementation of agreements on disarmament and arms control

The General Assembly,

Recalling its resolutions 50/70 M of 12 December 1995, 51/45 E of 10 December 1996, 52/38 E of 9 December 1997, 53/77 J of 4 December 1998, 54/54 S of 1 December 1999, 55/33 K of 20 November 2000, 56/24 F of 29 November 2001, 57/64 of 22 November 2002, 58/45 of 8 December 2003, 59/68 of 3 December 2004, 60/60 of 8 December 2005, 61/63 of 6 December 2006, 62/28 of 5 December 2007, 63/51 of 2 December 2008, 64/33 of 2 December 2009 and 65/53 of 8 December 2010,

Emphasizing the importance of the observance of environmental norms in the preparation and implementation of disarmament and arms limitation agreements,

Recognizing that it is necessary to take duly into account the agreements adopted at the United Nations Conference on Environment and Development, as well as prior relevant agreements, in the drafting and implementation of agreements on disarmament and arms limitation,

Taking note of the report of the Secretary-General submitted pursuant to resolution 65/53,

Noting that the Fifteenth Summit Conference of Heads of State and Government of the Movement of Non-Aligned Countries, held in Sharm el-Sheikh, Egypt, from 11 to 16 July 2009, and the Sixteenth Ministerial Conference and Commemorative Meeting of the Movement of Non-Aligned Countries, held in Bali, Indonesia, from 23 to 27 May 2011, welcomed the adoption by the General Assembly, without a vote, of resolutions 63/51 and 65/53, on the observance of environmental norms in the drafting and the implementation of agreements on disarmament and arms control,

Mindful of the detrimental environmental effects of the use of nuclear weapons,

1. *Reaffirms* that international disarmament forums should take fully into account the relevant environmental norms in negotiating treaties and agreements on disarmament and arms limitation and that all States, through their actions, should contribute fully to ensuring compliance with the aforementioned norms in the implementation of treaties and conventions to which they are parties;

2. *Calls upon* States to adopt unilateral, bilateral, regional and multilateral measures so as to contribute to ensuring the application of scientific and technological progress within the framework of international security, disarmament and other related spheres, without detriment to the environment or to its effective contribution to attaining sustainable development;

3. *Welcomes* the information provided by Member States on the implementation of the measures they have adopted to promote the objectives envisaged in the present resolution;

4. *Invites* all Member States to communicate to the Secretary-General information on the measures they have adopted to promote the objectives envisaged in the present resolution, and requests the Secretary-General to submit a report containing that information to the General Assembly at its sixty-seventh session;

5. *Decides* to include in the provisional agenda of its sixty-seventh session the item entitled "Observance of environmental norms in the drafting and implementation of agreements on disarmament and arms control".

Science and technology and disarmament

On 2 December (**decision 66/515**), the General Assembly decided to include in the provisional agenda of its sixty-seventh (2012) session the item entitled "Role of science and technology in the context of international security and disarmament".

Studies, research and training

UN Institute for Disarmament Research

The Secretary-General in July transmitted the report of the Director of the United Nations Institute for Disarmament Research (UNIDIR) [A/66/123] covering its activities from August 2010 to July 2011, as well as its proposed 2011–2012 programme of work and estimated budget, as approved by the Advisory Board on Disarmament Matters in its capacity as UNIDIR Board of Trustees. The Institute's programme of work was structured in five categories: weapons of mass destruction; weapons of societal disruption; security and society; emerging threats; and improving processes and creating synergies.

The Board of Trustees recommended that a subvention be provided for the Institute from the regular budget for the 2012–2013 biennium (cost-adjusted), and that efforts be made to increase the subvention. The Director also reported on the status of voluntary funds received from Governments and philanthropic foundations, which covered the majority of the Institute's budget and financed all of its operational activities. UNIDIR was seeking to expand its donor base as part of its resource mobilization strategy; however, due to the global financial crisis, contributions to its core functions continued to erode.

General Assembly action. The General Assembly, in section IV of **resolution 66/247** of 24 December (see p. 1393), having considered the Secretary-General's request [A/66/170] for a subvention to UNIDIR resulting from the recommendation of the Board of Trustees, and the related report of the Advisory Committee on Administrative and Budgetary Questions [A/66/7/Add.8], approved a subvention for the Institute in the amount of $577,800 from the UN regular budget for the 2012–2013 biennium.

Disarmament fellowships, training and advisory services

Twenty-five fellows participated in the 2011 UN disarmament fellowship, training and advisory services programme, which was offered by the United Nations Office for Disarmament Affairs (UNODA). The programme featured a study session in Geneva; study visits to intergovernmental organizations and Member States; and a study session at UN Headquarters.

Disarmament information programme

In 2011, the United Nations Disarmament Information Programme published its flagship publication, the *Disarmament Yearbook*, and an occasional paper, *Study on the Development of a Framework for Improving End-Use and End-User Control Systems* [Sales No. E.12.IX.5]. In December, UNODA published a booklet entitled *Delegitimizing Nuclear Weapons*, as part of the Critical Disarmament Issues series; released the Disarmament Study Series No. 33 on the subject of developments in information and telecommunications in the context of international security; and published the third edition of the booklet *Disarmament: A Basic Guide*, in collaboration with the NGO Committee on Disarmament. The Office embarked on making all its publications available in electronic formats. UNODA also organized the twenty-third United Nations Conference on Disarmament Issues (Matsumoto City, Japan, 27–29 July).

Regional disarmament

Positive developments in regional disarmament in 2011 included efforts to consolidate existing nuclear-weapon-free zones and facilitate the creation of new ones. The three UNODA regional centres continued their cooperation with Member States and regional organizations in implementing the United Nations Programme of Action to Prevent, Combat and Eradicate the Illicit Trade in Small Arms and Light Weapons in All Its Aspects (see p. 525), especially in building their legal and administrative capacities for tracing and marking such weapons.

GENERAL ASSEMBLY ACTION

On 2 December [meeting 71], the General Assembly, on the recommendation of the First Committee [A/66/412], adopted **resolution 66/36** without vote [agenda item 98 (*h*)].

Regional disarmament

The General Assembly,

Recalling its resolutions 45/58 P of 4 December 1990, 46/36 I of 6 December 1991, 47/52 J of 9 December 1992, 48/75 I of 16 December 1993, 49/75 N of 15 December 1994, 50/70 K of 12 December 1995, 51/45 K of 10 December 1996, 52/38 P of 9 December 1997, 53/77 O of 4 December 1998, 54/54 N of 1 December 1999, 55/33 O of 20 November 2000, 56/24 H of 29 November 2001, 57/76 of 22 November 2002, 58/38 of 8 December 2003, 59/89 of 3 December 2004, 60/63 of 8 December 2005, 61/80 of 6 December 2006, 62/38 of 5 December 2007, 63/43 of 2 December 2008, 64/41 of 2 December 2009 and 65/45 of 8 December 2010 on regional disarmament,

Believing that the efforts of the international community to move towards the ideal of general and complete disarmament are guided by the inherent human desire for genuine peace and security, the elimination of the danger of war and the release of economic, intellectual and other resources for peaceful pursuits,

Affirming the abiding commitment of all States to the purposes and principles enshrined in the Charter of the United Nations in the conduct of their international relations,

Noting that essential guidelines for progress towards general and complete disarmament were adopted at the tenth special session of the General Assembly,

Taking note of the guidelines and recommendations for regional approaches to disarmament within the context of global security adopted by the Disarmament Commission at its 1993 substantive session,

Welcoming the prospects of genuine progress in the field of disarmament engendered in recent years as a result of negotiations between the two super-Powers,

Taking note of the recent proposals for disarmament at the regional and subregional levels,

Recognizing the importance of confidence-building measures for regional and international peace and security,

Convinced that endeavours by countries to promote regional disarmament, taking into account the specific characteristics of each region and in accordance with the principle of undiminished security at the lowest level of armaments, would enhance the security of all States and would thus contribute to international peace and security by reducing the risk of regional conflicts,

1. *Stresses* that sustained efforts are needed, within the framework of the Conference on Disarmament and under the umbrella of the United Nations, to make progress on the entire range of disarmament issues;

2. *Affirms* that global and regional approaches to disarmament complement each other and should therefore be pursued simultaneously to promote regional and international peace and security;

3. *Calls upon* States to conclude agreements, wherever possible, for nuclear non-proliferation, disarmament and confidence-building measures at the regional and subregional levels;

4. *Welcomes* the initiatives towards disarmament, nuclear non-proliferation and security undertaken by some countries at the regional and subregional levels;

5. *Supports and encourages* efforts aimed at promoting confidence-building measures at the regional and subregional levels to ease regional tensions and to further disarmament and nuclear non-proliferation measures at the regional and subregional levels;

6. *Decides* to include in the provisional agenda of its sixty-seventh session the item entitled "Regional disarmament".

Conventional arms control at regional and subregional levels

In response to General Assembly resolution 65/46 [YUN 2010, p. 575] on conventional arms control at the regional and subregional levels, the Secretary-General in July submitted a report [A/66/154 & Add.1] containing the views of 15 Member States (Armenia, Colombia, Congo, El Salvador, Guyana, Jordan, Kazakhstan, Lebanon, Mexico, Montenegro, Norway, Portugal, Russian Federation, Turkmenistan, Ukraine) on the issue.

GENERAL ASSEMBLY ACTION

On 2 December [meeting 71], the General Assembly, on the recommendation of the First Committee [A/66/412], adopted **resolution 66/37** by recorded vote (175-1-2) [agenda item 98 (*i*)].

Conventional arms control at the regional and subregional levels

The General Assembly,

Recalling its resolutions 48/75 J of 16 December 1993, 49/75 O of 15 December 1994, 50/70 L of 12 December 1995, 51/45 Q of 10 December 1996, 52/38 Q of 9 December 1997, 53/77 P of 4 December 1998, 54/54 M of 1 December 1999, 55/33 P of 20 November 2000, 56/24 I of 29 November 2001, 57/77 of 22 November 2002, 58/39 of 8 December 2003, 59/88 of 3 December 2004, 60/75 of 8 December 2005, 61/82 of 6 December 2006, 62/44 of 5 December 2007, 63/44 of 2 December 2008, 64/42 of 2 December 2009 and 65/46 of 8 December 2010,

Recognizing the crucial role of conventional arms control in promoting regional and international peace and security,

Convinced that conventional arms control needs to be pursued primarily in the regional and subregional contexts since most threats to peace and security in the post-cold-war era arise mainly among States located in the same region or subregion,

Aware that the preservation of a balance in the defence capabilities of States at the lowest level of armaments would contribute to peace and stability and should be a prime objective of conventional arms control,

Desirous of promoting agreements to strengthen regional peace and security at the lowest possible level of armaments and military forces,

Noting with particular interest the initiatives taken in this regard in different regions of the world, in particular the commencement of consultations among a number of Latin American countries and the proposals for conventional arms control made in the context of South Asia, and recognizing, in the context of this subject, the relevance and value of the Treaty on Conventional Armed Forces in Europe, which is a cornerstone of European security,

Believing that militarily significant States and States with larger military capabilities have a special responsibility in promoting such agreements for regional security,

Believing also that an important objective of conventional arms control in regions of tension should be to prevent the possibility of military attack launched by surprise and to avoid aggression,

1. *Decides* to give urgent consideration to the issues involved in conventional arms control at the regional and subregional levels;

2. *Requests* the Conference on Disarmament to consider the formulation of principles that can serve as a framework for regional agreements on conventional arms control, and looks forward to a report of the Conference on this subject;

3. *Requests* the Secretary-General, in the meantime, to seek the views of Member States on the subject and to submit a report to the General Assembly at its sixty-seventh session;

4. *Decides* to include in the provisional agenda of its sixty-seventh session the item entitled "Conventional arms control at the regional and subregional levels".

RECORDED VOTE ON RESOLUTION 66/37:

In favour: Afghanistan, Albania, Algeria, Andorra, Angola, Antigua and Barbuda, Argentina, Armenia, Australia, Austria, Azerbaijan, Bahamas, Bahrain, Bangladesh, Barbados, Belarus, Belgium, Belize, Benin, Bolivia, Bosnia and Herzegovina, Botswana, Brazil, Brunei Darussalam, Bulgaria, Burkina Faso, Cambodia, Cameroon, Canada, Cape Verde, Chad, Chile, China, Colombia, Comoros, Congo, Costa Rica, Côte d'Ivoire, Croatia, Cyprus, Czech Republic, Democratic People's Republic of Korea, Denmark, Djibouti, Dominican Republic, Ecuador, Egypt, El Salvador, Estonia, Ethiopia, Fiji, Finland, France, Gabon, Georgia, Germany, Ghana, Greece, Grenada, Guatemala, Guinea, Guinea-Bissau, Guyana, Haiti, Honduras, Hungary, Iceland, Indonesia, Iran, Iraq, Ireland, Israel, Italy, Jamaica, Japan, Jordan, Kazakhstan, Kenya, Kyrgyzstan, Lao People's Democratic Republic, Latvia, Lebanon, Lesotho, Liberia, Libya, Liechtenstein, Lithuania, Luxembourg, Madagascar, Malawi, Malaysia, Maldives, Mali, Malta, Marshall Islands, Mauritania, Mauritius, Mexico, Micronesia, Monaco, Mongolia, Montenegro, Morocco, Mozambique, Myanmar, Namibia, Nepal, Netherlands, New Zealand, Nicaragua, Niger, Nigeria, Norway, Oman, Pakistan, Palau, Panama, Papua New Guinea, Paraguay, Peru, Philippines, Poland, Portugal, Qatar, Republic of Korea, Republic of Moldova, Romania, Saint Kitts and Nevis, Saint Lucia, Saint Vincent and the Grenadines, Samoa, San Marino, Sao Tome and Principe, Saudi Arabia, Senegal, Serbia, Seychelles, Sierra Leone, Singapore, Slovakia, Slovenia, Solomon Islands, South Africa, Spain, Sri Lanka, Suriname, Swaziland, Sweden, Switzerland, Syrian Arab Republic, Tajikistan, Thailand, the former Yugoslav Republic of Macedonia, Timor-Leste, Togo, Tonga, Trinidad and Tobago, Tunisia, Turkey, Turkmenistan, Tuvalu, Uganda, Ukraine, United Arab Emirates, United Kingdom, United Republic of Tanzania, United States, Uruguay, Uzbekistan, Vanuatu, Venezuela, Viet Nam, Yemen, Zambia, Zimbabwe.

Against: India.

Abstaining: Bhutan, Russian Federation.

Regional confidence-building measures

In June, the Secretary-General, in response to General Assembly resolution 65/47 [YUN 2010, p. 576] on confidence-building measures in the regional and subregional context, submitted a report [A/66/112 & Add.1] containing the views of 10 Member States (Armenia, Bolivia, Estonia, Germany, Guyana, Jordan, Portugal, Spain, Turkmenistan, Ukraine) on the issue.

Chapter VII: Disarmament

GENERAL ASSEMBLY ACTION

On 2 December [meeting 71], the General Assembly, on the recommendation of the First Committee [A/66/412], adopted **resolution 66/38** without vote [agenda item 98 (*j*)].

Confidence-building measures in the regional and subregional context

The General Assembly,

Guided by the purposes and principles enshrined in the Charter of the United Nations,

Recalling its resolutions 58/43 of 8 December 2003, 59/87 of 3 December 2004, 60/64 of 8 December 2005, 61/81 of 6 December 2006, 62/45 of 5 December 2007, 63/45 of 2 December 2008, 64/43 of 2 December 2009 and 65/47 of 8 December 2010,

Recalling also its resolution 57/337 of 3 July 2003 entitled "Prevention of armed conflict", in which it calls upon Member States to settle their disputes by peaceful means, as set out in Chapter VI of the Charter, inter alia, by any procedures adopted by the parties,

Recalling further the resolutions and guidelines adopted by consensus by the General Assembly and the Disarmament Commission relating to confidence-building measures and their implementation at the global, regional and subregional levels,

Considering the importance and effectiveness of confidence-building measures taken at the initiative and with the agreement of all States concerned, and taking into account the specific characteristics of each region, since such measures can contribute to regional stability,

Convinced that resources released by disarmament, including regional disarmament, can be devoted to economic and social development and to the protection of the environment for the benefit of all peoples, in particular those of the developing countries,

Recognizing the need for meaningful dialogue among States concerned to avert conflict,

Welcoming the peace processes already initiated by States concerned to resolve their disputes through peaceful means bilaterally or through mediation, inter alia, by third parties, regional organizations or the United Nations,

Recognizing that States in some regions have already taken steps towards confidence-building measures at the bilateral, subregional and regional levels in the political and military fields, including arms control and disarmament, and noting that such confidence-building measures have improved peace and security in those regions and contributed to progress in the socioeconomic conditions of their people,

Concerned that the continuation of disputes among States, particularly in the absence of an effective mechanism to resolve them through peaceful means, may contribute to the arms race and endanger the maintenance of international peace and security and the efforts of the international community to promote arms control and disarmament,

1. *Calls upon* Member States to refrain from the use or threat of use of force in accordance with the purposes and principles of the Charter of the United Nations;

2. *Reaffirms its commitment* to the peaceful settlement of disputes under Chapter VI of the Charter, in particular Article 33, which provides for a solution by negotiation, enquiry, mediation, conciliation, arbitration, judicial settlement, resort to regional agencies or arrangements or other peaceful means chosen by the parties;

3. *Reaffirms* the ways and means regarding confidence- and security-building measures set out in the report of the Disarmament Commission on its 1993 session;

4. *Calls upon* Member States to pursue these ways and means through sustained consultations and dialogue, while at the same time avoiding actions that may hinder or impair such a dialogue;

5. *Urges* States to comply strictly with all bilateral, regional and international agreements, including arms control and disarmament agreements, to which they are party;

6. *Emphasizes* that the objective of confidence-building measures should be to help to strengthen international peace and security and to be consistent with the principle of undiminished security at the lowest level of armaments;

7. *Encourages* the promotion of bilateral and regional confidence-building measures, with the consent and participation of the parties concerned, to avoid conflict and prevent the unintended and accidental outbreak of hostilities;

8. *Requests* the Secretary-General to submit a report to the General Assembly at its sixty-seventh session containing the views of Member States on confidence-building measures in the regional and subregional context;

9. *Decides* to include in the provisional agenda of its sixty-seventh session the item entitled "Confidence-building measures in the regional and subregional context".

Standing Committee on Security Questions in Central Africa

At its thirty-second meeting (Sao Tome and Principe, 12–16 March) [A/66/72-S/2011/225], the Standing Committee on Security Questions in Central Africa adopted the Sao Tome Declaration on a Central African Common Position on the Arms Trade Treaty, in preparation for the 2012 United Nations Conference on the Arms Trade Treaty (see p. 524).

In July [A/66/163], the Secretary-General submitted a report on the activities of the Committee, including its review of such recurrent issues considered at its ministerial meetings as progress made by member States in implementing the 2003 Brazzaville Programme of Priority Activities for combating the proliferation of small arms and light weapons in Central Africa, and the implementation of the Libreville Declaration, which stressed the need for all member States to make voluntary financial contributions to the Committee's Trust Fund. The Committee also considered the issue of maritime piracy in the Gulf of Guinea, and the implementation in Central Africa of numerous Security Council resolutions on women, peace and security, as well as of General Assembly resolution 65/69 on women, disarmament, non-proliferation and arms control [YUN 2010, p. 513].

New topics included the illegal exploitation of natural resources in Central Africa; the impact of climate change on peace and security in the subregion; the protection of widows and their children; and combating trafficking in persons, especially women and children, in Central Africa.

GENERAL ASSEMBLY ACTION

On 2 December [meeting 71], the General Assembly, on the recommendation of the First Committee [A/66/413], adopted **resolution 66/55** without vote [agenda item 99 (*f*)].

Regional confidence-building measures: activities of the United Nations Standing Advisory Committee on Security Questions in Central Africa

The General Assembly,

Recalling its previous relevant resolutions, in particular resolution 65/84 of 8 December 2010,

Recalling also the guidelines for general and complete disarmament adopted at its tenth special session, the first special session devoted to disarmament,

Bearing in mind the establishment by the Secretary-General on 28 May 1992 of the United Nations Standing Advisory Committee on Security Questions in Central Africa, the purpose of which is to encourage arms limitation, disarmament, non-proliferation and development in the subregion,

Reaffirming that the purpose of the Standing Advisory Committee is to conduct reconstruction and confidence-building activities in Central Africa among its member States, including through confidence-building and arms limitation measures,

Taking note of the Sao Tome Declaration on a Central African Common Position on the Arms Trade Treaty, adopted by the States members of the Standing Advisory Committee on 16 March 2011 at their thirty-second ministerial meeting, held in Sao Tome from 12 to 16 March 2011,

Convinced that the resources released by disarmament, including regional disarmament, can be devoted to economic and social development and to the protection of the environment for the benefit of all peoples, in particular those of developing countries,

Considering the importance and effectiveness of confidence-building measures taken on the initiative and with the participation of all States concerned and taking into account the specific characteristics of each region, since such measures can contribute to regional stability and to international peace and security,

Convinced that development can be achieved only in a climate of peace, security and mutual confidence both within and among States,

Recalling the Brazzaville Declaration on Cooperation for Peace and Security in Central Africa, the Bata Declaration for the Promotion of Lasting Democracy, Peace and Development in Central Africa and the Yaoundé Declaration on Peace, Security and Stability in Central Africa,

Bearing in mind resolutions 1196(1998) and 1197(1998), adopted by the Security Council on 16 and 18 September 1998, respectively, following its consideration of the report of the Secretary-General on the causes of conflict and the promotion of durable peace and sustainable development in Africa,

Emphasizing the need to strengthen the capacity for conflict prevention and peacekeeping in Africa, and welcoming the close cooperation established between the United Nations and the Economic Community of Central African States for that purpose,

Taking note with interest of the increasing focus of the Standing Advisory Committee on human security questions, such as trafficking in persons, especially in women and children, as an important consideration for subregional peace, stability and conflict prevention,

Expressing concern about the increasing impact of cross-border criminality, in particular the activities of the Lord's Resistance Army and increasing incidents of piracy in the Gulf of Guinea, on peace, security and development in Central Africa,

Considering the urgent need to prevent the possible movement of illicit weapons and mercenaries from the conflict in Libya into the neighbouring countries in the Central African region,

1. *Reaffirms its support* for efforts aimed at promoting confidence-building measures at the regional and subregional levels in order to ease tensions and conflicts in Central Africa and to further sustainable peace, stability and development in the subregion;

2. *Reaffirms* the importance of disarmament and arms limitation programmes in Central Africa carried out by the States of the subregion with the support of the United Nations, the African Union and other international partners;

3. *Renews its encouragement* to the States members of the United Nations Standing Advisory Committee on Security Questions in Central Africa and other interested States to provide financial support for the implementation of the Central African Convention for the Control of Small Arms and Light Weapons, Their Ammunition and All Parts and Components That Can Be Used for Their Manufacture, Repair and Assembly (Kinshasa Convention), adopted on 30 April 2010, at the thirtieth ministerial meeting of the Standing Advisory Committee, held in Kinshasa from 26 to 30 April 2010;

4. *Welcomes* the adoption by the States members of the Standing Advisory Committee of the Sao Tome Declaration on a Central African Common Position on the Arms Trade Treaty, encourages the Committee to take the necessary measures for the implementation of the steps identified in the Declaration, towards the continued active participation of its member States in the process for the arms trade treaty, and requests the United Nations Regional Office for Central Africa and international partners to support those measures;

5. *Also welcomes* the active participation of experts of States members of the Standing Advisory Committee in the open-ended meeting of governmental experts on the Implementation of the Programme of Action to Prevent, Combat and Eradicate the Illicit Trade in Small Arms and Light Weapons in All Its Aspects, held in New York from 9 to 13 May 2011;

6. *Encourages* the States members of the Standing Advisory Committee to carry out the programmes of activities adopted at their ministerial meetings;

7. *Also encourages* the States members of the Standing Advisory Committee to continue their efforts to render the early warning mechanism for Central Africa fully operational as an instrument for analysing and monitoring the political situation in the subregion within the framework of the prevention of crises and armed conflicts, and requests the Secretary-General to provide the assistance necessary for its smooth functioning;

8. *Welcomes* the signing of the Kinshasa Convention by all eleven States members of the Standing Advisory Committee, and appeals to them to ratify the Convention in a timely manner in order to facilitate its early entry into force and implementation;

9. *Appeals* to the international community to support the efforts undertaken by the States concerned to implement disarmament, demobilization and reintegration programmes;

10. *Requests* the United Nations Regional Office for Central Africa, in collaboration with the United Nations Regional Centre for Peace and Disarmament in Africa, to facilitate the efforts undertaken by the States members of the Standing Advisory Committee, in particular for their execution of the Implementation Plan for the Kinshasa Convention, as adopted on 19 November 2010 at their thirty-first ministerial meeting, held in Brazzaville from 15 to 19 November 2010;

11. *Requests* the Secretary-General and the Office of the United Nations High Commissioner for Refugees to continue to assist the countries of Central Africa in tackling the problems of refugees and displaced persons in their territories;

12. *Requests* the Secretary-General and the United Nations High Commissioner for Human Rights to continue to provide their full assistance for the proper functioning of the Subregional Centre for Human Rights and Democracy in Central Africa;

13. *Reminds* the States members of the Standing Advisory Committee of the commitments they undertook at the adoption of the Declaration on the Trust Fund of the United Nations Standing Advisory Committee on Security Questions in Central Africa (Libreville Declaration) on 8 May 2009, and invites those States members of the Committee that have not already done so to contribute to the Trust Fund;

14. *Urges* other Member States and intergovernmental and non-governmental organizations to support the activities of the Standing Advisory Committee effectively through voluntary contributions to the Trust Fund;

15. *Urges* the States members of the Standing Advisory Committee, in accordance with Security Council resolution 1325(2000) of 31 October 2000, to strengthen the gender component of the various meetings of the Committee relating to disarmament and international security;

16. *Expresses its satisfaction* to the Secretary-General for his support for the effective inauguration of the United Nations Regional Office for Central Africa in Libreville, welcomes the efforts made by the Office since its opening, and strongly encourages the States members of the Standing Advisory Committee and international partners to support the work of the Office;

17. *Welcomes* the efforts of the Standing Advisory Committee towards addressing cross-border security threats in Central Africa, including the fallout from the situation in Libya, and welcomes the role of the United Nations Regional Office for Central Africa in coordinating those efforts, working closely with the Economic Community of Central African States, the African Union and all relevant regional and international partners;

18. *Expresses its satisfaction* to the Secretary-General for his support for the revitalization of the activities of the Standing Advisory Committee, and requests him to continue to provide the assistance needed to ensure the success of its regular biannual meetings;

19. *Calls upon* the Secretary-General to submit to the General Assembly at its sixty-seventh session a report on the implementation of the present resolution;

20. *Decides* to include in the provisional agenda of its sixty-seventh session the sub-item entitled "Regional confidence-building measures: activities of the United Nations Standing Advisory Committee on Security Questions in Central Africa".

Regional centres for peace and disarmament

GENERAL ASSEMBLY ACTION

On 2 December [meeting 71], the General Assembly, on the recommendation of the First Committee [A/66/413], adopted **resolution 66/53** without vote [agenda item 99 (*b*)].

United Nations regional centres for peace and disarmament

The General Assembly,

Recalling its resolutions 60/83 of 8 December 2005, 61/90 of 6 December 2006, 62/50 of 5 December 2007, 63/76 of 2 December 2008, 64/58 of 2 December 2009 and 65/78 of 8 December 2010 regarding the maintenance and revitalization of the three United Nations regional centres for peace and disarmament,

Recalling also the reports of the Secretary-General on the United Nations Regional Centre for Peace and Disarmament in Africa, the United Nations Regional Centre for Peace and Disarmament in Asia and the Pacific and the United Nations Regional Centre for Peace, Disarmament and Development in Latin America and the Caribbean,

Reaffirming its decision, taken in 1982 at its twelfth special session, to establish the United Nations Disarmament Information Programme, the purpose of which is to inform, educate and generate public understanding and support for the objectives of the United Nations in the field of arms control and disarmament,

Bearing in mind its resolutions 40/151 G of 16 December 1985, 41/60 J of 3 December 1986, 42/39 D of 30 November 1987 and 44/117 F of 15 December 1989 on the regional centres for peace and disarmament in Nepal, Peru and Togo,

Recognizing that the changes that have taken place in the world have created new opportunities and posed new challenges for the pursuit of disarmament, and bearing in mind in this regard that the regional centres for peace and disarmament can contribute substantially to understanding and cooperation among States in each particular region in the areas of peace, disarmament and development,

Recalling that, in paragraph 127 of the Final Document of the Fifteenth Summit Conference of Heads of State and Government of the Movement of Non-Aligned Countries, held in Sharm el-Sheikh, Egypt, from 11 to 16 July 2009, and in paragraph 162 of the Final Document of the Sixteenth Ministerial Conference and Commemorative Meeting of the Movement of Non-Aligned Countries, held in Bali, Indonesia, from 23 to 27 May 2011, the Movement of Non-Aligned Countries emphasized the importance of United Nations activities at the regional level to increase the stability and security of its Member States, which could be promoted in a substantive manner by the maintenance and revitalization of the three regional centres for peace and disarmament,

1. *Reiterates* the importance of United Nations activities at the regional level to advance disarmament and to increase the stability and security of its Member States, which could be promoted in a substantive manner by the maintenance and revitalization of the three regional centres for peace and disarmament;

2. *Reaffirms* that, in order to achieve positive results, it is useful for the three regional centres to carry out dissemination and educational programmes that promote regional peace and security and that are aimed at changing basic attitudes with respect to peace and security and disarmament so as to support the achievement of the purposes and principles of the United Nations;

3. *Appeals* to Member States in each region that are able to do so, as well as to international governmental and non-governmental organizations and foundations, to make voluntary contributions to the regional centres in their respective regions in order to strengthen their activities and initiatives;

4. *Emphasizes* the importance of the activities of the Regional Disarmament Branch of the Office for Disarmament Affairs of the Secretariat;

5. *Requests* the Secretary-General to provide all necessary support, within existing resources, to the regional centres in carrying out their programmes of activities;

6. *Decides* to include in the provisional agenda of its sixty-seventh session the item entitled "United Nations regional centres for peace and disarmament".

Africa

In July [A/66/159], the Secretary-General reported on the activities of the United Nations Regional Centre for Peace and Disarmament in Africa (Lomé, Togo) during the period from July 2009 to June 2011. The Centre increased its assistance to Member States and intergovernmental and civil society organizations in Africa to promote peace and security through disarmament and arms regulation. It focused on assisting Member States in the region and cooperating with regional and subregional organizations to address the threats posed to peace, security and socioeconomic development by the proliferation of small arms and light weapons. The Centre helped the African Union (AU) Commission adopt an African strategy to control small arms and light weapons and in reaching an AU common position on the proposed arms trade treaty (see p. 524). The Centre shared its expertise and contributed to the project consolidation seminar of the Regional Centre on Small Arms and Light Weapons/African Union/European Union (Addis Ababa, 17–18 January), which produced a road map for activities for the remaining two years of the project. It also assisted the Government of Togo in implementing Security Council resolution 1325 [YUN 2000, p. 1113] by co-organizing with the Government training on issues related to violence against women for female officers of the gendarmerie and security forces (Lomé, January); and another with the United Nations Development Programme and the secretariat of the Geneva Declaration on Armed Violence and Development on promising practices in armed violence prevention and reduction in East and Central Africa (Nairobi, February).

In a later report [A/67/117], the Secretary-General indicated that early in 2011, the Centre, together with the Togolese Government and civil society, reinitiated efforts to develop a national action plan on the role of Togolese women in promoting security and peaceful conflict resolution, which was validated by Togolese Government officials and civil society members in October. As part of the African Union Regional Economic Communities Steering Committee on Small Arms, the Centre continued to assist the AU in developing a common strategy for the control of small arms and light weapons and a related action plan. At a meeting held in September in Lomé, AU governmental experts agreed to a draft strategy and action plan for strengthening their capacity to implement measures against the illicit proliferation, circulation and trafficking of small arms and light weapons, as well as to promote cooperation, coordination and exchange of information on the issue.

With the aim of harmonizing approaches to small arms and light weapons marking within West Africa, the Centre supported the Economic Community of West African States in adopting a new agreement on marking small arms and light weapons in early December. The Centre was requested by the secretariat of the Economic Community of Central African States in March to provide support in implementing the Kinshasa Convention on the control of small arms and light weapons [YUN 2010, p. 118]. In cooperation with the Friedrich-Ebert-Stiftung, the Centre started a project in October to assess small arms and light weapons trafficking within and among Benin, Ghana, Nigeria and Togo.

As at 31 December 2010, the reserves and fund balance of the Centre's trust fund stood at $219,877.

GENERAL ASSEMBLY ACTION

On 2 December [meeting 71], the General Assembly, on the recommendation of the First Committee [A/66/413], adopted **resolution 66/58** without vote [agenda item 99 (*a*)].

United Nations Regional Centre for Peace and Disarmament in Africa

The General Assembly,

Mindful of the provisions of Article 11, paragraph 1, of the Charter of the United Nations stipulating that a function of the General Assembly is to consider the general principles of cooperation in the maintenance of international peace and security, including the principles governing disarmament and arms limitation,

Recalling its resolutions 40/151 G of 16 December 1985, 41/60 D of 3 December 1986, 42/39 J of 30 November 1987 and 43/76 D of 7 December 1988 on the United Nations Regional Centre for Peace and Disarmament in Africa and its resolutions 46/36 F of 6 December 1991 and 47/52 G of 9 December 1992 on regional disarmament, including confidence-building measures,

Recalling also its resolutions 48/76 E of 16 December 1993, 49/76 D of 15 December 1994, 50/71 C of 12 December 1995, 51/46 E of 10 December 1996, 52/220 of 22 December 1997, 53/78 C of 4 December 1998, 54/55 B of 1 December 1999, 55/34 D of 20 November 2000, 56/25 D of 29 November 2001, 57/91 of 22 November 2002, 58/61 of 8 December 2003, 59/101 of 3 December 2004, 60/86 of 8 December 2005, 61/93 of 6 December 2006, 62/216 of 22 December 2007, 63/80 of 2 December 2008 and 64/62 of 2 December 2009,

Reaffirming the role of the Regional Centre in promoting disarmament, peace and security at the regional level,

Welcoming the continuing and deepening cooperation between the Regional Centre and the African Union, in particular its institutions in the fields of disarmament, peace and security, as well as between the Centre and relevant United Nations bodies and programmes in Africa, and considering the communiqué adopted by the Peace and Security Council of the African Union at its two-hundredth meeting, held in Addis Ababa on 21 August 2009,

Recalling the decision taken by the Executive Council of the African Union at its eighth ordinary session, held in Khartoum from 16 to 21 January 2006, in which the Council called upon member States to make voluntary contributions to the Regional Centre to maintain its operations,

Recalling also the call by the Secretary-General for continued financial and in kind support from Member States, which would enable the Regional Centre to discharge its mandate in full and to respond more effectively to requests for assistance from African States,

1. *Takes note* of the report of the Secretary-General;
2. *Welcomes* the continental dimension of the activities of the United Nations Regional Centre for Peace and Disarmament in Africa in response to the evolving needs of African Member States in the areas of disarmament, peace and security;
3. *Also welcomes* the undertaking by the Regional Centre to provide capacity-building, technical assistance programmes and advisory services to the African Union Commission and subregional organizations on the control of small arms and light weapons, including on stockpile management and destruction, the proposed arms trade treaty and issues related to weapons of mass destruction, as detailed in the report of the Secretary-General;
4. *Further welcomes* the contribution of the Regional Centre to continental disarmament, peace and security, in particular its assistance to the African Union Commission in the elaboration of the African Union Strategy on the Control of Illicit Proliferation, Circulation and Trafficking of Small Arms and Light Weapons and the ongoing process of seeking an African common position on the proposed arms trade treaty, and to the African Commission on Nuclear Energy in its implementation of the African Nuclear-Weapon-Free Zone Treaty (Treaty of Pelindaba);
5. *Notes with appreciation* the tangible achievements and impact of the Regional Centre at the regional level, including its assistance to Central African States in their elaboration of the Central African Convention for the Control of Small Arms and Light Weapons, Their Ammunition and All Parts and Components That Can Be Used for Their Manufacture, Repair and Assembly (Kinshasa Convention), to Central and West African States in the elaboration of their respective common positions on the proposed arms trade treaty, to West Africa on security sector reform initiatives, and to East Africa on programmes to control brokering of small arms and light weapons;
6. *Also notes with appreciation* the contribution of the Regional Centre to the "One United Nations" approach and to United Nations inter-agency mechanisms, including the United Nations Development Assistance Framework, the common country assessments and the poverty reduction strategy papers, in a number of African countries;
7. *Urges* all States, as well as international governmental and non-governmental organizations and foundations, to make voluntary contributions to enable the Regional Centre to carry out its programmes and activities and meet the needs of the African States;
8. *Urges*, in particular, States members of the African Union to make voluntary contributions to the Trust Fund for the United Nations Regional Centre for Peace and Disarmament in Africa in conformity with the decision taken by the Executive Council of the African Union in Khartoum in January 2006;
9. *Requests* the Secretary-General to continue to facilitate close cooperation between the Regional Centre and the African Union, in particular in the areas of disarmament, peace and security;
10. *Also requests* the Secretary-General to continue to provide the necessary support to the Regional Centre for greater achievements and results;
11. *Further requests* the Secretary-General to report to the General Assembly at its sixty-seventh session on the implementation of the present resolution;
12. *Decides* to include in the provisional agenda of its sixty-seventh session the sub-item entitled "United Nations Regional Centre for Peace and Disarmament in Africa".

Asia and the Pacific

As requested in General Assembly resolution 65/83 [YUN 2010, p. 578], the Secretary-General, in June [A/66/113], reported on the work of the United Nations Regional Centre for Peace and Disarmament in Asia and the Pacific (Kathmandu, Nepal) between July 2010 and June 2011. The Centre launched two new projects: on armed violence reduction and prevention, and on strengthening the media's role and capacity in advocating and promoting disarmament and non-proliferation in Asia and the Pacific. The Centre helped to organize the first regional best and promising practices seminar on armed violence reduction and prevention for South and South-East Asia (Kathmandu, March), and a regional workshop for East and South-East Asia on strengthening the capacity of the media in advocating and promoting peace and disarmament in the region (Beijing, January). It continued to organize annual conferences on disarmament and non-proliferation issues.

As at 31 December 2010, the reserves and fund balance of the Centre's trust fund stood at $636,078.

GENERAL ASSEMBLY ACTION

On 2 December [meeting 71], the General Assembly, on the recommendation of the First Committee [A/66/413], adopted **resolution 66/56** without vote [agenda item 99 (*e*)].

United Nations Regional Centre for Peace and Disarmament in Asia and the Pacific

The General Assembly,

Recalling its resolutions 42/39 D of 30 November 1987 and 44/117 F of 15 December 1989, by which it established the United Nations Regional Centre for Peace and Disarmament in Asia and renamed it the United Nations Regional Centre for Peace and Disarmament in Asia and the Pacific, with headquarters in Kathmandu and with the mandate of providing, on request, substantive support for the initiatives and other activities mutually agreed upon by the Member States of the Asia-Pacific region for the implementation of measures for peace and disarmament, through appropriate utilization of available resources,

Welcoming the physical operation of the Regional Centre from Kathmandu in accordance with General Assembly resolution 62/52 of 5 December 2007,

Recalling the mandate of the Regional Centre to provide, on request, substantive support for the initiatives and other activities mutually agreed upon by the Member States of the Asia-Pacific region for the implementation of measures for peace and disarmament,

Taking note of the report of the Secretary-General and expressing its appreciation to the Regional Centre for its important work in promoting confidence-building measures through the organization of meetings, conferences and workshops in the region, including conferences held on Jeju Island, Republic of Korea, on 2 and 3 December 2010 and in Matsumoto, Japan, from 27 to 29 July 2011, a regional workshop on strengthening the media's capacity in promoting disarmament held in Beijing on 20 and 21 January 2011 and a regional seminar on armed violence prevention held in Kathmandu from 16 to 18 March 2011,

Appreciating the timely execution by Nepal of its financial commitments for the physical operation of the Regional Centre,

1. *Expresses its satisfaction* for the activities carried out in the past year by the United Nations Regional Centre for Peace and Disarmament in Asia and the Pacific, and invites all States of the region to continue to support the activities of the Centre, including by continuing to take part in them, where possible, and by proposing items for inclusion in the programme of activities of the Centre, in order to contribute to the implementation of measures for peace and disarmament;

2. *Expresses its gratitude* to the Government of Nepal for its cooperation and financial support, which has enabled the Regional Centre to operate from Kathmandu;

3. *Expresses its appreciation* to the Secretary-General and the Office for Disarmament Affairs of the Secretariat for providing necessary support with a view to ensuring the smooth operation of the Regional Centre from Kathmandu and to enabling the Centre to function effectively;

4. *Appeals* to Member States, in particular those within the Asia-Pacific region, as well as to international governmental and non-governmental organizations and foundations, to make voluntary contributions, the only resources of the Regional Centre, to strengthen the programme of activities of the Centre and the implementation thereof;

5. *Reaffirms its strong support* for the role of the Regional Centre in the promotion of United Nations activities at the regional level to strengthen peace, stability and security among its Member States;

6. *Underlines* the importance of the Kathmandu process for the development of the practice of region-wide security and disarmament dialogues;

7. *Requests* the Secretary-General to report to the General Assembly at its sixty-seventh session on the implementation of the present resolution;

8. *Decides* to include in the provisional agenda of its sixty-seventh session the sub-item entitled "United Nations Regional Centre for Peace and Disarmament in Asia and the Pacific".

Latin America and the Caribbean

The United Nations Regional Centre for Peace, Disarmament and Development in Latin America and the Caribbean (Lima, Peru) focused on supporting Member States in addressing the illicit trafficking and use of firearms, ammunition and explosives, according to the Secretary-General's July report on the Centre's activities during the period from July 2010 to June 2011 [A/66/140], submitted in response to General Assembly resolution 65/79 [YUN 2010, p. 579]. The Centre supported countries in the adoption of a harmonized regional approach to addressing the threat, including robust firearms control measures. It implemented assistance packages in the Andean and Caribbean subregions, helping improve the security of firearms stockpiles and create national firearms commissions, as well as providing specialized training for law enforcement officials and comparative legislative studies on firearms control. It also offered capacity-building, training and policy, technical and legal assistance on firearms control and armed violence reduction and prevention. The Centre promoted the Secretary-General's five-point proposal on nuclear disarmament [YUN 2008, p. 565] by assisting Member States in organizing conferences and workshops to discuss actions towards a nuclear-weapon-free world and by providing expertise on capacity-building for State entities.

As at 31 December 2010, the reserves and fund balance of the Centre's trust fund stood at $1,645,138.

GENERAL ASSEMBLY ACTION

On 2 December [meeting 71], the General Assembly, on the recommendation of the First Committee [A/66/413], adopted **resolution 66/54** without vote [agenda item 99 (c)].

United Nations Regional Centre for Peace, Disarmament and Development in Latin America and the Caribbean

The General Assembly,

Recalling its resolutions 41/60 J of 3 December 1986, 42/39 K of 30 November 1987 and 43/76 H of 7 December 1988 on the United Nations Regional Centre for Peace, Disarmament and Development in Latin America and the Caribbean, with headquarters in Lima,

Recalling also its resolutions 46/37 F of 9 December 1991, 48/76 E of 16 December 1993, 49/76 D of 15 December 1994, 50/71 C of 12 December 1995, 52/220 of 22 December 1997, 53/78 F of 4 December 1998, 54/55 F of 1 December 1999, 55/34 E of 20 November 2000, 56/25 E of 29 November 2001, 57/89 of 22 November 2002, 58/60 of 8 December 2003, 59/99 of 3 December 2004, 60/84 of 8 December 2005, 61/92 of 6 December 2006, 62/49 of 5 December 2007, 63/74 of 2 December 2008, 64/60 of 2 December 2009 and 65/79 of 8 December 2010,

Recognizing that the Regional Centre has continued to provide substantive support for the implementation of regional and subregional initiatives and has intensified its contribution to the coordination of United Nations efforts towards peace and disarmament and for the promotion of economic and social development,

Reaffirming the mandate of the Regional Centre to provide, on request, substantive support for the initiatives and other activities of the Member States of the region for the implementation of measures for peace and disarmament and for the promotion of economic and social development,

Taking note of the report of the Secretary-General, and expressing its appreciation for the important assistance provided by the Regional Centre to many countries in the region, including through capacity-building and technical assistance programmes as well as outreach activities, for the development of plans to reduce and prevent armed violence from an arms control perspective, for promoting the implementation of relevant agreements and treaties and for capacity-building initiatives aimed at bolstering the efforts of the law enforcement community to combat illicit firearms trafficking,

Welcoming the support provided by the Regional Centre to Member States in the implementation of disarmament and non-proliferation instruments,

Emphasizing the need for the Regional Centre to develop and strengthen its activities and programmes in a comprehensive and balanced manner, in accordance with its mandate,

Welcoming the ongoing support provided by the Regional Centre to Member States in the implementation of the Programme of Action to Prevent, Combat and Eradicate the Illicit Trade in Small Arms and Light Weapons in All Its Aspects,

Welcoming also the initiative of the Regional Centre to conduct its first course specifically for women, in line with efforts to implement gender mainstreaming in promoting disarmament, non-proliferation and arms control, as called for in General Assembly resolution 65/69 of 8 December 2010,

Recalling the report of the Group of Governmental Experts on the relationship between disarmament and development, referred to in General Assembly resolution 59/78 of 3 December 2004, which is of utmost interest with regard to the role that the Regional Centre plays in promoting the issue in the region in pursuit of its mandate to promote economic and social development related to peace and disarmament,

Noting that security and disarmament issues have always been recognized as significant topics in Latin America and the Caribbean, the first inhabited region in the world to be declared a nuclear-weapon-free zone,

Emphasizing the importance of maintaining the support provided by the Regional Centre for strengthening the nuclear-weapon-free zone established by the Treaty for the Prohibition of Nuclear Weapons in Latin America and the Caribbean (Treaty of Tlatelolco), and its efforts in promoting peace and disarmament education,

Bearing in mind the important role of the Regional Centre in promoting confidence-building measures, arms control and limitation, disarmament and development at the regional level,

Bearing in mind also the importance of information, research, education and training for peace, disarmament and development in order to achieve understanding and cooperation among States,

1. *Reiterates its strong support* for the role of the United Nations Regional Centre for Peace, Disarmament and Development in Latin America and the Caribbean in the promotion of United Nations activities at the regional and subregional levels to strengthen peace, disarmament, stability, security and development among its member States;

2. *Expresses its satisfaction* for the activities carried out in the past year by the Regional Centre, and requests the Centre to continue to take into account the proposals to be submitted by the countries of the region for the promotion of, inter alia, confidence-building measures, arms control and limitation, transparency, the reduction and prevention of armed violence, disarmament and development at the regional and subregional levels;

3. *Expresses its appreciation* for the political support for and financial contributions to the Regional Centre, which are essential for its continued operation;

4. *Appeals* to Member States, in particular those within the Latin American and Caribbean region, and to international governmental and non-governmental organizations and foundations to make and to increase voluntary contributions in order to strengthen the Regional Centre, its programme of activities and the implementation thereof;

5. *Invites* all States of the region to continue to take part in the activities of the Regional Centre, proposing items for inclusion in its programme of activities and making greater and better use of the potential of the Centre to meet the current challenges facing the international community, with a view to fulfilling the aims of the Charter of the United Nations in the areas of peace, disarmament and development;

6. *Recognizes* that the Regional Centre has an important role in the promotion and development of regional and subregional initiatives agreed upon by the countries of Latin America and the Caribbean in the field of weapons of mass destruction, in particular nuclear weapons, and conventional arms, including small arms and light weapons, as well as in the relationship between disarmament and development;

7. *Encourages* the Regional Centre to further develop activities in all countries of the region in the important areas of peace, disarmament and development;

8. *Requests* the Secretary-General to report to the General Assembly at its sixty-seventh session on the implementation of the present resolution;

9. *Decides* to include in the provisional agenda of its sixty-seventh session the sub-item entitled "United Nations Regional Centre for Peace, Disarmament and Development in Latin America and the Caribbean".

Chapter VIII
Other political and security questions

In 2011, the United Nations continued to address political and security questions related to its support for democratization worldwide, the promotion of decolonization, the peaceful uses of outer space and the Organization's public information activities.

The Special Committee on the Situation with regard to the Implementation of the Declaration on the Granting of Independence to Colonial Countries and Peoples reviewed progress in implementing the 1960 Declaration, particularly the exercise of self-determination by the remaining Non-Self-Governing Territories. It organized a Caribbean regional seminar (Kingstown, Saint Vincent and the Grenadines, 31 May–2 June) to assess past contributions and expected accomplishments in the Decade for the Eradication of Colonialism (2011–2020).

In an April resolution, the General Assembly drew attention to the fiftieth anniversary of the Committee on the Peaceful Uses of Outer Space, which held a commemorative segment to mark the occasion. As part of its consideration of the recommendations of the Third (1999) United Nations Conference on the Exploration and Peaceful Uses of Outer Space, the Committee endorsed a paper on harnessing space-derived geospatial data for sustainable development and agreed that it would constitute its contribution to the United Nations Conference on Sustainable Development in 2012.

There was progress in implementing the United Nations Platform for Space-based Information for Disaster Management and Emergency Response (UN-SPIDER), including through the provision of technical advisory support to 23 countries and the support of emergency response activities in seven emergency situations. Coordination by UN-SPIDER of the collection of pre- and post-disaster space-based information following the earthquake in March off the east coast of Japan represented a significant source of information for national disaster relief efforts.

In May, the United Nations Scientific Committee on the Effects of Atomic Radiation held its fifty-eighth session in Vienna, where it took note of the twenty-fifth anniversary of the Chernobyl accident and considered, in terms of the levels and effects of radiation, the effects of the Fukushima Daiichi nuclear power plant accident that resulted from the earthquake in eastern Japan. Subsequently, the Secretary-General issued an August report with the findings of a UN system-wide study on the implications of the accident and convened, in September, a high-level meeting on strengthening nuclear safety and security.

Addressing developments in information and telecommunications in the context of international security, the Assembly in December called on Member States to promote consideration of existing and potential threats in the field of information security, as well as possible strategies to address the threats emerging in the field, consistent with the need to preserve the free flow of information.

The Committee on Information, at its session in April and May, continued to review UN information policies and activities, and the management and operation of the UN Department of Public Information (DPI). The Committee considered reports of the Secretary-General on DPI activities promoting the work of the United Nations to a global audience through strategic communications and news and outreach services.

General aspects of international peace and security

Support for democracies

UN system activities

In a September report [A/66/353] submitted in response to General Assembly resolution 64/12 [YUN 2009, p. 574], the Secretary-General made recommendations on cooperation between Member States, regional and intergovernmental organizations and the United Nations to strengthen programmes promoting and consolidating democracy. The report also reviewed the support provided by the UN system to new or restored democracies and provided an account of the observance of the International Day of Democracy, 15 September, as noted in resolutions 64/12 [ibid.] and 62/7 [YUN 2007, p. 605] and celebrated for the first time in 2008 [YUN 2008, p. 12].

With the vigorous call for democratic change across the Middle East and North Africa in 2011, UN action in support of democratic transitions assumed a renewed sense of urgency, and the Secretary-General made the promotion of democracy and human rights a key focus in his second term. UN assistance to new or restored democracies included strengthening democratic governance and the rule of law; protecting and promoting human rights; supporting constitution-making processes; electoral assistance; enabling civic engagement; and empowering women. The United Nations and regional and intergovernmental organizations broadened and deepened their cooperation; in particular, they strove to work in complementarity and to emphasize synergies in promoting, consolidating and strengthening democracy and democratic practices at the local, national and regional levels to avoid duplication and ensure the efficient use of scarce resources. Within the UN system, the Inter-Agency Working Group on Democracy of the Executive Committee on Peace and Security organized in New York a series of round tables and seminars on the linkages between democracy and peace and security, human rights and gender, respectively, which resulted in policy and operational recommendations.

The Secretary-General recommended that the international community be more ambitious in celebrating the International Day of Democracy. More Member States should regard the Day as an opportunity to encourage citizen engagement and highlight the benefits of living in free, democratic societies. As the Day was also a chance to reach out to the next generation of leaders, particular attention should be paid to youth. Building on the close cooperation of the United Nations with regional and intergovernmental organizations, the Secretary-General intended to focus on three key areas: facilitating the exchange of practices and lessons learned between Member States and other actors; strengthening the Organization's capacity to act as a resource for technical assistance and advice for Member States; and improving and refining the actions of the United Nations as implementer to assist Member States in transition. Finally, the Secretary-General recommended reviewing the role of and synergies between the International Conference of New or Restored Democracies and the Community of Democracies, with both movements enhancing peer support to countries undergoing democratic transition.

On 24 December, the General Assembly decided that the agenda item on support by the UN system of the efforts of Governments to promote and consolidate new or restored democracies would remain for consideration during its resumed sixty-sixth (2012) session (**decision 66/557**).

Regional aspects of international peace and security

Indian Ocean

In 2011, the Ad Hoc Committee on the Indian Ocean continued its efforts to reach agreement on ways forward in implementing the 1971 Declaration of the Indian Ocean as a Zone of Peace, as adopted by the General Assembly in resolution 2832(XXVI) [YUN 1971, p. 34]. The Committee held its formal session [A/66/29] in New York on 14 July, at which the Chair stated that the changing security and geopolitical scenarios of the Indian Ocean region continued to produce issues for Member States. New challenges in the arms trade and disarmament efforts had come to the fore, while sophisticated piracy and non-State players, including terrorist groups and transnational subversive elements, had emerged as threats to peace and security within and between States. There had also been positive developments, including growing regional cooperation in economic, technical and scientific disciplines; exponential growth in people-to-people contacts; socioeconomic development; and, in many countries, phenomenal economic growth. The Ad Hoc Committee had a continuing role to play on the basis of providing broad-based participation open to all Member States within the region and beyond, but Member States might wish to reflect on the scope of the Committee's work, including a revision of the Declaration in line with current regional realities. Members of the Committee should therefore consider how new approaches could be developed and how recommendations could be made to the General Assembly regarding a way forward. The Chair was requested to continue informal consultations with the members of the Committee and to report through the Committee to the General Assembly at its sixty-eighth (2013) session.

GENERAL ASSEMBLY ACTION

On 2 December [meeting 71], the General Assembly, on the recommendation of the First (Disarmament and International Security) Committee [A/66/403], adopted **resolution 66/22** by recorded vote (124-4-46) [agenda item 89].

Implementation of the Declaration of the Indian Ocean as a Zone of Peace

The General Assembly,

Recalling the Declaration of the Indian Ocean as a Zone of Peace, contained in its resolution 2832(XXVI) of 16 December 1971, and recalling also its resolutions 54/47 of 1 December 1999, 56/16 of 29 November 2001, 58/29 of 8 December 2003, 60/48 of 8 December 2005, 62/14 of 5 December 2007 and 64/23 of 2 December 2009 and other relevant resolutions,

Recalling also the report of the Meeting of the Littoral and Hinterland States of the Indian Ocean held in New York from 2 to 13 July 1979,

Recalling further paragraph 102 of the Final Document of the Thirteenth Conference of Heads of State or Government of Non-Aligned Countries, held at Kuala Lumpur in 24 and 25 February 2003, in which it was noted, inter alia, that the Chair of the Ad Hoc Committee on the Indian Ocean would continue his informal consultations on the future work of the Committee,

Emphasizing the need to foster consensual approaches that are conducive to the pursuit of such endeavours,

Noting the initiatives taken by countries of the region to promote cooperation, in particular economic cooperation, in the Indian Ocean area and the possible contribution of such initiatives to overall objectives of a zone of peace,

Convinced that the participation of all permanent members of the Security Council and the major maritime users of the Indian Ocean in the work of the Ad Hoc Committee is important and would assist the progress of a mutually beneficial dialogue to develop conditions of peace, security and stability in the Indian Ocean region,

Considering that greater efforts and more time are required to develop a focused discussion on practical measures to ensure conditions of peace, security and stability in the Indian Ocean region,

Having considered the report of the Ad Hoc Committee on the Indian Ocean,

1. *Takes note* of the report of the Ad Hoc Committee on the Indian Ocean;
2. *Reiterates its conviction* that the participation of all permanent members of the Security Council and the major maritime users of the Indian Ocean in the work of the Ad Hoc Committee is important and would greatly facilitate the development of a mutually beneficial dialogue to advance peace, security and stability in the Indian Ocean region;
3. *Requests* the Chair of the Ad Hoc Committee to continue his informal consultations with the members of the Committee and to report through the Committee to the General Assembly at its sixty-eighth session;
4. *Requests* the Secretary-General to continue to render, within existing resources, all necessary assistance to the Ad Hoc Committee, including the provision of summary records;
5. *Decides* to include in the provisional agenda of its sixty-eighth session the item entitled "Implementation of the Declaration of the Indian Ocean as a Zone of Peace".

RECORDED VOTE ON RESOLUTION 66/22:

In favour: Afghanistan, Algeria, Angola, Antigua and Barbuda, Argentina, Armenia, Australia, Azerbaijan, Bahamas, Bahrain, Bangladesh, Barbados, Belarus, Belize, Benin, Bhutan, Bolivia, Brazil, Brunei Darussalam, Burkina Faso, Cambodia, Cameroon, Cape Verde, Chad, Chile, China, Colombia, Comoros, Congo, Costa Rica, Côte d'Ivoire, Cuba, Democratic People's Republic of Korea, Djibouti, Dominican Republic, Ecuador, Egypt, Ethiopia, Fiji, Ghana, Guatemala, Guinea, Guinea-Bissau, Guyana, Haiti, Honduras, India, Indonesia, Iran, Iraq, Jamaica, Japan, Jordan, Kazakhstan, Kenya, Kuwait, Kyrgyzstan, Lao People's Democratic Republic, Lebanon, Lesotho, Liberia, Libya, Madagascar, Malawi, Malaysia, Maldives, Mali, Mauritania, Mauritius, Mexico, Mongolia, Morocco, Mozambique, Myanmar, Namibia, Nepal, New Zealand, Nicaragua, Niger, Nigeria, Oman, Pakistan, Panama, Papua New Guinea, Paraguay, Peru, Philippines, Qatar, Republic of Korea, Russian Federation, Saint Kitts and Nevis, Saint Lucia, Saint Vincent and the Grenadines, Samoa, Sao Tome and Principe, Saudi Arabia, Senegal, Seychelles, Sierra Leone, Singapore, Solomon Islands, South Africa, Sri Lanka, Sudan, Suriname, Swaziland, Syrian Arab Republic, Tajikistan, Thailand, Timor-Leste, Togo, Tonga, Tunisia, Turkmenistan, United Arab Emirates, United Republic of Tanzania, Uruguay, Uzbekistan, Vanuatu, Venezuela, Viet Nam, Yemen, Zambia, Zimbabwe.

Against: France, Israel, United Kingdom, United States.

Abstaining: Albania, Andorra, Austria, Belgium, Bosnia and Herzegovina, Bulgaria, Canada, Croatia, Cyprus, Czech Republic, Denmark, El Salvador, Estonia, Finland, Georgia, Germany, Greece, Hungary, Iceland, Ireland, Italy, Latvia, Liechtenstein, Lithuania, Luxembourg, Malta, Marshall Islands, Micronesia, Monaco, Montenegro, Netherlands, Norway, Palau, Poland, Portugal, Republic of Moldova, Romania, San Marino, Serbia, Slovakia, Slovenia, Spain, Sweden, the former Yugoslav Republic of Macedonia, Turkey, Ukraine.

Decolonization

The General Assembly's Special Committee on the Situation with regard to the Implementation of the Declaration on the Granting of Independence to Colonial Countries and Peoples (Special Committee on decolonization) held its annual session in New York in two parts: 24 February and 31 March (first part); and 13, 20, 21, 23 and 24 June (second part). The Special Committee considered various aspects of the implementation of the 1960 Declaration, adopted by the Assembly in resolution 1514(XV) [YUN 1960, p. 49], including general decolonization issues and the situation in the individual Non-Self-Governing Territories (NSGTs). The Special Committee adopted three resolutions and recommended eight draft resolutions for adoption by the General Assembly. In accordance with resolution 65/117 [YUN 2010, p. 585], the Special Committee reported to the Assembly on its activities [A/66/23].

Decade for the Eradication of Colonialism

Caribbean regional seminar

The Special Committee on decolonization organized a Caribbean regional seminar (Kingstown, Saint Vincent and the Grenadines, 31 May–2 June) [A/66/23] to hear the views of representatives of NSGTs, experts, members of civil society and other stakeholders who could assist in identifying policy approaches and practical measures that could be pursued in the UN decolonization process. The Seminar assessed past contributions and fresh goals, as well as expected accomplishments in the Third International Decade for the Eradication of Colonialism, 2011–2020, as declared by the General Assembly in resolution 65/119 [YUN 2010, p. 587]. The participants' contributions would be further considered at the Special Committee's substantive session (see above), with a view to submitting proposals to the Assembly concerning fulfilment of the objectives of the Third International Decade.

Participants identified a number of issues related to the process of decolonization during the Second International Decade for the Eradication of Colonialism (2001–2010) [YUN 2000, p. 548], including the impact of climate change, especially on small island NSGTs; the global economic and financial crisis; the role of regional cooperation; education and public awareness, including of indigenous peoples; the role of women; the empowerment of vulnerable people; and the capacity for full self-governance. They further discussed goals and expected accomplishments concerning the NSGTs in the Caribbean, the Pacific and other regions, including follow-up to the 2010 Pacific regional seminar [YUN 2010, p. 585]; and considered goals and expected accomplishments of the UN system in providing assistance to the NSGTs. With regard to the Third International Decade, seminar participants reconfirmed that the United Nations had a valid ongoing role in the process of decolonization; reaffirmed the role of the Special Committee as the primary vehicle for fostering decolonization as well as for monitoring the situation in the NSGTs; and affirmed that the Special Committee should continue to take stock of challenges and opportunities for decolonization and draw up a plan of action for the International Decade with a view to advancing the decolonization process.

Declaration on the Granting of Independence to Colonial Countries and Peoples

GENERAL ASSEMBLY ACTION

On 9 December [meeting 81], the General Assembly, on the recommendation of the Fourth (Special Political and Decolonization) Committee [A/66/434], adopted **resolution 66/91** by recorded vote (168-3-1) [agenda item 60].

Implementation of the Declaration on the Granting of Independence to Colonial Countries and Peoples

The General Assembly,

Having examined the report of the Special Committee on the Situation with regard to the Implementation of the Declaration on the Granting of Independence to Colonial Countries and Peoples for 2011,

Recalling its resolution 1514(XV) of 14 December 1960, containing the Declaration on the Granting of Independence to Colonial Countries and Peoples, and all its subsequent resolutions concerning the implementation of the Declaration, the most recent of which was resolution 65/117 of 10 December 2010, as well as the relevant resolutions of the Security Council,

Bearing in mind its resolution 65/119 of 10 December 2010, by which it declared the period 2011–2020 the Third International Decade for the Eradication of Colonialism, and the need to examine ways to ascertain the wishes of the peoples of the Non-Self-Governing Territories on the basis of resolution 1514(XV) and other relevant resolutions on decolonization,

Recognizing that the eradication of colonialism has been one of the priorities of the United Nations and continues to be one of its priorities for the decade that began in 2011,

Regretting that measures to eliminate colonialism by 2010, as called for in its resolution 55/146 of 8 December 2000, have not been successful,

Reiterating its conviction of the need for the eradication of colonialism, as well as racial discrimination and violations of basic human rights,

Noting with satisfaction the continued efforts of the Special Committee in contributing to the effective and complete implementation of the Declaration and other relevant resolutions of the United Nations on decolonization,

Stressing the importance of the formal participation of the administering Powers in the work of the Special Committee,

Noting with satisfaction the cooperation and active participation of certain administering Powers in the work of the Special Committee, and encouraging the others also to do so,

Noting that the Caribbean regional seminar was held in Kingstown from 31 May to 2 June 2011,

1. *Reaffirms* its resolution 1514(XV) and all other resolutions and decisions on decolonization, including its resolution 65/119, by which it declared the period 2011–2020 the Third International Decade for the Eradication of Colonialism, and calls upon the administering Powers, in accordance with those resolutions, to take all steps necessary to enable the peoples of the Non-Self-Governing Territories concerned to exercise fully as soon as possible their right to self-determination, including independence;

2. *Reaffirms once again* that the existence of colonialism in any form or manifestation, including economic exploitation, is incompatible with the Charter of the United Nations, the Declaration on the Granting of Independence to Colonial Countries and Peoples and the Universal Declaration of Human Rights;

3. *Reaffirms its determination* to continue to take all steps necessary to bring about the complete and speedy eradication of colonialism and the faithful observance by all States of the relevant provisions of the Charter, the Declaration on the Granting of Independence to Colonial Countries and Peoples and the Universal Declaration of Human Rights;

4. *Affirms once again its support* for the aspirations of the peoples under colonial rule to exercise their right to self-determination, including independence, in accordance with the relevant resolutions of the United Nations on decolonization;

5. *Calls upon* the administering Powers to cooperate fully with the Special Committee on the Situation with regard to the Implementation of the Declaration on the Granting of Independence to Colonial Countries and Peoples to develop and finalize, as soon as possible, a constructive programme of work on a case-by-case basis for the Non-Self-Governing Territories to facilitate the implementation of the mandate of the Special Committee and the relevant resolutions on decolonization, including resolutions on specific Territories;

6. *Recalls with satisfaction* the professional, open and transparent conduct of both the February 2006 and the October 2007 referendums to determine the future status of Tokelau, monitored by the United Nations;

7. *Requests* the Special Committee to continue to seek suitable means for the immediate and full implementation of the Declaration and to carry out the actions approved by the General Assembly regarding the Second and Third International Decades for the Eradication of Colonialism in all Territories that have not yet exercised their right to self-determination, including independence, and in particular:

(a) To formulate specific proposals to bring about an end to colonialism and to report thereon to the General Assembly at its sixty-seventh session;

(b) To continue to examine the implementation by Member States of resolution 1514(XV) and other relevant resolutions on decolonization;

(c) To continue to examine the political, economic and social situation in the Non-Self-Governing Territories, and to recommend, as appropriate, to the General Assembly the most suitable steps to be taken to enable the populations of those Territories to exercise their right to self-determination, including independence, in accordance with the relevant resolutions on decolonization, including resolutions on specific Territories;

(d) To develop and finalize, as soon as possible and in cooperation with the administering Power and the Territory in question, a constructive programme of work on a case-by-case basis for the Non-Self-Governing Territories to facilitate the implementation of the mandate of the Special Committee and the relevant resolutions on decolonization, including resolutions on specific Territories;

(e) To continue to dispatch visiting and special missions to the Non-Self-Governing Territories in accordance with the relevant resolutions on decolonization, including resolutions on specific Territories;

(f) To conduct seminars, as appropriate, for the purpose of receiving and disseminating information on the work of the Special Committee, and to facilitate participation by the peoples of the Non-Self-Governing Territories in those seminars;

(g) To take all steps necessary to enlist worldwide support among Governments, as well as national and international organizations, for the achievement of the objectives of the Declaration and the implementation of the relevant resolutions of the United Nations;

(h) To observe annually the Week of Solidarity with the Peoples of Non-Self-Governing Territories;

8. *Recalls* that the plan of action for the Second International Decade for the Eradication of Colonialism, updated as necessary, represents an important legislative authority for the attainment of self-government by the Non-Self-Governing Territories, and that the case-by-case assessment of the attainment of self-government in each Territory can make an important contribution to this process;

9. *Calls upon* all States, in particular the administering Powers, as well as the specialized agencies and other organizations of the United Nations system, to give effect within their respective spheres of competence to the recommendations of the Special Committee for the implementation of the Declaration and other relevant resolutions of the United Nations;

10. *Calls upon* the administering Powers to ensure that economic and other activities in the Non-Self-Governing Territories under their administration do not adversely affect the interests of the peoples but instead promote development, and to assist them in the exercise of their right to self-determination;

11. *Urges* the administering Powers concerned to take effective measures to safeguard and guarantee the inalienable rights of the peoples of the Non-Self-Governing Territories to their natural resources and to establish and maintain control over the future development of those resources, and requests the relevant administering Power to take all steps necessary to protect the property rights of the peoples of those Territories;

12. *Urges* all States, directly and through their action in the specialized agencies and other organizations of the United Nations system, to provide moral and material assistance, as needed, to the peoples of the Non-Self-Governing Territories, and requests the administering Powers to take steps to enlist and make effective use of all possible assistance, on both a bilateral and a multilateral basis, in the strengthening of the economies of those Territories;

13. *Requests* the Secretary-General, the specialized agencies and other organizations of the United Nations system to provide economic, social and other assistance to the Non-Self-Governing Territories and to continue to do so, as appropriate, after they exercise their right to self-determination, including independence;

14. *Reaffirms* that the United Nations visiting missions to the Territories are an effective means of ascertaining the situation in the Territories, as well as the wishes and aspirations of their inhabitants, and calls upon the administering Powers to continue to cooperate with the Special Committee in the discharge of its mandate and to facilitate visiting missions to the Territories;

15. *Calls upon* all the administering Powers to cooperate fully in the work of the Special Committee and to participate formally in its future sessions;

16. *Approves* the report of the Special Committee on the Situation with regard to the Implementation of the Declaration on the Granting of Independence to Colonial Countries and Peoples covering its work during 2011, including the programme of work envisaged for 2012;

17. *Requests* the Secretary-General to provide the Special Committee with the facilities and services required for the implementation of the present resolution, as well as the other resolutions and decisions on decolonization adopted by the General Assembly and the Special Committee.

RECORDED VOTE ON RESOLUTION 66/91:

In favour: Afghanistan, Albania, Algeria, Andorra, Angola, Antigua and Barbuda, Argentina, Armenia, Australia, Austria, Azerbaijan, Bahamas, Bahrain, Bangladesh, Barbados, Belarus, Belgium, Belize, Benin, Bhutan, Bolivia, Bosnia and Herzegovina, Botswana, Brazil, Brunei Darussalam, Bulgaria, Burkina Faso, Burundi, Cambodia, Cameroon, Canada, Cape Verde, Chad, Chile, China, Colombia, Comoros, Congo, Costa Rica, Côte d'Ivoire, Croatia, Cuba, Cyprus, Czech Republic, Democratic People's Republic of Korea, Denmark, Djibouti, Dominica, Dominican Republic, Ecuador, Egypt, El Salvador, Eritrea, Estonia, Ethiopia, Fiji, Finland, Germany, Ghana, Greece, Grenada, Guatemala, Guinea, Guinea-Bissau, Guyana, Haiti, Honduras, Hungary, Iceland, India, Indonesia, Iran, Iraq, Ireland, Italy, Jamaica, Japan, Jordan, Kazakhstan, Kenya, Kuwait, Kyrgyzstan, Lao People's Democratic Republic, Latvia, Lebanon, Lesotho, Liberia, Libya, Liechtenstein, Lithuania, Luxembourg, Madagascar, Malawi, Malaysia, Maldives, Mali, Malta, Marshall Islands, Mauritania, Mauritius, Mexico, Monaco, Mongolia, Montenegro, Morocco, Mozambique, Namibia, Nepal, Netherlands, New Zealand, Nicaragua, Norway, Oman, Pakistan, Panama, Papua New Guinea, Paraguay, Peru, Philippines, Poland, Portugal, Qatar, Republic of Korea, Republic of Moldova, Romania, Russian Federation, Saint Lucia, Saint Vincent and the Grenadines, Samoa, San Marino, Saudi

Arabia, Senegal, Serbia, Sierra Leone, Singapore, Slovakia, Slovenia, Solomon Islands, South Africa, Spain, Sri Lanka, Sudan, Swaziland, Sweden, Switzerland, Syrian Arab Republic, Tajikistan, Thailand, the former Yugoslav Republic of Macedonia, Timor-Leste, Togo, Tonga, Trinidad and Tobago, Tunisia, Turkey, Turkmenistan, Tuvalu, Uganda, Ukraine, United Arab Emirates, Uruguay, Uzbekistan, Vanuatu, Venezuela, Viet Nam, Yemen, Zambia, Zimbabwe.

Against: Israel, United Kingdom, United States.
Abstaining: France.

Implementation by international organizations

In a February report [A/66/63], the Secretary-General stated that he had brought General Assembly resolution 65/110 [YUN 2010, p. 590] to the attention of the specialized agencies and other international institutions associated with the United Nations and invited them to submit information regarding their implementation activities in support of NSGTs. Replies received from eight agencies or institutions were summarized in an April report [E/2011/73 & Add.1] of the Economic and Social Council President on his consultations with the Special Committee on decolonization. According to the information provided, several specialized agencies and other organizations of the UN system continued to provide support to the peoples of NSGTs, pursuant to the relevant resolutions and decisions of the Assembly, the Council and the Special Committee.

ECONOMIC AND SOCIAL COUNCIL ACTION

On 28 July [meeting 49], the Economic and Social Council adopted **resolution 2011/40** [draft: E/2011/L.45 & E/2011/SR.49] by roll-call vote (27-0-22) [agenda item 9].

Support to Non-Self-Governing Territories by the specialized agencies and international institutions associated with the United Nations

The Economic and Social Council,

Having examined the report of the Secretary-General and the report of the President of the Economic and Social Council containing the information submitted by the specialized agencies and other organizations of the United Nations system on their activities with regard to the implementation of the Declaration on the Granting of Independence to Colonial Countries and Peoples,

Having heard the statement by the representative of the Special Committee on the Situation with regard to the Implementation of the Declaration on the Granting of Independence to Colonial Countries and Peoples,

Recalling General Assembly resolutions 1514(XV) of 14 December 1960 and 1541(XV) of 15 December 1960, the resolutions of the Special Committee and other relevant resolutions and decisions, including, in particular, Economic and Social Council resolution 2010/30 of 23 July 2010,

Bearing in mind the relevant provisions of the final documents of the successive Conferences of Heads of State or Government of Non-Aligned Countries and of the resolutions adopted by the Assembly of Heads of State and Government of the African Union, the Pacific Islands Forum and the Caribbean Community,

Conscious of the need to facilitate the implementation of the Declaration on the Granting of Independence to Colonial Countries and Peoples, contained in General Assembly resolution 1514(XV),

Welcoming the current participation, in their capacity as observers, of those Non-Self-Governing Territories that are associate members of the regional commissions in the world conferences in the economic and social sphere, subject to the rules of procedure of the General Assembly and in accordance with relevant United Nations resolutions and decisions, including resolutions and decisions of the Assembly and the Special Committee on specific Non-Self-Governing Territories,

Noting that only some specialized agencies and organizations of the United Nations system have been involved in providing assistance to Non-Self-Governing Territories,

Welcoming the assistance extended to Non-Self-Governing Territories by certain specialized agencies and other organizations of the United Nations system, in particular the United Nations Development Programme,

Stressing that, because the development options of the small island Non-Self-Governing Territories are limited, they face special challenges in planning for and implementing sustainable development, and that they will be constrained in meeting those challenges without the continuing cooperation and assistance of the specialized agencies and other organizations of the United Nations system,

Stressing also the importance of securing the necessary resources for funding expanded programmes of assistance for the peoples concerned and the need to enlist the support of all the major funding institutions within the United Nations system in that regard,

Reaffirming the mandates of the specialized agencies and other organizations of the United Nations system to take all appropriate measures, within their respective spheres of competence, to ensure the full implementation of Assembly resolution 1514(XV) and other relevant resolutions,

Expressing its appreciation to the African Union, the Pacific Islands Forum, the Caribbean Community and other regional organizations for the continued cooperation and assistance they have extended to the specialized agencies and other organizations of the United Nations system in that regard,

Expressing its conviction that closer contacts and consultations between and among the specialized agencies and other organizations of the United Nations system and regional organizations help to facilitate the effective formulation of programmes of assistance for the peoples concerned,

Mindful of the imperative need to keep under continuous review the activities of the specialized agencies and other organizations of the United Nations system in the implementation of the various United Nations decisions relating to decolonization,

Bearing in mind the extremely fragile economies of the small island Non-Self-Governing Territories and their vulnerability to natural disasters, such as hurricanes, cyclones and sea-level rise, and recalling the relevant resolutions of the General Assembly,

Recalling General Assembly resolution 65/110 of 10 December 2010, entitled "Implementation of the Declaration on the Granting of Independence to Colonial Countries and Peoples by the specialized agencies and the international institutions associated with the United Nations",

1. *Takes note* of the report of the President of the Economic and Social Council and endorses the observations and suggestions arising therefrom;
2. *Also takes note* of the report of the Secretary-General;
3. *Recommends* that all States intensify their efforts within the specialized agencies and other organizations of the United Nations system of which they are members to ensure the full and effective implementation of the Declaration on the Granting of Independence to Colonial Countries and Peoples, contained in General Assembly resolution 1514(XV), and other relevant resolutions of the United Nations;
4. *Reaffirms* that the specialized agencies and other organizations and institutions of the United Nations system should continue to be guided by the relevant resolutions of the United Nations in their efforts to contribute to the implementation of the Declaration and all other relevant General Assembly resolutions;
5. *Also reaffirms* that the recognition by the General Assembly, the Security Council and other United Nations organs of the legitimacy of the aspirations of the peoples of the Non-Self-Governing Territories to exercise their right to self-determination entails, as a corollary, the extension of all appropriate assistance to those peoples;
6. *Expresses its appreciation* to those specialized agencies and other organizations of the United Nations system that have continued to cooperate with the United Nations and the regional and subregional organizations in the implementation of Assembly resolution 1514(XV) and other relevant resolutions of the United Nations, and requests all of the specialized agencies and other organizations of the United Nations system to implement the relevant provisions of those resolutions;
7. *Requests* the specialized agencies and other organizations of the United Nations system and international and regional organizations to examine and review conditions in each Non-Self-Governing Territory so that they may take appropriate measures to accelerate progress in the economic and social sectors of those Territories;
8. *Urges* those specialized agencies and organizations of the United Nations system that have not yet provided assistance to Non-Self-Governing Territories to do so as soon as possible;
9. *Requests* the specialized agencies and other organizations and bodies of the United Nations system and regional organizations to strengthen existing measures of support and to formulate appropriate programmes of assistance to the remaining Non-Self-Governing Territories, within the framework of their respective mandates, in order to accelerate progress in the economic and social sectors of those Territories;
10. *Recommends* that the executive heads of the specialized agencies and other organizations of the United Nations system formulate, with the active cooperation of the regional organizations concerned, concrete proposals for the full implementation of the relevant resolutions of the United Nations and submit those proposals to their governing and legislative organs;
11. *Also recommends* that the specialized agencies and other organizations of the United Nations system continue to review, at the regular meetings of their governing bodies, the implementation of Assembly resolution 1514(XV) and other relevant resolutions of the United Nations;
12. *Recalls* the preparation by the Department of Public Information and the Department of Political Affairs of the Secretariat, in consultation with the United Nations Development Programme, the specialized agencies and the Special Committee on the Situation with regard to the Implementation of the Declaration on the Granting of Independence to Colonial Countries and Peoples, of an informational leaflet on assistance programmes available to the Non-Self-Governing Territories and its updated online version, and requests that they be disseminated as widely as possible;
13. *Welcomes* the continuing efforts made by the United Nations Development Programme in maintaining a close liaison between the specialized agencies and other organizations of the United Nations system, including the Economic Commission for Latin America and the Caribbean and the Economic and Social Commission for Asia and the Pacific, and in providing assistance to the peoples of the Non-Self-Governing Territories;
14. *Encourages* the Non-Self-Governing Territories to take steps to establish and/or strengthen disaster preparedness and management institutions and policies;
15. *Requests* the administering Powers concerned to facilitate, when appropriate, the participation of appointed and elected representatives of Non-Self-Governing Territories in the relevant meetings and conferences of the specialized agencies and other organizations of the United Nations system, in accordance with relevant United Nations resolutions and decisions, including the resolutions and decisions of the General Assembly and the Special Committee on specific Territories, so that they may benefit from the related activities of those agencies and organizations;
16. *Recommends* that all Governments intensify their efforts within the specialized agencies and other organizations of the United Nations system of which they are members to accord priority to the question of providing assistance to the peoples of the Non-Self-Governing Territories;
17. *Draws the attention* of the Special Committee to the present resolution and to the discussion held on the subject at the substantive session of 2011 of the Economic and Social Council;
18. *Recalls* the adoption by the Economic Commission for Latin America and the Caribbean on 16 May 1998 of its resolution 574(XXVII), in which the Commission called for the mechanisms necessary for its associate members, including the Non-Self-Governing Territories, to participate, subject to the rules of procedure of the General Assembly, in the special sessions of the Assembly convened to review and assess the implementation of the plans of action of those United Nations world conferences in which the Territories had originally participated in their capacity as observers, and in the work of the Economic and Social Council and its subsidiary bodies;
19. *Requests* the President of the Council to continue to maintain close contact on those matters with the Chair of the Special Committee and to report thereon to the Council;
20. *Requests* the Secretary-General to follow up on the implementation of the present resolution, paying particular attention to cooperation and integration arrangements for maximizing the efficiency of the assistance activities undertaken by various organizations of the United Nations system, and to report thereon to the Council at its substantive session of 2012;
21. *Decides* to keep the above questions under continuous review.

ROLL-CALL VOTE ON RESOLUTION 2011/40:

In favour: Australia, Bahamas, Bangladesh, Cameroon, Chile, China, Côte d'Ivoire, Ecuador, Egypt, Ghana, Guatemala, India, Iraq, Mauritius, Mexico, Mongolia, Morocco, Namibia, Nicaragua, Pakistan, Peru, Philippines, Qatar, Saudi Arabia, Senegal, Venezuela Zambia.

Against: None.

Abstaining: Argentina, Belgium, Canada, Estonia, Finland, France, Germany, Hungary, Italy, Japan, Latvia, Malta, Norway, Republic of Korea, Russian Federation, Rwanda, Slovakia, Spain, Switzerland, Ukraine, United Kingdom, United States.

GENERAL ASSEMBLY ACTION

On 9 December [meeting 81], the General Assembly, on the recommendation of the Fourth Committee [A/66/432], adopted **resolution 66/84** by recorded vote (115-0-56) [agenda item 58].

Implementation of the Declaration on the Granting of Independence to Colonial Countries and Peoples by the specialized agencies and the international institutions associated with the United Nations

The General Assembly,

Having considered the item entitled "Implementation of the Declaration on the Granting of Independence to Colonial Countries and Peoples by the specialized agencies and the international institutions associated with the United Nations",

Having also considered the report of the Secretary-General and the report of the Economic and Social Council on the item,

Having examined the chapter of the report of the Special Committee on the Situation with regard to the Implementation of the Declaration on the Granting of Independence to Colonial Countries and Peoples for 2011 relating to the item,

Recalling its resolutions 1514(XV) of 14 December 1960 and 1541(XV) of 15 December 1960 and the resolutions of the Special Committee, as well as other relevant resolutions and decisions, including in particular Economic and Social Council resolution 2010/30 of 23 July 2010,

Bearing in mind the relevant provisions of the final documents of the successive Conferences of Heads of State or Government of Non-Aligned Countries and of the resolutions adopted by the Assembly of Heads of State and Government of the African Union, the Pacific Islands Forum and the Caribbean Community,

Conscious of the need to facilitate the implementation of the Declaration on the Granting of Independence to Colonial Countries and Peoples, contained in resolution 1514(XV),

Noting that the large majority of the remaining Non-Self-Governing Territories are small island Territories,

Welcoming the assistance extended to Non-Self-Governing Territories by certain specialized agencies and other organizations of the United Nations system, in particular the United Nations Development Programme,

Welcoming also the participation in the capacity of observers of those Non-Self-Governing Territories that are associate members of regional commissions in the world conferences in the economic and social spheres, subject to the rules of procedure of the General Assembly and in accordance with relevant resolutions and decisions of the United Nations, including resolutions and decisions of the Assembly and the Special Committee on specific Territories,

Noting that only some specialized agencies and other organizations of the United Nations system have been involved in providing assistance to Non-Self-Governing Territories,

Stressing that, because the development options of the small island Non-Self-Governing Territories are limited, there are special challenges to planning for and implementing sustainable development and that those Territories will be constrained in meeting the challenges without the continuing cooperation and assistance of the specialized agencies and other organizations of the United Nations system,

Stressing also the importance of securing the resources necessary for funding expanded programmes of assistance for the peoples concerned and the need to enlist the support of all major funding institutions within the United Nations system in that regard,

Reaffirming the mandates of the specialized agencies and other organizations of the United Nations system to take all appropriate measures, within their respective spheres of competence, to ensure the full implementation of General Assembly resolution 1514(XV) and other relevant resolutions,

Expressing its appreciation to the African Union, the Pacific Islands Forum, the Caribbean Community and other regional organizations for the continued cooperation and assistance they have extended to the specialized agencies and other organizations of the United Nations system in this regard,

Expressing its conviction that closer contacts and consultations between and among the specialized agencies and other organizations of the United Nations system and regional organizations help to facilitate the effective formulation of programmes of assistance to the peoples concerned,

Mindful of the imperative need to keep under continuous review the activities of the specialized agencies and other organizations of the United Nations system in the implementation of the various resolutions and decisions of the United Nations relating to decolonization,

Bearing in mind the extremely fragile economies of the small island Non-Self-Governing Territories and their vulnerability to natural disasters, such as hurricanes, cyclones and sea-level rise, and recalling the relevant resolutions of the General Assembly,

Recalling its resolution 65/110 of 10 December 2010 on the implementation of the Declaration by the specialized agencies and the international institutions associated with the United Nations,

1. *Takes note* of the report of the Secretary-General;
2. *Recommends* that all States intensify their efforts in the specialized agencies and other organizations of the United Nations system in which they are members to ensure the full and effective implementation of the Declaration on the Granting of Independence to Colonial Countries and Peoples, contained in General Assembly resolution 1514(XV), and other relevant resolutions of the United Nations;
3. *Reaffirms* that the specialized agencies and other organizations and institutions of the United Nations system should continue to be guided by the relevant resolutions of the United Nations in their efforts to contribute to the implementation of the Declaration and all other relevant resolutions of the General Assembly;

4. *Also reaffirms* that the recognition by the General Assembly, the Security Council and other United Nations organs of the legitimacy of the aspirations of the peoples of the Non-Self-Governing Territories to exercise their right to self-determination entails, as a corollary, the extension of all appropriate assistance to those peoples;

5. *Expresses its appreciation* to those specialized agencies and other organizations of the United Nations system that have continued to cooperate with the United Nations and the regional and subregional organizations in the implementation of General Assembly resolution 1514(XV) and other relevant resolutions of the United Nations, and requests all the specialized agencies and other organizations of the United Nations system to implement the relevant provisions of those resolutions;

6. *Requests* the specialized agencies and other organizations of the United Nations system to intensify their engagement with the work of the Special Committee on the Situation with regard to the Implementation of the Declaration on the Granting of Independence to Colonial Countries and Peoples as an important element for the implementation of General Assembly resolution 1514(XV), including possible participation at the regional seminars on decolonization, upon the invitation of the Special Committee;

7. *Requests* the specialized agencies and other organizations of the United Nations system and international and regional organizations to examine and review conditions in each Territory so as to take appropriate measures to accelerate progress in the economic and social sectors of the Territories;

8. *Urges* those specialized agencies and other organizations of the United Nations system that have not yet provided assistance to Non-Self-Governing Territories to do so as soon as possible;

9. *Requests* the specialized agencies and other organizations and institutions of the United Nations system and regional organizations to strengthen existing measures of support and formulate appropriate programmes of assistance to the remaining Non-Self-Governing Territories, within the framework of their respective mandates, in order to accelerate progress in the economic and social sectors of those Territories;

10. *Requests* the specialized agencies and other organizations of the United Nations system concerned to provide information on:

(*a*) Environmental problems facing the Non-Self-Governing Territories;

(*b*) The impact of natural disasters, such as hurricanes and volcanic eruptions, and other environmental problems, such as beach and coastal erosion and droughts, on those Territories;

(*c*) Ways and means to assist the Territories to fight drug trafficking, money-laundering and other illegal and criminal activities;

(*d*) Illegal exploitation of the marine and other natural resources of the Territories and the need to utilize those resources for the benefit of the peoples of the Territories;

11. *Recommends* that the executive heads of the specialized agencies and other organizations of the United Nations system formulate, with the active cooperation of the regional organizations concerned, concrete proposals for the full implementation of the relevant resolutions of the United Nations and submit the proposals to their governing and legislative organs;

12. *Also recommends* that the specialized agencies and other organizations of the United Nations system continue to review at the regular meetings of their governing bodies the implementation of General Assembly resolution 1514(XV) and other relevant resolutions of the United Nations;

13. *Recalls* the adoption by the Economic Commission for Latin America and the Caribbean of its resolution 574(XXVII) of 16 May 1998, calling for the necessary mechanisms for its associate members, including Non-Self-Governing Territories, to participate in the special sessions of the General Assembly, subject to the rules of procedure of the Assembly, to review and assess the implementation of the plans of action of those United Nations world conferences in which the Territories originally participated in the capacity of observer, and in the work of the Economic and Social Council and its subsidiary bodies;

14. *Requests* the Chair of the Special Committee on the Situation with regard to the Implementation of the Declaration on the Granting of Independence to Colonial Countries and Peoples to continue to maintain close contact on these matters with the President of the Economic and Social Council;

15. *Recalls* the publication by the Department of Public Information and the Department of Political Affairs of the Secretariat, in consultation with the United Nations Development Programme, the specialized agencies and the Special Committee, of an information leaflet on assistance programmes available to the Non-Self-Governing Territories, which was updated for the United Nations website on decolonization, and requests its continued updating and wide dissemination;

16. *Welcomes* the continuing efforts made by the United Nations Development Programme in maintaining close liaison among the specialized agencies and other organizations of the United Nations system, including the Economic Commission for Latin America and the Caribbean and the Economic and Social Commission for Asia and the Pacific, and in providing assistance to the peoples of the Non-Self-Governing Territories;

17. *Encourages* the Non-Self-Governing Territories to take steps to establish and/or strengthen disaster preparedness and management institutions and policies, inter alia, with the assistance of the relevant specialized agencies;

18. *Requests* the administering Powers concerned to facilitate, when appropriate, the participation of appointed and elected representatives of Non-Self-Governing Territories in the relevant meetings and conferences of the specialized agencies and other organizations of the United Nations system, in accordance with relevant resolutions and decisions of the United Nations, including resolutions and decisions of the General Assembly and the Special Committee on specific Territories, so that the Territories may benefit from the related activities of those agencies and organizations;

19. *Recommends* that all Governments intensify their efforts in the specialized agencies and other organizations of the United Nations system of which they are members to accord priority to the question of providing assistance to the peoples of the Non-Self-Governing Territories;

20. *Requests* the Secretary-General to continue to assist the specialized agencies and other organizations of the United Nations system in working out appropriate

measures for implementing the relevant resolutions of the United Nations and to prepare for submission to the relevant bodies, with the assistance of those agencies and organizations, a report on the action taken in implementation of the relevant resolutions, including the present resolution, since the circulation of his previous report;

21. *Commends* the Economic and Social Council for its debate and resolution on this question, and requests it to continue to consider, in consultation with the Special Committee, appropriate measures for the coordination of the policies and activities of the specialized agencies and other organizations of the United Nations system in implementing the relevant resolutions of the General Assembly;

22. *Requests* the specialized agencies to report periodically to the Secretary-General on the implementation of the present resolution;

23. *Requests* the Secretary-General to transmit the present resolution to the governing bodies of the appropriate specialized agencies and international institutions associated with the United Nations so that those bodies may take the measures necessary to implement it, and also requests the Secretary-General to report to the General Assembly at its sixty-seventh session on the implementation of the present resolution;

24. *Requests* the Special Committee to continue to examine the question and to report thereon to the General Assembly at its sixty-seventh session.

RECORDED VOTE ON RESOLUTION 66/84:

In favour: Afghanistan, Algeria, Angola, Antigua and Barbuda, Australia, Azerbaijan, Bahamas, Bahrain, Bangladesh, Barbados, Belarus, Belize, Benin, Bhutan, Bolivia, Botswana, Brazil, Brunei Darussalam, Burkina Faso, Burundi, Cambodia, Cameroon, Cape Verde, Chad, Chile, China, Colombia, Comoros, Congo, Costa Rica, Côte d'Ivoire, Cuba, Democratic People's Republic of Korea, Djibouti, Dominica, Dominican Republic, Ecuador, Egypt, El Salvador, Eritrea, Ethiopia, Fiji, Ghana, Grenada, Guatemala, Guinea, Guinea-Bissau, Guyana, Haiti, Honduras, India, Indonesia, Iraq, Jamaica, Jordan, Kenya, Kuwait, Kyrgyzstan, Lao People's Democratic Republic, Lebanon, Libya, Madagascar, Malawi, Malaysia, Maldives, Mali, Marshall Islands, Mauritania, Mauritius, Mexico, Morocco, Mozambique, Namibia, Nepal, New Zealand, Nicaragua, Oman, Pakistan, Panama, Papua New Guinea, Paraguay, Peru, Philippines, Qatar, Saint Lucia, Saint Vincent and the Grenadines, Samoa, Saudi Arabia, Senegal, Sierra Leone, Singapore, Solomon Islands, South Africa, Sri Lanka, Sudan, Swaziland, Syrian Arab Republic, Tajikistan, Thailand, Timor-Leste, Togo, Tonga, Trinidad and Tobago, Tunisia, Turkmenistan, Tuvalu, Uganda, United Arab Emirates, Uruguay, Uzbekistan, Venezuela, Viet Nam, Yemen, Zambia, Zimbabwe.

Against: None.

Abstaining: Albania, Andorra, Argentina, Armenia, Austria, Belgium, Bosnia and Herzegovina, Bulgaria, Canada, Croatia, Cyprus, Czech Republic, Denmark, Estonia, Finland, France, Germany, Greece, Hungary, Iceland, Ireland, Israel, Italy, Japan, Kazakhstan, Latvia, Liechtenstein, Lithuania, Luxembourg, Malta, Micronesia, Monaco, Mongolia, Montenegro, Netherlands, Norway, Palau, Poland, Portugal, Republic of Korea, Republic of Moldova, Romania, Russian Federation, San Marino, Serbia, Slovakia, Slovenia, Spain, Sweden, Switzerland, the former Yugoslav Republic of Macedonia, Turkey, Ukraine, United Kingdom, United States, Vanuatu.

Puerto Rico

In accordance with the Special Committee's 2010 resolution [YUN 2010, p. 593] concerning the self-determination and independence of Puerto Rico, the Committee's Rapporteur, in a March report [A/AC.109/2011/L.13], provided information on Puerto Rico, including recent political, military and economic developments and UN action.

Following its usual practice, the Committee [A/66/23] acceded to requests for hearings from representatives of a number of organizations, which presented their views on 20 June [A/AC.109/2011/SR.4,5]. The Committee adopted a resolution by which it reaffirmed the inalienable right of the people of Puerto Rico to self-determination and independence; urged the United States to return the occupied land and installations on Vieques Island and in Ceiba to the people of Puerto Rico and to respect fundamental human rights, such as the right to health and economic development; and requested the General Assembly to consider the question of Puerto Rico. The Rapporteur was requested to report in 2012 on the resolution's implementation.

Territories under review

Falkland Islands (Malvinas)

The Special Committee on decolonization [A/66/23] considered the question of the Falkland Islands (Malvinas) at two meetings held on 21 June. The Committee had before it a Secretariat working paper on the Territory [A/AC.109/ 2011/14 & Corr.1] that addressed constitutional and political developments, mine clearance, economic and social conditions, participation in international organizations and arrangements, and the future status of the Territory. Statements were heard from two members of the Legislative Assembly of the Falkland Islands; two petitioners representing the Malvinas Islands; and the Minister for Foreign Affairs, International Trade and Worship of Argentina. Further remarks were made by the representatives of 21 Member States [A/AC.109/2011/SR.6,7]. The Committee adopted a resolution requesting Argentina and the United Kingdom to consolidate the process of dialogue and cooperation by resuming negotiations towards finding a peaceful solution to the sovereignty dispute relating to the Territory as soon as possible.

Communications. The Secretary-General received a series of letters from Argentina and the United Kingdom on the dispute [A/65/683, A/65/684, A/65/689, A/65/751, A/65/753, A/65/789, A/65/793, A/65/850, A/65/868], which addressed topics such as the anniversary of the occupation of the Malvinas Islands by the United Kingdom; the Islanders' right to self-determination; the role of the Special Committee on decolonization; the exploration and exploitation of renewable and nonrenewable natural resources and conduct of military exercises in the Territory by the United Kingdom; action taken unilaterally by Argentina against the Falkland Islands and their economy; and the Day of Affirmation of Argentine Sovereignty over the Malvinas Islands and the Antarctic Sector. One letter [A/66/385] to the General Assembly President from the United Kingdom contained a response to remarks by the President of Argentina [A/66/PV.11] on 21 September during the the Assembly's general debate.

In further letters, Argentina transmitted to the Secretary-General the Declaration on the deployment of the frigate HMS *Montrose* to the Malvinas Islands, adopted by the States members of the Union of South American Nations (Asunción, Paraguay, 29 October) [A/66/548]; the Special communiqué on the question of the Malvinas Islands, adopted at the twenty-first Ibero-American Summit of Heads of State and Government (Asunción, Paraguay, 28–29 October) [A/66/549]; and the Special communiqué on the Malvinas Islands, adopted by the Heads of State and Government of Latin America and the Caribbean within the framework of the Summit of the Community of Latin American and Caribbean States (Caracas, Venezuela, 3 December) [A/66/606].

In a 6 April letter [A/65/812], Guyana reaffirmed the region's abiding interest in a peaceful and definitive solution to the sovereignty dispute and requested the Secretary-General to renew his efforts to bring about the resumption of negotiations.

On 24 December, the General Assembly decided that the agenda item on the question of the Falkland Islands (Malvinas) would remain for consideration during its resumed sixty-sixth (2012) session (**decision 66/557**).

Gibraltar

The Special Committee on decolonization [A/66/23] considered the question of Gibraltar on 13 June [A/AC.109/2011/SR.3]. It had before it a Secretariat working paper [A/AC.109/2011/13] describing political developments and economic and social conditions in the Territory, and presenting the positions of the United Kingdom (the administering Power), Gibraltar and Spain concerning Gibraltar's future status. Spain and the leader of the opposition in Gibraltar made statements at the meeting.

On 9 December (**decision 66/522**), the General Assembly, recalling its decision 65/521 of 10 December 2010 [YUN 2010, p. 594], as well as the statement agreed upon by Spain and the United Kingdom in Brussels on 27 November 1984 [YUN 1984, p. 1075] and the establishment of the tripartite Forum for Dialogue on Gibraltar in December 2004 [YUN 2004, p. 606], urged both Governments to reach a solution to the question of Gibraltar, in light of the relevant Assembly resolutions and applicable principles, and in the spirit of the UN Charter. The Assembly also welcomed the continuing commitment to the Forum for Dialogue, including in the six additional areas of cooperation announced in 2009 [YUN 2009, p. 589].

New Caledonia

The Special Committee on decolonization [A/66/23] considered the question of New Caledonia at its 23 June meeting [A/AC.109/2011/SR.8]. It had before it a Secretariat working paper [A/AC.109/2011/16] describing the political and socioeconomic conditions and developments in the Territory. A representative of the Front de libération national kanak socialiste made a statement at the meeting, as did the representatives of Papua New Guinea, Saint Lucia and Solomon Islands. The representative of Fiji, also speaking on behalf of co-sponsor Papua New Guinea, introduced a draft resolution, which was adopted by the Committee.

GENERAL ASSEMBLY ACTION

On 9 December [meeting 81], the General Assembly, on the recommendation of the Fourth Committee [A/66/434], adopted **resolution 66/87** without vote [agenda item 60].

Question of New Caledonia

The General Assembly,

Having considered the question of New Caledonia,

Having examined the chapter of the report of the Special Committee on the Situation with regard to the Implementation of the Declaration on the Granting of Independence to Colonial Countries and Peoples for 2011 relating to New Caledonia,

Reaffirming the right of peoples to self-determination as enshrined in the Charter of the United Nations,

Recalling General Assembly resolutions 1514(XV) of 14 December 1960 and 1541(XV) of 15 December 1960,

Noting the importance of the positive measures being pursued in New Caledonia by the French authorities, in cooperation with all sectors of the population, to promote political, economic and social development in the Territory, including measures in the area of environmental protection and action with respect to drug abuse and trafficking, in order to provide a framework for its peaceful progress to self-determination,

Noting also, in this context, the importance of equitable economic and social development, as well as continued dialogue among the parties involved in New Caledonia in the preparation of the act of self-determination of New Caledonia,

Noting further the visit of the Special Rapporteur on the rights of indigenous peoples to New Caledonia from 4 to 13 February 2011,

Noting with satisfaction the intensification of contacts between New Caledonia and neighbouring countries of the South Pacific region,

1. *Welcomes* the significant developments that have taken place in New Caledonia since the signing of the

Nouméa Accord on 5 May 1998 by the representatives of New Caledonia and the Government of France;

2. *Urges* all the parties involved, in the interest of all the people of New Caledonia, to maintain, in the framework of the Nouméa Accord, their dialogue in a spirit of harmony, and in this context welcomes the unanimous agreement, reached in Paris on 8 December 2008, on the transfer of powers to New Caledonia in 2009 and the conduct of provincial elections in May 2009;

3. *Notes* the relevant provisions of the Nouméa Accord aimed at taking more broadly into account the Kanak identity in the political and social organization of New Caledonia, and welcomes, in this context, the adoption on 18 August 2010 by the Government of New Caledonia of the law on the anthem, the motto and banknote designs;

4. *Also notes* the ongoing difficulties regarding the question of the flag and the ensuing Cabinet crisis;

5. *Acknowledges* those provisions of the Nouméa Accord relating to control of immigration and protection of local employment, and notes that unemployment remains high among Kanaks and that recruitment of foreign mine workers continues;

6. *Notes* the concerns expressed by a group of indigenous people in New Caledonia regarding their underrepresentation in the Territory's governmental and social structures;

7. *Also notes* the concerns expressed by representatives of indigenous people regarding incessant migratory flows and the impact of mining on the environment;

8. *Takes note* of the relevant provisions of the Nouméa Accord to the effect that New Caledonia may become a member or associate member of certain international organizations, such as international organizations in the Pacific region, the United Nations, the United Nations Educational, Scientific and Cultural Organization and the International Labour Organization, according to their regulations;

9. *Notes* the agreement between the signatories to the Nouméa Accord that the progress made in the emancipation process shall be brought to the attention of the United Nations;

10. *Recalls* the fact that the administering Power invited to New Caledonia, at the time the new institutions were established, a mission of information which comprised representatives of countries of the Pacific region;

11. *Notes* the continuing strengthening of ties between New Caledonia and both the European Union and the European Development Fund in such areas as economic and trade cooperation, the environment, climate change and financial services;

12. *Calls upon* the administering Power to continue to transmit to the Secretary-General information as required under Article 73 *e* of the Charter of the United Nations;

13. *Invites* all the parties involved to continue promoting a framework for the peaceful progress of the Territory towards an act of self-determination in which all options are open and which would safeguard the rights of all sectors of the population, according to the letter and the spirit of the Nouméa Accord, which is based on the principle that it is for the populations of New Caledonia to choose how to control their destiny;

14. *Recalls with satisfaction* the efforts of the French authorities to resolve the question of voter registration by adopting, in the French Congress of Parliament, on 19 February 2007, amendments to the French Constitution allowing New Caledonia to restrict eligibility to vote in local polls to those voters registered on the 1998 electoral rolls when the Nouméa Accord was signed, thus ensuring strong representation of the Kanak population;

15. *Notes* the efforts of the French authorities to address the Cabinet crisis;

16. *Welcomes* all measures taken to strengthen and diversify the New Caledonian economy in all fields, and encourages further such measures in accordance with the spirit of the Matignon and Nouméa Accords;

17. *Also welcomes* the importance attached by the parties to the Matignon and Nouméa Accords to greater progress in housing, employment, training, education and health care in New Caledonia;

18. *Notes* the financial assistance rendered by the Government of France to the Territory in areas such as health, education, payment of public-service salaries and funding development schemes;

19. *Takes note* of the conclusions of the eighteenth Melanesian Spearhead Group Leaders Summit, held in Suva on 31 March 2011, including the recommendations for the annual monitoring and assessment of the Nouméa Accord;

20. *Acknowledges* the contribution of the Melanesian Cultural Centre to the protection of the indigenous Kanak culture of New Caledonia;

21. *Notes* the positive initiatives aimed at protecting the natural environment of New Caledonia, including the "Zonéco" operation designed to map and evaluate marine resources within the economic zone of New Caledonia;

22. *Welcomes* the cooperation among Australia, France and New Zealand in terms of surveillance of fishing zones, in accordance with the wishes expressed by France during the France-Oceania Summits in July 2003, June 2006 and July 2009;

23. *Acknowledges* the close links between New Caledonia and the peoples of the South Pacific and the positive actions being taken by the French and territorial authorities to facilitate the further development of those links, including the development of closer relations with the countries members of the Pacific Islands Forum and the easing of short-stay visa procedures for countries of the South Pacific;

24. *Recalls with satisfaction*, in this regard, the participation of New Caledonia at the forty-first summit of the Pacific Islands Forum, held in Port Vila on 4 and 5 August 2010, following its accession to the Forum as an associate member in October 2006, and welcomes the support of the Government of France for the application by New Caledonia for a full membership in the Pacific Islands Forum;

25. *Recalls* the continuing high-level visits to New Caledonia by delegations from countries of the Pacific region and high-level visits by delegations from New Caledonia to countries members of the Pacific Islands Forum;

26. *Welcomes* the cooperative attitude of other States and Territories in the region towards New Caledonia, its economic and political aspirations and its increasing participation in regional and international affairs;

27. *Also welcomes* the reactivation of dialogue on New Caledonia by the Ministerial Committee of the Pacific Islands Forum in 2010 and the request of Forum leaders to the Forum secretariat to explore ways to expand the role and engagement of New Caledonia in the Forum;

28. *Recalls* the successful conclusion of the Pacific regional seminar of the Special Committee on the Situation with regard to the Implementation of the Declaration on

the Granting of Independence to Colonial Countries and Peoples, held in Nouméa from 18 to 20 May 2010;

29. *Decides* to keep under continuous review the process unfolding in New Caledonia as a result of the signing of the Nouméa Accord;

30. *Requests* the Special Committee to continue the examination of the question of the Non-Self-Governing Territory of New Caledonia and to report thereon to the General Assembly at its sixty-seventh session.

Tokelau

At its meeting on 24 June [A/AC.109/2011/SR.9], the Special Committee on decolonization [A/66/23] considered the question of Tokelau (the three small atolls of Nukunonu, Fakaofo and Atafu in the South Pacific), administered by New Zealand. Before it was a Secretariat working paper [A/AC.109/2011/3] covering constitutional and political developments, external relations and economic and social conditions in the Territory, and presenting the positions of New Zealand and Tokelau on the Territory's future status. Statements were made by the Ulu-o-Tokelau (titular head of the Territory's Government, a position rotated annually among the three Faipule, or representatives of each atoll), the Administrator of Tokelau, and the representatives of Fiji, Papua New Guinea and Saint Lucia. The representative of Papua New Guinea, also on behalf of Fiji, introduced a draft resolution on the question of Tokelau, which the Committee adopted. The resolution acknowledged the ongoing commitment of New Zealand to meeting the social and economic requirements of the people of Tokelau, as well as the support and cooperation of the United Nations Development Programme (UNDP), and called upon the administering Power and UN agencies to continue to provide assistance to Tokelau as it further developed. It also requested the Committee to examine the question of Tokelau and report to the Assembly at its sixty-seventh (2012) session.

GENERAL ASSEMBLY ACTION

On 9 December [meeting 81], the General Assembly, on the recommendation of the Fourth Committee [A/66/434], adopted **resolution 66/88** without vote [agenda item 60].

Question of Tokelau

The General Assembly,

Having considered the question of Tokelau,

Having examined the chapter of the report of the Special Committee on the Situation with regard to the Implementation of the Declaration on the Granting of Independence to Colonial Countries and Peoples for 2011 relating to Tokelau,

Recalling its resolution 1514(XV) of 14 December 1960, containing the Declaration on the Granting of Independence to Colonial Countries and Peoples, and all resolutions and decisions of the United Nations relating to Non-Self-Governing Territories, in particular General Assembly resolution 65/114 of 10 December 2010,

Noting with appreciation the continuing exemplary cooperation of New Zealand as the administering Power with regard to the work of the Special Committee relating to Tokelau and its readiness to permit access by United Nations visiting missions to the Territory,

Noting also with appreciation the collaborative contribution to the development of Tokelau by New Zealand and the specialized agencies and other organizations of the United Nations system, in particular the United Nations Development Programme,

Noting that, as a small island Territory, Tokelau exemplifies the situation of most remaining Non-Self-Governing Territories and that, as a case study pointing to successful cooperation for decolonization, Tokelau has wider significance for the United Nations as it seeks to complete its work in decolonization,

Noting also Tokelau's associate member status with the Food and Agriculture Organization of the United Nations,

Recalling that New Zealand and Tokelau signed in November 2003 a document entitled "Joint statement of the principles of partnership", which sets out the rights and responsibilities of the two partners,

Bearing in mind the decision of the General Fono at its meeting in November 2003, following extensive consultations undertaken in all three villages, to explore formally with New Zealand the option of self-government in free association and its decision in August 2005 to hold in February 2006 a referendum on self-determination on the basis of a draft constitution for Tokelau and a draft treaty of free association with New Zealand, and its subsequent decision to hold a further referendum in October 2007,

1. *Notes* that Tokelau and New Zealand remain firmly committed to the ongoing development of Tokelau for the long-term benefit of the people of Tokelau, with particular emphasis on the further development of facilities on each atoll that meet their current requirements;

2. *Welcomes* the progress made towards the devolution of power to the three taupulega (village councils), in particular the delegation of the Administrator's powers to the three taupulega with effect from 1 July 2004 and the assumption by each taupulega from that date of full responsibility for the management of all its public services;

3. *Recalls* the decision of the General Fono in November 2003, following extensive consultations in all three villages and a meeting of the Special Committee on the Constitution of Tokelau, to explore formally with New Zealand the option of self-government in free association, and the discussions subsequently held between Tokelau and New Zealand pursuant to the decision of the General Fono;

4. *Also recalls* the decision of the General Fono in August 2005 to hold a referendum on self-government on the basis of a draft constitution for Tokelau and a draft treaty of free association with New Zealand, and notes the enactment by the General Fono of rules for the referendum;

5. *Further recalls* that two referendums to determine the status of Tokelau, held in February 2006 and October 2007, did not produce the two-thirds majority of the valid votes cast required by the General Fono to change Tokelau's status from that of a Non-Self-Governing Territory under the administration of New Zealand;

6. *Commends* the professional and transparent conduct of both the February 2006 and the October 2007 referendums, monitored by the United Nations;

7. *Acknowledges* the decision of the General Fono that consideration of any future act of self-determination by Tokelau will be deferred and that New Zealand and Tokelau will devote renewed effort and attention to ensuring that essential services and infrastructure on the atolls of Tokelau are enhanced and strengthened, thereby ensuring an enhanced quality of life for the people of Tokelau;

8. *Also acknowledges* Tokelau's adoption of its National Strategic Plan for 2010–2015 and the fact that the Joint Commitment for Development between Tokelau and New Zealand 2011–2015 will focus on a viable transportation arrangement, infrastructure development, fisheries development, human resources capacity and the strengthening of governance;

9. *Further acknowledges* the ongoing and consistent commitment of New Zealand to meeting the social and economic requirements of the people of Tokelau, as well as the support and cooperation of the United Nations Development Programme;

10. *Acknowledges* Tokelau's need for continued support from the international community;

11. *Recalls with satisfaction* the establishment and operation of the Tokelau International Trust Fund to support the ongoing needs of Tokelau, and calls upon Member States and international and regional agencies to contribute to the Fund and thereby lend practical support to Tokelau in overcoming the problems of smallness, isolation and lack of resources;

12. *Welcomes* the cooperative attitude of the other States and territories in the region towards Tokelau, and their support for its economic and political aspirations and its increasing participation in regional and international affairs;

13. *Calls upon* the administering Power and United Nations agencies to continue to provide assistance to Tokelau as it further develops;

14. *Welcomes* the actions taken by the administering Power to transmit information regarding the political, economic and social situation of Tokelau to the Secretary-General;

15. *Also welcomes* the commitment of both Tokelau and New Zealand to continue to work together in the interests of Tokelau and its people;

16. *Requests* the Special Committee on the Situation with regard to the Implementation of the Declaration on the Granting of Independence to Colonial Countries and Peoples to continue to examine the question of the Non-Self-Governing Territory of Tokelau and to report thereon to the General Assembly at its sixty-seventh session.

Western Sahara

The Special Committee on decolonization [A/66/23] considered the question of Western Sahara on 13 June. A Secretariat working paper [A/AC.109/2011/1] described the Secretary-General's good offices with the parties concerned and actions taken by the General Assembly and the Security Council (see p. 289). The Committee granted a request for hearing to Ahmed Boukhari of the Frente Popular para la Liberación de Saguía el-Hamra y de Río de Oro (Frente Polisario), who made a statement [A/AC.109/2011/SR.3]. Cuba also made a statement at the meeting [ibid.].

The Special Committee transmitted the relevant documentation to the Assembly's sixty-sixth (2011) session to facilitate the Fourth Committee's consideration of the question. The Secretary-General submitted his report [A/66/260] to the Assembly in August.

By **resolution 66/86** of 9 December (see p. 293), the Assembly supported the process of negotiations initiated by the Security Council since 2007, with a view to achieving a political solution that would provide for the self-determination of the people of Western Sahara. It requested the Special Committee to continue to consider the situation in Western Sahara and report to the Assembly's sixty-seventh (2012) session.

Island Territories

On 21 and 23 June, the Special Committee on decolonization [A/66/23] considered working papers on American Samoa [A/AC.109/2011/12], Anguilla [A/AC.109/2011/2], Bermuda [A/AC.109/2011/5], the British Virgin Islands [A/AC.109/2011/6], the Cayman Islands [A/AC.109/2011/8], Guam [A/AC.109/2011/15], Montserrat [A/AC.109/2011/11], Pitcairn [A/AC.109/2011/4], Saint Helena [A/AC.109/2011/7], the Turks and Caicos Islands [A/AC.109/2011/10] and the United States Virgin Islands [A/AC.109/2011/9], describing political developments and economic and social conditions in each of those 11 island Territories. The United Kingdom and the United States, as the administering Powers concerned, did not participate in the Special Committee's consideration of the Territories under their administration. Petitioners made statements on Guam and the Turks and Caicos Islands [A/AC.109/2011/SR.7,8]. The Committee adopted a consolidated draft resolution, which it subsequently recommended for adoption by the General Assembly (see below).

GENERAL ASSEMBLY ACTION

On 9 December [meeting 81], the General Assembly, on the recommendation of the Fourth Committee [A/66/434], adopted **resolution 66/89 A** and **B** without vote [agenda item 60].

Questions of American Samoa, Anguilla, Bermuda, the British Virgin Islands, the Cayman Islands, Guam, Montserrat, Pitcairn, Saint Helena, the Turks and Caicos Islands and the United States Virgin Islands

A
GENERAL

The General Assembly,

Having considered the questions of the Non-Self-Governing Territories of American Samoa, Anguilla, Bermuda, the British Virgin Islands, the Cayman Islands, Guam, Montserrat, Pitcairn, Saint Helena, the Turks and Caicos Islands and the United States Virgin Islands, hereinafter referred to as "the Territories",

Having examined the relevant chapter of the report of the Special Committee on the Situation with regard to the Implementation of the Declaration on the Granting of Independence to Colonial Countries and Peoples for 2011,

Recalling all resolutions and decisions of the United Nations relating to those Territories, including, in particular, the resolutions adopted by the General Assembly at its sixty-fifth session on the individual Territories covered by the present resolutions,

Recognizing that all available options for self-determination of the Territories are valid as long as they are in accordance with the freely expressed wishes of the peoples concerned and in conformity with the clearly defined principles contained in General Assembly resolutions 1514(XV) of 14 December 1960, 1541(XV) of 15 December 1960 and other resolutions of the Assembly,

Recalling its resolution 1541(XV), containing the principles that should guide Member States in determining whether or not an obligation exists to transmit the information called for under Article 73 *e* of the Charter of the United Nations,

Expressing concern that fifty-one years after the adoption of the Declaration on the Granting of Independence to Colonial Countries and Peoples, there still remain a number of Non-Self-Governing Territories,

Conscious of the importance of continuing effective implementation of the Declaration, taking into account the target set by the United Nations to eradicate colonialism by 2020 and the plans of action for the Second and Third International Decades for the Eradication of Colonialism,

Recognizing that the specific characteristics and the aspirations of the peoples of the Territories require flexible, practical and innovative approaches to the options for self-determination, without any prejudice to territorial size, geographical location, size of population or natural resources,

Noting the stated position of the Government of the United Kingdom of Great Britain and Northern Ireland and the stated position of the Government of the United States of America on the Non-Self-Governing Territories under their administration,

Noting also the constitutional developments in some Non-Self-Governing Territories affecting the internal structure of governance about which the Special Committee has received information,

Convinced that the wishes and aspirations of the peoples of the Territories should continue to guide the development of their future political status and that referendums, free and fair elections and other forms of popular consultation play an important role in ascertaining the wishes and aspirations of the people,

Convinced also that any negotiations to determine the status of a Territory must take place with the active involvement and participation of the people of that Territory, under the aegis of the United Nations, on a case-by-case basis, and that the views of the peoples of the Non-Self-Governing Territories in respect of their right to self-determination should be ascertained,

Noting that a number of Non-Self-Governing Territories have expressed concern at the procedure followed by some administering Powers, contrary to the wishes of the Territories themselves, of amending or enacting legislation for application to the Territories, either through orders in council, in order to apply to the Territories the international treaty obligations of the administering Power, or through the unilateral application of laws and regulations,

Aware of the importance of the international financial services and tourism sectors for the economies of some of the Non-Self-Governing Territories,

Noting the continued cooperation of the Non-Self-Governing Territories at the local and regional levels, including participation in the work of regional organizations,

Mindful that United Nations visiting and special missions provide an effective means of ascertaining the situation in the Territories, that some Territories have not received a United Nations visiting mission for a long time and that no visiting missions have been sent to some of the Territories, and considering the possibility of sending further visiting missions to the Territories at an appropriate time, in consultation with the relevant administering Powers and in accordance with the relevant resolutions and decisions of the United Nations on decolonization,

Mindful also that, in order for the Special Committee to enhance its understanding of the political status of the peoples of the Territories and to fulfil its mandate effectively, it is important for it to be apprised by the relevant administering Powers and to receive information from other appropriate sources, including the representatives of the Territories, concerning the wishes and aspirations of the peoples of the Territories,

Acknowledging the regular transmission by the administering Powers to the Secretary-General of information called for under Article 73 *e* of the Charter,

Aware of the importance both to the Territories and to the Special Committee of the participation of elected and appointed representatives of the Territories in the work of the Committee,

Recognizing the need for the Special Committee to ensure that the appropriate bodies of the United Nations actively pursue a public awareness campaign aimed at assisting the peoples of the Territories in gaining a better understanding of the options for self-determination,

Mindful, in this connection, that the holding of regional seminars in the Caribbean and Pacific regions and at Headquarters, with the active participation of representatives of the Non-Self-Governing Territories, provides a helpful means for the Special Committee to fulfil its mandate, and that the regional nature of the seminars, which alternate between the Caribbean and the Pacific, is a crucial element in the context of a United Nations programme for ascertaining the political status of the Territories,

Noting the stated positions of the representatives of the Non-Self-Governing Territories before the Special Committee and at its regional seminars,

Mindful that the 2011 Caribbean regional seminar was held in Kingstown from 31 May to 2 June 2011,

Conscious of the particular vulnerability of the Territories to natural disasters and environmental degradation, and, in this connection, bearing in mind the applicability to the Territories of the programmes of action or outcome documents of all United Nations world conferences and special sessions of the General Assembly in the economic and social spheres,

Noting with appreciation the contribution to the development of some Territories by the specialized agencies and other organizations of the United Nations system, in particular the United Nations Development Programme, the Economic Commission for Latin America and the Caribbean and the Economic and Social Commission for Asia and the Pacific, as well as regional institutions such as the Caribbean Development Bank, the Caribbean Community, the Organization of Eastern Caribbean States, the Pacific Islands Forum and the agencies of the Council of Regional Organizations in the Pacific,

Noting the statement by the representative of the Economic Commission for Latin America and the Caribbean at the Caribbean regional seminar in Kingstown that all six Caribbean Non-Self-Governing Territories are active associate members of the Economic Commission,

Aware that the Human Rights Committee, as part of its mandate under the International Covenant on Civil and Political Rights, reviews the status of the self-determination process, including in small island Territories under examination by the Special Committee,

Recalling the ongoing efforts of the Special Committee in carrying out a critical review of its work with the aim of making appropriate and constructive recommendations and decisions to attain its objectives in accordance with its mandate,

Recognizing that the annual working papers prepared by the Secretariat on developments in each of the small Territories, as well as the substantive documentation and information furnished by experts, scholars, non-governmental organizations and other sources, have provided important inputs to update the present resolutions,

Recalling the report of the Secretary-General on the Second International Decade for the Eradication of Colonialism,

1. *Reaffirms* the inalienable right of the peoples of the Non-Self-Governing Territories to self-determination, in conformity with the Charter of the United Nations and with General Assembly resolution 1514(XV), containing the Declaration on the Granting of Independence to Colonial Countries and Peoples;

2. *Also reaffirms* that, in the process of decolonization, there is no alternative to the principle of self-determination, which is also a fundamental human right, as recognized under the relevant human rights conventions;

3. *Further reaffirms* that it is ultimately for the peoples of the Territories themselves to determine freely their future political status in accordance with the relevant provisions of the Charter, the Declaration and the relevant resolutions of the General Assembly, and in that connection reiterates its long-standing call for the administering Powers, in cooperation with the territorial Governments and appropriate bodies of the United Nations system, to develop political education programmes for the Territories in order to foster an awareness among the people of their right to self-determination in conformity with the legitimate political status options, based on the principles clearly defined in Assembly resolution 1541(XV) and other relevant resolutions and decisions;

4. *Stresses* the importance of the Special Committee on the Situation with regard to the Implementation of the Declaration on the Granting of Independence to Colonial Countries and Peoples being apprised of the views and wishes of the peoples of the Territories and enhancing its understanding of their conditions, including the nature and scope of the existing political and constitutional arrangements between the Non-Self-Governing Territories and their respective administering Powers;

5. *Requests* the administering Powers to continue to transmit regularly to the Secretary-General information called for under Article 73 *e* of the Charter;

6. *Calls upon* the administering Powers to participate in and cooperate fully with the work of the Special Committee in order to implement the provisions of Article 73 *e* of the Charter and the Declaration and in order to advise the Special Committee on the implementation of the provisions under Article 73 *b* of the Charter on efforts to promote self-government in the Territories, and encourages the administering Powers to facilitate visiting and special missions to the Territories;

7. *Reaffirms* the responsibility of the administering Powers under the Charter to promote the economic and social development and to preserve the cultural identity of the Territories, and, as a priority, to mitigate the effects of the current global financial crisis where possible, in consultation with the territorial Governments concerned, towards the strengthening and diversification of their respective economies;

8. *Requests* the Territories and the administering Powers to take all measures necessary to protect and conserve the environment of the Territories against any degradation, and once again requests the specialized agencies concerned to continue to monitor environmental conditions in the Territories and to provide assistance to those Territories, consistent with their prevailing rules of procedure;

9. *Welcomes* the participation of the Non-Self-Governing Territories in regional activities, including the work of regional organizations;

10. *Stresses* the importance of implementing the plans of action for the Second and Third International Decades for the Eradication of Colonialism, in particular by expediting the application of the work programme for the decolonization of each Non-Self-Governing Territory, on a case-by-case basis, as well as by ensuring that periodic analyses are undertaken of the progress and extent of the implementation of the Declaration in each Territory, and that the working papers prepared by the Secretariat on each Territory should fully reflect developments in those Territories;

11. *Urges* Member States to contribute to the efforts of the United Nations to usher in a world free of colonialism within the context of the International Decades for the Eradication of Colonialism, and calls upon them to continue to give their full support to the Special Committee in its endeavours towards that noble goal;

12. *Stresses* the importance of the various constitutional exercises in the respective Territories administered by the United Kingdom of Great Britain and Northern Ireland and the United States of America, and led by the territorial Governments, designed to address internal constitutional structures within the present territorial arrangements, and decides to follow closely the developments concerning the future political status of those Territories;

13. *Requests* the Secretary-General to continue to report to the General Assembly on a regular basis on the implementation of decolonization resolutions adopted since the declaration of the Third International Decade for the Eradication of Colonialism;

14. *Reiterates its request* that the Human Rights Committee collaborate with the Special Committee, within the framework of its mandate on the right to self-determination as contained in the International Covenant on Civil and Political Rights, with the aim of exchanging information,

given that the Human Rights Committee is mandated to review the situation, including political and constitutional developments, in many of the Non-Self-Governing Territories that are within the purview of the Special Committee;

15. *Requests* the Special Committee to continue to collaborate with the Economic and Social Council and its relevant subsidiary intergovernmental bodies, within the framework of their respective mandates, with the aim of exchanging information on developments in those Non-Self-Governing Territories which are reviewed by those bodies;

16. *Also requests* the Special Committee to continue to examine the question of the Non-Self-Governing Territories and to report thereon to the General Assembly at its sixty-seventh session and on the implementation of the present resolution.

B
INDIVIDUAL TERRITORIES

The General Assembly,

Referring to resolution A above,

I
American Samoa

Taking note of the working paper prepared by the Secretariat on American Samoa and other relevant information,

Noting the statement made by the representative of the Governor of American Samoa at the Caribbean regional seminar, held in Kingstown from 31 May to 2 June 2011, that the Territory's position that it should be removed from the United Nations list of Non-Self-Governing Territories continued to hold, that it was time to make political and economic progress while respecting the concerns of the administering Power and the United Nations, and that the administering Powers should be urged to transmit information on their respective Non-Self-Governing Territories for consideration by the Special Committee on the Situation with regard to the Implementation of the Declaration on the Granting of Independence to Colonial Countries and Peoples,

Aware that under United States law the Secretary of the Interior has administrative jurisdiction over American Samoa,

Noting the position of the administering Power and the statements made by representatives of American Samoa in regional seminars, including at the 2011 Caribbean regional seminar, inviting the Special Committee to send a visiting mission to the Territory,

Aware of the work of the Future Political Status Study Commission, completed in 2006, the release of its report, with recommendations, in January 2007, and the creation of the American Samoa Constitutional Review Committee in the Territory, as well as the holding in June 2010 of American Samoa's fourth Constitutional Convention,

Noting, in that regard, the statement made by the representative of the Governor of American Samoa at the 2011 Caribbean regional seminar and previous policy papers presented to the Special Committee stating that, against a backdrop of a decades-long popular preference for integration with the United States of America, the Territory wished to move forward on political status, local autonomy and self-governance issues,

Acknowledging the indication by the territorial Government, including at the 2011 Caribbean regional seminar, that the effects of certain federal laws on the Territory's economy are serious cause for concern,

Aware that American Samoa continues to be the only United States Territory to receive financial assistance from the administering Power for the operations of the territorial Government,

1. *Takes note* that, at the November 2010 general elections, voters defeated the proposed amendments to the 1967 revised Constitution of American Samoa adopted at the fourth Constitutional Convention, held in June 2010;

2. *Welcomes* the work of the territorial Government with respect to moving forward on political status, local autonomy and self-governance issues with a view to making political and economic progress;

3. *Expresses its appreciation* for the invitation extended in 2011 to the Special Committee on the Situation with regard to the Implementation of the Declaration on the Granting of Independence to Colonial Countries and Peoples by the Governor of American Samoa to send a visiting mission to the Territory, calls upon the administering Power to facilitate such a mission if the territorial Government so desires, and requests the Chair of the Special Committee to take all the steps necessary to that end;

4. *Requests* the administering Power to assist the Territory by facilitating its work concerning a public awareness programme, consistent with Article 73 *b* of the Charter of the United Nations, and, in that regard, calls upon the relevant United Nations organizations to provide assistance to the Territory, if requested;

5. *Calls upon* the administering Power to assist the territorial Government in the diversification and sustainability of the economy of the Territory and to address employment and cost-of-living issues;

6. *Welcomes* the invitation to American Samoa in 2011 to become Pacific Islands Forum observer;

II
Anguilla

Taking note of the working paper prepared by the Secretariat on Anguilla and other relevant information,

Recalling the holding of the 2003 Caribbean regional seminar in Anguilla, hosted by the territorial Government and made possible by the administering Power, the first time that the seminar had been held in a Non-Self-Governing Territory,

Recalling also the statement of the representative of Anguilla at the Caribbean regional seminar, held in Frigate Bay, Saint Kitts and Nevis, from 12 to 14 May 2009,

Noting the internal constitutional review process resumed by the territorial Government in 2006, the work of the Constitutional and Electoral Reform Commission, which prepared its report in August 2006, the holding of public and other consultative meetings in 2007 on proposed constitutional amendments to be presented to the administering Power, and the 2008 decision to set up a drafting team consisting of territorial Government officials, members of the House of Assembly and lawyers to draft a new constitution, as well as the presentation of the draft constitution for public consultation in the Territory in 2009 and the expectation that the draft text will be discussed with the United Kingdom of Great Britain and Northern Ireland, with the aim of seeking full internal self-government without prejudice to independence as an option,

Aware of certain difficulties in the relations between the territorial Government and the administering Power regarding budgetary and economic matters and of the intention of the territorial Government to continue its commitment to high-end tourism in an effort to promote local employment opportunities,

Noting the participation of the Territory as an associate member in the Caribbean Community, the Organization of Eastern Caribbean States and the Economic Commission for Latin America and the Caribbean,

Aware of the willingness expressed by the Prime Ministers of the States members of the Organization of Eastern Caribbean States in 2011 to assist in the resolution of difficulties being experienced by the territorial Government in respect of its relations with the Government of the United Kingdom of Great Britain and Northern Ireland,

1. *Once again welcomes* the presentation of a new constitution for public consultation in 2009 with the aim of further discussing the new constitution with the administering Power in 2010, and urges that constitutional discussions be concluded as soon as possible;

2. *Requests* the administering Power to assist the Territory in its current efforts with regard to advancing the internal constitutional review exercise, if requested;

3. *Stresses* the importance of the previously expressed desire of the territorial Government for a visiting mission by the Special Committee, calls upon the administering Power to facilitate such a mission, if the territorial Government so desires, and requests the Chair of the Special Committee to take all the necessary steps to that end;

4. *Requests* the administering Power to assist the Territory by facilitating its work concerning public consultative outreach efforts consistent with Article 73 *b* of the Charter of the United Nations, and, in this regard, calls upon the relevant United Nations organizations to provide assistance to the Territory, if requested;

5. *Calls upon* the administering Power to assist the territorial Government in strengthening its commitments in the economic domain, including budgetary matters, with regional support as needed and appropriate;

6. *Welcomes* the active participation of the Territory in the work of the Economic Commission for Latin America and the Caribbean;

III
Bermuda

Taking note of the working paper prepared by the Secretariat on Bermuda and other relevant information,

Recalling the statement of the representative of Bermuda at the Caribbean regional seminar, held in Frigate Bay, Saint Kitts and Nevis, from 12 to 14 May 2009,

Conscious of the different viewpoints of the political parties on the future status of the Territory, and noting a January 2011 survey by local media according to which 73 per cent of respondents did not wish to sever ties with the United Kingdom of Great Britain and Northern Ireland, the administering Power, and 14 per cent were in favour of independence,

Recalling the dispatch of the United Nations special mission to Bermuda in 2005, at the request of the territorial Government and with the concurrence of the administering Power, which provided information to the people of the Territory on the role of the United Nations in the process of self-determination, on the legitimate political status options as clearly defined in General Assembly resolution 1541(XV) and on the experiences of other small States that have achieved a full measure of self-government,

1. *Stresses* the importance of the 2005 report of the Bermuda Independence Commission, which provides a thorough examination of the facts surrounding independence, and continues to regret that the plans for public meetings and the presentation of a Green Paper to the House of Assembly followed by a White Paper outlining the policy proposals for an independent Bermuda have so far not materialized;

2. *Requests* the administering Power to assist the Territory by facilitating its work concerning public educational outreach efforts, consistent with Article 73 *b* of the Charter of the United Nations, and, in this regard, calls upon the relevant United Nations organizations to provide assistance to the Territory, if requested;

IV
British Virgin Islands

Taking note of the working paper prepared by the Secretariat on the British Virgin Islands and other relevant information,

Noting the statement of the representative of the British Virgin Islands at the Caribbean regional seminar, held in Kingstown from 31 May to 2 June 2011, that independence was not a matter regularly discussed among the people of the Territory as there had been no popular call for such a drastic change in the relationship with the administering Power and that the policy framework governing the relationship with the administering Power was being reviewed,

Recalling the 1993 report of the Constitutional Commissioners, the 1996 debate on the report in the Legislative Council of the Territory, the establishment of the Constitutional Review Commission in 2004, the completion in 2005 of its report providing recommendations on internal constitutional modernization and the debate held in 2005 on the report in the Legislative Council, as well as the negotiations between the administering Power and the territorial Government, which resulted in the adoption of the new Constitution of the Territory in 2007,

Noting the view expressed in the aforementioned statement made by the representative of the British Virgin Islands at the 2011 Caribbean regional seminar that there was scope for further constitutional review with respect to the practical and effective implementation of the provisions of the 2007 Constitution in the Territory,

Aware of the negative impact of the global economic slowdown on the growth of the Territory's financial and tourism services sectors, which was possibly somewhat less severe in 2010–2011,

Cognizant of the potential usefulness of regional ties for the development of a small island Territory,

1. *Recalls* the Constitution of the British Virgin Islands, which took effect in 2007, and stresses the importance of continued discussions on constitutional matters, to accord greater responsibility to the territorial Government for the effective implementation of the 2007 Constitution;

2. *Requests* the administering Power to assist the Territory by facilitating its work concerning public outreach efforts, consistent with Article 73 *b* of the Charter of the United Nations, and, in that regard, calls upon the relevant United Nations organizations to provide assistance to the Territory, if requested;

3. *Welcomes* the efforts made by the Territory to strengthen its financial services regulatory regime and to seek new, non-traditional markets for its tourism industry;

4. *Also welcomes* the active participation of the Territory in the work of the Economic Commission for Latin America and the Caribbean;

5. *Further welcomes* the holding, for the first time at the level of heads of territorial Government, on 12 May 2011, of the meeting of the Inter-Virgin Islands Council between the Territory and the United States Virgin Islands;

V
Cayman Islands

Taking note of the working paper prepared by the Secretariat on the Cayman Islands and other relevant information,

Recalling the statement made by the representative of the territorial Government at the Pacific regional seminar, held in Nouméa from 18 to 20 May 2010,

Aware of the 2002 report of the Constitutional Modernization Review Commission, which contained a draft constitution for the consideration of the people of the Territory, the 2003 draft constitution offered by the administering Power and the subsequent discussions between the Territory and the administering Power in 2003, and the reopening of discussions between the administering Power and the territorial Government on internal constitutional modernization, in 2006, which resulted in the finalization of a new draft constitution in February 2009, its subsequent acceptance by referendum in May 2009, and promulgation in November 2009,

Conscious of the work, under the 2009 Constitution, of the new Constitutional Commission, which serves as an advisory body on constitutional matters,

Acknowledging the view of the territorial Government that, in spite of the global economic downturn and unemployment issues, the Territory's financial services and tourism industries would help sustain a strong economy,

1. *Recalls* the Constitution, which took effect in 2009, and stresses the importance of the work of the new Constitutional Commission, including human rights education, in the Territory;

2. *Requests* the administering Power to assist the Territory by facilitating its work concerning public awareness outreach efforts, consistent with Article 73 *b* of the Charter of the United Nations, and, in this regard, calls upon the relevant United Nations organizations to provide assistance to the Territory, if requested;

3. *Welcomes* the Territory's active participation in the work of the Economic Commission for Latin America and the Caribbean;

4. *Also welcomes* the efforts made by the territorial Government to implement sectoral management policies such as investment facilitation and regulation and the promotion of medical and sports tourism, as well as unemployment alleviation programmes in various economic sectors;

VI
Guam

Taking note of the working paper prepared by the Secretariat on Guam and other relevant information,

Noting the statement made by the representative of the Governor of Guam at the Caribbean regional seminar, held in Kingstown from 31 May to 2 June 2011, that the territorial Government had a strong commitment to the inalienable right of the Chamorro people of Guam to self-determination, aspired to a partnership with the administering Power wherein all interests would be respected and considered, and generally considered militarism an impediment to decolonization,

Aware that under United States law the relations between the territorial Government and the federal Government in all matters that are not the programme responsibility of another federal department or agency are under the general administrative supervision of the Secretary of the Interior,

Recalling that, in a referendum held in 1987, the registered and eligible voters of Guam endorsed a draft Guam Commonwealth Act that would establish a new framework for relations between the Territory and the administering Power, providing for a greater measure of internal self-government for Guam and recognition of the right of the Chamorro people of Guam to self-determination for the Territory,

Recalling also the requests by the elected representatives and non-governmental organizations of the Territory, including at the 2011 Caribbean regional seminar, that Guam not be removed from the list of the Non-Self-Governing Territories with which the Special Committee is concerned, pending the self-determination of the Chamorro people and taking into account their legitimate rights and interests,

Aware that negotiations between the administering Power and the territorial Government on the draft Guam Commonwealth Act ended in 1997 and that Guam has subsequently established a non-binding plebiscite process for a self-determination vote by the eligible Chamorro voters,

Cognizant of the importance that the administering Power continues to implement its programme of transferring surplus federal land to the Government of Guam,

Noting that the people of the Territory have called for reform in the programme of the administering Power with respect to the thorough, unconditional and expeditious transfer of land property to the people of Guam,

Aware of the deep concerns expressed by civil society and others, including at the meetings of the Special Political and Decolonization Committee (Fourth Committee) of the General Assembly in October 2009 and 2010, at the Pacific regional seminar held in Nouméa from 18 to 20 May 2010, and at the 2011 Caribbean regional seminar, regarding the potential social, cultural, economic and environmental impacts of the planned transfer of additional military personnel of the administering Power to the Territory,

Conscious that immigration into Guam has resulted in the indigenous Chamorros becoming a minority in their homeland,

1. *Calls once again upon* the administering Power to take into consideration the expressed will of the Chamorro people as supported by Guam voters in the referendum of 1987 and as subsequently provided for in Guam law regarding Chamorro self-determination efforts, encourages the administering Power and the territorial Government to enter into negotiations on the matter, and stresses the need for continued close monitoring of the overall situation in the Territory;

2. *Requests* the administering Power, in cooperation with the territorial Government, to continue to transfer land to the original landowners of the Territory, to continue to recognize and to respect the political rights and the cultural and ethnic identity of the Chamorro people of Guam and to take all measures necessary to address the concerns of the territorial Government with regard to the question of immigration;

3. *Also requests* the administering Power to assist the Territory by facilitating public outreach efforts, consistent with Article 73 *b* of the Charter of the United Nations, and, in this regard, calls upon the relevant United Nations organizations to provide assistance to the Territory, if requested, and welcomes the recent outreach work by the territorial Government, including the convening in 2011 of a Chamorro forum;

4. *Further requests* the administering Power to cooperate in establishing programmes for the sustainable development of the economic activities and enterprises of the Territory, noting the special role of the Chamorro people in the development of Guam;

5. *Welcomes* the invitation to Guam in 2011 to become Pacific Islands Forum observer;

VII
Montserrat

Taking note of the working paper prepared by the Secretariat on Montserrat and other relevant information,

Recalling the statement of the representative of Montserrat at the Caribbean regional seminar, held in Frigate Bay, Saint Kitts and Nevis, from 12 to 14 May 2009,

Aware of the 2002 report of the Constitutional Review Commission, the convening of a committee of the House of Assembly in 2005 to review the report, the subsequent negotiating process with the administering Power on a draft constitution according greater autonomy to the territorial Government, the efforts of the newly elected 2010 territorial Government to continue the process of negotiating constitutional reforms with the administering Power, and the draft constitution agreed between the two parties and published for public consultation,

Noting the approval of a new Constitution in 2010 and the work of the territorial Government to update the relevant parts of the Territory's legislation so that the Constitution can enter into force in 2011,

Aware that Montserrat continues to receive budgetary aid from the administering Power for the operation of the territorial Government,

Recalling the statements made by participants at the 2009 Caribbean regional seminar encouraging the administering Power to commit sufficient resources to meet the Territory's special needs,

Noting with concern the continued consequences of the 1995 volcanic eruption, which led to the evacuation of three quarters of the Territory's population to safe areas of the island and to areas outside the Territory, which continues to have enduring consequences for the economy of the island,

Acknowledging the continued assistance provided to the Territory by States members of the Caribbean Community, in particular Antigua and Barbuda, which has offered safe refuge and access to educational and health facilities, as well as employment for thousands who have left the Territory,

Noting the continuing efforts of the administering Power and the territorial Government to deal with the consequences of the volcanic eruption,

1. *Recalls* the progress made by the territorial Government and the administering Power on concluding the negotiations to reform the Constitution of the Territory, and welcomes the approval of a new Constitution for the Territory;

2. *Requests* the administering Power to assist the Territory by facilitating its work concerning public outreach efforts, consistent with Article 73 *b* of the Charter of the United Nations, and, in this regard, calls upon the relevant United Nations organizations to provide assistance to the Territory, if requested;

3. *Welcomes* the active participation of the Territory in the work of the Economic Commission for Latin America and the Caribbean;

4. *Calls upon* the administering Power, the specialized agencies and other organizations of the United Nations system, as well as regional and other organizations, to continue to provide assistance to the Territory in alleviating the consequences of the volcanic eruption;

VIII
Pitcairn

Taking note of the working paper prepared by the Secretariat on Pitcairn and other relevant information,

Taking into account the unique character of Pitcairn in terms of population, area and access,

Aware that, following consultations in 2009, the Pitcairn Constitution Order 2010, including human rights provisions, came into force in the Territory in March 2010,

Aware also that the administering Power and the territorial Government have implemented a new governance structure to strengthen administrative capacity in the Territory, based on consultations with the people of the Territory, and that Pitcairn continues to receive budgetary aid from the administering Power for the operation of the territorial Government,

1. *Recalls* the entry into force of the Pitcairn Constitution Order 2010 in the Territory in March 2010, featuring a new constitutional framework and human rights provisions, and all efforts by the administering Power and the territorial Government that would further devolve operational responsibilities to the Territory, with a view to gradually expanding self-government, including through training of local personnel;

2. *Requests* the administering Power to assist the Territory by facilitating its work concerning public outreach efforts, consistent with Article 73 *b* of the Charter of the United Nations, and, in this regard, calls upon the relevant United Nations organizations to provide assistance to the Territory, if requested;

3. *Also requests* the administering Power to continue its assistance for the improvement of the economic, social, educational and other conditions of the population of the Territory and to continue its discussions with the territorial Government on how best to support socioeconomic security in Pitcairn;

IX
Saint Helena

Taking note of the working paper prepared by the Secretariat on Saint Helena and other relevant information,

Recalling the statement of the representative of Saint Helena at the Caribbean regional seminar, held in Frigate Bay, Saint Kitts and Nevis, from 12 to 14 May 2009,

Taking into account the unique character of Saint Helena in terms of its population, geography and natural resources,

Aware of the internal constitutional review process led by the territorial Government since 2001, the completion of a draft constitution following negotiations between the administering Power and the territorial Government in 2003 and 2004, the consultative poll with regard to a new Constitution, held in Saint Helena in May 2005, the subsequent preparation of a revised draft constitution and its publication in June 2008 for further public consultation, and the entry into force of the new Constitution for Saint Helena, Ascension and Tristan da Cunha on 1 September 2009,

Cognizant that Saint Helena continues to receive budgetary aid from the administering Power for the operation of the territorial Government,

Aware of the efforts of the administering Power and the territorial Government to improve the socioeconomic conditions of the population of Saint Helena, in particular in the areas of employment and transport and communications infrastructure,

Noting the efforts of the Territory to address the problem of unemployment on the island and the joint action of the administering Power and the territorial Government in dealing with it,

Noting also the importance of improving the infrastructure and accessibility of Saint Helena, and, in this regard, the administering Power's announcement in 2010 about plans for building an airport on the island of Saint Helena,

1. *Stresses* the importance of the Territory's 2009 Constitution;

2. *Requests* the administering Power to assist the Territory by facilitating its work concerning public outreach efforts, consistent with Article 73 *b* of the Charter of the United Nations, and, in that regard, calls upon the relevant United Nations organizations to provide assistance to the Territory, if requested;

3. *Requests* the administering Power and relevant international organizations to continue to support the efforts of the territorial Government to address the Territory's socioeconomic development challenges, including unemployment, and limited transport and communications infrastructure;

4. *Calls upon* the administering Power to take into account the unique geographical character of Saint Helena while resolving as soon as feasible any outstanding issues related to the airport construction;

X
Turks and Caicos Islands

Taking note of the working paper prepared by the Secretariat on the Turks and Caicos Islands and other relevant information,

Recalling the statement of the representative of the Turks and Caicos Islands at the Caribbean regional seminar, held in Frigate Bay, Saint Kitts and Nevis, from 12 to 14 May 2009,

Recalling also the dispatch of the United Nations special mission to the Turks and Caicos Islands in 2006, at the request of the territorial Government and with the concurrence of the administering Power,

Aware of the 2002 report of the Constitutional Modernization Review Body, and acknowledging the Constitution agreed between the administering Power and the territorial Government, which entered into force in 2006,

Noting the administering Power's decisions to suspend parts of the 2006 Constitution of the Turks and Caicos Islands, covering the constitutional right to trial by jury, ministerial Government, and the House of Assembly, following the recommendations of an independent Commission of Inquiry and the ruling of the administering Power's Court of Appeal, to present a draft constitution for public consultation in 2011, and to introduce a new constitution for the Territory,

Noting also the continued postponement of elections in the Territory,

Acknowledging the impact that the global economic slowdown and other relevant developments have had on tourism and related real estate development, the mainstays of the Territory's economy, and the 2010–2011 fiscal stabilization plan providing stimuli to the Territory's private sector,

1. *Notes with grave concern* the ongoing situation in the Turks and Caicos Islands, and notes the efforts of the administering Power to restore good governance, including through the introduction of a new 2011 constitution, and sound financial management in the Territory;

2. *Calls for* the restoration of constitutional arrangements providing for representative democracy through elected territorial Government as soon as possible;

3. *Notes* the positions and repeated calls of the Caribbean Community and the Movement of Non-Aligned Countries for the restoration of democratically elected territorial Government as a matter of urgency, and also notes the view expressed by the administering Power that elections should not be postponed any longer than necessary;

4. *Also notes* the extensive public consultations undertaken by the Constitutional and Electoral Reform Adviser and the continued debate on constitutional and electoral reform within the Territory, and stresses the importance of participation by all groups and interested parties in the consultation process;

5. *Stresses* the importance of having in place in the Territory a Constitution that reflects the aspirations and wishes of the people of the Territory, based on the mechanisms for popular consultation;

6. *Requests* the administering Power to assist the Territory by facilitating its work concerning public outreach efforts, consistent with Article 73 *b* of the Charter of the United Nations, and, in that regard, calls upon the relevant United Nations organizations to provide assistance to the Territory, if requested;

7. *Welcomes* the active participation of the Territory in the work of the Economic Commission for Latin America and the Caribbean;

8. *Also welcomes* the continuing efforts made by the territorial Government addressing the need for attention to be paid to the enhancement of socioeconomic development across the Territory;

XI
United States Virgin Islands

Taking note of the working paper prepared by the Secretariat on the United States Virgin Islands and other relevant information,

Aware that under United States law the relations between the territorial Government and the federal Government in all matters not the programme responsibility of another federal department or agency are under the general administrative supervision of the Secretary of the Interior,

Aware also of the fifth attempt of the Territory to review the existing Revised Organic Act, which organizes its internal governance arrangements, as well as its requests to the administering Power and the United Nations system for assistance to its public education programme,

Cognizant that a draft constitution was proposed in 2009 and subsequently forwarded to the administering Power, which in 2010 requested the Territory to consider its objections to the draft constitution,

Cognizant also of the potential usefulness of regional ties for the development of a small island Territory,

1. *Welcomes* the proposal of a draft constitution emanating from the Territory in 2009, as a result of the work of the United States Virgin Islands Fifth Constitutional Convention, for review by the administering Power, and requests the administering Power to assist the territorial Government in achieving its political, economic and social goals, in particular the successful conclusion of the ongoing internal Constitutional Convention exercise;

2. *Requests* the administering Power to facilitate the process for approval of the proposed territorial constitution in the United States Congress and its implementation, once agreed upon in the Territory;

3. *Also requests* the administering Power to assist the Territory by facilitating its work concerning a public education programme, consistent with Article 73 *b* of the Charter of the United Nations, and, in this regard, calls upon the relevant United Nations organizations to provide assistance to the Territory, if requested;

4. *Reiterates its call for* the inclusion of the Territory in regional programmes of the United Nations Development Programme, consistent with the participation of other Non-Self-Governing Territories;

5. *Welcomes* the active participation of the Territory in the work of the Economic Commission for Latin America and the Caribbean;

6. *Also welcomes* the holding, for the first time at the level of heads of territorial Government, on 12 May 2011, of the meeting of the Inter-Virgin Islands Council between the Territory and the British Virgin Islands.

Other issues

Military activities and arrangements in colonial countries

In accordance with General Assembly decision 57/525 [YUN 2002, p. 564], Secretariat working papers submitted to the Special Committee on decolonization on Bermuda [A/AC.109/2011/5] and Guam [A/AC.109/2011/15] contained information on, among other things, military activities and arrangements by the administering Powers in those Territories.

Economic and other activities affecting NSGTs

The Special Committee on decolonization, in June [A/66/23], continued its consideration of economic and other activities affecting the interests of the peoples of NSGTs. It had before it Secretariat working papers containing information on, among other topics, economic conditions in American Samoa [A/AC.109/2011/12], Anguilla [A/AC.109/2011/2], Bermuda [A/AC.109/2011/5], the British Virgin Islands [A/AC.109/2011/6], the Cayman Islands [A/AC.109/2011/8], the Falkland Islands (Malvinas) [A/AC.109/2011/14], Gibraltar [A/AC.109/2011/13], Guam [A/AC.109/2011/15], Montserrat [A/AC.109/2011/11], New Caledonia [A/AC.109/2011/16], Pitcairn [A/AC.109/2011/4], Saint Helena [A/AC.109/2011/7], Tokelau [A/AC.109/2011/3], the Turks and Caicos Islands [A/AC.109/2011/10], the United States Virgin Islands [A/AC.109/2011/9], and Western Sahara [A/AC.109/2011/1].

GENERAL ASSEMBLY ACTION

On 9 December [meeting 81], the General Assembly, on the recommendation of the Fourth Committee [A/66/431], adopted **resolution 66/83** by recorded vote (170-2-2) [agenda item 57].

Economic and other activities which affect the interests of the peoples of the Non-Self-Governing Territories

The General Assembly,

Having considered the item entitled "Economic and other activities which affect the interests of the peoples of the Non-Self-Governing Territories",

Having examined the chapter of the report of the Special Committee on the Situation with regard to the Implementation of the Declaration on the Granting of Independence to Colonial Countries and Peoples for 2011 relating to the item,

Recalling General Assembly resolution 1514(XV) of 14 December 1960, as well as all other relevant resolutions of the Assembly, including, in particular, resolutions 46/181 of 19 December 1991, 55/146 of 8 December 2000 and 65/119 of 10 December 2010,

Reaffirming the solemn obligation of the administering Powers under the Charter of the United Nations to promote the political, economic, social and educational advancement of the inhabitants of the Territories under their administration and to protect the human and natural resources of those Territories against abuses,

Reaffirming also that any economic or other activity that has a negative impact on the interests of the peoples of the Non-Self-Governing Territories and on the exercise of their right to self-determination in conformity with the Charter and General Assembly resolution 1514(XV) is contrary to the purposes and principles of the Charter,

Reaffirming further that the natural resources are the heritage of the peoples of the Non-Self-Governing Territories, including the indigenous populations,

Aware of the special circumstances of the geographical location, size and economic conditions of each Territory, and bearing in mind the need to promote the stability, diversification and strengthening of the economy of each Territory,

Conscious of the particular vulnerability of the small Territories to natural disasters and environmental degradation,

Conscious also that foreign economic investment, when undertaken in collaboration with the peoples of the Non-Self-Governing Territories and in accordance with their wishes, could make a valid contribution to the socioeconomic development of the Territories and also to the exercise of their right to self-determination,

Concerned about any activities aimed at exploiting the natural and human resources of the Non-Self-Governing Territories to the detriment of the interests of the inhabitants of those Territories,

Bearing in mind the relevant provisions of the final documents of the successive Conferences of Heads of State or Government of Non-Aligned Countries and of the resolutions adopted by the Assembly of Heads of State and Government of the African Union, the Pacific Islands Forum and the Caribbean Community,

1. *Reaffirms* the right of the peoples of the Non-Self-Governing Territories to self-determination in conformity with the Charter of the United Nations and with General Assembly resolution 1514(XV), containing the Declaration on the Granting of Independence to Colonial Countries and Peoples, as well as their right to the enjoyment of their natural resources and their right to dispose of those resources in their best interest;

2. *Affirms* the value of foreign economic investment undertaken in collaboration with the peoples of the Non-Self-Governing Territories and in accordance with their wishes in order to make a valid contribution to the socioeconomic development of the Territories, especially during times of economic and financial crisis;

3. *Reaffirms* the responsibility of the administering Powers under the Charter to promote the political, economic, social and educational advancement of the Non-Self-Governing Territories, and reaffirms the legitimate rights of their peoples over their natural resources;

4. *Reaffirms its concern* about any activities aimed at the exploitation of the natural resources that are the heritage of the peoples of the Non-Self-Governing Territories, including the indigenous populations, in the Caribbean, the Pacific and other regions, and of their human resources, to the detriment of their interests, and in such a way as to deprive them of their right to dispose of those resources;

5. *Reaffirms* the need to avoid any economic and other activities that adversely affect the interests of the peoples of the Non-Self-Governing Territories;

6. *Calls once again upon* all Governments that have not yet done so to take, in accordance with the relevant provisions of General Assembly resolution 2621(XXV) of 12 October 1970, legislative, administrative or other measures in respect of their nationals and the bodies corporate under their jurisdiction that own and operate enterprises in the Non-Self-Governing Territories that are detrimental to the interests of the inhabitants of those Territories, in order to put an end to such enterprises;

7. *Calls upon* the administering Powers to ensure that the exploitation of the marine and other natural resources in the Non-Self-Governing Territories under their administration is not in violation of the relevant resolutions of the United Nations, and does not adversely affect the interests of the peoples of those Territories;

8. *Invites* all Governments and organizations of the United Nations system to take all possible measures to ensure that the permanent sovereignty of the peoples of the Non-Self-Governing Territories over their natural resources is fully respected and safeguarded in accordance with the relevant resolutions of the United Nations on decolonization;

9. *Urges* the administering Powers concerned to take effective measures to safeguard and guarantee the inalienable right of the peoples of the Non-Self-Governing Territories to their natural resources and to establish and maintain control over the future development of those resources, and requests the administering Powers to take all steps necessary to protect the property rights of the peoples of those Territories in accordance with the relevant resolutions of the United Nations on decolonization;

10. *Calls upon* the administering Powers concerned to ensure that no discriminatory working conditions prevail in the Territories under their administration and to promote in each Territory a fair system of wages applicable to all the inhabitants without any discrimination;

11. *Requests* the Secretary-General to continue, through all means at his disposal, to inform world public opinion of any activity that affects the exercise of the right of the peoples of the Non-Self-Governing Territories to self-determination in conformity with the Charter and General Assembly resolution 1514(XV);

12. *Appeals* to trade unions and non-governmental organizations, as well as individuals, to continue their efforts to promote the economic well-being of the peoples of the Non-Self-Governing Territories, and also appeals to the media to disseminate information about the developments in this regard;

13. *Decides* to follow the situation in the Non-Self-Governing Territories so as to ensure that all economic activities in those Territories are aimed at strengthening and diversifying their economies in the interest of their peoples, including the indigenous populations, and at promoting the economic and financial viability of those Territories;

14. *Requests* the Special Committee on the Situation with regard to the Implementation of the Declaration on the Granting of Independence to Colonial Countries and Peoples to continue to examine this question and to report thereon to the General Assembly at its sixty-seventh session.

RECORDED VOTE ON RESOLUTION 66/83:

In favour: Afghanistan, Albania, Algeria, Andorra, Angola, Antigua and Barbuda, Argentina, Armenia, Australia, Austria, Azerbaijan, Bahamas, Bahrain, Bangladesh, Barbados, Belarus, Belgium, Belize, Benin, Bhutan, Bolivia, Bosnia and Herzegovina, Botswana, Brazil, Brunei Darussalam, Bulgaria, Burkina Faso, Burundi, Cambodia, Cameroon, Canada, Cape Verde, Chad, Chile, China, Colombia, Comoros, Congo, Costa Rica, Côte d'Ivoire, Croatia, Cuba, Cyprus, Czech Republic, Democratic People's Republic of Korea, Denmark, Djibouti, Dominica, Dominican Republic, Ecuador, Egypt, El Salvador, Eritrea, Estonia, Ethiopia, Fiji, Finland, Germany, Ghana, Greece, Grenada, Guatemala, Guinea, Guinea-Bissau, Guyana, Haiti, Honduras, Hungary, Iceland, India, Indonesia, Iran, Iraq, Ireland, Italy, Jamaica, Japan, Jordan, Kazakhstan, Kenya, Kuwait, Kyrgyzstan, Lao People's Democratic Republic, Latvia, Lebanon, Lesotho, Liberia, Libya, Liechtenstein, Lithuania,

Luxembourg, Madagascar, Malawi, Malaysia, Maldives, Mali, Malta, Marshall Islands, Mauritania, Mauritius, Mexico, Micronesia, Monaco, Mongolia, Montenegro, Morocco, Mozambique, Namibia, Nepal, Netherlands, New Zealand, Nicaragua, Norway, Oman, Pakistan, Palau, Panama, Papua New Guinea, Paraguay, Peru, Philippines, Poland, Portugal, Qatar, Republic of Korea, Republic of Moldova, Romania, Russian Federation, Saint Lucia, Saint Vincent and the Grenadines, Samoa, San Marino, Saudi Arabia, Senegal, Serbia, Sierra Leone, Singapore, Slovakia, Slovenia, Solomon Islands, South Africa, Spain, Sri Lanka, Sudan, Swaziland, Sweden, Switzerland, Syrian Arab Republic, Tajikistan, Thailand, the former Yugoslav Republic of Macedonia, Timor-Leste, Togo, Tonga, Trinidad and Tobago, Tunisia, Turkey, Turkmenistan, Tuvalu, Uganda, Ukraine, United Arab Emirates, Uruguay, Uzbekistan, Vanuatu, Venezuela, Viet Nam, Yemen, Zambia, Zimbabwe.

Against: Israel, United States.

Abstaining: France, United Kingdom.

Dissemination of information

On 13 June [A/66/23], the Special Committee on decolonization held consultations with representatives of the UN Department of Political Affairs and Department of Public Information on the dissemination of information on decolonization. It also considered a report of the Secretary-General on the subject, covering the period from April 2010 to March 2011 [A/AC.109/2011/17].

GENERAL ASSEMBLY ACTION

On 9 December [meeting 81], the General Assembly, on the recommendation of the Fourth Committee [A/66/434], adopted **resolution 66/90** by recorded vote (166-3-2) [agenda item 60].

Dissemination of information on decolonization

The General Assembly,

Having examined the chapter of the report of the Special Committee on the Situation with regard to the Implementation of the Declaration on the Granting of Independence to Colonial Countries and Peoples for 2011 relating to the dissemination of information on decolonization and publicity for the work of the United Nations in the field of decolonization,

Recalling General Assembly resolution 1514(XV) of 14 December 1960, containing the Declaration on the Granting of Independence to Colonial Countries and Peoples, and other resolutions and decisions of the United Nations concerning the dissemination of information on decolonization, in particular Assembly resolution 65/116 of 10 December 2010,

Recognizing the need for flexible, practical and innovative approaches towards reviewing the options of self-determination for the peoples of Non-Self-Governing Territories with a view to implementing the plan of action for the Third International Decade for the Eradication of Colonialism,

Reiterating the importance of dissemination of information as an instrument for furthering the aims of the Declaration, and mindful of the role of world public opinion in effectively assisting the peoples of Non-Self-Governing Territories to achieve self-determination,

Recognizing the role played by the administering Powers in transmitting information to the Secretary-General in accordance with the terms of Article 73 *e* of the Charter of the United Nations,

Recognizing also the role of the Department of Public Information of the Secretariat, through the United Nations information centres, in the dissemination of information at the regional level on the activities of the United Nations,

Recalling the issuance by the Department of Public Information, in consultation with the United Nations Development Programme, the specialized agencies and the Special Committee, of an information leaflet on assistance programmes available to the Non-Self-Governing Territories,

Aware of the role of non-governmental organizations in the dissemination of information on decolonization,

1. *Approves* the activities in the field of dissemination of information on decolonization undertaken by the Department of Public Information and the Department of Political Affairs of the Secretariat, in accordance with the relevant resolutions of the United Nations on decolonization, and recalls with satisfaction the publication, in accordance with General Assembly resolution 61/129 of 14 December 2006, of the information leaflet entitled "What the UN Can Do to Assist Non-Self-Governing Territories", which was updated for the United Nations website on decolonization in May 2009, and encourages continued updating and wide dissemination of the information leaflet;

2. *Considers it important* to continue and expand its efforts to ensure the widest possible dissemination of information on decolonization, with particular emphasis on the options for self-determination available for the peoples of Non-Self-Governing Territories, and, to this end, requests the Department of Public Information, through the United Nations information centres in the relevant regions, to actively engage and seek new and innovative ways to disseminate material to the Non-Self-Governing Territories;

3. *Requests* the Secretary-General to further enhance the information provided on the United Nations decolonization website and to continue to include the full series of reports of the regional seminars on decolonization, the statements and scholarly papers presented at those seminars and links to the full series of reports of the Special Committee on the Situation with regard to the Implementation of the Declaration on the Granting of Independence to Colonial Countries and Peoples;

4. *Requests* the Department of Public Information to continue its efforts to update web-based information on the assistance programmes available to the Non-Self-Governing Territories;

5. *Requests* the Department of Political Affairs and the Department of Public Information to implement the recommendations of the Special Committee and to continue their efforts to take measures through all the media available, including publications, radio and television, as well as the Internet, to give publicity to the work of the United Nations in the field of decolonization and, inter alia:

(*a*) To develop procedures to collect, prepare and disseminate, particularly to the Non-Self-Governing Territories, basic material on the issue of self-determination of the peoples of the Territories;

(*b*) To seek the full cooperation of the administering Powers in the discharge of the tasks referred to above;

(c) To explore further the idea of a programme of collaboration with the decolonization focal points of territorial Governments, particularly in the Pacific and Caribbean regions, to help improve the exchange of information;

(d) To encourage the involvement of non-governmental organizations in the dissemination of information on decolonization;

(e) To encourage the involvement of the Non-Self-Governing Territories in the dissemination of information on decolonization;

(f) To report to the Special Committee on measures taken in the implementation of the present resolution;

6. *Requests* all States, including the administering Powers, to accelerate the dissemination of information referred to in paragraph 2 above;

7. *Requests* the Special Committee to continue to examine this question and to report to the General Assembly at its sixty-seventh session on the implementation of the present resolution.

RECORDED VOTE ON RESOLUTION 66/90:

In favour: Afghanistan, Albania, Algeria, Andorra, Angola, Antigua and Barbuda, Argentina, Armenia, Australia, Austria, Azerbaijan, Bahamas, Bahrain, Bangladesh, Barbados, Belarus, Belize, Benin, Bhutan, Bolivia, Bosnia and Herzegovina, Botswana, Brazil, Brunei Darussalam, Bulgaria, Burkina Faso, Burundi, Cambodia, Cameroon, Canada, Cape Verde, Chad, Chile, China, Colombia, Comoros, Congo, Costa Rica, Côte d'Ivoire, Croatia, Cuba, Cyprus, Czech Republic, Democratic People's Republic of Korea, Denmark, Djibouti, Dominica, Dominican Republic, Ecuador, Egypt, El Salvador, Eritrea, Estonia, Ethiopia, Fiji, Finland, Germany, Ghana, Greece, Grenada, Guatemala, Guinea, Guinea-Bissau, Guyana, Haiti, Honduras, Hungary, Iceland, India, Indonesia, Iran, Iraq, Ireland, Italy, Jamaica, Japan, Jordan, Kazakhstan, Kenya, Kuwait, Kyrgyzstan, Lao People's Democratic Republic, Latvia, Lebanon, Lesotho, Liberia, Libya, Liechtenstein, Lithuania, Luxembourg, Madagascar, Malawi, Malaysia, Maldives, Mali, Malta, Marshall Islands, Mauritania, Mauritius, Mexico, Monaco, Mongolia, Montenegro, Morocco, Mozambique, Namibia, Nepal, Netherlands, New Zealand, Nicaragua, Norway, Oman, Pakistan, Panama, Papua New Guinea, Paraguay, Peru, Philippines, Poland, Portugal, Qatar, Republic of Korea, Republic of Moldova, Romania, Russian Federation, Saint Lucia, Saint Vincent and the Grenadines, Samoa, San Marino, Saudi Arabia, Senegal, Serbia, Sierra Leone, Singapore, Slovakia, Slovenia, Solomon Islands, South Africa, Spain, Sri Lanka, Sudan, Swaziland, Sweden, Switzerland, Syrian Arab Republic, Tajikistan, Thailand, the former Yugoslav Republic of Macedonia, Timor-Leste, Togo, Tonga, Trinidad and Tobago, Tunisia, Turkey, Turkmenistan, Tuvalu, Uganda, Ukraine, United Arab Emirates, Uruguay, Uzbekistan, Venezuela, Viet Nam, Yemen, Zambia, Zimbabwe.

Against: Israel, United Kingdom, United States.

Abstaining: Belgium, France.

Information on Territories

In response to General Assembly resolution 65/108 [YUN 2010, p. 607], the Secretary-General submitted a March report [A/66/65 & Add.1] indicating the dates of transmittal of information from the administering Powers on economic, social and educational conditions in NSGTs for 2010, under Article 73 *e* of the Charter of the United Nations.

GENERAL ASSEMBLY ACTION

On 9 December [meeting 81], the General Assembly, on the recommendation of the Fourth Committee [A/66/430], adopted **resolution 66/82** by recorded vote (170-0-4) [agenda item 56].

Information from Non-Self-Governing Territories transmitted under Article 73 *e* of the Charter of the United Nations

The General Assembly,

Recalling its resolution 1970(XVIII) of 16 December 1963, in which it requested the Special Committee on the Situation with regard to the Implementation of the Declaration on the Granting of Independence to Colonial Countries and Peoples to study the information transmitted to the Secretary-General in accordance with Article 73 *e* of the Charter of the United Nations and to take such information fully into account in examining the situation with regard to the implementation of the Declaration, contained in General Assembly resolution 1514(XV) of 14 December 1960,

Recalling also its resolution 65/108 of 10 December 2010, in which it requested the Special Committee to continue to discharge the functions entrusted to it under resolution 1970(XVIII),

Stressing the importance of timely transmission by the administering Powers of adequate information under Article 73 *e* of the Charter, in particular in relation to the preparation by the Secretariat of the working papers on the Territories concerned,

Having examined the report of the Secretary-General on information from Non-Self-Governing Territories transmitted under Article 73 *e* of the Charter,

1. *Reaffirms* that, in the absence of a decision by the General Assembly itself that a Non-Self-Governing Territory has attained a full measure of self-government in terms of Chapter XI of the Charter of the United Nations, the administering Power concerned should continue to transmit information under Article 73 *e* of the Charter with respect to that Territory;

2. *Requests* the administering Powers concerned, in accordance with their Charter obligations, to transmit or continue to transmit regularly to the Secretary-General for information purposes, subject to such limitation as security and constitutional considerations may require, statistical and other information of a technical nature relating to economic, social and educational conditions in the Territories for which they are respectively responsible, as well as the fullest possible information on political and constitutional developments in the Territories concerned, including the constitution, legislative act or executive order providing for the government of the Territory and the constitutional relationship of the Territory to the administering Power, within a maximum period of six months following the expiration of the administrative year in those Territories;

3. *Requests* the Secretary-General to continue to ensure that adequate information is drawn from all available published sources in connection with the preparation of the working papers relating to the Territories concerned;

4. *Requests* the Special Committee on the Situation with regard to the Implementation of the Declaration on the Granting of Independence to Colonial Countries and

Peoples to continue to discharge the functions entrusted to it under General Assembly resolution 1970(XVIII), in accordance with established procedures.

RECORDED VOTE ON RESOLUTION 66/82:

In favour: Afghanistan, Albania, Algeria, Andorra, Angola, Antigua and Barbuda, Argentina, Armenia, Australia, Austria, Azerbaijan, Bahamas, Bahrain, Bangladesh, Barbados, Belarus, Belgium, Belize, Benin, Bhutan, Bolivia, Bosnia and Herzegovina, Botswana, Brazil, Brunei Darussalam, Bulgaria, Burkina Faso, Burundi, Cambodia, Cameroon, Canada, Cape Verde, Chad, Chile, China, Colombia, Comoros, Congo, Costa Rica, Côte d'Ivoire, Croatia, Cuba, Cyprus, Czech Republic, Democratic People's Republic of Korea, Denmark, Djibouti, Dominica, Dominican Republic, Ecuador, Egypt, El Salvador, Eritrea, Estonia, Ethiopia, Fiji, Finland, Germany, Ghana, Greece, Grenada, Guatemala, Guinea, Guinea-Bissau, Guyana, Haiti, Honduras, Hungary, Iceland, India, Indonesia, Iran, Iraq, Ireland, Italy, Jamaica, Japan, Jordan, Kazakhstan, Kenya, Kuwait, Kyrgyzstan, Lao People's Democratic Republic, Latvia, Lebanon, Lesotho, Liberia, Libya, Liechtenstein, Lithuania, Luxembourg, Madagascar, Malawi, Malaysia, Maldives, Mali, Malta, Marshall Islands, Mauritania, Mauritius, Mexico, Micronesia, Monaco, Mongolia, Montenegro, Morocco, Mozambique, Namibia, Nepal, Netherlands, New Zealand, Nicaragua, Norway, Oman, Pakistan, Palau, Panama, Papua New Guinea, Paraguay, Peru, Philippines, Poland, Portugal, Qatar, Republic of Korea, Republic of Moldova, Romania, Russian Federation, Saint Lucia, Saint Vincent and the Grenadines, Samoa, San Marino, Saudi Arabia, Senegal, Serbia, Sierra Leone, Singapore, Slovakia, Slovenia, Solomon Islands, South Africa, Spain, Sri Lanka, Sudan, Swaziland, Sweden, Switzerland, Syrian Arab Republic, Tajikistan, Thailand, the former Yugoslav Republic of Macedonia, Timor-Leste, Togo, Tonga, Trinidad and Tobago, Tunisia, Turkey, Turkmenistan, Tuvalu, Uganda, Ukraine, United Arab Emirates, Uruguay, Uzbekistan, Vanuatu, Venezuela, Viet Nam, Yemen, Zambia, Zimbabwe.

Against: None.

Abstaining: France, Israel, United Kingdom, United States.

Study and training

In response to General Assembly resolution 65/111 [YUN 2010, p. 608], the Secretary-General submitted a March report [A/66/68 & Add.1] on offers of study scholarships and training facilities for inhabitants of NSGTs during the period from 18 March 2010 to 17 March 2011 by the following Member States: Algeria, Argentina, Australia, Canada, Mexico and the Philippines. Over the years, 60 Member States and one non-member State—the Holy See—had made such offers.

GENERAL ASSEMBLY ACTION

On 9 December [meeting 81], the General Assembly, on the recommendation of the Fourth Committee [A/66/433], adopted **resolution 66/85** without vote [agenda item 59].

Offers by Member States of study and training facilities for inhabitants of Non-Self-Governing Territories

The General Assembly,

Recalling its resolution 65/111 of 10 December 2010,

Having examined the report of the Secretary-General on offers by Member States of study and training facilities for inhabitants of Non-Self-Governing Territories, prepared pursuant to its resolution 845(IX) of 22 November 1954,

Conscious of the importance of promoting the educational advancement of the inhabitants of Non-Self-Governing Territories,

Strongly convinced that the continuation and expansion of offers of scholarships is essential in order to meet the increasing need of students from Non-Self-Governing Territories for educational and training assistance, and considering that students in those Territories should be encouraged to avail themselves of such offers,

1. *Takes note* of the report of the Secretary-General;
2. *Expresses its appreciation* to those Member States that have made scholarships available to the inhabitants of Non-Self-Governing Territories;
3. *Invites* all States to make or continue to make generous offers of study and training facilities to the inhabitants of those Territories that have not yet attained self-government or independence and, wherever possible, to provide travel funds to prospective students;
4. *Urges* the administering Powers to take effective measures to ensure the widespread and continuous dissemination in the Territories under their administration of information relating to offers of study and training facilities made by States and to provide all the necessary facilities to enable students to avail themselves of such offers;
5. *Requests* the Secretary-General to report to the General Assembly at its sixty-seventh session on the implementation of the present resolution;
6. *Draws the attention* of the Special Committee on the Situation with regard to the Implementation of the Declaration on the Granting of Independence to Colonial Countries and Peoples to the present resolution.

Visiting missions

In June [A/66/23], the Special Committee on decolonization considered the question of sending visiting missions to NSGTs. It adopted a resolution in which it stressed the need to dispatch periodic visiting missions to facilitate the full implementation of the 1960 Declaration on decolonization, and called upon administering Powers to receive those missions in the Territories under their administration. It also requested the administering Powers to cooperate with the Special Committee in exploring the possibility of undertaking visiting or special missions in furtherance of the decolonization mandate of the General Assembly. The Committee Chair was asked to consult with the administering Powers concerned and report on the results.

The Special Committee recommended to the Assembly for adoption draft resolutions on 11 small

NSGTS (see p. 564), on New Caledonia (see p. 561) and on Tokelau (see p. 563), endorsing a number of conclusions and recommendations concerning the sending of visiting and special missions to those Territories.

Peaceful uses of outer space

The Committee on the Peaceful Uses of Outer Space (Committee on Outer Space), at its fifty-fourth session (Vienna, 1–10 June) [A/66/20], discussed ways and means to maintain outer space for peaceful purposes; the spin-off benefits of space technology; space and society; space and water; space and climate change; the use of space technology in the UN system; and the future role of the Committee. It also considered the implementation of the recommendations of the Third (1999) United Nations Conference on the Exploration and Peaceful Uses of Outer Space (UNISPACE III) [YUN 1999, p. 556] and reviewed the work of its two subcommittees, one dealing with scientific and technical issues (see p. 578) and the other with legal questions (see p. 581).

International Day of Human Space Flight

On 25 March, 34 Member States submitted to the General Assembly a draft resolution entitled "International Day of Human Space Flight" (see below). On 7 April, 33 additional Member States sponsored the draft resolution. The Assembly noted [A/65/PV.85] that the International Day (12 April) would further the maintenance of outer space for peaceful purposes and commemorate the fiftieth anniversary of the Committee on the Peaceful Uses of Outer Space.

GENERAL ASSEMBLY ACTION

On 7 April [meeting 85], the General Assembly adopted **resolution 65/271** [draft: A/65/L.67 & Add.1] without vote [agenda item 50].

International Day of Human Space Flight

The General Assembly,

Deeply convinced of the common interest of mankind in promoting and expanding the exploration and use of outer space, as the province of all mankind, for peaceful purposes and in continuing efforts to extend to all States the benefits derived therefrom,

Attaching great importance to international cooperation in peaceful space activities, for which the United Nations should continue to provide a focal point,

Recalling that 12 April 1961 was the date of the first human space flight, carried out by Mr. Yuri Gagarin, a Soviet citizen born in Russia, and acknowledging that this historic event opened the way for space exploration for the benefit of all mankind,

Welcoming the fact that the Committee on the Peaceful Uses of Outer Space will celebrate at its fifty-fourth session the fiftieth anniversary of the first session of the Committee and the fiftieth anniversary of human space flight,

Declares 12 April as the International Day of Human Space Flight to celebrate each year at the international level the beginning of the space era for mankind, reaffirming the important contribution of space science and technology in achieving sustainable development goals and increasing the well-being of States and peoples, as well as ensuring the realization of their aspiration to maintain outer space for peaceful purposes.

Commemorative segment. On 1 June, the Committee on Outer Space held a commemorative segment on the occasion of the fiftieth anniversary of human space flight and the fiftieth anniversary of the Committee. Participants adopted a declaration (see p. 585) that called upon States to take measures at the national, regional, interregional and global levels to engage in the common efforts to use space science and technology and their applications to preserve planet Earth and its space environment for future generations.

Implementation of UNISPACE III recommendations

In response to General Assembly resolution 65/97 [YUN 2010, p. 614], the Committee on Outer Space [A/66/20] considered the implementation of the recommendations of UNISPACE III [YUN 1999, p. 556]. It noted with appreciation that the Action Team on Public Health had submitted its final report [A/AC.105/C.1/L.305], which the Secretariat would transmit to the World Health Organization with an invitation to report to the Scientific and Technical Subcommittee at its forty-ninth (2012) session on the possible development of long-term tele-epidemiology and tele-health activities. In addition, consideration would be given to the creation of an international committee on tele-epidemiology and tele-health. The Committee endorsed a conference room paper on harnessing space-derived geospatial data for sustainable development and agreed that it would constitute its contribution [A/AC.105/993] to the United Nations Conference on Sustainable Development, to be held in Rio de Janeiro, Brazil, in 2012. It noted that a regional centre for space science and technology education for Western Asia would be established in Jordan by the end of the year. The Committee had before it a report [A/AC.105/973] on international cooperation in promoting the use of space-derived geospatial data for sustainable development and noted that it was the final report under the agenda item, consideration of which had concluded at the Committee's fifty-third (2010) session [YUN 2010, p. 609]. The Committee endorsed the recommendations of the Scientific and Technical Subcommittee (see p. 578), as submitted to the Subcommittee by its Working Group of the Whole, which had been reconvened to consider, among other matters, the implementation of UNISPACE III.

Scientific and Technical Subcommittee

The Scientific and Technical Subcommittee of the Committee on Outer Space, at its forty-eighth session (Vienna, 7–18 February) [A/AC.105/987], considered the United Nations Programme on Space Applications and the implementation of the UNISPACE III recommendations. It also dealt with matters relating to remote sensing of the Earth by satellite, including applications for developing countries and monitoring of the Earth's environment; space debris; space-system-based disaster management support; developments in global navigation satellite systems (GNSS); the use of nuclear power sources in outer space; near-Earth objects; the International Space Weather Initiative (see p. 580); long-term sustainability of outer space activities; and the examination of the physical nature and technical attributes of the geostationary orbit and its utilization and applications.

UN Programme on Space Applications

The United Nations Programme on Space Applications, as mandated by General Assembly resolution 37/90 [YUN 1982, p. 163], continued to promote greater cooperation in space science and technology between developed and developing countries, as well as among developing countries, by providing long-term fellowships, training programmes and seminars, and by supporting pilot projects and offering technical advisory services in capacity-building and regional cooperation. The Programme increased the awareness of knowledge-based themes in space science, law and exploration through multi-year work plans and projects, and by convening outreach events and workshops.

The United Nations Expert on Space Applications [A/AC.105/1011] reported that the Programme continued to support training for capacity-building in developing countries through the regional centres for space science and technology education affiliated with the United Nations Office for Outer Space Affairs. The goal of the regional centres—located in Morocco and Nigeria for the African region, India for Asia and the Pacific, and Brazil and Mexico for Latin America and the Caribbean—was to develop an indigenous capability for research and applications in remote sensing and geographic information systems; satellite communications; satellite meteorology and global climate; and space and atmospheric science. Curricula for those disciplines had been developed through expert meetings held under the Programme, and two further model curricula were being developed in the areas of GNSS and space law. At its sixth meeting (Tokyo, 5–9 September) [A/AC.105/1000], the International Committee on Global Navigation Satellite Systems (ICG) continued reviewing and discussing developments in GNSS and addressed the following issues: compatibility and interoperability; enhancement of the performance of GNSS services; dissemination of information and capacity-building; and reference frames, timing and applications. The Programme was preparing to hold the fourth UN expert meeting on the regional centres for space science and technology education, at which efforts would be made to further develop educational curricula.

One symposium, one expert meeting, two international meetings and five workshops were conducted within the framework of the Programme. The United Nations/United Arab Emirates/United States of America Workshop on Applications of GNSS (Dubai, United Arab Emirates, 16–20 January) was organized to demonstrate the benefits of and opportunities offered by maximizing the use of multiple GNSS. The Second United Nations/Argentina International Conference on the Use of Space Technology for Water Management (Buenos Aires, Argentina, 14–18 March) explored applications of space technology that provided cost-effective solutions to enhance the management, protection and restoration of water resources, and also contributed to mitigating water-related emergencies, providing safe drinking water and fighting desertification. The Third United Nations/Austria/European Space Agency Symposium on Small Satellite Programmes for Sustainable Development (Graz, Austria, 13–16 September) focused on the technical, managerial, regulatory and legal issues related to implementing small satellite programmes. At the United Nations/International Astronautical Federation Workshop on Space for Human and Environmental Security (Cape Town, South Africa, 30 September–2 October), participants discussed space technologies, applications, information and services that contributed to sustainable economic and social development programmes supporting human and environmental security, as well as opportunities for increasing regional and international cooperation in that area. The United Nations/Viet Nam Workshop on Space Technology Applications for Socio-Economic Benefits (Hanoi, Viet Nam, 10–14 October) increased awareness of the socioeconomic benefits of space-technology applications at the national, regional and international levels, focusing on satellite remote sensing, satellite communications, GNSS, capacity-building and regional and international cooperation. At the United Nations/Nigeria Workshop on the International Space Weather Initiative (Abuja, Nigeria, 17–21 October), participants adopted the Abuja International Space Weather Initiative resolution, which called for the establishment of an international centre for space weather science and education at the Space Environment Research Centre of Kyushu University. The United Nations/Islamic Republic of Iran Regional Workshop on the Use of Space Technology for Improving Human Health (Tehran, Iran, 23–26 October) promoted awareness of the use of space technology applied to health care and reviewed the benefits of applications such as tele-epidemiology/telehealth/telemedicine and tele-education in medicine. The United Nations/Malaysia Expert Meeting on Human Space Technology (Putrajaya, Malaysia, 14–18 November) raised awareness about human space technology and its applications among Member States, and discussed how to promote the Human Space Technology Initiative. Finally, the United Nations and ICG sponsored the United Nations International Meeting on the Applications of GNSS (Vienna, 12–16 December), which marked 10 years of achievement of the United Nations in GNSS, as reflected in a November publication [ST/SPACE/55] of the Office for Outer Space Affairs.

Following its consideration of the report [A/AC.105/980] of the United Nations Expert on Space Applications describing 2010 activities, those scheduled for 2011 and the activities of UN-affiliated regional centres for space science and technology education scheduled for 2009–2012, the Subcommittee expressed concern over the Programme's limited financial resources and appealed to Member States for voluntary contributions.

The General Assembly, in resolution 66/71 (see p. 582), endorsed the Programme on Space Applications for 2012, as proposed by the Expert.

Scientific and technical issues

In 2011, the Scientific and Technical Subcommittee [A/AC.105/987] continued to consider matters relating to the collection of Earth observation satellite data for sustainable development and noted with satisfaction that significant efforts were being made to build the capacity of developing countries in using Earth observations to improve quality of life and advance their socioeconomic development. It took note of the number of continued launches of Earth observation satellites and the innovative research conducted using such satellites, data from which could be used to develop advanced, global-integrated Earth system models.

For its consideration of space debris, the Subcommittee had before it a Secretariat note [A/AC.105/978] containing replies from six Member States and one international organization on national research on space debris, as well as the safety of space objects with nuclear power sources (NPS) on board and problems relating to their collision with space debris. Also before the Subcommittee was a conference room paper [A/AC.105/C.1/2011/CRP.14] containing the report of the International Interdisciplinary Congress on Space Debris entitled "Towards long-term sustainability of space activities: overcoming the challenges of space debris". The Subcommittee noted that some States were implementing space debris mitigation measures consistent with the Space Debris Mitigation Guidelines of the Committee on the Peaceful Uses of Outer Space [YUN 2007, p. 604] and/or the Space Debris Mitigation Guidelines of the Inter-Agency Space Debris Coordination Committee, or that they had developed their own mitigation standards based on those guidelines. The Subcommittee agreed that Member States, in particular space-faring nations, should pay greater attention to the problem of collisions of space objects, including those with NPS on board, with space debris and to other aspects of space debris, including its re-entry into the atmosphere. It further agreed that research on space debris should continue and that Member States should make available to all interested parties the results of that research, including information on practices that had proved effective in minimizing the creation of space debris.

For its consideration of developments in GNSS, the Subcommittee had before it reports on the United Nations/Republic of Moldova/United States of America Workshop on Applications of GNSS [A/AC.105/974], and the United Nations/International Astronautical Federation Workshop on GNSS Applications for Human Benefit and Development [A/AC.105/984]. It expressed its appreciation to the Office for Outer Space Affairs, in its capacity as secretariat of ICG, for promoting the use of GNSS through capacity-building initiatives in developing countries. The Subcommittee had for its consideration a secretariat note on the Fifth (2010) Meeting of ICG [A/AC.105/982]. A March report [A/AC.105/996] of the secretariat took note of the 2010 activities carried out in the ICG framework.

The Subcommittee continued its consideration of the use of NPS in outer space and encouraged States and international intergovernmental organizations to begin or continue implementing the Safety Framework for Nuclear Power Source Applications in Outer Space [YUN 2009, p. 605]. The Subcommittee endorsed the report of the reconvened Working Group on the Use of Nuclear Power Sources in Outer Space, which was annexed to the Subcommittee's report and recalled the objectives of the Working Group's workplan for the period 2011–2015.

For its consideration of near-Earth objects, the Subcommittee had before it an interim report of the Action Team on Near-Earth Objects [A/AC.105/C.1/L.308], and a Secretariat note on information on research in the field of near-Earth objects carried out by member States of the Committee on Outer Space, international organizations and other entities [A/AC.105/976 & Add.1]. The Subcommittee agreed that national and international efforts to detect and track near-Earth objects should be continued and expanded. It reconvened its Working Group on Near-Earth Objects and endorsed the Working Group's report, which was annexed to the report of the Subcommittee and previewed the goals and intersessional activities of the Working Group for the period 2012–2013.

In accordance with resolution 65/97 [YUN 2010, p. 614], the Subcommittee considered the long-term sustainability of outer space activities. It had before it several conference room papers on the issue: three contained comments from member States and permanent observers of the Committee on Outer Space [A/AC.105/C.1/2011/CRP.9,17,20], and another provided a list of points of contact, as communicated to the Secretariat [A/AC.105/C.1/2011/CRP.10 & Add.1,2]. It reconvened its Working Group on the Long-term Sustainability of Outer Space Activities and considered a paper on the Working Group's terms of reference and working methods [A/AC.105/C.1/L.307], which were later adopted by the Committee on Outer Space at its fifty-fourth (2011) session. The report of the Working Group was endorsed by the Subcommittee and annexed to its report.

Also submitted to the Subcommittee were Secretariat notes on international cooperation in the peaceful uses of outer space [A/AC.105/977 & Add.1 & A/AC.105/C.1/2011/CRP.8] containing replies from 13 Member States on their space activities.

Space-based disaster management and emergency response

The Scientific and Technical Subcommittee, at its forty-eighth session in February [A/AC.105/987], had before it a report [A/AC.105/981] on the activities carried out in 2010 in the framework of the United Nations Platform for Space-based Information for Disaster Management and Emergency Response (UN-SPIDER), established by Assembly resolution 61/110 [YUN 2006, p. 748]; a report [A/AC.105/985] of the Secretariat on technical advisory support activities carried out in 2010 in the framework of UN-SPIDER; a Secretariat note [A/AC.105/C.1/2011/CRP.15] on the proposed UN-SPIDER workplan 2012–2013; and a report [A/AC.105/C.1/2011/CRP.16] on coordination activities carried out by the United Nations Office for Outer Space Affairs with mechanisms and initiatives supporting emergency response activities with space-based information. The Subcommittee heard a statement by the UN-SPIDER Programme Coordinator on activities carried out in 2010 and the implementation of activities planned for 2011. It noted with satisfaction the progress made with regard to the 2010 activities, including the support provided through the programme to emergency efforts in response to major disasters worldwide, as well as the activities of Member States that were increasing the availability and use of space-based solutions in support of disaster management. The Subcommittee reconvened its Working Group of the Whole and endorsed its report, which was annexed to the Subcommittee's report.

Three December reports, which were to be considered at the Subcommittee's forty-eighth (2012) session, dealt with the implementation of UN-SPIDER activities in 2011 [A/AC.105/1010]; technical advisory support activities carried out in 2011 in the UN-SPIDER framework [A/AC.105/1009]; and the 2011 activities of a one-year project on space-based information for crowdsource mapping being carried out in the UN-SPIDER framework [A/AC.105/1007]. The report on UN-SPIDER activities in 2011 highlighted several accomplishments, including the provision of technical advisory support to 23 countries, further improvement of the UN-SPIDER Knowledge Portal and the organization of or support to a number of international and regional workshops and expert meetings, such as the International Conference on Space-based Technologies for Disaster Risk Management: Best practices for risk reduction and rapid response mapping (Beijing, 22–25 November). The report on the provision of UN-SPIDER technical advisory support described such activities as they were carried out on a regional basis—namely, in Africa, Asia and the Pacific, Latin America and the Caribbean, West Asia, and small island developing States. It also summarized UN-SPIDER emergency response activities to assist Member States in the framework of the existing mechanisms and initiatives. Those activities were supported in seven emergency situations—namely, in the aftermath of the earthquakes in Japan and Pakistan, the floods in Ghana, Namibia, Nigeria and Thailand, and the severe drought experienced in the Horn of Africa. The report on crowdsource mapping noted that technological advancements had made it possible for volunteer and technical communities to provide increasing support to disaster preparedness and emergency response efforts through satellite imagery and other space-based technologies, such as telecommunications satellites and GNSS. Two international expert meetings (Vienna, 5–6 July and Geneva, 16 November) determined the areas in which UN-SPIDER could contribute to and harness support for established crowdsource mapping communities; that experts from those communities should be invited to participate in UN-SPIDER technical advisory missions and relevant meetings planned for 2012; and that UN-SPIDER should focus broadly on crowdsource mapping instead of just crisis mapping, ensuring the support of the volunteer and technical communities for the full disaster risk management cycle.

International Space Weather Initiative

In accordance with resolution 65/97 [YUN 2010, p. 614], the Scientific and Technical Subcommittee [A/AC.105/987] considered the International Space

Weather Initiative (2010–2012). The Subcommittee had before it a note [A/AC.105/979] by the Secretariat containing replies from seven Member States and four international organizations on regional and international activities related to the Initiative. The Subcommittee welcomed the fact that participation in the Initiative was open to all countries, and noted that the Initiative consisted of three elements: the instrument array programme to operate and deploy space weather instruments; the data coordination and analysis programme to develop predictive models using International Space Weather Initiative data; and training, education and public outreach programmes. A Steering Committee of 16 members, which served as the governing body of the Initiative, held its first meeting (Vienna, 9 February) to assess progress and establish priorities for the upcoming year.

Legal Subcommittee

The Legal Subcommittee, at its fiftieth session (Vienna, 28 March–8 April) [A/AC.105/990], considered the status and application of the five UN treaties on outer space (see p. 582); information on the activities of international organizations relating to space law; matters related to the definition and delimitation of outer space and the character and utilization of the geostationary orbit; the review and possible revision of the Principles Relevant to the Use of Nuclear Power Sources in Outer Space; the examination and review of developments concerning the draft protocol on matters specific to space assets to the Convention on International Interests in Mobile Equipment; capacity-building in space law; the exchange of information on national mechanisms relating to space debris mitigation measures; and the exchange of information on national legislation relevant to the peaceful exploration and use of outer space.

The Subcommittee reconvened its Working Group on the Status and Application of the Five United Nations Treaties on Outer Space [YUN 2001, p. 570], which recognized that its discussion should continue to include issues related to the Agreement Governing the Activities of States on the Moon and Other Celestial Bodies [YUN 1979, p. 111] and that it should reflect the actual needs of States conducting activities in outer space vis-à-vis the provisions of the relevant UN treaties. The Chair had prepared a questionnaire on matters relating to the status and application of the five UN treaties, which was welcomed as a good basis for discussion as it focused on questions of practical relevance and served to organize and rationalize the Working Group's work. The Working Group requested the Secretariat to prepare, for the fifty-first (2012) session of the Subcommittee, an updated version of its note on activities being carried out or to be carried out on the Moon and other celestial bodies, which it had considered at its forty-seventh (2008) session [YUN 2008, p. 693]. The Subcommittee endorsed the report of the Working Group and the recommendation that its mandate be extended for an additional year.

For its consideration of the activities of international intergovernmental organizations and non-governmental organizations (NGOs) relating to space law, the Subcommittee had before it a Secretariat note with information received from the Committee on Space Research, the European Centre for Space Law, Unidroit, the International Institute of Space Law, the International Law Association, Intersputnik, and the International Telecommunications Satellite Organization [A/AC.105/C.2/L.281 & Add.1]. The Subcommittee noted that the activities of intergovernmental organizations and NGOs relating to space law continued to contribute to the development of space law and agreed that it was important to continue the exchange of information on recent developments between the Subcommittee and those organizations.

For its consideration of capacity-building in space law, the Subcommittee had before it a report [A/AC.105/989] on the United Nations/Thailand Workshop on Space Law, the theme of which was "Activities of States in outer space in the light of new developments: meeting international responsibilities and establishing national legal and policy frameworks". Also before the Subcommittee were conference room papers containing a directory of education opportunities in space law [A/AC.105/C.2/2011/CRP.3]; the draft Education Curriculum on Space Law [A/AC.105/C.2/2011/CRP.5]; and information submitted by five member States on actions and initiatives to build capacity in space law [A/AC.105/C.2/2011/CRP.6,14]. The Subcommittee agreed that capacity-building, training and education in space law were of paramount importance to international, regional and national efforts to develop space activities and increase knowledge about their legal framework. It acknowledged the space law capacity-building efforts conducted by governmental and non-governmental entities and noted the work that was carried out by the Office for Outer Space Affairs, along with space law educators and representatives of the regional centres for space science and technology education, to develop the curriculum on space law.

The Subcommittee reconvened its Working Group on the Definition and Delimitation of Outer Space, which considered Secretariat notes on replies from Member States on questions on the definition and delimitation of outer space [A/AC.105/889/Add.7–9] and on related national legislation and practice [A/AC.105/865 & Add.8–10]. It also had before it a conference room paper [A/AC.105/C.2/2011/CRP.10] containing the replies of Austria and El Salvador. The Working Group noted that the Chair planned to present to the Legal Subcommittee, at its fifty-first (2012) session, a proposal on possible ways of finding a solution to matters relating to the definition and delimitation of outer space. The Subcommittee endorsed the report of the Working Group, which was annexed to its report.

For its discussion on the exchange of information on national legislation relevant to the peaceful exploration and use of outer space, the Subcommittee considered a Secretariat note [A/AC.105/957/Add.1] and two conference room papers [A/AC.105/C.2/2011/CRP.7,13] containing information from five Member States on national legislation governing their space activities. A further conference room paper [A/AC.105/C.2/2011/CRP.9] contained an overview of national regulatory frameworks for space activities. The Subcommittee reconvened its Working Group on National Legislation Relevant to the Peaceful Exploration and Use of Outer Space [YUN 2009, p. 607] and noted that the Working Group's discussions, which included information-sharing about the development of national space legislation, allowed States to gain an understanding of existing national regulatory frameworks. In light of the increasing number of space-related international cooperation programmes and projects, the Subcommittee also noted the importance of the development of space legislation, which played a significant role in regulating and promoting such cooperation activities. The Subcommittee endorsed the report of the Working Group, which was annexed to its report.

Treaties

Two space-related treaties were deposited with the Secretary-General: the 1974 Convention on Registration of Objects Launched into Outer Space [YUN 1974, p. 56], which entered into force in 1976 and had 55 States parties as at 31 December; and the 1979 Agreement Governing the Activities of States on the Moon and Other Celestial Bodies [YUN 1979, p. 111], which entered into force in 1984 and had 13 States parties.

The three other space-related treaties, also developed by the Legal Subcommittee, were the 1966 Treaty on Principles Governing the Activities of States in the Exploration and Use of Outer Space, including the Moon and Other Celestial bodies [YUN 1966, p. 41], which entered into force in 1967; the 1967 Agreement on the Rescue of Astronauts, the Return of Astronauts and the Return of Objects Launched into Outer Space [YUN 1967, p. 33], which entered into force in 1968; and the 1971 Convention for International Liability for Damage Caused by Space Objects [YUN 1971, p. 52], which entered into force in 1972.

UN system coordination

The Inter-Agency Meeting on Outer Space Activities, at its thirty-first session (Geneva, 16–18 March) [A/AC.105/992], discussed the coordination of UN system plans and programmes in the practical application of space technology; the use of spatial data and activities related to the United Nations Geographic Information Working Group and the United Nations Spatial Data Infrastructure; participation in the process of the Group on Earth Observations; and the operational framework and good practices in the use of space-based technologies for disaster risk reduction and emergency response.

Representatives of participating UN entities reported on their activities and plans for 2010 and 2011, the details of which were included in the Secretary-General's report [A/AC.105/961] on the coordination of space-related activities within the UN system: directions and anticipated results for the period 2010–2011.

In line with agreements made at its thirtieth session [YUN 2010, p. 611], the Inter-Agency Meeting submitted to its thirty-first (2011) session a special report [A/AC.105/991] on the use of space technology within the UN system to address climate change issues. The Meeting endorsed the special report, as amended, and noted that the report would be submitted for consideration to the Committee on the Peaceful Uses of Outer Space at its fifty-fourth (2011) session (see p. 577).

The Office for Outer Space Affairs, as the secretariat of the Inter-Agency Meeting, informed the Meeting about the work of the Committee on Outer Space and its subsidiary bodies; activities under the Basic Space Science Initiative and Human Space Technology Initiative of the United Nations Programme on Space Applications; and activities undertaken in the areas of global health, humanitarian assistance and water management. The Office also informed the Meeting about developments in the UN-SPIDER programme, including activities planned for 2011–2012.

GENERAL ASSEMBLY ACTION

On 9 December [meeting 81], the General Assembly, on the recommendation of the Fourth Committee [A/66/425], adopted **resolution 66/71** without vote [agenda item 51].

International cooperation in the peaceful uses of outer space

The General Assembly,

Recalling its resolutions 51/122 of 13 December 1996, 54/68 of 6 December 1999, 59/2 of 20 October 2004, 61/110 and 61/111 of 14 December 2006, 62/101 of 17 December 2007, 62/217 of 22 December 2007, 65/97 of 10 December 2010 and 65/271 of 7 April 2011,

Recognizing the extraordinary achievements made over the past fifty years in human space flight and space exploration for peaceful purposes, and recalling the unique platform at the global level for international cooperation in space activities represented by the Committee on the Peaceful Uses of Outer Space,

Deeply convinced of the common interest of mankind in promoting and expanding the exploration and use of outer space, as the province of all mankind, for peaceful purposes and in continuing efforts to extend to all States the benefits derived therefrom, and also of the importance of international cooperation in this field, for which the United Nations should continue to provide a focal point,

Reaffirming the importance of international cooperation in developing the rule of law, including the relevant norms of space law and their important role in international cooperation for the exploration and use of outer space for peaceful purposes, and of the widest possible adherence to international treaties that promote the peaceful uses of outer space in order to meet emerging new challenges, especially for developing countries,

Seriously concerned about the possibility of an arms race in outer space, and bearing in mind the importance of article IV of the Treaty on Principles Governing the Activities of States in the Exploration and Use of Outer Space, including the Moon and Other Celestial Bodies (Outer Space Treaty),

Recognizing that all States, in particular those with major space capabilities, should contribute actively to the goal of preventing an arms race in outer space as an essential condition for the promotion and strengthening of international cooperation in the exploration and use of outer space for peaceful purposes,

Recognizing also that space debris is an issue of concern to all nations,

Noting the progress achieved in the further development of peaceful space exploration and applications as well as in various national and cooperative space projects, which contributes to international cooperation, and the importance of further developing the legal framework to strengthen international cooperation in this field,

Convinced of the need to promote the use of space technology towards implementing the United Nations Millennium Declaration,

Seriously concerned about the devastating impact of disasters,

Desirous of enhancing international coordination and cooperation at the global level in disaster management and emergency response through greater access to and use of space-based services for all countries and facilitating capacity-building and institutional strengthening for disaster management, in particular in developing countries,

Deeply convinced that the use of space science and technology and their applications in areas such as telehealth, tele-education, disaster management, environmental protection and other Earth observation applications contribute to achieving the objectives of the global conferences of the United Nations that address various aspects of economic, social and cultural development, particularly poverty eradication,

Taking note, in that regard, of the fact that the 2005 World Summit recognized the important role that science and technology play in promoting sustainable development,

Having considered the report of the Committee on the Peaceful Uses of Outer Space on the work of its fifty-fourth session,

1. *Endorses* the report of the Committee on the Peaceful Uses of Outer Space on the work of its fifty-fourth session;

2. *Agrees* that the Committee on the Peaceful Uses of Outer Space, at its fifty-fifth session, should consider the substantive items recommended by the Committee at its fifty-fourth session, taking into account the concerns of all countries, in particular those of developing countries;

3. *Notes* that, at its fiftieth session, the Legal Subcommittee of the Committee on the Peaceful Uses of Outer Space continued its work, as mandated by the General Assembly in its resolution 65/97;

4. *Agrees* that the Legal Subcommittee, at its fifty-first session, should consider the substantive items and reconvene the working groups recommended by the Committee, taking into account the concerns of all countries, in particular those of developing countries;

5. *Urges* States that have not yet become parties to the international treaties governing the uses of outer space to give consideration to ratifying or acceding to those treaties in accordance with their domestic law, as well as incorporating them in their national legislation;

6. *Notes* that, at its forty-eighth session, the Scientific and Technical Subcommittee of the Committee on the Peaceful Uses of Outer Space continued its work, as mandated by the General Assembly in its resolution 65/97;

7. *Agrees* that the Scientific and Technical Subcommittee, at its forty-ninth session, should consider the substantive items and reconvene the working groups recommended by the Committee, taking into account the concerns of all countries, in particular those of developing countries;

8. *Notes with appreciation* that some States are already implementing space debris mitigation measures on a voluntary basis, through national mechanisms and consistent with the Space Debris Mitigation Guidelines of the Inter-Agency Space Debris Coordination Committee and with the Space Debris Mitigation Guidelines of the Committee on the Peaceful Uses of Outer Space, endorsed by the General Assembly in its resolution 62/217;

9. *Invites* other States to implement, through relevant national mechanisms, the Space Debris Mitigation Guidelines of the Committee on the Peaceful Uses of Outer Space;

10. *Considers* that it is essential that States pay more attention to the problem of collisions of space objects, including those with nuclear power sources, with space debris, and other aspects of space debris, calls for the continuation of national research on this question, for the development of improved technology for the monitoring of space debris and for the compilation and dissemination of data on space debris, also considers that, to the extent possible, information thereon should be provided to the Scientific and Technical Subcommittee, and agrees that international cooperation is needed to expand appropriate and affordable strategies to minimize the impact of space debris on future space missions;

11. *Urges* all States, in particular those with major space capabilities, to contribute actively to the goal of preventing an arms race in outer space as an essential condi-

tion for the promotion of international cooperation in the exploration and use of outer space for peaceful purposes;

12. *Endorses* the United Nations Programme on Space Applications for 2012, as proposed to the Committee by the Expert on Space Applications and endorsed by the Committee;

13. *Welcomes* the continuous progress made by the International Committee on Global Navigation Satellite Systems towards achieving compatibility and interoperability among global and regional space-based positioning, navigation and timing systems and in the promotion of the use of global navigation satellite systems and their integration into national infrastructure, particularly in developing countries, and notes with satisfaction that the International Committee held its sixth meeting in Tokyo from 5 to 9 September 2011;

14. *Notes with satisfaction* the progress made within the framework of the United Nations Platform for Space-based Information for Disaster Management and Emergency Response (UN-SPIDER) in the implementation of the workplan of the UN-SPIDER programme for the biennium 2010–2011, and encourages Member States to provide, on a voluntary basis, the programme with the necessary additional resources to ensure that greater support could be provided to Member States by UN-SPIDER and its regional support offices;

15. *Notes with appreciation* that the African regional centres for space science and technology education in the French and English languages, located in Morocco and Nigeria, respectively, as well as the Centre for Space Science and Technology Education in Asia and the Pacific and the Regional Centre for Space Science and Technology Education for Latin America and the Caribbean, affiliated to the United Nations, have continued their education programmes in 2011, and agrees that the regional centres should continue to report to the Committee on their activities;

16. *Emphasizes* that regional and interregional cooperation in the field of space activities is essential to strengthen the peaceful uses of outer space, assist States in the development of their space capabilities and contribute to the achievement of the goals of the United Nations Millennium Declaration and to that end requests relevant regional organizations to offer the assistance necessary so that countries can carry out recommendations of regional conferences;

17. *Recognizes*, in this regard, the important role played by conferences and other mechanisms in strengthening regional and international cooperation among States, such as the African Leadership Conference on Space Science and Technology for Sustainable Development, the Asia-Pacific Regional Space Agency Forum, the Asia-Pacific Space Cooperation Organization and the Space Conference of the Americas;

18. *Notes with satisfaction* that the Sixth Space Conference of the Americas was hosted by the Government of Mexico and held in Pachuca, Mexico, from 15 to 19 November 2010, welcomes the adoption of the Pachuca Declaration, and also notes with satisfaction that the Government of Mexico has assumed the pro tempore secretariat of the Conference for the period 2011–2013; that the fourth meeting of the Council of the Asia-Pacific Space Cooperation Organization was held in Pattaya, Thailand, on 26 and 27 January 2011; that the Fourth African Leadership Conference on Space Science and Technology for Sustainable Development was hosted by the Government of Kenya and held in Mombasa, Kenya, from 26 to 28 September 2011; and that the eighteenth session of the Asia-Pacific Regional Space Agency Forum will be jointly organized by the Singapore Space and Technology Association, the National University of Singapore and the Government of Japan and held in Singapore from 6 to 9 December 2011;

19. *Requests* the Committee to continue to consider, as a matter of priority, ways and means of maintaining outer space for peaceful purposes and to report thereon to the General Assembly at its sixty-seventh session, and agrees that during its consideration of the matter the Committee could continue to consider ways to promote regional and interregional cooperation and the role space technology could play in the implementation of recommendations of the World Summit on Sustainable Development;

20. *Recognizes* that space science and technology and their applications make important contributions to economic, social and cultural development and welfare, as indicated in the resolution entitled "The Space Millennium: Vienna Declaration on Space and Human Development", and its resolution 59/2, and notes with satisfaction that a number of the recommendations set out in the Plan of Action of the Committee on the Peaceful Uses of Outer Space on the implementation of the recommendations of the Third United Nations Conference on the Exploration and Peaceful Uses of Outer Space (UNISPACE III) have been implemented and that satisfactory progress is being made in implementing the outstanding recommendations through national and regional activities;

21. *Urges* all Member States to continue to contribute to the Trust Fund for the United Nations Programme on Space Applications to enhance the capacity of the Office for Outer Space Affairs of the Secretariat to provide technical and legal advisory services in accordance with the Plan of Action, while maintaining the priority thematic areas agreed by the Committee;

22. *Emphasizes* the need to increase the benefits of space technology and its applications and to contribute to an orderly growth of space activities favourable to sustained economic growth and sustainable development in all countries, including mitigation of the consequences of disasters, in particular in developing countries;

23. *Reiterates* that the benefits of space technology and its applications should continue to be brought to the attention, in particular, of the major United Nations conferences and summits for economic, social and cultural development and related fields and that the use of space technology should be promoted towards achieving the objectives of those conferences and summits and for implementing the United Nations Millennium Declaration;

24. *Welcomes* the increased efforts to strengthen further the Inter-Agency Meeting on Outer Space Activities and urges entities of the United Nations system, particularly those participating in the Inter-Agency Meeting, to continue to examine, in cooperation with the Committee, how space science and technology and their applications could contribute to implementing the United Nations Millennium Declaration on the development agenda, particularly in the areas relating to, inter alia, food security and increasing opportunities for education;

25. *Calls upon* the United Nations University and other institutions of the same nature, within the framework of their mandates, to provide training and to carry out research in the areas of international space law and, in particular, matters relating to disasters and emergencies;

26. *Agrees* that the Committee and its subsidiary bodies at their respective sessions in 2012 should elect their officers nominated for the period 2012–2013;

27. *Decides* that Azerbaijan shall become a member of the Committee;

28. *Endorses* the decision of the Committee to grant permanent observer status to the Association of Remote Sensing Centres in the Arab World;

29. *Notes* that each of the regional groups has the responsibility for actively promoting the participation in the work of the Committee and its subsidiary bodies of the States members of the Committee that are also members of the respective regional groups, and agrees that the regional groups should consider this Committee-related matter among their members;

30. *Notes with satisfaction* that a panel discussion was held at United Nations Headquarters on 11 October 2011 on the topic of the contribution of the Committee on the Peaceful Uses of Outer Space to the United Nations Conference on Sustainable Development, to be held in Rio de Janeiro, Brazil, in 2012, with attention given to the use of space-derived geospatial data for sustainable development and taking into account the previous panel discussions held on climate change, food security, global health and emergencies;

31. *Invites* the Group on Earth Observations to contribute to the preparatory process for the 2012 United Nations Conference on Sustainable Development by addressing issues related to the use of space-derived geospatial data for sustainable development;

32. *Requests* the entities of the United Nations system, other international organizations and the Secretary-General to continue and, where appropriate, to enhance their cooperation with the Committee and to provide it with reports on the issues dealt with in the work of the Committee and its subsidiary bodies, and to address the issues covered by the panel discussions held in conjunction with sessions of the General Assembly;

33. *Recalls* the fact that the General Assembly, by its resolution 65/271, declared 12 April the International Day of Human Space Flight;

34. *Notes with satisfaction* the commemorative segment of the fifty-fourth session of the Committee on the Peaceful Uses of Outer Space on the occasion of the fiftieth anniversary of human space flight and the fiftieth anniversary of the Committee on the Peaceful Uses of Outer Space, held at Vienna on 1 June 2011;

35. *Adopts* the Declaration on the Fiftieth Anniversary of Human Space Flight and the Fiftieth Anniversary of the Committee on the Peaceful Uses of Outer Space, set forth in the annex to the present resolution.

Annex

Declaration on the Fiftieth Anniversary of Human Space Flight and the Fiftieth Anniversary of the Committee on the Peaceful Uses of Outer Space

We, the States Members of the United Nations, in commemorating the fiftieth anniversary of human space flight and the fiftieth anniversary of the Committee on the Peaceful Uses of Outer Space,

1. *Recall* the launch into outer space of the first human-made Earth satellite, Sputnik I, on 4 October 1957, thus opening the way for space exploration;

2. *Also recall* that, on 12 April 1961, Yuri Gagarin became the first human to orbit the Earth, opening a new chapter of human endeavour in outer space;

3. *Further recall* the amazing history of human presence in outer space and the remarkable achievements since the first human spaceflight, in particular Valentina Tereshkova becoming the first woman to orbit the Earth on 16 June 1963, Neil Armstrong becoming the first human to set foot upon the surface of the Moon on 20 July 1969, and the docking of the Apollo and Soyuz spacecrafts on 17 July 1975, being the first international human mission in space, and recall that for the past decade humanity has maintained a multinational permanent human presence in outer space aboard the International Space Station;

4. *Respectfully recall* that the human exploration of outer space has not been without sacrifice, and remember the men and women who have lost their lives in the pursuit of expanding humanity's frontiers;

5. *Emphasize* the significant progress in the development of space science and technology and their applications that has enabled humans to explore the universe, and the extraordinary achievements made over the past fifty years in space exploration efforts, including deepening the understanding of the planetary system and the Sun and the Earth itself, in the use of space science and technology for the benefit of all humankind and in the development of the international legal regime governing space activities;

6. *Recall* the entry into force of the Treaty on Principles Governing the Activities of States in the Exploration and Use of Outer Space, including the Moon and Other Celestial Bodies (Outer Space Treaty) on 10 October 1967, which establishes the fundamental principles of international space law;

7. *Also recall* the first meeting of the permanent Committee on the Peaceful Uses of Outer Space, convened on 27 November 1961, which facilitated the adoption of General Assembly resolutions 1721 A to E (XVI) of 20 December 1961, including resolution 1721 A (XVI), in which the first legal principles were commended to States for their guidance in space activities, and resolution 1721 B (XVI), in which the Assembly expressed its belief that the United Nations should provide a focal point for international cooperation in the peaceful exploration and use of outer space;

8. *Recognize* that the Committee on the Peaceful Uses of Outer Space, assisted by the Office for Outer Space Affairs of the Secretariat, has for the past fifty years served as a unique platform at the global level for international cooperation in space activities and that the Committee and its subsidiary bodies stand at the forefront in bringing the world together in using space science and technology to preserve the Earth and the space environment and ensure the future of human civilization;

9. *Acknowledge* that significant changes have occurred in the structure and content of the space endeavour, as reflected in the emergence of new technologies and the increasing number of actors at all levels, and therefore note with satisfaction the progress made in strengthening international cooperation in the peaceful uses of outer space by

enhancing the capacity of States for economic, social and cultural development and by strengthening the regulatory frameworks and mechanisms to that effect;

10. *Reaffirm* the importance of international cooperation in developing the rule of law, including the relevant norms of space law, and of the widest possible adherence to the international treaties that promote the peaceful uses of outer space;

11. *Express our firm conviction* that space science and technology and their applications, such as satellite communications, Earth observation systems and satellite navigation technologies, provide indispensable tools for viable long-term solutions for sustainable development and can contribute more effectively to efforts to promote the development of all countries and regions of the world, to improve people's lives, to conserve natural resources and to enhance the preparedness for and mitigation of the consequences of disasters;

12. *Express our deep concern* about the fragility of the space environment and the challenges to the long-term sustainability of outer space activities, in particular the impact of space debris;

13. *Stress* the need to look more closely into how advanced space research and exploration systems and technologies could further contribute to meeting challenges, including that of global climate change, and to food security and global health, and endeavour to examine how the outcomes and spin-offs of scientific research in human space flight could increase the benefits, in particular for developing countries;

14. *Emphasize* that regional and interregional cooperation in the field of space activities is essential to strengthen the peaceful uses of outer space, assist States in the development of their space capabilities and contribute to the achievement of the goals of the United Nations Millennium Declaration;

15. *Confirm* the need for closer coordination between the Committee on the Peaceful Uses of Outer Space and other intergovernmental bodies involved in the global development agenda of the United Nations, including with respect to the major United Nations conferences and summits for economic, social and cultural development;

16. *Call upon* all States to take measures at the national, regional, interregional and global levels to engage in the common efforts to use space science and technology and their applications to preserve planet Earth and its space environment for future generations.

Effects of atomic radiation

Report of Scientific Committee. At its fifty-eighth session (Vienna, 23–27 May) [A/66/46], the United Nations Scientific Committee on the Effects of Atomic Radiation continued to undertake broad assessments of the sources of ionizing radiation and its effects on human health and the environment, including activities related to the Chernobyl accident of 1986 and the radiological situation in the Marshall Islands. In terms of the levels and effects of radiation, the Committee considered the implications of the nuclear power plant accident following the east-Japan earthquake and tsunami in March. The emergency situation was still in progress at the time of the session, and it was likely that data from the accident would take months to analyse. The Committee recommended that the compilation of all relevant data and information be started as soon as possible. It envisaged a preliminary document for consideration at its fifty-ninth (2012) session and a more complete report for its sixtieth (2013) session.

The Committee took note of the twenty-fifth anniversary of the Chernobyl accident and acknowledged that the secretariat had arranged for a presentation of the results of the Committee's 2008 assessment of health effects due to radiation from the accident at the international scientific conference entitled "Twenty-five years after the Chernobyl accident: safety for the future" (Kyiv, Ukraine, 20–22 April).

Recognizing that by resolution 65/96 [YUN 2010, p. 618] the General Assembly had requested the Secretary-General to report on the effects of atomic radiation in the Marshall Islands (see below), the Committee agreed to offer a summary of its assessments on the topic to the Secretary-General.

Reports of Secretary-General. Pursuant to General Assembly resolution 65/96 [YUN 2010, p. 618], the Secretary-General submitted a September report [A/66/378] on the effects of atomic radiation in the Marshall Islands, which summarized the assessments undertaken on the topic over several decades by the United Nations Scientific Committee on the Effects of Atomic Radiation and others. The Secretary-General concluded by reaffirming the objective of Assembly resolution 64/35 [YUN 2009, p. 518]: that every effort should be made to end nuclear tests in order to avert devastating and harmful effects on the lives and health of people and the environment, and that the end of nuclear tests was one of the key means of achieving the goal of a nuclear-weapon-free world.

Also in response to Assembly resolution 65/96 [YUN 2010, p. 618], the Secretary-General submitted an October report [A/66/524] on the objective criteria and indicators to be equitably applied to determine membership that would best support the work of the United Nations Committee on the Effects of Atomic Radiation, and on the financial implications of increased membership. The secretariat noted that any changes made to the membership of the Committee ought to be primarily aimed at enhancing the effectiveness of its substantive work, while maintaining its scientific authority and independence of judgement, and respecting the desire for equitable geographical distribution. It suggested that the Assembly consider the development of a two-phased approach, consisting of a decision on the maximum size of the Committee for its effectiveness and efficiency, and determining the basis for any future changes in membership; and a special decision regarding the six applicant countries that, in 2007, expressed their desire to become Committee members.

In December, by resolution 66/70 (see below), the General Assembly decided to increase the membership of the Scientific Committee from 21 to 27 States and invited Belarus, Finland, Pakistan, the Republic of Korea, Spain and Ukraine to become members.

High-level meeting. The Secretary-General convened a high-level meeting on nuclear safety and security on 22 September. In advance of the meeting, the Secretary-General issued a report [SG/HLM/2011/1] with the findings of a UN system-wide study on the implications of the 11 March accident at the Fukushima Daiichi nuclear power plant in Japan; the accident occurred when the plant was struck by a tsunami that was triggered by a major earthquake in the eastern part of the country. The report comprised contributions from 16 UN entities and was organized into three sections. The first section focused on peaceful uses of nuclear energy and nuclear safety by addressing International Atomic Energy Agency (IAEA) safeguards; agriculture and food security; the environment; health; and sustainable development and financing. The second section focused on nuclear safety and security, including the role of IAEA; the nexus between nuclear safety and security; natural disasters; and climate change. The third section discussed the international emergency response framework in the case of nuclear accidents and addressed the adequacy of disaster preparedness measures; cooperation between international organizations; and the development of new monitoring and scientific capabilities. In the summary of the high-level meeting [A/C.4/66/8], the Secretary-General underscored the need to ensure public confidence and trust through transparency and openness in all aspects of nuclear energy; to strengthen nuclear safety as well as the international framework by implementing and revising relevant conventions; to build a stronger connection between nuclear safety and nuclear security; to strengthen the link between the international nuclear response system and the international humanitarian coordination system; and for States to review and strengthen their emergency preparedness and response arrangements and capabilities.

Communication. In a letter dated 10 October [A/C.4/66/8], the Secretary-General transmitted the Chair's summary of the High-level Meeting on Nuclear Safety and Security (New York, 22 September) to the President of the General Assembly as a basis for consideration of the matter in the Fourth Committee and in plenary.

GENERAL ASSEMBLY ACTION

On 9 December [meeting 81], the General Assembly, on the recommendation of the Fourth Committee [A/66/424], adopted **resolution 66/70** without vote [agenda item 50].

Effects of atomic radiation

The General Assembly,

Recalling its resolution 913(X) of 3 December 1955, by which it established the United Nations Scientific Committee on the Effects of Atomic Radiation, and its subsequent resolutions on the subject, in which, inter alia, it requested the Scientific Committee to continue its work,

Concerned about the potentially harmful effects on present and future generations resulting from the levels of radiation to which mankind and the environment are exposed,

Conscious of the continuing need to examine and compile information about atomic and ionizing radiation and to analyse its effects on mankind and the environment, and conscious also of the increased volume, complexity and diversity of that information,

Acknowledging the concerns about the radiological consequences of an accident which were raised by the accident at the Fukushima Daiichi nuclear power station following the March 2011 earthquake and tsunami in Japan,

Recalling the twenty-fifth anniversary of the nuclear accident at Chernobyl,

Recalling also the High-level Meeting on Nuclear Safety and Security convened in New York on 22 September 2011,

Recalling further that the Secretary-General invited the General Assembly to provide the Scientific Committee with the necessary capacity and resources to accomplish its tasks,

Reaffirming the desirability of the Scientific Committee continuing its work, and welcoming the increased commitment of States members of the Scientific Committee,

Emphasizing the vital need for sufficient, assured and predictable funding, as well as efficient management, of the work of the secretariat of the Scientific Committee to arrange the annual sessions and coordinate the development of documents based on scientific reviews of the sources of ionizing radiation and its effects on human health and the environment,

Recalling the tenth preambular paragraph of its resolution 65/96 of 10 December 2010, and noting with appreciation that the new P-4 post for the secretariat of the Scientific Committee has been filled,

Recognizing the increasing importance of the scientific work of the Scientific Committee and the need to carry out unforeseen additional work in cases such as the nuclear accident in Japan,

Recognizing also the importance of voluntary contributions to the general trust fund established by the Executive Director of the United Nations Environment Programme to support the work of the Scientific Committee,

Considering that the high quality of the work of the Scientific Committee needs to be maintained in the future,

Recognizing the importance of disseminating results from the work of the Scientific Committee and widely publicizing scientific knowledge about atomic radiation, and recalling, in that context, principle 10 of the Rio Declaration on Environment and Development,

Acknowledging that Belarus, Finland, Pakistan, the Republic of Korea, Spain and Ukraine had informed the President of the General Assembly before 28 February 2007, in accordance with paragraph 14 of Assembly resolution 61/109 of 14 December 2006, of their desire to become members of the Scientific Committee,

Welcoming the attendance of Belarus, Finland, Pakistan, the Republic of Korea, Spain and Ukraine as observers at the fifty-sixth, fifty-seventh and fifty-eighth sessions of the Scientific Committee,

1. *Commends* the United Nations Scientific Committee on the Effects of Atomic Radiation for the valuable contribution it has been making since its inception to wider knowledge and understanding of the levels, effects and risks of ionizing radiation, and for fulfilling its original mandate with scientific authority and independence of judgement;

2. *Reaffirms* the decision to maintain the present functions and independent role of the Scientific Committee;

3. *Takes note with appreciation* of the work of the Scientific Committee and notes the report on its fifty-eighth session;

4. *Requests* the Scientific Committee to continue its work, including its important activities to increase knowledge of the levels, effects and risks of ionizing radiation from all sources, and to report thereon to the General Assembly at its sixty-seventh session;

5. *Endorses* the intentions and plans of the Scientific Committee for conducting its programme of work of scientific review and assessment on behalf of the General Assembly, in particular its decision to conduct a full assessment of the levels of exposure and radiation risks attributable to the accident following the great east-Japan earthquake and tsunami, calls upon the Scientific Committee to submit to the Assembly at its sixty-seventh session the report requested by the Assembly on the attributability of health effects from radiation exposure, encourages the Scientific Committee at its earliest convenience to submit the other related reports, including on assessments of levels of ionizing radiation from electrical energy production, as well as on the effects on human health and the environment, and requests the Scientific Committee to submit plans for its ongoing and future programme of work to the Assembly at its sixty-seventh session;

6. *Calls upon* the Secretariat to facilitate the timely publication of the reports of the Scientific Committee, inter alia, by continuing to streamline internal procedures as necessary, and to strive to publish the reports within the same calendar year as their approval;

7. *Re-emphasizes* the need for the Scientific Committee to hold regular sessions on an annual basis so that its report can reflect the latest developments and findings in the field of ionizing radiation and thereby provide updated information for dissemination among all States;

8. *Invites* the Scientific Committee to continue its consultations with scientists and experts from interested Member States in the process of preparing its future scientific reports, and requests the Secretariat to facilitate such consultations;

9. *Welcomes*, in this context, the readiness of Member States to provide the Scientific Committee with relevant information on the levels and effects of ionizing radiation, and invites the Scientific Committee to analyse and give due consideration to such information, particularly in the light of its own findings;

10. *Also welcomes* the strategy of the Scientific Committee to improve data collection, encourages in this regard Member States, the organizations of the United Nations system and non-governmental organizations concerned to provide further relevant data about doses, effects and risks from various sources of radiation, which would greatly help in the preparation of future reports of the Scientific Committee to the General Assembly, and further encourages the International Atomic Energy Agency, the World Health Organization and other relevant organizations to establish and coordinate with the Secretariat the arrangements for periodic collection and exchange of data on radiation exposures of workers, the general public, and, in particular, medical patients;

11. *Requests* the United Nations Environment Programme to continue and strengthen, as appropriate, support for the effective conduct of the work of the Scientific Committee and for the dissemination of its findings to the General Assembly, the scientific community and the public;

12. *Urges* the United Nations Environment Programme to continue to strengthen the funding of the Scientific Committee, pursuant to paragraph 11 of General Assembly resolution 65/96;

13. *Encourages* Member States to make voluntary contributions to the general trust fund established by the Executive Director of the United Nations Environment Programme and also to make contributions in kind in order to support the work of the Scientific Committee;

14. *Takes note* of the report of the Secretary-General regarding the effects of atomic radiation in the Marshall Islands;

15. *Also takes note* of the report of the Secretary-General on the objective criteria and indicators to determine membership that would best support the essential work of the Scientific Committee and the financial implications of increased membership;

16. *Decides* to increase the membership of the Scientific Committee from twenty-one to twenty-seven States, on the understanding that the increase in membership can be achieved from within existing resources for the biennium 2012–2013, and requests the Secretariat and Member States to use the budget and the meeting time allocated to the work of the Scientific Committee in the most efficient manner in order to best avoid additional budgetary implications of the increased membership in the future;

17. *Invites* Belarus, Finland, Pakistan, the Republic of Korea, Spain and Ukraine to become members of the Scientific Committee, and requests the Government of each of those States to designate one scientist, with alternates and consultants, as appropriate, to be its representative in the Committee;

18. *Requests* the Secretary-General to report to the General Assembly at its sixty-ninth session on the experience of the increase in the membership of the Scientific Committee to twenty-seven States regarding its effectiveness, quality of work and equitable geographical distribution, as well as on options for further increase procedures;

19. *Decides* to next consider reviewing the possible increase in the membership of the Scientific Committee at its seventy-second session, taking into account new expres-

sions of interest in membership received by the Secretary-General between the sixty-sixth and seventy-second sessions of the General Assembly, all previous resolutions of the Assembly and, as appropriate, all relevant reports of the Secretary-General on the Scientific Committee as well as the principle of equitable geographical distribution and the need to ensure the effectiveness and the quality of work of the Scientific Committee, with a view to establishing a procedure at the seventy-third session for the possible further increase in the membership, and requests the Secretary-General to duly inform all Member States about this procedure.

Information security

In response to General Assembly resolution 65/41 [YUN 2010, p. 620], the Secretary-General issued a report [A/66/152 & Add.1] transmitting the views of 12 Member States on their general appreciation of issues of information security; national efforts to strengthen information security and promote international cooperation in that field; the content of international concepts aimed at strengthening the security of global information and telecommunications systems; and possible measures the international community could take to strengthen information security at the global level.

Communication. A 12 September letter [A/66/359] to the Secretary-General from China, the Russian Federation, Tajikistan and Uzbekistan contained a draft resolution on an international code of conduct for information security and called for international deliberations on the code within the UN framework.

GENERAL ASSEMBLY ACTION

On 2 December [meeting 71], the General Assembly, on the recommendation of the First Committee [A/66/407], adopted **resolution 66/24** without vote [agenda item 93].

Developments in the field of information and telecommunications in the context of international security

The General Assembly,

Recalling its resolutions 53/70 of 4 December 1998, 54/49 of 1 December 1999, 55/28 of 20 November 2000, 56/19 of 29 November 2001, 57/53 of 22 November 2002, 58/32 of 8 December 2003, 59/61 of 3 December 2004, 60/45 of 8 December 2005, 61/54 of 6 December 2006, 62/17 of 5 December 2007, 63/37 of 2 December 2008, 64/25 of 2 December 2009 and 65/41 of 8 December 2010,

Recalling also its resolutions on the role of science and technology in the context of international security, in which, inter alia, it recognized that scientific and technological developments could have both civilian and military applications and that progress in science and technology for civilian applications needed to be maintained and encouraged,

Noting that considerable progress has been made in developing and applying the latest information technologies and means of telecommunication,

Affirming that it sees in this process the broadest positive opportunities for the further development of civilization, the expansion of opportunities for cooperation for the common good of all States, the enhancement of the creative potential of humankind and additional improvements in the circulation of information in the global community,

Recalling, in this connection, the approaches and principles outlined at the Information Society and Development Conference, held in Midrand, South Africa, from 13 to 15 May 1996,

Bearing in mind the results of the Ministerial Conference on Terrorism, held in Paris on 30 July 1996, and the recommendations that were made,

Bearing in mind also the results of the World Summit on the Information Society, held in Geneva from 10 to 12 December 2003 (first phase) and in Tunis from 16 to 18 November 2005 (second phase),

Noting that the dissemination and use of information technologies and means affect the interests of the entire international community and that optimum effectiveness is enhanced by broad international cooperation,

Expressing concern that these technologies and means can potentially be used for purposes that are inconsistent with the objectives of maintaining international stability and security and may adversely affect the integrity of the infrastructure of States to the detriment of their security in both civil and military fields,

Considering that it is necessary to prevent the use of information resources or technologies for criminal or terrorist purposes,

Noting the contribution of those Member States that have submitted their assessments on issues of information security to the Secretary-General pursuant to paragraphs 1 to 3 of resolutions 53/70, 54/49, 55/28, 56/19, 57/53, 58/32, 59/61, 60/45, 61/54, 62/17, 63/37, 64/25 and 65/41,

Taking note of the reports of the Secretary-General containing those assessments,

Welcoming the initiative taken by the Secretariat and the United Nations Institute for Disarmament Research in convening international meetings of experts in Geneva in August 1999 and April 2008 on developments in the field of information and telecommunications in the context of international security, as well as the results of those meetings,

Considering that the assessments of the Member States contained in the reports of the Secretary-General and the international meetings of experts have contributed to a better understanding of the substance of issues of international information security and related notions,

Bearing in mind that the Secretary-General, in fulfilment of resolution 60/45, established in 2009, on the basis of equitable geographical distribution, a group of governmental experts, which, in accordance with its mandate, considered existing and potential threats in the sphere of information security and possible cooperative measures to address them and conducted a study on relevant international concepts aimed at strengthening the security of global information and telecommunications systems,

Welcoming the effective work of the Group of Governmental Experts on Developments in the Field of Information and Telecommunications in the Context of International Security and the relevant report transmitted by the Secretary-General,

Taking note of the assessments and recommendations contained in the report of the Group of Governmental Experts,

1. *Calls upon* Member States to promote further at multilateral levels the consideration of existing and potential threats in the field of information security, as well as possible strategies to address the threats emerging in this field, consistent with the need to preserve the free flow of information;

2. *Considers* that the purpose of such strategies could be served through further examination of relevant international concepts aimed at strengthening the security of global information and telecommunications systems;

3. *Invites* all Member States, taking into account the assessments and recommendations contained in the report of the Group of Governmental Experts on Developments in the Field of Information and Telecommunications in the Context of International Security, to continue to inform the Secretary-General of their views and assessments on the following questions:

   (*a*) General appreciation of the issues of information security;

   (*b*) Efforts taken at the national level to strengthen information security and promote international cooperation in this field;

   (*c*) The content of the concepts mentioned in paragraph 2 above;

   (*d*) Possible measures that could be taken by the international community to strengthen information security at the global level;

4. *Requests* the Secretary-General, with the assistance of a group of governmental experts, to be established in 2012 on the basis of equitable geographical distribution, taking into account the assessments and recommendations contained in the above-mentioned report, to continue to study existing and potential threats in the sphere of information security and possible cooperative measures to address them, including norms, rules or principles of responsible behaviour of States and confidence-building measures with regard to information space, as well as the concepts referred to in paragraph 2 above, and to submit to the General Assembly at its sixty-eighth session a report on the results of this study;

5. *Decides* to include in the provisional agenda of its sixty-seventh session the item entitled "Developments in the field of information and telecommunications in the context of international security".

Information

UN public information

Oversight activities

OIOS report. In response to General Assembly resolution 62/236 [YUN 2007, p. 1447], the Office of Internal Oversight Services (oios) submitted a report [A/66/180] highlighting the results of a review of the organizational framework of the public information function of the Secretariat, including the resources dedicated to that sphere of work. The review covered all departments of the Secretariat and all duty stations, field missions and entities subject to oios oversight.

Oios found that the public information function and its organizational framework had grown larger than the original department established for that role, with 2,113 full-time posts and nearly $50 million dollars in non-post resources devoted to the function. Activities were undertaken by decentralized public information offices, providing information on respective mandates. They constituted the link between the public and the United Nations, particularly at field-based missions where public support was critical. While the coordination of public information was rated as efficient overall, it was largely informal and challenged by differing mandates, a lack of clear direction and vision from senior leadership, and the unclear role and lack of a coordination mandate of the Department of Public Information (DPI). Oios recommended that the Department develop and present to the Committee on Information (see below) an action plan that considered the roles and responsibilities for coordinating the public information function in the Secretariat, including the role of DPI; the role of other Secretariat entities; the priorities of coordination activities; the need for a strategic plan for public information and communications; and the need to maintain data on post and non-post resources with levels and funding sources dedicated to public information.

Committee on Information

The General Assembly's Committee on Information, at its thirty-third session (New York, 26 April–7 May) [A/66/21], continued to consider UN information policies and activities, and to evaluate and follow up on efforts made and progress achieved in information and communications.

The Committee had before it three reports of the Secretary-General on activities of DPI from July 2010 to February 2011, which addressed the following areas: strategic communications services [A/AC.198/2011/2], with a review of communications campaigns and UN information centre (UNIC) activities; news services [A/AC.198/2011/3], with a summary of news and media-related products, activities and services; and outreach services [A/AC.198/2011/4], with a presentation of the Department's work with civil society groups, Member States, young people and the general public.

DPI activities

In response to General Assembly resolution 65/107 B [YUN 2010, p. 624], the Secretary-General submitted an August report [A/66/261] on questions relating to information, covering the activities of DPI since his reports to the Committee on Information in February.

Leading up to the United Nations Conference on Sustainable Development in 2012, the strategic communications services of DPI promoted informed discussion on sustainable development and related issues, such as forests, oceans, biodiversity and climate change. By producing press and information materials and/or developing and launching websites, DPI also provided communications support to the High-level Meeting of the Joint United Nations Programme on HIV/AIDS (see p. 1135) and the fifty-fifth session of the Commission on the Status of Women (see p. 1092), including the "UNiTE to End Violence against Women" campaign of the Secretary-General. The Department supported the United Nations Entity for Gender Equality and the Empowerment of Women by promoting its launch at the end of February. Women's issues were further promoted by the United Nations Regional Information Centre (UNRIC) Brussels, UNIC Ankara and UNIC Sana'a. In the lead-up to the High-Level Meeting of the General Assembly on the Prevention and Control of Non-communicable Diseases (see p. 1146), the Department organized a media forum in partnership with the American Cancer Society. For the second observance of Nelson Mandela International Day, the Department focused its campaign on the theme "Take action! Inspire change" to encourage people to devote 67 minutes of their time to public service in honour of Nelson Mandela's 67-year struggle for freedom and equal rights. On the International Day for the Elimination of Racial Discrimination, in addition to a range of outreach activities by the UNIC network, a videoconference on racial discrimination with a special focus on people of African descent was organized at Headquarters for 200 middle- and high-school students from Canada, Trinidad and Tobago and the United States. The Department marked the seventeenth annual commemoration of the genocide in Rwanda under the theme "Rebuilding Rwanda: reconciliation and education", and organized a memorial ceremony at Headquarters in cooperation with the Permanent Mission of Rwanda. The international media seminar on peace in the Middle East (Budapest, Hungary, 12–13 July), which was organized by DPI and co-hosted by Hungary, brought together about 100 current and former policymakers from Israel and the Palestinian Authority. Participants examined the peace process in the light of the changing political landscape in the Arab world and discussed the role of new and visual media in promoting the peace agenda. With a focus on innovation and integration in the digital sphere and new recruitment policies for field staff, DPI, the Department of Peacekeeping Operations and the Department of Field Support held their eighth annual training workshop at the United Nations Regional Service Centre at Entebbe, Uganda from 18 to 21 April. Further communications support was provided to the New Partnership for Africa's Development and the commemoration of the International Year of Youth.

Outreach services and programmes included preparations for the sixty-fourth Annual United Nations Department of Public Information/Non-Governmental Organizations Conference, entitled "Sustainable societies; responsive citizens" (Bonn, Germany, 3–5 September). The Conference outcomes would contribute to the Assembly's special session on the tenth anniversary of the International Year of Volunteers (see p. 857). In the wake of the earthquake and tsunami of 11 March (see p. 963), a number of UN messengers of peace and goodwill ambassadors joined the Secretary-General in recording video messages of solidarity with the people of Japan. The messages, which were transmitted to the affected populations through Japanese broadcast and online partners, UNICs and the Organization's social media channels, were viewed over 200,000 times online. The United Nations Academic Impact [YUN 2009, p. 618] continued to expand. Over 660 institutions of higher education and research in 104 countries had entered into a global partnership with the United Nations by mid-July. To engage the nearly 1 million annual visitors who viewed the rotating roster of public exhibitions curated and installed by DPI in the Headquarters Visitors' Lobby, seven exhibitions were organized on the following topics: remembrance of the victims of slavery and the transatlantic slave trade; the work of the United Nations Mine Action Service to save lives and protect livelihoods; global progress in combating malaria; honouring victims of the Chernobyl accident 25 years after the disaster; democracy projects in five world regions; the importance of water to indigenous peoples' way of life; and UN peacekeeping efforts to improve the rule of law in war-torn countries. In addition, work continued on the expansion of the Department's e-publishing programme. This included entering into an e-book distribution agreement with JSTOR—a digital library of academic journals and books; the publication of 31 new e-books for mobile devices; and plans to convert more than 300 popular UN titles into formats suitable for those devices.

UN website, multilingualism and accessibility

In 2011, structural elements of the Organization's website were realigned to improve navigation and expand the use of common branding elements with a view to enhancing consistency and coherence of presentation. In addition, new web pages were created in the six UN official languages for observances mandated by the General Assembly. From the beginning of the year, reports on website traffic were based on data collected through the use of Google Analytics, which facilitated the analysis of usage trends by language, geographical region, specific sites and date ranges. The Department continued to build on cooperative arrangements established with universities in Belarus, China and Spain for the translation of web content into Russian, Chinese and Spanish, respectively. In collaboration with the Arabic Translation Service of the Department for General Assembly and Conference Management, the Arabic Website Unit of DPI provided translation into Arabic. As part of its efforts to ensure that the UN website was accessible to people with disabilities, including those with visual, hearing and motion impairments, DPI incorporated the use of captioning into the production of daily news videos on the Organization's home page and was working to extend captioning to other DPI videos.

Radio, television, video and photo services

UN Radio increased the frequency of updates to partners by sending e-mail alerts to radio stations promoting daily coverage. It also expanded its story coverage by adding spot reports from the field, in part by making greater use of the Skype application to conduct interviews. The Radio Section produced special features and related interviews on the International Day of Remembrance of the Victims of Slavery and the Transatlantic Slave Trade, the International Day of United Nations Peacekeepers and the High-level Meeting on HIV/AIDS (see p. 1135). A new radio interview feature called "From the field" was launched to enable UN officials to talk about completed missions.

UN Television provided live coverage of numerous events, including the High-level Meeting on HIV/AIDS and the Fourth United Nations Conference on the Least Developed Countries (see p. 827), which was broadcast live on Facebook—a first for a UN conference held away from Headquarters. The Department's flagship television news magazine series, *21st Century*, which was aired by more than 60 international broadcasters, continued to gain recognition. *UN in Action*, a short-format series produced in four UN languages, expanded the scope of its coverage to highlight the Organization's work in areas such as economic and social development, the environment, human rights and health. With the Office for the Coordination of Humanitarian Affairs, DPI co-produced *The World in a Day*, a film featuring the Secretary-General, as well as a video of a visit of the Secretary-General to Nigeria and Ethiopia to highlight the issue of maternal health. DPI continued to expand the reach of programmes produced by UN Television, including through the screening of several features on human rights and socioeconomic issues at the Latin American Studies department at Yale University; a feature story on the use of rape as a weapon of war in Bosnia and Herzegovina at a session of the Human Rights Council in Geneva, at the Munich Film Festival and in the context of the "UNiTE to End Violence against Women" campaign in New York; and a film about Afghan migrants in Greece at the United Nations Association of New York. The Centro Niemeyer in Asturias, Spain, organized a major UN film series that included historical and prize-winning films from the Organization's film and video archives. Through its live streaming service and by providing on-demand access to archival material, UN Webcast made available more than 1,100 video clips and played a key role in the production and distribution of the daily news videos for the UN home page. UN Photo covered nearly 650 events, including the visits of the Secretary-General to 33 countries; about 3,000 images were made available to the public.

Library and knowledge services

The Dag Hammarskjöld Library resumed training activities following the reopening of its training space. Between March and June, 1,370 UN staff members, delegates, representatives of NGOs and others participated in library training programmes. Initial results from the data-collection exercise for the review of UN depository libraries indicated that 87 per cent of the libraries wanted more training in the use of UN information resources. In response to users' needs for quality information at any time and at any location, the Library was transitioning from print collections to electronic resources and preparing new mechanisms for the delivery of electronic resources onto the desktops of staff members worldwide. At the same time, the Library continued to ensure the preservation and accessibility of the Organization's published records since 1946. Having completed the main series of Security Council documents, the digitization programme was shifting its focus to earlier General Assembly documentation. In the period from March through June, bibliographic metadata records were created for 6,600 UN documents and publications to ensure their easy retrieval; by 30 June, 860,700 bibliographic metadata records had been recorded in UNBISnet, providing a complete voting history on all Assembly and Council resolutions.

UN information centres

The UNIC network, composed of 63 information centres, services and components around the world, served as the DPI field presence. In 2011, the centres continued to: forge partnerships with Governments, media organizations, NGOs, academic institutions and other civil society entities; increase collaborative arrangements with national broadcasters; and organize training courses to build the communications capacity of dpi field staff. A monthly film screening—"Cine ONU"—and debate organized by unric Brussels expanded to other countries, including France, Germany, Iceland and Israel. Unic New Delhi held the eighth edition of the We Care Film Fest, an annual international festival of documentary films on disability issues launched by the ngo Brotherhood. With support from the UN Communications Group in Pakistan and in collaboration with Search for Common Ground, unic Islamabad broadcasted 12 feature radio programmes on UN priority issues throughout the country. Unic Mexico City concluded an agreement with the Instituto Latinoamericano de la Comunicación Educativa with the aim of improving the quality of education in Latin America. The Government of Angola advised dpi of the approval of plans for a unic in Luanda to serve the needs of the Portuguese-speaking countries in Africa. Vacancies for the new centre had been classified, the director's post had been advertised and the preparation of a host country agreement was under way.

GENERAL ASSEMBLY ACTION

On 9 December [meeting 81], the General Assembly, on the recommendation of the Fourth Committee [A/66/429], adopted **resolution 66/81 A** and **B** without vote [agenda item 55].

Questions relating to information

A

INFORMATION IN THE SERVICE OF HUMANITY

The General Assembly,

Taking note of the comprehensive and important report of the Committee on Information,

Taking note also of the report of the Secretary-General on questions relating to information,

Urges all countries, organizations of the United Nations system as a whole and all others concerned, reaffirming their commitment to the principles of the Charter of the United Nations and to the principles of freedom of the press and freedom of information, as well as to those of the independence, pluralism and diversity of the media, deeply concerned by the disparities existing between developed and developing countries and the consequences of every kind arising from those disparities that affect the capability of the public, private or other media and individuals in developing countries to disseminate information and communicate their views and their cultural and ethical values through endogenous cultural production, as well as to ensure the diversity of sources and their free access to information, and recognizing the call in this context for what in the United Nations and at various international forums has been termed "a new world information and communication order, seen as an evolving and continuous process":

(*a*) To cooperate and interact with a view to reducing existing disparities in information flows at all levels by increasing assistance for the development of communications infrastructures and capabilities in developing countries, with due regard for their needs and the priorities attached to such areas by those countries, and in order to enable them and the public, private or other media in developing countries to develop their own information and communications policies freely and independently and increase the participation of media and individuals in the communication process, and to ensure a free flow of information at all levels;

(*b*) To ensure for journalists the free and effective performance of their professional tasks and condemn resolutely all attacks against them;

(*c*) To provide support for the continuation and strengthening of practical training programmes for broadcasters and journalists from public, private and other media in developing countries;

(*d*) To enhance regional efforts and cooperation among developing countries, as well as cooperation between developed and developing countries, to strengthen communications capacities and to improve the media infrastructure and communications technology in the developing countries, especially in the areas of training and dissemination of information;

(*e*) To aim at, in addition to bilateral cooperation, providing all possible support and assistance to the developing countries and their media, public, private or other, with due regard to their interests and needs in the field of information and to action already adopted within the United Nations system, including:

(i) The development of the human and technical resources that are indispensable for the improvement of information and communications systems in developing countries and support for the continuation and strengthening of practical training programmes, such as those already operating under both public and private auspices throughout the developing world;

(ii) The creation of conditions that will enable developing countries and their media, public, private or other, to have, by using their national and regional resources, the communications technology suited to their national needs, as well as the necessary programme material, especially for radio and television broadcasting;

(iii) Assistance in establishing and promoting telecommunication links at the subregional, regional and interregional levels, especially among developing countries;

(iv) The facilitation, as appropriate, of access by the developing countries to advanced communications technology available on the open market;

(*f*) To provide full support for the International Programme for the Development of Communication of the United Nations Educational, Scientific and Cultural Organization, which should support both public and private media.

B

UNITED NATIONS PUBLIC INFORMATION POLICIES AND ACTIVITIES

The General Assembly,

Emphasizing that the Committee on Information is its main subsidiary body mandated to make recommendations to it relating to the work of the Department of Public Information of the Secretariat,

Reaffirming its resolution 13(I) of 13 February 1946, in which it established the Department of Public Information, with a view to promoting to the greatest possible extent an informed understanding of the work and purposes of the United Nations among the peoples of the world, and all other relevant resolutions of the General Assembly related to the activities of the Department,

Emphasizing that the contents of public information and communications should be placed at the heart of the strategic management of the United Nations and that a culture of communications and transparency should permeate all levels of the Organization as a means of fully informing the peoples of the world of the aims and activities of the United Nations, in accordance with the purposes and principles enshrined in the Charter of the United Nations, in order to create broad-based global support for the United Nations,

Stressing that the primary mission of the Department of Public Information is to provide, through its outreach activities, accurate, impartial, comprehensive, balanced, timely and relevant information to the public on the tasks and responsibilities of the United Nations in order to strengthen international support for the activities of the Organization with the greatest transparency,

Recalling its resolution 65/107 B of 10 December 2010, which provided an opportunity to take due steps to enhance the efficiency and effectiveness of the Department and to maximize the use of its resources,

Expressing its concern that the gap in information and communications technology between the developed and the developing countries has continued to widen and that vast segments of the population in developing countries are not benefiting from the information and communications technologies that are currently available, and, in this regard, underlining the necessity of rectifying the imbalances in the present development of information and communications technologies in order to make it more just, equitable and effective,

Recognizing that developments in information and communications technologies open vast new opportunities for economic growth and social development and can play an important role in the eradication of poverty in developing countries, and, at the same time, emphasizing that the development of these technologies poses challenges and risks and could lead to the further widening of disparities between and within countries,

Recalling its resolution 63/306 of 9 September 2009, on multilingualism, and emphasizing the importance of making use, to the fullest extent possible, of the official languages of the United Nations in the activities of the Department of Public Information, with the aim of eliminating the disparity between the use of English and the five other official languages,

I
Introduction

1. *Requests* the Secretary-General, in respect of the public information policies and activities of the United Nations, to continue to implement fully the recommendations contained in relevant resolutions;

2. *Reaffirms* that the United Nations remains the indispensable foundation of a peaceful and just world and that its voice must be heard in a clear and effective manner, and emphasizes the essential role of the Department of Public Information in this context;

3. *Stresses* the importance of the provision of clear, timely, accurate and comprehensive information by the Secretariat to Member States, upon their request, within the framework of existing mandates and procedures;

4. *Reaffirms* the central role of the Committee on Information in United Nations public information policies and activities, including the prioritization of those activities, and decides that recommendations relating to the programme of the Department of Public Information shall originate, to the extent possible, in the Committee and shall be considered by the Committee;

5. *Requests* the Department of Public Information, following the priorities laid down by the General Assembly in its resolution 65/244 of 24 December 2010, and recalling the United Nations Millennium Declaration and the 2005 World Summit Outcome, to pay particular attention to peace and security, development and human rights and to major issues such as the eradication of poverty, including the global food crisis, conflict prevention, sustainable development, the HIV/AIDS epidemic, combating terrorism in all its forms and manifestations, and the needs of the African continent;

6. *Requests* the Department of Public Information and its network of United Nations information centres to pay particular attention to progress in implementing the internationally agreed development goals, including those contained in the Millennium Declaration, and the outcomes of the major related United Nations summits and conferences in carrying out its activities, and calls upon the Department to play an active role in raising public awareness of the world financial and economic crisis and its impact on development, including the achievement of the Millennium Development Goals, and of the global challenge of climate change, in particular the actions taken within the framework of the United Nations Framework Convention on Climate Change, especially in the context of the principle of common but differentiated responsibilities, particularly in the context of the Conference of the Parties and of the Meetings of the Parties to the Kyoto Protocol;

II
General activities of the Department of Public Information

7. *Takes note* of the reports of the Secretary-General on the activities of the Department of Public Information;

8. *Requests* the Department of Public Information to maintain its commitment to a culture of evaluation and to continue to evaluate its products and activities with the objective of enhancing their effectiveness, and to continue to cooperate and coordinate with Member States and the Office of Internal Oversight Services of the Secretariat;

9. *Reaffirms* the importance of more effective coordination between the Department of Public Information and the Office of the Spokesperson for the Secretary-General, and requests the Secretary-General to ensure consistency in the messages of the Organization;

10. *Notes* the efforts of the Department of Public Information to continue to publicize the work and decisions of the General Assembly, and requests the Department to continue to enhance its working relationship with the Office of the President of the General Assembly;

11. *Encourages* continued collaboration between the Department of Public Information and the United Nations Educational, Scientific and Cultural Organization in the promotion of culture and in the fields of education and communication, bridging the existing gap between the developed and the developing countries;

12. *Notes with appreciation* the efforts of the Department of Public Information to work at the local level with other organizations and bodies of the United Nations system to enhance the coordination of their communications activities, and reiterates its request to the Secretary-General to report to the Committee on Information at its thirty-fourth session on progress achieved in this regard and on the activities of the United Nations Communications Group;

13. *Reaffirms* that the Department of Public Information must prioritize its work programme, while respecting existing mandates and in line with regulation 5.6 of the Regulations and Rules Governing Programme Planning, the Programme Aspects of the Budget, the Monitoring of Implementation and the Methods of Evaluation, to focus its message and better concentrate its efforts and to match its programmes with the needs of its target audiences, on the basis of improved feedback and evaluation mechanisms;

14. *Requests* the Secretary-General to continue to exert all efforts to ensure that publications and other information services of the Secretariat, including the United Nations website and the United Nations News Service, contain comprehensive, balanced, objective and equitable information in all official languages about the issues before the Organization and that they maintain editorial independence, impartiality, accuracy and full consistency with resolutions and decisions of the General Assembly;

15. *Reiterates its request* to the Department of Public Information and content-providing offices of the Secretariat to ensure that United Nations publications are produced in all official languages, as well as in an environmentally friendly and cost-neutral manner, and to continue to coordinate closely with all other entities, including all other departments of the Secretariat and funds and programmes of the United Nations system, in order to avoid duplication, within their respective mandates, in the issuance of United Nations publications;

16. *Emphasizes* that the Department of Public Information should maintain and improve its activities in the areas of special interest to developing countries and, where appropriate, other countries with special needs, and that the activities of the Department should contribute to bridging the existing gap between the developing and the developed countries in the crucial field of public information and communications;

17. *Reiterates its concern* that the issuance of daily press releases has not been expanded to all official languages, through cost-neutral cooperative arrangements with academic and other institutions, as requested in previous resolutions and in full respect of the principle of parity of all six official languages;

Multilingualism and public information

18. *Emphasizes* the importance of ensuring equitable treatment of all the official languages of the United Nations in all the activities of the Department of Public Information, whether based on traditional or new media, including in presentations to the Committee on Information, with the aim of eliminating the disparity between the use of English and the five other official languages;

19. *Reiterates its request* to the Secretary-General to ensure that the Department of Public Information has appropriate staffing capacity in all the official languages of the United Nations to undertake all its activities and to include this aspect in future programme budget proposals for the Department, bearing in mind the principle of parity of all six official languages, while respecting the workload in each official language;

20. *Welcomes* the ongoing efforts of the Department of Public Information to enhance multilingualism in all its activities, and stresses the importance of ensuring that the texts of all new public United Nations documents in all six official languages, information materials and all older United Nations documents are made available through the United Nations website and are accessible to Member States without delay, and further stresses the importance of fully implementing its resolution 63/306;

Bridging the digital divide

21. *Requests* the Department of Public Information to contribute to raising the awareness of the international community of the importance of the implementation of the outcome documents of the World Summit on the Information Society and of the possibilities that the use of the Internet and other information and communications technologies can bring to societies and economies, as well as of ways to bridge the digital divide, including by commemorating World Information Society Day on 17 May;

22. *Emphasizes* the importance of the network of United Nations information centres in enhancing the public image of the United Nations, in disseminating messages on the United Nations to local populations, especially in developing countries, bearing in mind that information in local languages has the strongest impact on local populations, and in mobilizing support for the work of the United Nations at the local level;

23. *Welcomes* the work done by the network of United Nations information centres in favour of the publication of United Nations information materials and the translation of important documents into languages other than the official languages of the United Nations, encourages the network of information centres to continue to develop web pages in local languages and the Department of Public Information to provide necessary resources and technical facilities, with a view to reaching the widest possible spectrum of audiences and extending the United Nations message to all the corners of the world, in order to strengthen international support for the activities of the Organization, and encourages the continuation of efforts in this regard;

24. *Stresses* the importance of rationalizing the network of United Nations information centres, and, in this regard, requests the Secretary-General to continue to make proposals in this direction, including through the redeployment of resources where necessary, and to report to the Committee on Information at its successive sessions;

25. *Reaffirms* that the rationalization of United Nations information centres must be carried out on a case-by-case basis in consultation with all concerned Member States in which existing information centres are located, the countries served by those information centres and other

interested countries in the region, taking into consideration the distinctive characteristics of each region;

26. *Recognizes* that the network of United Nations information centres, especially in developing countries, should continue to enhance its impact and activities, including through strategic communications support, and calls upon the Secretary-General to report on the implementation of this approach to the Committee on Information at its successive sessions;

27. *Requests* the Department of Public Information, through the United Nations information centres, to strengthen its cooperation with all other United Nations entities at the country level and in the context of the United Nations Development Assistance Framework, in order to enhance coherence in communications and to avoid duplication of work;

28. *Stresses* the importance of taking into account the special needs and requirements of developing countries in the field of information and communications technology for the effective flow of information in those countries;

29. *Also stresses* the importance of efforts to strengthen the outreach activities of the United Nations to those Member States remaining outside the network of United Nations information centres, and encourages the Secretary-General, within the context of rationalization, to extend the services of the network of information centres to those Member States;

30. *Further stresses* that the Department of Public Information should continue to review the allocation of both staff and financial resources to the United Nations information centres in developing countries, taking into account the specific needs of the least developed countries;

31. *Welcomes* the support by some Member States, including developing countries, in offering, inter alia, rent-free premises for the United Nations information centres because of lack of funding, bearing in mind that such support should not be a substitute for the full allocation of financial resources for the information centres in the context of the programme budget of the United Nations;

32. *Notes* the strengthening of the United Nations information centres in Cairo, Mexico City and Pretoria, and encourages the Secretary-General to explore the strengthening of other centres, especially in Africa, in cooperation with the Member States concerned and in a cost-neutral manner;

33. *Welcomes* General Assembly resolution 64/243 of 24 December 2009, in which the Assembly requested the Secretary-General to establish a United Nations information centre in Luanda as a contribution towards addressing the needs of Portuguese-speaking African countries, reiterates its request to the Secretary-General, in coordination with the Government of Angola, to take the measures necessary for the prompt establishment of the information centre, and requests the Secretary-General to report to the Committee on Information at its thirty-fourth session on the progress made in this regard;

34. *Encourages* the Secretary-General, when appointing directors to the United Nations information centres, to fully consider, inter alia, the experience of candidates in the field of information and communications technology as one of the highly desirable appointment criteria;

III
Strategic communications services

35. *Reaffirms* the role of the strategic communications services in devising and disseminating United Nations messages by developing communications strategies, in close collaboration with the substantive departments, United Nations funds and programmes and the specialized agencies, in full compliance with their legislative mandates;

Promotional campaigns

36. *Appreciates* the work of the Department of Public Information in promoting, through its campaigns, issues of importance to the international community, such as the United Nations Millennium Declaration and the progress made in implementing the internationally agreed development goals, United Nations reform, the eradication of poverty, conflict prevention, peacekeeping, peacebuilding, sustainable development, disarmament, decolonization, human rights, including the rights of women and children, persons with disabilities and migrant workers, strategic coordination in humanitarian relief, especially in natural disasters and other crises, HIV/AIDS, malaria, tuberculosis, non-communicable diseases and other diseases, the needs of the African continent, the nature of the critical economic and social situation in Africa and the priorities of the New Partnership for Africa's Development, the special needs of the least developed countries, the establishment of the permanent memorial to the victims of slavery and the transatlantic slave trade, combating terrorism in all its forms and manifestations, dialogue among civilizations, the culture of peace and tolerance and the consequences of the Chernobyl disaster, as well as prevention of genocide, and requests the Department, in cooperation with the countries concerned and with the relevant organizations and bodies of the United Nations system, to continue to take appropriate measures to enhance world public awareness of all these issues;

37. *Requests* the Department of Public Information to contribute to the observance of International Mother Language Day on 21 February, as proclaimed by the General Conference of the United Nations Educational, Scientific and Cultural Organization; the International Day of Remembrance of the Victims of Slavery and the Transatlantic Slave Trade on 25 March, in accordance with General Assembly resolution 62/122 of 17 December 2007; and Nelson Mandela International Day on 18 July, in accordance with Assembly resolution 64/13 of 10 November 2009, and to play a role in raising awareness and promoting these events in a cost-neutral manner, where appropriate;

38. *Commends* the role of the Secretariat, especially the Department of Public Information, in holding the first official ceremony commemorating the International Day of Nowruz, on 21 March 2011, organized jointly by all the sponsors of General Assembly resolution 64/253 of 23 February 2010;

39. *Requests* the Department of Public Information and its network of United Nations information centres to take appropriate measures to raise awareness of and disseminate information on the United Nations Conference on Sustainable Development to be held in 2012, and relevant sustainable development issues;

40. *Also requests* the Department of Public Information and its network of United Nations information cen-

tres to raise awareness of and disseminate information, in a cost-neutral manner, on the Third International Decade for the Eradication of Colonialism, declared by the General Assembly in its resolution 65/119 of 10 December 2010;

Role of the Department of Public Information in United Nations peacekeeping operations

41. *Requests* the Secretariat to continue to ensure the involvement of the Department of Public Information from the planning stage of future peacekeeping operations through interdepartmental consultations and coordination with other departments of the Secretariat, in particular with the Department of Peacekeeping Operations and the Department of Field Support;

42. *Requests* the Department of Public Information, the Department of Peacekeeping Operations and the Department of Field Support to continue their cooperation in raising awareness of the new realities, far-reaching successes and challenges faced by peacekeeping operations, especially multidimensional and complex ones, and the recent surge in United Nations peacekeeping activities, and welcomes efforts by the three Departments to develop and implement a comprehensive communications strategy on current challenges facing United Nations peacekeeping;

43. *Stresses* the importance of enhancing the public information capacity of the Department of Public Information in the field of peacekeeping operations and its role, in close cooperation with the Department of Peacekeeping Operations and the Department of Field Support, in the process of selecting public information staff for United Nations peacekeeping operations or missions and, in this regard, invites the Department of Public Information to second public information staff who have the skills necessary to fulfil the tasks of the operations or missions, taking into account the principle of equitable geographical distribution in accordance with Chapter XV, Article 101, paragraph 3, of the Charter of the United Nations, and to consider views expressed, especially by host countries, when appropriate, in this regard;

44. *Emphasizes* the importance of the peacekeeping gateway on the United Nations website, and requests the Department of Public Information to continue its efforts in supporting the peacekeeping missions to further develop their websites;

45. *Requests* the Department of Public Information and the Department of Peacekeeping Operations to continue to cooperate in implementing an effective outreach programme to explain the zero-tolerance policy of the Organization regarding sexual exploitation and abuse and to inform the public of the outcome of all such cases involving peacekeeping personnel, including cases where allegations are ultimately found to be legally unproven, and also to inform the public of the adoption by the General Assembly of the United Nations Comprehensive Strategy on Assistance and Support to Victims of Sexual Exploitation and Abuse by United Nations Staff and Related Personnel;

Role of the Department of Public Information in strengthening dialogue among civilizations and the culture of peace as means of enhancing understanding among nations

46. *Recalls* its resolutions on dialogue among civilizations and the culture of peace, and requests the Department of Public Information, while ensuring the pertinence and relevance of subjects for promotional campaigns under this issue, to continue to provide the support necessary for the dissemination of information pertaining to dialogue among civilizations and the culture of peace, as well as the initiative on the Alliance of Civilizations, and to take due steps in fostering the culture of dialogue among civilizations and promoting cultural understanding, tolerance, respect for and freedom of religion or belief and effective enjoyment by all of all human rights and civil, political, economic, social and cultural rights, including the right to development;

47. *Invites* the United Nations system, especially the Department of Public Information, to continue to encourage and facilitate dialogue among civilizations and to formulate ways and means to promote dialogue among civilizations in the activities of the United Nations in various fields, taking into account the Programme of Action of the Global Agenda for Dialogue among Civilizations, and, in this regard, looks forward to the report of the Secretary-General requested by the General Assembly in its resolution 60/4 of 20 October 2005, and also welcomes the decision of the President of the General Assembly at its sixty-fourth session to hold an informal thematic debate on this issue in 2010;

48. *Recognizes* the achievements of the Alliance of Civilizations and the efforts made by the High Representative of the Secretary-General for the Alliance of Civilizations, which it had welcomed in its resolution 64/14 of 10 November 2009, takes note of the broad range of initiatives and partnerships in the areas of youth, education, the media and migration to be launched at the fourth Alliance of Civilizations Forum, to be held in Doha from 11 to 13 December 2011, and welcomes the continuing support of the Department of Public Information for the work of the Alliance of Civilizations, including its ongoing projects;

IV
News services

49. *Stresses* that the central objective of the news services implemented by the Department of Public Information is the timely delivery of accurate, objective and balanced news and information emanating from the United Nations system in all four mass media, namely, print, radio, television and the Internet, to the media and other audiences worldwide, with the overall emphasis on multilingualism, and reiterates its request to the Department to ensure that all news-breaking stories and news alerts are accurate, impartial and free of bias;

50. *Emphasizes* the importance of the Department of Public Information continuing to draw the attention of world media to stories that do not obtain prominent coverage, through the initiative entitled "10 Stories the World Should Hear More About" and through video and audio coverage by United Nations Television and United Nations Radio;

Traditional means of communication

51. *Welcomes* the continuing initiative of United Nations Radio, which remains one of the most effective and far-reaching traditional media available to the Department of Public Information and an important instrument in United Nations activities, to enhance its live radio broadcasting service by making more frequently updated reports in all six official languages and features available to broadcasters on a daily basis on all United Nations activities,

and requests the Secretary-General to continue to make every effort to achieve parity in the six official languages in United Nations Radio productions;

52. *Also welcomes* the ongoing efforts being made by the Department of Public Information to disseminate programmes directly to broadcasting stations all over the world in the six official languages, with the addition of Portuguese and Kiswahili, as well as in other languages where possible;

53. *Requests* the Department of Public Information to continue building partnerships with local, national and regional broadcasters to extend the United Nations message to all the corners of the world in an accurate and impartial way, and requests the Radio and Television Service of the Department to continue to take full advantage of the technological infrastructure made available in recent years;

United Nations website

54. *Reaffirms* that the United Nations website is an essential tool for the media, non-governmental organizations, educational institutions, Member States and the general public and, in this regard, reiterates the continued need for strengthened efforts by the Department of Public Information to maintain and improve it;

55. *Recognizes* the efforts made by the Department of Public Information to implement the basic accessibility requirements for persons with disabilities to access the United Nations website, and calls upon the Department to continue to work towards compliance with accessibility requirements on all new and updated pages of the website, with the aim of ensuring its accessibility for persons with different kinds of disabilities;

56. *Notes* that the multilingual development and enrichment of the United Nations website has improved, and, in this regard, requests the Department of Public Information, in coordination with content-providing offices of the Secretariat, to further improve the actions taken to achieve full parity among the six official languages on the United Nations website, and especially reiterates its request to the Secretary-General to ensure the adequate distribution of financial and human resources within the Department allocated to the United Nations website among all official languages, taking into consideration the specificity of each official language;

57. *Recognizes* the cooperative arrangements undertaken by the Department of Public Information with academic institutions to increase the number of web pages available in some official languages, and reiterates its urgent request to the Secretary-General to extend those arrangements to all the official languages of the United Nations;

58. *Reiterates its request* that all content-providing offices of the Secretariat translate all English-language materials and databases posted on the United Nations website into all other official languages and make them available on the respective language websites in the most practical, efficient and cost-effective manner;

59. *Reaffirms* the need to enhance the technological infrastructure of the Department of Public Information on a continuous basis in order to widen the outreach of the Department and to continue to improve the United Nations website in a cost-neutral manner;

60. *Requests* the Secretary-General to continue to take full advantage of new developments in information technology in order to improve the expeditious dissemination of information on the United Nations in a cost-neutral manner, in accordance with the priorities established by the General Assembly in its resolutions and taking into account the linguistic diversity of the Organization, recognizes the e-mail news alerts service, and encourages the Department to consult with the Office of Information and Communications Technology in order to explore, as a matter of priority, the provision of the service in all official languages;

61. *Recognizes* that some official languages use non-Latin and bidirectional scripts and that technological infrastructures and supportive applications in the United Nations are based on Latin script, which leads to difficulties in processing non-Latin and bidirectional scripts, and urges the Office of Information and Communications Technology to further collaborate with the Department of Public Information and to continue its efforts to ensure that technological infrastructures and supportive applications in the United Nations fully support Latin, non-Latin and bidirectional scripts in order to enhance the equality of all official languages on the United Nations website;

62. *Calls upon* the Department of Public Information, recognizing the importance of audiovisual archives and the actions taken by the Dag Hammarskjöld Library to preserve the published record of the Organization as a common heritage, welcoming the completion of an inventory of sixty-five years of United Nations audiovisual history, stressing the urgency of digitization in order to prevent further deterioration of the unique historical archives, and taking note of efforts made by the Department thus far to develop a digitization strategy in consultation with other Departments, including the Office of Information and Communications Technology, to explore avenues of support for digitization, including working with interested partners, to ensure that such archives are preserved and are accessible;

V
Library services

63. *Also calls upon* the Department of Public Information to continue to lead the Steering Committee for the Modernization and Integrated Management of United Nations Libraries, and further commends the steps taken by the Dag Hammarskjöld Library and the other member libraries of the Steering Committee to align their activities, services and outputs more closely with the goals, objectives and operational priorities of the Organization;

64. *Reiterates* the need to maintain a multilingual collection of books, periodicals and other materials in hard copy, accessible to Member States, ensuring that the Library continues to be a broadly accessible resource for information about the United Nations and its activities;

65. *Calls upon* the Department of Public Information, recognizing the importance of audiovisual archives in preserving our common heritage, to continue to examine its policies and activities regarding the durable preservation of its radio, television, film and photographic archives and the action taken in ensuring that the archives are preserved and are accessible, including in the context of the construction work of the capital master plan within the overall budget of the plan;

66. *Notes* the initiative taken by the Dag Hammarskjöld Library, in its capacity as the focal point, to expand the scope of the regional training and knowledge-sharing workshops organized for the depository libraries in developing countries to include outreach in their activities;

67. *Acknowledges* the role of the Dag Hammarskjöld Library in enhancing knowledge-sharing and networking activities to ensure access to the vast store of United Nations knowledge for delegates, permanent missions of Member States, the Secretariat, researchers and depository libraries worldwide;

VI
Outreach services

68. *Also acknowledges* that the outreach services provided by the Department of Public Information continue to work towards promoting awareness of the role and work of the United Nations;

69. *Welcomes* the educational outreach activities of the Department of Public Information, through the United Nations Works programme and the Global Teaching and Learning Project, to reach educators and young people worldwide via a range of multimedia platforms, and encourages the United Nations Works programme to continue to develop further its partnerships with global media networks and celebrity advocates and the Global Teaching and Learning Project to further expand its activities to teachers and students in primary, intermediate and secondary schools;

70. *Notes* the launch of the United Nations Academic Impact, an initiative that aims to facilitate exchanges between the United Nations and institutions of higher education and to support the common principles and goals of the Organization;

71. *Also notes* the importance of the continued implementation by the Department of Public Information of the ongoing programme for broadcasters and journalists from developing countries and countries with economies in transition, as mandated by the General Assembly, and requests the Department to consider how best to maximize the benefits derived from the programme by extending, inter alia, its duration and the number of its participants;

72. *Welcomes* the movement towards educational outreach and the orientation of the *UN Chronicle*, both print and online editions, and, to this end, encourages the *UN Chronicle* to continue to develop co-publishing partnerships, collaborative educational activities and events with civil society organizations and institutions of higher learning;

73. *Requests* the Department of Public Information to continue the publication of the *UN Chronicle* with a view to improving it further in a cost-neutral manner and to report to the Committee on Information at its thirty-fourth session on progress in this matter, and reiterates its request to submit options for publishing the *UN Chronicle* in all six official languages;

74. *Notes* the efforts undertaken by the Department of Public Information in organizing exhibitions on important United Nations-related issues, within existing mandates, at United Nations Headquarters and at other United Nations offices as a useful tool for reaching out to the general public, reaffirms the important role that guided tours play as a means of reaching out to the general public, and requests the Secretary-General to continue his efforts to ensure that the guided tours provided at United Nations Headquarters and other United Nations duty stations are consistently available, in accordance with their income-generating nature, in particular in all the United Nations official languages;

75. *Also notes* the ongoing efforts of the Department of Public Information to strengthen its role as a focal point for two-way interaction with civil society relating to the priorities and concerns of the Organization identified by Member States;

76. *Commends*, in a spirit of cooperation, the United Nations Correspondents Association for its ongoing activities and for its Dag Hammarskjöld Memorial Scholarship Fund, which sponsors journalists from developing countries to come to United Nations Headquarters and report on the activities during the General Assembly, and further encourages the international community to continue its financial support for the Fund;

77. *Expresses its appreciation* for the efforts and contribution of United Nations Messengers of Peace, Goodwill Ambassadors and other advocates to promote the work of the United Nations and to enhance international public awareness of its priorities and concerns, and calls upon the Department of Public Information to continue to involve them in its communications and media strategies and outreach activities;

VII
Final remarks

78. *Requests* the Secretary-General to report to the Committee on Information at its thirty-fourth session and to the General Assembly at its sixty-seventh session on the activities of the Department of Public Information and on the implementation of all recommendations and requests contained in the present resolution;

79. *Also requests* the Secretary-General to make every effort to ensure that the level of services provided by the Department of Public Information is maintained throughout the period of the implementation of the capital master plan;

80. *Notes* the initiative taken by the Department of Public Information, in cooperation with the Department of Safety and Security and the Protocol and Liaison Service, during the general debate of the sixty-third session of the General Assembly, to issue special identification stickers to press officers of Member States to enable them to escort media covering the visits of high-level officials to restricted areas, and strongly urges the Secretary-General to continue to improve this practice by acceding to the request by Member States to provide the needed number of additional passes to press officers of Member States to allow their access to all areas that are deemed restricted, in order to effectively and comprehensively report on high-level meetings that include officials of delegations of Member States;

81. *Requests* the Committee on Information to report to the General Assembly at its sixty-seventh session;

82. *Decides* to include in the provisional agenda of its sixty-seventh session the item entitled "Questions relating to information".

PART TWO

Human rights

Chapter I
Promotion of human rights

In 2011, United Nations efforts to promote human rights were advanced by several developments. The review of the work and functioning of the Human Rights Council was completed, the text of the Optional Protocol to the Convention on the Rights of the Child on a communications procedure was finalized and the first meeting of States parties to the International Convention for the Protection of All Persons from Enforced Disappearance was convened. The Council examined the human rights record of 49 Member States through the universal periodic review mechanism, designed to assess the human rights record of all States every four years. By year's end, all 193 Member States had been reviewed, with a 100 per cent participation rate in the process, completing the first cycle and providing a framework within which each State had made public commitments in respect of recommendations to improve the human rights situation on the ground.

The Human Rights Council Advisory Committee, which provided expertise to the Council, held its sixth and seventh sessions and submitted nine recommendations, while the Council's complaint procedure, which consisted of the Working Group on Communications and the Working Group on Situations, addressed consistent patterns of gross and reliably attested human rights violations throughout the world.

During the year, the Council held three regular sessions (sixteenth, seventeenth and eighteenth), as well as four special sessions (fifteenth, sixteenth, seventeenth and eighteenth) that focused on the human rights situation in the Libyan Arab Jamahiriya and in the Syrian Arab Republic. In an unprecedented move, the Council, condemning the gross and systematic human rights violations in Libya, recommended in February the suspension of the country's membership in the Council, which the General Assembly endorsed in March. The membership rights of Libya were restored in November following the commitments made by the interim Government—the National Transitional Council—to uphold its obligations under international human rights law. Human rights were also promoted through the work of the treaty bodies—committees of experts monitoring States parties' compliance with the legally binding human rights treaties.

The Office of the High Commissioner for Human Rights provided support to the work of the Council and its mechanisms, including the treaty bodies and the special procedures. The Office strengthened its country engagement and expanded its presence at the country and regional levels.

In December, the General Assembly adopted the Optional Protocol to the Convention on the Rights of the Child on a communications procedure and the United Nations Declaration on Human Rights Education and Training. It reaffirmed the universal, indivisible, interrelated, interdependent and mutually reinforcing nature of all human rights and fundamental freedoms, and designated 21 March as World Down Syndrome Day. The International Year of People of African Descent, 2011 was also observed.

UN machinery

Human Rights Council

Council sessions

During the year the Human Rights Council held its sixteenth (28 February–25 March) [A/HRC/16/2], seventeenth (31 May–17 June) [A/HRC/17/2] and eighteenth (12–30 September and 21 October) [A/HRC/18/2] regular sessions. The Council also held four special sessions: its fifteenth (25 February) [A/HRC/S-15/1] on the situation of human rights in the Libyan Arab Jamahiriya (see p. 758); and its sixteenth (29 April) [A/HRC/S-16/2] (see p. 779), seventeenth (22–23 August) [A/HRC/S-17/2] (see p. 780) and eighteenth (2 December) [A/HRC/S-18/2] (see p. 781) on the situation of human rights in the Syrian Arab Republic. All sessions were held in Geneva.

The Council adopted 89 resolutions, 59 decisions and three President's statements, and brought to the attention of the General Assembly 12 resolutions for its consideration and possible action. The resolutions, decisions and statements adopted during the 2011 sessions were contained in its reports to the Assembly [A/66/53 & Add.1 & Corr.1 & Add.2 & Corr.1].

The General Assembly addressed revised estimates to the 2012–2013 budget resulting from resolutions and decisions adopted by the Council in section VIII of **resolution 66/247** of 24 December (see p. 1393).

GENERAL ASSEMBLY ACTION

On 19 December [meeting 89], the General Assembly, on the recommendation of the Third (Social, Humanitarian and Cultural) Committee [A/66/457], adopted **resolution 66/136** by recorded vote (122-3-59) [agenda item 64].

Report of the Human Rights Council

The General Assembly,

Recalling its resolution 60/251 of 15 March 2006, by which it established the Human Rights Council, and its resolution 65/281 of 17 June 2011 on the review of the Human Rights Council,

Recalling also its resolutions 62/219 of 22 December 2007, 63/160 of 18 December 2008, 64/143 of 18 December 2009 and 65/195 of 21 December 2010,

Having considered the recommendations contained in the report of the Human Rights Council,

Takes note of the report of the Human Rights Council, its addendum and its recommendations.

RECORDED VOTE ON RESOLUTION 66/136:

In favour: Afghanistan, Algeria, Angola, Antigua and Barbuda, Argentina, Armenia, Azerbaijan, Bahamas, Bahrain, Bangladesh, Barbados, Belize, Benin, Bhutan, Bolivia, Botswana, Brazil, Brunei Darussalam, Burkina Faso, Cambodia, Cape Verde, Central African Republic, Chad, Chile, China, Comoros, Congo, Côte d'Ivoire, Cuba, Democratic Republic of the Congo, Djibouti, Dominica, Dominican Republic, Ecuador, Egypt, El Salvador, Eritrea, Ethiopia, Fiji, Gabon, Gambia, Ghana, Grenada, Guatemala, Guinea, Guinea-Bissau, Guyana, Haiti, India, Indonesia, Iraq, Jamaica, Jordan, Kenya, Kuwait, Kyrgyzstan, Lao People's Democratic Republic, Lebanon, Lesotho, Liberia, Libya, Madagascar, Malawi, Malaysia, Maldives, Mali, Mauritania, Mauritius, Mexico, Mongolia, Morocco, Mozambique, Myanmar, Namibia, Nepal, Nicaragua, Niger, Nigeria, Oman, Pakistan, Papua New Guinea, Paraguay, Peru, Philippines, Qatar, Republic of Korea, Russian Federation, Saint Kitts and Nevis, Saint Lucia, Saint Vincent and the Grenadines, Sao Tome and Principe, Saudi Arabia, Senegal, Seychelles, Sierra Leone, Singapore, Solomon Islands, South Africa, South Sudan, Sri Lanka, Sudan, Suriname, Swaziland, Tajikistan, Thailand, Timor-Leste, Togo, Trinidad and Tobago, Tunisia, Turkey, Tuvalu, Uganda, United Arab Emirates, United Republic of Tanzania, Uruguay, Uzbekistan, Vanuatu, Venezuela, Viet Nam, Yemen, Zambia, Zimbabwe.

Against: Belarus, Democratic People's Republic of Korea, Syrian Arab Republic.

Abstaining: Albania, Andorra, Australia, Austria, Belgium, Bosnia and Herzegovina, Bulgaria, Canada, Colombia, Costa Rica, Croatia, Cyprus, Czech Republic, Denmark, Estonia, Finland, France, Georgia, Germany, Greece, Honduras, Hungary, Iceland, Iran, Ireland, Israel, Italy, Japan, Kazakhstan, Latvia, Liechtenstein, Lithuania, Luxembourg, Malta, Marshall Islands, Monaco, Montenegro, Netherlands, New Zealand, Norway, Palau, Panama, Poland, Portugal, Republic of Moldova, Romania, Samoa, San Marino, Serbia, Slovakia, Slovenia, Spain, Sweden, Switzerland, the former Yugoslav Republic of Macedonia, Tonga, Ukraine, United Kingdom, United States.

Election of Council members

On 20 May, by **decision 65/415**, the General Assembly, pursuant to resolution 60/251 [YUN 2006, p. 757], elected the following 15 countries as members of the Human Rights Council for a three-year term of office beginning on 19 June: Austria, Benin, Botswana, Burkina Faso, Chile, Congo, Costa Rica, the Czech Republic, India, Indonesia, Italy, Kuwait, Peru, the Philippines and Romania. They would fill the vacancies occurring on the expiration of the terms of office of Argentina, Bahrain, Brazil, Burkina Faso, Chile, France, Gabon, Ghana, Japan, Pakistan, the Republic of Korea, Slovakia, Ukraine, the United Kingdom and Zambia. The Council comprised 47 members.

Suspension and restoration of membership rights of Libya

In mid-February, participants in mass demonstrations in Libya called for democratic reform and the toppling of the regime of Colonel Muammar Qadhafi. The arrest on 15 February by Libyan internal security forces of Fathi Terbil, a well-known lawyer and human rights defender, sparked a mass protest with thousands gathering in front of the courthouse in Benghazi and spreading the following day to other towns, including Al-Bayda, Al-Quba, Darnah and Tobruk. Large-scale protests emerged in Tripoli on 20 February, leading to both Government use of significant force and protestors attacking Government buildings. Clashes intensified in Tripoli and fighting took place in other cities. On 22 February, Colonel Qadhafi announced on national television that he would lead millions to purge Libya until he purified the land. By 24 February, media reports indicated that protestors were in control of Benghazi, Misrata, Tobruk and Zuwarah.

Human Rights Council action (February). On 25 February, at its fifteenth special session (see p. 758), which addressed the situation of human rights in Libya [A/66/53 (res. S-15/1)], the Human Rights Council condemned the gross and systematic human rights violations committed in the country, including indiscriminate armed attacks against civilians, extrajudicial killings, arbitrary arrests, detention and torture of peaceful demonstrators. It reminded the Government to respect its commitment as a Council member to uphold the highest standards in the promotion and protection of human rights, and in an unprecedented move, recommended that the General Assembly, in view of the human rights violations committed by the authorities, consider applying the measures in paragraph 8 of Assembly resolution 60/251 [YUN 2000, p. 757]. That text provided for the suspension of a country's membership in the Council for committing such violations. The Council also decided to dispatch an independent international commission of inquiry to investigate alleged violations of international human rights law in Libya and report to the Council at its seventeenth (2011) session. It requested the High Commissioner to provide an oral update on the situation at the Council's sixteenth session and a follow-up report at its seventeenth session (see p. 75).

General Assembly consideration. On 1 March [A/65/PV.76], the General Assembly considered a draft resolution [A/65/L.60] introduced by 5 States (Botswana, Jordan, Lebanon, Nigeria, Qatar) and later sponsored by an additional 68 States [A/65/L.60/Add.1], proposing the suspension of Libya's membership in the Council. In his statement, the Secretary-General demanded an end to the violence against civilians and full respect for their fundamental human rights, including those of peaceful assembly and free speech. Reports from the ground indicated that the death toll from nearly two weeks of violence was unknown, but was likely to exceed 1,000; thousands had been injured. The Secretary-General expressed concern about the continued loss of life, the ongoing repression of the population and the clear incitement to violence against the civilian population by Colonel Qadhafi and his supporters. He welcomed the Council's recommendation to suspend Libya's membership as long as the violence continued, supported its decision to dispatch a commission of inquiry to investigate the alleged violations, and commended the Security Council's decision in **resolution 1970(2011)** (see p. 267) to refer the situation in Libya to the International Criminal Court (ICC). Those actions sent a strong message that there was no impunity and that those who committed crimes against humanity would be punished. In that context, he urged the Assembly to act decisively as well.

The Assembly adopted resolution 65/265 (see below) suspending Libya's rights of membership in the Human Rights Council.

GENERAL ASSEMBLY ACTION

On 1 March [meeting 76], the General Assembly adopted **resolution 65/265** [draft: A/65/L.60 & Add.1] without vote [agenda item 117].

Suspension of the rights of membership of the Libyan Arab Jamahiriya in the Human Rights Council

The General Assembly,

Recalling its resolution 60/251 of 15 March 2006, in particular paragraph 8, which states that the General Assembly may suspend the rights of membership in the Human Rights Council of a member of the Council that commits gross and systematic violations of human rights,

Noting Human Rights Council resolution S-15/1 of 25 February 2011,

Welcoming the statement issued by the League of Arab States on 22 February 2011 and the communiqué issued by the Peace and Security Council of the African Union on 23 February 2011,

Expressing deep concern about the human rights situation in the Libyan Arab Jamahiriya,

1. *Decides* to suspend the rights of membership in the Human Rights Council of the Libyan Arab Jamahiriya;
2. *Decides also* to review the matter, as appropriate.

Report of High Commissioner. In response to Human Rights Council resolution S-15/1 (see p. 604), the High Commissioner on 7 June [A/HRC/17/45] provided information on developments in the human rights situation in Libya. On 14 March, at the Council's sixteenth (2011) session, the Deputy High Commissioner had reported that the human rights situation had continued to deteriorate, with reports of intensified fighting and indiscriminate air strikes resulting in numerous civilian injuries and deaths. Humanitarian access to the war-affected areas remained hindered. On 15 March, the United Nations International Commission of Inquiry was established. Following the adoption on 17 March of Security Council **resolution 1973(2011)**, authorizing States and regional organizations to take all necessary measures to protect civilians (see p. 271), an international coalition commenced missile and air strikes against military installations, aircraft and other Government forces. On 2 May, the ICC Prosecutor stated that he had strong evidence that crimes against humanity were, and continued to be, committed by Colonel Qadhafi's regime. On 16 May, he requested ICC judges to issue arrest warrants for Muammar Qadhafi, his son Saif al-Islam Qadhafi and military intelligence chief Abdullah Al-Senussi on two types of crimes against humanity, murder and persecution. The High Commissioner concluded that the peaceful protests that erupted in February were violently suppressed by excessive use of force against the opposition, and that serious human rights violations had occurred on a widespread and protracted basis and continued to take place. She also pointed out that non-State actors that exercised government-like functions and control over a territory, such as the de facto National Transitional Council (NTC) established in Benghazi, were obliged to respect human right norms.

International Commission of Inquiry report. In response to Council resolution S-15/1 (see p. 604), the Commission submitted a report [A/HRC/17/44] describing its findings, which included an overview of the events from February, the categories of security groups participating in the events and its conclusions on violations alleged during the demonstrations and during the armed conflict. There was sufficient evidence to suggest that Government forces had engaged in excessive use of force against demonstrators, leading to significant deaths and injuries. While much remained to be done, particularly because the conflict was ongoing and alleged violations continued to be reported, the Commission had identified a number of violations which led it to conclude that international crimes, specifically crimes against humanity and war crimes, had been committed in Libya. It noted that the NTC had made a public undertaking in which it committed to build a constitutional democratic State based on the rule of law, respect for human rights and the guarantee of equal rights and opportunities for all its citizens. The Commission made a series of recommendations to the Government of Libya and to the NTC.

Human Rights Council action (June). On 17 June [A/66/53 (res. 17/17)], the Council condemned the continuing deterioration of the human rights situation in Libya since February; reiterated its call for the authorities to cease all human rights violations; took note of the NTC statements of its commitment to uphold international human rights law and underlined the importance of implementing those statements; and encouraged the Office of the High Commissioner for Human Rights (OHCHR) to identify ways to increase its engagement with Libya. It also extended the mandate of the Commission of Inquiry and requested it to provide an oral update at the Council's eighteenth (2011) session and a final written report at its nineteenth (2012) session.

Libyan interim government. In August, opposition forces captured the government-held city of Tripoli and the NTC issued the Constitutional Declaration. On 16 September [A/66/PV.2], the General Assembly, by **resolution 66/1 A** (see p. 1357), accepted the credentials and recognized the NTC as the legal representative of Libya, replacing the Qadhafi government.

International Commission of Inquiry update. On 19 September, pursuant to Human Rights Council resolution 17/17 (see above), the International Commission of Inquiry Chairman, Philippe Kirsch presented an oral report on the situation in Libya at the Council's eighteenth session [A/HRC/18/2]. Libya made statements as the country concerned.

Human Rights Council action (September). On 29 September [A/66/53/Add.1 (res. 18/9)], the Council welcomed the commitments made by Libya to uphold its obligations under international human rights law and recommended that the General Assembly lift the suspension of Libya's membership rights in the Human Rights Council.

On 18 November, by resolution 66/11, the Assembly restored those rights (see below).

GENERAL ASSEMBLY ACTION

On 18 November [meeting 60], the General Assembly adopted **resolution 66/11** [draft: A/66/L.9 & Add.1] by recorded vote (123-4-6) [agenda item 120].

Restoration of the rights of membership of Libya in the Human Rights Council

The General Assembly,

Recalling its resolution 60/251 of 15 March 2006,

Recalling also its resolution 65/265 of 1 March 2011, in which it decided to suspend the rights of membership of the Libyan Arab Jamahiriya in the Human Rights Council,

Recalling further its resolution 66/1 A of 16 September 2011, in which it accepted the credentials of the representatives to the sixty-sixth session of the General Assembly, including the credentials of the delegation of Libya,

Taking note of Human Rights Council resolution 18/9 of 29 September 2011,

Welcoming the commitments made by Libya to uphold its obligations under international human rights law, to promote and protect human rights, democracy and the rule of law, and to cooperate with relevant international human rights mechanisms, as well as the Office of the United Nations High Commissioner for Human Rights and the International Commission of Inquiry established by the Human Rights Council in its resolution S-15/1 of 25 February 2011,

Decides to restore the rights of membership of Libya in the Human Rights Council.

RECORDED VOTE ON RESOLUTION 66/11:

In favour: Afghanistan, Albania, Algeria, Andorra, Angola, Argentina, Armenia, Australia, Austria, Bahrain, Belgium, Belize, Benin, Bhutan, Bosnia and Herzegovina, Brazil, Burkina Faso, Canada, Cape Verde, Chad, Chile, China, Colombia, Comoros, Congo, Costa Rica, Côte d'Ivoire, Croatia, Cyprus, Czech Republic, Denmark, Djibouti, Dominican Republic, Egypt, Eritrea, Estonia, Ethiopia, Fiji, Finland, France, Gabon, Georgia, Germany, Ghana, Greece, Guatemala, Guinea, Guyana, Haiti, Honduras, Hungary, Iceland, India, Indonesia, Iran, Iraq, Ireland, Israel, Italy, Japan, Jordan, Kazakhstan, Kenya, Kuwait, Kyrgyzstan, Lao People's Democratic Republic, Latvia, Lebanon, Libya, Liechtenstein, Lithuania, Luxembourg, Malaysia, Maldives, Mali, Malta, Mauritius, Mexico, Monaco, Mongolia, Montenegro, Morocco, Myanmar, Nepal, New Zealand, Niger, Norway, Oman, Peru, Philippines, Poland, Portugal, Qatar, Republic of Moldova, Russian Federation, Saint Lucia, Samoa, San Marino, Saudi Arabia, Senegal, Serbia, Singapore, Slovakia, Slovenia, Spain, Sri Lanka, Sudan, Sweden, Switzerland, Tajikistan, Thailand, the former Yugoslav Republic of Macedonia, Togo, Trinidad and Tobago, Tunisia, Uganda, Ukraine, United Arab Emirates, United Kingdom, United Republic of Tanzania, United States, Uruguay, Yemen.

Against: Bolivia, Ecuador, Nicaragua, Venezuela.

Abstaining: Antigua and Barbuda, Bahamas, Barbados, Botswana, Cuba, Viet Nam.

Work of the Council

Review of work and functioning

Working Group. The open-ended intergovernmental working group on the review of the work and functioning of the Human Rights Council, established by Council resolution 12/1 [YUN 2009, p. 624], held its second session (Geneva, 7, 17–18 & 23–24 February) [A/HRC/WG.8/2/1]. The facilitators appointed to carry forward the review [YUN 2010, p. 637] presented their respective contribution on the state of the review process. On 14 February, on the basis of a compilation of those contributions, the Council President, as the chair of the working group, circulated a negotiating text to the Permanent Missions to the UN Office in Geneva and other stakeholders.

On 17 February, the working group took note of the paper "Update Report of the Coordinator to the Human Rights Council on Overlapping Issues", which would serve as a basis for consultations with the co-facilitators of the review process in New York. On 24 February, the working group adopted the draft "Outcome of the review of the work and functioning of the United Nations Human Rights Council".

Human Rights Council action. On 25 March [A/66/53 (res. 16/21)], the Council adopted the "Outcome of the review of the work and functioning of the United Nations Human Rights Council"; decided that the Outcome should be a supplement to the institution-building package contained in Council resolutions 5/1 and 5/2 of 18 June 2007 [YUN 2007, pp. 663 & 666], as well as in other related Council resolutions, decisions and President's statements; and submitted a draft resolution to the General Assembly for consideration.

General Assembly consideration. On 17 June [A/65/PV.100], the General Assembly considered draft resolution [A/65/L.78]. The Assembly President noted that the draft resolution was the conclusion of a coordinated process between Geneva and New York and that the text was as close as possible to a broad consensus. It proposed to align the cycle of the membership of the Council with the calendar year; recognized the role of the Council President; institutionalized the ad hoc arrangement on the allocation of the Council's report to both the plenary and the Third Committee; and recognized the need to provide adequate financing to fund unforeseen and extraordinary expenses arising from Council resolutions. The technical nature of the improvements underlined the fact that the majority of States perceived the Council as a strong and largely well-functioning organ, and that a major institutional overhaul was neither required nor desirable. The General Assembly would conduct another review of the Council in 10 to 15 years.

GENERAL ASSEMBLY ACTION

On 17 June [meeting 100], the General Assembly, adopted **resolution 65/281** [draft: A/65/L.78] by recorded vote (154-4-0) [agenda item 13 & 115].

Review of the Human Rights Council

The General Assembly,

Recalling its resolution 60/251 of 15 March 2006 establishing the Human Rights Council, and in particular paragraphs 1 and 16 thereof,

Recalling also its resolution 62/219 of 22 December 2007,

Recognizing that peace and security, development and human rights are the pillars of the United Nations system and the foundations for collective security and well-being,

Reaffirming that the Human Rights Council was created with the aim of ensuring effective enjoyment by all of all human rights, civil, political, economic, social and cultural rights, including the right to development, and that the Council is responsible for promoting universal respect for the protection of all human rights and fundamental freedoms for all, without distinction of any kind and in a fair and equal manner,

Recalling the competencies of the Third and Fifth Committees as the Main Committees of the General Assembly tasked with social, humanitarian and cultural issues and administrative and budgetary issues, respectively,

Taking note of Human Rights Council resolution 16/21 of 25 March 2011 containing the text entitled "Outcome of the review of the work and functioning of the Human Rights Council",

Recalling all its previous decisions on the allocation of the agenda item entitled "Report of the Human Rights Council",

Recalling also its resolution 63/263 of 24 December 2008 which endorses the relevant conclusions and recommendations of the Advisory Committee on Administrative and Budgetary Questions on the consideration of the financial requirements arising from resolutions and decisions of the Human Rights Council,

1. *Reaffirms* its resolution 60/251;
2. *Decides* that the present resolution shall supplement its resolution 60/251;
3. *Decides also* to maintain the status of the Human Rights Council as a subsidiary body of the General Assembly and to consider again the question of whether to maintain this status at an appropriate moment and at a time no sooner than ten years and no later than fifteen years;
4. *Decides further* that from 2013, the Human Rights Council will start its yearly membership cycle on 1 January;
5. *Decides* that, as a transitional measure, the period of office of members of the Human Rights Council ending in June 2012, June 2013 and June 2014 will exceptionally be extended until the end of the respective calendar year;
6. *Decides also* to continue its practice of allocating the agenda item entitled "Report of the Human Rights Council" to the plenary of the General Assembly and to the Third Committee, in accordance with its decision 65/503 A, with the additional understanding that the President of the Council will present the report in her or his capacity as President to the plenary of the General Assembly and the Third Committee and that the Third Committee will hold an interactive dialogue with the President of the Council at the time of her or his presentation of the report of the Council to the Third Committee;
7. *Decides further* that the annual report of the Human Rights Council shall cover the period from 1 October to 30 September, including the regular September session of the Council;
8. *Decides* to consider through its Fifth Committee all financial implications emanating from the resolutions and decisions contained in the annual report of the Human Rights Council, including those emanating from its September session;
9. *Recognizes* the need to provide adequate financing to fund unforeseen and extraordinary expenses arising from resolutions and decisions of the Human Rights Council, and in this regard requests the Secretary-General to present a report with options for consideration by the Fifth Committee at the main part of the sixty-sixth session of the General Assembly, taking into account the relevant conclu-

sions and recommendations of the Advisory Committee on Administrative and Budgetary Questions;

10. *Adopts* the text entitled "Outcome of the review of the work and functioning of the Human Rights Council" annexed to the present resolution.

ANNEX

Outcome of the review of the work and functioning of the Human Rights Council

I. Universal periodic review

A. Basis, principles and objectives of the review

1. The basis, principles and objectives of the universal periodic review as set forth in paragraphs 1 to 4 of the annex to Human Rights Council resolution 5/1 of 18 June 2007 shall be reaffirmed.

B. Periodicity and order of the review

2. The second cycle of the review shall begin in June 2012.

3. The periodicity of the review for the second and subsequent cycles will be four and a half years. This will imply the consideration of forty-two States per year during three sessions of the Working Group on the Universal Periodic Review.

4. The order of review established for the first cycle of the review shall be maintained for the second and subsequent cycles.

C. Process and modalities of the review

1. Focus and documentation

5. The review during the second and subsequent cycles will continue to be based on the three documents identified in paragraph 15 of the annex to Human Rights Council resolution 5/1.

6. The second and subsequent cycles of the review should focus on, inter alia, the implementation of the accepted recommendations and the developments in the human rights situation in the State under review.

7. The general guidelines for universal periodic review reports adopted by the Council in its decision 6/102 of 27 September 2007 shall be adjusted to the focus of the second and subsequent cycles before the eighteenth session of the Council.

8. Other relevant stakeholders are encouraged to include in their contributions information on the follow-up to the preceding review.

9. The summary of the information provided by other relevant stakeholders should contain, where appropriate, a separate section for contributions by the national human rights institution of the State under review that is accredited in full compliance with the principles relating to the status of national institutions for the promotion and protection of human rights ("the Paris Principles"), contained in the annex to General Assembly resolution 48/134 of 20 December 1993. Information provided by other accredited national human rights institutions will be reflected accordingly, as well as information provided by other stakeholders.

2. Modalities

10. The role of the group of three rapporteurs (troika) shall be maintained as set forth in the annex to Council resolution 5/1 and in the President's statement PRST/8/1.

11. Following the extension of the review cycle to four and a half years and within existing resources and workload, the duration of the Working Group meeting for the review will be extended from the present three hours and the modalities will be agreed upon at the seventeenth session of the Council, including the list of speakers, which shall be based on the modalities as appear in the Appendix.

12. The final outcome of the review will be adopted by the plenary of the Council. The modalities for the organization of the one-hour consideration of the outcome shall be in accordance with the President's statement PRST/9/2.

13. The national human rights institution of the State under review, consistent with the Paris Principles, shall be entitled to intervene immediately after the State under review during the adoption of the outcome of the review by the Council plenary.

14. The Universal Periodic Review voluntary trust fund to facilitate the participation of States, established by the Council in its resolution 6/17 of 28 September 2007, should be strengthened and operationalized in order to encourage a significant participation of developing countries, particularly least developing countries and small island developing States, in their review.

D. Outcome of the review

15. The recommendations contained in the outcome of the review should preferably be clustered thematically with the full involvement and consent of the State under review and the States that made the recommendations.

16. The State under review should clearly communicate to the Council, in a written format, preferably prior to the Council plenary meeting, its positions on all received recommendations, in accordance with the provisions of paragraphs 27 and 32 of the annex to Council resolution 5/1.

E. Follow-up to the review

17. While the outcome of the review, as a cooperative mechanism, should be implemented primarily by the State concerned, States are encouraged to conduct broad consultations with all relevant stakeholders in this regard.

18. States are encouraged to provide the Council, on a voluntary basis, with a midterm update on follow-up to accepted recommendations.

19. The voluntary fund for financial and technical assistance, established by the Council in its resolution 6/17, should be strengthened and operationalized in order to provide a source of financial and technical assistance to help countries, in particular least developed countries and small island developing States, to implement the recommendations emanating from their review. A board of trustees should be established in accordance with the rules of the United Nations.

20. States may request the United Nations representation at the national or regional level to assist them in the implementation of follow-up to their review, bearing in mind the provisions of paragraph 36 of the annex to Council resolution 5/1. The Office of the United Nations High Commissioner for Human Rights may act as a clearing house for such assistance.

21. Financial and technical assistance for the implementation of the review should support national needs and priorities, as may be reflected in national implementation plans.

II. Special procedures

A. Selection and appointment of mandate holders

22. To further strengthen and enhance transparency in the selection and appointment process of mandate holders envisaged in the annex to Council resolution 5/1, the following provisions will apply:

(*a*) In addition to entities specified in paragraph 42 of the annex to Council resolution 5/1, national human rights institutions in compliance with the Paris Principles may also nominate candidates as special procedure mandate holders;

(*b*) Individual candidates and candidates nominated by entities shall submit an application for each specific mandate, together with personal data and a motivation letter no longer than 600 words. The Office of the High Commissioner shall prepare a public list of candidates who applied for each vacancy;

(*c*) The consultative group established pursuant to paragraph 47 of the annex to Council resolution 5/1 will consider, in a transparent manner, candidates having applied for each specific mandate. However, under exceptional circumstances and if a particular post justifies it, the group may consider additional candidates with equal or more suitable qualifications for the post. The group shall interview shortlisted candidates to ensure equal treatment of all candidates;

(*d*) In implementing paragraph 52 of the annex to Council resolution 5/1, the President shall justify his or her decision if he or she decides not to follow the order of priority proposed by the consultative group.

B. Working methods

23. In line with Council resolution 5/2 of 18 June 2007, States should cooperate with and assist special procedures mandate holders in the performance of their tasks and it is incumbent on mandate holders to exercise their functions in accordance with their mandates and in compliance with the code of conduct.

24. The integrity and independence of the special procedures mandate holders and the principles of cooperation, transparency and accountability are integral to ensuring a robust system of special procedures that would enhance the capacity of the Council to address human rights situations on the ground.

25. The special procedures mandate holders shall continue to foster a constructive dialogue with States. The special procedures mandate holders shall also endeavour to formulate their recommendations in a concrete, comprehensive and action-oriented way and pay attention to the technical assistance and capacity-building needs of States in their thematic and country mission reports. The comments of the State concerned shall be included as an addendum to country mission reports.

26. States are urged to cooperate with and assist special procedures mandate holders by responding in a timely manner to requests for information and visits, and to study carefully the conclusions and recommendations addressed to them by the special procedures mandate holders.

27. The Council should streamline its requests to special procedures mandate holders, in particular with regard to reporting, to ensure a meaningful discussion of their reports. The Council should remain a forum for open, constructive and transparent discussion on cooperation between States and special procedures mandate holders, allowing for the identification and exchange of good practices and lessons learned.

28. The national human rights institution, consistent with the Paris Principles, of the country concerned shall be entitled to intervene immediately after the country concerned during the interactive dialogue, following the presentation of a country mission report by a special procedures mandate holder.

29. The Office of the High Commissioner will continue to maintain information on special procedures, such as mandates, mandate holders, invitations and country visits and responses thereto, as well as reports presented to the Council and the General Assembly, in a comprehensive and easily accessible manner.

30. The Council strongly rejects any act of intimidation or reprisal against individuals and groups who cooperate or have cooperated with the United Nations, its representatives and mechanisms in the field of human rights, and urges States to prevent and ensure adequate protection against such acts.

C. Resources and funding

31. The Council recognizes the importance of ensuring the provision of adequate and equitable funding, with equal priority accorded to civil and political rights and economic, social and cultural rights, including the right to development, to support all special procedures mandate holders according to their specific needs, including additional tasks entrusted to them by the General Assembly. This should be achieved through the regular budget of the United Nations.

32. The Council therefore requests the Secretary-General to ensure the availability of adequate resources within the regular budget of the Office of the High Commissioner to support the full implementation by special procedures mandate holders of their mandates.

33. The Council also recognizes the continued need for extrabudgetary funding to support the work related to the special procedures, and welcomes further voluntary contributions by Member States, emphasizing that these contributions should be, to the extent possible, non-earmarked.

34. The Council highlights the need for full transparency in the funding of the special procedures.

III. Human Rights Council Advisory Committee

35. The Council shall, within existing resources, strengthen its interaction with the Human Rights Council Advisory Committee and engage more systematically with it through work formats such as seminars, panels, working groups and sending feedback to the inputs of the Committee.

36. The Council shall endeavour to clarify specific mandates given to the Advisory Committee under relevant resolutions, including indicating thematic priorities, and provide specific guidelines for the Advisory Committee with a view to triggering implementation-oriented outputs.

37. In order to provide a proper setting for a better interaction between the Council and its Advisory Committee, the first annual session of the Committee shall henceforth be convened immediately prior to the March session of the Council, while the second session shall be held in August.

38. The annual report of the Advisory Committee shall be submitted to the Council at its September session, and be the subject of an interactive dialogue with the Committee Chair. The present provision does not exclude other interaction with the Committee should such opportunities arise and be deemed appropriate by the Council.

39. The Advisory Committee shall endeavour to enhance intersessional work between its members in order to give effect to the provisions of paragraph 81 of the annex to Council resolution 5/1.

IV. Agenda and framework for the programme of work

40. The agenda of the Council and the framework for the programme of work are as specified in the annex to Council resolution 5/1.

41. Council cycles will be aligned with the calendar year and be subject to any necessary transitional arrangements decided on by the General Assembly.

V. Methods of work and rules of procedure

A. Yearly panel discussion with United Nations agencies and funds

42. The Council shall hold a half-day panel discussion once a year to interact with the heads of governing bodies and secretariats of United Nations agencies and funds within their respective mandates on specific human rights themes, with the objective of promoting the mainstreaming of human rights throughout the United Nations system. The present provision does not preclude other opportunities that may arise for discussions between the Council and United Nations agencies and funds on the mainstreaming of human rights.

43. State or regional groups may propose issues to be discussed by the panel. On the basis of such proposals and consultation with all regional groups, the President of the Council will propose the theme of the panel discussion for the upcoming year for approval by the Council at its relevant organizational session.

44. The Office of the High Commissioner, in its capacity as secretariat of the Council, shall coordinate the preparation of the documentation required for the panel discussion.

B. Voluntary yearly calendar of resolutions

45. The Bureau shall establish a tentative yearly calendar for the thematic resolutions of the Council in consultation with the main sponsors. The yearly calendar will be established on a voluntary basis and without prejudice to the right of States as provided for in paragraph 117 of the annex to Council resolution 5/1.

46. The calendar should also contemplate the appropriate synchronization of schedules for resolutions, mandates and presentation of reports by the special procedures mandate holders, taking into account the need for balance among them.

47. The Bureau shall present a report to the Council at its eighteenth session.

C. Biennial and triennial thematic resolutions

48. In principle and on a voluntary basis, omnibus thematic resolutions should be considered on a biennial or triennial basis.

49. Thematic resolutions on the same issue to be presented in-between the above-mentioned intervals are expected to be shorter and focused on addressing the specific question or gap in standards that justified their presentation.

D. Transparency and extensive consultations for resolutions and decisions

50. The consultation process on, inter alia, resolutions and decisions of the Council shall observe the principles of transparency and inclusiveness.

E. Documentation

51. There is a need to ensure the availability of working documents in a timely manner and in all official languages of the United Nations.

F. Deadlines for the notification and submission of draft initiatives and information related to programme budget implications

52. There is a need for early submission of draft resolutions and decisions by the end of the penultimate week of the Council session.

53. Sponsors of initiatives are encouraged to contact the Office of the High Commissioner before the second week of the session with a view to facilitating the circulation of information on budgetary implications, if any.

G. Establishment of an Office of the President

54. In line with the procedural and organizational roles of the President, an Office of the President of the Human Rights Council shall be established, within existing resources, to support the President in the fulfilment of his or her tasks and to enhance efficiency, continuity and institutional memory in this regard.

55. The Office of the President shall be provided with adequate resources drawn from the regular budget, including staff, office space and necessary equipment required for the fulfilment of the tasks. The appointment of the staff of the Office shall promote equitable geographic distribution and gender balance. The staff of the Office shall be accountable to the President.

56. The composition, modalities and financial implications of the Office of the President shall be considered by the Council on the basis of the report of the secretariat, at its seventeenth session.

H. Human Rights Council secretariat services

57. The secretariat services to the Council and its mechanisms should continue to be improved to enhance the efficiency of the work of the Council.

I. Accessibility for persons with disabilities

58. There is a need to enhance accessibility for persons with disabilities to the Council and the work of its mechanisms, including its information and communications technology, Internet resources and documents, in accordance with international standards on accessibility for persons with disabilities.

J. Use of information technology

59. The Council shall explore the feasibility of using information technology, such as videoconferencing or videomessaging, to enhance access and participation by non-resident State delegations, specialized agencies, other intergovernmental organizations and national human rights institutions consistent with the Paris Principles, as well as by non-governmental organizations in consultative status, bearing in mind the need to ensure full compliance of such participation with the Council's rules of procedure and rules concerning accreditation.

60. The use of modern information technology, such as electronic circulation, is encouraged in order to reduce the circulation of paper.

K. Task force

61. The Council decides to establish a task force to study the issues envisaged in paragraphs 57 to 60 above, in consultation with Government representatives, the Office of the High Commissioner, the United Nations Office at Geneva and all relevant stakeholders, and to submit concrete recommendations to the Council at its nineteenth session.

L. Technical assistance trust fund

62. The Council will consider modalities for the establishment of a technical assistance trust fund to support the participation of least developed countries and small island developing States in the work of the Council at its nineteenth session.

APPENDIX

Modalities for establishing the list of speakers for the Working Group on the Universal Periodic Review

The established procedures, which allow speaking time of three minutes for Member States and two minutes for observer States, will continue to apply when all speakers can be accommodated within the number of minutes available to Member and observer States.

Should it not be possible to accommodate all speakers within the minutes available based on three minutes of speaking time for Member States and two minutes for observer States, the speaking time will be reduced to two minutes for all.

If all speakers still cannot be accommodated, the speaking time will be divided among all delegations inscribed so as to enable each and every speaker to take the floor.

Steps for drawing up the list of speakers

1. The list of speakers will open at 10 a.m. on the Monday of the week preceding the beginning of the session of the Working Group on the Universal Periodic Review and remain open for a period of four days. It will close on the Thursday at 6 p.m. A registration desk will be set up at the Palais des Nations. The exact location will be communicated to all permanent missions by the secretariat.

2. In all cases, regardless of speaking time, the delegations inscribed on the list of speakers will be arranged in alphabetical order of the country names in English. On the Friday morning preceding the beginning of the session, the President, in the presence of the Bureau, will draw by lot the first speaker on the list. The list of speakers will continue from the State drawn onwards. On the Friday afternoon, all delegations will be informed of the speaking order and of the speaking time available to delegations.

3. Speaking time limits during the review will be strictly enforced. Speakers who exceed their speaking time will have their microphones cut off. Speakers may therefore wish to deliver the essential part of their statements at the beginning.

4. All speakers will have the possibility of swapping places on the list of speakers under bilateral arrangement between speakers.

RECORDED VOTE ON RESOLUTION 65/281:

In favour: Afghanistan, Albania, Algeria, Andorra, Antigua and Barbuda, Argentina, Australia, Austria, Azerbaijan, Bahamas, Bahrain, Bangladesh, Barbados, Belarus, Belgium, Belize, Benin, Bolivia, Bosnia and Herzegovina, Botswana, Brazil, Brunei Darussalam, Bulgaria, Burkina Faso, Burundi, Cameroon, Chad, Chile, China, Colombia, Comoros, Costa Rica, Croatia, Cuba, Cyprus, Czech Republic, Democratic People's Republic of Korea, Democratic Republic of the Congo, Denmark, Djibouti, Dominican Republic, Ecuador, Egypt, Eritrea, Estonia, Ethiopia, Fiji, Finland, France, Gambia, Georgia, Germany, Ghana, Greece, Grenada, Guatemala, Guyana, Haiti, Honduras, Hungary, Iceland, India, Indonesia, Iran, Iraq, Ireland, Italy, Jamaica, Japan, Jordan, Kazakhstan, Kenya, Kuwait, Kyrgyzstan, Lao People's Democratic Republic, Latvia, Lebanon, Lesotho, Liberia, Liechtenstein, Lithuania, Luxembourg, Madagascar, Malawi, Malaysia, Maldives, Malta, Mauritius, Mexico, Monaco, Mongolia, Montenegro, Morocco, Myanmar, Namibia, Nepal, Netherlands, New Zealand, Nicaragua, Niger, Norway, Oman, Pakistan, Panama, Papua New Guinea, Paraguay, Peru, Philippines, Poland, Portugal, Qatar, Republic of Korea, Republic of Moldova, Romania, Russian Federation, Saint Lucia, Saint Vincent and the Grenadines, Samoa, San Marino, Saudi Arabia, Senegal, Serbia, Sierra Leone, Singapore, Slovakia, Slovenia, South Africa, Spain, Sri Lanka, Sudan, Suriname, Swaziland, Sweden, Switzerland, Syrian Arab Republic, Tajikistan, Thailand, the former Yugoslav Republic of Macedonia, Timor-Leste, Trinidad and Tobago, Turkey, Turkmenistan, Uganda, Ukraine, United Arab Emirates, United Kingdom, United Republic of Tanzania, Uruguay, Uzbekistan, Venezuela, Viet Nam, Yemen, Zambia, Zimbabwe.

Against: Canada, Israel, Palau, United States.

Abstaining: None.

Office of Council President. On 17 June [A/66/53 (dec. 17/118)], the Council established an Office of the President to support the President in fulfilling his or her tasks and to enhance efficiency and institutional memory. It further decided that the appointment should promote geographical distribution and gender balance; that the President would select, manage and renew the staff of the Office, in accordance with UN staff regulations and rules; that the staff of the Office should serve for a one-year term, on a renewable basis; and that the Office should be operational no later than the seventh cycle of the Council.

The General Assembly welcomed the establishment of the Office in section VIII of **resolution 66/247** of 24 December (see p. 1393).

Universal periodic review

The Human Rights Council established the universal periodic review (UPR) [YUN 2007, p. 663] as an instrument for assessing every four years the human rights records of all Member States. Each review, conducted by the Working Group on the UPR, was facilitated by groups of three States, or "troikas", acting as rapporteurs.

Working Group sessions. The Working Group on UPR, made up of the 47 Council members, held its tenth (24 January–4 February) [A/HRC/17/2], eleventh (2–13 May) [A/HRC/18/2] and twelfth (3–14 October) [A/HRC/19/2] sessions in Geneva. It reviewed 49 countries in the order of consideration determined by the Council in 2007 [YUN 2007, p. 663]. As provided for in Council resolution 5/1 [ibid.], the review was based on a national report prepared by the State under review; a compilation by OHCHR of information about the human rights situation in the State concerned, as reported by treaty bodies and special procedures; and a summary by OHCHR of credible information from other stakeholders, including non-governmental organizations (NGOs).

At its tenth session, the Working Group considered and adopted reports on Nauru [A/HRC/17/3], Rwanda [A/HRC/17/4], Nepal [A/HRC/17/5], Saint Lucia [A/HRC/17/6 & Corr.1], Oman [A/HRC/17/7], Austria [A/HRC/17/8], Myanmar [A/HRC/17/9], Australia [A/HRC/17/10], Georgia [A/HRC/17/11], Saint Kitts and Nevis [A/HRC/17/12], Sao Tome and Principe [A/HRC/17/13], Namibia [A/HRC/17/14 & Corr.1], the Niger [A/HRC/17/15], Mozambique [A/HRC/17/16], Estonia [A/HRC/17/17] and Paraguay [A/HRC/17/18]. The reports summarized the presentation by the State under review; the interactive dialogue in the Working Group between State and Council; the response by the State; and the conclusions and/or recommendations to the State under review. The outcome of the review comprised the report of the Working Group together with the views of the State under review about the recommendations and/or conclusions, as well as its voluntary commitments and its replies to questions or issues that were not sufficiently addressed during the interactive dialogue.

Responses were submitted by Nauru [A/HRC/17/3/Add.1], Rwanda [A/HRC/17/4/Add.1], Nepal [A/HRC/17/5/Add.1], Saint Lucia [A/HRC/17/6/Add.1], Oman [A/HRC/17/7/Add.1], Austria [A/HRC/17/8/Add.1], Myanmar [A/HRC/17/9/Add.1], Australia [A/HRC/17/10/Add.1], Georgia [A/HRC/17/11/Add.1], Saint Kitts and Nevis [A/HRC/17/12/Add.1], Namibia [A/HRC/17/14/Add.1 & Corr.1], the Niger [A/HRC/17/15/Add.1], Mozambique [A/HRC/17/16/Add.1], Estonia [A/HRC/17/17/Add.1] and Paraguay [A/HRC/17/18/Add.1].

At its eleventh session, the Working Group considered and adopted reports on Belgium [A/HRC/18/3], Denmark [A/HRC/18/4], Palau [A/HRC/18/5], Somalia [A/HRC/18/6 & Corr.1], Seychelles [A/HRC/18/7], Solomon Islands [A/HRC/18/8 & Corr.1], Latvia [A/HRC/18/9], Sierra Leone [A/HRC/18/10], Singapore [A/HRC/18/11], Suriname [A/HRC/18/12], Greece [A/HRC/18/13], Samoa [A/HRC/18/14], Saint Vincent and the Grenadines [A/HRC/18/15], the Sudan and South Sudan [A/HRC/18/16], Hungary [A/HRC/18/17] and Papua New Guinea [A/HRC/18/18 & Corr.1].

Responses were submitted by Denmark [A/HRC/18/4/Add.1], Palau [A/HRC/18/5/Add.1], Somalia [A/HRC/18/6/Add.1], Latvia [A/HRC/18/9/Add.1], Sierra Leone [A/HRC/18/10/Add.1], Singapore [A/HRC/18/11/Add.1], Suriname [A/HRC/18/12/Add.1], Greece [A/HRC/18/13/Add.1], Samoa [A/HRC/18/14/Add.1], Saint Vincent and the Grenadines [A/HRC/18/15/Add.1], the Sudan and South Sudan [A/HRC/18/16/Add.1 & Corr.1], Hungary [A/HRC/18/17/Add.1] and Papua New Guinea [A/HRC/18/18/Add.1].

At its twelfth session, the Working Group considered and adopted reports on Tajikistan [A/HRC/19/3], the United Republic of Tanzania [A/HRC/19/4], Antigua and Barbuda [A/HRC/19/5], Swaziland [A/HRC/19/6], Trinidad and Tobago [A/HRC/19/7], Thailand [A/HRC/19/8], Ireland [A/HRC/19/9], Togo [A/HRC/19/10], Syria [A/HRC/19/11], Venezuela [A/HRC/19/12], Iceland [A/HRC/19/13], Zimbabwe [A/HRC/19/14], Lithuania [A/HRC/19/15], Uganda [A/HRC/19/16], Timor-Leste [A/HRC/19/17], the Republic of Moldova [A/HRC/19/18] and Haiti [A/HRC/19/19].

Responses were submitted by Tajikistan [A/HRC/19/3/Add.1], Tanzania [A/HRC/19/4/Add.1], Antigua and Barbuda [A/HRC/19/5/Add.1 & Corr.1], Swaziland [A/HRC/19/6/Add.1], Trinidad and Tobago [A/HRC/19/7/Add.1], Thailand [A/HRC/19/8/Add.1], Ireland [A/HRC/19/9/Add.1], Togo [A/HRC/19/10/Add.1], Syria [A/HRC/19/11/Add.1], Venezuela [A/HRC/19/12/Add.1], Iceland [A/HRC/19/13/Add.1], Lithuania [A/HRC/19/15/Add.1], Uganda [A/HRC/19/16/Add.1], Timor-Leste [A/HRC/19/17/Add.1], Moldova [A/HRC/19/18/Add.1] and Haiti [A/HRC/19/19/Add.1].

Human Rights Council action. At its sixteenth session [A/HRC/16/2], the Council considered the outcome of the reviews conducted during the ninth session of the Working Group [YUN 2010, p. 635]. The Council adopted, through standardized decisions, the outcomes of the reviews on Liberia [dec. 16/101], Malawi [dec. 16/102], Mongolia [dec. 16/103], Panama [dec. 16/104], Maldives [dec.16/105], Andorra [dec. 16/106], Bulgaria [dec. 16/107], Honduras [dec. 16/108], Lebanon [dec. 16/109], Marshall Islands [dec. 16/110], Croatia [dec. 16/111], Jamaica [dec. 16/112], Micronesia [dec. 16/113], Mauritania [dec. 16/114] and the United States [dec. 16/115].

At its seventeenth session [A/HRC/17/2], the Council considered the outcome of the reviews conducted during the tenth session of the Working Group. The Council adopted the outcomes of the reviews of Nauru [dec. 17/101], Rwanda [dec. 17/102], Nepal [dec. 17/103], Saint Lucia [dec. 17/104], Oman [dec. 17/105], Austria [dec. 17/106], Myanmar [dec. 17/107], Australia [dec. 17/108], Georgia [dec. 17/109], Saint Kitts and Nevis [dec. 17/110], Sao Tome and Principe [dec. 17/111], Namibia [dec. 17/112], the Niger [dec. 17/113], Mozambique [dec. 17/114], Estonia [dec. 17/115] and Paraguay [dec. 17/116].

At its eighteenth session [A/HRC/18/2], the Council considered the outcome of the reviews conducted during the eleventh session of the Working Group. The Council adopted the outcomes of the reviews of Belgium [dec. 18/101], Denmark [dec. 18/102], Palau [dec. 18/103], Somalia [dec. 18/104], Seychelles [dec. 18/105], Solomon Islands [dec. 18/106], Latvia [dec. 18/107], Sierra Leone [dec. 18/108], Singapore [dec. 18/109], Suriname [dec. 18/110], Greece [dec. 18/111], Samoa [dec. 18/112], Saint Vincent and the Grenadines [dec. 18/113], the Sudan [dec. 18/114 A], South Sudan [dec. 18/114 B], Hungary [dec. 18/115] and Papua New Guinea [dec. 18/116].

Reports of High Commissioner. In her annual report [A/66/36], the United Nations High Commissioner for Human Rights, Navanethem Pillay (South Africa), noted that the first cycle of the UPR had provided a framework within which each State had made public commitments in respect of recommendations directed at improving the human rights situation on the ground. The second cycle should build on the initial review by following up on the achievements and pledges by States. In a further report [A/HRC/19/21], she noted that by the end of October all Member States had been reviewed, with a 100 per cent participation rate in the UPR.

Human Rights Council action. In follow-up to Human Rights Council resolution 16/21 on the review of its work and functioning (see p. 607), the Council, on 17 June [A/66/53 (dec. 17/119)], decided that the order of the review established for the first UPR cycle should be maintained for the second and subsequent cycles. It also decided on the general guidelines for the preparation of information under UPR; the duration of the review for each country; aspects relating to the list of speakers; and the revision of the terms of reference of the Voluntary Fund. A tentative timetable for the session of the Working Group on UPR as of the second cycle was annexed to the decision.

Human Rights Council Advisory Committee

The Human Rights Council Advisory Committee, a think-tank for the Council composed of 18 experts serving in their personal capacity held its sixth (17–21 January) [A/HRC/AC/6/3] and seventh (8–12 August) [A/HRC/AC/7/4] sessions in Geneva. At its sixth session, the Committee adopted four recommendations to be submitted to the Council on: missing persons; the study on discrimination in the context of the right to food (see p. 721); the drafting group on the promotion of the rights of peoples to peace; and the preliminary study on ways and means to further advance the right of people working in rural areas. It also adopted a recommendation on the drafting group on enhancement of international cooperation in the field of human rights. The Committee endorsed the final report on best practices in the matter of missing persons [A/HRC/AC/6/3 (rec. 6/1)], and pursuant to Council requests [YUN 2009, p. 626, YUN 2010, pp. 636 & 717], submitted to the Council, respectively, its final study on discrimination in the context of the right to food [rec. 6/2], its progress report on the draft declaration on the right of peoples to peace [rec. 6/3] (see p. 703) and a preliminary study on the advancement of the rights of peasants and other people working in rural areas [rec. 6/5]. The Committee also took note of the preparatory document submitted by the drafting group on enhancement of international cooperation in the field of human rights, established in 2010 [YUN 2010, p. 636] [rec. 6/4].

At its seventh session, the Advisory Committee adopted five recommendations on: a study on promoting human rights and fundamental freedoms through a better understanding of traditional values of humankind; human rights and international solidarity; the drafting group on the promotion of the rights of peoples to peace; the right to food; and the enhancement of international cooperation in the field of human rights. The Committee established a drafting group to prepare the aforementioned study [A/HRC/AC/7/4 (rec. 7/1)].

By a President's statement of 25 March [A/66/53 (PRST/16/1)], the Council President took note of the reports of the Committee on its fifth [YUN 2010, p. 636] and sixth sessions.

Human Rights Council action. In follow-up to Human Rights Council resolution 16/21 on the review of its work and functioning, the Council on 30 September [A/66/53/Add.1 (dec. 18/121)] decided to adjust the cycle of the Advisory Committee to run from 1 October to 30 September, to ensure that the annual reporting of the Committee to the Council and the interactive dialogue thereon would take place at the end of the cycle.

Complaint procedure

The complaint procedure of the Human Rights Council comprised the Working Group on Communications, which examined communications of alleged violations and assessed their merits, and the Working Group on Situations, which, on the recommendation of the Working Group on Communications, reported to the Council on consistent patterns of gross violations and recommended a course of action.

Working Group on Communications. The five-member Working Group on Communications held its eighth (11–15 April) [A/HRC/WG.5/8/R.2] and ninth (29 August–2 September) [A/HRC/WG.5/9/R.2] sessions in Geneva.

At its eighth session, the Working Group considered 34 files of communications concerning 27 countries. That included 21 new files containing communications and Government replies thereto in relation to 19 countries. A total of 33 replies to 34 files were received from Governments in relation to the communications. The Working Group also examined 10 files related to communications concerning 9 countries which, at its seventh session [YUN 2010, p. 636], it had decided to keep under review. Ten replies were received from concerned Governments in relation to those communications. The Working Group also had before it three files relating to communications concerning two countries, the consideration of which, at its seventh session, it had postponed. Three replies had been received from concerned Governments in relation to those communications.

The Working Group adopted 34 decisions. Decisions were taken on all the 21 new files registered under the complaint procedure between June and October 2010, as well as on 10 files of communications that had been kept under review and the 3 files of communications, the consideration of which had been postponed from the seventh session. The Working Group decided to transmit six files relating to six countries (Iraq, Kyrgyzstan, Lao People's Democratic Republic, Mexico, Syrian Arab Republic, Turkmenistan) to the Working Group on Situations. It decided to keep under review until its next session 13 files relating to 10 countries (Colombia, Egypt, Guatemala, Kenya, Maldives, Nigeria, Pakistan, Philippines, Togo, Yemen) and requested further information from the Governments concerned. The consideration of 15 files relating to 12 countries (Algeria, Bahrain, Bangladesh, Canada, India, Indonesia, Kazakhstan, Lao People's Democratic Republic, Mauritius, Nepal, Thailand, United States) was discontinued. The Working Group received Government replies to 33 of the 34 files before it.

At its ninth session, the Working Group considered 30 files of communications concerning 22 countries. That included 17 new files containing communications and Government replies thereto in relation to 13 countries. A total of 15 replies relating to 17 files were received from Governments in relation to the communications. The Working Group also examined 13 files related to communications concerning 10 countries which it had decided to keep under review from its eighth session. In relation to those communications, the Group had received 10 replies from concerned Governments.

The Working Group adopted 30 decisions. Decisions were taken on all 17 news files registered between November 2010 and March 2011, as well as on all 13 files of communications that had been kept under review at its eighth session. The Working Group transmitted one file relating to one country (Yemen) to the Working Group on Situations. It kept under review until its next session seven files relating to six countries (Canada, Kenya, Mexico, Nigeria, Philippines, Tunisia) and requested further information from the Governments concerned. Consideration was discontinued of 22 files relating to 17 countries (Bahrain, Bangladesh, Brazil, China, Colombia, Djibouti, Egypt, Guatemala, India, Iran, Maldives, Mexico, Pakistan, Philippines, Syria, Thailand, Togo). The Working Group received Government replies to 25 out of the 30 files before it.

Working Group on Situations. The five-member Working Group on Situations held its seventh (31 January–4 February) [A/HRC/16/R.1] and eighth (20–24 June) [A/HRC/18/R.1] sessions in Geneva.

At its seventh session, the Working Group had before it dossiers relating to the human rights situation in Colombia, the Democratic Republic of the Congo (DRC), the Gambia, Iraq, Nepal, Nigeria, Somalia, Tajikistan and Zimbabwe. The material consisted of texts of communications, together with Government replies and observations thereon. The Working Group referred the case concerning Tajikistan to the Human Rights Council. It decided to keep under review cases concerning Colombia, Iraq, Nepal and Zimbabwe, postponed the case concerning the DRC and dismissed cases concerning the Gambia, Nigeria and Somalia.

At its eighth session, the Working Group had before it dossiers relating to the human rights situation in Colombia, the DRC, Iraq, Kyrgyzstan, the Lao People's Democratic Republic, Mexico, Nepal, Syria, Turkmenistan and Zimbabwe. The Working Group referred the case concerning the DRC to the Human Rights Council. It decided to keep under review cases concerning Iraq, Kyrgyzstan, the Lao People's Democratic Republic, Nepal and Zimbabwe, postponed cases related to Colombia, Mexico and Turkmenistan and dismissed the case concerning Syria.

Human Rights Council action. In March [A/HRC/16/2], the Council held two closed meetings of the complaint procedure. It examined the human rights situation in Tajikistan and decided to keep the situation under review. In June [A/HRC/17/2], the Council held two closed meetings, examined the human rights situation in Tajikistan and decided to keep the situation under review. In September [A/HRC/18/2], the Council held two closed meetings of the complaint procedure and examined the human rights situations in the DRC and in Tajikistan. It decided to discontinue its consideration of the situation in Tajikistan and to keep the situation in the DRC under review.

Office of High Commissioner for Human Rights

Reports of High Commissioner. In her annual report to the General Assembly [A/66/36] covering activities since the previous report [YUN 2010, p. 637], the High Commissioner said that OHCHR sought to respond swiftly to human rights crises in many parts of the world. The year saw massive popular movements in North Africa and the Middle East, where people claimed their civil, cultural, economic, social and political rights and expressed their desire for sound governance. Developments in Bahrain, Egypt, Libya, Syria, Tunisia and Yemen, and other situations in Côte d'Ivoire and the Sudan, highlighted the need to develop sustainable ways to prevent the escalation of violence and protect civilians promptly and effectively. The OHCHR Rapid Response Section was called upon more than in any other year, including in regard to facilitating the implementation of resolutions of the Human Rights Council. The Council held special sessions on Libya and Syria, and established international commissions of inquiry to investigate violations of international humanitarian and human rights law.

During the period under review, two new thematic mandates were established: the Working Group on the elimination of discrimination against women in law and in practice [YUN 2010, p. 751] and the Special Rapporteur on the rights to freedom of peaceful assembly and association [ibid., p. 698]. Two new country mandates were established: the Special Rapporteur on the human rights situation in Iran (see p. 769) and the independent expert on Côte d'Ivoire. The Council also established the Working Group on human rights and transnational and other business enterprises (see p. 716). In other developments, by the end of May, 175 of 192 Member States had been reviewed through the universal periodic review (UPR) process (see p. 611), with a 100 per cent participation rate; the first cycle of UPR would be completed in March 2012. In June 2011, the General Assembly endorsed the outcome of the review by the Council of its work and functioning (see p. 608), which was completed in March.

The Office continued to implement its six thematic priorities for 2010–2013: strengthening human rights mechanisms and the development of international human rights law; countering discrimination; pursuing economic, social and cultural rights and combating inequalities and poverty, including in the context of the economic, food and climate crises; protecting human rights in the context of migration; combating impunity and strengthening accountability, the rule of law and democratic society; and protecting human rights in situations of armed conflict, violence and insecurity.

The General Assembly took note of the report on 19 December (**decision 66/537**).

In her annual report to the Human Rights Council [A/HRC/19/21] on the activities of OHCHR, covering 2011, the High Commissioner focused on the implementation of the six thematic priorities. As at December, OHCHR had 58 field presences: 12 regional offices, 13 country offices, 15 human rights components in UN peace missions and 18 human rights advisers in UN country teams. An OHCHR country office was established in Tunisia, and human rights staff were integrated into the United Nations Support Mission in Libya. With regard to efforts to strengthen the treaty body system, the High Commissioner noted the many varied proposals made through the nine consultations held since 2009 among different stakeholders, including States parties to international human rights treaties, treaty body experts, UN entities and specialized agencies, and civil society. She welcomed the increasing number of cross-regional initiatives undertaken by the Council, including the establishment of new mandates, which indicated the Council's determination to address multiple human rights issues and challenges. However, that determination carried significant resource implications. The High Commissioner pointed out the sharp increase in the tasks requested of OHCHR, including those arising from the steadily expanding system of human rights treaty bodies, commissions of inquiry and requests for assistance from States, that had tested the limits of OHCHR resources. Despite calls made during the Council review for a more rationalized programme of work and calendar of resolutions, the Council had continued to adopt record numbers of resolutions. In 2011 the Council had adopted 108 resolutions, compared to 80 adopted in 2010, resulting in the increase of new mandates, including reports, panels and other activities. It was increasingly difficult for the Office to give them all the attention that they deserved.

Human Rights Council action. In a 30 September statement [A/66/53/Add.1 (PRST/18/2)], the Council President acknowledged the need for dialogue between OHCHR and the Council; noted the need for regular and transparent exchanges of information; and recognized the progress made by the High Commissioner in presenting information on sources and allocation of funding to OHCHR in her annual report. The Council President also invited the High Commissioner to include in that report detailed information on allocations of the regular budget, according to programme and mandates; voluntary contributions received by OHCHR, including their specific allocation; allocation of earmarked and unearmarked contributions, according to programmes and mandates; and allocation of funding for the special procedures, which would be considered at a mutually agreed forum.

Composition of staff

Report of High Commissioner. As requested by the Human Rights Council in 2010 [YUN 2010, p. 638], the High Commissioner reported in January [A/HRC/16/35] on the composition of OHCHR staff and on further efforts to correct the imbalance and achieve equitable geographical representation. According to the report, as at 31 December 2010, OHCHR had 476 staff members in the Professional category and above: 234 from Western Europe and other States, 75 from Asia, 69 from Africa, 65 from Latin America and the Caribbean and 33 from Eastern Europe. Nationals from 113 countries were represented in the Professional and above workforce: of those nationalities, 6 were underrepresented, 90 were considered within range, while 16 were overrepresented. An analysis of data using regional methodology showed a steady, continuous and significant increase in the percentage of OHCHR staff from regions identified as requiring better representation within OHCHR over the previous four years. The High Commissioner concluded that noticeable and sustained progress had been achieved in increasing the geographical diversity of staff. OHCHR remained attentive to the need to maintain emphasis on the broadest possible geographical diversity of its staff, and would continue its efforts in that regard.

Human Rights Council action. On 24 March [A/66/53 (res. 16/10)], by a recorded vote of 31 to 13 with 2 abstentions, the Council expressed concern that despite the measures taken by OHCHR, the imbalance in the geographical representation of its composition remained prominent, and that a single region occupied more posts in both the professional and technical categories, as well as permanent and temporary categories, than the other four regions combined. It requested the High Commissioner to enhance the implementation of measures to achieve a better representation of unrepresented or underrepresented countries and regions, while considering applying a zero-growth cap on the representation of countries and regions already overrepresented; encouraged the General Assembly to consider further measures to promote desirable ranges of geographical balance in OHCHR; welcomed efforts made towards achieving a gender balance in the composition of the staff; and requested the High Commissioner to report to the Council's nineteenth (2012) session.

Joint workplan

A report of the Secretary-General issued in December [A/HRC/19/31-E/CN.6/2012/12] reviewed the cooperation between the United Nations Entity for Gender Equality and the Empowerment of Women (UN-Women) and OHCHR and provided the joint workplan for 2012.

Other aspects
Role of prevention

OHCHR report. Pursuant to Human Rights Council resolution 14/5 on the role of prevention in the promotion and protection of human rights [YUN 2010, p. 639], OHCHR in September submitted a report [A/HRC/18/24] providing information on the questionnaire circulated to States, national human rights institutions, NGOs and other stakeholders on the conceptual and practical dimensions of prevention, and a summary of the OHCHR workshop (Geneva, 20 May) convened to discuss the information gathered from the questionnaire, which generated 53 responses. The questionnaire and the workshop revealed four key findings: the need to further elaborate what prevention meant in practice; that a holistic and strategic action on human rights across all State functions would result in more effective prevention; the need for improved collection and disaggregation of statistics and data related explicitly to human rights; and that initiatives to tackle discrimination, particularly against vulnerable groups, should apply to the full range of vulnerable groups in the community. The report concluded with two main recommendations: that further research be undertaken on the different aspects of prevention and on consolidating the different definitions and approaches to prevention; and that practical tools be developed to support States and other actors in understanding the role of prevention and to guide them through the development of national prevention policies.

Human Rights Council action. On 29 September [A/66/53/Add.1 (res. 18/13)], the Council stressed the need to further develop and raise awareness of the concept of prevention of human rights violations in order to encourage its reflection in relevant policies and strategies at the national, regional and international levels; recognized the need for further research to assist States and stakeholders to integrate the role of prevention in human rights promotion and protection; and encouraged OHCHR to prepare a toolkit to support States and stakeholders in understanding the role of prevention, and present it to the Council's twenty-second (2013) session.

Nature of all human rights and fundamental freedoms

In 2011, the General Assembly, by resolution 66/151 (see below), encouraged States to take into account the universal, indivisible, interrelated, interdependent and mutually reinforcing nature of all human rights when integrating the promotion and protection of human rights into national policies and when promoting international cooperation in the field of human rights.

GENERAL ASSEMBLY ACTION

On 19 December [meeting 89], the General Assembly, on the recommendation of the Third Committee [A/66/462/Add.2], adopted **resolution 66/151** without vote [agenda item 69 (*b*)].

The universal, indivisible, interrelated, interdependent and mutually reinforcing nature of all human rights and fundamental freedoms

The General Assembly,

Reaffirming the purposes and principles set out in the Charter of the United Nations, including developing friendly relations among nations based on respect for the principle of equal rights and self-determination of peoples and achieving international cooperation in solving international problems of an economic, social, cultural or humanitarian character and in promoting and encouraging respect for human rights and fundamental freedoms for all,

Acknowledging that peace and security, development and human rights are the pillars of the United Nations system and the foundations for collective security and well-being, and recognizing that development, peace and security and human rights are interlinked and mutually reinforcing,

Reaffirming the Universal Declaration of Human Rights and the Vienna Declaration and Programme of Action, and recalling the International Covenant on Civil and Political Rights, the International Covenant on Economic, Social and Cultural Rights and other human rights instruments,

Recognizing that, in accordance with the Universal Declaration of Human Rights, the ideal of free human beings enjoying civil and political freedom and freedom from fear and want can be achieved only if conditions are created whereby everyone may enjoy her or his civil and political rights as well as her or his economic, social and cultural rights,

Recalling that the Vienna Declaration and Programme of Action reaffirmed the right to development, as established in the Declaration on the Right to Development, as a universal and inalienable right and an integral part of fundamental human rights, and the human person as the central subject of development, and recognizing that, while development facilitates the enjoyment of all human rights, the lack of development may not be invoked to justify the abridgement of internationally recognized human rights,

Recalling also that the work of the Human Rights Council is to be guided by the principles of universality, impartiality, objectivity and non-selectivity, constructive international dialogue and cooperation, with a view to enhancing the promotion and protection of all human rights, civil, political, economic, social and cultural rights, including the right to development,

Recognizing the efforts of the international community to ensure the universal, indivisible, interrelated, interdependent and mutually reinforcing nature of, and to give equal and fair treatment to, all human rights and fundamental freedoms, while acknowledging the important role played by enhanced international cooperation in the field of human rights in this regard,

1. *Reaffirms* that all human rights are universal, indivisible, interrelated, interdependent and mutually reinforcing and that all human rights, civil, political, economic, social and cultural rights must be treated in a fair and equal manner, on the same footing and with the same emphasis;

2. *Recalls*, in this regard, the importance of ensuring the universality, objectivity and non-selectivity of the consideration of human rights issues;

3. *Stresses* that democracy, development and respect for human rights and fundamental freedoms are interdependent and mutually reinforcing;

4. *Acknowledges* that good governance and the rule of law at the national and international levels are essential for sustained economic growth, sustainable development and the eradication of poverty and hunger;

5. *Stresses* that the existence of widespread extreme poverty inhibits the full and effective enjoyment of human rights, and reaffirms that States should take steps to eliminate obstacles to development resulting from failure to observe civil and political rights, as well as economic, social and cultural rights;

6. *Encourages* States to take into account the universal, indivisible, interrelated, interdependent and mutually reinforcing nature of all human rights when integrating the promotion and protection of all human rights into relevant national policies and when promoting international cooperation in the field of human rights, while recalling that the primary responsibility for promoting and protecting human rights rests with the State;

7. *Encourages* the United Nations system to continue to improve its efforts to take into account the universal, indivisible, interrelated, interdependent and mutually reinforcing nature of all human rights when mainstreaming human rights into its activities, with a view to contributing to the full enjoyment of, universal respect for and observance of all human rights and fundamental freedoms;

8. *Recognizes* the positive contribution of all relevant stakeholders, including civil society, to promoting the universal, indivisible, interrelated, interdependent and mutually reinforcing nature of all human rights, and encourages the continuation of efforts in this regard, as appropriate to their activities;

9. *Encourages* the United Nations High Commissioner for Human Rights, treaty bodies, special procedures of the Human Rights Council and other mandate holders to continue to improve their efforts to take into account the universal, indivisible, interrelated, interdependent and mutually reinforcing nature of all human rights in the fulfilment of their mandates;

10. *Requests* the Secretary-General to submit to the General Assembly at its sixty-eighth session a report on the implementation of the present resolution.

Human rights instruments

In 2011, nine UN human rights instruments were in force with expert bodies monitoring their implementation. Those instruments and their treaty bodies were: the 1965 International Convention on the Elimination of All Forms of Racial Discrimination [YUN 1965, p. 440, GA res. 2106 A (XX)] (Committee on the Elimination of Racial Discrimination); the 1966 International Covenant on Civil and Political Rights and the Optional Protocol thereto [YUN 1966, p. 423, GA res. 2200 A (XXI)] and the Second Optional Protocol aiming at the abolition of the death penalty [YUN 1989, p. 484, GA res. 44/128] (Human Rights Committee); the 1966 International Covenant on Economic, Social and Cultural Rights [YUN 1966, p. 419, GA res. 2200 A (XXI)] and the Optional Protocol thereto [YUN 2008, p. 729, GA res. 63/117] (Committee on Economic, Social and Cultural Rights); the 1979 Convention on the Elimination of All Forms of Discrimination against Women [YUN 1979, p. 895, GA res. 34/180] and the Optional Protocol thereto [YUN 1999, p. 1100, GA res. 54/4] (Committee on the Elimination of Discrimination against Women); the 1984 Convention against Torture and Other Cruel, Inhuman or Degrading Treatment or Punishment [YUN 1984, p. 813, GA res. 39/46] and the Optional Protocol thereto [YUN 2002, p. 631, GA res. 57/199] (Committee against Torture and Subcommittee on Prevention of Torture); the 1989 Convention on the Rights of the Child [YUN 1989, p. 560, GA res. 44/25] and the Optional Protocols on the involvement of children in armed conflict and on the sale of children, child prostitution and child pornography [YUN 2000, pp. 616 & 618, GA res. 54/263] (Committee on the Rights of the Child); the 1990 International Convention on the Protection of the Rights of All Migrant Workers and Members of Their Families [YUN 1990, p. 594, GA res. 45/158] (Committee on the Protection of the Rights of All Migrant Workers and Members of Their Families); the 2006 Convention on the Rights of Persons with Disabilities and the Optional Protocol thereto [YUN 2006, p. 785, GA res. 61/106] (Committee on the Rights of Persons with Disabilities); and the 2006 International Convention for the Protection of All Persons from Enforced Disappearance [ibid., p. 800, GA res. 61/177] (Committee on Enforced Disappearances).

The 1948 Convention on the Prevention and Punishment of the Crime of Genocide [YUN 1948–49, p. 959, GA res. 260 A (III)] did not establish a treaty body, but the mandate of the Office of the Special Adviser on the Prevention of Genocide [YUN 2004, p. 730] included collecting information on situations where there might be a risk of genocide, war crimes, ethnic cleansing and crimes against humanity; alerting relevant actors where such a risk existed; and advocating and mobilizing for appropriate action.

Effective implementation of international human rights instruments

Reports of Secretary-General. Pursuant to General Assembly resolutions 65/200 [YUN 2010, p. 641] and 65/204 [ibid., p. 645], the Secretary-General in September submitted a report [A/66/344] on measures to improve further the effectiveness, harmonization and reform of the treaty body system, which provided information on the workload faced by treaty bodies, reviewed the ongoing treaty body strengthening process, and pursuant to resolution 64/173 [YUN 2009, p. 646] contained recommendations for achieving equitable geographical distribution in the membership of human rights treaty bodies for consideration by the Assembly. The Secretary-General concluded that a lack of resources was weakening States parties' accountability under international human rights law and that all funding to the treaty bodies should come from the regular budget, as they were core activities mandated by international treaties. Although the treaty bodies had continued efforts to harmonize their working methods, there were limits to harmonization owing to the specificity of the respective treaties. The report presented two proposals: one on reducing the current backlogs through additional meeting time, and the other on establishing a calendar for long-term planning based on 100 per cent compliance with State party reporting obligations.

Pursuant to Human Rights Council resolution 9/8 [YUN 2008, p. 725], the Secretary-General in December submitted a report [A/HRC/19/28] that reviewed developments in the effective implementation of international human rights instruments, including recommendations for further improving, harmonizing and reforming the treaty body system. In 2011, human rights treaty bodies held 23 sessions amounting to 71 weeks in Geneva and New York, during which 115 State party reports were reviewed in plenary sessions. As at 1 December, treaty bodies had received 117 State party reports, including 12 common core documents. The treaty bodies and the Secretariat examined some 11,119 items of correspondence, and registered some 110 new individual complaints received by the treaty bodies. The Human Rights Committee, the Committee against Torture, the Committee on the Elimination of Racial Discrimination and the Committee on the Elimination of Discrimination against Women examined and adopted 129 final decisions concerning some 223 cases. They issued 45 requests for interim measures of protection in cases where lack of such protection might lead to irreparable harm for the petitioners. They also followed up on over 155 decisions relating to violations of the International Covenant on Civil and Political Rights, the Convention against torture and the Convention on the Elimination of Discrimination against Women.

The Secretary-General observed that at the time of the report only one third of States parties had complied in a timely manner with their reporting obligations, and even at that low level of compliance, treaty bodies were faced with serious structural difficulties to address their workload. In 2011, an average of 250 reports were pending consideration by treaty bodies. He pointed out that the two proposals presented in his September report (see above) to provide treaty bodies with sufficient meeting time to consider State party reports efficiently were mutually compatible. As no comprehensive review of the workload and resourcing of the treaty bodies had been conducted, the Secretary-General called on the General Assembly to undertake a review of the resources of the treaty body system as a whole, taking into account its current and projected needs.

Convention against racial discrimination

Accessions and ratifications

As at 31 December, the number of parties to the International Convention on the Elimination of All Forms of Racial Discrimination, adopted by the General Assembly in resolution 2106(XX) [YUN 1965, p. 440], stood at 175, with Djibouti becoming a party during the year.

The amendment to article 8 of the Convention, regarding the financing of the Committee on the Elimination of Racial Discrimination [YUN 1992, p. 714], had been accepted by 43 States parties as at 31 December. The amendment would enter into force when accepted by a two-thirds majority of States parties, comprising approximately 116 of the 175 States parties to the Convention.

Implementation

Monitoring body. The Committee on the Elimination of Racial Discrimination, established under article 8 of the Convention, held its seventy-eight (14 February–11 March) and seventy-ninth (8 August–2 September) sessions in Geneva [A/66/18]. It considered reports submitted by 21 countries (Albania, Armenia, Bolivia, Cuba, Czech Republic, Georgia, Ireland, Kenya, Lithuania, Maldives, Malta, Norway, Paraguay, Republic of Moldova, Rwanda, Serbia, Spain, Ukraine, United Kingdom, Uruguay, Yemen) and adopted concluding observations on them.

With regard to the Convention's implementation by States parties whose reports were seriously overdue, the Committee noted that 25 States were at least 10 years late in submitting their reports, and 16 States were at least 5 years late. At its seventy-ninth session, the Committee decided to postpone the scheduled review of the Convention's implementation in Jordan and Viet Nam as the States parties had submitted their reports prior to that session. It also decided to postpone the review scheduled in respect to Belize in the light of a commitment received from the State party to finalize its report in the near future.

Under article 14 of the Convention, the Committee considered communications from individuals or groups claiming violations by a State party of their rights as enumerated in the Convention. Fifty-four States parties had recognized the Committee's competence to do so.

Pursuant to article 15 of the Convention, which empowered the Committee to consider petitions, reports and other information relating to Trust and Non-Self-Governing Territories, the Committee noted, as it had done in the past, that it was difficult to fulfil its functions comprehensively, owing to the fact that the reports received contained only scant information directly relating to the principles and objectives of the Convention.

The Committee considered a number of situations under its early warning and urgent action procedure, including situations in Brazil, Chile, Colombia, Costa Rica, Ethiopia, India, Indonesia, Kyrgyzstan, Papua New Guinea, Paraguay, Peru, the Russian Federation, Slovakia, South Africa, Suriname, the United Kingdom, the United Republic of Tanzania and the United States. In the light of information received from Colombia, the Committee decided to remove the case from its early warning and urgent action procedure. Even though information on the situation of indigenous communities in the Chaco in Paraguay was submitted under the early warning and urgent action procedure, the Committee decided to address it during the interactive dialogue with the State party, the outcome of which was reflected in the concluding observations. It also decided to refer to the situation of the Romani and Irish Traveller community at Dale Farm, County of Essex, United Kingdom, in its concluding observations.

At its seventy-eighth and seventy-ninth sessions, the Committee adopted: a decision calling on Côte d'Ivoire to immediately halt inter-ethnic violence and clashes, investigate and punish the perpetrators and provide redress to the victims; a statement calling on the Secretary-General to seek urgent measures to ensure the protection of concerned populations and avoid the risk of inter-ethnic violence and divisions which might worsen the situation in Libya; a statement declaring that Syria was in breach of articles 2, 4(*a*) and 5 of the Convention and urging Syria to end the violence and serious human rights violations against the civilian population; and a statement calling on the United Kingdom to suspend the planned eviction of families at Dale Farm until culturally appropriate accommodation was provided.

Complementary standards

Committee session. Pursuant to a decision to adjourn its third session in November 2010 [YUN 2010, p. 641] and resume its work in 2011, the Ad Hoc Committee on the Elaboration of Complementary Standards held its resumed third session (Geneva, 11–21 April 2011) [A/HRC/18/36], holding preliminary substantive discussions on "Xenophobia" and on "Establishment, designation or maintaining of national mechanisms with competences to protect against and prevent all forms and manifestations of racism, racial discrimination, xenophobia and related intolerance". The Ad Hoc Committee was established by the Council in 2006 [YUN 2006, p. 774] to elaborate complementary standards to the Convention in the form of a convention or additional protocol(s), fill gaps in the treaty, and provide new normative standards for combating racism, racial discrimination, xenophobia and related intolerance.

OHCHR note. By a 1 December note [A/HRC/19/78], the OHCHR secretariat informed the Human Rights Council that the fourth session of the Ad Hoc Committee had been postponed and would be held from 10 to 20 April 2012.

(On the Organization's activities to combat racial discrimination, see also p. 651.)

Covenant on civil and political rights and optional protocols

Accessions and ratifications

As at 31 December, the parties to the International Covenant on Civil and Political Rights and the Optional Protocol thereto, adopted by the General Assembly in resolution 2200A(XXI) [YUN 1966, p. 423], numbered 167 and 114, respectively. During the year, Tunisia became party to the Optional Protocol.

The Second Optional Protocol, aimed at the abolition of the death penalty and adopted by the Assembly in resolution 44/128 [YUN 1989, p. 484], had 73 States parties.

Implementation

Monitoring body. The Human Rights Committee, established under article 28 of the Covenant, held three sessions in 2011: its 101st (New York, 14 March–1 April); 102nd (Geneva, 11-29 July) [A/66/40, Vol. I]; and 103rd (Geneva, 17 October–4 November) [A/67/40, Vol. I]. It considered reports submitted under article 40 from 11 States (Bulgaria, Ethiopia, Iran, Jamaica, Kazakhstan, Kuwait, Mongolia, Norway, Serbia, Slovakia, Togo) and adopted concluding observations on them.

The Committee adopted views on communications from individuals alleging violations of their rights under the Covenant, and decided that other such communications were inadmissible. Those views and decisions were annexed to the Committee's reports [A/66/40, Vol. II (Parts One & Two); A/67/40, Vol. II].

During its 102nd session, the Committee adopted General Comment No. 34 on article 19 (freedoms of opinion and expression) of the Covenant, which would replace General Comment No. 10 (1983).

At its 103rd session, the Committee amended rule 70 of its rules of procedure such that examinations of States parties in the absence of a report would be held in public, instead of private, session and that the resulting concluding observations would also be issued as public documents.

Pursuant to article 4 of the Covenant, certain States parties notified other States parties, through the intermediary of the Secretary-General, of the derogations of certain obligations under the Covenant due to public emergency. Guatemala, on 27 January, 31 May, 25 August and 12, 14 and 20 October, notified the other States parties that it had extended or declared a state of emergency in different provinces or parts of the country, during which certain rights would be suspended. On 25 February, Algeria notified the other States parties that it had lifted the state of emergency declared on 9 February 1992. On 12 May, Bahrain notified the other States parties that it had lifted the state of emergency declared on 15 March, and that all derogations of rights pursuant to that declaration had been terminated, effective as of 1 June 2011. On 28 September, Trinidad and Tobago notified the other States parties that it had declared a state of emergency on 21 August for a period of 15 days, with a further extension of three months. Peru, on 7 December, notified the other State parties that a state of emergency had been declared for a period of 60 days, starting 5 December, in certain provinces in the department of Cajamarca; on 22 December, Peru informed the States parties that the state of emergency had been lifted.

The General Assembly, on 19 December, took note of the Committee's report on its 100th [YUN 2010, p. 43] to 102nd sessions (**decision 66/537**).

(On the Organization's efforts to protect civil and political rights, see also p. 651.)

Covenant on economic, social and cultural rights and optional protocol

Accessions and ratifications

As at 31 December, there were 160 parties to the International Covenant on Economic, Social and Cultural Rights, adopted by the General Assembly in resolution 2200 A (XXI) [YUN 1966, p. 419].

The Optional Protocol to the Covenant, adopted by the Assembly in resolution 63/117 [YUN 2008, p. 729], established a procedure of individual communications for cases of alleged violations of economic, social and cultural rights. The Protocol would enter into force when ratified by 10 States. During the year, Argentina and El Salvador ratified the treaty, bringing the number of States parties to five as at 31 December.

Implementation

Monitoring body. The Committee on Economic, Social and Cultural Rights held its forty-sixth (2–20 May) and forty-seventh (14 November–2 December) sessions in Geneva [E/2012/22]. Its pre-sessional working group met in Geneva from 23 to 27 May and from 5 to 9 December to identify issues to be discussed with reporting States. The Committee examined reports submitted under articles 16 and 17 of the Covenant by Argentina, Cameroon, Estonia, Germany, Israel, the Republic of Moldova, the Russian Federation, Turkmenistan, Turkey and Yemen, and adopted concluding observations on them. On 20 May, the Committee adopted a statement on the obligations of States parties regarding the corporate sector and economic, social and cultural rights, and a statement on the importance and relevance of the right to development.

The Economic and Social Council, on 28 July and 5 December, respectively, deferred its consideration of the report of the Committee on its forty-fourth and forty-fifth sessions [YUN 2010, p. 644] (**decision 2011/264**) and deferred its consideration of the recommendations contained in that report until its 2012 substantive session (**decision 2011/279**).

(On the Organization's efforts to protect economic, social and cultural rights, see also p. 704.)

GENERAL ASSEMBLY ACTION

On 19 December [meeting 89], the General Assembly, on the recommendation of the Third Committee [A/66/462/Add.1], adopted **resolution 66/148** without vote [agenda item 69 (*a*)].

International Covenants on Human Rights

The General Assembly,

Recalling its resolution 64/152 of 18 December 2009,

1. *Welcomes* the annual report of the Human Rights Committee submitted to the General Assembly at its sixty-fifth session;

2. *Also welcomes* the reports of the Committee on Economic, Social and Cultural Rights on its forty-second and forty-third sessions and on its forty-fourth and forty-fifth sessions;

3. *Invites* the Chairs of the Committees to address and engage in an interactive dialogue with the General Assembly at its sixty-seventh and sixty-eighth sessions under the item entitled "Promotion and protection of human rights", within existing resources;

4. *Requests* the Secretary-General to keep the General Assembly informed of the status of the International Covenants on Human Rights and the Optional Protocols thereto, including all reservations and declarations, through the United Nations websites.

Convention on elimination of discrimination against women and optional protocol

(On the status of the Convention and Optional Protocol, see p. 1090. On the Special Rapporteur on violence against women, its causes and consequences, see p. 737.)

Convention against torture

Accessions and ratifications

As at 31 December, 149 States were parties to the 1984 Convention against Torture and Other Cruel, Inhuman or Degrading Treatment or Punishment, adopted by the General Assembly in resolution 39/46 [YUN 1984, p. 813]. Iraq and Vanuatu acceded to the Convention during the year.

States parties to the Optional Protocol to the Convention establishing an international inspection system for places of detention, adopted by the Assembly in resolution 57/199 [YUN 2002, p. 631] and entering into force in 2006 [YUN 2006, p. 776], rose to 61, with Bulgaria, Panama, Tunisia and Turkey becoming parties during the year.

As at 3 June, 56 parties had made the required declarations under articles 21 and 22, which recognized the competence of the Committee against Torture to receive and consider communications by which a State party claimed that another party was not fulfilling its obligations under the Convention, and from or on behalf of individuals who claimed to be victims of violations of the Convention's provisions by a State party. Four parties had made the declaration under article 21, concerning inter-State communications, bringing the number of declarations under that article to 60, while eight had done so under article 22, concerning individual communications, bringing the total under that article to 64.

Amendments to article 17 and 18, adopted in 1992 [YUN 1992, p. 735], had been accepted by 28 States parties as at year's end.

Implementation

Monitoring body. During the year, the Committee against Torture, established as a monitoring body under the Convention, held its forty-sixth (9 May–3 June) [A/66/44] and forty-seventh (31 October–25 November) [A/67/44] sessions in Geneva. Under article 19 of the Convention, it considered reports submitted by 16 countries (Belarus, Bulgaria, Djibouti, Finland, Germany, Ghana, Ireland, Kuwait, Madagascar, Mauritius, Monaco, Morocco, Paraguay, Slovenia, Sri Lanka, Turkmenistan) and adopted concluding observations on them.

The Committee continued, in accordance with article 20, to study reliable information that appeared to contain well-founded indications that torture was systematically practiced in a State party. The Rapporteur on article 20 encouraged States parties on which enquiries had been conducted to implement the Committee's related recommendations. Under article 22, the Committee considered communications submitted by individuals claiming that their rights under the Convention had been violated by a State party and who had exhausted all available domestic remedies.

On 19 December, the General Assembly took note of the Committee's report on its forty-fifth [YUN 2010, p. 645] and forty-sixth sessions (**decision 66/537**).

Subcommittee on prevention. The Subcommittee on Prevention of Torture and Other Cruel, Inhuman or Degrading Treatment or Punishment (Subcommittee on Prevention), established in 2006 [YUN 2006, p. 776] to carry out the functions laid down in the Optional Protocol adopted by resolution 57/199 [YUN 2002, p. 631], held its thirteenth (21–25 February), fourteenth (20–24 June) and fifteenth (14–18 November) sessions in Geneva. The mandate of the Subcommittee was to visit places where persons were or might be deprived of liberty and make recommendations to States parties on their protection; assist States parties in establishing national preventive mechanisms; provide support to such mechanisms; and cooperate with UN and other bodies in preventing ill-treatment.

The fifth annual report of the Subcommittee [CAT/C/48/3] covered its activities in 2011. The report was the first to cover the work of the expanded Subcommittee (from 10 of 25 members)—making the Subcommittee the largest of the UN human rights treaty bodies. The terms of office of the newly elected members started on 1 January 2011. In another development, in January, the Guidelines of the Subcommittee in relation to visits to States parties were issued [CAT/OP/12/4].

In 2011, the Subcommittee visited Ukraine (16–25 May) [CAT/OP/UKR/R.1], Brazil (19–30 September) [CAT/OP/BRA/1] and Mali (5–14 December) [CAT/OP/ML/1]. The visits were followed by the submission of a confidential report to the respective Governments that included recommendations. In March and October, Benin [CAT/OP/BEN/1/Add.1] and Mexico [CAT/OP/MEX/1/Add.1], respectively, submitted their replies relating to the Subcommittee's visits in 2008 [YUN 2008, p. 737]. In June, Paraguay [CAT/OP/PRY/2/Add.1] submitted replies relating to the Subcommittee's follow-up visit in 2010 [YUN 2010, p. 646].

Special Fund. Pursuant to General Assembly resolution 65/205 [YUN 2010, p. 708], the Secretary-General in August submitted a report [A/66/259] on the Special Fund established pursuant to article 26 of the Optional Protocol to the Convention against Torture. The Fund was established to help finance the implementation of the recommendations made by the Subcommittee on Prevention following visits to States parties, as well as education programmes of national preventive mechanisms. The General Assembly took note of report on 19 December (**decision 66/537**).

By a January note [A/HRC/16/74], the Secretary-General provided information on the status of the Special Fund as at 31 December 2010. By a December note [A/HRC/19/29], he informed the Human Rights Council that in 2010–2011, contributions had been received from the Czech Republic ($19,705), Spain ($26,774) and the United Kingdom ($855,263).

Convention on the rights of the child

Accessions and ratifications

As at 31 December, the number of States parties to the 1989 Convention on the Rights of the Child, adopted by the General Assembly in resolution 44/25 [YUN 1989, p. 560], stood at 193. States parties to the Optional Protocol to the Convention on the involvement of children in armed conflict, adopted by Assembly resolution 54/263 [YUN 2000, p. 615], rose to 143, with Djibouti, San Marino, Saudi Arabia and Saint Vincent and the Grenadines becoming parties during the year.

The Optional Protocol to the Convention on the sale of children, child prostitution and child pornography, also adopted by resolution 54/263, had 151 States parties, with Côte d'Ivoire, Djibouti, Guinea, Jamaica, Luxembourg, Mauritius, New Zealand, Pakistan and San Marino becoming parties during the year.

The Secretary-General reported on the status of the Convention and its Optional Protocols as at 1 July [A/66/230].

Implementation

Monitoring body. In 2011, the Committee on the Rights of the Child held its fifty-sixth (17 January–4 February), fifty-seventh (30 May–17 June) and fifty-eighth (19 September–7 October) sessions [A/67/41] in Geneva.

Under article 44 of the Convention, the Committee considered initial and periodic reports submitted by 22 countries (Afghanistan, Bahrain, Belarus, Cambodia, Costa Rica, Cuba, Czech Republic, Denmark, Egypt, Finland, Iceland, Italy, Lao People's Democratic Republic, Mexico, New Zealand, Panama, Republic of Korea, Seychelles, Singapore, Sweden, Syrian Arab Republic, Ukraine) and adopted concluding observations on them.

At its fifty-sixth session, the Committee adopted General Comment No. 13 on the right of the child to freedom from all forms of violence [CRC/C/GC/13].

On 30 September, in accordance with rule 79 of its rule of procedure, the Committee held its annual day of general discussion, which was devoted to the rights of children of incarcerated parents.

The Committee submitted to the General Assembly its biennial report [A/67/41] covering activities from its fifty-fourth to fifty-ninth sessions.

Optional protocol on communications

The Open-ended Working Group established in 2009 [YUN 2009, p. 637] and mandated to elaborate an optional protocol to the Convention on the Rights of the Child to provide a communications procedure, convened its second session in two parts (6–10 December 2010 and 10–16 February 2011) [A/HRC/17/36]. The first part was devoted to a debate on the proposal for a draft optional protocol prepared by the Chairperson [A/HRC/WG.7/2/2 & Corr.1] and the second part was devoted to discussions on the revised text of the proposal [A/HRC/WG.7/2/4]. The Working Group adopted by consensus the text of the draft optional protocol, which was transmitted to the Human Rights Council for consideration.

Human Rights Council action. On 17 June [A/66/53 (res. 17/18)], the Human Rights Council adopted the Optional Protocol to the Convention on the Rights of the Child on a communications procedure and recommended a resolution for adoption by the General Assembly.

GENERAL ASSEMBLY ACTION

On 19 December [meeting 89], the General Assembly, on the recommendation of the Third Committee [A/66/457], adopted **resolution 66/138** without vote [agenda item 64].

Optional Protocol to the Convention on the Rights of the Child on a communications procedure

The General Assembly,

Taking note with appreciation of the adoption by the Human Rights Council, through its resolution 17/18 of 17 June 2011, of the Optional Protocol to the Convention on the Rights of the Child on a communications procedure,

1. *Adopts* the Optional Protocol to the Convention on the Rights of the Child on a communications procedure as contained in the annex to the present resolution;

2. *Recommends* that the Optional Protocol be opened for signature at a signing ceremony to be held in 2012, and requests the Secretary-General and the United Nations High Commissioner for Human Rights to provide the necessary assistance.

ANNEX

Optional Protocol to the Convention on the Rights of the Child on a communications procedure

The States parties to the present Protocol,

Considering that, in accordance with the principles proclaimed in the Charter of the United Nations, the recognition of the inherent dignity and the equal and inalienable rights of all members of the human family is the foundation of freedom, justice and peace in the world,

Noting that the States parties to the Convention on the Rights of the Child (hereinafter referred to as "the Convention") recognize the rights set forth in it to each child within their jurisdiction without discrimination of any kind, irrespective of the child's or his or her parent's or legal guardian's race, colour, sex, language, religion, political or other opinion, national, ethnic or social origin, property, disability, birth or other status,

Reaffirming the universality, indivisibility, interdependence and interrelatedness of all human rights and fundamental freedoms,

Reaffirming also the status of the child as a subject of rights and as a human being with dignity and with evolving capacities,

Recognizing that children's special and dependent status may create real difficulties for them in pursuing remedies for violations of their rights,

Considering that the present Protocol will reinforce and complement national and regional mechanisms allowing children to submit complaints for violations of their rights,

Recognizing that the best interests of the child should be a primary consideration to be respected in pursuing remedies for violations of the rights of the child, and that such remedies should take into account the need for child-sensitive procedures at all levels,

Encouraging States parties to develop appropriate national mechanisms to enable a child whose rights have been violated to have access to effective remedies at the domestic level,

Recalling the important role that national human rights institutions and other relevant specialized institutions, mandated to promote and protect the rights of the child, can play in this regard,

Considering that, in order to reinforce and complement such national mechanisms and to further enhance the implementation of the Convention and, where applicable, the Optional Protocols thereto on the sale of children, child prostitution and child pornography and on the involvement of children in armed conflict, it would be appropriate to enable the Committee on the Rights of the Child (hereinafter referred to as "the Committee") to carry out the functions provided for in the present Protocol,

Have agreed as follows:

PART I
General provisions

Article 1
Competence of the Committee on the Rights of the Child

1. A State party to the present Protocol recognizes the competence of the Committee as provided for by the present Protocol.

2. The Committee shall not exercise its competence regarding a State party to the present Protocol on matters concerning violations of rights set forth in an instrument to which that State is not a party.

3. No communication shall be received by the Committee if it concerns a State that is not a party to the present Protocol.

Article 2
General principles guiding the functions of the Committee

In fulfilling the functions conferred on it by the present Protocol, the Committee shall be guided by the principle of the best interests of the child. It shall also have regard for the rights and views of the child, the views of the child being given due weight in accordance with the age and maturity of the child.

Article 3
Rules of procedure

1. The Committee shall adopt rules of procedure to be followed when exercising the functions conferred on it by the present Protocol. In doing so, it shall have regard, in particular, for article 2 of the present Protocol in order to guarantee child-sensitive procedures.

2. The Committee shall include in its rules of procedure safeguards to prevent the manipulation of the child by those acting on his or her behalf and may decline to examine any communication that it considers not to be in the child's best interests.

Article 4
Protection measures

1. A State party shall take all appropriate steps to ensure that individuals under its jurisdiction are not subjected to any human rights violation, ill-treatment or intimidation as a consequence of communications or cooperation with the Committee pursuant to the present Protocol.

2. The identity of any individual or group of individuals concerned shall not be revealed publicly without their express consent.

PART II
Communications procedure

Article 5
Individual communications

1. Communications may be submitted by or on behalf of an individual or group of individuals, within the jurisdiction of a State party, claiming to be victims of a violation by that State party of any of the rights set forth in any of the following instruments to which that State is a party:

(*a*) The Convention;

(*b*) The Optional Protocol to the Convention on the sale of children, child prostitution and child pornography;

(*c*) The Optional Protocol to the Convention on the involvement of children in armed conflict.

2. Where a communication is submitted on behalf of an individual or group of individuals, this shall be with their consent unless the author can justify acting on their behalf without such consent.

Article 6
Interim measures

1. At any time after the receipt of a communication and before a determination on the merits has been reached, the Committee may transmit to the State party concerned for its urgent consideration a request that the State party take such interim measures as may be necessary in exceptional circumstances to avoid possible irreparable damage to the victim or victims of the alleged violations.

2. Where the Committee exercises its discretion under paragraph 1 of the present article, this does not imply a determination on admissibility or on the merits of the communication.

Article 7
Admissibility

The Committee shall consider a communication inadmissible when:

(*a*) The communication is anonymous;

(*b*) The communication is not in writing;

(*c*) The communication constitutes an abuse of the right of submission of such communications or is incompatible with the provisions of the Convention and/or the Optional Protocols thereto;

(*d*) The same matter has already been examined by the Committee or has been or is being examined under another procedure of international investigation or settlement;

(*e*) All available domestic remedies have not been exhausted. This shall not be the rule where the application of the remedies is unreasonably prolonged or unlikely to bring effective relief;

(*f*) The communication is manifestly ill-founded or not sufficiently substantiated;

(*g*) The facts that are the subject of the communication occurred prior to the entry into force of the present Protocol for the State party concerned, unless those facts continued after that date;

(*h*) The communication is not submitted within one year after the exhaustion of domestic remedies, except in cases where the author can demonstrate that it had not been possible to submit the communication within that time limit.

Article 8
Transmission of the communication

1. Unless the Committee considers a communication inadmissible without reference to the State party concerned, the Committee shall bring any communication submitted to it under the present Protocol confidentially to the attention of the State party concerned as soon as possible.

2. The State party shall submit to the Committee written explanations or statements clarifying the matter and the remedy, if any, that it may have provided. The State party shall submit its response as soon as possible and within six months.

Article 9
Friendly settlement

1. The Committee shall make available its good offices to the parties concerned with a view to reaching a friendly settlement of the matter on the basis of respect for the ob-

ligations set forth in the Convention and/or the Optional Protocols thereto.

2. An agreement on a friendly settlement reached under the auspices of the Committee closes consideration of the communication under the present Protocol.

Article 10
Consideration of communications

1. The Committee shall consider communications received under the present Protocol as quickly as possible, in the light of all documentation submitted to it, provided that this documentation is transmitted to the parties concerned.

2. The Committee shall hold closed meetings when examining communications received under the present Protocol.

3. Where the Committee has requested interim measures, it shall expedite the consideration of the communication.

4. When examining communications alleging violations of economic, social or cultural rights, the Committee shall consider the reasonableness of the steps taken by the State party in accordance with article 4 of the Convention. In doing so, the Committee shall bear in mind that the State party may adopt a range of possible policy measures for the implementation of the economic, social and cultural rights in the Convention.

5. After examining a communication, the Committee shall, without delay, transmit its views on the communication, together with its recommendations, if any, to the parties concerned.

Article 11
Follow-up

1. The State party shall give due consideration to the views of the Committee, together with its recommendations, if any, and shall submit to the Committee a written response, including information on any action taken and envisaged in the light of the views and recommendations of the Committee. The State party shall submit its response as soon as possible and within six months.

2. The Committee may invite the State party to submit further information about any measures the State party has taken in response to its views or recommendations or implementation of a friendly settlement agreement, if any, including as deemed appropriate by the Committee, in the State party's subsequent reports under article 44 of the Convention, article 12 of the Optional Protocol to the Convention on the sale of children, child prostitution and child pornography or article 8 of the Optional Protocol to the Convention on the involvement of children in armed conflict, where applicable.

Article 12
Inter-State communications

1. A State party to the present Protocol may, at any time, declare that it recognizes the competence of the Committee to receive and consider communications in which a State party claims that another State party is not fulfilling its obligations under any of the following instruments to which the State is a party:

(*a*) The Convention;

(*b*) The Optional Protocol to the Convention on the sale of children, child prostitution and child pornography;

(*c*) The Optional Protocol to the Convention on the involvement of children in armed conflict.

2. The Committee shall not receive communications concerning a State party that has not made such a declaration or communications from a State party that has not made such a declaration.

3. The Committee shall make available its good offices to the States parties concerned with a view to a friendly solution of the matter on the basis of the respect for the obligations set forth in the Convention and the Optional Protocols thereto.

4. A declaration under paragraph 1 of the present article shall be deposited by the States parties with the Secretary-General of the United Nations, who shall transmit copies thereof to the other States parties. A declaration may be withdrawn at any time by notification to the Secretary-General. Such a withdrawal shall not prejudice the consideration of any matter that is the subject of a communication already transmitted under the present article; no further communications by any State party shall be received under the present article after the notification of withdrawal of the declaration has been received by the Secretary-General, unless the State party concerned has made a new declaration.

PART III
Inquiry procedure

Article 13
Inquiry procedure for grave
or systematic violations

1. If the Committee receives reliable information indicating grave or systematic violations by a State party of rights set forth in the Convention or in the Optional Protocols thereto on the sale of children, child prostitution and child pornography or on the involvement of children in armed conflict, the Committee shall invite the State party to cooperate in the examination of the information and, to this end, to submit observations without delay with regard to the information concerned.

2. Taking into account any observations that may have been submitted by the State party concerned, as well as any other reliable information available to it, the Committee may designate one or more of its members to conduct an inquiry and to report urgently to the Committee. Where warranted and with the consent of the State party, the inquiry may include a visit to its territory.

3. Such an inquiry shall be conducted confidentially, and the cooperation of the State party shall be sought at all stages of the proceedings.

4. After examining the findings of such an inquiry, the Committee shall transmit without delay these findings to the State party concerned, together with any comments and recommendations.

5. The State party concerned shall, as soon as possible and within six months of receiving the findings, comments and recommendations transmitted by the Committee, submit its observations to the Committee.

6. After such proceedings have been completed with regard to an inquiry made in accordance with paragraph 2 of the present article, the Committee may, after consultation with the State party concerned, decide to include a

summary account of the results of the proceedings in its report provided for in article 16 of the present Protocol.

7. Each State party may, at the time of signature or ratification of the present Protocol or accession thereto, declare that it does not recognize the competence of the Committee provided for in the present article in respect of the rights set forth in some or all of the instruments listed in paragraph 1.

8. Any State party having made a declaration in accordance with paragraph 7 of the present article may, at any time, withdraw this declaration by notification to the Secretary-General of the United Nations.

Article 14
Follow-up to the inquiry procedure

1. The Committee may, if necessary, after the end of the period of six months referred to in article 13, paragraph 5, invite the State party concerned to inform it of the measures taken and envisaged in response to an inquiry conducted under article 13 of the present Protocol.

2. The Committee may invite the State party to submit further information about any measures that the State party has taken in response to an inquiry conducted under article 13, including as deemed appropriate by the Committee, in the State party's subsequent reports under article 44 of the Convention, article 12 of the Optional Protocol to the Convention on the sale of children, child prostitution and child pornography or article 8 of the Optional Protocol to the Convention on the involvement of children in armed conflict, where applicable.

PART IV
Final provisions

Article 15
International assistance and cooperation

1. The Committee may transmit, with the consent of the State party concerned, to United Nations specialized agencies, funds and programmes and other competent bodies its views or recommendations concerning communications and inquiries that indicate a need for technical advice or assistance, together with the State party's observations and suggestions, if any, on these views or recommendations.

2. The Committee may also bring to the attention of such bodies, with the consent of the State party concerned, any matter arising out of communications considered under the present Protocol that may assist them in deciding, each within its field of competence, on the advisability of international measures likely to contribute to assisting States parties in achieving progress in the implementation of the rights recognized in the Convention and/or the Optional Protocols thereto.

Article 16
Report to the General Assembly

The Committee shall include in its report submitted every two years to the General Assembly in accordance with article 44, paragraph 5, of the Convention a summary of its activities under the present Protocol.

Article 17
Dissemination of and information on the Optional Protocol

Each State party undertakes to make widely known and to disseminate the present Protocol and to facilitate access to information about the views and recommendations of the Committee, in particular with regard to matters involving the State party, by appropriate and active means and in accessible formats to adults and children alike, including those with disabilities.

Article 18
Signature, ratification and accession

1. The present Protocol is open for signature to any State that has signed, ratified or acceded to the Convention or either of the first two Optional Protocols thereto.

2. The present Protocol is subject to ratification by any State that has ratified or acceded to the Convention or either of the first two Optional Protocols thereto. Instruments of ratification shall be deposited with the Secretary-General of the United Nations.

3. The present Protocol shall be open to accession by any State that has ratified or acceded to the Convention or either of the first two Optional Protocols thereto.

4. Accession shall be effected by the deposit of an instrument of accession with the Secretary-General.

Article 19
Entry into force

1. The present Protocol shall enter into force three months after the deposit of the tenth instrument of ratification or accession.

2. For each State ratifying the present Protocol or acceding to it after the deposit of the tenth instrument of ratification or instrument of accession, the present Protocol shall enter into force three months after the date of the deposit of its own instrument of ratification or accession.

Article 20
Violations occurring after the entry into force

1. The Committee shall have competence solely in respect of violations by the State party of any of the rights set forth in the Convention and/or the first two Optional Protocols thereto occurring after the entry into force of the present Protocol.

2. If a State becomes a party to the present Protocol after its entry into force, the obligations of that State vis-à-vis the Committee shall relate only to violations of the rights set forth in the Convention and/or the first two Optional Protocols thereto occurring after the entry into force of the present Protocol for the State concerned.

Article 21
Amendments

1. Any State party may propose an amendment to the present Protocol and submit it to the Secretary-General of the United Nations. The Secretary-General shall communicate any proposed amendments to States parties with a request to be notified whether they favour a meeting of States parties for the purpose of considering and deciding upon the proposals. In the event that, within four months of the date of such communication, at least one third of the States parties favour such a meeting, the Secretary-General shall convene the meeting under the auspices of the United Na-

tions. Any amendment adopted by a majority of two thirds of the States parties present and voting shall be submitted by the Secretary-General to the General Assembly for approval and, thereafter, to all States parties for acceptance.

2. An amendment adopted and approved in accordance with paragraph 1 of the present article shall enter into force on the thirtieth day after the number of instruments of acceptance deposited reaches two thirds of the number of States parties at the date of adoption of the amendment. Thereafter, the amendment shall enter into force for any State party on the thirtieth day following the deposit of its own instrument of acceptance. An amendment shall be binding only on those States parties that have accepted it.

Article 22
Denunciation

1. Any State party may denounce the present Protocol at any time by written notification to the Secretary-General of the United Nations. The denunciation shall take effect one year after the date of receipt of the notification by the Secretary-General.

2. Denunciation shall be without prejudice to the continued application of the provisions of the present Protocol to any communication submitted under articles 5 or 12 or any inquiry initiated under article 13 before the effective date of denunciation.

Article 23
Depositary and notification by the Secretary-General

1. The Secretary-General of the United Nations shall be the depositary of the present Protocol.

2. The Secretary-General shall inform all States of:

(*a*) Signatures, ratifications and accessions under the present Protocol;

(*b*) The date of entry into force of the present Protocol and of any amendment thereto under article 21;

(*c*) Any denunciation under article 22 of the present Protocol.

Article 24
Languages

1. The present Protocol, of which the Arabic, Chinese, English, French, Russian and Spanish texts are equally authentic, shall be deposited in the archives of the United Nations.

2. The Secretary-General of the United Nations shall transmit certified copies of the present Protocol to all States.

Also on 19 December [meeting 89], the General Assembly, on the recommendation of the Third Committee [A/66/458], adopted **resolution 66/141** without vote [agenda item 65 (*a*)].

Rights of the child

The General Assembly,

Reaffirming all its previous resolutions on the rights of the child in their entirety, the most recent of which is resolution 65/197 of 21 December 2010,

Emphasizing that the Convention on the Rights of the Child constitutes the standard in the promotion and protection of the rights of the child, and, bearing in mind the importance of the Optional Protocols to the Convention, calling for their universal ratification and effective implementation, as well as that of other human rights instruments,

Recalling the Convention on the Rights of Persons with Disabilities, the International Convention for the Protection of All Persons from Enforced Disappearance and the International Convention on the Protection of the Rights of All Migrant Workers and Members of Their Families,

Reaffirming that the general principles of the Convention on the Rights of the Child, including, inter alia, the best interests of the child, non-discrimination, participation and survival and development, provide the framework for all actions concerning children, including adolescents,

Reaffirming also the Vienna Declaration and Programme of Action, the United Nations Millennium Declaration and the outcome document of the twenty-seventh special session of the General Assembly on children, entitled "A world fit for children", and recalling the Copenhagen Declaration on Social Development and the Programme of Action, the Dakar Framework for Action adopted at the World Education Forum, the Declaration on Social Progress and Development, the Universal Declaration on the Eradication of Hunger and Malnutrition, the Declaration on the Right to Development and the Declaration of the commemorative high-level plenary meeting devoted to the follow-up to the outcome of the special session on children, held in New York from 11 to 13 December 2007, as well as the outcome document of the High-level Plenary Meeting of the General Assembly on the Millennium Development Goals, held in New York from 20 to 22 September 2010,

Taking note with appreciation of the reports of the Secretary-General on progress made towards achieving the commitments set out in the outcome document of the twenty-seventh special session of the General Assembly and on the status of the Convention on the Rights of the Child and the issues addressed in Assembly resolution 65/197, as well as the report of the Special Representative of the Secretary-General on Violence against Children and the report of the Special Representative of the Secretary-General for Children and Armed Conflict, whose recommendations should be carefully studied, taking fully into account the views of Member States,

Acknowledging the important role played by national governmental structures for children, including, where they exist, ministries and institutions in charge of child, family and youth issues and independent ombudspersons for children or other national institutions for the promotion and protection of the rights of the child,

Recognizing that the family has the primary responsibility for the nurturing and protection of children and that children, for the full and harmonious development of their personality, should grow up in a family environment and in an atmosphere of happiness, love and understanding,

Taking note with appreciation of the work to promote and protect the rights of the child carried out by all relevant organs, bodies, entities and organizations of the United Nations system, within their respective mandates, and relevant mandate holders and special procedures of the United Nations, as well as relevant regional organizations, where appropriate, and intergovernmental organizations, and recognizing the valuable role of civil society, including non-governmental organizations,

Profoundly concerned that the situation of children in many parts of the world has been negatively impacted by the world financial and economic crisis, and reaffirming that eradicating poverty continues to be the greatest global challenge facing the world today, recognizing its impact beyond the socioeconomic context,

Profoundly concerned also that the situation of children in many parts of the world remains critical, in an increasingly globalized environment, as a result of the persistence of poverty, social inequality, inadequate social and economic conditions, pandemics, in particular HIV/AIDS, malaria and tuberculosis, lack of access to safe drinking water and sanitation, environmental damage, natural disasters, armed conflict, foreign occupation, displacement, violence, terrorism, abuse, trafficking in children and their organs, all forms of exploitation, commercial sexual exploitation of children, child prostitution, child pornography and child sex tourism, neglect, illiteracy, hunger, intolerance, discrimination, racism, xenophobia, gender inequality, disability and inadequate legal protection, and convinced that urgent and effective national and international action is called for,

Gravely concerned about the devastating impact of some of the recent natural disasters, including on children, reaffirming the importance of providing speedy, sustainable and adequate humanitarian assistance in support of relief, early recovery, rehabilitation, reconstruction and development efforts of the affected countries, and reaffirming also the importance of ensuring that human rights, including child rights, are mainstreamed into these efforts,

Stressing the need for the full and effective implementation of the United Nations Global Plan of Action to Combat Trafficking in Persons, and expressing the view that it will, inter alia, contribute to the promotion and protection of the rights of children, enhance cooperation and better coordination of efforts in fighting trafficking in persons and promote increased ratification and full implementation of the United Nations Convention against Transnational Organized Crime and the Protocol to Prevent, Suppress and Punish Trafficking in Persons, Especially Women and Children, supplementing the United Nations Convention against Transnational Organized Crime,

I
Implementation of the Convention on the Rights of the Child and the Optional Protocols thereto

1. *Reaffirms* paragraphs 1 to 6 of its resolution 65/197, and urges States that have not yet done so to become parties to the Convention on the Rights of the Child, its Optional Protocol on the sale of children, child prostitution and child Pornography and its Optional Protocol on the involvement of children in armed conflict as a matter of priority and to implement them fully;

2. *Welcomes* the efforts of the Secretary-General to promote the universal ratification of the Optional Protocol to the Convention on the Rights of the Child on the sale of children, child prostitution and child pornography and the Optional Protocol on the involvement of children in armed conflict ahead of the tenth anniversary in 2012 of their entry into force, and calls for the effective implementation of the Convention and the above-mentioned Optional Protocols to ensure that all children may fully enjoy all their human rights and fundamental freedoms;

3. *Calls upon* States parties to withdraw reservations that are incompatible with the object and purpose of the Convention or the Optional Protocols thereto and to consider reviewing regularly other reservations with a view to withdrawing them in accordance with the Vienna Declaration and Programme of Action;

4. *Takes note with appreciation* of the adoption on 17 June 2011 by the Human Rights Council of an optional protocol to the Convention on the Rights of the Child providing a communications procedure complementary to the reporting procedure under the Convention on the Rights of the Child;

5. *Encourages* States parties, in implementing the provisions of the Convention and the Optional Protocols thereto, to take note of the recommendations, observations and general comments of the Committee on the Rights of the Child, including, inter alia, general comment No. 9 (2006) on the rights of children with disabilities;

6. *Welcomes* actions of the Committee to monitor the implementation by States parties of the Convention, and notes with appreciation its actions to follow up on its concluding observations and recommendations, and in this regard underlines, in particular, the regional workshops and the participation of the Committee in national-level initiatives;

II
Promotion and protection of the rights of the child and non-discrimination against children

Non-discrimination

7. *Reaffirms* paragraphs 9 to 11 of its resolution 63/241 of 24 December 2008, and calls upon States to ensure the enjoyment by all children of all their civil, political, cultural, economic and social rights without discrimination of any kind;

Registration, family relations and adoption or other forms of alternative care

8. *Also* reaffirms paragraphs 12 to 16 of its resolution 63/241, and urges all States parties to intensify their efforts to comply with their obligations under the Convention on the Rights of the Child to protect children in matters relating to registration, family relations and adoption or other forms of alternative care, and, in cases of international parental or familial child abduction, encourages States to facilitate, inter alia, the return of the child to the country in which he or she resided immediately before the removal or retention;

9. *Recalls* the Guidelines for the Alternative Care of Children, contained in the annex to its resolution 64/142 of 18 December 2009, as a set of orientations to help to inform policy and practice, and encourages States to take them into account;

Economic and social well-being of children, eradication of poverty, right to education, right to enjoyment of the highest attainable standard of physical and mental health and right to food

10. *Reaffirms* paragraphs 17 to 26 of its resolution 63/241, paragraphs 42 to 52 of its resolution 61/146 of 19 December 2006, on the theme of children and poverty, and paragraphs 37 to 42 of its resolution 60/231 of 23 December 2005, on the theme of children living with or affected by HIV and AIDS, and calls upon all States and the international community to create an environment in

which the well-being of the child is ensured, including by strengthening international cooperation in this field and by implementing their previous commitments relating to poverty eradication, the right to education, and measures to promote human rights education, in accordance with the evolving capacities of the child, the right to the enjoyment of the highest attainable standard of physical and mental health, including efforts to address the situation of children living with or affected by HIV and AIDS and to eliminate mother-to-child transmission of HIV, the right to food for all and the right to an adequate standard of living, including housing and clothing;

11. *Recognizes* the threat to the achievement of the internationally agreed development goals, including the Millennium Development Goals, posed by the global financial and economic crisis, which is connected to multiple, interrelated global crises and challenges, such as the food crisis and continuing food insecurity, volatile energy and commodity prices, environmental degradation and climate change, and calls upon States to address, in their response to these crises, the negative impact on the full enjoyment of the rights of children;

Elimination of violence against children

12. *Reaffirms* paragraphs 27 to 32 of its resolution 63/241 and paragraphs 47 to 62 of its resolution 62/141 of 18 December 2007, on the theme of elimination of violence against children, condemns all forms of violence against children, and urges all States to implement the measures set out in paragraph 27 of its resolution 63/241;

13. *Urges* States to take, or strengthen, as appropriate, legislative and other measures to effectively prevent, prohibit and eliminate all forms of violence against children, in all settings;

14. *Encourages* all States, requests United Nations entities and agencies, and invites regional organizations and civil society, including non-governmental organizations, to cooperate with the Special Representative of the Secretary-General on Violence against Children and to provide support, including financial support, to her for the effective and independent performance of her mandate, as set out in resolution 62/141, and in promoting the further implementation of the recommendations of the United Nations study on violence against children, while promoting and ensuring country ownership and national plans and programmes in this regard, and calls upon States and institutions concerned, and invites the private sector, to provide voluntary contributions for that purpose;

15. *Notes with appreciation* the consolidated partnerships promoted by the Special Representative of the Secretary-General on Violence against Children, in coordination with national Governments, United Nations agencies, regional organizations, human rights bodies and mechanisms and representatives of civil society and with the participation of children;

16. *Takes note with appreciation* of the joint report of the Special Rapporteur on the sale of children, child prostitution and child pornography and the Special Representative of the Secretary-General on Violence against Children, which provides an overview of accessible and child-sensitive counselling, complaint and reporting mechanisms to address incidents of violence, including sexual violence and exploitation;

Promoting and protecting the rights of children, including children in particularly difficult situations

17. *Reaffirms* paragraphs 34 to 42 of its resolution 63/241, and calls upon all States to promote and protect all human rights of all children in particularly difficult situations and to implement programmes and measures that provide them with special protection and assistance, including access to health care, education and social services, as well as, where appropriate and feasible, voluntary repatriation, reintegration, family tracing and family reunification, in particular for children who are unaccompanied, and to ensure that the best interests of the child are a primary consideration;

18. *Recalls* Human Rights Council resolution 16/12 of 24 March 2011 entitled "Rights of the child: a holistic approach to the protection and promotion of the rights of children working and/or living on the street", and calls for its full implementation;

Children alleged to have infringed or recognized as having infringed penal law and children of persons alleged to have infringed or recognized as having infringed penal law

19. *Reaffirms* paragraphs 43 to 47 of its resolution 63/241, and calls upon all States to respect and protect the rights of children alleged to have infringed or recognized as having infringed penal law, as well as children of persons alleged to have infringed or recognized as having infringed penal law;

Prevention and eradication of the sale of children, child prostitution and child pornography

20. *Also reaffirms* paragraphs 48 to 50 of its resolution 63/241, and calls upon all States to prevent, criminalize, prosecute and punish all forms of the sale of children, including for the purposes of the transfer of organs of the child for profit, child slavery, commercial sexual exploitation of children, child prostitution and child pornography, with the aim of eradicating those practices and the use of the Internet and other information and communications technologies for these purposes, to combat the existence of a market that encourages such criminal practices and take measures to eliminate the demand that fosters them, as well as to address the needs of victims effectively and take effective measures against the criminalization of children who are victims of exploitation;

21. *Calls upon* all States to develop and implement programmes and policies to protect children from abuse, sexual abuse, sexual exploitation, commercial sexual exploitation, child prostitution, child pornography, child sex tourism and child abduction, and calls upon States to implement strategies to locate and assist all children subject to these violations;

22. *Also calls upon* all States to enact and enforce necessary legislative or other measures, in cooperation with relevant stakeholders, to prevent the distribution over the Internet and in all other media of child pornography, including depictions of child sexual abuse, ensuring that adequate mechanisms are in place to enable the reporting and removal of such material and that its creators, distributors and collectors are prosecuted as appropriate;

Children affected by armed conflict

23. *Reaffirms* paragraphs 51 to 63 of its resolution 63/241, condemns in the strongest terms all violations and abuses committed against children affected by armed conflict, and in this regard urges all States and other parties to armed conflict that are engaged, in contravention of applicable international law, including humanitarian law, in the recruitment and use of children, in patterns of killing and maiming of children and/or rape and other sexual violence against children, and in recurrent attacks on schools and/or hospitals, as well as in all other violations and abuses against children, to take time-bound and effective measures to end them, and urges all States, United Nations agencies, funds and programmes, other relevant international and regional organizations and civil society to continue to give serious attention to, and to protect and assist child victims of, all violations and abuses committed against children in situations of armed conflict, in accordance with international humanitarian law, including the First to Fourth Geneva Conventions;

24. *Also reaffirms* the essential roles of the General Assembly, the Economic and Social Council and the Human Rights Council for the promotion and protection of the rights and welfare of children, including children affected by armed conflict, notes the increasing role played by the Security Council in ensuring protection for children affected by armed conflict, and also notes the activities undertaken by the Peacebuilding Commission, within its mandate, in areas that promote and contribute to the enjoyment of the rights and welfare of children;

25. *Notes with appreciation* the steps taken regarding Security Council resolutions 1539(2004) of 22 April 2004, 1612(2005) of 26 July 2005, 1882(2009) of 4 August 2009 and 1998(2011) of 12 July 2011, and the efforts of the Secretary-General to implement the monitoring and reporting mechanism on children and armed conflict in accordance with those resolutions, with the participation of and in cooperation with national Governments and relevant United Nations and civil society actors, including at the country level, requests the Secretary-General to ensure that information collected and communicated by the monitoring and reporting mechanism is accurate, objective, reliable and verifiable, and in this regard encourages the work and the deployment, as appropriate, of United Nations child protection advisers in peacekeeping operations and political and peacebuilding missions;

Child labour

26. *Reaffirms* paragraphs 64 to 80 of its resolution 63/241, on the theme of child labour, and calls upon all States to translate into concrete action their commitment to the progressive and effective elimination of child labour that is likely to be hazardous or to interfere with the child's education or to be harmful to the child's health or physical, mental, spiritual, moral or social development, and to eliminate immediately the worst forms of child labour;

27. *Notes with interest* the outcome of the Hague Global Child Labour Conference, including the Road Map for Achieving the Elimination of the Worst Forms of Child Labour by 2016;

28. *Calls upon* all States to take into account the global report of the Director-General of the International Labour Organization entitled "Accelerating action against child labour";

29. *Urges* all States that have not yet done so to consider ratifying both the Worst Forms of Child Labour Convention, 1999 (No. 182) and the Minimum Age Convention, 1973 (No. 138), of the International Labour Organization;

Implementing child rights in early childhood

30. *Reaffirms* paragraphs 28 to 45 of its resolution 65/197, reaffirming that early childhood is a critical phase for the realization of the rights enshrined in the Convention on the Rights of the Child, and urges all States to implement the measures set out in paragraph 43 of its resolution 65/197;

III
The rights of children with disabilities

31. *Also reaffirms* that all children with disabilities should have full enjoyment of their human rights and fundamental freedoms on an equal basis with other children, as enshrined in the Convention on the Rights of the Child and the Convention on the Rights of Persons with Disabilities, and that the full and effective implementation of these instruments is an important step to the realization of the rights of children with disabilities, including respect for their evolving capacities and respect for their right to preserve their identity;

32. *Stresses* the importance of international cooperation in supporting national efforts for the realization of the rights of children with disabilities, recognizing the importance of taking appropriate and effective measures among States that aim at facilitating and supporting capacity-building, including through the exchange and sharing of information, experiences, training programmes and best practices;

33. *Recognizes* that discrimination against any child on the basis of disability is a violation of the inherent dignity and worth of the child, and expresses grave concern that children with disabilities face violations of their human rights as well as discriminatory, attitudinal and environmental barriers to their participation and inclusion in society and in the community;

34. *Concerned* that children with disabilities, particularly girls, are often at greater risk, both within and outside the home, of physical or mental violence, injury or abuse, neglect or negligent treatment and maltreatment or exploitation, including sexual abuse;

35. *Reaffirms* that the eradication of poverty is essential to the achievement of all Millennium Development Goals and to the full realization of the rights of all children, including those with disabilities, and also reaffirms resolution 65/1 of 22 September 2010;

36. *Recognizes* that the majority of children with disabilities live in poverty and that equitable access to economic opportunities and social services, as close as possible to children's own communities, is an important part of relevant strategies for sustainable development;

37. *Also recognizes* that children with disabilities are often denied the right to a family environment and to live and be included in their communities, and in this regard reaffirms that they have equal rights with respect to family and community life and should not be separated from

their parents against their will, except when competent authorities subject to judicial review determine, in accordance with applicable laws and procedures, that such separation is necessary for the best interests of the child, and that in no case should separation be on the basis of a disability of either the child or one or both of the parents;

38. *Further recognizes* the importance of preventing the concealment, abandonment, neglect or segregation of children with disabilities, and in this regard encourages States to consider the introduction of a commitment towards replacing institutionalization with appropriate measures to support family and community care, and transferring resources to community-based support services and other forms of alternative care;

39. *Expresses concern* at the number of children with disabilities who continue to be denied the right to education, and in this regard reaffirms the right of children with disabilities to have effective access to education, on the basis of equal opportunity, in a manner conducive to their fullest possible social inclusion and individual development, including their cultural and spiritual development;

40. *Recognizes* also that early education is of high importance for children with disabilities, and that the measures taken to implement the right to education for children with disabilities should aim at their maximum inclusion in society, free from discrimination;

41. *Reaffirms* that States should take effective and appropriate measures to ensure, on an equal basis with others, that children with disabilities retain their fertility, and that adolescent boys and girls with disabilities have access to information and education, including on reproductive and family planning, that is age-appropriate and in an accessible format;

42. *Recognizes* that children with disabilities are particularly vulnerable in situations of risk, including situations of armed conflict, humanitarian emergencies and the occurrence of natural disasters, and reaffirms the obligations of States under international law, including international humanitarian law and international human rights law, to take all necessary measures to ensure their safety and protection in such situations, including by reviewing their emergency response programmes and support facilities to make them accessible for children with disabilities;

43. *Calls upon* all States to include, within the overall context of policies and programmes for the realization of the rights of the child, for all children within their jurisdiction, the relevant provisions for the realization of these rights for children with disabilities, in particular:

(*a*) Urges all States that have not yet done so to consider acceding to the Convention on the Rights of Persons with Disabilities and the Optional Protocol thereto, and to do so as a matter of priority, and invites regional integration organizations that have the relevant competence to do so, as defined in the Convention on the Rights of Persons with Disabilities, to consider accession to the Convention;

(*b*) To review on a regular basis relevant domestic laws, related regulations and policies in order to ensure that the rights of children with disabilities are fully respected, protected and fulfilled in line with the provisions of the Convention on the Rights of the Child and the Convention on the Rights of Persons with Disabilities;

(*c*) To prohibit discrimination on the basis of disability and guarantee to children with disabilities equal and effective legal protection against discrimination on all grounds;

(*d*) To ensure that children with disabilities have access to information on their rights, including through human rights education and training, enabling them to contribute to identifying, preventing and acting upon violations of their rights;

(*e*) To take appropriate measures to ensure that children with disabilities have access, on an equal basis with others, to the physical environment, to transportation, to information and communications technologies and systems and to other facilities and services open or provided to the public both in urban and in rural areas;

(*f*) To take all necessary measures to ensure the registration of children with disabilities immediately after birth, including by removing barriers that impede their registration, and to guarantee their right to a name, their right to a nationality and, as far as possible, their right to know and be cared for by their parents;

(*g*) To implement fully the commitments undertaken in General Assembly resolution 65/186 of 21 December 2010 entitled "Realizing the Millennium Development Goals for persons with disabilities towards 2015 and beyond", and to ensure that children with disabilities are rendered visible in the collection and analysis of data;

(*h*) To take measures to collect and disaggregate relevant information, including statistical and research data, as appropriate, in order to identify and address the barriers faced by children with disabilities in exercising their rights;

(*i*) To adopt, implement and/or strengthen appropriate policies aimed at ensuring the right to an adequate standard of living for children with disabilities and their families, along with equal access to quality and affordable services, especially health, nutrition, education, welfare, social protection, safe drinking water, sanitation and other services that are essential for the child's well-being, and, in this regard, to pay particular attention to the most vulnerable children with disabilities and to those living under especially difficult circumstances;

(*j*) To ensure that children with disabilities have access to the same range, quality and standard of free or affordable, gender-sensitive and age-appropriate health care and programmes as provided to other children, including in the area of sexual and reproductive health, and to take measures to prohibit the forced abortion and sterilization of children on grounds of disability;

(*k*) To ensure equal access for children with disabilities to appropriate, timely, affordable and high-quality rehabilitation within the existing health infrastructure, and strengthen the provision of community-based rehabilitation services consistent with the Convention on the Rights of Persons with Disabilities;

(*l*) To ensure that community and civil society institutions, services and facilities responsible for children with disabilities comply with national and local quality standards, especially in the areas of health and social protection, and to develop training programmes to ensure a quality, suitable and well-trained workforce for the inclusion of children with disabilities;

(*m*) To develop strategies, or include in existing strategies measures for the prevention and elimination of all forms of violence against children with disabilities, who are particularly vulnerable to, inter alia, cruel, inhuman, degrading treatment, medical or scientific experimentation, and sexual and physical violence, including bullying and cyberbullying, and to develop and introduce child- and gender-sensitive, accessible, safe and confidential reporting and complaints mechanisms;

(*n*) To adopt legislative and other appropriate measures, including cross-sectoral approaches, to ensure the full realization of the right to education for children with disabilities, including by ensuring that, on the basis of equal opportunity, accessibility and inclusiveness, they are not excluded from accessible, free and compulsory primary education directed to the development of their personality, talents and mental and physical abilities, from early childhood care and development to vocational training and preparation for work;

(*o*) To ensure that children with disabilities have equal access with other children to participation in play, recreation, culture, leisure and sporting activities, including in the preschool and school system;

(*p*) To ensure that children with disabilities have the right, on an equal basis with other children, to express their views freely on all matters affecting them, giving those views due weight in accordance with their age and maturity, and to be provided with disability- and age-appropriate assistance to realize that right;

(*q*) To take all appropriate measures to ensure the protection and safety of children with disabilities during and after situations of risk, including situations of armed conflict, humanitarian emergencies and natural disasters, including adopting and implementing programmes to ensure the physical and psychological recovery and social reintegration of children with disabilities, including children who acquire disability as a consequence of such situations of risk, and ensure that such recovery, reintegration and rehabilitation take place in an environment which fosters the well-being, health, self-respect and dignity of the child;

(*r*) To take all necessary measures to ensure that persons with disabilities, including children with disabilities, through their representative organizations, are closely consulted and actively involved in the development of legislation and policies to implement the Convention on the Rights of Persons with Disabilities, and in other decision-making processes concerning issues relating to persons with disabilities;

44. *Calls upon* all Member States, and invites the United Nations system, to strengthen international cooperation to ensure the realization of the rights of the child, including for children with disabilities, inter alia, by supporting national initiatives that give more emphasis to the development of children with disabilities, as appropriate, and by reinforcing international cooperation measures in fields of research or on the transfer of technology such as assistive technologies;

45. *Calls upon* the relevant entities, funds and programmes of the United Nations system, donor institutions, including the international financial institutions, and bilateral donors to support, inter alia, national initiatives, when requested, including development programmes for children with disabilities, financially and technically, as well as to enhance effective international cooperation and partnership to strengthen knowledge-sharing and capacity-building, with particular attention to policy development, programme development, research and professional training;

IV
Follow-up

46. *Recognizes* the work of the office of the Special Representative of the Secretary-General for Children and Armed Conflict, its increased level of activity and the progress achieved since the establishment of the mandate of the Special Representative, and, bearing in mind its resolution 63/241 and paragraphs 35 to 37 of resolution 51/77 of 12 December 1996, recommends that the Secretary-General extend the mandate of the Special Representative for a further period of three years;

47. *Decides:*

(*a*) To request the Secretary-General to submit to the General Assembly at its sixty-seventh session a comprehensive report on the rights of the child containing information on the status of the Convention on the Rights of the Child and the issues addressed in the present resolution, with a focus on indigenous children, bearing in mind relevant international norms and standards and regional and national particularities;

(*b*) To request the Special Representative of the Secretary-General for Children and Armed Conflict to continue to submit reports to the General Assembly and the Human Rights Council on the activities undertaken in the fulfilment of her mandate, including information on her field visits and on the progress achieved and the challenges remaining on the children and armed conflict agenda;

(*c*) To request the Special Representative of the Secretary-General on Violence against Children to continue to submit annual reports to the General Assembly and the Human Rights Council on the activities undertaken in the fulfilment of her mandate, including information on her field visits and on the progress achieved and the challenges remaining on the violence against children agenda;

(*d*) To request the Special Rapporteur on the sale of children, child prostitution and child pornography to continue to submit reports to the General Assembly and the Human Rights Council on the activities undertaken in the fulfilment of her mandate, including information on her field visits and on the progress achieved and the challenges remaining on the sale of children, child prostitution and child pornography agenda;

(*e*) To invite the Chair of the Committee on the Rights of the Child to present an oral report on the work of the Committee and engage in an interactive dialogue with the General Assembly at its sixty-seventh session under the item entitled "Promotion and protection of the rights of children";

(*f*) To continue its consideration of the question at its sixty-seventh session under the item entitled "Promotion and protection of the rights of children", focusing section III of the resolution entitled "Rights of the child" on indigenous children, bearing in mind relevant international norms and standards and regional and national particularities.

(On the Organization's efforts to protect the rights of the child, see also p. 740.)

Convention on migrant workers

Accessions and ratifications

As at 31 December, the number of States parties to the International Convention on the Protection of the Rights of All Migrant Workers and Members of Their Families, adopted by the General Assembly in resolution 45/158 [YUN 1990, p. 594] and entering into force in 2003 [YUN 2003, p. 676], rose to 45, with Bangladesh becoming party to the Convention in 2011.

Implementation

Monitoring body. The Committee on the Protection of the Rights of All Migrant Workers and Members of Their Families held its fourteenth (4–8 April) [A/66/48] and fifteenth (12–23 September) [A/67/48] sessions in Geneva. Under article 74 of the Convention, the Committee considered the reports of Argentina, Chile, Guatemala and Mexico and adopted concluding observations on them. The Committee noted with concern that many initial reports from States parties under article 73 of the Convention, which required them to report on measures taken to give effect to the provisions of the Convention, had not been received.

At its fourteenth session, in the context of the treaty bodies strengthening process, the Committee adopted a procedure whereby lists of issues focusing on priority issues would be adopted prior to the receipt of State party reports. The replies to those lists of issues by States parties would constitute their reports due under Article 73 of the Convention. The new procedure would apply only to periodic reports. At its fifteenth session, the Committee decided that, starting from 2014, it would examine States parties' reports according to a comprehensive reporting calendar, under which all States parties would be considered within a five-year reporting cycle. It also decided to adopt lists of issues prior to reporting at its sixteenth (2012) session in relation to those States parties with overdue second periodic reports.

(On the Organization's efforts to protect the rights of migrants, see also p. 666.)

Convention on rights of persons with disabilities

Accessions and ratifications

As at 31 December, the number of States parties to the Convention on the Rights of Persons with Disabilities, adopted by the General Assembly in resolution 61/106 [YUN 2006, p. 785], stood at 109. During the year, the Convention was ratified or acceded to by Bahrain, Belize, Cape Verde, Colombia, Cyprus, Indonesia, Luxembourg, Myanmar, Pakistan, Romania, the former Yugoslav Republic of Macedonia and Togo.

As at 31 December, the number of States parties to the Optional Protocol, which established an individual complaints mechanism, had increased to 65. During the year, the Protocol was ratified or acceded to by Cyprus, Luxembourg, the former Yugoslav Republic of Macedonia, Togo and Uruguay.

Pursuant to General Assembly resolution 64/154 [YUN 2009, p. 642], the Secretary-General, in July, submitted a report [A/66/121] on the status of the Convention, the activities of the Committee on the Rights of Persons with Disabilities and ongoing efforts by Governments towards ratification and implementation of the Convention.

Implementation

Monitoring body. The Committee on the Rights of Persons with Disabilities held its fifth (11–15 April) [CRPD/C/5/5] and sixth (19–23 September) [CRPD/C/6/2] sessions in Geneva. At its fifth session, the Committee held its first constructive dialogue with a State party on its report submitted under article 35 of the Convention. During the year, the Committee considered the initial reports of Tunisia [CRPD/C/TUN/1] and Spain [CRPD/C/ESP/1] and adopted concluding observations on them.

The Committee submitted to the General Assembly its first biennial report [A/66/55] covering activities from its first to its fourth sessions.

(On the Organization's efforts to protect the rights of persons with disabilities, see also p. 1029.)

GENERAL ASSEMBLY ACTION

On 24 December [meeting 93], the General Assembly, on the recommendation of the Third Committee [A/66/462/Add.1], adopted **resolution 66/229** without vote [agenda item 69 (a)].

Convention on the Rights of Persons with Disabilities and the Optional Protocol thereto

The General Assembly,

Recalling its previous relevant resolutions, the most recent of which was resolution 64/154 of 18 December 2009, as well as relevant resolutions of the Human Rights Council, the Commission for Social Development and the Commission on Human Rights,

Noting the request of the Committee on the Rights of Persons with Disabilities, contained in annex XVI to its report, that the General Assembly authorize an extension of its meeting time,

Noting also that document and translation costs for the reports of States parties constitute the largest part of the budget for the Committee,

Noting further that, while the Convention on the Rights of Persons with Disabilities has enjoyed a very high level of ratification in a short time, the Committee currently meets for only two sessions of one week per year, and noting that, in particular cases, members of the Committee may require reasonable accommodation, as defined in the Convention,

1. *Welcomes* the fact that, since the opening for signature of the Convention on the Rights of Persons with Disabilities and the Optional Protocol thereto on 30 March 2007, one hundred and fifty-three States have signed and one hundred and six States have ratified the Convention and ninety States have signed and sixty-four States have ratified the Optional Protocol, and that one regional integration organization has ratified the Convention;

2. *Calls upon* those States that have not yet done so to consider signing and ratifying the Convention and the Optional Protocol as a matter of priority;

3. *Welcomes* the holding of the third and fourth sessions of the Conference of States Parties to the Convention on the Rights of Persons with Disabilities and the work of the Committee on the Rights of Persons with Disabilities;

4. *Invites* States parties to adhere to the page limit established by the Committee for reports of States parties, and notes that this would reduce the operating costs of the Committee;

5. *Notes* the ongoing process of reform aimed at strengthening the treaty body system, including the report of the Secretary-General on measures to improve further the effectiveness, harmonization and reform of the treaty body system, and invites the Committee, in the context of this strengthening process, to continue to enhance its working methods and efficiency, including by sharing good practices with other treaty bodies;

6. *Decides* to authorize for the Committee an additional week of meeting time per year to be used consecutive to an existing regular session, bearing in mind the requirements of the Committee for reasonable accommodation, and without prejudice to the ongoing process of reform aimed at strengthening the treaty body system;

7. *Invites* the Chair of the Committee on the Rights of Persons with Disabilities to present an oral report on the work of the Committee and engage in an interactive dialogue with the General Assembly at its sixty-seventh and sixty-eighth sessions, under the item entitled "Promotion and protection of human rights", as a way to enhance communication between the Assembly and the Committee;

8. *Welcomes* the report of the Secretary-General and the activities undertaken in support of the Convention;

9. *Encourages* the Inter-Agency Support Group on the Convention on the Rights of Persons with Disabilities to continue its work to mainstream the Convention throughout the United Nations system through its Strategy and Plan of Action, approved in 2010, and calls upon the Department of Economic and Social Affairs of the Secretariat and the Office of the United Nations High Commissioner for Human Rights to continue strengthening their cooperation in this regard;

10. *Invites* the Secretary-General to intensify efforts to assist States to become parties to the Convention and the Optional Protocol, including by providing assistance with a view to achieving universal adherence;

11. *Requests* the Secretary-General to continue the progressive implementation of standards and guidelines for the accessibility of facilities and services of the United Nations system, taking into account relevant provisions of the Convention, in particular when undertaking renovations, including interim arrangements;

12. *Also requests* the Secretary-General to take further actions to promote the rights of persons with disabilities in the United Nations system in accordance with the Convention, including the retention and recruitment of persons with disabilities;

13. *Requests* United Nations agencies and organizations, and invites intergovernmental and non-governmental organizations, to continue to strengthen efforts undertaken to disseminate accessible information on the Convention and the Optional Protocol, including to children and young people to promote their understanding, and to assist States parties in implementing their obligations under those instruments;

14. *Requests* the Secretary-General to submit to the General Assembly at its sixty-seventh session a report on the status of the Convention and the Optional Protocol and on the implementation of the present resolution.

Convention for protection from enforced disappearance

Accessions and ratifications

As at 31 December, the International Convention for the Protection of All Persons from Enforced Disappearance, adopted by the General Assembly in resolution 61/177 [YUN 2006, p. 800], had 30 States parties. During the year Armenia, Belgium, Gabon, Montenegro, the Netherlands, Panama, Serbia, Tunisia and Zambia became parties to the Convention.

Pursuant to resolution 65/209 [YUN 2010, p. 654], the Secretary-General, in August, submitted a report [A/66/284] on the status of the Convention providing information on the first meeting of States parties (New York, 31 May), including the election of 10 members of the Committee on Enforced Disappearances, who assumed office on 1 July, and a panel discussion on ending impunity and preventing new victims.

Human Rights Council action. On 24 March [A/66/53 (res. 16/16)], the Council welcomed the entry into force of the International Convention for the Protection of All Persons from Enforced Disappearance on 23 December 2010 [YUN 2010, p. 654].

Implementation

Monitoring body. The Committee on Enforced Disappearances held its first session (Geneva, 8–11 November) [A/67/56], holding six plenary meetings and two days of induction training. Following its consideration of the provisional rules of procedure regarding the election of officers and the composition of the Bureau, the Committee elected the members of its Bureau, who would serve a two-year term. The Committee established three working groups to work on the rules of procedure, to develop reporting guidelines and to develop a "user manual" on individual communications, respectively. It further decided to appoint a special rapporteur, a deputy and an alternate to consider urgent action requests and issue interim or protection measures between sessions. It also confirmed the date of its second session, to be held from 26 to 30 March 2012.

(On the Organization's efforts to combat enforced or involuntary disappearances, see also p. 691.)

Financing

In April, the General Assembly considered the Secretary-General's report [A/65/628] on additional budgetary requirements of $836,500 (net) for the 2010–2011 biennium and $7,537,900 (net) for the 2012–2013 biennium resulting from the entry into force of the Convention. The Advisory Committee on Administrative and Budgetary Questions (ACABQ) [A/65/739] recommended that the Assembly approve the 2010–2011 requirements within the resources already appropriated for the biennium, and consider the 2012–2013 requirements in the context of the proposed programme budget for that biennium.

The Assembly, in section I of **resolution 65/268** of 4 April (see p. 1378), endorsed ACABQ's conclusions and recommendations, subject to the provisions of the resolution, and requested the Secretary-General to report in the context of the second performance report on the 2010–2011 programme budget.

GENERAL ASSEMBLY ACTION

On 19 December [meeting 89], the General Assembly, on the recommendation of the Third Committee [A/66/462/Add.2], adopted **resolution 66/160** without vote [agenda item 69 (b)].

International Convention for the Protection of All Persons from Enforced Disappearance

The General Assembly,

Reaffirming its resolution 61/177 of 20 December 2006, by which it adopted and opened for signature, ratification and accession the International Convention for the Protection of All Persons from Enforced Disappearance,

Recalling its resolution 47/133 of 18 December 1992, by which it adopted the Declaration on the Protection of All Persons from Enforced Disappearance as a body of principles for all States,

Recalling also its resolution 65/209 of 21 December 2010, as well as relevant resolutions adopted by the Human Rights Council, including resolution 16/16 of 24 March 2011, in which the Council took note of the report of the Working Group on Enforced or Involuntary Disappearances on best practices on enforced disappearances in domestic criminal legislation and encouraged States to give due consideration to the good practices identified in the report,

Recalling further that no exceptional circumstance whatsoever may be invoked as a justification for enforced disappearance,

Deeply concerned, in particular, by the increase in enforced or involuntary disappearances in various regions of the world, including arrest, detention and abduction, when these are part of or amount to enforced disappearances, and by the growing number of reports concerning harassment, ill-treatment and intimidation of witnesses of disappearances or relatives of persons who have disappeared,

Recalling that the Convention sets out the right of victims to know the truth regarding the circumstances of the enforced disappearance, the progress and results of the investigation and the fate of the disappeared person, and sets forth State party obligations to take appropriate measures in this regard,

Acknowledging that acts of enforced disappearance are recognized in the Convention as crimes against humanity, in certain circumstances,

Acknowledging also the valuable work of the International Committee of the Red Cross in promoting compliance with international humanitarian law in this field,

1. *Welcomes* the entry into force of the International Convention for the Protection of All Persons from Enforced Disappearance on 23 December 2010, and recognizes that its implementation will be a significant contribution to ending impunity and to promoting and protecting all human rights for all;

2. *Also welcomes* the fact that ninety States have signed the Convention and thirty have ratified or acceded to it, and calls upon States that have not yet done so to consider signing, ratifying or acceding to the Convention as a matter of priority, as well as to consider the option provided for in articles 31 and 32 of the Convention regarding the Committee on Enforced Disappearances;

3. *Further welcomes* the holding of the first meeting of the States parties to the Convention on 31 May 2011 and the election of the members of the Committee on Enforced Disappearances on that occasion, and welcomes the commencement of the work of the Committee;

4. *Welcomes* the report of the Secretary-General;

5. *Requests* the Secretary-General and the United Nations High Commissioner for Human Rights to continue their intensive efforts to assist States in becoming parties to the Convention, with a view to achieving universal adherence;

6. *Requests* United Nations agencies and organizations, and invites intergovernmental and non-governmental organizations and the Working Group on Enforced or Involuntary Disappearances, to continue making efforts to disseminate information on the Convention, to promote understanding of it and to assist States parties in implementing their obligations under this instrument;

7. *Invites* the Chair of the Committee on Enforced Disappearances and the Chair of the Working Group on Enforced or Involuntary Disappearances to address and engage in an interactive dialogue with the General Assembly at its sixty-seventh session under the item on the promotion and protection of human rights;

8. *Requests* the Secretary-General to submit to the General Assembly at its sixty-seventh session a report on the status of the Convention and the implementation of the present resolution.

Convention on genocide
Accessions and ratifications

As at 31 December, 142 States were parties to the 1948 Convention on the Prevention and Punishment of the Crime of Genocide, adopted by the General Assembly in resolution 260 A(III) [YUN 1948–49, p. 959]. Cape Verde became a party during the year.

Genocide prevention

Report of Secretary-General. Pursuant to General Assembly resolution 63/308 [YUN 2009, p. 50], in which the Assembly confirmed its intention "to continue its consideration of the responsibility to protect" as called for in the 2005 World Summit Outcome [YUN 2005, p. 62], the Secretary-General, in a June report [A/65/877], addressed the regional and subregional dimensions of the responsibility to protect in anticipation of the informal interactive dialogue on the topic in the General Assembly in July. He pointed out that his Special Advisers on the Prevention of Genocide and the Responsibility to Protect had been accelerating their contacts with regional groups on both thematic issues and specific country situations, and would look for ways to broaden and deepen those relationships as a matter of priority. The Joint Office of the two Special Advisers had provided training and awareness-raising programmes in many parts of the world as Governments, civil society and international secretariats had sought to forestall violent upheavals. The Secretary-General said that more of those sessions should be conducted in collaboration with regional and subregional organizations. He also observed that it would be helpful to UN work, including that of the Special Advisers, if focal points for the responsibility to protect, operating in various capitals around the world, mapped the capacities possessed by various States that could help to prevent genocide, war crimes, ethnic cleansing and crimes against humanity.

(For information on the responsibility to protect, see p. 49.)

General aspects
Human rights treaty body system

Meeting of Chairs. Pursuant to General Assembly resolution 57/202 [YUN 2002, p. 623], the Secretary-General in July submitted to the Assembly the report [A/66/175] on the twenty-third meeting of Chairs of human rights treaty bodies (Geneva, 30 June–1 July), which considered the follow-up to the recommendations of the twenty-second meeting [YUN 2010, p. 655] and reviewed developments relating to the work of the treaty bodies. Also discussed was the expertise and independence of treaty body members, as well as ways of enhancing the Chairs' annual meeting. The Chairs held informal consultations with representatives of 65 States parties on 30 June and adopted recommendations, which were annexed to the report. The Chairs also considered the report of the twelfth inter-committee meeting of the human rights treaty bodies (Geneva, 27–29 June), which focused on the structure of the dialogue with States parties, the format and length of concluding observations, and interactions with stakeholders, in particular NGOs and national human rights institutions.

The General Assembly took note of the report on 19 December (**decision 66/537**).

Meeting of Special Rapporteurs, independent experts and chairpersons. In July, the High Commissioner transmitted to the Human Rights Council the report [A/HRC/18/41] on the eighteenth meeting of special rapporteurs/representatives, independent experts and chairs of working groups of the special procedures of the Council (Geneva, 27 June–1 July). Mandate holders exchanged views with the High Commissioner, the Council President and the facilitator of the Council review segment on special procedures, and with States. The meeting convened a joint meeting with the twelfth inter-committee meeting of human rights treaty bodies (see above), and met with representatives of UN entities, OHCHR field presences, NGOs and national human rights institutions. Discussions focused on the independence of the special procedures, harmonization of working methods, the outcome of the Human Rights Council review and measures to enhance the engagement of mandate holders with various stakeholders in order to strengthen their effectiveness. Participants stressed the importance of increasing regular and extra-budgetary resources for special procedures and noted the appointment of 16 new mandate holders.

Membership of human rights treaty bodies

In 2011, the General Assembly, in accordance with resolution 64/173 [YUN 2009, p. 646], continued its consideration of the question of equitable geographical distribution in the membership of the human rights treaty bodies. In December, by resolution 66/153 (see below), the Assembly requested the High Commissioner to submit recommendations on implementation of that resolution and requested the Secretary-General to report on the question at its sixty-eighth (2013) session.

GENERAL ASSEMBLY ACTION

On 19 December [meeting 89], the General Assembly, on the recommendation of the Third Committee [A/66/462/Add.2], adopted **resolution 66/153** by recorded vote (135-54-1) [agenda item 69 (*b*)].

Promotion of equitable geographical distribution in the membership of the human rights treaty bodies

The General Assembly,

Recalling its previous resolutions on this question,

Reaffirming the importance of the goal of universal ratification of the United Nations human rights instruments,

Welcoming the significant increase in the number of ratifications of United Nations human rights instruments, which has especially contributed to their universality,

Reiterating the importance of the effective functioning of treaty bodies established pursuant to United Nations human rights instruments for the full and effective implementation of those instruments,

Recalling that, with regard to the election of the members of the human rights treaty bodies, the General Assembly as well as the former Commission on Human Rights recognized the importance of giving consideration in their membership to equitable geographical distribution, gender balance and representation of the principal legal systems and of bearing in mind that the members shall be elected and shall serve in their personal capacity, and shall be of high moral character, acknowledged impartiality and recognized competence in the field of human rights,

Reaffirming the significance of national and regional particularities and various historical, cultural and religious backgrounds, as well as of different political, economic and legal systems,

Recognizing that the United Nations pursues multilingualism as a means of promoting, protecting and preserving diversity of languages and cultures globally and that genuine multilingualism promotes unity in diversity and international understanding,

Recalling that the General Assembly as well as the former Commission on Human Rights encouraged States parties to United Nations human rights treaties, individually and through meetings of States parties, to consider how to give better effect, inter alia, to the principle of equitable geographical distribution in the membership of treaty bodies,

Expressing concern at the regional imbalance in the current composition of the membership of some of the human rights treaty bodies,

Reaffirming the importance of increasing efforts to address that imbalance,

Noting in particular that the status quo tends to be detrimental to the election of experts from some regional groups, in particular the African, Asian, Latin American and Caribbean and Eastern European groups,

Convinced that the goal of equitable geographical distribution in the membership of human rights treaty bodies is perfectly compatible and can be fully realized and achieved in harmony with the need to ensure gender balance and the representation of the principal legal systems in those bodies and the high moral character, acknowledged impartiality and recognized competence in the field of human rights of their members,

1. *Reiterates* that the States parties to the United Nations human rights instruments should take into account, in their nomination of members to the human rights treaty bodies, that these committees shall be composed of persons of high moral character and recognized competence in the field of human rights, consideration being given to the usefulness of the participation of some persons having legal experience, and to equal representation of women and men, and that members shall serve in their personal capacity, and also reiterates that, in the elections to the human rights treaty bodies, consideration shall be given to equitable geographical distribution of membership and to the representation of the different forms of civilization and of the principal legal systems;

2. *Encourages* the States parties to the United Nations human rights instruments to consider and adopt concrete actions, inter alia, the possible establishment of quota distribution systems by geographical region for the election of the members of the treaty bodies, thereby ensuring the paramount objective of equitable geographical distribution in the membership of those human rights bodies;

3. *Urges* the States parties to the United Nations human rights instruments, including the bureau members, to include this matter in the agenda of each meeting and/or Conference of States Parties to those instruments in order to initiate a debate on ways and means to ensure equitable geographical distribution in the membership of the human rights treaty bodies, based on previous recommendations of the Commission on Human Rights and the Economic and Social Council and the provisions of the present resolution;

4. *Recommends*, when considering the possible establishment of a quota by region for the election of the membership of each treaty body, the introduction of flexible procedures that encompass the following criteria:

(*a*) Each of the five regional groups established by the General Assembly must be assigned a quota of the membership of each treaty body in equivalent proportion to the number of States parties to the instrument that it represents;

(*b*) There must be provision for periodic revisions that reflect the relative changes in the geographical distribution of States parties;

(*c*) Automatic periodic revisions should be envisaged in order to avoid amending the text of the instrument when the quotas are revised;

5. *Stresses* that the process needed to achieve the goal of equitable geographical distribution in the membership of human rights treaty bodies can contribute to raising awareness of the importance of gender balance, the representation of the principal legal systems and the principle that the members of the treaty bodies shall be elected and shall serve in their personal capacity, and shall be of high moral character, acknowledged impartiality and recognized competence in the field of human rights;

6. *Requests* the Chairs of the human rights treaty bodies to consider at their next meeting the content of the present resolution and to submit, through the United Nations High Commissioner for Human Rights, specific recommendations for the achievement of the goal of equitable geographical distribution in the membership of the human rights treaty bodies, as well as an update on the implementation of the present resolution in their respective bodies;

7. *Requests* the High Commissioner to submit concrete recommendations on the implementation of the present resolution, and requests the Secretary-General to submit a comprehensive report in this regard, to the General Assembly at its sixty-eighth session;

8. *Decides* to continue its consideration of the question at its sixty-eighth session under the item entitled "Promotion and protection of human rights".

RECORDED VOTE ON RESOLUTION 66/153:

In favour: Afghanistan, Algeria, Angola, Antigua and Barbuda, Argentina, Azerbaijan, Bahamas, Bahrain, Bangladesh, Barbados, Belarus, Belize, Benin, Bhutan, Bolivia, Botswana, Brazil, Brunei Darussalam, Burkina Faso, Burundi, Cambodia, Cameroon, Cape Verde, Central African Republic, Chad, China, Colombia, Comoros, Congo, Costa Rica, Côte d'Ivoire, Cuba, Democratic People's Republic of Korea, Democratic Republic of the Congo, Djibouti, Dominica, Dominican Republic, Ecuador, Egypt, El Salvador, Equatorial Guinea, Eritrea, Ethiopia, Fiji, Gabon, Gambia, Ghana, Grenada, Guatemala, Guinea, Guinea-Bissau, Guyana, Haiti, Honduras, India, Indonesia, Iran, Iraq, Jamaica, Jordan, Kazakhstan, Kenya, Kuwait, Kyrgyzstan, Lao People's Democratic Republic, Lebanon, Lesotho, Liberia, Libya, Madagascar, Malawi, Malaysia, Maldives, Mali, Mauritania, Mauritius, Mexico, Mongolia, Morocco, Mozambique, Myanmar, Namibia, Nepal, Nicaragua, Niger, Nigeria, Oman, Pakistan, Panama, Papua New Guinea, Paraguay, Peru, Philippines, Qatar, Russian Federation, Rwanda, Saint Kitts and Nevis, Saint Lucia, Saint Vincent and the Grenadines, Samoa, Sao Tome and Principe, Saudi Arabia, Senegal, Seychelles, Sierra Leone, Singapore, Solomon Islands, Somalia, South Africa, South Sudan, Sri Lanka, Sudan, Suriname, Swaziland, Syrian Arab Republic, Tajikistan, Thailand, Timor-Leste, Togo, Tonga, Trinidad and Tobago, Tunisia, Turkmenistan, Tuvalu, Uganda, United Arab Emirates, United Republic of Tanzania, Uruguay, Uzbekistan, Vanuatu, Venezuela, Viet Nam, Yemen, Zambia, Zimbabwe.

Against: Albania, Andorra, Armenia, Australia, Austria, Belgium, Bosnia and Herzegovina, Bulgaria, Canada, Croatia, Cyprus, Czech Republic, Denmark, Estonia, Finland, France, Georgia, Germany, Greece, Hungary, Iceland, Ireland, Israel, Italy, Japan, Latvia, Liechtenstein, Lithuania, Luxembourg, Malta, Marshall Islands, Monaco, Montenegro, Netherlands, New Zealand, Norway, Palau, Poland, Portugal, Republic of Korea, Republic of Moldova, Romania, San Marino, Serbia, Slovakia, Slovenia, Spain, Sweden, Switzerland, the former Yugoslav Republic of Macedonia, Turkey, Ukraine, United Kingdom, United States.

Abstaining: Chile.

Other activities

Strengthening action to promote human rights

International cooperation in the field of human rights

Advisory Committee reports. Pursuant to Human Rights Council resolution 13/23 [YUN 2010, p. 656], the Advisory Committee in May submitted a report [A/HRC/AC/7/2] on enhancement of international cooperation in the field of human rights, which provided an update of the working document submitted at the Committee's sixth session (see p. 613), including new ideas that had emerged from discussions at that session. In December, the Advisory Committee submitted a further report [A/HRC/AC/8/3] on the topic.

Human Rights Council action. On 25 March [A/66/53 (res. 16/22)], the Council reaffirmed the importance of the enhancement of international cooperation for the promotion and protection of human rights; took note of the discussions held in the Human Rights Council Advisory Committee in fulfilment of the mandate given to explore ways and means to enhance international cooperation in the field of human rights; and decided to continue its consideration of the matter in 2012. It also requested OHCHR to provide an update on the operations of the UPR Voluntary Trust Fund and the Voluntary Fund for Financial and Technical Assistance and the resources available to them; seek the views of States and stakeholders on the contribution of the Voluntary Fund for Financial and Technical Assistance [YUN 2007, p. 664], in particular with regard to its sustainability and accessibility; and provide a compilation of those views at the Council's nineteenth (2012) session.

GENERAL ASSEMBLY ACTION

On 19 December [meeting 89], the General Assembly, on the recommendation of the Third Committee [A/66/462/Add.2], adopted **resolution 66/152** without vote [agenda item 69 (*b*)].

Enhancement of international cooperation in the field of human rights

The General Assembly,

Reaffirming its commitment to promoting international cooperation, as set forth in the Charter of the United Nations, in particular Article 1, paragraph 3, as well as relevant provisions of the Vienna Declaration and Programme of Action adopted by the World Conference on Human Rights on 25 June 1993 for enhancing genuine cooperation among Member States in the field of human rights,

Recalling its adoption of the United Nations Millennium Declaration on 8 September 2000 and of its resolution 64/171 of 18 December 2009, Human Rights Council resolution 16/22 of 25 March 2011 and the resolutions of the Commission on Human Rights on the enhancement of international cooperation in the field of human rights,

Recalling also the World Conference against Racism, Racial Discrimination, Xenophobia and Related Intolerance, held at Durban, South Africa, from 31 August to 8 September 2001, the Durban Review Conference, held at Geneva from 20 to 24 April 2009, and the political declaration of the high-level meeting of the General Assembly to commemorate the tenth anniversary of the adoption of the Durban Declaration and Programme of Action, and their role in the enhancement of international cooperation in the field of human rights,

Recognizing that the enhancement of international cooperation in the field of human rights is essential for the full achievement of the purposes of the United Nations, including the effective promotion and protection of all human rights,

Recognizing also that the promotion and protection of human rights should be based on the principle of cooperation and genuine dialogue and aimed at strengthening the capacity of Member States to comply with their human rights obligations for the benefit of all human beings,

Reaffirming that dialogue among religions, cultures and civilizations in the field of human rights could contribute greatly to the enhancement of international cooperation in this field,

Emphasizing the need for further progress in the promotion and encouragement of respect for human rights and fundamental freedoms through, inter alia, international cooperation,

Underlining the fact that mutual understanding, dialogue, cooperation, transparency and confidence-building are important elements in all activities for the promotion and protection of human rights,

Recalling the adoption of resolution 2000/22 of 18 August 2000, on the promotion of dialogue on human rights issues, by the Subcommission on the Promotion and Protection of Human Rights at its fifty-second session,

1. *Reaffirms* that it is one of the purposes of the United Nations and the responsibility of all Member States to promote, protect and encourage respect for human rights and fundamental freedoms through, inter alia, international cooperation;

2. *Recognizes* that, in addition to their separate responsibilities to their individual societies, States have a collective responsibility to uphold the principles of human dignity, equality and equity at the global level;

3. *Reaffirms* that dialogue among cultures and civilizations facilitates the promotion of a culture of tolerance and respect for diversity, and welcomes in this regard the holding of conferences and meetings at the national, regional and international levels on dialogue among civilizations;

4. *Urges* all actors on the international scene to build an international order based on inclusion, justice, equality and equity, human dignity, mutual understanding and promotion of and respect for cultural diversity and universal human rights, and to reject all doctrines of exclusion based on racism, racial discrimination, xenophobia and related intolerance;

5. *Reaffirms* the importance of the enhancement of international cooperation for the promotion and protection of human rights and for the achievement of the objectives of the fight against racism, racial discrimination, xenophobia and related intolerance;

6. *Considers* that international cooperation in the field of human rights, in conformity with the purposes and principles set out in the Charter of the United Nations and international law, should make an effective and practical contribution to the urgent task of preventing violations of human rights and fundamental freedoms;

7. *Reaffirms* that the promotion, protection and full realization of all human rights and fundamental freedoms should be guided by the principles of universality, non-selectivity, objectivity and transparency, in a manner consistent with the purposes and principles set out in the Charter;

8. *Emphasizes* the role of international cooperation in support of national efforts and in increasing the capacities of Member States in the field of human rights through, inter alia, the enhancement of their cooperation with human rights mechanisms, including through the provision of technical assistance, upon the request of and in accordance with the priorities set by the States concerned;

9. *Calls upon* Member States, the specialized agencies and intergovernmental organizations to continue to carry out a constructive dialogue and consultations for the enhancement of understanding and the promotion and protection of all human rights and fundamental freedoms, and encourages non-governmental organizations to contribute actively to this endeavour;

10. *Invites* States and relevant United Nations human rights mechanisms and procedures to continue to pay attention to the importance of mutual cooperation, understanding and dialogue in ensuring the promotion and protection of all human rights;

11. *Requests* the Secretary-General, in collaboration with the United Nations High Commissioner for Human Rights, to consult States and intergovernmental and non-governmental organizations on ways and means, as well as obstacles and challenges and possible proposals to overcome them, for the enhancement of international cooperation and dialogue in the United Nations human rights machinery, including the Human Rights Council;

12. *Decides* to continue its consideration of the question at its sixty-seventh session.

Also on 19 December [meeting 89], the General Assembly, on the recommendation of the Third Committee [A/66/462/Add.2], adopted **resolution 66/157** without vote [agenda item 69 (*b*)].

Strengthening United Nations action in the field of human rights through the promotion of international cooperation and the importance of non-selectivity, impartiality and objectivity

The General Assembly,

Bearing in mind that among the purposes of the United Nations are those of developing friendly relations among nations based on respect for the principle of equal rights and self-determination of peoples and taking other appropriate measures to strengthen universal peace, as well as achieving international cooperation in solving international problems of an economic, social, cultural or humanitarian character and in promoting and encouraging respect for human rights and fundamental freedoms for all without distinction as to race, sex, language or religion,

Desirous of achieving further progress in international cooperation in promoting and encouraging respect for human rights and fundamental freedoms,

Considering that such international cooperation should be based on the principles embodied in international law, especially the Charter of the United Nations, as well as the Universal Declaration of Human Rights, the International Covenants on Human Rights and other relevant instruments,

Deeply convinced that United Nations action in the field of human rights should be based not only on a profound understanding of the broad range of problems existing in all societies but also on full respect for the political, economic and social realities of each of them, in strict compliance with the purposes and principles of the Charter and for the basic purpose of promoting and encouraging respect for human rights and fundamental freedoms through international cooperation,

Recalling its previous resolutions in this regard,

Reaffirming the importance of ensuring the universality, objectivity and non-selectivity of the consideration of human rights issues, as affirmed in the Vienna Declaration and Programme of Action adopted by the World Conference on Human Rights on 25 June 1993, and the elimination of double standards;

Reaffirming also the importance of the objectivity, independence, impartiality and discretion of the special rapporteurs and representatives on thematic issues and on countries, as well as of the members of the working groups, in carrying out their mandates,

Underlining the obligation that Governments have to promote and protect human rights and to carry out the responsibilities that they have undertaken under international law, especially the Charter, as well as various international instruments in the field of human rights;

1. *Reiterates* that, by virtue of the principle of equal rights and self-determination of peoples enshrined in the Charter of the United Nations, all peoples have the right freely to determine, without external interference, their political status and to pursue their economic, social and cultural development, and that every State has the duty to respect that right within the provisions of the Charter, including respect for territorial integrity;

2. *Reaffirms* that it is a purpose of the United Nations and the task of all Member States, in cooperation with the Organization, to promote and encourage respect for human rights and fundamental freedoms and to remain vigilant with regard to violations of human rights wherever they occur;

3. *Calls upon* all Member States to base their activities for the promotion and protection of human rights, including the development of further international cooperation in this field, on the Charter of the United Nations, the Universal Declaration of Human Rights, the International Covenant on Economic, Social and Cultural Rights, the International Covenant on Civil and Political Rights and other relevant international instruments, and to refrain from activities that are inconsistent with that international framework;

4. *Considers* that international cooperation in this field should make an effective and practical contribution to the urgent task of preventing mass and flagrant violations of human rights and fundamental freedoms for all and to the strengthening of international peace and security;

5. *Reaffirms* that the promotion, protection and full realization of all human rights and fundamental freedoms for all, as a legitimate concern of the world community, should be guided by the principles of non-selectivity, impartiality and objectivity and should not be used for political ends;

6. *Requests* all human rights bodies within the United Nations system, as well as the special rapporteurs and representatives, independent experts and working groups, to take duly into account the contents of the present resolution in carrying out their mandates;

7. *Expresses its conviction* that an unbiased and fair approach to human rights issues contributes to the promotion of international cooperation as well as to the effective promotion, protection and realization of human rights and fundamental freedoms;

8. *Stresses*, in this context, the continuing need for impartial and objective information on the political, economic and social situations and events of all countries;

9. *Invites* Member States to consider adopting, as appropriate, within the framework of their respective legal systems and in accordance with their obligations under international law, especially the Charter, and international human rights instruments, the measures that they may deem appropriate to achieve further progress in international cooperation in promoting and encouraging respect for human rights and fundamental freedoms;

10. *Requests* the Human Rights Council to continue taking duly into account the present resolution and to consider further proposals for the strengthening of United Nations action in the field of human rights through the promotion of international cooperation and the importance of the principles of non-selectivity, impartiality and objectivity, including in the context of the universal periodic review;

11. *Requests* the Secretary-General to invite Member States and intergovernmental and non-governmental organizations to present further practical proposals and ideas that would contribute to the strengthening of United Nations action in the field of human rights through the promotion of international cooperation based on the principles of non-selectivity, impartiality and objectivity, and to submit a comprehensive report on the question to the General Assembly at its sixty-eighth session;

12. *Decides* to consider the matter at its sixty-eighth session under the item entitled "Promotion and protection of human rights".

Advisory services and technical cooperation

Board of Trustees report. Pursuant to Human Rights Council resolution 18/18 (see below), the Chairperson of the Board of Trustees of the United Nations Voluntary Fund for Technical Cooperation in the Field of Human Rights submitted a report [A/HRC/20/34] providing information on the Board's work in 2011, including an update on its activities since the previous report of the Secretary-General on advisory services and technical cooperation in the field of human rights [YUN 2010, p. 657]. Activities were carried out by OHCHR country offices in Bolivia, Kosovo, Mauritania, Mexico, the Occupied Palestinian Territory and Togo; the human rights components of UN peace missions in Afghanistan, the Central African Republic, Côte d'Ivoire, Darfur (Sudan), Guinea Bissau, Haiti, Liberia, Sierra Leone, Somalia, the Sudan and Timor-Leste; and human rights advisers in the Great Lakes Region (Burundi), Chad, Ecuador, South Caucasus (Georgia), Honduras, Kenya, Madagascar, Moldova, Niger, Paraguay, Papua New Guinea, the Russian Federation, Rwanda, Sri Lanka, Ukraine, Yemen and Zimbabwe.

At the end of 2011, the Voluntary Fund offered assistance in a wide range of activities undertaken in 34 countries and territories. Technical cooperation activities implemented through the Fund had been increasingly linked with international human rights monitoring mechanisms. The report also discussed technical cooperation with regard to trends, challenges, and synergies with other UN agencies, the work of the Human Rights Council and international treaty bodies and the special procedures.

Human Rights Council action. On 29 September [A/66/53/Add.1 (res. 18/18)], the Council decided to hold an annual thematic discussion to promote the sharing of experiences and best practices and technical cooperation; decided that the theme of the first discussion to be held at the Council's nineteenth (2012) session would be "Sharing of best practices and promoting technical cooperation: paving the way towards the second cycle of the universal periodic review"; and invited the Chairperson of the Board of Trustees to report on the Board's work on an annual basis, starting from the Council's twentieth (2012) session.

Voluntary Fund

The Board of Trustees of the United Nations Voluntary Fund for Technical Cooperation in the Field of Human Rights held its thirty-fourth (Burundi, 26–27 April and Kenya, 28–29 April) and thirty-fifth (Geneva, 31 October–3 November) [A/HRC/20/34] sessions. At its thirty-fourth session— the first time in its history that a session was organized outside of Geneva—the Board discussed technical cooperation activities by OHCHR in Burundi, activities by the Regional Human Rights Adviser for the Great Lakes, as well as activities by the Human Rights Adviser in Kenya; met with different organizations in Burundi and Kenya; and received an overview of the human rights situation in different parts of Somalia. During its thirty-fifth session, the Board was updated on the OHCHR 2012–2013 management plan; on implementation of activities funded by the Voluntary Fund across the regions; and on strategies being developed to address the challenges faced. It also received an overview on the use of the online performance monitoring system and briefings on the situations of human rights components of UN peace missions and on the situation of country offices. As at 31 December 2011, the estimated balance of the Fund was $17,920,195. For the 2010–2011 biennium, total income was $33,787,634 and total expenditure was $37,301,759.

Regional arrangements

Human Rights Council action. On 29 September [A/66/53/Add.1 (res. 18/14)], the Council welcomed the progress made by Governments in establishing regional and subregional arrangements for the promotion and protection of human rights; expressed appreciation for the efforts made by the member States of the Organization of Islamic Cooperation, as manifested by the establishment of the Independent Permanent Human Rights Commission; and requested the High Commissioner to hold a workshop in 2012 on regional arrangements to take stock of developments since the 2010 workshop [YUN 2010, p. 658], including a thematic discussion based on the experience of regional mechanisms, and to report on the discussions and progress in implementing the resolution at the Council's twenty-second (2013) session.

Africa

Report of Secretary-General. In accordance with General Assembly resolution 64/165 [YUN 2009, p. 650], the Secretary-General in August [A/66/325] reviewed the work carried out by the Subregional Centre for Human Rights and Democracy in Central Africa, based in Yaoundé, Cameroon. The report detailed activities from September 2009 to August 2011; presented the Centre's strategic thematic priorities for 2010–2013, and on the occasion of the tenth anniversary of the Centre's activities; and analysed the feedback on the Centre's work, impact and future directions received from an online survey addressed to Governments, subregional organizations, civil society organizations, the UN system and bilateral partners. It also provided an analysis of some of the Centre's experiences over the previous ten years and outlined its future direction. Among other initiatives, the Centre co-organized the first subregional dialogue on migration and human rights (Yaoundé, 6–8 December 2010); organized a subregional training and advocacy seminar on the Convention on the Rights of Persons with Disabilities and its Optional Protocol (Yaoundé, 23–25 November 2010); and organized a subregional workshop on national human rights institutions (Yaoundé, 27–29 June 2011) attended by representatives from nine countries.

GENERAL ASSEMBLY ACTION

On 19 December [meeting 89], the General Assembly, on the recommendation of the Third Committee [A/66/462/Add.2], adopted **resolution 66/162** without vote [agenda item 69 (*b*)].

**Subregional Centre for Human Rights
and Democracy in Central Africa**

The General Assembly,

Recalling its resolution 55/105 of 4 December 2000 concerning regional arrangements for the promotion and protection of human rights,

Recalling also its resolutions 55/34 B of 20 November 2000 and 55/233 of 23 December 2000, section III of its resolution 55/234 of 23 December 2000, its resolution 56/253 of 24 December 2001 and its resolutions 58/176 of 22 December 2003, 59/183 of 20 December 2004, 60/151 of 16 December 2005, 61/158 of 19 December 2006, 62/221 of 22 December 2007, 63/177 of 18 December 2008 and 64/165 of 18 December 2009 on the Subregional Centre for Human Rights and Democracy in Central Africa,

Recalling further that the World Conference on Human Rights recommended that more resources be made available for the strengthening of regional arrangements for the promotion and protection of human rights under the programme of technical cooperation in the field of human rights of the Office of the United Nations High Commissioner for Human Rights,

Recalling the report of the High Commissioner,

Taking note of the holding of the twenty-ninth, thirtieth, thirty-first and thirty-second ministerial meetings of the United Nations Standing Advisory Committee on Security Questions in Central Africa, in N'Djamena from 9 to 13 November 2009, in Kinshasa from 26 to 30 April 2010, in Brazzaville from 15 to 19 November 2010 and in Sao Tome from 12 to 16 March 2011,

Taking note also of the report of the Secretary-General,

Welcoming the 2005 World Summit Outcome, in particular the decision confirmed therein to double the regular budget of the Office of the High Commissioner over the subsequent five years,

1. *Welcomes* the activities of the Subregional Centre for Human Rights and Democracy in Central Africa at Yaoundé;

2. *Notes with satisfaction* the support provided for the establishment of the Centre by the host country;

3. *Also notes with satisfaction* the ongoing activities of the Centre in cooperation with the States members of the Economic Community of Central African States and Rwanda;

4. *Takes note* of the strategic thematic priorities of the Centre for the period 2012–2013, such as elimination of discrimination, focusing on the rights of indigenous populations, persons with disabilities, migrant workers and their families, women's human rights and gender issues; strengthening the rule of law and combating impunity; promotion of democracy and good governance; promotion and protection of economic, social and cultural rights; and strengthening national human rights institutions and cooperation with international and regional human rights mechanisms;

5. *Notes with satisfaction* the celebration of the tenth anniversary of the Centre;

6. *Encourages* the Centre to strengthen its cooperation and invest in relations with subregional organizations and bodies, including the African Union, the Economic Community of Central African States, the United Nations Regional Office for Central Africa and the United Nations country teams of the subregion;

7. *Encourages* the Regional Representative and Director of the Centre to continue to hold regular briefings for the ambassadors of Central African States based in Geneva and Yaoundé, as well as in countries of the subregion during visits of the Regional Representative, with the aim of exchanging information on the activities of the Centre and charting its direction;

8. *Notes* the efforts of the Secretary-General and the United Nations High Commissioner for Human Rights to ensure the full implementation of the relevant resolutions of the General Assembly in order to provide sufficient funds and human resources for the missions of the Centre;

9. *Requests* the Secretary-General and the High Commissioner to continue to provide additional funds and human resources within the existing resources of the Office of the High Commissioner to enable the Centre to respond positively and effectively to the growing needs in the promotion and protection of human rights and in developing a culture of democracy and the rule of law in the Central African subregion;

10. *Requests* the Secretary-General to submit to the General Assembly at its sixty-eighth session a report on the implementation of the present resolution.

National institutions

Reports of Secretary-General. Pursuant to General Assembly resolution 64/161 [YUN 2009, p. 651], the Secretary-General in August submitted a report [A/66/274] on national institutions for the promotion and protection of human rights, reviewing OHCHR activities to assist in establishing and strengthening those institutions; measures taken by Governments and national human rights institutions in that regard; support provided to international and regional activities of national human rights institutions; technical assistance provided with regard to those institutions; and cooperation between national institutions and international mechanisms to promote and protect human rights. The report also included information on the work of national human rights institutions in respect of specific thematic issues, such as the rights of indigenous peoples, the history, principles, roles and responsibilities of national human rights institutions and national human rights institutions in federal States.

Pursuant to Human Rights Council resolution 17/9 (see p. 643), the Secretary-General submitted a report [A/HRC/20/9] covering activities undertaken by OHCHR in 2011 to establish and strengthen national institutions for the promotion and protection of human rights; cooperation between those institutions and the international human rights system; and OHCHR support to regional networks of such institutions and the International Coordinating Committee of National Institutions for the Promotion and Protection of Human Rights. In addition to highlighting the main achievements, challenges and priorities regarding the establishment and strengthening of national institutions for human rights promotion and protection, the report also discussed activities of those institutions on thematic issues, such as business and human rights, older persons, persons with disabilities and the rights of indigenous peoples. In its capacity as secretariat of the International Coordinating Committee, OHCHR provided support to the twenty-fourth annual general meeting of the Committee (Geneva, 17–19 May).

In a further report [A/HRC/20/10], the Secretary-General provided information on the activities carried out in 2011 by the Subcommittee on Accreditation of the International Coordinating Committee of National Institutions for the Promotion and Protection of Human Rights in considering and reviewing applications for accreditation and in carrying out re-accreditation and accreditation reviews of those institutions. It also highlighted improvements in the accreditation process and provided information on the development of the general observations of the Subcommittee, aimed at a more rigorous but fairer and more transparent accreditation and review process. An annex to the report listed 69 national institutions that were in compliance with the Paris Principles, adopted by the General Assembly in 1993 [YUN 1993, p. 898]; 20 institutions not fully in compliance; 11 institutions that were non-compliant; and 2 institutions that had been suspended.

Human Rights Council action. On 16 June [A/66/53 (res. 17/9)], the Council welcomed the increasingly important role of national institutions for the promotion and protection of human rights in supporting cooperation between their Governments and the United Nations; encouraged States to establish effective, independent and pluralistic national institutions and to strengthen existing ones; encouraged national institutions to play an active role in preventing and combating human rights violations; and requested the Secretary-General to report to the Council's twentieth (2012) session on the implementation of the resolution and on the activities of the International Coordinating Committee in accrediting national institutions in compliance with the Paris Principles.

GENERAL ASSEMBLY ACTION

On 19 December [meeting 89], the General Assembly, on the recommendation of the Third Committee [A/66/462/Add.2], adopted **resolution 66/169** without vote [agenda item 69 (*b*)].

National institutions for the promotion and protection of human rights

The General Assembly,

Recalling its previous resolutions on national institutions for the promotion and protection of human rights, the most recent of which was resolution 64/161 of 18 December 2009, and those of the Commission on Human Rights and the Human Rights Council concerning national institutions and their role in the promotion and protection of human rights,

Welcoming the rapidly growing interest throughout the world in the creation and strengthening of independent, pluralistic national institutions for the promotion and protection of human rights,

Recalling the principles relating to the status of national institutions for the promotion and protection of human rights ("the Paris Principles"),

Reaffirming the important role that such national institutions play and will continue to play in promoting and protecting human rights and fundamental freedoms, in strengthening participation and the rule of law and in developing and enhancing public awareness of those rights and freedoms,

Recalling its resolution 65/207 of 21 December 2010 on the role of the Ombudsman, mediator and other national human rights institutions in the promotion and protection of human rights,

Recognizing the important role of the United Nations, in particular the Office of the United Nations High Commissioner for Human Rights, in assisting the development of independent and effective national human rights institutions, guided by the Paris Principles, and recognizing also in this regard the potential for strengthened and complementary cooperation among the United Nations, the International Coordinating Committee of National Institutions for the Promotion and Protection of Human Rights and those national institutions in the promotion and protection of human rights,

Recalling the Vienna Declaration and Programme of Action adopted by the World Conference on Human Rights on 25 June 1993, which reaffirmed the important and constructive role played by national human rights institutions, in particular in their advisory capacity to the competent authorities and their role in preventing and remedying human rights violations, in disseminating information on human rights and in education in human rights,

Reaffirming that all human rights are universal, indivisible, interrelated, interdependent and mutually reinforcing, and that all human rights must be treated in a fair and equal manner, on the same footing and with the same emphasis,

Bearing in mind the significance of national and regional particularities and various historical, cultural and religious backgrounds, and that all States, regardless of their political, economic and cultural systems, have the duty to promote and protect all human rights and fundamental freedoms,

Recalling the programme of action adopted by national institutions, at their meeting held in Vienna in June 1993 during the World Conference on Human Rights, for the promotion and protection of human rights, in which it was recommended that United Nations activities and programmes should be reinforced to meet the requests for assistance from States wishing to establish or strengthen their national institutions for the promotion and protection of human rights,

Taking note with appreciation of the report of the Secretary-General to the Human Rights Council on national institutions for the promotion and protection of human rights and on the accreditation process of the International Coordinating Committee,

Welcoming the strengthening in all regions of regional cooperation among national human rights institutions, and noting with appreciation the continuing work of the European Group of National Human Rights Institutions, the Network of National Institutions for the Promotion and Protection of Human Rights in the Americas, the Asia-Pacific Forum of National Human Rights Institutions and the Network of African National Human Rights Institutions,

1. *Takes note with appreciation* of the report of the Secretary-General and the conclusions contained therein;

2. *Reaffirms* the importance of the development of effective, independent and pluralistic national institutions for the promotion and protection of human rights, in accordance with the Paris Principles;

3. *Recognizes* the role of independent national institutions for the promotion and protection of human rights in working together with Governments to ensure full respect for human rights at the national level, including by contributing to follow-up actions, as appropriate, to the recommendations resulting from the international human rights mechanisms;

4. *Welcomes* the increasingly important role of national institutions for the promotion and protection of human rights in supporting cooperation between their Governments and the United Nations in the promotion and protection of human rights;

5. *Recognizes* that, in accordance with the Vienna Declaration and Programme of Action, it is the right of each State to choose the framework for national institutions that is best suited to its particular needs at the national level in order to promote human rights in accordance with international human rights standards;

6. *Encourages* Member States to establish effective, independent and pluralistic national institutions or, where they already exist, to strengthen them for the promotion and protection of all human rights and fundamental freedoms for all, as outlined in the Vienna Declaration and Programme of Action;

7. *Welcomes* the growing number of States establishing or considering the establishment of national institutions for the promotion and protection of human rights, and welcomes, in particular, the growing number of States that have accepted recommendations to establish national institutions compliant with the Paris Principles made through the universal periodic review and, where relevant, by treaty bodies and special procedures;

8. *Encourages* national institutions for the promotion and protection of human rights established by Member States to continue to play an active role in preventing and combating all violations of human rights as enumerated in the Vienna Declaration and Programme of Action and relevant international instruments;

9. *Recognizes* the role played by national institutions for the promotion and protection of human rights in the Human Rights Council, including its universal periodic review mechanism, in both preparation and follow-up, and the special procedures, as well as in the human rights treaty bodies, in accordance with Council resolutions 5/1 and 5/2 of 18 June 2007 and Commission on Human Rights resolution 2005/74 of 20 April 2005;

10. *Welcomes* the strengthening of opportunities to contribute to the work of the Human Rights Council for national human rights institutions compliant with the Paris Principles, as stipulated in the Council review outcome document adopted by the General Assembly by resolution 65/281 of 17 June 2011, and encourages national human rights institutions to make use of these participatory opportunities;

11. *Stresses* the importance of the financial and administrative independence and stability of national human rights institutions for the promotion and protection of human rights, and notes with satisfaction the efforts of those States that have provided their national institutions with more autonomy and independence, including by giving them an investigative role or enhancing such a role, and encourages other Governments to consider taking similar steps;

12. *Urges* the Secretary-General to continue to give high priority to requests from Member States for assistance in the establishment and strengthening of national human rights institutions;

13. *Underlines* the importance of the autonomy and independence of Ombudsman institutions, encourages increased cooperation between national human rights institutions and regional and international associations of Ombudsmen, and also encourages Ombudsman institutions to actively draw on the standards enumerated in international instruments and the Paris Principles to strengthen their independence and increase their capacity to act as national human rights protection mechanisms;

14. *Commends* the high priority given by the Office of the United Nations High Commissioner for Human Rights to work on national human rights institutions, encourages the High Commissioner, in view of the expanded activities relating to national institutions, to ensure that appropriate arrangements are made and budgetary resources provided to continue and further extend activities in support of national institutions, and invites Governments to contribute additional voluntary funds to that end;

15. *Encourages* all United Nations human rights mechanisms as well as agencies, funds and programmes to work within their respective mandates with Member States and national institutions in the promotion and protection of human rights with respect to, inter alia, projects in the area of good governance and the rule of law, and in this regard welcomes the efforts made by the High Commissioner to develop partnerships in support of national institutions, including the emerging tripartite partnership among the United Nations Development Programme, the Office of the High Commissioner and the International Coordinating Committee of National Institutions for the Promotion and Protection of Human Rights;

16. *Welcomes* the important role played by the International Coordinating Committee, in close cooperation with the Office of the High Commissioner, in assisting Governments, when requested, in the establishment and strengthening of national human rights institutions in accordance with the Paris Principles, in assessing the conformity of national human rights institutions with the Paris Principles and in providing technical assistance to strengthen national human rights institutions, upon request, with a view to enhancing their compliance with the Paris Principles;

17. *Encourages* national institutions, including Ombudsman and mediator institutions, to seek accreditation status through the International Coordinating Committee;

18. *Encourages* all Member States to take appropriate steps to promote the exchange of information and experience concerning the establishment and effective operation of national human rights institutions and to support the work of the International Coordinating Committee and its regional coordinating networks in this regard, including through support for the relevant technical assistance programmes of the Office of the High Commissioner;

19. *Requests* the Secretary-General to continue to provide the assistance necessary for holding international and regional meetings of national institutions, including meetings of the International Coordinating Committee, in cooperation with the Office of the High Commissioner;

20. *Also requests* the Secretary-General to report to the General Assembly at its sixty-eighth session on the implementation of the present resolution.

Human rights education

Declaration on human rights education and training

Working Group report. Pursuant to Human Rights Council resolution 13/15 [YUN 2010, p. 661], the Open-ended Working Group on the draft United Nations declaration on human rights education and training [ibid.] held a meeting (Geneva, 10–14 January) [A/HRC/WG.9/1/3] during which it finalized, adopted and submitted to the Council a draft declaration [A/HRC/WG.9/1/2].

Human Rights Council action. On 23 March [A/66/53 (res. 16/1)], the Council adopted the United Nations Declaration on Human Rights Education and Training and recommended its adoption by the General Assembly.

GENERAL ASSEMBLY ACTION

On 19 December [meeting 89], the General Assembly, on the recommendation of the Third Committee [A/66/457], adopted **resolution 66/137** without vote [agenda item 64].

United Nations Declaration on Human Rights Education and Training

The General Assembly,

Welcoming the adoption by the Human Rights Council, in its resolution 16/1 of 23 March 2011, of the United Nations Declaration on Human Rights Education and Training,

1. *Adopts* the United Nations Declaration on Human Rights Education and Training annexed to the present resolution;

2. *Invites* Governments, agencies and organizations of the United Nations system, and intergovernmental and non-governmental organizations to intensify their efforts to disseminate the Declaration and to promote universal respect and understanding thereof, and requests the Secretary-General to include the text of the Declaration in the next edition of *Human Rights: A Compilation of International Instruments.*

ANNEX

United Nations Declaration on Human Rights Education and Training

The General Assembly,

Reaffirming the purposes and principles of the Charter of the United Nations with regard to the promotion and encouragement of respect for all human rights and fundamental freedoms for all without distinction as to race, sex, language or religion,

Reaffirming also that every individual and every organ of society shall strive by teaching and education to promote respect for human rights and fundamental freedoms,

Reaffirming further that everyone has the right to education, and that education shall be directed to the full development of the human personality and the sense of its dignity, enable all persons to participate effectively in a free society and promote understanding, tolerance and friendship among all nations and all racial, ethnic or religious groups, and further the activities of the United Nations for the maintenance of peace, security and the promotion of development and human rights,

Reaffirming that States are duty-bound, as stipulated in the Universal Declaration of Human Rights, the International Covenant on Economic, Social and Cultural Rights and in other human rights instruments, to ensure that education is aimed at strengthening respect for human rights and fundamental freedoms,

Acknowledging the fundamental importance of human rights education and training in contributing to the promotion, protection and effective realization of all human rights,

Reaffirming the call of the World Conference on Human Rights, held in Vienna in 1993, on all States and institutions to include human rights, humanitarian law, democracy and rule of law in the curricula of all learning institutions, and its statement that human rights education should include peace, democracy, development and social justice, as set forth in international and regional human rights instruments, in order to achieve common understanding and awareness with a view to strengthening universal commitment to human rights,

Recalling the 2005 World Summit Outcome, in which Heads of State and Government supported the promotion of human rights education and learning at all levels, including through the implementation of the World Programme for Human Rights Education, and encouraged all States to develop initiatives in that regard,

Motivated by the desire to send a strong signal to the international community to strengthen all efforts in human rights education and training through a collective commitment by all stakeholders,

Declares the following:

Article 1

1. Everyone has the right to know, seek and receive information about all human rights and fundamental freedoms and should have access to human rights education and training.

2. Human rights education and training is essential for the promotion of universal respect for and observance of all human rights and fundamental freedoms for all, in accordance with the principles of the universality, indivisibility and interdependence of human rights.

3. The effective enjoyment of all human rights, in particular the right to education and access to information, enables access to human rights education and training.

Article 2

1. Human rights education and training comprises all educational, training, information, awareness-raising and learning activities aimed at promoting universal respect for and observance of all human rights and fundamental freedoms and thus contributing, inter alia, to the prevention of human rights violations and abuses by providing persons with knowledge, skills and understanding and developing their attitudes and behaviours, to empower them to contribute to the building and promotion of a universal culture of human rights.

2. Human rights education and training encompasses:

(*a*) Education about human rights, which includes providing knowledge and understanding of human rights norms and principles, the values that underpin them and the mechanisms for their protection;

(*b*) Education through human rights, which includes learning and teaching in a way that respects the rights of both educators and learners;

(*c*) Education for human rights, which includes empowering persons to enjoy and exercise their rights and to respect and uphold the rights of others.

Article 3

1. Human rights education and training is a lifelong process that concerns all ages.

2. Human rights education and training concerns all parts of society, at all levels, including preschool, primary, secondary and higher education, taking into account academic freedom where applicable, and all forms of education, training and learning, whether in a public or private, formal, informal or non-formal setting. It includes, inter alia, vocational training, particularly the training of trainers, teachers and State officials, continuing education, popular education, and public information and awareness activities.

3. Human rights education and training should use languages and methods suited to target groups, taking into account their specific needs and conditions.

Article 4

Human rights education and training should be based on the principles of the Universal Declaration of Human Rights and relevant treaties and instruments, with a view to:

(*a*) Raising awareness, understanding and acceptance of universal human rights standards and principles, as well as guarantees at the international, regional and national levels for the protection of human rights and fundamental freedoms;

(*b*) Developing a universal culture of human rights, in which everyone is aware of their own rights and responsibilities in respect of the rights of others, and promoting the development of the individual as a responsible member of a free, peaceful, pluralist and inclusive society;

(*c*) Pursuing the effective realization of all human rights and promoting tolerance, non-discrimination and equality;

(*d*) Ensuring equal opportunities for all through access to quality human rights education and training, without any discrimination;

(*e*) Contributing to the prevention of human rights violations and abuses and to the combating and eradication of all forms of discrimination, racism, stereotyping and incitement to hatred, and the harmful attitudes and prejudices that underlie them.

Article 5

1. Human rights education and training, whether provided by public or private actors, should be based on the principles of equality, particularly between girls and boys and between women and men, human dignity, inclusion and non-discrimination.

2. Human rights education and training should be accessible and available to all persons and should take into account the particular challenges and barriers faced by, and the needs and expectations of, persons in vulnerable and disadvantaged situations and groups, including persons with disabilities, in order to promote empowerment and human development and to contribute to the elimination of the causes of exclusion or marginalization, as well as enable everyone to exercise all their rights.

3. Human rights education and training should embrace and enrich, as well as draw inspiration from, the diversity of civilizations, religions, cultures and traditions of different countries, as it is reflected in the universality of human rights.

4. Human rights education and training should take into account different economic, social and cultural circumstances, while promoting local initiatives in order to encourage ownership of the common goal of the fulfilment of all human rights for all.

Article 6

1. Human rights education and training should capitalize on and make use of new information and communication technologies, as well as the media, to promote all human rights and fundamental freedoms.

2. The arts should be encouraged as a means of training and raising awareness in the field of human rights.

Article 7

1. States, and where applicable relevant governmental authorities, have the primary responsibility to promote and ensure human rights education and training, developed and implemented in a spirit of participation, inclusion and responsibility.

2. States should create a safe and enabling environment for the engagement of civil society, the private sector and other relevant stakeholders in human rights education and training, in which the human rights and fundamental freedoms of all, including of those engaged in the process, are fully protected.

3. States should take steps, individually and through international assistance and cooperation, to ensure, to the maximum of their available resources, the progressive implementation of human rights education and training by appropriate means, including the adoption of legislative and administrative measures and policies.

4. States, and where applicable relevant governmental authorities, should ensure adequate training in human rights and, where appropriate, international humanitarian law and international criminal law, of State officials, civil servants, judges, law enforcement officials and military personnel, as well as promote adequate training in human rights for teachers, trainers and other educators and private personnel acting on behalf of the State.

Article 8

1. States should develop, or promote the development of, at the appropriate level, strategies and policies and, where appropriate, action plans and programmes to implement human rights education and training, such as through its integration into school and training curricula. In so doing, they should take into account the World Programme for Human Rights Education and specific national and local needs and priorities.

2. The conception, implementation and evaluation of and follow-up to such strategies, action plans, policies and programmes should involve all relevant stakeholders, including the private sector, civil society and national human rights institutions, by promoting, where appropriate, multi-stakeholder initiatives.

Article 9

States should promote the establishment, development and strengthening of effective and independent national human rights institutions, in compliance with the principles relating to the status of national institutions for the promotion and protection of human rights ("the Paris Principles"), recognizing that national human rights institutions can play an important role, including, where necessary, a coordinating role, in promoting human rights education and training by, inter alia, raising awareness and mobilizing relevant public and private actors.

Article 10

1. Various actors within society, including, inter alia, educational institutions, the media, families, local communities, civil society institutions, including non-governmental organizations, human rights defenders and the private sector, have an important role to play in promoting and providing human rights education and training.

2. Civil society institutions, the private sector and other relevant stakeholders are encouraged to ensure adequate human rights education and training for their staff and personnel.

Article 11

The United Nations and international and regional organizations should provide human rights education and training for their civilian personnel and for military and police personnel serving under their mandates.

Article 12

1. International cooperation at all levels should support and reinforce national efforts, including, where applicable, at the local level, to implement human rights education and training.

2. Complementary and coordinated efforts at the international, regional, national and local levels can contribute to more effective implementation of human rights education and training.

3. Voluntary funding for projects and initiatives in the field of human rights education and training should be encouraged.

Article 13

1. International and regional human rights mechanisms should, within their respective mandates, take into account human rights education and training in their work.

2. States are encouraged to include, where appropriate, information on the measures that they have adopted in the field of human rights education and training in their reports to relevant human rights mechanisms.

Article 14

States should take appropriate measures to ensure the effective implementation of and follow-up to the present Declaration and make the necessary resources available in this regard.

Follow-up to International Year of Human Rights Learning

Report of Secretary-General. Pursuant to General Assembly resolution 64/82 [YUN 2009, p. 654], the Secretary-General in August submitted a report [A/66/225] providing information on international initiatives undertaken from August 2009 to June 2011 to advance human rights education and learning in follow-up to the International Year of Human Rights Learning, 2009, proclaimed by the General Assembly in 2007 [YUN 2007, p. 697]. The report highlighted activities carried out in the context of the World Programme for Human Rights Education [YUN 2009, p. 653] and the drafting and adoption by the Human Rights Council of the United Nations Declaration on Human Rights Education and Training (see above). The report concluded that UN initiatives contributed to increasing global awareness of human rights and the role of human rights education and learning as significant instruments in promoting and protecting human rights throughout the world.

GENERAL ASSEMBLY ACTION

On 19 December [meeting 89], the General Assembly, on the recommendation of the Third Committee [A/66/462/Add.2], adopted **resolution 66/173** without vote [agenda item 69 (*b*)].

Follow-up to the International Year of Human Rights Learning

The General Assembly,

Recalling that the purposes and principles set out in the Charter of the United Nations include promoting and encouraging respect for human rights and fundamental freedoms for all,

Reaffirming that all human rights are universal, indivisible and interdependent and that human rights learning can contribute to the understanding of their connectedness to people's daily lives,

Recalling its resolution 60/251 of 15 March 2006, in which it decided that the Human Rights Council should, inter alia, promote human rights education and learning as well as advisory services, technical assistance and capacity-building,

Recalling also the 2005 World Summit Outcome, in which Heads of State and Government expressed their support for the promotion of human rights education and learning at all levels, including through the implementation of the World Programme for Human Rights Education, as appropriate, and encouraged all States to develop initiatives in this regard,

Recalling further its resolutions 62/171 of 18 December 2007, 63/173 of 18 December 2008 and 64/82 of 10 December 2009 on the International Year of Human Rights Learning and its follow-up,

Welcoming Human Rights Council resolution 15/11 of 30 September 2010, in which the Council decided on the plan of action for the second phase (2010–2014) of the World Programme for Human Rights Education, and stressing the complementarity of human rights learning and human rights education,

Acknowledging that civil society, academia, the private sector, the media and, where appropriate, parliamentarians can play an important role at the national, regional and international levels in the development and facilitation of ways and means to promote and implement learning about human rights as a way of life at the community level,

Convinced that integrating human rights learning into all relevant development policies and programmes contributes to enabling people to participate as equals in the decisions that determine their lives,

Having considered the report of the Secretary-General,

1. *Reaffirms its conviction* that every woman, man, youth and child can realize his or her full human potential by, inter alia, learning about the comprehensive framework of human rights and fundamental freedoms, including the ability to act on that knowledge in order to ensure the effective realization of human rights and fundamental freedoms for all;

2. *Encourages* Member States to expand on efforts made beyond the International Year of Human Rights Learning and to consider devoting the financial and human resources necessary to further design and implement international, regional, national and local long-term human rights learning programmes of action aimed at broad-based and sustained human rights learning at all levels, in coordination with civil society, the media, the private sector, academia, parliamentarians and regional organizations, including the appropriate specialized agencies, funds and programmes of the United Nations system, and, where possible, to designate human rights cities;

3. *Calls upon* the United Nations High Commissioner for Human Rights and the Human Rights Council to support, cooperate and collaborate closely with civil society, the private sector, academia, regional organizations, the media and other relevant stakeholders, as well as with organizations, programmes and funds of the United Nations system, and relevant networks and bodies such as the Alliance of Civilizations, the United Nations Global Compact and the United Nations Office for Partnerships in efforts to develop, in particular, the design of strategies and international, regional, national and local programmes of action aimed at broad-based and sustained human rights learning at all levels;

4. *Welcomes* the adoption by the Human Rights Council of the United Nations Declaration on Human Rights Education and Training, and stresses the complementarity of human rights learning and the Declaration;

5. *Encourages* civil society organizations worldwide, in particular those working at the community level, to integrate human rights learning into dialogue and consciousness-raising programmes with groups working on education, development, poverty eradication, participation, children, indigenous peoples, gender equality, persons with disabilities, elder persons and migrants, as well as on other relevant political, civil, economic, social and cultural issues of concern;

6. *Encourages* relevant actors in civil society, including sociologists, anthropologists, members of academia and of the media and community leaders, to join in further developing the concept of human rights learning as a way to promote the full realization of all human rights and fundamental freedoms for all;

7. *Invites* relevant treaty bodies to take human rights learning into account in their interaction with States parties;

8. *Requests* the Secretary-General to submit to the General Assembly at its sixty-eighth session a report on the implementation of the present resolution.

World Down Syndrome Day

On 19 December, the General Assembly designated 21 March as World Down Syndrome Day, to be observed every year beginning in 2012. It encouraged States to take measures to raise awareness throughout society, including at the family level, regarding persons with Down syndrome.

GENERAL ASSEMBLY ACTION

On 19 December [meeting 89], the General Assembly, on the recommendation of the Third Committee [A/66/462/Add.1], adopted **resolution 66/149** without vote [agenda item 69 (*a*)].

World Down Syndrome Day

The General Assembly,

Recalling the 2005 World Summit Outcome and the United Nations Millennium Declaration, as well as the outcomes of the major United Nations conferences and summits in the economic, social and related fields,

Recalling also the Convention on the Rights of Persons with Disabilities, according to which persons with disabilities should enjoy a full and decent life, in conditions that ensure dignity, promote self-reliance and facilitate the person's active participation in the community and the full enjoyment of all human rights and fundamental freedoms on an equal basis with other persons, and by which States parties undertake to adopt immediate, effective and appropriate measures to raise awareness throughout society regarding persons with disabilities,

Affirming that ensuring and promoting the full realization of all human rights and fundamental freedoms for all persons with disabilities is critical to achieving internationally agreed development goals,

Aware that Down syndrome is a naturally occurring chromosomal arrangement that has always been a part of the human condition, exists in all regions across the globe and commonly results in variable effects on learning styles, physical characteristics or health,

Recalling that adequate access to health care, to early intervention programmes and to inclusive education, as well as appropriate research, are vital to the growth and development of the individual,

Recognizing the inherent dignity, worth and valuable contributions of persons with intellectual disabilities as promoters of the well-being and diversity of their communities, and the importance of their individual autonomy and independence, including the freedom to make their own choices,

1. *Decides* to designate 21 March as World Down Syndrome Day, to be observed every year beginning in 2012;
2. *Invites* all Member States, relevant organizations of the United Nations system and other international organizations, as well as civil society, including non-governmental organizations and the private sector, to observe World Down Syndrome Day in an appropriate manner, in order to raise public awareness of Down syndrome;
3. *Encourages* Member States to take measures to raise awareness throughout society, including at the family level, regarding persons with Down syndrome;
4. *Requests* the Secretary-General to bring the present resolution to the attention of all Member States and United Nations organizations.

International Day for the Right to the Truth

Report of Secretary-General. Pursuant to General Assembly resolution 65/196 [YUN 2010, p. 695], the Secretary-General in September submitted a report [A/66/335] on the observance of the International Day for the Right to the Truth concerning Gross Human Rights Violations for the Dignity of Victims (24 March), proclaimed by the Assembly in 2010 [YUN 2010, p. 695]. The report provided an account of the extent and nature of the observance of the International Day and concluded that there was a need for greater awareness about the International Day. An addendum [A/66/335/Add.1] covered observance activities in Argentina and Guatemala.

(For information on the right to the truth, see p. 685.)

International Year for People of African Descent

Working Group on people of African descent. At its tenth session (Geneva, 28 March–1 April) [A/HRC/18/45], the Working Group of Experts on People of African Descent engaged in a thematic discussion on the situation of people of African descent in the context of the International Year for People of African Descent, 2011, proclaimed by the General Assembly in resolution 64/169 [YUN 2009, p. 655]. The High Commissioner stressed that one of the most important goals of the Year was to raise awareness of the continuing problems facing people of African descent, especially those stemming from racism and racial discrimination. It was also an opportunity to recognize and celebrate the many contributions that Afro-descendants had made to their societies. The Working Group recommended that the international community declare an international decade for people of African descent to make the challenges they faced more visible, to identify solutions and to engage in a sustained campaign to eradicate structural discrimination. It also proposed that the theme for the International Year, which was widely accepted in the international community, should also be adopted as the theme of the decade, namely "People of African descent: recognition, justice and development".

Report of Secretary-General. Pursuant to General Assembly resolution 65/36 [YUN 2010, p. 661], the Secretary-General reported [A/66/342 & Add.1] on the programme of activities to mark the International Year for People of African Descent (2011), proclaimed by the Assembly in resolution 64/169 [YUN 2009, p. 655]. Views and recommendations on how to celebrate the International Year, as well as on activities planned, were received from 12 States (Bosnia and Herzegovina, Colombia, Costa Rica, Cuba, Dominican Republic, Ecuador, Jamaica, Lithuania, Mauritius, Serbia, Trinidad and Tobago, Ukraine), five UN bodies, two regional and other intergovernmental organizations, two civil society organizations and one national human rights institution. Ohchr, on 2 March, organized a panel discussion during the high-level segment of the Council's sixteenth session that focused on the full enjoyment of the human rights of people of African descent. On 21 March, the UN Department of Public Information organized a videoconference for middle and high school students on racial discrimination and the International Year. In April, the Office of the High Commissioner for Refugees in Ecuador provided support for the organization of a photo exhibition entitled "Let us never forget" as a joint effort with the municipality of Esmeraldas, the United Nations Educational, Scientific and Cultural Organization and the International Centre for Cultural Diversity.

Follow-up to 1993 World Conference

Report of Third Committee. On 29 November [A/66/462/Add.4], the Third Committee of the General Assembly reported on the implementation of and follow-up to the Vienna Declaration and Programme of Action, adopted at the 1993 World Conference on Human Rights [YUN 1993, p. 908]. It noted that on 16 September, the General Assembly, on the recommendation of the General Committee, decided to include in the agenda of its sixty-sixth (2011) session, under the item entitled "Promotion and protection of human rights", the sub-item entitled "Comprehensive implementation of and follow-up to the Vienna Declaration and Programme of Action" and to allocate it to the Third Committee. The Third Committee considered the sub-item on 18 October [A/C.3/66/SR.21 & 22]. No proposals were submitted under that sub-item.

The General Assembly took note of the report on 19 December (**decision 66/538**).

Chapter II

Protection of human rights

In 2011, the United Nations continued to protect human rights worldwide through several mechanisms. Its main organs—the General Assembly, the Security Council and the Economic and Social Council—remained engaged in protecting those rights. The Human Rights Council carried out its tasks as the central UN intergovernmental body responsible for promoting and protecting human rights and fundamental freedoms worldwide. The Council addressed violations, worked to prevent abuses, provided overall policy guidance, monitored the observance of human rights around the world and assisted States in fulfilling their human rights obligations.

Central to human rights protection were the special procedures of the Human Rights Council—independent experts with mandates to investigate, report and advise on human rights from a thematic or country-specific perspective. At the end of 2011, there were 45 special procedures (35 thematic mandates and 10 country or territory-related mandates) with 66 mandate-holders.

In 2011, special procedures submitted 136 reports to the Human Rights Council, including 62 country visit reports, and 26 reports to the General Assembly. They sent 605 communications to 124 States; 75 per cent of all communications were sent jointly by more than one mandate. Communications covered at least 1,298 individuals, 15 per cent of whom were women. Governments replied to 45 per cent of communications sent in 2011, and 19 per cent of communications were followed up by mandate-holders. Special procedures issued 270 news releases and public statements on situations of concern, including 30 statements issued jointly by two or more mandate-holders.

Special procedures conducted 82 country visits to 60 States and territories. Ninety countries had extended a standing invitation to special procedures as at 31 December.

The Council in 2011 established three thematic mandates: the independent expert on the promotion of a democratic and equitable international order; the special rapporteur on the promotion of truth, justice, reparation and guarantees of non-recurrence; and the working group on transnational corporations and other business enterprises.

Human rights were also protected through the network of human rights defenders in individual countries, operating within the framework of the 1998 Declaration on Human Rights Defenders.

Economic, social and cultural rights continued to be a major focus of activity. In December, the General Assembly adopted a resolution on human rights and cultural diversity, calling on States, international organizations and UN entities to recognize and promote respect for cultural diversity for the purpose of advancing peace, development and universally accepted human rights.

On 22 September, the General Assembly convened a high-level meeting on the theme "Victims of racism, racial discrimination, xenophobia and related intolerance: recognition, justice and development" to commemorate the tenth anniversary of the adoption of the Durban Declaration and Programme of Action.

Special procedures

Report of High Commissioner. In her annual report to the Human Rights Council [A/HRC/19/21], the United Nations High Commissioner for Human Rights, Navanethem Pillay (South Africa), noted that the role of special procedures remained essential in providing the Council with timely and reliable information. From January to November, special procedures mandate holders conducted 75 country visits and issued 543 communications. More States extended standing invitations to special procedures, increasing the number of invitations to 89 in November. Three new thematic mandates were established by the Council: a new working group on transnational corporations and other business enterprises; a special rapporteur on the promotion of truth, justice, reparation and guarantees of non-recurrence; and an independent expert on the promotion of a democratic and equitable international order. In all, there were 45 special procedures mandates (35 thematic and 10 geographically related). The Council also expanded the scope of the mandate on toxic waste to encompass the human rights obligations related to environmentally sound management and disposal of hazardous substances and waste.

Report of Secretary-General. In response to a Commission on Human Rights request [YUN 2004, p. 648] and a Human Rights Council decision [YUN 2006, p. 760], the Secretary-General submitted a December report [A/HRC/19/23] indicating that the special procedures' conclusions and recommendations contained in their 2011 reports to the Council's sixteenth, seventeenth and eighteenth sessions were available on the website of the Office of the High Commissioner.

Report of special procedures. In accordance with the decisions made by special procedures mandate holders at their sixteenth [YUN 2009, p. 645] and seventeenth [YUN 2010, p. 656] annual meetings, 29 mandate holders prepared and issued on 5 September a joint communications report [A/HRC/18/51 & Corr.1] containing summaries of communications and statistical information. The report covered all urgent appeals and letters of allegations sent by mandate holders from 1 December 2010 to 31 May 2011 and replies received between 1 February and 31 July 2011, including replies relating to communications sent prior to 1 December 2010.

Civil and political rights

Racism and racial discrimination

Follow-up to 2001 World Conference

During the year, efforts continued to implement the Durban Declaration and Programme of Action (DDPA) adopted by the 2001 World Conference against Racism, Racial Discrimination, Xenophobia and Related Intolerance [YUN 2001, p. 615]. In other activities, the General Assembly convened a high-level meeting to commemorate the tenth anniversary of the adoption of DDPA (see p. 652).

Intergovernmental Working Group. The Intergovernmental Working Group on the Effective Implementation of DDPA, established in 2002 [YUN 2002, p. 661] to make recommendations for its implementation and to prepare complementary standards, held its ninth session (Geneva, 17–28 October) [A/HRC/19/77]. The Working Group reviewed progress on the implementation of recommendations adopted at its previous session; shared experiences, including on good practices, implementation of the International Convention on the Elimination of All Forms of Racial Discrimination, DDPA and the outcome document of the 2009 Durban Review Conference [YUN 2009, p. 657]; and discussed best and good practices. Presentations by experts on the roles of sport and of education in combating racism, racial discrimination, xenophobia and related intolerance were followed by interactive discussions. The Working Group adopted conclusions and recommendations on the aforementioned themes.

Working Group on people of African descent. At its tenth session (Geneva, 28 March–1 April) [A/HRC/18/45], the Working Group of Experts on People of African Descent, established in 2002 [YUN 2002, p. 661] to consider problems of racial discrimination affecting people of African descent, in accordance with DDPA, engaged in a discussion on the situation of people of African descent in the context of the International Year for People of African Descent, 2011, as proclaimed by the General Assembly in resolution 64/169 [YUN 2009, p. 655] (see p. 649). Presentations were made on the topics of the tenth anniversary of DDPA, Durban+10; the current situation of and action to combat discrimination against people of African descent; the contribution made by people of African descent in global development; and the lack of knowledge of the culture, history and traditions of people of African descent by themselves and others.

Mission report. Following its mission to Portugal (16–20 May) [A/HRC/21/60/Add.1], the Working Group issued recommendations including implementation of national policies and programmes addressing racial discrimination faced by people of African descent; revision and harmonization of national legislation with international human rights norms; revision of Government policy that impeded collection of information disaggregated by ethnic or racial origin; adoption of special measures to remedy structural discrimination; and revision of school curricula. It also recommended the effective protection of the rights of children of African descent in line with the Convention on the Rights of the Child [YUN 1989, p. 560].

Human Rights Council action. On 30 September [A/66/53/Add.1 (res. 18/28)], the Council extended the Working Group's mandate for three years; decided that the Group would undertake a minimum of two country visits per year; and requested it to report annually on its activities.

Report of Secretary-General. In response to General Assembly resolution 65/240 [YUN 2010, p. 665], the Secretary-General in August [A/66/328] reported on global efforts for the total elimination of racism, racial discrimination, xenophobia and related intolerance and the comprehensive implementation of and follow-up to DDPA. The report summarized contributions on the topic received from 26 countries and four UN entities, and reviewed activities undertaken by UN bodies since the submission of the last report [YUN 2010, p. 664]. It concluded that some progress had been made in combating racism and related phenomena, yet stronger political will and urgent measures were needed to reverse increasingly hostile racist attitudes and violence. States were encouraged to invite the Working Group to carry out country visits, particularly in light of the fact that 2011 was the International Year for People of African Descent (see p. 649). The General Assembly took note of that report on 19 December (**decision 66/535**).

Human Rights Council action. On 29 September [A/66/53/Add.1 (res. 18/20)], by a recorded vote of 37 to 1, with 8 abstentions, the Council decided to convene at its twentieth (2012) session a panel discussion on the promotion and protection of human rights in a multicultural context, including through combating xenophobia, discrimination and intolerance. It requested the Office of the United Nations High Commissioner for Refugees (OHCHR) to liaise with States, special procedures and treaty bodies, and other stakeholders, including UN entities, to ensure their participation in the panel discussion; and to report on the discussion's outcome in the form of a summary.

General Assembly high-level meeting commemorating DDPA tenth anniversary

The General Assembly, in resolution 65/240 [YUN 2010, p. 665], decided to convene a one-day high-level meeting on the theme "Victims of racism, racial discrimination, xenophobia and related intolerance: recognition, justice and development" to commemorate the tenth anniversary of DDPA [YUN 2001, p. 615]. In that regard, on 13 June, the Assembly, by resolution 65/279 (see below), decided to hold the meeting on 22 September 2011.

GENERAL ASSEMBLY ACTION

On 13 June [meeting 96], the General Assembly adopted **resolution 65/279** [draft: A/65/L.76] without vote [agenda item 66 (*b*)].

Scope, modalities, format and organization of the high-level meeting of the General Assembly to commemorate the tenth anniversary of the adoption of the Durban Declaration and Programme of Action

The General Assembly,

Recalling its resolution 64/148 of 18 December 2009, in which it, inter alia, called for the commemoration of the tenth anniversary of the Durban Declaration and Programme of Action adopted by the World Conference against Racism, Racial Discrimination, Xenophobia and Related Intolerance,

Recalling also its resolution 65/240 of 24 December 2010, in which it decided to hold a one-day high-level meeting of the General Assembly, at the level of Heads of State and Government, on the second day of the general debate of the sixty-sixth session, on the theme "Victims of racism, racial discrimination, xenophobia and related intolerance: recognition, justice and development",

1. *Decides* that the high-level meeting of the General Assembly to commemorate the tenth anniversary of the adoption of the Durban Declaration and Programme of Action will be held on Thursday, 22 September 2011, and consist of an opening plenary meeting from 9 a.m. to 11 a.m., two consecutive round tables from 11 a.m. to 1 p.m. and from 3 p.m. to 6 p.m., and a closing plenary meeting from 6 p.m. to 7 p.m., and also decides that the morning meeting of the general debate on that day will be held from 11 a.m. to 1 p.m. and that that arrangement does not constitute a precedent;

2. *Also decides* that the speakers at the opening plenary will be the President of the General Assembly, the Secretary-General, the United Nations High Commissioner for Human Rights, the Head of State of South Africa, one speaker from each regional group and a representative of a non-governmental organization active in the field of racism, racial discrimination, xenophobia and related intolerance;

3. *Further decides* that the organizational arrangements of the round tables will be as follows:

(*a*) The round tables will address the overall theme of "Victims of racism, racial discrimination, xenophobia and related intolerance: recognition, justice and development";

(*b*) Each round table will be co-chaired by two Heads of State or Government to be invited by the President of the General Assembly after consultations with the regional groups;

(*c*) In order to promote a substantive and constructive dialogue, participation in each round table will include Member States, observers, representatives of entities of the United Nations system and experts, as well as selected representatives of civil society organizations and non-governmental organizations that are active in the field of racism, racial discrimination, xenophobia and related intolerance;

(*d*) Accredited delegates, observers and selected non-governmental organizations that are active in the field of racism, racial discrimination, xenophobia and related intolerance will be able to follow the proceedings of the round-table sessions in the overflow room;

(*e*) The proceedings of the round tables shall be webcast;

4. *Invites* the Holy See, in its capacity as observer State, Palestine, in its capacity as observer, and the European Union, in its capacity as observer, to participate in the preparatory activities and in the high-level meeting;

5. *Invites* the President of the General Assembly to draw up a list of representatives of civil society organizations, including non-governmental organizations active in the field of racism, racial discrimination, xenophobia and related forms of intolerance and, taking into account the principle of equitable geographical representation, to submit the list to Member States for consideration on a no-objection basis, for participation in the high-level meeting;

6. *Reiterates its call for* States to be represented at the high-level meeting, at the highest possible political level, including at the level of Heads of State and Government;

7. *Decides* that the closing plenary meeting will comprise the presentation of summaries of the discussions by the co-chairs of the round tables and the adoption of a short and concise political declaration aimed at mobilizing political will.

High-level meeting. At the High-level Meeting of the General Assembly on 22 September [A/66/PV.14], the Secretary-General said that in the ten years since the adoption of DDPA, new laws had been enacted, new institutions were pursuing justice, new initiatives were promoting dialogue, and new mindsets had taken hold. Nonetheless, intolerance had increased in many parts of the world. Noting that the global plan of action included recommendations for combating discrimination against persons of African and Asian descent, indigenous peoples, migrants, refugees, minorities, the Roma, and others, he called on the international community to do more to embrace diversity and safeguard the dignity of those groups. The High Commissioner for Human Rights pointed out that DDPA, together with the 2009 Review Conference outcome document, provided a comprehensive framework to address the scourge of racism, and that anti-discrimination work needed careful planning and a long-term focus. Highlighting the importance of developing national action plans as DDPA had envisaged—with the participation of victims and affected groups—she indicated that her Office had provided training and technical assistance in that area and stood ready to assist more States. The President of South Africa, Jacob Zuma, noted that there was much outstanding work to be done and called on States and the world in general to reaffirm their commitment at the national, regional and international levels to implement DDPA. At the conclusion of the opening meeting, the Assembly decided to adopt the draft political declaration entitled "United against racism, racial discrimination, xenophobia and related intolerance" (see below), instead of adopting it at the closing plenary meeting (**decision 66/504**).

GENERAL ASSEMBLY ACTION

On 22 September [meeting 14], the General Assembly adopted **resolution 66/3** [draft: A/66/L.2] without vote [agenda item 67 (*b*)].

United against racism, racial discrimination, xenophobia and related intolerance

The General Assembly

Adopts the following political declaration of the high-level meeting of the General Assembly to commemorate the tenth anniversary of the adoption of the Durban Declaration and Programme of Action:

United against racism, racial discrimination, xenophobia and related intolerance

We, Heads of State and Government and representatives of States and Governments, gathered at United Nations Headquarters in New York on 22 September 2011, on the occasion of the high-level meeting of the General Assembly to commemorate the tenth anniversary of the adoption of the Durban Declaration and Programme of Action,

1. Reaffirm that the Durban Declaration and Programme of Action, adopted in 2001, and the outcome document of the Durban Review Conference, adopted in 2009, provide a comprehensive United Nations framework and solid foundation for combating racism, racial discrimination, xenophobia and related intolerance;

2. Recall that the aim of this commemoration is to mobilize political will at the national, regional and international levels, and reaffirm our political commitment to the full and effective implementation of the Durban Declaration and Programme of Action and the outcome document of the Durban Review Conference, and their follow-up processes, at all these levels;

3. Welcome the progress made in many parts of the world in the fight against racism, racial discrimination, xenophobia and related intolerance since 2001;

4. Acknowledge that, in spite of concerted efforts by the international community in the past ten years, building on efforts of the past decades, the scourge of racism, racial discrimination, xenophobia and related intolerance, including their new forms and manifestations, still persists in all parts of the world and that countless human beings continue to the present day to be victims of racism, racial discrimination, xenophobia and related intolerance;

5. Reaffirm that racism, racial discrimination, xenophobia and related intolerance constitute a negation of the purposes and principles of the Charter of the United Nations and of the Universal Declaration of Human Rights and that equality and non-discrimination are fundamental principles of international law;

6. Recall, in that regard, the importance of the International Convention on the Elimination of All Forms of Racial Discrimination and the Committee on the Elimination of Racial Discrimination, as well as of universal ratification and effective implementation of the Convention;

7. Resolve to pursue our common goal of ensuring the effective enjoyment of all human rights and fundamental freedoms for all, especially for victims of racism, racial discrimination, xenophobia and related intolerance in all societies;

8. Welcome the initiative to erect a permanent memorial to honour the victims of slavery and the transatlantic slave trade;

9. Reiterate that the primary responsibility for effectively combating racism, racial discrimination, xenophobia and related intolerance lies with States;

10. Welcome the adoption of legislative measures and the establishment of specialized national mechanisms to combat racism, racial discrimination, xenophobia and related intolerance;

11. Call upon the United Nations system and international and regional organizations and invite all stakeholders, including parliaments, civil society and the private sector, to fully commit themselves and to intensify their efforts in the fight against racism, racial discrimination, xenophobia and related intolerance, and welcome the continued engagement of the United Nations High Commissioner for Human Rights in incorporating the implementation of the Durban Declaration and Programme of Action into the United Nations system;

12. Proclaim together our strong determination to make the fight against racism, racial discrimination, xenophobia and related intolerance, and the protection of the victims thereof, a high priority for our countries.

Human Rights Council action. On 30 September [A/66/53/Add.1 (res. 18/27)], by a recorded vote of 35 to 1, with 10 abstentions, the Council welcomed the political declaration adopted by the General Assembly during its High-level Meeting; decided that the Intergovernmental Working Group on the Effective Implementation of DDPA should convene its tenth session from 8 to 19 October 2012; and invited States, the UN system and stakeholders to intensify efforts to build support for DDPA. It requested the Secretary-General and OHCHR to establish an outreach programme and launch a public information campaign for the commemoration and follow-up thereto, including by distributing copies of DDPA widely; and requested the Secretary-General to make available at the Council's twentieth (2012) session his progress report submitted to the Assembly.

Sports and combating discrimination

The General Assembly, in resolution 65/240 [YUN 2010, p. 665] on global efforts to eliminate discrimination and to implement DDPA, called on States to take advantage of mass sporting events as outreach platforms to mobilize people and convey messages about equality and non-discrimination.

Human Rights Council action. On 30 September [A/66/53/Add.1 (res. 18/23)], the Council recognized the potential of sport as a universal language to educate people on the values of respect, diversity, tolerance and fairness, and as a means to combat all forms of discrimination. It welcomed the hosting of the 2012, 2014, 2016 and 2018 Winter or Summer Olympic and Paralympic Games in the cities of London, Sochi, Rio de Janeiro and Pyeong Chang, respectively. It stressed how the principles of the Olympic Charter—aimed at non-discrimination, equality, inclusion, respect and mutual understanding—related to the Universal Declaration of Human Rights and could translate into all aspects of society. The Council decided to convene, at its nineteenth (2012) session, a high-level interactive panel discussion on ways in which sport, in particular the Olympic and Paralympic Games, could be used to promote awareness and understanding of the Declaration. It requested OHCHR to liaise with special procedures, States and other stakeholders, including UN entities, to ensure their participation in the panel discussion, and to prepare a report on its outcome.

GENERAL ASSEMBLY ACTION

On 19 December [meeting 89], the General Assembly, on the recommendation of the Third (Social, Humanitarian and Cultural) Committee [A/66/460], adopted **resolution 66/144** by recorded vote (138-6-46) [agenda item 67 (*b*)].

Global efforts for the total elimination of racism, racial discrimination, xenophobia and related intolerance and the comprehensive implementation of and follow-up to the Durban Declaration and Programme of Action

The General Assembly,

Recalling its resolution 52/111 of 12 December 1997, in which it decided to convene the World Conference against Racism, Racial Discrimination, Xenophobia and Related Intolerance, and its resolutions 56/266 of 27 March 2002, 57/195 of 18 December 2002, 58/160 of 22 December 2003, 59/177 of 20 December 2004 and 60/144 of 16 December 2005, which guided the comprehensive follow-up to and effective implementation of the World Conference, and in this regard underlining the importance of their full and effective implementation,

Recalling also its resolutions 64/148 of 18 December 2009 and 65/240 of 24 December 2010, in which it, inter alia, called for the commemoration of the tenth anniversary of the Durban Declaration and Programme of Action adopted by the World Conference against Racism, Racial Discrimination, Xenophobia and Related Intolerance, which represented an important opportunity for the international community to reaffirm its commitment to the eradication of racism, racial discrimination, xenophobia and related intolerance, including by mobilizing political will at the national, regional and international levels, with a view to achieving concrete results,

Taking note of Human Rights Council decision 3/103 of 8 December 2006, by which, heeding the decision and instruction of the World Conference, the Council established the Ad Hoc Committee of the Human Rights Council on the Elaboration of Complementary Standards,

Bearing in mind the responsibility and commitments of the Human Rights Council emanating from the outcome document of the Durban Review Conference,

Reiterating that all human beings are born free and equal in dignity and rights and have the potential to contribute constructively to the development and well-being of their societies, and that any doctrine of racial superiority is scientifically false, morally condemnable, socially unjust and dangerous and must be rejected, together with theories that attempt to determine the existence of separate human races,

Convinced that racism, racial discrimination, xenophobia and related intolerance manifest themselves in a differentiated manner for women and girls and may be among the factors leading to a deterioration in their living conditions, poverty, violence, multiple forms of discrimination and the limitation or denial of their human rights, and recognizing the need to integrate a gender perspective into relevant policies, strategies and programmes of action against racism, racial discrimination, xenophobia and related intolerance in order to address multiple forms of discrimination,

Underlining the primacy of political will, international cooperation and adequate funding at the national, regional and international levels needed to address all forms and manifestations of racism, racial discrimination, xenophobia and related intolerance,

Emphasizing, while acknowledging the primary responsibility of States parties to implement their obligations under the International Convention on the Elimination of All Forms of Racial Discrimination, that international cooperation and technical assistance play an important role in assisting countries in the implementation of their obligations under the Convention,

Alarmed at the increase in racist violence and xenophobic ideas in many parts of the world, in political circles, in the sphere of public opinion and in society at large as a result, inter alia, of the resurgent activities of associations established on the basis of racist and xenophobic platforms and charters, and the persistent use of those platforms and charters to promote or incite racist ideologies,

Underlining the importance of urgently eliminating continuing and violent trends involving racism and racial discrimination, and conscious that any form of impunity for crimes motivated by racist and xenophobic attitudes plays a role in weakening the rule of law and democracy, tends to encourage the recurrence of such crimes and requires resolute action and cooperation for its eradication,

Recognizing that individuals belonging to vulnerable groups, such as migrants, refugees, asylum seekers and persons belonging to national or ethnic, religious and linguistic minorities, continue to be the main victims of violence and attacks perpetrated or incited by extremist political parties, movements and groups,

Acknowledging the central role of resource mobilization, effective global partnership and international cooperation in the context of paragraphs 157 and 158 of the Durban Programme of Action for the successful realization of the primary objectives and commitments undertaken at the World Conference,

Expressing grave concern at the lack of progress made in the implementation of the Durban Declaration and Programme of Action, in particular key paragraphs 157 to 159 of the Programme of Action,

Welcoming the continued commitment of the United Nations High Commissioner for Human Rights to profiling and increasing the visibility of the struggle against racism, racial discrimination, xenophobia and related intolerance, and recognizing the need for the High Commissioner to make this a cross-cutting issue in the activities and programmes of her Office,

Noting the work of the Intergovernmental Working Group on the Effective Implementation of the Durban Declaration and Programme of Action at its seventh and eighth sessions, held from 5 to 16 October 2009 and from 11 to 22 October 2010, respectively, and welcoming the adoption by the Human Rights Council of the conclusions and recommendations of the Working Group,

Noting also the progress made during the third session of the Ad Hoc Committee on the Elaboration of Complementary Standards, held in Geneva on 22 and 23 November 2010 and from 11 to 21 April 2011, and noting further the convening of the fourth session, to be held in Geneva during 2012,

Noting further the activities undertaken in the context of the International Year for People of African Descent, including the first World Summit of Afro-Descendants, held in La Ceiba, Honduras, in August 2011, and the high-level summit for people of African descent, held in Salvador, Brazil, in November 2011 to mark the tenth anniversary of the Durban outcome, and looking forward to the African Diaspora Summit, to be held in South Africa in 2012,

Recognizing the potential of sport as a universal language contributing to the education of people on the values of diversity, tolerance and fairness and as a means to combat racism, racial discrimination, xenophobia and related intolerance,

Welcoming the hosting of the 2010 and 2014 International Federation of Association Football World Cups in South Africa and Brazil, respectively, and stressing the importance of making continuing use of those events to promote understanding, tolerance and peace and to promote and strengthen efforts in the fight against racism, racial discrimination, xenophobia and related intolerance,

I
General principles

1. *Recognizes and affirms* that a global fight against racism, racial discrimination, xenophobia and related intolerance and all their abhorrent and evolving forms and manifestations is a matter of priority for the international community;

2. *Acknowledges* that no derogation from the prohibition of racial discrimination, genocide, the crime of apartheid or slavery is permitted, as defined in the obligations under the relevant human rights instruments;

3. *Expresses its profound concern about and its unequivocal condemnation* of all forms of racism and racial discrimination, including related acts of racially motivated violence, xenophobia and intolerance, as well as propaganda activities and organizations that attempt to justify or promote racism, racial discrimination, xenophobia and related intolerance in any form;

4. *Re-emphasizes* that international cooperation is a key principle in achieving the goal of the total elimination of racism, racial discrimination, xenophobia and related intolerance and the comprehensive follow-up to and effective implementation of the Durban Declaration and Programme of Action in this regard;

5. *Emphasizes* that the basic responsibility for effectively combating racism, racial discrimination, xenophobia and related intolerance lies with States, and to this end stresses that States have the primary responsibility to ensure the full and effective implementation of all commitments and recommendations contained in the Durban Declaration and Programme of Action as well as the outcome document of the Durban Review Conference, and in this regard welcomes the steps taken by numerous Governments;

6. *Expresses deep concern* at inadequate responses to emerging and resurgent forms of racism, racial discrimination, xenophobia and related intolerance, and urges States to adopt measures to address those scourges vigorously with a view to preventing their practice and protecting victims;

7. *Underlines* the imperative need to address all the contemporary forms and manifestations of racism, racial discrimination, xenophobia and related intolerance, which include, inter alia, incitement to such hatred, racial profiling and the propagation of racist and xenophobic acts through cyberspace, with a view to maximizing protection for victims, providing legal remedies and combating impunity;

8. *Stresses* that States and international organizations have a responsibility to ensure that measures taken in the struggle against terrorism do not discriminate in purpose or effect on grounds of race, colour, descent or national or ethnic origin, and urges all States to rescind or refrain from all forms of racial profiling;

9. *Recognizes* that States should implement and enforce appropriate and effective legislative, judicial, regulatory and administrative measures to prevent and protect against acts of racism, racial discrimination, xenophobia and related intolerance, thereby contributing to the prevention of human rights violations;

10. *Also recognizes* that racism, racial discrimination, xenophobia and related intolerance occur on the grounds of race, colour, descent or national or ethnic origin and that victims can suffer multiple or aggravated forms of discrimination based on other related grounds, such as sex, language, religion or belief, political or other opinion, social origin, property and birth or other status;

11. *Reaffirms* that any advocacy of national, racial or religious hatred that constitutes incitement to discrimination, hostility or violence shall be prohibited by law, and also reaffirms that the dissemination of ideas based on racial superiority or hatred, or incitement to racial discrimination, as well as all acts of violence or incitement to such acts, shall be declared offences punishable by law, in accordance with the international obligations of States, and that those prohibitions are consistent with freedom of opinion and expression;

12. *Emphasizes* that it is the responsibility of States to adopt effective measures to combat criminal acts motivated by racism, racial discrimination, xenophobia and related intolerance, including measures to ensure that such motivations are considered an aggravating factor for the purposes of sentencing, to prevent those crimes from going unpunished and to ensure the rule of law;

13. *Urges* all States to review and, where necessary, revise their immigration laws, policies and practices so that they are free of racial discrimination and compatible with their obligations under international human rights instruments;

14. *Calls upon* all States, in accordance with the commitments undertaken in paragraph 147 of the Durban Programme of Action, to take all measures necessary to combat incitement to violence motivated by racial hatred, including through the misuse of print, audiovisual and electronic media and new communications technologies, and, in collaboration with service providers, to promote the use of such technologies, including the Internet, to contribute to the fight against racism, in conformity with international standards of freedom of expression and taking all measures necessary to guarantee that right;

15. *Encourages* all States to include in their educational curricula and social programmes at all levels, as appropriate, knowledge of and tolerance and respect for all cultures, civilizations, religions, peoples and countries, as well as information on the follow-up to and implementation of the Durban Declaration and Programme of Action;

16. *Stresses* the responsibility of States to mainstream a gender perspective into the design and development of prevention, education and protection measures aimed at the eradication of racism, racial discrimination, xenophobia and related intolerance at all levels, to ensure that they effectively target the distinct situations of women and men;

II
International Convention on the Elimination of All Forms of Racial Discrimination

17. *Reaffirms* that universal adherence to and full implementation of the International Convention on the Elimination of All Forms of Racial Discrimination are of paramount importance for the fight against racism, racial discrimination, xenophobia and related intolerance, and for the promotion of equality and non-discrimination in the world;

18. *Expresses grave concern* that universal ratification of the Convention has not yet been reached, despite commitments under the Durban Declaration and Programme of Action, and calls upon those States that have not yet done so to accede to the Convention as a matter of urgency;

19. *Urges*, in the above context, the Office of the United Nations High Commissioner for Human Rights to maintain on its website and issue regular updates on a list of countries that have not yet ratified the Convention and to encourage those countries to ratify it at the earliest possible time;

20. *Expresses concern* at the serious delays in the submission of overdue reports to the Committee on the Elimination of Racial Discrimination, which impede the effectiveness of the Committee, makes a strong appeal to all States parties to the Convention to comply with their treaty obligations, and reaffirms the importance of the provision of technical assistance to requesting countries in the preparation of their reports to the Committee;

21. *Invites* States parties to the Convention to ratify the amendment to article 8 of the Convention on the financing of the Committee, and calls for adequate additional resources from the regular budget of the United Nations to enable the Committee to discharge its mandate fully;

22. *Urges* all States parties to the Convention to intensify their efforts to implement the obligations that they have accepted under article 4 of the Convention, with due regard to the principles of the Universal Declaration of Human Rights and article 5 of the Convention;

23. *Recalls* that the Committee holds that the prohibition of the dissemination of ideas based on racial superiority or racial hatred is compatible with the right to freedom of opinion and expression as outlined in article 19 of the Universal Declaration of Human Rights and in article 5 of the Convention;

24. *Welcomes* the work of the Committee in combating racism, racial discrimination, xenophobia and related intolerance in the follow-up to the World Conference against Racism, Racial Discrimination, Xenophobia and Related Intolerance and the measures recommended to strengthen the implementation of the Convention as well as the functioning of the Committee;

25. *Calls upon* Member States to do their utmost to ensure that their responses to the current financial and economic crisis do not lead to increased poverty and underdevelopment and, potentially, a rise in racism, racial discrimination, xenophobia and related intolerance against foreigners, immigrants and persons belonging to national or ethnic, religious and linguistic minorities all over the world;

26. *Reaffirms* that deprivation of citizenship on the basis of race or descent is a breach of State parties' obligations to ensure non-discriminatory enjoyment of the right to nationality;

III
Special Rapporteur on contemporary forms of racism, racial discrimination, xenophobia and related intolerance, and follow-up to his visits

27. *Takes note* of the reports of the Special Rapporteur on contemporary forms of racism, racial discrimination, xenophobia and related intolerance, and encourages relevant stakeholders to consider implementing the recommendations contained therein;

28. *Welcomes* Human Rights Council resolution 16/33 of 25 March 2011, by which the Council decided to extend the mandate of the Special Rapporteur for a period of three years;

29. *Reiterates its call* to all Member States, intergovernmental organizations, relevant organizations of the United Nations system and non-governmental organizations to cooperate fully with the Special Rapporteur, and calls upon States to consider responding favourably to his requests for visits so as to enable him to fulfil his mandate fully and effectively;

30. *Reaffirms* that any form of impunity condoned by public authorities for crimes motivated by racist and xenophobic attitudes plays a role in weakening the rule of law and democracy and tends to encourage the recurrence of such acts;

31. *Emphasizes* the obligations of States under international law to exercise due diligence to prevent crimes against migrants perpetrated with racist or xenophobic motivations, to investigate such crimes and to punish the

perpetrators and that not doing so violates, and impairs or nullifies the enjoyment of, the human rights and fundamental freedoms of victims, and urges States to reinforce measures in this regard;

32. *Recognizes with deep concern* the increase in anti-Semitism, Christianophobia and Islamophobia in various parts of the world, as well as the emergence of racial and violent movements based on racism and discriminatory ideas directed against Arab, Christian, Jewish and Muslim communities, as well as all religious communities, communities of people of African descent, communities of people of Asian descent, communities of indigenous people and other communities;

33. *Calls upon* States parties to fully implement legislation and other measures already in place to ensure that people of African descent are not discriminated against, and underlines in this regard the importance of supporting the programme of activities for the International Year for People of African Descent adopted by the General Assembly at its sixty-fifth session;

34. *Requests* the United Nations High Commissioner for Human Rights to continue to provide States, at their request, with advisory services and technical assistance to enable them to implement fully the recommendations of the Special Rapporteur;

35. *Requests* the Secretary-General to provide the Special Rapporteur with all the human and financial assistance necessary to carry out his mandate efficiently, effectively and expeditiously and to enable him to submit a report to the General Assembly at its sixty-seventh session;

36. *Requests* the Special Rapporteur, within his mandate, to continue giving particular attention to the negative impact of racism, racial discrimination, xenophobia and related intolerance on the full enjoyment of civil, cultural, economic, political and social rights;

37. *Invites* Member States to demonstrate greater commitment to fighting racism in sport by conducting educational and awareness-raising activities and by strongly condemning the perpetrators of racist incidents, in cooperation with national and international sports organizations;

38. *Recommends* that States engage in broad efforts to eliminate racism, racial discrimination, xenophobia and related intolerance and to promote respect for cultural, ethnic and religious diversity, and in that regard emphasizes the crucial role of education, including human rights education, training and learning, and a variety of awareness-raising measures which contribute to the creation of tolerant societies in which mutual understanding may be ensured;

39. *Also recommends* that all States give due attention to and closely monitor the way in which the concept of national, cultural and religious identity is debated within their societies, with a view to preventing it from being used as a tool to create artificial differences among some groups of the population;

40. *Expresses concern* at recent deeply marked tendencies within numerous societies to characterize migration as a problem and a threat to social cohesion, and in this context notes the numerous human rights challenges in combating racism, racial discrimination, xenophobia and related intolerance;

41. *Recommends* that States conduct human rights training, including on the challenges of racism, racial discrimination, xenophobia and related intolerance faced by migrants, refugees and asylum seekers, for law enforcement officials, especially immigration officials and border police, so that they may act in conformity with international human rights law;

42. *Also recommends* that States collect disaggregated data in order to design appropriate anti-racial discrimination legislation and policies and monitor their effectiveness, while abiding by some key principles, including self-identification, the right to privacy, and guaranteeing the consent of those individuals concerned, and the involvement of all groups of individuals concerned, in the design and implementation of the exercise;

IV
Outcomes of the 2001 World Conference against Racism, Racial Discrimination, Xenophobia and Related Intolerance, the 2009 Durban Review Conference and the commemoration of the tenth anniversary of the adoption of the Durban Declaration and Programme of Action (2011)

43. *Reaffirms* that the General Assembly is the highest intergovernmental mechanism for the formulation and appraisal of policy on matters relating to the economic, social and related fields, in accordance with Assembly resolution 50/227 of 24 May 1996, and that, together with the Human Rights Council, it shall constitute an intergovernmental process for the comprehensive implementation of and follow-up to the Durban Declaration and Programme of Action in combating racism, racial discrimination, xenophobia and related intolerance;

44. *Welcomes* the adoption of the political declaration of the high-level meeting of the General Assembly to commemorate the tenth anniversary of the adoption of the Durban Declaration and Programme of Action, whose aim is to mobilize political will at the national, regional and international levels;

45. *Reaffirms* the political commitment to the full and effective implementation of the Durban Declaration and Programme of Action, the outcome document of the Durban Review Conference, and their follow-up processes, at the national, regional and international levels, in combating racism, racial discrimination, xenophobia and related intolerance;

46. *Calls upon* all States that have not yet elaborated their national action plans on combating racism, racial discrimination, xenophobia and related intolerance to comply with their commitments undertaken at the World Conference against Racism, Racial Discrimination, Xenophobia and Related Intolerance of 2001;

47. *Calls upon* all States to formulate and implement without delay, at the national, regional and international levels, policies and plans of action to combat racism, racial discrimination, xenophobia and related intolerance, including their gender-based manifestations;

48. *Urges* States to support the activities of existing regional bodies or centres that combat racism, racial discrimination, xenophobia and related intolerance in their respective regions, and recommends the establishment of such bodies in all regions where they do not exist;

49. *Calls upon* those States that have not yet done so to consider signing and ratifying or acceding to the instruments enumerated in paragraph 78 of the Durban Programme of Action;

50. *Emphasizes* the fundamental and complementary role of national human rights institutions, regional bodies or centres and civil society, working jointly with States towards the elimination of all forms of racism and, in particular, towards the achievement of the objectives of the Durban Declaration and Programme of Action in this regard;

51. *Recognizes* the fundamental role of civil society in the fight against racism, racial discrimination, xenophobia and related intolerance, in particular in helping States to develop regulations and strategies, in taking measures and action against such forms of discrimination and through follow-up implementation;

52. *Reaffirms its commitment* to eliminating all forms of racism, racial discrimination, xenophobia and other forms of related intolerance against indigenous peoples, and in this regard notes the attention paid to the objectives of combating prejudice, eliminating discrimination and promoting tolerance, understanding and good relations among indigenous peoples and all other segments of society in the United Nations Declaration on the Rights of Indigenous Peoples;

53. *Acknowledges* that the World Conference of 2001, which was the third world conference against racism, was significantly different from the previous two conferences, as evidenced by the inclusion in its title of two important components relating to contemporary forms of racism, namely, xenophobia and related intolerance;

54. *Also acknowledges* that the outcomes of the World Conference and the Durban Review Conference have the same status as the outcomes of all the major United Nations conferences, summits and special sessions in the human rights and social fields;

55. *Emphasizes* the critical importance of increasing public support for the Durban Declaration and Programme of Action and the involvement of relevant stakeholders in its realization;

56. *Requests* the Department of Public Information of the Secretariat to compile and disseminate, within existing resources, in a single combined publication, the political declaration on the tenth anniversary of the adoption of the Durban Declaration and Programme of Action and the outcome document of the Durban Review Conference, with a view to increasing global support for and awareness of these documents, as well as to establish a programme of outreach through public information campaigns at all levels;

57. *Calls upon* Member States and the United Nations system to intensify efforts to widely distribute copies of the Durban Declaration and Programme of Action, and encourages efforts to ensure its translation and wide dissemination;

58. *Welcomes* the adoption of the laudable initiative led by the States members of the Caribbean Community and other Member States for the establishment of a permanent memorial at the United Nations to the victims of slavery and the transatlantic slave trade as a contribution towards the fulfilment of paragraph 101 of the Durban Declaration, expresses its appreciation for contributions made to the voluntary fund established in this regard, and urges other countries to contribute to the fund;

59. *Takes note* of the work of the mechanisms mandated to follow up on the World Conference and the Durban Review Conference, and underlines the importance of improving their effectiveness;

60. *Calls upon* the Human Rights Council to ensure that, upon the consideration and adoption of the conclusions and recommendations of the Intergovernmental Working Group on the Effective Implementation of the Durban Declaration and Programme of Action, the recommendations are brought to the attention of the relevant United Nations agencies for adoption and implementation within their respective mandates;

61. *Encourages* the Working Group of Experts on People of African Descent, further to the recommendation of the Working Group at its tenth session on the proclamation of a Decade for People of African Descent, to develop a programme of action, including a theme, for adoption by the Human Rights Council, with a view to proclaiming the decade starting in 2013 the Decade for People of African Descent;

62. *Encourages* the Office of the United Nations High Commissioner for Human Rights to continue mainstreaming the implementation of the Durban Declaration and Programme of Action and the outcome document of the Durban Review Conference in the whole United Nations system, and, in accordance with paragraphs 136 and 137 of the outcome document, which call for the establishment of an inter-agency task force, to update the Human Rights Council in this regard;

63. *Acknowledges* the central role of resource mobilization, effective global partnership and international cooperation in the context of paragraphs 157 and 158 of the Durban Programme of Action for the successful realization of commitments undertaken at the World Conference, and takes note of the mandate of the group of independent eminent experts on the implementation of the Durban Declaration and Programme of Action, especially in mobilizing the political will necessary for the successful implementation of the Declaration and Programme of Action;

64. *Requests* the Secretary-General to provide the resources necessary for the effective fulfilment of the mandates of the Intergovernmental Working Group on the Effective Implementation of the Durban Declaration and Programme of Action, the Working Group of Experts on People of African Descent, the group of independent eminent experts on the implementation of the Durban Declaration and Programme of Action and the Ad Hoc Committee on the Elaboration of Complementary Standards;

65. *Expresses concern* at the increasing incidence of racism in various sporting events, while noting with appreciation the efforts made by some governing bodies of the various sporting codes to combat racism, and in this regard invites all international sporting bodies to promote, through their national, regional and international federations, a world of sport free from racism and racial discrimination;

66. *Expresses serious concern* at past and recent incidents of racism in sport and at sporting events and, in this context, welcomes efforts of sports governing bodies to combat racism, including by pursuing anti-racism initiatives and by developing and applying disciplinary codes that impose sanctions for racist acts;

67. *Expresses its appreciation*, in this context, to the International Federation of Association Football for the initiative to introduce a visible theme on non-racism in football, and invites the Federation to continue this initiative at the 2014 World Cup soccer tournament to be held in Brazil;

68. *Calls upon* States to take advantage of mass sporting events as valuable outreach platforms for mobilizing people and conveying crucial messages about equality and non-discrimination;

69. *Acknowledges* the guidance and leadership role of the Human Rights Council and encourages it to continue overseeing the implementation of the Durban Declaration and Programme of Action, and requests the Office of the United Nations High Commissioner for Human Rights to continue to provide the Human Rights Council with all the support necessary for it to achieve its objectives in combating racism, racial discrimination, xenophobia and related intolerance;

V

Follow-up activities

70. *Reiterates its recommendation* that future meetings of the Human Rights Council and its relevant mechanisms focusing on the follow-up to the World Conference against Racism, Racial Discrimination, Xenophobia and Related Intolerance and the implementation of the Durban Declaration and Programme of Action be scheduled in a manner that allows broad participation and avoids overlap with the meetings devoted to the consideration of this item in the General Assembly;

71. *Requests* the Secretary-General to submit to the General Assembly at its sixty-seventh session a report on the implementation of the present resolution, with recommendations;

72. *Decides* to remain seized of this important matter at its sixty-seventh session under the item entitled "Elimination of racism, racial discrimination, xenophobia and related intolerance".

RECORDED VOTE ON RESOLUTION 66/144:

In favour: Afghanistan, Algeria, Angola, Antigua and Barbuda, Argentina, Azerbaijan, Bahamas, Bahrain, Bangladesh, Barbados, Belarus, Belize, Benin, Bhutan, Bolivia, Botswana, Brazil, Brunei Darussalam, Burkina Faso, Burundi, Cambodia, Cameroon, Cape Verde, Central African Republic, Chad, Chile, China, Colombia, Comoros, Congo, Costa Rica, Côte d'Ivoire, Cuba, Democratic People's Republic of Korea, Democratic Republic of the Congo, Djibouti, Dominica, Dominican Republic, Ecuador, Egypt, El Salvador, Equatorial Guinea, Eritrea, Ethiopia, Fiji, Gabon, Gambia, Ghana, Grenada, Guatemala, Guinea, Guinea-Bissau, Guyana, Haiti, Honduras, Iceland, India, Indonesia, Iran, Iraq, Jamaica, Jordan, Kazakhstan, Kenya, Kuwait, Kyrgyzstan, Lao People's Democratic Republic, Lebanon, Lesotho, Liberia, Libya, Liechtenstein, Madagascar, Malawi, Malaysia, Maldives, Mali, Mauritania, Mauritius, Mexico, Mongolia, Morocco, Mozambique, Myanmar, Namibia, Nepal, Nicaragua, Niger, Nigeria, Norway, Oman, Pakistan, Panama, Paraguay, Peru, Philippines, Qatar, Russian Federation, Rwanda, Saint Kitts and Nevis, Saint Lucia, Saint Vincent and the Grenadines, Sao Tome and Principe, Saudi Arabia, Senegal, Seychelles, Sierra Leone, Singapore, Solomon Islands, Somalia, South Africa, South Sudan, Sri Lanka, Sudan, Suriname, Swaziland, Switzerland, Syrian Arab Republic, Tajikistan, Thailand, Timor-Leste, Togo, Trinidad and Tobago, Tunisia, Turkey, Turkmenistan, Tuvalu, Uganda, United Arab Emirates, United Republic of Tanzania, Uruguay, Uzbekistan, Vanuatu, Venezuela, Viet Nam, Yemen, Zambia, Zimbabwe.

Against: Australia, Canada, Israel, Marshall Islands, Palau, United States.

Abstaining: Albania, Andorra, Armenia, Austria, Belgium, Bosnia and Herzegovina, Bulgaria, Croatia, Cyprus, Czech Republic, Denmark, Estonia, Finland, France, Georgia, Germany, Greece, Hungary, Ireland, Italy, Japan, Latvia, Lithuania, Luxembourg, Malta, Monaco, Montenegro, Netherlands, New Zealand, Papua New Guinea, Poland, Portugal, Republic of Korea, Republic of Moldova, Romania, Samoa, San Marino, Serbia, Slovakia, Slovenia, Spain, Sweden, the former Yugoslav Republic of Macedonia, Tonga, Ukraine, United Kingdom.

Contemporary forms of racism

Reports of Special Rapporteur. Pursuant to a Human Rights Council request [YUN 2008, p. 770], the Special Rapporteur on contemporary forms of racism, racial discrimination, xenophobia and related intolerance, Githu Muigai (Kenya), in May issued a report [A/HRC/17/40] that summarized his activities, presented an analysis of the racism and racial discrimination against Roma and addressed discrimination based on work and descent. The report focused on issues such as legal, political and institutional initiatives at the regional and national levels; persistent racism, discrimination and intolerance against Roma; addressing the reasons of the failure to eliminate discrimination against Roma; and discrimination based on caste and analogous systems of inherited status. The Rapporteur said that positive developments and good practices had been identified, yet were insufficient. He made recommendations on challenges faced by Roma with regard to education, employment, housing, health and the enjoyment of their civil and political rights. The Rapporteur encountered difficulties in researching the issue of discrimination based on work and descent due to the paucity of sources and lack of recent public information, and indicated that further study was necessary. In addition to a series of recommendations to States, Governments, institutions and civil society, the Rapporteur recommended that the full spectrum of special procedures address the issue of discrimination based on caste and other systems of inherited status in the context of their respective mandates.

An addendum to the report [A/HRC/17/40/Add.1] summarized 12 communications sent by the Rapporteur to 10 Governments between 1 March 2010 and 28 February 2011, eight replies received from seven Governments until 30 April 2011, and observations of the Rapporteur.

In July, pursuant to General Assembly resolution 65/199 [YUN 2010, p. 671], the Rapporteur submitted a report [A/HRC/18/44] on the implementation of that resolution, addressing the human rights and democratic challenges posed by extremist political parties, movements and groups, including neo-Nazis and skinhead groups, and similar extremist ideological movements. In that respect, he identified good practices developed by States and different stakeholders since the previous report [ibid., p. 670]. Among his recommendations, the Rapporteur called on States to ensure thorough and impartial investigation of racist and xenophobic crimes, and that those responsible were adequately sanctioned; engage with vulnerable groups at risk of such crimes, and reduce their fear, restore confidence in law enforcement officers and allow for better reporting of crimes; use new technologies, including the Internet, to promote equality, non-discrimination, diversity and democracy; and strengthen the capacity of law enforcement agents and the judiciary through human rights training, with a focus on crimes motivated by racist or xenophobic attitudes.

In August [A/66/312], the Secretary-General transmitted to the Assembly the Rapporteur's report on implementation of its resolution 65/199 on the inadmissibility of practices that contributed to fuelling contemporary forms of racism and related phenomena. The report summarized contributions from 14 States and views sent by five non-governmental organizations (NGOs) and the Office of the United Nations High Commissioner for Refugees, and put forward a number of recommendations.

Also in August, pursuant to General Assembly resolution 65/240 [YUN 2010, p. 665], the Secretary-General transmitted the Special Rapporteur's interim report [A/66/313] describing his activities, including country visits, and presenting issues he had addressed in annual reports, press releases, conferences, seminars and other meetings. The Rapporteur called on States to recognize the existence of racism and racial discrimination in society and in State institutions; collect ethnically disaggregated data and data on racist and xenophobic crimes perpetrated by individuals linked to extremist political parties and groups; redesign legislation, policies and programmes that had a disproportionate effect on the human rights of specific group; implement affirmative action measures; adopt strategies against racism, focusing on structural discrimination and the interrelation between racism and socioeconomic or political exclusion of certain parts of their population; invest in education, particularly in teaching the history of people of African descent, Roma and other communities; and involve victims of racism and racial discrimination in the design, decision-making, implementation and evaluation of national policies, especially those affecting them.

Mission report. Following his visit to Hungary (23–27 May) [A/HRC/20/33/Add.1], the Rapporteur recommended that the Government ensure adequate representation of ethnic and national minorities in Parliament and in political parties; reduce the high rate of Roma unemployment and increase efforts to eliminate discrimination and segregation of Roma in education; ensure the effective participation of Roma in political and public life; develop a national strategy to combat racial violence against Roma; carry out investigations into racist acts against Roma and ensure that responsible parties were prosecuted and sanctioned; take measures to condemn hate speech; and introduce safeguards against the anti-Roma and anti-Semitic discourse of the Jobbik political party which flouted human rights. He also recommended implementation of a strategy for early-stage integration of migrants, refugees and asylum seekers.

Human Rights Council action. On 29 September [A/66/53/Add.1 (res. 18/15)], the Council reaffirmed that any form of impunity condoned by public authorities for crimes motivated by racist and xenophobic attitudes played a role in weakening the rule of law and democracy and tended to encourage the recurrence of such acts; urged States to ensure that their political and legal systems reflected the multicultural diversity within their societies through promoting diversity, and making democratic institutions more participatory and inclusive; and urged States to fight against racism, racial discrimination, xenophobia and related intolerance as a way to strengthen democracy, the rule of law and transparent and accountable governance. The Council invited the High Commissioner for Human Rights to report to the Council at its twenty-first (2012) session on implementation of the resolution.

Communication. On 14 June [A/HRC/17/G/12], Singapore submitted its comments on the Special Rapporteur's 2010 mission to the country [YUN 2010, p. 671].

Mandate and appointment of Rapporteur. On 25 March [A/66/53 (res. 16/33)], the Council extended the mandate of the Rapporteur for three years and requested him/her to report annually to the Council and the General Assembly on all activities relating to the mandate.

During the Council's eighteenth (2011) session in September, Mutuma Ruteere (Kenya) was appointed as the new Special Rapporteur and took office on 1 November.

GENERAL ASSEMBLY ACTION

On 19 December [meeting 89], the General Assembly, on the recommendation of the Third Committee [A/66/460], adopted **resolution 66/143** by recorded vote (134-24-32) [agenda item 67 (a)].

Inadmissibility of certain practices that contribute to fuelling contemporary forms of racism, racial discrimination, xenophobia and related intolerance

The General Assembly,

Guided by the Charter of the United Nations, the Universal Declaration of Human Rights, the International Covenant on Civil and Political Rights, the International Convention on the Elimination of All Forms of Racial Discrimination and other relevant human rights instruments,

Recalling the provisions of Commission on Human Rights resolutions 2004/16 of 16 April 2004 and 2005/5 of 14 April 2005 and relevant Human Rights Council resolutions, in particular resolutions 7/34 of 28 March 2008 and 18/15 of 29 September 2011, as well as General Assembly resolutions 60/143 of 16 December 2005, 61/147 of

19 December 2006, 62/142 of 18 December 2007, 63/162 of 18 December 2008, 64/147 of 18 December 2009 and 65/199 of 21 December 2010 on this issue and resolutions 61/149 of 19 December 2006, 62/220 of 22 December 2007, 63/242 of 24 December 2008, 64/148 of 18 December 2009 and 65/240 of 24 December 2010, entitled "Global efforts for the total elimination of racism, racial discrimination, xenophobia and related intolerance and the comprehensive implementation of and follow-up to the Durban Declaration and Programme of Action",

Recalling also the Charter of the Nuremberg Tribunal and the Judgement of the Tribunal, which recognized, inter alia, the SS organization and all its integral parts, including the Waffen SS, as criminal and declared it responsible for many war crimes and crimes against humanity,

Recalling further the relevant provisions of the Durban Declaration and Programme of Action adopted by the World Conference against Racism, Racial Discrimination, Xenophobia and Related Intolerance on 8 September 2001, in particular paragraph 2 of the Declaration and paragraph 86 of the Programme of Action, as well as the relevant provisions of the outcome document of the Durban Review Conference, of 24 April 2009, in particular paragraphs 11 and 54,

Alarmed, in this regard, at the spread in many parts of the world of various extremist political parties, movements and groups, including neo-Nazis and skinhead groups, as well as similar extremist ideological movements,

Recalling that in 2010 the international community celebrated the sixty-fifth anniversary of victory in the Second World War, and welcoming in this regard the special solemn meeting of the sixty-fourth session of the General Assembly, held on 6 May 2010,

Recalling also that the sixty-sixth session of the General Assembly coincides with the sixty-fifth anniversary of the Judgement of the Nuremberg Tribunal,

Taking note of the report of the Special Rapporteur on contemporary forms of racism, racial discrimination, xenophobia and related intolerance submitted to the Human Rights Council in accordance with the request contained in General Assembly resolution 65/199,

1. *Reaffirms* the relevant provisions of the Durban Declaration and of the outcome document of the Durban Review Conference, in which States condemned the persistence and resurgence of neo-Nazism, neo-Fascism and violent nationalist ideologies based on racial and national prejudice and stated that those phenomena could never be justified in any instance or in any circumstances;

2. *Takes note with appreciation* of the report of the Special Rapporteur on contemporary forms of racism, racial discrimination, xenophobia and related intolerance prepared in accordance with the request contained in General Assembly resolution 65/199;

3. *Expresses its appreciation* to the United Nations High Commissioner for Human Rights for her commitment to maintaining the fight against racism, racial discrimination, xenophobia and related intolerance as one of the priority activities of her Office;

4. *Expresses deep concern* about the glorification of the Nazi movement and former members of the Waffen SS organization, including by erecting monuments and memorials and holding public demonstrations in the name of the glorification of the Nazi past, the Nazi movement and neo-Nazism, as well as by declaring or attempting to declare such members and those who fought against the anti-Hitler coalition and collaborated with the Nazi movement participants in national liberation movements;

5. *Expresses concern* at recurring attempts to desecrate or demolish monuments erected in remembrance of those who fought against Nazism during the Second World War, as well as to unlawfully exhume or remove the remains of such persons, and in this regard urges States to fully comply with their relevant obligations, inter alia, under article 34 of Additional Protocol I to the Geneva Conventions of 1949;

6. *Notes with concern* the increase in the number of racist incidents in several countries and the rise of skinhead groups, which have been responsible for many of these incidents, as well as the resurgence of racist and xenophobic violence targeting members of national, ethnic, religious or linguistic minorities, as observed by the Special Rapporteur in his latest report to the General Assembly;

7. *Reaffirms* that such acts may be qualified to fall within the scope of activities described in article 4 of the International Convention on the Elimination of All Forms of Racial Discrimination and that they may represent a clear and manifest abuse of the rights to freedom of peaceful assembly and of association as well as the rights to freedom of opinion and expression within the meaning of those rights as guaranteed by the Universal Declaration of Human Rights, the International Covenant on Civil and Political Rights and the International Convention on the Elimination of All Forms of Racial Discrimination;

8. *Stresses* that the practices described above do injustice to the memory of the countless victims of crimes against humanity committed in the Second World War, in particular those committed by the SS organization and those who fought against the anti-Hitler coalition and collaborated with the Nazi movement, and poison the minds of young people, and that failure by States to effectively address such practices is incompatible with the obligations of States Members of the United Nations under its Charter and is incompatible with the purposes and principles of the Organization;

9. *Also stresses* that such practices fuel contemporary forms of racism, racial discrimination, xenophobia and related intolerance and contribute to the spread and multiplication of various extremist political parties, movements and groups, including neo-Nazis and skinhead groups, and in this regard calls for increased political and legal vigilance;

10. *Emphasizes* the need to take the measures necessary to put an end to the practices described above, and calls upon States to take more effective measures in accordance with international human rights law to combat those phenomena and the extremist movements, which pose a real threat to democratic values;

11. *Recalls* the recommendation of the Special Rapporteur, made in his latest report to the General Assembly, to introduce into domestic criminal law a provision according to which committing an offence with racist or xenophobic motivations or aims constitutes an aggravating circumstance allowing for enhanced penalties, and encourages those States whose legislation does not contain such provisions to consider that recommendation;

12. *Reaffirms*, in this regard, the particular importance of all forms of education, including human rights education, as a complement to legislative measures, as outlined by the Special Rapporteur;

13. *Emphasizes* the recommendation of the Special Rapporteur regarding the importance of history classes in teaching the dramatic events and human suffering that resulted from the ideologies of Nazism and Fascism;

14. *Stresses* the importance of other positive measures and initiatives aimed at bringing communities together and providing them with space for genuine dialogue, such as round tables, working groups and seminars, including training seminars for State agents and media professionals, as well as awareness-raising activities, especially those initiated by civil society representatives which require continued State support;

15. *Underlines* the potentially positive role that relevant United Nations entities and programmes, in particular the United Nations Educational, Scientific and Cultural Organization, can play in the aforementioned areas;

16. *Reaffirms* that, according to article 4 of the International Convention on the Elimination of All Forms of Racial Discrimination, States parties to that instrument are under the obligation:

(a) To condemn all propaganda and all organizations that are based on ideas of racial superiority or that attempt to justify or promote racial hatred and discrimination in any form;

(b) To undertake to adopt immediate and positive measures designed to eradicate all incitement to, or acts of, such discrimination, with due regard to the principles embodied in the Universal Declaration of Human Rights and the rights expressly set forth in article 5 of the Convention;

(c) To declare as an offence punishable by law all dissemination of ideas based on racial superiority or hatred, and incitement to racial discrimination, as well as all acts of violence or incitement to such acts against any race or group of persons of another colour or ethnic origin, and also the provision of any assistance to racist activities, including the financing thereof;

(d) To declare illegal and prohibit organizations and organized and all other propaganda activities that promote and incite racial discrimination, and to recognize participation in such organizations or activities as an offence punishable by law;

(e) To prohibit public authorities or public institutions, national or local, from promoting or inciting racial discrimination;

17. *Also reaffirms* that, as underlined in paragraph 13 of the outcome document of the Durban Review Conference, any advocacy of national, racial or religious hatred that constitutes incitement to discrimination, hostility or violence should be prohibited by law, that all dissemination of ideas based on racial superiority or hatred, or incitement to racial discrimination as well as all acts of violence or incitement to such acts shall be declared offences punishable by law, in accordance with the international obligations of States, and that these prohibitions are consistent with freedom of opinion and expression;

18. *Expresses concern* about the use of the Internet to propagate racism, racial hatred, xenophobia, racial discrimination and related intolerance, as outlined in the latest report of the Special Rapporteur to the General Assembly, and in this regard calls upon States parties to the International Covenant on Civil and Political Rights to implement fully articles 19 and 20 of the Covenant, which guarantee the right to freedom of expression and set out the limitations thereto;

19. *Underlines*, at the same time, the positive role that the exercise of the right to freedom of opinion and expression, as well as full respect for the freedom to seek, receive and impart information, including through the Internet, can play in combating racism, racial discrimination, xenophobia and related intolerance;

20. *Encourages* those States that have made reservations to article 4 of the International Convention on the Elimination of All Forms of Racial Discrimination to give serious consideration to withdrawing such reservations as a matter of priority, as stressed by the Special Rapporteur in his report to the General Assembly at its sixty-fifth session;

21. *Notes* the importance of strengthening international cooperation at the regional and international levels with the aim of countering all manifestations of racism, racial discrimination, xenophobia and related intolerance, in particular regarding issues raised in the present resolution;

22. *Encourages* States parties to the International Convention on the Elimination of All Forms of Racial Discrimination to ensure that their legislation incorporates the provisions of the Convention, including those of article 4;

23. *Recalls* the request of the Commission on Human Rights, in its resolution 2005/5, that the Special Rapporteur continue to reflect on this issue, make relevant recommendations in his future reports and seek and take into account in this regard the views of Governments and non-governmental organizations;

24. *Requests* the Special Rapporteur to prepare, for submission to the General Assembly at its sixty-seventh session and to the Human Rights Council at its twentieth session, reports on the implementation of the present resolution, in particular regarding paragraphs 4, 5, 7, 8, 13 and 14 thereof, based on the views collected in accordance with the request of the Commission on Human Rights, as recalled by the Assembly in paragraph 23 above;

25. *Expresses its appreciation* to those Governments that have provided information to the Special Rapporteur in the course of the preparation of his report to the General Assembly;

26. *Also expresses its appreciation* to civil society actors that contribute to the fight against racism, racial discrimination, xenophobia and related intolerance in an impartial and unbiased manner;

27. *Stresses* that such information is important for the sharing of experiences and best practices in the fight against extremist political parties, movements and groups, including neo-Nazis and skinhead groups, as well as extremist ideological movements;

28. *Encourages* Governments and non-governmental organizations to cooperate fully with the Special Rapporteur in the exercise of the tasks outlined in paragraph 23 above;

29. *Encourages* Governments, non-governmental organizations and relevant actors to disseminate, as widely as possible, information regarding the contents of and the principles outlined in the present resolution, including through the media, but not limited to it;

30. *Decides* to remain seized of the issue.

RECORDED VOTE ON RESOLUTION 66/143:

In favour: Afghanistan, Algeria, Angola, Antigua and Barbuda, Argentina, Armenia, Azerbaijan, Bahamas, Bahrain, Bangladesh, Barbados, Belarus, Belize, Benin, Bhutan, Bolivia, Botswana, Brazil, Brunei Darussalam, Burkina Faso, Burundi, Cambodia, Cameroon, Cape Verde, Central African Republic, Chad, Chile, China, Colombia, Comoros, Congo, Costa Rica, Côte d'Ivoire, Cuba, Democratic People's Republic of Korea, Democratic Republic of the Congo, Djibouti, Dominica, Dominican Republic, Ecuador, Egypt, El Salvador, Equatorial Guinea, Eritrea, Ethiopia, Gabon, Gambia, Ghana, Grenada, Guatemala, Guinea, Guinea-Bissau, Guyana, Haiti, Honduras, India, Indonesia, Iran, Iraq, Israel, Jamaica, Jordan, Kazakhstan, Kenya, Kuwait, Kyrgyzstan, Lao People's Democratic Republic, Lebanon, Lesotho, Liberia, Libya, Madagascar, Malawi, Malaysia, Maldives, Mali, Mauritania, Mauritius, Mexico, Mongolia, Morocco, Mozambique, Myanmar, Namibia, Nepal, Nicaragua, Niger, Nigeria, Oman, Pakistan, Paraguay, Peru, Philippines, Qatar, Russian Federation, Rwanda, Saint Kitts and Nevis, Saint Vincent and the Grenadines, Sao Tome and Principe, Saudi Arabia, Senegal, Serbia, Seychelles, Sierra Leone, Singapore, Solomon Islands, Somalia, South Africa, South Sudan, Sri Lanka, Sudan, Suriname, Swaziland, Syrian Arab Republic, Tajikistan, Thailand, Timor-Leste, Togo, Trinidad and Tobago, Tunisia, Turkey, Turkmenistan, Tuvalu, Uganda, United Arab Emirates, United Republic of Tanzania, Uruguay, Uzbekistan, Vanuatu, Venezuela, Viet Nam, Yemen, Zambia, Zimbabwe.

Against: Albania, Belgium, Bulgaria, Canada, Czech Republic, Denmark, Estonia, France, Georgia, Hungary, Ireland, Latvia, Lithuania, Marshall Islands, Monaco, Netherlands, Palau, Poland, Romania, Slovakia, Spain, Sweden, United Kingdom, United States.

Abstaining: Andorra, Australia, Austria, Bosnia and Herzegovina, Croatia, Cyprus, Fiji, Finland, Germany, Greece, Iceland, Italy, Japan, Liechtenstein, Luxembourg, Malta, Montenegro, New Zealand, Norway, Panama, Papua New Guinea, Portugal, Republic of Korea, Republic of Moldova, Saint Lucia, Samoa, San Marino, Slovenia, Switzerland, the former Yugoslav Republic of Macedonia, Tonga, Ukraine.

Human rights defenders

Reports of Special Rapporteur. The Special Rapporteur on the situation of human rights defenders, Margaret Sekaggya (Uganda), described her activities during the reporting year in her third report [A/HRC/16/44 & Corr.1] to the Human Rights Council, submitted pursuant to a Council request [YUN 2008, p. 721]. She drew the attention of Member States to the 246 communications that were sent under the mandate during 2010. Focusing on the situation of women human rights defenders and those working on women's rights or gender issues, the risks and violations they faced, and the perpetrators involved, the Rapporteur made a series of recommendations to States, national human rights institutions, regional protection mechanisms and NGOs on guidelines regarding protection programmes for human rights defenders, particularly women human rights defenders, and other issues related to their security and protection.

An addendum [A/HRC/16/44/Add.1] summarized communications sent to 75 Governments from 11 December 2009 to 8 December 2010 and replies received before 7 February 2011. A further addendum [A/HRC/16/44/Add.3] presented the questionnaire on risks and challenges faced by women human rights defenders and those working on women's rights and gender issues sent by the Rapporteur to States on 3 November 2010, and reproduced the responses received from 36 Governments, NGOs and two regional groups.

In July, in response to General Assembly resolution 64/163 [YUN 2009, p. 666], the Secretary-General transmitted to the Assembly the report [A/66/203] of the Special Rapporteur which described the rights provided for in the Declaration on the Right and Responsibility of Individuals, Groups and Organs of Society to Promote and Protect Universally Recognized Human Rights and Fundamental Freedoms [YUN 1998, p. 608], known as the Declaration on human rights defenders. It analysed what the rights entailed as well as various aspects needed to ensure their implementation, addressed common restrictions and violations faced by human rights defenders, and made recommendations to facilitate implementation by States of each right. The report aimed to increase awareness among States of the rights provided for in the Declaration and to serve as a practical tool to human rights defenders.

Mission report. Following her visit to India (10–21 January) [A/HRC/19/55/Add.1], the Rapporteur described the legal and institutional framework for the promotion and protection of human rights and detailed the challenges faced by human rights defenders in the country in their legitimate activities. She pointed out that there was an array of laws in place that needed to be fully implemented, while laws that were outdated and not in conformity with international human rights standards needed to be repealed. Government authorities, including security forces, and the judiciary and human rights commissions, at the central and state levels, needed to do much more to ensure a safe and conducive environment for defenders. The Rapporteur made recommendations for the consideration of the central and state Governments and the legislature, the national and state human rights commissions, the judiciary, human rights defenders, the international community, donors, and all stakeholders.

Communication. On 23 February [A/HRC/16/G/7], Armenia submitted its comments on the Rapporteur's 2010 mission to the country [YUN 2010, p. 674].

Human Rights Council action. On 24 March [A/66/53 (res. 16/5)], the Council extended the mandate of the Rapporteur for three years, and requested him/her to report regularly to the Council and the General Assembly.

GENERAL ASSEMBLY ACTION

On 19 December [meeting 89], the General Assembly, on the recommendation of the Third Committee [A/66/462/Add.2], adopted **resolution 66/164** without vote [agenda item 69 (*b*)].

Promotion of the Declaration on the Right and Responsibility of Individuals, Groups and Organs of Society to Promote and Protect Universally Recognized Human Rights and Fundamental Freedoms

The General Assembly,

Recalling its resolution 53/144 of 9 December 1998, by which it adopted by consensus the Declaration on the Right and Responsibility of Individuals, Groups and Organs of Society to Promote and Protect Universally Recognized Human Rights and Fundamental Freedoms annexed to that resolution, and reiterating the importance of the Declaration and its promotion and implementation,

Recalling also all previous resolutions on this subject, in particular its resolution 64/163 of 18 December 2009 and Human Rights Council resolutions 13/13 of 25 March 2010 and 16/5 of 24 March 2011,

Noting with deep concern that in many countries persons and organizations engaged in promoting and defending human rights and fundamental freedoms frequently face threats and harassment and suffer insecurity as a result of those activities, including through restrictions on freedom of association or expression or the right to peaceful assembly, or abuse of civil or criminal proceedings,

Gravely concerned that, in some instances, national security and counter-terrorism legislation and other measures have been misused to target human rights defenders or have hindered their work and safety in a manner contrary to international law,

Gravely concerned also by the continuing high level of human rights violations committed against persons engaged in promoting and defending human rights and fundamental freedoms around the world and by the fact that in many countries impunity for threats, attacks and acts of intimidation against human rights defenders persists and that this has a negative impact on their work and safety,

Gravely concerned further by the targeting of human rights defenders for reporting and seeking information on human rights violations,

Gravely concerned by the considerable number of communications received by the Special Rapporteur of the Human Rights Council on the situation of human rights defenders that, together with the reports submitted by some of the other special procedure mechanisms, indicates the serious nature of the risks faced by human rights defenders, in particular women human rights defenders,

Stressing the important role that individuals, civil society organizations, non-governmental organizations, groups, organs of society and independent national institutions play in the promotion and protection of all human rights and fundamental freedoms for all, including in addressing all forms of human rights violations, combating impunity, fighting poverty and discrimination, and promoting access to justice, democracy, tolerance, human dignity and the right to development, and recalling that all have rights as well as responsibilities and duties within and towards the community,

Recognizing the substantial role that human rights defenders can play in supporting efforts to strengthen peace and development, through dialogue, openness, participation and justice, including by monitoring, reporting on and contributing to the promotion and protection of human rights,

Recognizing also that new forms of communication can serve as important tools for human rights defenders to promote and strive for the protection of human rights,

Recalling that, in accordance with article 4 of the International Covenant on Civil and Political Rights, certain rights are recognized as non-derogable in any circumstances and that any measures derogating from other provisions of the Covenant must be in accordance with that article in all cases, and underlining the exceptional and temporary nature of any such derogations, as stated in General Comment No. 29 on states of emergency adopted by the Human Rights Committee on 24 July 2001,

Welcoming the cooperation between the Special Rapporteur and other special procedures of the Human Rights Council, as well as other relevant United Nations bodies, offices, departments, specialized agencies and personnel, both at Headquarters and at the country level, within their mandates,

Welcoming also regional initiatives for the promotion and protection of human rights and the strengthened cooperation between international and regional mechanisms for the protection of human rights defenders, and encouraging further development in this regard,

Welcoming further the steps taken by some States towards adopting national policies or legislation for the protection of individuals, groups and organs of society engaged in promoting and defending human rights, including as follow-up to the universal periodic review mechanism of the Human Rights Council,

Recalling that the primary responsibility for promoting and protecting human rights rests with the State, reaffirming that national legislation consistent with the Charter of the United Nations and other international obligations of the State in the field of human rights and fundamental freedoms is the juridical framework within which human rights defenders conduct their activities, and noting with deep concern that the activities of some non-State actors pose a major threat to the security of human rights defenders,

Emphasizing the need for strong and effective measures for the protection of human rights defenders,

1. *Calls upon* all States to promote and give full effect to the Declaration on the Right and Responsibility of Individuals, Groups and Organs of Society to Promote and Protect Universally Recognized Human Rights and Fundamental Freedoms, including by taking, as appropriate, practical steps to that end;

2. *Welcomes* the reports of the Special Rapporteur of the Human Rights Council on the situation of human rights defenders and her contribution to the effective promotion of the Declaration and the improvement of the protection of human rights defenders worldwide;

3. *Condemns* all human rights violations committed against persons engaged in promoting and defending human rights and fundamental freedoms around the world, and urges States to take all appropriate action, consistent with the Declaration and all other relevant human rights instruments, to prevent and eliminate such human rights violations;

4. *Calls upon* all States to take all measures necessary to ensure the protection of human rights defenders, at both the local and the national levels, including in times of armed conflict and peacebuilding;

5. *Calls upon* States to respect, protect and ensure the rights to freedom of expression and association of human rights defenders and in this regard to ensure, where procedures governing registration of civil society organizations exist, that these are transparent, non-discriminatory, expeditious, inexpensive, allow for the possibility to appeal and avoid requiring re-registration, in accordance with national legislation, and are in conformity with international human rights law;

6. *Also calls upon* States to ensure that human rights defenders can perform their important role in the context of peaceful protests, in accordance with national legislation consistent with the Charter of the United Nations and international human rights law, and in this regard to ensure that no one is subject to excessive and indiscriminate use of force, arbitrary arrest and detention, torture and other cruel, inhuman or degrading treatment or punishment, enforced disappearance, abuse of criminal and civil proceedings or threats of such acts;

7. *Urges* States to ensure that any measures to combat terrorism and preserve national security are in compliance with their obligations under international law, in particular under international human rights law, and do not hinder the work and safety of individuals, groups and organs of society engaged in promoting and defending human rights;

8. *Also urges* States to take appropriate measures to address the question of impunity for attacks, threats and acts of intimidation committed by State and non-State actors, including cases of gender-based violence, against human rights defenders and their relatives, including by ensuring that complaints from human rights defenders are promptly investigated and addressed in a transparent, independent and accountable manner;

9. *Urges* all States to cooperate with and assist the Special Rapporteur in the performance of her mandate and to provide all information in a timely manner, as well as to respond without undue delay to communications transmitted to them by the Special Rapporteur;

10. *Calls upon* States to give serious consideration to responding favourably to the requests of the Special Rapporteur to visit their countries, and urges them to enter into a constructive dialogue with the Special Rapporteur with respect to the follow-up to and implementation of her recommendations, so as to enable the Special Rapporteur to fulfil her mandate even more effectively;

11. *Strongly encourages* States to translate the Declaration and to take measures to ensure its widest possible dissemination at the national and local levels, among public officials as well as individuals, groups, organs of society and other non-State actors;

12. *Encourages* States to promote awareness and training in regard to the Declaration in order to enable officials, agencies, authorities and members of the judiciary to observe the provisions of the Declaration and thus to promote better understanding and respect for individuals, groups and organs of society engaged in promoting and defending human rights, as well as for their work;

13. *Encourages* relevant United Nations bodies, including at the country level, within their respective mandates and working in cooperation with States, to give due consideration to the Declaration and to the reports of the Special Rapporteur, and in this context requests the Office of the United Nations High Commissioner for Human Rights to draw the attention of all relevant United Nations bodies, including at the country level, to the reports of the Special Rapporteur;

14. *Requests* the Office of the High Commissioner, as well as other relevant United Nations bodies, offices, departments and specialized agencies, within their respective mandates, to consider ways in which they can assist States in strengthening the role and security of human rights defenders, including in situations of armed conflict and peacebuilding;

15. *Requests* all concerned United Nations agencies and organizations, within their mandates, to provide all possible assistance and support to the Special Rapporteur for the effective fulfilment of her mandate, including through country visits;

16. *Requests* the Special Rapporteur to continue to report annually on her activities to the General Assembly and to the Human Rights Council in accordance with her mandate;

17. *Decides* to consider the question at its sixty-eighth session under the item entitled "Promotion and protection of human rights".

Reprisals for cooperation with human rights bodies

Report of Secretary-General. In a July report [A/HRC/18/19], submitted pursuant to Human Rights Council resolution 12/2 [YUN 2009, p. 668], the Secretary-General provided a compilation and analysis of information on alleged reprisals against individuals or groups who had cooperated or sought to cooperate with representatives of UN human rights bodies, as well as recommendations on how to address the issues of intimidation and reprisals. The report contained information gathered from 20 March 2010 to 15 June 2011 pertaining to cases in Bahrain, Bangladesh, Belarus, China, India, Kenya, Malawi, Rwanda, Saudi Arabia, Sri Lanka and the Sudan. It noted that in some instances it had not been possible to record additional cases due to security concerns or because the individuals exposed to reprisals had requested that their cases not be raised publicly. The report included summaries of communications sent to States by representatives of human rights mechanisms and the related replies. It provided follow-up information on cases included in previous reports on Colombia, Guatemala, Iran, Kenya, Mauritania, Myanmar, Uzbekistan, Venezuela and Yemen. The Secretary-General made recommendations for States to prevent intimidation and reprisals by publicly encouraging people to cooperate with UN human rights mechanisms; for the Human Rights Council to ensure that States investigate any alleged acts of intimidation and reprisal and inform the Council; for UN human rights mechanisms to develop good practices relating to responding to reprisals, for adoption by all human rights mechanisms; and for civil society to raise awareness about the current report.

Human Rights Council action. On 29 September [A/66/53/Add.1 (dec. 18/118)], the Council urged States to take measures to prevent the occurrence of reprisals and intimidation and to investigate any alleged acts of intimidation or reprisal; encouraged States to inform the Council of measures taken to address such acts, and preventive action and remedies, including prosecution, and to share best practices; decided to convene, at its twenty-first (2012) session, a panel discussion on the issue of intimidation or reprisal against individuals and groups who cooperated with the United Nations, its representatives and mechanisms in the field of human rights; and requested OHCHR to prepare a report on the outcome of the panel discussion.

Protection of migrants

Reports of Special Rapporteur. In response to a request by the Human Rights Council [YUN 2008, p. 773], the outgoing Special Rapporteur on the human rights of migrants, Jorge Bustamante (Mexico), in March [A/HRC/17/33] reported on his activities from August 2009 to February 2010. The Rapporteur's work focused on the themes of irregular migration and criminalization of migrants, protection of children in the migration process and the right to housing and health of migrants. He concluded that migrants were facing increasing intolerance and were becoming more vulnerable to racist or xenophobic outbreaks of violence. Migrants with an irregular status were often afraid or unable to seek protection and were left without access to basic social rights, particularly health care, education and housing. The Rapporteur stated that the two themes of migration in the context of climate change, and migrants' political participation and civil rights, required further consideration.

An addendum [A/HRC/17/33/Add.1] summarized 25 communications—urgent appeals and letters of allegations—addressed to 16 Governments between 1 April 2010 and 15 March 2011, as well as 13 replies received until 10 May 2011.

In response to General Assembly resolution 65/212 [YUN 2010, p. 676] and Human Rights Council resolution 8/10 [YUN 2008, p. 773], the Secretary-General in August transmitted to the Assembly the report of the Special Rapporteur [A/66/264], which reviewed his work as the mandate holder from August 2005 to July 2011 and summarized the activities carried out between 1 August 2010 and 31 July 2011. The Rapporteur noted that further discussion on the themes of migration in the context of climate change and the political participation and civil rights of migrants would allow the mandate to present innovative approaches. The themes also underlined the need for a human rights perspective in global discussions among stakeholders on migration. The Rapporteur stressed that migration could be an essential component of development and prosperity in all countries of origin, transit and destination.

On 19 December, the General Assembly took note of the report (**decision 66/537**).

Mission reports. Following his visit to South Africa (24 January–1 February) [A/HRC/17/33/Add.4], the Rapporteur noted that although the Government had taken measures to protect migrants, such as regularizing Zimbabwean migrants, addressing xenophobic attacks directed against migrants in townships, and striving to alleviate the impact of the economic crisis, other challenges remained. The integration of migrants into society was hampered by the absence of a comprehensive immigration policy and the lack of regional and multilateral agreements. The Rapporteur, noting the absence of a comprehensive immigration policy that respected migrants' human rights and ensured their integration in South African society, made a number of recommendations to the Government on the arrest and detention of foreign nationals, the need to develop thorough data and statistics based on the demand for the labour force, access of migrants to social services, particularly health care, and the situation of unaccompanied foreign children.

Following his visit to Albania (5–13 December) [A/HRC/20/24/Add.1], the recently appointed Special Rapporteur François Crépeau (see below) recognized that the Government had adopted an impressive set of laws, policies and strategies to ensure a comprehensive and rights-based approach to migration, in compliance with international and European standards and obligations. He also noted that a number of challenges remained, including a significant gap between policies and their practical implementation, which directly impacted on the capacities, resources and expertise of the State to ensure the full realization and protection of the human rights of migrants. The Rapporteur made several recommendations to the Government, including on strengthening the national protection system, the protection of the rights of Albanian migrants abroad, and Albanian returnees and foreign migrants in the country. He called on the European Union (EU) and other international organizations to continue supporting the country to address remaining challenges and to intensify cooperation with neighbouring countries and countries of destination in that regard.

Report of Secretary-General. In accordance with General Assembly resolution 65/212 [YUN 2010, p. 676], the Secretary-General in August submitted a report [A/66/253] summarizing information submitted by Governments on the implementation of that resolution and resolution 64/166 [YUN 2009, p. 670], both dealing with migrants' rights. The report provided information on the status of the International Convention on the Protection of the Rights of All Migrant Workers and Members of Their Families [YUN 1990, p. 593], as well as on the activities of the Committee on the Protection of the Rights of All Migrant Workers and Members of Their Families, the Special Rapporteur on the human rights of migrants, the universal periodic review process of the Human Rights Council, and OHCHR.

Appointment. On 17 June [A/66/53 (res. 17/12)], the Council extended the mandate of the Special Rapporteur on the human rights of migrants for a period of three years and requested that he/she report annually to the Council in accordance with its programme of work, and to the General Assembly at the request of the Council or the Assembly. The newly appointed Rapporteur, Francois Crépeau (Canada), assumed his functions on 1 August.

Human Rights Council action. On 30 September [A/66/53/Add.1 (res. 18/21)], the Council called on States to ensure that their immigration policies were consistent with their obligations under international human rights law, strengthen measures to protect the rights of migrant workers in times of humanitarian crisis, and protect migrants' rights relating to their conditions of work, regardless of their migratory status, particularly the right to equal pay for equal work. It requested the Rapporteur to support the building of synergies between States to strengthen cooperation for protecting the human rights of migrant workers and their families, and to report on best practices of States to protect those rights.

Migrants fleeing political unrest in North Africa

Unrest in North Africa beginning in early 2011 led to thousands of migrants and asylum seekers fleeing Libya, in particular to neighbouring countries.

(For information on the political and security situation in Libya, see p. 266.)

Human Rights Council action. On 17 June [A/66/53 (res. 17/22)], the Council, by a recorded vote of 32 to 14, with no abstentions, expressed alarm at the vulnerable situation of migrants and asylum seekers who had suffered hardship and death while attempting to flee the unrest in North Africa. Having been compelled to make dangerous journeys, the migrants had been subjected to life-threatening exclusion, detention, rejection and xenophobia. There had been reports of boats sinking, resulting in the death of several hundreds of people, mostly African citizens, and according to accounts, more than 1,200 people were missing. The Council recognized the efforts made by countries of destination on northern Mediterranean shores and by neighbouring north African countries to host migrants and asylum seekers. It called for a comprehensive inquiry by countries of destination into the allegations that sinking vessels carrying migrants and asylum seekers were abandoned to their fate, despite the ability of European ships in the vicinity to rescue them, and welcomed the 9 May call by the Council of Europe in that regard. The Council requested the High Commissioner to report on the situation of asylum seekers and migrants fleeing the events in North Africa at its eighteenth (2011) session. It also requested the Rapporteur to pay attention to the situation of persons fleeing by sea, including in North Africa, and who were denied assistance when approaching destination countries, and to report regularly thereon to the Council.

Report of High Commissioner. Pursuant to Human Rights Council resolution 17/22 (see above), the High Commissioner submitted a September report [A/HRC/18/54] on the situation of migrants and asylum seekers fleeing recent events in North Africa. The report described the human rights implications of their cross-border movement from January to August, including their displacement. It also described the international response to the situation and made recommendations on protecting the human rights of migrants and asylum seekers fleeing the events in North Africa.

GENERAL ASSEMBLY ACTION

On 19 December [meeting 89], the General Assembly, on the recommendation of the Third Committee [A/66/462/Add.2], adopted **resolution 66/172** without vote [agenda item 69 (*b*)].

Protection of migrants

The General Assembly,

Recalling all its previous resolutions on the protection of migrants, the most recent of which is resolution 65/212 of 21 December 2010, and recalling also Human Rights Council resolution 18/21 of 30 September 2011,

Reaffirming the Universal Declaration of Human Rights, which proclaims that all human beings are born free and equal in dignity and rights and that everyone is entitled to all the rights and freedoms set out therein, without distinction of any kind, in particular as to race, colour or national origin,

Reaffirming also that everyone has the right to freedom of movement and residence within the borders of each State and the right to leave any country, including his or her own, and to return to his or her country,

Recalling the International Covenant on Civil and Political Rights and the International Covenant on Economic, Social and Cultural Rights, the Convention against Torture and Other Cruel, Inhuman or Degrading Treatment or Punishment, the Convention on the Elimination of All Forms of Discrimination against Women, the Convention on the Rights of the Child, the International Convention on the Elimination of All Forms of Racial Discrimination, the Convention on the Rights of Persons with Disabilities, the Vienna Convention on Consular Relations and the International Convention on the Protection of the Rights of All Migrant Workers and Members of Their Families,

Recalling also the provisions concerning migrants contained in the outcome documents of all major United Nations conferences and summits, including the Outcome of the Conference on the World Financial and Economic Crisis and Its Impact on Development, which recognizes that migrant workers are among the most affected and vulnerable in the context of financial and economic crises,

Recalling further Commission on Population and Development resolutions 2006/2 of 10 May 2006 and 2009/1 of 3 April 2009,

Taking note with appreciation of the United Nations Development Programme *Human Development Report 2009: Overcoming Barriers—Human Mobility and Development*,

Taking note of advisory opinion OC-16/99 of 1 October 1999 on the Right to Information on Consular Assistance in the Framework of the Guarantees of the Due Process of Law and advisory opinion OC-18/03 of 17 September 2003 on the Juridical Condition and Rights of Undocumented Migrants, issued by the Inter-American Court of Human Rights,

Taking note also of the Judgment of the International Court of Justice of 31 March 2004 in the case concerning *Avena and Other Mexican Nationals* and the Judgment of the Court of 19 January 2009 regarding the request for interpretation of the *Avena* Judgment, and recalling the obligations of States reaffirmed in both decisions,

Underlining the importance of the Human Rights Council in promoting respect for the protection of the human rights and fundamental freedoms of all, including migrants,

Recognizing the increasing participation of women in international migration movements,

Recalling the High-level Dialogue on International Migration and Development, held in New York on 14 and 15 September 2006 for the purpose of discussing the multidimensional aspects of international migration and development, which, inter alia, recognized the relationship between international migration, development and human rights,

Noting that the fifth meeting of the Global Forum on Migration and Development, held in Geneva on 1 and 2 December 2011, drew together the results and conclusions of fourteen thematic meetings that took place worldwide from January to October 2011 on the central theme "Taking action on migration and development—coherence, capacity and cooperation" as a contribution to promoting international cooperation among States and between States and other actors in order to strengthen the capacity of States to address migration and development opportunities and challenges more effectively, and taking note with appreciation of the generous offer of Mauritius to assume the presidency of the Global Forum for 2012,

Recognizing the cultural and economic contributions made by migrants to receiving societies and their communities of origin, as well as the need to identify appropriate means of maximizing development benefits and responding to the challenges which migration poses to countries of origin, transit and destination, especially in the light of the impact of the financial and economic crisis, and committing to ensuring dignified, humane treatment with applicable protections and to strengthening mechanisms for international cooperation,

Emphasizing the global character of the migratory phenomenon, the importance of international, regional and bilateral cooperation and dialogue in this regard, as appropriate, and the need to protect the human rights of migrants, particularly at a time in which migration flows have increased in the globalized economy and take place in a context of new security concerns,

Bearing in mind the obligations of States under international law, as applicable, to exercise due diligence to prevent crimes against migrants and to investigate and punish perpetrators, and that not doing so violates and impairs or nullifies the enjoyment of the human rights and fundamental freedoms of victims,

Affirming that crimes against migrants, including trafficking in persons, continue to pose a serious challenge and require a concerted international assessment and response and genuine multilateral cooperation among countries of origin, transit and destination for their eradication,

Bearing in mind that policies and initiatives on the issue of migration, including those that refer to the orderly management of migration, should promote holistic approaches that take into account the causes and consequences of the phenomenon, as well as full respect for the human rights and fundamental freedoms of migrants,

Stressing the importance of regulations and laws regarding irregular migration, at all levels of government, being in accordance with the obligations of States under international law, including international human rights law,

Stressing also the obligation of States to protect the human rights of migrants regardless of their migration status, and expressing its concern at measures which, including in the context of policies aimed at reducing irregular migration, treat irregular migration as a criminal rather than an administrative offence where the effect of doing so is to deny migrants full enjoyment of their human rights and fundamental freedoms,

Aware that, as criminals take advantage of migratory flows and attempt to circumvent restrictive immigration policies, migrants become more vulnerable to, inter alia, kidnapping, extortion, forced labour, sexual exploitation, physical assault, debt servitude and abandonment,

Recognizing the contributions of young migrants to countries of origin and destination, and in that regard encouraging States to consider the specific circumstances and needs of young migrants,

Concerned about the large and growing number of migrants, especially women and children, who place themselves in a vulnerable situation by attempting to cross international borders without the required travel documents, and recognizing the obligation of States to respect the human rights of those migrants,

Stressing that penalties and the treatment given to irregular migrants should be commensurate with their infraction,

Recognizing the importance of having a comprehensive and balanced approach to international migration, and bearing in mind that migration enriches the economic, political, social and cultural fabric of States and the historical and cultural ties that exist among some regions,

Recognizing also the obligations of countries of origin, transit and destination under international human rights law,

Underlining the importance for States, in cooperation with non-governmental organizations and other relevant stakeholders, to undertake information campaigns aimed at clarifying opportunities, limitations, risks and rights in the event of migration, so as to enable everyone to make informed decisions and to prevent anyone from utilizing dangerous means to cross international borders,

1. *Calls upon* States to promote and protect effectively the human rights and fundamental freedoms of all migrants, regardless of their migration status, especially those of women and children, and to address international migration through international, regional or bilateral cooperation and dialogue and through a comprehensive and balanced approach, recognizing the roles and responsibilities of countries of origin, transit and destination in promoting and protecting the human rights of all migrants, and avoiding approaches that might aggravate their vulnerability;

2. *Expresses its concern* about the impact of financial and economic crises on international migration and migrants, and in that regard urges Governments to combat unfair and discriminatory treatment of migrants, particularly migrant workers and their families;

3. *Reaffirms* the rights set forth in the Universal Declaration of Human Rights and the obligations of States under the International Covenants on Human Rights, and in this regard:

(*a*) Strongly condemns the manifestations and acts of racism, racial discrimination, xenophobia and related intolerance against migrants and the stereotypes often applied to them, including on the basis of religion or belief, and urges States to apply and, where needed, reinforce the existing laws when xenophobic or intolerant acts, manifestations or expressions against migrants occur, in order to eradicate impunity for those who commit xenophobic and racist acts;

(*b*) Expresses concern about legislation adopted by some States that results in measures and practices that may restrict the human rights and fundamental freedoms of migrants, and reaffirms that, when exercising their sovereign right to enact and implement migratory and border security measures, States have the duty to comply with their obligations under international law, including international human rights law, in order to ensure full respect for the human rights of migrants;

(*c*) Calls upon States to ensure that their laws and policies, including in the areas of counter-terrorism and combating transnational organized crime, such as trafficking in persons and smuggling of migrants, fully respect the human rights of migrants;

(*d*) Calls upon States that have not done so to consider signing and ratifying or acceding to the International Convention on the Protection of the Rights of All Migrant Workers and Members of Their Families as a matter of priority, and requests the Secretary-General to continue his efforts to promote and raise awareness of the Convention;

(*e*) Takes note of the report of the Committee on the Protection of the Rights of All Migrant Workers and Members of Their Families on its thirteenth and fourteenth sessions;

4. *Also reaffirms* the duty of States to effectively promote and protect the human rights and fundamental freedoms of all migrants, especially those of women and children, regardless of their immigration status, in conformity with the Universal Declaration of Human Rights and the international instruments to which they are party, and therefore:

(*a*) Calls upon all States to respect the human rights and the inherent dignity of migrants and to put an end to arbitrary arrest and detention and, where necessary, to review detention periods in order to avoid excessive detention of irregular migrants, and to adopt, where applicable, alternative measures to detention;

(*b*) Urges all States to adopt effective measures to prevent and punish any form of illegal deprivation of liberty of migrants by individuals or groups;

(*c*) Notes with appreciation the measures adopted by some States to reduce detention periods in cases of undocumented migration in the application of domestic regulations and laws regarding irregular migration;

(*d*) Also notes with appreciation the successful implementation by some States of alternative measures to detention in cases of undocumented migration as a practice that deserves consideration by all States;

(*e*) Requests States to adopt concrete measures to prevent the violation of the human rights of migrants while in transit, including in ports and airports and at borders and migration checkpoints, to train public officials who work in those facilities and in border areas to treat migrants respectfully and in accordance with the law, and to prosecute, in conformity with applicable law, any act of violation of the human rights of migrants, inter alia, arbitrary detention, torture and violations of the right to life, including extrajudicial executions, during their transit from their country of origin to the country of destination and vice versa, including their transit through national borders;

(*f*) Underlines the right of migrants to return to their country of citizenship, and recalls that States must ensure that their returning nationals are duly received;

(*g*) Reaffirms emphatically the duty of States parties to ensure full respect for and observance of the Vienna Convention on Consular Relations, in particular with regard to the right of all foreign nationals, regardless of their immigration status, to communicate with a consular official of the sending State in case of arrest, imprisonment, custody or detention, and the obligation of the receiving State to inform the foreign national without delay of his or her rights under the Convention;

(*h*) Requests all States, in conformity with national legislation and applicable international legal instruments to which they are party, to enforce labour law effectively, including by addressing violations of such law, with regard to migrant workers' labour relations and working conditions, inter alia, those related to their remuneration and conditions of health, safety at work and the right to freedom of association;

(*i*) Encourages all States to remove unlawful obstacles, where they exist, that may prevent the safe, transparent, unrestricted and expeditious transfer of remittances, earnings, assets and pensions of migrants to their country of origin or to any other countries, in conformity with applicable legislation and agreements, and to consider, as appropriate, measures to solve other problems that may impede such transfers;

(*j*) Recalls that the Universal Declaration of Human Rights recognizes that everyone has the right to an effective remedy by the competent national tribunals for acts violating the fundamental rights granted to him or her;

5. *Emphasizes* the importance of protecting persons in vulnerable situations, and in this regard:

(a) Expresses its concern about the increase in the activities of transnational and national organized crime entities and others who profit from crimes against migrants, especially women and children, without regard for dangerous and inhumane conditions and in flagrant violation of domestic laws and international law and contrary to international standards;

(b) Also expresses its concern about the high level of impunity enjoyed by traffickers and their accomplices as well as other members of organized crime entities and, in this context, the denial of rights and justice to migrants who have suffered from abuse;

(c) Welcomes immigration programmes, adopted by some countries, that allow migrants to integrate fully into the host countries, facilitate family reunification and promote a harmonious, tolerant and respectful environment, and encourages States to consider the possibility of adopting these types of programmes;

(d) Encourages all States to develop international migration policies and programmes that include a gender perspective, in order to adopt the measures necessary to better protect women and girls against dangers and abuse during migration;

(e) Calls upon States to protect the human rights of migrant children, given their vulnerability, particularly unaccompanied migrant children, ensuring that the best interests of the child are a primary consideration in their policies of integration, return and family reunification;

(f) Encourages all States to prevent and eliminate discriminatory policies and legislation, at all levels of government, that deny migrant children access to education;

(g) Encourages States, while taking into account the best interests of the child as a primary consideration, to foster the successful integration of migrant children into the education system and the removal of barriers to their education in host countries and countries of origin;

(h) Urges States to ensure that repatriation mechanisms allow for the identification and special protection of persons in vulnerable situations, including persons with disabilities, and take into account, in conformity with their international obligations and commitments, the principle of the best interests of the child and family reunification;

(i) Urges States parties to the United Nations Convention against Transnational Organized Crime and supplementing protocols thereto, namely, the Protocol against the Smuggling of Migrants by Land, Sea and Air and the Protocol to Prevent, Suppress and Punish Trafficking in Persons, Especially Women and Children, to implement them fully, and calls upon States that have not done so to consider ratifying or acceding to them as a matter of priority;

6. *Takes note with appreciation* of the study of the Office of the United Nations High Commissioner for Human Rights on challenges and best practices in the implementation of the international framework for the protection of the rights of the child in the context of migration, and invites States to take into account the conclusions and recommendations of the study when designing and implementing their migration policies;

7. *Encourages* States to protect victims of national and transnational organized crime, including kidnapping, trafficking and, in some instances, smuggling, through, where applicable, the implementation of programmes and policies that guarantee protection and access to medical, psychosocial and legal assistance;

8. *Encourages* Member States that have not already done so to enact domestic legislation and to take further effective measures to combat international trafficking in persons and smuggling of migrants, recognizing that these crimes may endanger the lives of migrants or subject them to harm, servitude or exploitation, which may also include debt bondage, slavery, sexual exploitation or forced labour, and also encourages Member States to strengthen international cooperation to combat such trafficking and smuggling;

9. *Stresses* the importance of international, regional and bilateral cooperation in the protection of the human rights of migrants, and therefore:

(a) Requests all States, international organizations and relevant stakeholders to take into account in their policies and initiatives on migration issues the global character of the migratory phenomenon and to give due consideration to international, regional and bilateral cooperation in this field, including by undertaking dialogues on migration that include countries of origin, transit and destination, as well as civil society, including migrants, with a view to addressing, in a comprehensive manner, inter alia, its causes and consequences and the challenge of undocumented or irregular migration, granting priority to the protection of the human rights of migrants;

(b) Encourages States to take the measures necessary to achieve policy coherence on migration at the national, regional and international levels, including by ensuring coordinated child protection policies and systems across borders that are in full compliance with international human rights law;

(c) Also encourages States to further strengthen their cooperation in protecting witnesses in cases of smuggling of migrants and trafficking in persons;

(d) Calls upon the United Nations system and other relevant international organizations and multilateral institutions to enhance their cooperation in the development of methodologies for the collection and processing of statistical data on international migration and the situation of migrants in countries of origin, transit and destination and to assist Member States in their capacity-building efforts in this regard;

(e) Requests Member States, the United Nations system, international organizations, civil society and all relevant stakeholders, especially the United Nations High Commissioner for Human Rights and the Special Rapporteur of the Human Rights Council on the human rights of migrants, to ensure that the perspective of the human rights of migrants is included among the priority issues in the ongoing discussions on international migration and development within the United Nations system, and in this regard underlines the importance of adequately taking into account the human rights perspective as one of the priorities of the informal thematic debate on international migration and development, held in 2011, as well as in the High-level Dialogue on International Migration and Development, which will take place during the sixty-eighth session of the General Assembly, in 2013, as decided by the Assembly in its resolution 63/225 of 19 December 2008;

(f) Encourages States, relevant international organizations and civil society, including non-governmental organizations, to continue and to enhance their dialogue with a view to strengthening public policies aimed at promoting and respecting human rights, including those of migrants;

(g) Invites the Chair of the Committee on the Protection of the Rights of All Migrant Workers and Members of Their Families to address the General Assembly at its sixty-seventh session under the item entitled "Promotion and protection of human rights", within existing resources;

(h) Invites the Special Rapporteur on the human rights of migrants to submit his report to the General Assembly at its sixty-seventh session under the item entitled "Promotion and protection of human rights";

10. *Takes note* of the report of the Secretary-General, submitted to the General Assembly at its sixty-sixth session, on the implementation of resolution 65/212 and on how the International Convention on the Protection of the Rights of All Migrant Workers and Members of Their Families has influenced policy and practice, where applicable, to strengthen the protection of migrants;

11. *Requests* the Secretary-General to continue to pursue his efforts to gather information on the subject of the above-mentioned report, while encouraging Member States to provide information relating to the application of the Convention and recognizing States that have provided the requested information.

Also on 19 December, by **resolution 66/128** (see p. 1072), the General Assembly called on Governments to take action for the prevention and protection of migrant women against violence and discrimination, exploitation and abuse.

Discrimination against minorities

Report of independent expert. Pursuant to a Human Rights Council request [YUN 2008, p. 778], the independent expert on minority issues, Gay McDougall (United States), in her sixth and final annual report to the Council [A/HRC/16/45], reviewed her activities in 2010, including work to promote implementation of the Declaration on the Rights of Persons Belonging to National or Ethnic, Religious and Linguistic Minorities [YUN 1992, p. 722] and details on follow-up to the first [YUN 2008, p. 776], second [YUN 2009, p. 672] and third [YUN 2010, p. 679] sessions of the Forum on Minority Issues. The report also presented a thematic study on the role of minority rights protection in promoting stability and conflict prevention. The independent expert observed that attention to minority rights at an early stage—before grievances led to tensions and violence—would make an invaluable contribution to the culture of prevention within the United Nations, save countless lives and promote stability and development. Among a series of recommendations, she advocated that minority rights expertise be strengthened and integrated comprehensively across the UN system.

Mission reports. Following her visit to Rwanda (31 January–7 February) [A/HRC/19/56/Add.1], the independent expert affirmed that Government efforts to forge unity and social cohesion behind a Rwandan national identity and to diminish ethnicity as a destructive force in society were praiseworthy. Nevertheless, popular notions of ethnicity still existed in Rwandan society. Numerous communities that identified themselves as Batwa lived in poverty and hardship on the margins of mainstream society, were absent from the public life of the country, had no viable means of livelihood, and were categorized by the Government as "historically marginalized people". The independent expert made recommendations to the Government on establishing long-term reconciliation mechanisms, adopting anti-discrimination legislation, and ensuring the participation of all groups in the political arena. She also made recommendations to address the situation of the Batwa.

Following her mission to Bulgaria (4–11 July) [A/HRC/19/56/Add.2 & Corr.1], the independent expert noted the numerous laws, policies and programmes established by the Government to promote anti-discrimination, equality and the rights of minorities, including the Roma. In key areas, however, such as education, employment, health care and housing, the Roma remained at the bottom of the socioeconomic ladder. Government initiatives failed to address the entrenched discrimination, exclusion and poverty faced by many Roma. The independent expert called on the Government to match policies on Roma integration inspired by the EU and NGOs with Government-led implementation, concrete action on the ground and the financial resources necessary to improve the living conditions of the Roma. A new approach to Roma integration, designed and implemented in consultation with Roma organizations, was required to break the vicious circle of social exclusion and poverty. The expert made recommendations on access to education, employment discrimination, housing and living conditions, protecting Muslim and other religious minorities, the rights of Macedonians and Pomaks, the use of mother tongue languages, and strengthening national human rights institutions.

Mandate and appointment of independent expert. On 24 March [A/66/53 (res. 16/6)], the Council extended the mandate of the independent expert for a period of three years, requested the independent expert to submit annual reports on his/her activities to the Council, and invited OHCHR, the independent expert, UN agencies and States to explore possibilities for organizing activities to mark the twentieth anniversary of the Declaration on the Rights of Persons Belonging to National or Ethnic, Religious and Linguistic Minorities in 2012.

In June, the Human Rights Council appointed Rita Izsák (Hungary) as the new independent expert on minority issues and she assumed her functions on 1 August. By a 16 June note [A/HRC/17/G/13] referring thereto, Turkey transmitted to OHCHR a statement on its use of the word "minorities" as applied to Turkish citizens.

Communication. In a 3 March note [A/HRC/16/G/4], Viet Nam submitted its comments on the independent expert's 2010 mission to the country [YUN 2010, p. 680].

Human Rights Council action. On 29 September [A/66/53/Add.1 (res. 18/3)], the Council decided to convene, at its nineteenth (2012) session, a panel discussion to commemorate the twentieth anniversary of the Declaration, with a focus on its implementation, as well as on achievements, best practices and challenges. It requested OHCHR to liaise with the independent expert on minority issues, States, UN entities, civil society, NGOs and national human rights institutions to ensure their participation in the panel discussion, and to report on its outcome.

Forum on Minority Issues. The fourth session of the Forum on Minority Issues (Geneva, 29–30 November) focused on measures aimed at guaranteeing the rights of minority women and girls. The more than 400 participants included representatives of Governments, treaty bodies, UN specialized agencies, regional intergovernmental bodies, national human rights institutions and civil society. The Forum had before it a note by the independent expert on minority issues, Rita Izsák, on guaranteeing the rights of minority women [A/HRC/FMI/2011/2] and an OHCHR note providing draft recommendations on that topic [A/HRC/FMI/2011/3].

The Forum issued recommendations [A/HRC/19/71], including those addressing the thematic issues of minority women and girls and the right to education, effective political participation, and effective participation in economic, social and cultural life. The recommendations were directed to national, regional and local governments, parliaments, national human rights institutions, civil society, UN system and human rights mechanisms, the media, political parties, trade unions and civil society.

Report of High Commissioner. Pursuant to a Human Rights Council request [YUN 2010, p. 680], the High Commissioner submitted a December report [A/HRC/19/27] on developments in the work of UN human rights entities and on the activities undertaken by OHCHR in 2011 for promoting and implementing the rights provided for under the Declaration. Activities summarized in the report included consultations on policing and minority communities; a training workshop on minority rights; the OHCHR minorities fellowship programme; the seventh meeting of the Inter-Agency Group on Minorities; the fourth session of the Forum on Minority Issues (see above); regional and country engagement activities; and events in the context of the International Year for People of African Descent (see p. 649). The report provided an update on the work of human rights treaty bodies relating to minority rights.

GENERAL ASSEMBLY ACTION

On 19 December [meeting 89], the General Assembly, on the recommendation of the Third Committee [A/66/462/Add.2], adopted **resolution 66/166** without vote [agenda item 69 (*b*)].

Effective promotion of the Declaration on the Rights of Persons Belonging to National or Ethnic, Religious and Linguistic Minorities

The General Assembly,

Recalling its resolution 47/135 of 18 December 1992, by which it adopted the Declaration on the Rights of Persons Belonging to National or Ethnic, Religious and Linguistic Minorities annexed to that resolution, and bearing in mind article 27 of the International Covenant on Civil and Political Rights as well as other relevant existing international standards and national legislation,

Recalling also its subsequent resolutions on the effective promotion of the Declaration on the Rights of Persons Belonging to National or Ethnic, Religious and Linguistic Minorities, as well as Human Rights Council resolutions 6/15 of 28 September 2007, by which the Council established the Forum on Minority Issues, 16/6 of 24 March 2011 on the mandate of the Independent Expert on minority issues and 18/3 of 29 September 2011 on the panel to commemorate the twentieth anniversary of the adoption of the Declaration,

Affirming that the promotion and protection of the rights of persons belonging to national or ethnic, religious and linguistic minorities and dialogue between these minorities and the rest of society, as well as the constructive and inclusive development of practices and institutional arrangements to accommodate diversity within societies, contribute to political and social stability and the prevention and peaceful resolution of conflicts involving the rights of persons belonging to national or ethnic, religious and linguistic minorities,

Expressing concern at the frequency and severity of disputes and conflicts involving persons belonging to national or ethnic, religious and linguistic minorities in many countries and their often tragic consequences, and that they often suffer disproportionately from the effects of conflict resulting in the violation of their human rights and are particularly vulnerable to displacement through, inter alia, population transfers, refugee flows and forced relocation,

Emphasizing the important role that national institutions can play in the promotion and protection of the rights of persons belonging to national or ethnic, religious and linguistic minorities as well as in early warning and awareness-raising measures to address problems regarding minority situations,

Emphasizing also the need for reinforced efforts to meet the goal of the full realization of the rights of persons belonging to national or ethnic, religious and linguistic minorities, including by addressing economic and social conditions and marginalization, as well as to end any type of discrimination against them,

Emphasizing further the fundamental importance of human rights education, training and learning as well as of dialogue and interaction among all relevant stakeholders and members of society on the promotion and protection of the rights of persons belonging to national or ethnic, religious and linguistic minorities as an integral part of the development of society as a whole, including the sharing of best practices such as for the promotion of mutual understanding of minority issues, managing diversity by recognizing plural identities and promoting inclusive and stable societies as well as social cohesion therein,

Acknowledging that the United Nations has an important role to play regarding the protection of the rights of persons belonging to national or ethnic, religious and linguistic minorities by, inter alia, taking due account of, and giving effect to, the Declaration on the Rights of Persons Belonging to National or Ethnic, Religious and Linguistic Minorities,

Noting that 2012 will mark the twentieth anniversary of the adoption of the Declaration on the Rights of Persons Belonging to National or Ethnic, Religious and Linguistic Minorities,

Affirming that the anniversary offers an important opportunity to reflect on the promotion and protection of the rights of persons belonging to national or ethnic, religious and linguistic minorities, as well as on achievements, best practices and challenges with regard to implementation of the Declaration on the Rights of Persons Belonging to National or Ethnic, Religious and Linguistic Minorities,

Recognizing, in this context, the important role played by the Independent Expert on minority issues in promoting the implementation of the Declaration on the Rights of Persons Belonging to National or Ethnic, Religious and Linguistic Minorities,

1. *Reaffirms* the obligation of States to ensure that persons belonging to national or ethnic, religious and linguistic minorities may exercise fully and effectively all human rights and fundamental freedoms without any discrimination and in full equality before the law, as proclaimed in the Declaration on the Rights of Persons Belonging to National or Ethnic, Religious and Linguistic Minorities, and draws attention to the relevant provisions of the Durban Declaration and Programme of Action, including the provisions on forms of multiple discrimination;

2. *Urges* States and the international community to promote and protect the rights of persons belonging to national or ethnic, religious and linguistic minorities, as set out in the Declaration on the Rights of Persons Belonging to National or Ethnic, Religious and Linguistic Minorities, including through the encouragement of conditions for the promotion of their identity, the provision of adequate education and the facilitation of their participation in all aspects of the political, economic, social, religious and cultural life of society and in the economic progress and development of their country, without discrimination, and to apply a gender perspective while doing so;

3. *Urges* States to take all appropriate measures, inter alia, constitutional, legislative, administrative and other measures, for the promotion and implementation of the Declaration on the Rights of Persons Belonging to National or Ethnic, Religious and Linguistic Minorities, and appeals to States to cooperate bilaterally and multilaterally, in particular on the exchange of best practices and lessons learned, in accordance with the Declaration, in order to promote and protect the rights of persons belonging to national or ethnic, religious and linguistic minorities;

4. *Calls upon* States to give special attention to the situation and specific needs of women and children belonging to minorities while promoting and protecting the rights of persons belonging to national or ethnic, religious and linguistic minorities;

5. *Encourages* States, in their follow-up to the World Conference against Racism, Racial Discrimination, Xenophobia and Related Intolerance, to include aspects relating to persons belonging to national or ethnic, religious and linguistic minorities in their national plans of action and, in this context, to take forms of multiple discrimination fully into account;

6. *Takes note with appreciation* of the report of the Independent Expert on minority issues and its special focus on the role of the protection of minority rights in conflict prevention;

7. *Calls upon* States to integrate the promotion and protection of the rights of persons belonging to national or ethnic, religious and linguistic minorities, as well as effective non-discrimination and equality for all, into strategies for the prevention and resolution of conflicts involving these minorities, while ensuring their full and effective participation in the design, implementation and evaluation of such strategies;

8. *Calls upon* the Secretary-General to make available, at the request of Governments concerned, qualified expertise on minority issues, including in the context of the prevention and resolution of disputes, to assist in resolving existing or potential situations involving minorities;

9. *Commends* the Independent Expert on minority issues for the work that has been done and the important role played in raising the level of awareness of and in giving added visibility to the rights of persons belonging to national or ethnic, religious and linguistic minorities and for the ongoing efforts to promote and protect their rights in order to ensure equitable development and peaceful and stable societies, including through close cooperation with Governments, the relevant United Nations bodies and mechanisms and non-governmental organizations;

10. *Calls upon* all States to cooperate with and assist the Independent Expert on minority issues in the performance of the tasks and duties mandated to her, to provide her with all the necessary information requested and to seriously consider responding promptly and favourably to the requests of the Independent Expert to visit their countries in order to enable her to fulfil her duties effectively;

11. *Encourages* the specialized agencies, regional organizations, national human rights institutions and non-governmental organizations to develop regular dialogue and cooperation with the mandate holder as well as to continue to contribute to the promotion and protection of the rights of persons belonging to national or ethnic, religious and linguistic minorities;

12. *Expresses its appreciation* for the successful completion of the first three sessions of the Forum on Minority Issues, addressing the right to education, the right to effective political participation and the right to participation in economic life and which, through the widespread participation of stakeholders, provided an important platform for promoting dialogue on these topics, and encourages States to take into consideration, as appropriate, relevant recommendations of the Forum;

13. *Invites* States, United Nations mechanisms, bodies, specialized agencies, funds and programmes, regional, intergovernmental and non-governmental organizations and national human rights institutions as well as academics and experts on minority issues to continue to participate actively in the sessions of the Forum on Minority Issues;

14. *Welcomes* the decision of the Human Rights Council to convene at its nineteenth session a panel discussion to commemorate the twentieth anniversary of the adoption of the Declaration on the Rights of Persons Belonging to National or Ethnic, Religious and Linguistic Minorities, with a particular focus on its implementation as well as on achievements, best practices and challenges in this regard;

15. *Welcomes* the inter-agency cooperation among United Nations agencies, funds and programmes on minority issues, led by the Office of the United Nations High Commissioner for Human Rights, and urges them to further increase their cooperation by, inter alia, developing policies on the promotion and protection of the rights of persons belonging to minorities, drawing also on relevant outcomes of the Forum on Minority Issues;

16. *Requests* the United Nations High Commissioner for Human Rights to continue her efforts to improve coordination and cooperation among United Nations agencies, funds and programmes on activities related to the promotion and protection of the rights of persons belonging to national or ethnic, religious and linguistic minorities and to take the work of relevant regional organizations active in the field of human rights into account in her endeavours;

17. *Calls upon* the High Commissioner to continue to promote, within her mandate, the implementation of the Declaration on the Rights of Persons Belonging to National or Ethnic, Religious and Linguistic Minorities, and to engage in a dialogue with Governments for that purpose and regularly update and disseminate widely the United Nations Guide for Minorities;

18. *Invites* the High Commissioner to continue to seek voluntary contributions to facilitate the effective participation of representatives of non-governmental organizations and persons belonging to national or ethnic, religious and linguistic minorities, in particular those from developing countries, in minority-related activities organized by the United Nations, in particular the activities of its human rights bodies, and in doing so to give particular attention to ensuring the participation of young people and women;

19. *Invites* the human rights treaty bodies, when considering reports submitted by States parties as well as special procedures of the Human Rights Council, to continue to give attention, within their respective mandates, to situations and rights of persons belonging to national or ethnic, religious and linguistic minorities;

20. *Reaffirms* that the universal periodic review, as well as the United Nations human rights treaty bodies, constitute important mechanisms for the promotion and protection of human rights and fundamental freedoms, and in that regard calls upon States to effectively follow up on accepted universal periodic review recommendations related to the rights of persons belonging to national or ethnic, religious and linguistic minorities and further encourages States parties to give serious consideration to the follow-up to treaty body recommendations on the matter;

21. *Invites* the Independent Expert on minority issues to report annually to the General Assembly;

22. *Requests* the Secretary-General to submit to the General Assembly at its sixty-eighth session a report on the implementation of the present resolution, including information on activities undertaken by the Office of the High Commissioner, the Independent Expert on minority issues and relevant United Nations entities, within existing resources, as well as by Member States, to mark the twentieth anniversary of the adoption of the Declaration on the Rights of Persons Belonging to National or Ethnic, Religious and Linguistic Minorities;

23. *Decides* to continue consideration of the question at its sixty-eighth session under the item entitled "Promotion and protection of human rights".

Freedom of religion or belief

Reports of Special Rapporteur. Pursuant to a Human Rights Council request [YUN 2010, p. 681], the Special Rapporteur on freedom of religion or belief, Heiner Bielefeldt (Germany), submitted a report [A/HRC/16/53] reviewing his activities and discussing the theme of freedom of religion or belief and school education, focusing on international human rights documents, the elimination of stereotypes and prejudices, the issue of religious symbols in the school context and religious instruction in schools. The Rapporteur concluded that the issue was multifaceted and entailed significant opportunities as well as far-reaching challenges. He made recommendations for States, including providing teachers and students with voluntary opportunities for meetings and exchanges with their counterparts of different religions or beliefs; strengthening a non-discriminatory perspective in education in relation to freedom of religion or belief; reinforcing the protection of girls' right to education; taking measures against intolerance and discrimination based on religion or belief in school curricula, textbooks and teaching methods; and evaluating the curricula in public schools that touched upon religions and beliefs to determine if they promoted respect for freedom of religion or belief and were impartial, inclusive, age appropriate, and free of bias. He also emphasized the critical role of parents, families and legal guardians in the education of children in the field of religion or belief.

An addendum [A/HRC/16/53/Add.1] summarized cases transmitted to 25 Governments between 1 December 2009 and 30 November 2010 and replies received by 2 February 2011.

In response to General Assembly resolution 65/211 [YUN 2010, p. 681], the Secretary-General in July transmitted to the Assembly the Rapporteur's interim report [A/66/156], which reviewed activities carried out since the previous report [YUN 2010, p. 681] and focused on the role of the State in promoting interreligious communication—various forms of exchange of information, experiences and ideas of all kinds between individuals and groups belonging to different theistic, atheistic and non-theistic beliefs, or not professing any religion or belief. The Rapporteur encouraged States to take a constructive role in promoting interreligious communication and pointed to a number of possibilities for States, including encouraging interreligious communication by expressing appreciation for well-defined dialogue projects; facilitating dialogue among members of various religious or belief groups in the framework of the State itself; and developing forums for regular encounters of people of different religious or belief affiliations. He urged States to become more aware of the potential of informal interreligious communication that was not organized explicitly along denominational lines, such as informal settings in multicultural neighbourhoods, schools, clubs and other public services.

Mission reports. Following his mission to Paraguay (23–30 March) [A/HRC/19/60/Add.1], the Rapporteur appreciated the human rights commitment of the Government and the open, tolerant atmosphere in society at large. At the same time, he identified implementation deficits which might negatively affect the enjoyment of freedom of religion or belief by people living in situations of particular vulnerability. He encouraged the Government to ensure that the principle of non-discrimination on the grounds of religion or belief was implemented in a thorough and systematic manner; to reform the requirement of annual registration of non-Catholic religious or philosophical communities; to continue to support the Interreligious Forum; to pay attention to possible regional de facto monopolies of denominational schools run by one particular religious community, especially in rural areas; to review regulations concerning ceremonies in the police, the military and other State institutions to ensure that no member of those institutions was urged to attend religious practices against their will; and to pay more systematic attention to the structural vulnerability of members of indigenous peoples, especially in rural areas.

In his report [A/HRC/19/60/Add.2] on the mission to the Republic of Moldova (1–8 September), the Rapporteur noted that the Moldovan society continued to be in rapid transformation, which included the development of a sustainable human rights culture. The implementation of human rights standards ranked high on the Government's agenda and significant progress had been made. Nonetheless, challenges remained, such as the predominant position of the Orthodox Church, which enjoyed a privileged status at variance with the constitutional provision of a secular State. The Rapporteur observed that a public culture of appreciating diversity was needed. He recommended that the Government issue a robust anti-discrimination law, facilitate interreligious communication, elaborate education provisions to better meet diversity needs, speak out against incitement to religious hatred, and ensure the voluntary nature of religious instruction and that its registration procedure was in line with international human rights standards. He highlighted the responsibilities of religious communities and their leaders in encouraging religious tolerance, embracing diversity and defusing tensions.

Human Rights Council action. On 24 March [A/66/53 (res. 16/13)], the Council urged States to intensify efforts to protect and promote freedom of thought, conscience and religion or belief; stressed the importance of continued and strengthened dialogue in all forms to promote greater tolerance, respect and mutual understanding; called on States to make use of the potential of education for the eradication of prejudices and stereotypes against members of other religions or beliefs; and requested the Rapporteur to submit a report to the Council annually.

GENERAL ASSEMBLY ACTION

On 19 December [meeting 89], the General Assembly, on the recommendation of the Third Committee [A/66/462/Add.2], adopted **resolution 66/168** without vote [agenda item 69 (*b*)].

Elimination of all forms of intolerance and of discrimination based on religion or belief

The General Assembly,

Recalling its resolution 36/55 of 25 November 1981, by which it proclaimed the Declaration on the Elimination of All Forms of Intolerance and of Discrimination Based on Religion or Belief,

Recalling also article 18 of the International Covenant on Civil and Political Rights, article 18 of the Universal Declaration of Human Rights and other relevant human rights provisions,

Recalling further its previous resolutions on the elimination of all forms of intolerance and of discrimination based on religion or belief, including resolution 65/211 of 21 December 2010, and Human Rights Council resolution 16/13 of 24 March 2011,

Recognizing the important work carried out by the Human Rights Committee in providing guidance with respect to the scope of freedom of religion or belief,

Considering that religion or belief, for those who profess either, is one of the fundamental elements in their conception of life and that freedom of religion or belief should be fully respected and guaranteed,

Reaffirming that everyone has the right to freedom of thought, conscience and religion or belief, which includes the freedom to have or not to have, or to adopt, a religion or belief of one's own choice, and the freedom, either alone or in community with others and in public or private, to manifest one's religion or belief in teaching, practice, worship and observance,

Deeply concerned at continuing acts of intolerance and violence based on religion or belief against individuals and members of religious communities and religious minorities around the world and at the limited progress that has been made in the elimination of all forms of intolerance and of discrimination based on religion or belief, and believing that further intensified efforts are therefore required to promote and protect the right to freedom of thought, conscience and religion or belief and to eliminate all forms of hatred, intolerance and discrimination based on religion or belief, as also noted at the World Conference against Racism, Racial Discrimination, Xenophobia and Related Intolerance, held in Durban, South Africa, from 31 August to 8 September 2001, as well as at the Durban Review Conference, held in Geneva from 20 to 24 April 2009,

Concerned that acts of violence, or credible threats of violence, against persons belonging to religious communities and religious minorities are sometimes tolerated or encouraged by official authorities,

Concerned also at the increasing number of laws and regulations that limit the freedom of thought, conscience and religion or belief, and at the implementation of existing laws in a discriminatory manner,

Convinced of the need to address the rise in various parts of the world of religious extremism that affects the rights of individuals, the situations of violence and discrimination that affect many women and other individuals on the grounds or in the name of religion or belief or in accordance with cultural and traditional practices and the misuse of religion or belief for ends inconsistent with the Charter of the United Nations and other relevant instruments of the United Nations,

Seriously concerned about all attacks on religious places, sites and shrines in violation of international law, in particular human rights and humanitarian law, including any deliberate destruction of relics and monuments,

Emphasizing that States, regional organizations, non-governmental organizations, religious bodies and the media have an important role to play in promoting tolerance and respect for religious and cultural diversity and in the universal promotion and protection of human rights, including freedom of religion or belief,

Underlining the importance of education in the promotion of tolerance, which involves the acceptance by the public of, and its respect for, diversity, including with regard to religious expression, and underlining also the fact that education, in particular at school, should contribute in a meaningful way to promoting tolerance and the elimination of discrimination based on religion or belief,

1. *Strongly condemns* all forms of intolerance and of discrimination based on religion or belief, as well as violations of freedom of thought, conscience and religion or belief;

2. *Stresses* that the right to freedom of thought, conscience and religion or belief applies equally to all persons, regardless of their religion or belief and without any discrimination as to their equal protection by the law;

3. *Emphasizes* that, as underlined by the Human Rights Committee, restrictions on the freedom to manifest one's religion or belief are permitted only if limitations are prescribed by law, are necessary to protect public safety, order, health or morals or the fundamental rights and freedoms of others, are non-discriminatory and are applied in a manner that does not vitiate the right to freedom of thought, conscience and religion or belief;

4. *Also emphasizes* that freedom of religion or belief and freedom of expression are interdependent, interrelated and mutually reinforcing, and stresses further the role that these rights can play in the fight against all forms of intolerance and of discrimination based on religion or belief;

5. *Recognizes with deep concern* the overall rise in instances of intolerance and violence, regardless of the actors, directed against members of many religious and other communities in various parts of the world, including cases motivated by Islamophobia, anti-Semitism and Christianophobia;

6. *Strongly condemns* any advocacy of religious hatred that constitutes incitement to discrimination, hostility or violence, whether it involves the use of print, audiovisual or electronic media or any other means;

7. *Expresses concern* at the persistence of institutionalized social intolerance and discrimination practised against many on the grounds of religion or belief, and emphasizes that legal procedures pertaining to religious or belief-based groups and places of worship are not a prerequisite for the exercise of the right to manifest one's religion or belief and that such procedures, when legally required at the national or local level, should be non-discriminatory in order to contribute to the effective protection of the right of all persons to practise their religion or belief, either individually or in community with others and in public or private;

8. *Recognizes with concern* the situation of persons in vulnerable situations, including persons deprived of their liberty, refugees, asylum seekers and internally displaced persons, children, persons belonging to national or ethnic, religious and linguistic minorities and migrants, as regards their ability to freely exercise their right to freedom of religion or belief;

9. *Emphasizes* that States have an obligation to exercise due diligence to prevent, investigate and punish acts of violence against persons belonging to religious minorities, regardless of the perpetrator, and that failure to do so may constitute a human rights violation;

10. *Also emphasizes* that no religion should be equated with terrorism, as this may have adverse consequences on the enjoyment of the right to freedom of religion or belief of all members of the religious communities concerned;

11. *Deplores* the continued existence of instances of religious intolerance, as well as emerging obstacles to the enjoyment of the right to freedom of religion or belief, inter alia:

(*a*) Instances of intolerance and violence directed against members of many religious minorities and other communities in various parts of the world;

(*b*) Incidents of religious hatred, discrimination, intolerance and violence, which may be manifested by the derogatory stereotyping, negative profiling and stigmatization of persons based on their religion or belief;

(*c*) Attacks on or destruction of religious places, sites and shrines in violation of international law, in particular human rights and humanitarian law, as they have more than material significance for the dignity and lives of members of communities holding spiritual or religious beliefs;

(d) Instances, both in law and practice, that constitute violations of the fundamental right to freedom of religion or belief, including of the individual right to publicly express one's spiritual and religious beliefs, taking into account the relevant articles of the International Covenant on Civil and Political Rights, as well as other international instruments;

(e) Constitutional and legislative systems that fail to provide adequate and effective guarantees of freedom of thought, conscience and religion or belief to all without distinction;

12. *Urges* States to step up their efforts to protect and promote freedom of thought, conscience and religion or belief, and to this end:

(a) To ensure that their constitutional and legislative systems provide adequate and effective guarantees of freedom of thought, conscience and religion or belief to all without distinction, inter alia, by providing access to justice and effective remedies in cases where the right to freedom of thought, conscience and religion or belief or the right to freely practise one's religion, including the right to change one's religion or belief, is violated;

(b) To ensure that existing legislation is not implemented in a discriminatory manner or does not result in discrimination based on religion or belief, that no one within their jurisdiction is deprived of the right to life, liberty and security of person because of religion or belief and that no one is subjected to torture or other cruel, inhuman or degrading treatment or punishment, or arbitrary arrest or detention on that account and to bring to justice all perpetrators of violations of these rights;

(c) To end violations of the human rights of women and to devote particular attention to abolishing practices and legislation that discriminate against women, including in the exercise of their right to freedom of thought, conscience and religion or belief;

(d) To ensure that no one is discriminated against on the basis of his or her religion or belief when accessing, inter alia, education, medical care, employment, humanitarian assistance or social benefits and to ensure that everyone has the right and the opportunity to have access, on general terms of equality, to public services in their country, without any discrimination on the basis of religion or belief;

(e) To review, whenever relevant, existing registration practices in order to ensure that such practices do not limit the right of all persons to manifest their religion or belief, either alone or in community with others and in public or private;

(f) To ensure that no official documents are withheld from the individual on the grounds of religion or belief and that everyone has the right to refrain from disclosing information concerning their religious affiliation in such documents against their will;

(g) To ensure, in particular, the right of all persons to worship, assemble or teach in connection with a religion or belief and their right to establish and maintain places for these purposes, and the right of all persons to seek, receive and impart information and ideas in these areas;

(h) To ensure that, in accordance with appropriate national legislation and in conformity with international human rights law, the freedom of all persons and members of groups to establish and maintain religious, charitable or humanitarian institutions is fully respected and protected;

(i) To ensure that all public officials and civil servants, including members of law enforcement bodies, and personnel of detention facilities, the military and educators, in the course of fulfilling their official duties, respect freedom of religion or belief and do not discriminate for reasons based on religion or belief, and that all necessary and appropriate awareness-raising, education or training is provided;

(j) To take all necessary and appropriate action, in conformity with international standards of human rights, to combat hatred, discrimination, intolerance and acts of violence, intimidation and coercion motivated by intolerance based on religion or belief, as well as incitement to hostility and violence, with particular regard to members of religious minorities in all parts of the world;

(k) To promote, through education and other means, mutual understanding, tolerance, non-discrimination and respect in all matters relating to freedom of religion or belief by encouraging, in the society at large, a wider knowledge of different religions and beliefs and of the history, traditions, languages and cultures of the various religious minorities existing within their jurisdiction;

(l) To prevent any distinction, exclusion, restriction or preference based on religion or belief that impairs the recognition, enjoyment or exercise of human rights and fundamental freedoms on an equal basis and to detect signs of intolerance that may lead to discrimination based on religion or belief;

13. *Welcomes and encourages* initiatives by the media to promote tolerance and respect for religious and cultural diversity and the universal promotion and protection of human rights, including freedom of religion or belief;

14. *Stresses* the importance of a continued and strengthened dialogue in all its forms, including among and within religions or beliefs, and with broader participation, including of women, to promote greater tolerance, respect and mutual understanding, and welcomes different initiatives in this regard, including the Alliance of Civilizations initiative and the programmes led by the United Nations Educational, Scientific and Cultural Organization;

15. *Welcomes and encourages* the continuing efforts of all actors in society, including non-governmental organizations and bodies and groups based on religion or belief, to promote the implementation of the Declaration on the Elimination of All Forms of Intolerance and of Discrimination Based on Religion or Belief, and further encourages their work in promoting freedom of religion or belief, in highlighting cases of religious intolerance, discrimination and persecution and in promoting religious tolerance;

16. *Recommends* that States, the United Nations and other actors, including non-governmental organizations and bodies and groups based on religion or belief, in their efforts to promote freedom of religion or belief, ensure the widest possible dissemination of the text of the Declaration on the Elimination of All Forms of Intolerance and of Discrimination Based on Religion or Belief, in as many different languages as possible, and promote its implementation;

17. *Welcomes* the work and the interim report of the Special Rapporteur of the Human Rights Council on freedom of religion or belief, in particular his comments on interreligious communication;

18. *Urges* all Governments to cooperate fully with the Special Rapporteur, to respond favourably to his requests to visit their countries and to provide all information and follow-up necessary for the effective fulfilment of his mandate;

19. *Requests* the Secretary-General to ensure that the Special Rapporteur receives the resources necessary to fully discharge his mandate;

20. *Requests* the Special Rapporteur to submit an interim report to the General Assembly at its sixty-seventh session;

21. *Decides* to consider the question of the elimination of all forms of religious intolerance at its sixty-seventh session under the item entitled "Promotion and protection of human rights".

Combating intolerance, negative stereotyping, and incitement to violence

In 2011, the Human Rights Council considered intolerance, discrimination and violence on the basis of religion or belief in a wider framework of the open public debate of ideas, as well as intercultural and interfaith dialogue at the local, national and international levels.

Human Rights Council action. On 24 March [A/66/53 (res. 16/18)], the Council adopted a resolution on combating intolerance, negative stereotyping and stigmatization of, and discrimination, incitement to violence and violence against, persons based on religion or belief. It called on States to ensure that public functionaries did not discriminate against an individual on the basis of religion or belief; foster religious freedom and pluralism by promoting the ability of members of all religious communities to manifest their religion and contribute to society; encourage representation and participation of individuals, irrespective of their religion, in all sectors of society; counter religious profiling; and promote respect for and protection of places of worship and religious sites, cemeteries and shrines. The Council decided to convene a panel discussion on the issue at its seventeenth (2011) session.

Report of Secretary-General. In response to General Assembly resolution 65/224 [YUN 2010, p. 684], the Secretary-General submitted a September report [A/66/372] on combating defamation of religions, which focused on the implementation of that resolution, including the correlation between defamation of religions and the intersection of religion and race, the upsurge in incitement, intolerance and hatred in many parts of the world and steps taken by States to combat the phenomenon. The report contained information received from 15 States, the United Nations Alliance of Civilizations, OHCHR, UN human rights treaty bodies and special procedures of the Human Rights Council.

Communication. In a 29 March letter [A/65/802-S/2011/210], Tajikistan, on behalf of the Ambassadorial Group of the Organization of the Islamic Conference, transmitted to the Secretary-General the text of the statement issued by the Group at an emergency meeting (New York, 25 March) convened to discuss the burning of a copy of the Holy Koran by two pastors, following a mock trial in a church on 20 March in Florida, United States.

GENERAL ASSEMBLY ACTION

On 19 December [meeting 89], the General Assembly, on the recommendation of the Third Committee [A/66/462/Add.2], adopted **resolution 66/167** without vote [agenda item 69 (*b*)].

Combating intolerance, negative stereotyping, stigmatization, discrimination, incitement to violence and violence against persons, based on religion or belief

The General Assembly,

Reaffirming the commitment made by all States under the Charter of the United Nations to promote and encourage universal respect for and observance of all human rights and fundamental freedoms without distinction as to, inter alia, religion or belief,

Reaffirming also the obligation of States to prohibit discrimination on the basis of religion or belief and to implement measures to guarantee the equal and effective protection of the law,

Reaffirming further that all human rights are universal, indivisible, interdependent and interrelated,

Reaffirming that the International Covenant on Civil and Political Rights provides, inter alia, that everyone shall have the right to freedom of thought, conscience and religion or belief, which shall include freedom to have or to adopt a religion or belief of one's choice and freedom, either alone or in community with others and in public or private, to manifest one's religion or belief in worship, observance, practice and teaching,

Welcoming Human Rights Council resolution 16/18 of 24 March 2011,

Reaffirming the positive role that the exercise of the right to freedom of opinion and expression and the full respect for the freedom to seek, receive and impart information can play in strengthening democracy and combating religious intolerance,

Deeply concerned about incidents of intolerance, discrimination and violence against persons based on their religion or belief in all regions of the world,

Deploring any advocacy of discrimination or violence on the basis of religion or belief,

Strongly deploring all acts of violence against persons on the basis of their religion or belief, as well as any such acts directed against their homes, businesses, properties, schools, cultural centres or places of worship,

Strongly deploring, further, all attacks on and in religious places, sites and shrines in violation of international law, in particular human rights law and international humanitarian law, including any deliberate destruction of relics and monuments,

Concerned about actions that wilfully exploit tensions or target individuals on the basis of their religion or belief,

Noting with deep concern the instances of intolerance, discrimination and acts of violence occurring in many parts of the world, including cases motivated by discrimination against persons belonging to religious minorities, in addition to the negative projection of the followers of religions and the enforcement of measures that specifically discriminate against persons on the basis of religion or belief,

Expressing concern at manifestations of intolerance based on religion or belief that can generate hatred and violence among individuals composing different nations, and in this regard emphasizing the importance of respect for religious and cultural diversity, as well as interfaith and intercultural dialogue, which contribute to promoting a culture of tolerance and respect among individuals, societies and nations,

Recognizing the valuable contribution of people of all religions or beliefs to humanity and the contribution that dialogue among religious groups can make towards an improved awareness and understanding of the common values shared by all humankind,

Underlining the fact that States, regional organizations, non-governmental organizations, religious bodies and the media have an important role to play in promoting tolerance and respect for religious and cultural diversity and in the universal promotion and protection of human rights, including freedom of religion or belief,

Underlining also the importance of education in the promotion of tolerance, which involves the acceptance by the public of and its respect for religious and cultural diversity, including with regard to religious expression, and underlining further the fact that education, in particular at school, should contribute in a meaningful way to promoting tolerance and the elimination of discrimination based on religion or belief,

Recognizing that working together to enhance the implementation of existing legal regimes that protect individuals against discrimination and hate crimes, increase interfaith and intercultural efforts and expand human rights education is an important first step in combating incidents of intolerance, discrimination and violence against individuals on the basis of religion or belief,

Welcoming the establishment of the King Abdullah Bin Abdulaziz International Centre for Interreligious and Intercultural Dialogue in Vienna, initiated by King Abdullah of Saudi Arabia, on the basis of the purposes and principles enshrined in the Universal Declaration of Human Rights, and acknowledging the important role that the Centre is expected to play as a platform for the enhancement of interreligious and intercultural dialogue,

Welcoming also, in this regard, all international, regional and national initiatives aimed at promoting interreligious, intercultural and interfaith harmony and combating discrimination against individuals on the basis of religion or belief,

1. *Expresses deep concern* at the continued serious instances of derogatory stereotyping, negative profiling and stigmatization of persons based on their religion or belief, as well as programmes and agendas pursued by extremist organizations and groups aimed at creating and perpetuating negative stereotypes about religious groups, in particular when condoned by Governments;

2. *Expresses concern* that the number of incidents of religious intolerance, discrimination and related violence, as well as of negative stereotyping of individuals on the basis of religion or belief, continues to rise around the world, condemns, in this context, any advocacy of religious hatred against individuals that constitutes incitement to discrimination, hostility or violence, and urges States to take effective measures, as set forth in the present resolution and consistent with their obligations under international human rights law, to address and combat such incidents;

3. *Condemns* any advocacy of religious hatred that constitutes incitement to discrimination, hostility or violence, whether it involves the use of print, audiovisual or electronic media or any other means;

4. *Recognizes* that the open public debate of ideas, as well as interfaith and intercultural dialogue, at the local, national and international levels can be among the best protections against religious intolerance and can play a positive role in strengthening democracy and combating religious hatred, and expresses its conviction that a continuing dialogue on these issues can help to overcome existing misperceptions;

5. *Reiterates* the call made by the Secretary General of the Organization of the Islamic Conference at the fifteenth session of the Human Rights Council upon all States to take the following actions to foster a domestic environment of religious tolerance, peace and respect:

(*a*) Encouraging the creation of collaborative networks to build mutual understanding, promoting dialogue and inspiring constructive action towards shared policy goals and the pursuit of tangible outcomes, such as servicing projects in the fields of education, health, conflict prevention, employment, integration and media education;

(*b*) Creating an appropriate mechanism within Governments to, inter alia, identify and address potential areas of tension between members of different religious communities, and assisting with conflict prevention and mediation;

(*c*) Encouraging the training of Government officials in effective outreach strategies;

(*d*) Encouraging the efforts of leaders to discuss within their communities the causes of discrimination, and developing strategies to counter those causes;

(*e*) Speaking out against intolerance, including advocacy of religious hatred that constitutes incitement to discrimination, hostility or violence;

(*f*) Adopting measures to criminalize the incitement to imminent violence based on religion or belief;

(*g*) Understanding the need to combat denigration and the negative religious stereotyping of persons, as well as incitement to religious hatred, by strategizing and harmonizing actions at the local, national, regional and international levels through, inter alia, education and awareness-raising;

(*h*) Recognizing that the open, constructive and respectful debate of ideas, as well as interfaith and intercultural dialogue at the local, national and international levels, can play a positive role in combating religious hatred, incitement and violence;

6. *Calls upon* all States:

(*a*) To take effective measures to ensure that public functionaries, in the conduct of their public duties, do not discriminate against an individual on the basis of religion or belief;

(b) To foster religious freedom and pluralism by promoting the ability of members of all religious communities to manifest their religion and to contribute openly and on an equal footing to society;

(c) To encourage the representation and meaningful participation of individuals, irrespective of their religion or belief, in all sectors of society;

(d) To make a strong effort to counter religious profiling, which is understood to be the invidious use of religion as a criterion in conducting questioning, searches and other law enforcement investigative procedures;

7. *Also calls upon* all States to adopt measures and policies to promote the full respect for and protection of places of worship and religious sites, cemeteries and shrines, and to take measures in cases where they are vulnerable to vandalism or destruction;

8. *Calls for* strengthened international efforts to foster a global dialogue for the promotion of a culture of tolerance and peace at all levels, based on respect for human rights and diversity of religions and beliefs;

9. *Encourages* all States to consider providing updates on efforts made in this regard as part of ongoing reporting to the Office of the United Nations High Commissioner for Human Rights, and in this respect requests the United Nations High Commissioner for Human Rights to include those updates in her reports to the Human Rights Council;

10. *Requests* the Secretary-General to submit to the General Assembly at its sixty-seventh session a report on steps taken by States to combat intolerance, negative stereotyping, stigmatization, discrimination, incitement to violence and violence against persons, based on religion or belief, as set forth in the present resolution.

Right to self-determination

Report of Secretary-General. In response to General Assembly resolution 65/201 [YUN 2010, p. 688], the Secretary-General in July submitted a report [A/66/172] on the question of the universal realization of the right of peoples to self-determination. The report summarized developments relating to the consideration of that subject by the Human Rights Council and outlined the jurisprudence of the Human Rights Committee and the Committee on Economic, Social and Cultural Rights on the treaty-based human rights norms relating to the realization of that right. It also made references to the 9 January referendum by which 98.83 per cent of the people of South Sudan voted to secede from the rest of the Sudan (see p. 189) and the situation concerning Western Sahara, where the parties to the conflict, Morocco and the Frente Polisario, continued to meet at regular intervals, yet no progress had been made on the core issues of the future status of Western Sahara and the means by which the self-determination of the people of Western Sahara would occur (see p. 289).

GENERAL ASSEMBLY ACTION

On 19 December [meeting 89], the General Assembly, on the recommendation of the Third Committee [A/66/461], adopted **resolution 66/145** without vote [agenda item 68].

Universal realization of the right of peoples to self-determination

The General Assembly,

Reaffirming the importance, for the effective guarantee and observance of human rights, of the universal realization of the right of peoples to self-determination enshrined in the Charter of the United Nations and embodied in the International Covenants on Human Rights, as well as in the Declaration on the Granting of Independence to Colonial Countries and Peoples contained in General Assembly resolution 1514(XV) of 14 December 1960,

Welcoming the progressive exercise of the right to self-determination by peoples under colonial, foreign or alien occupation and their emergence into sovereign statehood and independence,

Deeply concerned at the continuation of acts or threats of foreign military intervention and occupation that are threatening to suppress, or have already suppressed, the right to self-determination of peoples and nations,

Expressing grave concern that, as a consequence of the persistence of such actions, millions of people have been and are being uprooted from their homes as refugees and displaced persons, and emphasizing the urgent need for concerted international action to alleviate their condition,

Recalling the relevant resolutions regarding the violation of the right of peoples to self-determination and other human rights as a result of foreign military intervention, aggression and occupation, adopted by the Commission on Human Rights at its sixty-first and previous sessions,

Reaffirming its previous resolutions on the universal realization of the right of peoples to self-determination, including resolution 65/201 of 21 December 2010,

Reaffirming also its resolution 55/2 of 8 September 2000, containing the United Nations Millennium Declaration, and recalling its resolution 60/1 of 16 September 2005, containing the 2005 World Summit Outcome, which, inter alia, upheld the right to self-determination of peoples under colonial domination and foreign occupation,

Taking note of the report of the Secretary-General on the right of peoples to self-determination,

1. *Reaffirms* that the universal realization of the right of all peoples, including those under colonial, foreign and alien domination, to self-determination is a fundamental condition for the effective guarantee and observance of human rights and for the preservation and promotion of such rights;

2. *Declares its firm opposition* to acts of foreign military intervention, aggression and occupation, since these have resulted in the suppression of the right of peoples to self-determination and other human rights in certain parts of the world;

3. *Calls upon* those States responsible to cease immediately their military intervention in and occupation of foreign countries and territories and all acts of repression, discrimination, exploitation and maltreatment, in particular the brutal and inhuman methods reportedly employed for the execution of those acts against the peoples concerned;

4. *Deplores* the plight of millions of refugees and displaced persons who have been uprooted as a result of the aforementioned acts, and reaffirms their right to return to their homes voluntarily in safety and with honour;

5. *Requests* the Human Rights Council to continue to give special attention to violations of human rights, especially the right to self-determination, resulting from foreign military intervention, aggression or occupation;

6. *Requests* the Secretary-General to report on the question to the General Assembly at its sixty-seventh session under the item entitled "Right of peoples to self-determination".

On the same date, the General Assembly took note of the Secretary-General's report on the right of peoples to self-determination (**decision 66/536**).

Right of Palestinians to self-determination

During the year, the General Assembly reaffirmed the right of the Palestinian people to self-determination, including the right to their independent State of Palestine, as well as the right of all States in the region to live in peace within secure and internationally recognized borders. States and UN system bodies were urged to assist Palestinians in the early realization of the right.

Human Rights Council action. On 25 March [A/66/53 (res. 16/30)], by a recorded vote of 45 to 1, with no abstentions, the Council urged Member States and UN system bodies to support and assist the Palestinian people in the early realization of their right to self-determination.

GENERAL ASSEMBLY ACTION

On 19 December [meeting 89], the General Assembly, on the recommendation of the Third Committee [A/66/461], adopted **resolution 66/146** by recorded vote (182-7-3) [agenda item 68].

The right of the Palestinian people to self-determination

The General Assembly,

Aware that the development of friendly relations among nations, based on respect for the principle of equal rights and self-determination of peoples, is among the purposes and principles of the United Nations, as defined in the Charter,

Recalling, in this regard, its resolution 2625(XXV) of 24 October 1970 entitled "Declaration on Principles of International Law concerning Friendly Relations and Cooperation among States in accordance with the Charter of the United Nations",

Bearing in mind the International Covenants on Human Rights, the Universal Declaration of Human Rights, the Declaration on the Granting of Independence to Colonial Countries and Peoples and the Vienna Declaration and Programme of Action adopted at the World Conference on Human Rights on 25 June 1993,

Recalling the Declaration on the Occasion of the Fiftieth Anniversary of the United Nations,

Recalling also the United Nations Millennium Declaration,

Recalling further the advisory opinion rendered on 9 July 2004 by the International Court of Justice on the *Legal Consequences of the Construction of a Wall in the Occupied Palestinian Territory*, and noting in particular the reply of the Court, including on the right of peoples to self-determination, which is a right *erga omnes*,

Recalling the conclusion of the Court, in its advisory opinion of 9 July 2004, that the construction of the wall by Israel, the occupying Power, in the Occupied Palestinian Territory, including East Jerusalem, along with measures previously taken, severely impedes the right of the Palestinian people to self-determination,

Expressing the urgent need for the resumption and accelerated advancement of negotiations within the Middle East peace process, based on the relevant resolutions of the United Nations, the Madrid terms of reference, including the principle of land for peace, the Arab Peace Initiative and the Quartet road map to a permanent two-State solution to the Israeli-Palestinian conflict, and for the speedy achievement of a just, lasting and comprehensive peace settlement between the Palestinian and Israeli sides,

Stressing the need for respect for and preservation of the territorial unity, contiguity and integrity of all of the Occupied Palestinian Territory, including East Jerusalem, and recalling in this regard its resolution 58/292 of 6 May 2004,

Recalling its resolution 65/202 of 21 December 2010,

Affirming the right of all States in the region to live in peace within secure and internationally recognized borders,

1. *Reaffirms* the right of the Palestinian people to self-determination, including the right to their independent State of Palestine;

2. *Urges* all States and the specialized agencies and organizations of the United Nations system to continue to support and assist the Palestinian people in the early realization of their right to self-determination.

RECORDED VOTE ON RESOLUTION 66/146:

In favour: Afghanistan, Albania, Algeria, Andorra, Angola, Antigua and Barbuda, Argentina, Armenia, Australia, Austria, Azerbaijan, Bahamas, Bahrain, Bangladesh, Barbados, Belarus, Belgium, Belize, Benin, Bhutan, Bolivia, Bosnia and Herzegovina, Botswana, Brazil, Brunei Darussalam, Bulgaria, Burkina Faso, Burundi, Cambodia, Cape Verde, Central African Republic, Chad, Chile, China, Colombia, Comoros, Congo, Costa Rica, Côte d'Ivoire, Croatia, Cuba, Cyprus, Czech Republic, Democratic People's Republic of Korea, Democratic Republic of the Congo, Denmark, Djibouti, Dominica, Dominican Republic, Ecuador, Egypt, El Salvador, Equatorial Guinea, Eritrea, Estonia, Ethiopia, Fiji, Finland, France, Gabon, Gambia, Georgia, Germany, Ghana, Greece, Grenada, Guatemala, Guinea, Guinea-Bissau, Guyana, Haiti, Honduras, Hungary, Iceland, India, Indonesia, Iran, Iraq, Ireland, Italy, Jamaica, Japan, Jordan, Kazakhstan, Kenya, Kuwait, Kyrgyzstan, Lao People's Democratic Republic, Latvia, Lebanon, Lesotho, Liberia, Libya, Liechtenstein, Lithuania, Luxembourg, Madagascar, Malawi, Malaysia, Maldives, Mali, Malta, Mauritania, Mauritius, Mexico, Monaco, Mongolia, Montenegro, Morocco, Mozambique, Myanmar, Namibia, Nepal, Netherlands, New Zealand, Nicaragua, Niger, Nigeria, Norway, Oman, Pakistan, Panama, Papua New Guinea, Paraguay, Peru, Philippines, Poland, Portugal, Qatar, Republic of Korea, Republic of Moldova, Romania, Russian Federation, Rwanda, Saint Kitts and Nevis, Saint Lucia, Saint Vincent and the Grenadines, Samoa, San Marino, Sao Tome and Principe, Saudi Arabia, Senegal, Serbia,

Seychelles, Sierra Leone, Singapore, Slovakia, Slovenia, Solomon Islands, Somalia, South Africa, Spain, Sri Lanka, Sudan, Suriname, Swaziland, Sweden, Switzerland, Syrian Arab Republic, Tajikistan, Thailand, the former Yugoslav Republic of Macedonia, Timor-Leste, Togo, Trinidad and Tobago, Tunisia, Turkey, Turkmenistan, Tuvalu, Uganda, Ukraine, United Arab Emirates, United Kingdom, United Republic of Tanzania, Uruguay, Uzbekistan, Vanuatu, Venezuela, Viet Nam, Yemen, Zambia, Zimbabwe.

Against: Canada, Israel, Marshall Islands, Micronesia, Nauru, Palau, United States.

Abstaining: Cameroon, South Sudan, Tonga.

Mercenaries

Reports of Working Group. In a July report [A/HRC/18/32], the Working Group on the use of mercenaries as a means of violating human rights and impeding the exercise of the right of peoples to self-determination described activities undertaken since its last report [YUN 2010, p. 689], covering communications sent between 18 April 2010 and 30 April 2011, as well as its activities over the previous six years. The Working Group identified challenges for the mandate, including new forms of mercenary activities; discussed the need for an international regulatory framework for private and military security companies (PMSCs) to ensure protection of human rights; and analysed the relationship between the draft convention elaborated by the Working Group, the Montreux Document on pertinent international legal obligations, and good practices for States related to operations of PMSCs during armed conflict, as well as the International Code of Conduct for Private Security Service Providers for those companies. The Working Group recommended that States adopt legislation to regulate PMSCs, ensure accountability of PMSCs for human rights violations, and provide a remedy for victims.

In response to a Human Rights Commission request [YUN 2005, p. 788], the Secretary-General in August [A/66/317] transmitted the Working Group's report, covering recent activities of mercenaries and PMSCs. As the events in Côte d'Ivoire (see p. 140) and the Libyan Arab Jamahiriya (see p. 266) had shown, mercenaries allegedly continued to be recruited and active. The Working Group was concerned about the reported involvement of mercenaries in serious human rights violations. Although the Working Group had seen some positive developments concerning PMSCs in several countries, as well as progress in efforts to prosecute employees of PMSCs for human rights violations, it remained concerned about the lack of transparency and accountability of those companies, and the absence of an international regulatory framework to monitor their activities. The report reviewed the Working Group's activities, including discussions held during the expert seminar on the State monopoly on the legitimate use of force (New York, 6–7 July), and took stock of its activities during the previous six years,

particularly a draft convention on PMSCs, which was being considered by member States.

Mission report. After its visit to Iraq (12–16 June) [A/HRC/18/32/Add.4], the Working Group learned that the number of incidents involving PMSCs had decreased, yet Iraq continued to grapple with the grant of legal immunity extended to private security contractors under Order 17 issued by the Coalition Provisional Authority, which prevented prosecutions in Iraqi courts. The Working Group expressed concern about the lack of accountability for violations committed between 2003 and 2009 and recalled that the victims were still waiting for justice. Four years after Nissour Square shooting, the case against the alleged perpetrators was still pending in United States courts. The Working Group made recommendations for consideration by Iraq and the United States.

Working Group. The open-ended intergovernmental working group to consider the possibility of elaborating an international regulatory framework on the regulation, monitoring and oversight of the activities of PMSCs held its first session (Geneva, 23–27 May) [A/HRC/WG.10/1/CRP.2]. At the session, the Working Group considered law and practice in relation to PMSCs, national legislation and practices, elements of an international regulatory framework, and accountability and right to an effective remedy for victims. The Working Group was established by the Human Rights Council in 2010 [YUN 2010, p. 690].

Human Rights Council action. On 29 September [A/66/53/Add.1 (res. 18/4)], the Council, by a recorded vote of 31 to 11, with 4 abstentions, requested States to exercise the utmost vigilance against any kind of recruitment, training, hiring or financing of mercenaries by private companies offering international military consultancy and security services, and to impose a ban on such companies intervening in armed conflicts or actions to destabilize constitutional regimes; noted the summary of the first session of the open-ended intergovernmental working group to consider the possibility of elaborating an international regulatory framework on the regulation, monitoring and oversight of the activities of PMSCs; and requested the Working Group to report at the sixty-seventh (2012) session of the General Assembly and the twenty-first (2012) session of the Council.

International Convention

The number of States parties to the 1989 International Convention against the Recruitment, Use, Financing and Training of Mercenaries remained at 32 as at 31 December. The Convention was adopted by the General Assembly in resolution 44/34 [YUN 1989, p. 825] and entered into force in 2001 [YUN 2001, p. 632].

GENERAL ASSEMBLY ACTION

On 19 December [meeting 89], the General Assembly, on the recommendation of the Third Committee [A/66/461], adopted **resolution 66/147** by recorded vote (130-53-6) [agenda item 68].

Use of mercenaries as a means of violating human rights and impeding the exercise of the right of peoples to self-determination

The General Assembly,

Recalling all of its previous resolutions on the subject, including resolution 65/203 of 21 December 2010, and Human Rights Council resolutions 15/12 of 30 September 2010, 15/26 of 1 October 2010 and 18/4 of 29 September 2011, as well as all resolutions adopted by the Commission on Human Rights in this regard,

Recalling also all of its relevant resolutions in which, inter alia, it condemned any State that permitted or tolerated the recruitment, financing, training, assembly, transit or use of mercenaries with the objective of overthrowing the Governments of States Members of the United Nations, especially those of developing countries, or of fighting against national liberation movements, and recalling further the relevant resolutions and international instruments adopted by the General Assembly, the Security Council, the Economic and Social Council and the Organization of African Unity, inter alia, the Organization of African Unity Convention for the elimination of mercenarism in Africa, as well as by the African Union,

Reaffirming the purposes and principles enshrined in the Charter of the United Nations concerning the strict observance of the principles of sovereign equality, political independence, the territorial integrity of States, the self-determination of peoples, the non-use of force or of the threat of use of force in international relations and non-interference in affairs within the domestic jurisdiction of States,

Reaffirming also that, by virtue of the principle of self-determination, all peoples have the right freely to determine their political status and to pursue their economic, social and cultural development and that every State has the duty to respect this right in accordance with the provisions of the Charter,

Reaffirming further the Declaration on Principles of International Law concerning Friendly Relations and Cooperation among States in accordance with the Charter of the United Nations,

Welcoming the establishment of the open-ended intergovernmental Working Group of the Human Rights Council with the mandate of considering the possibility of elaborating an international regulatory framework, including the option of elaborating a legally binding instrument on the regulation, monitoring and oversight of the activities of private military and security companies,

Alarmed and concerned at the danger that the activities of mercenaries constitute to peace and security in developing countries, in particular in Africa and in small States,

Deeply concerned at the loss of life, the substantial damage to property and the negative effects on the policy and economies of affected countries resulting from criminal mercenary activities,

Extremely alarmed and concerned about recent mercenary activities in some developing countries in various parts of the world, including in areas of armed conflict, and the threat they pose to the integrity of and respect for the constitutional order of the affected countries,

Concerned at the alleged involvement of mercenaries, as well as employees of some private military and security companies with mercenary-related activities, in serious human rights violations, including summary executions, enforced disappearances, rape, torture, cruel, inhuman or degrading treatment, arbitrary arrests and detentions, arson, pillaging and looting,

Convinced that a comprehensive, legally binding international regulatory instrument is important for regulating private military and security companies and, in this regard, for taking measures to ensure their accountability for human rights violations and monitor their activities,

Convinced also that, notwithstanding the way in which they are used or the form that they take to acquire some semblance of legitimacy, mercenaries or mercenary-related activities are a threat to peace, security and the self-determination of peoples and an obstacle to the enjoyment of all human rights by peoples,

1. *Takes note with appreciation* of the report of the Working Group on the use of mercenaries as a means of violating human rights and impeding the exercise of the right of peoples to self-determination, and expresses its appreciation for the work of the experts of the Working Group;

2. *Reaffirms* that the use of mercenaries and their recruitment, financing and training are causes for grave concern to all States and violate the purposes and principles enshrined in the Charter of the United Nations;

3. *Recognizes* that armed conflict, terrorism, arms trafficking and covert operations by third Powers, inter alia, encourage the demand for mercenaries on the global market;

4. *Urges once again* all States to take the steps necessary and to exercise the utmost vigilance against the menace posed by the activities of mercenaries and to take legislative measures to ensure that their territories and other territories under their control, as well as their nationals, are not used for the recruitment, assembly, financing, training, protection or transit of mercenaries for the planning of activities designed to impede the right of peoples to self-determination, to destabilize or overthrow the Government of any State or to dismember or impair, totally or in part, the territorial integrity or political unity of sovereign and independent States conducting themselves in compliance with the right of peoples to self-determination;

5. *Requests* all States to exercise the utmost vigilance against any kind of recruitment, training, hiring or financing of mercenaries by private companies offering international military consultancy and security services, as well as to impose a specific ban on such companies intervening in armed conflicts or actions to destabilize constitutional regimes;

6. *Encourages* States that import the military assistance, consultancy and security services provided by private companies to establish regulatory national mechanisms for the registering and licensing of those companies in order to ensure that imported services provided by those private companies neither impede the enjoyment of human rights nor violate human rights in the recipient country;

7. *Emphasizes its utmost concern* about the impact of the activities of private military and security companies on the enjoyment of human rights, in particular when operat-

ing in armed conflicts, and notes that private military and security companies and their personnel are rarely held accountable for violations of human rights;

8. *Calls upon* all States that have not yet done so to consider taking the action necessary to accede to or ratify the International Convention against the Recruitment, Use, Financing and Training of Mercenaries;

9. *Welcomes* the cooperation extended by those countries that received a visit by the Working Group and the adoption by some States of national legislation that restricts the recruitment, assembly, financing, training and transit of mercenaries;

10. *Condemns* recent mercenary activities in developing countries in various parts of the world, in particular in areas of conflict, and the threat they pose to the integrity of and respect for the constitutional order of those countries and the exercise of the right of their peoples to self-determination, and stresses the importance for the Working Group of looking into sources and root causes, as well as the political motivations of mercenaries and for mercenary-related activities;

11. *Calls upon* States to investigate the possibility of mercenary involvement whenever and wherever criminal acts of a terrorist nature occur and to bring to trial those found responsible or to consider their extradition, if so requested, in accordance with domestic law and applicable bilateral or international treaties;

12. *Condemns* any form of impunity granted to perpetrators of mercenary activities and to those responsible for the use, recruitment, financing and training of mercenaries, and urges all States, in accordance with their obligations under international law, to bring them, without distinction, to justice;

13. *Calls upon* Member States, in accordance with their obligations under international law, to cooperate with and assist the judicial prosecution of those accused of mercenary activities in transparent, open and fair trials;

14. *Requests* the Working Group to continue the work already done by the previous Special Rapporteurs on the strengthening of the international legal framework for the prevention and sanction of the recruitment, use, financing and training of mercenaries, taking into account the proposal for a new legal definition of a mercenary drafted by the Special Rapporteur in his report to the Commission on Human Rights at its sixtieth session, including the elaboration and presentation of concrete proposals on possible complementary and new standards aimed at filling existing gaps, as well as general guidelines or basic principles encouraging the further protection of human rights, in particular the right of peoples to self-determination, while facing current and emergent threats posed by mercenaries or mercenary-related activities;

15. *Requests* the Office of the United Nations High Commissioner for Human Rights, as a matter of priority, to publicize the adverse effects of the activities of mercenaries on the right of peoples to self-determination and, when requested and where necessary, to render advisory services to States that are affected by those activities;

16. *Expresses its appreciation* to the Office of the High Commissioner for its support for the holding of the five regional governmental consultations on traditional and new forms of mercenary activities as a means of violating human rights and impeding the exercise of the right of peoples to self-determination, in particular regarding the effects of the activities of private military and security companies on the enjoyment of human rights;

17. *Notes with appreciation* the work of the Working Group on the elaboration of concrete principles on the regulation of private companies offering military assistance, consultancy and other military security-related services on the international market, which it carried out after country visits and through the process of regional consultations, and in consultation with academics and intergovernmental and non-governmental organizations, and also notes its work on the draft convention on the regulation, monitoring and oversight of private military and security companies for consideration by Member States;

18. *Takes note* of the summary of the first session of the open-ended intergovernmental Working Group of the Human Rights Council to consider the possibility of elaborating an international regulatory framework on the regulation, monitoring and oversight of the activities of private military and security companies, expresses satisfaction regarding the participation of experts, including the members of the Working Group on the use of mercenaries, as resource persons at that session, and requests the Working Group on the use of mercenaries and other experts to continue to participate;

19. *Encourages* Member States to continue considering the proposal of the Working Group on the use of mercenaries regarding a possible convention for regulating private military and security companies, and recommends to all Member States, including those confronted with the phenomenon of private military and security companies, as contracting States, States of operations, home States or States whose nationals are employed to work for a private military and security company, to contribute to the work of the open-ended intergovernmental Working Group, taking into account the initial work done by the Working Group on the use of mercenaries;

20. *Urges* all States to cooperate fully with the Working Group on the use of mercenaries in the fulfilment of its mandate;

21. *Requests* the Secretary-General and the United Nations High Commissioner for Human Rights to provide the Working Group with all the assistance and support necessary for the fulfilment of its mandate, both professional and financial, including through the promotion of cooperation between the Working Group and other components of the United Nations system that deal with countering mercenary-related activities, in order to meet the demands of its current and future activities;

22. *Requests* the Working Group to consult States and intergovernmental and non-governmental organizations in the implementation of the present resolution and to report, with specific recommendations, to the General Assembly at its sixty-seventh session its findings on the use of mercenaries to undermine the enjoyment of all human rights and to impede the exercise of the right of peoples to self-determination;

23. *Decides* to consider at its sixty-seventh session the question of the use of mercenaries as a means of violating human rights and impeding the exercise of the right of peoples to self-determination under the item entitled "Right of peoples to self-determination".

RECORDED VOTE ON RESOLUTION 66/147:

In favour: Afghanistan, Algeria, Angola, Antigua and Barbuda, Argentina, Armenia, Azerbaijan, Bahamas, Bahrain, Bangladesh, Barbados, Belarus, Belize, Benin, Bhutan, Bolivia, Botswana, Brazil, Brunei Darussalam, Burkina Faso, Burundi, Cambodia, Cameroon, Cape Verde, Central African Republic, Chad, China, Comoros, Congo, Costa Rica, Côte d'Ivoire, Cuba, Democratic People's Republic of Korea, Democratic Republic of the Congo, Djibouti, Dominica, Dominican Republic, Ecuador, Egypt, El Salvador, Equatorial Guinea, Eritrea, Ethiopia, Gabon, Gambia, Ghana, Grenada, Guatemala, Guinea, Guinea-Bissau, Guyana, Haiti, Honduras, India, Indonesia, Iran, Iraq, Jamaica, Jordan, Kazakhstan, Kenya, Kuwait, Kyrgyzstan, Lao People's Democratic Republic, Lebanon, Lesotho, Liberia, Libya, Madagascar, Malawi, Malaysia, Maldives, Mali, Mauritania, Mauritius, Mongolia, Morocco, Mozambique, Myanmar, Namibia, Nepal, Nicaragua, Niger, Nigeria, Oman, Pakistan, Panama, Papua New Guinea, Paraguay, Peru, Philippines, Qatar, Russian Federation, Rwanda, Saint Kitts and Nevis, Saint Lucia, Saint Vincent and the Grenadines, Samoa, Sao Tome and Principe, Saudi Arabia, Senegal, Seychelles, Sierra Leone, Singapore, Solomon Islands, Somalia, South Africa, Sri Lanka, Sudan, Suriname, Swaziland, Syrian Arab Republic, Tajikistan, Thailand, Timor-Leste, Togo, Trinidad and Tobago, Tunisia, Tuvalu, Uganda, United Arab Emirates, United Republic of Tanzania, Uruguay, Uzbekistan, Vanuatu, Venezuela, Viet Nam, Yemen, Zambia, Zimbabwe.

Against: Albania, Andorra, Australia, Austria, Belgium, Bosnia and Herzegovina, Bulgaria, Canada, Croatia, Cyprus, Czech Republic, Denmark, Estonia, Finland, France, Georgia, Germany, Greece, Hungary, Iceland, Ireland, Israel, Italy, Japan, Latvia, Liechtenstein, Lithuania, Luxembourg, Malta, Marshall Islands, Micronesia, Monaco, Montenegro, Netherlands, New Zealand, Norway, Palau, Poland, Portugal, Republic of Korea, Republic of Moldova, Romania, San Marino, Serbia, Slovakia, Slovenia, Spain, Sweden, the former Yugoslav Republic of Macedonia, Turkey, Ukraine, United Kingdom, United States.

Abstaining: Chile, Colombia, Fiji, Mexico, Switzerland, Tonga.

Rule of law, democracy and human rights

Administration of justice

In 2011, the Human Rights Council continued its consideration of the question of human rights in the administration of justice, including the reports issued in 2010 by the Secretary-General and the High Commissioner [YUN 2010, p. 693]; the latter report also addressed juvenile justice.

Human Rights Council action. On 29 September [A/66/53/Add.1 (res. 18/12)], the Council adopted a resolution on human rights in the administration of justice, in particular juvenile justice, which called on States to ensure full implementation of UN standards on human rights in the administration of justice; urged them to integrate children's issues in their rule of law efforts, and to develop and implement a juvenile justice policy to prevent and address juvenile delinquency; called on States to consider establishing mechanisms to monitor and safeguard the rights of children, including children within their criminal justice systems; urged States to take measures to prevent and respond to violence against children within the justice system; invited OHCHR to collaborate with the United Nations Office on Drugs and Crime and the Special Representative of the Secretary-General on Violence against Children in organizing an expert consultation on prevention of and responses to violence against children within the juvenile justice system and to report thereon; and requested the High Commissioner to report on the protection of the human rights of juveniles deprived of their liberty at the Council's twenty-first (2012) session.

Transitional justice

Report of High Commissioner. Pursuant to a Human Rights Council request [YUN 2009, p. 685], the High Commissioner in July submitted a report [A/HRC/18/23] on human rights and transitional justice, which provided an update on OHCHR activities in that context, including by the human rights components of UN peacekeeping and political missions. OHCHR had supported transitional justice programmes in more than 20 countries worldwide in the design and implementation of transitional justice processes and capacity-building and partnership. The report also contained an analysis of the relationship between disarmament, demobilization and reintegration and transitional justice. The High Commissioner stated that the two processes were interrelated and coordination between them was essential for facilitating their coherence and mutual reinforcement.

Right to the truth

OHCHR report. Pursuant to a Human Rights Council request [YUN 2009, p. 685], OHCHR convened a seminar on the importance of archives as a means to guarantee the right to the truth (Geneva, 24–25 February) and submitted a report [A/HRC/17/21] on its outcome. The seminar's discussion focused on four themes: the preservation of archives and the right to the truth; using archives in criminal accountability processes; using archives in non-judicial truth-seeking processes; and the placement of archives of repressive rule. The report outlined the importance of archives to the ability of victims to realize their right to the truth, to judicial accountability and non-judicial truth-seeking processes, and for reparations. It recorded the views of participants regarding States' duties to protect and preserve information concerning human rights violations and States' obligations to ensure the preservation of archives and to enact laws to govern the management and access to archives. The report also presented possible initiatives for the preservation and management of archives during transitional periods.

International Day for the Right to the Truth. In accordance with General Assembly resolution 65/196 [YUN 2010, p. 695], which proclaimed 24 March as the International Day for the Right to the Truth concerning Gross Human Rights Violations and for the Dignity of Victims, the Secretary-General submitted a report [A/66/335] on the observance of the first International Day in 2011. The report provided an overview of the right to the truth and summarized information provided by States, the UN system and other international organizations, and civil society entities on activities commemorating the International Day. El Salvador hosted a panel discussion at UN Headquarters in New York, as well as a tribute in Geneva, dedicated to the memory and legacy of Monsignor Oscar Arnulfo Romero, of El Salvador, who was engaged in the promotion and protection of human rights in the country, particularly those of the most vulnerable populations, and had become a global symbol for human rights and a reminder that the violations he denounced should never be repeated. The International Day coincided with the thirty-first anniversary of the assassination of Monsignor Romero [YUN 1980, p. 828]. The report concluded that there was a need for greater awareness about the International Day at the global, national and local levels in order to enhance its observance.

In an addendum [A/66/335/Add.1] to the report, Argentina and Guatemala provided information on activities carried out in their countries in connection with the commemoration of the International Day.

The General Assembly took note of the report on 19 December (**decision 66/533**).

Truth, justice, reparation and non-recurrence

Establishment of new mandate. On 29 September [A/66/53/Add.1 (res. 18/7)], the Council decided to appoint, for a period of three years, a special rapporteur on the promotion of truth, justice, reparation and guarantees of non-recurrence, whose tasks would include gathering information on national situations, including on normative frameworks, national practices and experiences relating to the promotion of truth, justice, reparation and guarantees of non-recurrence in addressing gross violations of human rights and serious violations of international humanitarian law; studying trends, developments and challenges and making recommendations thereon; identifying, exchanging and promoting good practices and lessons learned; undertaking a study on the ways and means to implement the issues pertaining to the mandate; raising awareness concerning the value of a systematic approach when dealing with gross violations of human rights and serious violations of international humanitarian law, and making recommendations in that regard; and reporting annually to the Council and the General Assembly.

Independence of judges and lawyers

Reports of Special Rapporteur. In a report issued in April [A/HRC/17/30 & Corr.1], the Special Rapporteur on the independence of judges and lawyers, Gabriela Knaul (Brazil), reported on her activities in 2010 and focused on aspects of the relationship between gender and the judiciary, within the broader context of the administration of justice. The report addressed major obstacles to women's access to justice, including the feminization of poverty, as well as laws, policies and practices that discriminated against women; elaborated on the conditions required for the effective realization of women's rights to access to justice and for developing a gender-sensitive judiciary; and discussed the role of the judiciary in advancing women's human rights. The Rapporteur presented a number of good practices and made recommendations to Governments, the international community and other stakeholders.

An addendum of 19 May [A/HRC/17/30/Add.1] summarized 97 communications sent to 45 governmental authorities between 16 March 2010 and 15 March 2011 and replies received between 1 May 2010 and 10 May 2011.

In response to Human Rights Council resolution 17/2 (see p. 687), the Secretary-General in August transmitted to the General Assembly the interim report [A/66/289] of the Special Rapporteur, which addressed the need to integrate a gender perspective in the criminal justice system and in respect of the role to be played by judges and lawyers. Noting that the integration of a gender perspective meant integrating both women and men's perspectives and needs, the Rapporteur pointed out that more should be done to understand and challenge the effects that gender-based stereotypes, prejudices and discrimination had on both women and men in both their access to and engagement in the justice system and the criminal justice system. The Rapporteur recommended that States share best practices and common standards regarding the integration of a gender perspective in the criminal justice system; identify the occurrences and causes of gender-based discrimination in the criminal justice system and assess their impact on women's involvement with the system, whether as judicial actors, victims, witnesses or offenders; encourage qualified women to occupy high-level positions within the judiciary and in the justice system; and combat gender-based stereotyping, bias and prejudices in the criminal justice system.

On 19 December, the General Assembly took note of the report (**decision 66/537**).

Mission reports. During her visit to Romania (17–24 May) [A/HRC/20/19/Add.1], the Special Rapporteur examined judicial reform efforts, including the action plan for meeting the benchmarks established within the cooperation and verification mechanism of the European Commission, Law 202 of 2010, known as the "small reform," and the strategy for strengthening integrity within the judiciary (2011–2016). She addressed issues related to the independence of the courts and the legal professions, predictability of the judicial system, administration and oversight of the judiciary, and the judicial budget. She also examined the functioning of the prosecution service; free exercise of the legal profession by lawyers; access to justice; legal aid as well as aspects related to capacity-building and training of judges, prosecutors and other legal professionals; and various codes of law expected to enter into force in 2012 and 2013. The report concluded with recommendations for strengthening the judicial system and the independence of judges and lawyers.

Following her mission to Bulgaria (9–16 May) [A/HRC/20/19/Add.2], the Special Rapporteur examined judicial reform efforts as well as the court system, and addressed challenges relating to the independence and impartiality of the judiciary. She referred to issues that had an impact on the administration of justice and the independence of judges and lawyers, namely access to justice, legal aid, fair trial guarantees, and capacity-building and training for judges, prosecutors and investigators. The Rapporteur made several recommendations, particularly on judicial reform and enhancing the independence of the judiciary.

Following her visit to Turkey (10–14 October) [A/HRC/20/19/Add.3], the Rapporteur pointed out that as a whole, the reforms undertaken by the Government could be considered an improvement, yet challenges remained to guarantee the independence and impartiality of judges and prosecutors in practice. Reference was made in particular to the role of public prosecutors in the administration of courts; the position and functions of the Minister of Justice within the High Council of Judges and Prosecutors; the need for separation between the careers of judges and prosecutors; the excessively close relationship between judges and prosecutors; the appointment, transfer and rotation system for judges and prosecutors; the mindset of judges and prosecutors; and the issue of women in the administration of justice. She also examined the issue of access to justice and delayed proceedings, the lack of adequate infrastructure in the judiciary and long pretrial detention periods, as well as a widespread perception that lawyers were not treated in the same manner as judges and prosecutors and the difficulties they faced in defending their clients, especially in terrorism-related crimes. In some instances, lawyers had been criminally charged for activities carried out in the legitimate exercise of their profession when defending suspects accused of terrorism-related charges. The Rapporteur also made recommendations concerning the requirements for admission to the Bar and concluded with remarks in respect of capacity-building and legal human rights training for judges, prosecutors and lawyers.

Human Rights Council action. On 16 June [A/66/53 (res. 17/2)], the Council extended the mandate of the Special Rapporteur for a period of three years and requested the Rapporteur to report regularly to the Council and annually to the General Assembly.

Electoral processes

Report of Secretary-General. In response to General Assembly resolution 64/155 [YUN 2009, p. 687], the Secretary-General in August submitted a report [A/66/314] describing the activities of the UN system in providing electoral assistance to Member States over the previous two years. Assistance was provided to 57 countries and territories, 11 of them on the basis of a Security Council mandate. As the focal point for electoral assistance activities, the Under-Secretary-General for Political Affairs was responsible for the Organization's electoral policy and for ensuring system-wide coherence, and was supported by the Electoral Assistance Division, which assisted with the design and staffing of UN electoral activities and maintained the roster of electoral experts. In peacekeeping or post-conflict environments, electoral assistance was provided through components of field missions under the aegis of the Department of Peacekeeping Operations or the Department of Political Affairs. The United Nations Development Programme usually played a supporting role to electoral assistance provided by field missions. The report also discussed cooperation within and outside the UN system, and made observations aimed at strengthening the provision of electoral assistance by the UN system. Issues discussed in the report included progress in the coordination of electoral assistance; electoral assistance funding and the need for Member State contributions; gender and elections; women and underrepresented groups; and containing risks that could trigger violence or spark tensions during the electoral process. The report indicated that the demand from Member States for electoral assistance remained high, and concluded with an emphasis on governance, noting that investments in elections would not yield sustainable peace and development without independent and professional judiciaries; open, pluralistic media; a robust civil society; a credible government; and effective governance at all levels.

GENERAL ASSEMBLY ACTION

On 19 December [meeting 89], the General Assembly, on the recommendation of the Third Committee [A/66/462/Add.2], adopted **resolution 66/163** without vote [agenda item 69 (*b*)].

Strengthening the role of the United Nations in enhancing periodic and genuine elections and the promotion of democratization

The General Assembly,

Reaffirming that democracy is a universal value based on the freely expressed will of the people to determine their own political, economic, social and cultural systems and their full participation in all aspects of their lives,

Reaffirming also that, while democracies share common features, there is no single model of democracy and that democracy does not belong to any country or region, and reaffirming further the necessity of due respect for sovereignty and the right to self-determination,

Stressing that democracy, development and respect for all human rights and fundamental freedoms are interdependent and mutually reinforcing,

Reaffirming that Member States are responsible for organizing, conducting and ensuring free and fair electoral processes and that Member States, in the exercise of their sovereignty, may request that international organizations provide advisory services or assistance for strengthening and developing their electoral institutions and processes, including sending preliminary missions for that purpose,

Recognizing the importance of fair, periodic and genuine elections, including in new democracies and countries undergoing democratization, in order to empower citizens to express their will and to promote successful transition to long-term sustainable democracies,

Recognizing also that Member States are responsible for ensuring free and fair elections, free of intimidation, coercion and tampering of vote counts, and that all such acts are sanctioned accordingly,

Recalling its previous resolutions on the subject, in particular resolution 64/155 of 18 December 2009,

Reaffirming that United Nations electoral assistance and support for the promotion of democratization are provided only at the specific request of the Member State concerned,

Noting with satisfaction that increasing numbers of Member States are using elections as a peaceful means of discerning the will of the people, which builds confidence in representational governance and contributes to greater national peace and stability, and may contribute to regional stability,

Recalling the Universal Declaration of Human Rights, adopted on 10 December 1948, in particular the principle that the will of the people, as expressed through periodic and genuine elections, shall be the basis of government authority, as well as the right freely to choose representatives through periodic and genuine elections, which shall be by universal and equal suffrage and shall be held by secret vote or by equivalent free voting procedures,

Reaffirming the International Covenant on Civil and Political Rights, the Convention on the Elimination of All Forms of Discrimination against Women and the International Convention on the Elimination of All Forms of Racial Discrimination, in particular that citizens, without distinction of any kind, have the right and the opportunity to take part in the conduct of public affairs, directly or through freely chosen representatives, and to vote and to be elected in genuine periodic elections which shall be by universal and equal suffrage and shall be held by secret ballot, guaranteeing the free expression of the will of the electors,

Stressing the importance, generally and in the context of promoting fair and free elections, of respect for the freedom to seek, receive and impart information, in accordance with the International Covenant on Civil and Political Rights, and noting in particular the fundamental importance of access to information and media freedom,

Recognizing the need for strengthening democratic processes, electoral institutions and national capacity-building in requesting countries, including the capacity to administer fair elections, promote the participation of women on equal terms with men, increase citizen participation and provide civic education in requesting countries in order to consolidate and regularize the achievements of previous elections and support subsequent elections,

Noting the importance of ensuring orderly, open, fair and transparent democratic processes that preserve the right of peaceful assembly,

Noting also that the international community can contribute to creating conditions which could foster stability and security throughout the pre-election, election and post-election periods in transitional and post-conflict situations,

Reiterating that transparency is a fundamental basis for free and fair elections, which contribute to the accountability of Governments to their citizens, which, in turn, is an underpinning of democratic societies,

Acknowledging, in this regard, the importance of international election observation for the promotion of free and fair elections and its contribution to enhancing the integrity of election processes in requesting countries, to promoting public confidence and electoral participation and to mitigating the potential for election-related disturbances,

Acknowledging also that extending invitations regarding international electoral assistance and/or observation is the sovereign right of Member States, and welcoming the decisions of those States that have requested such assistance and/or observation,

Welcoming the support provided by Member States to the electoral assistance activities of the United Nations, inter alia, through the provision of electoral experts, including electoral commission staff, and observers, as well as through contributions to the United Nations Trust Fund for Electoral Assistance, the Democratic Governance Thematic Trust Fund of the United Nations Development Programme and the United Nations Democracy Fund,

Recognizing that electoral assistance, particularly through appropriate, sustainable and cost-effective electoral technology, supports the electoral processes of developing countries,

Recognizing also the coordination challenges posed by the multiplicity of actors involved in electoral assistance both within and outside the United Nations,

Welcoming the contributions made by international and regional organizations and also by non-governmental organizations to enhancing the effectiveness of the principle of periodic and genuine elections and the promotion of democratization,

1. *Welcomes* the report of the Secretary-General;

2. *Commends* the electoral assistance provided upon request to Member States by the United Nations, and requests that such assistance continue on a case-by-case basis in accordance with the evolving needs and legislation of requesting countries to develop, improve and refine their electoral institutions and processes, recognizing that the responsibility for organizing free and fair elections lies with Governments;

3. *Reaffirms* that the electoral assistance provided by the United Nations should continue to be carried out in an objective, impartial, neutral and independent manner;

4. *Requests* the Under-Secretary-General for Political Affairs, in his role as United Nations focal point for electoral assistance matters, to continue to inform Member States regularly about the requests received and the nature of any assistance provided;

5. *Requests* that the United Nations continue its efforts to ensure, before undertaking to provide electoral assistance to a requesting State, that there is adequate time to organize and carry out an effective mission for providing such assistance, including the provision of long-term technical cooperation, that conditions exist to allow a free and fair election and that the results of the mission will be reported comprehensively and consistently;

6. *Notes* the importance of adequate resources for the administration of efficient and transparent elections at the national and local levels, and recommends that Member States provide adequate resources for these elections, including to consider establishing internal funding where feasible;

7. *Recommends* that, throughout the timespan of the entire electoral cycle, including before and after elections, as appropriate, based on a needs assessment and in accordance with the evolving needs of requesting Member States, bearing in mind sustainability and cost-effectiveness, the United Nations continue to provide technical advice and other assistance to requesting States and electoral institutions in order to help to strengthen their democratic processes, also bearing in mind that the relevant office may additionally provide assistance in the form of mediation and good offices, upon the request of Member States;

8. *Notes with appreciation* the additional efforts being made to enhance cooperation with other international, governmental and non-governmental organizations in order to facilitate more comprehensive and needs-specific responses to requests for electoral assistance, encourages those organizations to share knowledge and experience in order to promote best practices in the assistance they provide and in their reporting on electoral processes, and expresses its appreciation to those Member States, regional organizations and non-governmental organizations that have provided observers or technical experts in support of United Nations electoral assistance efforts;

9. *Acknowledges* the aim of harmonizing the methods and standards of the many intergovernmental and non-governmental organizations engaged in observing elections, and in this regard expresses appreciation for the Declaration of Principles for International Election Observation and the Code of Conduct for International Election Observers, which elaborate guidelines for international electoral observation;

10. *Recalls* the establishment by the Secretary-General of the United Nations Trust Fund for Electoral Assistance, and, bearing in mind that the Fund is currently close to depletion, calls upon Member States to consider contributing to the Fund;

11. *Encourages* the Secretary-General, through the United Nations focal point for electoral assistance matters and with the support of the Electoral Assistance Division of the Department of Political Affairs of the Secretariat, to continue responding to the evolving nature of requests for assistance and the growing need for specific types of medium-term expert assistance aimed at supporting and strengthening the existing capacity of the requesting Government, in particular by enhancing the capacity of national electoral institutions;

12. *Requests* the Secretary-General to provide the Electoral Assistance Division with adequate human and financial resources to allow it to carry out its mandate, including to enhance the accessibility and diversity of the roster of electoral experts and the Organization's electoral institutional memory, and to continue to ensure that the Office of the United Nations High Commissioner for Human Rights is able to respond, within its mandate and in close coordination with the Division, to the numerous and increasingly complex and comprehensive requests from Member States for advisory services;

13. *Reiterates* the need for ongoing comprehensive coordination, under the auspices of the United Nations focal point for electoral assistance matters, between the Electoral Assistance Division and the United Nations Development Programme and the Department of Peacekeeping Operations and the Department of Field Support of the Secretariat to ensure coordination and coherence and avoid duplication of United Nations electoral assistance, and encourages further engagement of the Office of the United Nations High Commissioner for Human Rights in this context;

14. *Requests* the United Nations Development Programme to continue its democratic governance assistance programmes in cooperation with other relevant organizations, in particular those that promote the strengthening of democratic institutions and linkages between civil society and Governments;

15. *Reiterates* the importance of reinforced coordination within and outside the United Nations system, and reaffirms the clear leadership role within the United Nations system of the United Nations focal point for electoral assistance matters, including in ensuring system-wide coherence and consistency and in strengthening the institutional memory and the development, dissemination and issuance of United Nations electoral assistance policies;

16. *Requests* the Secretary-General to report to the General Assembly at its sixty-eighth session on the implementation of the present resolution, in particular on the status of requests from Member States for electoral assistance, and on his efforts to enhance support by the Organization for the democratization process in Member States.

Freedom of expression

Reports of Special Rapporteur. Pursuant to a Human Rights Council request [YUN 2008, p. 814], the Special Rapporteur on the promotion and protection of the right to freedom of opinion and expression, Frank La Rue (Guatemala), in May submitted a report [A/HRC/17/27] detailing his activities between March 2010 and March 2011 and exploring trends and challenges to the right of individuals to seek, receive and impart information and ideas through the Internet. The report underlined the applicability to the Internet, as a communication medium, of international human rights norms and standards on the right to freedom of opinion and expression and set out the exceptional circumstances under which the dissemination of certain types of information might be restricted; addressed access to Internet content and to the physical and technical infrastructure required to access the Internet; outlined ways in which States were increasingly censoring information online through blocking or filtering information and other means; and addressed the issue of universal access to the Internet. The Rapporteur concluded with recommendations on the main subjects of the report.

An addendum [A/HRC/17/27/Add.1 & Corr.1] summarized 195 communications sent to 71 Governments between 20 March 2010 and 31 March 2011 and replies received by 13 May 2011. Of the 195 communications, 188 were submitted jointly with other special procedures mandate holders.

In August [A/66/290], pursuant to a Human Rights Council request (see below), the Secretary-General transmitted another report of the Special Rapporteur to the General Assembly. The Rapporteur outlined his activities and examined the right of all individuals to seek, receive and impart information and ideas through the Internet, including access to online content and to Internet connection. The report outlined the types of expression that States were required to prohibit under international law and discussed impermissible restrictions, given the debate over regulation of content on the Internet. While Internet access was not yet recognized as a human right, the report focused on the obligation of States to facilitate the enjoyment of the right to freedom of expression via the Internet and summarized both challenges and initiatives to make the Internet available to all segments of society. It concluded with recommendations to ensure full access to online content free of censorship and access to Internet connection, particularly for marginalized and disadvantaged groups.

On 19 December, the General Assembly took note of that report (**decision 66/537**).

Mission reports. Following his visit to Algeria (10–17 April) [A/HRC/20/17/Add.1], the Special Rapporteur focused on legal action in relation to the exercise of freedom of expression; freedom of the press and the right to information; freedom of opinion and expression on the Internet; censorship on the import of books; freedom of peaceful assembly and demonstration; freedom of association; and the National Advisory Commission for the Promotion and Protection of Human Rights. He pointed out that Algeria had come a long way from the Black Decade, during which journalists paid a tremendously high price, and welcomed the lifting of the state of emergency, as well as the Government's decision to embark on political reforms. He cautioned, however, that the legal framework was still restrictive, coupled with practices inherited from the past that unduly restricted the right to freedom of opinion and expression, as well as the rights to freedom of peaceful assembly and of association. He made several recommendations on each of those issues to strengthen the democratic foundations of Algeria.

Following his mission to Israel and the Occupied Palestinian Territory (6–17 December) [A/HRC/20/17/Add.2], the Special Rapporteur outlined his main issues of concern in Israel, the West Bank, and Gaza vis-à-vis the respective obligations of the Israeli Government, the Palestinian Authority (PA) and the de facto authorities in Gaza. Those concerns included, in Israel, recent attempts to diminish the space for criticism within Israel regarding its occupation policies, as well as the discriminatory treatment of Palestinian citizens of Israel and attempts to curtail their right to freedom of opinion and expression; in the Occupied Palestinian Territory, restrictions on journalists' freedom of movement imposed by the Israeli Government, and the division between the PA in the West Bank and the de facto authorities in Gaza; in the West Bank, the increasing number of journalists, human rights defenders and bloggers who were arbitrarily detained and interrogated by PA security forces for expressing critical views, and undue restrictions imposed on freedom of assembly by the Israeli security forces; in Gaza, restrictions imposed by the de facto authorities on the rights to freedom of expression and of assembly; and in East Jerusalem, the restrictions imposed by the Israeli Government on the right of Palestinians to seek, receive and impart ideas and opinions. The report concluded with recommendations to the Israeli Government, the PA, and the de facto authorities in Gaza on the main issues of concern.

Human Rights Council action. On 24 March [A/66/53 (res. 16/4)], the Council extended the mandate of the Special Rapporteur for three years and requested him/her to submit an annual report to the Council and to the General Assembly.

On 29 September [A/66/53/Add.1 (dec. 18/119)], the Council took note of the Special Rapporteur's report on freedom of expression on the Internet, and decided to convene at its nineteenth (2012) session a panel discussion on the promotion and protection of freedom of expression on the Internet, with a particular focus on the ways and means to improve its protection in accordance with international human rights law.

Freedom of peaceful assembly and association

Human Rights Council action. Recognizing the need to reflect on the promotion and protection of human rights in the context of peaceful protests, the Council, on 17 June [A/66/53 (dec. 17/120)] decided to convene, at its eighteenth (2011) session, a panel discussion on the promotion and protection of human rights in the context of peaceful protests, with a focus on ways to improve the protection of those rights in such contexts in line with international human rights law. It requested OHCHR to prepare a summary report on the outcome of the discussion.

OHCHR report. An OHCHR report issued in December [A/HRC/19/40] summarized the panel discussion (Geneva, 13 September). Participants heard statements by the Deputy High Commissioner for Human Rights and the President of Maldives, contributions of panellists and concluding remarks by the Human Rights Council President. The summary also included issues raised by stakeholders.

Other issues

Capital punishment

Report of Secretary-General. In July [A/HRC/18/20], the Secretary-General reported on developments with regard to the death penalty from July 2010 to June 2011, as well as developments during the period January–June 2010 which were not included in his previous report [YUN 2010, p. 699]. At the time of the report, about 140 Member States were believed to have abolished the death penalty or introduced a moratorium. Djibouti and Gabon had abolished the death penalty for all crimes, and in the United States, the state of Illinois adopted a law abolishing the death penalty, becoming the sixteenth state in the country to do so. Bangladesh, China, the Gambia, Guyana and Kenya had restricted the scope of the death penalty or limited its use. Kyrgyzstan became the seventy-third State party to the Second Optional Protocol to the International Covenant on Civil and Political Rights, aiming at the abolition of the death penalty [YUN 1989, p. 484]. The report also drew attention to a number of phenomena, including the continuing trend towards abolition, the ongoing difficulties in gaining access to reliable information on executions, and various international efforts towards the universal abolition of the death penalty.

Human Rights Council action. On 28 September [A/66/53/Add.1 (dec. 18/117)], the Council requested the Secretary-General to continue to submit to the Council a yearly supplement to his quinquennial report on capital punishment and the implementation of the safeguards guaranteeing protection of the rights of those facing the death penalty, paying special attention to the imposition of the death penalty on persons younger than 18 years of age at the time of the offence, on pregnant women and on persons with mental or intellectual disabilities.

Communication. On 11 March, in reference to General Assembly resolution 65/206 [YUN 2010, p. 699] on the moratorium on the use of the death penalty, Egypt transmitted to the Secretary-General a note verbale [A/65/779] from 53 Member States that objected to any attempt to impose a moratorium on the use the death penalty or abolish it in contravention of stipulations under international law.

Disappearance of persons

Working Group activities. The five-member Working Group on Enforced or Involuntary Disappearances held three sessions in 2011: its ninety-third (Mexico City, 15–18 March), ninety-fourth (Geneva, 4–8 July) and ninety-fifth (Geneva, 1–11 November) [A/HRC/19/58/Rev.1]. In addition to its core mandate to assist families in determining the fate or whereabouts of family members who had been reportedly disappeared and to act as a communication channel between families and the Government concerned, the Group monitored compliance with the 1992 Declaration on the Protection of All Persons from Enforced Disappearance [YUN 1992, p. 744]. The total number of cases transmitted by the Group to Governments since its inception was 53,778. Cases under active consideration that had not been clarified, closed or discontinued totalled 42,759, concerning 82 States. The Group had clarified 448 cases over the past five years. Between 13 November 2010 and 11 November 2011, the Group transmitted 261 new cases of enforced disappearance to 25 Governments. Of those, 73 were sent under the urgent action procedure to 16 Governments. The Group also clarified 63 cases in 18 States. The Group's report summarized information on disappearances relating to 95 States and territories.

In 2011, the Group adopted one general comment on the right to recognition as a person before the law in the context of enforced disappearances.

The Working Group decided to amend the way in which its statistics were counted so that, in exceptional circumstances and for humanitarian reasons, cases might be included in the statistics of a different State from the one in which the enforced disappearance occurred. It also decided to deal with all enforced disappearances, regardless of the type of armed conflict in which they occurred. The revised methods of work, approved on 11 November, were annexed to the report and would come into effect on 1 January 2012.

Mission reports. Following its visit to Timor-Leste (7–14 February) [A/HRC/19/58/Add.1], the Group stated that much remained to be done to achieve the right to the truth, justice and reparation for the disappeared and their families. Recommendations included compliance with the recommendations made by the Commission for Reception, Truth and Reconciliation and the bilateral Commission on Truth and Friendship; the swift adoption of the draft laws on the establishment of the Memory Institute and a national reparations programme; the need to achieve more truth about what occurred in the past; a greater focus on the judicial process; and the incorporation of an autonomous crime of enforced disappearance into the criminal code.

Following its mission to Mexico (18–31 March) [A/HRC/19/58/Add.2], the Group acknowledged the efforts that Mexico had made in the field of human rights, including to combat enforced disappearances, and the challenges posed by the existing complex public security situation in the context of the fight against organized crime. The Group made recommendations relating to prevention, investigations, penalties and reparation for the victims of enforced disappearances, as well as on the protection of particularly vulnerable groups. Recommendations included ensuring that enforced disappearance was classified as an offence in the criminal codes of all the federal entities; that the definition of enforced disappearance in criminal legislation was brought into line with that of relevant international instruments; that civil courts had jurisdiction over all matters relating to enforced disappearances; that a national search programme for missing persons was established; and that the right to full reparation for the victims of enforced disappearance was guaranteed.

Following its visit to the Republic of the Congo (24 September–3 October) [A/HRC/19/58/Add.3], the Group welcomed the state of peace and sense of national unity that had resulted from the reconciliation between the different parts of Congolese society. It noted, however, that those responsible for the enforced disappearances had been neither identified nor punished, the fate of the disappeared was not known, and the compensation received by some families needed to be supplemented. Among its recommendations, the Group called on the authorities to continue the investigations, incorporate enforced disappearance into the Criminal Code as an autonomous offence, ban detention in secret or in unofficial places, and establish a national truth and reconciliation commission.

Human Rights Council action. On 24 March [A/66/53 (res. 16/16)], the Council extended the mandate of the Working Group for three years and, noting that 2012 would mark the twentieth anniversary of the adoption of the 1992 Declaration [YUN 1992, p. 744], encouraged States to translate the Declaration into their languages to assist its global dissemination and the ultimate goal of prevention of enforced disappearances.

Missing persons

Pursuant to a Human Rights Council request [YUN 2010, p. 701], the Human Rights Council Advisory Committee submitted a February report [A/HRC/16/70] on best practices in the matter of missing persons unaccounted for as a result of armed conflict, requested by the Council in 2008 [YUN 2008, p. 796]. The report addressed a number of topics, including respect for and implementation of international law; measures to prevent persons from going missing; missing persons and the restoration of family links; mechanisms established to clarify the fate of missing persons; the right of families to know the fate of missing relatives; criminal investigation and prosecution of human rights violations linked to missing persons; legal status of missing persons and support for families of missing persons; management of the dead and identification of human remains; information management and legal protection of personal data; and international cooperation to solve cases. The report concluded with a number of best practices and recommendations, including preparation of a draft model law on missing persons by the International Committee of the Red Cross, establishment of an information bureau and graves registration service, and establishment of a special rapporteur on missing persons to enhance the existing international mechanisms protecting the rights of missing persons and their families.

Extralegal executions

Reports of Special Rapporteur. Pursuant to a Human Rights Council request [YUN 2008, p. 803], the new Special Rapporteur on extrajudicial, summary or arbitrary executions, Christof Heyns (South Africa), in May submitted his first report [A/HRC/17/28] covering the activities of the mandate over the previous year. Focusing on protecting the right to life in the context of policing assemblies, it discussed the legal norms applicable to the use of lethal force during demonstrations; the domestic application of international norms; socio-legal approaches and understanding of crowd behavior; principles of policing protests; and assembly law reform. The Rapporteur noted that while both the maintenance of public order and protection of the rights of others were important, in some of the life-and-death situations presented by demonstrations, the emphasis on one of those two approaches would lead to different decisions on whether to use firearms. Based on a study covering 76 countries, he concluded that many domestic legal systems did not adhere to international standards in respect of the right to freedom of assembly, and the use of force during demonstrations. It was proposed that over time, the centrality of the norm of self-defence, as the guiding principle for the use of deadly force, should be asserted more strongly. Recommendations were made on action to be taken by UN bodies involved in human rights monitoring, the elaboration of basic principles for managing demonstrations, UN engagement with regional and domestic human rights initiatives to ensure conformity with international standards, and training and equipping of UN peacekeepers that might have to deal with protests.

A 27 May addendum [A/HRC/17/28/Add.1] reviewed 123 communications sent by the Special Rapporteur to 52 Governments and 3 actors, including 54 urgent appeals and 69 allegation letters, between 16 March 2010 and 15 March 2011, and replies received between 1 May 2010 and 30 April 2011. The main issues covered in the letters were attacks or killings (33), excessive use of force (30), the death penalty (24), deaths in custody (10), death threats (6), armed conflict (5), impunity (3) and other concerns (8). The Rapporteur received 43 responses and 5 acknowledgments, representing a 53 per cent response rate. Further addenda followed up on the Rapporteur's recommendations following his 2009 visit [A/HRC/17/28/Add.4] to Kenya [YUN 2009, p. 692] and his 2008 visits [A/HRC/17/28/Add.5] to the United States and [A/HRC/17/28/Add.6] to Afghanistan [YUN 2008, p. 804].

In August, pursuant to General Assembly resolution 65/208 [YUN 2010, p. 704], the Secretary-General transmitted the Special Rapporteur's report [A/66/330] focusing on the international standards relevant to the use of lethal force during arrest. Different models of how countries dealt with the issue were identified and discussed. A case study examined the legal framework applicable to targeted killing, where arrest could reasonably have been an option. The point was made that the frameworks established by international law provided sufficient room to deal with serious as well as less serious security threats. Recommendations were made to ensure greater domestic compliance with international norms.

On 19 December, the General Assembly took note of the report (**decision 66/537**).

Human Rights Council action. On 16 June [A/66/53 (res. 17/5)], the Council demanded that all States ensure that the practice of extrajudicial, summary or arbitrary executions was brought to an end and that they took effective action to combat and eliminate the phenomenon in all its forms; extended the Special Rapporteur's mandate for three years; and requested the Rapporteur to examine situations of extrajudicial, summary or arbitrary executions and to report annually to the Council and the General Assembly.

Torture and cruel treatment

Reports of Special Rapporteur. Pursuant to a Human Rights Council request [YUN 2008, p. 810], the Special Rapporteur on torture and other cruel, inhuman or degrading treatment or punishment, Juan E. Méndez (Argentina), in February [A/HRC/16/52] submitted his first report. He advocated a victim-centred approach to the work of his mandate and believed that all human rights standards were subject to the norm of "progressive development", in that they evolved in accordance with new repressive actions and features. In that regard, it was important to consolidate current interpretations of what constituted torture and cruel, inhuman and degrading treatment or punishment, and to insist on implementation of States' obligations to prevent and to punish violations. He observed that rather than torture, there were credible and human rights friendly forensic and other scientific alternatives which had been proven to achieve the desired results in law enforcement and crime prevention. Scientific advances had made possible the provision of evidence to corroborate evidence that torture has been administered; hence those new techniques were important tools for achieving accountability. He also intended to develop linkages between science and forensics as an alternative in law enforcement, countering terrorism and effective criminal prosecution. The report re-emphasized the mandate's position on pretrial detention, non-refoulement and diplomatic assurances, conditions in detention and torture in secret detention. It also highlighted issues requiring longer-term consideration and engagement with States.

An addendum [A/HRC/16/52/Add.1] summarized 66 letters of allegations of torture to 34 Governments and 137 urgent appeals to 53 Governments on behalf of persons who might be at risk of torture or other forms of ill-treatment sent between 21 December 2009 to 1 December 2010, as well as Government responses received up to 30 January 2011.

A further addendum [A/HRC/16/52/Add.2] addressed the follow-up to the Rapporteur's recommendations subsequent to visits to Azerbaijan, Brazil, China, Denmark, Equatorial Guinea, Georgia, Indonesia, Jordan, Kazakhstan, Moldova, Mongolia, Nepal, Nigeria, Paraguay, Spain, Sri Lanka, Togo, Uruguay and Uzbekistan.

In accordance with General Assembly resolution 65/205 [YUN 2010, p. 708], the Secretary-General in August transmitted the report [A/66/268] of the Special Rapporteur addressing issues of special concern and recent developments in the context of his mandate. He drew the Assembly's attention to his assessment that solitary confinement was practiced in a majority of States. He found that where the physical conditions and the prison regime of solitary confinement caused severe mental and physical pain or suffering—when used as a punishment, during pre-trial detention, indefinitely, prolonged, on juveniles or persons with mental disabilities—it could amount to cruel, inhuman or degrading treatment or punishment and even torture. In addition, the use of solitary confinement increased the risk that acts of torture and other cruel, inhuman or degrading treatment would go undetected and unchallenged. The report highlighted principles to guide States to re-evaluate and minimize the use of solitary confinement and, in certain cases, abolish the practice. Solitary confinement should be used only in exceptional circumstances, as a last resort, for as short a time as possible. The Rapporteur emphasized the need for minimum procedural safeguards to ensure that all persons deprived of their liberty were treated with humanity and respect for the inherent dignity of the human person.

Mission reports. Following his visit to Tunisia (15–22 May) [A/HRC/19/61/Add.1], the Special Rapporteur welcomed the high-level consensus across the political spectrum on the need to abolish torture and ill-treatment, and a series of positive steps taken towards restoring justice for past and recent acts of torture and ill-treatment. He observed that given the legacy of torture from the past regime, and the lack of timely investigations into allegations of torture and ill-treatment, it could not be said that a culture of impunity no longer prevailed. The Rapporteur identified two issues that needed the attention of the Government to ensure justice in times of a successful transition: prompt and thorough investigations into all cases of torture and ill-treatment, prosecution of the perpetrators, and the provision of effective remedies and reparations for all victims; and the establishment of safeguards against torture and ill-treatment through the introduction of constitutional, legislative and administrative reforms. He recommended that the fact-finding commission established to investigate the abuses committed during the revolution and its aftermath (17 December 2010–May 2011) complete its work as soon as possible and that its findings be followed by investigations and prosecutions, and that victims receive adequate reparation and rehabilitation. On the prevention of torture, he recommended that constitutional, legislative and administrative reforms be expedited.

During his mission to Kyrgyzstan (5–13 December) [A/HRC/19/61/Add.2], the Special Rapporteur was encouraged by concrete steps taken to curb torture, but remained concerned by a shortfall in legislation and law enforcement practices. The lack of effective legislative safeguards against torture and ill-treatment and the insignificant sanction provided for the crime of torture created an environment conducive to impunity. The general conditions in most places of detention visited amounted to inhuman and degrading treatment. Based on information provided in meetings with decision makers, victims and civil society representatives, the Rapporteur concluded that the use of torture and ill-treatment to extract confessions remained widespread. He recommended that the Government expedite legislative reforms to ensure the absolute prohibition of torture; establish safeguards against torture and ill-treatment in law and practice; initiate prompt investigations into allegations of torture and ill-treatment, and prosecute when warranted; establish an effective national preventive mechanism; and allocate sufficient resources to improve detention centre conditions.

Communication. In a 2 March note [A/HRC/16/G/3], Jamaica submitted its comments on the Special Rapporteur's 2010 mission to the country [YUN 2010, p. 707].

Human Rights Council action. On 25 March [A/66/53 (res. 16/23)], the Council extended the Special Rapporteur's mandate for three years and requested the Rapporteur to report to the General Assembly and to the Council. Among other actions, it called on States to prevent torture and other cruel treatment, particularly in places of detention, and to have all alleged cases of torture investigated.

Voluntary fund for torture victims

Report of Secretary-General. In his annual report [A/66/276] to the General Assembly on the status of the United Nations Voluntary Fund for Victims of Torture, the Secretary-General provided information on the recommendations of the Fund's Board of Trustees at its thirty-third [YUN 2010, p. 708] and thirty-fourth (31 January–4 February) sessions. At those sessions, the Board made recommendations for grants for 2011 for 280 ongoing and 23 new projects carried out by NGOs in over 70 countries, for an amount of $9,525,050. The High Commissioner for Human Rights approved those recommendations on behalf of the Secretary-General. Contributions from 20 countries from 5 August 2010 to 22 July 2011 amounted to $9,552,609, while pledges from three countries totalled $669,056.

The General Assembly took note of the report on 19 December (**decision 66/537**).

The Secretary-General further reported [A/HRC/19/26] that since the new Board of Trustees was appointed on 22 October, the Board's thirty-fifth session, originally planned for 17–21 October, had to be postponed to 25 January–3 February 2012. No additional session would be organized for the decisions and recommendations to be taken in 2012. The Board would hold its thirty-sixth session in October 2012.

GENERAL ASSEMBLY ACTION

On 19 December [meeting 89], the General Assembly, on the recommendation of the Third Committee [A/66/462/Add.1], adopted **resolution 66/150** without vote [agenda item 69 (a)].

Torture and other cruel, inhuman or degrading treatment or punishment

The General Assembly,

Reaffirming that no one shall be subjected to torture or other cruel, inhuman or degrading treatment or punishment,

Recalling that freedom from torture and other cruel, inhuman or degrading treatment or punishment is a non-derogable right under international law, including international human rights law and international humanitarian law, that must be respected and protected under all circumstances, including in times of international or internal armed conflict or disturbance or any other public emergency, that the absolute prohibition of torture and other cruel, inhuman or degrading treatment or punishment is affirmed in relevant international instruments and that legal and procedural safeguards against such acts must not be subject to measures that would circumvent this right,

Recalling also that the prohibition of torture is a peremptory norm of international law and that international, regional and domestic courts have held the prohibition of cruel, inhuman or degrading treatment or punishment to be customary international law,

Recalling further the definition of torture contained in article 1 of the Convention against Torture and Other Cruel, Inhuman or Degrading Treatment or Punishment, without prejudice to any international instrument or national legislation which contains or may contain provisions of wider application,

Emphasizing the importance of properly interpreting and implementing the obligations of States with respect to torture and other cruel, inhuman or degrading treatment or punishment and of abiding strictly by the definition of torture contained in article 1 of the Convention,

Noting that, under the Geneva Conventions of 1949, torture and inhuman treatment are a grave breach and that, under the statute of the International Tribunal for the Prosecution of Persons Responsible for Serious Violations of International Humanitarian Law Committed in the Territory of the Former Yugoslavia since 1991, the statute of the International Criminal Tribunal for the Prosecution of Persons Responsible for Genocide and Other Serious Violations of International Humanitarian Law Committed in the Territory of Rwanda and Rwandan Citizens Responsible for Genocide and Other Such Violations Committed in the Territory of Neighbouring States between 1 January and 31 December 1994 and the Rome Statute of the International Criminal Court, acts of torture can constitute crimes against humanity and, when committed in a situation of armed conflict, constitute war crimes,

Welcoming the entry into force of the International Convention for the Protection of All Persons from Enforced Disappearance, the implementation of which will make a significant contribution to the prevention and prohibition of torture, including by prohibiting secret places of detention, and encouraging all States that have not done so to consider signing, ratifying or acceding to the Convention,

Commending the persistent efforts of civil society organizations, including non-governmental organizations, national human rights institutions and national preventive mechanisms, and the considerable network of centres for the rehabilitation of victims of torture, to prevent and combat torture and to alleviate the suffering of victims of torture,

Deeply concerned with all acts which can amount to torture and other cruel, inhuman or degrading treatment or punishment committed against persons exercising their rights of peaceful assembly and freedom of expression in all regions of the world,

1. *Condemns* all forms of torture and other cruel, inhuman or degrading treatment or punishment, including through intimidation, which are and shall remain prohibited at any time and in any place whatsoever and can thus never be justified, and calls upon all States to implement fully the absolute and non-derogable prohibition of torture and other cruel, inhuman or degrading treatment or punishment;

2. *Emphasizes* that States must take persistent, determined and effective measures to prevent and combat all acts of torture and other cruel, inhuman or degrading treatment or punishment, stresses that all acts of torture must be made offences under domestic criminal law, and encourages States to prohibit under domestic law acts constituting cruel, inhuman or degrading treatment or punishment;

3. *Welcomes* the establishment of national preventive mechanisms to prevent torture and other cruel, inhuman or degrading treatment or punishment, urges States to consider establishing, appointing, maintaining or enhancing independent and effective mechanisms with qualified expertise to undertake monitoring visits to places of detention, inter alia with a view to preventing acts of torture or other cruel, inhuman or degrading treatment or punishment, and calls upon States parties to the Optional Protocol to the Convention against Torture and Other Cruel, Inhuman or Degrading Treatment or Punishment to fulfil their obligation to designate or establish truly independent and effective national preventive mechanisms;

4. *Emphasizes* the importance of States ensuring proper follow-up to the recommendations and conclusions of the relevant treaty bodies and mechanisms, including the Committee against Torture, the Subcommittee on Prevention of Torture and Other Cruel, Inhuman or Degrading Treatment or Punishment and the Special Rapporteur of the Human Rights Council on torture and other cruel, inhuman or degrading treatment or punishment;

5. *Condemns* any action or attempt by States or public officials to legalize, authorize or acquiesce in torture and other cruel, inhuman or degrading treatment or punishment under any circumstances, including on grounds of national security or through judicial decisions, and urges States to ensure accountability of those responsible for all such acts;

6. *Encourages* States to consider establishing or maintaining appropriate national processes to record allegations of torture and other cruel, inhuman or degrading treatment or punishment;

7. *Stresses* that an independent, competent domestic authority must promptly, effectively and impartially investigate all allegations of torture or other cruel, inhuman or degrading treatment or punishment, as well as wherever there is reasonable ground to believe that such an act has been committed, and that those who encourage, order, tolerate or perpetrate such acts must be held responsible, brought to justice and punished in a manner commensurate with the severity of the offence, including the officials in charge of any place of detention, or other place where persons are deprived of their liberty, where the prohibited act is found to have been committed;

8. *Recalls*, in this respect, the Principles on the Effective Investigation and Documentation of Torture and Other Cruel, Inhuman or Degrading Treatment or Punishment (the Istanbul Principles) as a useful tool in efforts to prevent and combat torture and the updated set of principles for the protection and promotion of human rights through action to combat impunity;

9. *Calls upon* all States to implement effective measures to prevent torture and other cruel, inhuman or degrading treatment or punishment, particularly in places of detention and other places where persons are deprived of their liberty, including legal and procedural safeguards, as well as education and training of personnel who may be involved in the custody, interrogation or treatment of any individual subjected to any form of arrest, detention or imprisonment;

10. *Urges* States, as an important element in preventing and combating torture and other cruel, inhuman or degrading treatment or punishment, to ensure that no authority or official orders, applies, permits or tolerates any sanction or other prejudice against any person or organization for having been in contact with any national or international monitoring or preventive body active in the prevention and combating of torture and other cruel, inhuman or degrading treatment or punishment;

11. *Calls upon* all States to adopt a gender-sensitive approach in the fight against torture and other cruel, inhuman or degrading treatment or punishment, paying special attention to gender-based violence;

12. *Calls upon* States to ensure that the rights of persons with disabilities, bearing in mind the Convention on the Rights of Persons with Disabilities, are fully integrated into torture prevention and protection, and welcomes the efforts of the Special Rapporteur in this regard;

13. *Encourages* all States to ensure that persons convicted of torture or other cruel, inhuman or degrading treatment or punishment have no subsequent involvement in the custody, interrogation or treatment of any person under arrest, detention, imprisonment or other deprivation of liberty and that persons charged with torture or other cruel, inhuman or degrading treatment or punishment have no involvement in the custody, interrogation or treatment of any person under arrest, detention, imprisonment or other deprivation of liberty while such charges are pending;

14. *Emphasizes* that acts of torture in armed conflict are serious violations of international humanitarian law and in this regard constitute war crimes, that acts of torture can constitute crimes against humanity and that the perpetrators of all acts of torture must be prosecuted and punished, and in this regard notes the efforts of the International Criminal Court to end impunity by seeking to ensure accountability and punishment of perpetrators of such acts, in accordance with the Rome Statute, bearing in mind its principle of complementarity, and encourages States that have not yet done so to consider ratifying or acceding to the Rome Statute;

15. *Strongly urges* States to ensure that no statement that is established to have been made as a result of torture is invoked as evidence in any proceedings, except against a person accused of torture as evidence that the statement was made, encourages States to extend that prohibition to statements made as a result of cruel, inhuman or degrading treatment or punishment, and recognizes that adequate corroboration of statements, including confessions, used as evidence in any proceedings constitutes one safeguard for the prevention of torture and other cruel, inhuman or degrading treatment or punishment;

16. *Stresses* that States must not punish personnel for not obeying orders to commit or conceal acts amounting to torture or other cruel, inhuman or degrading treatment or punishment;

17. *Urges* States not to expel, return ("refouler"), extradite or in any other way transfer a person to another State where there are substantial grounds for believing that the person would be in danger of being subjected to torture, stresses the importance of effective legal and procedural safeguards in this regard, and recognizes that diplomatic assurances, where used, do not release States from their obligations under international human rights, humanitarian and refugee law, in particular the principle of non-refoulement;

18. *Recalls* that, for the purpose of determining whether there are such grounds, the competent authorities shall take into account all relevant considerations, including, where applicable, the existence in the State concerned of a consistent pattern of gross, flagrant or mass violations of human rights;

19. *Calls upon* States parties to the Convention against Torture and Other Cruel, Inhuman or Degrading Treatment or Punishment to fulfil their obligation to submit for prosecution or extradite those alleged to have committed acts of torture, and encourages other States to do likewise, bearing in mind the need to fight impunity;

20. *Stresses* that national legal systems must ensure that victims of torture or other cruel, inhuman or degrading treatment or punishment obtain redress without suffering any retribution for bringing complaints or giving evidence, have access to justice, are awarded fair and adequate compensation and receive appropriate social, psychological, medical and other relevant specialized rehabilitation, and urges States to establish, maintain, facilitate or support rehabilitation centres or facilities where victims of torture can receive such treatment and where effective measures for ensuring the safety of their staff and patients are taken;

21. *Recalls* its resolution 43/173 of 9 December 1988 on the Body of Principles for the Protection of All Persons under Any Form of Detention or Imprisonment, and in this context stresses that ensuring that any individual arrested or detained is promptly brought before a judge or other independent judicial officer in person and permitting prompt and regular medical care and legal counsel as well as visits by family members and independent monitoring mechanisms are effective measures for the prevention of torture and other cruel, inhuman or degrading treatment or punishment;

22. *Reminds* all States that prolonged incommunicado detention or detention in secret places can facilitate the perpetration of torture and other cruel, inhuman or degrading treatment or punishment and can in itself constitute a form of such treatment, and urges all States to respect the safeguards concerning the liberty, security and dignity of the person and to ensure that secret places of detention and interrogation are abolished;

23. *Emphasizes* that conditions of detention must respect the dignity and human rights of detainees, highlights the importance of reflecting on this in efforts to promote respect for and protection of the rights of detainees, and notes in this regard concerns about solitary confinement when it amounts to torture or other cruel, inhuman or degrading treatment or punishment;

24. *Calls upon* all States to take appropriate effective legislative, administrative, judicial and other measures to prevent and prohibit the production, trade, export, import and use of equipment that have no practical use other than for the purpose of torture or other cruel, inhuman or degrading treatment or punishment;

25. *Urges* all States that have not yet done so to become parties to the Convention as a matter of priority, and calls upon States parties to give early consideration to signing and ratifying the Optional Protocol to the Convention;

26. *Urges* all States parties to the Convention that have not yet done so to make the declarations provided for in articles 21 and 22 concerning inter-State and individual communications, to consider the possibility of withdrawing their reservations to article 20 and to notify the Secretary-General of their acceptance of the amendments to articles 17 and 18 with a view to enhancing the effectiveness of the Committee as soon as possible;

27. *Urges* States parties to comply strictly with their obligations under the Convention, including, in view of the high number of reports not submitted in time, their obligation to submit reports in accordance with article 19 of the Convention, and invites States parties to incorporate a gender perspective and information concerning children and juveniles and persons with disabilities when submitting reports to the Committee;

28. *Welcomes* the work of the Committee and its report submitted in accordance with article 24 of the Convention, recommends that the Committee continue to include information on the follow-up by States to its recommendations, and supports the Committee in its intention to further improve the effectiveness of its working methods;

29. *Invites* the Chairs of the Committee and of the Subcommittee to present oral reports on the work of the committees and to engage in an interactive dialogue with the General Assembly at its sixty-seventh session under the sub-item entitled "Implementation of human rights instruments";

30. *Calls upon* the United Nations High Commissioner for Human Rights, in conformity with her mandate established by the General Assembly in its resolution 48/141 of 20 December 1993, to continue to provide, at the request of States, advisory services for the prevention of torture and other cruel, inhuman or degrading treatment or punishment, including for the preparation of national reports to the Committee and for the establishment and operation of national preventive mechanisms, as well as technical assistance for the development, production and distribution of teaching material for this purpose;

31. *Takes note with appreciation* of the interim report of the Special Rapporteur, and encourages the Special Rapporteur to continue to include in his recommendations proposals on the prevention and investigation of torture and other cruel, inhuman or degrading treatment or punishment, including its gender-based manifestations;

32. *Requests* the Special Rapporteur to continue to consider including in his report information on the follow-up by States to his recommendations, visits and communications, including progress made and problems encountered, and on other official contacts;

33. *Calls upon* all States to cooperate with and assist the Special Rapporteur in the performance of his task, to supply all necessary information requested by the Special Rapporteur, to fully and expeditiously respond to and follow up on his urgent appeals, to give serious consideration to responding favourably to requests by the Special Rapporteur to visit their countries and to enter into a constructive dialogue with the Special Rapporteur on requested visits to their countries as well as with respect to the follow-up to his recommendations;

34. *Stresses* the need for the continued regular exchange of views among the Committee, the Subcommittee, the Special Rapporteur and other relevant United Nations mechanisms and bodies, as well as for the pursuance of cooperation with relevant United Nations programmes, notably the United Nations crime prevention and criminal justice programme, with regional organizations and mechanisms, as appropriate, and with civil society organizations, including non-governmental organizations, with a view to enhancing further their effectiveness and cooperation on issues relating to the prevention and eradication of torture, inter alia, by improving their coordination;

35. *Recognizes* the global need for international assistance to victims of torture, stresses the importance of the work of the Board of Trustees of the United Nations Voluntary Fund for Victims of Torture, appeals to all States and organizations to contribute annually to the Fund, preferably with a substantial increase in the level of contributions, and encourages contributions to the Special Fund established by the Optional Protocol to help finance the implementation of the recommendations made by the Subcommittee as well as education programmes of the national preventive mechanisms;

36. *Requests* the Secretary-General to continue to transmit to all States the appeals of the General Assembly for contributions to the Funds and to include the Funds on an annual basis among the programmes for which funds are pledged at the United Nations Pledging Conference for Development Activities;

37. *Also requests* the Secretary-General to submit to the Human Rights Council and to the General Assembly at its sixty-seventh session a report on the operations of the Funds;

38. *Further requests* the Secretary-General to ensure, within the overall budgetary framework of the United Nations, the provision of adequate staff and facilities for the bodies and mechanisms involved in preventing and combating torture and assisting victims of torture or other cruel, inhuman or degrading treatment or punishment, including, in particular, the Committee, the Subcommittee and the Special Rapporteur, commensurate with the strong support expressed by Member States for preventing and combating torture and assisting victims of torture, in order to enable them to discharge their mandates in a comprehensive, sustained and effective manner and taking fully into account the specific nature of their mandates;

39. *Calls upon* all States, the Office of the United Nations High Commissioner for Human Rights and other United Nations bodies and agencies, as well as relevant intergovernmental and civil society organizations, including non-governmental organizations, to commemorate, on 26 June, the United Nations International Day in Support of Victims of Torture;

40. *Decides* to consider at its sixty-seventh session the reports of the Secretary-General, including the report on the United Nations Voluntary Fund for Victims of Torture and the Special Fund established by the Optional Protocol, the report of the Committee against Torture and the interim report of the Special Rapporteur on torture and other cruel, inhuman or degrading treatment or punishment.

Arbitrary detention

Working Group activities. The five-member Working Group on Arbitrary Detention held its sixtieth (2–6 May), sixty-first (29 August–2 September) and sixty-second (16–25 November) sessions in Geneva [A/HRC/19/57]. On 14 November, the Working Group celebrated its twentieth anniversary and, on that occasion, launched its database containing over 650 opinions on individual cases adopted since its establishment. The database was available in English, French and Spanish. Between 1 January and 30 November, the Group adopted 68 opinions concerning 105 persons in 31 States; the texts of 51 of those opinions were contained in an addendum [A/HRC/19/57/Add.1] and 17 in a later addendum [A/HRC/22/44/Add.1]. Between 18 November 2010 and 17 November 2011, the Group transmitted 108 urgent appeals to 45 States concerning 1,629 individuals, including 99 women and 4 minors. Governments and sources reported that 21 persons were released.

The States informed the Group that they had taken measures to remedy the situation of the detainees: in some cases, the detainees were released; in others, the Group was assured that the detainees concerned would be guaranteed a fair trial. The Group engaged in dialogue with the countries it visited, and recommended changes to legislation governing detention or the adoption of other measures. Information on the implementation of the Group's recommendations made in 2007 [YUN 2007, p. 739] and in 2008 [YUN 2008, p. 798] was received respectively from Angola and Colombia.

In 2011, the Working Group devoted its attention to pre-trial detention as an exceptional measure, and the human right of habeas corpus. It also discussed the need to revisit the definition and scope of arbitrary deprivation of liberty. In that connection, the Group held informal consultations with representatives of Governments and civil society in preparation of its Deliberation No. 9 on the definition and scope of arbitrary deprivation of liberty in customary international law. In its recommendations, the Group requested States to ensure that measures alternative to detention and less restrictive in character were available in domestic legal systems; to ensure the right to a habeas corpus in their domestic legislation; and to remedy arbitrary detention mainly by immediate release and compensation.

Mission reports. Following its visit to Georgia (15–24 June) [A/HRC/19/57/Add.2], the Working Group noted that many legislative reforms and positive initiatives had been undertaken to assist in safeguarding against the occurrences of deprivation of liberty. It drew the Government's attention to a number of issues, including the protection of the right to due process and a fair trial; the independence of the judiciary; excessive and harsh sentencing; the lack of use of alternatives to deprivation of liberty; the plea bargaining system; administrative detention; detention in the context of peaceful demonstrations; and issues relating to asylum seekers and irregular migrants. The Group made recommendations regarding those issues. In a later addendum [A/HRC/19/57/Add.4], Georgia submitted its comments on the Group's report.

Following its mission to Germany (26 September–5 October) [A/HRC/19/57/Add.3], the Working Group noted a number of positive aspects with respect to the institutions and laws safeguarding against occurrences of arbitrary deprivation of liberty. It drew attention to the State's inter-agency approach to addressing the socioeconomic causes of offences and its impact in reducing crime as one of vital importance that could be disseminated and shared beyond Germany. The report highlighted initiatives including collaboration between the police and education departments to respond to factors impacting criminality; the establishment in Hamburg of an independent special commission to investigate police officers in cases of alleged misconduct or ill-treatment; and the abrogation of the obligation of authorities to report children of migrants in an irregular situation receiving education or emergency medical treatment. Despite those achievements, the Working Group identified areas of concern, such as the preventive detention system, under which persons who had already served their sentences were deprived of their liberty as they were deemed to represent a danger to society; the uneven use of restraints, such as handcuffs and shackles; the disproportionate number of foreigners and Germans of foreign origin in detention; and aspects of the "fast-track" airport procedure, an accelerated process for asylum applicants from countries considered to be safe States. The Group made recommendations on those and other issues.

Communication. In a 9 March note [A/HRC/16/G/8], Malaysia submitted its comments on the Working Group's 2010 visit to the country [YUN 2010, p. 711].

Terrorism

Reports of Special Rapporteur. Pursuant to a Human Rights Council request [YUN 2010, p. 714], the Special Rapporteur on the promotion and protection of human rights and fundamental freedoms while countering terrorism, Martin Scheinin (Finland), submitted his sixth and final report [A/HRC/16/51], covering his activities from 1 August to 10 December 2010 and presenting a compilation of 10 areas of best practices in countering terrorism. The compilation was based on an analysis of his work conducted over six years and interaction with various stakeholders. The Rapporteur advocated the practices, which were annexed to the report, as concrete models for wider adoption and implementation by States. The areas addressed in the practices included: consistency of counter-terrorism law and of counter-terrorism practices with human rights, humanitarian law and refugee law; principles of normalcy and specificity; regular reviews of the operation of counter-terrorism law and practice; remedies provision; reparations and assistance to victims; definition of terrorism; offence of incitement to terrorism; listing of terrorist entities; and arrest and interrogation of terrorist suspects.

An addendum [A/HRC/16/51/Add.1] summarized 18 communications and three press releases transmitted to 12 Governments in 2010, and 10 replies received from 7 Governments.

In accordance with General Assembly resolution 65/221 [YUN 2010, p. 714], the Secretary-General in August transmitted to the Assembly the first report [A/66/310] of the Special Rapporteur, Ben Emmerson (United Kingdom). After an account of both the former and the new Rapporteur's activities between February and August 2011, the report highlighted areas of interest to the Rapporteur in the discharge of his mandate, in particular the rights of victims of terrorism, and the prevention of terrorism. In his conclusions, the Rapporteur pointed out his intention to build and elaborate on the 10 areas of best practice prepared by his predecessor (see above), to ensure that proportionate attention was paid to the rights of direct and indirect victims of terrorism, and to focus on the prevention of terrorism through promotion and protection of human rights, and in compliance with obligations under human rights law.

Mission report. Following his follow-up mission to Tunisia (22–26 May) [A/HRC/20/14/Add.1], the Special Rapporteur, Mr. Scheinin, recommended that the Government proceed to resolve the ambiguous status of the 2003 anti-terrorism law which had not been formally repealed at the time of his visit, but was qualified as "dormant" and still applied by courts in isolated cases; introduce a bill to replace the 2003 anti-terrorism law with a proper legal framework that complied with international human rights norms and standards; initiate amendments to legislation to the effect that persons deprived of their liberty had access to a lawyer immediately after apprehension; implement video and audio recording of interrogations to strengthen the safeguards against torture and other forms of ill-treatment; create an effective bail system; clarify the structures, responsibilities and powers of all internal security forces in publicly available laws; and establish an effective national preventive mechanism following the State's accession to the Optional Protocol to the Convention against Torture.

Report of Secretary-General. Pursuant to General Assembly resolution 65/221 [YUN 2010, p. 714], the Secretary-General in July [A/66/204] reported on developments within the UN system in relation to human rights and counter-terrorism, including through the activities of OHCHR, the Human Rights Council and its special procedures mandates, the human rights treaty bodies, the Counter-Terrorism Implementation Task Force and its Working Group on Protecting Human Rights while Countering Terrorism, and the Counter-Terrorism Committee and its Executive Directorate. He reported on the consideration by the UN human rights system of issues relating to countering terrorism, including compliance of legislation, policies and practices for countering terrorism with international human rights law. He urged States to ensure that their counter-terrorism measures complied with their obligations under international law and to take advantage of the basic human rights reference guides developed by the Working Group.

Report of High Commissioner. Pursuant to a Human Rights Council request [YUN 2010, p. 714], the High Commissioner submitted a report [A/HRC/16/50] on the protection of human rights and fundamental freedoms while countering terrorism. She expressed concern at the erosion of respect for due process in the context of counter-terrorism policies and practices and identified issues of concern and other practices which impeded the right to a fair trial, such as the use of intelligence in criminal justice processes. She made recommendations for the Counter-Terrorism Implementation Task Force to incorporate a human rights approach in all aspects of its work and step up its engagement with civil society, NGOs and human rights defenders, and for the Security Council to ensure that sanctions imposed against individuals and entities were accompanied by safeguards which guaranteed due process standards. Another recommendation was for States to develop and maintain a criminal justice system based on rule of law, and ensure that individuals suspected of terrorist activity were brought to justice with due process guarantees.

Human Rights Council action. Recognizing the need to reflect on the question of the human rights of victims of terrorist acts, the Council on 24 March [A/66/53 (dec. 16/116)] decided to convene a panel discussion at its seventeenth (2011) session on the human rights of victims of terrorism, taking into account the recommendations of the Secretary-General's 2008 Symposium on Supporting Victims of Terrorism [YUN 2009, p. 13]. It requested OHCHR to prepare a summary report on the outcome of the discussion.

OHCHR report. An OHCHR report [A/HRC/19/38] summarized the panel discussion (Geneva, 1 June). Participants examined various topics pertaining to victims of terrorism, including the need for a strengthened focus on their human rights; regional and domestic practices for the protection of their human rights; and proposals to enhance such protection.

Human Rights Council action. On 16 June [A/66/53 (res. 17/8)], the Council, deploring the suffering caused by terrorism to the victims and their families, recommended that the General Assembly proclaim 19 August the International Day of Remembrance and Tribute to the Victims of Terrorism.

OHCHR report. Pursuant to a Human Rights Council decision [YUN 2010, p. 714], a panel discussion on human rights in the context of action taken to address terrorist hostage-taking was held during the Council's sixteenth (2011) session (Geneva, 11 March). An OHCHR report [A/HRC/18/29] stated that participants examined various topics, including the primary responsibility of States to promote and protect human rights, strengthening cooperation to prevent and combat terrorism, and protecting the rights of victims of terrorism involved in hostage-taking.

Human Rights Council action. On 29 September [A/66/53/Add.1 (res. 18/10)], the Council recognized that the issue of hostage-taking by terrorist groups posed a number of challenges and had an adverse impact on the protection of hostages' human rights, as well on the rights of those living in local communities in the countries affected by hostage-taking. It requested the Human Rights Council Advisory Committee to prepare a study on the issue to promote awareness and understanding and to submit the study at the Council's twenty-third (2013) session and an interim report at its twenty-first (2012) session.

OHCHR note. In a 21 December note [A/HRC/19/62], the OHCHR secretariat stated that the Rapporteur's next report would be submitted to the Council's twentieth (2012) session.

GENERAL ASSEMBLY ACTION

On 19 December [meeting 89], the General Assembly, on the recommendation of the Third Committee [A/66/462/Add.2], adopted **resolution 66/171** without vote [agenda item 69 (*b*)].

Protection of human rights and fundamental freedoms while countering terrorism

The General Assembly,

Reaffirming the purposes and principles of the Charter of the United Nations,

Reaffirming also the Universal Declaration of Human Rights,

Reaffirming further the Vienna Declaration and Programme of Action,

Reaffirming the fundamental importance, including in response to terrorism and the fear of terrorism, of respecting all human rights and fundamental freedoms and the rule of law,

Reaffirming also that States are under the obligation to protect all human rights and fundamental freedoms of all persons,

Reaffirming further that terrorism cannot and should not be associated with any religion, nationality, civilization or ethnic group,

Reiterating the important contribution of measures taken at all levels against terrorism, consistent with international law, in particular international human rights, refugee and humanitarian law, to the functioning of democratic institutions and the maintenance of peace and security and thereby to the full enjoyment of human rights and fundamental freedoms, as well as the need to continue this fight, including through strengthening international cooperation and the role of the United Nations in this respect,

Deeply deploring the occurrence of violations of human rights and fundamental freedoms in the context of the fight against terrorism, as well as violations of international refugee and humanitarian law,

Noting with concern measures that can undermine human rights and the rule of law, such as the detention of persons suspected of acts of terrorism in the absence of a legal basis for detention and due process guarantees, the deprivation of liberty that amounts to placing a detained person outside the protection of the law, the trial of suspects without fundamental judicial guarantees, the illegal deprivation of liberty and transfer of individuals suspected of terrorist activities, and the return of suspects to countries without individual assessment of the risk of there being substantial grounds for believing that they would be in danger of subjection to torture, and limitations to effective scrutiny of counter-terrorism measures,

Stressing that all measures used in the fight against terrorism, including the profiling of individuals and the use of diplomatic assurances, memorandums of understanding and other transfer agreements or arrangements, must be in compliance with the obligations of States under international law, including international human rights, refugee and humanitarian law,

Stressing also that a criminal justice system based on respect for human rights and the rule of law, including due process and fair trial guarantees, is one of the best means for effectively countering terrorism and ensuring accountability,

Recalling article 30 of the Universal Declaration of Human Rights, and reaffirming that acts, methods and practices of terrorism in all its forms and manifestations are activities aimed at the destruction of human rights, fundamental freedoms and democracy, threatening the territorial integrity and security of States and destabilizing legitimately constituted Governments, and that the international community should take the necessary steps to enhance cooperation to prevent and combat terrorism,

Reaffirming its unequivocal condemnation of all acts, methods and practices of terrorism in all its forms and manifestations, wherever and by whomsoever committed, regardless of their motivation, as criminal and unjustifiable, and renewing its commitment to strengthen international cooperation to prevent and combat terrorism,

Recognizing that respect for all human rights, respect for democracy and respect for the rule of law are interrelated and mutually reinforcing,

Emphasizing the importance of properly interpreting and implementing the obligations of States with respect to torture and other cruel, inhuman or degrading treatment or punishment, and of abiding strictly by the definition of torture contained in article 1 of the Convention against

Torture and Other Cruel, Inhuman or Degrading Treatment or Punishment, in the fight against terrorism,

Recalling its resolution 65/221 of 21 December 2010 and Human Rights Council resolution 13/26 of 26 March 2010 and other relevant resolutions and decisions as stated in the preamble to resolution 65/221, and welcoming the efforts of all relevant stakeholders to implement those resolutions,

Recalling also its resolution 60/288 of 8 September 2006, by which it adopted the United Nations Global Counter-Terrorism Strategy, and its resolution 64/297 of 8 September 2010 on the review of the Strategy, and reaffirming that the promotion and protection of human rights for all and the rule of law are essential to the fight against terrorism, recognizing that effective counter-terrorism measures and the protection of human rights are not conflicting goals but complementary and mutually reinforcing, and stressing the need to promote and protect the rights of victims of terrorism,

Recalling further Human Rights Council resolution 15/15 of 30 September 2010, by which the Council decided to extend the mandate of the Special Rapporteur on the promotion and protection of human rights and fundamental freedoms while countering terrorism,

Recalling its resolution 64/115 of 16 December 2009 and the annex thereto entitled "Introduction and implementation of sanctions imposed by the United Nations", in particular the provisions of the annex regarding listing and delisting procedures,

1. *Reaffirms* that States must ensure that any measure taken to combat terrorism complies with their obligations under international law, in particular international human rights, refugee and humanitarian law;

2. *Deeply deplores* the suffering caused by terrorism to the victims and their families, expresses its profound solidarity with them, and stresses the importance of providing them with assistance;

3. *Expresses serious concern* at the occurrence of violations of human rights and fundamental freedoms, as well as of international refugee and humanitarian law, committed in the context of countering terrorism;

4. *Reaffirms* that all counter-terrorism measures should be implemented in accordance with international law, including international human rights, refugee and humanitarian law, thereby taking into full consideration the human rights of all, including persons belonging to national or ethnic, religious and linguistic minorities, and in this regard must not be discriminatory on grounds such as race, colour, sex, language, religion or social origin;

5. *Also reaffirms* the obligation of States, in accordance with article 4 of the International Covenant on Civil and Political Rights, to respect certain rights as non-derogable in any circumstances, recalls, in regard to all other Covenant rights, that any measures derogating from the provisions of the Covenant must be in accordance with that article in all cases, and underlines the exceptional and temporary nature of any such derogations, and in this regard calls upon States to raise awareness about the importance of these obligations among national authorities involved in combating terrorism;

6. *Urges* States, while countering terrorism:

(*a*) To fully comply with their obligations under international law, in particular international human rights, refugee and humanitarian law, with regard to the absolute prohibition of torture and other cruel, inhuman or degrading treatment or punishment;

(*b*) To take all steps necessary to ensure that persons deprived of liberty, regardless of the place of arrest or detention, benefit from the guarantees to which they are entitled under international law, including the review of the detention and other fundamental judicial guarantees;

(*c*) To ensure that no form of deprivation of liberty places a detained person outside the protection of the law, and to respect the safeguards concerning the liberty, security and dignity of the person, in accordance with international law, including international human rights and humanitarian law;

(*d*) To take all steps necessary to ensure the right of anyone arrested or detained on a criminal charge to be brought promptly before a judge or other officer authorized by law to exercise judicial power and the entitlement to trial within a reasonable time or release;

(*e*) To treat all prisoners in all places of detention in accordance with international law, including international human rights and humanitarian law;

(*f*) To respect the right of persons to equality before the law, courts and tribunals and to a fair trial as provided for in international law, including international human rights law, such as the International Covenant on Civil and Political Rights, and international humanitarian and refugee law;

(*g*) To safeguard the right to privacy in accordance with international law, and to take measures to ensure that interferences with the right to privacy are regulated by law, and subject to effective oversight and appropriate redress, including through judicial review or other means;

(*h*) To protect all human rights, including economic, social and cultural rights, bearing in mind that certain counter-terrorism measures may have an impact on the enjoyment of these rights;

(*i*) To ensure that guidelines and practices in all border control operations and other pre-entry mechanisms are clear and fully respect their obligations under international law, particularly international refugee and human rights law, towards persons seeking international protection;

(*j*) To fully respect non-refoulement obligations under international refugee and human rights law and, at the same time, to review, with full respect for these obligations and other legal safeguards, the validity of a refugee status decision in an individual case if credible and relevant evidence comes to light that indicates that the person in question has committed any criminal acts, including terrorist acts, falling under the exclusion clauses under international refugee law;

(*k*) To refrain from returning persons, including in cases related to terrorism, to their countries of origin or to a third State whenever such transfer would be contrary to their obligations under international law, in particular international human rights, humanitarian and refugee law, including in cases where there are substantial grounds for believing that they would be in danger of subjection to torture, or where their life or freedom would be threatened, in violation of international refugee law, on account of their race, religion, nationality, membership of a particular social group or political opinion, bearing in mind obligations that States may have to prosecute individuals not returned;

(*l*) Insofar as such an act runs contrary to their obligations under international law, not to expose individuals to cruel, inhuman or degrading treatment or punishment by way of return to another country;

(*m*) To ensure that their laws criminalizing acts of terrorism are accessible, formulated with precision, non-discriminatory, non-retroactive and in accordance with international law, including human rights law;

(*n*) Not to resort to profiling based on stereotypes founded on grounds of discrimination prohibited by international law, including on racial, ethnic and/or religious grounds;

(*o*) To ensure that the interrogation methods used against terrorism suspects are consistent with their international obligations and are reviewed on a regular basis to prevent the risk of violations of their obligations under international law, including international human rights, refugee and humanitarian law;

(*p*) To ensure that any person whose human rights or fundamental freedoms have been violated has access to an effective and enforceable remedy within a reasonable time and that victims of such violations receive adequate, effective and prompt reparations, where appropriate, including by bringing to justice those responsible for such violations;

(*q*) To ensure due process guarantees, consistent with all relevant provisions of the Universal Declaration of Human Rights, and their obligations under the International Covenant on Civil and Political Rights, the Geneva Conventions of 1949 and the Additional Protocols thereto, of 1977, and the 1951 Convention relating to the Status of Refugees and the 1967 Protocol thereto in their respective fields of applicability;

(*r*) To shape, review and implement all counter-terrorism measures in accordance with the principles of gender equality and non-discrimination;

7. *Also urges* States, while countering terrorism, to take into account relevant United Nations resolutions and decisions on human rights, and encourages them to give due consideration to the recommendations of the special procedures and mechanisms of the Human Rights Council and to the relevant comments and views of United Nations human rights treaty bodies;

8. *Welcomes* the entry into force of the International Convention for the Protection of All Persons from Enforced Disappearance, the implementation of which will make a significant contribution in support of the rule of law in countering terrorism, including by prohibiting places of secret detention, and encourages all States that have not yet done so to consider signing, ratifying or acceding to the Convention;

9. *Encourages* all States that have not yet done so to consider signing, ratifying or acceding to the Convention against Torture and Other Cruel, Inhuman or Degrading Treatment or Punishment and the Optional Protocol thereto, the implementation of which will make a significant contribution in support of the rule of law in countering terrorism;

10. *Calls upon* the United Nations entities involved in supporting counter-terrorism efforts to continue to facilitate the promotion and protection of human rights and fundamental freedoms, as well as due process and the rule of law, while countering terrorism;

11. *Recognizes* the need to continue ensuring that fair and clear procedures under the United Nations terrorism-related sanctions regime are strengthened in order to enhance their efficiency and transparency, and welcomes and encourages the ongoing efforts of the Security Council in support of these objectives, including by supporting the enhanced role of the office of the ombudsperson and continuing to review all the names of individuals and entities in the regime, while emphasizing the importance of these sanctions in countering terrorism;

12. *Urges* States, while ensuring full compliance with their international obligations, to ensure the rule of law and to include adequate human rights guarantees in their national procedures for the listing of individuals and entities with a view to combating terrorism;

13. *Requests* the Office of the United Nations High Commissioner for Human Rights and the Special Rapporteur of the Human Rights Council on the promotion and protection of human rights and fundamental freedoms while countering terrorism to continue to contribute to the work of the Counter-Terrorism Implementation Task Force, including by raising awareness, inter alia, through regular dialogue, about the need to respect human rights and the rule of law while countering terrorism and support the exchange of best practices to promote and protect human rights, fundamental freedoms and the rule of law in all aspects of counter-terrorism, including, as appropriate, those identified by the Special Rapporteur in his report submitted to the Human Rights Council pursuant to Council resolution 15/15;

14. *Welcomes* the ongoing dialogue established in the context of the fight against terrorism between the Security Council and its Counter-Terrorism Committee and the relevant bodies for the promotion and protection of human rights, and encourages the Security Council and its Counter-Terrorism Committee to strengthen the links, cooperation and dialogue with relevant human rights bodies, in particular with the Office of the United Nations High Commissioner for Human Rights, the Special Rapporteur on the promotion and protection of human rights and fundamental freedoms while countering terrorism, other relevant special procedures and mechanisms of the Human Rights Council, and relevant treaty bodies, giving due regard to the promotion and protection of human rights and the rule of law in their ongoing work relating to counter-terrorism;

15. *Calls upon* States and other relevant actors, as appropriate, to continue to implement the United Nations Global Counter-Terrorism Strategy, which, inter alia, reaffirms respect for human rights for all and the rule of law as the fundamental basis of the fight against terrorism;

16. *Requests* the Counter-Terrorism Implementation Task Force to continue its efforts to ensure that the United Nations can better coordinate and enhance its support to Member States in their efforts to comply with their obligations under international law, including international human rights, refugee and humanitarian law, while countering terrorism, and to encourage the Working Groups of the Task Force to incorporate a human rights perspective into their work;

17. *Encourages* relevant United Nations bodies and entities and international, regional and subregional organizations, in particular those participating in the Counter-Terrorism Implementation Task Force, which provide technical assistance, upon request, consistent with their mandates, related to the prevention and suppression of terrorism, to step up their efforts to ensure respect for international human rights, refugee and humanitarian law, as well as the rule of law, as an element of technical assistance, including in the adoption and implementation of legislative and other measures by States;

18. *Urges* relevant United Nations bodies and entities and international, regional and subregional organizations, including the United Nations Office on Drugs and Crime, within its mandate related to the prevention and suppression of terrorism, to step up their efforts to provide, upon request, technical assistance for building the capacity of Member States in the development and implementation of programmes of assistance and support for victims of terrorism in accordance with relevant national legislation;

19. *Calls upon* international, regional and subregional organizations to strengthen information-sharing, coordination and cooperation in promoting the protection of human rights, fundamental freedoms and the rule of law while countering terrorism;

20. *Takes note with appreciation* of the report of the Secretary-General on protecting human rights and fundamental freedoms while countering terrorism and the report of the Special Rapporteur of the Human Rights Council on the promotion and protection of human rights and fundamental freedoms while countering terrorism, submitted pursuant to resolution 65/221;

21. *Requests* the Special Rapporteur on the promotion and protection of human rights and fundamental freedoms while countering terrorism to continue to make recommendations, in the context of his mandate, with regard to preventing, combating and redressing violations of human rights and fundamental freedoms in the context of countering terrorism and to continue to report and engage in interactive dialogues on an annual basis with the General Assembly and the Human Rights Council in accordance with their programmes of work;

22. *Requests* all Governments to cooperate fully with the Special Rapporteur on the promotion and protection of human rights and fundamental freedoms while countering terrorism in the performance of the tasks and duties mandated, including by reacting promptly to the urgent appeals of the Special Rapporteur and providing the information requested, and to give serious consideration to responding favourably to his requests to visit their countries, as well as to cooperate with other relevant procedures and mechanisms of the Human Rights Council regarding the promotion and protection of human rights and fundamental freedoms while countering terrorism;

23. *Welcomes* the work of the United Nations High Commissioner for Human Rights to implement the mandate given to her in General Assembly resolution 60/158 of 16 December 2005, and requests her to continue her efforts in this regard;

24. *Requests* the Secretary-General to submit a report on the implementation of the present resolution to the Human Rights Council and to the General Assembly at its sixty-eighth session;

25. *Decides* to continue the consideration of the question at its sixty-eighth session under the item entitled "Promotion and protection of human rights".

Right to peace

Report of Advisory Committee. In response to a Human Rights Council request [YUN 2010, p. 717], the Human Rights Council Advisory Committee submitted an April progress report [A/HRC/17/39 & Corr.1] on the preparation of a draft declaration on the right of peoples to peace. The report proposed more than 40 possible standards for inclusion in the draft declaration, specific rationale for including them and relevant legal standards. After its sixth (2011) session (see p. 613), the Advisory Committee invited stakeholders to comment on the report in a questionnaire.

Human Rights Council action. On 17 June [A/66/53 (res. 17/16)], the Council, by a recorded vote of 32 to 14, with no abstentions, supported the need to further promote the realization of the right of peoples to peace; requested the Advisory Committee to present a draft declaration on that right and to report on progress at the Council's twentieth (2012) session; and requested OHCHR to retransmit the questionnaire prepared by the Advisory Committee on the issue of the right of peoples to peace, seeking the comments of States, civil society, academia and relevant stakeholders.

Traditional values

Human Rights Council action. On 24 March [A/66/53 (res. 16/3)], the Council, by a recorded vote of 24 to 14, with 7 abstentions, affirmed that all cultures and civilizations in their traditions, customs, religions and beliefs shared a common set of values that belonged to humankind in its entirety, and that dignity, freedom and responsibility were traditional values. The Council welcomed the holding of the workshop on traditional values and human rights in October 2010 and the High Commissioner's report summarizing the discussions at the workshop [YUN 2010, p. 719]. It requested its Advisory Committee to prepare a study on how a better understanding and appreciation of the traditional values of dignity, freedom and responsibility could contribute to the promotion and protection of human rights, and to present it to the Council before its twenty-first (2012) session.

Sexual orientation and gender identity

Human Rights Council action. On 17 June [A/66/53 (res. 17/19)], the Council, by a recorded vote of 23 to 19, with 3 abstentions, requested the High Commissioner to commission a study, to be finalized by December 2011, documenting discriminatory laws and practices and acts of violence against individuals based on their sexual orientation and gender identity, in all regions of the world, and how international human rights law could be used to end violence and related human rights violations based on sexual orientation and gender identity. It decided to convene a panel discussion during the Council's nineteenth (2012) session informed by the study, and that the panel would discuss the appropriate follow-up to the study's recommendations.

Report of High Commissioner. In response to Human Rights Council resolution 17/19 (see above), the High Commissioner issued a November report

[A/HRC/19/41] on discriminatory laws and practices and acts of violence against individuals based on their sexual orientation and gender identity, with a particular focus on critical human rights concerns that States had an obligation to address, and emerging responses. Drawing on UN sources, it included data and findings from regional organizations, national authorities and NGOs that revealed a pattern of human rights violations against lesbian, gay, bisexual and transgender persons. Governments and intergovernmental bodies had often overlooked violence and discrimination based on sexual orientation and gender identity. Further action was needed, especially at the national level, if individuals were to be better protected from such human rights violations. The High Commissioner made recommendations to Member States that drew on measures recommended by UN human rights mechanisms, as well as recommendations to the Human Rights Council.

Economic, social and cultural rights

Realizing economic, social and cultural rights

Reports of High Commissioner. As requested by the Human Rights Council [YUN 2010, p. 719], the High Commissioner in March [A/HRC/17/24 & Corr.1] reported on the 2010 activities of the Office of the United Nations High Commissioner for Human Rights (OHCHR), treaty bodies and special procedures in relation to economic, social and cultural rights. The report also covered OHCHR activities on assistance and technical cooperation to States, UN agencies, civil society and other actors.

Pursuant to General Assembly resolution 48/141 [YUN 1993, p. 906], the High Commissioner, in an April report [E/2011/90], focused on the use of indicators in realizing economic, social and cultural rights. The analysis included a description of human rights indicators and their role in implementing economic, social and cultural rights; the rationale for the use of indicators for implementing and monitoring those rights; and a summary of methodological, institutional and practical considerations for the effective use of human rights indicators.

The Economic and Social Council took note of the report on 28 July (**decision 2011/265**).

Right to development

Working Group activities. The Working Group on the Right to Development, at its twelfth session (Geneva, 14–18 November) [A/HRC/19/52 & Corr.1], considered the reports of the Chairperson-Rapporteur containing summaries of the submissions received from Governments, groups of Governments and regional groups [A/HRC/WG.2/12/2], and inputs from other stakeholders [A/HRC/WG.2/12/3], pursuant to Council resolution 15/25 [YUN 2010, p. 720]. It also had before it the summary of the Council's panel discussion on "The way forward in the realization of the right to development: between policy and practice" [A/HRC/WG.2/12/4], submitted pursuant to Council decision 16/117 (see below). The Working Group concluded that the right-to-development criteria and operational sub-criteria in the high-level task force's 2010 report [YUN 2010, p. 719] needed to be revised and refined. The Working Group requested OHCHR to make available on its website, and to the next session of the Working Group, all written submissions by Governments, groups of Governments and regional groups, as well as inputs by other stakeholders. It also invited the Chairperson-Rapporteur to hold informal consultations with the aforementioned parties and report to the thirteenth (2012) session of the Working Group.

Reports of Secretary-General and High Commissioner. In response to a General Assembly request in resolution 65/219 [YUN 2010, p. 720], the High Commissioner stated in a June secretariat note [A/HRC/18/22] that, due to established procedure and the timing of the reporting cycle, the consolidated report of the Secretary-General and the High Commissioner on the right to development would be submitted to the Council's nineteenth (2012) session.

In August, the Secretary-General submitted a consolidated report [A/66/216] providing an overview of OHCHR activities relating to the right to development and a compilation of the conclusions and recommendations adopted by the Working Group with a view to contributing to intergovernmental deliberations on future action in implementing the right to development. The Secretary-General concluded that new efforts were needed to overcome political and polarized debate; mobilize support from a wide public constituency; and encourage international organizations to integrate all human rights, including the right to development, into their work.

OHCHR note. In a 30 August note [A/HRC/18/39], the OHCHR secretariat informed the Human Rights Council that since the twelfth session of the Working Group was scheduled for November, the Group would submit the report on that session to the Council's nineteenth (2012) session.

Human Rights Council action. On 25 March [A/66/53 (dec. 16/117)], by a recorded vote of 45 to none, with 1 abstention, the Council decided to hold a panel during its eighteenth (2011) session to commemorate the twenty-fifth anniversary of the Declaration on the Right to Development [YUN 1986, p. 717]; requested OHCHR to organize the panel and invite relevant UN human rights mechanisms, specialized agencies, funds and programmes, as well as civil society and national human rights institutions; and requested the Office to prepare a summary of the panel discussions to be submitted to the Working Group on the Right to Development at its twelfth (2011) session and to the Council's nineteenth (2012) session.

Pursuant to that decision, the Council held a panel discussion on the theme "The way forward in the realization of the right to development: between policy and practice" (Geneva, 14 September), and in November, the High Commissioner issued a summary report [A/HRC/19/39] of the discussion. In a statement annexed to the report, UN system agencies and other international organizations, in support of policy coherence in the implementation of the right to development, recognized the political commitments made in the 2010 Millennium Development Goals (MDG) outcome document [YUN 2010, p. 815], resolved to work together to promote the economic and social advancement of peoples, and expressed their commitment to carry the vision forward and make the right to development a reality for all.

On 30 September [A/66/53/Add.1 (res. 18/26)], by a recorded vote of 45 to none, with 1 abstention, the Council welcomed the holding of the panel discussion, and noted that the consolidated report of the Secretary-General and the High Commissioner would be submitted to the Council's nineteenth (2012) session, and that the twelfth session of the Working Group was scheduled for 14 to 18 November 2011. It also decided that the list of right to development criteria and corresponding operational sub-criteria, once endorsed by the Working Group, should be used in elaborating a set of standards for implementing the right to development. The Working Group should also take steps to ensure the practical application of those standards, including guidelines on implementing the right to development, which could evolve into a basis for considering an international legal standard of a binding nature.

GENERAL ASSEMBLY ACTION

On 19 December [meeting 89], the General Assembly, on the recommendation of the Third Committee [A/66/462/Add.2], adopted **resolution 66/155** by recorded vote (154-6-29) [agenda item 69 (*b*)].

The right to development

The General Assembly,

Guided by the Charter of the United Nations, which expresses, in particular, the determination to promote social progress and better standards of life in larger freedom and, to that end, to employ international mechanisms for the promotion of the economic and social advancement of all peoples,

Recalling the Universal Declaration of Human Rights, as well as the International Covenant on Civil and Political Rights and the International Covenant on Economic, Social and Cultural Rights,

Recalling also the outcomes of all the major United Nations conferences and summits in the economic and social fields,

Recalling further that the Declaration on the Right to Development, adopted by the General Assembly in its resolution 41/128 of 4 December 1986, confirmed that the right to development is an inalienable human right and that equality of opportunity for development is a prerogative both of nations and of individuals who make up nations, and that the individual is the central subject and beneficiary of development,

Stressing that the Vienna Declaration and Programme of Action reaffirmed the right to development as a universal and inalienable right and an integral part of fundamental human rights, and the individual as the central subject and beneficiary of development,

Reaffirming the objective of making the right to development a reality for everyone, as set out in the United Nations Millennium Declaration, adopted by the General Assembly on 8 September 2000,

Deeply concerned that the majority of indigenous peoples in the world live in conditions of poverty, and recognizing the critical need to address the negative impact of poverty and inequity on indigenous peoples by ensuring their full and effective inclusion in development and poverty eradication programmes,

Reaffirming the universality, indivisibility, interrelatedness, interdependence and mutually reinforcing nature of all civil, cultural, economic, political and social rights, including the right to development,

Expressing deep concern over the lack of progress in the trade negotiations of the World Trade Organization, and reaffirming the need for a successful outcome of the Doha Development Round in key areas such as agriculture, market access for non-agricultural products, trade facilitation, development and services,

Recalling the outcome of the twelfth session of the United Nations Conference on Trade and Development, held in Accra from 20 to 25 April 2008, on the theme "Addressing the opportunities and challenges of globalization for development",

Recalling also all its previous resolutions, Human Rights Council resolution 18/26 of 30 September 2011, previous resolutions of the Council and those of the Commission on Human Rights on the right to development, in particular Commission resolution 1998/72 of 22 April 1998 on the urgent need to make further progress towards the realization of the right to development as set out in the Declaration on the Right to Development,

Recalling further that 2011 marks the twenty-fifth anniversary of the Declaration on the Right to Development,

Recalling the outcome of the eleventh session of the Working Group on the Right to Development of the Human Rights Council, held in Geneva from 26 to 30 April 2010, as contained in the report of the Working Group and as referred to in the report of the Secretary-General and the United Nations High Commissioner for Human Rights on the right to development,

Recalling also the Fifteenth Summit Conference of Heads of State and Government of the Movement of Non-Aligned Countries, held in Sharm el-Sheikh, Egypt, from 11 to 16 July 2009, and the previous summits and conferences at which the States members of the Movement stressed the need to operationalize the right to development as a priority,

Reiterating its continuing support for the New Partnership for Africa's Development as a development framework for Africa,

Expressing its appreciation for the efforts of the Chair-Rapporteur of the Working Group on the Right to Development of the Human Rights Council and the members of the high-level task force on the implementation of the right to development in completing the 2008–2010 three-phase road map established by the Council in its resolution 4/4 of 30 March 2007,

Noting with sadness the passing of the former Chair-Rapporteur of the Working Group, and welcoming the new mandate holder,

Deeply concerned about the negative impacts of the global economic and financial crises on the realization of the right to development,

Recognizing that, while development facilitates the enjoyment of all human rights, the lack of development may not be invoked to justify the abridgement of internationally recognized human rights,

Recognizing also that Member States should cooperate with each other in ensuring development and eliminating obstacles to development, that the international community should promote effective international cooperation for the realization of the right to development and the elimination of obstacles to development and that lasting progress towards the implementation of the right to development requires effective development policies at the national level, as well as equitable economic relations and a favourable economic environment at the international level,

Recognizing further that poverty is an affront to human dignity,

Recognizing that extreme poverty and hunger are one of the greatest global threats and require the collective commitment of the international community for its eradication, pursuant to Millennium Development Goal 1, and therefore calling upon the international community, including the Human Rights Council, to contribute towards achieving that goal,

Recognizing also that historical injustices have undeniably contributed to the poverty, underdevelopment, marginalization, social exclusion, economic disparity, instability and insecurity that affect many people in different parts of the world, in particular in developing countries,

Stressing that poverty eradication is one of the critical elements in the promotion and realization of the right to development and that poverty is a multifaceted problem that requires a multifaceted and integrated approach in addressing economic, political, social, environmental and institutional dimensions at all levels, especially in the context of the Millennium Development Goal of halving, by 2015, the proportion of the world's people whose income is less than one dollar a day and the proportion of people who suffer from hunger,

1. *Recognizes* the significance of all efforts under way and events held to commemorate the twenty-fifth anniversary of the Declaration on the Right to Development, including the panel discussion on the theme "The way forward in the realization of the right to development: between policy and practice", held during the eighteenth session of the Human Rights Council;

2. *Endorses* the conclusions and recommendations adopted by consensus by the Working Group on the Right to Development of the Human Rights Council at its eleventh session, and calls for their immediate, full and effective implementation by the Office of the United Nations High Commissioner for Human Rights and other relevant actors;

3. *Supports* the realization of the mandate of the Working Group, as renewed by the Human Rights Council in its resolution 9/3 of 24 September 2008, with the recognition that the Working Group will convene annual sessions of five working days and submit its reports to the Council;

4. *Emphasizes* the relevant provisions of General Assembly resolution 60/251 of 15 March 2006 establishing the Human Rights Council, and in this regard calls upon the Council to implement the agreement to continue to act to ensure that its agenda promotes and advances sustainable development and the achievement of the Millennium Development Goals, and also in this regard to lead to raising the right to development, as set out in paragraphs 5 and 10 of the Vienna Declaration and Programme of Action, to the same level as and on a par with all other human rights and fundamental freedoms;

5. *Notes* the efforts under way within the framework of the Working Group with a view to completing the tasks entrusted to it by the Human Rights Council in its resolution 4/4, and reaffirms the conclusions and recommendations of the Working Group agreed upon at its eleventh session;

6. *Also notes* the work of the high-level task force on the implementation of the right to development, the mandate of which ended in 2010, including its consolidation of findings and the list of right-to-development criteria and corresponding operational sub-criteria;

7. *Recalls* that the Working Group will consider at its twelfth session the two compilations of views received from Governments, groups of Governments and regional groups, and from other stakeholders on the work of the high-level task force;

8. *Stresses* that it is important that the views requested of Member States and relevant stakeholders on the work of the high-level task force and the way forward take into consideration the essential features of the right to development, using as a reference the Declaration on the Right to Development and resolutions on the right to development of the Commission on Human Rights, the Human Rights Council and the General Assembly;

9. *Also stresses* that the above-mentioned compilations of views, criteria and corresponding operational sub-criteria, once considered, revised and endorsed by the Working Group, should be used, as appropriate, in the elaboration of a comprehensive and coherent set of standards for the implementation of the right to development;

10. *Emphasizes* the importance of the Working Group taking appropriate steps to ensure respect for and practical application of the above-mentioned standards, which could take various forms, including the elaboration of guidelines on the implementation of the right to development, and evolve into a basis for consideration of an international legal

standard of a binding nature through a collaborative process of engagement;

11. *Stresses* the importance of the core principles contained in the conclusions of the Working Group at its third session, congruent with the purpose of international human rights instruments, such as equality, non-discrimination, accountability, participation and international cooperation, as critical to mainstreaming the right to development at the national and international levels, and underlines the importance of the principles of equity and transparency;

12. *Also stresses* that it is important that the Chair-Rapporteur and the Working Group, in the discharge of their mandates, take into account the need:

(a) To promote the democratization of the system of international governance in order to increase the effective participation of developing countries in international decision-making;

(b) To also promote effective partnerships such as the New Partnership for Africa's Development and other similar initiatives with the developing countries, particularly the least developed countries, for the purpose of the realization of their right to development, including the achievement of the Millennium Development Goals;

(c) To strive for greater acceptance, operationalization and realization of the right to development at the international level, while urging all States to undertake at the national level the necessary policy formulation and to institute the measures required for the implementation of the right to development as an integral part of all human rights and fundamental freedoms, and also urging all States to expand and deepen mutually beneficial cooperation in ensuring development and eliminating obstacles to development in the context of promoting effective international cooperation for the realization of the right to development, bearing in mind that lasting progress towards the implementation of the right to development requires effective development policies at the national level and a favourable economic environment at the international level;

(d) To consider ways and means to continue to ensure the operationalization of the right to development as a priority;

(e) To mainstream the right to development in the policies and operational activities of the United Nations and the specialized agencies, funds and programmes, as well as in the policies and strategies of the international financial and multilateral trading systems, bearing in mind in this regard that the core principles of the international economic, commercial and financial spheres, such as equity, non-discrimination, transparency, accountability, participation and international cooperation, including effective partnerships for development, are indispensable in achieving the right to development and preventing discriminatory treatment arising from political or other non-economic considerations in addressing the issues of concern to the developing countries;

13. *Encourages* the Human Rights Council to continue considering how to ensure follow-up to the work of the former Subcommission on the Promotion and Protection of Human Rights on the right to development, in accordance with the relevant provisions of the resolutions adopted by the General Assembly and the Commission on Human Rights and in compliance with decisions to be taken by the Council;

14. *Invites* Member States and all other stakeholders to participate actively in future sessions of the Social Forum, while recognizing the strong support extended to the Forum at its first four sessions by the Subcommission on the Promotion and Protection of Human Rights;

15. *Reaffirms* the commitment to implement the goals and targets set out in all the outcome documents of the major United Nations conferences and summits and their review processes, in particular those relating to the realization of the right to development, recognizing that the realization of the right to development is critical to achieving the objectives, goals and targets set in those outcome documents;

16. *Also reaffirms* that the realization of the right to development is essential to the implementation of the Vienna Declaration and Programme of Action, which regards all human rights as universal, indivisible, interdependent and interrelated, places the human person at the centre of development and recognizes that, while development facilitates the enjoyment of all human rights, the lack of development may not be invoked to justify the abridgement of internationally recognized human rights;

17. *Stresses* that the primary responsibility for the promotion and protection of all human rights lies with the State, and reaffirms that States have the primary responsibility for their own economic and social development and that the role of national policies and development strategies cannot be overemphasized;

18. *Reaffirms* the primary responsibility of States to create national and international conditions favourable to the realization of the right to development, as well as their commitment to cooperate with each other to that end;

19. *Also reaffirms* the need for an international environment that is conducive to the realization of the right to development;

20. *Stresses* the need to strive for greater acceptance, operationalization and realization of the right to development at the international and national levels, and calls upon all States to institute the measures required for the implementation of the right to development as an integral part of all human rights and fundamental freedoms;

21. *Emphasizes* the critical importance of identifying and analysing obstacles impeding the full realization of the right to development at both the national and the international levels;

22. *Affirms* that, while globalization offers both opportunities and challenges, the process of globalization remains deficient in achieving the objectives of integrating all countries into a globalized world, and stresses the need for policies and measures at the national and global levels to respond to the challenges and opportunities of globalization if this process is to be made fully inclusive and equitable;

23. *Recognizes* that, despite continuous efforts on the part of the international community, the gap between developed and developing countries remains unacceptably wide, that most of the developing countries continue to face difficulties in participating in the globalization process and that many risk being marginalized and effectively excluded from its benefits;

24. *Expresses its deep concern*, in this regard, about the negative impact on the realization of the right to development due to the further aggravation of the economic and social situation, in particular of developing countries, as a result of the ongoing international energy, food and financial crises, as well

as the increasing challenges posed by global climate change and the loss of biodiversity, which have increased vulnerabilities and inequalities and have adversely affected development gains, in particular in developing countries;

25. *Underlines* the fact that the international community is far from meeting the target set in the United Nations Millennium Declaration of halving the number of people living in poverty by 2015, reaffirms the commitment made to meet that target, and emphasizes the principle of international cooperation, including partnership and commitment, between developed and developing countries towards achieving the goal;

26. *Urges* developed countries that have not yet done so to make concrete efforts towards meeting the targets of 0.7 per cent of their gross national product for official development assistance to developing countries and 0.15 to 0.2 per cent of their gross national product to least developed countries, and encourages developing countries to build on the progress achieved in ensuring that official development assistance is used effectively to help to meet development goals and targets;

27. *Recognizes* the need to address market access for developing countries, including in the sectors of agriculture, services and non-agricultural products, in particular those of interest to developing countries;

28. *Calls once again for* the implementation of a desirable pace of meaningful trade liberalization, including in areas under negotiation in the World Trade Organization; the implementation of commitments on implementation-related issues and concerns; a review of special and differential treatment provisions, with a view to strengthening them and making them more precise, effective and operational; the avoidance of new forms of protectionism; and capacity-building and technical assistance for developing countries as important issues in making progress towards the effective implementation of the right to development;

29. *Recognizes* the important link between the international economic, commercial and financial spheres and the realization of the right to development; stresses in this regard the need for good governance and for broadening the base of decision-making at the international level on issues of development concern and the need to fill organizational gaps, as well as to strengthen the United Nations system and other multilateral institutions; and also stresses the need to broaden and strengthen the participation of developing countries and countries with economies in transition in international economic decision-making and norm-setting;

30. *Also recognizes* that good governance and the rule of law at the national level assist all States in the promotion and protection of human rights, including the right to development, and agrees on the value of the ongoing efforts being made by States to identify and strengthen good governance practices, including transparent, responsible, accountable and participatory government, that are responsive and appropriate to their needs and aspirations, including in the context of agreed partnership approaches to development, capacity-building and technical assistance;

31. *Further recognizes* the important role and the rights of women and the application of a gender perspective as a cross-cutting issue in the process of realizing the right to development, and notes in particular the positive relationship between the education of women and their equal participation in the civil, cultural, economic, political and social activities of the community and the promotion of the right to development;

32. *Stresses* the need for the integration of the rights of children, girls and boys alike, in all policies and programmes and for ensuring the promotion and protection of those rights, especially in areas relating to health, education and the full development of their capacities;

33. *Recalls* the Political Declaration on HIV and AIDS: Intensifying Our Efforts to Eliminate HIV and AIDS, adopted on 10 June 2011 at the High-level Meeting of the General Assembly on HIV/AIDS, stresses that further and additional measures must be taken at the national and international levels to fight HIV and AIDS and other communicable diseases, taking into account ongoing efforts and programmes, and reiterates the need for international assistance in this regard;

34. *Welcomes* the Political Declaration of the High-level Meeting of the General Assembly on the Prevention and Control of Non-communicable Diseases, adopted on 19 September 2011, with a particular focus on development and other challenges and social and economic impacts, particularly for developing countries;

35. *Recalls* the Convention on the Rights of Persons with Disabilities, which entered into force on 3 May 2008, and stresses the need to take into consideration the rights of persons with disabilities and the importance of international cooperation in support of national efforts in the realization of the right to development;

36. *Stresses its commitment* to indigenous peoples in the process of the realization of the right to development, and reaffirms the commitment to promote their rights in the areas of education, employment, vocational training and retraining, housing, sanitation, health and social security, in accordance with recognized international human rights obligations and taking into account, as appropriate, the United Nations Declaration on the Rights of Indigenous Peoples, adopted by the General Assembly in its resolution 61/295 of 13 September 2007;

37. *Recognizes* the need for strong partnerships with civil society organizations and the private sector in pursuit of poverty eradication and development, as well as for corporate social responsibility;

38. *Emphasizes* the urgent need for taking concrete and effective measures to prevent, combat and criminalize all forms of corruption at all levels, to prevent, detect and deter in a more effective manner international transfers of illicitly acquired assets and to strengthen international cooperation in asset recovery, consistent with the principles of the United Nations Convention against Corruption, particularly chapter V thereof, stresses the importance of a genuine political commitment on the part of all Governments through a firm legal framework, and in this context urges States to sign and ratify the Convention as soon as possible and States parties to implement it effectively;

39. *Also emphasizes* the need to strengthen further the activities of the Office of the United Nations High Commissioner for Human Rights in the promotion and realization of the right to development, including by ensuring effective use of the financial and human resources necessary to fulfil its mandate, and calls upon the Secretary-General to provide the Office of the High Commissioner with the necessary resources;

40. *Reaffirms* the request to the United Nations High Commissioner for Human Rights, in mainstreaming the right to development, to undertake effectively activities aimed at strengthening the global partnership for development among Member States, development agencies and the international development, financial and trade institutions and to reflect those activities in detail in her next report to the Human Rights Council;

41. *Reaffirms* the request to the Office of the High Commissioner, in consultation with States Members of the United Nations and other relevant stakeholders, to continue the commemoration of the twenty-fifth anniversary of the Declaration on the Right to Development in 2011;

42. *Calls upon* the United Nations funds and programmes, as well as the specialized agencies, to mainstream the right to development in their operational programmes and objectives, and stresses the need for the international financial and multilateral trading systems to mainstream the right to development in their policies and objectives;

43. *Requests* the Secretary-General to bring the present resolution to the attention of Member States, United Nations organs and bodies, specialized agencies, funds and programmes, international development and financial institutions, in particular the Bretton Woods institutions, and non-governmental organizations;

44. *Also requests* the Secretary-General to submit a report to the General Assembly at its sixty-seventh session and an interim report to the Human Rights Council on the implementation of the present resolution, including efforts undertaken at the national, regional and international levels in the promotion and realization of the right to development, and invites the Chair-Rapporteur of the Working Group to present a verbal update to the Assembly at its sixty-seventh session.

RECORDED VOTE ON RESOLUTION 66/155:

In favour: Afghanistan, Algeria, Andorra, Angola, Antigua and Barbuda, Argentina, Armenia, Austria, Azerbaijan, Bahamas, Bahrain, Bangladesh, Barbados, Belarus, Belize, Benin, Bhutan, Bolivia, Bosnia and Herzegovina, Botswana, Brazil, Brunei Darussalam, Burkina Faso, Burundi, Cambodia, Cameroon, Cape Verde, Central African Republic, Chad, Chile, China, Colombia, Comoros, Congo, Costa Rica, Côte d'Ivoire, Cuba, Cyprus, Democratic People's Republic of Korea, Democratic Republic of the Congo, Djibouti, Dominica, Dominican Republic, Ecuador, Egypt, El Salvador, Equatorial Guinea, Eritrea, Ethiopia, Fiji, France, Gabon, Gambia, Ghana, Greece, Grenada, Guatemala, Guinea, Guinea-Bissau, Guyana, Haiti, Honduras, India, Indonesia, Iran, Iraq, Ireland, Jamaica, Jordan, Kazakhstan, Kenya, Kuwait, Kyrgyzstan, Lao People's Democratic Republic, Lebanon, Lesotho, Liberia, Libya, Liechtenstein, Luxembourg, Madagascar, Malawi, Malaysia, Maldives, Mali, Malta, Mauritania, Mauritius, Mexico, Monaco, Mongolia, Montenegro, Morocco, Mozambique, Myanmar, Namibia, Nepal, Nicaragua, Niger, Nigeria, Oman, Pakistan, Panama, Papua New Guinea, Paraguay, Peru, Philippines, Portugal, Qatar, Russian Federation, Rwanda, Saint Kitts and Nevis, Saint Lucia, Saint Vincent and the Grenadines, Sao Tome and Principe, Saudi Arabia, Senegal, Serbia, Seychelles, Sierra Leone, Singapore, Slovenia, Solomon Islands, Somalia, South Africa, South Sudan, Spain, Sri Lanka, Sudan, Suriname, Swaziland, Switzerland, Syrian Arab Republic, Tajikistan, Thailand, Timor-Leste, Togo, Tonga, Trinidad and Tobago, Tunisia, Turkey, Turkmenistan, Tuvalu, Uganda, United Arab Emirates, United Republic of Tanzania, Uruguay, Uzbekistan, Vanuatu, Venezuela, Viet Nam, Yemen, Zambia, Zimbabwe.

Against: Canada, Israel, Netherlands, Palau, United Kingdom, United States.

Abstaining: Albania, Australia, Belgium, Bulgaria, Croatia, Czech Republic, Denmark, Estonia, Finland, Georgia, Germany, Hungary, Iceland, Italy, Japan, Latvia, Lithuania, New Zealand, Norway, Poland, Republic of Korea, Republic of Moldova, Romania, Samoa, San Marino, Slovakia, Sweden, the former Yugoslav Republic of Macedonia, Ukraine.

Human rights and international solidarity

Mandate of independent expert. On 25 March [A/66/53 (dec. 16/118)], the Council, by a recorded vote of 32 to 14, with no abstentions, postponed the renewal of the mandate of the independent expert on human rights and international solidarity to its seventeenth (2011) session, and for that reason extended the mandate until June 2011. In a 6 June note [A/HRC/18/34], the OHCHR secretariat informed the Council that the independent expert's report on implementation of Human Rights Council resolution 15/13 [YUN 2010, p. 724] that was to be submitted at the Council's eighteenth (2011) session would be submitted following the renewal of the independent expert's mandate and the Council's appointment of a new mandate holder.

On 16 June [A/66/53 (res. 17/6)], the Council, by a recorded vote of 32 to 14, with no abstentions, extended the mandate for three years and requested the independent expert to continue work on the preparation of a draft declaration on the right of peoples and individuals to international solidarity and to report to the Council on implementation of the resolution. The newly appointed independent expert, Virginia Dandan (Philippines), assumed her functions on 1 August.

Human Rights Council action. On 29 September [A/66/53/Add.1 (res. 18/5)], the Council, by a recorded vote of 33 to 12, with 1 abstention, requested the independent expert to continue her work in the preparation of a draft declaration on the right of peoples and individuals to international solidarity and in further developing guidelines, standards, norms and principles with a view to promoting and protecting that right by addressing existing and emerging obstacles to its realization; and asked its Advisory Committee, in cooperation with the expert, to prepare inputs to contribute to the elaboration of the draft declaration. It requested the High Commissioner to convene a workshop in 2012 on the gender implications of international solidarity, the impact of a right to international solidarity, the role of international solidarity in achieving the MDGs, and the realization of the right to development; and the independent expert to present a summary of the workshop's discussions to the Council, as well as to report on the implementation of the resolution at the Council's twenty-first (2012) session.

Democratic and equitable international order

In 2011, the Human Rights Council considered the question of a democratic and equitable international order. It affirmed that such an order fostered the full realization of all human rights for all, and that everyone was entitled to it. The Council urged all international stakeholders to build such an international order.

Establishment of new mandate. On 29 September [A/66/53/Add.1 (res. 18/6)], the Council, by a recorded vote of 29 to 12, with 5 abstentions, established, for a period of three years, a new special procedures mandate of independent expert on the promotion of a democratic and equitable international order to identify best practices in, and possible obstacles to, the promotion and protection of a democratic and equitable international order; submit proposals and/or recommendations to the Council on possible actions in that regard; raise awareness concerning the importance of promoting and protecting a democratic and equitable international order; report regularly to the Council and the General Assembly; and present a first report to the Council at its twenty-first (2012) session.

GENERAL ASSEMBLY ACTION

On 19 December [meeting 89], the General Assembly, on the recommendation of the Third Committee [A/66/462/Add.2], adopted **resolution 66/159** by recorded vote (130-54-6) [agenda item 69 (*b*)].

Promotion of a democratic and equitable international order

The General Assembly,

Recalling its previous resolutions on the promotion of a democratic and equitable international order, including resolution 65/223 of 21 December 2010, and taking note of Human Rights Council resolution 18/6 of 29 September 2011,

Reaffirming the commitment of all States to fulfil their obligations to promote universal respect for, and observance and protection of, all human rights and fundamental freedoms for all, in accordance with the Charter of the United Nations, other instruments relating to human rights and international law,

Affirming that the enhancement of international cooperation for the promotion and protection of all human rights should continue to be carried out in full conformity with the purposes and principles of the Charter and international law as set forth in Articles 1 and 2 of the Charter and, inter alia, with full respect for sovereignty, territorial integrity, political independence, the non-use of force or the threat of force in international relations and non-intervention in matters that are essentially within the domestic jurisdiction of any State,

Recalling the Preamble to the Charter, in particular the determination to reaffirm faith in fundamental human rights, in the dignity and worth of the human person and in the equal rights of men and women and of nations large and small,

Reaffirming that everyone is entitled to a social and international order in which the rights and freedoms set forth in the Universal Declaration of Human Rights can be fully realized,

Reaffirming also the determination expressed in the Preamble to the Charter to save succeeding generations from the scourge of war, to establish conditions under which justice and respect for the obligations arising from treaties and other sources of international law can be maintained, to promote social progress and better standards of life in larger freedom, to practise tolerance and good-neighbourliness, and to employ international machinery for the promotion of the economic and social advancement of all peoples,

Stressing that the responsibility for managing worldwide economic and social issues, as well as threats to international peace and security, must be shared among the nations of the world and should be exercised multilaterally, and that in this regard the central role must be played by the United Nations, as the most universal and representative organization in the world,

Considering the major changes taking place on the international scene and the aspirations of all peoples for an international order based on the principles enshrined in the Charter, including promoting and encouraging respect for human rights and fundamental freedoms for all and respect for the principle of equal rights and self-determination of peoples, peace, democracy, justice, equality, the rule of law, pluralism, development, better standards of living and solidarity,

Recognizing that the enhancement of international cooperation in the field of human rights is essential for the full achievement of the purposes of the United Nations, including the effective promotion and protection of all human rights,

Considering that the Universal Declaration of Human Rights proclaims that all human beings are born free and equal in dignity and rights and that everyone is entitled to all the rights and freedoms set out therein, without distinction of any kind, such as race, colour, sex, language, religion, political or other opinion, national or social origin, property, birth or other status,

Reaffirming that democracy, development and respect for human rights and fundamental freedoms are interdependent and mutually reinforcing, and that democracy is based on the freely expressed will of the people to determine their own political, economic, social and cultural systems and their full participation in all aspects of their lives,

Recognizing that the promotion and protection of human rights should be based on the principle of cooperation and genuine dialogue and aimed at strengthening the capacity of Member States to comply with their human rights obligations for the benefit of all human beings,

Emphasizing that democracy is not only a political concept, but that it also has economic and social dimensions,

Recognizing that democracy, respect for all human rights, including the right to development, transparent and accountable governance and administration in all sectors of society, and effective participation by civil society are an essential part of the necessary foundations for the realization of social and people-centred sustainable development,

Noting with concern that racism, racial discrimination, xenophobia and related intolerance may be aggravated by, inter alia, inequitable distribution of wealth, marginalization and social exclusion,

Reaffirming that dialogue among religions, cultures and civilizations could contribute greatly to the enhancement of international cooperation at all levels,

Underlining the fact that it is imperative for the international community to ensure that globalization becomes a positive force for all the world's people, and that only through broad and sustained efforts, based on our common humanity in all its diversity, can globalization be made fully inclusive and equitable,

Deeply concerned that the current global economic, financial, energy and food crises, resulting from a combination of several major factors, including macroeconomic and other factors, such as environmental degradation, desertification and global climate change, natural disasters and the lack of financial resources and the technology necessary to confront their negative impact in developing countries, particularly in the least developed countries and small island developing States, represent a global scenario that is threatening the adequate enjoyment of all human rights and widening the gap between developed and developing countries,

Stressing that efforts to make globalization fully inclusive and equitable must include policies and measures, at the global level, that correspond to the needs of developing countries and countries with economies in transition and are formulated and implemented with their effective participation,

Stressing also the need for adequate financing of and technology transfer to developing countries, in particular the landlocked developing countries and small island developing States, including to support their efforts to adapt to climate change,

Having listened to the peoples of the world, and recognizing their aspirations to justice, to equality of opportunity for all, to the enjoyment of their human rights, including the right to development, to live in peace and freedom and to equal participation without discrimination in economic, social, cultural, civil and political life,

Recalling Human Rights Council resolutions 5/1 on institution-building of the Council and 5/2 on the Code of Conduct for Special Procedures Mandate Holders of the Council, both of 18 June 2007, and stressing that all mandate holders shall discharge their duties in accordance with those resolutions and the annexes thereto,

Resolved to take all measures within its power to secure a democratic and equitable international order,

1. *Affirms* that everyone is entitled to a democratic and equitable international order;

2. *Also affirms* that a democratic and equitable international order fosters the full realization of all human rights for all;

3. *Calls upon* all Member States to fulfil their commitment expressed in Durban, South Africa, during the World Conference against Racism, Racial Discrimination, Xenophobia and Related Intolerance to maximize the benefits of globalization through, inter alia, the strengthening and enhancement of international cooperation to increase equality of opportunities for trade, economic growth and sustainable development, global communications through the use of new technologies and increased intercultural exchange through the preservation and promotion of cultural diversity, and reiterates that only through broad and sustained efforts to create a shared future based upon our common humanity and all its diversity can globalization be made fully inclusive and equitable;

4. *Affirms* that a democratic and equitable international order requires, inter alia, the realization of the following:

(*a*) The right of all peoples to self-determination, by virtue of which they can freely determine their political status and freely pursue their economic, social and cultural development;

(*b*) The right of peoples and nations to permanent sovereignty over their natural wealth and resources;

(*c*) The right of every human person and all peoples to development;

(*d*) The right of all peoples to peace;

(*e*) The right to an international economic order based on equal participation in the decision-making process, interdependence, mutual interest, solidarity and cooperation among all States;

(*f*) International solidarity, as a right of peoples and individuals;

(*g*) The promotion and consolidation of transparent, democratic, just and accountable international institutions in all areas of cooperation, in particular through the implementation of the principle of full and equal participation in their respective decision-making mechanisms;

(*h*) The right to equitable participation of all, without any discrimination, in domestic and global decision-making;

(*i*) The principle of equitable regional and gender-balanced representation in the composition of the staff of the United Nations system;

(*j*) The promotion of a free, just, effective and balanced international information and communications order, based on international cooperation for the establishment of a new equilibrium and greater reciprocity in the international flow of information, in particular correcting the inequalities in the flow of information to and from developing countries;

(*k*) Respect for cultural diversity and the cultural rights of all, since this enhances cultural pluralism, contributes to a wider exchange of knowledge and understanding of cultural backgrounds, advances the application and enjoyment of universally accepted human rights across the world and fosters stable, friendly relations among peoples and nations worldwide;

(*l*) The right of every person and all peoples to a healthy environment and to enhanced international cooperation that responds effectively to the needs for assistance of national efforts to adapt to climate change, particularly in developing countries, and that promotes the fulfilment of international agreements in the field of mitigation;

(*m*) The promotion of equitable access to benefits from the international distribution of wealth through enhanced international cooperation, in particular in economic, commercial and financial international relations;

(*n*) The enjoyment by everyone of ownership of the common heritage of mankind in connection to the public right of access to culture;

(*o*) The shared responsibility of the nations of the world for managing worldwide economic and social development, as well as threats to international peace and security, that should be exercised multilaterally;

5. *Stresses* the importance of preserving the rich and diverse nature of the international community of nations and peoples, as well as respect for national and regional particularities and various historical, cultural and religious

backgrounds, in the enhancement of international cooperation in the field of human rights;

6. *Also stresses* that all human rights are universal, indivisible, interdependent and interrelated and that the international community must treat human rights globally in a fair and equal manner, on the same footing and with the same emphasis, and reaffirms that, while the significance of national and regional particularities and various historical, cultural and religious backgrounds must be borne in mind, it is the duty of States, regardless of their political, economic and cultural systems, to promote and protect all human rights and fundamental freedoms;

7. *Urges* all actors on the international scene to build an international order based on inclusion, justice, equality and equity, human dignity, mutual understanding and promotion of and respect for cultural diversity and universal human rights, and to reject all doctrines of exclusion based on racism, racial discrimination, xenophobia and related intolerance;

8. *Reaffirms* that all States should promote the establishment, maintenance and strengthening of international peace and security and, to that end, should do their utmost to achieve general and complete disarmament under effective international control, as well as to ensure that the resources released by effective disarmament measures are used for comprehensive development, in particular that of the developing countries;

9. *Also reaffirms* the need to continue working urgently for the establishment of an international economic order based on equity, sovereign equality, interdependence, common interest and cooperation among all States, irrespective of their economic and social systems, which shall correct inequalities and redress existing injustices, make it possible to eliminate the widening gap between the developed and the developing countries and ensure steadily accelerating economic and social development and peace and justice for present and future generations;

10. *Further reaffirms* that the international community should devise ways and means to remove the current obstacles and meet the challenges to the full realization of all human rights and to prevent the continuation of human rights violations resulting therefrom throughout the world;

11. *Urges* States to continue their efforts, through enhanced international cooperation, towards the promotion of a democratic and equitable international order;

12. *Welcomes* the decision of the Human Rights Council in its resolution 18/6 to establish a new special procedures mandate of Independent Expert on the promotion of a democratic and equitable order and the mandate set out in the resolution;

13. *Requests* the Secretary-General and the United Nations High Commissioner for Human Rights to provide all the human and financial resources necessary for the effective fulfilment of the mandate of the Independent Expert;

14. *Calls upon* all Governments to cooperate with and assist the Independent Expert in his or her task, to supply all necessary information requested by him or her and to consider responding favourably to the requests of the Independent Expert to visit their countries to enable him or her to fulfil his or her mandate more effectively;

15. *Requests* the Human Rights Council, the human rights treaty bodies, the Office of the United Nations High Commissioner for Human Rights, the special mechanisms extended by the Council and the Human Rights Council Advisory Committee to pay due attention, within their respective mandates, to the present resolution and to make contributions towards its implementation;

16. *Calls upon* the Office of the High Commissioner to build upon the issue of the promotion of a democratic and equitable international order;

17. *Requests* the Secretary-General to bring the present resolution to the attention of Member States, United Nations organs, bodies and components, intergovernmental organizations, in particular the Bretton Woods institutions, and non-governmental organizations, and to disseminate it on the widest possible basis;

18. *Requests* the Independent Expert to submit to the General Assembly at its sixty-seventh session an interim report on the implementation of the present resolution and to continue his or her work;

19. *Decides* to continue consideration of the matter at its sixty-seventh session under the item entitled "Promotion and protection of human rights".

RECORDED VOTE ON RESOLUTION 66/159:

In favour: Afghanistan, Algeria, Angola, Antigua and Barbuda, Azerbaijan, Bahamas, Bahrain, Bangladesh, Barbados, Belarus, Belize, Benin, Bhutan, Bolivia, Botswana, Brazil, Brunei Darussalam, Burkina Faso, Burundi, Cambodia, Cameroon, Cape Verde, Central African Republic, Chad, China, Colombia, Comoros, Congo, Côte d'Ivoire, Cuba, Democratic People's Republic of Korea, Democratic Republic of the Congo, Djibouti, Dominica, Dominican Republic, Ecuador, Egypt, El Salvador, Equatorial Guinea, Eritrea, Ethiopia, Fiji, Gabon, Gambia, Ghana, Grenada, Guatemala, Guinea, Guinea-Bissau, Guyana, Haiti, Honduras, India, Indonesia, Iran, Iraq, Jamaica, Jordan, Kazakhstan, Kenya, Kuwait, Kyrgyzstan, Lao People's Democratic Republic, Lebanon, Lesotho, Liberia, Libya, Madagascar, Malawi, Malaysia, Maldives, Mali, Mauritania, Mauritius, Mongolia, Morocco, Mozambique, Myanmar, Namibia, Nepal, Nicaragua, Niger, Nigeria, Oman, Pakistan, Panama, Papua New Guinea, Paraguay, Philippines, Qatar, Russian Federation, Rwanda, Saint Kitts and Nevis, Saint Lucia, Saint Vincent and the Grenadines, Sao Tome and Principe, Saudi Arabia, Senegal, Seychelles, Sierra Leone, Singapore, Solomon Islands, Somalia, South Africa, South Sudan, Sri Lanka, Sudan, Suriname, Swaziland, Syrian Arab Republic, Tajikistan, Thailand, Timor-Leste, Togo, Tonga, Trinidad and Tobago, Tunisia, Turkmenistan, Tuvalu, Uganda, United Arab Emirates, United Republic of Tanzania, Uruguay, Uzbekistan, Vanuatu, Venezuela, Viet Nam, Yemen, Zambia, Zimbabwe.

Against: Albania, Andorra, Australia, Austria, Belgium, Bosnia and Herzegovina, Bulgaria, Canada, Croatia, Cyprus, Czech Republic, Denmark, Estonia, Finland, France, Georgia, Germany, Greece, Hungary, Iceland, Ireland, Israel, Italy, Japan, Latvia, Liechtenstein, Lithuania, Luxembourg, Malta, Marshall Islands, Monaco, Montenegro, Netherlands, New Zealand, Norway, Palau, Poland, Portugal, Republic of Korea, Republic of Moldova, Romania, Samoa, San Marino, Serbia, Slovakia, Slovenia, Spain, Sweden, Switzerland, the former Yugoslav Republic of Macedonia, Turkey, Ukraine, United Kingdom, United States.

Abstaining: Argentina, Armenia, Chile, Costa Rica, Mexico, Peru.

Globalization

Report of Secretary-General. In response to General Assembly resolution 65/216 [YUN 2010, p. 727], the Secretary-General in August submitted a report [A/66/293] that summarized the views on globalization and its impact on the full enjoyment of human rights received from eight Governments (Azerbaijan, Bulgaria, Cuba, Kuwait, Panama, Peru, Senegal, Serbia), as well as from the World Trade Organization. The report provided recommendations on ways to address the issue.

GENERAL ASSEMBLY ACTION

On 19 December [meeting 89], the General Assembly, on the recommendation of the Third Committee [A/66/462/Add.2], adopted **resolution 66/161** by recorded vote (137-54-0) [agenda item 69 (*b*)].

Globalization and its impact on the full enjoyment of all human rights

The General Assembly,

Guided by the purposes and principles of the Charter of the United Nations, and expressing, in particular, the need to achieve international cooperation in promoting and encouraging respect for human rights and fundamental freedoms for all without distinction,

Recalling the Universal Declaration of Human Rights, as well as the Vienna Declaration and Programme of Action adopted by the World Conference on Human Rights on 25 June 1993 and the Durban Declaration and Programme of Action adopted by the World Conference against Racism, Racial Discrimination, Xenophobia and Related Intolerance on 8 September 2001,

Recalling also the International Covenant on Civil and Political Rights and the International Covenant on Economic, Social and Cultural Rights,

Recalling further the Declaration on the Right to Development adopted by the General Assembly in its resolution 41/128 of 4 December 1986, and underlining that 2011 marks the twenty-fifth anniversary of the adoption of the Declaration,

Recalling the United Nations Millennium Declaration and the outcome documents of the twenty-third and twenty-fourth special sessions of the General Assembly, held in New York from 5 to 10 June 2000 and in Geneva from 26 June to 1 July 2000, respectively,

Recalling also its resolutions 64/174 of 18 December 2009 and 65/216 of 21 December 2010,

Recognizing that all human rights are universal, indivisible, interdependent and interrelated and that the international community must treat human rights globally in a fair and equal manner, on the same footing and with the same emphasis,

Realizing that globalization affects all countries differently and makes them more exposed to external developments, positive as well as negative, inter alia, in the field of human rights,

Realizing also that globalization is not merely an economic process, but that it also has social, political, environmental, cultural and legal dimensions, which have an impact on the full enjoyment of all human rights and fundamental freedoms,

Emphasizing the need to fully implement the global partnership for development and enhance the momentum generated by the 2005 World Summit in order to operationalize and implement the commitments made in the outcomes of the major United Nations conferences and summits, including the 2005 World Summit, in the economic, social and related fields, and reaffirming, in particular, the commitment contained in paragraphs 19 and 47 of the 2005 World Summit Outcome to promote fair globalization and the development of the productive sectors in developing countries to enable them to participate more effectively in and benefit from the process of globalization,

Realizing the need to undertake a thorough, independent and comprehensive assessment of the social, environmental and cultural impact of globalization on societies,

Recognizing in each culture a dignity and value that deserve recognition, respect and preservation, convinced that, in their rich variety and diversity and in the reciprocal influences that they exert on one another, all cultures form part of the common heritage belonging to all humankind, and aware of the risk that globalization poses more of a threat to cultural diversity if the developing world remains poor and marginalized,

Recognizing also that multilateral mechanisms have a unique role to play in meeting the challenges and opportunities presented by globalization,

Realizing the need to consider the challenges and opportunities linked to globalization with a view to addressing such challenges and building on possible opportunities in order to achieve the full enjoyment of all human rights,

Emphasizing the global character of the migratory phenomenon, the importance of international, regional and bilateral cooperation and the need to protect the human rights of migrants, particularly at a time in which migration flows have increased in the globalized economy,

Expressing grave concern at the negative impact of international financial turmoil on social and economic development and on the full enjoyment of all human rights, particularly in the light of the continuing global financial and economic crisis, which has an adverse impact on the realization of the internationally agreed development goals, particularly the Millennium Development Goals, and recognizing that developing countries are in a more vulnerable situation when facing such impact and that regional economic cooperation and development strategies and programmes can play a role in mitigating such impact,

Expressing deep concern at the negative impact of the continuing global food and energy crises and climate challenges on social and economic development and on the full enjoyment of all human rights for all,

Recognizing that globalization should be guided by the fundamental principles that underpin the corpus of human rights, such as equity, participation, accountability, non-discrimination at both the national and the international levels, respect for diversity, tolerance and international cooperation and solidarity,

Emphasizing that the existence of widespread extreme poverty inhibits the full realization and effective enjoyment of human rights and that its immediate alleviation and eventual elimination must remain a high priority for the international community,

Acknowledging that there is greater acceptance that the increasing debt burden faced by the most indebted developing countries is unsustainable and constitutes one of the principal obstacles to achieving sustainable development and poverty eradication and that, for many developing countries, excessive debt servicing has severely constrained their capacity to promote social development and to provide basic services to realize economic, social and cultural rights,

Strongly reiterating the determination to ensure the timely and full realization of the development goals and objectives agreed at the major United Nations conferences and summits, including those agreed at the Millennium Summit, that are described as the Millennium Development Goals, which have helped to galvanize efforts towards poverty eradication,

Gravely concerned at the inadequacy of measures to narrow the widening gap between the developed and the developing countries, and within countries, which has contributed to, inter alia, deepening poverty and has adversely affected the full enjoyment of all human rights, in particular in developing countries,

Emphasizing that transnational corporations and other business enterprises have a responsibility to respect all human rights,

Emphasizing also that human beings strive for a world that is respectful of human rights and cultural diversity and that, in this regard, they work to ensure that all activities, including those affected by globalization, are consistent with those aims,

1. *Recognizes* that, while globalization, by its impact on, inter alia, the role of the State, may affect human rights, the promotion and protection of all human rights is first and foremost the responsibility of the State;

2. *Emphasizes* that development should be at the centre of the international economic agenda and that coherence between national development strategies and international obligations and commitments is imperative for an enabling environment for development and an inclusive and equitable globalization;

3. *Reaffirms* that narrowing the gap between rich and poor, both within and between countries, is an explicit goal at the national and international levels, as part of the effort to create an enabling environment for the full enjoyment of all human rights;

4. *Also reaffirms* the commitment to create an environment at both the national and the global levels that is conducive to development and to the eradication of poverty by, inter alia, promoting good governance within each country and at the international level, eliminating protectionism, enhancing transparency in the financial, monetary and trading systems and committing to an open, equitable, rule-based, predictable and non-discriminatory multilateral trading and financial system;

5. *Recognizes* the impacts that the global financial and economic crisis is still having on the ability of countries, particularly developing countries, to mobilize resources for development and to address the impact of this crisis, and, in this context, calls upon all States and the international community to alleviate, in an inclusive and development-oriented manner, any negative impacts of this crisis on the realization and the effective enjoyment of all human rights;

6. *Also recognizes* that, while globalization offers great opportunities, the fact that its benefits are very unevenly shared and its costs unevenly distributed represents an aspect of the process that affects the full enjoyment of all human rights, in particular in developing countries;

7. *Welcomes* the report of the United Nations High Commissioner for Human Rights on globalization and its impact on the full enjoyment of human rights, which focuses on the liberalization of agricultural trade and its impact on the realization of the right to development, including the right to food, and takes note of the conclusions and recommendations contained therein;

8. *Reaffirms* the international commitment to eliminating hunger and to securing food for all, today and tomorrow, and reiterates that the relevant United Nations organizations should be assured the resources needed to expand and enhance their food assistance, and support social safety net programmes designed to address hunger and malnutrition, when appropriate, through the use of local or regional purchase;

9. *Calls upon* Member States, relevant agencies of the United Nations system, intergovernmental organizations and civil society to promote inclusive, equitable and environmentally sustainable economic growth for managing globalization so that poverty is systematically reduced and the international development targets are achieved;

10. *Recognizes* that the responsible operations of transnational corporations and other business enterprises can contribute to the promotion, protection and fulfilment of all human rights and fundamental freedoms, in particular economic, social and cultural rights;

11. *Also recognizes* that only through broad and sustained efforts, including policies and measures at the global level to create a shared future based upon our common humanity in all its diversity, can globalization be made fully inclusive and equitable and have a human face, thus contributing to the full enjoyment of all human rights;

12. *Underlines* the urgent need to establish an equitable, transparent and democratic international system to strengthen and broaden the participation of developing countries in international economic decision-making and norm-setting;

13. *Affirms* that globalization is a complex process of structural transformation, with numerous interdisciplinary aspects, which has an impact on the enjoyment of civil, political, economic, social and cultural rights, including the right to development;

14. *Also affirms* that the international community should strive to respond to the challenges and opportunities posed by globalization in a manner that promotes and protects human rights while ensuring respect for the cultural diversity of all;

15. *Underlines*, therefore, the need to continue to analyse the consequences of globalization for the full enjoyment of all human rights;

16. *Takes note* of the report of the Secretary-General, and requests him to continue to seek further the views of Member States and relevant agencies of the United Nations system and to submit to the General Assembly at its sixty-seventh session a substantive report on the subject based on these views, including recommendations on ways to address the impact of globalization on the full enjoyment of all human rights.

RECORDED VOTE ON RESOLUTION 66/161:

In favour: Afghanistan, Algeria, Angola, Antigua and Barbuda, Argentina, Armenia, Azerbaijan, Bahamas, Bahrain, Bangladesh, Barbados, Belarus, Belize, Benin, Bhutan, Bolivia, Botswana, Brazil, Brunei Darussalam, Burkina Faso, Burundi, Cambodia, Cameroon, Cape Verde, Central African Republic, Chad, Chile, China, Colombia, Comoros, Congo, Costa Rica, Côte d'Ivoire, Cuba, Democratic People's Republic of Korea, Democratic Republic of the Congo, Djibouti, Dominica, Dominican Republic, Ecuador, Egypt, El Salvador, Equatorial Guinea, Eritrea, Ethiopia, Fiji, Gabon, Gambia, Ghana, Grenada, Guatemala, Guinea, Guinea-Bissau, Guyana, Haiti, Honduras, India, Indonesia, Iran, Iraq, Jamaica, Jordan, Kazakhstan, Kenya, Kuwait, Kyrgyzstan, Lao People's Democratic Republic, Lebanon, Lesotho, Liberia, Libya, Madagascar, Malawi, Malaysia, Maldives, Mali, Mauritania, Mauritius, Mexico, Mongolia, Morocco, Mozambique, Myanmar, Namibia, Nepal, Nicaragua, Niger, Nigeria, Oman, Pakistan, Panama, Papua New Guinea, Paraguay, Peru, Philippines, Qatar, Russian Federation, Rwanda, Saint Kitts and Nevis, Saint Lucia, Saint Vincent and the Grenadines, Samoa, Sao Tome and Principe, Saudi Arabia, Senegal, Seychelles, Sierra Leone, Singapore, Solomon Islands, Somalia, South Africa, South Sudan, Sri Lanka, Sudan, Suriname, Swaziland, Syrian Arab Republic, Tajikistan, Thailand, Timor-Leste, Togo, Tonga, Trinidad and Tobago, Tunisia, Turkmenistan, Tuvalu, Uganda, United Arab Emirates, United Republic of Tanzania, Uruguay, Uzbekistan, Vanuatu, Venezuela, Viet Nam, Yemen, Zambia, Zimbabwe.

Against: Albania, Andorra, Australia, Austria, Belgium, Bosnia and Herzegovina, Bulgaria, Canada, Croatia, Cyprus, Czech Republic, Denmark, Estonia, Finland, France, Georgia, Germany, Greece, Hungary, Iceland, Ireland, Israel, Italy, Japan, Latvia, Liechtenstein, Lithuania, Luxembourg, Malta, Marshall Islands, Micronesia, Monaco, Montenegro, Netherlands, New Zealand, Norway, Palau, Poland, Portugal, Republic of Korea, Republic of Moldova, Romania, San Marino, Serbia, Slovakia, Slovenia, Spain, Sweden, Switzerland, the former Yugoslav Republic of Macedonia, Turkey, Ukraine, United Kingdom, United States.

Abstaining: None.

Foreign debt

Reports of independent expert. In response to a Human Rights Council request [YUN 2010, p. 730], the independent expert on the effects of foreign debt and other related international financial obligations of States on the full enjoyment of all human rights, particularly economic, social and cultural rights, Cephas Lumina (Zambia), in a report submitted in April [A/HRC/17/37], provided an update on the three regional multi-stakeholder consultations convened by OHCHR between June 2010 and February 2011 in Latin America and the Caribbean, Africa, and Asia and the Pacific on the draft general guidelines on foreign debt and human rights. The goal of the consultations was to generate ideas, based on regional experiences and perspectives, on the form and content of the draft guidelines in order to improve them and assist the independent expert in refining them. The report highlighted main and recurring themes of the consultations, including the consensus on the need for the guidelines; the need for the guidelines to be anchored in a rights-based framework; concern regarding the voluntary character of the guidelines; impact assessments as a critical part of due diligence to ensure respect for human rights; the oversight role of parliament and civil society in relation to loan contraction and debt management; and the adverse impact of incoherence in debt and trade policies on addressing the debt crisis and debt relief efforts. The last regional consultation was scheduled to be held in Geneva in June, followed by a final seminar in September to discuss a revised version of the guidelines and their operationalization. The independent expert would present a progress report and revised draft guidelines to the Council in 2012.

As requested by the Human Rights Council in 2008 [YUN 2008, p. 828] and in resolution 16/14 (see p. 716), the Secretary-General in August [A/66/271] transmitted the independent expert's report examining the issue of export credit and investment insurance agencies, commonly known as export credit agencies, which were collectively the principal source of public financing for foreign corporate involvement in large-scale industrial and infrastructure projects in developing countries and emerging economies. Export credit agencies had assumed an increasingly important role in the global economy, particularly in the context of the global financial crisis. Many projects supported by such agencies, however, had harmful environmental, social and human rights consequences and were not financially viable. Numerous reports had documented human rights violations arising from or associated with export credit agency projects, including forced displacement of local populations, violation of the rights of indigenous peoples, denial of access to basic services and environmental damage. Export credit agencies often lacked transparency and accountability in their funding decisions and operations. The report focused attention on the adverse impact of export credit agency-supported activities on sustainable development and the realization of human rights in the countries where such activities were undertaken. It examined the contribution of export credits to the debt burdens of those countries. The report called on States to address the negative impact of export credit agency-supported projects and made recommendations on measures to ensure that export credit agencies' activities did not undermine the human rights and other obligations of their home and host States and did not contribute to human rights violations.

The General Assembly took note of that report on 19 December (**decision 66/537**).

Mission reports. Following his visits to Australia (7–11 February) and Solomon Islands (14–18 February) [A/HRC/17/37/Add.1], the independent expert reported on Australia's development assistance programme and its impact on the realization of economic, social and cultural rights and the right to development, as well as the attainment of the MDGs in Pacific Island countries receiving Australian development assistance. In Solomon Islands, he assessed the effectiveness of bilateral and multilateral aid in supporting the realization of human rights and the achievement of the MDGs. The visits were linked in order to consider the issues from the perspective of provider and recipient of development assistance.

He noted the lack of a human rights-based approach to Australia's development programme and the over-reliance on technical assistance and private contractors to deliver the aid programme. Although foreign aid had helped Solomon Islands make progress towards achieving the MDGs and in restoring law and order, and fiscal and economic stability, a number of challenges remained, including ensuring sustainable capacity-building, aligning donor priorities with the Government's development agenda, ensuring accountability in the use and management of public resources, ensuring equitable distribution of the country's resources, and reducing aid dependency. The report concluded with recommendations to Governments and development partners.

Following his visit to Viet Nam (21–29 March) [A/HRC/20/23/Add.1], the independent expert remarked that Viet Nam had made remarkable progress towards the MDGs, having achieved the targets on poverty reduction, universal access to primary education and gender equality well ahead of schedule. It had made progress towards the other MDGs, and its Government showed a commitment to achieving them by the target date. Nonetheless, challenges remained, such as addressing the huge socioeconomic disparities between the ethnic minorities and the rest of the population, ensuring that the financing of the trade and budget deficits did not increase the external debt burden to an unsustainable level, addressing possible shortfalls of concessional financing, and addressing the impact of climate change. The expert concluded with recommendations to the Government and development partners.

Following his visit to the Democratic Republic of the Congo (25 July–5 August) [A/HRC/20/23/Add.2], the independent expert stated that country had made important socioeconomic progress since 2001, including reaching the completion point of the Heavily Indebted Poor Countries Initiative in 2010. Despite an increase in poverty-reducing spending, access to basic services was insufficient and the costs and quality of services remained a concern. The country also faced development challenges, such as the reconstruction and rehabilitation of its dilapidated socio-economic infrastructure, an unstable security situation in parts of the country, lack of transparency and accountability in public finance management, widespread corruption and ineffective domestic resource mobilization. The expert made recommendations to the Government and development partners.

Human Rights Council action. On 24 March [A/66/53 (res. 16/14)], the Council, by a recorded vote of 29 to 13, with 4 abstentions, extended the independent expert's mandate for three years and requested him/her to report regularly to the Council and the General Assembly; to explore further, in the annual report, the interlinkages with trade and other issues, including HIV/AIDS; and to seek the views of States, international organizations, UN entities, international and regional financial institutions and NGOs on the draft general guidelines [YUN 2010, p. 730] with a view to improving them, and to present the draft to the Council.

On 16 June [ibid. (res. 17/7)], the Council, by a recorded vote of 30 to 13, with 3 abstentions, requested the independent expert to continue to explore the interlinkages with trade and other issues, including HIV/AIDS, when examining the impact of structural adjustment and foreign debt; report to the Assembly on the issue of the effects of foreign debt and other related international financial obligations of States on the full enjoyment of all human rights, particularly economic, social and cultural rights; and submit a report on implementation of the resolution at the Assembly's sixty-sixth (2011) session and a revised draft of the guidelines on foreign debt and human rights to the Council in 2012. It reiterated its request to the High Commissioner to pay more attention to the debt burden of developing countries, and especially the social impact of the measures arising from foreign debt.

Transnational corporations

Reports of Special Representative. The Special Representative of the Secretary-General on the issue of human rights and transnational corporations and other business enterprises, John Ruggie (United States), in March submitted his final report [A/HRC/17/31] summarizing his work from 2005 to 2011, and presented the "Guiding Principles on Business and Human Rights: Implementing the United Nations 'Protect, Respect and Remedy' Framework" for consideration by the Council. The Framework rested on three pillars: the duty of the State to protect against human rights abuses by third parties, including business enterprises, through appropriate policies, regulation and adjudication; the corporate responsibility to respect human rights, which meant that business enterprises should act with due diligence to avoid infringing on the rights of others; and the need for greater access by victims to effective remedy, both judicial and non-judicial. Each pillar was an essential component in an interrelated system of preventative and remedial measures. The Guiding Principles' normative contribution was in elaborating the implications of existing standards and practices for States and businesses; integrating them within a single, coherent and comprehensive template; and identifying where the current regime fell short and how it should be improved. Each Principle was accompanied by a commentary, clarifying its meaning and implications. The Representative pointed out that the Principles were universally applicable, yet when it came to means for implementation, one size did not fit all.

In three further addenda, the Special Representative outlined key lessons learned from a pilot project conducted in 2009–2010 to test the applicability of the principles for non-judicial grievance mechanisms [A/HRC/17/31/Add.1 & Corr.1]; trends and observations from a cross-national study on human rights and corporate law [A/HRC/17/31/Add.2]; and the ten principles that could guide the integration of human rights risk management into contract negotiations [A/HRC/17/31/Add.3].

In a May report [A/HRC/17/32] on business and human rights in conflict-affected regions: challenges and options towards State responses, the Special Representative pointed out that the most egregious business-related human rights abuses took place in conflict-affected areas and other situations of widespread violence. Such situations required States to take action as a matter of urgency, but there remained a lack of clarity among States with regard to what innovative, proactive and practical policies and tools had the greatest potential for preventing or mitigating business-related abuses in situations of conflict. The Representative outlined policy options that home, host and neighbouring States had or could develop to prevent and deter corporate-related human rights abuses in conflict contexts. In his conclusions, he recommended that the advisory role of the State where businesses were involved in conflict-affected areas be strengthened; that States define what risks or activities should prompt a State response and what responses would be appropriate and necessary; and that standard-setting exercises be supported by multilateral agreements on risks and prohibited activities with respect to business in conflict or other high-risk situations.

Establishment of new working group. On 16 June [A/66/53 (res. 17/4)], the Council endorsed the Guiding Principles on Business and Human Rights (see p. 716); established a Working Group on the issue of human rights and transnational corporations and other business enterprises, consisting of five independent experts, for three years; requested the Working Group to promote dissemination and implementation of the Guiding Principles and to report annually to the Council and General Assembly; established a Forum on Business and Human Rights under the guidance of the Working Group to discuss trends and challenges in implementing the Principles, and promote cooperation on issues linked to business and human rights; and requested the Secretary-General to report on how the UN system could contribute to the advancement of the business and human rights agenda and the dissemination and implementation of the Principles at the Council's twenty-first (2012) session.

Unilateral coercive measures

OHCHR note. On 6 June, the OHCHR secretariat issued a note [A/HRC/18/28] informing the Human Rights Council that the thematic study on the impact of unilateral coercive measures on the enjoyment of human rights, including recommendations on actions aimed at ending such measures, was under preparation, would require additional time for completion, and would be submitted to the Council's nineteenth (2012) session.

Report of Secretary-General. In response to General Assembly resolution 65/217 [YUN 2010, p. 730], the Secretary-General in August submitted a report [A/66/272] that summarized information received from 11 Governments (Argentina, Belarus, Bosnia and Herzegovina, Burkina Faso, Cuba, Dominican Republic, Ecuador, Guatemala, Guyana, Iraq, Kuwait) on the impact of unilateral coercive measures on their populations.

Communication. On 29 June [A/65/896-S/2011/407], Egypt, on behalf of the Coordinating Bureau of the Non-Aligned Movement (NAM), transmitted to the Secretary-General the outcome documents of the sixteenth NAM Ministerial Conference (Bali, Indonesia, 23–27 May), which contained text on unilateral coercive measures.

Human Rights Council action. On 30 September [A/66/53/Add.1 (dec. 18/120)], the Council, by a recorded vote of 34 to 12, with no abstentions, noting that the thematic study (see above) was under preparation and would be submitted at the Council's nineteenth (2012) session, decided to examine that question in accordance with its annual programme of work under the same agenda item.

GENERAL ASSEMBLY ACTION

On 19 December [meeting 89], the General Assembly, on the recommendation of the Third Committee [A/66/462/Add.2], adopted **resolution 66/156** by recorded vote (137-54-0) [agenda item 69 (*b*)].

Human rights and unilateral coercive measures

The General Assembly,

Recalling all its previous resolutions on this subject, the most recent of which was resolution 65/217 of 21 December 2010, and Human Rights Council resolution 15/24 of 1 October 2010 and decision 18/120 of 30 September 2011, as well as previous resolutions of the Council and the Commission on Human Rights,

Reaffirming the pertinent principles and provisions contained in the Charter of Economic Rights and Duties of States proclaimed by the General Assembly in its resolution 3281(XXIX) of 12 December 1974, in particular article 32 thereof, in which it declared that no State may use or encourage the use of economic, political or any other type of measures to coerce another State in order to obtain from it the subordination of the exercise of its sovereign rights,

Taking note of the report of the Secretary-General submitted pursuant to General Assembly resolution 65/217, and recalling the reports of the Secretary-General on the implementation of Assembly resolutions 52/120 of 12 December 1997 and 55/110 of 4 December 2000,

Stressing that unilateral coercive measures and legislation are contrary to international law, international humanitarian law, the Charter of the United Nations and the norms and principles governing peaceful relations among States,

Recognizing the universal, indivisible, interdependent and interrelated character of all human rights, and in this regard reaffirming the right to development as an integral part of all human rights,

Recalling the Final Document of the Sixteenth Ministerial Conference and Commemorative Meeting of the Movement of Non-Aligned Countries, held in Bali, Indonesia, from 23 to 27 May 2011, the Final Document of the Fifteenth Summit Conference of Heads of State and Government of the Movement of Non-Aligned Countries, held in Sharm el-Sheikh, Egypt, from 11 to 16 July 2009, and those adopted at previous summits and conferences, in which States members of the Movement agreed to oppose and condemn those measures or laws and their continued application, persevere with efforts to effectively reverse them and urge other States to do likewise, as called for by the General Assembly and other United Nations organs, and request States applying those measures or laws to revoke them fully and immediately,

Recalling also that, at the World Conference on Human Rights, held in Vienna from 14 to 25 June 1993, States were called upon to refrain from any unilateral measure not in accordance with international law and the Charter that creates obstacles to trade relations among States and impedes the full realization of all human rights and also severely threatens the freedom of trade,

Bearing in mind all the references to this question in the Copenhagen Declaration on Social Development adopted by the World Summit for Social Development on 12 March 1995, the Beijing Declaration and Platform for Action adopted by the Fourth World Conference on Women on 15 September 1995, the Istanbul Declaration on Human Settlements and the Habitat Agenda adopted by the second United Nations Conference on Human Settlements (Habitat II) on 14 June 1996, and their five-year reviews,

Expressing concern about the negative impact of unilateral coercive measures on international relations, trade, investment and cooperation,

Expressing grave concern that, in some countries, the situation of children is adversely affected by unilateral coercive measures not in accordance with international law and the Charter that create obstacles to trade relations among States, impede the full realization of social and economic development and hinder the well-being of the population in the affected countries, with particular consequences for women, children, including adolescents, the elderly and persons with disabilities,

Deeply concerned that, despite the recommendations adopted on this question by the General Assembly, the Human Rights Council, the Commission on Human Rights and recent major United Nations conferences, and contrary to general international law and the Charter, unilateral coercive measures continue to be promulgated and implemented, with all their negative implications for the social humanitarian activities and economic and social development of developing countries, including their extraterritorial effects, thereby creating additional obstacles to the full enjoyment of all human rights by peoples and individuals under the jurisdiction of other States,

Bearing in mind all the extraterritorial effects of any unilateral legislative, administrative and economic measures, policies and practices of a coercive nature against the development process and the enhancement of human rights in developing countries, which create obstacles to the full realization of all human rights,

Reaffirming that unilateral coercive measures are a major obstacle to the implementation of the Declaration on the Right to Development,

Recalling article 1, paragraph 2, common to the International Covenant on Civil and Political Rights and the International Covenant on Economic, Social and Cultural Rights, which provides, inter alia, that in no case may a people be deprived of its own means of subsistence,

Noting the continuing efforts of the open-ended Working Group on the Right to Development of the Human Rights Council, and reaffirming in particular its criteria, according to which unilateral coercive measures are one of the obstacles to the implementation of the Declaration on the Right to Development,

1. *Urges* all States to cease adopting or implementing any unilateral measures not in accordance with international law, international humanitarian law, the Charter of the United Nations and the norms and principles governing peaceful relations among States, in particular those of a coercive nature, with all their extraterritorial effects, which create obstacles to trade relations among States, thus impeding the full realization of the rights set forth in the Universal Declaration of Human Rights and other international human rights instruments, in particular the right of individuals and peoples to development;

2. *Also urges* all States not to adopt any unilateral measures not in accordance with international law and the Charter that impede the full achievement of economic and social development by the population of the affected countries, in particular children and women, that hinder their well-being and that create obstacles to the full enjoyment of their human rights, including the right of everyone to a standard of living adequate for his or her health and well-being and his or her right to food, medical care and education and the necessary social services, as well as to ensure that food and medicine are not used as tools for political pressure;

3. *Strongly objects* to the extraterritorial nature of those measures which, in addition, threaten the sovereignty of States, and in this context calls upon all Member States neither to recognize those measures nor to apply them, as well as to take administrative or legislative measures, as appropriate, to counteract the extraterritorial applications or effects of unilateral coercive measures;

4. *Condemns* the continuing unilateral application and enforcement by certain Powers of unilateral coercive measures, and rejects those measures, with all their extraterritorial effects, as being tools for political or economic pressure against any country, in particular against developing countries, adopted with a view to preventing those countries from exercising their right to decide, of their own free will, their own political, economic and social systems, and because of the negative effects of those measures on the realization of all the human rights of vast sectors of their populations, in particular children, women, the elderly and persons with disabilities;

5. *Reaffirms* that essential goods such as food and medicines should not be used as tools for political coercion and that under no circumstances should people be deprived of their own means of subsistence and development;

6. *Calls upon* Member States that have initiated such measures to abide by the principles of international law, the Charter, the declarations of the United Nations and world conferences and relevant resolutions and to commit themselves to their obligations and responsibilities arising from the international human rights instruments to which they are parties by revoking such measures at the earliest possible time;

7. *Reaffirms*, in this context, the right of all peoples to self-determination, by virtue of which they freely determine their political status and freely pursue their economic, social and cultural development;

8. *Recalls* that, according to the Declaration on Principles of International Law concerning Friendly Relations and Cooperation among States in accordance with the Charter of the United Nations, contained in the annex to General Assembly resolution 2625(XXV) of 24 October 1970, and the relevant principles and provisions contained in the Charter of Economic Rights and Duties of States proclaimed by the Assembly in its resolution 3281(XXIX), in particular article 32 thereof, no State may use or encourage the use of economic, political or any other type of measures to coerce another State in order to obtain from it the subordination of the exercise of its sovereign rights and to secure from it advantages of any kind;

9. *Rejects* all attempts to introduce unilateral coercive measures, and urges the Human Rights Council to take fully into account the negative impact of those measures, including through the enactment of national laws and their extraterritorial application which are not in conformity with international law, in its task concerning the implementation of the right to development;

10. *Requests* the United Nations High Commissioner for Human Rights, in discharging her functions relating to the promotion, realization and protection of the right to development and bearing in mind the continuing impact of unilateral coercive measures on the population of developing countries, to give priority to the present resolution in her annual report to the General Assembly;

11. *Underlines* the fact that unilateral coercive measures are one of the major obstacles to the implementation of the Declaration on the Right to Development, and in this regard calls upon all States to avoid the unilateral imposition of economic coercive measures and the extraterritorial application of domestic laws that run counter to the principles of free trade and hamper the development of developing countries, as recognized by the Working Group on the Right to Development of the Human Rights Council;

12. *Recognizes* that, in the Declaration of Principles adopted at the first phase of the World Summit on the Information Society, held in Geneva from 10 to 12 December 2003, States were strongly urged to avoid and refrain from any unilateral measure not in accordance with international law and the Charter of the United Nations in building the information society;

13. *Reiterates its support* for the invitation of the Human Rights Council to all special rapporteurs and existing thematic mechanisms of the Council in the field of economic, social and cultural rights to pay due attention, within the scope of their respective mandates, to the negative impact and consequences of unilateral coercive measures;

14. *Reaffirms* the request of the Human Rights Council that the Office of the United Nations High Commissioner for Human Rights prepare a thematic study on the impact of unilateral coercive measures on the enjoyment of human rights, including recommendations on actions aimed at ending such measures, taking into account all previous reports, resolutions and relevant information available to the United Nations system in this regard, to be submitted to the Council at its nineteenth session;

15. *Requests* the Secretary-General to bring the present resolution to the attention of all Member States, to continue to collect their views and information on the implications and negative effects of unilateral coercive measures on their populations and to submit an analytical report thereon to the General Assembly at its sixty-seventh session, while reiterating once again the need to highlight the practical and preventive measures in this respect;

16. *Decides* to examine the question on a priority basis at its sixty-seventh session under the sub-item entitled "Human rights questions, including alternative approaches for improving the effective enjoyment of human rights and fundamental freedoms".

RECORDED VOTE ON RESOLUTION 66/156:

In favour: Afghanistan, Algeria, Angola, Antigua and Barbuda, Argentina, Armenia, Azerbaijan, Bahamas, Bahrain, Bangladesh, Barbados, Belarus, Belize, Benin, Bhutan, Bolivia, Botswana, Brazil, Brunei Darussalam, Burkina Faso, Burundi, Cambodia, Cameroon, Cape Verde, Central African Republic, Chad, Chile, China, Colombia, Comoros, Congo, Costa Rica, Côte d'Ivoire, Cuba, Democratic People's Republic of Korea, Democratic Republic of the Congo, Djibouti, Dominica, Dominican Republic, Ecuador, Egypt, El Salvador, Equatorial Guinea, Eritrea, Ethiopia, Fiji, Gabon, Gambia, Ghana, Grenada, Guatemala, Guinea, Guinea-Bissau, Guyana, Haiti, Honduras, India, Indonesia, Iran, Iraq, Jamaica, Jordan, Kazakhstan, Kenya, Kuwait, Kyrgyzstan, Lao People's Democratic Republic, Lebanon, Lesotho, Liberia, Libya, Madagascar, Malawi, Malaysia, Maldives, Mali, Mauritania, Mauritius, Mexico, Mongolia, Morocco, Mozambique, Myanmar, Namibia, Nepal, Nicaragua, Niger, Nigeria, Oman, Pakistan, Panama, Papua New Guinea, Paraguay, Peru, Philippines, Qatar, Russian Federation, Rwanda, Saint Kitts and Nevis, Saint Lucia, Saint Vincent and the Grenadines, Samoa, Sao Tome and Principe, Saudi Arabia, Senegal, Seychelles, Sierra Leone, Singapore, Solomon Islands, Somalia, South Africa, South Sudan, Sri Lanka, Sudan, Suriname, Swaziland, Syrian Arab Republic, Tajikistan, Thailand, Timor-Leste, Togo, Tonga, Trinidad and Tobago, Tunisia, Turkmenistan, Tuvalu, Uganda, United Arab Emirates, United Republic of Tanzania, Uruguay, Uzbekistan, Vanuatu, Venezuela, Viet Nam, Yemen, Zambia, Zimbabwe.

Against: Albania, Andorra, Australia, Austria, Belgium, Bosnia and Herzegovina, Bulgaria, Canada, Croatia, Cyprus, Czech Republic, Denmark, Estonia, Finland, France, Georgia, Germany, Greece, Hungary, Iceland, Ireland, Israel, Italy, Japan, Latvia, Liechtenstein, Lithuania, Luxembourg, Malta, Marshall Islands, Micronesia, Monaco, Montenegro, Netherlands, New Zealand, Norway, Palau, Poland, Portugal, Republic of Korea, Republic of Moldova, Romania, San Marino, Serbia, Slovakia, Slovenia, Spain, Sweden, Switzerland, the former Yugoslav Republic of Macedonia, Turkey, Ukraine, United Kingdom, United States.

Abstaining: None.

Non-repatriation of funds of illicit origin

In 2011, the Human Rights Council considered the question of non-repatriation of funds of illicit origin. It recognized that States continued to face challenges in fund and asset recovery of illicit origin, including legal challenges, and was convinced that corruption, including the transfer of funds and assets of illicit origin and their non-repatriation, was no longer a local matter but a transnational phenomenon affecting all societies and economies, making international cooperation essential to prevent and combat it.

Human Rights Council action. On 17 June [A/66/53 (res. 17/23)], the Council, by a recorded vote of 32 to 2, with 12 abstentions, requested the High Commissioner to prepare a comprehensive study on the negative impact of the non-repatriation of funds of illicit origin to the countries of origin on the enjoyment of human rights, in particular economic, social and cultural rights, and to report thereon to the Council's nineteenth (2012) session.

Social Forum

Human Rights Council action. On 25 March [A/66/53 (res. 16/26)], the Council took note of the report of the 2010 Social Forum [YUN 2010, p. 733]; decided that the Social Forum in 2011 would meet for three days in Geneva, focusing on the right to development; requested the High Commissioner to submit a background report for the dialogues and debates to be held at the Social Forum; and invited the Social Forum to submit a report to the Council.

Social Forum session. The Social Forum (Geneva, 3–5 October) [A/HRC/19/70], which was attended by Member States, UN bodies, intergovernmental organizations, NGOs, academic institutions and independent experts, had before it a background report [A/HRC/SF/2011/2] of the High Commissioner reviewing measures needed to implement the right to development at the local, national, regional and international levels, with particular focus on the role and contribution of civil society and NGOs. Participants heard expert presentations complemented by interactive exchanges of views, leading to recommendations on, among others, promoting social and environmental justice, accountability and justiciability; utilizing the right to development as a normative framework for policy coherence and systemic integration in international law; public budget monitoring; and implementing human rights obligations at the core of development agendas. Consideration was given to the proposal of the levy of a financial transaction tax that would ensure that resources thus generated were allocated to poverty alleviation and development. The report also discussed the role and contribution of civil society and international assistance and cooperation.

Extreme poverty

Report of independent expert. As requested by the Human Rights Council [YUN 2008, p. 833], the independent expert on the question of human rights and extreme poverty, Magdalena Sepúlveda Carmona (Chile), in March submitted a report [A/HRC/17/34] on recovery from the global economic and financial crisis, with a particular focus on the most vulnerable and marginalized groups. The independent expert identified the human rights framework that States must comply with when designing recovery measures; analysed a number of recovery measures from a human rights perspective, highlighting their potential to threaten the enjoyment of economic, social and cultural rights; and recommended measures that States should consider to facilitate a human rights-based recovery from the crisis. Those pertained to ensuring a social protection floor for all; promoting employment; ensuring gender-sensitive policies; implementing socially responsible taxation policies; enhancing regulation to protect individuals from abuse by private actors; strengthening State institutional capacity; improving data collection and poverty monitoring systems; creating a national dialogue; ensuring an environmentally sustainable recovery; and enhancing international assistance and cooperation.

Human Rights Council action. On 17 June [A/66/53 (res. 17/13)], the Council, welcoming the independent expert's work, extended the mandate of the current mandate holder as a special rapporteur for three years; requested the Special Rapporteur on extreme poverty and human rights to report annually to the General Assembly and to the Council; and invited the Rapporteur and relevant stakeholders to participate in the two-day consultation on the progress report on the draft guiding principles on extreme poverty and human rights that OHCHR would organize in Geneva on 22 and 23 June 2011 (see below).

Report of Special Rapporteur. As requested by the Council (see above), the Secretary-General in August transmitted to the General Assembly the report [A/66/265] of the Special Rapporteur (Ms. Carmona, previously the independent expert) that described the ways in which States and social forces penalizing those living in poverty were interconnected and multidimensional. She analysed several laws, regulations and practices that punished, segregated, controlled and undermined the autonomy of persons living in poverty, and identified four areas of concern: laws, regulations and practices restricting the performance of life-sustaining behaviours in public spaces by persons living in poverty; measures relating to the gentrification and privatization of public spaces that disproportionately affected persons living in poverty; conditions imposed on access to public services and social benefits that interfered with the autonomy, privacy and family life of persons living in poverty; and excessive and arbitrary use of detention and incarceration that threatened the liberty and personal security of persons living in poverty. She made recommendations addressing those concerns.

The General Assembly took note of the report on 19 December (**decision 66/537**).

OHCHR report. Pursuant to a Human Rights Council request [YUN 2010, p. 734], OHCHR submitted a report [A/HRC/19/32] summarizing the contributions of a multi-stakeholder consultation on the annotated outline of draft guiding principles on extreme poverty and human rights, as well as of oral statements made during a two-day meeting (Geneva, 22–23 June).

Mission reports. Following her visit to Ireland (10–15 January) [A/HRC/17/34/Add.2], the independent expert reported on the impact of the economic and financial crises on the country and noted that the crises had been severe, particularly for the most vulnerable segments of society. While Ireland had made impressive advances in poverty reduction over the past decade, those gains would be reversed if those living in poverty and social exclusion were not protected during the recovery. The independent expert urged Ireland to strengthen the legal and institutional framework by giving domestic legal effect to Ireland's international human rights obligations; review its Programme for Government and National Recovery to ensure that it complied with human rights principles and consider reversing measures that would disproportionately impact the most vulnerable, particularly reductions in social protection payments and funding to public services; strengthen the social protection system, infrastructure and social services to ensure the full enjoyment of all economic, social and cultural rights of the population; and remove barriers that prevented the most vulnerable from accessing their entitlements.

Following her visit to Timor-Leste (13–18 November) [A/HRC/20/25/Add.1], the Special Rapporteur said that she was concerned that poverty persisted despite notable efforts and several successful programmes in the ten years since independence. She pointed out that economic growth and development had not benefited all Timorese equally and that the poorest segments of society remained in a grave situation. She recommended that the Government concentrate its efforts on social and economic policies that ensured inclusive and equitable growth and development and strengthen efforts to diversify the non-oil economy, build sustainable industries, and ensure the preservation of its natural resources for future generations. She recommended several steps that Timor-Leste could take to strengthen its institutional and legal framework; improve access to justice, education, health and land rights; and enhance its social protection system.

Following her mission to Paraguay (11–16 December) [A/HRC/20/25/Add.2], the Special Rapporteur reported on a number of flagship programmes, including the Tekoporã conditional cash transfer programme, the Abrazo ("hug") Programme and the Family Health Units Programme. While acknowledging the magnitude of the challenges faced by Paraguay and the progress made in rights-based public policy planning, she expressed concern at the presence of striking economic and social inequalities, the high degree of concentration of land ownership, corruption, a regressive tax structure and environmental problems, which interfered with poor people's enjoyment of their rights. The report set forth recommendations for ensuring that the human rights of persons living in poverty were protected and that an inclusive form of growth was achieved.

Right to food

Reports of Special Rapporteur. As requested by the Human Rights Council [YUN 2010, p. 737], the Special Rapporteur on the right to food, Olivier De Schutter (Belgium), submitted a report [A/HRC/16/49] demonstrating why agriculture should be fundamentally redirected towards modes of production that were environmentally sustainable, socially just and contributed to the realization of the human right to adequate food, and how that could be achieved. He identified agroecology as a mode of agricultural development that showed strong conceptual connections with the right to food and had proven results for fast progress in the realization of that human right for many vulnerable groups in various countries and environments. Agroecology delivered advantages that were complementary to better-known conventional approaches and contributed to broader economic development. The Rapporteur concluded that moving towards sustainability was vital for future food security and an essential component of the right to food. Recommendations were made for States to implement public policies supporting the adoption of agroecological practices; for donors to engage in long-term relationships with partner countries supporting programmes and policies to scale up agroecological approaches for lasting change; and for the research community to increase the budget for agroecological research at the field level, train scientists and assess projects on the basis of a comprehensive set of performance criteria.

An addendum [A/HRC/16/49/Add.1] summarized communications sent to States by the Special Rapporteur from 5 December 2009 to 6 December 2010 and the responses received until 6 February 2011. During that period, the Rapporteur sent three communications to three Member States and received one reply, as well as four replies concerning communications summarized in previous reports.

In accordance with General Assembly resolution 65/220 [YUN 2010, p. 737], the Secretary-General in August submitted the interim report [A/66/262] of the Rapporteur, which identified the issues raised by the expansion of contract farming and noted seven areas in which Governments and firms could ensure that it resulted in pro-poor outcomes and contributed to the realization of the right to food. Contract farming rarely encouraged farmers to climb up the value chain and move into the packaging, processing or marketing of their produce. The report examined other business models that could be more inclusive, such as farmer-controlled enterprises, joint ventures or direct-to-consumer food marketing practices by farmers. The Rapporteur concluded that Governments had a key role to play in protecting individuals against the risks involved in alternative business models and in ensuring that contract farming and other business models supported the right to food of small producers, their local communities and the entire population. Recommendations for Governments related to supporting the organization of farmers into cooperatives and producers' organizations to improve their bargaining power, creating an enabling environment for the development of local markets benefiting small-scale farmers, and providing small-scale farmers with appropriate support.

In response to a Human Rights Council request [YUN 2010, p. 737] to explore ways of raising the capacity of countries, particularly developing countries, including least developed and net food-importing countries, to ensure the realization of the right to adequate food for their populations, the Rapporteur submitted a December report [A/HRC/19/59/Add.5] setting out guiding principles on human rights impact assessments of trade and investment agreements. The principles were intended to provide States with guidance on how best to ensure that the trade and investment agreements they concluded were consistent with their obligations under international human rights instruments.

Mission reports. Following his visit to Mexico (13–20 June) [A/HRC/19/59/Add.2], the Special Rapporteur pointed out the need to target agricultural support programmes to the needs of small-scale farmers in disadvantaged areas; explored efforts to strengthen social programmes, ensure a decent living for workers including agricultural labourers, ensure protection against the effects of development projects, and improve access to services for remote rural communities through "sustainable rural towns"; and addressed the growing problem of obesity and its relationship with food and nutrition policies. He also commented on the introduction of transgenic maize and on the need for a more sustainable use of water. The Rapporteur recommended that the Government ensure that its agricultural policies made a more effective contribution to combating rural poverty, set the minimum wage at a level that guaranteed all workers a living wage, conduct an independent assessment of the "sustainable rural towns" experience before expanding existing projects, and revise the 2010 national agreement for nutritional health.

During his mission to South Africa (7–15 July) [A/HRC/19/59/Add.3], the Rapporteur examined the state of food security in that country and the legal and policy framework guiding its efforts, and outlined a possible strategy that could ensure food availability for all through social assistance programmes and income opportunities. He commended South Africa for its efforts at building an adequate institutional and policy framework to move towards the full realization of the right to food. The report concluded with recommendations to the Government, including improving the collection of data on food security to monitor progress and inform policymaking; strengthening strategies and policies that related to food security; accelerating the creation of comprehensive rural development policies, which would progressively improve the right to food of vulnerable groups; strengthening the protection of farm workers; and stimulating a transition towards sustainable agricultural systems by supporting agroecological practices.

Following his visit to Madagascar (8–22 July) [A/HRC/19/59/Add.4], the Rapporteur examined the impact of recent natural disasters and the political crisis on food insecurity in the country; the strategic thrust of the national policy on nutrition; the public programmes that supported the agriculture and livestock farming sectors; land policies; policies on rice production and fisheries agreements signed with other States; and the impact of the international sanctions imposed after the 2009 coup d'état [YUN 2009 p. 310]. Recommendations were addressed to the Government, as well as to donors, lenders, international organizations and development partners.

Advisory Committee studies. As requested by the Human Rights Council in 2009 [YUN 2009, p. 626] and in 2010 [YUN 2010, p. 737], the Council's Advisory Committee in February submitted, respectively, a study [A/HRC/16/40] on discrimination in the context of the right to food, and a preliminary study [A/HRC/16/63] on the advancement of the rights of peasants and other people working in rural areas, in particular smallholders engaged in the production of food and/or other agricultural products.

Human Rights Council action. On 25 March [A/66/53 (res. 16/27)], the Council encouraged States to incorporate a human rights perspective in their national strategies for the realization of the right to food, to promote the conditions for everyone to be free from hunger, and to establish appropriate institutional mechanisms. The Council requested the Advisory Committee to continue work on the issue of discrimination in the context of the right to food; requested OHCHR to collect the views of Member States and other stakeholders on the Committee's final study on that issue, as well as on the preliminary study on ways and means to advance the rights of people working in rural areas, in particular the views of the Food and Agriculture Organization of the United Nations. The Committee was also requested to undertake studies on the urban poor and their right to food, rural women and their right to food, and the relationship between malnutrition and childhood diseases. The Council requested the Rapporteur to submit a report at its nineteenth (2012) session on implementation of the resolution.

GENERAL ASSEMBLY ACTION

On 19 December [meeting 89], the General Assembly, on the recommendation of the Third Committee [A/66/462/Add.2], adopted **resolution 66/158** without vote [agenda item 69 (*b*)].

The right to food

The General Assembly,

Reaffirming the Charter of the United Nations and its importance for the promotion and protection of all human rights and fundamental freedoms for all,

Reaffirming also all previous resolutions and decisions on the right to food adopted within the framework of the United Nations,

Recalling the Universal Declaration of Human Rights, which provides that everyone has the right to a standard of living adequate for her or his health and well-being, including food, the Universal Declaration on the Eradication of Hunger and Malnutrition and the United Nations Millennium Declaration, in particular Millennium Development Goal 1 on eradicating extreme poverty and hunger by 2015,

Recalling also the provisions of the International Covenant on Economic, Social and Cultural Rights, in which the fundamental right of every person to be free from hunger is recognized,

Bearing in mind the Rome Declaration on World Food Security and the World Food Summit Plan of Action and the Declaration of the World Food Summit: five years later, adopted in Rome on 13 June 2002,

Reaffirming the concrete recommendations contained in the Voluntary Guidelines to Support the Progressive Realization of the Right to Adequate Food in the Context of National Food Security, adopted by the Council of the Food and Agriculture Organization of the United Nations in November 2004,

Reaffirming also the Five Rome Principles for Sustainable Global Food Security contained in the Declaration of the World Summit on Food Security, adopted in Rome on 16 November 2009,

Reaffirming further that all human rights are universal, indivisible, interdependent and interrelated, and that they must be treated globally, in a fair and equal manner, on the same footing and with the same emphasis,

Reaffirming that a peaceful, stable and enabling political, social and economic environment, at both the national and the international levels, is the essential foundation that will enable States to give adequate priority to food security and poverty eradication,

Reiterating, as in the Rome Declaration on World Food Security and the Declaration of the World Food Summit: five years later, that food should not be used as an instrument of political or economic pressure, and reaffirming in this regard the importance of international cooperation and solidarity, as well as the necessity of refraining from unilateral measures that are not in accordance with international law and the Charter of the United Nations and that endanger food security,

Convinced that each State must adopt a strategy consistent with its resources and capacities to achieve its individual goals in implementing the recommendations contained in the Rome Declaration on World Food Security and the World Food Summit Plan of Action and, at the same time, cooperate regionally and internationally in order to organize collective solutions to global issues of food security in a world of increasingly interlinked institutions, societies and economies where coordinated efforts and shared responsibilities are essential,

Recognizing that the complex character of the global food crisis, in which the right to adequate food is threatened to be violated on a massive scale, is a combination of several major factors, such as the global financial and economic crisis, environmental degradation, desertification and the impacts of global climate change, as well as natural disasters and the lack in many countries of the appropriate technology, investment and capacity-building necessary to confront its impact, particularly in developing countries, least developed countries and small island developing States,

Resolved to act to ensure that the human rights perspective is taken into account at the national, regional and international levels in measures to address the global food crisis,

Expressing its deep concern at the number and scale of natural disasters, diseases and pests, as well as the negative impact of climate change, and their increasing impact in recent years, which have resulted in substantial loss of life and livelihood and threatened agricultural production and food security, in particular in developing countries,

Stressing the importance of reversing the continuing decline of official development assistance devoted to agriculture, both in real terms and as a share of total official development assistance,

Recognizing the importance of the protection and preservation of agrobiodiversity in guaranteeing food security and the right to food for all,

Recognizing also the role of the Food and Agriculture Organization of the United Nations as the key United Nations agency for rural and agricultural development and its work in supporting the efforts of Member States to achieve the full realization of the right to food, including through its provision of technical assistance to developing countries in support of the implementation of national priority frameworks,

Taking note of the final Declaration adopted at the International Conference on Agrarian Reform and Rural Development of the Food and Agriculture Organization of the United Nations in Porto Alegre, Brazil, on 10 March 2006,

Acknowledging the High-level Task Force on the Global Food Security Crisis established by the Secretary-General, and supporting the Secretary-General in his continuing efforts in this regard, including continued engagement with

Member States and the Special Rapporteur of the Human Rights Council on the right to food,

1. *Reaffirms* that hunger constitutes an outrage and a violation of human dignity and therefore requires the adoption of urgent measures at the national, regional and international levels for its elimination;

2. *Also reaffirms* the right of everyone to have access to safe, sufficient and nutritious food, consistent with the right to adequate food and the fundamental right of everyone to be free from hunger, so as to be able to fully develop and maintain his or her physical and mental capacities;

3. *Considers it intolerable* that, as estimated by the United Nations Children's Fund, more than one third of the children who die every year before the age of 5 do so from hunger-related illness, that, as estimated by the Food and Agriculture Organization of the United Nations, the number of people who are undernourished is about 925 million worldwide, and that an additional 1 billion people are suffering from serious malnutrition, including as a result of the global food crisis, while, according to the latter organization, the planet could produce enough food to feed everyone around the world;

4. *Expresses its concern* at the fact that the effects of the world food crisis continue to have serious consequences for the poorest and most vulnerable people, particularly in developing countries, which have been further aggravated by the world financial and economic crisis, and at the particular effects of this crisis on many net food-importing countries, especially on least developed countries;

5. *Also expresses its concern* that women and girls are disproportionately affected by hunger, food insecurity and poverty, in part as a result of gender inequality and discrimination, that in many countries, girls are twice as likely as boys to die from malnutrition and preventable childhood diseases and that it is estimated that almost twice as many women as men suffer from malnutrition;

6. *Encourages* all States to take action to address gender inequality and discrimination against women, in particular where it contributes to the malnutrition of women and girls, including measures to ensure the full and equal realization of the right to food and ensuring that women have equal access to resources, including income, land and water and their ownership, as well as full and equal access to education, science and technology, to enable them to feed themselves and their families;

7. *Encourages* the Special Rapporteur of the Human Rights Council on the right to food to continue mainstreaming a gender perspective in the fulfilment of his mandate, and encourages the Food and Agriculture Organization of the United Nations and all other United Nations bodies and mechanisms addressing the right to food and food insecurity to integrate a gender perspective into their relevant policies, programmes and activities;

8. *Reaffirms* the need to ensure that programmes delivering safe and nutritious food are inclusive of and accessible to persons with disabilities;

9. *Encourages* all States to take steps with a view to achieving progressively the full realization of the right to food, including steps to promote the conditions for everyone to be free from hunger and, as soon as possible, to enjoy fully the right to food, and to create and adopt national plans to combat hunger;

10. *Recognizes* the advances reached through South-South cooperation in developing countries and regions in connection with food security and the development of agricultural production for the full realization of the right to food;

11. *Stresses* that improving access to productive resources and public investment in rural development are essential for eradicating hunger and poverty, in particular in developing countries, including through the promotion of investments in appropriate small-scale irrigation and water management technologies in order to reduce vulnerability to droughts;

12. *Recognizes* that 80 per cent of hungry people live in rural areas and 50 per cent are small-scale farm-holders, and that these people are especially vulnerable to food insecurity, given the increasing cost of inputs and the fall in farm incomes; that access to land, water, seeds and other natural resources is an increasing challenge for poor producers; that sustainable and gender-sensitive agricultural policies are important tools for promoting land and agrarian reform, rural credit and insurance, technical assistance and other associated measures to achieve food security and rural development; and that support by States for small farmers, fishing communities and local enterprises, including through the facilitation of access of their products to national and international markets and empowerment of small producers, particularly women, in value chains, is a key element for food security and the provision of the right to food;

13. *Stresses* the importance of fighting hunger in rural areas, including through national efforts supported by international partnerships to stop desertification and land degradation and through investments and public policies that are specifically appropriate to the risk of drylands, and in this regard calls for the full implementation of the United Nations Convention to Combat Desertification in Those Countries Experiencing Serious Drought and/or Desertification, Particularly in Africa;

14. *Urges* States that have not yet done so to favourably consider becoming parties to the Convention on Biological Diversity and to consider becoming parties to the International Treaty on Plant Genetic Resources for Food and Agriculture as a matter of priority;

15. *Recalls* the United Nations Declaration on the Rights of Indigenous Peoples, acknowledges that many indigenous organizations and representatives of indigenous peoples have expressed in different forums their deep concerns over the obstacles and challenges they face for the full enjoyment of the right to food, and calls upon States to take special actions to combat the root causes of the disproportionately high level of hunger and malnutrition among indigenous peoples and the continuous discrimination against them;

16. *Notes* the need to further examine various concepts such as, inter alia, "food sovereignty" and their relation with food security and the right to food, bearing in mind the need to avoid any negative impact on the enjoyment of the right to food for all people at all times;

17. *Requests* all States and private actors, as well as international organizations within their respective mandates, to take fully into account the need to promote the effective realization of the right to food for all, including in the ongoing negotiations in different fields;

18. *Recognizes* the need to strengthen national commitment as well as international assistance, upon the request of and in cooperation with the affected countries, towards the full realization and protection of the right to food, and in particular to develop national protection mechanisms for people forced to leave their homes and land because of hunger or humanitarian emergencies affecting the enjoyment of the right to food;

19. *Stresses* the need to make efforts to mobilize and optimize the allocation and utilization of technical and financial resources from all sources, including external debt relief for developing countries, and to reinforce national actions to implement sustainable food security policies;

20. *Calls for* the early conclusion and a successful, development-oriented outcome of the Doha Round of trade negotiations of the World Trade Organization as a contribution to creating international conditions that permit the full realization of the right to food;

21. *Stresses* that all States should make all efforts to ensure that their international policies of a political and economic nature, including international trade agreements, do not have a negative impact on the right to food in other countries;

22. *Recalls* the importance of the New York Declaration on Action against Hunger and Poverty, and recommends the continuation of efforts aimed at identifying additional sources of financing for the fight against hunger and poverty;

23. *Recognizes* that the promises made at the World Food Summit in 1996 to halve the number of persons who are undernourished are not being fulfilled, while recognizing the efforts of Member States in this regard, and invites once again all international financial and development institutions, as well as the relevant United Nations agencies and funds, to give priority to and provide the necessary funding to realize the aim of halving by 2015 the proportion of people who suffer from hunger, as well as the right to food as set out in the Rome Declaration on World Food Security and the United Nations Millennium Declaration;

24. *Reaffirms* that integrating food and nutritional support, with the goal that all people at all times will have access to sufficient, safe and nutritious food to meet their dietary needs and food preferences for an active and healthy life, is part of a comprehensive effort to improve public health, including the response to the spread of HIV/AIDS, tuberculosis, malaria and other communicable diseases;

25. *Urges* States to give adequate priority in their development strategies and expenditures to the realization of the right to food;

26. *Stresses* the importance of international cooperation and development assistance as an effective contribution both to the expansion and improvement of agriculture and its environmental sustainability, food production, breeding projects on diversity of crops and livestock, and institutional innovations such as community seed banks, farmer field schools and seed fairs and to the provision of humanitarian food assistance in activities related to emergency situations, for the realization of the right to food and the achievement of sustainable food security, while recognizing that each country has the primary responsibility for ensuring the implementation of national programmes and strategies in this regard;

27. *Also stresses* that States parties to the World Trade Organization Agreement on Trade-Related Aspects of Intellectual Property Rights should consider implementing that agreement in a manner that is supportive of food security, while being mindful of the obligation of Member States to promote and protect the right to food;

28. *Calls upon* Member States, the United Nations system and other relevant stakeholders to support national efforts aimed at responding rapidly to the food crises currently occurring across Africa, in particular in the Horn of Africa, and expresses its deep concern that funding shortfalls are forcing the World Food Programme to cut operations across different regions, including Southern Africa;

29. *Invites* all relevant international organizations, including the World Bank and the International Monetary Fund, to continue to promote policies and projects that have a positive impact on the right to food, to ensure that partners respect the right to food in the implementation of common projects, to support strategies of Member States aimed at the fulfilment of the right to food and to avoid any actions that could have a negative impact on the realization of the right to food;

30. *Takes note with appreciation* of the interim report of the Special Rapporteur;

31. *Supports* the realization of the mandate of the Special Rapporteur, as extended by the Human Rights Council in its resolution 13/4 of 24 March 2010;

32. *Requests* the Secretary-General and the United Nations High Commissioner for Human Rights to provide all the human and financial resources necessary for the effective fulfilment of the mandate of the Special Rapporteur;

33. *Welcomes* the work already done by the Committee on Economic, Social and Cultural Rights in promoting the right to adequate food, in particular its General Comment No. 12 (1999) on the right to adequate food (article 11 of the International Covenant on Economic, Social and Cultural Rights), in which the Committee affirmed, inter alia, that the right to adequate food is indivisibly linked to the inherent dignity of the human person and is indispensable for the fulfilment of other human rights enshrined in the International Bill of Human Rights, and is also inseparable from social justice, requiring the adoption of appropriate economic, environmental and social policies, at both the national and the international levels, oriented to the eradication of poverty and the fulfilment of all human rights for all;

34. *Recalls* General Comment No. 15 (2002) of the Committee on Economic, Social and Cultural Rights on the right to water (articles 11 and 12 of the Covenant), in which the Committee noted, inter alia, the importance of ensuring sustainable access to water resources for human consumption and agriculture in realization of the right to adequate food;

35. *Reaffirms* that the Voluntary Guidelines to Support the Progressive Realization of the Right to Adequate Food in the Context of National Food Security, adopted by the Council of the Food and Agriculture Organization of the United Nations in November 2004, represent a practical tool to promote the realization of the right to food for all, contribute to the achievement of food security and thus provide an additional instrument in the attainment of internationally agreed development goals, including those contained in the United Nations Millennium Declaration;

36. *Welcomes* the continued cooperation of the High Commissioner, the Committee and the Special Rappor-

teur, and encourages them to continue their cooperation in this regard;

37. *Calls upon* all Governments to cooperate with and assist the Special Rapporteur in his task, to supply all necessary information requested by him and to give serious consideration to responding favourably to the requests of the Special Rapporteur to visit their countries to enable him to fulfil his mandate more effectively;

38. *Requests* the Special Rapporteur to submit to the General Assembly at its sixty-seventh session an interim report on the implementation of the present resolution and to continue his work, including by examining the emerging issues with regard to the realization of the right to food within his existing mandate;

39. *Invites* Governments, relevant United Nations agencies, funds and programmes, treaty bodies, civil society actors and non-governmental organizations, as well as the private sector, to cooperate fully with the Special Rapporteur in the fulfilment of his mandate, inter alia, through the submission of comments and suggestions on ways and means of realizing the right to food;

40. *Decides* to continue the consideration of the question at its sixty-seventh session under the item entitled "Promotion and protection of human rights".

Right to adequate housing

Reports of Special Rapporteur. As requested by the Human Rights Council [YUN 2007, p. 780], the Special Rapporteur on adequate housing as a component of the right to an adequate standard of living, and on the right to non-discrimination in that context, Raquel Rolnik (Brazil), submitted her report [A/HRC/16/42] in which she discussed the importance of integrating human rights standards in post-disaster and post-conflict reconstruction processes. The report focused on common issues between the two situations and on three key entry points: security of tenure; consultation and participation; and institutional coordination. Recommendations were addressed to States and the international community on how to improve prevention, relief and rehabilitation efforts by incorporating the right to adequate housing. The Rapporteur called on States to intensify efforts to respect, protect and fulfil the right to adequate housing in both urban and rural contexts; develop and implement land tenure reform policies and programmes that made suitably located, secure, safe and affordable housing accessible to all; and recognize and protect a variety of land tenure forms, instead of a predominant or exclusive focus on freehold ownership.

An addendum [A/HRC/16/42/Add.1] summarized 24 communications sent to 16 States between 23 December 2009 and 6 December 2010 and eight replies received from seven States between 4 February 2010 and 6 February 2011.

Pursuant to a Human Rights Council request [YUN 2010, p. 741], the Secretary-General transmitted to the General Assembly the August report of the Rapporteur [A/66/270] focusing on the right to adequate housing in post-disaster settings. The report assessed human rights standards and guidelines relevant to an approach to disaster response based on the right to adequate housing and discussed some existing limitations. It elaborated on challenges to the right in disaster response, including inattention to or discrimination against vulnerable and disadvantaged groups; the overemphasis on individual property ownership and the difficulty of addressing the multiple tenure forms equally in restitution and recovery programmes; the risks of approaching post-disaster reconstruction predominantly as a business or development opportunity that benefited only a few; and limitations in existing frameworks for reconstruction and recovery. The report concluded by outlining an approach to disaster response that comprehensively integrated the right to adequate housing.

The General Assembly took note of that report on 19 December (**decision 66/537**).

Mission reports. Following her mission to the World Bank (26 October–1 November 2010) [A/HRC/22/46/Add.3], the Special Rapporteur presented her observations and recommendations on the World Bank's safeguard policies, particularly on the right to adequate housing, in the context of its two-year consultative process to review and update its environmental and social safeguard policies. She recommended that the World Bank commit to undertake human rights due diligence in all of its activities, including investment lending, development policy lending and the newly adopted Program-for-Results. It should also ensure that mechanisms were in place to implement those policies and address actual and potential adverse human rights impacts.

Following her visit to Argentina (13–21 April) [A/HRC/19/53/Add.1], the Rapporteur identified factors impeding the realization of the right to adequate housing in the country, including the lack of market regulation for land transactions; real estate speculation; the lack of federal coordination in the formulation and implementation of housing policies; a legal framework for evictions that failed to guarantee due process; and a lack of comprehensive housing policies that were sufficiently diverse to provide long-term solutions to the various housing needs. Recommendations were provided in five priority areas: housing and land policies; informal settlements; evictions; the situation of indigenous peoples; and the situation of migrants. The Rapporteur observed that given the progress made in legislation and investment in housing and the economic growth of recent years, Argentina was able to draw up and implement a social pact on land use to ensure the implementation of the right to adequate housing for all its inhabitants.

Following her mission to Algeria (9–19 July) [A/HRC/19/53/Add.2], the Rapporteur reported on existing housing policies, the country's continuing housing crisis, and issues with accessibility and affordability. She noted that the idea of housing as a fundamental right was deeply rooted in Algerian society and that the State considered the question of housing as one of its main responsibilities vis-à-vis the population. The Rapporteur showed how a democratization of housing policy based on transparency and the direct involvement of citizens and civil society organizations in defining and implementing those policies would constitute an important step in shifting the focus from housing construction to the realization of the right to housing. Recommendations were made to assist the Government in its efforts to improve the enjoyment of that right.

Right to health

Reports of Special Rapporteur. As requested by the Human Rights Council [YUN 2010, p. 742], the Special Rapporteur on the right of everyone to the enjoyment of the highest attainable standard of physical and mental health, Anand Grover (India), in April [A/HRC/17/25] submitted a report that examined the ways in which the right to health framework could add value to development policies and programmes. Using the example of HIV/AIDS, he considered projects in which a human rights-based approach had been utilized, and explored the value added of that approach. The report identified a number of challenges that remained in incorporating human rights into development work. The Special Rapporteur warned against adoption of a "culture of evaluation" to the detriment of human rights-based approaches. He pointed out that it was difficult to conduct evidence-based evaluations of human rights-based health interventions with the same level of methodological rigour applied to, for instance, clinical drug trials. Given the difficulty of illustrating the cause and effect relationship between the realization of human rights and intended health outcomes—such as the empowerment of sex workers, their increased use of condoms, and the resultant lower levels of HIV infection—it was imperative that a broad range of evidence-informed practices were used when evaluating human rights-based interventions. The report concluded with recommendations to the United Nations and other actors in the development and human rights fields concerning ways to strengthen the integration of development and human rights.

An addendum [A/HRC/17/25/Add.1] summarized 46 communications sent to 29 States from 16 March 2010 to 15 March 2011, including three communications that originated prior to 16 March, as well as 21 replies received from 2 May 2010 to 1 May 2011.

In response to a Human Rights Council request [YUN 2009, p. 730], the Rapporteur in March submitted a report [A/HRC/17/43] summarizing the discussions and recommendations made at the expert consultation on access to medicines as a fundamental component of the right to health (Geneva, 11 October 2010). The issues discussed included the need for States to develop suitable national health legislation and policies and to strengthen their national health systems. States were called on to ensure the sustainable financing, availability and affordability of medicines, and to establish monitoring and accountability mechanisms.

As requested by the Human Rights Council [YUN 2010, p. 742], the Secretary-General in August transmitted to the General Assembly the Rapporteur's interim report [A/66/254], which examined the right to sexual and reproductive health. He considered the impact of criminal and other legal restrictions on abortion, conduct during pregnancy, contraception and family planning, and the provision of sexual and reproductive education and information. Some restrictions in each of those areas, which were often discriminatory in nature, violated the right to health by restricting access to quality goods, services and information, and infringed human dignity. Realization of the right to health required the removal of barriers that interfered with individual decision-making on health-related issues and with access to health services, education and information, in particular on health conditions that only affected women and girls. He recommended that States undertake reforms towards policies and programmes relating to sexual and reproductive health as required by international human rights law. In that context, he called on States to formulate public health policies and programmes that disseminated evidence-based information regarding sexual and reproductive health and provided for family planning; to decriminalize abortion, the supply and use of contraception, and the provision of information relating to sexual and reproductive health; and to ensure the availability, accessibility and quality of a full range of contraceptive methods.

The General Assembly took note of that report on 19 December (**decision 66/537**).

Mission reports. During his visit to Ghana (23–30 May) [A/HRC/20/15/Add.1], the Rapporteur examined the effect of the National Health Insurance Scheme (NHIS), including concerns regarding membership and coverage, the exclusion of some important goods and services, and the long-term sustainability of NHIS. Other areas of focus included the extreme under-resourcing of the mental health sector; women's health and maternal mortality, which had been declared a national emergency; efforts to reduce the spread of malaria; and issues relating to environmental and occupational health. The

Rapporteur observed that there were significant issues regarding occupational health and safety, particularly in the mining sector, which the Government should urgently address. He made recommendations to the Government pertaining to the overall health care system, HIV/AIDS, mental health, maternal mortality, malaria and occupational health.

During his mission to Viet Nam (24 November– 5 December) [A/HRC/20/15/Add.2], the Special Rapporteur examined health systems and financing within the country, noting that the increasing privatization of the health sector and the decentralization of health governance presented challenges pertaining to access to health care and increasing out-of-pocket expenditures. There were also concerns regarding the national social health insurance programme, including the scheme's coverage and quality of services. The report addressed access to medicine and high drug prices, which were a significant barrier to the availability of medicines, especially for the poor and near poor; the potential impact of the Trans-Pacific Partnership Agreement on access to medicines; issues related to HIV/AIDS prevention and control; and the detention and mandatory treatment of drug users and female sex workers in rehabilitation centres. He concluded the report with recommendations to the Government.

Human Rights Council action. On 17 June [A/66/53 (res. 17/14)], the Council urged States, UN entities and relevant stakeholders to promote the development, availability and affordability of new drugs for diseases disproportionately affecting developing countries. It requested the Rapporteur to prepare a study on existing challenges with regard to access to medicines in the context of the right to physical and mental health, as well as ways to overcome them and good practices, to be presented to the Council's twenty-third (2013) session.

Human rights and HIV/AIDS

Report of Secretary-General. Pursuant to a Human Rights Council request [YUN 2009, p. 730], the Secretary-General submitted a study [A/HRC/16/69] on steps taken to promote and implement programmes to address HIV/AIDS-related human rights. The study was based on survey responses received from Governments, UN entities and NGOs, as well as a 25 October 2010 consultation of States, NGOs and UN representatives in Geneva. Informants reported some success in strengthening human rights elements of national HIV responses, but also identified many politically difficult challenges to be overcome. HIV-related discrimination remained widespread in many sectors of society and was closely linked to HIV-related stigma, ignorance regarding modes of HIV transmission, and association of HIV with behaviours that were criminalized or considered immoral. The study highlighted the need for programmes to be adequately funded and implemented at a scale necessary to make a difference.

Human Rights Council action. On 25 March [A/66/53 (res. 16/28)], the Council called on States to establish participatory, gender-sensitive, transparent and accountable national HIV/AIDS policies and programmes and implement them at all levels; address the vulnerabilities faced by children and adolescents affected by and living with HIV; and take steps to eliminate laws that were counterproductive to HIV prevention, treatment, care and support, including laws mandating disclosure of HIV status. The Council requested OHCHR to engage with the 2011 General Assembly high-level meeting on AIDS (see p. 1135), providing a human rights-based perspective, and to inform the Council thereon. It decided to hold a panel discussion at its nineteenth (2012) session to give voice to people living with or affected by HIV/AIDS, particularly young people, women and orphaned children.

Report of High Commissioner. In response to a Human Rights Council request (see above), the High Commissioner submitted a report [A/HRC/19/37] reviewing the context and objectives of the Political Declaration on HIV and AIDS adopted at the high-level meeting on AIDS (see p. 1135), including information on the role OHCHR played in advocating for a human rights-based perspective, and an analysis of the Declaration from a human rights perspective. It highlighted that the 2011 Declaration represented an opportunity to chart a new course for the global AIDS response and to advance human rights by addressing discrimination associated with HIV-related stigma, vulnerability and risk behaviours.

Maternal mortality

OHCHR report. As requested by the Human Rights Council [YUN 2010, p. 742], OHCHR in July submitted a study [A/HRC/18/27 & Corr.1 & Corr.1/Rev.1] containing an analytical compilation of good and effective practices in adopting a human rights-based approach to eliminate preventable maternal mortality and morbidity. It identified the common features of such practices, analysed how they embodied a human rights-based approach, and highlighted good practices that had been effective in reducing maternal mortality and morbidity. The report remarked that interventions to reduce maternal mortality and morbidity were more effective when stakeholders applied principles of a human rights-based approach to address the needs of the most poor and marginalized. The interventions highlighted in the report demonstrated the need to incorporate a holistic and comprehensive human rights-based approach into integrated strategies to combat maternal mortality and morbidity.

Human Rights Council action. On 28 September [A/66/53/Add.1 (res. 18/2)], the Council encouraged States and other stakeholders, including national human rights institutions and NGOs, to address the interlinked root causes of maternal mortality and morbidity; requested OHCHR to convene an expert workshop to prepare technical guidance on the application of a human rights-based approach to the implementation of policies and programmes to reduce preventable maternal mortality and morbidity; and to present such guidance to the Council. It decided to continue considering the issue at its twenty-first (2012) session.

Health of older persons

Report of Special Rapporteur. In response to a Human Rights Council request [YUN 2010, p. 742], the Special Rapporteur on the right of everyone to the enjoyment of the highest attainable standard of physical and mental health, submitted a thematic study [A/HRC/18/37] on the realization of the right to health of older persons. Noting the significant pace of the world's ageing, the study urged a paradigm shift whereby society should move beyond a simple search for healthy ageing by its citizens and begin working towards active and dignified ageing. That shift required reframing society's concept of ageing and focusing on the continued participation of older persons in social, economic, cultural and civic life, as well as their continuous contributions to society. The report underscored that the right-to-health approach was indispensable for the design, implementation, monitoring and evaluation of health-related policies and programmes to mitigate consequences of an ageing society and to ensure the enjoyment of that human right by older persons. Encouraging older persons to remain physically, politically, socially and economically active for as long as possible would benefit not only the individual, but also society as a whole.

Water and sanitation

Reports of Special Rapporteur. As requested by the Human Rights Council (see below), the Special Rapporteur on the human right to safe drinking water and sanitation, Catarina de Albuquerque (Portugal), in July submitted a report [A/HRC/18/33] that focused on national and local planning for the implementation of the rights to water and sanitation, highlighting the importance of having a vision and political will to ensure the realization of those rights. She outlined existing frameworks for planning and the significance of integrating human rights throughout the planning process and identified factors for successful planning, including sound legal frameworks and institutions, access to justice and clear designation of responsibilities, adequate financing, participation and transparency, and nondiscrimination and equality. Her conclusions and recommendations pertained to providing a framework for prioritization; providing a framework for ambitious but realistic planning; ensuring sustainability; and emphasizing accountability.

In an addendum [A/HRC/18/33/Add.1], the Rapporteur presented a compilation of good practices for implementing the rights to water and sanitation of a range of stakeholders, including national and local State bodies, international agencies, service providers, NGOs and civil society, and covered many approaches to realizing those rights, including legislation, planning, service delivery, advocacy and capacity-building, monitoring and litigation.

As requested by the Human Rights Council [YUN 2010, p. 743], the Secretary-General in August transmitted to the General Assembly the report [A/66/255] of the Rapporteur, which reviewed the major issues surrounding the resources available for the realization of the rights to water and sanitation; considered sources of financing within the sectors; and offered concrete examples of how stakeholders could better utilize limited resources by keeping human rights principles in mind. The Rapporteur concluded that beyond the need for additional resources, existing resources should be better targeted to prioritize the most excluded and marginalized. She recommended that States prioritize funding for water and sanitation, ensure that household contributions remained affordable, increase the percentage of international aid allocated to water and sanitation, and ensure transparency of budgets and other funding for the sectors.

Mission reports. Following her visit to the United States (22 February–4 March) [A/HRC/18/33/Add.4], the independent expert (Ms. de Albuquerque, later the Special Rapporteur) observed that while the vast majority of people living in the country had access to clean and safe drinking water and sanitation, ageing and deteriorating water and sanitation infrastructure forced the question of whether nineteenth- and twentieth-century technology would carry the country into the next century. Estimates indicated an annual $4 billion to $6 billion funding gap for infrastructure in the sector. The expert recommended the development of a national water policy and plan of action guided by the normative content of the rights to water and sanitation, and concerted efforts to ensure targeting of policies and programmes to reach the hidden and poorest segments of the population.

Following her mission to Namibia (4–11 July) [A/HRC/21/42/Add.3], the Special Rapporteur outlined the legal framework of the rights to water and sanitation in the country; made a general assessment of the enjoyment of those rights, including in terms of water quality and pollution, sanitation and affordability; and examined specific issues related to rural areas, informal settlements, the mining sector, inadequate regulation and budget allocations. She concluded the report with recommendations addressed to the Government.

Following her visit to Senegal (14–21 November) [A/HRC/21/42/Add.1], the Rapporteur acknowledged progress in the expansion of access to safe water in the country and commitments to invest in sanitation, yet expressed concern at the inequalities between urban and rural areas, the limited affordability of water and sanitation in poor communities, and the low quality of water in some regions. She underlined the need for further investments in sanitation and in awareness-raising strategies on hygiene promotion. Recommendations to the Government focused on strengthening institutional and legal frameworks, expanding access to safe drinking water and sanitation, ensuring that water quality met international standards, and ensuring the affordability of water and sanitation. She affirmed that the international community must uphold and enhance its commitments to assist Senegal.

Human Rights Council action. On 24 March [A/66/53 (res. 16/2)], the Council welcomed the work of the independent expert, including the progress in collecting good practices for her compendium report [YUN 2010, p. 742]; extended for three years the mandate of the mandate holder as a special rapporteur on the human right to safe drinking water and sanitation; and requested the Special Rapporteur to report to the General Assembly and Council on an annual basis.

On 28 September [A/66/53/Add.1 (res. 18/1)], the Council, expressing concern that approximately 884 million people lacked access to improved water sources and that more than 2.6 billion people did not have access to improved sanitation, called on States to continuously monitor and analyse the status of the realization of the right to safe drinking water and sanitation on the basis of the criteria of availability, quality, acceptability, accessibility and affordability; and requested the Rapporteur to report annually to the Assembly and the Council.

Cultural rights

Report of independent expert. In response to a Human Rights Council request [YUN 2009, p. 724], the independent expert in the field of cultural rights, Farida Shaheed (Pakistan), submitted a March report [A/HRC/17/38] exploring the concept of cultural heritage from the perspective of human rights and presented a list of human rights issues related to cultural heritage. A compilation of references in international law on the rights of individuals and communities in relation to cultural heritage, a summary of information received from 30 States and 22 other stakeholders in response to a questionnaire disseminated by the expert, and input gathered from an experts' meeting convened by the expert on the right to access to and enjoyment of cultural heritage (Geneva, 8–9 February) were included in the report. The expert made recommendations for States to recognize and value the diversity of cultural heritages present in their territories and under their jurisdiction; respect the free development of cultural heritage; ensure access to the cultural heritage of one's own communities as well as that of others; and adopt measures to ensure access to and enjoyment of cultural heritage by all people regardless of gender, including people with scarce financial resources and those with disabilities.

Mission reports. Following her mission to Austria (5–15 April) [A/HRC/20/26/Add.1 & Corr.1], the expert pointed out initiatives taken to ensure the realization of cultural rights, including measures to increase access to culture by all, in particular youth, persons with disabilities and people with low incomes; support initiatives for promoting intercultural exchanges, cultural diversity and participation in cultural life; and protect and promote cultural rights of recognized national minorities. Nonetheless, further steps were needed. Measures to promote cultural diversity and cultural rights remained compartmentalized and lacked an institutional framework that would facilitate building upon valuable experience. Implementation of the rights of persons belonging to minorities and disadvantaged groups in the fields of education, culture and language, as well as their rights not to be discriminated against and to participate in the life of society, remained insufficient. The expert recommended establishing a unified framework and an institutional body, at the level of the Federal Government, to promote cultural diversity and intercultural understanding, and incorporating minority culture in school curricula.

During her visit to Morocco (5–16 September) [A/HRC/20/26/Add.2], the independent expert addressed the issue of the realization of cultural rights of various groups, including persons with disabilities and the Amazigh and Jewish communities. She observed that amendments to the Constitution had strengthened the protection of human rights, including those of the most vulnerable populations, placed greater importance on cultural rights and cultural diversity, and conferred official status to the Amazigh language. Yet some laws, policies and practices were still not in keeping with the State's international and constitutional commitment to recognize and respect cultural rights and cultural diversity. She concluded the report with recommendations to strengthen the promotion and protection of cultural rights for all in Morocco. The report included a separate chapter on the realization of cultural rights in Western Sahara.

Human Rights Council action. On 17 June [A/66/53 (res. 17/15)], the Council recognized that respect for cultural rights was essential for development, peace and the eradication of poverty, building social cohesion and promoting mutual respect, tolerance and understanding between individuals and groups; took note of the independent expert's work, including the questionnaire on access to cultural heritage and the holding of an experts' meeting on the topic; and requested the expert to present her next report to the Council's twentieth (2012) session.

Cultural diversity

Report of Secretary-General. Pursuant to General Assembly resolution 64/174 [YUN 2009, p. 724], the Secretary-General issued a July report [A/66/161] on human rights and cultural diversity, taking into account the views of States, UN agencies and NGOs. The report provided a summary of comments on the recognition and importance of cultural diversity among peoples and nations received from 16 States and one NGO. Comments from Governments focused on measures taken to promote cultural diversity and to protect and ensure access to cultural heritage.

GENERAL ASSEMBLY ACTION

On 19 December [meeting 89], the General Assembly, on the recommendation of the Third Committee [A/66/462/Add.2], adopted **resolution 66/154** by recorded vote (136-53-2) [agenda item 69 (*b*)].

Human rights and cultural diversity

The General Assembly,

Recalling the Universal Declaration of Human Rights, the International Covenant on Economic, Social and Cultural Rights and the International Covenant on Civil and Political Rights, as well as other pertinent human rights instruments,

Recalling also its resolutions 54/160 of 17 December 1999, 55/91 of 4 December 2000, 57/204 of 18 December 2002, 58/167 of 22 December 2003, 60/167 of 16 December 2005, 62/155 of 18 December 2007 and 64/174 of 18 December 2009, and recalling further its resolutions 54/113 of 10 December 1999, 55/23 of 13 November 2000 and 60/4 of 20 October 2005 concerning the United Nations Year of Dialogue among Civilizations,

Noting that numerous instruments within the United Nations system promote cultural diversity, as well as the conservation and development of culture, in particular the Declaration of the Principles of International Culture Cooperation proclaimed on 4 November 1966 by the General Conference of the United Nations Educational, Scientific and Cultural Organization at its fourteenth session,

Taking note of the report of the Secretary-General,

Recalling that, as stated in the Declaration on Principles of International Law concerning Friendly Relations and Cooperation among States in accordance with the Charter of the United Nations, contained in the annex to its resolution 2625(XXV) of 24 October 1970, States have the duty to cooperate with one another, irrespective of the differences in their political, economic and social systems, in the various spheres of international relations, in the promotion of universal respect for and observance of human rights and fundamental freedoms for all, and in the elimination of all forms of racial discrimination and all forms of religious intolerance,

Welcoming the adoption of the Global Agenda for Dialogue among Civilizations by its resolution 56/6 of 9 November 2001,

Welcoming also the contribution of the World Conference against Racism, Racial Discrimination, Xenophobia and Related Intolerance, held in Durban, South Africa, from 31 August to 8 September 2001, the Durban Review Conference, held in Geneva from 20 to 24 April 2009, and the high-level meeting of the General Assembly to commemorate the tenth anniversary of the adoption of the Durban Declaration and Programme of Action, held on 22 September 2011, to the promotion of respect for cultural diversity,

Welcoming further the Universal Declaration on Cultural Diversity of the United Nations Educational, Scientific and Cultural Organization, together with its Action Plan, adopted on 2 November 2001 by the General Conference of the United Nations Educational, Scientific and Cultural Organization at its thirty-first session, in which member States invited the United Nations system and other intergovernmental and non-governmental organizations concerned to cooperate with the United Nations Educational, Scientific and Cultural Organization in the promotion of the principles set forth in the Declaration and its Action Plan with a view to enhancing the synergy of actions in favour of cultural diversity,

Recalling the Ministerial Meeting on Human Rights and Cultural Diversity of the Movement of Non-Aligned Countries, held in Tehran on 3 and 4 September 2007,

Reaffirming that all human rights are universal, indivisible, interdependent and interrelated and that the international community must treat human rights globally in a fair and equal manner, on the same footing and with the same emphasis, and that, while the significance of national and regional particularities and various historical, cultural and religious backgrounds must be borne in mind, it is the duty of States, regardless of their political, economic and cultural systems, to promote and protect all human rights and fundamental freedoms,

Recognizing that cultural diversity and the pursuit of cultural development by all peoples and nations are a source of mutual enrichment for the cultural life of humankind,

Recognizing also the contribution that diverse cultures have been making to the development and promotion of human rights and fundamental freedoms,

Taking into account that a culture of peace actively fosters non-violence and respect for human rights and strengthens solidarity among peoples and nations and dialogue between cultures,

Recognizing that all cultures and civilizations share a common set of universal values,

Recognizing also that the promotion of the rights of indigenous people and their cultures and traditions will contribute to the respect for and observance of cultural diversity among all peoples and nations,

Considering that tolerance of cultural, ethnic, religious and linguistic diversities, as well as dialogue among and within civilizations, is essential for peace, understanding and friendship among individuals and people of different cultures and nations of the world, while manifestations of cultural prejudice, intolerance and xenophobia towards different cultures and religions generate hatred and violence among peoples and nations throughout the world,

Recognizing in each culture a dignity and value that deserve recognition, respect and preservation, and convinced that, in their rich variety and diversity, and in the reciprocal influences that they exert on one another, all cultures form part of the common heritage belonging to all humankind,

Convinced that the promotion of cultural pluralism and tolerance towards and dialogue among various cultures and civilizations would contribute to the efforts of all peoples and nations to enrich their cultures and traditions by engaging in a mutually beneficial exchange of knowledge and intellectual, moral and material achievements,

Acknowledging the diversity of the world, recognizing that all cultures and civilizations contribute to the enrichment of humankind, acknowledging the importance of respect and understanding for religious and cultural diversity throughout the world, and, in order to promote international peace and security, committing itself to advancing human welfare, freedom and progress everywhere, as well as to encouraging tolerance, respect, dialogue and cooperation among different cultures, civilizations and peoples,

1. *Affirms* the importance for all peoples and nations to hold, develop and preserve their cultural heritage and traditions in a national and international atmosphere of peace, tolerance and mutual respect;

2. *Emphasizes* the important contribution of culture to development and the achievement of national development objectives and internationally agreed development goals, including the Millennium Development Goals;

3. *Welcomes* the adoption on 8 September 2000 of the United Nations Millennium Declaration, in which Member States consider, inter alia, that tolerance is one of the fundamental values essential to international relations in the twenty-first century and that it should include the active promotion of a culture of peace and dialogue among civilizations, with human beings respecting one another in all their diversity of belief, culture and language, neither fearing nor repressing differences within and between societies but cherishing them as a precious asset of humanity;

4. *Recognizes* the right of everyone to take part in cultural life and to enjoy the benefits of scientific progress and its applications;

5. *Affirms* that the international community should strive to respond to the challenges and opportunities posed by globalization in a manner that ensures respect for the cultural diversity of all;

6. *Expresses its determination* to prevent and mitigate cultural homogenization in the context of globalization, through increased intercultural exchange guided by the promotion and protection of cultural diversity;

7. *Affirms* that intercultural dialogue essentially enriches the common understanding of human rights and that the benefits to be derived from the encouragement and development of international contacts and cooperation in the cultural fields are important;

8. *Welcomes* the recognition at the World Conference against Racism, Racial Discrimination, Xenophobia and Related Intolerance of the necessity of respecting and maximizing the benefits of diversity within and among all nations in working together to build a harmonious and productive future by putting into practice and promoting values and principles such as justice, equality and non-discrimination, democracy, fairness and friendship, tolerance and respect within and among communities and nations, in particular through public information and educational programmes to raise awareness and understanding of the benefits of cultural diversity, including programmes in which the public authorities work in partnership with international and non-governmental organizations and other sectors of civil society;

9. *Recognizes* that respect for cultural diversity and the cultural rights of all enhances cultural pluralism, contributing to a wider exchange of knowledge and understanding of cultural background, advancing the application and enjoyment of universally accepted human rights throughout the world and fostering stable, friendly relations among peoples and nations worldwide;

10. *Emphasizes* that the promotion of cultural pluralism and tolerance at the national, regional and international levels is important for enhancing respect for cultural rights and cultural diversity;

11. *Also emphasizes* that tolerance and respect for diversity facilitate the universal promotion and protection of human rights, including gender equality and the enjoyment of all human rights by all, and underlines the fact that tolerance and respect for cultural diversity and the universal promotion and protection of human rights are mutually supportive;

12. *Urges* all actors on the international scene to build an international order based on inclusion, justice, equality and equity, human dignity, mutual understanding and promotion of and respect for cultural diversity and universal human rights, and to reject all doctrines of exclusion based on racism, racial discrimination, xenophobia and related intolerance;

13. *Urges* States to ensure that their political and legal systems reflect the multicultural diversity within their societies and, where necessary, to improve democratic institutions so that they are more fully participatory and avoid marginalization and exclusion of, and discrimination against, specific sectors of society;

14. *Calls upon* States, international organizations and United Nations agencies and invites civil society, including non-governmental organizations, to recognize and promote respect for cultural diversity for the purpose of advancing the objectives of peace, development and universally accepted human rights;

15. *Stresses* the necessity of freely using the media and new information and communications technologies to create the conditions for a renewed dialogue among cultures and civilizations;

16. *Requests* the Office of the United Nations High Commissioner for Human Rights to continue to bear in mind fully the issues raised in the present resolution in the course of its activities for the promotion and protection of human rights;

17. *Also requests* the Office of the High Commissioner and invites the United Nations Educational, Scientific and Cultural Organization to support initiatives aimed at promoting intercultural dialogue on human rights;

18. *Urges* relevant international organizations to conduct studies on how respect for cultural diversity contributes to fostering international solidarity and cooperation among all nations;

19. *Requests* the Secretary-General to prepare a report on the implementation of the present resolution, includ-

ing efforts undertaken at the national, regional and international levels regarding the recognition and importance of cultural diversity among all peoples and nations in the world and taking into account the views of Member States, relevant United Nations agencies and non-governmental organizations, and to submit the report to the General Assembly at its sixty-eighth session;

20. *Decides* to continue consideration of the question at its sixty-eighth session under the sub-item entitled "Human rights questions, including alternative approaches for improving the effective enjoyment of human rights and fundamental freedoms".

RECORDED VOTE ON RESOLUTION 66/154:

In favour: Afghanistan, Algeria, Angola, Antigua and Barbuda, Argentina, Azerbaijan, Bahamas, Bahrain, Bangladesh, Barbados, Belarus, Belize, Benin, Bhutan, Bolivia, Botswana, Brazil, Brunei Darussalam, Burkina Faso, Burundi, Cambodia, Cameroon, Cape Verde, Central African Republic, Chad, Chile, China, Colombia, Comoros, Congo, Costa Rica, Côte d'Ivoire, Cuba, Democratic People's Republic of Korea, Democratic Republic of the Congo, Djibouti, Dominica, Dominican Republic, Ecuador, Egypt, El Salvador, Equatorial Guinea, Eritrea, Ethiopia, Fiji, Gabon, Gambia, Ghana, Grenada, Guatemala, Guinea, Guinea-Bissau, Guyana, Haiti, Honduras, India, Indonesia, Iran, Iraq, Jamaica, Jordan, Kazakhstan, Kenya, Kuwait, Kyrgyzstan, Lao People's Democratic Republic, Lebanon, Lesotho, Liberia, Libya, Madagascar, Malawi, Malaysia, Maldives, Mali, Mauritania, Mauritius, Mexico, Mongolia, Morocco, Mozambique, Myanmar, Namibia, Nepal, Nicaragua, Niger, Nigeria, Oman, Pakistan, Panama, Papua New Guinea, Paraguay, Peru, Philippines, Qatar, Russian Federation, Rwanda, Saint Kitts and Nevis, Saint Lucia, Saint Vincent and the Grenadines, Samoa, Sao Tome and Principe, Saudi Arabia, Senegal, Seychelles, Sierra Leone, Singapore, Solomon Islands, Somalia, South Africa, South Sudan, Sri Lanka, Sudan, Suriname, Swaziland, Syrian Arab Republic, Tajikistan, Thailand, Timor-Leste, Togo, Tonga, Trinidad and Tobago, Tunisia, Turkmenistan, Tuvalu, Uganda, United Arab Emirates, United Republic of Tanzania, Uruguay, Uzbekistan, Vanuatu, Venezuela, Viet Nam, Yemen, Zambia, Zimbabwe.

Against: Albania, Andorra, Australia, Austria, Belgium, Bosnia and Herzegovina, Bulgaria, Canada, Croatia, Cyprus, Czech Republic, Denmark, Estonia, Finland, France, Georgia, Germany, Greece, Hungary, Iceland, Ireland, Israel, Italy, Japan, Latvia, Liechtenstein, Lithuania, Luxembourg, Malta, Marshall Islands, Micronesia, Monaco, Montenegro, Netherlands, New Zealand, Norway, Palau, Poland, Portugal, Republic of Korea, Republic of Moldova, Romania, San Marino, Slovakia, Slovenia, Spain, Sweden, Switzerland, the former Yugoslav Republic of Macedonia, Turkey, Ukraine, United Kingdom, United States.

Abstaining: Armenia, Serbia.

Right to education

Reports of Special Rapporteur. In response to a Human Rights Council request [YUN 2008, p. 842], the newly appointed Special Rapporteur on the right to education, Kishore Singh (India) [YUN 2010, p. 745], in April submitted his first annual report [A/HRC/17/29 & Corr.1] to the Council, which focused on the promotion of equality of opportunity in education. It also provided an overview of concerns the Rapporteur intended to study in the course of his mandate.

Ensuring equality of opportunity in education was an overarching principle that was reflected in core human rights treaties. States had the duty to adopt measures to eradicate discrimination and ensure equal access for all to education. The report detailed core human rights standards provisions which established the obligation to promote equal opportunities in education, and described different sources of inequalities and different types of initiatives to address them. It concluded by formulating recommendations based on human rights standards.

An addendum [A/HRC/17/29/Add.1] summarized seven communications sent to seven Governments between 1 March 2010 and 29 April 2011, and five replies received between 15 April 2010 and 29 April 2011.

As requested by the Human Rights Council [YUN 2008, p. 842], the Secretary-General in August transmitted to the General Assembly the interim report [A/66/269] of the Rapporteur, which focused on the issue of domestic financing of basic education. It detailed human rights obligations for financing education and provided practical examples of national legal frameworks that ensured domestic financing. The report contained an update on the situation of education in emergencies, pursuant to General Assembly resolution 64/290 [YUN 2010, p. 745]. The Special Rapporteur underlined that the attention and funding dedicated to education in emergencies continued to be insufficient, and called for more investment in preventive efforts and for better protection of education during armed conflict.

The General Assembly took note of that report on 19 December (**decision 66/537**).

Mission reports. Following his visit to Senegal (8–14 January) [A/HRC/17/29/Add.2], the Rapporteur made recommendations aimed at modernizing legislation on education, establishing a legal basis for sustained investment in education, ending exclusion from education and inequality in educational opportunities, ensuring a protective school environment for girls, safeguarding public interest in education, placing greater priority on technical and vocational training, modernizing the *daaras* (traditional Koranic schools) and combating exploitation of children in all forms.

Following his mission to Kazakhstan (12–20 September) [A/HRC/20/21/Add.1], the Rapporteur pointed out the commitments made to protect the right to education through ratification of treaties and the fact that Kazakhstan had achieved almost universal enrolment at the primary and secondary levels and high literacy rates as a result of long-standing investments in education. Nevertheless, the Rapporteur noted that challenges remained with regard to quality of education and the promotion of equal opportunities in education. He underlined the need to continue investing in multilingual education, the need to invest in the integration of persons with disabilities into mainstream education, and the need to ensure education for migrants and refugees residing in the country.

Human Rights Council action. On 16 June [A/66/53 (res. 17/3)], the Council urged all States to give full effect to the right to education by promoting equality of opportunity in education in accordance with their human rights obligations; urged all relevant stakeholders to increase their efforts so that the goals of the Education for All [YUN 2000, p. 1081] agenda could be achieved by 2015; and extended the mandate of the Special Rapporteur for three years.

Environmental and scientific concerns

Human rights and the environment

In 2011, the Human Rights Council considered the question of human rights and the environment, including with regard to climate change. It also reaffirmed the MDGs, including Goal 7 on ensuring environmental sustainability.

Human Rights Council action. On 24 March [A/66/53 (res. 16/11)], the Council requested OHCHR, in consultation with States, international organizations and intergovernmental bodies, including the United Nations Environment Programme and multilateral environmental agreements, special procedures, treaty bodies and other stakeholders, to conduct a detailed analytical study on the relationship between human rights and the environment, to be submitted to the Council prior to its nineteenth (2012) session.

Climate change

Human Rights Council action. On 30 September [A/66/53/Add.1 (res. 18/22)], the Council reiterated its concern that climate change posed an immediate and far-reaching threat to people and communities around the world and had adverse implications for the full enjoyment of human rights; requested OHCHR to convene, prior to the Council's nineteenth (2012) session, a seminar on addressing the adverse impacts of climate change on human rights; decided that the seminar would build on the previous work of the Human Rights Council and its mechanisms; and requested OHCHR to submit a summary report to the Council's twentieth (2012) session on the seminar and make the report available to the Conference of the Parties to the United Nations Framework Convention on Climate Change [YUN 1992, p. 681] at its eighteenth (2012) session.

Toxic wastes

Reports of Special Rapporteur. As requested by the Human Rights Council [YUN 2008, p. 843], the newly appointed Special Rapporteur on the adverse effects of the movement and dumping of toxic and dangerous products and wastes on the enjoyment of human rights, Calin Georgescu (Romania) [YUN 2010, p. 748], in July submitted his first annual report [A/HRC/18/31], which focused on the adverse effects that the unsound management and disposal of medical waste had on the enjoyment of human rights. While approximately 75 to 80 per cent of the total waste generated by health-care establishments did not pose any particular risk to human health or the environment, the remaining waste was regarded as hazardous and could create a variety of health risks if not managed and disposed of in an appropriate manner. Hazardous health-care waste included infectious waste, sharps, anatomical and pathological waste, obsolete or expired chemical products and pharmaceuticals, and radioactive materials. Medical waste was often mixed with general household waste, and either disposed of in municipal waste facilities or dumped illegally. The report contained examples of the impact of improper management and disposal of medical waste in many countries. Nevertheless, the international community had paid little attention to the issue. In his recommendations, the Rapporteur called on relevant stakeholders, including States, international organizations and mechanisms, the donor community, public and private health-care facilities, the pharmaceutical industry and civil society to strengthen efforts to achieve safe and sustainable management of medical waste.

Mission report. During his visit to Poland (25–31 May) [A/HRC/18/31/Add.2], the Rapporteur examined progress made to ensure the safe and environmentally sound management and disposal of hazardous products and wastes. While welcoming Poland's progress in that area, he expressed concern that it had not yet taken the necessary measures to ensure that the International Covenant on Economic, Social and Cultural Rights [YUN 1966, p. 419] was given full effect in its domestic legal order and noted that some of the economic and social rights enshrined in the Constitution, including the right to safe and healthy working conditions and the right to a healthy environment, could not be directly invoked before national courts and tribunals. The Rapporteur recommended that the Government take measures to give full effect to the International Covenant and to ratify a number of International Labour Organization conventions on health and safety at work. He called on Poland to finalize, as a matter of priority, the adoption of the new Act on waste.

Human Rights Council action. On 29 September [A/66/53/Add.1 (res. 18/11)], the Council extended for three years the Rapporteur's mandate, with the new title of Special Rapporteur on the implications for human rights of the environmentally sound management and disposal of hazardous substances and wastes; requested the Special Rapporteur to include in his report to the Council information on the adverse effects that the improper management and disposal of hazardous substances and wastes might have on the enjoyment of human rights; and requested him to develop, in consultation with relevant stakeholders and ohchr, a set of best practices with regard to the implications for human rights of the environmentally sound management and disposal of hazardous substances and wastes, to be annexed to his final report.

Forensic genetics

Report of High Commissioner. As requested by the Human Rights Council [YUN 2010, p. 747], the High Commissioner in July submitted a report [A/HRC/18/25 & Corr.1] on the obligation of States to investigate serious violations of human rights, and the use of forensic genetics. It focused on the law pertaining to the obligation to investigate gross violations of human rights law and serious violations of international humanitarian law, through a survey of the applicable international and regional instruments and jurisprudence. Based on responses received from 14 States and three organizations, the report outlined State law and practice regarding initiatives taken in order to investigate human rights and international humanitarian law violations, particularly through the use of forensic genetics and the establishment of genetic databanks.

Genetic privacy

In response to Economic and Social Council decision 2010/259 [YUN 2010, p. 747], the Secretary-General in May [E/2011/108] transmitted to the Council a report of the Director-General of the United Nations Educational, Scientific and Cultural Organization (unesco) on genetic privacy and non-discrimination. Unesco assessed the situation at the national and international levels in that domain based on consultations with States and UN and international organizations, pointing to a diversity of national legislative and institutional measures to safeguard human rights from potential discrimination based on genetic information. The majority of responding countries identified the need to develop specific legislation in the areas of biobanking, management of electronic clinical files, forensic identification, biometrics and the sale of genetic tests over the counter.

On 26 July, by **decision 2011/242**, the Council took note of the report.

Slavery and related issues

Report of Special Rapporteur. As requested by the Human Rights Council [YUN 2007, p. 784], the Special Rapporteur on contemporary forms of slavery, including its causes and consequences, Gulnara Shahinian (Armenia), in July submitted a report [A/HRC/18/30 & Corr.1] covering her activities since her previous report [YUN 2010, p. 748] and focusing on child slavery in the artisanal mining and quarrying sector. The report discussed the international legal framework for combating child slavery; the root causes, manifestations and aggravating factors that led to child slavery in the mining and quarrying sector; the nature and impact of child slavery on the enjoyment of children's rights; and challenges in its prevention. The report concluded with best practices for eradicating and key strategies in tackling child slavery in the sector.

Mission reports. Following her visit to Peru (9–20 May) [A/HRC/18/30/Add.2], the Rapporteur provided information on existing legislation; institutional mechanisms, programmes, plans and activities aimed at combating contemporary forms of slavery; and highlighted positive measures. She drew attention to major challenges and made recommendations on addressing legislative gaps, strengthening law enforcement and institutional capacity, intensifying measures to address the worst forms of child labour, economic exploitation and domestic servitude of children, and providing remedies to victims of contemporary forms of slavery.

Following her mission to Lebanon (10–17 October) [A/HRC/21/41/Add.1], the Rapporteur provided information on existing policies, programmes, plans and activities aimed at combating domestic servitude and highlighted positive measures taken. She made recommendations regarding legislative gaps, strengthening law enforcement and institutional capacity, stepping up measures to protect migrant domestic workers, preventing domestic servitude and providing effective remedies to victims.

Fund on slavery

Report of Secretary-General. The Secretary-General in August [A/67/269] reported on the financial status of the United Nations Voluntary Trust Fund on Contemporary Forms of Slavery. At its sixteenth session (Geneva, 28 November–5 December), the Fund's Board of Trustees recommended 52 new project grants amounting to $497,000 to assist ngo projects in 41 countries. Nine countries and one entity had contributed $457,034 since the Board's fifteenth session [YUN 2010, p. 749]. The Board estimated that the Fund would need at least $1.5 million before its seventeenth session, scheduled for 3–7 December 2012. The High Commissioner approved the Board's recommendations on behalf of the Secretary-General on 30 December 2011.

On 19 December, the General Assembly took note of the Secretary-General's August 2010 report on the Fund's financial status [ibid.] (**decision 66/537**).

Slavery and transatlantic slave trade

Commemorative meeting. On 25 March, the General Assembly decided that the commemorative meeting on the occasion of the International Day of Remembrance of the Victims of Slavery and the Transatlantic Slave Trade, held on that day, would include a statement on behalf of the Caribbean Community (CARICOM), a statement by Ruth Simmons, President of Brown University, and cultural presentations (**decision 65/546**). The meeting was addressed by the Secretary-General, Member States on behalf of regional groups, and the representative of the host country [A/65/PV.81].

Report of Secretary-General. Pursuant to Assembly resolution 65/239 [YUN 2010, p. 750], the Secretary-General in September reported [A/66/382] on the programme of educational outreach on the transatlantic slave trade and slavery. Working in close collaboration with States Members of CARICOM and the African Group, the UN Department of Public Information (DPI) organized the fourth annual observance on 25 March of the International Day of Remembrance of the Victims of Slavery and the Transatlantic Slave Trade. The theme of the 2011 commemoration, "The Living Legacy of 30 Million Untold Stories", recalled the estimated 30 million Africans who were uprooted by the system of slavery and whose many stories under that system had not been told fully. It emphasized the importance of a more constructive portrayal in history and literature of the diverse skills which enslaved Africans brought to the homelands they were forced to adopt, and which were indispensable contributions to the economic foundation of the countries in the Americas and of the eighteenth century world economy. The DPI outreach strategy utilized its network of information centres to disseminate the message of the observance internationally, and promoted partnership activities with civil society organizations committed to building awareness of the dangers of racism and racial discrimination, as well as the continuing legacy of slavery and the slave trade.

On 24 December, by **decision 66/557**, the Assembly decided that the item "Follow-up to the commemoration of the two-hundredth anniversary of the abolition of the transatlantic slave trade" would remain for consideration during its resumed sixty-sixth (2012) session.

Permanent memorial

Report of Secretary-General. As requested by General Assembly resolution 65/239 [YUN 2010, p. 750], the Secretary-General in July [A/66/162] reported on the status of the United Nations Trust Fund for Partnerships—Permanent Memorial to and remembrance of the victims of slavery and the transatlantic slave trade. As at 30 June, $990,654 had been received in contributions to the Trust Fund comprising $944,645 in contributions from Member States, $28,057 in private donations and $17,952 in interest.

GENERAL ASSEMBLY ACTION

On 12 December [meeting 83], the General Assembly adopted **resolution 66/114** [draft: A/66/L.25 & Add.1] without vote [agenda item 119].

Permanent memorial to and remembrance of the victims of slavery and the transatlantic slave trade

The General Assembly,

Recalling its resolution 61/19 of 28 November 2006, entitled "Commemoration of the two-hundredth anniversary of the abolition of the transatlantic slave trade" and subsequent resolutions entitled "Permanent memorial to and remembrance of the victims of slavery and the transatlantic slave trade",

Recalling also the designation of 25 March as the annual International Day of Remembrance of the Victims of Slavery and the Transatlantic Slave Trade,

Recognizing how little is known about the transatlantic slave trade and its lasting consequences, felt throughout the world, and welcoming the increased attention that the annual commemoration by the General Assembly has brought to the issue, including raising awareness in many States,

Noting the initiatives undertaken by States in reaffirming their commitment to implement paragraphs 101 and 102 of the Durban Declaration of the World Conference against Racism, Racial Discrimination, Xenophobia and Related Intolerance, aimed at countering the legacy of slavery and contributing to the restoration of the dignity of the victims of slavery and the slave trade,

Recalling, in particular, paragraph 101 of the Durban Declaration, which, inter alia, invited the international community and its members to honour the memory of the victims,

Stressing the importance of educating and informing current and future generations about the causes, consequences and lessons of slavery and the transatlantic slave trade,

Recalling that the permanent memorial initiative complements the work being done at the United Nations Educational, Scientific and Cultural Organization on the Slave Route Project, including its commemorative activities,

1. *Endorses* the initiative of Member States to erect, at a place of prominence at United Nations Headquarters that is easily accessible to delegates, United Nations staff and visitors, a permanent memorial in acknowledgement of the tragedy and in consideration of the legacy of slavery and the transatlantic slave trade;

2. *Recalls* the establishment of a committee of interested States to oversee the permanent memorial project, drawn from all geographical regions of the world, with Member States from the Caribbean Community and the African Union playing a primary role, in collaboration with the United Nations Educational, Scientific and Cultural Organization, representatives of the Secretariat, the Schomburg Center for Research in Black Culture of the New York Public Library and civil society;

3. *Also recalls* the establishment of a trust fund for the permanent memorial, referred to as the United Nations Trust Fund for Partnerships—Permanent Memorial, administered by the United Nations Office for Partnerships, and notes the current status of contributions to the Trust Fund;

4. *Recognizes* the necessity of sustained voluntary contributions in order to achieve in a timely manner the goal of erecting a permanent memorial in honour of the victims of slavery and the transatlantic slave trade;

5. *Expresses sincere appreciation* to those Member States that have already made contributions to the Trust Fund, encourages additional contributions, and invites Member States and other interested parties that have not done so to do likewise;

6. *Requests* the Secretary-General to organize a series of activities annually to commemorate the International Day of Remembrance of the Victims of Slavery and the Transatlantic Slave Trade, including a commemorative meeting of the General Assembly at United Nations Headquarters and, as appropriate, activities through the network of United Nations information centres;

7. *Requests* the Department of Public Information of the Secretariat, in cooperation with the countries concerned and with relevant organizations and bodies of the United Nations system, to continue to take appropriate steps to enhance world public awareness of the commemorative activities and the permanent memorial initiative, and to facilitate efforts to erect the permanent memorial at United Nations Headquarters;

8. *Reiterates its request*, in resolution 64/15 of 16 November 2009, for Member States to develop, in accordance with their national legislation, educational programmes, including through school curricula, designed to educate and inculcate in future generations an understanding of the lessons, history and consequences of slavery and the slave trade, and to provide such information to the Secretary-General for inclusion in his report;

9. *Welcomes* the conclusion of the tripartite memorandum of understanding between the United Nations Office for Partnerships, the United Nations Educational, Scientific and Cultural Organization and the Permanent Memorial Committee to serve as the framework for cooperation in implementing the initiative to honour the victims of slavery and the transatlantic slave trade;

10. *Also welcomes* the recent launch of the international design competition for the permanent memorial, and encourages the broadest possible participation and submission of designs from all geographical regions of the world;

11. *Encourages* the United Nations Educational, Scientific and Cultural Organization to assist the Permanent Memorial Committee in identifying qualified candidates, including from its pool of international specialists, to serve on the independent international panel of judges to select the winning design;

12. *Takes note* of the report of the Secretary-General on the programme of educational outreach on the transatlantic slave trade and slavery relating to the diverse educational outreach strategy to increase awareness of and to educate future generations about the causes, consequences, lessons and legacy of the transatlantic slave trade and to communicate the dangers of racism and prejudice, and encourages continued action in this regard;

13. *Requests* the Secretary-General to report to the General Assembly at its sixty-sixth session on continued action to implement the programme of educational outreach, including actions taken by Member States in implementing the present resolution, as well as steps to enhance world public awareness of the commemorative activities and the permanent memorial initiative;

14. *Requests* the United Nations Office for Partnerships, through the Secretary-General, to submit a comprehensive report to the General Assembly at its sixty-seventh session on the status of the Trust Fund and, in particular, on contributions received and their utilization;

15. *Decides* to include in the provisional agenda of its sixty-seventh session the item entitled "Follow-up to the commemoration of the two-hundredth anniversary of the abolition of the transatlantic slave trade".

Vulnerable groups

Women

Violence against women

Reports of Special Rapporteur. Pursuant to a Human Rights Council request [YUN 2008, p. 848], the Special Rapporteur on violence against women, its causes and consequences, Rashida Manjoo (South Africa), in May submitted her first thematic report [A/HRC/17/26] highlighting her activities in 2010 and early 2011 and addressing the topic of multiple and intersecting forms of discrimination in the context of violence. The report acknowledged that while such discrimination had contributed to and exacerbated violence against women, information on the intersections between gender-based discrimination and other forms of discrimination were too often overlooked. In addition to analysing the forms, causes and consequences of multiple forms of discrimination, the report considered inter-gender and intra-gender differences, arguing that a one-size-fits-all programmatic approach was insufficient for combating gender-based violence. Even though all women were at risk of experiencing violence, not all women were equally susceptible to acts of violence. The report proposed a holistic approach to conceptualizing and addressing the issue by considering human rights as universal, interdependent and indivisible; situating violence against women on a continuum; acknowledging the structural aspects and factors of discrimination; and analysing social and/or economic hierarchies between women and men and also among women.

An addendum [A/HRC/17/26/Add.1] summarized 17 communications—eight allegation letters and nine urgent appeals—sent to 13 Member States from 21 March 2010 to 15 March 2011; many of them were sent jointly with other Human Rights Council mandate holders. The Rapporteur remained concerned that only three Governments had replied.

In response to General Assembly resolution 65/187 [YUN 2010, p. 1145], the Secretary-General in August transmitted the report [A/66/215] of the Special Rapporteur, which provided an overview of the mandate's work and main findings and the challenges it continued to encounter, and presented recommendations to address violence against women through a holistic framework based on States' obligations to respect, protect and fulfil the human rights of women and girls.

On 19 December, the General Assembly took note of the report (**decision 66/532**).

Mission reports. Following her visit to the United States (24 January–7 February) [A/HRC/17/26/Add.5 & Corr.1], the Rapporteur highlighted the positive legislative and policy initiatives undertaken by the Government to reduce the prevalence of violence against women, including the Violence against Women Act and the establishment of dedicated offices on violence against women at the highest level. Nevertheless, the lack of legally binding federal provisions providing substantive protective legislation and the inadequate implementation of existing laws, policies and programmes had resulted in continued prevalence of violence against women and the discriminatory treatment of victims, with a particularly detrimental impact on poor, minority and immigrant women. Multiple forms of discrimination against certain groups of women made them more vulnerable. The Rapporteur made recommendations to the Government on a legal framework; remedies for victims of domestic violence, sexual assault and stalking; military violence; violence against women in detention; and violence against native American women.

During her mission to Jordan (11–24 November) [A/HRC/20/16/Add.1], the Rapporteur examined the equality and non-discrimination rights of women, intimate partner violence, gender-motivated killings of women, and violence against migrant and refugee women. She pointed out that the Government had acknowledged the need to ensure equality and non-discrimination for women, and had taken steps to achieve their integration into education, employment and politics. Given the traditional roles that the majority of women had conventionally undertaken, however, a purely legal or programmatic approach would not be sufficient to achieve substantive and not just formal equality. Holistic solutions were required that addressed both the individual empowerment of women and the social, economic and cultural barriers that were a reality in their lives. Empowerment must be coupled with social transformation to address the systemic and structural causes of inequality and discrimination, which often led to violence against women. The Rapporteur made recommendations to the Government regarding law and policy reforms, societal change and awareness-raising, and statistics and data collection.

Following her mission to Somalia (9–16 December) [A/HRC/20/16/Add.3], the Special Rapporteur reported on the situation of violence against women in the country and discussed the responses of the State, UN agencies and donors to prevent such violence, to protect and provide remedies for women who had been subjected to violence, and to prosecute and punish the perpetrators. She concluded with recommendations addressed to Transitional Federal Government and local Governments, UN and international agencies and to civil society, the media and Somalis abroad.

OHCHR report. As requested by the Human Rights Council [YUN 2010, p. 752], OHCHR in April submitted a report [A/HRC/17/23] summarizing information submitted by stakeholders on efforts aimed at preventing violence against women, as well as related challenges. Written contributions were received from 42 States, one observer, seven UN bodies, two national human rights institutions and 36 civil society organizations and other institutions, groups or individuals. The report cited examples of good practices organized around three categories: legal measures, policy measures and operational measures.

Expert workshop. On 9 March, OHCHR issued a report [A/HRC/17/22] on the expert workshop held on the theme "The elimination of all forms of violence against women—challenges, good practices and opportunities" (Geneva, 24–25 November 2010) pursuant to Human Rights Council resolution 11/2 [YUN 2009, p. 734]. The workshop, with approximately 100 participants, considered the challenges, good practices and opportunities in relation to five cross-cutting aspects of the elimination of violence against women: investigating cases of violence against women; the prosecution of violence against women and punishment of perpetrators; reparation for women subject to violence; prevention of violence against women; and protection of women subject to violence.

Meeting of Expert Group. In response to Human Rights Council resolution 7/24 [YUN 2008, p. 882] and General Assembly resolution 65/281 (see p. 607), the Special Rapporteur convened an expert group meeting on gender-motivated killings of women (New York, 12 October) [A/HRC/20/16/Add.4] to inform her thematic report on the topic to the Council in 2012. The meeting brought together 25 experts from academia, civil society organizations and UN entities with technical and practical expertise on and experience in working on violence against women.

Human Rights Council action. On 24 March [A/66/53 (res. 16/7)], the Council extended the Rapporteur's mandate for three years and requested her to recommend measures for eliminating violence against women, report to the Council annually, and present an oral report to the Commission on the Status of Women annually.

On 17 June [ibid. (res. 17/11)], the Council urged States to take steps towards protecting women facing violence. It decided to include in the annual full-day discussion on women's human rights, at its twentieth (2012) session, the theme of remedies, with a focus on transformative and culturally sensitive reparations for women who had been subjected to violence, and requested OHCHR to prepare and disseminate a summary report of the proceedings. The Council also invited OHCHR to prepare a thematic analytical study on the issue of violence against women and girls and disability, and to report to the Council at its twentieth session.

Trafficking in women and girls

Reports of Special Rapporteur. In response to a Human Rights Council request [YUN 2008, p. 848], the Special Rapporteur on trafficking in persons, especially women and children, Joy Ngozi Ezeilo (Nigeria), submitted an April report [A/HRC/17/35] covering the period from 1 March 2010 until 1 March 2011. The Rapporteur reviewed her activities during the previous year and, in a thematic analysis of the right to an effective remedy for trafficked persons, outlined the international legal framework of that right and what it entailed in the context of trafficked persons. She analysed key components of the right, including restitution, recovery, compensation, satisfaction and guarantees of non-repetition, access to information, legal assistance, and regularization of residence status. She also identified special factors to be considered in realizing the right to an effective remedy for trafficked children. In addition to her conclusions and recommendations, the Special Rapporteur submitted the draft basic principles on the right to an effective remedy for trafficked persons.

An addendum [A/HRC/17/35/Add.1] summarized 10 communications sent to 10 countries from 1 April 2010 to 15 March 2011, and three Government replies received from 11 May 2010 to 1 May 2011.

As requested by the Council [YUN 2008, p. 848], the Secretary-General in August [A/66/283] transmitted to the General Assembly the interim report of the Rapporteur, covering the period from 1 August 2010 to 31 July 2011. The Rapporteur outlined her activities and focused on the right to an effective remedy for trafficked persons. She discussed different forms of substantive remedies, including restitution, recovery, compensation, satisfaction and guarantee of non-repetition, and highlighted the importance of procedural rights of access to those remedies, such as the provision of information, legal assistance, interpretation services and regularization of residence status. The Rapporteur concluded with recommendations to States in implementing the right to an effective remedy. The draft basic principles on the right to an effective remedy were annexed to the report.

The General Assembly took note of that report on 19 December (**decision 66/537**).

Expert meeting. The Rapporteur convened an expert meeting on the prosecution of trafficking in persons cases (Geneva, 4 July) [A/HRC/20/18/Add.3], which was organized to solicit the views of leading criminal justice practitioners from various States engaged in investigating, prosecuting and adjudicating trafficking cases, as well as those of representatives from international and regional organizations, in order to inform the Rapporteur's annual thematic report to the Human Rights Council's twentieth (2012) session. The participants discussed international legal standards and elements applicable to criminal justice responses to trafficking; observable progress and remaining challenges for States in adopting a rights-based approach to prosecuting trafficking cases; and good practices and lessons learned. It was agreed that there was a need for States to adopt comprehensive domestic legislation to criminalize trafficking and to protect victims using guidance from normative international legal frameworks.

Mission reports. Following her mission to Thailand (8–19 August) [A/HRC/20/18/Add.2], the Rapporteur highlighted the country's commitment and progress in combating trafficking in persons, as evidenced by its anti-trafficking legislation and the high level of regional and subregional cooperation in combating trafficking in persons. She nonetheless expressed concern regarding the lack of capacity and willingness of law enforcement authorities to properly identify trafficked persons; the arrest, detention and summary deportation of trafficked persons; the lack of adequate support for the recovery of trafficked persons in shelters; the low rate of prosecution and delays in prosecuting trafficking cases; and the insufficient efforts made to tackle the root causes, such as restrictive immigration policies and the abuse of migrants' human rights. The Rapporteur made recommendations to the Government, including increasing capacity-building activities for governmental officials; staffing shelters with psychologists, social workers, health professionals and interpreters; strengthening labour protection for all workers, including migrant workers; and creating more opportunities for safe labour migration.

Following her visit to Australia (17–30 November) [A/HRC/20/18/Add.1], the Rapporteur pointed out the country's strong commitment to combating trafficking in persons, including the high level of government engagement and partnership with civil society organizations. She observed, however, that trafficking statistics did not appear to account for the true nature and scale of the problem. She expressed concern regarding gaps in some services offered by the support programme for trafficked persons. She welcomed a draft bill that moved towards remedying many of the legislative shortcomings under the current legislative framework, and welcomed its imminent passage into law. She made recommendations to the Government with regard to developing a new framework for collecting data on trafficked persons, increasing capacity-building activities for government officials, addressing gaps in the support programme, and ensuring regional engagement to strengthen national responses and address the root causes of trafficking in sending countries, including the creation of more opportunities for safe labour migration.

Human Rights Council action. On 16 June [A/66/53 (res. 17/1)], the Council extended the mandate of the Rapporteur for three years and requested her to report annually to the Council and the General Assembly. The Council encouraged Governments to refer to the Recommended Principles and Guidelines on Human Rights and Human Trafficking developed by OHCHR in integrating a human rights-based approach into their responses to combat trafficking in persons.

Communication. In a 26 May letter [A/HRC/17/G/6], Belarus transmitted to the Council President a joint letter of a group of countries that had established in Geneva the Group of Friends United against Human Trafficking [YUN 2010, p. 1111].

Children

Violence against children

Reports of Special Representative. Pursuant to General Assembly resolution 65/197 [YUN 2010, p. 647], the Special Representative of the Secretary-General on violence against children, Marta Santos Pais (Portugal), in February submitted her second annual report [A/HRC/16/54] to the Human Rights Council. It reviewed progress in the priority areas of her mandate and highlighted initiatives she promoted to institutionalize regional governance structures and strengthen strategic alliances with key partners. In spite of a growing commitment across regions to address violence against children, that phenomenon continued to affect the lives of millions of children. The Special Representative identified areas of concern to be given special attention in 2011: promoting universal ratification of the Optional Protocols to the Convention on the Rights of the Child; conducting a global survey to assess progress in violence prevention and responses; and addressing violence in the context of education and the administration of justice.

In response to General Assembly resolution 65/197, the Secretary-General in August submitted to the Assembly the annual report [A/66/227] of the Special Representative, complementing her report to the Council. It reviewed developments and initiatives to advance progress in the follow-up to the UN study on violence against children [YUN 2006, p. 216] at the global, regional and national levels; institutionalize regional governance structures; and strengthen alliances to speed up global progress towards a world free from violence. The report identified areas to which the Special Representative would devote special attention.

Joint report. In response to Human Rights Council resolution 13/20 [YUN 2010, p. 754], the Special Representative and the Special Rapporteur on the sale of children, child prostitution and child pornography (see below) in March issued a joint report [A/HRC/16/56] on the fight against sexual violence against children. The report provided an overview of accessible and child-sensitive counselling, complaint and reporting mechanisms to address incidents of violence, including sexual violence and exploitation, and drew attention to positive developments and persisting challenges. It highlighted legal obligations, roles and responsibilities of State institutions and other key stakeholders, and made recommendations for strengthening those mechanisms to safeguard the right of children to freedom from all forms of violence.

Sale of children, child prostitution and child pornography

Reports of Special Rapporteur. Pursuant to a Human Rights Council request [YUN 2010, p. 754], the Special Rapporteur on the sale of children, child prostitution and child pornography, Najat Maalla M'jid (Morocco), submitted a report [A/HRC/16/57] covering the activities carried out since her previous report to the Council in 2009 [YUN 2009, p. 735], in particular country visits, conferences, seminars and consultations. The report complemented the joint report issued in March by the Special Rapporteur and the Secretary-General's Special Representative on Violence against Children (see above).

An addendum [A/HRC/16/57/Add.1 & Corr.1] summarized communications sent to nine countries between 16 June 2009 and 23 November 2010, and replies received from 16 June 2009 to 23 January 2011.

In accordance with General Assembly resolution 65/197 [YUN 2010, p. 647], the Secretary-General in August transmitted to the Assembly the report [A/66/228] of the Rapporteur on building rights-based and comprehensive national child protection systems to prevent and combat the sale of children, child prostitution and child pornography. The report was intended to be a tool for implementing the recommendations formulated since the beginning of the mandate by providing guiding principles and essential components of a rights-based child protection system aimed at preventing the sale of children, child prostitution and child pornography.

The General Assembly took note of the report on 19 December (**decision 66/534**).

Mission reports. Following her visit to Mauritius (1–11 May) [A/HRC/19/63/Add.1], the Rapporteur highlighted the scope and root causes of the sale of children, child prostitution and child pornography, as well as legislative, political and programmatic measures undertaken to prevent those practices and to protect children. She also examined international and regional cooperation, and partnerships with the private sector. The Rapporteur concluded with recommendations for strengthening efforts to build a rights-based and comprehensive national child protection strategy.

Following her mission to France (21 November–2 December) [A/HRC/19/63/Add.2], the Rapporteur highlighted the Government's efforts to protect children from sale, prostitution and child pornography, which had had encouraging results. She noted legal measures in tune with the main international and regional instruments, arrangements for prevention and protection, and many programmes of assistance, support and care for children in difficulty. Nonetheless, challenges remained, including the excessive legislation and the trend towards a punitive approach. In particular, children—often the most vulnerable children from dysfunctional and/or insecure families—slipped through the safety net, and unaccompanied foreign minors appeared to be the most disadvantaged and the most vulnerable to exploitation. Care of children remained fragmented and uneven, and suffered from a lack of intersectoral cooperation. The Rapporteur concluded with recommendations designed to consolidate and enhance the Government's efforts.

Economic and Social Council action. On 28 July, the Economic and Social Council adopted **resolution 2011/33** on prevention, protection and international cooperation against the use of new information technologies to abuse and/or exploit children (see p. 1209). It urged States to adopt measures designed to criminalize the misuse of technology to commit child sexual exploitation crimes, consider measures to detect and remove known child sexual abuse images from the Internet, and facilitate the identification of those responsible for the abuse and/or exploitation of children.

Rights of children working and/or living on the street

Human Rights Council action. On 24 March [A/66/53 (res. 16/12)], the Council called on States to give priority attention to the prevention of the phenomenon of children working and/or living on the street by addressing its diverse causes through economic, social, educational and empowerment strategies; requested the High Commissioner to prepare a summary of the full-day meeting on the rights of the child (see below), as a follow-up to Council resolution 7/29 [YUN 2008, p. 738], before the seventeenth (2011) session of the Council; decided to focus its next full-day meeting on children and the administration of justice; and extended the Special Rapporteur's mandate for three years.

Report of High Commissioner. Pursuant to Council resolutions 7/29 [ibid.] and 16/12 (see above), the High Commissioner submitted a summary of the full-day meeting on the protection and promotion of the rights of children working and/or living on the street (Geneva, 9 March) [A/HRC/17/46], which comprised two panels: one focused on the root causes and factors, and the other on prevention strategies and responses. The meeting aimed to raise awareness about the situation, reaffirm existing standards and commitments undertaken by Member States to protect children, highlight good practices and lessons learned, identify key challenges and recommend a way forward.

Children and armed conflict

Report of Secretary-General. As requested in Security Council presidential statement S/PRST/2010/10 [YUN 2010, p. 756], the Secretary-General in April submitted a report [A/65/820-S/2011/250] on children and armed conflict, covering developments in 2010. Pursuant to Security Council resolution 1882(2009) [YUN 2009, p. 739], the two annexes listing parties that recruited or used children included those parties to armed conflict that engaged in patterns of killing and maiming of children and/or rape and other sexual violence against children, in contravention of international law. The report outlined grave violations committed against children in armed conflict; reviewed progress made by parties to conflict on dialogue and on action plans to end violations and abuse against children; provided updates on the release of children associated with armed forces and armed groups; described progress made by the UN system in implementing Security Council requests; and examined grave violations related to attacks on schools and hospitals. It affirmed that grave violations had occurred in Afghanistan, Burundi, the Central African Republic, Chad, Colombia, Côte d'Ivoire, the Democratic Republic of the Congo, Haiti, India, Iraq, Lebanon, Myanmar, Nepal, the Occupied Palestinian Territory and Israel, Pakistan, the Philippines, Somalia, the Sudan, Sri Lanka, Thailand, Uganda and Yemen. The Secretary-General recommended that the Security Council ensure that schools and hospitals remained protected and continued to function. Special attention should be paid to the protection of girls' access to schools and hospitals, given the increased targeting of such facilities in some countries. He further recommended that the Council consider expanding the annexes to his report to include parties that attacked schools and/or hospitals. The Security Council was encouraged to continue considering targeted measures against perpetrators of grave violations against children who were listed in his reports.

Security Council consideration. On 12 July [S/PV.6581], the Council considered the Secretary-General's report (see p. 741) and a concept paper [S/2011/409] submitted by Germany. Following the adoption of resolution 1998(2011) (see below), the Secretary-General noted the signing of 15 action plans covering nine conflict areas since 2004. Those successes showed the value of naming and shaming. During the previous year, some 10,000 children associated with armed groups were released. The Secretary-General's Special Representative for Children and Armed Conflict, Radhika Coomaraswamy (Sri Lanka), noting that persistent violators of children were on the Secretary-General's list with little action taken against them, said that great challenges remained. The Council must deal with the issue in a comprehensive manner and find ways of dealing with perpetrators as well as devising means of prevention.

SECURITY COUNCIL ACTION

On 12 July [meeting 6581], the Security Council unanimously adopted **resolution 1998(2011)**. The draft [S/2011/425] was submitted by 54 States.

The Security Council,

Reaffirming its resolutions 1261(1999) of 25 August 1999, 1314(2000) of 11 August 2000, 1379(2001) of 20 November 2001, 1460(2003) of 30 January 2003, 1539(2004) of 22 April 2004, 1612(2005) of 26 July 2005 and 1882(2009) of 4 August 2009, and all relevant statements by its President, which contribute to a comprehensive framework for addressing the protection of children affected by armed conflict,

Reiterating its primary responsibility for the maintenance of international peace and security and, in this connection, its commitment to address the widespread impact of armed conflict on children,

Calling upon all parties to armed conflicts to comply strictly with the obligations applicable to them under international law for the protection of children in armed conflict, including those contained in the Convention on the Rights of the Child and the Optional Protocol thereto on the involvement of children in armed conflict, as well as the Geneva Conventions of 12 August 1949 and the Additional Protocols thereto, of 1977,

Acknowledging that the implementation of resolutions 1612(2005) and 1882(2009) has generated progress, resulting in the release and reintegration of children into their families and communities and in a more systematic dialogue with the United Nations country-level task forces on monitoring and reporting and parties to armed conflict on the implementation of time-bound action plans, while remaining deeply concerned over the lack of progress on the ground in some situations of concern where parties to conflict continue to violate with impunity the relevant provisions of applicable international law relating to the rights and protection of children in armed conflict,

Stressing the primary role of Governments in providing protection and relief to all children affected by armed conflict, and reiterating that all actions undertaken by United Nations entities within the framework of the monitoring and reporting mechanism must be designed to support and supplement, as appropriate, the protection and rehabilitation roles of national Governments,

Convinced that the protection of children in armed conflict should be an important aspect of any comprehensive strategy to resolve conflict,

Recalling the responsibilities of States to end impunity and to prosecute those responsible for genocide, crimes against humanity, war crimes and other egregious crimes perpetrated against children,

Stressing the need for alleged perpetrators of crimes against children in situations of armed conflict to be brought to justice through national justice systems and, where applicable, international justice mechanisms and mixed criminal courts and tribunals in order to end impunity,

Noting relevant provisions of the Rome Statute of the International Criminal Court,

Having considered the report of the Secretary-General of 23 April 2011, and stressing that the present resolution does not seek to make any legal determination as to whether situations which are referred to in the report of the Secretary-General are or are not armed conflicts in the context of the Geneva Conventions and the Additional Protocols thereto, nor does it prejudge the legal status of the non-State parties involved in those situations,

Expressing deep concern about attacks as well as threats of attacks in contravention of applicable international law against schools and/or hospitals and protected persons in relation to them as well as the closure of schools and hospitals in situations of armed conflict as a result of attacks and threats of attacks, and calling upon all parties to armed conflict to immediately cease such attacks and threats,

Recalling the provisions of the resolution of the General Assembly on the right to education in emergency situations related to children in armed conflict,

Noting that article 28 of the Convention on the Rights of the Child recognizes the right of the child to education and sets forth obligations for States parties to the Convention, with a view to progressively achieving this right on the basis of equal opportunity,

1. *Strongly condemns* all violations of applicable international law involving the recruitment and use of children by parties to armed conflict, as well as their re-recruitment, killing and maiming, rape and other sexual violence, abductions, attacks against schools or hospitals and the denial of humanitarian access by parties to armed conflict and all other violations of international law committed against children in situations of armed conflict;

2. *Reaffirms* that the monitoring and reporting mechanism will continue to be implemented in situations listed in annex I and annex II ("the annexes") to the reports of the Secretary-General on children and armed conflict, in line with the principles set out in paragraph 2 of resolution 1612(2005), and that its establishment and implementation shall not prejudice or imply a decision by the Security Council as to whether or not to include a situation on its agenda;

3. *Recalls* paragraph 16 of resolution 1379(2001), and requests the Secretary-General to also include in the annexes to his reports on children and armed conflict those parties to armed conflict that engage, in contravention of applicable international law:

(*a*) In recurrent attacks on schools and/or hospitals;

(b) In recurrent attacks or threats of attacks against protected persons in relation to schools and/or hospitals in situations of armed conflict, bearing in mind all other violations and abuses committed against children, and notes that the present paragraph will apply to situations in accordance with the conditions set out in paragraph 16 of resolution 1379(2001);

4. *Urges* parties to armed conflict to refrain from actions that impede children's access to education and to health services, and requests the Secretary-General to continue to monitor and report, inter alia, on the military use of schools and hospitals in contravention of international humanitarian law, as well as on attacks against and/or kidnapping of teachers and medical personnel;

5. *Invites* the Secretary-General, through the Special Representative of the Secretary-General for Children and Armed Conflict, to exchange appropriate information and maintain interaction from the earliest opportunity with the Governments concerned regarding violations and abuses committed against children by parties which may be included in the annexes to his periodic reports;

6. While noting that some parties to armed conflict have responded to its call upon them to prepare and implement concrete time-bound action plans to halt the recruitment and use of children in violation of applicable international law:

(a) *Reiterates its call upon* those parties to armed conflict listed in the annexes to the report of the Secretary-General on children and armed conflict that have not already done so to prepare and implement, without further delay, action plans to halt the recruitment and use of children and the killing and maiming of children, in violation of applicable international law, as well as rape and other sexual violence against children;

(b) *Calls upon* those parties that have existing action plans and have since been listed for multiple violations to prepare and implement separate action plans, as appropriate, to halt the killing and maiming of children, recurrent attacks on schools and/or hospitals, and recurrent attacks or threats of attacks against protected persons in relation to schools and/or hospitals, in violation of applicable international law, as well as rape and other sexual violence against children;

(c) *Calls upon* those parties listed in the annexes to the report of the Secretary-General on children and armed conflict that commit, in contravention of applicable international law, recurrent attacks on schools and/or hospitals, and recurrent attacks or threats of attacks against protected persons in relation to schools and/or hospitals, in situations of armed conflict, to prepare without delay concrete time-bound action plans to halt those violations and abuses;

(d) *Further calls upon* all parties listed in the annexes to the report of the Secretary-General on children and armed conflict to address all other violations and abuses committed against children and undertake specific commitments and measures in this regard;

(e) *Urges* those parties listed in the annexes to the report of the Secretary-General on children and armed conflict to implement the provisions contained in the present paragraph, in close cooperation with the Special Representative of the Secretary-General for Children and Armed Conflict and the United Nations country-level task forces on monitoring and reporting;

7. In this context, *encourages* Member States to devise ways, in close consultation with the United Nations country-level task forces on monitoring and reporting and United Nations country teams, to facilitate the development and implementation of time-bound action plans and the review and monitoring by the United Nations country-level task forces of obligations and commitments relating to the protection of children in armed conflict;

8. *Invites* the United Nations country-level task forces on monitoring and reporting to consider including in their reports the relevant information provided by the Governments concerned and to ensure that information collected and communicated by the mechanism is accurate, objective, reliable and verifiable;

9. *Reiterates its determination* to ensure respect for its resolutions on children and armed conflict, and in this regard:

(a) Welcomes the sustained activity and recommendations of the Security Council Working Group on Children and Armed Conflict, as called for in paragraph 8 of resolution 1612(2005), and invites the Working Group to continue reporting regularly to the Council;

(b) Expresses deep concern that certain parties persist in committing violations and abuses against children, and expresses its readiness to adopt targeted and graduated measures against persistent perpetrators, taking into account the relevant provisions of resolutions 1539(2004), 1612(2005) and 1882(2009);

(c) Requests enhanced communication between the Working Group on Children and Armed Conflict and relevant Security Council sanctions committees, including through the exchange of pertinent information on violations and abuses committed against children in armed conflict;

(d) Encourages its relevant sanctions committees to continue to invite the Special Representative of the Secretary-General for Children and Armed Conflict to brief them on specific information pertaining to her mandate that would be relevant to the work of the committees, encourages the sanctions committees to bear in mind the relevant recommendations of the reports of the Secretary-General on children and armed conflict, and encourages the Special Representative to share specific information contained in the reports of the Secretary-General with relevant sanctions committee expert groups;

(e) Expresses its intention, when establishing, modifying or renewing the mandate of relevant sanctions regimes, to consider including provisions pertaining to parties to armed conflict that engage in activities in violation of applicable international law relating to the rights and protection of children in armed conflict;

10. *Encourages* Member States that wish to do so to continue to communicate relevant information to the Council on the implementation of its resolutions on children and armed conflict;

11. *Calls upon* Member States concerned to take decisive and immediate action against persistent perpetrators of violations and abuses against children in situations of armed conflict, and further calls upon them to bring to justice those responsible for such violations that are prohibited under applicable international law, including with regard to the recruitment and use of children, killing and maiming, rape and other sexual violence, attacks on schools and/or

hospitals, and attacks or threats of attacks against protected persons in relation to schools and/or hospitals through national justice systems, and where applicable, international justice mechanisms and mixed criminal courts and tribunals, with a view to ending impunity for those committing crimes against children;

12. *Stresses* the responsibility of the United Nations country-level task forces on monitoring and reporting and United Nations country teams, consistent with their respective mandates, to ensure effective follow-up to Council resolutions on children and armed conflict, to monitor and report progress to the Secretary-General in close cooperation with his Special Representative for Children and Armed Conflict and to ensure a coordinated response to issues related to children and armed conflict;

13. *Reiterates its request* to the Secretary-General to ensure that, in all his reports on country-specific situations, the matter of children and armed conflict is included as a specific aspect of the report, and expresses its intention to give its full attention to the information provided therein, including the implementation of relevant Council resolutions and of the recommendations of the Working Group on Children and Armed Conflict, when dealing with those situations on its agenda;

14. *Reaffirms* its decision to continue to include specific provisions for the protection of children in the mandates of all relevant United Nations peacekeeping, peacebuilding and political missions, encourages the deployment of child protection advisers to such missions, and calls upon the Secretary-General to ensure that such advisers are recruited and deployed in line with the relevant country-specific resolutions of the Council and the Policy Directive on Mainstreaming the Protection, Rights and Well-being of Children Affected by Armed Conflict of the Department of Peacekeeping Operations of the Secretariat;

15. *Requests* Member States, United Nations peacekeeping, peacebuilding and political missions and United Nations country teams, within their respective mandates and in close cooperation with the Governments of the countries concerned, to establish appropriate strategies and coordination mechanisms for information exchange and cooperation on child protection concerns, in particular on cross-border issues, bearing in mind relevant conclusions of the Working Group on Children and Armed Conflict and paragraph 2 (*d*) of resolution 1612(2005);

16. *Welcomes* the progress achieved by the United Nations country-level task forces on monitoring and reporting, and stresses that a strengthened monitoring and reporting mechanism with adequate capacities is necessary to ensure an adequate follow-up to the recommendations of the Secretary-General and the conclusions of the Working Group on Children and Armed Conflict, in accordance with resolutions 1612(2005) and 1882(2009);

17. *Requests* the Secretary-General to continue to take the necessary measures, including, where applicable, to bring the monitoring and reporting mechanism to its full capacity, to allow for prompt advocacy and effective response to all violations and abuses committed against children and to ensure that information collected and communicated by the mechanism is accurate, objective, reliable and verifiable;

18. *Stresses* that effective disarmament, demobilization and reintegration programmes for children, building on best practices identified by the United Nations Children's Fund and other relevant child protection actors, including the International Labour Organization, are crucial for the well-being of all children who, in contravention of applicable international law, have been recruited or used by armed forces and groups, and are a critical factor for durable peace and security, and urges national Governments and donors to ensure that these community-based programmes receive timely, sustained and adequate resources and funding;

19. *Calls upon* Member States, United Nations entities, including the Peacebuilding Commission, and other parties concerned to ensure that the protection, rights, well-being and empowerment of children affected by armed conflict are integrated into all peace processes and that post-conflict recovery and reconstruction planning, programmes and strategies prioritize issues concerning children affected by armed conflict;

20. *Invites* the Special Representative of the Secretary-General for Children and Armed Conflict to brief the Council on the modalities of the inclusion of parties in the annexes to the periodic reports of the Secretary-General on children and armed conflict, enabling an exchange of views;

21. *Directs* the Working Group on Children and Armed Conflict, with the support of the Special Representative of the Secretary-General for Children and Armed Conflict, to consider, within one year, a broad range of options for increasing pressure on persistent perpetrators of violations and abuses against children in situations of armed conflict;

22. *Requests* the Secretary-General to submit a report by June 2012 on the implementation of its resolutions and the statements by its President on children and armed conflict, including the present resolution, which would include, inter alia:

(*a*) Annexed lists of parties in situations of armed conflict on the agenda of the Council or in other situations, in accordance with paragraph 19 (*a*) of resolution 1882(2009) and paragraph 3 of the present resolution;

(*b*) Information on measures taken by parties listed in the annexes to end all violations and abuses committed against children in situations of armed conflict;

(*c*) Information on progress made in the implementation of the monitoring and reporting mechanism established in resolution 1612(2005);

(*d*) Information on the criteria and procedures used for listing and de-listing parties to armed conflict in the annexes to his periodic reports, in accordance with paragraph 3 of the present resolution, bearing in mind the views expressed by all the members of the Working Group on Children and Armed Conflict during informal briefings to be held before the end of 2011;

23. *Decides* to remain actively seized of the matter.

Reports of Special Representative. Pursuant to General Assembly resolution 65/197 [YUN 2010, p. 647], the Secretary-General's Special Representative for Children and Armed Conflict in July submitted a report [A/HRC/18/38] to the Human Rights Council covering her activities from May 2010 to May 2011. The report described progress made in ratifying protocols on children in armed conflict and signing action plans to release children from armed groups. It addressed grave violations against children in armed conflict, highlighted the growing trend of attacks on schools and hospitals, discussed the issue of children and justice during and in the aftermath of armed conflict, and called for universal ratification of the Optional Protocol on the involvement of children in armed conflict. During the period under review, the Representative carried out field missions to Somalia (November 2010), Afghanistan (January–February 2011) and the Philippines (April 2011). The Representative made recommendations for States parties to the Convention on the Rights of the Child to strengthen measures for preventing the recruitment of children into the armed forces or armed groups and their use in hostilities; for the international community to continue to advocate for 18 years as the minimum age for recruitment into armed forces; and for States to ensure the participation of children in justice processes whenever grave child rights violations were committed during armed conflict. She urged States, the Security Council, the United Nations and civil society to launch a global campaign or partnership to ensure the protection of schools and hospitals during armed conflict. She also recommended the design and implementation of a strategy to halt and prevent further attacks on schools and hospitals.

As requested by the General Assembly in resolution 51/77 [YUN 1996, p. 665], the Representative submitted a report [A/66/256] covering the period from August 2010 to August 2011 that detailed progress made over the previous year, including on awareness-raising, partnership-building, information-collection and the release of children from armed forces and groups; highlighted remaining challenges in the context of the changing nature of conflict; and outlined other issues of concern. It described the way forward in terms of ending violations committed against children and described action taken to mainstream the children and armed conflict agenda within the UN system. The report presented recommendations on the protection of children affected by conflict for the Assembly's attention. The annex to the report set out suggested standard operating procedures outlining minimum measures that might be put in place by national armed forces, as well as multinational and peacekeeping forces, to ensure the protection of children in the course of military operations.

Working Group activities. In October [S/2011/610], the Chair of the Security Council Working Group on Children and Armed Conflict reported on the Group's activities since its last report [YUN 2010, p. 757]. The Group held four meetings in 2011 (25 February, 2 May, 22 June, 30 September), during which it adopted conclusions on children and armed conflict in Afghanistan [S/AC.51/2011/3], the Central African Republic [S/AC.51/2011/5], Chad [S/AC.51/2011/4], the Democratic Republic of the Congo [S/AC.51/2011/1], Iraq [S/AC.51/2011/6] and Somalia [S/AC.51/2011/2]. The Group undertook a mission to Afghanistan (4–7 June).

On the basis of the Working Group's conclusions, the Security Council President forwarded letters from the Chairman of the Working Group to the Secretary-General on Afghanistan (2 June) [S/2011/339], the Central African Republic (2 August) [S/2011/485], Chad (8 June) [S/2011/347], the Democratic Republic of the Congo (25 March 2011) [S/2011/194], Iraq (8 November) [S/2011/697] and Somalia (7 April) [S/2011/230].

Internally displaced persons

Reports of Special Rapporteur. Pursuant to Human Rights Council resolution 14/6 [YUN 2010, p. 759], the newly appointed Special Rapporteur on the human rights of internally displaced persons (IDPs), Chaloka Beyani (Zambia), submitted his first report [A/HRC/16/43] to the Council, detailing the activities of the previous mandate holder, Walter Kälin (Switzerland) and activities since he assumed his mandate on 1 November. It also presented the Rapporteur's methods of work and described the issues and challenges with regard to internal displacement which the Rapporteur had identified and prioritized in the initial phase of his mandate, including ratification and implementation of the African Union Convention for the Protection and Assistance of Internally Displaced Persons (Kampala Convention); natural disasters and climate change; women and internal displacement; and IDPs outside camps.

In accordance with General Assembly resolution 62/153 [YUN 2007, p. 793], the Secretary-General in August [A/66/285] submitted the report of the Rapporteur, which outlined his activities from August 2010 to July 2011 and reviewed the issue of climate change and internal displacement. The Rapporteur recommended that a human rights-based approach be used to inform and strengthen all actions at the local, regional, national and international levels to address climate change-related internal displacement. The Guiding Principles on Internal Displacement [YUN 1998, p. 675] provided a sound legal framework which States should implement through legislation, policies and institutions. The Rapporteur also made recommendations related to adaptation and mitigation measures; measures to enhance knowledge, develop guidance and strengthen global monitoring mechanisms; and cooperation and assistance, including increased international support.

The General Assembly took note of that report on 19 December (**decision 66/537**).

Mission reports. Following his visit to Maldives (16–21 July) [A/HRC/19/54/Add.1], the Rapporteur commended Government efforts at the domestic level, particularly with regard to disaster risk reduction and other prevention measures, and for making assistance to those displaced in the aftermath of the 2004 tsunami a national priority. He concluded that a national framework on IDPs in line with international human rights and the Guiding Principles was necessary to complement those initiatives. He urged the Government, with the support of the international community, to put in place policy, legislative and institutional frameworks to address current and potential situations of internal displacement in the country, whether due to sudden or slow-onset natural disasters.

During his mission to Kenya (19–27 September) [A/HRC/19/54/Add.2], the Rapporteur examined the situation of IDPs, including those displaced due to the 2007–2008 post-election violence, natural disasters, and development and environmental conservation projects. He commended the progress achieved, such as the development of a draft IDP policy and draft IDP bill, and the establishment of an institutional focal point on internal displacement. The Government had facilitated the return and resettlement of IDPs affected by post-election violence and had maintained constructive cooperation with the United Nations. Nonetheless, remaining challenges included the lack of a policy and legislative framework, of comprehensive and disaggregated data-collection systems, and of sufficient operational and institutional capacity. He highlighted the humanitarian need to address the dire living conditions and human rights of persons who remained displaced, and the need for a broader and more participatory approach to durable solutions. He encouraged the Government to address those concerns, ratify the Kampala Convention, and adopt the draft policy and draft bill on IDPs.

GENERAL ASSEMBLY ACTION

On 19 December [meeting 89], the General Assembly, on the recommendation of the Third Committee [A/66/462/Add.2], adopted **resolution 66/165** without vote [agenda item 69 (*b*)].

Protection of and assistance to internally displaced persons

The General Assembly,

Recalling that internally displaced persons are persons or groups of persons who have been forced or obliged to flee or to leave their homes or places of habitual residence, in particular as a result of or in order to avoid the effects of armed conflict, situations of generalized violence, violations of human rights or natural or human-made disasters, and who have not crossed an internationally recognized State border,

Recognizing that internally displaced persons are to enjoy, in full equality, the same rights and freedoms under international and domestic law as do other persons in their country,

Deeply disturbed by the alarmingly high numbers of internally displaced persons throughout the world, for reasons including armed conflict, violations of human rights and natural or human-made disasters, who receive inadequate protection and assistance, and conscious of the serious challenges that this is creating for the international community,

Recognizing that natural disasters are a cause of internal displacement, and concerned about factors, such as climate change, that are expected to exacerbate the impact of natural hazards, and climate-related events,

Recognizing also that the consequences of hazards can be prevented or substantially mitigated by integrating disaster risk reduction strategies into national development policies and programmes,

Conscious of the human rights and humanitarian dimensions of the problem of internally displaced persons, including in long-term displacement situations, and the responsibilities of States and the international community to strengthen further their protection and assistance,

Emphasizing that States have the primary responsibility to provide protection and assistance to internally displaced persons within their jurisdiction, as well as to address the root causes of the displacement problem in appropriate cooperation with the international community,

Reaffirming that all persons, including those internally displaced, have the right to freedom of movement and residence and should be protected against being arbitrarily displaced,

Noting the international community's growing awareness of the issue of internally displaced persons worldwide and the urgency of addressing the root causes of their displacement and finding durable solutions, including voluntary return in safety and with dignity, as well as voluntary local integration in the areas to which persons have been displaced or voluntary settlement in another part of the country,

Recalling the relevant norms of international law, including international human rights law, international humanitarian law and international refugee law, and recognizing that the protection of internally displaced persons has been strengthened by identifying, reaffirming and consolidating specific standards for their protection, in particular through the Guiding Principles on Internal Displacement,

Recalling also the relevance of international humanitarian law, including the Geneva Conventions of 1949 and the Additional Protocols thereto, of 1977, as a vital legal framework for the protection of and assistance to civilians in armed conflict and under foreign occupation, including internally displaced persons,

Noting with appreciation the adoption by the International Conference on the Great Lakes Region of the Protocol on the Protection of and Assistance to Internally Displaced Persons and the Protocol on the Property Rights of Returning Persons and the adoption of the African Union Convention for the Protection and Assistance of Internally Displaced Persons in Africa, as steps contributing to the strengthening of the regional normative framework for the protection of and assistance to internally displaced persons in Africa,

Welcoming the increasing dissemination, promotion and application of the Guiding Principles on Internal Displacement when dealing with situations of internal displacement,

Deploring practices of forced displacement and their negative consequences for the enjoyment of human rights and fundamental freedoms by large groups of populations, and recalling the relevant provisions of the Rome Statute of the International Criminal Court that define the deportation or forcible transfer of population as a crime against humanity, and the unlawful deportation, transfer, or ordering the displacement of the civilian population as war crimes,

Expressing its appreciation to those Governments and intergovernmental, regional and non-governmental organizations that have supported the work of the former Representative of the Secretary-General on the human rights of internally displaced persons and, according to their roles and responsibilities, have helped to provide protection and assistance to internally displaced persons,

Welcoming the continuing cooperation between the Special Rapporteur on the human rights of internally displaced persons and national Governments, the relevant offices and agencies of the United Nations as well as with other international and regional organizations, and encouraging further strengthening of this collaboration in order to promote better strategies for, protection of, assistance to and durable solutions for internally displaced persons,

Welcoming also the priorities set by the Special Rapporteur, contained in his report to the Human Rights Council,

Acknowledging with appreciation the important and independent contribution of the International Red Cross and Red Crescent Movement and other humanitarian agencies in protecting and assisting internally displaced persons, in cooperation with relevant international bodies,

Recalling the Vienna Declaration and Programme of Action adopted by the World Conference on Human Rights on 25 June 1993, regarding the need to develop global strategies to address the problem of internal displacement,

Recalling also its resolution 64/162 of 18 December 2009 and Human Rights Council resolution 14/6 of 17 June 2010,

1. *Takes note with appreciation* of the report of the Special Rapporteur on the human rights of internally displaced persons and the conclusions and recommendations contained therein;

2. *Commends* the Special Rapporteur for the activities undertaken so far, for the catalytic role that he plays in raising the level of awareness about the plight of internally displaced persons and for his ongoing efforts to address their development and other specific needs, including through the mainstreaming of the human rights of internally displaced persons into all relevant parts of the United Nations system;

3. *Encourages* the Special Rapporteur, through continuous dialogue with Governments and all intergovernmental and non-governmental organizations concerned, to continue his analysis of the root causes of internal displacement, the needs and human rights of those displaced, measures of prevention, including early warning, and ways to strengthen protection and assistance, as well as durable solutions for internally displaced persons, and, in the latter regard, to use in his activities the Framework on Durable Solutions for Internally Displaced Persons of the Inter-Agency Standing Committee, and also encourages the Special Rapporteur to continue to promote comprehensive strategies, taking into account the primary responsibility of States for the protection of and assistance to internally displaced persons within their jurisdiction;

4. *Recognizes* the adverse effects of climate change as contributors to environmental degradation and extreme weather events, which may, among other factors, contribute to human displacement, and encourages the Special Rapporteur, in close collaboration with States and intergovernmental and non-governmental organizations, to continue to explore the human rights implications and dimensions of disaster-induced internal displacement, with a view to supporting Member States in their efforts to build local resilience and capacity to prevent displacement or to provide assistance and protection to those who are forced to flee;

5. *Calls upon* States to provide durable solutions, and encourages strengthened international cooperation, including through the provision of resources and expertise to assist affected countries, in particular developing countries, in their national efforts and policies related to assistance, protection and rehabilitation for internally displaced persons;

6. *Welcomes* the adoption of the African Union Convention for the Protection and Assistance of Internally Displaced Persons in Africa during the summit of the African Union held in Kampala in October 2009, and invites African States to consider signing and/or ratifying the Convention;

7. *Recognizes* that Member States have the primary responsibility to promote durable solutions for internally displaced persons within their jurisdiction, thus contributing to their national, economic and social development processes, and encourages the international community, the United Nations system, the Special Rapporteur, relevant international and regional organizations and donor countries to continue to support international, regional and national efforts to meet the needs of internally displaced persons, on the basis of solidarity, the principles of international cooperation and the Guiding Principles on Internal Displacement, and ensure that humanitarian assistance efforts are appropriately funded;

8. *Expresses particular concern* at the grave problems faced by many internally displaced women and children, including violence and abuse, sexual exploitation, trafficking in persons, forced recruitment and abduction, and encourages the continued commitment of the Special Rapporteur to promote action to address their particular assistance, protection and development needs, as well as those of other groups with special needs, such as severely traumatized individuals, older persons and persons with disabilities, taking into account all relevant United Nations resolutions;

9. *Emphasizes* the importance of consultation with internally displaced persons and host communities by Governments and other relevant actors, in accordance with their specific mandates, during all phases of displacement, as well as the participation of internally displaced persons, where appropriate, in programmes and activities pertaining to them, taking into account the primary responsibility of States for the protection of and assistance to internally displaced persons within their jurisdiction;

10. *Notes* the importance of taking the human rights and the specific protection and assistance needs of internally displaced persons into consideration, when appropriate, in peace processes, and emphasizes that durable solutions for internally displaced persons, including through voluntary return, sustainable reintegration and rehabilitation processes and their active participation, as appropriate, in the peace process, are necessary elements of effective peacebuilding;

11. *Welcomes* the role of the Peacebuilding Commission in this regard, and continues to urge the Commission to intensify its efforts, within its mandate, in cooperation

with national and transitional Governments and in consultation with the relevant United Nations entities, to incorporate the rights and the specific needs of internally displaced persons, including their voluntary return in safety and with dignity, reintegration and rehabilitation, as well as related land and property issues, when advising on or proposing country-specific peacebuilding strategies for post-conflict situations in cases under consideration;

12. *Recognizes* the Guiding Principles on Internal Displacement as an important international framework for the protection of internally displaced persons, welcomes the fact that an increasing number of States, United Nations organizations and regional and non-governmental organizations are applying them as a standard, and encourages all relevant actors to make use of the Guiding Principles when dealing with situations of internal displacement;

13. *Welcomes* the use of the Guiding Principles on Internal Displacement by the Special Rapporteur in his dialogue with Governments, intergovernmental and non-governmental organizations and other relevant actors, and requests him to continue his efforts to further the dissemination, promotion and application of the Guiding Principles and to provide support for efforts to promote capacity-building and the use of the Guiding Principles, as well as the development of domestic legislation and policies;

14. *Encourages* States to continue to develop and implement domestic legislation and policies dealing with all stages of displacement, in an inclusive and non-discriminatory way, including through the identification of a national focal point within the Government for issues of internal displacement, and through the allocation of budget resources, and encourages the international community and national actors to provide financial support and cooperation to Governments, upon request, in this regard;

15. *Expresses its appreciation* that an increasing number of States have adopted domestic legislation and policies dealing with all stages of displacement;

16. *Urges* all Governments to continue to facilitate the activities of the Special Rapporteur, in particular Governments with situations of internal displacement, and to respond favourably to requests from the Special Rapporteur for visits so as to enable him to continue and enhance dialogue with Governments in addressing situations of internal displacement, and thanks those Governments that have already done so;

17. *Invites* Governments to give serious consideration, in dialogue with the Special Rapporteur, to the recommendations and suggestions addressed to them, in accordance with his mandate, and to inform him of measures taken thereon;

18. *Calls upon* Governments to provide protection and assistance, including reintegration and development assistance, to internally displaced persons, and to facilitate the efforts of the relevant United Nations agencies and humanitarian organizations in these respects, including by further improving access to internally displaced persons and by maintaining the civilian and humanitarian character of camps and settlements for internally displaced persons where they exist;

19. *Emphasizes* the central role of the Emergency Relief Coordinator for the coordination of protection of and assistance to internally displaced persons, inter alia, through the inter-agency cluster system, welcomes continued initiatives taken in order to ensure better protection, assistance and development strategies for internally displaced persons, as well as better coordination of activities regarding them, and emphasizes the need to strengthen the capacities of the United Nations organizations and other relevant actors to meet the immense humanitarian challenges of internal displacement;

20. *Encourages* all relevant United Nations organizations and humanitarian assistance, human rights and development organizations to enhance their collaboration and coordination, through the Inter-Agency Standing Committee and United Nations country teams in countries with situations of internal displacement, and to provide all possible assistance and support to the Special Rapporteur, and requests the continued participation of the Special Rapporteur in the work of the Inter-Agency Standing Committee and its subsidiary bodies;

21. *Notes with appreciation* the increased attention paid to the issue of internally displaced persons in the consolidated appeals process, and encourages further efforts in this regard;

22. *Also notes with appreciation* the increasing role of national human rights institutions in assisting internally displaced persons and in promoting and protecting their human rights;

23. *Recognizes* the relevance of the global database on internally displaced persons advocated by the Special Rapporteur, and encourages the members of the Inter-Agency Standing Committee and Governments to continue to collaborate on and support this effort, including by providing financial resources and relevant data on situations of internal displacement;

24. *Welcomes* the initiatives undertaken by regional organizations, such as the African Union, the International Conference on the Great Lakes Region, the Organization of American States and the Council of Europe, to address the protection, assistance and development needs of internally displaced persons and to find durable solutions for them, and encourages regional organizations to strengthen their activities and their cooperation with the Special Rapporteur;

25. *Requests* the Secretary-General to continue to provide the Special Rapporteur, from within existing resources, with all assistance necessary to carry out his mandate effectively, and encourages the Office of the United Nations High Commissioner for Human Rights, in close cooperation with the Emergency Relief Coordinator, the Office for the Coordination of Humanitarian Affairs of the Secretariat and the Office of the United Nations High Commissioner for Refugees and all other relevant United Nations offices and agencies, to continue to support the Special Rapporteur;

26. *Encourages* the Special Rapporteur to continue to seek the contributions of States, relevant organizations and institutions in order to create a more stable basis for his work;

27. *Requests* the Special Rapporteur to prepare, for the General Assembly at its sixty-seventh and sixty-eighth sessions, a report on the implementation of the present resolution;

28. *Decides* to continue its consideration of the question of protection of and assistance to internally displaced persons at its sixty-eighth session.

Persons with disabilities

Human Rights Council action. On 24 March [A/66/53 (res. 16/15)], the Council called on stakeholders to consider the findings and recommendations of the OHCHR thematic study on the role of international cooperation in support of national efforts for realizing the rights of persons with disabilities [YUN 2010, p. 759]; invited the High Commissioner to make the study available to the General Assembly's high-level meeting on ensuring accessibility for and inclusion of persons with disabilities in all aspects of development efforts at its sixty-seventh (2012) session; welcomed the initiative to promote a new multi-donor trust fund through the establishment of the UN partnership for the rights of persons with disabilities; invited OHCHR, within two years of the partnership's establishment, to provide information to the Council on its status and operation; decided that its next annual interactive debate on the rights of persons with disabilities would be held at its nineteenth (2012) session, and would focus on participation in political and public life; and requested OHCHR to prepare a study on the participation of persons with disabilities in political and public life and to make the study available on the OHCHR website prior to the Council's nineteenth session.

OHCHR study. In response to that request (see above), OHCHR in December submitted a study [A/HRC/19/36] on participation in political and public life by persons with disabilities. The study analysed relevant provisions of the Convention on the Rights of Persons with Disabilities, highlighted good practices in the field of participation of persons with disabilities in elections and in the conduct of public affairs, and identified the main challenges that prevented or limited the equal and effective participation of persons with disabilities in the political and public life of their countries.

Indigenous peoples

Reports of Special Rapporteur. In accordance with a Human Rights Council request [YUN 2010, p. 761], the Special Rapporteur on the rights of indigenous people, James Anaya (United States), in July submitted his fourth report [A/HRC/18/35] to the Council, summarizing his activities during the third year of his mandate, including cooperation with international and regional mechanisms in the field of indigenous rights, and the activities carried out in his four principal areas of work: promoting good practices; thematic studies; country reports; and communications relating to alleged violations. The report also analysed the impact of extractive industries operating within or near indigenous territories. Responses to a questionnaire on the issue revealed conflicting points of view on the potential adverse impact and benefits of extractive or development projects in indigenous territories; the practical implications in that context of international standards affirming the rights of indigenous peoples; and the kind of measures required to fulfil the responsibilities of States, corporate actors and indigenous peoples themselves. The Special Rapporteur observed that a number of State legal and institutional frameworks, domestic court decisions, business internal policies and pilot projects were relevant to indigenous peoples' rights in the context of extractive industries, and recommended that they be given careful consideration. He proposed to work towards the operationalization of the rights of indigenous peoples and related institutional guarantees in the context of natural resource extraction and development projects affecting indigenous territories, with the aim to present specific guidelines or principles to the Council in 2013.

An addendum [A/HRC/18/35/Add.1] summarized communications sent to Governments between 1 December 2010 and 31 May 2011, and replies received between 1 February and 31 July 2011.

In further addenda, the Rapporteur submitted reports on the situation of the rights of the indigenous people of Guatemala with relation to extraction projects in their traditional territories [A/HRC/18/35/Add.3] in follow-up to his 2010 visit [YUN 2010, p. 761] and on the situation of indigenous peoples affected by the El Diquís hydroelectric project in Costa Rica [A/HRC/18/35/Add.8].

As requested by the Human Rights Council [ibid.], the Secretary-General in August transmitted to the General Assembly the report [A/66/288] of the Rapporteur reviewing his activities during the first three-year term of his mandate, which began in May 2008. In addition to outlining the work undertaken in the spheres of promoting good practices, country reports, cases of alleged human rights violations and thematic studies, the report described studies on the duty of States to consult with and obtain the consent of indigenous peoples before adopting measures that affected them, the responsibility of corporations to respect the rights of indigenous peoples, and issues related to extractive industries in indigenous peoples' traditional territories.

Mission reports. Following his visits to New Caledonia (6–13 February) and to Paris (22–24 June) to meet with French officials on the situation of indigenous peoples in New Caledonia [A/HRC/18/35/Add.6], the Rapporteur made a number of recommendations to assist with advancing the rights of the Kanak people in the context of the implementation of the Nouméa Accord [YUN 1998, p. 574] and the United Nations-supported decolonization process. The Accord provided for the gradual, irreversible transfer of powers from France to New Caledonia with the possibility of full independence in the future, while at the same time recognizing the distinct identity of the Kanak people and the need to reverse historical trends of oppression against them, consistent with international standards on both decolonization and indigenous peoples. The Rapporteur recommended that concerted efforts be made to ensure that officials of both the French and New Caledonia Governments and members of the New Caledonia Congress, as well as New Caledonia society, were aware of the United Nations Declaration on the Rights of Indigenous Peoples [YUN 2007, p. 691] and its implications.

In response to a request by Suriname for technical and advisory assistance as it developed legislative and administrative measures to secure the territorial and other rights of the nation's indigenous and tribal peoples, the Rapporteur visited that country (3–16 March) [A/HRC/18/35/Add.7]. He outlined a process for moving towards developing legislation and related administrative measures to secure those rights. He included suggestions for the basic contents of the legislation, while emphasizing that the legislation should be the outcome of a participatory process, assisted by relevant international institutions, in which indigenous and tribal peoples were themselves involved.

Following his mission to Argentina (27 November–7 December) [A/HRC/21/47/Add.2], the Rapporteur highlighted the Government's actions to recognize the rights of indigenous peoples in the country, including reforms to the 1994 Constitution relating to indigenous peoples; the adoption of an act establishing a process to help regularize indigenous lands; the ratification of the International Labour Organization Indigenous and Tribal Peoples Convention, 1989 (No. 169); and the vote in the General Assembly in support of the United Nations Declaration on the Rights of Indigenous Peoples. A significant gap remained, however, between the established regulatory framework on indigenous issues and its actual implementation. The Rapporteur recommended that the Government prioritize and implement the human rights of indigenous peoples at both the federal and provincial levels. In particular, it should adopt clear public policies and develop guidelines for government officials, along with additional legislative and administrative measures to increase awareness of, and State action on, indigenous matters by all parties, including government officials.

Communications. In notes of 25 August [A/HRC/18/G/4] and 16 September [A/HRC/18/G/8], Guatemala and Costa Rica, respectively, submitted comments on the Special Rapporteur's report on the situation of indigenous peoples affected by mining and other projects and by the El Diquís hydroelectric project (see above).

Report of High Commissioner. As requested by the Human Rights Council [YUN 2010, p. 761], the High Commissioner in July [A/HRC/18/26 & Corr.1] reviewed information on developments of human rights bodies and mechanisms relating to the rights of indigenous peoples between May 2010 and April 2011. She also outlined the activities undertaken by OHCHR at headquarters and in the field that contributed to promoting and implementing the provisions of the United Nations Declaration of the Rights of Indigenous Peoples.

Human Rights Council action. On 29 September [A/66/53/Add.1 (res. 18/8)], the Council decided to hold on an annual basis a half-day panel on the rights of indigenous peoples and, at its 2012 session, a discussion on access to justice by indigenous peoples; welcomed the adoption of General Assembly resolution 65/198 [ibid., p. 763], in which the Assembly decided to organize a high-level plenary meeting to be known as the World Conference on Indigenous Peoples, in 2014; welcomed the establishment of the United Nations-Indigenous Peoples Partnership; requested the Secretary-General to prepare a document on the ways and means of promoting participation at the United Nations of recognized indigenous peoples' representatives on issues affecting them, and to present it to the Council's twenty-first (2012) session; requested the Rapporteur to report to the Assembly's sixty-seventh (2012) session; and requested the High Commissioner to submit to the Council an annual report on the rights of indigenous peoples containing information on developments in human rights bodies and mechanisms and activities undertaken by OHCHR.

Expert Mechanism

The Expert Mechanism on the Rights of Indigenous Peoples, at its fourth session (Geneva, 11–15 July) [A/HRC/18/43], discussed and adopted the final report on the study on indigenous peoples and the right to participate in decision-making [A/HRC/EMRIP/2011/2]. The Human Rights Council in 2009 [YUN 2009, p. 748] had requested the Expert Mechanism to carry out that study with a view to presenting a final text to the Council's eighteenth (2011) session. The Expert Mechanism also held a discussion on follow-up to thematic studies and advice, as well as discussions on proposals to be submitted to the Council and on the United Nations Declaration on the Rights of Indigenous Peoples. In addition to the five members of the Expert Mechanism, the session was attended by representatives of States, UN entities, NGOs, national human rights institutions, academics and indigenous peoples.

The Expert Mechanism in August [A/HRC/18/42] submitted to the Council the final report of the study, which focused on examples of good practices of indigenous peoples' participation in different levels of decision-making.

Human Rights Council action. On 29 September [A/66/53/Add.1 (res. 18/8)], the Council welcomed the Expert Mechanism's completion of its final study on indigenous peoples and decision-making; recommended that the Expert Mechanism adopt the practice of devoting time to the discussion of updates relevant to past mandated thematic studies on a permanent basis; encouraged all interested parties to consider the examples of good practices contained in the Expert Mechanism's final study as a practical guide on how to attain the goals of the United Nations Declaration on the Rights of Indigenous Peoples; and requested the Expert Mechanism to: prepare a study on the role of languages and culture in the promotion and protection of the rights and identity of indigenous peoples and to present it the Council's twenty-first (2012) session; seek the views of States on best practices regarding measures and implementation strategies to attain the goals of the United Nations Declaration on the Rights of Indigenous Peoples; and discuss the upcoming (2014) World Conference on Indigenous Peoples and to contribute to the exploration of the modalities for the meeting, including indigenous peoples' participation in the Conference and its preparations.

Voluntary Fund for Indigenous Populations

The Board of Trustees of the United Nations Voluntary Fund for Indigenous Populations, at its twenty-fourth session (Geneva, 7–11 February) [A/67/221], recommended 30 grants totalling $156,330 to enable indigenous representatives to attend the tenth session of the Permanent Forum on Indigenous Issues (see below) and another 24 travel grants totalling $78,937 to enable those representatives to attend the fourth session of the Expert Mechanism (see p. 750).

Voluntary Fund for International Decade

The Voluntary Fund for the Second International Decade of the World's Indigenous People, 2005–2014, established by General Assembly resolution 59/174 [YUN 2004, p. 799], continued to promote, support and implement the goals of the Second Decade in terms of promoting indigenous peoples' culture, education, health, human rights, environment and economic development. In May, the Bureau of the United Nations Permanent Forum on Indigenous Issues (see below), serving as the Advisory Group for the Fund, considered project proposals for funding received by the Secretariat, in accordance with resolution 59/174. It proposed to award grants to 16 projects being implemented by indigenous organizations and NGOs in 15 countries.

Permanent Forum on Indigenous Issues

The 16-member Permanent Forum on Indigenous Issues, established by Economic and Social Council resolution 2000/22 [YUN 2000, p. 731] to address indigenous issues relating to economic and social development, the environment, health, education and culture, and human rights, held its tenth session in 2011 (New York, 16–27 May) [E/2011/43 & Corr.1]. It did not consider a special theme during the session, as its working plan was to alternate a working method one year, followed by consideration of a special theme. It had before it reports submitted by its secretariat and subsidiary mechanisms, Governments, UN system bodies, intergovernmental organizations, regional organizations and NGOs [E/C.19/2011/1 & Rev.1, E/C.19/2011/2–13]. The Forum recommended three draft decisions for adoption by the Economic and Social Council on an international expert group meeting on the theme "Combating violence against indigenous women and girls: article 22 of the United Nations Declaration on the Rights of Indigenous Peoples"; venue and dates of the eleventh session of the Forum; and the provisional agenda for that session. The Forum identified proposals, objectives, recommendations and areas of possible action and, through the Council, recommended that States, UN system entities, intergovernmental organizations, indigenous peoples, the private sector and NGOs assist in their realization. The Forum issued recommendations on follow-up to the recommendations of the Permanent Forum on economic and social development, the environment and free, prior and informed consent; implementation of the United Nations Declaration on the Rights of Indigenous Peoples; the comprehensive dialogue with the United Nations Children's Fund; the half-day discussion on the right to water and indigenous people; and future work.

Economic and Social Council action. On 28 July [E/2011/99], the Council decided that the eleventh session of the Permanent Forum would be held in New York from 7 to 18 May 2012 (**decision 2011/267**). It authorized a three-day international expert group meeting on the theme "Combating violence against indigenous women and girls: article 22 of the United Nations Declaration on the Rights of Indigenous Peoples", and requested that the results of the meeting be reported to the eleventh session of the Permanent Forum, the fifty-sixth (2012) session of the Commission on the Status of Women and the sixty-seventh (2012) session of the General Assembly (**decision 2011/266**). On 29 July, the Council took note of the report of the Permanent Forum on its tenth session and approved the provisional agenda for its eleventh session (**decision 2011/277**).

Expert meetings and conferences

An international expert group meeting addressed the theme "Indigenous peoples and forests" (New York, 12–14 January) [E/C.19/2011/5], providing conclusions and recommendations to the Permanent Forum.

The 2011 meeting of the Inter-Agency Support Group on Indigenous Issues (Geneva, 16–17 September) [E/C.19/2011/10], hosted by the World Health Organization, considered the theme "Indigenous peoples' health".

GENERAL ASSEMBLY ACTION

On 19 December [meeting 89], the General Assembly, on the recommendation of the Third Committee [A/66/459], adopted **resolution 66/142** without vote [agenda item 66 (*a*)].

Rights of indigenous peoples

The General Assembly,

Recalling all relevant resolutions of the General Assembly, the Human Rights Council and the Economic and Social Council relating to the rights of indigenous peoples,

Reaffirming its resolution 65/198 of 21 December 2010, in which it decided to organize a high-level plenary meeting of the General Assembly, to be known as the World Conference on Indigenous Peoples, to be held in 2014,

Recalling its resolution 59/174 of 20 December 2004 on the Second International Decade of the World's Indigenous People (2005–2014),

Recalling also the 2007 United Nations Declaration on the Rights of Indigenous Peoples, which addresses their individual and collective rights,

Recalling further the United Nations Millennium Declaration, the 2005 World Summit Outcome and the outcome document of the High-level Plenary Meeting of the General Assembly on the Millennium Development Goals,

Recalling Human Rights Council resolution 18/8 of 29 September 2011 on human rights and indigenous peoples,

Recalling also the first Peoples' World Conference on Climate Change and the Rights of Mother Earth, hosted by the Plurinational State of Bolivia in Cochabamba from 20 to 22 April 2010,

Stressing the importance of promoting and pursuing the objectives of the United Nations Declaration on the Rights of Indigenous Peoples also through international cooperation to support national and regional efforts to achieve the ends of the Declaration, including the right to maintain and strengthen the distinct political, legal, economic, social and cultural institutions of indigenous peoples and the right to participate fully, if they so choose, in the political, economic, social and cultural life of the State,

Recognizing the value and the diversity of the cultures and the form of the social organization of indigenous peoples and their holistic traditional scientific knowledge of their lands, natural resources and environment,

Concerned about the extreme disadvantages that indigenous peoples have typically faced across a range of social and economic indicators and about the impediments to their full enjoyment of their rights,

Recalling its resolution 65/198, by which it decided to expand the mandate of the United Nations Voluntary Fund for Indigenous Populations so that it could assist representatives of indigenous peoples' organizations and communities to participate in sessions of the Human Rights Council and of human rights treaty bodies, on the basis of diverse and renewed participation and in accordance with relevant rules and regulations, including Economic and Social Council resolution 1996/31 of 25 July 1996, and urged States to contribute to the Fund,

1. *Welcomes* the work of the Expert Mechanism on the Rights of Indigenous Peoples and of the Special Rapporteur on the rights of indigenous peoples, takes note of his report on the rights of indigenous peoples, and encourages all Governments to respond favourably to his requests for visits;

2. *Urges* Governments and intergovernmental and non-governmental organizations to continue to contribute to the United Nations Voluntary Fund for Indigenous Populations and the Trust Fund for the Second International Decade of the World's Indigenous People, and invites indigenous organizations and private institutions and individuals to do likewise;

3. *Encourages* those States that have not yet ratified or acceded to the International Labour Organization Indigenous and Tribal Peoples Convention, 1989 (No. 169) to consider doing so and to consider supporting the United Nations Declaration on the Rights of Indigenous Peoples, and welcomes the increased support by States for the Declaration;

4. *Encourages* States, in consultation and cooperation with indigenous peoples, to take the appropriate measures, including legislative measures, to achieve the ends of the Declaration;

5. *Encourages* all interested parties, in particular indigenous peoples, to disseminate and consider good practices at different levels as a practical guide on how to attain the goals of the Declaration;

6. *Requests* the Secretary-General, in coordination with the United Nations Permanent Forum on Indigenous Issues, to convene, within existing resources, a high-level event during the eleventh session of the Forum to commemorate the fifth anniversary of the adoption of the United Nations Declaration on the Rights of Indigenous Peoples in order to raise awareness of the importance of pursuing its objectives;

7. *Stresses* that the result of that event could serve as an input for the preparation of the high-level plenary meeting of the General Assembly in 2014, to be known as the World Conference on Indigenous Peoples;

8. *Invites* Governments, indigenous peoples and other stakeholders, including the media, as well as relevant organizations and bodies of the United Nations system, to carry out activities focused on marking the fifth anniversary of the adoption of the Declaration, at the regional and national levels;

9. *Decides* to continue consideration of the question at its sixty-seventh session, under the item entitled "Rights of indigenous peoples".

Chapter III

Human rights country situations

In 2011, the General Assembly, the Human Rights Council, the Secretary-General, Special Rapporteurs and independent experts addressed the human rights situation in Member States.

In Africa, as the political stalemate in Côte d'Ivoire between elected President Alsassane Ouattara and former President Laurent Gbagbo and their supporters continued, the human rights situation worsened. Almost 300 people had been killed since the beginning of the crisis, and reports of abductions and illegal detention persisted. The security situation improved after President Ouattara was sworn into office, but serious human rights challenges remained. The situation failed to improve in the Democratic Republic of the Congo and in Somalia, and the situation in the Darfur region of the Sudan remained precarious. In Libya, systematic human rights violations were committed following demonstrations in a number of cities across the country in February. The Human Rights Council welcomed the creation of a national human rights commission in Burundi in January and the establishment of a human rights institution in May. In Tunisia, a wave of protests led to the departure of President Zine El-Abidine Ben Ali, and the transitional Government requested that the Office of the High Commissioner for Human Rights establish an office in the country.

In the Democratic People's Republic of Korea, the human rights and humanitarian situation deteriorated despite a change in the country's leadership. In Iran, the year was marked by a crackdown on human rights defenders, women's rights activists, journalists and Government opponents, as well as an increase in the application of the death penalty. In September, the Myanmar National Human Rights Commission was formed to promote and safeguard the fundamental rights of citizens.

In Belarus, the human rights situation declined rapidly following elections held the previous year. Six hundred peaceful protestors contesting the electoral process were arrested and detained.

The situation in the territories occupied by Israel worsened, despite the opening of the border with Egypt, which provided some relief to the citizens of Gaza. Following peaceful protests in Syria, the authorities used lethal violence and prevented access to medical treatment. A pattern of murder and disappearances, torture, deprivation of liberty and persecution by the Syrian military and security forces, and the uprising of armed non-State actors, resulted in gross violations of human rights and fundamental freedoms. Armed groups took control of large areas of Yemen during the year following the use of force on peaceful protesters. The authorities deliberately sought to punish the population by cutting off access to basis services, resulting in an increasingly dire humanitarian situation.

The Human Rights Council held four special sessions on particular situations—its fifteenth special session (25 February) on the situation of human rights in Libya; and its sixteenth (29 April), seventeenth (22–23 August) and eighteenth (2 December) special sessions on the situation in Syria.

General aspects

In the annual report on the activities undertaken by the Office of the High Commissioner for Human Rights (OHCHR) [A/HRC/19/21], the High Commissioner, Navanethem Pillay, reviewed the work of the Office at the country and regional levels, including its efforts to respond to deteriorating human rights situations. At the country level, its work was conducted through human rights field presences, support for human rights mechanisms and dialogue between the High Commissioner and Member States—including bilateral meetings, open or confidential communication, country visits by the High Commissioner and technical cooperation programmes.

In December, OHCHR had 58 field presences: 13 country/stand-alone offices, 15 human rights components of peace missions, 12 regional offices and 18 human rights advisers in UN country teams. Regional presences included: East Africa (Addis Ababa, Ethiopia); Southern Africa (Pretoria, South Africa); West Africa (Dakar, Senegal); South-East Asia (Bangkok, Thailand); the Pacific (Suva, Fiji); the Middle East (Beirut, Lebanon); Central Asia (Bishkek, Kyrgyzstan); Europe (Brussels, Belgium); Central America (Panama City); and South America (Santiago, Chile); as well as the United Nations Subregional Centre for Human Rights and Democracy in Central Africa (Yaoundé, Cameroon) and the United Nations Human Rights Training and Documentation Centre for South-West Asia and the Arab Region (Doha, Qatar). In 2011, OHCHR established a country office in Tunisia (see p. 615), and human rights staff were integrated into the United Nations Support Mission in Libya. Country offices were also located in Bolivia, Cambodia, Colombia, Guatemala, Guinea, Mauritania, Mexico, Nepal, Togo and Uganda. OHCHR maintained stand-alone offices in the Occupied Palestinian Territory and in Kosovo.

OHCHR had 18 human rights advisers in UN country teams in Chad, Ecuador, the Great Lakes region (based in Burundi), Honduras, Kenya, Madagascar, Moldova, Niger, Papua New Guinea, Paraguay, the Russian Federation, Rwanda, Serbia, Sri Lanka, the Southern Caucasus (based in Tbilisi and covering Armenia, Azerbaijan and Georgia), Tajikistan, the former Yugoslav Republic of Macedonia and Ukraine.

The High Commissioner concluded that human rights treaty bodies provided valuable advice for Member States and advocacy tools for national institutions and non-governmental organizations (NGOs); contributed to the integration of human rights considerations into the work of UN agencies and programmes; and provided the universal periodic review mechanism with the building blocks to ensure that the peer review was based on objective technical grounds. Efforts to strengthen the treaty body system were crucial but did not replace the need for human and financial resources essential to a well-functioning and credible treaty body system.

Africa

Burundi

Human Rights Council action. On 25 March [A/HRC/16/2 (res.16/34)], the Human Rights Council recognized the major changes in the Government and representation of Burundi following the elections held there from June to September 2010 [YUN 2010, p. 141] and resolved that the independent expert on the situation of human rights in the country would report to the Council at its seventeenth (2011) session.

Report of independent expert. On 31 May [A/HRC/17/50], the independent expert on the human rights situation in Burundi, Fatsah Ouguergouz (Algeria), reported to the Human Rights Council following his first visit to the country (8–17 November 2010). He noted that national consultations were held throughout the country on the establishment of a truth and reconciliation commission and a special tribunal to prosecute those responsible for serious violations of human rights. Significant advances were made towards the establishment of an independent national human rights commission. The independent expert reported on the main allegations of human rights violations brought to his attention, including violations of the right to life and to physical integrity, which were largely attributed to State officials. He noted, in particular, allegations of extrajudicial killings of at least nine persons by law enforcement officers. The freedom of expression of journalists and human rights defenders was also curtailed. The independent expert drew attention to the slowness of the justice system and the poor prison conditions observed.

The independent expert urged Burundi to bring to justice members of the defence and security forces and all other persons suspected of having perpetrated serious violations of human rights, and to intensify efforts to reform the justice system, particularly with regard to the recruitment and independence of the judiciary. He called on the Government to set up transitional justice mechanisms to promote national reconciliation. He called on the international community to increase its support to Burundi, particularly in the capacity-building of the justice system. The international community was encouraged to assist the Government in establishing the independent national human rights commission and transitional justice mechanisms.

Human Rights Council action. On 30 September [A/HRC/18/2 (res. 18/24)], the Human Rights Council welcomed the creation of an independent national human rights commission on 5 January and the establishment of a human rights institution on 23 May. It urged the international community to increase its technical and financial assistance to the Government with a view to supporting its efforts to promote and protect human rights.

Côte d'Ivoire

Report of High Commissioner. In a February report on the human rights situation in Côte d'Ivoire [A/HRC/16/79], submitted pursuant to Human Rights Council resolution S-14/1 [YUN 2010, p. 766], the High Commissioner for Human Rights stated that while the first round of the presidential elections, held on 31 October 2010, was conducted peacefully, the run-off round of 28 November was marred by a radicalization of political rhetoric that drove the country into turmoil. Following the announcement of divergent results by the Independent Electoral Commission and the Constitutional Council, elected President Alsassane Ouattara formed a Government, and Laurent Gbagbo tried to retain power [YUN 2010, p. 191]. The recruitment and use of youth groups, militias and alleged mercenaries following the election resulted in serious human rights violations, some of which were ethnically and politically motivated and produced victims on both sides, but mainly among supporters of Rassemblement des houphouëtistes pour la démocratie et la paix. As the political stalemate continued, the human rights situation became more precarious.

Almost 300 people had been killed since the beginning of the crisis, and there were continued reports of abductions, illegal detention and attacks against civilians. More than 35,000 people fled their homes to seek refuge elsewhere, including neighbouring countries. It was reported that thousands of youths were forcibly recruited and armed. The State-owned television corporation disseminated xenophobic messages inciting hatred and violence, and promoted ethnic division between the north and the south. The obstruction of the United Nations Operation in Côte d'Ivoire (UNOCI) limited its ability to verify the full extent of the human rights violations across the country.

The High Commissioner recommended that the Government conduct in-depth, independent and impartial investigations into all politically related violence; continue to seek a peaceful resolution of the crisis; and ensure that victims of sexual violence received adequate medical and psychological assistance and reparation, and that perpetrators were brought to justice. The High Commissioner also recommended that Mr. Gbagbo and his supporters end all infringement of the rights to life and physical integrity; respect the freedom of movement of, and fully cooperate with, the United Nations, the African Union (AU) and other partners for a peaceful resolution of the crisis; stop the recruitment, arming and use of youth groups, militias and mercenaries; end the harassment and persecution of supporters of other political parties and groups on the grounds of political opinion or ethnicity; refrain from unlawful action against unarmed civilians; ensure that the public and private media controlled by them stopped broadcasting inflammatory messages, including against the United Nations; and cease all actions, statements and other manipulations that incited the security forces to commit human rights violations.

Human Rights Council action. On 25 March [A/HRC/16/2 (res. 16/25)], the Human Rights Council expressed concern at the seriousness and extent of the abuses and violations of international human rights and humanitarian law; condemned all atrocities and other violations of human rights, threats and actions of intimidation, and acts of obstruction directed at UNOCI operations; urged all media outlets to refrain from inciting violence, hostility and the propaganda of hate speech; and called for an end to the violence. It called on all Ivorian parties to cooperate fully with the UN agencies and other actors working to assist refugees and internally displaced persons (IDPs), and on Member States, UN agencies and international financial institutions to provide technical assistance and capacity-building. The Council decided to dispatch an independent international commission of inquiry, appointed by the Council President, to investigate the allegations of serious abuses and violations of human rights committed in Côte d'Ivoire following the 2010 presidential election in order to identify those responsible and bring them to justice, and to present its findings to the Council at its seventeenth (2011) session. The Council also called on all parties to cooperate fully with the commission of inquiry.

Report of Commission of Inquiry. In a July report [A/HRC/17/48] submitted in response to Council resolution 16/25, the International Commission of Inquiry on Côte d'Ivoire stated that it had visited the country from 4 to 28 May and met with a number of Ivorian authorities, including President Ouattara, Prime Minister Guillaume Soro, political figures, national institutions, international organizations and civil society organizations. The conflict in the country stemmed from former President Gbagbo's refusal to accept the election results, along with the exploitation of the ethnic question, the manipulation by political figures of young Ivorians, and unresolved land issues. The Government indicated at the highest level that national reconciliation was a priority. The Commission recommended, among other measures, that the Government ensure that those responsible for violations of human rights and international humanitarian law were brought to justice; that the underlying causes of the crisis, in particular those relating to discrimination, were addressed; and that the initiatives taken towards reconciliation, in particular the establishment and operation of the Dialogue, Truth and Reconciliation Commission, complied with established international principles and good practices. The security of persons and property should be ensured, in particular through the disarmament of persons not belonging to the defence and security forces. The Government should develop lasting solutions for IDPs and ratify international statutes, charters, and conventions.

Report of High Commissioner. In a June report [A/HRC/17/49] covering events from February to May, the High Commissioner stated that direct attacks against civilians by the security forces had abated since the arrest of former President Gbagbo on 11 April. Nevertheless, the human rights situation remained precarious, with a pattern of violations, including summary executions; excessive use of force; enforced disappearances; rape; torture; cruel, inhumane and degrading treatment; arbitrary arrests and detentions; and looting. In addition, the health, agriculture and education sectors and the economy were severely affected by the post-electoral crisis, leading to the deterioration of the humanitarian situation. Armed confrontations between the Forces nouvelles (FN) and the security forces loyal to Mr. Gbagbo escalated as pro-Ouattara forces moved towards Abidjan, resulting in a major humanitarian crisis with serious human rights implications. On 17 March, President Ouattara signed a decree creating a new army, the Forces républicaines de Côte d'Ivoire (FRCI), which merged the FN and the Forces de défense et de sécurité. Although the presence of FRCI had a positive effect on the security situation, its arrival in most areas in the west and south also coincided with acts of looting, extortion, confiscation of private property, arbitrary arrest and detention, and summary executions. The High Commissioner recommended, among other measures, that the Government address the security gap to protect the civilian population, adopt a zero tolerance policy on serious human rights violations, including sexual violence, and bring to justice any elements of the security forces involved in such violations. The Government should establish or rebuild institutions, including the judiciary, police and correction services, and a national human rights institution, to ensure the protection of human rights; train and sensitize the police, the gendarmerie, the armed forces and the judiciary in dealing with sexual and gender-based violence; ensure that the conditions of detention of Mr. Gbagbo, his wife, former officials and any other detainees were in line with international standards; develop a comprehensive transitional justice strategy; and comprehensively address the root causes of the conflict.

Human Rights Council action. On 17 June [A/HRC/17/2 (res.17/21)], the Human Rights Council called for an immediate end to conflict in Côte d'Ivoire, including violence against women and localized violence, and for the respect for human rights and fundamental freedoms. It urged the Government to end human rights violations, including arbitrary detention and violence against women and children, and address the underlying causes of such violations; ensure that victims of sexual violence received adequate medical and psychological assistance and redress; and bring the perpetrators of such violence to justice. The Council called on UN agencies and other actors to continue to cooperate with the Government to protect human rights and facilitate the safe return of refugees and IDPs. It established, for one year, the mandate of the independent expert on the human rights situation in Côte d'Ivoire and requested the expert to report to the Council in 2012. The Council requested the High Commissioner to report at its eighteenth (2011) session.

Report of High Commissioner. In a September report [A/HRC/18/52] covering events from June to August, submitted pursuant to Council resolution 17/21, the High Commissioner found the security situation to be fragile, especially in Abidjan and the west. Civilians, particularly women and children, remained the primary victims of human rights violations and abuses and continued to face difficulties in accessing the criminal justice system, which was experiencing logistical and human resources challenges as a result of the conflict. Reports of human rights violations by FRCI continued, including extra-judicial and summary executions; torture; inhumane and degrading treatment; sexual and gender-based violence; arbitrary arrests and detention; and violations of economic and social rights through acts of extortion, threats and intimidation. While some corrective action had been taken in the form of arrests, the Government needed to intensify efforts to address human rights violations by FRCI, and was urged to address the impunity of FRCI. The High Commissioner recommended that the Government ensure that the Dialogue, Truth and Reconciliation Commission operated in accordance with international standards; ensure that efforts to end impunity were extended to international crimes and gross human rights violations committed in the country since 19 September 2002; and accelerate the establishment of a professional and inclusive security force. The international community should assist victims, support investigations of human rights violations and ensure that the perpetrators of such violations be held to account, including before the International Criminal Court (ICC).

Report of independent expert. In a later report [A/HRC/19/72], the independent expert on the human rights situation in Côte d'Ivoire, Doudou Diène (Senegal), following two visits to the country (14–25 November and 7–13 December), stated that the security situation had gradually improved since President Ouattara was sworn into office. Legislative elections held on 11 December were well organized, despite polarization stemming from a boycott of the elections by Mr. Gbagbo's party after the former president was transferred to the ICC on 30 November. Remaining challenges included restoring security throughout the country and along its borders; reforming the security sector; restoring the rule of law and justice; combating impunity; promoting reconciliation; strengthening social cohesion; restoring the State's sovereignty and re-establishing its services countrywide; reviving the economy; reducing poverty; and ensuring the protection, return and reintegration of displaced and refugee populations. The independent expert highlighted a continuation of violations of the right to life; acts of torture, degrading and inhuman treatment; arbitrary arrests; rapes; violations of freedom of expression; racketeering and extortion; attacks and violent acts against religious buildings and leaders; and violations of the right to education, health and food. The expert recommended that the Government focus on rebuilding democracy and consolidating the State apparatus; promote human rights and economic and social development; revitalize coexistence; and strengthen cooperation and regional and subregional solidarity. The Government should develop a rural land policy in cooperation with the concerned communities in order to break the link between land and ethnicity, and foster cooperation in land use for shared prosperity. A programme to educate people about human rights should be implemented. The independent expert also recommended that the arms embargo against Côte d'Ivoire be lifted in order to strengthen the effectiveness of the national security system.

Democratic Republic of the Congo

Report of independent experts. In the third joint report of the seven UN experts on the situation in the Democratic Republic of the Congo (DRC) [A/HRC/16/68], submitted in March pursuant to a 2010 Human Rights Council resolution [YUN 2010, p. 767], the experts stated that the human rights situation had not improved since 2008. The DRC had responded to less than 7 per cent of urgent appeals sent by the experts, and although they acknowledged the willingness of the authorities to improve human rights cooperation with the international community, such cooperation needed to be sustained to be fruitful. The experts were of the view that the current mandate given to a group of seven thematic special procedures mandate holders was not the most suitable mechanism to respond to the needs of the country. The experts welcomed the decision by a military court in eastern DRC, which, for the first time, sentenced a high-ranking commander for crimes against humanity for having sent troops to rape, beat and loot the population in Fizi on 1 January. The reporting period was, nevertheless, marked by an increase in violations against human rights defenders and media representatives. Human rights violations by armed groups and members of the national security forces continued, including acts of arbitrary execution, arrest and detention; rape; torture; cruel, inhumane and degrading treatment; looting; and the recruitment of children by the leaders of armed groups.

Communication. In an 8 March note to OHCHR [A/HRC/16/G/6], the DRC requested that its report on the situation of human rights in the country, which was annexed to the note, be published as a document of the sixteenth (2011) session of the Council.

Human Rights Council action. On 25 March [A/HRC/16/2 (res.16/35)], the Human Rights Council noted the commitment of the DRC to cooperate with OHCHR and the special procedures of the Council. It encouraged the Government to continue to ratify international and regional human rights instruments, and to complete the establishment of a national human rights commission. The Council called on the Government to ensure free and fair elections, protecting the rights of all citizens. It invited the High Commissioner to increase and enhance its technical assistance programmes and activities, and to report to the Council in 2012.

Report of High Commissioner. In a later report [A/HRC/19/48], the High Commissioner stated that, despite the Government's efforts to implement some of the recommendations made by OHCHR and other human rights mechanisms, with a view to fighting impunity, strengthening State institutions and improving the human rights situation, there was little improvement in the overall situation in 2011. The structural weaknesses of State institutions, in particular the judicial system and security forces, together with practices of corruption and the presence of armed groups, resulted in impunity and fostered systemic human rights violations. Prisoners were often detained in conditions susceptible to ill-treatment and torture, and high death rates in detention continued. The number of cases of sexual and gender-based violence remained high and several incidents of mass rapes took place during the reporting period. The enjoyment of socioeconomic rights was also impeded. In the run-up to the presidential and legislative elections, political opponents, journalists and human rights defenders continued to face various threats and human rights violations, including arbitrary and illegal arrest and detention. There was some improvement in bringing soldiers, agents and officers of the armed forces and of the national police to justice. The High Commissioner commended the adoption of the law criminalizing torture but noted that other necessary reform initiatives in the penitentiary and judicial systems had either stalled or were poorly implemented. She recommended that the DRC enhance its dialogue and cooperation with international human rights mechanisms.

Guinea

Human Rights Council action. On 25 March [A/HRC/16/2 (res.16/36)], the Human Rights Council noted that the human rights situation in Guinea had improved significantly since the adoption of Council resolution 13/21 [YUN 2010, p. 768]. It invited the authorities to pursue their efforts to implement the recommendations of the international commission of inquiry [YUN 2009, p. 230] relating to combating impunity; protecting the victims of acts of violence; the reform of the justice system and the security sector; the adoption of a national plan to combat discrimination; and the harmonization of national legislation with Security Council resolution 1820(2008) [YUN 2008, p. 1265] on violence against women and girls. The High Commissioner was invited to report to the Council in 2012.

Report of High Commissioner. In a later report [A/HRC/19/49], the High Commissioner stated that in 2011, the Government took steps towards implementing the recommendations made in her previous report [YUN 2010, p. 768], including on security sector reform. Nevertheless, reports continued to allege human rights violations, such as arbitrary arrest and detention, harassment and threats against human rights defenders, and breaches of the right to the freedoms of assembly and association. Most of the allegations of human rights violations were attributed to the security forces. The Government made progress towards launching a transitional justice process but major shortcomings remained in the follow-up to human rights violations. In particular, the Government's commitment to prioritize the fight against impunity had not been addressed, as illustrated by the slow rate of prosecution of the presumed authors of crimes against humanity committed during the events of 28 September 2009 [YUN 2009, p. 229]. The High Commissioner recommended that the Government combat impunity, and investigate and hold accountable the perpetrators of human rights violations. It should establish transitional justice mechanisms, in compliance with international human rights norms; establish a national human rights institution; develop close cooperation with civil society organizations, including women's organizations and victims' associations; accelerate the reform of the judiciary; ensure the integration of human rights into security sector reform; and increase its cooperation with international human rights mechanisms. The international community should provide adequate financial support to enable the Government to create and operationalize the proposed national human rights commission, and provide the necessary assistance to reduce poverty and improve the realization of economic, social and cultural rights.

Libya

Human Rights Council special session

In a 22 February letter [A/HRC/S-15/1], Hungary, on behalf of 51 other member States and observers of the Human Rights Council, requested the convening of a special session of the Council on 25 February to address the human rights situation in the Libyan Arab Jamahiriya.

Human Rights Council action. The Council, at its fifteenth special session, held on 25 February [A/HRC/S-15/1 (res. S-15/1)], condemned the gross and systematic human rights violations committed in Libya, including indiscriminate armed attacks against civilians, extrajudicial killings, arbitrary arrests, detention and torture of peaceful demonstrators. It called on the Government to protect its population; end human rights violations; stop attacks against civilians; and fully respect human rights and fundamental freedoms, including freedom of expression and assembly. The Council called for the release of arbitrarily detained persons and the cessation of intimidation, persecution and arbitrary arrests of individuals, including lawyers, human rights defenders and journalists. It urged the authorities to ensure the safety of civilians; refrain from any reprisals against people who took part in demonstrations; facilitate the departure of foreign nationals wishing to leave the country; allow the provision of humanitarian assistance to those in need; and cease the blocking of public access to the Internet and telecommunication networks. The Council called for an inclusive national dialogue aimed at systemic changes responding to the will of the Libyan people and the promotion and protection of their human rights. It called on the authorities to guarantee access to human rights and humanitarian organizations, including human rights monitors. The Council decided to dispatch an independent international commission of inquiry to investigate alleged violations of international human rights law in Libya, to establish the facts and circumstances of violations and of the crimes perpetrated, and to report to the Council at its seventeenth (2011) session. It called on the authorities to cooperate fully with the commission. The High Commissioner was asked to provide an oral update to the Council at its sixteenth session and submit a follow-up report to the seventeenth session. The Council recommended that the General Assembly, in view of the gross human rights violations by the Libyan authorities, consider the application of the measures concerning the suspension of the rights of membership in the Council foreseen in Assembly resolution 60/251 [YUN 2006, p. 757].

General Assembly action. By **resolution 65/265** of 1 March (see p. 605), the General Assembly suspended Libya's rights of membership in the Human Rights Council.

Follow-up to special session

On 11 March [A/HRC/16/2], the Human Rights Council President announced the members of the International Commission of Inquiry appointed to investigate alleged violations of international human rights law in Libya. On 14 March, the Deputy High Commissioner presented an update on the human rights situation in Libya, as requested by the Council in resolution S-15/1 (see above).

Report of International Commission of Inquiry. The International Commission of Inquiry to investigate alleged violations of international human rights law in Libya stated in its report to the Council [A/HRC/17/44] that it considered violations committed before, during and after the demonstrations witnessed in a number of cities in February. In the light of the armed conflict that developed in late February (see p. 266) and continued during the Commission's operations, the Commission looked into violations of human rights law as well as the relevant provisions of international humanitarian law, the *lex specialis* that applied during armed conflict. It also considered events in the light of international criminal law. It met with over 350 people during its field missions, including medical staff and patients in hospitals, those detained and persons displaced either within Libya or in transit points or refugee camps outside the country. The Commission called on the Government to cease acts of violence against civilians; investigate alleged violations, in particular cases of extrajudicial, summary or arbitrary executions, disappearances and torture; release unconditionally all people held as a result of participation in peaceful demonstrations; reveal the names of all people in custody to relieve the suffering of the relatives of the disappeared; grant reparations to the victims or their families; ensure unrestricted access to places of detention for humanitarian and human rights organizations; and bring laws and policies into conformity with international human rights standards. The National Transitional Council should ensure the implementation of applicable international humanitarian and international human rights law; investigate alleged violations; grant reparations to victims or their families; and ensure unrestricted access to places of detention. The Commission recommended that the Council extend the Commission's mandate or establish a mechanism with the ability to continue the investigations into the human rights and humanitarian law situations for one year.

Human Rights Council action. On 17 June [A/HRC/17/2 (res. 17/17)], the Human Rights Council condemned the deterioration of the human rights situation in Libya since February, including ongoing gross and systematic human rights violations, in particular indiscriminate armed attacks against civilians, extrajudicial killings, enforced disappearances, arbitrary detention, torture and sexual violence against women and children. It expressed concern at the arbitrary detention and killing of civilians, including human rights defenders, migrants and journalists; and reiterated its call on the authorities to cease all violations of human rights, protect its population, release all those arbitrarily detained and ensure unimpeded humanitarian access. It urged the authorities to take steps to ensure the safety of foreign nationals. The Council reiterated its call for a national dialogue aimed at systemic changes responding to the will of all Libyan people and at the promotion and protection of their human rights. It urged all parties to ensure the implementation of the recommendations contained in the report of the Commission of Inquiry and called on the authorities to cooperate fully with the Commission and all international human rights bodies and mechanisms. It extended the Commission's mandate and requested it to continue its work, provide an oral update to the Council at its eighteenth (2011) session, and a final report in 2012.

On 29 September [A/HRC/18/2 (res. 18/9)], the Human Rights Council welcomed commitments made by Libya to uphold its obligations under international human rights law, to promote and protect human rights, democracy and the rule of law, and to cooperate with international human rights mechanisms. It recommended that the General Assembly lift the suspension of the rights of membership of Libya at its current session.

General Assembly action. By **resolution 66/11** of 18 November (see p. 606), the Assembly restored the rights of membership of Libya in the Human Rights Council.

(For more information on the political and security situation in Libya, see p. 266.)

Somalia

Human Rights Council action. On 17 June [A/HRC/17/2 (res. 17/25)], the Human Rights Council expressed its concern at the human rights and humanitarian situation in Somalia; condemned and called for the cessation of the human rights abuses perpetrated against the civilian population by the Al-Shabaab insurgent group and its affiliates; called on Somalia to fulfil its obligations under international human rights and humanitarian law; and urged all parties to assist in effecting unhindered humanitarian access by opening up humanitarian corridors and spaces. The Council called on the Transitional Federal Government, and encouraged the African Union Mission in Somalia (AMISOM), to provide their security forces with training in international human rights and humanitarian law, with international support. The Government and its subnational authorities were encouraged to implement the recommendations presented during the session of the Working Group on the Universal Periodic Review (see p. 611). The Council extended the mandate of the independent expert on the situation of human rights in Somalia for one year, and requested him to report in 2012.

Report of independent expert. In an August report [A/HRC/18/48], the independent expert on the situation of human rights in Somalia, Shamsul Bari (Bangladesh), stated that drought, conflict and a denial of humanitarian assistance had resulted in a declaration of famine in two regions of south-central Somalia. Apart from drought and famine, the armed conflict between Islamist insurgents and the Transitional Federal Government, supported by AMISOM, continued to cause deaths and injury to the civilian population, due mainly to indiscriminate shelling and firing in urban areas, and suicide and improvised explosive attacks by Al-Shabaab. Poor command and control over Government forces and the loose integration of soldiers within militia and clan-based affiliations led to violence. Al-Shabaab continued to perpetrate serious violations of humanitarian and human rights law, including summary executions of civilians associated with the Government, unlawful arrest and detention, and acts amounting to torture and other inhumane, cruel and degrading practices. The widespread and systematic recruitment and use of children in armed conflict also continued. The weakness of the structures designed to administer justice, including law enforcement and the protection of human rights, continued to impede progress towards the establishment of rule-of-law mechanisms. Journalists continued to suffer injuries, and were subjected to arbitrary and unlawful arrests, threats and other forms of intimidation. Domestic and sexual violence, as well as harmful traditional practices, such as female genital mutilation, were reported across Somalia. In Somaliland, relative stability and functioning institutions permitted some positive developments. In January, the President promulgated an act establishing the Somaliland National Human Rights Commission. Somaliland also launched a five-year justice strategy to address its shortcomings in an open and cooperative relationship with the international community.

The independent expert recommended that the Government establish appropriate mechanisms to communicate with the Somali people on a regular basis; establish a national human rights commission; strengthen policy measures related to human rights, in line with the road map of the universal periodic review (see p. 612); ratify the core human rights conventions; take advantage of the constitution-making process; and adopt a human rights-based approach to security sector reform. The international community should contribute the necessary funds to the Government to avert further disaster related to drought and famine.

Sudan

Communication. In a 17 August letter [S/2011/522], the Sudan transmitted to the Security Council its comments on the thirteenth report of the High Commissioner on the situation of human rights in the Sudan, entitled "Preliminary report on violations of international human rights and humanitarian law in Southern Kordofan from 5 to 30 June 2011".

Reports of independent expert. In an August report [A/HRC/18/40], submitted pursuant to Council resolution 15/27 [YUN 2010, p. 770], the independent expert on the situation of human rights in the Sudan, Mohamed Chande Othman (United Republic of Tanzania), reviewed developments from September 2010 to June 2011. The independent expert visited the Sudan from 6 to 13 March and from 31 May to 8 June. He commended the Sudan and South Sudan for efforts to ensure a credible and peaceful referendum for the self-determination of South Sudan, which resulted in the independence of South Sudan on 9 July (see p. 196). Throughout the reporting period there were widespread allegations of arbitrary arrests and detention, torture, and lack of access to detention facilities, perpetrated by the national security services. The human rights situation in Darfur remained precarious, with continuing fighting and breaches of human rights and international humanitarian law by the parties to the conflict. Hundreds of thousands of civilians continued to suffer the effects of the armed conflict through direct attacks, displacements and limited access to humanitarian assistance. In Abyei, the independent expert noted the destruction of the town since fighting began in May, and the hundreds of thousands of civilians displaced. In Southern Kordofan, where the situation had deteriorated significantly since the outbreak of hostilities in June, the main concern was the welfare and security of civilians trapped in the fighting.

The independent expert recommended that the Sudan continue the review of national laws and reform aspects of the current statutory framework that infringed on political and civil rights and freedoms. The Government should investigate allegations of violations and bring perpetrators to justice. It should ensure that human rights defenders, humanitarian workers, members of the political opposition, journalists and other civil society members were not intimidated, arrested and detained, ill-treated or tortured; that its armed forces respected international human rights and humanitarian law; open dialogue with South Sudan; and guarantee unhindered access to all aid organizations. South Sudan should address impunity by ensuring that allegations of violations of human rights were thoroughly investigated; provide adequate means and resources to institutions responsible for the administration of justice and the rule of law; ensure that the State budget was adequately distributed among key sectors, such as education, health, social services, law enforcement and rule-of-law institutions; and ratify key international human rights treaties and conventions. Regarding Southern Kordofan, the independent expert called on the parties to the conflict to agree to a cessation of hostilities, and provide the United Nations and humanitarian organizations with unhindered access to the areas affected by the violence. The Human Rights Council was called on to order an independent investigation into alleged violations of human rights and humanitarian law during the hostilities in Southern Kordofan with a view to holding perpetrators to account.

In an addendum [A/HRC/18/40/Add.1], the independent expert reported on the status of implementation of the recommendations to the Sudan identified in the first report of the group of experts on the Sudan [YUN 2007, p. 806]. Based on the information received through dialogue with the Government, the independent expert concluded that the Government had not taken any significant steps towards the implementation of most of the recommendations since his previous report to the Council [YUN 2009, p. 758];

he therefore recommended that the Council continue its review process.

Human Rights Council action. On 29 September [A/HRC/18/2 (res. 18/16)], the Human Rights Council expressed its appreciation to the Sudan for its immediate recognition of the State of South Sudan; noted with concern the humanitarian situation in Southern Kordofan and Blue Nile provinces; and called on all parties to end violence and halt clashes. Member States, UN agencies and stakeholders were asked to support the Sudan in improving the human rights situation. The Council urged OHCHR to provide the Sudan with technical support and training; renewed the mandate of the independent expert; and requested the expert to submit a report at its twenty-first (2012) session.

South Sudan

On 29 September [A/HRC/18/2 (res. 18/17)], the Council welcomed South Sudan as a new State and Member of the United Nations. It called on the Government to strengthen cooperation with the United Nations Mission in South Sudan on issues pertaining to the promotion and protection of human rights, and prevent violence; called on Member States, UN agencies and international financial institutions to provide South Sudan with technical assistance and capacity-building to promote respect for human rights; and requested the High Commissioner to report to the Council in 2012.

Tunisia

A wave of protests in Tunisia led to the departure of President Zine El-Abidine Ben Ali on 14 January. Although it was acknowledged that the act of self-immolation of Mohamed Bouazizi on 17 December 2010 sparked the protests, the root causes included decades of repression, corruption, exclusion, denial of rights and injustice. The High Commissioner dispatched an assessment mission to the country from 26 January to 2 February to gain an understanding of human rights challenges and examine the possibilities for the advancement of rights.

The transitional Government, formed on 27 January, took positive action regarding freedom of expression and association; accountability and long-term reform; prisoners' rights; economic and social rights; and the ratification of international human rights treaties. On 10 February, the transitional Government requested the High Commissioner to open an OHCHR office in Tunisia. The mission concluded that human rights were at the root of the Tunisian people's calls for freedom, dignity and social justice. It identified 10 areas that required the attention of international and national actors, particularly the Tunisian authorities, in the process of democratic transition, including: ensuring that governing structures were participatory and inclusive; bringing the constitution in line with international human rights standards; ensuring freedom of expression and association; ensuring accountability for human rights violations; guaranteeing the independence of the commissions on political reform, human rights abuses since 17 December 2010, and corruption; establishing an independent account of events that took place in prisons during the period of unrest and taking remedial measures; adopting an inclusive approach to transitional justice; redressing disparities in living standards and social support structures; ensuring that development policies resulted from participatory processes; and enhancing Tunisia's cooperation with the UN human rights system.

Human Rights Council action. On 24 March [A/HRC/16/2 (res. 16/19)], the Human Rights Council welcomed the political transition in Tunisia and the commitment of the transitional Government to realize fully the universal values of human dignity, liberty, democracy and human rights. It took note of the decision to set up a country office in Tunisia. The Council encouraged the transitional Government to continue to implement the recommendations contained in the assessment mission report and ensure accountability for human rights violations. The UN system was invited to assist the transitional process in Tunisia.

Americas

Bolivia

Report of High Commissioner. The High Commissioner for Human Rights, in a report on the activities of the OHCHR office in Bolivia [A/HRC/19/21/Add.2], stated that the country continued to advance in implementing the reforms envisaged in the 2009 Constitution [YUN 2009, p. 758]. Significant progress was made in developing policies and measures to combat racism and discrimination. State human rights policies, including those pertaining to women's right to health and the right to education, showed positive trends. In October, the first elections of senior members of the judiciary and the Constitutional Court were held peacefully and with broad public participation, as a result of which the bodies reflected intercultural and gender equality. Nevertheless, the crisis in the administration of justice worsened in the period preceding the elections. Implementation of the rights of indigenous peoples stalled with respect to the right to be consulted on administrative or legislative proposals and measures likely to affect them. Several indigenous peoples organized demonstrations demanding respect for their rights. Afro-Bolivians established a national forum representing grass-roots organizations, but limitations on their enjoyment of economic, social and cultural rights persisted. Although the number of cases of lynching declined for the first time in four years, levels of violence against women remained a cause for concern. Isolated cases of excessive use of force by the police, violating victims' right to life or physical integrity, also occurred. The High Commissioner urged the Legislative Assembly to adopt an appropriate legislative framework for protecting women against all forms of violence, including trafficking and femicide. She encouraged the State to draw up and implement a plurinational human rights education plan and urged the Government to guarantee respect for indigenous peoples' right to consultation. The High Commissioner recommended, among other measures, that an impartial investigation be carried out into the human rights violations committed during the police operation against indigenous people marching in defence of the Isiboro Sécure National Park and Indigenous Territory; and that the law establishing a mechanism for the prevention of torture be adopted without delay.

Colombia

Communication. On 25 February [A/HRC/16/G/10], Colombia transmitted to OHCHR its observations on the 2010 report of the High Commissioner [YUN 2010, p. 771].

Report of High Commissioner. In a report on the human rights situation in Colombia [A/HRC/19/21/Add.3], the High Commissioner stated that Colombia pursued legislative and public policy initiatives, condemned human rights violations and took action against corruption and illegal land appropriation. The Government also took steps to address human rights violations of the magnitude of extrajudicial executions and illegal mass wiretapping conducted by intelligence agencies. A significant number of human rights and international humanitarian law violations were still committed, however, primarily by illegal armed groups, but also allegedly by State agents. Forced displacement, the recruitment of children and adolescents, and anti-personnel mine incidents continued, and impunity remained a structural problem. Nevertheless, despite isolated acts of violence, local elections were held in October in a calm environment, in contrast to the violence and reports of fraud and corruption during the campaign. OHCHR-Colombia continued to express concern about the number of attacks against human rights defenders; community, social, Afro-Colombian and indigenous leaders; trade union members; and journalists. The High Commissioner urged the Government to designate a focal point to manage the comprehensive protection programme provided for in the Victims' and Land Restitution Law; called on the Attorney General to establish a unit to investigate crimes related to land restitution; and called on the Government to complement land restitution processes with rural development and income-generation programmes. The Attorney General and the police were urged to strengthen mechanisms to investigate attacks against human rights defenders, and prosecute and punish such acts. The High Commissioner urged the Government to improve institutional and operational coordination to dismantle illegal armed groups and prosecute their members and collaborators.

Guatemala

Report of High Commissioner. In a report on OHCHR activities in Guatemala in 2011 [A/HRC/19/21/Add.1], the High Commissioner stated that OHCHR conducted monitoring activities and provided advisory and technical assistance to State institutions and civil society to assist in the implementation of Guatemala's international human rights obligations. She reaffirmed that, with a new Government taking office in January 2012, action should be taken to address long-standing gaps in the enjoyment of human rights, such as reducing the high levels of insecurity, impunity and poverty; putting an end to malnutrition; and eradicating discrimination and violence against women. The High Commissioner called on the Government to implement the recommendations made in previous reports and implement security and justice policies based on the respect for, and guarantee of, all human rights; and to guarantee the continuance of the unit for the analysis of attacks against human rights defenders. She urged Congress to ensure that reforms to the laws on professional careers in the judiciary and the public prosecutor's office were adopted. The High Commissioner reiterated to the Government the need to implement and adequately fund the National Plan for the Prevention of Domestic Violence and Violence against Women. Guatemala was urged to revert the patterns of discrimination and exclusion that affected indigenous peoples; promote a sustainable and inclusive rural development policy to guarantee food security; and implement a comprehensive and progressive tax reform to enable an expansion of fiscal resources, social expenditure and redistribution.

Haiti

Report of independent expert. In April [A/HRC/17/42], the independent expert on the situation of human rights in Haiti, Michel Forst (France), in response to Human Rights Council President's statement PRST/15/1 [YUN 2010, p. 772], reported on the human rights situation in Haiti during the period from March 2010 to March 2011. He drew the attention of Haiti and the international community to the lack of any strategy to deal with displaced persons. Since the beginning of the humanitarian crisis following the 2010 earthquake [YUN 2010, p. 916], the United Nations and national and international human rights organizations had reported on the phenomenon of domestic and inter-family violence, the role of gangs operating inside and around camps for internally displaced persons, and the impunity of perpetrators of violence against women. The independent expert also considered the situation of child victims of human trafficking in the country and abroad. Children continued to face the threats of abduction, illegal adoption and sexual violence, and cases of deportation or forcible return of Haitians from several countries in the region were documented. Since the outbreak of the cholera epidemic in October 2010 [YUN 2010, p. 327], at least 45 people had been lynched by mobs accusing them of practising witchcraft to spread the disease. The independent expert recommended that a study on the lack of reliable data on violence against women be undertaken to identify trends and verify figures on the problem. Illegal children's homes should be monitored and steps taken to close down facilities that failed to meet legal requirements. Action should be taken to combat child abduction, illegal adoption, sexual violence against children, and the use of children as household servants. Specialized care should be provided to people with spinal cord injuries and buildings should be made accessible to persons with disabilities. The lynching of cholera victims and people accused of witchcraft should be stopped; a strategy to curb the spread of unofficial camps should be adopted; and lighting should be provided throughout the camps. Forced returns of Haitians, where unavoidable, should be carried out in observance of legal norms and should not further burden the country. Regarding State institutions, the independent expert recommended that the Supreme Council of the Judiciary be established and supplied with trained staff and funding. The national system of legal aid should continue; initiatives dealing with prison overcrowding and ageing infrastructure should be strengthened; the provision of prison meals should be guaranteed; and convicted persons serving prison sentences and persons in pretrial detention should be kept physically apart.

Human Rights Council action. In a 30 September statement [A/HRC/18/2 (PRST 18/1)], the Council President extended the mandate of the independent expert on the situation of human rights in Haiti until 2012.

On 24 December (**decision 66/557**), the General Assembly decided that the agenda item on the situation of democracy and human rights in Haiti would remain for consideration during its resumed sixty-sixth (2012) session.

Asia

Afghanistan

Report of High Commissioner. In a report on the human rights situation in Afghanistan and technical assistance achievements in human rights [A/HRC/19/47], the High Commissioner stated that conflict-related violence continued to claim the lives of numerous civilians and increased displacement. Protection of civilians remained a crucial human rights issue, particularly with the transition of lead security responsibility from international forces to the Afghan National Security Forces, which began on 20 July 2011 and was scheduled to be completed by the end of 2014. Despite some gains in the education and health sectors, impunity and poor governance, characterized by corruption and an inability to provide essential services, disappointed the aspirations of the vast majority of Afghans. Violence against women and girls, including sexual violence and harmful traditional practices, remained widespread. Arbitrary detention and the lack of respect for due process continued to be major concerns. Impunity was also widespread and accountability for human rights violations was weak, affecting the Government's commitment to promote transitional justice. Capacity-building of national human rights institutions and civil society organizations was key to the development of human rights protection mechanisms. The High Commissioner recommended, among other measures, that the National Security Forces and international forces take all precautions to prevent and minimize the loss of civilian life, injury to civilians and damage to civilian objects. The Taliban and other anti-Government elements should prevent civilian casualties by complying with international law. The Government should ensure prosecution of all serious crimes of violence against women; promote an inclusive peace process; reaffirm its commitment to justice and combating impunity; uphold human rights values in all negotiations and efforts aimed at achieving reconciliation and lasting peace; investigate reports of torture and ill treatment at detention facilities; and prosecute and punish public officers found responsible for committing or condoning such practices.

Cambodia

Report of Special Rapporteur. In an August report [A/HRC/18/46], the Special Rapporteur on the human rights situation in Cambodia, Surya Subedi (Nepal), expressed concern about various human rights issues, especially freedom of expression and land and housing rights. Charges of incitement, defamation and dissemination of disinformation were brought against human rights defenders, land rights activists and members of communities defending their land and housing rights in the face of eviction. Cambodia had enacted laws to protect human rights but was lagging behind in implementation, and many laws fell short of the standards required by the rule-of-law principle. The Special Rapporteur made recommendations aimed at strengthening Parliament and enhancing the effectiveness of the Constitutional Council. Parliament should review the Penal Code to ensure its compliance with the permissible limitation to freedom of expression under international human rights law, and the judiciary should interpret the Code in line with human rights standards of freedom of expression. The Government was urged to address the pattern of violence by facilitating dialogue among potentially affected communities, authorities and private enterprise.

Communication. In a 21 September note [A/HRC/18/G/5], Cambodia transmitted to OHCHR its comments on the Special Rapporteur's report.

Report of Secretary-General. In a September report [A/HRC/18/47] issued in response to a 2010 Human Rights Council resolution [YUN 2010, p. 773], the Secretary-General described the role and achievements of OHCHR in Cambodia in assisting the Government and people of Cambodia in the promotion and protection of human rights during the period from July 2010 to June 2011. He stated that the legal and institutional framework of Cambodia had developed further, but the human rights situation remained uneven and in some quarters was regressing. The Government's sensitivity to criticism, particularly on human rights issues, stifled debate on issues of national importance. Disputes related to land, which seemed to be increasing, represented a major human rights challenge. OHCHR strengthened its focus on the rights to access information and on press freedom. The ability of individuals and groups to peacefully exercise their rights to freedom of expression, assembly and association, however, continued to be challenged. Under its Land and Housing Rights programme, OHCHR worked with all stakeholders to monitor, promote and implement the right to an adequate standard of living and housing, prevent forced eviction, and realize security of tenure. Nevertheless, demonstrations and protests in the capital and provinces were common, as a growing marginalized and dispossessed sector of the population attempted to take part in the decision-making process. The complexities of the legal framework and procedural requirements put indigenous communities at risk of land confiscation and of losing their livelihoods to deforestation. Despite the Government's legal and judicial reform strategy, progress towards reforming the court system, strengthening the independence of institutions and promoting a transparent legislative process remained slow.

Human Rights Council action. On 30 September [A/HRC/18/2 (res.18/25)], the Human Rights Council expressed its concern about some areas of the human rights situation in Cambodia and urged the Government to strengthen its efforts to establish the rule of law, continue its judicial reform work, combat corruption, and enhance efforts to resolve land ownership and tenure issues in a fair and open manner. The Council extended by two years the mandate of the Special Rapporteur, and requested the Rapporteur and the Secretary-General to report to the Council in 2012 and 2013.

Democratic People's Republic of Korea

Communication. The Democratic People's Republic of Korea (DPRK), in a 19 January letter to the Human Rights Council [A/HRC/16/G/2], rejected categorically the Special Rapporteur on the situation of human rights in the DPRK as a product of political confrontation and a plot against the country.

Report of Special Rapporteur. In February [A/HRC/16/58], the Special Rapporteur, Marzuki Darusman (Indonesia), submitted a report highlighting the deterioration of the human rights situation in the country, covering the second half of 2010 and the beginning of 2011. He noted with concern that the imposition of restrictions on the media and punishment of any form of association and expression deemed hostile to the Government seemed to continue. Human rights violations were committed in all correctional centres, and it was claimed that abuses, including deaths, were rampant. The Special Rapporteur emphasized the need for the DPRK to protect and promote human rights, focusing on freedom of movement, expression and opinion; the death penalty; torture; and cruel, inhumane and degrading treatment. He urged all parties to reconvene the six-party talks—involving China, the DPRK, Japan, the Republic of Korea, the Russian Federation and the United States [YUN 2007, p. 380]—to address issues such as regional peace and security and to create an environment of progress on human rights. The resumption of dialogue between the DPRK and the Republic of Korea was also encouraged. The Special Rapporteur called on the DPRK to recognize the need to cooperate with OHCHR to advance human rights policies and programmes. DPRK authorities were urged to address food scarcity by revisiting the public distribution system, channelling or reallocating financial resources of sectors that benefited the standard of living. The authorities should also address unresolved cases of abduction comprehensively, including accountability for agents responsible for abductions.

Human Rights Council action. On 24 March [A/HRC/16/2 (res.16/8)], the Human Rights Council, by a recorded vote of 30 to 3, with 11 abstentions, expressed concern at the ongoing grave, widespread and systematic human rights violations in the DPRK; extended the Special Rapporteur's mandate for one year; and urged the Government to cooperate fully with the Special Rapporteur and permit him unrestricted access to visit the country, and to ensure rapid, unimpeded access for humanitarian assistance. The Special Rapporteur was invited to submit regular reports to the Council and the General Assembly.

Report of Special Rapporteur. In August [A/66/322], the Special Rapporteur submitted a report on the human rights situation in the DPRK, focusing on asylum seekers and trafficking of persons, food security, the health system, freedom of expression and political prisons. Available statistics indicated that between January and April, close to 870 asylum seekers crossed over to Thailand after travelling through a number of countries in the region. While most asylum seekers were exploited by traffickers, women and children were particularly vulnerable. Women who were trafficked were often exposed to violence. In some cases, women had been sold to nationals of transit countries as sex slaves to work in brothels or bars, or forced to marry in order to avoid deportation. The Special Rapporteur urged the authorities to take action to prevent violence against women and hold accountable those responsible for such violence. He appealed to neighbouring countries to respect the rights of refugees, particularly the principle of non-refoulement and the human rights of asylum seekers and irregular immigrants. The Rapporteur called on the Government to provide greater space for independent media, free access to the Internet and freedom of movement by journalists. He urged the Government to introduce more extensive food security policies. The DPRK was called on to pay increased attention to providing adequate nutrition and health care to women and children; and release political prisoners, particularly those whose imprisonment was based on their association with their relatives. The Rapporteur reiterated his offer to provide assistance in improving the human rights situation in the country and urged the DPRK to accept the offer of OHCHR to engage in technical cooperation.

Report of Secretary-General. In a September report [A/66/343], the Secretary-General provided an overview of the deteriorating human rights and humanitarian situation in the country from August 2010 to August 2011. The report highlighted efforts by the Government in providing humanitarian assistance with the help of various UN offices, including the World Food Programme, the United Nations Population Fund, the Food and Agriculture Organization of the United Nations, the United Nations Children's Fund and the United Nations Development Programme. The Secretary-General urged the Government to secure the rights to food, water, sanitation and health, as well as take measures to respect the people's right to freedom of thought, conscience and religion, assembly, opinion and expression. The Government was called on to submit outstanding reports to treaty bodies on the implementation of the International Covenants on Civil and Political Rights, and on Economic, Social and Cultural Rights [YUN 1966, p. 406], and the Convention on the Elimination of All Forms of Discrimination against Women [YUN 1979, p. 889]. The Secretary-General urged the DPRK to engage with OHCHR and use its expertise to improve its human rights record. He called on the DPRK to communicate its position on the conclusions and recommendations of the universal periodic review to the Human Rights Council. The Secretary-General urged the Government to provide access to the Special Rapporteur and encouraged it to establish an independent national human rights institution. He also urged the international community to provide humanitarian aid, especially food and medical assistance, to the people of the DPRK.

GENERAL ASSEMBLY ACTION

On 19 December [meeting 89], the General Assembly, on the recommendation of the Third (Social, Humanitarian and Cultural) Committee [A/66/462/Add.3], adopted **resolution 66/174** by recorded vote (123-16-51) [agenda item 69 (c)].

Situation of human rights in the Democratic People's Republic of Korea

The General Assembly,

Reaffirming that States Members of the United Nations have an obligation to promote and protect human rights and fundamental freedoms and to fulfil the obligations that they have undertaken under the various international instruments,

Mindful that the Democratic People's Republic of Korea is a party to the International Covenant on Civil and Political Rights, the International Covenant on Economic, Social and Cultural Rights, the Convention on the Rights of the Child and the Convention on the Elimination of All Forms of Discrimination against Women,

Acknowledging the participation of the Democratic People's Republic of Korea in the universal periodic review process, expressing serious concern at the refusal of the Government of the Democratic People's Republic of Korea to articulate its position as to which recommendations included in the outcome report of its universal periodic review, adopted in March 2010, enjoy its support, and regretting the continuing lack of action by the Democratic People's Republic of Korea to implement the recommendations contained in the report,

Recalling the concluding observations of the treaty-monitoring bodies under the four treaties to which the Democratic People's Republic of Korea is a party,

Noting with appreciation the collaboration established between the Government of the Democratic People's

Republic of Korea and the United Nations Children's Fund and the World Health Organization in order to improve the health situation in the country, and the collaboration established with the United Nations Children's Fund in order to improve the quality of education for children,

Noting the decision on the resumption, on a modest scale, of the activities of the United Nations Development Programme in the Democratic People's Republic of Korea, and encouraging the engagement of the Government with the international community to ensure that the programmes benefit the persons in need of assistance,

Noting also the cooperation established between the Government of the Democratic People's Republic of Korea and the World Food Programme, the United Nations Children's Fund and the Food and Agriculture Organization of the United Nations for the purpose of conducting a rapid food security assessment in the country, as well as the letter of understanding signed with the World Food Programme, and emphasizing the importance of providing further access to all United Nations entities,

Recalling its resolutions 60/173 of 16 December 2005, 61/174 of 19 December 2006, 62/167 of 18 December 2007, 63/190 of 18 December 2008, 64/175 of 18 December 2009 and 65/225 of 21 December 2010, Commission on Human Rights resolutions 2003/10 of 16 April 2003, 2004/13 of 15 April 2004 and 2005/11 of 14 April 2005, Human Rights Council decision 1/102 of 30 June 2006 and Council resolutions 7/15 of 27 March 2008, 10/16 of 26 March 2009, 13/14 of 25 March 2010 and 16/8 of 24 March 2011, and mindful of the need for the international community to strengthen its coordinated efforts aimed at achieving the implementation of those resolutions,

Taking note of the report of the Special Rapporteur on the situation of human rights in the Democratic People's Republic of Korea, regretting that he still has not been allowed to visit the country and that he received no cooperation from the authorities of the Democratic People's Republic of Korea, and taking note also of the comprehensive report of the Secretary-General on the situation of human rights in the Democratic People's Republic of Korea submitted in accordance with resolution 65/225,

Noting the importance of the inter-Korean dialogue, which could contribute to the improvement of the human rights and humanitarian situation in the country,

Noting with regret that the reunion of separated families across the border, which is an urgent humanitarian concern of the entire Korean people, has been halted, and hoping that it will be resumed as early as possible and that necessary arrangements for further reunions on a larger scale and a regular basis will be made between the Democratic People's Republic of Korea and the Republic of Korea,

1. *Expresses its very serious concern* at:

(*a*) The persistence of continuing reports of systematic, widespread and grave violations of civil, political, economic, social and cultural rights in the Democratic People's Republic of Korea, including:

(i) Torture and other cruel, inhuman or degrading treatment or punishment, including inhuman conditions of detention, public executions, extrajudicial and arbitrary detention; the absence of due process and the rule of law, including fair trial guarantees and an independent judiciary; the imposition of the death penalty for political and religious reasons; collective punishments; and the existence of a large number of prison camps and the extensive use of forced labour;

(ii) Limitations imposed on every person who wishes to move freely within the country and travel abroad, including the punishment of those who leave or try to leave the country without permission, or their families, as well as punishment of persons who are returned;

(iii) The situation of refugees and asylum seekers expelled or returned to the Democratic People's Republic of Korea and sanctions imposed on citizens of the Democratic People's Republic of Korea who have been repatriated from abroad, leading to punishments of internment, torture, cruel, inhuman or degrading treatment or the death penalty, and in this regard strongly urges all States to respect the fundamental principle of non-refoulement, to treat those who seek refuge humanely and to ensure unhindered access to the United Nations High Commissioner for Refugees and his Office, with a view to protecting the human rights of those who seek refuge, and once again urges States parties to comply with their obligations under the 1951 Convention relating to the Status of Refugees and the 1967 Protocol thereto in relation to refugees from the Democratic People's Republic of Korea who are covered by those instruments;

(iv) All-pervasive and severe restrictions on the freedoms of thought, conscience, religion, opinion and expression, peaceful assembly and association, the right to privacy and equal access to information, by such means as the persecution of individuals exercising their freedom of opinion and expression, and their families, and the right of everyone to take part in the conduct of public affairs, directly or through freely chosen representatives, of his or her country;

(v) The violations of economic, social and cultural rights, which have led to severe malnutrition, widespread health problems and other hardship for the population in the Democratic People's Republic of Korea, in particular for persons belonging to particularly exposed groups, inter alia, women, children and the elderly;

(vi) Continuing violations of the human rights and fundamental freedoms of women, in particular the trafficking of women for the purpose of prostitution or forced marriage and the subjection of women to human smuggling, forced abortions, gender-based discrimination, including in the economic sphere, and gender-based violence and continuing impunity for such violence;

(vii) Continuing reports of violations of the human rights and fundamental freedoms of children, in particular the continued lack of access to basic economic, social and cultural rights for many children, and in this regard notes the particularly vulnerable situation faced by, inter alia, returned or repatriated children, street children, children with disabilities, children whose parents are detained, children living in detention or in institutions and children in conflict with the law;

(viii) Continuing reports of violations of the human rights and fundamental freedoms of persons with disabilities, especially on the use of collective camps and of coercive measures that target the rights of persons with disabilities to decide freely and responsibly on the number and spacing of their children;

(ix) Violations of workers' rights, including the right to freedom of association and collective bargaining, the right to strike as defined by the obligations of the Democratic People's Republic of Korea under the International Covenant on Economic, Social and Cultural Rights, and the prohibition of the economic exploitation of children and of any harmful or hazardous work of children as defined by the obligations of the Democratic People's Republic of Korea under the Convention on the Rights of the Child;

(b) The continued refusal of the Government of the Democratic People's Republic of Korea to recognize the mandate of the Special Rapporteur on the situation of human rights in the Democratic People's Republic of Korea or to extend cooperation to him, despite the renewal of the mandate by the Human Rights Council in its resolutions 7/15, 10/16, 13/14 and 16/8;

(c) The continued refusal of the Government of the Democratic People's Republic of Korea to articulate which recommendations enjoyed its support following its universal periodic review by the Human Rights Council or to express its commitment to their implementation, and regrets the lack of actions taken to date to implement the recommendations contained in the final outcome;

2. *Reiterates its very serious concern* at unresolved questions of international concern relating to abductions in the form of enforced disappearance, which violates the human rights of nationals of other sovereign countries, and in this regard strongly calls upon the Government of the Democratic People's Republic of Korea urgently to resolve these questions, including through existing channels, in a transparent manner, including by ensuring the immediate return of abductees;

3. *Expresses its very deep concern* at the precarious humanitarian situation, including a serious deterioration in the availability of and access to food, in the country, partly as a result of frequent natural disasters, compounded by structural weaknesses in agricultural production resulting in significant shortages of food, and the increasing State restrictions on the cultivation and trade in foodstuffs, as well as the prevalence of chronic and acute malnutrition, particularly among the most vulnerable groups, pregnant women, infants and the elderly, which, despite some progress, continues to affect the physical and mental development of a significant proportion of children, and urges the Government of the Democratic People's Republic of Korea, in this regard, to take preventive and remedial action, cooperating where necessary with international donor agencies and in accordance with international standards for monitoring humanitarian assistance;

4. *Commends* the Special Rapporteur for the activities undertaken so far and for his continued efforts in the conduct of his mandate despite the limited access to information;

5. *Strongly urges* the Government of the Democratic People's Republic of Korea to respect fully all human rights and fundamental freedoms and, in this regard:

(a) To immediately put an end to the systematic, widespread and grave violations of human rights mentioned above, inter alia, by implementing fully the measures set out in the above-mentioned resolutions of the General Assembly, the Commission on Human Rights and the Human Rights Council, and the recommendations addressed to the Democratic People's Republic of Korea by the Human Rights Council in the context of the universal periodic review and the United Nations special procedures and treaty bodies;

(b) To protect its inhabitants, address the issue of impunity and ensure that those responsible for violations of human rights are brought to justice before an independent judiciary;

(c) To tackle the root causes leading to refugee outflows and prosecute those who exploit refugees by human smuggling, trafficking and extortion, while not criminalizing the victims, and to ensure that citizens of the Democratic People's Republic of Korea expelled or returned to the Democratic People's Republic of Korea are able to return in safety and dignity, are humanely treated and are not subjected to any kind of punishment;

(d) To extend its full cooperation to the Special Rapporteur, including by granting him full, free and unimpeded access to the Democratic People's Republic of Korea, and to other United Nations human rights mechanisms so that a full needs assessment of the human rights situation may be made;

(e) To engage in technical cooperation activities in the field of human rights with the United Nations High Commissioner for Human Rights and her Office, as pursued by the High Commissioner in recent years, with a view to improving the situation of human rights in the country, and strive to implement the recommendations made in the universal periodic review by the Human Rights Council;

(f) To engage in cooperation with the International Labour Organization with a view to significantly improving workers' rights;

(g) To continue and reinforce its cooperation with United Nations humanitarian agencies;

(h) To ensure full, safe and unhindered access to humanitarian aid and take measures to allow humanitarian agencies to secure its impartial delivery to all parts of the country on the basis of need in accordance with humanitarian principles, as it pledged to do, and to ensure access to adequate food and implement more effective food security policies, including through sustainable agriculture, sound food production distribution measures and by allocating more funds to the food sector, and to ensure adequate monitoring of humanitarian assistance;

(i) To improve cooperation with the United Nations country team and development agencies so that they can directly contribute to improving the living conditions of the civilian population, including accelerating progress towards the achievement of the Millennium Development Goals, in accordance with international monitoring and evaluation procedures;

(*j*) To consider ratifying and acceding to remaining international human rights treaties, which would enable a dialogue with the human rights treaty bodies;

6. *Decides* to continue its examination of the situation of human rights in the Democratic People's Republic of Korea at its sixty-seventh session, and to this end requests the Secretary-General to submit a comprehensive report on the situation in the Democratic People's Republic of Korea and requests the Special Rapporteur to continue to report his findings and recommendations.

RECORDED VOTE ON RESOLUTION 66/174:

In favour: Afghanistan, Albania, Andorra, Antigua and Barbuda, Argentina, Australia, Austria, Bahamas, Bahrain, Barbados, Belgium, Belize, Benin, Bhutan, Bosnia and Herzegovina, Botswana, Brazil, Bulgaria, Burundi, Canada, Cape Verde, Central African Republic, Chile, Colombia, Costa Rica, Côte d'Ivoire, Croatia, Cyprus, Czech Republic, Denmark, Djibouti, El Salvador, Eritrea, Estonia, Fiji, Finland, France, Gabon, Gambia, Georgia, Germany, Ghana, Greece, Guatemala, Guinea-Bissau, Haiti, Honduras, Hungary, Iceland, Iraq, Ireland, Israel, Italy, Jamaica, Japan, Jordan, Kazakhstan, Kiribati, Kyrgyzstan, Latvia, Liberia, Libya, Liechtenstein, Lithuania, Luxembourg, Madagascar, Malawi, Maldives, Malta, Marshall Islands, Mauritius, Mexico, Micronesia, Monaco, Montenegro, Morocco, Nauru, Netherlands, New Zealand, Norway, Palau, Panama, Papua New Guinea, Paraguay, Peru, Philippines, Poland, Portugal, Republic of Korea, Republic of Moldova, Romania, Rwanda, Saint Lucia, Samoa, San Marino, Sao Tome and Principe, Saudi Arabia, Serbia, Seychelles, Sierra Leone, Slovakia, Slovenia, Solomon Islands, South Sudan, Spain, Sweden, Switzerland, Tajikistan, Thailand, the former Yugoslav Republic of Macedonia, Timor-Leste, Togo, Tonga, Tunisia, Turkey, Tuvalu, Ukraine, United Arab Emirates, United Kingdom, United Republic of Tanzania, United States, Uruguay, Vanuatu.

Against: Algeria, Belarus, China, Cuba, Democratic People's Republic of Korea, Egypt, Iran, Myanmar, Oman, Russian Federation, Sudan, Syrian Arab Republic, Uzbekistan, Venezuela, Viet Nam, Zimbabwe.

Abstaining: Angola, Armenia, Azerbaijan, Bangladesh, Bolivia, Brunei Darussalam, Burkina Faso, Cambodia, Cameroon, Chad, Comoros, Congo, Democratic Republic of the Congo, Dominica, Dominican Republic, Ecuador, Ethiopia, Grenada, Guinea, Guyana, India, Indonesia, Kenya, Kuwait, Lao People's Democratic Republic, Lesotho, Malaysia, Mali, Mauritania, Mozambique, Namibia, Nepal, Nicaragua, Niger, Nigeria, Pakistan, Qatar, Saint Kitts and Nevis, Saint Vincent and the Grenadines, Senegal, Singapore, Somalia, South Africa, Sri Lanka, Suriname, Swaziland, Trinidad and Tobago, Turkmenistan, Uganda, Yemen, Zambia.

Report of Special Rapporteur. In a later report [A/HRC/19/65], the Special Rapporteur stated that the human rights and humanitarian situation continued to deteriorate in the DPRK. In December, Kim Jong-Un succeeded his father, Kim Jong-il, as the new leader of the country.

Iran

Report of Secretary-General. In response to General Assembly resolution 65/226 [YUN 2010, p. 777], the Secretary-General submitted a March report on the human rights situation in Iran [A/HRC/16/75]. He stated that since his previous report [YUN 2010, p. 776], the situation had been marked by a crackdown on human rights defenders, women's rights activists, journalists and Government opponents. Concerns about torture, arbitrary detentions and unfair trials continued to be raised by UN human rights mechanisms. The Penal Code continued to allow amputation and flogging for a range of crimes, including theft, enmity against God, and certain sexual acts, and adultery was punishable by stoning. Application of the death penalty had increased, including in cases of political prisoners, since the beginning of the year; at least 66 people were executed in January alone. Public executions continued, suggesting that their ban, issued in January 2008, had not been effectively enforced. The age of criminal liability remained discriminatory between girls and boys and was very low by international standards; death sentences for juveniles were reported. Discrimination persisted against minority groups, in some cases amounting to persecution. The rights of the Arab, Azeri, Baloch and Kurdish communities were limited, particularly in the areas of housing, education, freedom of expression and religion, health and employment. Some positive developments were reported, however, including Iran's signing, in September 2010, of the Optional Protocol to the Convention on the Rights of the Child on the involvement of children in armed conflict [YUN 2000, p. 615]; the State's examination before the Committee for the Elimination of Racial Discrimination, in August 2010; and the conduct of a judicial colloquium together with OHCHR, in December 2010.

Human Rights Council action. On 24 March [A/HRC/16/2 (res.16/9)], the Human Rights Council, by a recorded vote of 22 to 7, with 14 abstentions, appointed a Special Rapporteur on the situation of human rights in Iran, to report to the General Assembly at its sixty-sixth (2011) session and to the Council in 2012. It called on Iran to cooperate fully with the Special Rapporteur and to permit access to the country.

Report of Secretary-General. In a September report [A/66/361], the Secretary-General highlighted areas of continuing concern for human rights in Iran, and noted reports of the increased number of executions, amputations, arbitrary arrests and detentions; unfair trials; torture and ill-treatment; and, in particular, a crackdown on human rights activists, lawyers, journalists and opposition activists. He encouraged Iran to address the concerns highlighted in the report and to guarantee freedom of expression and assembly. He called on Iran to institute a moratorium on executions, with a view to abolishing the death penalty. The Secretary-General expressed his concern at the low rate of replies to communications sent by the special procedures mandate holders alleging serious human rights violations and called on Iran to strengthen its collaboration with the Human Rights Council in that regard.

Report of Special Rapporteur. By a September note [A/66/374], the Secretary-General transmitted to the General Assembly the report of the Special Rapporteur on the situation of human rights in Iran, Ahmed Shaheed (Maldives), submitted in response to Human Rights Council resolution 16/9. The Special Rapporteur, who was appointed by the Council President on 17 June and assumed responsibility for the mandate on 1 August, notified the Secretariat that, owing to his late appointment, he was not in a position to present a substantive report. The report focused instead on his proposed methodology and recent trends in the human rights situation in Iran. The Special Rapporteur stressed the importance of freedom of expression and assembly for a democratic, open society, and encouraged Iran to refrain from repressing dissent. He urged Iran to prevent discrimination against women, as well as religious and ethnic minorities, and expressed concern about the well-being and health of prisoners. The Special Rapporteur requested that he be allowed to visit the country to either substantiate or lay to rest allegations of human rights violations.

GENERAL ASSEMBLY ACTION

On 19 December [meeting 89], the General Assembly, on the recommendation of the Third Committee [A/66/462/Add.3], adopted **resolution 66/175** by recorded vote (89-30-64) [agenda item 69 (c)].

Situation of human rights in the Islamic Republic of Iran

The General Assembly,

Guided by the Charter of the United Nations, as well as the Universal Declaration of Human Rights, the International Covenants on Human Rights and other international human rights instruments,

Recalling its previous resolutions on the situation of human rights in the Islamic Republic of Iran, the most recent of which is resolution 65/226 of 21 December 2010,

1. *Takes note* of the report of the Secretary-General submitted pursuant to resolution 65/226, which highlights further negative developments in the human rights situation in the Islamic Republic of Iran, and the report of the Special Rapporteur on the situation of human rights in the Islamic Republic of Iran submitted pursuant to Human Rights Council resolution 16/9 of 24 March 2011, which notes concern over reports of targeted violence and discrimination against minority groups and alarm at a documented dramatic increase in executions, including secret group executions carried out inside prisons;

2. *Expresses deep concern* at serious ongoing and recurring human rights violations in the Islamic Republic of Iran relating to, inter alia:

(*a*) Torture and cruel, inhuman or degrading treatment or punishment, including flogging and amputations;

(*b*) The continuing high incidence of and dramatic increase in the carrying out of the death penalty in the absence of internationally recognized safeguards, including public executions, notwithstanding a circular from the former head of the judiciary prohibiting public executions, and secret group executions, as well as reports of executions undertaken without the notification of the prisoner's family members or legal counsel;

(*c*) The continuing imposition and carrying out of the death penalty against minors and persons who at the time of their offence were under the age of 18, in violation of the obligations of the Islamic Republic of Iran under the Convention on the Rights of the Child and the International Covenant on Civil and Political Rights;

(*d*) The imposition of the death penalty for crimes that lack a precise and explicit definition, including *moharabeh* (enmity against God), or for crimes that do not qualify as the most serious crimes, in violation of international law;

(*e*) The practice of suspension strangulation as a method of execution, and the fact that persons in prison continue to face sentences of execution by stoning, notwithstanding a circular from the former head of the judiciary prohibiting stoning;

(*f*) The continuing and systematic targeting of human rights defenders, including, inter alia, lawyers, journalists and other media representatives, Internet providers and bloggers, who endure intimidation, interrogation, arrest and arbitrary detention as a result of their activities, noting, in particular, the continued harassment and detention of staff members of the Defenders of Human Rights Centre;

(*g*) Pervasive gender inequality and violence against women, including sexual violence, a continued crackdown on women's human rights defenders, arrests, violent repression and sentencing of women exercising their right to peaceful assembly and increased discrimination against women and girls in law and in practice;

(*h*) Continuing discrimination and other human rights violations, at times amounting to persecution, against persons belonging to ethnic, linguistic or other minorities, including, inter alia, Arabs, Azeris, Baluchis and Kurds and their defenders, noting, in particular, reports of the violent suppression and detention of ethnic Arabs and Azeris, the violent repression of environmental protests in Azeri territory and the high rate of executions of persons belonging to minority groups;

(*i*) Increased persecution and human rights violations against persons belonging to recognized religious minorities, including, inter alia, Christians, Jews, Sufis, Sunni Muslims and Zoroastrians and their defenders, noting, in particular, the widespread arrest and detention of Sufis and evangelical Christians and reports of harsh sentences against Christian pastors;

(*j*) Increased persecution and human rights violations against persons belonging to unrecognized religious minorities, particularly members of the Baha'i faith, including escalating attacks on Baha'is and their defenders, including in State-sponsored media, a significant increase in the number of Baha'is arrested and detained, including the targeted attack on the Baha'i educational institution, the reinstatement of twenty-year sentences against seven Baha'i leaders following deeply flawed legal proceedings, and renewed measures to deny Baha'is employment in the public and private sectors;

(k) The continuing and sustained house arrest of leading opposition figures from the 2009 presidential elections;

(l) Ongoing, systemic and serious restrictions of freedom of peaceful assembly and association and freedom of opinion and expression, including those imposed on the media, political opponents, human rights defenders, lawyers, journalists, Internet providers, Internet users, bloggers, clerics, artists, filmmakers, academics, students, labour leaders and trade unions, from all sectors of Iranian society;

(m) The continuing use of State security forces and Government-directed militias to forcibly disperse Iranian citizens engaged in the peaceful exercise of freedom of expression and freedom of peaceful assembly and association;

(n) Severe limitations and restrictions on the right to freedom of thought, conscience, religion or belief, including arbitrary arrest, indefinite detention and lengthy jail sentences, for those exercising this right, and the arbitrary demolition of places of worship and burial;

(o) Persistent failure to uphold due process of law, and violations of the rights of detainees, including defendants held without charge or held incommunicado, the systematic and arbitrary use of prolonged solitary confinement, the lack of access of detainees to legal representation of their choice, the refusal to consider granting bail to detainees, and the poor conditions of prisons, including the serious overcrowding and poor level of sanitation, as well as persistent reports of detainees being subjected to torture, including rape and other forms of sexual violence, harsh interrogation techniques and the use of pressure exerted upon their relatives and dependants, including through arrest, to obtain false confessions that are then used at trials;

(p) Continuing arbitrary or unlawful interference by State authorities with the privacy of individuals, in particular in relation to private homes, and with their correspondence, including voicemail and e-mail communications, in violation of international law;

3. *Expresses particular concern* at the failure of the Government of the Islamic Republic of Iran to conduct any comprehensive investigation or to launch an accountability process for alleged violations in the period following the presidential elections of 12 June 2009, and reiterates its call upon the Government to launch a process of credible, independent and impartial investigations into reports of human rights violations and to end impunity for such violations;

4. *Calls upon* the Government of the Islamic Republic of Iran to immediately and unconditionally release all those who have been arbitrarily arrested and detained for simply exercising their right to peaceful assembly and participating in peaceful protests about political, economic, environmental or other issues, including the conduct and results of the 2009 presidential elections;

5. *Strongly urges* the Government of the Islamic Republic of Iran to ensure free, fair, transparent and inclusive parliamentary elections in 2012 that reflect the will of the people and are consistent with the Universal Declaration of Human Rights, the International Covenant on Civil and Political Rights and all other relevant human rights instruments to which the State is a party, and calls upon the Government to allow independent observation, including by civil society and candidates, of the electoral process and to allow independent local and international journalists to freely observe and report on the elections as well as subsequent political developments;

6. *Calls upon* the Government of the Islamic Republic of Iran to address the substantive concerns highlighted in the report of the Secretary-General and the specific calls to action found in previous resolutions of the General Assembly, and to respect fully its human rights obligations, in law and in practice, in particular:

(a) To eliminate, in law and in practice, amputations, flogging and other forms of torture and other cruel, inhuman or degrading treatment or punishment;

(b) To abolish, in law and in practice, public executions and other executions carried out in the absence of respect for internationally recognized safeguards;

(c) To abolish, pursuant to its obligations under article 37 of the Convention on the Rights of the Child and article 6 of the International Covenant on Civil and Political Rights, executions of minors and persons who at the time of their offence were under the age of 18;

(d) To abolish the use of stoning and suspension strangulation as methods of execution;

(e) To eliminate, in law and in practice, all forms of discrimination and other human rights violations against women and girls;

(f) To eliminate, in law and in practice, all forms of discrimination and other human rights violations against persons belonging to religious, ethnic, linguistic or other minorities, recognized or otherwise, to refrain from monitoring individuals on the basis of their religious beliefs, and to ensure that the access of minorities to education and employment is on a par with that of all Iranians;

(g) To eliminate discrimination against, and exclusion of, women and members of certain groups, including members of the Baha'i faith, regarding access to higher education, and to eliminate the criminalization of efforts to provide higher education to Baha'i youth denied access to Iranian universities;

(h) To implement, inter alia, the 1996 report of the Special Rapporteur on religious intolerance, in which he recommended ways in which the Islamic Republic of Iran could emancipate the Baha'i community, and to accord the seven Baha'i leaders held since 2008 the due process of law and rights that they are constitutionally guaranteed, including the right to adequate legal representation without intimidation and the right to timely, fair and open legal proceedings;

(i) To end the harassment, intimidation and persecution of political opponents, human rights defenders, labour leaders, students, academics, journalists, other media representatives, bloggers, clerics, artists and lawyers, including by releasing persons imprisoned arbitrarily or on the basis of their political views;

(j) To end restrictions placed on Internet users and Internet providers that violate the rights to freedom of expression, association and privacy;

(k) To end restrictions on the press and media representatives, including the selective jamming of satellite broadcasts;

(l) To end the use of State security forces and Government-directed militias to forcibly disperse Iranian citizens engaged in the peaceful exercise of their rights to freedom of expression, peaceful assembly and association;

(m) To uphold, in law and in practice, procedural guarantees to ensure due process of law;

7. *Also calls upon* the Government of the Islamic Republic of Iran to strengthen its national human rights institutions in accordance with the principles relating to the status of national institutions for the promotion and protection of human rights ("the Paris Principles");

8. *Further calls upon* the Government of the Islamic Republic of Iran to consider ratifying or acceding to the international human rights treaties to which it is not already a party, to effectively implement those human rights treaties to which it is already a party, to withdraw any reservations it may have made upon signature or ratification of other international human rights instruments where such reservations are overly general, imprecise or could be considered incompatible with the object and purpose of the treaty, and to consider acting upon the concluding observations concerning the Islamic Republic of Iran adopted by the bodies of the international human rights treaties to which it is a party;

9. *Welcomes* the appointment of the Special Rapporteur on the situation of human rights in the Islamic Republic of Iran;

10. *Calls upon* the Government of the Islamic Republic of Iran to positively avail itself of the opportunity to cooperate fully with the Special Rapporteur and other international human rights mechanisms, including by allowing the Special Rapporteur unfettered access to the country to carry out his mandate;

11. *Encourages* the Government of the Islamic Republic of Iran to continue exploring cooperation on human rights and justice reform with the United Nations, including the Office of the United Nations High Commissioner for Human Rights;

12. *Expresses deep concern* that, despite the Islamic Republic of Iran's standing invitation to all thematic special procedures mandate holders, it has not fulfilled any requests from those special mechanisms to visit the country in six years and has left unanswered the vast majority of the numerous and repeated communications from those special mechanisms, and strongly urges the Government of the Islamic Republic of Iran to fully cooperate with the special mechanisms, including facilitating their visits to its territory, so that credible and independent investigations of all allegations of human rights violations can be conducted;

13. *Strongly encourages* the Government of the Islamic Republic of Iran to seriously consider all of the recommendations put forward at its universal periodic review by the Human Rights Council, with the full and genuine participation of civil society and other stakeholders;

14. *Strongly encourages* the thematic special procedures mandate holders to pay particular attention to, with a view to investigating and reporting on, the situation of human rights in the Islamic Republic of Iran, in particular the Special Rapporteur on extrajudicial, summary or arbitrary executions, the Special Rapporteur on torture and other cruel, inhuman or degrading treatment or punishment, the Special Rapporteur on the promotion and protection of the right to freedom of opinion and expression, the Special Rapporteur on the rights to freedom of peaceful assembly and of association, the Special Rapporteur on the situation of human rights defenders, the Special Rapporteur on freedom of religion or belief, the Special Rapporteur on the independence of judges and lawyers, the Special Rapporteur on violence against women, its causes and consequences, the Independent Expert on minority issues, the Working Group on Arbitrary Detention, the Working Group on Enforced or Involuntary Disappearances and the Working Group on Discrimination against Women in Law and in Practice;

15. *Requests* the Secretary-General to report to the General Assembly at its sixty-seventh session on the progress made in the implementation of the present resolution, including options and recommendations to improve its implementation, and to submit an interim report to the Human Rights Council at its nineteenth session;

16. *Decides* to continue its examination of the situation of human rights in the Islamic Republic of Iran at its sixty-seventh session under the item entitled "Promotion and protection of human rights".

RECORDED VOTE ON RESOLUTION 66/175:

In favour: Albania, Andorra, Argentina, Australia, Austria, Bahamas, Barbados, Belgium, Belize, Bosnia and Herzegovina, Botswana, Bulgaria, Canada, Cape Verde, Central African Republic, Chile, Colombia, Costa Rica, Croatia, Cyprus, Czech Republic, Denmark, Dominican Republic, El Salvador, Estonia, Finland, France, Gambia, Germany, Greece, Haiti, Honduras, Hungary, Iceland, Ireland, Israel, Italy, Japan, Kiribati, Latvia, Liberia, Libya, Liechtenstein, Lithuania, Luxembourg, Malawi, Maldives, Malta, Marshall Islands, Mexico, Micronesia, Monaco, Montenegro, Nauru, Netherlands, New Zealand, Norway, Palau, Panama, Papua New Guinea, Peru, Poland, Portugal, Republic of Korea, Republic of Moldova, Romania, Rwanda, Saint Lucia, Samoa, San Marino, Sao Tome and Principe, Senegal, Seychelles, Slovakia, Slovenia, Solomon Islands, South Sudan, Spain, Sweden, Switzerland, the former Yugoslav Republic of Macedonia, Timor-Leste, Tonga, Tunisia, Ukraine, United Kingdom, United Republic of Tanzania, United States, Vanuatu.

Against: Afghanistan, Algeria, Armenia, Bangladesh, Belarus, Bolivia, Brunei Darussalam, China, Cuba, Democratic People's Republic of Korea, Ecuador, India, Iran, Kazakhstan, Lebanon, Myanmar, Nicaragua, Oman, Pakistan, Qatar, Russian Federation, Sri Lanka, Sudan, Syrian Arab Republic, Tajikistan, Turkmenistan, Uzbekistan, Venezuela, Viet Nam, Zimbabwe.

Abstaining: Angola, Antigua and Barbuda, Bahrain, Benin, Bhutan, Brazil, Burkina Faso, Cambodia, Cameroon, Chad, Comoros, Congo, Côte d'Ivoire, Democratic Republic of the Congo, Djibouti, Dominica, Egypt, Ethiopia, Fiji, Gabon, Ghana, Grenada, Guatemala, Guinea, Guinea-Bissau, Guyana, Indonesia, Jamaica, Jordan, Kenya, Kuwait, Kyrgyzstan, Lao People's Democratic Republic, Lesotho, Malaysia, Mali, Mauritania, Mauritius, Mongolia, Morocco, Mozambique, Nepal, Niger, Nigeria, Paraguay, Philippines, Saint Kitts and Nevis, Saint Vincent and the Grenadines, Saudi Arabia, Serbia, Sierra Leone, Singapore, Somalia, South Africa, Suriname, Swaziland, Thailand, Togo, Trinidad and Tobago, Tuvalu, Uganda, United Arab Emirates, Uruguay, Zambia.

Kyrgyzstan

Report of High Commissioner. In April [A/HRC/17/41], the High Commissioner submitted, in response to Human Rights Council resolution 14/14 [YUN 2010, p. 779], a report on technical assistance and cooperation on human rights for Kyrgyzstan. The report, covering the period from June 2010 to February 2011, focused on developments in legislative and electoral processes, particularly in the human rights sphere. The High Commissioner said that the human rights concerns described in the report, including the lack of an independent and effective administration of justice, as well as gender-based violence and discriminatory practices towards women, might undermine the Government's efforts towards reconciliation. Among other measures, the High Commissioner recommended that the Government address deficiencies in the protection of fair trial rights for detainees, including those being tried in relation to the unrest of 7 April 2010 [YUN 2010, p. 779] and in cases related to the June 2010 interethnic violence in the south of the country. Law enforcement authorities should prevent illegal and arbitrary detentions, guarantee unrestricted access by civil society monitoring groups to all places of deprivation of liberty and ensure timely and effective investigation into allegations of torture. The Government should review and streamline its legislation and policies on housing to ensure their consistency with international human rights standards, and develop a comprehensive national housing strategy to ensure the inclusion of more diversified forms of housing for vulnerable groups. The authorities should provide resources to ensure that victims of gender-based violence had access to adequate medical and psychological care. The Government should emphasize that promotion and protection of minority rights were an integral part of peace and reconciliation. It should also ratify or accede to international human rights instruments to which it was not a party, including those that provided for individual complaints procedures.

Human Rights Council action. On 17 June [A/HRC/17/2 (res.17/20)], the Human Rights Council called on Kyrgyzstan to uphold its commitment to the Universal Declaration of Human Rights and to implement its international human rights obligations. It reaffirmed the need to uphold the rights and freedoms of peaceful assembly, expression and association; condemned the acts that resulted in the killing of protesters on 7 April 2010; and urged the Government to take special measures to ensure the protection of human rights. The Council also urged the Government to bring its judicial system into line with its international obligations and ensure that progress was made in improving the human rights situation in the areas of administration of justice, torture and arbitrary detention, the right to adequate housing, the rights of women, minority rights and human rights mechanisms. The Government was also urged to address arbitrary detentions, torture and corruption; and promote interethnic reconciliation. The Council requested the High Commissioner to continue to provide technical assistance through her office in Bishkek, and to report to the Council's twentieth (2012) session.

Myanmar

Report of Special Rapporteur. In a March progress report [A/HRC/16/59], the Special Rapporteur on the situation of human rights in Myanmar, Tomás Ojea Quintana (Argentina), stated that the human rights situation remained serious, but there were opportunities for positive developments. He urged the Government to release all remaining prisoners of conscience and encouraged it to include all parties in the national reconciliation and transition process. Regarding the right to education, the Special Rapporteur recommended that the Government significantly increase funding for education, pay teachers reasonable salaries and provide adequate training opportunities, review and reform the curricula and teaching methods, revise the language-instruction policy to reflect international standards regarding cultural rights, invest in children's health and nutrition, and strengthen education monitoring and evaluation mechanisms.

Communication. On 11 March [A/HRC/16/G/9], Myanmar forwarded to the Human Rights Council its comments on the report of the Special Rapporteur (see above).

Human Rights Council action. On 25 March [A/HRC/16/2 (res. 16/24)], the Human Rights Council condemned the ongoing, systematic violations of human rights and fundamental freedoms of the people of Myanmar. It welcomed the 2010 release of Daw Aung San Suu Kyi from house arrest [YUN 2010, p. 780] and urged Myanmar to begin an inclusive post-election national reconciliation process. It also urged the unconditional release for all prisoners of conscience and called on the Government to recognize the pre-election registration status of all political parties; lift restrictions on the freedom of assembly, association, movement and expression; and undertake a transparent, inclusive and comprehensive review of compliance of all national legislation with international human rights law. The Council urged the Government to ensure the independence and impartiality of the judiciary and expressed concern that calls to end impunity had not been heeded. It called on the Government to address reports of torture and ill-treatment of prisoners of conscience; ensure safe and unhindered access for the United Nations, international humanitarian organizations and their partners to all parts of Myanmar; and end the continuing grave violations of international human rights and humanitarian law, the systematic forced displacement of people within the country and to neighbouring countries and the recruitment and use of child soldiers. It expressed concern at the continuing discrimination, human rights violations, violence, displacement and economic deprivation affecting numerous ethnic minorities. The Council extended the mandate of the Special Rapporteur for one year. It requested him to submit a progress report and encouraged him to provide to the sixty-sixth (2011) session of the General Assembly an assessment of progress made by Myanmar regarding its transition to democracy.

Communication. In a 9 June note to the Human Rights Council [A/HRC/17/G/10], Myanmar transmitted its closing remarks to the Council at its seventeenth session.

Report of Secretary-General. In an August report on the human rights situation in Myanmar [A/66/267], submitted in response to General Assembly resolution 65/241 [YUN 2010, p. 780], the Secretary-General observed that the continued detention of political prisoners remained a concern. It was inconsistent with the Government's commitments and initial efforts towards greater openness and respect for fundamental freedoms and the rule of law, and was counterproductive to fostering peace and dialogue. Of equal concern were ongoing tensions and armed conflict with some ethnic groups. The Secretary-General's Special Adviser on Myanmar, Vijay Nambiar (India), urged the Government to cooperate with UN human rights mechanisms, including the Special Rapporteur, to address outstanding concerns about ongoing reports of violations and to strengthen governance capacity, including training, institutional reform and the rule of law. The Special Adviser visited Myanmar from 11 to 13 May, and again from 31 October to 4 November.

Report of Special Rapporteur. In a September report [A/66/365], the Special Rapporteur, who visited the country from 21 to 25 August, stated that the new Government had taken steps to improve the human rights situation and deepen the transition to democracy. On 5 September, the Myanmar National Human Rights Commission was formed by presidential decree with a mandate to promote and safeguard the fundamental rights of citizens described in the Constitution. Nevertheless, many serious human rights issues remained and needed to be addressed. He urged that priority be given to the release of all prisoners of conscience and recommended that the Government improve the conditions of detention and the treatment of prisoners; ensure respect for the freedoms of expression, assembly and association; accelerate the review and amendment of legislation and legal provisions that limited fundamental freedoms and contravened international standards; ratify core human rights conventions; ensure that investigations into gross and systematic human rights violations were conducted in an impartial and credible manner; and ensure that the new Myanmar Human Rights Commission was established in compliance with international standards. The Rapporteur called on the authorities and all armed groups to ensure the protection of civilians in conflict-affected areas and respect for international human rights and humanitarian law. The use of anti-personnel landmines should be prohibited and technical assistance from the international community should be sought in the area of judicial reform, capacity-building and training of judges and lawyers.

Communication. On 24 October [A/C.3/66/2], Myanmar transmitted to the Secretary-General a memorandum on the situation of human rights in the country.

GENERAL ASSEMBLY ACTION

On 24 December [meeting 93], the General Assembly, on the recommendation of the Third Committee [A/66/462/Add.3], adopted **resolution 66/230** by recorded vote (83-21-39) [agenda item 69 (*c*)].

Situation of human rights in Myanmar

The General Assembly,

Guided by the Charter of the United Nations and the Universal Declaration of Human Rights, and recalling the International Covenants on Human Rights and other relevant human rights instruments,

Reaffirming that all Member States have an obligation to promote and protect human rights and fundamental freedoms and the duty to fulfil the obligations they have undertaken under the various international instruments in this field,

Reaffirming also its previous resolutions on the situation of human rights in Myanmar, the most recent of which is resolution 65/241 of 24 December 2010, those of the Commission on Human Rights, and those of the Human Rights Council, the most recent of which are resolutions 13/25 of 26 March 2010 and 16/24 of 25 March 2011,

Welcoming the statements made by the President of the Security Council on 11 October 2007 and 2 May 2008, and the Security Council statements to the press of 22 May and 13 August 2009,

Welcoming also the report of the Secretary-General on the situation of human rights in Myanmar and the observations contained therein, and recalling his visit to the country on 3 and 4 July 2009 and the visits of his Special Adviser on Myanmar from 31 January to 3 February and on 26 and 27 June 2009, on 27 and 28 November 2010 and from 11 to 13 May and from 31 October to 4 November 2011, while urging the Government of Myanmar to continue to make progress in its cooperation with the good offices mission, including by facilitating further visits,

Welcoming further the visit to Myanmar of the Special Rapporteur on the situation of human rights in Myanmar from 21 to 25 August 2011 and the access granted to political and other actors, including prisoners, welcoming the reports of the Special Rapporteur, and urging the implementation of the recommendations contained therein and in previous reports,

Deeply concerned that many of the urgent calls contained in the above-mentioned resolutions, as well as the statements of other United Nations bodies concerning the situation of human rights in Myanmar, have not yet been acted upon,

Reaffirming the essential importance of a genuine process of dialogue and national reconciliation for a transition to democracy,

Acknowledging the publicly stated commitment of the President of Myanmar to implement reform, promote national reconciliation, safeguard human rights and fundamental freedoms and promote good governance, democracy and the rule of law, and acknowledging also the stated commitment of the President to addressing social, economic and environmental issues,

Welcoming the recent talks between the Government of Myanmar and Daw Aung San Suu Kyi, while urging the Government to take further steps to advance an effective and genuine dialogue with the broad spectrum of political parties, including the National League for Democracy, pro-democracy actors, ethnic minorities and other relevant stakeholders in a genuine process of dialogue, national reconciliation and transition to democracy,

Considering that democratic, transparent and inclusive elections must be the cornerstone of any democratic reform process, and deeply regretting that the 2010 general elections represent a missed opportunity in that regard, noting, in particular, the restrictions imposed by the electoral laws, limited access to the media, reported incidents of official intimidation, the cancellation of elections in certain ethnic areas and the lack of independence of the electoral commission, and expressing concern at the failure of the electoral commission to follow up on complaints about the electoral process, including about voting procedures,

Encouraging the continued cooperation of the Government of Myanmar with the international community in order to achieve concrete progress with regard to human rights and fundamental freedoms and political processes, and noting the stated intention of the Government to do so,

1. *Expresses grave concern* about the ongoing systematic violations of human rights and fundamental freedoms of the people of Myanmar, while recognizing the commitment made by the Government of Myanmar to implement reforms to address those violations;

2. *Welcomes* the recent talks between the Government of Myanmar and Daw Aung San Suu Kyi and opposition parties, and encourages the Government to develop the current talks into a substantive and regular dialogue while comprehensively engaging with the democratic opposition, including the National League for Democracy, and political, ethnic and civil society groups and actors in order to begin an all-inclusive and democratic reform process leading to national reconciliation and lasting peace in Myanmar;

3. *Calls upon* the Government of Myanmar to continue to ensure that no restrictions are placed on the exercise by Daw Aung San Suu Kyi of all her human rights and fundamental freedoms, in particular with regard to the freedom of movement and the right to participate fully in the political process, including through engagement with relevant stakeholders, and to take adequate measures to protect her physical safety;

4. *Welcomes* the release on 12 October 2011 of more than 200 prisoners of conscience, and strongly urges the Government of Myanmar to release without further delay and without conditions all prisoners of conscience, including the Chairman of the Shan Nationalities League for Democracy, U Hkun Htun Oo, the leader of the 88 Generation Students Group, U Min Ko Naing, one of the founders of the 88 Generation Students Group, Ko Ko Gyi, human rights defender U Myint Aye and the leader of the All Burma Monks' Alliance, U Gambira, and to allow their full participation in the political process, emphasizing that their unrestricted release is fundamental to national reconciliation, and strongly calls upon the Government to reveal the whereabouts of persons who are detained or have been subjected to enforced disappearance and to desist from further politically motivated arrests;

5. *Notes* the establishment of new national, regional and state legislatures in Myanmar and some steps taken to engage legislatures on issues relevant to the promotion and protection of human rights, and encourages further efforts in that regard;

6. *Calls upon* the Government of Myanmar to lift all restrictions imposed on the representatives of political parties as well as on other political and civil society actors in the country, including by amending the relevant laws, and to ensure that the upcoming by-elections are held in a participatory, inclusive and transparent manner, while recognizing the announcement of changes in the electoral law that would allow for wider participation, and urging that they be put into effect;

7. *Notes* the stated intention and first initiatives of the Government of Myanmar to carry out media reform and open up space for the press, and strongly calls upon the Government of Myanmar to lift restrictions on the freedom of assembly, association and movement and the freedom of expression, including for free and independent media, to improve the availability and accessibility of Internet and mobile telephone services, and to end the use of censorship, including the use of the Electronic Transactions Law to prevent the reporting of views critical of the Government;

8. *Acknowledges with appreciation* the formation of the Myanmar National Human Rights Commission, encourages the Government of Myanmar to ensure that it is established and mandated in such a way as to be an independent, credible and effective institution, in accordance with the principles relating to the status of national institutions for the promotion and protection of human rights ("the Paris Principles"), and, further, encourages the Commission to receive complaints and to investigate violations, and recommends that the Government seek technical assistance from the Office of the United Nations High Commissioner for Human Rights in the development of that new institution, noting some initial contacts in this regard;

9. *Expresses grave concern* at the continuing practice of arbitrary detention, enforced disappearance, rape and other forms of sexual violence, torture and cruel, inhuman or degrading treatment or punishment, and urges the Government of Myanmar to undertake without further delay a full, transparent, effective, impartial and independent investigation into all reports of human rights violations and to bring to justice those responsible in order to end impunity for violations of human rights, and, regretting that previous calls to that effect have not been heeded, calls upon the Government to do so as a matter of priority and, if necessary, drawing on the assistance of the United Nations;

10. *Takes note* of the recent steps taken by the Government of Myanmar to review some national legislation, and calls upon the Government to undertake a transpar-

ent, inclusive and comprehensive review of compliance of the Constitution and all national legislation with international human rights law, fully engaging with democratic opposition, civil society groups, ethnic groups and other stakeholders, while recalling once more that the procedures established for the drafting of the Constitution resulted in a de facto exclusion of opposition groups from the process;

11. *Urges* the Government of Myanmar to ensure the independence and impartiality of the judiciary and the independence of lawyers, to guarantee due process of law, and to fulfil earlier assurances made to the Special Rapporteur on the situation of human rights in Myanmar to begin a dialogue on judicial reform;

12. *Expresses its concern* about the conditions in prisons and other detention facilities and consistent reports of ill-treatment of prisoners of conscience, including torture, and about the moving of prisoners of conscience to isolated prisons far from their families where they cannot receive regular visits, or food and medicine, and calls upon the Government of Myanmar to ensure that proper investigations are conducted of all deaths in prison;

13. *Expresses deep concern* about the resumption of armed conflict and the breakdown of long-standing ceasefires in areas including Kachin and Shan States, as a result of continued pressures imposed by the national authorities on certain ethnic groups and the exclusion of some key ethnic political parties from the political process and from decisions affecting their lives, while noting some steps taken to establish ceasefires in other areas, and calls upon the Government of Myanmar to protect the civilian population in all parts of the country and for all concerned to use political means to re-establish ceasefire agreements, and also calls upon the Government to expand the offer of peace talks with armed groups on a nationwide basis;

14. *Strongly calls upon* the Government of Myanmar to take urgent measures to put an end to continuing grave violations of international human rights and humanitarian law, including the targeting of persons based on their belonging to particular ethnic groups, the targeting of civilians as such in military operations, and rape and other forms of sexual violence, and to end impunity for such acts;

15. *Also strongly calls upon* the Government of Myanmar to end the practice of systematic forced displacement of large numbers of persons within their country and other causes of refugee flows into neighbouring countries;

16. *Expresses its concern* about the continuing discrimination, human rights violations, violence, displacement and economic deprivation affecting numerous ethnic minorities, including, but not limited to, the Rohingya ethnic minority in Northern Rakhine State, and calls upon the Government of Myanmar to take immediate action to bring about an improvement in their respective situations, and to grant citizenship to the Rohingya ethnic minority;

17. *Urges* the Government of Myanmar to intensify its cooperation with the Office of the United Nations High Commissioner for Human Rights and other partners to conduct adequate human rights and international humanitarian law training for its armed forces, police and prison personnel, to ensure their strict compliance with international human rights law and international humanitarian law and to hold them accountable for any violations thereof;

18. *Calls upon* the Government of Myanmar to consider ratifying and acceding to remaining international human rights treaties, which would enable a dialogue with the other human rights treaty bodies, while noting some initial steps taken by the Government in this regard;

19. *Also calls upon* the Government of Myanmar to allow human rights defenders to pursue their activities unhindered and to ensure their safety, security and freedom of movement in that pursuit;

20. *Strongly calls upon* the Government of Myanmar to put an immediate end to the continuing recruitment and use of child soldiers by the armed forces and other armed groups, in violation of international law by all parties, to intensify measures to ensure the protection of children from armed conflict, to pursue its collaboration with the Special Representative of the Secretary-General for Children and Armed Conflict, to swiftly conclude and implement an effective joint action plan for the national armed forces, to facilitate access for dialogue on action plans with other parties listed in the annual report of the Secretary-General on children and armed conflict, and to allow unrestricted access to all areas where children are recruited for those purposes;

21. *Notes with appreciation* the prolongation of the supplementary understanding between the International Labour Organization and the Government of Myanmar on forced labour, and the reported progress on changes in law and practice to eliminate the use of forced labour, particularly in relation to awareness-raising, but expresses grave concern at the continuing practice of forced labour, including the reported use of civilian porters, including convict porters, and calls upon the Government to intensify its cooperation with the International Labour Organization on the basis of the understanding, with a view to extending action against forced labour as widely as possible throughout the country and to fully implementing with urgency the recommendations of the Commission of Inquiry of the International Labour Organization;

22. *Welcomes* the approval of the Labour Organizations Bill, and the prior constructive consultation on it with the International Labour Organization, and encourages its full implementation;

23. *Also welcomes* the positive steps taken by the Government of Myanmar to facilitate and improve humanitarian response, and calls upon the Government to take further measures to allow humanitarian assistance to reach all persons in need throughout the country by ensuring timely, safe, full and unhindered access to all parts of Myanmar, including conflict and border areas, for the United Nations, international humanitarian organizations and their partners, taking into account the need to process swiftly requests for visa and in-country travel permission;

24. *Further welcomes* the invitation extended to the International Committee of the Red Cross to provide some technical assistance in prisons, and encourages the Government of Myanmar to allow it to carry out other activities in accordance with its mandate, in particular by granting access to persons detained and to areas of internal armed conflict;

25. *Encourages* the Government of Myanmar to continue to cooperate with international health entities on HIV/AIDS, malaria and tuberculosis;

26. *Reaffirms its full support* for the good offices of the Secretary-General pursued through his Special Adviser on Myanmar, consistent with the report of the Secretary-General on the situation of human rights in Myanmar, and urges the Government of Myanmar to cooperate fully with the good offices mission, including by facilitating the visits of the Special Adviser to the country and granting him unrestricted access to all relevant stakeholders, including the highest level of leadership, political parties, human rights defenders, representatives of ethnic groups, student leaders and other opposition groups, and to respond substantively and without delay to the proposals of the Secretary-General, including the establishment of a United Nations office in support of the mandate of good offices;

27. *Welcomes* the role played by countries neighbouring Myanmar and members of the Association of Southeast Asian Nations in support of the good offices mission of the Secretary-General;

28. *Also welcomes* the continued contribution of the Group of Friends of the Secretary-General on Myanmar in support of the work of the good offices mission;

29. *Further welcomes* the visit of the Special Rapporteur to Myanmar from 21 to 25 August 2011 and the access granted to him, and urges the Government of Myanmar to implement the recommendations addressed to the Government in his report and to cooperate fully with the Special Rapporteur in the exercise of his mandate, including by facilitating further visits;

30. *Calls upon* the Government of Myanmar to engage in a dialogue with the Office of the High Commissioner with a view to ensuring full respect for all human rights and fundamental freedoms;

31. *Acknowledges* the participation by the Government of Myanmar in the universal periodic review in January 2011 as the State under review, and strongly encourages the Government to implement the recommendations accepted, including the recommendations to consider acceding to the International Covenant on Civil and Political Rights, the International Covenant on Economic, Social and Cultural Rights and other core human rights treaties, while also urging the Government to reconsider the many important recommendations which were rejected and to seek technical cooperation from the Office of the High Commissioner in this regard;

32. *Requests* the Secretary-General:

(a) To continue to provide his good offices and to pursue his discussions on the situation of human rights, the transition to democracy and the national reconciliation process with the Government and the people of Myanmar, involving all relevant stakeholders, including democracy and human rights groups, and to offer technical assistance to the Government in this regard;

(b) To give all necessary assistance to enable the Special Adviser and the Special Rapporteur to discharge their mandates fully, effectively and in a coordinated manner;

(c) To report to the General Assembly at its sixty-seventh session, as well as to the Human Rights Council, on the progress made in the implementation of the present resolution;

33. *Decides* to continue the consideration of the question at its sixty-seventh session, on the basis of the reports of the Secretary-General and the Special Rapporteur.

RECORDED VOTE ON RESOLUTION 66/230:

In favour: Afghanistan, Albania, Andorra, Argentina, Armenia, Australia, Austria, Bahamas, Barbados, Belgium, Bosnia and Herzegovina, Botswana, Bulgaria, Burundi, Canada, Chile, Costa Rica, Croatia, Cyprus, Czech Republic, Denmark, El Salvador, Estonia, Finland, France, Germany, Ghana, Greece, Honduras, Hungary, Iceland, India, Iraq, Ireland, Italy, Jamaica, Japan, Kazakhstan, Latvia, Lebanon, Liberia, Liechtenstein, Lithuania, Luxembourg, Maldives, Malta, Marshall Islands, Mauritius, Mexico, Micronesia, Monaco, Mongolia, Montenegro, Namibia, Netherlands, New Zealand, Norway, Palau, Panama, Peru, Poland, Portugal, Republic of Korea, Republic of Moldova, Romania, Samoa, San Marino, Serbia, Slovakia, Slovenia, Solomon Islands, Spain, Sweden, Switzerland, the former Yugoslav Republic of Macedonia, Tonga, Tunisia, Turkey, Ukraine, United Kingdom, United Republic of Tanzania, United States, Uruguay.

Against: Algeria, Bangladesh, Belarus, Brunei Darussalam, Cambodia, China, Cuba, Ecuador, Egypt, Iran, Lao People's Democratic Republic, Myanmar, Nicaragua, Oman, Russian Federation, Sri Lanka, Sudan, Syrian Arab Republic, Uzbekistan, Venezuela, Viet Nam.

Abstaining: Antigua and Barbuda, Bahrain, Benin, Bolivia, Brazil, Burkina Faso, Cameroon, Colombia, Comoros, Côte d'Ivoire, Djibouti, Dominican Republic, Ethiopia, Fiji, Guatemala, Indonesia, Jordan, Kenya, Kuwait, Kyrgyzstan, Madagascar, Malaysia, Mali, Morocco, Nepal, Pakistan, Philippines, Qatar, Saint Vincent and the Grenadines, Saudi Arabia, Singapore, South Africa, Thailand, Timor-Leste, Trinidad and Tobago, Turkmenistan, United Arab Emirates, Yemen, Zambia.

Nepal

Report of High Commissioner. In December [A/HRC/19/21/Add.4], the High Commissioner reported on the human rights situation and the activities of her office in Nepal. The High Commissioner reviewed the situation in relation to 10 priority human rights areas and major developments, and found that, while many challenges remained, some progress was made towards a successful conclusion of Nepal's peace process. Nepal decided not to renew the OHCHR mandate to operate a field presence in the country beyond 8 December 2011, but the office was ready to find modalities to continue to support Nepal in advancing the human rights agenda. In her recommendations, the High Commissioner urged the political parties in the Constituent Assembly to finalize the Constitution and to ensure that it complied with international human rights commitments undertaken by Nepal. She called on the Government to develop a comprehensive strategy to ensure gender equality and address gender-based violence; and ensure that cases of serious human rights violations moved expeditiously through the criminal justice system without political interference. In addition, political efforts to withdraw such cases from prosecution or allow for amnesties or pardons had to cease. The High Commissioner called for the comprehensive training of law enforcement officials on the new Untouchability Act; implementation should include ensuring that the police properly registered and investigated all cases of caste-based discrimination and ceased the practice of informally settling cases through ad-hoc and unsanctioned "mediations". She further called for a time-bound plan to be developed to provide reasonable accommodation for persons with disabilities, and for the implementation of a programme to protect human rights defenders and journalists at risk.

Yemen

Human Rights Council action. On 16 June [A/HRC/17/2 (dec. 17/117)], the Human Rights Council, welcoming Yemen's invitation to OHCHR to visit the country, requested the High Commissioner to report to the Council on the visit at its eighteenth (2011) session.

Report of High Commissioner. In September [A/HRC/18/21], the High Commissioner reported on the OHCHR Assessment Mission to Yemen (28 June–6 July). The Mission observed that many Yemenis who had peacefully called for greater freedoms, an end to corruption and respect for the rule of law were met with excessive and disproportionate use of lethal force by the State, which led to hundreds of people being killed and thousands suffering injuries. On 8 April, the Gulf Cooperation Council initiated the creation of a Cabinet of National Accord, according to which the President would transfer his powers to the Vice-President, followed by elections and the adoption of a new constitution. The initiative, however, remained stalled. When the Mission arrived in Yemen, a number of separate struggles were taking place in major cities. Armed opponents of President Ali Abdallah Saleh appeared to be in de facto control of parts of the country and the major cities. The Mission observed that some of those seeking to achieve or retain power deliberately sought to punish and cause severe hardship to the civilian population by cutting off access to basis services, including electricity, fuel and water. The deteriorating humanitarian situation adversely affected the majority of the population, but in particular the poorest and most vulnerable, including children, internally displaced persons (IDPs) and refugees.

The Mission recommended, among other measures, that the Government end attacks against civilians and civilian targets by security forces; unconditionally release all prisoners detained for peacefully exercising their freedom of expression and assembly; launch independent investigations into credible allegations of serious human rights violations committed by government security forces; provide reparation to victims who had suffered harm as a result of unlawful acts committed by government security forces or their affiliates; end the use and recruitment of children; and refrain from any action that would deprive the population of basic services. The Government should define and implement a comprehensive programme aimed at ensuring the protection of those affected by the conflict in the northern Sa'ada province, particularly IDPs; enhance cooperation with the United Nations, including implementing the recommendations of treaty bodies, the universal periodic review, and special procedures; establish a national human rights institution; take measures to preserve the gains made by women; and redress disparities in standards of living and access to health, education, employment and social support structures. All armed opposition groups should remove all weapons from public areas of peaceful demonstrations; ensure that no children participated in checkpoint activities or in the protection of protestors; cease acts of violence, harassment, threats and attempts to intimidate demonstrators expressing opposing points of view; release civilians held in detention centres; refrain from attacking targets that provided essential services to the civilian population; and cooperate with investigations into abuses that might have been committed by armed men under opposition command. The international community should call on all parties to refrain from using violence; ensure that international, independent and impartial investigations of incidents that had resulted in heavy loss of life and injuries were conducted; and heed the call for humanitarian assistance.

Communication. On 15 September [A/HRC/18/G/9], Yemen transmitted to the Human Rights Council its comments on the report of the OHCHR Assessment Mission.

Human Rights Council action. On 29 September [A/HRC/18/2 (res. 18/19)], the Human Rights Council condemned all violations of human rights in Yemen by all parties; called on all parties to move forward in negotiations on an inclusive, Yemeni-led process of political transition based on the Gulf Cooperation Council initiative; called on the Government and the High Commissioner to develop a framework for continued dialogue and strengthened cooperation on human rights; and requested OHCHR to present a progress report in 2012.

Report of High Commissioner. In a later report [A/HRC/19/51], the High Commissioner stated that OHCHR deployed a delegation to Yemen from 20 to 27 December to assess the human rights situation and report on the implementation of recommendations made by the Office following its previous assessment mission. The delegation noted that on 15 November, the Government established a framework for the implementation of Human Rights Council resolution 18/19 and the recommendations made by the OHCHR Assessment Mission, including the establishment of a national commission of investigation. On 23 November, the Government and members of the opposition signed an agreement in Riyadh, Saudi Arabia, on the transition process, in accordance with the Gulf Cooperation Council initiative; the agreement led to the scheduling of elections in February 2012. Nevertheless, Yemenis peacefully calling for greater freedoms, an end to corruption and respect for the rule of law continued to be victimized by the excessive and disproportionate use of lethal force in situations where non-lethal measures should have been used. In addition, insufficient steps were taken to investigate allegations of serious human rights violations. The delegation reiterated many of the recommendations contained in the report of the Assessment Mission, including that the Government should end attacks against civilians and civilian targets by security forces. In addition, the delegation recommended that the Government disallow amnesties that prevented accountability of persons responsible for serious human rights violations; release remaining detainees and publish the names of persons released, those still detained, and the justification for their detention; and refrain from any action intended to deprive the population of basic services. Armed groups should ease restrictions on movement.

Europe and the Mediterranean

Belarus

Communications. On 10 May [A/HRC/17/G/3], the European Union (EU) and Hungary transmitted to the Human Rights Council an 18 February letter to Belarus from Canada, Croatia, Moldova, Norway, Switzerland, the United States and the EU expressing concern regarding several reports of human rights violations that followed presidential elections that took place in Belarus in December 2010. Of particular concern were reports on the arrest of presidential candidates, activists, journalists and civil society representatives, as well as the detention and harassment of members of the opposition and others on political grounds. Belarus was invited to participate, in cooperation with the High Commissioner, in an informal briefing on the human rights situation in the country. Belarus did not respond to that invitation.

In a 23 May letter to the Council [A/HRC/17/G/4], Belarus stated that on 19 December 2010, it took forceful measures to subdue an attempted coup d'état.

Human Rights Council action. On 17 June [A/HRC/17/2 (res. 17/24)], the Human Rights Council, by a recorded vote of 21 to 5, with 19 abstentions, condemned the human rights violations occurring before, during and in the aftermath of the presidential elections of 19 December 2010. It urged Belarus to end politically motivated persecution and harassment of opposition leaders, representatives of civil society, human rights defenders, lawyers, independent media, students and those defending them; comply with international standards for due process and fair trial; release and rehabilitate all political prisoners; and investigate allegations of disproportionate use of force and violations of human rights, including the use of torture and ill-treatment of detainees in connection with the events of 19 December 2010. Belarus was urged to respect freedom of expression, association and assembly; implement commitments made with the Organization for Security and Cooperation in Europe; and allow international monitors and cease the detention and expulsion of those monitors. The Council requested the High Commissioner to monitor the human rights situation and present an oral report at its eighteenth (2011) session, and a comprehensive report in 2012. Relevant thematic special procedures mandate holders were encouraged to contribute to the High Commissioner's report with recommendations on how to redress the human rights situation. The Council called on Belarus to cooperate fully with all mechanisms of the Council, the High Commissioner and human rights treaty bodies; permit access to visit the country; and provide all necessary information. It decided to consider further steps in 2012.

Communication. A 13 September note from Belarus to the Human Rights Council [A/HRC/18/G/7] contained comments on the events of 19 December 2010 and the post-electoral period. Belarus stated, among other things, that accusations of violations of the rights to freedom of expression and peaceful assembly were groundless in the context of the mass disorder of 19 December 2010.

Cyprus

Communications. In an 18 January letter [A/HRC/16/G/5], Cyprus brought to the attention of the Human Rights Council President what it called a "grave human rights violation" that occurred on 25 December 2010, when security forces of the subordinate local administration of Turkey interrupted a religious service in an Orthodox church located in the town of Rizokarpaso, ordered the churchgoers to evacuate and sealed the church. At the same time, the regime did not allow a Christmas mass to be held in a church located in the nearby town of Yialoussa. In a 25 March 2011 letter to the Council President [A/HRC/16/G/14], Turkey said that the allegations made by Cyprus reflected neither the realities of the case nor the general facts regarding the exercise of freedom of religion in North Cyprus.

On 3 March [A/HRC/16/G/11], Turkey transmitted to the Council a 1 March letter reflecting the Turkish Cypriot views on the report of the Secretary-General on the question of human rights in Cyprus [YUN 2010, p. 783]. In a 1 April letter to the Council [A/HRC/16/G/16], Cyprus addressed the views presented in Turkey's letter.

Turkey, in notes of 25 March [A/HRC/16/G/15] and 16 June [A/HRC/16/G/19], and Cyprus, in an 18 May letter [A/HRC/16/G/18], presented to the Human Rights Council their views regarding the situation in Cyprus.

Report of High Commissioner. In response to a Human Rights Council resolution [YUN 2006, p. 760], the Secretary-General transmitted to the Council an OHCHR report on the question of human rights in Cyprus covering the period from 1 December 2010 to 30 November 2011 [A/HRC/19/22]. The report reviewed human rights concerns in Cyprus, including the right to life and the question of missing persons, the principle of non-discrimination, freedom of movement, property rights, freedom of religion and cultural rights, freedom of opinion and expression, and the right to education. Positive developments included the extension of the deadline for applications of Greek Cypriots to the Immovable Property Commission and measures to allow Turkish Cypriots to participate more effectively in public affairs and social, economic and cultural life. The division of the island continued to constitute an obstacle to the full enjoyment of all human rights and fundamental freedoms by the entire population of Cyprus. The Secretary-General hoped that the efforts made by the Greek Cypriot and Turkish Cypriot leaders to negotiate a comprehensive settlement of the Cyprus problem would improve the human rights situation.

Middle East

Syrian Arab Republic

Human Rights Council special session (April). On 27 April, the United States, with the support of 15 Council members, requested the convening of a special session of the Council on 29 April to address the human rights situation in the Syrian Arab Republic.

The Council held its sixteenth special session on 29 April [A/HRC/S-16/2]. In a resolution adopted by a recorded vote of 26 to 9, with 7 abstentions [A/HRC/S-16/2 (res. S-16/1)], the Council expressed its regret at the death of hundreds of people in connection with the political protests in Syria that began in March and concern at alleged deliberate killings, arrests and instances of torture of peaceful protesters by the Syrian authorities. It condemned the use of lethal violence against protesters and the hindrance of access to medical treatment, and urged Syria to end human rights violations, protect its population and respect human rights and fundamental freedoms, including freedom of expression and assembly. The Council called on Syria to release prisoners of conscience and arbitrarily detained persons, including those detained before the protests, and cease any intimidation, persecution and arbitrary arrests of individuals, including lawyers, human rights defenders and journalists. The authorities were urged to refrain from reprisals against people who took part in peaceful demonstrations; allow the provision of assistance to those in need; and enlarge the scope of political participation aimed at ensuring civil liberties and enhancing social justice. The Council stressed the need for the authorities to launch credible and impartial investigations, and prosecute those responsible for attacks on peaceful protesters. The High Commissioner was requested to dispatch a mission to Syria to investigate alleged violations of international human rights law; establish the facts and circumstances of such violations and the crimes perpetrated, with a view to avoiding impunity and ensuring full accountability; provide a preliminary report and oral update to the Human Rights Council at its seventeenth session; and submit a follow-up report at the Council's eighteenth (2011) session. Syria was called on to cooperate fully with mission personnel.

Report of High Commissioner. In June, in response to Council resolution S-16/1 (see above), the High Commissioner submitted a preliminary report on the human rights situation in Syria [A/HRC/17/CRP.1]. Allegations of widespread human rights violations by Syrian security forces had been reported, including excessive use of force in quelling demonstrators; arbitrary detentions; summary executions, torture and other cruel or inhuman treatment; and violations of the rights to freedom of assembly, expression and movement, and to food and health. The High Commissioner established a fact-finding mission headed by the Deputy High Commissioner for Human Rights, Kyung-wha Kang, to investigate human rights violations in Syria. By notes of 6 and 20 May, and 7 June, she formally requested Syria to cooperate with the mission and ensure full access to the country, but received no response. Nevertheless, the mission began its work on 23 May, gathering information from a range of sources inside and outside of Syria.

Communication. On 4 July [A/HRC/18/G/1], Syria transmitted to the Human Rights Council a note it had sent on 27 June to the High Commissioner detailing what it called misinformation and fallacies contained in her preliminary report on the human rights situation in the country.

Report of High Commissioner. The High Commissioner issued a report on the human rights situation in Syria covering the period from 15 March to 15 July [A/HRC/18/53]. Syria's failure to cooperate with OHCHR with regard to access to the country significantly hampered the work of the fact-finding mission established by resolution S-16/1; the report, therefore, did not cover all major geographical areas where protests took place, and addressed only the most serious violations. Nevertheless, the mission found a pattern of violations that constituted widespread or systematic attacks against the civilian population, which might amount to crimes against humanity under the Rome Statute of the International Criminal Court (ICC) [YUN 1998, p. 1209]. Violations included murder and disappearances, torture, deprivation of liberty and persecution. The High Commissioner recommended that Syria end gross human rights violations; take immediate steps to end impunity; ensure the unconditional release of detainees held on the basis of their participation in peaceful demonstrations, as well as the safe and voluntary return of refugees and internally displaced persons (IDPs); allow safe and unrestricted access to journalists to investigate and report on the situation; ensure full and unhindered access for humanitarian workers to provide aid and assistance to those in need; allow OHCHR access to conduct investigations into human rights abuses; and invite the special procedures of the Council to visit Syria in order to monitor and report on the human rights situation. The High Commissioner recommended that the Council ensure that the situation remained on its agenda through the establishment of appropriate monitoring and investigating mechanisms, and that the League of Arab States (LAS) remained engaged in calling for concerted action for the protection of human rights in the country.

Security Council action. The Security Council, in presidential statement **S/PRST/2011/16** of 3 August (see p. 469), condemned the widespread violations of human rights and the use of force against civilians by the Syrian authorities.

Human Rights Council special session (August). On 17 August [A/HRC/S-17/1], Poland and the EU requested the convening of a special session of the Human Rights Council on 22 August to address the question of the situation of human rights in Syria. The request was supported by 24 Council members.

The Council held its seventeenth special session from 22 to 23 August [A/HRC/S-17/2]. In a resolution adopted by a recorded vote of 33 to 4, with 9 abstentions [A/HRC/S-17/2 (res. S-17/1)], the Council condemned the continued grave and systematic human rights violations by the Syrian authorities, such as arbitrary executions; excessive use of force and the killing and persecution of protesters and human rights defenders; arbitrary detention; enforced disappearances; and torture and ill-treatment of detainees, including children. It expressed concern about the findings contained in the report of the fact-finding mission established pursuant to resolution S-16/1, and deplored the continued indiscriminate attacks on the population. The Commission called on the authorities to end human rights violations and release prisoners of conscience and arbitrarily detained persons. It urged Syria to allow independent media to operate without undue restrictions, and ensure timely, safe and unhindered access for humanitarian agencies and workers, as well as the safe passage of humanitarian and medical supplies into the country. The Council called for a Syrian-led political process and for an inclusive national dialogue conducted in an environment without fear and intimidation. It reinforced its call on the authorities to cooperate fully with OHCHR and human rights mechanisms. The Council encouraged thematic special procedures mandate holders to continue to pay particular attention to the situation of human rights in Syria, and urged the authorities to cooperate with mandate holders. It decided to dispatch an independent international commission of inquiry to investigate alleged violations since March; establish the facts and circumstances that might amount to such violations; and where possible, identify those responsible with a view to ensuring that perpetrators of violations, including those that might constitute crimes against humanity, were held accountable. The Council requested that the report of the commission of inquiry be made public before the end of November. The High Commissioner was asked to report on the implementation of the resolution in 2012.

Report of commission of inquiry. In response to Council resolution S-17/1 (see above), the independent international commission of inquiry on Syria submitted its report in November [A/HRC/S-17/2/Add.1]. The commission met with Member States from all regional groups, regional organizations, NGOs, human rights defenders, journalists and experts. It interviewed 223 victims and witnesses of alleged human rights violations, including civilians and defectors from the military and security forces. The commission documented patterns of summary executions, arbitrary arrest, enforced disappearances, torture—including sexual violence—and violations of children's rights. The body of evidence gathered indicated that the military and security forces had committed gross violations of human rights since the beginning of the protests in March. The commission recommended that Syria end human rights violations; initiate prompt, independent and impartial investigations; suspend alleged perpetrators of serious human rights violations from the military; and ratify the Rome Statute of ICC. Syria should release all persons arbitrarily detained and provide international monitoring bodies and the International Committee of the Red Cross with access to all places of detention; allow full access for the commission and outside observers; grant access to affected areas and provide international organizations with full cooperation for the purpose of protecting the population and providing humanitarian assistance; and ensure full access for media. The commission of inquiry also recommended that Syria abolish legislation granting military and security forces immunity; support hospitals and clinics to ensure the provision of adequate health care; establish a mechanism to investigate disappearances, as well as a reparation fund for victims of serious human rights violations; implement political and legal reforms; respect human rights defenders; and facilitate the voluntary return of Syrian refugees. Opposition groups should ensure respect for international human rights law. The commission recommended that the Human Rights Council establish the mandate of special rapporteur on the situation of human rights in Syria and invite the High Commissioner to report periodically on the human rights situation. The High Commissioner should establish a field presence in the country with a protection and promotion mandate. States and regional organizations, particularly LAS, should support efforts to protect the population, end gross human rights violations and suspend the provision of arms to all parties; assist Syria in addressing institutional weaknesses by strengthening the independence of its judiciary and reforming its security sector; and provide Syrian nationals seeking protection with refuge.

Human Rights Council special session (December). On 30 November [A/HRC/S-18/1], Poland and the EU requested the convening of a special session of the Human Rights Council on 2 December to examine the human rights situation in Syria in the light of the report of the commission of inquiry established by the Council in resolution S-17/1 (see p. 780). The request was supported by 28 Council members.

On 2 December [A/HRC/S-18/2 (res. S-18/1)], the Human Rights Council, by a recorded vote of 37 to 4, with 6 abstentions, condemned the continued widespread, systematic and gross violations of human rights and fundamental freedoms by the Syrian authorities, attacks against civilians, extensive violations of children's rights, sexual violence against civilians and the obstruction and denial of medical assistance to the injured and sick. It urged the Government to meet its responsibility to protect its population; release all prisoners of conscience and those arbitrarily detained; initiate impartial investigations to end impunity, ensure accountability and bring perpetrators to justice; suspend from the military and the security forces all alleged perpetrators of serious human rights violations; guarantee unhindered access to medical care; allow independent and international media to operate in the country; respect human rights defenders; ensure access for humanitarian actors; and facilitate the voluntary return of Syrian refugees and IDPs. It urged the authorities to respect the will of the people and cooperate with OHCHR. The Council decided to establish the mandate of Special Rapporteur on the situation of human rights in Syria, once the mandate of the commission of inquiry ended, to monitor the human rights situation, as well as the implementation of the commission's recommendations and the Council's resolutions. Syria was called on to cooperate fully with the Special Rapporteur. The Council invited UN agencies and regional organizations to support efforts to protect the population of Syria and assist Syria in strengthening the independence of its judiciary and reforming its security sector. It requested the Special Rapporteur to report to the Council and the General Assembly within 12 months. The Council invited the High Commissioner to report periodically on the situation. The Secretary-General was invited to contribute to a peaceful solution and requested to report to the Council in 2012.

GENERAL ASSEMBLY ACTION

On 19 December [meeting 89], the General Assembly, on the recommendation of the Third Committee [A/66/462/Add.3], adopted **resolution 66/176** by recorded vote (133-11-43) [agenda item 69 (*c*)].

Situation of human rights in the Syrian Arab Republic

The General Assembly,

Guided by the Charter of the United Nations,

Reaffirming the purposes and principles of the Charter, the Universal Declaration of Human Rights and relevant international human rights treaties, including the International Covenants on Human Rights,

Recalling Human Rights Council resolution S-16/1 of 29 April 2011, and recalling also Human Rights Council resolution S-17/1 of 23 August 2011, which established an independent international commission of inquiry to investigate all alleged violations of international human rights law since March 2011 in the Syrian Arab Republic, and regretting the lack of cooperation of the Syrian authorities with the commission of inquiry,

Welcoming all efforts made by the League of Arab States to address all aspects of the situation in the Syrian Arab Republic, and the steps undertaken by the League of Arab States to ensure the implementation of its Plan of Action, including those aimed at ending all human rights violations and all acts of violence,

Expressing concern about the continuing lack of commitment by the Syrian authorities to fully and immediately implement the Plan of Action of the League of Arab States of 2 November 2011,

Welcoming the decisions of the League of Arab States of 12 and 16 November 2011 on the developments in respect of the situation in the Syrian Arab Republic,

Expressing deep concern about the ongoing human rights violations and use of violence by the Syrian authorities against their population,

Reaffirming that all States Members of the United Nations should refrain in their international relations from the threat or use of force against the territorial integrity or political independence of any State, or in any other manner inconsistent with the purposes of the United Nations,

1. *Strongly condemns* the continued grave and systematic human rights violations by the Syrian authorities, such as arbitrary executions, excessive use of force and the persecution and killing of protesters and human rights defend-

ers, arbitrary detention, enforced disappearances, torture and ill-treatment of detainees, including children;

2. *Calls upon* the Syrian authorities to immediately put an end to all human rights violations, to protect their population and to fully comply with their obligations under international human rights law, and calls for an immediate end to all violence in the Syrian Arab Republic;

3. *Also calls upon* the Syrian authorities to implement the Plan of Action of the League of Arab States in its entirety without further delay;

4. *Invites* the Secretary-General, in accordance with his functions, to provide support, if requested, to the League of Arab States observer mission in the Syrian Arab Republic, consistent with the decisions of the League of Arab States of 12 and 16 November 2011;

5. *Calls upon* the Syrian authorities to comply with Human Rights Council resolutions S-16/1 and S-17/1, including by cooperating fully and effectively with the independent international commission of inquiry.

RECORDED VOTE ON RESOLUTION 66/176:

In favour: Afghanistan, Albania, Andorra, Antigua and Barbuda, Argentina, Australia, Austria, Azerbaijan, Bahamas, Bahrain, Barbados, Belgium, Belize, Benin, Bosnia and Herzegovina, Botswana, Brazil, Bulgaria, Burkina Faso, Burundi, Cambodia, Canada, Cape Verde, Central African Republic, Chile, Colombia, Comoros, Congo, Costa Rica, Côte d'Ivoire, Croatia, Cyprus, Czech Republic, Denmark, Dominican Republic, Egypt, El Salvador, Estonia, Ethiopia, Finland, France, Georgia, Germany, Greece, Grenada, Guatemala, Guinea, Guinea-Bissau, Guyana, Haiti, Honduras, Hungary, Iceland, Indonesia, Iraq, Ireland, Israel, Italy, Jamaica, Japan, Jordan, Kazakhstan, Kiribati, Kuwait, Kyrgyzstan, Latvia, Liberia, Libya, Liechtenstein, Lithuania, Luxembourg, Madagascar, Malawi, Maldives, Malta, Marshall Islands, Mauritius, Mexico, Micronesia, Monaco, Mongolia, Montenegro, Morocco, Nauru, Netherlands, New Zealand, Nigeria, Norway, Oman, Palau, Panama, Papua New Guinea, Paraguay, Peru, Poland, Portugal, Qatar, Republic of Korea, Republic of Moldova, Romania, Rwanda, Saint Lucia, Samoa, San Marino, Sao Tome and Principe, Saudi Arabia, Senegal, Serbia, Seychelles, Sierra Leone, Slovakia, Slovenia, Solomon Islands, South Sudan, Spain, Sudan, Sweden, Switzerland, Thailand, the former Yugoslav Republic of Macedonia, Timor-Leste, Togo, Tonga, Trinidad and Tobago, Tunisia, Turkey, Tuvalu, Ukraine, United Arab Emirates, United Kingdom, United States, Uruguay, Vanuatu.

Against: Belarus, Cuba, Democratic People's Republic of Korea, Ecuador, Iran, Myanmar, Nicaragua, Syrian Arab Republic, Uzbekistan, Venezuela, Zimbabwe.

Abstaining: Algeria, Angola, Armenia, Bangladesh, Bhutan, Bolivia, Brunei Darussalam, Cameroon, Chad, China, Djibouti, Dominica, Fiji, Gambia, Ghana, India, Kenya, Lao People's Democratic Republic, Lebanon, Lesotho, Malaysia, Mali, Mauritania, Mozambique, Nepal, Niger, Pakistan, Philippines, Russian Federation, Saint Kitts and Nevis, Saint Vincent and the Grenadines, Singapore, Somalia, South Africa, Sri Lanka, Swaziland, Tajikistan, Turkmenistan, Uganda, United Republic of Tanzania, Viet Nam, Yemen, Zambia.

Communication. On 15 December [A/66/623-S/2011/775], Syria transmitted identical letters to the General Assembly and the Security Council regarding a statement on the human rights situation in the country, delivered by the High Commissioner during a closed meeting of the Security Council held on 12 December. Syria said that the statement was politicized, unprofessional and lacking in objectivity.

Report of High Commissioner. In a December report [A/HRC/19/79], the High Commissioner provided information on the implementation of Human Rights Council resolution S-17/1.

(For more information on the political and security situation in Syria, see p. 468.)

Territories occupied by Israel

In 2011, the Human Rights Council addressed cases of human rights violations in the territories occupied by Israel following the 1967 hostilities in the Middle East. Political and other issues in the region were considered by the Security Council, the General Assembly, the Special Committee to Investigate Israeli Practices Affecting the Human Rights of the Palestinian People and Other Arabs of the Occupied Territories (Committee on Israeli Practices) and other bodies (see PART ONE, Chapter VI).

Human Rights Council action. On 25 March, the Human Rights Council adopted three resolutions concerning the territories occupied by Israel. By recorded vote of 30 to 1, with 15 abstentions [A/HRC/16/2 (res.16/29)], the Council demanded that Israel end its occupation of the Palestinian land occupied since 1967 and respect its commitments within the peace process towards the establishment of an independent Palestinian State. It condemned the continuous Israeli military attacks and operations in the Occupied Palestinian Territory, as well as the indiscriminate rocket and mortar fire from Gaza against civilians. The Council demanded that Israel stop targeting civilians and halt practices that coerced Palestinian citizens to leave East Jerusalem; respect religious and cultural rights in the occupied Palestinian territories; cease all excavation work beneath and around the Al-Aqsa mosque compound; ensure the respect of internationally recognized sports principles, particularly the free movement of Palestinian sports teams and athletes; stop the demolition of Palestinian houses in East Jerusalem; release Palestinian prisoners and detainees; and lift the siege imposed on Gaza and allow the free access of fuel, humanitarian needs and medicine. The Council called for the international protection of the Palestinian people in the Occupied Palestinian Territory.

By a recorded vote of 45 to 1, with no abstentions [A/HRC/16/2 (res. 16/30)], the Council reaffirmed the inalienable, permanent and unqualified rights of the Palestinian people to self-determination, including their right to establish a sovereign and contiguous State, as well as its support for the solution of two States, Palestine and Israel, living side by side in peace and security. It urged Member States and UN system bodies to support and assist the Palestinian people in the early realization of their right to self-determination.

By a recorded vote of 45 to 1, with no abstentions [A/HRC/16/2 (res.16/31)], the Human Rights Council condemned Israeli announcements of the construction of new housing units for Israeli settlers in and around occupied East Jerusalem. It expressed its concern at planned Israeli settlement construction in the vicinity of the Adam settlement in the occupied West Bank; the so-called E-1 plan, aimed at expanding the Israeli settlement of Maale Adumim and building the wall around it; the implications of Israel's announcement that it would retain the major settlement blocks in the Occupied Palestinian Territory; the Israeli decision to establish and operate a tramway between West Jerusalem and the Israeli settlement of Pisgat Zeev, in violation of international law and UN resolutions; the continued closures of and within the Territory, and the restriction of the freedom of movement of people and goods; the continued construction, contrary to international law, of the wall inside the Territory; and Israeli plans to demolish hundreds of houses in East Jerusalem, resulting in the displacement of more than 2,000 Palestinian residents. The Council urged Israel to reverse the settlement policy in the Territory and prevent any new installation of settlers, and implement the 2005 Agreement on Movement and Access [YUN 2005, p. 519]. It also called on Israel to prevent violence by Israeli settlers, and demanded that it comply with its legal obligations under the 2004 advisory opinion of the International Court of Justice (ICJ) [YUN 2004, p. 452] on the legal consequences of the construction of a wall in the Occupied Palestinian Territory. The parties were urged to give renewed impetus to the peace process.

Report of Special Rapporteur. On 13 September [A/66/358], the Secretary-General transmitted to the General Assembly the report of the Special Rapporteur on the situation of human rights in the Palestinian territories occupied since 1967, Richard Falk (United States). The report, submitted in response to Human Rights Council resolution 5/1 [YUN 2007, p. 664], focused on the right of Palestinians to self-determination; the situation of Palestinian prisoners detained by Israel; Israeli settlements in the occupied Palestinian territories; violence by Israeli settlers against Palestinians and their property; the vulnerable situation of children in the occupied territories; and the impact of the blockade by Israel on Gaza. The Special Rapporteur remained unable to obtain cooperation from Israel in discharging his obligations under the mandate, and was thus unable to visit the West Bank and East Jerusalem. Changed circumstances in Egypt, however, had created the prospect of access to Gaza by way of the Rafah Crossing, which would be kept open for both entry and exit of persons.

As a result, for the first time in its 43 years of existence, the Special Committee to Investigate Israeli Practices Affecting the Human Rights of the Palestinian People and Other Arabs of Occupied Territories was able to gain entry to Gaza. The Special Rapporteur recommended that Israel adopt the guidelines of the Israeli human rights organization B'Tselem for the protection of Palestinian children living under occupation who were arrested or detained; allow entry into Gaza of materials for repair of water and electricity infrastructure to avoid further deterioration in the health of the civilian population, especially children; develop and implement appropriate detention and imprisonment policies and practices for Palestinians; and lift the unlawful blockade of Gaza. The General Assembly should request that ICJ issue an advisory opinion on the legal status of prolonged occupation.

Report of High Commissioner. In response to Human Rights Council resolutions S-9/1 [YUN 2009, p. 780] and S-12/1 [ibid., p. 787], the High Commissioner issued, in December [A/HRC/19/20], the fourth report on the human rights situation in the Occupied Palestinian Territory, covering the period from 1 December 2010 to 15 November 2011. The report highlighted issues of concern with regard to each of the three main duty-bearers in the Territory, namely the de facto authorities in Gaza, Israel and the Palestinian Authority (PA). Regarding the de facto authorities, issues of concern included the indiscriminate firing of rockets and mortar shells at Israel by Palestinian armed groups; arbitrary detention and ill-treatment of detainees by security forces and alleged enforced disappearances; and curtailment of the freedom of expression, opinion and assembly. Regarding Israel, human rights concerns related to law enforcement in the West Bank and the right to life; discriminatory practices in the expansion of Israeli settlements and impunity for settler violence; the construction of the wall in the Territory; the transfer of Bedouin communities living in Area C of the West Bank; and the blockade of Gaza, which continued to adversely affect the human rights situation there. OHCHR continued to receive reports of arbitrary detention and ill-treatment of detainees by security forces of the PA, and some Palestinian actors sought to curtail civil rights.

The report addressed recommendations to the de facto authorities in Gaza, Israel and the PA. The de facto authorities should ensure respect for international humanitarian law by members of its armed groups and groups under its control, in particular in relation to the prohibition of targeting civilians and ending the use of indiscriminate weapons; issue clear orders to security forces in Gaza prohibiting the use of torture and/or cruel, inhuman or degrading treatment; and end the use of military tribunals to try civilians. Israel should prevent the excessive use of force during law enforcement operations;

ensure the accountability of its security forces and compensate victims of violations; cease the transfer of its civilian population into occupied territory; prevent attacks by Israeli settlers against Palestinian civilians and their property in the West Bank, including East Jerusalem; ensure that Palestinian victims of alleged crimes by Israeli settlers could file and follow up on complaints; cancel any plans to transfer Bedouin communities from the West Bank that might amount to forced transfer and/or forced evictions; and lift the blockade of Gaza and ensure that materials for reconstruction could be delivered. The PA should ensure that its law enforcement agencies/security services refrain from arbitrary arrests, and that civil society organizations, human rights defenders and journalists be able to carry out their work in a safe and secure environment.

Occupied Syrian Golan

Communication. On 18 March [A/HRC/16/G/12], the Syrian Arab Republic forwarded a 14 March letter from Syria to the Human Rights Council regarding the sentencing of two Syrian citizens to prison.

Human Rights Council action. On 24 March [A/HRC/16/2 (res. 16/17)], the Human Rights Council, by a recorded vote of 29 to 1, with 16 abstentions, called on Israel to comply with the relevant resolutions of the General Assembly, Security Council and the Human Rights Council concerning the occupied Syrian Golan. It also called on Israel to desist from building settlements; changing the physical character, demographic composition, institutional structure and legal status of the occupied Syrian Golan; imposing Israeli citizenship and Israeli identity cards on Syrian citizens; and carrying out repressive measures and practices that obstructed the enjoyment of their fundamental rights. Displaced persons of the occupied Syrian Golan should be allowed to return to their homes and recover their property. Israel was further called on to allow the Syrian population of the occupied Syrian Golan to visit their families and relatives in the Syrian motherland through the Quneitra checkpoint under the supervision of the International Committee of the Red Cross (ICRC) and rescind its decision to prohibit such visits; release the Syrian detainees in Israeli prisons, some of whom had been detained for more than 25 years, and treat them in conformity with international humanitarian law; and allow ICRC delegates to visit Syrian prisoners of conscience and detainees in Israeli prisons accompanied by specialized physicians to assess the state of their physical and mental health and to protect their lives. It determined that all legislative and administrative measures and actions taken by Israel that sought to alter the character and legal status of the occupied Syrian Golan were null and void; constituted a violation of international law and of the Geneva Convention relative to the Protection of Civilian Persons in Time of War, of 12 August 1949; and had no legal effect. The Council requested Member States not to recognize any of the above-mentioned legislative or administrative measures. The Secretary-General was asked to disseminate the resolution as widely as possible and report to the Council on the matter at its next main session.

Report of Secretary-General. In response to resolution 16/17, the Secretary-General submitted to the Human Rights Council a December report [A/HRC/19/46] and later addendum [A/HRC/19/46/Add.1] containing information received from Syria, Algeria and Cuba on the implementation of the resolution.

Follow-up to 2009 Fact-Finding Mission on the Gaza Conflict

Human Rights Council action. On 25 March, the Human Rights Council, by a recorded vote of 27 to 3, with 16 abstentions, adopted a resolution [A/HRC/16/2 (res.16/32)] on follow-up to the report of the United Nations Fact-Finding Mission on the Gaza Conflict [YUN 2009, p. 783]. The Council regretted the non-cooperation by Israel with the members of the committee of independent experts in international humanitarian and human rights law, and its failure to comply with the calls of the Council and the General Assembly to conduct independent and credible investigations into the serious violations of international humanitarian and international human rights law reported by the Mission. It called on the High Commissioner to follow up on the determination of modalities for the establishment of an escrow fund for the provision of reparations to Palestinians who suffered loss and damage as a result of unlawful acts attributable to Israel during the military operations conducted from December 2008 to January 2009, also taking into consideration Israelis who suffered loss and damage as a result of unlawful acts attributable to the Palestinian side. The Council reiterated its call to the Assembly to promote a discussion on the future legality of the use of certain munitions, as referred to in the report of the Mission. It recommended that the Assembly reconsider the report and urged it to submit the report to the Security Council for appropriate action. The Human Rights Council requested the Secretary-General to present to the Council at its eighteenth (2011) session a progress report on the implementation of the Mission's recommendations. The High Commissioner was asked to submit to the Council's eighteenth session a report on the implementation of the resolution.

Report of Committee of independent experts. In a May report [A/HRC/16/24] submitted in response to Human Rights Council resolution 15/6 [YUN 2010, p. 788], the Committee of independent experts in international humanitarian and human rights law established pursuant to Council resolution 13/9 [ibid., p. 787] found that Israel had dedicated significant resources to the investigation of over 400 allegations of operational misconduct in Gaza reported by the Fact-Finding Mission and others; in 19 investigations completed by the Israeli authorities, no violations were found to have been committed. Non-governmental organizations, victims and their legal representatives, however, had difficulty accessing information about progress in investigations. The Committee had strong reservations regarding the promptness of some investigations of individual incidents, and it was concerned that the duration of the ongoing investigations into the allegations contained in the Mission's report could impair their effectiveness and, therefore, the prospects of achieving accountability and justice. With regard to the PA, the Committee reported that the Palestinian Independent Investigation Commission was unable to investigate rocket and mortar attacks against Israel and other human rights violations in the Gaza Strip, and thus complete its mandate, as it had not received positive responses to requests for access from either Israel or the de facto authorities in Gaza. The Committee was concerned that criminal accountability mechanisms had not been duly activated in relation to many of the allegations of serious violations in the Mission's report. The Committee acknowledged that the de facto authorities had made efforts to provide information concerning criminal investigations into alleged human rights violations committed by their security forces, and was aware that it was not uncommon for such cases to be resolved through out-of-court settlements. The Committee remained concerned, however, that the de facto authorities had not investigated the launching of rocket and mortar attacks against Israel, and recommended that those authorities make serious efforts to conduct criminal inquiries into all the allegations of grave violations of international law implicated by those attacks.

Report of High Commissioner. In an August report [A/HRC/18/50], the High Commissioner provided information on the status of implementation of Human Rights Council resolution 16/32 (see p. 784). The High Commissioner was not aware that any action had been taken by Israel or the Palestinian side.

Report of Secretary-General. In a September report [A/HRC/18/49] issued in response to Council resolution 16/32, the Secretary-General provided information on the status of the implementation of the recommendations contained in the report of the Fact-Finding Mission, including action by the Human Rights Council, the Security Council, the Prosecutor of the ICC, the General Assembly, Israel, Palestinian armed groups, responsible Palestinian authorities and the international community.

Follow-up to 2010 fact-finding mission on humanitarian flotilla incident

Report of High Commissioner. In March [A/HRC/16/73/Add.1], the High Commissioner issued an addendum to her 2010 report on follow-up to the report of the independent international fact-finding mission [YUN 2010, p. 786] on the humanitarian flotilla incident, in which Israel, on 31 May 2010, intercepted a convoy bound for Gaza, resulting in the deaths of nine people and the wounding of several others [ibid., p. 439]. The addendum provided information received from Palestine and Turkey on the implementation of Human Rights Council resolution 15/1 concerning the incident [ibid., p. 786].

Human Rights Council action. On 25 March [A/HRC/16/2 (res. 16/20)], the Council, by a recorded vote of 37 to 1, with 8 abstentions, stated that it regretted the non-cooperation of Israel with the fact-finding mission; called on concerned parties to ensure the implementation of the conclusions contained in the mission's report; and requested the High Commissioner to report to the Council's seventeenth (2011) session on the status of implementation.

Report of High Commissioner. In May [A/HRC/17/47], the High Commissioner reported on the status of implementation of Council resolution 16/20.

Human Rights Council action. On 17 June [A/HRC/17/2 (res. 17/10)], the Council, by a recorded vote of 36 to 1, with 8 abstentions, requested the High Commissioner to bring to the Secretary-General's attention the conclusions contained in the report of the fact-finding mission, as well as the follow-up reports, and submit to the Council's twentieth (2012) session a final report on the implementation of the conclusions.

PART THREE

Economic and social questions

Chapter I

Development policy and international economic cooperation

In 2011, the recovery of the global economy continued, with strong output growth in developing countries and a weaker economic performance in developed countries. Economic progress, however, failed to translate into employment opportunities, and joblessness and poverty remained key challenges. For the United Nations, sustained and inclusive growth for a fair and more equitable globalization, including job creation, as well as steps for advancing the development agenda beyond 2015, were major focus areas in development policy and international economic cooperation. With regard to other priorities, such as food insecurity and climate change, the United Nations examined policy responses, as well as the potential of science and technology, to address global challenges. New development concepts were also assessed, including happiness and well-being and people's empowerment and development.

Sustainable development remained a priority for the UN system. Preparations were under way for the United Nations Conference on Sustainable Development (Rio+20), to be held in Rio de Janeiro, Brazil, in 2012. The Commission on Sustainable Development reviewed progress in the follow-up to the 2002 World Summit on Sustainable Development and the implementation of Agenda 21—the action plan on sustainable development adopted by the 1992 United Nations Conference on Environment and Development. The Commission's high-level segment in May addressed the thematic cluster for its 2010–2011 implementation cycle: transport, chemicals, waste management, mining and a 10-year framework of programmes on sustainable consumption and production patterns. There was broad agreement that concrete actionable decisions on the five themes were fundamental to achieving the goals of sustainable development and the Millennium Development Goals (MDGs).

The UN system continued to work towards the eradication of poverty and the achievement of the MDGs. The General Assembly reviewed progress made in implementing the Second United Nations Decade for the Eradication of Poverty (2008–2017), and the Economic and Social Council, with the adoption of its multi-year programme of work for the annual ministerial reviews 2012–2014, reaffirmed its commitment to the achievement of the MDGs.

The Council, at its high-level segment in July, discussed the theme "Current global and national trends and challenges and their impact on education" and held a high-level policy dialogue with the international financial and trade institutions on developments in the world economy.

At its session in May, the Commission on Science and Technology for Development considered progress made in implementing and following up on the outcomes of the World Summit on the Information Society. It also dealt with measuring the impact of information and communications technology for development and technologies to confront challenges in areas such as agriculture and water.

The Committee for Development Policy, at its session in March, addressed three themes: education for all, issues related to the least developed countries (LDCs), and migration and development. The Committee of Experts on Public Administration, at its session in April, considered public governance for results, particularly with regard to post-conflict and post-disaster countries, including social protection for vulnerable populations.

The UN system continued to focus on the development problems of groups of countries in special situations. At the Fourth United Nations Conference on the Least Developed Countries, held in Istanbul in May, participants adopted the Istanbul Declaration and the Programme of Action for the Least Developed Countries for the Decade 2011–2020. The Declaration renewed global partnership and solidarity with LDCs, and the Programme of Action set as its overarching goal to overcome the structural challenges faced by LDCs in order to eradicate poverty, achieve internationally agreed development goals and enable graduation from the LDC category.

The General Assembly reviewed UN system support to small island developing States as well as progress in implementing the 1994 Barbados Programme of Action for the Sustainable Development of Small Island Developing States, the follow-up 2005 Mauritius Strategy and the 2003 Almaty Programme of Action for assisting landlocked developing countries.

International economic relations

The *World Economic and Social Survey 2011: The Great Green Technological Transformation* [Sales No. E.11.II.C.1; overview E/2011/50], published by the UN Department of Economic and Social Affairs (DESA), analysed the options and challenges associated with the shift to more efficient and renewable energy technologies; with transforming agricultural technologies so as to guarantee food security without further degrading land and water resources; and with applying the technology required to adapt to climate change and reduce risks to human populations from natural hazards.

The *Survey* noted that the enormous progress in improving welfare over the previous two centuries had come at the lasting cost of degradation of the environment. It stressed the need for new development pathways that would ensure environmental sustainability and reverse ecological destruction, while providing a decent livelihood for present and future generations. Due to the exponential growth in world population, human activity was threatening to surpass the limits of the Earth's capacity as a source of natural resources and a sink for waste, hence requiring a fundamental technological overhaul.

The main challenges lay in the improvement of techniques needed for a green economy, the accessibility and affordability of those technologies for developing countries, and the limited time period given due to pressures on the ecosystem. Governments had to assume a more central role, and intense international cooperation had to be facilitated. The *Survey* proposed the creation of "green national innovation systems" that would reorient sector-specific innovation systems towards a focus on green technologies, and ensure consistency among green technology, industrial and demand-side policies. Targets aimed at a global energy transformation would have to take into account differences in levels of development of countries, and green energy policies would have to be coherent along production and consumption chains. With regard to food security, the report affirmed that the main policy focus on the supply side should be promotion and development of sustainable agriculture as practiced by small farm holders in developing countries. A comprehensive approach to food security was essential and had to be supported by an enabling institutional environment.

The report found that the frequency of climate-related disasters—from which developing countries tended to suffer more—had increased, and pointed out that disaster risk management should be an integral part of national development strategies. Finally, multilateral trading rules and international finance needed to be "greened"; an effective global technology development and diffusion regime needed to be established; the intellectual property rights regime needed to be changed; multilateral trading rules should grant greater flexibility to developing countries in conducting industrial policy; financing of green technology transfer required financial reforms; and global governance capabilities needed to be strengthened.

The *World Economic Situation and Prospects 2011* [Sales No. E.11.II.C.2; update E/2011/113], jointly produced by desa, the United Nations Conference on Trade and Development (unctad) and the five United Nations regional commissions, found that the recovery of the global economy continued, with strong output growth in developing countries and a weaker economic performance in developed countries. Higher energy and food prices had created upward pressure on inflation rates, underpinning the tightening of monetary policy, especially in many developing countries. Employment trends had improved, but major challenges such as rising long-term unemployment and high youth unemployment in a number of economies remained. World trade of goods and services had expanded more than expected, marking a strong rebound from the severe contraction in 2009. Developing countries—particularly Asian economies with large shares in trade of manufactured goods—led the recovery.

Net private capital inflows to emerging economies continued to recover from their pronounced decline during the global financial crisis. The outlook pointed to a number of risks, however, including problems regarding the sustainability of public finances in developed economies, the remaining vulnerability of the private financial sector, continued high and volatile commodity prices and the possible collapse of the United States dollar. In the area of policymaking, numerous challenges remained, such as how to time the unwinding of fiscal support, the redesign of fiscal policy to promote employment and sustainable development, greater synergy between monetary and fiscal policy, the provision of sufficient funding to developing countries and more effective international policy coordination.

The unctad *Trade and Development Report 2012* [Sales No. E.12.II.D.6] (see p. 902) focused on policies for inclusive and balanced growth.

The *Human Development Report 2011* [Sales No. 11.III.B.1] (see p. 844), prepared by the United Nations Development Programme (undp), had as its theme sustainability and equity.

Development and international economic cooperation

International economic cooperation issues were considered by various UN bodies, including the General Assembly and the Economic and Social Council.

On 10 and 11 March, the Council held in New York its special high-level meeting with the Bretton Woods institutions (the World Bank Group and the International Monetary Fund), the World Trade Organization and the United Nations Conference on Trade and Development, addressing the theme

"Coherence, coordination and cooperation on financing for development" (see p. 921).

On 26 April, the Council adopted the themes for its annual ministerial reviews 2012–2014 (**decision 2011/208**). The themes were "Promoting productive capacity, employment and decent work to eradicate poverty in the context of inclusive, sustainable and equitable economic growth at all levels for achieving the Millennium Development Goals" (2012); "Science, technology and innovation, and the potential of culture, for promoting sustainable development and achieving the Millennium Development Goals" (2013); and "Addressing ongoing and emerging challenges for meeting the Millennium Development Goals in 2015 and for sustaining development gains in the future" (2014).

On 22 December, the Assembly took note of the report of the Second (Economic and Financial) Committee on its discussion of macroeconomic policy questions [A/66/438] (**decision 66/542**).

Parliamentary hearing. In February [A/65/728], the General Assembly President transmitted a summary report of the 2010 parliamentary hearing (New York, 2–3 December 2010), organized by the International Parliamentary Union, which addressed the theme "Towards economic recovery: rethinking development, retooling global governance". The annual event was attended by some 160 parliamentarians from 50 countries and five regional parliamentary organizations.

The Economic and Social Council took note of the report on 22 July (**decision 2011/218**).

High-level segment of Economic and Social Council

In accordance with its decision 2010/262 [YUN 2010, p. 1132], the Economic and Social Council, at the high-level segment of its 2011 substantive session (Geneva, 4–8 July) [A/66/3/Rev.1], discussed the theme of "Current global and national trends and challenges and their impact on education". Following its annual ministerial review on the topic, the Council, on 8 July, adopted the ministerial declaration of the high-level segment, entitled "Implementing the internationally agreed goals and commitments in regard to education" (see p. 1056). It held a special event to mark the twenty-fifth anniversary of the Declaration on the Right to Development [YUN 1986, p. 717] and a special event on the humanitarian situation in the Horn of Africa.

The Council had before it a May report [E/2011/15] of the Secretary-General on regional cooperation in the economic, social and related fields, submitted in response to General Assembly resolution 1823(XVII) [YUN 1962, p. 293] and Council resolution 1817(LV) [YUN 1973, p. 449]. The report examined the progress made by different regions in moving towards a new development paradigm of inclusive and sustainable development, and covered regional contributions to the International Year of Youth, the Fourth United Nations Conference on the Least Developed Countries and the Rio+20 Conference to be held in 2012. It also covered developments in selected areas of regional and interregional cooperation, including policy matters addressed during the regional commissions' ministerial sessions, and efforts to promote coherence at the regional level, including through the Regional Coordination Mechanisms convened by the regional commissions, as well as interregional cooperation among the commissions. The Council also had before it the 2011 world economic and social survey [E/2011/50] (see p. 789) and a report on the world economic situation and prospects as of mid-2011 [E/2011/113] (see p. 790).

Policy dialogue. On 5 July [A/66/3/Rev.1], the Council held a high-level policy dialogue with the international financial and trade institutions of the UN system on developments in the world economy.

Communications. On 25 January [S/2011/215], the League of Arab States transmitted to the Secretary-General the resolutions adopted by the Arab Economic, Development and Social Summit at its second session (Sharm el-Sheikh, Egypt, 19 January), including the Sharm el-Sheikh Declaration, which renewed commitments regarding development strategies and focused on the advancement of the human, economic, social and technological development of Arab societies.

On 1 June [A/66/87], Namibia, as President of the Inter-Parliamentary Union (IPU), transmitted to the Secretary-General the text of a resolution adopted by the 124th Assembly of IPU (Panama City, 15–20 April) on the role of parliaments in ensuring sustainable development through the management of natural resources, agricultural production and demographic change.

On 8 July [A/65/903], Kazakhstan transmitted to the Secretary-General the Astana Declaration on "Peace, Cooperation and Development", adopted at the thirty-eighth session of the Organization of Islamic Cooperation Council of Foreign Ministers (Astana, Kazakhstan, 28–30 June).

On 27 September [A/66/388], Argentina transmitted to the Secretary-General the Ministerial Declaration adopted at the thirty-fifth annual meeting of the Ministers for Foreign Affairs of the Group of 77 and China (New York, 23 September), which reviewed the world economic situation and addressed challenges facing developing countries.

Globalization and interdependence

In response to Assembly resolution 65/168 [YUN 2010, p. 793], the Secretary-General submitted an August report [A/66/223] on sustained, inclusive and equitable economic growth for a fair and more equitable globalization for all, including job creation. The report reviewed globalization in the wake of the global financial and economic crisis and addressed economic growth and policies to make growth more sustained, inclusive and equitable. It found that the frequency and severity of financial crises had increased over the previous three decades—usually preceded by large capital movements, rising commodity prices and interest rate hikes—and noted that significant problems, such as macroeconomic instability, financial volatility and boom-bust cycles, associated with financial liberalization and unrestricted private capital flows, which particularly affected developing countries, remained unsolved. It further examined new and emerging developments in globalization with regard to economic growth, income poverty, employment, inequality, international trade, financial flows, debt relief and distress, food security, environment and climate change, as well as information and communications technology. The report emphasized the need for more equitable growth and employment through land reforms, social policies and productive job creation.

The Secretary-General recommended increased policy coherence and coordination at the international level to prevent and mitigate the effects of future financial crises. Developing countries needed enhanced policy space, and the international community should provide further assistance to developing countries in terms of managing development processes, strengthening social protection and building human capital and capacity. As for financial support, the Secretary-General underlined the importance of commitments to official development assistance and suggested that debt relief be provided by extending the heavily indebted poor countries initiative to all low-income countries with debt problems.

GENERAL ASSEMBLY ACTION

On 22 December [meeting 91], the General Assembly, on the recommendation of the Second Committee [A/66/442/Add.1], adopted **resolution 66/210** without vote [agenda item 21 (*a*)].

Role of the United Nations in promoting development in the context of globalization and interdependence

The General Assembly,

Recalling its resolutions 62/199 of 19 December 2007, 63/222 of 19 December 2008, 64/210 of 21 December 2009 and 65/168 of 20 December 2010 on the role of the United Nations in promoting development in the context of globalization and interdependence,

Reaffirming the central role of the United Nations in promoting international cooperation for development and policy coherence on global development issues, including in the context of globalization and interdependence,

Recognizing that globalization and interdependence imply that the economic performance of a country is increasingly affected by factors outside its geographical borders and that maximizing in an equitable manner the benefits of globalization requires responses to globalization to be developed through a strengthened global partnership for development to achieve the internationally agreed development goals, including the Millennium Development Goals,

Reaffirming its strong support for fair and inclusive globalization and the need to translate growth into poverty reduction and, in this regard, its resolve to make the goals of full and productive employment and decent work for all, including for women and young people, a central objective of relevant national and international policies as well as national development strategies, including poverty reduction strategies, as part of efforts to achieve the Millennium Development Goals,

Expressing deep concern about the ongoing adverse impacts, particularly on development, of the world financial and economic crisis, cognizant that the global economy is entering a challenging new phase with significant downside risks, including turbulence in global financial and commodity markets and widespread fiscal strains, which threaten the global economic recovery, and stressing the need to continue to address systemic fragilities and imbalances and the need for continuing efforts to reform and strengthen the international financial system,

Taking note of the report of the Secretary-General entitled "Globalization and interdependence: sustained, inclusive and equitable economic growth for a fair and more equitable globalization for all, including job creation",

1. *Reaffirms* the need for the United Nations to play a fundamental role in the promotion of international cooperation for development and the coherence, coordination and implementation of development goals and actions agreed upon by the international community, and resolves to strengthen coordination within the United Nations system in close cooperation with all other multilateral financial, trade and development institutions in order to support sustained economic growth, poverty eradication and sustainable development;

2. *Also reaffirms* the need to strengthen the central role of the United Nations in enhancing the global partnership for development, with a view to creating a supportive global environment for the attainment of the Millennium Development Goals, including accelerating efforts to deliver and fully implement existing global partnership for development commitments;

3. *Recognizes* that the scaling-up of successful policies and approaches in the implementation and the achievement of the Millennium Development Goals needs to be complemented by a strengthened global partnership for development;

4. *Also recognizes* that the increasing interdependence of national economies in a globalizing world and the emergence of rules-based regimes for international economic relations have meant that the space for national economic policy, that is, the scope for domestic policies, especially in the areas of trade, investment and international devel-

Chapter I: Development policy and international economic cooperation

opment, is now often framed by international disciplines, commitments and global market considerations and that it is for each Government to evaluate the trade-off between the benefits of accepting international rules and commitments and the constraints posed by the loss of policy space;

5. *Further recognizes* that policies which link economic and social development can contribute to reducing inequalities within and among countries with a view to guaranteeing that the poor and those living in the most vulnerable situations maximize their benefits from economic growth and development;

6. *Decides* to include in the provisional agenda of its sixty-eighth session the item entitled "Globalization and interdependence", and requests the Secretary-General to submit to the General Assembly a report on the sub-item entitled "Role of the United Nations in promoting development in the context of globalization and interdependence".

Development cooperation with middle-income countries

In response to resolution 64/208 [YUN 2009, p. 795], the Secretary-General submitted an August report [A/66/220] on development cooperation with middle-income countries. Representing more than 70 per cent of the world population and almost 43 per cent of world gross product, and with a number of economies sustaining rapid growth over the preceding decade, middle-income countries had been increasingly reshaping patterns of global production, trade, capital flows, technology and labour conditions. The report addressed challenges for the development of middle-income countries, including macroeconomic trends, poverty and inequality and policy challenges. It further examined achievements in development cooperation of the UN system with middle-income countries, along with the engagement of international financial institutions. According to the Secretary-General, the UN system needed to develop a more specific policy framework for middle-income countries, taking into account the diversity among and within those countries. Technical cooperation should enhance the capacities of those countries to promote higher value-added, knowledge-based industrial and modern service economies; diversify exports; increase employment; promote social inclusion and investment in social development; ensure a consistently countercyclical macrofinancial framework and policies; strengthen prudential national financial regulation; and ensure economic, social and environmental policy coherence by means of national development strategies.

GENERAL ASSEMBLY ACTION

On 22 December [meeting 91], the General Assembly, on the recommendation of the Second Committee [A/66/442/Add.3], adopted **resolution 66/212** without vote [agenda item 21 (*c*)].

Development cooperation with middle-income countries

The General Assembly,

Recalling the outcomes of the United Nations major international conferences and summits, including the United Nations Millennium Declaration and the 2005 World Summit Outcome, as well as the relevant provisions of General Assembly resolutions,

Reaffirming its resolution 62/208 of 19 December 2007, entitled "Triennial comprehensive policy review of operational activities for development of the United Nations system", in which it recognized that middle-income developing countries still face significant challenges in the area of poverty eradication and that efforts to address those challenges should be supported in order to ensure that achievements made to date are sustained, including through support to the effective development of comprehensive cooperation policies,

Recalling its resolutions 63/223 of 19 December 2008 and 64/208 of 21 December 2009,

1. *Takes note* of the report of the Secretary-General;
2. *Stresses* the importance of the continued substantive consideration of the issue of development cooperation with middle-income countries;
3. *Requests* the Secretary-General to submit to the General Assembly at its sixty-eighth session a report on development cooperation with middle-income countries, and decides to include in the provisional agenda of the session, under the item entitled "Globalization and interdependence" the sub-item entitled "Development cooperation with middle-income countries".

Development through partnerships

In compliance with resolution 64/223 [YUN 2009, p. 796], the Secretary-General submitted an August report [A/66/320] on the implementation of the proposed modalities for enhanced cooperation between the United Nations and all relevant partners, in particular the private sector. The report reviewed the concept of partnerships, the role of Member States, developments at the system level, trends at the level of agencies, funds and programmes and measures to address key operational challenges. The Secretary-General recommended that the UN system strengthen the enabling environment for partnerships with the private sector through more strategic approaches and new partnership models, thus achieving greater impact and scale. Further recommendations included improving capacity-building at all levels, improving partner selection and engagement processes and taking into account the recommendations of the Global Compact LEAD Working Group, launched at the Private Sector Forum in September.

JIU report. In July [A/66/137 & Corr.1], the Secretary-General transmitted a Joint Inspection Unit (JIU) report entitled "United Nations corporate partnerships: the role and functioning of the Global Compact", which examined the role and degree of success of the Global Compact and the risks associated with the use of the United Nations brand by companies that might benefit from their association with the Organization without having to prove their conformity with UN core values and principles.

JIU found that, while the Global Compact initiative evolved quickly under the aegis of the Secretary-General, the lack of a clear mandate had resulted in blurred focus and impact, while the absence of adequate entry criteria and an effective monitoring system had drawn some criticism and reputational risk for the Organization. The inspectors further noted the absence of a regulatory and institutional framework, as well as the lack of an effective screening and monitoring system to verify the engagement of the participants and their actual implementation of the Global Compact principles. At times, the flexibility granted to the Global Compact Office (GCO) in terms of financing and staffing had led to the bypassing of regulations and to an unbalanced funding structure. The report further identified a costly and ineffective governance structure without central decision-making, and stressed the need for an independent performance evaluation mechanism.

JIU recommended the preparation of a long-term strategic framework in accordance with a clear mandate for the GCO, and the regrouping of the latter with the United Nations Office for Partnerships under one umbrella. In terms of participants, it requested a more equal composition by category and geographic region, and a selection process based on preset criteria. Further recommendations concerned the strengthening of accountability, transparency, funding structure and evaluation mechanisms.

In October [A/66/137/Add.1], the Secretary-General transmitted his comments on the JIU report. He generally agreed on the remarks of the inspectors and stated that many of the recommendations had already been implemented or were being implemented.

GENERAL ASSEMBLY ACTION

On 22 December [meeting 91], the General Assembly, on the recommendation of the Second Committee [A/66/447], adopted **resolution 66/223** without vote [agenda item 26].

Towards global partnerships

The General Assembly,

Recalling its resolutions 55/215 of 21 December 2000, 56/76 of 11 December 2001, 58/129 of 19 December 2003, 60/215 of 22 December 2005, 62/211 of 19 December 2007 and 64/223 of 21 December 2009,

Reiterating that sustainable development is a key element of the overarching framework for United Nations activities, in particular for achieving the internationally agreed development goals, including the Millennium Development Goals, and those contained in the Plan of Implementation of the World Summit on Sustainable Development ("Johannesburg Plan of Implementation"),

Recalling the objectives formulated in the United Nations Millennium Declaration, notably the Millennium Development Goals, and the reaffirmation they received in the 2005 World Summit Outcome, and the outcome document of the High-level Plenary Meeting of the General Assembly on the Millennium Development Goals in 2010, particularly in regard to developing partnerships through the provision of greater opportunities to the private sector, non-governmental organizations and civil society in general so as to enable them to contribute to the realization of the goals and programmes of the Organization, in particular in the pursuit of development and the eradication of poverty,

Underlining the fact that cooperation between the United Nations and all relevant partners, including the private sector, shall serve the purposes and principles embodied in the Charter of the United Nations, and shall be undertaken in a manner that maintains and promotes the integrity, impartiality and independence of the Organization,

Taking note of the further increase in the number of public-private partnerships worldwide,

Welcoming the contribution of all relevant partners, including the private sector, non-governmental organizations and civil society, to the implementation of the outcomes of the United Nations conferences and summits and their reviews in the economic, social, environmental and related fields, as well as the realization of the internationally agreed development goals, including the Millennium Development Goals,

Emphasizing that the United Nations, together with the private sector and all other relevant partners, can contribute in multiple ways to addressing the obstacles confronted by developing countries in mobilizing the resources needed to finance their sustainable development and to the realization of the internationally agreed development goals,

Welcoming the efforts and encouraging further efforts by all relevant partners, including the private sector, to engage as reliable and consistent partners in the development process and to take into account not only the economic and financial but also the developmental, social, human rights, gender and environmental implications of their undertakings and, in general, towards implementing corporate social and environmental responsibility, that is, bringing such values and responsibilities to bear on their conduct and policy premised on profit incentives, in conformity with national laws and regulations,

Recalling that the 2005 World Summit welcomed the positive contributions of the private sector and civil society, including non-governmental organizations, foundations and academia, in the promotion and implementation of development and human rights programmes, and also recalling that the 2005 World Summit resolved to enhance the contribution of non-governmental organizations, civil society, the private sector and other stakeholders in national development efforts, as well as in the promotion of the global partnership for development, and encouraged public-private partnerships in a wide range of areas, with the aim of eradicating poverty and promoting full employment and social integration,

Noting that private sector partnerships can play an important role in support of the humanitarian assistance activities of the United Nations system, taking into account the primary role of the affected State in the initiation, organization, coordination and implementation of such assistance within its territory,

Recognizing the contribution of the private sector to the provision of resources and expertise on the policy environment, technical programmes, advocacy and communication, knowledge management and resource mobilization in many areas, in accordance with national legislation and development plans and priorities,

Noting that the financial and economic crisis, inter alia, has demonstrated the need for values and principles in business, including for sustainable business practices, and the promotion of full and productive employment and decent work for all, which in turn has led to broader private sector engagement in support of United Nations goals,

Reaffirming the principles of sustainable development, and underlining the need for a global consensus on the key values and principles that will promote sustainable, fair, equitable and sustained economic development, and that corporate social and environmental responsibility are important elements of such a consensus,

Recognizing the importance of promoting a gender perspective in global partnerships, welcoming in this context the establishment of the United Nations Entity for Gender Equality and the Empowerment of Women (UN-Women), and taking note with appreciation of the joint United Nations Global Compact/UN-Women initiative "Women's Empowerment Principles: Equality Means Business",

Taking note with appreciation of the progress achieved in the work of the United Nations on partnerships, notably in the framework of various United Nations organizations, agencies, funds, programmes, task forces, commissions and initiatives, and taking note of the establishment of partnerships at the field level, entered into by various United Nations agencies, non-public partners and Member States,

Noting with appreciation the advancement of the concept of corporate social responsibility through the United Nations Global Compact,

Recognizing the vital role that the United Nations Global Compact Office continues to play with regard to strengthening the capacity of the United Nations to partner strategically with the private sector in accordance with its General Assembly mandate to advance United Nations values and responsible business practices within the United Nations system and among the global business community,

1. *Takes note* of the report of the Secretary-General, the report of the Joint Inspection Unit and the comments of the Secretary-General thereon;

2. *Stresses* that partnerships are voluntary and collaborative relationships between various parties, both public and non-public, in which all participants agree to work together to achieve a common purpose or undertake a specific task and, as mutually agreed, to share risks and responsibilities, resources and benefits;

3. *Also stresses* the importance of the contribution of voluntary partnerships to the achievement of the internationally agreed development goals, including the Millennium Development Goals, while reiterating that they are a complement to, but not intended to substitute for, the commitment made by Governments with a view to achieving those goals;

4. *Further stresses* that partnerships should be consistent with national laws and national development strategies and plans, as well as the priorities of countries where they are implemented, bearing in mind the relevant guidance provided by Governments;

5. *Emphasizes* the vital role played by Governments in promoting responsible business practices, including providing the necessary legal and regulatory frameworks, where appropriate, and invites them to continue to provide support to United Nations efforts to engage with the private sector, as appropriate and bearing in mind the activities undertaken by the United Nations Global Compact Local Networks;

6. *Recognizes* the vital role that the private sector plays in development, including through engaging in various partnership models and by generating decent employment and investment, giving access to and developing new technologies, as well as stimulating sustained, inclusive and equitable economic growth, while bearing in mind the need to ensure that their activities conform fully with the principle of national ownership of development strategies;

7. *Also recognizes* the need for effective accountability and transparency in the implementation of such public-private partnerships by the United Nations;

8. *Calls upon* the international community to continue to promote multi-stakeholder approaches in addressing the challenges of development in the context of globalization;

9. *Encourages* the United Nations system to continue to develop, for those partnerships in which it participates, a common and systemic approach, which places greater emphasis on impact, transparency, coherence, accountability and sustainability, without imposing undue rigidity in partnership agreements, and with due consideration being given to the following partnership principles: common purpose, transparency, bestowing no unfair advantages upon any partner of the United Nations, mutual benefit and mutual respect, accountability, respect for the modalities of the United Nations, striving for balanced representation of relevant partners from developed and developing countries and countries with economies in transition, sectoral and geographic balance, and not compromising the independence and neutrality of the United Nations;

10. *Also encourages* the United Nations system to continue to find innovative and additional ways to achieve lasting impact by identifying and replicating successful partnership models and pursuing new forms of collaboration;

11. *Requests* the United Nations Global Compact Local Networks to promote the Women's Empowerment Principles and to create awareness of the many ways in which business can promote gender equality in the workplace, marketplace and community;

12. *Underlines*, in this context, the importance of integrity measures as taken and advocated by the United Nations Global Compact;

13. *Requests* the Secretary-General to promote effective implementation of the revised United Nations guidelines for partnerships between the United Nations and the private sector, including through the effective implementation of the revised Guidelines on Cooperation between the United Nations and the Business Sector, thus promoting a

culture of transparency and performance, and invites the Secretary-General to create an internal advisory group in the Secretariat, which will use innovative and cost-effective working methods to ensure coherent brand management across the United Nations and to make recommendations on partnership best practices and lessons learned;

14. *Invites* the United Nations system, when considering partnerships, to seek to engage in a more coherent manner with private sector entities, including small and medium-sized enterprises, that support the core values of the United Nations as reflected in the Charter and other relevant conventions and treaties and that commit to the principles of the United Nations Global Compact by translating them into operational corporate policies, codes of conduct and management, monitoring and reporting systems;

15. *Encourages* the international community to strengthen global partnerships for the integration and implementation of the International Labour Organization Global Jobs Pact in partnerships, in accordance with national plans and priorities;

16. *Takes note with appreciation* of the convening of an annual United Nations Private Sector Forum since 2008;

17. *Also takes note with appreciation* of the introduction of the private sector track at the Fourth United Nations Conference on the Least Developed Countries, held in Istanbul, Turkey, from 9 to 13 May 2011;

18. *Recognizes* the work of the United Nations Global Compact Local Networks, as well as the importance of cooperation between the United Nations system at the local level and the United Nations Global Compact Local Networks, to support, as appropriate and in a manner complementary to existing networks, the coordination and application of global partnerships locally;

19. *Acknowledges* the holding of annual meetings of United Nations system private sector focal points, which bring together United Nations entities to share best practices and lessons learned in order to improve partnerships and create conditions for effective scaling up;

20. *Notes* the progress made in further facilitating the collaboration between the United Nations and the private sector and enhancing transparency by the launching of the United Nations business website, which links private sector resources with the needs of the United Nations system;

21. *Requests* the Secretary-General to submit to the General Assembly at its sixty-eighth session a report on specific progress on integrity measures, on the implementation of the revised United Nations guidelines for partnerships between the United Nations and the private sector and on the strengthening of the United Nations Global Compact Local Networks.

Happiness and well-being

Introducing on 19 July [A/65/PV.109] a draft resolution [A/65/L.86] entitled "Happiness: towards a holistic approach to development", Bhutan noted that an increasing number of thinkers, economists and political leaders were searching for ways to make development more sustainable, humane and holistic, and that several Member States had taken initiatives to develop indicators for happiness and well-being.

The draft resolution invited Member States to elaborate additional measures that better reflected happiness and well-being, with a view to guiding their public policies.

GENERAL ASSEMBLY ACTION

On 19 July [meeting 109], the General Assembly adopted **resolution 65/309** [draft: A/65/L.86 & Add.1] without vote [agenda item 13].

Happiness: towards a holistic approach to development

The General Assembly,

Bearing in mind the purposes and principles of the United Nations, as set forth in the Charter of the United Nations, which include the promotion of the economic advancement and social progress of all peoples,

Conscious that the pursuit of happiness is a fundamental human goal,

Cognizant that happiness as a universal goal and aspiration embodies the spirit of the Millennium Development Goals,

Recognizing that the gross domestic product indicator by nature was not designed to and does not adequately reflect the happiness and well-being of people in a country,

Conscious that unsustainable patterns of production and consumption can impede sustainable development, and recognizing the need for a more inclusive, equitable and balanced approach to economic growth that promotes sustainable development, poverty eradication, happiness and well-being of all peoples,

Acknowledging the need to promote sustainable development and achieve the Millennium Development Goals,

1. *Invites* Member States to pursue the elaboration of additional measures that better capture the importance of the pursuit of happiness and well-being in development with a view to guiding their public policies;

2. *Invites* those Member States that have taken initiatives to develop new indicators, and other initiatives, to share information thereon with the Secretary-General as a contribution to the United Nations development agenda, including the Millennium Development Goals;

3. *Welcomes* the offer of Bhutan to convene during the sixty-sixth session of the General Assembly a panel discussion on the theme of happiness and well-being;

4. *Invites* the Secretary-General to seek the views of Member States and relevant regional and international organizations on the pursuit of happiness and well-being and to communicate such views to the General Assembly at its sixty-seventh session for further consideration.

People's empowerment and development

In a letter of 13 August [A/66/197] to the Secretary-General, Bangladesh requested the inclusion in the agenda of the sixty-sixth (2011) session of the General Assembly of a supplementary item entitled "People's empowerment and a peace-centric development model". According to an attached explanatory memorandum, interlinked and mutually reinforcing elements of peace and empowerment included eradicating poverty and hunger, reducing inequality, mitigating deprivation, creating jobs for all, including excluded people, accelerating human development and fighting terrorism of all kinds.

GENERAL ASSEMBLY ACTION

On 22 December [meeting 91], the General Assembly, on the recommendation of the Second Committee [A/66/448], adopted **resolution 66/224** without vote [agenda item 29].

People's empowerment and development

The General Assembly,

Guided by the purposes and principles enshrined in the Charter of the United Nations,

Expressing concern about the crippling effects of poverty, inequality and disparity all over the globe, and recognizing that people should be the focus of all plans, programmes and policies, at all levels,

Recognizing that the empowerment of people is essential to achieving development,

Appreciating the efforts of the Prime Minister of Bangladesh, Sheikh Hasina, in articulating the linkages between people's empowerment and development,

1. *Notes* the proposal of the Prime Minister of Bangladesh on integrating the interlinked and mutually reinforcing elements of people's empowerment and development, expressed as eradicating poverty and hunger, reducing inequality, mitigating deprivation, creating jobs for all, including excluded people, accelerating human development and fighting terrorism in all its forms and manifestations in accordance with international law;

2. *Also notes* the offer of the Government of Bangladesh to convene an international conference on people's empowerment and development during the first half of 2012 to seek the views of Member States on the subject.

Human security

In resolution 64/291 [YUN 2010, p. 806], the General Assembly took note of the ongoing efforts to define the notion of human security and requested the Secretary-General to seek the views of Member States in that regard. In a July note [A/66/160], the Secretariat stated that extensive consultations with all relevant stakeholders were expected to take place throughout 2011 in order to propose a possible definition.

Sustainable development

In 2011, various UN bodies, including the General Assembly, the Economic and Social Council and the Commission on Sustainable Development, considered the implementation of the outcomes of the 2002 World Summit on Sustainable Development [YUN 2002, p. 821], particularly the Johannesburg Declaration and Plan of Implementation, which outlined actions and targets for stepping up implementation of Agenda 21—a programme of action for sustainable development worldwide, adopted at the 1992 United Nations Conference on Environment and Development [YUN 1992, p. 672]—and of the Programme for the Further Implementation of Agenda 21, adopted by the Assembly at its nineteenth special session in 1997 [YUN 1997, p. 792]. Further steps were taken to prepare for the United Nations Conference on Sustainable Development, to be held in Rio de Janeiro, Brazil, in 2012.

In presidential statement **S/PRST/2011/4** of 11 February (see p. 41), the Security Council highlighted the interdependence between security and development and underlined the importance of close cooperation with the Economic and Social Council in accordance with Article 65 of the UN Charter.

Commission on Sustainable Development

As the main body responsible for coordinating and monitoring implementation of the Summit outcomes, the Commission on Sustainable Development held its nineteenth session in New York (14 May 2010 and 2–13 May 2011) [E/2011/29], electing members of the Bureau at its first meeting on 14 May 2010.

Intersessional events. An intersessional senior expert group meeting on "Sustainable development of lithium resources in Latin America: emerging issues and opportunities" (Santiago, Chile, 10–11 November 2010) [E/CN.17/2011/16] concluded that greater international cooperation, including scientific, technological and financial cooperation, was needed to enhance national and regional sustainable development.

An intersessional consultative meeting on "Solid waste management in Africa" (Rabat, Morocco, 25–26 November 2010) [E/CN.17/2011/15], organized by the Department of Economic and Social Affairs (DESA) in partnership with the United Nations Human Settlements Programme and the United Nations Environment Programme (UNEP), sought to identify the special needs of the African continent and to build a coalition for reducing the negative impacts of improper waste management. In the resulting Rabat Declaration, participants stated that enhanced waste management through partnerships would offer multiple benefits for Africa.

DESA and UNEP held a high-level intersessional meeting [E/CN.17/2011/13] on a 10-year framework of programmes on sustainable consumption and production patterns (Panama City, 13–14 January 2011). The Commission recognized that the framework could provide a platform for the sharing of best practices and thus enable replication and monitoring of goals and objectives.

An intersessional conference on building partnerships for moving towards zero waste (Tokyo, 16–18 February) [E/CN.17/2011/14], organized by DESA, the United Nations Centre for Regional Development and the Ministry of the Environment of Japan, addressed the rising volume and complexity of waste streams and called for an international partnership to respond to that challenge.

Preparatory meeting. The Intergovernmental Preparatory Meeting for the Commission's nineteenth session (New York, 28 February–4 March) [E/CN.17/2011/19] had before it the Secretary-General's reports on policy options and actions for expediting progress in implementation on interlinkages and cross-cutting issues [E/CN.17/2011/3], transport [E/CN.17/2011/4], chemicals [E/CN.17/2011/5], waste management [E/CN.17/2011/6], mining [E/CN.17/2011/7] and a 10-year framework of programmes on sustainable consumption and production patterns [E/CN.17/2011/8]. Also before the Meeting was a Secretariat note [E/CN.17/2011/12] on priorities for actions of major groups concerning transport, chemicals, waste management, mining and a 10-year framework of programmes on sustainable consumption and production patterns.

Following discussions on those themes, the Chair proposed a draft negotiating document to be transmitted to the Commission. Participants took note of the document on 4 March.

Communication. Thailand submitted to the nineteenth session a summary of the Fifth Regional Environmentally Sustainable Transport Forum in Asia (Bangkok, 23–25 August 2010) [E/CN.17/2011/18], jointly organized by Thailand, Japan, the United Nations Centre for Regional Development and the Economic and Social Commission for Asia and the Pacific.

Policy session. At its nineteenth session—the policy session of the 2010–2011 implementation cycle—the Commission discussed the thematic cluster for the cycle: transport, chemicals, waste management, mining and a 10-year framework of programmes on sustainable consumption and production patterns. There was broad agreement among the delegates that concrete decisions on those five themes were of fundamental importance to achieving the goals of sustainable development and the Millennium Development Goals (MDGs). Full agreement on elements of a decision on the transport and mining themes as well as on a 10-year framework of programmes on sustainable consumption and production patterns was reached; however, consensus was not achieved on the themes related to chemicals and waste management.

The Commission recommended to the Economic and Social Council for adoption one draft decision on the provisional agenda for its twentieth session and another on the adoption of the report on the Commission's nineteenth session. It also took note of the draft programme of work for the biennium 2012–2013 for the DESA Division for Sustainable Development [E/CN.17/2011/11]. The Commission brought to the attention of the Council the Chair's summary, "Proposed outcome document on policy options and practical measures to expedite implementation in transport, chemicals, waste management, mining, and a 10-year framework of programmes on sustainable consumption and production patterns".

High-level segment. The Commission's high-level segment (11–13 May) addressed the five thematic areas under consideration. Interactive ministerial round tables were held on developing programmes and a framework to accelerate the shift towards sustainable consumption and production, enhancing access to sustainable urban and rural transport, moving towards zero waste and sound management of chemicals and creating an enabling environment for sustainable mining. Delegations indicated the need to achieve concrete policy actions and measures that would expedite the implementation of the sustainable development agenda with clear means of implementation and political will. Building partnerships and strengthening cooperation, including South-South and South-North cooperation, were also suggested.

The interactive ministerial dialogue of 13 May was opened by the Secretary-General, who stressed that the United Nations Conference on Sustainable Development (Rio+20) should provide the opportunity to make a fundamental transformation in consumption patterns, lifestyles and values, while addressing the need for equity in institutions and policies.

During the partnerships fair (2–6 May), registered partnerships for sustainable development reported on progress achieved, lessons learned and opportunities explored to network with existing and potential partners and to create synergies among partnerships. The Learning Centre offered 14 courses in which participants had the opportunity to gain knowledge, acquire practical know-how, share national experiences and discuss best practices with regard to the five themes, as well as cross-cutting issues such as monitoring, education and partnerships.

The Economic and Social Council, on 27 July, took note of the Commission's report on its nineteenth session (**decision 2011/244**) and approved the provisional agenda for the Commission's twentieth session (**decision 2011/243**).

Implementation of Agenda 21, the Programme for the Further Implementation of Agenda 21 and the Johannesburg Plan of Implementation

In response to General Assembly resolution 65/152 [YUN 2010, p. 803], the Secretary-General submitted an August report [A/66/287] on the implementation of Agenda 21, the Programme for the Further Implementation of Agenda 21 and the outcomes of the World Summit on Sustainable Development, reviewing actions taken by Governments, UN system organizations and major groups in implementing sustainable development goals and targets, including through partnerships.

The report elaborated ways to promote closer convergence among the three pillars of sustainable development—economic growth, social improvement and environmental protection—and examined challenges related to poverty eradication, adverse impacts on nature and natural resources, and international commitment. It identified as priorities the sectors of energy, water, food security and sustainable agriculture, urbanization, biodiversity and oceans; stressed the importance of institutions and governance regarding sustainable development; and reviewed preparations for the 2012 United Nations Conference on Sustainable Development.

The declared goal of establishing a renewable low-carbon energy system on a global scale remained elusive; the Secretary-General recommended common efforts to expand access to clean energy, enhance industrial energy efficiency and promote green industry. More investment in water infrastructure and better management of water were required to enhance agricultural productivity and meet growing demand. While the proportion of the urban population living in slums had decreased, the absolute numbers had risen from 767 million to some 828 million over the previous decade, pointing to the need for equitable planning and adequate economic policies. The report stressed the fact that nearly 17,000 species of plants and animals were threatened with extinction, and requested strategic planning and greater efficiency in the use of natural resources in order to prevent further human-induced biodiversity loss. Moreover, newly emerging threats such as ocean acidification, ocean noise and plastics, microplastics and marine debris had to be addressed. The Secretary-General stated that the institutional framework needed to support the integration of the three pillars of sustainable development, avoid duplication and strengthen coherence and synergies.

On 24 December, the General Assembly decided that the agenda item on sustainable development would remain for consideration during its resumed sixty-sixth (2012) session (**decision 66/557**).

Preparations for UN Conference on Sustainable Development

In accordance with General Assembly resolution 64/236 [YUN 2009, p. 802], the Preparatory Committee for the United Nations Conference on Sustainable Development held its second session (New York, 7–8 March) [A/CONF.216/PC/9]. It considered progress achieved and remaining gaps in the implementation of the outcomes of the major summits in the area of sustainable development; analysed the themes of the Conference; and addressed organizational and procedural matters.

The Committee had before it the Secretary-General's report on the objective and themes of the Conference [A/CONF.216/PC/7] and a related note by the Secretariat [A/CONF.216/PC/8].

The Committee held two interactive discussions on the themes of the Conference: "Green economy in the context of sustainable development and poverty eradication" and "Institutional framework for sustainable development". On 8 March, the Committee adopted a decision on the process for the preparation of the draft outcome document for the Conference.

Meeting on 12 September, the Bureau of the Preparatory Committee prepared a set of recommendations for the organization of work of the Conference. On 4 October [A/C.2/66/2], the Co-Chairs of the Bureau—Antigua and Barbuda and the Republic of Korea—transmitted those recommendations to the Secretary-General for consideration by the Second Committee and possible inclusion in the final resolution on the modalities of the Conference.

GENERAL ASSEMBLY ACTION

On 22 December [meeting 91], the General Assembly, on the recommendation of the Second Committee [A/66/440/Add.1], adopted **resolution 66/197** without vote [agenda item 19 (*a*)].

Implementation of Agenda 21, the Programme for the Further Implementation of Agenda 21 and the outcomes of the World Summit on Sustainable Development

The General Assembly,

Recalling its resolutions 55/199 of 20 December 2000, 56/226 of 24 December 2001, 57/253 and 57/270 A of 20 December 2002 and 57/270 B of 23 June 2003, as well as its resolutions 64/236 of 24 December 2009 and 65/152 of 20 December 2010 and all other relevant resolutions on the implementation of Agenda 21, the Programme for the Further Implementation of Agenda 21 and the outcomes of the World Summit on Sustainable Development,

Recalling also the Rio Declaration on Environment and Development, Agenda 21, the Programme for the Further Implementation of Agenda 21, the Johannesburg Declaration on Sustainable Development and the Plan of Implementation of the World Summit on Sustainable Development ("Johannesburg Plan of Implementation"), as well as the Monterrey Consensus of the International Conference on Financing for Development, the Doha Declaration on Financing for Development: outcome document of the Follow-up International Conference on Financing for Development to Review the Implementation of the Monterrey

Consensus and the outcome document of the High-level Plenary Meeting of the General Assembly on the Millennium Development Goals,

Recalling further its decision to hold the United Nations Conference on Sustainable Development in Brazil in 2012,

1. *Takes note* of the report of the Secretary-General;

2. *Also takes note* of the report of the Preparatory Committee for the United Nations Conference on Sustainable Development on its second session, and endorses its decision 2/1, entitled "Process for the preparation of the draft outcome document for the United Nations Conference on Sustainable Development", as contained in chapter VI of the report;

3. *Decides* that the United Nations Conference on Sustainable Development shall be held from 20 to 22 June 2012 in Rio de Janeiro, Brazil, and recommends for adoption by the Conference the provisional agenda of the Conference as set forth in annex I to the present resolution;

4. *Encourages* Member States to be represented at the Conference at the highest possible level, including Heads of State or Government;

5. *Decides* that the Conference shall be composed of six plenary meetings, on the basis of two meetings a day, and four high-level round-table sessions, to be held in concurrence with the plenary meetings, except during the opening and closing plenary meetings;

6. *Also decides* that the Conference shall be organized in accordance with the organization of work set forth in annex II to the present resolution;

7. *Notes* the need to expedite the process for conclusion of the draft provisional rules of procedure of the Conference as early as possible in 2012 and, in this regard, notes the decision of the Bureau of the Preparatory Committee to initiate informal consultations on this matter to be concluded in a timely manner;

8. *Calls upon* all Member States to continue to actively engage in the preparatory process, and in the Conference itself, with a view to reaching a successful outcome of the Conference;

9. *Decides* that the third session of the Preparatory Committee shall be held from 13 to 15 June 2012 in Rio de Janeiro;

10. *Strongly encourages* Member States to conclude negotiations on the draft outcome document at the third session of the Preparatory Committee;

11. *Reiterates its request* to the Secretary-General to continue to provide all appropriate support to the work of the preparatory process of the Conference and to the Conference itself and to ensure inter-agency cooperation and effective participation and coherence within the United Nations system, as well as the efficient use of resources, so that the objective and the two themes of the Conference can be addressed;

12. *Invites* Member States, observers and all relevant stakeholders, including the regional commissions, United Nations organizations and bodies, other relevant intergovernmental and regional organizations, international financial institutions and major groups involved in sustainable development, to participate fully and effectively in the Conference and to provide ideas and proposals reflecting their experiences and lessons learned as a contribution to the preparatory process of the Conference, as agreed in the preparatory process by Member States;

13. *Encourages* Governments, in their national preparations for the Conference, to continue to actively involve and to coordinate inputs from all national agencies responsible for economic development, social development and environmental protection;

14. *Emphasizes* the importance of the support of the United Nations development system, as appropriate, for national preparations for the Conference, upon the request of national authorities;

15. *Reiterates its deep concern* that the resources available in the voluntary Trust Fund to Support the Work of the Commission on Sustainable Development are insufficient to fund the participation of representatives from developing countries, as well as representatives of major groups, in the meetings of the preparatory process of the Conference and in the Conference itself;

16. *Urges* international and bilateral donors and other countries and entities in a position to do so to provide contributions to the voluntary Trust Fund for the Conference in a timely manner and requests the Secretary-General to make further efforts to use the limited resources in the Trust Fund in an efficient, effective and transparent manner in order to enhance the active participation of representatives from developing countries in the preparatory process of the Conference (comprising the remaining intersessional meetings, informal informal negotiations and the third session of the Preparatory Committee), and in the Conference itself, and in this regard encourages the Secretary-General, when using the resources of the Trust Fund, to prioritize the coverage of economy-class air tickets, daily subsistence and terminal expenses;

17. *Requests* the Secretary-General to submit a report on the outcome of the Conference to the General Assembly at its sixty-seventh session;

18. *Decides* to include in the provisional agenda of its sixty-seventh session, under the item entitled "Sustainable development", the sub-item entitled "Implementation of Agenda 21, the Programme for the Further Implementation of Agenda 21 and the outcomes of the World Summit on Sustainable Development", taking into account the outcome of the Conference.

Annex I

Provisional agenda of the United Nations Conference on Sustainable Development, Rio de Janeiro, Brazil, 20 to 22 June 2012

1. Opening of the Conference.
2. Election of the President.
3. Adoption of the rules of procedure.
4. Adoption of the agenda of the Conference.
5. Election of officers other than the President.
6. Organization of work, including the establishment of subsidiary bodies, and other organizational matters.
7. Credentials of representatives to the Conference:
   (*a*) Appointment of the members of the Credentials Committee;
   (*b*) Report of the Credentials Committee.
8. General debate.
9. Reports of the round tables.
10. Outcome of the Conference.
11. Adoption of the report of the Conference.
12. Closure of the Conference.

ANNEX II
Proposed organization of work of the United Nations Conference on Sustainable Development, Rio de Janeiro, Brazil, 20 to 22 June 2012

1. The arrangements set out below have been formulated pursuant to General Assembly resolution 64/236.

2. The United Nations Conference on Sustainable Development will be held in Rio de Janeiro, Brazil, from 20 to 22 June 2012.

I. Organization of work
A
Plenary meetings

3. The United Nations Conference on Sustainable Development will consist of a total of six high-level plenary meetings to be held, as follows:

Wednesday, 20 June 2012: from 10 a.m. to 1 p.m. and from 3 to 6 p.m.

Thursday, 21 June 2012: from 10 a.m. to 1 p.m. and from 3 to 6 p.m.

Friday, 22 June 2012: from 10 a.m. to 1 p.m. and from 3 to 6 p.m.

Evening sessions may be held, if required. All plenary meetings will be held at the Riocentro Exhibition and Convention Center.

4. The list of speakers for the plenary meetings will be established by the drawing of lots, in accordance with the customary protocol that ensures that Heads of State or Government speak first, followed by other heads of delegation. The Holy See, in its capacity as observer State, Palestine, in its capacity as observer, and the European Union, in its capacity as observer, will be included in the list of speakers. Statements will be limited to five minutes. Detailed arrangements will be communicated in a timely manner through a note by the Secretariat, prepared in close consultations with the host country and the Bureau of the Preparatory Committee.

5. The formal opening plenary meeting, to be held during the morning of Wednesday, 20 June, will consider all procedural and organizational matters, including the adoption of the rules of procedure and of the agenda, the election of the President of the Conference, the election of officers, the establishment of a Main Committee, the appointment of the members of the Credentials Committee and arrangements for the preparation of the report of the Conference, and other matters. The plenary meeting will also hear statements from the President of the Economic and Social Council and the nine major groups.

6. At the ceremonial opening of the Conference, which will be held on Wednesday, 20 June, during the afternoon plenary meeting, statements will be made by the President of the Conference, the President of the General Assembly, the Secretary-General of the United Nations and the Secretary-General of the Conference.

7. The closing plenary meeting, to be held during the afternoon of Friday, 22 June, is expected to conclude with the presentation of the summaries by the Rapporteurs of the high-level round tables and the adoption of the outcome document and the report of the Conference.

B
Main Committee

8. A Main Committee, established in accordance with the rules of procedure of the Conference, will meet, if necessary, in parallel with plenary meetings except during the opening and closing meetings. The Main Committee would be seized with finalizing any outstanding matters.

C
High-level round tables

9. The United Nations Conference on Sustainable Development will hold four high-level round-table sessions in parallel with the plenary meetings, as follows:

Wednesday, 20 June 2012: from 4.30 to 7.30 p.m.

Thursday, 21 June 2012: from 10 a.m. to 1 p.m. and from 3 to 6 p.m.

Friday, 22 June 2012: from 10 a.m. to 1 p.m.

10. The four high-level round-table sessions will have a common theme: "Looking at the way forward in implementing the expected outcomes of the Conference".

11. Each high-level round table will have two Co-Chairs and a Rapporteur, to be appointed by the President of the Conference from among the Heads of State or Government and ministers attending the Conference, in accordance with the principle of equitable geographical distribution and taking into account invitations for nominations to be extended to the Chairs of regional groups.

12. The outcomes of the round tables should be reflected in the summaries by the Rapporteurs, which should be submitted to the closing plenary meeting of the Conference and included in the final report of the Conference.

13. The four round-table sessions will be interactive and multi-stakeholder in nature, with seventy seats each: up to fifty for Government delegations and at least twenty for other participants, including representatives of observers, entities of the United Nations system and other accredited intergovernmental organizations and major groups. Member States and other participants are encouraged to be represented at the round tables at the highest possible level. Participants will be invited by the Secretariat to sign up for participation in one of the round tables in advance of the Conference, bearing in mind the total number of participants outlined above. The opening of the inscription for participation in the round tables will be announced in the *Journal of the United Nations*.

14. Any given State, observer, entity of the United Nations system or other accredited intergovernmental organization or representative of a major group may participate in only one of the round tables. Each participant may be accompanied by one adviser.

15. The list of participants in each round-table session will be made available prior to the meeting.

16. The proceedings of the round tables will be telecast in an "overflow room" which will be open to the media and all other accredited participants.

II. Credentials of representatives to the Conference: appointment of the members of the Credentials Committee

17. A Credentials Committee will be appointed according to the rules of procedure of the Conference.

III. Participants

A
Member States and observers

18. The Conference, including the plenary and informal meetings, will be open to participation by all States Members of the United Nations, the Holy See, in its capacity as observer State, Palestine, in its capacity as observer, and the European Union, in its capacity as observer, as well as intergovernmental organizations and other entities having received a standing invitation from the General Assembly to participate as observers in the sessions and the work of all international conferences convened under its auspices, in accordance with the rules of procedure of the Conference.

B
Institutional stakeholders

19. Other relevant intergovernmental organizations that were accredited to the World Summit on Sustainable Development and to the Commission on Sustainable Development, as well as relevant organizations of the United Nations system, may participate in the deliberations of the Conference, as appropriate, in accordance with the rules of procedure of the Conference.

20. In addition, interested intergovernmental organizations that were not accredited to the World Summit on Sustainable Development or to the Commission on Sustainable Development may apply to the General Assembly for accreditation following the established accreditation procedure. Online registration and accreditation forms will be available at the Conference website.

C
Major groups

21. Non-governmental organizations and other major groups that were accredited to the World Summit on Sustainable Development and those that are in consultative status with the Economic and Social Council are invited to participate in the deliberations of the Conference, as appropriate, in accordance with the rules of procedure of the Conference.

22. In addition, interested non-governmental organizations and other major groups that are not in consultative status with the Economic and Social Council or were not accredited to the World Summit on Sustainable Development or to the Commission on Sustainable Development may apply to the General Assembly for accreditation following the established accreditation procedure.

IV. Secretariat

23. The Secretary-General of the Conference serves as focal point within the Secretariat of the United Nations for providing support to the organization of the Conference, in cooperation with the host country authorities.

V. Documentation

24. In accordance with the practice followed at previous United Nations conferences, the official documentation of the Conference will include documents issued before, during and after the Conference.

25. In accordance with the practice followed at previous United Nations conferences, it is recommended that the report of the Conference consist of the decisions of the Conference, a brief account of the proceedings and a reportorial account of the work of the Conference and the action taken at the plenary meetings.

26. Summaries of the plenary meetings and high-level round-table discussions should also be included in the report of the Conference.

VI. Organization of parallel meetings and other events of the Conference

27. Parallel meetings and other events, including a partnership forum and learning centres, will be held during the same hours as the plenary meetings and the round tables, if they are held in the main building. The partnership forum and learning centres will constitute an official part of the Conference. Interpretation for such meetings will be provided on an as-available basis.

VII. Side events

28. Special events, including briefings, seminars, workshops and panel discussions on issues related to sustainable development, will be organized by Member States, organizations of the United Nations system and accredited institutional and non-institutional stakeholders for the benefit of the participants in the Conference. Guidelines for organizing special events and the calendar of those events will be made available at the Conference website.

VIII. Media coverage

29. Press materials will be prepared by the Department of Public Information of the Secretariat for journalists covering the Conference. In addition, regular press releases will be issued on the results of plenary meetings, round tables and other events. All relevant documentation will be made available electronically at the Conference website.

30. The plenary meetings and round tables, as well as press conferences, will be broadcast live to the media area. A programme of special media briefings and press conferences will be announced.

On 22 December, the General Assembly adopted a decision on arrangements for accreditation and participation of non-governmental organizations (NGOs) and other major groups in the United Nations Conference on Sustainable Development and its preparatory process (**decision 66/544A**).

Agricultural technology for development

In response to General Assembly resolution 64/197 [YUN 2009, p. 807], the Secretary-General, in August, submitted a report [A/66/304] on agricultural technology for development.

The report reviewed the progress in making appropriate sustainable agricultural technologies available and affordable, especially to smallholder farmers, and making agriculture more resilient, including to climate change. Boosting agricultural productivity was one of the most effective ways of addressing global poverty and food and nutrition insecurity, which particularly affected smallholder and family farmers. The Secretary-General recommended a holistic approach to raise productivity and the resilience of agriculture and examined the progress made in terms of national policies and strategies, agricultural research and development, technology transfer and extension services as well as market and financing services. He suggested reforming the agricultural sector to integrate sustainable agriculture and support to smallholders, including women farmers, into national policies and strategies; devoting greater efforts and resources towards agricultural technologies for effective adaptation to climate change and natural resource scarcities; and increasing investment in reducing post-harvest waste. Further recommendations included addressing the deficit of women in key education, research and extension services and acknowledging their role as main food producers.

GENERAL ASSEMBLY ACTION

On 22 December [meeting 91], the General Assembly, on the recommendation of the Second Committee [A/66/440], adopted **resolution 66/195** by recorded vote (141-2-33) [agenda item 19].

Agricultural technology for development

The General Assembly,

Recalling its resolution 64/197 of 21 December 2009 on agricultural technology for development,

Recalling also the Rio Declaration on Environment and Development, Agenda 21, the Programme for the Further Implementation of Agenda 21, the Johannesburg Declaration on Sustainable Development and the Plan of Implementation of the World Summit on Sustainable Development ("Johannesburg Plan of Implementation"),

Recalling further the 2005 World Summit Outcome,

Recalling its resolution 65/178 of 20 December 2010 on agriculture development and food security,

Noting the previous work done by the Commission on Sustainable Development, in particular at its sixteenth and seventeenth sessions, highlighting the thematic focus on agriculture,

Acknowledging the work performed by the High-level Task Force on the Global Food Security Crisis, established by the Secretary-General in 2008, and specifically its call for increased investment, as appropriate, in the development of agricultural technology as well as for the transfer and use of existing technologies, on mutually agreed terms, especially for smallholder farmers, in particular rural women, and recalling the World Summit on Food Security, convened by the Food and Agriculture Organization of the United Nations in Rome from 16 to 18 November 2009, and underlining the importance of advancing and implementing agricultural technologies,

Welcoming the commitments set out in the Joint Statement on Global Food Security, adopted in L'Aquila, Italy, on 10 July 2009, which focused on sustainable agriculture development,

Recalling the High-level Plenary Meeting of the General Assembly on the Millennium Development Goals, held in New York from 20 to 22 September 2010, and its outcome document, reaffirming its commitment to achieve the Millennium Development Goals, and recognizing the beneficial impact that the adoption of agricultural technologies can have for the achievement of many of those goals, including for eradicating extreme poverty and hunger, empowering women and ensuring environmental sustainability, while remaining concerned about the pace of progress to date in achieving those goals, particularly in the least developed countries and in Africa,

Taking note of the Programme of Action for the Least Developed Countries for the Decade 2011–2020 adopted at the Fourth United Nations Conference on the Least Developed Countries, held in Istanbul, Turkey, from 9 to 13 May 2011, and recognizing the need to continue to work towards fulfilling the commitments made in the Programme of Action,

Acknowledging the importance of the forthcoming United Nations Conference on Sustainable Development,

Stressing the critical role of women in the agricultural sector and their contribution to enhancing agricultural and rural development, improving food security and nutrition and eradicating rural poverty, and underlining the fact that meaningful progress in agricultural development necessitates, inter alia, closing the gender gap and ensuring that women have equal access to agricultural technologies, related services and inputs and all the necessary productive resources, as well as to education and training, social services, health care, health services and financial services and access to and participation in markets,

Acknowledging the role and work of civil society and the private sector in furthering progress in developing countries, in promoting the use of sustainable agricultural technology and the training of smallholder farmers, in particular rural women,

Considering the increasing need to innovate in agri-food chains in order to respond to the challenges posed by, inter alia, climate change, the depletion and scarcity of natural resources, urbanization and globalization, and recognizing that agricultural research and sustainable agricultural technologies can greatly contribute to agricultural, rural and economic development, the adaptation of agriculture and food security and nutrition and help to mitigate the negative impact of climate change, land degradation and desertification,

1. *Welcomes* the report of the Secretary-General on agricultural technology for development;

2. *Urges* Member States, relevant United Nations organizations and other stakeholders to strengthen efforts to improve the development of appropriate sustainable agricultural technologies and their transfer and dissemination under fair, transparent and mutually agreed terms to developing countries, especially the least developed countries, in particular at the bilateral and regional levels, and to support national efforts to foster the utilization of local know-how and agricultural technologies, promote agricultural technology research and access to knowledge and information through suitable communication for development strategies and enable rural women, as well as men and youth, to increase sustainable agricultural productivity, reduce post-harvest losses and enhance food and nutritional security;

3. *Encourages* international, regional and national efforts to strengthen the capacity of developing countries, especially their smallholder farmers, in particular rural women, in order to enhance the productivity and nutritional quality of food crops, to promote sustainable practices in pre-harvest and post-harvest agricultural activities and to enhance food security and nutrition-related pro-

grammes and policies that take into consideration the specific needs of women and youth;

4. *Calls upon* Member States and relevant United Nations organizations and other stakeholders to mainstream gender into agricultural policies and projects and to focus on closing the gender gap to achieve equal access for women to labour-saving technologies, agricultural technology information and know-how, equipment, decision-making forums and associated agricultural resources to ensure that agriculture, food security and nutrition-related programmes and policies take into consideration the specific needs of women and youth;

5. *Underlines* the importance of supporting and advancing research in improving and diversifying crop varieties and seed systems as well as supporting the establishment of sustainable agricultural systems and management practices, such as conservation agriculture and integrated pest management, in order to make agriculture more resilient and, in particular, to make crops and farm animals, including livestock, more tolerant to diseases, pests and environmental stresses, including drought and climate change, in a manner consistent with national regulations and relevant international agreements;

6. *Also underlines* the importance of the sustainable use and management of water resources to increase and ensure agricultural productivity, and calls for further efforts to develop and strengthen irrigation facilities and water-saving technology;

7. *Encourages* Member States, civil society and public and private institutions to develop partnerships to support financial and market services, including training, capacity-building, infrastructure and extension services, and calls for further efforts by all stakeholders to include smallholder farmers, in particular rural women, in planning and taking decisions about making appropriate sustainable agricultural technologies and practices available and affordable to them;

8. *Calls upon* Member States to include sustainable agricultural development as an integral part of their national policies and strategies, notes the positive impact that North-South, South-South and triangular cooperation can have in this regard, and urges the relevant bodies of the United Nations system to include elements of agricultural technology, research and development in efforts to achieve the Millennium Development Goals, with a focus on the research and development of technology that is affordable, durable and sustainable and that can be easily used by and disseminated to smallholder farmers, in particular rural women;

9. *Requests* relevant United Nations organizations, including the Food and Agriculture Organization of the United Nations and the International Fund for Agricultural Development, to promote, support and facilitate the exchange of experience among Member States on ways to augment sustainable agriculture and management practices, such as conservation agriculture, and increase the use of agricultural technologies that have a positive impact on the entire value chain, including technology for post-harvest crop storage and transportation, especially in pressing environmental circumstances;

10. *Underlines* the instrumental role of agricultural technology, agricultural research and technology transfer on mutually agreed terms, as well as the sharing of knowledge and practices, in furthering sustainable development and in achieving the Millennium Development Goals, calls, therefore, upon Member States and encourages relevant international bodies to support sustainable agricultural research and development, and in this regard calls for continued support to the international agricultural research system, including the Consultative Group on International Agricultural Research and other relevant international organizations and initiatives;

11. *Requests* the Secretary-General to submit to the General Assembly at its sixty-eighth session a report on the implementation of the present resolution.

RECORDED VOTE ON RESOLUTION 66/195:

In favour: Albania, Andorra, Angola, Antigua and Barbuda, Argentina, Armenia, Australia, Austria, Azerbaijan, Bahamas, Barbados, Belarus, Belgium, Belize, Benin, Bhutan, Bosnia and Herzegovina, Botswana, Brazil, Bulgaria, Burkina Faso, Burundi, Cameroon, Canada, Cape Verde, Central African Republic, Chad, Chile, China, Colombia, Comoros, Congo, Costa Rica, Côte d'Ivoire, Croatia, Cyprus, Czech Republic, Denmark, Dominica, Dominican Republic, El Salvador, Eritrea, Estonia, Ethiopia, Fiji, Finland, France, Georgia, Germany, Greece, Grenada, Guatemala, Guinea, Guinea-Bissau, Guyana, Haiti, Honduras, Hungary, Iceland, India, Ireland, Israel, Italy, Jamaica, Japan, Kazakhstan, Kenya, Kyrgyzstan, Latvia, Lesotho, Liberia, Liechtenstein, Lithuania, Luxembourg, Madagascar, Malawi, Maldives, Mali, Malta, Marshall Islands, Mauritius, Mexico, Micronesia, Monaco, Mongolia, Montenegro, Mozambique, Myanmar, Namibia, Nauru, Nepal, Netherlands, New Zealand, Nigeria, Norway, Palau, Panama, Papua New Guinea, Paraguay, Peru, Philippines, Poland, Portugal, Republic of Korea, Republic of Moldova, Romania, Russian Federation, Saint Lucia, Saint Vincent and the Grenadines, San Marino, Senegal, Serbia, Sierra Leone, Singapore, Slovakia, Slovenia, Solomon Islands, Spain, Sri Lanka, Suriname, Sweden, Switzerland, Tajikistan, Thailand, the former Yugoslav Republic of Macedonia, Timor-Leste, Togo, Tonga, Trinidad and Tobago, Turkey, Tuvalu, Uganda, Ukraine, United Kingdom, United Republic of Tanzania, United States, Uruguay, Uzbekistan, Viet Nam, Zambia, Zimbabwe.

Against: South Africa, Venezuela.

Abstaining: Afghanistan, Algeria, Bahrain, Bangladesh, Bolivia, Brunei Darussalam, Cuba, Democratic People's Republic of Korea, Djibouti, Ecuador, Egypt, Gabon, Indonesia, Iraq, Jordan, Kuwait, Lebanon, Libya, Malaysia, Morocco, Nicaragua, Niger, Oman, Pakistan, Qatar, Saudi Arabia, Somalia, Sudan, Swaziland, Syrian Arab Republic, Tunisia, United Arab Emirates, Yemen.

Sustainable tourism

Regional events. The Central American Tourism Council of the Central American Integration System (SICA), in cooperation with the World Tourism Organization, held its first workshop on sustainable tourism (Roatán, Honduras, 24 June). At the meeting, Central American Ministers of Tourism highlighted the importance of the biodiversity of natural resources and the environment as well as their fragility and vulnerability, and urged the international community to support sustainable tourism.

The Heads of State and Government of SICA, at their thirty-seventh meeting (San Salvador, El Salvador, 22 July), declared 2012 as the Year of Sustainable Tourism.

GENERAL ASSEMBLY ACTION

On 22 December [meeting 91], the General Assembly, on the recommendation of the Second Committee [A/66/440], adopted **resolution 66/196** without vote [agenda item 19].

Sustainable tourism and sustainable development in Central America

The General Assembly,

Recalling all relevant resolutions of the General Assembly on this matter,

Recalling also the Manila Declaration on World Tourism, the Rio Declaration on Environment and Development and Agenda 21, the Amman Declaration on Peace through Tourism, the Johannesburg Declaration on Sustainable Development and the Plan of Implementation of the World Summit on Sustainable Development ("Johannesburg Plan of Implementation"), the Declaration of Barbados and the Programme of Action for the Sustainable Development of Small Island Developing States, the Mauritius Declaration and the Mauritius Strategy for the Further Implementation of the Programme of Action for the Sustainable Development of Small Island Developing States, and the Istanbul Declaration and the Programme of Action for the Least Developed Countries for the Decade 2011–2020,

Recalling further the outcome document of the High-level Plenary Meeting of the General Assembly on the Millennium Development Goals,

Recognizing the important dimension and role of sustainable tourism as a positive instrument towards the eradication of poverty, the protection of the environment and the improvement of quality of life and its contribution to achieving sustainable development, especially in developing countries,

Welcoming the efforts of the Marrakech Process on sustainable consumption and production, the achievements of the International Task Force on Sustainable Tourism Development and the objectives of the Global Partnership for Sustainable Tourism, launched in 2011 as a permanent successor to the International Task Force,

Taking note of the outcome document of the first workshop on sustainable tourism, adopted by the Central American Tourism Council of the Central American Integration System on 24 June 2011, at a meeting organized in cooperation with the World Tourism Organization in Roatan, Honduras, in the framework of the United Nations Conference on Sustainable Development, to be held in Rio de Janeiro, Brazil, from 20 to 22 June 2012,

Taking note also of the Joint Declaration, the Plan of Action and the declaration of 2012 as the Year of Sustainable Tourism in Central America, adopted at the thirty-seventh meeting of Heads of State and Government of the Central American Integration System, held in San Salvador on 22 July 2011, and the Declaration of the Central American Tourism Council, adopted at its eighty-second meeting, held in Guanacaste, Costa Rica, on 7 July 2011,

Emphasizing that sustainable tourism in Central America is a fundamental pillar of regional integration and an engine of social and economic development, given its significant contribution in terms of jobs, income, investment and hard currency, and therefore contributes to the achievement of the Millennium Development Goals,

1. *Invites* States Members of the United Nations and other stakeholders, and the World Tourism Organization, to continue to support the activities undertaken by the Central American countries for the promotion of responsible and sustainable tourism in the region, including in the context of emergency preparedness and response to natural disasters, as well as for capacity-building in order to achieve the internationally agreed development goals, including the Millennium Development Goals, by extending the benefits of tourism to all sectors of society, in particular the most vulnerable and marginalized groups of the population;

2. *Takes note* of the work of the Central American Governments in the implementation of existing programmes designed to launch and promote sustainable tourism throughout the region, in coordination with the Central American Commission for Environment and Development, and welcomes their contribution to the United Nations Conference on Sustainable Development in this regard;

3. *Encourages* the Central American countries, through the Central American Tourism Council and the Central American Tourism Integration Secretariat, to continue to support sustainable tourism with policies that foster responsive and inclusive tourism, strengthen regional identity and protect the natural and cultural heritage, especially their ecosystems and biodiversity and notes that existing initiatives, such as the Global Partnership for Sustainable Tourism, among other international initiatives, can deliver direct and focused support to Governments to this end;

4. *Recognizes* the need to promote the development of sustainable tourism, in particular through the consumption of sustainable tourism products and services, and to strengthen the development of ecotourism, taking into account the declaration of 2012 as the Year of Sustainable Tourism in Central America, while maintaining the culture and environmental integrity of indigenous and local communities and enhancing the protection of ecologically sensitive areas and the natural heritage, and to promote the development of sustainable tourism and capacity-building in order to contribute to the strengthening of rural and local communities and small and medium-sized enterprises, taking into account the need to address, inter alia, the challenges of climate change and the need to halt the loss of biodiversity;

5. *Requests* the Secretary-General to report to the General Assembly at its sixty-eighth session on developments related to the implementation of the present resolution, taking into account the reports prepared by the World Tourism Organization in this field.

Eradication of poverty

Second UN Decade for the Eradication of Poverty

In response to General Assembly resolution 65/174 [YUN 2010, p. 810], the Secretary-General submitted an August report [A/66/221] on the implementation of the Second United Nations Decade for the Eradication of Poverty (2008–2017). The report addressed the challenges to poverty eradication and some key policy measures for poverty reduction. It also highlighted the growing policy coherence within the framework of the Second Decade and described efforts to enhance coordination in support of the Global Jobs Pact [YUN 2009, p. 1062] and the Social Protection Floor Initiative.

Challenges to poverty eradication included the lack of sustained, inclusive and equitable economic growth; slow employment creation; increasing global food prices and weak agricultural development; as well as climate change and conflict. While strong growth in China and other countries of East and South-East Asia had helped to reduce poverty significantly, low and volatile growth in the least developed countries had entailed stagnant levels of poverty. The number of jobless persons reached 205 million in 2010, and the World Bank estimated that an additional 44 million people had fallen into poverty due to the rise in food prices that year. Furthermore, people who lived in poverty were often ill-equipped to resist or mitigate the adverse effects of climate change and conflict.

The Secretary-General stressed the need for a coordinated response leading to sustained, inclusive and equitable economic growth and macroeconomic policies promoting the creation of productive employment and supporting stronger social protection. He further underlined the importance of agricultural investments and rural development for poverty reduction and improved food security. The Second United Nations Decade for the Eradication of Poverty provided a framework for action to enhance coherence and synergy among UN system-wide activities, but required additional efforts and further collaboration by Member States, civil society and other partners.

Communication. In a 13 June letter [A/65/864], Japan transmitted to the Secretary-General the statement of the Chair of the Millennium Development Goals follow-up meeting (Tokyo, 2–3 June), which discussed ways to accelerate progress towards the achievement of the goals.

GENERAL ASSEMBLY ACTION

On 22 December [meeting 91], the General Assembly, on the recommendation of the Second Committee [A/66/444/Add.1], adopted **resolution 66/215** without vote [agenda item 23 (a)].

Second United Nations Decade for the Eradication of Poverty (2008–2017)

The General Assembly,

Recalling its resolutions 47/196 of 22 December 1992, 48/183 of 21 December 1993, 50/107 of 20 December 1995, 56/207 of 21 December 2001, 57/266 of 20 December 2002, 58/222 of 23 December 2003, 59/247 of 22 December 2004, 60/209 of 22 December 2005, 61/213 of 20 December 2006, 62/205 of 19 December 2007, 63/230 of 19 December 2008, 64/216 of 21 December 2009 and 65/174 of 20 December 2010,

Recalling also the United Nations Millennium Declaration, adopted by Heads of State and Government on the occasion of the Millennium Summit, as well as the international commitment to eradicate extreme poverty and to halve, by 2015, the proportion of the world's people whose income is less than one dollar a day and the proportion of people who suffer from hunger,

Recalling further the 2005 World Summit Outcome,

Recalling the Programme of Action for the Least Developed Countries for the Decade 2011–2020, adopted in May 2011 at the Fourth United Nations Conference on the Least Developed Countries with a main aim of enabling half the number of the least developed countries to meet the criteria for graduation by 2020,

Recalling also its resolution 60/265 of 30 June 2006 on the follow-up to the development outcome of the 2005 World Summit, including the Millennium Development Goals and the other internationally agreed development goals, its resolution 61/16 of 20 November 2006 on the strengthening of the Economic and Social Council and its resolution 63/303 of 9 July 2009 entitled "Outcome of the Conference on the World Financial and Economic Crisis and Its Impact on Development",

Welcoming the poverty-related discussions in the annual ministerial reviews held by the Economic and Social Council, which play an important supporting role in the implementation of the Second United Nations Decade for the Eradication of Poverty (2008–2017),

Noting with appreciation the ministerial declaration adopted at the high-level segment of the substantive session of 2006 of the Economic and Social Council on creating an environment at the national and international levels conducive to generating full and productive employment and decent work for all, and its impact on sustainable development, and also Economic and Social Council resolution 2011/37 of 28 July 2011 entitled "Recovering from the world financial and economic crisis: a Global Jobs Pact",

Recalling the International Conference on Financing for Development and the Doha Declaration on Financing for Development: outcome document of the Follow-up International Conference on Financing for Development to Review the Implementation of the Monterrey Consensus,

Recalling also the outcomes of the World Summit for Social Development and the twenty-fourth special session of the General Assembly,

Recalling further the High-level Plenary Meeting of the General Assembly on the Millennium Development Goals and its outcome document,

Underlining the fact that, in the face of the ongoing adverse impacts of the multiple, interrelated global crises and challenges, such as the financial and economic crisis, the food crisis, volatile energy and commodity prices and climate change, cooperation and increased commitment by all relevant partners, including the public sector, the private sector and civil society, are needed more than ever, and recognizing in this context the urgent need to achieve the internationally agreed development goals, including the Millennium Development Goals,

Expressing concern that, while there has been progress in reducing poverty, especially in some middle-income countries, this progress has been uneven and the number of people living in poverty in some countries continues to increase, with women and children constituting the majority of the most affected groups, especially in the least developed countries and particularly in sub-Saharan Africa,

Recognizing that rates of economic growth vary among countries and that these differences must be addressed by, among other actions, promoting pro-poor growth and social protection,

Concerned at the global nature of poverty and inequality, and underlining the fact that the eradication of poverty and hunger is an ethical, social, political and economic imperative of all humankind,

Reaffirming that eradicating poverty is one of the greatest global challenges facing the world today, particularly in Africa and in least developed countries and in some middle-income countries, and underlining the importance of accelerating sustainable, broad-based and inclusive economic growth, including full, productive employment generation and decent work,

Recognizing that mobilizing financial resources for development at the national and international levels and the effective use of those resources are central to a global partnership for development in support of the achievement of the internationally agreed development goals, including the Millennium Development Goals,

Recognizing also the contributions of South-South and triangular cooperation to the efforts of developing countries to eradicate poverty and to pursue sustainable development,

Acknowledging that good governance at the national and international levels and sustained, inclusive and equitable economic growth, supported by full employment and decent work, rising productivity and a favourable environment, including public and private investment and entrepreneurship, are necessary to eradicate poverty, achieve the internationally agreed development goals, including the Millennium Development Goals, and realize a rise in living standards, and that corporate social responsibility initiatives play an important role in maximizing the impact of public and private investment,

Underlining the priority and urgency given by Heads of State and Government to the eradication of poverty, as expressed in the outcomes of the major United Nations conferences and summits in the economic and social fields,

Recalling that the theme of the 2012 annual ministerial review to be held by the Economic and Social Council will be "Promoting productive capacity, employment and decent work to eradicate poverty in the context of inclusive, sustainable and equitable economic growth at all levels for achieving the Millennium Development Goals",

1. *Takes note* of the report of the Secretary-General on the implementation of the Second United Nations Decade for the Eradication of Poverty (2008–2017), under the theme "Full employment and decent work for all";

2. *Reaffirms* that the objective of the Second United Nations Decade for the Eradication of Poverty (2008–2017) is to support, in an efficient and coordinated manner, the follow-up to the implementation of the internationally agreed development goals, including the Millennium Development Goals, relating to the eradication of poverty and to coordinate international support to that end;

3. *Also reaffirms* that each country must take primary responsibility for its own development and that the role of national policies and strategies cannot be overemphasized for the achievement of sustainable development and poverty eradication, and recognizes that increased effective national efforts should be complemented by concrete, effective and supportive international programmes, measures and policies aimed at expanding the development opportunities of developing countries, while taking into account national conditions and ensuring respect for national ownership, strategies and sovereignty;

4. *Calls upon* the international community, including Member States, to address the root causes of extreme poverty and hunger;

5. *Emphasizes* the need to accord the highest priority to poverty eradication within the United Nations development agenda, while stressing the importance of addressing the causes and challenges of poverty through integrated, coordinated and coherent strategies at the national, intergovernmental and inter-agency levels;

6. *Reiterates* the need to strengthen the leadership role of the United Nations in promoting international cooperation for development and its role at the regional level, which is critical for the eradication of poverty;

7. *Calls upon* the international community to continue to give priority to the eradication of poverty, and calls upon donor countries in a position to do so to support the effective national efforts of developing countries in this regard, through adequate, predictable financial resources on bilateral and multilateral bases;

8. *Stresses* the importance of ensuring, at the national, intergovernmental and inter-agency levels, coherent, comprehensive and integrated activities for the eradication of poverty in accordance with the outcomes of the major United Nations conferences and summits in the economic, social and related fields;

9. *Reaffirms* the commitment to promote opportunities for full, freely chosen and productive employment, including for the disadvantaged, as well as decent work for all, with full respect for fundamental principles and rights at work under conditions of equity, equality, security and dignity, and also reaffirms that macroeconomic policies should, inter alia, support employment creation, taking fully into account the social and environmental impact and dimensions of globalization, and that these concepts are key elements of sustainable development for all countries and are therefore a priority objective of international cooperation;

10. *Emphasizes* that education and training are among the critical factors in empowering those living in poverty, while recognizing the complexity of the challenge of poverty eradication, and in this regard recognizes the role of the United Nations Educational, Scientific and Cultural Organization in coordinating the Education for All partners and in promoting the development of sector-wide education policies by, inter alia, elaborating pedagogical tools for grass-roots organizations and policymakers;

11. *Recognizes* the role of other specialized agencies and United Nations funds and programmes, including the United Nations Children's Fund and the United Nations Development Programme, in contributing to international advocacy for eradicating poverty, including through education and training;

12. *Encourages* the international community to enhance international cooperation in support of agricultural and rural development and food production in developing countries, particularly in least developed countries;

13. *Reaffirms* the need to fulfil all official development assistance commitments, including the commitments by many developed countries to achieve the target of 0.7 per cent of gross national product for official development assistance to developing countries by 2015 and to reach a level of at least 0.5 per cent of gross national product for official development assistance by 2010, as well as a target of 0.15 per cent to 0.20 per cent of gross national product for official development assistance to the least developed countries;

14. *Welcomes* the increasing efforts to improve the quality of official development assistance and to increase its development impact, recognizes the Development Cooperation Forum of the Economic and Social Council and notes other initiatives such as the high-level forums on aid effectiveness, which produced the 2005 Paris Declaration on Aid Effectiveness and the 2008 Accra Agenda for Action, that make important contributions to the efforts of those countries which have made commitments to them, including through the adoption of the fundamental principles of national ownership, alignment, harmonization and managing for results, and bears in mind that there is no one-size-fits-all formula that will guarantee effective assistance and that the specific situation of each country needs to be fully considered;

15. *Resolves* to work to operationalize the World Solidarity Fund established by the General Assembly, and invites Member States, international organizations, the private sector, relevant institutions, foundations and individuals to make voluntary contributions to the Fund;

16. *Recognizes* that sustained, inclusive and equitable economic growth is essential for eradicating poverty and hunger, in particular in developing countries, and stresses that national efforts in this regard should be complemented by an enabling international environment and by ensuring greater coherence among macroeconomic, trade and social policies at all levels;

17. *Calls upon* Member States to continue their ambitious efforts to strive for more inclusive, equitable, balanced, stable and development-oriented sustainable socioeconomic approaches to overcoming poverty and inequality;

18. *Recognizes* that poverty is multidimensional and invites national Governments, supported by the international community, to consider developing complementary measures which better reflect this multidimensionality;

19. *Invites* all stakeholders, including Member States, relevant organizations of the United Nations system and civil society organizations, to share good practices of programmes and policies which address inequalities for the benefit of those living in extreme poverty and promote the active participation of those living in extreme poverty in the design and implementation of such programmes and policies, with the aim of accelerating progress towards achieving the Millennium Development Goals and informing the discussions on the way forward after 2015, and in this regard takes note of the outcomes of the Millennium Development Goals follow-up meeting, held in Tokyo on 2 and 3 June 2011, and requests the Secretary-General to include in his annual report on progress in the implementation of the Millennium Development Goals a compilation of such good practices;

20. *Reiterates its call* to the relevant organizations of the United Nations system to consider activities to implement the Second Decade, in consultation with Member States and other relevant stakeholders;

21. *Recalls* the inter-agency system-wide plan of action for poverty eradication involving more than twenty-one agencies, funds, programmes and regional commissions, and requests the Secretary-General to provide details on the implementation of the plan of action to Member States;

22. *Reaffirms* the need to give the highest priority to its consideration of the question of poverty eradication, and in that regard reiterates its decision, in resolution 63/230, as a contribution to the Second Decade, to convene, at its sixty-eighth session, a meeting of the General Assembly at the highest appropriate political level centred on the review process devoted to the theme relating to the issue of poverty eradication, and stresses that the meeting and the preparatory activities should be carried out within the budget level proposed by the Secretary-General for the biennium 2012–2013 and should be organized in the most effective and efficient manner;

23. *Notes with concern* the continuing high levels of unemployment and underemployment, particularly among young people, as a consequence of the global financial and economic crisis, recognizes that decent work remains one of the best routes out of poverty, and in this regard invites donor countries, multilateral organizations and other development partners to continue to assist Member States, in particular developing countries, in adopting policies consistent with the Global Jobs Pact adopted by the International Labour Conference at its ninety-eighth session, as a general framework within which each country can formulate policy packages specific to its situation and national priorities in order to promote a job-intensive recovery and sustainable development;

24. *Urges* Member States to address the global challenge of youth unemployment by developing and implementing strategies that give young people everywhere a real chance to find decent and productive work, and, in this context, stresses the need for the development of a global strategy on youth employment with a focus on youth unemployment;

25. *Urges* the international community, including the United Nations system, to implement the outcome documents relating to the internationally agreed development goals, including the Millennium Development Goals;

26. *Also urges* the international community, including the United Nations system, to implement the Outcome of the Conference on the World Financial and Economic Crisis and Its Impact on Development in support of the objectives of the Second Decade;

27. *Calls upon* the relevant organizations of the United Nations system, within their respective mandates and resources, to support Member States, at their request, in strengthening their macroeconomic policy capacity and national development strategies so as to contribute to achieving the objectives of the Second Decade;

28. *Encourages* greater inter-agency convergence and collaboration within the United Nations system in sharing

knowledge, promoting policy dialogue, facilitating synergies, mobilizing funds, providing technical assistance in the key policy areas underlying the decent work agenda and strengthening system-wide policy coherence on employment issues, including by avoiding duplication of effort;

29. *Decides* to include in the provisional agenda of its sixty-seventh session, under the item entitled "Eradication of poverty and other development issues", the sub-item entitled "Implementation of the Second United Nations Decade for the Eradication of Poverty (2008–2017)", and requests the Secretary-General to submit to the General Assembly at its sixty-seventh session a report on the implementation of the present resolution.

Also on 22 December, the Assembly took note of report of the Second Committee [A/66/444] on eradication of poverty and other development issues (**decision 66/547**).

Legal empowerment of the poor and eradication of poverty

Pursuant to General Assembly resolution 64/215 [YUN 2009, p. 811] on the legal empowerment of the poor and eradication of poverty, the Secretary-General in September submitted a report [A/66/341] on the resolution's implementation that underlined the importance of expanding access to justice and the rule of law in order to reduce poverty and achieve the internationally agreed development goals. According to the Secretary-General, legal empowerment of the poor required improvements in the administration of justice and expansion of identity and birth registration, as well as the repeal of laws that impeded the poor from exercising their rights. Further recommendations related to pro-poor property rights; access to land and assets; employment policy and regulatory frameworks that protected labour and increased employment; a fair, inclusive and socially responsible private sector; and quality education and training that targeted vulnerable populations. International cooperation should be conducive to the legal empowerment of the poor. National and local contexts, including traditional or informal dispute resolution mechanisms, had to be considered in any reforms aimed at empowering people living in poverty.

Millennium Development Goals

The *Millennium Development Goals Report 2011*, published by desa [Sales No. E.11.I.10], evaluated the progress made on mdg indicators. Despite setbacks after the 2008–2009 economic downturn, exacerbated by the food and energy crisis, the world was still on track to reach the poverty-reduction target, mainly due to rapid economic growth in Eastern Asia, especially China. Economic recovery after the crisis, however, had failed to translate into employment opportunities and a slowdown in progress against poverty was reflected in the number of working poor. There was a disconnect between poverty reduction and the persistence of hunger and, based on current trends, sub-Saharan Africa would be unable to meet the hunger-reduction target by 2015. Nevertheless, the sub-Saharan region showed the best record for improvement in primary school enrolment.

The report further portrayed gaps in the achievement of main targets related to nutrition, gender equality, maternal health and sanitation, and found worrisome regional trends regarding hiv/aids, despite the decline in new infections. While forests were disappearing rapidly in Africa and South America, Asia was able to register net gains of forests, and the world was likely to surpass the drinking water target of 89 per cent coverage. Although official development assistance (oda) to developing countries was at a record high, it fell short of promises made in 2005.

Report of Secretary-General. In response to General Assembly resolution 65/10 [YUN 2010, p. 829], the Secretary-General submitted a July report [A/66/126] on accelerating progress towards the mdgs: options for sustained and inclusive growth and issues for advancing the UN development agenda beyond 2015. The report discussed progress made towards achieving the mdgs and outstanding challenges en route to the 2015 targets. It found that the global economic crisis had a far-reaching impact on all mdgs, with the cost of their achievement potentially rising by up to 1.5 per cent of gross domestic product annually. The report further stated that progress had been uneven, often with modest impact on the poorest and most vulnerable, and stressed the need for sustained, equitable, inclusive and job-intensive growth that provided opportunities to everyone—including women, young people and disadvantaged groups. That could be accomplished through a development-oriented macroeconomic framework; the adoption of green technologies and sustainable resource management strategies; coherent and inclusive social policies; and human rights protection and good governance.

The Secretary-General stressed the need for a stronger global partnership for development—goal 8 of the mdgs—and pointed out that oda had continued to fall short of commitments in 2010. He recommended the advancement of the Doha Round of trade negotiations, enhanced debt restructuring and relief modalities, and increased access to medicine at low cost for the poor, facilitated through global mechanisms. Issues that should be central to the United Nations development agenda post-2015 included sustainable development, equality, respect for nature, solidarity, freedom and tolerance, and sharing responsibilities.

Science and technology for development

Commission on Science and Technology for Development

At its fourteenth session (Geneva, 23–27 May) [E/2011/31], the Commission on Science and Technology for Development (CSTD) considered progress made in the implementation of and follow-up to the outcomes of the World Summit on the Information Society (WSIS) [YUN 2003, p. 857 & YUN 2005, p. 933] at the regional and international levels. It also addressed its two priority themes: measuring the impact of information and communications technology for development, and technologies to address challenges in areas such as agriculture and water. The session included two ministerial round tables on: the review of progress made in the implementation of WSIS outcomes and harnessing science and technology for development.

The Commission had before it reports of the Secretary-General on the priority themes [E/CN.16/2011/2 & 3] and on progress made in implementing and following up on WSIS outcomes at the regional and international levels [A/66/64]; a report of the Chair of the Working Group on Improvements to the Internet Governance Forum [A/66/67]; a note by the United Nations Conference on Trade and Development (UNCTAD) on methods of work of the Commission [E/CN.16/2011/4]; and a summary report by UNCTAD on the Commission's intersessional panel meeting (Geneva, 15–17 December 2010) [E/CN.16/2011/CRP.1].

The Secretary-General underscored the need to review agricultural science, technology and innovation systems with a view to strengthening the support to smallholder farmers through sustainable agriculture, and integrating a gender perspective in the design of those policies [E/CN.16/2011/2]. He also called for enhanced international efforts on measuring the impact of information and communication technologies (ICTs) under the aegis of CSTD and the Partnership on Measuring ICT for Development [E/CN.16/2011/3].

The Commission recommended two draft resolutions and six draft decisions for adoption by the Economic and Social Council (see below).

On 26 July (**decision 2011/240**), the Council took note of the Commission's report on its fourteenth session and approved the provisional agenda and documentation for its fifteenth (2012) session.

Also on 26 July, the Economic and Social Council extended the mandate of the Commission's Gender Advisory Board for a further three years, beginning on 1 January 2012, to allow it to complete its programme of work within the extrabudgetary resources allocated for that purpose (**decision 2011/235**).

Participation in Commission work

On 26 July, the Economic and Social Council invited NGOs and civil society entities that were not in consultative status with the Council but that had received accreditation to WSIS to participate in the work of the Commission on Science and Technology for Development until 2015 (**decision 2011/236**). It extended the arrangements for the participation of academic and technical entities (**decision 2011/237**) and business sector entities, including the private sector (**decision 2011/238**), in the work of the Commission until 2015. It also requested the secretariat of the Commission to propose to the Council, for approval, lists of NGOs and civil society entities not accredited to WSIS that had expressed the wish to participate in the work of the Commission, to enable them to participate in that work until 2015, on an exceptional basis (**decision 2011/239**).

ECONOMIC AND SOCIAL COUNCIL ACTION

On 26 July [meeting 44], the Economic and Social Council, on the recommendation of the Commission on Science and Technology for Development [E/2011/31], adopted **resolution 2011/17** without vote [agenda item 13 (*b*)].

Science and technology for development

The Economic and Social Council,

Recognizing the role of the Commission on Science and Technology for Development as the United Nations torchbearer for science, technology and innovation for development,

Recognizing also the critical role of innovation in maintaining national competitiveness in the global economy and in realizing sustainable development,

Recalling the 2005 World Summit Outcome, which recognizes that the role of science and technology, including information and communications technologies, are vital for the achievement of the internationally agreed development goals, and reaffirming the commitments contained therein, especially the commitment to support the efforts of developing countries, individually and collectively, to harness new agricultural technologies in order to increase agricultural productivity through environmentally sustainable means,

Recalling also that the United Nations Conference on Trade and Development is the secretariat of the Commission,

Recalling further the work of the Commission on science, technology and engineering for innovation and capacity-building in education and research and on development-oriented policies for a socio-economically inclusive information society, including policies relating to access, infrastructure, and an enabling environment,

Welcoming the work of the Commission on its two current priority themes, "Technologies to address challenges in areas such as agriculture and water" and "Measuring the impact of information and communications technology for development",

Recognizing the important role that information and communications technologies play in promoting innovation in science and technology for development,

Recognizing also the importance of science, technology and innovation policy reviews in assisting developing countries to strengthen their national development plans and improve their innovation systems,

Recalling the agreed conclusions of the Commission on the Status of Women on access and participation of women and girls in education, training and science and technology, including for the promotion of women's equal access to full employment and decent work, adopted at its fifty-fifth session, in which it, inter alia, highlighted the need for the sharing of good practice examples in mainstreaming a gender perspective into science, technology and innovation policies and programmes, with a view to replicating and scaling up successes, and recalling further the call of the Commission on the Status of Women upon the Commission on Science and Technology for Development for concrete steps in this respect,

Taking note of the report of the intersessional panel meeting of the Commission on Science and Technology for Development, held in Geneva in December 2010, and of the summary report prepared by the secretariat of the United Nations Conference on Trade and Development,

Taking note also of the reports of the Secretary-General of the United Nations to the Commission on Science and Technology for Development,

Extending its appreciation to the Secretary-General of the United Nations Conference on Trade and Development for his role in helping to complete the aforementioned reports in a timely manner,

Noting that science, technology and innovation, and information and communications technologies are essential to raising agricultural productivity and to soil, water and watershed management, particularly to support smallholder farmers,

Noting with concern that there has been a decline of investment in publicly funded agricultural research and development in many countries, as well as a decrease in donor support for agricultural research,

Noting that agricultural research, education and extension services in many countries do not adequately address local, social needs, especially those related to the poor, including smallholder farmers,

Recognizing the key role played by women in agriculture and water management at the domestic and farm levels, while noting their lack of access to credit, land, knowledge and skills that are essential to raising productivity and reducing poverty,

Recognizing also that increased investments in watershed management, agricultural knowledge, water and soil management, and science and technology, particularly when complemented by investments in rural development in such areas as infrastructure, telecommunications and processing facilities, can increase productivity and yield high economic rates of return, reduce poverty and have positive environmental, social, health and cultural benefits,

Taking note of the outcome documents adopted at the Fourth United Nations Conference on the Least Developed Countries, held in Istanbul, Turkey, from 9 to 13 May 2011, namely, the Istanbul Declaration and the Programme of Action,

Extending its appreciation to the Government of Turkey for its initiative to set up an International Science, Technology and Innovation Centre with a view to helping to build the technological capabilities of the least developed countries,

Decides to make the following recommendations for consideration by national Governments, the Commission on Science and Technology for Development and the United Nations Conference on Trade and Development:

(*a*) Governments are encouraged to take into account the findings of the Commission and take the following actions:

   (i) Review their agricultural science, technology and innovation systems with a view to strengthening policies for more sustainable agricultural practices, particularly for smallholder farmers, while integrating a gender perspective in the design of these policies;

   (ii) Consider increasing the share and improving the effectiveness of public expenditure for agricultural research and development;

   (iii) Target public investment towards improving physical and research and development infrastructures (including rural road networks, power and Internet connections, education, training and health), linkages among farmers, agricultural research, agricultural product processing and marketing, and extension services, supporting sustainable, regenerative production methods;

   (iv) Review research and education systems to ensure that they adequately address the challenges faced by smallholder farmers to achieve more sustainable agricultural practices;

   (v) Encourage participatory research which engages farmers, agricultural workers, especially women, and other stakeholders;

   (vi) Support sustainable agriculture by introducing mechanisms and policies that prevent land degradation and the overuse of pesticides, fertilizers, water and energy, especially fossil fuels, as well as consider the health, environmental and social costs of agricultural production processes;

   (vii) Support research on irrigation and soil improvement technologies, as well as the application of affordable information and communication technologies and other technologies, to lower costs and make agriculture more profitable for smallholder farmers;

   (viii) Consider improving market access for developing country producers;

(*b*) The Commission on Science and Technology for Development is encouraged to:

   (i) Provide technical and policy support and advice, upon request, on how to strengthen and stimulate innovation in sustainable agricultural and water management systems, including extension services, in collaboration with the United Nations Conference on Trade and Development, the Food and Agriculture Organization of the United Nations and other relevant international and regional organizations;

(ii) Promote an integrated, international and collaborative approach in these areas, particularly to meet the needs of smallholder farmers;
  (iii) Promote the exchange, dissemination and diffusion of best practice examples in the area of agricultural science, technology and innovation and promote cooperation between countries in order to face common challenges in matters of science and technology;
  (iv) Facilitate new science, technology and innovation policy reviews, as requested by member countries, to emphasize science and technology and information and communications technologies in building human capacity and infrastructure to foster innovation in national development plans and programmes, in close collaboration with the United Nations Educational, Scientific and Cultural Organization, the World Bank and other relevant international development banks and institutions, and consider new modalities to monitor progress for their implementation;
  (v) In particular, the Commission should identify opportunities and best practices and synergies in and between e-science, e-engineering and e-education programmes worldwide in the course of performing science, technology and innovation policy reviews;
  (vi) Complete and disseminate the new science, technology and innovation policy methodology guidelines and share outcomes and best practices resulting from their implementation;
  (vii) Examine new metrics to assess and document outcomes of investments in science and technology and engineering research and development, education and infrastructure, in collaboration with the United Nations Educational, Scientific and Cultural Organization, the World Bank and member countries that have established programmes in this field of research;
  (viii) Continue to provide a forum, in collaboration with its Gender Advisory Board, to share good practice examples and lessons learned in integrating a gender perspective in science, technology and innovation policymaking and implementation;
  (ix) Consider, on an annual basis, an award, in collaboration with the World Summit on the Information Society World Summit Awards and the International Center for New Media, in Salzburg, Austria, for the innovative application of information and communications technologies in the fields of science, technology and engineering that support development.

Report of Secretary-General. In response to General Assembly resolution 64/212 [YUN 2009, p. 816], the Secretary-General submitted a July report [A/66/208] on science and technology for development that reviewed the work carried out by CSTD in areas such as agriculture, rural development, ICT and environmental management. It also provided information on activities carried out by UNCTAD and other organizations to assist developing countries in integrating science, technology and innovation policies in their national development plans and strategies.

The CSTD report Implementing WSIS Outcomes: Experience to Date and Prospects for the Future [UNCTAD/DTL/STICT/2011/3] summarized progress at the midpoint between the second phase of WSIS and the comprehensive review of implementation scheduled for 2015. It observed that, while substantial progress had been made towards achieving the universal availability and use of basic telecommunications, there was an increasing concern about the divergence in the quality of access to communications, including the Internet, and the value derived from it.

UNCTAD had launched a new series of studies entitled The Technology and Innovation Report, which sought to address issues in science, technology and innovation that were both topical and important for developing countries, with an emphasis on policy-relevant analysis and conclusions.

UNCTAD convened the third expert meeting on enterprise development policies and capacity-building in science, technology and innovation (Geneva, 19–21 January 2011). It also convened an expert meeting on green and renewable technologies as energy solutions for rural development (Geneva, 9–11 February 2010).

Intersessional panel meeting. The CSTD intersessional panel meeting (Manila, Philippines, 13–15 December 2011) [E/CN.16/2012/CRP.1] addressed innovation, research, technology transfer for mutual advantage, entrepreneurship and collaborative development in the information society; open access, virtual science libraries, geospatial analysis and other complementary ICT and science, technology, engineering and mathematics assets to address development issues; and follow-up to WSIS.

GENERAL ASSEMBLY ACTION

On 22 December [meeting 91], the General Assembly, on the recommendation of the Second Committee [A/66/442/Add.2], adopted **resolution 66/211** without vote [agenda item 21 (*b*)].

Science and technology for development

The General Assembly,

Recalling its resolutions 58/200 of 23 December 2003, 59/220 of 22 December 2004, 60/205 of 22 December 2005, 61/207 of 20 December 2006, 62/201 of 19 December 2007 and 64/212 of 21 December 2009,

Taking note of Economic and Social Council resolutions 2006/46 of 28 July 2006 and 2009/8 of 24 July 2009,

Recalling the 2005 World Summit Outcome,

Recalling also the outcomes of the World Summit on the Information Society,

Taking note of the report of the Commission on Science and Technology for Development on its fourteenth session,

Recalling its resolutions 64/208 of 21 December 2009 and 65/280 of 17 June 2011,

Recalling also the agreed conclusions of the Commission on the Status of Women on access and participation of women and girls in education, training and science and technology, adopted at its fifty-fifth session,

Recognizing the vital role that science and technology, including environmentally sound technologies, can play in development and in facilitating efforts to eradicate poverty, achieve food security, fight diseases, improve education, protect the environment, accelerate the pace of economic diversification and transformation, and improve productivity and competitiveness,

Concerned that many developing countries lack affordable access to information and communications technologies and that for the majority of the poor the promise of science and technology remains unfulfilled, and emphasizing the need to effectively harness technology to bridge the digital divide,

Recognizing that international support can help developing countries to benefit from technological advances and enhance their productive capacity,

Reaffirming the need to enhance the science and technology programmes of the relevant entities of the United Nations system,

Noting with appreciation the collaboration between the Commission on Science and Technology for Development and the United Nations Conference on Trade and Development in establishing the Network of Centres of Excellence in science and technology for developing countries and in designing and carrying out science, technology and innovation policy reviews,

Taking note with interest of the establishment of the inter-agency cooperation network on biotechnology, UN-Biotech,

Taking note of the report of the Secretary-General,

Encouraging the development of initiatives to promote private sector engagement in technology transfer and technological and scientific cooperation,

1. *Reaffirms its commitment*:

(*a*) To strengthen and enhance existing mechanisms and to support initiatives for research and development, including through voluntary partnerships between the public and private sectors, to address the special needs of developing countries in the areas of health, agriculture, conservation, sustainable use of natural resources and environmental management, energy, forestry and the impact of climate change;

(*b*) To promote and facilitate, as appropriate, access to, and development, transfer and diffusion of, technologies, including environmentally sound technologies and the corresponding know-how, to developing countries;

(*c*) To assist developing countries in their efforts to promote and develop national strategies for human resources and science and technology, which are primary drivers of national capacity-building for development;

(*d*) To promote and support greater efforts to develop renewable sources of energy, including appropriate technology;

(*e*) To implement policies at the national and international levels to attract both public and private investment, domestic and foreign, that enhances knowledge, transfers technology on mutually agreed terms and raises productivity;

(*f*) To support the efforts of developing countries, individually and collectively, to harness new agricultural technologies in order to increase agricultural productivity through environmentally sustainable means;

2. *Recognizes* that science and technology, including information and communications technologies, are vital for the achievement of the internationally agreed development goals, including the Millennium Development Goals, and for the full participation of developing countries in the global economy;

3. *Notes* that full and equal access to and participation in science and technology for women of all ages is imperative for achieving gender equality and the empowerment of women, and underlines that addressing barriers to equal access for women and girls to science and technology requires a systematic, comprehensive, integrated, sustainable, multidisciplinary and multisectoral approach;

4. *Requests* the Commission on Science and Technology for Development to provide a forum within which to continue to assist the Economic and Social Council as the focal point in the system-wide follow-up to the outcomes of the World Summit on the Information Society and to address within its mandate, in accordance with Council resolution 2006/46, the special needs of developing countries in areas such as agriculture, rural development, information and communications technologies and environmental management;

5. *Encourages* the United Nations Conference on Trade and Development, in collaboration with relevant partners, to continue to undertake science, technology and innovation policy reviews, with a view to assisting developing countries and countries with economies in transition in identifying the measures that are needed to integrate science, technology and innovation policies into their national development strategies;

6. *Encourages* the United Nations Conference on Trade and Development and other relevant organizations to assist developing countries in their efforts to integrate science, technology and innovation policies into national development strategies;

7. *Encourages* Governments to strengthen and foster investment in research and development for environmentally sound technologies and to promote the involvement of the business and financial sectors in the development of those technologies, and invites the international community to support those efforts;

8. *Encourages* existing arrangements and the further promotion of regional, subregional and interregional joint research and development projects, where feasible, by mobilizing existing scientific and research and development resources and by networking sophisticated scientific facilities and research equipment;

9. *Encourages* the international community to continue to facilitate, in view of the difference in level of development between countries, an adequate diffusion of scientific and technical knowledge and transfer of, access to and acquisition of technology for developing countries, under fair, transparent and mutually agreed terms, in a manner conducive to social and economic welfare for the benefit of society;

10. *Reiterates its call for* continued collaboration between United Nations entities and other international organizations, civil society and the private sector in implementing the outcomes of the World Summit on the Information Society, with a view to putting the potential of information and communications technologies at the service of development through policy research on the digital divide and on new challenges of the information society, as well as technical assistance activities, involving multi-stakeholder partnerships;

11. *Requests* the Secretary-General to submit to the General Assembly at its sixty-eighth session a report on the implementation of the present resolution and recommendations for future follow-up, including lessons learned in integrating science, technology and innovation policies into national development strategies.

Information and communication technologies

During 2011, the United Nations continued to ensure that the benefits of new technologies, especially ICTs, were available to all, in keeping with recommendations contained in the ministerial declaration adopted by the Economic and Social Council at its 2000 high-level segment [YUN 2000, p. 799]; the Millennium Declaration [ibid., p. 49]; the 2003 Declaration of Principles and Plan of Action adopted at the first phase of WSIS [YUN 2003, p. 857]; and the 2005 Tunis Commitment and the Tunis Agenda adopted at its second phase [YUN 2005, p. 933].

Inter-Agency Round Table on Communication for Development

The Secretary-General transmitted the report [A/67/207] of the Director-General of the United Nations Educational, Scientific and Cultural Organization (UNESCO) on the implementation of Assembly resolution 50/130 [YUN 1995, p. 1438], including the recommendations of the twelfth United Nations Inter-Agency Round Table on Communication for Development (New Delhi, India, 14–17 November). The Round Table, entitled "The role of communication for development in empowering adolescent girls", focused on the potential of communication for development principles and practices to advance the rights of adolescent girls and communities. Participants recommended strengthening advocacy efforts throughout all available UN agency and inter-agency mechanisms; enhancing capacity development through broad-based partnerships; strengthening research, monitoring and evaluation of communication; and enhancing knowledge management and information-sharing.

Cooperation on public policy issues pertaining to the Internet

In response to Council resolution 2010/2 [YUN 2010, p. 837], the Chair of the Working Group on Improvements to the Internet Governance Forum submitted an April report [A/66/67-E/2011/79] presenting the outcome of the two meetings held by the Working Group (Montreux, Switzerland, 25–26 February and Geneva, 24–25 March). The Working Group was established on 17 December 2010 during the CSTD intersessional panel. The Group reviewed inputs from member States and other stakeholders on improvements to the Forum. The wealth of information, the complexity and political sensitivity of the subject and a significant divergence of views among member States on a number of proposals did not allow the Working Group to finalize a set of recommendations on improving the Forum. It was therefore suggested that the Working Group extend its deliberations beyond the fourteenth session of the Commission.

The Council took note of the report on 29 July (**decision 2011/275**).

Also in response to Council resolution 2010/2, the Secretary-General in May submitted a report [A/66/77-E/2011/103] on enhanced cooperation on public policy issues pertaining to the Internet, which summarized the outcome of consultations on the topic organized by the Under-Secretary-General for Economic and Social Affairs between September and December 2010. Contributors reflected on the public policy issues of concern, on international cooperation mechanisms to address those issues and on the role of the United Nations and other entities in facilitating enhanced cooperation. Contributors identified a wide range of public policy issues, underscoring the interdisciplinary nature of Internet governance and its relevance to development. Diverging views emerged on procedural aspects of enhanced cooperation. Contributors generally agreed that cooperation was already taking place in many respects; that specific issues of concern could be identified and discussed; that progress had not been the same on all issues since the holding of WSIS in 2005; and that cooperation mechanisms should be used to the extent that they were helpful.

The Council took note of the report on 29 July (**decision 2011/275**).

Internet Governance Forum. The sixth meeting of the Internet Governance Forum (Nairobi, 27–30 September) focused on the overall theme of "The Internet as a catalyst for change: access, development, freedoms and innovation". Sessions were held on Internet governance for development; emerging issues; access and diversity; security, openness and privacy; managing critical Internet resources; and taking stock and the way forward.

Economic and Social Council action. On 28 July, by **resolution 2011/33** (see p. 1209), the Council encouraged Member States to address the misuse of new ICTs to abuse and exploit children.

Follow-up to World Summit on the Information Society

In response to Economic and Social Council resolution 2006/46 [YUN 2006, p. 1001], the Secretary-General in March [A/66/64-E/2011/77] reported on progress made in the implementation of and follow-up to the WSIS outcomes at the regional and international levels.

One of the key trends consisted of continued growth and change in mobile connectivity, with mobile telephone networks being available to 90 per cent of the world's population. While broadband access was growing, that process had been faster in developed countries than in developing countries, raising concerns of a new digital divide based on the quality of available access. Much attention was being paid to the spread of new mobile applications, particularly in the sectors of mobile health and mobile transactions, which potentially offered substantial added value to end users, including in developing countries. The report underlined the impact of social networking and the growth of user-generated content, called "Web 2.0", and raised concerns over data privacy and security, risks to national security, commercial confidentiality, industrial espionage, the exploitation of personal data by government agencies and businesses, and the risk of identity theft and other abuse.

The regional commissions continued to support WSIS implementation through regional action plans. Activities included regional conferences and workshops, facilitation of the sharing of best practice experiences, support to Governments in policy development, and capacity-building.

At the international level, the International Telecommunication Union (ITU) hosted the 2010 WSIS Forum (Geneva, 10–14 May 2010), featuring high-level sessions on WSIS and the MDGs, broadband implementation and applications, social networking, ICTs for disaster management and cybersecurity. During the event, the United Nations Group on the Information Society [YUN 2006, p. 1000] organized an interactive session entitled "Financing mechanisms for ICT for development".

The Partnership on Measuring ICT for Development, a collaborative forum for the United Nations and other agencies to address challenges of data collection and analysis concerning ICT for development and WSIS outcomes, had published 50 core indicators for ICT infrastructure and access, the use of ICTs by households and enterprises, the ICT sector and trade in ICT goods, and ICTs in education. Formed in 2004, the partnership comprised 11 member organizations.

The Secretary-General concluded that the digital divide raised new challenges, and underlined the need for investment in infrastructure and innovative services that made use of broadband. UN agencies further emphasized the importance of e-government in realizing a global information society, the challenge of capacity-building and the importance of engaging the private sector.

ECONOMIC AND SOCIAL COUNCIL ACTION

On 26 July [meeting 44], the Economic and Social Council, on the recommendation of the Commission on Science and Technology for Development [E/2011/31], adopted **resolution 2011/16** without vote [agenda item 13 (*b*)].

Assessment of the progress made in the implementation of and follow-up to the outcomes of the World Summit on the Information Society

The Economic and Social Council,

Recalling the outcome documents of the World Summit on the Information Society,

Recalling also its resolution 2006/46 of 28 July 2006 on the follow-up to the World Summit on the Information Society and review of the Commission on Science and Technology for Development, and the mandate that it gave to the Commission,

Recalling further its resolution 2010/2 of 19 July 2010 on the assessment of the progress made in the implementation of and follow-up to the outcomes of the World Summit,

Recalling General Assembly resolution 65/141 of 20 December 2010 on information and communications technologies for development,

Taking note with satisfaction of the report of the Secretary-General on the progress made in the implementation of and follow-up to the outcomes of the World Summit at the regional and international levels,

Taking note of the report of the Secretary-General entitled "Improvements and innovations in existing financing mechanisms: information and communication technology for development",

Noting the submission of the report entitled *Implementing WSIS Outcomes: Experience to Date and Prospects for the Future*, by the Commission as an information document,

Expressing its appreciation to the Secretary-General of the United Nations Conference on Trade and Development for his role in helping to ensure completion of the aforementioned reports in a timely manner,

Taking stock: reviewing the implementation of the outcomes of the World Summit on the Information Society

1. *Notes* the ongoing implementation of the outcomes of the World Summit on the Information Society, emphasizing in particular its multi-stakeholder nature, the roles played in this regard by leading agencies as action line facilitators and the roles of the regional commissions and the United Nations Group on the Information Society, and expresses its appreciation for the role of the Commission on Science and Technology for Development in assisting the Economic and Social Council as the focal point in the system-wide follow-up to the World Summit;

2. *Takes note* of the respective reports of many United Nations entities, with their own executive summaries, submitted as inputs for the elaboration of the annual report of the Secretary-General to the Commission, and published on the website of the Commission as mandated in Economic and Social Council resolution 2007/8 of 25 July 2007, and recalls the importance of close coordination among the leading action line facilitators and with the secretariat of the Commission;

3. *Notes* the implementation of the outcomes of the World Summit at the regional level facilitated by the regional commissions, as observed in the report of the Secretary-General on progress made in the implementation of and follow-up to the outcomes of the World Summit at the regional and international levels, including the steps taken in this respect, and emphasizes the need to continue to address issues of specific interest to each region, focusing on the challenges and obstacles that each may be facing with regard to the implementation of all goals and principles established by the World Summit, with particular attention to information and communications technology for development;

4. *Reiterates* the importance of maintaining a process of coordinating the multi-stakeholder implementation of the outcomes of the World Summit through effective tools, with the goal of exchanging information among action line facilitators, identifying issues that need improvement and discussing the modalities of reporting the overall implementation process, encourages all stakeholders to continue to contribute information to the stocktaking database on the implementation of the goals established by the World Summit, maintained by the International Telecommunication Union, and invites United Nations entities to update information on their initiatives in the stocktaking database;

5. *Highlights* the urgent need for the incorporation of the recommendations of the outcome documents of the World Summit in the revised guidelines for United Nations country teams on preparing the common country assessments and United Nations Development Assistance Frameworks, including the addition of an information and communications technology for development component;

6. *Notes* the holding in Geneva from 16 to 20 May 2011 of the World Summit on the Information Society Forum 2011, organized by the International Telecommunication Union, the United Nations Educational, Scientific and Cultural Organization, the United Nations Conference on Trade and Development and the United Nations Development Programme as a multi-stakeholder platform for the implementation of the outcomes of the World Summit and to facilitate the implementation of the World Summit action lines;

7. *Calls upon* all States, in building the information society, to take steps to avoid and to refrain from taking any unilateral measure not in accordance with international law and the Charter of the United Nations that impedes the full achievement of economic and social development by the population of the affected countries and that hinders their well-being;

8. *Welcomes* the progress highlighted in the report of the Secretary-General regarding the implementation of and follow-up to the outcomes of the World Summit, in particular the fact that the rapid growth in mobile telephony since 2005 has meant that more than half of the world's inhabitants will have access to information and communications technologies within their reach, in line with one of the World Summit targets; the value of this progress is enhanced by the advent of new services and applications, including m-health, m-transactions, e-government, e-business and developmental services, which offer great potential to the development of the information society;

9. *Notes with great concern* that many developing countries lack affordable access to information and communications technologies and that for the majority of the poor, the promise of science and technology, including information and communications technologies, remains unfulfilled, and emphasizes the need to effectively harness technology, including information and communications technologies, to bridge the digital divide;

10. *Recognizes* that information and communications technologies present new opportunities and challenges and that there is a pressing need to address the major impediments that developing countries face in accessing the new technologies, such as lack of resources, infrastructure, education, capacity, investment and connectivity and issues related to technology ownership, standards and flows, and in this regard calls upon all stakeholders to provide adequate resources, enhanced capacity-building and transfer of technology to developing countries, particularly the least developed countries;

11. *Also recognizes* the rapid growth in broadband access networks, especially in developed countries, and notes with concern that there is a growing digital divide in the availability, affordability, quality of access and use of broadband networks between high-income countries and other regions, with least developed countries and Africa as a continent lagging behind the rest of the world;

12. *Further recognizes* that the transition to a mobile-led communications environment is leading to significant changes in operators' business models and that it requires significant rethinking of the ways in which individuals and communities make use of networks and devices, of Government strategies and of ways in which communications networks can be used to achieve development objectives;

13. *Recognizes* that, even with all the developments and the improvement observed in some respects, in numerous developing countries information and communications technologies and their applications are still not affordable for the majority of people, particularly those living in rural areas;

14. *Also recognizes* that the number of Internet users is growing and that in some instances the digital divide is also changing in character from one based on whether access is available to one based on the quality of access, information and skills that users can obtain, and the value they can derive from it, and recognizes in this regard that there is a need to prioritize the use of information and communications technologies through innovative approaches, including multi-stakeholder approaches, within national and regional development strategies;

15. *Welcomes* the report of the Broadband Commission for Digital Development, submitted to the Secretary-General of the United Nations in New York on 19 September 2010, and notes that the report includes the Declaration of Broadband Inclusion for All of the Commission;

16. *Notes* that, while a solid foundation for capacity-building in information and communications technology has been laid in many areas with regard to building the information society, there is still a need for continuing efforts to address the ongoing challenges, especially those faced by developing countries and the least developed countries, and draws attention to the positive impact of broadened capacity development that involves institutions, organizations and entities dealing with information and communications technologies and Internet governance issues;

17. *Recognizes* the need to focus on capacity development policies and sustainable support to further enhance the impact of activities and initiatives at the national and local levels aimed at providing advice, services and support with a view to building a people-centred, inclusive and development-oriented information society;

18. *Notes* that topics that were not central at the first and second phases of the World Summit continue to emerge, such as the potential of information and communications technologies to combat climate change, social networking, virtualization and cloud computing, the protection of online privacy and the empowerment and protection, especially against cyberexploitation and abuse, of vulnerable groups of society, in particular children and young people;

19. *Reiterates* the importance of information and communications technology indicators as a monitoring and evaluation tool for measuring the digital divide between countries and within societies and in informing decision makers when formulating policies and strategies for social, cultural and economic development, and emphasizes that the standardization and harmonization of reliable and regularly updated information and communications technology indicators that capture the performance, efficiency, affordability and quality of goods and services is essential for implementing information and communications technology policies;

Internet governance

20. *Reaffirms* paragraph 21 of its resolution 2010/2 of 19 July 2010 and paragraph 16 of General Assembly resolution 65/141 of 20 December 2010;

21. *Reaffirms also* paragraphs 35 to 37 and paragraphs 67 to 72 of the Tunis Agenda for the Information Society;

Enhanced cooperation

22. *Recalls* its resolution 2010/2, in which it invited the Secretary-General of the United Nations to convene open and inclusive consultations involving all Member States and all other stakeholders with a view to assisting the process towards enhanced cooperation, in order to enable Governments on an equal footing to carry out their roles and responsibilities in respect of international public policy issues pertaining to the Internet but not in respect of the day-to-day technical and operational matters that do not impact upon those issues, through a balanced participation of all stakeholders in their respective roles and responsibilities, as stated in paragraph 35 of the Tunis Agenda;

23. *Notes with appreciation* the open and inclusive consultations convened by the Secretary-General, through the Department of Economic and Social Affairs of the Secretariat, from September to December 2010, including the meeting held in New York on 14 December 2010;

24. *Decides* to forward the report of the Secretary-General on enhanced cooperation on public policy issues pertaining to the Internet regarding the outcome of those consultations to the General Assembly for consideration at its sixty-sixth session in order to enable Governments on an equal footing to carry out their roles and responsibilities in respect of international public policy issues pertaining to the Internet but not in respect of the day-to-day technical and operational matters that do not impact upon those issues;

Internet Governance Forum

25. *Recalls* General Assembly resolution 65/141 on information and communications technologies for development, in which it extended the mandate of the Internet Governance Forum for a further five years, while recognizing the need for improvements;

26. *Takes note with appreciation* of the report on the outcomes of the Working Group on Improvements to the Internet Governance Forum, and expresses its gratitude to all the members of the Working Group for their time and valuable efforts in this endeavour, as well as to all Member States and other relevant stakeholders that have submitted inputs to the Working Group consultation process;

27. *Notes* that the wealth of information and the complexity and political sensitivity of the subject as well as a divergence of views among members of the Working Group on a number of concrete proposals did not, within the short time frame that it had, allow the Working Group to finalize a set of recommendations, as appropriate, on improving the Forum;

28. *Agrees* to extend the mandate of the Working Group on Improvements to the Internet Governance Forum until the fifteenth session of the Commission on Science and Technology for Development, and invites it to complete its task on the basis of the work already accomplished;

29. *Urges* that the Working Group be reconvened at the earliest possible time to enable timely submission of its recommendations to the Commission at its fifteenth session, which shall constitute an input from the Commission to the General Assembly, through the Economic and Social Council;

The road ahead

30. *Urges* the United Nations entities still not actively cooperating in the implementation of and follow-up to the outcomes of the World Summit through the United Nations system to take the necessary steps and commit to a people-centred, inclusive and development-oriented information society and to catalyse the attainment of the internationally agreed development goals, including those contained in the United Nations Millennium Declaration;

31. *Calls upon* all stakeholders to keep the goal of bridging the digital divide, in its different forms, an area of priority concern, put into effect sound strategies that contribute to the development of e-government and continue to focus on pro-poor information and communications technology policies and applications, including with regard to broadband access at the grass-roots level, with a view to narrowing the digital divide between and within countries;

32. *Urges* all stakeholders to prioritize the development of innovative approaches that will stimulate the provision

of universal access to affordable broadband infrastructure for developing countries and the use of relevant broadband services in order to ensure the development of a people-centred, inclusive and development-oriented and information society, and to minimize the digital divide;

33. *Calls upon* international and regional organizations to continue to assess and report on a regular basis on the universal accessibility of nations to information and communications technologies, with the aim of creating equitable opportunities for the growth of the information and communications technology sectors of developing countries;

34. *Urges* all countries to make concrete efforts to fulfil their commitments under the Monterrey Consensus of the International Conference on Financing for Development;

35. *Calls upon* United Nations organizations and other relevant organizations and forums, in accordance with the outcomes of the World Summit, to periodically review and modify the methodologies for information and communications technology indicators, taking into account different levels of development and national circumstances, and therefore:

(*a*) Endorses the work of the Partnership on Measuring Information and Communication Technologies for Development;

(*b*) Calls upon United Nations organizations and other relevant organizations and forums to study the implications of the current world economic situation on information and communications technology deployment, particularly information and communications technology connectivity through broadband, and its economic sustainability;

(*c*) Calls upon the Partnership on Measuring Information and Communication Technologies for Development to further its work on measuring the impact of information and communications technologies, particularly in developing countries, by creating practical guidelines, methodologies and indicators;

(*d*) Encourages Governments to collect relevant data at the national level on information and communications technologies, to share information about country case studies and to collaborate with other countries in capacity-building exchange programmes;

(*e*) Encourages United Nations organizations and other relevant organizations and forums to promote impact assessment of information and communications technologies on poverty and in key sectors to identify the knowledge and skills needed to boost impacts;

(*f*) Calls upon international development partners to provide financial support to further facilitate capacity-building and technical assistance in developing countries;

36. *Invites* the international community to make voluntary contributions to the special trust fund established by the United Nations Conference on Trade and Development to support the review and assessment work of the Commission on Science and Technology for Development regarding follow-up to the World Summit, while acknowledging with appreciation the financial support provided by the Governments of Finland and Switzerland to this fund;

37. *Requests* the Secretary-General to submit to the Commission, on a yearly basis, a report on the implementation of the recommendations contained in Economic and Social Council resolutions on the assessment of the quantitative and qualitative progress made in the implementation of and follow-up to the outcomes of the World Summit;

38. *Urges* the Secretary-General to ensure the continued functioning of the Internet Governance Forum and its structures in preparation for the fifth meeting of the Forum, to be held in Nairobi from 27 to 30 September 2011, and future meetings of the Forum, without prejudice to the improvements that may be proposed by the Working Group on Improvements to the Internet Governance Forum;

39. *Invites* all stakeholders to contribute to the open consultation of the United Nations Group on the Information Society on the overall review of the implementation of the World Summit outcomes, in order to ensure that their views and needs are reflected in the outcomes of that consultation, that is, the Action Plan, which shall be presented to the United Nations System Chief Executives Board for Coordination at its meeting in April 2012, and requests the Group to provide a report on the open consultation for consideration by the Commission at its fifteenth session in May 2012.

Other events. The World Summit on the Information Society Forum 2011 (Geneva, 16–20 May), organized by ITU, UNESCO, UNCTAD and the United Nations Development Programme (UNDP), was attended by more than 1,150 WSIS stakeholders and included several high-level dialogues, meetings, interactive sessions and thematic workshops on topics such as social media, digital inclusion and cyberspace.

The Broadband Commission for Digital Development, established in 2010 by ITU and UNESCO, held a Broadband Leadership Summit (Geneva, 24–25 October), during which it set targets for making broadband policy universal and for boosting broadband affordability and uptake.

GENERAL ASSEMBLY ACTION

On 22 December [meeting 91], the General Assembly, on the recommendation of the Second Committee [A/66/437], adopted **resolution 66/184** without vote [agenda item 16].

Information and communications technologies for development

The General Assembly,

Recalling its resolutions 56/183 of 21 December 2001, 57/238 of 20 December 2002, 57/270 B of 23 June 2003, 59/220 of 22 December 2004, 60/252 of 27 March 2006, 62/182 of 19 December 2007, 63/202 of 19 December 2008, 64/187 of 21 December 2009, 65/141 of 20 December 2010 and other relevant resolutions,

Recalling also Economic and Social Council resolutions 2006/46 of 28 July 2006, 2008/3 of 18 July 2008, 2009/7 of 24 July 2009 and 2010/2 of 19 July 2010, and taking note of Economic and Social Council resolution 2011/16 of 26 July 2011 on the assessment of the progress made in the implementation of and follow-up to the outcomes of the World Summit on the Information Society,

Recalling further the Declaration of Principles and the Plan of Action adopted by the World Summit on the Information Society at its first phase, held in Geneva from 10 to 12 December 2003, and endorsed by the General Assembly, and the Tunis Commitment and the Tunis Agenda for the Information Society, adopted by the Summit at its second phase, held in Tunis from 16 to 18 November 2005, and endorsed by the General Assembly,

Recalling the 2005 World Summit Outcome,

Recalling also the High-level Plenary Meeting of the General Assembly on the Millennium Development Goals and its outcome document,

Taking note of the report of the Secretary-General on progress made in the implementation of and follow-up to the outcomes of the World Summit on the Information Society at the regional and international levels,

Noting the organization of the World Summit on the Information Society Forum 2011 in Geneva from 16 to 20 May 2011,

Noting also the establishment of the Broadband Commission for Digital Development at the invitation of the Secretary-General of the International Telecommunication Union and the Director-General of the United Nations Educational, Scientific and Cultural Organization, and taking note of the "Broadband targets for 2015", established by the Commission at its Broadband Leadership Summit, held in Geneva on 24 and 25 October 2011, which set targets for making broadband policy universal and for increasing affordability and broadband uptake towards the attainment of the internationally agreed development goals, including the Millennium Development Goals, to ensure that the potential of broadband connectivity and content are at the service of development,

Recognizing the role of the Commission on Science and Technology for Development in assisting the Economic and Social Council as the focal point in the system-wide follow-up, in particular the review and assessment of the progress made in implementing the outcomes of the World Summit on the Information Society, while at the same time maintaining its original mandate on science and technology for development,

Noting the holding of the fourteenth session of the Commission on Science and Technology for Development in Geneva from 23 to 27 May 2011,

Noting also that cultural diversity is the common heritage of humankind and that the information society should be founded on and stimulate respect for cultural identity, cultural and linguistic diversity, traditions and religions and foster dialogue among cultures and civilizations, and noting also that the promotion, affirmation and preservation of diverse cultural identities and languages, as reflected in relevant agreed United Nations documents, including the Universal Declaration on Cultural Diversity of the United Nations Educational, Scientific and Cultural Organization, will further enrich the information society,

Acknowledging the positive trends in global connectivity and affordability in the field of information and communications technologies, in particular the steady increase in Internet access to one third of the world's population, the rapid diffusion of mobile telephony, the increased availability of multilingual content and Internet addresses and the advent of new services and applications, including m-health, mobile transactions, e-government, e-education, e-business and developmental services, which offer great potential for the development of the information society,

Emphasizing, however, that in spite of recent progress, there remains an important digital divide, recognizing in this regard that currently only 26 per cent of the population in developing countries uses the Internet, compared with 74 per cent in developed countries, and stressing the need to reduce the digital divide, including with regard to such issues as international interconnection charges for Internet use, and to ensure that the benefits of new technologies, especially information and communications technologies, are available to all,

Reaffirming the need to harness the potential of information and communications technologies to promote the achievement of the internationally agreed development goals, including the Millennium Development Goals, through sustained, inclusive and equitable economic growth and sustainable development,

Expressing concern about the ongoing adverse impacts of the world financial and economic crisis on the positive trends in the diffusion of information and communications technologies and the investment needed to ensure universal access to such technologies,

Expressing concern also about the growing gap in broadband provision between developed and developing countries, as well as about the new dimensions that the digital divide has taken on,

Recognizing that the lack of capacity-building for the productive use of information and communications technologies needs to be addressed in order to overcome the digital divide,

Recognizing also that the number of Internet users is growing and that the digital divide is also changing in character from one based on whether access is available to one based on the quality of access, the information and skills that users can obtain and the value they can derive from it, and recognizing in this regard that there is a need to prioritize the use of information and communications technologies through innovative approaches, including multi-stakeholder approaches, within national and regional development strategies,

Reaffirming paragraphs 4, 5 and 55 of the Declaration of Principles adopted in Geneva in 2003, and recognizing that freedom of expression and the free flow of information, ideas and knowledge are essential for the information society and are beneficial to development,

Conscious of the challenges faced by States, in particular developing countries, in combating cybercrime, and emphasizing the need to reinforce technical assistance and capacity-building activities for the prevention, prosecution and punishment of the use of information and communications technologies for criminal purposes,

Acknowledging that the Internet is a central element of the infrastructure of the information society and is a global facility available to the public,

Recognizing that the international management of the Internet should be multilateral, transparent and democratic, with the full involvement of Governments, the private sector, civil society and international organizations, as stated in the Tunis Agenda for the Information Society,

Recognizing also the importance of the Internet Governance Forum and its mandate as a forum for multi-stakeholder dialogue on various matters, including public policy issues related to key elements of Internet governance, in order to foster the sustainability, robustness, security, stability and development of the Internet, as well as its role in building partnerships among different stakeholders so as to help in addressing the various issues of Internet governance, while acknowledging the calls for improvements in its working methods,

Recalling its decision that the desirability of the continuation of the Internet Governance Forum will be considered again by Member States in the General Assembly in the context of a ten-year review of the implementation of the outcome of the World Summit on the Information Society in 2015,

Reiterating the significance and urgency of the process towards enhanced cooperation in full consistency with the mandate provided in the Tunis Agenda and the need for enhanced cooperation to enable Governments, on an equal footing, to carry out their roles and responsibilities in respect of international public policy issues pertaining to the Internet but not in respect of the day-to-day technical and operational matters that have no impact on those issues,

Reaffirming that the outcomes of the World Summit on the Information Society relating to Internet governance, namely, the process towards enhanced cooperation and the convening of the Internet Governance Forum, are to be pursued by the Secretary-General through two distinct processes, and recognizing that the two processes may be complementary,

Reaffirming also paragraphs 35 to 37 and 67 to 72 of the Tunis Agenda,

Welcoming the efforts undertaken by the host countries in organizing the meetings of the Internet Governance Forum, held in Athens in 2006, in Rio de Janeiro, Brazil, in 2007, in Hyderabad, India, in 2008, in Sharm el-Sheikh, Egypt, in 2009, in Vilnius in 2010 and in Nairobi in 2011,

Recognizing the pivotal role of the United Nations system in promoting development, including with respect to enhancing access to information and communications technologies, inter alia, through partnerships with all relevant stakeholders,

Welcoming, in view of the existing gaps in information and communications technologies infrastructure, the Connect Africa summits held in Kigali in 2007 and in Cairo in 2008, the Connect the Commonwealth of Independent States summit held in Minsk in 2009, the meeting of Commonwealth countries held in Colombo in 2010, the First Digital Agenda Assembly of the European Union held in Brussels on 16 and 17 June 2011 and the annual European Dialogue on Internet Governance, which are regional initiatives aimed at mobilizing human, financial and technical resources to accelerate the implementation of the connectivity goals of the World Summit on the Information Society,

1. *Recognizes* that information and communications technologies have the potential to provide new solutions to development challenges, particularly in the context of globalization, and can foster sustained, inclusive and equitable economic growth and sustainable development, competitiveness, access to information and knowledge, poverty eradication and social inclusion that will help to expedite the integration of all countries, especially developing countries, in particular the least developed countries, into the global economy;

2. *Expresses concern* regarding the digital divide in access to information and communications technologies and broadband connectivity between countries at different levels of development, which affects many economically and socially relevant applications in such areas as government, business, health and education, and further expresses concern with regard to the special challenges faced in the area of broadband connectivity by developing countries, including the least developed countries, small island developing States and landlocked developing countries;

3. *Acknowledges* that a gender divide exists as part of the digital divide, and encourages all stakeholders to ensure the full participation of women in the information society and women's access to and use of information and communications technologies for their overall empowerment and benefit;

4. *Stresses* that, for the majority of the poor, the development promise of science and technology, including information and communications technologies, remains unfulfilled, and emphasizes the need to effectively harness technology, including information and communications technologies, to bridge the digital divide;

5. *Also stresses* the important role of Governments in the design of their national public policies and in the provision of public services responsive to national needs and priorities through, inter alia, the effective use of information and communications technologies, including on the basis of a multi-stakeholder approach, to support national development efforts;

6. *Recognizes* that, in addition to financing by the public sector, financing of information and communications technologies infrastructure by the private sector has come to play an important role in many countries and that domestic financing is being augmented by North-South flows and complemented by South-South cooperation, and also recognizes that South-South and triangular cooperation can be useful tools for promoting the development of information and communications technologies;

7. *Also recognizes* that information and communications technologies present new opportunities and challenges and that there is a pressing need to address the major impediments that developing countries face in accessing the new technologies, such as insufficient resources, infrastructure, education, capacity, investment, connectivity and issues related to technology ownership, standards and flows, and in this regard calls upon all stakeholders to provide adequate resources, enhanced capacity-building and technology transfer, on mutually agreed terms, to developing countries, particularly the least developed countries;

8. *Further recognizes* the immense potential that information and communications technologies have in promoting the transfer of technologies in a wide spectrum of socioeconomic activity;

9. *Encourages* strengthened and continuing cooperation between and among stakeholders to ensure the effective implementation of the outcomes of the Geneva and Tunis phases of the World Summit on the Information Society through, inter alia, the promotion of national, re-

gional and international multi-stakeholder partnerships, including public-private partnerships, and the promotion of national and regional multi-stakeholder thematic platforms in a joint effort and dialogue with developing countries, including the least developed countries, development partners and actors in the information and communications technologies sector;

10. *Reaffirms* the role of the General Assembly in the overall review of the implementation of the outcomes of the World Summit on the Information Society, to be held by the end of 2015, as recognized in paragraph 111 of the Tunis Agenda for the Information Society, and further decides to consider the modalities for this review process at its sixty-seventh session;

11. *Welcomes* the efforts undertaken by Tunisia, host of the second phase of the World Summit on the Information Society, in collaboration with the United Nations Conference on Trade and Development, the International Telecommunication Union and other relevant international and regional organizations, for organizing annually the ICT 4 All Forum and technological exhibition as a platform within the framework of the follow-up to the Summit to promote a dynamic business environment for the information and communications technologies sector worldwide;

12. *Notes* the progress that has been made by United Nations entities in cooperation with national Governments, regional commissions and other stakeholders, including non-governmental organizations and the private sector, in the implementation of the action lines contained in the outcome documents of the World Summit on the Information Society, and encourages the use of those action lines for the achievement of the Millennium Development Goals;

13. *Also notes* the implementation of the outcomes of the World Summit on the Information Society at the regional level, facilitated by the regional commissions, as observed in the report of the Secretary-General on progress made in the implementation of and follow-up to the outcomes of the World Summit at the regional and international levels;

14. *Encourages* the United Nations funds and programmes and the specialized agencies, within their respective mandates and strategic plans, to contribute to the implementation of the outcomes of the World Summit on the Information Society, and emphasizes the need for resources in this regard;

15. *Recognizes* the urgent need to harness the potential of knowledge and technology, and in this regard encourages the United Nations development system to continue its effort to promote the use of information and communications technologies as a critical enabler of development and a catalyst for the achievement of the internationally agreed development goals, including the Millennium Development Goals;

16. *Also recognizes* the role of the United Nations Group on the Information Society as an inter-agency mechanism of the United Nations System Chief Executives Board for Coordination designed to coordinate United Nations implementation of the outcomes of the World Summit on the Information Society;

17. *Notes* the report of the Chair of the Working Group on Improvements to the Internet Governance Forum, and takes note of the decision of the Economic and Social Council, in paragraphs 27 to 29 of its resolution 2011/16, to extend the mandate of the Working Group until the fifteenth session of the Commission on Science and Technology for Development in order for it to complete its task in accordance with its mandate, and urges the Working Group to submit its recommendations to the Commission at its fifteenth session, which shall constitute an input from the Commission to the General Assembly, through the Economic and Social Council;

18. *Stresses* the need for the enhanced participation of all developing countries, in particular the least developed countries, in all Internet Governance Forum meetings, and in this regard invites Member States, as well as other stakeholders, to support the participation of Governments and all other stakeholders from developing countries in the Forum itself, as well as in the preparatory meetings;

19. *Recalls* paragraph 22 of its resolution 65/141, takes note of the report of the Secretary-General on enhanced cooperation on public policy issues pertaining to the Internet, in particular of the consultations convened by the Secretary-General through the Department of Economic and Social Affairs of the Secretariat, including the meeting held in New York on 14 December 2010, invites the Chair of the Commission on Science and Technology for Development to convene, in conjunction with the fifteenth session of the Commission, a one-day open, inclusive and interactive meeting involving all Member States and other stakeholders, particularly those from developing countries, including the private sector, civil society and international organizations, with a view to identifying a shared understanding of enhanced cooperation on public policy issues pertaining to the Internet, in accordance with paragraphs 34 and 35 of the Tunis Agenda, and requests the Secretary-General to include information on the outcome of the meeting when preparing his report on the status of the implementation of and follow-up to the present resolution;

20. *Requests* the Secretary-General to submit to the General Assembly at its sixty-seventh session, through the Commission on Science and Technology for Development and the Economic and Social Council, a report on the status of the implementation of and follow-up to the present resolution, as part of his annual reporting on the progress made in the implementation of and follow-up to the outcomes of the World Summit on the Information Society at the regional and international levels;

21. *Decides* to include in the provisional agenda of its sixty-seventh session the item entitled "Information and communications technologies for development".

Development policy and public administration

Committee for Development Policy

The Committee for Development Policy, at its thirteenth session (New York, 21–25 March) [E/2011/33

& Corr.1], addressed three themes: education for all, issues related to the least developed countries (including monitoring of the development progress of Equatorial Guinea and Samoa), and migration and development.

Regarding the theme of the 2011 annual ministerial review, entitled "Implementing the internationally agreed goals and commitments in regard to education", the Committee noted that many developing countries had achieved significant progress towards meeting the internationally agreed targets on education, including the provision of universal primary education. Urgent improvements, however, were needed in terms of quality of education, including the enhancement of cognitive skills.

In preparation for the triennial review of the list of least developed countries to be undertaken in 2012, the Committee reviewed the criteria and indicators used to identify such countries, and proposed further refinements. Samoa, scheduled for graduation in 2014, was recovering from the economic and financial crisis as well as the tsunami disaster of 2009 and was expected to return to its sustainable development path. The economic prospects of Equatorial Guinea, whose graduation was endorsed by the Council in 2009, continued to be favourable.

During its evaluation of the interaction between development and migration, the Committee found that international migration had a significant impact on the development and functioning of modern economies. It called for increased international cooperation and clearer progress towards creating an international framework for the regulation of migration flows, and for the promotion of measures to enhance the positive developmental impacts of migration and minimize its negative effects.

For its forthcoming fourteenth (2012) session, the Committee would undertake work on the theme of the 2012 annual ministerial review of the Economic and Social Council, entitled "Promoting productive capacity, employment and decent work to eradicate poverty in the context of inclusive, sustainable and equitable economic growth at all levels for achieving the Millennium Development Goals".

ECONOMIC AND SOCIAL COUNCIL ACTION

On 27 July [meeting 47], the Economic and Social Council adopted **resolution 2011/20** [draft: E/2011/L.34] without vote [agenda item 13 (*a*)].

Report of the Committee for Development Policy on its thirteenth session

The Economic and Social Council,

Recalling General Assembly resolution 59/209 of 20 December 2004 on a smooth transition strategy for countries graduating from the list of least developed countries, resolution 65/286 of 29 June 2011 on implementing the smooth transition strategy for countries graduating from the list of least developed countries and resolution 61/16 of 20 November 2006 on strengthening of the Economic and Social Council,

Recalling also General Assembly resolution 65/280 of 17 June 2011 on the Programme of Action for the Least Developed Countries for the Decade 2011–2020,

Recalling further its resolutions 1998/46 of 31 July 1998, 2007/34 of 27 July 2007, 2009/35 of 31 July 2009 and 2010/9 of 22 July 2010,

Expressing its conviction that no country graduating from the least developed countries category should have its positive development disrupted or reversed, but that it should be able to continue and sustain its progress and development,

Acknowledging the contribution that the Committee for Development Policy can make to further strengthen the work of the Economic and Social Council by broadening and deepening the use of the expertise available in the Committee,

1. *Takes note* of the report of the Committee for Development Policy on its thirteenth session;

2. *Requests* the Committee, at its fourteenth session, to examine and make recommendations on the themes chosen by the Economic and Social Council for the high-level segment of its substantive session of 2012;

3. *Takes note* of the proposals made by the Committee regarding its future programme of work, in particular to monitor the development progress of Cape Verde and Maldives and review the existing smooth transition mechanisms to identify how they can be further strengthened or improved and better monitored;

4. *Recalls* its endorsement of the recommendation of the Committee that Equatorial Guinea be graduated from the list of least developed countries;

5. *Reiterates* its recommendation that the General Assembly take note of the recommendation of the Committee that Equatorial Guinea be graduated from the list of least developed countries;

6. *Welcomes* the outcome of the Fourth United Nations Conference on the Least Developed Countries, and notes the contributions of the Committee to the Conference;

7. *Requests* the Committee to monitor the development progress of countries graduating from the list of least developed countries and to include its findings in its annual report to the Council;

8. *Reiterates* the importance for development and trading partners to implement concrete measures in support of the transition strategy for ensuring durable graduation;

9. *Decides* to engage in, within existing resources, more frequent interactions with the Committee, and invites the Chair and, as necessary, other members of the Committee to meet with the Council, including, as appropriate:

(*a*) To discuss, prior to the annual substantive session of the Council, the views and recommendations on the themes of the high-level segment and other relevant issues contained in the annual report of the Committee to the Council;

(*b*) To exchange views, during the general segment, on the programme of work of the Committee on the themes to be addressed by the Council at the high-level segment of its following substantive session and on other pertinent issues that the Committee wishes to bring to the attention of the Council.

Public administration

The Committee of Experts on Public Administration, at its tenth session (New York, 4–8 April) [E/2011/44], considered the component on post-conflict and post-disaster countries, including social protection for vulnerable populations, of the current year's theme—public governance for results. The Committee had before it Secretariat notes on public governance for results: a conceptual and operational framework [E/C.16/2011/2]; State capacity for post-conflict and post-disaster reconstruction and social protection policies [E/C.16/2011/3]; and a review of the United Nations Programme in Public Administration and Finance [E/C.16/2011/4]. The Committee submitted a draft resolution to the Economic and Social Council for adoption (see p. 824).

The Committee recommended to the Secretariat and the Council that they assist Governments, including through better practice guides, mechanisms for constant monitoring and review, and building organizations with a learning culture. They should ensure that the United Nations had the capacity to provide independent information, such as on the MDGs, in order to facilitate independent performance evaluation.

With regard to post-conflict and post-disaster countries, the Committee noted a lack of assistance on governance capacities for development and recommended that those be developed to complement ongoing assistance in peace and security carried out by UNDP and the Department of Peacekeeping Operations. Programmes of public sector development should move from technical assistance provided by expatriate advisers to the creation of a locally rooted public administration.

The Committee urged DESA to contribute to an international mechanism for financing adjustments to the environmental crisis, and to provide technical support to address agricultural losses and food insecurity. It further recommended assisting countries in the radical restructuring of public administration and development management to meet the challenges of the cumulative impact of successive disasters.

As to social protection, the safeguard of vulnerable groups should be a priority for any Government, with strategies including criteria such as affordability; national values on an ethic of social solidarity; vertical and horizontal equity; support from non-State actors; gender; sustainability over time; the possibility of phasing out when appropriate so as to avoid individual dependency as well as fiscal traps; and administrative efficiency. Special attention should be paid to vulnerable groups excluded from mainstream social protection programmes. The Committee called on the United Nations to work with Member States to forge a global agenda for social protection, linked more closely with national development agendas beyond the targeted year of 2015.

Regarding performance management in governance, the Committee recommended that Member States place priority on training senior managers and civil servants; improve the compensation system for government employees; establish an effective performance appraisal system; and recognize the importance of education on citizenship and a culture of responsibility.

ECONOMIC AND SOCIAL COUNCIL ACTION

On 26 April [meeting 9], the Economic and Social Council, on the recommendation of the Committee of Experts on Public Administration [E/2010/44], adopted **resolution 2011/2** [draft: E/2011/L.5] without vote [agenda item 2].

Report of the Committee of Experts on Public Administration on its ninth session

The Economic and Social Council,
Recalling its resolutions 2002/40 of 19 December 2002, 2003/60 of 25 July 2003, 2005/3 of 31 March 2005, 2005/55 of 21 October 2005, 2006/47 of 28 July 2006, 2007/38 of 4 October 2007, 2008/32 of 25 July 2008 and 2009/18 of 29 July 2009, all on public administration and development,

Referring to General Assembly resolutions 50/225 of 19 April 1996, 56/213 of 21 December 2001, 57/277 of 20 December 2002, 58/231 of 23 December 2003, 59/55 of 2 December 2004 and 60/34 of 30 November 2005 on public administration and development, and resolutions 63/202 of 19 December 2008 and 64/187 of 21 December 2009 on information and communication technologies for development,

Taking note of the support being provided by the United Nations Programme in Public Administration and Finance to Member States for institutional and human resource capacity development in the public sector, electronic and mobile government development, development management and citizen engagement,

Taking note also of the work of the Committee of Experts on Public Administration in providing advice to the Economic and Social Council aimed at the advancement of the internationally agreed development goals, including the Millennium Development Goals, within the context of its mandate,

Underscoring the importance of strengthening effective public administration institutions, human resources, management processes and tools and citizen involvement in policymaking with a view to addressing the challenges posed by global crises,

1. *Takes note* of the report of the Committee of Experts on Public Administration on its ninth session, which dealt with the challenges to and opportunities for public administration in the context of the financial and economic crisis, a review of the United Nations Programme in Public Administration and Finance and the public administration perspective on implementing the internationally agreed goals and commitments in regard to gender equality and empowerment of women;

2. *Takes note with appreciation* of the work of the International Organization of Supreme Audit Institutions in promoting greater transparency, accountability and efficient and effective receipt and use of public resources for the benefit of citizens and of the 1977 Lima Declaration of Guidelines on Auditing Precepts and the 2007 Mexico Declaration on Supreme Audit Institutions Independence, which set out the principles of independence in government auditing, and encourages the wide dissemination of these principles;

3. *Recognizes* the key role of public administration and public governance in implementing the internationally agreed development goals, including the Millennium Development Goals, and in addressing the challenges posed by global crises;

4. *Also recognizes* that information and communications technology provides a potent tool for advancing gender equality and women's empowerment, as well as the importance of e-government for development;

5. *Requests* the Secretariat:

(a) To give due recognition to innovative public sector initiatives by Member States through the promotion and strengthening of the United Nations Public Service Day and the Public Service Awards;

(b) To support further development of the United Nations Public Administration Network for partnership-building, knowledge-sharing and the exchange of best practices in the area of public administration;

(c) To assist in the implementation of the Plan of Action on e-government-related issues adopted by the World Summit on the Information Society at its first phase, held in Geneva from 10 to 12 December 2003;

(d) To assist countries in public institutional and human resources development and development management in order to strengthen national ownership and capacity for the articulation of national development strategies, their effective implementation and full citizen engagement, with a special focus on developing countries, Africa, countries in transition and the least developed countries;

(e) To collect data on gender equality in public administration and high-level civil service positions, within its existing mandate;

(f) To continue to develop its online and offline training tools for capacity development and consolidate the products and services of its online information resources on public administration country studies.

On 27 July [meeting 47], the Economic and Social Council, on the recommendation of the Committee of Experts on Public Administration [E/2011/44], adopted **resolution 2011/22** [draft: E/2011/L.23] without vote [agenda item 13 (g)].

Report of the Committee of Experts on Public Administration on its tenth session

The Economic and Social Council,

Recalling its resolutions 2002/40 of 19 December 2002, 2003/60 of 25 July 2003, 2005/3 of 31 March 2005, 2005/55 of 21 October 2005, 2006/47 of 28 July 2006, 2007/38 of 4 October 2007, 2008/32 of 25 July 2008, 2009/18 of 29 July 2009 and 2011/2 of 26 April 2011, all on public administration and development,

Recalling also General Assembly resolutions 50/225 of 19 April 1996, 56/213 of 21 December 2001, 57/277 of 20 December 2002, 58/231 of 23 December 2003, 59/55 of 2 December 2004 and 60/34 of 30 November 2005, all on public administration and development,

Recognizing the work of the Committee of Experts on Public Administration in providing policy advice and programmatic guidance to the Economic and Social Council on issues related to governance and public administration in development,

Taking note of the support being provided by the United Nations Programme in Public Administration and Finance to Member States for institutional and human resource capacity-building, development management, electronic and mobile government development, and citizen engagement in the public sector,

Taking note also of the discussions held during the tenth session of the Committee on post-conflict and post-disaster countries as well as on social protection for vulnerable populations, and having considered the recommendations made therein,

1. *Takes note* of the report of the Committee of Experts on Public Administration on its tenth session and of the focus of the Committee on "Local public governance and administration for results: how local public administration should be improved to support the implementation of the internationally agreed development agenda, including the Millennium Development Goals" as the theme of its eleventh session, in 2012;

2. *Requests* the Secretariat:

(a) To continue to support the development of the United Nations Public Administration Network for partnership-building, knowledge dissemination and the exchange of knowledge, best practices and lessons learned in the area of public administration;

(b) To continue to develop and promote the United Nations Public Administration Country Studies, which contains analytical and case studies, guidelines and other knowledge-sharing outputs on best practices and lessons learned in governance for development, including for post-conflict countries and countries facing the cumulative effects of successive disasters;

(c) To better publicize the opportunity represented by the United Nations Public Service Awards, to disseminate information on good practices and innovation from the awards and to strive to better promote and utilize innovative public administration initiatives, including those identified within the context of the awards;

(d) To continue to enhance, within existing resources, its support for capacity-building in the public sector, including in human resource development, promoting participatory governance institutions with a view to making public administration more open, transparent, accountable and responsive to citizens in all countries, and use case studies, as appropriate, in capacity-building and training activities, and assess the impact of those case studies;

(e) To continue to assist in analysis, policy options and capacity-building, including for post-conflict countries, particularly on their governance capacities for development;

(f) To continue to provide countries in post-disaster situations with policy advice, capacity-building actions and tools for engaging citizens, civil society organizations and the private sector in recovery and reconstruction efforts, deepening public accountability and preventing corruption;

(g) To continue activities around the themes of public service delivery and the engagement of citizens in accountability and preventing corruption;

(h) To continue to assist in capacity-building and technical cooperation for e-government, including through the further development of the Measurement and Evaluation Tool for E-Government Readiness;

3. *Encourages* the Committee to focus its efforts to achieve fully developed, consensus-based views and recommendations on issues related to public administration.

On 27 July, the Council decided that the eleventh session of the Committee of Experts on Public Administration would be held at UN Headquarters from 16 to 20 April 2012 and approved the provisional agenda for the session (**decision 2011/252**).

Improving public administration

On 10 November [A/C.2/66/SR.34], Austria, on behalf of 30 countries, introduced a draft resolution entitled "Promoting the efficiency, transparency and accountability of public administration by strengthening supreme audit institutions" [A/C.2/66/L.16]. The sponsors believed that building strong institutions was a central development challenge and that supreme audit institutions played a critical role, as they helped promote sound financial management and thus accountable and transparent government.

GENERAL ASSEMBLY ACTION

On 22 December [meeting 91], the General Assembly, on the recommendation of the Second Committee [A/66/442], adopted **resolution 66/209** without vote [agenda item 21].

Promoting the efficiency, accountability, effectiveness and transparency of public administration by strengthening supreme audit institutions

The General Assembly,

Recalling Economic and Social Council resolution 2011/2 of 26 April 2011,

Recalling also its resolutions 59/55 of 2 December 2004 and 60/34 of 30 November 2005 and its previous resolutions on public administration and development,

Recalling further the United Nations Millennium Declaration,

Emphasizing the need to improve the efficiency, accountability, effectiveness and transparency of public administration,

Emphasizing also that efficient, accountable, effective and transparent public administration has a key role to play in the implementation of the internationally agreed development goals, including the Millennium Development Goals,

Stressing the need for capacity-building as a tool to promote development, and welcoming the cooperation of the International Organization of Supreme Audit Institutions with the United Nations in this regard,

1. *Recognizes* that supreme audit institutions can accomplish their tasks objectively and effectively only if they are independent of the audited entity and are protected against outside influence;

2. *Also recognizes* the important role of supreme audit institutions in promoting the efficiency, accountability, effectiveness and transparency of public administration, which is conducive to the achievement of national development objectives and priorities as well as the internationally agreed development goals, including the Millennium Development Goals;

3. *Takes note with appreciation* of the work of the International Organization of Supreme Audit Institutions in promoting greater efficiency, accountability, effectiveness, transparency and efficient and effective receipt and use of public resources for the benefit of citizens;

4. *Also takes note with appreciation* of the Lima Declaration of Guidelines on Auditing Precepts of 1977 and the Mexico Declaration on Supreme Audit Institutions Independence of 2007, and encourages Member States to apply, in a manner consistent with their national institutional structures, the principles set out in those Declarations;

5. *Encourages* Member States and relevant United Nations institutions to continue and to intensify their cooperation, including in capacity-building, with the International Organization of Supreme Audit Institutions in order to promote good governance by ensuring efficiency, accountability, effectiveness and transparency through strengthened supreme audit institutions.

Groups of countries in special situations

On 16 September [A/66/443], the General Assembly, on the recommendation of the General Committee, included in the agenda of its sixty-sixth session the item entitled "Groups of countries in special situations", covering least developed, landlocked and transit developing countries, and allocated it to the Second Committee.

On 22 December, the Assembly took note of the report of the Second Committee (**decision 66/545**).

Least developed countries

The special problems of the officially designated least developed countries (LDCs) were considered in several UN forums in 2011, particularly at the Fourth United Nations Conference on the Least Developed Countries (LDC-IV) (Istanbul, Turkey, 9–13 May). The Conference adopted the Istanbul Declaration and the Programme of Action for LDCs for the Decade 2011–2020. The Committee for Development Policy (CDP), UNCTAD and the United Nations Office of the High Representative for the Least Developed Countries, Landlocked Developing Countries and Small Island Developing States (UN-OHRLLS) also considered LDC-related issues.

The *Least Developed Countries Report 2011* [Sales No. E.11.II.D.5], published by UNCTAD, examined the potential role of South-South cooperation for inclusive and sustainable development. It stated that LDCs needed to go beyond business as usual in order to promote development and suggested how South-South cooperation supported such a transformational agenda. The report showed that despite strong gross domestic product growth during the previous decade, the benefits of growth were neither inclusive nor sustainable, mainly because growth was not complemented by structural transformation and employment creation. Most LDCs continued to deepen their specialization in exports of primary commodities and low-value, labour-intensive manufacturing, rather than diversifying into more sophisticated products. The benefits of South-South cooperation would be greatest when the policies of catalytic developmental States in LDCs and South-South cooperation reinforced each other in a continual process of change and development.

LDC list

In preparation for the triennial review of the list of LDCs to be undertaken in 2012 [E/2011/33], CDP re-examined the criteria and indicators used to identify such countries. CDP defined LDCs as low-income countries suffering from the most severe structural impediments to sustainable development. While confirming the reliability of the criteria used for identification, it proposed further refinements to the indicators, in particular to better reflect the structural vulnerability of countries to climate change.

Maldives graduated from the LDC category on 1 January, after a long transition period. Graduation was endorsed in 2004 by the Economic and Social Council [YUN 2004, p. 855] and noted by the General Assembly [ibid.], and was scheduled to take place in 2007. Due to the devastation caused by the Indian Ocean tsunami of 26 December 2004 [ibid., p. 952], the Assembly, by resolution 60/33 [YUN 2005, p. 942], deferred graduation to 1 January 2011.

CDP recommended the graduation of Equatorial Guinea in March 2009 [YUN 2009, p. 829]. That recommendation was endorsed by the Council [ibid., p. 829] but had not been confirmed by the General Assembly.

The list of LDCs comprised the following 48 countries: Afghanistan, Angola, Bangladesh, Benin, Bhutan, Burkina Faso, Burundi, Cambodia, the Central African Republic, Chad, the Comoros, the Democratic Republic of the Congo, Djibouti, Equatorial Guinea, Eritrea, Ethiopia, the Gambia, Guinea, Guinea-Bissau, Haiti, Kiribati, the Lao People's Democratic Republic, Lesotho, Liberia, Madagascar, Malawi, Mali, Mauritania, Mozambique, Myanmar, Nepal, the Niger, Rwanda, Samoa, Sao Tome and Principe, Senegal, Sierra Leone, Solomon Islands, Somalia, the Sudan, Timor-Leste, Togo, Tuvalu, Uganda, the United Republic of Tanzania, Vanuatu, Yemen and Zambia.

Smooth transition strategy

According to the Istanbul Programme of Action (see p. 828), a smooth transition of countries graduating from LDC status was vital to ensure that those countries were eased onto a sustainable development path without any disruption to their development plans, programmes and projects. The Programme invited the Assembly to establish an ad hoc working group to further study and strengthen the smooth transition process. The Assembly, in resolution 66/213 (see p. 830), requested its President to establish the working group.

The President of the Assembly, on 23 December [A/66/PV.91], said that support for the working group would be provided by UN-OHRLLS as the secretariat of the group, as well as by DESA, CDP and its secretariat.

On 22 December, the Assembly adopted the terms of reference of the Ad Hoc Working Group to further study and strengthen the smooth transition process for countries graduating from the LDC category (**decision 66/553**).

GENERAL ASSEMBLY ACTION

On 29 June [meeting 105], the General Assembly adopted **resolution 65/286** [draft: A/65/L.66/Rev.1 & Add.1] without vote [agenda item 23].

Implementing the smooth transition strategy for countries graduating from the list of least developed countries

The General Assembly,

Recalling its resolutions 46/206 of 20 December 1991 and 59/209 of 20 December 2004,

Recalling also Economic and Social Council resolutions 2006/1 of 7 February 2006, 2007/34 of 27 July 2007 and 2009/35 of 31 July 2009 as they relate to the need for monitoring the progress of countries graduating from least developed country status, and to the importance of taking into consideration the nature and extent of this progress in determining a smooth transition strategy for these countries,

Recalling further Economic and Social Council decision 2004/299 of 23 July 2004, which highlighted the proposals of the Secretary-General for concrete mechanisms to implement a smooth transition strategy for graduating countries, as well as the recommendations on possible features of a smooth transition strategy contained in the report of the Committee for Development Policy on its tenth session,

Recalling the Istanbul Declaration and the Programme of Action for the Least Developed Countries for the Decade 2011–2020, adopted at the Fourth United Nations Conference on the Least Developed Countries held in Istanbul, Turkey, from 9 to 13 May 2011, in which Member States committed to assisting the least developed countries with an overarching goal of enabling half of them to meet the criteria for graduation by 2020,

1. *Reiterates* the importance of ensuring that the graduation of a country from least developed country status does not cause disruption in the development progress that country has achieved;

2. *Urges* graduating countries and all bilateral and multilateral development and trading partners to pursue or intensify their efforts, consistent with World Trade Organization rules, to contribute to the full implementation of resolution 59/209, with a view to ensuring the smooth transition of graduating least developed countries;

3. *Looks forward*, in accordance with General Assembly resolution 65/171 of 20 December 2010, to the report of the Secretary-General to the Assembly at its sixty-seventh session on the support measures effectively provided by development and trading partners for the countries that have graduated or will be graduating from least developed country status and on possible ways to better ensure their smooth transition;

4. *Decides* that the long-standing benefit of travel-related support that has been made available by the United Nations to the least developed countries will be extended, if requested, within existing resources, to Cape Verde and Maldives for a period appropriate to the development situation of the country and for a maximum of three years, beginning immediately after the adoption of the present resolution, and that the same benefit will be granted, also if requested, within existing resources, and for a period appropriate to the development situation of the country and for a maximum of three years, to any other country that graduates from least developed country status;

5. *Urges* the Committee for Development Policy, with assistance and support from other relevant entities, to continue its monitoring of the development progress of graduated countries as a complement to its triennial review of the list of least developed countries, to pay particular attention to the effectiveness of smooth transition for graduated countries, and to report thereon to the Economic and Social Council at its substantive session.

Review of the Programme of Action (2001–2010)

In response to General Assembly resolution 65/171 [YUN 2010, p. 846] and Economic and Social Council resolution 2010/27 [ibid., p. 844], the Secretary-General in February submitted a report [A/66/66-E/2011/78] on the ten-year appraisal and review of the implementation of the Brussels Programme of Action for LDCs for the Decade 2001–2010 [YUN 2001, p. 770]. The report, to be submitted to LDC-IV, identified lessons learned and best practices, as well as structural constraints and handicaps encountered, resource requirements and resource gaps in achieving the objectives of the Programme of Action. In accordance with Assembly resolution 63/227 [YUN 2008, p. 944], the report also evaluated actions and initiatives needed to overcome obstacles and identified effective international and domestic policies in the light of the outcome of the appraisal.

The report outlined progress achieved with respect to the Programme's main objectives, including economic development; poverty, hunger and other targets related to the MDGs; good governance; mobilization of financial resources; and progress towards graduation. The report concluded that economic and social development in LDCs had been better during the implementation period of the Programme of Action than in the previous decade—albeit with significant differences among individual LDCs—but that the specific goals and objectives had not been fully attained. The structural transformation that would put LDCs on a path of sustainable growth had not occurred. The Secretary-General called for greater ownership and leadership in the implementation of a programme of action, and advised LDCs to identify authorities to oversee the execution of development strategies. Recommendations for a new programme of action included considering new players, including large and influential developing countries; focusing on structural transformation through increasing productive capacity and diversification; tapping the enormous human resources potential of LDCs, especially the large youth population; increasing financial resources; and ensuring mutual accountability between LDCs and their national, regional and global partners.

The Assembly took note of the report on 22 December (**decision 66/546**).

Fourth UN Conference on Least Developed Countries

Preparatory process

In accordance with General Assembly resolutions 64/213 [YUN 2009, p. 835] and 65/171 [YUN 2010, p. 846], the Intergovernmental Preparatory Committee for LDC-IV held its first (10–14 January) [A/CONF.219/IPC/6] and second substantive sessions (4–8 April) [A/CONF.219/4] in New York. On 8 April, the Preparatory Committee adopted four decisions, including on the draft provisional agenda [A/CONF.219/IPC/8] and the draft rules of procedure [A/CONF.219/IPC/L.2].

Pre-conference events were held [A/CONF.219.IPC/10] on science, technology and innovation: setting priorities, shaping and implementing policies for LDCs (Istanbul, 7–8 February); building a knowledge base for innovation and creativity to promote development (Geneva, 14–15 February); harnessing the positive contribution of South-South cooperation for LDC development (New Delhi, 18–19 February); reducing vulnerability due to climate change, climate variability and extremes, land degradation and biodiversity loss: challenges and opportunities (New York, 28 February); digital inclusion for LDCs: innovation, growth and sustainability (Geneva, 8–9 March); promoting universal access to essential services (New York, 10 March); and growth, employment and decent work in LDCs (New York, 29 March) [A/CONF.219/7].

A summit-level meeting of LDCs was held in Istanbul on 8 May on the eve of the Conference.

Conference

In accordance with Assembly resolutions 64/213 and 65/171, LDC-IV (Istanbul, 9–13 May) [A/CONF.219/7] sought to comprehensively appraise the implementation of the Brussels Programme of Action; identify effective international and domestic policies; reaffirm the global commitment to addressing the special needs of LDCs; and mobilize additional international support measures and action in favour of LDCs.

In the course of the general debate, statements were made by 121 Member States, 13 UN bodies and eight intergovernmental organizations. The Conference featured six high-level interactive thematic debates and 45 special events organized by Member States, UN bodies and other organizations. The Conference also featured a Parliamentary Forum (8 May), a Civil Society Forum (7–13 May) and a private sector track. On 13 May, the Conference adopted the Istanbul Declaration and the Programme of Action for LDCs for the Decade 2011–2020.

Istanbul Declaration. In the Istanbul Declaration, Governments committed to the overarching goal of enabling half of LDCs to meet the criteria for graduation through the eradication of poverty and the achievement of accelerated, sustained, inclusive and equitable growth and sustainable development. The Declaration renewed global partnership and solidarity with LDCs and affirmed the importance of the fulfilment of ODA commitments by donor countries. At the same time, Governments underscored that ownership, leadership and primary responsibility for development rested with LDCs themselves. In order to facilitate productive capacity-building as a development multiplier, priority should be given to infrastructure services; the private sector, particularly small and medium-sized enterprises; mobilization of domestic and external financial resources; science and technology transfer; agriculture and rural development policies; and regional economic integration. The Declaration further recognized the potential of international trade, new innovative finance mechanisms and South-South cooperation; addressed challenges such as climate change and the high debt burden of many LDCs; and underlined the importance of effective and efficient monitoring of the Istanbul Programme of Action.

Programme of Action (2011–2020). In accordance with the Istanbul Declaration, the Programme of Action for LDCs for the Decade 2011–2020 (Istanbul Programme of Action) [A/CONF.219/3/Rev.1] set as its overarching goal to overcome the structural challenges faced by LDCs in order to eradicate poverty, achieve internationally agreed development goals and enable graduation from the LDC category.

The following objectives were to be pursued by international support measures and LDC national policies: achieve sustained, equitable and inclusive economic growth by strengthening LDC productive capacity; build human capacities by fostering sustained, equitable and inclusive human and social development, gender equality and the empowerment of women; reduce the vulnerability of LDCs to economic, natural and environmental shocks and disasters through strengthening their resilience; ensure enhanced financial resources for the development of LDCs; and enhance good governance by strengthening democratic processes, institutions and the rule of law.

The Programme of Action was based on principles such as country ownership and leadership; an integrated approach to development; genuine partnership and solidarity; peace and security, development and human rights; equity at all levels; voice and representation; and a balanced role of the State and market considerations, taking into account the significant role of the Government in achieving economic growth. The actions taken by LDCs and their development partners were to be focused on eight interlinked priority areas, namely productive capacity; agriculture, food security and rural development; trade; commodities; human and social development; multiple crises and other emerging challenges; mobilization of financial resources for development and capacity-building; and good governance at all levels.

The Programme of Action further stressed the importance of South-South cooperation as a complement to North-South cooperation and of a smooth transition strategy for countries graduating from LDC status. Efficient follow-up and monitoring mechanisms were considered as crucial for such implementation, with particular emphasis on national-level arrangements.

Trade and Development Board action. At its forty-eighth annual session [TD/B/58/9], the Trade and Development Board took action on the report of the UNCTAD secretariat on the implementation of the outcome of LDC-IV [TD/B/58/7] (see p. 906).

GENERAL ASSEMBLY ACTION

On 17 June [meeting 100], the General Assembly adopted **resolution 65/280** [draft: A/65/L.75] without vote [agenda item 23 (*a*)].

Programme of Action for the Least Developed Countries for the Decade 2011–2020

The General Assembly,

Recalling its resolution 63/227 of 19 December 2008, in which it decided to convene the Fourth United Nations Conference on the Least Developed Countries at a high level in 2011, as well as its resolutions 64/213 of 21 December 2009 and 65/171 of 20 December 2010,

1. *Expresses its profound gratitude* to the Government and the people of the Republic of Turkey for hosting the Fourth United Nations Conference on the Least Developed Countries in Istanbul from 9 to 13 May 2011, and for providing all the necessary support;

2. *Endorses* the Istanbul Declaration and the Programme of Action for the Least Developed Countries for the Decade 2011–2020, adopted by the Fourth United Nations Conference on the Least Developed Countries, and calls upon all the relevant stakeholders to commit to implementing the Programme of Action.

Briefing by High Representative. On 22 July [E/2011/SR.40], the High Representative for the Least Developed Countries, Landlocked Developing Countries and Small Island Developing States briefed the Economic and Social Council on the outcome of LDC-IV.

ECONOMIC AND SOCIAL COUNCIL ACTION

On 22 July [meeting 40], the Economic and Social Council adopted **resolution 2011/9** [draft: E/2011/L.31] without vote [agenda item 6 (*b*)].

Programme of Action for the Least Developed Countries for the Decade 2011–2020

The Economic and Social Council,

Recalling the Istanbul Declaration and the Programme of Action for the Least Developed Countries for the Decade 2011–2020, adopted by the Fourth United Nations Conference on the Least Developed Countries, held in Istanbul, Turkey, from 9 to 13 May 2011, and endorsed by the General Assembly in resolution 65/280 of 17 June 2011, in which the Assembly called upon all the relevant stakeholders to commit to implementing the Programme of Action,

Reaffirming the overarching goal of the Programme of Action of overcoming the structural challenges faced by the least developed countries in order to eradicate poverty, achieve the internationally agreed development goals and enable graduation from the least developed country category,

Recalling its resolution 2010/27 of 23 July 2010 on the implementation of the Programme of Action for the Least Developed Countries for the Decade 2001–2010,

1. *Takes note* of the oral report of the High Representative for the Least Developed Countries, Landlocked Developing Countries and Small Island Developing States on the implementation of the Programme of Action for the Least Developed Countries for the Decade 2011–2020;

2. *Expresses its profound gratitude* to the Government and the people of the Republic of Turkey for hosting the Fourth United Nations Conference on the Least Developed Countries and for providing all the necessary support, and expresses its gratitude to other donors and contributors for their generous contributions to the Conference and its preparatory process;

3. *Welcomes with appreciation* the decisions taken by the Executive Boards of the United Nations Development Programme/United Nations Population Fund/United Nations Office for Project Services, the United Nations Children's Fund and the United Nations Entity for Gender Equality and the Empowerment of Women (UN-Women) at their 2011 annual sessions to integrate the Programme of Action within their respective programmes of work;

4. *Invites* all other organizations of the United Nations system and other multilateral organizations, including the Bretton Woods institutions and international and regional financial institutions, to contribute to the implementation of the Programme of Action and to integrate it into their programmes of work, as appropriate and in accordance with their respective mandates, and to participate fully in its review at the national, subregional, regional and global levels;

5. *Invites* its subsidiary bodies, including the functional commissions and regional commissions, to make effective contributions to the implementation and review of the Programme of Action, in accordance with their respective mandates;

6. *Decides* to include the Programme of Action as part of its review of the implementation of and follow-up to major United Nations conferences and summits;

7. *Calls upon* the least developed countries, with the support of their development partners, to promote implementation of the Programme of Action, including by integrating its provisions into their national policies and development framework and conducting regular reviews with the full involvement of all key stakeholders;

8. *Also calls upon* the least developed countries, in cooperation with their development partners, to broaden their existing country review mechanisms, including those for the achievement of the Millennium Development Goals, and the implementation of poverty reduction strategy papers, common country assessments and United Nations Development Assistance Frameworks, and the existing consultative mechanisms to cover the review of the Programme of Action;

9. *Calls upon* the development partners and all other relevant actors to implement the Programme of Action by integrating it into their respective national cooperation pol-

icy frameworks, programmes and activities, as appropriate, to ensure enhanced, predictable and targeted support to the least developed countries, as set out in the Programme of Action, and the delivery of their commitments, and to consider appropriate measures to overcome shortfalls or shortcomings, if any;

10. *Underlines* the need to take the steps necessary to ensure mutual accountability of least developed countries and their development partners for delivering their commitments undertaken under the Programme of Action;

11. *Decides* to include in its annual ministerial review, in 2015, the review of the implementation of the Programme of Action;

12. *Also decides* that the Development Cooperation Forum should take into consideration the Programme of Action when it reviews the trends in international development cooperation, as well as policy coherence for development;

13. *Requests* the Secretary-General to submit to the Economic and Social Council at its substantive session of 2012, under the sub-item entitled "Review and coordination of the implementation of the Istanbul Programme of Action for the Least Developed Countries for the Decade 2011–2020", a progress report on the implementation of the Programme of Action.

Report of Secretary-General. In accordance with Assembly resolution 65/171 [YUN 2010, p. 846], the Secretary-General submitted a July report [A/66/134] on the outcome of LDC-IV. The report provided an overview of the Istanbul Programme of Action (see p. 828) and endorsed the active role ascribed to the UN system, particularly UN-OHRLLS, in the implementation process as well as the follow-up and monitoring of the implementation of the Programme of Action.

Ministerial meeting. The Annual Ministerial Meeting of LDCs (New York, 26 September) focused on global development challenges, including the famine in the Horn of Africa, and their links to sustainable development. Addressing the meeting, the Secretary-General underlined the role of the Istanbul Programme of Action as a development compact and said that the next generation of development targets beyond 2015 should reflect the sustainability dimension more prominently.

GENERAL ASSEMBLY ACTION

On 22 December [meeting 91], the General Assembly, on the recommendation of the Second Committee [A/66/443/Add.1], adopted **resolution 66/213** without vote [agenda item 22 (*a*)].

Fourth United Nations Conference on the Least Developed Countries

The General Assembly,

Recalling the Istanbul Declaration and the Programme of Action for the Least Developed Countries for the Decade 2011–2020, adopted at the Fourth United Nations Conference on the Least Developed Countries and endorsed by the General Assembly through its resolution 65/280 of 17 June 2011, in which the Assembly called upon all the relevant stakeholders to commit to implementing the Programme of Action,

Reaffirming the overarching goal of the Istanbul Programme of Action of overcoming the structural challenges faced by the least developed countries in order to eradicate poverty, achieve internationally agreed development goals and enable graduation from the least developed country category,

Recalling Economic and Social Council resolution 2011/9 of 22 July 2011 on the Programme of Action for the Least Developed Countries for the Decade 2011–2020,

Recalling also General Assembly resolutions 59/209 of 20 December 2004 and 65/286 of 29 June 2011 on the importance of a smooth transition for countries graduating from the list of least developed countries, and reaffirming the aim of enabling half the least developed countries to meet the criteria for graduation by 2020,

Taking note of the Ministerial Declaration adopted at the Ministerial Meeting of the Least Developed Countries, held in New York on 26 September 2011,

Taking note also of the report of the Fourth United Nations Conference on the Least Developed Countries, held in Istanbul, Turkey, from 9 to 13 May 2011,

Recognizing the important contribution of civil society, the private sector and parliamentarians to the Fourth United Nations Conference on the Least Developed Countries and the preparatory process for the Conference,

1. *Takes note* of the report of the Secretary-General on the outcome of the Fourth United Nations Conference on the Least Developed Countries;

2. *Calls upon* the least developed countries, with the support of their development partners, to fulfil their commitments and to promote implementation of the Istanbul Programme of Action, including by integrating its provisions into their national policies and development framework and conducting regular reviews with the full involvement of all key stakeholders, and in this regard, invites the Office of the High Representative for the Least Developed Countries, Landlocked Developing Countries and Small Island Developing States, the subsidiary bodies of the Economic and Social Council, including United Nations regional and functional commissions, the United Nations resident coordinator system and the United Nations country teams to actively support the integration and the implementation of the Istanbul Programme of Action;

3. *Also calls upon* the least developed countries, in cooperation with their development partners, to broaden their existing country review mechanisms, including those for the achievement of the Millennium Development Goals, the implementation of poverty reduction strategy papers, common country assessments and United Nations Development Assistance Frameworks, and the existing consultative mechanisms to cover the review of the Istanbul Programme of Action;

4. *Calls upon* the development partners to integrate the Istanbul Programme of Action into their respective national cooperation policy frameworks, programmes and activities, as appropriate, to ensure enhanced, predictable and targeted support to the least developed countries, as set out in the Istanbul Programme of Action, and the delivery of

their commitments, and to consider appropriate measures to overcome shortfalls or shortcomings, if any;

5. *Invites* all organizations of the United Nations system and other multilateral organizations, including the Bretton Woods institutions and international and regional financial institutions, to contribute to the implementation of the Istanbul Programme of Action and to integrate it into their programmes of work, as appropriate and in accordance with their respective mandates, and to participate fully in its review at the national, subregional, regional and global levels;

6. *Calls upon* the developing countries, guided by the spirit of solidarity and consistent with their capabilities, to provide support for the effective implementation of the Istanbul Programme of Action in mutually agreed areas of cooperation within the framework of South-South cooperation, which is a complement to, but not a substitute for, North-South cooperation;

7. *Invites* the private sector, civil society and foundations to contribute to the implementation of the Istanbul Programme of Action in their respective areas of competence in line with the national priorities of the least developed countries;

8. *Welcomes with appreciation* the decisions taken by the Executive Boards of the United Nations Development Programme, the United Nations Population Fund, the United Nations Office for Project Services, the United Nations Children's Fund, the United Nations Entity for Gender Equality and the Empowerment of Women (UN-Women) and the World Food Programme at their 2011 annual sessions to integrate the Istanbul Programme of Action within their respective programmes of work, welcomes with appreciation the adoption of a resolution by the Assemblies of States members of the World Intellectual Property Organization to mainstream the relevant parts of the Istanbul Programme of Action into various programmes of the organization, also welcomes the decision of the Trade and Development Board of the United Nations Conference on Trade and Development to mainstream the relevant provisions of the Istanbul Programme of Action into the work of the secretariat and its intergovernmental machinery, and in this regard invites the governing bodies of all other United Nations funds and programmes and multilateral organizations to do the same in an expeditious manner, as appropriate and in accordance with their respective mandates;

9. *Calls upon* the least developed countries, their development partners, the United Nations system and all other actors to fully and effectively implement the commitments that have been made in the Istanbul Programme of Action in its eight priority areas, namely, productive capacity, agriculture, food security and rural development, trade, commodities, human and social development, multiple crises and other emerging challenges, mobilizing financial resources for development and capacity-building, and good governance at all levels, in a coordinated, coherent and expeditious manner;

10. *Expresses concern* that the ongoing impact of the economic and financial crisis demonstrates the need for appropriate regional and international support to be deployed in a timely and targeted manner to complement the efforts of the least developed countries aimed at building resilience in the face of economic shocks and mitigating their effects;

11. *Notes with appreciation* the efforts made by the United Nations system and other international and regional organizations, including the work of the Inter-Agency Consultative Group and the development of a road map to coordinate the activities of the relevant organizations of the United Nations system for the implementation of the Istanbul Programme of Action;

12. *Underlines* the need for giving particular attention to the issues and concerns of the least developed countries in all major United Nations conferences and processes;

13. *Notes* the ongoing preparatory process for the United Nations Conference on Sustainable Development, to be held in Rio de Janeiro, Brazil, from 20 to 22 June 2012;

14. *Requests* the Secretary-General to take the steps necessary to undertake a joint gap and capacity analysis on a priority basis by 2013 with the aim of establishing a technology bank and science, technology and innovation supporting mechanism dedicated to least developed countries, building on the existing international initiatives;

15. *Recalls* that a smooth transition of countries graduating from least developed country status is vital to ensure that those countries are eased onto a path towards sustainable development without any abrupt disruption to their development plans, programmes and projects;

16. *Requests* the President of the General Assembly to establish, in consultation with Member States and the Secretary-General, an ad hoc working group to further study and strengthen the smooth transition process for the countries graduating from the least developed country category and to submit a report to the Assembly at its sixty-seventh session with specific recommendations, consistent with the Istanbul Programme of Action;

17. *Encourages* Governments, intergovernmental and non-governmental organizations, major groups and other donors to contribute to the Trust Fund in a timely manner to support the implementation, follow-up and monitoring of the Istanbul Programme of Action as well as the participation of the representatives from the least developed countries in the annual review meeting on the implementation of the Istanbul Programme of Action by the Economic and Social Council as well as in other relevant forums, and in this regard, expresses its appreciation to those countries that have made voluntary contributions to the Trust Fund;

18. *Stresses* that the Office of the High Representative for the Least Developed Countries, Landlocked Developing Countries and Small Island Developing States should continue to fulfil its functions to assist the Secretary-General for the effective follow-up and monitoring of the implementation of the Istanbul Programme of Action and the full mobilization and coordination of all parts of the United Nations system, with a view to facilitating the coordinated implementation of and coherence in the follow-up and monitoring of the Istanbul Programme of Action at the country, regional and global levels, and to assist in mobilizing international support and resources for the implementation of the Istanbul Programme of Action, and to this end, it should continue its awareness-raising and advocacy work in favour of least developed countries in partnership with the relevant part of the United Nations, as well as with parliaments, civil society, the media, academia and foundations, and provide appropriate support to group consultations of least developed countries;

19. *Underlines* that the Office of the High Representative for the Least Developed Countries, Landlocked Developing Countries and Small Island Developing States should be provided with the necessary support to fulfil its mandate for the timely and effective implementation of the Istanbul Programme of Action, and recognizes that the report of the Secretary-General to the General Assembly at its sixty-seventh session, as requested in paragraph 155 of the Istanbul Programme of Action, will facilitate, inter alia, consideration by the Assembly of the ongoing resource requirements of the Office of the High Representative;

20. *Requests* the Secretary-General to submit to the General Assembly at its sixty-seventh session a progress report on the implementation of the Programme of Action for the Least Developed Countries for the Decade 2011–2020.

On 24 December (**decision 66/557**), the General Assembly decided that the agenda item on groups of countries in special situations: follow-up to LDC-IV would remain for consideration during its resumed sixty-sixth (2012) session.

Small island developing States

During 2011, UN bodies continued to review progress in the implementation of the Programme of Action for the Sustainable Development of Small Island Developing States (Barbados Programme of Action), adopted in 1994 [YUN 1994, p. 783]. Member States also reviewed the Mauritius Strategy for Further Implementation of the Programme of Action for the Sustainable Development of Small Island Developing States, adopted by the 2005 International Meeting to Review the Implementation of the 1994 Programme of Action [YUN 2005, p. 946].

Commission on Sustainable Development consideration. At the nineteenth session of the Commission on Sustainable Development [E/2011/29], many delegates indicated that, according to the High-level Review Meeting on the Implementation of the Mauritius Strategy for the Further Implementation of the Programme of Action for the Sustainable Development of Small Island Developing States [YUN 2010, p. 850], the progress of those States towards sustainable development was inadequate and there were shortcomings in the institutional support for those States. A group of countries argued that a more formal, holistic coordination mechanism was essential for delivering UN and non-UN support to those States and that there was a need for more technical data and analysis to address their unique vulnerabilities. It was also proposed that regional mechanisms be developed to protect the ocean and coastal zones of small island developing States (SIDS) from ship-generated waste and to address the challenges posed by transboundary movement of hazardous material.

UN support for SIDS

In response to Economic and Social Council resolution 2010/34 [YUN 2010, p. 849] and General Assembly resolution 65/2 [ibid., p. 850], the Secretary-General, in May [E/2011/110] and August [A/66/218], respectively, submitted reports to the Council and the Assembly that provided an integrated analysis of UN system support to SIDS and reviewed UN system support to those States.

The reports reviewed the progress made by the UN system in integrating the Barbados Programme of Action and the Mauritius Strategy into its mandates, programmes and processes, with a view to promoting the coherence and coordination of UN support to SIDS. The reports formulated recommendations on how such support could be more targeted, efficient and effective. The analysis of the support provided by the UN system focused on the mandates of relevant UN entities, with reference to institutional issues, financial contributions, and four particular domains of support—normative support, technical cooperation and support for capacity-building, analytical support and coordination mechanisms. The reports concluded that the UN system had provided SIDS with a wide range of targeted support in the implementation of the Mauritius Strategy. There was, however, room for improvement and enhancement in the delivery of coordinated and coherent programmes. The Secretary-General recommended the integration of issues of concern to SIDS into the work of the UN system; the strengthening of coordination and coherence of support; and the identification of focal points within every UN entity to ensure such support. He further underlined the need for effective knowledge management, a strong voice for SIDS at the global level, and enhanced collaboration within the UN system. Analytical work to address the special vulnerabilities of those States and to explore ways in which to help build their resilience should be continued.

On 29 July, the Council deferred action on the draft resolution entitled "Review of United Nations support for small island developing States" until its resumed substantive session (**decision 2011/274**).

ECONOMIC AND SOCIAL COUNCIL ACTION

On 5 December [meeting 54], the Economic and Social Council adopted **resolution 2011/44** [draft: E/2011/L.52 & E/2011/SR.54] without vote [agenda item 13 (*a*)].

Review of United Nations support for small island developing States

The Economic and Social Council,

Recalling the Declaration of Barbados, the Programme of Action for the Sustainable Development of Small Island Developing States and the Mauritius Strategy for the Further Implementation of the Programme of Action for the Sustainable Development of Small Island Developing States,

Recalling also its resolutions 2009/17 of 29 July 2009 and 2010/34 of 23 July 2010 on the review of United Nations support for small island developing States,

Recalling further General Assembly resolution 65/2 of 25 September 2010 on the outcome document of the High-level Review Meeting on the Implementation of the Mauritius Strategy for the Further Implementation of the Programme of Action for the Sustainable Development of Small Island Developing States,

Recalling the report of the Committee for Development Policy on its twelfth session containing the Committee's independent views and perspectives on United Nations support for small island developing States,

Recalling also that the unique and particular vulnerabilities and development needs of small island developing States have been acknowledged by the international community,

Acknowledging that small island developing States have demonstrated their commitment to promoting sustainable development and will continue to do so, as well as the long-standing support provided by the international community,

Noting that the High-level Review Meeting on the Implementation of the Mauritius Strategy highlighted some shortcomings in the institutional support for small island developing States, as well as other constraints on the full and effective implementation of the Mauritius Strategy and the Barbados Programme of Action,

1. *Requests* the Committee for Development Policy, within existing resources, to submit to the Economic and Social Council, prior to its substantive session of 2013, a report providing the independent views and perspectives of the Committee on how to further the full and effective implementation of the Barbados Programme of Action and the Mauritius Strategy, including by refocusing efforts towards a results-oriented approach and considering what improved and additional measures might be needed to more effectively address the unique and particular vulnerabilities and development needs of small island developing States;

2. *Recommends* that the report requested in paragraph 1 above be considered a contribution to the ongoing review process initiated under paragraph 33 of General Assembly resolution 65/2;

3. *Invites* the Secretary-General to facilitate the work of the Committee for Development Policy as requested in paragraph 1 above, upon the request of the Committee;

4. *Notes* the recommendations to the Economic and Social Council contained in the related report of the Secretary-General.

Mauritius Strategy

In a report [A/66/278] submitted in August in accordance with General Assembly resolution 65/2 [YUN 2010, p. 850], the Secretary-General provided concrete recommendations to enhance the implementation of the Barbados Programme of Action and the Mauritius Strategy. The report summarized the views and recommendations received from Member States, experts and UN entities on how to address some of the key vulnerabilities faced by SIDS. Suggested measures to address the vulnerability and development needs of those States covered climate change adaptation, disaster risk management, preservation of biodiversity, energy challenges, economic structural disadvantages, food security, sustainable tourism and debt sustainability. Responses from Member States recommended greater communication between the UN system and SIDS; a comprehensive review of financial support mechanisms; improvement in the collection and analysis of data; the development of renewable energy resources; and greater political commitment to the education system. Recommendations from UN entities and intergovernmental organizations were complementary and included debt relief, resource mobilization and the strengthening of self-reliance.

GENERAL ASSEMBLY ACTION

On 22 December [meeting 91], the General Assembly, on the recommendation of the Second Committee [A/66/440/Add.2], adopted **resolution 66/198** without vote [agenda item 19 (*b*)].

Follow-up to and implementation of the Mauritius Strategy for the Further Implementation of the Programme of Action for the Sustainable Development of Small Island Developing States

The General Assembly,

Reaffirming the Declaration of Barbados and the Programme of Action for the Sustainable Development of Small Island Developing States, the Mauritius Declaration and the Mauritius Strategy for the Further Implementation of the Programme of Action for the Sustainable Development of Small Island Developing States, and the Plan of Implementation of the World Summit on Sustainable Development ("Johannesburg Plan of Implementation"), including chapter VII on the sustainable development of small island developing States,

Recalling the outcome document of the High-level Review Meeting on the Implementation of the Mauritius Strategy for the Further Implementation of the Programme of Action for the Sustainable Development of Small Island Developing States, held in New York on 24 and 25 September 2010, General Assembly resolution 65/156 of 20 December 2010 and all its other previous resolutions on the subject, as well as the report of the Secretary-General on the five-year review of the Mauritius Strategy,

Acknowledging the importance of the upcoming United Nations Conference on Sustainable Development,

1. *Notes* the report of the Secretary-General on concrete recommendations to enhance the implementation of the Programme of Action for the Sustainable Development of Small Island Developing States and the Mauritius Strategy for the Further Implementation of the Programme of Action for the Sustainable Development of Small Island Developing States, prepared in response to the request contained in the outcome document of the High-level Review Meeting on the Implementation of the Mauritius Strategy;

2. *Also notes* the report of the Secretary-General on the review of United Nations system support to small island developing States;

3. *Further notes* the ongoing preparatory process for the United Nations Conference on Sustainable Development to be held in Rio de Janeiro, Brazil, from 20 to 22 June 2012;

4. *Stresses* the importance of the continued substantive consideration of the follow-up to and implementation of the Mauritius Strategy for the Further Implementation of the Programme of Action for the Sustainable Development of Small Island Developing States;

5. *Decides* to include in the provisional agenda of its sixty-seventh session, under the item entitled "Sustainable development", the sub-item entitled "Follow-up to and implementation of the Mauritius Strategy for the Further Implementation of the Programme of Action for the Sustainable Development of Small Island Developing States";

6. *Also decides* to consider, at its sixty-seventh session, the reports of the Secretary-General on concrete recommendations to enhance the implementation of the Programme of Action for the Sustainable Development of Small Island Developing States and the Mauritius Strategy for the Further Implementation of the Programme of Action for the Sustainable Development of Small Island Developing States and on the review of United Nations system support to small island developing States, issued for the sixty-sixth session.

Landlocked developing countries

Report of Secretary-General. In response to General Assembly resolution 65/172 [YUN 2010, p. 856], the Secretary-General in July submitted a report [A/66/205] on the implementation of the Almaty Programme of Action: Addressing the Special Needs of Landlocked Developing Countries within a New Global Framework for Transit Transport Cooperation for Landlocked and Transit Developing Countries [YUN 2003, p. 875]. The report provided an update on progress made in the implementation and the efforts undertaken by the UN system and other international organizations. It also identified the major challenges encountered and made recommendations to accelerate implementation of the Programme.

While the landlocked developing countries (LLDCs) as a group were on their way to economic recovery after suffering from setbacks caused by the global financial and economic crisis, they were facing challenges related to international trade, poverty, unemployment, food insecurity and deforestation. Despite considerable progress achieved in several priority areas, the report identified several gaps: ratification of conventions to facilitate international trade by LLDCs had been slow; the percentage of paved roads remained low; railways remained an underutilized form of transport; energy infrastructure was insufficient and unreliable; nine LLDCs were not members of the World Trade Organization; and the geographic distribution of foreign direct investment remained uneven.

The report concluded that being landlocked imposed a major constraint to economic growth and the attainment of development objectives. The economies of LLDCs remained fragile because of their vulnerability to external shocks, owing to limited export diversification, limited productive capacities, lack of export competitiveness and high transport and transit costs.

The Secretary-General recommended increased financial support by the international community; prioritization of resource allocation for the maintenance and rehabilitation of transit transport infrastructure; and ratification and implementation of international agreements on transport and trade facilitation. He further suggested LLDCs that be supported in strengthening their analytical capacities to develop and implement coherent and comprehensive transport policies and in sharpening their negotiation skills for effective participation in international trade.

Communications. On 25 April [E/ESCAP/67/22], Mongolia transmitted to the Economic and Social Commission for Asia and the Pacific the Ulaanbaatar Declaration, adopted by the High-level Asia-Pacific Policy Dialogue on the Implementation of the Almaty Programme of Action and other Development Gaps Faced by the Landlocked Developing Countries (Ulaanbaatar, Mongolia, 12–14 April).

On 27 September [A/66/392], Paraguay, as Chair of the Group of Landlocked Developing Countries, transmitted to the Secretary-General the communiqué adopted at the Tenth Annual Ministerial Meeting of Landlocked Developing Countries (New York, 23 September).

GENERAL ASSEMBLY ACTION

On 22 December [meeting 91], the General Assembly, on the recommendation of the Second Committee [A/66/443/Add.2], adopted **resolution 66/214** without vote [agenda item 22 (*b*)].

Specific actions related to the particular needs and problems of landlocked developing countries: outcome of the International Ministerial Conference of Landlocked and Transit Developing Countries and Donor Countries and International Financial and Development Institutions on Transit Transport Cooperation

The General Assembly,

Recalling its resolutions 58/201 of 23 December 2003, 60/208 of 22 December 2005, 61/212 of 20 December 2006, 62/204 of 19 December 2007, 63/228 of 19 December 2008, 64/214 of 21 December 2009 and 65/172 of 20 December 2010,

Recalling also the United Nations Millennium Declaration,

Recalling further the High-level Plenary Meeting of the General Assembly on the Millennium Development Goals and its outcome document,

Recalling the Almaty Declaration and the Almaty Programme of Action: Addressing the Special Needs of Landlocked Developing Countries within a New Global Framework for Transit Transport Cooperation for Landlocked and Transit Developing Countries,

Recalling also its resolution 63/2 of 3 October 2008, by which it adopted the Declaration of the high-level meeting of the sixty-third session of the General Assembly on the midterm review of the Almaty Programme of Action,

Taking note of the Ezulwini Declaration adopted at the Third Meeting of Trade Ministers of Landlocked Developing Countries, held in Ezulwini, Swaziland, on 21 and 22 October 2009,

Taking note also of the Ulaanbaatar Declaration as an outcome of the High-level Asia-Pacific Policy Dialogue on the Implementation of the Almaty Programme of Action and Other Development Gaps Faced by the Landlocked Developing Countries, organized jointly by the Government of Mongolia and the Secretariat of the Economic and Social Commission for Asia and the Pacific and held in Ulaanbaatar from 12 to 14 April 2011,

Taking note further of the communiqué of the Tenth Annual Ministerial Meeting of Landlocked Developing Countries, held at United Nations Headquarters on 23 September 2011,

Recognizing that the lack of territorial access to the sea, aggravated by remoteness from world markets, and prohibitive transit costs and risks continue to impose serious constraints on export earnings, private capital inflow and domestic resource mobilization of landlocked developing countries and therefore adversely affect their overall growth and socioeconomic development,

Expressing concern that inadequate transport, telecommunications and energy infrastructure remains a major obstacle to trade and inhibits growth in landlocked developing countries,

Expressing support to those landlocked developing countries that are emerging from conflict, with a view to enabling them to rehabilitate and reconstruct, as appropriate, political, social and economic infrastructure and to assisting them in achieving their development priorities in accordance with the goals and targets of the Almaty Programme of Action,

Recognizing that the primary responsibility for establishing effective transit systems rests with landlocked and transit developing countries,

Reaffirming that the Almaty Programme of Action constitutes a fundamental framework for genuine partnerships between landlocked and transit developing countries and their development partners at the national, bilateral, subregional, regional and global levels,

1. *Takes note* of the report of the Secretary-General entitled "Implementation of the Almaty Programme of Action: Addressing the Special Needs of Landlocked Developing Countries within a New Global Framework for Transit Transport Cooperation for Landlocked and Transit Developing Countries";

2. *Reaffirms* the right of access of landlocked countries to and from the sea and freedom of transit through the territory of transit countries by all means of transport, in accordance with the applicable rules of international law;

3. *Also reaffirms* that transit countries, in the exercise of their full sovereignty over their territory, have the right to take all measures necessary to ensure that the rights and facilities provided for landlocked countries in no way infringe upon their legitimate interests;

4. *Calls upon* landlocked and transit developing countries to take all appropriate measures, as set out in the Declaration of the high-level meeting of the sixty-third session of the General Assembly on the midterm review of the Almaty Programme of Action, to speed up the implementation of the Almaty Programme of Action, and calls upon landlocked developing countries to take greater ownership of the Almaty Programme of Action by further mainstreaming it into their national development strategies;

5. *Calls upon* development partners and multilateral and regional financial and development institutions to provide landlocked and transit developing countries with appropriate, substantial and better-coordinated technical and financial assistance, particularly in the form of grants or concessional loans, for the implementation of the Almaty Programme of Action;

6. *Reaffirms its full commitment* to urgently address the special development needs of and the challenges faced by landlocked developing countries through the full, timely and effective implementation of the Almaty Programme of Action, as contained in the Declaration on the midterm review;

7. *Acknowledges* that landlocked and transit developing countries in Africa, Asia, Europe and Latin America have strengthened their policy and governance reform efforts and that development partners, including international financial and development institutions, have paid greater attention to the establishment of efficient transit systems;

8. *Notes with concern* that, despite the progress made in implementing the priorities of the Almaty Programme of Action, landlocked developing countries continue to be marginalized in international trade, have serious capacity-building needs in the area of trade and transport facilitation, and face challenges in their efforts to establish efficient transit transport systems which prevent them from fully harnessing the potential of trade as an engine of sustained economic growth and development to achieve the internationally agreed development goals, including the Millennium Development Goals;

9. *Invites* Member States, including development partners, organizations of the United Nations system and other relevant international, regional and subregional organizations, to speed up further the implementation of the specific actions in the five priorities agreed upon in the Almaty Programme of Action and those contained in the Declaration on the midterm review, in a better-coordinated manner, in particular for the construction, maintenance and improvement of their transport, storage and other transit-related facilities, including alternative routes, completion of missing links and improved communications and energy infrastructure, so as to enhance intraregional connectivity, and strengthen analytical capacities to assist in the development and implementation of coherent and comprehensive transport policies to support the transit corridors needed to facilitate trade, and, in this regard, encourages enhanced regional, subregional and bilateral cooperation which offers more appropriate, direct and effective solutions in addressing landlocked and transit country issues;

10. *Expresses concern* that the economic growth and social well-being of landlocked developing countries remain highly vulnerable to external shocks and to the multiple challenges faced by the international community, and

invites the international community to assist landlocked developing countries in strengthening their resilience and in protecting the advances made towards the realization of the Millennium Development Goals and the priorities of the Almaty Programme of Action;

11. *Encourages* the relevant international organizations, including the Office of the High Representative for the Least Developed Countries, Landlocked Developing Countries and Small Island Developing States, and the United Nations regional commissions, as well as relevant research institutions, to assist the landlocked developing countries, as appropriate, in undertaking research on the vulnerability of landlocked developing countries to external shocks, through the development of a set of vulnerability indicators that can be used by the landlocked developing countries for early warning purposes;

12. *Underlines* the importance of international trade and trade facilitation as one of the priorities of the Almaty Programme of Action, notes that the ongoing negotiations of the World Trade Organization on trade facilitation are particularly important for landlocked developing countries to gain a more efficient flow of goods and services as well as improved international competitiveness resulting from lower transaction costs, and calls upon the international community to ensure that the agreement on trade facilitation in the final outcome of the Doha Round fulfils the objective of lowering transaction costs by, inter alia, reducing transport time and enhancing certainty in transborder trade;

13. *Calls upon* development partners to implement effectively the Aid for Trade initiative, giving adequate consideration to the special needs and requirements of landlocked developing countries, including capacity-building for the formulation of trade policies, participation in trade negotiations and implementation of trade facilitation measures, as well as the diversification of export products through private-sector involvement, including the development of small and medium-sized enterprises, with a view to increasing the competitiveness of the products of landlocked developing countries in export markets;

14. *Recognizes* that the economies of many landlocked developing countries are still reliant on a few export commodities, which often have low value addition, and encourages the international community to enhance efforts to support landlocked developing countries in diversifying their economic base, to encourage, on mutually agreed terms, the transfer of technologies related to transit transport systems, including information and communications technology, and to enhance value addition to their exports through the development of their productive capacities;

15. *Encourages* the further strengthening of South-South cooperation and triangular cooperation, as well as cooperation among subregional and regional organizations, in support of the efforts of landlocked and transit developing countries towards achieving the full and effective implementation of the Almaty Programme of Action;

16. *Underlines* the prominent role that foreign direct investment plays in accelerating development and poverty reduction through employment, the transfer of managerial and technological know-how and non-debt-creating flows of capital, recognizes the considerable role and potential of private-sector involvement in infrastructure development for transport, telecommunications and utilities for landlocked developing countries, and in this regard encourages Member States to facilitate foreign direct investment flows to landlocked developing countries and calls upon landlocked and transit developing countries to promote an enabling environment so as to attract foreign direct investment and private sector involvement;

17. *Recognizes* that broader and more effective cooperation among landlocked developing countries and between landlocked and transit developing countries is necessary to ensure a harmonized approach to the design, implementation and monitoring of trade and transport facilitation policy reforms across borders, and in this regard encourages landlocked and transit developing countries to ratify and to implement effectively, as appropriate, international conventions and agreements and regional and subregional agreements on transport and trade facilitation;

18. *Calls upon* the relevant organizations of the United Nations system, and invites other international organizations, including the World Bank, the regional development banks, the World Customs Organization, the World Trade Organization, regional economic integration organizations and other relevant regional and subregional organizations, to further integrate the Almaty Programme of Action into their relevant programmes of work, taking full account of the Declaration on the midterm review, and encourages them to continue, as appropriate, within their respective mandates, their support to landlocked and transit developing countries, through, inter alia, well-coordinated and coherent technical assistance programmes in transit transport and trade facilitation;

19. *Welcomes* the efforts made by Member States, including development partners, and the United Nations system, including the regional commissions, in providing infrastructure development and connectivity and the integration of regional rail and road networks and in strengthening the legal frameworks of landlocked and transit developing countries, encourages them to continue providing their support, and in this regard welcomes the ongoing efforts made by the Office of the High Representative and the Economic Commission for Africa, in cooperation with the African Union Commission and other relevant international and regional organizations, towards assisting in the elaboration of the intergovernmental agreement on the Trans-African Highway;

20. *Urges* landlocked developing countries to sign and ratify, at their earliest convenience, the Multilateral Agreement for the Establishment of an International Think Tank for Landlocked Developing Countries in order to bring the think tank to full operation, and invites the Office of the High Representative and relevant organizations of the United Nations system, Member States, including development partners, and relevant international and regional organizations to support the think tank so that it can undertake its role;

21. *Decides* to hold a comprehensive ten-year review conference on the implementation of the Almaty Programme of Action in 2014, in accordance with paragraph 49 of the Almaty Programme of Action and paragraph 32 of the Declaration on the midterm review, preceded, where necessary, by regional and global as well as thematic preparations in a most effective, well-structured and broad participatory manner; underlines that intergovernmental mechanisms at the global and regional levels, including those of the United Nations regional commissions, as well as relevant substantive material and statistical data,

should be effectively utilized in the review process; recalls that, also in accordance with the aforesaid paragraph 49, the Office of the High Representative is designated as the United Nations system-wide focal point for the preparatory review process; and notes that United Nations system organizations, including the United Nations Conference on Trade and Development, the United Nations Development Programme, the regional commissions and relevant international and regional organizations, within their respective mandates, should provide necessary support and actively contribute to the preparatory review process and the comprehensive ten-year review conference itself;

22. *Also decides* to take a decision, at its sixty-seventh session, on the organizational aspects, venue, duration and dates of the comprehensive ten-year review conference on the Almaty Programme of Action and of possible intergovernmental preparatory committee meetings, to be held in 2014 in a most effective manner;

23. *Encourages* Member States, including development partners, as well as private entities, to make voluntary contributions to the Trust Fund established by the Secretary-General to support the activities related to the follow-up to the implementation of the outcome of the Almaty International Ministerial Conference, as well as the participation of landlocked developing countries in the preparatory process and in the comprehensive ten-year review conference itself;

24. *Requests* the Secretary-General to submit to the General Assembly at its sixty-seventh session a report on the implementation of the Almaty Programme of Action and on the progress made in the preparatory process for the comprehensive ten-year review conference;

25. *Decides* to include in the provisional agenda of its sixty-seventh session, under the item entitled "Groups of countries in special situations", the sub-item entitled "Specific actions related to the particular needs and problems of landlocked developing countries: outcome of the International Ministerial Conference of Landlocked and Transit Developing Countries and Donor Countries and International Financial and Development Institutions on Transit Transport Cooperation".

Chapter II

Operational activities for development

The Millennium Development Goals (MDGs), with their target date of 2015, continued to provide an overall framework for the development activities of the UN system in 2011. Various organizations delivered development assistance to developing countries and to countries with economies in transition. The United Nations Development Programme (UNDP)—the central UN body for technical assistance, in its dual role as the lead development agency and coordinator of the UN development system—had as its focus areas poverty reduction and achievement of the MDGs; democratic governance; crisis prevention; and environment and sustainable development. In 2011, the Programme saw its income decrease to $5.54 billion from the 2010 level of $5.95 billion. Total expenditures also decreased to $5.57 billion, from $5.99 billion in 2010.

Development assistance was also provided through the UN Department of Economic and Social Affairs, which funded technical cooperation projects worth some $65.9 million in 2011; the United Nations Fund for International Partnerships, with allocations to projects totalling $1.19 billion; the United Nations Office for Project Services, which implemented projects worth $1.06 billion on behalf of its partners; and the United Nations Capital Development Fund, which spent some $60 million in the least developed countries.

Contributions for operational activities for development of the UN system as a whole amounted to some $22.8 billion, about the same as in 2010 in nominal terms and 6.9 per cent less in real terms. Total contributions were equivalent to about 15 per cent of total official development assistance, excluding debt relief. Some 67 per cent of funding was directed to longer-term development activities, against 33 per cent to activities with a humanitarian assistance focus.

Of the total expenditures for operational activities for development, over 70 per cent focused on programme activities at the country level, of which 47 per cent, worth $8.5 billion, were in Africa. The remainder related to global and regional programme activities and programme support and management. About half of the development-related expenditures—excluding local resources—at the country level were spent in low-income countries.

The UNDP-administered United Nations Volunteers programme, with 7,303 volunteers, carried out 7,708 assignments in 132 countries. Those operations, supported by UNDP regular resources, amounted to $236 million. In December, the General Assembly observed the tenth anniversary of the first International Year of Volunteers.

System-wide activities

Operational activities segment of the Economic and Social Council

On 15 February, the Economic and Social Council decided that the operational activities segment of its substantive session of 2011 should be devoted to progress on and implementation of General Assembly resolution 62/208 [YUN 2007, p. 877] regarding the triennial comprehensive policy review of operational activities for development of the UN system and follow-up resolutions of the Assembly and the Council concerning operational activities for development of the UN system (**decision 2011/206**).

In accordance with that decision, the Council discussed the question at meetings of its substantive session on 14, 15 and 18 July [A/66/3/Rev.1]. It also considered follow-up to policy recommendations of the Assembly and the Council, as well as the following reports: report of the UNDP Administrator and the Executive Director of the United Nations Population Fund (UNFPA) [E/2011/5]; annual report of the Executive Board of the United Nations Children's Fund (UNICEF) [E/2011/6]; annual report of the World Food Programme (WFP) for 2010 [E/2011/14]; report of the UNICEF Executive Board on the work of its first regular session of 2011 [E/2011/34/Rev.1], plus an addendum on the joint meeting of the Executive Boards of UNDP/UNFPA/United Nations Office for Project Services (UNOPS), UNICEF, the United Nations Entity for Gender Equality and the Empowerment of Women (UN-Women) and WFP [E/2011/34 (Part I)/Add.1]; report of the UNDP/UNFPA Executive Board on its work in 2010 [E/2011/35]; report of the WFP Executive Board on its first and second regular sessions and annual session of 2010 [E/2011/36]; and an extract from the report of the UNICEF Executive Board on its 2011 annual session containing the decisions adopted at that session [E/2011/L.18]. The Council took note of those reports on 18 July (**decision 2011/215**).

The Council also had before it reports of the Secretary-General on: analysis of the funding of operational activities for development of the UN system for 2009 [A/66/79-E/2011/107]; the functioning of the resident coordinator system, including costs and benefits [E/2011/86]; simplification and harmonization of the UN development system [E/2011/88]; and results achieved and measures and processes implemented in follow-up to Assembly resolution 62/208 [E/2011/112] (see below).

On 14 July, the Council held a panel discussion on the theme "2012 Quadrennial comprehensive policy review of the General Assembly—what are the expectations: issues, process and outcome?". On 15 July, the Council held a panel discussion on the theme "Strengthening the leadership of the United Nations resident coordinator: the role of accountability frameworks, resources and results reporting"; a discussion on progress in the independent evaluation of the initiative "Delivering as one"; and a dialogue with the executive heads of the UN funds and programmes on the theme "Looking to the future of operational activities for development of funds and programmes: strengths, weaknesses, opportunities and threats". On 18 July, the Council held a special dialogue on defining the concept of 'critical mass of core resources'.

Operational activities for development

Reports of Secretary-General. In a May report [E/2011/112], the Secretary-General reviewed progress in implementing General Assembly resolution 62/208 [YUN 2007, p. 877] on the 2007 triennial comprehensive policy review of operational activities for development of the UN system. The report, prepared in consultation with the organizations of the UN system and inter-agency mechanisms, examined the role and functioning of UN development cooperation; funding for the operational activities for development of the UN system; the contribution of UN operational activities to national capacity development and development effectiveness; improved functioning of the UN development system; and action taken by the UN system to implement resolution 62/208. An annex summarized progress on actions taken and targets set by the UN system to implement the resolution.

Also in May [A/66/79-E/2011/107], the Secretary-General submitted an analysis of the funding of operational activities for development of the UN system for 2009, stating that total contributions to those activities amounted to some $21.9 billion, the same in real terms as in 2008, and accounted for about 18 per cent of total official development assistance (ODA), excluding debt relief. The decline in humanitarian assistance-related funding was offset by an increase in development-related funding. About 65 per cent of funding was directed to longer-term development-related activities against 35 per cent to activities with a humanitarian assistance focus. Contributions for development-related activities—excluding local resources from programme countries—increased by 8.1 per cent in real terms in 2009. Funding for humanitarian assistance, however, declined by 7.8 per cent.

From 1994 to 2009, total contributions for operational activities for development of the UN system grew at a faster rate than both total ODA and ODA from the States members of the Development Assistance Committee of the Organization for Economic Co-operation and Development (OECD/DAC). Total ODA in 2009—excluding debt relief—was $124 billion. Between 1994 and 2009, the share of contributions provided by multilateral organizations (excluding the European Commission) and private sources increased from 7 to 19 per cent, while the share of OECD/DAC countries declined from 76 to 63 per cent. Some 33 per cent of all direct contributions by OECD/DAC countries to the multilateral system were channelled through the UN development system, making the Organization the largest multilateral partner of DAC countries. Contributions from developing countries grew by some 75 per cent in real terms between 2005 and 2009. Ten OECD/DAC countries accounted for some 65 per cent of total core resources for development-related activities.

Some 27 per cent of total funding was in the form of core resources, with the remaining 73 per cent in the form of non-core contributions characterized by varying degrees of restrictions with regard to their application and use. Some 88 per cent of non-core funding was single donor and programme- and project-specific, thereby contributing to the fragmentation of resources flows, with a consequent impact on programme coherence, efficiencies and transaction costs.

Of the total expenditures of $22.1 billion for operational activities for development—both for development and humanitarian assistance—in 2009, some 69 per cent related to programme activities at the country level, with low-income countries accounting for 65 per cent of that share. The remaining 31 per cent of expenditures related to global and regional programme activities and programme support and management.

Some $13.6 billion of the total expenditures were for development-related activities (excluding local resources from programme countries), of which 57 per cent, or $7.7 billion, was in the form of country programmable resources. The remaining 43 per cent related to global and regional programme activities (19 per cent), programme support and management (17 per cent) and various other activities. Some $1.1 billion were spent at the country level in the form of local resources from programme countries themselves. Low-income countries were the destination of some 71 per cent of total country programmable resources.

The UN development system was moderately concentrated, with 43 programme countries, or 30 per cent of the total, accounting for some 80 per cent of all country-level expenditures in 2009. The report made a number of recommendations to the Economic and Social Council for action.

In an April report on the functioning of the resident coordinator system, including costs and benefits [E/2011/86], the Secretary-General stated that the organizations of the UN system had endeavoured to strengthen the role of the resident coordinators by institutionalizing their lead role; establishing frameworks for cooperation in the UN country team; creating incentives for collaboration; and establishing clear lines of accountability. Nevertheless, the management and accountability system remained a work in progress. There was room for improvement of the instruments that empowered the resident coordinator. While the use of innovative funding mechanisms such as multi-donor trust funds was important, the UN system needed to accelerate the implementation of other innovative instruments to strengthen the relevance of its contribution to programme countries. The report contained recommendations submitted to the Council for action, including acceleration of the implementation of reform and improvement of the United Nations Development Assistance Framework and other instruments in support of the resident coordinator system.

In response to Assembly resolution 62/208 [YUN 2007, p. 877], the Secretary-General submitted to the Council an April report [E/2011/88] on simplification and harmonization of the UN development system, stating that considerable progress had been made over the preceding three years. A large number of innovations were initiated at the country level, leading to efficiency gains and cost savings. Lessons learned informed inter-agency guidance, which was increasingly country-driven. Nonetheless, there was limited scope for experimentation at the country level without commensurate adjustment of headquarters procedures and practices. Procurement and human resources management were seen as the priority for simplification and harmonization.

Underlying the different business practices were different business models, which responded to organization-specific mandates and programme activities guided by governing bodies. There was potential for simplification and harmonization within existing business models, for example, in procurement and human resources management. A staged approach was required, first by striving to achieve major progress without major structural transformations and showing quick wins, efficiency gains and savings. Firmer commitment might then be achieved for more fundamental changes involving the decision-making of governing bodies. Subsequent steps should give more attention to simplification. Recommendations to the Council included that UN system organizations be encouraged to establish indicators and mechanisms to track and demonstrate efficiency gains and cost savings.

ECONOMIC AND SOCIAL COUNCIL ACTION

On 18 July [meeting 34], the Economic and Social Council adopted **resolution 2011/7** [draft: E/2011/L.35] without vote [agenda item 3].

Progress in the implementation of General Assembly resolution 62/208 on the triennial comprehensive policy review of operational activities for development of the United Nations system

The Economic and Social Council,

Recalling General Assembly resolutions 62/208 of 19 December 2007 on the triennial comprehensive policy review of operational activities for development of the United Nations system, 63/232 of 19 December 2008, 64/220 of 21 December 2009 and 65/177 of 20 December 2010 on operational activities for development of the United Nations system, and 64/289 of 2 July 2010 on system-wide coherence and Economic and Social Council resolutions 2008/2 of 18 July 2008, 2009/1 of 22 July 2009 and 2010/22 of 23 July 2010 on progress in the implementation of Assembly resolution 62/208,

Reaffirming the importance of the comprehensive policy review of operational activities for development, through which the General Assembly establishes key system-wide policy orientations for the development cooperation and country-level modalities of the United Nations system,

Acknowledging the importance of delivering assistance in order to overcome the challenges to improving human life by implementing General Assembly resolution 62/208,

Recalling the role of the Economic and Social Council in providing coordination and guidance to the United Nations system so as to ensure that policy orientations established by the General Assembly are implemented on a system-wide basis in accordance with Assembly resolutions 57/270 B of 23 June 2003, 61/16 of 20 November 2006, 62/208 and other relevant resolutions,

Taking note with appreciation of the reports of the Secretary-General submitted to the Council at the operational activities segment of its substantive session of 2011,

Funding of operational activities for development of the United Nations development system

1. *Takes note* of the report of the Secretary-General on the analysis of the funding of operational activities for development of the United Nations system for 2009, and recalls the section of General Assembly resolution 64/289 on improving the funding system of operational activities for development of the United Nations system, and looks forward to its implementation;

Results achieved and measures and processes implemented in follow-up to General Assembly resolution 62/208

2. *Notes* the steps taken by the United Nations development system to implement General Assembly resolution 62/208;

3. *Welcomes* the establishment of the United Nations Entity for Gender Equality and the Empowerment of Women (UN-Women), invites the United Nations country teams, in that context, to elaborate the division of labour among themselves in order to better address the needs of countries in improving gender equality and the empowerment of women, and calls upon the United Nations Development Group to support efforts to evaluate more systematically, including through joint evaluations, the impact of the growing number of joint initiatives, such as joint programming and programmes, on bringing agencies together to contribute to gender equality and the empowerment of women, in accordance with their respective mandates;

4. *Invites* the United Nations system and the relevant international financial institutions, including the Bretton Woods institutions, to explore further ways to enhance cooperation, collaboration and coordination, including in countries in transition from relief to development, including through the greater harmonization of strategic frameworks, instruments, modalities and partnership arrangements, in full accordance with the priorities of the recipient Governments, and in that regard emphasizes the importance of ensuring, under the leadership of national authorities, greater consistency between the strategic frameworks developed by the United Nations agencies, funds and programmes and the relevant international financial institutions, including the Bretton Woods institutions, while maintaining the institutional integrity and organizational mandates of each organization and the national poverty reduction strategies, including poverty reduction strategy papers, where they exist;

5. *Welcomes* the intergovernmental meetings of programme pilot countries, held in Maputo in May 2008, in Kigali in October 2009 and in Hanoi in June 2010, takes note with appreciation of the Maputo, Kigali and Hanoi declarations, and looks forward to the outcome of the intergovernmental conference on "delivering as one" in Montevideo in November 2011, taking into account the principle of national ownership and "no one size fits all";

Functioning of the resident coordinator system, including costs and benefits

6. *Invites* United Nations system organizations to redouble their efforts to implement the management and accountability system of the United Nations development and resident coordinator system, including the functional firewall for the resident coordinator system, so as to ensure that the resident coordinator system is functioning in an optimal way that reflects the inputs of the United Nations system as a whole and reinforces the implementation of the principle of mutual accountability within the United Nations country team;

7. *Encourages* United Nations system organizations to improve the linkages between the United Nations Development Assistance Framework and their agency-specific programming and project documents, taking into consideration their specialized mandates and business models, and notes in this context the efforts of some programme countries to improve linkages through the development of common country programmes;

8. *Invites* the United Nations Development Group to conduct a review of existing funding modalities in support of the resident coordinator system, including appropriate burden-sharing arrangements among relevant United Nations organizations, and to make recommendations to improve the provision of resources and support to the resident coordinator system at the country level, to be reported by the Secretary-General to the Economic and Social Council;

9. *Calls upon* the Secretary-General to ensure that both the Emergency Relief Coordinator and the Administrator of the United Nations Development Programme enhance their consultations before presenting final recommendations in the selection process for resident coordinators in countries likely to require significant humanitarian response operations;

10. *Urges* the High-level Committee on Management and the United Nations Development Group to review regulations and policies relating to human resources and interagency staff mobility to ensure that they are supportive of the careers of United Nations system staff who serve as resident coordinators, and to establish a system-wide policy to support qualified staff from various geographical and agency backgrounds applying for resident coordinator assessment;

Simplification and harmonization of the United Nations system

11. *Urges* United Nations system organizations to identify and accelerate the implementation of those business processes that promise the highest return from simplification and harmonization, in compliance with relevant intergovernmental mandates;

12. *Encourages* United Nations system organizations, within their existing planning, budget and evaluation systems, to report on their cost savings resulting from improvement of their business operations, and in that regard requests the United Nations Development Group to support United Nations country teams in developing their country-level indicators for their efficient business practices as part of the process launched by the United Nations Development Group in 2010;

13. *Urges* United Nations Headquarters to pay renewed attention to the needs of United Nations country teams and to take bold initiatives to remove bottlenecks and create sufficient ground for innovations at the country level;

Guidelines for the quadrennial comprehensive policy review in 2012

14. *Requests* the Secretary-General to pay particular attention, in the report for the 2012 quadrennial comprehensive policy review of operational activities for development of the United Nations system, to:

(*a*) The status of implementation of the actions mandated by the Assembly in its resolution 62/208;

(*b*) The identification of specific measures, actions and decisions required to further improve the relevance and impact of operational activities for development of the United Nations system at the country, regional and global levels as well as their effectiveness, efficiency and coherence, taking into consideration the findings of the independent evaluation of "delivering as one" as well as the reports of the country-led evaluations;

(*c*) A review of progress made by the United Nations development system to ensure national ownership and leadership of United Nations operational activities, including through the use of national administrative systems and the identification of further steps needed in that regard;

(d) An assessment of the functioning of the resident coordinator system, including its ability to represent and support the entire United Nations system at the country level, in alignment with national development priorities, and, if needed, recommendations for measures in that regard;

(e) Further proposals to ensure adequate, predictable and stable funding for United Nations operational activities for development;

(f) Reporting on discussions held by the governing bodies of United Nations funds and programmes on attaining a critical mass of core resources;

(g) Agency reviews of the current policies regarding recovery of support costs for non-core funding, including information as to whether core resources have subsidized non-core funding;

(h) A review of progress made by the United Nations development system to improve results-based strategic planning and management in order to improve accountability and transparency, and identification of measures to further improve its long-term delivery and results;

(i) An analysis of how the characteristics, approaches and strategic and programming frameworks of United Nations system operational activities should evolve to respond to various country situations, based on the principles of national ownership and leadership, and to the evolving international development cooperation environment;

(j) A review of progress at the country level in improving coordination on mainstreaming gender equality and the empowerment of women in United Nations system operational activities;

(k) An assessment of the United Nations Development Assistance Frameworks to determine, inter alia, their alignment with national priorities, their focus on the internationally agreed development goals, including the Millennium Development Goals, and the effectiveness of their process, building on the review conducted by the United Nations Development Group;

15. *Encourages* the Secretary-General, in preparing the report for the quadrennial comprehensive policy review, to make full use of the outcomes of the survey on the effectiveness, efficiency and relevance of the support of the United Nations system and the comprehensive review of the existing institutional framework for the system-wide evaluation of operational activities for development of the United Nations system;

16. *Requests* the Secretary-General to submit to the General Assembly, through the Economic and Social Council, a comprehensive report on the analysis of the implementation of Assembly resolution 62/208 and a report on the analysis of funding of operational activities for development, as well as to submit directly to the Assembly a report with recommendations for the quadrennial comprehensive policy review.

Communications. On 29 June [A/65/896-S/2011/407], Egypt, as Chair of the Coordinating Bureau of the Non-Aligned Movement, transmitted to the Secretary-General the final document of the sixteenth Ministerial Conference of the Non-Aligned Movement (Bali, Indonesia, 23–27 May), which addressed, among other matters, operational activities for development of the UN system.

Argentina, on 27 September [A/66/388], transmitted to the Secretary-General the Ministerial Declaration adopted at the thirty-fifth annual meeting of the Ministers for Foreign Affairs of the Group of 77 developing countries and China (New York, 23 September), which addressed, among other topics, operational activities for development of the UN system.

Pledging Conference. The 2011 United Nations Pledging Conference for Development Activities was held in New York on 8 November [A/CONF.208/2011/3], with 20 Member States pledging approximately $265 million for 2012. In August [A/CONF.208/2011/2], the Secretary-General provided a statement of contributions pledged or paid at the 2010 Pledging Conference to 23 funds and programmes, and to two trust funds.

Delivering as one. The participants at the fourth High-level Intergovernmental Conference on Delivering as one (Montevideo, Uruguay, 8–10 November) reaffirmed the continuing relevance of the 2006 report of the High-level Panel on United Nations System-wide Coherence [YUN 2006, p. 1584], in which the "Delivering as one" initiative was proposed. They recognized that the impact of implementing the initiative in the field in eight pilot and 11 "self-starter" countries had been positive and recommended that the "Delivering as one" process should serve as a model for the UN membership at large.

Aid effectiveness. The outcome document of the Fourth High-level Forum on Aid Effectiveness (Busan, Republic of Korea, 29 November–1 December) [E/2012/11] addressed the issues of realizing change: complementary actions to achieve common goals; from effective aid to cooperation for effective development; and the road ahead: partnering for progress towards and beyond the Millennium Development Goals (MDGs).

GENERAL ASSEMBLY ACTION

On 22 December [meeting 91], the General Assembly, on the recommendation of the Second (Economic and Financial) Committee [A/66/445/Add.1], adopted **resolution 66/218** without vote [agenda item 24 (a)].

Operational activities for development of the United Nations system

The General Assembly,

Recalling its resolutions 62/208 of 19 December 2007, 63/232 of 19 December 2008, 64/220 of 21 December 2009, 64/289 of 2 July 2010 and 65/177 of 20 December 2010, as well as Economic and Social Council resolutions 2008/2 of 18 July 2008, 2009/1 of 22 July 2009, 2010/22 of 23 July 2010 and 2011/7 of 18 July 2011,

Recalling also the High-level Plenary Meeting of the General Assembly on the Millennium Development Goals and its outcome document,

Chapter II: Operational activities for development

Reaffirming the importance of the comprehensive policy review of operational activities for development, through which the General Assembly establishes key system-wide policy orientations for development cooperation and country-level modalities of the United Nations system,

Acknowledging the importance of delivering assistance in order to overcome the challenges to improving human life by implementing resolution 62/208,

Recalling the role of the Economic and Social Council in providing coordination and guidance to the United Nations system so as to ensure that policy orientations established by the General Assembly are implemented on a system-wide basis in accordance with Assembly resolutions 57/270 B of 23 June 2003, 61/16 of 20 November 2006, 62/208 and other relevant resolutions,

Taking note with appreciation of the reports of the Secretary-General submitted to the Economic and Social Council at the operational activities segment of its substantive session of 2011,

1. *Takes note* of the report of the Secretary-General on the analysis of the funding of operational activities for development of the United Nations system for 2009, recalls the section of resolution 64/289 on improving the funding system of operational activities for development of the United Nations system for enhanced system-wide coherence and looks forward to its implementation, and notes the progress made in broadening and improving reporting, in line with paragraph 28 of resolution 62/208;

2. *Recognizes* the importance of strengthening strategies for operational activities for development of the United Nations system, in order to contribute to the achievement of the Millennium Development Goals by 2015, especially in the least developed countries and other developing countries that are lagging behind in meeting the targets;

3. *Takes note* of the report of the High-level Committee on South-South Cooperation on its sixteenth session, and looks forward to the outcome of its seventeenth session, to be held in 2012;

4. *Recalls* Economic and Social Council decision 2009/214 of 22 July 2009 on operational activities for development and Council resolutions 2010/22 and 2011/7 on progress in the implementation of General Assembly resolution 62/208, and expresses appreciation for the guidance provided by the Council on the further implementation of Assembly resolution 62/208 as contained in Council resolution 2010/22 and for the guidelines for the quadrennial comprehensive policy review in 2012 contained in Council resolution 2011/7;

5. *Also recalls* that, in its resolution 63/232, the General Assembly decided to hold its next comprehensive policy review of operational activities for development of the United Nations system in 2012 and subsequent reviews on a quadrennial basis, and reiterates its request to the Secretary-General to postpone to its sixty-seventh session the submission, through the Economic and Social Council, of the comprehensive analysis of the implementation of resolution 62/208, to be prepared in accordance with the guidance contained in paragraph 143 of that resolution.

The Assembly, on 22 December, took note of the report of the Second Committee [A/66/445] on operational activities for development (**decision 66/548**).

Technical cooperation through UNDP

UNDP/UNFPA/UNOPS Executive Board

The UNDP/UNFPA/UNOPS Executive Board held two regular sessions (31 January–3 February and 6–9 September) and an annual session (6–17 June) [E/2011/35], all in New York.

The Board adopted 42 decisions, including those providing an overview of action taken at its January/February [E/2011/35 (dec. 2011/13)], June [dec. 2011/30] and September [dec. 2011/42] sessions. Other decisions dealt with the work of UNDP, UNFPA (see p. 1005), UNOPS (see p. 856) and the United Nations Capital Development Fund (UNCDF) (see p. 860); and with the least developed and middle-income countries (see p. 845).

The Economic and Social Council, by **decision 2011/215** of 18 July, took note of the UNDP/UNFPA Board's report on its work in 2010 [YUN 2010, p. 867].

Revised rules of procedure

At its January/February session, the Executive Board considered its revised rules of procedure [DP/2011/18; Sales No. E.11.I.14].

On 31 January [E/2011/35 (dec. 2011/1)], the Board, recalling General Assembly resolution 65/176 [YUN 2010, p. 868] wherein the Assembly changed the name of the Executive Board of UNDP/UNFPA to the Executive Board of UNDP/UNFPA/UNOPS, approved the revised rules of procedure.

UNDP/UNFPA activities

On 3 February [dec. 2011/13], the UNDP/UNFPA/UNOPS Executive Board took note of the 2010 joint report of the UNDP Administrator and the UNFPA Executive Director to the Economic and Social Council [YUN 2010, p. 869].

An August joint UNDP/UNFPA report [DP/2011/40-DP/FPA/2011/12] described the implementation of the decisions and recommendations of the Programme Coordinating Board of the Joint United Nations Programme on HIV/AIDS (UNAIDS) (see p. 1011), focusing on selected results achieved by UNDP and UNFPA in addressing HIV. It also reviewed the decisions and recommendations relevant to UNDP and UNFPA adopted at the twenty-seventh and twenty-eighth meetings of the Programme Coordinating Board of UNAIDS, held in December 2010 and June 2011, respectively.

On 9 September [dec. 2011/41], the Board requested UNDP and UNFPA to ensure that their strategic plans and results frameworks for 2014–2017 were consistent with UNAIDS strategies and frameworks; requested UNFPA, until the adoption of the next strategic plan, to integrate the objectives and deliverables outlined in the UNAIDS strategies and the UNAIDS unified budget, results and accountability framework into the update of the UNFPA strategic guidance on HIV and relevant strategies and policies; and requested UNDP, until the adoption of the next strategic plan, to update its corporate strategy on AIDS to reflect UNAIDS strategies and to integrate the UNAIDS unified budget, results and accountability framework into the relevant strategies and policies related to results.

Human Development Report

The *Human Development Report 2011* [Sales No. E.11.III.B.1], prepared by UNDP, had as its theme sustainability and equity. The *Report* examined the global challenge of sustainable development and its relationship to rising inequality within and among countries, and identified polices that would make development both more sustainable and more equitable. It recognized that the world's most disadvantaged people suffered the most from environmental degradation and disproportionately lacked political power, making it harder for the world community to reach agreement on needed global policy changes. The *Report* also outlined ways in which sustainability and equity could be jointly advanced. It concluded with a call for new approaches to global development financing and environmental controls, arguing that those measures were both essential and feasible.

On 3 February [dec. 2011/12], the Executive Board called on the UNDP Human Development Report Office, charged with preparing the *Report*, to improve the consultation process with Member States on the *Report* in an inclusive and transparent manner. It emphasized the need to take into account the discussions conducted at the UN Statistical Commission in 2010 [YUN 2010, p. 1266] on the sound use of indicators and methodologies, in order to enhance the usefulness of the *Report*. The UNDP Administrator was asked to report to the Board's 2011 annual session on the measures taken to ensure implementation of General Assembly resolution 57/264 [YUN 2002, p. 841] and corresponding decisions of the Executive Board.

In response to that decision, an update [DP/2011/25] on *Human Development Report* preparations and consultations was submitted to the Board's June session. In order to address the concerns of the Board and the Statistical Commission, the Statistical Advisory Panel had been reactivated, and the Office had liaised with national statistical offices and international data providers and held consultations with experts, policymakers and civil leaders. Informal consultations had also taken place with the Executive Board.

On 16 June [dec. 2011/17], the Board took note of the actions taken by the Office to engage with the international statistical community on statistical matters related to the *Report*, and requested the Office to hold regular consultations with stakeholders to ensure that the *Report* contributed effectively to internationally agreed development goals, including the MDGs.

UNDP operational activities

Country and regional programmes

At its January/February session [dec. 2011/13], the UNDP/UNFPA/UNOPS Executive Board took note of the draft common country programme document for the United Republic of Tanzania and of the first one-year extension of the country programme for Peru. It also approved eight country programmes on a no-objection basis.

In June [dec. 2011/30], the Board approved the common country programme document for Tanzania that was presented at its January/February session; the second one-year extension of the country programme for South Africa; and the two-year extensions of the country programmes for Croatia, Madagascar and Paraguay. It took note of the first one-year extensions of the country programmes for Egypt, Guinea, Haiti, Mauritius, the Republic of Moldova, Tunisia and the United Arab Emirates. It also took note of 22 draft country programmes and the comments made on them, and of the draft common country programme document for Albania and the draft subregional programme document for Barbados and the Organization of Eastern Caribbean States.

By an 11 August note [DP/2011/41], the UNDP Administrator informed the Board that, further to South Sudan becoming a UN Member State on 14 July (see p. 1354), the Government had requested recipient country status on 5 August. The Board, on 9 September [dec. 2011/31], welcomed South Sudan as a new programme country for UNDP, UNFPA and UNOPS and authorized the UNDP Administrator and the Executive Directors of UNFPA and UNOPS to proceed with programme development in the country in close cooperation with the Government and other stakeholders. On 8 September [dec. 2011/40], the Board noted South Sudan's request to present, on an exceptional basis, the UNDP and UNFPA draft country programme documents to the Board's first regular session in 2012; decided to discuss those documents at an informal consultation prior to that session; and approved the request to present the final UNDP and UNFPA country programme documents for South Sudan to the Board for approval, on an exceptional basis, at that session.

The Board, in September [dec. 2011/42], approved 24 country programmes. It approved the one-year extensions of the country programmes for Egypt, Guinea,

Haiti, Mauritius, Moldova, Tunisia and the United Arab Emirates. It took note of the two-year extension of the Fourth Cooperation Framework for South-South Cooperation and the one-year extensions of the country programmes for Eritrea and the Syrian Arab Republic. It also took note of 18 draft country programme documents and the comments made thereon.

Assistance to Myanmar

The Board, in September, had before it a UNDP Administrator's note on assistance to Myanmar [DP/2011/38], presenting the conclusions, recommendations and strategic challenges identified in the 2011 independent assessment of the Human Development Initiative, phase 4, for the period June 2010–May 2011. A three-member international independent mission carried out its work from 24 April to 3 June 2011. The mission concluded that the Initiative was in compliance with the Executive Board mandate and made recommendations on implementing the Initiative. To conclude consultations with all development partners, UNDP requested a one-year extension of phase 4 until the end of 2012.

On 8 September [dec. 2011/35], the Board endorsed the proposed one-year extension of phase 4 of the Initiative until 2012. It authorized the UNDP Administrator to allocate for the revised period (2008–2012) an estimated $55.9 million from regular (core) resources, and to mobilize other (non-core) resources up to $85 million.

Programme matters

On 17 June [dec. 2011/28], the Board welcomed the Istanbul Declaration and the Programme of Action for the Least Developed Countries for the Decade 2011–2020 (see p. 828), adopted in May at the Fourth United Nations Conference on the Least Developed Countries, and invited the UNDP Administrator and the Executive Directors of UNFPA and UNOPS to integrate the implementation of the Programme of Action into their programmes of work. It invited the Chair of the United Nations Development Group (UNDG) to integrate the implementation of the Programme of Action into the workplans of UNDG.

Also on 17 June [dec. 2011/29], the Board requested UNDP to provide support to the national development strategies of middle-income countries on a case-by-case basis.

UNDP programme results

UNDP activities under the 2008–2013 strategic plan, endorsed by the UNDP/UNFPA Executive Board in 2007 [YUN 2007, p. 898], updated in 2008 [YUN 2008, p. 975] and extended in 2009 to 2013 [YUN 2009, p. 862], were conducted in four focus areas: poverty reduction and MDG achievement; democratic governance; crisis prevention and recovery; and environment and sustainable development. The annual report of the UNDP Administrator on the strategic plan: performance and results for 2011 [DP/2012/7] and its annexes provided an overview of UNDP results and contributions across the four focus areas, together with an in-depth analysis of nine corporate outcomes. The nine selected outcomes represented all focus areas, emphasizing employment, social protection, access to justice, citizen security, citizen participation and electoral processes.

Together with UN partners, UNDP in 2011 provided over $170 million to 39 countries towards food security. In low-income countries, UNDP assistance focused on expanding access to food by supporting increases in food production, establishing resilience mechanisms to protect crops and livestock in areas prone to drought and natural disasters, and stimulating the food industry for commerce as a means to increase income. Sixteen targeted countries in Africa increased resilience and capacity to respond to crises.

In response to the HIV epidemic, UNDP provided $275 million in assistance to 46 countries. More than 70 per cent of countries reporting on HIV highlighted contributions to gender results, including increased attention to women and girls in national HIV plans and budgets, strengthened leadership of women living with HIV, and improved maternal health. Several high-prevalence countries in Africa witnessed significant drops in prevalence rates and increased coverage of life-saving drugs and preventative measures.

UNDP served as a principal recipient for the Global Fund to Fight AIDS, Tuberculosis and Malaria in 32 countries, enabling national partners to access resources for improving health outcomes and providing life-saving treatment and prevention services to millions of people in need.

UNDP, in many cases working with UNCDF, spent close to $300 million in strategic and operational support to 62 countries on job creation and livelihoods enhancement, directly benefiting 1.6 million individuals worldwide. It worked with Governments to establish temporary employment through public works as a way to secure livelihoods. In 2011, more than 5.2 million workdays were generated through UNDP-supported emergency and short-term employment schemes involving over 170,000 skilled and unskilled workers, close to 40 per cent of whom were women or were from other vulnerable groups.

Working primarily with ministries of justice and the interior, UNDP assisted 90 countries in strengthening institutions, providing access to justice to individuals and communities and guaranteeing the rule of law. In 34 conflict-affected or vulnerable settings, integrated actions across the penal chain strengthened criminal investigation techniques, legal assistance for local populations, and logistical support to mobile court systems and police investigators.

UNDP programme delivery in South Sudan was approximately $97 million, including help in preparing the country for independence. UNDP contributions included assistance for training, logistics and financial management for the conduct of the referendum on self-determination in January; state-building to perform core functions; and extension of the rule of law and law enforcement to the remotest parts of the country.

UNDP contributed to pro-poor economic growth based on sound environmental management. Thirty-eight countries—20 of which demonstrated increased access to under-served populations—adopted policies or strategies for sustainable energy services. Integrated approaches to water and coastal resources management were applied in 109 countries, increasing access to safe water and basic sanitation services, and supporting the governance of over 20 of the most important trans-boundary freshwater and marine systems in the world. Sound biodiversity and ecosystems management helped to improve livelihoods in 140 countries, while 30 countries carried out land management interventions, improving the productivity and rehabilitation of 19 million hectares and benefiting 300,000 land users.

UNDP supported 140 countries in addressing the impact of climate change, formulating and implementing low-emission, climate-resilient development strategies; overcoming market and institutional barriers to climate change adaptation; and undertaking the investment assessments required for mitigation or adaptation measures in key sectors.

In support of public transparency and accountability for the use of aid, 79 countries developed national aid policies, joint assistance strategies or similar policy tools, and 86 countries implemented aid management systems.

Poverty reduction and MDG achievement

UNDP contributions in the poverty and MDGs focus area were made primarily through the policy and implementation dimensions. That focus area represented, on average, 31 per cent of UNDP development expenditures from 2008 to 2011, covering approximately 99 per cent of programme countries. Accelerated implementation of the MDGs—to which UNDP contributed by brokering new partnerships and changes in attitudes—appeared to be taking hold.

Thirteen countries supported by UNDP adopted country-led action plans to accelerate achievement of the MDGs, targeting marginalized populations. Implementation of those policies started in nine of the countries, five of which demonstrated that objectives were being achieved. Seven countries improved coverage of women, youth and vulnerable groups through employment support initiatives or social protection schemes.

Twenty-six countries supported by UNDP adopted policies promoting the development of small enterprises and women's entrepreneurship, increasing access to productive assets and financial services for the poor; 17 among them implemented those policies and reported increased access by youth, women and vulnerable groups. Twenty countries adopted policies in support of private-public initiatives to improve public services; 13 of them started implementing those policies, and four demonstrated positive change.

Democratic governance

UNDP responded to country needs in democratic governance primarily through contributions in the policy and awareness dimensions. That focus area represented on average 36 per cent of total development expenditures from 2008 to 2011, covering some 95 per cent of UNDP programme countries.

UNDP provided electoral support to 58 countries —28 in Africa, 10 in Latin America and the Caribbean, 9 in Asia and the Pacific, 6 in the Arab States, and 5 in Europe and the Commonwealth of Independent States. In Africa alone, 16 countries held national elections, all of which benefited from UNDP assistance. Seventeen countries adopted initiatives to increase the percentage of eligible voters included in voter registries, 15 of which demonstrated an increase in voter registration. Electoral management bodies adopted measures to advance gender equality in 12 countries, of which 6 monitored gender impact in their operations.

Regarding governance, 28 countries developed initiatives to increase access to formal and informal justice to strengthen women's and men's legal rights; 22 showed positive change. Twenty-one countries adopted policies or programmes to prevent and respond to gender-based violence; 14 demonstrated progress. Twenty countries adopted law reform initiatives; six of those demonstrated that objectives were being reached. In 18 countries, public administration bodies adopted measures to advance gender equality; 11 implemented the measures, and seven of those demonstrated that objectives were being achieved.

Crisis prevention and recovery

UNDP addressed challenges in disaster risk reduction and recovery and support to countries in special development situations. Those countries accounted for $1.6 billion of expenditures in 2011; the focus area represented about 22 per cent of UNDP development expenditures from 2008 to 2011, covering approximately 62 per cent of programme countries.

Contributions focused on re-establishing justice and security services in the aftermath of crisis; building national capacity to improve the responsiveness and accountability of justice and security institutions; and supporting community empowerment and citizen security, with a focus on women's security and access to justice. Five countries supported by UNDP adopted an initiative to increase the number of properly processed justice cases, which was implemented in all five countries and resulted in an increase in cases processed with due diligence. In two of the countries, a new or revised policy or programme on citizen security or the prevention of armed violence was adopted, and there was evidence of progress in both.

UNDP contributed to strengthened access to justice and the protection of citizens, particularly women, by building up legal and penal capacity. It helped to address gender-based violence in 22 countries. Lessons from its three-pronged approach—institution building, security and justice delivery, and policy interventions—used in Iraq, Sierra Leone and Somalia, served to drive programmes in other countries.

Energy and the environment

UNDP accelerated efforts to advance an integrated approach to sustainable development based on responsible growth and equity. That focus area represented about 11 per cent of UNDP development expenditures from 2008 to 2011, covering approximately 91 per cent of programme countries. From 2008 to 2011 the UNDP portfolio increased by 19 per cent, with climate change-specific work growing by 300 per cent. Small island developing States were particularly affected by climate change and environmental threats; they all requested UNDP support. UNDP contributed many innovative solutions to the integration of environmental concerns into all sectors.

The primary UNDP engagement in the area related to the policy dimension, followed by the resilience dimension. Eighty-five countries integrated environmental and climate change considerations into development plans and programmes; 41 of them demonstrated that outcomes were being reached. Initiatives to increase access to clean, renewable energy by the poor and vulnerable were adopted in 56 countries, 40 of which demonstrated increased access.

Thirty-four countries adopted policies or strategies for improved sustainable energy services, 25 of which had been implemented, and outcomes were being reached in 17. Initiatives to overcome market or institutional barriers to climate change adaptation were adopted by 29 countries; 22 implemented them and 17 demonstrated that objectives were being met.

Gender equality

At the January/February session of the Executive Board, the UNDP Administrator gave an oral report on the implementation of the UNDP gender equality strategy and a briefing on UNDP achievements in gender in 2010.

On 3 February [dec. 2011/2], the Board welcomed the results of UNDP in promoting gender-responsive economic policy management; incorporating sex-disaggregated data in the *Human Development Report*; improving measures for gender equality and the empowerment of women; promoting political participation of women; advocating for adequate resource allocations for gender equality in post-conflict recovery and reconstruction; and ensuring that women benefited equally from climate change finance mechanisms. The Board took note of the first results of the "gender marker", which revealed that progress had been achieved and that challenges remained for mainstreaming gender, and encouraged UNDP to integrate that tool in its planning, monitoring, evaluation and reporting systems. Welcoming the work of the Gender Steering and Implementation Committee in reviewing results in gender mainstreaming and in advancing gender equality, the Board urged UNDP to ensure that management staff were made accountable for implementing the gender strategy, and called for the Committee to be replicated at the regional level. The Board urged UNDP to work closely with UN-Women (see p. 1093) and requested it to increase its investments to accelerate the strengthening of capacity and the delivery of programming for gender equality and the empowerment of women. The UNDP Administrator was asked to provide an oral report annually on the implementation of the gender equality strategy for the remainder of the period of the UNDP strategic plan.

Programming arrangements

Midterm review of UNDP strategic plan, 2008–2013

At its June session, the UNDP/UNFPA/UNOPS Executive Board considered the midterm review of the UNDP strategic plan and the annual report of the UNDP Administrator on performance and results for 2010 [DP/2011/22 & Corr.1], including the revised development results framework, the development effectiveness matrix and the revised institutional framework. The review sought to optimize the contributions of UNDP to development outcomes around the globe and affirmed that its primary contribution to advancing human development was through programming that supported inclusiveness, resilience and sustainability. UNDP proposed adjustments to the development and institutional results frameworks for the second half of the strategic plan period. An annex presented revised results frameworks and an addendum [DP/2011/22/Add.2] contained statistics on UNDP activities.

On 17 June [dec. 2011/14], the Executive Board requested the Administrator to implement the proposed changes during the remaining months of 2011 and to report, through the annual report of the Administrator starting from the annual session 2012, on the basis of the new revised frameworks. It requested UNDP to enhance its annual reports by including descriptions of challenges and steps taken to address them; gender-equality and capacity-development results reporting; a comprehensive narrative of UNDP contributions to development; and clearer statements on the development results generated by UNDP contributions. Taking note of the revised integrated financial resources framework for 2011–2013, the Board encouraged the Administrator to seek efficiencies by exercising budgetary discipline in elaborating the draft institutional budget for 2012–2013. The Board requested the Administrator, when preparing the 2014–2017 strategic plan, to establish a clear focus and role for the work of UNDP; develop a results frameworks template providing clear explanations of its approach and definitions and how they linked to reporting; develop robust results frameworks; include in the frameworks clear, measurable indicators for monitoring results; and improve data-collection systems for results-based management and reporting. The Board requested UNDP to present at the second regular session of 2011 a conference room paper outlining a road map that identified milestones and time frames for making progress in achieving the objectives identified. It requested the Administrator to present a cumulative review of the strategic plan at the 2013 annual session in order to capture results and data for 2012, and endorsed the decision for a combined cumulative review and annual report, with an improved reporting format, so that the review and the report better addressed development changes generated by UNDP contributions.

As requested by the Executive Board (see above), UNDP, in September, submitted a conference room paper [DP/2011/CRP.5] that included the milestones and time frames relating to the remainder of the 2008–2013 strategic plan and the road map leading to the 2014–2017 strategic plan. The Board, on 9 September [dec. 2011/36], requested the UNDP Administrator to update and consult with the Board on progress, as foreseen in the road map.

Midterm review of UNDP global programme, 2009–2013

In June, the Executive Board considered a report on the midterm review of the UNDP Global Programme, 2009–2013 [DP/2011/27], which presented the main findings of the midterm review and proposals for the way forward. The stated objective of the Global Programme remained to support programme countries in achieving the internationally agreed development goals, including the MDGs.

The Board, on 16 June [dec. 2011/18], urged the Global Programme to build on the results achieved in the first half of the Programme, including by providing global policy leadership on inclusive, resilient and sustainable human development, advancing new standards for policy advisory services, and increasing focus on multi-practice initiatives to enhance the integration of policy services to tackle complex development challenges. It requested that a final report on the Global Programme's performance and results be submitted to the Board's 2013 annual session, with an assessment of the progress of multi-practice policy advisory services, including in the areas of sustaining progress towards the MDGs, preparing for the 2012 United Nations Conference on Sustainable Development (Rio+20), and advancing the local development and local governance agenda.

Monitoring and evaluation

At its January/February session, the UNDP/UNFPA/UNOPS Executive Board considered a report [DP/2011/3] containing the revised UNDP evaluation policy, which sought to establish a common institutional basis for the evaluation function. On 3 February [dec. 2011/3], the Board approved the revised evaluation policy; urged UNDP to improve the preparation, submission and tracking of management responses to independent and decentralized evaluations, and to incorporate lessons learned from those evaluations in the design, presentation and implementation of programmes; requested UNDP to include an overview of the status of the implementation of management responses in the annual report of the Administrator; called on UNDP to better track and guide the quality of decentralized evaluations through the regional bureaux in order to ensure that all evaluations met the minimum quality standards defined by the Evaluation Office; and requested UNDP to include an overview of the quality assessment of decentralized evaluations in its annual report on evaluation.

The Board also considered five thematic evaluations carried out by the Evaluation Office on the UNDP contribution to disaster prevention and recovery [DP/2011/4]; strengthening national capacities [DP/2011/6]; environmental management for poverty reduction: the poverty-environment nexus [DP/2011/8]; strengthening local governance [DP/2011/10]; and development and corporate results at the regional level [DP/2011/12]. Management responses to those evaluations were contained in five other documents [DP/2011/5, DP/2011/7, DP/2011/9, DP/2011/11 and DP/2011/13], respectively.

On 3 February, the Board took action on the evaluation of the UNDP contribution to disaster prevention and recovery, and the management response [dec. 2011/4]; strengthening national capacities, and the management response [dec. 2011/5]; environmental management for poverty reduction: the poverty-environment nexus, and the management response [dec. 2011/6]; strengthening local governance, and the management response [dec. 2011/7]; and development and corporate results at the regional level, and the management response [dec. 2011/8].

In June, the Executive Board considered the annual report on evaluation in UNDP [DP/2011/24], which assessed the progress made in fulfilling the evaluation function. The report also presented findings and lessons learned from independent evaluations conducted by the Evaluation Office in 2010, as well as the Office's programme of work for 2011 and 2012. During 2010–2011, the Evaluation Office conducted 14 assessments of development results in Bangladesh, Brazil, Egypt, El Salvador, Ghana, Jamaica, the Lao People's Democratic Republic, Malawi, Mongolia, Paraguay, Senegal, Somalia, Thailand and Tunisia. It also completed five thematic evaluations on the work of UNDP (see p. 848). In the 2010 reporting period, 88 country offices completed 185 evaluations—35 outcome evaluations, 130 project evaluations and 20 other evaluations.

On 16 June [dec. 2011/16], the Board requested UNDP to address the issues raised by the independent evaluations. It noted with concern that while the number of country offices having conducted at least one evaluation had increased, the overall number of outcome evaluations continued to decline in 2010 and country office compliance with evaluation plans and in conducting outcome evaluations continued to be low; it requested UNDP to address obstacles limiting compliance with evaluation plans and outcome evaluations. The Board requested UNDP to strengthen the capacity for decentralized evaluation and to address obstacles limiting both the quality of decentralized evaluations and compliance with evaluation plans and outcome evaluations. It approved the Evaluation Office's revised programme of work for 2011 and the tentative programme of work for 2012.

Financial and administrative matters

The UNDP Administrator, in the annual review of the financial situation [DP/2012/17 & Corr.1,2 & Add.1], reported that, in 2011, total income—which comprised contributions, interest and other income—dropped by 7 per cent to $5.54 billion, from $5.95 billion in 2010. Total contributions decreased by 7 per cent to $5.11 billion, from $5.49 billion in 2010. Total expenditures also decreased by 7 per cent to $5.57 billion, from $5.99 billion in 2010, yet remained above the level of total income by drawing from unspent resource balances.

Following three consecutive years of decline, contributions to regular (core) resources increased slightly to $975 million, 1 per cent above the 2010 level of $967 million. UNDP expenditures related to regular resources decreased by 9 per cent to $983 million, from $1.08 billion in 2010.

Other (non-core) resources contributions consisted of funding from programme country Governments, which increased by 25 per cent, from $0.69 billion in 2010 to $0.86 billion; contributions from bilateral partners, which decreased by 10 per cent from $1.76 billion to $1.59 billion; and contributions from multilateral partners, which decreased by 11 per cent to $1.54 billion, from $1.74 billion in 2010. Total other resources contributions decreased by 5 per cent to $4.08 billion, from $4.31 billion in 2010. The overall decrease was mainly attributable to programmes in countries with special development situations. Contributions for such programmes dropped by 30 per cent to $1.17 billion, from $1.66 billion in 2010. Other resources expenditures amounted to $4.53 billion, a 3 per cent decrease compared to $4.67 billion in 2010, while remaining above the level of total contributions. Of the $4.53 billion in other resources expenditures, $0.86 billion was funded from programme-country Governments, compared to $0.69 billion in 2010.

Other or "earmarked" resources comprised an important complement to the regular or "unearmarked" resource base. In 2011, UNDP was funded by 80 per cent "earmarked" resources and 19 per cent "unearmarked" resources, with UNCDF making up the remaining 1 per cent.

The ability of UNDP to fulfil its mandate was contingent on a viable mix of predictable core and non-core resources, which allowed UNDP to pursue management and programming focused on long-term effectiveness and sustainability.

The value of fund flows to multi-donor trust funds, joint programmes and other UN organizations totalled $1.5 billion, compared to $1.15 billion in 2010. The increase was due primarily to a rise in contributions to multi-donor trust funds and joint programmes, from $610 million in 2010 to $887 million in 2011, in large part due to a significant increase in contributions to three multi-donor trust funds.

The comparative figures for 2010 contained figures for the entire year for the United Nations Women's Fund, which became part of UN-Women on 2 July 2010. That change increased the magnitude of the comparative changes, representing approximately 4 per cent of the drop in income and expenditures when comparing 2011 with 2010.

The Executive Board, on 8 September [dec. 2011/34], took note of the annual review of the financial situation in 2010 [YUN 2010, p. 879]. It urged all Member States to support UNDP in its efforts to reach its targets for regular resource contributions, and to make contributions to UNDP regular resources for 2011 and onwards, if possible through multi-year pledges.

The UNDP Administrator submitted to the Board's September session proposed amendments to the UNDP financial regulations and rules [DP/2011/36]. The changes were being effected as a result of the upcoming adoption of the International Public Sector Accounting Standards (IPSAS) on 1 January 2012 and new cost classifications under the integrated budget approved by the Executive Board in 2010 [YUN 2010, p. 882]. Other proposed changes were intended to reflect organizational structures and working methods, and to enhance the consistency and clarity of terminology.

In a July report [DP/2011/37], the Advisory Committee on Administrative and Budgetary Questions (ACABQ) said that, subject to comments made in the report, it had no objection to the Board's approval of the proposed amendments.

The Executive Board, on 9 September [dec. 2011/33], approved the proposed amended financial regulations and took note of the amended financial rules. It requested UNDP to keep it informed on the implementation of IPSAS.

Regular funding commitments to UNDP

In a May report [DP/2011/23], UNDP provided information on the status of regular funding commitments to the Programme and its associated funds and programmes for 2011 and onward, and a summary of the provisional income for regular and other resources received in 2010. The report stated that while overall contributions in 2010 had increased to $5 billion, contributions to regular resources decreased to $0.97 billion and, thus, did not meet the 2010 funding target for regular resources set out in the strategic plan, 2008–2013. It was estimated that the 10 largest donors in 2010 (Netherlands, Norway, United States, Sweden, United Kingdom, Japan, Denmark, Switzerland, Canada, Spain) would provide close to 82 per cent of regular resources in 2011.

On 17 June [dec. 2011/15], the Executive Board reiterated that regular resources, by their untied nature, formed the bedrock of UNDP finances; requested countries to provide contributions to regular resources for 2011; and encouraged Member States to announce pledges, on a multi-year basis if feasible, and payment schedules, and to adhere to such pledges and payment schedules thereafter.

Biennial budget, 2012–2013

The Executive Board, at its September session, considered a report of the Administrator [DP/2011/34] on UNDP institutional budget estimates for 2012–2013. The estimates reflected an unprecedented level of $120.1 million or 12.3 per cent in volume reductions in comparison to the 2010–2011 gross budget of $980.9 million approved in 2010 [YUN 2010, p. 881]. Those reductions offset $31.1 million (3.2 per cent) in non-discretionary cost increases and $40 million (4.1 per cent) in proposed investments, resulting in a net budget reduction of $49.3 million or 5 per cent. Thus, in gross terms, the institutional budget estimates for 2012–2013 were $931.9 million. An increase of $0.3 million in income that offset the gross budget estimates was also projected, raising total income offsets to $75.4 million. In net terms, therefore, the institutional budget estimates for 2012–2013 were $856.5 million. As had been the case in the past two budgetary periods, the Administrator requested exceptional authority during 2012–2013 to disburse, if needed, up to $15 million in regular resources for security measures, the use of which would be limited to new and emerging security mandates as defined in UN Department of Safety and Security (DSS) directives.

ACABQ in August submitted its comments and recommendations on the report [DP/2011/35].

On 9 September [dec. 2011/32], the Executive Board approved, with modifications, the presentation of activities and associated costs reflected in the Administrator's report. It approved gross regular resources in the amount of $931.9 million, representing the institutional budget for 2012–2013. The Board endorsed the Administrator's request for exceptional authority to access up to an additional $15 million in regular resources for security measures, and decided that UNDP would limit the use of those funds to new and emerging security mandates, as defined in DSS directives. It requested UNDP to make, in consultation with UNFPA and UNICEF, an informal presentation on the timetable for the review and analysis of harmonized cost recovery rates at the first regular session in 2012, and further requested that UNDP, in consultation with UNFPA and UNICEF, address in the review whether fixed indirect costs should continue to be fully covered by regular resources.

Integrated budget for UNDP, UNFPA and UNICEF

At its January/February session, the Executive Board considered a joint informal note of UNDP, UNFPA and UNICEF on the road map to an integrated budget: cost classification and results-based budgeting, prepared in response to a 2010 Board decision [YUN 2010, p. 882]. The note contained information on differences in the categorization of costs into cost classifications, and a mock-up illustrating the format of key budget tables and accompanying explanations.

On 3 February [dec. 2011/10], the Executive Board requested UNDP and UNFPA to present their 2012–2013 biennial budget documents in line with the format of the key budget tables and accompanying explanations presented in the note, including the results of the joint review of the impact of cost definitions and classifications of activities on cost recovery.

In September, the Executive Board considered a joint note of UNDP, UNFPA and UNICEF, which provided information on the status of the road map to an integrated budget and contained a proposal to provide informally to the Board at its 2012 second regular session: the results of the joint review of the impact on harmonized cost recovery rates within the context of the integrated budget and new strategic plans from 2014 onwards; a mock integrated budget; and steps taken and progress achieved towards the integrated budget. The three agencies renewed their commitment to present an integrated budget from 2014 onwards.

Audit reports

At its January/February session, the Executive Board considered a report of the Administrator on the implementation of the recommendations of the United Nations Board of Auditors for the biennium 2008–2009 [DP/2011/14], which reviewed the implementation of the 89 audit recommendations made by the Board of Auditors for that biennium. UNDP had implemented all recommendations targeted for completion by the third quarter of 2010. The report also reviewed progress made in addressing the top 11 audit priorities for 2008–2009, and outlined management plans to address the revised set of top 10 audit-related management priorities for the 2010–2011 biennium. The revised list reflected progress and positive gains noted by the Board of Auditors between the issuance of the original top 15 list—for the 2006–2007 biennium—and the issuance of the revised top 11 list.

The report recalled that in July 2010, the Board of Auditors had issued an unqualified or "clean" audit opinion on the financial statements of UNDP for the biennium ended 31 December 2009 [YUN 2010, p. 889]. While that was the second consecutive biennium that UNDP had been awarded such a positive audit opinion, UNDP management shared the view of its Audit Advisory Committee that positive gains derived from key management initiatives begun in recent years could be easily reversed if those gains were not protected or if underlying systemic issues were not addressed.

On 3 February [dec. 2011/9], the Executive Board requested the managements of UNDP, UNFPA and UNOPS to ensure full compliance with the recommendations of the Board of Auditors and to address recurring issues that the Board raised in its report, in particular issues affecting the management and oversight of expenditures in high-risk environments and programme-execution modalities, as well as with regard to the introduction of IPSAS. The Board noted the significant increase in the number of complaints in cases of fraud and presumptive fraud in UNDP and UNFPA, and requested the two organizations to elaborate, in their 2010 annual internal audit reports to the Executive Board and in their management responses, the steps taken to address those issues. The Board expressed concern regarding the high level of the UNDP cash balance and requested it to provide to the 2011 annual session detailed information on the level of unspent funds, including on the reasons why funds were unspent, as well as on the UNDP investment policy and practices, and the steps taken to ensure a more appropriate level of liquidity.

The Executive Board, in June, considered a report on internal audit and investigations [DP/2011/29] that reviewed the activities of the Office of Audit and Investigations (OAI) for 2010. The report contained information on the adequacy of resources available for audit and investigations, and, in particular, on how appropriate and timely capacity for investigations was ensured; a multi-year trend analysis of audit issues over the period 2006–2010; and the results of the follow-up efforts for implementing the 18-month-old recommendations. It also contained an analysis of findings from country office audits relating to programme and project management. The annual report of the Audit Advisory Committee was appended to the report.

In 2010, OAI issued 69 audit reports comprising 10 Headquarters audits, 57 country office audits and 2 inter-agency audits. The 10 Headquarters audit reports included two consolidated reports on audits of grants from the Global Fund to Fight AIDS, Tuberculosis and Malaria. The two inter-agency audits referred to the consolidated report on the coordinated audits of the Common Humanitarian Fund for Sudan and the report on the joint audit of the harmonized approach to cash transfers in Viet Nam. The 57 country office audits consisted of 26 comprehensive office audits, 10 audits of directly implemented projects, 7 follow-up audits and 10 audits of Global Fund projects; four audits focused on the procurement function at the country office level. Since most of the 2010 audit reports covered operations in 2009, the audit outcomes generally reflected the status of operations in that year. The 57 country office audits, as well as the audits of regional centres, accounted for about $1.6 billion (38 per cent) of the $4.2 billion in expenditures that UNDP incurred at the field level in 2009. An additional $1.8 billion in expenditures was covered by audits of projects executed by non-governmental organizations (NGOs) and/or Governments. The 57 country office audit reports contained 649 recommendations, of which 49 per cent were ranked high priority, in that action was considered imperative to ensure that UNDP was not exposed to high risks. Procurement, with 22 per cent of the total, accounted for the largest share of the recommendations, followed by finance, governance and strategic management, and project management.

Of 69 audit reports, 7 contained an "unsatisfactory" rating: those were all country office audits. OAI closely monitored country offices and Headquarters units rated "unsatisfactory" by conducting on-site follow-up audits within one year, in addition to the ongoing desk reviews of the implementation status of audit recommendations. OAI experienced a further increase in its caseload in 2010, receiving 215 complaints. Together with 110 open cases carried over from 2009, that constituted a caseload of 325 in 2010. Of those 325 cases, 132 were closed after a preliminary assessment determined that no investigation was warranted, 18 cases were referred to other UNDP offices, and 16 cases were referred to other organizations. Sixty cases were closed after full investigation; 36 of the cases investigated resulted in an investigation report establishing evidence of misconduct; 76 cases were undergoing preliminary assessment and 23 cases were undergoing investigation. Complaints relating to financial irregularities, such as procurement fraud, theft, embezzlement and entitlements fraud, continued to be the largest category of cases handled, followed by allegations of improper recruitment and cases related to other staffing decisions.

On 17 June [dec. 2011/22], the Executive Board expressed its support for enhancing the internal audit and investigative capacities of OAI by reprioritizing resources from elsewhere in the biennial budget, and requested UNDP to ensure that sufficient resources were allocated for such purposes when the 2012–2013 biennial budget was presented to the Board. The Board welcomed the descriptions of cases of fraud and presumptive fraud, and requested UNDP to improve reporting on such cases, with emphasis on actions taken in cases of misconduct.

In June, the Executive Board considered the UNDP report on the recommendations of the Joint Inspection Unit (JIU) in 2010 [DP/2011/22/Add.1]. During that year, JIU issued seven reports with 75 recommendations. Of those, 48 recommendations—including 14 directed to the Executive Board—were relevant to UNDP. The report reviewed the management responses to the recommendations and provided an update on the implementation of the recommendations contained in reports issued by JIU in 2008 and 2009. The Board took note of the report on 17 June [dec. 2011/30].

Information disclosure

The Executive Board in June considered a report by UNDP, UNFPA and UNOPS on responding to the emerging demand from institutional donors for greater information disclosure of internal audit reports [DP-FPA-OPS/2011/1]. On 17 June [dec. 2011/23], the Board decided that the UNDP Administrator and the Executive Directors of UNFPA and UNOPS could, upon request, disclose to a donor intergovernmental organization and the Global Fund to Fight AIDS, Tuberculosis and Malaria internal audit reports pertaining to a project to which the said donor was financially contributing, exercising discretion and protecting the legitimate rights of the programme country. The Board requested UNDP, UNFPA and UNOPS to explore options to facilitate the viewing of internal audit reports, including technological options, and further requested them to present to the Board's second regular session of 2011 a proposal for the remote viewing of those reports, providing secure access and proper safeguards for the confidentiality of the information.

In September, UNDP, UNFPA and UNOPS submitted a joint information note containing a proposal for remote viewing of internal audit reports. The Executive Board took note of that proposal [dec. 2011/42].

Ethics Office

In June, the Executive Board considered the third report of the UNDP Ethics Office [DP/2011/30], covering its activities in 2010. The Office focused on institutionalizing its work within UNDP so that ethical considerations permeated decision-making, both at the corporate and individual levels. The ever-increasing number of requests for services suggested that such institutionalization might be occurring: the Office, established in 2007, received 186 requests for services in 2008, 392 in 2009 and 483 in 2010. There was a dramatic increase in the number of requests from 2008 to 2009 (110 per cent) and a smaller increase from 2009 to 2010 (23 per cent). The activities of the Office included standard-setting and policy support; training, education and outreach; advice and guidance; the financial disclosure policy; and protection of staff against retaliation for reporting misconduct and for cooperating with audits or investigations. The 483 requests received in 2010 dealt with ethics advice (270); financial disclosure programme advice (75); general information (67); requests for protection against retaliation (6); training (17); standard-setting and policy-input (21); and system-wide coherence (27).

On 17 June [dec. 2011/24], the Board encouraged the managements of UNDP, UNFPA and UNOPS to strengthen the functions of their ethics offices and to provide them with sufficient resources.

Other matters

At its January/February session, the Executive Board considered a note by the UNDP Administrator [DP/2011/17] requesting the Board to adopt two amendments to the Instrument for the Establishment of the Restructured Global Environment Facility (GEF). The amendments concerned a revision of the process for appointing the Chief Executive Officer/Chairperson and the lengthening of the term of that position to four years; and confirmation of the availability of GEF to serve as a financial mechanism of the 1994 United Nations Convention to Combat Desertification in Countries Experiencing Serious Drought and/or Desertification, Particularly in Africa [YUN 1994, p. 944]. The two amendments had been approved at the fourth meeting of the GEF Assembly [YUN 2010, p. 1018]. In accordance with the GEF Instrument, the amendments could become effective only after adoption by the GEF Implementing Agencies (UNDP, United Nations Environment Programme, World Bank) and the Trustee (World Bank).

On 3 February [dec. 2011/11], the Board adopted the amendments.

Also at its January/February session, the Executive Board considered a report on human resources management in UNDP [DP/2011/16], which reviewed the human resources management priorities for the period of the UNDP strategic plan (2008–2013). The report focused on progress made in implementing the human resources strategy entitled "Human Resources in UNDP—A People-Centred Strategy 2008–2011" and of the action plan project "Managing performance and developing staff", as well as on challenges encountered. The Board took note of the report [dec. 2011/13].

Other technical cooperation

Development Account

In response to General Assembly resolution 56/237 [YUN 2001, p. 810], the Secretary-General, in May, submitted the seventh progress report on the implementation of projects financed from the Development Account [A/66/84]. The report reviewed progress made and results achieved in implementing projects funded from the Account since the sixth progress report [YUN 2009, p. 867] and provided updates on the management and coordination of the Account. Established by the Assembly in resolution 52/12 B [YUN 1997, p. 1392], the Account helped countries strengthen their macroeconomic capacities and supported transparent and accountable governance, sustainable development, the advancement of women, finance and trade, statistical capacity-building, national development strategies and social inclusion. Together with the UN regular programme of technical cooperation and extrabudgetary resources, the Account provided essential funding for the operational activities for development of UN Secretariat entities. The budget for the Account for the 2010–2011 biennium was $23.6 million. As most of the implementing entities were non-resident, the Account enabled Member States to tap the resources and capacities of UN departments that were not represented at the country level. Those resources and capacities came from their normative and analytical work, which was a major part of the mandate of the executing entities.

All the projects funded under the first five tranches had been completed. The report assessed the fifth tranche projects implemented during the period 2006–2009, comprising 24 projects initially approved in 2005 and 6 projects that were added following an additional allocation in 2007, totalling 30 projects. Of those projects, 8 addressed all the MDGs and 22 addressed one or more MDGs. Almost half of the projects sought to deliver outputs—such as methodologies and data gathering tools—aimed at strengthening countries' capacities for policy development. Methodologies were either adapted or developed by local experts to suit national contexts. Nine projects were geared towards strengthening the performance of countries in one sector with expected results in poverty reduction and global partnership for development. Their main output was frequently in the form of assistance to the development of systems, such as in the areas of trade information flow, e-commerce and e-business; updating manuals used by national law enforcement facilities; and researching best practices to be used by project beneficiaries.

The review of the fifth tranche projects demonstrated that the projects aimed at the broadest possible impact: addressing all the MDGs, or targeting the overarching goal of poverty reduction. A fundamental goal for the Account was to ensure capacity-building in developing countries. Over two thirds of the projects reviewed aimed at developing the capacities of institutions, and the remainder aimed at developing an enabling environment through support to policies and strategies.

In December, by **resolution 66/246** (see p. 1383), the Assembly decided to appropriate an additional $6 million for the Development Account.

UN activities

Department of Economic and Social Affairs

During 2011, the Department of Economic and Social Affairs (DESA) had approximately 387 technical cooperation projects under execution, with a total project expenditure of $65.9 million. Projects financed by UNDP represented $1.6 million; projects financed by UNFPA represented $0.06 million; and those financed by trust funds, $64.2 million. On a geographical basis, the DESA technical cooperation programme included expenditures of $36.9 million for interregional and global programmes; $23.5 million in Asia and the Pacific; $3.7 million in Africa; $1 million in the Middle East; and $0.9 million in the Americas.

Distribution of expenditures by substantive sectors was as follows: associate expert programme, $27 million; programme support, $24.2 million; regional development, $3.6 million; public administration capacity, $3.1 million; water and energy, $2.8 million; statistics, $2.7 million; development management, $1 million; e-government, $0.9 million; small island developing States, $0.6 million; the United Nations Forum on Forests, $0.02 million; and social policy and development, $0.02 million. Of the total delivery of $65.9 million, the associate expert programme comprised 41 per cent; programme support, 36.7 per cent; regional development, 5.5 per cent; and public administration capacity, 4.7 per cent. On a component basis, the Department's delivery included: $56.9 million for project personnel; $4.2 million for subcontracts; $2.7 million for training; $1.2 million for equipment; and $0.9 million for miscellaneous expenses.

Total expenditure for DESA against the United Nations regular programme of technical cooperation was $6.7 million. Distribution of expenditure by Division was as follows: public administration and development management, $1.6 million; statistics, $1.2 million; sustainable development, $3.1 million; administrative support, $0.3 million; and social policy and development, $1 million. On a geographical basis, the activities of DESA were interregional and global in scope.

Total expenditure for DESA against the United Nations Development Account was $2.7 million. Distribution of expenditures by Division was as follows: statistics, $0.5 million; development policy and analysis, $0.4 million; sustainable development, $0.4 million; public administration and development management, $0.7 million; Office for Economic and Social Council Support and Coordination, $0.4 million; the United Nations Forum on Forests, $0.2 million; and population, $0.1 million.

OIOS evaluation

In a March evaluation [E/AC.51/2011/2], the Office of Internal Oversight Services (OIOS) stated that DESA had effectively supported intergovernmental decision-making, the global statistical system and progress towards the MDGs, but had fallen short in its system-wide coordination work and was challenged by low visibility and weak internal synergies.

The evaluation showed that DESA did many things well. Its role in supporting the Economic and Social Council and related intergovernmental bodies was the one most appreciated by Member States and other stakeholders. The Department's support for the global statistical system was one of the areas in which its role and effectiveness were seen most clearly. DESA contributed to the achievement of the MDGs, including monitoring their progress, and its publications were generally well regarded. In fulfilling those functions, DESA had been able to adapt to changes in the priorities of Member States. In other functions, however, its role was less clearly defined. DESA operated in crowded territory, with responsibility for development shared within the UN system with UNDP and a range of specialized agencies. While it had sometimes been described as the United Nations think-tank on economic and social issues, it was not the only entity to fill such a role. The Department's impact was felt the most when it focused on its areas of greatest strength. What differentiated DESA, and remained the source of its comparative advantage, was its support for the policy and normative work of the intergovernmental bodies, the global scope of its work, its convening power and its role as analyst rather than advocate.

Fostering coherence within the Department was an ongoing management challenge. Opportunities for cross-divisional collaboration and complementarities had not been fully exploited. Where such opportunities had been seized, the benefits had been acknowledged, but a more systematic approach to the identification of such synergies was needed. Intellectual leadership was not always supported by effective management practices. Staff concerns about the transparency and consistency of decisions, as well as the quality of consultation and communication within DESA, were evident. OIOS recommended that DESA sharpen its strategic focus; improve coordination with partners; develop a Department-wide publication and outreach strategy; and strengthen internal coordination and communication.

UN Office for Partnerships

The United Nations Office for Partnerships, formed in 2006 [YUN 2006, p. 1046], served as a gateway for public-private partnerships with the UN system in furtherance of the MDGs. It oversaw the United Nations Fund for International Partnerships and the United Nations Democracy Fund, and provided partnership advisory services and outreach.

Reporting to the General Assembly in July on the activities of the Office [A/66/188], the Secretary-General said that while the operations of the two Funds remained the core work of the Office for Partnerships, it also provided advisory services to a wide range of non-State actors who sought to partner with the UN system. The Office worked in collaboration with the United Nations Foundation to promote and implement partnership advisory services and outreach initiatives, as well as to foster strategies for engaging global corporations, foundations and leading philanthropists with the UN system.

The Assembly took note of the report on 24 December (**decision 66/554**).

UN Fund for International Partnerships

The United Nations Fund for International Partnerships (UNFIP) was established in 1998 [YUN 1998, p. 1297] to serve as the interface between the UN system and the United Nations Foundation, the public charity responsible for administering Robert E. Turner's $1 billion contribution in support of UN causes. At the end of 2011, the cumulative allocations provided by the United Nations Foundation through UNFIP to projects implemented by the UN system reached approximately $1.19 billion. Of that amount, $0.4 billion (37 per cent) represented core Turner funds, and $0.7 billion (63 per cent) was generated from other co-financing partners. The total number of UN projects and programmes supported through the end of 2011 by the United Nations Foundation through UNFIP stood at 524. Collectively, those projects had been implemented by 43 UN entities in 124 countries.

Grant-making continued to be an important aspect of the work of the United Nations Foundation. However, it had evolved from pure grant-making to also receiving grants and third-party co-financing. The main areas of activity were global health, with emphasis on children's health; women and population; and energy and climate change. Over time, investments in children's health proved to be one of the most promising avenues for attracting a wide variety of partner support. The successful campaigns on polio, measles and malaria helped to channel hundreds of millions of additional dollars in support of UN global health efforts. The programme on women and population promoted gender equality and empowered women and girls, with a particular focus on reproductive and sexual health and rights. Support was also provided to the Sustainable Energy for All initiative, a partnership of Governments, the private sector and civil society that mobilized action around three objectives for 2030: ensuring universal access to modern energy services; doubling the global rate of improvement in energy efficiency; and doubling the share of renewable energy in the global energy mix.

UN Democracy Fund

The United Nations Democracy Fund (UNDEF) was established by the Secretary-General in 2005 [YUN 2005, p. 655] to support democratization around the world. It focused on strengthening the voice of civil society, promoting human rights and ensuring the participation of all groups in democratic processes. Through UNDEF, the United Nations Office for Partnerships channelled approximately $110 million to more than 400 projects in 150 countries. They ranged from strengthening civil society leadership skills and promoting the participation of women and youth, to media programmes allowing civil society to project its voice.

In 2011, the Fund began funding its fifth round of projects: 65 projects were funded, at a cost of $14 million. Projects covered: community development (33 per cent); women's empowerment (26 per cent); youth (15 per cent); media (9 per cent); strengthening instrumentalities of government (8 per cent); rule of law and human rights (6 per cent); and tools for democratization (3 per cent). The Fund financed an initiative in Egypt to support integrity in the administrative apparatus of the Ministries of the Interior, Housing, Health, Social Solidarity, Education and Justice; a project in Guinea to develop the integrity and capacity of the judicial system; an initiative in China to strengthen the role of marginalized rural women in village-level governance; and a project in Azerbaijan to create the first women's parliament. An initiative in the Russian Federation sought to develop the democratic participation of northern indigenous peoples. In Latin America, the Fund was financing a project to train legal professionals to litigate before the Inter-American Court of Human Rights.

Partnership advisory services and outreach

The United Nations Office for Partnerships provided advice to entities, including academic institutions, companies, foundations, government agencies, media groups and civil society organizations on how best to develop and implement public-private partnerships. Investment in high-impact initiatives was encouraged by providing advice to potential partners regarding procedures and best practices; assisting in the design of programmes and projects; helping to establish and manage global and regional networks; and promoting the MDGs as a framework for action.

In 2011, a wide spectrum of companies, foundations and NGOs approached the Office to offer assistance and seek advice on how to join the United Nations in finding sustainable solutions to some of the world's most challenging problems. The majority of non-State actors offered assistance in programmes focused on poverty reduction, gender equality, the empowerment of women and girls, education and health in the global South.

UN Office for Project Services

The United Nations Office for Project Services (UNOPS) was established in 1995 [YUN 1995, p. 900], in accordance with General Assembly decision 48/501 [YUN 1994, p. 806], as a separate, self-financing entity of the UN system to act as a service provider to UN organizations. It offered a broad range of services, from overall project management to the provision of single inputs.

2011 activities

The UNOPS Executive Director, in his annual report on UNOPS activities [DP/OPS/2012/4], informed the UNDP/UNFPA/UNOPS Executive Board that, in 2011, the Office had made good progress in implementing its 2010–2013 strategic plan with respect to management and operational results. Four goals defined the work of UNOPS for 2010–2013. Goal one, rebuilding peace and stability after conflict, accounted for 37 per cent of work on behalf of partners in 2011; goal two, early recovery of communities affected by natural disasters, 5.5 per cent; goal three, the ability of people to develop local economies and obtain social services, 49 per cent; and goal four, environmental sustainability and adaptation to climate change, 8.5 per cent.

In 2011, UNOPS implemented 1,049 projects worth $1.06 billion on behalf of its partners, down 16 per cent in value from the record level achieved a year earlier. Despite the lower overall figure, UNOPS operations increased in low-income countries and countries affected by conflict.

In 2011, 60.9 per cent of project delivery was on behalf of the UN system. UNDP continued to be the most important partner: the volume of delivery for UNDP was $334 million, or 31.4 per cent of the total.

Key operational results completed on behalf of partners included constructing or renovating 74 schools, 14 hospitals, 33 police stations, 2,300 kilometres of roads and over 45,000 shelters and camp facilities. More than half a million people were trained in various fields; 219 events were organized; 2.2 million pieces of equipment were procured; and mine action work was supported in 14 countries.

In post-conflict and post-disaster settings, UNOPS helped partners construct or maintain more than 12,400 emergency relief structures, such as shelters, and 32,300 other relief facilities. UNOPS-supported projects generated more than 7.4 million days of paid work for local people. Over 1 million people were assessed or treated for disease, and more than 496,000 were reached with disease-prevention initiatives. Support in environmental management was provided to 46 countries, and support in managing national parks was provided to 7 countries.

The UNDP/UNFPA/UNOPS Executive Board, on 17 June [dec. 2011/21], took note of the Executive Director's annual report on UNOPS activities in 2010 [YUN 2010, p. 887].

Financial, administrative and operational matters

Budget estimates

A July report [DP/OPS/2011/5] outlined UNOPS budget estimates for the 2012–2013 biennium, which totalled $148.7 million. The resources were geared towards implementing the UNOPS 2010–2013 strategic plan [YUN 2009, p. 870]. For UNOPS, a fully replenished operational reserve represented a significant measure of financial sustainability and viability as a fully self-financing service provider in the United Nations. The transition to the International Public Sector Accounting Standards (IPSAS) in 2012 added to the challenges associated with the preparation of the budget. It was estimated that the introduction of IPSAS would affect actual net revenue for 2012–2013 by approximately $13 million, owing mainly to delayed revenue recognition. With those budget estimates, UNOPS was aiming at generating margins sufficient to keep the operational reserves above the minimum requirement at the end of 2013, in spite of the effect on actual results of IPSAS-related accounting treatments. That translated into a target of zero net revenue for the upcoming biennium after accounting for IPSAS implications and regular provisions. The format of the budget aligned with the harmonized budget approach of UNDP, UNFPA and UNICEF.

Also in July, ACABQ submitted its comments and recommendations on the UNOPS budget estimates [DP/OPS/2011/6].

On 9 September [dec. 2011/38], the UNDP/UNFPA/UNOPS Executive Board approved the budget estimates and, in particular, the net revenue target, recognizing the one-time accounting effects of the transition to IPSAS.

Audit report

The April activity report for 2010 of the UNOPS Internal Audit and Investigations Group [DP/OPS/2011/2] stated that 52 reports had been released in 2010, compared with 61 in 2009. The combined 2010 audit reports contained 796 audit recommendations for improving internal controls and organizational efficiency and effectiveness. Of those, 279 pertained to internal audit reports, 264 to project audit reports and 253 to Small Grants and Mine Action Programme audit reports. The top four areas of audit recommendations were organizational issues (18 per cent), procurement (18 per cent), project management (17 per cent) and finance (17 per cent). Almost all audit recommendations issued in or prior to 2007 had been implemented as of mid-March 2011, as had 88 per cent of those issued in 2008, 73 per cent of those issued in 2009 and 43 per cent of those issued in 2010.

On 17 June [dec. 2011/22], the Executive Board encouraged the initiative for jointly auditing "Delivering as one" programmes, and encouraged UNOPS to intensify the implementation of audit recommendations older than 18 months.

Procurement in UN system

An annual statistical report on the procurement activities of UN system organizations for 2010 [DP/OPS/2011/4] stated that total UN system procurement under all sources of funding during 2010 was $14.5 billion—an increase of $747 million over 2009. The share of procurement from developing countries increased by 2.9 percentage points, to 57.7 per cent.

The report compiled information supplied by 36 UN organizations. The overall procurement volume (goods and services combined) of those entities in 2010 increased to $14.5 billion, from $13.8 billion in 2009—a gain of 5.4 per cent. The total procurement of goods increased to $681 million, an increase of 10.7 per cent, while procurement of services grew by $66 million, an increase of 0.9 per cent. Ten countries—United States, Switzerland, Afghanistan, Sudan, India, Russian Federation, United Kingdom, Denmark, Pakistan, France—supplied 45.5 per cent of procurement. Procurement from suppliers from developing countries and countries with economies in transition grew by 62.6 per cent between 2006 and 2010, reaching $8,402 million in 2010. A thematic supplement to the report focused on procurement and its contribution to the MDGs.

On 8 September [dec. 2011/37], the UNDP/UNFPA/UNOPS Executive Board welcomed the data presentation and analysis contained in the report, as well as the relevance of the thematic supplement.

UN Volunteers

In 2011 [DP/2012/17], 7,303 United Nations volunteers, representing 162 nationalities, worked for the UNDP-administered United Nations Volunteers (UNV) programme, compared with 7,765 in 2010. The volunteers carried out 7,708 assignments in 132 countries. Those operations, supported by UNDP regular resources, amounted to $236 million. Of that, 10 per cent was covered from contributions made directly to the UNV programme; the rest was covered by direct charges to programmes of the United Nations and its organizations, funds and programmes, including UNDP.

UN volunteers contributed to the strategic objectives of 23 UN entities and 18 UN missions, often serving in challenging and remote locations and post-conflict situations. Forty-six per cent of international UN volunteers recruited in 2011 were female. Almost one third of volunteers were nationals of the countries in which they served. The UNV Online Volunteering service expanded significantly, engaging the skills of over 10,000 people yearly over the Internet.

The commemoration of the tenth anniversary of the 2001 International Year of Volunteers (see below) gave UNV the opportunity to join forces with many partners, notably with the sustainable development-focused NGO community. The annual UN Department of Public Information/NGO Conference (Bonn, Germany, 3–5 September) brought a substantive contribution to the debate on volunteerism. The first Global Volunteer Conference: Volunteering for a Sustainable Future (Budapest, Hungary, 15–17 September) adopted a declaration that called on all sectors of society to prioritize volunteerism.

Anniversary of International Year of Volunteers

In accordance with General Assembly resolution 63/153 [YUN 2008, p. 987], the tenth anniversary of the International Year of Volunteers [YUN 2001, p. 814] was observed in 2011.

On 16 June [dec. 2011/20], the UNDP/UNFPA/UNOPS Executive Board took note of the significant role played by UNV as the focal point for the marking of the tenth anniversary of the International Year. It congratulated UNV on its fortieth anniversary and on the achievements of the programme over all those years.

On 5 December, which was also the International Volunteer Day for Economic and Social Development, the Assembly devoted two plenary meetings to the follow-up to the International Year [A/66/PV.73 & 74] and adopted resolution 66/67 on the topic (see below). The commemoration of the tenth anniversary included the launch of the first *State of the World's Volunteerism Report* [Sales No. E.11.I.12].

GENERAL ASSEMBLY ACTION

On 5 December [meeting 73], the General Assembly, on the recommendation of the Third (Social, Humanitarian and Cultural) Committee [A/66/454 (Part I)], adopted **resolution 66/67** without vote [agenda item 27].

Tenth anniversary of the International Year of Volunteers

The General Assembly,

Recalling its resolution 63/153 of 18 December 2008 on the follow-up to the implementation of the International Year of Volunteers and the commemoration of its tenth anniversary,

Noting that the momentum created by the International Year has contributed to the vibrancy of volunteerism globally with the involvement of more people, from a broader cross-section of societies,

Recognizing that volunteerism is an important component of any strategy aimed at, inter alia, such areas as poverty reduction, sustainable development, health, youth empowerment, climate change, disaster prevention and management, social integration, humanitarian action, peacebuilding and, in particular, overcoming social exclusion and discrimination,

Acknowledging the existing contribution of the organizations of the United Nations system in support of volunteering, especially the work of the United Nations Volunteers programme around the world, and acknowledging also the efforts of the International Federation of Red Cross and Red Crescent Societies to promote volunteerism throughout its global network,

Bearing in mind the need for an integrated and coordinated follow-up to the International Year to be pursued in the relevant parts of the United Nations system,

1. *Welcomes* the successful observance of the tenth anniversary of the International Year of Volunteers in 2011, and also welcomes the growth and development of volunteerism since the International Year, in 2001;

2. *Acknowledges* that the tenth anniversary has provided the opportunity and impetus for an increased and unprecedented level of collaboration among Governments, the United Nations system, civil society, private sector partners and people from a broad cross-section of societies all over the world, and reaffirms the need for further efforts to achieve the goals of the International Year in the areas of the recognition, facilitation, networking and promotion of volunteerism worldwide;

3. *Commends* the contributions from national and international volunteers for their fundamental role in disaster prevention and recovery, most recently evidenced by their performance in the aftermath of natural catastrophes in many parts of the world, such as mass landslides and floods in south-eastern Brazil and the devastating earthquake that struck eastern Japan in March 2011;

4. *Also commends* the increasing link between volunteerism and sports, which, through the invaluable contributions of national and international volunteers to the preparation and organization of major sport events such as the Olympic and the Paralympic Games, contributes to the promotion of the ideal of peace;

5. *Recognizes* the valuable contribution of volunteering, including traditional forms of mutual aid and self-help and other forms of civic participation, to social and economic development, thus benefiting society at large, communities and volunteer networks;

6. *Encourages* Member States to support the setting-up of knowledge and information platforms, as well as focal points at the international, regional, national and local levels, in order to foster the sharing of resources and good practices of volunteerism that could be adapted, implemented, replicated and scaled up on a sustained basis;

7. *Encourages* Member States and volunteers to take appropriate steps to enhance the protection of volunteers, and also encourages the adoption of good practices in the promotion and management of volunteerism;

8. *Reaffirms* the need to recognize and promote all forms of volunteerism in order to engage and benefit all segments of society, including women, children, young persons, older persons, persons with disabilities, minorities, migrants and those who remain excluded for social or economic reasons;

9. *Acknowledges* the importance of civil society organizations to the promotion of volunteerism, and in that respect recognizes that strengthening the dialogue and interaction among Member States, the United Nations and civil society contributes to the expansion of volunteerism;

10. *Takes note* that volunteerism contributes to human development, and invites Governments to integrate volunteering more fully into peace and development programmes and initiatives, which offer opportunities to build strong and cohesive volunteer coalitions around shared goals at the local, national, regional and international levels;

11. *Also takes note* of the actions taken by Governments to support and promote volunteerism, and reiterates its call upon them to continue such action;

12. *Calls upon* the relevant organizations and bodies of the United Nations system to further recognize and integrate volunteerism in its various forms into their policies, programmes and reports, recognizes the contributions of volunteers and volunteer organizations, and encourages their participation in future United Nations and other relevant international conferences;

13. *Recognizes* the importance of further involving all relevant partners, including civil society, and facilitating their coordination and cooperation towards creating an enabling environment where individuals can engage in volunteer activities and promoting the well-being of volunteers, welcomes in this regard the expanding involvement of the private sector in support of volunteerism, and encourages its further engagement through the expansion of corporate volunteering and employee volunteer activities;

14. *Welcomes* the work of the United Nations Volunteers as the focal point for the tenth anniversary of the International Year in support of Member States, including by co-hosting regional consultations for the tenth anniversary of the International Year, held in Quito, Ankara, Manila and Dakar, preparatory to the Global Volunteer Conference co-hosted with the International Federation of Red Cross and Red Crescent Societies, held in Budapest from 15 to 17 September 2011, as well as the Department of Public Information/Non-Governmental Organizations Conference, held in Bonn, Germany, from 3 to 5 September 2011, and requests the United Nations Volunteers to continue their efforts to promote volunteerism, including through the mobilization of national and international volunteers and the development of newer and innovative recruitment modalities such as online volunteering;

15. *Emphasizes* that people-to-people relations are the core value of volunteerism, and encourages further efforts to build and strengthen networks among volunteers and all relevant partners at the national, regional and international levels, including the World Volunteer Web as a global networking hub;

16. *Welcomes* the active engagement of national committees and coordinating bodies in the promotion of the tenth anniversary of the International Year, and emphasizes the importance of further enhancing this global network for building their partnership and sharing experiences and good practices;

17. *Recognizes* the need to further strengthen the link between domestic volunteers and international volunteer-sending organizations in order to facilitate the globalization of volunteer opportunities;

18. *Emphasizes* the important contribution of volunteering to the achievement of the Millennium Development Goals, and calls for a people-centred, holistic approach to the promotion of volunteering;

19. *Also emphasizes* the important contribution of volunteering and the participation of individuals and communities to the achievement of sustainable development and related initiatives;

20. *Further emphasizes* that volunteerism offers valuable opportunities for youth engagement and leadership to contribute to the development of peaceful and inclusive societies, while also allowing youth to acquire skills, build their capacities and increase their employability;

21. *Requests* Governments and the United Nations system to work together with other volunteer-involving organizations to support efforts to enhance the security and protection of volunteers;

22. *Encourages* the preparedness of volunteer-involving organizations and volunteers for respecting national and local norms and customs in performing their responsibilities;

23. *Decides* that two plenary meetings devoted to the follow-up to the International Year and the commemoration of its tenth anniversary shall be held as follows:

(a) At the opening of the plenary meeting to be held at 10 a.m. on 5 December 2011, statements will be made by the President of the General Assembly, the Secretary-General, the chairs of the five regional groups, the representative of the host country and the Executive Coordinator of the United Nations Volunteers;

(b) Following the opening of the plenary meetings, the launch of the first *State of the World's Volunteerism Report* will be held until 1 p.m., with the participation of the Administrator of the United Nations Development Programme, the chief author of the report and two selected United Nations Volunteers;

(c) At the plenary meeting to be held from 3 p.m. to 6 p.m., statements will be made by Member States and those with a standing invitation to participate as observers in the sessions and the work of the General Assembly;

24. *Looks forward* to a full report on the marking of the tenth anniversary of the International Year, as well as recommendations to further integrate volunteering in peace and development during the next decade and beyond, bearing in mind the request to the Secretary-General to report on this subject to the General Assembly at its sixty-seventh session under the item entitled "Social development".

Economic and technical cooperation among developing countries

South-South cooperation

In response to General Assembly resolution 64/221 [YUN 2009, p. 874], the Secretary-General, in an August report on the state of South-South cooperation [A/66/229], highlighted the changing nature of South-South interactions and how they affected development opportunities across the global South. Covering the period from 2009 to 2011, in the wake of the 2008–2009 economic crisis, the report presented data showing a more resilient South, which had embraced deeper and more institutionalized integration, resulting in more robust economic, political and social interactions. Those increased connections had led to stronger demand for multilateral support to South-South and triangular cooperation, called for by both developed and developing countries, which required further coordination and deeper and more targeted financial resources.

There had been a marked deepening of relations in the area of South-South and triangular cooperation, the Secretary-General said. Governments sought to consolidate the legal foundations of cooperation while multilateral bodies played a brokering role between developing and developed countries. New partnerships, innovative funding and support mechanisms were established to address a range of social and economic challenges. The United Nations and other multilateral organizations spurred partnerships and dialogue, and articulated principles to guide South-South cooperation.

Regardless of the development level or size of an economy, every developing country had something to offer. Together, the global South possessed a wealth of information and data, effective knowledge-sharing systems, proven development policy options, tested institutional capacity-building solutions and affordable and appropriate technologies in areas such as food security, climate change and HIV/AIDS research. That knowledge could be more broadly shared, replicated and scaled up across the South.

GENERAL ASSEMBLY ACTION

On 22 December [meeting 91], the General Assembly, on the recommendation of the Second Committee [A/66/445/Add.2], adopted **resolution 66/219** without vote [agenda item 24 (b)].

South-South cooperation

The General Assembly,

Reaffirming its resolution 64/222 of 21 December 2009, in which it endorsed the Nairobi outcome document of the High-level United Nations Conference on South-South Cooperation,

Recalling its resolutions 33/134 of 19 December 1978, 57/270 B of 23 June 2003, 60/212 of 22 December 2005, 62/209 of 19 December 2007, 63/233 of 19 December 2008, 64/1 of 6 October 2009, 64/221 of 21 December 2009 and other resolutions relating to South-South cooperation,

Recalling also the 2005 World Summit Outcome,

1. *Takes note* of the report of the Secretary-General on the state of South-South cooperation;

2. *Decides* to hold the seventeenth session of the High-level Committee on South-South Cooperation from 22 to

25 May 2012, preceded by an organizational meeting on 3 May 2012 to elect the President and Bureau of the seventeenth session of the High-level Committee;

3. *Also decides* to include in the provisional agenda of its sixty-seventh session, under the item entitled "Operational activities for development", the sub-item entitled "South-South cooperation", and requests the Secretary-General to submit to it at the session a comprehensive report on the state of South-South cooperation.

Pérez-Guerrero Trust Fund

On 22 December, the General Assembly renamed the Pérez-Guerrero Trust Fund for Economic and Technical Cooperation among Developing Countries [YUN 1986, p. 437] the "Pérez-Guerrero Trust Fund for South-South Cooperation" (**decision 66/549**).

UN Day for South-South Cooperation

The General Assembly, on 22 December (**decision 66/550**), decided that, beginning in 2012, the observance of the United Nations Day for South-South Cooperation would be changed from 19 December to 12 September to mark the day in 1978 when the United Nations Conference on Technical Cooperation among Developing Countries adopted the Buenos Aires Plan of Action for Promoting and Implementing Technical Cooperation among Developing Countries [YUN 1978, p. 467]. The Day was proclaimed by resolution 58/220 [YUN 2003, p. 913].

UN Capital Development Fund

The United Nations Capital Development Fund (UNCDF), the capital investment organization of the United Nations for the least developed countries (LDCs), specialized in public and private financing mechanisms to catalyse economic growth and make it more inclusive and sustainable. Combining capital and technical assistance, UNCDF programmes helped local governments strengthen public investment and basic service delivery and ensure that financial services reached more poor people and small businesses.

A report on results achieved in 2011 [DP/2012/11] stated that UNCDF had a strong year in 2011. It operated in 42 of the 48 LDCs, focusing particularly on post-conflict countries. Contributions grew to $52 million, up 27 per cent from 2010. Programme delivery grew to roughly $60 million, up 22 per cent from 2010 and more than double the 2006 figure. Sixty-three per cent of programme delivery was in Africa, 30 per cent in Asia and the Pacific, and 7 per cent in the Arab States and Haiti. Programmes supporting local development accounted for 60 per cent of total delivery; programmes supporting financial services for the poor accounted for 40 per cent.

Several programme initiatives took shape in 2011. Building on the successful Pacific Financial Inclusion Programme, UNCDF developed and received initial funding for a global initiative designed to bring "mobile money" to additional LDCs in Africa and Asia. The "local climate adaptive living" facility, a new programme designed to help local governments finance climate change adaptation measures, began pilot activities in Bhutan and Cambodia. Clean Start, designed to enable poor households to finance clean energy solutions, approached its pilot phase. The Fund refined its "local authorities financial and institutional analysis" system and developed a "making access to finance possible" diagnostic and action framework.

UNCDF operated local development country programmes in 30 LDCs and provided technical assistance on behalf of UNDP in 5 non-LDCs. It strove to improve local government capacities to plan, allocate and manage resources; increase local government access to investment capital; and strengthen the policy and institutional environment.

The Fund supported finance programmes for the poor in 27 LDCs and supported such UNDP activities in seven countries where UNCDF did not have its own programmes, serving 4,062,161 people in all. Given that households on average comprised five persons, that represented a positive impact on the lives of some 20.3 million people. The Fund strove to increase access to financial services; increase the sustainability of the financial service providers it supported; and strengthen the policy and institutional environment.

UNCDF met most of its 2011 targets for improving local government capacities to plan, allocate and manage resources, as well as for increasing access to financial services and improving the sustainability of service providers. The results for influencing wider policy and institutional environments were mixed, with further efforts in that regard planned for 2012.

On 16 June [dec. 2011/19], the UNDP/UNFPA/UNOPS Executive Board took note of the report on results achieved by UNCDF in 2010 [YUN 2010, p. 891]. It encouraged UNCDF to mobilize contributions to its regular resources or multi-year thematic contributions and to expand to more LDCs, and encouraged Member States to contribute to UNCDF regular resources.

Chapter III

Humanitarian and special economic assistance

In 2011, 302 natural disasters resulted in 29,780 deaths and economic loss of $366 billion—the highest on record. The United Nations, through the Office for the Coordination of Humanitarian Affairs (OCHA), continued to mobilize and coordinate humanitarian assistance to respond to international emergencies. During the year, consolidated inter-agency and flash appeals were launched for Afghanistan, the Central African Republic, Chad, the Democratic Republic of the Congo, Djibouti, El Salvador, Haiti, Kenya, the Libyan Arab Jamahiriya, Namibia, Nicaragua, Niger, Pakistan, Somalia, South Sudan, Sri Lanka, the Sudan, Yemen and Zimbabwe as well as the Occupied Palestinian Territory and West Africa. The appeals sought $8.9 billion to assist some 56 million people. About $5.6 billion was made available, meeting 63 per cent of requirements.

OCHA received contributions for natural disaster assistance totalling $1.5 billion to respond to 35 disaster events worldwide. The Central Emergency Response Fund continued to allow for the rapid provision of assistance to populations affected by sudden-onset disasters and underfunded emergencies. About $465 million was allocated to 473 projects in 45 countries.

During the year, the Economic and Social Council considered ways to strengthen UN humanitarian assistance coordination, including support to South Sudan. The General Assembly adopted resolutions on improving the effectiveness and coordination of military and civil defence assets for natural disaster response; emergency humanitarian assistance for the rehabilitation and reconstruction of Belize, Costa Rica, El Salvador, Guatemala, Honduras, Nicaragua and Panama; assistance in mine action; strengthening humanitarian assistance, emergency relief and rehabilitation in the Horn of Africa; the rehabilitation and economic development of the Semipalatinsk region of Kazakhstan; and the International Strategy for Disaster Reduction.

Humanitarian assistance

Coordination

Humanitarian affairs segment of the Economic and Social Council

In accordance with Council **decision 2011/210**, the humanitarian affairs segment of the Economic and Social Council (19–21 July) [A/66/3/Rev.1] considered the theme "Working in partnership to strengthen coordination of humanitarian assistance in a changing world". It also convened panels on strengthening resilience, preparedness and capacities for humanitarian response and on preparing for the future: predictable, effective, flexible and adequate humanitarian financing and its accountable use to meet the evolving needs and challenges in the delivery of humanitarian assistance. On 18 May, the Council decided to hold an informal event on 19 July to discuss transition from relief to development, namely the role of the United Nations and the international community in supporting the capacity of the Government of South Sudan to manage the transition (**decision 2011/212**).

The Council considered the Secretary-General's May report [A/66/81-E/2011/117] on strengthening the coordination of UN emergency humanitarian assistance, submitted in response to General Assembly resolutions 46/182 [YUN 1991, p. 421] and 65/133 [YUN 2010, p. 897] and Council resolution 2010/1 [ibid., p. 894]. The report described the major humanitarian trends and challenges over the previous year and analysed two thematic issues of concern: strengthening resilience, preparedness and capacities for humanitarian response; and humanitarian financing.

Humanitarian needs continued to increase as a result of new and ongoing conflicts, the increasing frequency and intensity of natural disasters, and the impact of global challenges including food and energy price volatility. During the reporting period, from June 2010 to May 2011, the United Nations responded to more than 30 emergencies. At the end of 2010, an estimated 27.5 million people remained internally displaced by armed conflict globally, with children accounting for up to 50 per cent. Africa had the highest number of internally displaced persons (IDPs), an estimated 11.1 million. New or renewed conflicts across sub-Saharan Africa, in particular in Côte d'Ivoire, the Democratic Republic of the Congo and Somalia, accounted for an increase in the number of refugees under the mandate of the Office of the United Nations High Commissioner for Refugees (UNHCR) by an estimated 140,000 to 10.5 million by the end of 2010.

Nearly 297,000 people were killed in 373 natural disasters—compared with 328 recorded in 2009—affecting almost 208 million others and causing an estimated $110 billion in damages. Food price increases in the second half of 2010, compounded by fuel price spikes, resulted in a net increase of some 44 million in the number of people in low and middle income countries living in extreme poverty.

On humanitarian financing, the Secretary-General reported that despite the effects of the global recession, in 2010 humanitarian aid contributions from Member States and the private sector continued to increase. At least 140 countries, as well as private sector organizations and individuals, contributed towards a total of $15.6 billion in funding both within and outside the consolidated appeals process framework. That represented an increase of $4 billion compared with the funding levels reported in 2009, and was in part accounted for by the high levels of support for humanitarian emergencies in Haiti and Pakistan. A growing number of Member States were providing resources for humanitarian action, including some that were aid recipients themselves. However, overall funding in relation to need (as measured by contributions to the consolidated appeals process) declined from 73 per cent in 2006 to 63 per cent in 2010.

Other topics addressed by the report included humanitarian coordination with regard to capacity and coordination in the field, humanitarian leadership, accountability to affected people, harmonizing needs assessments, emergency rules and procedures for rapid humanitarian response, and humanitarian civil-military coordination. On harmonizing needs assessments, the Secretary-General reported that the United Nations and its partners, through the Inter-Agency Standing Committee Needs Assessment Task Force, finalized the operational guidance on coordinated assessments in emergencies, which provided a framework and tools for the coordination of needs assessments and the consolidation of assessment information. The Secretary-General concluded with a series of recommendations for consideration by States, non-State actors, humanitarian organizations and the UN system.

ECONOMIC AND SOCIAL COUNCIL ACTION

On 21 July [meeting 39], the Economic and Social Council adopted **resolution 2011/8** [draft: E/2011/L.33] without vote [agenda item 5].

Strengthening of the coordination of emergency humanitarian assistance of the United Nations

The Economic and Social Council,

Reaffirming General Assembly resolution 46/182 of 19 December 1991 and the guiding principles contained in the annex thereto, and recalling other relevant resolutions of the Assembly and relevant resolutions and agreed conclusions of the Economic and Social Council,

Reaffirming also the principles of neutrality, humanity, impartiality and independence for the provision of humanitarian assistance and the need for all actors engaged in the provision of humanitarian assistance in situations of complex emergencies and natural disasters to promote and fully respect those principles,

Recalling its decision to consider the theme "Working in partnership to strengthen coordination of humanitarian assistance in a changing world" at the humanitarian affairs segment of its substantive session of 2011,

Recalling also its decision to convene two panels, on the themes "Preparing for the future: predictable, effective, flexible and adequate humanitarian financing and its accountable use to meet the evolving needs and challenges in the delivery of humanitarian assistance" and "Strengthening resilience, preparedness and capacities for humanitarian response", and its decision to hold an informal event on the theme "The role of the United Nations and the international community in supporting the capacity of the Government of South Sudan to manage the transition",

Welcoming the commemoration of the twentieth anniversary of the adoption of General Assembly resolution 46/182 on 19 December 1991,

Expressing grave concern at the increase in the number of people affected by humanitarian emergencies, including those associated with natural hazards and complex emergencies, at the increased impact of natural disasters and at the displacement resulting from humanitarian emergencies,

Reiterating the need to mainstream a gender perspective into humanitarian assistance in a comprehensive and consistent manner,

Expressing its deep concern at the increasing challenges facing Member States and the United Nations humanitarian response capacity posed by the consequences of natural disasters, including those related to the continuing impact of climate change, by the ongoing impact of the financial and economic crisis, and by the global food crisis and continuing food insecurity, and the potential of those challenges to increase the need for resources for disaster risk reduction, preparedness and humanitarian assistance, including in developing countries,

Condemning the increasing number of attacks and other acts of violence against humanitarian personnel, facilities, assets and supplies, and expressing deep concern about the negative implications of such attacks for the provision of humanitarian assistance to affected populations,

Noting with grave concern that violence, including sexual and gender-based violence, and violence against children, continues to be deliberately directed against civilian populations in many emergency situations,

Emphasizing that building and strengthening national and local preparedness, prevention, resilience, mitigation and response capacity is critical to saving lives, reducing suffering and providing a more predictable and effective delivery of assistance and relief,

Acknowledging the benefits of investing in preparedness, prevention, resilience and mitigation measures and of studying the possibility of developing tools to guide investments that are in line with the national priorities of Member States, in order to save lives, reduce suffering and mitigate the damage to property caused by disasters,

Recognizing the clear relationship between emergency response, rehabilitation and development, and reaffirming that, in order to ensure a smooth transition from relief to rehabilitation and development, emergency assistance must be provided in ways that will be supportive of recovery and long-term development, and that emergency measures should be seen as a step towards sustainable development,

Noting the contribution, as appropriate, of relevant regional and subregional organizations in the provision of humanitarian assistance within their region, upon the request of the affected State,

Taking note of the fact that the United Nations and its partners, through the Inter-Agency Standing Committee Needs Assessment Task Force, have finalized the operational guidance on coordinated assessments in emergencies, which provides a framework and tools for the coordination of needs assessments and the consolidation of assessment information,

1. *Takes note* of the report of the Secretary-General;
2. *Stresses* that the United Nations system should continue to enhance existing humanitarian capacities, knowledge and institutions, including, as appropriate, through the transfer of technology and expertise to developing countries, and encourages the international community to support efforts of Member States aimed at strengthening their capacity to build resilience, mitigate disaster risks, and prepare for and respond to disasters;
3. *Welcomes* the convening of the third session of the Global Platform for Disaster Risk Reduction, in Geneva from 8 to 13 May 2011, and urges Member States to assess their progress in strengthening preparedness levels for humanitarian response, with a view to increasing efforts to develop, update and strengthen disaster preparedness and risk reduction measures at all levels, in accordance with the Hyogo Framework for Action, in particular priority 5 thereof, taking into account their own circumstances and capacities and in coordination with relevant actors, as appropriate, and encourages the international community and relevant United Nations entities, including the International Strategy for Disaster Reduction, to give increased priority to preparedness and disaster risk reduction activities, in particular by supporting national and local efforts in that regard;
4. *Encourages* Member States, as well as relevant regional and international organizations, in accordance with their specific mandates, to support adaptation to the effects of climate change and to strengthen disaster risk reduction and early warning systems in order to minimize the humanitarian consequences of natural disasters, including those related to the continuing impact of climate change, takes note of the *2011 Global Assessment Report on Disaster Risk Reduction: Revealing risk, redefining development*, and encourages relevant entities to continue research on the humanitarian implications;
5. *Encourages* Member States to create and strengthen an enabling environment for the capacity-building of their national and local authorities, national societies of the International Red Cross and Red Crescent Movement, and national and local non-governmental and community-based organizations in providing timely humanitarian assistance, and also encourages the international community, the relevant entities of the United Nations system and other relevant institutions and organizations to support national authorities in their capacity-building programmes, including through technical cooperation and long-term partnerships, based on recognition of their important role in providing humanitarian assistance;
6. *Welcomes* the initiatives undertaken at the regional and national levels in relation to the implementation of the Guidelines for the Domestic Facilitation and Regulation of International Disaster Relief and Initial Recovery Assistance adopted at the thirtieth International Conference of the Red Cross and Red Crescent, held in Geneva from 26 to 30 November 2007, and encourages Member States and, where applicable, regional organizations to take further steps to strengthen operational and legal frameworks for international disaster relief, taking into account, as appropriate, those Guidelines;
7. *Encourages* efforts to enhance cooperation and coordination of United Nations humanitarian entities, other relevant humanitarian organizations and donor countries with the affected State, with a view to planning and delivering emergency humanitarian assistance in ways that are supportive of early recovery as well as sustainable rehabilitation, reconstruction and development efforts;
8. *Also encourages* efforts to provide education in humanitarian emergencies, including in order to contribute to a smooth transition from relief to development;
9. *Requests* the Emergency Relief Coordinator to continue to lead the efforts to strengthen the coordination of humanitarian assistance, and urges relevant United Nations organizations and other relevant intergovernmental organizations, as well as other humanitarian and relevant development actors, including civil society, to continue to work with the Office for the Coordination of Humanitarian Affairs of the Secretariat to enhance the coordination, effectiveness and efficiency of humanitarian assistance;
10. *Encourages* Member States to improve cooperation with the Office for the Coordination of Humanitarian Affairs to enhance the coordination, effectiveness and efficiency of humanitarian assistance;
11. *Encourages* United Nations humanitarian organizations and other relevant organizations, while strengthening the coordination of humanitarian assistance in the field, to continue to work in close coordination with national Governments, taking into account the primary role of the affected State in the initiation, organization, coordination and implementation of such assistance within its territory;
12. *Welcomes* the continued efforts to strengthen the humanitarian response capacity in order to provide a timely, predictable, coordinated and accountable response to humanitarian needs, and requests the Secretary-General to continue efforts in that regard, in consultation with Member States, including by strengthening support to and improving the identification, selection and training of United Nations resident/humanitarian coordinators;
13. *Requests* the United Nations system and other relevant actors to continue to improve and strengthen humanitarian coordination mechanisms, notably at the field level, including the existing cluster coordination mechanism, and by improving partnership and coordination with national and local authorities, including the use of national/local coordination mechanisms, where possible;
14. *Expresses concern* at the challenges related to, inter alia, safe access to and use of fuel, firewood, alternative energy, water and sanitation, shelter, food and health-care services in humanitarian emergencies, and takes note with appreciation of initiatives at the national and international levels that promote effective cooperation in that regard;

15. *Recognizes* the benefits for the effectiveness of the humanitarian response of the engagement of and coordination with relevant humanitarian actors, and encourages the United Nations to continue to pursue efforts to strengthen partnerships at the global level with the International Red Cross and Red Crescent Movement, relevant humanitarian non-governmental organizations and other participants in the Inter-Agency Standing Committee;

16. *Requests* United Nations humanitarian organizations, in consultation with Member States, as appropriate, to strengthen the evidence base for humanitarian assistance by further developing common mechanisms to improve the quality, transparency and reliability of, and make further progress towards, common humanitarian needs assessments, to assess their performance in assistance and to ensure the most effective use of humanitarian resources by those organizations;

17. *Requests* the United Nations to continue to identify solutions to strengthen its ability to recruit and deploy appropriately senior, skilled and experienced humanitarian staff quickly and flexibly, giving paramount consideration to the highest standards of efficiency, competence and integrity, while paying due regard to gender equality and to recruiting on as wide a geographical basis as possible; to further develop specialist technical expertise and capacity to fill gaps in critical humanitarian programming; and to procure emergency relief material rapidly and cost-effectively, and locally when appropriate, in order to support Governments and United Nations country teams in the coordination and provision of international humanitarian assistance;

18. *Calls upon* the United Nations and its humanitarian partners to enhance accountability to Member States, including affected States, and all other stakeholders, and to further strengthen humanitarian response efforts, including by monitoring and evaluating the provision of their humanitarian assistance, incorporating lessons learned into programming, and consulting with the affected populations so that their needs are appropriately addressed;

19. *Urges* all actors engaged in the provision of humanitarian assistance to fully commit to and duly respect the guiding principles contained in the annex to General Assembly resolution 46/182, including the humanitarian principles of humanity, impartiality and neutrality, as well as the principle of independence as recognized by the Assembly in its resolution 58/114 of 17 December 2003;

20. *Calls upon* all States and parties in complex humanitarian emergencies, in particular in armed conflict and in post-conflict situations, in countries in which humanitarian personnel are operating, in conformity with the relevant provisions of international law and national laws, to cooperate fully with the United Nations and other humanitarian agencies and organizations and to ensure the safe and unhindered access of humanitarian personnel and delivery of supplies and equipment, in order to allow humanitarian personnel to perform efficiently their task of assisting affected civilian populations, including refugees and internally displaced persons;

21. *Calls upon* all parties to armed conflicts to comply with their obligations under international humanitarian law, human rights law and refugee law;

22. *Calls upon* all States and parties to comply fully with the provisions of international humanitarian law, including all the Geneva Conventions of 12 August 1949, in particular the Geneva Convention relative to the Protection of Civilian Persons in Time of War, in order to protect and assist civilians in occupied territories, and in that regard urges the international community and the relevant organizations of the United Nations system to strengthen humanitarian assistance to civilians in those situations;

23. *Urges* Member States to continue to take the steps necessary to ensure the safety and security of humanitarian personnel, premises, facilities, equipment, vehicles and supplies operating within their borders, and in other territories under their effective control, recognizes the need for appropriate collaboration between humanitarian actors and relevant authorities of the affected State in matters related to the safety and security of humanitarian personnel, requests the Secretary-General to expedite his efforts to enhance the safety and security of personnel involved in United Nations humanitarian operations, and urges Member States to ensure that perpetrators of crimes committed against humanitarian personnel in their territory or in other territories under their effective control do not operate with impunity and are brought to justice as provided for by national laws and in accordance with obligations under international law;

24. *Encourages* the United Nations and other relevant humanitarian actors to include as part of their risk management strategy the building of good relations and trust with national and local governments, and to promote acceptance by local communities and all relevant actors, in order to enable humanitarian assistance to be provided in accordance with humanitarian principles;

25. *Emphasizes* the fundamentally civilian character of humanitarian assistance, and, in situations in which military capacity and assets are used to support the implementation of humanitarian assistance, reaffirms the need for their use to be undertaken with the consent of the affected State and in conformity with international law, including international humanitarian law, as well as humanitarian principles;

26. *Requests* Member States, relevant United Nations organizations and other relevant actors to ensure that all aspects of humanitarian response address the specific needs of women, girls, men and boys, taking into consideration age and disability, including through improved collection, analysis and reporting of sex- and age-disaggregated data, taking into account, inter alia, the information provided by States;

27. *Urges* Member States to continue to prevent, investigate and prosecute acts of sexual and gender-based violence in humanitarian emergencies, calls upon Member States and relevant organizations to strengthen support services for victims of such violence, and calls for a more effective response in that regard;

28. *Notes* the increasing challenges facing Member States, in particular developing countries, and the international humanitarian response system in responding effectively to all humanitarian emergencies, in particular the underfunded and forgotten emergencies, and in that regard stresses the need to enhance existing and build new partnerships, strengthen financing mechanisms, broaden the

donor base and engage other partners to ensure adequate resources for the provision of humanitarian assistance;

29. *Encourages* Member States, the private sector, civil society and other relevant entities to make contributions and to consider increasing and diversifying their contributions to humanitarian funding mechanisms, including consolidated and flash appeals, the Central Emergency Response Fund and other funds, based on and in proportion to assessed needs, as a means of ensuring flexible, predictable, timely, needs-based and, where possible, multi-year, non-earmarked and additional resources to meet global humanitarian challenges, encourages donors to adhere to the Principles and Good Practice of Humanitarian Donorship, and reiterates that contributions for humanitarian assistance should be provided in a way that is not to the detriment of resources made available for international cooperation for development;

30. *Recognizes* that building preparedness is a long-term investment that will contribute to the achievement of humanitarian and development objectives, including a reduction in the need for humanitarian response, and therefore further encourages Member States and other relevant actors to provide effective, predictable, flexible and adequate funding for preparedness activities, and stresses that international preparedness efforts reinforce national and local response capacities and support existing national and local institutions;

31. *Requests* the Secretary-General to reflect the progress made in the implementation of and follow-up to the present resolution in his next report to the Economic and Social Council and the General Assembly on the strengthening of the coordination of emergency humanitarian assistance of the United Nations.

Central Emergency Response Fund

The Central Emergency Response Fund (CERF), a cash-flow mechanism for the initial phase of humanitarian emergencies established in 1992 [YUN 1992, p. 584], continued to allow for the rapid provision of assistance to populations affected by sudden-onset disasters and underfunded emergencies. The Fund was upgraded by General Assembly resolution 60/124 [YUN 2005, p. 991] to include a grant element, targeted at $450 million, to ensure the availability of immediate resources to address humanitarian crises. CERF helped millions of people in 45 countries in 2011, by jump-starting critical relief operations and ensuring that life-saving programmes did not stall due to lack of funding. The Fund responded to almost every major crisis worldwide in 2011, and some $465 million in CERF funds were allocated to 473 projects by about a dozen UN agencies. Humanitarian emergencies in Africa received two-thirds of all CERF grants, totalling $284 million, followed by emergencies in Asia and the Pacific, which received slightly more than one-fifth of CERF funding.

Report of Secretary-General. In response to General Assembly resolution 65/133 [YUN 2010, p. 897], the Secretary-General in September [A/66/357] reported on the Central Emergency Response Fund, covering the period from 1 July 2010 to 30 June 2011. He indicated that the Emergency Relief Coordinator allocated $342 million from the Fund to support life-saving activities in 43 countries and territories, of which $215.6 million was made available from the Fund's rapid response window and $126.5 million from the underfunded emergencies window. Funding for conflict-related emergencies accounted for $194 million and $120 million was made available for natural disaster-related emergencies. Geographically, the resources of the Fund continued to focus primarily on Africa (59 per cent) and Asia and the Caucasus (28 per cent), while the Middle East and the Caribbean and Latin America received 7 per cent and 6 per cent, respectively. A range of agencies involved with emergency response received support from the Fund during the reporting period, including the World Food Programme ($112 million; 33 per cent of total CERF funding), the United Nations Children's Fund ($80 million; 23 per cent) and the Office of the United Nations High Commissioner for Refugees ($39 million; 11 per cent). The Fund's loan element maintained a reserve of $50 million to provide rapid access to funding for agencies while they were waiting for donor pledges to be disbursed. A single loan of $9.9 million was disbursed to OCHA in December 2010 and was repaid at the end of June 2011.

Five-Year Evaluation. In response to General Assembly resolution 63/139 [YUN 2008, p. 996], the Secretary-General commissioned an independent comprehensive review [A/66/357] of CERF activities from 2006 to 2010. The evaluation took place over nine months, beginning in October 2010 and ending in July 2011. Key findings of the evaluation concerned added value, operational management, achievements, accountability, and effectiveness of the Fund. A total of 19 recommendations were presented: 6 to the Emergency Relief Coordinator; 4 to the secretariat of the Fund; 2 to the Office of the Controller; 2 to donors; 2 to cluster lead agencies; and 3 to the agencies. Many changes proposed in the plan were already under way at the time of reporting.

Advisory Group meetings. At its April meeting [A/65/907] (Nairobi, 27–29 April), the CERF Advisory Group, established by Assembly resolution 60/124 [YUN 2005, p. 991], reviewed the efforts of the secretariat of the Fund to identify options for the loan facility. It requested the secretariat to provide options on how to reduce the balance of the loan facility, to integrate the recommendations and conclusions resulting from the country reviews into the performance and accountability framework, and to report back on the cost of producing print and video public service announcements for the Fund.

At a later meeting [A/66/613] (New York, 26–27 October), the Advisory Group noted that the five-year evaluation highlighted some general inefficiencies in the humanitarian system and the need to enhance responsibility for collective results at the country level. It endorsed the recommendation to reduce the CERF loan fund to $30 million and to transfer the balance to the grant window. The Group also considered a number of policy issues, including the timeliness of CERF-funded activities, the quality of reporting on results, and the potential role of CERF in funding preparedness activities.

On 15 December, the General Assembly, by resolution 66/119 (see below), took note of the findings of the five-year evaluation, decided to reduce the size of the loan element of the Fund to $30 million, and requested that the balance of any funds above that amount be placed in the grant element of the Fund and used for that purpose.

GENERAL ASSEMBLY ACTION

On 15 December [meeting 86], the General Assembly adopted **resolution 66/119** [draft: A/66/L.28 & Add.1] without vote [agenda item 70 (*a*)].

Strengthening of the coordination of emergency humanitarian assistance of the United Nations

The General Assembly,

Reaffirming its resolution 46/182 of 19 December 1991 and the guiding principles contained in the annex thereto, other relevant General Assembly and Economic and Social Council resolutions and agreed conclusions of the Council,

Noting the reports of the Secretary-General on the strengthening of the coordination of emergency humanitarian assistance of the United Nations and on the Central Emergency Response Fund,

Reaffirming the principles of neutrality, humanity, impartiality and independence for the provision of humanitarian assistance, and reaffirming also the need for all actors engaged in the provision of humanitarian assistance in situations of complex emergencies and natural disasters to promote and fully respect these principles,

Deeply concerned about global challenges such as the ongoing adverse impact of the world financial and economic crisis and the negative impact of the excessively volatile food prices on food security and about their effect on the increasing vulnerability of populations and impact on the need for and provision of humanitarian assistance,

Emphasizing the need to mobilize adequate, predictable, timely and flexible resources for humanitarian assistance based on and in proportion to assessed needs, with a view to ensuring fuller coverage of the needs in all sectors and across humanitarian emergencies, and recognizing, in this regard, the achievements of the Central Emergency Response Fund,

Reiterating the need for Member States, relevant United Nations organizations and other relevant actors to mainstream a gender perspective into humanitarian assistance, including by addressing the specific needs of women, girls, boys and men in a comprehensive and consistent manner, and to take into account the needs of affected populations, including persons with disabilities,

Expressing its deep concern about the increasing challenges faced by Member States and the United Nations humanitarian response system and their capacities as a result of the consequences of natural disasters, including those related to the continuing impact of climate change, and reaffirming the importance of implementing the Hyogo Framework for Action 2005–2015: Building the Resilience of Nations and Communities to Disasters, inter alia, by providing adequate resources for disaster risk reduction, including investment in disaster preparedness, and by working towards building back better in all phases from relief to development,

Recognizing the challenges posed by the magnitude and complexity of recent humanitarian emergencies, in particular to the capacity and coordination of the humanitarian response system,

Recognizing also that building national and local preparedness and response capacity is critical to a more predictable and effective response and contributes to the achievement of humanitarian and development objectives, including enhanced resilience and a reduced need for humanitarian response,

Emphasizing that enhancing international cooperation on emergency humanitarian assistance is essential, and reaffirming its resolution 65/264 of 28 January 2011 on international cooperation on humanitarian assistance in the field of natural disasters,

Emphasizing also the fundamentally civilian character of humanitarian assistance, and, in situations in which military capacity and assets are used to support the implementation of humanitarian assistance, reaffirming the need for their use to be undertaken with the consent of the affected State and in conformity with international law, including international humanitarian law, as well as humanitarian principles,

Condemning the increasing number of deliberate threats and violent attacks against humanitarian personnel and facilities, and noting the negative implications for the provision of humanitarian assistance to populations in need,

Recognizing the high numbers of persons affected by humanitarian emergencies, including internally displaced persons, bearing in mind their particular needs, and welcoming in this regard the adoption and ongoing process of ratification of the African Union Convention for the Protection and Assistance of Internally Displaced Persons in Africa, which marks a significant step towards strengthening the national and regional normative framework for the protection of and assistance to internally displaced persons in Africa,

Recognizing also the importance of the Geneva Conventions of 1949, which include a vital legal framework for the Protection of Civilian Persons in Time of War, including the provision of humanitarian assistance,

Noting with grave concern that violence, including gender-based violence, particularly sexual violence, and violence against children, continues to be deliberately directed against civilian populations in many emergency situations,

Noting with appreciation the efforts that the United Nations continues to make to improve humanitarian response, including by strengthening humanitarian response capacities, improving humanitarian coordination, enhancing predictable and adequate funding and strengthening the accountability of all stakeholders, and recognizing the importance of strengthening emergency administrative procedures and funding to allow for an effective and needs-based response to emergencies,

Recognizing that, in strengthening the coordination of humanitarian assistance in the field, United Nations organizations should continue to work in close coordination with national Governments,

Welcoming the sixtieth anniversary of the 1951 Convention relating to the Status of Refugees and the fiftieth anniversary of the 1961 Convention on the Reduction of Statelessness,

Reaffirming the importance of humanitarian assistance by the United Nations system, and welcoming the twentieth anniversary of its resolution 46/182,

1. *Welcomes* the outcome of the fourteenth humanitarian affairs segment of the Economic and Social Council at its substantive session of 2011;

2. *Requests* the Emergency Relief Coordinator to continue her efforts to strengthen the coordination and accountability of humanitarian assistance and leadership within the United Nations humanitarian response system, including through the Inter-Agency Standing Committee, and calls upon relevant United Nations organizations and other relevant intergovernmental organizations, as well as other humanitarian and development actors, to continue to work with the Office for the Coordination of Humanitarian Affairs of the Secretariat to enhance the coordination, effectiveness and efficiency of humanitarian assistance;

3. *Also requests* the Emergency Relief Coordinator to improve dialogue with Member States on the relevant processes, activities and deliberations of the Inter-Agency Standing Committee;

4. *Calls upon* the relevant organizations of the United Nations system and, as appropriate, other relevant humanitarian actors to continue efforts to improve the humanitarian response to natural and man-made disasters and complex emergencies by further strengthening humanitarian response capacities at all levels, by continuing to strengthen the provision and coordination of humanitarian assistance at the global and field level, including through existing cluster coordination mechanisms, and in support of national authorities of the affected State, as appropriate, and by further enhancing efficiency, transparency, performance and accountability;

5. *Recognizes* the benefits of engagement and coordination with relevant humanitarian actors to the effectiveness of humanitarian response, and encourages the United Nations to continue to pursue efforts to strengthen partnerships at the global level with the International Red Cross and Red Crescent Movement, relevant humanitarian non-governmental organizations and other participants in the Inter-Agency Standing Committee;

6. *Requests* the Secretary-General to continue strengthening the support provided to United Nations resident/humanitarian coordinators and to United Nations country teams, including by providing necessary training, identifying resources and improving the identification of and the selection process for United Nations resident/humanitarian coordinators, and enhancing their performance accountability;

7. *Calls upon* the Chair of the United Nations Development Group and the Emergency Relief Coordinator to enhance their consultations before presenting final recommendations on the selection process for resident coordinators in countries likely to require significant humanitarian response operations;

8. *Reaffirms* the importance of implementing the Hyogo Framework for Action 2005–2015: Building the Resilience of Nations and Communities to Disasters, and takes note with appreciation of the midterm review of the Hyogo Framework for Action, the outcome of the third session of the Global Platform for Disaster Risk Reduction, held in Geneva from 8 to 13 May 2011, and the 2011 Global Assessment Report on Disaster Risk Reduction;

9. *Calls upon* Member States and the international community to increase resources for disaster risk reduction measures, including by providing effective, predictable, flexible and adequate funding, where possible, for prevention, mitigation and preparedness for effective response and contingency planning in order to, inter alia, further strengthen national and local capacities to prepare for and respond to humanitarian emergencies, and furthermore encourages closer cooperation between national stakeholders and humanitarian and development actors in this regard;

10. *Urges* Member States, the United Nations and other relevant organizations to take further steps to provide a coordinated emergency response to the food and nutrition needs of affected populations, while aiming to ensure that such steps are supportive of national strategies and programmes aimed at improving food security;

11. *Expresses concern* about the challenges related to, inter alia, safe access to and use of fuel, firewood, alternative energy, water and sanitation, shelter and food and healthcare services in humanitarian emergencies, and takes note with appreciation of initiatives at the national and international levels that promote effective cooperation in this regard;

12. *Encourages* the international community, including relevant United Nations organizations and the International Federation of Red Cross and Red Crescent Societies, to support efforts of Member States aimed at strengthening their capacity to prepare for and respond to disasters and to support efforts, as appropriate, to strengthen systems for identifying and monitoring disaster risk, including vulnerability and natural hazards;

13. *Welcomes* the initiatives at the regional and national levels related to the implementation of the Guidelines for the Domestic Facilitation and Regulation of International Disaster Relief and Initial Recovery Assistance, adopted at the Thirtieth International Conference of the Red Cross and Red Crescent, held in Geneva from 26 to 30 November 2007, and encourages Member States and, where applicable, regional organizations to take further steps to strengthen operational and legal frameworks for international disaster relief, taking into account the Guidelines, as appropriate;

14. *Encourages* States to create an enabling environment for the capacity-building of local authorities and of national and local non-governmental and community-based organizations in order to ensure better preparedness in providing timely, effective and predictable humanitarian assistance, and encourages the United Nations and humanitarian organizations to provide support to such efforts, including, as appropriate, through the transfer of technology and expertise to developing countries and

through support to programmes aimed at enhancing the coordination capacities of affected States;

15. *Calls upon* United Nations humanitarian entities, other relevant humanitarian organizations, development partners, the private sector, donor countries and the affected State to enhance cooperation and coordination and to continue to utilize and develop appropriate tools with a view to planning and delivering humanitarian assistance in ways that are supportive of early recovery as well as of sustainable rehabilitation and reconstruction efforts;

16. *Encourages* the United Nations system and humanitarian organizations to continue their efforts to mainstream early recovery into humanitarian programming, acknowledges that early recovery should receive further funding, and encourages the provision of timely, flexible and predictable funding for early recovery, including through established humanitarian instruments;

17. *Takes note* of the efforts of Member States, the United Nations system and the international community to strengthen preparedness and local, national and regional humanitarian response capacity, and calls upon the United Nations and relevant partners to continue support in this regard;

18. *Encourages* efforts to provide education in humanitarian emergencies, including in order to contribute to a smooth transition from relief to development;

19. *Calls upon* relevant United Nations organizations to support the improvement of the consolidated appeals process, inter alia, by engaging in the preparation of common needs assessments and common humanitarian action plans, including through a better analysis of gender-related allocations, in order to further the development of the process as an instrument for United Nations strategic planning and prioritization, and by involving other relevant humanitarian organizations in the process, while reiterating that consolidated appeals should be prepared in consultation with affected States;

20. *Requests* Member States, relevant humanitarian organizations of the United Nations system and other relevant humanitarian actors to ensure that all aspects of humanitarian response, including disaster preparedness and needs assessments, take into account the specific needs of the affected population, recognizing that giving appropriate consideration to, inter alia, gender, age and disability is part of a comprehensive and effective humanitarian response, and in this regard encourages efforts to ensure gender mainstreaming in the delivery of humanitarian assistance;

21. *Calls upon* United Nations humanitarian organizations, in consultation with Member States, as appropriate, to strengthen the evidence base for humanitarian assistance by further developing common mechanisms to improve the quality, transparency and reliability of, and make further progress towards, common humanitarian needs assessments, including through improved collection, analysis and reporting of sex-, age- and disability-disaggregated data to assess their performance in assistance and to ensure the most effective use of humanitarian resources by these organizations;

22. *Calls upon* the United Nations and its humanitarian partners to enhance accountability to Member States, including affected States, and all other stakeholders, and to further strengthen humanitarian response efforts, including by monitoring and evaluating the provision of their humanitarian assistance, incorporating lessons learned into programming and consulting with the affected populations so that their needs are appropriately addressed;

23. *Calls upon* donors to provide adequate, timely, predictable and flexible resources based on and in proportion to assessed needs, including for underfunded emergencies, to consider providing early and multi-year commitments to pooled humanitarian funds and to continue to support diverse humanitarian funding channels, encourages efforts to adhere to the Principles and Good Practice of Humanitarian Donorship, and in this respect encourages the private sector, civil society and other relevant entities to make relevant contributions, complementary to those of other sources;

24. *Welcomes* the important achievements of the Central Emergency Response Fund in ensuring a more timely and predictable response to humanitarian emergencies, and stresses the importance of continuing to improve the functioning of the Fund in order to ensure that resources are used in the most efficient, effective, accountable and transparent manner possible;

25. *Takes note with appreciation* of the findings of the five-year evaluation of the Central Emergency Response Fund carried out in 2011, in this regard decides to reduce the size of the loan element of the Fund to 30 million United States dollars, and requests that the balance of any funds, including interest earned, above 30 million dollars be placed in the grant element of the Fund and used for that purpose;

26. *Decides* to authorize, in exceptional circumstances and on a time-bound basis, the Emergency Relief Coordinator and relevant operational agencies under the leadership of the Coordinator to utilize the loan element of the Central Emergency Response Fund to enhance, within their respective mandates, rapid response coordination where insufficient capacity exists at the field level;

27. *Calls upon* all Member States and invites the private sector and all concerned individuals and institutions to consider increasing their voluntary contributions to the Central Emergency Response Fund, and emphasizes that contributions should be additional to current commitments to humanitarian programming and should not be to the detriment of resources made available for international cooperation for development;

28. *Reiterates* that the Office for the Coordination of Humanitarian Affairs should benefit from adequate and more predictable funding, and calls upon all Member States to consider increasing voluntary contributions;

29. *Reaffirms* the obligation of all States and parties to an armed conflict to protect civilians in armed conflicts in accordance with international humanitarian law, and invites States to promote a culture of protection, taking into account the particular needs of women, children, older persons and persons with disabilities;

30. *Calls upon* States to adopt preventive measures and effective responses to acts of violence committed against civilian populations in armed conflicts and to ensure that those responsible are promptly brought to justice, in accordance with national law and their obligations under international law;

31. *Urges* all Member States to address gender-based violence in humanitarian emergencies and to ensure that their laws and institutions are adequate to prevent, promptly investigate and prosecute gender-based violence,

and calls upon States, the United Nations and all relevant humanitarian organizations to improve coordination, harmonize response and strengthen capacity, with a view to reducing such violence and ensuring support services to victims of such violence;

32. *Recognizes* the Guiding Principles on Internal Displacement as an important international framework for the protection of internally displaced persons, encourages Member States and humanitarian agencies to continue to work together, in collaboration with host communities, in endeavours to provide a more predictable response to the needs of internally displaced persons, and in this regard calls for continued and enhanced international support, upon request, for the capacity-building efforts of States;

33. *Calls upon* all States and parties in complex humanitarian emergencies, in particular in armed conflict and in post-conflict situations, in countries in which humanitarian personnel are operating, in conformity with the relevant provisions of international law and national laws, to cooperate fully with the United Nations and other humanitarian agencies and organizations and to ensure the safe and unhindered access of humanitarian personnel, as well as delivery of supplies and equipment, in order to allow such personnel to efficiently perform their task of assisting affected civilian populations, including refugees and internally displaced persons;

34. *Welcomes* the progress made towards further enhancing the security management system of the United Nations, and supports the approach taken by the Secretary-General to focus the security management system on enabling the United Nations system to deliver on its mandates, programmes and activities by effectively managing the risks to which personnel are exposed, including in the provision of humanitarian assistance;

35. *Requests* the Secretary-General to report on actions taken to enable the United Nations to continue to strengthen its ability to recruit and deploy staff quickly and flexibly, to procure emergency relief materials and services rapidly, cost-effectively and locally, where applicable, and to quickly disburse funds in order to support Governments and United Nations country teams in the coordination of international humanitarian assistance;

36. *Also requests* the Secretary-General to report to the General Assembly at its sixty-seventh session, through the Economic and Social Council at its substantive session of 2012, on progress made in strengthening the coordination of emergency humanitarian assistance of the United Nations and to submit a report to the Assembly on the detailed use of the Central Emergency Response Fund.

On 24 December, the Assembly decided that the agenda item on strengthening of the coordination of UN emergency humanitarian assistance would remain for consideration during its sixty-sixth (2012) session (**decision 66/557**).

Disaster response

In 2011, 302 natural disasters resulted in 29,780 deaths and economic loss of $366 billion—the highest on record. In the Horn of Africa, a prolonged drought affected 10.4 million people. In Asia, a 9.0 magnitude earthquake hit the north-eastern region of Japan on 11 March, followed by a 10-metre-high tsunami, killing more than 14,700 people as of 1 May. In New Zealand, a 6.3 magnitude earthquake hit on 22 February, causing 166 deaths and destroying and damaging more than 100,000 homes. A series of storms, torrential rains and floods hit Cambodia, the Lao People's Democratic Republic, Sri Lanka, Thailand and Viet Nam, causing hundreds of deaths and leaving millions of people homeless. In the Philippines, 19 tropical cyclones were reported in 2011, compared with 11 in 2010. Tropical storm Washi struck northern Mindanao in December, affecting 624,600 people, causing 1,495 deaths and destroying nearly 40,000 homes. In Pakistan, torrential monsoon rains triggered severe flooding, affecting over 9.2 million people, including an estimated 5.2 million who needed humanitarian assistance. In the Americas, the ongoing efforts to recover from the devastating earthquake of January 2010 in Haiti were further hampered by a cholera outbreak that began in October 2010. By May 2011, the epidemic had stabilized in many areas and the mortality rate had declined to 1.7 per cent nationwide; the epidemic had caused over 4,800 deaths, with a total of more than 280,000 cases. Ocha received contributions for natural disaster assistance totalling $1.5 billion in response to 35 disaster events worldwide.

International cooperation

In January, the General Assembly considered the Secretary-General's 2010 report on humanitarian assistance in the field of natural disasters, from relief to development [YUN 2010, p. 924].

GENERAL ASSEMBLY ACTION

On 28 January [meeting 75], the General Assembly adopted **resolution 65/264** [draft: A/65/L.59 & Add.1] without vote [agenda item 69 (*a*)].

International cooperation on humanitarian assistance in the field of natural disasters, from relief to development

The General Assembly,

Reaffirming its resolution 46/182 of 19 December 1991, the annex to which contains the guiding principles for the strengthening of the coordination of emergency humanitarian assistance of the United Nations system, as well as all its resolutions on international cooperation on humanitarian assistance in the field of natural disasters, from relief to development, and recalling the resolutions of the humanitarian segments of the substantive sessions of the Economic and Social Council,

Reaffirming also the principles of neutrality, humanity, impartiality and independence for the provision of humanitarian assistance,

Reaffirming further the Hyogo Declaration, the Hyogo Framework for Action 2005–2015: Building the Resilience of Nations and Communities to Disasters and the common statement of the special session on the Indian Ocean disaster: risk reduction for a safer future, as adopted by the World Conference on Disaster Reduction, held in Kobe, Hyogo, Japan, from 18 to 22 January 2005,

Looking forward to the third session of the Global Platform for Disaster Risk Reduction, to be held in Geneva from 8 to 13 May 2011, the report of the forthcoming Hyogo Framework for Action midterm review and the Global Assessment Report on Disaster Risk Reduction, due in 2011,

Emphasizing that the affected State has the primary responsibility in the initiation, organization, coordination and implementation of humanitarian assistance within its territory and in the facilitation of the work of humanitarian organizations in mitigating the consequences of natural disasters,

Emphasizing also the responsibility of all States to undertake disaster risk reduction, including through preparedness, as well as response and early recovery efforts, in order to minimize the impact of natural disasters, while recognizing the importance of international cooperation in support of the efforts of affected countries which may have limited capacities in this regard,

Expressing its deep concern at the increasing challenges to Member States and to the United Nations humanitarian response capacity to deal with the consequences of natural disasters, given the effects of global challenges, including the impact of climate change, the global financial and economic crisis, and the humanitarian implications of the global food crisis and continuing food insecurity,

Concerned about the challenges posed by the magnitude of some natural disasters, in particular to the capacity and coordination of the humanitarian response system,

Expressing its deep concern that rural and urban poor communities in the developing world are the hardest hit by the effects of increased disaster risk,

Acknowledging the impacts of rapid urbanization in the context of natural disasters and that urban disaster preparedness and responses require appropriate disaster risk reduction strategies, including in urban planning, early recovery strategies implemented from the initial stage of relief operations, as well as rehabilitation and development strategies,

Noting that local communities are the first responders in most disasters, underlining the critical role played by in-country capacities in disaster risk reduction, including preparedness, as well as response and recovery, and acknowledging the need to support efforts of Member States to develop and enhance national and local capacities which are fundamental to improving the overall delivery of humanitarian assistance,

Recognizing the high numbers of persons affected by natural disasters, including in this respect internally displaced persons, and the need to address the humanitarian needs arising from internal displacement throughout the world owing to natural disasters,

Reaffirming the importance of international cooperation in support of the efforts of the affected States in dealing with natural disasters in all their phases, in particular in preparedness, response and the early recovery phase, and of strengthening the response capacity of countries affected by disaster,

Recognizing the progress made by the United Nations Platform for Space-based Information for Disaster Management and Emergency Response (UN-SPIDER) in its mission, encouraging Member States to provide all support necessary, on a voluntary basis, to UN-SPIDER, including financial support, to enable it to carry out its workplan for 2010–2011, and reiterating the importance of enhancing international coordination and cooperation at the global level in disaster management and emergency response through greater access to and use of space-based services for all countries and by facilitating capacity-building and institutional strengthening for disaster management, in particular in developing countries,

Taking note of the proposal to establish the Global Framework for Climate Services to develop and provide science-based climate information and prediction for climate risk management and for adaptation to climate variability and change, and looking forward to its implementation,

Welcoming the important role played by Member States, including developing countries, that have granted necessary and continued generous assistance to countries and peoples stricken by natural disasters,

Recognizing the significant role played by national Red Cross and Red Crescent societies, as part of the International Red Cross and Red Crescent Movement, in disaster preparedness and risk reduction, disaster response, rehabilitation and development,

Emphasizing the need to address vulnerability and to integrate disaster risk reduction, including preparedness, into all phases of natural disaster management, post-natural disaster recovery and development planning,

Recognizing that efforts to achieve economic growth, sustainable development and internationally agreed development goals, including the Millennium Development Goals, can be adversely affected by natural disasters, and noting the positive contribution that those efforts can make in strengthening the resilience of populations to such disasters,

Recognizing also the clear relationship between emergency response, rehabilitation and development, and reaffirming that, in order to ensure a smooth transition from relief to rehabilitation and development, emergency assistance must be provided in ways that will be supportive of recovery and long-term development and that emergency measures should be seen as a step towards sustainable development,

Emphasizing, in this context, the important role of development organizations in supporting national efforts to mitigate the consequences of natural disasters,

1. *Takes note* of the report of the Secretary-General;
2. *Expresses its deep concern* at the increasing impact of natural disasters, resulting in massive losses of life and property worldwide, in particular in vulnerable societies lacking adequate capacity to mitigate effectively the long-term negative social, economic and environmental consequences of natural disasters;
3. *Calls upon* States to fully implement the Hyogo Declaration and the Hyogo Framework for Action 2005–2015: Building the Resilience of Nations and Communities to Disasters, in particular those commitments related to assistance for developing countries that are prone to natural disasters and for disaster-stricken States in the transition phase towards sustainable physical, social and economic recovery, for risk-reduction activities in post-disaster recovery and for rehabilitation processes;

4. *Calls upon* Member States, the United Nations system and other relevant humanitarian and development actors to accelerate the implementation of the Hyogo Framework for Action, emphasizes the promotion and strengthening of disaster preparedness activities at all levels, in particular in hazard-prone areas, and encourages them to increase funding and cooperation for disaster risk reduction activities, including disaster preparedness;

5. *Calls upon* all States to adopt, where required, and to continue to implement effectively, necessary legislative and other appropriate measures to mitigate the effects of natural disasters and integrate disaster risk reduction strategies into development planning, and in this regard requests the international community to continue to assist developing countries as well as countries with economies in transition, as appropriate;

6. *Acknowledges* that global climate change, among other factors, contributes to the increase in intensity and frequency of natural disasters, which amplify natural disaster risk, and in this regard encourages Member States, as well as relevant regional and international organizations, in accordance with their specific mandates, to support adaptation to the adverse effects of climate change and to strengthen disaster risk reduction and early warning systems in order to minimize the humanitarian consequences of natural disasters, including through the provision of technology and support for capacity-building in developing countries;

7. *Welcomes* the initiatives at the regional and national levels related to the implementation of the Guidelines for the Domestic Facilitation and Regulation of International Disaster Relief and Initial Recovery Assistance, adopted at the Thirtieth International Conference of the Red Cross and Red Crescent, held in Geneva from 26 to 30 November 2007, and encourages Member States and, where applicable, regional organizations to take further steps to strengthen operational and legal frameworks for international disaster relief, taking into account the Guidelines, as appropriate;

8. *Also welcomes* the effective cooperation among the affected States, relevant bodies of the United Nations system, donor countries, regional and international financial institutions and other relevant organizations, such as the International Red Cross and Red Crescent Movement, and civil society, in the coordination and delivery of emergency relief, and stresses the need to continue such cooperation and delivery throughout relief operations and medium- and long-term rehabilitation and reconstruction efforts, in a manner that reduces vulnerability to future natural hazards;

9. *Reiterates* the commitment to support, as a matter of priority, the efforts of countries, in particular developing countries, to strengthen their capacities at all levels in order to reduce risks, prepare for and respond rapidly to natural disasters and mitigate their impact;

10. *Urges* Member States to develop, update and strengthen early warning systems, disaster preparedness and risk reduction measures at all levels, in accordance with the Hyogo Framework for Action, taking into account their own circumstances and capacities and in coordination with relevant actors, as appropriate, and encourages the international community and relevant United Nations entities to continue to support national efforts in this regard;

11. *Encourages* Member States to consider elaborating and presenting to the International Strategy for Disaster Reduction secretariat their national platforms for disaster reduction in accordance with the Hyogo Framework for Action, and also encourages States to cooperate with each other to reach this objective;

12. *Stresses* that, to increase further the effectiveness of humanitarian assistance, particular international cooperation efforts should be undertaken to enhance and broaden further the utilization of national and local capacities and, where appropriate, of regional and subregional capacities for disaster preparedness and response, which may be made available in closer proximity to the site of a disaster, and more efficiently and at lower cost;

13. *Also stresses*, in this context, the importance of strengthening international cooperation, particularly through the effective use of multilateral mechanisms, in the timely provision of humanitarian assistance through all phases of a disaster, from relief and recovery to development, including the provision of adequate resources;

14. *Encourages* all Member States to facilitate, to the extent possible, the transit of emergency humanitarian assistance and development assistance, provided in the context of international efforts, including in the phase from relief to development, in full accordance with the provisions of resolution 46/182 and the annex thereto, and in full respect of the humanitarian principles of humanity, neutrality, impartiality and independence, and their obligations under international law, including international humanitarian law;

15. *Takes note* of the recommendation of the Secretary-General, and decides that the Central Register of Disaster Management Capacities should be discontinued;

16. *Reaffirms* the important role of the Office for the Coordination of Humanitarian Affairs of the Secretariat as the focal point within the overall United Nations system for advocacy for and coordination of humanitarian assistance among United Nations humanitarian organizations and other humanitarian partners;

17. *Welcomes*, so as to increase further the effectiveness of humanitarian assistance, the incorporation of experts from developing countries that are prone to natural disasters into the United Nations Disaster Assessment and Coordination system, and the work of the International Search and Rescue Advisory Group in assisting such countries in strengthening urban search and rescue capacities and establishing mechanisms for improving their coordination of national and international response in the field;

18. *Recalls* its resolution 57/150 of 16 December 2002 entitled "Strengthening the effectiveness and coordination of international urban search and rescue assistance", and welcomes the holding of the first global meeting of the International Search and Rescue Advisory Group, in Kobe, Japan, from 14 to 16 September 2010;

19. *Urges* Member States, the United Nations system and other humanitarian actors to consider the specific and differentiated consequences of natural disasters both in rural and urban areas, when designing and implementing disaster risk reduction, preparedness, humanitarian assistance and early recovery strategies, giving special emphasis to addressing the needs of those living in rural and urban poor areas prone to natural disasters;

20. *Recognizes* that information and telecommunication technology can play an important role in disaster response, encourages Member States to develop emergency

response telecommunication capacities, and encourages the international community to assist the efforts of developing countries in this area, where needed, including in the recovery phase;

21. *Encourages* Member States that have not acceded to or ratified the Tampere Convention on the Provision of Telecommunication Resources for Disaster Mitigation and Relief Operations, to consider doing so;

22. *Encourages* the further use of space-based and ground-based remote-sensing technologies, including as provided by UN-SPIDER, as well as the sharing of geographical data, for the prevention, mitigation and management of natural disasters, where appropriate, and invites Member States to continue to provide their support to the consolidation of the United Nations capability in the area of satellite-derived geographical information for early warning, preparedness, response and early recovery;

23. *Encourages* Member States, relevant United Nations organizations and international financial institutions to enhance the global capacity for sustainable post-disaster recovery in areas such as coordination with traditional and non-traditional partners, identification and dissemination of lessons learned, development of common tools and mechanisms for recovery needs assessment, strategy development and programming, and incorporation of risk reduction into all recovery processes, and welcomes the ongoing efforts to this end;

24. *Encourages* Member States and the United Nations system to support national initiatives that address the possible differentiated impacts of natural disasters on the affected population, including through the collection and analysis of data disaggregated, inter alia, by sex, age and disability, using, inter alia, the existing information provided by States, and through the development of tools, methods and procedures that will result in more timely and useful initial needs assessments;

25. *Calls upon* United Nations humanitarian organizations, in consultation with Member States, as appropriate, to strengthen the evidence base for humanitarian assistance by further developing common mechanisms to improve the quality, transparency and reliability of, and make further progress towards, common humanitarian needs assessments, to assess their performance in assistance and to ensure the most effective use of humanitarian resources by these organizations;

26. *Stresses* the importance of the full and equal participation of women in decision-making and of gender mainstreaming in developing and implementing disaster risk reduction, preparedness, response and recovery strategies, and in this regard requests the Secretary-General to continue ensuring that gender mainstreaming is better taken into account in all aspects of humanitarian responses and activities;

27. *Encourages* Member States and relevant regional and international organizations to identify and improve the dissemination of best practices for improving disaster preparedness, response and early recovery and to scale up successful local initiatives, as appropriate;

28. *Requests* the United Nations system to improve its coordination of disaster recovery efforts, from relief to development, inter alia, by strengthening institutional, coordination and strategic planning efforts in disaster recovery, in support of national authorities;

29. *Calls upon* relevant United Nations humanitarian and development organizations to continue efforts to ensure continuity and predictability in their response and to further improve coordination in recovery processes in support of the efforts of national authorities;

30. *Calls upon* the United Nations system and other humanitarian actors to improve the dissemination of tools and services to support enhanced disaster risk reduction, in particular preparedness, and early recovery;

31. *Calls upon* relevant United Nations humanitarian and development organizations, in consultation with Member States, to strengthen tools and mechanisms to ensure that early recovery needs and support are integrated into the planning and implementation of disaster preparedness, humanitarian response and development cooperation activities, as appropriate;

32. *Acknowledges* that early recovery should receive further funding, and encourages the provision of timely, flexible and predictable funding for early recovery, including through established humanitarian instruments;

33. *Encourages* the United Nations system and other relevant humanitarian and development actors to support humanitarian coordinators and resident coordinators, in order to strengthen their capacity, inter alia, to support the host Government in implementing preparedness measures and to coordinate preparedness activities of country teams in support of national efforts, and also encourages the United Nations system and other relevant humanitarian actors to further strengthen the ability to quickly and flexibly deploy humanitarian professionals to support Governments and country teams in the immediate aftermath of a disaster;

34. *Emphasizes* the need to mobilize adequate, flexible and sustainable resources for recovery, preparedness and disaster risk reduction activities in order to ensure predictable and timely access to resources for humanitarian assistance in emergencies resulting from disasters associated with natural hazards;

35. *Welcomes* the achievements of the Central Emergency Response Fund and its contribution to the promotion and enhancement of early humanitarian response, calls upon all Member States and invites the private sector and all concerned individuals and institutions to consider increasing voluntary contributions to the Fund, including, when possible, through multi-year and early commitments, and emphasizes that contributions should be additional to current commitments to humanitarian programming and not to the detriment of resources made available for international cooperation for development;

36. *Invites* Member States, the private sector and all concerned individuals and institutions to consider voluntary contributions to other humanitarian funding mechanisms;

37. *Requests* the Secretary-General to continue to improve the international response to natural disasters and to report thereon to the General Assembly at its sixty-sixth session, and to include in his report recommendations on how to ensure that humanitarian assistance is provided in ways supportive of the transition from relief to development, as well as on the lessons learned on strengthening the coordination and response capacity when facing natural disasters of large magnitude.

Report of Secretary-General. Pursuant to General Assembly resolution 65/264 (see above), the Secretary-General submitted a September report [A/66/339] that reviewed the occurrence of disasters associated with natural hazards and highlighted emerging trends in the period from 1 June 2010 to 31 May 2011. The report found that the highest burden of natural disaster-related mortality and risk continued to be concentrated in countries with low gross domestic product and weak governance, and that poverty and lack of resources increased vulnerability. New evidence confirmed that disaster losses especially affected child welfare and development, with droughts having a particularly detrimental impact on child malnutrition rates.

The report examined key challenges, such as preparedness for emergency response, the transition from relief to development, and humanitarian response in urban settings, and evaluated advancement in humanitarian assistance in the field of disasters. While the United Nations had made significant progress in using country-based pooled funds and the CERF with increasing effectiveness, funding for preparedness remained ad hoc and inconsistent. Furthermore, the ability of humanitarian actors to access affected populations continued to be jeopardized in many humanitarian crisis situations. While protection concerns were often acute in natural disasters, the international community lacked predictable and effective leadership and coordination in that regard. With respect to civil-military relations in natural disaster response, the Secretary-General encouraged Member States that engaged their military forces to liaise with humanitarian coordination mechanisms from the early stages of emergency and at all levels. As for the role of technology, he acknowledged the possibility for disaster-affected populations to transmit critical information, thereby increasing the speed, relevance and effectiveness of assistance provided, but also pointed out challenges such as questions of privacy, relevance and verification of information.

The Secretary-General stressed the importance of disaster preparedness and the need to support strengthening the response capacity of local, regional and national actors; to include development actors in strategic planning at an earlier stage; and to take into account the unique consequences of natural disasters in urban areas. He urged the UN system and other humanitarian actors to increase funding for disaster preparedness and early recovery activities, and called on Member States to facilitate the rapid and unimpeded passage of humanitarian personnel and supplies to disaster-affected communities.

UN-SPIDER programme. The Committee on the Peaceful Uses of Outer Space (see p. 577) submitted a report [A/AC.105/1010] on the 2011 activities of the United Nations Platform for Space-based Information for Disaster Management and Emergency Response (UN-SPIDER). Major accomplishments included the provision of technical advisory support to 23 countries; improving the UN-SPIDER knowledge portal; and organizing international and regional workshops and expert meetings, including the International Conference on Space-based Technologies for Disaster Risk Management "Best practices for risk reduction and rapid response mapping" (Beijing, 22–25 November).

On 9 December, in **resolution 66/71** (see p. 582), the General Assembly noted the progress made in the implementation of the workplan of the UN-SPIDER programme for the 2010–2011 biennium.

GENERAL ASSEMBLY ACTION

On 23 December [meeting 92], the General Assembly adopted **resolution 66/227** [draft: A/66/L.33 & Add.1] without vote [agenda item 70 (a)].

International cooperation on humanitarian assistance in the field of natural disasters, from relief to development

The General Assembly,

Reaffirming its resolution 46/182 of 19 December 1991, the annex to which contains the guiding principles for the strengthening of the coordination of emergency humanitarian assistance of the United Nations system, as well as all its resolutions on international cooperation on humanitarian assistance in the field of natural disasters, from relief to development, and recalling the resolutions of the humanitarian segments of the substantive sessions of the Economic and Social Council,

Reaffirming also the principles of neutrality, humanity, impartiality and independence for the provision of humanitarian assistance,

Reaffirming further the Hyogo Declaration, the Hyogo Framework for Action 2005–2015: Building the Resilience of Nations and Communities to Disasters and the common statement of the special session on the Indian Ocean disaster: risk reduction for a safer future, as adopted by the World Conference on Disaster Reduction, held in Kobe, Hyogo, Japan, from 18 to 22 January 2005,

Taking note with appreciation of the midterm review of the Hyogo Framework for Action, the outcome of the third session of the Global Platform for Disaster Risk Reduction, held in Geneva from 8 to 13 May 2011, and the 2011 Global Assessment Report on Disaster Risk Reduction,

Emphasizing the fundamentally civilian character of humanitarian assistance,

Emphasizing also that the affected State has the primary responsibility in the initiation, organization, coordination and implementation of humanitarian assistance within its territory and in the facilitation of the work of humanitarian organizations in mitigating the consequences of natural disasters,

Emphasizing further the primary responsibility of each State to undertake disaster risk reduction, including through the implementation of and follow-up to the Hyogo Framework for Action, as well as response and early recovery efforts, in order to minimize the impact of natural disasters, while recognizing the importance of international cooperation in support of the efforts of affected countries which may have limited capacities in this regard,

Expressing its deep concern at the increasing challenges to Member States and to the United Nations humanitarian response capacity to deal with the consequences of natural disasters, given the effects of global challenges, including the impact of climate change, the ongoing adverse impact of the global financial and economic crisis and the negative impact of excessively volatile food prices on food security, and other key factors that exacerbate the risk of natural disasters,

Also expressing its deep concern that rural and urban poor communities in the developing world are the hardest hit by the effects of increased disaster risk,

Acknowledging the impacts of rapid urbanization in the context of natural disasters and that urban disaster preparedness and responses require appropriate disaster risk reduction strategies, including in urban planning, early recovery strategies implemented from the initial stage of relief operations, as well as mitigation, rehabilitation and sustainable development strategies,

Noting that local communities are the first responders in most disasters, underlining the critical role played by in-country capacities in disaster risk reduction, including preparedness, as well as response and recovery, and acknowledging the need to support efforts of Member States to develop and enhance national and local capacities which are fundamental to improving the overall delivery of humanitarian assistance,

Recognizing the high numbers of persons affected by natural disasters, including in this respect internally displaced persons, and the need to address the humanitarian and development needs arising from internal displacement throughout the world owing to natural disasters, and encouraging all relevant actors to consider making use of the Guiding Principles on Internal Displacement when dealing with situations of internal displacement,

Reaffirming the importance of international cooperation in support of the efforts of the affected States in dealing with natural disasters in all their phases, in particular in preparedness, response and the early recovery phase, and of strengthening the response capacity of countries affected by disaster,

Recognizing the progress made by the United Nations Platform for Space-based Information for Disaster Management and Emergency Response (UN-SPIDER) in its mission, encouraging Member States to provide all support necessary, on a voluntary basis, to UN-SPIDER, including financial support, to enable it to carry out its workplan for 2012–2013, and reiterating the importance of enhancing international coordination and cooperation at the global level in disaster management and emergency response through greater access to and use of space-based services for all countries and by facilitating capacity-building and institutional strengthening for disaster management, in particular in developing countries,

Taking note of the progress in the establishment of the Global Framework for Climate Services to develop and provide science-based climate information and prediction for climate risk management and for adaptation to climate variability and change, and looking forward to its implementation,

Welcoming the important role played by Member States, including developing countries, that have granted necessary and continued generous assistance to countries and peoples stricken by natural disasters,

Recognizing the significant role played by national Red Cross and Red Crescent societies, as part of the International Red Cross and Red Crescent Movement, in disaster preparedness and risk reduction, disaster response, rehabilitation and development,

Emphasizing the need to address vulnerability and to integrate disaster risk reduction, including preparedness, into all phases of natural disaster management, post-natural disaster recovery and development planning, through close collaboration of all relevant actors and sectors,

Recognizing that efforts to achieve economic growth, sustainable development and internationally agreed development goals, including the Millennium Development Goals, can be adversely affected by natural disasters, and noting the positive contribution that those efforts can make in strengthening the resilience of populations to such disasters,

Recognizing also the clear relationship between emergency response, rehabilitation and development, and reaffirming that, in order to ensure a smooth transition from relief to rehabilitation and development, emergency assistance must be provided in ways that will be supportive of short- and medium-term recovery and long-term development and that emergency measures should be seen as a step towards sustainable development,

Emphasizing, in this context, the important role of development organizations in supporting national efforts to mitigate the consequences of natural disasters,

1. *Takes note* of the report of the Secretary-General;

2. *Expresses its deep concern* at the increasing impact of natural disasters, resulting in massive losses of life and property worldwide, in particular in vulnerable societies lacking adequate capacity to mitigate effectively the long-term negative social, economic and environmental consequences of natural disasters;

3. *Calls upon* States to fully implement the Hyogo Declaration and the Hyogo Framework for Action 2005–2015: Building the Resilience of Nations and Communities to Disasters, in particular those commitments related to assistance for developing countries that are prone to natural disasters and for disaster-stricken States in the transition phase towards sustainable physical, social and economic recovery, for risk-reduction activities in post-disaster recovery and for rehabilitation processes;

4. *Calls upon* Member States, the United Nations system and other relevant humanitarian and development actors to accelerate the implementation of the Hyogo Framework for Action, emphasizes the promotion and strengthening of disaster preparedness activities at all levels, in particular in hazard-prone areas, and encourages them to increase funding and cooperation for disaster risk reduction activities, including disaster preparedness;

5. *Calls upon* all States to adopt, where required, and to continue to implement effectively, necessary legislative and other appropriate measures to mitigate the effects of natural disasters and integrate disaster risk reduction strategies into development planning, and in this regard requests the international community to continue to assist developing countries as well as countries with economies in transition, as appropriate;

6. *Acknowledges* that climate change, among other factors, contributes to environmental degradation and to the

increase in the intensity and frequency of extreme weather events, both of which amplify natural disaster risk, and in this regard encourages Member States, as well as relevant regional, subregional and international organizations, in accordance with their specific mandates, to support adaptation to the adverse effects of climate change and to strengthen disaster risk reduction and early warning systems in order to minimize the humanitarian consequences of natural disasters, including through the provision of technology and support for capacity-building in developing countries;

7. *Welcomes* the initiatives at the regional and national levels related to the implementation of the Guidelines for the Domestic Facilitation and Regulation of International Disaster Relief and Initial Recovery Assistance, as reported to the Thirty-first International Conference of the Red Cross and Red Crescent, held in Geneva from 28 November to 1 December 2011, and encourages Member States and, where applicable, regional organizations to take further steps to strengthen operational and legal frameworks for international disaster relief, taking into account the Guidelines, as appropriate;

8. *Also welcomes* the effective cooperation among the affected States, relevant bodies of the United Nations system, donor countries, regional and international financial institutions and other relevant organizations, such as the International Red Cross and Red Crescent Movement, and civil society, in the coordination and delivery of emergency relief, and stresses the need to continue such cooperation and delivery throughout relief operations and medium- and long-term rehabilitation and reconstruction efforts, in a manner that reduces vulnerability to future natural hazards;

9. *Reiterates* the commitment to support, as a matter of priority, the efforts of countries, in particular developing countries, to strengthen their capacities at all levels in order to reduce risks, prepare for and respond rapidly to natural disasters and mitigate their impact;

10. *Urges* Member States to develop, update and strengthen early warning systems, disaster preparedness and risk reduction measures at all levels, in accordance with the Hyogo Framework for Action, taking into account their own circumstances and capacities and in coordination with relevant actors, as appropriate, and encourages the international community and relevant United Nations entities to continue to support national efforts in this regard;

11. *Also urges* Member States to improve their response to early warning information in order to ensure that early warning leads to early action, and encourages all stakeholders to support the efforts of Member States in this regard;

12. *Encourages* Member States to consider elaborating and presenting to the International Strategy for Disaster Reduction secretariat their national platforms for disaster reduction in accordance with the Hyogo Framework for Action, and also encourages States to cooperate with each other to reach this objective;

13. *Recognizes* the importance of applying a multi-hazard approach to preparedness, and encourages Member States, taking into account their specific circumstances, and the United Nations system to continue to apply the approach to their preparedness activities, including by giving due regard to, inter alia, secondary environmental hazards stemming from industrial and technological accidents;

14. *Stresses* that, to increase further the effectiveness of humanitarian assistance, particular international cooperation efforts should be undertaken to enhance and broaden further the utilization of national and local capacities and, where appropriate, of regional and subregional capacities for disaster preparedness and response, which may be made available in closer proximity to the site of a disaster, and more efficiently and at lower cost;

15. *Also stresses*, in this context, the importance of strengthening international cooperation, particularly through the effective use of multilateral mechanisms, in the timely provision of humanitarian assistance through all phases of a disaster, from relief and recovery to development, including the provision of adequate resources;

16. *Encourages* all Member States to facilitate, to the extent possible, the transit of emergency humanitarian assistance and development assistance, provided in the context of international efforts, including in the phase from relief to development, in full accordance with the provisions of resolution 46/182 and the annex thereto, and in full respect of the humanitarian principles of humanity, neutrality, impartiality and independence, and their obligations under international law, including international humanitarian law;

17. *Reaffirms* the leading role of the Office for the Coordination of Humanitarian Affairs of the Secretariat as the focal point within the overall United Nations system for advocacy for and coordination of humanitarian assistance among United Nations humanitarian organizations and other humanitarian partners;

18. *Welcomes* the important contribution of the United Nations Disaster Assessment and Coordination system and the International Search and Rescue Advisory Group to the effectiveness of humanitarian assistance, and the support provided to the coordination of national and international response in the field, and encourages the continued incorporation of experts from developing countries that are prone to natural disasters into those mechanisms;

19. *Urges* Member States, the United Nations system and other humanitarian actors to consider the specific and differentiated consequences of natural disasters both in rural and urban areas when designing and implementing disaster risk reduction, prevention and mitigation, preparedness, humanitarian assistance and early recovery strategies, giving special emphasis to addressing the needs of those living in rural and urban poor areas prone to natural disasters;

20. *Recognizes* that information and telecommunication technology can play an important role in disaster response, encourages Member States to develop emergency response telecommunication capacities and encourages the international community to assist the efforts of developing countries in this area, where needed, including in the recovery phase, and in this regard encourages Member States that have not acceded to or ratified the Tampere Convention on the Provision of Telecommunication Resources for Disaster Mitigation and Relief Operations to consider doing so;

21. *Encourages* the further use of space-based and ground-based remote-sensing technologies, including as provided by UN-SPIDER, as well as the sharing of geographical data, for the prevention, mitigation and management of natural disasters, where appropriate, and invites Member States to continue to provide their support to the consolidation of the United Nations capability in the area of satellite-derived geographical information for early warning, preparedness, response and early recovery;

22. *Recognizes* the opportunities for new technologies, when utilized in a coordinated fashion and based on humanitarian principles, potentially to improve the effectiveness and accountability of humanitarian response, and encourages Member States, the United Nations and its humanitarian partners to consider engaging, inter alia, with the volunteer and technical communities in order to make use of the variety of data and information available during emergencies and disaster risk efforts;

23. *Encourages* Member States, relevant United Nations organizations and international financial institutions to enhance the global capacity for sustainable post-disaster recovery in areas such as coordination with traditional and non-traditional partners, identification and dissemination of lessons learned, development of common tools and mechanisms for recovery needs assessment, strategy development and programming, and incorporation of risk reduction into all recovery processes, and welcomes the ongoing efforts to this end;

24. *Encourages* Member States and the United Nations system to support national initiatives that address the possible differentiated impacts of natural disasters on the affected population, including through the collection and analysis of data disaggregated, inter alia, by sex, age and disability, using, inter alia, the existing information provided by States, and through the development of tools, methods and procedures that will result in more timely and useful initial needs assessments;

25. *Calls upon* United Nations humanitarian organizations, in consultation with Member States, as appropriate, to strengthen the evidence base for humanitarian assistance by further developing common mechanisms to improve the quality, transparency and reliability of, and make further progress towards, common humanitarian needs assessments, to assess their performance in assistance and to ensure the most effective use of humanitarian resources by these organizations;

26. *Stresses* the importance of the full and equal participation of women in decision-making and of gender mainstreaming in developing and implementing disaster risk reduction, preparedness, response and recovery strategies, and in this regard requests the Secretary-General to continue ensuring that gender mainstreaming is better taken into account in all aspects of humanitarian responses and activities;

27. *Encourages* Member States and relevant regional and international organizations to identify and improve the dissemination of best practices for improving disaster preparedness, response and early recovery and to scale up successful local initiatives, as appropriate;

28. *Requests* the United Nations humanitarian and development organizations to improve their coordination of disaster recovery efforts, from relief to development, inter alia, by strengthening institutional, coordination and strategic planning efforts in disaster preparedness, resilience-building and recovery, in support of national authorities, and by ensuring that development actors participate in strategic planning at an early stage;

29. *Calls upon* the United Nations system and other humanitarian actors to improve the dissemination of tools and services to support enhanced disaster risk reduction, in particular preparedness, and early recovery;

30. *Calls upon* relevant United Nations humanitarian and development organizations, in consultation with Member States, to strengthen tools and mechanisms to ensure that early recovery needs and support are integrated into the planning and implementation of disaster preparedness, humanitarian response and development cooperation activities, as appropriate;

31. *Encourages* the United Nations system and humanitarian organizations to continue their efforts to mainstream early recovery into humanitarian programming, acknowledges that early recovery should receive further funding, and encourages the provision of timely, flexible and predictable funding for early recovery, including through established humanitarian instruments;

32. *Encourages* the United Nations system and other relevant humanitarian and development actors to support humanitarian coordinators and resident coordinators, in order to strengthen their capacity, inter alia, to support the host Government in implementing preparedness measures and to coordinate preparedness activities of country teams in support of national efforts, and also encourages the United Nations system and other relevant humanitarian actors to further strengthen the ability to quickly and flexibly deploy humanitarian professionals to support Governments and country teams in the immediate aftermath of a disaster;

33. *Emphasizes* the need to mobilize adequate, flexible and sustainable resources for recovery, preparedness and disaster risk reduction activities in order to ensure predictable and timely access to resources for humanitarian assistance in emergencies resulting from disasters associated with natural hazards;

34. *Welcomes* the achievements of the Central Emergency Response Fund and its contribution to the promotion and enhancement of early humanitarian response, calls upon all Member States and invites the private sector and all concerned individuals and institutions to consider increasing voluntary contributions to the Fund, including, when possible, through multi-year and early commitments, and emphasizes that contributions should be additional to current commitments to humanitarian programming and not to the detriment of resources made available for international cooperation for development;

35. *Invites* Member States, the private sector and all concerned individuals and institutions to consider voluntary contributions to other humanitarian funding mechanisms;

36. *Requests* the Secretary-General to continue to improve the international response to natural disasters and to report thereon to the General Assembly at its sixty-seventh session, and to include in his report recommendations on how to ensure that humanitarian assistance is provided in ways supportive of the transition from relief to development.

International Strategy for Disaster Reduction

Global Assessment Report. The *2011 Global Assessment Report on Disaster Risk Reduction: Revealing Risk, Redefining Development*, a collaborative effort of the International Strategy for Disaster Reduction system partners, highlighted the relationship between disasters and poverty. At the same time, incidents in Australia, New Zealand and Japan were reminders that developed countries were also exposed and at risk. The report found that, while the risk of being killed by a cyclone or flood was lower than it had been 20 years earlier, economic loss risk continued to increase across all regions and threatened the economies of low-income countries. Drought was the disaster that was most associated with inappropriate social and economic policy choices, and often with the instability caused by conflict. Progress was being made in early warning, preparedness and response, but countries were struggling to address the underlying risk drivers, and gender and public awareness were not being adequately addressed. The report recommended a redefinition of development in terms of sensitivity to disaster and climate risk, and the location of overall responsibility for disaster risk management in a central ministry with a high level of political authority, to ensure the coherence of policy and planning.

Midterm review of Hyogo Framework for Action. The midterm review of the Hyogo Framework for Action 2005–2015 [YUN 2005, p. 1016]—facilitated by the secretariat of the United Nations Office for Disaster Risk Reduction—highlighted progress achieved over the previous five years in disaster risk reduction and the role the Framework had played in promoting that progress. It confirmed that the progress was uneven across the world, reflecting broad economic and institutional differences among regions and countries. An analysis of government reports indicated that progress took place in the passing of national legislation, setting up early warning systems, and strengthening disaster preparedness and response. Concerns remained about the lack of systematic multi-hazard risk assessments and early warning systems, factoring in social and economic vulnerabilities, the integration of disaster risk reduction into sustainable development policies and planning at the national and international level, and the insufficient level of implementation of the Framework at the local level.

The review recommended that national and international institutions, including bilateral aid organizations and the United Nations, integrate disaster risk reduction in their development, climate change adaptation, environmental and humanitarian planning, and execution and accountability frameworks to safeguard development gains and investments; improve governance for the implementation of the Framework at the national and international level; assess the effectiveness of National Platforms in informing and supporting the executive level of decision-making; and develop accountability mechanisms to measure action and progress.

Global Platform for Disaster Risk Reduction. The Global Platform for Disaster Risk Reduction, the main global forum for strategic advice coordination and partnership development for disaster reduction, held its third session (Geneva, 8–13 May), which was attended by over 2,600 delegates representing 168 Governments, 25 intergovernmental organizations and 65 non-governmental organizations. The session stressed the importance of ensuring the further implementation of the Framework, while discussions concerning the post-2015 disaster risk reduction framework unfolded. In that context, the Government of Japan made an offer to host the Third World Conference on Disaster Risk Reduction in 2015 to coincide with the end date of the Hyogo Framework for Action 2005–2015. As an integral component of the third session, the first World Reconstruction Conference—organized by the Global Facility for Disaster Reduction and Recovery, the World Bank and the Strategy secretariat—focused on how to develop an effective recovery framework, more reliable financing and knowledge practice, stressing the integration of risk reduction into all post-disaster actions.

Report of Secretary-General. In response to General Assembly resolution 65/157 [YUN 2010, p. 925], the Secretary-General, in an August report [A/66/301], reviewed the implementation of the International Strategy for Disaster Reduction, adopted by the programme forum of the International Decade for Natural Disaster Reduction (1990–2000) in 1999 [YUN 1999, p. 859] and endorsed by the Assembly in resolution 54/219 [ibid., p. 861]. Disaster risk was accumulating faster than economic growth, hampering development and the achievement of the Millennium Development Goals. Risk management systems and decision-making required further development, including disaster loss accounting and integrated risk modelling, to support sound development and investment planning. Based on the findings of the *2011 Global Assessment Report*, the midterm review of the Hyogo Framework for Action and the deliberations at the third session of the Global Platform for Disaster Risk Reduction (see above), the Secretary-General recommended that any future framework for sustainable development include a clear prescription for incorporation of disaster and climate risk management; that national disaster loss registers, disaster risk mapping and financial tracking systems be established and developed to support development planning and investment choices; and that national mechanisms for disaster risk reduction be better used for advocacy, knowledge and cooperation. He asked Member States and organizations to scale up their financial, human and technology investments for disaster risk reduction.

GENERAL ASSEMBLY ACTION

On 22 December [meeting 91], the General Assembly, on the recommendation of the Second (Economic and Financial) Committee [A/66/440/Add.3], adopted **resolution 66/199** without vote [agenda item 19 (c)].

International Strategy for Disaster Reduction

The General Assembly,

Recalling its decision 57/547 of 20 December 2002 and its resolutions 44/236 of 22 December 1989, 49/22 A of 2 December 1994, 49/22 B of 20 December 1994, 53/185 of 15 December 1998, 54/219 of 22 December 1999, 56/195 of 21 December 2001, 57/256 of 20 December 2002, 58/214 and 58/215 of 23 December 2003, 59/231 and 59/233 of 22 December 2004, 60/195 and 60/196 of 22 December 2005, 61/198 and 61/200 of 20 December 2006, 62/192 of 19 December 2007, 63/216 and 63/217 of 19 December 2008, 64/200 of 21 December 2009 and 65/157 of 20 December 2010 as well as Economic and Social Council resolutions 1999/63 of 30 July 1999 and 2001/35 of 26 July 2001, and taking into consideration its resolution 57/270 B of 23 June 2003 on the integrated and coordinated implementation of and follow-up to the outcomes of the major United Nations conferences and summits in the economic and social fields,

Acknowledging the importance of the forthcoming United Nations Conference on Sustainable Development,

1. *Takes note* of the report of the Secretary-General on the implementation of resolutions 64/200 and 65/157;

2. *Notes* the ongoing preparatory process for the United Nations Conference on Sustainable Development, to be held in Rio de Janeiro, Brazil, from 20 to 22 June 2012;

3. *Stresses* the importance of the continued substantive consideration of the issue of disaster risk reduction, and encourages Member States and the relevant United Nations bodies to take into consideration the important role of disaster risk reduction activities for, inter alia, the achievement of sustainable development;

4. *Recognizes* that the Global Platform for Disaster Risk Reduction was confirmed at its third session, held in Geneva from 8 to 13 May 2011, as being the main forum at the global level for strategic advice coordination and partnership development for disaster risk reduction;

5. *Takes note with appreciation* of the results of the midterm review of the Hyogo Framework for Action 2005–2015: Building the Resilience of Nations and Communities to Disaster, calls upon Member States, United Nations funds and programmes and the specialized agencies, within their mandates, to accelerate the implementation of the Hyogo Framework for Action and requests the secretariat of the International Strategy for Disaster Reduction to facilitate the development of a post-2015 framework for disaster risk reduction;

6. *Also takes note with appreciation* of the efforts made by the Secretary-General to strengthen the secretariat of the Strategy, including through the extension until 2015 of the post of Assistant Secretary-General for Disaster Risk Reduction and Special Representative of the Secretary-General for the Implementation of the Hyogo Framework for Action;

7. *Requests* the Secretary-General, in consultation with Member States, to look, in an inclusive, open and transparent manner, into other measures to ensure that the secretariat of the Strategy can discharge its cross-cutting mandate with efficiency and effectiveness;

8. *Welcomes* the offer made by the Government of Japan to host the Third World Conference on Disaster Risk Reduction in 2015;

9. *Decides* to include in the provisional agenda of its sixty-seventh session, under the item entitled "Sustainable development", the sub-item entitled "International Strategy for Disaster Reduction";

10. *Requests* the Secretary-General to submit to the General Assembly at its sixty-seventh session a report on the implementation of the present resolution and to include therein an update on what progress has been made and what the opportunities are for making further progress in mainstreaming disaster risk reduction more effectively across the whole United Nations system.

Military and civil response

Communications. In a letter [A/65/772] dated 28 February, Qatar informed the General Assembly about the HOPEFOR initiative, proposed by the Government and launched in June 2010 in New York at the International Peace Institute, with the intention to improve the use of military and civil defence assets in humanitarian response. In a subsequent letter [A/67/661], Qatar and Turkey transmitted the recommendations of the first International Conference on the HOPEFOR initiative (Doha, Qatar, 27–29 November), which focused on the strengthening of institutional systems and frameworks and areas for cooperation, as well as capacity-building and preparedness.

GENERAL ASSEMBLY ACTION

On 1 July [meeting 107], the General Assembly adopted **resolution 65/307** [draft: A/65/L.82 & Add.1] without vote [agenda item 69 (*a*)].

Improving the effectiveness and coordination of military and civil defence assets for natural disaster response

The General Assembly,

Reaffirming its resolution 46/182 of 19 December 1991 and the guiding principles contained in the annex thereto, other relevant resolutions of the General Assembly and the Economic and Social Council and agreed conclusions of the Council,

Recalling the aim to improve the predictability and the effective use of civil and military defence assets for natural disaster response, based on humanitarian principles, while emphasizing the fundamentally civilian character of humanitarian assistance, and reaffirming the leading role of civilian organizations in implementing humanitarian assistance,

Recognizing that building national and local preparedness and response capacity is critical to a more predictable and effective response,

Recognizing also the importance of promoting preparedness for disaster response through regional and international partnerships,

Taking note in this regard of the letter from Sheikh Hamad bin Jassim bin Jabr Al-Thani, Prime Minister and Minister for Foreign Affairs of Qatar, to the President of the General Assembly and the concept paper attached thereto, entitled "HOPEFOR initiative: a global cooperative framework to improve the effectiveness of military and civil defence assets in relief operations",

Taking note of the calls by Mr. Leonel Fernández Reyna, President of the Dominican Republic, and Mr. Abdullah Gül, President of Turkey, at the general debate of the sixty-fifth session of the General Assembly, on 23 September 2010, on the need to more effectively address the issue of disaster response,

1. *Reaffirms* the principles of neutrality, humanity, impartiality and independence for the provision of humanitarian assistance;

2. *Emphasizes* the fundamentally civilian character of humanitarian assistance, and reaffirms the need in situ-

ations of natural disaster in which military capacity and assets are used to support the implementation of humanitarian assistance, for such use to be undertaken with the consent of the affected State and in conformity with international law, including international humanitarian law, as well as humanitarian principles;

3. *Recalls in this regard* the revised guidelines on the use of military and civil defence assets in disaster relief, and stresses the value of their use and of the development by the United Nations, in consultation with States and other relevant actors, of further guidance on civil-military relations in the context of humanitarian activities;

4. *Takes note with appreciation* of the initiative of Qatar, the Dominican Republic and Turkey, to reflect, in close coordination with the Emergency Relief Coordinator, on improving the effectiveness and coordination of military and civil defence assets for natural disaster response;

5. *Also takes note with appreciation* of the HOPEFOR initiative by Qatar, which aims to improve humanitarian civil-military coordination and ensure that the use of military and civil defence assets in support of natural disaster relief operations is undertaken in an appropriate, effective and coordinated manner, in accordance with the principles contained in paragraph 2 of the present resolution, and as the last resort as defined in the Oslo Guidelines;

6. *Takes note with interest* of the decision of Qatar, the Dominican Republic and Turkey to co-convene an international conference, to be held in Doha in 2011, to discuss the concept of the HOPEFOR initiative and consider the options outlined in the paper thereon and steps for their implementation, as appropriate, in close collaboration with Member States, regional and international organizations and the Emergency Relief Coordinator.

Mine action

Pursuant to General Assembly resolution 64/84 [YUN 2009, p. 891], the Secretary-General in August submitted a report [A/66/292] on the implementation of that resolution and on follow-up to previous resolutions on assistance in mine clearance and mine action, including on relevant United Nations policies and activities, covering the period from August 2009 to July 2011. The report stressed the impact of mine action in the five major areas of United Nations work—peace and security, humanitarian affairs, economic development, human rights, and international law—and described the efforts of the United Nations Mine Action Team to integrate mine action in all five areas.

At the Second Review Conference of States Parties to the Convention on the Prohibition of the Use, Stockpiling, Production and Transfer of Anti-Personnel Mines and on Their Destruction [YUN 2009, p. 554], participants adopted the Cartagena Declaration "A shared commitment for a mine-free world" and the Cartagena Action Plan 2010–2014, which provided guidance and a framework for the implementation and universalization of the Convention. The Tenth Meeting of States Parties to the Anti-Personnel Mine Ban Convention [YUN 2010, p. 562] reviewed the intersessional work programme for 2011 and established a new Standing Committee on Resources, Cooperation and Assistance. The First Meeting of States Parties to the Convention on Cluster Munitions [ibid.] adopted the Vientiane Declaration and Action Plan, guiding its implementation.

The Secretary-General further examined the integration of mine action in the UN system, coordination and partnerships, servicing the mine action community, and resource mobilization and allocation. During the reporting period, increased focus was placed on integrating mine action within UN peacekeeping, humanitarian and development efforts. In 2009, in recognition of the critical role of standing capacities in the planning and start-up of missions, the United Nations Mine Action Service (UNMAS) established its Standing Mine Action Capacity mechanism to provide immediate response to emergency situations, reinforce existing programmes and conduct needs assessments and programme evaluations. A survey—conducted for 49 mine action programmes that had received support from UNMAS for implementing the United Nations Inter-Agency Mine Action Strategy 2006–2010—revealed the decreasing rate of civilian deaths and injuries, the positive correlation between mine action and enhanced humanitarian and development responses, the integration of mine action into national development and reconstruction plans, and the establishment of national mine action authorities.

The Secretary-General noted progress in the field of mine action including the establishment of concrete international norms and the application of proven solutions; however, he expressed concern about the continued landmine use reported in Afghanistan, Colombia, Myanmar, Pakistan and Yemen, as well as new usage in the Libyan Arab Jamahiriya, Somalia and the Sudan. He called upon the international community to provide continued political and financial support for the elimination of landmines and explosive remnants of war.

GENERAL ASSEMBLY ACTION

On 9 December [meeting 81], the General Assembly, on the recommendation of the Fourth (Special Political and Decolonization) Committee [A/66/423], adopted **resolution 66/69** without vote [agenda item 49].

Assistance in mine action

The General Assembly,

Recalling its resolution 64/84 of 10 December 2009 and all its previous resolutions on assistance in mine clearance and on assistance in mine action, all adopted without a vote,

Recalling also all relevant treaties and conventions and their review processes,

Noting with appreciation the extent to which the International Day for Mine Awareness and Assistance in Mine Action has been commemorated worldwide,

Reaffirming its deep concern at the tremendous humanitarian and development problems caused by the presence of mines and explosive remnants of war, which have serious and lasting social and economic consequences for the populations of countries affected by them,

Bearing in mind the serious threat that mines and explosive remnants of war pose to the safety, health and lives of local civilian populations, as well as of personnel participating in humanitarian, peacekeeping, rehabilitation and mine-clearance programmes and operations,

Deeply alarmed by the number of mines that continue to be laid each year as well as the presence of a decreasing but still very large number of, and area of square kilometres infested by, mines and explosive remnants of war as a result of armed conflicts, and therefore remaining convinced of the necessity and urgency of strengthening mine-action efforts by the international community with a view to eliminating the threat of landmines and explosive remnants of war to civilians as soon as possible,

Recognizing that, in addition to the primary role of States, the United Nations has a significant role to play in the field of assistance in mine action through the United Nations Mine Action Team, including the United Nations Mine Action Service, and considering mine action to be an important and integrated component of United Nations humanitarian and development activities, as well as noting the integration of mine action in numerous United Nations peacekeeping operations,

Noting with appreciation the enhanced cooperation of the United Nations Mine Action Team with non-governmental organizations and other stakeholders through meetings of the Committee on Mine Action, and progress in active involvement in the humanitarian coordination mechanism,

Recognizing the valuable mine-action efforts of national and international mine-action practitioners, including United Nations personnel and peacekeepers, enabling local communities to resume normal lives and reclaim their livelihoods by regaining access to previously contaminated lands,

Stressing the pressing need to urge non-State actors to halt immediately and unconditionally new deployments of mines, improvised explosive devices and other associated explosive devices,

Noting the ongoing efforts to develop a new United Nations Inter-Agency Mine Action Strategy for the period 2011–2015,

1. *Takes note* of the report of the Secretary-General on assistance in mine action;

2. *Calls*, in particular, for the continuation of the efforts of States, with the assistance of the United Nations and relevant organizations involved in mine action, as appropriate, to foster the establishment and development of national mine-action capacities in countries in which mines and explosive remnants of war constitute a serious threat to the safety, health and lives of the local civilian population or an impediment to social and economic development efforts at the national and local levels;

3. *Urges* all States, in particular those that have the capacity to do so, as well as the United Nations system and other relevant organizations and institutions involved in mine action, to support mine-affected States and territories, as appropriate, by providing:

(*a*) Assistance to countries affected by mines and explosive remnants of war for the establishment and development of national mine-action capacities, including, where appropriate, in the fulfilment of the relevant international obligations of those countries;

(*b*) Support for national programmes, where appropriate, in cooperation with the relevant bodies of the United Nations system and relevant regional, governmental and non-governmental organizations, to reduce the risks posed by landmines and explosive remnants of war, taking into consideration the different needs of women, girls, boys and men;

(*c*) Reliable, predictable and timely contributions for mine-action activities, including through national mine-action efforts and mine-action programmes of non-governmental organizations, including those relating to victim assistance and mine risk education, especially at the local level, as well as through relevant national, regional and global trust funds, including the Voluntary Trust Fund for Assistance in Mine Action;

(*d*) Necessary information and technical, financial and material assistance to locate, remove, destroy and otherwise render ineffective minefields, mines, booby traps, other devices and explosive remnants of war, in accordance with international law, as soon as possible;

(*e*) Technological assistance (i) to countries affected by mines and explosive remnants of war; and (ii) to promote user-oriented scientific research on and development of mine-action techniques and technology that are effective, sustainable, appropriate and environmentally sound;

4. *Encourages* efforts to conduct all mine-action activities in accordance with the International Mine Action Standards (IMAS) or IMAS-compliant national standards, and emphasizes the importance of using an information management system, such as the Information Management System for Mine Action, to help facilitate mine-action activities;

5. *Urges* all mine-affected States, pursuant to applicable international law, to identify all areas, as appropriate, under their jurisdiction or control containing mines and other explosive remnants of war in the most efficient manner possible and to employ land release techniques, including non-technical survey, technical survey and clearance when appropriate;

6. *Encourages* mine-affected States, with support from relevant development partners as appropriate, to proactively mainstream mine action and victim assistance requirements into development plans and processes to ensure that development priorities include mine action and that mine action is predictably funded;

7. *Encourages* all relevant multilateral, regional and national programmes and bodies to include activities related to mine action, including clearance, in their humanitarian, rehabilitation, reconstruction and development assistance activities, where appropriate, bearing in mind the need to ensure national and local ownership, sustainability and capacity-building, as well as to include a gender and age-appropriate perspective in all aspects of such activities;

8. *Encourages* Member States, as appropriate, and relevant organizations involved in mine action to continue

efforts to ensure that mine-action programmes are gender- and age-sensitive, so that women, girls, boys and men can benefit equally from them, and encourages the participation of all stakeholders in the programming of mine action;

9. *Stresses* the importance of cooperation and coordination in mine action, and emphasizes the primary responsibility of national authorities in that regard, also stresses the supporting role of the United Nations and other relevant organizations in that regard, and looks forward to the imminent completion of the evaluation by the Joint Inspection Unit of the scope, organization, effectiveness and approach of the work of the United Nations in mine action, as requested in its resolution 64/84;

10. *Recognizes* the importance of explicitly incorporating references to mine action, when appropriate, in ceasefire and peace agreements in the light of the potential that mine action can have as a peace and confidence-building measure in post-conflict situations among the parties concerned;

11. *Requests* the Secretary-General to submit to the General Assembly at its sixty-eighth session a report on the implementation of the present resolution and on follow-up to previous resolutions on assistance in mine clearance and on assistance in mine action, including on relevant United Nations policies and activities as well as in regard to the evaluation by the Joint Inspection Unit of the scope, organization, effectiveness and approach of the work of the United Nations in mine action;

12. *Decides* to include in the provisional agenda of its sixty-eighth session the item entitled "Assistance in mine action".

Humanitarian action

The consolidated appeals process (CAP), an inclusive and coordinated programme cycle for analysing context, assessing needs and planning prioritized humanitarian response, was the humanitarian sector's main strategic planning and programming tool. In 2011, the United Nations and its humanitarian partners issued consolidated and flash appeals seeking $8.9 billion in assistance to 56 million people in Afghanistan, the Central African Republic, Chad, the Democratic Republic of the Congo, Djibouti, El Salvador, Haiti, Kenya, Libya, Namibia, Nicaragua, Niger, Pakistan, Somalia, South Sudan, Sri Lanka and the Sudan, as well as the Occupied Palestinian Territory and the West Africa subregion (Benin, Burkina Faso, Cape Verde, Côte d'Ivoire, Gambia, Ghana, Guinea, Guinea-Bissau, Liberia, Mali, Mauritania, Nigeria, Senegal, Sierra Leone, Togo), Yemen and Zimbabwe. About 63 per cent ($5.6 billion) of requirements was met.

The General Assembly, in **resolution 66/117** of 15 December, called on Governments and parties in complex humanitarian emergencies to cooperate fully with the United Nations and other humanitarian agencies and organizations, and to ensure the safe and unhindered access of humanitarian personnel (see p. 1435).

Africa

Central Africa and Great Lakes region

Central African Republic

The UN Consolidated Appeal for the Central African Republic in 2011 sought $141.9 million, of which 46 per cent ($65.2 million) was received.

The security situation, and hence humanitarian access, deteriorated in the north and north-east of the country at the beginning of the year with the resurgence of the armed conflict between the Convention des Patriotes pour la Justice et la Paix (CPJP) and Government forces and their allies of the Union des Forces Démocratiques pour le Redressement. More worrying, criminal groups in the Haute Kotto, Vakaga and Bamingui Bangoran provinces increasingly targeted humanitarian workers and assets. Although CPJP signed a ceasefire agreement with the Government on 12 June, humanitarian programmes continued to be affected by persistent criminal threat. A few milestones were reached during the year, including the successful presidential and parliamentary electoral process and the set-up of a new Government, as well as progress made in disarmament, demobilization and reintegration. As at the end of October, the number of people affected by displacement in the country was estimated at 171,751, of which 105,206 were internally displaced persons (IDPs) and 66,545 were returnees. The decrease in funding over the previous two years was a major concern for the humanitarian community. Given the limited available funding, the Humanitarian Country Team aimed to maximize the strategic use of financing mechanisms such as the Central Emergency Response Fund (CERF) and the Common Humanitarian Fund (CHF) by targeting the highest-priority projects. The CHF emergency reserve was activated to support the cholera outbreak in October. In 2011, the country received $5 million from the CERF underfunded window. About $13.7 million was channeled through the CHF. The three main objectives under the common humanitarian strategy for the country remained saving lives, protection and early recovery.

Chad

The UN Consolidated Appeal for Chad in 2011 sought $535.3 million, of which 59 per cent ($314.1 million) was received.

The severe and large-scale malnutrition and food insecurity crisis in the west and the centre of Chad and the continuing but slow return of IDPs required a major humanitarian response in 2011. More displaced people accessing humanitarian assistance in eastern Chad; outbreaks of cholera, polio and meningitis which threatened some 3 million people; the continued major presence of refugees in eastern and south-eastern Chad; and the prevalence of vulnerable households affected by previous disasters such as floods and droughts all together accounted for more than 3.8 million vulnerable people who continued to need protection and assistance. Since the signing of the peace agreement between Chad and the Sudan [YUN 2010, p. 158] and the subsequent departure of the United Nations Mission in the Central African Republic and Chad in 2010 [ibid., p. 168], Chad had experienced a period of relative stability with the absence of armed conflict within its borders. While humanitarian actors still faced criminal attacks and therefore moved with armed escorts, those incidents remained isolated and humanitarian access was generally available. However, security in the border areas between Chad and the Sudan was fragile. The strategic objectives of the humanitarian community focused on the continuation of life-saving assistance to people affected by crises, while seeking the integration of durable solutions wherever possible. Transition from emergency assistance towards early recovery was a key concern for humanitarian actors, especially in the light of the lack of financial resources dedicated to early recovery interventions.

Democratic Republic of Congo

The Humanitarian Action Plan for the Democratic Republic of the Congo (DRC) sought $735.8 million, of which 66 per cent ($487.4 million) was received.

The population in the east of the DRC continued to be affected by armed conflicts and violent incidents conducted by various armed forces. The number of IDPs remained high at 1.7 million, including 128,782 newly displaced in the first quarter of the year. The Lord's Resistance Army (LRA), which continued to commit serious human and humanitarian rights violations, represented a major threat in the border regions with the Central African Republic and South Sudan. Between January and August, 254 attacks by LRA against civilians were reported, and some 440,000 people were considered as displaced or refugees at the end of the year due to LRA activities. In the south-west, along the border with Angola, the humanitarian situation remained alarming due to the expulsion of Congolese immigrants by Angolan authorities. The result of humanitarian assistance fell short of expectations, mainly due to constraints such as insecurity, inaccessibility of territories, and lack of infrastructure and funding.

Namibia

On 29 March, the Government of Namibia declared a national emergency to respond to large-scale flooding in its seven northern regions (Caprivi, Kavango, Kunene, Ohangwena, Omusati, Oshana, Oshikoto) and requested support from partners. At the onset of the floods, the Government provided 30 million Namibian dollars (approximately $4.5 million) and established the Floods Emergency Management Coordination to synchronize the emergency response in the affected regions. Agencies carried out a joint rapid assessment, the results of which underpinned the initial Flash Appeal launched on 14 April, requesting $2,310,450 for emergency response. The amount was later revised to $3,798,201, of which 44 per cent ($1,682,185) was received. As of August, 134,219 people were affected, amounting to 31 per cent of the total population in the concerned regions. A total of 106 people were reported drowned and about 40,600 people were displaced, with up to 17,500 people in 78 relocation centres. Agriculture—the main livelihood of most of the affected communities—was disrupted and basic economic infrastructure was damaged. While initial intervention in the relocation camps helped to avert a potential health crisis due to possible disease outbreak, some of the health services were inaccessible and immunization programmes disrupted. After floodwaters receded in July, humanitarian efforts focused on providing basic life-saving assistance to those in relocation sites, and assisting returnees in reconstructing their livelihoods.

South Sudan

The UN Consolidated Appeal for South Sudan in 2011 sought $619.7 million, of which 61 per cent ($377.8 million) was received.

South Sudan's January referendum and the subsequent preparations for secession on 9 July dominated the political landscape in the first half of the year. The post-independence period ushered in a number of changes, including the appointment of a new government and the deployment of a new peacekeeping mission (see p. 189). A number of issues related to the Comprehensive Peace Agreement [YUN 2005, p. 301] were still pending, including border demarcation, agreement on wealth-sharing and agreement on the status of Abyei. The situation remained fragile, with increased insecurity, ongoing displacement, underlying vulnerability and rising food security concerns generating high humanitarian needs throughout the year. The humanitarian community continued to operate across the country's ten states and responded to new emergencies, including the influx of over 110,000 displaced people from the Abyei area in May and more than 347,300 South Sudanese returnees from the Sudan, high levels of insecurity-induced displacement, and outbreaks of diseases. The majority of the received funds were directed towards food security and livelihoods; health; common services and coordination; non-food items and emergency shelter; nutrition; and water, sanitation and hygiene. The operating environment remained challenging, and a rise in interference in aid operations, primarily by military actors, imposed serious costs on the relief effort in terms of delays, lost funds and lost supplies, and by affecting the safety and security of humanitarian personnel.

Sudan

The UN Consolidated Appeal for Sudan in 2011 sought $1.1 billion, of which 65 per cent ($741.5 million) was received.

The Sudan faced significant socioeconomic, political and security challenges during the year. While the separation of South Sudan in July was relatively peaceful and Southern Sudanese residing in the Sudan continued to return, outbreaks of fighting in Abyei, Southern Kordofan and Blue Nile states led to large-scale displacement and severely affected local populations. The bulk of humanitarian needs continued to be concentrated in Darfur, the three Protocol Areas, Khartoum state and parts of Eastern Sudan. Fighting between the Sudanese armed forces and armed movements reportedly resulted in 355 fatalities between January and October. Up to 1.9 million people were estimated to remain displaced throughout Darfur, relying on humanitarian agencies to provide basic services. Humanitarian actors continued to face varying constraints on humanitarian access—particularly in areas under the control of armed opposition movements—as well as restrictions on the movement of humanitarian personnel and assets, including medical supplies, fuel, and other items necessary to sustain humanitarian activities.

Uganda

Based on consultations with the Government of Uganda, the United Nations, the non-governmental community and donor representatives, the Humanitarian Country Team decided in August 2010 that the humanitarian situation in Uganda would no longer warrant a CAP. Instead, it was agreed that an Inter-Agency Working Group, with participation of the Office of the Prime Minister, should develop a humanitarian profile for Uganda as a tool to guide decisions on humanitarian action.

As at November, there were no terrorist attacks in Uganda despite several alerts. The February–March national and local government elections were accompanied by some localized violence but concluded as planned. Although the natural disasters experienced in 2011 were less severe than those of the previous year, vulnerability to natural disasters remained a key humanitarian concern, with 15,650 households affected by flooding and landslides. In line with the overall improvement of the humanitarian situation, ocha Uganda phased down and closed its country office at the end of the year.

Zimbabwe

The UN Consolidated Appeal for Zimbabwe in 2011 sought $478.6 million, of which 46 per cent ($221.7 million) was received.

The humanitarian situation continued to be stable, but elements of fragility remained cause for concern in key sectors such as food security, health and nutrition, and water, sanitation and hygiene. The food security situation improved slightly during the year due to increased acreage and timely agricultural inputs and extension support provided by all humanitarian stakeholders. Uneven rainfall distribution and a dry spell in the agricultural season, however, affected six of the country's ten provinces. Hence, rates for chronic and acute child malnutrition stood at 35 per cent and 2.4 per cent, respectively. A third of rural Zimbabweans continued to drink from unprotected water sources and were thus exposed to water-borne diseases. Key priorities of humanitarian assistance were improving food security levels; addressing the needs of asylum seekers, migrants and other vulnerable groups; prevention of and rapid response to disease outbreaks; and response to natural disasters.

West Africa

The UN Consolidated Appeal for West Africa in 2011 sought $712.2 million to assist Benin, Burkina Faso, Cape Verde, Côte d'Ivoire, the Gambia, Ghana, Guinea, Guinea-Bissau, Liberia, Mali, Mauritania, Nigeria, Senegal, Sierra Leone and Togo. Forty per cent ($286.8 million) of the requested amount was received, leaving the regional CAP for West Africa one of the least-funded appeals in 2011.

Communities in West Africa continued to be threatened by the compounded effects of climate change; natural disasters like floods and droughts; demographic change; epidemics; urbanization; acute and chronic malnutrition; chronic poverty; and violent conflicts related to political, social and economic tensions. Countries in the region struggled to build capacities to better respond to humanitarian needs and accelerate overall human development by addressing issues of stability, rehabilitation from conflict and natural disasters, and securing resources for short- and long-term needs. From the beginning of the year, the political crisis in Côte d'Ivoire (see p. 140) was prominent on the humanitarian agenda. As of 3 June, and despite large scale efforts of the humanitarian community, approximately 500,000 IDPs, 135,000 third-country nationals and 212,000 refugees needed humanitarian aid in Côte d'Ivoire and neighbouring countries, such as Ghana, Guinea, Liberia, Mali and

Togo. To address the needs of the affected populations, humanitarian actors developed two separate Emergency Humanitarian Action Plans to complement the Regional CAP: the Emergency Humanitarian Action Plan for Côte d'Ivoire and four of its neighbouring countries (Burkina Faso, Ghana, Guinea and Mali) and the Emergency Humanitarian Action Plan Liberia (see below).

Côte d'Ivoire and neighbouring countries

The Emergency Humanitarian Action Plan for Côte d'Ivoire, Burkina Faso, Ghana, Guinea and Mali, requesting $292 million, was designed to allow humanitarian actors to reinforce their logistical capacities, level of preparedness, and coordination so as to respond to the actual and potential humanitarian needs of up to two million people in Côte d'Ivoire, as well as up to 100,000 refugees and other vulnerable groups, including 420,000 returnees and third country nationals. Despite significant improvements in the security situation in most parts of Côte d'Ivoire following the arrest of former President Laurent Gbagbo on 11 April and the swearing-in of President Alassane Ouattara, violent attacks on civilians by militia remnants and inter-ethnic confrontations continued in the south-west along the border with Liberia. According to the Office of the United Nations High Commissioner for Refugees, the number of asylum seekers in Ghana increased almost five-fold from 3,240 people at the end of March to 16,720 people as of 15 June. Access to food, proper health care, education, clean water, sanitation and income-generating activities was of great concern for the displaced populations and also for host communities. Humanitarian activities focused on four strategic objectives: reducing excess mortality and morbidity in crisis situations, reinforcing livelihoods of the ones most affected by slow or sudden-onset crisis, ensuring humanitarian access and improving protection of vulnerable people, and strengthening coordination and preparedness of emergencies at national and regional levels.

Liberia

The UN Emergency Humanitarian Action Plan for Liberia sought $166.7 million, of which 59 per cent ($99 million) was received.

The ongoing post-electoral crisis in Côte d'Ivoire had huge humanitarian implications for the lives and livelihoods of people in the region as a whole, and Liberia in particular. The humanitarian community immediately intervened to support the Government in addressing the needs of thousands of Ivorian families seeking refuge along the Liberian border. While life-saving assistance was being scaled up to meet the primary needs of the refugees, the political crisis in Côte d'Ivoire further deteriorated. As at 24 March, over 93,000 Ivorian refugees had been registered in Liberia, with more than half of them crossing since 24 February. UNHCR and the Government, together with other humanitarian actors, worked to provide clean water, shelter, food, health, protection, sanitation, education and security. The arrest of former Ivorian President Gbagbo resulted in the voluntary return of up to 96,000 registered Ivorian refugees between April and October. Nevertheless, by mid-November, some 47,500 refugees were still in camps and relocation villages, while about 90,000 refugees were residing in host families.

Niger

The UN Consolidated Appeal for Niger sought $215.9 million, of which 54 per cent ($116.1 million) was received.

In 2011, Niger occupied rank 186 of 187 according to the Human Development Index, with 43.1 per cent of the population living below the poverty line. An insufficient agricultural performance in 2009 had led to a further deterioration of Niger's fragile agricultural sector and exposed nearly half of the population to moderate or severe food insecurity. Efforts by the Government and its technical and financial partners and a better agricultural performance in 2010–2011 helped improve the food security situation. In February, however, a new humanitarian issue emerged as a result of the armed conflict and social turmoil in Côte d'Ivoire, Libya and Nigeria. Niger was particularly affected from mid-February to mid-October, when some 246,900 Nigerien migrants were forced to return to their country. The situation was further exacerbated by recurring factors such as diseases, floods and bushfires. In addition, during the first five months of the year, some 1,200 people were affected by meningitis, 2,100 by cholera and 10,500 by measles. Despite efforts to foster development, a significant part of the population remained dependent on humanitarian assistance.

Horn of Africa

In 2011, the Horn of Africa experienced the year's most severe food crisis in the world, with over 12 million people in Djibouti, Ethiopia, Kenya and Somalia severely affected and in urgent need of humanitarian aid. The United Nations declared famine in parts of Somalia, and large parts of Djibouti, Ethiopia and Kenya were suffering from severe food insecurity as a result of drought, high food prices, and significant inflows of refugees fleeing the drought in Somalia. With most of the elements of the humanitarian plans already in place (see p. 885), drafting a new, regional, consolidated appeal for the emergency was not recommended.

International meetings. International efforts in response to the drought included the Organization of Islamic Cooperation pledging meeting on Somalia (Istanbul, Turkey, 17 August), and the African Union Pledging Conference (Addis Ababa, Ethiopia, 25 August), where leaders made pledges of more than $350 million.

The Intergovernmental Authority on Development (IGAD) and the Heads of State of the East African Community, at a joint Summit on the Horn of Africa crisis (Nairobi, 8–9 September), adopted a Joint Declaration, launching the Initiative to End Drought Emergencies in the Horn of Africa and mandating IGAD to lead and coordinate its implementation through the Regional Disaster Resilience and Sustainability Platform. The Platform was designed to play a key role in mobilizing human, physical and financial resources and coordinating the implementation of priority regional disaster risk reduction and dry land development projects. The Summit also supported the Dry land Initiative that was launched by six countries (Djibouti, Ethiopia, Kenya, Somalia, South Sudan, Uganda) to promote integrated rural development.

More than $200 million in new aid was pledged at a United Nations mini-summit (New York, 24 September) held to raise awareness on the region's humanitarian crisis and help tackle the root causes of its recurring drought-related food shortages.

Furthermore, IGAD and the African Development Bank held a joint workshop on livestock development and drought preparedness in the Horn of Africa (Djibouti, 4–15 November).

GENERAL ASSEMBLY ACTION

On 15 December [meeting 86], the General Assembly adopted **resolution 66/120** [draft: A/66/L.29 & Add.1] without vote [agenda item 70].

Strengthening humanitarian assistance, emergency relief and rehabilitation in response to the severe drought in the Horn of Africa region

The General Assembly,

Recalling its resolution 46/182 of 19 December 1991 and other relevant General Assembly and Economic and Social Council resolutions,

Reaffirming the principles of neutrality, humanity, impartiality and independence for the provision of humanitarian assistance, and the need for all actors engaged in the provision of humanitarian assistance in situations of complex emergencies and natural disasters to promote and fully respect these principles,

Emphasizing that the affected State has primary responsibility for the initiation, organization, coordination and implementation of humanitarian assistance within its territory and for facilitation of the work of humanitarian organizations in mitigating the consequences of natural disasters,

Recalling the Updated Comprehensive Framework for Action produced by the United Nations system High-level Task Force on the Global Food Security Crisis which, among other things, emphasized the twin-track approach of addressing both the immediate humanitarian food crisis and the need for building long-term resilience to contribute to food and nutrition security,

Deeply concerned about the critical humanitarian situation in the Horn of Africa region, where the United Nations has declared a state of famine in parts of Somalia, while other parts of Somalia and parts of Ethiopia, Kenya and Djibouti are suffering severe food insecurity and, altogether, over 13 million people are in need of assistance that saves lives and reduces suffering,

Deeply concerned also about the protracted armed conflict in Somalia, including acts by armed groups to prevent affected populations from receiving or, where necessary, seeking humanitarian assistance, as well as to obstruct or prevent humanitarian personnel and United Nations and associated personnel from discharging their humanitarian functions,

Deeply regretting the loss of human lives and suffering, and conscious of the huge loss in crops and livestock sustained and the negative impact on the environment of the drought and famine situation in the Horn of Africa region,

Underlining the urgent need for humanitarian assistance and continued relief, rehabilitation and livelihood assistance, based on assessed needs of members of vulnerable communities, such as destitute pastoralists and farmers, refugees and internally displaced persons,

Highlighting the fact that the humanitarian crisis in the Horn of Africa, although exceptionally acute at this time, is a protracted crisis that requires continued commitments by host Governments, the United Nations, international and regional organizations, civil society groups and donors to address humanitarian and developmental challenges,

Welcoming the efforts of the Governments and people of the Horn of Africa region to protect and provide humanitarian assistance to the victims of drought and famine, and welcoming also regional initiatives to address the present humanitarian crisis, build resilience and prevent drought disasters, including the Intergovernmental Authority on Development and East African Community joint summit on the Horn of Africa crisis, held in Nairobi on 8 and 9 September 2011, the African Union pledging conference for the Horn of Africa, held in Addis Ababa on 25 August 2011, and the Organization of Islamic Cooperation pledging meeting on Somalia, held in Istanbul, Turkey, on 17 August 2011, and their outcomes,

Welcoming also the holding and outcome of the ministerial mini-summit on the humanitarian response to the Horn of Africa crisis, held in New York on 24 September 2011,

Welcoming further the efforts and assistance of the international community, including donors, the United Nations system, regional organizations, international agencies, and the International Red Cross and Red Crescent Movement, as well as non-governmental organizations and private sector entities, in providing relief and in supplementing the efforts of the Governments and people of the Horn of Africa region to combat famine and other effects of drought and food insecurity,

Recognizing that in strengthening the coordination of humanitarian assistance in the field, United Nations organizations should continue to work in close coordination with national Governments,

1. *Expresses its solidarity, sympathy and support* for the people and Governments of the Horn of Africa region affected by the drought and famine conditions;

2. *Commends* steps taken by the Governments of those affected countries to accommodate refugees, and calls upon the United Nations to continue to work closely with the Governments concerned and other partners in providing necessary assistance to refugees and support to host communities, as appropriate;

3. *Expresses its appreciation* to the international community, including Governments, the United Nations system, regional organizations, international agencies and the International Red Cross and Red Crescent Movement, as well as non-governmental organizations and private sector entities, that are providing emergency relief to the affected populations;

4. *Expresses its appreciation* to the Secretary-General, the Emergency Relief Coordinator, the Office for the Coordination of Humanitarian Affairs of the Secretariat and the United Nations funds and programmes, as well as other humanitarian organizations, for their response, and underlines the urgent need to continue to scale up assistance aimed at alleviating the consequences of the drought in the most affected areas in the Horn of Africa region and to build resilience in the longer term;

5. *Urges* the international community, including relevant international and regional organizations, as well as the private sector and civil society, to continue providing humanitarian assistance and to make contributions to humanitarian funding mechanisms, in response to relevant appeals;

6. *Requests* the Emergency Relief Coordinator to continue to lead the efforts to strengthen the coordination of humanitarian assistance and promote partnerships among humanitarian and development actors, and urges relevant United Nations and other relevant intergovernmental organizations, as well as other humanitarian and relevant development actors, including civil society, to continue to work with the Office for the Coordination of Humanitarian Affairs to enhance the coordination, effectiveness and efficiency of humanitarian assistance;

7. *Encourages* States and other actors providing humanitarian assistance to improve cooperation with the Office for the Coordination of Humanitarian Affairs so as to enhance the coordination, effectiveness and efficiency of humanitarian assistance to the Horn of Africa;

8. *Requests* the Secretary-General and all the organs and bodies of the United Nations system, international financial institutions and development agencies to assist the countries of the Horn of Africa region whenever possible through continued effective humanitarian, technical and financial assistance that contributes to building resilience and overcoming the humanitarian situation, in particular food insecurity and chronic water deficiency in the short, medium and long term, in conformity with the priorities identified at the national level;

9. *Calls upon* all States to maintain the momentum and political commitment shown at the joint summit on the Horn of Africa crisis to addressing the underlying causes of vulnerability in drought-prone areas and strengthening the resilience of members of drought-affected communities, including pastoralists and agro-pastoralists, through the prioritization and integration of risk-reduction activities, including water management, agricultural development and social protection, into development policies, planning and national resource allocations, and in this regard calls upon the international community to continue to support those efforts;

10. *Requests* the relevant organs and organizations of the United Nations system and other multilateral organizations to continue to maintain appropriate support and assistance to national and regional efforts towards strengthening disaster risk reduction, including early warning, disaster preparedness and health and nutrition surveillance capacities of the countries affected;

11. *Strongly condemns* the expulsion of humanitarian organizations, the ban on the activities of humanitarian personnel, and the targeting, hindering or prevention of the delivery of humanitarian assistance in Somalia by armed groups, and deplores any attacks on humanitarian personnel;

12. *Calls upon* all States and parties to cooperate fully with the United Nations and other humanitarian agencies and organizations, in conformity with the relevant provisions of international law and national laws, and to ensure the safe and unhindered access of humanitarian personnel, as well as delivery of supplies and equipment, in order to allow such personnel to save lives and efficiently perform their task of assisting affected civilian populations, including refugees and internally displaced persons;

13. *Requests* the Secretary-General to report to the General Assembly at its sixty-seventh session on the implementation of the present resolution under the sub-item entitled "Strengthening of the coordination of emergency humanitarian assistance of the United Nations".

Djibouti

The Djibouti Drought Appeal, which started in October 2010 and was designed to run for 15 months sought $33.3 million, of which 58 per cent ($19.4 million) was received.

In 2011, insufficient rainfall since 2005 [YUN 2005, p. 1031] had had a direct and life-threatening impact upon the most vulnerable, particularly pastoralists and rural dwellers. Consecutive drought led to further depletion of water reserves, massive loss of livestock, increased malnutrition (especially among children under five), and associated health problems. Furthermore, the country was confronted with a significant rise in the number of refugees due to the increasing violence and instability in south-central Somalia, as well as continued high prices of food staples, exacerbating the problem of malnutrition. The Drought Appeal for Djibouti was based on three main strategic priorities: providing humanitarian assistance to the severely drought-affected population; ensuring their socioeconomic stability; and strengthening the resilience, preparedness and response capacity of the drought-affected communities.

Kenya

In 2011, as the crisis in Somalia escalated and drought conditions in Kenya intensified, humanitarian partners revised the 2011+Kenya Emergency Humanitarian Response Plan launched in 2010 [YUN

2010, p. 903] to request $741.8 million—the largest amount ever requested for Kenya through a consolidated appeal mechanism—of which 71 per cent ($529.5 million) was received. On 30 May, the Government declared the drought a national disaster, as malnutrition rates exceeded emergency thresholds in a number of districts. The humanitarian partners developed a longer-term appeal strategy covering three years, from 2011 to 2013, for Kenya to address immediate emergency priorities as well as medium- to longer-term requirements. The cumulative effects of poor or failed rainfall seasons, volatile food and fuel prices, constant refugee influx with its impact on host communities, and overall protection and security concerns remained challenges for the humanitarian situation throughout the year.

Somalia

The Consolidated Appeal for Somalia, which sought $1 billion in 2011, received 87 per cent ($868.1 million) of the requested amount.

The year 2011 marked 20 years of crisis in Somalia [YUN 1991, p. 427]. During that period, the country lacked a central government, was embroiled in civil war and a large part of the population suffered from a humanitarian crisis. In 2011, Somalia began sliding deeper into crisis due to a combination of drought, rising food prices and conflict, which led to population displacement and increased vulnerability. Drought was the main reason for displacement in July and August. Additionally, fighting erupted between Transitional Federal Government allied forces and Al Shabaab in parts of southern Somalia, resulting in a number of insecurity-related displacements and loss of livelihoods. On 20 July, the United Nations declared famine for the first time since 1991–1992 [YUN 1992, p. 593] in two regions of Somalia, where acute malnutrition rates among children exceeded 30 per cent. By September 2011, the United Nations declared famine in four more regions, as the situation became the worst humanitarian emergency in the world. Four million Somalis, accounting for almost two thirds of the population, were in urgent need of humanitarian assistance. Due to timely support from donors, humanitarian response was scaled up significantly in the second half of the year, and by November, three regions were lifted out of famine.

North Africa

Libyan Arab Jamahiriya

The UN Regional Flash Appeal for the Libyan Crisis, operating from March to December, sought $336.2 million, of which 83 per cent ($279.2 million) was received.

The uprising in Libya (see p. 266) that began on 16 February led to a continuing political and security crisis wherein the Government maintained partial control of the western part of the country, while the eastern part was largely under the control of anti-government forces. As of 18 May, over 803,000 people had fled the country since the start of the conflict, including 296,500 Libyans, 94,884 Egyptians, 58,904 Nigeriens, 41,322 Tunisians, 24,365 Chadians and over 271,200 third-country nationals. While the initial appeal of 7 March focused on evacuation, new information about the crisis led the Humanitarian Country Team to reprioritize its actions and strategic objectives in mid-May. The revised focus was placed on addressing the crisis inside Libya, while taking into account the needs of people who had left the country or were stranded at borders, and communities that were hosting displaced people. Restricted access into Libya limited the humanitarian community's ability to assess needs and develop a meaningful understanding of the situation inside the country. Following an agreement reached with the Government on 17 April, the United Nations established a humanitarian presence in both Benghazi and Tripoli; however, following crowd attacks on UN and diplomatic buildings on 1 May, the UN international presence in Tripoli had to be relocated for security reasons.

Asia

Afghanistan

The 2011 UN Consolidated Appeal for Afghanistan sought $582.3 million, of which 73 per cent ($422.8 million) was received.

The appeal took into account the root causes of humanitarian crises in Afghanistan, including ongoing conflict [YUN 2001, p. 255] and endemic natural disasters, combined with limited humanitarian access, human rights abuses, lack of good governance and widespread corruption, as well as a slow-moving economy and underdevelopment.

An estimated 450,000 individuals were displaced as at September as a result of the protracted conflict. Furthermore, UNHCR observed that more than 43 per cent of UNHCR-assisted refugee returnee hosting villages failed to reintegrate and had poor living standards. While the initial CAP placed greater emphasis on life-saving and livelihood-saving activities as well as strengthening emergency preparedness and contingency planning, an Emergency Revision was launched on 30 September. The revised appeal responded to a drought in the north, northeast and west of Afghanistan, which left an estimated 2.6 million people facing acute food security needs. The drought-related projects amounted to $142 million, inclusive of the clusters food security and agriculture; water, sanitation and hygiene; nutrition; health; and emergency shelter and non-food items. Thirty-one new projects were added toward the provision of humanitarian assistance and protection to victims of conflict and natural disasters. Access to most parts of the country was impaired by the high levels of insecurity combined with a rugged landscape, severe climate and the chronically under-developed basic infrastructure, and thus remained one of the main challenges for humanitarian actors.

Iraq

The 2011 Regional Response Plan for Iraqi Refugees (RRP) sought $292 million, of which 35 per cent ($103 million) was received by 30 June.

The RRP provided a comprehensive and strategic framework for responding to the immediate needs of Iraqi refugees in 12 countries: Egypt, Iran, Jordan, Lebanon, Syria, Turkey and the Gulf Cooperation Council countries. In 2011, all countries experienced new arrivals, especially Jordan, Lebanon and Syria, which continued to host the vast majority of the Iraqi refugees. As of 31 October, 176,982 Iraqis were registered with UNHCR. Although the situation in Iraq had substantially improved since 2008, targeted attacks against individuals and the withdrawal of United States forces raised further questions amongst refugees in relation to the viability of return.

Occupied Palestinian Territory

The UN Consolidated Appeal for the Occupied Palestinian Territory, which sought $536.9 million in 2011, received 57 per cent ($305.4 million) of the requested amount.

The appeal focused on the humanitarian situation of Palestinian communities in the Gaza Strip, East Jerusalem, Area C of the West Bank and areas isolated by the Barrier. The year was marked by significant political developments in the region and in the Occupied Palestinian Territory. Those included a reconciliation agreement reached between the two main political factions, Fatah and Hamas, in May (see p. 406), a Palestine application for full membership at the United Nations in September (see p. 409), and a subsequent campaign to join individual UN organizations. The main features of the Israeli occupation, however, remained in place and consequently the humanitarian needs in the Occupied Palestinian Territory did not fundamentally change. Serious protection and human rights issues, limited access to essential services and entrenched levels of food insecurity continued to characterize the lives of many Palestinians. Two-thirds of the Palestinians in Gaza and one-third in the West Bank were unable to secure an adequate diet without assistance. Between 1 January and 30 September, 98 Palestinians were killed and 1,727 were injured in direct conflict-related incidents, which represented a nearly 30 per cent increase in deaths and injuries from the same period in 2010. Eleven Israelis were killed and 106 injured in violent attacks by and clashes with Palestinians. Humanitarian agencies faced significant obstacles regarding staff movement and day-to-day operations in the territory, hampering the provision of aid and undermining the effectiveness of assistance to vulnerable Palestinians.

Pakistan

Report of Secretary-General. In response to General Assembly resolution 64/294 [YUN 2010, p. 933], the Secretary-General in March submitted a report [A/65/773] on strengthening emergency relief, rehabilitation, reconstruction and prevention in the wake of devastating floods in Pakistan. The report covered the period from August 2010 to February 2011 and described the impact of the disaster, focusing on the humanitarian relief, rehabilitation and reconstruction assistance supplied by the United Nations and its partners. It also described some of the critical humanitarian challenges as well as efforts in disaster risk reduction and preparedness.

Over the course of the 2010 July and August monsoon season, Pakistan experienced the worst floods in its history [YUN 2010, p. 933]. At the request of the Government, the international community stepped in to support the national response efforts. The United Nations exhibited its solidarity with and commitment to Pakistan with a number of high-level visits. The Secretary-General visited the flood-affected areas in August and appointed Rauf Engin Soysal (Turkey) to succeed Jean-Maurice Ripert (France) as his Special Envoy for Assistance to Pakistan in September to oversee the coordination of international assistance. High-level meetings included the 110th plenary meeting of the sixty-fourth session of the General Assembly, held on 19 August 2010, and the High-level Ministerial Meeting of Member States on the flood emergency in Pakistan, held on 19 September 2010. The Third Ministerial Meeting of the Friends of Democratic Pakistan (Brussels, 15 October 2010) dedicated part of its discussions to the floods, as did the Pakistan Development Forum (Islamabad, 14–15 November 2010). The Pakistan Initial Floods Emergency Response Plan, launched on 11 August 2010, had sought $459 million to respond to the immediate relief needs of flood-affected people. The Pakistan Floods Relief and Early Recovery Response Plan [YUN 2010, p. 933], a revision of the Initial Plan, sought $1.93 billion to support the Government in addressing the residual relief needs for six months and early recovery needs of flood-affected families for 12 months up to August 2011. United Nations organizations in Pakistan had received over $51 million from the Central Emergency Response Fund in 2010—the largest amount allocated to a single country over the course of one year.

As at 31 January 2011, approximately 6 million people had received food assistance, 9.3 million people had essential medication needs covered, and almost 900,000 households had been provided with emergency shelter.

In January, the Government shifted the focus from relief to recovery and declared the relief phase of the response plan to be at an end. The United Nations, through the One UN Disaster Risk Management Programme, continued to provide technical support in establishing and strengthening policy, legal and institutional arrangements for disaster risk management.

Flood Rapid Response Plan. In August and September, heavy rains affected 5.4 million people in Pakistan, particularly in Sindh, where all 23 districts were afflicted. The Government, through the National Disaster Management Authority and the Armed Forces' logistical capacity, deployed rescue and life-saving relief operations. Access issues due to damaged infrastructure and continuing heavy rain, however, hampered the delivery of aid. In response to the Government's request for assistance on 6 September, the Humanitarian Country Team developed a Rapid Response Plan to address the needs of the population in support to the Government's relief interventions. The Plan sought $356.8 million, of which 44 per cent ($157.1 million) was received. The first phase focused on critical needs of the severely affected families in the areas of food security, safe drinking water and purification materials, sanitation and hygiene, emergency health services, and non-food items, along with critical early recovery, community restoration and capacity-building needs. The second phase was designed to provide a revised plan based on data collected from needs assessments.

Philippines

The Humanitarian Action Plan for Conflict-Affected Provinces of Mindanao sought $33.3 million, of which 54 per cent ($18 million) was received. It was launched in February to support humanitarian activities in six provinces of the southern Philippine island of Mindanao: Maguindanao, Lanao del Sur, Lanao del Norte, Sultan Kudarat, North Cotabato and South Cotabato, and mainly targeted IDPs displaced by the conflict that began in August 2008. After the suspension of military actions in July 2009, the security situation improved markedly, furthering the return and resettlement of IDPs. While the focus of humanitarian actions was on assistance in return sites, some people remained displaced due to security and safety concerns, lack of access to basic services, and lack of resources to rebuild damaged houses and livelihoods. In addition to the recurring displacements, many of the conflict-affected areas were prone to natural disasters.

On 16 December 2011, Tropical Storm Washi made landfall on the north-eastern coast of Mindanao. According to a 20 December report from the National Disaster Risk Reduction and Management Council, the storm and accompanying floods killed 957 people, with a further 49 reported missing and 1,582 injured. The Government and Humanitarian Country Team carried out joint rapid assessments, based on which the emergency revision of the initial 2012 Humanitarian Action Plan issued in December sought $28.6 million to support the Government in addressing the needs of those affected.

Sri Lanka

The UN Flash Appeal for Sri Lanka, operating from January to June, sought $46.4 million, of which 57 per cent ($26.6 million) was received.

Following the heavy rains in December 2010 that devastated districts throughout eastern, northern and north-central Sri Lanka, further rainfall after 30 January 2011 seriously damaged crops, farm and transportation infrastructure, and housing. According to the Disaster Management Centre of the Ministry of Disaster Management, over 1.1 million people were affected in the January floods, followed by 1.2 million in February; a total of 62 deaths were reported for both disasters. The Centre coordinated the flood response, and on 10 January, the Government officially requested UN relief assistance. An initial appeal was launched on 18 January based on joint Government-UN rapid needs assessments in the worst affected areas. The Appeal was later revised, focusing on immediate life-saving needs for the flood-affected people through June in five sectors: food, agriculture and livelihoods; WASH (water, sanitation and hygiene); shelter; health and nutrition; and education.

Joint Plan for Assistance. The Joint Plan for Assistance 2011 for the Northern Province of Sri Lanka sought $289.7 billion, of which 34 per cent ($99.5 million) was received. The Plan was jointly designed by the Government, the United Nations and its agencies, national and international non-governmental organizations (NGOs), and international organizations. Since the end of the conflict in May 2009 [YUN 2009, p. 898], the humanitarian community worked in support of the Government to ensure the safe and dignified return of IDPs. Activities included maintenance of welfare centres and an effective return process leading to permanent resettlement.

Yemen

The UN Consolidated Appeal for Yemen in 2011 sought $292.3 million, of which 67 per cent ($194.4 million) was received.

The appeal identified five key drivers of humanitarian need: continuing and unpredictable civil unrest; ongoing conflict in northern and southern Yemen; the continually increasing presence of refugees, migrants and third-country nationals; rises in the cost of living; and a crisis in provision of basic services. From February, the Government was confronted with nationwide protests, in some instances involving serious levels of violence, calling for regime change and reform. In the north, six rounds of conflict between the Al Houthi group and the Government led to the displacement of more than 300,000 people, while in the south, fighting between Government security forces and insurgents from June caused nearly 90,000 new displacements. Furthermore, essential Government services were reduced or eliminated, which exacerbated severe and widespread chronic vulnerabilities in the country, particularly with regard to nutrition, food security, and access to water, social welfare and health care. Despite the political instability, the influx of refugees and asylum seekers from the Horn of Africa continued unabated in 2011, with 73,000 new arrivals as at September. They received assistance in the form of protection, shelter, water and sanitation, health, education, livelihoods and community services. Life-saving assistance was provided to 269,500 IDPs and returnees throughout the year, and slightly over one million food-insecure people were assisted between June and October.

Latin America and the Caribbean

Haiti

The UN Consolidated Appeal for Haiti in 2011 sought $382.4 million, of which 56 per cent ($214.7 million) was received.

The overall situation in Haiti continued to be one of large-scale displacement. The 2010 earthquake [YUN 2010, p. 907] had displaced around 2.1 million people, of whom 1.3 million were still residing in settlements at the end of 2010. During 2011, the food security situation deteriorated significantly, with 45 per cent of the population—4.5 million people—facing food insecurity. The CAP aimed to ensure continued humanitarian aid to the earthquake-affected people, to support the return of thousands of IDPs, and to contribute to the transition from emergency to longer-term recovery programmes. Following the cholera outbreak in October 2010 [ibid., p. 327], UN agencies and NGO partners issued an inter-cluster cholera response plan on 11 November, requesting $164 million in support of the efforts of the Government to mitigate the impact of the cholera outbreak. The emergency response fund received $81.6 million from 40 donors. As of June 2011, $74.8 million had been disbursed to fund 80 projects implemented by 51 partners. Due to joint efforts in sectors such as health, water, hygiene and sanitation, the mortality rate dropped from over 2.4 per cent in November 2010 to 1.4 per cent in September 2011.

Central America

On 10 October, Tropical Depression E-12 arrived in Central America, bringing unprecedented heavy rainfall. Almost two million people were affected by floods and landslides across the region, including in Costa Rica, El Salvador, Guatemala, Honduras, Mexico, Nicaragua and Panama. The Governments of El Salvador, Guatemala, Honduras and Nicaragua declared states of emergency.

El Salvador was particularly affected. According to the Economic Commission for Latin America and the Caribbean (ECLAC), damages and losses were estimated at over $840 million, equivalent to almost 4 per cent of the gross domestic product (GDP). The storm left 35 people dead, 59,854 people evacuated, and 54,903 people in emergency shelters. Following the request for international assistance by the Government, a Flash Appeal was launched on 25 October, seeking $14.8 million, of which 40 per cent ($6 million) was received.

The Government of Nicaragua requested assistance from the international community after declaring a state of emergency on 17 October. A Flash Appeal seeking $14.8 million—of which 36 per cent ($5.4 million) was received—was launched on 28 October. Main areas targeted by the appeal were related to water and sanitation in the shelters, health, food aid, agricultural livelihoods and early recovery.

Special Summit. In the wake of the disaster, the Heads of State and Government of the members of the Central American Integration System held a special summit (San Salvador, El Salvador, 25 October). Participants adopted the Declaration of Comalapa, which included the commitment to develop a permanent framework for the construction and reconstruction of infrastructure, taking into account the increasing impact of climate change. They further urged industrialized countries to significantly reduce their greenhouse gas emissions and to provide financial support for capacity-building and technology transfer in order to facilitate climate change mitigation and adaptation.

GENERAL ASSEMBLY ACTION

On 11 November [meeting 58], the General Assembly adopted **resolution 66/9** [draft: A/66/L.7 & Add.1] without vote [agenda item 70 (*a*)].

Emergency humanitarian assistance for the rehabilitation and reconstruction of Belize, Costa Rica, El Salvador, Guatemala, Honduras, Nicaragua and Panama

The General Assembly,

Recalling all relevant resolutions of the General Assembly on emergency humanitarian assistance, and reaffirming the principles of humanity, neutrality, impartiality and independence for the provision of humanitarian assistance,

Deeply disturbed by the loss of life that brought grief to so many families in Central America and by just how many people were affected by the Pacific tropical depression E-12 and the intense rainfall in Belize, Costa Rica, El Salvador, Guatemala, Honduras, Nicaragua and Panama from 10 to 19 October 2011,

Aware of the extensive material damage to crops, housing, basic infrastructure and tourist and other areas, which, inter alia, poses a severe threat to the food security of the people of Central America, particularly the poorest families, and of the adverse effects on economic activity and trade in the isthmus,

Also aware that the geography of Central American countries makes them especially vulnerable to the adverse effects of meteorological phenomena associated with climate change and other factors which, in recent years, have given rise to new risk scenarios, plunging the most vulnerable populations deeper into poverty and undermining efforts to reach the Millennium Development Goals and promote more sustainable development for the people of Central America,

Recognizing the efforts of the Central American Governments to minimize loss of life and provide speedy assistance to the stricken population,

Considering the Declaration of Comalapa adopted at the special summit of Heads of State and Government of the countries members of the Central American Integration System, held in San Salvador on 25 October 2011,

Also considering the enormous effort needed to rebuild the stricken areas and to address the serious situation left in the wake of a natural disaster which, over nine days, produced some of the heaviest rains ever seen in Central America, with twice the amount of rain recorded during hurricane Mitch in 1998, and that this effort will require the broad, coordinated and sustained support of the international community,

1. *Expresses its solidarity with and support* for the Governments and peoples of Belize, Costa Rica, El Salvador, Guatemala, Honduras, Nicaragua and Panama;

2. *Expresses its appreciation* to the members of the international community that have already provided timely assistance for rescue and aid efforts targeted at the stricken population, in particular, the Office for the Coordination of Humanitarian Affairs of the Secretariat and the United Nations Development Programme, and commends the efforts of the Emergency Relief Coordinator to strengthen the coordination of humanitarian assistance;

3. *Acknowledges* the efforts and progress made by Central American countries in strengthening their disaster-preparedness capacity, emphasizes the importance of investing in disaster risk reduction, and encourages the international community to continue to cooperate with the affected Governments towards this end;

4. *Appeals* to all Member States and all organs and agencies of the United Nations system, as well as the international financial and development institutions, to continue to cooperate with Belize, Costa Rica, El Salvador, Guatemala, Honduras, Nicaragua and Panama in their relief, rehabilitation and humanitarian assistance efforts and in rebuilding the region;

5. *Requests* the relevant organizations and bodies of the United Nations system and other multilateral organizations to support and assist national and regional capacity-building in the areas of natural disaster preparedness, prevention and mitigation and risk management in the above-mentioned countries according to needs and in the specialized institution of the Central American Integration System, the Coordination Centre for Natural Disaster Prevention in Central America;

6. *Requests* the Secretary-General to report to the General Assembly at its sixty-seventh session on the implementation of the present resolution and progress made in relief, rehabilitation and reconstruction efforts in the stricken countries.

Special economic assistance

African economic recovery and development

New Partnership for Africa's Development

The General Assembly in 2002, by resolution 57/7 [YUN 2002, p. 910], endorsed the Secretary-General's recommendation [ibid., p. 909] that the New Partnership for Africa's Development (NEPAD), adopted in 2001 by the Assembly of Heads of State and Government of the Organization of African Unity [YUN 2001, p. 900], should be the framework within which the international community should concentrate its efforts for Africa's development. During 2011, efforts continued to focus on UN and international support for NEPAD and its implementation.

Implementation and support for NEPAD

Report of Secretary-General. In response to a request of the Committee for Programme and Coordination (CPC) [YUN 2005, p. 1004], the Secretary-General in March submitted a report [E/AC.51/2011/4] on UN system support for NEPAD, which detailed work undertaken by various entities of the UN system since June 2010. The report was organized around nine thematic clusters corresponding to the Partnership's priorities and strategies: infrastructure development; governance; peace and security; agriculture, food security and rural development; industry, trade and market access; environment, population and urbanization; social and human development; science and technology; and communications, advocacy and outreach. In addition, four selected policy issues in the implementation of NEPAD were examined: strengthening of the cluster system and enhanced cooperation between the United Nations and the African Union; support for the mobilization of financial resources for NEPAD implementation; institutional support; and cross-cutting issues, such as the preparatory process of the Fourth United Nations Conference on the Least Developed Countries, gender-based violence and gender mainstreaming. The report also identified challenges and constraints faced by the UN system, in particular in the light of the recent crises in African countries.

The Secretary-General observed that the report coincided with the tenth anniversary of the adoption of NEPAD. Recommendations included ensuring appropriate human and financial resources to effectively implement cluster activities, strengthening UN system synergy through sharing of best practices and know-how, ensuring effective and results-based monitoring of the impact of cluster activities, and strengthening of the collaboration with non-United Nations development partners.

CPC action. CPC, at its fifty-first session (6 June–1 July) [A/66/16], noted that the Office of the Special Adviser on Africa was still not being led at the legislatively mandated level of Under-Secretary-General and urged the Secretary-General to fill the vacant post. It reaffirmed the urgent need for the Office of the Special Adviser to pursue the principles underpinning South-South cooperation in its efforts to advance the African agenda and the NEPAD objectives.

GENERAL ASSEMBLY ACTION

On 22 June [meeting 102], the General Assembly adopted **resolution 65/284** [draft: A/65/L.69/Rev.1 & Add.1] without vote [agenda item 62 (*a*)].

New Partnership for Africa's Development: progress in implementation and international support

The General Assembly,

Recalling its resolution 57/2 of 16 September 2002 on the United Nations Declaration on the New Partnership for Africa's Development,

Recalling also its resolution 57/7 of 4 November 2002 on the final review and appraisal of the United Nations New Agenda for the Development of Africa in the 1990s and support for the New Partnership for Africa's Development and resolutions 58/233 of 23 December 2003, 59/254 of 23 December 2004, 60/222 of 23 December 2005, 61/229 of 22 December 2006, 62/179 of 19 December 2007, 63/267 of 31 March 2009 and 64/258 of 16 March 2010 entitled "New Partnership for Africa's Development: progress in implementation and international support",

Recalling further the 2005 World Summit Outcome, including the recognition of the need to meet the special needs of Africa, and recalling also its resolution 60/265 of 30 June 2006,

Recalling the political declaration on Africa's development needs, adopted at the high-level meeting on Africa's development needs on 22 September 2008,

Recalling also the High-level Plenary Meeting of the General Assembly on the Millennium Development Goals and its outcome document, including the recognition that more attention should be given to Africa, especially to those countries most off track to achieve the Millennium Development Goals by 2015,

Bearing in mind that African countries have primary responsibility for their own economic and social development and that the role of national policies and development strategies cannot be overemphasized, and bearing in mind also the need for their development efforts to be supported by an enabling international economic environment, and in this regard recalling the support given by the International Conference on Financing for Development to the New Partnership,

Emphasizing that a favourable national and international environment for Africa's growth and development is important for progress in the implementation of the New Partnership,

Stressing the need to implement all commitments by the international community regarding the economic and social development of Africa,

1. *Welcomes* the eighth consolidated report of the Secretary-General;
2. *Takes note* of the report of the Secretary-General on a monitoring mechanism to review commitments towards Africa's development needs;
3. *Reaffirms its full support* for the implementation of the New Partnership for Africa's Development;
4. *Reaffirms its commitment* to the full implementation of the political declaration on Africa's development needs, as reaffirmed in the Doha Declaration on Financing for Development, adopted as the outcome document of the Follow-up International Conference on Financing for Development to Review the Implementation of the Monterrey Consensus, held in Doha from 29 November to 2 December 2008;
5. *Recognizes* the progress made in the implementation of the New Partnership as well as regional and international support for the New Partnership, while acknowledging that much needs to be done in its implementation;
6. *Takes note* of the Political Declaration on HIV and AIDS: Intensifying Our Efforts to Eliminate HIV and AIDS, adopted at the high-level meeting on HIV/AIDS on 10 June 2011;
7. *Recognizes* that HIV/AIDS, malaria, tuberculosis and other infectious diseases pose severe risks for the entire world and serious challenges to the achievement of development goals;
8. *Recalls*, in this regard, the commitment to pursue all necessary efforts to scale up support for nationally driven, sustainable and comprehensive responses in Africa to achieve broad multisectoral coverage for prevention, treatment, care and support, with the full and active participation of people living with HIV, vulnerable groups, most affected communities, civil society and the private sector, towards achieving the goal of universal access to comprehensive prevention programmes, treatment, care and support by 2010, in line with the Political Declaration on HIV/AIDS of 2 June 2006;

9. *Reaffirms its commitment* to redouble efforts to achieve universal access to HIV/AIDS prevention, treatment, care and support services as an essential step in achieving Millennium Development Goal 6 and as a contribution to reaching the other Millennium Development Goals;

10. *Reaffirms* the resolve to provide assistance for prevention and care, with the aim of ensuring an HIV/AIDS-, malaria- and tuberculosis-free Africa, by addressing the needs of all, in particular the needs of women, children and young people, and by achieving as closely as possible the goal of universal access to comprehensive HIV/AIDS prevention programmes, treatment, care and support in African countries, to accelerate and intensify efforts to expand access to affordable and quality medicines in Africa, including antiretroviral drugs, inter alia, by encouraging pharmaceutical companies to make drugs available, and to ensure strengthened global partnership and increased bilateral and multilateral assistance, where possible on a grant basis, to combat HIV/AIDS, malaria, tuberculosis and other infectious diseases in Africa through the strengthening of health systems;

11. *Expresses deep concern* about the ongoing adverse impacts of crises, including the global financial and economic crisis, volatile energy and food prices and ongoing concerns over food security, as well as the increasing challenges posed by climate change, drought, land degradation, desertification and the loss of biodiversity, and the serious challenges these impacts pose to the fight against poverty and hunger, which could further undermine the achievement of the internationally agreed development goals, including the Millennium Development Goals, particularly in Africa;

12. *Expresses grave concern* that Africa is among the hardest hit by the impact of the world financial and economic crisis, recognizes that, while growth is returning, there is a need to sustain the recovery, which is fragile and uneven, and therefore reaffirms that it will continue to support the special needs of Africa and take action to mitigate the multidimensional impacts of the crisis on the continent;

13. *Expresses concern* at Africa's disproportionately low share in the volume of international trade, which stands at only 2 per cent, and also expresses concern that, despite an overall increase in the nominal volume and share of official development assistance to Africa, such assistance will likely rise by just 1 per cent a year in real terms, compared to the average 13 per cent rate of growth over the past three years, and that, at this rate, any additional aid to African countries will be outpaced by population growth, the increased debt burden of some African countries, the rising unemployment rate, the fall in capital inflows and the significant fall in remittances to the continent as a result of the world financial and economic crisis, which have a negative impact on the hard-earned socio-economic and political gains that Africa has achieved in recent years;

14. *Notes* that foreign direct investment is a major source of financing for development, and in this regard calls upon developed countries to continue to devise source-country measures to encourage and facilitate the flow of foreign direct investment, inter alia, through the provision of export credits and other lending instruments, risk guarantees and business development services;

15. *Calls upon* developing countries and countries with economies in transition to continue their efforts to create a domestic environment conducive to attracting investments by, inter alia, achieving a transparent, stable and predictable investment climate with proper contract enforcement and respect for property rights;

16. *Stresses* the importance of enhancing efforts to mobilize investments from all sources in human resources and physical, environmental, institutional and social infrastructure;

17. *Reaffirms* the need to enhance the voice and participation of developing countries, including African countries, in international economic decision-making and norm-setting, notes recent steps being taken in this regard, and emphasizes in this context that the efforts to address the ongoing impact of the world economic and financial crisis should not lead to further marginalization of the African continent;

I

Actions by African countries and organizations

18. *Welcomes* the progress made by African countries in fulfilling their commitments in the implementation of the New Partnership to deepen democracy, human rights, good governance and sound economic management, and encourages African countries, with the participation of stakeholders, including civil society and the private sector, to continue their efforts in this regard by developing and strengthening institutions for governance, creating an environment conducive to involving the private sector, including small and medium-sized enterprises, in the New Partnership implementation process and to attracting foreign direct investment for the development of the region;

19. *Also welcomes* the integration of the New Partnership into the African Union structures and processes and the establishment of its Planning and Coordinating Agency as a technical body of the African Union;

20. *Notes with appreciation* the efforts exerted by the African Union and the regional economic communities in the area of economic integration, as well as ongoing efforts by the African Union in the operationalization of the provision contained in General Assembly resolutions 59/213 of 20 December 2004, 61/296 of 17 September 2007 and 63/310 of 14 September 2009, and stresses the key role of the United Nations system in supporting the African Union, in the social, economic and political fields and in the area of peace and security;

21. *Welcomes* the commendable progress that has been achieved in implementing the African Peer Review Mechanism, in particular the completion of the peer review process in thirteen countries, and welcomes the progress in implementing the national programmes of action resulting from these reviews, and in this regard urges African States that have not yet done so to consider joining the Mechanism process and to strengthen the Mechanism process for its efficient performance;

22. *Welcomes and appreciates* the continuing and increasing efforts of African countries in mainstreaming a gender perspective and the empowerment of women in the implementation of the New Partnership;

23. *Recognizes* the need for African countries to continue to coordinate, in accordance with their respective national strategies and priorities, all types of external support in order to integrate effectively such assistance into their development processes;

24. *Encourages* African countries to accelerate the achievement of the objective of food security in Africa, and welcomes the commitment made by African leaders to raise the share of agriculture and rural development in their budget expenditures, and in this regard reaffirms its support for, inter alia, the Comprehensive Africa Agriculture Development Programme and the outcome of the post-Abuja meeting of the International Technical Committee of the Food Security Summit, held in Addis Ababa in May 2007;

25. *Recognizes* the important role that African regional economic communities can play in the implementation of the New Partnership, and in this regard encourages African countries and the international community to give regional economic communities the support necessary to strengthen their capacity;

26. *Welcomes* the collaboration between the African Private Sector Forum and the United Nations Global Compact, and encourages the strengthening of this partnership in conjunction with the African Union Commission in support of the development of the African private sector and the promotion of public-private partnership projects and the achievement of the Millennium Development Goals, in line with the relevant executive decisions of the African Union;

27. *Encourages* African countries to design a coordinated and comprehensive continent-wide communications and outreach strategy to further enhance public awareness of the objectives and goals of the New Partnership;

28. *Also encourages* African countries to strengthen and expand local and transit infrastructure and to continue sharing best practices with a view to strengthening regional integration, and in this regard notes with appreciation the work of the high-level subcommittee of the African Union on the Presidential Infrastructure Champion Initiative, which seeks to further strengthen the development of infrastructure on the African continent in collaboration with relevant development partners;

II

Response of the international community

29. *Welcomes* the efforts by development partners to strengthen cooperation with the New Partnership;

30. *Recognizes* the important role that North-South, South-South and triangular cooperation can play in supporting Africa's development efforts, including in the implementation of the New Partnership, while bearing in mind that South-South cooperation is not a substitute for but rather a complement to North-South cooperation;

31. *Welcomes* the various important initiatives established between African countries and their development partners, as well as other initiatives, and emphasizes in this regard the importance of coordination in such initiatives on Africa and the need for their effective implementation;

32. *Urges* continued support of measures to address the challenges of poverty eradication and hunger, job creation and sustainable development in Africa, including, as appropriate, debt relief, improved market access, support for the private sector and entrepreneurship, fulfilment of commitments on official development assistance and increased flows of foreign direct investment, and transfer of technology;

33. *Recognizes* that Africa, which contributes the least to climate change, is one of the regions most vulnerable and most exposed to its adverse impacts, and in this regard calls upon the international community, in particular developed countries, to support Africa in its adaptation and sustainable development efforts through, inter alia, the transfer and deployment of technology, capacity-building and the provision of adequate and predictable new resources;

34. *Reiterates* the important role of trade as an engine of growth and development and its contribution to the attainment of the Millennium Development Goals, and emphasizes the need to resist protectionist tendencies and to rectify any trade-distorting measures already taken that are inconsistent with World Trade Organization rules, while recognizing the right of countries, in particular developing countries, to fully utilize their flexibilities consistent with their World Trade Organization commitments and obligations, and recognizes that the early and successful conclusion of the Doha Round of trade negotiations with a balanced, ambitious, comprehensive and development-oriented outcome would provide a much-needed impetus to international trade and contribute to economic growth and development;

35. *Also reiterates* the need for all countries and relevant multilateral institutions to continue efforts to enhance coherence in their trade policies towards African countries, and acknowledges the importance of efforts to fully integrate African countries into the international trading system and to build their capacity to compete through such initiatives as aid for trade and, given the world economic and financial crisis, the provision of assistance to address the adjustment challenges of trade liberalization;

36. *Calls for* a comprehensive and sustainable solution to the external debt problems of African countries, including cancellation or restructuring, as appropriate, and on a case-by-case basis, for heavily indebted African countries not part of the Heavily Indebted Poor Countries Initiative that have unsustainable debt burdens, and emphasizes the importance of debt sustainability;

37. *Recognizes* that the negative impact of the world financial and economic crisis on development is still unfolding and entails the possibility of undoing the progress towards achieving the Millennium Development Goals by 2015 and that it may threaten debt sustainability in some developing countries, inter alia, through its impact on the real economy and through the increase in borrowing undertaken in order to mitigate the negative impacts of the crisis;

38. *Expresses deep concern* at the fact that the commitment to double aid to Africa by 2010, as articulated at the Summit of the Group of Eight held at Gleneagles from 6 to 8 July 2005, was not entirely reached, and in this regard stresses the need to make rapid progress in order to fulfil the Gleneagles and other donors' substantial commitments to increase aid through a variety of means;

39. *Acknowledges* efforts by developed countries to increase resources for development, including commitments by some developed countries to increase official development assistance, and calls for the fulfilment of all official development assistance commitments, including the commitments by many developed countries to achieve the target of 0.7 per cent of gross national income for official development assistance to developing countries by 2015 and to reach the level of at least 0.5 per cent of gross national income for official development assistance by 2010, as well as the target of 0.15 to 0.20 per cent of gross national income for official development assistance to least developed

countries, and urges those developed countries that have not yet done so to make concrete efforts in this regard in accordance with their reiterated commitments;

40. *Welcomes* the efforts of some developed countries, which are on target to meet the commitments made in terms of increased official development assistance;

41. *Also welcomes* recent efforts and initiatives to enhance the quality of aid and to increase its impact, including the Paris Declaration on Aid Effectiveness and the Accra Agenda for Action, and the resolve to take concrete, effective and timely action in implementing all agreed commitments on aid effectiveness, with clear monitoring and deadlines, including by further aligning assistance with countries' strategies, by building institutional capacities, by reducing transaction costs and eliminating bureaucratic procedures, by making progress on untying aid, by enhancing the absorptive capacity and financial management of recipient countries and by strengthening the focus on development results;

42. *Recognizes* the need for the international community to align its efforts more specifically towards supporting the Comprehensive Africa Agriculture Development Programme, and in this regard takes note of the Declaration of the World Summit on Food Security;

43. *Also recognizes* the need for the international community to make continued efforts to increase the flow of new and additional resources for financing for development from all sources, public and private, domestic and foreign, to support the development of African countries;

44. *Invites* all of Africa's development partners, in particular developed countries, to support African countries in promoting and maintaining macroeconomic stability, to help African countries to attract investments and promote policies conducive to attracting domestic and foreign investment, for example by encouraging private financial flows, to promote investment by their private sectors in Africa, to encourage and facilitate the transfer of the technology needed to African countries on favourable terms, including on concessional and preferential terms, as mutually agreed, and to assist in strengthening human and institutional capacities for the implementation of the New Partnership, consistent with its priorities and objectives and with a view to furthering Africa's development at all levels;

45. *Stresses* that conflict prevention, management and resolution and post-conflict consolidation are essential for the achievement of the objectives of the New Partnership, and welcomes in this regard the cooperation and support granted by the United Nations and development partners to the African regional and subregional organizations in the implementation of the New Partnership;

46. *Welcomes* the continued efforts of the United Nations Peacebuilding Commission in assisting post-conflict countries in Africa and the strengthening of the relationship between the Peacebuilding Commission and the African Union, and appreciates in this regard the visit by the Chair of the Organizational Committee of the Peacebuilding Commission and the Chairs of the country-specific configurations to African Union headquarters on 9 November 2009;

47. *Requests* the United Nations system to continue to provide assistance to the Planning and Coordinating Agency of the New Partnership and to African countries in developing projects and programmes within the scope of the priorities of the New Partnership and to place greater emphasis on monitoring, evaluation and dissemination of the effectiveness of its activities in support of the New Partnership;

48. *Welcomes* the Basic Education in Africa Programme of the United Nations Educational, Scientific and Cultural Organization, which seeks to prioritize education and which supports holistic and comprehensive reform;

49. *Invites* the Secretary-General, as a follow-up to the 2005 World Summit, to urge the United Nations development system to assist African countries in implementing quick-impact initiatives through, inter alia, the Millennium Villages Project, and requests the Secretary-General to include in his report an assessment of those quick-impact initiatives;

50. *Requests* the Secretary-General to promote greater coherence in the work of the United Nations system in support of the New Partnership, on the basis of the agreed clusters of the Regional Coordination Mechanism for Africa, and in this regard calls upon the United Nations system to continue to mainstream the special needs of Africa in all its normative and operational activities;

51. *Reaffirms* the commitment by all States to establish a monitoring mechanism to follow up on all commitments related to the development of Africa, as stipulated in paragraph 39 of the political declaration on Africa's development needs, and in this regard requests the President of the General Assembly to continue informal consultations, led by Member States with the participation of relevant stakeholders, on the nature, scope, priorities and institutional arrangements for a monitoring mechanism that builds on existing mechanisms as well as on the recommendations contained in the report of the Secretary-General, with a view to making it operational by the end of the sixty-sixth session of the Assembly;

52. *Requests* the Secretary-General to continue to take measures to strengthen the Office of the Special Adviser on Africa in order to enable it to effectively fulfil its mandate, including monitoring and reporting on progress related to meeting the special needs of Africa;

53. *Also requests* the Secretary-General to submit a comprehensive report on the implementation of the present resolution to the General Assembly at its sixty-sixth session on the basis of inputs from Governments, organizations of the United Nations system and other stakeholders in the New Partnership.

Report of Secretary-General. In response to General Assembly resolution 65/284 (see p. 892), the Secretary-General in July submitted the ninth consolidated report [A/66/202] on progress achieved to implement and support NEPAD, which highlighted action taken by African countries and organizations; the response of the international community in building on the momentum of international support for Africa's development; and support provided by the UN system in NEPAD implementation in areas ranging from official development assistance, debt relief and foreign direct investment to trade and South-South cooperation. In the sector of infrastructure, focus was placed on power, transport and water. The establishment of the NEPAD Planning and Coordinating Agency (NPCA) in 2010 and its integration into the structures and processes of the African Union (AU) led to strengthened coherence and coordination of development efforts. Progress on the implementation of commitments under the Comprehensive Africa Agriculture Development Programme at both country and regional levels continued, with an increasing number of countries designing programmes to deliver on the 6 per cent agricultural productivity target. Progress had been most notable in meeting the target of 10 per cent of the budget invested in agriculture. Ten countries had met the target, compared to only five countries in 2009, and nine countries had invested between 5 and 10 per cent of the budget. To ensure the availability of affordable, safe and effective medicine, NEPAD led the African Medicines Regulatory Harmonization Initiative, which mobilized financial and technical resources, advocated for reviews of the regulation of medicines, and coordinated capacity-building initiatives for regulation. Additionally, NPCA continued to promote human resource development for nurses and midwives. The report also discussed the activities of the Regional Coordination Mechanism of UN entities and organizations working in Africa in support of the AU and NEPAD, as well as progress achieved with the Millennium Villages Project and the peer review process.

The Secretary-General concluded with a number of recommendations including: African countries allocating more resources to NEPAD projects and promoting private sector development, while development partners take urgent steps to honour their commitments to Africa; strengthening mechanisms for the participation, inclusion and empowerment of all segments of society in the political and development processes; improving the investment climate; integrating climate change issues into economic planning and management; mainstreaming of environmental policy into productive sectors; and strengthening of the national health systems and research infrastructure in the field of HIV/AIDS. The Secretary-General further urged development partners to substantially scale up aid disbursements and conclude the Doha Round of multilateral trade negotiations.

Social dimensions of NEPAD

The Commission for Social Development, at its forty-ninth session (New York, 19 February 2010 and 9–18 February 2011) [E/2011/26-E/CN.5/2011/12], recommended to the Economic and Social Council for adoption a resolution on the social dimensions of NEPAD. In resolution 2011/26 (see below), the Council decided that the Commission for Social Development should continue to give prominence to and raise awareness of the social dimensions of NEPAD during its fiftieth (2012) session. It also requested the Secretary-General to submit a report on the subject for the aforementioned session.

ECONOMIC AND SOCIAL COUNCIL ACTION

On 28 July [meeting 48], the Economic and Social Council adopted **resolution 2011/26** [E/2011/26] without vote [agenda item 14 (*b*)].

Social dimensions of the New Partnership for Africa's Development

The Economic and Social Council,

Recalling the outcomes of the World Summit for Social Development, held in Copenhagen from 6 to 12 March 1995, and of the twenty-fourth special session of the General Assembly entitled "World Summit for Social Development and beyond: achieving social development for all in a globalizing world", held in Geneva from 26 June to 1 July 2000,

Reaffirming the United Nations Millennium Declaration of 8 September 2000, the United Nations Declaration on the New Partnership for Africa's Development of 16 September 2002 and General Assembly resolution 57/7 of 4 November 2002 on the final review and appraisal of the United Nations New Agenda for the Development of Africa in the 1990s and support for the New Partnership for Africa's Development,

Noting the conclusions of the African Union Extraordinary Summit on Employment and Poverty Alleviation in Africa, held in Ouagadougou on 8 and 9 September 2004,

Recognizing the commitments made with regard to meeting the special needs of Africa at the 2005 World Summit and reaffirmed in the political declaration on Africa's development needs adopted at the high-level meeting held at United Nations Headquarters on 22 September 2008,

Remaining concerned that Africa is the only continent currently not on track to achieve any of the goals set out in the Millennium Declaration by 2015, and in this regard emphasizing that concerted efforts and continued support are required to fulfil the commitments to address the special needs of Africa,

Expressing deep concern that attainment of the social development objectives may be hindered by the financial and economic crisis, as well as by challenges brought about by the food and energy crises and climate change,

Recognizing that capacity-building, knowledge-sharing and best practices are essential for the successful implementation of the New Partnership for Africa's Development, and recognizing also the need for continued support from the international community, New Partnership for Africa's Development partners and United Nations agencies,

Bearing in mind that African countries have primary responsibility for their own economic and social development, that the role of national policies and development strategies cannot be overemphasized and that the development efforts of such countries need to be supported by an enabling international economic environment, and in this regard recalling the support given by the International Conference on Financing for Development to the New Partnership,

1. *Takes note* of the report of the Secretary-General;
2. *Welcomes* the progress made by African countries in fulfilling their commitments in the implementation of the New Partnership for Africa's Development to deepen democracy, human rights, good governance and sound economic management, and encourages African countries, with the participation of stakeholders, including civil soci-

ety and the private sector, to intensify their efforts in this regard by developing and strengthening institutions for governance and by creating an environment conducive to attracting foreign direct investment for the development of the region;

3. *Also welcomes* the progress that has been made in implementing the African Peer Review Mechanism, as reflected in particular by the number of countries that have signed up to participate in the Mechanism, the completion of the peer review process and the progress in implementing the recommendations of those reviews in some countries and the completion of the self-assessment process, the hosting of country support missions and the launching of the national preparatory process for the peer review in others, and urges African States that have not yet done so to join the Mechanism, as a matter of priority, and to strengthen the peer review process so as to ensure its efficient performance;

4. *Welcomes in particular* the organization of the first session of the African Union Conference of Ministers in charge of Social Development, held in Windhoek from 27 to 31 October 2008, and recalls in this regard the African Common Position on Social Integration and the Social Policy Framework for Africa, both of which have been endorsed by Africa's Heads of State;

5. *Welcomes* the efforts made by African countries and regional and subregional organizations, including the African Union, to mainstream a gender perspective and the empowerment of women in the implementation of the New Partnership, including through the implementation of the Protocol to the African Charter on Human and Peoples' Rights on the Rights of Women in Africa;

6. *Emphasizes* that the African Union and the regional economic communities have a critical role to play in the implementation of the New Partnership, and in this regard encourages African countries, with the assistance of their development partners, to increase and coordinate effectively their support for enhancing the capacities of those institutions and to promote regional cooperation and social and economic integration in Africa;

7. *Also emphasizes* that progress in the implementation of the New Partnership depends also on a national and international environment favourable to Africa's growth and development, including measures to promote a policy environment conducive to private sector development and entrepreneurship;

8. *Further emphasizes* that democracy, respect for all human rights and fundamental freedoms, including the right to development, transparent and accountable governance and administration in all sectors of society, and effective participation by civil society, including non-governmental and community-based organizations, and by the private sector are among the indispensable foundations for the realization of social and people-centred sustainable development;

9. *Emphasizes* that the increasing unacceptably high levels of poverty and social exclusion faced by most African countries require a comprehensive approach to the development and implementation of social and economic policies, inter alia, to reduce poverty, to promote economic activity, growth and sustainable development, to ensure employment creation and decent work for all, to promote education, health and social protection and to enhance social inclusion, political stability, democracy and good governance and the promotion and protection of human rights and fundamental freedoms, so as to ensure the achievement of Africa's social and economic objectives;

10. *Recognizes* that, while social development is primarily the responsibility of Governments, international cooperation and assistance are essential for the full achievement of that goal;

11. *Also recognizes* the contribution made by Member States to the implementation of the New Partnership in the context of South-South cooperation, and encourages the international community, including the international financial institutions, to support the efforts of African countries, including through trilateral cooperation;

12. *Welcomes* the various important initiatives of Africa's development partners in recent years, and in this regard emphasizes the importance of coordination in such initiatives on Africa by ensuring the effective implementation of existing commitments, including through the African Union/New Partnership for Africa's Development African Action Plan 2010–2015: Advancing Regional and Continental Integration in Africa;

13. *Recognizes* the regional coordination mechanism of United Nations agencies and organizations working in Africa in support of the African Union and its New Partnership for Africa's Development Programme of Action, which aims to ensure coordination and coherence in the delivery of support for greater effectiveness and impact through increased joint programming and joint implementation of activities;

14. *Urges* continuous support for measures to address the challenges of poverty eradication and sustainable development in Africa, with special emphasis on the Millennium Development Goals related to poverty and hunger, health, education, empowerment of women and gender equality, including, as appropriate, debt relief, improved market access, support for the private sector and entrepreneurship, enhanced official development assistance, increased foreign direct investment and transfer of technology on mutually agreed terms, empowerment of women in all aspects, including economic and political aspects, the promotion of social protection systems and the conclusion of the round of negotiations of the World Trade Organization;

15. *Recognizes* that the implementation of the commitments made by Governments during the First United Nations Decade for the Eradication of Poverty (1997–2006) has fallen short of expectations, and welcomes the proclamation of the Second Decade (2008–2017) by the General Assembly in its resolution 62/205 of 19 December 2007 in order to support, in an efficient and coordinated manner, the internationally agreed development goals related to poverty eradication, including the Millennium Development Goals;

16. *Encourages* all development partners to implement the principles of aid effectiveness, as recalled in the Doha Declaration on Financing for Development adopted by the Follow-up International Conference on Financing for Development to Review the Implementation of the Monterrey Consensus on 2 December 2008;

17. *Recognizes* the need for national Governments and the international community to make continued efforts to increase the flow of new and additional resources for financing for development from all sources, public and private, domestic and foreign, to support the development of African countries;

18. *Acknowledges* the activities of the Bretton Woods institutions and the African Development Bank in African

countries, and invites those institutions to continue their support for the implementation of the priorities and objectives of the New Partnership;

19. *Encourages* Africa's development partners to continue to integrate the priorities, values and principles of the New Partnership into their development assistance programmes;

20. *Encourages* African countries and their development partners to place people at the centre of government development action and to secure core investment spending in health, education and social safety nets;

21. *Notes* the growing collaboration among the entities of the United Nations system in support of the New Partnership, and requests the Secretary-General to promote greater coherence in the work of the United Nations system in support of the New Partnership, on the basis of the agreed clusters;

22. *Emphasizes* the importance for the communication, advocacy and outreach cluster to continue to muster international support for the New Partnership and to urge the United Nations system to demonstrate more evidence of cross-sectoral synergies in order to promote a comprehensive approach regarding successive phases of planning and implementation of social development programmes in Africa;

23. *Invites* the Secretary-General, as a follow-up to the 2005 World Summit, to urge the organizations and bodies of the United Nations system to assist African countries in implementing quick-impact initiatives, based on their national development priorities and strategies, to enable them to achieve the Millennium Development Goals, and in this respect acknowledges commitments made by development partners;

24. *Encourages* the international community to support African countries in addressing the challenges of climate change by providing the financial and technological resources and capacity-building needed to support adaptation and mitigation action;

25. *Requests* the Secretary-General to continue to take measures to strengthen the Office of the Special Adviser on Africa, and requests the Office to collaborate with the Department of Economic and Social Affairs of the Secretariat and to include the social dimensions of the New Partnership in its comprehensive reports to the General Assembly at its sixty-sixth session;

26. *Requests* the Commission for Social Development to discuss in its annual programme of work those regional programmes that promote social development so as to enable all regions to share experiences and best practices, with the agreement of the countries concerned, and in this regard requests that the programmes of work of the Commission include the priority areas of the New Partnership, as appropriate;

27. *Decides* that the Commission for Social Development should continue to give prominence to and raise awareness of the social dimensions of the New Partnership during its fiftieth session;

28. *Requests* the Secretary-General, in collaboration with the Office of the Special Adviser on Africa, taking into consideration General Assembly resolutions 62/179 of 19 December 2007, 63/267 of 31 March 2009 and 64/258 of 16 March 2010 entitled "New Partnership for Africa's Development: progress in implementation and international support", to submit to the Commission for Social Development for its consideration at its fiftieth session a report on the social dimensions of the New Partnership.

Report of Secretary-General. Pursuant to Economic and Social Council resolution 2011/26 (see p. 896), the Secretary-General submitted a November report [E/CN.5/2012/2] on the social dimensions of NEPAD, which examined the progress made and challenges faced in improving governance; eradicating poverty; creating decent jobs; and investing in human resource development, food security and infrastructure, as called for by NEPAD. The report also discussed financing mechanisms for social development and key policy responses aimed at further improving and consolidating Africa's social development gains. The Secretary-General noted that the architecture of global economic governance constrained the development potential of NEPAD, and that African countries had a limited role in norm-setting and decision-making in relation to the international policies that had a strong bearing on the region's development prospects. He called for adequate representation of African countries in all global groupings, including the G-20, in order to ensure that the continent was not marginalized in global economic governance. Recommendations to the Commission for Social Development included greater coherence between macroeconomic strategies and social policies; stronger focus on structural transformation with regard to the composition and sustainability of growth; the support of small- and medium-sized enterprises in order to raise agricultural productivity; concerted efforts to protect and sustain social investments; and the promotion of universal access to basic social protection and social services.

African countries emerging from conflict

On 13 June, the Economic and Social Council and the Peacebuilding Commission convened an informal joint event, "Promoting Durable Peace and Sustainable Development in the Sudan and South Sudan", to highlight the importance of development to peace, the need for effective international support to the Sudan and South Sudan, and the importance of regional cooperation. Two panel sessions were held under the theme "Development and State-building priorities in South Sudan" and "Promoting durable peace and sustainable development in the Sudan and South Sudan: a regional perspective". Participants underscored the need for political stability and basic security for development, as well as the importance of national ownership and an inclusive and participatory approach to governance to restore confidence and create legitimacy for the new State.

Following South Sudan's independence on 9 July, the country was admitted as a Member State of the United Nations by General Assembly **resolution 65/308** (see p. 1354).

ECONOMIC AND SOCIAL COUNCIL ACTION

On 29 July [meeting 50], the Economic and Social Council adopted **resolution 2011/43** [draft: E/2011/L.51] without vote [agenda item 7 (*f*)].

Support to the Republic of South Sudan

The Economic and Social Council,

Recalling its resolution 2009/32 of 31 July 2009,

Welcoming General Assembly resolution 65/308 of 14 July 2011 on the admission of the Republic of South Sudan to membership in the United Nations,

Recognizing that development, peace, security and human rights are interlinked and mutually reinforcing,

Recalling the informal joint event of the Economic and Social Council and the Peacebuilding Commission on the theme "Promoting durable peace and sustainable development in the Sudan and South Sudan", held in New York on 13 June 2011,

Recalling also Security Council resolution 1996(2011) of 8 July 2011 establishing the United Nations Mission in South Sudan,

1. *Welcomes* the independence of South Sudan, which took place on 9 July 2011;
2. *Acknowledges* the enormous humanitarian, peacebuilding and development challenges facing the country;
3. *Reaffirms* the need to strengthen the synergy between the economic and social development programmes of South Sudan and its peace and security agenda;
4. *Expresses its appreciation* to the Chair of the Peacebuilding Commission for providing insights and information on best practices, particularly on lessons learned from its experiences, that are relevant for addressing the economic and social challenges of peacebuilding in other African countries emerging from conflict;
5. *Encourages* all Member States to contribute to the socio-economic development of South Sudan;
6. *Requests* the Secretary-General and all relevant organs and bodies of the United Nations system, as well as the international financial institutions and development agencies, to assist South Sudan, whenever possible, through continued effective humanitarian, peacebuilding and predictable development assistance, in conformity with national priorities, including the promotion of capacity-building, in order to lay a solid foundation for long-term development;
7. *Invites*, in particular, the governing bodies of the United Nations funds and programmes to pay particular attention to the situation in South Sudan and to the coordination of their activities in the country;
8. *Requests* the Secretary-General to report to the Economic and Social Council, at its substantive session of 2012, on how the United Nations development system is implementing integrated, coherent and coordinated support to South Sudan, consistent with national priorities, while ensuring clarity of roles and responsibilities in the implementation of United Nations operational activities;
9. *Decides* to consider this matter at its substantive session of 2012 under the agenda sub-item entitled "African countries emerging from conflict".

On 22 July [E/2011/SR.41], during the 2011 substantive session of the Economic and Social Council (see p. 1359), the Chairman of the Organizational Committee of the Peacebuilding Commission addressed the Economic and Social Council via videoconference on the question of African countries emerging from conflict. He underlined that the Economic and Social Council could play a decisive role in ensuring that socioeconomic development remained central to the international community's support and commitment to countries emerging from conflict. Since July 2010, two more African countries—Guinea and Liberia—had been added to the four countries already on the Commission's agenda: Burundi, the Central African Republic, Guinea-Bissau and Sierra Leone (see p. 47).

Other economic assistance

Haiti

Report of Ad Hoc Advisory Group. In response to Economic and Social Council resolution 2010/28 [YUN 2010, p. 917], the Ad Hoc Advisory Group on Haiti reported in July [E/2011/133] on the Group's visit to Haiti from 15 to 18 June; the recovery process of the country and the challenges faced; aid effectiveness; and development policy options for strengthening recovery and reconstruction, and establishing a long-term economic plan for the country. The Group reported that important developments had occurred since its visit at the same time the previous year, such as close to 50,000 people leaving IDP camps every month to settle in permanent or semi-permanent shelters; tons of debris having been removed as a result of, for example, the cash-for-work and food-for-work programmes; UN agencies supporting the Government to rehabilitate areas by setting up recycling systems in a sustainable manner, and thus creating small enterprises and a significant number of jobs; and cholera cases having diminished in numbers. Reconstruction and recovery efforts, however, were overshadowed by the political and electoral situation as well as persistent poverty that had affected about two thirds of the population (see p. 298).

The Group considered it imperative for Haiti to remain on the international agenda and to receive appropriate support, in particular through a strong UN presence on the ground, in the form of the United Nations Stabilization Mission in Haiti and the UN country team. It recommended that the UN system foster the sustainability of all reconstruction projects through an increased focus on national capacity-building; systematize its joint programmes, pool their resources and coordinate their implementation; and continue to promote the rule of law and its cross-cutting dimension in the work of both Haitian stakeholders and development partners. Further recommendations were addressed to the Government, donors and the international community.

On 28 July (**decision 2011/268**), the Council welcomed the report of the Advisory Group and requested it to report on its activities in support of the country's recovery, reconstruction and development efforts to the Council at its 2012 substantive session.

Communications. In letters dated 20 December 2010 [E/2011/8], 3 February 2011 [E/2011/69] and 24 March [E/2011/80] respectively, the Bahamas, the United States and France expressed their wishes to become members of the Ad Hoc Advisory Group. On 17 February, the Economic and Social Council decided to appoint the Bahamas and the United States as members (**decision 2011/207**), and on 26 April, it further appointed France as a member of the Group (**decision 2011/211**).

Report of Secretary-General. Pursuant to General Assembly resolution 65/135 [YUN 2010, p. 918], the Secretary-General in September submitted a report [A/66/332] on humanitarian assistance, emergency relief, rehabilitation, recovery and reconstruction in response to the humanitarian emergency in Haiti, including the devastating effects of the earthquake. During the reporting period from October 2010 to July 2011, humanitarian assistance responding to displacement, emergency shelter needs, food insecurity and malnutrition was provided to people affected by the earthquake and cholera crises [YUN 2010, p. 327]. Underlying structural poverty, insecurity, political instability and recurrent natural disasters, however, remained serious challenges, and long-term solutions were desperately needed.

Within days of the cholera outbreak in October 2010, a humanitarian response was put in place under the leadership of the Ministry of Health and Population, and the number of cholera treatment centres increased substantially. Awareness-raising on cholera prevention and treatment together with the distribution of water, sanitation and hygiene items helped to reduce incidences and mortality rates and to mitigate the impact of the epidemic. Due to serious gaps in Haiti's basic service coverage, in particular water and sanitation systems, however, longer-term behaviour change and the addressing of disparities between urban and rural areas were needed and would require sustained investment in social mobilization and health and hygiene education.

Chernobyl

In a letter dated 26 April [A/65/828] addressed to the Secretary-General on the observance of the twenty-fifth anniversary of the disaster at the Chernobyl nuclear power plant [YUN 1986, p. 584], Cuba stated that as part of its 21-year-old humanitarian programme, provided in response to the request for international aid, 25,392 persons from various countries had been treated in Cuba, including 21,340 children, most of them Ukrainian.

Kazakhstan

In response to General Assembly resolution 63/279 [YUN 2009, p. 905], the Secretary-General in September submitted a report [A/66/337] on international cooperation and coordination for the human and ecological rehabilitation and economic development of the Semipalatinsk region, a former nuclear testing range in Kazakhstan (the Polygon). The report outlined progress made towards accelerating the development of the area from 2008 to 2011, through programmes and actions of the Government and the international community, including UN agencies.

The year 2011 marked the twentieth anniversary of the closing of the Semipalatinsk nuclear testing site. During the reporting period, the Government developed a number of ministerial programmes aimed at resolving the problems in the Semey region, including the Zhasyl Damu programme which incorporated activities to ensure radiation security, rehabilitation of the environment and transfer of territories for land-use activities. A new regional development programme for 2011–2015 entitled "Raising competitiveness of the region through innovative approaches to regional planning and social services", jointly funded by the Government and UN agencies, was approved and launched. International assistance, such as the UN project on enhancing human security in the former nuclear test site, addressed a variety of socio-economic, environmental and health-related problems.

The Government, supported by UN agencies, the Comprehensive Nuclear-Test-Ban Treaty Organization and the International Atomic Energy Agency, organized an international conference (Astana, Kazakhstan, 26 August 2010), dedicated to the International Day against Nuclear Tests. The conference set forth future priorities in the socioeconomic, environmental and health sector, including strengthening data collection, analysis and monitoring of the socio-economic situation in the area; ensuring a gradual decrease of technogenic influence on the population and the environment; and developing a long-term plan for improving mother and child health, as well as improving quality control systems in health services. The Secretary-General called on the international community to support the development programme for 2011–2015, with a view to increasing the effectiveness of assistance to the affected region and to enhancing the overall positive impact on people's lives.

GENERAL ASSEMBLY ACTION

On 22 December [meeting 91], the General Assembly, on the recommendation of the Second Committee [A/66/440], adopted **resolution 66/193** without vote [agenda item 19].

International cooperation and coordination for the human and ecological rehabilitation and economic development of the Semipalatinsk region of Kazakhstan

The General Assembly,

Recalling its resolutions 52/169 M of 16 December 1997, 53/1 H of 16 November 1998, 55/44 of 27 November 2000, 57/101 of 25 November 2002, 60/216 of 22 December 2005 and 63/279 of 24 April 2009,

Recognizing that the Semipalatinsk nuclear testing ground, inherited by Kazakhstan and closed in 1991, remains a matter of serious concern for the people and Government of Kazakhstan with regard to the long-term consequences of its activity for the lives and health of the people, especially children and other vulnerable groups, as well as for the environment of the region,

Taking into account the fact that a number of international programmes in the Semipalatinsk region have been completed since the closure of the nuclear testing ground, but that serious social, economic and ecological problems continue to exist,

Taking into consideration the results of the International Conference on Semipalatinsk, held in Tokyo on 6 and 7 September 1999, which have promoted the effectiveness of the assistance provided to the population of the region,

Acknowledging the progress made towards accelerating the development of the Semipalatinsk region during the period 2008–2011, through programmes and actions of the Government of Kazakhstan and the international community, including United Nations agencies,

Recognizing the important role of national development policies and strategies in the rehabilitation of the Semipalatinsk region,

Recognizing also the challenges that Kazakhstan faces in the rehabilitation of the Semipalatinsk region, in particular in the context of the efforts by the Government of Kazakhstan to ensure the effective and timely achievement of the internationally agreed development goals, including the Millennium Development Goals, in particular with regard to health care and environmental sustainability,

Recognizing further that the Government of Kazakhstan may call upon the United Nations Resident Coordinator in Kazakhstan to render assistance in conducting consultations for establishing a multi-stakeholder mechanism, with the participation of various government bodies, local governments, civil society, the donor community and international organizations, to improve governance and enable the more efficient use of resources allocated for the rehabilitation of the Semipalatinsk region, in particular regarding the areas of radiation safety, socioeconomic development and health and environmental protection, and for the provision of information on risks to the population,

Emphasizing the importance of support by donor States and international development organizations for the efforts of Kazakhstan to improve the social, economic and environmental situation in the Semipalatinsk region, and the need for the international community to continue to pay due attention to the rehabilitation of the Semipalatinsk region,

Taking note of the need to utilize modern technologies to minimize and mitigate radiological, health, socioeconomic, psychological and environmental challenges in the Semipalatinsk region,

Considering the importance of cooperation with the United Nations in establishing a coherent framework for coordination in addressing the needs of the region to introduce innovative approaches to the regional planning and social assistance to the population, especially to its most vulnerable groups, of the Semipalatinsk region aimed at improving their quality of life,

Emphasizing the importance of the new development-oriented approach in tackling problems in the Semipalatinsk region in the medium to long term,

Expressing appreciation to donor countries and organizations, United Nations agencies, funds and programmes, the specialized agencies and related organizations mentioned in the report of the Secretary-General for their contribution to the rehabilitation of the Semipalatinsk region,

1. *Takes note* of the report of the Secretary-General on the implementation of resolution 63/279 and the information contained therein on measures taken to solve the health, ecological, economic and humanitarian problems in the Semipalatinsk region;

2. *Welcomes and recognizes* the important role of the Government of Kazakhstan in providing domestic resources to help to meet the needs of the Semipalatinsk region, implementing measures for optimizing public administration of the territory and facilities of the former Semipalatinsk nuclear test site, ensuring radiation safety and environmental rehabilitation and reintegrating the use of the nuclear test site into the national economy;

3. *Urges* the international community to provide assistance to Kazakhstan in formulating and implementing special programmes and projects for the treatment and care of the affected population as well as in efforts to ensure economic growth and sustainable development in the Semipalatinsk region, including increasing effectiveness of existing programmes;

4. *Calls upon* Member States, relevant multilateral financial organizations and other entities of the international community, including academia and non-governmental organizations, to share knowledge and experience in order to contribute to the human and ecological rehabilitation and economic development of the Semipalatinsk region;

5. *Requests* the Secretary-General to continue pursuing a consultative process, with the participation of interested States and relevant United Nations agencies, on modalities for mobilizing and coordinating the necessary support to seek appropriate solutions to the problems and needs of the Semipalatinsk region, including those prioritized in his report;

6. *Calls upon* the Secretary-General to continue his efforts to enhance world public awareness of the problems and needs of the Semipalatinsk region;

7. *Requests* the Secretary-General to report to the General Assembly at its sixty-ninth session, under the item entitled "Sustainable development", on progress made in the implementation of the present resolution.

On 24 December, the General Assembly decided that the agenda item on special economic assistance to individual countries or regions would remain for consideration during its resumed sixty-sixth (2012) session (**decision 66/557**).

Chapter IV
International trade, finance and transport

In 2011, the work of the United Nations on international trade, finance and transport focused on multilateral efforts to stimulate and sustain the global recovery from the world economic and financial crisis of 2008; and to consider new measures to prevent such crises in the future, even as the role of international trade as an engine for development remained under threat due to increased use of protectionist measures as a reaction to the prevailing economic uncertainties.

During the year, international trade was not able to revive the growth conditions of the preceding decade that had been particularly supportive of economic and social progress in the developing world. International trade expansion slowed to only 5.5 per cent in 2011. In most developed economies—particularly in the euro zone—trade volumes did not recover to their pre-crisis levels. Faced with weak external demand from developed countries and heightened global uncertainties, export growth in developing countries and economies in transition also registered a deceleration to 7 and 6 per cent, respectively. Commodity prices remained high and volatile.

In March, a special high-level meeting of the Economic and Social Council with the Bretton Woods institutions (the World Bank Group and the International Monetary Fund), the World Trade Organization (wto) and the United Nations Conference on Trade and Development (unctad) addressed coherence, coordination and cooperation on financing for development.

At its annual session in September, the Trade and Development Board—the governing body of unctad—took action on fostering industrial development in Africa, unctad technical cooperation activities and their financing, and an evaluation of the unctad programme of assistance to the Palestinian people.

In December, the General Assembly held its Fifth High-level Dialogue on Financing for Development on the status of implementation and the tasks ahead for the Monterrey Consensus and Doha Declaration on financing for development. As it became clear that efforts by wto member States to conclude the Doha Round of Trade Negotiations had failed, the Eighth wto Ministerial Conference recognized that it was unlikely that all elements of the Doha Round could be concluded simultaneously in the near future, and that there was a need to explore different negotiating approaches while respecting the principles of transparency and inclusiveness.

International trade and development

According to the *Trade and Development Report, 2012* [Sales No. E.12.II.D.6], prepared by the United Nations Conference on Trade and Development, the world economy, which continued to suffer from the fallout of the financial crisis that began in late 2007 and the meltdown in September 2008 [YUN 2008, p. 934], was not able in 2011 to revive the growth conditions of the preceding decade that had been particularly supportive of economic and social progress in the developing world. International trade expansion slowed to only 5.5 per cent. In most developed economies—particularly in the euro zone—trade volumes had not recovered to their pre-crisis levels. Exports from the United States continued to grow at a faster rate than those from Japan, as the latter were affected by supply disruptions due to natural disasters in 2011. In the European Union, intraregional trade, which accounted for a large proportion of member countries' trade, suffered as a result of the region's economic recession. Faced with weak external demand from developed countries and heightened global uncertainties, export growth in developing countries and economies in transition also registered a deceleration to 7 and 6 per cent, respectively. Sluggish demand from developed countries primarily affected exporters of manufactures in developing countries, although increased South-South trade partly counterbalanced that deceleration.

Commodity prices remained high and volatile, peaking during the first months of the year—oil being an exception—and briefly rebounding at the end of 2011. Price movements continued to be heavily influenced by the presence of financial investors in commodity markets. Price reductions were accompanied by a large decline in positions taken by financial investors. The year was the weakest for commodity investment flows since 2002, and also the most volatile.

Multilateral trading system

In response to General Assembly resolution 65/142 [YUN 2010, p. 939], the Secretary-General submitted a July report [A/66/185 & Add.1] on international trade and development. The report discussed relevant trends in the topic; developments in the multilateral trading system; the way forward, including duty-free quota-free market access, reduction and elimination of cotton subsidies and tariffs, a services waiver, accession to the World Trade Organization (WTO) and a least developed country-plus package; and regional trade agreements. According to the report, the multilateral trading system was facing major uncertainties regarding the prospect of the closing of the Doha Round of trade negotiations, launched a decade earlier [YUN 2001, p. 1432], which came on top of a series of changes in the structure and direction of international trade. The growth of trade in intermediate goods, which was linked to the spread of international production, was accelerating and often included a strong regional component. Favourable economic realities had also contributed to increased South-South trade and cooperation, which if properly harnessed could contribute to inclusive and sustainable development.

The Secretary-General observed that a dynamic trade and investment nexus had over the past two decades been a key driver of growth and structural transformation in some developing countries. That dynamism had begun to change the economic landscape in favour of complementary policies required to strengthen productive capacities, expand employment opportunities in support of inclusive and sustainable development and better cope with external shocks. Greater attention needed to be given to the agriculture and services sectors, as integrated and coherent trade, industrial, labour market and social policies could contribute to a more equitable sharing of wealth and opportunities within and across countries. The Secretary-General called for the reinvigoration of the multilateral trading system and the conclusion of the Doha Round with a strong development dimension; for the least developed country (LDC) package to make an important contribution to the implementation of the Istanbul Programme of Action (see p. 828); and attention to be given to realizing Millennium Development Goal (MDG) 8 on an open, equitable, rule-based, predictable and non-discriminatory multilateral trading and financial system. Development imperatives under rapidly changing economic conditions needed to be factored into the norms and instruments of the international trading system, such as through enhanced policy space for development and achieving greater coherence between the multilateral trading system and regional trade agreements, as well as between the international trade and financial systems.

WTO report. According to the WTO *Annual Report 2012*, WTO members, recognizing that the Doha Round could not be completed in its entirety by the end of 2011, embarked in May on a process aimed at delivering a smaller package by the Ministerial Conference in December (see below). In July, however, the Chair of the negotiating group reported that a package was not turning out as members had wished.

Meanwhile, the Third Global Review of Aid for Trade, hosted by WTO (Geneva, 18–19 July), brought together high-level participation from organizations, donors and partner countries involved in building capacity to trade in developing countries, with a focus on resource mobilization, mainstreaming trade into development plans, strengthening regional cooperation, improving monitoring and evaluation, and promoting greater dialogue with the private sector. In October, the Chair of the negotiating group reported that while no member was ready to give up on the Doha objectives, there was a collective sense that they needed to explore different approaches from those employed previously.

WTO Ministerial Conference. The Eighth Ministerial Conference of WTO (Geneva, 15–17 December) recognized that it was unlikely that all elements of the Doha Round could be concluded simultaneously in the near future, and that there was a need to explore different negotiating approaches while respecting the principles of transparency and inclusiveness. The Conference also approved the accession of Montenegro, the Russian Federation and Samoa; agreed on the revision of the Plurilateral Government Procurement Agreement; and adopted a waiver to permit preferential treatment of service suppliers from LDCs.

GENERAL ASSEMBLY ACTION

On 22 December [meeting 91], the General Assembly, on the recommendation of the Second (Economic and Financial) Committee [A/66/438/Add.1], adopted **resolution 66/185** without vote [agenda item 17 (*a*)].

International trade and development

The General Assembly,

Recalling its resolutions 56/178 of 21 December 2001, 57/235 of 20 December 2002, 58/197 of 23 December 2003 and 63/203 of 19 December 2008 on international trade and development,

Noting its resolutions 59/221 of 22 December 2004, 60/184 of 22 December 2005, 61/186 of 20 December 2006, 62/184 of 19 December 2007, 64/188 of 21 December 2009 and 65/142 of 20 December 2010 on international trade and development,

Recalling the United Nations Millennium Declaration, as well as the outcomes of the International Conference on Financing for Development and the World Summit on Sustainable Development, the 2005 World Summit Outcome and the Doha Declaration on Financing for Development: outcome document of the Follow-up International Conference on Financing for Development to Review the Implementation of the Monterrey Consensus,

Recalling also the Conference on the World Financial and Economic Crisis and Its Impact on Development and its outcome document,

Recalling further the High-level Plenary Meeting of the General Assembly on the Millennium Development Goals and its outcome document,

Recalling the Fourth United Nations Conference on the Least Developed Countries and its outcome documents,

Reaffirming the value of multilateralism to the global trading system and the commitment to achieving a universal, rules-based, open, non-discriminatory and equitable multilateral trading system that contributes to growth, sustainable development and employment generation in all sectors, and emphasizing that bilateral and regional trading arrangements should contribute and be complementary to the goals of the multilateral trading system,

Reiterating that development concerns form an integral part of the Doha Development Agenda, which places the needs and interests of all developing countries, including least developed countries, at the heart of the Doha Work Programme,

Reaffirming that agriculture remains a fundamental and key sector for the overwhelming majority of developing countries, and stressing the importance of a successful conclusion of the Doha Work Programme in this regard,

Expressing deep concern about the ongoing adverse impacts, particularly on development, of the world financial and economic crisis, cognizant that the global economy is entering a challenging new phase with significant downside risks, including the turbulence in global financial and commodity markets and widespread fiscal strains, that threaten the global economic recovery, and stressing the need to continue to address systemic fragilities and imbalances and the need for continuing efforts to reform and strengthen the international financial system,

Noting that while some developing countries have been the main contributors to recent global economic growth, the economic crisis has reduced their capacity to withstand further shocks, recalling the commitments made to support strong, sustainable, balanced and inclusive growth, and reaffirming the need to work cooperatively to meet development commitments to achieve the Millennium Development Goals by 2015,

1. *Takes note* of the report of the Trade and Development Board and the report of the Secretary-General;

2. *Reaffirms* that international trade is an engine for development and sustained economic growth, and also reaffirms the critical role that a universal, rules-based, open, non-discriminatory and equitable multilateral trading system, as well as meaningful trade liberalization, can play in stimulating economic growth and development worldwide, thereby benefiting all countries at all stages of development;

3. *Emphasizes* the need to resist protectionist tendencies and to rectify any trade-distorting measures already taken that are inconsistent with World Trade Organization rules, recognizing the right of countries, in particular developing countries, to fully utilize flexibilities consistent with their World Trade Organization commitments and obligations;

4. *Expresses serious concern* at the lack of progress in the Doha Round of World Trade Organization negotiations, reiterates the call for the necessary flexibility and political will in order to break the current impasse in the negotiations, and in this regard calls for a balanced, ambitious, comprehensive and development-oriented outcome of the Doha Development Agenda multilateral trade negotiations, in keeping with the development mandate of the Doha Ministerial Declaration, the decision of 1 August 2004 of the General Council of the World Trade Organization and the Hong Kong Ministerial Declaration adopted by the World Trade Organization in 2005;

5. *Welcomes* the convening of the Eighth Ministerial Conference of the World Trade Organization, to be held in Geneva in December 2011, and looks forward to its outcome;

6. *Reaffirms* the commitments made at the Fourth Ministerial Conference of the World Trade Organization relating to the least developed countries, and encourages developed countries and developing countries, declaring themselves in a position to do so, to take steps towards the goal of realizing the timely implementation of duty-free and quota-free market access on a lasting basis for all least developed countries, consistent with the Hong Kong Ministerial Declaration;

7. *Emphasizes* the full, timely and effective implementation of the relevant provisions of the Programme of Action for the Least Developed Countries for the Decade 2011–2020;

8. *Reaffirms* the Marrakesh Ministerial Decision on Measures Concerning the Possible Negative Effects of the Reform Programme on Least Developed and Net Food-importing Developing Countries;

9. *Stresses* the need to remove food export restrictions and extraordinary taxes on food purchased for non-commercial, humanitarian purposes by the World Food Programme, and to not impose them in the future;

10. *Recognizes* the particular challenges that may be faced by small, vulnerable economies to fully benefit from the multilateral trading system in a manner commensurate with their special circumstances, and in this regard encourages progress in the implementation of the World Trade Organization work programme on small economies, as mandated in the 2001 Doha Ministerial Declaration and the 2005 Hong Kong Ministerial Declaration, which supports their efforts towards sustainable development;

11. *Reaffirms* the commitment to address the special development needs of and the challenges faced by landlocked developing countries, and calls for the full, timely and effective implementation of the Almaty Programme of Action: Addressing the Special Needs of Landlocked Developing Countries within a New Global Framework for Transit Transport Cooperation for Landlocked and Transit Developing Countries, in accordance with the Declaration of the high-level meeting of the sixty-third session of the General Assembly on the midterm review of the Almaty Programme of Action;

12. *Expresses concern* about the adoption of unilateral actions that are not consistent with the rules of the World Trade Organization, harm the exports of all countries, in particular those of developing countries, and have a considerable bearing on the ongoing World Trade Organization negotiations and on the achievement and further enhancement of the development dimension of the trade negotiations;

13. *Notes* the holding in Geneva on 18 and 19 July 2011 of the Third Global Review of Aid for Trade, aimed at reviewing progress achieved and identifying additional measures needed to support developing and least developed countries in building their supply and export capacities, and stresses the need to implement the aid-for-trade commitments;

14. *Recognizes* that South-South trade should be strengthened, notes that enhanced market access between developing countries can play a positive role in stimulating South-South trade, and in this regard, inter alia, takes note of the conclusion of the third round of the Global System of Trade Preferences among Developing Countries, by the adoption, on 15 December 2010, of the São Paulo Round Protocol;

15. *Reiterates* the important role of the United Nations Conference on Trade and Development as the focal point within the United Nations system for the integrated treatment of trade and development and interrelated issues in the areas of finance, technology, investment and sustainable development, invites the Conference to continue working to enhance its contribution in its three major pillars, namely, consensus-building, research and policy analysis, and technical assistance, and calls upon the international community to work towards the strengthening of the Conference;

16. *Invites* the United Nations Conference on Trade and Development to continue, in accordance with its mandate, to monitor and assess the evolution of the international trading system and of trends in international trade from a development perspective, and in particular to analyse issues of concern to developing countries, placing greater emphasis on practical solutions, to undertake policy analysis, to work with all relevant stakeholders and to support developing countries in building productive national capacities and international competitiveness, including through technical assistance activities;

17. *Welcomes* the convening of the thirteenth session of the United Nations Conference on Trade and Development in Doha from 21 to 26 April 2012 on the theme "Development-centred globalization: Towards inclusive and sustainable growth and development", and looks forward to its successful outcome;

18. *Recognizes* the role of the Enhanced Integrated Framework for Trade-related Technical Assistance to Least Developed Countries;

19. *Requests* the Secretary-General, in collaboration with the secretariat of the United Nations Conference on Trade and Development, to submit to the General Assembly at its sixty-seventh session a report on the implementation of the present resolution and developments in the multilateral trading system, under the sub-item entitled "International trade and development" of the item entitled "Macroeconomic policy questions";

20. *Also requests* the Secretary-General to transmit the present resolution to the Director-General of the World Trade Organization.

On 22 December (**decision 66/542**), the General Assembly took note of the report of the Second Committee [A/66/438 & Add.1–4] on its discussion of macroeconomic policy questions, including those related to international trade and development.

United Nations Conference on Trade and Development

Trade and Development Board

In 2011, the Trade and Development Board (TDB)—the governing body of the United Nations Conference on Trade and Development (UNCTAD)—met in one annual session (fifty-eighth, 12–23 and 28 September [A/66/15 (Part IV)]) and three executive sessions (fifty-second, 11–12 and 14 April) [A/66/15 (Part II)]; fifty-third, 27–28 June and 11 July [A/66/15 (Part III)]; and fifty-fourth, 28–29 November) [TD/B/EX(54)2], all in Geneva).

At its fifty-second executive session, TDB approved as the theme of the Thirteenth United Nations Conference on Trade and Development (UNCTAD-XIII)—to be held in Doha, Qatar, from 16 to 22 April 2012—development-centred globalization: towards inclusive and sustainable growth and development. The Board also approved the sub-themes of the conference and its preparatory process, and addressed institutional, organizational, administrative and related matters.

At its fifty-third executive session [A/66/15 (Part III)], TDB decided to align the modalities for its cooperation with the Inter-Parliamentary Union (IPU) with the practices of the General Assembly, remove IPU from the list of non-governmental organizations (NGOs) having status with UNCTAD, and list it as an observer international organization of parliamentarians [decision 506(EX-53) (A/66/15 (Part III))]. It also decided that national, regional and subregional NGOs, as well as the national affiliates of international NGOs already in status with UNCTAD, were eligible to apply for consultative status with UNCTAD in accordance with existing applicable procedures and practices [decision 507(EX-53)]; and to adopt the same arrangements for the accreditation and participation of civil society in UNCTAD-XIII and its preparatory meetings as at past conferences, and that two hearings with civil society, parliamentarians and the private sector would be convened within the framework of the Preparatory Committee for UNCTAD-XIII [decision 508(EX-53)]. In other action, the Board took note of the report of the Trade and Development Commission on its third session [TD/B/C.I/21], endorsed the agreed conclusions and postponed the fourth session of the Commission until late 2012; took note of the report of the Investment, Enterprise and Development Commission on its third session [TD/B/C.II/15)] and postponed its fourth session until late 2012; and took note of the reports of the Working Party on the Strategic Framework and the Programme Budget on its fifty-seventh [TD/B/WP/227] and fifty-eighth [TD/B/WP/230] sessions. Also at the session, TDB held a panel discussion on "Enhancing aid effectiveness: From Paris to Busan", for which the Board had before it a secretariat note [TD/B/EX(53)/3] that reviewed progress in strengthening aid effectiveness and highlighted measures that could be taken by both donors and recipients to ensure better development outcomes in Africa from aid.

At its fifty-eighth annual session, TDB adopted agreed conclusions on the UNCTAD contribution to the implementation of the outcome from the Fourth United Nations Conference on the Least Developed Countries (see p. 827), economic development in Africa (see p. 906), and the report of the independent evaluator on the UNCTAD programme of assistance to the Palestinian people (see p. 906). Taking note of the technical cooperation activities carried out by UNCTAD

[TD/B/WP/232 & Add.1,2 & Corr.1], TDB also, inter alia, expressed its concern at the decrease registered in 2010 in the delivery of technical cooperation in support of LDCs; urged the secretariat to continue to ensure that priority was assigned to LDCs; and called on development partners to continue contributing to the LDC Trust Fund [decision 510(LVIII) (A/66/15 (Part IV))]. In other action, the Board established an open-ended Preparatory Committee and approved the draft provisional agenda for UNCTAD-XIII [TD/B/58/CRP.3]; took note of the forty-fourth annual report of the United Nations Commission on International Trade Law [A/66/17]; took note of the reports of the Joint Advisory Group on the International Trade Centre on its forty-fourth [ITC/AG(XLIV)/238] and forty-fifth [ITC/AG(XLV)/242] sessions; took note of the report of the Working Party on the Strategic Framework and the Programme Budget on its fifty-ninth session and endorsed the agreed conclusions [TD/B/WP/236]; and took note of the report by the President of the Advisory Body set up in accordance with paragraph 166 of the Bangkok Plan of Action [TD/B/58/CRP.4]. The Board also took action on institutional and administrative and related matters.

At its fifty-fourth executive session, TDB took note of the UNCTAD *Least Developed Countries Report 2011* [Sales No. E.11.II.D.5] and the report of the Working Party on the Strategic Framework and Programme Budget on its sixtieth session [TD/B/WP/238]; agreed to postpone the sixty-first session of the Working Party until after UNCTAD-XIII, and requested the UNCTAD secretariat to identify a suitable week in late June or early July 2012 for that session; and approved the draft provisional agenda for the sixty-first session of the Working Party.

Implementation of the outcome from LDC-IV

At its fifty-eighth annual session [A/66/15 (Part IV)], TDB had before it a report [TD/B/58/7] of the UNCTAD secretariat on the implementation of the outcome from the Fourth United Nations Conference on the Least Developed Countries (LDC-IV) (see p. 827). The report assessed the resultant Istanbul Programme of Action, the situation of LDCs in relation to the quantitative goals and targets of the Programme of Action, and the implications of the Programme for its own work. According to the Programme, UNCTAD should conduct intergovernmental consensus-building, provide technical assistance to LDCs, and maintain its institutional capacity in research and analysis of LDCs. The report stressed the need to improve the statistical capacity of LDCs, enhance data collection and ensure implementation of the Programme of Action by all stakeholders.

TDB took note of the report and urged LDCs and their development partners to pursue the implementation of the agreed priorities and targets contained in the Programme of Action. Noting the continued commodity overdependence of LDCs, the Board requested the UNCTAD secretariat, in cooperation with other relevant agencies, to assist LDCs to address the negative impact of commodity price volatility on their economies [agreed conclusions 508(LVIII)].

Industrial development in Africa

At its fifty-eighth annual session [A/66/15 (Part IV)], TDB had before it the UNCTAD *Economic Development in Africa Report 2011: Fostering Industrial Development in Africa in the New Global Environment* [Sales No. E.11.II.D.14].

Taking note of the key message of the report—that Africa needed a new industrial policy to induce economic transformation, create employment and reduce poverty—the Board, inter alia, acknowledged that the State, while designing industrial policy, should give priority to consultations with the private sector and entrepreneurs, among other stakeholders; noted that promoting scientific and technological innovation, creating inter-sectoral linkages in the domestic economy, promoting entrepreneurship, and enhancing coherence between industrial and other economic policies were important in fostering industrial development in Africa; stressed that the promotion of industry should not be at the expense of the agricultural sector; and requested UNCTAD to continue to undertake policy-oriented research on economic development issues and challenges facing African countries, and to strengthen efforts to disseminate its research findings [agreed conclusions 509(LVIII)].

Evaluation

At its fifty-eighth annual session [A/66/15 (Part IV)], TDB had before it a report of the independent evaluator on the UNCTAD programme of assistance to the Palestinian people [TD/B/58/6 & Add.1], which recommended that UNCTAD develop new strategies with appropriate resources toward a more effective engagement in the occupied Palestinian territories, as well as the management response thereto [TD/B/58/CRP.2]. The Board requested the UNCTAD secretariat to take the recommendations contained in the report into account in its continuing implementation of the Accra Accord [agreed conclusions 511(LVIII)].

Subsidiary bodies

During the year, the Trade and Development Commission held its third session (Geneva, 6–10 June) [TD/B/C.I/21] (see p. 907). The Investment, Enterprise and Development Commission held its third session (Geneva, 2–6 May) [TD/B/C.II/15] (see p. 907). The Intergovernmental Group of Experts on

Competition Law and Policy held its eleventh session (Geneva, 19–21 July) [TD/B/C.I/CLP/12] (see p. 930). The Intergovernmental Working Group of Experts on International Standards of Accounting and Reporting held its twenty-eighth session (Geneva, 12–14 October) [TD/B/C.II/ISAR/61] (see p. 931). The Working Party on the Strategic Framework and the Programme Budget held its fifty-eighth (Geneva, 14–15 and 29 March) [TD/B/WP/230], fifty-ninth (Geneva, 5–7 September) [TD/B/WP/236] and sixtieth sessions (Geneva, 21–23 and 29 November) [TD/B/WP/238] (see p. 908).

Trade and Development Commission

The Trade and Development Commission, at its third session [TD/B/C.I/21], took note of the reports of the following: the Multi-year Expert Meeting on Commodities and Development on its third session [TD/B/C.I/MEM.2/16]; the Multi-year Expert Meeting on Services, Development and Trade: the Regulatory and Institutional Dimension, on its third session [TD/B/C.I/MEM.3/9]; the Multi-year Expert Meeting on International Cooperation: South-South Cooperation and Regional Integration, on its third session [TD/B/C.II/MEM.2/9]; the Multi-year Expert Meeting on Transport and Trade Facilitation on its third session [TD/B/C.I/MEM.1/9]; and the Expert Meeting on Maximizing the Development Impact of Remittances [TD/B/C.I/EM.4/3].

The Commission had before it UNCTAD secretariat notes on assessing the evolution of the international trading system and enhancing its contribution to development and economic recovery [TD/B/C.I/15]; the integration of developing countries in global supply chains, including through adding value to their exports [TD/B/C.I/16]; and progress reports on the implementation of the provisions of the Accra Accord [YUN 2008, p. 1042] related to key trade and development issues [TD/B/C.I/17], commodities [TD/B/C.I/18], transport and trade facilitation [TD/B/C.I/19], and cross-divisional capacity-building [TD/B/C.I/20].

In agreed conclusions, the Commission expressed concern over the uneven trade and economic recovery from the global economic crisis; recognized that trade and trade policies needed to be streamlined and augmented with complementary policies for building competitive and diversified agricultural, industrial and services productive capacities; emphasized that trade policies should contribute to both the quantity and quality of employment; stressed the importance of building services supply capacities, including infrastructure services, to promote diversification, competitiveness, employment creation and increased trade; emphasized the importance of the WTO Doha Round of trade negotiation; and highlighted the increase and significance of South-South trade. The Commission encouraged UNCTAD to analyse the evolution of global supply chains; and continue its research and analysis on the contribution of migrants' remittances to development. UNCTAD was asked to pursue its mandate on trade and development issues as contained in the Accra Accord, and to reinforce assistance to developing countries, in particular LDCs.

TDB, at its fifty-third executive session [A/66/15 (Part III)], took note of the report of the Commission and endorsed the agreed conclusions contained therein.

Investment, Enterprise and Development Commission

The Investment, Enterprise and Development Commission, at its third session [TD/B/C.II/15], addressed two main themes: best practices in infrastructure investment; and enhancing productive capacities through entrepreneurship, science and innovation policies.

The Commission took note of the reports of the following: the Multi-year Expert Meeting on Enterprise Development Policies and Capacity-building in Science, Technology and Innovation on its third session [TD/B/C.II/MEM.1/10]; the Multi-year Expert Meeting on Investment for Development on its third session [TD/B/C.II/MEM.3/9]; the Multi-year Expert Meeting on International Cooperation: South-South Cooperation and Regional Integration, on its third session [TD/B/C.II/MEM.2/9]; the Intergovernmental Working Group of Experts on International Standards of Accounting and Reporting on its twenty-seventh session [TD/B/C.II/ISAR/57]; and the Expert Meeting on the Contribution of Foreign Direct Investment to the Transfer and Diffusion of Technology and Know-how for Sustainable Development in Developing Countries, Especially Least Developed Countries [TD/B/C.II/EM.2/3]. It also reviewed the investment policy of Guatemala [UNCTAD/DIAE/PCB/2010/9].

The Commission had before it an UNCTAD secretariat note [TD/B/C.II/14] on the implementation of the provisions of the Accra Accord related to the areas of work on science, technology and innovation, and information and communication technologies.

In agreed conclusions, the Commission stressed the importance of investment in agriculture; recognized the importance of an enabling external environment and coherence of policies at the national and international levels; noted the significance of information and communication technologies (ICTs) for development and encouraged UNCTAD to continue its work on ICTs for development; emphasized the need to intensify activities in the area of International Investment Agreements, especially on investor-State dispute prevention and settlement; and observed the growing opportunities for investment in new technologies in developing countries.

TDB, at its fifty-third executive session [A/66/15 (Part III)], took note of the report of the Commission and endorsed the agreed conclusions contained therein.

Working Party on the Strategic Framework and the Programme Budget

The Working Party on the Strategic Framework and the Programme Budget, at its fifty-eighth session [TD/B/WP/230], took note of a report on the implementation of the UNCTAD communications strategy and publications policy [TD/B/WP/229]. It was noted that there were no agreed conclusions. The Working Group, however, reached consensus on the following: appreciation of the progress made in the implementation of the communications strategy and the publications policy; the importance of translation for outreach, and the need for timely translation of UNCTAD publications as a matter of priority; and the need for the UNCTAD Secretary-General to pursue his efforts to ensure an effective multilingual approach to the UNCTAD communications strategy. In the absence of agreed conclusions, the secretariat would continue implementing the agreed conclusions from the previous year's meeting [YUN 2010, p. 965] where those conclusions remained applicable.

During its fifty-ninth session [TD/B/WP/236], the Working Party reviewed the technical cooperation activities of UNCTAD and their financing, and considered the in-depth evaluation of the UNCTAD programme on science and technology for development [TD/B/WP/234]. In agreed conclusions, the Working Party requested that member States further discuss the recommendations of the UNCTAD evaluation report at the next Working Party on technical cooperation in the second half of 2012; and called on development partners in a position to do so to continue to contribute to the LDC Trust Fund.

At its sixtieth session [TD/B/WP/238], the Working Party reviewed the proposed UNCTAD Biennial Programme Plan for the period 2014–2015 [TD/B/WP(60)/CRP.1/Rev.1]. It was also noted that the practice and principle of agreed conclusions in the Working Party would continue after UNCTAD-XIII.

At its fifty-third executive session [A/66/15 (Part III)], TDB took note of the reports of the Working Party on its fifty-seventh [YUN 2010, p. 965] and fifty-eighth sessions. At its fifty-eighth annual session [A/66/15 (Part IV)], TDB took note of the report of the Working Party on its fifty-ninth session and endorsed the agreed conclusions. At its fifty-fourth executive session [TD/B/EX(54)/2], TDB took note of the report of the sixtieth session of the Working Party; agreed to postpone the sixty-first session of the Working Party until after UNCTAD-XIII, and requested the UNCTAD secretariat to identify a suitable week in late June or early July 2012 for that session; and approved the draft provisional agenda for the sixty-first session of the Working Party.

International Trade Centre

The joint UNCTAD/WTO International Trade Centre (ITC), as set forth in its Annual Report 2011 [ITC/AG(XLVI)/243], continued to design programmes and reinvent its services towards the following five strategic objectives: building awareness and improving the availability and use of trade intelligence; strengthening trade support institutions; enhancing policies for the benefit of exporting enterprises; building the export capacity of enterprises to respond to market opportunities; and mainstreaming inclusiveness and sustainability into trade promotion and export development policies. In 2010–2011, ITC provided programme support enabling 1,620 enterprises to meet potential buyers with whom they subsequently had business transactions. It also created and implemented 51 export development strategies, representing a 55 per cent increase over the previous biennium. ITC assisted an average of 36 trade support institutions each year during the 2010–2011 biennium, and in 2011 it had 224 active projects and delivered more trade-related technical assistance than ever before. It continued working with WTO on the joint Programme on Trade Capacity for Acceding Least Developed Countries. By facilitating consensus-building and public-private dialogue on accession issues, ITC supported two LDCs—Samoa and Vanuatu—in gaining WTO membership in 2011. Those were among the 11 LDCs that ITC had assisted with WTO accession since 2010.

During the year, the distribution of extra-budgetary ITC expenditure on programme delivery by region was as follows: sub-Saharan Africa, 60 per cent; Arab States, 13 per cent; Asia-Pacific, 12 per cent; Eastern Europe and Central Asia, 4 per cent; and Latin America and the Caribbean, 11 per cent. In aggregate, 55 per cent of expenditure was on programmes in LDCs, sub-Saharan Africa, landlocked developing countries (LLDCs), and small island developing States (SIDS).

Joint Advisory Group

The Joint Advisory Group (JAG) on ITC, at its forty-fifth session (Geneva, 30 June–1 July) [ITC/AG(XLV)/242], discussed ITC activities based on the Centre's Annual Report 2010 [YUN 2010, p. 942], and made recommendations to the UNCTAD Trade and Development Board and WTO General Council. Discussing the Fourth United Nations Conference on the Least Developed Countries (LDC-IV) (p. 827), the WTO Director-General stated that the outcome highlighted the importance of the service sector to the economies of developing countries and LDCs, starting with tourism. The UNCTAD Secretary-General stressed the importance of ITC support to the private sector in LDCs, especially to develop tourism. JAG commended ITC on its technical assistance programmes and progress in implementing results-based management. A number of delegates from donor countries recommended a stronger linking of ITC projects to strategic objectives, a sharper assessment of results and outcomes, and a demonstration of value for money. Delegates welcomed the introduction of quality-assurance mechanisms to enhance ITC performance. They also applauded the increased focus of ITC on delivery to the most vulnerable countries—LDCs, LLDCs, SIDS and sub-Saharan African States—although some delegates from countries outside those categories expressed the hope that donors would not overlook their need for ITC support. Some delegates expressed concern that certain regions continued to attract few resources, namely, the Caribbean, Eastern Europe and Central Asia, and Latin America. Delegates acknowledged that changes brought about by the so-called "Arab Spring" would make the work of ITC even more important, to help countries rebuild their economies and make the transition to democracy and competitive market conditions. There was a call for ITC to follow up on LDC-IV, and several countries commended ITC for organizing, parallel to the Conference, the World Export Development Forum, which focused on tourism, the private sector and poor communities. All the countries involved in the Enhancing Arab Capacity for Trade Programme, ENACT, spoke about its importance and positive impact and urged the main donor, Canada, to continue its support. Countries emphasized the importance of the work of ITC in mainstreaming gender into its activities at headquarters and in the field, and welcomed the launch of the Women and Trade programme.

TDB, at its fifty-eighth session [A/66/15 (Part IV)], took note of the reports of the Group on its forty-fourth [YUN 2010, p. 943] and forty-fifth sessions.

Administrative and budgetary matters

Pursuant to General Assembly resolution 59/276 [YUN 2004, p. 1383], the Secretary-General, in April, submitted a preliminary budget for the ITC programme of activities for the biennium 2012–2013 [A/66/6 (Sect.13)], and, in September, detailed estimated resource requirements and projected income for that biennium [A/66/6 (Sect. 13)/Add.1)]. The budget was to be funded equally by WTO and the United Nations, acting through UNCTAD. The overall resources required for the biennium 2012–2013 for ITC amounted to SwF 74,679,600 before re-costing, representing an increase of SwF 1,081,900, or 1.5 per cent, compared with the biennium 2010–2011. The proposed resources were partially offset by a projected income of SwF 500,000, leaving a net amount of SwF 74,179,600 to be shared equally between WTO and the United Nations. The regular budget resources for the biennium were to be supplemented by extra-budgetary resources amounting to approximately $88,957,100, equivalent to SwF 96,518,500. That represented an increase of approximately 8 per cent of the total extra-budgetary resources available for the biennium 2010–2011. The Advisory Committee on Administrative and Budgetary Questions issued its recommendation in an October report [A/66/7/Add.5] to the General Assembly.

On 24 December, the Assembly, in section VI of **resolution 66/247** (see p. 1393), approved resources for ITC in the amount of $41,337,700 (corresponding to the United Nations share equivalent of SwF 38,072,000) for the biennium 2012–2013.

Other matters

Public Symposium

The third UNCTAD Public Symposium (Geneva, 22–24 June) [TD/B/58/8], organized in cooperation with the UN Non-Governmental Liaison Service and other partners, brought together over 250 representatives of civil society, the private sector, governments, parliaments, academia, the media, UN agencies and other international organizations. Participants discussed how to make trade and finance work for full and productive employment and to reduce inequalities; how to make financial and monetary reforms to ensure sustainable economic growth; and how the transition to a green economy, in the context of sustainable development and poverty eradication, could be fair and equitable. The Symposium called for more reforms in global governance; maintaining the focus of development on poverty reduction; reforms at the Bretton Woods institutions (the World Bank Group and the International Monetary Fund); securing greater capital to fund development; income redistribution policies as a way of reducing the costs of volatility in markets; stabilizing exchange rate regimes through the use of reserve funds and loans from regional banks; fostering the transition towards a green, fair and equitable economy; policies to increase the creation of employment opportunities; national legislation to encourage the use of renewable energies posing no threat to food security; and better coordination of macroeconomic policies at the global level. Partnerships with civil society were considered crucial to bringing about change in world consumption, production, trade and finance patterns, and to building support for achieving sustainable and inclusive development.

Commodities

In response to General Assembly resolution 64/192 [YUN 2009, p. 926], the Secretary-General transmitted a report [A/66/207] prepared by the UNCTAD secretariat on world commodity trends and prospects, including an analysis of the causes of excessive commodity price volatility. The report stated that commodity prices reached record levels in 2011 with exceptionally high price volatility. Prices of crude oil, minerals and precious metals more than doubled their end-of-year 2008 levels. The prices of key agricultural commodities, including coffee, maize, cotton, oats and sugar (although not rice), also surpassed their previously reported levels.

The UNCTAD food price index reached a peak in February 2011 and averaged 269 points from January to May, up 21 per cent from the same period in 2010. The world food-price inflation in developing countries exceeded 9 per cent in February 2011. The burden of high and volatile food prices fell disproportionately on low-income developing countries. Surging commodity prices contributed to popular uprisings and food riots in some countries during 2010–2011, as food-price inflation and rising energy costs took their toll.

The majority of the price hikes in agrifood and non-agrifood commodities could be explained by market fundamentals such as rising demand for commodities in emerging economies, especially China and India; adverse weather patterns due to greater climatic variability; low yields and declining productivity growth rates in some regions; low inventories or stock levels; increasing scarcity of arable farmland and water; supply shortages in mineral markets due to insufficient investment in exploration and new technologies during the 1990s; depreciation of the United States dollar; government policies, such as subsidies and export restrictions; and biofuels mandates which might have diverted key staples and agricultural land away from food production and towards the production of fuel. Geopolitical tensions in oil-producing countries in the Middle East and North Africa further fuelled the upward trajectory in crude oil and gasoline prices during the first quarter of 2011. The high prices drew speculative investors—such as hedge funds and commodity-index and exchange-traded funds—into commodity markets.

The episodes of extreme volatility in commodity markets prompted collaborative global action. Agriculture ministers from the Group of Twenty (G-20) leading economies met in Paris on 22–23 June and established a five-point Action Plan on Food Price Volatility and Agriculture, the centrepiece of which was an Agricultural Market Information System designed to address high and volatile food prices.

According to the report, ensuring that price volatility would not impede growth, development, and poverty eradication efforts required innovative and coherent policies at national, regional and international levels. The extreme vulnerability of mineral resource-endowed developing countries would require prudent fiscal policies and management, institutional mechanisms and market strategies, such as stabilization funds and diversification against dependence on a limited number of commodities. Tighter regulation and greater transparency were important for reducing excessive price volatility in "financialized" commodity markets; and policy measures should aim to improve market functioning and increase resilience of countries to shocks.

GENERAL ASSEMBLY ACTION

On 22 December [meeting 91], the General Assembly, on the recommendation of the Second Committee [A/66/438/Add.4], adopted **resolution 66/190** without vote [agenda item 17 (*d*)].

Commodities

The General Assembly,

Recalling its resolutions 59/224 of 22 December 2004, 61/190 of 20 December 2006, 63/207 of 19 December 2008 and 64/192 of 21 December 2009 on commodities,

Recalling also the United Nations Millennium Declaration adopted by Heads of State and Government on 8 September 2000, the 2005 World Summit Outcome adopted on 16 September 2005 and its resolution 60/265 of 30 June 2006 on the follow-up to the development outcome of the 2005 World Summit, including the Millennium Development Goals and the other internationally agreed development goals, and the High-level Plenary Meeting of the General Assembly on the Millennium Development Goals and its outcome document,

Recalling further the Programme of Action for the Least Developed Countries for the Decade 2011–2020,

Taking note of the targets set out in the Declaration of the World Summit on Food Security, held in Rome from 16 to 18 November 2009, which reaffirms the pledge to end hunger and poverty,

Recalling the Conference on the World Financial and Economic Crisis and Its Impact on Development and its outcome,

Recalling also the International Conference on Financing for Development, held in Monterrey, Mexico, from 18 to 22 March 2002, and the Follow-up International Conference on Financing for Development to Review the Implementation of the Monterrey Consensus, held in Doha from 29 November to 2 December 2008,

Taking note of the Accra Accord, adopted by the United Nations Conference on Trade and Development at its twelfth session, containing far-reaching recommendations on commodity issues, and of further decisions and agreed conclusions on commodities adopted by the Trade and Development Board and its subsidiary bodies in 2010 and 2011, including the evaluation and review of the implementation by the Conference of the Accra Accord, and looking forward to the thirteenth session of the United Nations Conference on Trade and Development, to be held in Doha from 21 to 26 April 2012,

Taking note also of the Political Declaration of the High-level Meeting on Africa's Development Needs, held in New York on 22 September 2008,

Taking note further of the Arusha Declaration and Plan of Action on African Commodities adopted at the African Union Conference of Ministers of Trade on Commodities, held in Arusha, United Republic of Tanzania, from 21 to 23 November 2005, and endorsed by the Executive Council of the African Union at its eighth ordinary session, held in Khartoum from 16 to 21 January 2006,

Recalling the Plan of Implementation of the World Summit on Sustainable Development ("Johannesburg Plan of Implementation"),

Recognizing that many developing countries continue to be highly dependent on primary commodities as their principal source of export revenues, employment, income generation and domestic savings, and as the driving force of investment, economic growth and social development, including poverty eradication,

Taking note of the comprehensive policy report entitled "Price Volatility in Food and Agricultural Markets: Policy Responses", issued on 2 June 2011 by the Food and Agriculture Organization of the United Nations, the International Fund for Agricultural Development, the International Monetary Fund, the Organization for Economic Cooperation and Development, the United Nations Conference on Trade and Development, the World Food Programme, the World Bank, the World Trade Organization, the International Food Policy Research Institute and the High-level Task Force on the Global Food Security Crisis,

Deeply concerned by episodes of commodity price booms and subsequent busts and by the fact that many commodity-dependent developing countries and economies in transition continue to be highly vulnerable to price fluctuations, and recognizing the need to improve the regulation, functioning and transparency of financial and commodity markets, which can address excessive commodity price volatility,

Recognizing the impact of factors such as climate change on the production of agricultural commodities,

Recognizing also that uncertainty in global commodity markets reinforces the need to comprehensively deal with the commodity problematique, inter alia, the demand for commodities, supply capacities, commodity revenues and investments in commodity-dependent economies, while taking due account of the diversity of each country's individual situation and needs and the promotion of their sustainable development, and to strengthen the nexus between trade, food, finance, investment in sustainable agriculture, energy and industrialization,

Stressing the importance of policies to address longer-term structural issues of the commodity economy and integrate commodity policies into wider development and poverty eradication strategies at all levels,

Taking note of all relevant voluntary initiatives aimed at improving transparency in commodity markets and mitigating the impact of excessive price volatility,

Underlining the importance of timely, accurate and transparent information in helping to address excessive food price volatility, and in this regard, taking note of the Agricultural Market Information System hosted by the Food and Agriculture Organization of the United Nations, and urging the participating international organizations, private sector actors and Governments to ensure the public dissemination of timely and quality food market information,

1. *Takes note* of the note by the Secretary-General transmitting the report on world commodity trends and prospects prepared by the secretariat of the United Nations Conference on Trade and Development;

2. *Underlines* the need for further efforts to address excessive commodity price volatility, in particular by assisting producers, especially small-scale producers, in managing risk;

3. *Calls upon* the international community to support the efforts of commodity-dependent developing countries to address the factors that create structural barriers to international trade and impede, inter alia, diversification, including tariff and non-tariff barriers, limited access to financial services resulting in scarce resources for investing in the commodity sector, weak infrastructure, particularly as regards both the cost and availability of transportation and storage, and lack of skills in producing and marketing alternative products;

4. *Calls for*, in that regard, the successful conclusion of the Doha Development Round of trade negotiations with a development-oriented outcome that ensures, inter alia, greater market access for products from developing countries;

5. *Also calls for* a coherent set of policy actions at the national, regional and international levels to address excessive price volatility and support commodity-dependent developing countries in mitigating negative impacts, in particular by facilitating value addition and enhancing their participation in commodity and related product value chains, by supporting large-scale diversification of these economies and by encouraging the use and further development of market-oriented risk management tools, instruments and strategies;

6. *Recognizes* the potential for innovation, productivity improvements and promotion of non-traditional exports in most commodity-dependent developing countries, particularly in Africa, and calls for enhanced support by the international community as well as exchanges of experience in these areas within the framework of South-South economic cooperation;

7. *Calls upon* the international community to work closely with commodity-dependent economies to identify trade-related policies and instruments as well as investment and financial policies as key elements of the development strategies of those economies;

8. *Underlines* the importance of increased investments in infrastructure as a means of promoting agricultural development and enhancing commodity diversification and trade, and urges the international community to assist commodity-dependent developing countries and to invest in and support research and development of agricultural productivity;

9. *Expresses concern* over the large-scale land acquisitions in developing countries by, among others, transnational corporations, that incur risk to development efforts, stresses the importance of promoting responsible international investment in agriculture, urges the Committee on World Food Security to finalize the voluntary guidelines on the responsible governance of tenure of land, fisheries and forests in the context of national food security, and invites the United Nations Conference on Trade and Development, in cooperation with other relevant international organizations, to continue its research and analysis on this issue;

10. *Stresses* that technical assistance and capacity-building aimed at improving the commodity export competitiveness of producers is particularly important, especially in Africa, and invites the donor community to provide necessary resources for commodity-specific, financial and technical assistance, in particular for human and institutional capacity-building, as well as infrastructure development of developing countries, with a view to reducing their institutional bottlenecks and transaction costs and enhancing their commodity trade and development in accordance with national development plans;

11. *Also stresses* that the Aid for Trade initiative should aim to help developing countries, particularly least developed countries, to build the supply-side capacity and trade-related infrastructure that they need to assist them to implement and benefit from World Trade Organization agreements and, more broadly, to expand their trade;

12. *Underlines* the important contribution of the commodities sector to rural development, in particular to providing rural employment and income, and to the efforts for achieving food security;

13. *Emphasizes* the importance of international measures and national strategies to improve the performance of the agricultural sector, including the functioning of markets and trading systems, to ensure a better supply-side response from producers, in particular small farmers, in order to incentivize them to take the risks inherent in investing in increased and diversified production;

14. *Stresses* the importance of managing excessive price volatility, including, inter alia, through the development of appropriate non-trade-distorting tools at the international level and the improvement of transparency in the international market;

15. *Recalls* the agreement to keep under regular review, by the Ministerial Conference and appropriate organs of the World Trade Organization, the impact of the results of the Uruguay Round on the least developed countries as well as on the net food-importing developing countries, with a view to fostering positive measures to enable them to achieve their development objectives, and in this regard calls for the implementation of the Marrakesh Decision on Measures Concerning the Possible Negative Effects of the Reform Programme on Least-Developed and Net Food-Importing Developing Countries;

16. *Encourages* developed countries that have not already done so and developing countries declaring themselves in a position to do so to take steps towards the goal of realizing timely implementation of duty-free and quota-free market access on a lasting basis for all least developed countries, consistent with the Hong Kong Ministerial Declaration adopted by the World Trade Organization in 2005;

17. *Calls upon* international financial institutions and development banks to assist developing countries, in particular commodity-dependent developing countries, in managing the effects of excessive price volatility;

18. *Reaffirms* that every State has and shall freely exercise full permanent sovereignty over all its wealth, natural resources and economic activities;

19. *Recognizes* the importance of increasing efficiency, effectiveness and transparency in the management of public and private sector revenues in developed and developing countries derived from all commodities and commodities-related industries, including final processed goods, in support of development;

20. *Also recognizes* the important contributions of the Common Fund for Commodities and other international commodities organizations, and encourages them, in cooperation with the International Trade Centre, the United Nations Conference on Trade and Development, the United Nations Industrial Development Organization and other relevant bodies, to continue to strengthen coordination among themselves and study ways to establish greater stability in the commodities market as well as to enhance activities in developing countries to improve access to markets and reliability of supply, enhancing diversification and addition of value, improving the competitiveness of commodities, strengthening the market chain, improving market structures, broadening the export base and ensuring the effective participation of all stakeholders;

21. *Stresses* that the United Nations Conference on Trade and Development and its partners, in the spirit of inter-agency cooperation and multi-stakeholder partnerships and within their respective mandates, should continue to engage actively in collaborative research and analysis of the commodity problematique and related capacity and consensus-building activities with a view to providing regular analysis and policy advice relevant to the sustainable development of commodity-dependent developing countries, particularly low-income countries;

22. *Underlines* the urgent need for the provision of, and access to, trade finance to commodity-dependent developing countries, given the tightened access to all types of credit and noting debt sustainability;

23. *Stresses* the importance of the continuing substantive consideration of the sub-item entitled "Commodities", and decides to include the sub-item in the provisional agenda of its sixty-eighth session, under the item entitled "Macroeconomic policy questions";

24. *Requests* the Secretary-General, in collaboration with the secretariat of the United Nations Conference on Trade and Development, to submit to the General Assembly at its sixty-eighth session a report presenting an updated assessment of commodity trends and prospects, ways to strengthen coordination among international commodities organizations and other relevant international organizations and the causes of excessive commodity price volatility.

On 22 December (**decision 66/542**), the General Assembly took note of the report of the Second Committee [A/66/438 & Add.1–4] on its discussion of macroeconomic policy questions, including commodities.

Individual commodities

Cocoa. On 14 December 2010, the Secretary-General issued a depositary notification [C.N.810.2010. TREATIES-2] drawing the attention of parties to an error in article 62 (3) of the authentic text of the International Cocoa Agreement, 2010 [YUN 2010, p. 944] as well as the certified true copies circulated by the depositary notification of 30 September 2010 [C.N.497.2010. TREATIES-2], whereby the term "fifth cocoa year" should have read "tenth cocoa year". In accordance with the established depositary practice, a period of 90 days from the date of the notification was set for any objection to be communicated to the Secretary-General. No objections were received and the proposed correction was effected to the text of the Agreement.

As at 31 December, there were 18 parties to the International Cocoa Agreement, 2001 [YUN 2001, p. 880]. The International Cocoa Agreement, 2010 [YUN 2010, p. 994] had one signatory (Switzerland).

Sugar. On 2 June, the International Sugar Council decided to extend the International Sugar Agreement, 1992 [YUN 1992, p. 625] until 31 December 2013. As at 31 December 2011, the Agreement had 60 parties. Indonesia became a party during the year.

Tropical Timber. On 7 December 2011, the International Tropical Timber Agreement, 2006 [YUN 2006, p. 1124] entered into force, following ratification of the Agreement by the Government of Benin on that date. As at 31 December 2011, there were 60 parties to the Agreement. During the year, Albania, Benin, Estonia, Greece, Guatemala, Honduras and Myanmar became parties.

Common Fund for Commodities

At the end of 2011, the Common Fund for Commodities (CFC)—established in 1990 to realize the potential of commodity production, processing, manufacturing, and trade for the benefit of the poor [YUN 1980, p. 621]—had 116 parties. During the year, the ad hoc Working Group of the CFC Executive Board held two meetings, and the Governing Council established a Reform Committee to come to a decision in 2012 regarding the future role and mandate of the Fund and its long-term financial sustainability.

Coercive economic measures

Pursuant to General Assembly resolution 64/189 [YUN 2009, p. 921], the Secretary-General submitted a July report [A/66/138] on unilateral economic measures as a means of political and economic coercion against developing countries. The report summarized replies received from 18 Member States (Armenia, Brunei Darussalam, Colombia, Cuba, Egypt, Gabon, Guatemala, Lebanon, Malaysia, Malta, Mauritius, Mexico, Myanmar, Oman, Qatar, Sudan, Ukraine and Viet Nam) expressing their views on the imposition of such measures; and two United Nations bodies and one other international organization reporting the continued application of such measures against eight Member States (Belarus, Cuba, Democratic People's Republic of Korea, Islamic Republic of Iran, Libyan Arab Jamahiriya, Myanmar, the Sudan and the Syrian Arab Republic) as well as the Occupied Palestinian Territory.

Communications. On 24 June [A/65/876], Iran transmitted to the Secretary-General a document concerning new unilateral sanctions against some Iranian companies and individuals. On 25 August [A/66/323], Belarus transmitted to the Secretary-General a document concerning unilateral sanctions against Belarusian enterprises. On 17 October [A/C.2/66/4], Syria transmitted to the Secretary-General a document concerning unilateral sanctions targeted at the Syrian economic, financial and banking sectors.

GENERAL ASSEMBLY ACTION

On 22 December [meeting 91], the General Assembly, on the recommendation of the Second Committee [A/66/438/Add.1], adopted **resolution 66/186** by recorded vote (122-2-53) [agenda item 17 (*a*)].

Unilateral economic measures as a means of political and economic coercion against developing countries

The General Assembly,

Recalling the relevant principles set forth in the Charter of the United Nations,

Reaffirming the Declaration on Principles of International Law concerning Friendly Relations and Cooperation among States in accordance with the Charter of the United Nations, which states, inter alia, that no State may use or encourage the use of unilateral economic, political or any other type of measures to coerce another State in order to obtain from it the subordination of the exercise of its sovereign rights,

Bearing in mind the general principles governing the international trading system and trade policies for development contained in relevant resolutions, rules and provisions of the United Nations and the World Trade Organization,

Recalling its resolutions 44/215 of 22 December 1989, 46/210 of 20 December 1991, 48/168 of 21 December 1993, 50/96 of 20 December 1995, 52/181 of 18 December 1997, 54/200 of 22 December 1999, 56/179 of 21 December 2001, 58/198 of 23 December 2003, 60/185 of 22 December 2005, 62/183 of 19 December 2007 and 64/189 of 21 December 2009,

Gravely concerned that the use of unilateral coercive economic measures adversely affects the economy and development efforts of developing countries in particular and has a general negative impact on international economic cooperation and on worldwide efforts to move towards a non-discriminatory and open multilateral trading system,

Recognizing that such measures constitute a flagrant violation of the principles of international law as set forth in the Charter, as well as the basic principles of the multilateral trading system,

1. *Takes note* of the report of the Secretary-General;
2. *Urges* the international community to adopt urgent and effective measures to eliminate the use of unilateral coercive economic measures against developing countries that are not authorized by relevant organs of the United Nations or are inconsistent with the principles of international law as set forth in the Charter of the United Nations and that contravene the basic principles of the multilateral trading system;

3. *Calls upon* the international community to condemn and reject the imposition of the use of such measures as a means of political and economic coercion against developing countries;

4. *Requests* the Secretary-General to continue to monitor the imposition of measures of this nature and to study the impact of such measures on the affected countries, including the impact on trade and development;

5. *Also requests* the Secretary-General to submit to the General Assembly at its sixty-eighth session a report on the implementation of the present resolution.

RECORDED VOTE ON RESOLUTION 66/186:

In favour: Afghanistan, Algeria, Angola, Antigua and Barbuda, Argentina, Armenia, Azerbaijan, Bahamas, Bahrain, Bangladesh, Barbados, Belarus, Belize, Benin, Bhutan, Bolivia, Botswana, Brazil, Brunei Darussalam, Burkina Faso, Burundi, Cambodia, Cameroon, Cape Verde, Central African Republic, Chad, Chile, China, Colombia, Comoros, Congo, Costa Rica, Côte d'Ivoire, Cuba, Democratic People's Republic of Korea, Djibouti, Dominica, Dominican Republic, Ecuador, Egypt, El Salvador, Eritrea, Ethiopia, Fiji, Gabon, Grenada, Guatemala, Guinea, Guinea-Bissau, Guyana, Honduras, India, Indonesia, Iran, Iraq, Jamaica, Jordan, Kazakhstan, Kenya, Kuwait, Kyrgyzstan, Lao People's Democratic Republic, Lebanon, Lesotho, Liberia, Libya, Madagascar, Malawi, Malaysia, Maldives, Mali, Mauritius, Mexico, Mongolia, Morocco, Mozambique, Myanmar, Namibia, Nepal, Nicaragua, Niger, Nigeria, Oman, Pakistan, Panama, Papua New Guinea, Paraguay, Qatar, Russian Federation, Saint Lucia, Saint Vincent and the Grenadines, Saudi Arabia, Senegal, Sierra Leone, Singapore, Solomon Islands, Somalia, South Africa, Sri Lanka, Sudan, Suriname, Swaziland, Syrian Arab Republic, Tajikistan, Thailand, Timor-Leste, Togo, Tonga, Trinidad and Tobago, Tunisia, Turkmenistan, Tuvalu, Uganda, United Arab Emirates, United Republic of Tanzania, Uruguay, Uzbekistan, Venezuela, Viet Nam, Yemen, Zambia, Zimbabwe.

Against: Israel, United States.

Abstaining: Albania, Andorra, Australia, Austria, Belgium, Bosnia and Herzegovina, Bulgaria, Canada, Croatia, Cyprus, Czech Republic, Denmark, Estonia, Finland, France, Georgia, Germany, Greece, Hungary, Iceland, Ireland, Italy, Japan, Latvia, Liechtenstein, Lithuania, Luxembourg, Malta, Marshall Islands, Monaco, Montenegro, Netherlands, New Zealand, Norway, Palau, Peru, Philippines, Poland, Portugal, Republic of Korea, Republic of Moldova, Romania, San Marino, Serbia, Slovakia, Slovenia, Spain, Sweden, Switzerland, the former Yugoslav Republic of Macedonia, Turkey, Ukraine, United Kingdom.

International financial system and development

In response to General Assembly resolution 65/143 [YUN 2010, p. 947], the Secretary-General submitted a July report [A/66/167] on the international financial system and development. The report stated that during the financial and economic crisis, in the last quarter of 2008 and early 2009, the aggregate international reserve holding of developing countries fell by about $300 billion. Reserve holding by developing countries and economies in transition totalled about $5.4 trillion at the end of 2009, to which an additional $500 billion was added in 2010. A large proportion of that holding was accumulated by developing countries in Asia, particularly China, which was holding about $2.6 trillion in foreign-exchange reserves at the end of 2010. Net private capital flows to developing countries were estimated to have risen from about $325 billion in 2009 to about $392 billion in 2010, as stronger growth and higher interest rates in developing countries had attracted investors. The foreign direct investment portion of net private flows to developing countries was estimated at over $300 billion in 2010.

In 2010, total net official development assistance (ODA) from the member countries of the Development Assistance Committee (DAC) of the Organization for Economic Cooperation and Development reached $129 billion, the highest level ever, representing 0.32 per cent of their combined gross national income (GNI). Net bilateral ODA to Africa was $29 billion, an increase of 4 per cent in real terms over 2009. Net ODA/GNI ratios of many large donors were below the internationally agreed target of 0.7 per cent, while five countries (Denmark, Luxembourg, the Netherlands, Norway and Sweden) continued to exceed that target. Although aid delivery to least developed countries (LDCs) increased from $12 billion in 2000 to $37 billion in 2009, the improvement of DAC member countries' aggregated ODA/GNI ratio (from 0.05 per cent to 0.10 per cent) was not sufficient to achieve the LDC target of 0.15–0.20 per cent. Despite the increase in the volume of aid, the overall ODA delivery in 2010 fell short by $21 billion of the pledges made at the 2005 G-8 Gleneagles Summit. The shortfall regarding Africa was $18 billion. About half (8 out of 15) of the DAC/European Union (EU) members met the ambitious EU ODA/GNI target of 0.51 per cent set for 2010.

As for strengthening the international financial architecture, the report stated that important priorities were the implementation of Basel III [YUN 2010, p. 945], new rules for systemically important financial institutions and adequate regulation of the shadow banking system. It was vital to ensure that regulations and their implementation as well as supervisory practices were driven by the goal of bolstering global financial stability and development, rather than by interests of narrow groups of private financial institutions and/or markets. The International Monetary Fund (IMF) needed to pay more attention to spillovers from the policies of major countries on the rest of the world. Enhancing international coherence and promoting coordination among national economic policies towards improved financial stability and sustainable global growth should become a central objective of the IMF agenda. Given the reality of financial globalization, there was a need for some form of international framework for assessing policies to manage cross-border capital flows. An international framework for sovereign debt restructuring was suggested as a means of addressing the rising public debt in developed countries. Furthermore, there was scope for further enhancing multilateral liquidity, and for creating a multilateral mechanism to provide financing in systemic crises, in conjunction with bilateral and regional liquidity support arrangements. The need to explore options for reform of the international monetary system was now broadly accepted.

Communication. On 3 October [A/C.2/66/3], Singapore, on behalf of the Global Governance Group (3G), comprised of 29 UN Member States, transmitted to the Secretary-General a document entitled "Global Governance Group inputs to the G-20 on global governance". The 3G recognized the important role played by the G-20 in stemming the worst effects of the 2008 global economic and financial crisis and in addressing aspects of global economic governance. The United Nations was the only global body with universal participation and unquestioned legitimacy, but effectiveness was necessary to deal with time-sensitive problems that could have serious global consequences. The 3G advocated crafting solutions to urgent global challenges by involving varying subsets of countries which either had specific interests or established expertise in the subject matter, thus ensuring swift response, broad perspectives and transparency.

GENERAL ASSEMBLY ACTION

On 22 December [meeting 91], the General Assembly, on the recommendation of the Second Committee [A/66/438/Add.2], adopted **resolution 66/187** without vote [agenda item 17 (*b*)].

International financial system and development

The General Assembly,

Recalling its resolutions 55/186 of 20 December 2000 and 56/181 of 21 December 2001, both entitled "Towards a strengthened and stable international financial architecture responsive to the priorities of growth and development, especially in developing countries, and to the promotion of economic and social equity", as well as its resolutions 57/241 of 20 December 2002, 58/202 of 23 December 2003, 59/222 of 22 December 2004, 60/186 of 22 December 2005, 61/187 of 20 December 2006, 62/185 of 19 December 2007, 63/205 of 19 December 2008, 64/190 of 21 December 2009 and 65/143 of 20 December 2010,

Recalling also the United Nations Millennium Declaration and its resolution 56/210 B of 9 July 2002, in which it endorsed the Monterrey Consensus of the International Conference on Financing for Development, the Rio Declaration on Environment and Development, Agenda 21, the Programme for the Further Implementation of Agenda 21 and the Plan of Implementation of the World Summit on Sustainable Development ("Johannesburg Plan of Implementation"),

Recalling further the Doha Declaration on Financing for Development: outcome document of the Follow-up International Conference on Financing for Development to Review the Implementation of the Monterrey Consensus, held in Doha from 29 November to 2 December 2008,

Recalling the Conference on the World Financial and Economic Crisis and Its Impact on Development and its outcome document,

Recalling also the High-level Plenary Meeting of the General Assembly on the Millennium Development Goals and its outcome document,

Recognizing the work undertaken by the Ad Hoc Open-ended Working Group of the General Assembly to follow up on the issues contained in the Outcome of the Conference on the World Financial and Economic Crisis and Its Impact on Development, and taking note of its progress report,

Expressing deep concern about the ongoing adverse impacts, particularly on development, of the world financial and economic crisis, cognizant that the global economy is entering a challenging new phase with significant downside risks, including the turbulence in global financial and commodity markets and widespread fiscal strains, which threaten the global economic recovery, and stressing the need to continue to address systemic fragilities and imbalances and the need for continuing efforts to reform and strengthen the international financial system,

Noting that, while some developing countries have been the main contributors to recent global economic growth, the economic crisis has reduced their capacity to withstand further shocks, recalling the commitments made to support strong, sustainable, balanced and inclusive growth, and reaffirming the need to work cooperatively to meet development commitments to achieve the Millennium Development Goals by 2015,

Reaffirming the purposes of the United Nations, as set forth in its Charter, including to achieve international cooperation in solving international problems of an economic, social, cultural or humanitarian character and to be a centre for harmonizing the actions of nations in the attainment of common ends, and reiterating the need to strengthen the leadership role of the United Nations in promoting development,

Reiterating that the international financial system should support sustained, inclusive and equitable economic growth, sustainable development, and hunger and poverty eradication efforts in developing countries, while allowing for the coherent mobilization of all sources of financing for development,

Recalling the Fourth United Nations Conference on the Least Developed Countries and the Programme of Action for the Least Developed Countries for the Decade 2011–2020, and recognizing, in this context, that the international financial system should be supportive, as appropriate, of the special needs and priorities of the least developed countries,

Stressing the importance of commitment to ensuring sound domestic financial sectors, which make a vital contribution to national development efforts, as an important component of an international financial architecture that is supportive of development,

  1. *Takes note* of the report of the Secretary-General;
  2. *Recognizes* the need to continue to enhance the coherence and consistency of the international monetary, financial and trading systems and the importance of ensuring their openness, fairness and inclusiveness in order to complement national development efforts to ensure sustained, inclusive and equitable economic growth and the

achievement of the internationally agreed development goals, including the Millennium Development Goals;

3. *Stresses* the need to act decisively to tackle the challenges confronting the global economy in order to ensure balanced, sustainable, inclusive and equitable global growth with full and productive employment and quality jobs;

4. *Notes*, in this regard, the important efforts undertaken nationally, regionally and internationally to respond to the challenges posed by the financial and economic crisis, including the efforts to reinforce the banking sector by increasing its transparency and accountability;

5. *Also notes* that the United Nations, on the basis of its universal membership and legitimacy, provides a unique and key forum for discussing international economic issues and their impact on development, and reaffirms that the United Nations is well positioned to participate in various reform processes aimed at improving and strengthening the effective functioning of the international financial system and architecture, while recognizing that the United Nations and the international financial institutions have complementary mandates which make the coordination of their actions crucial;

6. *Recalls*, in this regard, the resolve to strengthen the coordination of the United Nations system and multilateral financial, trade and development institutions so as to support economic growth, poverty eradication and sustainable development worldwide, on the basis of a clear understanding of and respect for their mandates and governance structures;

7. *Also recalls* that countries must have the flexibility necessary to implement countercyclical measures and to pursue tailored and targeted responses to the crisis, and calls for conditionalities to be streamlined to ensure that they are timely, tailored and targeted and that they support developing countries in the face of financial, economic and development challenges;

8. *Further recalls*, in this regard, the improvement of the lending framework of the International Monetary Fund through, inter alia, streamlined conditions and the creation of more flexible instruments, such as a precautionary and liquidity line, while also noting that new and ongoing programmes should not contain unwarranted procyclical conditionalities;

9. *Recognizes* the role of private capital flows in mobilizing financing for development, stresses the challenges posed by excessive short-term capital inflows to many developing countries, encourages further review of the benefits and disadvantages of macroprudential measures available to mitigate the impact of volatile capital flows, and requests the Secretary-General to take this into account in preparing his report on the implementation of the present resolution;

10. *Notes* that countries can seek to negotiate, as a last resort, on a case-by-case basis and through existing frameworks, agreements on temporary debt standstills between debtors and creditors in order to help to mitigate the adverse impacts of the crisis and to stabilize macroeconomic developments;

11. *Reaffirms* the importance of broadening and strengthening the participation of developing countries in international economic decision-making and norm-setting, and in this regard takes note of recent important decisions on reform of the governance structures, quotas and voting rights of the Bretton Woods institutions, better reflecting current realities and enhancing the voice and participation of developing countries, and reiterates the importance of the reform of the governance of those institutions in order to deliver more effective, credible, accountable and legitimate institutions;

12. *Notes*, in this regard, the decisions taken by the World Bank Group on voice and participation and further institutional reforms to meet new challenges, and the addition of the twenty-fifth Chair to the Boards of Executive Directors of the World Bank Group, and looks forward to progress in its institutional reforms, calls for the swift implementation of the 2010 quota and governance reform of the International Monetary Fund, and reiterates the importance of an open, transparent and merit-based process for selecting the heads of the International Monetary Fund and other international financial institutions;

13. *Recognizes* the role of special drawing rights as an international reserve asset, and acknowledges that recent special drawing rights allocations helped to supplement international reserves in response to the world financial and economic crisis, thus contributing to the stability of the international financial system and global economic resilience;

14. *Reiterates* that effective, inclusive multilateral surveillance should be at the centre of crisis prevention efforts, and stresses the need to continue strengthening surveillance of economic policies of countries;

15. *Invites* the international financial and banking institutions to continue enhancing the transparency of risk-rating mechanisms, noting that sovereign risk assessments made by the private sector should maximize the use of strict, objective and transparent parameters, which can be facilitated by high-quality data and analysis, and encourages relevant institutions, including the United Nations Conference on Trade and Development, to continue their work on the issue, including its potential impact on the development prospects of developing countries;

16. *Calls upon* the multilateral, regional and subregional development banks and development funds to continue to play a vital role in serving the development needs of developing countries and countries with economies in transition, including through coordinated action, as appropriate, stresses that strengthened regional development banks and subregional financial institutions can add flexible financial support to national and regional development efforts, thus enhancing their ownership and overall efficiency, and in this regard welcomes recent capital increases at multilateral and regional development banks and, in addition, encourages efforts to ensure that subregional development banks are adequately funded;

17. *Encourages* enhanced regional and subregional cooperation, including through regional and subregional development banks, commercial and reserve currency arrangements and other regional and subregional initiatives;

18. *Stresses* the need to continuously improve standards of corporate and public sector governance, including those related to accounting, auditing and measures to ensure transparency, noting the disruptive effects of inadequate policies;

19. *Requests* the Secretary-General to submit to the General Assembly at its sixty-seventh session a report on the implementation of the present resolution, to be prepared in cooperation with the Bretton Woods institutions and other relevant stakeholders;

20. *Decides* to include in the provisional agenda of its sixty-seventh session, under the item entitled "Macroeconomic policy questions", the sub-item entitled "International financial system and development".

Also on 22 December (**decision 66/542**), the General Assembly took note of the report of the Second Committee [A/66/438 & Add.1–4] on its discussion of macroeconomic policy questions, including those related to the international financial system and development.

Debt situation of developing countries

In response to General Assembly resolution 65/144 [YUN 2010, p. 950], the Secretary-General submitted a July report [A/66/164] that analysed the external debt situation and debt-servicing problems of developing countries and countries with economies in transition. The total external debt of developing countries and countries with economies in transition stood at approximately $3.5 trillion by the end of 2009. The growth rate of total external debt slowed from 8 per cent in 2007–2008 to 3.5 per cent in 2008–2009. The UNCTAD secretariat estimated that debt grew by approximately 10 per cent during 2010, bringing total external debt to nearly $3.9 trillion. The average debt service to export ratio of developing countries decreased from 12 per cent in 2009 to an estimated 9.2 per cent in 2010, and their average external debt to gross national income (GNI) ratio decreased from 21.8 per cent in 2009 to an estimated 20.2 per cent in 2010. Improvements in debt ratios were driven by the fact that developing countries, as a group, were running large current account surpluses, and had provided a net transfer of financial resources to developed countries of approximately $557 billion during 2010. Even though a number of developing countries with emerging financial markets did not need foreign financing, private capital continued to flow to those countries. Net private capital inflows to such countries were estimated to have surpassed $900 billion in 2010, a 50 per cent increase over 2009 flows, and were projected to reach $1 trillion by 2012.

In 2010, total international reserves of developing countries surpassed $5.5 trillion, corresponding to 1.5 times the total external debt of developing countries. Private capital flows of the "carry trade" type continued to countries with high interest rates. Those flows were not caused by scarcity of funds but rather by attempts of central banks to fight inflation in growing economies. Such enormous gross capital flows were seen as having the potential to lead to a situation in which the exchange rate value was driven by speculative capital flows rather than by market fundamentals. Such "carry trade" activities could plant the seed for a currency crisis.

In 2010, debt service represented less than 4 per cent of exports in East Asia and the Pacific, more than 22 per cent of exports in Eastern Europe and Central Asia, 5.3 per cent in sub-Saharan Africa, 5.8 per cent in the Middle East and North Africa, 6.8 per cent in South Asia and 14 per cent in Latin America and the Caribbean. External debt was close to 40 per cent of GNI in Eastern Europe and Central Asia and 12 per cent of GNI in East Asia and the Pacific, approximately 14 per cent in the Middle East and North Africa, 18 per cent in sub-Saharan Africa and South Asia and 24 per cent in Latin America and the Caribbean. Even in the presence of large regional differences, debt ratios improved in almost all developing regions. Debt ratios varied across countries and reserve coverage was limited and rapidly decreasing in some small and vulnerable economies. In 2009, the total debt of the 49 LDCs stood at 32 per cent of the group's GNI, 10 percentage points higher than the average for all developing countries. Estimates for 2010 indicated that the average debt of LDCs would drop to 28 per cent of GNI, 8 percentage points higher than the estimate for the average developing country.

The report concluded that responsible and prudent lending and borrowing was the first line of defence against the emergence of debt problems. Further discussion and consensus-building around a set of draft principles on responsible sovereign lending and borrowing, released by UNCTAD in May, would contribute to the prevention of debt crises in the future.

GENERAL ASSEMBLY ACTION

On 22 December [meeting 91], the General Assembly, on the recommendation of the Second Committee [A/66/438/Add.3], adopted **resolution 66/189** without vote [agenda item 17 (*c*)].

External debt sustainability and development

The General Assembly,

Recalling its resolutions 58/203 of 23 December 2003, 59/223 of 22 December 2004, 60/187 of 22 December 2005, 61/188 of 20 December 2006, 62/186 of 19 December 2007, 63/206 of 19 December 2008, 64/191 of 21 December 2009 and 65/144 of 20 December 2010,

Recalling also the United Nations Millennium Declaration, adopted on 8 September 2000,

Recalling further the 2005 World Summit Outcome,

Recalling the International Conference on Financing for Development and its outcome document and the Doha Declaration on Financing for Development: outcome document of the Follow-up International Conference on Financing for Development to Review the Implementation of the Monterrey Consensus,

Recalling also the Conference on the World Financial and Economic Crisis and Its Impact on Development and its outcome document,

Recalling further the High-level Plenary Meeting of the General Assembly on the Millennium Development Goals and its outcome document,

Recalling the Fourth United Nations Conference on the Least Developed Countries and the Istanbul Declaration and the Programme of Action for the Least Developed Countries for the Decade 2011–2020,

Recalling also its resolution 57/270 B of 23 June 2003,

Recalling further its resolution 60/265 of 30 June 2006 on the follow-up to the development outcome of the 2005 World Summit, including the Millennium Development Goals and the other internationally agreed development goals,

Emphasizing that debt sustainability is essential for underpinning growth, underlining the importance of debt sustainability and effective debt management to the efforts to achieve national development goals, including the Millennium Development Goals, and acknowledging that sovereign debt crises tend to be costly and disruptive, including for employment and productive investment, and tend to be followed by cuts in public spending, including on health and education, affecting in particular the poor and vulnerable,

Reaffirming that each country has primary responsibility for its own development and that the role of national policies and development strategies, including in the area of debt management, cannot be overemphasized for the achievement of sustainable development, and recognizing that national efforts, including to achieve development goals and to maintain debt sustainability, should be complemented by supportive global programmes, measures and policies aimed at expanding the development opportunities of developing countries, while taking into account national conditions and ensuring respect for national ownership, strategies and sovereignty,

Reaffirming also that multilateral institutions, including entities within the United Nations system and other relevant organizations, should continue to play an important role, given their respective mandates, in assisting countries in achieving and maintaining debt sustainability,

Reiterating that debt sustainability depends on a confluence of many factors at the international and national levels, and emphasizing that country-specific circumstances and the impact of external shocks, such as those derived from the world financial and economic crisis, should continue to be taken into account in debt sustainability analyses,

Expressing deep concern about the ongoing adverse impacts, particularly on development, of the world financial and economic crisis, cognizant that the global economy is entering a challenging new phase with significant downside risks, including turbulence in global financial and commodity markets and widespread fiscal strains, which threaten the global economic recovery, and stressing the need to continue to address systemic fragilities and imbalances and the need for continuing efforts to reform and strengthen the international financial system,

Recognizing the importance of efforts undertaken at the national, regional and international levels in response to the challenges posed by the world financial and economic crisis, and acknowledging that the impacts of the crisis on development continue, entail the possibility of undermining the progress made towards achieving the internationally agreed development goals, including the Millennium Development Goals, and threaten debt sustainability in many countries, especially developing countries, through, inter alia, the consequences on the real economy and government revenue and the increase in borrowing to mitigate the negative impacts of the crisis,

Recognizing also the important role, on a case-by-case basis, of debt relief, including debt cancellation, as appropriate, and debt restructuring as debt crisis prevention and management tools for mitigating the impact of the world financial and economic crisis in developing countries,

Recognizing further the role of private capital flows in mobilizing financing for development, stressing the challenges posed by excessive short-term capital inflows to many developing countries, including to their debt sustainability, and encouraging further review of the benefits and disadvantages of the macroprudential measures available to mitigate the impact of volatile capital flows,

Expressing concern that some low-income countries face increased challenges in servicing their debt,

Expressing deep concern that, in spite of international efforts, many least developed countries still struggle with a high debt burden,

Noting with appreciation that the Heavily Indebted Poor Countries Initiative, the Multilateral Debt Relief Initiative and bilateral donors have provided substantial debt relief to thirty-two countries that have reached the completion point under the Heavily Indebted Poor Countries Initiative, which has considerably reduced their debt vulnerability and enabled them to increase their investments in social services, while acknowledging with concern that some post-completion point countries remain classified as being at high risk of debt distress and need to avoid rebuilding unsustainable debt burdens,

Convinced that enhanced market access for goods and services of export interest to developing countries contributes significantly to debt sustainability in those countries,

1. *Takes note* of the report of the Secretary-General;
2. *Emphasizes* the special importance of a timely, effective, comprehensive and durable solution to the debt problems of developing countries in order to promote their economic growth and development;
3. *Stresses* the importance of responsible lending and borrowing, emphasizes that creditors and debtors must share responsibility for preventing unsustainable debt situations, and encourages Member States, the Bretton Woods institutions, the regional development banks and other relevant multilateral financial institutions and stakeholders to continue the ongoing discussions on this issue, inter alia, within the framework of the initiative of the United Nations Conference on Trade and Development to promote responsible sovereign lending and borrowing;
4. *Acknowledges* the role played by the Debt Sustainability Framework for Low-Income Countries, jointly developed by the International Monetary Fund and the World Bank, to guide borrowing and lending decisions, and encourages continued review of the Framework, with the full engagement of borrower Governments, in an open and transparent manner;
5. *Reiterates* that no single indicator should be used to make definitive judgements about a country's debt sustainability, and, in this regard, while acknowledging the need to use transparent and comparable indicators, invites the International Monetary Fund and the World Bank, in their assessment of debt sustainability, to continue to take into account a country's structural weaknesses and the fundamental changes caused by, inter alia, natural disasters, conflicts and changes in global growth prospects or in the terms of trade, especially for commodity-dependent developing countries, as well as by the impact of developments

in financial markets, and to provide information on this issue to Member States, using the appropriate frameworks;

6. *Recognizes* that the long-term sustainability of debt depends on, inter alia, economic growth, mobilization of domestic and international resources, export prospects of debtor countries, responsible debt management, sound macroeconomic policies, transparent and effective regulatory frameworks and success in overcoming structural development problems, and hence on the creation of an enabling international environment that is conducive to development;

7. *Also recognizes* the enormity and the multidimensional nature of the world financial and economic crisis, which caused a sharp deterioration of the debt ratios in several developing countries, stresses the need to continue to assist developing countries in avoiding a build-up of unsustainable debt so as to reduce the risk of relapsing into another debt crisis, takes note in this regard of the additional resources made available during and since the crisis through the International Monetary Fund and the multilateral development banks, and calls for the continued provision of concessional and grant-based financing to low-income countries to enable them to respond to the consequences of the crisis;

8. *Further recognizes* the roles of the United Nations and the international financial institutions in accordance with their respective mandates, and encourages them to continue to support global efforts towards sustained, inclusive and equitable growth, sustainable development and the external debt sustainability of developing countries, including through continued monitoring of global financial flows and their implications in this regard;

9. *Emphasizes* the need for coordinated policies aimed at fostering debt financing, debt relief and debt restructuring, recalls, in this regard, the improvement of the lending framework of the International Monetary Fund through, inter alia, streamlined conditions and the creation of more flexible instruments, such as a precautionary and liquidity line, while noting that new and ongoing programmes should not contain unwarranted procyclical conditionalities, and urges the multilateral development banks to continue to move forward on flexible, concessional, fast-disbursing and front-loaded assistance that will substantially and quickly assist developing countries facing financing gaps in their efforts to achieve the Millennium Development Goals, taking into consideration the individual absorptive capacities and debt sustainability of those countries;

10. *Notes* the provision by the International Monetary Fund of interest relief to low-income countries in the form of zero-interest payments on financing from concessional lending facilities until the end of 2011, and invites the Fund to consider extending its concessional loan facilities for low-income countries for the post-2011 period;

11. *Also notes* that countries can seek to negotiate, as a last resort, on a case-by-case basis and through existing frameworks, agreements on temporary debt standstills between debtors and creditors in order to help mitigate the adverse impacts of the crisis and stabilize macroeconomic developments;

12. *Further notes* the progress made under the Heavily Indebted Poor Countries Initiative and the Multilateral Debt Relief Initiative, while expressing concern that some countries have yet to reach decision or completion points, calls for the full and timely implementation of those Initiatives and for continued support to the remaining eligible countries in completing the Heavily Indebted Poor Countries Initiative process, and encourages all parties, both creditors and debtors, to fulfil their commitments as rapidly as possible in order to complete the debt relief process;

13. *Welcomes and encourages* the efforts of the heavily indebted poor countries, calls upon them to continue to strengthen their domestic policies to promote economic growth and poverty eradication through, inter alia, the creation of a domestic environment conducive to private-sector development, a stable macroeconomic framework and transparent and accountable systems of public finance, and invites the international financing institutions and the donor community to continue to provide adequate and sufficiently concessional financing;

14. *Encourages* the international financial institutions to review the implementation and the impact of debt relief initiatives to better understand why some countries still face persisting debt problems after completion of the Heavily Indebted Poor Countries Initiative, and calls for the consideration of strategies to address them;

15. *Underlines* the fact that heavily indebted poor countries eligible for debt relief will not be able to enjoy its full benefits unless all creditors, both public and private, contribute their fair share and become involved in the international debt resolution mechanisms to ensure the debt sustainability of those countries, invites creditors, both private and public, that are not yet fully participating in debt relief initiatives to substantially increase their participation, including through providing comparable treatment to the extent possible to debtor countries that have concluded sustainable debt relief agreements with creditors;

16. *Stresses* that debt relief can play a key role in liberating resources that should be directed towards activities consistent with poverty eradication, sustained economic growth, economic development and the internationally agreed development goals, including the Millennium Development Goals, and in this regard urges countries to direct the resources freed through debt relief, in particular through debt cancellation and reduction, towards those objectives, according to their national priorities and strategies;

17. *Encourages* donor countries to take steps to ensure that resources provided for debt relief under the Heavily Indebted Poor Countries Initiative and the Multilateral Debt Relief Initiative do not detract from official development assistance resources intended to be available for developing countries;

18. *Notes with concern* that some low- and middle-income developing countries that are not part of existing debt relief initiatives may have large debt burdens that may create constraints on mobilizing the resources needed to achieve the internationally agreed development goals, including the Millennium Development Goals, indicating a possible need to consider debt relief initiatives for those countries on a case-by-case basis, and encourages the consideration of medium- and long-term sustainability as well as new approaches to deal with bilateral and private non-Paris Club debt;

19. *Encourages* the Paris Club, in dealing with the debt of low- and middle-income debtor countries that are not part of the Heavily Indebted Poor Countries Initiative, to take into account their medium-term debt sustainability in addition to their financing gaps, and notes with appreciation the Evian approach of the Paris Club in providing dif-

ferent terms of debt relief in order to respond to the specific needs of debtor countries while preserving debt cancellation for heavily indebted poor countries;

20. *Stresses* the need for the international community to remain vigilant in monitoring the debt situation of the least developed countries and to continue to take effective measures, preferably within existing frameworks, to address the debt problem of those countries, including through the cancellation of the multilateral and bilateral debt owed by least developed countries to creditors, both public and private;

21. *Welcomes* the efforts of and calls upon the international community to provide flexibility, and stresses the need to continue those efforts in helping post-conflict developing countries, especially those that are heavily indebted and poor, to achieve initial reconstruction for economic and social development;

22. *Also welcomes* the efforts of and invites creditors to provide flexibility to developing countries affected by natural disasters so as to allow them to address their debt concerns, while taking into account their specific situations and needs;

23. *Calls for* the consideration of additional measures and initiatives aimed at ensuring long-term debt sustainability through increased grant-based and other forms of concessional financing, the cancellation of 100 per cent of the eligible official multilateral and bilateral debt of heavily indebted poor countries and, where appropriate and on a case-by-case basis, significant debt relief or restructuring for developing countries with an unsustainable debt burden that are not part of the Heavily Indebted Poor Countries Initiative;

24. *Invites* donor countries, taking into account country-specific debt sustainability analyses, to continue their efforts to increase bilateral grants to developing countries, which could contribute to debt sustainability in the medium to long term, and recognizes the need for countries to be able to promote employment and productive investment and to invest in, inter alia, health and education while maintaining debt sustainability;

25. *Calls for* the intensification of efforts to prevent and mitigate the prevalence and cost of debt crises by enhancing international financial mechanisms for crisis prevention and resolution, encourages the private sector to cooperate in this regard, and invites creditors and debtors to further explore, where appropriate and on a mutually agreed, transparent and case-by-case basis, the use of new and improved debt instruments and innovative mechanisms such as debt swaps, including debt for equity in Millennium Development Goal projects, as well as debt indexation instruments;

26. *Also calls for* the consideration of enhanced approaches to sovereign debt restructuring and debt resolution mechanisms, based on existing frameworks and principles, with the broad participation of creditors and debtors, the comparable treatment of all creditors and an important role for the Bretton Woods institutions and other relevant organizations within the United Nations system, and in this regard calls upon all countries to promote and contribute to the discussions, within the United Nations and other appropriate forums, on the need for and feasibility of a more structured framework for international cooperation in this area;

27. *Decides* to devote one of the special events of the Second Committee during the sixty-seventh session of the General Assembly to lessons learned from debt crises and to the ongoing work on sovereign debt restructuring and debt resolution mechanisms, with the participation of all relevant stakeholders, including multilateral financial institutions;

28. *Notes* the changing composition of the sovereign debt of some countries, which has shifted increasingly from official to commercial borrowing and from external to domestic public debt, although for most low-income countries external finance is still largely official, also notes that the levels of domestic debt and the significantly increased number of creditors, both official and private, could create other challenges for macroeconomic management and public debt sustainability, and stresses the need to address the implications of these changes, including through improved data collection and analysis;

29. *Recognizes* concerns about vulture fund litigation and that some debtor countries may experience difficulties in obtaining comparable treatment from non-Paris Club creditors, as required by the standard clause included in Paris Club agreements, and encourages the continued provision by the relevant institutions of mechanisms and legal assistance to debtor countries to solve litigation issues;

30. *Stresses* the need to increase information-sharing, transparency and the use of objective criteria in the construction and evaluation of debt scenarios, including an assessment of domestic public and private debt, in order to ensure the achievement of development goals, recognizes that credit-rating agencies play a significant role in the provision of information, including the assessment of corporate and sovereign risks, and in this regard invites the President of the General Assembly at its sixty-sixth session to convene a thematic debate on the role of credit rating agencies in the international financial system and requests the Secretary-General to continue to report on this issue when preparing his report on the implementation of the present resolution;

31. *Invites* the international community to continue efforts to increase support, including financial and technical assistance, for institutional capacity-building in developing countries to enhance sustainable debt management as an integral part of national development strategies, including by promoting transparent and accountable debt management systems and negotiation and renegotiation capacities and through supporting legal advice in relation to tackling external debt litigation and debt data reconciliation between creditors and debtors so that debt sustainability may be achieved and maintained;

32. *Invites* the United Nations Conference on Trade and Development, the International Monetary Fund and the World Bank, in cooperation with the regional commissions, regional development banks and other relevant multilateral financial institutions and stakeholders, to continue and intensify cooperation in respect of capacity-building activities in developing countries in the area of debt management and debt sustainability;

33. *Encourages* further improvement of the mutual exchange of information, on a voluntary basis, on borrowing and lending among all creditors and borrowers;

34. *Acknowledges* that timely and comprehensive data on the level and composition of debt are a condition necessary for, inter alia, building early warning systems aimed at limiting the impact of debt crises, calls for debtor and

creditor countries to intensify their efforts to collect data, and calls for donors to consider increasing their support for technical cooperation programmes aimed at increasing the statistical capacity of developing countries in that regard;

35. *Calls upon* all Member States and the United Nations system, and invites the Bretton Woods institutions and the private sector, to take appropriate measures and actions for the implementation of the commitments, agreements and decisions of the major United Nations conferences and summits, in particular those related to the question of the external debt sustainability of developing countries;

36. *Requests* the Secretary-General to submit to the General Assembly at its sixty-seventh session a report on the implementation of the present resolution and to include in the report a comprehensive and substantive analysis of the external debt situation of developing countries;

37. *Decides* to include in the provisional agenda of its sixty-seventh session, under the item entitled "Macroeconomic policy questions", the sub-item entitled "External debt sustainability and development".

Also on 22 December (**decision 66/542**), the Assembly took note of the report of the Second Committee [A/66/438 & Add.1–4] on its discussions of macroeconomic policy questions, including those related to external debt sustainability and development.

Financing for development

In 2011, the General Assembly and the Economic and Social Council as well as other UN bodies continued to follow up on the outcomes of the 2002 International Conference on Financing for Development, held in Monterrey, Mexico [YUN 2002, p. 953] and the 2008 Follow-up International Conference on Financing for Development to Review the Implementation of the Monterrey Consensus, held in Doha, Qatar [YUN 2008, p. 1076].

Follow-up to the International Conference on Financing for Development and 2008 Review Conference

Special high-level meeting of the Economic and Social Council

On 15 February (**decision 2011/202**), the Economic and Social Council, recalling its resolution 2009/30 [YUN 2009, p. 941], decided that its special high-level meeting with the Bretton Woods institutions (the World Bank Group and the International Monetary Fund (imf)), the World Trade Organization (wto) and the United Nations Conference on Trade and Development (unctad) on coherence, coordination and cooperation on financing for development would be held at UN Headquarters in New York on 10–11 March.

Participating in the meeting were high-level governmental officials in the areas of finance, foreign affairs and development cooperation, as well as senior staff of UN system organizations and other international organizations, along with representatives of civil society and the business sector. The four sub-themes addressed were: follow-up to the outcome of the 2010 High-level Plenary Meeting of the General Assembly on the Millennium Development Goals (mdgs) [YUN 2010, p. 813]; the role of the UN system in global economic governance; financial support for development efforts of least developed countries (ldcs); and financial support for development efforts of middle-income countries. Each thematic debate included presentations by the World Bank, wto, unctad, the UN Department of Economic and Social Affairs and Government representatives, followed by interactive discussions.

The meeting had before it a note by the Secretary-General [E/2011/74], prepared in consultation with the major institutional stakeholders involved in financing for development, which provided background information and suggested points for reflection and discussion on the four sub-themes. According to the Secretary-General, the world financial and economic crisis had adversely affected development gains and slowed or reversed progress in economic and social development in many countries. Although a deeper and prolonged recession seemed to have been averted through unprecedented coordinated actions by major developed and emerging economies, the recovery was still tepid, fragile and uneven. In addition to challenges in respect of the governance structures of multilateral bodies, the overall system of global economic governance continued to suffer from a deficit of coherence, coordination and cooperation. The creation of a more effective UN framework for coordination, coherence and cooperation should be at the forefront of efforts to reform the existing system of global economic governance. The higher level of vulnerability of ldcs constrained their capacity to mobilize domestic resources and absorb external shocks, and their limited access to private capital made oda the most vital source of development finance for achieving the mdgs and other development goals. Concerted efforts were needed to conclude the Doha Round of multilateral trade negotiations with a strong development outcome. Priority areas of development cooperation for middle-income countries as a group should be in poverty eradication and reduction of economic and social inequality, strengthened governance, production diversification, increased resilience to external financial and trade shocks, external debt sustainability and strengthened financial and technological capacity for climate change adaptation and mitigation.

In his opening remarks, the President of the Economic and Social Council—who also prepared a summary of the meeting [A/66/75-E/2011/87]—cautioned that in the absence of effective policy coordination and cooperation, there was a risk of a new global recession, as the fragile and uneven recovery had been challenged by the recent increases in food and energy prices. Developing countries were still facing the social and economic effects of the crisis, which constituted a major setback on the way towards attaining the MDGs by 2015. The President stressed the need to build a stronger global partnership for the achievement of the MDGs, called for enhanced engagement of the Group of Twenty (G-20) with the United Nations, and urged the international community to maintain financial support for LDCs by fulfilling the ODA commitments. He also called for strengthening the cooperation of the UN system with middle-income countries by aligning it with country priorities and development strategies and taking advantage of increased South-South and triangular cooperation.

In his address, the Secretary-General called for charting a course for sustainable and equitable development to overcome the challenges faced by the international community, namely, rising debt, high unemployment, growing inequality and poverty, devastating natural disasters as well as the impacts of climate change, and the volatility of food prices. He highlighted the uneven progress towards the MDGs, with inadequate results in job creation, food production, infrastructure development and green technology. Accelerating progress required strengthening the global partnership for development based on mutual accountability, and extending the partnership beyond aid, to debt relief, access to essential medicines and technologies as well as access to global markets. Turning to LDCs, the Secretary-General stressed their high levels of poverty and hunger and vulnerability to climate change and food price shocks. He urged all countries to participate at the highest level at the Fourth United Nations Conference on the Least Developed Countries (see p. 827). He called for attention to the needs and development concerns of middle-income countries and underscored that further efforts were needed to improve social safety nets and economic security in those countries. The Secretary-General further called for strengthening the role of the United Nations in global economic governance and for improving coordination, accountability and effectiveness within the UN system.

The meeting was also addressed by the President of the UNCTAD Trade and Development Board, the Acting Secretary of the Development Committee of the World Bank and IMF, and the Secretary of the International Monetary and Financial Committee of IMF.

ECONOMIC AND SOCIAL COUNCIL ACTION

On 28 July [meeting 49], the Economic and Social Council adopted **resolution 2011/38** [draft: E/2011/L.40] without vote [agenda item 6 (*a*)].

Follow-up to the International Conference on Financing for Development

The Economic and Social Council,

Recalling the International Conference on Financing for Development, held in Monterrey, Mexico, from 18 to 22 March 2002, and the Follow-up International Conference on Financing for Development to Review the Implementation of the Monterrey Consensus, held in Doha from 29 November to 2 December 2008,

Recalling also the Outcome of the Conference on the World Financial and Economic Crisis and Its Impact on Development,

Recalling further the High-level Plenary Meeting of the General Assembly on the Millennium Development Goals and its outcome document,

Taking note of the Istanbul Declaration and the Programme of Action for the Least Developed Countries for the Decade 2011–2020, adopted at the Fourth United Nations Conference on the Least Developed Countries, held in Istanbul, Turkey, from 9 to 13 May 2011,

Recalling General Assembly resolution 65/145 of 20 December 2010 on the follow-up to the International Conference on Financing for Development and resolution 65/146 of 20 December 2010 on innovative mechanisms of financing for development, as well as Economic and Social Council resolution 2009/30 of 31 July 2009 on a strengthened and more effective intergovernmental inclusive process to carry out the financing for development follow-up and resolution 2010/26 of 23 July 2010 on the follow-up to the International Conference on Financing for Development and the 2008 Review Conference, and all other relevant resolutions of the General Assembly and Economic and Social Council,

Recalling also General Assembly resolution 65/285 of 29 June 2011 on the review of the implementation of Assembly resolution 61/16 on the strengthening of the Economic and Social Council,

Taking note of the summary by the President of the Economic and Social Council of the special high-level meeting of the Council with the Bretton Woods institutions, the World Trade Organization and the United Nations Conference on Trade and Development, held in New York on 10 and 11 March 2011,

Taking note also of the note by the Secretary-General on coherence, coordination and cooperation on financing for development,

Reaffirming the Monterrey Consensus of the International Conference on Financing for Development in its entirety, its integrity and its holistic approach, recalling the resolve to take concrete action to implement the Monterrey Consensus and address the challenges of financing for development in the spirit of global partnership and solidarity in support of the achievement of the internationally agreed development goals, including the Millennium Development Goals,

Reaffirming also that each country must take primary responsibility for its own development and that the role of national policies and development strategies cannot be overemphasized for the achievement of sustainable development, and recognizing that national efforts should be complemented by supportive global programmes, measures and policies aimed at expanding the development opportunities of developing countries, while taking into account national conditions and ensuring respect for national ownership strategies and sovereignty,

Deeply concerned about the ongoing adverse impacts of the global financial and economic crisis on development, including on the capacity of developing countries to mobilize resources for development, recognizing that, while global growth is returning, there is a need to sustain the recovery, which is fragile and uneven, and acknowledging that an effective response to the impacts of the crisis requires the timely implementation of all development commitments, including existing aid commitments,

1. *Reaffirms* the importance of staying fully engaged, nationally, regionally and internationally, in ensuring proper and effective follow-up to the implementation of the Monterrey Consensus of the International Conference on Financing for Development, as reaffirmed in the Doha Declaration on Financing for Development, and of continuing unremitting efforts to build bridges between all relevant stakeholders within the holistic agenda of the financing for development process;

2. *Reiterates* the role played by the United Nations as a focal point for the financing for development follow-up process and the need to maintain that role to ensure the continuity and dynamism of the process, while reaffirming the need to further intensify the engagement of all stakeholders, including the United Nations system, the World Bank, the International Monetary Fund and the World Trade Organization, in the follow-up to and implementation of the commitments made at Monterrey and Doha;

3. *Also reiterates* that the Economic and Social Council should continue to strengthen its role in promoting coherence, coordination and cooperation in the implementation of the Monterrey Consensus and the Doha Declaration and as a forum for multi-stakeholder involvement;

4. *Emphasizes* that the financing for development follow-up process should constitute a continuum of events, each contributing to and feeding into the next, ensuring the holistic nature of the process and making better and more effective use of existing mechanisms and resources;

5. *Welcomes* the substantive discussions undertaken during the special high-level meeting of the Council, and emphasizes that those discussions are an integral and mutually reinforcing part of the financing for development follow-up process;

6. *Also welcomes* the increased interaction and coordination at the staff level with the institutions involved prior to the high-level meeting of the Council;

7. *Recognizes* the efforts of the President of the Council, in consultation with Member States, to continue to work with the appropriate representatives of the Bretton Woods institutions, the World Trade Organization and the United Nations Conference on Trade and Development to improve the agenda and the format of the high-level meeting of the Council, considering innovative approaches that are conducive, inter alia, to the high-level participation of those institutions;

8. *Takes note*, in that regard, of the recommendations on the special high-level meeting of the Council with the Bretton Woods institutions, the World Trade Organization and the United Nations Conference on Trade and Development contained in the note by the President of the General Assembly of 20 June 2011;

9. *Stresses* the need to further improve the dialogue between Member States and representatives of the Bretton Woods institutions, the World Trade Organization and the United Nations Conference on Trade and Development during the special high-level meeting of the Council, as part of a forum for multi-stakeholder dialogue, and requests the President of the Council to seek a more interactive, dynamic and substantive discussion on key issues related to the financing for development framework;

10. *Encourages* the President of the Council to continue consultations with the appropriate representatives of the World Trade Organization, with a view to further strengthening their participation in the special high-level meeting of the Council;

11. *Welcomes* the efforts undertaken to give more prominence to the consideration of the agenda item on financing for development during the annual substantive session of the Council, including the allocation of the item to its coordination segment;

12. *Stresses its resolve* to continue improving those modalities in accordance with its resolutions 2009/30 and 2010/26;

13. *Encourages* all relevant stakeholders to consider organizing seminars, panel discussions and briefings as part of the preparations for and contribution to the above-mentioned events in order to raise visibility, attract interest and participation and promote substantive discussions on a continuing basis;

14. *Notes* the ongoing discussions on innovative mechanisms of financing for development, while reiterating that such voluntary mechanisms should supplement and not be a substitute for traditional sources of financing;

15. *Reiterates* the importance of further improving cooperation between the United Nations, the Bretton Woods institutions and the World Trade Organization in the implementation of the Monterrey Consensus and the Doha Declaration, based on a clear understanding and respect for their respective mandates and governance structures;

16. *Welcomes*, in that regard, the invitation by the Bretton Woods institutions to the President of the Council to participate in the meeting of the Development Committee of the Bretton Woods institutions, and notes that the participation of the President of the Council in meetings of the intergovernmental bodies of the international organizations, as appropriate, can contribute to the financing for development follow-up process;

17. *Encourages* the Department of Economic and Social Affairs of the Secretariat, especially the Financing for Development Office, to maintain regular interaction at the staff level with the World Bank, the International Monetary Fund, the World Trade Organization and the United Nations Conference on Trade and Development in the interest of greater coherence, coordination and cooperation, each acting in accordance with its respective intergovernmental mandates;

18. *Acknowledges* the efforts undertaken to strengthen the financing for development follow-up process, and underscores the fact that the modalities of the process should be reviewed, as appropriate, in accordance with the provisions contained in paragraph 30 of General Assembly resolution 65/145;

19. *Recalls* the decision to consider the need to hold a follow-up conference on financing for development by 2013, as appropriate;

20. *Reiterates its appeal* to Member States and other potential donors to consider contributing generously to the Trust Fund for the Follow-up to the International Conference on Financing for Development, which would facilitate the implementation of a strengthened and more effective intergovernmental inclusive process to carry out the financing for development follow-up.

Report of Secretary-General. In response to General Assembly resolution 65/145 [YUN 2010, p. 956], the Secretary-General submitted an August report [A/66/329] on follow-up to and implementation of the Monterrey Consensus [YUN 2002, p. 953] and the Doha Declaration on Financing for Development [YUN 2008, p. 1069]. The report presented recent developments in six thematic areas: mobilizing domestic financial resources for development; mobilizing international resources for development: foreign direct investment and other private flows; international trade as an engine for development; increasing international financial and technical cooperation for development; external debt; and addressing systemic issues: enhancing the coherence and consistency of the international monetary, financial and trading systems in support of development. The strengthening of the financing for development intergovernmental follow-up process was also reviewed.

Mobilization of domestic financial resources for development was hampered by the continuing impact of the global economic and financial crisis. The average savings rate, as compared to gross domestic product (GDP), in low-and middle-income countries dropped to 28 per cent in 2009 from its high of nearly 31 per cent achieved in the 2000–2007 period. Savings rates were uneven among countries, with savings stagnating in sub-Saharan Africa and soaring in East Asia and the Pacific. Increasing internal public revenue remained a critical but challenging component of domestic resource mobilization in a number of developing countries. During the crisis, government revenue in emerging economies and developing countries fell from 29 per cent in 2007/2008 to 27 per cent in 2010 compared to the average of 36 per cent in advanced economies. Net private capital flows rose from an estimated $325 billion in 2009 to $392 billion in 2010, as investors were attracted by stronger growth and higher interest rates in developing countries. There was concern, however, that sharp short-term capital flows could complicate developing country policy to curb inflation and manage exchange rates, and expose them to sharp capital reversals. Official recorded remittances to developing countries were estimated to have totalled $325 billion in 2010, a 6 per cent increase from 2009, constituting more than 20 per cent of the GDP of a number of low-income countries. This reflected a positive impact of diaspora in resource mobilization.

The role of international trade as an engine of development was under threat due to increased use of protectionist measures as a reaction to economic uncertainties, as well as a lack of attention of policy makers to the Doha Round of multilateral trade negotiations. G-20 Governments introduced more trade barriers between mid-October 2010 and the end of April 2011 than in the previous periods since the crisis began, while new import-restrictive measures taken by G-20 economies over the period from October 2010 to April 2011 doubled to 0.6 per cent of total G-20 imports compared to the previous six months.

Aid flows to developing countries increased to a record $129 billion in 2010, even though that amount was below the level of commitments. As for external debt, debt indicators improved in many developing countries in 2010 despite an increase in nominal external debt of 8 per cent due to a recovery in growth and exports; the ratio of external debt to GDP decreased from 23.7 per cent in 2009 to 21.6 per cent in 2010; and estimates for the ratio of external debt service to exports of goods and services for 2010 also showed a return to pre-crisis levels for all income groups, reaching 6.5 per cent in low-income countries, 19 per cent in lower-middle-income countries and 35 per cent in upper-middle-income countries.

GENERAL ASSEMBLY ACTION

On 22 December [meeting 91], the General Assembly, on the recommendation of the Second Committee [A/66/439], adopted **resolution 66/191** without vote [agenda item 18].

Follow-up to the International Conference on Financing for Development

The General Assembly,

Recalling the International Conference on Financing for Development, held in Monterrey, Mexico, from 18 to 22 March 2002, and the Follow-up International Conference on Financing for Development to Review the Implementation of the Monterrey Consensus, held in Doha from 29 November to 2 December 2008, and its resolutions 56/210 B of 9 July 2002, 57/250, 57/272 and 57/273 of 20 December 2002, 57/270 B of 23 June 2003, 58/230 of 23 December 2003, 59/225 of 22 December 2004, 60/188 of 22 December 2005, 61/191 of 20 December 2006, 62/187 of 19 December 2007, 63/239 of 24 December 2008, 64/193 of 21 December 2009 and 65/145 and 65/146 of 20 December 2010, as well as Economic and Social Council resolutions 2002/34 of 26 July 2002, 2003/47 of 24 July 2003, 2004/64 of 16 September 2004, 2006/45 of 28 July 2006, 2007/30 of 27 July 2007, 2008/14 of 24 July 2008, 2009/30 of 31 July 2009, 2010/26 of 23 July 2010 and 2011/38 of 28 July 2011,

Recalling also the 2005 World Summit Outcome,

Recalling further the Conference on the World Financial and Economic Crisis and Its Impact on Development and its outcome document,

Recalling the High-level Plenary Meeting of the General Assembly on the Millennium Development Goals and its outcome document,

Taking note of the summary by the President of the Economic and Social Council of the special high-level meeting of the Council with the Bretton Woods institutions, the World Trade Organization and the United Nations Conference on Trade and Development, held in New York on 10 and 11 March 2011,

Taking note also of the report of the Secretary-General on the follow-up to and implementation of the Monterrey Consensus and the Doha Declaration on Financing for Development,

Taking note further of the report of the Secretary-General on innovative mechanisms of financing for development,

Recalling the progress report of the Ad Hoc Open-ended Working Group of the General Assembly to follow up on the issues contained in the Outcome of the Conference on the World Financial and Economic Crisis and Its Impact on Development,

Expressing deep concern about the ongoing adverse impacts, particularly on development, of the world financial and economic crisis, cognizant that the global economy is entering a challenging new phase with significant downside risks, including the turbulence in global financial and commodity markets and widespread fiscal strains, which threaten global economic recovery, and stressing the need to continue to address systemic fragilities and imbalances and the need for continuing efforts to reform and strengthen the international financial system,

1. *Reaffirms* the Monterrey Consensus of the International Conference on Financing for Development in its entirety, its integrity and its holistic approach, and recalls the resolve to take concrete action to implement the Monterrey Consensus and to address the challenges of financing for development in the spirit of global partnership and solidarity in support of the achievement of the internationally agreed development goals, including the Millennium Development Goals;

2. *Also reaffirms* that each country has primary responsibility for its own development and that the role of national policies and development strategies cannot be overemphasized for the achievement of sustainable development, and recognizes that national efforts should be complemented by supportive global programmes, measures and policies aimed at expanding the development opportunities of developing countries, while taking into account national conditions and ensuring respect for national ownership, strategies and sovereignty;

3. *Reaffirms its determination* to advance and strengthen the global partnership for development as the centrepiece of cooperation in the years ahead, as reaffirmed in the United Nations Millennium Declaration, the Monterrey Consensus, the Plan of Implementation of the World Summit on Sustainable Development ("Johannesburg Plan of Implementation"), the 2005 World Summit Outcome, the Doha Declaration on Financing for Development: outcome document of the Follow-up International Conference on Financing for Development to Review the Implementation of the Monterrey Consensus, and the outcome document of the High-level Plenary Meeting of the General Assembly on the Millennium Development Goals, entitled "Keeping the promise: united to achieve the Millennium Development Goals";

4. *Recalls* the importance of the overall commitment to just and democratic societies for development, as spelled out in the Monterrey Consensus;

5. *Reaffirms* the importance of the implementation of the commitment to sound policies, good governance at all levels and the rule of law;

6. *Recognizes* that the mobilization of financial resources for development and the effective use of all of those resources are central to the global partnership for development, including in support of the achievement of the internationally agreed development goals, including the Millennium Development Goals, and also recognizes that the mobilization of domestic and international resources and an enabling domestic and international environment are key drivers for development;

7. *Recalls* the resolve of Member States to enhance and strengthen domestic resource mobilization and fiscal space, including, where appropriate, through modernized tax systems, more efficient tax collection, the broadening of the tax base and the effective combating of tax evasion and capital flight, and reiterates that, while each country is responsible for its tax system, it is important to support national efforts in these areas by strengthening technical assistance and enhancing international cooperation and participation in addressing international tax matters;

8. *Expresses deep concern* about the ongoing adverse impacts of the global financial and economic crisis on development, including on the capacity of developing countries to mobilize resources for development, recognizes that there is a need to promote the recovery, and acknowledges that an effective response to the impacts of the crisis requires timely implementation of all development commitments, including existing aid commitments;

9. *Recalls* that the ongoing fight against corruption at all levels is a priority, reaffirms the need to take urgent and decisive steps to continue to combat corruption in all its manifestations in order to reduce obstacles to effective resource mobilization and allocation and to prevent the diversion of resources away from activities that are vital for development, recalls that this requires strong institutions at all levels, including, in particular, effective legal and judicial systems, and enhanced transparency, recognizes the efforts and achievements of developing countries in this regard, notes the increased commitment of States that have already ratified or acceded to the United Nations Convention against Corruption, and in this regard urges all States that have not yet done so to consider ratifying or acceding to the Convention;

10. *Reaffirms* the importance of implementing measures to curtail illicit financial flows at all levels, enhancing disclosure practices and promoting transparency in financial information, and in this regard notes that strengthening national and multinational efforts to address this issue is crucial, including through support and technical assistance to developing countries to enhance their capacities;

11. *Emphasizes* the need for more effective government involvement so as to ensure an appropriate regulation of the market that promotes the public interest, and also recognizes the need to better regulate financial markets;

12. *Recognizes* that a dynamic, inclusive, well-functioning and socially responsible private sector is a valuable instrument for generating economic growth and reducing poverty, emphasizes the need to pursue, at the national level and in a manner consistent with national laws, appropriate policy and regulatory frameworks through which to encourage public and private initiatives, including at the local level, and to foster a dynamic and well-functioning business sector, while improving income growth and distribution, raising productivity, empowering while improving empowerment of women, and protecting labour rights and the environment, and reiterates the importance of ensuring that the benefits of growth reach all people by empowering individuals and communities;

13. *Reiterates* that the mobilization of domestic and international resources for social development is an essential

component for the implementation of the commitments made at the World Summit for Social Development, held in Copenhagen from 6 to 12 March 1995, and in this regard requests the Secretary-General, in cooperation with the Chair of the Commission for Social Development at its fiftieth session, to organize a special event in 2012 on the financing of social development;

14. *Notes* that foreign direct investment is a major source of financing for development, and in this regard calls upon developed countries to continue to devise source-country measures to encourage and facilitate the flow of foreign direct investment, inter alia, through the provision of export credits and other lending instruments, risk guarantees and business development services; calls upon developing countries to continue their efforts to create a domestic environment conducive to attracting investments by, inter alia, achieving a transparent, stable and predictable investment climate with proper contract enforcement and respect for property rights; and stresses the importance of enhancing efforts to mobilize investment from all sources in human resources and physical, environmental, institutional and social infrastructure;

15. *Reaffirms* that international trade is an engine for development and sustained economic growth, and also reaffirms the critical role that a universal, rules-based, open, non-discriminatory and equitable multilateral trading system, as well as meaningful trade liberalization, can play in stimulating economic growth and development worldwide, thereby benefiting all countries at all stages of development;

16. *Emphasizes* the need to resist protectionist tendencies and to rectify any trade-distorting measures already taken that are inconsistent with World Trade Organization rules, recognizing the right of countries, in particular developing countries, to fully utilize their flexibilities consistent with their World Trade Organization commitments and obligations, and that the successful conclusion of the Doha Round with a balanced, ambitious, comprehensive and development-oriented outcome would provide much-needed impetus to international trade and contribute to economic growth and development;

17. *Underlines* the fact that the fulfilment of all official development assistance commitments is crucial, including the commitments by many developed countries to achieve the target of 0.7 per cent of gross national product for official development assistance to developing countries by 2015 as well as the target of 0.15 per cent to 0.20 per cent of gross national product for official development assistance to least developed countries, and urges developed countries that have not yet done so to fulfil their commitments for official development assistance to developing countries;

18. *Stresses* the essential role that official development assistance plays in complementing, leveraging and sustaining financing for development in developing countries and in facilitating the achievement of development objectives, including the internationally agreed development goals, in particular the Millennium Development Goals, reiterates that official development assistance can play a catalytic role in assisting developing countries in removing constraints on sustained, inclusive and equitable growth by, inter alia, enhancing social, institutional and physical infrastructure, promoting foreign direct investment, trade and technological innovations, improving health and education, fostering gender equality, preserving the environment and eradicating poverty, and welcomes steps to improve the effectiveness and quality of aid based on the fundamental principles of national ownership, alignment, harmonization, managing for results and mutual accountability;

19. *Also stresses* the need to strengthen and support South-South cooperation, while stressing further that South-South cooperation is not a substitute for, but rather a complement to, North-South cooperation, and calls for the effective implementation of the Nairobi outcome document of the High-level United Nations Conference on South-South Cooperation, held in Nairobi from 1 to 3 December 2009;

20. *Recognizes* that human development remains a key priority, that human resources are the most precious and valuable asset that countries possess, and that the realization of full and productive employment and decent work for all is essential, and reiterates the importance of investment in human capital, inter alia, in health and education, through inclusive social policies, in accordance with national strategies and priorities;

21. *Considers* that innovative mechanisms of financing can make a positive contribution towards assisting developing countries in mobilizing additional resources for financing for development on a voluntary basis and that such financing should supplement and not be a substitute for traditional sources of financing, and, while highlighting the considerable progress on innovative sources of financing for development achieved to date, stresses the importance of scaling up present initiatives and developing new mechanisms, as appropriate;

22. *Takes note* of the ongoing discussions on innovative mechanisms of financing for development, and requests the President of the Economic and Social Council to organize a special event on innovative mechanisms of financing for development with the participation of relevant stakeholders during the substantive session of 2012 of the Council;

23. *Emphasizes* the special importance of a timely, effective, comprehensive and durable solution to the debt problems of developing countries for promoting their economic growth and development;

24. *Also emphasizes* that debt sustainability is essential for underpinning growth, underlining in this regard the importance of debt sustainability and effective debt management to the efforts to achieve national development goals, including the Millennium Development Goals, and acknowledges that sovereign debt crises tend to be costly and disruptive, including for employment and productive investments, and tend to be followed by cuts in public spending, including on health and education, affecting, in particular, the poor and vulnerable;

25. *Stresses* that the financial and economic crisis has highlighted the need for reform as well as added new impetus to ongoing international discussions on the reform of the international financial system and architecture, including on issues related to mandate, scope, governance, responsiveness and development orientation, as appropriate, and in this regard encourages continued open, inclusive and transparent dialogue;

26. *Notes* the important efforts undertaken nationally, regionally and internationally to respond to the challenges posed by the financial and economic crisis, in order to ensure a full return to growth with quality jobs, to reform and strengthen financial systems and to create strong, sustainable and balanced global growth;

27. *Recognizes* the need to continue to enhance the coherence and consistency of the international monetary, financial and trading systems and the importance of ensuring their openness, fairness and inclusiveness as complements to national development efforts to ensure sustained, inclusive and equitable economic growth and the achievement of the internationally agreed development goals, including the Millennium Development Goals;

28. *Reaffirms* the importance of broadening and strengthening the participation of developing countries in international economic decision-making and norm-setting, and in this regard takes note of recent important decisions on the reform of the governance structures, quotas and voting rights of the Bretton Woods institutions, better reflecting current realities and enhancing the voice and participation of developing countries, and reiterates the importance of the reform of the governance of those institutions for delivering more effective, credible, accountable and legitimate institutions;

29. *Also reaffirms* that the United Nations funds and programmes and the regional commissions, and the specialized agencies of the United Nations system, in accordance with their respective mandates, have an important role to play in advancing development and protecting development gains, in accordance with national strategies and priorities, including progress towards achieving the Millennium Development Goals, and further reaffirms its determination to continue to take steps for a strong, well-coordinated, coherent, effective and efficient United Nations system in support of the Goals;

30. *Further reaffirms* the need to further intensify the engagement of regional commissions in the financing for development follow-up process, including through the provision of technical advice and analyses to be made available to Member States;

31. *Reiterates* the importance of ensuring a strengthened, and more effective, intergovernmental inclusive process for carrying out the financing for development follow-up;

32. *Acknowledges* the efforts undertaken to strengthen the financing for development follow-up process, and reiterates that the modalities of the process should be reviewed, as appropriate, in accordance with the provisions set out in paragraph 30 of General Assembly resolution 65/145;

33. *Decides*, in accordance with paragraph 90 of the Doha Declaration on Financing for Development, to consider the need to hold a follow-up financing for development conference by 2013, and in this regard decides to hold informal consultations with a view to taking a final decision on the need for such a conference by 2013;

34. *Recognizes* the work of the Financing for Development Office of the Secretariat, and encourages the Office, in collaboration with experts from the public and private sectors, academia and civil society, to continue its work in accordance with its mandate;

35. *Reiterates its appeal* to Member States and other potential donors to consider contributing generously to the Trust Fund for the Follow-up to the International Conference on Financing for Development, which would facilitate the implementation of a strengthened and more effective intergovernmental inclusive process for carrying out the financing for development follow-up;

36. *Decides* to include in the provisional agenda of its sixty-seventh session the item entitled "Follow-up to and implementation of the outcome of the 2002 International Conference on Financing for Development and the 2008 Review Conference", and requests the Secretary-General to submit, under the item, an annual analytical assessment of the status of implementation of the Monterrey Consensus and the Doha Declaration on Financing for Development, and of the present resolution, which is to be prepared in full collaboration with the major institutional stakeholders.

High-level Dialogue on Financing for Development

In response to General Assembly resolution 65/145 [YUN 2010, p. 956], by which the Assembly decided to hold its fifth High-level Dialogue on Financing for Development at UN Headquarters in New York from 7–8 December, the Secretary-General issued a June note [A/65/897] on the proposed organization of work of the Dialogue. The meeting, to be held on the theme "The Monterrey Consensus and Doha Declaration on Financing for Development: Status of Implementation and tasks ahead", would consist of plenary and informal meetings, three interactive multi-stakeholder round tables and an informal interactive dialogue. The round tables would focus on reform of the international monetary and financial system and its implications for development; the impact of the world financial and economic crisis on foreign direct investment and other private flows, external debt and international trade; and the role of financial and technical development cooperation. The informal dialogue would examine the link between financing for development and achieving internationally agreed development goals, including the MDGs.

GENERAL ASSEMBLY ACTION

On 12 September [meeting 118], the General Assembly adopted **resolution 65/314** [draft: A/65/L.91] without vote [agenda item 19].

Modalities for the fifth High-level Dialogue on Financing for Development

The General Assembly,

Recalling the International Conference on Financing for Development, held in Monterrey, Mexico, from 18 to 22 March 2002, the Follow-up International Conference on Financing for Development to Review the Implementation of the Monterrey Consensus, held in Doha from 29 November to 2 December 2008, and its resolutions 56/210 B of 9 July 2002, 57/250 of 20 December 2002, 57/270 B of 23 June 2003, 57/272 and 57/273 of 20 December 2002, 58/230 of 23 December 2003, 59/225 of 22 December 2004, 60/188 of 22 December 2005, 61/191 of 20 December 2006, 62/187 of 19 December 2007, 63/239 of 24 December 2008, 64/193 of 21 December 2009 and 65/145 of 20 December 2010, as well as Economic and Social Council resolutions 2002/34 of 26 July 2002, 2003/47 of 24 July 2003, 2004/64 of 16 September 2004, 2006/45 of 28 July 2006, 2007/30 of 27 July 2007, 2008/14 of 24 July 2008, 2010/26 of 23 July 2010 and 2011/38 of 28 July 2011,

1. *Decides* to hold its fifth High-level Dialogue on Financing for Development on 7 and 8 December 2011 at United Nations Headquarters;

2. *Takes note* of the note by the Secretary-General on the proposed organization of work of the fifth High-level Dialogue;

3. *Decides* that the overall theme of the fifth High-level Dialogue will be "The Monterrey Consensus and Doha Declaration on Financing for Development: status of implementation and tasks ahead";

4. *Stresses* the importance of the full involvement of all relevant stakeholders in the implementation of the Monterrey Consensus at all levels, and also stresses the importance of their full participation in the financing for development follow-up process, in accordance with the rules of procedure of the General Assembly, in particular the accreditation procedures and modalities of participation utilized at the Monterrey and Doha Conferences;

5. *Decides* that the modalities for the fifth High-level Dialogue will be the same as those used for the fourth High-level Dialogue, as described in General Assembly resolution 64/194 of 21 December 2009;

6. *Decides also* that the fifth High-level Dialogue will consist of a series of plenary and informal meetings, three interactive multi-stakeholder round tables and an informal interactive dialogue;

7. *Decides further* that the themes of the round tables and of the informal interactive dialogue will be as follows:

(*a*) Round table 1: The reform of the international monetary and financial system and its implications for development;

(*b*) Round table 2: The impact of the world financial and economic crisis on foreign direct investment and other private flows, external debt and international trade;

(*c*) Round table 3: The role of financial and technical development cooperation, including innovative sources of development finance, in leveraging the mobilization of domestic and international financial resources for development;

(*d*) Informal interactive dialogue: The link between financing for development and achieving the internationally agreed development goals, including the Millennium Development Goals;

8. *Decides* that the fifth High-level Dialogue will result in a summary by the President of the General Assembly, which will be issued as a document of the Assembly.

Summary by President of General Assembly. As set forth in a later summary of the event prepared by the President of the General Assembly [A/66/678] in accordance with resolution 65/314 (see above), participants at the fifth High-level Dialogue on Financing for Development expressed concern about the impact of the global economic situation on trade, capital flows and economic development; and reaffirmed the relevance of the financing for development agenda in the post-2015 development framework.

In his opening remarks, delivered by the Acting President of the Assembly, the President expressed concern about factors contributing to the uncertainty in the global economic environment, including the sovereign debt crises in Europe, the continuing jobs crisis in developed countries, weaknesses in the financial sector, climate change, and volatile food and energy prices. Donors needed to deliver on their ODA commitments despite fiscal pressures and explore the potential of innovative financing to provide additional resources. After almost a decade of multilateral trade negotiations, the share of the LDCs in world trade remained extremely low. It was important for the international community to provide duty-free and quota-free access for all products originating from LDCs and increase resources for aid for trade to enable poorer countries to enhance their trade competitiveness.

The Deputy Secretary-General emphasized that economic recovery remained fragile and uneven, unemployment and vulnerable employment persisted, poverty was on the rise, and famine threatened more than 13 million people in the Horn of Africa. As a result, many developing countries needed additional assistance to cope with the impact of the crisis and to expand their social safety nets. Yet most donor countries, faced with mounting debts, were tightening their budgets. In that difficult environment, it was critical that donor countries fulfil their commitments regarding ODA. Development cooperation was not charity but rather smart investment in security and prosperity.

The President of the Economic and Social Council highlighted the importance of the Monterrey Consensus and the Doha Declaration for the achievement of the internationally agreed development goals, including those contained in the Millennium Declaration. It was also important to address the development needs of middle-income countries and to better align international support with national priorities in that group of States.

Innovative mechanisms of financing for development

Communication. On 16 March [A/65/818], France, on behalf of the Leading Group on Innovative Financing for Development, transmitted the Chair's summary of its eighth plenary meeting (Tokyo, 16–17 December 2010). The group expressed its support for the growing attention to innovative financing for development on the UN agenda, and pledged to work within the United Nations to foster the follow-up of the General Assembly resolution on the subject [YUN 2010, p. 959].

Report of Secretary-General. In response to Assembly resolution 65/146 [YUN 2010, p. 959], the Secretary-General submitted a September report [A/66/334] on innovative mechanisms of financing for development. The Secretary-General observed that there was an absence of an internationally agreed definition and classification of innovative financing, as the two existing classification schemes by the Organization for Economic Cooperation and Development (OECD) and the World Bank differed in their coverage and, as a result, their estimates were not strictly comparable. The report estimated that funds raised under the various innovative financing mechanisms since the Monterrey Consensus [YUN 2002, p. 953] amounted to some $37 billion under the OECD framework, $57 billion under the World Bank framework, or close to $60 billion when both were used in conjunction. The report reviewed the contribution of innovative financing mechanisms in the areas of health and climate change and environment. Within the health sector, the main global programmes were delivered by the GAVI Alliance; the Global Fund to Fight AIDS, Tuberculosis and Malaria; and UNITAID, the International Drug Purchase Facility. In climate change and environment, programmes operated mainly through carbon emission trading. Direct financing programmes included climate markets, the Adaptation Fund, and World Bank's Eco 3PlusNote and Green Bond trading. The report also discussed major new innovative financing proposals under consideration and highlighted a variety of other proposals for new vertical funds to channel resources to sectors including education; health; climate change and environment; and food security and agriculture.

The report concluded that while the potential to raise additional resources for development remained significant, considerable progress had been made in raising resources through innovative financing since the Monterrey Consensus. There was a need, however, to fully align interventions with national systems; and the case for general budget support remained strong. The Secretary-General called for consideration to be given to allocation through globally inclusive institutions such as the United Nations. He recommended that the General Assembly might wish to consider setting up a working group on innovative mechanisms of financing for development to examine the potential of existing and proposed mechanisms and make recommendations for increasing their scale and predictability; improving delivery and monitoring; and enhancing their effectiveness in contributing to development goals, including the MDGs, as well as climate change mitigation and adaptation.

Follow-up to conference on world financial and economic crisis

Recovering from the crisis

In 2011, the General Assembly decided to explore, at its sixty-sixth session, the most efficient modalities for the follow-up to the 2009 Conference on the World Financial and Economic Crisis and Its Impact on Development [YUN 2009, p. 947].

GENERAL ASSEMBLY ACTION

On 12 September [meeting 118], the General Assembly adopted **resolution 65/313** [draft: A/65/L.42/Rev.1] without vote [agenda item 13].

Follow-up to the Conference on the World Financial and Economic Crisis and Its Impact on Development

The General Assembly,

Recalling its resolution 63/303 of 9 July 2009, in which it endorsed the Outcome of the Conference on the World Financial and Economic Crisis and Its Impact on Development, held in New York from 24 to 30 June 2009,

Recalling also its resolution 63/305 of 31 July 2009, in which it decided to establish an ad hoc open-ended working group of the General Assembly to follow up on the issues contained in the Outcome of the Conference on the World Financial and Economic Crisis and Its Impact on Development,

Recalling further its decision of 13 September 2010 to take note of the progress report of the Ad Hoc Open-ended Working Group of the General Assembly to follow up on the issues contained in the Outcome of the Conference on the World Financial and Economic Crisis and Its Impact on Development,

Expressing deep concern about the ongoing adverse impact, particularly on development, of the world financial and economic crisis, recognizing that global growth is returning and that there is a need to sustain the recovery, which is fragile and uneven, and stressing the need to continue to address systemic fragilities and imbalances,

Taking note of the important efforts undertaken nationally, regionally and internationally to respond to the challenges posed by the financial and economic crisis, in order to ensure a full return to growth with quality jobs, to reform and strengthen financial systems and to create strong, sustainable and balanced global growth,

Recognizing the need to ensure proper follow-up to the outcomes of the Conference on the World Financial and Economic Crisis and Its Impact on Development,

Decides to explore further, at its sixty-sixth session, the most efficient modalities for the intergovernmental follow-up process of the Conference on the World Financial and Economic Crisis and Its Impact on Development, and in this regard requests the President of the General Assembly to hold open, inclusive, timely and transparent consultations with all Member States.

Ad hoc panel of experts

In 2011, the Economic and Social Council, pursuant to its decision 2010/264 [YUN 2010, p. 961], continued consultations on how to implement the mandates assigned to it regarding the UN response to the global financial and economic crisis. The Council undertook consultations regarding General Assembly consideration of establishing an ad hoc panel of experts on the crisis and its impact on development, taking into account various related processes, including the Ad Hoc Open-ended Working Group of the General Assembly to follow up on the issues contained in the Outcome of the Conference on the World Financial and Economic Crisis and Its Impact on Development [YUN 2010, p. 960], as well as Assembly deliberations on the role of the United Nations in global economic governance and development, and on the modalities of the financing for development follow-up process.

While the Council, by resolution 2011/39 (see below), recommended, inter alia, that the possible establishment of an ad hoc panel of experts on the global financial and economic crisis and its impact on development be considered further by the Assembly, by the close of the year, the latter had not yet resumed the relevant discussions.

ECONOMIC AND SOCIAL COUNCIL ACTION

On 28 July [meeting 49], the Economic and Social Council adopted **resolution 2011/39** [draft: E/2011/L.4] without vote [agenda item 6 (*a*)].

Follow-up to the Outcome of the Conference on the World Financial and Economic Crisis and Its Impact on Development: consideration of the possible establishment of an ad hoc panel of experts

The Economic and Social Council,

Recalling the International Conference on Financing for Development and its outcome document and the Follow-up International Conference on Financing for Development to Review the Implementation of the Monterrey Consensus and its outcome document,

Recalling also the Conference on the World Financial and Economic Crisis and Its Impact on Development and its Outcome,

Mindful of the ongoing discussions in the General Assembly regarding the Ad Hoc Open-ended Working group of the General Assembly to follow up on the issues contained in the Outcome of the Conference on the World Financial and Economic Crisis and Its Impact on Development,

Recognizing that, in accordance with General Assembly resolution 65/94 of 8 December 2010, the Assembly will consider at its sixty-sixth session the role of the United Nations in global governance, focusing on global economic governance and development,

Expressing deep concern about the ongoing adverse impact, particularly on development, of the world financial and economic crisis, recognizing that global growth is returning and there is a need to sustain the recovery, which is fragile and uneven, and stressing the need to continue to address systemic fragilities and imbalances,

Recognizing the valuable contribution of the United Nations system as well as the contribution of various independent bodies, such as the Commission of Experts of the President of the Sixty-third Session of the General Assembly on Reforms of the International Monetary and Financial System, in informing and providing intellectual support to the intergovernmental work of Member States,

Stressing the need to maximize the effectiveness, the transparency, the efficiency and the coherence of the United Nations system,

Recalling the consultation process in the Economic and Social Council on the follow-up to the Outcome of the Conference on the World Financial and Economic Crisis and Its Impact on Development, including the request to consider and make recommendations to the General Assembly regarding the possible establishment of an ad hoc panel of experts on the world economic and financial crisis and its impact on development,

1. *Affirms* the need to examine the most efficient modalities to provide independent technical expertise and analysis on issues relating to the world financial and economic crisis and its impact on development, to be made available to the Economic and Social Council and the General Assembly, which could contribute to informing international action and political decision-making and to fostering constructive dialogue and exchanges among policymakers, academics, institutions and civil society;

2. *Recommends*, in that regard, that the possible establishment of an ad hoc panel of experts on the world economic and financial crisis and its impact on development should be further considered by the General Assembly, taking into account the outcomes of the various related processes, including the Ad Hoc Open-ended Working Group of the General Assembly to follow up on the issues contained in the Outcome of the Conference on the World Financial and Economic Crisis and Its Impact on Development, as well as the forthcoming deliberations in the Assembly on the role of the United Nations in global economic governance and development, and on the modalities of the financing for development follow-up process;

3. *Requests* the Secretary-General to explore options in that respect, taking into account the need to make full use of existing United Nations bodies, including the regional commissions, and to report to the General Assembly through existing reporting mechanisms.

Other matters

Competition law and policy

Group of experts

At its eleventh session (Geneva, 19–21 July) [TD/B/C.I/CLP/12], the Intergovernmental Group of Experts on Competition Law and Policy considered the following topics: the foundations of an effective competition agency; capacity-building in the area of competition policy; the importance of coherence between competition policies and government policies; the peer review of Serbian competition law and policy; and the review of the experience gained so far in enforcement cooperation, including at the regional level.

In agreed conclusions, the Group reaffirmed the fundamental role of competition law and policy for sound economic development; noted that competition law and policy was one of the key instruments for addressing globalization; and recognized the need to strengthen UNCTAD work on competition law and policy. It encouraged further promotion of competition policy as a tool that contributed to development and supported economic growth, structural change, inclusive development and poverty reduction, and called upon UNCTAD to promote and support young competition agencies. UNCTAD was asked to undertake further voluntary peer reviews on the competition law and policy of member States or regional groupings of States, and provide feedback on the follow-up of the peer reviews. The Group recommended that its twelfth session hold a voluntary peer review of the United Republic of Tanzania, Zambia and Zimbabwe, and requested the UNCTAD secretariat to organize and report on three round tables at that session on the following topics: competition policy and public procurement; knowledge and human resource management for effective enforcement of competition law; and cross-border anti-competitive practices.

International Standards of Accounting and Reporting

Group of experts

At its twenty-eighth session (Geneva, 12–14 October) [TD/B/C.II/ISAR/61], the Intergovernmental Working Group of Experts on International Standards of Accounting and Reporting (ISAR) underscored the importance of a comprehensive and integrated approach to capacity-building for high-quality corporate reporting. The Group noted with concern the continuing challenges to corporate reporting that had arisen in the course of the global financial crisis; reiterated the importance of consistent implementation and enforcement of global standards and codes of corporate reporting as a precondition for realizing the benefits of such standards to the global economy; and discussed the importance of assessing and measuring the progress in building capacity in that area.

The Group took into consideration the UNCTAD secretariat draft questionnaire on measurement methodologies [TD/B/C.II/ISAR/59]. The UNCTAD secretariat was asked to incorporate into the questionnaire comments received at the twenty-eighth session of the Group, and additional input that member States might provide; conduct pilot tests of the capacity-building measurement methodology during the intersessional period; and report on its findings at the next session. The Group also requested UNCTAD to continue contributing to the field of environmental reporting frameworks, particularly those related to climate change issues, with a view to promoting a harmonized approach among member States. It reiterated the importance of corporate governance disclosure for promoting sustainable economic development, and considered the results of two country case studies of corporate governance disclosure relating to the Russian Federation and Trinidad and Tobago. The Group requested UNCTAD to continue providing technical guidance to local institutions wishing to produce similar standardized country case studies using the ISAR benchmarks on good practices in corporate governance disclosure.

International cooperation in tax matters

Committee of experts

In response to Economic and Social Council resolution 2010/33 [YUN 2010, p. 962], the Secretary-General submitted a March report [E/2011/76] on strengthening institutional arrangements to promote international cooperation in tax matters, including the Committee of Experts on International Cooperation in Tax Matters. The report reviewed existing institutional arrangements, including the Committee, and the work of other international forums on tax matters; summarized views provided by Member States; and presented options for consideration by the Council.

The report stated that there was no entity with the global legitimacy, resources and expertise to serve as a single coordinating body for international tax co-operation. While each country was responsible for its own tax system, the universal membership and legitimacy of the United Nations could serve as a catalyst for increased international cooperation in tax matters to the benefit of developed and developing countries alike. Since the majority of UN Member States were members of neither the OECD nor the Group of 20, the United Nations had a key role to play towards ensuring the active participation of developing countries in relevant activities. The Secretary-General recommended that the Council might wish to consider strengthening the existing arrangements within the United Nations while retaining the current format of the Committee; converting the Committee into an intergovernmental commission on international cooperation in tax matters serving as a subsidiary body of the Council; or creating an intergovernmental commission and retaining the current Committee as a subsidiary body of that commission.

ECONOMIC AND SOCIAL COUNCIL ACTION

On 27 July [meeting 47], the Economic and Social Council adopted **resolution 2011/23** [draft: E/2011/L.26] without vote [agenda item 13 (*h*)].

Committee of Experts on International Cooperation in Tax Matters

The Economic and Social Council,

Recalling its resolution 2004/69 of 11 November 2004,

Recognizing the call made in the Monterrey Consensus of the International Conference on Financing for Development for the strengthening of international tax cooperation through enhanced dialogue among national tax authorities and greater coordination of the work of the concerned multilateral bodies and relevant regional organizations, giving special attention to the needs of developing countries and countries with economies in transition,

Recalling the request to the Economic and Social Council made in the Doha Declaration on Financing for Development and the Outcome of the Conference on the World Financial and Economic Crisis and Its Impact on Development to examine the strengthening of the institutional arrangements to promote international cooperation in tax matters, including the Committee of Experts on International Cooperation in Tax Matters,

Recognizing that, while each country is responsible for its tax system, it is important to support efforts in these areas by strengthening technical assistance and enhancing international cooperation and participation in addressing international tax matters, including in the area of double taxation,

Recognizing also the need for an inclusive, participatory and broad-based dialogue on international cooperation in tax matters,

Noting the activities developing within the concerned multilateral bodies and relevant subregional and regional organizations, and recognizing the need to promote collaboration between the United Nations and other international bodies dealing with cooperation in tax matters,

Welcoming the discussion in the Economic and Social Council on 26 April 2011 on international cooperation in tax matters,

Taking note of the report of the Committee on its sixth session,

1. *Welcomes* the work of the Committee of Experts on International Cooperation in Tax Matters to implement the mandate given to it in Economic and Social Council resolution 2004/69, and encourages the Committee to continue its efforts in this regard;

2. *Takes note with appreciation* of the report of the Secretary-General on the strengthening of institutional arrangements to promote international cooperation in tax matters, including the Committee, and acknowledges the need for enhanced dialogue among national tax authorities on issues related to international cooperation in tax matters;

3. *Recognizes* the need for continued consultations to explore options with regard to the strengthening of institutional arrangements to promote international cooperation in tax matters, including on the issue of the conversion of the Committee into an intergovernmental subsidiary body of the Economic and Social Council;

4. *Emphasizes* that it is important for the Committee to enhance its collaboration with other international organizations active in the area of international tax cooperation, including the International Monetary Fund, the World Bank and the Organization for Economic Cooperation and Development;

5. *Requests* the Secretary-General to submit to the Economic and Social Council a report on the role and work of the Committee in promoting international cooperation in tax matters, including further options to strengthen the work of the Committee and its cooperation with concerned multilateral bodies and relevant regional and subregional organizations;

6. *Decides* to hold a one-day meeting in 2012 in conjunction with the special high-level meeting of the Economic and Social Council with the Bretton Woods institutions, the World Trade Organization and the United Nations Conference on Trade and Development to consider international cooperation in tax matters, including institutional arrangements to promote such cooperation;

7. *Encourages* the President of the Economic and Social Council to issue invitations to representatives of national tax authorities to attend the meeting;

8. *Stresses* the need for appropriate funding for the subsidiary bodies of the Committee to enable those bodies to fulfil their mandates;

9. *Reiterates*, in this regard, its appeal to Member States, relevant organizations and other potential donors to consider contributing generously to the Trust Fund for International Cooperation in Tax Matters established by the Secretary-General in order to supplement regular budgetary resources, and invites the Secretary-General to intensify efforts to that end.

Also on 27 July (**decision 2011/253**), the Economic and Social Council decided to convene the seventh session of the Committee of Experts on International Cooperation in Tax Matters in Geneva from 24 to 28 October, and to approve the provisional agenda for the session.

Committee session. The central topics of the seventh session of the Committee of Experts on International Cooperation in Tax Matters (Geneva, 24–28 October) [E/2011/45-E/C.18/2011/6] were the update of the United Nations Model Double Taxation Convention between Developed and Developing Countries [E/C.18/2011/CRP.2 & Add.1–3], which represented the culmination of the work of the Committee and of the previous Ad Hoc Group of Experts in the 10 years since the previous update [YUN 1999, p. 904]; the practical manual on transfer pricing for developing countries [E/C.18/2011/5 & E/C.18/2011/CRP.10]; article 13: capital gains; taxation of development projects; tax treatment of development projects; tax treatment of services [E/C.18/2011/CRP.7]; concept of beneficial ownership; revision of the Manual for the Negotiation of Bilateral Tax Treaties between Developed and Developing Countries [E/C.18/2011/CRP.11 & Add.1–7]; capacity-building; and tax cooperation and its relevance to major environmental issues, particularly climate change [E.C.18/2011/CRP.9].

Transport

Maritime transport

The *Review of Maritime Transport, 2012* [Sales No. E.12.II.D.17], prepared by the UNCTAD secretariat, reported that world seaborne trade grew by 4 per cent in 2011—reaching an estimated 8.7 billion tons—whereas the tonnage of the world fleet grew by a greater rate of almost 10 per cent, as ship owners took delivery of vessels that had been ordered before the economic crisis began. China, Japan and the Republic of Korea built more than 93 per cent of tonnage delivered in 2011.

With supply outstripping demand, freight rates fell even further, to unprofitable levels for most shipping companies. For importers and exporters, however, the low freight rates helped reduce transaction costs, which was important for reviving global trade. World container port throughput increased in 2011 by an estimated 5.9 per cent to 572.8 million 20-foot equivalent units, its highest level ever.

Legal and regulatory developments during the year included the adoption of amendments to the 1996 Protocol to the Convention on Limitation of Liability for Maritime Claims, 1976 [YUN 1996, p. 1431] regarding compensation limits, as well as a set of technical and operational measures to increase energy efficiency and reduce greenhouse gas emissions from international shipping, adopted under the auspices of the International Maritime Organization in July and expected to enter into force in 2013.

Developing countries continued to expand their participation in different maritime sectors, including shipbuilding, ownership, registration, operation, scrapping and manning. Ship owners of one third of the world fleet and 12 of the top 20 container operators were from developing countries. Almost 42 per cent of the world fleet was registered in Liberia, the Marshall Islands and Panama, and more than 92 per cent of scrapping in 2011 took place in Bangladesh, China, India and Pakistan.

Transport of dangerous goods

Committee of experts

In response to Economic and Social Council resolution 645 G (XXIII) [YUN 1957, p. 194], the Secretary-General submitted an April report [E/2011/91] on the work of the Committee of Experts on the Transport of Dangerous Goods and on the Globally Harmonized System of Classification and Labelling of Chemicals, focusing on the biennium 2009–2010 and on the implementation of Council resolution 2009/19 [YUN 2009, p. 960].

The secretariat had published the sixteenth revised edition of the *Recommendations on the Transport of Dangerous Goods: Model Regulations* [Sales No. E.09.VIII.2], the fifth revised edition of the *Recommendations on the Transport of Dangerous Goods: Manual of Tests and Criteria* [Sales No. E.09.VIII.2] and the third revised edition of the *Globally Harmonized System of Classification and Labelling of Chemicals* [Sales No. E.09.II.E.10]. All of the main legal instruments and codes governing the international transport of dangerous goods by sea, air, road, rail or inland waterway had been amended accordingly, with effect from 1 January 2011, and many Governments had transposed the provisions of the Model Regulations into their own legislation for domestic traffic for application from 2011. Numerous Governments and international organizations had also revised or taken steps to revise existing national and international legislation in order to implement the Globally Harmonized System as soon as possible.

The Committee adopted amendments to the Model Regulations and the Manual of Tests and Criteria that consisted mainly of new or revised provisions concerning the security of transport of high-consequence radioactive material; listing and classification of dangerous goods and related packing and test methods; transport of dangerous goods packed in limited and excepted quantities; transport in packages and cargo transport units containing substances presenting a risk of asphyxiation when used for cooling or conditioning purposes; the use of salvage pressure receptacles and the use, design, construction, inspection, testing and handling of flexible bulk containers; and the use of electronic data interchange for documentation purposes. Amendments to the Globally Harmonized System adopted by the Committee included various new or revised provisions concerning, inter alia, new hazard categories for chemically unstable gases and non-flammable aerosols; the further rationalization of precautionary statements; and the further clarification of criteria to avoid differences in their interpretation.

The Committee adopted a programme of work for the biennium 2011–2012, planning its sessions and those of the Subcommittee of Experts on the Transport of Dangerous Goods and the Subcommittee of Experts on the Globally Harmonized System of Classification and Labelling of Chemicals in accordance with Economic and Social Council resolution 1999/65 [YUN 1999, p. 906]. It recommended a draft resolution for adoption by the Economic and Social Council (see below).

ECONOMIC AND SOCIAL COUNCIL ACTION

On 27 July [meeting 47], the Economic and Social Council adopted **resolution 2011/25** [draft: E/2011/L.22] without vote [agenda item 13 (*m*)].

Work of the Committee of Experts on the Transport of Dangerous Goods and on the Globally Harmonized System of Classification and Labelling of Chemicals

The Economic and Social Council,

Recalling its resolutions 1999/65 of 26 October 1999 and 2009/19 of 29 July 2009,

Having considered the report of the Secretary-General on the work of the Committee of Experts on the Transport of Dangerous Goods and on the Globally Harmonized System of Classification and Labelling of Chemicals during the biennium 2009–2010,

A. Work of the Committee regarding the transport of dangerous goods

Recognizing the importance of the work of the Committee of Experts on the Transport of Dangerous Goods and on the Globally Harmonized System of Classification and Labelling of Chemicals for the harmonization of codes and regulations relating to the transport of dangerous goods,

Bearing in mind the need to maintain safety standards at all times and to facilitate trade, as well as the importance of these issues to the various organizations responsible for modal regulations, while meeting the growing concern for the protection of life, property and the environment through the safe and secure transport of dangerous goods,

Noting the ever-increasing volume of dangerous goods being introduced into worldwide commerce and the rapid expansion of technology and innovation,

Recalling that, while the major international instruments governing the transport of dangerous goods by the various modes of transport and many national regulations are now better harmonized with the Model Regulations annexed to the Committee's recommendations on the transport of dangerous goods, further work on harmonizing these instruments is necessary to enhance safety and to facilitate trade, and recalling also that uneven progress in the updating of national inland transport legislation in some countries of the world continues to present serious challenges to international multimodal transport,

Noting with concern that, despite the recommendations contained in chapter 5.5 of the *Recommendations on the Transport of Dangerous Goods: Model Regulations*, intended to alert workers involved in opening and unloading transport units containing general cargo that has been fumigated prior to shipment for phytosanitary purposes and who may be unfamiliar with the substantial risks of asphyxiation, intoxication and death when such units have not been ventilated, accidents during such operations are still reported in port areas and inland container depots,

1. *Expresses its appreciation* for the work of the Committee of Experts on the Transport of Dangerous Goods and on the Globally Harmonized System of Classification and Labelling of Chemicals with respect to matters relating to the transport of dangerous goods, including their security in transport;

2. *Requests* the Secretary-General:

(*a*) To circulate the new and amended recommendations on the transport of dangerous goods to the Governments of Member States, the specialized agencies, the International Atomic Energy Agency and other international organizations concerned;

(*b*) To publish the seventeenth revised edition of the *Recommendations on the Transport of Dangerous Goods: Model Regulations* and amendment 1 to the fifth revised edition of the *Recommendations on the Transport of Dangerous Goods: Manual of Tests and Criteria* in all the official languages of the United Nations, in the most cost-effective manner, no later than the end of 2011;

(*c*) To make those publications available on the website of the Economic Commission for Europe, which provides secretariat services to the Committee, and on CD-ROM;

3. *Invites* all Governments, the regional commissions, the specialized agencies, the International Atomic Energy Agency and the other international organizations concerned to transmit to the secretariat of the Committee their views on the work of the Committee, together with any comments that they may wish to make on the recommendations on the transport of dangerous goods;

4. *Invites* all interested Governments, the regional commissions, the specialized agencies and the international organizations concerned to take into account the recommendations of the Committee when developing or updating appropriate codes and regulations;

5. *Invites*, in particular, the Governments of Member States, the International Labour Organization and the International Maritime Organization to draw the attention of authorities and other entities concerned with workplace safety to the warning, marking, documentation and training provisions contained in chapter 5.5 of the *Recommendations on the Transport of Dangerous Goods: Model Regulations* or in the *International Maritime Dangerous Goods Code*, concerning fumigated cargo transport units, and to take appropriate steps to ensure their implementation and workers' awareness;

6. *Requests* the Committee to study, in consultation with the International Maritime Organization, the International Civil Aviation Organization, the regional commissions and the intergovernmental organizations concerned, the possibilities of improving the implementation of the Model Regulations on the transport of dangerous goods in all countries for the purposes of ensuring a high level of safety and eliminating technical barriers to international trade, including through the further harmonization of international agreements or conventions governing the international transport of dangerous goods;

7. *Invites* all Governments, as well as the regional commissions and organizations concerned, the International Maritime Organization and the International Civil Aviation Organization to provide feedback to the Committee regarding differences between the provisions of national, regional or international legal instruments and those of the Model Regulations, in order to enable the Committee to develop cooperative guidelines for enhancing consistency between these requirements and reducing unnecessary impediments; to identify existing substantive and international, regional and national differences, with the aim of reducing those differences in modal treatment to the greatest extent practical and ensuring that, where differences are necessary, they do not pose impediments to the safe and efficient transport of dangerous goods; and to undertake an editorial review of the Model Regulations and various modal instruments with the aim of improving clarity, user friendliness and ease of translation;

B. Work of the Committee regarding the Globally Harmonized System of Classification and Labelling of Chemicals

Bearing in mind that, in paragraph 23 (*c*) of the Plan of Implementation of the World Summit on Sustainable Development ("Johannesburg Plan of Implementation"), countries were encouraged to implement the Globally Harmonized System of Classification and Labelling of Chemicals as soon as possible with a view to having the system fully operational by 2008,

Bearing in mind also that the General Assembly, in its resolution 57/253 of 20 December 2002, endorsed the Johannesburg Plan of Implementation and requested the

Economic and Social Council to implement the provisions of the Plan relevant to its mandate and, in particular, to promote the implementation of Agenda 21 by strengthening system-wide coordination,

Noting with satisfaction:

(*a*) That the Economic Commission for Europe and all United Nations programmes and specialized agencies concerned with chemical safety in the field of transport or of the environment, in particular the United Nations Environment Programme, the International Maritime Organization and the International Civil Aviation Organization, have already taken appropriate steps to amend or update their legal instruments in order to give effect to the Globally Harmonized System of Classification and Labelling of Chemicals or are considering amending them as soon as possible,

(*b*) That the International Labour Organization, the Food and Agriculture Organization of the United Nations and the World Health Organization are also taking appropriate steps to adapt their existing chemical safety recommendations, codes and guidelines to the Globally Harmonized System, in particular in the areas of occupational health and safety, pesticide management and the prevention and treatment of poisoning,

(*c*) That the Globally Harmonized System has been in force in Mauritius since 2004,

(*d*) That New Zealand, where the first edition of the Globally Harmonized System has been in force since 2001, is updating its national legislation in accordance with the provisions of the third revised edition,

(*e*) That, in the European Union, the first adaptation to technical progress of its "Classification, Labelling and Packaging Regulation" implementing the Globally Harmonized System in its member States and in the European Economic Area, entered into force on 25 September 2009 and that a second adaptation, intended to bring the "Classification, Labelling and Packaging Regulation" in line with the provisions of the third revised edition of the Globally Harmonized System, is expected to be published in the first half of 2011,

(*f*) That, in Serbia, national legislation implementing the Globally Harmonized System entered into force on 18 September 2010,

(*g*) That, in the United States of America, the Occupational Safety and Health Administration of the Department of Labor published on 30 September 2009 a proposed rule to modify its existing Hazard Communication Standard to conform with the third revised edition of the Globally Harmonized System;

(*h*) That implementation of the Globally Harmonized System has started in the Republic of Korea, Singapore and Viet Nam,

(*i*) That other Member States (for example, Australia, Brazil, Canada, China, Japan, Malaysia, the Russian Federation, South Africa and Switzerland) participating in the activities of the Subcommittee of Experts on the Globally Harmonized System of Classification and Labelling of Chemicals are actively preparing revisions of national legislation or have developed or already issued standards applicable to chemicals in implementation of the Globally Harmonized System,

(*j*) That a number of United Nations programmes and specialized agencies and regional organizations, in particular the United Nations Institute for Training and Research, the International Labour Organization, the World Health Organization, the Economic Commission for Europe, the Asia-Pacific Economic Cooperation, the Organization for Economic Cooperation and Development and the European Union, Governments and non-governmental organizations representing the chemical industry, have organized or contributed to multiple workshops, seminars and other capacity-building activities at the international, regional, subregional and national levels in order to raise administration, health sector and industry awareness and to prepare for or support the implementation of the Globally Harmonized System,

Aware that effective implementation will require further cooperation between the Subcommittee of Experts on the Globally Harmonized System of Classification and Labelling of Chemicals and the international bodies concerned, continued efforts by the Governments of Member States, cooperation with the industry and other stakeholders, and significant support for capacity-building activities in countries with economies in transition and developing countries,

Recalling the particular significance for building capacities at all levels of the Global Partnership for Capacity-building to Implement the Globally Harmonized System of Classification and Labelling of Chemicals of the United Nations Institute for Training and Research, the International Labour Organization and the Organization for Economic Cooperation and Development,

1. *Commends* the Secretary-General on the publication of the third revised edition of the *Globally Harmonized System of Classification and Labelling of Chemicals* in the six official languages of the United Nations, in book form and on CD-ROM, and its availability, together with related informational material, on the website of the Economic Commission for Europe, which provides secretariat services to the Committee of Experts on the Transport of Dangerous Goods and on the Globally Harmonized System of Classification and Labelling of Chemicals;

2. *Expresses its deep appreciation* to the Committee, the Economic Commission for Europe, United Nations programmes, specialized agencies and other organizations concerned for their fruitful cooperation and their commitment to the implementation of the Globally Harmonized System;

3. *Requests* the Secretary-General:

(*a*) To circulate the amendments to the third revised edition of the *Globally Harmonized System of Classification and Labelling of Chemicals* to the Governments of Member States, the specialized agencies and other international organizations concerned;

(*b*) To publish the fourth revised edition of the *Globally Harmonized System of Classification and Labelling of Chemicals* in all the official languages of the United Nations in the most cost-effective manner, no later than the end of 2011, and to make it available on CD-ROM and on the website of the Economic Commission for Europe;

(*c*) To continue to make information on the implementation of the Globally Harmonized System available on the website of the Economic Commission for Europe;

4. *Invites* Governments that have not yet done so to take the necessary steps, through appropriate national procedures and/or legislation, to implement the Globally Harmonized System as soon as possible;

5. *Reiterates its invitation* to the regional commissions, United Nations programmes, specialized agencies and other organizations concerned to promote the implementation of the Globally Harmonized System and, where relevant, to amend their respective international legal instruments addressing transport safety, workplace safety, consumer protection or the protection of the environment, so as to give effect to the Globally Harmonized System through such instruments;

6. *Invites* Governments, the regional commissions, United Nations programmes, specialized agencies and other organizations concerned to provide feedback to the Subcommittee of Experts on the Globally Harmonized System on the steps taken for the implementation of the Globally Harmonized System in all relevant sectors, through international, regional or national legal instruments, recommendations, codes and guidelines, including, when applicable, information about the transitional periods for its implementation;

7. *Encourages* Governments, the regional commissions, United Nations programmes, specialized agencies and other relevant international organizations and non-governmental organizations, in particular those representing industry, to strengthen their support for the implementation of the Globally Harmonized System by providing financial contributions and/or technical assistance for capacity-building activities in developing countries and countries with economies in transition;

C. Programme of work of the Committee

Taking note of the programme of work of the Committee of Experts on the Transport of Dangerous Goods and on the Globally Harmonized System of Classification and Labelling of Chemicals for the biennium 2011–2012 as contained in paragraphs 48 and 49 of the report of the Secretary-General,

Noting the relatively poor level of participation of experts from developing countries and countries with economies in transition in the work of the Committee and the need to promote their wider participation in its work,

1. *Decides* to approve the programme of work of the Committee of Experts on the Transport of Dangerous Goods and on the Globally Harmonized System of Classification and Labelling of Chemicals;

2. *Stresses* the importance of the participation of experts from developing countries and from countries with economies in transition in the work of the Committee, calls in that regard for voluntary contributions to facilitate their participation, including through support for travel and daily subsistence, and invites Member States and international organizations in a position to do so to contribute;

3. *Requests* the Secretary-General to submit to the Economic and Social Council in 2013 a report on the implementation of the present resolution, the recommendations on the transport of dangerous goods and the Globally Harmonized System of Classification and Labelling of Chemicals.

Chapter V

Regional economic and social activities

The five UN regional commissions in 2011 continued to provide technical cooperation, including advisory services, promote programmes and projects and provide training to enhance national capacity-building. Three of those bodies held regular sessions during the year—the Economic Commission for Africa (ECA), the Economic and Social Commission for Asia and the Pacific (ESCAP), and the Economic Commission for Europe (ECE). The Economic Commission for Latin America and the Caribbean (ECLAC) and the Economic and Social Commission for Western Asia (ESCWA) did not meet in 2011. The Executive Secretaries of the commissions held periodic meetings to exchange views and coordinate activities and positions on major development issues.

ECA met in March on the theme "Governing development in Africa" and adopted a ministerial statement on a wide range of issues. ESCAP held its sixty-seventh session in May on the theme "Beyond the crises: long-term perspectives on social protection and development in Asia and the Pacific". ECE, at its sixty-fourth session in March, discussed economic integration and the role of regional integration and cooperation for promoting sustainable development.

The regional commissions also addressed the economic and social effects of the global economic and financial crisis that had begun in 2008. Within the context of their mandates, the commissions took action to mitigate the effects of the crisis in their regions and to support stabilization and economic recovery.

Regional cooperation

In 2011, the United Nations continued to strengthen cooperation among its regional commissions, between them and other UN entities, and with regional and international organizations.

On 26 April (**decision 2011/209**), the Economic and Social Council decided that the theme for the item on regional cooperation of its 2011 substantive session would be "Regional cooperation as a catalyst for development: examples from the regions". The Council held a dialogue on the issue with the Executive Secretaries of the regional commissions on 8 July.

On 18 May (**decision 2011/213**), the Council took note of the report of the Secretary-General on regional cooperation in the economic, social and related fields [YUN 2010, p. 968].

The Council considered regional cooperation during its general segment on 25 July, adopting two resolutions and two decisions.

By **decision 2011/223** of 25 July, the Council took note of the report on the economic situation in the Economic Commission for Europe region in 2010–2011 [YUN 2010, p. 983]; the overview of economic and social conditions in Africa, 2011 [ibid., p. 968]; the summary of the *Economic and Social Survey of Asia and the Pacific, 2011* [ibid., p. 974]; the report on the economic situation and outlook in Latin America and the Caribbean, 2010–2011 [ibid., p. 988]; and the summary of the *Survey of Economic and Social Developments in the ESCWA Region, 2010–2011*.

Meetings of Executive Secretaries. The Executive Secretaries held four meetings throughout the year: in Santiago, Chile, in January, hosted by the Executive Secretary of the Economic Commission for Latin America and the Caribbean; in New York, in February; at the margins of the substantive session of the Economic and Social Council in Geneva, in July; and at the margins of their dialogue with the General Assembly's Second Committee in New York, in October [E/2011/15 & E/2012/15]. They focused on the regional commissions' support to UN system-wide coherence at the regional and global levels; regional perspectives and contributions towards achieving the Millennium Development Goals (MDGs); promotion of policies leading to greater inclusion and equity; regional contributions to the United Nations Conference on Sustainable Development (Rio+20) process (see p. 799); and regional cooperation as a tool for development.

Cooperation in the economic, social and related fields

In accordance with General Assembly resolution 1823(XVII) [YUN 1962, p. 293] and Economic and Social Council resolution 1817(LV) [YUN 1973, p. 449], the Secretary-General in May submitted a report [E/2011/15] on regional cooperation in the economic, social and related fields. The report examined the progress made by different regions in moving towards a new development paradigm of inclusive and sustainable development; regional contributions to the International Year of Youth and the Fourth United Nations Conference on the Least Developed Countries (LDCs); and regional contributions towards the Rio+20 Conference to be held in 2012. The report covered developments in selected areas of regional and interregional cooperation, including policy matters addressed during the regional commission ministerial sessions, efforts to promote coherence at the regional level, including through the Regional Coordination Mechanism convened by the regional commissions, as well as inter-regional cooperation among the commissions.

Two addendums [E/2011/15/Add.1,2] contained resolutions and decisions adopted at the regular sessions of the regional commissions.

The Economic and Social Council took note of the report on 25 July (**decision 2011/223**).

Africa

The Economic Commission for Africa (ECA) organized its annual session as part of the joint meetings of the African Union (AU) Conference of Ministers of Economy and Finance and the ECA Conference of African Ministers of Finance, Planning and Economic Development, in accordance with Economic and Social Council resolution 2007/4 [YUN 2007, p. 1014]. ECA held its forty-fourth session/Fourth Joint Annual Meetings of the AU and ECA Conference of Ministers (Addis Ababa, Ethiopia, 28–29 March) [E/ECA/CM/44/6] under the theme "Governing development in Africa". The session considered an overview of economic and social conditions in Africa in 2010 [E/ECA/COE/30/2], a review of progress on regional and continental integration [E/ECA/COE/30/10/Rev.1] and a report on progress in achieving the MDGs in Africa [E/ECA/COE/30/9].

The session adopted 10 resolutions and a ministerial statement [E/ECA/CM/44/3], in which Ministers noted that Africa's recovery in the aftermath of the global crisis had been swift and strong compared to previous downturns due to structural reforms. Ministers committed to taking a direct and active role in development, promoting inclusive public policy processes, deepening the mobilization of additional support among African member States, improving the quality of statistical information, mobilizing financial resources, advocating for LDCs, deepening regional integration, combating illicit financial flows, addressing the impact of climate change, supporting the Mutual Review of Development Effectiveness and the African Peer Review Mechanism, supporting investment in science and technology, implementing the Comprehensive African Agricultural Development Programme and supporting ECA subregional offices.

The Committee of Experts of the AU-ECA fourth annual meeting met from 24 to 27 March [E/ECA/CM/44/2/Rev.1].

The activities of the Commission were summarized in the ECA annual report [E/ECA/COE/31/21].

Economic trends

Africa's growth momentum slowed sharply in 2011, primarily due to political unrest in North Africa and a continued slump in the developed economies, with growth falling to 2.7 per cent, down from 4.6 per cent in 2010 [E/2012/17]. The intensity and persistence of the social and political turmoil in North Africa increased investor risk aversion, prompting capital inflows and private investment to decline. Production and exports of oil were also disrupted, especially in Libya, and tourism collapsed. Consequently, North Africa recorded zero growth, down from 4.2 per cent in 2010.

Outside North Africa, economic activity was buoyant with solid growth of 4.5 per cent reinforcing the recovery of 4.8 per cent in 2010. Per capita real gross domestic product (GDP) increased by 2.2 per cent outside North Africa, similar to the growth rate seen in 2010. For the first time in five years, the growth of the continent's oil exporters lagged behind that of oil importers, with the oil-exporting group decelerating from 5.1 per cent in 2010 to 1.5 per cent; however, in oil-importing countries, a boom in public infrastructure spending and increased agricultural production helped growth rise to 4.2 per cent, from 4 per cent in 2010.

Despite experiencing drought and famine, East Africa registered 5.8 per cent growth, close to the 6 per cent of 2010. Conversely, in West Africa, economic activity moderated, affected by contraction in Côte d'Ivoire: growth fell to 5.6 per cent, from 6.9 per cent in 2010, weighed down by Côte d'Ivoire's 0.4 per cent contraction caused by post-election violence and a collapse of exports. Lower oil production by Nigeria also contributed. Economic activity in Central Africa remained fairly robust, although output declined from 5.2 per cent in 2010 to 4.2 per cent in 2011. Growth was underpinned by large public investment in infrastructure, strong performance of services sectors and increased timber exports. Southern Africa's output expanded by 3.8 per cent, up from 3.5 per cent in 2010, with considerable variations in the subregion.

The Economic Report on Africa, a joint publication of ECA and the AU, devoted its 2011 edition to the theme "Governing development in Africa—the role of the State in economic transformation".

Activities

The ECA programme of work in 2011 was organized under ten subprogrammes: macroeconomic analysis, finance and economic development; food security and sustainable development; governance and public administration; information and science and technology for development; regional integration, infrastructure and trade; gender and women in development; subregional activities for development; development planning and administration; statistics; and social development [E/ECA/COE/31/21]. In other activities, ECA continued to support the AU and the New Partnership for Africa's Development (NEPAD) [YUN 2001, p. 899].

Macroeconomic analysis, finance and economic development

ECA activities aimed at strengthening the capacity of States to design and implement policies and programmes to achieve sustained growth for poverty reduction. In the area of macroeconomic analysis, ECA focused on the role of the State and development planning frameworks as critical means for addressing Africa's development challenges. In the area of MDGs and LDCs, ECA provided assistance to States in capacity-building on MDG consistent planning; participants from national planning agencies from over 30 countries benefited from training workshops during the year. ECA, together with the AU Commission (AUC) and the African Development Bank (AfDB), embarked on an initiative to articulate an African position on the post-2015 agenda.

In the area of financing for development, ECA worked closely with other regional development institutions, such as AUC, AfDB and the United Nations Development Programme (UNDP), to coordinate and build consensus on the challenges of financing Africa's development. The Regional Forum on Financing for Development: Mobilizing Resources for Economic Transformation in Africa (Addis Ababa, 18–20 May), organized by ECA in collaboration with AUC and AfDB, adopted an outcome document representing an African common position on issues related to financing for development for the Fourth High-level Forum on Aid Effectiveness (Busan, Republic of Korea, 29 November–1 December) and the fifth High-level Dialogue on Financing for Development (see p. 921).

New Partnership for Africa's Development

As the coordinator of UN agencies and organizations working in Africa in support of NEPAD, a programme for the continent's development initiated by African leaders in 2001 [YUN 2001, p. 899], ECA supported the coordination and coherence of UN activities in Africa through the Regional Coordination Mechanism (RCM). Projects and activities included an expert group meeting on coordinating development in Africa; a group training on the implementation and appraisal of NEPAD-related projects; the provision of capacity-building support to various AU organs; the organization of the twelfth session of RCM; the strengthening of the RCM secretariat; participation in the Intergovernmental Committee of Experts organized by the ECA Subregional Office for Eastern Africa; and experience and knowledge-sharing among subregional offices on the establishment of subregional coordination mechanisms.

In February [E/ECA/COE/30/16], the ECA secretariat submitted a report on United Nations support to the AU and its NEPAD programme from March 2010 to March 2011.

(For information on NEPAD, see p. 891).

Food security and sustainable development

ECA strengthened the capacity of States to formulate and implement policies, strategies and programmes for achieving food security and sustainable development. ECA prepared a report, Food Security in Africa: challenges, opportunities and policy options, which reviewed policy options for security within the context of structural changes in the global food market and developed recommendations for the formulation of food security policies. In close collaboration with AUC, a draft Africa Bioenergy Policy Framework and Guidelines was developed, to serve as a technical tool for promoting the sustainable development of bioenergy within the framework of NEPAD and global conventions on bioenergy. In preparation for Rio+20, ECA, in collaboration with AUC, AfDB, UNDP and the United Nations Environment Programme (UNEP), organized workshops on institutional and strategic frameworks for sustainable development (Addis Ababa, 7–9 March) and on a sustainable development indicator framework for Africa (Addis Ababa, 10–11 March). The first workshop, attended by more than 90 policymakers and experts, examined institutions, policies and strategies for sustainable development, while the second, attended by over 100 policymakers and experts, adopted the proposed Sustainable Development Indicator Framework for Africa.

As part of the preparatory process for Rio+20, a regional preparatory meeting (Addis Ababa, 20–25 October) resulted in the adoption of the *Africa Consensus Statement to Rio+20* [E/ECA/CFSSD/7/Min./3] which addressed a wide range of sustainable development topics of relevance to Africa, including the need to reinforce and integrate the economic, social and environmental pillars of sustainable development; the green economy within the context of sustainable development and poverty reduction; and the institutional framework for sustainable development.

Climate change

The seventeenth Conference of the Parties to the United Nations Framework Convention on Climate Change (Durban, South Africa, 28 November –11 December) delivered on the two priority issues of Africa: the adoption of the governing instrument of the Green Climate Fund and the second commitment period to the Kyoto Protocol.

The Conference launched the Durban Platform, which aimed to prevent a temperature rise beyond acceptable levels. A number of issues, however, required further negotiation. Africa should play an enhanced role; negotiations should draw insights from the report by the working group appointed by the Secretary-General; the Fund should be adequately capitalized; representatives of Africa and LDCs on the Board should ensure that the Fund mobilize financial resources; and the review of long-term temperature goal agreed at the Cancún Conference [YUN 2010, p. 1019] should ensure that the global goal of temperature rise would not expose Africa to unacceptable risks.

Governance and public administration

ECA launched a number of reports, including the 2011 Mutual Review of Development Effectiveness Report, launched on 30 November during the Fourth High-level Forum on Aid Effectiveness, and Public Financial Management with a View to Improving Domestic Resources Mobilization, which examined the various policy-related conceptual frameworks and methods in public financial management and resource mobilization. The second meeting of the Committee on Governance and Popular Participation (CGPP) (Addis Ababa, 9–10 March), reviewed and evaluated the activities of ECA in the area of governance and public administration and proposed activities for the 2012–2013 biennium; suggested how ECA could improve its governance and public administration activities and working relations with continental, subregional and national institutions; and adopted the new Statutes of the CGPP. Support was provided to national anti-corruption institutions through the AU Advisory Board on Corruption (AUABC); in collaboration with the AU, ECA prepared the Regional Anti-corruption Programme for Africa for 2011–2016, which was approved by the AUABC in Mombasa, Kenya, in October. ECA held an expert group meeting (Addis Ababa, 7–8 March) to review the technical publication Assessment of the Impact and Effectiveness of Civil Society Organizations and Non-governmental Organizations in Promoting Governance in Africa.

Information and science and technology for development

ECA provided support on policy and strategy development to Burkina Faso, Ethiopia, the Gambia, Ghana, Mali, the Niger, Nigeria and Rwanda, increasing the number of countries that had developed national and sectoral plans and strategies on information and communications technology (ICT). ECA undertook a study in Cameroon, Ethiopia, the Gambia, Morocco and Mozambique to take stock of the situation in ICT policy development and implementation, which helped identify priority areas for those countries. Capacity-building among national statistical offices involved 17 francophone African countries and focused on collecting, analysing and disseminating ICT statistics through training courses organized in collaboration with the International Telecommunication Union and the United Nations Conference on Trade and Development in the framework of the international Partnership on Measuring ICT for Development. In the area of library and information management services, capacity-building and resources development were provided to States, as well as clients throughout the region.

Regional integration, infrastructure and trade

ECA organized a high-level symposium (Addis Ababa, April) that brought together representatives of civil society to discuss their role in deepening regional integration; an expert group meeting on the establishment of the Intra-Regional Economic Community Free Trade Agreement (Addis Ababa, 31 May–1 June) that looked at the potential impact of free trade agreements on African economies; and the seventh session of the Committee on Trade, Regional Cooperation and Integration (Addis Ababa, 2–3 June), which examined fast-tracking a continental free trade area and accelerating the process towards a Continental Customs Union and African Common Market. ECA presented a paper on boosting intra-African trade as a basis for discussion among the ministers and high-level officials at the seventh ordinary session of the AU Conference of Ministers of Trade (Accra, Ghana, November).

In the area of energy, ECA, with the AUC Department of Infrastructure and Energy, organized an expert group meeting to validate two reports on bioenergy policy and technology options (Addis Ababa, 21–23 November), which reviewed the key findings and formulated recommendations for policy options and instruments. ECA continued to enhance the capacities for African countries to participate effectively in multilateral trade negotiations, Aid for Trade and the African Growth and Opportunity Act (AGOA); and, in partnership with AUC, conducted a continental survey of 104 respondents in over half of AGOA beneficiaries on their experiences and expectations of AGOA. The results were presented to the AGOA Midterm Review (Lusaka, Zambia, May). ECA helped to prepare a study entitled "African Case Stories: A Snapshot of Aid for Trade on the Ground in Africa", which was launched at the third Global Review on Aid for Trade (Geneva, July).

In March, the ECA secretariat submitted a report [E/ECA/COE/30/10/Rev.1] on progress towards regional and continental integration in Africa.

Europe-Africa fixed link

An April report [E/2011/21] on the project for a Europe-Africa fixed link through the Strait of Gibraltar, prepared jointly by ECE and ECA pursuant to Economic and Social Council resolution 2009/11 [YUN 2009, p. 971], summarized the work done under the authority of the Spanish-Moroccan Joint Committee by two engineering firms. The period 2006–2011 was devoted to updating the project's feasibility and undertaking an evaluation. The 2011–2013 phase would focus on the preliminary project study and on a wider programme of research to identify and analyse a technically feasible option.

ECONOMIC AND SOCIAL COUNCIL ACTION

On 25 July [meeting 42], the Economic and Social Council adopted **resolution 2011/12** [draft: E/2011/L.14] without vote [agenda item 10].

Europe-Africa fixed link through the Strait of Gibraltar

The Economic and Social Council,

Recalling its resolutions 1982/57 of 30 July 1982, 1983/62 of 29 July 1983, 1984/75 of 27 July 1984, 1985/70 of 26 July 1985, 1987/69 of 8 July 1987, 1989/119 of 28 July 1989, 1991/74 of 26 July 1991, 1993/60 of 30 July 1993, 1995/48 of 27 July 1995, 1997/48 of 22 July 1997, 1999/37 of 28 July 1999, 2001/29 of 26 July 2001, 2003/52 of 24 July 2003, 2005/34 of 26 July 2005, 2007/16 of 26 July 2007 and 2009/11 of 28 July 2009,

Referring to resolution 912(1989), adopted on 1 February 1989 by the Parliamentary Assembly of the Council of Europe, regarding measures to encourage the construction of a major traffic artery in south-western Europe and to study thoroughly the possibility of a fixed link through the Strait of Gibraltar,

Referring also to the Barcelona Declaration adopted at the Euro-Mediterranean Ministerial Conference, held in Barcelona, Spain, on 27 and 28 November 1995, and to the work programme annexed thereto, which is aimed at connecting Mediterranean transport networks to the trans-European network in order to ensure their interoperability,

Referring further to the European Commission communication of 31 January 2007 on strengthening transport cooperation with neighbouring countries, established on the basis of the conclusions of the report of November 2005 of the High-level Group on the Extension of the Major Trans-European Transport Axes to the Neighbouring Countries and Regions, and to the conclusions of the first Euro-Mediterranean Ministerial Conference on Transport, held in Marrakech, Morocco, on 15 December 2005, as well as to the Regional Transport Action Plan for the Mediterranean Region 2007–2013, adopted by the Euro-Mediterranean Transport Forum at its eighth meeting, held in Brussels on 29 and 30 May 2007,

Referring to the final declaration of the Ministerial Conference of the "Barcelona Process: Union for the Mediterranean", held in Marseille, France, on 3 and 4 November 2008, and the emphasis placed on transport projects in the Joint Declaration of the Paris Summit for the Mediterranean of 13 July 2008,

Referring also to the meeting held in Luxembourg on 8 June 2008 between the Ministers of Transport of Morocco and Spain and the Vice-President of the European Commission and Commissioner for Transport with regard to the official presentation to the European institutions of the project for a fixed link,

Taking note of the follow-up report prepared jointly by the Economic Commission for Europe and the Economic Commission for Africa in accordance with Economic and Social Council resolution 2009/11,

Noting the conclusions of the studies carried out by the Western Mediterranean Transport Group on Europe-Maghreb transport and cooperation agreements and on transport conditions for nationals of Maghreb origin when they travel to the Western Mediterranean in the summer, and the action plan for the period 2009–2011, adopted at the sixth Conference of Ministers of Transport of the Western Mediterranean, held in Rome on 20 May 2009,

Noting also the conclusions of the studies carried out by the European Commission (INFRAMED, MEDA TEN-T, REG-MED and DESTIN) for the development of an integrated transport network in the Mediterranean basin,

Taking note of the Regional Transport Action Plan which constitutes a road map for intensifying cooperation in the Mediterranean with regard to infrastructure planning and the reform of transport service regulations, as well as the list of priority projects annexed thereto, including the fixed link through the Strait of Gibraltar,

Taking note also of the conclusions of the global evaluation of the project, carried out in 2010 by an independent consortium of international consultants, which indicate that the geostrategic component of the project and the potential for the development of mass-transit networks offered by long-distance rail transportation weigh significantly in favour of its implementation and the involvement of the international community, especially regarding its financing,

1. *Welcomes* the cooperation on the project for the link through the Strait of Gibraltar between the Economic Commission for Africa, the Economic Commission for Europe, the Governments of Morocco and Spain, and specialized international organizations;

2. *Also welcomes* the progress made in the project studies as a result, in particular, of deep-sea drilling, which has given a decisive impetus to geological and geotechnical exploration and to the technical, economic and traffic update studies currently being finalized;

3. *Further welcomes* the organization by the International Tunnelling Association, under the auspices of the Economic Commission for Europe and the Economic Commission for Africa, of the seminar held in Madrid in January 2005 entitled "Soundings and treatments: new developments relating to geological formations";

4. *Commends* the Economic Commission for Europe and the Economic Commission for Africa for the work done in preparing the project follow-up report requested by the Economic and Social Council in its resolution 2009/11;

5. *Renews its invitation* to the competent organizations of the United Nations system and to specialized governmental and non-governmental organizations to participate

in the studies and work on the fixed link through the Strait of Gibraltar;

6. *Requests* the Executive Secretaries of the Economic Commission for Africa and the Economic Commission for Europe to continue to take an active part in the follow-up to the project and to report to the Economic and Social Council at its substantive session of 2013 on the progress made on the project studies;

7. *Requests* the Secretary-General to provide formal support and, to the extent that priorities permit, the resources necessary, from within the regular budget, to the Economic Commission for Europe and the Economic Commission for Africa, to enable them to carry out the activities mentioned above.

Gender and women in development

ECA supported and strengthened the capacity of States to address gender equality and women's advancement concerns through action towards achieving internationally agreed goals, including the MDGs. The seventh session of the Committee on Women and Development (Addis Ababa, May) reviewed the work undertaken by the secretariat and considered how national machineries on gender could effectively use the tools and products.

The Committee considered a report on recent trends in national mechanisms for gender equality in Africa and on the status of gender inequality in the social, economic and political sector; the African Women's Human Rights Observatory; the e-network of African gender machineries; the interregional project on enhancing capacities to eradicate violence against women; and the 2010 Compendium of Good Practices in Gender Mainstreaming, focusing on gender, conflict and peace.

In its work on a gender-aware macroeconomic model, the secretariat produced a study, Gender Sensitive Policies: Simulations from the Gender Aware Macroeconomic Model, which discussed how the production of the household sector was accounted for in official national accounts and presented a framework for a comprehensive accounting of household production. In line with the recommendation from the forty-first session of the United Nations Statistical Commission [YUN 2010, p. 1262] on the formulation of a regional strategy on gender statistics, ECA organized a series of meetings that improved understanding of the conceptual and methodological approaches of satellite accounts on household production, its feasibility in the African context, and its importance in evidence-based development policy and programme formulation; improved understanding of the module for collecting data on violence against women; and developed an Africa Programme on Gender Statistics for submission to the third meeting of the Statistical Commission for Africa in 2012.

In the area of violence against women, and as part of the Secretary General's campaign "UNiTE to End Violence against Women", ECA, in collaboration with other regional commissions and UN agencies, initiated a project on enhancing capacities to eradicate violence against women through networking of local knowledge communities. The project included strengthening the capacity of countries to measure violence against women in order to obtain a baseline and an up-to-date analysis. A regional workshop on enhancing capacity of African countries to eradicate violence against women (Addis Ababa, 5–7 October) looked at the nature, prevalence, causes, consequences and impact of violence against women and identified gaps in data and statistics, based on a seven-country study undertaken by the secretariat.

Subregional development activities

In 2011, the five ECA subregional offices, located in Central Africa (Yaoundé, Cameroon), East Africa (Kigali, Rwanda), North Africa (Rabat, Morocco), Southern Africa (Lusaka, Zambia) and West Africa (Niamey, Niger), worked with other partners to provide technical assistance to address development challenges and accelerate regional integration through capacity-building, advisory services, training workshops and the implementation of field projects. The offices also served as catalysts to operationalize the analytical and normative work of ECA at the subregional and country levels.

Development planning and administration

The 2011 Conference of Ministers considered a February report of the African Institute for Economic Development and Planning (IDEP) [E/ECA/COE/30/20]. Against the background of the internal organizational reforms carried out during 2009, the year 2010 was in many ways the year of full revival for the Institute. In terms of the range of substantive programme activities, IDEP had never had a fuller and more diversified year, especially as regards its training activities but also with reference to its policy research work and policy dialogue initiatives. Through its programmes and activities, the Institute covered all the subregions while consolidating its standing in its host country, Senegal, as a foremost centre of advanced training for government officials.

The Conference of Ministers in March adopted resolution 889(XLIV) on the Institute (see p. 943).

ECONOMIC AND SOCIAL COUNCIL ACTION

On 25 July [meeting 42] the Economic and Social Council adopted **resolution 2011/13** [draft: E/2011/15/Add.1, as orally amended] without vote [agenda item 10].

African Institute for Economic Development and Planning

The Economic and Social Council,

Taking note of resolution 889(XLIV) adopted by the Conference of African Ministers of Finance, Planning and Economic Development annexed to the present resolution,

Recognizing the important role of the African Institute for Economic Development and Planning in capacity-building, as well as the pressing need to restore planning frameworks across the African continent,

1. *Notes* the invitation to the Economic and Social Council by the Conference of African Ministers of Finance, Planning and Economic Development to lend its support to a significant increase in the United Nations grant to the African Institute for Economic Development and Planning;

2. *Invites* the General Assembly to consider increasing the Organization's grant to the African Institute for Economic Development and Planning and other options to allow the Institute to effectively carry out its mission in supporting the capacity-building efforts of its member States;

3. *Requests* the Secretary-General to facilitate the implementation of the present resolution.

ANNEX
Resolution 889(XLIV) on the African Institute for Economic Development and Planning

The Conference of Ministers,

Recalling its resolution 875(XLIII) on the repositioning of the African Institute for Economic Development and Planning,

Having received with great satisfaction the report submitted to it on the work of the Institute over the past year showing the commendable progress that has been made in programme delivery and management,

Taking note of the steps taken to physically renovate the Institute building and efforts made for vigorous outreach,

Acknowledging the substantially upscaled level of contributions to the Institute from a record number of countries as well as from development partners,

Recognizing the important role of the Institute in capacity-building, as well as the pressing need to restore planning frameworks across the continent,

Recalling its endorsement of the request by the Governing Council of the Institute for a significant increase in the Organization's annual grant to the Institute,

1. *Commends* the Governing Council and management of the African Institute for Economic Development and Planning for the achievements recorded to restore the Institute's capacity to deliver on its programmes;

2. *Calls upon* the management of the Economic Commission for Africa to continue with the full programmatic integration of the Institute into its programme of work;

3. *Notes with appreciation* that the States members and partners of the Institute have renewed their commitments to the Institute and that many of them have paid their contributions, and urges member States and partners to continue to show support to the Institute by continuing to pay their assessed contributions and any outstanding arrears;

4. *Reiterates its request* that the Organization's grant to the Institute be significantly increased, and invites the Secretary-General to take all the necessary measures to implement this request, including by bringing the present resolution to the attention of the Economic and Social Council;

5. *Invites* the Economic and Social Council to lend its support to the request to increase the Organization's grant to the Institute so as to allow it to effectively carry out its mission in supporting the capacity-building efforts of its member States;

6. *Reiterates its request* to the Governing Council of the Institute to continue to furnish it with an annual report on the progress made in the work of the Institute.

General Assembly action. On 24 December, the General Assembly, in section 18 of **resolution 66/246** (see p. 1383), increased the grant of the Institute to $2.6 million per biennium.

Statistics

ECA advocated for an enhanced participation of African countries during the current round of population and housing censuses. Twenty-nine countries had already conducted their censuses. As a result of ECA advocacy, Botswana, Madagascar, Morocco, Namibia, South Africa, the Sudan and Tunisia adopted the global and regional implementation strategies on the 2008 System of National Accounting (SNA), with support from UN country teams. In the Sudan, the technical support and the strategies were helpful in separating the accounts and GDP between South Sudan and the Sudan. ECA and AfDB designed a five-year regional programme for the implementation of the 2008 SNA along with the Africa Group on National Accounts. ECA prepared the Compendium of Intra-African and Related Foreign Trade Statistics to provide quality and timely merchandise statistics, as well as to support regional economic, monetary, and social integration. ECA, AfDB and AUC produced the third joint African Statistical Yearbook, a leading source of statistical information on Africa. As of December, 29 countries were implementing their national strategy for the development of statistics, while 16 countries had finalized the design and were awaiting approval and funding to start implementation.

Social development

ECA produced its first African Social Development Report, which addressed social protection, and a report on strengthening capacities to promote gender-sensitive social protection policies in African countries, which provided policymakers with evidence from nine countries and recommendations to enable the integration of social protection policies and gender into national and subregional development plans and frameworks. It also organized a consultative training workshop to operationalize and use accountability indices for accelerating implementation of commitments on HIV/AIDS.

ECA delivered a technical discussion paper on youth employment policies for the meeting of the AU Ministers of Labour and Social Affairs, and supported the second training of the AU Youth Volunteer Corps, where 138 young Africans from 27 countries were provided with skills for deployment in various countries across the continent.

The Committee on Human and Social Development convened its second session (Addis Ababa, October), under the theme "Implementing Social Policy for Sustainable Development", which was attended by 90 representatives from 36 States. ECA submitted reports on health to the AU Ministers of Health meeting (Windhoek, Namibia, May), which focused on the theme "The Impact of Climate Change on Health in Africa", and reports on international migration and development to the Committee on Human and Social Development and to the Africa Regional Dialogue on International Migration. ECA also published the *African Social Development Review*, which focused on promoting and supporting the social development priorities of ECA, AUC and the AU-NEPAD programme.

Programme and organizational questions
Programme of work, 2012–2013

The thirtieth meeting of the Committee of Experts (Addis Ababa, 24–27 March) [E/ECA/CM/44/2/Rev.1] had before it the proposed programme of work and priorities for the 2012–2013 biennium [E/ECA/COE/30/18], which aimed at assisting African countries to formulate and implement the policies and programmes that would lead to sustainable economic growth and social development, with particular emphasis on poverty reduction. The proposed biennial programme was shaped around two thematic pillars, promoting regional integration and helping meet Africa's special needs and global challenges, and activities conducted through the ten subprogrammes.

The Committee took note of the document. The Conference of Ministers endorsed the programme of work and priorities at its Joint Annual Meeting [E/ECA/CM/44/6 (res. 888(XLIV))].

Construction of office facilities

Pursuant to resolution 63/263 [YUN 2008, p. 1545], the Secretary-General in September provided an update [A/66/351] on the status of the construction of additional office facilities at ECA. The construction was scheduled for completion in August 2012, followed by an interior set-up lasting approximately six months. Discrepancies resulting from an error on the part of the architecture and construction management consultant were found in the execution of the contract. The costs of the discrepancies, provisionally estimated at $734,000, resulted in increased costs and substantial depletion of the budgeted contingency, thereby increasing the risk to the project. The latest cost estimates amounted to $15,333,244.

In October [A/66/7/Add.3], the Advisory Committee on Administrative and Budgetary Questions submitted its comments and recommendations. The Committee urged the Secretary-General to closely monitor project expenditures and ensure that the project was delivered within the approved budget.

General Assembly action. The General Assembly, by section VII of **resolution 66/247** of 24 December (see p. 1393), requested the Secretary-General, through the Office of Central Support Services, to take into account lessons learned and best practices from past construction projects in implementing future construction projects.

(For information on the construction of office facilities at ECA, see p. 1427.)

Asia and the Pacific

The Economic and Social Commission for Asia and the Pacific (ESCAP) held its sixty-seventh session (Bangkok, Thailand, 19–25 May) [E/2011/39] in two segments: the senior officials segment (19–21 May) and the ministerial segment (23–25 May). The theme of the session was "Beyond the crises: long-term perspectives on social protection and development in Asia and the Pacific".

The Commission adopted 15 resolutions. It discussed issues pertinent to the Special Body on Least Developed and Landlocked Developing Countries; the Commission's subsidiary structure; management issues; activities of the Advisory Committee of Permanent Representatives and Other Representatives Designated by Members of the Commission; policy issues for the region; and the dates, venue and theme of the Commission's sixty-eighth session.

The activities of the Commission were summarized in the ESCAP annual reports [E/2011/39 & E/2012/39].

Economic trends

The summary [E/2012/18] of the *Economic and Social Survey of Asia and the Pacific, 2012* [Sales No. E.12.II.F.9] stated that the "V-shaped" recovery from the global economic crisis seen in 2010 was short-lived, as the world economy entered the second stage of crisis in 2011, with sharp deterioration in the global environment. The growth rate of the developing economies in the region declined to 7.0 per cent, from a robust rate of 8.8 per cent in 2010, with a further slowdown forecast in 2012, emanating from a slackening demand for the region's exports in advanced economies and higher costs of capital. Of even greater concern were the serious and growing inequalities between and within countries. Despite the slowdown, the region would remain the fastest-growing globally and an anchor of stability in the world economy. An increasing concern of policymakers was the imposition of various trade restrictive measures by crisis-affected countries. Another challenge for the region was high and volatile commodity prices. The commodity boom presented risks as well as opportunities. The less developed economies should resist the impulse towards commodity specialization, which, in turn, could delay industrialization and economic diversification. Challenges for policymakers included the need to better manage the balance between growth and inflation; coping with capital flows and exchange rate volatility; addressing jobless growth and unemployment; and tackling inequality.

Policy issues

The Commission had before it a summary of the *Economic and Social Survey of Asia and the Pacific, 2011* [E/ESCAP/67/19], prepared by the ESCAP secretariat, which stated that economies of the region faced fresh challenges throughout the year, including the return of food and fuel crises that were threatening hard-won development gains, sluggish recovery in the advanced economies and a deluge of short-term capital flows, leading to volatility in capital markets, the build-up of asset bubbles and the appreciation of exchange rates. Furthermore, the devastation wrought by the earthquake and tsunami in Japan provided another stark reminder of the region's vulnerability to natural disasters. In addition to addressing short-term risks, policymakers had to meet the challenge of rebalancing the region's economies in favour of domestic and regional investment and consumption. Some of the areas that needed policy attention were improved transport linkages, regional institution-building, streamlined transport and trade facilitation, and progress towards a regional energy framework.

At its 2011 session, the Commission considered the *Economic and Social Survey of Asia and the Pacific, 2011* [Sales No. E.11.II.F.2].

Activities

Least developed and landlocked developing countries

The Commission had before it a note by the secretariat [E/ESCAP/67/1] on addressing development gaps, including the implementation of the Almaty Programme of Action; the Programme of Action for the Least Developed Countries for the Decade 2011–2020, which was adopted by the Fourth United Nations Conference on the Least Developed Countries (Istanbul, Turkey, 9–13 May) (see p. 826); and a note from Mongolia [E/ESCAP/67/22] transmitting the Ulaanbaatar Declaration adopted by the High-level Asia-Pacific Policy Dialogue on the Implementation of the Almaty Programme of Action and other Development Gaps Faced by the Landlocked Developing Countries (Ulaanbaatar, Mongolia, 12–14 April).

Taking note of the Ulaanbaatar Declaration on 25 May [E/2011/39 (res. 67/1)], the Commission requested the Executive Secretary to assist landlocked developing countries in the region in implementing the Declaration, and to report to the Commission's sixty-ninth (2013) session.

Macroeconomic policy, poverty reduction and development

The Commission had before it the report of the Centre for the Alleviation of Poverty through Sustainable Agriculture (CAPSA) [E/ESCAP/67/4]. The Commission noted the new challenges facing the region, including high food and fuel prices and expressed concern about the impact of those challenges on the efforts of countries to reduce poverty and achieve the MDGs. The Commission welcomed the efforts of the secretariat to promote a coordinated regional voice through the organization of the High-level Consultation on the G-20 Seoul Summit in 2010. The Commission commended the work of CAPSA and suggested that it continue policy-oriented work and revive its focus on cross-country studies while broadening the coverage of studies.

Trade and investment

The Commission had before it the reports of the Asian and Pacific Centre for Transfer of Technology [E/ESCAP/67/5] and the United Nations Asian and Pacific Centre for Agricultural Engineering and Machinery (UNAPCAEM) [E/ESCAP/67/6]. The Commission reaffirmed the importance of the multilateral trading system and the need for a fair, equitable and rule-based multilateral regime to achieve inclusive and sustainable development. It emphasized the importance of deeper regional cooperation on trade and investment, while also noting the proliferation of regional and bilateral trade agreements. The Commission expressed its support for the work of UNAPCAEM, in particular South-South cooperation for technology transfer in the agricultural sector, and commended its work in the area of rice production technology. It endorsed the recommendations of the UNAPCAEM Governing Council, particularly that the focus of the Centre should remain agricultural machinery and engineering; land and water management; agro-industrial development; application of ICT in the agricultural sector; post-harvest technology and food chain quality control; bio-resources, including biomass and bio-energy; and climate-resilient technology.

The second session of the Committee on Trade and Investment (Bangkok, 27–29 July) [E/ESCAP/CTI(2)/6] focused on capturing emerging trade and investment opportunities.

Transport

The Commission had before it the report of the Committee on Transport on its second session (Bangkok, 1–3 November 2010) [E/ESCAP/67/7]. The Commission commended the work of ESCAP in supporting the development of transport infrastructure in the region, recognized that the Asian Highway and Trans-Asian Railway had served as major building blocks for regional connectivity and encouraged the secretariat to foster better transport connectivity among countries to promote regional cooperation and integration. The Commission expressed its appreciation to the secretariat for its work on drafting an intergovernmental agreement on dry ports, as requested by the Committee on Transport at its second session, and noted the development of logistics villages and parks to undertake cargo handling, distribution, processing and packaging away from major cities to reduce traffic congestion and distribution costs. The Commission expressed its commitment to the Decade of Action for Road Safety, 2011–2020, launched on 11 May.

Environment and development

The Commission had before it the report of the Ministerial Conference on Environment and Development on its sixth session [YUN 2010, p. 976]. The secretariat was commended for its work in promoting green growth, including the holding of the First National Seminar on Green Growth Policy Tools for Low Carbon Development in Thailand (Bangkok, 23–24 February), and in promoting sustainable urban development, including the publication of the *State of Asian Cities 2010/11*, the completion of the Kitakyushu Initiative for a Clean Environment, the regional project on pro-poor housing finance, and the technical assistance programme on integrated resource recovery centres in urban areas.

On 25 May, in a resolution [E/2011/39 (res. 67/3)] on the Sixth Ministerial Conference on Environment and Development in Asia and the Pacific [YUN 2010, p. 976], the Commission encouraged States to implement the outcome documents of the Conference, formulate programmes and strategies, encourage the private sector and civil society to participate in activities related to the Astana "Green Bridge" Initiative [ibid., p. 984], facilitate joint research on the development and application of policies and tools, promote knowledge-sharing networks and support the flow of new technologies.

Also on 25 May, the Commission adopted a resolution [E/2011/39 (res. 67/2)] on promoting regional cooperation for enhanced energy security and the sustainable use of energy in Asia and the Pacific and submitted it to the Economic and Social Council (see below).

ECONOMIC AND SOCIAL COUNCIL ACTION

On 25 July [meeting 42], the Economic and Social Council adopted **resolution 2011/14** [draft: E/2011/15/Add.2] without vote [agenda item 10].

Promoting regional cooperation for enhanced energy security and the sustainable use of energy in Asia and the Pacific

The Economic and Social Council,

Taking note of resolution 67/2 of 25 May 2011, adopted at the sixty-seventh session of the Economic and Social Commission for Asia and the Pacific, annexed to the present resolution, in which it, inter alia, requests the Executive Secretary to convene, in 2013, the Asian and Pacific Energy Forum at the ministerial level to discuss the progress achieved in the Asia-Pacific region in addressing the energy security challenges at the regional, national and household levels and to facilitate continuous dialogue among member States with a view to enhancing energy security and working towards sustainable development,

Endorses Economic and Social Commission for Asia and the Pacific resolution 67/2 on promoting regional cooperation for enhanced energy security and the sustainable use of energy in Asia and the Pacific, as set out in the annex to the present resolution.

ANNEX

67/2. Promoting regional cooperation for enhanced energy security and the sustainable use of energy in Asia and the Pacific

The Economic and Social Commission for Asia and the Pacific,

Recalling the Plan of Implementation of the World Summit on Sustainable Development ("Johannesburg Plan of Implementation"), in particular those parts which concern energy, and General Assembly resolution 65/151 of 20 December 2010, in which the Assembly decided to declare 2012 as the International Year of Sustainable Energy for All,

Recalling also its resolution 63/6 of 23 May 2007 on the implementation of intercountry energy cooperation to enhance energy security for sustainable development with a view to widening access to energy services in least developed countries, landlocked developing countries and small island developing States and resolution 64/3 of 30 April 2008 on promoting renewable sources of energy for energy security and sustainable development in Asia and the Pacific,

Taking note of the Ministerial Declaration on Environment and Development in Asia and the Pacific, 2010, adopted on 2 October 2010 by the Sixth Ministerial Conference on Environment and Development in Asia and the Pacific,

Recognizing that energy security is a key development issue for all countries in the Asia-Pacific region, in particular for the least developed countries, landlocked developing countries and small island developing States,

Recognizing also that nearly 1 billion people in the Asia-Pacific region today do not have access to modern affordable energy services,

Emphasizing the need to improve access to reliable, affordable and environmentally sound energy resources for the achievement of the internationally agreed development goals, including the Millennium Development Goals,

Recognizing that energy demand in the Asia-Pacific region is rising faster than in other regions and is projected to almost double by the year 2030 and that fossil fuels are likely to remain the main source of energy for meeting that demand,

Expressing concern that volatile oil prices may threaten the region's nascent recovery from the global economic crisis and its prospects for achieving the Millennium Development Goals by 2015,

Recognizing the potential of various new and renewable energy technologies to meet the challenges presented by unmet energy demand,

Expressing appreciation for the work of the secretariat of the Economic and Social Commission for Asia and the Pacific in promoting subregional energy cooperation with a view to enhancing energy security and sustainable development,

Welcoming the ongoing efforts of Governments to promote regional and interregional cooperation for enhanced energy security and sustainable use of energy resources,

1. *Calls upon* all members and associate members to further promote regional cooperation in addressing energy security challenges and to formulate and implement coherent energy policies based on comprehensive assessments of their environmental and social impacts;

2. *Urges* members and associate members, as appropriate, to give due attention to supply-side constraints, the management of energy demand and the consequences of price volatility and potential disruptions to energy supply;

3. *Calls upon* members and associate members to cooperate proactively in the development and deployment of cost-effective new and renewable energy technologies and to promote cooperation in increasing energy efficiency, in particular, in the context of South-South cooperation;

4. *Encourages* all members and associate members to develop and strengthen efficient policy and regulatory structures at the national and subnational levels that will encourage private sector investment in energy products;

5. *Also encourages* members and associate members to actively engage the private sector in order to enhance investments, to generate innovations and to take a leadership role as a partner in creating a sustainable energy future;

6. *Invites* Governments, donor countries, relevant United Nations bodies, agencies, international and subregional organizations, international and regional financial institutions, as well as the private sector and civil society, to actively consider contributing towards the implementation of the present resolution;

7. *Requests* the Executive Secretary:

(*a*) To strengthen the role and capacity of the secretariat of the Economic and Social Commission for Asia and the Pacific in the area of energy security;

(*b*) To ensure effective coordination with other United Nations bodies and agencies, in particular through UN-Energy, and with multilateral agencies and subregional organizations in working towards enhancing the capacity of States members of the Commission;

(*c*) To collaborate effectively with development partners in order to mobilize financial and technical support to promote regional cooperation for enhanced energy security;

(*d*) To assist members and associate members in meeting their energy security challenges through: (i) the collaborative development of energy security scenarios; and (ii) the organization of meetings and regional networking arrangements aimed at promoting the exchange of experiences and information;

(*e*) To convene, in 2013, the Asian and Pacific Energy Forum at the ministerial level to discuss the progress achieved in the Asia-Pacific region in addressing the energy security challenges at the regional, national and household levels and to facilitate continuous dialogue among member States with a view to enhancing energy security and working towards sustainable development;

(*f*) To report to the Commission at its seventieth session on the progress in the implementation of the present resolution.

Information and communications technology

The Commission had before it the report of the Committee on Information and Communications Technology on its second session (24–26 November 2010) [E/ESCAP/67/9] and the report of the Asian and Pacific Training Centre for Information and Communication Technology for Development (APCICT) [E/ESCAP/67/10]. The importance of regional cooperation in addressing challenges and gaps related to ICT access and connectivity, infrastructure-building for ICT and the expansion of broadband connectivity was acknowledged, as was the need to address the availability, affordability and reliability of the services. The Commission recognized the importance of developing content and applications for the delivery of education, public health, the protection of personal information and property, the preservation of culture and moral values, environmental protection, disaster monitoring and the promotion of modern lifestyles. It noted that expanding broadband and mobile networks in the region would provide new opportunities for ESCAP to foster socioeconomic development. It supported the intent of the secretariat to develop innovative projects that made use of ICT and space technology in the areas of transport and trade, and requested the secretariat to prepare studies and proposals relating to those areas for presentation to the Committee on Information and Communications Technology at its third (2012) session. The Commission underlined the need to expand the ICT capacity-building initiatives of APCICT, including the Academy of ICT Essentials for Government Leaders programme, in order to help bridge the digital divide and assist members in utilizing ICT for socioeconomic development.

Disaster risk reduction

The Commission had before it a note from Iran [E/ESCAP/67/21] introducing a revised draft resolution on the establishment of the Asian and Pacific Centre for the Development of Disaster Information Management in Iran; the report of the ESCAP/World Meteorological Organization (WMO) Typhoon Committee on its forty-third session (Jeju, Republic of Korea, 17–22 January) [E/ESCAP/67/INF/6]; and the report of the thirty-eighth session of the WMO/ESCAP Panel on Tropical Cyclones (New Delhi, India, 21–25 February) [E/ESCAP/67/INF/7]. The Commission expressed appreciation for the efforts of the secretariat in promoting regional cooperation in disaster risk reduction, in collaboration with international organizations and regional stakeholders. It expressed appreciation for the work of the secretariat in facilitating the implementation of the Hyogo Framework for Action 2005–2015: Building the Resilience of Nations and Communities to Disasters [YUN 2005, p. 1016] and introducing the Asia-Pacific Gateway for Disaster Risk Reduction and Development.

On 25 May [E/2011/39 (res. 67/4)], the Commission decided to initiate the process for the establishment of the Asian and Pacific Centre for the Development of Disaster Information Management in Iran. It requested the Executive Secretary to support the process for the establishment of the Centre.

Social development

The Commission had before it the report of the Committee on Social Development on its second session (Bangkok, 19–21 October 2010) [E/ESCAP/67/11]. The Commission emphasized the role of social development in regional efforts to combat poverty, promote inclusive development and achieve the MDGs. It emphasized the role of social protection in addressing the needs of the most vulnerable groups, especially persons with disabilities, older persons, economically dependent women, people living with HIV and AIDS, and those living in remote and rural communities. The Commission welcomed the Regional Forum on Elderly Care Services in Asia and the Pacific (Nanjing, China, January), organized by ESCAP, which addressed ageing issues in the region. The Commission also noted the convening, by ESCAP and the Joint United Nations Programme on HIV/AIDS, of the Asia-Pacific Regional Consultation on Universal Access to HIV Prevention, Treatment, Care and Support (March) as a regional contribution to the General Assembly High-level Meeting on AIDS in June.

On 25 May, the Commission adopted resolutions on the full and effective implementation of the Madrid International Plan of Action on Ageing [E/2011/39 (res. 67/5)]; enhancing accessibility for persons with disabilities at ESCAP [res. 67/6]; the role of cooperatives in social development [res. 67/7]; strengthening social protection systems [res. 67/8]; and Asia-Pacific regional reviews of the progress achieved in realizing the Declaration of Commitment on HIV/AIDS and the Political Declaration on HIV/AIDS [res. 67/9].

Statistics

The Commission had before it the report of the Committee on Statistics on its second session (Bangkok, 15–17 December 2010) [E/ESCAP/67/12] and the report of the Statistical Institute for Asia and the Pacific [E/ESCAP/67/13 & Corr.1]. The Commission recognized the importance of promoting the development of official statistics in support of inclusive and sustainable development, including the achievement of the MDGs.

On 25 May, the Commission adopted resolutions on a core set of economic statistics to guide the improvement of basic economic statistics [E/2011/39 (res. 67/10)]; strengthening statistical capacity [res. 67/11]; improving civil registration and vital statistics [res. 67/12]; and the revision of the statute of the Statistical Institute for Asia and the Pacific [res. 67/13] (see below).

ECONOMIC AND SOCIAL COUNCIL ACTION

On 25 July [meeting 42], the Economic and Social Council adopted **resolution 2011/15** [draft: E/2011/15/Add.2] without vote [agenda item 10].

Revision of the statute of the Statistical Institute for Asia and the Pacific

The Economic and Social Council,

Taking note of resolution 67/13 of 25 May 2011, adopted at the sixty-seventh session of the Economic and Social Commission for Asia and the Pacific, annexed to the present resolution, in which it adopts a revised statute for the Statistical Institute for Asia and the Pacific, the text of which is annexed to the said resolution, to, inter alia, provide for the term of the members of the Governing Council to be changed to a period of three years from the current five years,

Endorses resolution 67/13 on the revision of the statute of the Statistical Institute for Asia and the Pacific, as set out in the annex to the present resolution.

ANNEX
**67/13. Revision of the statute
of the Statistical Institute for Asia and the Pacific**

The Economic and Social Commission for Asia and the Pacific,

Recalling its resolution 61/2 of 18 May 2005 on the statute of the Statistical Institute for Asia and the Pacific,

Noting the suggestion made by members of the Commission at the sixth session of the Governing Council of the Institute,

Recognizing the fact that both the members of the Governing Council and non-members have participated in the discussion on the Institute's activities,

Recognizing also the desirability of increasing the frequency with which the election to the Governing Council takes place in order to enhance the scope of countries in the region to influence the make-up of the Council and the direction of the Institute's operations,

1. *Decides*, in this regard, to adopt a revised statute for the Statistical Institute for Asia and the Pacific, annexed to the present resolution, to provide for the term of the members of the Governing Council to be changed to a period of three years from the current five years;

2. *Also decides* that the revised statute shall be applied to the term of the current members of the Governing Council, which is changed from five years to three years, accordingly, effective as of the date of its adoption by the Commission.

ANNEX TO RESOLUTION 67/13
Statute of the Statistical Institute for Asia and the Pacific

Establishment

1. The Statistical Institute for Asia and the Pacific (hereinafter "the Institute"), established in May 1970 as the Asian Statistical Institute, and accorded the legal status of a subsidiary body of the Economic and Social Commission for Asia and the Pacific (hereinafter "the Commission") pursuant to Commission resolutions 50/5 of 13 April 1994 and 51/1 of 1 May 1995, shall continue in existence under the same title and under the terms of the present statute.

2. Participation in the training and other activities of the Institute is open to all members and associate members of the Commission.

3. The Institute has the status of a subsidiary body of the Commission.

Objectives

4. The objectives of the Institute are to strengthen, through practically oriented training of official statisticians, the capability of the developing members and associate members and economies in transition of the region to collect, analyse and disseminate statistics as well as to produce timely and high-quality statistics that can be utilized for economic and social development planning, and to assist those developing members and associate members and economies in transition in establishing or strengthening their statistical training capability and other related activities.

Functions

5. The Institute will achieve the above objectives by undertaking such functions as:

(*a*) Training of official statisticians, utilizing existing centres and institutions for training available in member States;

(*b*) Networking and partnership with other international organizations and key stakeholders;

(*c*) Dissemination of information.

Status and organization

6. The Institute shall have a Governing Council (hereinafter "the Council"), a Director and staff. The Commission shall keep separate accounts for the Institute.

7. The Institute is located in the Tokyo Metropolitan Area.

8. The activities of the Institute shall be in line with relevant policy decisions adopted by the General Assembly, the Economic and Social Council and the Commission. The Institute shall be subject to the financial and staff regulations and rules of the United Nations and the applicable administrative instructions.

Governing Council

9. The Institute shall have a Governing Council consisting of a representative designated by the Government of Japan and eight representatives nominated by other members and associate members of the Economic and Social Commission for Asia and the Pacific elected by the Commission. The members and associate members to be elected by the Commission shall be elected for a period of three years but shall be eligible for re-election. The Executive Secretary of the Commission or his or her representative shall attend meetings of the Council.

10. The Director of the Institute shall serve as Secretary of the Council.

11. Representatives of (*a*) States that are not members of the Council, (*b*) United Nations bodies and specialized and related agencies and (*c*) such other organizations as the Council may deem appropriate, as well as experts in fields of interest to the Council, may be invited by the Executive Secretary to attend meetings of the Council.

12. The Council shall meet at least once a year and shall adopt its own rules of procedure. Sessions of the Council shall be convened by the Executive Secretary of the Commission, who may propose special sessions of the Council at his or her own initiative and shall convene special sessions at the request of a majority of the Council members.

13. A quorum for meetings of the Council shall be a majority of its members.

14. The nine representatives constituting the Council under paragraph 9 of the present statute shall have one vote each. Decisions and recommendations of the Council shall be made by consensus or, when this is not possible, by a majority of the members present and voting.

15. The Council shall, at each regular session, elect a Chair and Vice-Chair, who shall hold office until the next regular session of the Council. The Chair or, in his or her absence, the Vice-Chair shall preside at meetings of the Council. If the Chair is unable to serve for the full term for which he or she has been elected, the Vice-Chair shall act as Chair for the remainder of that term.

16. The Council shall review the administration and financial status of the Institute and the implementation of its programme of work. The Executive Secretary of the Commission shall submit an annual report, as adopted by the Council, to the Commission at its annual sessions.

17. The Council shall review and endorse annual and long-term workplans consistent with the programme of work.

Director and staff

18. The Institute shall have a Director and staff, who shall be staff members of the Commission appointed under the appropriate United Nations regulations, rules and administrative instructions. The Council will be invited to nominate candidates for the position of Director, once the vacancy is announced, and to provide advice, as appropriate. Other members and associate members of the Commission may also submit nominations for the post.

The Director and Professional staff shall be appointed for a total term, in principle, not exceeding five years. All appointments shall be for a fixed duration and shall be limited to service with the Institute.

19. The Director shall be responsible to the Executive Secretary of the Commission for the administration of the Institute, the preparation of annual and long-term workplans and the implementation of the programme of work.

Resources of the Institute

20. All members and associate members of the Commission should be encouraged to make a regular annual contribution to the operations of the Institute. The United Nations shall administer a joint contribution trust fund for the Institute, as referred to in paragraph 6, in which these contributions shall be deposited and utilized solely for the activities of the Institute, subject to paragraph 22 of the present statute.

21. United Nations bodies and specialized agencies and other entities should also be encouraged to make voluntary contributions to the operations of the Institute. The United Nations shall maintain separate trust funds for voluntary contributions for technical cooperation projects or other extraordinary voluntary contributions for activities of the Institute.

22. The financial resources of the Institute shall be administered in accordance with the Financial Regulations and Rules of the United Nations.

Amendments

23. Amendments to the present statute shall be adopted by means of a resolution of the Commission.

Matters not covered by the present statute

24. In the event of any procedural matter arising that is not covered by the present statute or rules of procedure adopted by the Governing Council under paragraph 12 of this statute, the pertinent part of the rules of procedure of the Commission shall apply.

Entry into force

25. The present statute shall enter into force on the date of its adoption by the Commission.

Technical cooperation

The Commission had before it an overview of the secretariat's technical cooperation activities and extrabudgetary contributions in 2010 [E/ESCAP/67/16]. Total cash contributions received in 2010 for technical cooperation from the regular budget and voluntary sources amounted to approximately $16.8 million. The total volume of technical cooperation delivery in 2010 was approximately $13.9 million. Activities aimed at promoting regional connectivity; developing capacities in international trade research, investment and technology transfer; operationalizing green growth; fostering disaster risk reduction and ICT for development; striving towards achieving the MDGs in the context of the global financial crisis; building social foundations for more inclusive and resilient societies; and building statistical capacity.

The Executive Secretary informed the Commission that the secretariat had shifted its technical cooperation work towards a capacity development approach. Key to the approach was the development of a limited number of integrated capacity development project documents for each subprogramme for the period 2011–2013.

Programme and organizational questions

Proposed programme of work, 2012–2013

The Commission had before it the draft programme of work for the 2012–2013 biennium [E/ESCAP/67/14] and a secretariat note summarizing progress in the implementation of Commission resolutions [E/ESCAP/67/3 & Corr.1].

On 25 May, the Commission adopted a resolution on cooperation between ESCAP and other United Nations and regional and subregional organizations serving the region [E/2011/39 (res. 67/14)] and a resolution on the midterm review of the functioning of the conference structure of the Commission [res. 67/15].

ESCAP subregional offices

The Commission expressed support for the work of the Subregional Office for the Pacific, based in Suva, Fiji, in addressing the unique development challenges faced by Pacific small island developing States. The Commission noted that the objective of the Subregional Office for East and North-East Asia, inaugurated in 2010 in Incheon, Republic of Korea, was to achieve sustainable economic and social development in the subregion, covering challenges such as environmental issues, promotion of knowledge-sharing and strengthening partnerships with civil society and other key development partners. The Commission noted the progress made in establishing the Subregional Office for North and Central Asia, including the signing of the host country agreement between the United Nations and Kazakhstan. The Subregional Office for South and South-West Asia was inaugurated in December in New Delhi.

ESCAP sixty-eighth session

The Commission, having considered a note by the secretariat on the dates, venue and theme for the sixty-eighth session of the Commission [E/ESCAP/67/18], decided to hold its sixty-eighth session in Bangkok in April or May of 2012 and endorsed the theme, "Enhancing regional economic integration in the Asia-Pacific region".

Europe

The Economic Commission for Europe (ECE) at its sixty-fourth session (Geneva, 29–31 March) [E/2011/37-E/ECE/1462], discussed two main issues: the economic integration in the ECE region: developments and new challenges in light of the economic crisis; and the role of regional integration and cooperation for promoting sustainable development in the ECE region. The Commission adopted one decision and six conclusions. Panel discussions were held on promoting economic integration and global competitiveness in the ECE region; improving energy networks; and energy efficiency and diversification of energy sources. The Commission decided that its next session would be held in 2013.

The activities of the Commission were summarized in the ECE Report 2011 [ECE/INF/2011/1].

Economic trends

A report on the economic situation in the ECE region: Europe, North America and the Commonwealth of Independent States (CIS) [E/2012/16] indicated that economic growth in most of the region had been very slow, the Central Asian economies being the exception. Numerous economies had real GDP below that achieved prior to the start of the global crisis and the subsequent recession that began in 2008. In addition, much of the region had experienced high unemployment and increasing poverty. Both the financial crisis in 2008–2009 and the timid recovery in 2010–2011 represented policy failures. The crisis was largely the result of insufficient and improper regulation of the financial sector in the advanced economies of North America and Europe and the excessive reliance on external capital for developmental finance in the economies in transition and the new member States of the European Union (EU). Although the fiscal and monetary stimulus policies enacted in the immediate aftermath of the crisis were a vast improvement over the responses in the 1930s and prevented a world depression, macroeconomic policy in 2010 shifted prematurely to austerity, thereby extending and, in some cases, worsening the economic downturn. What was needed was stimulus in the short run combined with an agenda for consolidating finances in the long run, but the political processes in the advanced economies were unable to achieve that outcome. In some cases, the austerity measures implemented to improve the debt situation actually worsened it by significantly reducing economic growth. The Eurozone crisis had raised fundamental questions about the desirability and sustainability of designing a monetary union without integrated financial supervision, a fiscal union and a central bank that could act as a lender of last resort.

Real GDP growth in the region was expected to decline in 2012 to 1.3 per cent from 2.1 per cent in 2011 and 2.8 per cent in 2010. Growth in European advanced economies was expected to be close to zero in 2012, as many of them experienced recessions; growth in North America would increase slightly to 2.1 per cent, as recoveries in Canada and the United States gathered strength; and growth in the European emerging economies would remain moderate at 3.2 per cent.

Activities
Trade

The Committee on Trade, at its fourth session (Geneva, 14–15 June) [ECE/TRADE/C/2011/14], featured a joint high-level segment with UNDP to discuss Aid for Trade (AfT) priorities in the countries of the South Caucasus and Western CIS. The discussions were based on the findings of the ECE trade needs assessment for Belarus, and the results of the UNDP AfT reviews for Armenia, Belarus, Georgia, the Republic of Moldova and Ukraine. An afternoon was devoted to Belarus, where both AfT priorities and technical and procedural barriers to trade were discussed.

The Committee endorsed reports of the 2009 and 2010 plenary sessions of the United Nations Centre for Trade Facilitation and Electronic Business (UN/CEFACT) [ECE/TRADE/C/CEFACT/2009/28 & ECE/TRADE/C/CEFACT/2010/25]; the programme of work of UN/CEFACT for 2010–2011 [ECE/TRADE/C/2009/17]; the reports of the 2009 and 2010 sessions of the ECE Working Party on Regulatory Cooperation and Standardization Policies [ECE/TRADE/C/WP.6/2009/19 & ECE/TRADE/C/WP.6/2010/20]; the terms of reference of the Group of Experts on Risk Management in Regulatory Systems [ECE/TRADE/C/WP.6/2010/2]; the reports of the 2009 and 2010 sessions of the Working Party on Agricultural Quality Standards [ECE/TRADE/C/WP.7/2009/24 & ECE/TRADE/C/WP.7/2010/16]; and the biennial evaluation plan for the Trade Sub-Programme for 2010–2011 [ECE/TRADE/C/2011/9].

At its sixty-fourth session in March [E/2011/37], the Commission requested that work be undertaken, in cooperation with the World Trade Organization (WTO) and other organizations, to ensure the participation of countries with economies in transition in the WTO AfT initiative. The Commission requested the secretariat to work with WTO and other organizations to support the follow-up to the 2010 AfT Roadmap Ministerial Conference of the United Nations Special Programme for the Economies of Central Asia (SPECA), and ensure the participation and involvement of SPECA countries in the WTO AfT initiative.

Timber

The joint sixty-ninth session of the Timber Committee and thirty-sixth session of the European Forestry Commission (Antalya, Turkey, 10–14 October) [ECE/TIM/2011/20] focused on forests in a green economy. It was attended by 120 participants from the region and 160 national experts. The Committee discussed: the report on the State of Europe's Forests 2011 [ECE/TIM/2011/2]; an outlook study on the future of forests in Europe [ECE/TIM/2011/INF/4]; the ECE/Food and Agriculture Organization of the United Nations (FAO) Action Plan for the Forest Sector in a Green Economy [ECE/TIM/2011/3]; guidelines to facilitate interactive discussions during the special segment on the green economy [ECE/TIM/2011/4]; a summary of the ECE/FAO Forest Products Annual Market Review 2010–2011 [ECE/TIM/2011/5]; ECE and FAO in a changing international environment: briefing and discussion of recent developments [ECE/TIM/2011/7]; proposed revisions of the terms of reference for the Joint ECE/FAO Working Party on Forest Economics and Statistics [ECE/TIM/2011/8]; Towards the 2013 Strategic Review of the Integrated Programme of Work on Forestry and Timber [ECE/TIM/2011/9]; a review of activities and the programme of work for 2011 [ECE/TIM/2011/10]; a review of activities during the International Year of Forests (2011) [ECE/TIM/2011/11]; and matters arising from the sixty-fourth session of ECE [ECE/TIM/2011/12]. The Committee also discussed FAO climate change activities since the thirty-fifth session of the Commission [ECE/TIM/2011/14]; preparation of a long-term strategy for the Global Forest Resource Assessment programme [ECE/TIM/2011/15]; the FAO Committee on Forestry Multi-Year Programme of Work for 2012–2015 [ECE/TIM/2011/16]; and a review of the mandate and modus operandi of the European Forestry Commission Working Party on the Management of Mountain Watersheds [ECE/TIM/2011/17].

Transport

The seventy-third session of the Inland Transport Committee (Geneva, 1–3 March) [ECE/TRANS/221] discussed commitments and opportunities related to the ECE session in 2011, the Commission on Sustainable Development and the review process of achieving the MDGs; the transport situation in ECE countries and emerging trends; climate change and transport; intelligent transport systems; assistance to countries with economies in transition; and the Transport, Health and Environment Pan-European Programme. It also discussed action taken by its working parties on issues such as road traffic safety, transport and competitiveness, strengthening border crossing facilitation, inland transport security, fuel standards, intermodal transport and logistics, and transport of people with reduced mobility. The Committee reviewed issues related to the harmonization of vehicle regulation, transport of dangerous goods and transport of perishable foodstuffs.

The Committee considered a review of the transport situation in 2010 and emerging trends in the ECE and its neighbouring regions [ECE/TRANS/2011/1 & Corr.1]; a report on assistance to countries with economies in transition [ECE/TRANS/2011/2 & Corr.1]; a position paper by the Working Party on Rail Transport [ECE/TRANS/2011/3 & Corr.1]; a report of the Working Party on Rail Transport on its sixty-fourth session (Vienna, 18–19 November 2010) [ECE/TRANS/SC.2/214]; the activities of the secretariat and Contracting Parties with a view to strengthening the TIR Convention and ensuring transparency in managing the TIR system [ECE/TRANS/2011/4]; the results of the meetings held by the Bureau of the Inland Transport Committee in 2010 [ECE/TRANS/2011/5]; and a white paper on efficient and sustainable inland water transport in Europe [ECE/TRANS/SC.3/189].

Energy

The twentieth session of the Committee on Sustainable Energy (Geneva, 16–18 November) [ECE/ENERGY/87], attended by over 150 representatives from 35 ECE member States, discussed securing affordable and sustainable energy; the International Year for Sustainable Energy for All (2012); activities of the Committee; cooperation and coordination with other sectoral committees and with other intergovernmental and non-governmental organizations; review of the work of the Committee and its subsidiary bodies; the programme of work in the field of energy for 2012–2013; and the Regional Advisory Services Programme in the field of energy. Participants explored the imperatives for the United Nations to enable policies and investments that could place the world on a path to a sustainable energy future, and ways to activate the public and private sectors to act at the scale needed to deal with the energy challenges.

The Committee considered studies under the Working Party on Gas [ECE/ENERGY/2011/6] and under the Ad Hoc Group of Experts on Cleaner Electricity Production from Coal and Other Fossil Fuels [ECE/ENERGY/2011/7], and reports on the review of the work of the Committee and its subsidiary bodies [ECE/ENERGY/2011/1], the regional advisory services programme in the field of energy [ECE/ENERGY/2011/2], cooperation and coordination with other intergovernmental and non-governmental organizations [ECE/ENERGY/2011/3], the twenty-second session of the Steering Committee of the Energy Efficiency 21 Programme (Geneva, 21 April) [ECE/ENERGY/

WP.4/2011/2], the Expert Group on Resource Classification (Geneva, 6–8 April) [ECE/ENERGY/GE.3/2011/2], the seventh session of the Ad Hoc Group of Experts on Coal Mine Methane (Krakow, Poland, 11 October) [ECE/ENERGY/GE.4/2011/2] and the twelfth session the Group of Experts on the Supply and Use of Gas (Geneva, 20 January) [ECE/ENERGY/WP.3/GE.5/2011/2].

The Economic Commission for Europe in March [E/2011/37 (dec. A(64))] endorsed the Best Practice Guidance for Effective Methane Drainage and Use in Coal Mines [Sales No. E.10.II.E.2] and proposed to the Economic and Social Council that it recommend its application to all countries.

Economic and Social Council action. Welcoming the Commission's endorsement of the Best Practice Guidance for Effective Methane Drainage and Use in Coal Mines, the Council on 25 July invited Member States, international organizations and the regional commissions to ensure the application of the Guidance in countries worldwide (**decision 2011/222**).

Environment

Two special sessions of the Committee on Environmental Policy were held during the year (Geneva, 24–27 May) [ECE/CEP/S/2011/2] and (Astana, Kazakhstan, 20 September) [ECE/CEP/S/2011/8] in preparation for the seventh "Environment for Europe" (EfE) Ministerial Conference (Astana, 21–23 September) [ECE/ASTANA.CONF/2011/2]. The Conference, which gathered more than 1,500 participants from Governments, civil society, business and the media, discussed two main themes: sustainable management of water and water-related ecosystems; and greening the economy: mainstreaming the environment into economic development. Participants adopted the Astana Ministerial Declaration [ECE/ASTANA.CONF/2011/2/Add.1], in which ministers confirmed their commitment to improving environmental protection and promoting sustainable development in the region. The Chair's summary [ECE/ASTANA.CONF/2011/2/Add.2] outlined the results of the Conference.

The sixth meeting of the Steering Committee on Education for Sustainable Development (Geneva, 7–8 April) [ECE/CEP/AC.13/2011/2] considered the implementation of the ECE Strategy for Education for Sustainable Development. The third session of the Joint Task Force on Environmental Indicators (Geneva, 11–13 July) [ECE/CEP-CES/GE.1/2011/2] undertook an initial reading of proposed additional indicators for inland and seawater. The fourth session of the Joint Task Force on Environmental Indicators (Geneva, 18–20 October) [ECE/CEP-CES/GE.1/2011/4] considered biodiversity indicators. The twelfth session of the Working Group on Environmental Monitoring and Assessment (Geneva, 20–21 October) [ECE/CEP/AC.10/2011/2] considered the outcomes of the EfE Ministerial Conference.

Economic cooperation and integration

The sixth session of the Committee on Economic Cooperation and Integration (Geneva, 30 November–2 December) [ECE/CECI/2011/2] focused on the innovation performance review of Kazakhstan and on the ECE Public-Private Partnership Initiative. The Committee reviewed the implementation of its programme of work and the work of its subsidiary bodies, took note of developments under the Public-Private Partnerships Initiative and adopted its programme of work for 2012–2013.

The Committee considered the report on the third session of the Team of Specialists on Public-Private Partnerships (Geneva, 18–19 April) [ECE/CECI/PPP/2011/2]; the report on the fourth session of the Team of Specialists on Innovation and Competitiveness Policies (Geneva, 12–13 May) [ECE/CECI/ICP/2011/2]; the report on the fifth session of the Team of Specialists on Intellectual Property (Geneva, 7–8 July) [ECE/CECI/IP/2011/2]; and the report on the international conference Promoting Eco-innovation: Policies and Opportunities (Tel Aviv, Israel, 11–13 July) [ECE/CECI/CONF.10/2].

Housing and land management

The seventy-second session of the Committee on Housing and Land Management (Geneva, 3–4 October) [ECE/HBP/167] discussed country profiles on the housing sector; improvement of urban environmental performance; land registration and land markets; housing modernization and management; and affordable, healthy and ecological housing.

The Committee considered the report on the second meeting of the Working Group on a Possible Legally Binding Instrument on Affordable, Healthy and Ecological Housing in the ECE Region (Geneva, 5–6 July) [ECE/HBP/AC.1/2011/4] and the report of the Working Party on Land Administration on its seventh session (Geneva, 30 June–1 July) [ECE/HBP/WP.7/2011/8].

Statistics

The fifty-ninth plenary session of the Conference of European Statisticians (Geneva, 14–16 June) [ECE/CES/81] considered the implications of the meetings of its parent bodies—the March session of ECE and the February session of the United Nations Statistical Commission (see p. 1215). Two seminars focused on measuring human capital, and on the organization of data collection and sharing and the management challenges for implementing statistical data and metadata exchange. The Conference addressed, among other issues, the coordination of international statistical work in the ECE region. It endorsed the Guide on the Impact of Globalization on National Accounts and adopted the second edition of the Canberra Group Handbook on Household Income Statistics, and requested the secretariat to publish them.

Other events included the meeting of the High-level Group for Strategic Developments in Business Architecture (Luxembourg, 9 February); the third meeting of the Joint Task Force on Measuring Sustainable Development (Geneva, 19–20 May) [ECE/CES/2012/19/Add.14]; the meeting on the management of statistical information systems (Luxembourg, 23–25 May) [ECE/CES/2011/47]; the twelfth session of the Group of Experts on Business Registers (Paris, 14–15 September) [ECE/CES/GE.42/2011/2]; the work session on statistical data confidentiality (Tarragona, Spain, 26–28 October) [ECE/CES/2012/19/Add.7]; and the sixth session of the Group of Experts on Measuring Quality of Employment (Geneva, 31 October–2 November) [ECE/CES/GE.12/2011/2].

Programme and organizational questions
Programme of work

ECE in March [E/2011/37] considered new directions and initiatives in its programme of work. It had before it secretariat notes that provided information on areas of work that were relatively new or recently launched, namely on new directions and initiatives in the United Nations Special Programme for the Economies of Central Asia (SPECA) and in the field of innovation [E/ECE/1456], on global road safety and inland water transport [E/ECE/1457], on new directions and initiatives in the fields of forests and housing [E/ECE/1458] and on the seventh "Environment for Europe" Ministerial Conference, the Environment and Health Process, Measuring sustainable development [E/ECE/1459 & Corr.1].

The Commission [E/2011/37 (dec. A(64))] welcomed progress in the SPECA programme and reiterated the need to strengthen synergies at the pan-European level on work on forests.

ECE Reform

The Commission [E/2011/37 (dec. A(64))] reaffirmed the strategic directions adopted by the 2005 ECE reform [YUN 2005, p. 1114], welcomed their implementation and achievements, and underlined the importance of its first five-year review scheduled to take place in 2011–2012.

Latin America and the Caribbean

The Economic Commission for Latin America and the Caribbean (ECLAC) did not meet in 2011. The Commission's thirty-fourth session was to be held in 2012.

ECLAC activities in 2011 were described in its biennial report [E/2012/40].

Economic trends

According to the report Latin America and the Caribbean: economic situation and outlook, 2011–2012 [E/2012/19], economic growth in the region slowed to 4.3 per cent after a brisk rebound of 5.9 per cent in 2010. However, economic performance across the subregions was uneven: GDP growth was 4.5 per cent in South America, 4.1 per cent in Central America and just 0.7 per cent in the Caribbean. The shift in external conditions experienced during the year was reflected in aggregate domestic demand in the region, dampening growth expectations and generating fresh challenges for the authorities. The rebound in the labour markets continued more moderately; the urban unemployment rate was estimated to have fallen to 6.8 per cent and inflation rose only slightly, to 6.9 per cent. Amid weaker global growth, greater uncertainty and increased volatility in international financial markets, the region's growth rate was projected to slacken again in 2012, to 3.7 per cent.

Activities

ECLAC activities in 2011 were organized under 12 subprogrammes: linkages with the global economy, regional integration and cooperation; production and innovation; macroeconomic policies and growth; social development and equality; mainstreaming the gender perspective in regional development; population and development; planning of public administration; environment and human settlements; natural resources and infrastructure; statistics and economic projections; subregional activities in Mexico and Central America; and subregional activities in the Caribbean.

Global economy, regional integration and cooperation

During the 2010–2011 biennium, the work of the subprogramme was conducted along two lines: first, contributing, through the ECLAC Division of International Trade and Integration, to the improvement of the region's linkages with the global economy by developing trade, integration and cooperation schemes; second, strengthening the role of ECLAC as a partner for assistance and technical advice as well as a forum for building consensus. The subprogrammes's work was organized around three subject areas: economic and commercial trends in Latin American international relations; internationalization strategies for Latin America and Caribbean countries with an emphasis on competitiveness, and negotiation and administration of trade agreements; and regional integration and cooperation, trade and climate change, and the promotion of linkages between trade and poverty reduction efforts and gender equality.

Documents published under the subprogramme included the flagship publication *Latin America and the Caribbean in the World Economy 2010–2011: The region in the decade of the emerging economies* [Sales No. E.11.II.G.5]; *Invertir en integración: Los retornos de la complementariedad entre hardware y software*, prepared for the fourth Meeting of Ministers of Finance of America and the Caribbean (Calgary, Canada, 26 March); and *Latin America and the Caribbean and the European Union: Striving for a Renewed Partnership*, prepared for the seventh EU-Latin America and Caribbean Summit, due to take place in Santiago in 2012. The Division organized a conference on labour markets and the global economy (Santiago, 14–15 June) to improve understanding of the mechanisms by which trade interacts with employment.

Production and innovation

The ECLAC Production, Productivity and Management Division provided research, technical assistance and a forum for regional dialogue on production activities. The 2011 edition of the flagship publication *Foreign Direct Investment in Latin America and the Caribbean* registered over 180,000 downloads between May and December. The Regional Dialogue on Broadband, an ECLAC initiative designed to allow countries to exchange knowledge and best practices for developing broadband policies, requested ECLAC to design and implement a statistical tool to analyse the broadband market. ECLAC set up a Regional Broadband Information Observatory on 27 May, in time for the Regional Dialogue's fourth meeting (October), which was attended by senior officials representing the 10 participating countries. At the request of the Ministry of Industry of Argentina, ECLAC analysed 10 different value chains in the country and organized round tables with the main public and private stakeholders in each value chain. The diagnosis formed the basis for Argentina's Agri-Food and Agribusiness Strategic Planning 2020, which was launched on 4 October.

Macroeconomic policies and growth

The challenges that arose from the increased capital inflows to the region and the commodity price boom, as well as the policy dilemmas faced by Governments and the policy alternatives, were analysed at a high-level meeting in April and in the 2010–2011 edition of the Economic Development Division's flagship publication, *Economic Survey of Latin America and the Caribbean*. The 2011 edition of the *Preliminary Overview of the Economies of Latin America and the Caribbean* provided a regional overview from a global and a sectoral perspective. ECLAC contributed to the debate on the role of fiscal policy in the region and beyond in the context of the global crisis through the organization of a workshop on regional financial architecture: challenges to promote economic development (Santiago, 28 November), attended by participants from Latin America, the Caribbean and the EU. The Division disseminated technical and policy documents on stimulus measures, fostering of sustainable development, protection of the most vulnerable sectors of the population and efforts to achieve greater social cohesion.

Social development and equality

During the biennium, the region experienced solid economic growth and job creation that contributed to poverty reduction. However, social vulnerability remained high and socioeconomic gaps large. Consequently, the work of the subprogramme focused on strengthening social protection and care provisions with a redistribution emphasis, improving social expenditure and child poverty analysis, studying and promoting the positive impact of ICT on health and education, and disseminating innovative social development projects. The Social Development Division's flagship publication *Social Panorama of Latin America* took an in-depth look at the chain that produced and reproduced social gaps, and focused on how structural heterogeneity, labour segmentation and gaps in social protection were linked along the chain. In June, ECLAC hosted three seminars to consider the challenges posed by the construction of integrated inclusive social protection in Latin America, including analysis of the role of protection systems within integrated systems of social information. ECLAC also organized a seminar on social protection in Chile from the Latin American perspective and a seminar on inclusive social protection in the region.

Mainstreaming gender in regional development

The ECLAC Division for Gender Affairs generated knowledge to support the development and monitoring of public policies for gender equality, and to incorporate that knowledge into capacity-building for national mechanisms for the advancement of women and national statistical institutes. The formulation of public policies and programmes promoting gender equality was strengthened through generation of information on measurement of women's unpaid work, participation of women in decision-making and gender-based violence; strengthening of national capacities to produce gender statistics; and generation of innovative approaches to develop a gender-based approach to poverty reduction. The Gender Equality Observatory for Latin America and the Caribbean was consolidated, allowing easy access to systematized information through a web portal in four languages. The international seminar Policies on Time, Time for Policies took place in the framework of the forty-sixth meeting of the Presiding Officers of the Regional Conference on Women in Latin America and the Caribbean (Santiago, 28–30 December), where experts and government representatives assessed information on time use in the region and discussed implications and recommendations for care policies. ECLAC, UN-Women and Mexico's National Institute of Statistics and Geography and National Women's Institute held the twelfth international meeting on gender statistics: empowerment, economic autonomy and public policy (Aguascalientes, Mexico, 5–7 October), which was attended by 175 participants and representatives of 16 countries. In the area of monitoring gender violence, the virtual course "Measurement of violence against women through statistical surveys" took place from 3 October to 10 December as part of the interregional project on enhancing capacities to eradicate violence against women through networking of local knowledge communities.

Population and development

The ECLAC Latin American and Caribbean Demographic Centre (CELADE)-Population Division engaged in technical support to enhance national census capacities, and provided workshops and reference publications on census topics, such as living conditions, household equipment, environment, demographic and socioeconomic characteristics, as well as the training of enumerators, use of new technologies, data coherence and demographic analysis. An executable and portable version of the Regional System of Indicators on Ageing was developed and distributed to users. It allowed for analyses on population ageing and the situation of older persons; it also offered urban/rural disaggregation, as well as growth rates, indicators on sociodemographic conditions, indicators on MDGs and thematic maps for cities with one million or more inhabitants. CELADE implemented the second phase of the International Development Research Centre–funded project on national transfers accounts, which measured consumption and labour earnings by age as well as the flows of resources between ages and across generations. ECLAC, with ECE and ECA, organized a workshop on strengthening national capacities to deal with international migration (Geneva, 22–23 September), which was attended by government delegates, experts on migration and representatives of civil society from the three regions.

Public administration

The Latin American and Caribbean Institute for Economic and Social Planning (ILPES) provided policy advice on development strategies and public-sector economics to improve performance of public policies, programmes and projects and to strengthen knowledge networks. It promoted and supported the creation of new instruments for budgetary policymaking and evaluation, and disseminated results-based management practices for incorporation into the public-policy cycle. It organized international courses on planning, government and development, electronic government, and MDGs at the municipal level. ILPES publications on planning and budgeting, which provided policy analysis and recommendations for action, had registered over 1.3 million downloads. A major publication, *Espacios iberoamericanos: Hacia una nueva arquitectura del Estado para el desarrollo*, was released in 2011. The twenty-third regional seminar on fiscal policy, organized by ILPES and attended by some 150 participants from 20 countries (Santiago, January), focused on the impact of expenditure and tax systems on income distribution. The first regional meeting of the National Public Investment Systems Network, organized by the Dominican Republic with the collaboration of ILPES and the World Bank (Santo Domingo, Dominican Republic, 13–14 April), focused on the development of national systems of public investment appraisal.

Environment and human settlements

The ECLAC Sustainable Development and Human Settlements Division worked on interrelationships among economic growth, environmental protection, urban development and social equity, also consolidating work on the economics of climate change. The Division organized the Latin American and Caribbean Regional Meeting Preparatory to the United Nations Conference on Sustainable Development (Rio+20) (Santiago, September), attended by representatives of 34 States and nearly 100 civil society members. The meeting resulted in a set of conclusions for the region, which served as input in the preparatory process for Rio+20. As part of the ECLAC contribution to support sustainable development conferences, the Division presented a preliminary assessment on sustainable development in the region at the regional preparatory meeting for Rio+20 and contributed to the Issue

Management Group on a Green Economy publication, *Working Towards a Balanced and Inclusive Green Economy: A United Nations System-wide Perspective*, which was completed in December. ECLAC also conducted a mission to estimate the socioeconomic and environmental impact of the flooding in Colombia.

Natural resources and infrastructure

The ECLAC Natural Resources and Infrastructure Division organized several events to disseminate the results of its research, including a regional conference on building commitment, efficiency and equity for sustainable drinking water and sanitation services (Santiago, March), which resulted in the formulation of public policy guidelines for the water supply and sanitation sector; and the regional session on Latin America and the Caribbean at the international conference Water in the Green Economy in Practice: Towards Rio+20 (Zaragoza, Spain, October), which sought to position the water agenda as a key element for advancing towards a green economy. It also contributed to the seventh Inter-American Dialogue on Water Management (Medellin, Colombia, 13–19 November).

Two events were organized on biofuel issues: a policy dialogue on institutional development and innovation in biofuels (Santiago, March), which discussed innovation systems needed to promote biofuels production, patents and intellectual property topics, as well as sustainability assessment tools for the production and use of biofuels; and a regional forum on biofuels (San Salvador, El Salvador, 30 November–1 December), which offered an opportunity to exchange experiences, promote research and analyse the challenges of sustainable development in biofuels use and production. The Division organized a high-level seminar (Santiago, November) that analysed the impact of infrastructure policies on economic and social development and outlined the need to coordinate a regional strategy for sustainable transport; and the international seminar Latin American Dialogue on Financing of Low-carbon Electricity, jointly with the Department of Economic and Social Affairs (DESA) and the Global Sustainable Electricity Partnership (Santiago, 22–23 August). National authorities, the private sector and maritime researchers from 40 countries in Africa, America, Asia, Europe and Oceania participated in the annual conference of the International Association of Maritime Economists (25–28 October) held at ECLAC headquarters.

Statistics and economic projections

The ECLAC Statistics and Economic Projections Division provided support to the region's countries in their effort to build, strengthen and harmonize statistical information and the decision-making systems underlying the design, monitoring and assessment of development policies. Events organized during the year included a regional seminar on the implementation of the 2008 recommendations on national accounts (Santiago, October); a workshop on satellite accounts on health (Santiago, November); two regional seminars on the Millennium indicators (February and December); and a coordination meeting of the Statistical Conference of the Americas Working Group on the Monitoring of Progress towards the MDGs (Buenos Aires, Argentina, July). Technical missions to various countries to analyse their price and national accounts statistics were also completed. Price-taking activities began in the first part of the year and the first price validation meeting was held in May. A project on satellite accounts and indicators on water began in late 2010 and two launching meetings were held in May 2011, in Colombia and in Ecuador. Within the project, technical workshops on collecting and validating information were held in both countries.

Subregional activities

Mexico and Central America

The ECLAC subregional headquarters in Mexico assisted the Governments and stakeholders of the countries it served—Costa Rica, Cuba, Dominican Republic, El Salvador, Guatemala, Haiti, Honduras, Mexico, Nicaragua, Panama—to strengthen their capacities to address economic and social issues, as well as to design or evaluate policies and measures in the areas of trade, integration and sustainable development. In the area of economic development, the subregional headquarters organized a seminar for high-level authorities of central banks and regulatory bodies on the implications of the adoption of the Basel III criteria (Mexico City, 30 June–1 July). In the area of social development, the subregional headquarters released the 2011 edition of its biennial publication, *Social Development Indicators*, which updated key social indicators in 10 thematic areas of social development for the countries of the subregion. Training workshops in the use of specialized trade databases, such as the Module to Analyse the Growth of International Commerce (MAGIC Plus), were held. A Train the Trainers course was conducted at the request of Guatemala's Ministry of Economic Affairs (Guatemala City, 11–14 April) and a course of MAGIC Plus was given for Nicaraguan officials (15–16 November). A study on energy and climate change in Central America was completed, and the findings were presented to authorities and officials from the environment sector at the Regional Congress on Clean Electricity (San José, Costa Rica, March), the meeting of directors of energy and hydrocarbons of the Central American Integration System countries (Guatemala City, May), the Clean Energy Summit (Guatemala City, May) and the workshop on climate change and energy for the Government of El Salvador. A mission was conducted in September to assist the Haitian Institute of Statistics (IHSI) in building a monthly indicator of economic activity. The subregional headquarters backed the attendance of representatives from IHSI at the sixth meeting of the Statistical Conference of the Americas (Dominican Republic, November) to present Haiti's short- and medium-term statistical challenges and gather regional support. In July, technical assistance was provided to the Central American Agricultural Council to present and discuss the estimated effects and costs of climate change on agriculture in the subregion. From 25 October to 19 November, a team of experts provided technical assistance to Costa Rica, El Salvador, Guatemala, Honduras and Nicaragua on the evaluation of the economic, social and environmental damages and losses resulting from Tropical Depression E-12.

Caribbean

The ECLAC subregional headquarters for the Caribbean in Port of Spain, Trinidad and Tobago, strengthened the capacity of policymakers and other stakeholders to formulate and implement economic and social development measures and to improve opportunities for integration in the Caribbean, as well as between the Caribbean and the wider Latin American region. The Caribbean Development and Cooperation Committee held the fifteenth meeting of its Monitoring Committee (Port of Spain, 12 September) and discussed progress in implementing the 2010–2011 biennium work programme. The first Caribbean Development Round Table, a forum for development experts to examine new approaches and challenges to the sustainable development of small developing countries, examined how the Caribbean could develop new policies and strategies to meet challenges related to growth, social equity, vulnerability and environmental sustainability in small economies. ECLAC conducted the third meeting of the Technical Advisory Committee of the Regional Coordination Mechanism, which served to strengthen ECLAC collaboration with the Small Island Development States (SIDS) Unit of DESA, resulting in Caribbean SIDS having greater knowledge of global action in relation to the Mauritius Strategy and increasing their cooperation.

Western Asia

The Economic and Social Commission for Western Asia (ESCWA) did not meet in 2011, in accordance with its decision in 2005 [YUN 2005, p. 1120] to hold its biennial sessions in even years. The Commission's twenty-seventh session was to be held in 2012.

ESCWA 2010–2011 activities were described in its annual report [E/ESCWA/OES/2012/1] and biennial report [E/ESCWA/27/5(Part I)].

Economic trends

The summary of the *Survey of Economic and Social Developments in the ESCWA Region, 2011–2012* [E/2012/20] stated that the impact of the global downturn on countries of the region varied depending on their integration with Europe, the United States and the rest of the world.

Since the start of the year, uncertainty had returned to the region as the Arab Spring social movement spread across the Arab world; however, due to high oil prices, growth was expected to be 4.8 per cent. Growth in the member countries of the Cooperation Council for the Arab States of the Gulf (Gulf Cooperation Council) was estimated to reach 5.7 per cent, up from 4.4 per cent in 2010, while growth in more diversified economies fell to 2.3 per cent, from 5.7 per cent in 2010. Growth in the more diversified economies was mainly driven by Iraq, which was expected to boast double-digit growth rates.

Activities

ESCWA activities in 2011 were organized under seven subprogrammes: integrated management of natural resources for sustainable development; social development; economic development and integration; ICT for regional integration; statistics for evidence-based policymaking; advancement of women; and conflict mitigation and development.

Natural resources management for sustainable development

The subprogramme, implemented by the ESCWA Sustainable Development and Productivity Division, aimed at improving the sustainable management and use of natural resources, and promoting regional cooperation in the management of water, energy and the production sectors. Within the framework of the Regional Initiative for the Assessment of the Impact of Climate Change on Water Resources and Socio-Economic Vulnerability in the Arab Region, ESCWA prepared a guidance document, A Methodological Framework for Pursuing an Integrated Assessment, which reviewed global and regional climate models, hydrological models and vulnerability assessment tools. The document was discussed during an expert general meeting of ESCWA, the League of Arab States and the UNEP Regional Office for West Asia in July. The Division also organized a training workshop on partnerships between the private and public sectors in renewable energy projects for Syrian officials. ESCWA contributed to increasing the competitiveness of small and medium-sized enterprises (SMEs) through advocacy and capacity-building activities that increased SME awareness and understanding of green jobs and available opportunities in the production and use of environmental goods and services within a green economy context, which led to the adoption, by SME associations, of measures for increased competitiveness: Green Help Desk (Lebanon), green economy action plan (Syrian Arab Republic), improving SME competitiveness (Jordan) and developing green jobs (Lebanon).

A draft legal framework for shared water resources in the Arab region was finalized at two intergovernmental consultative meetings, in May and December. The progress achieved was reported to the third session of the Arab Ministerial Water Council in June.

Social development

The subprogramme, implemented by the Social Development Division, aimed to strengthen national social policies that were specific to the region and culturally sensitive, and to encourage community development with a view to reducing social inequity and enhancing social stability. ESCWA supported Jordan, Lebanon and Oman in the consideration of their social protection schemes; it devised social protection mapping and developed country profiles with a view to generating discussions in all member countries on integrated social protection mechanisms. ESCWA contributed to the capacity of countries to adopt policies to address the implications of demographic changes, which resulted in follow-up measures indicating increased understanding of the sociodemographic implications of the youth bulge for migration and development. Iraq established a youth parliament and Palestine took action to reinforce the analytical skills of policymakers to enable them to publish a national youth report. Workshops and seminars were held to enhance the role of civil society in development and to promote a dynamic public-civic relationship. ESCWA followed up on the repercussions, causes and dynamics of the Arab uprisings and issued remedying measures, action plans and technical input for a dynamic civic engagement in the process of change and transition towards democratization.

Economic development and integration

The subprogramme, implemented by the Economic Development and Globalization Division, aimed to strengthen macroeconomic policymaking for short-term economic growth and sustainable economic development, facilitation of trade and negotiation of trade and investment agreements. The *Survey of Economic and Social Developments in the ESCWA Region, 2009–2010* was issued in December. The twelfth session of the Transport Committee (Beirut, Lebanon, 17–19 May) discussed the progress achieved in implementing the components of the Integrated Transport System in the Arab Mashreq, with a focus on the Decade of Action for Road Safety 2011–2020. An expert group meeting on transport and trade facilitation (Beirut, 1–2 March) called on countries to activate national transport and trade facilitation committees through executive workplans. A regional workshop on requirements for the establishment of Single Windows for handling export/import procedures and formalities in the ESCWA region focused on enhancing the knowledge on the Single Window concept, its benefits and its relationship to trade facilitation, and on enhancing the capacity of countries on Single Window for international trade requirements. Participants discussed the study on Single Window for Handling Export/Import Procedures and Formalities in ESCWA member countries.

ICT for regional integration

The subprogramme, implemented by the Information and Communication Technology Division, aimed to narrow the digital divide to build an inclusive development-oriented information society and knowledge-based economy. ESCWA assisted countries in accelerating ICT development through its Regional Technology Centre in Amman, Jordan. Expert group meetings were held on a regional road map for Internet governance, which resulted in a Call for Arab Stakeholders; on an enabling environment for the development of Arabic e-services, which provided a platform for sharing experiences and best practices; and on promoting South-South cooperation in technology transfer, which produced a collaboration framework for technology development, management, maintenance and service, also sharing best practices for cooperation and successful technology transfer case studies in water, energy, agriculture and ICT. ESCWA prepared a Regional Profile of the Information Society in Western Asia, 2011, the fifth in a series that provided essential information on the status of the information society in member countries. A study on Information Society Measurement: Building a Common Benchmarking Model for the ESCWA Region explored the interplay between the value of evidence-based decision making, the limitations of available data, the evaluation of existing models and the diverse contexts throughout the region.

Statistics

The subprogramme, implemented by the Statistics Division, aimed to improve the production and use of harmonized and comparable economic, social and sectoral statistics, including gender-disaggregated data, thereby allowing for informed and evidence-based decision making. Progress was made in implementing the Fundamental Principles of Official Statistics, and in complying with data dissemination standards of the International Monetary Fund. The average availability of the MDG indicators in the countries of the region had improved by about 17 per cent since 2008, indicating significant progress in data compilation and dissemination to monitor MDGs. The System of Environmental Economic Accounting for Water had been implemented in Egypt, Jordan and Oman.

Advancement of women

The subprogramme, implemented by the ESCWA Centre for Women, aimed to increase the focus on women and gender issues, with a view to reducing the gender imbalance and empowering women. The Centre released a report on progress in the achievement of the MDGs in the ESCWA region and organized an expert group meeting on the same topic to assist countries in integrating a gender perspective in MDG implementation, reporting, monitoring and evaluation.

The Committee on Women, at its fifth session (Beirut, 19–21 December) [E/ESCWA/ECW/2011/IG.1/7/Report], considered steps taken by Arab countries to implement the recommendations made by the Committee at its fourth session; the activities of the Centre since the fourth session of the Committee; and the ESCWA programme of work for the 2012–2013 biennium in the area of the advancement of women. The Committee also took up issues of importance to women's progress and empowerment, including gender mainstreaming into the policies, programmes and activities of public institutions; progress achieved in implementing the Convention on the Elimination of All Forms of Discrimination against Women in Arab countries; innovative initiatives to end violence against women; women's participation in political leadership and decision-making; and the role of the media and communications in empowering women in the Arab world. Those discussions resulted in the adoption of the Beirut Declaration, which called on countries to promote the role of women in decision-making and empower rural women by integrating their priorities into national planning.

ECONOMIC AND SOCIAL COUNCIL ACTION

On 18 May [meeting 11], the Economic and Social Council adopted **resolution 2011/4** [draft: E/2010/15/Add.1, as orally amended] without vote [agenda item 3].

Upgrading the Economic and Social Commission for Western Asia Centre for Women to the level of a division and follow-up to the implementation of the Beijing Platform for Action in the Arab countries after fifteen years: Beijing+15

The Economic and Social Council,

Noting the adoption by the Economic and Social Commission for Western Asia at its twenty-sixth session, held in Beirut from 17 to 20 May 2010, of the resolution on upgrading the Centre for Women to the level of a division and follow-up to the implementation of the Beijing Platform for Action in the Arab countries after fifteen years: Beijing+15,

Takes note of the Economic and Social Commission for Western Asia resolution on upgrading the Centre for Women to the level of a division and follow-up to the implementation of the Beijing Platform for Action in the Arab countries after fifteen years: Beijing+15, as set out in the annex to the present resolution.

ANNEX
Upgrading the Economic and Social Commission for Western Asia Centre for Women to the level of a division and follow-up to the implementation of the Beijing Platform for Action in the Arab countries after fifteen years: Beijing+15

The Economic and Social Commission for Western Asia,

Recalling the Beijing Declaration and Platform for Action, the outcome documents of the twenty-third special session of the General Assembly entitled "Women 2000: gender equality, development and peace for the twenty-first century", the declaration of the Commission on the Status of Women on the occasion of the tenth anniversary of the Fourth World Conference on Women and the resolutions of the Arab Regional Conference Ten Years after Beijing: Call for Peace,

Recalling also the Millennium Development Goals, in particular Goal 3 on promoting gender equality and empowering women, and its relevance to combating poverty and stimulating sustainable development,

Guided by the Convention on the Elimination of All Forms of Discrimination against Women, and reaffirming General Assembly resolutions 60/230 of 23 December 2005 and 62/218 of 22 December 2007 on the Convention, and all other relevant international resolutions,

Recalling that the Commission on the Status of Women reaffirmed the Beijing Declaration and Platform for Action which stressed the importance of the role assumed by the United Nations regional commissions in coordinating between member countries in order to harmonize positions and enable the national machineries for the advancement of women to contribute effectively to accelerating the implementation of the Beijing Platform for Action and all relevant follow-up activities,

Recalling also its resolution 240(XXII) of 17 April 2003 on the establishment within the Economic and Social Commission for Western Asia of a committee on women and a centre for women at the Commission, to act as the secretariat of the committee,

Noting the international efforts and the bases established by General Assembly resolution 63/311 of 14 September 2009 on system-wide coherence, which called for strengthening institutional arrangements in support of gender equality and the empowerment of women through all United Nations entities concerned with the advancement of women, bearing in mind the expected impact of the resolution on the role and mandates of the centres and divisions for the advancement of women at the regional commissions,

Taking into account the recommendation of the Committee on Women at its third session, held in Abu Dhabi on 14 and 15 March 2007, that the Economic and Social Commission for Western Asia undertake a central role in increasing cooperation, integration and exchange of expertise among member countries and providing support for building the institutional and human capacity of national machineries for the advancement of women, in cooperation and coordination with the United Nations Development Fund for Women, the League of Arab States, the Arab Women Organization and the Center of Arab Women for Training and Research,

Noting the efforts exerted by the Economic and Social Commission for Western Asia for the empowerment of women by building the capacity of national machineries for the advancement of women to integrate women into national policies and implement international conventions and other relevant international resolutions, in particular the Convention on the Elimination of All Forms of Discrimination against Women,

1. *Calls upon* member countries to adopt the resolution on the follow-up to implementation of the Beijing Platform for Action in the Arab States after fifteen years: Beijing+15, which was adopted by the Committee on Women at its fourth session, held in Beirut from 21 to 23 October 2009, and the outcome of the fifty-fourth session of the Commission on the Status of Women;

2. *Requests* member countries to adopt the recommendation made by the Committee on Women at its fourth session on supporting the Centre for Women with additional human resources in order to upgrade it to the level of a division, similar to other divisions of the Economic and Social Commission for Western Asia, with the aim of increasing its efforts in assisting member countries in the area of empowerment of women;

3. *Requests* the secretariat to complete administrative procedures related to the upgrading of the Centre for Women to the level of a division;

4. *Requests* the Executive Secretary to submit to the Economic and Social Commission for Western Asia at its twenty-seventh session a report on progress achieved in the implementation of the present resolution.

Conflict mitigation and development

The subprogramme, implemented by the Section for Emerging and Conflict-related Issues, aimed to increase understanding by countries of the impact of conflict and enhance their capacity to identify, assess, predict and respond to challenges posed by conflict, with a view to reducing its impact on development.

ESCWA participated in the Fourth United Nations Conference on the Least Developed Countries (Istanbul, 9–13 May), co-organizing the special event on Delivering for Development in Conflict-affected LDCs: The role of Governance and State-building.

ESCWA focused on strengthening national capacities in assessing governance limitations and priority areas, identifying policy recommendations, and developing action plans for the establishment of a more efficient distribution of power and competencies between the central and local levels of government to achieve equitable access to essential services. In that regard, ESCWA implemented the first phases of a project to assist Lebanon to create a path towards sustainable development and lasting peace, and carried out a national assessment in Iraq on perceptions and contributing factors undermining nation-building, citizenship and the adoption of tolerance, human rights values and gender equality.

ECONOMIC AND SOCIAL COUNCIL ACTION

On 18 May [meeting 11], the Economic and Social Council adopted **resolution 2011/3** [draft: E/2010/15/Add.1, as orally amended] without vote [agenda item 3].

Upgrading the Economic and Social Commission for Western Asia Section for Emerging and Conflict-related Issues to the level of a division and establishing a governmental committee on emerging issues and development in conflict settings

The Economic and Social Council,

Noting the adoption by the Economic and Social Commission for Western Asia at its twenty-sixth session, held in Beirut from 17 to 20 May 2010, of the resolution on upgrading the Section for Emerging and Conflict-related Issues to the level of a division and establishing a governmental committee on emerging issues and development in conflict settings,

Takes note of the Economic and Social Commission for Western Asia resolution on upgrading the Section for Emerging and Conflict-related Issues to the level of a division and establishing a governmental committee on emerging issues and development in conflict settings, as set out in the annex to the present resolution.

ANNEX

Upgrading the Section for Emerging and Conflict-related Issues to the level of a division and establishing a governmental committee on emerging issues and development in conflict settings

The Economic and Social Commission for Western Asia,

Cognizant of the repercussions of successive conflicts in the region, in particular occupation and its negative impact on economic and social development in member countries, the importance of addressing that impact and adopting an approach that takes into account the realities of the region in solving development problems,

Emphasizing the need to sustain economic and social development efforts in all circumstances, in particular under conditions of crisis and occupation, as economic and social development represents a basic instrument for peacebuilding,

Guided by the 2005 World Summit Outcome, which stressed the correlation between development, human rights and peace, as no element can be realized without the others,

Guided also by the report of the Secretary-General on peacebuilding in the immediate aftermath of conflict in which he calls for enhancement of the conflict management capacity of regional commissions, strengthening regional capacity in peacebuilding and creating employment opportunities, and building the capacity of the public sector and its institutions,

Recalling Commission resolutions 282(XXV) of 29 May 2008 and 271(XXIV) of 11 May 2006 on mitigating the impact on development of conflict, occupation and instability in the Commission region and strengthening the role of the Commission in that regard,

Noting the recommendation of the Technical Committee at its third meeting on the establishment at the Commission of a governmental committee on emerging issues and development in conflict settings, and the outcome of the consultations held between the secretariat and member countries participating in the working group charged with studying the issue,

Noting also peacebuilding efforts exerted by the Commission through its programmes to mitigate the impact on development of conflict and occupation, and build the capacity of member countries to address the challenges stemming from conflict, emerging issues and instability,

1. *Declares its commitment* to the inalienable rights of the Palestinian people and its support to the efforts of the Palestinian people and the Palestinian Authority towards the establishment of an independent State of Palestine, based on United Nations resolutions and its condemnation of the Israeli actions that violate the rights of Palestinians, including: changing the demography of the occupied city of Jerusalem; imposing a siege on Gaza; building the annexation and expansion wall on Palestinian territory; and obstructing efforts to achieve development and build Palestinian institutions;

2. *Calls upon* member countries:

(*a*) To continue to seek the achievement of peace and stability in the region and remedy the root causes of conflict within a framework of economic and social development programmes;

(*b*) To enhance development efforts, in particular in countries affected by conflict and occupation, in order to achieve the Millennium Development Goals;

(*c*) To promote public sector institutional capacity-building efforts in view of the contribution of such efforts to addressing emerging issues and conflict, developing regional cooperation and coordination in that area;

(*d*) To intensify efforts to monitor and analyse potential sources of conflict and develop plans and programmes to address them;

(*e*) To formulate policies, programmes and strategies at the national and regional level with a view to addressing the repercussions of conflict and instability in member countries, preventing potential conflict and addressing the roots of such conflict and instability;

(*f*) To contribute to the mobilization of financial and human resources to support development efforts in situations of instability and foster preparedness of member countries to address potential future conflict;

3. *Decides* to establish a committee on emerging issues and development in conflict settings comprising member country representatives with functions and mandates to be determined after further consultation with member countries;

4. *Requests* the secretariat:

(*a*) To provide the necessary support for subprogramme 7 of the Commission in terms of financial and human resources and upgrade the section responsible for its implementation to the level of a division similar to other subprogrammes of the Commission, with a view to meeting the needs of member countries and intensifying its activities in the following areas:

(i) **Emerging issues**: monitoring and analysing emerging issues and presenting recommendations, proposals and practical programmes to deal with them;

(ii) **Development in situations of conflict and instability**: designing and implementing programmes, projects and activities aimed at mitigating the repercussions of conflict and instability, and contributing to peacebuilding;

(iii) **Development in the least developed countries**: defining and meeting institutional needs in order to achieve the Millennium Development Goals;

(iv) **Development of public sector institutions**: designing and implementing projects and programmes for institutional development in member countries in all planning and management areas with a view to enabling them to address present and potential future crises and challenges;

(*b*) To provide organizational and technical support to the committee on emerging issues and development in conflict settings;

(*c*) To promote the effective participation of the Commission and member countries in regional and international events and forums relating to conflict and emerging issues;

(*d*) To promote cooperation with international and regional organizations in the field of peacebuilding and development in conflict settings, build the institutional capacity of member countries, and design programmes and policies pursuant to international recommendations on development in conflict settings;

5. *Requests* the Executive Secretary to follow up on the implementation of the present resolution and submit to the Commission at its twenty-seventh session a report on progress achieved in that regard.

Chapter VI

Energy, natural resources and cartography

Among the several UN bodies dedicated to the conservation, development and use of energy and natural resources, the International Atomic Energy Agency (IAEA), in addition to its work on the nonproliferation of nuclear weapons, in 2011 continued to address global challenges related to nuclear technology, including energy security, human health and food security, water resources management, as well as nuclear safety and security. In response to the Fukushima Daiichi accident—a nuclear disaster caused by a tsunami triggered by an earthquake that hit eastern Japan on 11 March—IAEA in June convened a Ministerial Conference on Nuclear Safety. In September, the IAEA Action Plan on Nuclear Safety was endorsed by the fifty-fifth session of the General Conference. A major event during the year in the area of food security was the declaration of global freedom from rinderpest by the Food and Agriculture Organization of the United Nations (FAO) and the World Organization for Animal Health. IAEA had supported Member States for more than 25 years in their efforts to control and eradicate that disease.

Through World Water Day (22 March) and World Water Week (21–27 August), UN-Water focused on the challenges of urban water supply, particularly water quality and sanitation.

In July, the Economic and Social Council established a Committee of Experts on Global Geospatial Information Management to provide a forum for coordination and dialogue on enhanced cooperation in the field of global geospatial information. The Committee held its first meeting in October.

In December, the General Assembly adopted resolution 66/206 inviting Member States, as well as the UN system and other stakeholders to raise global awareness of the importance of new and renewable sources of energy and low-emission technologies, as well as promote greater access to modern, reliable, affordable and sustainable energy services.

Energy and natural resources

Energy
Nuclear energy
International Atomic Energy Agency

According to the 2011 annual report [GC(56)/2] of the International Atomic Energy Agency (IAEA), the Agency continued to address global challenges related to nuclear technology, including energy security, human health and food security, water resources management, nuclear safety and security, and nonproliferation (see PART ONE, Chapter VII). The fifty-fifth session of the IAEA General Conference (Vienna, 19–23 September) adopted resolutions on strengthening international cooperation in nuclear, radiation, transport and waste safety; nuclear security; strengthening technical cooperation activities; strengthening activities related to nuclear science, technology and applications; implementing the Treaty on the Non-Proliferation of Nuclear Weapons safeguards agreement between the Agency and the Democratic People's Republic of Korea; and applying IAEA safeguards in the Middle East. During the year, the General Conference approved the membership of Dominica, the Lao People's Democratic Republic and Tonga, bringing the Agency's membership to 152 States at the end of the year.

In June [A /66/95], the Secretary-General transmitted to the General Assembly the 2010 IAEA annual report [YUN 2010, p. 999], of which the Assembly took note on 22 December (resolution 66/206) (see p. 966).

Activities

At the end of 2011, there were 435 nuclear power reactors in operation with a total capacity of 369 gigawatts-electric, 2 per cent less than at the beginning of the year. The decrease was due to the permanent retirement of 13 reactors, including 12 following the accident at Tokyo Electric Power Company's Fukushima Daiichi nuclear power plant. On 11 March, an earthquake in eastern Japan triggered a tsunami that caused the nuclear accident. Of the 64 new power reactors under construction at the end of 2011, 26 were in China, 10 in the Russian Federation, 6 in India and 5 in the Republic of Korea. Some countries, such as Germany, decided to phase out and discontinue the use of nuclear power while others, such as Belgium, Italy and Switzerland, re-evaluated their nuclear programmes. In the wake of the Fukushima Daiichi accident, the Agency expanded the scope of its guidance and assistance for long-term operation.

IAEA continued to assist Member States in applying nuclear technology in the areas of food and agriculture, health, water resources, the environment and industry. By year's end, the Agency was coordinating research activities in Member States through 130 research projects involving 1,667 research, technical and doctoral contracts and agreements. Of particular note was the eradication—announced by FAO and the World Organization for Animal Health (OIE) in early 2011—of rinderpest (cattle plague), a highly contagious viral disease of cattle, buffalo, yak and other wildlife species that had caused immense livestock losses over many decades. The Agency, in collaboration with FAO, OIE and other partners, had supported Member States for more than 25 years in their efforts to control and eradicate the disease. During the year, the Agency's research activities resulted in the adoption of 14 irradiation treatments pertaining to the health of plants for quarantined pests under the International Plant Protection Convention. The Political Declaration of the High-level Meeting of the UN General Assembly on the Prevention and Control of Non-communicable Diseases (NCDs) (see p. 1146) formally recognized the Agency's role in the fight against NCDs, particularly cancer and heart diseases. The Agency enhanced its collaboration with the World Health Organization and other UN agencies on its cancer initiatives. During the fifty-fifth session of the General Conference in September, a two-day scientific forum highlighted the importance of water on the international agenda and the role that nuclear techniques played in addressing key water and climate issues.

Regarding nuclear safety and security, an international meeting in May on the Code of Conduct on the Safety of Research Reactors concluded that the Code was the principal reference of Member State activities in the area of reactor safety research and provided recommendations to address common safety issues such as regulatory supervision and ageing management. The first draft of an action plan for the review of the Agency's safety standards was prepared by the Secretariat and submitted to the Commission on Safety Standards at its meeting in November.

IAEA also convened a five-day Ministerial Conference on Nuclear Safety (Vienna, 20–24 June) in response to the Fukushima Daiichi accident. The Conference adopted a Ministerial Declaration requesting the IAEA Director General to prepare a draft Action Plan on Nuclear Safety. In September, the Action Plan—a framework of actions to strengthen global nuclear safety—was endorsed by the fifty-fifth session of the General Conference.

In Africa, the technical cooperation programme focused on the sustainable application of nuclear techniques to achieve increased food security, improved nutrition and health services, along with better management of groundwater resources, improved energy development planning, quality control in industrial development and a cleaner and safer environment. In Asia and the Pacific, the focus on strengthening human and institutional capacity to apply nuclear technology in the health, agriculture and industry sectors continued. Also following the Fukushima Daiichi accident, the IAEA secretariat coordinated a new regional co-operative agreement project to enhance national capacities for monitoring radioactive substances in the marine environment in the Asia and the Pacific region. In Europe, technical cooperation activities concentrated on support for countries planning a nuclear power programme, and on the use of radiation in health care. Ensuring that appropriate levels of safety and security in all aspects of the peaceful use of nuclear technology were maintained was a key component of the Agency's technical cooperation projects. In Latin America, emphasis was placed on promoting technical excellence, leadership and cooperation among Member States, particularly through trilateral cooperation arrangements within regional projects planned for the 2012–2013 technical co-operation programme cycle. In 2011, approximately €83.3 million from the Technical Cooperation Fund (TCF) was disbursed to 123 countries or territories, of which 30 were least developed countries. The nuclear fuel cycle (predisposal and disposal of nuclear fuel waste) accounted for 27 per cent of TCF resources, followed by human health at 18.3 per cent, and nuclear safety at 16.1 per cent.

On 1 November [A/66/PV.46], Yukiya Amano, Director General of IAEA, presented the Agency's updated 2010 annual report [YUN 2010, p. 999] to the General Assembly.

High-level meeting on nuclear safety and security. In response to the Fukushima Daiichi nuclear disaster (see p. 963), the Secretary-General convened a high-level meeting on nuclear safety and security (New York, 22 September), which focused on strengthening the global nuclear safety regime and ensuring maximum nuclear safety standards. In advance of the meeting, the Secretary-General in August released a UN system-wide study on the implications of the Fukushima Daiichi accident [SG/HLM/2011/1]. In October, the Secretary-General transmitted to the General Assembly the Chair's summary of the high-level meeting [A/C.4/66/8].

GENERAL ASSEMBLY ACTION

On 2 November [meeting 48], the General Assembly adopted **resolution 66/7** [draft: A/66/L.6 & Add.1] without vote [agenda item 86].

Report of the International Atomic Energy Agency

The General Assembly,

Having received the report of the International Atomic Energy Agency for 2010,

Taking note of the statement by the Director General of the International Atomic Energy Agency, in which he provided additional information on the main developments in the activities of the Agency during 2011,

Recognizing the importance of the work of the Agency,

Recognizing also the cooperation between the United Nations and the Agency and the Agreement governing the relationship between the United Nations and the Agency as approved by the General Conference of the Agency on 23 October 1957 and by the General Assembly in the annex to its resolution 1145(XII) of 14 November 1957,

1. *Takes note with appreciation* of the report of the International Atomic Energy Agency;

2. *Takes note* of resolutions GC(55)/RES/9 on measures to strengthen international cooperation in nuclear, radiation, transport and waste safety; GC(55)/RES/10 on nuclear security; GC(55)/RES/11 on the strengthening of the Agency's technical cooperation activities; GC(55)/RES/12 on strengthening the Agency's activities related to nuclear science, technology and applications, comprising GC(55)/RES/12 A on non-power nuclear applications and GC(55)/RES/12 B on nuclear power applications; GC(55)/RES/13 on the implementation of the Agreement between the Agency and the Democratic People's Republic of Korea for the application of safeguards in connection with the Treaty on the Non-Proliferation of Nuclear Weapons; GC(55)/RES/14 on the application of Agency safeguards in the Middle East; and GC(55)/RES/15 on personnel matters, comprising GC(55)/RES/15 A on the staffing of the Agency's Secretariat and GC(55)/RES/15 B on women in the Secretariat; and decisions GC(55)/DEC/10 on the amendment to article XIV.A of the Statute of the Agency; GC(55)/DEC/11 on strengthening the effectiveness and improving the efficiency of the safeguards system and application of the Model Additional Protocol; and GC(55)/DEC/12 on the amendment to article VI of the Statute, adopted by the General Conference of the Agency at its fifty-fifth regular session, held from 19 to 23 September 2011;

3. *Reaffirms its strong support* for the indispensable role of the Agency in encouraging and assisting the development and practical application of atomic energy for peaceful uses, in technology transfer to developing countries and in nuclear safety, verification and security;

4. *Appeals* to Member States to continue to support the activities of the Agency;

5. *Requests* the Secretary-General to transmit to the Director General of the Agency the records of the sixty-sixth session of the General Assembly relating to the activities of the Agency.

New and renewable sources of energy

In response to General Assembly resolution 65/151 [YUN 2010, p. 1001], the Secretary-General in August submitted a report [A/66/306] on the promotion of new and renewable sources of energy including an overview of status and prospects; national and international efforts in the promotion of new and renewable sources of energy; and options for coordinated global energy strategies.

The Secretary-General stressed the need for a transformation of global energy systems that would sustainably satisfy the rapid growth in energy demand, particularly in developing countries, and diminish the negative impacts of global climate change. He noted that the growth of the renewable energy industry over the previous five years had been driven by accelerated deployment of new technologies. Despite record investments being made by countries competing for leadership in those new markets, many poor countries with largely rural populations had seen relatively low growth in the use and commercialization of renewable energy technologies. Most of the growth had occurred in developed countries, and in a number of developing countries with emerging economies.

The Secretary-General also noted that in some regions, onshore wind, geothermal, small hydropower and biomass technologies were becoming economically competitive. Solar photovoltaic and concentrated solar power, however, remained expensive though their costs were dropping rapidly. Unfortunately, the costs for most rural off-grid renewable energy, including solar home systems and village-scale mini-grids, also remained high.

Much more cooperation and action were needed to substantially increase the contribution of new technologies to the global energy system. A coordinated global energy strategy needed to be adopted, in conjunction with consistent and stable national policies, to bring down the cost of renewable energy technologies, including off-grid systems, for use by the poorest segments of the population living in rural areas. International support was necessary to help remove the financial, technological, infrastructural and institutional barriers to creating the enabling environments.

International institutional arrangements, including the various organizations of the UN system, international financial institutions and international organizations, such as the International Renewable Energy Agency, continued to play an important role in promoting international cooperation through capacity-building and technical cooperation. UN-Energy was leading global efforts to create awareness and was coordinating activities undertaken by the United Nations to increase the share of renewable energy and reduce the intensity of energy use.

New and renewable sources of energy were a major priority for the upcoming United Nations Conference on Sustainable Development in 2012. The Conference would present an opportunity to garner international support for the promotion of effective use of new and renewable sources of energy. The Secretary-General called for a coordinated global energy strategy that would enable progress toward a transition into low-carbon economies.

By **resolution 2011/14** (see p. 946), the Economic and Social Council took note of Economic and Social Commission for Asia and the Pacific resolution 67/2 on promoting regional cooperation for enhanced energy security and the sustainable use of energy in Asia and the Pacific.

GENERAL ASSEMBLY ACTION

On 22 December [meeting 91], the General Assembly, on the recommendation of the Second (Economic and Financial) Committee [A/66/440/Add.10], adopted **resolution 66/206** without vote [agenda item 19 (*j*)].

Promotion of new and renewable sources of energy

The General Assembly,

Recalling its resolutions 53/7 of 16 October 1998, 54/215 of 22 December 1999 and 55/205 of 20 December 2000, and recalling also its resolutions 56/200 of 21 December 2001, 58/210 of 23 December 2003, 60/199 of 22 December 2005, 62/197 of 19 December 2007 and 64/206 of 21 December 2009 on the promotion of new and renewable sources of energy and its resolution 65/151 of 20 December 2010 on the International Year of Sustainable Energy for All,

1. *Takes note* of the report of the Secretary-General;
2. *Notes* the ongoing preparatory process for the United Nations Conference on Sustainable Development, to be held in Rio de Janeiro, Brazil, from 20 to 22 June 2012;
3. *Welcomes* the efforts by Governments and institutions that have embarked on policies and programmes that seek to expand the use of new and renewable sources of energy for sustainable development, and recognizes the contributions of regional initiatives, institutions and regional economic commissions in supporting the efforts of countries, in particular developing countries and countries with economies in transition, in this respect;
4. *Invites* Member States, as well as the United Nations system and all other relevant stakeholders, to use the opportunity offered by the International Year of Sustainable Energy for All to raise global awareness of the importance of new and renewable sources of energy and low-emission technologies, the more efficient use of energy, greater reliance on advanced energy technologies, including cleaner fossil fuel technologies, and the environment-friendly use of traditional energy resources, as well as the promotion of access to modern, reliable, affordable and sustainable energy services, and notes in this regard the initiative of the Secretary-General "Sustainable Energy for All";
5. *Notes with appreciation* regional and multilateral mechanisms and initiatives for energy cooperation and integration to encourage the use of new and renewable sources of energy, such as the PetroCaribe Alternative Energy Source Financing Fund, the Mesoamerican Integration and Development Project, the Caribbean Renewable Energy Development Programme, the energy initiative of the New Partnership for Africa's Development, the Mediterranean Solar Plan, Energy+, the European Union Energy Initiative for Poverty Eradication and Sustainable Development, the Paris-Nairobi Climate Initiative on Clean Energy for All in Africa, the Africa-European Union Energy Partnership, the Baltic Sea Region Energy Cooperation, the International Partnership for Energy Efficiency Cooperation, the Energy and Climate Partnership of the Americas, the Global Bioenergy Partnership, the International Renewable Energy Agency, the Global Alliance for Clean Cookstoves, the Clean Energy Ministerial and the Union of South American Nations strategy on energy;
6. *Stresses* the importance of the continued substantive consideration of the issue of the promotion of new and renewable sources of energy;
7. *Requests* the Secretary-General to submit to the General Assembly at its sixty-seventh session a report on the implementation of the present resolution;
8. *Decides* to include in the provisional agenda of its sixty-seventh session, under the item entitled "Sustainable development", the sub-item entitled "Promotion of new and renewable sources of energy".

International Year of Sustainable Energy for All (2012)

In September, in response to General Assembly resolution 65/151 [YUN 2010, p. 1001], as set forth in a later report [A/67/314], the Secretary-General launched his "Sustainable Energy for All" initiative, guided by a High-level Group in line with his vision statement on the topic [A/66/645], to mobilize action towards three objectives to be achieved by 2030: providing universal access to modern energy services; doubling the global rate of improvement in energy efficiency; and doubling the share of renewable energy in the global energy mix.

Natural resources

Water resources

UN-Water

Throughout the year, UN-Water focused on urban water challenges.

World Water Day, hosted in Cape Town, South Africa, on 22 March under the theme "Water and Urbanization", focused on the impact of rapid urban population growth, industrialization and climate change, and how conflict and natural disasters affected urban water systems.

UN-Water organized World Water Week (Stockholm, Sweden, 21–27 August), on the theme "Water in an Urbanising World". UN-Water was among the key organizers of the conference, Towards the United Nations Conference on Sustainable Development (Rio+20): Water Cooperation Issues (Dushanbe, Tajikistan, 19–20 October), which addressed transboundary water disputes. UN-Water also hosted a conference entitled, Water in the Green Economy in Practice: Towards Rio+20 (Zaragoza, Spain, 3–5 October) to outline the role of water in economic models emphasizing environmental sustainability, along with the tools that turned such models into practical realities.

With the support of the Municipality of Zaragoza, Spain, the UN-Water Decade Programme on Advocacy and Communication launched the online United Nations Documentation Centre on Water and Sanitation, an authoritative and readily accessible source for a wide range of materials on water and sanitation produced by the UN system, with over 1,200 UN publications available for download.

Communications. On 28 March [A/65/811], Saudi Arabia transmitted to the Secretary-General the Charter of the International Energy Forum, which was approved at the extraordinary ministerial meeting held in Riyadh, Saudi Arabia, on 22 February.

On 8 April [A/65/817], Tajikistan transmitted to the Secretary-General the summary report of the side event of World Water Day 2011 on the theme "Water challenges and problems for cities".

On 16 May [A/65/842], Uzbekistan transmitted a report on the measures it had taken to ensure the rational use of water resources in Central Asia, and on the international conference, Towards the Sixth World Water Forum—Joint Action Towards Water Security. On 6 June [A/65/863], Tajikistan responded that the report subjectively examined the use of water resources and the development of hydropower in the Aral Sea basin and was a one-sided reflection of the outcome of the conference.

Cartography

Global geospatial information management

In accordance with Economic and Social Council decision 2010/240 [YUN 2010, p. 1004], the Secretary-General submitted a May report on global geospatial information management [E/2011/89], which described the activities of the United Nations in the field of geospatial information; major initiatives at the national, regional and global levels; and the need for a global mechanism on global geographic information management.

The report stressed the importance of geospatial information in addressing humanitarian, peace and security, environmental and development challenges and suggested the establishment of a global mechanism to discuss issues on geospatial information management. The report also addressed the need for better UN-facilitated coordination and made recommendations on the way forward, including the creation of a committee of experts on global geospatial information management. The committee was expected to play a leadership role in setting the agenda for the management of global geospatial information and provide a vehicle for coordination between Member States and international organizations.

ECONOMIC AND SOCIAL COUNCIL ACTION

On 27 July [meeting 47], the Economic and Social Council adopted **resolution 2011/24** [draft: E/2011/L.53] without vote [agenda item 13 (*k*)].

Committee of Experts on Global Geospatial Information Management

The Economic and Social Council,

Recalling its decision 2010/240 of 21 July 2010, in which it requested the Secretary-General to submit to it at its substantive session of 2011 a report on global geographic information management,

Recalling also Statistical Commission decision 41/110 of 26 February 2010, in which the Commission requested the Statistics Division of the Department of Economic and Social Affairs of the Secretariat to convene a meeting of an international expert group to address global geographic information management issues, including reviewing the existing mechanisms and exploring the possibility of creating a global forum,

Recalling further the resolution on global geographic information management adopted by the eighteenth United Nations Regional Cartographic Conference for Asia and the Pacific, in which the Conference requested the Secretary-General and the Secretariat to initiate discussions and prepare a report, for submission to the Economic and Social Council, on global coordination of geographic information management, including consideration of the possible creation of a United Nations global forum for the exchange of information between countries and other interested parties, and in particular for sharing best practices in legal and policy instruments, institutional management models, technical solutions and standards, interoperability of systems and data, and sharing mechanisms that guarantee easy and timely accessibility of geographic information and services,

Recognizing the importance of integrating cartographic and statistical information, as well as spatial data, with a view to fostering location-based geospatial information, applications and services,

Recognizing also the role of the United Nations in promoting international cooperation on cartography, geographical names and geospatial information, including through the organization of conferences, expert meetings, technical publications, training courses and cooperation projects,

Taking into account the urgent need to take concrete action to strengthen international cooperation in the area of global geospatial information,

1. *Takes note* of the report of the Secretary-General on global geospatial information management and the recommendations contained therein;

2. *Recognizes* the need to promote international cooperation in the field of global geospatial information;

3. *Decides*, in this regard, to establish the Committee of Experts on Global Geospatial Information Management, in accordance with the terms of reference contained in the annex to the present resolution, to be established and administered within existing resources and organized accordingly, and requests the Committee to present to the Economic and Social Council, in 2016, a comprehensive review of all aspects of its work and operations, in order to allow Member States to assess its effectiveness;

4. *Encourages* Member States to hold regular high-level, multi-stakeholder discussions on global geospatial information, including through the convening of global forums, with a view to promoting a comprehensive dialogue with all relevant actors and bodies;

5. *Emphasizes* the importance of promoting national, regional and global efforts to foster the exchange

of knowledge and expertise, to assist developing countries in building and strengthening national capacities in this field.

ANNEX

Terms of reference of the Committee of Experts on Global Geospatial Information Management

Objectives and functions

1. The objectives and functions of the Committee of Experts on Global Geospatial Information Management will be:

(*a*) To provide a forum for coordination and dialogue among Member States, and between Member States and relevant international organizations, including the United Nations regional cartographic conferences and their permanent committees on spatial data infrastructures, on enhanced cooperation in the field of global geospatial information;

(*b*) To propose workplans and guidelines with a view to promoting common principles, policies, methods, mechanisms and standards for the interoperability and interchangeability of geospatial data and services;

(*c*) To provide a platform for the development of effective strategies on how to build and strengthen national capacity concerning geospatial information, especially in developing countries, and, in this regard, to assist interested countries in developing the full potential of geospatial information and the underlying technology;

(*d*) To compile and disseminate best practices and experiences of national, regional and international bodies on geospatial information related, inter alia, to legal instruments, management models and technical standards, thus contributing to the establishment of spatial data infrastructures, while allowing for flexibility in the development of national geospatial activities;

(*e*) In performing its functions, the Committee should build upon and make use of the existing work of other forums and mechanisms in related fields.

Membership, composition and terms of office

2. The Committee will comprise experts from all Member States, as well as experts from international organizations as observers. In appointing their national representatives, Member States will seek to designate experts with specific knowledge drawn from the interrelated fields of surveying, geography, cartography and mapping, remote sensing, land/sea and geographic information systems and environmental protection.

3. The Committee will elect two Co-Chairs during each session from among its members, respecting geographical balance and representation.

4. The Committee may establish, as and when needed, informal working groups or subcommittees to deal with specific issues related to its work programme.

Reporting procedure

5. The Committee will report to the Economic and Social Council.

Frequency of meetings

6. The Committee will normally meet once a year and may hold, under exceptional circumstances, additional meetings, as appropriate.

Secretariat

7. The Committee will be supported by the Statistics Division of the Department of Economic and Social Affairs and the Cartographic Section of the Department of Field Support.

Meeting documentation

8. Meeting documentation will include an agenda, the previous report of the Committee, thematic notes prepared by working groups or subcommittees, notes by the Secretariat, and other relevant documents prepared by external experts or expert groups.

Committee report. The inaugural session of the United Nations Committee of Experts on Global Geospatial Information Management (Seoul, Republic of Korea, 26 October) [E/2011/46] adopted decisions on its terms of reference, rules of procedure, contribution to the United Nations Conference on Sustainable Development (Rio+20) and inventory of issues. The Committee took note of the oral statement of the Chair of the High-level Forum on Global Geospatial Information Management, which summarized the main findings and recommendations of the Forum, held from 24 to 26 October, as well as the Seoul Declaration adopted at the Forum. It also took note of the report of the Secretary-General on the UNmap project [E/C.20/2011/6].

The Committee decided to create a task force to prepare a contribution to the Rio+20 Conference as well as a working group to elaborate an inventory of issues and propose a five-year workplan for the Committee to consider at its second session.

It further decided to recommend to the Council that its second session be held in New York from 13 to 15 August 2012.

Standardization of geographical names

At its twenty-sixth session (Vienna, 2–6 May) [E/2011/119 & Corr.1], the United Nations Group of Experts on Geographical Names considered reports from 14 of its 23 linguistic/geographical divisions and 10 working groups; the liaison officers and international organizations; and the Coordinator Task Team for Africa. The session also discussed preparations for the Tenth United Nations Conference on the Standardization of Geographical Names, scheduled to be held in New York from 7 to 16 August 2012, as well as the agenda for the twenty-seventh session of the Group, planned for 6 and 17 August 2012 in conjunction with the Tenth Conference.

On 27 July, by **decision 2011/251**, the Economic and Social Council took note of the report of the Group of Experts on its twenty-sixth session; decided that its twenty-seventh session would be held in New York on 6 and 17 August 2012; and further decided that the Tenth United Nations Conference on the Standardization of Geographical Names would be held in New York from 7 to 16 August 2012.

UN Regional Cartographic Conference for Asia and the Pacific

On 29 July (**decision 2011/276**), the Economic and Social Council decided to hold the Nineteenth United Nations Regional Cartographic Conference for Asia and the Pacific in Bangkok from 29 October to 2 November 2012.

Chapter VII

Environment and human settlements

In 2011, the United Nations worked with the international community to protect the natural environment and improve living conditions for people residing in cities through legally binding instruments and other commitments, as well as by means of the United Nations Environment Programme (UNEP) and the United Nations Human Settlements Programme (UN-Habitat).

Ministerial consultations at the twenty-sixth session of the UNEP Governing Council/Global Ministerial Environment Forum, held in February, addressed the UNEP contribution to the preparatory process for the United Nations Conference on Sustainable Development, to be held in 2012, focusing on the two interlinked topics of the green economy and international environmental governance. The Council/Forum adopted 17 decisions addressing global environmental challenges. In addition, the first session of the plenary meeting to determine modalities and institutional arrangements for an intergovernmental science-policy platform on biodiversity and ecosystem services met in Nairobi in October.

The ninth session of the United Nations Forum on Forests, convened in February, focused on the topic of forests for people. The Forum adopted a ministerial declaration on the occasion of the launch of the International Year of Forests, 2011.

On 20 September, the General Assembly convened a high-level meeting on the theme "Addressing desertification, land degradation and drought in the context of sustainable development and poverty eradication". The tenth session of the Conference of the Parties to the United Nations Convention to Combat Desertification, held in October, adopted decisions designed to make the Convention a global authority on scientific and technical knowledge pertaining to desertification, land degradation and drought.

The tenth meeting of the Conference of the Parties to the Basel Convention on the Control of Transboundary Movements of Hazardous Wastes and their Disposal, held in October, adopted the Cartagena Declaration on the Prevention, Minimization and Recovery of Hazardous Wastes and Other Wastes, which reaffirmed that the Convention was the primary global legal instrument for guiding the environmentally sound management of hazardous and other wastes and their disposal.

The Conference of the Parties to the United Nations Framework Convention on Climate Change, at its seventeenth session, held in November and December, agreed on a second commitment period under the Kyoto Protocol, to start in January 2013, and affirmed the mitigation pledges under the Convention made by 89 countries, regulating 80 per cent of global emissions until 2020. It also agreed on how and by when developed and developing countries would report on their mitigation efforts, and identified a path towards the future legal climate framework that would be applicable to all.

The United Nations Decade on Biodiversity 2011–2020 was launched at the end of the year. Recognizing that millions of the world's inhabitants depended on the health of coral reefs and related ecosystems, the General Assembly, in December, adopted a resolution on the protection of coral reefs for sustainable livelihoods and development.

UN-Habitat continued to support the implementation of the 1996 Habitat Agenda and the Millennium Development Goals. The twenty-third session of the UN-Habitat Governing Council, held in April, adopted 18 resolutions addressing issues related to housing and urban development. By a December resolution, the Assembly decided to convene in 2016 a third United Nations conference on housing and sustainable urban development (Habitat III) in order to reinvigorate the global commitment to sustainable urbanization.

Environment

UN Environment Programme

Governing Council/Ministerial Forum

The twenty-sixth session of the Governing Council/Global Ministerial Environment Forum (GC/GMEF) of the United Nations Environment Programme (UNEP) was held in Nairobi from 21 to 24 February [A/66/25]. Ministerial-level consultations (21–22 February) focused on the UNEP contribution to the preparatory process for the United Nations Conference on Sustainable Development, to be held in Rio de Janeiro, Brazil, in 2012 (Rio+20), addressing under that overarching theme the two interlinked topics of the green economy and international environmental governance. The Committee of the Whole, established by the Council/Forum, held eight meetings to consider the agenda items assigned to it. At the first plenary meeting, the UNEP Executive Director delivered a policy statement that was summarized in the report of the session [UNEP/GC.26/19]. Annexed thereto was also a summary of the views expressed during the ministerial consultations on each topic, as presented by the President of the Council/Forum on 24 February. On the same date, GC/GMEF decided to hold its twelfth special session in 2012 from 20 to 22 February at a venue to be determined, and its twenty-seventh session in 2013 from 18 to 22 February in Nairobi. It also approved the provisional agendas for those sessions [A/66/25 (dec. 26/17)].

On 27 July (**decision 2011/246**), the Economic and Social Council took note of the GC/GMEF report on its twenty-sixth session.

The General Assembly took note of the report in resolution 66/203 of 22 December (see p. 975).

Subsidiary body

The twenty-sixth (2011) session of the Council/Forum had before it a December 2010 note by the UNEP Executive Director [UNEP/GC.26/INF/4] on the work of the Committee of Permanent Representatives—open to representatives of all UN Member States and members of specialized agencies—since the twenty-fifth (2009) GC/GMEF session [YUN 2009, p. 1002].

In 2011, the Committee held an extraordinary meeting on 3 February [UNEP/CPR/114/3] and regular meetings on 15 March [UNEP/CPR/115/2], 23 June [UNEP/CPR/116/2], 22 September [UNEP/CPR/117/2] and 19 December [UNEP/CPR/118/2]. The Committee discussed, among other subjects, the outcome of the twenty-sixth GC/GMEF session and preparations for its twelfth (2012) special session; work on the fifth Global Environment Outlook report—a review of the state of the planet; the International Resource Panel; and preparations for Rio+20.

Ministerial consultations

Preparatory process for the United Nations Conference on Sustainable Development

In January, the UNEP Executive Director submitted to GC/GMEF a discussion paper [UNEP/GC.26/17] for the ministerial consultations on the UNEP contribution to the preparatory process for Rio+20. The paper outlined the genesis of the Conference, including the Nusa Dua Declaration [YUN 2010, p. 1009], by which Governments clarified their commitment to UNEP playing an active role in the Conference; the organization, preparatory process and calendar for the Conference; the mechanisms in place for the UNEP contribution; and UNEP engagement in the preparatory process, in particular through its work on the green economy and international environmental governance.

Green economy

In January, the Executive Director submitted for the ministerial consultations at the twenty-sixth GC/GMEF session a background paper [UNEP/GC.26/17/Add.1] on benefits, challenges and risks associated with a transition to a green economy. The paper provided an overview of the context and concept of a green economy; national green economy initiatives; key green economy policy messages; and steps that Governments and other stakeholders could take in promoting a green economy. He also submitted a note summarizing international developments in relation to the green economy and describing related UNEP activities in 2010 [YUN 2010, p. 1014].

International environmental governance

The Council/Forum had before it notes by the Executive Director on the work of the Consultative Group of Ministers or High-Level Representatives on International Environmental Governance [YUN 2010, p. 1009], which contained the Nairobi-Helsinki Outcome, and on incremental reforms of and changes to international environmental governance [ibid.]. Also before it were notes containing inputs from major groups and stakeholders on the topic [UNEP/GC.26/INF/19] and another on environment in the UN system [UNEP/GC.26/INF/23] that outlined how various UN system entities were engaged in performing the key objectives and functions being considered in the reform of the international environmental governance system.

For the ministerial consultations on international environmental governance, the Executive Director also prepared a discussion paper [UNEP/GC.26/17/Add.2] that addressed the fragmented governance structure and relatively meagre financial means of the environmental pillar of sustainable development vis-à-vis its social and economic pillars. The briefing highlighted the need to strengthen environmental governance and create incentives for effective implementation of existing environmental laws and policies, as well as for strengthening the coordination of sustainable development. It also suggested key messages for Rio+20.

The Council/Forum [A/66/25 (dec. 26/1)] requested the Executive Director, in cooperation with other interested UN entities, to organize informal meetings in New York for governmental representatives on the Nairobi-Helsinki Outcome in the context of discussions on the institutional framework for sustainable development; and to submit for its consideration at its twelfth (2012) special session a draft decision on incremental improvements in international environmental governance. The Council/Forum invited the Preparatory Committee for the United Nations Conference on Sustainable Development to consider the options for broader institutional reform identified in the Nairobi-Helsinki Outcome and initiate an analysis of the financial, structural and legal implications and comparative advantages of those options.

Programme areas

Chemicals and waste

Waste management. The Council/Forum [A/66/25 (dec. 26/3)], having before it reports of the Executive Director on chemicals and waste management [YUN 2010, p. 1040] and on chemicals management, including mercury [UNEP/GC.26/5/Rev.1], as well as a summary of the outcome of the second session of the intergovernmental negotiating committee to prepare a legally binding instrument on mercury (Chiba, Japan, 24–28 January) [UNEP/GC.26/5/Rev.1/Add.1], recommended that the issue of integrated waste management be further dealt with as a key priority area under the "Delivering as one" initiative [YUN 2006, p. 1584]. It took note of the UNEP initiative to set up a global partnership on waste management, and requested the UNEP Executive Director to strengthen cooperation and coordination within relevant UN and other international institutions in the area of waste management. The Executive Director was also asked to ensure coherence and complementarity and avoid duplication with relevant work under the United Nations and other international institutions and arrangements. By the same decision, the Council/Forum requested the Executive Director to submit input on chemicals and wastes management as part of the UNEP contribution to the Preparatory Committee for the United Nations Conference on Sustainable Development. It also addressed issues related to lead and cadmium, mercury, and the Strategic Approach to International Chemicals Management [YUN 2006, p. 1246].

Also submitted to the Council/Forum were reports on the need for global action in relation to lead and cadmium [UNEP/GC.26/INF/11]; the final reviews of scientific information on lead [UNEP/GC.26/INF/11/Add.1] and cadmium [UNEP/GC.26/INF/11/Add.2], along with an overview of existing and future national actions, including legislation, relevant to both elements, respectively; the health and environmental effects of the movement of products containing lead, cadmium and mercury in Latin America and the Caribbean [UNEP/GC.26/INF/11/Add.3] as well as Asia and the Pacific [UNEP/GC.26/INF/11/Add.4]; other UNEP activities related to lead and cadmium [UNEP/GC.26/INF/11/Add.5]; and progress of the UNEP Global Mercury Partnership from January 2009 to June 2010 [YUN 2010, p. 1039].

Financing options. The Council/Forum [A/66/25 (dec. 26/7)], having considered the report by the Executive Director on the consultative process on financing options on chemicals and wastes [YUN 2010, p. 1041], and an addendum summarizing the outcome of the third meeting in the process (Pretoria, South Africa, 10–11 January) [UNEP/GC.26/11/Add.1], requested UNEP to continue to support the process.

Cooperation and coordination. The Council/Forum [A/66/25 (dec. 26/12)], having considered the report by the Executive Director on efforts to enhance cooperation and coordination in the chemicals and waste cluster [YUN 2010, p. 1041], requested the Executive Director to provide input on the consultative process on financing options for chemicals and wastes to the Preparatory Committee for the United Nations Conference on Sustainable Development.

Monitoring and assessment

The Council/Forum considered reports by the Executive Director on: the state of the environment and the UNEP contribution to meeting substantive environmental challenges, which summarized key policy issues emanating from UNEP assessment and early warning activities [YUN 2010, p. 1010]; an inventory of all assessments led and supported by UNEP since 2009 [ibid.]; and the requirements for a migration to targeted assessments in thematic priority areas and, in particular, UNEP-Live as a supporting framework for such assessments [ibid.]. On 24 February [A/66/25 (dec. 26/2)], the Council/Forum requested the Executive Director to continue to improve the coherence of assessments and their scientific rigour, as well as assist countries in capacity development; facilitate the finalization of the fifth report in the Global Environment Outlook process and the summary for policymakers in time to contribute to Rio+20; and to proceed with the development of UNEP-Live.

Regarding global water quality monitoring and assessment, the Council/Forum [A/66/25 (dec. 26/14)] requested the Executive Director to facilitate the development of the Global Environment Monitoring System/Water Programme [YUN 2005, p. 1137] in order to ensure that it provided scientifically credible water quality data that met the needs of the United Nations.

Sustainable consumption and production

The Council/Forum had before it a report by the UNEP Executive Director on sustainable consumption and production [UNEP/GC.26/7]. The report provided an account of good practices in promoting sustainable consumption and production adopted since the 1992 UN Conference on Environment and Development and described UNEP work on sustainable consumption and production and resource efficiency.

It also discussed the work of the Marrakech Process on Sustainable Consumption and Production, which was launched in response to a request made in the 2002 Johannesburg Plan of Implementation of the World Summit on Sustainable Development [YUN 2002, p. 821] to develop a 10-year framework of programmes to support the shift to sustainable consumption and production patterns; and addressed the question of why a 10-year framework of programmes on sustainable consumption and production was needed. An addendum to the report [UNEP/GC.26/7/Add.1] presented the outcome of the high-level intersessional meeting of the Commission on Sustainable Development (CSD) on a 10-year framework of programmes dealing with sustainable consumption and production (Panama City, 13–14 January) (see p. 797).

On 24 February [A/66/25 (dec. 26/5)], the Council/Forum recognized that the 10-year framework of programmes on sustainable consumption and production, as considered by CSD, could serve as an input to the preparatory process for Rio+20 and requested the Executive Director to ensure that UNEP played a lead role, with the UN Department of Economic and Social Affairs, in developing and implementing a 10-year framework of such programmes. The Executive Director was also asked to submit a report on the implementation of the decision to the Council/Forum at its twelfth (2012) special session in anticipation of its contribution to Rio+20.

South-South cooperation

The Council/Forum [A/66/25 (dec. 26/13)] took note of the reports by the UNEP Executive Director on progress made in promoting South-South cooperation to achieve sustainable development [YUN 2010, p. 1012]; activities undertaken by the UNEP Programme on South-South cooperation for achieving sustainable development [ibid., p. 1032]; and regional and national activities to promote South-South cooperation [ibid., p. 1012]. It requested the Executive Director to strengthen results-based management in UNEP.

In a separate decision [dec. 26/16], the Council/Forum, having before it a note [UNEP/CBD/COP/10/18/Add.1/Rev.1] from the Executive Secretary of the Convention on Biological Diversity on the Multi-year Plan of Action for South-South Cooperation on Biodiversity for Development, adopted by the Group of 77 developing counties and China at the tenth meeting of the Conference of the Parties to the Convention on Biological Diversity [YUN 2010, p. 1023], encouraged member States and other Governments to contribute further to the development of the Plan. It invited parties, other Governments, regional and international organizations, UN bodies—including UNEP—and others to do the same.

UN system coordination and cooperation

The Council/Forum [A/66/25 (dec. 26/11)], having before it the report of the Executive Director [YUN 2010, p. 1013] on enhanced coordination across the UN system, including the Environment Management Group (EMG) [YUN 1998, p. 981], and a report [YUN 2010, p. 1013] on progress made in implementing the memorandum of understanding concluded in 2008 [YUN 2008, p. 1151] between UNEP and the United Nations Development Programme (UNDP), encouraged EMG to prepare UN system contributions to the tenth (2011) session of the Conference of the Parties to the United Nations Convention to Combat Desertification in Those Countries Experiencing Serious Drought and/or Desertification, Particularly in Africa (see p. 982); to the nineteenth (2011) session of the Commission on Sustainable Development (see p. 797); and, identifying existing studies on the green economy, to the preparatory process for Rio+20 (see p. 971).

UNEP/UN-Habitat cooperation. The joint progress report of the Executive Directors of UNEP and the United Nations Human Settlements Programme (UN-Habitat) [UNEP/GC.26/INF/10] provided an overview of the cooperation between the two Programmes in the 2009–2010 period. The report also set forth their planned cooperation in the subsequent biennium, which would be focused on cities and climate change, particularly climate change assessments; ecosystem-based adaptation in coastal cities; harnessing the mitigation potential of buildings, housing and construction; and low-carbon cities: transport and urban planning.

Environmental emergencies

The Council/Forum [A/66/25 (dec. 26/15)], having before it a report of the Executive Director on the proposed biennial programme of work and budget for 2012–2013 [UNEP/GC.26/13], including the subprogramme on disasters and conflicts, requested the Executive Director to coordinate, in cooperation with the Office for the Coordination of Humanitarian Affairs (OCHA), within the following 12 months, the preparation of a baseline document on existing roles, responsibilities and divisions of labour among international organizations involved in responding to environmental emergencies, identifying key gaps and opportunities. The Executive Director was asked to ensure, in cooperation with OCHA, over the coming three years, that key organizations involved in responding to environmental emergencies had a clear and mutually agreed understanding of their respective roles and responsibilities in various scenarios. The Council/Forum decided, in cooperation with OCHA, UNDP and other actors, to continue to contribute to strengthening the UN response mechanism for the coordination and mobilization of international assistance to countries facing environmental risks and impacts from natural and man-made disasters through, in particular, the UNEP disasters and conflicts subprogramme and the collaborative partnership between UNEP and OCHA. It requested the Executive Director to continue, in cooperation with the International Strategy for Disaster Reduction, UNDP, the United Nations Educational, Scientific and Cultural Organization (UNESCO) and other actors, to strengthen integrated approaches to reducing the risk of natural and man-made disasters and adapting to the impacts of climate change. The Executive Director was also asked to organize, in consultation with OCHA, the International Strategy for Disaster Reduction and other partners, regular meetings on environmental emergencies to promote among member States the application of voluntary guidelines for environmental emergencies.

Advisory Group. The ninth meeting of the Advisory Group on Environmental Emergencies (Bern, Switzerland, 18–19 May) initiated two studies: on the implications of climate change and urbanization for environmental emergency preparedness and response; and on the integration of environmental emergencies into preparedness and contingency planning.

Biodiversity and ecosystem services

The Council/Forum [A/66/25 (dec. 26/4)], having considered the report of the Executive Director on the intergovernmental science-policy platform on biodiversity and ecosystem services called for in the Busan outcome, endorsed the outcomes of the third and final ad hoc intergovernmental and multi-stakeholder meeting on the issue [YUN 2010, p. 1029]. It decided, based on the request by the General Assembly in resolution 65/162 [ibid., p. 1006], to convene a plenary meeting providing for the participation of all member States, in particular representatives from developing countries, to determine modalities and institutional arrangements for the platform at the earliest opportunity; and requested the Executive Director, in cooperation with UNESCO, the Food and Agriculture Organization of the United Nations (FAO) and UNDP, to convene the meeting in 2011 and to facilitate any ensuing process to implement the platform, until such time as a secretariat was established.

Plenary meeting. The first session of the plenary meeting to determine modalities and institutional arrangements for an intergovernmental science-policy platform on biodiversity and ecosystem services [UNEP/IPBES.MI/1/8] took place at UNEP headquarters in Nairobi, Kenya, from 3 to 7 October. It had before it, among other documents, reports of an international expert meeting on such a platform and capacity-building (Trondheim, Norway, 25–27 May) [UNEP/IPBES.MI/1/INF/10], co-convened by Brazil and Norway; a meeting of scientific organizations on the generation-of-knowledge function of such a platform (Paris, 10 June) [UNEP/IPBES.MI/1/INF/11], convened by the International Council for Science and hosted by UNESCO; and an international science workshop on assessments for such a platform (Tokyo, 25–29 July) [UNEP/IPBES.MI/1/INF/12], co-convened by Japan and South Africa and hosted by the United Nations University. The session discussed legal issues related to the establishment and operationalization of the platform; functions and operating principles of the platform; functions and structures of bodies that might be established under the platform; rules of procedure for platform meetings; the process and criteria for selecting the host institution or institutions and the physical location of the platform's secretariat; and the work programme of the platform. The session had before it corresponding documents on those and related issues [UNEP/IPBES.MI/1/3, UNEP/IPBES.MI/1/4, UNEP/IPBES.MI/1/5, UNEP/IPBES.MI/1/6, UNEP/IPBES.MI/1/7, UNEP/IPBES.MI/1/INF/3 & Add.1, UNEP/IPBES.MI/1/INF/4 & Add.1, UNEP/IPBES.MI/1/INF/5, UNEP/IPBES.MI/1/INF/6 & Add.1, UNEP/IPBES.MI/1/INF/8, UNEP/IPBES.MI/1/INF/9, UNEP/IPBES.MI/1/INF/14]. The first session determined that it was not possible to proceed regarding the platform's legal status without consensus. The remaining matters discussed were to be considered further at the second (2012) plenary session.

Marine and coastal ecosystems

The Council/Forum [A/66/25 (dec. 26/6)] took note of the report by the Executive Director on UNEP activities to protect marine and coastal ecosystems [YUN 2010, p. 1032] and requested the Executive Director to organize the third session of the Intergovernmental Review Meeting on the Implementation of the Global Programme of Action for the Protection of the Marine Environment from Land-based Activities, to be held in 2012.

Governance, work programme and budget

Programme of work and budget for 2012–2013

The Executive Director submitted for the consideration of the Council/Forum during its twenty-sixth session a report [UNEP/GC.26/13] on the proposed biennial programme of work and budget for 2012–2013 that reviewed the likely availability of resources in the Environment Fund during that period. The report set out UNEP objectives for the biennium, expected accomplishments, indicators of achievement and performance measures; outputs; and resource requirements. It also described work programme resource requirements and management. The report included six subprogramme narratives on climate change; disasters and conflicts; ecosystem management; environmental guidance; harmful substances and hazardous waste; and resource efficiency and sustainable consumption and production.

The Council/Forum [A/66/25 (dec. 26/9)], having considered the proposed biennial work programme and budget and the related report of the Advisory Committee on Administrative and Budgetary Questions (ACABQ) [UNEP/GC.26/13/Add.1], as well as notes by the Executive Director on the implementation of the programme of work and budgets, including information on support provided to Africa, for January–December 2010 [UNEP/GC.26/INF/6/Add.1], and on the relationship between UNEP and the multilateral environmental agreements that it administered [YUN 2010, p. 1018], approved the programme and support budget for the 2012–2013 biennium and appropriations for the Environment Fund in the amount of $191 million.

The Council/Forum [dec. 26/13] also requested the Executive Director to continue to strengthen results-based management in UNEP and, wherever possible, to provide an account of relevant activities in a results-based report to the Governing Council on the implementation of the work programmes and budgets.

Trust funds

The Council/Forum [A/66/25 (dec. 26/10)], having before it a report by the Executive Director on the management of trust funds and earmarked contributions [YUN 2010, p. 1017], approved the establishment of three technical cooperation trust funds since its twenty-fifth (2009) session, and the extension of four general trust funds and three technical cooperation trust funds, all in support of the UNEP work programme. It also approved the establishment of one technical cooperation trust fund since its twenty-fifth session and the extension of twelve general trust funds and three technical cooperation trust funds, all in support of regional seas programmes, conventions, protocols and special funds.

Additional reports

Other reports by the Executive Director submitted to the Council/Forum for its twenty-sixth session concerned resolutions adopted by the General Assembly at its sixty-fifth session of relevance to UNEP and measures for the implementation of Assembly resolution 62/208 [YUN 2007, p. 877] [UNEP/GC.26/INF/3]; statements and recommendations from major groups and stakeholders [UNEP/GC.26/INF/5]; the status of the Environment Fund and other sources of UNEP funding [UNEP/GC.26/INF/6]; the report of the Board of Auditors on the audit of the accounts of the Environment Fund for the biennium ended 31 December 2009 [YUN 2010, p. 1017]; changes in the status of ratification of and accession to conventions and protocols in the field of the environment [UNEP/GC.26/INF/8]; corporate memorandums of understanding concerning cooperation between UNEP and other UN system bodies [YUN 2010, p. 1013]; the report of the International Panel for Sustainable Resource Management [UNEP/GC.26/INF/16]; the UNEP contribution to CSD at its nineteenth (2011) session [UNEP/GC.26/INF/18]; the integrated assessment of black carbon and tropospheric ozone [UNEP/GC.26/INF/20]; and the Joint Inspection Unit report on the environmental profile of UN system organizations and their in-house environmental management policies and practices [YUN 2010, p. 1043].

GENERAL ASSEMBLY ACTION

On 22 December [meeting 91], the General Assembly, on the recommendation of the Second (Economic and Financial) Committee [A/66/440/Add.7], adopted **resolution 66/203** without vote [agenda item 19 (g)].

Report of the Governing Council of the United Nations Environment Programme on its twenty-sixth session

The General Assembly,

Recalling its resolutions 2997(XXVII) of 15 December 1972, 53/242 of 28 July 1999, 55/200 of 20 December 2000, 57/251 of 20 December 2002, 64/204 of 21 December 2009, 65/162 of 20 December 2010 and other previous resolutions relating to the Governing Council/Global Ministerial Environment Forum of the United Nations Environment Programme,

Taking into account Agenda 21 and the Plan of Implementation of the World Summit on Sustainable Development ("Johannesburg Plan of Implementation"),

Reaffirming the Rio Declaration on Environment and Development and its principles,

Recalling the 2005 World Summit Outcome,

Recalling also the Bali Strategic Plan for Technology Support and Capacity-building,

Reaffirming its commitment to strengthening the role of the United Nations Environment Programme as set out in the Nairobi Declaration on the Role and Mandate of the United Nations Environment Programme of 7 February 1997 and in the Nusa Dua Declaration of 26 February 2010,

Acknowledging the importance of the upcoming United Nations Conference on Sustainable Development,

Noting that 2012 marks the fortieth anniversary of the United Nations Environment Programme,

1. *Takes note* of the report of the Governing Council of the United Nations Environment Programme on its twenty-sixth session and the decisions contained therein;

2. *Notes* the ongoing preparatory process for the United Nations Conference on Sustainable Development, to be held in Rio de Janeiro, Brazil, from 20 to 22 June 2012;

3. *Stresses* the importance of the continued substantive consideration of the work of the Governing Council of the United Nations Environment Programme;

4. *Reiterates* the continuing need for the United Nations Environment Programme to conduct up-to-date, comprehensive, scientifically credible and policy-relevant global environment assessments, in close consultation with Member States, in order to support decision-making processes at all levels, and in this regard notes that the fifth report in the Global Environment Outlook series and its related summary for policymakers is currently under development, and stresses the need to enhance the policy relevance of the Outlook by, inter alia, identifying policy options to speed up the achievement of the internationally agreed goals and to inform global and regional processes and meetings where progress towards the agreed goals will be discussed, including the United Nations Conference on Sustainable Development;

5. *Welcomes* the approval of the programme of work and the budget for the period 2012–2013;

6. *Reiterates* the need for stable, adequate and predictable financial resources for the United Nations Environment Programme, and, in accordance with resolution 2997(XXVII), underlines the need to consider the adequate reflection of all the administrative and management costs of the Programme in the context of the United Nations regular budget;

7. *Takes note* of United Nations Environment Programme Governing Council decision 26/1 of 24 February 2011 on international environmental governance, and of the Nairobi-Helsinki Outcome;

8. *Reiterates* the importance of the Nairobi headquarters location of the United Nations Environment Programme, and requests the Secretary-General to keep the resource needs of the Programme and the United Nations Office at Nairobi under review so as to permit the delivery, in an effective manner, of necessary services to the Programme and to the other United Nations organs and organizations in Nairobi;

9. *Decides* to include in the provisional agenda of its sixty-seventh session, under the item entitled "Sustainable development", a sub-item entitled "Report of the Governing Council of the United Nations Environment Programme on its twelfth special session".

Other matters

Cooperation with UN Scientific Committee on the Effects of Atomic Radiation

The General Assembly, in **resolution 66/70** of 9 December (see p. 587), requested UNEP to continue supporting the work of the United Nations Scientific Committee on the Effects of Atomic Radiation and for the dissemination of its findings to the Assembly, the scientific community and the public. The Assembly urged UNEP to continue to strengthen the Committee's funding, and encouraged Member States to make voluntary contributions to the UNEP general trust fund to support the Committee's work.

UNEP Year Book

The *UNEP Year Book 2011: Emerging issues in our global environment* provided information on international environmental events and developments during 2010, and highlighted three emerging issues: plastic debris in the ocean; phosphorus and food production; and forest biodiversity. It also presented data and trends regarding environmental indicators, including those related to the depletion of the ozone layer, climate change, natural resource use, biodiversity loss, waste, water and environmental governance.

Global Environment Facility

The Global Environment Facility (GEF) united 182 member Governments in partnership with international institutions, non-governmental organizations (NGOs) and the private sector to address environmental issues. The GEF partnership comprised 10 UN bodies: UNEP, UNDP, the World Bank, FAO, the United Nations Industrial Development Organization, the African Development Bank, the Asian Development Bank, the European Bank for Reconstruction and Development, the Inter-American Development Bank and the International Fund for Agricultural Development. GEF served as the financial mechanism for the 1992 Convention on Biological Diversity [YUN 1992, p. 683], the 1992 United Nations Framework Convention on Climate Change (UNFCCC) [ibid., p. 681], the 1994 United Nations Convention to Combat Desertification in Those Countries Experiencing Serious Drought and/or Desertification, Particularly in Africa (UNCCD) [YUN 1994, p. 944], and the 2001 Stockholm Convention on Persistent Organic Pollutants [YUN 2001, p. 971].

In 2010–2011, GEF provided $326 million in new grants in conjunction with $2.04 billion in co-financing for a total of $2.4 billion. GEF allocations per focal area amounted to $84.41 million ($1,676.71 million in co-financing) for climate change; $24.60 million ($50.41 million in co-financing) for biodiversity; $17.37 million ($64.44 million in co-financing) for persistent organic pollutants; $5.40 million ($17.90 million in co-financing) for land degradation; and $2.60 million ($5.55 million in co-financing) for ozone-depleting substances. In addition, $192.11 million ($227.48 million in co-financing) was allocated for the multifocal area.

At its twenty-sixth session, the UNEP Council/Forum [A/66/25 (dec. 26/8)] took note of the report of the Executive Director and supporting material on amendments to the Instrument for the Establishment of the Restructured Global Environment Facility [YUN 2010, p. 1018]. It adopted the amendment by which GEF would be made available to serve as a financial mechanism for UNCCD; and the amendment to paragraph 21 of the Instrument relating to the appointment and term of the GEF Chief Executive Officer/Chairperson.

In its report [FCCC/CP/2011/7] to the seventeenth (2011) session of the Conference of the Parties to UNFCCC (see below), GEF described its achievements since its establishment in 1991, including, among other efforts, recent activities related to climate change mitigation, technology transfer, climate change adaptation, and enabling activities funded from the GEF Trust Fund, the Least Developed Countries Fund and the Special Climate Change Fund; and on responses to Convention guidance and the sixteenth (2010) Conference of the Parties [YUN 2010, p. 1019]. GEF reported on its strategies, programmes and projects for financing the agreed incremental costs of activities concerning desertification [ICCD/CRIC(10)/23] to the tenth session of the Conference of the Parties to UNCCD (see p. 982). In its report to the fifth (2011) meeting of the Conference of the Parties to the Stockholm Convention (see p. 984), the Facility set forth its activities in the area covered by the Convention from 1 November 2008 to 30 June 2010 and provided responses to Convention guidance, particularly GEF-related decisions from the fourth (2009) session of the Conference of the Parties [YUN 2009, p. 1035] [UNEP/POPS/COP.5/24].

International conventions and mechanisms

In response to General Assembly resolutions 65/159 [YUN 2010, p. 1020], 65/160 [ibid., p. 1026] and 65/161 [ibid., p. 1023], the Secretary-General, in an August note [A/66/291], transmitted reports submitted by the secretariats of the United Nations Framework Convention on Climate Change (see below), the United Nations Convention to Combat Desertification in Those Countries Experiencing Serious Drought and/or Desertification, Particularly in Africa (see p. 981), and the Convention on Biological Diversity (see p. 980)—collectively known as the 'Rio Conventions'.

Joint Liaison Group. The eleventh meeting of the Joint Liaison Group of the Rio Conventions (Bonn, Germany, 11 April) discussed activities undertaken by the Group; support for the coordination of national planning and reporting processes; cooperation on gender mainstreaming; plans for events at the United Nations Conference on Sustainable Development, to be held in 2012 (Rio+20); and outreach and communication initiatives. The Group agreed to formalize its terms of reference and modus operandi; identified a set of joint high-level activities for the Conference and for the twentieth anniversary of the conventions in 2012; and decided on new and revised joint publications on climate change adaptation, forests and gender.

Convention on climate change

As at 31 December, 194 States and the European Union (EU) were parties to the United Nations Framework Convention on Climate Change (UNFCCC), which was opened for signature in 1992 [YUN 1992, p. 681] and entered into force in 1994 [YUN 1994, p. 938]. Andorra acceded to the Convention during the year.

At year's end, 191 States and the EU were parties to the Kyoto Protocol to the Convention [YUN 1997, p. 1048], which entered into force in 2005 [YUN 2005, p. 1146]. There were 26 parties to the 2006 amendment to annex B of the Protocol [YUN 2006, p. 1220], which had not yet entered into force. Cuba, Georgia and Kazakhstan deposited their instruments of ratification in 2011.

Pursuant to General Assembly resolution 65/159 [YUN 2010, p. 1020], the Secretary-General, in his August note [A/66/291] on the implementation of UN environmental conventions, transmitted to the Assembly the report of the UNFCCC secretariat. The report recapitulated the outcomes of the sixteenth (2010) session of the Conference of the Parties to the Convention [ibid.] and the sixth (2010) session of the Conference of the Parties serving as the Meeting of the Parties to the Kyoto Protocol [ibid.]. It also reviewed progress in implementing the Cancún Agreements [ibid., p. 1019], as parties continued their negotiations on such matters as the technology mechanism; mitigation; the United Nations Collaborative Programme on Reducing Emissions from Deforestation and Forest Degradation in Developing Countries, including the role of conservation, the sustainable management of forests, and enhancement of forest carbon stocks (REDD+); finance; and further commitments for annex I parties under the Kyoto Protocol.

Communication. By an 8 June letter [A/65/862], Ecuador transmitted a proposed new market ("Net Avoided Emissions") mechanism for mitigation.

Conference of parties. The seventeenth session of the Conference of the Parties to UNFCCC (Durban, South Africa, 28 November–9 December 2011) [FCCC/CP/2011/9 & Add.1,2] adopted 19 decisions, including, most critically, decisions concerning a second commitment period under the Kyoto Protocol, to start in January 2013; affirming the mitigation pledges under the Convention covering the period until 2020 made by 89 countries, both industrialized and developing, and covering 80 per cent of global emissions; reaching agreement on how and by when developed and developing countries would report on those mitigation efforts, as well as on the details of verifying them; and identifying a path towards the future legal climate framework that would be applicable to all. Countries set a deadline of 2015 for the conclusion of those negotiations and a deadline of 2020 for the entry into force of the new agreement. The Conference of the Parties also agreed on the need to increase the level of ambition to curb greenhouse gases, as informed by the review of the adequacy of the global temperature goal of 2 degrees Celsius to be carried out during the 2013–2015 period, as well as by the next assessment report of the Intergovernmental Panel on Climate Change.

The Conference also adopted decisions concerning results-based financing for activities related to reducing emissions from deforestation and forest degradation in developing countries (REDD); REDD+; the Green Climate Fund; the operationalization of the Technology Mechanism, including the terms of reference for the Climate Technology Centre and Network; modalities and procedures for the Technology Executive Committee; and collaboration with GEF.

Meeting of Protocol parties. The seventh session of the Conference of the Parties serving as the Meeting of the Parties to the Kyoto Protocol [FCCC/KP/CMP/2011/10 & Add.1,2], held concurrently with the seventeenth session of the Conference of the Parties to UNFCCC, adopted 17 decisions. It agreed that the second commitment period under the Protocol was to begin on 1 January 2013 and was to last for a period of five or eight years, with the latter to be decided in 2012, and that countries that would participate in the second commitment period would convert their emission reduction targets into quantified objectives. Other decisions concerned land use, land-use change and forestry; emissions trading and the project-based mechanisms; greenhouse gases, sectors and source categories, common metrics to calculate the carbon dioxide equivalence of anthropogenic emissions by sources and removals by sinks, and other methodological issues; and information on potential environmental, economic and social consequences, including spillover effects, of tools, policies, measures and methodologies available to annex I parties.

In November [FCCC/KP/CMP/2011/3 (Part I, II)], the Executive Board of the Protocol's clean development mechanism issued its annual report covering its work from 15 October 2010 to 26 October 2011.

Subsidiary bodies. During the year, the Subsidiary Body for Scientific and Technological Advice held its thirty-fourth (Bonn, Germany, 6–16 June) [FCCC/SBSTA/2011/2] and thirty-fifth (Durban, South Africa, 28 November–3 December) [FCCC/SBSTA/2011/5] sessions. The Subsidiary Body for Implementation also held its thirty-fourth (Bonn, 6–17 June) [FCCC/SBI/2011/7 & Add.1] and thirty-fifth (Durban, 28 November–3 December) [FCCC/SBI/2011/17] sessions.

Security Council consideration. On 20 July [S/PV.6587], the Security Council held an open debate on the impact of climate change in the context of the maintenance of international peace and security. The Council had before it a concept note prepared by Germany [S/2011/408]; another was submitted by Nauru [S/2011/436]. The Secretary-General, addressing the Council, said that the agreements reached in the context of UNFCCC in Copenhagen [YUN 2009, p. 1015] and Cancún [YUN 2010, p. 1019] provided a foundation for action on reducing greenhouse gas emissions enabling countries to adapt, but operationalization of the agreements, including those on protecting forests, adaptation and technology, had to be accelerated. Ambitious targets were needed to ensure that any increase in global average temperature remained below 2 degrees Celsius. The Council could play a vital role in making clear the link between climate change, peace and security and mobilizing action. The UNEP Executive Director also addressed the Council.

SECURITY COUNCIL ACTION

On 20 July [meeting 6587], following consultations among the Security Council members, the President made statement **S/PRST/2011/15** on behalf of the Council:

The Security Council reaffirms its primary responsibility under the Charter of the United Nations for the maintenance of international peace and security. The Council stresses the importance of establishing strategies of conflict prevention.

The Council recognizes the responsibility for sustainable development issues, including climate change, conferred upon the General Assembly and the Economic and Social Council.

The Council underlines General Assembly resolution 63/281 of 3 June 2009, which reaffirms that the United Nations Framework Convention on Climate Change is the key instrument for addressing climate change, recalls the provisions of the Convention, including the acknowledgement that the global nature of climate change calls for the widest possible cooperation by all countries and their participation in an effective and appropriate international response, in accordance with their common but differentiated responsibilities and respective capabilities and their social and economic conditions, and invites the relevant organs of the United Nations, as appropriate and within their respective mandates, to intensify their efforts in considering and addressing climate change, including its possible security implications.

The Council notes General Assembly resolution 65/159 of 20 December 2010 entitled 'Protection of global climate for present and future generations of humankind'.

The Council notes that, in response to the request contained in General Assembly resolution 63/281, the Secretary-General submitted a report to the Assembly on climate change and its possible security implications.

The Council expresses its concern that possible adverse effects of climate change may, in the long run, aggravate certain existing threats to international peace and security.

The Council expresses its concern that possible security implications of loss of territory of some States caused by sea-level rise may arise, in particular in small low-lying island States.

The Council notes that, in matters relating to the maintenance of international peace and security under its consideration, conflict analysis and contextual information on, inter alia, possible security implications of climate change is important, when such issues are drivers of conflict, represent a challenge to the implementation of Council mandates or endanger the process of consolidation of peace. In this regard, the Council requests the Secretary-General to ensure that his reporting to the Council contains such contextual information.

GENERAL ASSEMBLY ACTION

On 22 December [meeting 91], the General Assembly, on the recommendation of the Second Committee [A/66/440/Add.4], adopted **resolution 66/200** without vote [agenda item 19 (*d*)].

Protection of global climate for present and future generations of humankind

The General Assembly,

Recalling its resolutions 43/53 of 6 December 1988, 54/222 of 22 December 1999, 62/86 of 10 December 2007, 63/32 of 26 November 2008, 64/73 of 7 December 2009 and 65/159 of 20 December 2010 and other resolutions and decisions relating to the protection of the global climate for present and future generations of humankind,

Recalling also the principles and provisions of the United Nations Framework Convention on Climate Change,

Recalling further the United Nations Millennium Declaration, the Johannesburg Declaration on Sustainable Development and the Plan of Implementation of the World Summit on Sustainable Development ("Johannesburg Plan of Implementation"), the 2005 World Summit Outcome, the outcome of the thirteenth session of the Conference of the Parties to the United Nations Framework Convention and of the third session of the Conference of the Parties serving as the Meeting of the Parties to the Kyoto Protocol, held in Bali, Indonesia, from 3 to 15 December 2007, and the outcomes of all the sessions, the Programme of Action for the Sustainable Development of Small Island Developing States, the Mauritius Declaration and the Mauritius Strategy for the Further Implementation of the Programme of Action for the Sustainable Development of Small Island Developing States, and the Programme of Action for the Least Developed Countries for the Decade 2011–2020, adopted at the Fourth United Nations Conference on the Least Developed Countries, held in Istanbul, Turkey, from 9 to 13 May 2011,

Reaffirming its commitment to the ultimate objective of the Convention, namely, to stabilize greenhouse gas concentrations in the atmosphere at a level that prevents dangerous anthropogenic interference with the climate system, and also reaffirming that such a level should be achieved within a time frame sufficient to allow ecosystems to adapt naturally to climate change, to ensure that food production is not threatened and to enable economic development to proceed in a sustainable manner,

Reaffirming the financial obligations of developed country parties and other developed parties included in annex II to the Convention under the Convention and the Kyoto Protocol,

1. *Recalls* the outcome of the sixteenth session of the Conference of the Parties to the United Nations Framework Convention on Climate Change and of the sixth session of the Conference of the Parties serving as the Meeting of the Parties to the Kyoto Protocol, hosted in Cancun, Mexico, by the Government of Mexico from 29 November to 10 December 2010;
2. *Recognizes* the need to build on the existing political momentum with a view to further advancing climate change negotiations;
3. *Takes note* of the report of the Executive Secretary of the United Nations Framework Convention on Climate Change on the United Nations Climate Change Conference and its follow-up;
4. *Underlines* the importance of achieving an ambitious, substantive, holistic and balanced outcome through the ongoing negotiations at the Conference of the Parties to the Convention and the Meeting of the Parties to the Kyoto Protocol;
5. *Notes with appreciation* that the Government of South Africa hosted the seventeenth session of the Conference of the Parties to the Convention and the seventh session of the Conference of the Parties serving as the Meeting of the Parties to the Kyoto Protocol in Durban from 28 November to 9 December 2011;
6. *Notes* the ongoing preparatory process for the United Nations Conference on Sustainable Development, to be held in Rio de Janeiro, Brazil, from 20 to 22 June 2012;
7. *Invites* the secretariat of the Convention to report, through the Secretary-General, to the General Assembly at its sixty-seventh session on the work of the Conference of the Parties;
8. *Requests* the Secretary-General to make provisions for the sessions of the Conference of the Parties to the Convention and its subsidiary bodies in his proposal for the programme budget for the biennium 2012–2013;
9. *Decides* to include in the provisional agenda of its sixty-seventh session, under the item entitled "Sustainable development", the sub-item entitled "Protection of global climate for present and future generations of humankind".

Vienna Convention and Montreal Protocol

As at 31 December, 195 States and the eu were parties to the 1985 Vienna Convention for the Protection of the Ozone Layer [YUN 1985, p. 804], which entered into force in 1988 [YUN 1988, p. 810].

The number of parties to the Montreal Protocol on Substances that Deplete the Ozone Layer, which was adopted in 1987 [YUN 1987, p. 686], included 195 States and the eu. Parties to the 1990 Amendment to the Protocol [YUN 1990, p. 522] numbered 195 States and the eu. Parties to the 1992 Amendment [YUN 1992, p. 684] numbered 193 States and the eu, with Angola and Kazakhstan becoming parties during the year. Parties to the 1997 Amendment [YUN 1997, p. 1049] numbered 184 States and the eu, with Angola, Kazakhstan and Vanuatu becoming parties. Parties to the 1999 Amendment [YUN 1999, p. 986] numbered 171 States and the EU, with Angola, Bosnia and Herzegovina, Cabo Verde, Georgia, Solomon Islands and Vanuatu becoming parties.

Conference of parties and Meeting of Protocol parties. The combined ninth meeting of the Conference of the Parties to the Vienna Convention and the twenty-third meeting of the Parties to the Montreal Protocol (Bali, Indonesia, 21–25 November) [UNEP/OzL.Conv.9/7-UNEP/OzL.Pro.23/11] adopted 4 and 33 decisions, respectively, concerning the ratification status of the Convention, Protocol and amendments; essential-use nominations for controlled substances for 2012; essential-use exemption for chlorofluorocarbon-113 for aerospace applications in the Russian Federation; critical-use exemptions for methyl bromide for 2013, and its quarantine and pre-shipment uses; global laboratory and analytical-use exemptions; carbon tetrachloride; alternatives to and destruction technologies for ozone-depleting substances; the Technology and Economic Assessment Panel and its subsidiary bodies; non-compliance and non-reporting by parties; requests for the revision of baseline data; and administrative and financial matters.

Subsidiary bodies. The Open-ended Working Group of the Parties to the Montreal Protocol held its thirty-first meeting (Montreal, Canada, 1–5 August) [UNEP/OzL.Pro.WG.1/31/6]; and the Implementation Committee under the Non-Compliance Procedure for the Montreal Protocol held its forty-sixth (Montreal, 7–8 August) [UNEP/OzL.Pro/ImpCom/46/5] and forty-seventh (Bali, 18–19 November) [UNEP/OzL.Pro/ImpCom/47/6] sessions.

Convention on air pollution

As at 31 December, the number of parties to the 1979 Convention on Long-range Transboundary Air Pollution [YUN 1979, p. 710], which entered into force in 1983 [YUN 1983, p. 645], remained at 50 States and the EU. Eight protocols to the Convention dealt with the programme for monitoring and evaluation of pollutants in Europe (1984); the reduction of sulphur emissions or their transboundary fluxes by at least 30 per cent (1985); the control of emissions of nitrogen oxides or their transboundary fluxes (1988); the control of volatile organic compounds or their transboundary fluxes (1991); the further reduction of sulphur emissions (1994); heavy metals (1998); persistent organic pollutants (1998); and the abatement of acidification, eutrophication and ground-level ozone (1999). Amendments to the protocol on persistent organic pollutants were adopted in 2009 [YUN 2009, p. 1018].

The twenty-ninth session of the Executive Body for the Convention (Geneva, 12–16 December) [ECE/EB.AIR/109 & Cor.1 & Add.1] adopted 14 decisions concerning the review and revision of protocols; compliance by numerous parties with their protocol obligations; reporting of persistent organic pollutants emissions; and the Action Plan for the Implementation of the Long-term Strategy for the Convention. It also adopted the 2012–2013 work plan for the implementation of the Convention [ECE/EB.AIR/109/Add.2].

Convention on Biological Diversity

As at 31 December, 192 States and the EU were parties to the 1992 Convention on Biological Diversity [YUN 1992, p. 683], which entered into force in 1993 [YUN 1993, p. 810].

At year's end, the number of parties to the Cartagena Protocol on Biosafety, which was adopted in 2000 [YUN 2000, p. 973] and entered into force in 2003 [YUN 2003, p. 1051], rose to 161 States and the EU. Morocco and Uruguay became parties during the year.

In his August note [A/66/291] on the implementation of UN environmental conventions, the Secretary-General, pursuant to resolution 65/161 [YUN 2010, p. 1023], transmitted to the General Assembly the report submitted by the secretariat of the Convention. The report recapitulated the outcome of the tenth (2010) meeting of the Conference of the Parties to the Convention [ibid., p. 1022] and that of the fifth (2010) meeting of the Conference of the Parties to the Convention serving as the Meeting of the Parties to the Cartagena Protocol on Biosafety to the Convention on Biological Diversity [ibid., p. 1023], as well as meetings of subsidiary organs; activities undertaken in the context of the International Year of Biodiversity [YUN 2010, p. 1030] and other UN observances; and collaboration with the UNFCCC and UNCCD secretariats and other conventions related to biodiversity.

Subsidiary bodies. The seventh meeting of the Ad Hoc Open-ended Inter-Sessional Working Group on Article 8(j) and Related Provisions of the Convention on Biological Diversity (Montreal, 31 October–4 November) [UNEP/CBD/COP/11/7] made eight recommendations to the Conference of the Parties at its eleventh (2012) meeting concerning progress in the implementation of article 8(j) relating to traditional knowledge; mechanisms to promote the participation of indigenous and local communities in Convention work; the revised multi-year programme of work; benefit-sharing from and the unlawful appropriation of traditional knowledge; the development of elements of sui generis systems for the protection of traditional knowledge; customary sustainable use as a new major component of the Article 8(j) work programme; the development of indicators relevant to traditional knowledge and customary sustainable use; and recommendations of the United Nations Permanent

Forum on Indigenous Issues and terms of reference for the development of guidelines on repatriation.

The fifteenth meeting of the Subsidiary Body on Scientific, Technical and Technological Advice (Montreal, 7–11 November) [UNEP/CBD/COP/11/2] adopted eight recommendations to the eleventh (2012) Conference of the Parties concerning indicators and other tools for assessing progress in implementing the Strategic Plan for Biodiversity 2011–2020; ecosystem restoration; the capacity-building strategy for the Global Taxonomy Initiative; invasive alien species; the biological diversity of inland water ecosystems; the sustainable use of biodiversity; Arctic biodiversity; and improving the effectiveness of the Subsidiary Body.

Communication. By a 28 September letter [A/66/391], Switzerland transmitted the Geneva Call for Urgent Action on the Implementation of the Successful Nagoya Outcomes, which resulted from the annual high-level meeting of past, present and future Convention Presidents (Chateau Bossey, Switzerland, 3 September).

UN Decade on Biodiversity

The Executive Secretary of the Convention on Biological Diversity, in his report on the work of the Conference of the Parties to the Convention in 2011, contained in a note by the Secretary-General [A/67/295], provided information on the United Nations Decade on Biodiversity 2011–2020, declared by the General Assembly in resolution 65/161 [YUN 2010, p. 1023]. In September, the Convention secretariat signed a memorandum of cooperation with 27 international agencies, organizations and multilateral environmental conventions with respect to activities to be carried out under the aegis of the Decade in support of the Strategic Plan for Biodiversity 2011–2020 and the Aichi Biodiversity Targets, adopted in 2010 [YUN 2010, p. 1023]. UNESCO organized an event on the margins of its 2011 General Conference (Paris, 25 October–11 November) to mark the organization's new biodiversity strategy and its contribution to the Decade. Following numerous regional events, the global launch of the Decade took place from 17 to 19 December in Japan.

GENERAL ASSEMBLY ACTION

On 22 December [meeting 91], the General Assembly, on the recommendation of the Second Committee [A/66/440/Add.6], adopted **resolution 66/202** without vote [agenda item 19 (*f*)].

Convention on Biological Diversity

The General Assembly,

Recalling its resolutions 64/203 of 21 December 2009 and 65/161 of 20 December 2010 and previous resolutions relating to the Convention on Biological Diversity,

Acknowledging the importance of the upcoming United Nations Conference on Sustainable Development,

1. *Takes note* of the report of the Executive Secretary of the Convention on Biological Diversity on the progress of work of the Conference of the Parties to the Convention;
2. *Notes* the ongoing preparatory process for the United Nations Conference on Sustainable Development, to be held in Rio de Janeiro, Brazil, from 20 to 22 June 2012;
3. *Stresses* the importance of the continued substantive consideration of the issue of biological diversity;
4. *Notes with appreciation* the offer of the Government of India to host the eleventh meeting of the Conference of the Parties to the Convention from 8 to 19 October 2012, and the sixth meeting of the Conference of the Parties serving as the Meeting of the Parties to the Cartagena Protocol on Biosafety from 1 to 5 October 2012;
5. *Invites* the secretariat of the Convention to report, through the Secretary-General, to the General Assembly at its sixty-seventh session on the work of the Conference of the Parties;
6. *Decides* to include in the provisional agenda of its sixty-seventh session, under the item entitled "Sustainable development", the sub-item entitled "Convention on Biological Diversity".

Convention to combat desertification

As at 31 December, the number of parties to the 1994 United Nations Convention to Combat Desertification in Those Countries Experiencing Serious Drought and/or Desertification, Particularly in Africa (UNCCD) [YUN 1994, p. 944], which entered into force in 1996 [YUN 1996, p. 958], stood at 193 States and the EU.

In his August note on the implementation of UN environmental conventions [A/66/291], the Secretary-General transmitted to the General Assembly the report of the Convention secretariat. The report reviewed the preparations for the high-level meeting on the theme "Addressing desertification, land degradation and drought in the context of sustainable development and poverty eradication" (see p. 982); meetings of subsidiary bodies; activities undertaken in the context of the Decade for Deserts and the Fight against Desertification (2010–2020), declared by the Assembly in resolution 62/195 [YUN 2007, p. 1046], and other UN observances; and collaboration with GEF, UNFCCC and the Convention on Biodiversity.

Subsidiary bodies. The ninth session of the Committee for the Review of the Implementation of the Convention (CRIC) (Bonn, Germany, 21–25 February) [ICCD/CRIC(9)/16], considered issues relating to preliminary analyses of information contained in the reports of parties, UN agencies, intergovernmental organizations, and civil society organizations on implementation of the Convention against performance indicators; best practices in the implementation of the Convention; and improving the procedures for communication of information.

The second special session of the Committee on Science and Technology (CST) (Bonn, 16–25 February) [ICCD/CST(S-2)/9] considered the status of work on methodologies and baselines for the effective use of the subset of impact indicators on strategic objectives 1, 2 and 3 of the 10-year Strategic Plan and Framework [YUN 2007, p. 1064] to enhance the implementation of the Convention, along with an assessment of the outcome of the first Scientific Conference [YUN 2009, p. 1022]; preparations for the second Scientific Conference; the role of science and technology correspondents; and progress made on the implementation of the knowledge-management system.

The tenth sessions of CRIC and CST took place concurrently with the tenth session of the Conference of the Parties to UNCCD in October (see below).

High-level meeting. Pursuant to resolution 65/160 [YUN 2010, p. 1026] the General Assembly, on 20 September [A/66/PV.6], convened a high-level meeting on the theme "Addressing desertification, land degradation and drought in the context of sustainable development and poverty eradication". The meeting, which included two panel discussions, had before it a June note by the Secretary-General [A/65/861] transmitting a report submitted by the UNCCD secretariat in preparation for the meeting. The Secretary-General asked meeting participants to resolve to reverse the trend of land degradation and recognize that resisting desertification, preserving drylands and nurturing the communities that depended on them lay at the core of sustainable development. The Assembly President, in his concluding statement [A/66/PV.9], said that participants had decided that if arid land was to become a source of common prosperity, land use and policy had to be addressed in accordance with sustainable development principles. Prevention was the most effective way to cope with land degradation; such efforts had to go hand-in-hand with those aimed at poverty eradication and contribute to the realization of the Millennium Development Goals. Many world leaders called for strengthening the scientific base of the Convention with a view to better understanding desertification, land degradation and drought; promoting the implementation of the Convention as a global policy and monitoring framework for addressing issues of land and soil degradation in all ecosystems affected by land degradation; and setting up a measurable sustainable development goal and targets related to land degradation.

Conference of parties. The tenth session of the Conference of the Parties to UNCCD (Changwon City, Republic of Korea, 10–21 October) [ICCD/COP(10)/31 & Add.1] adopted 39 decisions, among which were decisions on the implementation of the Convention, including issues related to science, technology and knowledge, with a view to making the Convention a global authority on scientific and technical knowledge pertaining to desertification, land degradation and drought. Other decisions concerned the 10-year strategic plan and framework (2008–2018) for enhancing UNCCD implementation; the governance and institutional arrangements of the Global Mechanism; collaboration with GEF; the high-level meeting of the General Assembly to address desertification, land degradation and drought (see above); and preparations for Rio+20. Three round tables addressed desertification, land degradation and drought and food security; UNCCD in the context of Rio+20; and harnessing science and knowledge for combating desertification, land degradation and drought.

GENERAL ASSEMBLY ACTION

On 22 December [meeting 91], the General Assembly, on the recommendation of the Second Committee [A/66/440/Add.5], adopted **resolution 66/201** without vote [agenda item 19 (e)].

Implementation of the United Nations Convention to Combat Desertification in Those Countries Experiencing Serious Drought and/or Desertification, Particularly in Africa

The General Assembly,

Recalling its resolutions 58/211 of 23 December 2003, 61/202 of 20 December 2006, 62/193 of 19 December 2007, 63/218 of 19 December 2008, 64/202 of 21 December 2009 and 65/160 of 20 December 2010, as well as other resolutions relating to the implementation of the United Nations Convention to Combat Desertification in Those Countries Experiencing Serious Drought and/or Desertification, Particularly in Africa,

Concerned by the negative economic impacts of desertification, land degradation and drought, and in this regard welcoming the organization of the second United Nations Convention to Combat Desertification Scientific Conference, on the theme "Economic assessment of desertification, sustainable land management and resilience of arid, semi-arid and dry subhumid areas", to be held by March 2013 at the latest,

Concerned also by the increasing frequency and severity of dust storms and sandstorms affecting arid and semi-arid regions and their negative impact on the environment and the economy,

Noting the need for enhanced cooperation among the secretariats of the United Nations Convention to Combat Desertification, the United Nations Framework Convention on Climate Change and the Convention on Biological Diversity, while respecting their individual mandates,

Underlining the cross-sectoral nature of desertification, land degradation and drought mitigation, and in this regard inviting all relevant United Nations organizations to cooperate with the secretariat of the United Nations Convention to Combat Desertification in supporting an effective response to those challenges,

Expressing its deep appreciation to the Government of the Republic of Korea for hosting the tenth session of the Conference of the Parties to the Convention in Changwon City from 10 to 21 October 2011,

Taking note of the high-level meeting of the General Assembly on the theme "Addressing desertification, land degradation and drought in the context of sustainable development and poverty eradication", which emphasized that the United Nations Convention to Combat Desertification serves as a tool for achieving, inter alia, food security, poverty eradication and sustainable development, for promoting sustainable land use in drylands, and for enhancing the scientific process so that desertification, land degradation and drought issues are better understood, and acknowledging the comprehensive work carried out by the focal point and the secretariat of the United Nations Convention to Combat Desertification in organizing the high-level meeting,

Acknowledging the importance of the upcoming United Nations Conference on Sustainable Development,

1. *Takes note* of the report of the Secretary-General on the implementation of resolution 65/160 and on the implementation of the United Nations Convention to Combat Desertification in Those Countries Experiencing Serious Drought and/or Desertification, Particularly in Africa;

2. *Expresses deep concern* about the critical situation in the Horn of Africa region, which is experiencing one of the worst droughts in history, and underlines that this situation highlights the need for the effective implementation of the Convention and its ten-year strategic plan and framework to enhance the implementation of the Convention (2008–2018), through short-, medium- and long-term measures;

3. *Welcomes* the outcomes of the tenth session of the Conference of the Parties to the Convention, and emphasizes the need to implement the decisions adopted at the session;

4. *Also welcomes* the effort by the Conference of the Parties to the Convention to find lasting solutions with respect to the governance and institutional arrangements of the Global Mechanism, as a follow-up to various external assessments undertaken, including the 2009 report of the Joint Inspection Unit, with a view to better servicing the Conference of the Parties;

5. *Recommends* the strengthening of the advisory role of the Committee for the Review of the Implementation of the Convention and the Committee on Science and Technology, through their recommendations, in order to monitor effectively the decisions of the Conference of the Parties to the Convention;

6. *Notes* the continuing need for strengthening the scientific basis of the Convention and the decision of the Conference of the Parties to the Convention at its tenth session to establish an ad hoc working group, taking into consideration regional balance, to further discuss options for the provision of scientific advice focusing on desertification, land degradation and drought issues, taking into account the regional approach of the Convention;

7. *Also notes* the efforts under way for the development and implementation of scientifically based and sound methods for monitoring and assessing desertification;

8. *Invites* the Global Environment Facility, in further enhancing resource allocation during future replenishments, to consider increasing allocations to the land degradation focal area, depending on the availability of resources;

9. *Notes* the importance of the participation of civil society organizations and other stakeholders in the sessions of the Conference of the Parties to the Convention and its subsidiary bodies in accordance with the rules of procedure of the Conference of the Parties, as well as the involvement of these stakeholders in the implementation of the Convention and the ten-year strategic plan and framework to enhance the implementation of the Convention;

10. *Reaffirms its resolve* to support and strengthen the implementation of the Convention, with a view to addressing causes of desertification, land degradation and drought, as well as poverty resulting from land degradation, through, inter alia, the mobilization of adequate and predictable financial resources, the transfer of technology on mutually agreed terms and capacity-building;

11. *Notes* the ongoing preparatory process for the United Nations Conference on Sustainable Development, to be held in Rio de Janeiro, Brazil, from 20 to 22 June 2012;

12. *Reaffirms* the continuation of the current institutional linkage and related administrative arrangements between the Convention secretariat and the United Nations Secretariat for a further five-year period, to be reviewed by both the General Assembly and the Conference of the Parties to the Convention no later than 31 December 2017, as decided by the Conference of the Parties at its tenth session;

13. *Decides* to include in the United Nations calendar of conferences and meetings for the biennium 2012–2013 the sessions of the Conference of the Parties to the Convention and its subsidiary bodies envisaged for the biennium and requests the Secretary-General to make provisions for the sessions of the Conference of the Parties and its subsidiary bodies when submitting the proposed programme budget for the biennium 2012–2013;

14. *Also decides* to include in the provisional agenda of its sixty-seventh session, under the item entitled "Sustainable development", the sub-item entitled "Implementation of the United Nations Convention to Combat Desertification in Those Countries Experiencing Serious Drought and/or Desertification, Particularly in Africa";

15. *Requests* the Secretary-General to submit to the General Assembly at its sixty-seventh session a report on the implementation of the present resolution.

Basel Convention

As at 31 December, 177 States and the EU were parties to the 1989 Basel Convention on the Control of Transboundary Movements of Hazardous Wastes and their Disposal [YUN 1989, p. 420], which entered into force in 1992 [YUN 1992, p. 685]. Iraq, Palau and Suriname became parties during the year. The 1995 amendment to the Convention [YUN 1995, p. 1333], not yet in force, had been ratified, accepted or approved by 72 parties, with Argentina, Malta and Zambia becoming parties in 2011. The number of parties to the 1999 Basel Protocol on Liability and Compensation for Damage resulting from Transboundary Movement of Hazardous Wastes and Their Disposal [YUN 1999, p. 998], not yet in force, remained at 10.

Conference of parties. The tenth meeting of the Conference of the Parties to the Convention (Cartagena de Indias, Colombia, 17–21 October) [UNEP/CHW.10/28] adopted the Cartagena Declaration on the Prevention, Minimization and Recovery of Hazardous Wastes and Other Wastes, which reaffirmed that the Basel Convention was the primary global legal instrument for guiding the environmentally sound management of hazardous and other wastes and their disposal. Among the 29 decisions adopted were those concerning the strategic framework for the implementation of the Convention for 2012–2021; operation of the Convention regional and coordinating centres; technical guidelines; cooperation with the International Maritime Organization and World Customs Organization; cooperation and coordination among the Basel, Rotterdam and Stockholm conventions; national legislation, enforcement of the Convention and efforts to combat illegal traffic; environmentally sound dismantling of ships; the Partnership Programme, the Partnership for Action on Computing Equipment and the Mobile Phone Partnership Initiative; capacity-building for the implementation of the Convention; and administrative and budgetary matters.

Rotterdam Convention

As at 31 December, 145 States and the EU were parties to the 1998 Rotterdam Convention on the Prior Informed Consent Procedure for Certain Hazardous Chemicals and Pesticides in International Trade [YUN 1998, p. 997], which entered into force in 2004 [YUN 2004, p. 1063]. Honduras, Israel, Montenegro, Morocco, the Russian Federation and Zambia became parties during the year.

The Chemical Review Committee, at its seventh meeting (Rome, 28 March–1 April) [UNEP/FAO/RC/CRC.7/15], recommended to the Conference of the Parties to the Rotterdam Convention (see below) that two pesticides—endosulfan and azinphos methyl—and one severely hazardous pesticide formulation—Gramoxone Super—be included in the Convention's Prior Informed Consent procedure. It also recommended for inclusion three industrial chemicals: perfluorooctane sulfonate (PFOS), its salts and precursors; pentaBDE commercial mixtures; and octaBDE commercial mixtures.

Conference of parties. The fifth meeting of the Conference of the Parties to the Convention (Geneva, 20–24 June) [UNEP/FAO/RC/COP.5/26] adopted 14 decisions, concerning the listing of alachlor, aldicarb and endosulfan in Annex III to the Convention; financial rules and financial mechanisms; notifications of final regulatory actions; procedures and mechanisms on compliance with the Convention; Chemical Review Committee appointments; information exchange; cooperation and coordination among the Basel, Rotterdam and Stockholm conventions; cooperation with the World Trade Organization; technical assistance: workplan for the biennium 2012–2013; and financing and budget for the biennium 2012–2013.

Stockholm Convention

As at 31 December, 174 States and the EU were parties to the 2001 Stockholm Convention on Persistent Organic Pollutants (POPs) [YUN 2001, p. 971], which entered into force in 2004 [YUN 2004, p. 1066]. Montenegro, Palau, the Russian Federation and Suriname became parties during the year.

Conference of parties. The fifth meeting of the Conference of the Parties to the Stockholm Convention (Geneva, 25–29 April) [UNEP/POPS/COP.5/36] marked the tenth anniversary of the adoption of the Convention. Among the 29 decisions adopted, parties agreed to list endosulfan in Annex A to the Convention, with specific exemptions. Other decisions concerned further steps in enhancing cooperation and coordination among the Basel, Rotterdam and Stockholm conventions; the continued need for the pesticide DDT for disease vector control; and the endorsement of seven new Convention regional centres—in Algeria, India, Iran, Kenya, Senegal and South Africa as well as the Russian Federation, conditional on that country's ratification of the Convention.

The seventh meeting of the Persistent Organic Pollutants Review Committee (Geneva, 10–14 October) [UNEP/POPS/POPRC.7/19 & Add.1] adopted decisions concerning hexabromocyclododecane; chlorinated naphthalenes; hexachlorobutadiene; alternatives to endosulfan, to perfluorooctane sulfonic acid in open applications, to perfluorooctane sulfonate and its derivatives, and to DDT; the evaluation of brominated diphenyl ethers and the work programme on brominated diphenyl ethers and perfluorooctane sulfonic acid, its salts and perfluorooctane sulfonyl fluoride; toxic interactions; debromination of brominated flame retardants; climate change and persistent organic pollutants; and the Committee's work.

Environmental topics

The atmosphere

Intergovernmental Panel on Climate Change

In 2011, the Intergovernmental Panel on Climate Change (IPCC) held its thirty-third (Abu Dhabi, United Arab Emirates, 10–13 May) and thirty-fourth (Kampala, Uganda, 18–19 November) sessions. At its thirty-third session, the Panel adopted decisions related to the review of IPCC procedures; governance and management; the conflict of interest policy; the IPCC communications strategy; and the trust fund programme and revised 2011 and proposed 2012 budgets. Progress reports were presented on Working Group I and II contributions to the Fifth Assessment Report [YUN 2008, p. 1164]; scenario development and coordination with the scientific community; communications and outreach; the IPCC scholarship programme; IPCC joint expert meetings and workshops; and the Special Report on Managing the Risks of Extreme Events and Disasters to Advance Climate Change Adaptation (SREX).

At its thirty-fourth session, the Panel adopted decisions related to its procedures and conflict of interest policy. Progress reports were presented on Working Group I, II and III contributions to the Fifth Assessment Report; IPCC joint expert meetings and workshops; the task force on national greenhouse gas inventories; the task group on data and scenario support for impact and climate analysis; and the Special Report on Renewable Energy Sources and Climate Change Mitigation (SRREN) and SREX. During the year, IPCC released SRREN, which reviewed the potential of bioenergy, direct solar energy, geothermal energy, hydropower, ocean energy and wind energy; and SREX, which addressed the interaction of climatic, environmental, and human factors that could lead to impacts and disasters, options for managing the risks posed by impacts and disasters, and the role played by non-climatic factors in determining impacts.

Terrestrial ecosystems

Forests

United Nations Forum on Forests

The United Nations Forum on Forests (UNFF), at its ninth session (New York, 1 May 2009 and 24 January–4 February 2011) [E/2011/42], focused on the theme "forests for people". It recommended to the Economic and Social Council draft decisions on the ministerial declaration of the high-level segment of the session; the dates and venue for its tenth session; and its report on the ninth session and provisional agenda for its tenth (2013) session, respectively. UNFF also brought to the attention of the Council its resolution on forests for people, livelihoods and poverty eradication, and its decision to grant accreditation to the intergovernmental organization African Forest Forum to participate as an observer at its ninth and future sessions. Annexed to the report of the session were summaries by the Chairs of the multi-stakeholder dialogue among Member States, major groups and members of the Collaborative Partnership on Forests; and the high-level round tables held during the session.

The Forum had before it reports of the Secretary-General on: the assessment of progress made on the implementation of the non-legally binding instrument on all types of forests [YUN 2007, p. 1072] and towards the achievement of the four global objectives on forests [E/CN.18/2011/2]; regional and subregional inputs [E/CN.18/2011/3]; community-based forest management [E/CN.18/2011/4]; cultural and social values of forests and social development [E/CN.18/2011/5]; conclusions and recommendations for addressing key challenges of forests for people, livelihoods and poverty eradication [E/CN.18/2011/6]; preparations for the International Year of Forests, 2011 [YUN 2010, p. 1031]; the high-level ministerial segment and policy dialogue with heads of international organizations (see below) [E/CN.18/2011/8]; enhanced cooperation and cross-sectoral policy and programme coordination [E/CN.18/2011/10]; and the means of implementation for sustainable forest management [E/CN.18/2011/12 & Corr.1]. It had before it notes by the Secretariat on multi-stakeholder dialogue [E/CN.18/2011/9]; UN trust funds to support UNFF [E/CN.18/2011/14]; and the accreditation of the African Forest Forum [E/CN.18/2011/18]. UNFF also had before it discussion papers submitted by the major groups on social development and indigenous and other local and forest-dependent communities [E/CN.18/2011/9/Add.1] and on forests and culture [E/CN.18/2011/9/Add.2], as well as a paper on the Community Forestry Programme in Nepal [E/CN.18/2011/9/Add.3]; an information document [E/CN.18/2011/11] on the Collaborative Partnership on Forests Framework 2009 and 2010; and the report of the first meeting of the Open-ended Intergovernmental Ad Hoc Expert Group on Forest Financing [YUN 2010, p. 1031].

Communication. In addition to communications submitted earlier [YUN 2010, p. 1031], UNFF had before it at its ninth session an 11 January letter from China [E/CN.18/2011/19] transmitting a summary of an international expert meeting on forests for people (Guilin, China, 17–20 November 2009).

High-level segment. At the high-level segment of the ninth session of UNFF (New York, 2–3 February), four round tables focused on the topics of forests for people; finance for forest-dependent communities; forests-plus: a cross-sectoral and cross-institutional approach; and forests and Rio+20. The high-level dialogue with the heads of the member organizations of the Collaborative Partnership on Forests addressed promoting the International Year of Forests, 2011; forest finance and implementation of the non-legally binding instrument on all types of forests and achievement of the global objectives on forests; and forests and Rio+20. During the segment, the Forum adopted a ministerial declaration on the occasion of the launch of the International Year of Forests, 2011 (see below).

On 27 July, the Economic and Social Council took note of the UNFF report on its ninth session and approved the provisional agenda of its tenth session (**decision 2011/250**); and accepted the offer of Turkey to host the tenth session in Istanbul from 8 to 19 April 2013 (**decision 2011/249**). On the same date, the Council took note of the ministerial declaration of the high-level segment of the ninth UNFF session and decided to transmit it to the General Assembly for its endorsement, as a contribution of the Forum to Rio+20 (**decision 2011/248**).

On 22 December (**decision 66/543**), the Assembly endorsed the ministerial declaration adopted at the high-level segment of the ninth UNFF session on the occasion of the launch of the International Year of Forests, 2011, and decided to transmit it as a contribution of the Forum to Rio+20.

International Year of Forests, 2011

In a later report [E/CN.18/2013/9], the Secretary-General provided an overview of activities held in celebration of the International Year of Forests, 2011, which was launched as a platform to share success stories related to sustainable forest management around the world. The report described lessons learned from awareness-raising activities—including the Forest Heroes awards programme established by the Forum to identify and honour the efforts of people who nurtured, protected and managed forests around the world— and related trends based on information submitted by 70 countries and regional and subregional entities.

Mountains

In response to General Assembly resolution 64/205 [YUN 2009, p. 1028], the Secretary-General submitted an August report [A/66/294] prepared by FAO on the status of sustainable mountain development. The report addressed issues related to biodiversity and mountain ecosystems; climate change; desertification; mountain water; watershed management; disaster risk management; indigenous peoples; gender; payment for environmental services; high-quality mountain products; tourism; policy and law; education; research; and communications and networking regarding sustainable mountain development. In addition to activities at the national level that promoted sustainable mountain development, the report described UN system contributions, including a June meeting on mountain initiatives organized by FAO and the Mountain Partnership, originally known as the International Partnership for Sustainable Development in Mountain Regions, which was launched as an outcome of the 2002 World Summit on Sustainable Development [YUN 2002, p. 821]; a July course of the International Programme on Research and Training on Sustainable Management of Mountain Areas on natural hazards and disaster risk management in mountain areas, organized by the Mountain Partnership and the University of Turin, Italy; and the Second World Landslide Forum held in October, organized by the International Consortium on Landslides and hosted by FAO. The report concluded with recommendations for promoting and sustaining development in mountain regions around the world through international processes, policies, financial mechanisms, awareness-raising and research.

GENERAL ASSEMBLY ACTION

On 22 December [meeting 91], the General Assembly, on the recommendation of the Second Committee [A/66/440/Add.9], adopted **resolution 66/205** without vote [agenda item 19 (*i*)].

Sustainable mountain development

The General Assembly,

Recalling its resolution 53/24 of 10 November 1998, by which it proclaimed 2002 the International Year of Mountains, and noting, in this regard, the Bishkek Mountain Platform, the outcome document of the Global Mountain Summit, held in Bishkek from 28 October to 1 November 2002,

Recalling also its resolutions 55/189 of 20 December 2000, 57/245 of 20 December 2002, 58/216 of 23 December 2003, 59/238 of 22 December 2004, 60/198 of 22 December 2005, 62/196 of 19 December 2007 and 64/205 of 21 December 2009,

Reaffirming chapter 13 of Agenda 21 and all relevant paragraphs of the Plan of Implementation of the World Summit on Sustainable Development ("Johannesburg Plan of Implementation"), in particular paragraph 42 thereof, as the overall policy frameworks for sustainable development in mountain regions,

Noting the International Partnership for Sustainable Development in Mountain Regions ("Mountain Partnership"), launched during the World Summit on Sustainable Development, with benefits from the committed support of fifty countries, sixteen intergovernmental organizations and one hundred and thirteen organizations from major groups, as an important multi-stakeholder approach to addressing the various interrelated dimensions of sustainable development in mountain regions,

Noting also the Global Change and the World's Mountains Conference, held in Perth, United Kingdom of Great Britain and Northern Ireland in 2010, the Lucerne World Mountain Conference, held in Lucerne, Switzerland in 2011, and its regional assessment reports on progress in sustainable mountain development since 1992 and its Call for Action, and the International Conference on Green Economy and Sustainable Mountain Development, held in Kathmandu in 2011,

Acknowledging that despite the progress that has been made in promoting sustainable development of mountain regions, poverty, food insecurity, social exclusion and environmental degradation are still high,

Acknowledging also the importance of the upcoming United Nations Conference on Sustainable Development,

1. *Takes note* of the report of the Secretary-General;
2. *Notes with appreciation* that a growing network of Governments, organizations, major groups and individuals around the world recognize the importance of the sustainable development of mountain regions for poverty eradication, and recognizes the global importance of mountains as

the source of most of the Earth's fresh water, as repositories of rich biological diversity and other natural resources, including timber and minerals, as providers of some sources of renewable energy, as popular destinations for recreation and tourism and as areas of important cultural diversity, knowledge and heritage, all of which generate positive, unaccounted economic benefits;

3. *Recognizes* that mountains provide sensitive indications of climate change through phenomena such as modifications of biological diversity, the retreat of mountain glaciers and changes in seasonal runoff that are having an impact on major sources of fresh water in the world, and stresses the need to undertake actions to minimize the negative effects of these phenomena and promote adaptation measures;

4. *Also recognizes* that sustainable mountain development is a key component in achieving the Millennium Development Goals in many regions of the world;

5. *Encourages* greater consideration of sustainable mountain development issues in intergovernmental discussions on climate change, biodiversity loss and combating desertification in the context of the United Nations Framework Convention on Climate Change, the Convention on Biological Diversity, the United Nations Convention to Combat Desertification in Those Countries Experiencing Serious Drought and/or Desertification, Particularly in Africa and the United Nations Forum on Forests;

6. *Notes with concern* that there remain key challenges to achieving sustainable development, eradicating poverty in mountain regions and protecting mountain ecosystems, and that populations in mountain regions are frequently among the poorest in a given country;

7. *Encourages* Governments to adopt a long-term vision and holistic approaches in their sustainable development strategies, and to promote integrated approaches to policies related to sustainable development in mountain regions;

8. *Also encourages* Governments to integrate mountain sustainable development in national, regional and global policymaking and development strategies, including through incorporating mountain-specific requirements in sustainable development policies or through specific mountain policies;

9. *Notes* that the growing demand for natural resources, including water, the consequences of erosion, deforestation and watershed degradation, the frequency and scale of natural disasters, as well as increasing out-migration, the pressures of industry, transport, tourism, mining and agriculture and the consequences of climate change and loss of biodiversity are some of the key challenges in fragile mountain ecosystems to implementing sustainable development and eradicating poverty in mountain regions, consistent with the Millennium Development Goals;

10. *Underlines* the importance of sustainable forest management, the avoidance of deforestation and the restoration of lost and degraded forest ecosystems of mountains in order to enhance the role of mountains as natural carbon and water regulators, and notes that International Mountain Day is devoted in 2011 to the theme "Mountains and forests", as a contribution to the observance of the International Year of Forests, 2011;

11. *Notes* that sustainable agriculture in mountain regions is important for the protection of the mountain environment and the promotion of the local economy, and appreciates the important role of the Food and Agriculture Organization of the United Nations in the United Nations system in promoting sustainable agricultural development and forestry and its beneficial impact on sustainable mountain development through its field programme, normative activities and support to international processes;

12. *Expresses deep concern* at the number and scale of natural disasters and their increasing impact in recent years, which have resulted in massive loss of life and long-term negative social, economic and environmental consequences for vulnerable societies throughout the world, in particular in mountain regions, especially those in developing countries, and urges the international community to take concrete steps to support national and regional efforts to ensure the sustainable development of mountains, and, in this regard, notes with appreciation the Second World Landslide Forum, which was organized by the International Consortium on Landslides and hosted by the Food and Agriculture Organization of the United Nations in October 2011, and the course on disaster risk management in mountain areas of the International Programme on Research and Training on Sustainable Management of Mountain Areas, organized by the Mountain Partnership Secretariat and the University of Turin, Italy;

13. *Encourages* Governments, the international community and other relevant stakeholders to develop or improve disaster risk management strategies to cope with the increasing adverse impact of disasters in mountain regions, such as flash floods, including glacial lake outburst floods, as well as landslides, debris flows and earthquakes;

14. *Calls upon* Governments, with the collaboration of the scientific community, mountain communities and intergovernmental organizations, where appropriate, to study, with a view to promoting sustainable mountain development, the specific concerns of mountain communities, including the adverse impact of climate change on mountain environments and biological diversity, in order to elaborate sustainable adaptation strategies and subsequently implement adequate measures to cope with the adverse effects of climate change;

15. *Underlines* the fact that action at the national level is a key factor in achieving progress in sustainable mountain development, welcomes its steady increase in recent years with a multitude of events, activities and initiatives, and invites the international community to support the efforts of developing countries to develop and implement strategies and programmes, including, where required, enabling policies and laws for the sustainable development of mountains, within the framework of national development plans;

16. *Encourages* the further establishment of committees or similar multi-stakeholder institutional arrangements and mechanisms at the national and regional levels, where appropriate, to enhance intersectoral coordination and collaboration for sustainable development in mountain regions;

17. *Also encourages* the increased involvement of local authorities, as well as other relevant stakeholders, in particular the rural population, indigenous peoples, civil society and the private sector, in the development and implementation of programmes, land-use planning and land tenure arrangements, and activities related to sustainable development in mountains;

18. *Underlines* the need for improved access to resources, including land, for women in mountain regions, as well as the need to strengthen the role of women in mountain regions in decision-making processes that affect their communities, cultures and environments, and encourages Governments and intergovernmental organizations to integrate the gender dimension, including gender-disaggregated data, in mountain development activities, programmes and projects;

19. *Stresses* that indigenous cultures, traditions and knowledge, including in the field of medicine, are to be fully considered, respected and promoted in development policy, programmes and planning in mountain regions, and underlines the importance of promoting the full participation and involvement of mountain communities in decisions that affect them and of integrating indigenous knowledge, heritage and values in all development initiatives;

20. *Recalls with appreciation* the adoption by the Conference of the Parties to the Convention on Biological Diversity of a programme of work on mountain biological diversity;

21. *Invites* States and other stakeholders to strengthen implementation of the programme of work on mountain biological diversity, including through the establishment of appropriate multi-stakeholder institutional arrangements and an appropriate multi-stakeholder institutional mechanism;

22. *Recognizes* that many developing countries, as well as countries with economies in transition, need to be assisted in the formulation and implementation of national strategies and programmes for sustainable mountain development, through bilateral, multilateral and South-South cooperation, as well as through other collaborative approaches;

23. *Emphasizes* the importance of the exchange of best practices, information and appropriate environmentally sound technologies for sustainable mountain development, and encourages Member States and relevant organizations in this regard;

24. *Notes* that funding for sustainable mountain development has become increasingly important, especially in view of the greater recognition of the global importance of mountains and the high levels of extreme poverty, food insecurity and hardship that mountain communities face, and, in this respect, invites Governments, the United Nations system, the international financial institutions, the Global Environment Facility, all relevant United Nations conventions and their funding mechanisms, within their respective mandates, and all relevant stakeholders from civil society and the private sector to consider providing support, including through voluntary financial contributions, to local, national and international programmes and projects for sustainable development in mountain regions, particularly in developing countries;

25. *Underlines* the need to explore a wide range of funding sources, such as public-private partnerships, increased opportunities for microfinance, including microcredit and microinsurance, small housing loans, savings, education and health accounts, and support for entrepreneurs seeking to develop small and medium-sized businesses and, where appropriate, on a case-by-case basis, debt for sustainable development swaps;

26. *Encourages* the further development of sustainable agricultural value chains and the improvement of access to and participation in markets for mountain farmers and agro-industry enterprises, with a view to substantially increasing the income of farmers, in particular smallholders and family farmers;

27. *Welcomes* the growing contribution of sustainable tourism initiatives in mountain regions as a way to enhance environmental protection and socioeconomic benefits to local communities, and the fact that consumer demand is increasingly moving towards responsible and sustainable tourism;

28. *Notes* that public awareness needs to be raised with respect to the positive and unaccounted economic benefits that mountains provide not only to highland communities, but also to a large portion of the world's population living in lowland areas, and underlines the importance of enhancing the sustainability of ecosystems that provide essential resources and services for human well-being and economic activity and of developing innovative means of financing for their protection;

29. *Recognizes* that mountain ranges are usually shared among several countries, and in this context encourages transboundary cooperation approaches where the States concerned agree to the sustainable development of mountain ranges and information-sharing in this regard;

30. *Notes with appreciation*, in this context, the Convention on the Protection of the Alps which promotes constructive new approaches to the integrated, sustainable development of the Alps, including through its thematic protocols on spatial planning, mountain farming, conservation of nature and landscape, mountain forests, tourism, soil protection, energy and transport, as well as the Declaration on Population and Culture, the Action Plan on Climate Change in the Alps, cooperation with other convention bodies on relevant subjects and activities in the context of the Mountain Partnership;

31. *Also notes with appreciation* the Framework Convention on the Protection and Sustainable Development of the Carpathians, adopted and signed by the seven countries of the region to provide a framework for cooperation and multisectoral policy coordination, a platform for joint strategies for sustainable development and a forum for dialogue between all involved stakeholders;

32. *Further notes with appreciation* the work of the International Centre for Integrated Mountain Development, which promotes transboundary cooperation among the eight member countries of the Himalaya Hindu Kush to foster action and change for overcoming the economic, social and physical vulnerability of mountain peoples;

33. *Notes with appreciation* the contribution of the Sustainable Agriculture and Rural Development in Mountain Regions project of the Food and Agriculture Organization of the United Nations and the statement of the Adelboden Group in promoting specific policies, appropriate institutions and processes for mountain regions and the positive, unaccounted economic benefits they provide;

34. *Stresses* the importance of building capacity, strengthening institutions and enhancing higher and continuing education on mountain issues in order to expand opportunities and encourage the retention of skilled people, including youth, in mountain areas, and stresses also

the importance of promoting educational and advocacy programmes in order to foster sustainable mountain development at all levels, to enhance awareness of sustainable development issues in mountain regions and of the nature of relationships between highland and lowland areas and to take full advantage of the opportunities provided annually by International Mountain Day on 11 December in this regard;

35. *Encourages* Member States to collect at the local, national and regional levels, as appropriate, disaggregated scientific data on mountain areas through systematic monitoring, including of trends in progress and change, based on relevant criteria, to support interdisciplinary research programmes and projects and to improve decision-making and planning;

36. *Encourages* all relevant entities of the United Nations system, within their respective mandates, to further enhance their constructive efforts to strengthen inter-agency collaboration to achieve more effective implementation of the relevant chapters of Agenda 21, including chapter 13, and paragraph 42 and other relevant paragraphs of the Johannesburg Plan of Implementation, taking into account the need for the further involvement of the United Nations system, in particular the Food and Agriculture Organization of the United Nations, the United Nations Environment Programme, the United Nations University, the United Nations Development Programme, the United Nations Educational, Scientific and Cultural Organization and the United Nations Children's Fund, as well as international financial institutions and other relevant international organizations;

37. *Recognizes* the efforts of the Mountain Partnership implemented in accordance with Economic and Social Council resolution 2003/61 of 25 July 2003, invites the international community and other relevant stakeholders, including civil society and the private sector, to consider participating actively in the Mountain Partnership to increase its value, and invites the Partnership secretariat to report on its activities and achievements to the Commission on Sustainable Development at its twentieth session, in 2013, at which "mountains" will be one of the thematic clusters to come under revision;

38. *Notes with appreciation*, in this context, the efforts of the Mountain Partnership to cooperate with existing multilateral instruments relevant to mountains, such as the Convention on Biological Diversity, the United Nations Convention to Combat Desertification in Those Countries Experiencing Serious Drought and/or Desertification, Particularly in Africa, the United Nations Framework Convention on Climate Change, the International Strategy for Disaster Reduction and mountain-related regional instruments such as the Convention on the Protection of the Alps and the Framework Convention on the Protection and Sustainable Development of the Carpathians;

39. *Notes* the ongoing preparatory process for the United Nations Conference on Sustainable Development, to be held in Rio de Janeiro, Brazil, from 20 to 22 June 2012;

40. *Notes with appreciation* the ongoing efforts to improve strategic cooperation among the institutions and initiatives dealing with mountain development, such as the Mountain Forum, the Mountain Partnership, the Mountain Research Initiative, the International Mountain Society, the Global Mountain Biodiversity Assessment, the International Centre for Integrated Mountain Development and the Consortium for Sustainable Development of the Andean Ecoregion;

41. *Requests* the Secretary-General to report to the General Assembly at its sixty-eighth session on the implementation of the present resolution under the sub-item entitled "Sustainable mountain development" of the item entitled "Sustainable development".

Marine ecosystems

Coral reefs

In response to General Assembly resolution 65/150 [YUN 2010, p. 1032], the Secretary-General submitted an August report [A/66/298 and Corr.1] that enumerated efforts designed to protect and manage coral reefs towards enhancing the sustainable development of marine and coastal areas. The report addressed the importance of protecting coral reefs and related ecosystems for sustainable livelihoods and development; the economic, social and environmental benefits of protecting coral reefs, in the context of the themes and objectives of Rio+20; and the role of national legislation in protecting coral reefs, including the importance of involving indigenous and local communities. The Secretary-General set forth potential action, consistent with international law, needed to protect coral reefs and related ecosystems, and proposed coordinated and coherent action across the UN system, including an expanded role for UN-Oceans as a coordination mechanism on ocean and coastal issues. He also recommended steps related to minimizing global carbon dioxide emissions; reducing unsustainable fishing practices; decreasing watershed-based sedimentation and pollution; reducing marine-based pollution and damage; improving coastal development; increasing the coverage and effectiveness of managed and protected marine areas; reinforcing regional and international collaboration; promoting best practices; implementing sustainable tourism and ecotourism; encouraging data collection and scientific research; and promoting education.

GENERAL ASSEMBLY ACTION

On 22 December [meeting 91], the General Assembly, on the recommendation of the Second Committee [A/66/440], adopted **resolution 66/194** without vote [agenda item 19].

Protection of coral reefs for sustainable livelihoods and development

The General Assembly,

Recalling the Rio Declaration on Environment and Development and Agenda 21, the Programme of Action for the Sustainable Development of Small Island Developing

States, the Plan of Implementation of the World Summit on Sustainable Development ("Johannesburg Plan of Implementation"), the Mauritius Declaration and the Mauritius Strategy for the Further Implementation of the Programme of Action for the Sustainable Development of Small Island Developing States, the United Nations Millennium Declaration, and the United Nations Framework Convention on Climate Change,

Reaffirming the United Nations Convention on the Law of the Sea, which provides the overall legal framework for ocean activities, and emphasizing its fundamental character, conscious that the problems of ocean space are closely interrelated and need to be considered as a whole through an integrated, interdisciplinary and intersectoral approach,

Recalling the Convention on Biological Diversity as an important instrument in the conservation and sustainable use of marine biodiversity,

Recalling also biodiversity-related conventions and organizations, including the Convention on International Trade in Endangered Species of Wild Fauna and Flora, the Convention on Wetlands of International Importance especially as Waterfowl Habitat, the Convention on the Conservation of Migratory Species of Wild Animals, the United Nations Educational, Scientific and Cultural Organization and the Food and Agriculture Organization of the United Nations,

Recognizing the role of national legislation in the context of the protection of coral reefs and related ecosystems within national jurisdictions,

Recalling its annual resolutions on oceans and the law of the sea and on sustainable fisheries, including resolutions 61/105 of 8 December 2006, 64/71 and 64/72 of 4 December 2009, 65/37 A of 7 December 2010 and 65/37 B of 4 April 2011, as well as its resolution 65/159 of 20 December 2010 on the protection of global climate for present and future generations of humankind, its resolution 64/236 of 24 December 2009, in which it decided to organize the United Nations Conference on Sustainable Development, its resolution 65/155 of 20 December 2010 entitled "Towards the sustainable development of the Caribbean Sea for present and future generations", its resolution 65/161 of 20 December 2010 on the Convention on Biological Diversity and other relevant resolutions,

Noting the Manado Ocean Declaration adopted by the World Ocean Conference on 14 May 2009 and the Jakarta Mandate on Marine and Coastal Biological Diversity of 1995,

Noting also the work under the Convention on Biological Diversity on marine and coastal biodiversity, in particular on coral reefs and related ecosystems, and in this connection the outcome of the tenth meeting of the Conference of the Parties to the Convention, held in Nagoya, Japan, from 18 to 29 October 2010, including in relation to the updating and revision of the strategic plan for the post-2010 period,

Noting further the request of the Conference of the Parties, at its tenth meeting, to the Executive Secretary of the Convention to prepare, subject to the availability of financial resources, a report on the progress made in the implementation of the specific workplan on coral bleaching adopted by the Conference of the Parties in its decision VII/5,

Noting with concern that coral reef degradation will likely lead to the loss of significant economic and social benefits, in particular for States which are highly vulnerable to coral reef loss and have a low capacity to respond,

Recognizing that millions of the world's inhabitants depend on the health of coral reefs and related ecosystems for sustainable livelihoods and development as they are a primary source of food and income, add to the aesthetic and cultural dimensions of communities and also provide for protection from storms, tsunamis and coastal erosion,

Expressing grave concern about the adverse impact of climate change and ocean acidification on the health and survival of coral reefs and related ecosystems around the world, including through sea-level rise, increase in the severity and incidence of coral bleaching, rising sea surface temperature and higher storm intensity, combined with the synergistic negative effects of waste run-off, overfishing, destructive fishing practices, alien invasive species and coral mining,

Maintaining that the United Nations Framework Convention on Climate Change is the primary international, intergovernmental forum for negotiating the global response to climate change, and calling upon States to take urgent global action to address climate change in accordance with the principles identified in the Convention, including the principle of common but differentiated responsibilities and respective capabilities,

Acknowledging that, in many countries, indigenous and local communities have a distinctive relationship with marine and coastal environments, including coral reefs and related ecosystems, and in some cases ownership thereof, in accordance with national legislation, and that such peoples have an important role to play in the protection, management and preservation of those reefs and related ecosystems,

Acknowledging also the leadership role in tropical marine ecosystems management provided by the International Coral Reef Initiative, a partnership of Governments, international organizations and non-governmental organizations,

Welcoming regional initiatives that address serious threats to coral reefs which are transboundary in nature and, in this regard, welcoming regional initiatives, including the Coral Triangle Initiative on Coral Reefs, Fisheries and Food Security, the Micronesia Challenge, the Caribbean Challenge, the Pacific Oceanscape Framework, the Eastern Tropical Pacific Seascape Project, the Western Indian Ocean Partnership, the West African Conservation Challenge and the Regional Initiative for the Conservation and Wise Use of Mangroves and Coral Reefs in the Americas,

Welcoming also the efforts of the agencies, programmes and funds of the United Nations system in the field of the protection of marine biodiversity and, in particular, coral reefs and related ecosystems,

Taking note of the report of the Secretary-General on the protection of coral reefs for sustainable livelihoods and development, requested in its resolution 65/150 of 20 December 2010,

Acknowledging the importance of the upcoming United Nations Conference on Sustainable Development, to be held in Rio de Janeiro, Brazil, from 20 to 22 June 2012,

1. *Urges* States, within their national jurisdictions and the competent international organizations, within their respective mandates, given the imperative for action, to take

practical steps at all levels to protect coral reefs and related ecosystems for sustainable livelihoods and development, including immediate and concerted global, regional and local action to respond to the challenges and to address the adverse impact of climate change, including through mitigation and adaptation, as well as of ocean acidification, on coral reefs and related ecosystems;

2. *Also urges* States to formulate, adopt and implement integrated and comprehensive approaches for the management of coral reefs and related ecosystems under their jurisdiction, encourages regional cooperation in accordance with international law regarding the protection and enhancement of the resilience of coral reefs, and in that respect calls upon development partners to support such efforts in developing countries, including through the provision of financial resources, capacity-building, environmentally sound technologies and know-how on mutually agreed terms, as well as the exchange of relevant scientific, technical, socioeconomic and legal information, to enable developing countries to take all action necessary for the protection of their coral reefs and related ecosystems, as appropriate;

3. *Further urges* States to identify relevant measures or tools for the protection of coral reefs within their national jurisdiction as an urgent sustainable development priority to address, inter alia, poverty eradication, food security, sustainable livelihoods and ecosystem conservation and, in this regard, encourages States to implement and integrate them, as appropriate, into broader sustainable development strategies;

4. *Stresses* the need to improve the understanding of the economic, social and environmental benefits of coral reefs and related ecosystems, in order to develop and enhance measures to protect coral reefs, reinforce their resilience and strengthen the ability of coastal communities to adapt to environmental changes and coral reef degradation;

5. *Encourages* Member States and other stakeholders to address, as appropriate, the protection of coral reefs for sustainable livelihoods and development;

6. *Notes* the ongoing preparatory process for the United Nations Conference on Sustainable Development, to be held in Rio de Janeiro, Brazil, from 20 to 22 June 2012.

Waste from chemical munitions dumped at sea

By a 9 November letter [A/C.2/66/6], Lithuania transmitted the summary of the follow-up seminar to General Assembly resolution 65/149 [YUN 2010, p. 1037] entitled "Cooperative measures to assess and increase awareness of environmental effects related to waste originating from chemical munitions dumped at sea" (Vilnius, Lithuania, 20 September).

Other matters

Oil slick in Lebanon

In response to General Assembly resolution 65/147 [YUN 2010, p. 1015], the Secretary-General submitted an August report [A/66/297] reviewing progress in implementing resolutions 61/194 [YUN 2006, p. 1215], 62/188 [YUN 2007, p. 1053], 63/211 [YUN 2008, p. 1150] and 64/195 [YUN 2010, p. 1011] on the oil slick on Lebanese shores that resulted from the destruction by Israel of oil storage tanks in Lebanon following the outbreak of hostilities between Israel and the paramilitary group Hizbullah in 2006 [YUN 2006, p. 574]. Some 15,000 tons of fuel oil were released into the Mediterranean Sea, contaminating about 150 kilometres of coastline in Lebanon and the Syrian Arab Republic. The Secretary-General remained concerned at the lack of implementation of the relevant provisions of the Assembly resolutions on the subject vis-à-vis reparations and compensation to the Government and people of Lebanon and Syria affected by the oil spill. He encouraged States and the international donor community to make contributions to the Eastern Mediterranean Oil Spill Restoration Trust Fund hosted by the Lebanon Recovery Fund.

GENERAL ASSEMBLY ACTION

On 22 December [meeting 91], the General Assembly, on the recommendation of the Second Committee [A/66/440], adopted **resolution 66/192** by recorded vote (165-8-6) [agenda item 19].

Oil slick on Lebanese shores

The General Assembly,

Recalling its resolutions 61/194 of 20 December 2006, 62/188 of 19 December 2007, 63/211 of 19 December 2008, 64/195 of 21 December 2009 and 65/147 of 20 December 2010 on the oil slick on Lebanese shores,

Reaffirming the outcome of the United Nations Conference on the Human Environment, especially principle 7 of the Declaration of the Conference, in which States were requested to take all possible steps to prevent pollution of the seas,

Emphasizing the need to protect and preserve the marine environment in accordance with international law,

Taking into account the 1992 Rio Declaration on Environment and Development, especially principle 16, in which it was stipulated that the polluter should, in principle, bear the cost of pollution, and taking into account also chapter 17 of Agenda 21,

Noting with great concern the environmental disaster caused by the destruction by the Israeli Air Force on 15 July 2006 of the oil storage tanks in the direct vicinity of the Jiyeh electric power plant in Lebanon, resulting in an oil slick that covered the entirety of the Lebanese coastline, extended to the Syrian coastline and hindered efforts to achieve sustainable development, as already highlighted by the General Assembly in its resolutions 61/194, 62/188, 63/211, 64/195 and 65/147,

Noting that the Secretary-General expressed grave concern at the lack of any acknowledgement on the part of the Government of Israel of its responsibilities vis-à-vis reparations and compensation to the Government and people of Lebanon and the Syrian Arab Republic affected by the oil spill,

Recalling that, in paragraph 4 of its resolution 65/147, it requested the Government of Israel to assume responsibility for prompt and adequate compensation to the Government of Lebanon and other countries directly affected by the oil slick, such as the Syrian Arab Republic, whose shores have been partially polluted, and recognizing the conclusion of the Secretary-General that this request of the Assembly has yet to be implemented,

Acknowledging that the Secretary-General concluded that this oil spill is not covered by any of the international oil spill compensation funds and thus merits special consideration, and recognizing that further consideration needs to be given to the option of securing the relevant compensation from the Government of Israel,

Noting the observation of the Secretary-General that the experience of the United Nations Compensation Commission in handling claims for compensation for environmental damage resulting from the unlawful invasion and occupation of Kuwait by Iraq may be of some value in terms of defining environmental damage in a case such as the present oil slick, in measuring and quantifying the damage sustained and in determining the amount of compensation payable in respect of it,

Noting again with appreciation the assistance offered by donor countries and international organizations for the clean-up operations and the early recovery and reconstruction of Lebanon through bilateral and multilateral channels, including the Athens Coordination Meeting on the response to the marine pollution incident in the Eastern Mediterranean, held on 17 August 2006, as well as the Stockholm Conference for Lebanon's Early Recovery, held on 31 August 2006,

Acknowledging that the Secretary-General has welcomed the agreement of the Lebanon Recovery Fund to host the Eastern Mediterranean Oil Spill Restoration Trust Fund, under its existing mechanism, and expressing concern that to date no contributions have been made to the Trust Fund,

1. *Takes note* of the report of the Secretary-General on the implementation of General Assembly resolution 65/147 on the oil slick on Lebanese shores;

2. *Reiterates*, for the sixth consecutive year, its deep concern about the adverse implications of the destruction by the Israeli Air Force of the oil storage tanks in the direct vicinity of the Lebanese Jiyeh electric power plant, for the achievement of sustainable development in Lebanon;

3. *Considers* that the oil slick has heavily polluted the shores of Lebanon and partially polluted Syrian shores and consequently has had serious implications for livelihoods and the economy of Lebanon, owing to the adverse implications for natural resources, biodiversity, fisheries and tourism, and for human health, in the country;

4. *Reiterates its request* to the Government of Israel to assume responsibility for prompt and adequate compensation to the Government of Lebanon and other countries directly affected by the oil slick, such as the Syrian Arab Republic whose shores have been partially polluted, for the costs of repairing the environmental damage caused by the destruction, including the restoration of the marine environment, in particular in the light of the conclusion contained in the report of the Secretary-General that there remains grave concern at the lack of implementation of the relevant provisions of the resolutions of the General Assembly on the subject vis-à-vis reparations and compensation to the Government and people of Lebanon and the Syrian Arab Republic affected by the oil spill;

5. *Requests* the Secretary-General to give further consideration to the option of securing the relevant compensation from the Government of Israel;

6. *Also requests* the Secretary-General to explore the value of the experience of the United Nations Compensation Commission in terms of defining environmental damage in a case such as the present oil slick, in measuring and quantifying the damage sustained and in determining the amount of compensation payable in respect of it;

7. *Reiterates its appreciation* for the efforts of the Government of Lebanon and those of Member States, regional and international organizations, regional and international financial institutions, non-governmental organizations and the private sector in the initiation of clean-up and rehabilitation operations on the polluted shores, and encourages Member States and the above-mentioned entities to continue their financial and technical support to the Government of Lebanon towards achieving the completion of clean-up and rehabilitation operations, with the aim of preserving the ecosystem of Lebanon and that of the Eastern Mediterranean Basin;

8. *Welcomes* the agreement of the Lebanon Recovery Fund to host the Eastern Mediterranean Oil Spill Restoration Trust Fund, based on voluntary contributions, to provide assistance and support to the States directly adversely affected in their integrated environmentally sound management, from clean-up to safe disposal of oily waste, of this environmental disaster resulting from the destruction of the oil storage tanks at the Jiyeh electric power plant;

9. *Notes* that in his report the Secretary-General urged Member States, international organizations, international and regional financial institutions, non-governmental organizations and the private sector to continue their support for Lebanon in this matter, in particular for rehabilitation activities on the Lebanese coast and in the broader recovery efforts, and stated that such international effort should be intensified, since Lebanon is still engaged in the treatment of wastes and the monitoring of recovery, and reiterates its invitation to States and the international donor community to make voluntary financial contributions to the Trust Fund, and in this regard requests the Secretary-General to mobilize international technical and financial assistance, in order to ensure that the Trust Fund has sufficient and adequate resources;

10. *Recognizes* the multidimensionality of the adverse impact of the oil slick, and requests the Secretary-General to submit to the General Assembly at its sixty-seventh session a report on the implementation of the present resolution under the item entitled "Sustainable development".

RECORDED VOTE ON RESOLUTION 66/192:

In favour: Afghanistan, Albania, Algeria, Andorra, Angola, Antigua and Barbuda, Argentina, Armenia, Austria, Azerbaijan, Bahamas, Bahrain, Bangladesh, Barbados, Belarus, Belgium, Belize, Benin, Bhutan, Bolivia, Bosnia and Herzegovina, Botswana, Brazil, Brunei Darussalam, Bulgaria, Burkina Faso, Burundi, Cambodia, Cape Verde, Chad, Chile, China, Comoros, Congo, Costa Rica, Côte d'Ivoire, Croatia, Cuba, Cyprus, Czech Republic, Democratic People's Republic of Korea, Denmark, Djibouti, Dominica, Dominican Republic, Ecuador, Egypt, El Salvador, Eritrea, Estonia, Ethiopia, Fiji, Finland, France, Georgia, Germany, Greece, Grenada, Guatemala, Guinea, Guinea-Bissau, Guyana, Haiti, Honduras, Hungary,

Iceland, India, Indonesia, Iran, Iraq, Ireland, Italy, Jamaica, Japan, Jordan, Kazakhstan, Kenya, Kuwait, Kyrgyzstan, Lao People's Democratic Republic, Latvia, Lebanon, Lesotho, Liberia, Libya, Liechtenstein, Lithuania, Luxembourg, Madagascar, Malawi, Malaysia, Maldives, Mali, Malta, Mauritius, Mexico, Monaco, Mongolia, Montenegro, Morocco, Mozambique, Myanmar, Namibia, Nepal, Netherlands, New Zealand, Nicaragua, Niger, Nigeria, Norway, Oman, Pakistan, Papua New Guinea, Paraguay, Peru, Philippines, Poland, Portugal, Qatar, Republic of Korea, Republic of Moldova, Romania, Russian Federation, Saint Lucia, Saint Vincent and the Grenadines, San Marino, Saudi Arabia, Senegal, Serbia, Sierra Leone, Singapore, Slovakia, Slovenia, Solomon Islands, Somalia, South Africa, Spain, Sri Lanka, Sudan, Suriname, Swaziland, Sweden, Switzerland, Syrian Arab Republic, Tajikistan, Thailand, the former Yugoslav Republic of Macedonia, Timor-Leste, Togo, Trinidad and Tobago, Tunisia, Turkey, Tuvalu, Uganda, Ukraine, United Arab Emirates, United Kingdom, United Republic of Tanzania, Uruguay, Uzbekistan, Venezuela, Viet Nam, Yemen, Zambia, Zimbabwe.

Against: Australia, Canada, Israel, Marshall Islands, Micronesia, Nauru, Palau, United States.

Abstaining: Cameroon, Central African Republic, Colombia, Gabon, Panama, Tonga.

Harmony with nature

In response to General Assembly resolution 65/164 [YUN 2010, p. 1043], the Secretary-General submitted an August report [A/66/302] on harmony with nature. The report focused on the evolving relationship of humankind with nature as reflected in environmental legislation. As requested by the Assembly in resolution 65/164, the Secretary-General convened an interactive dialogue in commemoration of International Mother Earth Day on 20 April, with the participation of Member States, UN organizations, independent experts and other stakeholders, as a contribution to the preparatory process of the United Nations Conference on Sustainable Development, to be held in Rio de Janeiro, Brazil, in 2012. The dialogue addressed ways to promote sustainable development in harmony with nature and sharing national experiences on indicators for measuring such development. The report contained recommendations drawn from the interactive dialogue designed to facilitate further consideration of the theme by Member States.

GENERAL ASSEMBLY ACTION

On 22 December [meeting 91], the General Assembly, on the recommendation of the Second Committee [A/66/440/Add.8], adopted **resolution 66/204** without vote [agenda item 19 (*h*)].

Harmony with Nature

The General Assembly,

Reaffirming the Rio Declaration on Environment and Development, Agenda 21, the Programme for the Further Implementation of Agenda 21, the Johannesburg Declaration on Sustainable Development and the Plan of Implementation of the World Summit on Sustainable Development ("Johannesburg Plan of Implementation"),

Recalling its resolutions 64/196 of 21 December 2009 and 65/164 of 20 December 2010 on Harmony with Nature and its resolution 63/278 of 22 April 2009, by which it designated 22 April as International Mother Earth Day,

Recalling also the 1982 World Charter for Nature,

Recalling further its resolution 64/253 of 23 February 2010, entitled "International Day of Nowruz", and its resolution 65/309 of 19 July 2011, entitled "Happiness: towards a holistic approach to development",

Taking note of the interactive dialogue of the General Assembly on Harmony with Nature, which was held on 20 April 2011, to commemorate International Mother Earth Day by discussing ways to promote a holistic approach to sustainable development in harmony with nature and sharing national experiences on criteria and indicators for measuring sustainable development in harmony with nature,

Noting the first Peoples' World Conference on Climate Change and the Rights of Mother Earth, hosted by the Plurinational State of Bolivia in Cochabamba from 20 to 22 April 2010,

Acknowledging the importance of the United Nations Conference on Sustainable Development, to be held in Rio de Janeiro, Brazil, from 20 to 22 June 2012,

Expressing concern about documented environmental degradation and the negative impact on nature resulting from human activity, and recognizing the need to strengthen scientific knowledge on the effects of human activities on ecosystems,

Recognizing that gross domestic product was not designed as an indicator for measuring environmental degradation resulting from human activity and the need to overcome this limitation with regard to sustainable development and the work carried out in this regard,

Recognizing also the uneven availability of statistical basic data under the three pillars of sustainable development and the need to improve their quality and quantity,

Reaffirming that fundamental changes in the way societies produce and consume are indispensable for achieving global sustainable development and that all countries should promote sustainable consumption and production patterns, with the developed countries taking the lead and with all countries benefiting from the process, taking into account the Rio principles, including the principle of common but differentiated responsibilities, as set out in principle 7 of the Rio Declaration on Environment and Development,

Recognizing that many ancient civilizations and indigenous cultures have a rich history of understanding the symbiotic connection between human beings and nature that fosters a mutually beneficial relationship,

Recognizing also the work undertaken by civil society, academia and scientists in regard to signalling the precariousness of life on Earth, as well as their efforts to devise more sustainable models for production and consumption,

Considering that sustainable development is a holistic concept that requires the strengthening of interdisciplinary linkages in the different branches of knowledge,

1. *Takes note* of the second report of the Secretary-General on Harmony with Nature;

2. *Requests* the President of the General Assembly to convene, at the sixty-sixth session of the Assembly, an interactive dialogue, to be held at the plenary meetings to be convened during the commemoration of International Mother Earth Day on 23 April 2012, with the participation of Member States, United Nations organizations, independent experts and other stakeholders, to discuss the scientific findings on how human activities are affecting the Earth's ecosystem;

3. *Requests* the Secretary-General to establish a trust fund for the participation of independent experts in the interactive dialogue to be held at the plenary meetings to be convened during the commemoration of International Mother Earth Day on 23 April 2012, and invites Member States and other relevant stakeholders to consider contributing to this fund;

4. *Also requests* the Secretary-General to continue making use of the existing information portal on sustainable development maintained by the secretariat of the United Nations Conference on Sustainable Development and the Division for Sustainable Development of the Department of Economic and Social Affairs of the Secretariat to gather information and contributions on ideas and activities to promote a holistic approach to sustainable development in harmony with nature being undertaken to advance the integration of scientific interdisciplinary work, including success stories on the use of traditional knowledge, and existing national legislation, taking into account that such a portal will be launched by 2012;

5. *Notes* the ongoing preparatory process for the United Nations Conference on Sustainable Development, to be held in Rio de Janeiro, Brazil, from 20 to 22 June 2012;

6. *Encourages* all countries and the relevant bodies of the United Nations system to develop and strengthen the quality and quantity of basic statistical data on the three pillars of sustainable development, and invites the international community and the pertinent bodies of the United Nations system to assist the efforts of developing countries by providing capacity-building and technical support;

7. *Invites* the relevant entities of the United Nations system to work with other relevant actors, including non-governmental organizations, experts and the academic community, as appropriate, both to identify new ways and means to overcome the limitations of gross domestic product with regard to sustainable development and to better measure the environmental degradation resulting from human activity;

8. *Requests* the Secretary-General to submit to the General Assembly at its sixty-seventh session a report on the implementation of the present resolution.

Human settlements

UN-Habitat

Governing Council

The twenty-third session of the Governing Council of the United Nations Human Settlements Programme (UN-Habitat) was held in Nairobi, Kenya, from 11 to 15 April [A/66/8]. Summaries by the President of the Council of the high-level segment on UN-Habitat activities, the work programme and the budget for the biennium 2012–2013, as well as of the dialogue on the special theme for the session—sustainable urban development through expanding equitable access to land, housing, basic service and infrastructure—were annexed to the proceedings of the session [HSP/GC/23/7]. The Committee of the Whole, established by the Council, held four meetings to consider the agenda items assigned to it. At the first plenary meeting, the UN-Habitat Executive Director delivered a policy statement that was summarized in the proceedings. On 15 April, the Council approved the provisional agenda of its twenty-fourth (2013) session [A/66/8 (dec. 23/1)].

Subsidiary body

The twenty-third session of the Council had before it a March report on the work of the Committee of Permanent Representatives [HSP/GC/23/3] since the twenty-second (2009) session of the Council [YUN 2009, p. 1042], covering the Committee's work during its thirty-third, thirty-fourth and thirty-fifth regular meetings (11 June, 24 September, 7 December 2009, respectively); its thirty-sixth, thirty-seventh, thirty-eighth, thirty-ninth regular meetings (5 March, 14 June, 15 September, 16 December 2010, respectively); and its fortieth (2 March 2011) regular meeting. An addendum to the report [HSP/GC/23/3/Add.1] contained draft resolutions prepared by the Committee.

Programme areas

The Governing Council had before it a January report by the Executive Director [HSP/GC/23/2] on activities undertaken by UN-Habitat in response to the resolutions adopted by the Council at its twenty-second session [YUN 2009, p. 1042]. The report highlighted major outcomes and achievements, including the publication of flagship reports such as the *Global Report on Human Settlements 2009* and *State of the World's Cities 2010/2011*; the World Urban Campaign, launched at the fifth World Urban Forum [YUN 2010, p. 1045]; and UN participation, coordinated by UN-Habitat, at the 2010 Shanghai World Exposition [ibid., p. 1046].

UN-Habitat/UNEP cooperation. The Governing Council also had before it the joint progress report on cooperation between UN-Habitat and UNEP for the period 2009–2010 [HSP/GC/23/2/Add.6] (see p. 973).

Gender equality

The Governing Council [A/66/8 (res. 23/1)], having before it a report by the Executive Director on the implementation of the gender equality action plan 2008–2013 [HSP/GC/23/5/Add.6], requested the Executive Director to strengthen the Gender Mainstreaming Unit and, with the Unit, to manage a unified system of gender focal points and a gender task force effective throughout UN-Habitat. The Executive Director was also asked to set up an advisory group to advise the Executive Director on all issues related to gender mainstreaming in the work of UN-Habitat and to provide oversight regarding the implementation of the gender equality action plan. The group would consist of representatives of women's organizations, academic institutions, the private sector, local authorities, and government policymakers and decision makers.

Human settlements development in the Occupied Palestinian Territory

The Governing Council [A/66/8 (res. 23/2)] called on UN-Habitat to focus on improving the housing conditions of Palestinians, addressing urbanization challenges, supporting the building of a Palestinian State and fostering humanitarian action and peacebuilding in the areas where there were acute humanitarian and development needs. The Executive Director was requested to establish and chair an advisory board to the Special Human Settlements Programme for the Palestinian People and the Technical Cooperation Trust Fund, comprising representatives to the United Nations of contributing member States, in order to provide policy guidance to the Programme.

Support for pro-poor housing

The Governing Council, addressing the need for adequate housing in Iraq [A/66/8 (res. 23/3)], encouraged the Executive Director to secure technical assistance to support housing and pro-poor housing initiatives in all stages of planning and implementation, and secure capacity-building in the fields of project management and provision of infrastructure.

Public spaces

In consideration of the importance of green, safe and socially inclusive public spaces, the Governing Council [A/66/8 (res. 23/4)] requested the Executive Director to advance the agenda on place-making and public spaces in a way that would consolidate local and international approaches to creating inclusive cities; enhance the knowledge of UN-Habitat partners and local authorities concerning place-making, public spaces and the quality of urban life; and facilitate and implement exchange, cooperation and research between partners working in that field. The Executive Director was also asked to develop, in collaboration with Habitat Agenda partners, a policy approach on the role that place-making could play in meeting the challenges of the rapidly urbanizing world, to disseminate that policy and its results widely and to develop a plan for ensuring its application internationally.

World Urban Forum

The Governing Council [A/66/8 (res. 23/5)], having before it the report of the Executive Director on the fifth World Urban Forum [YUN 2010, p. 1045], as well as the UN-Habitat management response [HSP/GC/23/2/Add.3] to the review of the first four sessions of the Forum [HSP/GC/23/INF/3], requested the Executive Director to implement, in consultation with the Committee of Permanent Representatives, the main findings resulting from the lessons learned from the review and the UN-Habitat evaluation of the fifth session in which there was concurrence. He was also asked to improve and define a timely planning process based on a results-based framework.

African Ministerial Conference on Housing and Urban Development

On 15 April [A/66/8 (res. 23/6)], the Governing Council welcomed the Bamako Declaration and Action Plan, adopted by the African Ministerial Conference on Housing and Urban Development (Bamako, Mali, 22–24 November 2010), by which African Governments committed themselves to stimulating land policy, administration and management to tackle housing and sustainable urban development challenges. It also welcomed the decision of the Conference at its special session (Nairobi, 9–10 April 2011) to establish a permanent secretariat and accept Kenya's offer to host that secretariat. The Council requested UN-Habitat and the Government of South Africa to continue supporting preparations for the establishment of the Conference secretariat in Kenya.

Urban youth development

The Council [A/66/8 (res. 23/7)], having before it a report of the Executive Director on the Opportunities Fund for Urban Youth-led Development [HSP/GC/23/5/Add.5], encouraged the Executive Director to strengthen the programme's financial basis and human resources, establish an independent youth unit, outsource grant management of the Urban Youth Fund to regional offices, and align the thematic focuses of the Fund with those of the key UN-Habitat work programmes, as recommended in the evaluation of the Youth Empowerment Programme. The Executive Director was requested to continue mainstreaming young people in UN-Habitat work. He was also asked to evaluate the operation of the Urban Youth

Fund after five years and present the results to the Governing Council in 2015.

Habitat III

The Governing Council [A/66/8 (res. 23/8)] took note of the report of the Executive Director on the question of convening, in 2016, a third United Nations conference on housing and sustainable urban development (Habitat III) [HSP/GC/23/2/Add.4] and invited the Secretary-General to include the proposals set forth therein in his report, which was to be considered by the General Assembly at its sixty-sixth (2011) session (see p. 999). The purposes of such a conference would include reviewing past policies, achievements and obstacles; putting in place a new urban development agenda capable of responding to the new urban challenges and opportunities, such as climate change and urban safety and security, in addition to advancing a new role for cities and local authorities; and finding ways of strengthening the institutional framework for land governance, housing and sustainable urban development.

The Assembly took action on the question of convening a third UN conference on housing and sustainable urban development in resolution 66/207 of 22 December (see p. 999).

Improving the lives of slum dwellers

The Governing Council adopted a resolution [A/66/8 (res. 23/9)] on global and national strategies and frameworks for improving the lives of slum dwellers beyond the Millennium Development Goals (MDG) target to achieve a significant improvement in the lives of at least 100 million slum dwellers by 2020 [YUN 2000, p. 52]. It invited Governments and regional and local authorities to assess their slum population levels and trends and set targets to be attained by 2020 through national urban development strategies that prioritized improved access to adequate housing and basic services and infrastructure for slum dwellers. It requested UN-Habitat to provide technical and advisory assistance to those ends.

Urban economy and financial mechanisms

The Governing Council had before it a February report of the Executive Director on the evaluation of the experimental reimbursable seeding operations programme and other innovative financial mechanisms field-tested for financing housing, infrastructure and upgrading for the urban poor [HSP/GC/23/5/Add.4]. On 15 April [A/66/8 (res. 23/10)], it requested the Executive Director to: shift the focus of UN-Habitat work in the area of human settlements financing towards strengthening its normative approaches to urban economy and the promotion of finance for urban upgrading, housing and basic services for the urban poor; explore a partnership model with development finance institutions for future lending, guarantee and financial advisory services in the urban upgrading and housing finance sectors; and transfer either the experimental reimbursable seeding operations programme portfolio or the management of that portfolio and the technical loan guarantee oversight responsibilities of the slum upgrading facility programme to an appropriate external development finance partner. The Council called on Governments to support UN-Habitat efforts to maximize its comparative advantage around normative work, partnership and regional presence.

Guidelines

Having before it a report of the Executive Director on coordinated implementation of the guidelines on access to basic services for all and the guidelines on decentralization and strengthening of local authorities [YUN 2010, p. 1050], the Governing Council [A/66/8 (res. 23/12)], inter alia, urged UN-Habitat to place special emphasis in all its programmes related to decentralization and access to basic services on enhancing national and regional exchanges on implementing the guidelines. UN-Habitat was called on to enhance partnerships with local authorities and their international associations for the implementation of best practices of the guidelines on decentralization. The Council also called on UN-Habitat to strengthen the human and financial capacities dedicated to facilitating the development of instruments for operationalizing the two sets of guidelines and to assist countries, in particular developing countries, to implement the guidelines.

Urban crime prevention

In a resolution on sustainable urban development policies for safer cities and urban crime prevention [A/66/8 (res. 23/14)], the Council requested UN-Habitat, in cooperation with UN bodies, in particular the United Nations Office on Drugs and Crime, and specialized organizations, to compile best practices on policies, norms and institutional conditions related to urban crime prevention within the context of sustainable human settlements and urban development, focusing on the respective roles and responsibilities of national governments and local authorities on that specific policy area. It called on UN-Habitat to mainstream the issue of crime prevention, urban safety and social cohesion as a primary component of sustainable urban development, and to draft guidelines on access to and delivery of urban crime prevention within the context of sustainable urban development. The Council requested UN-Habitat to promote triangular, South-South and city-to-city cooperation in the area of crime prevention through exchanges of experts, best practices and policy options.

Country activities

The Governing Council [A/66/8 (res. 23/15)] welcomed the 2011 edition of the UN-Habitat report on country activities [HSP/GC/23/INF/4], which set forth UN-Habitat global and interregional programmes as well as its activities in Africa, the Arab States, Asia and the Pacific, Latin America and the Caribbean, and Europe. The Council requested the Executive Director to mobilize and devote adequate core resources to the preparation, implementation, monitoring and evaluation of country activities aligned with the focus areas of the medium-term strategic and institutional plan, and to contribute to post-disaster and post-conflict rehabilitation and reconstruction efforts in affected countries. The Executive Director was also asked to improve the dissemination of best practices and lessons learned from country activities and ensure that they fed into the global normative work of UN-Habitat, with the goal of strengthening its accountability and effectiveness. He was further requested to develop subregional, regional and interregional programmes as mechanisms to promote South-South cooperation, including triangular cooperation.

Global housing

The Governing Council [A/66/8 (res. 23/16)], taking note of the report of the fifth session of the World Urban Forum [YUN 2010, p. 1045], requested the Executive Director, in consultation with Governments, including through the Committee of Permanent Representatives, and with relevant local government executing agencies of housing projects funded by UN-Habitat, to review the implementation of the Global Strategy for Shelter to the Year 2000 [YUN 1991, p. 520] and to formulate a new global housing strategy.

Equitable access

The Governing Council [A/66/8 (res. 23/17)] took note of the January paper of the Executive Director on the dialogue on the special theme for the twenty-third session of the Council: sustainable urban development through expanding equitable access to land, housing, basic services and infrastructure [HSP/GC/23/4]. The paper highlighted three sub-themes: sustainable urban development; integrated delivery of land, housing, basic services and infrastructure; the green economy in the context of sustainable urban development and eradication of urban poverty, and the institutional framework for sustainable urban development. The Council requested the Executive Director, in consultation with the Committee of Permanent Representatives, to ensure the involvement of UN-Habitat in the preparatory process for the United Nations Conference on Sustainable Development, to be held in 2012 (Rio+20).

Natural disaster risk reduction

In a resolution on natural disaster risk reduction, preparedness, prevention and mitigation as a contribution to sustainable urban development [A/66/8 (res. 23/18)], the Governing Council requested UN-Habitat to support the implementation of urban risk reduction and early warning programmes, including the production of guidelines and training programmes and the collection and dissemination of best practices.

Governance, work programme and budget

Governance

The Governing Council [A/66/8 (res. 23/13)] took note of the January report of the Executive Director on the review of the UN-Habitat governance structure [HSP/GC/23/2/Add.1], in which he reported on work conducted through 31 January; and an April secretariat note on the review of the UN-Habitat governance structure, phase III [HSP/GC/23/INF/7], which proposed a set of governance options based on how various governance systems could contribute to tackling the challenges arising from UN-Habitat efforts to implement its medium-term strategic and institutional plan and improve its governance structure. The Council requested the Executive Director, jointly with the Committee of Permanent Representatives, to examine those options further.

Work programme and budget for 2012–2013

The Governing Council had before it the proposed work programme and budget of UN-Habitat for the 2012–2013 biennium [HSP/GC/23/5]. The work programme and budget was based on the six-year medium-term strategic and institutional plan 2008–2013 endorsed by the Council in 2007 [YUN 2007, p. 1086] and built on the biennial strategic framework for 2012–2013, which was endorsed by the Committee on Programme and Coordination in June 2010 and included four subprogrammes: shelter and sustainable human settlements development, monitoring the Habitat Agenda, regional and technical cooperation, and human settlements financing. Also before the Council was the related ACABQ report [HSP/GC/23/5/Add.1].

On 15 April [A/66/8 (res. 23/11)], the Council approved the proposed work programme and budget for 2012–2013; approved the general-purpose budget of $70,221,500 and endorsed the special-purpose budget of $110,524,800 for the 2012–2013 biennium detailed in the proposed work programme and budget for 2012–2013; and approved an increase in the general-purpose statutory reserve from $6,619,500 to $7,022,150. It requested the Executive Director, in consultation with the Committee of Permanent Representatives, to develop a strategic plan for 2014–2019, including a road map for preparatory work, taking into account the recommendations of the peer review and other reviews of the medium-term strategic and institutional plan for 2008–2013, for presentation to and approval by the Council at its twenty-fourth (2013) session.

Additional reports

Other reports by the Executive Director submitted to the Governing Council for consideration during its twenty-third session included a report on cooperation with agencies and organizations within the UN system, intergovernmental organizations outside the UN system and NGOs [HSP/GC/23/2/Add.7]; a progress report on the implementation of the medium-term strategic and institutional plan for the period 2008–2013 [HSP/GC/23/5/Add.2] and the midterm review of implementation [HSP/GC/23/5/Add.3]; the report of the fifth session of the World Urban Forum [YUN 2010, p. 1045]; a report on the status of voluntary contributions to UN-Habitat as at 28 February 2011 [HSP/GC/23/INF/5]; and the UN-Habitat financial report for the biennium ended 31 December 2009 and report of the Board of Auditors [YUN 2010, p. 1048].

Follow-up to the 1996 UN Conference on Human Settlements (Habitat II)

An August report [A/66/281] submitted by the Secretary-General in response to General Assembly resolution 65/165 [YUN 2010, p. 1047] described the activities of UN-Habitat over the previous twelve months in implementing the Habitat Agenda [YUN 1996, p. 994], adopted by the 1996 United Nations Conference on Human Settlements (Habitat II) [ibid., p. 992], and the strengthening of UN-Habitat. The report provided an overview of the action taken during the twenty-third session of the UN-Habitat Governing Council (see p. 994); progress in implementing the substantive work of UN-Habitat; budgetary and financial issues; and other significant developments. The report highlighted the midterm review of the medium-term strategic and institutional plan for the period 2008–2013 and approval of the UN-Habitat work programme and budget for the 2012–2013 biennium, as well as progress on issues related to adequate shelter and slum upgrading. It also addressed issues related to the guidelines on decentralization and strengthening of local authorities; cities and climate change; post-disaster and post-conflict reconstruction; other financial and budgetary matters; flagship UN-Habitat reports, including the *Global Report on Human Settlements 2011—Cities and Climate Change*; regional ministerial meetings; and organizational and programmatic reforms.

The Secretary-General stated that it was important that Governments review the effectiveness of the policies set forth in the 1996 Habitat Agenda; put in place a new agenda for responding to the new and predominantly urban challenges; and strengthen the existing institutional framework for human settlements development. He concluded that it was time for the General Assembly to support the convening of a third United Nations conference on housing and sustainable urban development (Habitat III) in 2016. He recommended that Governments include sustainable urban development and the role of cities and local authorities in the outcome of the United Nations Conference on Sustainable Development in 2012. Although the MDG target on slums [YUN 2000, p. 52] had been achieved in advance of the 2020 target date, 828 million people were still living in slums, and the world's slum population was increasing at an estimated annual rate of almost 60 million. The Secretary-General therefore recommended that the Assembly support UN-Habitat Governing Council resolution 23/9 (see p. 996) on improving the lives of slum dwellers beyond the MDG target.

Coordinated implementation of Habitat Agenda

In a May report [E/2011/106] submitted in response to Economic and Social Council decision 2010/236 [YUN 2010, p. 1047], the Secretary-General described activities undertaken by UN-Habitat—including the nature of cooperation across and outside of the UN system—in the coordinated implementation of the Habitat Agenda at the global, regional, national and thematic levels. Key issues raised in flagship UN-Habitat reports were also highlighted. The Secretary-General called for an early decision by Governments on the convening, in 2016, of a third UN conference on housing and sustainable urban development (Habitat III), and for support by Governments and UN agencies for UN-Habitat Governing Council resolution 23/9 (see p. 996) on improving the lives of slum dwellers beyond the MDG target. He also requested Governments to include sustainable urban development and the role of cities and local authorities in their contributions to the preparatory process for and deliberations at Rio+20; and the Economic and Social Council to include sustainable urbanization, urban poverty reduction and slum upgrading as a cross-cutting issue in the preparations for and follow-up to the outcomes of relevant summits and major international conferences.

Chapter VII: Environment and human settlements

ECONOMIC AND SOCIAL COUNCIL ACTION

On 27 July [meeting 47], the Economic and Social Council adopted **resolution 2011/21** [draft: E/2011/L.48] without vote [agenda item 13 (*d*)].

Human settlements

The Economic and Social Council,

Recalling its relevant resolutions and decisions on the coordinated implementation of the Habitat Agenda,

Acknowledging the work of the United Nations Human Settlements Programme (UN-Habitat) towards attaining the goal of sustainable urban development and the implementation of the Habitat Agenda,

1. *Takes note* of the report of the Secretary-General on the coordinated implementation of the Habitat Agenda;

2. *Encourages* the inclusion, where appropriate, of sustainable urbanization, including urban poverty reduction, slum upgrading, the role of local authorities, as well as urban resilience to natural disasters and the impact of climate change, as a cross-cutting issue in the preparations for, as well as the follow-up to, the outcome of relevant summits and major international conferences, including the United Nations Conference on Sustainable Development, to be convened in 2012;

3. *Takes note* of the report of the Executive Director of UN-Habitat on a third United Nations conference on housing and sustainable urban development, prepared in accordance with General Assembly resolutions 64/207 of 21 December 2009 and 65/165 of 20 December 2010, in which it requested the Secretary-General to prepare a report on the question of convening, in 2016, a third United Nations conference on housing and sustainable urban development (Habitat III), in collaboration with the Governing Council of UN-Habitat, for consideration by the Assembly at its sixty-sixth session, and welcomes resolution 23/8 of 15 April 2011 of the Governing Council of UN-Habitat, in which it invited the Assembly to deliberate at its sixty-sixth session on the question of convening, in 2016, a third United Nations Conference on housing and sustainable urban development (Habitat III);

4. *Invites* Governments and regional and local authorities, in accordance with national legislation, to enumerate the populations living in slums in their countries, regions and urban areas and, on that basis, to set, with the support of the international community, voluntary and realistic national, regional and local targets, to be attained by 2020, with regard to improving significantly the lives of slum-dwellers, in line with resolution 23/9 of 15 April 2011 of the Governing Council of UN-Habitat, entitled "Global and national strategies and frameworks for improving the lives of slum-dwellers beyond the Millennium Development Goals target";

5. *Decides* to transmit to the General Assembly for consideration at its sixty-sixth session the report of the Secretary-General on the coordinated implementation of the Habitat Agenda;

6. *Invites* countries in a position to do so and relevant organizations to provide voluntary funding for promoting the participation of developing countries in the meetings of the Governing Council of UN-Habitat and in the World Urban Forum, as well as in other relevant conferences on sustainable urbanization;

7. *Requests* the Secretary-General to submit to the Economic and Social Council for its consideration at its substantive session of 2012 a report on the coordinated implementation of the Habitat Agenda.

In response to resolution 2011/21, the Secretary-General, by an August note [A/66/326], transmitted his May report to the Assembly.

Third UN Conference on housing and sustainable urban development (Habitat III)

In an August report [A/66/282], submitted in response to resolution 64/207 [YUN 2009, p. 1040] and UN-Habitat Governing Council resolution 23/8 (see p. 996), the Secretary-General recommended convening a third UN conference on housing and sustainable urban development (Habitat III) as a means of examining key developments that had emerged since the 1996 UN Conference on Human Settlements, including: the demographic dominance of cities, which had come to accommodate more than half of the world's population, and their dominant role as engines of national economic growth and development; the rapid spatial expansion of urban settlements, which led to the emergence of megacities, mega-urban regions, as well as increasing spatial and social fragmentation, poverty and inequality within cities; and the emergence of new global issues and forces, including high levels of internal and transnational migration, globalization, sustainable urban development, climate change, rising urban insecurity and crime, the increasing destruction of human settlements by natural and human-caused disasters and conflicts, and rising informality within cities. The conference would also allow consideration of a resurgence of the role of the public sector in urban planning and development and the significantly increased frequency, intensity and impacts on cities of human-caused and natural disasters, and the larger volume of operational work undertaken by UN-Habitat in post-disaster and post-conflict reconstruction and rehabilitation. The report concluded with recommendations on the preparatory process for the proposed Habitat III conference, which should outline a new development agenda that could respond to the new challenges and role of cities.

GENERAL ASSEMBLY ACTION

On 22 December [meeting 91], the General Assembly, on the recommendation of the Second Committee [A/66/441], adopted **resolution 66/207** without vote [agenda item 20].

Implementation of the outcome of the United Nations Conference on Human Settlements (Habitat II) and strengthening of the United Nations Human Settlements Programme (UN-Habitat)

The General Assembly,

Recalling its resolution 65/165 of 20 December 2010 and all other previous resolutions on the implementation of the outcome of the United Nations Conference on Human Settlements (Habitat II) and strengthening of the United Nations Human Settlements Programme (UN-Habitat),

Recalling also Economic and Social Council resolution 2011/21 of 27 July 2011 and all other previous resolutions of the Council on human settlements,

Recalling further the goal contained in the United Nations Millennium Declaration and the 2005 World Summit Outcome of achieving a significant improvement in the lives of at least 100 million slum dwellers by 2020 and the goal contained in the Plan of Implementation of the World Summit on Sustainable Development ("Johannesburg Plan of Implementation") to halve, by 2015, the proportion of people who lack access to safe drinking water and sanitation,

Recalling the Habitat Agenda, the Declaration on Cities and Other Human Settlements in the New Millennium, the Johannesburg Plan of Implementation and the Monterrey Consensus of the International Conference on Financing for Development,

Expressing concern about the continuing increase in the number of slum dwellers in the world, despite the attainment of the Millennium Development Goal target of achieving a significant improvement in the lives of at least 100 million slum dwellers by 2020,

Taking note of the outcome document of the High-level Plenary Meeting of the General Assembly on the Millennium Development Goals, in particular paragraph 77 (*k*), in which Heads of State and Government committed themselves to working towards cities without slums, beyond current targets, by reducing slum populations and improving the lives of slum dwellers, with adequate support of the international community, by prioritizing national urban planning strategies with the participation of all stakeholders, by promoting equal access for people living in slums to public services, including health, education, energy, water and sanitation and adequate shelter, and by promoting sustainable urban and rural development, and encouraging UN-Habitat to continue providing the necessary technical assistance,

Taking note also of resolution 23/9 of 15 April 2011 of the Governing Council of UN-Habitat, entitled "Global and national strategies and frameworks for improving the lives of slum dwellers beyond the Millennium Development Goals target",

Recognizing the negative impacts of environmental degradation, including climate change, desertification and loss of biodiversity, on human settlements,

Welcoming with appreciation the important contribution of UN-Habitat, within its mandate, to more cost-effective transitions between emergency relief, recovery and reconstruction, and also its participation in the Inter-Agency Standing Committee,

Welcoming the progress being made by UN-Habitat in the implementation of its medium-term strategic and institutional plan for the period 2008–2013 and its efforts, as a non-resident agency, in helping programme countries to mainstream the Habitat Agenda into their respective development frameworks,

Welcoming also the offer of the Government of Italy and the city of Naples to host the sixth session of the World Urban Forum from 1 to 7 September 2012,

Recognizing the continuing need for adequate and predictable financial contributions to the United Nations Habitat and Human Settlements Foundation so as to ensure timely, effective and concrete global implementation of the Habitat Agenda, the Declaration on Cities and Other Human Settlements in the New Millennium and the relevant internationally agreed development goals,

Taking note of resolution 23/10 of 15 April 2011 of the Governing Council of UN-Habitat, entitled "Future activities by the United Nations Human Settlements Programme in urban economy and financial mechanisms for urban upgrading, housing and basic services for the urban poor",

Recalling its resolution 64/207 of 21 December 2009, in which it took note of the recommendation made by the Governing Council of UN-Habitat in its resolution 22/1 of 3 April 2009 and, having considered the question of convening, in 2016, a third United Nations conference on housing and sustainable urban development (Habitat III), requested the Secretary-General to prepare a report on that question, in collaboration with the Governing Council, for its consideration at its sixty-sixth session,

Recalling also that, in its resolution 65/165, it encouraged the Secretary-General, in consultation with the Governing Council of UN-Habitat and in discussion with all the partners of the Habitat Agenda, to consider the possibility of integrating the two themes of "housing finance systems" and "sustainable urbanization" into the preparatory process for Habitat III,

1. *Takes note* of the reports of the Secretary-General on the coordinated implementation of the Habitat Agenda, on the implementation of the outcome of the United Nations Conference on Human Settlements (Habitat II) and strengthening of the United Nations Human Settlements Programme (UN-Habitat) and on the third United Nations conference on housing and sustainable urban development (Habitat III);

2. *Decides* to convene in 2016, in line with the bi-decennial cycle (1976, 1996 and 2016), a third United Nations conference on housing and sustainable urban development (Habitat III) to reinvigorate the global commitment to sustainable urbanization that should focus on the implementation of a "New Urban Agenda", which should build on the Habitat Agenda, the Declaration on Cities and Other Human Settlements in the New Millennium and the relevant internationally agreed development goals, including those contained in the United Nations Millennium Declaration, and the Johannesburg Declaration on Sustainable Development and the Johannesburg Plan of Implementation, and the outcomes of other major United Nations conferences and summits;

3. *Acknowledges*, in this regard, the importance of the forthcoming United Nations Conference on Sustainable Development, to be held in Rio de Janeiro, Brazil, from 20 to 22 June 2012;

4. *Emphasizes* that the Conference and the preparatory process should take full advantage of planned meetings by aligning with the twenty-fourth and twenty-fifth sessions

of the Governing Council of UN-Habitat and with the sixth and seventh sessions of the World Urban Forum, and encourages the regular regional ministerial conferences on housing and urban development and other relevant expert group meetings to support the activities of the preparatory process, taking into account that the Conference and the preparatory process should be carried out in the most inclusive, efficient, effective and improved manner;

5. *Decides* to consider before the end of 2012 the scope, modalities, format and organization of the third United Nations conference on housing and sustainable urban development (Habitat III), in a most efficient and effective manner;

6. *Invites* the Secretary-General to appoint the Executive Director of UN-Habitat to serve as Secretary-General of the third United Nations conference on housing and sustainable urban development and to act as focal point on behalf of the United Nations system;

7. *Invites* Governments and regional and local authorities, in accordance with national legislation, to enumerate the populations living in slums in their countries, regions and urban areas and, on that basis, to set, with the support of the international community, voluntary and realistic national, regional and local targets, to be attained by 2020, with regard to improving significantly the lives of slum dwellers, in line with resolution 23/9 of the Governing Council of UN-Habitat;

8. *Invites* UN-Habitat to provide, within its current budget and in line with its medium-term strategic and institutional plan for the period 2008–2013, or its subsequent strategic plan, technical and advisory assistance to Governments and regional and local authorities wishing to assess their slum population levels and trends, set voluntary national, regional and local 2020 targets, prepare national, regional and local slum prevention and upgrading strategies and plans, formulate and implement slum upgrading and housing programmes and monitor the progress of implementation, and to report periodically to the Governing Council and the General Assembly;

9. *Welcomes* the progress made by UN-Habitat in the implementation of its medium-term strategic and institutional plan for the period 2008–2013, and takes note of the conclusions of the midterm review of the implementation of the plan submitted to the Governing Council of UN-Habitat at its twenty-third session;

10. *Encourages* UN-Habitat to continue to work on the strategic plan for 2014–2019 in consultation with the Committee of Permanent Representatives, in an open and transparent manner, setting realistic and achievable goals for the period it covers;

11. *Takes note* of the report of the Executive Director on the review of the governance structure of the United Nations Human Settlements Programme, and encourages UN-Habitat to move this process forward, in cooperation with the Committee of Permanent Representatives, in order to continue on its path towards the improvement of its transparency, accountability, efficiency and effectiveness;

12. *Notes* the request made by the Governing Council of UN-Habitat in its resolution 23/10 that the Executive Director, in building on the lessons learned from the experimental reimbursable seeding operations and slum upgrading facility programmes, shift the focus of the work of UN-Habitat in the area of human settlements financing towards strengthening its normative approaches to urban economy and the promotion of finance for urban upgrading, housing and basic services for the urban poor, while taking into account geographical and regional balance, as well as the request to explore as expeditiously as possible and to select, in consultation with the Committee of Permanent Representatives, a partnership model with development finance institutions for future lending, guarantee and financial advisory services in the urban upgrading and housing finance sectors;

13. *Reiterates its encouragement* to UN-Habitat to continue, within its mandate and in line with its medium-term strategic and institutional plan for the period 2008–2013, its existing cooperation on issues related to cities and climate change and to continue to play a complementary role in matters related to climate change within the United Nations system, in particular in addressing the vulnerability of cities to climate change, including through further normative work and expansion of its technical assistance to towns and cities on local action for the mitigation of urban-based greenhouse gas emissions and adaptation to climate change, with a focus on vulnerable urban populations, slum dwellers, the urban poor and at-risk populations;

14. *Stresses* the importance of timely action by UN-Habitat in response to natural and human-made disasters, in particular through its work in addressing post-disaster and post-conflict housing and infrastructure needs through its normative and operational work as part of the continuum from emergency relief to recovery and to urban development through effective urban planning;

15. *Reiterates its support* for the dissemination and implementation of the guidelines on decentralization and strengthening of local authorities and the guidelines on access to basic services for all, approved by the Governing Council of UN-Habitat in its resolutions 21/3 of 20 April 2007 and 22/8 of 3 April 2009, respectively, and reaffirmed by the Governing Council in its resolution 23/12 of 15 April 2011;

16. *Invites* the international donor community and financial institutions to contribute generously to UN-Habitat through increased voluntary financial contributions to the United Nations Habitat and Human Settlements Foundation, including the Water and Sanitation Trust Fund and the technical cooperation trust funds, and invites Governments in a position to do so and other stakeholders to provide predictable multi-year funding and increased non-earmarked contributions;

17. *Requests* the Secretary-General to submit to the General Assembly at its sixty-seventh session a report on the implementation of the present resolution;

18. *Decides* to include in the provisional agenda of its sixty-seventh session the item entitled "Implementation of the outcome of the United Nations Conference on Human Settlements (Habitat II) and strengthening of the United Nations Human Settlements Programme (UN-Habitat)".

Chapter VIII

Population

In 2011, world population passed the 7 billion threshold. Life expectancy reached 70 years in all of the world's regions except Africa. The world was both older—with 893 million people over the age of 60—and younger—there were 1.8 billion people between the ages of 10 and 24, the largest youth cohort in history. Nearly 2,000 communities declared their abandonment of female genital mutilation/cutting during the year, and there was a sizeable unmet need for contraception in at least 46 countries.

UN population activities continued to be guided by the Programme of Action adopted at the 1994 International Conference on Population and Development (ICPD) and the key actions for its implementation adopted at the twenty-first special session of the General Assembly in 1999. The Commission on Population and Development—the body responsible for monitoring, reviewing and assessing implementation of the Programme of Action—considered as its special theme "Fertility, reproductive health and development". The Population Division of the UN Department of Economic and Social Affairs continued to analyse and report on world demographic trends and policies.

The United Nations Population Fund (UNFPA) assisted countries in implementing the ICPD agenda and the Millennium Development Goals through their use of population data to formulate sound policies and programmes. In 2011, UNFPA provided assistance to 156 countries, areas and territories, with emphasis on expanding access to maternal and newborn health, increasing availability of family planning, strengthening HIV-prevention services, advocating for gender equality and reproductive rights, and increasing young people's access to services. As the world population approached 7 billion, UNFPA launched the 7 Billion Actions campaign to promote dialogue on what it meant to live in a world with so many people and encourage action on issues that affected everyone.

Commission on Population and Development

The Commission on Population and Development, at its forty-fourth session (New York, 16 April 2010 and 11–15 April 2011) [E/2011/25], considered as its special theme "Fertility, reproductive health and development", adopted a resolution [res. 2011/1] on the special theme, and discussed follow-up actions to the recommendations of the 1994 ICPD [YUN 1994, p. 955].

The Commission considered the report of its Bureau on its three intersessional meetings (New York, 5 November 2010, 6 and 20 January 2011) [E/CN.9/2011/2] and took note [E/2011/25 (dec. 2011/102)] of the Secretary-General's report on programme implementation and progress of work in the field of population [YUN 2010, p. 1063] and of a Secretariat note on the draft programme of work of the Population Division for the 2012–2013 biennium [E/CN.9/2011/CRP.1/Rev.1]. The Commission also had before it four reports of the Secretary-General [E/CN.9/2011/3–6] (see below) and 10 statements submitted by non-governmental organizations (NGOs) in consultative status with the Economic and Social Council [E/CN.9/2011/NGO/1–10].

The Commission held general debates on: national experience in population matters: fertility, reproductive health and development; the further implementation of the ICPD Programme of Action in the light of its twentieth anniversary; and the contribution of population and development issues to the theme of the annual ministerial review of the Economic and Social Council (see p. 1056).

Reports of Secretary-General. In a January report [E/CN.9/2011/3] on fertility, reproductive health and development, the Secretary-General indicated that reductions in fertility could contribute to development and concluded—by looking at the diverse experiences of low-fertility, intermediate-fertility and high-fertility countries—that high-fertility countries tended to score poorly in most outcomes related to reproductive health. The report addressed different aspects of reproductive health, focusing on ways to accelerate the achievement of the goals and objectives of the ICPD Programme of Action. Global fertility, measured as the average number of children women would bear at current fertility rates, had dropped from 4.9 children per woman in 1950 to an estimated 2.5 children per woman in 2005–2010. Fifty-six per cent of women of reproductive age who were married or in a union used modern contraceptive methods, and 9 out of 10 developing country Governments provided support to family planning programmes.

Declining fertility had induced beneficial changes in the age distribution of the population, ushering in a period when the number of potential workers grew faster than the number of dependants and boosting savings. Countries that used those savings to increase investment, generate more jobs and improve child health and education had reaped benefits in economic growth and human development. Between 1960 and 1995, declining fertility had accounted for an estimated 20 per cent of per capita output growth in both developed and developing countries. The report concluded that slowing fertility rates—by ensuring universal access to reproductive health-care services, meeting the need for family planning and accelerating the improvement of maternal and child health—could be beneficial for development.

A report issued in January [E/CN.9/2011/4] on the monitoring of population programmes focused on fertility, reproductive health and development. It reviewed the interrelations between fertility, sexual and reproductive health, development and human rights, and examined work in progress. The report also identified challenges of programme implementation, including governance issues; inadequate funding; the global financial crisis; weakened health systems; gender inequalities; opposition from faith-based organizations; and inequities in the delivery of services to the poor. The report highlighted knowledge of what worked and summarized 12 key elements needed to speed up progress on universal access to sexual and reproductive health.

The Secretary-General's January report [E/CN.9/2011/5] on the flow of financial resources for assisting in the implementation of the ICPD Programme of Action, submitted in accordance with General Assembly resolutions 49/128 [YUN 1994, p. 963] and 50/124 [YUN 1995, p. 1094], stated that although donor assistance had been increasing steadily over the previous few years, reaching $10.4 billion in 2008, the upward trend had stalled, and funding remained virtually unchanged in 2009. It was expected to increase slightly to under $10.5 billion in 2010 and to $10.8 billion in 2011. Resources for population activities mobilized by developing countries, as a group, were estimated at $29.8 billion for 2009 and were expected to increase to $31 billion in 2010 and $34 billion in 2011. Funding levels remained below the targets necessary to implement the goals of the Programme of Action and to achieve the Millennium Development Goals (MDGs); that was true for all four components of the costed population package—family planning; reproductive health; sexually transmitted diseases and HIV/AIDS; and basic research, data and population and development policy analysis. Funding was not expected to increase to levels required to meet current needs, given the global financial situation. It was therefore essential for Governments of donor and developing countries to mobilize the resources required to meet current needs.

The Secretary-General's biennial report [E/CN.9/2011/6] on world demographic trends, submitted in accordance with Economic and Social Council resolution 1996/2 [YUN 1996, p. 976], reviewed the results of six population-projection scenarios prepared in order to explore the implications of different fertility trends for population growth and population ageing over the next three centuries. The scenarios underscored the importance of reaching replacement-level fertility in all countries to avoid unsustainable increases or decreases of the population and provided a rationale for addressing current population imbalances and reinforcing policies that fostered fertility reductions in countries where fertility was still above replacement level. According to the scenarios, current population dynamics would produce excessive population growth if maintained over the long run. To stabilize world population, fertility had to drop to below-replacement level and maintain that level for a lengthy period to counterbalance the expected increases in longevity. Eventually, fertility had to regain replacement level. Such a path underpinned the medium scenario, by which world population peaked at 9.4 billion in 2070, declined to 7.9 billion in 2195 and rose to 8.3 billion in 2300. There was no guarantee that the scenario would become a reality as high-fertility countries might not reduce their fertility sufficiently or countries with intermediate fertility levels might see them stagnate above replacement level.

Commission action. The Commission adopted and brought to the attention of the Economic and Social Council a resolution on fertility, reproductive health and development [E/2011/25 (res. 2011/1)], by which it reaffirmed its commitment to the full implementation of the ICPD Programme of Action and welcomed the General Assembly's decision in resolution 65/234 [YUN 2010, p. 1053] to extend the Programme beyond 2014. The Commission urged Governments to promote full respect for human rights and fundamental freedoms, including by eliminating all forms of discrimination against girls and women; to redouble efforts to eliminate preventable maternal morbidity and mortality by ensuring that universal access to reproductive health was achieved by 2015; and to strengthen health systems and ensure that they prioritized universal access to sexual and reproductive information and health-care services. Governments were also urged to strengthen basic infrastructure, human and technical resources and the provision of health facilities, and to enact laws concerning the minimum legal age of consent and the minimum age for marriage.

The Commission decided that the special theme for its forty-sixth (2013) session would be "New trends in migration: demographic aspects" and that its forty-seventh (2014) session would be devoted to an assessment of the status of implementation of the ICPD Programme of Action [E/2011/25 (dec. 2011/101)]. It also adopted the provisional agenda for its forty-fifth (2012) session.

By **decision 2011/247** of 27 July, the Economic and Social Council took note of the report of the Commission on its forty-fourth (2011) session and approved the provisional agenda for the forty-fifth (2012) session.

In preparation for its forty-fifth session, the Commission's Bureau held two meetings in 2011 (New York, 7 September and Yogyakarta, Indonesia, 18 October) [E/CN.9/2012/3].

Communication. On 24 May [E/CN.9/2012/1], Indonesia transmitted to the Secretary-General the Yogyakarta Declaration on Family Planning, Maternal Health and Poverty Alleviation, adopted at the International Conference on Promoting Family Planning and Maternal Health for Poverty Alleviation (Yogyakarta, 26–27 October 2010).

International migration and development

Global Forum meeting. The fifth meeting of the Global Forum on Migration and Development (Geneva, 1–2 December) [A/67/73] focused on the theme "Taking Action on Migration and Development—Coherence, Capacity and Cooperation". The Forum—a State-led, informal consultative process open to UN Member States and observers—addressed the plight of the approximately 214 million international migrants worldwide and the challenge to achieve humane and secure circumstances for migrants as well as prosperity for their host societies and countries of origin. Attended by some 600 delegates from 160 countries and 36 observers, as well as about 120 civil society representatives, the Forum featured a meeting of civil society (29–30 November), followed by the governmental meeting (1–2 December). Three working sessions focused on labour mobility and development; addressing irregular migration through coherent migration-and-development strategies; and tools for evidence-based migration and development policies. The Forum made recommendations for: Governments in destination countries to offer companies seeking to invest in emerging markets incentives to help train the local workforce; destination countries with large numbers of unemployed migrant workers to cooperate with companies in the country of origin in providing jobs for returning workers; countries of origin and of destination to establish partnerships to address the multiple aspects of irregular migration; and Governments of destination countries to establish schemes designed to prevent xenophobia and group enmity towards migrants.

On 4 November, Mexico transmitted to the Secretary-General the report [YUN 2010, p. 1054] of the fourth meeting of the Global Forum on Migration and Development (Puerto Vallarta, Mexico, 8–11 November 2010).

General Assembly informal thematic debate. Pursuant to General Assembly resolution 63/225 [YUN 2008, p. 1186], the General Assembly President convened an informal thematic debate on international migration and development (New York, 19 May) [A/65/944], which sought to take stock of and contribute to the ongoing dialogue on the issue, including the process leading to the Assembly's second High-level Dialogue on International Migration and Development in 2013. Two panel debates were held: one on the contribution of migrants to development, and the other on improving international cooperation on international migration and development. In his summary of the debate, the President concluded that international migration deserved continued attention, both because international cooperation was necessary to take advantage of the opportunities it generated and because its impact was likely to increase. Every effort should be made to continue the dialogue, strengthen partnerships, support capacity-development and safeguard the rights of migrants. By showcasing good practices and sharing innovative policies, the debate had set a useful basis for the consideration of those issues in 2013.

Ninth Meeting on International Migration. In response to General Assembly resolution 58/208 [YUN 2003, p. 1087], the UN Population Division organized the Ninth Coordination Meeting on International Migration (New York, 17–18 February) [ESA/P/WP.219], attended by some 100 representatives of UN system bodies, intergovernmental organizations and NGOs, as well as invited experts and representatives of Member States. Participants reviewed the latest evidence on emerging topics; discussed recent initiatives on capacity-building and training on international migration; and, in a two-part session on measuring the impact of migration, focused on new approaches to assess the contribution of international migration to countries of origin and destination, and on measuring migrant integration in developed and developing countries. Twenty-three organizations reported on their migration activities during the coordination segment.

By **resolution 66/172** of 19 December (see p. 667), the General Assembly called on States to promote and protect the human rights and fundamental freedoms of migrants and to ratify the International Convention on the Protection of the Rights of All Migrant Workers and Members of Their Families [YUN 1990, p. 594]. On the same date, by **resolution 66/128** (see p. 1072), the Assembly called on Governments to adopt or strengthen measures to protect the human rights of women migrant workers and to expand dialogue among States on devising innovative methods to promote legal channels of migration.

United Nations Population Fund

Activities

Executive Board. The Executive Board of the United Nations Development Programme (UNDP), the United Nations Population Fund (UNFPA) and the United Nations Office for Project Services (UNOPS) held its first regular session (31 January–3 February), annual session (6–17 June) and second regular session (6–9 September) [E/2011/35] in New York.

On 17 June [E/2011/35 (dec. 2011/25)], the Executive Board took note of the documents that made up the UNFPA Executive Director's 2010 report [DP/FPA/2011/3 (Part I & Add.1, Part II)] [YUN 2010, p. 1058]. It encouraged UNFPA to report on the development and implementation of programmes that sought to provide assistance to adolescents and youth; supported UNFPA in improving policies on adolescents and youth, and in ensuring the inclusion of adolescents and youth in policies and programmes; and emphasized the need for UNFPA to enable the exchange of best practices and effective adolescent and youth policies.

By **decision 2011/215** of 18 July, the Economic and Social Council took note of the UNDP/UNFPA report to the Council [ibid.]; and the report of the UNDP/UNFPA Executive Board on its work during 2010 [YUN 2010, p. 867].

Reports of Executive Director. In a report [DP/FPA/2012/6 (Part I)] to the Executive Board, the UNFPA Executive Director reviewed progress made by UNFPA in 2011 in implementing its 2008–2013 strategic plan, focusing on outcomes in population and development, reproductive health and rights, and gender equality. While leading the global review of ICPD, UNFPA focused on the cohort of young people and MDG 5 on maternal health, which showed the least progress compared with other MDGs.

With regard to the 2008–2011 strategic plan indicators, trend data were available for 23 of the 26 indicators and targets set for 2011 had been achieved for 9 indicators. Progress for 14 of the 23 indicators was lagging behind, although in a number of countries there were positive signs that investment was making a difference. On programme performance at the country level, 83 per cent of country programmes had implemented 75 per cent of planned annual workplan outputs as compared with the 2007 baseline of 51 per cent. Total UNFPA expenditures in the focus area of reproductive health and rights remained the highest (58 per cent), followed by those in population and development (16.3 per cent), gender equality (12.4 per cent), and programme coordination and assistance (13.3 per cent).

An addendum [DP/FPA/2012/6 (Part I)/Add.1] provided a statistical and financial review for 2011. The report stated that from 2010 to 2011, total UNFPA revenue increased by $52.4 million, or 6 per cent, to $929.1 million due to increases of $96 million in cofinancing revenue, $3.9 million in other revenue and a 9.5 per cent decrease in regular resource revenue of $47.4 million; regular resources revenue totalled $484 million. Total expenses increased from $823.9 million to $824.5 million and the balance of unexpended regular resources—a total of $49.8 million—was available for programming in 2012. The operational reserve was decreased in accordance with UNFPA Financial Regulations and Rules. UNFPA closed the year in robust financial health.

Midterm review. In July, pursuant to a 2009 Executive Board decision [YUN 2009, p. 1049], the Executive Director submitted a report [DP/FPA/2011/11] on the midterm review of the UNFPA 2008–2013 strategic plan. The report examined the changing context within which UNFPA operated, and reviewed the progress, achievements and challenges in implementing the strategic plan from 2008 to 2010. The review concluded that while UNFPA had much to be proud of, its full potential was still to be realized. The report identified challenges relating to the organization's ability to deliver both development and management results. A proposed revised strategic direction and results frameworks addressed those challenges, strengthening the organization's focus and prioritizing issues in a streamlined set of seven outcomes and outputs: linking population dynamics and development plans; expanding access to maternal and newborn health; increasing availability of family planning; strengthening HIV-prevention services; advocating for gender equality and reproductive rights; increasing young people's access to services; and harnessing the power of data. An integrated financial resources framework laid out the estimated resources needed to implement the remainder of the plan.

On 9 September [E/2011/35 (dec. 2011/39)], the Executive Board took note of the report, welcomed its strategic direction and requested UNFPA to reflect the priorities of the revised strategic plan in the

2012–2013 institutional budget. It also requested UNFPA to submit in 2013 the cumulative report on the 2008–2013 UNFPA strategic plan at the Board's annual session and the new strategic plan at its second regular session.

JIU recommendations. The Executive Director reported [DP/FPA/2012/6 (Part II)] on UNFPA management's responses to the recommendations of the Joint Inspection Unit (JIU). In 2011, JIU issued four reports that were relevant to UNFPA concerning the review of the medical service in the UN system [JIU/REP/2011/1]; South-South and triangular cooperation in the UN system [JIU/REP/2011/3]; accountability frameworks in the UN system [JIU/REP/2011/5]; and business continuity in the UN system [JIU/REP/2011/6]. Out of 35 recommendations issued by JIU in 2011, 16 pertained to UNFPA management and five were directed to legislative organs. The report provided UNFPA management responses to those recommendations, as well as an update of the implementation status of JIU recommendations issued in 2009 [YUN 2009, p. 1049] and in 2010 [YUN 2010, p. 1058].

State of World Population report. The Fund's *State of World Population 2011* report [Sales No. E.10.III.H.1] was entitled "*People and Possibilities in a World of 7 Billion*". Looking at the dynamics behind the numbers, the report explained the trends that were defining a world of 7 billion.

Population and development

In 2011, UNFPA programme assistance in population and development totalled $76 million from core resources and $35.7 million from other resources. As the world population approached 7 billion, UNFPA, on World Population Day (11 July), launched the 7 Billion Actions campaign to promote dialogue on what it meant to live in a world with so many people and encourage action on related issues. The worldwide advocacy effort continued through 31 October. UNFPA also worked to ensure that population issues were addressed in MDGs reviews and the follow-up to major UN conferences.

At the national level, support for integrating population dynamics and related population matters in development strategies and plans was mainly provided through capacity-development activities. The target for 2011 of 90 per cent was partially met. UNFPA continued to empower young people to advocate for the inclusion of their rights and needs in public policies through capacity development, strengthening youth-led organizations, and developing institutional structures for youth participation, with a particular focus on those most marginalized.

Countries were progressing on census operations. By the end of 2011, 63 per cent of programme countries receiving UNFPA assistance had completed their population and housing censuses as planned with significant support from UNFPA. The Fund also worked to raise awareness, build a knowledge base, and strengthen national capacity to incorporate emerging population issues such as ageing, migration, urbanization, the environment and climate change into national development plans, tailored to address the growing needs of countries in those areas. Slightly more than half of the newly approved national development plans/poverty reduction strategy papers addressed such emerging population issues, indicating limited progress.

Population statistics. In 2011, the 7 billionth person was projected to have been born on 26 October. Life expectancy reached 70 years in all of the world's regions except Africa. Children were healthier and more of them were surviving into adulthood. The world was both older, with 893 million people over the age of 60, and younger—there were 1.8 billion people between the ages of 10 and 24, the largest youth cohort in history. About one in two people lived in a city.

Reproductive health and rights

In 2011, UNFPA programme assistance in reproductive health totalled $158.5 million from core resources and $239.3 million from other resources. The year saw strong leadership, increased momentum and decisive action in relation to reproductive health. The Secretary-General's Global Strategy on Women's and Children's Health continued to elevate reproductive health and reproductive rights at the international level and in policies and programmes at the national level. Over 100 new commitments were made, ranging from increasing access to modern contraceptives (Afghanistan, Bangladesh, Cambodia, Kyrgyzstan, Myanmar, Nepal, Nigeria); increasing the budget allocated to maternal, neonatal and child care by 50 per cent by 2015 (Senegal); increasing human resources for maternal and newborn health (Afghanistan, Bangladesh, Lao People's Democratic Republic, Myanmar, Nepal); providing free deliveries (Indonesia, Lao People's Democratic Republic, Nepal); and reducing adolescent pregnancies (Bangladesh). Efforts were scaled up in Afghanistan, Bangladesh, Burkina Faso, the Democratic Republic of the Congo, Sierra Leone, Zambia and Zimbabwe to enhance financing, strengthen policy and improve service delivery for women's and children's health.

The Campaign on Accelerated Reduction of Maternal Mortality in Africa continued to expand, with 36 countries engaged in it. The UNFPA maternal health thematic fund scaled up support to 33 priority countries for maternal health, including for midwifery, and to 43 countries for the Campaign to End Fistula.

The midwifery programme, led by UNFPA in partnership with the International Confederation of Midwives, supported 30 countries, with 22 midwifery advisers in 19 countries.

UNFPA intensified efforts to close the gap between the number of individuals who used contraceptives and those who wished to space or limit the number of their children, garnering donor support and directing funds to strengthen the capacity of health systems and procure essential reproductive health supplies. Community-based distribution played a key role in reaching underserved communities. The proportion of countries with service delivery points offering at least three modern methods of contraception continued to improve and the number of couples using modern methods was increasing dramatically. UNFPA was a leading partner in the Reproductive Health Supplies Coalition. The Fund played a critical role in supporting the Andean Plan for the Prevention of Adolescent Pregnancy, an initiative of Bolivia, Chile, Colombia, Ecuador, Peru and Venezuela to address adolescent pregnancy.

UNFPA continued to lead activities to increase the demand, access to, and utilization of HIV- and sexually transmitted infections-prevention services, especially for women, young people and other vulnerable groups. Expanding access to condoms was a central focus. Some 86 countries were implementing the UNFPA 10-step strategic approach to comprehensive condom programming and developing national condom strategies, policies and plans. Among the development partners, UNFPA was the largest supplier of both male and female condoms to low-income countries in 2010. The Fund also continued to strengthen capacities to deliver and scale up adolescent sexual and reproductive health/HIV information, education and services. Support was provided in 87 countries to strengthen youth-friendly services in those fields.

Gender equality and women's empowerment

In 2011, UNFPA programme assistance in gender equality and women's empowerment totalled $41.8 million from core resources and $43.2 million from other resources. The Fund provided technical assistance for strengthening national capacities to ensure that national development policies and funding frameworks incorporated gender equality and the human rights of women and adolescent girls, particularly their reproductive rights. In Eritrea, Gabon, Myanmar, Sri Lanka and Uganda, UNFPA built national capacity for gender mainstreaming and for raising awareness of the Convention on the Elimination of All Forms of Discrimination against Women [YUN 1979, p. 895] and other human rights conventions. UNFPA also worked with partners, in particular UN-Women [YUN 2010, p. 1178], to strengthen gender mainstreaming in the UN system.

UNFPA strategies sought to increase a supportive environment for male participation in the elimination of harmful practices. In Bangladesh, Cambodia, China, Malawi and South Africa, UNFPA and its partners mobilized men and boys and initiated new programmes on gender-based violence (GBV) prevention and improved response. UNFPA engagement with male parliamentarians in several countries, including Indonesia, Myanmar and Sri Lanka, through regional networks helped raise awareness and support for enabling policies and legal frameworks.

The UNFPA-United Nations Children's Fund (UNICEF) Joint Programme on Female Genital Mutilation/Cutting contributed to the accelerated abandonment of the practice in some 15 countries. Efforts against the practice yielded encouraging results. Throughout Africa, more than 18,000 community education sessions were held and about 3,000 religious leaders publicly declared that the practice should end. Consequently, almost 2,000 communities declared their abandonment of the practice during 2011. In addition, two countries—Guinea-Bissau and Kenya—issued legislation on the practice, bringing to 18 the number of countries banning it in Africa.

UNFPA supported parliaments and government departments in developing national legislation relating to women's human rights and reproductive rights in Gabon, Mali and Zambia. The Fund convened a global meeting on prenatal sex selection (Ha Noi, Viet Nam, 5–6 October) with high-level participation from Asian countries and some Eastern European countries. UNFPA supported South-South collaboration on addressing sex selection and lessons learned from China and India, and provided technical assistance to Eastern European countries.

UNFPA continued to address GBV, particularly domestic and sexual violence, in collaboration with other UN agencies and in the context of inter-agency partnerships. With UNFPA support, Angola adopted a law against domestic violence; Zimbabwe developed the 2011–2015 national GBV strategy; Maldives finalized the Domestic Violence Bill drafted in 2010; and the Sudan incorporated the national GBV strategy in the national five-year strategic plan. Armenia developed and promoted a national GBV action plan.

Country and intercountry programmes

UNFPA programme expenditures for country, global and regional activities in 2011 totalled $358.6 million, compared with $366.3 million in 2010, according to the Executive Director's statistical and financial review [DP/FPA/2012/6 (Part I)/Add.1]. The 2011 figure included $274.2 million for country/

territory programmes (compared with $282.6 million in 2010) and $84.4 million for global and regional programmes (compared with $83.7 million in 2010).

Africa. Provisional data for UNFPA expenditures for programmes in sub-Saharan Africa totalled $136.8 million in 2011, compared to $137.4 million in 2010. Most of that amount was spent on reproductive health (43.3 per cent), followed by population and development (21.5 per cent), programme coordination and assistance (21.5 per cent), and gender equality and women's empowerment (13.7 per cent).

On 3 February [E/2011/35 (dec. 2011/13)], the Executive Board, at its first regular session of 2011, approved the UNFPA country programme documents on Burkina Faso and Zambia, and took note of the draft common country programme document for the United Republic of Tanzania. On 17 June [dec. 2011/30], at its annual session, the Board took note of the draft country programme documents for Ethiopia, Gabon, Ghana, Mauritania, Sao Tome and Principe, Senegal and Zimbabwe. It took note of the one-year programme extension for Guinea; approved the two-year programme extension for Madagascar; approved the second one-year programme extension for South Africa; and approved the UNFPA results and resources framework of the common country programme document for Tanzania. On 9 September [dec. 2011/31], at its second regular session of 2011, the Board welcomed South Sudan as a new programme country for UNDP, UNFPA and UNOPS, and authorized the UNDP Administrator and the UNFPA and UNOPS Executive Directors to proceed with programme development in the country. On the same day [dec. 2011/40], the Board noted the request by South Sudan to present, on an exceptional basis, the UNDP and UNFPA draft country programme documents to the Board at its first regular session of 2012; decided that it would discuss those documents at an informal consultation prior to that session; and decided to approve, on an exceptional basis, the final UNDP and UNFPA country programme documents for South Sudan at that session. Also on 9 September [dec. 2011/42], the Board took note of the one-year country programme extension for Eritrea; the draft common country programme for Cape Verde; and the draft country programme documents for the Central African Republic, Chad, the Gambia, Malawi and Mozambique. The Board also approved the country programmes for Ethiopia, Gabon, Ghana, Mauritania, Sao Tome and Principe, Senegal and Zimbabwe on a no-objection basis.

Arab States. Provisional expenditures for UNFPA programmes in the Arab States totalled $26.4 million in 2011, compared with $25.8 million in 2010. Most of that amount was spent on reproductive health (48.5 per cent), followed by programme coordination and assistance (21.2 per cent), population and development (17.8 per cent), and gender equality and women's empowerment (4.3 per cent).

On 3 February [E/2011/35 (dec. 2011/13)], the Executive Board approved the UNFPA country programme document on Somalia. On 17 June [dec. 2011/30], the Board took note of the draft country programme document for Morocco and of the one-year programme extension for Tunisia. On 9 September [dec. 2011/42], the Board took note of the one-year programme extensions for Egypt and the Syrian Arab Republic, and of the draft country programme documents for Algeria and Yemen. It also approved the country programme for Morocco on a no-objection basis.

Asia and the Pacific. Provisional expenditures for UNFPA programmes in Asia and the Pacific totalled $94.3 million in 2011, compared with $96 million in 2010. Most of that amount was spent on reproductive health (59.1 per cent), followed by population and development (19.5 per cent), programme coordination and assistance (12 per cent), and gender equality and women's empowerment (9.4 per cent).

On 3 February [E/2011/35 (dec. 2011/13)], the Executive Board approved the UNFPA country programme documents on Indonesia and Maldives. On 17 June [dec. 2011/30], the Board took note of the draft country programme documents for Bangladesh, the Lao People's Democratic Republic, Mongolia and the Philippines. On 9 September [dec. 2011/42], the Board took note of the draft country programme documents for Iran, Myanmar, Papua New Guinea, Thailand and Viet Nam. It also approved the country programmes for Bangladesh, the Lao People's Democratic Republic, Mongolia and the Philippines on a no-objection basis.

Eastern Europe and Central Asia. Provisional expenditures for UNFPA programmes in Eastern Europe and Central Asia totalled $16.2 million in 2011, compared with $16.9 million in 2010. Most of that amount was spent on reproductive health (40.1 per cent), followed by programme coordination and assistance (29 per cent), population and development (19.8 per cent), and gender equality and women's empowerment (11.1 per cent).

On 17 June [E/2011/35 (dec. 2011/30)], the Board took note of the draft country programme documents for Albania, Kyrgyzstan and Ukraine, and of the one-year programme extension for Moldova. On 9 September [dec. 2011/42], the Board approved the country programmes for Albania, Kyrgyzstan and Ukraine on a no-objection basis.

Latin America and the Caribbean. Provisional expenditures for UNFPA programmes in Latin America and the Caribbean totalled $33.2 million in 2011, compared with $38.5 million in 2010. Most of that amount was spent on reproductive health (38.8 per cent), followed by population and development (25 per cent), programme coordination and assistance

(18.7 per cent), and gender equality and women's empowerment (17.5 per cent).

On 3 February [E/2011/35 (dec. 2011/13)], the Executive Board approved the UNFPA country programme document on Uruguay. On 17 June [dec. 2011/30], it took note of the draft country programme documents for El Salvador and Honduras; the draft multi-country programme document for the English-speaking and Dutch-speaking Caribbean countries; the one-year programme extension for Haiti; and the two-year programme extension for Paraguay. On 9 September [dec. 2011/42], the Board took note of the draft country programme documents for Brazil, the Dominican Republic, Panama and Peru. It also approved the country programmes for El Salvador, the English-speaking and Dutch-speaking Caribbean countries and Honduras on a no-objection basis.

Global programme. Provisional expenditures for the UNFPA global programme totalled $51.7 million in 2011, the same as in 2010. Most of that amount was spent on programme coordination and assistance (48.3 per cent), followed by population and development (23.2 per cent), reproductive health (21.9 per cent), and gender equality and women's empowerment (6.6 per cent).

Financial and management questions

Financing

UNFPA income from all sources totalled $929.1 million in 2011, compared with $876.7 million in 2010 [DP/FPA/2012/6 (Part I)/Add.1], comprising $450.7 million from regular resources, $439.8 million from other resources and other income of $38.7 million. Expenditures totalled $824.5 million, up from $823.9 million in 2010, resulting in a net surplus of $104.6 million.

On 3 February [E/2011/35 (dec. 2011/10)], the Executive Board took note of a joint informal note of UNDP, UNFPA and UNICEF on the road map to an integrated budget: cost classification and results-based budgeting; endorsed the results-based budgeting approach contained in the note; and requested UNDP and UNFPA to present their 2012–2013 biennial budget documents in line with the format presented in the note, including the results of the joint review of the impact of cost definitions and classifications of activities on cost recovery.

On 17 June [dec. 2011/27], the Board decided to consider the UNFPA 2012–2013 biennial budget at its first regular session of 2012; approved an interim, one-month budget allocation for January 2012, in the amount of $11.5 million, pending final approval of that budget; and agreed that the allocation would be part of, and not incremental to, the UNFPA 2012–2013 biennial budget.

In November [DP/FPA/2012/1], UNFPA submitted the 2012–2013 institutional budget proposal totalling $292.2 million gross ($245 million). UNFPA had provided the strategic context of the budget in the midterm review of its 2008–2013 strategic plan (see p. 1005). It linked the management results framework in the revised strategic plan with the resources contained in the institutional budget, based on the harmonized results-based budgeting methodology approved by the Executive Board in decision 2011/10 (see above). The financial context of the budget was based on 2012–2013 income estimates of $1,718.8 million.

In December [DP/FPA/2012/2], the Advisory Committee on Administrative and Budgetary Questions (ACABQ) recommended the Board's approval of the proposed appropriation of $292.2 million for the 2012–2013 institutional budget, subject to its comments and recommendations.

Audit and oversight

The Executive Board on 3 February took note of the November 2010 report [YUN 2010, p. 1062] on UNFPA follow-up to recommendations of the United Nations Board of Auditors for the 2008–2009 biennium [E/2011/35 (dec. 2011/9)]. It requested UNFPA management to ensure full compliance with the Auditors' recommendations and to address recurring issues that the Board of Auditors had raised in its reports, particularly issues affecting the management and oversight of expenditures in high-risk environments and programme-execution modalities. The Executive Board requested UNFPA to elaborate, in its 2010 annual internal audit report to the Executive Board and in its management responses, the steps taken to address the significant increase in the number of complaints in cases of fraud and presumptive fraud. It also requested UNFPA to update the Board on the development and implementation of its internal control framework.

In April, the Director of the UNFPA Division for Oversight Services reported on internal audit and oversight activities in 2010 [DP/FPA/2011/5], including audits of nine country offices—six in Africa and three in the Arab States. The report sought to inform the Board of the risks that could impact the work of the Fund in a development environment marked by change and challenges. The document included the annual report of the UNFPA Audit Advisory Committee and management's response.

The Executive Board took note of the report and the corresponding management response on 17 June [E/2011/35 (dec. 2011/22)]. It noted with concern the critical findings of the Division for Oversight Services and requested the Executive Director to improve the implementation of an internal control framework; implement enterprise risk management; address human resources issues; promote the use of evidence-based programming; reduce the number of partners and workplans at the country level; and ensure a smooth transition to the International Public Sector Accounting Standards (IPSAS), adopted by General Assembly resolution 60/283 [YUN 2006, p. 1580]. The Executive Director was further requested to develop a comprehensive plan of action to address the 15 recommendations contained in the report.

Also on 17 June [dec. 2011/23], the Executive Board took note of a coordinated paper [DP-FPA-OPS/2011/1] by UNDP, UNFPA and UNOPS on responding to the emerging demand for greater information disclosure of internal audit reports. The Board decided that the UNDP Administrator and the Executive Directors of UNFPA and UNOPS could, upon request, disclose to a donor intergovernmental organization and the Global Fund to Fight AIDS, Tuberculosis and Malaria internal audit reports pertaining to a given project in which the donor was financially contributing, exercising discretion and protecting the rights of the programme country. It requested UNDP, UNFPA and UNOPS to explore options to facilitate the viewing of internal audit reports, and to present to the Board's second regular (2011) session a proposal for the remote viewing of internal audit reports providing secure access and proper safeguards for the confidentiality of the information disclosed. It also requested UNDP, UNFPA and UNOPS to continue to report, in their annual reports on internal audit and investigation, on the internal audit reports disclosed; to inform the Board on requests from organizations not covered by the decision for disclosure of internal audit reports; and to seek guidance from the Executive Board on such requests for disclosure.

The UNFPA Executive Director in November submitted to the Executive Board the second report [DP/FPA/2012/5] on UNFPA follow-up to the recommendations of the Board of Auditors for the 2008–2009 biennium [YUN 2010, p. 1062]. The report provided an update on UNFPA actions to implement the recommendations and indicated the priority accorded to each of the audit recommendations. As at 30 September, UNFPA had implemented 73 of the 93 recommendations. It had established dedicated mechanisms to follow up on audit recommendations and was addressing the root causes of the problems identified by the Board of Auditors.

Ethics Office

In June, the Executive Board had before it an April report of the UNFPA Ethics Office [DP/FPA/2011/6], reviewing its activities in 2010 and describing the progression of the ethics function in UNFPA since the establishment of the Office in 2008 [YUN 2008, p. 1188].

On 17 June [E/2011/35 (dec. 2011/24)], the Board took note of the report and encouraged UNFPA management to further strengthen the functions of the Office and to provide it with sufficient resources.

Other financial and administrative issues

In a report on funding commitments to UNFPA [DP/FPA/2011/4], the Executive Director analysed contributions by States and others and revenue projections for 2011 and future years. UNFPA considered a stable base of regular resources as critical to enable it to support countries in implementing the ICPD Programme of Action and achieving the MDGs. In line with General Assembly resolution 62/208 [YUN 2007, p. 877], UNFPA recognized that non-core (co-financing) resources represented an important supplement to the Fund's regular resource base.

In 2010, UNFPA income was $866.5 million—$507.7 million in regular resources and $358.8 million in co-financing resources, inclusive of interest and other income. Out of the 150 donor Governments, eight countries belonged to the Organization for Economic Cooperation and Development/Development Assistance Committee, and 33 programme countries increased their contributions. The top 10 donor countries were the Netherlands, Sweden, Norway, the United States, Denmark, Finland, the United Kingdom, Japan, Spain and Germany.

As at 1 March 2011, the projected regular contribution from donor countries for 2011 was estimated at $444.2 million, a decrease of $47 million from 2010. Sixty pledges for 2011 had been received, 29 of which were multi-year commitments.

The Executive Board took note of the report on 16 June [E/2011/35 (dec. 2011/26)] and encouraged countries to make multi-year pledges and to make contributions by the first half of the year.

In December, the Executive Director reported [DP/FPA/2012/3] on the revision of UNFPA Financial Regulations and Rules. In response to Executive Board decision 2009/27 [YUN 2009, p. 1053], effective 1 January 2010, UNFPA had issued a revised set of Financial Regulations and Rules that allowed the organization to change some of its accounting policies under the UN System Accounting Standards, and move to full compliance in 2012 under IPSAS. In 2011, UNFPA participated in a joint exercise with UNDP and UNICEF to identify revisions to their regulations and rules. UNFPA identified new definitions and new regulations and rules to allow the organization to adopt in 2012 the new cost classification categories approved by Executive Board decision 2010/32 [YUN 2010, p. 1061]. UNFPA updated the definitions and aligned its Financial Regulations and Rules based on Executive Board decisions, terminology updates, accounting policies and business practices.

In December [DP/FPA/2012/2], ACABQ recommended the Board's approval of the revised Financial Regulations and Rules, subject to its recommendations.

Other issues. On 31 January [E/2011/35 (dec. 2011/1)], the Board, recalling that the General Assembly, by resolution 65/176 [YUN 2010, p. 868], had decided that the name of the UNDP/UNFPA Executive Board should be changed to the UNDP/UNFPA/UNOPS Executive Board and recognizing that the resolution necessitated a revision of the Rules of Procedure of the Board, approved the Revised Rules of Procedure of the UNDP/UNFPA/UNOPS Executive Board [DP/2011/18].

At its first regular (2011) session, the Executive Board had before it a report on UNFPA human resources management [YUN 2010, p. 1062], of which it took note on 3 February [E/2011/35 (dec. 2011/13)].

Joint UN Programme on HIV/AIDS

A joint UNDP/UNFPA report was issued in August [DP/2011/40-DP/FPA/2011/12] on implementation of the decisions and recommendations of the Programme Coordinating Board of the Joint United Nations Programme on HIV/AIDS (UNAIDS). The report focused on selected results of UNDP and UNFPA in addressing HIV and provided an update on the decisions and recommendations relevant to UNFPA and UNDP from the twenty-seventh and twenty-eighth meetings of the Programme Coordinating Board, held in December 2010 and June 2011, respectively.

On 9 September [E/2011/35 (dec. 2011/41)], the Executive Board took note of the report and requested UNDP and UNFPA to ensure that the relevant aspects of their 2014–2017 strategic plans and results frameworks were consistent with UNAIDS strategies and frameworks. It requested UNFPA, until the adoption of the next strategic plan, to integrate the objectives and deliverables outlined in the strategies of UNAIDS and the UNAIDS unified budget, results and accountability framework, into the update of the UNFPA strategic guidance on HIV and the relevant strategies and policies.

United Nations Population Award

The 2011 United Nations Population Award was presented to Professor Mohammad Jalal Abbasi-Shavazi of Iran in the individual category and to the Institut de formation et de recherche démographique, based in Cameroon, in the institutional category.

The Award was established by General Assembly resolution 36/201 [YUN 1981, p. 792], to be presented annually to individuals and institutions for outstanding contributions to increasing awareness of population problems and to their solutions. In August, the Secretary-General transmitted to the Assembly the report of the UNFPA Executive Director on the Population Award [A/66/263].

Other population activities

UN Population Division

In a report on programme implementation and work progress of the UN Population Division in 2011 [E/CN.9/2012/7], the Secretary-General described the Division's activities dealing with the analysis of fertility, mortality and international migration; the preparation of world population estimates and projections; the monitoring of population policies; the analysis of the interrelations between population and development; and the monitoring and dissemination of population information.

In the area of fertility and family planning, the Division issued the *World Fertility Report 2009*, an analysis of fertility trends and their main proximate determinants, which included key indicators of fertility, nuptiality, contraceptive use and population policies regarding childbearing for 196 countries or areas, with data points around 1970, around 1995 and the most recent data. While total fertility fell in all but three of the 185 countries or areas for which data was available for all three time periods, major differences in fertility levels persisted across countries. Total fertility was below replacement level (2.1 children per woman) in 32 of 102 developing countries or areas with data available, yet remained above 4 children per woman in 10 countries or areas. The Division published the wallchart *World Contraceptive Use 2011*, showing the latest data available on contraceptive prevalence, method-specific use and unmet need for family planning. It indicated that in at least 46 countries, 20 per cent or more of the women of reproductive age who were married or in a union had an unmet need for contraception. To raise awareness about changes in union formation and the timing of marriage, the Division produced the fact sheet "World marriage patterns" (*Population Facts* No. 2011/1), which showed that marriage in adolescence had been declining worldwide, but remained high in some countries despite laws setting the minimum age for marriage without parental consent at 18 or over. In collaboration with UNFPA, the Division continued to report on three indicators of universal access to reproductive health that were part of the revised framework for tracking progress towards the achievement of the MDGs: contraceptive prevalence (indicator 5.3), the adolescent birth rate (indicator 5.4) and the unmet need for family planning (indicator 5.6).

In the area of health and mortality, the Division released the report *Sex Differentials in Childhood Mortality*, the first global review of sexual differentials in infant and child mortality produced by the United Nations in over a decade. In many areas of the world, advances in survival appeared to be accruing relatively equitably to girls and boys and, in many less developed regions, girls' past disadvantage in mortality at ages 1–4 appeared to be easing. Several countries showed an unusually high gender imbalance in infant mortality rates, suggesting a greater than expected degree of male disadvantage in survival. In China and India, however, there was evidence that girls were not benefiting as much as boys from the national trends of mortality decline. The Division released the *World Mortality Report 2007*, which provided a comprehensive set of mortality estimates for the world's countries and their aggregates, along with levels and trends of selected mortality indicators for 195 countries and areas. The *World Mortality Report 2009* was released as an update to the 2007 report and provided an overview of levels and trends of mortality since 1950 at the world level, for development groups and major areas. The Division published the wallchart *World Mortality 2011*, which presented key indicators of mortality at the global, regional and country levels, highlighting variations among countries in annual deaths; crude death rates; life expectancy at birth by sex; infant mortality; under-five mortality; and the probabilities of dying from birth to age 15, from age 15 to age 60 and from birth to age 60. The Division organized an expert group meeting on "Mortality crises: conflicts, violence, famine, natural disasters and the growing burden of non-communicable diseases" (New York, 14–15 November), which reviewed the state of the art with regard to evidence and understanding of crises that caused significant rises in mortality levels, and discussed how current knowledge on the issue could inform the preparation of the UN mortality estimates.

Regarding international migration, the Division provided substantive servicing for the General Assembly's informal thematic debate on the issue (see p. 1004) and organized the Ninth Coordination Meeting on International Migration (ibid.). In response to a growing demand for disaggregated migration data, the Division produced several outputs on the sex and age distributions of international migrants and their implications for migration policy. It issued the data set *Trends in International Migrant Stock: Migrants by Age and Sex*, which provided estimates and projections of the number of international migrants in 196 countries as at mid-2010 for the years 1990, 2000 and 2010. The Division also produced the wallchart *The Age and Sex of Migrants 2011*, the technical paper No. 2011/1, entitled "International migration in a globalizing world: the role of youth", the data set *International Migration Flows to and from Selected Countries: The 2010 Revision* and the *International Migration Report 2009: A Global Assessment*, which analysed the sex and age of the global migrant stock, discussed trends in international migration flows and summarized trends in global net migration estimates and projections.

The Division continued to prepare the official UN population estimates and projections for all countries and areas of the world. The results were used throughout the UN system by all entities requiring population data and were distributed as part of widely used, Internet-accessible databases, including the World Development Indicators database maintained by the World Bank; the data portal of the United Nations (UNdata) maintained by the UN Statistics Division; and FAOSTAT, the statistics database maintained by the Food and Agriculture Organization of the United Nations. The Division issued the results of the *2010 Revision* of *World Population Prospects*, which confirmed that the world population was close to 7 billion. That information was used by UNFPA and many international organizations and media to raise awareness of population issues in the 7 Billion Actions campaign.

Regarding population policies, the Division published two wallcharts for 192 Member and 3 non-member States of the United Nations: *World Abortion Policies 2011*, which provided information on abortion policies (legal grounds on which induced abortion was permitted); and *World Fertility Policies 2011*, which provided information on government views and policies on the level of fertility, including adolescent fertility, and fertility-related factors, such as the legal age for marriage and support for family planning.

Regarding population and development, the Division organized an expert group meeting on adolescents and youth and development (New York, 21–22 July) and published the wallcharts *Rural Population, Development and the Environment 2011* and *Urban Population, Development and the Environment 2011*, with selected indicators for 196 countries or areas.

Regarding monitoring, coordination and dissemination of population information, the Division continued to distribute MORTPAK for Windows, the Division's software package for demographic measurement.

The Division's programme of technical cooperation focused on building and strengthening capacity in developing countries to analyse demographic information needed to guide the formulation and implementation of population policy. The Division organized an expert group meeting on strengthening capacity in the production and use of national transfer accounts (Belo Horizonte, Brazil, 6–7 December).

Chapter IX

Social policy, cultural development and human resources development

In 2011, the United Nations continued to promote social policy and cultural and human resources development, and to implement its programmes of action pertaining to the situation of social groups including persons with disabilities, youth, ageing, and the family.

The Commission for Social Development, in February, considered as its priority theme "Poverty eradication". In July, the Economic and Social Council, in considering recovery from the global economic and financial crisis, requested UN funds, programmes and specialized agencies to take into account the International Labour Organization's Global Jobs Pact in their policies and programmes. Also in the field of social policy and cultural issues, the General Assembly considered implementation of the outcome of the 1995 World Summit for Social Development and of the further initiatives adopted at the Assembly's twenty-fourth (2000) special session.

UN bodies continued to monitor the implementation of the 1982 World Programme of Action concerning Disabled Persons, the 1993 Standard Rules on the Equalization of Opportunities for Persons with Disabilities, and the 2006 Convention on the Rights of Persons with Disabilities. In July, the Economic and Social Council adopted a resolution on equalizing opportunities by, for and with persons with disabilities and mainstreaming disability issues in the development agenda, and in December, the General Assembly decided to convene a high-level meeting in 2013 on "The way forward: a disability-inclusive development agenda towards 2015 and beyond".

During the year, Member States, civil society organizations and UN entities continued to support the International Year of Youth; and at the Assembly's High-level Meeting on Youth, the Secretary-General requested the international community to expand the horizons of opportunity for young women and men, and to answer their demands for dignity and decent work.

In the area of cultural development, the United Nations Educational, Scientific and Cultural Organization (UNESCO), as the lead agency for the 2005–2014 United Nations Decade of Education for Sustainable Development, supported Member States in integrating the principles of sustainable development into inclusive education policies and plans. The Director-General of UNESCO launched a global partnership for girls' and women's education at a high-level forum in May. The Alliance of Civilizations continued to call on its members to develop good governance of cultural diversity through national plans, and held its Fourth Annual Forum in Doha, Qatar, in December. The General Assembly adopted resolutions on follow-up to the Declaration and Programme of Action on a Culture of Peace; the promotion of interreligious and intercultural dialogue, understanding and cooperation for peace; building a peaceful and better world through sport and the Olympic ideal; and culture and development.

In the field of human resources development, the annual ministerial review of the Economic and Social Council was held on the theme "Implementing the internationally agreed goals and commitments in regard to education". In its ministerial declaration on the topic, the Council called for a people-centred, holistic approach to the development of education systems, and for prioritizing education in national development strategies.

Social policy

Social development

Follow-up to 1995 World Summit and General Assembly special session

In response to General Assembly resolution 65/185 [YUN 2010, p. 1066], the Secretary-General submitted a July report [A/66/124] on the implementation of the Copenhagen Declaration on Social Development and the Programme of Action, adopted at the 1995 World Summit for Social Development [YUN 1995, p. 1113], and of the further initiatives for social development, adopted by the Assembly's twenty-fourth (2000) special session [YUN 2000, p. 1012]. The report assessed the social impact of the global crisis, taking into account the discussion held during the forty-ninth session of the Commission for Social Development (see p. 1020). The Secretary-General made several recommendations to prevent losing further ground in poverty eradication and other areas of social development, and to accelerate progress to meet the Millennium Development Goals (MDGs) targets before 2015. In particular, he recommended that macroeconomic and social policies take into consideration and address inequality; the creation of employment opportunities and decent jobs be integral to macroeconomic policy objectives; and Government policies be consistently counter-cyclical, and fiscal resources be conserved during boom periods to support expansionary measures in times of need. Furthermore, universal social protection systems and active employment generation programmes should become permanent measures as part of a policy mix to advance the decent work agenda, eradicate poverty and foster social cohesion. To enhance implementation of the outcome of the World Summit for Social Development and of the Assembly's twenty-fourth special session, the Secretary-General recommended that Member States launch country-led initiatives on creating inclusive societies by sharing lessons learned and best practices, including ways to enhance political support for social issues; and that the General Assembly promote broader and more focused engagement of UN system organizations and all stakeholders in the work of the Commission for Social Development, and promote greater coherence in the implementation and response of UN system organizations.

On 19 December, by **decision 66/531**, the General Assembly took note of the report of the Secretary-General.

GENERAL ASSEMBLY ACTION

On 19 December [meeting 89], the General Assembly, on the recommendation of the Third (Social, Humanitarian and Cultural) Committee [A/66/454 (Part II)], adopted **resolution 66/125** without vote [agenda item 27 (a)].

Implementation of the outcome of the World Summit for Social Development and of the twenty-fourth special session of the General Assembly

The General Assembly,

Recalling the World Summit for Social Development, held at Copenhagen from 6 to 12 March 1995, and the twenty-fourth special session of the General Assembly entitled "World Summit for Social Development and beyond: achieving social development for all in a globalizing world", held at Geneva from 26 June to 1 July 2000,

Reaffirming that the Copenhagen Declaration on Social Development and the Programme of Action and the further initiatives for social development adopted by the General Assembly at its twenty-fourth special session, as well as a continued global dialogue on social development issues, constitute the basic framework for the promotion of social development for all at the national and international levels,

Recalling the United Nations Millennium Declaration and the development goals contained therein, as well as the commitments made at major United Nations summits, conferences and special sessions, including the commitments made at the 2005 World Summit and at the High-level Plenary Meeting of the General Assembly on the Millennium Development Goals,

Recalling also its resolution 57/270 B of 23 June 2003 on the integrated and coordinated implementation of and follow-up to the outcomes of the major United Nations conferences and summits in the economic and social fields,

Recalling further its resolution 60/209 of 22 December 2005 on the implementation of the first United Nations Decade for the Eradication of Poverty (1997–2006),

Recalling its resolution 63/303 of 9 July 2009 on the Outcome of the Conference on the World Financial and Economic Crisis and Its Impact on Development,

Reaffirming Economic and Social Council resolution 2008/18 of 24 July 2008 on promoting full employment and decent work for all and Council resolution 2010/12 of 22 July 2010 on promoting social integration, and welcoming the decision of the Commission for Social Development to have "Poverty eradication" as the priority theme for the 2011–2012 review and policy cycle,

Noting with appreciation the ministerial declaration adopted at the high-level segment of the substantive session of 2006 of the Economic and Social Council, entitled "Creating an environment at the national and international levels conducive to generating full and productive employment and decent work for all, and its impact on sustainable development",

Noting that the decent work agenda of the International Labour Organization, with its four strategic objectives, has an important role to play in achieving the objective of full and productive employment and decent work for all, including its objective of social protection, as reaffirmed in the International Labour Organization Declaration on Social Justice for a Fair Globalization, in which the particular role of the Organization in promoting fair globalization and its responsibility to assist its members in their efforts were acknowledged, as well as in the Global Jobs Pact,

Emphasizing the need to enhance the role of the Commission for Social Development in the follow-up to and review of the World Summit for Social Development and the outcome of the twenty-fourth special session of the General Assembly,

Recognizing that the three core themes of social development, namely, poverty eradication, full and productive employment and decent work for all and social integration are interrelated and mutually reinforcing, and that an enabling environment therefore needs to be created so that all three objectives can be pursued simultaneously,

Recognizing also that a people-centred approach must be at the centre of economic and social development,

Expressing deep concern that attainment of the social development objectives is being hindered by the ongoing adverse impact of the world financial and economic crisis, volatile energy and food prices and the challenges posed by climate change,

Recognizing the complex character of the current global food crisis and ongoing food insecurity, including food price volatility, as a combination of several major factors, both structural and conjunctural, which is also negatively affected by, inter alia, environmental degradation, drought and desertification, global climate change, natural disasters and the lack of the necessary technology, and recognizing also that a strong commitment from national Governments and the international community as a whole is required to confront the major threats to food security and to ensure that policies in the area of agriculture do not distort trade and worsen the food crisis,

Deeply concerned that extreme poverty persists in all countries of the world, regardless of their economic, social and cultural situation, and that its extent and its manifestations, such as hunger, trafficking in human beings, disease, lack of adequate shelter and illiteracy, are particularly severe in developing countries, while acknowledging the significant progress made in several parts of the world in combating extreme poverty,

Recognizing the importance of the international community in supporting national capacity-building efforts in the area of social development, while recognizing the primary responsibility of national Governments in this regard,

Affirming its strong support for fair globalization and the need to translate growth into eradication of poverty and commitment to strategies and policies that aim to promote full, freely chosen and productive employment and decent work for all and that these should constitute a fundamental component of relevant national and international policies as well as national development strategies, including poverty reduction strategies, and reaffirming that employment creation and decent work should be incorporated into macroeconomic policies, taking fully into account the impact and social dimension of globalization, the benefits and costs of which are often unevenly shared and distributed,

Recognizing the need to enhance access to the benefits of trade, including agricultural trade, for developing countries in order to foster social development,

Recognizing also that social inclusion is a means for achieving social integration and is crucial for fostering stable, safe, harmonious, peaceful and just societies and for improving social cohesion so as to create an environment for development and progress,

1. *Takes note* of the report of the Secretary-General;

2. *Welcomes* the reaffirmation by Governments of their will and commitment to continue implementing the Copenhagen Declaration on Social Development and the Programme of Action, in particular to eradicate poverty, promote full and productive employment and foster social integration to achieve stable, safe and just societies for all;

3. *Recognizes* that the implementation of the Copenhagen commitments and the attainment of the internationally agreed development goals, including the Millennium Development Goals, are mutually reinforcing and that the Copenhagen commitments are crucial to a coherent people-centred approach to development;

4. *Reaffirms* that the Commission for Social Development continues to have the primary responsibility for the follow-up to and review of the World Summit for Social Development and the outcome of the twenty-fourth special session of the General Assembly and that it serves as the main United Nations forum for an intensified global dialogue on social development issues, and calls upon Member States, the relevant specialized agencies, funds and programmes of the United Nations system and civil society to enhance their support for its work;

5. *Expresses deep concern* that the ongoing adverse impact of the world financial and economic crisis, volatile energy and food prices and food insecurity and the challenges posed by climate change, as well as the lack of results so far in the multilateral trade negotiations, have negative implications for social development;

6. *Stresses* the importance of the policy space of national Governments, in particular in the areas of social expenditure and social protection programmes, and calls upon international financial institutions and donors to support developing countries in achieving their social development, in line with their national priorities and strategies by, among other things, providing debt relief;

7. *Recognizes* that the broad concept of social development affirmed by the World Summit for Social Development and the twenty-fourth special session of the General Assembly has not been fully implemented in national and international policymaking and, although poverty eradication is a central part of development policy and discourse, further attention should be given to the other commitments agreed to at the Summit, in particular those concerning employment and social integration, which have also suffered from a general disconnect between economic and social policymaking;

8. *Acknowledges* that the first United Nations Decade for the Eradication of Poverty (1997–2006), launched after the World Summit for Social Development, has provided the long-term vision for sustained and concerted efforts at the national and international levels to eradicate poverty;

9. *Recognizes* that the implementation of the commitments made by Governments during the first Decade has fallen short of expectations, and welcomes the proclamation of the Second United Nations Decade for the Eradication of Poverty (2008–2017) by the General Assembly in its resolution 62/205 of 19 December 2007 in order to support, in an efficient and coordinated manner, the internationally agreed development goals related to poverty eradication, including the Millennium Development Goals;

10. *Emphasizes* that the major United Nations conferences and summits, including the Millennium Summit, the 2005 World Summit, the High-level Plenary Meeting of the General Assembly on the Millennium Development Goals and the International Conference on Financing for Development, in its Monterrey Consensus, have reinforced the priority and urgency of poverty eradication within the United Nations development agenda;

11. *Also emphasizes* that poverty eradication policies should attack poverty by addressing its root and structural causes and manifestations, and that equity and the reduction of inequalities need to be incorporated in those policies;

12. *Reaffirms* that each country has the primary responsibility for its own economic and social development and that the role of national policies and development strategies cannot be overemphasized, and underlines the importance of adopting effective measures, including new financial mechanisms, as appropriate, to support the efforts of developing countries to achieve sustained economic growth, sustainable development, poverty eradication and the strengthening of their democratic systems;

13. *Stresses* that an enabling environment is a critical precondition for achieving equity and social development and that, while economic growth is essential, entrenched inequality and marginalization are an obstacle to the broad-based and sustained growth required for sustainable, inclusive and people-centred development, and recognizes the need to balance and ensure complementarity between measures to achieve growth and measures to achieve economic and social equity in order for there to be an impact on overall poverty levels;

14. *Also stresses* that stability in global financial systems and corporate social responsibility and accountability,

as well as national economic policies that have an impact on other stakeholders, are essential in creating an enabling international environment to promote economic growth and social development;

15. *Recognizes* the need to promote respect for all human rights and fundamental freedoms in order to address the most pressing social needs of people living in poverty, including through the design and development of appropriate mechanisms to strengthen and consolidate democratic institutions and governance;

16. *Reaffirms* the commitment to gender equality and the empowerment of women, as well as to the mainstreaming of a gender perspective into all development efforts, recognizing that these are critical for achieving sustainable development and for efforts to combat hunger, poverty and disease and to strengthen policies and programmes that improve, ensure and broaden the full participation of women in all spheres of political, economic, social and cultural life, as equal partners, and to improve their access to all resources needed for the full exercise of all their human rights and fundamental freedoms by removing persistent barriers, including ensuring equal access to full and productive employment and decent work, as well as strengthening their economic independence;

17. *Encourages* Governments to promote effective participation of people in civic, social, economic and political activities, as well as in the planning and implementation of social integration policies and strategies, in order to better achieve the goals of poverty eradication, full employment and decent work and social integration;

18. *Reaffirms* the commitment to promote opportunities for full, freely chosen and productive employment, including for the most disadvantaged, as well as decent work for all, in order to deliver social justice combined with economic efficiency, with full respect for fundamental principles and rights at work under conditions of equity, equality, security and dignity, and further reaffirms that macroeconomic policies should, inter alia, support employment creation, taking fully into account the social impact and dimension of globalization;

19. *Also reaffirms* that there is an urgent need to create an environment at the national and international levels that is conducive to the attainment of full and productive employment and decent work for all as a foundation for sustainable development and that an environment that supports investment, growth and entrepreneurship is essential to the creation of new job opportunities, and further reaffirms that opportunities for men and women to obtain productive work in conditions of freedom, equity, security and human dignity are essential to ensuring the eradication of hunger and poverty, the improvement of economic and social well-being for all, the achievement of sustained economic growth and sustainable development of all nations and a fully inclusive and equitable globalization;

20. *Stresses* the importance of removing obstacles to the realization of the right of peoples to self-determination, in particular of peoples living under colonial or other forms of alien domination or foreign occupation, which adversely affect their social and economic development, including their exclusion from labour markets;

21. *Reaffirms* the need to address all forms of violence in its many manifestations, including domestic violence, particularly against women, children, older persons and persons with disabilities, and discrimination, including xenophobia, recognizes that violence increases challenges to States and societies in the achievement of poverty eradication, full and productive employment and decent work for all and social integration, and further recognizes that terrorism, trafficking in arms, organized crime, trafficking in persons, money-laundering, ethnic and religious conflict, civil war, politically motivated killing and genocide present fundamental threats to societies and pose increasing challenges to States and societies in the attainment of conditions conducive to social development, and that they further present urgent and compelling reasons for action by Governments individually and, as appropriate, jointly to foster social cohesion while recognizing, protecting and valuing diversity;

22. *Requests* the United Nations funds, programmes and agencies to mainstream the goal of full and productive employment and decent work for all in their policies, programmes and activities, as well as to support efforts of Member States aimed at achieving this objective, and invites financial institutions to support efforts in this regard;

23. *Recognizes* that promoting full employment and decent work also requires investing in education, training and skills development for women and men, and girls and boys, strengthening social protection and health systems and applying international labour standards;

24. *Also recognizes* that full and productive employment and decent work for all, which encompass social protection, fundamental principles and rights at work, tripartism and social dialogue, are key elements of sustainable development for all countries and are therefore a priority objective of international cooperation;

25. *Encourages* States to design and implement policies and strategies for poverty eradication, full employment and decent work for all, including the creation of full and productive employment that is appropriately and adequately remunerated, as well as policies and strategies for social integration that promote gender equality and the empowerment of women and address the specific needs of social groups such as young people, persons with disabilities, older persons, migrants and indigenous peoples, taking into account the concerns of these groups in the planning, implementation and evaluation of development programmes and policies;

26. *Stresses* the need to allocate adequate resources for the elimination of all forms of discrimination against women in the workplace, including unequal access to labour market participation and wage inequalities, as well as reconciliation of work and private life for both women and men;

27. *Acknowledges* the important nexus between international migration and social development, and stresses the importance of enforcing labour law effectively with regard to migrant workers' labour relations and working conditions, inter alia, those related to their remuneration and conditions of health, safety at work and the right to freedom of association;

28. *Recognizes* that, since the convening of the World Summit for Social Development in Copenhagen in 1995, advances have been made in addressing and promoting social integration, including through the adoption of the

Madrid International Plan of Action on Ageing, 2002, the World Programme of Action for Youth, the Convention on the Rights of Persons with Disabilities, the United Nations Declaration on the Rights of Indigenous Peoples and the Beijing Declaration and Platform for Action;

29. *Stresses* that the benefits of economic growth should be distributed more equitably and that, in order to close the gap of inequality and avoid any further deepening of inequality, comprehensive social policies and programmes, including appropriate social transfer and job creation programmes and social protection systems, are needed;

30. *Recognizes* the importance of providing social protection schemes for the formal and informal economy as instruments to achieve equity, inclusion and stability and cohesion of societies, and emphasizes the importance of supporting national efforts aimed at bringing informal workers into the formal economy;

31. *Stresses* that poverty eradication policies should, inter alia, ensure that people living in poverty have access to education, health, water and sanitation and other public and social services, as well as access to productive resources, including credit, land, training, technology, knowledge and information, and ensure that citizens and local communities participate in decision-making on social development policies and programmes in this regard;

32. *Recognizes* that the social integration of people living in poverty should encompass addressing and meeting their basic human needs, including nutrition, health, water, sanitation, housing and access to education and employment, through integrated development strategies;

33. *Reaffirms* that social integration policies should seek to reduce inequalities, promote access to basic social services, education for all and health care, eliminate discrimination, increase the participation and integration of social groups, particularly young people, older persons and persons with disabilities, and address the challenges posed by globalization and market-driven reforms to social development in order for all people in all countries to benefit from globalization;

34. *Urges* Governments, with the cooperation of relevant entities, to develop systems of social protection and to extend or broaden, as appropriate, their effectiveness and coverage, including for workers in the informal economy, recognizing the need for social protection systems to provide social security and support labour-market participation, invites the International Labour Organization to strengthen its social protection strategies and policies on extending social security coverage, and urges Governments, while taking account of national circumstances, to focus on the needs of those living in, or vulnerable to, poverty and give particular consideration to universal access to basic social security systems, recognizing that social protection floors can provide a systemic base to address poverty and vulnerability;

35. *Requests* the United Nations system to continue to support national efforts of Member States to achieve inclusive social development in a coherent and coordinated manner;

36. *Reaffirms* the commitment to promote the rights of indigenous peoples in the areas of education, employment, housing, sanitation, health and social security, and notes the attention paid to those areas in the United Nations Declaration on the Rights of Indigenous Peoples;

37. *Recognizes* the need to formulate social development policies in an integral, articulated and participative manner, recognizing poverty as a multidimensional phenomenon, calls for interlinked public policies on this matter, and underlines the need for public policies to be included in a comprehensive development and well-being strategy;

38. *Acknowledges* the role that the public sector can play as an employer and its importance in developing an environment that enables the effective generation of full and productive employment and decent work for all;

39. *Also acknowledges* the vital role that the private sector can play in generating new investments, employment and financing for development and in advancing efforts towards full employment and decent work;

40. *Recognizes* that steps should be taken to anticipate and offset the negative social and economic consequences of globalization, giving priority to agricultural and non-farm sectors, and to maximize its benefits for poor people living and working in rural areas, while paying special attention to the development of microenterprises and small and medium-sized enterprises, particularly in rural areas, as well as subsistence economies, to secure their safe interaction with larger economies;

41. *Also recognizes* the need to pay necessary attention to the social development of people in urban areas, especially the urban poor;

42. *Further recognizes* the need to give priority to investing in and further contributing to sustainable agricultural development and microenterprises, small and medium-sized enterprises and entrepreneurship cooperatives and other forms of social enterprises and the participation and entrepreneurship of women as means to promote full and productive employment and decent work for all;

43. *Reaffirms* the commitments made in respect of meeting the special needs of Africa at the 2005 World Summit, underlines the call of the Economic and Social Council for enhanced coordination within the United Nations system and the ongoing efforts to harmonize the current initiatives on Africa, and requests the Commission for Social Development to continue to give due prominence in its work to the social dimensions of the New Partnership for Africa's Development;

44. *Also reaffirms*, in this context, that international cooperation has an essential role in assisting developing countries, including the least developed countries, in strengthening their human, institutional and technological capacity;

45. *Stresses* that the international community shall enhance its efforts to create an enabling environment for social development and poverty eradication through increasing market access for developing countries, technology transfer on mutually agreed terms, financial aid and a comprehensive solution to the external debt problem;

46. *Also stresses* that international trade and stable financial systems can be effective tools to create favourable conditions for the development of all countries and that trade barriers and some trading practices continue to have negative effects on employment growth, particularly in developing countries;

47. *Acknowledges* that good governance and the rule of law at the national and international levels are essential for sustained economic growth, sustainable development and the eradication of poverty and hunger;

48. *Urges* developed countries that have not yet done so in accordance with their commitments to make concrete efforts towards meeting the targets of 0.7 per cent of their gross national product for official development assistance to developing countries and 0.15 to 0.2 per cent of their gross national product to least developed countries, and encourages developing countries to build on the progress achieved in ensuring that official development assistance is used effectively to help to meet development goals and targets;

49. *Urges* Member States and the international community to fulfil all their commitments to meet the demands for social development, including social services and assistance, that have arisen from the global financial and economic crisis, which particularly affects the poorest and most vulnerable;

50. *Welcomes* the contribution to the mobilization of resources for social development by the initiatives taken on a voluntary basis by groups of Member States based on innovative financing mechanisms, including those that aim to provide further drug access at affordable prices to developing countries on a sustainable and predictable basis, such as the International Drug Purchase Facility, UNITAID, as well as other initiatives such as the International Finance Facility for Immunization and the Advance Market Commitments for Vaccines, and notes the New York Declaration of 20 September 2004, which launched the Action against Hunger and Poverty initiative and called for further attention to raise funds urgently needed to help to meet the Millennium Development Goals and to complement and ensure the long-term stability and predictability of foreign aid;

51. *Reaffirms* that social development requires the active involvement of all actors in the development process, including civil society organizations, corporations and small businesses, and that partnerships among all relevant actors are increasingly becoming part of national and international cooperation for social development, and also reaffirms that, within countries, partnerships among the Government, civil society and the private sector can contribute effectively to the achievement of social development goals;

52. *Underlines* the responsibility of the private sector, at both the national and the international levels, including small and large companies and transnational corporations, regarding not only the economic and financial implications but also the development, social, gender and environmental implications of their activities, their obligations towards their workers and their contributions to achieving sustainable development, including social development, and emphasizes the need to take concrete actions on corporate responsibility and accountability, including through the participation of all relevant stakeholders, inter alia, for the prevention or prosecution of corruption;

53. *Stresses* the importance of promoting corporate social responsibility and accountability, encourages responsible business practices, such as those promoted by the Global Compact, invites the private sector to take into account not only the economic and financial implications but also the development, social, human rights, gender and environmental implications of its undertakings, and underlines the importance of the International Labour Organization Tripartite Declaration of Principles concerning Multinational Enterprises and Social Policy;

54. *Invites* the Secretary-General, the Economic and Social Council, the regional commissions, the relevant specialized agencies, funds and programmes of the United Nations system and other intergovernmental forums, within their respective mandates, to continue to integrate into their work programmes and give priority attention to the Copenhagen commitments and the Declaration on the tenth anniversary of the World Summit for Social Development, to continue to be actively involved in their follow-up and to monitor the achievement of those commitments and undertakings;

55. *Invites* the Commission for Social Development to emphasize in its review of the implementation of the Copenhagen Declaration on Social Development and the Programme of Action the increased exchange of national, regional and international experiences, the focused and interactive dialogues among experts and practitioners and the sharing of best practices and lessons learned, and to address, inter alia, the impact of the world financial and economic crisis and the world food and energy crises on social development goals;

56. *Decides* to include in the provisional agenda of its sixty-seventh session the sub-item entitled "Implementation of the outcome of the World Summit for Social Development and of the twenty-fourth special session of the General Assembly", and requests the Secretary-General to submit a report on the question to the Assembly at that session.

Recovering from the economic and financial crisis: a Global Jobs Pact

In response to Economic and Social Council resolution 2010/25 [YUN 2010, p. 1071], the Secretary-General submitted a May report [E/2011/92] prepared by the International Labour Organization on recovering from the global economic and financial crisis, which reviewed national and international support for the implementation of the Global Jobs Pact [YUN 2009, p. 1062]. Support for the Pact continued to grow, having received endorsement from the General Assembly, the Economic and Social Council, the Group of 20 and various regional and national bodies, and was recognized as an effective tool to help accelerate progress towards development goals, including the MDGs.

The report stated that achieving full employment and decent work for all remained a challenge. The crisis had led to a two-speed recovery in the labour market, with a continued rise in unemployment in developed economies and the European Union, contrasted by slight employment growth and sustained high levels of vulnerable employment and working poverty in developing regions. Globally, the crisis had particularly affected youth, with approximately 77.7 million, or 12.6 per cent, unemployed. While employment recovery was weak, recovery was seen in several macroeconomic indicators, including real global gross domestic product, private consumption, gross fixed investment and world trade, which underlined the fact that employment was not necessarily a derivative of economic growth.

Several international and regional initiatives were undertaken in support of the Pact, such as the Tripartite Caribbean Symposium (Barbados, 25–26 January); the second African Decent Work Symposium (Yaoundé, Cameroon, 6–8 October 2010); and the Oslo Conference on the challenges of growth, employment and social cohesion (Oslo, Norway, 13 September 2010). The report also reviewed examples of support for the Pact at the national level, together with suggested policy options aimed at promoting a job-intensive recovery, as well as efforts to build policy coherence in support of the Pact through the UN system.

The report concluded that the principles and objectives of the Global Jobs Pact aimed to address the root causes of the crisis, so that growth was strong, equitable, job-rich and sustainable. To support the rebalancing of the global development agenda, structural change and increased investment was needed to address labour market deficiencies while improving the quantity and quality of jobs. The way forward should focus on closer correlation between sound fiscal and monetary targets of macroeconomic policy together with employment, social and environmental policies; addressing declining wage shares; closing the income inequality gap; and promoting job-rich growth through social dialogue.

ECONOMIC AND SOCIAL COUNCIL ACTION

On 28 July [meeting 49], the Economic and Social Council adopted **resolution 2011/37** [draft: E/2011/L.21/Rev.1] without vote [agenda item 6 (*a*)].

Recovering from the world financial and economic crisis: a Global Jobs Pact

The Economic and Social Council,

Expressing deep concern about the ongoing adverse impact, particularly on development, of the world financial and economic crisis, recognizing that global growth is returning and there is a need to sustain the recovery, which is fragile and uneven, and stressing the need to continue to address systemic fragilities and imbalances,

Observing that unemployment and underemployment levels remain persistently high in many countries, particularly among the younger generations,

Conscious of the need to promote sustained, inclusive and equitable economic growth that generates employment, leads to poverty eradication, fosters sustainable development and strengthens social cohesion,

Recalling the Outcome of the Conference on the World Financial and Economic Crisis and Its Impact on Development,

Recalling also the Global Jobs Pact, adopted by the International Labour Conference on 19 June 2009, which is intended to promote a job-intensive recovery from the crisis and to promote sustainable growth,

Recalling further its resolutions on recovering from the crisis: a Global Jobs Pact, adopted in 2009 and 2010,

Recalling its decision that the theme of the 2012 annual ministerial review should be "Promoting productive capacity, employment and decent work to eradicate poverty in the context of inclusive, sustainable and equitable economic growth at all levels for achieving the Millennium Development Goals",

1. *Takes note* of the report of the Secretary-General;

2. *Reiterates* that the Global Jobs Pact is a general framework within which each country can formulate policy packages specific to its situation and priorities, and encourages Member States to continue to promote and make full use of the Pact and implement policy options contained therein;

3. *Also reiterates* that giving effect to the recommendations and policy options of the Global Jobs Pact requires consideration of financing and capacity-building and that least developed and developing countries and countries with economies in transition that lack the fiscal space to adopt appropriate response and recovery policies require particular support, and invites donor countries, multilateral organizations and other development partners to consider providing funding, including existing crisis resources, for the implementation of those recommendations and policy options;

4. *Recognizes* the need to universally respect, promote and realize fundamental principles and rights at work, in accordance with the International Labour Organization Declaration on Fundamental Principles and Rights at Work;

5. *Also recognizes* the need to promote and realize at least basic social protection in order to achieve decent work and nationally designed social protection floors, in all countries, in line with national priorities and circumstances;

6. *Welcomes* the efforts by the international financial institutions and other relevant organizations, as well as by the United Nations development system, to integrate into their activities policy measures mentioned in the Global Jobs Pact;

7. *Requests* the United Nations funds and programmes and the specialized agencies to continue to take into account the Global Jobs Pact in their respective policies and programmes, through their appropriate decision-making processes, and invites them to integrate, as appropriate, information on progress made to date into their regular reporting;

8. *Reiterates* that the agenda contained in the Global Jobs Pact requires policy coherence and international coordination;

9. *Requests* the Secretary-General, in coordination with the International Labour Organization, to assess and review job-intensive investment and strategies and to report to the Economic and Social Council at its substantive session of 2012, with a view to supporting job creation and promoting sustained, inclusive and equitable economic growth;

10. *Also requests* the Secretary-General, in his report to the annual ministerial review of the Council at its substantive session of 2012, to report on the use of the Global Jobs Pact by the United Nations system and on progress made in implementing the present resolution;

11. *Encourages* the High-level Committee on Programmes of the United Nations System Chief Executives Board for Coordination to consider further measures to promote system-wide policy coherence in the area of decent work and sustained, inclusive and equitable economic growth.

Commission for Social Development

The Commission for Social Development, at its forty-ninth session (New York, 19 February 2010 and 9–18 February 2011) [E/2011/26 & Corr.1], considered the priority theme of poverty eradication, taking into account its interrelationship with social integration and full employment and decent work for all. The Commission recommended for adoption by the Economic and Social Council four draft resolutions on the social dimensions of the New Partnership for Africa's Development (see p. 896); mainstreaming disability in the development agenda (see p. 1031); the second review and appraisal of the Madrid International Plan of Action on Ageing (see p. 1028); and the twentieth anniversary of the International Year of the Family (see p. 1039). It also recommended one draft decision for adoption by the Council on the Commission's report on its forty-ninth session and provisional agenda and documentation for the fiftieth session. The Commission requested the Council to confirm the nomination of members of the Board of the United Nations Research Institute for Social Development (UNRISD) [dec. 49/101]; and brought to the attention of the Council its adoption of one resolution on policies and programmes involving youth [res. 49/1] and one decision on documents considered by the Commission at its forty-ninth session [dec. 49/102]. The Commission held high-level panel discussions on the priority theme of poverty alleviation and on the emerging issue of social protection. In recognition of its priority theme, the Commission was addressed by the independent expert on human rights and extreme poverty of the Human Rights Council. The Commission was also briefed by the Special Rapporteur on disability on his report (see p. 1030), in connection with its review of United Nations plans and programmes of action pertaining to the situation of social groups.

For its consideration of the priority theme, the Commission had before it a report of the Secretary-General on poverty eradication [E/CN.5/2011/3], prepared in response to Council resolution 2010/10 [YUN 2010, p. 1076], which presented progress achieved in poverty eradication and reviewed challenges related to sustained, inclusive growth; employment creation; inequality; and economic shocks, climate change and conflict. It also examined major policy challenges in the areas of economic growth and employment; social protection; and social policy and structural transformation. The report noted that sustained economic growth with sufficient increases in productive employment and decent work had led to fast poverty declines in some countries; however, in many other nations, work had not brought about income security and social protection. Rising income inequalities, which overlapped with gender inequalities and other forms of marginalization and social exclusion, further limited the effectiveness of economic growth in reducing poverty, and the burden of conflict, weather-related disasters and other climate change impacts added to the lack of economic opportunities. The Secretary-General stated that the social consequences of such shocks were most severe in countries where social protection systems were weakest. Universal access to basic social protection and social services, especially health and education, were necessary to break the intergenerational cycle of poverty, and should be complemented by broader interventions that addressed discrimination, access to resources, and their redistribution.

The Commission took note [dec. 49/102] of the documents of the Secretary-General and the Secretariat that were before it at the forty-ninth session relating to: promoting social integration; poverty eradication; the emerging issue of social protection; the report of the Board of UNRISD on the work of the Institute during 2009 and 2010; and the nomination of members of the Board of UNRISD.

On 28 July, the Council took note of the Commission's report on its forty-ninth session and approved the provisional agenda and documentation for its fiftieth (2012) session (**decision 2011/255**).

Other Commission reports. Other documents issued in 2011, to be considered during the Commission's fiftieth (2012) session, included reports on the preparations for and observance of the twentieth anniversary of the International Year of the Family in 2014 [A/67/61-E/2012/3]; the provisional annotated agenda and proposed organization of work of the Commission [E/CN.5/2012/1]; social dimensions of the New Partnership for Africa's Development [E/CN.5/2012/2]; poverty eradication [E/CN.5/2012/3]; modalities of the second review and appraisal of the Madrid International Plan of Action on Ageing, 2002 [E/CN.5/2012/5]; mainstreaming disability in the development agenda [E/CN.5/2012/6]; and monitoring of the implementation of the Standard Rules on the Equalization of Opportunities for Persons with Disabilities [E/CN.5/2012/7]; together with a note on youth: poverty and unemployment

[E/CN.5/2012/8]; and statements submitted by non-governmental organizations in consultative status with the Economic and Social Council [E/CN.5/2012/NGO/1–28].

Social integration

In response to Economic and Social Council resolution 2010/12 on promoting social integration [YUN 2010, p. 1073], the Secretary-General submitted a report [E/CN.5/2011/2] on the implementation of that resolution, which reviewed national policies and programmes towards social integration in different regions, taking into consideration their relation to poverty eradication. Many Governments were increasingly recognizing the importance of social integration in advancing social development, and several countries had shifted from implementing fragmented or ad hoc programmes to adopting cross-sectoral policies that were more closely aligned with national development goals and poverty reduction strategies. The report also discussed effective interventions in promoting social integration, which varied in their scope and focus, including social protection, employment and group-specific interventions; and social integration through broad-based participation of citizens and communities in the design, monitoring and implementation of social policies.

The Secretary-General stated that country experiences had shown that social protection programmes were progressively being seen as an effective means to reduce poverty, inequality and social exclusion, as well as increase income-generating opportunities and promote social integration. Nonetheless, persistent prejudice, stereotyping and discrimination prevented full participation of citizens in the social, cultural and political life of a society. Although many countries had adopted or amended their legislation to address the needs of vulnerable groups and ensure their inclusion, implementation of those provisions was frequently hampered by a weak institutional capacity for programme delivery and outreach, as well as insufficient regulatory frameworks. The Secretary-General recommended, among other things, that Governments strengthen policies and interventions targeting specific social groups, while mainstreaming social integration and inclusion objectives in all policies and programmes; promote universal access to basic social services; promote policies and strategies for achieving full employment and decent work that fostered the social integration of vulnerable groups and promoted gender equality; increase participation of citizens and communities in the planning and implementation of social integration policies and strategies; and strengthen institutional mechanisms to promote their involvement.

GENERAL ASSEMBLY ACTION

On 19 December [meeting 89], the General Assembly, on the recommendation of the Third Committee [A/66/454 (Part II)], adopted **resolution 66/122** without vote [agenda item 27 (*b*)].

Promoting social integration through social inclusion

The General Assembly,

Recalling the World Summit for Social Development, held at Copenhagen from 6 to 12 March 1995, and the twenty-fourth special session of the General Assembly entitled "World Summit for Social Development and beyond: achieving social development for all in a globalizing world", held at Geneva from 26 June to 1 July 2000,

Recalling also Economic and Social Council resolution 2010/12 of 22 July 2010 on promoting social integration,

Recalling further the outcome document of the High-level Plenary Meeting of the General Assembly on the Millennium Development Goals, in which Heads of State and Government acknowledged the significant importance of promoting comprehensive systems of social protection that provide universal access to essential social services, consistent with national priorities and circumstances, to meet internationally agreed development goals, including the Millennium Development Goals,

Taking note with appreciation of the study by the United Nations Children's Fund entitled *Narrowing the Gaps to Meet the Goals*, released on 7 September 2010, which shows that an equity-focused approach to child survival and development, focusing on reaching the most deprived and vulnerable children, proves to be a practical and effective strategy for meeting the health Millennium Development Goals for children,

Reaffirming the commitment of the international community to realizing the universal right to work, an adequate standard of living, necessary social services and social security,

Stressing that the promotion of sustained, inclusive and equitable economic growth is necessary to achieve poverty eradication and should be complemented, as appropriate, by effective social protection policies, including social inclusion policies,

Recognizing that the gains of economic growth should benefit also those who are in vulnerable or marginalized situations,

Recognizing also that social inclusion policies and systems play a critical role in promoting an inclusive society, and are also crucial for fostering stable, safe, harmonious, peaceful and just societies and for improving social cohesion and inclusion so as to create an environment for development and progress,

Reaffirming the important role of corporate social responsibility and accountability in contributing to an enabling environment to promote economic growth and social integration,

Recognizing that social inclusion policies also strengthen the democratic process,

Stressing that social inclusion policies should promote gender equality and the empowerment of women and equal access to opportunities and social protection for all, in particular for those who are in vulnerable or marginalized situations,

Acknowledging that the participation of persons in vulnerable or marginalized situations is crucial to formulating and implementing social inclusion policies that effectively achieve social integration, as appropriate,

Recognizing the important role played by civil society, including non-governmental organizations, in promoting social integration, inter alia, through social programmes and support for the development of socially inclusive policies,

Stressing the importance of an enabling international environment, in particular enhanced international cooperation to support national efforts towards promoting social integration through social inclusion in every country, including the fulfilment of all commitments on official development assistance, debt relief, market access, financial and technical support and capacity-building,

Expressing concern that, in times of economic and financial crisis and ongoing concern about energy and food insecurity, social exclusion can be exacerbated; in this regard sustainable and reliable social inclusion policies and programmes can play a positive role,

1. *Stresses* that States, which bear the main responsibility for social integration and social inclusion, should prioritize the creation of a "society for all" based on respect for all human rights and the principles of equality among individuals, the access to basic social services and the promotion of the active participation of every member of society, in particular those in vulnerable or marginalized situations, in all aspects of life, including civic, social, economic and political activities, as well as participation in decision-making processes;

2. *Calls upon* States to promote a more equitable participation in and access to economic growth gains through, inter alia, policies that ensure inclusive labour markets and by implementing socially responsive macroeconomic policies in which employment has a key role, and social inclusion strategies which promote social integration ensuring social protection floors for those who are in vulnerable or marginalized situations, as defined by each country in accordance with its individual circumstances, including on a demand-driven basis, and the promotion and protection of their social and economic rights;

3. *Encourages* States to consider, when appropriate, the creation of national institutions or agencies for promoting, implementing and evaluating social inclusion programmes and mechanisms at the national and local levels;

4. *Also encourages* States, together with relevant United Nations entities, to continue monitoring progress towards the relevant Millennium Development Goals, in particular regarding their indicators, as their achievement is an essential element to shape and promote national policies for social inclusion;

5. *Invites* Member States, and encourages regional organizations, to support national efforts to achieve inclusive societies, in particular in developing countries, upon their request, by providing, inter alia, financial and technical cooperation for the design and implementation of sound social inclusion policies;

6. *Encourages* Member States to mainstream social integration objectives into social inclusion policies, promoting the participation of persons in vulnerable or marginalized situations in planning, implementing and monitoring processes, in collaboration, as appropriate, with relevant organizations of the United Nations development system, regional organizations, international and regional financial institutions, development and social partners, the private sector and civil society organizations;

7. *Invites* States, relevant organizations of the United Nations development system, regional organizations, international and regional financial institutions, development and social partners, the private sector and civil society organizations to exchange views and share information on sound social inclusion policies and best practices;

8. *Requests* the Secretary-General to submit a report on the implementation of the present resolution to the General Assembly at its sixty-eighth session;

9. *Decides* to consider the question further at its sixty-eighth session under the item entitled "Social development".

Report on world social situation

An August report [A/66/226] of the Secretary-General provided the General Assembly with an overview of the world social situation in 2011, which considered the causes and transmission of the financial and economic crisis of 2009, as well as its ongoing adverse social consequences. The report noted that while a deeper, more prolonged global recession had been averted through coordinated stimulus measures, recovery was fragile and uneven. The economic slowdown had reduced social spending in most developing countries, while the turn towards fiscal austerity had undermined social spending in developed countries and threatened nascent recovery. In developed economies, increased unemployment was the dominant social impact of the crisis. While the informal economy and peasant agricultural sector in developing economies had absorbed much of the impact of formal sector job losses, many more workers were subject to weaker employment conditions. The loss of jobs also increased the vulnerability of populations, especially in developing countries without comprehensive social protection, with tens of millions of people falling into or trapped in extreme poverty as a result of the crisis. Given the fragility of the economic recovery and uneven progress in major economies, social conditions were expected to recover slowly. The report also reviewed measures to address the crisis, including the role of Government; a focus on employment growth; social protection systems; and food and agricultural development.

The Secretary-General stated that the crisis was an opportunity to rethink the role of social policy and social investment, by transforming policy responses to the crisis into opportunities to strengthen social development and achieve more sustained, inclusive and equitable development. He recommended that Governments pursue counter-cyclical policies in a consistent manner in order to stabilize income and employment as well as to protect the gains made, and take into account the likely social implications of their economic policies. Universal social protection systems and active employment programmes should become permanent features of national crisis response measures, and social investments should be accorded priority in recovery strategies and development policies.

On 19 December, the General Assembly took note of the report of the Secretary-General on the world social situation 2011: the global social crisis (**decision 66/531**).

The full version of the report was published as *The Global Social Crisis: Report on the World Social Situation 2011* [Sales No. E.10.IV.12].

Cooperatives in social development

In response to resolution 64/136 [YUN 2009, p. 1065], by which the General Assembly proclaimed the year 2012 the International Year of Cooperatives, the Secretary-General submitted a July report [A/66/136] on cooperatives in social development and the implementation of the International Year, which was officially launched on 31 October 2011. The report highlighted the contribution of cooperatives to socioeconomic development, food security, inclusive finance and social protection, as well as to the strengthening of societies through peacebuilding and disaster recovery. As member-owned business enterprises, cooperatives enabled the self-empowerment of the poor and other marginalized groups, and promoted community self-reliance, collaboration and cohesion. The report also examined how cooperatives could be strengthened, and highlighted some of the practices of successful cooperatives, including sound governance; capable leadership; management and market knowledge; the provision of training; mainstreaming cooperatives in education; and information databases and sound research to support policy recommendations. The report also reviewed activities planned for the observance of the International Year of Cooperatives at the international, regional and national levels, and noted the support received from Governments through the establishment of national steering committees across all regions.

The Secretary-General stated that special attention should be given to strengthening the internal capacities of cooperatives, as well as to a supportive regulatory framework. He presented recommendations for promoting and strengthening cooperatives, including with regard to generating public awareness of cooperatives and their values; promoting the growth of financial and agricultural cooperatives; expanding the availability of research on the operations and contribution of cooperatives; and improving legislation and State regulatory capacity to provide an enabling environment for cooperative formation.

On 31 October [A/66/PV.45], the General Assembly, on the proposal of its President, decided to invite Gordon Brown, former Prime Minister of the United Kingdom, to make a statement at that meeting (**decision 66/508**), devoted to the launch of the International Year.

GENERAL ASSEMBLY ACTION

On 19 December [meeting 89], the General Assembly, on the recommendation of the Third Committee [A/66/454 (Part II)], adopted **resolution 66/123** without vote [agenda item 27 (*b*)].

Cooperatives in social development

The General Assembly,

Recalling its resolutions 47/90 of 16 December 1992, 49/155 of 23 December 1994, 51/58 of 12 December 1996, 54/123 of 17 December 1999, 56/114 of 19 December 2001, 58/131 of 22 December 2003, 60/132 of 16 December 2005, 62/128 of 18 December 2007, 64/136 of 18 December 2009 and 65/184 of 21 December 2010 concerning cooperatives in social development,

Recognizing that cooperatives, in their various forms, promote the fullest possible participation in the economic and social development of all people, including women, youth, older persons, persons with disabilities and indigenous peoples, are becoming a significant factor of economic and social development and contribute to the eradication of poverty,

Recognizing also the important contribution and potential of all forms of cooperatives to the follow-up to the World Summit for Social Development, the Fourth World Conference on Women and the second United Nations Conference on Human Settlements (Habitat II), including their five-year reviews, the World Food Summit, the Second World Assembly on Ageing, the International Conference on Financing for Development, the World Summit on Sustainable Development and the 2005 World Summit,

Noting with appreciation the potential role of cooperative development in the improvement of the social and economic conditions of indigenous peoples and rural communities,

1. *Takes note* of the report of the Secretary-General;
2. *Welcomes* the proclamation of the year 2012 as the International Year of Cooperatives and the launch of the Year on 31 October 2011;
3. *Encourages* all Member States, as well as the United Nations and all other relevant stakeholders, to take advantage of the International Year of Cooperatives as a way of promoting cooperatives and raising awareness of their contribution to social and economic development and to share good practices on the implementation of the activities carried out during the Year;
4. *Invites* Governments and international organizations, in partnership with cooperatives and cooperative organizations, to consider developing a road map or plan of action for the promotion of cooperatives for sustainable

socioeconomic development beyond the International Year of Cooperatives and to submit it to the General Assembly at its sixty-seventh session so as to ensure a focused and effective follow-up to the activities of the Year;

5. *Draws the attention* of Governments to the recommendation contained in the report of the Secretary-General to focus support on cooperatives as sustainable and successful business enterprises that contribute directly to employment generation, poverty reduction and social protection, across a variety of economic sectors in urban and rural areas;

6. *Encourages* Governments to keep under review, as appropriate, the legal and administrative provisions governing the activities of cooperatives in order to enhance the growth and sustainability of cooperatives in a rapidly changing socioeconomic environment by, inter alia, providing a level playing field for cooperatives vis-à-vis other business and social enterprises, including appropriate tax incentives and access to financial services and markets;

7. *Urges* Governments, relevant international organizations and the specialized agencies, in collaboration with national and international cooperative organizations, to give due consideration to the role and contribution of cooperatives in the implementation of and follow-up to the outcomes of the World Summit for Social Development, the Fourth World Conference on Women and the second United Nations Conference on Human Settlements (Habitat II), including their five-year reviews, the World Food Summit, the Second World Assembly on Ageing, the International Conference on Financing for Development, the World Summit on Sustainable Development and the 2005 World Summit by, inter alia:

(*a*) Utilizing and developing fully the potential and contribution of cooperatives for the attainment of social development goals, in particular the eradication of poverty, the generation of full and productive employment and the enhancement of social integration;

(*b*) Encouraging and facilitating the establishment and development of cooperatives, including taking measures aimed at enabling people living in poverty or belonging to vulnerable groups, including women, youth, persons with disabilities, older persons and indigenous peoples, to fully participate, on a voluntary basis, in cooperatives and to address their social service needs;

(*c*) Taking appropriate measures aimed at creating a supportive and enabling environment for the development of cooperatives by, inter alia, developing an effective partnership between Governments and the cooperative movement through joint consultative councils and/or advisory bodies and by promoting and implementing better legislation, research, sharing of good practices, training, technical assistance and capacity-building of cooperatives, especially in the fields of management, auditing and marketing skills;

(*d*) Raising public awareness of the contribution of cooperatives to employment generation and to socioeconomic development, promoting comprehensive research and statistical data-gathering on the activities, employment and overall socioeconomic impact of cooperatives at the national and international levels and promoting sound national policy formulation by harmonizing statistical methodologies;

8. *Invites* Governments, in collaboration with the cooperative movement, to develop programmes aimed at enhancing capacity-building of cooperatives, including by strengthening the organizational, management and financial skills of their members, while respecting the principles of gender equality and the empowerment of women, and to introduce and support programmes to improve the access of cooperatives to new technologies;

9. *Invites* Governments and international organizations, in collaboration with cooperatives and cooperative organizations, to promote, as appropriate, the growth of agricultural cooperatives through easy access to affordable finance, adoption of sustainable production techniques, investments in rural infrastructure and irrigation, strengthened marketing mechanisms and support for the participation of women in economic activities;

10. *Also invites* Governments and international organizations, in collaboration with cooperatives and cooperative organizations, to promote, as appropriate, the growth of financial cooperatives to meet the goal of inclusive finance by providing easy access to affordable financial services for all;

11. *Encourages* Governments to intensify and expand the availability and accessibility of research on the operations and contribution of cooperatives and to establish methodologies for the collection and dissemination of comparable global data on and the good practices of cooperative enterprises, in collaboration with all stakeholders;

12. *Invites* Governments, relevant international organizations, the specialized agencies and local, national and international cooperative organizations to continue to observe the International Day of Cooperatives annually, on the first Saturday of July, as proclaimed by the General Assembly in its resolution 47/90;

13. *Requests* the Secretary-General, in cooperation with the relevant United Nations and other international organizations and national, regional and international cooperative organizations, to continue rendering support to Member States, as appropriate, in their efforts to create a supportive environment for the development of cooperatives, providing assistance for human resources development, technical advice and training and promoting an exchange of experience and best practices through, inter alia, conferences, workshops and seminars at the national and regional levels;

14. *Also requests* the Secretary-General to submit to the General Assembly at its sixty-eighth session a report on the implementation of the present resolution, including an overview of the activities that have been implemented during the International Year of Cooperatives.

Ageing persons

Follow-up to Second World Assembly on Ageing (2002)

In response to General Assembly resolution 65/182 [YUN 2010, p. 1194] on follow-up to the Second World Assembly on Ageing [YUN 2002, p. 1193], the Secretary-General submitted a July report [A/66/173] on the implementation of that resolution, particularly with regard to the situation of the rights of older persons. The report outlined the situation of and challenges faced by older persons in all regions of the world; reviewed the existing international framework, including some of the principles, standards and obligations of States parties that were applicable to older persons; and presented examples of national responses to human rights issues.

The report stated that by 2050, more than 20 per cent of the world's population would be aged 60 or older. As a result, greater attention to the needs and challenges faced by many older people was required, as well as to the continuing essental contribution they could make to the functioning of society if adequate guarantees were in place. While older persons faced numerous challenges around the world, the most pressing were poverty and inadequate living conditions; age-related discrimination; violence and abuse; and a lack of special measures, mechanisms and services to cope with increasing demands. A large number of older persons confronted critical human rights issues such as homelessness, malnutrition, unattended chronic diseases, a lack of access to safe drinking water and sanitation, unaffordable medicines and treatments, and income insecurity. Furthermore, while the essential role older persons could play as custodians of culture and history was recognized, many contributions to the report acknowledged that prejudice against and stigmatization of older persons were broadly tolerated in societies across the world. Age discrimination in relation to the enjoyment of all rights was compounded by other forms of discrimination, including those based on health conditions, sex, disabilities and ethnic origin. While national measures to protect the human rights of older persons were multiple and diverse, and some Governments were paying attention to normative gaps and the need to afford special protection to older persons, those policies were inconsistent across the globe and did not indicate the presence of comprehensive legal, policy and institutional frameworks. At the international level, there was no dedicated international protection regime for the human rights of older persons, and existing mechanisms lacked a systematic and comprehensive approach to the specific circumstances of older men and women.

The Secretary-General recommended that the General Assembly consider continuing the work of the Open-ended Working Group on Ageing, established in 2010 by resolution 65/182 [YUN 2010, p. 1194], in order to address existing gaps at the international level in the protection of the human rights of older persons, as well as consider the feasibility of further instruments and measures. He also recommended that Member States enhance their capacity to collect data, statistics and qualitative information to better assess the situation of older persons and to set adequate monitoring mechanisms for programmes and policies; and implement more effective multisectoral policies and programmes. In addition, States parties to international instruments should incorporate the situation of older persons more explicitly in their reporting.

World Elder Abuse Awareness Day

In December, by resolution 66/127 (see below), the General Assembly designated 15 June as World Elder Abuse Awareness Day, and invited Member States, the UN system, international and regional organizations, and civil society to observe the Day as appropriate.

GENERAL ASSEMBLY ACTION

On 19 December [meeting 89], the General Assembly, on the recommendation of the Third Committee [A/66/454 (Part II)], adopted **resolution 66/127** without vote [agenda item 27 (c)].

Follow-up to the Second World Assembly on Ageing

The General Assembly,

Recalling its resolution 57/167 of 18 December 2002, in which it endorsed the Political Declaration and the Madrid International Plan of Action on Ageing, 2002, its resolution 58/134 of 22 December 2003, in which it took note, inter alia, of the road map for the implementation of the Madrid Plan of Action, and its resolutions 60/135 of 16 December 2005, 61/142 of 19 December 2006, 62/130 of 18 December 2007, 63/151 of 18 December 2008, 64/132 of 18 December 2009 and 65/182 of 21 December 2010,

Recognizing that, in many parts of the world, awareness of the Madrid Plan of Action remains limited or non-existent, which limits the scope of implementation efforts,

Taking note of the report of the Secretary-General,

Recognizing that, by 2050, more than 20 per cent of the world's population will be 60 years old or older, and recognizing also that the increase in the number of older people will be greatest and most rapid in the developing world,

Deeply concerned that the situation of older persons in many parts of the world has been negatively affected by the world financial and economic crisis,

Recognizing the essential contribution that the majority of older men and women can continue to make to the functioning of society if adequate guarantees are in place,

Noting that older women outnumber older men, and noting with concern that older women often face multiple forms of discrimination resulting from their gender-based roles in society, compounded by their age, disability or other grounds, which affect the enjoyment of their human rights,

1. *Reaffirms* the Political Declaration and the Madrid International Plan of Action on Ageing, 2002;

2. *Encourages* Governments to pay greater attention to building capacity to eradicate poverty among older persons, in particular older women, by mainstreaming ageing issues into poverty eradication strategies and national development plans, and to include both ageing-specific policies and ageing-mainstreaming efforts in their national strategies;

3. *Encourages* Member States to strengthen their efforts to develop national capacity to address their national implementation priorities identified during the review and

appraisal of the Madrid Plan of Action, and invites Member States that have not done so to consider a step-by-step approach to developing capacity that includes the setting of national priorities, the strengthening of institutional mechanisms, research, data collection and analysis and the training of necessary personnel in the field of ageing;

4. *Also encourages* Member States to overcome obstacles to the implementation of the Madrid Plan of Action by devising strategies that take into account the entirety of the human life course and foster intergenerational solidarity in order to increase the likelihood of greater success in the years ahead;

5. *Further encourages* Member States to place particular emphasis on choosing national priorities that are realistic, sustainable and feasible and have the greatest likelihood of being achieved in the years ahead and to develop targets and indicators to measure progress in the implementation process;

6. *Encourages* all Member States to further implement the Madrid Plan of Action as an integral part of their national development plans and poverty eradication strategies;

7. *Invites* Member States to identify key priority areas for the remainder of the first decade of implementation of the Madrid Plan of Action, including empowering older persons and promoting their rights, raising awareness of ageing issues and building national capacity to address ageing;

8. *Recommends* that Member States increase awareness-raising of the Madrid Plan of Action, including by strengthening networks of national focal points on ageing, working with the regional commissions and enlisting the help of the Department of Public Information of the Secretariat to seek increased attention for ageing issues;

9. *Encourages* Governments that have not done so to designate focal points for handling follow-up of national plans of action on ageing;

10. *Invites* Governments to conduct their ageing-related policies through inclusive and participatory consultations with relevant stakeholders and social development partners, in the interest of developing effective policies creating national policy ownership and consensus-building;

11. *Recommends* that Member States enhance their capacity regarding more effective data collection, statistics and qualitative information, disaggregated when necessary by relevant factors, including sex and disability, in order to better assess the situation of older persons and to set adequate monitoring mechanisms for programmes and policies geared towards protecting the full and equal enjoyment of all human rights and fundamental freedoms by older persons;

12. *Also recommends* that States parties to existing international human rights instruments address the situation of older persons, where appropriate, more explicitly in their reports, and encourages treaty body monitoring mechanisms and special procedures mandate holders, in accordance with their mandates, to pay more attention to the situation of older persons in their dialogue with Member States, in their consideration of the reports or in their country missions;

13. *Calls upon* Governments to ensure, as appropriate, conditions that enable families and communities to provide care and protection to persons as they age, and to evaluate improvements in the health status of older persons, including on a gender-specific basis, and to reduce disability and mortality;

14. *Encourages* Governments to continue their efforts to implement the Madrid Plan of Action and to mainstream the concerns of older persons into their policy agendas, bearing in mind the crucial importance of family intergenerational interdependence, solidarity and reciprocity for social development and the realization of all human rights for older persons, and to prevent age discrimination and provide social integration;

15. *Recognizes* the importance of strengthening intergenerational partnerships and solidarity among generations, and in this regard calls upon Member States to promote opportunities for voluntary, constructive and regular interaction between young people and older generations in the family, the workplace and society at large;

16. *Encourages* Member States to adopt social policies that promote the development of community services for older persons, taking into account the psychological and physical aspects of ageing and the special needs of older women;

17. *Also encourages* Member States to ensure that older persons have access to information about their rights so as to enable them to participate fully and justly in their societies and to claim full enjoyment of all human rights;

18. *Calls upon* Member States to develop their national capacity for monitoring and enforcing the rights of older persons, in consultation with all sectors of society, including organizations of older persons, through, inter alia, national institutions for the promotion and protection of human rights where applicable;

19. *Also calls upon* Member States to strengthen and incorporate a gender and disability perspective into all policy actions on ageing, as well as to address and eliminate discrimination on the basis of age, gender or disability, and recommends that Member States engage with all sectors of society, in particular with relevant organizations with an interest in the matter, including organizations of older persons, of women and of persons with disabilities, in changing negative stereotypes about older persons, in particular older women and older persons with disabilities, and promote positive images of older persons;

20. *Further calls upon* Member States to address the well-being and adequate health care of older persons, as well as any cases of neglect, abuse and violence against older persons, by designing and implementing more effective prevention strategies and stronger laws and policies to address these problems and their underlying factors;

21. *Decides* to designate 15 June as World Elder Abuse Awareness Day, and invites all Member States, organizations of the United Nations system and other international and regional organizations, as well as civil society, including non-governmental organizations and individuals, to observe it in an appropriate manner;

22. *Calls upon* Member States to take concrete measures to further protect and assist older persons in emergency situations, in accordance with the Madrid Plan of Action;

23. *Stresses* that, in order to complement national development efforts, enhanced international cooperation is essential to support developing countries in implementing the Madrid Plan of Action, while recognizing the importance of assistance and the provision of financial assistance;

24. *Encourages* the international community, including international and bilateral donors, to enhance international cooperation to support national efforts to eradicate poverty, in keeping with internationally agreed goals, in order to achieve sustainable social and economic support for older persons, while bearing in mind that countries have the primary responsibility for their own economic and social development;

25. *Also encourages* the international community to support national efforts to forge stronger partnerships with civil society, including organizations of older persons, academia, research foundations, community-based organizations, including caregivers, and the private sector, in an effort to help to build capacity on ageing issues;

26. *Encourages* the international community and the relevant agencies of the United Nations system, within their respective mandates, to support national efforts to provide funding for research and data-collection initiatives on ageing, as appropriate, in order to better understand the challenges and opportunities presented by population ageing and to provide policymakers with more accurate and more specific information on gender and ageing;

27. *Recognizes* the important role of various international and regional organizations that deal with training, capacity-building, policy design and monitoring at the national and regional levels in promoting and facilitating the implementation of the Madrid Plan of Action, and acknowledges the work that is undertaken in various parts of the world, as well as regional initiatives, and by institutes such as the International Institute on Ageing in Malta and the European Centre for Social Welfare Policy and Research in Vienna;

28. *Recommends* that Member States reaffirm the role of United Nations focal points on ageing, increase technical cooperation efforts, expand the role of the regional commissions on ageing issues, especially in the review and appraisal of progress in the implementation of the Madrid Plan of Action during the tenth anniversary of its adoption in 2012, and provide added resources for those efforts, facilitate the coordination of national and international non-governmental organizations on ageing and enhance cooperation with academia on a research agenda on ageing;

29. *Reiterates* the need for additional capacity-building at the national level in order to promote and facilitate further implementation of the Madrid Plan of Action, as well as the results of its first review and appraisal cycle, and in this regard encourages Governments to support the United Nations Trust Fund for Ageing to enable the Department of Economic and Social Affairs of the Secretariat to provide expanded assistance to countries, upon their request;

30. *Requests* the United Nations system to strengthen its capacity to support, in an efficient and coordinated manner, national implementation of the Madrid Plan of Action, where appropriate;

31. *Recommends* that the situation of older persons be taken into account in the ongoing efforts to achieve the internationally agreed development goals, including those contained in the United Nations Millennium Declaration;

32. *Takes note with appreciation* of the work of the Open-ended Working Group on Ageing, established by General Assembly in paragraph 28 of resolution 65/182, and recognizes the positive contributions of Member States, as well as relevant bodies and organizations of the United Nations, intergovernmental and relevant non-governmental organizations, national human rights institutions and invited panellists during the first two working sessions of the Open-ended Working Group;

33. *Invites* States and relevant bodies and organizations of the United Nations system, including relevant human rights mandate holders and treaty bodies and the regional commissions, as well as intergovernmental and relevant non-governmental organizations with an interest in the matter, to continue to make contributions to the work entrusted to the Open-ended Working Group, as appropriate;

34. *Requests* the Secretary-General to continue to provide all necessary support to the Open-ended Working Group, within existing resources;

35. *Also requests* the Secretary-General to submit to the General Assembly at its sixty-seventh session a report on the implementation of the present resolution, in particular on the integration of older persons, including older women, in social development and the promotion of the full and equal enjoyment of all human rights and fundamental freedoms by older persons.

Open-ended Working Group on Ageing

The Open-ended Working Group on Ageing, established by General Assembly resolution 65/182 [YUN 2010, p. 1194], held its first organizational session [A/AC.278/2011/2] (New York, 15 February), at which it adopted a draft decision on the modalities of participation of non-governmental organizations in the work of the Group. At its first working session [A/AC.278/2011/4 & Corr.1] (New York, 18–21 April), the Working Group considered the current situation of the human rights of older persons; existing international instruments and mechanisms; the work of regional human rights systems in addressing the rights of older persons; and the identification of gaps and measures to address them. At its second working session [A/AC.278/2011/5] (New York, 1–4 August), the Group considered five topics, namely, discrimination and multiple discrimination; the right to the enjoyment of the highest attainable standard of physical and mental health; violence and abuse; social protection and the right to social security; and age and social exclusion.

Implementation of Madrid Plan of Action

Pursuant to Economic and Social Council resolution 2010/14 [YUN 2010, p. 1196], the Secretary-General submitted a report [E/CN.5/2011/7] to the forty-ninth session of the Commission for Social Development, which was prepared to facilitate the Commission's discussions on the organization of the second review and appraisal of the Madrid Plan of Action [YUN 2002, p. 1194]. The report outlined the process and modalities of the first review and appraisal and their continuing relevance for the second review and appraisal;

a preliminary list and timeline of initiatives of the UN system and civil society in preparation for the second process; and lessons learned from the first review and appraisal. The report stated that following the first review, certain shortcomings in the process became apparent, such as a lack of capacity in qualitative and quantitative data collection and a lack of participation of civil society. In regions where demographic ageing was more advanced, there was a greater interest in the review and appraisal process, as well as more resource availability by both Member States and regional commissions. In contrast, the participation of most Member States with a younger demographic profile, which usually correlated with a greater array of development challenges, remained limited. The UN system was working to expand national data collection in developing and transition countries; however, more action was required by Member States, with the assistance of national, regional and global research institutes and organizations, as well as the UN system. Furthermore, the involvement of civil society was critical in bringing the voice of older persons into the process, as well as in providing an alternate source of information and knowledge in countries with limited capacity for data collection, research and information on the social situation and rights of older persons. The Secretary-General stated that provisions should be made for holding civil society forums in all regions as part of the regional review and appraisal process. He also proposed a calendar for the second review and appraisal, beginning at the national and regional levels in 2011 and leading up to the global segment at the fifty-first session of the Commission for Social Development in 2013.

Commission action. At its February session [E/2011/26 & Corr.1], the Commission for Social Development recommended a draft resolution for adoption by the Economic and Social Council on modalities for the second review and appraisal of the Madrid International Plan of Action on Ageing, 2002 (see below).

ECONOMIC AND SOCIAL COUNCIL ACTION

On 28 July [meeting 48], the Economic and Social Council, on the recommendation of the Commission for Social Development [E/2011/26 & Corr.1], adopted **resolution 2011/28** without vote [agenda item 14 (*b*)].

Modalities for the second review and appraisal of the Madrid International Plan of Action on Ageing, 2002

The Economic and Social Council,

Recalling that, in the Madrid International Plan of Action on Ageing, 2002, adopted by the Second World Assembly on Ageing, held in Madrid from 8 to 12 April 2002, the systematic review of its implementation by Member States was requested as being essential for its success in improving the quality of life of older persons,

Recalling also that the Economic and Social Council, in its resolution 2003/14 of 21 July 2003, invited Governments, the United Nations system and civil society to participate in a bottom-up approach to the review and appraisal of the Madrid Plan of Action,

Bearing in mind that the Commission for Social Development, in its resolution 42/1 of 13 February 2004, decided to undertake the review and appraisal of the Madrid Plan of Action every five years,

Recalling that, in its resolution 2010/14 of 22 July 2010, it decided that the procedure for the second review and appraisal of the Madrid Plan of Action would follow the set procedure of the first review and appraisal exercise, further decided to conduct the second global review and appraisal of the Madrid Plan of Action in 2013 at the fifty-first session of the Commission for Social Development and endorsed the theme "Full implementation of the Madrid International Plan of Action on Ageing: social situation, well-being and dignity, development and the full realization of all human rights for older persons" for the second review and appraisal exercise,

Recalling General Assembly resolution 65/182 of 21 December 2010, on the follow-up to the Second World Assembly on Ageing, in which the Assembly established an open-ended working group, open to all States Members of the United Nations, for the purpose of strengthening the protection of the human rights of older persons by considering the existing international framework of the human rights of older persons and identifying possible gaps and how best to address them, including by considering, as appropriate, the feasibility of further instruments and measures,

Taking note with appreciation of the report of the Secretary-General,

1. *Endorses* the timeline for carrying out the second review and appraisal of the Madrid International Plan of Action on Ageing, 2002, as outlined in the report of the Secretary-General;

2. *Invites* Member States to identify actions they have taken since the first review and appraisal exercise, with the aim of presenting this information to the regional commissions during 2012, and invites each Member State to decide for itself the actions or activities it intends to review, utilizing a bottom-up participatory approach;

3. *Encourages* Member States to establish or strengthen a national coordinating body or mechanism, as appropriate, to, inter alia, facilitate the implementation of the Madrid Plan of Action, including its review and appraisal;

4. *Also encourages* Member States to utilize more fully, within their specific national circumstances, a bottom-up participatory approach to the review and appraisal process, and invites Member States to consider utilizing in their national review and appraisal exercise, if they so desire, a combination of quantitative and participatory qualitative data-gathering and analysis, including, where appropriate, sharing of best practices in such data collection;

5. *Encourages* the regional commissions to continue to facilitate the review and appraisal exercise at the regional level, including through consultation with relevant regional bodies, as appropriate, by:

(*a*) Promoting networking and the sharing of information and experiences;

(*b*) Assisting and providing advice to Governments in the gathering, synthesis and analysis of information, as well as in the presentation of the findings of national reviews and appraisals;

(c) Providing an analysis of the main findings, identifying key priority action areas and good practices and suggesting policy responses by 2012;

6. *Requests* the United Nations system to continue to support Member States in their national efforts for review and appraisal by providing, upon their request, technical assistance for capacity-building;

7. *Encourages* the international community, including international and bilateral donors, to enhance international cooperation, in keeping with internationally agreed goals, to support national efforts to eradicate poverty in order to ensure sustainable social and economic support for older persons, including by strengthening national capacity in the area of policy development and implementation with regard to older persons, while bearing in mind that countries have the primary responsibility for their own economic and social development;

8. *Encourages* Member States and United Nations organizations, where appropriate, to provide support to regional commissions in facilitating the review and appraisal process and organizing regional conferences to review national review and appraisal results in 2012;

9. *Requests* the Secretary-General to submit to the Commission for Social Development at its fiftieth session, in 2012, a report, including an analysis of the preliminary findings of the second review and appraisal exercise, together with an identification of prevalent and emerging issues and related policy options;

10. *Also requests* the Secretary-General to submit to the Commission at its fifty-first session, in 2013, a report, including conclusions of the second review and appraisal exercise, together with the identification of prevalent and emerging issues and related policy options.

Persons with disabilities

World Programme of Action

Pursuant to General Assembly resolution 65/186 [YUN 2010, p. 1078], the Secretary-General submitted a July report [A/66/128] on the realization of the Millennium Development Goals (MDGs) and other internationally agreed development goals for persons with disabilities. The report reviewed progress made to integrate the disability perspective in development processes, while noting that the rights and concerns of persons with disabilities remained to be integrated into mainstream development processes. Since the adoption in 2006 of the Convention on the Rights of Persons with Disabilities [YUN 2006, p. 785], which reinforced the overarching principles and goals promoted in the World Programme of Action concerning Disabled Persons [YUN 1982, p. 981], there had been renewed vigour to address the rights and concerns of persons with disabilities in society and development. An increasing number of Governments were strengthening national frameworks on disability through the implementation of the Convention, with efforts including exploring policy options for including disability in the mainstream development agenda; promoting accessibility; empowering persons with disabilities; and building national capacities and institutional frameworks to incorporate the disability perspective at all levels of decision-making. In addition, multi-stakeholder partnerships within and outside the UN system had explored the linkages between disability and other issues, such as gender, child poverty, mental health, peace and security, and emergency and disaster management.

The report also considered the socioeconomic aspects of disability, stating that the exclusion of persons with disabilities resulted in significant costs to society. At the individual level, social exclusion often contributed to further discrimination and rendered persons with disabilities disproportionately likely to live in poverty. Access to employment was the most cost-effective method of reducing poverty among persons with disabilities, their families and their communities, and efforts should also be scaled up to reach out to the millions of children excluded from schools. The Secretary-General outlined priority areas for action, namely the equalization of opportunities for persons with disabilities in all aspects of society and development; collection, analysis and use of disability data and statistics; capacity-building of stakeholders; promoting international development cooperation; and building on existing mechanisms and networks for disability-inclusive development. He also highlighted opportunities to ensure the inclusion of disability in the global development agenda towards and beyond 2015, recommending, among other things, that the international community intensify efforts to include disability in the MDGs; and that Governments and the UN system assess the impact of all policies and programmes on persons with disabilities related to the MDGs, and facilitate the participation of persons with disabilities in the preparatory processes leading to a post-2015 development framework.

GENERAL ASSEMBLY ACTION

On 19 December [meeting 89], the General Assembly, on the recommendation of the Third Committee [A/66/454 (Part II)], adopted **resolution 66/124** without vote [agenda item 27 (*b*)].

High-level Meeting of the General Assembly on the realization of the Millennium Development Goals and other internationally agreed development goals for persons with disabilities

The General Assembly,

Recalling the World Programme of Action concerning Disabled Persons, the Standard Rules on the Equalization of Opportunities for Persons with Disabilities and the Convention on the Rights of Persons with Disabilities, in which persons with disabilities are recognized as both development agents and beneficiaries in all aspects of development,

Recalling also its previous resolutions on the internationally agreed development goals, including the Millennium Development Goals, in which it recognized the collective responsibility of Governments to uphold the principles of human dignity, equality and equity at the global level, and stressing the duty of Member States to achieve greater justice and equality for all, in particular persons with disabilities,

Noting that persons with disabilities, who face a greater risk of living in absolute poverty, make up an estimated 15 per cent of the world's population, of whom 80 per cent live in developing countries, and recognizing the importance of international cooperation and its promotion in support of national efforts, in particular for developing countries,

Recalling its resolution 65/186 of 21 December 2010, by which it requested the Secretary-General to submit information on the implementation of the resolution, with a view to convening, within existing resources, a high-level meeting at the sixty-seventh session of the General Assembly on strengthening efforts to ensure accessibility for and inclusion of persons with disabilities in all aspects of development efforts,

1. *Takes note with appreciation* of the report of the Secretary-General entitled "Realization of the Millennium Development Goals and other internationally agreed development goals for persons with disabilities";

2. *Decides* to convene a one-day High-level Meeting of the General Assembly, at the level of Heads of State and Government, on 23 September 2013, the Monday before the start of the general debate of the sixty-eighth session of the Assembly, with the overarching theme "The way forward: a disability-inclusive development agenda towards 2015 and beyond", which shall be funded within existing resources, in order to strengthen efforts to ensure accessibility for and inclusion of persons with disabilities in all aspects of development efforts;

3. *Also decides* that the organizational arrangements for the High-level Meeting should be as follows:

(*a*) The High-level Meeting will comprise a plenary meeting and two consecutive informal interactive round tables, the round tables to be chaired by Member States at the invitation of the President of the General Assembly, and the themes for the round tables will be decided by the President of the Assembly in consultation with Member States;

(*b*) The opening plenary meeting will feature statements by the President of the General Assembly, the Secretary-General, the Chair of the Committee on the Rights of Persons with Disabilities, an eminent person actively engaged in disability issues and a representative of non-governmental organizations in consultative status with the Economic and Social Council, both of whom will be chosen by the President of the Assembly;

(*c*) The Chairs of the round tables will present summaries of the discussions at the closing plenary meeting;

(*d*) In order to promote interactive and substantive discussions, participation in each round table will include Member States, observers and representatives of entities of the United Nations system, as well as selected representatives of civil society, organizations of persons with disabilities and the private sector;

4. *Further decides* that the High-level Meeting will result in a concise, action-oriented outcome document in support of the aims of the Convention on the Rights of Persons with Disabilities and the realization of the Millennium Development Goals and other internationally agreed development goals for persons with disabilities, and requests the President of the General Assembly to produce a draft text, in consultation with Member States, taking into account input from organizations of persons with disabilities, and to convene informal consultations, within existing resources, at an appropriate date in order to enable sufficient consideration and agreement by Member States prior to the Meeting;

5. *Calls upon* Member States to consider including in their delegations to the High-level Meeting persons with disabilities, bearing in mind the principles of gender balance and non-discrimination and the fact that there are disability and age diversities;

6. *Invites* the President of the General Assembly to draw up a list of representatives of non-governmental organizations in consultative status with the Economic and Social Council who will participate in the High-level Meeting;

7. *Also invites* the President of the General Assembly, following appropriate consultations with Member States, to draw up a list of representatives of other non-governmental organizations, organizations of persons with disabilities, relevant civil society organizations and the private sector who might participate in the High-level Meeting, taking into account the principle of equitable geographical representation, and to submit the list to Member States for consideration on a no-objection basis and bring to the attention of the Assembly the finalized list;

8. *Encourages* all Member States, intergovernmental and non-governmental organizations, private sector entities and other relevant stakeholders to consider supporting the participation of representatives from developing countries, in particular, to give a prominent role to delegates who are persons with disabilities and representatives of non-governmental organizations and civil society organizations from those countries, in order to promote the broadest possible participation, and requests the Secretary-General to take, within existing resources, all necessary measures in this regard, including the accessibility of the High-level Meeting;

9. *Requests* the President of the General Assembly, in consultation with Member States, to finalize the organizational arrangements for the High-level Meeting, taking into account the length of the meetings, the identification of the eminent person actively engaged in disability issues and the representative of non-governmental organizations in consultative status with the Economic and Social Council to speak at the opening plenary meeting, the identification of a representative of a non-governmental organization in consultative status with the Economic and Social Council active in disability issues to speak at the first round table and the identification of Chairs for the round tables, bearing in mind the level of representation and equitable geographical representation.

Equalization of opportunities

Pursuant to Economic and Social Council resolution 2008/20 [YUN 2008, p. 1212], the Secretary-General submitted to the Commission for Social Development a note transmitting the first report of the Special Rapporteur on Disability of the Commission, Shuaib Chalklen (South Africa), on monitoring implementation of the Standard Rules on the Equalization of Opportunities for Persons with Disabilities [E/CN.5/2011/9].

The report outlined the work and priorities of the Special Rapporteur in the period from February to October 2010, which were built on relevant human rights and development instruments, including the MDGs; other internationally agreed development goals and international commitments and standards; and the three instruments on disability, namely the World Programme of Action concerning Disabled Persons, adopted by resolution 37/52 [YUN 1982, p. 981], the Standard Rules on the Equalization of Opportunities for Persons with Disabilities [YUN 1993, p. 977], and the Convention on the Rights of Persons with Disabilities [YUN 2006, p. 785]. The activities of the Rapporteur focused on monitoring the implementation of the Standard Rules and synergy among the disability-specific instruments; the mainstreaming of disability in development, including a priority focus on disability-inclusive development in Africa; fostering international cooperation; promoting the instruments on disability and other international development instruments; and vulnerable groups within the disability community.

The Special Rapporteur stated that the Convention, together with the World Programme of Action, strengthened the international normative framework on promoting disability rights. However, there was a persistent gap between commitments and policy and practices, with the most common barriers to inclusive development including negative attitudes; lack of resources; lack of political will; poor support for inclusion among development professionals; absence of a clear legal framework; and lack of capacity to implement policies. The Rapporteur recommended that Member States and the UN system urgently address the lack of statistics and data on disability and analysis of the situation of persons with disabilities in economic and social development; and that Member States share good practices and examples of promoting disability-inclusive development and the mainstreaming of disability in development. Further recommendations included the establishment of a multi-donor trust fund or similar entity under the auspices of the United Nations, to promote disability rights in development and support the efforts of Member States in implementing internationally agreed development goals, including the MDGs and the Convention; the establishment of disability focal points in each of the UN agencies; the empowerment of persons with disability and their organizations; and better coordination among disability coalitions.

Commission action. At its February session [E/2011/26 & Corr.1], the Commission for Social Development recommended a draft resolution for adoption by the Economic and Social Council on the further promotion of equalization of opportunities by, for and with persons with disabilities, and mainstreaming disability in the development agenda (see below).

ECONOMIC AND SOCIAL COUNCIL ACTION

On 28 July [meeting 48], the Economic and Social Council, on the recommendation of the Commission for Social Development [E/2011/26 & Corr.1], adopted **resolution 2011/27** without vote [agenda item 14 (*b*)].

Further promotion of equalization of opportunities by, for and with persons with disabilities and mainstreaming disability issues in the development agenda

The Economic and Social Council,

Recalling the outcomes of the World Summit for Social Development, held in Copenhagen from 6 to 12 March 1995, and of the twenty-fourth special session of the General Assembly entitled "World Summit for Social Development and beyond: achieving social development for all in a globalizing world", held at Geneva from 26 June to 1 July 2000,

Recalling also the World Programme of Action concerning Disabled Persons, the Standard Rules on the Equalization of Opportunities for Persons with Disabilities and the Convention on the Rights of Persons with Disabilities, in which persons with disabilities are recognized as both development agents and beneficiaries in all aspects of development,

Recalling further its previous resolutions concerning persons with disabilities and further promotion of equalization of opportunities and mainstreaming of disability issues in the development agenda and the relevant resolutions adopted by the General Assembly,

Welcoming the fact that, since the opening for signature on 30 March 2007 of the Convention on the Rights of Persons with Disabilities and the Optional Protocol thereto, one hundred and forty-eight States and one regional integration organization have signed and one hundred and two States have ratified or acceded to and one regional integration organization has formally confirmed the Convention and ninety States have signed and sixty-two States have ratified or acceded to the Optional Protocol, and encouraging all States that have not yet done so to consider signing and ratifying the Convention and the Optional Protocol,

Acknowledging that the majority of the 690 million persons with disabilities in the world live in conditions of poverty, and in this regard recognizing the critical need to address the impact of poverty on persons with disabilities,

Noting that persons with disabilities make up an estimated 10 per cent of the world's population, of whom 80 per cent live in developing countries, and recognizing the important role of international cooperation in supporting national efforts to mainstream disability issues in the development agenda, in particular for developing countries,

Emphasizing the importance of the collection and compilation of national data and information regarding the situation of persons with disabilities, following existing guidelines on disability statistics, that are disaggregated by gender and age, which could be used by Governments to enable their development policy planning, monitoring, evaluation and implementation to be disability-sensitive, in particular in the achievement of the Millennium Development Goals for persons with disabilities, while reiterating the request to the United Nations system to facilitate technical assistance within existing resources, including the provision of assistance, in particular to developing countries, for capacity-building and for the collection and compilation of national and regional data and statistics on disabilities,

Convinced that addressing the profound social, cultural and economic disadvantage and exclusion experienced by many persons with disabilities, and that promoting the use of universal design as appropriate, as well as the progressive removal of barriers to their full and effective participation in all aspects of development, and promoting their economic, social and cultural rights, will further the equalization of opportunities and contribute to the realization of a "society for all" in the twenty-first century,

Stressing that the Convention on the Rights of Persons with Disabilities emphasizes the importance of international cooperation for improving the living conditions of persons with disabilities in every country, particularly in developing countries, and promotes the full realization of the civil, political, economic, social and cultural rights of persons with disabilities,

Underlining the importance of mobilizing resources at all levels for the successful implementation of the Standard Rules on the Equalization of Opportunities for Persons with Disabilities, the World Programme of Action concerning Disabled Persons and the Convention on the Rights of Persons with Disabilities, and recognizing the importance of international cooperation and its promotion in support of national efforts, in particular in developing countries,

1. *Welcomes* the outcome document of the High-level Plenary Meeting of the General Assembly on the Millennium Development Goals, particularly the recognition that policies and actions must also focus on persons with disabilities so that they benefit from progress towards achieving the Goals;

2. *Calls upon* Member States and United Nations bodies and agencies to include disability issues and persons with disabilities in reviewing progress towards achieving the Millennium Development Goals and to step up efforts to include in their assessment the extent to which persons with disabilities are able to benefit from efforts to achieve the Goals;

3. *Calls upon* Member States to enable persons with disabilities to participate as agents and beneficiaries of development, in particular in all efforts towards eradicating extreme poverty and hunger, achieving universal primary education, promoting gender equality and the empowerment of women, reducing child mortality, improving maternal health, combating HIV/AIDS, malaria and other diseases, ensuring environmental sustainability and developing a global partnership for development, are inclusive of and accessible to persons with disabilities;

4. *Encourages* all Member States, concerned intergovernmental organizations, international and regional organizations and civil society, in particular organizations of persons with disabilities, and the private sector, to engage in cooperative arrangements aimed at providing the necessary technical and expert assistance to enhance capacities in mainstreaming disability issues, including the perspective of persons with disabilities, in the development agenda, and in this regard encourages the Secretariat and other relevant bodies to find improved ways to enhance international technical cooperation;

5. *Welcomes* the work of the Special Rapporteur on disability of the Commission for Social Development, and takes note of his report;

6. *Decides* to extend the mandate of the Special Rapporteur for the period from 2012 to 2014, in accordance with the provisions set down in section IV of the Standard Rules on the Equalization of Opportunities for Persons with Disabilities to further their promotion and monitoring, including the human rights dimension of disability, and with the provisions of the present resolution, and in this regard reaffirms paragraph 3 of Economic and Social Council resolution 2008/20 of 24 July 2008;

7. *Requests* the Special Rapporteur to further:

(*a*) Raise awareness of the Convention on the Rights of Persons with Disabilities, the World Programme of Action concerning Disabled Persons and the Standard Rules;

(*b*) Promote the inclusion of persons with disabilities and the mainstreaming of disability issues in development programmes and strategies at the national, regional and international levels;

(*c*) Promote international cooperation, including technical cooperation, that is inclusive of and accessible to persons with disabilities, as well as the exchange and sharing of expertise and best practices on disability issues;

(*d*) Collaborate, in fulfilment of the above tasks, with all relevant stakeholders, including organizations of persons with disabilities;

8. *Requests* the Special Rapporteur to contribute to the planned high-level meeting of the sixty-seventh session of the General Assembly and its preparation, taking account of the priorities of the international community in strengthening efforts to ensure accessibility for and inclusion of persons with disabilities in all aspects of development efforts;

9. *Expresses concern* at the lack of sufficient resources for the Special Rapporteur, and recognizes the importance of providing adequate resources for the implementation of his mandate;

10. *Encourages* Member States, intergovernmental organizations, non-governmental organizations and the private sector to continue to contribute to the United Nations Voluntary Fund on Disability in order to support the activities of the Special Rapporteur as well as new and expanded initiatives to strengthen national capacities for the equalization of opportunities by, for and with persons with disabilities;

11. *Requests* the Special Rapporteur to submit to the Commission for Social Development at its fiftieth session an annual report on his activities in implementing the present resolution.

Youth

World Programme of Action for Youth

In 2011, UN policies and programmes on youth continued to focus on efforts to implement the World Programme of Action for Youth to the Year 2000 and Beyond, adopted by the General Assembly in resolution 50/81 [YUN 1995, p. 1211] and covering 10 priority issues for youth: education; employment; hunger and poverty; health; environment; drug abuse; juvenile delinquency; leisure-time activities; girls and young women; and participation in society and decision-making. In resolution 60/2 [YUN 2005, p. 1296], the Assembly added five additional priority areas: the mixed impact of globalization on young women and men; the use of and access to information and communication technologies; the increase in the incidence of HIV infection among young people and the impact of the epidemic on their lives; the involvement of young people in armed conflict, both as victims and as perpetrators; and the importance of addressing intergenerational issues in an ageing society.

Report of Secretary-General. In response to Assembly resolution 64/134 [YUN 2009, p. 1187], the Secretary-General reported [A/66/129] on key activities and initiatives undertaken by Member States, civil society organizations and UN entities in support of the International Year of Youth, which commenced on 12 August 2010 [YUN 2010, p. 1192]. Pursuant to a request by the Commission for Social Development [YUN 2009, p. 1185], the Secretary-General reported [YUN 2010, p. 1193] on mechanisms for coordination and collaboration of UN entities in their work related to youth.

GENERAL ASSEMBLY ACTION

On 19 December [meeting 89], the General Assembly, on the recommendation of the Third Committee [A/66/454 (Part II)], adopted **resolution 66/121** without vote [agenda item 27 (*b*)].

Policies and programmes involving youth

The General Assembly,

Recalling the World Programme of Action for Youth, adopted by the General Assembly in its resolutions 50/81 of 14 December 1995 and 62/126 of 18 December 2007,

Recalling also the outcome document of the High-level Meeting of the General Assembly on Youth: Dialogue and Mutual Understanding, adopted by the General Assembly on 26 July 2011,

Recalling further the Outcome of the Conference on the World Financial and Economic Crisis and Its Impact on Development,

Welcoming the initiative of the Government of Sri Lanka to host in 2014 a world conference on youth in Colombo, with a focus on the participation and involvement of youth in achieving the internationally agreed development goals, including the Millennium Development Goals,

Welcoming also the participation of young representatives in national delegations at the General Assembly,

Profoundly concerned that the situation of youth, especially girls and young women, in many parts of the world has been negatively impacted by the world financial and economic crisis, and reaffirming that eradicating poverty continues to be among the greatest global challenges facing the world today, recognizing its impact beyond the socio-economic context,

Recognizing that the ways in which young people are able to address their aspirations and challenges and fulfil their potential will influence current social and economic conditions and the well-being and livelihood of future generations, and stressing the need for further efforts to promote the interests of youth, including the full enjoyment of their human rights, inter alia, by supporting young people in developing their potential and talents and tackling obstacles facing youth,

Recognizing also that the international community has been challenged by multiple and interrelated crises, including the ongoing impact of the financial and economic crisis, volatile energy and food prices and ongoing concerns over food security, as well as the increasing challenges posed by climate change and the loss of biodiversity, all of which have increased vulnerabilities and inequalities and have adversely affected development gains, in particular in developing countries, and calling for enhanced cooperation and concerted action to address those challenges, taking into account the positive role that education can play in that respect,

1. *Reaffirms* the World Programme of Action for Youth, including its fifteen interrelated priority areas, and calls upon Member States to continue its implementation at the local, national, regional and international levels;

2. *Takes note with appreciation* of the report of the Secretary-General entitled "International Year of Youth: Dialogue and Mutual Understanding";

3. *Also takes note with appreciation* of the report of the Secretary-General entitled "Implementation of the World Programme of Action for Youth: United Nations system coordination and collaboration related to youth", and welcomes the recent increased collaboration among the United Nations entities in the area of youth development;

4. *Expresses deep concern* that the attainment of the social development objectives may be hindered by the multiple and interrelated crises, including the ongoing impact of the financial and economic crisis, volatile energy and food prices and ongoing concerns over food security, as well as the increasing challenges posed by climate change and the loss of biodiversity;

5. *Recognizes* that young people in all countries are both a major human resource for development and key agents for social change, economic development and technological innovation, and affirms that investment in youth development and education is crucial for sustainable social and economic development;

6. *Reaffirms* that the strengthening of international cooperation regarding youth, including through the fulfilment of all official development assistance commitments, the transfer of appropriate technology, capacity-building, the enhancement of dialogue, mutual understanding and the active participation of young people are crucial elements of efforts towards achieving the eradication of poverty, full employment and social integration;

7. *Urges* Member States to promote the full and effective participation of young people and youth-led organizations in relevant decision-making processes, including in developing, implementing and monitoring policies, programmes and activities at all times, especially in times of crisis;

8. *Also urges* Member States to specifically address youth development in their economic and financial recovery measures by emphasizing youth employment and promoting entrepreneurship, volunteerism and the devel-

opment of formal, informal and non-formal educational and training systems in line with the needs of young people and their societies, and encourages all relevant stakeholders, including academia, the private sector, trade unions and financial institutions, to promote social responsibility and to develop partnerships in this regard;

9. *Calls upon* Member States to promote the well-being of young people, particularly the poor and the marginalized, through comprehensive policies and action plans and, in particular, to address poverty, employment and social integration as fundamental aspects of their national development agendas, and encourages the international community and the United Nations system to support Member States in this regard;

10. *Stresses* the potential of information and communications technology to improve the quality of life of young people in order to enable them to better participate in the global economy, and in this regard calls upon Member States, with the support of the United Nations system, donors, the private sector and civil society, to ensure universal, non-discriminatory, equitable, safe and affordable access to information and communications technology, especially in schools and public places, and to remove the barriers to bridging the digital divide, including through the transfer of technology on mutually agreed terms and international cooperation, as well as to promote the development of locally relevant content and implement measures to equip young people with the knowledge and skills to use information and communications technology appropriately and safely;

11. *Also stresses* that young people are particularly vulnerable in the labour market in times of crisis, and, in order to meet the needs of youth in a rapidly changing labour market, recognizes that promoting full employment, decent work and entrepreneurship requires investing in education, training and skills development for young women and men, strengthening social protection and health systems, applying internationally agreed labour standards, paying special attention to young people employed in the informal economy and the progressive and effective elimination of child labour;

12. *Recognizes* that youth employment and job opportunities for youth contribute to social stability, cohesion and inclusion and that States have an important role in addressing the demands of youth in this regard, notes that the Global Jobs Pact provides recommendations and policy options for States, and invites donor countries, multilateral organizations and other stakeholders to support national efforts aimed at enhancing employment for youth;

13. *Urges* Member States to address the challenges of girls and young women, as well as gender stereotypes that perpetuate discrimination against girls and young women and stereotypic roles of men and women that are preclusive of social development, by reaffirming the commitment to the empowerment of women and gender equality, as well as to the mainstreaming of a gender perspective into all development efforts, recognizing that these are critical for achieving sustainable development and for efforts to combat hunger, poverty and disease, and to strengthen policies and programmes that improve, ensure and broaden the full participation of young women in all spheres of political, economic, social and cultural life, as equal partners, and to improve their access to all resources needed for the full exercise of all their human rights and fundamental freedoms by removing persistent barriers, including ensuring equal access to full and productive employment and decent work, as well as strengthening their economic independence;

14. *Recognizes* the ongoing impact of the financial and economic crisis on the quality of life and health of young people, and in this regard encourages Member States to promote health education and health literacy among young people, including through evidence-based education and information strategies and programmes in and out of schools and through public campaigns, as well as to increase the access of youth to affordable, safe and effective health care by paying special attention to, and raising awareness regarding, nutrition, including eating disorders and obesity, the effects of non-communicable and communicable diseases and sexual and reproductive health, as well as measures to prevent sexually transmitted diseases, including HIV and AIDS;

15. *Urges* Member States to increase efforts, including to address the ongoing social impact of the crises, to improve the quality of education and promote universal access to education, particularly for young women, out-of-school youth, youth with disabilities, indigenous youth, youth in rural areas, young migrants and youth living with HIV and affected by AIDS, without discrimination on any basis, to ensure that they can acquire the knowledge, capacities, skills and ethical values needed, including by appropriate access to scholarships and other mobility programmes, non-formal education, and technical and vocational education and training, in order to further develop their contributions to societies as relevant actors to promote development;

16. *Also urges* Member States to take concerted actions in conformity with international law to remove the obstacles to the full realization of the rights of young people living under foreign occupation to promote the achievement of the Millennium Development Goals;

17. *Further urges* Member States to take effective measures in conformity with international law to protect young people affected or exploited by terrorism and incitement;

18. *Urges* Member States to promote equal opportunities for all, to combat all forms of discrimination against young people, including that based on race, colour, sex, language, religion, political or other opinion, national or social origin, property, birth or other status, and to foster social integration for social groups such as young persons with disabilities, young migrants and indigenous youth on an equal basis with others;

19. *Encourages* Member States to consider including youth representatives in their delegations at all relevant discussions in the General Assembly and the Economic and Social Council and its functional commissions and at relevant United Nations conferences, as appropriate, bearing in mind the principle of gender balance and non-discrimination, and, inter alia, to consider establishing a national youth delegate programme, and emphasizes that such youth representatives should be selected through a transparent process which ensures that they have a suitable mandate to represent young people in their countries;

20. *Calls upon* donors, including Member States and intergovernmental and non-governmental organizations, to actively contribute to the United Nations Youth Fund in order to facilitate the participation of youth representatives from developing countries in the activities of the United Nations, taking into account the need for greater geograph-

ical balance of youth representation, as well as to accelerate the implementation of the World Programme of Action for Youth and to support the production of the *World Youth Report*, and in this regard requests the Secretary-General to take appropriate action to encourage contributions to the Fund;

21. *Reiterates its request* to the Secretary-General to strengthen the United Nations Programme on Youth within the existing resources of the Department of Economic and Social Affairs of the Secretariat so as to meet the increasing demands on the Programme;

22. *Requests* that the United Nations entities enhance their coordination and intensify efforts towards a more coherent, comprehensive and integrated approach to youth development through, inter alia, the Inter-Agency Network on Youth Development, calls upon the United Nations entities and relevant partners to develop additional measures to support national, regional and international efforts in addressing challenges hindering youth development, and in this regard encourages close collaboration with Member States and other relevant stakeholders, including civil society, particularly youth-led organizations.

High-level meeting on youth

As part of the International Year of Youth: Dialogue and Mutual Understanding, declared by resolution 64/134 [YUN 2009, p. 1187], the General Assembly decided to hold a high-level meeting on youth, under the overarching theme "Youth: dialogue and mutual understanding" (New York, 25–26 July).

GENERAL ASSEMBLY ACTION

On 15 March [meeting 78], the General Assembly adopted **resolution 65/267** [draft: A/65/L.63] without vote [agenda item 27 (*b*)].

Organization of the High-level Meeting on Youth

The General Assembly,

Recalling its resolution 64/134 of 18 December 2009, by which it proclaimed the year commencing on 12 August 2010 the International Year of Youth: Dialogue and Mutual Understanding and decided to organize, under the auspices of the United Nations, a world youth conference as the highlight of the Year,

Recalling also its resolutions 50/81 of 14 December 1995 and 62/126 of 18 December 2007, by which it adopted the World Programme of Action for Youth, as contained in the annexes thereto, and acknowledging that the Programme of Action provides Member States with a useful policy framework and practical guidelines for improving the situation of youth,

Bearing in mind that youth represent a significant proportion of the world's population and that the way in which the challenges and potential of young people are addressed will influence social and economic conditions and the well-being and livelihood of future generations,

Recognizing that the International Year of Youth provides an important opportunity to enhance dialogue and mutual understanding among youth worldwide, to promote youth participation at all levels, and to increase the commitment and investment from Governments and the international community in addressing the challenges that hinder youth,

1. *Decides* that the world youth conference shall take the form of a high-level meeting of the General Assembly, to be held at United Nations Headquarters in New York on 25 and 26 July 2011, and shall be funded within existing resources and through voluntary contributions;

2. *Also decides* that the High-level Meeting shall have as its overarching theme "Youth: dialogue and mutual understanding";

3. *Calls upon* Member States to pay due attention to relevant internationally agreed development goals, including the Millennium Development Goals, and relevant outcomes and programmes of action, including the World Programme of Action for Youth and General Assembly resolution 62/126;

4. *Decides* that the organizational arrangements for the High-level Meeting shall be as follows:

(*a*) The High-level Meeting will comprise plenary meetings and two consecutive informal interactive round tables, with the round tables to be chaired by Member States at the invitation of the President of the General Assembly and to address the following themes:

  (i) Round table 1: Strengthening international co-operation regarding youth and enhancing dialogue, mutual understanding and active youth participation as indispensable elements of efforts towards achieving social integration, full employment and the eradication of poverty;

  (ii) Round table 2: Challenges to youth development and opportunities for poverty eradication, employment and sustainable development;

(*b*) The opening plenary meeting will feature statements by the President of the General Assembly, the Secretary-General and an eminent person actively engaged in youth issues, and a youth representative of non-governmental organizations in consultative status with the Economic and Social Council, both of whom will be chosen by the President of the Assembly;

(*c*) The Chairs of the round tables will present summaries of the discussions at the closing plenary meeting;

(*d*) In order to promote interactive and substantive discussions, participation in each round table will include Member States, observers and representatives of entities of the United Nations system, civil society, youth organizations and the private sector, without a list of speakers being maintained in this regard;

5. *Also decides* that the High-level Meeting shall result in a concise action-oriented outcome document, and requests the President of the General Assembly to produce a draft text, in consultation with Member States, taking into account input from youth-led organizations, and to convene informal consultations at an appropriate date in order to enable sufficient consideration and agreement by Member States prior to the Meeting;

6. *Invites* Member States and observers to be represented at a high level at the High-level Meeting;

7. *Invites* the Holy See, in its capacity as observer State, and Palestine, in its capacity as observer, to participate in the preparatory activities and in the High-level Meeting;

8. *Calls upon* Member States to consider including in their delegation to the High-level Meeting young people who suitably and broadly represent youth in their countries, bearing in mind the principles of gender balance and non-discrimination;

9. *Invites* the President of the General Assembly to draw up a list of representatives of non-governmental organizations in consultative status with the Economic and Social Council who may participate in the High-level Meeting;

10. *Also invites* the President of the General Assembly to draw up a list of representatives of other non-governmental organizations, relevant civil society organizations and the private sector who may participate in the High-level Meeting, taking into account the principle of equitable geographical representation, and to submit the list to Member States for consideration on a no-objection basis;

11. *Encourages* all Member States, intergovernmental and non-governmental organizations, private sector entities, and other relevant stakeholders to consider supporting the participation of representatives from developing countries, in particular youth delegates and representatives of non-governmental organizations and civil society organizations from those countries, including by making voluntary contributions to the United Nations Youth Fund, in order to ensure the broadest possible participation, and requests the Secretary-General to take all necessary measures in this regard;

12. *Requests* the President of the General Assembly, in consultation with Member States, to finalize the organizational arrangements of the meetings, taking into account the length of the meetings, the identification of the eminent person and the youth representative to speak at the opening plenary meeting and the identification of Chairs for the round tables, bearing in mind the level of representation as well as equitable geographical representation.

The High-Level Meeting on Youth conducted two informal interactive panel discussions on 25 July, and two plenary meetings on 26 July [A/65/PV.110-112]. In his remarks at the Meeting, the Secretary-General stated that the international community must work to expand the horizons of opportunity for young women and men, and to answer their legitimate demands for dignity and decent work. Ahead of the Rio+20 United Nations Conference on Sustainable Development in 2012, he underlined that youth must play a central role in bringing new ideas, fresh thinking and energy to the Rio+20 process. That could be achieved through the Youth Delegates Programme of the United Nations, which provided young people with the opportunity to represent themselves meaningfully on the international stage. The Secretary-General stated that while the International Year of Youth was coming to a close, obligations to young people remained, including promoting a culture of dialogue and mutual understanding, and confronting the pressing issues of climate change, nuclear disarmament, women's and children's health, strengthening democracy, achieving the MDGs, and ensuring sustainable development.

GENERAL ASSEMBLY ACTION

On 26 July [meeting 111], the General Assembly adopted **resolution 65/312** [draft: A/65/L.87] without vote [agenda item 27 (*b*)].

Outcome document of the High-level Meeting of the General Assembly on Youth: Dialogue and Mutual Understanding

The General Assembly,

Recalling its resolution 64/134 of 18 December 2009, in particular paragraph 3 thereof, and its resolution 65/267 of 15 March 2011, in particular paragraph 1 thereof,

Adopts the following outcome document of the High-level Meeting of the General Assembly on Youth: Dialogue and Mutual Understanding:

Outcome document of the High-level Meeting of the General Assembly on Youth: Dialogue and Mutual Understanding

We, Heads of State and Government, Ministers and representatives of Member States, gathered at a high-level meeting at United Nations Headquarters in New York on 25 and 26 July 2011 on the theme "Youth: dialogue and mutual understanding",

1. Stress the need to disseminate and foster among young people and educate them about the ideals of peace, freedom, justice, tolerance, respect for human rights and fundamental freedoms, solidarity and dedication to the objectives of progress and development;

2. Recall resolution 64/134 of 18 December 2009, by which the General Assembly proclaimed the year commencing on 12 August 2010 the International Year of Youth: Dialogue and Mutual Understanding, and acknowledge the significance of the High-level Meeting as the highlight of the International Year of Youth;

3. Reaffirm the World Programme of Action for Youth, including its fifteen interrelated priority areas, and call upon Member States to continue its implementation at the local, national, regional and international levels;

4. Encourage Member States to develop comprehensive policies and action plans that focus on the best interests of youth, particularly the poor and marginalized, and address all aspects of youth development, and also encourage the international community and the United Nations system to support national youth programmes and further develop and improve the existing international framework on youth, including the World Programme of Action for Youth, in order to fully address all current challenges affecting youth;

5. Also encourage Member States to promote gender equality and the empowerment of women in all aspects of youth development, recognizing the vulnerability of girls and young women, and the important role of boys and young men in ensuring gender equality;

6. Note with appreciation the activities, special events, contributions and inputs of Member States and all stakeholders, including youth-led organizations, the private sector, civil society and the media, as well as United Nations entities, and take into account the input from youth-led organizations to the outcome document of the High-level Meeting;

7. Recognize that the ways in which young people are able to address their aspirations and challenges and fulfil their potential will influence current social and economic conditions and the well-being and livelihood of future generations, and stress the need for further efforts to promote the interests of youth, including the full enjoyment of their human rights, inter alia, by supporting young people in developing their potential and talents and tackling obstacles facing youth;

8. Recall the commitment to achieving the internationally agreed development goals, including the Millennium Development Goals, and to implementing the outcomes of global conferences and summits and relevant programmes;

9. Stress the important role of effective sectoral and cross-sectoral national youth policies, reflecting youth in all its diversity, as well as of international cooperation in promoting the achievement of the internationally agreed development goals, including the Millennium Development Goals;

10. Invite Member States to review and evaluate the implementation of their commitments to relevant internationally agreed development goals, including the Millennium Development Goals, and the relevant outcomes and programmes of action, including the World Programme of Action for Youth, and request the United Nations regional commissions to assist Member States in sharing information on national experiences, lessons learned and good practices in that regard;

11. Encourage Member States to continue developing, implementing, monitoring and evaluating effective national youth policies, taking into account their cultural context regarding youth development, as well as to promote relevant regional programmes on youth;

12. Reaffirm our determination to give priority attention to the promotion of youth and their interests and to address the challenges that hinder youth development, in particular through poverty eradication, the promotion of sustained economic growth, sustainable development and full and productive employment and decent work for all, and call for increased participation of youth and youth-led organizations in the formulation of, as appropriate, local, national, regional and international development strategies and policies;

13. Reaffirm the need for young people to be protected from all forms of violence, including gender-based violence, trafficking in persons, bullying and cyberbullying, as well as from involvement and manipulation in criminal activities such as drug-related crimes, and recognize the need for the development of safe and youth-friendly counselling and complaint and reporting mechanisms for the redress of violations of their rights;

14. Reaffirm that the strengthening of international cooperation regarding youth, including through the fulfilment of all official development assistance commitments, the transfer of appropriate technology, capacity-building, the enhancement of dialogue, mutual understanding and the active participation of youth, are crucial elements of efforts towards achieving the eradication of poverty, full employment and social integration;

15. Welcome the ongoing efforts by Member States to implement their pledges to achieve the internationally agreed development goals, including the Millennium Development Goals, and acknowledge the contributions of Member States, the United Nations entities, civil society organizations, including youth-led organizations, and the private sector to improve the situation of young people; note with concern, however, that, despite these efforts, substantial numbers of young people reside in areas where poverty constitutes a major challenge and access to basic social services is limited, especially for girls and young women, and that youth development remains hindered by the economic and financial crisis, as well as by challenges brought about by the food crisis and continued food insecurity, the energy crisis and climate change; and also note with concern that the overall progress towards achieving the internationally agreed development goals, including the Millennium Development Goals, in particular on issues relevant to youth, has been uneven;

16. Recognize that the majority of the world's youth live in developing countries and that development constraints pose additional challenges to youth owing to their limited access to resources, education and training, health care, employment and broader socio-economic development opportunities, and therefore request United Nations entities to take into account these development constraints when designing and implementing their programmes on youth in order to ensure that benefits reach young people living in developing countries equally;

17. Condemn the recruitment and use of youth in armed conflict, in contravention of applicable international law, deplore the negative consequences it has on the youth involved, and call upon Member States, in cooperation with the United Nations entities, to take concrete measures and continue to support programmes to ensure the effective social and economic reintegration and rehabilitation of demobilized young people;

18. Recognize the importance of preventing and addressing youth crime, including drug-related crime, and its impact on youth and the socio-economic development of societies, as well as of protecting young victims and witnesses and supporting the rehabilitation, reintegration and inclusion of young offenders in society with a view to them assuming constructive roles;

19. Invite Member States, following the celebration of the International Year of Youth, to continue to place greater emphasis on, and expand their activities at the national, regional and international levels in promoting, including through human rights education and learning, a culture of dialogue and mutual understanding among and with youth, as agents of development, social inclusion, tolerance and peace;

20. Reiterate that the full and effective participation of young people and youth-led organizations in relevant decision-making processes through appropriate channels is key to, inter alia, achieving the internationally agreed development goals, including the Millennium Development Goals, and to implementing the outcomes of global conferences and summits, as well as the World Programme of Action for Youth;

21. Recognize the positive contribution that youth representatives make to the General Assembly and other United Nations entities and their role in serving as an important channel of communication between young people and the United Nations, and in this regard request the Secretary-General to adequately support existing instru-

ments so that they can continue to facilitate their effective participation in meetings;

22. Encourage Member States, in cooperation with relevant actors, to promote dialogue and mutual understanding to better address youth-related issues, particularly as regards active youth participation, youth work, gender equality and the empowerment of women, social integration, full employment and decent work for all, access to quality education, the development of scientific and innovative capacities, scholarships and training, access to and safe use of information and communications technology, in particular in the interest of the protection of children and young people, access to health care, the elimination of discrimination, protection from all forms of violence, intergenerational solidarity, and the impacts of financial, economic and other crises;

23. Request the United Nations agencies, and invite the international community and civil society, as well as the private sector, to promote the broader youth development agenda and to strengthen international cooperation and the exchange of good practices in order to support Member States in their efforts to achieve such progress, taking into account the fact that the primary responsibility for ensuring youth development lies with States;

24. Urge the United Nations entities, including specialized agencies, funds and programmes, in accordance with their mandates, to support, upon request, the strengthening of national capacities and efforts in the development and implementation of national plans, policies and programmes that can accelerate the achievement of internationally agreed development goals, including the Millennium Development Goals, and the relevant outcomes and programmes of action, including the World Programme of Action for Youth;

25. Request the United Nations entities to enhance their coordination and intensify efforts towards a more coherent, comprehensive and integrated approach to youth development through, inter alia, the Inter-Agency Network on Youth Development, call upon the United Nations entities and relevant partners to develop additional measures to support national, regional and international efforts in addressing challenges hindering youth development, and in this regard encourage close collaboration with Member States as well as other relevant stakeholders, including civil society;

26. Request the Secretary-General to submit a report, with due regard to existing reporting obligations, to the Commission for Social Development at its fifty-first session, on national experiences, lessons learned and good practices on how to address problems affecting youth, which report shall also evaluate the achievements and shortcomings of ongoing United Nations programmes related to youth and put forward concrete recommendations on how to more effectively address the challenges hindering the development and participation of youth, including through volunteer activities; how to improve the United Nations programmes and structures related to youth, including their coherence; how to better foster dialogue and mutual understanding among youth worldwide; and how to assess progress in these fields, and should be prepared in consultation with Member States, as well as the relevant specialized agencies, funds and programmes, and regional commissions, taking into account the work done by the United Nations system; and also request the Secretariat to consult, as appropriate, with youth-led and youth-focused organizations to ensure that various youth inputs are duly shared with the Commission for Social Development during its deliberations;

27. Reiterate our request to the Secretary-General to propose a set of possible indicators linked to the World Programme of Action for Youth and the proposed goals and targets, in order to assist Member States in assessing the situation of youth, encouraging continued consultations with Member States;

28. Renew our resolve to fulfil our commitments to promote youth development, dialogue and mutual understanding, paying due attention to the relevant internationally agreed development goals, including the Millennium Development Goals, and relevant outcomes and programmes of action, including the World Programme of Action for Youth. Therefore, we pledge to commit to the following actions:

(a) Call upon the international community to continue to support the efforts of Member States, together with civil society, including youth-led organizations, the private sector and other parts of society, to anticipate and offset the negative social and economic consequences of globalization and to maximize its benefits for young people;

(b) Also call upon donors, including Member States and intergovernmental and non-governmental organizations, to support the efforts of Member States in the implementation of this outcome document as well as the World Programme of Action for Youth;

(c) Address the high rates of youth unemployment, underemployment, vulnerable employment and informal employment by developing and implementing targeted and integrated national youth employment policies for inclusive job creation; improved employability; skill development and vocational training to meet specific labour market needs of youth, including young migrants; and increased entrepreneurship, including the development of networks of young entrepreneurs at the local, national, regional and global levels, which foster knowledge among young people about their rights and responsibilities in society; and in this regard request donors, specialized United Nations entities and the private sector to continue to provide assistance, including technical and funding support, as required;

(d) Urge Member States to address the global challenge of youth unemployment by developing and implementing strategies that give young people everywhere a real chance to find decent and productive work, and, in this context, consider undertaking efforts towards the development of a global strategy on youth employment with a focus on youth unemployment, and encourage Member States, employers' organizations, trade unions, the private sector, institutions of education at all levels, youth organizations and civil society, with the support of the international community, all relevant stakeholders, including financial institutions, and the United Nations system, as appropriate, to develop partnerships in this regard to foster inclusive employment opportunities in the labour market, including through the promotion of youth entrepreneurship, taking into account regional and national particularities;

(e) Undertake appropriate measures, in cooperation with civil society, including youth-led organizations, educational institutions and the private sector, in order to strengthen international, regional and national partnerships to foster mutual respect, tolerance and understanding among young people with different racial, cultural and religious backgrounds;

(f) Increase efforts to improve the quality of education and promote universal access to education, particularly for young women, out-of-school youth, youth with disabilities, indigenous youth, youth in rural areas, young migrants, and youth living with HIV and affected by AIDS, without discrimination on any basis, to ensure that they can acquire the knowledge, capacities, skills and ethical values needed, including by appropriate access to scholarships and other mobility programmes, non-formal education, as well as technical and vocational education and training, to develop and to participate fully in the process of social, economic and political development, since knowledge and education are key factors for youth participation, dialogue and mutual understanding;

(g) Promote and provide human rights education and learning for youth, taking particular account of young women, and develop initiatives in that regard, in order to promote dialogue and mutual understanding, tolerance and friendship among youth of all nations;

(h) Urge Member States to take effective measures in conformity with international law to protect young people affected or exploited by terrorism and incitement;

(i) Adopt appropriate laws and develop strategies for the prevention and elimination of all forms of violence against youth, in all settings, and to ensure the implementation of policies and adequately resourced programmes on ending violence against youth, including initiatives to support youth action to end violence through youth-led organizations and networks;

(j) Strengthen the use of information and communications technology to improve the quality of life of young people, and, with the support of the United Nations system, donors, the private sector and civil society, promote universal, non- discriminatory, equitable, safe and affordable access to information and communications technology, especially in schools and public places, and remove the barriers to bridging the digital divide, including through transfer of technology and international cooperation, as well as promote the development of locally relevant content and implement measures to equip young people with the knowledge and skills needed to use information and communications technology appropriately and safely;

(k) Ensure that young people enjoy the highest attainable standard of physical and mental health by providing youth with access to sustainable health systems and social services without discrimination and by paying special attention to, and raising awareness regarding, nutrition, including eating disorders and obesity, the effects of non-communicable and communicable diseases and sexual and reproductive health, as well as measures to prevent sexually transmitted diseases, including HIV and AIDS;

(l) Promote youth participation in training and capacity-building for environmental issues, including climate change adaptation and mitigation, tackling desertification and other challenges, particularly for those who are engaged in agricultural production and play a vital role in providing food security, which is threatened by climate change;

(m) Promote and protect effectively the human rights and fundamental freedoms of all migrants, especially young people, regardless of their migration status, address international migration through international, regional or bilateral cooperation and dialogue and through a comprehensive and balanced approach, recognizing the roles and responsibilities of countries of origin, transit and destination in promoting and protecting the human rights of all migrants, especially young people, and address the root causes of youth migration, while avoiding approaches that might aggravate their vulnerability;

(n) Urge Member States to take concerted actions in conformity with international law to remove the obstacles to the full realization of the rights of young people living under foreign occupation to promote the achievement of the Millennium Development Goals;

(o) Encourage Member States, the international community, the United Nations system and the private sector to support youth-led organizations in achieving openness and inclusiveness and to strengthen their capacity to participate in national and international development activities;

(p) Encourage Member States to strengthen mechanisms for partnerships with civil society, including youth-led organizations, as contributions to youth development, and create effective channels of cooperation, dialogue and information exchange among young people, including rural and urban youth, their national Governments and other relevant decision makers, as appropriate;

(q) Call upon donors, including Member States and intergovernmental and non-governmental organizations, to actively contribute to the United Nations Youth Fund in order to support catalytic and innovative actions in the field of youth and to facilitate the participation of youth representatives from developing countries in the activities of the United Nations Programme on Youth, taking into account the need for a greater geographic balance of youth representation, and, in this regard, request the Secretary-General to take appropriate action to encourage contributions to the Fund as well as synergy with other youth-related funds of United Nations entities.

Family

Twentieth anniversary of the International Year of the Family, 2014

Pursuant to General Assembly resolution 64/133 [YUN 2009, p. 1066], the Secretary-General reported [YUN 2010, p. 1081] on the follow-up to the tenth anniversary in 2004 of the International Year of the Family [YUN 1994, p. 1144], and preparations for the twentieth anniversary of the Year, to be held in 2014.

Commission action. At its February session [E/2011/6 & Corr.1], the Commission for Social Development recommended a draft resolution for adoption by the Economic and Social Council on preparation for and observance of the twentieth anniversary of the International Year of the Family (see below).

ECONOMIC AND SOCIAL COUNCIL ACTION

On 28 July [meeting 48], the Economic and Social Council, on the recommendation of the Commission for Social Development [E/2011/26 & Corr.1], adopted **resolution 2011/29** without vote [agenda item 14 (b)].

Preparation for and observance of the twentieth anniversary of the International Year of the Family

The Economic and Social Council,

Recalling General Assembly resolutions 44/82 of 8 December 1989, 47/237 of 20 September 1993, 50/142 of 21 December 1995, 52/81 of 12 December 1997, 54/124 of 17 December 1999, 56/113 of 19 December 2001, 57/164 of 18 December 2002, 58/15 of 3 December 2003, 59/111 of 6 December 2004, 59/147 of 20 December 2004, 60/133 of 16 December 2005, 62/129 of 18 December 2007 and 64/133 of 18 December 2009 concerning the proclamation of the International Year of the Family and the preparations for, observance of and follow-up to the tenth anniversary of the International Year of the Family,

Recognizing that the preparations for and observance of the twentieth anniversary of the International Year of the Family provide a useful opportunity to draw further attention to the objectives of the Year for increasing cooperation at all levels on family issues and for undertaking concerted actions to strengthen family-centred policies and programmes as part of an integrated and comprehensive approach to development,

Recognizing also that the follow-up to the International Year of the Family is an integral part of the agenda and of the multi-year programme of work of the Commission for Social Development until 2014,

Noting the active role of the United Nations in enhancing international coopcration in family-related issues, in particular in the areas of research and information, including the compilation, analysis and dissemination of data,

Noting also the importance of designing, implementing and monitoring family-oriented policies, especially in the areas of poverty eradication, full employment and decent work, work-family balance, social integration and intergenerational solidarity,

Recognizing that the overall objectives of the International Year of the Family and its follow-up processes continue to guide national and international efforts to improve family well-being worldwide,

Emphasizing that it is necessary to increase coordination of the activities of the United Nations system on family-related issues in order to contribute fully to the effective implementation of the objectives of the International Year of the Family and its follow-up processes,

1. *Welcomes* the report of the Secretary-General on the follow-up to the tenth anniversary of the International Year of the Family and the preparations for the twentieth anniversary of the Year and the recommendations contained therein;

2. *Urges* Member States to view 2014 as a target year, by which concrete efforts will be taken to improve family well-being through the implementation of effective national policies, strategies and programmes;

3. *Requests* the Commission for Social Development to review annually the preparations for the twentieth anniversary of the International Year of the Family as part of its agenda and of its multi-year programme of work until 2014;

4. *Also requests* the Commission to consider the following themes to guide the preparations for the twentieth anniversary of the International Year of the Family: (*a*) poverty eradication: confronting family poverty and social exclusion; (*b*) full employment and decent work: ensuring work-family balance; and (*c*) social integration: advancing social integration and intergenerational solidarity;

5. *Invites* Member States to consider undertaking activities in preparation for the twentieth anniversary of the International Year of the Family at the national level;

6. *Encourages* Member States to continue their efforts to develop appropriate policies to address family poverty, social exclusion and work-family balance and to share good practices in those areas;

7. *Encourages* United Nations agencies and bodies, including the regional commissions, as well as intergovernmental and non-governmental organizations and research and academic institutions, to work closely with the Department of Economic and Social Affairs of the Secretariat in a coordinated manner on family-related issues, including the upcoming preparations for the twentieth anniversary of the International Year of the Family;

8. *Encourages* the regional commissions, within their respective mandates and resources, to participate in the preparatory process for the twentieth anniversary of the International Year of the Family and to play an active role in facilitating regional cooperation in this regard, and invites Member States, non-governmental organizations and academic institutions to support, as appropriate, the preparations for regional meetings in observance of the twentieth anniversary of the Year;

9. *Requests* the Secretary-General to submit a report to the General Assembly at its sixty-seventh session, through the Commission and the Economic and Social Council, on the implementation of the present resolution, including a description of the state of the preparations for the observance of the twentieth anniversary of the International Year of the Family at all levels.

Report of Secretary-General. In response to Economic and Social Council resolution 2011/29 (see p. 1039), the Secretary-General submitted a November report [A/67/61-E/2012/3] on preparations for the observance of the twentieth anniversary of the International Year of the Family in 2014. The report reviewed family policy development and implementation by Member States, focusing on the areas proposed as themes for the observance, namely, confronting family poverty and social exclusion; ensuring work-family balance; and advancing social integration and intergenerational solidarity. It also outlined developments in preparation for the observance, including regional, national and international initiatives, and civil society initiatives. The Secretary-General stated that the forthcoming anniversary of the International Year offered an opportunity to revisit family-oriented policies as part of overall development efforts. He recommended, among other things, that Governments establish or strengthen national agencies or governmental bodies to design, evaluate and monitor family policies; analyse how families affected and were affected by policies; and promote families as a priority subject for study, investment, partnership and political action. Governments were encouraged to adopt effective and equitable means of delivering family-centred benefits, including social protection and cash transfers, in order to reduce family poverty, address gender discrimination and prevent the intergenerational transfer of poverty. He recommended that Governments and the private sector strengthen provisions relating to work-life balance, such as parental leave, flexible work and part-time arrangements, paternal involvement and support for childcare arrangements; and that Governments and other stakeholders invest in intergenerational solidarity through the provision of social pensions, support of volunteering programmes aimed at youth and older persons, investment in cross-generational community centres, and the promotion of intergenerational communication at work through job-sharing and mentoring programmes. On the observance of the twentieth anniversary, the Secretary-General recommended that Governments, UN agencies and bodies, civil society organizations and academic institutions share good practices and data on family policy development, and that Governments collaborate with civil society, private enterprises and academic institutions to support family-oriented policy and programme design, implementation and evaluation.

GENERAL ASSEMBLY ACTION

On 19 December [meeting 89], the General Assembly, on the recommendation of the Third Committee [A/66/454 (Part II)], adopted **resolution 66/126** without vote [agenda item 27 (*b*)].

Preparations for and observance of the twentieth anniversary of the International Year of the Family

The General Assembly,

Recalling its resolutions 44/82 of 8 December 1989, 50/142 of 21 December 1995, 52/81 of 12 December 1997, 54/124 of 17 December 1999, 56/113 of 19 December 2001, 57/164 of 18 December 2002, 58/15 of 3 December 2003, 59/111 of 6 December 2004, 59/147 of 20 December 2004, 60/133 of 16 December 2005, 62/129 of 18 December 2007 and 64/133 of 18 December 2009, concerning the proclamation of the International Year of the Family and the preparations for, observance of and follow-up to the tenth anniversary of the International Year,

Noting that in paragraph 5 of its resolution 59/111 and paragraph 2 of its resolution 59/147, respectively, the General Assembly underlined the need to realize the objectives of the International Year and to develop concrete measures and approaches to address national priorities in dealing with family issues,

Noting also the importance of designing, implementing and monitoring family-oriented policies, especially in the areas of poverty eradication, full employment and decent work, work-family balance, social integration and intergenerational solidarity,

Recognizing that the preparations for and observance of the twentieth anniversary of the International Year in 2014 provide a useful opportunity to draw further attention to the objectives of the International Year for increasing cooperation at all levels on family issues and for undertaking concerted actions to strengthen family-centred policies and programmes as part of an integrated comprehensive approach to development,

Aware that a major objective of the International Year is to address the major concern of strengthening the capacity of national institutions to formulate, implement and monitor policies in respect of families,

Noting that the family-related provisions of the outcomes of the major United Nations conferences and summits of the 1990s and their follow-up processes continue to provide policy guidance on ways to strengthen family-centred components of policies and programmes as part of an integrated comprehensive approach to development,

Convinced of the necessity of ensuring an action-oriented follow-up to the tenth anniversary of the International Year beyond 2004,

Recognizing the important catalytic and supportive role of United Nations bodies, the specialized agencies and the regional commissions in ensuring an action-oriented follow-up in the field of the family, including their positive contribution to strengthening national capacities in family policymaking,

Cognizant of the need for continued inter-agency cooperation on family issues in order to generate greater awareness of this subject among the governing bodies of the United Nations system,

Convinced that civil society, including research and academic institutions, has a pivotal role in advocacy, promotion, research and policymaking in respect of family policy development and capacity-building,

Noting that, in its resolution 59/111, the General Assembly decided to celebrate the anniversary of the International Year on a ten-year basis,

Taking note with appreciation of the report of the Secretary-General,

1. *Encourages* Governments to continue to make every possible effort to realize the objectives of the International Year of the Family and to integrate a family perspective into national policymaking;

2. *Invites* Governments and regional intergovernmental entities to provide for more systematic national and regional data on family well-being and to identify and ensure support for constructive family policy developments, including the exchange of information on good policies and practices;

3. *Urges* Member States to view 2014 as a target year by which concrete efforts will be made to improve family well-being through the implementation of effective national policies, strategies and programmes;

4. *Encourages* Member States to adopt holistic approaches to policies and programmes that address family poverty, social exclusion and work-family balance and that share good practices in those areas, and invites Member States to stimulate public debate and consultations on family-oriented and gender- and child-sensitive social protection policies, in accordance with the objectives of the International Year;

5. *Also encourages* Member States to promote policies and programmes supporting intergenerational solidarity at the family and community levels and geared to reducing the vulnerability of younger and older generations through various social protection strategies;

6. *Urges* Member States to create a conducive environment to strengthen and support all families, recognizing that equality between women and men and respect for all the human rights and fundamental freedoms of all family members are essential to family well-being and to society at large, noting the importance of reconciliation of work and family life and recognizing the principle that both parents have common responsibilities for the upbringing and development of the child;

7. *Invites* Governments to continue to develop strategies and programmes aimed at strengthening national capacities to address national priorities relating to family issues, and encourages the United Nations Programme on the Family, within its mandate, to assist Governments in this regard, including through the provision of technical assistance to build and develop national capacities in the area of formulating, implementing and monitoring family policies;

8. *Invites* Member States to consider undertaking activities in preparation for the twentieth anniversary of the International Year at the national level;

9. *Encourages* Governments to support the United Nations Trust Fund on Family Activities to enable the Department of Economic and Social Affairs of the Secretariat to provide expanded assistance to countries, upon their request;

10. *Recommends* that United Nations agencies and bodies, intergovernmental and non-governmental organizations, research and academic institutions and the private sector play a supportive role in promoting the objectives of the International Year;

11. *Requests* the Secretary-General to submit a report to the General Assembly at its sixty-eighth session, through the Commission for Social Development and the Economic and Social Council, on the implementation of the present resolution, including a description of the state of preparation for the observance of the twentieth anniversary of the International Year at all levels;

12. *Decides* to consider the topic "Preparations for and observance of the twentieth anniversary of the International Year of the Family" at its sixty-seventh session under the sub-item entitled "Social development, including questions relating to the world social situation and to youth, ageing, disabled persons and the family".

Cultural development

Culture of peace

Follow-up to the Declaration and Programme of Action on a Culture of Peace

Pursuant to General Assembly resolution 65/11 [YUN 2010, p. 1083], the Secretary-General transmitted an August report [A/66/273] by the Director-General of the United Nations Educational, Scientific and Cultural Organization (UNESCO) on the implementation of the Declaration and Programme of Action on a Culture of Peace [YUN 1999, p. 594]. The report summarized actions taken by UNESCO and other UN entities to implement the Programme of Action, particularly in the eight action areas of education; sustainable economic and social development; human rights; equality between men and women; democratic participation; understanding, tolerance and solidarity; communication and information; and international peace and security. The report also outlined recommendations for future action in promoting a culture of peace and non-violence.

Among its activities, UNESCO supported its Member States in providing quality, inclusive education that promoted the values of peace, human rights, tolerance, intercultural understanding, democracy, non-violence and respect. As the lead agency for the 2005–2014 United Nations Decade of Education for Sustainable Development, proclaimed by General Assembly resolution 57/254 [YUN 2002, p. 826], UNESCO supported Member States in integrating the principles, values and practices of sustainable development into inclusive education policies and plans, including climate change education, teacher development policies, textbook and curriculum revision and renewal of pedagogical approaches. It promoted the right to education through its work in implementing the World Programme for Human Rights Education [YUN 2004, p. 678], including by developing a series of materials to assist Member States in integrating education for peace and human rights into school systems. The Director-General launched a new global partnership for girls' and women's education at a high-level forum on 26 May, which focused on reaching illiterate or semi-illiterate adolescent girls and scaling up women's literacy programmes through partnerships with corporations. In the area of communication and information, UNESCO worked to underline the role that the media played in dialogue, democracy and development processes and for the protection of human rights, including by supporting the capacities of media professionals in the areas of journalism safety, conflict-sensitive reporting and reporting on elections. The organization supported countries in post-conflict and post-disaster situations through a dedicated Intersectoral Platform, which assisted in reconstructing educational systems, providing policy advice and expertise on resolving conflicts that might arise over natural resources, revitalizing in-country research facilities, integrating disaster prevention and mitigation efforts into post-conflict and post-disaster responses, and protecting and rehabilitating damaged cultural and natural heritage. During the reporting period, UNESCO assisted Member States affected by natural disasters, namely, the earthquake in Haiti, the floods in Benin and Pakistan, the tsunami and volcanic eruption in Indonesia, and the earthquake and tsunami in Japan, as well as countries in post-conflict environments, such as Afghanistan, the Democratic Republic of the Congo, Iraq, the Occupied Palestinian Territory and several countries in West Africa.

The report also reviewed the work of UNESCO in developing, in consultation with Member States, a consolidated programme of action for a culture of peace and non-violence, which built on lessons learnt from the International Decade for a Culture of Peace and Non-Violence for the Children of the World, 2001–2010 [YUN 2001, p. 609], and the International Year for the Rapprochement of Cultures, 2010 (see p. 1044). It aimed to strengthen the global movement to promote a culture of peace and non-violence at national, regional and international levels, and would develop programmes by harnessing the multidisciplinary expertise of UNESCO in education, the sciences, culture, and communications and information. The General Conference of UNESCO, at its thirty-sixth (2011) session (Paris, 25 October–10 November), adopted the programme of action.

GENERAL ASSEMBLY ACTION

On 12 December [meeting 83], the General Assembly adopted **resolution 66/116** [draft: A/66/L.23 & Add.1] without vote [agenda item 15].

Follow-up to the Declaration and Programme of Action on a Culture of Peace

The General Assembly,

Bearing in mind the Charter of the United Nations, including the purposes and principles contained therein, and especially the dedication to saving succeeding generations from the scourge of war,

Recalling the Constitution of the United Nations Educational, Scientific and Cultural Organization, which states that, "since wars begin in the minds of men, it is in the minds of men that the defences of peace must be constructed",

Recalling also its previous resolutions on a culture of peace, in particular resolution 52/15 of 20 November 1997 proclaiming 2000 the International Year for the Culture of Peace, resolution 53/25 of 10 November 1998 proclaiming the period 2001–2010 the International Decade for a Culture of Peace and Non-Violence for the Children of the World, and resolutions 56/5 of 5 November 2001, 57/6 of 4 November 2002, 58/11 of 10 November 2003, 59/143 of 15 December 2004, 60/3 of 20 October 2005, 61/45 of 4 December 2006, 62/89 of 17 December 2007, 63/113 of 5 December 2008, 64/80 of 7 December 2009 and 65/11 of 23 November 2010, adopted under its agenda item entitled "Culture of peace",

Recognizing the importance of the Declaration and Programme of Action on a Culture of Peace, which serve as the universal mandate for the international community, particularly the United Nations system, for the promotion of a culture of peace and non-violence that benefits humanity, in particular future generations,

Reaffirming the United Nations Millennium Declaration which calls for the active promotion of a culture of peace,

Taking note of the 2005 World Summit Outcome adopted at the high-level plenary meeting of the General Assembly,

Welcoming the observance of 2 October as the International Day of Non-Violence, as proclaimed by the United Nations,

Recognizing that all efforts made by the United Nations system in general and the international community at large for peacekeeping, peacebuilding, the prevention of conflicts, disarmament, sustainable development, the promotion of human dignity and human rights, democracy, the rule of law, good governance and gender equality at the national and international levels contribute greatly to the culture of peace,

Noting that its resolution 57/337 of 3 July 2003 on the prevention of armed conflict could contribute to the further promotion of a culture of peace,

Taking into account the "Manifesto 2000" initiative of the United Nations Educational, Scientific and Cultural Organization promoting a culture of peace, which has received over seventy-five million signatures of endorsement throughout the world,

Recognizing the importance of respect and understanding for religious and cultural diversity throughout the world, of choosing negotiations over confrontation and of working together and not against each other,

Welcoming the report of the Director General of the United Nations Educational, Scientific and Cultural Organization on the implementation of resolution 65/11, as transmitted by the Secretary-General,

Welcoming also the report of the Secretary-General on intercultural, interreligious and intercivilizational dialogue,

Recalling the proclamation by the United Nations Educational, Scientific and Cultural Organization of 21 February as the International Mother Language Day, which aims at protecting, promoting and preserving linguistic and cultural diversity, and multilingualism, in order to foster and enrich a culture of peace, social harmony, cross-cultural dialogue and mutual understanding,

Appreciating the increased ongoing efforts of the United Nations Alliance of Civilizations in promoting a culture of peace through a number of practical projects in the areas of youth, education, media and migrations, in collaboration with Governments, international organizations, foundations and civil society groups, as well as media and corporate leaders,

Welcoming the adoption by the General Conference of the United Nations Educational, Scientific and Cultural Organization at its thirty-sixth session of a programme of action for a culture of peace and non-violence, and noting that the objectives of that programme of action are in line with the Declaration and Programme of Action on a Culture of Peace adopted by the General Assembly,

Encouraging the continued and increasing efforts and activities on the part of civil society organizations throughout the world in advancing the culture of peace as envisaged in the Programme of Action,

1. *Reiterates* that the objective of the effective implementation of the Programme of Action on a Culture of Peace is to strengthen further the global movement for a culture of peace following the observance of the International Decade for a Culture of Peace and Non-Violence for

the Children of the World, 2001–2010, and calls upon all concerned to renew their attention to this objective;

2. *Invites* Member States to continue to place greater emphasis on and expand their activities promoting a culture of peace at the national, regional and international levels and to ensure that peace and non-violence are fostered at all levels;

3. *Invites* the entities of the United Nations system, within their existing mandates, to integrate, as appropriate, the action areas of the Programme of Action in their programmes of activities, focusing on promoting a culture of peace and non-violence at the regional, national and international levels;

4. *Commends* the United Nations Educational, Scientific and Cultural Organization, for which the promotion of a culture of peace is the expression of its fundamental mandate, for further strengthening the activities it has undertaken to promote a culture of peace, including the promotion of peace education and the dissemination of the Declaration on a Culture of Peace and the Programme of Action and related materials in various languages across the world;

5. *Invites* the United Nations Educational, Scientific and Cultural Organization to consider the feasibility of creating a special fund under the Organization to cater to the country-specific projects for the effective promotion of a culture of peace;

6. *Commends* the relevant United Nations bodies, in particular the United Nations Children's Fund, the United Nations Entity for Gender Equality and the Empowerment of Women (UN-Women) and the University for Peace, for their activities in further promoting a culture of peace and non-violence, including the promotion of peace education and activities related to specific areas identified in the Programme of Action, and encourages them to continue and further strengthen and expand their efforts;

7. *Encourages* the Peacebuilding Commission to continue to promote peacebuilding activities and advance a culture of peace and non-violence in post-conflict peacebuilding efforts at the country level;

8. *Urges* the appropriate authorities to provide age-appropriate education, in children's schools, that includes lessons in mutual understanding, tolerance, active citizenship, human rights and the promotion of a culture of peace;

9. *Encourages* the involvement of media, especially the mass media, in promoting a culture of peace and non-violence, with particular regard to children and young people;

10. *Commends* civil society, non-governmental organizations and young people for their activities in further promoting a culture of peace and non-violence, including through their campaign to raise awareness on a culture of peace;

11. *Encourages* civil society and non-governmental organizations to further strengthen their efforts to promote a culture of peace, inter alia, by adopting their own programme of activities to complement the initiatives of Member States, the organizations of the United Nations system and other international and regional organizations, in line with the Declaration and Programme of Action;

12. *Stresses* the role of the United Nations Educational, Scientific and Cultural Organization in mobilizing all relevant stakeholders within and outside the United Nations system in support of cultural diversity, intercultural dialogue and a culture of peace, and invites the Organization to continue to enhance communication and outreach, including through the culture of peace website, in order to promote the objectives of the newly adopted programme of action for a culture of peace and non-violence at the regional, national and global levels;

13. *Invites* Member States, all parts of the United Nations system and civil society organizations, including the International Day of Peace Non-Governmental Organization Committee at the United Nations, to accord increasing attention to their observance of the International Day of Peace on 21 September each year as a day of global ceasefire and non-violence, in accordance with General Assembly resolution 55/282 of 7 September 2001;

14. *Invites* the Secretary-General, within existing resources, in consultation with the Member States and taking into account the observations of civil society organizations, to explore mechanisms and strategies for the implementation of the Declaration and Programme of Action and to initiate outreach efforts to increase global awareness of the Programme of Action and its eight areas of action aimed at their implementation;

15. *Requests* the Secretary-General to submit to the General Assembly at its sixty-seventh session a report on actions undertaken to implement the present resolution and on heightened activities by the United Nations and its affiliated agencies to implement the Programme of Action and to promote a culture of peace and non-violence;

16. *Decides* to include in the provisional agenda of its sixty-seventh session the item entitled "Culture of peace".

On 24 December, the Assembly decided that the agenda item on a culture of peace would remain for consideration at its resumed sixty-sixth (2012) session (**decision 66/557**).

Interreligious and intercultural understanding

In response to General Assembly resolution 65/138 [YUN 2010, p. 1085], the Secretary-General submitted an August report [A/66/280] on intercultural, interreligious and intercivilizational dialogue, which outlined the main activities carried out by the UN system in support of dialogue among cultures, civilizations and religions. In particular, the report reviewed lessons learned from the International Year for the Rapprochement of Cultures, 2010, declared by General Assembly resolution 62/90 [YUN 2007, p. 1122], for which UNESCO served as the lead agency. The main objective of the Year was to help dissipate any confusion stemming from ignorance, prejudice and exclusion that created tension, insecurity, violence or conflict, with the ultimate aim of integrating the principles of dialogue into policies at all levels. Member States and various partners, including the Alliance of Civilizations and civil society stakeholders, considered various activities in support of the Year, which focused on providing greater opportunities for research and activities such as meetings and public debates; promoting the role of creativity; improving access to formal and non-formal education; maximizing the contributions of the media and of new information and communications technology; and recognizing and respecting knowledge, including traditional knowledge systems and the knowledge of indigenous peoples. Numerous projects were launched, and the Year's activities underlined the need to focus on the links between cultural diversity, dialogue, development, security and peace.

The report summarized a range of activities undertaken by the UN system to promote dialogue among cultures. UNESCO contributed to the celebration of the International Day of Nowruz on 21 March, declared by General Assembly resolution 64/253 [YUN 2010, p. 1087], and launched the annual International Festival of Cultural Diversity. As part of the International Day of the World's Indigenous People, observed on 9 August, the secretariat of the United Nations Permanent Forum on Indigenous Issues organized a special event in honour of indigenous filmmakers for their work in raising sensitivity and awareness about the culture, history and everyday life of indigenous peoples around the world. The UN system engaged with faith-based organizations and involved them in its policy and advocacy activities, including initiatives by the United Nations Population Fund and the United Nations Children's Fund. UN entities also supported a rights-based approach to dialogue among cultures, civilizations and religions, pursuant to General Assembly resolution 65/138 [YUN 2010, p. 1085], including the United Nations High Commissioner for Human Rights, the Special Rapporteur on freedom of religion or belief, and the independent expert of the Human Rights Council on the right of access to and enjoyment of cultural heritage. The first observance of World Interfaith Harmony Week, proclaimed by the General Assembly in its resolution 65/5 [YUN 2010, p. 1088], was marked by over 200 events in more than 40 countries.

GENERAL ASSEMBLY ACTION

On 23 December [meeting 92], the General Assembly adopted **resolution 66/226** [draft: A/66/L.32 & Add.1] without vote [agenda item 15].

Promotion of interreligious and intercultural dialogue, understanding and cooperation for peace

The General Assembly,

Reaffirming the purposes and principles enshrined in the Charter of the United Nations and the Universal Declaration of Human Rights, in particular the right to freedom of thought, conscience and religion,

Recalling its resolution 65/138 of 16 December 2010, on the promotion of interreligious and intercultural dialogue, understanding and cooperation for peace and its other related resolutions,

Recalling also its resolution 64/14 of 10 November 2009, on the Alliance of Civilizations, in which it welcomed efforts to promote greater understanding and respect among people from different civilizations, cultures and religions,

Bearing in mind the valuable contribution that interreligious and intercultural dialogue can make to an improved awareness and understanding of the common values shared by all humankind,

Noting that interreligious and intercultural dialogue has made significant contributions to mutual understanding, tolerance and respect, as well as to the promotion of a culture of peace and an improvement of overall relations among people from different cultural and religious backgrounds and among nations,

Recognizing that cultural diversity and the pursuit of cultural development by all peoples and nations are sources of mutual enrichment for the cultural life of humankind,

Emphasizing the importance of culture for development in achieving the Millennium Development Goals, and in this regard noting the close links between cultural diversity, dialogue and development,

Noting the various initiatives at the national, regional and international levels for enhancing dialogue, understanding and cooperation among religions, cultures and civilizations, which are mutually reinforcing and interrelated,

Welcoming the establishment of the King Abdullah Bin Abdulaziz International Centre for Interreligious and Intercultural Dialogue in Vienna, initiated by King Abdullah of Saudi Arabia, on the basis of the purposes and principles enshrined in the Universal Declaration of Human Rights, and acknowledging the important role that the Centre is expected to play as a platform for the enhancement of interreligious and intercultural dialogue,

Acknowledging the tenth anniversary of the 2001 Universal Declaration on Cultural Diversity, and welcoming the commemoration of the International Year for the Rapprochement of Cultures in 2010 and the proclamation by the General Conference of the United Nations Educational, Scientific and Cultural Organization at its thirty-sixth session of an international decade for the rapprochement of cultures (2013–2022),

Encouraging activities aimed at promoting interreligious and intercultural dialogue in order to enhance social stability, respect for diversity and mutual respect in diverse communities and to create, at the global level, and also at the regional, national and local levels, an environment conducive to peace and mutual understanding,

Recognizing the contributions of the media and of new information and communications technology to changing peoples' perceptions of different cultures and religions, including through the promotion of dialogue,

Reaffirming the importance of sustaining the process of engaging all stakeholders, including young men and women as relevant actors, in interreligious and intercultural dialogue within the appropriate initiatives at various levels which aims to challenge preconceived ideas and improve mutual understanding,

Recognizing the commitment of all religions to peace and the need for voices of moderation from all religions and beliefs to work together in order to build a more secure and peaceful world,

1. *Reaffirms* that mutual understanding and interreligious and intercultural dialogue constitute important

dimensions of the dialogue among civilizations and of the culture of peace;

2. *Takes note* of the report of the Secretary-General on intercultural, interreligious and intercivilizational dialogue;

3. *Notes* the continuing work of the United Nations Educational, Scientific and Cultural Organization on intercultural and interreligious dialogue and its efforts to promote dialogue among civilizations, cultures and peoples, as well as activities related to a culture of peace, and welcomes in particular the adoption of its new programme of action for a culture of peace and non-violence and its focus on concrete actions at the global, regional and subregional levels;

4. *Reaffirms* the solemn commitment of all States to fulfil their obligations to promote universal respect for, and observance and protection of, all human rights and fundamental freedoms for all in accordance with the Charter of the United Nations, the Universal Declaration of Human Rights and other instruments relating to human rights and international law, the universal nature of these rights and freedoms being beyond question;

5. *Welcomes* the efforts by the media to promote interreligious and intercultural dialogue, encourages the further promotion of dialogue among the media from all cultures and civilizations, emphasizes that everyone has the right to freedom of expression, and reaffirms that the exercise of this right carries with it special duties and responsibilities and may therefore be subject to certain restrictions, but that these shall be only such as are provided by law and necessary for respect of the rights or reputations of others, protection of national security or of public order, or of public health or morals;

6. *Also welcomes* the efforts to use information and communications technology, including the Internet, to promote interreligious and intercultural dialogue, and in this regard acknowledges with appreciation the establishment by the Movement of Non-Aligned Countries of the Interfaith Dialogue e-Portal pursuant to commitments made during the Special Non-Aligned Movement Ministerial Meeting on Interfaith Dialogue and Cooperation for Peace and Development, held in Manila from 16 to 18 March 2010;

7. *Encourages* Member States to consider, as and where appropriate, initiatives that identify areas for practical action in all sectors and levels of society for the promotion of interreligious and intercultural dialogue, tolerance, understanding and cooperation, inter alia, the ideas suggested during the High-level Dialogue on Interreligious and Intercultural Understanding and Cooperation for Peace, held in New York on 4 and 5 October 2007, including the idea of an enhanced process of dialogue among world religions;

8. *Calls upon* Member States to consider, as appropriate and where applicable, interreligious and intercultural dialogue as an important tool in efforts aimed at achieving peace and the full realization of the Millennium Development Goals;

9. *Recognizes* the efforts by relevant stakeholders to foster peaceful and harmonious coexistence within societies by promoting respect for religious and cultural diversity, including by engendering sustained and robust interaction among various segments of society;

10. *Acknowledges* the active engagement of the United Nations system with faith-based organizations in the promotion of interreligious and intercultural dialogue and in bringing together people of different faiths to discuss common issues and objectives;

11. *Also acknowledges* the important role of civil society, including academia, in fostering interreligious and intercultural dialogue, and encourages support for practical measures that mobilize civil society, including building capacities, opportunities and frameworks for cooperation;

12. *Invites* Member States to further promote reconciliation to help to ensure durable peace and sustained development, including through reconciliatory measures and acts of service and by encouraging forgiveness and compassion among individuals;

13. *Recognizes* that the Office for Economic and Social Council Support and Coordination in the Department of Economic and Social Affairs of the Secretariat plays a valuable role as focal point within the Secretariat on the issue, and encourages it to continue to interact and coordinate with the relevant entities of the United Nations system and coordinate their contribution to the intergovernmental process;

14. *Requests* the Secretary-General to report to the General Assembly at its sixty-seventh session on the implementation of the present resolution.

Alliance of Civilizations

Report of High Representative. By a letter of 11 August [A/66/305], the Secretary-General transmitted to the General Assembly the fourth annual report of the High Representative for the Alliance of Civilizations, together with the third implementation plan of the Alliance (2011–2013), and highlighted the main activities carried out between August 2010 and July 2011 in accordance with the second implementation plan (2009–2011). During the period under review, the main achievements were the adoption of the Alliance's Regional Strategy for the Mediterranean at a regional conference hosted by the Government of Malta in November 2010, as well as the launching of its action plan in July 2011. The report outlined activities in support of the reporting period's main priority to consolidate the Alliance as a global platform for intercultural dialogue and cooperation, noting that support for the Alliance continued to grow, with membership of the Group of Friends increasing to 130, comprising 108 countries and 22 international organizations. A major civil society consultation was organized in Doha, Qatar (3–4 May) as a pre-forum event of the Fourth Forum of the Alliance (see p. 1047), and efforts increased to build and/or consolidate interfaith networks and networks targeting specific groups, and to set up partnerships involving the private sector. The High Representative intensified action to develop the Alliance as a soft-power tool of cultural and preventive diplomacy, including by furthering contacts and dialogue with political, religious, media and civil society representatives. Furthermore, various initiatives continued during the reporting period to support the Alliance's objectives, including national plans and regional strategies, and multi-stakeholder initiatives in fields such as education, youth, media, and migration and integration. Building upon the trends and initiatives of the period, the Alliance's programme of action for the 2011–2013 period would take into consideration the new context in the Middle East and North Africa; the reconciliation of diversity and cohesion in European societies; the influence of religion on peace, security and development; reinforcing the Alliance as a United Nations soft-power tool for dialogue and peace by working more closely with non-State actors; and focusing the Fourth Annual Forum on the connections between the Alliance's mission and the MDGs.

Fourth Annual Forum. The Fourth Annual Forum of the United Nations Alliance of Civilizations (Doha, Qatar, 11–13 December) was held under the theme "Intercultural Dialogue to Boost Development", and brought together more than 2,500 participants to consider the main topic of the role of culture, cultural diversity and intercultural dialogue to foster sustainable development, taking into consideration the efforts made since the turn of the century by the international community to achieve the agenda of the MDGs. The Forum's plenary sessions considered that theme through three sub-topics, namely, the contributions of cultural diversity to development; promoting trust and tolerance to advance development goals; and new strategies for intercultural dialogue, understanding and cooperation. A side event focused on the prevailing challenges facing Arab states in transitions, and a group of young leaders met at the Youth Preparatory Event on 10 December to debate the Forum's main theme as well as their role in achieving the Alliance's objectives. The discussions resulted in the drafting of Youth Recommendations to world leaders on specific policies that affected the lives of young people, which were presented during the Forum's opening plenary.

International Day of Friendship

The General Assembly declared 30 July the International Day of Friendship in resolution 65/275 (see below), introduced by Paraguay and sponsored by many Member States, during the Assembly's consideration of the agenda item on a culture of peace [A/65/PV.88].

GENERAL ASSEMBLY ACTION

On 3 May [meeting 88], the General Assembly adopted **resolution 65/275** [draft: A/65/L.72 & Add.1] without vote [agenda item 15].

International Day of Friendship

The General Assembly,

Recalling the goals and objectives of the Declaration and Programme of Action on a Culture of Peace, and the International Decade for a Culture of Peace and Non-Violence for the Children of the World (2001–2010), and all its relevant resolutions,

Recognizing the relevance and importance of friendship as a noble and valuable sentiment in the lives of human beings around the world,

Bearing in mind that friendship between peoples, countries, cultures and individuals can inspire peace efforts and presents an opportunity to build bridges between communities, honouring cultural diversity,

Affirming that friendship can contribute to the efforts of the international community, in accordance with the Charter of the United Nations, towards the promotion of dialogue among civilizations, solidarity, mutual understanding and reconciliation,

Convinced of the importance of involving youth and future leaders in community activities aimed at the inclusion of and respect between different cultures, while promoting international understanding, respect for diversity and a culture of peace, in accordance with the Declaration and Programme of Action on a Culture of Peace,

Noting that friendship-related activities, events and initiatives are observed each year in many countries,

1. *Decides* to designate 30 July as the International Day of Friendship;
2. *Invites* all Member States, organizations of the United Nations system and other international and regional organizations, as well as civil society, including non-governmental organizations and individuals, to observe the International Day of Friendship in an appropriate manner, in accordance with the culture and other appropriate circumstances or customs of their local, national and regional communities, including through education and public awareness-raising activities;
3. *Requests* the Secretary-General to bring the present resolution to the attention of all Member States and organizations of the United Nations system.

Sport for peace and development

Olympic Truce and ideal

The General Assembly, pursuant to resolution 64/4 [YUN 2009, p. 1075], considered the sub-item on "Building a peaceful and better world through sport and the Olympic ideal" prior to the Games of the XXX Olympiad and the XIV Paralympic Games to be held in London in 2012.

GENERAL ASSEMBLY ACTION

On 17 October [meeting 34], the General Assembly adopted **resolution 66/5** [draft: A/66/L.3 & Add.1] without vote [agenda item 11 (*a*)].

Building a peaceful and better world through sport and the Olympic ideal

The General Assembly,

Recalling its resolution 64/4 of 19 October 2009, in which it decided to include in the provisional agenda of its sixty-sixth session the sub-item entitled "Building a peaceful and better world through sport and the Olympic ideal", and recalling also its prior decision to consider the sub-item every two years, in advance of each Summer and Winter Olympic Games,

Recalling also its resolution 48/11 of 25 October 1993, which, inter alia, revived the ancient Greek tradition of *ekecheiria* ("Olympic Truce") calling for a truce during the Olympic Games that would encourage a peaceful environment and ensure the safe passage and participation of athletes and relevant persons at the Games, thereby mobilizing the youth of the world to the cause of peace,

Recalling further that the core concept of *ekecheiria*, historically, was the cessation of hostilities from seven days before until seven days after the Olympic Games, which, according to the legendary oracle of Delphi, was to replace the cycle of conflict with a friendly athletic competition every four years,

Reaffirming the value of sport in promoting education, health, development and peace,

Recalling the inclusion in the United Nations Millennium Declaration of an appeal for the observance of the Olympic Truce now and in the future and for support for the International Olympic Committee in its efforts to promote peace and human understanding through sport and the Olympic ideal,

Acknowledging the valuable contribution that the appeal launched by the International Olympic Committee for an Olympic Truce could make towards advancing the purposes and principles of the Charter of the United Nations,

Noting that the Games of the XXX Olympiad will take place from 27 July to 12 August 2012, and that the XIV Paralympic Games will take place from 29 August to 9 September 2012, in London,

Welcoming the granting of observer status to the International Olympic Committee in the General Assembly pursuant to the adoption of resolution 64/3 on 19 October 2009 and the participation of the Committee in the sessions and work of the Assembly,

Acknowledging the joint endeavours of the International Olympic Committee, the International Paralympic Committee, the Office of the Special Adviser to the Secretary-General on Sport for Development and Peace, and the United Nations system in such fields as human development, poverty alleviation, humanitarian assistance, health promotion, HIV and AIDS prevention, child and youth education, gender equality, peacebuilding and sustainable development,

Noting the successful conclusion of the first Youth Olympic Games, held in Singapore from 14 to 26 August 2010, and welcoming the first Youth Winter Olympic Games, to be held in Innsbruck, Austria, from 13 to 22 January 2012, and the second Youth Olympic Games, to be held in Nanjing, China, from 16 to 28 August 2014,

Recalling the articles on leisure, recreation, sport and play of relevant international conventions, including article 30 of the Convention on the Rights of Persons with Disabilities recognizing the right of persons with disabilities to take part on an equal basis with others in cultural life, recreation, leisure and sport, and noting that the 1948 Olympic Games, held in London, inspired the staging of the first organized sporting event for patients with spinal cord injuries, in Stoke Mandeville, near London, heralding the birth of a new global sporting movement for athletes with disabilities; the establishment of the Paralympic Games; and plans to stage integrated and inclusive Games for Everyone in 2012,

Recalling also that the main themes of the Olympic and Paralympic Games in London in 2012 are to host genuinely sustainable Games that deliver long-term social, economic, environmental and sporting benefits, helping to promote more stable, inclusive and peaceful communities and urban regeneration, addressing climate change, enhancing international relations and cooperation, and changing attitudes towards disability; and to inspire young people around the world to enrich their lives through sport, for example through the introduction of International Inspiration, the London 2012 international legacy programme,

Welcoming the commitment made by various States Members of the United Nations to developing national and international programmes which promote peace and conflict resolution and the Olympic and Paralympic values through sport and through culture, education, sustainable development and wider public engagement,

Recognizing the humanitarian opportunities presented by the Olympic Truce and by other initiatives supported by the United Nations to achieve the cessation of conflict, such as the International Day of Peace, established by General Assembly resolution 36/67 of 30 November 1981,

Noting with satisfaction the flying of the United Nations flag at the Olympic Park,

1. *Urges* Member States to observe, within the framework of the Charter of the United Nations, the Olympic Truce, individually and collectively, throughout the period beginning with the start of the Games of the XXX Olympiad and ending with the close of the XIV Paralympic Games;

2. *Welcomes* the work of the International Olympic Committee and the International Paralympic Committee to mobilize international sports organizations and the National Olympic Committees and National Paralympic Committees of Member States to undertake concrete actions at the local, national, regional and international levels to promote and strengthen a culture of peace based on the spirit of the Olympic Truce, and invites those organizations and national committees to share information and best practices, as appropriate;

3. *Also welcomes* the leadership of Olympic and Paralympic athletes in promoting peace and human understanding through sport and the Olympic ideal;

4. *Calls upon* all Member States to cooperate with the International Olympic Committee and the International Paralympic Committee in their efforts to use sport as a tool to promote peace, dialogue and reconciliation in areas of conflict during and beyond the period of the Olympic and Paralympic Games;

5. *Welcomes* the cooperation among Member States, the United Nations and the specialized agencies, funds and programmes, and the International Olympic Committee and, where appropriate, the International Paralympic Committee, to work towards a meaningful and sustainable contribution through sport to raising awareness of and to the achievement of the Millennium Development Goals, and encourages the Olympic and Paralympic movements to work closely with national and international sports organizations on the use of sport to contribute to the Millennium Development Goals;

6. *Requests* the Secretary-General and the President of the General Assembly to promote the observance of the Olympic Truce among Member States and support for human development initiatives through sport and to cooperate with the International Olympic Committee, the International Paralympic Committee and the sporting community in general in the realization of those objectives;

7. *Decides* to include in the provisional agenda of its sixty-eighth session the sub-item entitled "Building a peaceful and better world through sport and the Olympic ideal" and to consider the sub-item before the XXII Olympic Winter Games and the XI Paralympic Winter Games, to be held in Sochi, Russian Federation, in 2014.

On 24 December, the Assembly decided that the agenda item on sport for peace and development: building a peaceful and better world through sport and the Olympic ideal would remain for consideration during its resumed sixty-sixth (2012) session (**decision 66/557**).

Communication. In July [A/65/904], Uzbekistan transmitted to the Secretary-General a report on the promotion of sport as a key social priority of its Government.

Culture and development

Pursuant to General Assembly resolution 65/166 [YUN 2010, p. 1090], the Secretary-General transmitted a July report [A/66/187] of the UNESCO Director-General on progress made in implementing that resolution through the work undertaken by 18 UN entities. The report included an assessment of the value and desirability of organizing a United Nations conference on culture and development, stating that such a conference would address the impact of culture on sustainable development to better inform the development agenda towards achieving the MDGs. The report also considered the aim, level, format, timing and budgetary implications of the conference.

The Director-General stated that resolution 65/166 was instrumental in revitalizing the debate on the impact of culture on sustainable development at a time when international development actors were assessing gaps in achieving development objectives. It also encouraged the compilation of data and best practices on the linkages between culture and development to demonstrate the impact of culture on the social and economic well-being of peoples and societies; facilitated greater integration of culture into United Nations Development Assistance Frameworks; and fostered international partnerships in the field of culture and development, such as the memorandum of understanding signed on 1 July by UNESCO and the World Bank, which included a framework for technical work in the areas of preservation and rehabilitation of historic cities, conservation of natural heritage sites, cultural indicators, the economics of culture and the promotion of cultural diversity.

The Director-General recommended a number of actions to reinforce implementation of the resolution, including supporting efforts by all UN entities to enhance understanding of the nexus between culture and sustainable development; encouraging studies that documented the qualitative impact of culture on the well-being of society and showcased the potential of human rights-based cultural approaches to foster sustainable peace; and pursuing the operationalization of the culture and development approach initiated under projects funded by the Millennium Development Goals Achievement Fund.

GENERAL ASSEMBLY ACTION

On 22 December [meeting 91], the General Assembly, on the recommendation of the Second (Economic and Financial) Committee [A/66/442], adopted **resolution 66/208** without vote [agenda item 21].

Culture and development

The General Assembly,

Guided by the purposes and principles enshrined in the Charter of the United Nations,

Recalling its resolutions 41/187 of 8 December 1986, 46/158 of 19 December 1991, 51/179 of 16 December 1996, 52/197 of 18 December 1997, 53/184 of 15 December 1998, 55/192 of 20 December 2000, 57/249 of 20 December 2002, and 65/166 of 20 December 2010, concerning culture and development,

Recalling also the adoption by the General Conference of the United Nations Educational, Scientific and Cultural Organization of the Universal Declaration on Cultural Diversity and the Action Plan for its implementation, on 2 November 2001, and the Convention on the Protection and Promotion of the Diversity of Cultural Expressions, as well as other international conventions of that organization that acknowledge the important role of cultural diversity for social and economic development, and welcoming the commemoration of the tenth anniversary of the Universal Declaration on Cultural Diversity at the thirty-sixth session of the General Conference,

Recognizing that culture is an essential component of human development, represents a source of identity, innovation and creativity for the individual and the community and is an important factor in social inclusion and poverty eradication, providing for economic growth and ownership of development processes,

Acknowledging that cultural diversity is a source of enrichment for humankind and an important contributor to the sustainable development of local communities, peoples and nations, empowering them to play an active and unique role in development initiatives,

Recalling the concerns expressed in the Beijing Declaration and the Platform for Action on the underrepresentation of women in decision-making positions in the area of culture, which has prevented women from having a significant impact in the area of culture and development,

Recalling also the importance of the promotion of national cultures, artistic creation in all its forms and international and regional cultural cooperation, and reaffirming in this regard the relevance of strengthening national efforts and regional and international cooperation mechanisms for cultural action and artistic creation,

Recognizing the linkages between cultural and biological diversity and the positive contribution of local and indigenous traditional knowledge in addressing environmental challenges in a sustainable manner,

Noting with satisfaction that, in its resolution 65/1 of 22 September 2010, entitled "Keeping the promise: united to achieve the Millennium Development Goals", the General Assembly emphasized the importance of culture for development and its contribution to the achievement of the Millennium Development Goals and, in that respect, encouraged international cooperation in the cultural field, aimed at achieving development objectives,

Taking note of the note by the Secretary-General transmitting the report prepared by the United Nations Educational, Scientific and Cultural Organization, and, in this regard, acknowledging the work undertaken by United Nations agencies to optimize the contributions of culture to sustainable development,

Acknowledging the importance of the forthcoming United Nations Conference on Sustainable Development,

1. *Emphasizes* the important contribution of culture to the achievement of sustainable development and of national development objectives and internationally agreed development goals, including the Millennium Development Goals;

2. *Recognizes* that culture contributes to the development of innovative creative capacities in people and is an important component of modernization and innovations in economic and social life;

3. *Invites* all Member States, intergovernmental bodies, organizations of the United Nations system, relevant non-governmental organizations and all other relevant stakeholders:

(*a*) To raise public awareness of the importance of cultural diversity for sustainable development, promoting its positive value through education and media tools;

(*b*) To ensure a more visible and effective integration and mainstreaming of culture into social, environmental and economic development policies and strategies at all levels;

(*c*) To promote capacity-building, where appropriate, at all levels for the development of a dynamic cultural and creative sector, in particular by encouraging creativity, innovation and entrepreneurship, supporting the development of cultural institutions and cultural industries, providing technical and vocational training for culture professionals and increasing employment opportunities in the cultural and creative sector for sustained, inclusive and equitable economic growth and development;

(*d*) To actively support the emergence of local markets for cultural goods and services and to facilitate the effective and licit access of such goods and services to international markets, taking into account the expanding range of cultural production and consumption and, for States parties to it, the provisions of the Convention on the Protection and Promotion of the Diversity of Cultural Expressions;

(*e*) To enhance women's active share in cultural decision-making with men and to undertake activities that promote women's empowerment and the perception of attitudes and a culture favourable to equality;

(*f*) To preserve and maintain local and indigenous traditional knowledge and community practices of environmental management, which are valuable examples of culture as a vehicle for sustainable development, and to foster synergies between modern science and technology and local and indigenous knowledge, practices and innovation;

(*g*) To promote global awareness of the linkages between cultural and biological diversity, including through the protection and encouragement of the customary use of biological resources, in accordance with traditional cultural practices, as a key element of a comprehensive approach to sustainable development;

(*h*) To support national legal frameworks and policies for the protection and preservation of cultural heritage and cultural property, the fight against illicit trafficking in cultural property and the return of cultural property, in accordance with national legislation and applicable international legal frameworks, including by promoting international cooperation to prevent the misappropriation of cultural heritage and products, recognizing the importance of intellectual property rights in sustaining those involved in cultural creativity;

(*i*) To note that, in achieving these objectives, innovative mechanisms of financing can make a positive contribution in assisting developing countries in mobilizing additional resources for development on a stable, predictable and voluntary basis, and to reiterate that such voluntary mechanisms should be effective, should aim to mobilize resources that are stable and predictable, should supplement and not be a substitute for traditional sources of financing, should be disbursed in accordance with the priorities of developing countries and should not unduly burden such countries;

4. *Encourages* all Member States, intergovernmental bodies, organizations of the United Nations system, relevant non-governmental organizations and all other relevant stakeholders to enhance international cooperation in supporting the efforts of developing countries for the development and consolidation of cultural industries, cultural tourism and culture-related microenterprises and to assist those countries in developing the necessary infrastructure and skills, as well as in mastering information and communications technologies and in gaining access to new technologies on mutually agreed terms;

5. *Invites* the organizations of the United Nations system, in particular the United Nations Educational, Scientific and Cultural Organization, to continue to provide support, to facilitate financing and to assist Member States, upon their request, in developing their national capacities to assess how best to optimize the contribution of culture to development, including through information-sharing, exchange of best practices, data collection, research and study, and the use of appropriate evaluation indicators, as well as to implement applicable international cultural conventions, taking into account the relevant resolutions of the General Assembly;

6. *Invites* the United Nations Educational, Scientific and Cultural Organization and other relevant United Nations bodies to continue to assess the contribution of culture to the achievement of sustainable development through the compilation of quantitative data, including indicators and

statistics, with a view to informing development policies and relevant reports, where appropriate;

7. *Requests* the Secretary-General to ensure that United Nations country teams continue to further integrate and mainstream culture into their programming exercises, in particular United Nations Development Assistance Frameworks, in consultation with relevant national authorities, when assisting countries in the pursuit of their development objectives;

8. *Encourages* all Member States, intergovernmental bodies, organizations of the United Nations system, relevant non-governmental organizations and all other relevant stakeholders to take into consideration the contribution of culture to the achievement of development in the formulation of national, regional and international development policies and international cooperation instruments;

9. *Requests* the Secretary-General to submit to the General Assembly at its sixty-eighth session a progress report on the implementation of the present resolution and to assess, in consultation with relevant United Nations funds and programmes and specialized agencies of the United Nations development system, in particular the United Nations Educational, Scientific and Cultural Organization and the United Nations Development Programme, the feasibility of various measures, including a possible United Nations conference, to take stock of the contribution of culture to development and to formulate a consolidated approach to culture and development and, in this context, takes note of the annual ministerial review on the theme "Science, technology and innovation, and the potential of culture, for promoting sustainable development and achieving the Millennium Development Goals" to be held by the Economic and Social Council in 2013;

10. *Encourages* Member States to share with the Secretary-General information and lessons learned on the contribution of culture to the achievement of development as a contribution to the United Nations development agenda, including the Millennium Development Goals;

11. *Decides* to include in the provisional agenda of its sixty-eighth session, under the item entitled "Globalization and interdependence", a sub-item entitled "Culture and development".

Human resources development

Pursuant to General Assembly resolution 64/218 [YUN 2009, p. 1107], the Secretary-General submitted a July report [A/66/206] on the impact of the global financial and economic crisis on human resources development. The crisis continued to have significant implications in almost all countries, with advanced economies experiencing an increase in unemployment and a decrease in budgetary resources devoted to government education and training programmes. In developing countries, pre-existing socioeconomic challenges were expected to affect long-term human resources development in view of a "job-poor" economic recovery, high youth unemployment, and volatile food and energy prices, among other things. The report reviewed emerging national challenges and opportunities in human resources development, as well as examples of strategies for sustaining and developing human resources, including approaches by countries to address longer-term needs in areas such as information and communications technology; the green economy; intellectual property; the design of social protection programmes; education and health services; and productive agriculture and rural development. The report also highlighted the role of the international community in formulating and implementing national human resources development strategies.

The Secretary-General stated that human resources development was at the heart of economic, social and environmental development. At the national level, he recommended, among other things, that Governments place human resources development at the core of economic and social development and intervene effectively to reduce the share of the population in low-productivity jobs; strengthen social protection systems; better align education and training systems and labour market needs; and strengthen labour institutions and regulations to respond in a timely manner to economic downturns by preserving jobs and protecting workers in vulnerable jobs. Measures should be devised to reduce unemployment and underemployment among young men and women; efforts should be made to reduce barriers to unemployment, particularly gender barriers; and the interlinkages among human resources development, energy, food security, agriculture and rural development should be better understood and addressed. At the international level, bilateral and multilateral donors should support developing countries in enhancing national human resources development, including through North-South, South-South and triangular cooperation, and UN entities and civil society actors should shift their approach from training individuals to building institutional capacity to address long-term national human resources development needs.

GENERAL ASSEMBLY ACTION

On 22 December [meeting 91], the General Assembly, on the recommendation of the Second Committee [A/66/444/Add.3], adopted **resolution 66/217** without vote [agenda item 23 (*c*)].

Human resources development

The General Assembly,

Recalling its resolutions 52/196 of 18 December 1997, 54/211 of 22 December 1999, 56/189 of 21 December 2001, 58/207 of 23 December 2003, 60/211 of 22 December 2005, 62/207 of 19 December 2007 and 64/218 of 21 December 2009,

Stressing that human resources development lies at the heart of economic, social and environmental development and that health and education are at the core of human resources development,

Stressing also that human resources development is key to the efforts to achieve the internationally agreed development goals, including the Millennium Development Goals, and to expand opportunities for people, in particular for the most vulnerable groups of the population,

Welcoming the considerable efforts made over the years, yet recognizing that many countries continue to face formidable challenges in developing a sufficient pool of human resources capable of meeting national economic and social needs and that the formulation and implementation of effective human resources strategies often require resources and capacities not always available in developing countries,

Stressing that human resources development is even more critical in view of the current global challenges, including the ongoing adverse impacts, particularly on development, of the global financial and economic crisis, in order to tackle the negative effects of the global crisis, and set the basis for sustained, inclusive and equitable growth and recovery,

Recognizing that the benefits of human resources development are best realized in national and international environments that support equal opportunity, access to education and non-discrimination and maintain an enabling environment for job creation,

Recognizing also that the ongoing adverse impacts, particularly on development, of the global financial and economic crisis continue to diminish the ability of many countries, especially developing countries, to cope with and address human resources development challenges and to formulate and implement effective strategies for poverty eradication and sustainable development,

Acknowledging the important nexus between international migration and development and the need to deal with the challenges and opportunities that migration presents to countries of origin, transit and destination, recognizing that migration brings benefits as well as challenges to the global community, and stressing that the brain drain continues to be a severe problem in many developing and transitioning countries, undermining efforts in the area of human resources development,

Reaffirming that gender equality is of fundamental importance for achieving sustained economic growth, poverty eradication and sustainable development, in accordance with the relevant General Assembly resolutions and United Nations conferences, and that investing in the development of women and girls has a multiplier effect, in particular on productivity, efficiency and sustained economic growth, in all sectors of the economy, especially in key areas such as agriculture, industry and services,

Recognizing that education is the key to promoting the development of human potential, equality and understanding among peoples, as well as to sustaining economic growth and eradicating poverty, and recognizing also that, to achieve those ends, it is essential that quality education be available to all, including indigenous peoples, girls and women, rural inhabitants and persons with disabilities,

Stressing that Governments have the primary responsibility for defining and implementing appropriate policies for human resources development, and the need for continued support from the international community for the national efforts of developing countries,

1. *Takes note* of the report of the Secretary-General;

2. *Calls upon* Member States to place human resources development at the core of economic and social development and develop short-, medium- and long-term strategies to effectively enhance their human resources capacities, as educated, healthy, capable, productive and flexible workforces are the foundation for achieving sustained, inclusive and equitable economic growth and development;

3. *Stresses* the need for Member States to emphasize and integrate human resources development into national development strategies, including national development policies and strategies to eradicate poverty and achieve the Millennium Development Goals, in order to address structural and multidimensional challenges to enhancing national productive capacities and to ensure that human resources development implications are taken into account by all national development stakeholders;

4. *Encourages* Member States to adopt and implement comprehensive human resources development strategies premised on national development objectives that ensure a strong link between education, training and employment, help to maintain a productive and competitive workforce and are responsive to the needs of the economy;

5. *Emphasizes* the need for Member States to adopt cross-sectoral approaches and mechanisms to identify human resources development needs in the medium and long term for all sectors of the economy and to formulate and implement policies and programmes to address those needs;

6. *Stresses* that investment in human resources development should be an integral part of national development policies and strategies, and in this regard calls for the adoption of policies to facilitate investment focused on physical and social infrastructure, including education, in particular skills upgrading and vocational training in areas such as science and technology, including information and communications technology, as well as in capacity development, health and sustainable development;

7. *Encourages* Member States, as appropriate, to continue to strengthen comprehensive social protection systems, to adopt policies that strengthen existing safety nets and protect vulnerable groups and to take other appropriate actions, including boosting domestic consumption and production, recognizes that social protection floors, defined according to national priorities and the individual circumstances of Member States, can provide systemic approaches to address poverty and vulnerability and can contribute significantly to successful human resources development strategies, acknowledges in this regard that many developing countries lack the necessary financial resources and capacity to implement such countercyclical measures, and in this regard recognizes the need for continued mobilization of additional domestic and international resources, as appropriate;

8. *Encourages* Member States in a position to do so to consider implementing, and the States members of the International Labour Organization to implement, policies consistent with the International Labour Organization Declaration on Fundamental Principles and Rights at Work and their obligations under all relevant ratified conventions of the International Labour Organization, and recalls the importance of promoting decent work for all and of increas-

ing quality jobs, including through measures aimed at ensuring occupational health and safety and through working relationships based on effective social dialogue;

9. *Stresses* that human resources development strategies should include measures to reduce unemployment and underemployment among young men and women and the long-term unemployed, who have been disproportionately affected by slow growth in jobs recovery, and to integrate underutilized human resources into the labour market through policies that promote skills development and productivity and reduce barriers to employment, particularly gender barriers, including by providing incentives for recruiting, retaining and retooling, assistance in job-finding and job-matching and vocational and on-the-job training, and by promoting, inter alia, youth entrepreneurship;

10. *Stresses also* the need for Member States to retain and further enhance national human resources by boosting job-rich recovery and promoting decent work, including by adopting policies and incentives that enhance labour productivity and stimulate private investment and entrepreneurship and that strengthen the role of labour administration and institutions in order to foster job creation and increase the participation of vulnerable groups, including workers in informal sectors;

11. *Emphasizes* the need to address the interlinkages among human resources development, energy and food security, agriculture and rural development, and encourages Member States to strengthen capacity in agriculture and rural development;

12. *Stresses* that sustainable development is dependent, inter alia, on healthy human resources, calls upon Member States to continue their efforts to strengthen national health systems, urges the further strengthening of international cooperation in the area of health, inter alia, through the exchange of best practices in the areas of health system strengthening, access to medicines, training of health personnel, transfer of technology and production of affordable, safe, effective and good-quality medicine, and in this regard stresses that international cooperation and assistance, in particular external funding, need to become more predictable and to be better aligned with national priorities and channelled to recipient countries in ways that strengthen national health systems;

13. *Calls upon* the international community, including the entities of the United Nations system, to support the efforts of developing countries to address the adverse effects of HIV/AIDS, malaria, tuberculosis and other infectious diseases, in particular in Africa, as well as the prevention and control of non-communicable diseases, which is a challenge of epidemic proportions, and their effects on human resources;

14. *Calls upon* relevant United Nations entities to support national efforts to build institutional capacities to address long-term national human resources development needs in addition to providing training to individuals;

15. *Calls upon* the international community to assist developing countries in the implementation of national human resources development strategies, and encourages the international community, including the private sector and relevant civil society actors, to provide and mobilize financial resources, capacity-building, technical assistance, transfer of technology and supply of expertise from all sources, as appropriate;

16. *Calls for* steps to integrate gender perspectives into human resources development, including through policies, strategies and targeted actions aimed at promoting women's capacities and access to productive activities, and in this regard emphasizes the need to ensure the full participation of women in the formulation and implementation of such policies, strategies and actions;

17. *Stresses* the important contributions of the public and private sectors, respectively, in meeting national training and educational needs to support the efficient functioning of enterprises and matching the needs of a rapidly changing economy, and encourages the integration of those contributions, including through the greater use of public-private partnerships and incentives;

18. *Calls for* actions at the national, regional and international levels that will give high priority to improving and expanding literacy, as well as science proficiency, including by providing tertiary, technical-vocational and adult education, and stresses the need to ensure that, by 2015, children everywhere, boys and girls alike, will be able to complete a full course of primary schooling and will have equal access to all levels of education;

19. *Encourages* Governments to consider appropriate measures at the national level, such as upgrading human skills, better aligning educational and training systems to labour market needs, and strengthening labour institutions and regulations to respond to economic downturns;

20. *Encourages* States in a position to do so to maintain or consider enhancing measures to boost a job-rich recovery, such as policies and incentives to enhance labour productivity and stimulate private investment, besides making efforts to reduce budget deficits in the long term, as appropriate;

21. *Encourages* efforts by Member States and the international community to promote a balanced, coherent and comprehensive approach to international migration and development, in particular by building partnerships and ensuring coordinated action to develop capacities, including for the management of migration, and in this regard reiterates the need to consider innovative measures to maximize the benefits of migration while minimizing the negative effects of the migration of both highly skilled and low-skilled workers from developing countries;

22. *Requests* the Secretary-General to submit to the General Assembly at its sixty-eighth session a report on the implementation of the present resolution, including an assessment of the contribution of science, technological knowledge and innovation to human resources development in developing countries;

23. *Decides* to include in the provisional agenda of its sixty-eighth session, under the item entitled "Eradication of poverty and other development issues", the sub-item entitled "Human resources development".

UN research and training institutes

UN Institute for Training and Research

In response to Economic and Social Council resolution 2009/27 [YUN 2009, p. 1109], the Secretary-General submitted a May report [E/2011/115] on the

United Nations Institute for Training and Research (UNITAR), the second to be prepared and submitted to the Council in compliance with General Assembly resolution 62/210 [YUN 2007, p. 1150], by which the Assembly established a streamlined reporting arrangement for UNITAR. Since January 2010, the Institute had embarked on a set of new strategic priorities that aimed to bring it closer to its goal of becoming a centre of excellence in the fields of training, capacity development and research on knowledge systems. In 2010, the Institute's overall beneficiary outreach increased by 33 per cent and its organization of events by 5.7 per cent compared to 2009. The use of technology-enhanced tools increased, and achievements were made in enhancing the diversity and quality of the Institute's products and services, and in results-based management. UNITAR was also implementing a new business model that had self-generated income at its core, and continued to register growth in financial performance; however, non-earmarked contributions to the General Fund to support institutional reforms remained at low and unpredictable levels, with a 20 per cent decrease in 2010 compared to 2008. The weak levels of those contributions had delayed the activities and investments that were instrumental in implementing the Institute's new business model and advancing other reforms, such as enhancing the quality of training, improving evaluation practices and making progress in the area of knowledge management. Other challenges included limited contributions to the newly created Fellowship Fund and office space limitations. The Secretary-General recommended that Member States provide full support to the Institute in implementing its strategic reforms, including financial contributions to the General Fund and Fellowship Fund, and the means to address the office space challenges that were likely to stop growth and the achievement of strategic goals.

ECONOMIC AND SOCIAL COUNCIL ACTION

On 22 July [meeting 41], the Economic and Social Council adopted **resolution 2011/11** [draft: E/2011/L.39] without vote [agenda item 15].

United Nations Institute for Training and Research

The Economic and Social Council,

Recalling its resolution 2009/27 of 30 July 2009,

Recalling also General Assembly resolutions 57/268 of 20 December 2002, 58/223 of 23 December 2003, 59/252 of 22 December 2004, 60/213 of 22 December 2005, 62/210 of 19 December 2007 and section I of Assembly resolution 64/260 of 29 March 2010,

Acknowledging the progress made by the United Nations Institute for Training and Research on the establishment of results-based management and quality standards and the expanded use of technology-enhanced tools,

Acknowledging also the efficiency gains realized by the Institute through increased e-learning course offerings and the emphasis placed on multiplier effects, with a view to facilitating knowledge transfer through the development of training capacities in national and regional organizations,

Acknowledging further the leadership role the Institute has been playing in its responses to thematic priorities for training, such as system-wide coherence and United Nations operational activities for development, as well as through its active collaboration with agencies, inter alia on climate change, peacekeeping, international migration and development-related issues,

Encouraged by the growth in beneficiary outreach through increased training and knowledge-sharing events and by the expanded presence of the Institute in developing countries,

Encouraged also by the growth in earmarked voluntary contributions to the Institute and the implementation of a new business model with self-generated income to diversify sources of funding,

Concerned, however, over the low levels of non-earmarked voluntary contributions to the Institute and the negative effects that such low levels have on the efforts to pursue strategic reforms and meet the training and capacity-development needs of developing countries,

Welcoming the establishment of the Fellowship Fund to ensure that fee-based training services will remain accessible to developing countries,

1. *Takes note* of the report of the Secretary-General;
2. *Welcomes* the strategic plan of the United Nations Institute for Training and Research for the period 2010–2012;
3. *Calls upon* the Institute to pursue its innovations in the field of capacity development;
4. *Encourages* the Institute to continue improving its effectiveness and the high quality of its output, in order to consolidate its important role in the training of beneficiaries;
5. *Calls upon* the Institute to pursue its efforts to enhance the capabilities of learning centres in developing countries with innovative methodologies, as well as to contribute to better coordination of United Nations research and training institutes;
6. *Invites* Member States to identify concrete actions, including different ways of enhancing non-earmarked voluntary contributions, to respond to the challenges referred to in paragraphs 61 and 62 of the report of the Secretary-General, as well as to strengthen the Institute to contribute more effectively to United Nations development cooperation;
7. *Requests* the Secretary-General to report to the Economic and Social Council at its substantive session of 2013 on the implementation of the present resolution.

UNITAR financing

In the financial report and audited financial statements of UNITAR for the year ended 31 December

2011 [A/67/5/Add.4], the Board of Auditors reviewed the financial transactions and operations at the headquarters of unitar in Geneva. For the biennium 2010–2011, the total income of the Institute was $42.05 million, with total expenditures amounting to $42.62 million. At the end of the biennium, total assets amounted to $16.77 million, and total liabilities were $9.34 million. The Board made several recommendations based on its audit, in particular, that unitar disclose the information about the programme support income, including the definition, scope and calculation methodology in the notes to the financial statements, to enable users to better understand the financial statements; clearly articulate the definition, scope and percentage of programme support cost and administrative cost to make the financial statements more transparent and understandable; and intensify its efforts to ensure the timely implementation of the International Public Sector Accounting Standards.

United Nations University

In July, the Council of the United Nations University (unu) submitted to the Economic and Social Council a report [E/2011/129] on the work of the University in 2010. Its projects and activities focused on the five thematic clusters defined by the unu Strategic Plan 2009–2012 [YUN 2009, p. 1110], namely, peace, security and human rights; human and socio-economic development and good governance; global health, population and sustainable livelihoods; global change and sustainable development; and science, technology, innovation and society. Within the scope of those clusters, the University undertook the functions of research and study, teaching and capacity development, and knowledge-sharing and transfer. Highlights during the year included the welcoming of 14 new Council members to replace those whose six-year tenure ended in 2010, as well as three new institute directors. The Iceland-based unu Land Restoration Training Programme became operational, as well as the unu Institute for Sustainability and Peace Sustainable Cycles operating unit in Germany. With regard to institutional priorities, the Office of the Rector designated five strategic priority initiatives within the framework set out in the Strategic Plan for 2010, specifically, postgraduate programmes; twin institutes, whereby each unu Institute would have two locations, one in a developed country and the other in a developing country; quality assurance; communications; and fund-raising.

The Economic and Social Council took note of the report on 22 July (**decision 2011/221**).

UNU Council annual session. At its fifty-eighth session (Bruges, Belgium, 28 November–1 December), the unu Council heard and discussed the Rector's annual "State of the University report"; the financial overview of the University; and the programme and budget estimates for the 2012–2013 biennium. It also considered a range of strategic issues, including developments regarding the twin institute concept; the operation and activities of the unu institutes and programmes; ongoing and new initiatives; and the University's postgraduate programme.

UN System Staff College

In response to General Assembly resolution 60/214 [YUN 2005, p. 1527], the Secretary-General, in May [E/2011/116], transmitted to the Economic and Social Council the report of the Director of the United Nations System Staff College, covering the work of the College since the previous report in 2009 [YUN 2009, p. 1112]. The report reviewed the training and learning activities carried out during the reporting period with regard to fostering a cohesive management culture in the UN system; reinforcing system-wide coherence; strengthening knowledge-sharing in the system; and supporting the peace, security and staff safety efforts of the United Nations. It also outlined the College's partnership strategy with various entities in the UN system, which contributed to the introduction of 11 courses and the development of three knowledge products in 2010. That year also saw the establishment of a tripartite alliance among the College, the Departments of Peacekeeping Operations and Field Support, and the United Nations Institute for Training and Research.

In 2010, overall income increased by 18 per cent over the preceding year, while expenditure increased by 21 per cent. An increase in self-generated income from 56 per cent of total income in 2009 to 70 per cent in 2010 reflected the College's strategy of lessening its donor dependency. Encouraging results were achieved in all programmatic areas, with a delivery rate of more than 89 per cent in terms of the results-based budget for 2010, and an increase of 23 per cent in the number of beneficiaries reached by the College's training and learning activities compared with 2009. The College worked to improve the quality of its services and its internal management structure, which had led it to become a key ally of inter-agency policymaking bodies such as the United Nations System Chief Executives Board for Coordination, as well as the High-level Committees on Programmes and on Management, which relied on the College's inter-agency work for the implementation of training across the system. The year 2010 marked the final stage of the reform process of the College governance structure, enabling the College to deliver more efficiently and effectively against its mandate. The Director concluded by encouraging Member States to designate the College as the focal point for UN-wide learning and leadership skills-building through references in relevant resolutions.

ECONOMIC AND SOCIAL COUNCIL ACTION

On 22 July [meeting 41], the Economic and Social Council adopted **resolution 2011/10** [draft: E/2011/L.25] without vote [agenda item 15].

United Nations System Staff College in Turin, Italy

The Economic and Social Council,

Recalling General Assembly resolutions 54/228 of 22 December 1999, 55/207 of 20 December 2000, 55/258 of 14 June 2001, 55/278 of 12 July 2001, 58/224 of 23 December 2003 and 60/214 of 22 December 2005,

Recalling also its resolution 2009/10 of 27 July 2009, in which it approved amendments to the statute of the United Nations System Staff College,

Reaffirming the role of the Staff College as an institution for system-wide knowledge management, training and continuous learning for the staff of the United Nations system, in particular in the areas of economic and social development, peace and security and internal management,

Having considered the report of the Secretary-General, submitted pursuant to paragraph 8 of resolution 60/214,

1. *Takes note* of the report of the Secretary-General;
2. *Welcomes* the progress made by the United Nations System Staff College, over the past two years, in providing high-quality learning and training to the United Nations system;
3. *Calls upon* all organizations of the United Nations system to make full and effective use of the services provided by the Staff College;
4. *Encourages* Member States to continue to support the Staff College by recognizing its unique inter-agency mandate and its important role in fostering system-wide coherence and strategic leadership.

Education

Annual ministerial review. From 4 to 7 July, during the high-level segment of its 2011 substantive session [A/66/3/Rev.1] (see p. 1359), the Economic and Social Council held its annual ministerial review on the theme "Implementing the internationally agreed goals and commitments in regard to education". The Council had before it national reports on the subject by Bangladesh [E/2011/96]; Belarus [E/2011/98]; Germany [E/2011/97]; Malawi [E/2011/120]; Mauritius [E/2011/94]; Mexico [E/2011/95 & Add.1]; Qatar [E/2011/93]; Senegal [E/2011/126]; Thailand [E/2011/121]; and Venezuela [E/2011/118]. It also had before it a 6 June letter by Argentina [E/2011/125] transmitting the report of the Latin America and the Caribbean regional preparatory meeting on key education challenges in the region: teachers, quality and equity (Buenos Aires, 12–13 May), as well as a 22 June letter from Togo [E/2011/124] transmitting the report of the African regional preparatory meeting on the right to education for all in Africa: reinforcing quality and equity (Lomé, 12 April).

The Council had before it an April report [E/2011/83] of the Secretary-General on the theme of the annual ministerial review, which reviewed progress towards implementing the internationally agreed goals and commitments related to education. It considered trends in achieving international Education for All goals; examined the quality of education and the relevance of learning gaps across and within countries, as well as teacher shortages and deployment and inequitable patterns of teacher deployment. The report highlighted measures that had proven effective in overcoming inequality in access and participation in education, and in ensuring a more equitable distribution of higher levels of learning outcomes. The Secretary-General made recommendations on an integrated and holistic approach to development; policy coherence; strengthening coordination and cooperation; adopting a broader vision of education for development beyond universal primary education; spending on education; accountability and transparency; inclusive policies and targeted interventions; strategic planning and implementation; working conditions and teacher training; and the quality and relevance of learning.

The Council also had before it an April report [E/2011/82] of the Secretary-General, which highlighted global trends and challenges and their impact on education, including with regard to the global economy; job insecurity and rising inequalities; food insecurity; migration patterns; climate change and disaster risks; conflict and human insecurity; and technological innovations. It stated that many of those trends required policy responses to mitigate negative effects on education and learning, and made recommendations on securing stable education expenditure; building resilience to income shocks; developing skills for twenty-first century challenges and opportunities; promoting migration for education; revitalizing the global commitment to education; and supporting peacebuilding through education.

Thematic discussion. In the context of its discussion on the theme "Current global and national trends and challenges and their impact on education", the Council held special policy dialogues on accelerating education for all: mobilizing resources and partnerships; education for sustainable development; and education challenges in Africa and the least developed countries. It further conducted a special debate on education, human rights and conflict; a thematic round table on education for the future: changing needs; and a discussion on the challenge to achieve education for all: Germany's approach.

Ministerial declaration. On 8 July, the Council adopted the draft ministerial declaration entitled "Implementing the internationally agreed goals and commitments in regard to education" [E/2011/L.28].

Chapter X

Women

In 2011, United Nations efforts to advance the status of women worldwide continued to be guided by the Beijing Declaration and Platform for Action, adopted at the Fourth (1995) World Conference on Women, and the outcome of the General Assembly's twenty-third (2000) special session (Beijing+5), which reviewed progress in their implementation.

On 1 January, the United Nations Entity for Gender Equality and the Empowerment of Women (UN-Women), established by General Assembly resolution 64/289, became operational. It combined the mandates and assets of the United Nations Development Fund for Women, the Office of the Special Adviser to the Secretary-General on Gender Issues and Advancement of Women, the Division for the Advancement of Women, and the International Research and Training Institute for the Advancement of Women, with the aim to provide guidance and technical support to Member States on gender equality, the empowerment of women and gender mainstreaming. With transitional arrangements completed by the end of 2010, the core elements for the functioning of the new entity were in place. The UN-Women Executive Board adopted the financial rules and regulations in April; the strategic plan, 2011–2013—which set out the entity's vision, mission and priorities—in June; and the institutional budget for the biennium 2012–2013 in December.

The Commission on the Status of Women, at its fifty-fifth session, held a high-level round table and panel discussions on its priority theme, "Access and participation of women and girls in education, training and science and technology, including for the promotion of women's equal access to full employment and decent work", and decided to transmit to the Economic and Social Council the summaries of those discussions, together with agreed conclusions related to the priority theme, as input to the Council's annual ministerial review. The Commission further brought to the Council's attention resolutions it had adopted on mainstreaming gender equality and promoting empowerment of women in climate change policies and strategies; and women, the girl child and HIV and AIDS. It also recommended to the Council the adoption of a draft resolution on the situation of and assistance to Palestinian women, which the Council adopted in July.

Issues central to women's lives on which the General Assembly adopted resolutions included follow-up to the Fourth World Conference on Women and full implementation of the Beijing Declaration and Platform for Action and the outcome of its twenty-third special session; women in development; women in rural areas; violence against women migrant workers; women and political participation; and the girl child.

A Security Council presidential statement in October on women and peace and security underlined the importance of women's participation in conflict prevention and resolution efforts, including in the negotiation and implementation of peace agreements. It encouraged Member States, and international and regional organizations to take measures to increase the numbers of women involved in mediation efforts and the numbers of women in representative roles in regional and international organizations.

Follow-up to the Fourth World Conference on Women and Beijing+5

During 2011, the Commission on the Status of Women, the Economic and Social Council and the General Assembly considered follow-up to the 1995 Fourth World Conference on Women, particularly the implementation of the Beijing Declaration and Platform for Action [YUN 1995, p. 1170] and the political declaration and further actions and initiatives to implement both instruments adopted at the twenty-third (2000) special session of the Assembly (Beijing+5) by resolution S/23-2 [YUN 2000, p. 1084]. The Declaration had reaffirmed the commitment of Governments to the goals and objectives of the Fourth World Conference and to the implementation of the 12 critical areas of concern outlined in the Platform for Action: women and poverty; education and training of women; women and health; violence against women; women and armed conflict; women and the economy; women in power and decision-making; institutional mechanisms for the advancement of women; human rights of women; women and the media; women and the environment; and the girl child. The issue of mainstreaming a gender perspective into UN policies and programmes continued to be addressed (see below).

Report of Secretary-General. In response to General Assembly resolution 65/191 [YUN 2010, p. 1136], the Secretary-General, in a July report [A/66/211], reviewed the follow-up to and the implementation of the Beijing Declaration and Platform for Action and the outcomes of the Assembly's twenty-third special session. He focused on selected UN intergovernmental processes, including advances made during the sixty-fifth (2010) session of the Assembly and the 2010 sessions of the Economic and Social Council and its functional commissions, and assessed the extent to which they integrated a gender perspective. The report further evaluated preparatory documentation for, and, when applicable, outcomes of the 2011 Fourth United Nations Conference on the Least Developed Countries (see p. 827), the 2012 United Nations Conference on Sustainable Development (see p. 799), and the 2013 review and appraisal of the Madrid International Plan of Action on Ageing, 2002 (see p. 1027).

The analysis suggested that there had been some progress in incorporating a gender perspective into the intergovernmental processes examined, particularly in ensuring that reports of the Secretary-General to the Assembly and to the Economic and Social Council reflected a gender perspective, while progress had been more limited with respect to resolutions. High-level events continued to offer good opportunities for incorporating a gender perspective into intergovernmental processes and for reflecting them in major outcome documents. The review of intergovernmental documents indicated that in most cases, the inclusion of a gender perspective reflected a genuine focus on gender equality issues. However, the share of resolutions of the General Assembly, the Economic and Social Council, and the functional commissions of the Council that included a gender perspective remained low, and even high-level events did not always give sufficient attention to gender equality issues. References to gender equality and empowerment of women issues continued to be most strongly evidenced in the intergovernmental processes focusing on social and economic issues, namely, in the processes of the Second (Economic and Financial) and Third (Social, Humanitarian and Cultural) Committees.

The Secretary-General suggested that the General Assembly consider reiterating its call to UN intergovernmental bodies to mainstream a gender perspective into all issues under their consideration and within their mandates, including in all UN summits, conferences and special sessions and in their follow-up processes; requesting the Secretary-General to ensure that his reports systematically included a gender perspective through gender analysis and the provision of sex- and age-disaggregated quantitative data; encouraging Governments to improve the collection, analysis and dissemination of data disaggregated by sex, and age, to enhance capacity development in that regard, and to develop relevant gender-sensitive indicators to support policymaking; and calling upon Governments and the UN system to encourage and support the participation of women's groups and non-governmental organizations specialized in gender equality issues in intergovernmental processes through increased outreach, funding and capacity development.

GENERAL ASSEMBLY ACTION

On 19 December [meeting 89], the General Assembly, on the recommendation of the Third (Social, Humanitarian and Cultural) Committee [A/66/455 & Corr.1], adopted **resolution 66/132** without vote [agenda item 28 (*b*)].

Follow-up to the Fourth World Conference on Women and full implementation of the Beijing Declaration and Platform for Action and the outcome of the twenty-third special session of the General Assembly

The General Assembly,

Recalling its previous resolutions on the question, including resolution 65/191 of 21 December 2010, and recalling also the section of resolution 64/289 of 2 July 2010 entitled "Strengthening the institutional arrangements for support of gender equality and the empowerment of women",

Deeply convinced that the Beijing Declaration and Platform for Action and the outcome of the twenty-third special session of the General Assembly entitled "Women 2000: gender equality, development and peace for the twenty-first century" are important contributions to the achievement of gender equality and the empowerment of women and must be translated into effective action by all States, the United Nations system and other organizations concerned,

Reaffirming the commitments to gender equality and the advancement of women made at the Millennium Summit, the 2005 World Summit, the High-level Plenary Meeting of the General Assembly on the Millennium Development Goals and other major United Nations summits, conferences and special sessions, and reaffirming also that their full, effective and accelerated implementation is integral to achieving the internationally agreed development goals, including the Millennium Development Goals,

Welcoming progress made towards achieving gender equality, but stressing that challenges and obstacles remain in the implementation of the Beijing Declaration and Platform for Action and the outcome of the twenty-third special session,

Recognizing that the responsibility for the implementation of the Beijing Declaration and Platform for Action and the outcome of the twenty-third special session rests primarily at the national level and that strengthened efforts are necessary in this respect, and reiterating that enhanced international cooperation is essential for full, effective and accelerated implementation,

Welcoming the work of the Commission on the Status of Women in reviewing the implementation of the Beijing Declaration and Platform for Action, and taking note with appreciation of all its agreed conclusions, including the latest, on access and participation of women and girls in education, training and science and technology, including for the promotion of women's equal access to full employment and decent work, adopted by the Commission at its fifty-fifth session,

Welcoming also the full operationalization of the United Nations Entity for Gender Equality and the Empowerment of Women (UN-Women) on 1 January 2011,

Recognizing that the participation and contribution of civil society, in particular women's groups and other non-governmental organizations, are important to the implementation of the Beijing Declaration and Platform for Action and the outcome of the twenty-third special session,

Reaffirming that gender mainstreaming is a globally accepted strategy for promoting the empowerment of women and achieving gender equality by transforming structures of inequality, and reaffirming also the commitment to actively promote the mainstreaming of a gender perspective into the design, implementation, monitoring and evaluation of policies and programmes in all political, economic and social spheres, as well as the commitment to strengthen the capabilities of the United Nations system in the area of gender equality,

Reaffirming also the commitments in regard to gender equality and the empowerment of women in the Doha Declaration on Financing for Development: outcome document of the Follow-up International Conference on Financing for Development to Review the Implementation of the Monterrey Consensus,

Bearing in mind the challenges and obstacles to changing discriminatory attitudes and gender stereotypes, which perpetuate discrimination against women and stereotypic roles of men and women, and stressing that challenges and obstacles remain in the implementation of international standards and norms to address the inequality between men and women,

Reaffirming the Declaration of Commitment on HIV/AIDS and the Political Declaration on HIV and AIDS: Intensifying Our Efforts to Eliminate HIV and AIDS adopted at the High-level Meeting on AIDS, held on 10 June 2011, in which, inter alia, the promotion of gender equality and the empowerment of women were recognized as fundamental for reducing the vulnerability of women to HIV,

Expressing serious concern that the urgent goal of 50/50 gender balance in the United Nations system, especially at senior and policymaking levels, with full respect for the principle of equitable geographical distribution, in conformity with Article 101, paragraph 3, of the Charter of the United Nations, remains unmet, and that the representation of women in the United Nations system has remained almost static, with negligible improvement in some parts of the system, as reflected in the report of the Secretary-General on the improvement of the status of women in the United Nations system,

Reaffirming the important role of women in the prevention and resolution of conflicts and in peacebuilding,

Recalling Security Council resolutions 1325(2000) of 31 October 2000, 1820(2008) of 19 June 2008, 1888(2009) of 30 September 2009, 1889(2009) of 5 October 2009 and 1960(2010) of 16 December 2010 on women and peace and security and resolution 1882(2009) of 4 August 2009 on children and armed conflict,

1. *Takes note with appreciation* of the report of the Secretary-General on the measures taken and progress achieved in follow-up to the implementation of the Beijing Declaration and Platform for Action and the outcome of the twenty-third special session of the General Assembly;

2. *Reaffirms* the Beijing Declaration and Platform for Action adopted at the Fourth World Conference on Women and the outcome of the twenty-third special session of the General Assembly, as well as the declaration adopted on the occasion of the fifteen-year review of the implementation of the Beijing Declaration and Platform for Action at the fifty-fourth session of the Commission on the Status of Women, and also reaffirms its commitment to their full, effective and accelerated implementation;

3. *Also reaffirms* the primary and essential role of the General Assembly and the Economic and Social Council, as well as the catalytic role of the Commission on the Status of Women, in promoting gender equality and the empowerment of women based on the full implementation of the Beijing Declaration and Platform for Action and the outcome of the twenty-third special session and in promoting and monitoring gender mainstreaming within the United Nations system;

4. *Recognizes* that the implementation of the Beijing Declaration and Platform for Action and the fulfilment of the obligations of States parties under the Convention on the Elimination of All Forms of Discrimination against Women are mutually reinforcing in respect of achieving gender equality and the empowerment of women, and in this regard welcomes the contributions of the Committee on the Elimination of Discrimination against Women to promoting the implementation of the Platform for Action and the outcome of the twenty-third special session, and invites States parties to the Convention to include information on measures taken to enhance implementation at the national level in their reports to the Committee under article 18 of the Convention;

5. *Calls upon* States parties to comply fully with their obligations under the Convention on the Elimination of All Forms of Discrimination against Women and the Optional Protocol thereto and to take into consideration the concluding observations as well as the general recommendations of the Committee, urges States parties to consider limiting the extent of any reservations that they lodge to the Convention, to formulate any reservations as precisely and narrowly as possible and to regularly review such reservations with a view to withdrawing them so as to ensure that no reservation is incompatible with the object and purpose of the Convention, also urges all Member States that have not yet ratified or acceded to the Convention to consider doing so, and calls upon those Member States that have not yet done so to consider signing and ratifying or acceding to the Optional Protocol;

6. *Welcomes* the progress made in the effective functioning of UN-Women in regard to its governance structure, as well as administration, budgeting and human resources;

7. *Reaffirms* the important role of UN-Women in leading, coordinating and promoting accountability of the United Nations system in its work on gender equality and the empowerment of women;

8. *Calls upon* UN-Women to continue to support gender mainstreaming across the United Nations system as an integral part of its work and, in that regard, to place a strong and more systematic focus on support for gender mainstreaming across the United Nations system;

9. *Welcomes* the commitment of UN-Women to support Member States in their efforts to develop and

strengthen norms, policies and standards on gender equality and the empowerment of women as well as to integrate gender perspectives into sectoral policy and normative frameworks;

10. *Urges* Member States to increase funding for the budget of UN-Women by providing, when legislative and budgetary provisions allow, core, multi-year, predictable, stable and sustainable voluntary contributions, recognizing the importance of adequate funding in enabling UN-Women to implement its strategic plan promptly and effectively, and recognizing also that the mobilization of financial resources for achieving its goals still remains a challenge;

11. *Encourages* all actors, inter alia, Governments, the United Nations system, other international organizations and civil society, to continue to support the work of the Commission on the Status of Women in fulfilling its central role in the follow-up to and review of the implementation of the Beijing Declaration and Platform for Action and the outcome of the twenty-third special session, and, as applicable, to carry out the recommendations of the Commission, and welcomes in this regard the Commission's continued sharing of experiences, lessons learned and good practices in overcoming challenges to full implementation at the national and international levels and the evaluation of progress in the implementation of priority themes;

12. *Calls upon* Governments and the organs and relevant funds, programmes and specialized agencies of the United Nations system, within their respective mandates, and other international and regional organizations, including financial institutions, and all relevant actors of civil society, including non-governmental organizations, to intensify action to achieve the full and effective implementation of the Beijing Declaration and Platform for Action and the outcome of the twenty-third special session;

13. *Reaffirms* that States have an obligation to exercise due diligence to prevent violence against women and girls, provide protection to the victims and investigate, prosecute and punish the perpetrators of violence against women and girls and that failure to do so violates and impairs or nullifies the enjoyment of their human rights and fundamental freedoms, calls upon Governments to elaborate and implement laws and strategies to eliminate violence against women and girls, encourages and supports men and boys in taking an active part in the prevention and elimination of all forms of violence, encourages increased understanding among men and boys of how violence harms girls, boys, women and men and undermines gender equality, encourages all actors to speak out against any violence against women, and in this regard encourages Member States to continue to support the Secretary-General's ongoing campaign "UNITE to End Violence against Women" and the UN-Women social mobilization and advocacy platform "Say NO–UNITE to End Violence against Women";

14. *Reiterates its call* to the United Nations system, including the main organs, their main committees and subsidiary bodies, functions such as the annual ministerial review and the Development Cooperation Forum of the Economic and Social Council, and the funds, programmes and specialized agencies, to increase efforts to fully mainstream a gender perspective into all issues under their consideration and within their mandates, as well as in all United Nations summits, conferences and special sessions and in their follow-up processes, including the United Nations Conference on Sustainable Development in 2012 and the review and appraisal of the Madrid International Plan of Action on Ageing, 2002, at the fifty-first session of the Commission for Social Development, in 2013;

15. *Requests* the entities of the United Nations system systematically to incorporate the outcomes of the Commission on the Status of Women into their work within their mandates, inter alia, to ensure effective support for the efforts of Member States towards the achievement of gender equality and the empowerment of women, and in this regard welcomes the commitment of UN-Women to establish concrete results-based reporting mechanisms, as well as to ensure coherence, consistency and coordination between the normative and operational aspects of its work;

16. *Strongly encourages* Governments to continue to support the role and contribution of civil society, in particular non-governmental organizations and women's organizations, in the implementation of the Beijing Declaration and Platform for Action and the outcome of the twenty-third special session;

17. *Calls upon* Governments and the United Nations system to encourage women's groups and other non-governmental organizations specializing in gender equality and the empowerment of women to participate in intergovernmental processes, including through increased outreach, funding and capacity-building;

18. *Calls upon* intergovernmental bodies of the United Nations to systematically request the inclusion of a gender perspective in reports of the Secretary-General and other inputs to intergovernmental processes;

19. *Requests* that reports of the Secretary-General submitted to the General Assembly and the Economic and Social Council and their subsidiary bodies systematically address gender perspectives through qualitative gender analysis and the provision of sex- and age-disaggregated data and, where available, quantitative data, in particular through concrete conclusions and recommendations for further action on gender equality and the empowerment of women, in order to facilitate gender-sensitive policy development, and in this regard requests the Secretary-General to convey the importance of reflecting a gender perspective to all stakeholders who provide inputs to his reports;

20. *Encourages* Member States, with the support of, as appropriate, United Nations entities, including UN-Women, international and regional organizations and other relevant actors, to prioritize the strengthening of national data collection and monitoring capacities with regard to statistics disaggregated by sex and age, as well as national tracking indicators for gender equality and the empowerment of women through multisectoral efforts and partnerships;

21. *Calls upon* all parts of the United Nations system to continue to play an active role in ensuring the full, effective and accelerated implementation of the Beijing Declaration and Platform for Action and the outcome of the twenty-third special session, through, inter alia, the maintenance of gender specialists in all entities of the United Nations system, as well as by ensuring that all personnel, especially in the field, receive training and appropriate follow-up, including tools, guidance and support, for accelerated gender mainstreaming, and reaffirms the need to strengthen

the capabilities of the United Nations system in the area of gender;

22. *Requests* the Secretary-General to review and redouble his efforts to make progress towards achieving the goal of 50/50 gender balance at all levels throughout the United Nations system, with full respect for the principle of equitable geographical distribution, in conformity with Article 101, paragraph 3, of the Charter of the United Nations, considering, in particular, women from developing and least developed countries, from countries with economies in transition and from unrepresented or largely underrepresented Member States, and to ensure managerial and departmental accountability with respect to gender balance targets, and strongly encourages Member States to identify and regularly submit more women candidates for appointment to positions in the United Nations system, especially at more senior and policymaking levels, including in peacekeeping operations;

23. *Calls upon* the United Nations system to continue its efforts towards achieving the goal of gender balance, including with the active support of gender focal points, and requests the Secretary-General to provide an oral report to the Commission on the Status of Women at its fifty-sixth session and to report to the General Assembly at its sixty-seventh session on the improvement of the status of women in the United Nations system, under the item entitled "Advancement of women", and on progress made and obstacles encountered in achieving gender balance, with recommendations for accelerating progress, and up-to-date statistics, including the number and percentage of women and their functions and nationalities throughout the United Nations system, and information on the responsibility and accountability of the offices of human resources management and the secretariat of the United Nations System Chief Executives Board for Coordination for promoting gender balance;

24. *Encourages* increased efforts by Governments and the United Nations system to enhance accountability for the implementation of commitments to gender equality and the empowerment of women at the international, regional and national levels, including by improved monitoring and reporting on progress in relation to policies, strategies, resource allocations and programmes and by achieving gender balance;

25. *Reaffirms* that Governments bear the primary responsibility for the achievement of gender equality and the empowerment of women and that international cooperation has an essential role in assisting developing countries in progressing towards the full implementation of the Beijing Declaration and Platform for Action;

26. *Requests* the Secretary-General to continue to report annually to the General Assembly under the item entitled "Advancement of women", as well as to the Commission on the Status of Women and the Economic and Social Council, on the follow-up to and progress made in the implementation of the Beijing Declaration and Platform for Action and the outcome of the twenty-third special session, with an assessment of progress in gender mainstreaming, including information on key achievements, lessons learned and good practices, and recommendations on further measures to enhance implementation.

Critical areas of concern

Women and poverty

Women in development

Pursuant to General Assembly resolution 64/217 [YUN 2009, p. 1120], the Secretary-General submitted an August report [A/66/219] on integrating a gender perspective into national development strategies. The report reviewed measures taken by Governments, support provided by the UN system, and the role of donors and the new aid effectiveness agenda [YUN 2008, p. 942]. It also highlighted gender-responsive budgeting and planning as a good practice example.

The Secretary-General noted that despite progress towards achieving the Millennium Development Goals (MDGs), significant gaps remained between urban and rural areas and for those who were the most disadvantaged economically or because of sex, age, disability or ethnicity. The majority of maternal deaths continued to be concentrated in sub-Saharan Africa and Southern Asia, and children from the poorest households, living in rural or in conflict areas, especially girls, were the most likely not to be attending school. Access to secondary education remained restricted for girls in some regions, and worldwide, women's access to employment, resources and decision-making positions remained a challenge. Progress in improving the share of women in non-agricultural paid employment was particularly slow. Intergovernmental bodies continued to reaffirm the importance of gender-sensitive national policies for progress towards the MDGs, gender equality and the empowerment of women—essential for development and poverty eradication—was reflected as a priority area of the Istanbul Programme of Action for the Least Developed Countries for the Decade 2011–2020 (see p. 828), and, in that context, least developed countries had committed to establishing and continuing to implement national development plans that took into account the needs of women and girls.

The report concluded that Governments had undertaken many initiatives, such as identifying gender issues as a priority or cross-cutting subject that was systematically mainstreamed across all sectors in all stages of the policy process. Nevertheless, in some countries, gender perspectives were only partially integrated in specific sectoral areas. Beyond awareness-raising, capacity-building and training activities, concerted efforts were needed for the effective incorporation of gender perspectives into national development policies and strategies. Common strategies included developing capacity and expertise in line ministries as well as in national mechanisms for gender equality; strengthening accountability, monitoring and evaluation mechanisms; ensuring sufficient human and financial resources; and promoting the participation of civil society, particularly women's organizations, in the national development planning processes. With respect to the role of the UN system and donors, emphasis should be placed on integrating gender perspectives in all development cooperation work and building on the national ownership of gender-mainstreaming initiatives. Measures should include mechanisms to track resources allocated to achieve gender equality goals; coordination mechanisms with a gender equality focus; and accountability mechanisms to measure and track performance. The Secretary-General suggested that the General Assembly call on Member States and relevant actors to undertake actions related to gender mainstreaming efforts; participation and accountability; resource allocation and tracking; measures and tools; and least developed countries.

GENERAL ASSEMBLY ACTION

On 22 December [meeting 91], the General Assembly, on the recommendation of the Second (Economic and Financial) Committee [A/66/444/Add.2], adopted **resolution 66/216** without vote [agenda item 23 (*b*)].

Women in development

The General Assembly,

Recalling its resolutions 52/195 of 18 December 1997, 54/210 of 22 December 1999, 56/188 of 21 December 2001, 58/206 of 23 December 2003, 59/248 of 22 December 2004, 60/210 of 22 December 2005, 62/206 of 19 December 2007 and 64/217 of 21 December 2009, and all its other resolutions on the integration of women in development, and the relevant resolutions and agreed conclusions adopted by the Commission on the Status of Women, including the Declaration adopted at its forty-ninth session,

Reaffirming the Beijing Declaration and Platform for Action and the outcome of the twenty-third special session of the General Assembly, entitled "Women 2000: gender equality, development and peace for the twenty-first century",

Reaffirming also the commitments to gender equality and the advancement of women made at the Millennium Summit, the 2005 World Summit and other major United Nations summits, conferences and special sessions, and reaffirming further that their full, effective and accelerated implementation is integral to achieving the internationally agreed development goals, including the Millennium Development Goals,

Reaffirming further the United Nations Millennium Declaration, which affirms that the equal rights and opportunities of women and men must be assured, and calls for, inter alia, the promotion of gender equality and the empowerment of women as being effective in and essential to eradicating poverty and hunger, combating diseases and stimulating development that is truly sustainable,

Recalling the outcomes of the International Conference on Financing for Development and the World Summit on Sustainable Development, the Doha Declaration on Financing for Development: outcome document of the Follow-up International Conference on Financing for Development to Review the Implementation of the Monterrey Consensus, the Outcome of the Conference on the World Financial and Economic Crisis and Its Impact on Development, and the outcomes of the High-level Plenary Meeting of the General Assembly on the Millennium Development Goals, the high-level meeting on HIV and AIDS, the High-level Meeting of the General Assembly on the Prevention and Control of Non-communicable Diseases, the Fourth United Nations Conference on the Least Developed Countries and the high-level meeting on Africa's development needs,

Welcoming the full operationalization of the United Nations Entity for Gender Equality and the Empowerment of Women (UN-Women) on 1 January 2011, noting that its establishment and the conduct of its work should lead to more effective coordination, coherence and gender mainstreaming across the United Nations, and recognizing its role to assist Member States and the United Nations system in progressing more effectively and efficiently towards the goals of achieving gender equality and the empowerment of women,

Noting the importance of the organizations and bodies of the United Nations system, in particular its funds and programmes, and the specialized agencies, in facilitating the advancement of women in development,

Reaffirming that gender equality is of fundamental importance for achieving sustained and inclusive economic growth, poverty eradication and sustainable development, in accordance with the relevant resolutions of the General Assembly and United Nations conferences, and that investing in the development of women and girls has a multiplier effect, in particular on productivity, efficiency and sustained and inclusive economic growth, in all sectors of the economy, especially in key areas such as agriculture, industry and services,

Recognizing that access to basic affordable health care, preventive health-care information and the highest standard of health, including in the areas of sexual and reproductive health, is critical to women's economic advancement, that lack of economic empowerment and independence increases women's vulnerability to a range of negative consequences, including the risk of contracting HIV/AIDS, and that the neglect of women's full enjoyment of human rights severely limits their opportunities in public and private life, including the opportunities for receiving an education and for achieving economic and political empowerment,

Reaffirming the need to eliminate gender disparities in primary and secondary education by the earliest possible date and at all levels by 2015, and reaffirming also that equal access to education and training at all levels, in particular in business, trade, administration, information and communications technology and other new technologies, and fulfilment of the need to eliminate gender inequalities at all levels are essential for gender equality, the empowerment of women and poverty eradication and to allowing women's full and equal contribution to, and equal opportunity to benefit from, development,

Reaffirming also the significant contributions that women make to the economy, that women are key contributors to the economy and to combating poverty and inequalities through both remunerated and unremunerated work at home, in the community and in the workplace, and that the empowerment of women is a critical factor in the eradication of poverty,

Recognizing that the difficult socioeconomic conditions that exist in many developing countries, in particular the least developed countries, have contributed to the feminization of poverty,

Recognizing also, in this context, the importance of respect for all human rights, including the right to development, and of a national and international environment that promotes, inter alia, justice, gender equality, equity, civil and political participation and civil, political, economic, social and cultural rights and fundamental freedoms for the advancement and empowerment of women,

Bearing in mind the challenges and obstacles to changing discriminatory attitudes and gender stereotypes, which perpetuate discrimination against women and stereotypic roles of men and women, and stressing that challenges and obstacles remain in the implementation of international standards and norms to address the inequality between men and women,

Recognizing that poverty eradication and the achievement and preservation of peace are mutually reinforcing, and recognizing also that peace is inextricably linked to equality between women and men and to development,

1. *Takes note* of the report of the Secretary-General on integrating a gender perspective into national development strategies;

2. *Calls upon* Member States, the United Nations system and other international and regional organizations, within their respective mandates, and all sectors of civil society, including non-governmental organizations, as well as all women and men, to fully commit themselves and to intensify their contributions to the implementation of the Beijing Declaration and Platform for Action and the outcome of the twenty-third special session of the General Assembly;

3. *Recognizes* the mutually reinforcing links between gender equality and poverty eradication and the achievement of all of the Millennium Development Goals, as well as the need to elaborate and implement, where appropriate, in consultation with all relevant stakeholders, comprehensive gender-sensitive poverty eradication strategies that address social, structural and macroeconomic issues;

4. *Emphasizes* the need to link policies on economic and social development to ensure that all people, including those living in poverty and in vulnerable situations, benefit from inclusive economic growth and development, in accordance with the goals of the Monterrey Consensus of the International Conference on Financing for Development and the Doha Declaration on Financing for Development: outcome document of the Follow-up International Conference on Financing for Development to Review the Implementation of the Monterrey Consensus;

5. *Urges* Member States, the United Nations system and non-governmental organizations to accelerate their efforts and provide adequate resources to increase the voice and full and equal participation of women in all decision-making bodies at the highest levels of government and in the governance structures of international organizations, including through eliminating gender stereotyping in appointments and promotions, to build women's capacity as agents of change and to empower them to participate actively and effectively in the design, implementation, monitoring, evaluation and reporting of national development, poverty eradication and environmental policies, strategies and programmes;

6. *Encourages* Member States to continue to increase, as appropriate, the participation of civil society, including women's organizations, in Government decision-making in national development policy areas;

7. *Encourages* Member States and the United Nations system to ensure systematic attention to, recognition of and support for the crucial role of women in the prevention and resolution of conflict, in mediation and peacebuilding efforts and in the rebuilding of post-conflict society, inter alia, through promoting women's capacity, leadership and engagement in political and economic decision-making;

8. *Stresses* the importance of the adoption by Member States, international organizations, including the United Nations, the private sector, non-governmental organizations, trade unions and other stakeholders of appropriate measures to identify and address the ongoing adverse impacts of the world financial and economic crisis, volatile energy prices and the food crisis, and the challenges posed by climate change for women and girls, and of maintaining adequate levels of funding for the achievement of gender equality and the empowerment of women;

9. *Also stresses* the importance of the creation by Member States, international organizations, including the United Nations, the private sector, non-governmental organizations, trade unions and other stakeholders of a favourable and conducive national and international environment in all areas of life for the effective integration of women in development, and of their undertaking and disseminating a gender analysis of policies and programmes related to macroeconomic stability, structural reform, taxation, investments, including foreign direct investment, and all relevant sectors of the economy;

10. *Urges* the donor community, Member States, international organizations, including the United Nations, the private sector, non-governmental organizations, trade unions and other stakeholders to strengthen the focus and impact of development assistance targeting gender equality and the empowerment of women and girls through gender mainstreaming, the funding of targeted activities and enhanced dialogue between donors and partners, and to also strengthen the mechanisms needed to measure effectively the resources allocated to incorporating gender perspectives in all areas of development assistance;

11. *Urges* Member States to incorporate a gender perspective, commensurate with gender-equality goals, into the design, implementation, monitoring, evaluation and reporting of national development strategies, to ensure alignment between national action plans on gender equality and national development strategies, and to encourage the involvement of men and boys in the promotion of gender equality, and in this regard calls upon the United Nations system to support national efforts to develop methodologies and tools and to promote capacity-building and evaluation;

12. *Encourages* Member States to ensure inclusive and more effective participation of national mechanisms for gender equality and women's empowerment in the formulation of national development strategies, including strategies

aimed at eradicating poverty and reducing inequalities, and calls upon the United Nations system to support national efforts in this regard;

13. *Also encourages* Member States, as appropriate, to strengthen capacities for gender mainstreaming by allocating adequate financial and human resources to national women's machineries as well as to and within line ministries, establishing and/or strengthening dedicated units for gender equality and the empowerment of women, and providing capacity development for technical staff, and developing tools and guidelines;

14. *Encourages* Member States, the United Nations system and donor countries to strengthen gender-responsive planning and budgeting processes and to develop and strengthen methodologies and tools for this purpose as well as for the monitoring and evaluation of investments for gender-equality results, as appropriate, and encourages donors to mainstream a gender perspective in their practices, including joint coordination and accountability mechanisms;

15. *Encourages* Member States to adopt and implement legislation and policies designed to promote the reconciliation of work and family responsibilities, including through increased flexibility in working arrangements, such as part-time work, and the facilitation of breastfeeding for working mothers, to provide care facilities for children and other dependants, and to ensure that both women and men have access to maternity or paternity, parental and other forms of leave and are not discriminated against when availing themselves of such benefits;

16. *Expresses deep concern* about the pervasiveness of violence against women and girls, reiterates the need to further intensify efforts to prevent and eliminate all forms of violence against women and girls, and recognizes that violence against women and girls is one of the obstacles to the achievement of the objectives of equality, development and peace and that women's poverty and lack of political, social and economic empowerment, as well as their marginalization, may result from their exclusion from social policies for and the benefits of sustainable development and can place them at increased risk of violence;

17. *Encourages* Governments, the private sector, non-governmental organizations and other actors of civil society to promote and protect the rights of women workers, to take action to remove structural and legal barriers to, as well as eliminate stereotypic attitudes towards, gender equality at work, and to initiate positive steps towards promoting equal pay for equal work or for work of equal value;

18. *Urges* Governments to develop, adequately resource and implement active labour-market policies on full and productive employment and decent work for all, including the full participation of women and men in both rural and urban areas;

19. *Calls upon* Governments to strengthen efforts to protect the rights of, and ensure decent work conditions for, domestic workers, including migrant women, in relation to, inter alia, working hours, conditions and wages, and to promote access to health-care services and other social and economic benefits;

20. *Encourages* Member States to adopt and/or review and to fully implement gender-sensitive legislation and policies that reduce, through specifically targeted measures, horizontal and vertical occupational segregation and gender-based wage gaps;

21. *Urges* all Member States to undertake a gender analysis of national labour laws and standards and to establish gender-sensitive policies and guidelines for employment practices, including for transnational corporations, with particular attention to export-processing zones, building in this regard on multilateral instruments, including the Convention on the Elimination of All Forms of Discrimination against Women and conventions of the International Labour Organization;

22. *Stresses* the importance of developing national strategies for the promotion of sustainable and productive entrepreneurial activities, and encourages Governments to create a climate that is conducive to increasing the number of women entrepreneurs and the size of their businesses by giving them equal access to financial instruments, providing them with training and advisory services in business, administration and information and communications technology, facilitating networking and information-sharing and increasing their participation on advisory boards and in other forums so as to enable them to contribute to the formulation and review of policies and programmes being developed by financial institutions;

23. *Urges* all Member States to take all appropriate measures to eliminate discrimination against women with regard to their access to all types of financial services and products, including bank loans, bank accounts, mortgages and other forms of financial credit, regardless of their economic and social status, to support women's access to legal assistance and to encourage the financial sector to mainstream gender perspectives in their policies and programmes;

24. *Recognizes* the role of microfinance, including microcredit, in the eradication of poverty, the empowerment of women and the generation of employment, notes in this regard the importance of sound national financial systems, and encourages the strengthening of existing and emerging microcredit institutions and their capacities, including through the support of international financial institutions;

25. *Urges* Governments to ensure that microfinance programmes focus on developing savings products that are safe, convenient and accessible to women and support women's efforts to retain control over their savings;

26. *Urges* all Governments to eliminate discrimination against women in the field of education and ensure their equal access to all levels of education;

27. *Urges* Member States to adopt and review legislation and policies to ensure women's equal access to and control over land, housing and other property, including through inheritance, land reform programmes and land markets, and to take measures to implement those laws and policies;

28. *Urges* Governments to take measures to facilitate equitable access to land and property rights by providing training designed to make the judicial, legislative and administrative system more responsive to gender-equality issues, to provide legal aid for women seeking to claim their rights, to support the efforts of women's groups and networks and to carry out awareness campaigns so as to draw attention to the need for women's equal rights to land and property;

29. *Recognizes* the need to empower women, particularly poor women, economically and politically, and in this regard encourages Governments, with the support of their development partners, to invest in appropriate infrastructure and other projects, including the provision of water and sanitation to rural areas and urban slums, to increase health and well-being, relieve the workloads of women and girls and release their time and energy for other productive activities, including entrepreneurship;

30. *Also recognizes* the central role of agriculture in development, and stresses the importance of reviewing agricultural policies and strategies to ensure that women's critical role in food and nutritional security is recognized and addressed as an integral part of both short- and long-term responses to food insecurity, excessive price volatility and food crises in developing countries;

31. *Further recognizes* the critical role and contribution of rural women, including indigenous women, and their traditional knowledge, in enhancing agricultural and rural development, improving food security and eradicating rural poverty;

32. *Expresses concern* at the overall expansion of the HIV and AIDS epidemic and the fact that women and girls are still the most affected by HIV and AIDS, that they are more easily infected, that they bear a disproportionate share of the caregiving burden and that they are more vulnerable to violence, stigmatization and discrimination, poverty and marginalization from their families and communities as a result of HIV and AIDS, and taking into account that despite substantial progress, the 2010 deadline of universal access has not been met, calls upon Governments and the international community to urgently scale up responses towards achieving the goal of universal access to comprehensive HIV prevention programmes, treatment, care and support and, in line with the 2011 Political Declaration on HIV and AIDS: Intensifying Our Efforts to Eliminate HIV and AIDS, to ensure that national responses to HIV and AIDS meet the specific needs of women and girls, including those living with and affected by HIV and AIDS across their lifespan;

33. *Reaffirms* the commitment to achieve universal access to reproductive health by 2015, as set out at the International Conference on Population and Development, by integrating this goal into strategies for attaining the internationally agreed development goals, including those contained in the United Nations Millennium Declaration aimed at reducing maternal mortality, improving maternal health, reducing child mortality, promoting gender equality, combating HIV and AIDS and eradicating poverty;

34. *Urges* Governments and all sectors of society to promote and to pursue gender-based approaches to the prevention and control of non-communicable diseases based on data disaggregated by sex and age in their effort to address the critical differences in the rapidly growing magnitude of non-communicable diseases, including cardiovascular diseases, cancers, chronic respiratory diseases and diabetes, which affect people of all ages, gender, race and income levels, as noted in the Political Declaration of the High-level Meeting of the General Assembly on the Prevention and Control of Non-communicable Diseases, and notes that poor populations and those living in vulnerable situations, in particular in developing countries, bear a disproportionate burden and that non-communicable diseases can affect women and men differently, because, inter alia, women bear a disproportionate share of the burden of caregiving;

35. *Expresses deep concern* that maternal health remains one area constrained by some of the largest health inequities in the world, and over the uneven progress in improving child and maternal health, and in this context calls upon States to implement their commitments to preventing and reducing child and maternal mortality and morbidity, and welcomes in that regard the Secretary-General's Global Strategy for Women's and Children's Health as well as national, regional and international initiatives contributing to the reduction in the number of maternal deaths and deaths of the newborn and children under age 5;

36. *Recognizes* that there is a need for all donors to maintain and deliver on their existing bilateral and multilateral official development assistance commitments and targets, and that the full implementation of those commitments will substantially boost resources available to push forward the international development agenda;

37. *Also recognizes* the need to strengthen the capacity of Governments to incorporate a gender perspective into policies and decision-making, and encourages all Governments, international organizations, including the United Nations system, and other relevant stakeholders to assist and support the efforts of developing countries in integrating a gender perspective into all aspects of policymaking, including through the provision of technical assistance and financial resources;

38. *Encourages* the international community, the United Nations system, the private sector and civil society to continue to provide the financial resources necessary to assist Governments in their efforts to meet the development targets and benchmarks agreed upon at the World Summit for Social Development, the Fourth World Conference on Women, the International Conference on Population and Development, the Millennium Summit, the International Conference on Financing for Development, the World Summit on Sustainable Development, the Second World Assembly on Ageing, the twenty-third and twenty-fourth special sessions of the General Assembly and other relevant United Nations conferences and summits;

39. *Urges* multilateral donors, and invites international financial institutions, within their respective mandates, and regional development banks to review and implement policies that support national efforts to ensure that a higher proportion of resources reaches women, in particular in rural and remote areas;

40. *Stresses* the importance of improving and systematizing the collection, analysis and dissemination of data disaggregated by sex and age, and of developing gender-sensitive indicators that are specific and relevant with respect to supporting policymaking and national systems for monitoring and reporting on progress and impact, and in that regard encourages developed countries and relevant entities of the United Nations system to provide support and assistance to developing countries, upon their request, with respect to establishing, developing and strengthening their databases and information systems;

41. *Calls upon* all organizations of the United Nations system, within their organizational mandates, to mainstream a gender perspective and to pursue gender equality in their country programmes, planning instruments and sector-wide programmes and to articulate specific country-

level goals and targets in this domain in accordance with national development strategies, and welcomes the work of UN-Women with United Nations country teams in assisting Member States, at their request, in integrating a gender perspective into national development policies and strategies, in accordance with their national priorities, and stresses its important role in leading, coordinating and promoting the accountability of the United Nations system so as to ensure that the commitment to gender equality and gender mainstreaming translates into effective action throughout the world;

42. *Calls upon* the organizations of the United Nations development system, within their organizational mandates, to further improve their institutional accountability mechanisms and to include intergovernmentally agreed gender-equality results and gender-sensitive indicators in their strategic frameworks;

43. *Requests* the Secretary-General to submit to the General Assembly at its sixty-eighth session a report on the progress made in the implementation of the present resolution, including on integrating a gender perspective into national development strategies;

44. *Decides* to include in the provisional agenda of its sixty-eighth session, under the item entitled "Eradication of poverty and other development issues", the sub-item entitled "Women in development".

Women in rural areas

Pursuant to General Assembly resolution 64/140 [YUN 2009, p. 1125], the Secretary-General submitted a July report [A/66/181] on improvement of the situation of women in rural areas, which reviewed the activities undertaken by Member States and UN entities to empower rural women.

The report noted that Member States and UN entities had taken measures to improve the situation of rural women and girls as far as expanding their access to local services, land rights, technologies, and employment and entrepreneurship; and had taken steps to protect indigenous and local knowledge, promote women's contribution to climate change adaptation and mitigation, and recognize, reduce and redistribute women's disproportionate burden of unpaid care work. These initiatives benefited only a small number of communities, however, and rural women continued to be economically and socially disadvantaged because of their limited access to economic resources and opportunities and their exclusion from planning and decision-making. While there was growing recognition that rural women, including indigenous women, were critical agents in poverty reduction, food security, environmental sustainability and other aspects related to achievement of the MDGs, insufficient attention was paid to the factors that deepened inequalities between rural women and men, and inadequate action was taken to eliminate discrimination and overcome the structural disadvantages faced by women. According to the Secretary-General, achievement of the MDGs in rural areas required a more coherent, systematic and strategic integration of the economic empowerment of women and girls in rural areas into national development strategies and plans, including in the areas of rural development, infrastructure and local governance. Noting that the Commission on the Status of Women would consider the empowerment of rural women as its priority theme in 2012, the Secretary-General concluded with a set of further recommendations for consideration by the General Assembly.

GENERAL ASSEMBLY ACTION

On 19 December [meeting 89], the General Assembly, on the recommendation of the Third Committee [A/66/455 & Corr.1], adopted **resolution 66/129** without vote [agenda item 28 (*a*)].

Improvement of the situation of women in rural areas

The General Assembly,

Recalling its resolutions 56/129 of 19 December 2001, 58/146 of 22 December 2003, 60/138 of 16 December 2005, 62/136 of 18 December 2007 and 64/140 of 18 December 2009,

Welcoming the decision of the Commission on the Status of Women to consider the empowerment of rural women and their role in poverty and hunger eradication, development and current challenges as its priority theme at its fifty-sixth session, in 2012,

Recognizing that rural women are critical agents in poverty reduction, that they are crucial to the achievement of food and nutritional security in poor and vulnerable households and to environmental sustainability and that, in other ways, they are also critical to the achievement of all the Millennium Development Goals, and concerned that rural women continue to be economically and socially disadvantaged because of their limited access to economic resources and opportunities, their limited or lack of access to land, water and other resources, their limited or lack of access to credit, extension services and agricultural inputs, their exclusion from planning and decision-making and their disproportionate burden of unpaid care work,

1. *Takes note* of the report of the Secretary-General;

2. *Urges* Member States, in collaboration with the organizations of the United Nations and civil society, as appropriate, to continue their efforts to implement the outcome of and to ensure an integrated and coordinated follow-up to the relevant United Nations conferences and summits, including their reviews, and to attach greater importance to the improvement of the situation of rural women, including indigenous women, in their national, regional and global development strategies by, inter alia:

(*a*) Creating an enabling environment for improving the situation of rural women and ensuring systematic attention to their needs, priorities and contributions, including through enhanced cooperation and a gender perspective, and their full participation in the development, implementation and follow-up of macroeconomic policies, including development policies and programmes and poverty eradication strategies, including poverty reduction strategy papers, where they exist, based on internationally agreed development goals, including the Millennium Development Goals;

(b) Pursuing the political and socioeconomic empowerment of rural women and supporting their full and equal participation in decision-making at all levels, including through affirmative action, where appropriate, and support for women's organizations, labour unions or other associations and civil society groups promoting rural women's rights;

(c) Promoting consultation with and the participation of rural women, including indigenous women and women with disabilities, through their organizations and networks, in the design, development and implementation of gender equality and rural development programmes and strategies;

(d) Ensuring that perspectives of rural women are taken into account and that they participate in the design, implementation, follow-up and evaluation of policies and activities related to emergencies, including natural disasters, humanitarian assistance, peacebuilding and post-conflict reconstruction, and taking appropriate measures to eliminate all forms of discrimination against rural women in this regard;

(e) Integrating a gender perspective into the design, implementation and evaluation of and follow-up to development policies and programmes, including budget policies, paying increased attention to the needs of rural women so as to ensure that they benefit from policies and programmes adopted in all spheres and that the disproportionate number of rural women living in poverty is reduced;

(f) Strengthening measures, including resource generation, to accelerate progress towards the achievement of Millennium Development Goal 5 on improving maternal health by addressing the specific health needs of rural women and taking concrete measures to enhance and provide access to the highest attainable standards of health for women in rural areas, as well as quality, affordable and universally accessible primary health care and support services, including in such areas of sexual and reproductive health as prenatal and postnatal health care, emergency obstetric care, family planning information and increasing knowledge, awareness and support for the prevention of sexually transmitted diseases, including HIV/AIDS;

(g) Promoting sustainable infrastructure, access to safe and clean drinking water and sanitation and safe cooking and heating practices, to improve the health of rural women and children;

(h) Investing in and strengthening efforts to meet the basic needs of rural women, including needs relating to their food and nutritional security and that of their families, and to promote adequate standards of living for them as well as decent conditions for work and access to local, regional and global markets through improved availability, access to and use of critical rural infrastructure, such as energy and transport, science and technology, local services, capacity-building and human resources development measures and the provision of a safe and reliable water supply and sanitation, nutritional programmes, affordable housing programmes, education and literacy programmes, and health and social support measures, including in the areas of sexual and reproductive health, and HIV/AIDS prevention, treatment, care, including psychosocial aspects, and support services;

(i) Designing and implementing national policies that promote and protect the enjoyment by rural women and girls of all human rights and fundamental freedoms and creating an environment that does not tolerate violations or abuses of their rights, including domestic violence, sexual violence and all other forms of gender-based violence;

(j) Ensuring that the rights of older women in rural areas are taken into account with regard to their equal access to basic social services, appropriate social protection/social security measures, equal access to and control of economic resources, and empowerment of older women through access to financial and infrastructure services, with special focus on support to older women, including indigenous women, who often have access to few resources and are more vulnerable;

(k) Promoting the rights of women and girls with disabilities in rural areas, including by ensuring access on an equal basis to productive employment and decent work, economic and financial resources and disability-sensitive infrastructure and services, in particular in relation to health and education, as well as by ensuring that their priorities and needs are fully incorporated into policies and programmes, inter alia, through their participation in decision-making processes;

(l) Developing specific assistance programmes and advisory services to promote economic skills of rural women in banking, modern trading and financial procedures, and providing microcredit and other financial and business services to a greater number of women in rural areas, in particular female heads of households, for their economic empowerment;

(m) Mobilizing resources, including at the national level and through official development assistance, for increasing women's access to existing savings and credit schemes, as well as targeted programmes that provide women with capital, knowledge and tools that enhance their economic capacities;

(n) Integrating increased employment opportunities for rural women into all international and national development strategies and poverty eradication strategies, including by, inter alia, expanding non-agricultural employment opportunities, improving working conditions and increasing access to productive resources;

(o) Investing in infrastructure and in time- and labour-saving technologies, especially in rural areas, benefiting women and girls by reducing their burden of domestic activities, affording the opportunity for girls to attend school and women to engage in self-employment or participate in the labour market;

(p) Taking steps towards ensuring that women's unpaid work and contributions to on-farm and off-farm production, including income generated in the informal sector, are recognized, and supporting remunerative non-agricultural employment of rural women, improving working conditions and increasing access to productive resources;

(q) Promoting programmes and services to enable rural women and men to reconcile their work and family responsibilities and to encourage men to share, equally with women, household, childcare and other care responsibilities;

(r) Developing strategies to decrease women's vulnerability to environmental factors while promoting rural women's role in protecting the environment;

(s) Considering the adoption, where appropriate, of national legislation to protect the knowledge, innovations and practices of women in indigenous and local communities relating to traditional medicines, biodiversity and indigenous technologies;

(t) Addressing the lack of timely, reliable and sex-disaggregated data, including by intensifying efforts to include women's unpaid work in official statistics, and developing a systematic and comparative research base on rural women that will inform policy and programme decisions;

(u) Strengthening the capacity of national statistical offices to collect, analyse and disseminate comparable sex-disaggregated data, including on time use, and gender statistics in rural areas to serve as a basis for gender-responsive policy design and strategy development in rural areas;

(v) Designing, revising and implementing laws to ensure that rural women are accorded full and equal rights to own and lease land and other property, including through the equal right to inheritance, and undertaking administrative reforms and all necessary measures to give women the same right as men to credit, capital, appropriate technologies and access to markets and information, and to ensure equal access to justice and legal support;

(w) Supporting a gender-sensitive education system that considers the specific needs of rural women in order to eliminate gender stereotypes and discriminatory tendencies affecting them, including through community-based dialogue involving women and men, and girls and boys;

(x) Promoting education, training and relevant information programmes for rural and farming women through the use of affordable and appropriate technologies and the mass media;

(y) Developing the capacity of personnel working in the areas of national development strategies, rural development, agricultural development, poverty eradication and implementation of the Millennium Development Goals to identify and address the challenges and constraints facing rural women, including through training programmes and the development and dissemination of methodologies and tools, while acknowledging technical assistance of relevant United Nations agencies;

3. *Strongly encourages* Member States, United Nations entities and all other relevant stakeholders to take measures to identify and address any negative impact of the current global crises on women in rural areas, including on legislation, policies and programmes that strengthen gender equality and the empowerment of women;

4. *Requests* the relevant organizations and bodies of the United Nations system, in particular those dealing with issues of development, to address and support the empowerment of rural women and their specific needs in their programmes and strategies;

5. *Stresses* the need to identify the best practices for ensuring that rural women have access to and full participation in the area of information and communications technology, to address the priorities and needs of rural women and girls as active users of information and to ensure their participation in developing and implementing global, regional and national information and communications technology strategies, taking appropriate educational measures to eliminate gender stereotypes regarding women in the field of technology;

6. *Calls upon* Member States to consider the concluding observations and recommendations of the Committee on the Elimination of Discrimination against Women concerning their reports to the Committee when formulating policies and designing programmes focused on the improvement of the situation of rural women, including those to be developed and implemented in cooperation with relevant international organizations;

7. *Invites* Governments to promote the economic empowerment of rural women, to adopt gender-responsive rural development strategies, including budget framework and relevant assessment measures, and to ensure that the needs and priorities of rural women and girls are systematically addressed and that they can effectively contribute to poverty alleviation, hunger eradication and food and nutritional security;

8. *Encourages* Governments and international organizations to integrate the perspective of women in rural areas, including indigenous women, into the preparations for and outcome of the United Nations Conference on Sustainable Development, to be held in Rio de Janeiro, Brazil, from 20 to 22 June 2012, with a view to accelerating progress on gender equality and women's empowerment in rural areas;

9. *Invites* Governments, relevant international organizations and the specialized agencies to continue to observe the International Day of Rural Women annually, on 15 October, as proclaimed by the General Assembly in its resolution 62/136;

10. *Requests* the Secretary-General to report to the General Assembly at its sixty-eighth session on the implementation of the present resolution.

Education and training of women

Reports of Secretary-General. In accordance with Economic and Social Council resolution 2009/15 [YUN 2009, p. 1155], the Secretary-General submitted a report [E/CN.6/2011/3] on access and participation of women and girls in education, training, science and technology, including for the promotion of women's equal access to full employment and decent work.

The report underlined that ensuring women's equal access to scientific and technological knowledge and skills was a rights issue, inasmuch as education was a basic human right, but also an economic imperative, as doing so would widen the pool of human resources available to apply technology and carry out research and development. Progress had been made in expanding access to basic education for girls—a prerequisite for acquiring literacy and numeracy skills, basic scientific knowledge and technological competencies—but evidence suggested that vocational education was marked by strong gender segregation, with women underrepresented in technical subject areas. As far as employment, women remained underrepresented in the field of research and development; few women were leaders at scientific institutions, members of scientific boards or headed large technology companies; and women scientists and engineers faced difficulty in gaining recognition for their work and progressing in their career. The report also noted the importance of ensuring that the focus of science and its applications responded to women's needs and situations, and that national and international research priorities benefited women and men equally.

The Secretary-General concluded that greater attention must be paid to gender-equality issues in science, technology and innovation. Increasing women's access to scientific knowledge and technology; promoting women's participation in science and technology education; and ensuring that women contributed to science, technology and innovation could contribute to accelerating development. He recommended that the Commission on the Status of Women call on Governments, the UN system and other stakeholders to mainstream a gender perspective in all science, technology and innovation policies and programmes; develop national strategies to increase the participation of women and girls in science and technology education and training and employment; promote a positive image of careers in science and technology for women; and ensure gender parity in decision-making positions in science academies, funding institutions, academia and the public and private sector.

Also in accordance with resolution 2009/15 [YUN 2009, p. 1155], the Secretary-General submitted a report [E/CN.6/2011/5] on progress in mainstreaming a gender perspective in the development, implementation and evaluation of national policies and programmes, with a particular focus on access and participation of women and girls in education, training, science and technology, including for the promotion of women's equal access to full employment and decent work.

Despite an expansion of educational opportunities in the preceding decades, which included a larger share of the world's population accessing formal education and a steady improvement in the global ratio of girls' to boys' enrolment, gender gaps remained in education access. Particularly in sub-Saharan Africa, Western Asia and Southern Asia, access to post-primary education remained restricted for women and girls. Gender disparities in terms of access and occupational segregation were often more pronounced in technical and vocational education than in general education, and women and girls remained overrepresented in the humanities and social sciences and underrepresented in science and engineering. Narrowed gaps in education access were visible in countries that undertook reforms to address the disadvantages faced by girls, which included financial and cultural barriers. Initiatives included recruiting female teachers, providing incentives for their deployment to rural areas, giving teachers gender-sensitization training and building satellite schools. Financial incentives for families with limited resources helped increase girls' enrolment, as did awareness-raising campaigns to convince parents of the importance of girls' education. As early marriage or pregnancy could force girls to drop out of school, Government measures included education code revisions allowing teenage mothers to return to school. Concerns about girls' safety, particularly their vulnerability to sexual violence on the way to or within school, were addressed by some Governments through investment in water, energy or transportation infrastructure. Non-formal training—a complement to formal education that could reach out-of-school women and girls—was of particular importance to emergency-affected countries, while non-formal education remained a critical tool for eradicating illiteracy among adult women.

Women's labour force participation increased, but not on par with educational gains, and the quality of women's employment had not much improved. Among the 20- to 24-year-old population, women continued to lag behind men in all regions. South Asia recorded the greatest gap, with 82 per cent of men employed or seeking employment compared with 27 per cent of women. Furthermore, progress towards full employment was not always connected to decent work. Women entered the labour market, but in jobs that paid less, and did not guarantee worker's rights, extend social protection or promote social dialogue.

The Secretary-General highlighted the need to regularly evaluate the impact of initiatives at the national level to determine the most effective way of reducing gender gaps in education. More attention to the transition by young women from school to work was needed to ensure that gains in education translated into employment opportunities. He suggested that the Commission consider calling on Governments, the UN system and other relevant actors to systematically mainstream a gender perspective in all education and employment policies and programmes, and monitor and evaluate the impact on women and men; take measures to eliminate inequalities related to age, poverty, geographical location, language, ethnicity, religion and disability affecting women and girls in accessing and participating in education at all levels; remove economic barriers to girls' education; ensure women's and girls' equal access to technical and vocational training; and ensure that secondary and tertiary institutions equip women and girls with job readiness skills and provide career guidance.

Commission action. On 22 February, as part of the priority theme for its fifty-fifth session [E/2011/27], the Commission on the Status of Women held a high-level round table on access and participation of women and girls in education, training, science and technology, including for the promotion of women's equal access to full employment and decent work. On 23 February, the Commission held two panel discussions on key policy initiatives and capacity-building on gender mainstreaming; one focused on science and technology and the other on education and training.

In its agreed conclusions on the priority theme, the Commission underlined that addressing the barriers to equal access of women and girls to education, training and science and technology required a systematic, comprehensive, integrated, sustainable, multidisciplinary and multisectoral approach, including policy, legislative and programmatic interventions and gender-responsive budgeting. It urged Governments and other stakeholders to strengthen national legislation, policies and programmes; expand access and participation in education; strengthen gender-sensitive education and training, including in science and technology; support the transition from education to full employment and decent work; increase retention and progression of women in science and technology employment; and make science and technology responsive to women's needs.

Extension of Gender Advisory Board. On 26 July, the Economic and Social Council extended the mandate of the Gender Advisory Board of the Commission on Science and Technology for Development [YUN 1995, p. 850] for a further three years, beginning on 1 January 2012 (**decision 2011/235**).

Women and health

Women, the girl child and HIV/AIDS

Report of Secretary-General. Pursuant to Commission on the Status of Women resolution 54/2 [YUN 2010, p. 1140], the Secretary-General submitted a report [E/CN.6/2011/7] on women, the girl child and HIV and AIDS, which provided information on the activities undertaken by Member States and within the UN system to implement that resolution. He reported that many Member States had integrated gender perspectives into their national HIV/AIDS response, or included measures on HIV and AIDS in gender equality strategies and action plans. Legislation, strategies, policies and programmes on HIV and AIDS needed to address the gender dimension of the epidemic and prioritize women's needs, with corresponding budget allocations. Efforts to improve access for women to HIV prevention, treatment, care and support should be scaled up, including through strengthening the accessibility of quality public health care, such as integrated HIV and sexual and reproductive health services. Although many Member States had taken measures to prevent mother-to-child transmission, including by providing antiretroviral treatment for pregnant women and offering HIV testing, women continued to lack access to those services. Furthermore, there should be continued efforts among Member States to increase antiretroviral treatment coverage among women and girls, including at-risk populations, and ensure the initiation of treatment at an early stage of the disease. The Secretary-General also recommended that awareness-raising efforts by Governments and other stakeholders on HIV and AIDS and sexual and reproductive health be continued and directed at the general public, students, and health and other professionals; and also be targeted at specific groups such as men and boys and high-risk groups of women, including female sex workers. Governments and other stakeholders should take measures to create enabling environments that empowered women and girls and reduced their vulnerability to HIV. While efforts had been made to better understand the gender dimensions of the epidemic, more information related to HIV and AIDS and its impact on women and girls was needed, and efforts had to be strengthened to collect and analyse such data.

Commission action. On 4 March, the Commission on the Status of Women adopted a resolution [E/2011/27 (res. 55/2)] on women, the girl child and HIV and AIDS, which stressed the need to increase and coordinate political and financial commitments to address gender equality and equity in national HIV and AIDS responses, and urged Governments to reflect in their national policies, strategies and budgets the gender dimension of the pandemic. It urged Governments and stakeholders to address the increased vulnerability to HIV faced by women and girls living with disabilities; the challenges faced by older women in accessing HIV treatment, care and support; and the situation faced by girls caring for people living with or affected by HIV and AIDS. It called upon Governments to develop and implement policies and programmes to eliminate HIV-related stigma and discrimination; create an environment for the empowerment of women and girls to enable them to protect themselves from HIV infection; integrate HIV prevention and voluntary counselling and testing into other health services; and promote the participation of people living with HIV, young people and civil society, particularly women's organizations, in addressing all aspects of HIV and AIDS.

Eliminating maternal mortality

On 1 March, the Commission on the Status of Women [E/2011/27], in response to its resolution 54/5 [YUN 2010, p. 1143], convened an expert panel on the elimination of preventable maternal mortality and morbidity and the empowerment of women. The panel was an opportunity to gauge progress in addressing maternal mortality; identify good practices and successful interventions; and discuss ways and means for accelerating action on measurably reducing and eliminating maternal mortality and achieving MDG 5 (a three-quarters reduction in maternal mortality and universal access to reproductive health). Participants noted that the average annual percentage decline in the global maternal mortality ratio was 2.3 per cent, well short of the 5.5 per cent annual decline needed to meet the MDG target. Large disparities between regions remained. In sub-Saharan Africa, a woman's risk of dying from preventable or treatable complications of pregnancy and childbirth over the course of her lifetime was 1 in 31, compared with 1 in 4,300 in developed regions.

Participants addressed measures and initiatives such as investment in education; investment in the economic empowerment of women; effective leadership and strategic partnerships, including multi-stakeholder partnerships; and the Secretary-General's Global Strategy for Women and Children's Health [YUN 2010, p. 1140], whose Information and Accountability Commission issued a May report, *Keeping Promises, Measuring Results*, presenting an accountability framework to measure and track the Global Strategy's results and resources. The panel agreed that greater focus should be placed on developing and strengthening national-level leadership and partnerships, and that—as financial resources remained inadequate—donor countries had to meet their pledges, and official development assistance needed to be invested in social services that benefited the health needs of women and girls.

Violence against women

On 1 August, pursuant to General Assembly resolution 65/187 [YUN 2010, p. 1145], the Special Rapporteur on violence against women, its causes and consequences submitted to the General Assembly her first written report [A/66/215], which reviewed the mandate's work, main findings and challenges, and presented recommendations to address violence against women through a framework based on States' obligations to respect, protect and fulfil the human rights of women and girls (see p. 737).

Trust Fund activities. In response to General Assembly resolution 50/166 [YUN 1995, p. 1188], the Secretary-General transmitted to the Human Rights Council and the Commission on the Status of Women a December report [A/HRC/19/30-E/CN.6/2012/13] of UN-Women (see p. 1093) on the 2011 activities of the United Nations Trust Fund in Support of Actions to Eliminate Violence against Women. Guided by its 2010–2015 strategic plan, "Vision 2015" [YUN 2010, p. 1145], the Fund awarded $17.1 million in new grants to 22 initiatives in 34 countries. This included close to $4 million in support for five new projects in conflict and post-conflict settings, and, for the first time, the provision of grants to projects in Iraq and South Sudan. Most new grants (81 per cent) were awarded to civil society organizations, followed by governmental organizations (13 per cent) and UN country teams (6 per cent). Grants distributed during the fifteenth (2011) grant-making cycle were expected to reach over 6 million beneficiaries between 2011 and 2014.

By the end of the year, the Fund had a portfolio of 96 active grants covering 86 countries and territories with a total value of more than $61 million. Africa had the largest portfolio (32 per cent), followed by Asia and the Pacific (25 per cent), Latin America and the Caribbean (19 per cent), Central and Eastern Europe and the Commonwealth of Independent States (12 per cent), and the Arab States region (5 per cent). Cross-regional programmes accounted for 7 per cent of the entire portfolio.

Violence against women migrant workers

Pursuant to General Assembly resolution 64/139 [YUN 2009, p. 1134], the Secretary-General submitted a July report [A/66/212] on measures taken by 23 Member States, 5 UN entities and the International Organization for Migration (IOM) to address and prevent violence and discrimination against women migrant workers. States also provided information on anti-trafficking policies and programmes.

The global number of international migrants was estimated at 214 million in 2010, with women accounting for 49 per cent. Many migrant women were at risk for gender-based violence, discrimination and exploitation, and those with irregular immigration status, limited access to information or language skills, restrictions on their freedom of movement by employers, lack of access to justice, or who were starting out in destination countries in a state of debt and dependency, were particularly vulnerable. Violence against women migrant workers had an adverse affect on social and economic development, to which they actively contributed in their countries of origin and destination.

The report noted that States, sometimes with the support of UN entities and IOM, continued to strengthen legal frameworks, policies, national action plans and strategies that contributed to preventing violence and discrimination against women migrant workers. Promising actions included extending labour laws to cover domestic workers; introducing standardized contractual arrangements for domestic workers; regulating and monitoring recruitment agencies to prevent abusive and illegal practices; disseminating information to potential migrant women to promote legal migration; training officials; raising public awareness about combating violence, racism and xenophobia against women migrant workers; and providing services to women migrant workers who were victims of violence. Bilateral and multilateral agreements and cooperation provided a strong basis for addressing discrimination and violence against women migrant workers. At the same time, key gaps persisted in respect of implementing global normative and policy frameworks related to protecting women migrant workers against discrimination, violence and violations of their rights. The knowledge base remained inadequate, and gaps persisted in data collection and dissemination, and in the research and analysis needed to inform policy and programme interventions. There was also little reporting on the impact of measures taken and results achieved in regard to women migrant workers.

The Secretary-General concluded that national labour laws should protect women migrant workers—including domestic workers—and that immigration laws should incorporate gender perspectives to prevent discrimination against women. States should ensure policy coherence among gender-sensitive and rights-based policies and programmes on migration, labour and anti-trafficking; and facilitate effective action in law enforcement and prosecution, prevention, capacity-building, victim protection and the support and exchange of information and good practices. Education programmes, awareness-raising and other prevention efforts directed at migrant women, recruiting and employment agencies, employers, the media, public officials and the general population should continue in origin and destination countries. The Secretary-General recommended that States continue to ratify and implement international instruments, with a special focus on early ratification of the Convention No. 189 concerning Decent Work for Domestic Workers and the accompanying Recommendation No. 201, adopted by the General Conference of the International Labour Organization on 16 June. The new Convention, a major addition to the international human rights framework relevant to women migrant workers, proposed measures to protect domestic workers against violence, harassment and abuse; promote and protect their labour rights; and encouraged States to conclude bilateral, regional or multilateral agreements to further protect overseas domestic workers.

GENERAL ASSEMBLY ACTION

On 19 December [meeting 89], the General Assembly, on the recommendation of the Third Committee [A/66/455 & Corr.1], adopted **resolution 66/128** without vote [agenda item 28 (*a*)].

Violence against women migrant workers

The General Assembly,

Recalling all of its previous resolutions on violence against women migrant workers and those adopted by the Commission on the Status of Women, the Commission on Human Rights and the Commission on Crime Prevention and Criminal Justice, and the Declaration on the Elimination of Violence against Women;

Reaffirming the provisions concerning women migrant workers contained in the outcome documents of the World Conference on Human Rights, the International Conference on Population and Development, the Fourth World Conference on Women and the World Summit for Social Development and their reviews,

Welcoming the establishment of the United Nations Entity for Gender Equality and the Empowerment of Women (UN-Women), and expressing the hope that it will robustly support national efforts to increase women's access to economic opportunities, especially for those who are most excluded, including women migrant workers, and to end violence against women migrant workers, in the light of the UN-Women strategic plan, 2011–2013, which has among its six goals increasing women's access to economic opportunities, and preventing violence against women and girls and expanding access to survivor services, and the policy and programmatic work of UN-Women on empowering women migrant workers,

Welcoming also the agreed conclusions adopted by the Commission on the Status of Women during its fifty-fifth session, and taking note, in particular, of the commitment, as appropriate, to implement gender-sensitive policies and programmes for women migrant workers, to ensure that all women, including care workers, are legally protected against violence and exploitation, to provide safe and legal channels that recognize women migrant workers' skills and education and fair labour conditions, and to facilitate their productive employment and decent work and integration into the labour force,

Recalling the discussions during the High-level Dialogue on International Migration and Development, held on 14 and 15 September 2006, which recognized, inter alia, the need for special protection for migrant women, and noting that another high-level dialogue on the same theme will be held in 2013,

Welcoming the adoption of Convention No. 189 and Recommendation No. 201 on decent work for domestic workers by the International Labour Conference on 16 June 2011, at its one-hundredth session, noting the importance of the early entry into force of Convention No. 189 and encouraging States to consider ratifying it, encouraging States parties to the Convention on the Elimination of All Forms of Discrimination against Women to take note of and consider general recommendation No. 26 on women migrant workers adopted by the Committee on the Elimination of Discrimination against Women in November 2008, and encouraging States parties to the International Convention on the Protection of the Rights of All Migrant Workers and Members of Their Families to take note of and consider general comment No. 1 on migrant domestic workers adopted by the Committee on the Protection of the Rights of All Migrant Workers and Members of Their Families in December 2010, acknowledging that they are complementary and mutually reinforcing,

Recognizing the increasing participation of women in international migration, driven in large part by socioeconomic factors, and that this feminization of migration requires greater gender sensitivity in all policies and efforts related to the subject of international migration,

Stressing the shared responsibility of all stakeholders, in particular countries of origin, transit and destination, relevant regional and international organizations, the private sector and civil society, in promoting an environment that prevents and addresses violence against women migrant workers, including in the context of discrimination, through targeted measures, and in this regard recognizing the importance of joint and collaborative approaches and strategies at the national, bilateral, regional and international levels,

Recognizing that women migrant workers are important contributors to social and economic development, through the economic and social impacts, as a result of their work, on countries of origin and destination, and underlining the value and dignity of their labour, including the labour of domestic workers,

Recognizing also the particular vulnerability of women and their children at all stages of the migration process, extending from the moment of deciding to migrate, and including transit, engagement in formal and informal employment, and integration into the host society, as well as during their return to and reintegration in their countries of origin,

Expressing deep concern at the continuing reports of grave abuses and violence committed against migrant women and girls, including gender-based violence, in particular sexual violence, domestic and family violence, racist and xenophobic acts, abusive labour practices, exploitative conditions of work, and contemporary forms of slavery, including all forms of forced labour, and trafficking in persons,

Recognizing that the intersection of, inter alia, gender, age, class and ethnic discrimination and stereotypes can compound the discrimination faced by women migrant workers, and that gender-based violence is a form of discrimination,

Reaffirming the commitment to protect and promote the human rights of all women, including, without discrimination, indigenous women who migrate for work, and in this regard noting the attention paid in the United Nations Declaration on the Rights of Indigenous Peoples to the elimination of all forms of violence and discrimination against indigenous women, as appropriate,

Noting that the priority theme of the fifty-sixth session of the Commission on the Status of Women will be "The empowerment of rural women and their role in poverty and hunger eradication, development and current challenges", and in this regard recognizing the role and contribution of rural women migrant workers towards poverty eradication and development in their communities,

Concerned that many migrant women who are employed in the informal economy and in less skilled work are especially vulnerable to abuse and exploitation, underlining in this regard the obligation of States to protect the human rights of migrants so as to prevent and address abuse and exploitation, and observing with concern that many women migrant workers take on jobs for which they may be overqualified and in which, at the same time, they may be more vulnerable because of poor pay and inadequate social protection,

Emphasizing the need for objective, comprehensive and broad-based information, including sex- and age-disaggregated data and statistics, and gender-sensitive indicators for research and analysis, and a wide exchange of experience and lessons learned by individual Member States and civil society in the formulation of targeted policies and concrete strategies to specifically address violence against women migrant workers, including in the context of discrimination,

Realizing that the movement of a significant number of women migrant workers may be facilitated and made possible by means of fraudulent or irregular documentation and sham marriages with the object of migration, that this may be facilitated through, inter alia, the Internet and that those women migrant workers are more vulnerable to abuse and exploitation,

Recognizing the importance of exploring the link between migration and trafficking in persons in order to further efforts towards protecting women migrant workers from violence, discrimination, exploitation and abuse,

Encouraged by some measures adopted by some countries of destination to alleviate the plight of women migrant workers residing in their areas of jurisdiction and to promote access to justice, such as the establishment of gender-sensitive protection mechanisms for migrant workers, facilitating their access to mechanisms for reporting complaints or providing assistance during legal proceedings,

Underlining the important role of relevant United Nations treaty bodies in monitoring the implementation of human rights conventions, and the relevant special procedures, within their respective mandates, in addressing the problem of violence against women migrant workers and in protecting and promoting their human rights and welfare,

1. *Takes note with appreciation* of the report of the Secretary-General;

2. *Encourages* Member States to consider signing and ratifying or acceding to relevant International Labour Organization conventions and to consider signing and ratifying or acceding to the International Convention on the Protection of the Rights of All Migrant Workers and Members of Their Families, the Protocol to Prevent, Suppress and Punish Trafficking in Persons, Especially Women and Children, supplementing the United Nations Convention against Transnational Organized Crime, the Protocol against the Smuggling of Migrants by Land, Sea and Air, supplementing the United Nations Convention against Transnational Organized Crime, the 1954 Convention relating to the Status of Stateless Persons and the 1961 Convention on the Reduction of Statelessness, as well as all other human rights treaties that contribute to the protection of the rights of women migrant workers, and also encourages Member States to implement the United Nations Global Plan of Action to Combat Trafficking in Persons;

3. *Takes note* of the report of the Special Rapporteur of the Human Rights Council on violence against women, its causes and consequences, entitled "Political economy of women's human rights", submitted to the Council at its eleventh session, in particular her elaboration in that report of the current issues of the exploitation and violence that women migrants face in the context of the current global economic trends and crises;

4. *Encourages* all United Nations special rapporteurs on human rights whose mandates touch on the issues of violence against women migrant workers to improve the collection of information on and analysis of those areas within their mandates relating to the current challenges

facing women migrant workers, and also encourages Governments to cooperate with the special rapporteurs in this regard;

5. *Calls upon* all Governments to incorporate a human rights, gender-sensitive and people-centred perspective in legislation, policies and programmes on international migration and on labour and employment, consistent with their human rights obligations and commitments under human rights instruments, for the prevention of and protection of migrant women against violence and discrimination, exploitation and abuse, to take effective measures to ensure that such migration and labour policies do not reinforce discrimination, and, where necessary, to conduct impact assessment studies of such legislation, policies and programmes in order to identify the impact of measures taken and the results achieved in regard to women migrant workers;

6. *Calls upon* Governments to adopt or strengthen measures to protect the human rights of women migrant workers, regardless of their immigration status, including in policies that regulate the recruitment and deployment of women migrant workers, and to consider expanding dialogue among States on devising innovative methods to promote legal channels of migration, inter alia, in order to deter illegal migration, to consider incorporating a gender perspective into immigration laws in order to prevent discrimination and violence against women, including in independent, circular and temporary migration, and to consider permitting, in accordance with national legislation, women migrant workers who are victims of violence to apply for residency permits independently of abusive employers or spouses;

7. *Urges* Governments to enhance bilateral, regional, interregional and international cooperation to address violence against women migrant workers, fully respecting international law, including international human rights law, as well as to strengthen efforts to reduce the vulnerability of women migrant workers by facilitating effective access to justice and effective action in the areas of law enforcement, prosecution, prevention, capacity-building, and victim protection and support, by exchanging information and good practices in combating violence and discrimination against women migrant workers and by fostering sustainable development alternatives to migration in countries of origin;

8. *Also urges* Governments to take into account the best interests of the child by adopting or strengthening measures to promote and protect the human rights of migrant girls, including unaccompanied girls, regardless of their immigration status, so as to prevent labour and economic exploitation, discrimination, sexual harassment, violence and sexual abuse in the workplace, including in domestic work;

9. *Further urges* Governments to strongly encourage all stakeholders, especially the private sector, including employment agencies involved in recruiting women migrant workers, to strengthen the focus on and funding support for the prevention of violence against women migrant workers, in particular by promoting the access of women to meaningful and gender-sensitive information and education on, inter alia, the costs and benefits of migration, rights and benefits to which they are entitled in the countries of origin and employment, overall conditions in countries of employment and procedures for legal migration, as well as to ensure that laws and policies governing recruiters, employers and intermediaries promote adherence to and respect for the human rights of migrant workers, particularly women;

10. *Encourages* all States to remove obstacles that may prevent the transparent, safe, unrestricted and expeditious transfer of remittances of migrants to their countries of origin or to any other countries, including, where appropriate, by reducing transaction costs and implementing woman-friendly remittance transfer, savings and investment schemes, including diaspora investment schemes, in conformity with applicable national legislation, and to consider, as appropriate, measures to solve other problems that may impede women migrant workers' access to and management of their economic resources;

11. *Calls upon* Governments to recognize the right of women migrant workers, regardless of their immigration status, to have access to emergency health care, and in this regard to ensure that women migrant workers are not discriminated against on the grounds of pregnancy and childbirth and, in accordance with national legislation, to address the vulnerabilities to HIV experienced by migrant populations and support their access to HIV prevention, treatment, care and support;

12. *Urges* States that have not yet done so to adopt and implement legislation and policies that protect all women migrant domestic workers and to include therein, and improve where necessary, relevant monitoring and inspection measures in line with applicable International Labour Organization conventions and other instruments to ensure compliance with international obligations, and to grant women migrant workers in domestic service access to gender-sensitive, transparent mechanisms for bringing complaints against employers, while stressing that such instruments should not punish women migrant workers, and calls upon States to promptly investigate and punish all violations of their rights;

13. *Calls upon* Governments, in cooperation with international organizations, non-governmental organizations, the private sector and other stakeholders, to provide women migrant workers who are victims of violence, irrespective of their immigration status, in line with domestic legislation, with the full range of emergency assistance and protection and, to the extent possible, gender-sensitive services that are culturally and linguistically appropriate, in accordance with relevant international human rights instruments and applicable conventions;

14. *Also calls upon* Governments, in particular those of the countries of origin and destination, to put in place penal and criminal sanctions in order to punish perpetrators of violence against women migrant workers and intermediaries, and gender-sensitive redress and justice mechanisms that victims can access effectively and that allow their views and concerns to be presented and considered at appropriate stages of proceedings, including other measures that will allow victims to be present during the judicial process, when possible, and to protect women migrant workers who are victims of violence from revictimization, including by authorities;

15. *Urges* all States to adopt effective measures to put an end to the arbitrary arrest and detention of women migrant workers and to take action to prevent and punish any form of illegal deprivation of the liberty of women migrant workers by individuals or groups;

16. *Encourages* Governments to formulate and implement training programmes for their law enforcers, immigration officers and border officials, diplomatic and consular officials, prosecutors and service providers, with a view to sensitizing those public-sector workers to the issue of violence against women migrant workers and imparting to them the necessary skills and attitude to ensure the delivery of proper, professional and gender-sensitive interventions;

17. *Also encourages* Governments to promote coherence between migration, labour and anti-trafficking policies and programmes concerning women migrant workers, based on a human rights, gender-sensitive and people-centred perspective, to ensure that the human rights of women migrant workers are protected throughout the migration process, and to enhance efforts to prevent violence against women migrant workers, prosecute perpetrators and protect and support victims and their families;

18. *Calls upon* States, in accordance with the provisions of article 36 of the Vienna Convention on Consular Relations, to ensure that, if a woman migrant worker is arrested or committed to prison or custody pending trial, or is detained in any other manner, the competent authorities respect her freedom to communicate with and have access to the consular officials of the country of her nationality, and in this regard to inform without delay, if that woman migrant worker so requests, the consular post of her State of nationality;

19. *Invites* the United Nations system and other concerned intergovernmental and non-governmental organizations to cooperate with Governments, within existing resources, towards a better understanding of the issues concerning women and international migration, and to improve the collection, dissemination and analysis of sex- and age-disaggregated data and information in order to assist in the formulation of migration and labour policies that are, inter alia, gender-sensitive and that protect human rights, as well as to aid in policy assessment and to continue to support national efforts to address violence against women migrant workers in a coordinated way that ensures effective implementation, enhances their impact and strengthens positive outcomes for women migrant workers;

20. *Encourages* Governments to formulate national policies concerning women migrant workers that are based on up-to-date, relevant sex-disaggregated data and analysis in close consultation with women migrant workers and relevant stakeholders throughout the policy process, and also encourages Governments to ensure that such process is adequately resourced and that the resulting policies have measurable targets and indicators, timetables and monitoring and accountability measures, in particular for employment agencies, employers and public officials, and provide for impact assessments and ensure multi-sector coordination within and between countries of origin, transit and destination through appropriate mechanisms;

21. *Encourages* concerned Governments, in particular those of the countries of origin, transit and destination, to avail themselves of the expertise of the United Nations, including the Statistics Division of the Department of Economic and Social Affairs of the Secretariat, and UN-Women, to develop and enhance appropriate sex-disaggregated national data-collection, analysis and dissemination methodologies that will generate comparable data, and tracking and reporting systems on violence against women migrant workers and, wherever possible, violations of their rights at all stages of the migration process, and:

(*a*) To further study the costs of violence against women, including migrant workers, to the women themselves, their families and their communities;

(*b*) To analyse the opportunities available to women migrant workers and their impact on development;

(*c*) To support the improvement of macrodata on remittances, for appropriate policy formulation and implementation;

22. *Requests* the Secretary-General to provide a comprehensive, analytical and thematic report to the General Assembly at its sixty-eighth session on the problem of violence against women migrant workers and on the implementation of the present resolution, specifically with regard to access to justice for women migrant workers, highlighting the impact of legislation, policies and programmes on women migrant workers, taking into account updated information from the organizations of the United Nations system, in particular the International Labour Organization, the United Nations Development Programme, UN-Women and the United Nations Office on Drugs and Crime, as well as the reports of special rapporteurs that refer to the situation of women migrant workers and other relevant sources, such as the International Organization for Migration, including non-governmental organizations.

Violence against indigenous women and girls

At its tenth session (16–27 May, New York) [E/2011/43], the Permanent Forum on Indigenous Issues (see p. 751) recommended to the Economic and Social Council the adoption of a draft decision on violence against indigenous women and girls.

On 28 July, by **decision 2011/266**, the Council decided to authorize a three-day international expert group meeting on the theme "Combating violence against indigenous women and girls: article 22 of the United Nations Declaration on the Rights of Indigenous Peoples", and requested that the results of the meeting be reported to the Permanent Forum on Indigenous Issues at its eleventh (2012) session; the General Assembly at its sixty-seventh (2012) session; and the Commission on the Status of Women at its fifty-sixth (2012) session.

Women and armed conflict

Women, peace and security

Pursuant to presidential statement S/PRST/2010/22 [YUN 2010, p. 1161], made in connection with the tenth anniversary of Security Council resolution 1325(2000) [YUN 2000, p. 1113], the Secretary-General submitted a September report [S/2011/598] on women and peace and security. The report was based on contributions from 38 Member States, 4 regional organizations and 27 entities of the UN system and focused on four broad action areas: prevention, participation, protection, and relief and recovery.

The Secretary-General expressed concern about the uneven implementation of resolution 1325(2000) and called for proactive steps to accelerate implementation of key elements of the agenda, such as strengthening women's engagement in conflict resolution and deterring widespread and systematic abuses of women's rights during conflict. He welcomed the creation of the UN-Women and expected it to improve coherence and coordination, as well as galvanize innovation and ensure accountability in those areas of work. The report stated that gender equality and women's empowerment issues must be addressed in all UN support for mediation efforts, peace agreement implementation and post-conflict elections. The Secretary-General also committed to ensuring that all UN commissions of inquiry and related investigative bodies and UN-supported truth commissions had gender expertise and access to sexual violence investigative capacity, drawing on UN-Women support. The Secretary-General called on UN entities and Member States to offer, in conflict and post-conflict situations, technical and financial support to women's organizations, which were key to strengthening constituencies for peace and building the leverage of women engaged in conflict resolution and peacebuilding. Periodic review of the indicators on women and peace and security [YUN 2010, p. 1160] and progress in meeting the targets of the strategic results framework would provide information on the achievement of gender-related results in conflict and post-conflict situations. To address the low numbers of women in conflict resolution and the implementation of peace agreements, the Secretary-General recommended that Member States supporting peace processes offer negotiating parties incentives to ensure women's inclusion on delegations. He urged Member States to increase the number of women in their foreign service and national security establishments, and in their security forces so as to increase the pool available for deployment as peacekeepers. He further recommended that Member States—particularly those in conflict and post-conflict situations—develop and implement national action plans on women and peace and security; and identify means for bringing justice, redress and assistance to women and girls for war crimes they have suffered, ending impunity for those atrocities.

Communication. In a letter [S/2011/654] dated 20 October, Nigeria informed the Secretary-General that the Security Council was scheduled to hold an open debate on women and peace and security on 25 October (see below).

SECURITY COUNCIL ACTION

On 28 October [meeting 6642], following consultations among Security Council members, the President made statement **S/PRST/2011/20** on behalf of the Council:

The Security Council reaffirms its commitment to the full and effective implementation of resolutions 1325(2000), 1820(2008), 1888(2009), 1889(2009) and 1960(2010) on women and peace and security and all relevant statements by its President.

The Council urges all parties to fully comply with their obligations under the Convention on the Elimination of All Forms of Discrimination against Women, of 1979 and the Optional Protocol thereto, of 1999 and strongly encourages States that have not ratified or acceded to the Convention and Optional Protocol to consider doing so.

The Council recalls the 2005 World Summit Outcome, the Beijing Declaration and Platform for Action, the outcome documents of the twenty-third special session of the General Assembly entitled "Women 2000: gender equality, development and peace for the twenty-first century", and the declaration of the fifty-fourth session of the Commission on the Status of Women.

The Council welcomes the report of the Secretary-General of 29 September 2011 on women and peace and security, and takes note of the analysis and recommendations it contains on progress in implementing commitments on women and peace and security, including on the representation and participation of women in decision-making forums, institutions and mechanisms related to the prevention and resolution of armed conflict and to peacebuilding.

The Council welcomes the commitments and efforts of Member States, regional organizations and the Secretary-General to implement its resolutions on women and peace and security. The Council, however, remains concerned about the persistence of gaps and challenges that seriously hinder the implementation of resolution 1325(2000), including the continued low number of women in formal institutions of conflict prevention and resolution, particularly in preventive diplomacy and mediation efforts.

The Council stresses the importance of promoting and protecting the human rights of women and girls in the context of the implementation of resolution 1325(2000), fully implementing international humanitarian law and human rights law in armed conflict and post-conflict situations, increasing women's participation in conflict prevention, resolution and peacebuilding and incorporating a gender perspective into United Nations field missions.

The Council welcomes the contributions and role of the United Nations Entity for Gender Equality and the Empowerment of Women (UN-Women) in implementing resolutions on women and peace and security. The Council expresses its intention to welcome briefings by the Under-Secretary-General and Executive Director of UN-Women. The Council notes with satisfaction the increased coordination and coherence in policy and programming for women and girls within the United Nations system since the creation of UN-Women. In this regard, the Council underlines the importance of the mandates of the Special Representative of the Secretary-General on Sexual Violence in Conflict and the Special Representative of the Secretary-General for Children and Armed Conflict, which contribute to the work on the women and peace and security agenda.

The Council reiterates its strong condemnation of all violations of applicable international law committed against women and girls in armed conflict and post-conflict situations and urges the complete cessation by all parties of such acts with immediate effect. The Council also urges Member States to bring to justice those responsible for crimes of this nature.

The Council notes that the fight against impunity for the most serious crimes of international concern committed against women and girls has been strengthened through the work of the International Criminal Court, ad hoc and mixed tribunals, as well as specialized chambers in national tribunals. The Council reiterates its intention to enhance its efforts to fight impunity and uphold accountability for serious crimes against women and girls with appropriate means and draws attention to the full range of justice and reconciliation mechanisms to be considered, including national, international and mixed criminal courts and tribunals, truth and reconciliation commissions as well as national reparation programmes for victims, institutional reforms and traditional dispute resolution mechanisms.

The Council welcomes the efforts of Member States to implement resolution 1325(2000) at the national level, including the increase in the number of States that have formulated or revised national action plans and strategies. The Council reiterates its call to Member States to continue to implement resolution 1325(2000), including through the development of national action plans or other national-level strategies.

The Council recalls the statement by its President of 22 September 2011 on preventive diplomacy, in which it, inter alia, recognized the important role of women in the prevention and resolution of conflicts and in peacebuilding, and reiterated its call to increase the equal participation, representation and full involvement of women in preventive diplomacy efforts. The Council recalls General Assembly resolution 65/283 on strengthening the role of mediation in the peaceful settlement of disputes, conflict prevention and resolution and the encouragement it contains to promote equal, full and effective participation of women in all forums and at all levels of the peaceful settlement of disputes, conflict prevention and resolution, particularly at the decision-making level.

The Council encourages efforts by Member States, the United Nations Secretariat, United Nations field missions, United Nations agencies, funds and programmes, international financial institutions and regional and subregional organizations to, as appropriate, provide support and strengthen the capacities of relevant government institutions and women's organizations engaged in issues related to armed conflict or post-conflict situations. The Council underlines the importance of the participation of women in conflict prevention and resolution efforts, including in the negotiation and implementation of peace agreements, as well as international dialogues, contact groups, engagement conferences and donor conferences in support of conflict resolution. In this regard, the Council reiterates the need to support, as appropriate, local women's peace initiatives, processes for conflict resolution and initiatives that involve women in implementation mechanisms of the peace agreements, including through the local-level presence of United Nations field missions.

The Council acknowledges the significant contribution that women can have in conflict prevention and mediation efforts and encourages Member States and international and regional organizations to take measures to increase the number of women involved in mediation efforts and the number of women in representative roles in regional and international organizations. The Council therefore stresses the importance of creating enabling conditions for women's participation during all stages of peace processes and for countering negative societal attitudes regarding full and equal participation of women in conflict resolution and mediation.

The Council continues to encourage Member States to deploy greater numbers of female military and police personnel to United Nations peacekeeping operations and reiterates that all military and police personnel should be provided with adequate training to carry out their responsibilities.

The Council encourages negotiating parties and mediation teams to adopt a gender perspective in negotiating and implementing peace agreements and to facilitate increased representation of women in peacebuilding forums. In this regard, the Council requests the Secretary-General and relevant United Nations entities to assist, as appropriate, in enabling regular consultations between women's groups and relevant participants in conflict mediation and peacebuilding processes. The Council also requests the Secretary-General to ensure that regular briefings are provided to his mediators and their teams on gender issues relevant to peace agreement provisions and specific obstacles to full and equal political participation of women.

The Council recognizes the need for more systematic attention to and implementation of women and peace and security commitments in its own work and expresses its willingness to ensure that measures to enhance women's engagement in conflict prevention and resolution and peacebuilding are advanced in its work, including on preventive diplomacy. The Council welcomes the intention of the Ad Hoc Working Group on Conflict Prevention and Resolution in Africa to incorporate a gender perspective in its work.

The Council reiterates its intention to convene a high-level review in 2015 to assess progress at the global, regional and national levels in implementing resolution 1325(2000), renew commitments and address obstacles and constraints that have emerged in the implementation of resolution 1325(2000).

The Council requests the Secretary-General in his next annual report on resolution 1325(2000) to include, inter alia, a comprehensive overview of specific actions, achievements and challenges to the implementation of the present statement, in particular those concerning the participation of women in mediation and preventive diplomacy.

Women in power and decision-making

Women and political participation

In 2011, the General Assembly considered the issue of women and political participation. By resolution 66/130 (see p. 1078), the Assembly called upon all States to enhance the political participation of women; accelerate the achievement of equality between men and women; and, in all situations, promote and protect the human rights of women, including in situations of political transition. It requested the Secretary-General to report on the implementation of the resolution at its sixty-eighth (2013) session.

GENERAL ASSEMBLY ACTION

On 19 December [meeting 89], the General Assembly, on the recommendation of the Third Committee [A/66/455 & Corr.1], adopted **resolution 66/130** without vote [agenda item 28 (*a*)].

Women and political participation

The General Assembly,

Reaffirming the obligations of all States to promote and protect human rights and fundamental freedoms as stated in the Charter of the United Nations, and guided by the purposes and principles of human rights instruments,

Reaffirming also the Universal Declaration of Human Rights, which states that everyone has the right to take part in the Government of his or her country directly, or through freely chosen representatives, and the right of equal access to public service,

Guided by the Convention on the Elimination of All Forms of Discrimination against Women, which affirms human rights and fundamental freedoms and equality for women around the world, and which states, inter alia, that States parties shall take all appropriate measures to eliminate discrimination against women in the political and public life of the country,

Reaffirming the Beijing Declaration and Platform for Action and the outcome of the twenty-third special session of the General Assembly entitled "Women 2000: gender equality, development and peace for the twenty-first century",

Recognizing the central role of the United Nations Entity for Gender Equality and the Empowerment of Women (UN-Women) in leading and coordinating action to promote gender equality and the empowerment of women within the United Nations system, as well as in supporting all countries' efforts to promote gender equality and the empowerment of women,

Recognizing also the important contributions that women have made towards the achievement of representative, transparent and accountable Governments in many countries,

Stressing the critical importance of women's political participation in all contexts, including in times of peace and of conflict and at all stages of political transition, concerned that many obstacles still prevent women from participating in political life on equal terms with men, and noting in that regard that situations of political transition may provide a unique opportunity to address such obstacles,

Recognizing the essential contributions that women around the world continue to make to the achievement and maintenance of international peace and security and to the full realization of all human rights, to the promotion of sustainable development and economic growth, and to the eradication of poverty, hunger and disease,

Reaffirming that the active participation of women, on equal terms with men, at all levels of decision-making is essential to the achievement of equality, sustainable development, peace and democracy,

Highly concerned that women in every part of the world continue to be largely marginalized from the political sphere, often as a result of discriminatory laws, practices, attitudes and gender stereotypes, low levels of education, lack of access to health care and the disproportionate effect of poverty on women,

Recognizing the importance of empowering all women through education and training in government, public policy, economics, civics, information technology and science to ensure that they develop the knowledge and skills needed to make full contributions to society and the political process,

Reaffirming the important role of women in the prevention and resolution of conflicts and in peacebuilding and the need for Member States and the United Nations system to increase the role of women in decision-making with regard to conflict prevention and resolution and the rebuilding of post-conflict societies, in accordance with Security Council resolution 1325(2000) of 31 October 2000 and its subsequent follow-up resolutions, as well as other relevant United Nations resolutions,

Noting with appreciation the establishment by the Human Rights Council of the Working Group on Discrimination against Women in Law and in Practice,

1. *Reaffirms* its resolution 58/142 of 22 December 2003 on women and political participation, and calls upon all States to implement it fully;

2. *Calls upon* all States to eliminate laws, regulations and practices that, in a discriminatory manner, prevent or restrict women's participation in the political process;

3. *Also calls upon* all States to enhance the political participation of women, to accelerate the achievement of equality between men and women and, in all situations, including in situations of political transition, to promote and protect the human rights of women with respect to:

   (*a*) Engaging in political activities;
   (*b*) Taking part in the conduct of public affairs;
   (*c*) Associating freely;
   (*d*) Assembling peacefully;
   (*e*) Expressing their opinions and seeking, receiving and imparting information and ideas freely;
   (*f*) Voting in elections and public referendums and being eligible for election to publicly elected bodies on equal terms with men;
   (*g*) Participating in the formulation of government policy and the implementation thereof, holding public office and performing public functions at all levels of government;

4. *Calls upon* States in situations of political transition to take effective steps to ensure the participation of women on equal terms with men in all phases of political reform, from decisions on whether to call for reforms in existing institutions to decisions regarding transitional governments, to the formulation of government policy, to the means of electing new democratic governments;

5. *Urges* all States to comply fully with their obligations under the Convention on the Elimination of All Forms of Discrimination against Women, urges States that

have not yet ratified or acceded to the Convention to do so, and urges States parties to the Convention to consider signing, ratifying or acceding to the Optional Protocol thereto;

6. *Also urges* all States to take, inter alia, the following actions to ensure women's equal participation, and encourages the United Nations system and other international and regional organizations, within their existing mandates, to enhance their assistance to States in their national efforts:

(*a*) To review the differential impact of their electoral systems on the political participation of women and their representation in elected bodies and to adjust or reform those systems where appropriate;

(*b*) To take all appropriate measures to eliminate prejudices that are based on the idea of the inferiority or the superiority of either of the sexes or on stereotyped roles for men and women and that constitute a barrier to women's access to and participation in the political sphere, and to adopt inclusive approaches to their political participation;

(*c*) To strongly encourage political parties to remove all barriers that directly or indirectly discriminate against the participation of women, to develop their capacity to analyse issues from a gender perspective, and to adopt policies, as appropriate, to promote the ability of women to participate fully at all levels of decision-making within those political parties;

(*d*) To promote awareness and recognition of the importance of women's participation in the political process at the community, local, national and international levels;

(*e*) To develop mechanisms and training to encourage women to participate in the electoral process, political activities and other leadership activities, and empower women to assume public responsibilities by developing and providing appropriate tools and skills, in consultation with women;

(*f*) To implement appropriate measures within governmental bodies and public sector institutions to eliminate direct or indirect barriers to and enhance women's participation in all levels of political decision-making;

(*g*) To accelerate the implementation of strategies, as appropriate, that promote gender balance in political decision-making, and take all appropriate measures to encourage political parties to ensure that women have a fair and equal opportunity to compete for all elective public positions;

(*h*) To improve and broaden women's access to information and communications technologies, including e-government tools, in order to enable political participation and to promote engagement in broader democratic processes, while also improving the responsiveness of these technologies to women's needs, including those of marginalized women;

(*i*) To investigate allegations of violence, assault or harassment of women elected officials and candidates for political office, create an environment of zero tolerance for such offences and, to ensure accountability, take all appropriate steps to prosecute those responsible;

(*j*) To encourage greater involvement of women who may be marginalized, including indigenous women, women with disabilities, women from rural areas and women of any ethnic, cultural or religious minority, in decision-making at all levels, and address and counter the barriers faced by marginalized women in accessing and participating in politics and decision-making at all levels;

(*k*) To encourage the promotion of programmes geared towards the sensitization and orientation of youth and children, in particular young women and girls, on the importance of the political process and women's participation in politics;

(*l*) To ensure that measures to reconcile family and professional life apply equally to women and men, bearing in mind that equitable sharing of family responsibilities between women and men and reduction of the double burden of paid and unpaid work can help to create an enabling environment for women's political participation;

(*m*) To promote the granting of appropriate maternity and paternity leave in order to facilitate women's political participation;

(*n*) To take proactive measures to address factors preventing or hindering women from participating in politics, such as violence, poverty, lack of access to quality education and health care, and gender stereotypes;

(*o*) To monitor and evaluate progress in the representation of women in decision-making positions;

7. *Encourages* States to ensure an expanded role for women in the prevention, management and resolution of conflict and in mediation and peacebuilding efforts, as called for in Security Council resolution 1325(2000) and subsequent relevant resolutions;

8. *Also encourages* States to appoint women to posts within all levels of their Governments, including, where applicable, bodies responsible for designing constitutional, electoral, political or institutional reforms;

9. *Further encourages* States to commit themselves to establishing the goal of gender balance in governmental bodies and committees, as well as in public administrative entities, and in the judiciary, including, inter alia and as appropriate, setting specific targets and implementing measures to substantially increase the number of women with a view to achieving equal representation of women and men, if necessary through positive action, in all governmental and public administration positions;

10. *Encourages* States and relevant civil society organizations to support programmes that facilitate women's participation in political and other leadership activities, including peer support and capacity development for new office holders, and to promote public/private civil society partnerships for women's empowerment;

11. *Invites* States to exchange experience and best practices on women's political participation in all phases of the political process, including in times of political change and reform;

12. *Notes with interest* the focus, inter alia, on the political participation of women, including the issues raised in the present resolution, in the work of the Human Rights Council Working Group on Discrimination against Women in Law and in Practice;

13. *Encourages* States to disseminate the present resolution among all relevant institutions, in particular national, regional and local authorities, as well as among political parties;

14. *Requests* the Secretary-General to submit to the General Assembly at its sixty-eighth session a report on the implementation of the present resolution, and encourages Governments to provide precise data on the political participation of women at all levels, including, where appropriate, information on the political participation of women in times of political transition.

Institutional mechanisms for the advancement of women

Inter-Agency Network. The United Nations Inter-Agency Network on Women and Gender Equality (IANWGE), at its tenth annual session (New York, 16–18 February) [IANWGE/2011/Report], discussed UN system coordination to accelerate gender equality and the empowerment of women, including the role of UN-Women; matters related to the fifty-fifth session of the Commission on the Status of Women; matters related to the Committee on the Elimination of Discrimination against Women; progress on and remaining obstacles for women's economic empowerment; current interagency work on women and peace and security in view of Security Council presidential statement S/PRST/2010/22 [YUN 2010, p. 1161]; addressing violence against women in a coordinated manner through the Secretary-General's UNiTE to End Violence against Women campaign; status and prospects in the UN system with regard to gender equality and empowerment of women in the workplace; new and emerging issues such as developments in the Middle East and their impact on women and girls; ensuring effective coordination of gender mainstreaming and capacity development to that end; capacity development for effective gender mainstreaming; and updates on and review of the work of IANWGE Task Forces.

Participants decided to establish an Inter-Agency Working Group on Policy Dialogue on Women's Economic Empowerment; to replace the Task Force on Violence against Women by a Standing Committee; to abolish the Task Force on Gender, Water and Sanitation; to establish time-bound Task Forces on Rural Women and Women's Access to Justice; and to maintain the Task Forces on Women and Peace and Security, Gender and Trade, and Gender and the MDGs.

Report of Secretary-General. In response to Economic and Social Council resolution 2010/29 [YUN 2010, p. 1169], the Secretary-General, in a May report [E/2011/114], assessed progress in implementing the gender mainstreaming strategy within the UN system, focusing on the areas of design, implementation, monitoring and evaluation. The report emphasized progress at the country level, particularly through the United Nations Development Assistance Framework process, and reflected on advances made in terms of UN staff capacity development and on the coordination strategy of UN-Women.

The report found that most UN entities included accountability for gender mainstreaming in overall institutional accountability frameworks; monitoring, evaluation and oversight mechanisms; and staff performance appraisals. They also continued to pay attention to gender dimensions in their design, implementation, monitoring and evaluation of policies and programmes. With regard to capacity development and training, an increasing number of entities made specific commitments to ensure that all policies, strategies and action plans were gender-sensitive and gender-responsive. Nevertheless, gaps and challenges continued to impede full implementation of gender mainstreaming in UN system entities. These included a lack of consistent integration of gender perspectives in strategic plans; lack of staff with gender expertise and their strategic placement; limited application and/or access to data disaggregated by sex and gender-sensitive indicators; limited funding; and lack of accountability mechanisms. The Secretary-General underlined the need to pay more focused attention to the practical implementation of gender mainstreaming, as several important linkages continued to manifest weakness between the intergovernmental normative framework governing gender equality and the development and implementation of corresponding programmes at the country level; between the stated organizational priorities and institutional workplans; and between the decisions to strengthen accountability and the slow development of common tools for assessing progress and gaps both at the programme and the managerial and staff performance levels. He suggested that the Economic and Social Council call upon UN entities to increase human and financial resources to support gender-sensitive policies and programmes and improved tracking and monitoring; use the establishment of UN-Women to create new opportunities for engagement and action on gender mainstreaming, including through enhanced joint programming; draw on the expertise of UN-Women to assist in the preparation of the United Nations Development Assistance Framework and other development frameworks to ensure gender dimensions are addressed; provide ongoing capacity development on gender mainstreaming for resident coordinators and UN country teams to ensure they are better able to assist national partners in integrating a gender perspective in their development frameworks; and focus more on deliverables in programming activities to ensure that attention was paid to the needs and priorities of women and girls at the country level.

ECONOMIC AND SOCIAL COUNCIL ACTION

On 14 July [meeting 29], the Economic and Social Council adopted **resolution 2011/6** [draft: E/2011/L.30] without vote [agenda item 7 (*e*)].

Mainstreaming a gender perspective into all policies and programmes in the United Nations system

The Economic and Social Council,

Reaffirming its agreed conclusions 1997/2 of 18 July 1997 on mainstreaming a gender perspective into all policies and programmes in the United Nations system, and recalling its resolutions 2001/41 of 26 July 2001, 2002/23 of 24 July 2002, 2003/49 of 24 July 2003, 2004/4 of 7 July 2004, 2005/31 of 26 July 2005, 2006/36 of 27 July 2006, 2007/33 of 27 July 2007, 2008/34 of 25 July 2008, 2009/12 of 28 July 2009 and 2010/29 of 23 July 2010,

Reaffirming also the commitment made at the 2005 World Summit to actively promote the mainstreaming of a gender perspective in the design, implementation, monitoring and evaluation of policies and programmes in all political, economic and social spheres and to further undertake to strengthen the capabilities of the United Nations system in the area of gender,

Reaffirming further that gender mainstreaming is a globally accepted strategy for achieving gender equality and the empowerment of women and constitutes a critical strategy in the full, effective and accelerated implementation of the Beijing Declaration and Platform for Action and the outcome documents of the twenty-third special session of the General Assembly,

Welcoming the establishment of the United Nations Entity for Gender Equality and the Empowerment of Women (UN-Women) which consolidates the mandates and functions of the Office of the Special Adviser on Gender Issues and Advancement of Women, the Division for the Advancement of Women, the United Nations Development Fund for Women and the International Research and Training Institute for the Advancement of Women, with the additional role of leading, coordinating and promoting the accountability of the United Nations system in its work on gender equality and the empowerment of women, as established under General Assembly resolution 64/289 of 2 July 2010,

1. *Takes note with appreciation* of the report of the Secretary-General and the recommendations contained therein, and calls for further and continued efforts to mainstream a gender perspective into all policies and programmes of the United Nations in accordance with all relevant resolutions of the Economic and Social Council;

2. *Stresses* that the Inter-Agency Network on Women and Gender Equality constitutes a key forum for achieving more effective coordination, coherence and gender mainstreaming across the United Nations system, the exchange and cross-fertilization of ideas and practical experience on gender mainstreaming within the United Nations system, and looks forward to the continued implementation of the policy and strategy for gender mainstreaming within the United Nations system;

3. *Requests* the United Nations system, including its agencies, funds and programmes, within their respective mandates, to continue mainstreaming the issue of gender in accordance with previous Council resolutions, in particular resolution 2008/34, and General Assembly resolution 64/289, including mainstreaming a gender perspective into all operational mechanisms, inter alia the United Nations Development Assistance Framework and other development frameworks, ensuring that managers provide leadership and support, within the United Nations system, to advance gender mainstreaming, strengthening monitoring, reporting and evaluation so as to allow system-wide assessment of progress in gender mainstreaming, and using existing training resources, including institutions and infrastructure, to assist in the development and application of unified training modules and tools on gender mainstreaming and to promote the collection, analysis and use of accurate, reliable, comparable and relevant data, disaggregated by sex and age, during programme development and the evaluation of gender mainstreaming in order to assess progress towards achieving gender equality and the empowerment of women;

4. *Requests* the United Nations system to continue to support Member States, with their agreement and consent, in the implementation of national policies for the achievement of gender equality and the empowerment of women, inter alia, by providing support and capacity development to national machineries for the advancement of women;

5. *Recognizes* that large gaps remain between policy and practice and that building United Nations staff capacities alone is not sufficient for the entire United Nations system to meet its commitments and obligations with respect to gender mainstreaming;

6. *Calls upon* the United Nations Entity for Gender Equality and the Empowerment of Women (UN-Women), in accordance with General Assembly resolution 64/289:

(*a*) To ensure that its work leads to more effective coordination, coherence and gender mainstreaming across the United Nations system;

(*b*) To fully assume its role in leading, coordinating and promoting the accountability of the United Nations system in its work on gender equality and the empowerment of women;

(*c*) To continue to support gender mainstreaming across the United Nations system as an integral part of its work;

(*d*) To establish concrete results-based reporting mechanisms, as well as to ensure coherence, consistency and coordination between the normative and operational aspects of its work;

(*e*) In the context of its work at the field level, to operate as part of the resident coordinator system, within the United Nations country team, leading and coordinating the work of the country team on gender equality and the empowerment of women, under the overall leadership of the resident coordinator;

(*f*) Based on the principle of universality, to provide, through its normative support functions and operational activities, guidance and technical support to all Member States, across all levels of development and in all regions, at their request, on gender equality, the empowerment and rights of women and gender mainstreaming;

7. *Requests* the United Nations system, including its agencies, funds and programmes within their respective organizational mandates, to continue working collaboratively to enhance gender mainstreaming within the United Nations system, including by:

(*a*) Ensuring effective coordination on gender mainstreaming and gender equality and the empowerment of women, within existing coordination mechanisms, including the United Nations System Chief Executives Board for Coordination, the High-Level Committee on Programmes, the High-Level Committee on Management, the United

Nations Development Group and the Inter-Agency Network on Women and Gender Equality, led by UN-Women, with clear roles and responsibilities designated for all parts of the system;

(b) Ensuring strong leadership at the Headquarters level, and providing clear guidance and improved collaboration within the United Nations country teams;

(c) Enhancing resource mobilization capacity and increasing the predictability of both human and financial resources for gender equality and the empowerment of women;

(d) Enhancing and strengthening the various accountability frameworks of the United Nations system to ensure more coherent, accurate and effective management, monitoring, evaluation and reporting of each United Nations entity's gender equality results, including tracking of gender-related resource allocation and expenditure, and results-based approaches within the United Nations system;

(e) Improving the application of a gender perspective in programming work and enhancing a broader approach to capacity development for all United Nations staff, including the Secretariat staff, including by working on guidelines which could provide specialized instructions on gender mainstreaming and serve as performance indicators against which staff could be assessed;

(f) Ensuring greater focus on deliverables and the development of clear gender equality outcomes and outputs in programming activities, including in the United Nations development framework, such as the United Nations Development Assistance Framework, so as to ensure that attention is paid to the needs and priorities of women and girls at the country level;

(g) Ensuring support from United Nations country teams for national efforts to accelerate progress towards achieving the internationally agreed development goals and other commitments related to gender equality and the empowerment of women;

(h) Ensuring that all personnel, especially in the field, receive training and appropriate follow-up, including tools, guidance and support, for accelerated gender mainstreaming, including by providing ongoing capacity development for resident coordinators and the United Nations country teams to ensure that they are better able to assist national partners in achieving gender equality and the empowerment of women through their development frameworks;

(i) Enhancing the use of data disaggregated by sex by the United Nations country teams in the preparation of indicators to measure progress, including, where used, the United Nations Development Assistance Framework;

(j) Ensuring progress, including through managerial and departmental accountability, towards achieving the goal of a 50/50 gender balance at all levels in the Secretariat and throughout the United Nations system, with due regard to the representation of women from developing countries and keeping in mind the principle of equitable geographical representation, in conformity with Article 101, paragraph 3, of the Charter of the United Nations;

8. *Requests* the Secretary-General to submit to the Economic and Social Council at its substantive session of 2012 a report on the implementation of the present resolution, with particular emphasis on progress in promoting system-wide accountability on gender equality and the empowerment of women at both the global and country levels.

Human rights of women

UN-Women and OHCHR activities

During the year, cooperation intensified between UN-Women and the Office of the High Commissioner for Human Rights (OHCHR) with the goal of achieving equality between women and men and promoting and protecting women's human rights. In a December report [A/HRC/19/31–E/CN.6/2012/12], the Secretary-General reviewed cooperation in 2011 with respect to inter-agency mechanisms and initiatives; human rights treaty bodies; human rights special procedures; country-level cooperation; intergovernmental bodies; information dissemination; and the development of tools in support of national policies, laws and programmes designed to operationalize human rights standards. The report further presented the joint workplan for 2012 and recommendations for new and strengthened modalities for cooperation between UN-Women and OHCHR.

Palestinian women

In accordance with Economic and Social Council resolution 2010/6 [YUN 2010, p. 482], a report of the Secretary-General [E/CN.6/2011/6] reviewed the situation of and assistance to Palestinian women from September 2009 to September 2010 (see p. 451).

On 4 March, the Commission on the Status of Women adopted a resolution on the subject and recommended the text to the Economic and Social Council for adoption.

On 26 July, the Council took action on the situation of and assistance to Palestinian women in **resolution 2011/18** (see p. 452).

Women and the environment

Gender equality and sustainable development

On 1 March, the Commission on the Status of Women [E/2011/27] held an expert panel discussion on the emerging issue of gender equality and sustainable development. Participants noted that women's contributions to sustainable development were both undervalued and underutilized, and measures were needed to ensure that women fully participated in the discourse on economic development, social progress and environmental protection and management, including with regard to climate change adaptation and mitigation. Recommendations from the discussion included ensuring women's effective participation in the processes leading up to the United Nations Conference on Sustainable Development, to be held in Rio de Janeiro in May 2012; promoting participatory dialogues among Governments, civil society and the private sector with respect to developing and implementing gender-responsive policy and budget frameworks for sustainable development; ensuring that international conventions on environmental issues integrated the issues of gender equality and women's empowerment and full participation; identifying opportunities for women to turn green practices into profitable business opportunities; and conducting an assessment of women's opportunities and participation in a green economy within the context of sustainable development and poverty eradication.

Women and climate change policies

On 4 March, the Commission on the Status of Women adopted a resolution [E/2011/27 (res. 55/1)] on mainstreaming gender equality and promoting empowerment of women in climate change policies and strategies, which called upon Governments to integrate a gender perspective in environmental and climate change policies, and to strengthen mechanisms and provide adequate resources to ensure women's full and equal participation in decision-making at all levels on environmental issues, in particular on strategies related to the impact of climate change on the lives of women and girls. The Commission also called upon Governments to support and empower rural women, who were engaged in agricultural production and played a vital role in providing food security threatened by climate change, by enhancing their access to and control of resources. It encouraged Governments to strengthen international cooperation in such areas as training, capacity-building and technology transfer in order to address the challenges faced by women and girls in the context of climate change; and called upon Governments to continue to incorporate a gender perspective and make efforts to ensure the effective participation of women in the ongoing climate change talks leading to the seventeenth Conference of the Parties to the United Nations Framework Convention on Climate Change (see p. 939).

The girl child

On 25 February, the Commission on the Status of Women [E/2011/27] held an expert panel discussion on the elimination of all forms of discrimination and violence against the girl child to evaluate progress in the implementation of the agreed conclusions on the subject adopted by the Commission at its fifty-first (2007) session [YUN 2007, p. 1173]. Participants noted that despite some progress, discrimination and violation of the human rights of girls persisted and there was a need to reinforce, expand and replicate good practices, and to use them as the basis for designing and ensuring the implementation of better laws, policies and programmes. Recommended actions included strengthening girls' knowledge of their rights and promoting their empowerment and participation in the development of public policy and decision-making; enhancing efforts to address discriminatory attitudes and gender stereotypes and to transform power relations through curriculum revision and teacher training in the education sector; and expanding interventions to engage boys and men in ending discrimination and violence against girls into systematic, large-scale and coordinated programmes, targeting young boys in particular.

Report of Secretary-General. Pursuant to General Assembly resolution 64/145 [YUN 2009, p. 1147], an August report of the Secretary-General [A/66/257] reviewed international obligations and commitments with respect to the girl child stemming from human rights treaties and international conferences, as well as legal and policy development. It assessed the negative impact on the girl child by poverty and the global economic crisis; violence, abuse and exploitation; gender disparities in education; inadequate water, sanitation and hygiene; inadequate nutrition and the prevalence of anaemia; HIV/AIDS; gender-based health risks, particularly in adolescence; disabilities; humanitarian crises; and a lack of participation opportunities. It also highlighted actions taken to address child and forced marriage.

Despite the international legal and normative obligations of States regarding the human rights of the girl child, girls continued to suffer not only from the effects of poverty and disease, but also from social and cultural norms that reinforced gender inequality; discrimination on the basis of ethnicity; and social, geographical and income inequities; all of which made them extremely vulnerable to further deprivation and marginalization. In reviewing progress towards ending child marriage, the report noted that the practice had been decreasing, albeit slowly. Data indicated significant inequities, with child marriage strongly associated with girls who had little formal education and taking place in communities where the marrying of a girl child was part of a cluster of gender norms and attitudes reflecting the low value accorded to the human rights of girls. Several countries enacted legislation setting the minimum age of marriage at 18, while others increased the minimum age of marriage to 18 and eliminated differences in the legal age between boys and girls. More comprehensive policies and programmes addressed the needs of adolescents who were already married while supporting actions to end the practice, which required an approach that—in addition to legislation—involved community discussions to collectively explore better alternatives.

The report cited progress in promoting the rights of girls in a number of areas. Numerous States adopted laws and policies addressing multiple forms of violence against girls, including human trafficking, sexual violence and exploitation, and female genital mutilation; and the humanitarian community continued to invest in tools and guidelines towards ensuring that inter-agency coordination mechanisms responded to the needs of girls affected by crisis situations. To build on those efforts, the Secretary-General requested action by Governments, supported by development agencies, non-governmental organizations and civil society, with the engagement of girls, boys, men and women. He called for the promotion of girls' participation and empowerment, including by involving girls in the design and delivery of development programmes; supporting programmes to develop their leadership skills; and facilitating girls' access to social networks and safe spaces where they could gain essential information and health and protective services. Where inequalities and discrimination against girls were entrenched, social change and transformation of power relations were essential to achieving gender equality. Governments, communities and households were accountable for shaping environments that did not tolerate discrimination or violence against girls. In the context of ensuring that girls start and stay in school, efforts were needed to identify and reach out to girls who were most excluded, including girls from the poorest households; rural, slum and remote areas; socially excluded groups, including children with disabilities; and indigenous and disadvantaged minority populations. He further recommended investing in the rights and protection of adolescent girls to ensure they were no longer neglected in development policies and programmes; and expanding and improving health, nutrition and other services to address the needs and rights of girls. On 19 December, the General Assembly took note of the report of the Secretary-General on the girl child (**decision 66/534**).

GENERAL ASSEMBLY ACTION

On 19 December [meeting 89], the General Assembly, on the recommendation of the Third Committee [A/66/458], adopted **resolution 66/140** without vote [agenda item 65 (a)].

The girl child

The General Assembly,

Reaffirming its resolution 64/145 of 18 December 2009 and all relevant resolutions, including the agreed conclusions of the Commission on the Status of Women, in particular those relevant to the girl child,

Reaffirming also the equal rights of women and men as enshrined in the Charter of the United Nations,

Recalling all human rights and other instruments relevant to the rights of the child, in particular the girl child, including the Convention on the Rights of the Child, the Convention on the Elimination of All Forms of Discrimination against Women, the Convention on the Rights of Persons with Disabilities, the Optional Protocols thereto and the Convention on Consent to Marriage, Minimum Age for Marriage and Registration of Marriages,

Reaffirming the internationally agreed development goals, including the Millennium Development Goals, as well as the commitments relevant to the girl child made at the 2005 World Summit, and welcoming the outcome document of the High-level Plenary Meeting of the General Assembly on the Millennium Development Goals, entitled "Keeping the promise: united to achieve the Millennium Development Goals",

Reaffirming also the outcome document of the twenty-seventh special session of the General Assembly on children, entitled "A world fit for children", the Declaration of Commitment on HIV/AIDS adopted at the twenty-sixth special session of the General Assembly on HIV/AIDS, entitled "Global Crisis—Global Action", and the Political Declaration on HIV/AIDS of 2006,

Reaffirming further all other relevant outcomes of major United Nations summits and conferences relevant to the girl child, as well as their five- and ten-year reviews, including the Beijing Declaration and Platform for Action adopted at the Fourth World Conference on Women, the outcome of the twenty-third special session of the General Assembly entitled "Women 2000: gender equality, development and peace for the twenty-first century", the Programme of Action of the International Conference on Population and Development and the Programme of Action of the World Summit for Social Development, as well as the agreed conclusions adopted by the Commission on the Status on Women at its fifty-fifth session, at which it considered "Access and participation of women and girls in education, training and science and technology, including for the promotion of women's equal access to full employment and decent work" as its priority theme,

Welcoming the adoption by the Commission on the Status of Women of the declaration on the occasion of the fifteenth anniversary of the Fourth World Conference on Women, and reiterating that full and effective implementation of the Beijing Declaration and Platform for Action, in particular the strategic objectives relating to the girl child, is essential to achieving the internationally agreed development goals, including the Millennium Development Goals,

Recalling the outcomes of the recent high-level meetings of the General Assembly relevant to the girl child,

Recalling also the Secretary-General's 2008–2015 campaign "UNiTE to End Violence against Women" and the call upon Governments, civil society, women's organizations, young people, the private sector, the media and the entire United Nations system to join forces in addressing the global pandemic of violence against women and girls,

Reaffirming the importance of gender mainstreaming across the United Nations system, including in relation to the girl child,

Recognizing that chronic poverty remains the single biggest obstacle to meeting the needs of and promoting and protecting the rights of children and that urgent national and international action is therefore required to eliminate it, and noting that the burden of the global financial and economic crisis, the energy crisis, the food crisis and the continuing food insecurity as a result of various factors is felt directly by households, especially those depending on income from the informal sector, and particularly by women and girls,

Recognizing also that girl children are often at greater risk of being exposed to and encountering various forms of discrimination and violence, which continue to hinder efforts towards the achievement of the Millennium Development Goals, and reaffirming the need to achieve gender equality to ensure a just and equitable world for girls, including through partnering with men and boys, as an important strategy for advancing the rights of the girl child,

Recognizing further that progress has been made in the adoption of national legislation that affirms the equality of girls and boys and that corresponding measures have not been taken to effectively implement such legislation, and recognizing the continuing existence of discrimination against women and girls throughout the world and that addressing this situation will require additional efforts to strengthen policy implementation, including through international cooperation,

Recognizing that the empowerment of and investment in girls, which is critical for economic growth, and the achievement of all Millennium Development Goals, including the eradication of poverty and extreme poverty, as well as the meaningful participation of girls in decisions that affect them, are key in breaking the cycle of discrimination and violence and in promoting and protecting the full and effective enjoyment of their human rights, and recognizing also that empowering girls requires their active participation in decision-making processes and the active support and engagement of their parents, legal guardians, families and care providers, boys and men, as well as the wider community,

Deeply concerned about all forms of violence against children, in particular the phenomena that disproportionately affect girls, such as commercial sexual exploitation and child pornography, child and forced marriages, rape, sexual abuse, domestic violence and trafficking in persons and, in addition, about the corresponding lack of accountability and impunity, which reflect discriminatory norms reinforcing the lower status of girls in society,

Deeply concerned also that violence against women and girls is underrecognized, particularly at the community level, and underreported or unrecorded because of stigma, fear, social tolerance and the often illegal and covert nature of such activities,

Deeply concerned further about discrimination against the girl child and the violation of the rights of the girl child, which often result in less access for girls to education, and to quality education, nutrition and physical and mental health care, in girls enjoying fewer of the rights, opportunities and benefits of childhood and adolescence than boys, and in leaving them more vulnerable than boys to the consequences of unprotected and premature sexual relations and often being subjected to various forms of cultural, social, sexual and economic exploitation and violence, abuse, rape, incest, honour-related crimes and harmful traditional practices, such as female infanticide, child and forced marriages, prenatal sex selection and female genital mutilation,

Deeply concerned that child and forced marriages expose young married girls to greater risk of HIV and sexually transmitted infections, often lead to early childbearing and increase the risk of disability, stillbirth and maternal death, and reduce their opportunities to complete their education, gain comprehensive knowledge, participate in the community or develop employable skills, and violate and impair the full enjoyment of the human rights of women and girls,

Deeply concerned also that early pregnancy and early childbearing and limited access to sexual and reproductive health care, including in the area of skilled birth attendance and emergency obstetric care, cause high prevalences of obstetric fistula and high levels of maternal mortality and morbidity and furthermore entail complications during pregnancy and childbirth which often lead to death, particularly for young women and girls,

Recognizing that progress towards ending child and forced marriages can have a positive impact on indicators related to girls' education, maternal health and child health, thereby contributing to the achievement of the Millennium Development Goals,

Deeply concerned that, despite their widespread practice, child and forced marriages are still underreported, and recognizing that this requires further attention,

Deeply concerned also that female genital mutilation violates and impairs the full enjoyment of the human rights of women and girls and that it is an irreparable and irreversible harmful practice, and that the goal of ending female genital mutilation by 2010, set out in the document entitled "A world fit for children", remains unmet,

Deeply concerned further that, in situations of poverty, war and armed conflict, girl children are among those most affected and furthermore become the victims of sexual violence, abuse and exploitation and sexually transmitted infections and diseases, including HIV and AIDS, which have a serious impact on the quality of their lives and leave them open to further discrimination, violence and neglect, thus limiting their potential for full development,

Emphasizing that increased access to education for young people, especially girls, including in the areas of sexual and reproductive health, dramatically lowers their vulnerability to preventable diseases, in particular HIV infection and sexually transmitted diseases,

Recognizing that early childbearing continues to be an impediment to the improvement of the educational and social status of girls in all parts of the world and that, overall, child and forced marriages and early motherhood can severely curtail their educational opportunities and are likely to have a long-term, adverse impact on their employment opportunities and on their and their children's quality of life,

Convinced that racism, racial discrimination, xenophobia and related intolerance reveal themselves in a differentiated manner for women and girls and can be among the factors leading to a deterioration in their living conditions, poverty, violence, multiple forms of discrimination and limitation or denial of their human rights,

Recognizing that women and girls with disabilities are subject to multiple forms of discrimination, including in respect of their access to education and employment, and the importance of the implementation of the Convention on the Rights of Persons with Disabilities in this regard,

Noting with concern that, in some parts of the world, men outnumber women as a result, in part, of harmful attitudes and practices, such as female genital mutilation, son preference, which results in female infanticide and prenatal sex selection, early marriage, including child marriage, violence against women, sexual exploitation, sexual abuse and discrimination against girls in food allocation and in other practices related to health and well-being, with the result that fewer girls than boys survive into adulthood,

Deeply concerned that the phenomenon of child-headed households, in particular those headed by girls, is becoming a serious social problem,

Deeply concerned also that the impact of the HIV and AIDS epidemic, including illness and mortality, erosion of the extended family, exacerbation of poverty, unemployment and underemployment, and migration, as well as urbanization, have contributed to the increase in the number of child-headed households,

Recognizing that women and girls bear the disproportionate burden of caring for and supporting those living with and affected by HIV and AIDS, and that this impacts negatively on girls by depriving them of their childhood and diminishing their opportunities to receive an education,

1. *Stresses* the need for full and urgent implementation of the rights of the girl child as provided to her under human rights instruments, and urges States to consider signing and ratifying or acceding to the Convention on the Rights of the Child, the Convention on the Elimination of All Forms of Discrimination against Women, the Convention on the Rights of Persons with Disabilities and the Optional Protocols thereto as a matter of priority;

2. *Urges* all States that have not yet signed and ratified or acceded to the Minimum Age Convention, 1973 (No. 138) and the Worst Forms of Child Labour Convention, 1999 (No. 182), of the International Labour Organization to consider doing so;

3. *Urges* all Governments and the United Nations system to strengthen efforts bilaterally and with international organizations and private sector donors in order to achieve the goals of the World Education Forum, in particular that of eliminating gender disparities in primary and secondary education by 2005, which have not been fully met, and to implement the United Nations Girls' Education Initiative as a means of reaching this goal, and calls for the implementation of and reaffirms the commitments contained in the Education for All goals and the Millennium Development Goals, particularly those related to gender and education;

4. *Calls upon* all States to place enhanced emphasis on quality education for the girl child, including catch-up and literacy education for those who did not receive formal education, to promote access to skills and entrepreneurial training for young women and to tackle male and female stereotypes in order to ensure that young women entering the labour market have opportunities to obtain full and productive employment and decent work;

5. *Encourages* States to promote the development of gender-sensitive curricula for educational programmes at all levels and to take concrete measures to ensure that educational materials portray women and men, youth, girls and boys in positive and non-stereotypic roles, particularly in the teaching of scientific and technological subjects, in order to address the root causes of segregation in working life;

6. *Calls upon* States and the international community to recognize the right to education on the basis of equal opportunity and non-discrimination by making primary education compulsory and available free to all children, and ensuring that all children have access to education of good quality, as well as making secondary education generally available and accessible to all, in particular through the progressive introduction of free education, bearing in mind that special measures to ensure equal access, including affirmative action, contribute to achieving equal opportunity and combating exclusion, and ensuring school attendance, in particular for girls and children from low-income families;

7. *Calls upon* States, with the support of international organizations, civil society and non-governmental organizations, as appropriate, to develop policies and programmes, giving priority to formal and informal education programmes, including age-appropriate sex education, with appropriate direction and guidance from parents and legal guardians, that support girls and enable them to acquire knowledge, develop self-esteem and take responsibility for their own lives, and to place special focus on programmes to educate women and men, especially parents, about the importance of girls' physical and mental health and well-being, including the elimination of discrimination against girls in child and forced marriages;

8. *Calls upon* all States and international and non-governmental organizations, individually and collectively, to implement further the Beijing Platform for Action, in particular the strategic objectives relating to the girl child, and the further actions and initiatives to implement the Beijing Declaration and Platform for Action, and to mobilize all necessary resources and support in order to achieve the goals and strategic objectives and actions set out in the Beijing Declaration and Platform for Action;

9. *Calls upon* all States to take measures to address the obstacles that continue to affect the achievement of the goals set forth in the Beijing Platform for Action, as contained in paragraph 33 of the further actions and initiatives, where appropriate, including the strengthening of national mechanisms to implement policies and programmes for the girl child and, in some cases, to enhance coordination among responsible institutions for the realization of the human rights of girls, as indicated in the further actions and initiatives;

10. *Urges* States to strengthen efforts to urgently eradicate all forms of discrimination against women and girls and, where applicable, to remain dedicated to the implementation of the Convention on the Elimination of All Forms of Discrimination against Women and the Optional Protocol thereto;

11. *Also urges* States to fulfil the pledges that they made at the Fourth World Conference on Women and at the twenty-third special session of the General Assembly to modify or abolish remaining laws that discriminate against women and girls;

12. *Further urges* States to improve the situation of girl children living in poverty, deprived of nutrition, water and sanitation facilities, with limited or no access to basic physical and mental health-care services, shelter, education, participation and protection, taking into account that, while a severe lack of goods and services hurts every human being, it is most threatening and harmful to the girl child, leaving her unable to enjoy her rights, to reach her full potential and to participate as a full member of society;

13. *Urges* States to ensure that the applicable requirements of the International Labour Organization for the employment of girls and boys are respected and effectively

enforced and that girls who are employed have equal access to decent work, and equal payment and remuneration, are protected from economic exploitation, discrimination, sexual harassment, violence and abuse in the workplace, are aware of their rights and have access to formal and non-formal education, skills development and vocational training, and also urges States to develop gender-sensitive measures, including national action plans, where appropriate, to eliminate the worst forms of child labour, including commercial sexual exploitation, slavery-like practices, forced and bonded labour, trafficking and hazardous forms of child labour;

14. *Recognizes* the importance of strengthening health systems, in particular primary health care and the need to integrate the HIV response into it, and notes that weak health systems, which already face many challenges, including a lack of trained health workers and insufficient retention of skilled health workers, are among the biggest barriers to accessing health care;

15. *Calls upon* States, with the support of relevant stakeholders including the private sector, civil society, non-governmental organizations and community-based organizations, as appropriate, to take all measures necessary to ensure the right of girls to the enjoyment of the highest attainable standard of health, including sexual and reproductive health, and to develop sustainable health systems and social services;

16. *Urges* all States to promote gender equality and equal access to basic social services, such as education, nutrition, birth registration, health care, including sexual and reproductive health, vaccinations and protection from diseases representing the major causes of mortality, including non-communicable diseases, and to mainstream a gender perspective in all development policies and programmes, including those relating to children as well as those specific to the girl child;

17. *Calls upon* States, with the support of international organizations and civil society, including non-governmental organizations, and the media, to take appropriate measures to address the root factors of child and forced marriages, including by undertaking educational activities to raise awareness regarding the negative aspects of such practices;

18. *Urges* all States to enact and strictly enforce laws to ensure that marriage is entered into only with the free and full consent of the intending spouses, and, in addition, to enact and strictly enforce laws concerning the minimum legal age of consent and the minimum age for marriage and raise the minimum age for marriage where necessary, and to develop and implement comprehensive policies, plans of action and programmes for the survival, protection, development and advancement of the girl child in order to promote and protect the full enjoyment of her human rights and to ensure equal opportunities for girls, including by making such plans an integral part of her total development process;

19. *Urges* States to ensure that efforts to enact and implement legislation to end child and forced marriages engage all stakeholders and agents of change and ensure that the information on the legislation against the practice is well known and generates social support for the enforcement of such laws and legislation;

20. *Calls upon* States to support community workshops and discussion sessions to enable communities to collectively explore ways to prevent and address child and forced marriages, provide information through stakeholders who are credible to the community, such as medical personnel and local, community and religious leaders, regarding the harm associated with these marriages, give greater voice to girls and ensure consistence of message throughout the entire community, and encourage the much-needed strong engagement of men and boys;

21. *Also calls upon* States to support and implement, including with dedicated resources, multisectoral policies and programmes that end the practice of child and forced marriages and ensure the provision of viable alternatives and institutional support, especially educational opportunities for girls, with an emphasis on keeping girls in school through post-primary education, including those who are already married or pregnant, ensuring physical access to education, including by establishing safe residential facilities, increasing financial incentives to families, promoting the empowerment of girls, improving educational quality and ensuring safe and hygienic conditions in schools;

22. *Further calls upon* States to strengthen research, data collection and analysis on the girl child, disaggregated by sex, age and geographical location, in order to provide a better understanding of the situations of girls, especially of the multiple forms of discrimination that they face, and to develop necessary policies and programme responses, which should take a holistic approach to addressing the full range of the forms of discrimination that girls may face, in order to protect their rights effectively;

23. *Urges* States to take all measures necessary to ensure the full enjoyment by girls with disabilities of all human rights and fundamental freedoms on an equal basis with other children, and to adopt, implement and strengthen appropriate policies and programmes designed to address their needs;

24. *Urges* all States to enact and enforce legislation to protect girls from all forms of violence and exploitation, including female infanticide and prenatal sex selection, female genital mutilation, rape, domestic violence, incest, sexual abuse, sexual exploitation, child prostitution and child pornography, trafficking and forced migration, forced labour and forced marriage, as well as marriage under legal age, and to develop age-appropriate safe, confidential and disability-accessible programmes and medical, social and psychological support services to assist girls who are subjected to violence and discrimination;

25. *Urges* States to complement punitive measures with educational activities designed to promote a process of consensus towards the abandonment of harmful practices such as female genital mutilation and to provide appropriate services for those affected by the practices;

26. *Calls upon* all States to enact and enforce the necessary legislative or other measures, in cooperation with relevant stakeholders, to prevent the distribution over the Internet of child pornography, including depictions of child sexual abuse, ensuring that adequate mechanisms are in place to enable reporting and removal of such material and that its creators, distributors and collectors are prosecuted as appropriate;

27. *Urges* States to formulate comprehensive, multidisciplinary and coordinated national plans, programmes or strategies to eliminate all forms of discrimination and

violence against women and girls, which should be widely disseminated and should provide targets and timetables for implementation, as well as effective domestic enforcement procedures through the establishment of monitoring mechanisms involving all parties concerned, including consultations with women's organizations, giving attention to the recommendations relating to the girl child of the Special Rapporteurs of the Human Rights Council on violence against women, its causes and consequences, and on trafficking in persons, especially women and children, and of the Special Representative of the Secretary-General on Violence against Children;

28. *Also urges* States to ensure that the right of children to express themselves and to participate in all matters affecting them, in accordance with their age and maturity, is fully and equally enjoyed by girls;

29. *Further urges* States to involve girls, including girls with special needs, and their representative organizations, in decision-making processes, as appropriate, and to include them as full and active partners in identifying their own needs and in developing, planning, implementing and assessing policies and programmes to meet those needs;

30. *Recognizes* that a considerable number of girl children are particularly vulnerable, including orphans, children living on the street, internally displaced and refugee children, children affected by trafficking and sexual and economic exploitation, children living with or affected by HIV and AIDS, and children who are incarcerated who live without parental support, and therefore urges States, with the support of the international community, where relevant, to take appropriate measures to address the needs of such children by implementing national policies and strategies to build and strengthen governmental, community and family capacities to provide a supportive environment for such children, including by providing appropriate counselling and psychosocial support, and ensuring their enrolment in school and access to shelter, good nutrition and health and social services on an equal basis with other children;

31. *Encourages* States to promote actions, including through bilateral and multilateral technical cooperation and financial assistance, for the social reintegration of children in difficult situations, in particular girls, considering, inter alia, views, skills and capacities that those children have developed in the conditions in which they lived and, where appropriate, with their meaningful participation;

32. *Urges* all States and the international community to respect, promote and protect the rights of the girl child, taking into account the particular vulnerabilities of the girl child in pre-conflict, conflict and post-conflict situations, as well as in other humanitarian emergencies, and further urges States to take special measures for the protection of girls, in particular to protect them from sexually transmitted infections, including HIV infection, gender-based violence, including rape, sexual abuse and sexual exploitation, torture, abduction and forced labour, paying special attention to refugee and displaced girls, and to take into account their special needs in the delivery of humanitarian assistance and disarmament, demobilization, rehabilitation assistance and reintegration processes;

33. *Deplores* all cases of sexual exploitation and abuse of women and children, especially girls, in humanitarian crises, including those cases involving humanitarian workers and peacekeepers, and urges States to take effective measures to address gender-based violence in humanitarian emergencies and to make all possible efforts to ensure that their laws and institutions are adequate to prevent, promptly investigate and prosecute acts of gender-based violence;

34. *Also deplores* all acts of sexual exploitation, abuse of and trafficking in women and children by military, police and civilian personnel involved in United Nations operations, welcomes the efforts undertaken by United Nations agencies and peacekeeping operations to implement a zero-tolerance policy in this regard, and requests the Secretary-General and personnel-contributing countries to continue to take all appropriate action necessary to combat these abuses by such personnel, including through the full implementation without delay of those measures adopted in the relevant General Assembly resolutions based on recommendations of the Special Committee on Peacekeeping Operations;

35. *Urges* Member States, the United Nations and other international, regional and subregional organizations, as well as civil society, including non-governmental organizations, the private sector and the media, to fully and effectively implement the relevant provisions of the United Nations Global Plan of Action to Combat Trafficking in Persons and the activities outlined therein, and expresses its view that it will, inter alia, contribute to the promotion of the rights of the girls and enhance cooperation and a better coordination of efforts in fighting trafficking in persons and promote increased ratification and full implementation of the United Nations Convention against Transnational Organized Crime and the Protocol to Prevent, Suppress and Punish Trafficking in Persons, Especially Women and Children, supplementing the United Nations Convention against Transnational Organized Crime;

36. *Calls upon* Member States to devise, enforce and strengthen effective child- and youth-sensitive measures to combat, eliminate and prosecute all forms of trafficking in women and girls, including for sexual and economic exploitation, as part of a comprehensive anti-trafficking strategy within wider efforts to eliminate all forms of violence against women and girls, including by taking effective measures against the criminalization of girls who are victims of exploitation and ensuring that girls who have been exploited receive access to the necessary psychosocial support;

37. *Calls upon* Governments, civil society, including the media, and non-governmental organizations to promote human rights education and full respect for and the enjoyment of the human rights of the girl child, inter alia, through the translation, production and dissemination of age-appropriate and gender-sensitive information material on those rights to all sectors of society, in particular to children;

38. *Requests* the Secretary-General, as Chair of the United Nations System Chief Executives Board for Coordination, to ensure that all organizations and bodies of the United Nations system, individually and collectively, in particular the United Nations Children's Fund, the United Nations Educational, Scientific and Cultural Organization, the World Food Programme, the United Nations Population Fund, the United Nations Entity for Gender Equality and the Empowerment of Women (UN-Women), the World Health Organization, the United Nations Development Programme, the Office of the United Nations High

Commissioner for Refugees and the International Labour Organization, take into account the rights and the particular needs of the girl child in country programmes of cooperation in accordance with national priorities, including through the United Nations Development Assistance Framework;

39. *Requests* all human rights treaty bodies and the human rights mechanisms of the Human Rights Council, including the special procedures, to adopt regularly and systematically a gender perspective in the implementation of their mandates and to include in their reports information on the qualitative analysis of violations of the human rights of women and girls, and encourages the strengthening of cooperation and coordination in that regard;

40. *Requests* States to ensure that, in all policies and programmes designed to provide comprehensive HIV and AIDS prevention, treatment, care and support, particular attention and support are given to the girl child at risk, living with or affected by HIV, including pregnant girls and young and adolescent mothers and girls with disabilities, with a view to achieving Millennium Development Goal 6, in particular to halt and begin to reverse by 2015 the spread of HIV;

41. *Invites* States to promote initiatives aimed at reducing the prices of antiretroviral drugs, especially second-line drugs, available to the girl child, including bilateral and private sector initiatives as well as initiatives on a voluntary basis taken by groups of States, including those based on innovative financing mechanisms that contribute to the mobilization of resources for social development, including those that aim to provide further access to drugs at affordable prices to developing countries on a sustainable and predictable basis, and in this regard takes note of the International Drug Purchase Facility, UNITAID;

42. *Calls upon* all States to integrate food and nutritional support with the goal that children, especially girl children, have access at all times to sufficient, safe and nutritious food to meet their dietary needs and food preferences, for an active and healthy life, as part of a comprehensive response to HIV and AIDS, other communicable diseases and non-communicable diseases;

43. *Urges* States and the international community to increase resources at all levels, particularly in the education and health sectors, so as to enable young people, especially girls, to gain the knowledge, attitudes and life skills that they need to overcome their challenges, including the prevention of HIV infection and early pregnancy, and to enjoy the highest attainable standard of physical and mental health, including sexual and reproductive health;

44. *Stresses* the need to strengthen the commitment of States and the United Nations system in their responsibility to mainstream the promotion and protection of the rights of the child, in particular the girl child, in the development agenda at the national, regional and international levels;

45. *Urges* States, the international community, the relevant United Nations entities, civil society and international financial institutions to continue to actively support, through the allocation of increased human and financial resources, targeted innovative programmes that address ending female genital mutilation and developing and providing education programmes, such as the United Nations Population Fund-United Nations Children's Fund joint programme on accelerating the abandonment of female genital mutilation, and sensitization workshops on the dire consequences of this harmful practice for the health of the girl, and to provide training programmes for those who perform the harmful procedure so that they may adopt an alternative profession;

46. *Stresses* that a common coordinated approach that promotes positive social change at the community, national and international levels could lead to the abandonment of female genital mutilation within a generation, with some of the main achievements being obtained by 2015, in line with the Millennium Development Goals;

47. *Urges* States, the international community, the relevant United Nations entities, civil society and the international financial institutions to actively support, through the allocation of increased human and financial resources, efforts to end child and forced marriages;

48. *Calls upon* States to strengthen the capacity of national health systems, and in this regard calls upon the international community to assist national efforts, including by allocation of adequate resources in order to provide essential services needed to prevent obstetric fistula and to treat those cases that occur by providing the continuum of services, including family planning, prenatal and postnatal care, skilled birth attendance, emergency obstetric care and post-partum care, to adolescent girls, including those living in poverty and in underserved rural areas where obstetric fistula is most common;

49. *Calls upon* States and the international community to create an environment in which the well-being of the girl child is ensured, inter alia, by cooperating, supporting and participating in global efforts for poverty eradication at the global, regional and country levels, recognizing that strengthened availability and effective allocation of resources are required at all levels, in order to ensure that all the internationally agreed development and poverty eradication goals, including those set out in the United Nations Millennium Declaration, are realized within their time framework, and reaffirming that investment in children, particularly girls, and the realization of their rights are among the most effective ways to eradicate poverty;

50. *Requests* the Secretary-General to submit a report to the General Assembly at its sixty-eighth session on the implementation of the present resolution, including an emphasis on child-headed households: causes, effects and prospects, using information provided by Member States, the organizations and bodies of the United Nations system and non-governmental organizations, with a view to assessing the impact of the present resolution on the well-being of the girl child.

International Day of the Girl Child

GENERAL ASSEMBLY ACTION

On 19 December [meeting 89], the General Assembly, on the recommendation of the Third Committee [A/66/462/Add.2], adopted **resolution 66/170** without vote [agenda item 69 (*b*)].

International Day of the Girl Child

The General Assembly,

Recalling its resolution 64/145 of 18 December 2009 and all other relevant resolutions, including the agreed conclusions of the Commission on the Status of Women, in particular those relevant to the girl child,

Recalling also all human rights and other instruments relevant to the rights of the child, in particular the girl child, including the Convention on the Rights of the Child, the Convention on the Elimination of All Forms of Discrimination against Women, the Convention on the Rights of Persons with Disabilities and the Optional Protocols thereto,

Recognizing that empowerment of and investment in girls, which are critical for economic growth, the achievement of all Millennium Development Goals, including the eradication of poverty and extreme poverty, as well as the meaningful participation of girls in decisions that affect them, are key in breaking the cycle of discrimination and violence and in promoting and protecting the full and effective enjoyment of their human rights, and recognizing also that empowering girls requires their active participation in decision-making processes and the active support and engagement of their parents, legal guardians, families and care providers, as well as boys and men and the wider community,

1. *Decides* to designate 11 October as the International Day of the Girl Child, to be observed every year beginning in 2012;

2. *Invites* all Member States, relevant organizations of the United Nations system and other international organizations, as well as civil society, to observe the International Day of the Girl Child, and to raise awareness of the situation of girls around the world;

3. *Requests* the Secretary-General to bring the present resolution to the attention of all Member States and United Nations organizations.

UN machinery

Convention on the elimination of discrimination against women

As at 31 December, 187 States were parties to the 1979 Convention on the Elimination of All Forms of Discrimination against Women, adopted by the General Assembly in resolution 34/180 [YUN 1979, p. 895]. Nauru acceded on 23 June. At year's end, 65 States had accepted the amendment to article 20, paragraph 1, of the Convention in respect of the meeting time of the Committee on the Elimination of Discrimination against Women (CEDAW), which was adopted by States parties in 1995 [YUN 1995, p. 1178]. In 2011, Albania, the Czech Republic, Ecuador, Kuwait and Nauru accepted the amendment, which would enter into force when accepted by a two-thirds majority of States parties.

The Optional Protocol to the Convention, adopted by the Assembly in resolution 54/4 [YUN 1999, p. 1100] and which entered into force in 2000 [YUN 2000, p. 1123], had 103 States parties as at 31 December. Cabo Verde acceded on 10 October, Ghana on 3 February and Seychelles on 1 March.

In accordance with General Assembly resolution 64/138 [YUN 2009, p. 1153], the Secretary-General submitted a June report [A/66/99] on the status of the Convention from 24 August 2009 to 1 July 2011. The report covered the working methods of CEDAW (see below); efforts to encourage universal ratification of the Convention and its Optional Protocol, and acceptance of the amendment to article 20, paragraph 1 of the Convention; technical assistance to States parties; and dissemination of the Convention, its Optional Protocol and information on CEDAW work.

CEDAW

In 2011, the Committee on the Elimination of Discrimination against Women (CEDAW), established in 1982 [YUN 1982, p. 1149] to monitor compliance with the 1979 Convention, held three regular sessions [A/66/38 & A/67/38].

At its forty-eighth session (Geneva, 17 January– 4 February) [A/66/38], CEDAW considered and prepared concluding observations on the initial or periodic reports of Bangladesh, Belarus, Israel, Kenya, Liechtenstein, South Africa and Sri Lanka on measures taken to implement the Convention. CEDAW also considered a Secretary-General's report on the status of submission of reports by States parties under article 18 of the Convention [CEDAW/C/48/2]; a note by the Secretary-General on reports provided by specialized agencies on the implementation of the Convention in areas falling within the scope of their activities [CEDAW/C/48/3]; and a report of the United Nations Educational, Scientific and Cultural Organization (UNESCO) [CEDAW/C/48/3/Add.1]. The Committee elected its chair [A/66/38, (dec. 48/I)] and its remaining officers [dec. 48/II]; confirmed the members of the Working Group on Communications under the Optional Protocol to the Convention on the Elimination of All Forms of Discrimination against Women [dec. 48/III]; confirmed the members of the pre-session working group for the fifty-first session [dec. 48/IV]; expanded the working group on harmful practices [dec. 48/V]; confirmed the members of the working group on women in armed conflict and post-conflict situations [dec. 48/VI]; and decided to elaborate a general recommendation on access to justice and establish a working group in that regard [dec. 48/VII]. On 3 February [dec. 48/VIII], the Committee endorsed the revised draft outline of the general recommendation on harmful practices—developed jointly by CEDAW and the Committee on the Rights of the Child—and authorized the working group on harmful practices to start production of the draft. The Committee also established a task force to study a working paper prepared by the Office of the United Nations High Commissioner for Refugees on gender equality in the context of displacement and statelessness [dec. 48/IX].

On 28 July, by **decision 2011/254**, the Economic and Social Council took note of the Secretariat note [E/2011/105] transmitting the outcomes of the forty-sixth [YUN 2010, p. 1176], forty-seventh [ibid.] and forty-eighth sessions of CEDAW.

At its forty-ninth session (New York, 11–29 July) [A/67/38], CEDAW considered and prepared concluding observations on the initial or periodic reports of Costa Rica, Djibouti, Ethiopia, Italy, Nepal, the Republic of Korea, Singapore and Zambia. The Committee also considered a report of the Secretary-General on the status of submission of reports by States parties under article 18 of the Convention [CEDAW/C/48/2], and notes by the Secretary-General on reports provided by the specialized agencies on the implementation of the Convention in areas falling within the scope of their activities [CEDAW/C/49/3]; ways and means of expediting the work of the Committee [CEDAW/C/49/4]; and containing the reports of UNESCO [CEDAW/C/49/3/Add.2] and the International Labour Organization (ILO) [CEDAW/C/49/3/Add.4]. CEDAW decided to lift, on an indefinite basis, the simultaneous distribution policy with respect to its documentation [A/67/38 (dec. 49/I)]; to hold, on 18 July, a day of discussion on the draft general recommendation on women in armed conflict and post-conflict situations [dec. 49/II]; to send letters to Egypt and Tunisia on the rights of women in the democratization process [dec. 49/III]; and to confirm its practice of referring to comments received from States parties relating to concluding observations of the Committee without reproducing them in its report [dec. 49/IV]. The Committee decided to respond to the note verbale from Belarus dated 23 May, noting that the practice of the Committee in regard to recording comments from States parties was to refer to them in its reports to the General Assembly [dec. 49/V]. CEDAW confirmed the members of the pre-session working group for the fifty-second session [dec. 49/VI]; adopted a decision on the adoption procedure of general recommendations Nos. 27 and 28 [dec. 49/VII]; and adopted a statement with respect to the Working Group on Working Methods, in which it proposed that the task force on working methods be transformed into a standing working group [dec. 49/VIII]. It also adopted a statement on the list of issues, which proposed measures for enhanced prioritization and keeping replies as concise as possible [dec. 49/IX].

At its fiftieth session (Geneva, 3–21 October) [A/67/38], CEDAW considered and prepared concluding observations on the initial or periodic reports of Chad, Côte d'Ivoire, Kuwait, Lesotho, Mauritius, Montenegro, Oman and Paraguay. The Committee also considered a report of the Secretary-General on the status of submission of reports by States parties under article 18 of the Convention [CEDAW/C/48/2], an ILO report [CEDAW/C/50/3], and a UNESCO report [CEDAW/C/50/4]. The Committee established task forces to enhance the constructive dialogue with States parties, as a pilot project, during the fifty-first and fifty-second sessions, and to evaluate the impact of the task force approach during its fifty-second session [A/67/38 (dec. 50/I)]. In a decision on strengthening the role of the country rapporteur [dec. 50/II], the Committee stated that rapporteurs should have a more prominent role in providing guidance to experts in the preparation of and during the constructive dialogues, and that they should conduct informal consultations with experts in order to ensure full coverage of main areas of concern in the country and to prevent overlap. CEDAW further established an open-ended task force on inquiries [dec. 50/III], a joint working group with the Human Rights Committee [dec. 50/IV], and a working group on rural women [dec. 50/VII]. The task force on gender equality in the context of asylum, statelessness and natural disasters would be transformed into a working group [dec. 50/VIII]. The Committee appointed Dubravka Šimonović as focal point for the United Nations Entity for Gender Equality and the Empowerment of Women [dec. 50/IX] and Zohra Rasekh as focal point for HIV and gender equality [dec. 50/X]. It also adopted statements on rural women [dec. 50/VI] and the anniversaries of the adoptions of the 1951 Convention relating to the Status of Refugees [YUN 1951, p. 520] and the 1961 Convention on the Reduction of Statelessness [YUN 1961, p. 533] [dec. 50/V].

GENERAL ASSEMBLY ACTION

On 19 December [meeting 89], the General Assembly, on the recommendation of the Third Committee [A/66/455 & Corr.1], adopted **resolution 66/131** without vote [agenda item 28 (*a*)].

Convention on the Elimination of All Forms of Discrimination against Women

The General Assembly,

Recalling its resolution 64/138 of 18 December 2009,

1. *Welcomes* the report of the Secretary-General on the status of the Convention on the Elimination of All Forms of Discrimination against Women;

2. *Also welcomes* the reports of the Committee on the Elimination of Discrimination against Women on its forty-fourth and forty-fifth and forty-sixth to forty-eighth sessions;

3. *Invites* the Chair of the Committee on the Elimination of Discrimination against Women to address and engage in an interactive dialogue with the General Assembly at its sixty-seventh and sixty-eighth sessions under the item on the advancement of women;

4. *Requests* the Secretary-General to submit to the General Assembly at its sixty-eighth session a report on the status of the Convention.

Commission on the Status of Women

The Commission on the Status of Women, at its fifty-fifth session (New York, 12 March 2010, 22 February–4 March and 14 March 2011) [E/2011/27], recommended to the Economic and Social Council the adoption of a draft resolution on the situation of and assistance to Palestinian women (see p. 452) and a draft decision on the report of the Commission's fifty-fifth session and provisional agenda and documentation for its fifty-sixth (2012) session. As part of its priority theme, "Access and participation of women and girls in education, training and science and technology, including for the promotion of women's equal access to full employment and decent work", the Commission held a high-level round table and several panel discussions on the topic. It decided to transmit to the Council the summaries of those discussions [E/2011/27 (dec. 55/101)], together with agreed conclusions related to the priority theme, as an input to the annual ministerial review of 2011 (see p. 1056). The Commission brought to the Council's attention resolutions it had adopted on mainstreaming gender equality and promoting empowerment of women in climate change policies and strategies [res. 55/1] (see p. 1083), and on women, the girl child and HIV and AIDS [res. 55/2] (see p. 1070). It also brought to the Council's attention a decision by which it took note of the report of the Executive Director of UN-Women [E/CN.6/2011/2], a note by the Secretary-General transmitting the report of the United Nations Development Fund for Women on its activities to eliminate violence against women [A/HRC/16/34-E/CN.6/2011/9], and reports of the Secretary-General on the priority theme [E/CN.6/2011/3] (see p. 1068); on progress in mainstreaming a gender perspective into the development, implementation and evaluation of national policies and programmes [E/CN.6/2011/5] (see p. 1069); on women, the girl child and HIV and AIDS [E/CN.6/2011/7] (see p. 1070); and on the joint workplan of the Division for the Advancement of Women, now part of UN-Women, and the Office of the United Nations High Commissioner for Human Rights [A/HRC/16/33-E/CN.6/2011/8].

By **decision 2011/241** of 26 July, the Economic and Social Council took note of the Commission's report on its fifty-fifth session and approved the provisional agenda for its fifty-sixth (2012) session.

Communication. In a 21 November letter [E/CN.6/2012/14] to the Commission Chairperson, the Economic and Social Council President summarized the outcome of the Council's 2011 substantive session and annual ministerial review (see p. 1056) and attached a list of resolutions adopted by the Council calling for action by its functional commissions.

Other reports. Documents issued in 2011, to be addressed during the Commission's 2012 session, included reports of the Secretary-General on the release of women and children taken hostage [E/CN.6/2012/7]; female genital mutilation [E/CN.6/2012/8]; maternal mortality and morbidity [E/CN.6/2012/9]; women's economic empowerment [E/CN.6/2012/10]; women, the girl child and HIV and AIDS [E/CN.6/2012/11]; the situation of and assistance to Palestinian women [E/CN.6/2012/6]; the empowerment of rural women and their role in poverty and hunger eradication [E/CN.6/2012/3]; the role of gender-responsive governance and institutions in the empowerment of rural women [E/CN.6/2012/4]; and a note by the Secretariat on promoting employment and decent work to eradicate poverty in the context of the MDGs [E/CN.6/2012/15].

Communications on the status of women

At a closed meeting on 2 March [E/2011/27], the Commission considered the report of the Working Group on Communications concerning the Status of Women [E/CN.6/2011//CRP.2]. The Working Group had considered 52 confidential communications received by UN-Women and noted that there were 36 replies from Governments, 34 of which concerned the 2011 list of communications while two concerned the list of the previous year [YUN 2010, p. 1177]. No non-confidential communications were received. The Group observed that the communications most frequently concerned sexual violence, including rape, gang rape, forced prostitution, threats of rape, sexual harassment, including in the workplace, and failure by States to prevent such violations, provide protection and support for victims, and punish the perpetrators; other forms of violence, including domestic violence, and harmful traditional practices, including forced and early marriage, with a lack of due diligence by States to investigate, prosecute and punish the perpetrators, provide adequate protection and support for victims, and ensure access to justice; trafficking for the purposes of forced labour, in particular for domestic servitude, and commercial sexual exploitation, and failure by States to prevent such violations and investigate, prosecute and punish perpetrators, including those fuelling the demand for sexual exploitation; abuse of power by military, security and law enforcement personnel, humiliation, lack of due process and delays in proceedings, arbitrary arrest and detention, and failure to grant a fair trial and impunity; physical and psychological threats and pressure on victims of violence, their families and witnesses by private individuals and law enforcement officials; inhuman treatment in detention and inadequate conditions of imprisonment for women; serious violations of human rights, some of which targeted specific groups, such as girls with disabilities, widows, and asylum-seeking and refugee women; intimidation, harassment, detention of, and death threats against, women human rights defenders and their families; and violations of the right to health, including sexual and reproductive health.

During its consideration of communications, the Working Group expressed concern about violence against women and girls and the mistreatment and detention of women human rights defenders and their families; harmful traditional practices, such as forced and early marriage; violations of the right of women to health, including sexual and reproductive health; the increasing number of cases of trafficking in women and girls; the climate of impunity and abuse of power, including where violence against women was perpetrated by law enforcement; the failure by States to exercise due diligence to prevent and respond to violence against women and girls; the persistence of gender stereotypes, including through the media; and discrimination and violence against specific groups, such as widows, asylum-seeking, refugee and internally displaced women, and girls with disabilities.

The Working Group was encouraged that some Governments had investigated the allegations and taken measures, including enacting new legislation; conducting legal reform; introducing policies and services, such as health-related services, to better protect and assist women, including victims of violence; developing national plans of action; prosecuting and punishing perpetrators of violence; and introducing targeted measures for the promotion of women's rights, including through gender-sensitive budgeting and public awareness-raising activities to promote gender equality and the advancement of women.

UN-Women

On 1 January, the United Nations Entity for Gender Equality and the Empowerment of Women (UN-Women), established by General Assembly resolution 64/289 [YUN 2010, p. 1396], became fully operational. The entity combined the mandates and assets of the four existing gender equality entities—namely, the United Nations Development Fund for Women (UNIFEM), the Office of the Special Adviser to the Secretary-General on Gender Issues and Advancement of Women the Division for the Advancement of Women, and the International Research and Training Institute for the Advancement of Women (INSTRAW). Its work was guided by the Convention on the Elimination of All Forms of Discrimination against Women [YUN 1979, p. 889], the Beijing Declaration and Platform for Action [YUN 1995, p. 1170], Security Council resolution 1325(2000) [YUN 2000, p. 1113] on women, peace and security, and the Millennium Declaration [YUN 2000, p. 49] and Millennium Development Goals. Geared towards delivering results on gender equality, the empowerment of women and gender mainstreaming, UN-Women conducted its work in three functional areas. Its operational activities responded to the needs and priorities of Member States at the national level; its normative support to intergovernmental processes strengthened the global policy framework; and its role in the UN system enhanced the coordination and accountability of UN work on gender. The General Assembly, Economic and Social Council, and Commission on the Status of Women provided governance and policy guidance for UN-Women's normative support function, while the Assembly, the Council and the UN-Women Executive Board provided governance and policy guidance on the entity's operational activities.

Economic and Social Council coordination segment. At the coordination segment of its substantive session (11–14 and 28 July), the Economic and Social Council focused on the role of the UN system in promoting implementation of the ministerial declaration on gender equality and the empowerment of women, adopted by the Council during its 2010 annual ministerial review [YUN 2010, p. 1135]. The Council had before it a May report [E/2011/85] of the Secretary-General on the topic, which addressed ways in which the system could strengthen its capacity to ensure coordinated action, with UN-Women in the leadership role.

The report noted that prior to the establishment of UN-Women, a number of gaps in the existing architecture had been identified, including weak coordination between intergovernmental decision- and policy-making and implementation at the country level; lack of a recognized driver with the authority and positioning to lead; lack of representation in high-level policy decision-making; and lack of accountability, political will and support for gender equality. Expectations were high that UN-Women would address these challenges in line with paragraph 52 of its founding resolution [YUN 2010, p. 1396].

The report also reviewed progress made by the UN system on the following cross-cutting issues identified in the ministerial declaration: discriminatory attitudes and gender stereotypes, including in the education sector; ending all forms of discrimination and violence against women and girls across all sectors; full empowerment of women, including equal participation of women and men in decision-making; the critical role of men and boys for the achievement of gender equality and women's empowerment; full integration of women into the formal economy; measures to ensure that women and girls with disabilities were not subject to multiple or aggravated forms of discrimination; the crucial role and contribution of rural women, including indigenous women; and the need to accelerate progress on women's health.

The Secretary-General concluded that it was important for all relevant actors to focus on lessons learned and good practices, and summarized some areas for further work by the relevant UN bodies, with the support of Governments and other stakeholders. These included requiring the full and equal participation of women in all political and economic decision-making processes; linking girls' and women's educational gains with employment opportunities; implementing a systematic and comprehensive approach aimed at eliminating all forms of violence against women, including in humanitarian settings; increasing proactive measures to put an end to discriminatory practices and gender stereotypes; mobilizing civil society towards stronger engagement of men and boys; promoting decent work for rural women; and increasing investment in well-functioning health systems and empowering women and communities to access them.

Institutional arrangements. In response to resolution 64/289 [YUN 2010, p. 1396], the Secretary-General submitted a July report [A/66/120] on strengthening the institutional arrangements for the support of gender equality and the empowerment of women, which covered progress with regard to the general principles of UN-Women; governance of the entity; administration and human resources; financing; and transitional arrangements. In January, as a first step in defining the UN-Women workplan, the Executive Director launched her "Vision and 100-day action plan", which set out the core principles and priorities for the building of a strong organization. In addition, the first UN-Women strategic plan, 2011–2013 (see p. 1096)—based on consultations with approximately 5,000 partners from national Governments, civil society, academia, the UN system and international development organizations—set out the entity's vision, mission and priorities. With regard to its coordination role, UN-Women made progress in developing a strategy that built on existing UN coordination mechanisms, such as the United Nations System Chief Executives Board for Coordination; the High-Level Committee on Programmes; the High-Level Committee on Management; and the Inter-Agency Network on Women and Gender Equality (see p. 1080). The strategy also covered the entity's approach to regional- and country-level coordination. In order to maintain and forge effective partnerships with civil society and coordinate and facilitate the participation of non-governmental organizations in the annual sessions of the Commission on the Status of Women, a Civil Society Section was created.

All transitional arrangements were successfully completed by the end of 2010, enabling UN-Women to become fully operational on 1 January without disrupting the activities of the four former entities. The Secretary-General concluded that the core elements for the effective functioning of the entity were in place, particularly its governance structure, with the establishment of the UN-Women Executive Board and the preparation of key planning and budgeting instruments and decisions thereon by the relevant intergovernmental bodies. While UN-Women had made excellent progress in putting in place the necessary administrative frameworks, consolidating its staff resources, and initiating the consolidation and strengthening of its field office structure, it had yet to fully establish its presence on the ground. Drawing attention to the need for further elaboration of the role of UN-Women in leading, coordinating and promoting the accountability of United Nations work for gender equality, the Secretary-General noted that the mobilization of necessary resources for achieving the entity's goals remained a challenge.

ECONOMIC AND SOCIAL COUNCIL ACTION

On 14 July [meeting 29], the Economic and Social Council adopted **resolution 2011/5** [draft: E/2011/L.29] without vote [agenda item 4].

The role of the United Nations system in implementing the internationally agreed goals and commitments in regard to gender equality and the empowerment of women

The Economic and Social Council,

Recalling the United Nations Millennium Declaration and the 2005 World Summit Outcome,

Recalling also the ministerial declaration adopted at the high-level segment of its substantive session of 2010 and its resolution 2008/29 of 24 July 2008,

Reaffirming that the full and effective implementation of the Beijing Declaration and Platform for Action and the outcome documents of the twenty-third special session of the General Assembly, the Convention on the Elimination of All Forms of Discrimination against Women by States parties, Member States' commitments under the Programme of Action of the International Conference on Population and Development, the outcomes of other relevant United Nations summits and conferences, and relevant resolutions, is part of an interconnected framework that underpins the work undertaken to advance gender equality and the empowerment of women and produces essential contributions to the achievement of the internationally agreed development goals, including those contained in the United Nations Millennium Declaration,

Welcoming the establishment of the United Nations Entity for Gender Equality and the Empowerment of Women (UN-Women) by the General Assembly in resolution 64/289 of 2 July 2010,

Reaffirming its agreed conclusions 1997/2 of 18 July 1997 on mainstreaming a gender perspective into all policies and programmes in the United Nations system and subsequent resolutions adopted on the same topic,

1. *Takes note with appreciation* of the report of the Secretary-General on the theme of the coordination segment;

2. *Recognizes* efforts made by the United Nations system to promote more robust and better coordinated

efforts to achieve gender equality and the empowerment of women, and encourages further efforts in that regard;

3. *Stresses* that the establishment of the United Nations Entity for Gender Equality and the Empowerment of Women (UN-Women) creates an opportunity and a responsibility for the whole United Nations system to scale up its efforts aimed at promoting gender equality and the empowerment of women, and to increase the attention paid to gender issues throughout the work of the United Nations system, and urges UN-Women to leverage effectively on its unique role as a United Nations entity that supports both normative processes and operational activities;

4. *Calls upon* UN-Women to fully assume, in accordance with the principle of universality, its role of leading, coordinating and promoting the accountability of the United Nations system in its work on gender equality and the empowerment of women, and of ensuring more effective coordination, coherence and gender mainstreaming within the United Nations system, and to continue to follow up on and support United Nations entities to advance effectively their work in that regard;

5. *Urges* all Member States and other stakeholders to enhance UN-Women and other United Nations system-wide efforts to promote gender equality and the empowerment of women through predictable, stable and sustainable financial support and encourages them to increase such financial support, and encourages UN-Women to seek to expand its financial support base;

6. *Encourages* UN-Women to use existing mechanisms, including the Inter-Agency Network on Women and Gender Equality and the United Nations System Chief Executives Board for Coordination, in a proactive and effective way in order to ensure the mainstreaming of a gender perspective across all areas of the United Nations work and, especially, to promote system-wide accountability on gender equality and the empowerment of women at the global, regional and country levels;

7. *Urges* the United Nations system, including agencies, funds and programmes, to recognize gender equality and the empowerment of women and girls as essential for achieving all the internationally agreed development goals, including the Millennium Development Goals, and to support action to address the cross-cutting issues identified in the ministerial declaration adopted at the high-level segment of its substantive session of 2010, so as to close implementation gaps that still persist in the achievement of gender equality and the empowerment of women in that respect;

8. *Calls upon* the United Nations system to give priority to the economic empowerment of women, with UN-Women to play a coordinating role in accordance with its mandate, including through promoting economic and social policies that uphold the rights of women and provide them with opportunities to fully participate in the formal labour force, to receive equal pay for equal work or work of equal value and to benefit from social protections on a non-discriminatory basis, and that promote the equal sharing of responsibilities between women and men;

9. *Also calls upon* the United Nations system to give priority to programmes that support girls' and women's transition from school to work by, inter alia, promoting their equal access to education at all levels, including technical and vocational training, expanding employment opportunities, including in new and non-traditional fields, supporting women's opportunities in business, trade, information and communications technology and entrepreneurial areas, and facilitating access to job search support services;

10. *Calls upon* United Nations entities, in their respective areas of competence and in accordance with their mandates, to strengthen women's participation in international trade, and to promote the contribution that Aid for Trade, including the Enhanced Integrated Framework for Trade-related Technical Assistance to Least Developed Countries, can make to that end;

11. *Encourages* all relevant United Nations entities to contribute towards the achievement of gender equality and the empowerment of women in the agricultural sector in order to enhance agricultural productivity, rural and agricultural development, improve food security and eradicate poverty, by promoting full employment and decent work for rural women and men, supporting rural women's equal access to land and other productive resources, including credit and technology, strengthening rural institutions and women's groups and enhancing rural women's and girls' productive capacities, as well as supporting rural women's, including indigenous women's, participation in planning and decision-making, so that they can realize their full potential;

12. *Encourages* the United Nations system, including the Bretton Woods institutions, in accordance with their mandates, to include a gender perspective in all responses to the financial and economic crisis, including recovery and stimulus packages, and to put in place appropriate mechanisms to ensure that resources and support reach women;

13. *Calls upon* the United Nations system, in particular the Food and Agriculture Organization of the United Nations, the International Fund for Agricultural Development and the World Food Programme, to ensure that responses to volatile food prices and ongoing concerns over food security consistently integrate a gender perspective, so as to prevent and mitigate any disproportionate negative impact on women;

14. *Urges* the United Nations system to work towards the active involvement of men and boys in promoting gender equality and the empowerment of women and the elimination of violence against women, and to make efforts to engage civil society organizations to that end;

15. *Requests* the World Health Organization, the United Nations Population Fund, the United Nations Children's Fund and other relevant United Nations entities to invest in and enhance national capacities to ensure well-functioning health systems that fully address the needs of women and girls and empower women, girls and communities to access them, and to scale up maternal and child mortality reduction strategies and strengthen family planning programmes, which are key to achieving the Millennium Development Goals, and in that regard welcomes the Secretary-General's Global Strategy for Women's and Children's Health;

16. *Encourages* United Nations entities, including the World Health Organization, to pay increased attention to the gender dimension in responses to HIV/AIDS and other communicable diseases, and non-communicable diseases, including through supporting national multisectoral initiatives that increase the capacity of women and girls to protect themselves from contracting these diseases;

17. *Urges* UN-Women and all United Nations entities to promote the full and equal participation of women in decision-making processes at all levels, including in political and economic decision-making processes, and to ensure that programmes and activities carried out by the United Nations system take into account the needs of women and girls, and men and boys;

18. *Calls upon* the United Nations system, upon request by Member States to support their efforts, including through national machineries for the advancement of women, to eliminate gender stereotypes in all spheres of life, including in public and political life, to foster the positive portrayal of women and girls as leaders and decision makers at all levels and in all areas and to promote the equal sharing of responsibilities between women and men;

19. *Calls upon* UN-Women and all other relevant United Nations entities, in their respective areas of competence and in accordance with their mandates, to strengthen efforts at all levels to end all forms of discrimination and violence against women and girls, including through an increased focus on prevention and the training of public officials, in particular those in law enforcement and judicial systems and health service providers, and effective support for victims and survivors, while addressing the linkages between violence against women and other issues;

20. *Urges* the United Nations system, including all its entities, to take further measures, in accordance with their agreed mandates, to improve women's participation during all stages of peace processes, and to support the efforts of Member States in that regard, with their agreement and consent, in post-conflict planning and peacebuilding, including by enhancing women's engagement in political and economic decision-making, including at early stages of recovery processes, and in that regard, to strengthen efforts to increase the number of women special representatives and special envoys;

21. *Urges* UN-Women and other United Nations entities to continue to promote the collection and analysis of relevant, accurate and reliable data, disaggregated by sex and age, to ensure that public policies are effectively grounded and targeted to reach all women, including women living in poverty, older women, migrant women, indigenous women, women with disabilities, women affected by HIV/AIDS, women living in rural or remote areas and women living in urban slums;

22. *Requests* the Under-Secretary-General and Executive Director of UN-Women to include information on the implementation of the present resolution in future presentations to be made to the Economic and Social Council or in relevant documentation to be submitted to the Council, including at its substantive session of 2012.

Executive Board

At its first regular session of the year (New York, 24–26 January) [UNW/2011/8], the Executive Board approved the report [UNW/2011/1] and decisions [UNW/2011/2] of the 2010 organizational session [YUN 2010, p. 1182]; the tentative workplan for its 2011 annual session in June (see below); and the tentative annual workplan for 2011. The Board also approved a decision on the 2010–2011 biennial support budget for UN-Women (see p. 1098); adopted its draft rules of procedure [UNW/2011/6]; and postponed consideration of the proposed financial regulations and rules of UN-Women to its resumed first regular session in order to take into account the views of the Advisory Committee on Administrative and Budgetary Questions.

At its resumed first regular session (21 March and 8 April) [UNW/2011/8/Add.1], the Executive Board adopted a decision on proposed financial regulations and rules of UN-Women (see p. 1100), and postponed its second regular session of 2011 to 5–7 December, thereby allowing the consideration of the support budget for the biennium 2012–2013 to take into account the result of the Executive Board's discussions on the strategic plan, 2011–2013, at its annual session.

At the annual session (New York, 27–30 June) [UNW/2011/10], the Executive Board adopted decisions on the UN-Women strategic plan, 2011–2013 (see below) and the Istanbul Programme of Action (see p. 828). With regard to financial, budgetary and administrative matters, three sub-items were introduced and addressed: the implementation of approved resource allocations; the harmonization of budget methodologies; and funding commitments to UN-Women. During the session, two side events were hosted by UN-Women: an interactive panel on best practices from the field, and a briefing on the use of social media by UN-Women.

At its second regular session of 2011 (New York, 5–7 December) [UNW/2012/2], the Executive Board adopted the report on its annual session in June; the tentative workplan for its first regular session of 2012, to be held in January; and the proposed annual workplan of the Executive Board for 2012. The Board also approved a decision on the UN-Women biennial institutional budget 2012–2013 (see p. 1099).

Functional areas

Operational activities

UN-Women strategic plan. In May, the Executive Director submitted to the Executive Board the UN-Women strategic plan, 2011–2013 [UNW/2011/9], which set out the vision, mission and priorities of the organization in supporting Member States and the UN system. The plan, which was driven by a longer-term vision and goals and results to 2017, contained three interrelated components—a development results framework, a management results framework and an integrated resources framework. The development results framework comprised the following six main areas of work, each supported by defined outcomes, targets and indicators: increase women's leadership and participation in all areas that affected their lives; increase women's access to economic empowerment and opportunities, especially for those who were most excluded; prevent violence against women and girls and expand access to survivor services; increase women's leadership in peace and security and humanitarian response; and strengthen the responsiveness of plans and budgets at all levels to gender equality. The sixth goal involved support for a comprehensive set of global norms, policies and standards on gender equality and women's empowerment that responded to new and emerging issues, challenges and opportunities and provided a firm basis for action by Governments and other stakeholders. The management results framework presented four system-level output clusters that were essential to UN-Women support for development results. These were to drive more effective and efficient UN system coordination and strategic partnerships; to institutionalize a strong culture of results-based management, reporting, knowledge management and evaluation; to enhance organizational effectiveness; and to mobilize and leverage adequate resources. The integrated resources framework showed the planned projected total income of UN-Women for the strategic plan, 2011–2013, and indicated how these funds were apportioned. The report addressed the modalities for launching the strategic plan at country, regional and global levels and stressed the need to adapt the organizational structure of UN-Women to support efficient and effective implementation.

The Executive Director presented the strategic plan, 2011–2013, at the annual session of the Executive Board (New York, 27–30 June) [UNW/2011/10]. Overall, delegations were satisfied with the plan and many speakers noted that it was a step towards achieving gender equality and closing the gap between global norms and the daily realities faced by women worldwide. On 30 June, the Executive Board adopted a decision [UNW/2011/10 (dec. 2011/3)] endorsing the UN-Women strategic plan, 2011–2013, and requesting the Executive Director to emphasize the importance of education and training as an enabling instrument for women's empowerment and leadership; mobilize relevant UN bodies and stakeholders to strengthen the provision of specialized education and training, in particular by using existing modalities and mechanisms; and submit to the Board, beginning at its annual session in 2012, an annual progress report on the strategic plan, 2011–2013, and provide updates at its regular sessions in 2012 and 2013. Recognizing the strategic plan's results-based approach, the Board requested that UN-Women further develop the results frameworks and present a timetable for consultations with Member States on the matter, in order to improve the linkages between outputs and outcomes, and also requested the Executive Director to present the revised results frameworks to the Executive Board prior to its 2013 annual session.

Least developed countries. On 30 June [UNW/2011/10 (dec. 2011/4)], the Executive Board adopted a decision welcoming the General Assembly's endorsement of the Istanbul Declaration and Programme of Action for the Least Developed Countries for the Decade 2011–2020 (see p. 828), adopted at the Fourth United Nations Conference on the Least Developed Countries (Istanbul, 9–13 May). The Board stressed the need for UN-Women to give special attention to the implementation of the Istanbul Programme of Action in its support of the least developed countries, and invited the Executive Director to integrate the implementation of the Programme of Action into the activities of UN-Women in accordance with its mandate.

Report of Executive Director. In December, the UN-Women Executive Director submitted to the Executive Board her first annual report [UNW/2012/1] on the entity's operational activities, in response to resolution 64/289 [YUN 2010, p. 1396]. The Executive Director noted that in 2011—a year of transition for UN-Women—a vision for the entity was articulated, a field capacity assessment was carried out and the strategic plan was endorsed and being implemented. A strong staffing base was established at Headquarters and the process was being extended to the field. In addition, a resource mobilization strategy had been outlined to ensure that UN-Women could deliver on the high expectations of stakeholders.

In order to secure more robust and predictable funding for its operational activities, three approaches would be used: (*a*) widen the donor base by sustaining and enlarging core contributions from current Government donors providing the largest contributions, targeting Government donors who may be able to make greater contributions and strengthening efforts to solicit contributions from emerging donors; (*b*) identify new opportunities for cost-sharing resources to complement the core resource base, including for the two trust funds managed by UN-Women—the United Nations Trust Fund in Support of Actions to Eliminate Violence against Women (see p. 1071) and the Fund for Gender Equality, which completed its first grant-making cycle at the end of 2010; and (*c*) expand the non-traditional partnerships of UN-Women, especially with the private sector, foundations and the national committees. On the entity's contribution to national capacity development—discussed in the context of each of the main areas of work identified in the UN-Women strategic plan, 2011–2013 (see p. 1096)—a multitude of approaches were adopted, including training, the dissemination of knowledge resources, the posting of experts or advisers on gender equality in key institutions, South-South exchange and cooperation, convening or mobilizing networks and providing financial or technical support. UN-Women promoted new initiatives and strengthened UN-system-wide accountability mechanisms for gender equality, including the adoption of a gender marker to track resources for gender equality and performance indicators to assess the gender responsiveness of common country programming. Towards ensuring the programming capacity of UN country teams, UN-Women monitored the coverage of gender issues in the annual reports of Resident Coordinators, which showed an overall trend towards stronger support for gender equality and the empowerment of women. As joint programming had become a preferred UN-country-team programming modality, the number of joint programmes in which UN-Women participated had steadily increased to a total of 104. UN-Women was present in all "Delivering as one" pilot countries, and such pilots had contributed important lessons on how the United Nations could provide coordinated support to Member States on achieving national priorities on gender equality. The Executive Director noted that while the entity could not support a physical presence in all countries seeking its technical and advisory support, it would continue to extend its reach through investment in online portals addressing the needs of specific practitioner communities, and offer access to knowledge products informed by evaluations, research and training conducted by UN-Women and its partners.

Normative support

In response to resolution 64/289 [YUN 2010, p. 1396], the Executive Director of UN-Women reported [E/CN.6/2012/2] to the Commission on the Status of Women on the normative aspects of the entity's work, in particular its support for gender-specific intergovernmental processes and efforts to increase attention to gender equality aspects in sectoral intergovernmental processes. In 2011, key objectives of the work of UN-Women included the delivery of critical support and forward-looking recommendations to intergovernmental discussions, as well as the leveraging of such discussions to help shape a results-oriented and actionable agenda for gender equality and the empowerment of women. Those efforts resulted in greater coherence between the support UN-Women provided to normative processes and the operational support it provided to partners at the national level.

UN-Women supported the Commission's fifty-fifth session, which resulted in a set of agreed conclusions (see p. 1092) that expanded the global normative framework in a number of key areas, including national legislation and programmes; access to and participation in education; gender-sensitive education and training; the transition from education to full employment and decent work; and women in science and technology employment. UN-Women's engagement with the work of the Economic and Social Council (see p. 1093) focused on the Council's role with regard to gender mainstreaming and operational activities. In the reports prepared to support the Third Committee's deliberations on a number of thematic questions to advance the gender equality agenda, UN-Women flagged areas where further progress was needed and proposed recommendations that proved useful in negotiation processes and outcomes on issues including gender-responsive budgeting and support for women migrant workers. In the field of security, UN-Women sought to support Member States in the implementation of policy commitments pertaining to women's needs during and after conflict, and ensure that women were empowered to participate as key actors in conflict prevention and resolution and long-term peacebuilding. To promote attention to gender equality issues that could be leveraged for results on the ground, UN-Women strategically targeted three major UN intergovernmental processes and a global event—the high-level meeting on AIDS in June (see p. 1135), the Conference of the Parties to the United Nations Framework Convention on Climate Change in December, the United Nations Conference on Sustainable Development, to be held in 2012, and the Fourth High-level Forum on Aid Effectiveness in November (see p. 939). In its engagements, UN-Women linked its normative support function with its operational experience and expertise, and moved to implement the normative guidance of intergovernmental bodies. Priority emphasis was placed on supporting the work of Member States, intergovernmental bodies, to further refine and expand the normative framework, as well as on helping to close the implementation gap between the policy commitments of Member States and women's daily realities.

Administrative and budgetary matters

UN-Women governance

Bureau of the Executive Board. At its 2010 organizational session [YUN 2010, p. 1182], the UN-Women Executive Board decided that its Bureau should be elected from among representatives of all its members, taking into consideration equitable geographical representation, and should consist of a President and four Vice-Presidents. It further decided that the presidency should rotate each year to a different regional group in alphabetical order beginning with Africa, and elected the members of the Bureau for 2011 [UNW/2011/1 (dec. 2010/1)].

Biennial budget 2010–2011

Pursuant to General Assembly resolution 64/289 [YUN 2010, p. 1396], the UN-Women Executive Director submitted to the Executive Board a January report [UNW/2011/3] on proposals for the use of voluntary resources for the support budget for the biennium 2010–2011. The report indicated how the Executive Director proposed to build the capacity required by UN-Women to deliver results that met its mandates and the demands for support from Member States. The proposed budget assumed that an amount of $500 million would be the total resources used by UN-Women in 2011, of which $413 million would be allocated for development programmes, $76 million for the support budget, $8 million for one-off costs for change management and the move of UN-Women headquarters to consolidated office premises, and $3 million for security and other costs mandated by the Assembly. The Executive Director proposed to use a share of the support budget to fund 160 posts, thereby establishing the basic institutional capacity needed to provide a minimum package of support services in at least 40 countries by year's end, and to create 95 new posts to provide the capacity required to implement the new United Nations coordination, gender mainstreaming and accountability functions and for increasing the scale of in-country operations in response to demand.

ACABQ report. In a January report [UNW/2011/4], the Advisory Committee on Administrative and Budgetary Questions (ACABQ) considered the proposals of the UN-Women Executive Director. The Committee supported the goal of maximizing funds for programme activities, but was of the view that the approach set out in the budget proposal should be clarified and further considered. It recommended that a revised support budget estimate be submitted for consideration by the Executive Board in June. As the priority was to ensure that UN-Women was provided with the necessary resources to meet its immediate operational requirements and to complete the ongoing planning and review processes, ACABQ recommended approval of the following elements of the proposed support budget: 97 posts currently funded from the biennium support budgets of UNIFEM and INSTRAW; the position of Assistant Secretary-General to head the Programme and Policy pillar; $8 million proposed for one-time costs related to the change management process; $6,189,000 in respect of non-post resources, together with an additional $2 million to meet priority requirements during the first six months of the year; and the provisions proposed for security, after-service health insurance and requirements relating to International Public Sector Accounting Standards. As the Committee was of the view that the migration of existing programme-funded posts should await the completion in February of the field capacity assessment and approval of the strategic plan, it did not recommend approval of new posts or the migration of posts related to field capacity to the support budget at that time.

Management response. In her response [UNW/2011/4/Add.1] to the ACABQ report, the Executive Director, concerning field capacity, did not agree that no action should be taken pending completion of the strategic plan and field capacity assessment. She set out elements of the support budget that she considered to require immediate approval.

Executive Board action. On 26 January [UNW/2011/8 (dec. 2011/1)], the Executive Board approved gross voluntary resources in the amount of $51.5 million; the additional amount of $2.5 million from voluntary core resources to cover UN-mandated security costs and $0.3 million for costs related to the adoption of the International Public Sector Accounting Standards and enhancement of the Atlas system; and the additional amounts of $5 million to support change management and $3 million for the move of premises and related technology installation.

Biennial budget 2012–2013

In an October report [UNW/2011/11], the Executive Director presented the institutional budget estimates for UN-Women for the biennium 2012–2013. The budget had been prepared in accordance with the harmonized results-based-budgeting and cost classification methodology applied by the United Nations Development Programme (UNDP), the United Nations Children's Fund, and the United Nations Population Fund (UNFPA), and was estimated at $140.8 million gross ($132.3 million net). In accordance with General Assembly resolution 64/289 [YUN 2010, p. 1396], the resources required to support the intergovernmental normative processes were being proposed by the Secretary-General in the context of the proposed UN programme budget (see p. 1375).

The budget provided for the institutional resources needed to implement the strategic plan (see p. 1096), and reflected the principal priority of strengthening the capacity of UN-Women to support countries in their pursuit of nationally owned priorities in gender equality and the empowerment of women. To that end, it provided for the phased development of 21 new country presences in 2012–2013, as well as the strengthening of UN-Women capacity in the 17 country presences for which the Executive Board had approved institutional budget resources for 2011. The budget represented 19.1 per cent of envisaged resource utilization. Over 86.3 per cent of resources would be devoted to development activities, while the share devoted to management activities would be 10.8 per cent.

ACABQ report. In its consideration [UNW/2011/12] of the proposed institutional budget for UN-Women, ACABQ recognized that the 2012–2013 institutional budget, being the first proposed biennial budget, served as a foundation for successive UN-Women budgets. While the Advisory Committee had no objection to the use of a "net" appropriation, it nonetheless noted that the majority of anticipated income had not been applied to offset the budget. Further explanation should be provided directly to the Executive Board as to why a larger contribution from extrabudgetary income should not be made towards the cost of the institutional budget. Should the balance of income be received, the Committee requested that clarification also be provided to the Board on how that income would be utilized and what role, if any, the Board would have in that process. ACABQ considered that the full support costs should have been clearly set out in the proposed budget and recommended that they be presented in future budgets with greater clarity and transparency. The Committee also noted that proposals for posts in the UN-Women institutional budget were not sufficiently based on workload indicators and requested that future budgetary submissions contain full justification for the posts requested. Concluding, ACABQ recognized that the proposal for the first UN-Women biennial institutional budget was more realistic than previous projections, taking into account the difficult economic circumstances and their potential impact on the level of voluntary contributions, and recommended its approval.

Management response. On 20 December, UN-Women provided a management response [UNW/2011/12/Add.1] to selected comments and recommendations of the Advisory Committee.

Executive Board action. On 7 December [UNW/2012/2 (dec. 2011/5)], the Executive Board approved a gross appropriation of $140.8 million for the institutional budget for 2012–2013; noted that funding from core voluntary resources was estimated at $132.3 million and funding from other resources and trust funds at $8.5 million; and recognized that additional extrabudgetary income earned should be used for the institutional budget.

Proposed financial regulations

Pursuant to General Assembly resolution 64/289 [YUN 2010, p. 1396], the Executive Director submitted for consideration by the Executive Board the proposed financial regulations and rules for UN-Women [UNW/2011/5 & Rev.1], taking into account the views expressed by the Office of the Controller and the Office of Legal Affairs, and incorporating the changes recommended by ACABQ (see below). The proposed financial regulations and rules were drawn primarily from the UNFPA financial regulations and rules; some were drawn from those of UNDP. The addendum to the report contained a comparison between the proposed financial regulations and rules and those of UNDP and UNFPA [UNW/2011/5/Add.1], providing explanations for deviations from those documents.

ACABQ report. In its consideration of the proposed financial regulations and rules [UNW/2011/7], the Advisory Committee was of the view that they provided an appropriate framework for governing the financial management of UN-Women but that adjustments to a number of the proposed regulations and rules were necessary to provide greater clarity, particularly in the sections relating to the preparation and submission of requests for funding under the biennial programme budget (the regular budget). ACABQ also recommended deleting certain proposed regulations and rules and including a provision that addressed the area of programme budget implications.

Executive Board action. On 8 April, the Executive Board took note of the report on the proposed financial regulations and rules for UN-Women and the related ACABQ report, and adopted the UN-Women financial rules and regulations [UNW/2011/8/Add.1 (dec. 2011/2)].

Chapter XI
Children

In 2011, climate-related disasters, humanitarian emergencies, conflicts and economic turbulence all took their toll on children, especially the poorest. The United Nations Children's Fund (UNICEF) responded with its partners to alleviate the worst suffering, and help communities rebuild and strengthen resilience.

More broadly, UNICEF deepened implementation of its equity agenda, putting first the rights of those children who were the most marginalized and most in need of assistance. The Fund cooperated with 151 countries, areas and territories focusing on five main issues: young child survival and development; basic education and gender equality; HIV/AIDS and children; child protection from violence, exploitation and abuse; and policy advocacy and partnerships for children's rights. In 2011, UNICEF programme assistance expenditure totalled $3,472 million.

The UNICEF global network of field offices strove to reach the poorest and most remote communities with life-saving interventions and supplies. At the country level, UNICEF supported the efforts of Governments to increase routine immunization, improve the quality of education, boost school enrolment and expand access to vital health services, including measures to prevent transmission of HIV from mother to child.

The General Assembly in December took action to strengthen collaboration on child protection within the UN system.

Follow-up to 2002 General Assembly special session on children

In response to General Assembly resolutions 58/157 [YUN 2003, p. 781] and 58/282 [YUN 2004, p. 1175], the Secretary-General in August submitted his ninth report [A/66/258] on the follow-up to the Assembly's twenty-seventh (2002) special session on children [YUN 2002, p. 1168]. He reviewed progress achieved in realizing the commitments set out in the Declaration and Plan of Action contained in the session's final document, "A world fit for children", adopted in resolution S-27/2 [ibid., p. 1169]. Failure to achieve the commitments would undermine efforts to attain the Millennium Development Goals (MDGs) by 2015 and beyond. The Secretary-General considered progress and room for growth in the four major areas of the Plan of Action: promoting healthy lives; providing quality education; protecting against abuse, exploitation and violence; and combating HIV/AIDS.

Within the area of health, the mortality rate for children under the age of five in developing countries declined from 99 deaths per 1,000 live births in 1990 to 66 deaths per 1,000 live births in 2009, representing the lowest number on record. From 2000 to 2008, the combination of improved immunization coverage and the opportunity for a second vaccine dose contributed to a 78 per cent drop in deaths caused by measles globally; however, neonatal mortality reduction continued to be slower. The transmission of polio continued in Afghanistan, India, Nigeria and Pakistan. As at early 2011, only 58 of 118 countries with data available were on track to meet the target of halving the number of underweight children. Vitamin A supplementation coverage had more than doubled in the least developed countries and progress had been made in eliminating iodine deficiency disorders. Progress in infant and young child feeding, however, had been modest. The Secretary-General's High-level Task Force on the Global Food Security Crisis [YUN 2008, p. 1343] made significant efforts to improve the nutrition of children and women in developing countries. The 2010 World Conference on Early Childhood Care and Education, organized by the United Nations Educational, Scientific and Cultural Organization (UNESCO) [YUN 2010, p. 1184], focused on equity and inclusion, and called for the extension of quality care for young children. The Secretary-General's Global Strategy for Women's and Children's Health [ibid., p. 1140] outlined the key areas where action was required to enhance financing, strengthen policy and improve service delivery.

In the area of education, considerable progress was made in terms of increased enrolments, narrowed gender gaps and extended opportunities for children in disadvantaged groups, although an estimated 67 million children of primary school age were out of school in 2008. Forty-two per cent of those children lived in poor countries affected by conflict. A key achievement in terms of policy development in 2010 was the adoption of the Dakar Declaration on Accelerating Girls' Education and Gender Equality. The Education for All Fast Track Initiative had been successful in leveraging funds for country education sector plans and the development of plans; however, the quality of education was lagging behind improvement in school enrolment ratios.

Establishing a protective environment for children, especially for girls, had become an integral part of quality education.

In developing countries, nearly half of children under age five were not registered and were, therefore, beyond the reach of protection and basic services. Strengthening child protection systems continued to be a major focus, with an estimated 131 countries engaged in reinforcing social welfare and justice systems. UNICEF and other partners worked with legislators and policymakers to improve legal and policy frameworks around child protection. There was a growing trend in aligning national policies with international standards for alternative care, including those recommended by the 2009 Guidelines for the Alternative Care for Children [YUN 2009, p. 1161]. A Road Map for Achieving the Elimination of the Worst Forms of Child Labour by 2016, a result of the International Labour Organization's Global Child Labour Conference in 2010, would track progress through 2016.

In 2009, there were 2.5 million children under age 15 living with HIV. Globally, HIV treatment coverage was notably lower for children than for adults; however, an array of cost-effective antiretroviral formulations for children was available. From 2005 to 2009, the number of children orphaned by AIDS increased from 14.6 million to 16.6 million. Routine and voluntary HIV testing and counselling of all pregnant women were considered the key entry points for services in the prevention of mother-to-child HIV transmission.

The Secretary-General recommended an equity-focused approach to achieving the MDGs, with efforts concentrating on the most vulnerable and disadvantaged children and families.

Promotion and protection of the rights of children

General Assembly action. The General Assembly, by **resolution 66/138** of 19 December (see p. 623), adopted the Optional Protocol to the Convention on the Rights of the Child on a communications procedure. That would allow the Committee on the Rights of the Child to receive complaints about violations and to organize country visits to investigate cases of grave and systematic violations of children's rights. By **resolution 66/141** of 19 December (see p. 627), the Assembly urged States to become parties to the 1990 Convention on the Rights of the Child [YUN 1990, p. 614], its Optional Protocol on the sale of children, child prostitution and child pornography [YUN 2000, p. 618], and its Optional Protocol on the involvement of children in armed conflict [ibid., p. 616].

GENERAL ASSEMBLY ACTION

On 19 December [meeting 89], the General Assembly, on the recommendation of the Third (Social, Humanitarian and Cultural) Committee [A/66/458], adopted **resolution 66/139** without vote [agenda item 65 (*a*)].

Strengthening collaboration on child protection within the United Nations system

The General Assembly,

Reaffirming the purposes and principles of the Charter of the United Nations,

Recalling the Convention on the Rights of the Child and its Optional Protocols, and reaffirming all its previous resolutions on the rights of the child,

Recognizing the primary role and responsibility of the State in the promotion and protection of the rights of the child, including child protection, bearing in mind the importance of relevant actors of the United Nations supporting the State in this regard,

Reaffirming that the best interest of the child, non-discrimination, participation and survival and development provide the framework for all actions concerning children, including those of a State and all relevant actors of the United Nations dealing with the promotion and protection of the rights of the child, including child protection,

Recognizing the important role and the continuing work of the United Nations system and all its relevant actors in the promotion and protection of the rights of the child, including child protection, and recognizing also the role and contribution of civil society in this regard,

Stressing that further strengthening collaboration within the United Nations system on the promotion and protection of the rights of the child, including child protection, is important for continuing to support efforts of Member States in the realization of the rights of the child, and in this regard reaffirms the important role that the General Assembly continues to play in strengthening collaboration and coherence within the United Nations system,

1. *Welcomes* the existing collaboration among relevant actors of the United Nations working on the promotion and protection of the rights of the child, including child protection, and encourages them, within existing resources and mandates, to highlight information on such collaboration in their existing reports to the General Assembly and to also address this issue within the framework of the existing Third Committee interactive dialogue under the item entitled "Promotion and protection of the rights of children", and invites these United Nations actors to further enhance their collaboration;

2. *Reiterates* the importance of all relevant actors of the United Nations on child protection to continue to exercise their functions in a fully independent manner and to act in full observance of their respective mandates;

3. *Underlines* the importance of sustained, adequate resources and support for the work of the United Nations system on the promotion and protection of the rights of the child, including child protection, and in this regard strongly encourages enhanced voluntary contributions to support the work of all relevant actors of the United Nations, so as to support technical assistance and capacity-building in the area of child protection;

4. *Requests* the Secretary-General to submit a report to the General Assembly at its sixty-eighth session on the current collaboration within the United Nations system on child protection, taking into account information provided by Member States and relevant actors of the United Nations.

(For more information on the protection of the rights of the child, see p. 622.)

United Nations Children's Fund

In 2011, UNICEF remained committed to achieving the MDGs [YUN 2000, p. 51] and the goals set out by the General Assembly's twenty-seventh (2002) special session on children [YUN 2002, p. 1168] in the document "A world fit for children" [ibid., p. 1169]. The work of UNICEF was also guided by the 1989 Convention on the Rights of the Child, adopted by the Assembly in resolution 44/25 [YUN 1989, p. 560], and its Optional Protocols. In line with its twice-extended medium-term strategic plan (MTSP), 2006–2013, UNICEF addressed five focus areas: young child survival and development; basic education and gender equality; HIV/AIDS and children; child protection from violence, exploitation and abuse; and policy advocacy and partnerships for children's rights.

The annual UNICEF flagship publication, *The State of the World's Children 2011* [Sales No. E.11.XX.1], focused on adolescents, highlighting the challenges they faced and the imperative of investing in adolescents to break the cycles of poverty and inequity. Adolescents around the world were generally healthier than in the past, largely because of investments in early and middle childhood; however, many threats to children continued to be at their height during adolescence. Secondary education was cited as critical to adolescent development and well-being, and the right of children to express their views freely on matters affecting them was deemed vital to their survival, development and education. Global challenges of adolescents included climate change, especially since nine out of ten adolescents lived in developing countries; poverty, unemployment and globalization; juvenile crime and violence; and lack of peace and security in conflict and emergency situations. To seize the opportunity of adolescence, the report suggested investing in data collection and analysis; education and training; mechanisms for participation; a supportive environment for adolescent rights; and addressing poverty and inequity.

UNICEF cooperated with 151 countries, areas and territories: 45 in sub-Saharan Africa, 35 in Latin America and the Caribbean, 35 in Asia, 16 in the Middle East and North Africa, and 20 in Central and Eastern Europe and the Commonwealth of Independent States. The bulk of UNICEF support continued to go to initiatives for young child survival and development, and to sub-Saharan Africa.

UNICEF operations in 2011 were described in the *UNICEF Annual Report 2011*, the UNICEF annual report to the Economic and Social Council [E/2012/6] and the annual report of the Executive Director on progress and achievements against the Fund's extended 2006–2013 MTSP [E/ICEF/2012/10].

The UNICEF Executive Board held its first regular session (8–11 February), its annual session (20–23 June) and its second regular session (12–15 September), all in New York [E/2011/34/Rev.1], during which it adopted 24 decisions.

By **decision 2011/215** of 18 July, the Economic and Social Council took note of the annual report of UNICEF covering 2010 [E/2011/6]; the report of the UNICEF Executive Board on its first regular session [E/2011/34 (Part I)] and the addendum to the report on the joint meeting of the Executive Boards of the United Nations Development Programme (UNDP)/United Nations Population Fund (UNFPA)/United Nations Office for Project Services (UNOPS), UNICEF, the United Nations Entity for Gender Equality and the Empowerment of Women (UN-Women) and the World Food Programme (WFP) [E/2011/34 (Part I)/Add.1]; and the extract from the Board's report on its annual session of 2011 [E/2011/L.18].

On 15 September, the Executive Board adopted the programme of work for its 2012 sessions [E/2011/34/Rev.1 (dec. 2011/14)].

Programme policies

The UNICEF Executive Director, in his annual report to the Economic and Social Council covering 2011 [E/2012/6], reviewed achievements against the MTSP for 2006–2013. He provided updates on funding for operational activities; strategic partnerships; and contributions to national capacity development and development effectiveness, including South-South cooperation, the transition from relief to development, and gender mainstreaming. The report also described progress made to improve the functioning of the UN development system and to evaluate operational activities, as well as to follow up on international conferences.

On 23 June [E/2011/34/Rev.1 (dec. 2011/10)], the Executive Board welcomed the endorsement, by the General Assembly in **resolution 65/280** (see p. 829), of the Istanbul Declaration and the Programme of Action for the Least Developed Countries for the Decade 2011–2020. The Board invited the Executive Director to integrate the implementation of the Programme of Action in the programme of UNICEF and to report on its implementation.

On the same day [dec. 2011/11], the Executive Board encouraged regional groups to recommend candidates for the Board's Bureau during the second regular session of 2011. It decided to convene in early January of each year, starting in 2012, the first meeting of its subsequent first regular session for the sole purpose of electing a new President and other members of the Bureau.

Medium-term strategic plan (2006–2013)

The Executive Director, in his annual report on progress and achievements against the MTSP [E/ICEF/2012/10], focused on the need to address disparities among children. The report presented results and analysed progress in each of the five focus areas. It also covered humanitarian action, supporting and cross-cutting strategies, and the Fund's organizational performance in 2011.

Many achievements in 2011 contributed to the well-being of children, including the progress achieved towards the child-related MDGs. Under-five child mortality fell to 7.6 million deaths in 2010, down from 8.5 million in 2005. The MDG target of halving the proportion of people without sustainable access to an improved drinking water source was met; however, disparities between and within countries in some cases grew wider. Poorer areas of some countries had less than 20 per cent coverage of improved drinking water. Though near-parity had been achieved between girls and boys in primary school enrolment, children from ethnic minorities, children with disabilities and children living in remote areas remained excluded from education in many countries. The situation of children from the poorest quintile, when compared to the richest in the same country, was worse in many social indicators. More work was needed to address those and other disparities. The refocus on equity held promise for children, especially through faster and more economical achievement of the MDGs. UNICEF emphasized the implementation of the refocus in partnership with Governments, civil society organizations and UN partners.

On 23 June [dec. 2011/12], the Board reiterated the need for UNICEF to improve its results-oriented reporting to the Board, and requested UNICEF to present a road map towards the MTSP for 2014–2017 at the first regular session of 2012. The Board urged UNICEF to support the efforts of Governments and other national partners to protect children from violence, abuse and exploitation, and encouraged information-sharing in that regard. The Board further requested UNICEF to introduce lessons learned and recommendations for future strategies in annual reports of the Executive Director.

Medium-term financial plan (2011–2014)

In September, the Executive Board considered the planned financial estimates for 2011–2014 [E/ICEF/2011/AB/L.5], which UNICEF recommended for approval. Total income was forecast to be $3,228 million in 2011, and was projected to remain in the same range in 2012. Total expenditure was estimated at $3,417 million in 2011; it was expected to increase by 3 per cent in 2012 and remain steady in 2013 and 2014. UNICEF also recommended approving the preparation of programme expenditure submissions to the Board of up to $1,236 million from regular resources in 2012, subject to the availability of resources and the continued validity of planned financial estimates. In addition, the Board was requested to suspend the annual transfer of $30 million to the after-service health insurance reserve for 2011 due to the global economic downturn.

The Board approved those recommendations on 15 September [dec. 2011/22] and requested that UNICEF continue to make annual transfers to the after-service health insurance reserve if end-of-year working capital from regular resources so permitted.

Programme matters

In February, the Executive Board considered the draft common country programme document for the United Republic of Tanzania [DP/FPA-ICEF-WFP/DCCP/2011/TZA/1], which integrated the requirements of the United Nations Development Assistance Framework with the country programme documents of UNDP, UNFPA, UNICEF and WFP, and particularly with the country programme actions plans signed by the Government of Tanzania.

The Executive Board, on 11 February [dec. 2011/2], approved the aggregate indicative budget for the common country programme document for Tanzania, covering the period from July 2011 to June 2015, in the amounts of $74,692,000 from regular resources, subject to the availability of funds, and $73,308,000 from other resources, subject to the availability of specific-purpose contributions.

The UNICEF secretariat at the annual session in June informed the Board [E/ICEF/2011/P/L.29] of the one-year extensions of country programmes approved by the Executive Director for Belize, Bhutan, Guinea, Haiti, Madagascar, the Republic of Moldova and Tunisia. It also presented the reasons for the proposed two-year extension of the country programme for Paraguay and the second one-year extension for South Africa, and requested the Board to approve them. The Board, on 23 June [dec. 2011/9], took note of the one-year extensions of the country programmes approved by the Executive Director and approved the two-year extension for Paraguay, as well as the second one-year extension for South Africa.

Welcoming South Sudan as a new programme country for UNICEF, the Executive Board, on 15 September [dec. 2011/16], noted that country's request to present, on an exceptional basis, the country programme document for South Sudan to the Board's first regular session of 2012; decided that the document would be discussed at an informal consultation of the Board, to take place prior to the first regular session of 2012; and decided to consider the document for approval, on an exceptional basis, at that session.

At the second regular session in September, the Executive Board considered a report [E/ICEF/2011/P/L.46] that recommended allocating $31,600,000 in regular resources and $633,910,000 for other resources, subject to the availability of specific-purpose contributions, for advocacy and programme development during the 2012–2013 biennium for headquarters and regional offices and intercountry programmes. The Board approved those recommendations on 15 September [dec. 2011/17].

Also in September, the UNICEF secretariat informed the Board [E/ICEF/2011/P/L.48] of the one-year extensions of country programmes approved by the Executive Director for Egypt and the Syrian Arab Republic, of which the Board took note on 15 September [dec. 2011/19].

Joint programming

The joint meeting of the Executive Boards of UNDP/UNFPA/UNOPS, UNICEF, UN-Women and WFP (New York, 4 and 7 February) [E/2011/34 (Part I)/Add.1] discussed equity in the context of achieving the MDGs; mainstreaming gender through the work of agencies and envisaged collaboration with UN-Women; lessons learned about the efficiency of emergency response and the transition to recovery and long-term development; and the "Delivering as one" initiative.

The UNICEF Executive Director stressed that an equity approach, with efforts focused on the most vulnerable and hard-to-reach children and families, was the most cost-effective and quickest way to achieve the MDGs. The Executive Director of UN-Women emphasized the need to build partnerships across the UN system and to create more opportunities for each organization to support gender equality, based on comparative advantages. The WFP Deputy Executive Director for Operations stated that the six agencies were present and active before, during and after a crisis. While there was agreement that the cluster approach had led to greater coherence, cluster response needed to be strengthened during megacrises. Presentations were made by the Under-Secretary to the Presidency of Uruguay and the Vice Minister for Foreign Affairs and Cooperation of Mozambique on the experiences of the two countries as part of the "Delivering as one" initiative.

The Executive Board, on 11 February [dec. 2011/6], took note of the joint informal note of UNDP, UNFPA and UNICEF on the road map to an integrated budget: cost classification and results-based budgeting, prepared in response to a request [YUN 2010, p. 882] of the UNDP/UNFPA Executive Board and a request [ibid., p. 1186] of the UNICEF Executive Board. The Board endorsed the results-based budgeting approach contained in the note, and requested UNICEF to present its 2012–2013 budget document in line with the format presented in the note.

Gender equality

In response to an Executive Board decision [YUN 2010, p. 1189], UNICEF reported [E/ICEF/2011/10] on the progress of its work on gender equality. The report covered strengthened institutional system and capacity, current performance, partnerships and emerging lessons, and the way forward.

Taking note of the report on 23 June [dec. 2011/13], the Executive Board requested UNICEF to work closely with UN-Women to advance gender equality and the empowerment of women. It requested UNICEF to report on the progress of its gender-equality work during the annual Board session.

Programmes by region

In 2011 [E/ICEF/2012/10], UNICEF programme assistance expenditure totalled $3,472 million, of which $1,974 million (57 per cent) went to sub-Saharan Africa, $824 million (23.7 per cent) to Asia, $275 million (7.9 per cent) to the Americas and the Caribbean, $136 million (3.9 per cent) to the Middle East and North Africa, and $101 million (2.9 per cent) to Central and Eastern Europe and the Commonwealth of Independent States, while $162 million (4.7 per cent) was spent interregionally. Approximately 57 per cent was spent in least developed countries.

In September [E/2011/34/Rev.1], the Executive Board had before it the summaries of the midterm reviews of country programmes in Eastern and Southern Africa [E/ICEF/2011/P/L.30], West and Central Africa [E/ICEF/2011/P/L.31], Latin America and the Caribbean [E/ICEF/2011/P/L.32], East Asia and the Pacific [E/ICEF/2011/P/L.33], South Asia [E/ICEF/2011/P/L.34], and the Middle East and North Africa [E/ICEF/2011/P/L.35]. The reports reviewed progress made, resources used, constraints faced and adjustments made in country programmes.

Field visits

A delegation of members of the Executive Boards of UNDP/UNFPA/UNOPS, UNICEF and WFP visited the Philippines (26 March–2 April) [E/ICEF/2011/CRP.13 & Corr.1] to enable Board members to witness operations and programmes. The Philippines was selected for the joint field visit as a result of several innovative developments related to conflict prevention and recovery and humanitarian approaches. Despite the attainment of lower-middle-income country status, the country continued to face challenges, particularly in fostering equitable, inclusive and sustained economic growth. As at 2010, the Philippines was not likely to meet MDGs 1, 2, 5 and 6. More people lived under the poverty line than when the Philippines was classified as a low-income-status country. The delegation concluded that there was a high level of development capacity in the Government and that the support of the UN system would remain central to advancing the country's development agenda.

In a visit to Bolivia (11–15 April) [E/ICEF/2011/CRP.12], a delegation of the Bureau of the Executive Board met with local government representatives, civil society organizations, other community members and UNICEF staff. The visit included a field trip to the province of Cochabamba, where the delegation observed various projects in the Chuñu Chuñuni community. It was noted that UNICEF placed a greater emphasis on cooperation and coordination with governmental authorities than with UN organizations, donor agencies and non-governmental organizations (NGOs). The delegation felt that UNICEF should attach enough importance to working jointly with other such partners. It was further observed that Bolivia was undergoing profound reforms, offering an opportunity for UNICEF to work on the "equity approach" in an innovative manner, as well as assist authorities in targeting the most vulnerable groups. Participants witnessed social unrest, and the delegation was informed that civil participation and protests were common. The UNICEF country office concluded that the visit had encouraged the team to more precisely identify the country programme's priorities, and to make the work of UNICEF more systemic and evidence-based.

The UNICEF Executive Board undertook a field visit to Ghana (9–14 May) [E/ICEF/2011/CRP.14] to better understand the challenges faced by children and women in the country. The visit included field trips to the Northern Region and a field trip to urban households in James Town. Ghana's population included 10.7 million children, of which an estimated 3.4 million were living in poverty. The country was on track to meet many of the MDGs but was facing challenges in achieving progress on Goals 5 and 7. The delegation noted that the challenges would need to be addressed using a collaborative approach. The delegation recognized the importance of focusing on equity and disparities, particularly between the south and the north, and between the population groups of large cities. The Board noted with satisfaction that all UNICEF programmes and activities were aligned with the priorities of the MTSP.

Programmes by sector

In 2011, UNICEF programme assistance expenditure, which was linked to the five focus areas established in 2005 under the 2006–2009 MTSP [YUN 2005, p. 1284], totalled $3,472 million, a 4 per cent increase over 2010. The largest share of expenditure, $1,822 million (52 per cent), went to young child survival and development, followed by basic education and gender equality ($709 million, or 21 per cent), policy advocacy and partnerships for children's rights ($359 million, or 11 per cent), child protection from violence, exploitation and abuse ($339 million, or 9.7 per cent), HIV/AIDS and children ($152 million, or 4 per cent), and other interventions ($91 million, or less than 4 per cent). Programme support, management and administration, and other costs, amounted to an additional $322 million, representing an increase of $46 million over 2010.

Young child survival and development

In the area of young child survival and development, child mortality continued to decline across all parts of the world. Pneumonia, diarrhoea and malaria, however, continued to cause over one third of deaths among children older than one month, while HIV was a leading killer of children in large parts of Africa. Polio eradication remained a priority, as well as creating awareness about stunting, which affected 27 per cent of children under five. Countries that had succeeded in reducing childhood disease faced the challenges of newborn mortality, poor developmental outcomes for children, high levels of malnutrition and insufficient early childhood development interventions.

UNICEF recognized that scaling up essential interventions focused on the most marginalized would allow countries to accelerate progress in achieving the MDGs. UNICEF contributed to vaccinating 10 million children in measles campaigns and to providing double doses of vitamin A supplement for 350 million children. Fifty-three out of 90 countries that had data showed progress in exclusive breastfeeding among infants of 0 to 6 months of age. UNICEF and its partners provided support in implementing the "Every Woman, Every Child" strategy in five African countries in an effort to improve maternal and newborn health services. In addition, UNICEF continued efforts to tackle cholera in West and Central Africa and responded to water-related emergencies, which occurred in 78 countries.

Basic education and gender equality

The UNICEF education agenda focused on gender, equity and human rights-based programming to support improved access to quality basic education for the most vulnerable children. Since 2009, the focus on equity resulted in 579,000 child-friendly schools (CFS) receiving support in 99 countries, and 86 countries developing quality standards based on CFS or similar models. By 2011, the CFS Global Capacity Development Programme had reached 603 participants from 107 countries.

UNICEF was the coordinating agency in 21 out of 46 Global Partnership for Education-endorsed countries, the implementing agency in Guinea and Madagascar, and the supervising entity in Afghanistan. UNICEF was also the co-chair of the Global Impact on Learning programme, which helped to define global metrics for learning. Seventy-one countries reported the development and implementation of national policies on Early Childhood Development/School Readiness compared to 65 in 2010. In partnership with the World Bank, UNICEF developed the Simulation for Equity in Education Model to identify and estimate costs of strategies addressing educational barriers.

HIV/AIDS and children

The UNICEF response to AIDS contributed to three result areas: prevention of mother-to-child transmission of HIV and paediatric HIV treatment; prevention of HIV among adolescents and young people; and protection of children and families affected by HIV and AIDS. Treatment for children living with HIV increased from 6 per cent in 2005 to 23 per cent in 2010. An estimated 5 million young people (aged 15–24) were living with HIV in 2010, a 12 per cent reduction since 2002.

Under the Global Plan to Eliminate New HIV Infections in Children by 2015 and Keeping Their Mothers Alive, launched by the Joint United Nations Programme on HIV/AIDS in June, UNICEF and the World Health Organization coordinated technical assistance, and developed implementation guidance and monitoring of country progress to achieve the Global Plan targets. Twenty-two countries, which collectively accounted for 90 per cent of new HIV infections in children, were prioritized for intensified support. As it entered its second phase (2011–2015), the Unite for Children, Unite against AIDS campaign [YUN 2005, p. 1290] emphasized eliminating mother-to-child transmission and halving new infections among young people.

Child protection from violence, exploitation and abuse

In the area of child protection from violence, exploitation and abuse, UNICEF prioritized prevention across four areas: strengthening systems through better laws, policies, regulations and services; addressing harmful practices; ensuring that interventions to protect children in emergencies strengthened systems and promoted social change; and expanding monitoring, evaluation and research to inform programmes and policies. That strategic approach showed results in birth registration, trafficking and migration, alternative care, disability, justice for children, violence against children, child marriage, female genital mutilation/cutting, child labour, mine action, and the protection of children affected by emergencies. In 2011, 23.8 million births were registered, more than 120 countries strengthened mechanisms to protect children, and the UNFPA-UNICEF programme on female genital mutilation/cutting in 15 countries showed a 30 per cent increase from 2010 in the number of villages that had abandoned the practice.

Policy advocacy and partnerships for children's rights

In the area of policy advocacy and partnerships for children's rights, UNICEF promoted policies and budgets that provided support to the poorest and most deprived. To increase impact, the Fund invested in the development of new data, tools and analyses, and in more extensive leveraging of partners' resources. Those innovations contributed to the scaling up of national social protection programmes, including cash transfer, by 93 countries, and a more intensive focus on children in national development plans and budgets in 102 countries.

The Fund made investments in knowledge networks to facilitate the sharing of ideas and information, including the Child Poverty and the "Recovery for All" networks with more than 3,000 members. It provided legal, institutional, budgetary and sectoral reform advice in 124 countries, in addition to developing a training programme on socioeconomic policies for child rights with equity, which attracted approximately 5,000 online participants. The World Bank and UNICEF developed a joint guidance note on integrating a child focus into poverty and social impact analysis in order to promote child-sensitive policies and reforms.

Humanitarian action

In 2011, UNICEF responded to 292 humanitarian situations of varying scales in 80 countries, further stretching the Fund's human and financial resources and requiring the reprogramming of resources in some contexts. Following the emergencies in Haiti and Pakistan in 2010, UNICEF improved its procedures to better deliver results.

In emergency, humanitarian, recovery or fragile situations, UNICEF assisted an estimated 1.8 million severely malnourished children aged 6 to 59 months through therapeutic feeding programmes; vaccinated 52.3 million children aged 6 months to 15 years against measles; helped to provide over 18.5 million people with access to safe water and 4.86 million people with access to appropriately designed toilets; helped 8.76 million school-aged children, including adolescents, to access formal and non-formal basic education; and provided 835,000 pregnant women with access to HIV/AIDS prevention. Over 11,600 children formerly associated with armed forces or groups were reintegrated into their families and communities.

Security incidents affecting UNICEF staff increased significantly, including the deaths of three staff members as a result of a deliberate attack on UN premises in Nigeria. A new approach to security management was implemented, and the Fund fostered a better understanding of international humanitarian law and risk management throughout the organization.

Organizational matters

Evaluation system

In accordance with the UNICEF evaluation policy [YUN 2008, p. 1287] and relevant Executive Board decisions, UNICEF in July submitted an annual report [E/ICEF/2011/15] on the Fund's evaluation function and major evaluations in UNICEF. The report reviewed global developments in evaluation and the state of the evaluation function in UNICEF at country, regional and global levels, outlining progress in strengthening the decentralized evaluation function. The report also summarized selected major evaluations conducted at the country, regional and global levels within the focus area of basic education and gender equality, outlining the sufficiencies and gaps within that area.

The Fund maintained an instrumental role in the United Nations Evaluation Group (UNEG), advocating for a strong evaluation function across the UN system and leading the substantive work of UNEG in several areas. A consolidated set of key performance indicators based on recent experiments in measuring system performance was provided for the first time.

Taking note of the report on 15 September [dec. 2011/20], the Board encouraged UNICEF to strengthen the link between evaluation and research functions. It requested the Fund to prepare a management response to the thematic analysis section of future annual reports of the Evaluation Office.

Ethics Office

In compliance with an Executive Board decision [YUN 2010, p. 1190], the UNICEF Office of Ethics, in July, submitted its second annual report [E/ICEF/2011/11], covering activities in 2010. The report provided information on the Office's mandated areas of work: standard setting and policy support; training, education and outreach; advice and guidance; the financial disclosure programme; protection of staff against retaliation; and participation in the United Nations Ethics Committee. As in 2008 and 2009, the Office's main activities were the management and administration of the Financial Disclosure Programme, in which major improvements were made. The programme matured in 2010 based on the work on new systems in 2009. The Office received 1,055 queries, 879 of which were related to the Financial Disclosure Programme, the largest category of queries. There were 102 requests for ethics advice in 2010, aside from those linked to the Financial Disclosure Programme; most of them dealt with employment-related concerns (53 per cent), including questions of fairness in the workplace and queries from supervisors on how to manage staff misconduct.

Taking note of the report on 23 June [dec. 2011/7], the Executive Board encouraged UNICEF management to strengthen the functions of the Ethics Office in its organization and to provide sufficient resources for the Office to carry out its programme of work.

JIU reports

In February, the Executive Board had before it a report [E/ICEF/2011/4] summarizing the response of UNICEF to recommendations contained in seven reports of the Joint Inspection Unit (JIU) issued from September 2009 through August 2010. According to the report, UNICEF had continued to work with JIU on the different reviews being conducted under its auspices as well as on the follow-up to recommendations issued by JIU. That dialogue and interaction had increased the relevance of the reports, improved implementation of recommendations and enhanced transparency.

The Executive Board took note of the report at its first regular session in February.

Knowledge management and research

In February, the Executive Board had before it an oral report [E/ICEF/2011/CRP.2] on the knowledge management and research functions of UNICEF. Major improvements had been made in knowledge management over the previous three years, the report stated, but further work was needed to better coordinate the research and knowledge management functions in a streamlined manner. Regarding the research function, the report noted that the Fund's potential as a knowledge-based organization was not fully exploited, as it had not sufficiently integrated learning from research and evidence.

Taking note of the report on 11 February [dec. 2011/3], the Board requested that the Fund submit at the Board's first regular session of 2012 a strategic integrated framework for research and knowledge management, as well as clear mechanisms for setting research priorities. UNICEF was requested to inform the Board at that session on concrete steps taken to improve knowledge management at headquarters and in the field.

Finances

In 2011, UNICEF income totalled $3,711 million, a 1 per cent increase compared with 2010 despite the struggling global economy; however, overall income was short of planned programme expenditures. Total income exceeded the financial estimate for 2011 by $483 million. UNICEF derived its income mainly from Governments, which contributed $2,260 million (60.9 per cent), and from the private sector and NGOs, which contributed $1,089 million (29.3 per cent). The balance came from inter-organizational arrangements, with contributions of $307 million (8.3 per cent), and other sources, with contributions of $55 million (1.5 per cent).

Total expenditure increased by 4 per cent compared with 2010 and amounted to $3,819 million. Expenditure on programme assistance amounted to $3,472 million. Combined expenditure on programme support ($215 million), management and administration ($89 million) and centrally shared security costs ($18 million) amounted to $322 million, an increase of $46 million compared to 2010.

Budget appropriations

In June, the Executive Board had before it 26 draft country and common country programme documents for approval. On 23 June [dec. 2011/8], the Board approved the aggregate indicative budgets for those programmes, amounting to the following totals of regular and other resources, respectively, by region: Central and Eastern Europe and the Commonwealth of Independent States: $16,175,000 and $91,436,000; East Asia and the Pacific: $27,105,000 and $136,938,000; Eastern and Southern Africa: $179,216,000 and $607,709,000; Middle East and North Africa: $6,045,000 and $30,400,000; South Asia: $112,410,000 and $333,000,000; the Americas and the Caribbean: $30,250,000 and $51,600,000; and West and Central Africa: $167,560,000 and $423,975,000.

In July [E/ICEF/2011/P/L.47], UNICEF requested additional regular resources in the amount of $117,982,062 for 25 approved country programmes, which—as a result of the modified system for the allocation of regular resources and revised projections of global levels of regular resources available for country programmes—required resources beyond the levels originally approved. The Board approved that request on 15 September [dec. 2011/18].

On 15 September [dec. 2011/15], the Board approved the aggregate indicative budget for 14 country and common country programmes of cooperation. The authorized budget amounted to the following totals for regular and other resources, respectively, by region: Eastern and Southern Africa: $110,986,000 and $379,000,000; East Asia and the Pacific: $26,487,000 and $165,940,000; Middle East and North Africa: $38,594,000 and $59,400,000; the Americas and the Caribbean: $21,750,000 and $168,350,000; and West and Central Africa: $3,750,000 and $2,000,000.

The Board in September had before it a document [E/ICEF/2011/AB/L.2] containing the institutional budget for 2012–2013. It was based on the results-based budgeting approach and presented in the format agreed upon by UNICEF, UNDP and UNFPA. The proposed budget was $966 million: of that, it was estimated that $628 million would be funded from regular resources and $338 million from other resources and trust funds. The budget reflected a 5.3 per cent decrease over the budget for 2010–2011.

A related report [E/ICEF/2011/AB/L.3] contained the comments of the Advisory Committee on Administrative and Budgetary Questions (ACABQ).

The Executive Board on 15 September [dec. 2011/23] approved an appropriation of $966 million for the institutional budget for 2012–2013. It took note of the results-based budgeting approach used to formulate the budget, and of the revised presentation of the budget, in line with Board decisions. The Board requested UNICEF to make, in consultation with UNDP and UNFPA, an informal presentation on the timetable for the review and analysis of harmonized cost recovery rates at the first regular session of 2012.

Resource mobilization

In 2011, UNICEF continued to collaborate with the public and private sectors to mobilize regular and other resources. A total of 92 Governments contributed to UNICEF resources. Total income from public-sector donors—Governments, intergovernmental organizations and inter-organizational arrangements—amounted to $2,567 million, a $128 million increase from 2010. Private-sector contributions, however, mainly comprising resources from UNICEF National Committees, individual donors, NGOs and foundations, decreased by 8 per cent to $1,089 million in the same period.

Thematic funding, which supported the achievement of the five MTSP focus areas by allowing long-term planning, sustainability and savings in transaction costs for both UNICEF and donors, decreased by 23 per cent, from $241 million in 2010 to $187 million in 2011. Thematic humanitarian assistance decreased by 44 per cent.

Income for humanitarian assistance decreased by 6 per cent to $963 million, which was largely attributed to the decline in private-sector income. The Fund requested funding support for emergencies and sought $1.6 billion for its humanitarian interventions.

Private Fundraising and Partnerships

In February, the Executive Board had before it a report on the 2011 Private Fundraising and Partnerships (PFP) workplan and proposed budget [E/ICEF/2011/AB/L.1 & Corr.1], according to which the PFP in 2011 would generate a projected $854.6 million in net consolidated income, of which $404.6 million would be for regular resources and $450 million for other resources. That would be achieved with expenditures of $153.9 million.

On 11 February [dec. 2011/5], the Executive Board approved budgeted expenditures of $153.9 million for 2011 and authorized UNICEF to increase expenditures up to $113.7 million, should the apparent proceeds from fundraising or card and gift sales increase, and to reduce expenditures to the extent necessary, should the net proceeds decrease. The Board authorized UNICEF to redeploy resources among the various budget lines up to a maximum of 10 per cent of the amounts approved and, when necessary, to spend an additional amount between Board sessions up to the amount caused by currency fluctuations. The Board also renewed investment funds, with $42 million established for 2011. It authorized UNICEF to incur expenditures in 2011 related to the cost of goods and inventory overhead (production and purchase of raw materials, cards and other products) for 2012 up to $15.8 million, as indicated in the financial projections of the PFP Strategic Plan 2011–2013. The Board also approved an interim one-month allocation for January 2011 in the amount of $15.4 million, to be absorbed in the annual PFP budget for 2011.

According to a report on private fundraising issued in July [E/ICEF/2011/AB/L.11], the PFP net income in 2010 amounted to $1,023.2 million, an increase of $248 million (32 per cent) over 2009. That included private fundraising ($317.3 million), sales of UNICEF cards and products ($16.8 million) and fundraising for other resources ($689.1 million).

Audits

The Executive Board, on 11 February [dec. 2011/4], took note of the report of the Board of Auditors [YUN 2010, p. 1442] and the report of the Secretary-General on the implementation of the recommendations of the Board of Auditors on the financial statements of the United Nations funds and programmes for the financial period ended 31 December 2009 [ibid., p. 1443].

In the annual report [E/ICEF/2011/AB/L.9 & Corr.1] to the Executive Board on internal audit activities, covering 2010, the Office of Internal Audit (OIA) stated that the 20 country office audits conducted that year focused on the functional areas of governance, management of programmes and operations management. The audits contained 345 observations, of which 39 were rated as high risk and 306 as medium risk. OIA also completed seven audits of headquarters, regional offices and thematic areas, and issued three summary analysis reports of all country office audits conducted in the previous year. Thirty per cent of country offices audited in 2010 were rated overall satisfactory, compared to 41 per cent in 2009; 60 per cent partially satisfactory, compared to 41 per cent in 2009; and 10 per cent unsatisfactory, compared to 18 per cent in 2009. OIA issued 347 audit observations to county offices in 2010; 252 of those cases remained open as at 31 December. OIA also issued 86 audit observations to headquarters units and regional offices in 2010; 66 of those cases remained open as at 31 December.

Taking note of the report and the UNICEF management response to it [E/ICEF/2011/AB/L.10], the Executive Board, on 15 September [dec. 2011/21], welcomed the focus on risk-based audit planning. The Board requested that OIA include information comparing the overall conclusions of completed audits of the organizational units, processes, systems and thematic areas of UNICEF in future annual reports. It decided that the UNICEF Executive Director could, upon request, disclose to approved non-member State donors internal audit reports pertaining to a programme or service to which the donor was financially contributing.

International Public Sector Accounting Standards

In response to Executive Board decision 2011/4 of 11 February, UNICEF submitted to the September session of the Board a progress report [E/ICEF/2011/AB/L.4] on the implementation of the recommendations of the Board of Auditors on the UNICEF accounts for the biennium 2008–2009. The report provided an update on implementation of the 21 main recommendations out of the 50 contained in the 2010 Report of the Board of Auditors [YUN 2010, p. 1442] and the strategic implications of the recommendations for the management and strategy of UNICEF. As of 30 April, 10 of the 21 main recommendations were fully implemented and 10 were under implementation. The report noted that the adoption of International Public Sector Account Standards (IPSAS) by January 2012 would improve the quality of UNICEF financial reporting. Areas of change resulting from the adoption of IPSAS would include management of inventory, premises, equipment and revenue; accounting for cash transfer; recording of expenses on delivery of goods and services; and reporting information related to employee benefits.

In June, UNICEF submitted a report [E/ICEF/2011/AB/L.8] presenting amendments to its Financial Regulations for approval and Financial Rules for information to allow for compliance with IPSAS and to update the cost categories for budgeting terminology.

ACABQ did not have any objection, subject to its comments, to approval by the Executive Board of the proposed amendments [E/ICEF/2011/AB/L.12].

Taking note of the ACABQ report on 15 September [dec. 2011/24], the Executive Board approved the proposed changes to the Financial Regulations, to take effect on 1 January 2012, and took note of the proposed changes to the Financial Rules. It requested UNICEF to keep the Board informed on the implementation of IPSAS, beginning with the first regular session of 2012.

Chapter XII
Refugees and displaced persons

In 2011, the number of people of concern to the Office of the United Nations High Commissioner for Refugees (UNHCR) stood at 35.4 million, including 10.4 million refugees, of which 7.2 million were living in protracted situations of exile. The number of people displaced within their own country as a result of conflict was an estimated 26.4 million, of whom 15.5 million benefited from UNHCR protection and assistance. The number of identifiable stateless persons stood at 3.5 million. An estimated 532,000 refugees were able to return home voluntarily.

During the year, UNHCR commemorated the sixtieth anniversary of the 1951 Convention relating to the Status of Refugees and the fiftieth anniversary of the 1961 Convention on the Reduction of Statelessness—the fundamental instruments on international protection—with 149 States parties to one or both treaties at the end of the year. The commemoration culminated in December with a ministerial-level event in Geneva, which brought together 155 Member States. More than 100 States made pledges during the meeting and renewed their commitment to persons in need of international protection, including through a ministerial communiqué. Also in December, the General Assembly encouraged States not parties to the Conventions to consider acceding to them, underlined the importance of the principle of non-refoulement—prohibiting the expulsion of or refusal to entry to a refugee—and recognized that a number of States not parties to the international refugee instruments had shown a generous approach to hosting refugees.

The year was marked by a rapid succession of large-scale humanitarian crises unfolding against a backdrop of political and social turmoil. Conflicts in Côte d'Ivoire, Libya, Somalia and the Sudan forced more than 800,000 refugees into neighbouring countries—the highest number in over a decade. The Middle East continued to experience turbulence, with more than 127,000 persons from the Syrian Arab Republic having sought refuge in neighbouring countries, primarily Iraq, Jordan, Lebanon and Turkey, in addition to more than 1 million displaced internally. Furthermore, an estimated 3.5 million people were newly displaced within the borders of their countries, one fifth more than in 2010. UNHCR estimated that some 43.7 million people in the world were displaced across or within borders by violence and persecution. To respond to those unprecedented challenges, the Office deployed 780 emergency staff globally. UNHCR was often required to operate in hazardous environments. Six staff members were killed in Afghanistan, the Democratic Republic of the Congo, South Sudan and Syria.

While new situations of conflict continued to multiply, old ones failed to be resolved, such as those in Afghanistan, the Democratic Republic of the Congo and Iraq. The Somali conflict—already 20 years old—degenerated further and, combined with the worst drought in decades, drove close to 300,000 refugees into neighbouring Kenya, Ethiopia, Djibouti and Yemen, bringing the number of Somali refugees in the region to some 950,000 by year's end.

Other issues that remained high on the UNHCR agenda were mixed migration, which intensified during the year; the growing concern of States for their national security, which continued to threaten protection; and detention of asylum seekers, for which the Office tried to identify alternatives.

In April, UNHCR launched the Global Resettlement Solidarity Initiative, which called on States to consider contributing resettlement places for non-Libyan refugees coming from Libya, who were hosted on the borders of Egypt and Tunisia, as well as for long-term refugees living in urban centres in Egypt.

In December, the General Assembly increased the membership of the UNHCR Executive Committee from 85 to 87 States.

Office of the United Nations High Commissioner for Refugees

Programme policy
Executive Committee

At its sixty-second session (Geneva, 3–7 October) [A/66/12/Add.1], the Executive Committee of the UNHCR Programme adopted decisions on administrative, financial and programme matters; on a revision of financial rules for voluntary funds administered by UNHCR; the 2012 programme of work of its Standing Committee; observer participation in the Standing Committee's 2011–2012 meetings; and the provisional agenda for its sixty-third (2012) session.

The General Debate of the session focused on the agency's commitment to international protection and burden-sharing; internal reform efforts; the interministerial event to commemorate the sixtieth and fiftieth anniversaries of the Convention relating to the Status of Refugees [YUN 1951, p. 520] and the Convention on the Reduction of Statelessness [YUN 1961, p. 533], respectively; the refugee situations in North Africa and the Horn of Africa; and protracted refugee situations.

In his opening statement [A/AC.96/SR.648] as well as in a later report [A/67/12] to the Committee, the High Commissioner, António Guterres, discussed the emergencies in Côte d'Ivoire, Libya and Somalia. Following the disputed election at the end of 2010, more than 200,000 Ivorians had fled their country seeking asylum mainly in Liberia, while hundreds of thousand had been internally displaced. In Libya, due to the conflict that had led to the fall of Muammar Qadhafi's regime, around 1.5 million people, including migrants and refugees, had left the country. A humanitarian operation organized jointly by the International Organization for Migration (IOM) and UNHCR helped 157,000 third-country nationals living in Libya to return home. Tens of thousands of refugees and migrants had fled by boat across the Mediterranean, many of them perishing on the way. Those most vulnerable to the violence in Libya were people from sub-Saharan Africa, many of them from war-torn countries. The High Commissioner appealed to Libya's National Transitional Council to ensure their safety, stressing that refugees and migrant workers must not be confused with mercenaries. The drought in Somalia, a country already worn down by a protracted conflict, had come on top of those two crises. During the year, close to 300,000 refugees entered neighbouring countries, bringing the number of Somali refugees in the region to 950,000. Together with another 1.5 million internally displaced Somalis, nearly a third of the country's population had been forced from their homes. Kenya, Ethiopia, Yemen and Djibouti had borne the burden of that mass exodus. UNHCR led the protection cluster and provided internally displaced persons (IDPs) with emergency relief, reaching nearly 400,000 people.

During the first nine months of 2011, UNHCR deployed more than 600 emergency staff to 36 countries—two and a half times as many as in previous years—and airlifted 70 tons of shelter and other relief items each week, more than triple the volume dispatched in 2010. By the end of the year, the Office had deployed 780 emergency staff globally. UNHCR was often required to operate in hazardous environments. Six staff members were killed in Afghanistan, the Democratic Republic of the Congo, South Sudan and Syria.

Displacement continued to grow worldwide as new conflicts multiplied and old ones were protracted, the High Commissioner said. In 2011, an estimated 3.5 million people were newly displaced, including 750,000 refugees—one fifth more than in 2010. As at 3 October, some 43.7 million people were uprooted due to conflict and persecution, the highest number in some 15 years. More than 7 million people—70 per cent of refugees of concern to UNHCR—lived in prolonged situations of exile. In all situations, the High Commissioner said, the solution was political and could not be achieved without the involvement of all actors. On the positive side, the determination of the Governments of Bosnia and Herzegovina, Croatia, Montenegro and Serbia to resolve the refugee situation in the region was encouraging.

Voluntary repatriation figures were at their lowest in 20 years because of old and new conflicts: fewer than 200,000 refugees chose to return home in 2010, compared with an annual average of over 1 million in the previous two decades. Resettlement had, therefore, become even more vital, although resettlement opportunities fell far short of needs. To avoid further backlog, in 2010 UNHCR reduced the number of resettlement submissions to 108,000 from 128,000 in 2009. Only 73,000 refugees departed for resettlement in 2010—14 per cent less than in 2009. The High Commissioner suggested that resettlement countries establish a pool of emergency slots to be activated during dramatic outflows. UNHCR also supported self-reliance programmes that allowed refugees to contribute to the development of their host countries, such as the multi-year strategy for Afghan refugees being developed with the Governments of Afghanistan, Iran and Pakistan. Local integration and self-reliance solutions posed enormous challenges for host countries, particularly considering that developing countries hosted 8 out of 10 refugees. Development assistance targeting refugee-hosting States was essential to ensuring better burden-sharing. There had been intense discussions about the role that UNHCR should play in protecting people displaced by natural disasters. As agreement had not been reached on a more predictable engagement in leading the protection cluster at country level in natural disasters, UNHCR continued to operate on a case-by-case basis.

The internal reform process of the agency begun five years earlier had reduced headquarters costs from 14 to 9 per cent of overall expenditure, and staff costs from 41 to 27 per cent. To strengthen protection and emergency response capacities, 42 new protection posts were created worldwide in early 2011, in addition to the 46 established in late 2010. Significant savings on airlifts had been attained and staff deployment mechanisms had been broadened. The agency was developing a more structured transition to the post-emergency phase in crisis areas.

Donors had provided unprecedented levels of contributions, but more donor flexibility was needed to ensure assistance across operations. Only around 18 per cent of income in 2010 had been totally unrestricted, while 55 per cent had been tightly earmarked. In 2011, UNHCR had almost 900 implementing partners —60 per cent of them national non-governmental organizations (NGOs)—using approximately 38 per cent of the agency's budget.

As for cooperation with other UN agencies, a memorandum of understanding with the World Food Programme (WFP) was updated to include new priorities and lessons learned, and a new framework was agreed with the United Nations Children's Fund to strengthen the predictability and effectiveness of collaboration in refugee emergencies.

The High Commissioner concluded that UNHCR had made considerable efforts to put statelessness—an issue confronting an estimated 12 to 15 million people—more prominently on the international agenda, and that countries could contribute with simple steps, such as ensuring that women could transmit their nationality to their children.

GENERAL ASSEMBLY ACTION

On 19 December [meeting 89], the General Assembly, on the recommendation of the Third (Social, Humanitarian and Cultural) Committee [A/66/456], adopted **resolution 66/133** without vote [agenda item 62].

Office of the United Nations High Commissioner for Refugees

The General Assembly,

Having considered the report of the United Nations High Commissioner for Refugees on the activities of his Office and the report of the Executive Committee of the Programme of the United Nations High Commissioner for Refugees on the work of its sixty-second session and the decisions contained therein,

Recalling its previous annual resolutions on the work of the Office of the United Nations High Commissioner for Refugees since its establishment by the General Assembly,

Expressing its appreciation for the leadership shown by the High Commissioner, commending the staff and implementing partners of the Office of the High Commissioner for the competent, courageous and dedicated manner in which they discharge their responsibilities, and underlining its strong condemnation of all forms of violence to which humanitarian personnel and United Nations and associated personnel are increasingly exposed,

1. *Endorses* the report of the Executive Committee of the Programme of the United Nations High Commissioner for Refugees on the work of its sixty-second session;

2. *Welcomes* the sixtieth anniversary of the 1951 Convention relating to the Status of Refugees and the fiftieth anniversary of the 1961 Convention on the Reduction of Statelessness, and welcomes in this context the convening and facilitation by the United Nations High Commissioner for Refugees of an intergovernmental commemorative event at the ministerial level as a recognition by States of the importance of respecting and upholding the values and principles enshrined in those two instruments;

3. *Also welcomes* the important work undertaken by the Office of the United Nations High Commissioner for Refugees and its Executive Committee in the course of the year, which is aimed at strengthening the international protection regime and at assisting Governments in meeting their protection responsibilities;

4. *Reaffirms* the 1951 Convention relating to the Status of Refugees and the 1967 Protocol thereto as the foundation of the international refugee protection regime, recognizes the importance of their full and effective application by States parties and the values they embody, notes with satisfaction that one hundred and forty-eight States are now parties to one instrument or to both, encourages States not parties to consider acceding to those instruments, underlines, in particular, the importance of full respect for the principle of non-refoulement, and recognizes that a number of States not parties to the international refugee instruments have shown a generous approach to hosting refugees;

5. *Notes* that seventy States are now parties to the 1954 Convention relating to the Status of Stateless Persons and that forty-two States are parties to the 1961 Convention on the Reduction of Statelessness, encourages States that have not done so to give consideration to acceding to those instruments, notes the work of the High Commissioner in regard to identifying stateless persons, preventing and reducing statelessness and protecting stateless persons, and urges the Office of the High Commissioner to continue to work in this area in accordance with relevant General Assembly resolutions and Executive Committee conclusions;

6. *Re-emphasizes* that the protection of refugees is primarily the responsibility of States, whose full and effective cooperation, action and political resolve are required to enable the Office of the High Commissioner to fulfil its mandated functions, and strongly emphasizes, in this context, the importance of active international solidarity and burden- and responsibility-sharing;

7. *Also re-emphasizes* that prevention and reduction of statelessness are primarily the responsibility of States, in appropriate cooperation with the international community;

8. *Further re-emphasizes* that protection of and assistance to internally displaced persons are primarily the responsibility of States, in appropriate cooperation with the international community;

9. *Encourages* the Office of the High Commissioner to pursue its efforts to strengthen its capacity to respond adequately to emergencies and thereby ensure a more predictable response to inter-agency commitments in case of emergency;

10. *Takes note* of the current activities of the Office of the High Commissioner related to protection of and assistance to internally displaced persons, including in the context of inter-agency arrangements in this field, emphasizes that such activities should be consistent with relevant General Assembly resolutions and should not undermine the refugee mandate of the Office and the institution of asylum, and encourages the High Commissioner to continue his dialogue with States on the role of his Office in this regard;

11. *Encourages* the Office of the High Commissioner to work in partnership and in full cooperation with relevant national authorities, United Nations offices and agencies, international and intergovernmental organizations, re-

gional organizations and non-governmental organizations to contribute to the continued development of humanitarian response capacities at all levels, and recalls the role of the Office as the cluster lead for protection, camp coordination and management, and emergency shelter in complex emergencies;

12. *Also encourages* the Office of the High Commissioner, among other relevant United Nations and other relevant intergovernmental organizations and humanitarian and development actors, to continue to work with the Office for the Coordination of Humanitarian Affairs of the Secretariat to enhance the coordination, effectiveness and efficiency of humanitarian assistance and to contribute, in consultation with States, as appropriate, to making further progress towards common humanitarian needs assessments, as stated, among other important issues, in General Assembly resolution 65/133 of 15 December 2010 on the strengthening of the coordination of emergency humanitarian assistance of the United Nations;

13. *Further encourages* the Office of the High Commissioner to engage in and implement in full the objectives of the "Delivering as one" initiative;

14. *Notes with appreciation* the progress made in the implementation of the process of structural and management change, including the global needs assessment initiative, undertaken by the Office of the High Commissioner, and encourages the Office to consolidate the various aspects of the reform process, including the results-based management and accountability framework and strategy, and to focus on continuous improvement in order to enable a more efficient response to the needs of beneficiaries and to ensure the effective and transparent use of its resources;

15. *Strongly condemns* attacks on refugees, asylum seekers and internally displaced persons as well as acts that pose a threat to their personal security and well-being, and calls upon all States concerned and, where applicable, parties involved in an armed conflict to take all measures necessary to ensure respect for human rights and international humanitarian law;

16. *Expresses deep concern* about the increasing number of attacks against humanitarian aid workers and convoys and, in particular, the loss of life of humanitarian personnel working in the most difficult and challenging conditions in order to assist those in need;

17. *Emphasizes* the need for States to ensure that perpetrators of attacks committed on their territory against humanitarian personnel and United Nations and associated personnel do not operate with impunity and that the perpetrators of such acts are promptly brought to justice as provided for by national laws and obligations under international law;

18. *Deplores* the refoulement and unlawful expulsion of refugees and asylum seekers, and calls upon all States concerned to ensure respect for the relevant principles of refugee protection and human rights;

19. *Emphasizes* that international protection of refugees is a dynamic and action-oriented function that is at the core of the mandate of the Office of the High Commissioner and that it includes, in cooperation with States and other partners, the promotion and facilitation of, inter alia, the admission, reception and treatment of refugees in accordance with internationally agreed standards and the ensuring of durable, protection-oriented solutions, bearing in mind the particular needs of vulnerable groups and paying special attention to those with specific needs, and notes in this context that the delivery of international protection is a staff-intensive service that requires adequate staff with the appropriate expertise, especially at the field level;

20. *Affirms* the importance of age, gender and diversity mainstreaming in analysing protection needs and in ensuring the participation of refugees and other persons of concern to the Office of the High Commissioner, as appropriate, in the planning and implementation of programmes of the Office and State policies, also affirms the importance of according priority to addressing discrimination, gender inequality and the problem of sexual and gender-based violence, recognizing the importance of addressing the protection needs of women and children in particular, welcomes, in this context, the series of dialogues with women and girls initiated by the Office, in this anniversary year, as an important move towards increasing understanding and improving the protection of women and girls, and underlines the importance of continuing to work on this issue;

21. *Strongly reaffirms* the fundamental importance and the purely humanitarian and non-political character of the function of the Office of the High Commissioner of providing international protection to refugees and seeking permanent solutions to refugee problems, and recalls that those solutions include voluntary repatriation and, where appropriate and feasible, local integration and resettlement in a third country, while reaffirming that voluntary repatriation, supported, as necessary, by rehabilitation and development assistance to facilitate sustainable reintegration, remains the preferred solution;

22. *Expresses concern* about the particular difficulties faced by the millions of refugees in protracted situations, and emphasizes the need to redouble international efforts and cooperation to find practical and comprehensive approaches to resolving their plight and to realize durable solutions for them, consistent with international law and relevant General Assembly resolutions;

23. *Recognizes* the importance of achieving durable solutions to refugee problems and, in particular, the need to address in this process the root causes of refugee movements in order to avert new flows of refugees;

24. *Recalls* the important role of effective partnerships and coordination in meeting the needs of refugees and in finding durable solutions to their situations, welcomes the efforts under way, in cooperation with countries hosting refugees and countries of origin, including their respective local communities, relevant United Nations agencies, international and intergovernmental organizations, regional organizations, as appropriate, non-governmental organizations and development actors, to promote a framework for durable solutions, particularly in protracted refugee situations, which includes an approach to sustainable and timely return that encompasses repatriation, reintegration, rehabilitation and reconstruction activities, and encourages States, in cooperation with relevant United Nations agencies, international and intergovernmental organizations, regional organizations, non-governmental organizations and development actors, to support, inter alia, through the allocation of funds, the implementation of such a framework to facilitate an effective transition from relief to development;

25. *Recognizes* that no solution to displacement can be durable unless it is sustainable, and therefore encourages the Office of the High Commissioner to support the sustainability of return and reintegration;

26. *Notes with appreciation* the efforts that an increasing number of States are making to create opportunities for resettlement as a durable solution, recognizes the need to increase the number of resettlement places, invites interested States, the Office of the High Commissioner and other relevant partners to make use of the Multilateral Framework of Understandings on Resettlement, where appropriate and feasible, and, in this context, commends the efforts in launching the Global Resettlement Solidarity Initiative in April 2011 by the Office and by those States that have responded generously in this respect;

27. *Also notes with appreciation* the activities undertaken by States to strengthen the regional initiatives that facilitate cooperative policies and approaches on refugees, and encourages States to continue their efforts to address, in a comprehensive manner, the needs of the people who require international protection in their respective regions, including the support provided for host communities that receive large numbers of persons who require international protection;

28. *Notes* the importance of States and the Office of the High Commissioner discussing and clarifying the role of the Office in mixed migratory flows, in order to better address protection needs in the context of mixed migratory flows, including by safeguarding access to asylum for those in need of international protection, and notes the readiness of the High Commissioner, consistent with his mandate, to assist States in fulfilling their protection responsibilities in this regard;

29. *Emphasizes* the obligation of all States to accept the return of their nationals, calls upon States to facilitate the return of their nationals who have been determined not to be in need of international protection, and affirms the need for the return of persons to be undertaken in a safe and humane manner and with full respect for their human rights and dignity, irrespective of the status of the persons concerned;

30. *Expresses concern* about the challenges associated with climate change and environmental degradation to the protection activities of the Office of the High Commissioner and the assistance it provides to vulnerable populations of concern across the globe, particularly in the least developed countries, and urges the Office to continue to address such challenges in its work, within its mandate, and in consultation with national authorities and in cooperation with competent agencies in its operations;

31. *Urges* all States and relevant non-governmental and other organizations, in conjunction with the Office of the High Commissioner, in a spirit of international solidarity and burden- and responsibility-sharing, to cooperate and to mobilize resources with a view to enhancing the capacity of and reducing the heavy burden borne by host countries, whose generosity is appreciated, in particular those that have received large numbers of refugees and asylum seekers, calls upon the Office to continue to play its catalytic role in mobilizing assistance from the international community to address the root causes as well as the economic, environmental and social impact of large-scale refugee populations in developing countries, in particular the least developed countries, and countries with economies in transition, and notes with appreciation those donor States, organizations and individuals that contribute to improving the condition of refugees who remain vulnerable members of society;

32. *Expresses deep concern* about the existing and potential challenges posed by the world financial and economic crisis to the activities of the Office of the High Commissioner;

33. *Calls upon* the Office of the High Commissioner to further explore ways and means to broaden its donor base, so as to achieve greater burden-sharing by reinforcing cooperation with governmental donors, non-governmental donors and the private sector;

34. *Recognizes* that adequate and timely resources are essential for the Office of the High Commissioner to continue to fulfil the mandate conferred upon it through its statute and by subsequent General Assembly resolutions on refugees and other persons of concern, recalls its resolutions 58/153 of 22 December 2003, 58/270 of 23 December 2003, 59/170 of 20 December 2004, 60/129 of 16 December 2005, 61/137 of 19 December 2006, 62/124 of 18 December 2007, 63/148 of 18 December 2008, 64/127 of 18 December 2009 and 65/194 of 21 December 2010 concerning, inter alia, the implementation of paragraph 20 of the statute of the Office, and urges Governments and other donors to respond promptly to annual and supplementary appeals issued by the Office for requirements under its programmes;

35. *Requests* the High Commissioner to report on his activities to the General Assembly at its sixty-seventh session.

Enlargement of Executive Committee

On 28 July, the Economic and Social Council took note of the requests of Azerbaijan [E/2011/75] and Rwanda [E/2011/130] to become members of the Executive Committee, and recommended that the Assembly decide on enlarging the membership of the Committee from 85 to 87 States (**decision 2011/263**).

GENERAL ASSEMBLY ACTION

On 19 December [meeting 89], the General Assembly, on the recommendation of the Third Committee [A/66/456], adopted **resolution 66/134** without vote [agenda item 62].

Enlargement of the Executive Committee of the Programme of the United Nations High Commissioner for Refugees

The General Assembly,

Taking note of Economic and Social Council decision 2011/263 of 28 July 2011 concerning the enlargement of the Executive Committee of the Programme of the United Nations High Commissioner for Refugees,

Taking note also of the request regarding the enlargement of the Executive Committee contained in the letter dated 1 March 2011 from the Permanent Representative of Azerbaijan to the United Nations addressed to the Secretary-General and the letter dated 11 July 2011 from the Chargé d'affaires a.i. of the Permanent Mission of Rwanda to the United Nations Office and other international organizations in Geneva addressed to the President of the Economic and Social Council,

1. *Decides* to increase the number of members of the Executive Committee of the Programme of the United Nations High Commissioner for Refugees from eighty-five States to eighty-seven States;

2. *Requests* the Economic and Social Council to elect the additional members at its resumed organizational session for 2012.

Standing Committee

The Standing Committee held three meetings in 2011 (Geneva, 1–3 March [A/AC.96/1097]; 21–23 June [A/AC.96/1104]; and 20 September [A/AC.96/1105]). It adopted decisions regarding programme budgets and funding for 2011; funding end-of-service and post-retirement liabilities; the establishment of an Independent Audit and Oversight Committee; and a proposed revision of the financial rules for voluntary funds administered by the High Commissioner. The Committee's work was summarized in an October secretariat report [A/AC.96/1106].

In October [A/66/12/Add.1], the Executive Committee adopted a decision on the programme of work of the Standing Committee in 2012, requesting that Committee to report on its work to the sixty-third session (2012) of the Executive Committee. It also approved applications by Governments as well as intergovernmental and international organizations to participate as observers in Standing Committee meetings in 2011 and 2012.

Refugee protection and assistance

In his annual report covering 2011 [A/67/12], the High Commissioner said that the Intergovernmental Event at the Ministerial Level of United Nations Member States on the occasion of the sixtieth anniversary of the 1951 Convention relating to the Status of Refugees and the fiftieth anniversary of the 1961 Convention on the Reduction of Statelessness (Geneva, 7–8 December) brought together 155 Member States. More than 100 of those made pledges relating to the protection of refugees, IDPs and stateless people. To enhance the Office's efficiency and effectiveness, reforms had been undertaken to reduce overall expenditures while addressing UNHCR volume of activities, which had nearly doubled in the previous five years. Investments were also made to improve the UNHCR ability to deliver. During the year, more than 40 protection positions were created and protection learning for both UNHCR staff and partners was strengthened. Among the major challenges to delivering protection, the report highlighted emergency situations, waning political will, threats of refoulement, sexual and gender-based violence, and the protection of refugees and asylum seekers at sea. More than 1,500 people, including potential asylum seekers, drowned or went missing while attempting to cross the Mediterranean in 2011. The High Commissioner underlined the complexity of modern migration, as people with international protection needs often travelled irregularly alongside other groups. Assisting States and other partners to develop protection strategies to address mixed migration remained a priority for UNHCR. In that context, activities included the update of the 10-Point Plan of Action on Refugee Protection and Mixed Migration [YUN 2006, p. 1390]; initiatives to enhance inter-State cooperation for the protection of refugees at sea; and efforts to address the protection needs of trafficked persons.

Other activities included assistance to persons of southern Sudanese origin in the Sudan, including operational support for issuing identity documentation to citizens of the new State of South Sudan (see p. 196). During the Libyan crisis, UNHCR and IOM jointly implemented a large-scale evacuation programme, which helped more than 300,000 third-country nationals to return to their homelands. UNHCR continued to provide protection and assistance to the Sahrawi refugees in the camps near Tindouf, Algeria. At the end of 2011, over 42,600 persons had registered for the confidence-building measures programme in the Sahrawi camps in Tindouf and in Western Sahara, which was aimed at bringing together families that had been separated for some 37 years. Some 12,300 persons had already benefited from the programme. Also in 2011, UNHCR assisted 61,600 refugees to resettle in a number of countries. The top three countries of asylum from which refugees departed for resettlement with UNHCR assistance remained Nepal, Thailand and Malaysia.

In a June report on international protection [A/AC/96/1098], the High Commissioner reflected on the manifold dimensions of the 1951 Refugee Convention and its 1967 Protocol, and reviewed the different facets of international protection: its historical and contemporary as well as legislative and security dimensions, and aspects related to human dignity, age and gender, along with proposed solutions. The Convention, which had international protection at its heart, had proven to be capable of adapting to a wide range of sociopolitical contexts. Forms of persecution related to gender discrimination, for example, had been accepted as falling within the definition of "refugee", and in the Council of Europe's Convention on Preventing and Combating Violence against Women and Domestic Violence, adopted in May, UNHCR ensured that language on gender-related persecution and gender-sensitive asylum procedures was properly reflected.

The principles of non-discrimination and non-refoulement were central to the 1951 Convention, as was UNHCR role in supervising States' implementation of their treaty obligations and in providing advice and technical support to Governments as they drafted their laws and policies. In addition to legislative frameworks, properly functioning asylum systems were a prerequisite for fulfilling obligations under the 1951 Convention. Supervising the implementation and monitoring the quality of national asylum procedures was a focus of UNHCR work in 2010. Many States had improved their asylum systems. The Republic of Korea, for example, shortened the refugee status determination period from over one year to within six months. UNHCR launched a project on Further Developing Asylum Quality, focusing on four southern and five central European countries.

The High Commissioner underlined how displacement-migration trends were increasingly set within other global trends, including climate change, population pressures and urbanization, as well as food, water and energy insecurity. The rise of terrorist attacks had led to more restrictive measures towards asylum seekers and refugees, who were often the target of xenophobia and discrimination.

A note by the High Commissioner on statelessness [A/AC.96/1098/Add.1], covering the period since the latest update of June 2009 [YUN 2009, p. 1203], took stock of challenges, outlined the Office's efforts and reviewed progress made, while also pointing to major trends and developments. Fifty years after the adoption of the 1961 Convention on the Reduction of Statelessness, up to 12 million people remained stateless. Statelessness was not merely a legal issue but also one requiring good governance and political determination. Arbitrary denial or deprivation of nationality resulting in statelessness continued to have a major impact worldwide, as the children and grandchildren of those affected generally became stateless at birth, thereby perpetuating the problem. The UNHCR statelessness budget in 2011 grew to $63 million, compared to 38.5 million in 2010 and $12 million in 2009. Baseline data on stateless populations had gradually improved through cooperation with national authorities in undertaking censuses and surveys. Gaps in baseline population data were a major impediment to establishing an effective response. In January, UNHCR organized a workshop for staff and partners on measuring statelessness. The Office launched a campaign to promote accession to the 1961 Convention on the Reduction of Statelessness and the 1954 Convention relating to the Status of Stateless Persons. UNHCR carried out initiatives to prevent statelessness through documentation, birth registration and legal aid in 25 countries, assisting people at risk of statelessness to acquire birth certificates and other identity documents needed to establish their nationality.

In many States, recognition of statelessness was the entry point for gaining a status that included residence and other rights. Yet procedures to determine statelessness existed in relatively few countries. UNHCR encouraged the establishment of such procedures and provided technical advice in 39 States, a jump from the 20 States where such activities were undertaken in the previous reporting period. In the context of the fiftieth anniversary of the 1961 Convention, UNHCR launched a series of meetings with governmental, United Nations, NGO and academic experts. Two of those meetings focused on the definition of a stateless person, determination procedures and status granted to stateless individuals under the 1954 Convention; a third meeting looked at safeguards to prevent statelessness among children under the 1961 Convention. Guidelines taking into account the conclusions of such meetings were being drafted.

The annual High Commissioner's Dialogue on Protection Challenges did not take place in 2011.

Populations of concern

According to the High Commissioner's annual report [A/67/12], the global population of concern at the end of 2011 was 35.4 million, including 10.4 million refugees. The latter number was approximately 144,000 less than in 2010 due to a reduction of about 16 per cent in the estimates of Afghan and Iraqi refugee populations in Iran, Pakistan and Syria, as well as to the fact that a number of refugees found durable solutions, mainly voluntary repatriation. The number of people displaced within their country as a result of conflict was an estimated 26.4 million, of whom 15.5 million had benefited from UNHCR protection and assistance, representing an increase of almost 800,000 compared to 2010. With regard to statelessness, UNHCR identified 3.5 million stateless persons in 2011, the same as in 2010. By the end of the year, statistics on stateless populations were available for 64 countries, compared to 30 countries in 2004, when the Office had started to systematically collect data. UNHCR was unable to provide comprehensive global statistics; however, the number of stateless persons worldwide was estimated at over 12 million. During 2011, about 876,100 individual claims for asylum or refugee status were submitted to Governments or UNHCR in 171 countries or territories—a 3 per cent increase compared to the 850,300 claims of 2010. UNHCR registered 11 per cent of the global total. The highest number of new claims came from asylum seekers from Zimbabwe (52,500), Afghanistan (43,000), Somalia (35,900), Côte d'Ivoire (33,000), the Democratic Republic of the Congo (31,500), Myanmar (29,800) and Iraq (29,100).

The generosity of countries hosting refugees remained fundamental to the UNHCR ability to carry out its mandate. Lower- and middle-income States accommodated the largest proportion of the world's refugees. While humanitarian agencies worked to ensure protection and provide essential services, refugees were sustained by the resources and support of their host Governments and communities. Pakistan remained the country hosting the largest number of refugees, followed by Iran—both countries hosting mainly Afghans. In Syria, the third largest hosting country, Iraqi refugees made up the main refugee population. Other important host countries included Kenya and Jordan. To better understand the contributions of hosting States, the Office convened a Steering Committee on the Cost and Impact of Hosting Refugees, comprised of interested members of the Executive Committee.

Protection issues

Refugee women

In June [A/AC.96/1104], the Standing Committee considered a document [EC/62/SC/CRP.14] on protecting refugee women, which discussed UNHCR progress in supporting women and girls in five areas: sexual and gender-based violence (SGBV); participation in decision-making and leadership; economic self-reliance; education; and access to sanitary materials. Women and girls represented 49 per cent of the UNHCR population of concern.

Among UNHCR initiatives aimed to reduce the exposure of women and girls to SGBV—in particular during darkness and when they searched for firewood—was the provision of solar lights and lamps in refugee camps in the Central African Republic, Djibouti, Ethiopia, Kenya, Rwanda and Uganda, as well as fuel-efficient and solar cookers in Chad and Nepal. In Kenya, a mobile court visited refugee camps on a monthly basis to ensure that women could obtain legal advice and legal representation.

Following the UNHCR commitment to supporting equal participation of women in decision-making bodies, women were increasingly assuming responsibilities in the public sphere and accounted for 40 per cent of refugee camp committee members. That progress was not matched, however, in urban settings, where people of concern were dispersed over large areas. The agency continued to work with communities to ensure that women's leadership was understood and accepted by all community members.

To support women of concern worldwide in addressing the daily struggle they faced in securing some form of income for themselves and their families, UNHCR advocated for refugees to be granted permits to work legally. The inability to work in the formal sector put women in situations of greater vulnerability to both economic and sexual exploitation. UNHCR engaged in small income-generation projects for women in a number of countries: a community centre for refugee women and children in Morocco provided a combination of mental health support, recreational activities, vocational training and business start-up opportunities.

UNHCR undertook initiatives to increase access to education for refugee girls, improve its quality and enhance the protection available in schools, providing incentives that promoted enrolment and improved retention rates in primary and secondary schools. In cooperation with the World Food Programme (WFP), the Office implemented school feeding programmes in Algeria, Colombia, Djibouti, Iran, the Sudan and Yemen, and increased the number of trained and qualified female teachers.

The lack of access to sanitary materials often had health implications resulting in girls missing school or women being unable to leave the house and perform daily activities. UNHCR responded to the financial and logistical obstacles to the delivery of sanitary pads to women by promoting the local purchase and provision of environmentally friendly sanitary materials as a means to reduce transport costs, promote self-reliance and develop local manufacturing capacity.

To provide assistance in creating safe environments and mitigating the risk of SGBV, UNHCR issued in June the publication *Action against Sexual and Gender-based Violence: An Updated Strategy*.

Refugees and HIV/AIDS

In 2011, many countries still did not mention refugees and IDPs in their national HIV strategies. UNHCR continued to advocate for refugees and IDPs to have access to national HIV and AIDS programmes and services. At its June meeting, the Standing Committee provided an update [EC/62/SC/CRP.15/Rev.1] on the Office's HIV and AIDS activities, in line with the UNHCR Strategic Plan for HIV and AIDS, 2008–2012, and reviewed progress made with respect to the UNHCR role as a co-sponsor of the Joint United Nations Programme on HIV/AIDS (UNAIDS). The Strategic Plan was aimed at guiding operations in camp, urban and non-camp settings, as well as in local integration and returnee situations, and was based on lessons learned from the previous Strategic Plans for 2002–2004 and 2005–2007. Progress had been made in improving access to antiretroviral therapy. As at June 2011, approximately 87 per cent of refugees had access to treatment programmes that were established for surrounding populations or host communities. Access to initiatives to prevent mother-to-child transmission increased to 75 per cent. Regarding inter-agency response in the context of UNAIDS, UNHCR worked together with WFP in addressing HIV in emergency situations. The Office played a steering role to ensure that HIV-related needs during humanitarian emergencies were identified and addressed from the early stages, as well as throughout the post-emergency phases.

Community services

As part of its protection policy, UNHCR pursued a community development approach, designed to enable staff to empower refugees by working with them in identifying measures that made a difference to the life of their host community. According to a document [EC/62/SC/CRP.16] considered by the Standing Committee in June, UNHCR was transitioning from a community services function to a sharper focus on community development. The Office focused on promoting the rights of groups that often faced discrimination—such as older persons and persons with disabilities—while identifying and making the best use of their capacities. For instance, a pilot outreach counselling centre had been established in Syria; it was run by some 130 trained refugees who provided support to refugees with mental health and disability issues, including those that were related to aging.

Role of host countries

A May report [EC/62/SC/CRP.18] on the role on host countries regarding the cost and impact of hosting refugees questioned the traditional distinction between "donor States" and "refugee-hosting States", and suggested that the notion of "contributing countries" would be more equitable. The view according to which refugees were a burden on the countries where they had taken up residence needed to be changed, especially considering that when refugees were provided with an opportunity to make use of their capacities, they made a positive contribution to their host communities.

Natural disasters

Following consultations among the three protection-mandated agencies—UNHCR, the International Federation of Red Cross and Red Crescent Societies and IOM—and the Emergency Relief Coordinator, the Inter-Agency Standing Committee, in early 2011, proposed to pilot a new arrangement in which UNHCR would assume a more predictable protection cluster leadership role in natural disaster situations. In June [A/AC.96/1104], the Standing Committee considered a report [EC/62/SC/CRP.19] reviewing UNHCR experience in addressing the basis for the Office's intervention, as well as the nature of the protection provided to populations affected by natural disasters, as compared with regular refugee operations; identifying key responsibilities and activities arising from the distinct roles of cluster lead agency and of operational partner in protection in natural disasters; exploring the most common protection issues arising in natural disasters; and providing a policy framework outlining UNHCR engagement in natural disasters.

The majority of the Standing Committee members declared, however, that they were not convinced by the information provided, and called for postponing any designation of responsibility as lead agency for protection in situations of natural disaster until outstanding questions were answered.

Staff security

In June [A/AC.96/1104], the Standing Committee considered a review of staff safety and security issues, including refugee security [EC/62/SC/CRP.17], which followed the 2009 audit on security governance undertaken by the Office of Internal Oversight Services [YUN 2009, p. 1198]. The political volatility in the Middle East and North Africa had underscored the importance of enhancing overall security preparedness in anticipation of a wide range of scenarios and threats. The UNHCR Field Safety Section (FSS) spearheaded efforts in that direction, while supporting the large volume of emergency needs arising from incidents in the field. FSS at headquarters and UNHCR safety advisers in the field assisted operations by providing security risk assessments, technical advice, training and input for inter-agency security management. In 2010, missions to the field totalled 413 days. During the first half of 2011, the pace accelerated with deployments to Côte d'Ivoire, Egypt, Liberia, Libya and Tunisia, as well as to the Western Sahara operation. With regard to information gathering and analysis, the UNHCR security management strategy emphasized the proactive use of information tools and resources to better understand and manage risk, and ultimately to enable country programmes to operate safely. Despite the continued efforts to improve its security information system, technical challenges remained concerning the efficient capturing of data. UNHCR continued to review and evaluate security management in the field through channels such as the United Nations Minimum Operating Security Standards (MOSS) [YUN 2004, p. 720]. At the end of 2010, UNHCR estimated that 82 per cent of its offices were MOSS-compliant.

At the meeting, delegations expressed appreciation for the UNHCR efforts to assure the safety and security of staff and persons of concern, welcoming in particular the presence of field safety advisers. They also asked for more information on remote management in high-risk operations; the apparent decrease in the rate of compliance with MOSS in field offices and the estimated costs involved; and the impact of changes in the UN security management system from a "when to leave" to a "how to stay" approach.

Protracted situations and durable solutions

According to the High Commissioner's annual report [A/67/12], some 7.2 million refugees were living in protracted situations of exile. Afghans constituted the largest protracted refugee population in the world with nearly 3 million registered refugees, most of whom had been living in Pakistan and Iran for over 30 years. In Africa, three of the most protracted refugee situations were drawing to a close, as the comprehensive solution strategies for Angolan, Liberian and Rwandan refugees were being implemented along with the cessation of refugee status. UNHCR worked with different partners to enable conditions conducive to the three traditional durable solutions to protracted situations: voluntary repatriation, local integration and resettlement. The agency argued that such solutions should be used in a complementary manner and should be put in place from the onset of displacement.

The number of displaced people returning home voluntarily had fallen steadily since 2004. That trend was reversed in 2011, with 532,000 refugees returning to their country of origin. UNHCR sought to ensure that, in addition to being voluntary, returns were safe, and that refugees received individual counselling prior to return. Once home, returnees were helped to reintegrate into their societies so that they could fully enjoy their political, social and economic rights. Approximately 68,200 Afghans returned to their country voluntarily with UNHCR assistance in 2011—49,200 from Pakistan and 18,900 from Iran. In the Western Balkans, UNHCR played a key role in supporting the Governments of Bosnia and Herzegovina, Croatia, Montenegro and Serbia to draw up a regional plan to resolve displacement stemming from the 1991–1995 conflict. Those Governments agreed to provide housing for the most vulnerable among the displaced, many of whom still lived in collective centres. The plan sought to provide durable solutions for 73,000 vulnerable refugees in the region. In Central Asia, UNHCR drew up a regional strategy for long-staying urban refugees in Kazakhstan, Kyrgyzstan, Tajikistan, Turkmenistan and Uzbekistan.

As for local integration, in Latin America the Cities of Solidarity framework was designed to contribute to the self-reliance of refugees, mostly in urban areas, while allowing them to gain access to health care, education, employment and housing services. The Philippines continued to allow some refugees to acquire citizenship through naturalization.

With regard to resettlement, in April, UNHCR launched the Global Resettlement Solidarity Initiative, which called on States to add more resettlement places to their existing quotas for refugees from Libya living at the borders of Egypt and Tunisia. Resettlement countries responded positively to the initiative: 13 countries pledged 1,700 places. Almost a third of those places were in addition to annual resettlement programmes, helping to preserve the places allocated to other emergency situations. During the year, UNHCR presented more than 90,000 refugees for resettlement consideration, a 15 per cent drop from 2010. Some 11 per cent of those submissions were for women and girls at risk. Approximately 61,000 refugees departed for resettlement in 2011. The top three countries of asylum from which refugees departed remained the same as in 2010: Nepal (18,150), Thailand (9,600) and Malaysia (8,400). By nationality, the main beneficiaries were refugees from Bhutan, Myanmar and Iraq.

A new version of the *UNHCR Resettlement Handbook* was issued at the Annual Tripartite Consultations on Resettlement, held in Geneva in July.

International instruments

In 2011, with the accession of Nauru to both the 1951 Convention relating to the Status of Refugees [YUN 1951, p. 520] and its 1967 Protocol [YUN 1967, p. 477], the number of parties to those instruments increased to 145 and 146, respectively.

The number of States parties to the 1954 Convention relating to the Status of Stateless Persons [YUN 1954, p. 416] rose to 71, with the ratification of the Philippines and the accession of Benin, Georgia, Nigeria, Panama and Turkmenistan. The number of parties to the 1961 Convention on the Reduction of Statelessness [YUN 1961, p. 533] also increased to 42 with the accession of Benin, Croatia, Nigeria, Panama and Serbia.

Regional activities

Africa

In 2011, conflicts in Côte d'Ivoire, Libya, Somalia and the Sudan forced more than 800,000 refugees into neighbouring countries—the highest number in over a decade. The population of concern to UNHCR in sub-Saharan Africa increased significantly from slightly over 10 million in January to over 12 million by the end of the year. The total comprised some 2.7 million refugees, 236,000 returned refugees, 367,000 asylum seekers, 6.9 million IDPs, 1.7 million returned IDPs, 21,000 stateless persons, as well as some 174,000 other persons of concerns.

According to the *UNHCR Global Report 2011*, the Office responded to major emergencies involving thousands of people fleeing post-election turmoil in Côte d'Ivoire, violence and famine in Somalia and armed clashes in areas disputed by the Sudan and South Sudan. UNHCR accelerated the implementation of its comprehensive strategies to bring to a close the protracted Angolan, Liberian and Rwandan refugee situations.

In Liberia, UNHCR extended protection and assistance to some 224,000 Ivorian refugees. Initially, most were welcomed in several villages along the border. As refugee numbers increased, however, UNHCR was obliged to set up five refugee camps in eastern Liberia so as to ensure a more effective delivery of services. In the second half of the year, UNHCR concluded tripartite agreements on voluntary repatriation with Côte d'Ivoire, Ghana, Liberia and Togo. By the end of the year, some 135,000 Ivorian refugees had returned, including 96,000 from Liberia.

UNHCR worked with 464 governmental, United Nations and NGO partners in the continent, 160 of whom were national NGOs. The Office supported the establishment of a secretariat for the African NGO Task Force, a coordinating platform for the continent's NGOs. The first training session on the UNHCR programmes took place in December in Burkina Faso and was attended by representatives of 12 West African NGOs.

On 20 April, UNHCR launched the Global Resettlement Solidarity Initiative, which called on States to consider contributing resettlement places for non-Libyan refugees coming from Libya and who were hosted on the borders of Egypt and Tunisia, as well as for long-term refugees living in urban centres in Egypt.

Report of Secretary-General. Pursuant to General Assembly resolution 65/193 [YUN 2010, p. 1207], the Secretary-General in August submitted a report [A/66/321] on UN assistance to refugees, returnees and displaced persons in Africa, covering 2010 and the first half of 2011.

The complex humanitarian situation in Somalia continued to dominate the humanitarian environment in East Africa and the Horn of Africa, said the report. During the reporting period, approximately 270,000 Somalis were forced to flee to neighbouring Ethiopia, Djibouti and Kenya. In June alone, 62,000 Somalis sought refuge in the region, while 65,000 fled internally to Mogadishu, bringing the total number of IDPs to 1.5 million. Kenya and Ethiopia continued to receive large numbers of refugees from Somalia and passed new laws that benefited asylum seekers and refugees. In the Sudan, the referendum of January resulted in a vote for the independence of Southern Sudan (see p. 196). Between 30 October 2010 and mid-June 2011, 365,000 southern Sudanese moved back to South Sudan. To increase assistance to IDPs, UNHCR expanded its presence along the major return routes in the states of Abyei, South Kordofan and Blue Nile, and in Southern Sudan.

In West Africa, the political deadlock following the 2010 presidential elections in Côte d'Ivoire had resulted in vast internal displacement and the movement of some 170,000 refugees into neighbouring Liberia, Guinea and Ghana. UNHCR coordinated the protection and assistance response for refugees, working closely with national authorities in the countries of asylum. With the end of the political crisis in April 2011, refugees and IDPs began to return, although new displacement and refugee flows continued.

With regard to Central Africa and the Great Lakes Region, the Central African Republic at the end of 2010 was hosting 22,000 refugees, mainly from Chad, the Sudan and the Democratic Republic of the Congo, while 176,000 people were internally displaced as a result of clashes between Government forces and rebel movements. Assuring protection and assistance for refugees and IDPs was difficult, and attacks against aid workers in early 2011 resulted in the suspension of activities and limited movement within the region. The withdrawal of the United Nations Mission in the Central African Republic and Chad on 31 December 2010 [YUN 2010, p. 168], at the request of the Chadian Government, proceeded without negative effects on security in and around refugee and IDP camps, helping to create an environment conducive to the return of some 50,000 IDPs. Nevertheless, the overall security context remained fragile. In the Democratic Republic of the Congo (DRC), fighting and insecurity brought the number of IDPs to 1.7 million. The progressive drawdown of the United Nations Organization Stabilization Mission in the Democratic Republic of the Congo, coupled with the absence of effective State authority and of a well-trained army or police force, hampered access to people of concern, undermining efforts to protect Rwandan refugees and IDPs in the provinces of North and South Kivu, Katanga, Equateur and Orientale. A series of tripartite agreements between UNHCR, the DRC and neighbouring States set the stage for an increase in returns to the country. More than 85,000 Congolese refugees had returned home from the United Republic of Tanzania since 2005, and the repatriation operation in Zambia concluded with the return of 40,000 Congolese refugees.

In Southern Africa, mixed migration was straining humanitarian resources along the southward route from East Africa, the Horn of Africa and the Great Lakes region. Public confusion over the difference between refugees and asylum seekers in need of protection and migrants on the move for economic or other reasons was undermining support for asylum and giving rise to restrictive protection policies. During the year, 107,000 individual asylum claims were submitted in South Africa. While that represented a significant decline compared to 2010, it was still the highest number of such applications received worldwide in 2011.

By subregion, UNHCR spent $527.9 million for East Africa and the Horn of Africa, where there were some 7.0 million people of concern. In Central Africa and the Great Lakes Region, $173.3 million were spent on 3.7 million people of concern, while in West Africa $109.8 million were spent on some 1.0 million people of concern. In Southern Africa, where approximately 449,000 people were of concern, UNHCR expended $46.7 million.

GENERAL ASSEMBLY ACTION

On 19 December [meeting 89], the General Assembly, on the recommendation of the Third Committee [A/66/456], adopted **resolution 66/135** without vote [agenda item 62].

Assistance to refugees, returnees and displaced persons in Africa

The General Assembly,

Recalling the Organization of African Unity Convention governing the specific aspects of refugee problems in Africa of 1969 and the African Charter on Human and Peoples' Rights,

Reaffirming that the 1951 Convention relating to the Status of Refugees, together with the 1967 Protocol thereto, as complemented by the Organization of African Unity Convention of 1969, remains the foundation of the international refugee protection regime in Africa,

Welcoming the adoption, and the ongoing ratification process, of the African Union Convention for the Protection and Assistance of Internally Displaced Persons in Africa, which marks a significant step towards strengthening the national and regional normative framework for the protection of and assistance to internally displaced persons,

Recognizing the particular vulnerability of women and children among refugees and other persons of concern, including exposure to discrimination and sexual and physical abuse, and in this regard acknowledging the importance of preventing and responding to sexual and gender-based violence,

Gravely concerned about the rising number of refugees in various parts of the continent,

Acknowledging the efforts of Member States, the United Nations High Commissioner for Refugees and other stakeholders in improving the situation of refugees, and expressing grave concern about the deteriorating living conditions in many refugee camps in Africa,

Recognizing that refugees, internally displaced persons and, in particular, women and children are at an increased risk of exposure to HIV and AIDS, malaria and other infectious diseases,

Recalling the regional dialogues that the Office of the United Nations High Commissioner for Refugees undertook on protection challenges and solutions with refugee women and girls in Uganda and Zambia in March and April 2011, respectively,

Welcoming the ministerial mini-summit on the humanitarian response to the Horn of Africa crisis, held in New York on 24 September 2011, the African Union pledging conference for the Horn of Africa, held in Addis Ababa on 25 August 2011, and the Organization for Islamic Cooperation pledging meeting on Somalia, held in Istanbul, Turkey, on 17 August 2011, as well as the Intergovernmental Authority on Development and East African Community joint summit on the Horn of Africa crisis on the theme "Ending Drought Emergencies: A Commitment to Sustainable Solutions", held in Nairobi on 8 and 9 September 2011, dedicated to raising awareness and mobilizing resources to address the crisis in the Horn of Africa, and in this context expressing appreciation for the valuable contributions of countries and international, regional and subregional organizations, as well as other relevant partners,

Noting with appreciation the Joint Declaration adopted at the joint summit on the Horn of Africa crisis, which, inter alia, expressed concern about the mass exodus of refugees into neighbouring countries, as well as the increased number of internally displaced persons due to the current humanitarian crises of drought and famine in the Horn of Africa,

Noting with appreciation also the Pact on Security, Stability and Development in the Great Lakes Region, adopted by the International Conference on the Great Lakes Region in 2006, and its instruments, in particular two of the protocols to the Pact, which are relevant to the protection of displaced persons, namely, the Protocol on the Protection of and Assistance to Internally Displaced Persons and the Protocol on the Property Rights of Returning Persons,

Acknowledging with appreciation the generosity, hospitality and spirit of solidarity of African countries that continue to host the influx of refugees due to recent humanitarian crises and protracted refugee situations and, in this regard, expressing particular appreciation for the commitment and efforts of neighbouring countries in the recent humanitarian crises in Côte d'Ivoire, Libya and the Horn of Africa, and further acknowledging with appreciation the coordination of humanitarian assistance by the United Nations as well as the continuing efforts of donors, the United Nations system, including the Office of the United Nations High Commissioner for Refugees, regional organizations, international agencies, non-governmental organizations and other partners, with regard to, inter alia, voluntary return, reintegration and resettlement, in addressing the plight of refugees during the emergency,

Recognizing that host States have the primary responsibility for the protection of and assistance to refugees on their territory, and the need to redouble efforts to develop and implement comprehensive durable solution strategies, in appropriate cooperation with the international community, and burden- and responsibility-sharing,

Emphasizing that States have the primary responsibility to provide protection and assistance to internally displaced persons within their jurisdiction, as well as to address the root causes of the displacement problem, in appropriate cooperation with the international community,

Welcoming the sixtieth anniversary of the 1951 Convention relating to the Status of Refugees and the fiftieth anniversary of the 1961 Convention on the Reduction of Statelessness, and welcoming in this context the convening, by the Office of the High Commissioner, of an intergovernmental event at the ministerial level on 7 and 8 December 2011 to commemorate these anniversaries,

1. *Takes note* of the reports of the Secretary-General and the United Nations High Commissioner for Refugees;

2. *Calls upon* African Member States that have not yet signed or ratified the African Union Convention for the Protection and Assistance of Internally Displaced Persons in Africa to consider doing so as early as possible in order to ensure its early entry into force and implementation;

3. *Notes* the need for African Member States to address resolutely the root causes of all forms of forced displacement in Africa and to foster peace, stability and prosperity throughout the African continent so as to forestall flows of refugees;

4. *Notes with great concern* that, despite all of the efforts made so far by the United Nations, the African Union and others, the situation of refugees and displaced persons in Africa remains precarious, and calls upon States and other parties to armed conflict to observe scrupulously the letter and spirit of international humanitarian law, bearing in mind that armed conflict is one of the principal causes of forced displacement in Africa;

5. *Welcomes* decisions EX.CL/Dec.629(XVIII) and EX.CL/Dec.653(XIX) on the humanitarian situation in Africa, insofar as they relate to refugees, returnees and displaced persons, adopted by the Executive Council of the African Union at its eighteenth ordinary session, held in Addis Ababa from 24 to 28 January 2011, and at its nineteenth ordinary session, held in Malabo from 23 to 28 June 2011, respectively;

6. *Expresses its appreciation* for the leadership shown by the Office of the United Nations High Commissioner for Refugees, and commends the Office for its ongoing efforts, with the support of the international community, to assist African countries of asylum, including by providing support to vulnerable local host communities, and to respond to the protection and assistance needs of refugees, returnees and displaced persons in Africa;

7. *Notes with appreciation* the initiatives taken by the African Union, the Subcommittee on Refugees, Returnees and Internally Displaced Persons of its Permanent Representatives Committee, and the African Commission on Human and Peoples' Rights, in particular the role of its Special Rapporteur on Refugees, Asylum Seekers, Migrants and Internally Displaced Persons in Africa, to ensure the protection of and assistance to refugees, returnees and displaced persons in Africa;

8. *Recalls* the adoption by the Executive Committee of the Programme of the United Nations High Commissioner for Refugees of the conclusion on refugees with disabilities and other persons with disabilities protected and assisted by the Office of the High Commissioner, at its sixty-first session, held from 4 to 8 October 2010, and endorses its report on the work of its sixty-second session, held from 3 to 7 October 2011;

9. *Acknowledges* the important contribution of age, gender and diversity mainstreaming in identifying, through a participatory approach, the protection risks faced by the different members of the refugee communities, in particular the non-discriminatory treatment and protection of women, children, persons with disabilities and the elderly;

10. *Affirms* that children, because of their age, social status and physical and mental development, are often more vulnerable than adults in situations of forced displacement, recognizes that forced displacement, return to post-conflict situations, integration in new societies, protracted situations of displacement and statelessness can increase child protection risks, taking into account the particular vulnerability of refugee children to forcible exposure to the risks of physical and psychological injury, exploitation and death in connection with armed conflict, and acknowledges that wider environmental factors and individual risk factors, particularly when combined, may generate different protection needs;

11. *Recognizes* that no solution to displacement can be durable unless it is sustainable, and therefore encourages the Office of the High Commissioner to support the sustainability of voluntary return, reintegration and resettlement;

12. *Also recognizes* the importance of early registration and effective registration systems and censuses as a tool of protection and as a means to the quantification and assessment of needs for the provision and distribution of humanitarian assistance and to implement appropriate durable solutions;

13. *Recalls* the conclusion on registration of refugees and asylum seekers adopted by the Executive Committee of the Programme of the High Commissioner at its fifty-second session, notes the many forms of harassment faced by refugees and asylum seekers who remain without any form of documentation attesting to their status, recalls the responsibility of States to register refugees on their territories and, as appropriate, the responsibility of the Office of the High Commissioner or mandated international bodies to do so, reiterates in this context the central role that early and effective registration and documentation can play, guided by protection considerations, in enhancing protection and supporting efforts to find durable solutions, and calls upon the Office, as appropriate, to help States to conduct this procedure should they be unable to register refugees on their territory;

14. *Calls upon* the international community, including States and the Office of the High Commissioner and other relevant United Nations organizations, within their respective mandates, to take concrete action to meet the protection and assistance needs of refugees, returnees and displaced persons and to contribute generously to projects and programmes aimed at alleviating their plight, facilitating durable solutions for refugees and displaced persons and supporting vulnerable local host communities;

15. *Reaffirms* the importance of timely and adequate assistance and protection for refugees, returnees and displaced persons, also reaffirms that assistance and protection are mutually reinforcing and that inadequate material assistance and food shortages undermine protection, notes the importance of a rights- and community-based approach in engaging constructively with individual refugees, returnees and displaced persons and their communities so as to achieve fair and equitable access to food and other forms of material assistance, and expresses concern in regard to situations in which minimum standards of assistance are not

met, including those in which adequate needs assessments have yet to be undertaken;

16. *Also reaffirms* that respect by States for their protection responsibilities towards refugees is strengthened by international solidarity involving all members of the international community and that the refugee protection regime is enhanced through committed international cooperation in a spirit of solidarity and burden- and responsibility-sharing among all States;

17. *Further reaffirms* that host States have the primary responsibility to ensure the civilian and humanitarian character of asylum, calls upon States, in cooperation with international organizations, within their mandates, to take all measures necessary to ensure respect for the principles of refugee protection and, in particular, to ensure that the civilian and humanitarian nature of refugee camps is not compromised by the presence or the activities of armed elements or used for purposes that are incompatible with their civilian character, and encourages the High Commissioner to continue efforts, in consultation with States and other relevant actors, to ensure the civilian and humanitarian character of camps;

18. *Condemns* all acts that pose a threat to the personal security and well-being of refugees and asylum seekers, such as refoulement, unlawful expulsion and physical attacks, calls upon States of refuge, in cooperation with international organizations, where appropriate, to take all measures necessary to ensure respect for the principles of refugee protection, including the humane treatment of asylum seekers, notes with interest that the High Commissioner has continued to take steps to encourage the development of measures to better ensure the civilian and humanitarian character of asylum, and encourages the High Commissioner to continue those efforts, in consultation with States and other relevant actors;

19. *Deplores* the continuing violence and insecurity which constitute an ongoing threat to the safety and security of staff members of the Office of the High Commissioner and other humanitarian organizations and an obstacle to the effective fulfilment of the mandate of the Office and the ability of its implementing partners and other humanitarian personnel to discharge their respective humanitarian functions, urges States, parties to conflict and all other relevant actors to take all measures necessary to protect activities related to humanitarian assistance, prevent attacks on and kidnapping of national and international humanitarian workers and ensure the safety and security of the personnel and property of the Office and that of all humanitarian organizations discharging functions mandated by the Office, and calls upon States to investigate fully any crime committed against humanitarian personnel and bring to justice the persons responsible for such crimes;

20. *Calls upon* the Office of the High Commissioner, the African Union, subregional organizations and all African States, in conjunction with agencies of the United Nations system, intergovernmental and non-governmental organizations and the international community, to strengthen and revitalize existing partnerships and forge new ones in support of the protection system for refugees, asylum seekers and internally displaced persons;

21. *Calls upon* the Office of the High Commissioner, the international community and other entities concerned to continue and, where appropriate, intensify their support to African Governments through appropriate capacity-building activities, including training of relevant officers, disseminating information about refugee instruments and principles, providing financial, technical and advisory services to accelerate the enactment or amendment and implementation of legislation relating to refugees, strengthening emergency response and enhancing capacities for the coordination of humanitarian activities, in particular those Governments that have received large numbers of refugees and asylum seekers;

22. *Reaffirms* the right of return and the principle of voluntary repatriation, appeals to countries of origin and countries of asylum to create conditions that are conducive to voluntary repatriation, and recognizes that, while voluntary repatriation remains the pre-eminent solution, local integration and third-country resettlement, where appropriate and feasible, are also viable options for dealing with the situation of African refugees who, owing to prevailing circumstances in their respective countries of origin, are unable to return home;

23. *Also reaffirms* that voluntary repatriation should not necessarily be conditioned on the accomplishment of political solutions in the country of origin in order not to impede the exercise of the refugees' right to return, recognizes that the voluntary repatriation and reintegration process is normally guided by the conditions in the country of origin, in particular that voluntary repatriation can be accomplished in conditions of safety and dignity, and urges the High Commissioner to promote sustainable return through the development of durable and lasting solutions, particularly in protracted refugee situations;

24. *Calls upon* the international donor community to provide financial and material assistance that allows for the implementation of community-based development programmes that benefit both refugees and host communities, as appropriate, in agreement with host countries and consistent with humanitarian objectives;

25. *Appeals* to the international community to respond positively, in the spirit of solidarity and burden- and responsibility-sharing, to the third-country resettlement needs of African refugees, notes in this regard the importance of using resettlement strategically, as part of situation-specific comprehensive responses to refugee situations, and to this end encourages States, the Office of the High Commissioner and other relevant partners to make full use of the Multilateral Framework of Understandings on Resettlement, where appropriate and feasible; and in this context commends recent efforts by the Office of the High Commissioner in launching the Global Resettlement Solidarity Initiative in April 2011 and by States that have responded generously in this respect;

26. *Calls upon* the international donor community to provide material and financial assistance for the implementation of programmes intended for the rehabilitation of the environment and infrastructure affected by refugees in countries of asylum as well as internally displaced persons, where appropriate;

27. *Urges* the international community, in the spirit of international solidarity and burden-sharing, to continue to fund generously the refugee programmes of the Office of the High Commissioner and, taking into account the substantially increased needs of programmes in Africa, inter alia, as a result of repatriation possibilities, to ensure that

Africa receives a fair and equitable share of the resources designated for refugees;

28. *Encourages* the Office of the High Commissioner and interested States to identify protracted refugee situations which might lend themselves to resolution through the development of specific, multilateral, comprehensive and practical approaches to resolving such refugee situations, including the improvement of international burden- and responsibility-sharing and the realization of durable solutions, within a multilateral context;

29. *Expresses grave concern* about the plight of internally displaced persons in Africa, notes the efforts of African States in strengthening the regional mechanisms for the protection of and assistance to internally displaced persons, calls upon States to take concrete action to pre-empt internal displacement and to meet the protection and assistance needs of internally displaced persons, recalls in that regard the Guiding Principles on Internal Displacement, takes note of the current activities of the Office of the High Commissioner related to the protection of and assistance to internally displaced persons, including in the context of inter-agency arrangements in this field, emphasizes that such activities should be consistent with relevant General Assembly resolutions and should not undermine the refugee mandate of the Office and the institution of asylum, and encourages the High Commissioner to continue his dialogue with States on the role of his Office in this regard;

30. *Invites* the Special Rapporteur on the human rights of internally displaced persons to continue his ongoing dialogue with Member States and the intergovernmental and non-governmental organizations concerned, in accordance with his mandate, and to include information thereon in his reports to the Human Rights Council and the General Assembly;

31. *Requests* the Secretary-General to submit a comprehensive report on assistance to refugees, returnees and displaced persons in Africa to the General Assembly at its sixty-seventh session, taking fully into account the efforts expended by countries of asylum, under the item entitled "Report of the United Nations High Commissioner for Refugees, questions relating to refugees, returnees and displaced persons and humanitarian questions".

The Americas

In Latin America, while countries had strong regional and national instruments for protecting persons of concern to UNHCR, the growing attention paid by States to their national security continued to threaten protection. The Mexico Plan of Action to Strengthen the International Protection of Refugees in Latin America [YUN 2004, p. 1210] and the Brasilia Declaration on the Protection of Refugees and Stateless Persons in the Americas [YUN 2010, p. 1210] continued to guide the strategies of UNHCR operations in the region. The Office, however, faced obstacles posed by pre-admissibility procedures. Those challenges were compounded by a rise in violence, discrimination, xenophobia and risks of human trafficking vis-à-vis asylum seekers and refugees. More than 70 per cent of the total refugee population lived in urban areas, where competition for scarce resources was high. As voluntary repatriation was not a viable option for most refugees, local integration needed to be strengthened. Through the Cities of Solidarity programme, more than 50 agreements had been signed in prior years to facilitate the access of asylum seekers, refugees and IDPs to education, health and employment services. In 2011, the city of Arica, Chile, became the latest to participate in the initiative.

Displacement due to violence and conflict at the hands of irregular armed groups and criminal gangs plagued different parts of Colombia. More than 143,000 new IDPs were registered in 2011. Despite the Government's efforts to provide solutions to displacement, including through the adoption of the Law on Victims and Land Restitution, returns were hindered by difficulties in guaranteeing effective law enforcement and security. Furthermore, the spillover of the Colombian conflict into Ecuador and Venezuela exposed refugees and host communities to higher levels of insecurity and had an impact on the delivery of protection. In Colombia and Ecuador, UNHCR began the implementation of a five-year plan to prevent and respond to sexual and gender-based violence (SGBV). During the year, displaced women and girls in Colombia participated in a series of dialogues on the High Commissioner's Five Commitments to Refugee Women. Ecuador continued to be the country in Latin America with the highest number of refugees and asylum seekers, with some 55,000 individuals recognized as refugees. It was estimated that up to 1,500 people crossed the border from Colombia into Ecuador each month, putting a strain on efforts to comply with international protection standards.

In Central America and Mexico, an increase in insecurity and displacement, due to intensified activities by transnational criminal organizations, irregular armed groups as well as human smugglers and traffickers made it more difficult to deliver protection. In the Caribbean, with a continuous flow of people travelling in small and often unseaworthy vessels, who were intercepted or rescued at sea, maritime accidents remained a concern. UNHCR advocacy contributed to the adoption in Panama of a law creating a mechanism for persons covered by the temporary humanitarian protection regime to apply for permanent residence. The law helped to end the protracted situation of some 860 Colombians living in vulnerable conditions in the Darien border region. Costa Rica established an administrative migratory tribunal to provide a second-instance review body for asylum claims. In Haiti, UNHCR worked in partnership with local organizations to prevent statelessness through birth registration and documentation projects, and supported the establishment of safe houses and income-generating activities for SGBV survivors. In June, the agency and the Office of the United Nations High Commissioner for Human Rights issued a joint advisory on returns to Haiti, appealing to Governments to renew residence permits and other mechanisms allowing Haitians to remain in their countries on humanitarian grounds. A positive example of governmental action in that regard was Brazil's decision to award more than 400 permanent residence visas to Haitians who had arrived in the country after the 2010 earthquake requesting asylum.

In North America, resettlement programmes in the United States and Canada were well developed thanks to the investment of substantial resources and a large pool of expertise. Although there was no advancement in the United States Congress on refugee-related legislation, the country took in 74 per cent of all refugees resettled by UNHCR during the year. Stricter security-screening measures slowed processing and departures.

Total UNHCR expenditures in the Americas were $57.4 million for a population of concern of 4.8 million.

Asia and the Pacific

In 2011, some 9.6 million people, representing about a quarter of the total number of persons of concern to UNHCR, lived in countries of the Asia and Pacific region. Of those, fewer than 1.3 million were in refugee camps, with the majority residing in urban environments. Despite the major disasters experienced in the region during the year—the earthquake and tsunami in Japan, the floods in South-East Asia and Typhoon Sendong in the Philippines—UNHCR was able to make substantial progress towards safeguarding protection and asylum space, including in the context of mixed migration and urban settings; finding solutions for protracted refugee situations; and ensuring protection and durable solutions for IDPs.

The dialogue between UNHCR and concerned States on a regional approach to refugees and irregular movements led to the endorsement of a regional cooperation framework in the context of the 2002 Bali Process on People Smuggling, Trafficking in Persons and Related Transnational Crime. Discussions on making the framework operational through the establishment of a regional support office continued throughout the year.

Afghanistan, Iran and Pakistan, together with UNHCR, agreed on a multi-year Solutions Strategy for Afghan Refugees to support voluntary repatriation, sustainable reintegration and assistance to host countries. More than 68,200 refugees repatriated voluntarily to Afghanistan under the auspices of the Office: some 49,200 from Pakistan, 18,900 from Iran and 100 from other countries. UNHCR offered grants to cover their transport and meet initial return needs. Returning refugees were processed through voluntary repatriation centres in countries of asylum and upon arrival to ensure that their decision to return was voluntary and well informed. The returnees were provided with access to health and social services and were offered mine-risk and legal counselling. In Iran, prolonged stay was made possible for approximately 900,000 registered refugees, and some 350,000 refugees benefited from health insurance. In August, a second wave of monsoon floods inundated vast areas of Pakistan's Sindh and Baluchistan provinces, affecting more than 7.4 million people. UNHCR provided life-saving assistance to some 1.7 million affected people.

The first Ministerial Conference on Refugee Protection and International Migration in Central Asia (Almaty, Kazakhstan, 15–16 March) adopted the Almaty Declaration as the basis for the regional cooperation framework and action plan. In Kyrgyzstan, UNHCR programmes strengthened the rights of people of concern and their access to services, and promoted reconciliation between communities through peacebuilding projects. Turkmenistan granted citizenship to more than 3,300 stateless persons during the year.

In South Asia, the UNHCR resettlement programme in Nepal remained the largest such initiative worldwide. During the year, some 18,100 refugees, originally from Bhutan, left Nepal for their new homes in eight different resettlement countries. In Sri Lanka, some 144,600 IDPs and more than 1,700 refugees uprooted during the civil war returned to their places of origin. In India, the Government maintained protection space for nearly 190,000 refugees and asylum seekers, of whom approximately 21,000 were registered with the Office. In July, UNHCR began issuing new identity cards with encrypted smart chips to enhance the protection of urban refugees in India.

In South-East Asia, UNHCR concluded its seven-year-old programme in Cambodia for refugees of the Montagnard ethnic minority from Viet Nam. A total of 1,800 members of that group had been assisted: some 800 of them returned to Viet Nam, while 1,000 resettled in a third country. The Office continued its efforts to help the Cambodian Government develop a national asylum system. In Bangladesh, 29,000 refugees from Myanmar's northern Rakhine State residing in two camps benefited from UNHCR assistance. The agency encountered constraints, however, in addressing the situation of an estimated 200,000 undocumented persons from Myanmar residing outside the camps. In Indonesia, UNHCR remained the primary provider of protection for refugees and asylum seekers, undertaking responsibility for their registration, the determination of their refugee status and the search for durable solutions.

In East Asia and the Pacific, the detention of asylum seekers, often for long periods, occurred in several countries and remained the main protection challenge.

UNHCR encouraged States to identify alternatives to detention. The growth in the number of boat movements and maritime incidents shaped asylum debates in the region, alerting States and international organizations to the necessity of developing cooperative regional approaches. In October, Australia announced that it would expand the use of "bridging visas" to allow more asylum seekers to live outside detention while their claims were being processed. The Republic of Korea adopted a Refugee Act in December, a milestone for the whole region. UNHCR also welcomed the adoption of the first resolution on refugee protection and assistance by the Japanese Diet.

UNHCR expenditures in Asia and the Pacific amounted to $386.0 million, for a population of concern of 9.6 million.

Middle East and North Africa

In 2011, social and political changes in the Middle East caused massive displacement, adding to the already large number of refugees and IDPs. More than 127,000 persons from Syria sought refuge in neighbouring countries, primary Iraq, Jordan, Lebanon and Turkey, in addition to more than 1 million displaced internally. According to the UNHCR *Global Report 2011*, despite the lack of well-established national asylum systems, countries in the region continued to host refugees—including approximately 165,000 from Iraq—and provide them with access to basic services.

As resettlement continued to be the main durable solution for Iraqi refugees in the region, UNHCR supported resettlement countries in the sectors of health, education, food and social services. During the year, Syria alone hosted around 110,000 refugees, mainly from Iraq. Applications for a total of 133,500 Iraqi refugees had been submitted for resettlement to various countries since 2007—16,000 in 2011 alone—and some 69,000 had left for their new homes.

The region continued to experience mixed migration flows through the Gulf of Aden, the Red Sea and the Mediterranean, with the Arab Gulf countries and Europe as the main destinations. Yemen received a record number of more than 100,000 new arrivals during the year. UNHCR assisted many of the new arrivals through its transit and reception centres on Yemen's coasts.

Mixed migration flows across the Sinai and into Israel, propelled by a human smuggling network reaching into East Africa, intensified during the year. The flow of new arrivals into Israel—mostly Eritreans—continued at an average rate of 2,000 people per month. The number of asylum seekers in Israel stood at approximately 50,000. The influx of asylum seekers spurred the Israeli Government to take measures to staunch the flow of arrivals, including the construction of a barrier along the border with Egypt and of a camp to house 10,000 people in the south of the country.

UNHCR advanced its partnerships in the countries of the Gulf Cooperation Council—Bahrain, Kuwait, Oman, Qatar, Saudi Arabia and the United Arab Emirates—focusing on fundraising and the promotion of refugee concerns among pan-Arab media outlets based in the Gulf. States such as Jordan, Lebanon and Syria continued to provide protection to people of concern to UNHCR, despite regional and domestic challenges. The protection space for refugees was generally upheld by the respective Governments and, in certain respects, expanded. Saudi Arabia, following an appeal by UNHCR, issued a decree halting the deportation of Somalis living illegally in the country until the situation in Somalia became conducive to return. In Kuwait, the Government announced that it would provide services and documents to refugees and naturalize some 34,000 Bedouins. UNHCR offered assistance and technical expertise to help address the Bedouin situation.

In North Africa, the crisis in Libya forced nearly 1 million Libyans and third-country nationals to flee to neighbouring States, with Tunisia and Egypt receiving the majority. UNHCR and IOM jointly implemented a large-scale evacuation programme in Tunisia and Egypt that assisted more than 300,000 third-country nationals to return to their homelands. In addition, more than 550,000 Libyans were internally displaced. Throughout the conflict, UNHCR provided protection and assistance to the affected population at the Tunisian and Egyptian borders.

Following the fifteenth meeting (Dakar, Senegal, October) of the Tripartite Commission, composed of Mauritania, Senegal and UNHCR, the voluntary repatriation of the remaining Mauritanian refugees in Senegal resumed in November. By the end of the year, the number of refugees who had returned to Mauritania since the operation began in 2008 stood at 22,000. Since 2004, some 42,000 Sahrawis from the refugee camps in Tindouf, Algeria, and Western Sahara, had registered to take part in family visits. Because of the limited carrying capacity of the aircraft available for that purpose, however, only some 12,000 persons had benefited from such visits by the end of 2011. UNHCR proposed an expansion of the programme to include transportation by land or by means of a larger aircraft. The Office organized a seminar (Madeira, Portugal, September) on the theme of Hassaniya culture to promote an exchange of views between the two Sahrawi communities.

In the Middle East, UNHCR spent $272.2 million for a population of concern of 4.1 million. In North Africa, it spent $90.2 million for a population of concern of some 843,000 people.

Europe

In 2011, Europe remained an important destination, with some 326,000 people applying for asylum, 85 per cent of whom sought asylum in European Union (EU) countries. That represented a 19 per cent increase Europe-wide and a 15 per cent increase in the EU over 2010. The largest increase was reported by the Southern European countries, with an 87 per cent rise, mainly due to boat arrivals in Italy and Malta. In the Nordic countries, however, the number of newly registered asylum seekers fell by 10 per cent to the same level observed in 2007 and 2008. The top places of origin of applicants in Europe were Afghanistan, Iraq, Serbia/Kosovo, the Russian Federation and Pakistan. The EU continued its efforts to create a Common European Asylum System and, in that context, UNHCR established firm cooperative links with the European Asylum Support Office. To assure access to territory and asylum for those in need of protection, UNHCR worked with States and other partners to institute protection-sensitive border management procedures and safeguards for asylum seekers, as well as to promote solidarity and responsibility-sharing among European countries. An example of such cooperation was the Further Developing Asylum Quality project, which involved UNHCR and 12 EU countries working together to establish mechanisms in national asylum structures that ensured high standards in the implementation of asylum procedures. With detention of asylum seekers being a growing concern, the Office monitored conditions of detention and advocated for effective safeguards, improved conditions and alternative solutions. Emphasis was placed on campaigns to foster tolerance and awareness as a means of addressing the xenophobia and racism to which refugees were often subject.

Large-scale internal displacement remained a reality in Eastern Europe, with nearly 1 million IDPs in the Caucasus region. Although some positive developments were observed in legislative frameworks in Turkey and Ukraine, and in the reception of asylum-seekers in the Russian Federation, the frequent reshuffling of government departments handling asylum, migration and border management posed particular problems in the subregion. Malfunctioning asylum systems prompted irregular onward movements of people of concern—many of whom became victims of human trafficking—particularly towards EU countries. The Office provided direct assistance grants to the most vulnerable asylum seekers and refugees, ensuring their protection and helping them to meet their immediate needs pending decisions on their status or the provision of a durable solution. Statelessness remained an issue throughout the subregion. Precise numbers were unknown, but could be as high as 120,000. In Armenia, UNHCR provided assistance to build a national asylum system through workshops and on-the-job training. In Azerbaijan, some 1,670 people benefited from monthly subsistence allowances to alleviate the most urgent household needs. In Ukraine, UNHCR continued to provide legal and material assistance to people of concern.

In South-Eastern Europe, UNHCR expressed support for a joint ministerial declaration signed by Bosnia and Herzegovina, Croatia, Montenegro and Serbia reflecting a commitment to find solutions for some 74,000 individuals displaced by the 1991–1995 conflict in the Balkans who were still without durable housing. A five-year Regional Housing Project was designed to address their needs. UNHCR and the United Nations Development Programme sought to pursue durable solutions for the people displaced as a result of the Kosovo conflict, whose situation was not addressed by the joint declaration or the Regional Housing Project. A Conference on the Provision of Civil Documentation and Registration in South-Eastern Europe (Zagreb, Croatia, 26–27 October), organized jointly by UNHCR and the Organization for Security and Cooperation in Europe (OSCE) and supported by the EU, resulted in the Zagreb Declaration, aimed at improving civil status documentation and registration for minorities, including Roma, and to reduce the number of stateless people and those at risk of statelessness. UNHCR provided technical support to improve the legislative and administrative frameworks on asylum and prevention of statelessness in Bosnia and Herzegovina, Croatia, Montenegro, the former Yugoslav Republic of Macedonia and Serbia.

In Central Europe, UNHCR continued to promote and support resettlement, including through an EU-funded joint project on reception and integration. Other efforts in Central Europe included support for integration programmes in the Czech Republic and Romania. Bulgaria, Hungary, Poland, Romania and Slovakia participated in the Further Developing Asylum Quality project, which was completed during the year. Amid increasing concerns over the rise in administrative detention of asylum seekers, UNHCR strengthened its monitoring of the practice of detention in Central Europe.

In Northern, Western, and Southern Europe, UNHCR worked with Governments to ensure that persons fleeing events in North Africa and seeking protection had access to asylum procedures, particularly in Italy and Malta, where many of those rescued at sea in the Mediterranean disembarked. UNHCR stepped up efforts to support capacity-building, solidarity and responsibility-sharing among States in the region. That included the relocation within the EU of 230 refugees from Malta. Resettlement places for some 1,370 refugees were identified in 10 European countries. UNHCR also gave operational support to the Greek Government's efforts to reform its asylum system, a challenging task in the light of the country's economic crisis. UNHCR also completed a project to improve the quality of the asylum system in Sweden.

UNHCR spent $128.2 million for Europe for a population of concern of 4.0 million.

Communication. On 15 November [A/66/624], Serbia transmitted to the General Assembly the Joint Declaration on Ending Displacement and Ensuring Durable Solutions for Vulnerable Refugees and Internally Displaced Persons, adopted by Bosnia and Herzegovina, Croatia, Montenegro and Serbia at the Ministerial Review Conference on Solving the Refugee Situation in the Western Balkans (Belgrade, Serbia, 7 November).

Policy development and cooperation

Partnerships and coordination

According to the High Commissioner's annual report [A/67/12], UNHCR in 2011 cooperated with a wide range of entities to fulfil its mandated objectives, with NGOs making up nearly 80 per cent of the Office's implementing partners. UNHCR channelled $677 million of its expenditures through 151 international and 611 national NGOs—a 20 per cent increase over 2010. The High Commissioner initiated a dialogue with key partners to achieve more transparent and results-oriented relationships. UNHCR was engaged in the work of the Inter-Agency Standing Committee and, under the leadership of the Emergency Relief Coordinator, participated in the development of the Transformative Agenda to strengthen humanitarian leadership in emergencies. In October, the Secretary General's Policy Committee [YUN 2005, p. 1513] adopted a decision on durable solutions, which provided a new framework aimed at strengthening the UN response to durable solutions for returning refugees and IDPs.

The Office strengthened partnerships with regional organizations, including the Economic Community of West African States, to which the Office provided financial and technical support for the convening of the first Ministerial Conference on Humanitarian Assistance and Internal Displacement in West Africa (Abuja, Nigeria, 7 July); the Organization of American States (OAS), with which the Office organized a course on International Refugee Law for Permanent Missions to the OAS; the Bali Process to address irregular migration and refugee protection in the Asia-Pacific region; OSCE in Central Asia and Europe on asylum and migration issues; and the Organization of Islamic Cooperation in preparing the Ministerial Conference on Refugees in the Muslim World, which was to take place in 2012 in Turkmenistan. Goodwill Ambassadors continued to provide support to the Office, helping to raise awareness, influence political action and advocate for the rights of persons of concern.

UNHCR bolstered partnership with corporations and foundations. Corporate partners gave the Office a record level of support in 2011—more than $35 million. The IKEA Foundation pledged a three-year contribution of $62 million to assist refugees in the Horn of Africa.

Evaluation activities

In October, the Executive Committee had before it a report [A/AC.96/1103] of the High Commissioner on the activities of the UNHCR Policy Development and Evaluation Service (PDES) from mid-2010 to mid-2011, which focused on urban areas; protracted refugee situations; durable solutions; emergencies and natural disasters; age, gender and diversity; refugee education; mixed migration; the changing context of humanitarian action; refugee activities and aspirations; results-based management; and publications.

In the past year, members of the PDES team had been deployed to emergency operations in Tunisia and to the joint UNHCR/IOM Humanitarian Evacuation Cell, operative in March in the context of the humanitarian situation in Libya and its neighbouring countries. With regard to urban areas, in June PDES organized an inter-agency workshop on effective practices in urban refugee programmes, co-hosted by UN-Habitat and the International Rescue Committee. By mid-2011, reviews on protracted refugee situations had been completed in Bangladesh, Croatia and Serbia, eastern Sudan and Tanzania. The Service also published studies on repatriation to Liberia and South Sudan, the resettlement of Bhutanese and Sudanese refugees in the United States, and refugee integration in Ghana. PDES published a review of the UNHCR response to the 2010 emergency in Kyrgyzstan and Uzbekistan [YUN 2010, p. 906], and completed a compilation of lessons learned from UNHCR involvement in emergency operations during the previous decade. PDES also published two reports on refugees and asylum seekers with disabilities and one on the protection of children against witchcraft accusations. As of mid-2011, reviews on the state of refugee education were being conducted in Malaysia, Mauritania and Uganda. PDES prepared a paper for the regional conference on mixed migration in the region spreading from the Horn of Africa to South Africa, convened by UNHCR and IOM (Dar es Salaam, Tanzania, 6–7 September 2010). The Service completed a review of the implementation of results-based management in UNHCR, involving missions to Georgia, the Sudan, Tanzania and Yemen.

Inspections

In his annual report [A/67/12], the High Commissioner noted that cooperation between internal oversight entities as well as with UN system entities, such as the Office of Internal Oversight Services (OIOS) and the Joint Inspection Unit, facilitated UNHCR work. In 2011, an Independent Audit and Oversight Committee was established to assist UNHCR and the Executive Committee on audit and oversight, as well as financial management. The UNHCR Inspector General's Office (IGO) focused on three core functions: inspections related to the quality of management of operations; investigations of allegations of misconduct by UNHCR personnel; and inquiries into attacks on UNHCR personnel and operations. Over the previous year, seven standard inspections of field operations were conducted in Africa, Asia, the Americas and Europe. Closure memorandums were issued for 25 standard inspections that had been conducted between 2007 and 2010. The rate of compliance with recommendations made by the IGO Inspection Service remained high, at 84 per cent. With regard to investigations, IGO registered 1,137 complaints over the previous year, 782 of which were related to protection and assistance, while 180 involved allegations of misconduct; the remainder did not directly concern IGO. The complaints of misconduct were assessed and sufficient grounds were found to open 61 cases. Meanwhile, 96 cases were closed, 15 of which resulted in referral to human resources management for further action, including determination of possible disciplinary measures. An ad hoc inquiry was undertaken in December, following an attack on the UNHCR office in Kandahar, Afghanistan, in which three staff members were killed. IGO convened a meeting with nine of the key UNHCR implementing partners to explore ways of cooperating on investigations.

In October, the Executive Committee had before it a July report [A/AC.96/1102] covering IGO activities between July 2010 and the end of June 2011. IGO, in early 2011, established an internal monitoring and compliance unit to build upon the existing risk-based mechanism and to follow up on recommendations from standard and ad hoc inspection reports, management implications reports and ad hoc inquiries.

Since its report to the Committee's sixty-first session [YUN 2010, p. 1214], IGO had conducted nine standard inspections of field locations and one of a headquarters unit. In addition, two ad hoc inspections were carried out. The Inspection Review Board mechanism, whose advice improved the quality of inspection reports, was extended and expanded to comprise 11 members.

OIOS activities. In July, OIOS submitted to the Executive Committee a report [A/AC.96/1101 & Corr.1] on its audit activities in respect of UNHCR for the period from 1 July 2010 to 30 June 2011 in the areas of planning, reporting and monitoring; staffing and funding; cooperation and coordination; and advisory services. During the reporting period, 15 reports were issued, as compared to 30 and 21 final reports published in the two prior periods, the difference being attributable to the OIOS vacancy rate, which was around 40 per cent. Recommendations covered the supply chain (69), programme and project management (47), human resources (24), information and technology (18), finance and administration (17), strategic management and governance (16) and safety and security (6). A later OIOS report [A/AC.96/1113] reviewed its internal audit activities in respect of UNHCR from 1 July 2011 to 30 June 2012.

Financial and administrative questions

In 2011 [A/67/12], the UNHCR budget amounted to $3.8 billion, comprising an initial approved budget of $3.3 billion and $500.9 million for six supplementary budgets created during the course of the year. The latter were established to address unforeseen emergency situations and included Pakistan ($121.5 million), Kyrgyzstan ($11.5 million), North Africa and the Mediterranean ($110.0 million), the Côte d'Ivoire situation ($126.0 million), the Sudan situation ($60.6 million), and the Somali displacement crisis ($71.3 million). Despite the persistence of the global financial and economic crisis, the Office received strong support from its donors, reaching a record $2.1 billion in contributions. Nevertheless, over one-third of the comprehensive needs of persons of concern remained unmet during the year.

UNHCR continued to diversify its funding sources, including from pooled funds and development sources, the private sector and individual donors. Private donors provided $111 million to the Office—an increase of 53 per cent over 2010. An additional 75,000 donors joined the list of UNHCR individual donors, bringing the total to nearly 488,000.

Biennial programme budget 2012–2013. In September [A/AC.96/1100 & Corr.1,2], the High Commissioner presented the proposed 2012–2013 biennial programme budget, amounting to $3,591.2 million for 2012 and $3,418.6 million for 2013, as well as the final 2010 budget and the 2011 revised budget approved by the Executive Committee at its sixty-first session in October 2010 [YUN 2010, p. 1215]. The proposed programme budget was based on a global needs assessment of all persons of concern to UNHCR and took into account the feasibility of programme implementation, including such issues as access to persons of concern and staffing. Planned activities were prioritized in line with the global strategic priorities.

In October [A/66/12/Add.1], the Executive Committee approved the total revised requirements for 2011 amounting to $3,780.5 million, and authorized the High Commissioner, within those appropriations, to effect adjustments in regional programmes, global programmes and headquarters budgets. The Committee also approved the 2012–2013 biennial programme budget amounting to $3,310.3 million for 2012 and $3,145.9 million for 2013, including the UN regular budget contribution; an operational reserve of $248.8 million in 2012 and $240.7 million in 2013; and an amount of $20 million for the "New or additional activities—mandate-related" reserve in both 2012 and 2013, respectively. The Committee noted that those provisions, together with those of $12.0 million for Junior Professional Officers in both 2012 and 2013, respectively, brought total requirements for 2012 to $3,591.2 million and for 2013 to $3,418.6 million; and authorized the High Commissioner to make adjustments as needed. The Committee requested the High Commissioner to respond flexibly and efficiently to the needs indicated under the biennial programme budget; and to create supplementary budgets and issue special appeals in case of new emergency needs that could not be met from the operational reserve.

The Advisory Committee on Administrative and Budgetary Questions (ACABQ) in September [A/AC.96/1100/Add.1] responded to the report on the biennial programme budget, the proposed revision of the UNHCR financial rules, as well as to the documents relating to the UNHCR accounts for the year ended 31 December 2010 (see p. 1131). The Committee recalled that since the biennium 2010–2011, the Office had presented its biennial programme budget in a new structure, consisting of four components (global refugee programme, global stateless programme, global reintegration projects and global IDP projects), and since then the budget had been based on an assessment of needs rather than on the expected availability of funds. While ACABQ had no objection to how UNHCR proposed to allocate resources to each component for 2012, the projection to fund the totality of the assessed needs by 2015 appeared to be ambitious. The Committee noted that UNHCR actions undertaken following the recommendations of the Board of Auditors [A/66/5/Add.5] were not explicitly expressed in the proposed budget for 2012–2013; it requested that future reports on follow-up actions by UNHCR to implement the recommendations of the Board of Auditors be made available to the Advisory Committee at the time of its consideration of the UNHCR biennial programme budgets. ACABQ did not have major objections with regard to the UNHCR proposed revision of its financial rules [EC/62/SC/CRP.27] in the matter of voluntary funds.

Accounts (2010)

The audited financial statements of voluntary funds administered by UNHCR for the year ending 31 December 2010 [A/66/5/Add.5] showed a total expenditure of $1.923 billion and total income of $1.992 billion, with a negative reserve balance of $72.3 million.

The Board of Auditors noted that the financial statements presented fairly the financial position of the voluntary funds administered by UNHCR and its financial performance and cash flows as at 31 December 2010, in accordance with the UN system accounting standards. With regard to the multi-year structural and management change process [YUN 2006, p. 1392], in which the Office had embarked in 2006 to reinforce its capacity to deliver assistance and to align working practices towards results-based management, the Board expected UNHCR to be able to demonstrate tangible benefits, but as yet it could not. The Board had identified significant concerns about important aspects of UNHCR financial, risk and performance management. The Board found UNHCR underprepared for the financial audit, which reflected deficiencies in the system in place to prepare financial statements. The Board found weaknesses in control and financial management oversight. For example, in 2010, 82 bank accounts (with a total balance of $50.3 million) and 17 investment accounts (with a total balance of $325 million) had lacked up-to-date reconciliations—a key financial control—which, combined with an excessive number of bank accounts, was exposing the Office to an increased risk of misappropriation and fraud. The Board found errors in the UNHCR expendable property (inventory) system. Expendable property had an approximate value of $130 million, but was not disclosed in the 2010 accounts because of concerns about the accuracy of its valuation. In addition, there was a risk that UNHCR would not be able to finalize the new policies and practices to implement the International Public Sector Accounting Standards (IPSAS) in 2012. Even if UNHCR achieved IPSAS-compliant financial statements, the benefits from IPSAS would be delayed because the Office had not established arrangements to realize the gains of IPSAS implementation. UNHCR performance reporting from its country network did not enable management to make effective judgements as to the cost-effectiveness of projects and activities or to hold local managers accountable for performance. Furthermore, the process of selecting implementing partners lacked rigour and transparency, increasing the risk of fraud, inefficiency and poor partner performance. The Board found little evidence of any competitive selection process, benchmarking of cost and performance against alternatives. The Global Plan of Action on protracted refugee situations had no senior accountable owner or indicators to measure progress.

The Board recommended that UNHCR implement an effective process for the preparation of year-end financial statements, including a detailed management review; centralize its banking arrangements, close any unnecessary bank accounts and improve bank reconciliation procedures; strengthen its preparation for IPSAS implementation by engaging with the Board on revised financial rules and regulations, and cleansing its accounting records; require country operations to document their justification for partner selection and assess the market for alternative partners; and establish a single senior point of ownership for protracted refugee situations to address progress and to hold country operations to account.

In September [A/AC.96/1099/Add.1], the High Commissioner described measures taken or proposed in response to the Board's recommendations.

General Assembly action. The General Assembly on 24 December decided that the item on financial reports and audited financial statements, and reports of the Board of Auditors: voluntary funds administered by the United Nations High Commissioner for Refugees would remain for consideration during its resumed sixty-sixth (2012) session (**decision 66/557**).

Management and administrative change

At the October meeting of the Standing Committee [A/AC.96/1105], the Deputy High Commissioner provided an update [EC/62/SC/CRP.29] on the UNHCR structural and management change process. Based on the implementation of the change process launched five years earlier [YUN 2006, p. 1392], the review of structures and tools was continuing in order to reinforce the Office's capacity to deliver assistance, protection and solutions to people of concern. The results framework [YUN 2009, p. 1200] was reviewed, focusing on improving the formulation of objectives and outputs, as well as by modifying indicators to enhance measurability. The revised framework was incorporated within the 2012–2013 planning exercise. Progress was also made in setting the global strategic priorities (GSPs) for 2012–2013, which were more limited in number and more focused than the 2010–2011 GSPs. Steps were undertaken to strengthen the understanding and use of results-based management within UNHCR, as well as its supporting software tool Focus. In that context, an e-learning programme on results-based management was launched; 12 workshops were organized in various locations during the first quarter of 2011, attended by some 300 staff; and 10 regional workshops took place for some 320 UNHCR staff from 114 countries who led planning exercises in the field. That training also provided an opportunity to review the incorporation of 2012–2013 GSPs at the country level.

A revised policy and procedures on assignments of international professional staff had been implemented since the September 2010 Compendium, and simplifications were made without affecting the integrity of the new policy. Simplification measures included reducing documentation required; facilitating rapid re-advertisement of vacant positions; facilitating the work of the UNHCR Joint Review Board; and adjusting the role of career management officers to ensure that their support for the assignments procedure did not detract from their prime career guidance role. With the processing of vacancies announced in the March 2011 Compendium, a more effective use of staff time and a streamlined process had been realized. The restructuring of the Division of Information Services and Technology (DIST) was almost completed. In that context, progress had been made in measuring the performance of information and communication technology (ICT) in UNHCR and the restructuring of DIST. A global ICT survey was conducted early in the year to establish credible baselines. The Division of Emergency, Security and Supply had, since its creation in 2009 [YUN 2009, p. 1202], engaged in a review and analysis of UNHCR procedures and mechanisms for emergency management to improve the quality and predictability of emergency responses. With regard to oversight, the Standing Committee had endorsed in June the establishment of the Independent Audit and Oversight Committee and recruitment had started. The High Commissioner asked the Deputy High Commissioner to take the lead in pursuing management priorities, with a view to simplifying processes; mapping out UNHCR initiatives for innovation; proposing an "innovation road map"; connecting with the private sector; and strengthening the internal communication system.

Global needs assessment

The Standing Committee discussed the global needs assessment (GNA) introduced in 2009 [YUN 2009, p. 1201] at its March [A/AC.96/1097] and September [A/AC.96/1105] meetings. On both occasions, delegations commented on the steady increase in funding needs, and there was a call for a detailed analysis of the GNA process. Concerns were expressed over the adequacy of funding allocations to cover the needs of refugees in Africa in 2012–2013. Contrary to other UN system organizations, since 2009 the UNHCR biennial programme budget was based on GNA rather than on resource availability.

Chapter XIII
Health, food and nutrition

The year 2011 marked thirty years since the HIV/AIDS epidemic was recognized. The June high-level meeting of the General Assembly on HIV/AIDS reviewed progress achieved in realizing the 2001 Declaration of Commitment and the 2006 Political Declaration on HIV/AIDS, and adopted a new political declaration on intensifying efforts to eliminate the disease. During the year, the Assembly also convened a high-level meeting on non-communicable diseases (NCDs), at which Member States addressed the prevention and control of NCDs, focusing on developmental challenges and social and economic impact, particularly for developing countries.

In April, the World Health Organization (WHO) launched the *Global status report on non-communicable diseases 2010*—its first publication on the worldwide epidemic of cardiovascular diseases, cancer, diabetes and chronic respiratory diseases.

Also in April, the General Assembly adopted a resolution on consolidating gains and accelerating efforts to control and eliminate malaria in developing countries, particularly in Africa, calling on Member States to scale up efforts to achieve the internationally agreed targets of near-zero deaths from malaria by 2015. In December, the Assembly adopted resolutions on agriculture development and food security, and on excessive price volatility in food and related financial and commodity markets. During the year, the World Food Programme provided food assistance for 99.1 million beneficiaries in 75 countries and commemorated its fiftieth anniversary.

Health

AIDS prevention and control

Implementation of Declaration of Commitment and Political Declaration

Report of Secretary-General. In March, the Secretary-General submitted a report [A/65/797] highlighting that 2011 marked thirty years since the HIV/AIDS epidemic was recognized. During that period, AIDS had claimed more than 25 million lives and over 60 million people had become infected with HIV. Nevertheless, HIV programmes were now bearing fruit, with global HIV incidence declining, treatment access expanding and an unparalleled global movement mobilizing to demand respect for the dignity and human rights of everyone affected by HIV. While promising, those accomplishments were insufficient and in jeopardy. The epidemic continued to outpace the response. Bold decisions were needed to reach zero new HIV infections, zero discrimination and zero AIDS-related deaths. The report contained five recommendations for achieving those goals: end new HIV infections by focusing efforts on the populations that accounted for the largest share of new infections, ensuring that legal, political and social environments enabled effective HIV responses and scaling up research investments; share responsibility by exercising inclusive and accountable leadership, meeting fair-share commitments to reach investment needs and strengthening national institutions, community systems and human resources for health; break the upward trajectory of treatment costs by encouraging, in cooperation with the pharmaceutical industry, the development of more affordable and longer-acting drug regimens, and maximizing efficiency in non-drug-related costs; ensure that responses to HIV promoted the health, human rights, security and dignity of women and girls; and ensure accountability by forging robust mechanisms for the translation of commitments into action.

The report also outlined the Joint United Nations Programme on HIV/AIDS (UNAIDS) strategy for 2011–2015, presenting a number of ambitious goals to be attained by 2015: reducing by 50 per cent sexual transmission of HIV; ensuring that 13 million people received HIV treatment; reducing by 50 per cent tuberculosis deaths among people with HIV; eliminating mother-to-child transmission of HIV; ensuring that children affected by AIDS stayed in school; and reducing by 50 per cent the number of countries with HIV-related restrictions on entry, stay and residence.

The progress and gaps in response to the epidemic analysed in the report were based on data submitted by 182 countries and on national and regional reviews on universal access to HIV prevention, treatment, care and support. In 2009, an estimated 33.3 million people were living with HIV, a 27 per cent increase from 1999. Globally, nearly 23 per cent of all people living with HIV were younger than 24, and youths between 15 and 24 accounted for 35 per cent of all people becoming newly infected. In 2009, women represented about 60 per cent of all people living with HIV in sub-Saharan Africa, where young women and adolescent girls were several times more likely to be living with the virus than males of the same age.

HIV prevention globally and especially in that region required concrete progress towards gender equality. Despite those inadequacies, as at December 2009, 15 countries had achieved the target set in the 2001 Declaration of Commitment on HIV/AIDS [YUN 2001, p. 1126] of at least 80 per cent coverage of antiretroviral prophylaxis among pregnant women living with HIV and an additional seven countries in sub-Saharan Africa had reported coverage between 50 per cent and 80 per cent. Countries in Eastern Europe and Central Africa had achieved especially high coverage. As a result of scaled-up prevention services, the number of children newly infected had declined by 24 per cent globally from 2004 to 2009. Trends indicated that young people were playing an increasingly vital role in HIV prevention.

By **resolution 1983(2011)** of 7 June (see p. 39), the Security Council, taking note of the Secretary-General's report, underlined that urgent and coordinated international action continued to be required to curb the impact of the HIV epidemic in conflict and post-conflict situations.

High-level meeting on HIV/AIDS. Pursuant to resolution 65/180 [YUN 2010, p. 1219], the General Assembly held on 8 April an interactive hearing on the high-level meeting on HIV/AIDS [A/65/835] planned for 8–10 June with representatives of non-governmental organizations, civil society and the private sector. Participants discussed the importance of sufficient financial resources to sustain an effective response and to advance progress towards universal access to HIV prevention, treatment, care and support; strategies to maximize collaboration between constituencies and sectors to strengthen HIV response; and strategies to forge enhanced linkages and coalitions between HIV and other global movements.

On 18 April (**decision 65/547**), the Assembly approved for participation in the high-level meeting the list of civil society representatives. On 20 May (**decision 65/548**), the Assembly decided that the opening plenary meeting of the review of the progress achieved in realizing the 2001 Declaration of Commitment on HIV/AIDS [YUN 2001, p. 1126] and the 2006 Political Declaration on HIV/AIDS [YUN 2006, p. 1411] would be held on 8 June.

Opening the high-level meeting, the President of the Assembly said that ten years earlier the Assembly had adopted an ambitious declaration to reverse the epidemic at a time when the situation seemed hopeless. In the previous five years, the number of people worldwide with access to treatment had increased tenfold. He urged world leaders to integrate the AIDS response into broader development programmes. In his remarks, the Secretary-General asserted that the challenge had now changed from reducing HIV infection to achieving zero new infections, zero stigma and zero AIDS-related deaths.

The meeting included five round tables focusing on shared responsibility; prevention; innovation and new technologies; women, girls and HIV; and integrating the HIV/AIDS response with broader health and development agendas.

On 10 June, the Assembly adopted a Political Declaration on HIV and AIDS entitled "Intensifying our Efforts to Eliminate HIV and AIDS", in which Member States committed themselves to ending the epidemic with renewed political will and to working in partnership with all stakeholders in such areas as prevention; treatment, care and support; human rights; resources; strengthening health systems; research and development; and coordination, monitoring and accountability. Member States also committed themselves to redoubling efforts to achieve, by 2015, universal access to HIV prevention, treatment, care and support.

GENERAL ASSEMBLY ACTION

On 10 June [meeting 95], the General Assembly adopted **resolution 65/277** [draft: A/65/L.77] without vote [agenda item 10].

Political Declaration on HIV and AIDS: Intensifying Our Efforts to Eliminate HIV and AIDS

The General Assembly

Adopts the political declaration on HIV and AIDS annexed to the present resolution.

ANNEX
Political Declaration on HIV and AIDS: Intensifying Our Efforts to Eliminate HIV and AIDS

1. We, Heads of State and Government and representatives of States and Governments assembled at the United Nations from 8 to 10 June 2011 to review progress achieved in realizing the 2001 Declaration of Commitment on HIV/AIDS and the 2006 Political Declaration on HIV/AIDS, with a view to guiding and intensifying the global response to HIV and AIDS by promoting continued political commitment and engagement of leaders in a comprehensive response at the community, local, national, regional and international levels to halt and reverse the HIV epidemic and mitigate its impact;

2. Reaffirm the sovereign rights of Member States, as enshrined in the Charter of the United Nations, and the need for all countries to implement the commitments and pledges in the present Declaration consistent with national laws, national development priorities and international human rights;

3. Reaffirm the 2001 Declaration of Commitment on HIV/AIDS and the 2006 Political Declaration on HIV/AIDS and the urgent need to scale up significantly our efforts towards the goal of universal access to comprehensive prevention programmes, treatment, care and support;

4. Recognize that, although HIV and AIDS are affecting every region of the world, each country's epidemic is distinctive in terms of drivers, vulnerabilities, aggravating factors and the populations that are affected, and therefore the responses from both the international community and

the countries themselves must be uniquely tailored to each particular situation, taking into account the epidemiological and social context of each country concerned;

5. Acknowledge the significance of this high-level meeting, which marks three decades since the first report of AIDS, ten years since the adoption of the Declaration of Commitment on HIV/AIDS and its time-bound measurable goals and targets, and five years since the adoption of the Political Declaration on HIV/AIDS and its commitment to urgently scale up responses towards achieving the goal of universal access to comprehensive prevention programmes, treatment, care and support by 2010;

6. Reaffirm our commitment to the achievement of all the Millennium Development Goals, in particular Goal 6, and, recognizing the importance of rapidly scaling up efforts to integrate HIV and AIDS prevention, treatment, care and support with efforts to achieve those Goals, in this regard welcome the outcome document of the 2010 High-level Plenary Meeting of the General Assembly on the Millennium Development Goals, entitled "Keeping the promise: united to achieve the Millennium Development Goals";

7. Recognize that HIV and AIDS constitute a global emergency, pose one of the most formidable challenges to the development, progress and stability of our respective societies and the world at large and require an exceptional and comprehensive global response that takes into account the fact that the spread of HIV is often a consequence and a cause of poverty;

8. Note with deep concern that, despite substantial progress over the three decades since AIDS was first reported, the HIV epidemic remains an unprecedented human catastrophe inflicting immense suffering on countries, communities and families throughout the world, that more than 30 million people have died from AIDS, with another estimated 33 million people living with HIV, that more than 16 million children have been orphaned because of AIDS, that over 7,000 new HIV infections occur every day, mostly among people in low- and middle-income countries, and that less than half of the people living with HIV are believed to be aware of their infection;

9. Reiterate with profound concern that Africa, in particular sub-Saharan Africa, remains the worst-affected region and that urgent and exceptional action is required at all levels to curb the devastating effects of this epidemic, and recognize the renewed commitment of African Governments and regional institutions to scale up their own HIV and AIDS responses;

10. Express deep concern that HIV and AIDS affect every region of the world and that the Caribbean continues to have the highest prevalence outside sub-Saharan Africa, while the number of new HIV infections is increasing in Eastern Europe, Central Asia, North Africa, the Middle East and parts of Asia and the Pacific;

11. Welcome the leadership and commitment shown in every aspect of the HIV and AIDS response by Governments, people living with HIV, political and community leaders, parliaments, regional and subregional organizations, communities, families, faith-based organizations, scientists, health professionals, donors, the philanthropic community, the workforce, the business sector, civil society and the media;

12. Welcome the exceptional efforts at the national, regional and international levels to implement the 2001 Declaration of Commitment on HIV/AIDS and the 2006 Political Declaration on HIV/AIDS and the important progress being made, including a more than 25 per cent reduction in the rate of new HIV infections in over 30 countries, the significant reduction in mother-to-child transmission of HIV and the unprecedented expansion of access to HIV antiretroviral treatment to over 6 million people, resulting in the reduction of AIDS-related deaths by more than 20 per cent in the past five years;

13. Recognize that the worldwide commitment to the global HIV epidemic has been unprecedented since the 2001 Declaration of Commitment on HIV/AIDS and the 2006 Political Declaration on HIV/AIDS, represented by an over eight-fold increase in funding from 1.8 billion United States dollars in 2001 to 16 billion dollars in 2010, the largest amount dedicated to combating a single disease in history;

14. Express deep concern that funding devoted to HIV and AIDS responses is still not commensurate with the magnitude of the epidemic either nationally or internationally and that the global financial and economic crisis continues to have a negative impact on the HIV and AIDS response at all levels, including the fact that, for the first time, international assistance has not increased from the levels in 2008 and 2009, and in this regard welcome the increased resources that are being made available as a result of the establishment by many developed countries of timetables to achieve the target of 0.7 per cent of gross national product for official development assistance by 2015, stressing also the importance of complementary innovative sources of financing, in addition to traditional funding, including official development assistance, to support national strategies, financing plans and multilateral efforts aimed at combating HIV and AIDS;

15. Stress the importance of international cooperation, including the role of North-South, South-South and triangular cooperation, in the global response to HIV and AIDS, bearing in mind that South-South cooperation is not a substitute for, but rather a complement to, North-South cooperation, and recognize the shared but differentiated responsibilities and respective capacities of Governments and donor countries, as well as civil society, including the private sector, while noting that national ownership and leadership are absolutely indispensable in this regard;

16. Commend the secretariat and the Co-sponsors of the Joint United Nations Programme on HIV/AIDS for their leadership role on HIV and AIDS policy and coordination and for the support they provide to countries through the Joint Programme;

17. Commend the Global Fund to Fight AIDS, Tuberculosis and Malaria for the vital role it is playing in mobilizing and providing funding for national and regional HIV and AIDS responses and in improving the predictability of financing over the long term, and welcome the commitment of over 30 billion dollars in funding from donors to date, including the significant pledges made by donors at the Global Fund replenishment conference held on 4 and 5 October 2010; note with concern that, while these pledges represent an increase in financing, they fall short of the amounts targeted by the Global Fund to further accelerate progress towards universal access, and recognize that to reach that goal it is imperative that the work of the Global Fund be supported and also that it be adequately funded;

18. Commend the work of the International Drug Purchase Facility, UNITAID, based on innovative financing and focusing on accessibility, quality and price reductions of antiretroviral drugs;

19. Welcome the Secretary General's Global Strategy for Women's and Children's Health, undertaken by a broad coalition of partners in support of national plans and strategies, to significantly reduce the number of maternal, newborn and under-five child deaths, as a matter of immediate concern, including by scaling up a priority package of high-impact interventions and integrating efforts in sectors such as health, education, gender equality, water and sanitation, poverty reduction and nutrition;

20. Recognize that agrarian economies are heavily affected by HIV and AIDS, which debilitate their communities and families with negative consequences for poverty eradication, that people die prematurely from AIDS because, inter alia, poor nutrition exacerbates the impact of HIV on the immune system and compromises its ability to respond to opportunistic infections and diseases, and that HIV treatment, including antiretroviral treatment, should be complemented with adequate food and nutrition;

21. Remain deeply concerned that, globally, women and girls are still the most affected by the epidemic and that they bear a disproportionate share of the caregiving burden, and that the ability of women and girls to protect themselves from HIV continues to be compromised by physiological factors, gender inequalities, including unequal legal, economic and social status, insufficient access to health care and services, including for sexual and reproductive health, and all forms of discrimination and violence, including sexual violence and exploitation;

22. Welcome the establishment of the United Nations Entity for Gender Equality and the Empowerment of Women (UN-Women) as a new stakeholder that can play an important role in global efforts to combat HIV by promoting gender equality and the empowerment of women, which are fundamental for reducing the vulnerability of women to HIV, and the appointment of the first Executive Director of UN-Women;

23. Welcome the adoption of the Convention on the Rights of Persons with Disabilities, and recognize the need to take into account the rights of persons with disabilities as set forth in that Convention, in particular with regard to health, education, accessibility and information, in the formulation of our global response to HIV and AIDS;

24. Note with appreciation the efforts of the Inter-Parliamentary Union in supporting national parliaments to ensure an enabling legal environment supportive of effective national responses to HIV and AIDS;

25. Express grave concern that young people between the ages of 15 and 24 years account for more than one third of all new HIV infections, with some 3,000 young people becoming infected with HIV each day, and note that most young people still have limited access to good quality education, decent employment and recreational facilities, as well as limited access to sexual and reproductive health programmes that provide the information, skills, services and commodities they need to protect themselves, that only 34 per cent of young people possess accurate knowledge of HIV, and that laws and policies in some instances exclude young people from accessing sexual health-care and HIV-related services, such as voluntary and confidential HIV testing, counselling and age-appropriate sex and HIV-prevention education, while also recognizing the importance of reducing risk-taking behaviour and encouraging responsible sexual behaviour, including abstinence, fidelity and correct and consistent use of condoms;

26. Note with alarm the rise in the incidence of HIV among people who inject drugs and that, despite continuing increased efforts by all relevant stakeholders, the drug problem continues to constitute a serious threat to, among other things, public health and safety and the well-being of humanity, in particular children and young people and their families, and recognize that much more needs to be done to effectively combat the world drug problem;

27. Recall our commitment that prevention must be the cornerstone of the global HIV and AIDS response, but note that many national HIV-prevention programmes and spending priorities do not adequately reflect this commitment, that spending on HIV prevention is insufficient to mount a vigorous, effective and comprehensive global HIV-prevention response, that national prevention programmes are often not sufficiently coordinated and evidence-based, that prevention strategies do not adequately reflect infection patterns or sufficiently focus on populations at higher risk of HIV, and that only 33 per cent of countries have prevalence targets for young people and only 34 per cent have specific goals in place for condom programming;

28. Note with concern that national prevention strategies and programmes are often too generic in nature and do not adequately respond to infection patterns and the disease burden; for example, where heterosexual sex is the dominant mode of transmission, married or cohabitating individuals, including those in sero-discordant relationships, account for the majority of new infections but are not sufficiently targeted with testing and prevention interventions;

29. Note that many national HIV-prevention strategies inadequately focus on populations that epidemiological evidence shows are at higher risk, specifically men who have sex with men, people who inject drugs and sex workers, and further note, however, that each country should define the specific populations that are key to its epidemic and response, based on the epidemiological and national context;

30. Note with grave concern that, despite the near elimination of mother-to-child transmission of HIV in high-income countries and the availability of low-cost interventions to prevent transmission, approximately 370,000 infants were estimated to have been infected with HIV in 2009;

31. Note with concern that prevention, treatment, care and support programmes have not been adequately targeted or made accessible to persons with disabilities;

32. Recognize that access to safe, effective, affordable, good quality medicines and commodities in the context of epidemics such as HIV is fundamental to the full realization of the right of everyone to enjoy the highest attainable standard of physical and mental health;

33. Express grave concern that the majority of low- and middle-income countries did not meet their universal access to HIV treatment targets, despite the major achievement of expansion in providing access to antiretroviral treatment to over 6 million people living with HIV in low- and middle-income countries, that there are at least 10 million people living with HIV who are medically eligible to start antiretroviral treatment now, that discontinued treatment is a threat to treatment efficacy, and that the sustain-

ability of providing life-long HIV treatment is threatened by factors such as poverty, lack of access to treatment and insufficient and unpredictable funding and by the fact that the number of new HIV infections is outpacing the number of people starting HIV treatment by a factor of two to one;

34. Recognize the pivotal role of research in underpinning progress in HIV prevention, treatment, care and support, and welcome the extraordinary advances in scientific knowledge about HIV and its prevention and treatment, but note with concern that most new treatments are not available or accessible in low- and middle-income countries and that even in developed countries there are often significant delays in accessing new HIV treatments for people not responding to currently available treatment, and affirm the importance of social and operational research in improving our understanding of factors that influence the epidemic and actions that address it;

35. Recognize the critical importance of affordable medicines, including generics, in scaling up access to affordable HIV treatment, and further recognize that protection and enforcement measures for intellectual property rights should be compliant with the World Trade Organization Agreement on Trade-Related Aspects of Intellectual Property Rights (TRIPS Agreement) and should be interpreted and implemented in a manner supportive of the right of Member States to protect public health and, in particular, to promote access to medicines for all;

36. Note with concern that regulations, policies and practices, including those that limit legitimate trade in generic medicines, may seriously limit access to affordable HIV treatment and other pharmaceutical products in low- and middle-income countries, and recognize that improvements can be made, inter alia through national legislation, regulatory policy and supply chain management, noting that reductions in barriers to affordable products could be explored in order to expand access to affordable and good quality HIV prevention products, diagnostics, medicine and treatment commodities for HIV, including for opportunistic infections and co-infections;

37. Recognize that there are additional means to reverse the global epidemic and avert millions of HIV infections and AIDS-related deaths, and in this context also recognize that new and potential scientific evidence is available that could contribute to the effectiveness and scaling up of prevention, treatment, care and support programmes;

38. Reaffirm the commitment to fulfil obligations to promote universal respect for and the observance and protection of all human rights and fundamental freedoms for all in accordance with the Charter, the Universal Declaration of Human Rights and other instruments relating to human rights and international law; and emphasize the importance of cultural, ethical and religious values, the vital role of the family and the community and, in particular, of people living with and affected by HIV, including their families, and the need to take into account the particularities of each country in sustaining national HIV and AIDS responses, reaching all people living with HIV, delivering HIV prevention, treatment, care and support and strengthening health systems, in particular primary health care;

39. Reaffirm that the full realization of all human rights and fundamental freedoms for all is an essential element in the global response to the HIV epidemic, including in the areas of prevention, treatment, care and support, recognize that addressing stigma and discrimination against people living with, presumed to be living with or affected by HIV, including their families, is also a critical element in combating the global HIV epidemic, and recognize also the need, as appropriate, to strengthen national policies and legislation to address such stigma and discrimination;

40. Recognize that close cooperation with people living with HIV and populations at higher risk of HIV infection will facilitate the achievement of a more effective HIV and AIDS response, and emphasize that people living with and affected by HIV, including their families, should enjoy equal participation in social, economic and cultural activities, without prejudice and discrimination, and that they should have equal access to health care and community support as all members of the community;

41. Recognize that access to sexual and reproductive health has been and continues to be essential for HIV and AIDS responses and that Governments have the responsibility to provide for public health, with special attention to families, women and children;

42. Recognize the importance of strengthening health systems, in particular primary health care and the need to integrate the HIV response into it, and note that weak health systems, which already face many challenges, including a lack of trained health workers and a lack of retention of skilled health workers, are among the biggest barriers to accessing HIV and AIDS-related services;

43. Reaffirm the central role of the family, bearing in mind that in different cultural, social and political systems various forms of the family exist, in reducing vulnerability to HIV, inter alia in educating and guiding children, and take account of cultural, religious and ethical factors to reduce the vulnerability of children and young people by ensuring access of both girls and boys to primary and secondary education, including HIV and AIDS in curricula for adolescents, ensuring safe and secure environments, especially for young girls, expanding good quality youth-friendly information and sexual health education and counselling services, strengthening reproductive and sexual health programmes, and involving families and young people in planning, implementing and evaluating HIV and AIDS prevention and care programmes, to the extent possible;

44. Recognize the role that community organizations play, including those run by people living with HIV, in sustaining national and local HIV and AIDS responses, reaching all people living with HIV, delivering prevention, treatment, care and support services and strengthening health systems, in particular the primary health-care approach;

45. Acknowledge that the current trajectory of costs of HIV programmes is not sustainable and that programmes must become more cost-effective and evidence-based and deliver better value for money, and that poorly coordinated and transaction-heavy responses and a lack of proper governance and financial accountability impede progress;

46. Note with concern that evidence-based responses, which must be informed by data disaggregated by incidence and prevalence, including by age, sex and mode of transmission, continue to require stronger measuring tools, data management systems and improved monitoring and evaluation capacity at the national and regional levels;

47. Note the relevant strategies on HIV and AIDS of the Joint United Nations Programme on HIV/AIDS and the World Health Organization;

48. Recognize that the deadlines for achieving key targets and goals set out in the 2001 Declaration of Commitment on HIV/AIDS and the 2006 Political Declaration on HIV/AIDS have now expired, while noting with deep concern that many countries have been unable to fulfil their pledges to achieve them, and stress the urgent need to recommit to those targets and goals and commit to new, ambitious and achievable targets and goals building on the impressive advances of the past ten years and addressing barriers to progress and new challenges through a revitalized and enduring HIV and AIDS response;

49. Therefore, we solemnly declare our commitment to end the epidemic with renewed political will and strong, accountable leadership and to work in meaningful partnership with all stakeholders at all levels to implement bold and decisive actions as set out below, taking into account the diverse situations and circumstances in different countries and regions throughout the world;

Leadership: uniting to end the HIV epidemic

50. Commit to seize this turning point in the HIV epidemic and, through decisive, inclusive and accountable leadership, to revitalize and intensify the comprehensive global HIV and AIDS response by recommitting to the commitments made in the 2001 Declaration of Commitment on HIV/AIDS and the 2006 Political Declaration on HIV/AIDS and by fully implementing the commitments, goals and targets contained in the present Declaration;

51. Commit to redouble efforts to achieve, by 2015, universal access to HIV prevention, treatment, care and support as a critical step towards ending the global HIV epidemic, with a view to achieving Millennium Development Goal 6, in particular to halt and begin to reverse, by 2015, the spread of HIV;

52. Reaffirm our determination to achieve all the Millennium Development Goals, in particular Goal 6, and recognize the importance of rapidly scaling up efforts to integrate HIV prevention, treatment, care and support with efforts to achieve these goals;

53. Pledge to eliminate gender inequalities and gender-based abuse and violence, increase the capacity of women and adolescent girls to protect themselves from the risk of HIV infection, principally through the provision of health care and services, including, inter alia, sexual and reproductive health, as well as full access to comprehensive information and education, ensure that women can exercise their right to have control over, and decide freely and responsibly on, matters related to their sexuality, including their sexual and reproductive health, free of coercion, discrimination and violence, in order to increase their ability to protect themselves from HIV infection, and take all necessary measures to create an enabling environment for the empowerment of women and to strengthen their economic independence, and, in this context, reiterate the importance of the role of men and boys in achieving gender equality;

54. Commit to update and implement, by 2012, through inclusive, country-led and transparent processes, multisectoral national HIV and AIDS strategies and plans, including financing plans, which include time-bound goals to be reached in a targeted, equitable and sustained manner, to accelerate efforts to achieve universal access to HIV prevention, treatment, care and support by 2015, and address unacceptably low prevention and treatment coverage;

55. Commit to increase national ownership of HIV and AIDS responses, while calling upon the United Nations system, donor countries, the Global Fund to Fight AIDS, Tuberculosis and Malaria, the business sector and international and regional organizations to support Member States in ensuring that nationally driven, credible, costed, evidence-based, inclusive and comprehensive national HIV and AIDS strategic plans are, by 2013, funded and implemented with transparency, accountability and effectiveness in line with national priorities;

56. Commit to encouraging and supporting the active involvement and leadership of young people, including those living with HIV, in the fight against the epidemic at the local, national and global levels, and agree to work with these new leaders to help to develop specific measures to engage young people about HIV, including in communities, families, schools, tertiary institutions, recreation centres and workplaces;

57. Commit to continue engaging people living with and affected by HIV in decision-making and planning, implementing and evaluating the response, and to partner with local leaders and civil society, including community-based organizations, to develop and scale up community-led HIV services and to address stigma and discrimination;

Prevention: expanding coverage, diversifying approaches and intensifying efforts to end new HIV infections

58. Reaffirm that prevention of HIV must be the cornerstone of national, regional and international responses to the HIV epidemic;

59. Commit to redouble HIV-prevention efforts by taking all measures to implement comprehensive, evidence-based prevention approaches, taking into account local circumstances, ethics and cultural values, including through, but not limited to:

(*a*) Conducting public awareness campaigns and targeted HIV education to raise public awareness about HIV;

(*b*) Harnessing the energy of young people in helping to lead global HIV awareness;

(*c*) Reducing risk-taking behaviour and encouraging responsible sexual behaviour, including abstinence, fidelity and consistent and correct use of condoms;

(*d*) Expanding access to essential commodities, particularly male and female condoms and sterile injecting equipment;

(*e*) Ensuring that all people, particularly young people, have the means to exploit the potential of new modes of connection and communication;

(*f*) Significantly expanding and promoting voluntary and confidential HIV testing and counselling and provider-initiated HIV testing and counselling;

(*g*) Intensifying national testing promotion campaigns for HIV and other sexually transmitted infections;

(*h*) Giving consideration, as appropriate, to implementing and expanding risk- and harm-reduction programmes, taking into account the *WHO, UNODC, UNAIDS Technical Guide for Countries to Set Targets for Universal Access to HIV Prevention, Treatment and Care for Injecting Drug Users*, in accordance with national legislation;

(*i*) Promoting medical male circumcision where HIV prevalence is high and male circumcision rates are low;

(*j*) Sensitizing and encouraging the active engagement of men and boys in promoting gender equality;

(*k*) Facilitating access to sexual and reproductive health-care services;

(*l*) Ensuring that women of childbearing age have access to HIV-prevention-related services and that pregnant women have access to antenatal care, information, counselling and other HIV services, and increasing the availability of and access to effective treatment for women living with HIV and infants;

(*m*) Strengthening evidence-based health sector prevention interventions, including in rural and hard-to-reach places;

(*n*) Deploying new biomedical interventions as soon as they are validated, including female-initiated prevention methods such as microbicides, HIV treatment prophylaxis, earlier treatment as prevention and an HIV vaccine;

60. Commit to ensure that financial resources for prevention are targeted to evidence-based prevention measures that reflect the specific nature of each country's epidemic by focusing on geographic locations, social networks and populations vulnerable to HIV infection, according to the extent to which they account for new infections in each setting, in order to ensure that resources for HIV prevention are spent as cost-effectively as possible and to ensure that particular attention is paid to women and girls, young people, orphans and vulnerable children, migrants and people affected by humanitarian emergencies, prisoners, indigenous people and people with disabilities, depending on local circumstances;

61. Commit to ensure that national prevention strategies comprehensively target populations at higher risk and that systems of data collection and analysis about these populations are strengthened, and to take measures to ensure that HIV services, including voluntary and confidential HIV testing and counselling, are accessible to these populations so that they are encouraged to access HIV prevention, treatment, care and support;

62. Commit to working towards reducing sexual transmission of HIV by 50 per cent by 2015;

63. Commit to working towards reducing transmission of HIV among people who inject drugs by 50 per cent by 2015;

64. Commit to working towards the elimination of mother-to-child transmission of HIV and substantially reducing AIDS-related maternal deaths by 2015;

Treatment, care and support: eliminating AIDS-related illness and death

65. Pledge to intensify efforts that will help to increase the life expectancy and quality of life of all people living with HIV;

66. Commit to accelerate efforts to achieve the goal of universal access to antiretroviral treatment for those eligible based on World Health Organization HIV treatment guidelines that indicate timely initiation of quality assured treatment for its maximum benefit, with the target of working towards having 15 million people living with HIV on antiretroviral treatment by 2015;

67. Commit to support the reduction of unit costs and improve HIV treatment delivery, through, inter alia, provision of good quality, affordable, effective, less toxic and simplified treatment regimens that avert drug resistance, simple, affordable diagnostics at point of care, cost reductions for all major elements of treatment delivery, mobilization and capacity-building of communities to support treatment scale-up and patient retention, programmes that support improved treatment adherence, directing particular efforts towards hard-to-reach populations far from physical health-care facilities and programmes and those in informal settlement settings and other locations where health-care facilities are inadequate and recognizing the supplementary prevention benefits from treatment alongside other prevention efforts;

68. Commit to develop and implement strategies to improve infant HIV diagnosis, including through access to diagnostics at point of care, significantly increase and improve access to treatment for children and adolescents living with HIV, including access to prophylaxis and treatments for opportunistic infections, as well as increased support to children and adolescents through increased financial, social and moral support for their parents, families and legal guardians, and promote a smooth transition from paediatric to young adult treatment and related support and services;

69. Commit to promote services that integrate prevention, treatment and care of co-occurring conditions, including tuberculosis and hepatitis and improve access to quality, affordable primary health care, comprehensive care and support services, including those which address physical, spiritual, psychosocial, socio-economic and legal aspects of living with HIV, and palliative care services;

70. Commit to take immediate action at the national and global levels to integrate food and nutritional support into programmes directed to people affected by HIV in order to ensure access to sufficient, safe and nutritious food to enable people to meet their dietary needs and food preferences, for an active and healthy life as part of a comprehensive response to HIV and AIDS;

71. Commit to remove before 2015, where feasible, obstacles that limit the capacity of low- and middle-income countries to provide affordable and effective HIV prevention and treatment products, diagnostics, medicines and commodities and other pharmaceutical products, as well as treatment for opportunistic infections and co-infections, and to reduce costs associated with life-long chronic care, including by amending national laws and regulations, as deemed appropriate by respective Governments, so as to optimize:

(*a*) The use, to the full, of existing flexibilities under the Agreement on Trade-Related Aspects of Intellectual Property Rights specifically geared to promoting access to and trade in medicines, and, while recognizing the importance of the intellectual property rights regime in contributing to a more effective AIDS response, ensure that intellectual property rights provisions in trade agreements do not undermine these existing flexibilities, as confirmed in the Doha Declaration on the TRIPS Agreement and Public Health, and call for early acceptance of the amendment to article 31 of the TRIPS Agreement adopted by the General Council of the World Trade Organization in its decision of 6 December 2005;

(*b*) Addressing barriers, regulations, policies and practices that prevent access to affordable HIV treatment by promoting generic competition in order to help to reduce costs associated with life-long chronic care and by encouraging all States to apply measures and procedures for enforcing intellectual property rights in such a manner as to avoid creating barriers to the legitimate trade in medicines, and to provide for safeguards against the abuse of such measures and procedures;

(c) Encouraging the voluntary use, where appropriate, of new mechanisms such as partnerships, tiered pricing, open-source sharing of patents and patent pools benefiting all developing countries, including through entities such as the Medicines Patent Pool, to help to reduce treatment costs and encourage development of new HIV treatment formulations, including HIV medicines and point-of-care diagnostics, in particular for children;

72. Urge relevant international organizations, upon request and in accordance with their respective mandates, such as, where appropriate, the World Intellectual Property Organization, the United Nations Industrial Development Organization, the United Nations Development Programme, the United Nations Conference on Trade and Development, the World Trade Organization and the World Health Organization, to provide national Governments of developing countries with technical and capacity-building assistance for the efforts of those Governments to increase access to HIV medicines and treatment, in accordance with the national strategies of each Government, consistent with, and including through the use of, existing flexibilities under the Agreement on Trade-Related Aspects of Intellectual Property Rights, as confirmed by the Doha Declaration on the TRIPS Agreement and Public Health;

73. Commit by 2015 to address factors that limit treatment uptake and contribute to treatment stock-outs and delays in drug production and delivery, inadequate storage of medicines, patient dropout, including inadequate and inaccessible transportation to clinical sites, lack of accessibility of information, resources and sites, especially for persons with disabilities, sub-optimal management of treatment-related side effects, poor adherence to treatment, out-of-pocket expenses for non-drug components of treatment, loss of income associated with clinic attendance and inadequate human resources for health care;

74. Call upon pharmaceutical companies to take measures to ensure timely production and delivery of affordable, good quality and effective antiretroviral medicines so as to contribute to maintaining an efficient national system of distribution of these medicines;

75. Expand efforts to combat tuberculosis, which is a leading cause of death among people living with HIV, by improving tuberculosis screening, tuberculosis prevention, access to diagnosis and treatment of tuberculosis and drug-resistant tuberculosis and access to antiretroviral therapy, through more integrated delivery of HIV and tuberculosis services in line with the Global Plan to Stop TB 2011–2015, and commit by 2015 to work towards reducing tuberculosis deaths among people living with HIV by 50 per cent;

76. Commit to reduce the high rates of HIV and hepatitis B and C co-infection by developing, as soon as practicable, an estimate of the global treatment need, increasing efforts towards the development of a vaccine for hepatitis C and rapidly expanding access to appropriate vaccination for hepatitis B and to diagnostics and treatment of HIV and hepatitis co-infections;

Advancing human rights to reduce stigma, discrimination and violence related to HIV

77. Commit to intensify national efforts to create enabling legal, social and policy frameworks in each national context in order to eliminate stigma, discrimination and violence related to HIV and promote access to HIV prevention, treatment, care and support and non-discriminatory access to education, health care, employment and social services, provide legal protections for people affected by HIV, including inheritance rights and respect for privacy and confidentiality, and promote and protect all human rights and fundamental freedoms, with particular attention to all people vulnerable to and affected by HIV;

78. Commit to review, as appropriate, laws and policies that adversely affect the successful, effective and equitable delivery of HIV prevention, treatment, care and support programmes to people living with and affected by HIV and to consider their review in accordance with relevant national review frameworks and time frames;

79. Encourage Member States to consider identifying and reviewing any remaining HIV-related restrictions on entry, stay and residence in order to eliminate them;

80. Commit to national HIV and AIDS strategies that promote and protect human rights, including programmes aimed at eliminating stigma and discrimination against people living with and affected by HIV, including their families, including by sensitizing the police and judges, training health-care workers in non-discrimination, confidentiality and informed consent, supporting national human rights learning campaigns, legal literacy and legal services, as well as monitoring the impact of the legal environment on HIV prevention, treatment, care and support;

81. Commit to ensuring that national responses to HIV and AIDS meet the specific needs of women and girls, including those living with and affected by HIV, across their lifespan, by strengthening legal, policy, administrative and other measures for the promotion and protection of women's full enjoyment of all human rights and the reduction of their vulnerability to HIV through the elimination of all forms of discrimination, as well as all types of sexual exploitation of women, girls and boys, including for commercial reasons, and all forms of violence against women and girls, including harmful traditional and customary practices, abuse, rape and other forms of sexual violence, battering and trafficking in women and girls;

82. Commit to strengthen national social and child protection systems and care and support programmes for children, in particular for the girl child, and adolescents affected by and vulnerable to HIV, as well as their families and caregivers, including through the provision of equal opportunities to support the development to their full potential of orphans and other children affected by and living with HIV, especially through equal access to education, the creation of safe and non-discriminatory learning environments, supportive legal systems and protections, including civil registration systems, and the provision of comprehensive information and support to children and their families and caregivers, especially age-appropriate HIV information, to assist children living with HIV as they transition through adolescence, consistent with their evolving capacities;

83. Commit to promoting laws and policies that ensure the full realization of all human rights and fundamen-

tal freedoms for young people, particularly those living with HIV and those at higher risk of HIV infection, so as to eliminate the stigma and discrimination they face;

84. Commit to address, according to national legislation, the vulnerabilities to HIV experienced by migrant and mobile populations and support their access to HIV prevention, treatment, care and support;

85. Commit to mitigate the impact of the epidemic on workers, their families, their dependants, workplaces and economies, including by taking into account all relevant conventions of the International Labour Organization, as well as the guidance provided by the relevant International Labour Organization recommendations, including the Recommendation on HIV and AIDS and the World of Work, 2010 (No. 200), and call upon employers, trade and labour unions, employees and volunteers to eliminate stigma and discrimination, protect human rights and facilitate access to HIV prevention, treatment, care and support;

Resources for the AIDS response

86. Commit to working towards closing, by 2015, the global HIV and AIDS resource gap, currently estimated by the Joint United Nations Programme on HIV/AIDS to be 6 billion dollars annually, through greater strategic investment and continued domestic and international funding to enable countries to access predictable and sustainable financial resources and through sources of innovative financing and by ensuring that funding flows through country finance systems, where appropriate and available, and is aligned with accountable and sustainable national HIV and AIDS and development strategies that maximize synergies and deliver sustainable programmes that are evidence-based and implemented with transparency, accountability and effectiveness;

87. Commit to breaking the upward trajectory of costs through the efficient utilization of resources, addressing barriers to the legal trade in generics and other low-cost medicines, improving the efficiency of prevention by targeting interventions to deliver more efficient, innovative and sustainable programmes for the HIV and AIDS response, in accordance with national development plans and priorities, and ensuring that synergies are exploited between the HIV and AIDS response and the efforts to achieve the internationally agreed development goals, including the Millennium Development Goals;

88. Commit, by 2015, through a series of incremental steps and through our shared responsibility, to reach a significant level of annual global expenditure on HIV and AIDS, while recognizing that the overall target estimated by the Joint United Nations Programme on HIV/AIDS is between 22 billion and 24 billion dollars in low- and middle-income countries, by increasing national ownership of HIV and AIDS responses through greater allocations from national resources and traditional sources of funding, including official development assistance;

89. Strongly urge those developed countries that have pledged to achieve the target of 0.7 per cent of their gross national product for official development assistance by 2015, and urge those developed countries that have not yet done so, to make additional concrete efforts to fulfil their commitments in this regard;

90. Strongly urge African countries that adopted the Abuja Declaration and Framework for Action for the fight against HIV/AIDS, Tuberculosis and Other Related Infectious Diseases to take concrete measures to meet the target of allocating at least 15 per cent of their annual budget to the improvement of the health sector, in accordance with the Abuja Declaration and Framework for Action;

91. Commit to enhance the quality of aid by strengthening national ownership, alignment, harmonization, predictability, mutual accountability and transparency, and results orientation;

92. Commit to supporting and strengthening existing financial mechanisms, including the Global Fund to Fight AIDS, Tuberculosis and Malaria and relevant United Nations organizations, through the provision of funds in a sustained and predictable manner, in particular to those countries with low and middle incomes with a high disease burden or a large number of people living with and affected by HIV;

93. Recommit to fully implementing the enhanced Heavily Indebted Poor Countries Initiative and agree to cancel all eligible bilateral official debts of qualified countries within the Initiative that reach the completion point under the Initiative, in particular the countries most affected by HIV and AIDS, and urge the use of debt service savings, inter alia, to finance poverty eradication programmes, particularly for prevention, treatment, care and support for HIV and AIDS and other infections;

94. Commit to scaling up new, voluntary and additional innovative financing mechanisms to help to address the shortfall of resources available for the global HIV and AIDS response and to improving the financing of the HIV and AIDS response over the long term, and to accelerating efforts to identify innovative financing mechanisms that will generate additional financial resources for HIV and AIDS to complement national budgetary allocations and official development assistance;

95. Appreciate that the Global Fund to Fight AIDS, Tuberculosis and Malaria is a pivotal mechanism for achieving universal access to prevention, treatment, care and support by 2015, recognize the programme for reform of the Global Fund, and encourage Member States, the business community, including foundations, and philanthropists to provide the highest level of support for the Global Fund, taking into account the funding targets to be identified at the 2012 midterm review of the Global Fund replenishment process;

Strengthening health systems and integrating HIV and AIDS with broader health and development

96. Commit to redouble efforts to strengthen health systems, including primary health care, particularly in developing countries, through measures such as allocating national and international resources, appropriate decentralization of HIV and AIDS programmes to improve access for communities, including rural and hard-to-reach populations, integration of HIV and AIDS programmes into primary health care, sexual and reproductive health-care services and specialized infectious disease services, improving planning for institutional, infrastructure and human resource needs, improving supply chain management within health systems and increasing human resource capacity for the response, including by scaling up the training and retention of human resources for health policy and planning, health-care personnel, consistent with the World Health Organization voluntary Global Code of Practice on

the International Recruitment of Health Personnel, community health workers and peer educators, with support from and in partnership with international and regional organizations, the business sector and civil society, as appropriate;

97. Support and encourage, through domestic and international funding and the provision of technical assistance, the substantial development of human capital, development of national and international research infrastructures, laboratory capacity and improved surveillance systems, and data collection, processing and dissemination, and training of basic and clinical researchers, social scientists and technicians, with a focus on those countries most affected by HIV and/or experiencing or at risk of a rapid expansion of the epidemic;

98. Commit, by 2015, to working with partners to direct resources to and strengthen the advocacy, policy and programmatic links between HIV and tuberculosis responses, primary health-care services, sexual and reproductive health, maternal and child health, hepatitis B and C, drug dependence, non-communicable diseases and overall health systems, leveraging health-care services to prevent mother-to-child transmission of HIV, strengthening the interface between HIV services, related sexual and reproductive health care and services and other health services, including maternal and child health, eliminating parallel systems for HIV-related services and information where feasible and strengthening linkages among national and global efforts concerned with human and national development, including poverty eradication, preventative health care, enhanced nutrition, access to safe and clean drinking water, sanitation, education and the improvement of livelihoods;

99. Commit to supporting all national, regional and global efforts to achieve the Millennium Development Goals, including those undertaken through North-South, South-South and triangular cooperation, to improve comprehensive and integrated HIV prevention, treatment, care and support programmes, as well as tuberculosis, sexual and reproductive health, malaria and maternal and child health care;

Research and development: the key to preventing, treating and curing HIV

100. Commit to investing in accelerated basic research on the development of sustainable and affordable HIV and tuberculosis diagnostics and treatments for HIV and its associated co-infections, microbicides and other new prevention technologies, including female-controlled prevention methods, rapid diagnostic and monitoring technologies, as well as biomedical operations and social, cultural and behavioural and traditional medicine research, and continuing to build national research capacity, especially in developing countries, through increased funding and public-private partnerships, and creating a conducive environment for research and ensuring that it is based on the highest ethical and scientific standards, and strengthening national regulatory authorities;

101. Commit to accelerate research and development for a safe, affordable, effective and accessible vaccine and for a cure for HIV, while ensuring that sustainable systems for vaccine procurement and equitable distribution are also developed;

Coordination, monitoring and accountability: maximizing the response

102. Commit to having effective evidence-based operational monitoring and evaluation and mutual accountability mechanisms between all stakeholders to support multisectoral national strategic plans for HIV and AIDS to fulfil the commitments in the present Declaration, with the active involvement of people living with, affected by and vulnerable to HIV, and other relevant civil society and private sector stakeholders;

103. Commit to revise by the end of 2012 the recommended framework of core indicators that reflect the commitments made in the present Declaration and to develop additional measures, where necessary, to strengthen national, regional and global coordination and monitoring mechanisms of HIV and AIDS responses through inclusive and transparent processes with the full involvement of Member States and other relevant stakeholders, with the support of the Joint United Nations Programme on HIV/AIDS;

Follow-up: sustaining progress

104. Encourage and support the exchange among countries and regions of information, research, evidence and experiences for implementing the measures and commitments related to the global HIV and AIDS response, in particular those contained in the present Declaration, facilitate intensified North-South, South-South and triangular cooperation, as well as subregional, regional and interregional cooperation and coordination, and in this regard continue to encourage the Economic and Social Council to request the regional commissions, within their respective mandates and resources, to support periodic, inclusive reviews of national efforts and progress made in their respective regions to combat HIV;

105. Request the Secretary-General to provide to the General Assembly an annual report on progress achieved in realizing the commitments made in the present Declaration and, with support from the Joint United Nations Programme on HIV/AIDS, to report to the Assembly on progress in accordance with global reporting on the Millennium Development Goals at the 2013 review of the Goals and subsequent reviews.

In September (**decision 65/551**), the Assembly included in the draft agenda of its sixty-sixth session an item entitled "Implementation of the Declaration of Commitment on HIV/AIDS and the Political Declarations on HIV and AIDS", and in December (**decision 66/557**), decided that that item would remain for consideration during its resumed sixty-sixth (2012) session.

Joint UN Programme on HIV/AIDS

The Joint United Nations Programme on HIV/AIDS (UNAIDS) advocated global action to fight HIV/AIDS. UNAIDS had 10 co-sponsors: the United Nations Population Fund; the United Nations Children's Fund; the World Food Programme (WFP); the United Nations Educational, Scientific and Cultural Organization; the International Labour Organization; the World Health Organization (WHO); the World Bank; the United Nations Development Programme; the Office of the United Nations High Commissioner for Refugees; and the United Nations Office on Drugs and Crime.

Report of Executive Director. In response to Economic and Social Council resolution 2009/6 [YUN 2009, p. 1220], the Secretary-General transmitted in May the report of the UNAIDS Executive Director [E/2011/109], which described the results achieved in the response to the HIV/AIDS pandemic since the 2009 report. Globally, the number of adults newly infected with HIV had declined by nearly 20 per cent since 1999, AIDS deaths had fallen by 19 per cent between 2004 and 2009, and the number of children newly infected with HIV was 24 per cent lower in 2009 than in 2004. The number of people receiving antiretroviral treatment continued to increase. Research breakthroughs occurred in 2010, with clinical trials demonstrating the partial efficacy of a vaginal microbicide and pre-exposure antiretroviral prophylaxis. Efforts had been made to increase the number of circumcised adult males, although faster progress was needed to help reduce sexual transmission. The percentage of countries reporting the existence of laws and regulations protecting people living with HIV from discrimination increased from 56 per cent in 2006 to 71 per cent in 2010. Those gains, however, were fragile, since the global financial and economic downturn had caused HIV financing to flatten. Although HIV incidence had declined globally, new infections were on the rise in Eastern Europe, Central Asia, the Middle East, North Africa and some high-income countries.

Following the release of the final report of the second independent evaluation of UNAIDS in 2009, the Joint Programme undertook steps to implement the recommendations of that assessment, with particular focus on actions to enhance the coordination and effectiveness of UNAIDS support to HIV responses. A new UNAIDS vision was formulated, envisaging zero new infections, zero AIDS-related deaths and zero discrimination. UNAIDS developed a new strategy for 2011–2015 reflecting that new vision. Work began on outlining a unified budget, results and accountability framework, to become effective in January 2012.

Since its last report, the Joint Programme had focused on achieving results in the 10 priority areas and across the six cross-cutting strategies set out in *Joint Action for Results: UNAIDS Outcome Framework 2009–2011* [YUN 2009, p. 1219]. Those areas were: reducing sexual transmission of HIV; preventing mothers from dying and babies from becoming infected with HIV; ensuring that people with HIV received treatment; preventing people with HIV from dying of tuberculosis; protecting drug users from becoming infected with HIV; empowering key populations to protect themselves from HIV infection and to access antiretroviral therapy; eliminating laws, practices and stigma that impeded effective responses to AIDS; meeting the HIV needs of women and girls and stopping gender-based violence; empowering young people to protect themselves from HIV; and enhancing social protection for people affected by HIV. The six cross-cutting strategies were: bringing AIDS planning and action into national development policy and broader accountability frameworks; optimizing UN support for applications to and programme implementation of the Global Fund to Fight AIDS, Tuberculosis and Malaria; improving country-by-country information generation, analysis and use; assessing and realigning the management of technical assistance programmes; developing shared messages for sustained political commitment, leadership development and advocacy; and strengthening engagement with communities, civil society and networks of people living with HIV.

ECONOMIC AND SOCIAL COUNCIL ACTION

On 26 July [meeting 45], the Economic and Social Council adopted **resolution 2011/19** [draft: E/2011/L.46] without vote [agenda item 7 (*g*)].

Joint United Nations Programme on HIV/AIDS

The Economic and Social Council,

Recalling its resolution 2009/6 of 24 July 2009,

Having considered the report of the Executive Director of the Joint United Nations Programme on HIV/AIDS,

Welcoming the Political Declaration on HIV and AIDS: Intensifying our Efforts to Eliminate HIV and AIDS adopted by the General Assembly at the high-level meeting on HIV/AIDS, held from 8 to 10 June 2011, as a key reference for the 2011–2015 Strategy of the Joint Programme,

Noting the adoption by the Programme Coordinating Board of the Joint Programme, in December 2010, of the 2011–2015 Strategy: Getting to Zero,

1. *Encourages* Governments, the United Nations system, civil society and the private sector to scale up efforts on an urgent basis to achieve the goals and targets contained in the Political Declaration on HIV and AIDS: Intensifying our Efforts to Eliminate HIV and AIDS;

2. *Urges* the Joint United Nations Programme on HIV/AIDS to support the full and effective implementation of the 2011 Political Declaration on HIV and AIDS;

3. *Also urges* the Joint Programme, while implementing the 2011–2015 Strategy: Getting to Zero, to support Governments in strengthening their national responses to the epidemic in accordance with their specific epidemiological situation, national contexts and priorities, while taking into due account the 2011 Political Declaration on HIV and AIDS;

4. *Calls upon* the United Nations system, in collaboration with all relevant stakeholders, to further strengthen coordinated action, in particular at the country level;

5. *Requests* the Secretary-General to transmit to the Economic and Social Council, at its substantive session of 2013, a report prepared by the Executive Director of the Joint Programme, in collaboration with its co-sponsors and other relevant organizations and bodies of the United Nations system, on progress made in implementing a coordinated response by the United Nations system to the HIV/AIDS epidemic.

Programme Coordinating Board. At its twenty-eighth meeting (Geneva, 21–23 June), the UNAIDS Programme Coordinating Board (PCB) [UNAIDS/PCB(28)/11.15] considered the report of its twenty-seventh meeting [YUN 2010, p. 1221], the report of the Executive Director [UNAIDS/PCB(28)/11.2] and that of the Committee of Cosponsoring Organizations [UNAIDS/PCB(28)/11.3]. As a follow-up to the thematic segment from the twenty-seventh PCB meeting, PCB requested UNAIDS to conduct a stocktaking exercise of both national nutrition and food security and HIV/AIDS strategies to identify gaps and propose relevant action. PCB approved its 2012–2015 unified budget, results and accountability framework, $485 million as the core budget for 2012–2013 and the proposed allocation between the 10 cosponsors and the Secretariat; decided that the General Assembly Political Declaration on HIV/AIDS (see p. 1135) served as a key reference to implement the unified budget, results and accountability framework; agreed that the theme for the thirtieth PCB meeting would be "Combination prevention: Addressing the urgent need to reinvigorate HIV prevention responses globally by scaling up and achieving synergies to halt and begin to reverse the spread of the AIDS epidemic"; and set the dates for the thirtieth (5–7 June 2012), thirty-first (11–13 December 2012), thirty-second (25–27 June 2013) and thirty-third (10–12 December 2013) meetings.

The Board's twenty-ninth meeting (Geneva, 13–15 December 2011) [UNAIDS/PCB(29)/11.28] took note of a paper [UNAIDS/PCB(29)/11.19] on the follow-up to the 2011 General Assembly High-level Meeting on AIDS (see p. 1135) and requested UNAIDS to launch a process of inclusive consultations to consider approaches to strategic investment, including the new investment framework for the global HIV response referenced by the Executive Director in his report [UNAIDS/PCB(29)/11.17]; requested UNAIDS at its thirtieth meeting to report on changes to indicators and developments concerning the Monitoring and Evaluation Reference Group, following the adoption of the 2011 Political Declaration; requested the establishment of a time-limited consultative process to better define UNAIDS technical support based upon its coordination role, and areas of core competency and strengths, reporting back to the thirtieth PCB; agreed that the theme for the thirty-first PCB meeting would be "Non-discrimination"; and set the dates for the thirty-fourth (17–19 June 2014) and thirty-fifth (9–11 December 2014) meetings.

UNAIDS 2011 World AIDS Day report

The 2011 *World AIDS Day Report*, released in November, stated that new HIV infections and AIDS-related deaths had fallen since the peak of the epidemic in the mid-2000s and that 6.6 million people were receiving treatment in low- and middle-income countries—nearly half those eligible. In order to reach the new targets set by the General Assembly in its 2011 Political Declaration on HIV/AIDS—achieving, by 2015, universal access to HIV prevention, treatment, care and support—the report stressed that the AIDS response must accelerate and be transformed from a short-term, piecemeal approach to a long-term strategic response with matching investment. Together with its partners, UNAIDS had mapped a new framework for AIDS investments, focusing on high-impact, high-value strategies. The framework aimed at maximizing the benefits of the HIV response; using country-specific epidemiology to ensure rational resource allocation; encouraging countries to implement the most effective programmes based on local context; and increasing efficiency in HIV prevention, treatment, care and support. The report called on countries and donors to use the tools available for HIV prevention and treatment, focus on the most effective programmes and invest accordingly.

Non-communicable diseases

Prevention and control of non-communicable diseases

In recognition of the threat posed by non-communicable diseases (NCDs), various UN entities in 2011 worked to facilitate an effective response. In April, WHO launched the *Global status report on non-communicable diseases 2010*—the first publication on the worldwide epidemic of cardiovascular diseases, cancer, diabetes and chronic respiratory diseases, as well as on their risk factors and determinants. The report provided a road map for reversing the epidemic including by strengthening national and global monitoring and surveillance; scaling up the implementation of measures to reduce risk factors like tobacco use, unhealthy diet, physical inactivity and harmful alcohol use; and improving access to cost-effective health-care interventions to prevent complications, disabilities and premature death.

At the sixty-fourth World Health Assembly (Geneva, 16–24 May) [WHA64/2011/REC/1], WHO expressed concern about the global threat posed by NCDs, particularly in developing countries, and called for urgent global action. WHO also discussed preparations for the 2011 High-level Meeting of the General Assembly on the Prevention and Control of Non-communicable Diseases (see p. 1146).

Pursuant to Assembly resolution 65/238 [YUN 2010, p. 1223], an informal interactive hearing [A/65/940] with non-governmental organizations, civil society organizations, the private sector and academia was held on 16 June at UN Headquarters to provide an input to the preparatory process of the 2011 High-level Meeting.

By **decision 65/549** of 28 July, the Assembly approved for participation in the High-level Meeting the list of civil society representatives drawn up by the Assembly President pursuant to paragraph 15 of resolution 65/238 [YUN 2010, p. 1223].

Report of the Secretary-General. Pursuant to General Assembly resolutions 64/265 and 65/238 [YUN 2010, pp. 1222 & 1223], the Secretary General submitted a May report [A/66/83] that reviewed the NCDs status, outlined the burden NCDs imposed on global health and socioeconomic development, and provided recommendations to counteract such diseases. Worldwide, NCDs were responsible for more deaths than all other causes combined. While the international community had focused on communicable diseases such as HIV/AIDS, malaria and tuberculosis, NCDs—commonly known as chronic or lifestyle-related diseases—had gone relatively unnoticed in the developing world and were becoming a global epidemic.

The data provided in the report were based on the WHO *Global status report on non-communicable diseases 2010* (see p. 1145). In 2008, 36 million people died from NCDs, representing 63 per cent of the 57 million global deaths that year. Cardiovascular diseases were responsible for the largest proportion of NCD-related deaths under the age of 70 (39 per cent), followed by cancers (27 per cent). The epidemic also appeared to affect the genders differently. In 2008, NCDs killed 4.9 million men and 3.3 million women between the ages of 15 and 59 worldwide; however, more women of the same age group died of NCDs in Africa than in high-income countries. The risk for men of dying from NCDs exceeded that of women in all age groups, a phenomenon that was attributed to men's greater exposure to risk factors such as tobacco and the harmful use of alcohol, and their lower use of preventive health care.

While NCDs had traditionally afflicted mainly high-income populations, evidence showed that the spread of such diseases was associated with increasing levels of development. Death and disease from NCDs outstripped communicable diseases in every region except Africa, where the rate was quickly rising. Such diseases, however, could be significantly reduced and prevented through proven and affordable measures, many of which were complementary to global health efforts under way. The report concluded with recommendations such as the inclusion of prevention and control of NCDs among priorities in national health strategies and plans; the engagement of non-health sectors; the implementation of international agreements to reduce risk factors; the promotion of healthy behaviour through wellness programmes and insurance plans for workers; and the accessibility of healthy foods.

Communication. In June [A/65/859], the Russian Federation transmitted the Moscow Declaration, adopted at the First Global Ministerial Conference on Healthy Lifestyles and Non-communicable Disease Control (Moscow, 28–29 April), during which participants affirmed their commitment to addressing the challenges posed by NCDs and outlined their action at the national and international levels.

High-level meeting on non-communicable diseases. Pursuant to resolution 64/265 and 65/238 [YUN 2010, pp. 1222 & 1223], the General Assembly held a high-level meeting on the prevention and control of non-communicable diseases (New York, 19–20 September), during which Heads of State and Government identified key issues, reviewed the changing landscape for global health and development, acknowledged the growing burden of NCDs, particularly in developing countries, and charted a way forward to strengthen national capacities and foster international cooperation.

The meeting included plenary sessions and three round tables. The opening plenary session featured statements by the President of the General Assembly and the Secretary-General. The Secretary-General stated that three out of five people on Earth died from NCDs. He also said that while treating the diseases could be affordable, preventing them could cost next to nothing. World leaders should encourage individuals to make smart choices that protected their health, such as exercising, eating well, limiting alcohol consumption and quitting smoking. The themes of the round tables were the challenges and impact of NCDs and their risk factors; strengthening national capacities to address NCD prevention and control; and fostering international cooperation. The closing plenary adopted the Political Declaration of the High-level Meeting of the General Assembly on the Prevention and Control of Non-communicable Diseases. Proclaiming the spread of NCDs a socioeconomic and development challenge of epidemic proportions, world leaders committed to reducing risk factors and creating health-promoting environments; strengthening national policies and health systems, international cooperation, country-level surveillance and monitoring systems; and promoting research and development for the prevention and control of NCDs in a sustainable and cost-effective manner.

GENERAL ASSEMBLY ACTION

On 19 September [meeting 3], the General Assembly adopted **resolution 66/2** [draft: A/66/L.1] without vote [agenda item 117].

Political Declaration of the High-level Meeting of the General Assembly on the Prevention and Control of Non-communicable Diseases

The General Assembly

Adopts the Political Declaration of the High-level Meeting of the General Assembly on the Prevention and Control of Non-communicable Diseases annexed to the present resolution.

ANNEX
Political Declaration of the High-level Meeting of the General Assembly on the Prevention and Control of Non-communicable Diseases

We, Heads of State and Government and representatives of States and Governments, assembled at the United Nations on 19 and 20 September 2011, to address the prevention and control of non-communicable diseases worldwide, with a particular focus on developmental and other challenges and social and economic impacts, particularly for developing countries,

1. Acknowledge that the global burden and threat of non-communicable diseases constitutes one of the major challenges for development in the twenty-first century, which undermines social and economic development throughout the world and threatens the achievement of internationally agreed development goals;

2. Recognize that non-communicable diseases are a threat to the economies of many Member States and may lead to increasing inequalities between countries and populations;

3. Recognize the primary role and responsibility of Governments in responding to the challenge of non-communicable diseases and the essential need for the efforts and engagement of all sectors of society to generate effective responses for the prevention and control of non-communicable diseases;

4. Recognize also the important role of the international community and international cooperation in assisting Member States, particularly developing countries, in complementing national efforts to generate an effective response to non-communicable diseases;

5. Reaffirm the right of everyone to the enjoyment of the highest attainable standard of physical and mental health;

6. Recognize the urgent need for greater measures at the global, regional and national levels to prevent and control non-communicable diseases in order to contribute to the full realization of the right of everyone to the highest attainable standard of physical and mental health;

7. Recall the relevant mandates of the General Assembly, in particular resolutions 64/265 of 13 May 2010 and 65/238 of 24 December 2010;

8. Note with appreciation the World Health Organization Framework Convention on Tobacco Control, reaffirm all relevant resolutions and decisions adopted by the World Health Assembly on the prevention and control of non-communicable diseases, and underline the importance for Member States to continue addressing common risk factors for non-communicable diseases through the implementation of the World Health Organization 2008–2013 Action Plan for the Global Strategy for the Prevention and Control of Non-communicable Diseases as well as the Global Strategy on Diet, Physical Activity and Health and the Global Strategy to Reduce the Harmful Use of Alcohol;

9. Recall the ministerial declaration adopted at the 2009 high-level segment of the Economic and Social Council, in which a call was made for urgent action to implement the Global Strategy for the Prevention and Control of Non-communicable Diseases and its related Action Plan;

10. Take note with appreciation of all the regional initiatives undertaken on the prevention and control of non-communicable diseases, including the Declaration of the Heads of State and Government of the Caribbean Community entitled "Uniting to stop the epidemic of chronic non-communicable diseases", adopted in September 2007, the Libreville Declaration on Health and Environment in Africa, adopted in August 2008, the statement of the Commonwealth Heads of Government on action to combat non-communicable diseases, adopted in November 2009, the declaration of commitment of the Fifth Summit of the Americas, adopted in June 2009, the Parma Declaration on Environment and Health, adopted by the member States in the European region of the World Health Organization in March 2010, the Dubai Declaration on Diabetes and Chronic Non-communicable Diseases in the Middle East and Northern Africa Region, adopted in December 2010, the European Charter on Counteracting Obesity, adopted in November 2006, the Aruba Call for Action on Obesity of June 2011, and the Honiara Communiqué on addressing non-communicable disease challenges in the Pacific region, adopted in July 2011;

11. Take note with appreciation also of the outcomes of the regional multisectoral consultations, including the adoption of ministerial declarations, which were held by the World Health Organization in collaboration with Member States, with the support and active participation of regional commissions and other relevant United Nations agencies and entities, and served to provide inputs to the preparations for the high-level meeting in accordance with resolution 65/238;

12. Welcome the convening of the first Global Ministerial Conference on Healthy Lifestyles and Non-communicable Disease Control, which was organized by the Russian Federation and the World Health Organization and held in Moscow on 28 and 29 April 2011, and the adoption of the Moscow Declaration, and recall resolution 64.11 of the World Health Assembly;

13. Recognize the leading role of the World Health Organization as the primary specialized agency for health, including its roles and functions with regard to health policy in accordance with its mandate, and reaffirm its leadership and coordination role in promoting and monitoring global action against non-communicable diseases in relation to the work of other relevant United Nations agencies, development banks and other regional and international organizations in addressing non-communicable diseases in a coordinated manner;

A challenge of epidemic proportions and its socioeconomic and developmental impacts

14. Note with profound concern that, according to the World Health Organization, in 2008, an estimated 36 million of the 57 million global deaths were due to non-communicable diseases, principally cardiovascular diseases, cancers, chronic respiratory diseases and diabetes, including about 9 million deaths before the age of 60, and that nearly 80 per cent of those deaths occurred in developing countries;

15. Note also with profound concern that non-communicable diseases are among the leading causes of preventable morbidity and of related disability;

16. Recognize further that communicable diseases, maternal and perinatal conditions and nutritional deficiencies are currently the most common causes of death in Africa, and note with concern the growing double burden of disease, including in Africa, caused by the rapidly rising in-

cidence of non-communicable diseases, which are projected to become the most common causes of death by 2030;

17. Note further that there is a range of other non-communicable diseases and conditions, for which the risk factors and the need for preventive measures, screening, treatment and care are linked with the four most prominent non-communicable diseases;

18. Recognize that mental and neurological disorders, including Alzheimer's disease, are an important cause of morbidity and contribute to the global non-communicable disease burden, for which there is a need to provide equitable access to effective programmes and health-care interventions;

19. Recognize that renal, oral and eye diseases pose a major health burden for many countries and that these diseases share common risk factors and can benefit from common responses to non-communicable diseases;

20. Recognize that the most prominent non-communicable diseases are linked to common risk factors, namely tobacco use, harmful use of alcohol, an unhealthy diet and lack of physical activity;

21. Recognize that the conditions in which people live and their lifestyles influence their health and quality of life and that poverty, uneven distribution of wealth, lack of education, rapid urbanization, population ageing and the economic social, gender, political, behavioural and environmental determinants of health are among the contributing factors to the rising incidence and prevalence of non-communicable diseases;

22. Note with grave concern the vicious cycle whereby non-communicable diseases and their risk factors worsen poverty, while poverty contributes to rising rates of non-communicable diseases, posing a threat to public health and economic and social development;

23. Note with concern that the rapidly growing magnitude of non-communicable diseases affects people of all ages, gender, race and income levels, and further that poor populations and those living in vulnerable situations, in particular in developing countries, bear a disproportionate burden and that non-communicable diseases can affect women and men differently;

24. Note with concern the rising levels of obesity in different regions, particularly among children and youth, and note that obesity, an unhealthy diet and physical inactivity have strong linkages with the four main non-communicable diseases and are associated with higher health costs and reduced productivity;

25. Express deep concern that women bear a disproportionate share of the burden of caregiving and that, in some populations, women tend to be less physically active than men, are more likely to be obese and are taking up smoking at alarming rates;

26. Note also with concern that maternal and child health is inextricably linked with non-communicable diseases and their risk factors, specifically as prenatal malnutrition and low birth weight create a predisposition to obesity, high blood pressure, heart disease and diabetes later in life, and that pregnancy conditions, such as maternal obesity and gestational diabetes, are associated with similar risks in both the mother and her offspring;

27. Note with concern the possible linkages between non-communicable diseases and some communicable diseases, such as HIV/AIDS, call for the integration, as appropriate, of responses to HIV/AIDS and non-communicable diseases, and in this regard call for attention to be given to people living with HIV/AIDS, especially in countries with a high prevalence of HIV/AIDS, in accordance with national priorities;

28. Recognize that smoke exposure from the use of inefficient cooking stoves for indoor cooking or heating contributes to and may exacerbate lung and respiratory conditions, with a disproportionate effect on women and children in poor populations whose households may be dependent on such fuels;

29. Acknowledge also the existence of significant inequalities in the burden of non-communicable diseases and in access to non-communicable disease prevention and control, both between countries, and within countries and communities;

30. Recognize the critical importance of strengthening health systems, including health-care infrastructure, human resources for health, and health and social protection systems, particularly in developing countries, in order to respond effectively and equitably to the health-care needs of people with non-communicable diseases;

31. Note with grave concern that non-communicable diseases and their risk factors lead to increased burdens on individuals, families and communities, including impoverishment from long-term treatment and care costs, and to a loss of productivity that threatens household income and leads to productivity loss for individuals and their families and to the economies of Member States, making non-communicable diseases a contributing factor to poverty and hunger, which may have a direct impact on the achievement of the internationally agreed development goals, including the Millennium Development Goals;

32. Express deep concern at the ongoing negative impacts of the financial and economic crisis, volatile energy and food prices and ongoing concerns over food security, as well as the increasing challenges posed by climate change and the loss of biodiversity, and their effect on the control and prevention of non-communicable diseases, and emphasize in this regard the need for prompt and robust, coordinated and multisectoral efforts to address those impacts, while building on efforts already under way;

**Responding to the challenge:
a whole-of-government and a whole-of-society effort**

33. Recognize that the rising prevalence, morbidity and mortality of non-communicable diseases worldwide can be largely prevented and controlled through collective and multisectoral action by all Member States and other relevant stakeholders at the local, national, regional and global levels, and by raising the priority accorded to non-communicable diseases in development cooperation by enhancing such cooperation in this regard;

34. Recognize that prevention must be the cornerstone of the global response to non-communicable diseases;

35. Recognize also the critical importance of reducing the level of exposure of individuals and populations to the common modifiable risk factors for non-communicable diseases, namely, tobacco use, unhealthy diet, physical inactivity and the harmful use of alcohol, and their determinants, while at the same time strengthening the capacity of individuals and populations to make healthier choices and follow lifestyle patterns that foster good health;

36. Recognize that effective non-communicable disease prevention and control require leadership and multisectoral approaches for health at the government level, including, as appropriate, health in all policies and whole-of-government approaches across such sectors as health, education, energy, agriculture, sports, transport, communication, urban planning, environment, labour, employment, industry and trade, finance, and social and economic development;

37. Acknowledge the contribution of and important role played by all relevant stakeholders, including individuals, families and communities, intergovernmental organizations and religious institutions, civil society, academia, the media, voluntary associations and, where and as appropriate, the private sector and industry, in support of national efforts for non-communicable disease prevention and control, and recognize the need to further support the strengthening of coordination among these stakeholders in order to improve the effectiveness of these efforts;

38. Recognize the fundamental conflict of interest between the tobacco industry and public health;

39. Recognize that the incidence and impacts of non-communicable diseases can be largely prevented or reduced with an approach that incorporates evidence-based, affordable, cost-effective, population-wide and multisectoral interventions;

40. Acknowledge that resources devoted to combating the challenges posed by non-communicable diseases at the national, regional and international levels are not commensurate with the magnitude of the problem;

41. Recognize the importance of strengthening local, provincial, national and regional capacities to address and effectively combat non-communicable diseases, particularly in developing countries, and that this may entail increased and sustained human, financial and technical resources;

42. Acknowledge the need to put forward a multisectoral approach for health at all government levels, to address non-communicable disease risk factors and underlying determinants of health comprehensively and decisively;

Non-communicable diseases can be prevented and their impacts significantly reduced, with millions of lives saved and untold suffering avoided. We therefore commit to:

Reduce risk factors and create health-promoting environments

43. Advance the implementation of multisectoral, cost-effective, population-wide interventions in order to reduce the impact of the common non-communicable disease risk factors, namely tobacco use, unhealthy diet, physical inactivity and harmful use of alcohol, through the implementation of relevant international agreements and strategies, and education, legislative, regulatory and fiscal measures, without prejudice to the right of sovereign nations to determine and establish their taxation policies and other policies, where appropriate, by involving all relevant sectors, civil society and communities, as appropriate, and by taking the following actions:

(*a*) Encourage the development of multisectoral public policies that create equitable health-promoting environments that empower individuals, families and communities to make healthy choices and lead healthy lives;

(*b*) Develop, strengthen and implement, as appropriate, multisectoral public policies and action plans to promote health education and health literacy, including through evidence-based education and information strategies and programmes in and out of schools and through public awareness campaigns, as important factors in furthering the prevention and control of non-communicable diseases, recognizing that a strong focus on health literacy is at an early stage in many countries;

(*c*) Accelerate implementation by States parties of the World Health Organization Framework Convention on Tobacco Control, recognizing the full range of measures, including measures to reduce consumption and availability, and encourage countries that have not yet done so to consider acceding to the Convention, recognizing that substantially reducing tobacco consumption is an important contribution to reducing non-communicable diseases and can have considerable health benefits for individuals and countries and that price and tax measures are an effective and important means of reducing tobacco consumption;

(*d*) Advance the implementation of the Global Strategy on Diet, Physical Activity and Health, including, where appropriate, through the introduction of policies and actions aimed at promoting healthy diets and increasing physical activity in the entire population, including in all aspects of daily living, such as giving priority to regular and intense physical education classes in schools, urban planning and re-engineering for active transport, the provision of incentives for work-site healthy-lifestyle programmes, and increased availability of safe environments in public parks and recreational spaces to encourage physical activity;

(*e*) Promote the implementation of the Global Strategy to Reduce the Harmful Use of Alcohol, while recognizing the need to develop appropriate domestic action plans, in consultation with relevant stakeholders, for developing specific policies and programmes, including taking into account the full range of options as identified in the Global Strategy, as well as raise awareness of the problems caused by the harmful use of alcohol, particularly among young people, and call upon the World Health Organization to intensify efforts to assist Member States in this regard;

(*f*) Promote the implementation of the World Health Organization Set of Recommendations on the Marketing of Foods and Non-alcoholic Beverages to Children, including foods that are high in saturated fats, trans-fatty acids, free sugars or salt, recognizing that research shows that food advertising geared to children is extensive, that a significant amount of the marketing is for foods with a high content of fat, sugar or salt and that television advertising influences children's food preferences, purchase requests and consumption patterns, while taking into account existing legislation and national policies, as appropriate;

(*g*) Promote the development and initiate the implementation, as appropriate, of cost-effective interventions to reduce salt, sugar and saturated fats and eliminate industrially produced trans-fats in foods, including through discouraging the production and marketing of foods that contribute to unhealthy diet, while taking into account existing legislation and policies;

(*h*) Encourage policies that support the production and manufacture of, and facilitate access to, foods that contribute to healthy diet, and provide greater opportunities for utilization of healthy local agricultural products and foods, thus contributing to efforts to cope with the challenges and take advantage of the opportunities posed by globalization and to achieve food security;

(i) Promote, protect and support breastfeeding, including exclusive breastfeeding for about six months from birth, as appropriate, as breastfeeding reduces susceptibility to infections and the risk of undernutrition, promotes the growth and development of infants and young children and helps to reduce the risk of developing conditions such as obesity and non-communicable diseases later in life, and in this regard strengthen the implementation of the International Code of Marketing of Breast-milk Substitutes and subsequent relevant World Health Assembly resolutions;

(j) Promote increased access to cost-effective vaccinations to prevent infections associated with cancers, as part of national immunization schedules;

(k) Promote increased access to cost-effective cancer screening programmes, as determined by national situations;

(l) Scale up, where appropriate, a package of proven, effective interventions, such as health promotion and primary prevention approaches, and galvanize actions for the prevention and control of non-communicable diseases through a meaningful multisectoral response, addressing risk factors and determinants of health;

44. With a view to strengthening its contribution to non-communicable disease prevention and control, call upon the private sector, where appropriate, to:

(a) Take measures to implement the World Health Organization set of recommendations to reduce the impact of the marketing of unhealthy foods and non-alcoholic beverages to children, while taking into account existing national legislation and policies;

(b) Consider producing and promoting more food products consistent with a healthy diet, including by reformulating products to provide healthier options that are affordable and accessible and that follow relevant nutrition facts and labelling standards, including information on sugars, salt and fats and, where appropriate, trans-fat content;

(c) Promote and create an enabling environment for healthy behaviours among workers, including by establishing tobacco-free workplaces and safe and healthy working environments through occupational safety and health measures, including, where appropriate, through good corporate practices, workplace wellness programmes and health insurance plans;

(d) Work towards reducing the use of salt in the food industry in order to lower sodium consumption;

(e) Contribute to efforts to improve access to and affordability of medicines and technologies in the prevention and control of non-communicable diseases;

Strengthen national policies and health systems

45. Promote, establish or support and strengthen, by 2013, as appropriate, multisectoral national policies and plans for the prevention and control of non-communicable diseases, taking into account, as appropriate, the 2008–2013 Action Plan for the Global Strategy for the Prevention and Control of Non-communicable Diseases and the objectives contained therein, and take steps to implement such policies and plans:

(a) Strengthen and integrate, as appropriate, non-communicable disease policies and programmes into health-planning processes and the national development agenda of each Member State;

(b) Pursue, as appropriate, comprehensive strengthening of health systems that support primary health care and deliver effective, sustainable and coordinated responses and evidence-based, cost-effective, equitable and integrated essential services for addressing non-communicable disease risk factors and for the prevention, treatment and care of non-communicable diseases, acknowledging the importance of promoting patient empowerment, rehabilitation and palliative care for persons with non-communicable diseases and of a life course approach, given the often chronic nature of non-communicable diseases;

(c) According to national priorities, and taking into account domestic circumstances, increase and prioritize budgetary allocations for addressing non-communicable disease risk factors and for surveillance, prevention, early detection and treatment of non-communicable diseases and the related care and support, including palliative care;

(d) Explore the provision of adequate, predictable and sustained resources, through domestic, bilateral, regional and multilateral channels, including traditional and voluntary innovative financing mechanisms;

(e) Pursue and promote gender-based approaches for the prevention and control of non-communicable diseases founded on data disaggregated by sex and age in an effort to address the critical differences in the risks of morbidity and mortality from non-communicable diseases for women and men;

(f) Promote multisectoral and multi-stakeholder engagement in order to reverse, stop and decrease the rising trends of obesity in child, youth and adult populations, respectively;

(g) Recognize where health disparities exist between indigenous peoples and non-indigenous populations in the incidence of non-communicable diseases and their common risk factors, and that these disparities are often linked to historical, economic and social factors, and encourage the involvement of indigenous peoples and communities in the development, implementation and evaluation of non-communicable disease prevention and control policies, plans and programmes, where appropriate, while promoting the development and strengthening of capacities at various levels and recognizing the cultural heritage and traditional knowledge of indigenous peoples and respecting, preserving and promoting, as appropriate, their traditional medicine, including conservation of their vital medicinal plants, animals and minerals;

(h) Recognize further the potential and contribution of traditional and local knowledge, and in this regard respect and preserve, in accordance with national capacities, priorities, relevant legislation and circumstances, the knowledge and safe and effective use of traditional medicine, treatments and practices, appropriately based on the circumstances in each country;

(i) Pursue all necessary efforts to strengthen nationally driven, sustainable, cost-effective and comprehensive responses in all sectors for the prevention of non-communicable diseases, with the full and active participation of people living with these diseases, civil society and the private sector, where appropriate;

(j) Promote the production, training and retention of health workers with a view to facilitating adequate deployment of a skilled health workforce within countries and regions, in accordance with the World Health Organization

Global Code of Practice on the International Recruitment of Health Personnel;

(k) Strengthen, as appropriate, information systems for health planning and management, including through the collection, disaggregation, analysis, interpretation and dissemination of data and the development of population-based national registries and surveys, where appropriate, to facilitate appropriate and timely interventions for the entire population;

(l) According to national priorities, give greater priority to surveillance, early detection, screening, diagnosis and treatment of non-communicable diseases and prevention and control, and to improving accessibility to safe, affordable, effective and quality medicines and technologies to diagnose and to treat them; provide sustainable access to medicines and technologies, including through the development and use of evidence-based guidelines for the treatment of non-communicable diseases, and efficient procurement and distribution of medicines in countries; and strengthen viable financing options and promote the use of affordable medicines, including generics, as well as improved access to preventive, curative, palliative and rehabilitative services, particularly at the community level;

(m) According to country-led prioritization, ensure the scaling-up of effective, evidence-based and cost-effective interventions that demonstrate the potential to treat individuals with non-communicable diseases, protect those at high risk of developing them and reduce risk across populations;

(n) Recognize the importance of universal coverage in national health systems, especially through primary health care and social protection mechanisms, to provide access to health services for all, in particular for the poorest segments of the population;

(o) Promote the inclusion of non-communicable disease prevention and control within sexual and reproductive health and maternal and child health programmes, especially at the primary health-care level, as well as other programmes, as appropriate, and also integrate interventions in these areas into non-communicable disease prevention programmes;

(p) Promote access to comprehensive and cost-effective prevention, treatment and care for the integrated management of non-communicable diseases, including, inter alia, increased access to affordable, safe, effective and quality medicines and diagnostics and other technologies, including through the full use of trade-related aspects of intellectual property rights (TRIPS) flexibilities;

(q) Improve diagnostic services, including by increasing the capacity of and access to laboratory and imaging services with adequate and skilled manpower to deliver such services, and collaborate with the private sector to improve affordability, accessibility and maintenance of diagnostic equipment and technologies;

(r) Encourage alliances and networks that bring together national, regional and global actors, including academic and research institutes, for the development of new medicines, vaccines, diagnostics and technologies, learning from experiences in the field of HIV/AIDS, among others, according to national priorities and strategies;

(s) Strengthen health-care infrastructure, including for procurement, storage and distribution of medicine, in particular transportation and storage networks to facilitate efficient service delivery;

International cooperation, including collaborative partnerships

46. Strengthen international cooperation in support of national, regional and global plans for the prevention and control of non-communicable diseases, inter alia, through the exchange of best practices in the areas of health promotion, legislation, regulation and health systems strengthening, training of health personnel, development of appropriate health-care infrastructure and diagnostics, and by promoting the development and dissemination of appropriate, affordable and sustainable transfer of technology on mutually agreed terms and the production of affordable, safe, effective and quality medicines and vaccines, while recognizing the leading role of the World Health Organization as the primary specialized agency for health in that regard;

47. Acknowledge the contribution of aid targeted at the health sector, while recognizing that much more needs to be done. We call for the fulfilment of all official development assistance-related commitments, including the commitments by many developed countries to achieve the target of 0.7 per cent of gross national income for official development assistance by 2015, as well as the commitments contained in the Programme of Action for the Least Developed Countries for the Decade 2011–2020, and strongly urge those developed countries that have not yet done so to make additional concrete efforts to fulfil their commitments;

48. Stress the importance of North-South, South-South and triangular cooperation, in the prevention and control of non-communicable diseases, to promote at the national, regional and international levels an enabling environment to facilitate healthy lifestyles and choices, bearing in mind that South-South cooperation is not a substitute for, but rather a complement to, North-South cooperation;

49. Promote all possible means to identify and mobilize adequate, predictable and sustained financial resources and the necessary human and technical resources, and to consider support for voluntary, cost-effective, innovative approaches for a long- term financing of non-communicable disease prevention and control, taking into account the Millennium Development Goals;

50. Acknowledge the contribution of international cooperation and assistance in the prevention and control of non-communicable diseases, and in this regard encourage the continued inclusion of non-communicable diseases in development cooperation agendas and initiatives;

51. Call upon the World Health Organization, as the lead United Nations specialized agency for health, and all other relevant United Nations system agencies, funds and programmes, the international financial institutions, development banks and other key international organizations to work together in a coordinated manner to support national efforts to prevent and control non-communicable diseases and mitigate their impacts;

52. Urge relevant international organizations to continue to provide technical assistance and capacity-building to developing countries, especially to the least developed countries, in the areas of non-communicable disease prevention and control and promotion of access to medicines for all, including through the full use of trade-related aspects of intellectual property rights flexibilities and provisions;

53. Enhance the quality of aid by strengthening national ownership, alignment, harmonization, predictability, mutual accountability and transparency, and results orientation;

54. Engage non-health actors and key stakeholders, where appropriate, including the private sector and civil society, in collaborative partnerships to promote health and to reduce non-communicable disease risk factors, including through building community capacity in promoting healthy diets and lifestyles;

55. Foster partnerships between government and civil society, building on the contribution of health-related non-governmental organizations and patients' organizations, to support, as appropriate, the provision of services for the prevention and control, treatment and care, including palliative care, of non-communicable diseases;

56. Promote the capacity-building of non-communicable-disease-related non-governmental organizations at the national and regional levels, in order to realize their full potential as partners in the prevention and control of non-communicable diseases;

Research and development

57. Promote actively national and international investments and strengthen national capacity for quality research and development, for all aspects related to the prevention and control of non-communicable diseases, in a sustainable and cost-effective manner, while noting the importance of continuing to incentivize innovation;

58. Promote the use of information and communications technology to improve programme implementation, health outcomes, health promotion, and reporting and surveillance systems and to disseminate, as appropriate, information on affordable, cost-effective, sustainable and quality interventions, best practices and lessons learned in the field of non-communicable diseases;

59. Support and facilitate non-communicable-disease-related research, and its translation, to enhance the knowledge base for ongoing national, regional and global action;

Monitoring and evaluation

60. Strengthen, as appropriate, country-level surveillance and monitoring systems, including surveys that are integrated into existing national health information systems and include monitoring exposure to risk factors, outcomes, social and economic determinants of health, and health system responses, recognizing that such systems are critical in appropriately addressing non-communicable diseases;

61. Call upon the World Health Organization, with the full participation of Member States, informed by their national situations, through its existing structures, and in collaboration with United Nations agencies, funds and programmes and other relevant regional and international organizations, as appropriate, building on continuing efforts to develop, before the end of 2012, a comprehensive global monitoring framework, including a set of indicators, capable of application across regional and country settings, including through multisectoral approaches, to monitor trends and to assess progress made in the implementation of national strategies and plans on non-communicable diseases;

62. Call upon the World Health Organization, in collaboration with Member States through the governing bodies of the World Health Organization, and in collaboration with United Nations agencies, funds and programmes, and other relevant regional and international organizations, as appropriate, building on the work already under way, to prepare recommendations for a set of voluntary global targets for the prevention and control of non-communicable diseases, before the end of 2012;

63. Consider the development of national targets and indicators based on national situations, building on guidance provided by the World Health Organization, to focus on efforts to address the impacts of non-communicable diseases and to assess the progress made in the prevention and control of non-communicable diseases and their risk factors and determinants;

Follow-up

64. Request the Secretary-General, in close collaboration with the Director General of the World Health Organization, and in consultation with Member States, United Nations funds and programmes and other relevant international organizations, to submit by the end of 2012 to the General Assembly, at its sixty-seventh session, for consideration by Member States, options for strengthening and facilitating multisectoral action for the prevention and control of non-communicable diseases through effective partnership;

65. Request the Secretary-General, in collaboration with Member States, the World Health Organization and relevant funds, programmes and specialized agencies of the United Nations system to present to the General Assembly at its sixty-eighth session a report on the progress achieved in realizing the commitments made in this Political Declaration, including on the progress of multisectoral action, and the impact on the achievement of the internationally agreed development goals, including the Millennium Development Goals, in preparation for a comprehensive review and assessment in 2014 of the progress achieved in the prevention and control of non-communicable diseases.

Tobacco

The World Health Organization Framework Convention on Tobacco Control, adopted by the World Health Assembly in 2003 [YUN 2003, p. 1251], entered into force in 2005. At the end of 2011, 173 States and the European Union were parties to the Convention.

WHO issued its *Report on the Global Tobacco Epidemic, 2011*, the third in a series of WHO reports that tracked the status of the tobacco epidemic and the impact of interventions implemented to stop it. The report established that tobacco use remained the leading cause of preventable death, killing nearly 6 million people and causing hundreds of billions of dollars in economic damage globally each year. The burden was particularly felt in low- and middle-income countries. It was projected that by 2030, 80 per cent of the estimated 8 million tobacco-related deaths per year would occur in such countries. The report emphasized the need for action and highlighted the impact of the so-called MPOWER measures—a package of six tobacco control measures introduced in 2008 and corresponding to one or more articles of the WHO Framework Convention—designed to assist countries in the implementation of effective intervention to reduce the demand for tobacco. On tobacco product packaging, the report stated that many countries could easily improve policies by increasing the size of warning labels, making warnings more specific, and including pictures rather than only text, to increase smokers' awareness of health risks—all at virtually no cost to Governments.

The report also provided, for the first time, systematically collected information about anti-tobacco mass media campaigns, which had proved to be a highly effective method of warning the public about the dangers of tobacco. The data revealed that more than 1 billion people lived in countries with legislation that required large graphic health warnings on every cigarette pack sold, and 1.9 billion people lived in the 23 countries that had aired high-quality national anti-tobacco mass media campaigns within the previous two years. While substantial progress had been made, the tobacco epidemic continued to expand because of ongoing tobacco industry marketing, population growth in countries where tobacco use was increasing, and the extreme addictiveness of tobacco. Tobacco control measures were among the core components of the outcome document of the UN High-level Meeting on Non-communicable Diseases (see p. 1146).

Malaria
Roll Back Malaria initiative

At its resumed sixty-fifth session (2011), the General Assembly had before it the WHO report [A/65/210] entitled "2001–2010: Decade to Roll Back Malaria in Developing Countries, Particularly in Africa" [YUN 2010, p. 1227].

GENERAL ASSEMBLY ACTION

On 18 April [meeting 86], the General Assembly adopted **resolution 65/273** [draft: A/65/L.70 & Add.1, as orally revised] without vote [agenda item 12].

Consolidating gains and accelerating efforts to control and eliminate malaria in developing countries, particularly in Africa, by 2015

The General Assembly,

Recalling that the period 2001–2010 was proclaimed the Decade to Roll Back Malaria in Developing Countries, Particularly in Africa, by the General Assembly, and that combating HIV/AIDS, malaria, tuberculosis and other diseases is included in the internationally agreed development goals, including the Millennium Development Goals,

Recalling also the malaria-related goals and commitments in the outcome document of the High-level Plenary Meeting of the General Assembly on the Millennium Development Goals,

Recalling further its resolution 64/79 of 7 December 2009 and all previous resolutions concerning the struggle against malaria in developing countries, particularly in Africa,

Recalling resolution 60.18, adopted by the World Health Assembly on 23 May 2007, urging a broad range of national and international actions to scale up malaria control programmes, and resolution 61.18 of 24 May 2008 on monitoring of the achievement of health-related Millennium Development Goals,

Bearing in mind the relevant resolutions of the Economic and Social Council relating to the struggle against malaria and diarrhoeal diseases, in particular resolution 1998/36 of 30 July 1998,

Taking note of all declarations and decisions on health issues, in particular those related to malaria, adopted by the Organization of African Unity and the African Union, including the Abuja call for accelerated action towards universal access to HIV and AIDS, tuberculosis and malaria services in Africa, issued by the Heads of State and Government of the African Union at the special summit of the African Union on HIV and AIDS, tuberculosis and malaria, held in Abuja from 2 to 4 May 2006, and taking note of the decision adopted by the Assembly of the African Union at its fifteenth ordinary session, held in Kampala from 25 to 27 July 2010, to extend the Abuja call to 2015 to coincide with the Millennium Development Goals,

Welcoming the leadership provided by the African Leaders Malaria Alliance and the continued commitment to help to achieve the 2015 targets, and encouraging them to continue to provide political leadership at the highest level in the fight against malaria in Africa,

Welcoming also the Secretary-General's Global Strategy for Women's and Children's Health, undertaken by a broad coalition of partners, in support of national plans and strategies, in order to significantly reduce the number of maternal, newborn and under-five child deaths as a matter of immediate concern by scaling up a priority package of high-impact interventions and integrating efforts in sectors such as health, education, gender equality, water and sanitation, poverty reduction and nutrition,

Recognizing the linkages in efforts being made to reach the targets set at the Extraordinary Summit of Heads of State and Government of the Organization of African Unity, held in Abuja on 24 and 25 April 2000, as necessary and important for the attainment of the "Roll Back Malaria" goal and the targets of the Millennium Development Goals by 2010 and 2015, respectively, and welcoming in this regard the commitment of Member States to respond to the specific needs of Africa,

Recognizing also that malaria-related ill health and deaths throughout the world can be substantially reduced with political commitment and commensurate resources if the public is educated and sensitized about malaria and appropriate health services are made available, particularly in countries where the disease is endemic,

Recognizing further that malaria control interventions have a positive impact on overall child and maternal mortality rates and could help African countries to reach Millennium Development Goals 4 and 5 of reducing child mortality and improving maternal health, respectively, by 2015,

Acknowledging the progress made in parts of Africa in reversing the high burden of malaria through political engagement and sustainable national malaria control programmes, as well as the progress being made towards achieving by 2015 the goals concerning malaria control set by the World Health Assembly and the Roll Back Malaria Partnership,

Recognizing that, despite the fact that increased global and national investments in malaria control have yielded significant results in decreasing the burden of malaria in many countries, and that some countries are moving towards elimination of malaria, many countries continue to have unacceptably high burdens of malaria and in order to reach internationally agreed development goals, including the health-related Millennium Development Goals, must rapidly increase malaria prevention and control efforts, which rely heavily on medicines and insecticides whose utility is continuously threatened by the development of resistance in humans to antimalarial agents, as well as resistance of mosquitoes to insecticides,

Recognizing also the challenges relating to counterfeit and substandard medicines, as well as poor malaria microscopy services,

Expressing concern about the continued morbidity, mortality and debility attributed to malaria, and recalling that more efforts are needed if the Abuja malaria targets and the malaria and Millennium Development Goal targets for 2015 are to be reached on time,

Emphasizing the importance of strengthening health systems to effectively sustain malaria control and elimination,

Commending the efforts of the World Health Organization, the United Nations Children's Fund, the Roll Back Malaria Partnership, the Global Fund to Fight AIDS, Tuberculosis and Malaria, the World Bank and other partners to fight malaria over the years,

Taking note with appreciation of the Global Malaria Action Plan developed by the Roll Back Malaria Partnership,

1. *Welcomes* the report prepared by the World Health Organization, and calls for support for the recommendations contained therein;

2. *Encourages* Member States, relevant organizations of the United Nations system, international institutions, non-governmental organizations, the private sector and civil society to continue to observe World Malaria Day in order to raise public awareness of and knowledge about the prevention, control and treatment of malaria as well as the importance of meeting the Millennium Development Goals, and stresses the importance of engaging local communities in this regard;

3. *Encourages* the Special Envoy of the Secretary-General for Malaria to continue raising the issue in collaboration with other United Nations organizations already working on those issues on the international political and development agendas and to work with national and global leaders to help to secure the political will, the partnerships and the funds to drastically reduce malaria deaths by 2015 through increased access to prevention, diagnosis and treatment, especially in Africa;

4. *Welcomes* the increased funding for malaria interventions and for research and development of preventive, diagnostic and control tools from the international community, through funding from multilateral and bilateral sources and from the private sector, as well as by making predictable financing available through appropriate and effective aid modalities and in-country health financing mechanisms aligned with national priorities, which are key to strengthening health systems, including malaria surveillance, and promoting universal and equitable access to high-quality malaria prevention, diagnostic and treatment services, and notes in this regard that a high level of external assistance per person at risk for malaria is associated with a decrease in the incidence of the disease;

5. *Urges* the international community, together with United Nations agencies and private organizations and foundations, to support the implementation of the Global Malaria Action Plan, including through support for programmes and activities at the country level in order to achieve internationally agreed targets on malaria;

6. *Calls upon* the international community to continue to support the secretariat of the Roll Back Malaria Partnership and partner organizations, including the World Health Organization, the World Bank and the United Nations Children's Fund, as vital complementary sources of support for the efforts of malaria-endemic countries to combat the disease;

7. *Appeals* to the international community to work in a spirit of cooperation towards effective, increased, harmonized, predictable and sustained bilateral and multilateral assistance to combat malaria, including support for the Global Fund to Fight AIDS, Tuberculosis and Malaria, in order to assist States, in particular malaria-endemic countries, to implement sound national health and sanitation plans, including malaria control strategies and integrated management of childhood illnesses, in a sustained and equitable way that, inter alia, contributes to strengthening health system development approaches at the district level;

8. *Appeals* to the malaria partners to resolve the financial supply chain and delivery bottlenecks that are responsible for stock-outs of long-lasting insecticide-treated nets, rapid diagnostic tests and artemisinin-based combination therapies at the national level, whenever they occur, including through the strengthening of malaria programme management at the country level;

9. *Welcomes* the contribution to the mobilization of additional and predictable resources for development by voluntary innovative financing initiatives taken by groups of Member States, and in this regard notes the International Drug Purchase Facility, UNITAID, the International Finance Facility for Immunization, the advance market commitments for vaccines, the Global Alliance for Vaccines and Immunization and phase one of the Affordable Medicines Facility for Malaria, and takes note of the work of the Leading Group on Innovative Financing for Development and its special task force on innovative financing for health which was set up recently;

10. *Urges* malaria-endemic countries to work towards financial sustainability, to increase, to the extent possible, domestic resource allocation to malaria control and to create favourable conditions for working with the private sector in order to improve access to good-quality malaria services;

11. *Urges* Member States to assess and respond to the needs for integrated human resources at all levels of the health system, in order to achieve the targets of the Abuja Declaration on Roll Back Malaria in Africa and the internationally agreed development goals, including the Millennium Development Goals, to take actions, as appropriate, to effectively govern the recruitment, training and retention of skilled health personnel, and to give particular focus to the availability of skilled personnel at all levels to meet technical and operational needs as increased funding for malaria control programmes becomes available;

12. *Calls upon* the international community, inter alia, by helping to meet the financial needs of the Global Fund to Fight AIDS, Tuberculosis and Malaria and through country-led initiatives with adequate international support, to intensify access to affordable, safe and effective antimalarial combination treatments, intermittent preventive treatment in pregnancies, adequate diagnostic facilities, long-lasting insecticide-treated mosquito nets, including, where appropriate, through the free distribution of such nets and, where appropriate, to insecticides for indoor residual spraying for malaria control, taking into account relevant international rules, including the Stockholm Convention on Persistent Organic Pollutants standards and guidelines;

13. *Requests* relevant international organizations, in particular the World Health Organization and the United Nations Children's Fund, to assist efforts of national Governments to provide universal access to malaria control interventions to address all at-risk populations, in particular young children and pregnant women, in malaria-endemic countries, particularly in Africa, as rapidly as possible, with due regard to ensuring proper use of those interventions, including long-lasting insecticide nets, and sustainability through full community participation and implementation through the health system;

14. *Calls upon* Member States, in particular malaria-endemic countries, with the support of the international community, to establish and/or strengthen national policies and operational plans, with a view to scaling up efforts to achieve internationally agreed malaria targets for 2015, in accordance with the technical recommendations of the World Health Organization;

15. *Commends* those African countries that have implemented the recommendations of the Abuja Summit in 2000 to reduce or waive taxes and tariffs for nets and other products needed for malaria control, and encourages other countries to do the same;

16. *Calls upon* United Nations agencies and their partners to continue to provide the technical support necessary to build and enhance the capacity of Member States to implement the Global Malaria Action Plan and meet the internationally agreed goals, including the Millennium Development Goals;

17. *Expresses its concern* about the increase in resistant strains of malaria in several regions of the world, and calls upon Member States, with support from the World Health Organization and other partners, to implement the Organization's Global Plan for Artemisinin Resistance Containment to strengthen and implement surveillance systems for drug and insecticide resistance, and upon the World Health Organization to coordinate a global network for the monitoring of drug and insecticide resistance and ensure that drug and insecticide testing is fully operational in order to enhance the use of current insecticide- and artemisinin-based combination therapies, and stresses that the data gathered should be utilized for further research and development of safe and effective therapies;

18. *Urges* all Member States to prohibit the marketing and use of oral artemisinin-based monotherapies and to replace them with oral artemisinin-based combination therapies, as recommended by the World Health Organization, and to develop the necessary financial, legislative and regulatory mechanisms in order to introduce artemisinin combination therapies at affordable prices in both public and private facilities;

19. *Recognizes* the importance of the development of safe and cost-effective vaccines and new medicines to prevent and treat malaria and the need for further and accelerated research, including into safe, effective and high-quality therapies, using rigorous standards, including by providing support to the Special Programme for Research and Training in Tropical Diseases and through effective global partnerships, such as the various malaria vaccine initiatives and the Medicines for Malaria Venture, where necessary stimulated by new incentives to secure their development and through effective and timely support towards prequalification of new antimalarials and their combinations;

20. *Calls upon* the international community, including through existing partnerships, to increase investment in and efforts towards research to optimize current tools, develop and validate new, safe and affordable malaria-related medicines, products and technologies, such as vaccines, rapid diagnostic tests, insecticides and delivery modes, to prevent and treat malaria, especially for at-risk children and pregnant women, and testing opportunities for integration in order to enhance effectiveness and delay the onset of resistance;

21. *Calls upon* malaria-endemic countries to assure favourable conditions for research institutions, including allocation of adequate resources and development of national policies and legal frameworks, where appropriate, with a view to, inter alia, informing policy formulation and strategic interventions on malaria;

22. *Reaffirms* the right to use, to the fullest extent, the provisions contained in the World Trade Organization Agreement on Trade-Related Aspects of Intellectual Property Rights (TRIPS Agreement), the Doha Declaration on the TRIPS Agreement and Public Health, the decision of the General Council of the World Trade Organization of 30 August 2003 on the implementation of paragraph 6 of the Doha Declaration on the TRIPS Agreement and Public Health, and, when formal acceptance procedures are completed, the amendment to article 31 of the Agreement, which provide flexibilities for the protection of public health, and in particular to promote access to medicines for all and to encourage the provision of assistance to developing countries in this regard, and calls for broad and timely acceptance of the amendment to article 31 of the Agreement, as proposed by the General Council of the World Trade Organization in its decision of 6 December 2005;

23. *Calls upon* the international community to support ways to expand access to affordable and safe products and treatments, such as vector control measures, including indoor residual spraying, long-lasting insecticide-treated

nets, including through the free distribution of such nets, adequate diagnostic facilities, intermittent preventive treatment in pregnancies and artemisinin-based combination therapy for populations at risk of falciparum malaria infection in endemic countries, particularly in Africa, including through additional funds and innovative mechanisms, inter alia, for the financing and scaling up of artemisinin production and procurement, as appropriate, to meet the increased need;

24. *Welcomes* the increased level of public-private partnerships for malaria control and prevention, including the financial and in-kind contributions of private sector partners and companies operating in Africa, as well as the increased engagement of non-governmental service providers;

25. *Encourages* the producers of long-lasting insecticide-treated nets to accelerate technology transfer to developing countries, and invites the World Bank and regional development funds to consider supporting malaria-endemic countries in establishing factories to scale up production of long-lasting insecticide-treated nets;

26. *Calls upon* Member States and the international community, including malaria-endemic countries, in accordance with existing guidelines and recommendations of the World Health Organization and the requirements of the Stockholm Convention related to the use of DDT, to become fully knowledgeable about the Organization's technical policies and strategies and the provisions in the Stockholm Convention, including for indoor residual spraying, long-lasting insecticide-treated nets and case management, intermittent preventive treatment for pregnant women and monitoring of in vivo resistance studies to artemisinin-based combination therapy treatment, as well as to increase capacity for the safe, effective and judicious use of indoor residual spraying and other forms of vector control, including quality control measures, in accordance with international rules, standards and guidelines;

27. *Requests* the World Health Organization, the United Nations Children's Fund and donor agencies to provide support to those countries which choose to use DDT for indoor residual spraying so as to ensure that it is implemented in accordance with international rules, standards and guidelines, and to provide all possible support to malaria-endemic countries to manage the intervention effectively and prevent the contamination, in particular, of agricultural products with DDT and other insecticides used for indoor residual spraying;

28. *Encourages* the World Health Organization and its member States, with the support of the parties to the Stockholm Convention, to continue to explore possible alternatives to DDT as a vector control agent;

29. *Calls upon* malaria-endemic countries to encourage regional and intersectoral collaboration, both public and private, at all levels, especially in education, health, agriculture, economic development and the environment, to advance malaria control objectives;

30. *Calls upon* the international community to support the strengthening of health systems, national pharmaceutical policies and national drug regulatory authorities, to monitor and fight against the trade in counterfeit and substandard antimalarial medicines and prevent their distribution and use, and to support coordinated efforts, inter alia, by providing technical assistance to improve surveillance, monitoring and evaluation systems and their alignment with national plans and systems so as to better track and report changes in coverage, the need for scaling up recommended interventions and the subsequent reductions in the burden of malaria;

31. *Urges* Member States, the international community and all relevant actors, including the private sector, to promote the coordinated implementation and enhance the quality of malaria-related activities, including via the Roll Back Malaria Partnership, in accordance with national policies and operational plans that are consistent with the technical recommendations of the World Health Organization and recent efforts and initiatives, including, where appropriate, the Paris Declaration on Aid Effectiveness and the Accra Agenda for Action, adopted during the Third High-level Forum on Aid Effectiveness, held in Accra from 2 to 4 September 2008;

32. *Requests* the Secretary-General, in close collaboration with the Director-General of the World Health Organization and in consultation with Member States, to report to the General Assembly at its sixty-sixth session on implementation of the present resolution, and specifically on progress towards achieving the 2015 targets of the Abuja Declaration and those of the Global Malaria Action Plan and Millennium Development Goal 6, including identification of best practices and successes, as well as specific challenges limiting the achievement of the targets, and, taking these into account, to provide recommendations to ensure that the targets are reached by 2015.

Report of Secretary-General. In July, pursuant to General Assembly resolution 65/273 (p. 1153), the Secretary-General transmitted a WHO report [A/66/169] on controlling and eliminating malaria in developing countries, particularly in Africa, by 2015, which highlighted progress made in achieving the goals set by that resolution. In June, revised objectives, targets and priorities of the Global Malaria Action Plan—created by the Roll Back Malaria Partnership—were released. International funding for malaria control had risen steeply in the previous decade with disbursements reaching their highest-ever levels in 2009 at $1.5 billion, but new financial commitments appeared to have stagnated thereafter. Between 2008 and the end of 2010, approximately 289 million long-lasting insecticide-treated nets were delivered to sub-Saharan Africa, enough to cover 76 per cent of the 765 million persons at risk of malaria. It was estimated that 42 per cent of households in Africa owned at least one insecticide-treated net in mid-2010, and that 35 per cent of children slept under such a net. The percentage of children using insecticide-treated nets was, however, still below the World Health Assembly target of 80 per cent. Since the lifespan of a long-lasting net was estimated to be three years, nets delivered in 2006 and 2007 were due for replacement, and those delivered between 2008 and 2010 would be soon. Failure to replace those nets could lead to a resurgence of malaria cases and deaths. Indoor residual spraying programmes had also expanded in recent years, with the number of people protected in sub-Saharan Africa increasing from 13 million in 2005 to 75 million in 2009, corresponding to protection for approximately 10 per cent of the at-risk population in 2009.

Two challenges were parasite resistance to antimalarial medicines and mosquito resistance to insecticides. One of the factors contributing to parasite resistance was the use of artemisinin-based monotherapies—which WHO had appealed to halt—instead of artemisinin-based combination therapies. In early 2011, WHO and the Roll Back Malaria Partnership released the Global Plan for Artemisinin Resistance Containment, whose objective was to preserve artemisinin-based combination therapies as an effective treatment for falciparum malaria.

The report concluded with recommendations for the consideration of the Assembly, including disbursing to malaria-endemic countries adequate financial resources, strengthening health systems capable of delivering vector-control interventions, and developing routine surveillance systems for malaria and for parasite and mosquito resistance.

Global public health

The sixty-fourth session of the World Health Assembly (Geneva, 16–24 May) [WHA64/2011/REC/1] discussed topics such as child health, chronic diseases, malaria and maternal health, as well as the WHO programme budget, and administration and management matters. Resolutions adopted by the Assembly concerned the implementation of the International Health Regulations, WHO reform, budgetary and administrative questions, health conditions in the Occupied Palestinian Territory, pandemic influenza preparedness, the strengthening of the health workforce, nursing and midwifery, national health policies and strategies, and national disaster management. The Assembly also adopted resolutions on preparations for the High-level Meeting on the Prevention and Control of Non-communicable Diseases (see p. 1146), the WHO role in achieving the Millennium Development Goals, perinatal and neonatal mortality, malaria and dracunculiasis.

Global health and foreign policy

In October, pursuant to General Assembly resolution 65/95 [YUN 2010, p. 1231], the Secretary-General transmitted a report [A/66/497] by the WHO Director-General on global health and foreign policy. The report described efforts taken by the international community to improve the coordination, coherence and effectiveness of governance for global health; explored the extent to which governance and the priority-setting of non-health sectors supported global health; and presented examples of how Governments and the multilateral system were working with a number of sectors to address health issues in order to attain better health outcomes. The conclusions acknowledged the continuing need for the foreign policy community to address global health issues, the need for greater and more in-depth understanding of that relationship and the importance of coherence between health and foreign policies within Member States in order to implement international accords.

GENERAL ASSEMBLY ACTION

On 12 December [meeting 83], the General Assembly adopted **resolution 66/115** [draft: A/66/L.24 & Add.1] without vote [agenda item 126].

Global health and foreign policy

The General Assembly,

Recalling its resolutions 63/33 of 26 November 2008, 64/108 of 10 December 2009 and 65/95 of 9 December 2010,

Recalling also the outcomes of the major United Nations conferences and summits in the economic, social and related fields, especially those related to global health,

Reaffirming the commitment to the achievement of all the Millennium Development Goals, in particular Goals 4, 5 and 6, as expressed in the outcome document of the High-level Plenary Meeting of the General Assembly on the Millennium Development Goals entitled "Keeping the promise: united to achieve the Millennium Development Goals", and in this regard welcoming the report of the Commission on Information and Accountability for Women's and Children's Health,

Welcoming the Political Declaration on HIV and AIDS: Intensifying Our Efforts to Eliminate HIV and AIDS, the outcome of the High-level Meeting of the General Assembly on HIV and AIDS, held in New York, from 8 to 10 June 2011, and reaffirming the political will to effectively implement the commitments contained therein,

Welcoming also the Political Declaration of the High-level Meeting of the General Assembly on the Prevention and Control of Non-communicable Diseases, adopted by the General Assembly on 19 September 2011, and reaffirming the political will to effectively implement the commitments contained therein,

Welcoming further the Rio Political Declaration on Social Determinants of Health, adopted at the World Conference on Social Determinants of Health, held in Rio de Janeiro, Brazil, from 19 to 21 October 2011,

Noting with concern that for millions of people throughout the world, the right of everyone to the enjoyment of the highest attainable standard of physical and mental health, including access to medicines, still remains a distant goal and that in many cases, especially for children and people living in poverty, the likelihood of achieving this goal is becoming increasingly remote,

Acknowledging that inequities in access to health care can increase during times of crisis, particularly for persons living with disabilities, and that special efforts should be made to maintain public health-care and primary health-care functions during these periods,

Acknowledging also that improvement of unfavourable social and economic conditions is primarily a social and economic policy issue and that most of the underlying risk factors for tuberculosis, malaria, HIV and AIDS and maternal and infant mortality, as well as for non-communicable diseases, are associated with social and economic conditions,

Recognizing that health inequities arise from social determinants of health, that is, the societal conditions in which people are born, grow, live, work and age, and that these determinants include experiences in their early years, education, economic status, employment and decent work, housing and environment, and effective systems of preventing and treating ill health,

Bearing in mind the long-term health consequences of exposure to nuclear radiation for the affected populations and the need for the international community to be better prepared to respond collectively, including through the full implementation of the International Health Regulations,

Recalling that, according to the report of the Intergovernmental Panel on Climate Change in 2007, projected exposure to climate change is likely to affect the health status of millions of people, particularly those with low adaptive capacity,

Noting the role of the Foreign Policy and Global Health Initiative in promoting synergy between foreign policy and global health, as well as the contribution of the Oslo Ministerial Declaration, which was reaffirmed, with renewed actions and commitments, by the ministerial declaration of 22 September 2010,

Welcoming the adoption by the sixty-fourth World Health Assembly on 24 May 2011 of resolution 64.5 on pandemic influenza preparedness: sharing of influenza viruses and access to vaccines and other benefits,

1. *Notes with appreciation* the note by the Secretary-General transmitting the report of the Director General of the World Health Organization and the recommendations contained in the report on improving coordination, coherence and effectiveness of governance for global health and addressing the social determinants of health;

2. *Calls for* more attention to health as an important cross-cutting policy issue on the international agenda;

3. *Encourages* Member States to continue to consider the close relationship between global health and foreign policy and to recognize that global health challenges entail concerted and sustained efforts to further promote a global policy environment supportive of global health;

4. *Invites* Member States to adopt a multisectoral approach, while taking into consideration the social determinants of health, with a view to reducing health inequities and enabling sustainable development, and stresses the urgent need to act on social determinants for the final push towards the achievement of the Millennium Development Goals, to protect economic and social development and to recognize the importance of universal coverage in national health systems, especially through primary health-care and social protection mechanisms, including nationally determined social protection floors, so as to provide access to health services for all, in particular the poorest segments of the population;

5. *Reiterates* the need to fully implement the International Health Regulations, as part of the emergency responses to health and environment-related issues;

Health and the environment

6. *Reaffirms* that human beings are at the centre of concerns related to sustainable development and are entitled to a healthy and productive life in harmony with nature;

7. *Also reaffirms* the leading role of the World Health Organization and the important role of the United Nations system in meeting the challenges of global health in a changing environment and enhancing the visibility of health issues in the different international forums;

8. *Further reaffirms* the United Nations Framework Convention on Climate Change, and the objectives and principles set out therein, and the commitment to enable the full, effective and sustained implementation of the Convention, in order to achieve its ultimate objective;

9. *Urges* Member States to intensify efforts to address, as appropriate, the social determinants of exposure to environmental hazards and their current and projected consequences on health;

10. *Calls for* more attention to health-related issues in the global environmental agenda as well as for more attention to environmental issues in the health agenda, and calls upon the international community to acknowledge the direct linkages between health and the environment;

11. *Urges* Member States to promote at all levels the integration of health concerns, including of people living in vulnerable situations, into strategies, policies and programmes for poverty eradication and sustainable development;

12. *Encourages* the development of multisectoral policies with a view to limiting not only the detrimental impact of human intervention and environmental degradation on but also the current and projected consequences of climate change for health;

13. *Encourages* Member States to link health and the environment in their national development plans and, through education and training at all levels, to develop national capacities to better prevent diseases related to the environment;

14. *Reaffirms* that the development of national and international policies on environmental protection has a beneficial effect on health;

15. *Stresses* the need to foster research on environmental risk factors and social determinants of health;

16. *Also stresses* the need to strengthen national monitoring mechanisms for measuring the impacts of the environment on health, identifying emerging risks and evaluating the progress made and to strengthen national risk assessment and early warning mechanisms for identifying, assessing and addressing health vulnerabilities posed by environmental degradation;

17. *Calls for* increased international, regional and subregional cooperation and assistance, including through the mobilization of resources and the transfer of knowledge, technology and expertise, on mutually agreed terms, so as to enhance the capacity of developing countries to manage risks, including through the development and sustainability of the infrastructure and scientific, technological, technical and institutional capacities needed to research, observe, analyse, map and, where possible, forecast natural and environmental hazards, vulnerabilities and disaster impacts;

18. *Reiterates* the importance of launching international capacity-building initiatives that assess health and environmental linkages and use the knowledge gained to create more effective national and regional policy responses to environmental threats to human health;

19. *Encourages*, in this regard, greater international cooperation on sharing best practices and providing technical assistance and assistance in capacity-building to developing countries in the implementation of their national policies;

20. *Encourages* Member States to take into consideration the important role of health for the achievement of sustainable development, including in the context of the United Nations Conference on Sustainable Development;

Health and natural disasters

21. *Expresses grave concern* at the increase in the number of people affected by natural disasters, and stresses the need to address their health needs;

22. *Underlines* the crucial role of health in emergency preparedness and response to natural disasters, as well as the need to fully integrate health into strategies for disaster risk reduction and sustainable recovery;

23. *Recognizes* the primary role of national and local authorities in responding to disasters and the leading role of the World Health Organization, as the lead of the Global Health Cluster, in the provision of humanitarian assistance by the United Nations system, and as a partner of the International Strategy for Disaster Reduction, in supporting relief efforts and enhancing disaster preparedness;

24. *Also recognizes* the clear relationship between emergency response, rehabilitation and development, and reaffirms that, in order to ensure a smooth transition from relief to rehabilitation and development, emergency assistance in natural disasters must be provided in ways that will be supportive of recovery and long-term development and that emergency measures should be seen as a step towards sustainable development;

25. *Welcomes* the adoption by the sixty-fourth World Health Assembly on 24 May 2011 of resolution 64.10 on strengthening national health emergency and disaster management capacities and resilience of health systems, on 20 May 2011 of resolution 64.1 on implementation of the International Health Regulations (2005) and on 24 May 2011 of resolution 64.24 on drinking water, sanitation and health;

26. *Stresses* the continued need for coordination in natural disasters among the Office for the Coordination of Humanitarian Affairs of the Secretariat, the World Health Organization, other relevant United Nations organizations, humanitarian organizations, the World Bank and regional development banks so as to enhance effectiveness of health responses and to strengthen preparedness and response capacity of national and local health authorities, in close coordination with national Governments, taking into account the primary and leading role of the affected State in the initiation, organization, coordination and implementation of such assistance within its territory;

27. *Recognizes* the important role of the International Strategy for Disaster Reduction in monitoring the implementation of the Hyogo Framework for Action 2005–2015: Building the Resilience of Nations and Communities to Disasters, including in the health sector;

28. *Encourages* Member States to strengthen all-hazards health emergency and disaster risk-management programmes, including disaster risk reduction, emergency preparedness and response, water and sanitation and epidemic control, and to integrate them into national and international health plans;

29. *Urges* Member States to intensify efforts, as appropriate, to address the social determinants of vulnerabilities to disasters and their current and projected consequences for health;

30. *Underlines* the importance of strengthening the preparedness of health systems for emergencies, including through programmes on safe and prepared hospitals and training for health-care workers;

31. *Encourages* Member States to strengthen the involvement of communities in disaster preparedness and response in order to enhance their resilience;

Follow-up actions

32. *Urges* Member States to continue to consider health issues in the formulation of foreign policy;

33. *Requests* the Secretary-General, in close collaboration with the Director General of the World Health Organization and with the participation of relevant programmes, funds and specialized agencies of the United Nations system, as well as other relevant multilateral institutions, as appropriate, and in consultation with Member States, to give high priority to generating and collecting comparable and reliable data on the interlinkages between health and environment, and health and natural disasters, and to submit to the General Assembly at its sixty-seventh session, under the item entitled "Global health and foreign policy", a report which reflects on these interlinkages and contains recommendations for improving the management of health risks arising from environmental disasters.

Road safety

WHO report. In September, the Secretary-General transmitted a report on improving global road safety [A/66/389], prepared by WHO in consultation with the UN regional commissions and other partners of the United Nations Road Safety Collaboration. The report, covering the period October 2009–August 2011, stated that since the previous report [YUN 2009, p. 1229], the two most notable road safety events were the hosting of the First Global Ministerial Conference on Road Safety by the Russian Federation (Moscow, 19–20 November 2009) and the launch of the Decade of Action for Road Safety [YUN 2010, p. 1233] in May 2011, both of which had drawn attention to the issue at the highest political levels in many countries, resulting in the development of plans and targets to address the problem.

The report recalled that nearly 1.3 million people in the world died each year of road crashes, 90 per cent of them in low- and middle-income countries. Another 20 to 50 million people suffered serious injuries. Road traffic injuries were also the leading cause of death for people between the ages of 10 and 24. Significant numbers of road traffic fatalities and injuries could be prevented by addressing the leading causes, which included excess speed, lack of seat belt and child restraint use, drinking and driving, lack of helmet use by riders on two- and three-wheel motorized vehicles, poorly designed and inadequately maintained roads, unsafe infrastructure and vehicles, and inadequate trauma care.

WHO and the UN regional commissions, in cooperation with partners of the Road Safety Collaboration, developed a Global Plan for the Decade of Action for Road Safety (2011–2020), providing a framework for activities and proposing to tackle road safety issues in the context of five major categories: road safety management; safer roads and mobility; safer vehicles; safer road users; and post-crash response. The Plan also proposed indicators to measure progress in each of those areas.

During the reporting period, the harmonization of international standards in the area of road traffic safety continued at the Economic Commission for Europe. As at August 2011, the 1949 and 1968 Conventions on Road Traffic [YUN 1948–49, p. 489 & YUN 1968, p. 664] had 96 and 70 contracting parties, respectively, while the European Agreement concerning the Work of Crews of Vehicles engaged in International Road Transport [YUN 1962, p. 497] had 50. The 1997 Agreement concerning the Adoption of Uniform Conditions for Periodical Technical Inspections of Wheeled Vehicles and the Reciprocal Recognition of such Inspections [YUN 1997, p. 1353], lagged behind, with only 12 contracting parties.

Since 2010, three resolutions related to road safety had been adopted by the World Health Assembly on the following topics: reducing the harmful use of alcohol [YUN 2010, p. 1228]; child injury prevention; and youth and health risks. Among the global initiatives undertaken in 2011 were the establishment of the Global New Car Assessment Programme, a non-profit organization promoting safer car manufacture; and the launch by WHO and the United States National Highway Traffic Safety Administration of a publication drawing attention to the problem of driver distraction linked to the increasing use of mobile phones.

The report recommended, among other actions, that the General Assembly call on Member States to, develop national plans and strengthen national road safety legislation; accede to and implement UN road safety legal instruments; and promote awareness-raising initiatives such as the observance of the World Day of Remembrance for Road Traffic Victims [YUN 2005, p. 1334] and the United Nations Global Road Safety Week [ibid.].

Food and agriculture

Food aid

World Food Programme

The Executive Board of the World Food Programme (WFP) held its first regular (14–16 February), annual (6–9 June) and second regular (14–17 November) sessions in Rome, during which it decided on organizational and programme matters and approved a number of projects. On 15 November, the Board approved its 2012–2013 biennial programme of work [WFP/EB.2/2011/11].

The Economic and Social Council, by **decision 2011/215** of 18 July, took note of the report of the Executive Board [E/2011/36] on its first and second regular sessions and annual session of 2010, as well as the WFP annual report for 2010 [E/2011/14], transmitted by the Secretary-General in February.

WFP activities

As the Annual Performance Report for 2011 [WFP/EB.A/2012/4] underscored, the year 2011 marked the fiftieth anniversary of the founding of the WFP, as well as the enhancement of the WFP governance structure and its commitment to institutional accountability and transparency. As a part of the latter, WFP created the Executive Management Council to identify risks and mitigating actions at the highest level. The Programme also adopted the internal control system of the Committee of Sponsoring Organizations of the Treadway Commission, a recognized global best practice.

According to the report, in 2011, WFP provided food assistance for 99.1 million people in 75 countries, with women and children accounting for 84 per cent of the beneficiaries. WFP reported significant progress in the reduction of chronic hunger and undernutrition for the first time ever. The number of malnourished children receiving special nutritional support was 11 million, compared with 8.5 million in 2010, even as food prices reached their twelve-year peak and WFP purchasing power declined by 25 per cent. High food and oil prices were the most significant challenges facing WFP and its beneficiaries. The report stated that 2011 was the costliest year in history in terms of damages caused by natural disasters. WFP implemented new mechanisms in response to the worst drought in 60 years in the Horn of Africa. The operational response had been significant and immediate, mobilizing 130 staff from other locations to expand operations quickly. Moreover, the wave of popular uprising across North Africa and the Middle East that started in late 2010 and the March earthquake in Japan had required WFP to respond to emergencies in countries where it had a limited presence, underlining the importance of the Programme's reach. The year had also demonstrated how crucial partnerships and new technologies were in the fight against hunger. Irrespective of the type of intervention, WFP staff continued to work in operational environments with significant health and psychosocial risks. In 2011, four WFP staff members lost their lives in the line of duty as a result of armed attacks in Ethiopia, Somalia and South Sudan.

WFP spent $1.23 billion on food in 2011 compared with $1.25 billion in 2010, but the volume of food purchased fell by 25 per cent from 3.2 million metric tons to 2.4 million metric tons. WFP had improved its operational efficiency by collaborating with the Food and Agriculture Organization of the United Nations (FAO) on 86 projects in 50 countries. WFP also cooperated with the International Fund for Agricultural Development (IFAD) on 11 projects in nine countries.

At the regional level, sub-Saharan Africa received the largest share of WFP assistance, with 58 per cent of operational expenditures for 42 countries; Asia received 21 per cent for 15 countries; Latin America and the Caribbean, 7 per cent for 17 countries; the Middle East and North Africa, 7 per cent for 10 countries; and Eastern Europe and the Commonwealth of Independent States, 1 per cent for 7 countries.

Administrative and financial matters

Amendments to General Regulations

Pursuant to resolution 53/223 [YUN 1999, p. 1153], a review of the distribution of seats in the WFP Executive Board was carried out in 2011. As a result, by resolution 2011/1 of 18 February (see below), the Economic and Social Council recommended to the General Assembly the adoption of a draft resolution entitled "Revision of the General Regulations of the World Food Programme". The Assembly approved the revision by resolution 65/266 of 7 March (see below).

ECONOMIC AND SOCIAL COUNCIL ACTION

On 18 February [meeting 4], the Economic and Social Council adopted **resolution 2011/1** [draft: E/2011/L.3] without vote [agenda item 2].

Revision of the General Regulations of the World Food Programme

The Economic and Social Council

Recommends to the General Assembly the adoption of the following draft resolution:

[For text, see General Assembly resolution 65/266 below.]

GENERAL ASSEMBLY ACTION

On 7 March [meeting 77], the General Assembly adopted **resolution 65/266** [draft: A/65/768] without vote [agenda item 9].

Revision of the General Regulations of the World Food Programme

The General Assembly,

Recalling its resolutions 48/162 of 20 December 1993, 50/8 of 1 November 1995 and 53/223 of 7 April 1999,

1. *Decides*, subject to the concurrence of the Conference of the Food and Agriculture Organization of the United Nations, that the members of the Executive Board of the World Food Programme shall be elected for a term of three years from among the States included in the lists set out in the Basic Texts of the World Food Programme, in accordance with the following distribution of seats, it being understood that this allocation of seats creates no precedent for the composition of other United Nations bodies of limited membership:

(*a*) Eight members from the States included in list A, four members to be elected by the Economic and Social Council and four by the Council of the Food and Agriculture Organization of the United Nations;

(*b*) Seven members from the States included in list B, four members to be elected by the Economic and Social Council and three by the Council of the Food and Agriculture Organization of the United Nations;

(*c*) Five members from the States included in list C, two members to be elected by the Economic and Social Council and three by the Council of the Food and Agriculture Organization of the United Nations;

(*d*) Twelve members from the States included in list D, six members to be elected by the Economic and Social Council and six by the Council of the Food and Agriculture Organization of the United Nations;

(*e*) Three members from the States included in list E, two members to be elected by the Economic and Social Council and one by the Council of the Food and Agriculture Organization of the United Nations;

(*f*) One additional member rotating among the States included in lists A, B and C to be elected by the Council of the Food and Agriculture Organization of the United Nations; the pattern of rotation shall be as follows:

(i) A State from list A to be elected to occupy the additional seat every other term, starting from 1 January 2012;

(ii) A State from list B to be elected to occupy the additional seat every fourth term, starting from 1 January 2015;

(iii) A State from list C to be elected to occupy the additional seat every fourth term, starting from 1 January 2021;

2. *Also decides* that the rotating seat shall henceforth rotate on a permanent basis among the States included in lists A, B and C, as described in paragraph 1 (*f*) above, without the need for a further review, unless such a review is requested by a majority of the Executive Board members and, in any event, not before the completion of one full rotation scheme of four terms;

3. *Further decides* that, subject to the concurrence of the Conference of the Food and Agriculture Organization of the United Nations, the revised General Regulations shall enter into force on 1 January 2012.

On 7 June [E/2011/131], the Executive Board expressed its desire to move from a biennial WFP management plan and budget cycle to a three-year management plan with a one-year budget appropriation and requested endorsement from the Economic and Social Council. Following Council **decision 2011/270** of 29 July, the General Assembly, by **decision 65/550** of 12 September, recommended that the WFP General Regulations be amended by replacing the word "biennial" in article XIV.6 (*a*) with the word "annual".

Resources and financing

WFP operational expenditure in 2011 was $4.02 billion—5 per cent less than in 2010. Total revenue was $3.74 billion, 12 per cent less than the 2010 total of $4.27 billion. Actual contribution revenue fell from 58 per cent in 2010 to 55 per cent in 2011. The decline in contribution revenue could be partly attributed to a tighter fiscal policy in some donor countries.

Food security
Food and Agriculture Organization of the United Nations

The 2011 edition of *The State of Food Insecurity in the World* focused on food price volatility. By using previously unavailable data sources and studies, it investigated what happened to domestic markets following the world food crisis of 2006–2008. The report emphasized that the impact of world price fluctuations on household food security and nutrition was context-specific, depending on factors such as commodities, national policies, and the demographic and production characteristics of different households. That diversity of impacts indicated a need for improved data and analysis so that Governments could implement better policies, thus leading to reduced food insecurity and domestic price volatility.

The report also highlighted the importance of a twin-track approach, aiming at improving short-term access to food and food production in the medium term while achieving long-lasting improvements in food security. In the short term, it was critical to ensure that the right targeted assistance was delivered to the right people at the right time. In the long term, investment in agriculture and the improvement of farmers' resilience were essential to providing sustained access to food for all and reducing vulnerability to price volatility and natural disasters.

Committee on World Food Security. By a May note [A/66/76-E/2011/102], the Secretary-General transmitted to the General Assembly and the Economic and Social Council a report on the reform of the Committee on World Food Security and on progress made towards its implementation. The report set forth the key features of the reform: expanded participation to ensure that all stakeholders were heard, increased focus on intersessional activities, strengthening of linkages at all levels, and the creation of a high-level panel of experts on food security and nutrition. The reform was based on the principles of inclusiveness, linkages to realistic situations on the ground, and flexibility in implementation. The report provided an update on progress made since the thirty-sixth session [YUN 2010, p. 1236] of the Committee, covering issues including food price volatility; land tenure and international investment in agriculture; development of a global strategic framework on food security and nutrition; work of the High-level Panel of Experts on Food Security and Nutrition; food security at the country level; engagement of the private sector in activities of the Committee; and organization of a round table to review methods of hunger measurement.

The Economic and Social Council took note of the report by **decision 2011/218** of 22 July.

On the same day, by **decision 2011/217**, the Council decided to discontinue its quadrennial consideration of reports on progress in the implementation of the World Food Summit Plan of Action [YUN 1996, p. 1129], with effect from 2011; and invited the Chair of the Committee on World Food Security to transmit to the Council every year, starting in 2012, a report on the main decisions and policy recommendations made, as well as on the results achieved by the Committee in the area of food security and nutrition, in accordance with its new roles and vision.

Agriculture development and food security

Report of Secretary-General. In August, the Secretary-General issued a report on agriculture development and food security [A/66/277], pursuant to General Assembly resolution 65/178 [YUN 2010, p. 1237]. The report stated that reducing the number of people who suffered from hunger and malnutrition was one of the most difficult challenges. Higher and more volatile food and fuel prices, political conflict and persistent underinvestment in agriculture, food and nutrition compounded the problem. Many countries lacked the social safety nets necessary to avert disasters. More than 38 million people had been displaced by sudden climate-related disasters in 2010, undermining their livelihoods and food security. The report projected that by 2050, as many as 20 per cent more people could be at risk of hunger owing to climate-related losses in productivity. The most severe food and nutrition security emergency in the world was occurring in the Horn of Africa, where one of the worst droughts since 1950 caused crop failure and critical livestock mortality, resulting in very high food prices—up to 270 per cent higher in certain areas of Somalia. Long-term investments in sustainable agriculture, interlinked with efforts to adapt to and mitigate climate change, alleviate poverty, empower women, improve market access, and manage ecosystems and natural resources were not happening quickly enough. Country-led responses supported by the international community needed to be intensified to meet the internationally agreed goals by 2015.

National budgets were the primary source of public spending on agriculture, which fell to an average of around 7 per cent in developing countries—even less in Africa. The pattern was, however, changing, especially due to the Comprehensive Africa Agriculture Development Programme [YUN 2004, p. 30], established by the New Partnership for Africa's Development in 2003. The number of people who suffered from hunger decreased from 1 billion in 2009 to about 925 million in 2010. Much, however, was left to be done to reach the Millennium Development Goal 1 target to reduce by half the proportion of people who suffered from hunger. The vast majority of the world's undernourished people—98 per cent—lived in the developing world, with two thirds of them living in seven countries: Bangladesh, China, the Democratic Republic of the Congo, Ethiopia, India, Indonesia and Pakistan.

Among the short-term safety nets, the report mentioned nutrition interventions, food- or cash-for-work initiatives, school feeding programmes and emergency food assistance. The international community also had to address the issues of how to support long-term sustainable development through different measures: the integration of sustainable agriculture and policymaking incorporating a gender perspective—women were the majority of smallholder farmers and rural entrepreneurs—as well as the development of agricultural value chains bringing together different players who produced, traded, processed and marketed agricultural products; sound water management; and the strengthening of early warning systems to help predict, prevent and address the impact of climate change and extreme weather events.

In June, the Agricultural Market Information System was launched as a network of countries, organizations and the private sector, including FAO, IFAD, the International Food Policy Research Institute, the Organization for Economic Cooperation and Development, the United Nations Conference on Trade and Development, WFP, the World Trade Organization, the World Bank and the High-level Task Force on the Global Food Security Crisis. It aimed to provide a global food market early warning system issuing alerts to price surges and helping ensure better preparedness and more rapid and consistent policy responses in times of crisis. The report concluded that with increasingly concerted action by the international community, the mobilization of all stakeholders and the fulfilment of funding pledges, the 2015 target for reducing by half the world's hungry could still be achieved.

On 22 December, the Assembly adopted **resolution 66/195** (see p. 803) on agricultural technology for development, by which it stressed the role of women in the agricultural sector and their contribution to enhancing agricultural and rural development, improving food security and nutrition.

GENERAL ASSEMBLY ACTION

On 22 December [meeting 91], the General Assembly, on the recommendation of the Second (Economic and Financial) Committee [A/66/446], adopted **resolution 66/220** without vote [agenda item 25].

Agriculture development and food security

The General Assembly,

Recalling the Declaration of the World Summit on Food Security, particularly the Five Rome Principles for Sustainable Global Food Security,

Recalling also the Rio Declaration on Environment and Development, Agenda 21, the Programme for the Further Implementation of Agenda 21, the Johannesburg Declaration on Sustainable Development and the Plan of Implementation of the World Summit on Sustainable Development ("Johannesburg Plan of Implementation"), the Monterrey Consensus of the International Conference on Financing for Development, the 2005 World Summit Outcome and the Doha Declaration on Financing for Development: outcome document of the Follow-up International Conference on Financing for Development to Review the Implementation of the Monterrey Consensus, the outcome document of the High-level Plenary Meeting of the General Assembly on the Millennium Development Goals and the Programme of Action for the Least Developed Countries for the Decade 2011–2020, as well as its resolutions 64/224 of 21 December 2009 and 65/178 of 20 December 2010,

Recalling further the Rome Declaration on World Food Security and the World Food Summit Plan of Action, the Declaration of the World Food Summit: five years later, including the goal of achieving food security for all through an ongoing effort to eradicate hunger in all countries, with an immediate view to reducing by half the number of undernourished people no later than 2015, as well as the commitment to achieving the goals set out in paragraph 19 of the United Nations Millennium Declaration,

Acknowledging the work undertaken by the High-level Task Force on the Global Food Security Crisis,

Welcoming the outcome of the thirty-seventh session of the Committee on World Food Security, held in Rome from 17 to 22 October 2011,

Noting the ongoing process of developing principles for responsible agricultural investment that respects rights, livelihoods and resources, as well as the inclusive process for the development of voluntary guidelines on the responsible governance of tenure of land, fisheries and forests in the context of national food security,

Reiterating that the multiple and complex causes of the global food crisis in developing countries, especially for net food importers, and its consequences for food security and nutrition require a comprehensive and coordinated response in the short, medium and long terms by national Governments and the international community, and remaining concerned that high and excessively volatile food prices pose a serious challenge to the fight against poverty and hunger and to the efforts of developing countries to attain food security and nutrition and to achieve the objective of reducing by half the number of undernourished people no later than 2015, as well as other internationally agreed development goals, including the Millennium Development Goals,

Recalling the agreement to keep under regular review, by the Ministerial Conference and appropriate organs of the World Trade Organization, the impact of the results of the Uruguay Round on the least developed countries as well as on the net food-importing developing countries, with a view to fostering positive measures to enable them to achieve their development objectives, and in this regard calls for the implementation of the Marrakesh Decision on Measures Concerning the Possible Negative Effects of the Reform Programme on Least Developed and Net Food-Importing Developing Countries,

Stressing the need to increase investment in agriculture and rural development, including through international cooperation, with a view to increasing the agricultural production of developing countries, many of which have become net food importers,

Welcoming national, regional and international initiatives and commitments aimed at improving food security and nutrition,

Recalling the commitments made to achieve global food security and provide adequate and predictable resources through bilateral and multilateral channels, including the financial and policy commitments set out in the Aquila Food Security Initiative,

Recognizing the importance of an enabling international and national environment to increase and sustain investment in the agriculture sector of developing countries and to create a more level playing field in agriculture through greater market access, a substantial reduction in trade-distorting domestic support and the parallel elimination of all forms of export subsidies and disciplines on all export measures with equivalent effect in accordance with the mandate from the Doha Work Programme of the World Trade Organization,

Recognizing also that agriculture plays a crucial role in addressing the needs of a growing global population and is inextricably linked to poverty eradication, especially in developing countries, and stressing that integrated and sustainable agriculture and rural development approaches are therefore essential to achieving enhanced food security in an environmentally sustainable way,

Recognizing further the importance and positive role of smallholder farmers, including women, cooperatives and indigenous and local communities in developing countries, and their knowledge and practices, in the preservation, conservation and sustainable use of traditional crops and biodiversity for present and future generations as an important contribution to the achievement of food security, as well as in the implementation of development goals in such fields as employment policy, social integration, regional and rural development, agriculture and environmental protection,

Recognizing that smallholder farmers, including women and indigenous peoples, may not have the equitable access to tools, markets and land tenure rights that is needed for them to reach their productive potential,

Reaffirming the right of everyone to have access to safe, sufficient and nutritious food, consistent with the right to adequate food and the fundamental right of everyone to be free from hunger, so as to be able to fully develop and maintain his or her physical and mental capacities,

Reaffirming also the need to strive for a comprehensive twin-track approach to food security that consists of direct action to immediately tackle hunger for the most vulnerable and medium- and long-term sustainable agriculture, food security, nutrition and rural development programmes to eliminate the root causes of hunger and poverty, including through the progressive realization of the right to adequate food,

Stressing the importance of the preservation of the natural resource base for food security,

Noting with appreciation the work undertaken by relevant international bodies and organizations, including the Food and Agriculture Organization of the United Nations, the International Fund for Agricultural Development and the World Food Programme, on agricultural development and on enhancing food security and nutrition,

Recognizing the need to strengthen international coordination and governance for food security through the Global Partnership for Agriculture, Food Security and Nutrition, of which the Committee on World Food Security is a central component, and reiterating that it is essential to enhance global governance, building on existing institutions and fostering effective partnerships,

Expressing concern that the number of people living in extreme poverty and hunger has reached nearly one billion, which is an unacceptable blight on the lives, livelihoods and dignity of many of the world's people, mostly in developing countries, and noting that the effects of long-standing underinvestment in food security, agriculture and rural development have recently been further exacerbated by the food, financial and economic crises, among other factors,

Remaining deeply concerned about starvation and the humanitarian disaster on an unimaginable scale being faced by millions of people in the Horn of Africa,

Expressing concern about the negative impact of high and excessively volatile food prices on food security and nutrition, particularly on the poor and people in vulnerable situations, which has undermined the prospect of developing countries for economic growth and poverty alleviation, including the goal to halve the proportion of people who suffer from hunger by 2015,

1. *Takes note* of the report of the Secretary-General;
2. *Welcomes* the note by the Chair of the Committee on World Food Security on the progress made in implementing the reform of the Committee, and urges Member States and encourages civil society and the private sector to strongly support such reform and the aims and endeavours of the Committee;
3. *Reiterates* the need to adequately and urgently address agriculture development and food security in the context of national, regional and international development policies, taking into account the importance of enhancing synergies between sustainable agriculture, biodiversity, food security, nutrition and development policies;
4. *Also reiterates* the importance of developing countries determining their own food security strategies, that food security is a national policy responsibility and that any plans for addressing food security challenges and the eradication of poverty in relation to food security must be

nationally articulated, designed, owned and led and built in consultation with all key stakeholders at the national level, and urges Member States, especially those that suffer from food insecurity, to make food security a high priority and to reflect this in their national programmes and budgets;

5. *Acknowledges* that the achievement of food security and improved nutrition outcomes are closely interlinked, and underlines the need to make special efforts to meet the nutritional needs of women, children, older persons and persons with disabilities, as well as those living in vulnerable situations, through targeted and effective programming;

6. *Reaffirms* the importance of adopting forward-looking economic policies that lead to sustained, inclusive and equitable economic growth and sustainable development and which increase employment opportunities, promote agriculture development and reduce poverty;

7. *Remains deeply concerned* by food crises and their negative impact on health and nutrition, especially in the Horn of Africa and other vulnerable regions, and, in this regard, underlines the urgent need for joint efforts at all levels to respond in a coherent and effective manner to these crises;

8. *Welcomes* the Declaration of the Summit on the Horn of Africa Crisis, held in Nairobi on 8 and 9 September 2011, which encouraged farmers and investors in agriculture to put more resources into agriculture in the high potential and arid and semi-arid lands to enhance food security and, in this regard, supported the Dry Land Initiative that was launched by six Horn of Africa countries to promote integrated rural development, as well as regional projects to address the underlying causes of vulnerability in drought-prone areas, with particular emphasis on pastoralists and agro-pastoralists, and to promote disaster risk reduction, ecosystem rehabilitation and sustainable livelihood practices;

9. *Also welcomes*, in this context, the strong leadership shown by African countries in undertaking initiatives to address the challenges of sustainable agriculture development and to achieve food security, such as the Comprehensive Africa Agriculture Development Programme of the New Partnership for Africa's Development, that can provide a framework through which support for agriculture and food security can be coordinated, and calls upon the international community to support Africa in the implementation of the various programmes under the New Partnership for Africa's Development;

10. *Recognizes* that underdevelopment, desertification and land degradation, as well as extreme weather events, inter alia, have contributed to undermining the livelihoods of the poor and people in vulnerable situations in the Horn of Africa and other vulnerable regions, and calls for an integrated approach at all levels in the form of immediate and medium- and long-term actions to address food security and nutrition;

11. *Promotes* a significant expansion of research on food and agriculture, and its funding, including by strengthening the work of the reformed Consultative Group on International Agricultural Research, supporting national research systems, public universities and research institutions, and promoting technology transfer, sharing of knowledge and practices and research to adapt to and mitigate climate change and improve equitable access to research results and technologies at the national, regional and international levels, while giving due consideration to the preservation of genetic resources;

12. *Stresses* the need to address the root causes of excessive food price volatility, including its structural causes, at all levels, and the need to manage the risks linked to high and excessively volatile prices in agriculture commodities and their consequences for global food security and nutrition, as well as for smallholder farmers and poor urban dwellers;

13. *Recognizes* the need to support a comprehensive and coordinated response to address the multiple and complex causes of the global food crisis, including the adoption of political, economic, social, financial and technical solutions in the short, medium and long terms by national Governments and the international community, including for mitigating the impact of high and excessively volatile food prices on developing countries; the relevant United Nations organizations have an important role to play in this regard;

14. *Underlines* the importance of timely, accurate and transparent information in helping to address excessive food price volatility, and in this regard takes note of the Agricultural Market Information System hosted by the Food and Agriculture Organization of the United Nations and urges the participating international organizations, private sector actors and Governments to ensure the public dissemination of timely and quality food market information products;

15. *Urges* Member States and international organizations to pursue policies and strategies that improve the functioning of domestic, regional and international markets and ensure equitable access for all to those markets, especially smallholder and women farmers in developing countries, notes the importance of non-trade-distorting special measures that are consistent with the rules of the World Trade Organization aimed at creating incentives for smallholder farmers in developing countries to enable them to increase their productivity and to compete on a more equal footing in world food markets, and urges Member States to refrain from taking measures that are inconsistent with the rules of the World Trade Organization and that have adverse impacts on global, regional and national food security;

16. *Stresses* that a universal, rules-based, open, non-discriminatory and equitable multilateral trading system will promote agriculture and rural development in developing countries and contribute to world food security, and urges national, regional and international strategies to promote the participation of farmers, especially smallholder farmers, including women, in community, domestic, regional and international markets;

17. *Also stresses* the need to remove food export restrictions or extraordinary taxes for food purchased for non-commercial humanitarian purposes by the World Food Programme, and not to impose them in the future;

18. *Calls upon* Member States and the World Trade Organization to take measures to promote trade policies that would be capable of promoting further trade in agriculture products, identifying the obstacles to trade which have the most serious impact on the world's poor and contributing to supporting small-scale and marginalized producers in developing countries;

19. *Recognizes* the urgency of, and reaffirms its commitment to, reaching an early and successful conclusion

of the Doha Round of World Trade Organization negotiations with a balanced, ambitious, comprehensive and development-oriented outcome as a key action to improve food security;

20. *Encourages* efforts at all levels to establish and strengthen social protection measures and programmes, including national safety nets and protection programmes for the needy and vulnerable such as food- and cash-for-work, cash-transfer and voucher programmes, school feeding programmes and mother-and-child nutrition programmes;

21. *Reaffirms* the need to include prevention and mitigation measures for the poor and smallholder farmers, particularly women in developing countries, appropriate to their national context and circumstances and in accordance with their capacities, especially when excessive food price volatility causes access and market disruptions in the short, medium and long term within the context of local, national, regional and international development policies, taking into account World Trade Organization rules and provisions;

22. *Supports* concrete initiatives aimed at improving protection for the most vulnerable against excessive price volatility through risk management strategies, tools and instruments, such as the development of the pilot project led by the Economic Community of West African States for a targeted regional emergency humanitarian food reserve, consistent with annex 2 to the World Trade Organization agreements;

23. *Recognizes* the importance of smallholder farmers in developing countries, including women and local and indigenous communities, in ensuring food security and nutrition, reducing poverty and preserving ecosystems, and the need to assist their development;

24. *Notes* the challenges faced by indigenous peoples in the context of food security, and in this regard calls upon States to take special actions to combat the root causes of the disproportionately high level of hunger and malnutrition among indigenous peoples;

25. *Stresses* the need to strengthen the capacity of smallholder and women farmers as a strategy to enhance agriculture development and food security by promoting equitable access to land, water, financial resources and technologies in accordance with national legislation, as well as improving smallholder farmers' participation in and access to sustainable agriculture value chains and markets;

26. *Underlines* the need for substantial additional investment and better policies in support of sustainable agricultural development, especially smallholder agriculture, in order for many of the poorest countries to reach the poverty and hunger targets of the Millennium Development Goals;

27. *Stresses* the need to increase sustainable agricultural production to augment the availability and quality of food, including through long-term investment, equitable access of smallholder farmers, including women, to markets, credit and inputs, improved land-use planning, crop diversification, commercialization, development of an adequate rural infrastructure and enhanced market access for developing countries, as well as sound water management, including efficient irrigation, water harvesting and storage and the appropriate management of relevant facilities, and the development of strong agriculture value chains and investment in rural infrastructure, which are critical to accelerating progress in order to achieve the hunger-related Millennium Development Goals;

28. *Recognizes* the urgent need to finalize the negotiations on the voluntary guidelines on the responsible governance of tenure of land, fisheries and forests in the context of national food security, which will underpin smallholder investment in agriculture;

29. *Also recognizes* the importance of agricultural investment, including foreign direct investment, through, inter alia, the private sector in enhancing agriculture development and food security as well as the need to promote responsible international investment in agriculture, and therefore calls for all investors to conduct agricultural practices in accordance with national legislation, taking into account national sovereignty over natural resources, environmental sustainability and the importance of promoting the well-being and improving the livelihood of local communities and indigenous peoples, as appropriate;

30. *Supports* an inclusive consultation process for the development and the broader ownership of principles for responsible agricultural investment that enhances food security and nutrition, and acknowledges that the first step of this consultation process will be to develop terms of reference that include the scope, purpose, intended recipients and structure of those principles as well as the format of the consultation process, taking into account existing frameworks, such as the principles for responsible agricultural investment developed by the Food and Agriculture Organization of the United Nations, the International Fund for Agricultural Development, the United Nations Conference on Trade and Development and the World Bank;

31. *Encourages* international, regional and national efforts to strengthen the capacity of developing countries, in particular their small-scale producers, in order to enhance the productivity and nutritional quality of food crops and to promote sustainable practices in pre-harvest and post-harvest agricultural activities;

32. *Underlines* the need to achieve food security and nutrition through sustainable agriculture in a manner that addresses the multiplicity of social needs, without jeopardizing options for future generations;

33. *Also underlines* the need to continue to take into account sustainable agriculture development and food security as an integral part of the three pillars of sustainable development as identified at the 2005 World Summit (economic development, social development and environmental protection);

34. *Stresses* the need to continue to strengthen cooperation among the Food and Agriculture Organization of the United Nations, the International Fund for Agricultural Development, the World Food Programme, regional commissions and all other relevant entities of the United Nations system and other intergovernmental organizations, the international financial institutions and international trade, financial and economic institutions, in accordance with their respective mandates, in order to increase their effectiveness, as well as to strengthen cooperation with non-governmental organizations and the private sector in promoting and strengthening efforts towards agriculture development and food security and nutrition;

35. *Requests* the Secretary-General to continue to ensure that a coordinated follow-up to the 2009 World Summit on Food Security is undertaken at the field level in

the context of the resident coordinator system, taking into account the coordinated follow-up to major international conferences of the United Nations;

36. *Invites* the Chair of the Committee on World Food Security to report, as part of the Committee's report to the General Assembly at its sixty-seventh session, through the Economic and Social Council, on the implementation of the reform of, and on progress made towards achieving the vision of, the Committee;

37. *Requests* the Secretary-General to report to the General Assembly at its sixty-seventh session on developments related to issues highlighted in the present resolution and on the progress in the implementation of the outcome of the 2009 World Summit on Food Security;

38. *Decides* to include in the provisional agenda of its sixty-seventh session the item entitled "Agriculture development and food security".

Also on 22 December [meeting 91], the General Assembly, on the recommendation of the Second Committee [A/66/438/Add.2], adopted **resolution 66/188** without vote [agenda item 17 (*b*)].

Addressing excessive price volatility in food and related financial and commodity markets

The General Assembly,

Recalling the Universal Declaration of Human Rights, which provides that everyone has the right to a standard of living adequate for her or his health and well-being, including food, the Universal Declaration on the Eradication of Hunger and Malnutrition and the United Nations Millennium Declaration, in particular Millennium Development Goal 1 on eradicating extreme poverty and hunger by 2015,

Bearing in mind the Rome Declaration on World Food Security and the World Food Summit Plan of Action and the Declaration of the World Summit on Food Security,

Recalling its resolution 56/210 B of 9 July 2002, in which it endorsed the Monterrey Consensus of the International Conference on Financing for Development, and recalling also the Plan of Implementation of the World Summit on Sustainable Development ("Johannesburg Plan of Implementation"),

Recalling also the Doha Declaration on Financing for Development: outcome document of the Follow-up International Conference on Financing for Development to Review the Implementation of the Monterrey Consensus,

Recalling further the Conference on the World Financial and Economic Crisis and Its Impact on Development and its outcome document,

Taking note of the work undertaken by the Food and Agriculture Organization of the United Nations, including the Committee on World Food Security, and by the United Nations Conference on Trade and Development, particularly its recent work on the financialization of commodity markets,

Taking note also of recent initiatives that aim to help Governments, firms and farmers to mitigate and build capacity to manage the risks associated with excessive food price volatility, in particular in the poorest countries,

Recognizing the need to support a comprehensive and coordinated response in order to address the multiple and complex causes of excessive price volatility of food and related commodities in financial markets,

Deeply concerned by excessive volatility of commodity prices and by the impact that excessive price volatility has on food security and sustainable development in developing countries, and, in particular, by the fact that many commodity-dependent developing countries and economies in transition continue to be highly vulnerable to excessive price fluctuations, and recognizing the need to improve the adequate regulation, functioning and transparency of financial and commodity markets in order to address excessive commodity price volatility,

Reiterating that the international financial system should support sustained, inclusive and equitable economic growth, sustainable development, and hunger and poverty eradication efforts in developing countries, while allowing for the coherent mobilization of all sources of financing for development,

Taking note of the report of the Secretary-General entitled "Agriculture development and food security: progress on the implementation of the outcome of the World Summit on Food Security", which inter alia, highlights the significant increase in the financialization of commodity markets since about 2004, as reflected in rising volumes of financial investments in commodity derivatives markets,

Taking note also of the policy report entitled "Price Volatility in Food and Agricultural Markets: Policy Responses", issued on 2 June 2011 by the Food and Agriculture Organization of the United Nations, the International Fund for Agricultural Development, the International Monetary Fund, the Organization for Economic Cooperation and Development, the United Nations Conference on Trade and Development, the World Food Programme, the World Bank, the World Trade Organization, the International Food Policy Research Institute and the High-level Task Force on the Global Food Security Crisis,

1. *Recognizes* the initiative of Leonel Fernández Reyna, President of the Dominican Republic, "Towards Reaching an International Consensus that Aims to Reduce Excessive Price Volatility and Speculation in Commodity Markets";

2. *Stresses* the need to take active measures to reduce excessive food price volatility, while acknowledging that there is an incomplete understanding of its causes and that more research needs to be done, and in this regard underlines the need to promote greater transparency and market information at all levels;

3. *Underlines* the importance of timely, accurate and transparent information in helping to address excessive food price volatility, and in this regard takes note of the Agricultural Market Information System hosted by the Food and Agriculture Organization of the United Nations, and urges the participating international organizations, private-sector actors and Governments to ensure the public dissemination of timely and quality food market information products;

4. *Requests* the President of the General Assembly at the sixty-sixth session to convene a high-level thematic debate, to be held in plenary meeting, with the participation of Member States, independent experts and other stakeholders, to promote an exchange of views on addressing excessive price volatility in food and related financial and commodity markets, while taking into account relevant work done at the national, regional and international levels;

5. *Invites* all relevant United Nations agencies and other international organizations, in particular the Food and Agriculture Organization of the United Nations and the United Nations Conference on Trade and Development, as well as other relevant United Nations agencies and international organizations, to participate actively in the high-level thematic debate and to continue their research and analysis on this matter;

6. *Recognizes* the importance of considering, in this dialogue, the needs of developing countries, and stresses that special attention should be given to the needs of net-food-importing developing countries in addressing excessive price volatility in food and related financial and commodity markets to achieve their food security;

7. *Requests* the Secretary-General to consider the outcomes of the high-level thematic debate in relevant reports to be submitted under the item entitled "Macroeconomic policy questions" and other relevant agenda items.

On 19 December, the General Assembly adopted **resolution 66/158** (see p. 723) on the right to food, which reaffirmed the concrete recommendations contained in the 2004 Voluntary Guidelines to Support the Progressive Realization of the Right to Adequate Food in the Context of National Food Security [YUN 2004, p. 1226].

International Years

The thirty-seventh session (Rome, 25 June–2 July) of the FAO Conference adopted resolutions on 2 July concerning the observance of the International Year of Quinoa in 2013, and of Family Farming in 2014, and requested the FAO Director-General to transmit the resolutions to the Secretary-General with a view to having the General Assembly take action (see below).

International Year of Quinoa, 2013

GENERAL ASSEMBLY ACTION

On 22 December [meeting 91], the General Assembly, on the recommendation of the Second Committee [A/66/446], adopted **resolution 66/221** without vote [agenda item 25].

International Year of Quinoa, 2013

The General Assembly,

Noting that quinoa is a natural food high in nutritional value,

Recognizing that Andean indigenous peoples, through their traditional knowledge and practices of living well, in harmony with nature, have maintained, controlled, protected and preserved quinoa in its natural state, including its many varieties and landraces, as food for present and future generations,

Affirming the need to focus world attention on the role that quinoa biodiversity can play, owing to the nutritional value of quinoa, in providing food security and nutrition and in the eradication of poverty in support of the achievement of the internationally agreed development goals, including the Millennium Development Goals, and of the outcome document of the High-level Plenary Meeting of the General Assembly on the Millennium Development Goals,

Recalling resolution 15/2011 adopted on 2 July 2011 by the Conference of the Food and Agriculture Organization of the United Nations at its thirty-seventh session,

Recalling also the Rome Declaration on World Food Security and the World Food Summit Plan of Action, the Declaration of the World Food Summit: five years later and the Declaration of the World Summit on Food Security,

Recalling further Economic and Social Council resolution 1980/67 of 25 July 1980 on international years and anniversaries and General Assembly resolutions 53/199 of 15 December 1998 and 61/185 of 20 December 2006 on the proclamation of international years,

Affirming the need to heighten public awareness of the nutritional, economic, environmental and cultural properties of quinoa,

1. *Decides* to declare 2013 the International Year of Quinoa;

2. *Invites* the Food and Agriculture Organization of the United Nations, mindful of the provisions of the annex to Economic and Social Council resolution 1980/67, to facilitate the implementation of the International Year of Quinoa, in collaboration with Governments and relevant organizations of the United Nations system, as well as indigenous peoples' organizations and non-governmental organizations, and also invites the Food and Agriculture Organization of the United Nations to keep the General Assembly informed of progress made in this regard;

3. *Stresses* that any activities that may arise from the implementation of the present resolution should be met through extrabudgetary resources;

4. *Calls upon* Governments and relevant regional and international organizations to make voluntary contributions and lend other forms of support to the Year, and invites non-governmental organizations, other relevant stakeholders and the private sector to make voluntary contributions to and support the Year.

International Year of Family Farming, 2014

On 22 December [meeting 91], the General Assembly, on the recommendation of the Second Committee [A/66/446], also adopted **resolution 66/222** without vote [agenda item 25].

International Year of Family Farming, 2014

The General Assembly,

Recalling resolution 16/2011 adopted on 2 July 2011 by the Conference of the Food and Agriculture Organization of the United Nations at its thirty-seventh session,

Recalling also General Assembly resolution 65/178 of 20 December 2010 on agriculture development and food security,

Noting the Declaration of the World Summit on Food Security, adopted on 18 November 2009, expressing, inter alia, support for the special needs of smallholder farmers, many of whom are women,

Recalling Economic and Social Council resolution 1980/67 of 25 July 1980 on international years and anniversaries and General Assembly resolutions 53/199 of 15 December 1998 and 61/185 of 20 December 2006 on the proclamation of international years,

Affirming that family farming and smallholder farming are an important basis for sustainable food production aimed at achieving food security,

Recognizing the important contribution that family farming and smallholder farming can play in providing food security and eradicating poverty in the attainment of the internationally agreed development goals, including the Millennium Development Goals,

1. *Decides* to declare 2014 the International Year of Family Farming;

2. *Invites* the Food and Agriculture Organization of the United Nations, mindful of the provisions of the annex to Economic and Social Council resolution 1980/67, to facilitate the implementation of the International Year of Family Farming, in collaboration with Governments, the United Nations Development Programme, the International Fund for Agricultural Development, the Consultative Group on International Agricultural Research and other relevant organizations of the United Nations system, as well as relevant non-governmental organizations, also invites the Food and Agriculture Organization of the United Nations to keep the General Assembly informed of progress made in this regard, and stresses that the costs of all activities that may arise from the implementation of the present resolution above and beyond activities currently within the mandate of the implementing agency should be met from voluntary contributions;

3. *Encourages* Member States to undertake activities within their respective national development programmes in support of the International Year of Family Farming.

Nutrition

Standing Committee on Nutrition

In 2011, the United Nations System Standing Committee on Nutrition continued to support the Scaling Up Nutrition (SUN) Movement—launched at the 1,000 Days: Change a Life, Change the Future event hosted by the United States and Ireland in September 2010. The SUN Movement focused on the critical 1,000-day window between pregnancy and a child's second birthday, in which proper nutrition could mean the difference between health and sickness, and life and death.

At the high-level event on nutrition (New York, 20 September), held alongside the High-level Meeting on the Prevention and Control of Non-communicable Diseases (see p. 1146), the Secretary-General appealed for leadership, funds and global solidarity to support the movement. A workshop was organized for about 150 participants from government Ministries, donor agencies, the private sector, civil society, UN agencies and others to assess progress one year after the launch of the SUN Movement, discuss challenges and agree on future steps to strengthen the movement.

UNU activities

The United Nations University Food and Nutrition Programme for Human and Social Development (UNU-FNP) (Ithaca, New York, United States), continued to contribute—through collaborative research and education, dissemination and advisory services—to efforts to resolve the pressing global problems of human survival, development and welfare. UNU-FNP continued to generate and provide access to new food and nutrition information.

UNU-FNP had created a global network of institutions engaged in capacity development in global health and nutrition in the context of higher education. In cooperation with North-West University (South Africa), the University of Venda (South Africa) and Wageningen University (Netherlands), UNU-FNP organized the African Nutrition Leadership Programme to develop the leadership skills of future leaders in the field of human nutrition in Africa.

The African Nutrition Graduate Students Network (AGSNet) met in Nigeria in September as part of the second conference of the Federation of African Nutrition Societies. AGSNet was positioning itself to collaborate with "similar-minded" institutions to find solutions to alleviate malnutrition on the African continent. UNU-FNP continued its support of the quarterly *Food and Nutrition Bulletin*.

Chapter XIV

International drug control and crime prevention

In 2011, the United Nations, through the Commission on Narcotic Drugs (CND), the International Narcotics Control Board (INCB), the Commission on Crime Prevention and Criminal Justice (CCPCJ) and the United Nations Office on Drugs and Crime (UNODC), continued to strengthen international cooperation in countering transnational organized crime, corruption, drugs and international terrorism. UNODC developed a number of new thematic and regional programmes, such as that on action against transnational organized crime and illicit trafficking, including drug trafficking, for the period 2011–2013, complemented by a comprehensive strategy to combat trafficking in persons and the smuggling of migrants. The Office provided technical assistance, legal advice and research to the main UN policymaking bodies in drug control and crime prevention, and assisted Member States in developing domestic legislation and in implementing the international drug control and crime prevention conventions. A UN system task force on transnational organized crime and drug trafficking, established by the Secretary-General and co-chaired by UNODC and the Department for Political Affairs, started its work on strengthening UN system coordination and response to illicit trafficking and organized crime.

In 2011, according to UNODC, between 167 and 315 million people aged 15–64 were estimated to have used an illicit substance in the preceding year. That corresponded to between 3.6 and 6.9 per cent of the adult population. The number of drug-related deaths in 2011 was estimated at 211,000.

CND—the main UN policymaking body dealing with drug control—held its fifty-fourth session in March, during which it recommended one resolution and three decisions for adoption by the Economic and Social Council. It also adopted 15 resolutions on topics such as drug-affected driving, rehabilitation and reintegration strategies in response to drug use disorders, and adequate availability of internationally controlled narcotic drugs and psychotropic substances for medical and scientific purposes.

INCB reviewed the issue of social cohesion, social disorganization and illegal drugs, and noted that countries throughout the world were faced with the challenge posed by marginalized communities, which were vulnerable to drug-related problems. INCB continued to oversee the implementation of the international drug control conventions, analyse the global drug situation and draw the attention of Governments to weaknesses in national control and treaty compliance, making recommendations for improvements at the national and international levels.

CCPCJ—the principal UN policymaking body in the field of crime prevention and criminal justice—held its twentieth session in April, during which it recommended to the Economic and Social Council four resolutions for adoption by the General Assembly, and four resolutions and two decisions for adoption by the Council. It also adopted seven resolutions and one decision on topics such as the United Nations Global Plan of Action to Combat Trafficking in Persons, transnational organized crime, fraudulent medicines and cybercrime.

Member States expressed differing positions regarding Bolivia's 2009 proposal to delete a provision of the Single Convention on Narcotic Drugs of 1961, as amended by the 1972 Protocol, aimed at abolishing coca leaf chewing, an ancestral practice of the Andean indigenous peoples. Bolivia on 29 June notified the Secretary-General that it had decided to denounce the Convention.

In December, the General Assembly noted that the world drug problem continued to constitute a threat to public health and safety and the well-being of humanity, and that it undermined socioeconomic and political stability and sustainable development. The Assembly called on States to take the measures necessary to implement the actions and attain the goals and targets set out in the 2009 Political Declaration and Plan of Action on International Cooperation towards an Integrated and Balanced Strategy to Counter the World Drug Problem.

UN Office on Drugs and Crime

The United Nations Office on Drugs and Crime (UNODC) addressed the interrelated issues of transnational organized crime, corruption, drugs and international terrorism, and offered global solutions for those problems within the broader multilateral framework of the United Nations. UNODC built on its comparative advantages based on three interconnected pillars, namely research, implementation of the UN conventions on drug control and crime prevention, and technical cooperation. The Office carried out a broad range of initiatives—including alternative development projects, illicit crop monitoring and anti-money laundering programmes—and worked with Member States to strengthen the rule of law, promote stable and viable criminal justice systems, and combat the growing threats of transnational organized crime and corruption.

In accordance with General Assembly resolutions 46/185 C [YUN 1991, p. 870] and 61/252 [YUN 2006, p. 1614], the Commission on Narcotic Drugs (CND) and the Commission on Crime Prevention and Criminal Justice (CCPCJ) functioned as the Office's governing bodies, and provided guidance in their respective areas to Member States and UNODC. In 2011, CND held its fifty-fourth (21–25 March and 12–13 December) [E/2011/28 & Add.1] and CCPCJ its twentieth session (11–15 April and 12–13 December) [E/2011/30 & Add.1], in Vienna.

The UNODC Executive Director described the Office's activities in 2011 in a later report to the two Commissions [E/CN.7/2012/3-E/CN.15/2012/3]. Those activities were conducted under the framework of its regional and thematic programmes, including drug control; combating transnational organized crime, corruption and terrorism; criminal justice; and research, trend analysis, and scientific and forensic support.

By the end of the year, UNODC regional programmes had been developed for East Africa, West Africa, the Arab States, Central America, East Asia and the Pacific, South-Eastern Europe, and Afghanistan and neighbouring countries. Those programmes helped to create effective regional mechanisms and stimulate the political will to fight organized crime and trafficking, facilitating the integration of development, the rule of law and human rights into UN peace and security activities, and providing support to countries, including fragile States.

The Office provided support to African States in their efforts to combat the world drug problem, including through strengthening their capacity to collect, analyse and share intelligence for use in the fight against drug trafficking and organized crime; providing operational support through the Global Programme against Money-Laundering and the Container Control Programme; and providing support to several countries to increase the coverage and improve the quality of drug abuse prevention and treatment and of rehabilitation and care services for drug abusers.

Some 90 per cent of the world's illicit opium continued to be produced in Afghanistan, fuelling local instability, transnational crime and illicit drug use in the region and worldwide. The Office assisted in the creation of several initiatives, including the Triangular Initiative between Afghanistan, Iran and Pakistan; the Targeted Anti-trafficking Regional Communication, Expertise and Training Operation to control precursor chemicals; and the Central Asian Regional Information and Coordination Centre, an intelligence body comprising Azerbaijan, Kazakhstan, Kyrgyzstan, the Russian Federation, Tajikistan, Turkmenistan and Uzbekistan. The Office launched a new regional programme for Afghanistan and neighbouring countries for the period 2011–2014, focusing on counter-narcotics and the rule of law.

In Central America, UNODC expanded its strategic interventions in response to transnational organized crime. Key areas included precursor control, container control and countering money-laundering, as well as drug abuse prevention and treatment for drug abusers. In Bolivia, Colombia and Peru, the Office continued its programmes on alternative development to facilitate the reintegration of former coca farmers into the licit economy.

In Asia and the Pacific, activities focused on drug data analysis, cross-border cooperation and drug demand reduction. The Office continued its activities in Bangladesh, Bhutan, India, Maldives, Nepal and Sri Lanka, focusing on HIV prevention among drug abusers, including in prisons, and on drug law enforcement.

With regard to sustainable livelihoods, UNODC redoubled its efforts to address illicit crop cultivation through development-oriented drug control programmes in Afghanistan, Bolivia, Colombia, the Lao People's Democratic Republic, Myanmar and Peru. To support drug supply reduction, the Office focused on strengthening national capacities and assisting in the creation of regional and international centres to foster cross-border law enforcement cooperation. During the year, UNODC increased its emphasis on compassionate and ethical demand reduction, rehabilitation and related health-protection measures as part of its efforts to put a health-centred and humanitarian approach at the heart of drug control policy.

The Executive Director concluded his report with a series of recommendations to the Commissions.

During the year, the Office published: *World Drug Report 2011* [Sales No. E.11.XI.10]; *Afghanistan Opium Survey 2010; Afghanistan Opium Survey 2011–Winter Rapid Assessment all regions; Afghanistan Opium Survey 2011–Summary findings; Afghanistan Cannabis Survey 2010; The Global Afghan Opium Trade: A Threat Assessment; Estado Plurinacional de Bolivia: Monitoreo de Cultivos de Coca 2010; Colombia: Monitoreo de Cultivos de Coca 2010; Peru: Monitoreo de Cultivos de Coca 2010; Patterns and Trends of Amphetamine-Type Stimulants and Other Drugs: Asia and the Pacific, 2011; South-East Asia: Opium Survey 2011;* and *Estimating Illicit Financial Flows resulting from Drug Trafficking and other Transnational Organized Crimes.*

Regional programmes

The Economic and Social Council in July considered a report of the Executive Director [YUN 2010, p. 1243] on support for the development and implementation of the regional programmes of the Office.

ECONOMIC AND SOCIAL COUNCIL ACTION

On 28 July [meeting 48], the Economic and Social Council, on the recommendation of the Commission on Crime Prevention and Criminal Justice [E/2011/30], adopted **resolution 2011/34** without vote [agenda item 14 (c)].

Support for the development and implementation of an integrated approach to programme development at the United Nations Office on Drugs and Crime

The Economic and Social Council,

Recalling General Assembly resolutions 63/197 of 18 December 2008 entitled "International cooperation against the world drug problem" and 64/179 of 18 December 2009 entitled "Strengthening the United Nations Crime Prevention and Criminal Justice Programme, in particular its technical cooperation capacity",

Recalling also the strategy for the period 2008–2011 for the United Nations Office on Drugs and Crime, which provides a clear framework for the work of the Office,

Recalling further its resolution 2009/23 of 30 July 2009 entitled "Support for the development and implementation of the regional programmes of the United Nations Office on Drugs and Crime" and its resolution 2010/20 of 22 July 2010 entitled "Support for the development and implementation of an integrated approach to programme development at the United Nations Office on Drugs and Crime",

1. *Welcomes* the report of the Executive Director of the United Nations Office on Drugs and Crime on support for the development and implementation of the regional programmes of the Office;

2. *Expresses its appreciation* for increased national ownership and participation in regional programmes, and encourages Member States in other subregions to engage with the United Nations Office on Drugs and Crime in the preparation of similar subregional programmes;

3. *Requests* the Secretariat to promote a culture of evaluation throughout the Organization, to mainstream the use of relevant monitoring and evaluation tools in programme planning and implementation and to provide adequate training, as appropriate and within available resources, to staff both at Headquarters and in field offices;

4. *Requests* that all regional and thematic programmes include provisions for evaluation, including an evaluation budget, an evaluation report and evaluation skills capacity development, and that already existing programmes be supplemented with annexes containing such provisions;

5. *Welcomes* the launch of the United Nations Office on Drugs and Crime Quality Control and Oversight Unit, which monitors programme and office performance of field offices and aims to ensure financial accountability is demonstrated through transparency and documented records, assisting both United Nations Office on Drugs and Crime headquarters and field offices in financial oversight and quality assurance;

6. *Encourages* Member States to continue to support the regional and thematic programmes of the United Nations Office on Drugs and Crime through unearmarked voluntary contributions, preferably through the general-purpose funds, when feasible, thereby supporting national ownership and regional prioritization;

7. *Welcomes* the progress made so far in the operationalization of the Central American Integration System/United Nations Office on Drugs and Crime Mechanism and its corresponding progressive development;

8. *Notes* the ongoing efforts with regard to the thematic and regional programmes developed with the support of the United Nations Office on Drugs and Crime and the launching of the regional programmes for West Africa and East Africa, as well as supporting the ongoing work of the regional programmes for East Asia and the Pacific, South-Eastern Europe, and Central America and the Caribbean, and also notes the presentation of the regional programme for the Arab States during the meeting of the standing open-ended intergovernmental working group on improving the governance and financial situation of the United Nations Office on Drugs and Crime, held on 18 February 2011, and of its inauguration;

9. *Looks forward* to the development of regional programmes for Afghanistan and neighbouring countries and Southern Africa, in consultation with the Member States of those regions, in the course of 2011;

10. *Welcomes* the establishment of centres of excellence in different countries of Latin America and the Caribbean as an important component for the effective implementation of regional and thematic programmes and the possible establishment of such centres of excellence or similar institutions in other countries in the region;

11. *Supports* the work of the United Nations Office on Drugs and Crime in leading the development of the integrated programme approach, in close cooperation with Member States;

12. *Encourages* increased joint activities among entities of the United Nations system, development agencies and regional organizations, within their respective mandates;

13. *Encourages* Member States, where appropriate, to draw on the technical assistance activities outlined in the regional programmes of the United Nations Office on Drugs and Crime and to use the regional programmes as a vehicle for increasing regional cooperation on thematic strategies;

14. *Encourages* the United Nations Office on Drugs and Crime to engage with bilateral and multilateral aid agencies and financial institutions to continue to support the implementation of the regional and thematic programmes of the Office;

15. *Requests* the United Nations Office on Drugs and Crime to continue to give high priority to and to support the implementation of the integrated regional and thematic programme approach, including by informing the open-ended intergovernmental working group of progress made, and to report on progress made in such implementation to the Commission on Narcotic Drugs at its fifty-fifth session and the Commission on Crime Prevention and Criminal Justice at its twenty-first session.

Administrative and budgetary matters

Administration

JIU report. By a note [E/CN.7/2011/14-E/CN.15/2011/20] dated 22 February, the Secretariat transmitted to CND and to CCPCJ a report [JIU/REP/2010/10] of the Joint Inspection Unit (JIU), which reviewed UNODC management and administration. It evaluated the Office with respect to its governance and financial framework, executive management, human resource management and oversight.

The inspectors noted that the trend for expansion of substantive and technical cooperation activities to new and diversified areas had diluted the strategic vision and the prioritization functions within the Office, and recommended conducting a thorough mandate review and a prioritization exercise on those mandates and related activities. The inspectors recommended that the Commissions hold joint reconvened sessions that would serve as an integrated governing body tasked with overseeing the budgetary and programmatic activities of the Office; encouraged increased efficiency and streamlining of financial management; and stated that opportunities to merge the two trust funds should be explored. Recommendations to the Executive Director included the institution of a corporate mechanism to oversee the financial situation of the Office and determine overall resource allocation, and the formulation of a fundraising strategy to enlarge the donor base of the Office.

The Secretary-General transmitted the note to the General Assembly on 19 August [A/66/315], and his own comments on the note on 16 September [A/66/315/Add.1 & Corr.1].

Commission action. CND on 22 March [E/2011/28 (res. 54/10)] and CCPCJ on 13 April [E/2011/30 (res. 20/1)] requested the Secretariat and the standing open-ended intergovernmental working group on improving the governance and financial situation of UNODC to submit an updated strategy for the period 2012–2015 to the reconvened sessions of the Commissions in December. They further requested the working group to consider the observations and recommendations made in that report, with a view to presenting recommendations for follow-up to the Commissions in the second half of 2011.

Intergovernmental working group. Pursuant to Economic and Social Council decision 2009/251 [YUN 2009, p. 1253] and requests by CND [ibid., p. 1252] and CCPCJ [ibid., p. 1082], a March Secretariat note [E/CN.7/2011/9-E/CN.15/2011/9] described the activities of the standing open-ended intergovernmental working group on improving the governance and financial situation of UNODC from 30 October 2010 to 10 March 2011.

On 28 July, the Economic and Social Council extended the mandate of the working group until the first half of 2013, at which time the Commissions would review its functioning and consider extending its mandate (**decision 2011/258**).

An October Secretariat note [E/CN.7/2011/9/Add.1-E/CN.15/2011/9/Add.1] outlined the working group's activities between 17 June and 6 October, including the consideration of the observations and recommendations of JIU. With respect to the recommendation to hold joint reconvened sessions, a draft decision was transmitted to the Economic and Social Council after the Chairs of the Commissions had consulted on it with all Member States. As a result, the Council, on 28 July, adopted **decision 2011/259**, pursuant to which the Commissions, starting in December, would hold joint meetings during their reconvened sessions to provide the Office with integrated policy directives on administrative, budgetary and strategic management issues.

In November [E/CN.7/2011/9/Add.2-E/CN.15/2011/9/Add.2], the Secretariat submitted a draft strategy for the period 2012–2015 in response to Commission resolutions 54/10 and 20/1 (see above). The strategy was based on the results of the strategy for the period 2008–2011 and included seven subprogrammes: countering transnational organized crime, illicit trafficking and illicit drug trafficking; countering corruption; terrorism prevention; justice; prevention, treatment and reintegration, and alternative development; research, trend analysis and forensics; and policy support.

Commission action. On 13 December [E/2011/30/Add.1 (res. 20/9) & E/2011/28/Add.1 (res. 54/17)], the Commissions requested the working group to explore with UNODC the creation of an internal system to monitor the implementation of recommendations made by relevant oversight bodies, including the Office of Internal Oversight Services, JIU, the Board of Auditors and the Independent Evaluation Unit, and to report to the Commissions in 2012.

Realignment of UNODC functions

In response to General Assembly resolution 65/227 [YUN 2010, p. 1244], the Secretary-General reported [E/CN.7/2011/3-E/CN.15/2011/3] on the realignment of the functions of the UNODC Division for Treaty Affairs and the Division for Operations.

Following consultations with Member States in 2009, UNODC realigned the Divisions by establishing thematic clusters—namely organized crime and illicit trafficking, corruption, justice, health, and terrorism prevention—around its key mandates. The realignment enabled the Office to acquire an integrated regional and thematic perspective and resulted in real gains in terms of improved policy; strategy; mobilization of resources; implementation of programmatic work; and partnerships with UN entities, multilateral and bilateral bodies and other stakeholders.

Following that realignment, it became necessary to bring the third substantive division of UNODC, the Division for Policy Analysis and Public Affairs, in line with the new approach of thematic clusters and integrated programming. Accordingly, in April 2010, the United Nations Office at Vienna/UNODC Executive Committee decided to adjust the structure of that Division to cluster, on the one hand, the Laboratory and Scientific Section, the Statistics and Survey Section and the Studies and Threat Analysis Section under the Research and Trend Analysis Branch; and, on the other hand, the Advocacy Section, the Co-Financing and Partnership Section and the Strategic Planning Unit under the Public Affairs and Policy Support Branch.

Budget

In February [E/CN.7/2011/11-E/CN.15/2011/11], the Executive Director identified adjustments to the UNODC consolidated budget for the biennium 2010–2011 [YUN 2009, p. 1253] as a result of revised requirements and changes in costing parameters. For the Fund of the United Nations International Drug Control Programme, Member States were requested to approve revised estimates for general-purpose funds totalling at least $16,378,300. Member States were also requested to endorse revised estimates for programme support cost funds totalling $22,970,500 and for special-purpose funds totalling $240,741,700. For the United Nations Crime Prevention and Criminal Justice Fund, Member States were requested to approve revised estimates for general-purpose funds totalling at least $4,250,900. They were also requested to endorse revised estimates for programme support cost funds totalling $8,211,500 and for special-purpose funds totalling $173,254,200.

In October, the Executive Director submitted to the Commissions the UNODC consolidated budget for the biennium 2012–2013 [E/CN.7/2011/16-E/CN.15/2011/22].

In November [E/CN.7/2011/17-E/CN.15/2011/23], the Advisory Committee on Administrative and Budgetary Questions submitted its comments and recommendations on that report. The Committee commended UNODC for the measures it had taken to stabilize its financial situation, expected it to closely monitor general-purpose funds income and expenditure, and encouraged it to further broaden its donor base.

Commission action. At its March session [E/2011/28 (res. 54/1)], CND approved the revised projected use of general-purpose funds in the biennium 2010–2011, and invited Member States to provide contributions totalling at least $16,378,300. It also endorsed the revised estimates for the programme support cost fund and special-purpose funds for the Fund of the United Nations International Drug Control Programme totalling $281,143,900. On 13 December [E/2011/28/Add.1 (res. 54/16)], the Commission approved the projected use of general-purpose funds in the biennium 2012–2013, and invited Member States to provide contributions totalling at least $12,648,300. It also endorsed the programme support cost fund and special-purpose estimates for the Fund of the United Nations International Drug Control Programme totalling $243,191,600.

At its April session [E/2011/30 (res. 20/2)], CCPCJ approved the revised projected use of general-purpose funds in the biennium 2010–2011, and invited Member States to provide contributions totalling at least $4,250,900. It also endorsed the revised estimates for the programme support cost funds and special-purpose funds for the United Nations Crime Prevention and Criminal Justice Fund totalling $186,118,700. On 13 December [E/2011/30/Add.1 (res. 20/8)], the Commission approved the projected use of general-purpose funds in the biennium 2012–2013, and invited Member States to provide contributions totalling at least $8,479,500. It also endorsed the programme support cost and special-purpose estimates for the United Nations Crime Prevention and Criminal Justice Fund totalling $232,290,900.

International drug control

Commission on Narcotic Drugs

At its fifty-fourth session (Vienna, 2 December 2010 and 21–25 March 2011) [E/2011/28], the Commission on Narcotic Drugs recommended one resolution and three decisions for adoption by the Economic and Social Council (see below). It also adopted 15 resolutions, which it brought to the attention of the Council (see below).

At its reconvened fifty-fourth session (Vienna, 12–13 December) [E/2011/28/Add.1], the Commission recommended one resolution and one decision for adoption by the Council. It also adopted two resolutions, which it brought to the attention of the Council: one on the budget for the biennium 2012–2013 for the Fund of the United Nations International Drug Control Programme, and one on the work of the standing open-ended intergovernmental working group on improving the governance and financial situation of UNODC.

In accordance with Economic and Social Council **decision 2011/259** of 28 July, one meeting of the Commission was held jointly with the Commission on Crime Prevention and Criminal Justice on 12 December.

The Economic and Social Council on 28 July took note of the Commission's report on its reconvened fifty-third session [E/2010/28/Add.1] and approved the provisional agenda for the fifty-fourth (2011) session (**decision 2011/260**). Also on 28 July, the Council took note of the Commission's report on its fifty-fourth session [E/2011/28] and approved the provisional agenda for the fifty-fifth (2012) session (**decision 2011/261**).

Drug demand reduction and drug abuse

The Commission considered a January report by the Secretariat [E/CN.7/2011/2] that reviewed the world situation with regard to drug abuse and the global demand for illicit drugs. The report noted that while there were stabilizing or decreasing trends for traditional drugs of abuse (heroin and cocaine) in regions of greatest consumption, that gain was being offset by the considerable increase in the use of synthetic and prescription drugs. Globally, cannabis remained the most consumed illicit drug. In terms of harm associated with use, however, opiates ranked highest. While cannabis use, particularly among young people, was stabilizing or declining in Western Europe, North America and parts of Oceania, consumption had increased in other parts of the world, particularly in Africa. The use of opioids, cocaine and amphetamine-type stimulants (ATS) in high-consumption countries was stabilizing or decreasing. The use of ATS was, however, increasing in Asia, with methamphetamine use increasing in parts of East and South-East Asia and amphetamine abuse increasing in the Near and Middle East. Abuse of prescription drugs was also a growing health problem in a number of developed and developing countries. Provision of treatment and care remained a challenge, with 11–33.5 million problem drug users estimated to have an unmet need for treatment. The lack of sustainable drug information and monitoring systems hindered the monitoring of changing and emerging trends, the implementation of evidence-based responses and the ability to assess the effectiveness of those responses.

A January report by the Executive Director [E/CN.7/2011/13] summarized replies from 50 Governments on measures they had taken to protect children and young people from drug abuse.

Preventing drug-affected driving. On 25 March [E/2011/28 (res. 54/2)], the Commission urged Member States to develop national responses to address the issue of drug-affected driving by assessing and monitoring the magnitude of that phenomenon and by exchanging information and best practices on effective responses, including through engagement with the international scientific and legal communities. The Commission requested UNODC to participate in international efforts to implement the Global Plan for the Decade of Action for Road Safety 2011–2020 (see p. 1159), and to incorporate public awareness of drug-affected driving into its public awareness programmes.

Alternative development. On 25 March [res. 54/4], the Commission noted that Peru and Thailand remained committed to jointly organizing an international workshop and an international conference on alternative development. It also noted that the aim of the events was to gather inputs and contributions and to assess efforts for developing a set of international guiding principles to serve as guidelines for alternative development programmes in drug-producing areas, to be considered at the international conference. The Commission urged Member States, UNODC, international financial institutions, donors, international organizations and other stakeholders to participate in the international workshop and the international conference.

Following up on that resolution, the Secretariat in December reported that, as the first part of the International Workshop and Conference on Alternative Development, Thailand, in association with Peru and in collaboration with UNODC, organized an International Workshop on Alternative Development (Chiang Mai and Chiang Rai, Thailand, 6–11 November) [E/CN.7/2012/8]. Participants agreed on the inputs for the draft International Guiding Principles on Alternative Development, which were annexed to the report.

Strategies for drug use disorders. On 25 March [res. 54/5], the Commission urged Member States to identify and counter discrimination against drug users while offering access to counselling, treatment and rehabilitation services directed at promoting health and well-being among individuals, families and communities. States were further urged to focus on prevention, treatment, care and support services for drug users suffering from a drug-related disorder, as well as for their families; and to develop interventions that would lead to social reintegration, including supporting programmes to facilitate the employment of people in treatment and recovery. The Commission requested UNODC to include rehabilitation- and reintegration-oriented modules for drug dependence treatment in its technical assistance and training programmes, and urged the Office to provide Member States with guidance and assistance in developing programmes of intervention as part of their overall drug demand reduction strategies. The Executive Director was requested to report to the Commission's fifty-fifth (2012) session on the implementation of the resolution.

Role of civil society in world drug problem. On 25 March [res. 54/11], the Commission encouraged

Member States to ensure that civil society played a participatory role, through consultation, in the development and implementation of drug control programmes and policies, in particular with regard to aspects of demand reduction; to cultivate an environment that promoted innovation; and to take into account promising approaches pursued by civil society to assist Governments in their efforts to address the world drug problem. It further encouraged States to provide to UNODC their experiences in working with civil society in UN forums and to provide suggestions with a view to improving the participatory role of civil society in addressing the world drug problem.

Principle of common and shared responsibility. On 25 March [res. 54/12], the Commission called on the international community to engage in cooperation and practical action in order to address the world drug problem on the basis of the principle of shared responsibility. The Commission requested UNODC to facilitate the exchange of experiences and good practices among Member States with respect to strategies to reduce illicit drug supply and demand and drug trafficking, and with respect to international cooperation to promote technical assistance projects aimed at addressing the world drug problem. The Commission also invited Member States to provide UNODC with information on such cooperation activities with a view to identifying priority areas in which cooperation might be strengthened, and requested the Office to report to the Commission's fifty-sixth (2013) session on the implementation of the resolution.

Achieving zero new HIV infections. On 25 March [res. 54/13], the Commission noted the provisions of the 2011–2015 Joint United Nations Programme on HIV/AIDS strategy "Getting to zero" [YUN 2010, p. 1222]; urged Member States to ensure continued political commitment to combating HIV/AIDS as one of the adverse consequences of drug abuse; requested UNODC to scale up evidence-based interventions to prevent HIV infection among people who used drugs, in particular injecting drug users; and requested the Office to provide advice and guidance on measures targeting the populations most at risk, such as injecting drug users, including measures to reduce stigmatization and discrimination.

Illicit cultivation, manufacture and trafficking

A Secretariat report on the world situation with regard to drug trafficking [E/CN.7/2012/4] reviewed the latest trends in illicit drug production and trafficking worldwide. In respect of seizure statistics, the report focused on 2009 and 2010; with regard to illicit drug crop cultivation and drug production, it focused on the period 2009–2011.

Cannabis continued to be the most widely produced, trafficked and used plant-based drug worldwide. While cannabis herb production was found in most countries, production of cannabis resin was concentrated in just a few countries, among which Afghanistan and Morocco were the most prominent examples. Global seizures of cannabis herb continued to be dominated by the quantities seized in the Americas. Large quantities of cannabis resin were smuggled out of Morocco into Europe, as well as out of Afghanistan into neighbouring countries.

In 2011, opium poppy cultivation in Afghanistan increased marginally, while the decline in opium production observed in 2010, caused by a disease affecting the opium poppy crop, was largely reversed. In 2010, coca bush cultivation remained concentrated in Bolivia, Colombia and Peru; the most marked shift was a continued decline in the area under cultivation in Colombia. While North America and Western and Central Europe continued to be the major destinations for cocaine smuggled out of South America, the scale of the cocaine phenomenon appeared to be contained in both of those well-established illicit markets. Conversely, various countries with a limited illicit market for cocaine showed indications of an increased availability of the drug.

In 2010, the global supply chain of amphetamine-type stimulants continued to evolve in terms of the extent of manufacture, patterns in trafficking routes and the nature of substances involved. Methamphetamine remained widely available in North America and Asia and the Pacific, but also appeared to spread to new markets, with global seizures increasing significantly. The availability of methylenedioxymethamphetamine (MDMA, commonly known as "ecstasy") had declined significantly between 2007 and 2009.

A January report of the Executive Director on promoting international cooperation in addressing the involvement of women and girls in drug trafficking, especially as couriers [E/CN.7/2011/7], summarized the data reported by Member States on women and girls involved as drug traffickers.

Cooperation against the world drug problem

International cooperation

Commission on Narcotic Drugs. On 23 and 24 March [E/2011/28], the Commission considered the implementation of the Political Declaration and Plan of Action on International Cooperation towards an Integrated and Balanced Strategy to Counter the World Drug Problem [YUN 2009, p. 1237]. Many speakers welcomed the stabilization of the level of use of amphetamine-type stimulants, cannabis, cocaine and opioids in many regions, but expressed concern over the increase in the use of new synthetic and prescription drugs. Participants noted the high prevalence of drug abuse among women and children, and underlined the need to monitor their situation and address their needs with respect to drug abuse prevention, treatment and care services. Representatives stressed the need to respond to new challenges related to illicit drug use, particularly among youth, such as new synthetic substances and the non-medical use of prescription drugs; the importance of a health-related approach and drug demand reduction as indispensable pillars of drug control; the need to base policies on scientific evidence and respect for the human rights and dignity of individuals in need; the need for increased resources and collaboration; the importance of evaluating interventions; and the crucial role played by non-governmental organizations (NGOs) and civil society. With respect to supply reduction and related measures, speakers referred to the need for States to accurately collect and share data on drug supply in order to effectively address drug trafficking. They discussed the need for enhanced international efforts to reduce illicit cannabis plant cultivation, the provision of resources and technical assistance, the sharing of best practices and lessons learned, and the importance of addressing the growing links between drug trafficking and organized crime. Several speakers noted the importance of fighting money-laundering, which had become increasingly sophisticated and transnational in nature, and called for the strengthening of regional and international cooperation and compliance with international standards.

Paris Pact initiative. On 25 March [res. 54/7], the Commission welcomed the decision taken by the reconvened meeting of the Paris Pact Policy Consultative Group (Vienna, 17 March) to convene in Vienna in the second half of 2011 an international ministerial conference in continuation of the Paris Pact initiative—an international partnership to counter Afghan opiates trafficking and consumption that emerged from the Paris Statement, adopted at the first Ministerial Conference on Drug Routes from Central Asia to Europe (Paris, 21–22 May 2003) [YUN 2003, p. 1263]. The Commission encouraged the international conference to strengthen the commitment of Member States to combating the illicit trade in Afghan opiates. It requested the Executive Director to facilitate the organization and holding of the conference and to report thereon to the Commission at its fifty-fifth (2012) session.

Measures to support African States. On 25 March [E/2011/28 (res. 54/14)], the Commission invited Member States to mobilize resources to enhance the implementation of the revised African Union Plan of Action on Drug Control and Crime Prevention (2007–2012) and UNODC regional programmes, as well as national strategies of African countries, to support those countries in their efforts to combat the world drug problem. The Commission requested UNODC to support the African Union in implementing its Plan of Action; called on the Governments of the region to raise awareness among the population, in particular among youth, of the dangers of drug abuse; and urged African national authorities to strengthen their legal systems, administrative procedures, training and technical support to exercise effective control over illicit drugs and precursor chemicals. The Commission requested the Executive Director to report to its fifty-fifth (2012) session on the implementation of the resolution.

Cooperation to assist transit States. On 25 March [res. 54/15], the Commission requested the international community, in particular countries of destination, to provide technical assistance and support to the most affected transit States in order to promote their capacities to counter the flow of illicit drugs. It requested UNODC, when developing regional and thematic programmes, to consider the needs of and consult with the States most affected by the transit of drugs, including technical and financial assistance. The Commission requested the Executive Director to report to its fifty-sixth (2013) session on the implementation of the resolution.

Data collection, reporting and analysis. On 25 March [res. 54/9], the Commission noted with concern the Secretariat report on the world situation with regard to drug abuse [E/CN.7/2011/2] (see p. 1175), which raised concern about the lack of current information on most of the epidemiological indicators on drug use. The Commission invited Member States to invest in capacity-building and quality-enhancing activities for the collection and reporting of information, and to participate in joint cooperation efforts, organized by UNODC and by other organizations and bodies, aimed at the exchange of technical knowledge of experts in the area of data collection, analysis and evaluation. The Commission requested the Executive Director to examine ways and means of utilizing expertise and know-how on drug-related data collection from scientific institutions and networks to inform quality assurance standards, capacity-building activities and a comprehensive understanding of the global drug situation, and to report thereon to the Commission's fifty-fifth (2012) session.

Security Council consideration. The Security Council met on 24 June [S/PV.6565] to consider the item "Threats to international peace and security" and to hear a briefing by the UNODC Executive Director, Yury Fedotov. He reported that a UN system task force on transnational organized crime and drug trafficking, established by the Secretary-General and co-chaired by UNODC and the Department for Political Affairs, had started its work. He noted that illicit drugs undermined stability, security and health in many parts of the world, and suggested four potential areas of response from the perspective of UNODC: concerted political will on the part of Member States to suppress organized crime; strengthening regional capacity to assist fragile States; consistent and proactive investments in the criminal justice institutions of weak States; and, with regard to adopting a comprehensive and cross-disciplinary strategy, addressing the challenges posed by organized crime and illicit trafficking in a coordinated and holistic way. Fifteen countries made statements at the meeting.

Report of Secretary-General. Pursuant to General Assembly resolution 65/233 [YUN 2010, p. 1252], the Secretary-General in June submitted a report [A/66/130] on international cooperation against the world drug problem. The report reviewed the world drug situation and examined the status of implementation of the mandates relating to international drug control by the Commission and by UNODC, other parts of the UN system and international organizations.

The Secretary-General noted that illicit drugs and associated crime and corruption were major threats to security, stability, public health and development around the globe, and that a balanced and comprehensive approach was the only effective way to eliminate or reduce illicit drug demand, supply and trafficking. A significant amount of work remained to be done, both by Governments and the international community, in ensuring that the objectives of the international drug conventions were achieved, namely that the use of narcotic drugs was limited to medical and scientific purposes; that there was adequate availability of narcotic drugs for such purposes; and that the illicit cultivation and production of, trafficking in and use of narcotic drugs were prevented.

GENERAL ASSEMBLY ACTION

On 19 December [meeting 89], the General Assembly, on the recommendation of the Third (Social, Humanitarian and Cultural) Committee [A/66/464], adopted **resolution 66/183** without vote [agenda item 108].

International cooperation against the world drug problem

The General Assembly,

Reaffirming the Political Declaration adopted by the General Assembly at its twentieth special session, the Declaration on the Guiding Principles of Drug Demand Reduction, the Action Plan on International Cooperation on the Eradication of Illicit Drug Crops and on Alternative Development, the Action Plan for the Implementation of the Declaration on the Guiding Principles of Drug Demand Reduction and the joint ministerial statement adopted at the ministerial segment of the forty-sixth session of the Commission on Narcotic Drugs,

Recalling that, in its resolution 64/182 of 18 December 2009, the General Assembly adopted the Political Declaration and Plan of Action on International Cooperation towards an Integrated and Balanced Strategy to Counter the World Drug Problem, as adopted by the Commission on Narcotic Drugs at the high-level segment of its fifty-second session, and called upon States to take the measures necessary to fully implement the actions set out therein, with a view to attaining, in a timely manner, their goals and targets,

Recalling also its resolution 53/115 of 9 December 1998, in which it urged Governments, the relevant United Nations bodies, the specialized agencies and other international organizations to assist and support, upon request, transit States, in particular developing countries in need of such assistance and support, aiming at enhancing their capacity to fight the illicit trafficking in narcotic drugs and psychotropic substances,

Recalling further the United Nations Millennium Declaration, the provisions of the 2005 World Summit Outcome addressing the world drug problem, the Political Declaration on HIV/AIDS and other relevant United Nations resolutions, including General Assembly resolution 65/233 of 21 December 2010 and those on regional and international cooperation to prevent the diversion and smuggling of precursors,

Recalling the adoption by the Economic and Social Council of its resolutions 2010/17 and 2010/21 of 22 July 2010 on the realignment of the functions of the United Nations Office on Drugs and Crime and changes to the strategic framework,

Noting with appreciation the efforts of the Secretary-General to develop, within the United Nations system, an effective and comprehensive approach to transnational organized crime and the world drug problem, and reaffirming the crucial role of Member States in this regard,

Welcoming the efforts made by Member States to comply with the provisions of the Single Convention on Narcotic Drugs of 1961 as amended by the 1972 Protocol, the Convention on Psychotropic Substances of 1971 and the United Nations Convention against Illicit Traffic in Narcotic Drugs and Psychotropic Substances of 1988,

Welcoming also the fiftieth anniversary of the adoption of the Single Convention on Narcotic Drugs,

Recognizing the importance both of the universality of the three international drug control conventions against the illicit use and trafficking of drugs and of their implementation,

Welcoming the measures taken by the United Nations Office on Drugs and Crime to develop a thematic and regional programme approach to its activities, and noting the progress in the implementation of such an approach,

Recalling all resolutions adopted by the Commission on Narcotic Drugs at its fifty-fourth session,

Gravely concerned that, despite continuing increased efforts by States, relevant organizations, civil society and non-governmental organizations, the world drug problem continues to constitute a serious threat to public health and safety and the well-being of humanity, in particular children and young people and their families, and to the national security and sovereignty of States, and that it undermines socioeconomic and political stability and sustainable development,

Deeply concerned about the need to take all appropriate measures, including legislative, administrative, social and educational measures, to protect children and young people against the illicit use of narcotic drugs and psychotropic substances as defined in the relevant treaties, and to prevent the use of children and young people in the illicit production of and trafficking in such substances, and urging Governments to implement Commission on Narcotic Drugs resolution 53/10 of 12 March 2010,

Noting with grave concern the global increased abuse of certain drugs and the proliferation of new substances, such as those indicated in Commission on Narcotic Drugs resolution 53/13 of 12 March 2010, as well as the increasing sophistication of the transnational organized criminal groups engaged in their manufacture and distribution,

Noting with grave concern also the global increased abuse and manufacture of amphetamine-type stimulants as well as the proliferation of chemical precursors used in the illicit manufacture of narcotic drugs and psychotropic substances, and the emergence of new methods of diversion used by organized criminal groups,

Recognizing that the use of substances that are not controlled under the international drug control treaties and that may pose potential public-health risks has emerged in recent years in several regions of the world, and noting the increasing number of reports about the production or manufacture of substances, most commonly herbal mixtures, including synthetic cannabinoid receptor agonists that have psychoactive effects similar to those produced by cannabis, and psychoactive substances marketed as bath salts,

Recognizing also the critical importance of forensic and scientific laboratory and treatment centre data and qualitative information in understanding the problem of illicit synthetic drugs and the range of products available on the illicit market,

Noting the need to promote adequate availability of internationally controlled narcotic drugs and psychotropic substances for medical and scientific purposes while preventing their diversion and abuse, in line with the Single Convention on Narcotic Drugs of 1961 as amended by the 1972 Protocol and the Convention on Psychotropic Substances of 1971, and recalling in that regard Commission on Narcotic Drugs resolutions 53/4 of 12 March 2010 and 54/6 of 25 March 2011,

Recognizing that sustained and collective efforts through international cooperation in demand reduction and supply reduction have shown that positive results can be achieved, and expressing its appreciation for the initiatives at the regional and international levels in this regard,

Recognizing also the principal role of the Commission on Narcotic Drugs and its subsidiary bodies, together with the International Narcotics Control Board, as the United Nations organs with prime responsibility for drug control matters, and recognizing further the need to promote and facilitate the effective implementation of and follow-up to the Political Declaration and Plan of Action on International Cooperation towards an Integrated and Balanced Strategy to Counter the World Drug Problem,

Reaffirming that countering the world drug problem in all its aspects requires a political commitment to reducing supply, as an integral component of a balanced and comprehensive drug control strategy, in accordance with the principles enshrined in the Political Declaration adopted by the General Assembly at its twentieth special session and the measures to enhance international cooperation to counter the world drug problem, including the Action Plan on International Cooperation on the Eradication of Illicit Drug Crops and on Alternative Development, also adopted at that session,

Reaffirming equally that reducing illicit drug use and its consequences requires a political commitment to efforts to reduce demand, which must be demonstrated by sustained widespread demand reduction initiatives that integrate a comprehensive public-health approach spanning the spectrum of prevention, education, early detection and intervention, treatment, care and related support services, recovery support, rehabilitation and social reintegration efforts, and that are age- and gender-sensitive, in full compliance with the three international drug control conventions and in accordance with the Declaration on the Guiding Principles of Drug Demand Reduction, adopted by the General Assembly at its twentieth special session, and with the Political Declaration and Plan of Action on International Cooperation towards an Integrated and Balanced Strategy to Counter the World Drug Problem, adopted by the Commission on Narcotic Drugs at the high-level segment of its fifty-second session, and other relevant General Assembly resolutions,

Recalling the recommendations contained in its resolution 64/182 that the Economic and Social Council devote one of its high-level segments to a theme related to the world drug problem and that the General Assembly hold a special session to address the world drug problem,

Conscious of the need to raise public awareness of the risks and threats posed to all societies by the different aspects of the world drug problem,

Reaffirming that the world drug problem remains a common and shared responsibility that requires effective and increased international cooperation and demands an integrated, multidisciplinary, mutually reinforcing and balanced approach to supply and demand reduction strategies,

1. *Reiterates its call upon* States to take, in a timely manner, the measures necessary to implement the actions and attain the goals and targets set out in the Political Declaration and Plan of Action on International Cooperation towards an Integrated and Balanced Strategy to Counter the World Drug Problem, adopted by the General Assembly at its sixty-fourth session;

2. *Reaffirms* that countering the world drug problem is a common and shared responsibility that must be addressed in a multilateral setting, requires an integrated and balanced approach and must be carried out in full conformity with the purposes and principles of the Charter of the United Nations and other provisions of international law, the Universal Declaration of Human Rights and the Vienna Declaration and Programme of Action on human rights, and, in particular, with full respect for the sovereignty and territorial integrity of States, for the principle of non-intervention in the internal affairs of States and for all human rights and fundamental freedoms, and on the basis of the principles of equal rights and mutual respect;

3. *Calls upon* Member States to engage in effective cooperation and practical action aimed at addressing the world drug problem on the basis of the principle of common and shared responsibility;

4. *Undertakes* to promote bilateral, regional and international cooperation, including through intelligence-sharing and cross-border cooperation, aimed at countering the world drug problem more effectively, in particular by encouraging and supporting such cooperation by those States most directly affected by illicit crop cultivation and the illicit production, manufacture, transit, trafficking, distribution and abuse of narcotic drugs and psychotropic substances;

5. *Reiterates* the commitment of Member States to promoting, developing, reviewing or strengthening effective, comprehensive, integrated drug demand reduction programmes, based on scientific evidence and covering a range of measures, including primary prevention, education, early detection and intervention, treatment, care and related support services, recovery support, rehabilitation and social reintegration efforts, aimed at promoting health and social well-being among individuals, families and communities and reducing the adverse consequences of drug abuse for individuals and society as a whole, taking into account the specific needs of women and the particular challenges posed by high-risk drug users, in full compliance with the three international drug control conventions and in accordance with national legislation, and commits Member States to investing increased resources in ensuring access to those interventions on a non-discriminatory basis, including in detention facilities, bearing in mind that those interventions should also consider vulnerabilities that undermine human development, such as poverty and social marginalization;

6. *Recommends* that the Economic and Social Council devote one of its high-level segments to a theme related to the world drug problem, and also recommends that the General Assembly hold a special session to address the world drug problem;

7. *Notes with great concern* the adverse consequences of drug abuse for individuals and society as a whole, reaffirms the commitment of all Member States to tackling those problems in the context of comprehensive, complementary and multisectoral drug demand reduction strategies, in particular such strategies targeting children, young people and their families, also notes with great concern the alarming rise in the incidence of HIV/AIDS and other blood-borne diseases among injecting drug users, reaffirms the commitment of all Member States to working towards the goal of universal access to comprehensive prevention programmes and treatment, care and related support services, in full compliance with the international drug control conventions and in accordance with national legislation, taking into account all relevant General Assembly resolutions and, when applicable, the *WHO, UNODC, UNAIDS Technical Guide for Countries to Set Targets for Universal Access to HIV Prevention, Treatment and Care for Injecting Drug Users*, and requests the United Nations Office on Drugs and Crime to carry out its mandate in this area in close cooperation with relevant organizations and programmes of the United Nations system, such as the World Health Organization, the United Nations Development Programme and the Joint United Nations Programme on HIV/AIDS;

8. *Urges* Member States, where appropriate, to develop national responses to address the issue of drug-affected driving by, inter alia, exchanging information and best practices on effective responses, including through engagement with the international scientific and legal communities;

9. *Encourages* Member States to promote, in accordance with Commission on Narcotic Drugs resolutions 53/4 and 54/6, the adequate availability of internationally controlled narcotic drugs and psychotropic substances for medical and scientific purposes while preventing their diversion and abuse, and requests the United Nations Office on Drugs and Crime and the International Narcotics Control Board to continue their efforts in that regard;

10. *Acknowledges* the continuing efforts made and the progress achieved in countering the world drug problem, notes with great concern the continuing illicit production of and trafficking in opium, the continuing illicit manufacture of and trafficking in cocaine, the increasing illicit production of and trafficking in cannabis, the ongoing global spread of the illicit manufacture of amphetamine-type stimulants and the increasing diversion of precursors, as well as the related distribution and use of illicit drugs, and stresses the need to strengthen and intensify joint efforts at the national, regional and international levels to tackle those global challenges in a more comprehensive manner, in accordance with the principle of common and shared responsibility, including by means of enhanced and better-coordinated technical and financial assistance;

11. *Invites* Member States to take appropriate measures so as to strengthen international cooperation and the exchange of information regarding the identification of new routes and modi operandi of organized criminal groups dedicated to the diversion or smuggling of substances frequently used in the illicit manufacture of narcotic drugs and psychotropic substances, in particular with respect to their trafficking via the Internet, and to continue to notify the International Narcotics Control Board of such information;

12. *Continues to encourage* Member States to promote, in accordance with Commission on Narcotic Drugs resolution 53/11 of 12 March 2010, the sharing of information on the potential abuse of and trafficking in synthetic cannabinoid receptor agonists;

13. *Recognizes* the need to collect relevant data and information regarding international cooperation for countering the world drug problem at all levels, and urges Member States to support dialogue through the Commission on Narcotic Drugs in order to address this issue;

14. *Also recognizes* that:

(*a*) Sustainable crop control strategies targeting the illicit cultivation of crops used for the production of narcotic drugs and psychotropic substances require international cooperation based on the principle of shared responsibility and an integrated and balanced approach, taking into account the rule of law and, where appropriate, security concerns, with full respect for the sovereignty and territorial integrity of States, the principle of non-intervention in the internal affairs of States and all human rights and fundamental freedoms;

(*b*) Such crop control strategies include, inter alia, alternative development and, where appropriate, preventive alternative development programmes, eradication and law enforcement measures;

(*c*) Such crop control strategies should be in full conformity with article 14 of the United Nations Convention against Illicit Traffic in Narcotic Drugs and Psychotropic

Substances of 1988 and appropriately coordinated and phased in accordance with national policies in order to achieve the sustainable eradication of illicit crops, noting furthermore the need for Member States to undertake to increase long-term investment in such strategies, coordinated with other development measures, in order to contribute to the sustainability of social and economic development and poverty eradication in affected rural areas, taking due account of the traditional licit uses of crops where there is historical evidence of such use and giving due consideration to the protection of the environment;

15. *Further recognizes* the significant role played by developing countries with extensive expertise in alternative development in promoting best practices and lessons learned from such programmes, and invites them to continue sharing those best practices with States affected by illicit crop cultivation, including those emerging from conflict, with a view to using them, where appropriate, in accordance with the national specificities of each State;

16. *Urges* Member States to intensify their cooperation with and assistance to transit States affected by illicit drug trafficking, directly or through the competent regional and international organizations, in accordance with article 10 of the United Nations Convention against Illicit Traffic in Narcotic Drugs and Psychotropic Substances of 1988, and on the basis of the principle of shared responsibility and the need for all States to promote and implement measures to counter the drug problem in all its aspects with an integrated and balanced approach;

17. *Requests* the international community, in particular the countries of destination, to provide, on the basis of the principle of shared responsibility, urgent and sufficient technical assistance and support to the most affected transit States in order to promote the capacities of such States to counter the flow of illicit drugs;

18. *Reiterates* the urgent need for Member States to strengthen international and regional cooperation in order to respond to the serious challenges posed by the increasing links between drug trafficking, money-laundering, corruption and other forms of organized crime, including trafficking in persons, smuggling of migrants, trafficking in firearms, cybercrime and, in some cases, terrorism and the financing of terrorism, and to the significant challenges faced by law enforcement and judicial authorities in responding to the ever-changing means used by transnational criminal organizations to avoid detection and prosecution;

19. *Recognizes* the increasing links between drug trafficking and the illicit manufacturing of and trafficking in firearms in some regions of the world and the need to prevent the spread of that problem to other regions, and urges Member States to take adequate measures, consistent with their international treaty obligations and other relevant international standards, to fully cooperate in preventing the acquisition and use of firearms and ammunition by criminal organizations involved in drug trafficking and in combating the illicit manufacturing of and trafficking in such firearms and ammunition;

20. *Reaffirms* the importance of the United Nations Office on Drugs and Crime and its regional offices in building capacity at the local level in the fight against transnational organized crime and drug trafficking, and urges the Office to consider regional vulnerabilities, projects and impact in the fight against drug trafficking, in particular in developing countries, when deciding to close and allocate offices, with a view to maintaining an effective level of support for national and regional efforts in combating the world drug problem;

21. *Urges* the United Nations Office on Drugs and Crime to increase collaboration with intergovernmental, international and relevant regional organizations involved in combating and addressing the world drug problem, as appropriate, in order to share best practices and scientific standards, and to maximize the benefits from their unique comparative advantage;

22. *Requests* the United Nations Office on Drugs and Crime, upon request, to continue providing technical assistance to Member States so as to enhance capacity in countering the world drug problem, including enhancing the analytical work of laboratories, by carrying out training programmes to develop indicators and instruments for the collection and analysis of accurate, reliable and comparable data on all relevant aspects of the world drug problem and, where appropriate, enhance or develop new national indicators and instruments, and invites Member States to invest, where necessary and taking into account specific needs and available resources, in capacity-building and quality-enhancing activities for the collection and reporting of information, and to participate in joint cooperation efforts organized by the United Nations Office on Drugs and Crime and/or by other national, regional or international organizations and bodies, aimed at the exchange of technical knowledge of experts in the area of data collection, analysis and evaluation and of practical experience in the area of drug data;

23. *Invites* the Commission on Narcotic Drugs, as the central policymaking body of the United Nations system on drug-related matters, to strengthen the capacity of the United Nations Office on Drugs and Crime to collect, analyse, use and disseminate accurate, reliable, objective and comparable data and to reflect such information in the *World Drug Report*;

24. *Encourages* the United Nations Office on Drugs and Crime to continue its efforts in supporting States to establish, upon request, operational frameworks essential for communication within and across national borders and in facilitating the exchange of information on and analysis of drug trafficking trends, with a view to increasing knowledge about the world drug problem at the national, regional and international levels, recognizes the importance of integrating laboratories and providing scientific support to drug control frameworks and of treating quality analytical data as a primary source of information worldwide, and urges coordination with other international entities, including the International Criminal Police Organization (INTERPOL);

25. *Urges* all Governments to provide the fullest possible financial and political support to the United Nations Office on Drugs and Crime by widening its donor base and increasing voluntary contributions, in particular general-purpose contributions, so as to enable it to continue, expand, improve and strengthen, within its mandates, its operational and technical cooperation activities, including with a view to the full implementation of the Political Declaration adopted by the General Assembly at its twentieth special session and the Political Declaration and Plan of Action on International Cooperation towards an Integrated

and Balanced Strategy to Counter the World Drug Problem adopted by the Commission on Narcotic Drugs at the high-level segment of its fifty-second session, as well as, where appropriate, relevant resolutions adopted by the Commission at that session, and recommends that a sufficient share of the regular budget of the United Nations continue to be allocated to the Office to enable it to carry out its mandates in a consistent and stable manner;

26. *Takes note* of Commission on Narcotic Drugs resolution 54/10 of 25 March 2011 on the recommendations of the standing open-ended intergovernmental working group on improving the governance and financial situation of the United Nations Office on Drugs and Crime, and encourages Member States and the Office to continue addressing the issues within the mandate of the working group in a pragmatic, results-oriented, efficient and cooperative manner;

27. *Encourages* the Commission on Narcotic Drugs, as the principal policymaking organ of the United Nations on matters of international drug control and as the governing body of the drug programme of the United Nations Office on Drugs and Crime, and the International Narcotics Control Board to strengthen their useful work on the control of precursors and other chemicals used in the illicit manufacture of narcotic drugs and psychotropic substances, and, in accordance with Commission resolution 54/8 of 25 March 2011, urges the Board to further strengthen communication with Member States and to work with them in identifying opportunities for more effective control and monitoring of the trade in precursor chemicals frequently used in the illicit manufacture of narcotic drugs and psychotropic substances;

28. *Urges* States that have not done so to consider ratifying or acceding to, and States parties to implement, as a matter of priority, all the provisions of the Single Convention on Narcotic Drugs of 1961 as amended by the 1972 Protocol, the Convention on Psychotropic Substances of 1971, the United Nations Convention against Illicit Traffic in Narcotic Drugs and Psychotropic Substances of 1988, the United Nations Convention against Transnational Organized Crime and the Protocols thereto and the United Nations Convention against Corruption;

29. *Takes note* of the resolutions adopted by the Commission on Narcotic Drugs at its fifty-fourth session, the *World Drug Report 2011* of the United Nations Office on Drugs and Crime and the most recent report of the International Narcotics Control Board, and calls upon States to strengthen international and regional cooperation to counter the threat to the international community caused by the illicit production of and trafficking in drugs, especially those in the opium group, as well as other aspects of the world drug problem, and to continue to take concerted measures within the framework of the Paris Pact and other relevant international initiatives;

30. *Notes* that the International Narcotics Control Board needs sufficient resources to carry out all its mandates, reaffirms the importance of its work, encourages it to continue to carry out its work in accordance with its mandates, urges Member States to commit themselves in a common effort to assigning, where possible, adequate and sufficient budgetary resources to the Board, in accordance with Economic and Social Council resolution 1996/20 of 23 July 1996, emphasizes the need to maintain its capacity, inter alia, through the provision of appropriate means by the Secretary-General and adequate technical support from the United Nations Office on Drugs and Crime, and calls for enhanced cooperation and understanding between Member States and the Board to enable it to implement all its mandates under the international drug control conventions;

31. *Emphasizes* the important role played by civil society, in particular non-governmental organizations, in addressing the world drug problem, notes with appreciation their important contribution to the review process, and also notes that representatives of affected populations and civil society entities, where appropriate, should be enabled to play a participatory role in the formulation and implementation of drug demand and supply reduction policy;

32. *Encourages* Member States to ensure that civil society plays a participatory role, where appropriate, through consultation in the development and implementation of drug control programmes and policies, in particular with regard to aspects of demand reduction;

33. *Encourages* the meetings of Heads of National Drug Law Enforcement Agencies and of the Subcommission on Illicit Drug Traffic and Related Matters in the Near and Middle East of the Commission on Narcotic Drugs to continue to contribute to the strengthening of regional and international cooperation, and in this regard acknowledges the discussions conducted at the twenty-first meeting of Heads of National Drug Law Enforcement Agencies, Africa, held in Addis Ababa from 5 to 9 September 2011, and Latin America and the Caribbean, held in Santiago from 3 to 7 October 2011;

34. *Welcomes* the ongoing efforts to strengthen cooperation in combating illicit trafficking in drugs, addressing supply, demand and the diversion of precursor chemicals undertaken by regional organizations and transregional initiatives such as the members of the Commonwealth of Independent States, the Triangular Initiative, the Shanghai Cooperation Organization, the Economic Cooperation Organization, the Collective Security Treaty Organization, the Eurasian Group on Combating Money-Laundering and Financing of Terrorism and other relevant subregional and regional organizations and initiatives, including the counter-narcotics strategy of the Shanghai Cooperation Organization for the period 2011–2016, the Inter-American Drug Abuse Control Commission of the Organization of American States, the European pacts to combat international drug trafficking and against synthetic drugs and the Association of Southeast Asian Nations Senior Officials on Drug Matters workplan to combat illicit drug production, trafficking and use (2009–2015) with the aim of achieving a drug-free South-East Asia by 2015, as well as the recent intensification of partnering between the States members of the Caribbean Community, the Dominican Republic and the United States of America within the framework of the Caribbean Basin Security Initiative, which aims, inter alia, to substantially reduce illicit trafficking in narcotic drugs;

35. *Invites* Member States, in close consultation with the United Nations Office on Drugs and Crime, donors and other relevant international organizations, to continue assisting African States in addressing health problems and raising awareness of the dangers associated with the abuse of all drugs, in accordance with Commission on Narcotic Drugs resolution 54/14 of 25 March 2011, and in this regard welcomes the signing of the memorandum of under-

standing between the United Nations Office on Drugs and Crime and the African Union Commission, in which the two organizations agreed to work towards enhancing the complementarities of their activities;

36. *Calls upon* the relevant United Nations agencies and entities and other international organizations, and invites international financial institutions, including regional development banks, to mainstream drug control issues into their programmes, and calls upon the United Nations Office on Drugs and Crime to maintain its leading role by providing relevant information and technical assistance;

37. *Takes note* of the report of the Secretary-General, and requests the Secretary-General to submit to the General Assembly at its sixty-seventh session a report on the implementation of the present resolution.

Regional cooperation

A Secretariat report [E/CN.7/2012/5] described action taken by five subsidiary bodies of the Commission in 2011. Each of the bodies reviewed trends in drug trafficking and regional and subregional cooperation, addressed drug law enforcement issues of priority in its region, and reviewed the implementation of previous recommendations. The report included the recommendations made by the subsidiary bodies.

The Ninth Meeting of Heads of National Drug Law Enforcement Agencies (HONLEA), Europe (Vienna, 28 June–1 July) [UNODC/HONEURO/9/6], adopted recommendations on regional cooperation in combating the illicit drug trade in Europe; licit trade in precursor chemicals: additional elements of effective control; and coercion to cohesion: alternative models of demand reduction. The Twenty-first Meeting of HONLEA, Africa (Addis Ababa, Ethiopia, 5–9 September) [UNODC/HONLAF/21/5], made recommendations with respect to controlled delivery operations; operations to counter drug trafficking; and precursor control: Africa's developing challenge. At the Twenty-first Meeting of HONLEA, Latin America and the Caribbean (Santiago, Chile, 3–7 October) [UNODC/HONLAC/21/5], recommendations were made on building partnerships with the chemical industry to strengthen precursor control, implementing effective border controls, and addressing the proceeds of drug trafficking. The Thirty-fifth Meeting of HONLEA, Asia and the Pacific (Agra, India, 22–25 November) [UNODC/HONLAP/35/5], made recommendations with regard to precursor chemicals: developing industry partnerships and meeting the challenges of substitute chemicals; the response of Asia and the Pacific to increased heroin production; and meeting the challenge of effective border controls. The forty-sixth session of the Subcommission on Illicit Drug Traffic and Related Matters in the Near and Middle East (Vienna, 19–22 December) [UNODC/SUBCOM/46/5] made recommendations regarding the ongoing impact of illicit drug production in Afghanistan, illicit manufacture of and trafficking in amphetamine-type stimulants in the region, and supporting models of drug demand reduction.

Pursuant to Economic and Social Council resolution 1992/28 [YUN 1992, p. 909], the Secretariat in May submitted a note [UNODC/HONEURO/9/5] that reviewed responses by Member States to a questionnaire on the functioning of the subsidiary bodies of the Commission. The assessment was based on the 67 replies received by the Secretariat from the members of the bodies and was undertaken to enhance the contributions of Member States to combating illicit drug trafficking, related crime and other forms of serious organized crime, and to identify ways and means of ensuring that the meetings met the needs and expectations of participating countries.

The Secretariat recommended to the Commission that it consider the recommendations adopted by the subsidiary bodies during the sessions of the Commission; recommend improvements to the format of the meetings; and recommend the establishment of informal groups of friends of the Chairpersons of the meetings, which could meet to support the work of each subsidiary body by discussing preparations, as well as to examine follow-up action, including the drafting of resolutions and decisions for the consideration of the Commission.

Conventions

International efforts to control narcotic drugs were governed by three global conventions: the 1961 Single Convention on Narcotic Drugs [YUN 1961, p. 382], which, with some exceptions of detail, replaced earlier narcotics treaties and was amended by the 1972 Protocol [YUN 1972, p. 397] to strengthen the role of the International Narcotics Control Board (INCB); the 1971 Convention on Psychotropic Substances [YUN 1971, p. 380]; and the 1988 United Nations Convention against Illicit Traffic in Narcotic Drugs and Psychotropic Substances [YUN 1988, p. 690].

As at 31 December, 184 States were Parties to the 1961 Convention, as amended by the 1972 Protocol. Afghanistan and Chad continued to be parties to the Convention in its unamended form only. Bolivia on 29 June notified the Secretary-General that it had decided to denounce the Convention. In accordance with article 46 (2) of the Convention, the denunciation would take effect on 1 January 2012. Bolivia also announced its intention to re-accede to the Convention but with a reservation allowing for the traditional use of the coca leaf (see p. 1184).

The number of parties to the 1971 Convention remained at 183 as at 31 December.

At year's end, 184 States and the European Union were parties to the 1988 Convention.

Commission action. On 22 and 23 March [E/2011/28], the Commission reviewed the implementation of the international drug control treaties. It had before it INCB reports for 2010 [YUN 2010, p. 1257] on the availability of internationally controlled drugs for ensuring adequate access for medical and scientific purposes [ibid.], and on the implementation of Article 12 of the United Nations Convention against Illicit Traffic in Narcotic Drugs and Psychotropic Substances [ibid., p. 1258].

On 25 March, the Commission adopted a resolution [E/2011/28 (res. 54/3)] on ensuring the availability of reference and test samples of controlled substances at drug testing laboratories for scientific purposes. It requested Member States, in consultation with INCB and UNODC, to review national procedures in order not to impair access to reference and test samples of internationally controlled substances for scientific purposes. It invited INCB and UNODC to work closely on mechanisms that would facilitate the provision of reference and test samples of controlled substances to drug testing laboratories in order to support their analytical and quality assurance work. The Commission requested UNODC to support Member States in enhancing the analytical work of laboratories and the training of experts.

Also on 25 March, the Commission adopted a resolution [res. 54/6] on promoting adequate availability of internationally controlled narcotic drugs and psychotropic substances for medical and scientific purposes. It requested UNODC to update its model laws to ensure that they reflected an appropriate balance between ensuring adequate access to internationally controlled drugs and preventing their diversion and abuse. It further requested UNODC to develop a technical guide explaining the revised model laws to support training and awareness-raising activities for its personnel in regional and country offices, and to ensure that the model laws were accessible and readily understood by Member States. The Commission invited Member States, UNODC and international organizations to facilitate the provision of technical assistance to developing countries, including through support for South-South cooperation.

Also on 25 March, the Commission adopted a resolution [res. 54/8] on strengthening international cooperation and regulatory and institutional frameworks for the control of precursor chemicals used in the illicit manufacture of synthetic drugs. It called on INCB to strengthen communication with Member States and to work with them in identifying opportunities for more effective control and monitoring of the trade in precursor chemicals frequently used in the illicit manufacture of narcotic drugs and psychotropic substances. The Commission urged Member States to strengthen, update or establish national legislation and mechanisms relating to the control of precursors, and requested them to submit to UNODC information related to cases of illicit traffic that they considered important because of new trends disclosed, the quantities involved, the sources from which the substances were obtained or the methods employed.

INCB report. In its report covering 2011 [E/INCB/2011/1, Sales No. E.12.XI.5], INCB requested those States that were not parties to the international drug control treaties to accede to them without delay. With regard to treaty implementation and control measures, Governments that did not submit statistical reports on internationally controlled substances were encouraged to improve their reporting performance. The Board further called on States parties to ensure that state and provincial policies and measures did not undermine efforts to combat drug abuse and trafficking in narcotic drugs, psychotropic substances and precursor chemicals. INCB encouraged Governments to implement the recommendations contained in its report on the availability of internationally controlled drugs (see above), and to collect reliable data on consumption levels of psychotropic substances. The Board called on Governments to ensure implementation of the system of estimates and assessments, extend the import and export authorization requirement to all substances in Schedules III and IV of the 1971 Convention, and verify the authenticity of all import orders that they considered to be suspicious. It also requested Governments to investigate the sources of substances diverted from domestic distribution channels, and encouraged them to examine whether the penalties foreseen under their national drug control legislation were sufficient to deter such diversion. INCB urged Governments of countries in which buprenorphine was used for licit purposes to adopt appropriate control measures, while making the substance available for use in medical treatment. With regard to precursors, Governments were urged to make sure that they were informed of any proposed export of precursors and to provide pre-export notifications. Exporting countries were urged to ensure that their exports would not violate the applicable laws and regulations of the importing countries.

Proposed amendment to Convention

In 2009, Bolivia submitted a proposal to amend article 49, paragraphs 1 (*c*) and 2 (*e*), of the Single Convention on Narcotic Drugs of 1961 as amended by the 1972 Protocol [YUN 2009, p. 1241]. The proposal was aimed at deleting a provision on abolishing coca leaf chewing, an ancestral practice of the Andean indigenous people.

The Economic and Social Council, by decision 2009/250 [ibid.], decided, in accordance with the Convention as amended, to ask the parties whether they accepted the proposed amendment, also asking them to submit to the Council any comments on the proposal.

Pursuant to the Council's decision, the Secretary-General in January and February transmitted to the Council notes from countries that rejected the proposed amendment. Such notes were submitted by the United States [E/2011/47], Sweden [E/2011/48], the United Kingdom [E/2011/49], Latvia [E/2011/52], Japan [E/2011/54], Canada [E/2011/51], Germany [E/2011/53], Estonia [E/2011/55], France [E/2011/56], Bulgaria [E/2011/57], Italy [E/2011/58], Slovakia [E/2011/62], Denmark [E/2011/67], Mexico [E/2011/60], the Russian Federation [E/2011/61], Singapore [E/2011/63], Malaysia [E/2011/66] and Ukraine [E/2011/71].

Colombia [E/2011/59], by a note of 31 January, stated that the Government had decided to withdraw its 2010 note [YUN 2010, p. 1257] in which it had rejected the amendment. Ecuador [E/2011/64] stated that it supported the amendment proposed by Bolivia: the prohibition was unjustifiable and discriminated against indigenous peoples who maintained that ancestral practice. Uruguay [E/2011/65] expressed support for Bolivia's right to develop its own strategy for voluntary eradication and endorsed the country's right to propose a re-evaluation of the coca leaf by international agencies. Costa Rica [E/2011/68] said that it had no objections to the amendment, provided that it related to identifiable ancestral practices, exclusively in indigenous territories, that were recognized by domestic legislation.

The former Yugoslav Republic of Macedonia did not accept the proposed amendment [E/2011/10] and subsequently withdrew its objections [E/2011/12].

Venezuela, by a letter of 28 January [A/65/714-E/2011/70] referred to the presidential declarations made at the Sixth Extraordinary Summit of the Bolivarian Alliance for the Peoples of Our America–Peoples' Trade Agreement (ALBA-TCP) (Maracay, Venezuela, 24 June 2009) and at the Seventh Summit of ALBA-TCP (Cochabamba, Bolivia, 17 October 2009). Both declarations, signed by the Heads of State and Government of the countries members of ALBA-TCP (Antigua and Barbuda, Bolivia, Cuba, Dominica, Ecuador, Honduras, Nicaragua, Saint Vincent and the Grenadines, Venezuela), supported Bolivia's proposal.

Ecuador, on 31 January [E/2011/81], as a member of the Union of South American Nations (UNASUR), transmitted the Georgetown Declaration of 26 November 2010, in which the member States of UNASUR "taking into account the claim of the values of peoples, ... acknowledged that the chewing of coca leaves is an ancestral cultural expression of the people of Bolivia that should be respected by the international community".

International Narcotics Control Board

INCB held its 100th (31 January–4 February), 101st (2–13 May) and 102nd (24 October–11 November) sessions, all in Vienna.

In accordance with the tasks assigned to it under the international conventions, the Board monitored the implementation of the international drug control treaties and maintained a permanent dialogue with Governments. The information received from Governments was used to identify the enforcement of treaty provisions requiring them to limit to medical and scientific purposes the licit manufacture of, trade in, and distribution and use of narcotic drugs and psychotropic substances. The Board, which was required by the treaties to report annually on the drug control situation worldwide, noted gaps and weaknesses in national control and treaty compliance, and made recommendations for improvements at the national and international levels.

The Board's 2011 report [E/INCB/2011/1, Sales No. E.12.XI.5] addressed the topics of social cohesion, social disorganization and illegal drugs, and noted that countries throughout the world were faced with the challenge posed by marginalized communities, which were vulnerable to drug-related problems. It described how, in some communities, drug abuse had become almost endemic, part of a vicious cycle involving a wide array of social problems relating to violence, organized crime, corruption, unemployment, poor health and poor education. Threats to social cohesion included social inequality, migration, political and economic transformation, an emerging culture of excess, the growth of individualism and consumerism, shifting traditional values, conflict, rapid urbanization, a breakdown in respect for the law, and the existence of an illicit drug economy.

According to the Board, it was important to respond to the needs of communities experiencing social disintegration and to involve local people at every stage of any intervention. Governments should ensure the provision of drug abuse prevention services; ensure that young people and families had access to educational, employment and leisure opportunities; and ensure that high-quality drug treatment and rehabilitation services were easily accessible. The Board underlined the importance of international cooperation in the building of capacity; the provision of technical assistance; and the sharing of best practices in rehabilitating those marginalized communities by investing in social cohesion, services and infrastructure.

The Board's recommendations to Governments addressed treaty accession; treaty implementation and control measures; and prevention of illicit drug production, manufacture, trafficking and abuse. Other recommendations were directed to UNODC and the World Health Organization.

The Board's report was supplemented by the following reports: Narcotic Drugs: Estimated World Requirements for 2012–Statistics for 2010 [E/INCB/

2011/2]; Psychotropic Substances: Statistics for 2010–Assessments of Annual Medical and Scientific Requirements for Substances in Schedules II, III and IV of the Convention on Psychotropic Substances of 1971 [E/INCB/2011/3]; and Precursors and Chemicals Frequently Used in the Illicit Manufacture of Narcotic Drugs and Psychotropic Substances: Report of the International Narcotics Control Board for 2011 on the Implementation of Article 12 of the United Nations Convention against Illicit Traffic in Narcotic Drugs and Psychotropic Substances of 1988 [E/INCB/2011/4].

The Economic and Social Council on 28 July took note of the INCB report for 2010 [YUN 2010, p. 1257] (**decision 2011/262**).

World drug situation

In its 2011 report [E/INCB/2011/1, Sales No. E.12.XI.5], INCB presented a regional analysis of world drug abuse trends and control efforts to keep Governments aware of situations that might endanger the objectives of international drug control treaties. The report provided information for each region on major developments; regional cooperation; national legislation, policy and action; cultivation, production, manufacture and trafficking; and abuse and treatment.

Africa

While cannabis remained the most widely cultivated, trafficked and abused drug in Africa, the smuggling of cocaine from South America through Africa and into Europe had emerged as a major threat. Furthermore, the increasing flow of heroin entering Africa had led to increased drug abuse throughout the region, particularly in East Africa and Southern Africa. Concerns that the illicit manufacture of amphetamine-type stimulants (ATS) might take hold in West Africa were confirmed by the seizure of a large methamphetamine laboratory in Lagos in June.

The African Union continued to implement its Plan of Action on Drug Control and Crime Prevention (2007–2012) [YUN 2007, p. 1286], while its Commission worked on the main components for the Plan of Action 2013–2018. The efforts of member States of the Economic Community of West African States (ECOWAS) to prevent drug trafficking and abuse were coordinated within the framework of the ECOWAS action plan against drug trafficking, organized crime and drug abuse. At the Twenty-first Meeting of HONLEA, Africa (Addis Ababa, 5–9 September), participants agreed on action to counter drug trafficking, including the use of controlled delivery operations, and the diversion of precursor chemicals, particularly substances used in the illicit manufacture of ATS.

Americas

Central America and the Caribbean. The region of Central America and the Caribbean continued to be used as a major transit area for smuggling drugs from South America into North America. Some Mexican drug cartels moved their drug trafficking operations to Central America, leading to increased levels of violence, kidnapping, bribery, torture and homicide in the subregion. The drug problem also led to drug-related corruption, which increasingly weakened the criminal justice systems.

UNODC supported the launching of a centre of excellence on drug demand reduction and treatment in the Dominican Republic in June, which would examine problems related to drug demand reduction in communities and prison settings.

North America. North America continued to have the world's largest illicit drug market in 2010, showing high levels of illicit drug production, manufacture, trade and consumption. In Mexico, drug trafficking organizations resorted to unprecedented levels of violence, and drug syndicates sought to undermine the state apparatus through the use of corruption, threats and intimidation. Prescription drug abuse was the fastest-growing drug problem in the United States.

Building upon their February declaration entitled "Beyond the border: shared vision for perimeter security and economic competitiveness", Canada and the United States in March released the United States-Canada Joint Border Threat and Risk Assessment, which aimed at providing policymakers, law enforcement officials and other stakeholders with information regarding established threats along the border. The third meeting of the United States-Mexico Merida High-Level Consultative Group on Bilateral Cooperation against Transnational Criminal Organizations (Washington, D.C., 29 April) aimed to increase bilateral cooperation and coordinate action against transnational organized crime by building upon the implementation framework developed under the Merida Initiative [YUN 2008, p. 1361]. In July, the Canadian Centre on Substance Abuse, in partnership with the Office of National Drug Control Policy of the United States, the European Monitoring Centre for Drugs and Drug Addiction, and the United States National Institute on Drug Abuse, hosted the International Drugs and Driving Symposium, with the purpose of building upon CND resolution 54/2 (see p. 1175).

South America. In 2010, the total area under illicit coca bush cultivation in South America was 6 per cent less than in 2009. The area under illicit cultivation in Colombia decreased by 15 per cent, while in Peru it increased by 2 per cent. There was no significant change in coca bush cultivation in Bolivia; the area under cultivation in the country accounted for 20 per cent of illicit coca bush cultivation in the region.

At its forty-ninth regular session (Paramaribo, Suriname, 4–6 May), the Inter-American Drug Abuse Control Commission adopted the Hemispheric Plan of Action on Drugs 2011–2015. In the area of demand reduction, the Plan of Action proposed the strengthening of the relationship between national authorities, academic institutions, research and specialized non-governmental organizations in order to generate evidence regarding demand for drugs. Developing effective and sustainable measures to reduce illicit drug crop cultivation and promoting alternative development and environmental protection programmes were among the objectives of the Plan of Action in the area of drug supply reduction.

Asia

East and South-East Asia. Illicit opium poppy cultivation and opium production continued to increase in the region in 2010, particularly in Myanmar—the world's second largest opium producer—and the Lao People's Democratic Republic. The Board urged the two countries to take the necessary action to reduce illicit opium poppy cultivation and called on the international community to provide assistance. Seizures of methamphetamine continued to increase in 2010, and large-scale illicit trafficking was reported, particularly in the area encompassing China, the Lao People's Democratic Republic, Myanmar and Thailand. Trafficking in and increasing abuse of ketamine, a substance not under international control, was a prominent problem in the region. Indonesia was facing an emerging challenge posed by the illicit manufacture and abuse of "ecstasy".

At the ministerial meeting of the Signatory Countries of the 1993 Memorandum of Understanding on Drug Control (Vientiane, Lao People's Democratic Republic, 24 May), representatives of Cambodia, China, the Lao People's Democratic Republic, Myanmar, Thailand and Viet Nam reviewed the latest trends in drug trafficking and abuse and endorsed the Subregional Action Plan on Drug Control (revision VIII) for the period 2011–2013, which provided a strategic outline for the collaborative efforts of the six signatory countries and UNODC in addressing the challenges posed by illicit drugs. The Association of Southeast Asian Nations (ASEAN) continued to promote cooperation pertaining to drug control in the region. At the eleventh meeting of ASEAN Senior Officials on Transnational Crime (Singapore, 25–29 July), combating drug trafficking, in particular trafficking in methamphetamine, was highlighted as a priority of ASEAN.

South Asia. South Asia experienced increasing problems related to the abuse of and trafficking in prescription drugs and over-the-counter pharmaceutical preparations containing narcotic drugs and psychotropic substances. Although all the countries of South Asia had a regulatory regime in place that included prescription requirements for controlled pharmaceuticals, gaps remained in the implementation and monitoring of compliance by pharmacies. The abuse of drugs by injection, including heroin, prescription opioids and mixtures with other controlled substances, reached significant proportions in Bangladesh, India and Nepal, contributing to an increase in HIV and hepatitis C infection rates. International drug trafficking organizations continued to use the region as a base for illicit manufacture of and trafficking in ATS, largely because of the wide availability of precursor chemicals.

South Asian countries participated in cooperative drug control activities organized by the Colombo Plan for Cooperative Economic and Social Development in Asia and the Pacific. Cooperation between India and Pakistan in drug-related matters continued. In September, the Narcotics Control Bureau of India and the Anti-Narcotics Force of Pakistan signed a memorandum of understanding on the reduction of illicit drug demand and the prevention of trafficking in narcotic drugs, psychotropic substances and precursor chemicals. The United Nations Regional Task Force on Injecting Drug Use and HIV/AIDS for Asia and the Pacific held a meeting (New Delhi, India, 10–11 February), which addressed the regional strategy for harm reduction for the period 2010–2015 and the increasing abuse of pharmaceutical drugs in the region.

West Asia. West Asia remained the epicentre of illicit opium poppy cultivation, accounting for nearly two thirds of global cultivation. It was also a significant hub for cannabis cultivation. There were indications of increased trafficking in various types of stimulants, and several countries in the region reported large seizures of cocaine in 2010 and in the first quarter of 2011. In addition, the non-medical use of prescription drugs containing internationally controlled substances was a growing problem reported in many countries in the Middle East.

As part of the UNODC-facilitated Triangular Initiative, Afghanistan, Iran and Pakistan held the sixth meeting of senior officials (Tehran, Iran, 31 May) to review the progress made in implementing the recommendations and actions agreed upon at the ministerial meeting held in November 2010, to discuss joint operations and the establishment of border liaison offices, and to examine a cross-border communication plan. During a meeting of the Board of Directors of the Gulf Cooperation Council's Criminal Information Centre to Combat Drugs (Doha, Qatar, 6–8 June), discussions focused on drug trafficking and cooperation among the member States of the Council in combating drug-related problems. Participants stressed the need to strengthen the collection of information, the exchange of law enforcement information, and the storage, analysis and sharing of such information. At the quadrilateral meeting of the Presidents of Afghanistan, Pakistan, the Russian Federation and Tajikistan (Dushanbe, Tajikistan, 2 September), the Heads of State agreed to cooperate with each other in the fight against the illicit production, smuggling and abuse of drugs, and to prevent traffickers from using Afghanistan as a transit country and country of destination for precursors.

Europe

There was not much evidence of a decrease in the level of cannabis abuse in most countries in Europe. The illicit cultivation of cannabis plants in Western and Central Europe increased dramatically. Cannabis plants were increasingly being illicitly cultivated on an industrial scale, mainly indoors, and with the involvement of organized criminal groups. While the abuse of cocaine had stabilized—although at a relatively high level—in most countries in Western and Central Europe, it appeared to have continued in South-Eastern and Eastern Europe. Cocaine was the primary drug of abuse in almost one fifth of new treatment cases in the European Union, and Europe remained the world's second-largest cocaine market. The abuse of MDMA remained stable and the known manufacture of "ecstasy" decreased. The illicit manufacture of amphetamine, however, was increasing. While amphetamine remained the most abused ATS, seizures of methamphetamine in Western and Central Europe had increased fivefold between 2004 and 2009.

In June, operation Channel West was carried out under the aegis of the Collective Security Treaty Organization. More than 46,300 law enforcement officers and special service agents from Belarus, Kazakhstan, Latvia, Lithuania, Poland, the Russian Federation and Ukraine were involved in the operation, establishing 4,437 joint operational groups in border areas and at rail stations, airports and road transport facilities. Their joint efforts led to the seizure of about three tons of drugs and more than 197 kilograms of precursor chemicals. In the political declaration adopted at the Group of Eight Ministerial Meeting on the Fight against Transatlantic Cocaine Trafficking (Paris, 10 May), States made a commitment to intensifying cooperation regarding the global drug problem, including drug trafficking and transatlantic trafficking in cocaine. Participants adopted an action plan aimed at strengthening cooperation, calling for effective implementation of the international drug control conventions, improving the sharing of intelligence, intensifying maritime cooperation, addressing the destabilizing effects of drug trafficking, and improving international legal cooperation mechanisms to target and confiscate criminal assets.

Oceania

An increase in the smuggling of cocaine into Oceania posed a new challenge to drug control efforts in the region. In Australia, the number of cocaine-related offences increased significantly. Large shipments of cocaine from South and Central America continued to be detected at the Australian border. New Zealand, Fiji and Tonga also reported an increase in cocaine seizures. Organized crime syndicates were involved in drug trafficking in the region, with West African drug syndicates trafficking heroin and methamphetamine into Australia and New Zealand, and Mexican, Central American and South American crime syndicates smuggling large shipments of cocaine into Australia. East and South-East Asian organized crime groups maintained an advantage in smuggling crystalline methamphetamine. Increased abuse of pharmaceutical preparations for non-medical purposes was another notable trend in Oceania.

The annual meeting of the Pacific Drug and Alcohol Research Network (Fiji, 9–11 August) was attended by representatives from 12 countries in the region and delegates from the World Health Organization and research institutes. Participants highlighted the importance of strengthening drug-related research and data collection and analysis, including by conducting a regional cannabis survey with the assistance of UNODC and regional organizations.

Crime prevention and criminal justice

Commission on Crime Prevention and Criminal Justice

At its twentieth session (Vienna, 3 December 2010 and 11–15 April 2011) [E/2011/30], the Commission on Crime Prevention and Criminal Justice (CCPCJ) recommended to the Economic and Social Council four draft resolutions for adoption by the General Assembly. It also recommended four draft resolutions and two draft decisions for adoption by the Council. The Commission further recommended for adoption by the Council two draft decisions: one on the report of the Commission's 2011 session, the agenda for its 2012 session and the organization of work of its future sessions; and one on extending the mandate of the standing open-ended intergovernmental working group on improving the UNODC governance and financial situation.

The Commission adopted seven resolutions and one decision, which it brought to the attention of the Council. In addition to a thematic discussion on protecting children in a digital age, the Commission also considered management, budgetary and administrative questions; integration and coordination of efforts with Member States; world crime trends; follow-up to the Twelfth United Nations Congress on Crime Prevention and Criminal Justice [YUN 2010, p. 1094] and preparations for the Thirteenth Congress; UN standards and norms in crime prevention and criminal justice; and the provisional agenda for its 2012 session.

At its reconvened session (Vienna, 12–13 December) [E/2011/30/Add.1], ccpcj recommended for adoption by the Council one draft resolution on the unodc strategy for the period 2012–2015, and one draft decision on the Commission's report on its reconvened twentieth session. The Commission also adopted two resolutions on budgetary matters and the unodc governance and financial situation, and brought them to the attention of the Council.

In accordance with Economic and Social Council **decision 2011/259** of 28 July, one meeting of the Commission was held jointly with the Commission on Narcotic Drugs on 12 December.

On 14 April [E/2011/30 (dec. 20/1)], the Commission decided that, at future sessions, on an experimental basis, the deadline for submitting draft resolutions to the part of the session held in the first half of the year would be one month prior to the commencement of that part of the session.

The Economic and Social Council, by **decision 2011/256** of 28 July, took note of the ccpcj report on its reconvened nineteenth session [YUN 2010, p. 1101]. Also on 28 July (**decision 2011/257**), the Council took note of the Commission's report on its twentieth session; decided that the prominent theme for the Commission's twenty-first (2012) session would be violence against migrants, migrant workers and their families; and approved the provisional agenda and documentation for that session.

Follow-up to the Twelfth United Nations Crime Congress

In response to General Assembly resolution 65/230 [YUN 2010, p. 1095], the Secretary-General in February submitted a report [E/CN.15/2011/15] on the follow-up to the Twelfth United Nations Congress on Crime Prevention and Criminal Justice and preparations for the Thirteenth Congress. The report provided information on follow-up to the Salvador Declaration on Comprehensive Strategies for Global Challenges: Crime Prevention and Criminal Justice Systems and Their Development in a Changing World, adopted by the Twelfth United Nations Congress on Crime Prevention and Criminal Justice (Salvador, Brazil, 12–19 April 2010) [YUN 2010, p. 1094], and analysed ways and means of improving the efficiency of the process involved in the UN congresses on crime prevention and criminal justice. It further included information on action taken by Member States to implement the Declaration and proposals made by them for ways and means of ensuring follow-up to the Declaration, as well as proposals for future unodc activity.

Report of Secretary-General. Also pursuant to General Assembly resolution 65/230, the Secretary-General in June submitted a report [A/66/91] on action taken to implement that resolution. The report reviewed follow-up to the Salvador Declaration, and contained information on the views and proposals of Member States for ways and means of improving the efficiency of the process involved in the UN congresses on crime prevention and criminal justice, an issue that was discussed at the twentieth session of the Commission. As a result, the Commission recommended to the Economic and Social Council the approval of a draft resolution for adoption by the General Assembly on follow-up to the Twelfth United Nations Congress on Crime Prevention and Criminal Justice and preparations for the Thirteenth Congress (see below). With respect to issues pertaining to the operationalization of the Salvador Declaration, an open-ended intergovernmental expert group was established to conduct a study of the problem of cybercrime and responses to it by Member States, the international community and the private sector. The expert group met to discuss substantive and methodological aspects of the study (Vienna, 17–21 January) [E/CN.15/2011/19].

The General Assembly took note of the report on 19 December (**decision 66/539**).

ECONOMIC AND SOCIAL COUNCIL ACTION

On 28 July [meeting 48], the Economic and Social Council, on the recommendation of the Commission on Crime Prevention and Criminal Justice [E/2011/30], adopted **resolution 2011/30** without vote [agenda item 14 (c)].

Follow-up to the Twelfth United Nations Congress on Crime Prevention and Criminal Justice and preparations for the Thirteenth United Nations Congress on Crime Prevention and Criminal Justice

The Economic and Social Council

Recommends to the General Assembly the adoption of the following draft resolution:

[For text, see General Assembly resolution 66/179 below.]

GENERAL ASSEMBLY ACTION

On 19 December [meeting 89], the General Assembly, on the recommendation of the Third Committee [A/66/463], adopted **resolution 66/179** without vote [agenda item 107].

Follow-up to the Twelfth United Nations Congress on Crime Prevention and Criminal Justice and preparations for the Thirteenth United Nations Congress on Crime Prevention and Criminal Justice

The General Assembly,

Recalling its resolution 56/119 of 19 December 2001 on the role, function, periodicity and duration of the United Nations congresses on the prevention of crime and the treatment of offenders, in which it stipulated the guidelines in accordance with which, beginning in 2005, the congresses, pursuant to paragraphs 29 and 30 of the statement of principles and programme of action of the United Nations crime prevention and criminal justice programme, should be held,

Emphasizing the responsibility assumed by the United Nations in the field of crime prevention and criminal justice in pursuance of Economic and Social Council resolution 155 C (VII) of 13 August 1948 and General Assembly resolution 415(V) of 1 December 1950,

Acknowledging that the United Nations congresses on crime prevention and criminal justice, as major intergovernmental forums, have influenced national policies and practices and promoted international cooperation in that field by facilitating the exchange of views and experience, mobilizing public opinion and recommending policy options at the national, regional and international levels,

Recalling its resolution 57/270 B of 23 June 2003 on the integrated and coordinated implementation of and follow-up to the outcomes of the major United Nations conferences and summits in the economic and social fields, in which it stressed that all countries should promote policies consistent and coherent with the commitments of the major United Nations conferences and summits, emphasized that the United Nations system had an important responsibility to assist Governments to stay fully engaged in the follow-up to and implementation of agreements and commitments reached at the major United Nations conferences and summits and invited its intergovernmental bodies to further promote the implementation of the outcomes of the major United Nations conferences and summits,

Recalling also its resolution 65/230 of 21 December 2010, in which it endorsed the Salvador Declaration on Comprehensive Strategies for Global Challenges: Crime Prevention and Criminal Justice Systems and Their Development in a Changing World, as adopted by the Twelfth United Nations Congress on Crime Prevention and Criminal Justice, and requested the Commission on Crime Prevention and Criminal Justice to consider at its twentieth session options to improve the efficiency of the process involved in the United Nations congresses on crime prevention and criminal justice,

1. *Takes note* of the report of the Secretary-General;
2. *Reiterates its invitation* to Governments to take into consideration the Salvador Declaration on Comprehensive Strategies for Global Challenges: Crime Prevention and Criminal Justice Systems and Their Development in a Changing World and the recommendations adopted by the Twelfth United Nations Congress on Crime Prevention and Criminal Justice when formulating legislation and policy directives and to make all efforts, where appropriate, to implement the principles contained therein, taking into account the economic, social, legal and cultural specificities of their respective States;
3. *Recalls* its resolution 62/173 of 18 December 2007, in which it endorsed the recommendations made by the Intergovernmental Group of Experts on Lessons Learned from United Nations Congresses on Crime Prevention and Criminal Justice at its meeting, held in Bangkok from 15 to 18 August 2006;
4. *Invites* Member States to provide their suggestions in relation to the overall theme, the agenda items and the topics for the workshops of the Thirteenth United Nations Congress on Crime Prevention and Criminal Justice, and requests the Secretary-General to report to the Commission on Crime Prevention and Criminal Justice at its twenty-first session on the suggestions made by Member States;
5. *Recommends*, in order to strengthen the outcome of future crime congresses, that the number of their agenda items and workshops be limited, and encourages the holding of side events that are focused on and complement the agenda items and workshops;
6. *Requests* the Commission to approve at its twenty-first session the overall theme, the agenda items and the topics for the workshops of the Thirteenth Congress.

Crime prevention programme

At its twentieth session [E/2011/30], CCPCJ considered the UNODC Executive Director's report on the Office's 2010 activities in the areas of the rule of law; prevention, treatment and reintegration; research, trend analysis and scientific and forensic support; and executive direction and management [E/CN.7/2011/3-E/CN.15/2011/3]. During the period under review, the Office supported Member States through research, normative work and field-based technical cooperation programmes. The report also provided information on the follow-up to the Political Declaration and Plan of Action on International Cooperation towards an Integrated and Balanced Strategy to Counter the World Drug Problem [YUN 2009, p. 1237].

Key priorities for UNODC included improving dialogue with Member States, partner international organizations, civil society and the private sector, and enhancing the policy profile of UNODC in line with its mandates. Over the preceding two years, Governments, with the assistance and expertise of the Secretariat, had launched a number of regional programmes to promote security and the rule of law, which were aligned with regional and national policies and priorities, and promoted ownership by partner countries.

In the area of transnational organized crime, UNODC tackled new and emerging forms by enhancing regional and national responses to cybercrime and environmental crime, and by increasing the capacity of States to prosecute maritime piracy. The Office in 2010 carried out technical assistance activities addressing trafficking in persons and smuggling of migrants in all regions, providing assistance to over 80 countries. Further to the adoption of the United

Nations Global Plan of Action to Combat Trafficking in Persons, annexed to General Assembly resolution 64/293 [YUN 2010, p. 1111], UNODC established the United Nations Voluntary Trust Fund for Victims of Trafficking in Persons, Especially Women and Children. The Office also provided expertise and technical assistance to promote integrity and combat corruption, in accordance with the four pillars of the United Nations Convention against Corruption: prevention, criminalization and law enforcement, international cooperation, and asset recovery.

In the field of international cooperation against terrorism, 32 countries were assisted directly by the Terrorism Prevention Branch of UNODC, 85 countries were reached through 19 regional or subregional workshops and over 1,500 criminal justice officials were trained. The crime prevention and criminal justice technical cooperation programmes continued to grow, covering 36 countries, with the most significant growth in programmes on penal reform and alternatives to imprisonment. Further programmes were developed and implemented in the areas of juvenile justice, access to legal aid, police oversight, violence against women and crime and violence prevention. With respect to law enforcement, assisting States to strengthen their capacity to investigate organized crime remained integral to the programme of technical assistance.

The UNODC Executive Director recommended to Member States, the Commission on Crime Prevention and Criminal Justice, and the Commission on Narcotic Drugs to support UNODC programmes in awareness-raising, capacity-building and investigation in response to the growing interest of organized crime in environmental crime; to develop domestic legislation, national action plans and capacity-building to tackle migrant smuggling networks; to support international initiatives to combat money-laundering and the financing of terrorism; and to support UNODC work in the area of crime prevention and criminal justice.

A further report of the Executive Director [E/CN.7/2012/3-E/CN.15/2012/3] described the activities of the Office in 2011. UNODC developed a number of new programmes, including the thematic programme on action against transnational organized crime and illicit trafficking, including drug trafficking, for the period 2011–2013, complemented by a comprehensive strategy to combat trafficking in persons and smuggling of migrants. A new regional programme for Afghanistan and neighbouring countries was launched. The Office organized a symposium on the theme "Taking stock and defining the way forward: strengthening the response to terrorism by addressing connections with related criminal activities" (Vienna, 16–17 March). The first grants were awarded to NGOs under the United Nations Voluntary Trust Fund for Victims of Trafficking in Persons, Especially Women and Children. UNODC conducted a series of joint missions with other UN agencies to assess the emerging threat of piracy in the Gulf of Guinea and the security situation in the Sahel countries and its impact on political developments in North Africa. The Office helped States to tackle new and emerging forms of transnational organized crime by enhancing responses to cybercrime and offences against cultural property. The Global Programme against Money-Laundering assisted and provided technical guidance to 79 States. At a UNODC conference (Djibouti, 14–15 December) on illicit financial flows stemming from Somali piracy, participants made recommendations in support of information-sharing, law enforcement cooperation and financial mapping. The Office assisted over 80 States in addressing trafficking in persons and smuggling of migrants. The first global database of case law relating to trafficking in persons was launched. To combat corruption, the Office helped to establish legal and policy frameworks to strengthen anti-corruption bodies and to support Government institutions in international cooperation and the recovery of assets. The Office provided direct assistance to 31 countries to combat terrorism; 85 countries were reached through 22 regional or subregional workshops and over 1,600 criminal justice officials were trained. Significant progress was made in implementing in-depth counter-terrorism regional and country programmes, including those for Afghanistan, Colombia and the Sahel region. UNODC further worked on a series of transnational organized threat assessments in order to address new and emerging issues such as piracy, cybercrime, trafficking in fraudulent medicines and the involvement of criminal groups in the handling of electronic waste. In the area of crime prevention and criminal justice, UNODC implemented 49 projects in 26 countries.

The Executive Director recommended that Member States develop multilateral strategies addressing specific transnational organized criminal markets on the basis of international threat assessments and joint response planning, in collaboration with UNODC; address the cross-border movement of money derived from drug trafficking and organized crime, including by ensuring that their border agencies were well trained in identifying and investigating the criminal groups involved; review border controls at principal trade ports of entry and encourage national authorities to participate in the UNODC Container Control Programme; and implement awareness-raising strategies to combat trafficking in persons, based on the UNODC Blue Heart Campaign.

During the year, the Office published: *Transnational Organized Crime Threat Assessments; 2011 Global Study on Homicide; Organized Crime and Instability in Central Africa–A Threat Assessment; The Criminal*

Justice Response to Support Victims of Acts of Terrorism; Handbook on Identity-related Crime; Corruption in the Western Balkans: bribery as experienced by the population; Estimating Illicit Financial Flows Resulting from Drug Trafficking and other Transnational Organized crimes; Smuggling of Migrants by Sea; Responses to Human Trafficking in Bangladesh, India, Nepal and Sri Lanka; and *The Role of Organized Crime in the Smuggling of Migrants from West Africa to the European Union.*

International cooperation

In response to Economic and Social Council resolution 2010/243 [YUN 2010, p. 1101], the Executive Director in January submitted a report [E/CN.15/2011/5] on international cooperation in combating transnational organized crime and corruption (see p. 1203). The report reviewed UNODC activities in the fight against transnational organized crime and corruption. It recommended that the Commission continue supporting the work of the Conference of the Parties to the United Nations Convention against Transnational Organized Crime and the work of the Conference of the States Parties to the United Nations Convention against Corruption, maintain and strengthen the political momentum necessary for the Conferences and their working groups to perform their functions, and urge Member States to ratify or accede to the Conventions and ensure their implementation.

Strengthening technical cooperation

In response to General Assembly resolutions 64/293 [YUN 2010, p. 1111] and 65/232 [ibid., p. 1104], the Secretary-General in July submitted a report [A/66/303] on implementation of the mandates of the United Nations crime prevention and criminal justice programme, covering the period from November 2009 to June 2011, with particular reference to the technical cooperation activities of UNODC. The report summarized the work of the Office in supporting Member States to counter transnational organized crime, corruption and terrorism, as well as to prevent crime and reinforce criminal justice systems. Support was provided to States addressing the interlinkages between money-laundering and organized crime. UNODC deployed experts in Southern Africa, West Africa, South-East Asia and Central Asia to help strengthen asset confiscation procedures, build procedures to counter money-laundering and combat the financing of terrorism, and establish financial intelligence units. Anti-corruption capacity-building projects were implemented in Afghanistan, Indonesia, Iraq and Nigeria. In the area of crime prevention and criminal justice reform, UNODC supported African States to engage in police reform (Kenya, Mauritius, Nigeria), to promote access to justice and legal aid (Burkina Faso, Cape Verde, Ghana, Guinea-Bissau, Liberia, Mali, Mauritania, Sierra Leone, Sudan, Togo), to strengthen the judiciary (Cape Verde, Guinea-Bissau, Nigeria) and prosecution services (Kenya), and to devise responses to violence against women (South Africa). In Asia, UNODC provided legislative assistance, capacity-building for lawyers and juvenile justice-related assistance in Afghanistan. Programmes were implemented on police reform in Pakistan, prevention of domestic violence and legal aid in Viet Nam, juvenile justice in Cambodia, and strengthening judicial integrity and capacity in Indonesia. In Latin America, crime prevention programmes for young people were implemented in Ecuador, Honduras and Peru, and programmes aimed at citizen security and safety audits were carried out in Brazil and Panama. Assistance was also rendered to Egypt, Jordan and the Libyan Arab Jamahiriya, especially in the areas of juvenile justice, prison reform and victims of family violence. The Office contributed to the international response to the threat of piracy off the coast of Somalia. While focusing on Kenya and Seychelles, the Office also supported Maldives, Mauritius, the United Republic of Tanzania and Yemen. Capacity-building measures included support for legal reform and ongoing trials, as well as enhancing the capacity of law enforcement, judicial bodies and prison services through technical assistance, improvements to infrastructure and the provision of essential equipment. The report provided recommendations aimed at enhancing the programme's activities.

GENERAL ASSEMBLY ACTION

On 19 December [meeting 89], the General Assembly, on the recommendation of the Third Committee [A/66/463], adopted **resolution 66/181** without vote [agenda item 107].

Strengthening the United Nations crime prevention and criminal justice programme, in particular its technical cooperation capacity

The General Assembly,

Reaffirming its resolutions 46/152 of 18 December 1991, 60/1 of 16 September 2005, 65/169 of 20 December 2010 and 65/190 and 65/232 of 21 December 2010,

Reaffirming also its resolutions relating to the urgent need to strengthen international cooperation and technical assistance in promoting and facilitating the ratification and implementation of the United Nations Convention against Transnational Organized Crime and the Protocols thereto, the United Nations Convention against Corruption and all the international conventions and protocols against terrorism, including those that recently entered into force,

Reaffirming further the commitments undertaken by Member States in the United Nations Global Counter-

Terrorism Strategy adopted on 8 September 2006, and its successive reviews of 4 and 5 September 2008 and of 8 September 2010,

Emphasizing that its resolution 65/187 of 21 December 2010 on the intensification of efforts to eliminate all forms of violence against women and its resolution 65/228 of 21 December 2010 on strengthening crime prevention and criminal justice responses to violence against women, by which it adopted the updated Model Strategies and Practical Measures on the Elimination of Violence against Women in the Field of Crime Prevention and Criminal Justice, have considerable implications for the United Nations crime prevention and criminal justice programme and its activities,

Recalling the adoption of its resolution 65/229 of 21 December 2010 on the United Nations Rules for the Treatment of Women Prisoners and Non-custodial Measures for Women Offenders (the Bangkok Rules), and encouraging in this regard efforts of Member States to conduct further study with a view to utilizing these practical measures,

Recalling also the adoption of its resolution 65/230 of 21 December 2010 on the Twelfth United Nations Congress on Crime Prevention and Criminal Justice, in which it endorsed the Salvador Declaration on Comprehensive Strategies for Global Challenges: Crime Prevention and Criminal Justice Systems and Their Development in a Changing World,

Taking into consideration all relevant Economic and Social Council resolutions, in particular resolutions 2011/33, 2011/34, 2011/35 and 2011/36 of 28 July 2011 and all those relating to the strengthening of international cooperation, as well as the technical assistance and advisory services of the United Nations crime prevention and criminal justice programme of the United Nations Office on Drugs and Crime in the fields of crime prevention and criminal justice, promotion and reinforcement of the rule of law and reform of criminal justice institutions, including with regard to the implementation of technical assistance,

Recalling its resolutions 58/17 of 3 December 2003, 61/52 of 4 December 2006 and 64/78 of 7 December 2009 on the return or restitution of cultural property to the countries of origin and Economic and Social Council resolutions 2003/29 of 22 July 2003 on the prevention of crimes that infringe on the cultural heritage of peoples in the form of movable property, 2004/34 of 21 July 2004 and 2008/23 of 24 July 2008 on protection against trafficking in cultural property, 2010/19 of 22 July 2010 on crime prevention and criminal justice responses to protect cultural property, especially with regard to its trafficking, and 2011/42 of 28 July 2011 on strengthening crime prevention and criminal justice responses to protect cultural property, especially with regard to its trafficking,

Recalling also the adoption of its resolution 64/293 of 30 July 2010 entitled "United Nations Global Plan of Action to Combat Trafficking in Persons", reaffirming the need for the full implementation of the Global Plan of Action, expressing the view that it will, inter alia, enhance cooperation and better coordination of efforts in fighting trafficking in persons and promote increased ratification and full implementation of the United Nations Convention against Transnational Organized Crime and the Protocol to Prevent, Suppress and Punish Trafficking in Persons, Especially Women and Children, supplementing the United Nations Convention against Transnational Organized Crime, and welcoming the launch of the United Nations Voluntary Trust Fund for Victims of Trafficking in Persons, Especially Women and Children,

Noting with appreciation the efforts of the Secretary-General to develop within the United Nations system an effective and comprehensive approach to transnational organized crime and drug trafficking, and reaffirming the crucial role of Member States in this regard,

Expressing its grave concern at the negative effects of transnational organized crime, including smuggling of and trafficking in human beings, narcotic drugs and small arms and light weapons, on development, peace and security and human rights, and at the increasing vulnerability of States to such crime,

Convinced of the importance of preventing youth crime, supporting the rehabilitation of young offenders and their reintegration into society, protecting child victims and witnesses, including efforts to prevent their revictimization, and addressing the needs of children of prisoners, and stressing that such responses should take into account the human rights and best interests of children and young people, as called for in the Convention on the Rights of the Child and the Optional Protocols thereto, where applicable, and in other relevant United Nations standards and norms in juvenile justice, where appropriate,

Concerned by the serious challenges and threats posed by the illicit trafficking in firearms, their parts and components and ammunition, and concerned about its links with other forms of transnational organized crime, including drug trafficking and other criminal activities, including terrorism,

Deeply concerned about the connections, in some cases, between some forms of transnational organized crime and terrorism, and emphasizing the need to enhance cooperation at the national, subregional, regional and international levels in order to strengthen responses to this evolving challenge,

Concerned about the growing degree of penetration of criminal organizations and their proceeds into the economy,

Recognizing that actions against transnational organized crime and terrorism are a common and shared responsibility, and stressing the need to work collectively to prevent and combat transnational organized crime, corruption and terrorism in all its forms and manifestations,

Emphasizing that transnational organized crime must be addressed in full respect for the principle of the sovereignty of States and in accordance with the rule of law as part of a comprehensive response to promote durable solutions through the promotion of human rights and more equitable socioeconomic conditions,

Encouraging Member States to develop, as appropriate, comprehensive crime prevention policies based on an understanding of the multiple factors that contribute to crime and to address such factors in a holistic manner,

Recognizing the need to maintain a balance in the technical cooperation capacity of the United Nations Office on Drugs and Crime between all relevant priorities identified by the General Assembly and the Economic and Social Council,

Recognizing also that, thanks to its broad membership and wide scope of application, the United Nations Convention against Transnational Organized Crime offers an important basis for international cooperation, inter alia for extradition, mutual legal assistance and confiscation, and represents in this regard a useful tool that should be further utilized,

Mindful of the need to ensure universal adherence to and full implementation of the United Nations Convention against Transnational Organized Crime and the Protocols thereto, and urging States parties to make full and effective use of these instruments,

Welcoming the adoption by the United Nations Office on Drugs and Crime of a regional approach to programming, based on continuing consultations and partnerships at the national and regional levels, particularly on its implementation, and focused on ensuring that the Office responds in a sustainable and coherent manner to the priorities of Member States,

Recognizing the general progress made by the United Nations Office on Drugs and Crime in the delivery of advisory services and assistance to requesting Member States in the areas of corruption, organized crime, money-laundering, terrorism, kidnapping and trafficking in persons, including the support and protection, as appropriate, of victims, their families and witnesses, as well as drug trafficking and international cooperation, with special emphasis on extradition and mutual legal assistance,

Reiterating its concern regarding the overall financial situation of the United Nations Office on Drugs and Crime,

1. *Takes note with appreciation* of the report of the Secretary-General prepared pursuant to resolution 65/232;

2. *Reaffirms* the importance of the United Nations Convention against Transnational Organized Crime and the Protocols thereto as the main tools of the international community to fight transnational organized crime;

3. *Notes with appreciation* that the number of States parties to the United Nations Convention against Transnational Organized Crime has reached one hundred and sixty-four, which is a significant indication of the commitment shown by the international community to combat transnational organized crime;

4. *Urges* Member States that have not yet done so to consider ratifying or acceding to the United Nations Convention against Transnational Organized Crime and the Protocols thereto, the United Nations Convention against Corruption and the international conventions and protocols related to terrorism;

5. *Encourages* States parties and signatories to the United Nations Convention against Transnational Organized Crime to support the activities of the open-ended intergovernmental working group established by the Conference of the Parties to the United Nations Convention against Transnational Organized Crime at its fifth session to develop a mechanism or mechanisms for the review of the implementation of the Convention and the Protocols thereto, and looks forward to the possible adoption of the terms of reference for such a review mechanism or mechanisms at the sixth session of the Conference of the Parties;

6. *Notes with appreciation* the convening of an open-ended intergovernmental expert group to conduct a comprehensive study of the problem of cybercrime and responses to it by Member States, the international community and the private sector, including the exchange of information on national legislation, best practices, technical assistance and international cooperation, with a view to examining options to strengthen existing and to propose new national and international, legal or other responses to cybercrime;

7. *Reaffirms* the importance of the United Nations crime prevention and criminal justice programme in promoting effective action to strengthen international cooperation in crime prevention and criminal justice, as well as of the work of the United Nations Office on Drugs and Crime in the fulfilment of its mandate in crime prevention and criminal justice, including providing to Member States, upon request and as a matter of high priority, technical cooperation, advisory services and other forms of assistance, and coordinating with and complementing the work of all relevant and competent United Nations bodies and offices;

8. *Recommends* that Member States, as appropriate to their national contexts, adopt a comprehensive and integrated approach to crime prevention and criminal justice reform, based on baseline assessments and data collection and focusing on all sectors of the justice system, and develop crime prevention policies, strategies and programmes, and requests the United Nations Office on Drugs and Crime to continue to provide technical assistance, upon request, to Member States for this purpose;

9. *Encourages* all States to have national and local action plans for crime prevention in order to take into account, in a comprehensive, integrated and participatory manner, inter alia, factors that place certain populations and places at higher risk of victimization and/or of offending and to ensure that such plans are based on the best available evidence and good practices, and stresses that crime prevention should be considered an integral element of strategies to foster social and economic development in all States;

10. *Calls upon* Member States to strengthen their efforts to cooperate, as appropriate, at the bilateral, subregional, regional and international levels to counter transnational organized crime effectively;

11. *Requests* the United Nations Office on Drugs and Crime to enhance its efforts, within existing resources and within its mandate, in providing technical assistance and advisory services for the implementation of its regional and subregional programmes in a coordinated manner with relevant Member States and regional and subregional organizations;

12. *Also requests* the United Nations Office on Drugs and Crime to continue to provide, within its mandate, technical assistance to Member States, upon their request, in the areas of crime prevention and criminal justice, with a view to strengthening the capacity of national criminal justice systems to investigate and prosecute all forms of crime and to protect the human rights and fundamental freedoms of defendants, as well as the legitimate interests of victims and witnesses;

13. *Urges* the United Nations Office on Drugs and Crime to continue to provide technical assistance to Member States to combat money-laundering and the financing of terrorism through the Global Programme against Money-Laundering, Proceeds of Crime and the Financing of Terrorism, in accordance with United Nations-related instruments and internationally accepted standards, including, where applicable, recommendations of relevant intergovernmental bodies, inter alia, the Financial Action

Task Force and relevant initiatives of regional, interregional and multilateral organizations against money-laundering;

14. *Urges* Member States to strengthen bilateral, regional and international cooperation to enable the return of assets illicitly acquired from corruption to the countries of origin, upon their request, in accordance with the provisions of the United Nations Convention against Corruption for asset recovery, in particular chapter V, and requests the United Nations Office on Drugs and Crime, within its existing mandate, to continue providing assistance to bilateral, regional and international efforts for that purpose, and also urges Member States to combat and penalize corruption, as well as the laundering of its proceeds;

15. *Requests* the United Nations Office on Drugs and Crime to continue to foster international and regional cooperation, including by facilitating the development of regional networks active in the field of legal and law enforcement cooperation in the fight against transnational organized crime, where appropriate, and by promoting cooperation among all such networks, including by providing technical assistance where it is required;

16. *Urges* the United Nations Office on Drugs and Crime to increase collaboration with intergovernmental, international and regional organizations that have transnational organized crime mandates, as appropriate, in order to share best practices and to take advantage of their unique and comparative advantage;

17. *Recognizes* the efforts made by the United Nations Office on Drugs and Crime to assist Member States in developing abilities and strengthening their capacity to prevent and combat kidnapping, and requests the Office to continue to provide technical assistance with a view to fostering international cooperation, in particular mutual legal assistance, aimed at countering effectively this growing serious crime;

18. *Draws attention* to the emerging policy issues identified in the report of the Secretary-General on the implementation of the mandates of the United Nations crime prevention and criminal justice programme, with particular reference to the technical cooperation activities of the United Nations Office on Drugs and Crime, namely, piracy, cybercrime, abuse and exploitation of children, trafficking in cultural property, illicit financial flows and illicit trafficking in endangered species of wild fauna and flora, and invites the Office to explore, within its mandate, ways and means of addressing those issues, bearing in mind Economic and Social Council resolutions 2007/12 of 25 July 2007 and 2007/19 of 26 July 2007 on the strategy for the period 2008–2011 for the Office;

19. *Requests* the United Nations Office on Drugs and Crime, within its existing mandate, to strengthen the collection, analysis and dissemination of accurate, reliable and comparable data and information to enhance knowledge on crime trends and support Member States in designing appropriate responses in specific areas of crime, in particular in their transnational dimension, taking into account the need to make the best possible use of existing resources;

20. *Urges* Member States and relevant international organizations to develop national and regional strategies, as appropriate, and other necessary measures, in cooperation with the United Nations crime prevention and criminal justice programme, to address effectively transnational organized crime, including trafficking in persons, the smuggling of migrants and illicit manufacturing of and trafficking in firearms, as well as corruption and terrorism;

21. *Urges* States parties to use the United Nations Convention against Transnational Organized Crime for broad cooperation in preventing and combating criminal offences against cultural property, especially in returning such proceeds of crime or property to their legitimate owners, in accordance with article 14, paragraph 2, of the Convention, and invites States parties to exchange information on all aspects of criminal offences against cultural property, in accordance with their national laws, and to coordinate administrative and other measures taken, as appropriate, for the prevention, early detection and punishment of such offences;

22. *Urges* the United Nations Office on Drugs and Crime to continue to assist Member States, upon request, in combating the illicit trafficking in firearms, their parts and components and ammunition, and to support them in their efforts to address its links with other forms of transnational organized crime, through, inter alia, technical assistance;

23. *Reaffirms* the importance of the United Nations Office on Drugs and Crime and its regional offices in building capacity at the local level in the fight against transnational organized crime and drug trafficking, and urges the Office to consider regional vulnerabilities, projects and impact in the fight against transnational organized crime, in particular in developing countries, when deciding to close and allocate offices, with a view to maintaining an effective level of support to national and regional efforts in those areas;

24. *Encourages* Member States to support the United Nations Office on Drugs and Crime in continuing to provide targeted technical assistance, within its existing mandate, to enhance the capacity of affected States, upon their request, to combat piracy by sea, including by assisting Member States in creating an effective law enforcement response and strengthening their judicial capacity;

25. *Welcomes* the progress achieved by the Conference of the Parties to the United Nations Convention against Transnational Organized Crime and the Conference of the States Parties to the United Nations Convention against Corruption in the implementation of their respective mandates;

26. *Encourages* States parties to continue to provide full support to the Conference of the Parties to the United Nations Convention against Transnational Organized Crime and the Conference of the States Parties to the United Nations Convention against Corruption, including providing information to the conferences regarding compliance with the treaties;

27. *Requests* the Secretary-General to continue to provide the United Nations Office on Drugs and Crime with adequate resources to promote, in an effective manner, the implementation of the United Nations Convention against Transnational Organized Crime and the United Nations Convention against Corruption and to discharge its functions as the secretariat of the conferences of the parties to the conventions, the Commission on Crime Prevention and Criminal Justice and the Commission on Narcotic Drugs, in accordance with its mandate;

28. *Notes with appreciation* the establishment and successful functioning of the Mechanism for the Review of Implementation of the United Nations Convention against Corruption, and encourages States parties and signatories to the Convention to provide full support to the Mechanism, adopted by the Conference of the States Parties to the Convention;

29. *Welcomes* the conclusion of the fourth session of the Conference of the States Parties to the United Nations Convention against Corruption, held in Marrakech, Morocco, from 24 to 28 October 2011, and the resolutions adopted at the session, including the Marrakech declaration on the prevention of corruption, and requests the Secretary-General to transmit to the General Assembly a report on the fourth session of the Conference of the States Parties to the Convention;

30. *Reiterates its request* to the United Nations Office on Drugs and Crime to enhance its technical assistance to Member States, upon request, to strengthen international cooperation in preventing and combating terrorism through the facilitation of the ratification and implementation of the universal conventions and protocols related to terrorism, in close consultation with the Counter-Terrorism Committee and its Executive Directorate, as well as to continue to contribute to the work of the Counter-Terrorism Implementation Task Force, and invites Member States to provide the Office with appropriate resources for its mandate;

31. *Requests* that the United Nations Office on Drugs and Crime continue to provide technical assistance to Member States, upon request, to strengthen the rule of law, taking also into account the work undertaken by the Rule of Law Coordination and Resource Group of the Secretariat and other relevant United Nations bodies;

32. *Encourages* Member States to take relevant measures, as appropriate to their national contexts, to ensure the diffusion, use and application of the United Nations standards and norms in crime prevention and criminal justice, including the consideration and, where they deem it necessary, dissemination of existing manuals and handbooks developed and published by the United Nations Office on Drugs and Crime;

33. *Reiterates* the importance of providing the United Nations crime prevention and criminal justice programme with sufficient, stable and predictable funding for the full implementation of its mandates, in conformity with the high priority accorded to it and in accordance with the increasing demand for its services, in particular with regard to the provision of increased assistance to developing countries, countries with economies in transition and countries emerging from conflict, in the area of crime prevention and criminal justice reform;

34. *Requests* the Secretary-General to submit a report to the General Assembly at its sixty-seventh session on the implementation of the mandates of the United Nations crime prevention and criminal justice programme, reflecting also emerging policy issues and possible responses;

35. *Also requests* the Secretary-General to include in the report referred to in paragraph 34 above information on the status of ratifications or accessions to the United Nations Convention against Transnational Organized Crime and the Protocols thereto.

Crime Prevention and Criminal Justice Programme network

Pursuant to Economic and Social Council resolutions 1992/22 [YUN 1992, p. 842], 1994/21 [YUN 1994, p. 1174] and 1999/23 [YUN 1999, p. 1054], and Council decision 2010/243 [YUN 2010, p. 1101], the Secretary-General in January reported to CCPCJ [E/CN.15/2011/7] on the activities carried out in 2010 by the institutes comprising the United Nations crime prevention and criminal justice programme network, which included the United Nations Interregional Crime and Justice Research Institute (UNICRI), 14 regional and affiliated institutes, and the International Scientific and Professional Advisory Council of the United Nations Crime Prevention and Criminal Justice Programme.

United Nations Interregional Crime and Justice Research Institute

In January [E/CN.15/2011/7], the Secretary-General informed the Commission that, pursuant to the statute of the United Nations Interregional Crime and Justice Research Institute, annexed to Economic and Social Council resolution 1989/56 [YUN 1989, p. 637], the Board of Trustees of the Institute would submit a report to the Commission that would include information on the activities undertaken by the Institute in 2010.

United Nations African crime prevention institute

In response to General Assembly resolution 65/231 [YUN 2010, p. 1108], the Secretary-General in June submitted a report [A/66/131] on the activities undertaken by the Uganda-based United Nations African Institute for the Prevention of Crime and the Treatment of Offenders to offer African countries technical support in crime prevention and the strengthening of criminal justice systems. The report further outlined practical measures proposed by the Institute, emphasizing collaboration while taking into account the role of local and outsourced resources. The Secretary-General highlighted the challenges Africa faced in litigation and the management of correctional institutions, especially with regard to sophisticated crime trends. Also covered were the difficulties that limited the capacity of the Institute for smooth operation and delivery of services. The income of the Institute for 2010 was $462,637, some 25 per cent less than the previous year.

The report concluded that the concept of globalization was relevant to challenges brought about by crime, which were spilling over all continents with disastrous effects. An approach that included appropriate legislation, effective criminal justice, sensitization of the population, training of criminal justice personnel, and research to identify emerging threats would help to keep the activities of criminal organizations in check. Good practices in Africa should be explored and developed, with a view to incorporating them in mainstream legislative mechanisms.

GENERAL ASSEMBLY ACTION

On 19 December [meeting 89], the General Assembly, on the recommendation of the Third Committee [A/66/463], adopted **resolution 66/182** without vote [agenda item 107].

United Nations African Institute for the Prevention of Crime and the Treatment of Offenders

The General Assembly,

Recalling its resolution 65/231 of 21 December 2010 and all other relevant resolutions,

Taking note of the report of the Secretary-General,

Bearing in mind that weaknesses in crime prevention lead to subsequent difficulties at the level of crime control mechanisms, and bearing in mind also the urgent need to establish effective crime prevention strategies for Africa, as well as the importance of law enforcement agencies and the judiciary at the regional and subregional levels,

Aware of the devastating impact of new and more dynamic crime trends on the national economies of African States, such as the high levels of transnational organized crime being recorded in Africa, including the utilization of digital technology to commit all types of cybercrime, illicit trafficking in cultural property and drugs, piracy and money-laundering, and of the fact that crime is a major obstacle to harmonious and sustainable development in Africa,

Noting with concern that in most African countries the existing criminal justice system does not have sufficiently skilled personnel and adequate infrastructure and is therefore ill-equipped to manage the emergence of new crime trends, and acknowledging the challenges that Africa faces in litigation processes and the management of correctional institutions,

Recognizing that the United Nations African Institute for the Prevention of Crime and the Treatment of Offenders is a focal point for all professional efforts aimed at promoting the active cooperation and collaboration of Governments, academics, institutions and scientific and professional organizations and experts in crime prevention and criminal justice,

Bearing in mind the Revised African Union Plan of Action on Drug Control and Crime Prevention (2007–2012), aimed at encouraging Member States to participate in and own the regional initiatives for effective crime prevention and good governance and strengthened justice administration,

Recognizing the importance of promoting sustainable development as a complement to crime prevention strategies,

Emphasizing the need to create necessary coalitions with all partners in the process of achieving effective crime prevention policies,

Noting that the financial situation of the Institute has greatly affected its capacity to deliver its services to African Member States in an effective and comprehensive manner,

1. *Commends* the United Nations African Institute for the Prevention of Crime and the Treatment of Offenders for its efforts to promote and coordinate regional technical cooperation activities related to crime prevention and criminal justice systems in Africa;

2. *Also commends* the initiative of the United Nations Office on Drugs and Crime in strengthening its working relationship with the Institute by supporting and involving the Institute in the implementation of a number of activities, including those contained in the Revised African Union Plan of Action on Drug Control and Crime Prevention (2007–2012), on strengthening the rule of law and criminal justice systems in Africa;

3. *Reiterates* the need to strengthen further the capacity of the Institute to support national mechanisms for crime prevention and criminal justice in African countries;

4. *Notes* the efforts of the Institute to establish contacts with organizations in those countries which are promoting crime prevention programmes and its maintenance of close links with regional and subregional political entities, such as the African Union Commission, the East African Community, the Commission of the Economic Community of West African States, the Intergovernmental Authority on Development and the Southern African Development Community;

5. *Encourages* the Institute, in cooperation with relevant United Nations agencies, to take into account the various planning authorities in the region that focus attention on the coordination of activities that promote development based on sustainable agricultural production and preservation of the environment in developing its crime prevention strategies;

6. *Urges* the States members of the Institute to continue to make every possible effort to meet their obligations to the Institute;

7. *Welcomes* the decision of the Governing Board of the Institute, at its eleventh ordinary session, held in Nairobi on 27 and 28 April 2011, to carry out a review of the Institute to ensure that it can fulfil its mandate and assume a more prominent role in dealing with existing crime;

8. *Also welcomes* the introduction by the Institute of a cost-sharing initiative in its execution of various programmes with Member States, partners and United Nations entities;

9. *Urges* all Member States and non-governmental organizations and the international community to continue adopting concrete practical measures to support the Institute in the development of the requisite capacity and in the implementation of its programmes and activities aimed at strengthening crime prevention and criminal justice systems in Africa;

10. *Urges* all States that have not already done so to consider ratifying or acceding to the United Nations Convention against Transnational Organized Crime and the Protocols thereto, as well as the United Nations Convention against Corruption;

11. *Requests* the Secretary-General to intensify efforts to mobilize all relevant entities of the United Nations system to provide the necessary financial and technical support to the Institute to enable it to fulfil its mandate, bearing in mind that the precarious financial situation of the Institute greatly undermines its capacity to deliver services effectively;

12. *Also requests* the Secretary-General to continue his efforts to mobilize the financial resources necessary to maintain the Institute with the core professional staff required to enable it to function effectively in the fulfilment of its mandated obligations;

13. *Encourages* the Institute to consider focusing on specific and general vulnerabilities of each programme country and to maximize the use of available initiatives to address crime problems with existing funds, as well as available capacity, by creating useful coalitions with regional and local institutions;

14. *Calls upon* the United Nations Office on Drugs and Crime to continue to work closely with the Institute;

15. *Requests* the Secretary-General to enhance the promotion of regional cooperation, coordination and collaboration in the fight against crime, especially in its transnational dimension, which cannot be dealt with adequately by national action alone;

16. *Also requests* the Secretary-General to continue making concrete proposals, including for the provision of additional core professional staff, to strengthen the programmes and activities of the Institute and to report to the General Assembly at its sixty-seventh session on the implementation of the present resolution.

Crime data collection

In response to Economic and Social Council resolution 2009/25 [YUN 2009, p. 1090], the Executive Director in January reported [E/CN.15/2011/17] on the activities of the open-ended intergovernmental expert group on improving the collection, reporting and analysis of crime data. UNODC used the recommendations of the first meeting of the expert group [YUN 2010, p. 1109] to guide and inform its subsequent work on the development of its data-collection system, including the United Nations Survey of Crime Trends and Operations of Criminal Justice Systems, covering 2009.

The Executive Director recommended to CCPCJ that it encourage Member States to appoint a focal point to coordinate the responses to future Survey questionnaires, to provide complete and timely responses to the latest and future Surveys, and to provide timely responses to the forthcoming UNODC data-gathering exercise on trafficking in persons.

A Secretariat note on world crime trends and emerging issues and responses in the field of crime prevention and criminal justice [E/CN.15/2011/10], prepared pursuant to Economic and Social Council resolution 1990/18 [YUN 1990, p. 727] and decision 2010/243 [YUN 2010, p. 1101], provided information on preliminary results from the Twelfth United Nations Survey of Crime Trends and Operations of Criminal Justice Systems; statistics and analysis on trends in intentional homicide and on crime and victimization in Africa; and findings from a series of surveys on the nature and extent of corruption.

Transnational organized crime

UN convention against transnational organized crime

The United Nations Convention against Transnational Organized Crime, adopted by General Assembly resolution 55/25 [YUN 2000, p. 1048], and its three supplementary Protocols—the Protocol to Prevent, Suppress and Punish Trafficking in Persons, Especially Women and Children [ibid., p. 1063]; the Protocol against the Smuggling of Migrants by Land, Sea and Air [ibid., p. 1067]; and the Protocol against the Illicit Manufacturing of and Trafficking in Firearms, Their Parts and Components and Ammunition, adopted by the Assembly in resolution 55/255 [YUN 2001, p. 1036]—continued to attract adherence. As at 31 December, 164 States and the European Union (EU) were parties to the Convention, 146 States and the EU were parties to the trafficking in persons Protocol, 128 States and the EU were parties to the migrants Protocol, and 90 States were parties to the firearms Protocol.

Conference of Parties. In June [A/66/92], the Secretary-General transmitted to the General Assembly the report of the Conference of the Parties to the United Nations Convention against Transnational Organized Crime on its fifth session [YUN 2010, p. 1110]. The Assembly took note of that report on 19 December (**decision 66/539**).

Intergovernmental working group. The Conference of the Parties, at its fifth (2010) session [YUN 2010, p. 1110], established an open-ended intergovernmental working group to explore options and make proposals for the establishment of a mechanism or mechanisms to assist the Conference in reviewing the implementation of the Convention and the Protocols thereto, as well as to prepare terms of reference for such a proposed review mechanism or mechanisms, guidelines for governmental experts and a blueprint for the country review reports, for consideration and possible adoption by the Conference at its sixth (2012) session. The working group held its first session (Vienna, 17–19 May) [CTOC/COP/WG.5/2011/6].

Commission action. On 15 April [E/2011/30 (res. 20/4)], the Commission called on Member States to ratify or accede to the United Nations Convention against Transnational Organized Crime and the Protocols thereto, and requested UNODC to continue to provide technical assistance to facilitate its ratification and implementation. The Commission further requested the Office to provide support to the Conference of the Parties to the Convention and its working groups; to develop global analyses of the threats and modalities of transnational organized crime; to study new forms and dimensions of transnational organized crime; and to analyse new and emerging challenges, in order to support evidence-based policy guidance.

At the same session [res. 20/5], the Commission urged Member States to strengthen international cooperation in combating transnational organized crime committed at sea. It requested UNODC to convene an expert meeting to survey the challenges to the criminal justice system in the investigation and prosecution of cases arising from organized criminal activities at sea. The Executive Director was requested to report to the Commission's twenty-second (2013) session on the implementation of the resolution.

Trafficking in persons

In April [E/2011/30 (res. 20/3)], the Commission urged Member States to contribute to the implementation of the Global Plan of Action to Combat Trafficking in Persons [YUN 2010, p. 1111], including by strengthening cooperation and improving coordination among themselves in achieving that goal. It also urged States to consider ratifying or acceding to the United Nations Convention against Transnational Organized Crime [YUN 2000, p. 1048] and the Protocol to Prevent, Suppress and Punish Trafficking in Persons, Especially Women and Children [ibid., p. 1063]. The Commission requested the Executive Director to strengthen the capacity of UNODC in the fight against trafficking in persons. It requested UNODC to promote public-private partnerships to counter trafficking in persons, especially women and children, including for the purpose of organ removal; and to strengthen its capacity to collect and analyse information and to report biennially, starting in 2012, on patterns, forms and flows of trafficking in persons.

The Working Group on Trafficking in Persons, established by the fourth (2008) session of the Conference of Parties to the United Nations Convention against Transnational Organized Crime [YUN 2008, p. 1234], held its third meeting (Vienna, 10–12 October) [CTOC/COP/WG.4/2011/8].

Communication. By a letter of 27 September [A/66/398], Belarus, on behalf of the Group of Friends United against Human Trafficking (Bahrain, Bangladesh, Belarus, Bolivia, Ecuador, Egypt, India, Kazakhstan, Kyrgyzstan, Libya, Nicaragua, Nigeria, Philippines, Qatar, Russian Federation, Singapore, Tajikistan, Turkmenistan, United Arab Emirates, Uzbekistan, Venezuela), transmitted to the Secretary-General the Declaration on the Global Efforts to Combat Trafficking in Persons, adopted at the second ministerial meeting of the Group (26 September), convened on the margins of the sixty-sixth session of the General Assembly.

Trafficking in cultural property

At its session in April [E/2011/30], the Commission discussed the work of UNODC with respect to the ratification and implementation of the United Nations Convention against Transnational Organized Crime and the Protocols thereto. The Commission highlighted the application of the Convention to new and emerging forms of transnational organized crime, in particular to trafficking in cultural property whenever there was involvement of organized criminal groups.

ECONOMIC AND SOCIAL COUNCIL ACTION

On 28 July [meeting 49], the Economic and Social Council, on the recommendation of the Commission on Crime Prevention and Criminal Justice [E/2011/30], adopted **resolution 2011/42** without vote [agenda item 14 (c)].

Strengthening crime prevention and criminal justice responses to protect cultural property, especially with regard to its trafficking

The Economic and Social Council
Recommends to the General Assembly the adoption of the following draft resolution:

[For text, see General Assembly resolution 66/180 below.]

GENERAL ASSEMBLY ACTION

On 19 December [meeting 89], the General Assembly, on the recommendation of the Third Committee [A/66/463], adopted **resolution 66/180** without vote [agenda item 107].

Strengthening crime prevention and criminal justice responses to protect cultural property, especially with regard to its trafficking

The General Assembly,
Recalling its resolutions 58/17 of 3 December 2003, 61/52 of 4 December 2006 and 64/78 of 7 December 2009 on the return or restitution of cultural property to the countries of origin, Economic and Social Council resolutions 2003/29 of 22 July 2003 entitled "Prevention of crimes that infringe on the cultural heritage of peoples in the form of movable property", 2004/34 of 21 July 2004 and 2008/23 of 24 July 2008 entitled "Protection against trafficking in cultural property" and 2010/19 of 22 July 2010 entitled "Crime prevention and criminal justice responses to protect cultural property, especially with regard to its trafficking", and the Salvador Declaration on Comprehensive Strategies for Global Challenges: Crime Prevention and Criminal Justice Systems and Their Development in a Changing World,
Recalling also the United Nations Convention against Transnational Organized Crime, adopted by the General Assembly in its resolution 55/25 of 15 November 2000, as well as the United Nations Convention against Corruption, adopted by the Assembly in its resolution 58/4 of 31 October 2003,
Recalling further the Convention on the Means of Prohibiting and Preventing the Illicit Import, Export and

Transfer of Ownership of Cultural Property, adopted by the General Conference of the United Nations Educational, Scientific and Cultural Organization on 14 November 1970, the Convention on Stolen or Illegally Exported Cultural Objects, adopted by the International Institute for the Unification of Private Law on 24 June 1995, and the Convention for the Protection of Cultural Property in the Event of Armed Conflict, adopted at The Hague on 14 May 1954, and the two Protocols thereto, adopted on 14 May 1954 and 26 March 1999, and reaffirming the necessity for those States that have not done so to consider ratifying or acceding to and, as States parties, implementing those international instruments,

Reiterating the significance of cultural property as part of the common heritage of humankind and as unique and important testimony of the culture and identity of peoples and the necessity of protecting it, and reaffirming in that regard the need to strengthen international cooperation in preventing, prosecuting and punishing all aspects of trafficking in cultural property,

Concerned that demand for stolen, looted and illicitly exported or imported cultural property is growing and fuels further looting, destruction, removal and theft of and trafficking in such unique property, and recognizing that urgent and commensurate legislative and administrative measures are required to discourage demand for illicitly acquired cultural property in the market,

Alarmed at the growing involvement of organized criminal groups in all forms and aspects of trafficking in cultural property and related offences, and observing that cultural property is increasingly being sold through markets, including in auctions, in particular over the Internet, and that such property is being unlawfully excavated and illicitly exported or imported, with the facilitation of modern and sophisticated technologies,

Inviting Member States to protect cultural property and prevent trafficking in such property by introducing appropriate legislation, including, in particular, procedures for its seizure, recovery and return, as well as by promoting education, launching awareness-raising campaigns, locating and inventorying such property, adopting adequate security measures, developing the capacities and human resources of monitoring institutions, such as the police and customs services, and of the tourism sector, involving the media and disseminating information on the theft and pillaging of cultural property,

Acknowledging the important contribution of the International Scientific and Professional Advisory Council of the United Nations crime prevention and criminal justice programme network in this field,

Recognizing the indispensable role of crime prevention and criminal justice responses in combating all forms and aspects of trafficking in cultural property and related offences in a comprehensive and effective manner,

1. *Welcomes* Economic and Social Council resolution 2010/19, as well as resolution 5/7 of 22 October 2010 entitled "Combating transnational organized crime against cultural property", adopted by the Conference of the Parties to the United Nations Convention against Transnational Organized Crime at its fifth session, held in Vienna from 18 to 22 October 2010;

2. *Urges* Member States that are parties to the aforementioned conventions, including the United Nations Convention against Transnational Organized Crime and the United Nations Convention against Corruption, to fully implement them, encourages those Member States that have not yet done so to consider becoming parties to those conventions, and encourages Member States and relevant international organizations to strengthen crime prevention and criminal justice responses to protect cultural property, especially with regard to its trafficking, within the framework of relevant United Nations conventions and resolutions, for the purpose of providing the widest possible international cooperation to address such crimes, including for extradition, mutual legal assistance and the confiscation and return of stolen cultural property to its rightful owner;

3. *Welcomes* the decision taken by the Economic and Social Council in its resolution 2010/19 to convene at least one additional meeting of the open-ended intergovernmental expert group on protection against trafficking in cultural property established within the framework of the Commission on Crime Prevention and Criminal Justice, and encourages Member States and other donors to support the convening of that expert group meeting and to submit to the Commission at its twenty-second session practical proposals for implementing, where appropriate, the recommendations made by the expert group at its meeting held in Vienna from 24 to 26 November 2009, with due attention to aspects of criminalization, international cooperation and mutual legal assistance;

4. *Also welcomes* the request made by the Conference of the Parties to the United Nations Convention against Transnational Organized Crime at its fifth session to its Working Group on International Cooperation and its Open-ended Interim Working Group of Government Experts on Technical Assistance to examine the relevant recommendations and outcomes of the meetings of the expert group and to make recommendations for consideration by the Conference of the Parties in order to promote the practical application of the Convention, by considering the extent and adequacy of existing norms, as well as other normative developments, with due attention to aspects of criminalization and international cooperation, including mutual legal assistance and extradition, in this regard;

5. *Urges* Member States and relevant institutions, as appropriate, to reinforce and fully implement mechanisms to strengthen international cooperation, including mutual legal assistance, in order to combat all forms and aspects of trafficking in cultural property and related offences, such as the theft, looting, damage, removal, pillage and destruction of cultural property, and to facilitate the recovery and return of stolen cultural property, and requests the Conference of the Parties to the United Nations Convention against Transnational Organized Crime and the Commission on Crime Prevention and Criminal Justice to continue their efforts to effectively strengthen crime prevention and criminal justice responses to protect cultural property, especially with regard to its trafficking, bearing in mind, in particular, paragraph 12 of Economic and Social Council resolution 2010/19;

6. *Urges* Member States to consider, among other effective measures within the framework of their national legislation, criminalizing activities related to all forms and aspects of trafficking in cultural property and related offences by using a broad definition that can be applied to all stolen, looted, unlawfully excavated and illicitly exported or

imported cultural property, and invites them to make trafficking in cultural property, including stealing and looting at archaeological and other cultural sites, a serious crime, as defined in article 2 of the United Nations Convention against Transnational Organized Crime, with a view to fully utilizing that Convention for the purpose of extensive international cooperation in fighting all forms and aspects of trafficking in cultural property and related offences;

7. *Also urges* Member States to take all appropriate steps and effective measures to strengthen legislative and administrative measures aimed at countering trade in stolen, looted and illicitly exported or imported cultural property, including appropriate domestic measures to maximize the transparency of activities of traders in cultural property in the market, in particular through effective regulations and supervision of dealers in antiquities, intermediaries and similar institutions, in accordance with their national law and other applicable law;

8. *Invites* Member States to continue to submit, in writing, comments on the model treaty for the prevention of crimes that infringe on the cultural heritage of peoples in the form of movable property, including views on its potential utility and on whether any improvements to it should be considered at the earliest possible date, in order to assist the Secretariat in preparing an analysis and a report to be presented to the expert group on protection against trafficking in cultural property at its next meeting, as well as to the Commission on Crime Prevention and Criminal Justice at its twenty-second session;

9. *Requests* the United Nations Office on Drugs and Crime, within its mandate, in consultation with Member States and in close cooperation, as appropriate, with the United Nations Educational, Scientific and Cultural Organization, the International Criminal Police Organization (INTERPOL) and other competent international organizations:

(*a*) To further explore the development of specific guidelines for crime prevention and criminal justice responses with respect to trafficking in cultural property;

(*b*) To explore possibilities for the collection, analysis and dissemination of data specifically addressing the relevant aspects of trafficking in cultural property;

(*c*) To continue to collect, analyse and disseminate information on crime trends through the United Nations Survey of Crime Trends and Operations of Criminal Justice Systems;

(*d*) To promote good practices, including in international cooperation;

(*e*) To assist Member States, upon request, in strengthening crime prevention and criminal justice responses to protect cultural property, especially with regard to its trafficking;

(*f*) To consider, where appropriate, addressing trafficking in cultural property in its regional, interregional and thematic programmes;

10. *Requests* the Secretary-General to report to the Commission on Crime Prevention and Criminal Justice at its twenty-second session on the implementation of the present resolution;

11. *Invites* Member States and other donors to provide extrabudgetary resources for the purposes of the present resolution, in accordance with the rules and procedures of the United Nations.

Trafficking in endangered species

On 8 April, Chile, Costa Rica, Guatemala and Mexico introduced at the CCPCJ session a draft resolution [E/CN.15/2011/L.5] on crime prevention and criminal justice responses against illicit trafficking in endangered species of wild fauna and flora (see below). The Commission on 15 April recommended the draft resolution for adoption by the Economic and Social Council.

ECONOMIC AND SOCIAL COUNCIL ACTION

On 28 July [meeting 48], the Economic and Social Council, on the recommendation of the Commission on Crime Prevention and Criminal Justice [E/2011/30], adopted **resolution 2011/36** without vote [agenda item 14 (*c*)].

Crime prevention and criminal justice responses to illicit trafficking in endangered species of wild fauna and flora

The Economic and Social Council,

Recalling its resolutions 2001/12 of 24 July 2001 and 2003/27 of 22 July 2003 concerning illicit trafficking in protected species of wild fauna and flora and its resolution 2008/25 of 24 July 2008 concerning international cooperation in preventing and combating illicit international trafficking in forest products, including timber, wildlife and other forest biological resources,

Recalling also General Assembly resolution 62/98 of 17 December 2007, in which the Assembly adopted a non-legally binding instrument on all types of forests, by which Member States and others were called upon to enhance bilateral, regional and international cooperation to address illicit international trafficking in forest products through the promotion of forest law enforcement and good governance at all levels, as well as to strengthen, through enhanced bilateral, regional and international cooperation, the capacity of countries to combat effectively illicit international trafficking in forest products, including timber, wildlife and other forest biological resources,

Recalling further the Convention on International Trade in Endangered Species of Wild Fauna and Flora, of 1973 and efforts made by parties to the Convention to implement it,

Reaffirming Commission on Crime Prevention and Criminal Justice resolution 16/1 of 27 April 2007, in which, inter alia, the Commission strongly encouraged Member States to cooperate at the bilateral, regional and international levels to prevent, combat and eradicate such illicit international trafficking in forest products, including timber, wildlife and other forest biological resources, where appropriate, through the use of international legal instruments such as the United Nations Convention against Transnational Organized Crime and the United Nations Convention against Corruption,

Conscious of the importance of promoting public-private partnerships to address illicit trafficking in endangered species of wild fauna and flora, especially as regards the adoption of preventive measures,

Welcoming General Assembly resolution 65/230 of 21 December 2010 on the Twelfth United Nations Congress on Crime Prevention and Criminal Justice, in which the Assembly endorsed the Salvador Declaration on Comprehensive Strategies for Global Challenges: Crime Prevention and Criminal Justice Systems and Their Development in a Changing World and invited Governments to take it into consideration when formulating legislation and policy directives and to make every effort, where appropriate, to implement the principles contained therein, taking into account the economic, social, legal and cultural specificities of their respective States,

Bearing in mind paragraph 14 of the Salvador Declaration, in which Member States acknowledged the challenge posed by emerging forms of crime that have a significant impact on the environment, encouraged Member States to strengthen their national crime prevention and criminal justice legislation, policies and practices in this area and invited Member States to enhance international cooperation, technical assistance and the sharing of best practices in this area, and also invited the Commission on Crime Prevention and Criminal Justice, in coordination with the relevant United Nations bodies, to study the nature of the challenge and ways to deal with it effectively,

Concerned by the involvement of organized criminal groups in all aspects of illicit trafficking in endangered species of wild fauna and flora, and underscoring in that regard the usefulness of the United Nations Convention against Transnational Organized Crime in reinforcing international cooperation in the fight against such crime,

Recognizing the efforts made at the bilateral, regional and international levels and the work of the International Consortium on Combating Wildlife Crime, a collaboration among the secretariat of the Convention on International Trade in Endangered Species of Wild Fauna and Flora, the International Criminal Police Organization (INTERPOL), the United Nations Office on Drugs and Crime, the World Bank and the World Customs Organization, as well as the work of the United Nations Environment Programme, the Food and Agriculture Organization of the United Nations, the World Trade Organization and the United Nations Conference on Trade and Development, in combating illicit trafficking in endangered species of wild fauna and flora,

Recalling the importance of effective cooperation between the United Nations Office on Drugs and Crime and relevant international organizations in combating illicit trafficking in endangered species of wild fauna and flora and for organizing, upon request, the provision of technical assistance to States in the areas of crime prevention and criminal justice,

1. *Strongly encourages* Member States to take appropriate measures to prevent and combat illicit trafficking in endangered species of wild fauna and flora, including the adoption, where appropriate, of the necessary legislation for the prevention, investigation and prosecution of such illicit trafficking, in accordance with the Convention on International Trade in Endangered Species of Wild Fauna and Flora, including its fundamental principles;

2. *Urges* Member States to strengthen international, regional and bilateral cooperation, including for purposes of extradition, mutual legal assistance, identification, and seizure and confiscation of proceeds of crime, and invites them to reinforce and develop relevant mechanisms for such purposes, in order to combat all forms and aspects of illicit trafficking in endangered species of wild fauna and flora and to facilitate the confiscation and/or return of such species, consistent with applicable international instruments;

3. *Also urges* Member States in that regard to consider, as appropriate, reviewing their legal frameworks with a view to providing the most extensive international cooperation possible to fully address all aspects of illicit trafficking in endangered species of wild fauna and flora, particularly with regard to extradition and mutual legal assistance for investigation and prosecution;

4. *Calls upon* Member States to fully utilize the United Nations Convention against Transnational Organized Crime and the United Nations Convention against Corruption for preventing and combating illicit trafficking in endangered species of wild fauna and flora, and in that regard calls upon Member States that have not done so to consider becoming parties to those Conventions, and calls for their full and effective implementation by States parties;

5. *Invites* Member States to consider making illicit trafficking in endangered species of wild fauna and flora a serious crime, in accordance with their national legislation and article 2, paragraph (*b*), of the United Nations Convention against Transnational Organized Crime, especially when organized criminal groups are involved;

6. *Encourages* Member States to identify opportunities to enhance law enforcement cooperation and information-sharing, by such means as exchanging law enforcement personnel, holding joint law enforcement activities and using existing law enforcement networks;

7. *Also encourages* Member States to share their experiences and best practices in the detection and prosecution of illicit trafficking in endangered species of wild fauna and flora, including in the thematic discussion to be held during the twenty-second session of the Commission on Crime Prevention and Criminal Justice;

8. *Requests* the United Nations Office on Drugs and Crime, within its mandate, to join the relevant international organizations in promoting and organizing meetings, seminars, similar events and all types of relevant cooperation to which the Office can contribute as regards the crime prevention and criminal justice aspect of protection against illicit trafficking in endangered species of wild fauna and flora;

9. *Also requests* the United Nations Office on Drugs and Crime, in consultation with Member States, in accordance with its mandate and in close cooperation with the competent international organizations referred to above in the present resolution, to explore ways and means to contribute to ongoing efforts to collect, analyse and disseminate relevant data, specifically addressing the scope, prevalence and other relevant aspects of illicit trafficking in endangered species of wild fauna and flora;

10. *Further requests* the United Nations Office on Drugs and Crime, within its mandate, in cooperation with Member States, relevant international organizations and the private sector, to continue to provide, upon request, technical assistance to States, particularly as regards the prevention, investigation and prosecution of illicit trafficking in endangered species of wild fauna and flora through, inter alia, the development of tools and capacity-building activities and through education and awareness-raising campaigns;

11. *Invites* Member States and other donors to provide extrabudgetary resources, where necessary and in accordance with the rules and procedures of the United Nations, for the implementation of the relevant paragraphs of the present resolution;

12. *Requests* the Secretary-General to prepare and submit to the Commission on Crime Prevention and Criminal Justice at its twenty-second session a report on the implementation of the present resolution.

Trafficking of fraudulent medicines

On 15 April [E/2011/30 (res. 20/6)], CCPCJ urged Member States and international and regional institutions to strengthen and implement measures and mechanisms to prevent trafficking in fraudulent medicines, and to strengthen international cooperation, including through the UNODC legal and operational technical assistance programmes, to increase the effectiveness of authorities in identifying and responding to such trafficking. The Commission further urged States to prevent trafficking by introducing legislation covering offences related to fraudulent medicines, such as money-laundering, corruption and smuggling, as well as the confiscation and disposal of criminal assets, extradition and mutual legal assistance. The Executive Director was requested to report on the implementation of the resolution at the Commission's twenty-second (2013) session.

Corruption

International cooperation

In response to Economic and Social Council resolution 2010/243 [YUN 2010, p. 1101], the Executive Director in January submitted a report [E/CN.15/2011/5] on international cooperation in combating transnational organized crime and corruption. The report reviewed UNODC activities in the fight against transnational organized crime and corruption. It also provided information on the work of the Mechanism for the Review of Implementation of the United Nations Convention against Corruption [YUN 2009, p. 1096], the working groups established by the Conference of the States Parties to the United Nations Convention against Corruption, and technical assistance.

UN Convention against corruption

As at 31 December, 157 States and the EU were parties to the United Nations Convention against Corruption, adopted by the General Assembly in 2003 [YUN 2003, p. 1127].

Conference of States Parties. The Conference of States Parties to the United Nations Convention against Corruption, at its fourth session (Marrakech, Morocco, 24–28 October) [CAC/COSP/2011/14], adopted six resolutions and two decisions on a range of issues, including international cooperation, prevention of corruption and asset recovery.

The Working Group on Asset Recovery, established by the first (2006) session of the Conference of States Parties [YUN 2006, p. 1303], held its fifth intersessional meeting (Vienna, 25–26 August) [CAC/COSP/WG.2/2011/5].

The Implementation Review Group, established by the third session (2009) of the Conference of States Parties [YUN 2009, p. 1096], held its second (Vienna, 30 May–2 June) [CAC/COSP/IRG/2011/4], resumed second (Vienna, 7–9 September) [CAC/COSP/IRG/2011/4/Add.1] and continued resumed second session (Marrakech, 25 October) [CAC/COSP/IRG/2011/4/Add.2].

The Open-ended Intergovernmental Working Group on the Prevention of Corruption, established by the third session of the Conference of States Parties [YUN 2009, p. 1096], held its second intersessional meeting (Vienna, 22–24 August) [CAC/COSP/WG.4/2011/4].

Communication. In a letter dated 30 May [E/2011/123], the Chair of the International Anti-Corruption Academy (IACA) International Transition Team transmitted to the Economic and Social Council an application for observer status for IACA with the Council. The Council granted observer status on 29 July (**decision 2011/269**).

Terrorism

International conventions related to terrorism

In a January report [E/CN.15/2011/4] on assistance in implementing the universal conventions and protocols related to terrorism, the Secretary-General informed the Commission about progress made in 2010 by UNODC, in particular by its Terrorism Prevention Branch, in delivering technical assistance on counter-terrorism. The report highlighted efforts made and challenges faced in responding to the evolving needs of Member States regarding criminal justice aspects of countering terrorism, and emphasized the need for enhanced governmental support to meet those challenges.

The Terrorism Prevention Branch provided support to countries in ratifying and implementing the international legal instruments against terrorism and in strengthening the capacity of national criminal justice systems to implement those instruments. In response to the increased demand for capacity-building assistance, the Branch offered sustained, tailor-made assistance to domestic criminal justice practitioners; assistance for strengthening international cooperation related to terrorist cases; and expertise-building in specialized areas, including through the development of tools and publications.

Assistance was provided to 43 countries. The Branch worked closely with the national authorities responsible for drafting national counter-terrorism strategies and action plans that required continuous local engagement by UNODC to support implementation; and developed in-depth counter-terrorism programmes for a number of countries, including Afghanistan, Algeria and Yemen. In addition, a regional counter-terrorism programme was developed for countries in the Sahel, and UNODC undertook regional programming for East Asian, South-East Asian and Pacific countries.

The Branch expanded its work in specific thematic areas, including strengthening international cooperation in criminal matters pertaining to counter-terrorism; addressing transportation-related security; suppressing the financing of terrorism; preventing nuclear, chemical, biological and radiological terrorism; enhancing procedural aspects of countering terrorism; and countering the use of the Internet for terrorist purposes. The delivery of technical assistance was fostered through enhanced coordination and partnerships with other entities and organizations, including the Counter-Terrorism Committee of the Security Council and that Committee's Executive Directorate, the Counter-Terrorism Implementation Task Force, and recipient and donor countries.

The report concluded with a set of recommendations for consideration by the Commission.

On 9 December, the General Assembly adopted **resolution 66/105** on measures to eliminate international terrorism (see p. 1285).

(For more information on terrorism, see also PART ONE, Chapter I).

Technical assistance for implementing counter-terrorism conventions

ECONOMIC AND SOCIAL COUNCIL ACTION

On 28 July [meeting 48], the Economic and Social Council, on the recommendation of the Commission on Crime Prevention and Criminal Justice [E/2011/30], adopted **resolution 2011/31** without vote [agenda item 14 (c)].

Technical assistance for implementing the international conventions and protocols related to counter-terrorism

The Economic and Social Council

Recommends to the General Assembly the adoption of the following draft resolution:

[For text, see General Assembly resolution 66/178 below.]

GENERAL ASSEMBLY ACTION

On 19 December [meeting 89], the General Assembly, on the recommendation of the Third Committee [A/66/463], adopted **resolution 66/178** without vote [agenda item 107].

Technical assistance for implementing the international conventions and protocols related to counter-terrorism

The General Assembly,

Reaffirming all General Assembly and Security Council resolutions related to technical assistance in countering terrorism,

Stressing again the need to strengthen international, regional and subregional cooperation to effectively prevent and combat terrorism, in particular by enhancing the national capacity of States through the provision of technical assistance, based on the needs and priorities identified by requesting States,

Recalling its resolution 65/232 of 21 December 2010, in which it, inter alia, reiterated its request to the United Nations Office on Drugs and Crime to enhance its technical assistance to Member States, upon request, to strengthen international cooperation in preventing and combating terrorism through the facilitation of the ratification and implementation of the universal conventions and protocols related to terrorism,

Recalling also its resolution 64/297 of 8 September 2010, in which it reaffirmed the United Nations Global Counter-Terrorism Strategy and underlined the importance of greater cooperation among United Nations entities and of the work of the Counter-Terrorism Implementation Task Force to ensure overall coordination and coherence in the counter-terrorism efforts of the United Nations system, as well as the need to continue to promote transparency and to avoid duplication,

Recalling further the Salvador Declaration on Comprehensive Strategies for Global Challenges: Crime Prevention and Criminal Justice Systems and Their Development in a Changing World, adopted by the Twelfth United Nations Congress on Crime Prevention and Criminal Justice,

Reiterating all aspects of the United Nations Global Counter-Terrorism Strategy and the need for States to continue to implement it,

Reaffirming its resolution 65/221 of 21 December 2010,

Reaffirming also its resolution 65/232, in which it, inter alia, expressed deep concern about the connections, in some cases, between some forms of transnational organized crime and terrorism and emphasized the need to enhance cooperation at the national, subregional, regional and international levels in order to strengthen responses to that evolving challenge,

Reiterating that it is the primary responsibility of Member States to implement the United Nations Global Counter-Terrorism Strategy, and recognizing the need to enhance the important role that the United Nations plays, in coordination with other international, regional and subregional organizations, in facilitating coherence in the implementation of the Strategy at the national, regional and global levels and in providing assistance, especially in the area of capacity-building,

Taking note of the Convention on the Suppression of Unlawful Acts Relating to International Civil Aviation and the Protocol Supplementary to the Convention for the Suppression of Unlawful Seizure of Aircraft, both adopted on 10 September 2010 at the International Conference on Air Law, held in Beijing from 30 August to 10 September 2010,

1. *Urges* Member States that have not yet done so to consider becoming parties to the existing international con-

ventions and protocols related to terrorism, and requests the United Nations Office on Drugs and Crime, within its mandate, in close coordination with the relevant entities of the Counter-Terrorism Implementation Task Force, to continue to provide technical assistance to Member States for the ratification and legislative incorporation of those international legal instruments;

2. *Urges* Member States to continue to strengthen international coordination and cooperation in order to prevent and combat terrorism in accordance with international law, including the Charter of the United Nations, and, when appropriate, by entering into bilateral and multilateral treaties on extradition and mutual legal assistance, and to ensure adequate training of all relevant personnel in executing international cooperation, and requests the United Nations Office on Drugs and Crime, within its mandate, to provide technical assistance to Member States to that end, including by continuing and enhancing its assistance related to international legal cooperation pertaining to terrorism;

3. *Stresses* the importance of the development and maintenance of fair and effective criminal justice systems, in accordance with applicable international law, as a fundamental basis of any strategy to counter terrorism, and requests the United Nations Office on Drugs and Crime, whenever appropriate, to take into account in its technical assistance to counter terrorism the elements necessary for building national capacity in order to strengthen criminal justice systems and the rule of law;

4. *Requests* the United Nations Office on Drugs and Crime, within its mandate, to continue to develop specialized legal knowledge in the area of counter-terrorism and pertinent thematic areas of relevance to the mandate of the Office and to provide assistance to requesting Member States with regard to criminal justice responses to terrorism, including, where appropriate, nuclear terrorism, the financing of terrorism and the use of the Internet for terrorist purposes, as well as assistance to and support for victims of terrorism;

5. *Calls upon* the United Nations Office on Drugs and Crime, within its mandate, to continue to develop its technical assistance programmes, in consultation with Member States, to assist them in ratifying and implementing the international legal instruments related to terrorism;

6. *Also calls upon* the United Nations Office on Drugs and Crime to continue to provide technical assistance for building the capacity of Member States to ratify and implement the international conventions and protocols related to terrorism, including through targeted programmes and the training of relevant criminal justice officials, upon request, the development of and participation in relevant initiatives and the elaboration of technical tools and publications;

7. *Urges* the United Nations Office on Drugs and Crime, in coordination with the Counter-Terrorism Committee and its Executive Directorate and the Counter-Terrorism Implementation Task Force, to strengthen its cooperation with international organizations and relevant entities of the United Nations system, as well as with regional and subregional organizations and arrangements, in the delivery of technical assistance, whenever appropriate;

8. *Requests* the United Nations Office on Drugs and Crime to continue to give high priority to the implementation of an integrated approach through the promotion of its regional and thematic programmes;

9. *Encourages* Member States to cooperate and to address, as appropriate, including through the effective exchange of information and sharing of experiences, connections between terrorism and related criminal activities in order to enhance criminal justice responses to terrorism, and calls upon the United Nations Office on Drugs and Crime, within its relevant mandates, to support the efforts of Member States in this regard, upon request;

10. *Expresses its appreciation* to Member States that have supported the technical assistance activities of the United Nations Office on Drugs and Crime, including through financial contributions, and invites Member States to consider making additional voluntary financial contributions, as well as providing in kind support, especially in view of the need for enhanced and effective delivery of technical assistance to assist Member States with the implementation of relevant provisions of the United Nations Global Counter-Terrorism Strategy;

11. *Requests* the Secretary-General to provide the United Nations Office on Drugs and Crime with sufficient resources to carry out activities, within its mandate, to assist Member States, upon request, in the implementation of the relevant elements of the United Nations Global Counter-Terrorism Strategy;

12. *Also requests* the Secretary-General to submit to the General Assembly at its sixty-seventh session a report on the implementation of the present resolution.

Illicit financial flows

On 10 April, Argentina and Peru introduced at the CCPCJ session a draft resolution [E/CN.15/2011/L.10] on strengthening international cooperation in combating the harmful effects of illicit financial flows resulting from transnational organized crime and drug trafficking and related offences (see below). The Commission on 15 April recommended that the Economic and Social Council approve the draft resolution for adoption by the General Assembly.

ECONOMIC AND SOCIAL COUNCIL ACTION

On 28 July [meeting 48], the Economic and Social Council, on the recommendation of the Commission on Crime Prevention and Criminal Justice [E/2011/30], adopted **resolution 2011/32** without vote [agenda item 14 (c)].

Strengthening international cooperation in combating the harmful effects of illicit financial flows resulting from criminal activities

The Economic and Social Council

Recommends to the General Assembly the adoption of the following draft resolution:

[For text, see General Assembly resolution 66/177 below.]

GENERAL ASSEMBLY ACTION

On 19 December [meeting 89], the General Assembly, on the recommendation of the Third Committee [A/66/463], adopted **resolution 66/177** without vote [agenda item 107].

Strengthening international cooperation in combating the harmful effects of illicit financial flows resulting from criminal activities

The General Assembly,

Concerned about the links between various types of transnational organized crime, including, as appropriate, drug trafficking and related offences provided for in the United Nations Convention against Transnational Organized Crime, and their impact on development as well as, in some cases, on security,

Concerned also that transnational organized criminal groups expand their activities to various sectors of economies with a view, inter alia, to legalizing proceeds of various types of crime and utilizing them for criminal purposes,

Concerned further about cases of transnational organized crime, including, as appropriate, drug trafficking and related offences provided for in the United Nations Convention against Transnational Organized Crime, that involve vast quantities of assets, which may exceed the resources of some States, and that may weaken governance systems, national economies and the rule of law, and bearing in mind in this regard, inter alia, paragraph 50 of the Plan of Action on International Cooperation towards an Integrated and Balanced Strategy to Counter the World Drug Problem,

Conscious of the need to enhance international cooperation to effectively prevent, detect and deter international transfers of illicitly acquired assets resulting from transnational organized crime, including, as appropriate, drug trafficking and related offences provided for in the United Nations Convention against Transnational Organized Crime,

Recognizing that the United Nations Convention against Transnational Organized Crime, the United Nations Convention against Corruption and other relevant instruments, including the United Nations Convention against Illicit Traffic in Narcotic Drugs and Psychotropic Substances of 1988, as well as relevant resolutions of other United Nations bodies, contribute to a global framework for preventing and countering the illicit flow of funds, including through money-laundering,

Recognizing also that the United Nations Convention against Transnational Organized Crime, the United Nations Convention against Corruption and the United Nations Convention against Illicit Traffic in Narcotic Drugs and Psychotropic Substances of 1988 provide a fundamental global framework of international standards for States parties for preventing and combating money-laundering,

Recalling its resolution 65/232 of 21 December 2010 on strengthening the United Nations crime prevention and criminal justice programme, and welcoming, in particular, the use of its technical cooperation capacity for preventing and countering the illicit flow of funds,

Recalling also paragraph 23 of the Salvador Declaration on Comprehensive Strategies for Global Challenges: Crime Prevention and Criminal Justice Systems and Their Development in a Changing World, adopted by the Twelfth United Nations Congress on Crime Prevention and Criminal Justice, in which Member States were encouraged to consider developing strategies or policies to combat illicit financial flows,

Noting with interest the work undertaken in countering money-laundering within the framework of relevant specialized regional and international bodies, such as the World Bank, the International Monetary Fund, the Egmont Group of Financial Intelligence Units, the Financial Action Task Force, regional bodies similar to the Task Force, the Organization for Economic Cooperation and Development, the International Criminal Police Organization (INTERPOL) and the World Customs Organization,

Noting with interest also the work of the United Nations Office on Drugs and Crime on the Global Programme against Money-Laundering, Proceeds of Crime and the Financing of Terrorism and the evaluation of the Global Programme by the Independent Evaluation Unit,

Convinced that technical assistance can play an important role in enhancing the ability of States, including by strengthening capacity- and institution-building, to prevent, detect and deter illicit financial flows originating from transnational organized crime, including, as appropriate, drug trafficking and related offences provided for in the United Nations Convention against Transnational Organized Crime,

Aware that the availability of information on illicit financial flows resulting from transnational organized crime, including, as appropriate, drug trafficking and related offences provided for in the United Nations Convention against Transnational Organized Crime, is very limited, and aware of the need to improve the quality, scope and completeness of such information,

Noting the many methods used by transnational organized criminal groups for laundering proceeds of crime, including through illicit trafficking in precious metals and the associated raw materials, and welcoming further research by Member States and other entities to study such methods,

Taking note of the analytical work of the United Nations Office on Drugs and Crime, which provides a preliminary overview of different forms of emerging criminal activity and their negative impact on the sustainable development of societies,

Noting with interest the efforts made within the framework of the Paris Pact initiative regarding work on illicit financial flows as a key issue in the drug economy,

Recognizing that the strengthening of national and international measures against the laundering of proceeds of crime derived from transnational organized crime, including, as appropriate, drug trafficking and related offences provided for in the United Nations Convention against Transnational Organized Crime, will contribute to weakening the economic power of criminal organizations,

Recognizing also the pertinence of the review of implementation mechanisms for the United Nations Convention against Corruption to the prevention of illicit financial flows as well as to a possible mechanism or mechanisms for the implementation of the United Nations Convention against Transnational Organized Crime,

Aware of the need to enhance international cooperation in the seizure and confiscation of proceeds of crime derived from or obtained directly or indirectly through the commission of crimes, including by means of the smuggling of cash,

1. *Urges* States parties to the United Nations Convention against Illicit Traffic in Narcotic Drugs and Psychotropic Substances of 1988, the United Nations Convention against Transnational Organized Crime and the United Nations Convention against Corruption to apply fully the provisions of those Conventions, in particular measures

to prevent and combat money-laundering, including by criminalizing the laundering of proceeds of transnational organized crime, including, as appropriate, drug trafficking and related offences provided for in the United Nations Convention against Transnational Organized Crime, and invites Member States that have not yet done so to consider becoming parties to those Conventions;

2. *Encourages* Member States to fully implement applicable standards, as appropriate, in order to adopt the comprehensive range of measures required to prevent and combat money-laundering and the financing of terrorism;

3. *Urges* Member States, in accordance with national laws, to require financial institutions and other businesses or members of any profession subject to obligations with regard to countering money-laundering to report promptly to the competent authorities any funds transaction in which they have reasonable grounds to suspect that the assets are proceeds of crime and money-laundering resulting from transnational organized crime, including, as appropriate, drug trafficking and related offences provided for in the United Nations Convention against Transnational Organized Crime;

4. *Also urges* Member States to consider taking all measures necessary to ensure that they do not provide a safe haven for wanted fugitives who have accumulated or are harbouring in their possession proceeds of crime derived from transnational organized crime, including, as appropriate, drug trafficking and related offences provided for in the United Nations Convention against Transnational Organized Crime, or who finance organized crime or criminal organizations, in particular by extraditing or prosecuting such fugitives, and urges Member States, in accordance with national laws and international law obligations, to fully cooperate with each other in this regard;

5. *Encourages* Member States to afford other countries the greatest possible measure of legal assistance and information exchange in connection with relevant investigations, inquiries and proceedings related to tracing illicit financial flows and seeking to identify illicitly acquired assets resulting from transnational organized crime, including, as appropriate, drug trafficking and related offences provided for in the United Nations Convention against Transnational Organized Crime;

6. *Also encourages* Member States to cooperate in confiscation-related investigations and proceedings, including through the recognition and enforcement of foreign temporary judicial orders and confiscation judgements, management of assets and implementation of asset-sharing measures, in accordance with their laws and applicable treaties;

7. *Urges* Member States to establish or, where applicable, strengthen national institutions specializing in financial intelligence by allowing them to receive, obtain, analyse and disseminate financial information relevant to preventing, detecting and deterring illicit financial flows resulting from transnational organized crime, including, as appropriate, drug trafficking and related offences provided for in the United Nations Convention against Transnational Organized Crime, and to ensure that such institutions have the ability to facilitate the exchange of such information with relevant international partners, in accordance with relevant domestic procedures;

8. *Also urges* Member States to consider related global and regional initiatives to facilitate the tracing of proceeds of crime resulting from transnational organized crime, including, as appropriate, drug trafficking and related offences provided for in the United Nations Convention against Transnational Organized Crime;

9. *Encourages* Member States to consider implementing measures, in accordance with the fundamental principles of their legal systems and consistent with their national legal frameworks, for the confiscation of assets absent a criminal conviction, in cases where it can be established that the subject assets are the proceeds of crime and a criminal conviction is not possible;

10. *Considers* that the review by the International Narcotics Control Board of the implementation of the United Nations Convention against Illicit Traffic in Narcotic Drugs and Psychotropic Substances of 1988 is also relevant to the work of the Commission on Crime Prevention and Criminal Justice in the area of money-laundering;

11. *Requests* the United Nations Office on Drugs and Crime, in close cooperation and consultation with Member States and in cooperation with relevant international organizations, to strengthen, simplify and make more efficient the collection and reporting of accurate, reliable and comparable data on transnational organized crime;

12. *Calls upon* the United Nations Office on Drugs and Crime to continue providing technical assistance, upon request, to Member States, in order to enhance their capacity to collect, analyse and report data on illicit financial flows resulting from transnational organized crime, including, as appropriate, drug trafficking and related offences provided for in the United Nations Convention against Transnational Organized Crime, as well as to prevent, detect and deter illicit financial flows and money-laundering resulting from such criminal activities;

13. *Urges* the United Nations Office on Drugs and Crime to continue providing technical assistance to Member States to combat money-laundering and the financing of terrorism through the Global Programme against Money-Laundering, Proceeds of Crime and the Financing of Terrorism, in accordance with related United Nations instruments and internationally accepted standards, including, where applicable, recommendations of relevant intergovernmental bodies, inter alia, the Financial Action Task Force, and relevant initiatives of regional, interregional and multilateral organizations against money-laundering;

14. *Requests* the United Nations Office on Drugs and Crime to continue, in consultation with Member States, its research on transnational organized crime, including illicit financial flows;

15. *Calls upon* the United Nations Office on Drugs and Crime to strengthen the Global Programme against Money-Laundering, Proceeds of Crime and the Financing of Terrorism, inter alia, in line with the recommendations made by the Independent Evaluation Unit in its review of the Global Programme;

16. *Requests* the United Nations Office on Drugs and Crime to strengthen its cooperation with other appropriate international and regional organizations engaged in combating the harmful effects of illicit financial flows resulting from transnational organized crime, including, as appropriate, drug trafficking and related offences provided for in the United Nations Convention against Transnational Organized Crime, for the purposes of providing technical assistance in this regard;

17. *Invites* Member States and other donors to provide extrabudgetary resources for these purposes, in accordance with the rules and procedures of the United Nations;

18. *Requests* the Executive Director of the United Nations Office on Drugs and Crime to report to the Commission on Crime Prevention and Criminal Justice at its twenty-second session on measures taken and progress achieved in the implementation of the present resolution.

Economic fraud and identity-related crime

In response to Economic and Social Council resolution 2009/22 [YUN 2009, p. 1101], the Secretary-General in January submitted a report [E/CN.15/2011/16] on international cooperation in the prevention, investigation, prosecution and punishment of economic fraud and identity-related crime, and on efforts of Member States to implement that resolution. It also provided information on UNODC action to promote mutual understanding and the exchange of views between public and private sector entities on issues related to economic fraud and identity-related crime by supporting and servicing the meetings of the core group of experts on identity-related crime held in 2010 (see below). It further contained information on the technical assistance provided in that regard.

Thirty-seven Member States provided information and relevant material on the implementation of resolution 2009/22: Algeria, Armenia, Australia, Belarus, Belgium, Bosnia and Herzegovina, Brunei Darussalam, Canada, China, Cyprus, Czech Republic, Egypt, El Salvador, Germany, Ghana, Guatemala, Japan, Jordan, Mauritius, Mexico, Moldova, Morocco, the Netherlands, Norway, Panama, the Philippines, Poland, the Russian Federation, Serbia, the Sudan, Sweden, Switzerland, Thailand, Togo, Trinidad and Tobago, Ukraine and the United Kingdom.

The core group of experts on identity-related crime held two meetings (Vienna, 18–22 January and 6–8 December 2010), which brought together representatives from Member States, the private sector, international organizations and academia in order to pool experiences, develop strategies, facilitate research and agree on practical action against that crime.

The Secretary-General recommended to the Commission that it take into account the information provided by Member States on national efforts to implement measures and policies aimed at preventing, investigating, prosecuting and punishing economic fraud and identity-related crime. In doing so, it could provide further guidance to UNODC regarding the delivery of technical assistance to Member States, with a view to structuring legislative responses to those crimes; developing and maintaining robust investigation and law enforcement mechanisms; adopting best practices and schemes for the protection of victims; and ensuring international cooperation to curb related offences.

ECONOMIC AND SOCIAL COUNCIL ACTION

On 28 July [meeting 48], the Economic and Social Council, on the recommendation of the Commission on Crime Prevention and Criminal Justice [E/2011/30], adopted **resolution 2011/35** without vote [agenda item 14 (*c*)].

International cooperation in the prevention, investigation, prosecution and punishment of economic fraud and identity-related crime

The Economic and Social Council,

Concerned about substantial increases in the volume, rate of transnational occurrence and range of offences relating to economic fraud and identity-related crime,

Concerned also about the use of identity-related crime to further the commission of other illicit activities,

Concerned further about the role played by information, communications and computer technologies in the evolution of economic fraud and identity-related crime,

Convinced of the need to develop comprehensive, multifaceted and coherent strategies and measures, including both reactive and preventive measures, to counter such forms of crime,

Convinced also of the importance of partnerships and synergies between Member States and civil society, in particular when they are developing their respective strategies and measures,

Convinced further of the need for Member States to explore the development of appropriate and timely support and services for victims of economic fraud and identity-related crime,

Bearing in mind the Salvador Declaration on Comprehensive Strategies for Global Challenges: Crime Prevention and Criminal Justice Systems and Their Development in a Changing World, in which serious concerns were expressed about the challenge posed by economic fraud and identity-related crime and their links to other criminal and, in some cases, terrorist activities, and in which Member States were invited to take appropriate legal measures to prevent, prosecute and punish economic fraud and identity-related crime and to continue to support the work of the United Nations Office on Drugs and Crime in that area and were encouraged to enhance international cooperation in that area, including through the exchange of relevant information and best practices, as well as through technical and legal assistance,

Acknowledging the efforts of the United Nations Office on Drugs and Crime to facilitate the work of the core group of experts on identity-related crime as a platform to bring together, on a regular basis, representatives of Governments, private sector entities, international and regional organizations and academia to pool experience, develop strategies, facilitate further research and agree on practical action against identity-related crime,

Noting the work of the core group of experts at its meetings held in Vienna from 18 to 22 January and from 6 to 8 December 2010,

Recalling that, in its resolutions 2007/20 of 26 July 2007 and 2009/22 of 30 July 2009, the Economic and Social Council requested the United Nations Office on Drugs and Crime to provide, upon request and subject to the availability of extrabudgetary resources, legal expertise or other forms of technical assistance to Member States reviewing or updating their laws dealing with transnational fraud and identity-related crime, in order to ensure that appropriate legislative responses to such offences were in place,

1. *Takes note* of the report of the Secretary-General, containing information on the efforts of reporting Member States to implement Economic and Social Council resolution 2009/22 and their strategies for responding to the problems posed by such forms of crime;

2. *Recommends* that the work of the core group of experts on identity-related crime be taken into account by the open-ended intergovernmental expert group, established in accordance with paragraph 42 of the Salvador Declaration on Comprehensive Strategies for Global Challenges: Crime Prevention and Criminal Justice Systems and Their Development in a Changing World, to conduct a comprehensive study of the problem of cybercrime and responses to it by Member States, the international community and the private sector, including the exchange of information on national legislation, best practices, technical assistance and international cooperation, with a view to examining options to strengthen existing and propose new national and international legal or other responses to cybercrime;

3. *Welcomes* the elaboration by the United Nations Office on Drugs and Crime and distribution to Member States of the *Handbook on Identity-related Crime*, including a practical guide to international cooperation to combat identity-related crime, expresses its gratitude to the Government of Canada for its financial support of that work, and encourages the use of the *Handbook* in technical assistance activities, in line with the mandates arising from Economic and Social Council resolutions 2004/26 of 21 July 2004, 2007/20 of 26 July 2007 and 2009/22 of 30 July 2009;

4. *Also welcomes* the work on victim issues in the field of identity-related crime undertaken in the framework of the United Nations crime prevention and criminal justice programme and its component institutions and, in particular, the release of a manual providing guidelines to law enforcement agents and prosecutors on the protection of victims of identity-related crime, and invites the United Nations Office on Drugs and Crime, through the core group of experts and subject to the availability of extrabudgetary resources, to work jointly with the International Centre for Criminal Law Reform and Criminal Justice Policy, with a view to expanding the manual, where appropriate, for use in different legal systems;

5. *Urges* Member States to cooperate effectively at the bilateral, regional and international levels, including on matters of extradition, mutual legal assistance, and confiscation of proceeds of crime and property and their return, in connection with economic fraud and identity-related crime;

6. *Encourages* Member States to study, at the national level, the specific short- and long-term effects of economic fraud and identity-related crime on society and on victims of such forms of crime and to develop strategies or programmes to combat those forms of crime;

7. *Requests* the United Nations Office on Drugs and Crime to continue its efforts, in consultation with the United Nations Commission on International Trade Law, to promote mutual understanding and the exchange of views between public and private sector entities on issues related to economic fraud and identity-related crime and, in particular, to focus the future work of the core group of experts on, among other things, the various issues raised by engaging the resources and expertise of the private sector in the development and delivery of technical assistance in this field;

8. *Invites* the United Nations Office on Drugs and Crime to cooperate with other international organizations active in this field, including the International Telecommunication Union and its Lead Study Group on Identity Management, as well as the International Criminal Police Organization (INTERPOL) and the International Civil Aviation Organization, in areas such as the setting of technical standards for documents, the forensic examination of fraudulent documents and the compilation of data that could be used for pattern analysis and the prevention of identity-related crime;

9. *Requests* the United Nations Office on Drugs and Crime to continue its efforts, including through the core group of experts, to collect information and data on the challenges posed by economic fraud and identity-related crime in different geographical regions;

10. *Requests* the Secretary-General to report to the Commission on Crime Prevention and Criminal Justice at its twenty-second session on the implementation of the present resolution.

Protecting children in a digital age

The Commission in April [E/2011/30] held a thematic discussion on protecting children in a digital age: the misuse of technology in the abuse and exploitation of children. The Secretariat submitted a note [E/CN.15/2011/2] as a discussion guide.

ECONOMIC AND SOCIAL COUNCIL ACTION

On 28 July [meeting 48], the Economic and Social Council, on the recommendation of the Commission on Crime Prevention and Criminal Justice [E/2011/30], adopted **resolution 2011/33** without vote [agenda item 14 (*c*)].

Prevention, protection and international cooperation against the use of new information technologies to abuse and/or exploit children

The Economic and Social Council,

Recalling General Assembly resolutions 55/63 of 4 December 2000, 56/121 of 19 December 2001 and 64/211 of 21 December 2009 concerning combating the criminal misuse of information technologies, as well as other relevant United Nations resolutions,

Reaffirming its resolution 2004/26 of 21 July 2004 entitled "International cooperation in the prevention, investigation, prosecution and punishment of fraud, the criminal misuse and falsification of identity and related crimes" and its resolution 2007/20 of 26 July 2007 entitled "International cooperation in the prevention, investigation, prosecution and punishment of economic fraud and identity-related crime",

Reaffirming also Commission on Crime Prevention and Criminal Justice resolution 16/2 of 27 April 2007 entitled "Effective crime prevention and criminal justice responses to combat sexual exploitation of children",

Taking note of resolution 9 of 7 September 1990, on computer-related crimes, adopted by the Eighth United Nations Congress on the Prevention of Crime and the

Treatment of Offenders, in which States were called upon to intensify their efforts to more effectively combat computer-related abuses,

Taking into consideration the outcome of the Tenth United Nations Congress on the Prevention of Crime and the Treatment of Offenders on meeting the challenges of the twenty-first century in combating crime and promoting justice,

Underscoring the importance of paragraph 42 of the Salvador Declaration on Comprehensive Strategies for Global Challenges: Crime Prevention and Criminal Justice Systems and Their Development in a Changing World, adopted by the Twelfth United Nations Congress on Crime Prevention and Criminal Justice, in which the Congress invited the Commission to consider convening an open-ended intergovernmental expert group to conduct a comprehensive study of the problem of cybercrime and responses to it by Member States, the international community and the private sector, and welcoming the meeting of that expert group held in Vienna from 17 to 21 January 2011,

Recognizing the work of the Commission in combating cybercrime,

Bearing in mind that the United Nations Convention against Transnational Organized Crime represents a major step forward in combating crimes relating to the use of new information and communications technologies,

Expressing concern that increasingly rapid technological advances have created new possibilities for the criminal misuse of new information and communications technologies,

Recalling the Convention on the Rights of the Child and the Optional Protocol to the Convention on the Rights of the Child on the sale of children, child prostitution and child pornography,

Reaffirming that the Worst Forms of Child Labour Convention, 1999 (No. 182), of the International Labour Organization requires States parties to take immediate and effective measures to secure the prohibition and elimination of the use, procuring or offering of a child for prostitution, for the production of pornography or for pornographic performances,

Reaffirming also Commission on Crime Prevention and Criminal Justice resolution 19/1 of 21 May 2010 entitled "Strengthening public-private partnerships to counter crime in all its forms and manifestations", and taking into consideration the outcome of the United Nations Office on Drugs and Crime symposium on public-private partnerships against transnational organized crime, held in Vienna on 8 April 2011, in which States called for effective cooperation with the private sector to combat sexual exploitation of children in a digital age,

Taking into account the fact that social spaces created using new information and communications technologies are heavily used by children for social interaction,

Stressing that new information and communications technologies and applications are being misused to commit child sexual exploitation crimes and that technical developments have permitted the appearance of crimes such as the production, distribution or possession of child sexual abuse images, audio or video, the exposure of children to harmful content, the grooming, harassment and sexual abuse of children and cyberbullying,

Bearing in mind the potential risks associated with certain content found on the Internet and virtual social networks and that easy contact with criminals online may affect the integral development of children,

Noting that, as a result of the technological advances of recent years, material that violates the integrity and rights of children is available to an increasing number of persons,

Expressing concern that new information and communications technologies have made it possible for criminals to contact children easily and in ways that were not previously possible,

Aware that new information and communications technologies make it possible to construct false identities that facilitate the abuse and/or exploitation of children by criminals,

Reaffirming that children should be afforded the same protection in cyberspace as in the physical world,

Underscoring the importance of cooperation between States and the private sector in combating the use of new information and communications technologies to abuse and/or exploit children,

Underscoring also the importance of international cooperation and coordination in effectively combating the criminal misuse of new information and communications technologies for the purpose of abusing and/or exploiting children,

Recognizing that gaps in the access to and use of new information and communications technologies by States can diminish the effectiveness of international cooperation in combating the use of those technologies to abuse and/or exploit children,

Noting the thematic discussion entitled "Protecting children in a digital age: the misuse of technology in the abuse and exploitation of children" held by the Commission at its twentieth session,

1. *Urges* those States that have not yet done so to consider ratifying the Convention on the Rights of the Child and the Optional Protocol to the Convention on the Rights of the Child on the sale of children, child prostitution and child pornography, the Worst Forms of Child Labour Convention, 1999 (No. 182), of the International Labour Organization, the United Nations Convention against Transnational Organized Crime and the Protocol to Prevent, Suppress and Punish Trafficking in Persons, Especially Women and Children, supplementing the United Nations Convention against Transnational Organized Crime;

2. *Urges* Member States to establish, develop and implement public policies and good practices aimed at protecting and defending the rights of the child, referring to security, privacy and intimacy in spaces created using new information and communications technologies;

3. *Encourages* Member States to involve ministries responsible for telecommunications, agencies responsible for data protection and representatives of the information and communications technology industry in intersectoral mechanisms for addressing the misuse of new information and communications technologies to abuse and/or exploit children, with a view to offering comprehensive solutions for such misuse and avoiding the violation of the rights of the child;

4. *Urges* Member States to adopt measures, including, where appropriate, legislation, designed to criminalize all aspects of the misuse of technology to commit child sexual exploitation crimes and to consider, in accordance with national and international law, appropriate measures to detect and remove known child sexual abuse images from the

Internet and to facilitate the identification of those responsible for the abuse and/or exploitation of children;

5. *Encourages* Member States to promote the creation and application of adequate verification measures to protect children online;

6. *Urges* Member States to specify the production, distribution, dissemination, voluntary receipt and possession of child sexual abuse and exploitation images, along with deliberate and repeated access to websites containing such images and viewing this type of content stored online, as a criminal offence in their legal systems;

7. *Also urges* Member States, consistent with their national legal frameworks, to cooperate closely with Internet service providers, mobile telephone companies and other key actors to establish appropriate and efficient mechanisms, possibly including legislation, for the reporting of child sexual abuse images and materials to the relevant authorities, to block websites with child sexual abuse images and to cooperate with law enforcement in the investigation and prosecution of the offenders responsible;

8. *Encourages* Member States to incorporate in their national legislation, in conformity with their legal systems, measures for saving and ensuring rapid access to electronic data during criminal investigations relating to the use of new information and communications technologies to abuse and/or exploit children;

9. *Urges* Member States to provide adequate resources to carry out their tasks effectively to the offices responsible for investigating and prosecuting the perpetrators of crimes committed using new information and communications technologies to violate the rights of the child;

10. *Encourages* Member States to implement awareness-raising activities to provide children with information on the mechanisms through which they can seek protection and assistance and report cases of abuse and/or exploitation in spaces created using new information and communications technologies, as well as awareness-raising activities aimed at parents and educators to prevent such crimes;

11. *Invites* Member States to implement effective reporting mechanisms whereby their citizens can report websites and/or virtual activities related to child sexual exploitation crimes;

12. *Urges* Member States to conduct campaigns to raise awareness among the general public of the risks of misuse of new information and communications technologies;

13. *Encourages* Member States to create and implement mechanisms for the appropriate authority to identify children who are abused and/or exploited through new information and communications technologies and to establish procedures for protecting them;

14. *Urges* Member States to promote the drafting and adoption of codes of conduct and other mechanisms of corporate social responsibility for Internet service providers, mobile telephone companies, Internet cafes and other relevant key actors;

15. *Requests* the United Nations Office on Drugs and Crime, taking into account, where appropriate, relevant data collected by the open-ended intergovernmental expert group to conduct a comprehensive study on the problem of cybercrime, to carry out a study facilitating the identification, description and evaluation of the effects of new information technologies on the abuse and exploitation of children, while taking into account relevant studies carried out by regional organizations and other organizations within the United Nations system, such as the United Nations Children's Fund, the International Telecommunication Union and the Office of the United Nations High Commissioner for Human Rights, with a view to promoting the exchange of experience and good practices;

16. *Also requests* the United Nations Office on Drugs and Crime, taking into account, where appropriate, relevant data collected by the expert group, to design and carry out an assessment of the needs of States for training in the investigation of offences against children committed by using new information and communications technologies and, on the basis of the results of that survey, to design a training and technical assistance programme to assist Member States in combating such offences more effectively, subject to the availability of resources and not duplicating the efforts of the International Criminal Police Organization (INTERPOL);

17. *Urges* Member States to increase their coordination and cooperation and to exchange information regarding good practices and successful experiences in combating the use of new information and communications technologies to abuse and/or exploit children;

18. *Encourages* Member States to take advantage of the knowledge and efforts, as well as the prevention initiatives, of the United Nations, other international organizations, regional organizations, civil society and the private sector to combat the criminal misuse of new information and communications technologies;

19. *Urges* Member States to ensure that mutual assistance regimes ensure the timely exchange of evidence in cases relating to the use of new information and communications technologies to abuse and/or exploit children;

20. *Invites* Member States to provide technical assistance and technology transfer, including training on investigational tools, particularly for the benefit of developing countries, with a view to enabling those countries to develop national capacity to effectively combat the activities of criminals who use new information and communications technologies to violate the rights of the child;

21. *Requests* the Secretary-General to report to the Commission on Crime Prevention and Criminal Justice at its twenty-third session on the implementation of the present resolution;

22. *Invites* Member States and other donors to provide extrabudgetary resources for implementation of the relevant paragraphs of the present resolution, in accordance with the rules and procedures of the United Nations.

Combating cybercrime

The open-ended intergovernmental expert group on the comprehensive study of the problem of cybercrime, established by CCPCJ in line with the Salvador Declaration on Comprehensive Strategies for Global Challenges [YUN 2010, p. 1097], held its first meeting (Vienna, 17–21 January) [E/CN.15/2011/19]. The group addressed the question of a comprehensive study of the problem of cybercrime and responses to it by Member States, the international community and the private sector, including the exchange of information on legislation, best practices, technical assistance and international cooperation, with a view to examining options to strengthen existing and to propose new national and international legal or other responses to cybercrime. The group adopted an outcome document, annexed to the report, entitled "Collection of topics for consideration in a comprehensive study on impact of and response to cybercrime".

Taking note of the outcome of the session, the Commission on 15 April [E/2011/30 (res. 20/7)] invited the expert group to finalize the report on the deliberations of its first session. The Commission requested UNODC to provide technical assistance and training to States with regard to the prevention, detection, investigation and prosecution of cybercrime. It further requested UNODC to strengthen cooperation with Member States, organizations such as the International Criminal Police Organization, the European Police Office, the International Telecommunication Union, the European Commission, the Council of Europe, the Shanghai Cooperation Organization and the Commonwealth of Independent States, as well as with the private sector, including computer companies and Internet service providers, on combating cybercrime. The Secretary-General was requested to report to the twenty-second (2013) session of the Commission on the implementation of the resolution.

Civilian private security services

Pursuant to Commission resolution 18/2 [YUN 2009, p. 1107], the Secretariat in January submitted a note on civilian private security services: their oversight and their role in and contribution to crime prevention and community safety [E/CN.15/2011/14]. In most of the 43 Member States that had submitted information, there seemed to be an adequate legal oversight of private security services with a responsible department for authorization and also for oversight and surveillance. A few States, however, reported their legal oversight over civilian private security services to be deficient. The note concluded that the role of civilian private security services was subsidiary in most of the responding States, while primary responsibility for public order, safety and security rested with the States.

The note also contained information regarding the decision of the Commission to establish an expert group to study the role of private security services and their contribution to crime prevention and community safety. With the financial support of the United Arab Emirates, UNODC organized a planning meeting (Abu Dhabi, 10–11 May 2010) [E/CN.15/2011/CRP.2], attended by experts in their personal capacity, to start preparatory work for the expert group.

Piracy

Pursuant to Commission resolution 19/6, the Executive Director in February submitted a report [E/CN.15/2011/18] on countering maritime piracy off the coast of Somalia. The report reviewed the UNODC response to the threat of maritime piracy off the coast of Somalia, and explained the strategy and main achievements of the Office in terms of technical assistance and capacity-building to strengthen the criminal justice systems of requesting States in East Africa and the Horn of Africa and in Somalia itself.

The 1982 United Nations Convention on the Law of the Sea [YUN 1982, p. 246] served as the primary international legal framework applicable to piracy. Some acts of piracy could also constitute offences under other international legal instruments, such as the Convention for the Suppression of Unlawful Acts against the Safety of Maritime Navigation [YUN 1988, p. 969], the International Convention against the Taking of Hostages [YUN 1979, p. 1144] and the United Nations Convention against Transnational Organized Crime [YUN 2000, p. 1048].

With regard to action at sea, the effectiveness of naval operations was increasing, resulting in growing numbers of arrests and prosecutions. It was estimated, however, that 90 per cent of pirates captured by naval forces had not been prosecuted, but had been released after their firearms and other equipment were seized. The principal reason cited was lack of evidence to support prosecution. The report of the Special Adviser to the Secretary-General on legal issues related to piracy off the coast of Somalia noted that the "catch and release" policy that allowed pirates to go free without prosecution consolidated their impunity, and because of the potential benefits, the risks involved did not act as a deterrent. In 2009, UNODC had launched the Counter-Piracy Programme from its Regional Office for Eastern Africa, with the short-term objective to build the criminal justice capacity of States willing to prosecute pirates to ensure that suspected pirates handed over by other States were afforded a fair and efficient trial and humane imprisonment. The medium- and long-term objectives of the programme were to build criminal justice capacity in Somalia. In January 2010, at the request of the member States of the Contact Group on Piracy off the Coast of Somalia, the Secretary-General had established the Trust Fund to Support Initiatives of States Countering Piracy off the Coast of Somalia [YUN 2010, p. 287]. UNODC engaged with the Trust Fund as both the manager of the Trust Fund and beneficiary of its funding for carrying out substantive projects. Since its inception, the Fund had approved 10 projects with a total value of $4,220,371, including UNODC initiatives aimed at strengthening criminal justice systems in Kenya, Seychelles and Somalia to fight piracy.

The Executive Director recommended to the Commission that it encourage more States in the region to prosecute suspected pirates captured off the coast of Somalia, and request UNODC to increase the volume of its activities and report to the Commission's twenty-first (2012) session on the implementation of the Counter-Piracy programme and the administration of the Trust Fund.

(For more information on piracy off the coast of Somalia, see also p. 243.)

UN standards and norms

The Commission considered a January report [E/CN.15/2011/12] of the Secretary-General on the use and application of UN standards and norms in crime prevention and criminal justice. The report reviewed progress made by UNODC in 2010 in support of the use and application of such standards and norms. It reviewed UNODC technical assistance efforts and described partnerships formed to promote the work of the Office in those areas.

UNODC supported Member States in the review of existing standards and norms and the development of new ones. The body of standards and norms, which included more than 50 instruments, was grouped into four clusters: persons in custody, non-custodial sanctions, juvenile justice and restorative justice; legal, institutional and practical arrangements for international cooperation; crime prevention and victim issues; and good governance, the independence of the judiciary and the integrity of criminal justice personnel. UNODC achieved progress in all four clusters.

In the area of prevention of crime and violence, the Office was implementing projects in Bolivia, Brazil, El Salvador and Honduras, and was implementing components of conflict prevention projects funded by the Millennium Development Goals Achievement Fund in Bolivia, Brazil, Honduras, Mauritania, Mexico and Panama. Projects for preventing violence against women were being implemented in the countries of the Southern Cone, Southern Africa and Viet Nam. UNODC was implementing prison reform projects in nine countries, and prison assessments were conducted in 11 countries in 2010.

To provide knowledge on crime trends and increase the availability of regional and international data, UNODC strengthened its key data collection instrument, the United Nations Survey of Crime Trends and Operations of Criminal Justice Systems. At the international level, the key crime indicator of "rate of intentional homicide" was gaining prominence.

With regard to technical assistance, the UNODC portfolio featured 45 programmes in 36 countries, with a pledged budget of $96 million. Notable developments occurred in the areas of penal reform and alternatives to imprisonment in all regions, juvenile justice in the Middle East and North Africa, access to justice and legal aid in Africa, police reform in Eastern Africa, and crime and violence prevention in Latin America and the Caribbean.

The Office was part of the United Nations Rule of Law Coordination and Resource Group [YUN 2006, p. 48], composed of 11 UN entities and agencies working on rule-of-law issues and tasked to assist in the development of strategies for rule-of-law assistance, ensure that the United Nations responded effectively to requests from States, and assist in mobilizing resources.

The Secretary-General recommended to CCPCJ that it accord high priority to the use and application of the UN standards and norms in crime prevention and criminal justice and encourage the development of new ones. The Commission should recommend to Member States that they adopt a comprehensive and integrated approach to crime prevention and criminal justice reform, based on baseline assessments and data collection; develop crime prevention policies, strategies and programmes based on an understanding of the root causes of crime, respond to the concerns of citizens, and build on available capacities and resources; build national and regional crime prevention and criminal justice reforms on international standards, including human rights treaties and UN standards and norms; and address the needs of children, youth, women, and vulnerable and at-risk groups when developing or reviewing national policies, strategies and programmes.

Child justice reform

The Commission considered a report of the Secretary-General [E/CN.15/2011/13], submitted pursuant to Economic and Social Council resolution 2009/26 [YUN 2009, p. 1104], on national and international efforts for child justice reform, in particular through improved coordination in technical assistance. The report contained information provided by Member States, the secretariat of the Interagency Panel on Juvenile Justice and the members of the Panel. It described trends towards legal and policy reform, the establishment of data collection and information management systems, the strengthening of institutional capacity, and child-sensitive procedures and institutions. It also described progress made in the coordination and joint provision of technical assistance to Member States by the UN system and NGOs.

The number of responses received pursuant to a note by the Secretariat, which requested Member States to provide information on their national efforts for child justice reform, provided an insufficient basis for drawing general or global conclusions. Three responses were received from Africa (all of them from North Africa), three from the Americas (one each from North America, Central America and South America), two from Asia, seven from States of Western, Central and Eastern Europe, and three from the Middle East.

With regard to technical assistance provided through UN system-wide coordination, the Interagency Panel on Juvenile Justice [YUN 1997, p. 1158] facilitated and enhanced coordination at the country and global levels of the provision of technical assistance from the members of the Panel in the area of child justice. The report described the activities of Defence for Children International, unicef, unodc and the World Organization against Torture.

The Secretary-General recommended to the Commission that it encourage States to integrate children's issues into their overall rule-of-law efforts, develop and implement a comprehensive juvenile justice policy, and benefit from the technical advice and assistance provided by UN agencies and programmes. The Executive Director was requested to report to the Commission's twenty-third (2014) session on the implementation of the resolution.

Strengthening the rule of law

Pursuant to Commission resolution 17/2 [YUN 2008, p. 1244], the Secretary-General in January submitted to the Commission a report [E/CN.15/2011/8] on strengthening the rule of law through improved integrity and capacity of prosecution services. The report contained information received from Member States and an overview of the Secretariat's work in the implementation of the resolution and the use of the Standards of Professional Responsibility and Statement of the Essential Duties and Rights of Prosecutors, developed by the International Association of Prosecutors and annexed to the resolution. It examined the potential for developing further the technical assistance support provided to Member States in strengthening the integrity and impartiality of their prosecution services, thus fostering the rule of law and respect for human rights.

Unodc expanded its technical assistance portfolio to cover activities aimed at enhancing the integrity of prosecutors and building their capacity in regard to both substantive issues and issues related to integrity and professional conduct. The Office continued to develop technical assistance and guidance tools addressing the needs of prosecutorial authorities. Information on efforts to implement the resolution was received from 16 Member States, and was related to the status of prosecution services within criminal justice systems; norms and standards governing professional conduct of prosecutors; appointment, tenure and conditions of service; disciplinary measures against prosecutors; and the prosecutors' role in criminal proceedings.

The Secretary-General concluded that the Standards had been used by many States as guidance to promote fair, effective and impartial prosecution services. They provided a widely accepted yardstick for the professional conduct of prosecutors and were an important tool for enhancing the integrity of prosecutorial services throughout the world. He recommended to the Commission that it invite Member States to continue using the United Nations Guidelines on the Role of Prosecutors [YUN 1990, p. 701] as a guiding tool for the organization and operation of their prosecutorial services; and request Member States to conduct surveys regularly on the integrity of judicial services, including the prosecutor's office.

Chapter XV

Statistics

In 2011, the United Nations continued its work on statistics, mainly through the Statistical Commission and the Statistics Division of the UN Department of Economic and Social Affairs. In February, the Commission adopted international recommendations for energy statistics—the first recommendations that provided a coherent basis for the production of energy statistics in the context of all economic statistics—and endorsed the main elements of its proposed implementation programme. The Commission further endorsed the recommendations of its Bureau on statistics of human development, while expressing concern on the sources and methods used for the *Human Development Report* and stressing the need for an authoritative agency in the UN system to coordinate statistical activities. The Commission also endorsed the way forward for the work of the Inter-Agency and Expert Group on Millennium Development Goals Indicators, and requested the Statistics Division to establish a group of experts to provide assistance to resolve specific data-related issues; requested the Statistics Division to formulate a proposal for designating World Statistics Day as a regular observance; and requested the expansion of the scope of work of the Inter-Agency and Expert Group on Gender Statistics to include serving as the coordination mechanism for the global programme on gender statistics.

Statistical Commission

The Statistical Commission held its forty-second session in New York from 22 to 25 February [E/2011/24] in accordance with Economic and Social Council decision 2010/235 [YUN 2010, p. 1262]. The 15 decisions adopted during the session and brought to the attention of the Council included the first World Statistics Day, held on 20 October 2010; gender statistics; national accounts; environmental-economic accounting; energy statistics; integrated economic statistics; short-term economic indicators; the International Comparison Programme; development indicators; statistics of human development; implementation of the Fundamental Principles of Official Statistics; statistical capacity-building; and regional statistical development in Western Asia. The Commission also took note of 19 reports considered during the session [E/2011/24 (dec. 42/115)].

By **decision 2011/245** of 27 July, the Economic and Social Council took note of the Commission's report on its forty-second session; decided that the forty-third session would be held in New York from 28 February to 2 March 2012; and approved the provisional agenda and documentation for that session.

Other reports. Other reports issued in December 2011, to be addressed during the Commission's 2012 session, covered the following subjects: population and housing censuses [E/CN.3/2012/2]; crime statistics [E/CN.3/2012/3]; national accounts [E/CN.3/2012/4, E/CN.3/2012/5]; agricultural statistics [E/CN.3/2012/6, E/CN.3/2012/7]; environmental-economic accounting [E/CN.3/2012/8]; environment statistics [E/CN.3/2012/9]; natural gas statistics [E/CN.3/2012/10]; statistics for economies based on natural resources [E/CN.3/2012/11]; information and communications technology statistics [E/CN.3/2012/12]; national quality assurance frameworks [E/CN.3/2012/13]; implementation of the Fundamental Principles of Official Statistics [E/CN.3/2012/14]; coordination of statistical activities [E/CN.3/2012/15, E/CN.3/2012/27]; efforts in initiating a plan of action on statistical development [E/CN.3/2012/16]; regional statistical development for Europe [E/CN.3/2012/18]; statistics of human development [E/CN.3/2012/17]; gender statistics [E/CN.3/2012/19, E/CN.3/2012/20]; disability statistics [E/CN.3/2012/21]; international merchandise trade statistics [E/CN.3/2012/22]; international trade in services [E/CN.3/2012/23]; finance statistics [E/CN.3/2012/24]; International Comparison Programme [E/CN.3/2012/25]; price indices [E/CN.3/2012/26]; international economic and social classifications [E/CN.3/2012/28]; development indicators for monitoring the Millennium Development Goals [E/CN.3/2012/29]; policy decisions of the General Assembly and the Economic and Social Council relevant to the work of the Commission [E/CN.3/2012/30]; global geospatial information management [E/CN.3/2012/31]; World Statistics Day [E/CN.3/2012/32]; and the draft multi-year programme of work 2012–2015 [E/CN.3/2012/33].

Demographic and social statistics

Population and housing censuses

The Secretary-General reported [E/CN.3/2011/21] on the implementation, since 2005, of the 2010 World Programme on Population and Housing Censuses, including the preparation and dissemination of international census guidelines, workshops, technical assistance, website development, and future initiatives relating to the Programme. As at the end of 2010, 121 countries or areas had already undertaken the 2010 round of population and housing censuses, which spanned from 2005 to 2014.

The Statistics Division developed a software package, CensusInfo, to help countries disseminate census data. To supplement the *Principles and Recommendations for Population and Housing Censuses, Revision 2* [YUN 2007, p. 1318], the Division issued, inter alia, the *Handbook on Population and Housing Census Editing, Revision 1* (2010) [Sales No. E.09.XVII.11], providing an overview of census data editing methodology; a report on guidelines for census evaluation; and the *Handbook on Geospatial Infrastructure in Support of Census Activities* (2009) [Sales No. E.09.XVIII.8], supplying tools for the application of census-mapping operations.

To strengthen capacity for planning and carrying out censuses, and in collaboration with regional commissions and subregional organizations, the Division had conducted 33 workshops with some 1,000 participants from over 140 countries and areas; five regional workshops on census evaluation in 2009 and 2010; and training workshops on CensusInfo for census data managers from 56 countries, as well as two regional seminars on strategies and technologies for census data dissemination.

Since the beginning of the 2010 census round, the Division also maintained the website on the 2010 World Population and Housing Census Programme with information on census-related activities across the world, including the Census Knowledge Base—a repository of census methodology guidelines and documents pertaining to country best practices in census-taking.

The Commission took note of the report on 24 February [dec. 42/115].

Health statistics

A report of the Intersecretariat Working Group on Health Statistics [E/CN.3/2011/22] described the Group's progress in drafting a framework for health statistics. The framework, which outlined the content of health statistics and the relationship between content and the most common sources of health data, was developed in response to the lack of core health statistics for use by countries and for cross-national comparisons. Work on the framework had progressed slowly, but several members of the Working Group had been involved in efforts by related groups that would provide input into the framework.

The Commission took note of the report on 24 February [dec. 42/115].

Education statistics

A report of the United Nations Educational, Scientific and Cultural Organization (UNESCO) on education statistics [E/CN.3/2011/23] addressed the revision and implementation of the International Standard Classification of Education (ISCED), and the establishment of an intersecretariat working group on education statistics. The proposed revisions included an extension and renaming of the lowest education level to encompass programmes for children aged 0 to 3 years; extensive definitions of types of education, in particular formal and non-formal education; a simplification of programme orientation; the introduction of new concepts of successful completion of ISCED levels; new coding systems for educational programmes and educational attainment; the introduction of qualifications as a derived variable within ISCED; the redefinition of education at the tertiary level; and a new governance procedure for adopting and implementing the new ISCED. Following consultations and feedback from regional and international experts, a draft text was finalized in 2010 and sent to UNESCO member States for comments.

The report also described the activities of the UNESCO Institute for Statistics in establishing an intersecretariat working group on education statistics, to be led by the Institute, in order to improve coordination mechanisms, promote the development of international standards and minimize duplication of efforts among international agencies.

The Commission took note of the report on 24 February [dec. 42/115].

Gender statistics

The Statistical Commission had before it three reports on gender statistics. The first summarized activities of the Statistics Division on gender statistics [E/CN.3/2011/4], among them, the publication of *The World's Women 2010: Trends and Statistics* [Sales No. E.10.XVII.11], which covered population and families, health, education, work, power and decision-making, violence against women, environment and poverty. The Division also co-organized the third Global Forum on Gender Statistics (Manila, Philippines, 11–13 October 2010), which focused on the gender dimensions of health statistics. The Forum recommended that countries and international organizations strengthen national capacity for data analysis and dissemination with a focus on gender perspective; improve the use of gender-based health statistics for policies; strengthen registration systems for producing vital statistics; harmonize data from different sources—administrative records, civil registration and surveys; and promote the use of data-collection tools for gender-based violence. The third meeting of the Inter-Agency and Expert Group on Gender Statistics (Manila, 14 October 2010) reiterated the need for a core set of indicators on gender statistics that countries could use to assess progress towards international commitments relating to gender equality, and urged the Division to complete the manual on gender statistics. In addition, the Division continued its work in compiling and disseminating gender statistics, maintaining a website providing sex-disaggregated data in the fields of population, women and men in families, health, education, work and political decision-making. The report also set out the Division's workplan for 2011–2012.

In response to a request by the Statistical Commission [YUN 2009, p. 1262], the Friends of the Chair reported on indicators on violence against women [E/CN.3/2011/5], presenting the conclusions and proposals of its last meeting (Aguascalientes, Mexico, 9–11 December 2009). The meeting reiterated a preference for collecting statistics on violence against women by a separate and dedicated statistical sample survey. The group concluded that there was a need to further explore administrative sources that could provide those statistics, such as police offices, courts, hospitals and safe houses; identified a set of core indicators for surveys on violence against women; and endorsed the development of guidelines for producing statistics on violence against women.

The third report [E/CN.3/2011/3], from the Ghana Statistical Service, contained a programme review of gender statistics prepared in collaboration with the statistical authorities of the Philippines. The report summarized the challenges faced by countries and the types of support provided by institutions for developing gender statistics. It called on the Statistics Division to assume the leading role in developing gender statistics. It also suggested that the Commission agree on proposed follow-up actions; collaborate with the Commission on the Status of Women to establish a minimum set of gender indicators; expand the terms of reference of the Inter-Agency and Expert Group on Gender Statistics to identify gaps and areas for consolidation; encourage the development of gender statistics programmes within national statistical systems; and recommend that the Division strengthen its gender statistics programme.

On 25 February [dec. 42/102], the Commission acknowledged the strategic role of the Inter-Agency and Expert Group on Gender Statistics and requested the expansion of its scope of work to include reviewing gender statistics with the aim of establishing a minimum set of gender indicators; guiding the development of manuals and methodological guidelines for the production and use of gender statistics; and serving as the coordination mechanism for the global programme on gender statistics. It also requested the Statistics Division, the regional commissions, the World Bank and the United Nations Population Fund to work with Member States to develop in-country support and to assist them in establishing a sound national programme on gender statistics; the Division to consult with the United Nations translation services to provide appropriate translations of the term "gender", taking into account the work that had been carried out by the Economic and Social Commission for Western Asia in that regard; and the donor community to devote adequate resources to the proposed gender statistics programme. It further requested that the Division and the Inter-Agency and Expert Group report to the Statistical Commission at its forty-third session (2012) on their proposed workplans and strategies for strengthening the global gender statistics programme.

Economic statistics

National accounts

The Statistical Commission considered a report [E/CN.3/2011/6] of the Intersecretariat Working Group on National Accounts, which provided an update on the printing and distribution of the English version of the *System of National Accounts 2008* (2008 SNA) [YUN 2008, p. 1379] and the translation into the other UN official languages; reassessed the research agenda of the 2008 SNA, taking into account issues that emerged during the SNA update, including the treatment of emission allowances and permits in national accounts, the treatment of financial intermediation services indirectly measured (FISIM) and the production of indicators recommended in the report of the Commission on the Measurement of Economic Performance and Social Progress (the Stiglitz report) (see p. 1224).

The report described the mandate and governance of the Intersecretariat Working Group on National Accounts and the Advisory Expert Group on National Accounts; and the establishment in 2010 of the Friends of the Chair Group on the impediments to the implementation of the 1993 SNA. The Group was tasked with assisting the Commission in identifying the causes of the slow and limited adoption of the 1993 SNA and to make suggestions for the way forward, given that the 1993 SNA had been superseded by the 2008 SNA. It was composed of experts on production of national accounts from developed and developing countries.

In response to the global economic and financial crisis, countries and international organizations, including UN entities, had launched coordinated statistical initiatives. The report stated that the SNA was recognized as the overarching framework for economic statistics, while its 2008 update provided for a better understanding of the structural aspects of the financial and economic crisis. It provided an assessment of whether the coordinated initiatives of the Statistics Division and Eurostat with Member States on the development of a data template of high-frequency and composite business cycle indicators and the initiatives of the Inter-Agency Group on Economic and Financial Statistics could be integrated into the implementation programme of the 2008 SNA. The report also described the progress of the Implementation Programme for the System of National Accounts 2008 and Supporting Statistics, a global statistical initiative assisting countries to develop their statistical capacity and switch from the 1968 or 1993 SNA to the 2008 SNA.

On 25 February [dec. 42/103], the Commission requested the Intersecretariat Working Group on National Accounts to consider, in consultation with the Advisory Expert Group, guidance on incorporating the contribution of the informal sector for an exhaustive measure of gross domestic product, on household sector issues and on related issues; requested the establishment of a dedicated knowledge base of training material for implementation of the 2008 SNA, covering the source data and implementation procedure; and urged the Friends of the Chair Group to complete its work, taking into account the implementation programme of the Intersecretariat Working Group for the 2008 SNA and the impediments faced by Member States in the transition to the 2008 SNA.

Agricultural statistics

On 24 February [dec. 42/115], the Commission took note of a report of the Friends of the Chair on Agricultural Statistics [E/CN.3/2011/24] on progress in developing the implementation plan of the Global Strategy to Improve Agricultural and Rural Statistics—prepared by the World Bank and the Food and Agriculture Organization of the United Nations with substantial input from the Friends of the Chair—which the Commission had endorsed at its forty-first session [YUN 2010, p. 1265]. The purpose of the Global Strategy was to provide a framework to enable national and international statistical systems to produce the information needed to guide decision-making in the twenty-first century. The Strategy was based on three pillars: establishing a minimum set of core data, integrating agriculture into national statistical systems, and fostering the sustainability of agricultural statistical systems. A regional approach had been adopted taking into account the different regional levels of statistical development, and ensuring ownership by regional institutions. A technical assistance programme, a training programme and a research agenda had been developed. A governance framework with coordinating structures at the global, regional and national levels was proposed, along with a strategy for mobilizing resources and technical support from developed countries, the donor community and international organizations.

The first drafts of the global and Africa implementation plans were discussed at the Fifth International Conference on Agricultural Statistics (Kampala, Uganda, 13–15 October 2010). The report described the technical components of the implementation plan: country assessment, training, technical assistance and methodological research.

Business registers

On 24 February [dec. 42/115], the Statistical Commission took note of the Wiesbaden Group on Business Registers' report [E/CN.3/2011/25] on its twenty-second meeting (Tallinn, Estonia, 27–30 September 2010), hosted by Statistics Estonia. The meeting focused on the following themes: country progress reports; the impact of economic globalization on the production, collection and interpretation of business data; profiling as a method for identifying the legal, operational and accounting structures of an enterprise in order to establish the statistical units within it; the dependence of statistical business registers on administrative data from sources such as tax authorities; the interactions of "producers" and "consumers" of business register information; improvement of business register coverage in agriculture, public sector and non-profit institutions; technical developments of the registers (re-engineering); and business registers and business statistics in developing countries. In view of the great diversity of business register designs, the Economic Commission for Europe urged the Wiesbaden Group to initiate preparation of international guidelines on business registers.

Energy statistics

The Secretary-General reported on energy statistics [E/CN.3/2011/8], describing the revision of the international recommendations for energy statistics (IRES), providing an overview of the draft revised recommendations and outlining the implementation programme. The revised IRES were the first recommendations that provided a coherent basis for producing energy statistics in the context of all economic statistics, linking them to existing standards, as well as a set of internationally agreed and harmonized definitions of energy products. IRES were prepared by the Statistics Division in cooperation with the Oslo Group on Energy Statistics and the Intersecretariat Working Group on Energy Statistics, and in consultation with countries worldwide. As a first step in the implementation of the international recommendations, several activities were planned, including the preparation of the Energy Statistics Compilers Manual, intended to contain further explanations of the recommendations and provide practical guidance.

On 25 February [dec. 42/105], the Commission adopted the international recommendations for energy statistics and endorsed the main elements of the proposed implementation programme.

Also transmitted to the Commission was a report [E/CN.3/2011/9] of the Oslo Group on Energy Statistics on its activities in 2009–2010, its contributions to the international recommendations for energy statistics, and its planned undertakings. Two meetings of the Group focused on the discussion and revision of IRES.

Tourism statistics

On 24 February [dec. 42/115], the Statistical Commission took note of a report [E/CN.3/2011/26] of the United Nations World Tourism Organization (UNWTO) on tourism statistics, issued in response to the Commission's request to develop an implementation programme for tourism statistics, including the preparation of a compilation guide and the organization of training workshops [YUN 2008, p. 1382]. The report stated that regional capacity-building programmes for tourism statistics were developed and implemented in Africa, Central America and Europe, and additional training workshops were conducted in Asia and the Commonwealth of Independent States region. In 2010, UNWTO prepared an updated version of the *Compendium of Tourism Statistics* for international comparability of tourism activity.

International Comparison Programme

The Commission considered a report [E/CN.3/2011/12] of the World Bank on the International Comparison Programme (ICP), which summarized the status of preparations for the 2011 round of the Programme. The ICP was in a sound financial position and the ICP Executive Board had approved the beginning of price surveys and national account activities in January. The report suggested, however, that several countries might struggle to complete pricing and provide the national account data being sought, and the Commission might wish to review country participation issues, as well as the workplan and time frame.

The ICP Global Office at the World Bank had coordinated regional initiatives and methodological development activities and prepared operational material for the price surveys and the compilation of detailed gross domestic product (GDP) expenditures. Regional and national coordinators had helped finalize the global core list of household product specifications and developed their own lists of items. The global core list of 601 items to be priced for the main survey on household consumption was developed. In 2010, the ICP Executive Board held two meetings (New York, 21 February; Washington, D.C., 18 October).

In the context of country participation in the Programme, the report mentioned specifically singleton countries, such as Argentina, Georgia, Iran and Turkmenistan; and States with dual participation, such as Egypt and the Sudan, operating under the coordination of the African Development Bank and the UN Economic and Social Commission for Western Asia; as well as regions undertaking ICP price data collection in 2011–2012, such as the Caribbean and Asia and the Pacific.

On 25 February [dec. 42/108], the Commission urged the Executive Board, the Global Office and the ICP regional coordinating units to continue to undertake consultations with Member States on the methodology of the Programme, in particular in the global linking process and on the use of purchasing power parity data and their computation. It acknowledged the significance of ICP in developing the capacity of countries to collect and compute price data and compile national accounts, and urged the World Bank to take additional steps to assist them in that respect.

Price statistics

On 24 February [dec. 42/115], the Commission took note of a report of the Intersecretariat Working Group on Price Statistics [E/CN.3/2011/27] on its organization and work, and providing updates of its terms of reference [YUN 2005, p. 1371]. Activities included the publication of the *Practical Guide to Producing Consumer Price Indices* and the *Export and Import Price Index Manual: Theory and Practice*; and the availability online of the *Consumer Price Index Manual*, as well as of the *Producer Price Index Manual*. An updated version of the Price Index Processor Software had been developed by the International Monetary Fund (IMF) and made available online. The report also gave an overview of the general objectives of the Group—such as developing handbooks on concepts and methods of price statistics, and coordinating the work of international organizations in implementing best practices—as well as of membership, activities and procedures for the production and publications of manuals.

Integrated economic statistics

A report of the Friends of the Chair on integrated economic statistics [E/CN.3/2011/10] provided information on progress in developing more extensive and practical guidelines on integrated economic statistics including case studies, which had been requested at the Commission's thirty-ninth session (2008) [YUN 2008, p. 1385]. The report requested the Commission to express its views on the guidelines and provide advice on their finalization. The guidelines focused on consistency and coherence in the full chain of economic statistics, from short-term indicators to national and international macroeconomic statistics based thereon. They gave practical advice for reconciling economic statistics from highly centralized as well as decentralized statistical agencies. Also discussed were the guiding principles and building blocks of integrated economic statistics; strategic planning for integrating those statistics; specific tools that countries could use in producing those statistics; good practices and communication examples for data dissemination; and practical issues related to compiling an integrated set of accounts.

On 25 February [dec. 42/106], the Commission welcomed the draft guidelines and requested that the final guidelines address further critical areas including, among others, governance issues and integration of source data. It requested the Statistics Division to develop and maintain a web-based knowledge portal even after the finalization of the guidelines in order to provide a single access point to a broad range of case studies and information material.

Short-term economic indicators

The Statistical Commission considered a report by the Secretary-General on short-term economic indicators [E/CN.3/2011/11] describing a joint initiative undertaken by the Statistics Division and Eurostat in collaboration with national statistical services to formulate an international programme of work on short-term statistics, as a part of a response to the economic and financial crisis. Recommendations for that programme were developed at three international seminars for official statisticians, academics and policymakers (Ottawa, Canada, 27–29 May 2009; Scheveningen, Netherlands, 14–16 December 2009; and Moscow, 17–19 November 2010). Four working groups were created to prepare thematic programmes of work for 2011–2012 in rapid estimates; business cycle composite indicators; tendency surveys; and data template and analytical indicators.

The Secretary-General requested the Commission to provide guidance on the overall programme; encourage countries to create national central data hubs with a single access point in their national statistical system; and submit their practices and usage of short-term economic indicators to the Division for inclusion in the Knowledge Base on Economic Statistics—an inventory of methodological guidance and country practices for economic statistics.

On 25 February [dec. 42/107], the Commission requested that the requirements of national accounts, the national statistical system and other national governance arrangements be taken into account in the implementation of the programme of work, and that due attention be given to the issue of source data improvement; and that the Statistics Division appoint an interregional adviser to assist countries in training and capacity-building for the programme on short-term statistics and work closely with the regional commissions in that area.

Natural resources and environment statistics

Environment statistics

The Secretary-General reported [E/CN.3/2011/28] on the conclusions and recommendations of the Expert Group on the Revision of the Framework for the Development of Environment Statistics, established by the Statistics Division in 2010 [YUN 2010, p. 1264]. At its first meeting (New York, 8–10 November 2010), the Expert Group concluded that the revision of the 1984 *Framework for the Development of Environment Statistics* [YUN 1984, p. 969] must start, although an agreement on a single scientific theory, on which the framework could be based, had not been found. It invited the Division to initiate the revision and development of a core set of environment statistics, and proposed that a subgroup be formed to assist the Division in that regard. It also invited Statistics Canada to elaborate on its proposal to apply the natural capital theory—according to which the environment contributes to human development through material and service flows—to developing a conceptual framework for environment statistics with the assistance of another subgroup. The Division was requested to put into operation the electronic discussion forum on the Expert Group's website, with the aim of engaging a wider range of experts, including representatives of the scientific and user communities. A timeline of the revision of the *Framework* and the establishment of the core set of environment statistics, as well as the expected outputs and responsibilities concluded the report.

The Commission took note of the report on 24 February [dec. 42/115].

Environmental-economic accounting

The Statistical Commission considered a report [E/CN.3/2011/7] of the Committee of Experts on Environmental-Economic Accounting that described its work in revising the System of Environmental-Economic Accounting (SEEA), focusing on the finalization of the recommendations for the 21 issues to be included in volume 1 of the revised SEEA; the promotion of SEEA in statistical communities; and the coordination of activities of entities and expert groups working within the mandate of the Committee.

The report presented an update on the progress in the preparation of seea-Energy, a subsystem of seea providing further elaboration of the concepts, classifications and accounts related to energy already included in seea. The Committee reiterated the importance of completing the drafting of seea-Energy, and welcomed the resumed work on it, made possible by the financial assistance of the Federal Statistical Office of Germany.

On 25 February [dec. 42/104], the Commission took note of the recommendations and requested the Committee of Experts to develop, in consultation with Member States and the regional commissions, an implementation plan for seea and to set priorities for Member States.

Other activities

Coordination and integration of statistical programmes

The Secretary-General reported on the work of the Committee for the Coordination of Statistical Activities [E/CN.3/2011/29], summarizing the conclusions of its fifteenth (New York, 22 February 2010) and sixteenth (Vienna, 1–3 September 2010) sessions. Subjects discussed included the global statistical system and the role of the Committee; the global inventory on statistical standards; coordination of capacity-building activities of international organizations in developing countries; the reporting mechanism on statistical capacity-building activities; use of non-official data in imputations/estimations made by international organizations; dissemination of microdata by international organizations; establishment of a network of statisticians working in international organizations; the Conference on Data Quality for International Organizations (Helsinki, Finland, 4–6 May 2010); and the first World Statistics Day.

The Commission took note of the report on 24 February [dec. 42/115].

Statistics of human development

In response to a Statistical Commission request [YUN 2010, p. 1266] at its forty-first session, the Secretary-General transmitted the reports of the Commission's Bureau [E/CN.3/2011/14] and of the United Nations Development Programme (undp) [E/CN.3/2011/15]. The former presented the findings and recommendations of an expert group meeting on the Human Development Index (hdi) (New York, 24–25 March 2010), which was called to assess the methodological soundness and appropriateness of the data used for the undp *Human Development Report*. The group reviewed the three dimensions of the classic hdi—income, education and health; proposals to modify the construction of the index; and proposals to introduce new adjusted indices, including gender inequality. The report noted that the multidimensional poverty index, subsequently included in the *Human Development Report 2010* [YUN 2010, p. 870], was not presented for discussion at that meeting by undp. The report invited the Commission to endorse the recommendations regarding the use of official statistics, the full transparency of all data sources and methodologies, and the reactivation of the Statistical Advisory Panel.

The undp report provided details about measurement innovations introduced in the 2010 *Report*, namely revisions to the hdi and the introduction of new indices. While hdi, since its introduction in 1990, had been widely regarded as the main alternative to measures based only on income, it had also been subjected to a range of criticisms. Efforts were made to refine the measures through use of better data with reasonable country coverage. The revisions concerned the measures of a decent standard of living and knowledge and education, as well as methodology, data sources for the hdi and hdi country coverage. While the Human Development Report Office relied largely on UN entities and international organizations to collect data, it also made use of data series from alternative renowned sources where official statistics were not available. Data availability determined hdi country coverage, and for the 2010 *Report*, a number of countries were missing data from international sources for one or more of the Index components. To address some of the limitations of the existing indices, three new measures were introduced in the 2010 *Report*: the inequality-adjusted hdi, the gender inequality index and the multidimensional poverty index. The report also provided information on the data sources of the new indices, while noting the limitation of the microdata, which were sparsely available in internationally harmonized databases. The report concluded that the Office intended to refine measures as more quality data became available; welcomed opportunities to work with the Commission to develop new data series and to encourage countries to extend the range and type of data available through more regular internationally harmonized household surveys; and had responded to all proposals of the expert group, providing transparency about data sources and estimation procedures, conducting advance consultations with country experts, and expanding the advisory panel with statistical experts including theoreticians and practitioners.

A report [E/CN.3/2011/16] by Brazil, Morocco and South Africa summarized the debate on Member States' concerns about country level statistical indicators released by international organizations, focusing on the concerns of those three countries about the choice of indicators and their methodology, and the use of source data. The report provided examples for discrepancies and problems that could arise from such discrepancies. The Commission was invited to advise on the consultation mechanism between Member States and the international agencies on those concerns; and to request the Statistics Division to enhance coordination among UN organizations in the selection and quality assessment of development indicators.

On 25 February [dec. 42/110], the Commission endorsed the recommendations of its Bureau and the concerns expressed in the report of Brazil, Morocco and South Africa. It expressed concern about the statistical sources and methods used for the *Human Development Report* and strong dissatisfaction that the UNDP Human Development Report Office did not respond adequately to the recommendations of the Expert Group on HDI prior to the release of the 2010 *Report*, which resulted in countries being omitted from the *Report* due to lack of data, discrepancies between the data in the *Report* and the data available from national sources, as well as the use of unapproved non-official data. The Commission stressed the relevance of the Fundamental Principles of Official Statistics and of the Principles Governing International Statistical Activities, and urged UNDP to review the Principles and subscribe to them. While recognizing that the choice of the theme and of the indicators for the *Report* was the prerogative of UNDP, the issue of data quality and adequacy fell within the purview of the Statistical Commission and prior consultation was necessary. The Commission reiterated the need for UNDP to be fully transparent in its methods of statistical work in preparing the *Report*, called for consultation with all parties concerned, and requested UNDP to report to the Commission within three months on the issues raised. It further urged the Statistics Division to assist Member States in addressing issues of data discrepancies and inconsistency with international organizations, and stressed the need for an authoritative agency in the UN system to coordinate statistical activities.

Implementation of Fundamental Principles of Official Statistics

The Secretary-General submitted a report [E/CN.3/2011/17] on the implementation of the Fundamental Principles of Official Statistics, adopted in 1994 [YUN 1994, p. 1265], and sought the Statistical Commission's guidance on how to better implement them. Due to violations of the intent and provisions of the Principles, questions had arisen regarding whether it was desirable to redraft and periodically review them; and whether the Commission should take specific actions on how countries implemented them. The report invited the Commission to consider appropriate mechanisms to refine or reformulate the Principles and to strengthen their implementation; and to consider appropriate actions to commemorate their twentieth anniversary in 2014.

On 25 February [dec. 42/111], the Commission acknowledged that the Fundamental Principles were still relevant and that no revision of the principles themselves was necessary. It recommended, however, that the Statistics Division facilitate the formation of a Friends of the Chair group to revise and update the language of the preamble of the Principles, assess how they could be re-enforced and develop a practical guide for their implementation. It requested the Division to submit the Principles, with the revised preamble, to the General Assembly and the Economic and Social Council for endorsement before 2014.

Standards on data and metadata exchange

On 24 February [dec. 42/115], the Commission took note of the progress report of the Task Force to Establish Standards on Data and Metadata Exchange [E/CN.3/2011/31], which noted that the Statistical Data and Metadata Exchange (SDMX) [YUN 2004, p. 1261] technical standards 2.0 were being revised. The SDMX 2.1 was intended to fix bugs and improve technical features relating to web services, structure queries and registry interface reconciliation, code lists, and the SDMX data formats. The report also stated that a decision to convene a working group for technical standards and another for content-oriented guidelines was reached, and further progress had been made in implementing SDMX standards and guidelines in statistical organizations.

The SDMX Global Conference 2011 (Washington, D.C., 2–4 May), co-hosted by IMF and the World Bank, included a review of SDMX activities over the previous 10 years, a business case for adopting SDMX, a showcasing of SDMX implementation in national and international organizations and examples of how to get started with SDMX. During the conference, the results of the SDMX 2011 Global Survey, which aimed to measure acceptance level, challenges and implementation plans of SDMX in official statistics, were presented.

Statistical capacity-building

The Secretary-General reported on the work of the Statistics Division to support State efforts in building national statistical capacity [E/CN.3/2011/18]. The report gave an overview of the Division's response to requests by the General Assembly and the Economic and Social Council and described its capacity-building approach, aimed at strengthening national statistical systems by improving the quality and relevance of statistical production, and by transferring professional knowledge to national statisticians. Other activities organized by the Division included fellowships, workshops and study visits for statisticians from developing countries. From 2006 to 2010, the Division organized 164 workshops, expert group meetings and seminars attended by 7,937 professionals. The Division continued its work on MDG indicators, population and housing censuses, gender statistics, economic and trade statistics, environment and energy statistics, data management and dissemination, geospatial information, and national statistical systems.

On 25 February [dec. 42/112], the Commission welcomed the organization of an event on the strategy of statistical capacity development at the fourth High-level Forum on Aid Effectiveness, to be held in November in the Republic of Korea, and requested the World Bank to report to the Commission at its forty-third (2012) session on this initiative and on progress towards implementing the Marrakech Action Plan for Statistics [YUN 2004, p. 1261].

The Commission also received a report of the Partnership in Statistics for Development in the 21st Century (PARIS21) [E/CN.3/2011/19] outlining its efforts to promote the use of better statistics and describing its 2010 activities. Those included supporting developing countries in producing data for the MDG indicators; helping States create national booklets on their statistical systems; and organizing advocacy seminars or donor round tables. PARIS21 continued to implement, along with the World Bank, the Accelerated Data Program and the International Household Survey Network (IHSN). It also assisted 33 countries in national strategy processes and in conducting peer reviews.

The Commission took note of the report at its forty-second session [dec. 42/115].

Development indicators

The Secretary-General reported [E/CN.3/2011/13] on progress made by the Statistics Division and the Inter-Agency and Expert Group on Millennium Development Goals Indicators in addressing concerns raised by the Statistical Commission in relation to the production of MDG indicators and the ability of countries to undertake their own monitoring. The Group and the Division worked to improve methods for the monitoring of progress towards the achievement of the Goals, resolve differences between national and international data sets, identify ways to increase capacity-building efforts for tracking MDGs, and define strategies to assist countries in improving coordination of MDG data reporting and monitoring. The report presented an assessment of data availability to monitor progress towards MDGs and described the preparation of the annual reports on that progress.

On 25 February [dec. 42/109], the Commission requested the Statistics Division to establish a group of experts to provide assistance to resolve specific MDG data-related issues and endorsed the way forward for the Inter-Agency and Expert Group, including the provision of further training for national and subnational monitoring.

Follow-up to Economic and Social Council policy decisions

The Statistical Commission had before it a note from the Secretary-General [E/CN.3/2011/32] briefing it on Economic and Social Council and General Assembly policy decisions adopted in 2010 that were relevant to the work of the Commission. The policy decisions concerned World Statistics Day; follow-up to the High-level Plenary Meeting of the sixty-fifth session of the General Assembly on the MDGS [YUN 2010, p. 813]; the multi-year programme of work for annual ministerial reviews of the Economic and Social Council; follow-up to Economic and Social Council resolutions on strengthening national capacity in statistics and on the 2010 World Population and Housing Census Programme; global geospatial information management; and improving the collection, reporting and analysis of data on ageing and people with disabilities. The report also indicated actions taken and proposed to be taken by the Commission and the Statistics Division in response to requests made by the Council and the Assembly.

The Commission took note of the report on 24 February [dec. 42/115].

Regional statistical development

The Statistical Commission had before it a report of the Economic and Social Commission for Western Asia (ESCWA) on regional statistical development in Western Asia [E/CN.3/2011/20], which outlined challenges to and priorities for official statistics for the region as well as issues of regional coordination, focusing on consistency of data published by national statistical offices and by international organizations.

On 25 February [dec. 42/113], the Commission urged ESCWA to play a greater role in coordination among different bodies active in the field of statistics in the region and urged the development partners to provide full support, in collaboration with regional entities such as the Arab Institute for Training and Research in Statistics, for the capacity-building efforts of the countries in the region.

National quality assurance frameworks

On 24 February [dec. 42/115], the Commission took note of the Secretary-General's report [E/CN.3/2011/33] summarizing the activities of the United Nations Expert Group on National Quality Assurance Frameworks—constituted in August 2010 [YUN 2010, p. 1269]—and presenting its programme of work for 2011.

Global geospatial information management

In response to a Statistical Commission request [YUN 2010, p. 1268], the Secretary-General reported on global geospatial information management (GGIM) [E/CN.3/2011/34], describing activities in the field and the findings of the second preparatory meeting (New York, 10–11 May 2010) on the proposed United Nations Committee of Experts on Global Geospatial Information Management. The report discussed the mandate of the Economic and Social Council for work on GGIM and the subsequent preparation of a draft mission statement and terms of reference for the proposed Committee of Experts; and outlined plans for 2011, including the third preparatory meeting on the proposed Committee and the first UN forum on GGIM.

The Commission took note of the report on 24 February [dec. 42/115].

By **resolution 2011/24** of 27 July (see p. 967), the Economic and Social Council established the Committee of Experts on Global Geospatial Information Management.

Inventory of global statistical standards

The Commission had before it a report of the Committee for the Coordination of Statistical Activities on the inventory of global statistical standards [E/CN.3/2011/30], highlighting progress in establishing an inventory to provide a knowledge centre and a reference system for international statistical standards, based on a system originally developed by the National Institute of Statistics and Geography of Mexico. The report discussed issues including the coverage of the system, classification, information contents, functionality, languages, maintenance, platform and the development of a prototype.

The Commission took note of the report on 24 February [dec. 42/115].

World Statistics Day

The Commission considered a report on the first World Statistics Day [E/CN.3/2011/2], held on 20 October 2010. The report provided an overview of the activities undertaken to mark the observance, including the launch of reports such as *The World's Women 2010: Trends and Statistics* [Sales No. E.10.XVII.11] by the Statistics Division and *The World in 2010: ICT facts and figures* by the International Telecommunications Union; and the involvement of UN information centres. World Statistics Day was deemed successful in raising the profile of official statistics, as well as in motivating statistical communities in many countries.

On 25 February [dec. 42/101], the Commission expressed its appreciation that the observance of World Statistics Day had made a positive impact in advocating the importance of official statistics and requested the Division to formulate, in consultation with the Commission's Bureau, a proposal for designating World Statistics Day as a regular observance.

Measurement of economic performance and social progress

On 24 February [dec. 42/115], the Commission took note of a report [E/CN.3/2011/35] prepared by the Institut National de la statistique et des études économiques in France outlining the country's initiatives in implementing the 12 recommendations included in the report of the Commission on the Measurement of Economic Performance and Social Progress (the Stiglitz Commission) one year after the publication of the report, which called for the sustainable reform of the entire domain of official statistics, both in France and at the international level. The Stiglitz Commission was established in 2008 on the initiative of the President of France to identify the limitations of using GDP in measuring economic performance and social progress and consider what additional information could give a more accurate picture.

Programme questions

On 25 February [dec. 42/114], the Commission took note of the oral report by the Director of the Statistics Division concerning the activities, plans and priorities of the Division and the draft programme of work of the Division for the 2012–2013 biennium. It also approved the adjustments to the list of outputs for the 2010–2011 programme and authorized the Bureau to approve further adjustments as necessary.

On the same day, the Commission considered and approved its draft multi-year programme of work for 2011–2014 [E/CN.3/2011/36], and approved the provisional agenda and documentation for its forty-third session, to be held in New York from 28 February to 2 March 2012.

PART FOUR

Legal questions

Chapter I

International Court of Justice

In 2011, the International Court of Justice (ICJ) delivered four Judgments, made 10 Orders, and had 16 contentious cases and one advisory procedure pending before it. In a 26 October address to the General Assembly, the ICJ President, Judge Hisashi Owada, noted that during the period from 1 August 2010 to 31 July 2011, the cases that the Court was entrusted to deal with involved States from all regions of the world and raised a broad range of legal questions. He added that a firm reliance on international law must underpin any future developments on the global stage and that the ICJ, as guardian of international law, was proud to play a vital role in an increasingly globalized world.

Judicial work of the Court

During 2011, the Court delivered its Judgment on the merits in the case concerning *Application of the Interim Accord of 13 September 1995 (the former Yugoslav Republic of Macedonia v. Greece)*, a Judgment on the preliminary objections raised by the Russian Federation in the case concerning *Application of the International Convention on the Elimination of All Forms of Racial Discrimination (Georgia v. Russian Federation)*, a Judgment on the request for the indication of provisional measures submitted by Costa Rica in the case concerning *Certain Activities carried out by Nicaragua in the Border Area (Costa Rica v. Nicaragua)*, and two Judgments on the applications of Costa Rica and Honduras for permission to intervene in the case concerning *Territorial and Maritime Dispute (Nicaragua v. Colombia)*.

The Court was seized of two new cases: *Request for Interpretation of the Judgment of 15 June 1962 in the Case concerning the Temple of Preah Vihear (Cambodia v. Thailand)*, and *Construction of a Road in Costa Rica along the San Juan River (Nicaragua v. Costa Rica)*.

The Court held public hearings in the cases concerning *Application of the Interim Accord of 13 September 1995 (the former Yugoslav Republic of Macedonia v. Greece)*, *Jurisdictional Immunities of the State (Germany v. Italy; Greece intervening)*, *Certain Activities carried out by Nicaragua in the Border Area (Costa Rica v. Nicaragua)*, and *Request for Interpretation of the Judgment of 15 June 1962 in the Case concerning the Temple of Preah Vihear (Cambodia v. Thailand)*.

The Court or its President made Orders on the conduct of the proceedings in the cases concerning *Ahmadou Sadio Diallo (Guinea v. Democratic Republic of the Congo)*; *Aerial Herbicide Spraying (Ecuador v. Colombia)*; *Jurisdictional Immunities of the State (Germany v. Italy; Greece intervening)*; *Questions relating to the Obligation to Prosecute or Extradite (Belgium v. Senegal)*; *Certain Activities carried out by Nicaragua in the Border Area (Costa Rica v. Nicaragua)*; and *Request for Interpretation of the Judgment of 15 June 1962 in the Case concerning the Temple of Preah Vihear (Cambodia v. Thailand)*. It also made an Order in relation to the request for an advisory opinion on the question of *Judgment No. 2867 of the Administrative Tribunal of the International Labour Organization upon a complaint filed against the International Fund for Agricultural Development*.

In the cases *Ahmadou Sadio Diallo (Guinea v. Democratic Republic of the Congo)*, *Maritime Dispute (Peru v. Chile)*, *Questions relating to the Obligation to Prosecute or Extradite (Belgium v. Senegal)*, and *Certain Activities carried out by Nicaragua in the Border Area (Costa Rica v. Nicaragua)*, pleadings were submitted within the fixed time limits, as was the request for an advisory opinion on the question of *Judgment No. 2867 of the Administrative Tribunal of the International Labour Organization upon a complaint filed against the International Fund for Agricultural Development*.

While there were no new developments in the case concerning *Gabcikovo-Nagymaros Project (Hungary/Slovakia)* [YUN 1998, p. 1186], the parties kept the Court informed of progress made in their negotiations. In the case *Armed Activities on the Territory of the Congo (Democratic Republic of the Congo v. Uganda)* [YUN 1999, p. 1209], the parties transmitted to the Court information concerning their negotiations to settle the question of reparation, as referred to in the 2005 Judgment [YUN 2005, p. 1381]. Both cases remained pending.

In the case *Jurisdiction and Enforcement of Judgments in Civil and Commercial Matters (Belgium v. Switzerland)*, Belgium informed the Court that it was discontinuing its proceedings against Switzerland; the case was subsequently removed from the Court's General List. The Court also granted Greece permission to intervene as a non-party in the case concerning *Jurisdictional Immunities of the State (Germany v. Italy)*.

ICJ activities in 2011 were covered in two reports to the General Assembly, for the periods 1 August 2010 to 31 July 2011 [A/66/4] and 1 August 2011 to 31 July 2012 [A/67/4]. The Assembly took note of the 2010/2011 report on 26 October (**decision 66/507**). The Assembly on 24 December decided that the agenda item "Report of the International Court of Justice" would remain for consideration during its resumed sixty-sixth (2012) session (**decision 66/557**).

Contentious proceedings

Ahmadou Sadio Diallo
(Guinea v. Democratic Republic of the Congo)

On 28 December 1998 [YUN 1998, p. 1190], Guinea instituted proceedings against the Democratic Republic of the Congo (DRC) by an Application in which it requested the Court to condemn the DRC for the serious breaches of international law allegedly perpetrated upon the person of a Guinean national, Ahmadou Sadio Diallo.

According to Guinea, Mr. Diallo, a businessman who had been a resident of the DRC for 32 years, was unlawfully imprisoned by the authorities of the DRC for two and a half months, divested from his investments, companies, bank accounts and properties, then expelled. The expulsion took place on 2 February 1996, as a result of his attempts to recover sums owed to him by the DRC (especially by Gécamines, a State enterprise and mining monopoly) and by oil companies operating in that country (Zaïre Shell, Zaïre Mobil and Zaïre Fina), by virtue of contracts concluded with businesses owned by him, namely Africom-Zaïre and Africontainers-Zaïre.

As a basis of the Court's jurisdiction, Guinea invoked its own declaration of acceptance of the compulsory jurisdiction of the Court of 11 November 1998 and a declaration of the DRC of 8 February 1989. Guinea filed its memorial within the time limit as extended by the Court [YUN 2000, p. 1213].

On 3 October 2002 [YUN 2002, p. 1266], the DRC filed preliminary objections to the admissibility of Guinea's Application; the proceedings on the merits were accordingly suspended.

By an Order of 7 November 2002 [ibid.], the Court fixed 7 July 2003 as the time limit within which Guinea might present a statement of its observations and submissions on the preliminary objections raised by the DRC; the statement was filed within the time limit.

Public hearings on the preliminary objections were held from 27 November to 1 December 2006 [YUN 2006, p. 1479], during which the parties presented final submissions to the Court. The DRC requested the Court to adjudge and declare that the Application of Guinea was inadmissible on the grounds that Guinea had no status to exercise diplomatic protection in the proceedings, since its Application sought essentially to secure reparation for injury suffered on account of the violation of rights of companies which did not possess its nationality, and, in any event, neither the companies in question nor Mr. Diallo had exhausted the local remedies available in the DRC. Guinea requested the Court to reject the preliminary objections raised by the DRC, declare its Application admissible, and fix time limits for further proceedings.

On 24 May 2007 [YUN 2007, p. 1327], the Court rendered a Judgment, by two separate votes of 14 to 1, declaring the Application of Guinea to be admissible insofar as it concerned protection of Mr. Diallo's rights as an individual and of his direct rights as *associé* in Africom-Zaïre and Africontainers-Zaïre, but inadmissible insofar as it concerned protection of Mr. Diallo in respect of alleged violations of the rights of Africom-Zaïre and Africontainers-Zaïre.

By an Order of 27 June 2007 [ibid., p. 1328], the Court fixed 27 March 2008 as the time limit for the filing of a counter-memorial by the DRC, which was filed within the time limit.

By an Order of 5 May 2008 [YUN 2008, p. 1394], the Court authorized the submission of a reply by Guinea and a rejoinder by the DRC. It fixed 19 November 2008 and 5 June 2009 as the respective time limits for the filing of those pleadings, which were filed within those limits.

Public hearings were held from 19 to 29 April 2010 [YUN 2010, p. 1273]. At the conclusion of their oral arguments, the parties presented their final submissions to the Court. Guinea requested the Court to adjudge and declare that, in carrying out arbitrary arrests of Mr. Diallo, and expelling him; in not respecting his right to the benefit of the provisions of the 1963 Vienna Convention on Consular Relations; in submitting him to humiliating and degrading treatment; in depriving him of the exercise of his rights of ownership, oversight and management in respect of the companies which he founded in the DRC and in which he was the sole *associé*; in preventing him from pursuing recovery of the numerous debts owed to those companies by the DRC and by other contractual partners; and in expropriating de facto Mr. Diallo's property, the DRC had committed internationally wrongful acts which engaged its responsibility to Guinea. The DRC was accordingly bound to make full reparation on account of the injury suffered by Mr. Diallo or by Guinea in the person of its national. Guinea further requested the Court to authorize it to submit an assessment of the amount of the compensation due to it on that account from the DRC in a subsequent phase of the proceedings in the event that the two parties should be unable to agree on such amount within six months following delivery of the Judgment.

The DRC, in the light of the arguments it had made and of the Court's Judgment of 24 May 2007, whereby the Court declared the application of Guinea to be inadmissible insofar as it concerned protection of Mr. Diallo in respect of alleged violations of the rights of Africom-Zaïre and Africontainers-Zaïre, requested the Court to adjudge and declare that the DRC had not committed any internationally wrongful acts towards Guinea in respect of Mr. Diallo's individual rights, or in respect of his direct rights as *associé* in Africom-Zaïre and Africontainers-Zaïre; accordingly, the application of Guinea was unfounded and no reparation was due.

The Court delivered its Judgment on 30 November 2010. By 8 votes to 6, it found that that the claim of Guinea concerning the arrest and detention of Mr. Diallo in 1988–1989 was inadmissible. The Court unanimously found that in respect of the circumstances in which Mr. Diallo was expelled from Congolese territory on 31 January 1996, the DRC violated article 13 of the International Covenant on Civil and Political Rights and article 12 of the African Charter on Human and Peoples' Rights; that, in respect of the circumstances in which Mr. Diallo was arrested and detained in 1995–1996 with a view to his expulsion, the DRC violated article 9 of the International Covenant on Civil and Political Rights and article 6 of the African Charter on Human and Peoples' Rights. By 13 votes to 1, the Court found that, by not informing Mr. Diallo without delay, upon his detention in 1995–1996, of his rights under article 36 of the Vienna Convention on Consular Relations, the DRC violated its obligations under that article. By 12 votes to 2, the Court rejected all other submissions by Guinea relating to the circumstances in which Mr. Diallo was arrested and detained with a view to his expulsion. By 9 votes to 5, it found that the DRC had not violated Mr. Diallo's direct rights as *associé* in Africom-Zaïre and Africontainers-Zaïre. The Court unanimously found that that the DRC was under obligation to make reparation, in the form of compensation, to Guinea for the injurious consequences of its violations of international obligations. It unanimously decided that, failing agreement between the parties on the matter within six months from the date of the Judgment, the question of compensation should be settled by the Court.

Appended to the Judgment was a joint declaration by five judges and another by two judges; separate opinions by one judge and one ad hoc judge; a joint dissenting opinion by two judges; and dissenting opinions by one judge and an ad hoc judge.

By an Order of 20 September 2011, the Court noted that the time limit fixed in its Judgment of 30 November 2010 had expired on 30 May 2011. It recalled that it had decided in that Judgment that, having been sufficiently informed of the facts of the case, a single exchange of pleadings by the parties would be sufficient in order for it to decide on the amount of compensation due to Guinea. The Court fixed 6 December 2011 and 21 February 2012 as the time limits for the filing of a memorial by Guinea and a counter-memorial by the DRC. The pleading by Guinea was filed within the time limit.

Application of the Convention on the Prevention and Punishment of the Crime of Genocide (Croatia v. Serbia)

On 2 July 1999 [YUN 1999, p. 1210], Croatia instituted proceedings before the Court against Serbia, then known as the Federal Republic of Yugoslavia, for alleged violations of the 1948 Convention on the Prevention and Punishment of the Crime of Genocide [YUN 1948–49, p. 959] committed between 1991 and 1995. In its Application, Croatia contended that by directly controlling the activity of its armed forces, intelligence agents, and various paramilitary detachments on the territory of Croatia, Serbia was liable for ethnic cleansing of Croatian citizens. It requested the Court to adjudge and declare that Serbia had breached its legal obligations to Croatia under the Genocide Convention and that it had an obligation to pay to Croatia, in its own right and as *parens patriae* for its citizens, reparations for damages to persons and property, as well as to the Croatian economy and environment caused by those violations of international law in a sum to be determined by the Court.

As basis for the Court's jurisdiction, Croatia invoked article IX of the Genocide Convention, to which, it claimed, both States were parties.

By an Order of 14 September 1999 [YUN 1999, p. 1210], the Court fixed 14 March and 14 September 2000 as the respective time limits for the filing of a memorial by Croatia and a counter-memorial by Serbia. Those limits were twice extended by Orders made during 2000 [YUN 2000, p. 1219]. Croatia filed its memorial within the extended time limit. On 11 September 2002 [YUN 2002, p. 1268], within the extended time limit for filing its counter-memorial, Serbia filed certain preliminary objections on jurisdiction and admissibility. The proceedings on the merits were suspended, in accordance with Article 79 of the Rules of Court. Croatia filed a statement of its observations and submissions on Serbia's preliminary objections on 25 April 2003 [YUN 2003, p. 1304], within the time limit fixed by the Court.

At the conclusion of public hearings on the preliminary objections on jurisdiction and admissibility, held from 26 to 30 May 2008, the parties presented final submissions to the Court [YUN 2008, p. 1395].

In its Judgment, rendered on 18 November 2008 [ibid.], the Court found that, subject to its statement concerning the second preliminary objection raised by Serbia, it had jurisdiction, on the basis of article IX of the Genocide Convention, to entertain Croatia's application, adding that Serbia's second preliminary objection did not possess an exclusively preliminary character. It then rejected the third preliminary objection submitted by Serbia.

By an Order of 20 January 2009 [YUN 2009, p. 1269], the President of the Court fixed 22 March 2010 as the time limit for the filing of the counter-memorial of Serbia. That pleading, containing counter-claims, was filed within the time limit.

By an Order of 4 February 2010 [YUN 2010, p. 1275], the Court directed the submission of a reply by Croatia and a rejoinder by Serbia concerning the claims presented by the parties. It fixed 20 December 2010 and 4 November 2011, respectively, as the time limits for the filing of those pleadings. The pleadings were filed within the time limits.

Territorial and Maritime Dispute (Nicaragua v. Colombia)

On 6 December 2001 [YUN 2001, p. 1195], Nicaragua instituted proceedings against Colombia in respect of a dispute concerning a group of related legal issues subsisting between the two States concerning title to territory and maritime delimitation in the western Caribbean. In its application, Nicaragua requested the Court to adjudge and declare, first, that Nicaragua had sovereignty over the islands of Providencia, San Andrés and Santa Catalina and all the appurtenant islands and keys, and also over the Roncador, Serrana, Serranilla and Quitasueño keys (insofar as they were capable of appropriation); and, second, in the light of the determinations concerning the title requested above, asked the Court to determine the course of the single maritime boundary between the areas of the continental shelf and the exclusive economic zone appertaining respectively to Nicaragua and Colombia. Nicaragua reserved the right to claim compensation for unjust enrichment consequent upon Colombian possession of the islands of San Andrés and Providencia, as well as the keys and maritime spaces up to the 82nd meridian, in the absence of lawful title.

As basis for the Court's jurisdiction, Nicaragua invoked article XXXI of the 1948 American Treaty on Pacific Settlement (Pact of Bogotá), to which both countries were parties, as well as the declarations of the two countries recognizing the compulsory jurisdiction of the Court.

By an Order of 26 February 2002 [YUN 2002, p. 1271], the Court fixed 28 April 2003 and 28 June 2004, respectively, as the time limits for the filing of a memorial by Nicaragua and of a counter-memorial by Colombia. The memorial of Nicaragua was filed within the time limit.

On 21 July 2003 [YUN 2003, p. 1305], Colombia filed preliminary objections to the jurisdiction of the Court; under Article 79 of the Rules of Court, proceedings on the merits were accordingly suspended. Nicaragua filed a statement of its observations and submissions on the preliminary objections raised by Colombia within the time limit of 26 January 2004 [YUN 2004, p. 1268], fixed by the Court by an Order of 24 September 2003.

Public hearings on the preliminary objections were held from 4 to 8 June 2007 [YUN 2007, p. 1329]. At the conclusion of those hearings, the parties presented their final submissions to the Court.

On 13 December 2007 [ibid., p. 1330], the Court rendered its Judgment on the preliminary objections. It found that Nicaragua's application was admissible insofar as it concerned sovereignty over the maritime features claimed by the parties other than the islands of San Andrés, Providencia and Santa Catalina, and in respect of the maritime delimitation between the parties.

Appended to the Judgment were dissenting opinions by the Vice-President and one judge; separate opinions by two judges; and declarations by four judges and an ad hoc judge.

By an Order of 11 February 2008 [YUN 2008, p. 1396], the President of the Court fixed 11 November 2008 as the time limit for the filing of the counter-memorial of Colombia, which was filed within that time limit.

By an Order of 18 December 2008 [ibid.], the Court directed Nicaragua to submit a reply and Colombia to submit a rejoinder. It fixed 18 September 2009 and 18 June 2010 as the respective time limits for the filing of those pleadings, which were filed within those limits.

On 25 February 2010 [YUN 2010, p. 1276], Costa Rica filed an application for permission to intervene in the case, stating that both Nicaragua and Colombia, in their boundary claims against each other, claimed maritime area to which Costa Rica was entitled. It made clear that it was seeking to intervene in the proceedings as a non-party State. The Court informed Nicaragua and Colombia of Costa Rica's application, and fixed 26 May 2010 as the time limit for filing their observations. The observations were filed within the time limit.

On 10 June 2010, Honduras also filed an application for permission to intervene in the case. It asserted that Nicaragua, in its dispute with Colombia, was putting forward maritime claims that lay in an area of the Caribbean Sea in which Honduras had rights and interests. Honduras stated that it was seeking primarily to intervene in the proceedings as a party. The application of Honduras was communicated to Nicaragua and Colombia. The President of the Court fixed 2 September 2010 as the time limit for those two States to furnish observations, which were filed within the time limit.

Public hearings on the admission of the application of Costa Rica for permission to intervene were held from 11 to 15 October 2010. Public hearings on the admission of the application of Honduras for permission to intervene took place from 18 to 22 October 2010.

On 4 May 2011, the Court delivered its Judgment on the admission of the application for permission to intervene filed by Costa Rica under article 62 of the Statute of the Court. By 9 votes to 7, it found that the application could not be granted.

Appended to the Judgment were declarations by one judge and one ad hoc judge; dissenting opinions by three judges; and a joint dissenting opinion by two judges.

On 4 May 2011, the Court delivered its Judgment on the admission of the application for permission to intervene filed by Honduras under article 62 of the Statute of the Court. By 13 votes to 2, it found that the application for permission to intervene could not be granted.

Appended to the Judgment were declarations by two judges; a joint declaration by two judges; and dissenting opinions by two judges.

Maritime Dispute (Peru v. Chile)

On 16 January 2008 [YUN 2008, p. 1399], Peru filed an application instituting proceedings against Chile concerning a dispute in relation to the delimitation of the boundary between the maritime zones of the two States in the Pacific Ocean, beginning at a point on the coast called Concordia, the terminal point of the land boundary established pursuant to the Treaty of 3 June 1929; and in relation to the recognition in favour of Peru of a maritime zone lying within 200 nautical miles of its coast, and thus appertaining to Peru, but which Chile considered to be part of the high seas.

Peru maintained that the maritime zones between Chile and Peru had never been delimited by agreement or otherwise. Peru stated that, since the 1980s, it had consistently endeavoured to negotiate the issues in dispute, but had constantly met with a refusal from Chile to enter into negotiations. It asserted that a note of 10 September 2004 from the Minister for Foreign Affairs of Chile to the Minister for Foreign Affairs of Peru made further attempts at negotiation impossible.

Peru consequently requested the Court to determine the course of the boundary between the maritime zones of the two States, and to adjudge and declare that Peru possessed exclusive sovereign rights in the maritime area situated within the limit of 200 nautical miles from its coast, but outside Chile's exclusive economic zone or continental shelf.

As the basis for the Court's jurisdiction, Peru invoked article XXXI of the Pact of Bogotá of 1948, to which both States were parties.

By an Order of 31 March 2008 [YUN 2008, p. 1399], the Court fixed 20 March 2009 and 9 March 2010 as the respective time limits for the filing of a memorial by Peru and a counter-memorial by Chile. Those pleadings were filed within the time limits. Bolivia, Colombia and Ecuador requested copies of the pleadings and annexed documents produced in the case. The Court, after ascertaining the views of the parties, acceded to those requests.

By an Order of 27 April 2010 [YUN 2010, p. 1279], the Court authorized the submission of a reply by Peru and a rejoinder by Chile. It fixed 9 November 2010 and 11 July 2011 as the respective time limits for the filing of those pleadings. The pleadings were filed within the time limits.

Aerial Herbicide Spraying (Ecuador v. Colombia)

On 31 March 2008 [YUN 2008, p. 1399], Ecuador filed an application instituting proceedings against Colombia in respect of a dispute concerning the alleged aerial spraying by Colombia of toxic herbicides at locations near, at and across its border with Ecuador. Ecuador maintained that the spraying had caused serious damage to people, crops, animals and the environment on the Ecuadorian side of the frontier, and posed a risk of further damage. It contended that it had made repeated efforts to negotiate an end to the fumigations, without success.

Ecuador accordingly requested the Court to adjudge and declare that Colombia had violated its obligations under international law by causing or allowing the deposit of toxic herbicides on the territory of Ecuador that had caused damage to human health, property and the environment; and that Colombia should indemnify Ecuador for any loss or damage caused by its internationally unlawful acts, and in particular the death or injury to the health of any person or persons arising from the use of such herbicides, any loss of or damage to the property or livelihood or human rights of such persons, environmental damage or the depletion of natural resources, the costs of monitoring to identify and assess future risks to public health, human rights and the environment resulting from the use of herbicides, and any other loss or damage. It further requested the Court to adjudge and declare that Colombia should respect the sovereignty and territorial integrity of Ecuador; prevent, on any part of its territory, the use of any toxic herbicides in such a way that they could be deposited onto the territory of Ecuador; and prohibit the use, by means of aerial dispersion, of such herbicides in Ecuador, or on or near any part of its border with Ecuador.

As the basis for the Court's jurisdiction, Ecuador invoked article XXXI of the 1948 Pact of Bogotá, to which both States were parties. Ecuador also relied on article 32 of the United Nations Convention against Illicit Traffic in Narcotic Drugs and Psychotropic Substances [YUN 1988, p. 688], to which both countries were parties.

Ecuador reaffirmed its opposition to the export and consumption of illegal narcotics, but stressed that the issues it presented to the Court related exclusively to the methods and locations of Colombia's operations to eradicate illicit coca and poppy plantations, and the harmful effects in Ecuador of such operations.

By an Order of 30 May 2008 [YUN 2008, p. 1400], the Court fixed 29 April 2009 and 29 March 2010 as the respective time limits for the filing of a memorial by Ecuador and a counter-memorial by Colombia. Those pleadings were filed within the time limits.

By an Order of 25 June 2010 [YUN 2010, p. 1279], the Court directed the submission of a reply by Ecuador and a rejoinder by Colombia. It fixed 31 January 2011 and 1 December 2011, respectively, as the time limits for the filing of those pleadings. The reply of Ecuador was filed within the time limit.

By an Order of 19 October 2011, the Court extended from 1 December 2011 to 1 February 2012 the time limit for the filing of a rejoinder by Colombia. That pleading was filed within the time limit.

Application of the International Convention on the Elimination of All Forms of Racial Discrimination (Georgia v. Russian Federation)

On 12 August 2008 [YUN 2008, p. 1401], Georgia instituted proceedings against the Russian Federation on the grounds of its actions on and around the territory of Georgia in breach of the International Convention on the Elimination of All Forms of Racial Discrimination [YUN 1965, p. 433]. In its application, Georgia also sought to ensure that the individual rights under the Convention of all persons on the territory of Georgia were fully respected and protected.

Georgia claimed that the Russian Federation, through its State organs, State agents, and other persons and entities exercising governmental authority, and through the South Ossetian and Abkhaz separatist forces and other agents acting on the instructions of, and under the direction and control of the Russian Federation, was responsible for serious violations of its fundamental obligations under the Convention. According to Georgia, the Russian Federation had violated those obligations during three distinct phases of its interventions in South Ossetia and Abkhazia from 1990 to August 2008. Georgia requested the Court to order the Russian Federation to comply with those obligations.

As the basis for the Court's jurisdiction, Georgia relied on article 22 of the Convention, to which both countries were party.

Georgia's application was accompanied by a request for the indication of provisional measures, in order to preserve its rights under the Convention "to protect its citizens against violent discriminatory acts by Russian armed forces, acting in concert with separatist militia and foreign mercenaries".

Public hearings on the request for the indication of provisional measures were held from 8 to 10 October 2008 [YUN 2008, p. 1401]. The Court on 15 October handed down an Order indicating provisional measures, adopted by 8 votes to 7. Both parties, within South Ossetia and Abkhazia and adjacent areas in Georgia, should refrain from any act of racial discrimination against persons, groups of persons or institutions; abstain from sponsoring, defending or supporting racial discrimination by any persons or organizations; ensure security of persons, the right to freedom of movement and residence within the border of the State, and the protection of the property of displaced persons and refugees; and ensure that public authorities and public institutions under their control or influence did not engage in acts of racial discrimination.

By an Order of 2 December 2008 [YUN 2008, p. 1402], the President fixed 2 September 2009 as the time limit for the filing of a memorial by Georgia and 2 July 2010 as the time limit for the filing of a counter-memorial by the Russian Federation. The memorial of Georgia was filed within that time limit.

On 1 December 2009, the Russian Federation filed preliminary objections in respect of jurisdiction. Pursuant to Article 79 of the Rules of Court, the proceedings on the merits were then suspended.

By an Order of 11 December 2009 [YUN 2009, p. 1273], the Court fixed 1 April 2010 as the time limit for the filing by Georgia of a statement containing its observations and submissions on the preliminary objections in respect of jurisdiction raised by the Russian Federation. Georgia filed that statement within the time limit.

Public hearings on the preliminary objections were held from 13 to 17 September 2010 [YUN 2010, p. 1280]. At the end of the hearings, the Russian Federation requested the Court to adjudge and declare that it lacked jurisdiction over the claims brought by Georgia against the Russian Federation. Georgia requested the Court to dismiss the preliminary objections presented by the Russian Federation and to hold that the Court had jurisdiction to hear the claims presented by Georgia and that those claims were admissible.

On 1 April 2011, the Court delivered its Judgment on the preliminary objections raised by the Russian Federation. By 12 votes to 4, it rejected the first preliminary objection raised by the Russian Federation. By 10 votes to 6, it upheld the second preliminary objection raised by the Russian Federation. By 10 votes to 6, it found that it had no jurisdiction to entertain the application filed by Georgia.

In its Judgment, the Court, recalling its Order of 15 October 2008 [YUN 2008, p. 1401] indicating provisional measures, stated that the Order had ceased to be operative upon the delivery of the Judgment on the preliminary objections. It added, however, that the parties had a duty to comply with their obligations under the International Convention on the Elimination of All Forms of Racial Discrimination, of which they were reminded in that Order.

Application of the Interim Accord of 13 September 1995 (the former Yugoslav Republic of Macedonia v. Greece)

On 17 November 2008 [YUN 2008, p. 1402], the former Yugoslav Republic of Macedonia (FYROM) instituted proceedings against Greece for what it described as a flagrant violation of Greece's obligations under article 11 of the Interim Accord signed by the parties on 13 September 1995. In its application, FYROM requested the Court to protect its rights under the Interim Accord and to ensure that it was allowed to exercise its rights as an independent State acting in accordance with international law, including the right to pursue membership of international organizations. It contended that Greece violated its rights under the Accord by objecting, in April 2008, to its application to join the North Atlantic Treaty Organization (NATO). FYROM contended, in particular, that Greece vetoed its application to join NATO because Greece desired to resolve the difference between the parties concerning the constitutional name of FYROM as a precondition for its membership of NATO.

By an Order of 20 January 2009 [YUN 2009, p. 1274], the Court fixed 20 July 2009 as the time limit for the filing of a memorial by FYROM and 20 January 2010 as the time limit for the filing of a counter-memorial by Greece. Those pleadings were filed within the time limit.

By an Order of 12 March 2010 [YUN 2010, p. 1281], the Court authorized the submission of a reply by FYROM and a rejoinder by Greece. It fixed 9 June 2010 and 27 October 2010 as the respective time limits for the filing of those pleadings. The pleadings were filed within those time limits.

Public hearings were held from 21 to 30 March 2011. At the end of those hearings, the parties presented their final submissions. FYROM requested the Court to reject Greece's objections as to the jurisdiction of the Court and the admissibility of FYROM's claims; to adjudge and declare that Greece had violated its obligations under article 11 of the Interim Accord; and to order that Greece comply with its obligations under that article, and cease and desist from objecting to FYROM's membership of NATO and of any other international, multilateral and regional organization and institution of which Greece was a member, in circumstances where FYROM was to be referred to in such organization or institution by the designation provided for in paragraph 2 of Security Council resolution 817(1993) [YUN 1993, p. 208].

Greece requested the Court to adjudge and declare that the case brought by FYROM did not fall within the Court's jurisdiction and that the claims of FYROM were inadmissible; in the event that the Court found that it had jurisdiction and that the claims were admissible, that the claims were unfounded.

In its Judgment of 5 December 2011, the Court found, by 14 votes to 2, that it had jurisdiction to entertain the application filed by FYROM and that the application was admissible. By 15 votes to 1, it found that Greece, by objecting to the admission of FYROM to NATO, had breached its obligation under article 11 of the Interim Accord. By 15 votes to 1, it rejected all other submissions made by FYROM.

One judge and one ad hoc judge appended dissenting opinions to the Judgment; one judge appended a separate opinion; and one judge and one ad hoc judge appended declarations.

Jurisdictional Immunities of the State (Germany v. Italy; Greece intervening)

On 23 December 2008 [YUN 2008, p. 1402], Germany instituted proceedings against Italy, alleging that through its judicial practice Italy had infringed and continued to infringe its obligations towards Germany under international law.

In its application, Germany contended that Italian judicial bodies had repeatedly disregarded the jurisdictional immunity of Germany as a sovereign State. After Italy's Corte di Cassazione in 2004 rendered its judgment in the *Ferrini* case, where that court declared that Italy held jurisdiction with regard to a claim brought by a person who during the Second World War had been deported to Germany to perform forced labour in the armaments industry, numerous other proceedings were instituted against Germany before Italian courts by persons who had also suffered injury as a consequence of the armed conflict.

Germany requested the Court to adjudge and declare that Italy had failed to respect Germany's jurisdictional immunity under international law by allowing civil claims to be brought against Germany based on violations of international humanitarian law by the German Reich during the Second World War; by taking measures of constraint against Villa Vigoni, a German State property used for government non-commercial purposes; and by declaring Greek judgments based on similar occurrences enforceable in Italy. Accordingly, Germany requested the Court to adjudge and declare that Italy had to ensure that all decisions of Italian courts and other judicial authorities infringing Germany's immunity become unenforceable, and that in the future Italian courts would not entertain legal actions against Germany founded on the occurrences described.

As the basis for the Court's jurisdiction, Germany invoked article 1 of the European Convention for the Peaceful Settlement of Disputes of 1957, ratified by Italy on 29 January 1960 and by Germany on 18 April 1961.

By an Order of 29 April 2009 [YUN 2009, p. 1274], the Court fixed 23 June 2009 and 23 December 2009 as the time limits, respectively, for the filing of a memorial by Germany and a counter-memorial by Italy. Those pleadings were filed within the time limits.

In its counter-memorial, Italy, referring to article 80 of the Rules of Court, made a counter-claim and asked the Court to adjudge and declare that, considering the existence under international law of an obligation of reparation owed to the victims of war crimes and crimes against humanity perpetrated by the Third Reich, Germany had violated that obligation with regard to Italian victims of such crimes by denying them reparation; and that Germany must offer reparation to those victims, by means of its own choosing, as well as through the conclusion of agreements with Italy.

On 6 July 2010 [YUN 2010, p. 1281], the Court made an Order on the admissibility of Italy's counter-claim. The Court examined whether it had jurisdiction *ratione temporis* under the 1957 European Convention for the Peaceful Settlement of Disputes. It could only have jurisdiction if the dispute that Italy sought to submit by way of its counter-claim related to facts or situations occurring after the entry into force of the Convention as between the parties on 18 April 1961. That was not the case, and the dispute which Italy sought to submit was therefore excluded from the temporal scope of the Convention. By its Order, the Court, by 13 votes to 1, found that the counter-claim presented by Italy was inadmissible and did not form part of the proceedings. The Court then authorized the submission of a reply by Germany and a rejoinder by Italy, and fixed 14 October 2010 and 14 January 2011 as the respective time limits for the filing of those pleadings. The pleadings were submitted within the time limits.

On 12 January 2011, Greece filed an application for permission to intervene in the case under article 62 of the Court's Statute. In that application, Greece stated that it did not seek to become a party to the case.

By an Order of 4 July 2011, the Court authorized Greece to intervene in the case as a non-party, in so far as that intervention was limited to the decisions of Greek courts.

Public hearings were held from 12 to 16 September 2011, at the end of which the parties presented their final submissions to the Court.

Germany requested the Court to adjudge and declare that Italy, by allowing civil claims based on violations of international humanitarian law by the German Reich during the Second World War to be brought against Germany, had committed violations of obligations under international law in that it had failed to respect the jurisdictional immunity which Germany enjoyed under international law; by taking measures of constraint against Villa Vigoni had also committed violations of Germany's jurisdictional immunity; and by declaring Greek judgments based on occurrences similar to those defined above enforceable in Italy had committed a further breach of Germany's jurisdictional immunity.

Accordingly, Germany requested the Court to adjudge and declare that Italy must ensure that all the decisions of its courts and other judicial authorities infringing Germany's sovereign immunity become unenforceable, and that in the future Italian courts do not entertain legal actions against Germany founded on the occurrences described.

Italy requested the Court to adjudge and hold the claims of Germany to be unfounded. That request was subject to the qualification that Italy had no objection to any decision by the Court obliging Italy to ensure that the mortgage on Villa Vigoni inscribed at the land registry was cancelled.

Greece presented its observations to the Court on 14 September 2011.

Questions relating to the Obligation to Prosecute or Extradite (Belgium v. Senegal)

On 19 February 2009 [YUN 2009, p. 1274], Belgium instituted proceedings against Senegal, on the grounds that a dispute existed between them regarding Senegal's compliance with its obligation to prosecute the former President of Chad, Hissène Habré, or to extradite him to Belgium for criminal proceedings. Belgium also submitted a request for the indication of provisional measures, in order to protect its rights pending the Court's Judgment on the merits.

In its application, Belgium maintained that Senegal, where Mr. Habré had been living in exile since 1990, had taken no action on Belgium's repeated requests to see the former President prosecuted in Senegal, failing his extradition to Belgium, for acts including crimes of torture and crimes against humanity.

To found the Court's jurisdiction, Belgium first invoked the unilateral declarations recognizing the Court's compulsory jurisdiction made by the parties on 17 June 1958 (Belgium) and 2 December 1985 (Senegal). Moreover, Belgium indicated that the two States had been parties to the 1984 Convention against Torture since 21 August 1986 (Senegal) and 25 June 1999 (Belgium). Article 30 of that Convention provided that any dispute between two States parties concerning the interpretation or application of the Convention which it had not been possible to settle through negotiation or arbitration might be submitted to the ICJ by one of the States. Belgium contended that negotiations between the two States had continued unsuccessfully since 2005, and that it had reached the conclusion that those negotiations had failed. Belgium stated, moreover, that it had suggested recourse to arbitration to Senegal and that the latter had failed to respond, whereas Belgium had persistently confirmed that a dispute on that subject continued to exist.

Belgium requested the Court to adjudge and declare that the Court had jurisdiction to entertain the dispute; Belgium's claim was admissible; Senegal was obliged to bring criminal proceedings against Mr. Habré for acts including crimes of torture and crimes against humanity which were alleged against him as perpetrator, co-perpetrator or accomplice; and failing the prosecution of Mr. Habré, Senegal was obliged to extradite him to Belgium to answer for those crimes before the Belgian courts.

Belgium's application was accompanied by a request for the indication of provisional measures. It explained therein that while Mr. Habré was under house arrest in Dakar, Senegal might lift his house arrest if it failed to find the budget necessary to hold his trial. In such an event, it would be easy for Mr. Habré to leave Senegal and avoid prosecution, which would cause irreparable prejudice to the rights conferred on Belgium by international law and violate the obligations which Senegal must fulfil.

Public hearings were held from 6 to 8 April 2009 [YUN 2009, p. 1274] to hear the observations of the parties on Belgium's request for the indication of provisional measures. At the close of the hearings, Belgium asked the Court to request as provisional measures that Senegal keep Mr. Habré under the control and surveillance of the Senegalese authorities, so that the rules of international law with which Belgium requested compliance could be applied. Senegal asked the Court to reject the provisional measures.

In its Order made on 28 May 2009 [ibid.], the Court found, by 13 votes to 1, that the circumstances, as they presented themselves to the Court, were not such as to require the exercise of its power under article 41 of the Court's Statute to indicate provisional measures.

By an Order of 9 July 2009 [ibid.], the Court fixed 9 July 2010 and 11 July 2011 as the time limits, respectively, for the filing of a memorial by Belgium and a counter-memorial by Senegal. The memorial of Belgium was filed within the time limit.

By an Order of 11 July 2011, the President of the Court extended the time limit for the filing of the counter-memorial of Senegal from 11 July 2011 to 29 August 2011. The counter-memorial was filed within the time limit.

Jurisdiction and Enforcement of Judgments in Civil and Commercial Matters (Belgium v. Switzerland)

On 21 December 2009 [YUN 2009, p. 1276], Belgium initiated proceedings against Switzerland in respect of a dispute concerning the interpretation and application of the Lugano Convention of 16 September 1988 on jurisdiction and the enforcement of judgments in civil and commercial matters and the application of the rules of general international law governing the exercise of State authority, in particular in the judicial domain, and relating to the decision by Swiss courts not to recognize a decision by Belgian courts and not to stay proceedings later initiated in Switzerland on the subject of the same dispute.

In its application, Belgium stated that the dispute had arisen out of the pursuit of parallel judicial proceedings in Belgium and Switzerland in respect of the civil and commercial dispute between the main shareholders in Sabena, the former Belgian airline now in bankruptcy. The Swiss shareholders in question were SAirGroup (formerly Swissair) and its subsidiary SAirLines; the Belgian shareholders were the Belgian State and three companies in which it held the shares.

To found the Court's jurisdiction, Belgium cited the unilateral declarations recognizing the compulsory jurisdiction of the Court made by the parties on 17 June 1958 (Belgium) and 28 July 1948 (Switzerland).

By an Order of 4 February 2010 [YUN 2010, p. 1283], the Court fixed 23 August 2010 as the time limit for the filing of a memorial by Belgium and 25 April 2011 as the time limit for the filing of a counter-memorial by Switzerland.

By an Order of 10 August 2010 [ibid.], the President of the Court, at the request of Belgium and after having ascertained the views of Switzerland, extended the time limits for the filing of the memorial of Belgium and the counter-memorial of Switzerland to 23 November 2010 and 24 October 2011, respectively. The memorial of Belgium was filed within the time limit.

On 18 February 2011, Switzerland raised preliminary objections to the Court's jurisdiction and to the admissibility of the application in the case.

By a letter dated 21 March 2011, Belgium, referring to Article 89 of the Rules of Court, informed the Court that its Government, in concert with the Commission of the European Union, considered that it could discontinue the proceedings instituted against Switzerland, and requested the Court to make an Order recording Belgium's discontinuance of the proceedings and directing that the case be removed from the Court's General List. Belgium explained that it had taken note that, in its preliminary objections, Switzerland had stated that the reference by the Swiss Federal Supreme Court in its 30 September 2008 judgment to the non-recognizability of a future Belgian judgment did not have the force of res judicata and did not bind either the lower cantonal courts or the Federal Supreme Court itself, and that there was therefore nothing to prevent a Belgian judgment from being recognized in Switzerland. A copy of the letter from Belgium was communicated to Switzerland, which was informed that the time limit within which Switzerland might state whether it opposed the discontinuance of the proceedings had been fixed as 28 March 2011.

Since Switzerland did not oppose such discontinuance within the time limit, the Court ordered that the case be removed from the List on 5 April 2011.

Whaling in the Antarctic (Australia v. Japan)

On 31 May 2010 [YUN 2010, p. 1284], Australia instituted proceedings against Japan, alleging that Japan's continued pursuit of a large-scale programme of whaling under the second phase of its Japanese Whale Research Program under Special Permit in the Antarctic (JARPA II) was in breach of obligations assumed by Japan under the International Convention for the Regulation of Whaling, as well as its other international obligations for the preservation of marine mammals and the marine environment.

Australia requested the Court to adjudge and declare that Japan was in breach of its international obligations in implementing JARPA II in the Southern Ocean, and to order that Japan cease implementation of JARPA II; revoke any authorisations, permits or licences allowing the activities which were the subject of the application to be undertaken; and provide assurances and guarantees that it would not take any further action under JARPA II or any similar programme until such programme had been brought into conformity with its obligations under international law.

As the basis for the Court's jurisdiction, Australia referred to the declarations recognizing the Court's jurisdiction as compulsory made by Australia on 22 March 2002 and by Japan on 9 July 2007.

By an Order of 13 July 2010 [ibid.], the Court fixed 9 May 2011 as the time limit for the filing of a memorial by Australia and 9 March 2012 as the time limit for the filing of a counter-memorial by Japan. Australia filed its memorial within the time limit.

Frontier Dispute (Burkina Faso/Niger)

On 20 July 2010 [YUN 2010, p. 1284], Burkina Faso and the Niger jointly submitted a frontier dispute between them to the Court.

By a joint letter dated 12 May, the two States notified to the Court a Special Agreement signed in Niamey on 24 February 2009, which entered into force on 20 November 2009. Under the terms of article 1 of the Special Agreement, the parties had agreed to submit their frontier dispute to the Court, and each of them would choose an ad hoc judge. Article 2 of the Special Agreement indicated the subject of the dispute: the Court was requested to determine the course of the boundary between the two countries in the sector from the astronomic marker of Tong-Tong (latitude 14° 25' 04" N; longitude 00° 12' 47" E) to the beginning of the Botou bend (latitude 12° 36' 18" N; longitude 01° 52' 07" E).

The Court was further requested to place on record the parties' agreement on the results of the work of the Joint Technical Commission on demarcation of the Burkina Faso-Niger boundary with regard to the following sectors: the sector from the heights of N'Gouma to the astronomic marker of Tong-Tong, and the sector from the beginning of the Botou bend to the River Mekrou. In article 3, the parties requested the Court to authorize the following proceedings: a memorial filed by each party not later than nine months after the seizing of the Court; a counter-memorial filed by each party not later than nine months after exchange of the memorials; and any other pleading whose filing, at the request of either of the parties, should be authorized or directed by the Court. Under article 7 of the Special Agreement, the parties accepted the Judgment of the Court as final and binding. From the day on which the Judgment was rendered, the parties would have 18 months in which to commence the work of demarcating the boundary. In case of difficulty in implementing the Judgment, either party could seize the Court pursuant to article 60 of its Statute. The parties requested the Court to nominate, in its Judgment, three experts to assist them in the demarcation.

Lastly, article 10 contained the following "Special undertaking": pending the Judgment of the Court, the parties undertook to maintain peace, security and tranquillity among the populations of the two States in the frontier region, refraining from any act of incursion into the disputed areas and organizing regular meetings of administrative officials and the security services. With regard to the creation of socioeconomic infrastructure, the parties undertook to hold preliminary consultations prior to implementation. The Special Agreement was accompanied by an exchange of notes dated 29 October and 2 November 2009 embodying the agreement between the two States on the delimited sectors of the frontier.

By an Order of 14 September 2010 [YUN 2010, p. 1285], the Court fixed 20 April 2011 and 20 January 2012 as the respective time limits for the filing of a memorial and a counter-memorial by each of the parties. The memorials were filed within the time limits. The parties did not consider it necessary to submit additional pleadings and the case became ready for hearing.

Certain Activities carried out by Nicaragua in the Border Area (Costa Rica v. Nicaragua)

On 18 November 2010 [YUN 2010, p. 1285], Costa Rica instituted proceedings against Nicaragua in respect of an alleged incursion into, occupation of and use by Nicaragua's army of Costa Rican territory as well as alleged breaches of Nicaragua's obligations towards Costa Rica under a number of international treaties and conventions.

Costa Rica charged Nicaragua with having occupied, in two separate incidents, the territory of Costa Rica in connection with the construction of a canal across Costa Rican territory from the San Juan River to Laguna los Portillos (also known as Harbor Head Lagoon), and with having carried out related works of dredging on the San Juan River. Costa Rica stated that the ongoing and planned dredging and the construction of the canal would seriously affect the flow of water to the Colorado River of Costa Rica, and would cause further damage to Costa Rican territory, including the wetlands and national wildlife protected areas in the region.

Costa Rica accordingly requested the Court to adjudge and declare that Nicaragua was in breach of its international obligations regarding the incursion into and occupation of Costa Rican territory, the damage inflicted to its protected rainforests and wetlands, and the damage intended to the Colorado River, wetlands and protected ecosystems, as well as the dredging and canalization activities being carried out by Nicaragua on the San Juan River. In particular, the Court was requested to adjudge and declare that, by its conduct, Nicaragua had breached the territory of Costa Rica, as agreed and delimited by the 1858 Treaty of Limits, the Cleveland Award and the first and second Alexander Awards; the fundamental principles of territorial integrity and the prohibition of use of force under the UN Charter and the Charter of the Organization of American States; the obligation imposed upon Nicaragua by article IX of the 1858 Treaty of Limits not to use the San Juan River to carry out hostile acts; the obligation not to damage Costa Rican territory; the obligation not to artificially channel the San Juan River away from its natural watercourse without Costa Rica's consent; the obligation not to prohibit the navigation on the San Juan River by Costa Rican nationals; the obligation not to dredge the San Juan River if that caused damage to Costa Rican territory, including the Colorado River, in accordance with the 1888 Cleveland Award; the obligations under the Ramsar Convention on Wetlands; and the obligation not to aggravate and extend the dispute by adopting measures against Costa Rica, including the expansion of the invaded and occupied Costa Rican territory. The Court was also requested to determine the reparation to be made by Nicaragua.

As the basis for the Court's jurisdiction, Costa Rica invoked article 36, paragraph 1, of the Statute of the Court by virtue of the operation of article XXXI of the American Treaty on Pacific Settlement of 1948 (Pact of Bogotá), as well as the declarations of acceptance of the compulsory jurisdiction of the Court made by Costa Rica on 20 February 1973 and by Nicaragua on 24 September 1929 (modified on 23 October 2001).

Also on 18 November 2010 Costa Rica requested the Court to order provisional measures so as to rectify the ongoing breach of its territorial integrity and to prevent further irreparable harm to its territory, pending the determination of the case on the merits.

Public hearings on the request for the indication of provisional measures were held from 11 to 13 January 2011.

On 8 March 2011, the Court delivered its decision on Costa Rica's request for the indication of provisional measures. In its Order, it indicated the following provisional measures: it unanimously found that each party should refrain from sending to, or maintaining in the disputed territory, including the caño (the canal cut by Nicaragua), any personnel, whether civilian, police or security. By 13 votes to 4, it found that notwithstanding the point above, Costa Rica could dispatch civilian personnel charged with protecting the environment to the disputed territory, including the caño, but only insofar as it was necessary to avoid irreparable prejudice being caused to the part of the wetland where that territory was situated; Costa Rica should consult with the Secretariat of the Ramsar Convention in regard to those actions, give Nicaragua prior notice of them and find common solutions with Nicaragua in that respect. It unanimously found that each party should refrain from any action which might aggravate or extend the dispute or make it more difficult to resolve. It further unanimously found that each party should inform the Court as to its compliance with the provisional measures.

Appended to the Order were separate opinions by two judges and an ad hoc judge, and declarations by three judges and an ad hoc judge.

By an Order of 5 April 2011, the Court, taking account of the views of the parties, fixed 5 December 2011 and 6 August 2012, respectively, as the time limits for the filing of a memorial by Costa Rica and a counter-memorial by Nicaragua. The memorial of Costa Rica was filed within the time limit.

Request for Interpretation of the Judgment of 15 June 1962 in the Case concerning the Temple of Preah Vihear (Cambodia v. Thailand)

On 28 April 2011, Cambodia submitted a request for interpretation of the Judgment rendered by the Court on 15 June 1962 in the case concerning the *Temple of Preah Vihear (Cambodia* v. *Thailand)* [YUN 1962, p. 467].

In its application, Cambodia indicated the points in dispute as to the meaning or scope of the Judgment, as stipulated by Article 98 of the Rules of Court. It stated that according to Cambodia, the Court's 1962 Judgment was based on the prior existence of an international boundary established and recognized by both States; according to Cambodia, that boundary was defined by the map which enabled the Court to find that Cambodia's sovereignty over the Temple was a direct and automatic consequence of its sovereignty over the territory on which the Temple was situated. According to Cambodia, Thailand was under an obligation, pursuant to the Judgment, to withdraw any military or other personnel from the vicinity of the Temple on Cambodian territory. That was a general and continuing obligation deriving from the statements concerning Cambodia's territorial sovereignty recognized by the Court. Cambodia asserted that Thailand disagreed with all of those points.

Cambodia sought to base the Court's jurisdiction on article 60 of the Statute of the Court, which provided that in the event of dispute as to the meaning or scope of a Judgment, the Court would construe it upon the request of any party. Cambodia also invoked Article 98 of the Rules of Court.

Cambodia explained that, while Thailand did not dispute Cambodia's sovereignty over the Temple—and only over the Temple itself—it did, however, call into question the 1962 Judgment in its entirety.

Cambodia contended that in 1962, the Court had placed the Temple under Cambodian sovereignty, because the territory on which it was situated was on the Cambodian side of the boundary, and that to refuse Cambodia's sovereignty over the area beyond the Temple as far as its "vicinity" was to say to the Court that the boundary line which it recognized in 1962 was wholly erroneous, including in respect of the Temple itself.

Cambodia emphasized that the purpose of its request was to seek an explanation from the Court regarding the meaning and scope of its Judgment. Such an explanation, which would be binding on Cambodia and Thailand, could then serve as a basis for a resolution of the dispute through negotiation or any other peaceful means.

Cambodia asked the Court to adjudge and declare that the obligation incumbent upon Thailand to withdraw any military or police forces, or other guards or keepers, stationed at the Temple, or in its vicinity on Cambodian territory (point 2 of the operative clause of the Court's 1962 Judgment) was a consequence of the general and continuing obligation to respect the integrity of the territory of Cambodia, that territory having been delimited in the area of the Temple and its vicinity by the line on the map referred to on page 21 of the Judgment, on which the Judgment was based.

Also on 28 April, Cambodia filed a request for the indication of provisional measures. It explained that since 22 April 2011, serious incidents had occurred in the area of the Temple, as well as at several locations along that boundary between the two States, causing fatalities, injuries and the evacuation of local inhabitants. Cambodia stated that serious armed incidents were continuing at the time of filing its request for interpretation, for which Thailand was entirely responsible.

Cambodia requested the Court to indicate the following provisional measures, pending the delivery of its Judgment: an immediate and unconditional withdrawal of all Thai forces from those parts of Cambodian territory situated in the area of the Temple; a ban on all military activity by Thailand in the area of the Temple; and that Thailand refrain from any act or action which could interfere with the rights of Cambodia or aggravate the dispute.

Public hearings on Cambodia's request for the indication of provisional measures were held on 30 and 31 May 2011.

At the close of the second round of oral observations, Cambodia reiterated its request for the indication of provisional measures. Thailand, for its part, in accordance with Article 60 of the Rules of Court and having regard to Cambodia's request for the indication of provisional measures and its oral pleadings, requested the Court to remove the case from the General List.

On 18 July 2011, the Court delivered its Order on the request for the indication of provisional measures. Unanimously rejecting Thailand's request to remove the case from the General List, the Court indicated provisional measures: by 11 votes to 5, that both parties immediately withdraw their military personnel from the provisional demilitarized zone, as defined in paragraph 62 of the Order, and refrain from any military presence within that zone and from any armed activity directed at that zone; by 15 votes to 1, that Thailand not obstruct Cambodia's free access to the Temple of Preah Vihear or Cambodia's provision of fresh supplies to its non-military personnel in the Temple; by 15 votes to 1, that both parties continue their cooperation within the Association of Southeast Asian Nations (ASEAN) and allow the observers appointed by ASEAN to have access to the provisional demilitarized zone; by 15 votes to 1, that both parties refrain from any action that might aggravate or extend the dispute or make it more difficult to resolve; by 15 votes to 1, that each party inform the Court as to its compliance with the provisional measures; by 15 votes to 1, that until the Court rendered its Judgment on the request for interpretation, it would remain seized of the matters which formed the subject of the Order.

Appended to the Order were dissenting opinions by the President, three judges and an ad hoc judge; a separate opinion by one judge; and declarations by one judge and an ad hoc judge.

By letters dated 24 November 2011, the Registrar of the Court informed the parties that the Court had decided to afford them the opportunity of furnishing further explanations, and had fixed 8 March 2012 and 21 June 2012 as the respective time limits for the filing by Cambodia and Thailand of such explanations.

(For more information on political and security development, see p. 375.)

Construction of a Road in Costa Rica along the San Juan River (Nicaragua v. Costa Rica)

On 22 December 2011, Nicaragua instituted proceedings against Costa Rica with regard to violations of Nicaraguan sovereignty and major environmental damages to its territory. Nicaragua contended that Costa Rica was carrying out major construction works along most of the border area between the two countries with grave environmental consequences.

In its application, Nicaragua claimed that Costa Rica's unilateral actions threatened to destroy the San Juan de Nicaragua River and its fragile ecosystem, including the adjacent biosphere reserves and internationally protected wetlands that depended upon the clean and uninterrupted flow of the river for their survival. According to Nicaragua, the most immediate threat to the river and its environment was posed by Costa Rica's construction of a road running parallel and in close proximity to the southern bank of the river, and extending for at least 120 kilometres, from Los Chiles in the west to Delta in the east. It was also stated that those works had caused and would continue to cause significant economic damage to Nicaragua.

Nicaragua accordingly requested the Court to adjudge and declare that Costa Rica had breached its obligation not to violate Nicaragua's territorial integrity as delimited by the 1858 Treaty of Limits, the Cleveland Award of 1888 and the five Awards of the Umpire Edward Porter Alexander of 30 September 1897, 20 December 1897, 22 March 1898, 26 July 1899 and 10 March 1900; its obligation not to damage Nicaraguan territory; and its obligations under international law and environmental conventions, including the Ramsar Convention on Wetlands, the Agreement over the Border Protected Areas between Nicaragua and Costa Rica (International System of Protected Areas for Peace Agreement), the Convention on Biological Diversity and the Convention for the Conservation of the Biodiversity and Protection of the Main Wild Life Sites in Central America. Furthermore, Nicaragua requested the Court to adjudge and declare that Costa Rica must restore the situation to the status quo ante; pay for all damages caused, including the costs added to the dredging of the San Juan River; and not undertake any future development in the area without an appropriate transboundary environmental impact assessment, to be presented to Nicaragua for its analysis and reaction.

Finally, Nicaragua requested the Court to adjudge and declare that Costa Rica should cease all the constructions under way that affected or might affect the rights of Nicaragua; and produce and present to Nicaragua an adequate environmental impact assessment with all the details of the works.

As the basis for the Court's jurisdiction, Nicaragua invoked article 36, paragraph 1, of the Statute of the Court by virtue of the operation of article XXXI of the American Treaty on Pacific Settlement of 1948 (Pact of Bogotá), as well as the declarations of acceptance of the compulsory jurisdiction of the Court made by Nicaragua on 24 September 1929 (modified on 23 October 2001) and by Costa Rica on 20 February 1973. Nicaragua further asserted that Costa Rica had repeatedly refused to give it appropriate information on the construction works and had denied that it had any obligation to provide to Nicaragua an environmental impact assessment allowing for an evaluation of the works. Nicaragua therefore requested the Court to order Costa Rica to produce such a document and to communicate it to Nicaragua. It added that in all circumstances, and particularly if that request did not produce results, it reserved its right to request provisional measures.

Nicaragua also stated that as the legal and factual grounds of the application were connected to the ongoing case concerning *Certain Activities carried out by Nicaragua in the Border Area (Costa Rica v. Nicaragua)*" (see p. 1237), it reserved its rights to consider whether to request that the proceedings in both cases should be joined.

Advisory proceedings

Judgment No. 2867 of the Administrative Tribunal of the International Labour Organization upon a complaint filed against the International Fund for Agricultural Development

On 26 April 2010 [YUN 2010, p. 1287], the Court received a request for an advisory opinion from the International Fund for Agricultural Development (IFAD), aimed at obtaining the reversal of a judgment rendered by an administrative court, the Administrative Tribunal of the International Labour Organization (ILO).

In its Judgment No. 2867 (S-G. v. IFAD), delivered on 3 February 2010, the Tribunal found that it had jurisdiction under the terms of article II of its statute to rule on the merits of a complaint against IFAD introduced by Ms. S-G., a former staff member of the Global Mechanism of the United Nations Convention to Combat Desertification in those Countries Experiencing Serious Drought and/or Desertification, Particularly in Africa. Ms. S-G. held a fixed-term contract of employment which was due to expire on 15 March 2006. By a memorandum of 15 December 2005, the Managing Director of the Global Mechanism informed her that, due to a budget reduction, her post would be abolished and her contract would not be renewed.

Ms. S-G. filed an appeal with the IFAD Joint Appeals Board, which recommended in December 2007 that she be reinstated within the Global Mechanism for a two-year period and paid an amount equivalent to all the salaries, allowances and entitlements she had lost since March 2006. The President of IFAD rejected that decision in April 2008. Ms. S-G. filed a complaint against IFAD with the Tribunal on 8 July 2008. In its Judgment, the Tribunal decided that the decision of the President of IFAD should be set aside, and made orders for the payment of damages and costs.

The IFAD Executive Board, by a resolution adopted on 22 April 2010, acting within the framework of article XII of the annex of the statute of the Tribunal, decided to challenge the judgment of the Tribunal and to refer the question of the validity of that judgment to the Court for an advisory opinion.

The President of the IFAD Executive Board transmitted to the Court a request for an advisory opinion by a letter of 23 April 2010, which contained nine questions.

By letters dated 26 April 2010, the Registrar of the Court gave notice of the request for an advisory opinion to all States entitled to appear before the Court.

By an Order of 29 April 2010 [ibid.], the Court decided that IFAD and its Member States entitled to appear before the Court, the States parties to the United Nations Convention to Combat Desertification entitled to appear before the Court and those UN specialized agencies which had made a declaration recognizing the jurisdiction of the ILO Administrative Tribunal pursuant to article II of the statute of the Tribunal were considered likely to be able to furnish information on the questions submitted to the Court; fixed 29 October 2010 as the time limit within which statements on those questions could be presented to the Court; fixed 31 January 2011 as the time limit within which States and organizations having presented statements could submit comments on the other statements; decided that the President of IFAD should transmit to the Court any statement which the complainant might wish to bring to the attention of the Court; and fixed 29 October 2010 as the time limit within which any statement by the complainant could be presented to the Court and 31 January 2011 as the time limit within which any comments by the complainant could be presented to the Court.

On 26 October 2010, the General Counsel of IFAD submitted its statement and a statement setting forth the views of the complainant. On 28 October 2010, Bolivia submitted a statement.

By an Order of 24 January 2011, the Court extended to 11 March 2011 the time limit within which States and organizations having presented statements could submit comments on the other statements, as well as the time limit within which any comments by the complainant could be presented to the Court. The time limits were extended in response to a request made by the General Counsel of IFAD. The comments of IFAD and those of the complainant were presented within that limit.

Other questions

Functioning and organization of the Court

Composition of the Court

Election of judges

On 26 July [A/66/182-S/2011/452], the Secretary-General notified the General Assembly and the Security Council that the terms of office of five members of the Court would expire on 5 February 2012, and therefore the Assembly and the Council should elect five judges for a nine-year term of office beginning on 6 February 2012. On the same date [A/66/183-S/2011/453 & A/66/184-S/2011/454], the Secretary-General submitted the list of candidates nominated by national groups and their curricula vitae.

On 10 November, the Assembly and the Council elected four members of the Court to fill the vacancies occurring on 5 February 2012. On 13 December, the Assembly and the Council elected one additional member to fill the remaining vacancy (**decision 66/404A**).

Trust Fund to Assist States in the Settlement of Disputes

In August [A/66/295], the Secretary-General reported on the activities and status of the Trust Fund to Assist States in the Settlement of Disputes through the ICJ since the submission of his 2010 report [YUN 2010, p. 1289]. The Fund, established in 1989 [YUN 1989, p. 818], provided financial assistance to States for expenses incurred in connection with a dispute submitted to the Court by way of a special agreement or the execution of a judgment resulting from such an agreement. A further purpose of the Fund was to help States parties to a dispute to comply with Judgments rendered by the Court.

Between 1 July 2010 and 30 June 2011, the Fund did not receive any applications for financial assistance from States. One State contributed to the Fund, which as at 30 June had a balance of $891,205.79. Noting that the Fund had a decreasing level of resources since its inception, and that the number of contributions remained low, the Secretary-General urged States and other entities to consider making contributions to the Fund.

Chapter II

International tribunals and court

In 2011, the International Tribunal for the Prosecution of Persons Responsible for Serious Violations of International Humanitarian Law Committed in the Territory of the Former Yugoslavia since 1991 (ICTY) continued to expedite its proceedings, in keeping with its completion strategy. During the year, ICTY rendered three Trial Chamber judgements. Significant advances were made during the year with the arrests and transfer to The Hague of fugitives Ratko Mladić and Goran Hadžić.

The International Criminal Tribunal for the Prosecution of Persons Responsible for Genocide and Other Serious Violations of International Humanitarian Law Committed in the Territory of Rwanda and Rwandan Citizens Responsible for Genocide and Other Such Violations Committed in the Territory of Neighbouring States between 1 January and 31 December 1994 (ICTR) continued to work towards its completion strategy. In 2011, it rendered six Trial Chamber judgements and six Appeals Chamber judgements. One fugitive was arrested, yet nine remained at large. For the first time, ICTR referred a case to the courts of Rwanda for trial.

The International Criminal Court (ICC) continued its proceedings with respect to situations of concern in seven countries. On 26 February, the Security Council referred the situation in the Libyan Arab Jamahiriya since 15 February 2011 to the ICC Prosecutor. In June, arrest warrants were issued against Libyan leader Muammar Qadhafi, his son Saif al-Islam Qadhafi, Libyan Government Spokesman, and Abdullah Al-Senussi, Director of Military Intelligence, for crimes against humanity. In October, an arrest warrant was issued against Laurent Gbagbo, former President of Côte d'Ivoire, for crimes against humanity. Mr. Gbagbo was surrendered to the Court on 30 November. Eleven arrest warrants were outstanding at year's end.

International Tribunal for the Former Yugoslavia

In 2011, the International Tribunal for the Former Yugoslavia (ICTY), established by Security Council resolution 827(1993) [YUN 1993, p. 440] and based in The Hague, continued efforts to implement its completion strategy [YUN 2002, p. 1275], which was endorsed by Council resolution 1503(2003) [YUN 2003, p. 1330].

The Tribunal worked at full capacity to finalize the remaining trials and appeals and continuously re-evaluated its working methods to identify ways to expedite the proceedings. The Office of the Prosecutor continued to seek the cooperation of the States of the former Yugoslavia and other States to fulfil its mandate. The Registry played a crucial role in the provision of administrative and judicial support.

On 19 October, Judge Theodor Meron (United States) and Judge Carmel Agius (Malta) were elected to the position of President and Vice-President of the Tribunal, respectively, taking office on 17 November. The Registrar, John Hocking, and the Prosecutor, Serge Brammertz, continued to fulfil their duties. The Security Council adopted two resolutions—1993(2011) and 2007(2011)—addressing, among other issues, the extension of the terms of office of the judges and the Prosecutor.

ICTY President Meron informed the Security Council on 7 December [S/PV.6678] that the Tribunal continued to work as rapidly as possible, given the constraints imposed by limited resources and the need to ensure the highest standards of procedural fairness. Proceedings were ongoing against 35 persons—18 at the trial level in seven cases and 17 at the appellate level in six cases. It was anticipated that judgements in six trials would be issued in 2012, with the Karadzić judgement issued during 2014. He noted that it was impossible to predict when judgements would be issued in the cases of Ratko Mladić and Goran Hadžić, who were arrested during the year. One appeal judgement was expected to be delivered in 2012, with a further five delivered in 2013, including the two multi-accused cases of Šainović et al. and Popović et al.

The activities of ICTY were covered in two reports to the Security Council and the General Assembly, for the periods from 1 August 2010 to 31 July 2011 [A/66/210-S/2011/473] and from 1 August 2011 to 31 July 2012 [A/67/214-S/2012/592].

The Assembly took note of the 2010/2011 report on 11 November (**decision 66/512**).

The Chambers

During the year, the Tribunal's three Trial Chambers rendered three judgements involving five accused, while the Appeals Chamber rendered no judgements. Judicial activities included first instance and appeals proceed-

Chapter II: International tribunals and court

ings against judgements, interlocutory decisions, State requests for review, and contempt cases. As at 31 July, ICTY had 25 judges from 23 countries, including 13 permanent judges, two permanent judges from the International Criminal Tribunal for Rwanda serving in the Appeals Chamber, and 10 ad litem (short-term) judges.

New arrests and indictments

In 2011, significant advances were made in establishing accountability for the crimes committed during the wars in the former Yugoslavia. Foremost among them were the arrests of Ratko Mladić on 26 May and Goran Hadžić on 20 July. They were the last fugitives remaining at large out of the 161 persons indicted by the Tribunal.

Ratko Mladić had evaded capture for 16 years and was transferred to The Hague on 31 May. His initial appearance was held on 3 June and he did not enter a plea. A further appearance was held on 4 July, at which the presiding judge entered a plea of not guilty on his behalf.

Goran Hadžić was a fugitive of justice for seven years and was transferred to The Hague on 22 July. His initial appearance was held on 25 July and pre-trial preparations were under way.

Security Council action. The Security Council welcomed the arrest of Ratko Mladić by a press statement of 27 May [SC/10265]. Congratulating the Serbian authorities on the arrest, the Council shared the hope that the development would help to bring the Western Balkans closer to reconciliation and to their European perspective.

The Council, by a press statement of 20 July [SC/10334], welcomed the arrest of Goran Hadžić, the final fugitive sought by ICTY. Commending the Serbian authorities on his arrest, the Council recognized that it was an important moment for international justice and for the victims of war crimes in the former Yugoslavia.

Ongoing cases and trials

In the case against Ante Gotovina, Ivan Čermak, and Mladen Markač, the judgement was rendered on 15 April. Trial Chamber I convicted Messrs. Gotovina and Markač on eight counts of crimes against humanity and violations of the laws or customs of war and sentenced them to 24 and 18 years' imprisonment, respectively. The Trial Chamber acquitted Mr. Čermak on all counts. Their trial commenced on 10 March 2008 [YUN 2008, p. 1407]. The indictment against Mr. Gotovina, a former high-ranking Croatian military official, was unsealed in 2001 [YUN 2001, p. 1199]. After evading arrest for almost four years, he was arrested in 2005 in the Canary Islands by the Spanish authorities and transferred to The Hague [YUN 2005, p. 1388]. He was charged with crimes against humanity and violations of the laws or customs of war allegedly committed in Croatia in 1995 [YUN 1995, p. 580]. On 14 July 2006 [YUN 2006, p. 1489], the Trial Chamber joined two cases involving Mr. Gotovina and Messrs. Čermak and Markač [YUN 2004, p. 1276] in one indictment and accepted proposed amendments to the indictment. The three were charged with persecutions, deportation, inhumane acts, plunder of public or private property, wanton destruction of cities, towns or villages, murder and cruel treatment, all allegedly committed against Serbs in 1995, during and in the aftermath of a Croatian military offensive. At that time, Mr. Gotovina and Mr. Čermak were senior military commanders, while Mr. Markač was the commander of the Croatian Special Police. All three pleaded not guilty [YUN 2007, p. 1335].

In the case against Momčilo Perišić, the defence concluded its case on 11 January 2011. Final briefs were filed on 4 March and final arguments were heard on 28 March. The judgement was rendered on 6 September. Trial Chamber I found Mr. Perišić guilty of crimes against humanity and violations of the laws or customs of war, for crimes committed in Bosnia and Herzegovina and Croatia between August 1993 and November 1995. He was sentenced to 27 years' imprisonment. According to the indictment, Mr. Perišić, Chief of the General Staff of the Yugoslav Army, had aided and abetted the planning, preparation, or execution of a military campaign of artillery and mortar shelling and sniping onto civilian areas of Sarajevo, killing and wounding thousands of civilians. His trial commenced on 2 October 2008 [YUN 2008, p. 1409].

Radovan Karadžić, former President of Republika Srpska and Supreme Commander of its armed forces, was charged under 11 counts with genocide, crimes against humanity and violations of the laws or customs of war allegedly committed in Bosnia and Herzegovina between 1992 and 1995. The trial commenced on 26 October 2009 [YUN 2009, p. 1282]. The case was hearing the prosecution's case-in-chief.

Vojislav Šešelj was charged with nine counts of crimes against humanity and violations of the laws or customs of war, for acts allegedly committed in Croatia, Bosnia and Herzegovina, and Serbia between August 1991 and September 1993 [YUN 2003, p. 1311 & YUN 2004, p. 1277]. After the close of the prosecution's case-in-chief, Trial Chamber III on 4 May 2011 ruled that there was enough evidence to support the counts alleged in the indictment. On 9 June, the Chamber ordered Mr. Šešelj to file the lists of witnesses he intended to call and exhibits he intended to tender as evidence during his defence case. On 23 August, Mr. Šešelj confirmed that he would not present a defence case.

On 23 February, Trial Chamber II issued its judgement in the case of Vlastimir Đorđević, a former senior Serbian police official, finding him guilty of five counts of crimes against humanity and violations of the laws or customs of war committed through his participation in a joint criminal enterprise and for having aided and abetted the murder of 724 Kosovo Albanians, the deportation and forcible transfer of hundreds of thousands of Kosovo Albanians from more than 60 locations, and the destruction of Kosovo Albanian religious and cultural property. The Chamber sentenced him to 27 years' imprisonment. Mr. Đorđevic was arrested on 17 June 2007 [YUN 2007, p. 1337] and his trial commenced on 27 January 2009 [YUN 2009, p. 1280].

In the trial of Jadranko Prlić, Bruno Stojić, Slobodan Praljak, Milivoj Petković, Valentin Ćorić and Berislav Pušić, the parties filed their final briefs on 7 January 2011. Closing arguments were heard between 7 February and 2 March. Prlić et al. were charged with 26 counts of crimes against humanity and violations of the laws or customs of war for acts allegedly committed against Serbs and Muslims in the Croatian-held part of Bosnia and Herzegovina between November 1991 and April 1994 [YUN 2004, p. 1276]. The trial commenced on 26 April 2006 [YUN 2006, p. 1487].

In 2010, the Appeals Chamber had granted the prosecution's request for a reversal of the Trial Chamber's decision to acquit Ramush Haradinaj, Idriz Balaj and Lahi Brahimaj on certain counts in the indictment, ordering a partial retrial of the case [YUN 2010, p. 1292]. Their retrial commenced on 18 August 2011. The three accused were charged with six counts of violations of the laws or customs of war for acts allegedly committed in Kosovo in 1998. In a judgement of 3 April 2008 [YUN 2008, p. 1407], Mr. Brahimaj had been sentenced to six years of imprisonment, while Messrs. Haradinaj and Balaj had been acquitted.

In the trial of Jovica Stanišić and Franko Simatović, the prosecution concluded its case on 5 April. The defence for Mr. Stanišić commenced its case on 14 June and the defence for Mr. Simatović commenced its case on 13 December. Both were charged with crimes against humanity and violations of the laws or customs of war for acts allegedly committed in Croatia and Bosnia and Herzegovina between April 1991 and December 1995. Their trial commenced on 28 April 2008 and was adjourned by order of the Appeals Chamber of 16 May 2008 because of the ill health of Mr. Stanišić [YUN 2008, p. 1408]. The trial recommenced on 2 June 2009 [YUN 2009, p. 1281].

In the trial of Mićo Stanišić and Stojan Župljanin, the prosecution closed its case on 1 February 2011 and the defence concluded its case on 8 December. Both were charged with 10 counts of crimes against humanity and violations of the laws or customs of war for acts allegedly committed in 1992 in Bosnia and Herzegovina. Their trial commenced on 14 September 2009 [YUN 2009, p. 1281].

Zdravko Tolimir was charged with genocide, conspiracy to commit genocide, crimes against humanity, and a violation of the laws or customs of war allegedly committed in Bosnia and Herzegovina in 1995 [YUN 2008, p. 1409]. The trial commenced on 26 February 2010 [YUN 2010, p. 1291], and the prosecution's case-in-chief was close to completion.

Trial proceedings against Vojislav Šešelj, charged with contempt for having disclosed in a book information which might identify 11 protected witnesses, began on 22 February 2011 and ended on 8 June. On 9 May, Trial Chamber II issued an order in lieu of indictment charging Mr. Šešelj with contempt for failing to remove from his website confidential information in violation of an order of a Chamber. The initial appearance was held on 6 July.

In the trial of Shefqet Kabashi, Trial Chamber I on 31 August accepted his guilty plea to two charges of contempt for his failure to testify before the Tribunal in the case of Ramush Haradinaj et al. (see above). On 16 September, the Chamber sentenced Mr. Kabashi to two months' imprisonment.

The trial of Dragomir Pećanac was held on 30 November and 1 December. He was convicted of one count of contempt for his failure to appear at the Tribunal when subject to a subpoena in the Tolimir case (see above). On 9 December, Trial Chamber II sentenced Mr. Pećanac to three months' imprisonment.

Judges of the Court

Extension of terms of office

General Assembly action. Following up on Security Council resolution 1954(2010) [YUN 2010, p. 1295], the General Assembly, on 14 January, authorized Judge Kevin Parker and Judge Uldis Kinis to complete their cases, taking note of the Tribunal's intention to complete the cases by the end of February 2011 and March 2011, respectively (**decision 65/413 A**).

ICTY request for extension. On 27 June, the Secretary-General transmitted to the Security Council [S/2011/392] and to the General Assembly [A/65/893] a letter of 8 June from the ICTY President requesting the extension of the terms of office of ICTY judges, as the terms of office of the judges of the Trial Chambers and the Appeals Chamber would expire on 31 December 2011 and 31 December 2012, respectively. The President also requested that eight ad litem judges be permitted to serve beyond the cumulative period of three years provided for under the statute of the Tribunal.

SECURITY COUNCIL ACTION

On 29 June [meeting 6571], the Security Council unanimously adopted **resolution 1993(2011)**. The draft [S/2011/395] was submitted by Portugal.

The Security Council,

Taking note of the letter dated 27 June 2011 from the Secretary-General to the President of the Security Council attaching a letter dated 8 June 2011 from the President of the International Tribunal for the Former Yugoslavia ("the International Tribunal"),

Recalling its resolutions 827(1993) of 25 May 1993, 1503(2003) of 28 August 2003 and 1534(2004) of 26 March 2004, and its previous resolutions concerning the International Tribunal,

Recalling in particular its resolution 1966(2010) of 22 December 2010, by which the Council established the International Residual Mechanism for Criminal Tribunals ("the Mechanism") and requested the International Tribunal to take all possible measures to expeditiously complete all its remaining work no later than 31 December 2014, to prepare its closure and to ensure a smooth transition to the Mechanism,

Taking note of the assessments by the International Tribunal in its completion strategy report,

Recalling that in its resolution 1931(2010) of 29 June 2010 the Council underlined its intention to extend, by 30 June 2011, the terms of office of the trial judges at the International Tribunal based on the International Tribunal's projected trial schedule and requested the President of the International Tribunal to submit to the Council an updated trial and appeals schedule, and taking note of the updated trial and appeals schedule submitted by the President of the International Tribunal,

Noting the concerns expressed by the President of the International Tribunal about staffing, and reaffirming that staff retention is essential for the timely completion of the work of the International Tribunal,

Noting with concern the risk that there will be insufficient capacity for the enforcement of sentences imposed by the International Tribunal,

Urging the International Tribunal to take all possible measures to complete its work expeditiously as requested in resolution 1966(2010),

Acting under Chapter VII of the Charter of the United Nations,

1. *Decides* to extend the term of office of the following permanent judges at the International Tribunal, who are members of the Trial Chambers, until 31 December 2012 or until the completion of the cases to which they are assigned, if sooner:
—Mr. Jean-Claude Antonetti (France)
—Mr. Guy Delvoie (Belgium)
—Mr. Christoph Flügge (Germany)
—Mr. Burton Hall (Bahamas)
—Mr. O-gon Kwon (Republic of Korea)
—Mr. Bakone Melema Moloto (South Africa)
—Mr. Howard Morrison (United Kingdom of Great Britain and Northern Ireland)
—Mr. Alphonsus Martinus Maria Orie (Netherlands);

2. *Decides also* to extend the term of office of the following ad litem judges at the International Tribunal, who are members of the Trial Chambers, until 31 December 2012 or until the completion of the cases to which they are assigned, if sooner:
—Mr. Melville Baird (Trinidad and Tobago)
—Ms. Elizabeth Gwaunza (Zimbabwe)
—Mr. Frederik Harhoff (Denmark)
—Ms. Flavia Lattanzi (Italy)
—Mr. Antoine Kesia-Mbe Mindua (Democratic Republic of the Congo)
—Ms. Prisca Matimba Nyambe (Zambia)
—Ms. Michèle Picard (France)
—Mr. Árpád Prandler (Hungary)
—Mr. Stefan Trechsel (Switzerland);

3. *Reaffirms* the necessity of trial of persons indicted by the International Tribunal, reiterates its call upon all States, especially the States of the former Yugoslavia, to intensify cooperation with and render all necessary assistance to the International Tribunal, and, in particular, calls for the arrest of Mr. Goran Hadžić;

4. *Reiterates* the importance of the International Tribunal being adequately staffed to complete its work expeditiously, calls upon relevant United Nations bodies to intensify cooperation with the Secretariat and the Registrar of the International Tribunal and to take a flexible approach in order to find practicable solutions to address this issue as the International Tribunal approaches the completion of its work, and at the same time calls upon the International Tribunal to renew its efforts to focus on its core functions;

5. *Commends* States that have concluded agreements for the enforcement of sentences of persons convicted by the International Tribunal or have otherwise accepted such convicted persons to serve their sentences in their territories, and calls upon States to renew their commitment to the enforcement of sentences and to look positively on requests from the International Tribunal in this regard;

6. *Calls upon* States that have not concluded agreements for the enforcement of sentences of persons convicted by the International Tribunal or otherwise accepted such convicted persons to serve their sentences in their respective territories and that are able to do so to consider concluding these agreements or accepting such persons;

7. *Decides* to remain seized of the matter.

On 29 June [A/65/894], the Security Council President drew the General Assembly President's attention to Council resolution 1993(2011).

General Assembly action. On 19 July, the Assembly extended the terms of office of eight permanent judges who were members of the Trial Chambers, until 31 December 2012 or until the completion of the cases to which they were assigned, as well as the terms of office of nine ad litem judges who were members of the Trial Chambers, until 31 December 2012 or until the completion of the cases to which they were assigned (**decision 65/413 B**).

Nomination for reappointment. By a letter of 13 September to the Security Council [S/2011/566], the Secretary-General nominated Serge Brammertz for reappointment as ICTY Prosecutor for a four-year term effective 1 January 2012.

SECURITY COUNCIL ACTION

On 14 September [meeting 6613], the Security Council unanimously adopted **resolution 2007(2011)**. The draft [S/2011/569] was submitted by Portugal.

The Security Council,

Recalling its resolution 1786(2007) adopted on 28 November 2007,

Having regard to article 16 of the statute of the International Tribunal for the Former Yugoslavia,

Having considered the nomination by the Secretary-General of Mr. Serge Brammertz for reappointment as Prosecutor of the International Tribunal,

Recalling that in its resolution 1966(2010) of 22 December 2010 it called upon the International Tribunal to take all possible measures to expeditiously complete all its remaining work as provided for in that resolution no later than 31 December 2014,

Decides to reappoint Mr. Serge Brammertz as Prosecutor of the International Tribunal for the Former Yugoslavia, notwithstanding the provisions of article 16, paragraph 4, of the statute of the International Tribunal related to the length of office of the Prosecutor, for a term with effect from 1 January 2012 until 31 December 2014, which is subject to an earlier termination by the Security Council upon the completion of the work of the International Tribunal.

On 24 December, the Assembly decided that the agenda item on ICTY would remain for consideration during its resumed sixty-sixth (2012) session (**decision 66/557**).

Office of the Prosecutor

In 2011, the Office of the Prosecutor made significant advances in establishing accountability for the crimes committed during the wars in the former Yugoslavia. Foremost among them were the arrests of Ratko Mladić on 26 May and Goran Hadžić on 20 July. They were the last fugitives remaining at large out of the 161 persons indicted by the Tribunal. The prosecution expressed its commitment to moving ahead expeditiously with the trials.

Serge Brammertz continued his duties as Prosecutor [YUN 2008, p. 1412].

As at 31 July, the prosecution had finalized a large component of its trial work. The presentation of the prosecution's case-in-chief was completed in all but four cases, three cases were in the defence phase of the proceedings, and two cases had concluded and were awaiting judgement. That progress was achieved notwithstanding problematic rates of staff attrition in the Office of the Prosecutor, which had left remaining staff to shoulder heavy burdens. The Prosecutor expressed concern that staffing difficulties would likely escalate given the absence of incentives for staff to remain.

The Office began shifting its attention and resources to the appeals phase of proceedings to ensure that it was positioned to deal with the upcoming appellate caseload. The Office also worked at full capacity to finalize the remaining trials and appeals. The prosecution continuously re-evaluated its working methods to identify ways to expedite the proceedings. A consistent methodology was applied across all cases for streamlining the presentation of evidence in court: that methodology focused on narrowing the issues in dispute with defence teams as much as possible and presenting evidence in written form. Efficient use was made of key evidence contained in the wartime notebooks and associated tapes of Ratko Mladić, which had been located by the Serbian authorities in 2010. The Office established a task force to handle issues related to those materials.

With the completion of trial activities, the Office abolished corresponding posts and proceeded with downsizing. At the same time, preparations began for the transition of functions to the International Residual Mechanism for Criminal Tribunals, in accordance with Security Council resolution 1966(2010) [YUN 2010, p. 1306].

Regarding international cooperation, with the arrests of Ratko Mladić and Goran Hadžić and their transfer to the The Hague, Serbia had met a key obligation towards the Tribunal. The Office acknowledged the important work done by the Serbian authorities who brought about the arrests, particularly the National Security Council, the Action Team established to track the fugitives, and the operatives from the security services. The Prosecutor recognized Serbia's genuine commitment to cooperating with the Tribunal. He also encouraged Serbia to provide information on how the fugitives were able to evade justice for so long and help the public to understand why they had to stand trial. Serbia's National Council for Cooperation continued to improve cooperation among different government bodies handling requests from the Office of the Prosecutor. The Council facilitated prosecution requests to reclassify Supreme Defence Council documents in the Perišić case as public documents. As a result, the Prosecutor in March informed the Perišić Trial Chamber that those documents could be made public.

With regard to cooperation with Croatia, the Office of the Prosecutor reported that Croatia was generally responsive to its requests. Nevertheless, the Office's long-standing request for important military documents relating to Operation Storm—requested for the Gotovina et al. case—remained outstanding. The inter-agency task force established in 2009

[YUN 2009, p. 1285] to locate or account for the missing documents continued its administrative investigation. The Prosecutor asked Croatia to address inconsistencies and questions in connection with the task force's findings, which remained unresolved. The Prosecutor expressed disappointment that in the aftermath of the Gotovina et al. judgement, the highest State officials had failed to comment objectively on the outcome of the case.

The authorities of Bosnia and Herzegovina responded promptly and adequately to requests for documents, as well as access to archives and witnesses, and were asked to step up efforts against fugitive networks. The Office supported the work of the State Prosecutor and the Special Department for War Crimes in processing cases and investigative files transferred by the Tribunal. Structural difficulties, however, impeded the implementation of the National War Crimes Strategy. Political initiatives in Bosnia and Herzegovina that sought to undermine the work of the State Prosecutor's Office and the State War Crimes Court were of deep concern.

Cooperation in judicial matters among the States of the former Yugoslavia remained critical to completing the Tribunal's mandate. Judicial institutions in those States faced challenges in coordinating their activities, which in turn imperilled the rule of law and reconciliation in the region. There were some improvements in war crimes information and evidence-sharing between prosecutors in Bosnia and Herzegovina, Croatia and Serbia. Legal barriers to the extradition of suspects and the transfer of evidence across borders, however, as well as parallel investigations, obstructed proceedings. While regional prosecutors expressed a commitment to addressing the problem of parallel investigations, the Prosecutor called for action at the political and operational levels as well.

The fact that convicted war criminal Radovan Stanković, transferred from the Tribunal to Bosnia and Herzegovina pursuant to rule 11 bis, remained at large almost four years after he escaped from prison in Foča [YUN 2007, p. 392] was identified as a concern. The Prosecutor encouraged Bosnia and Herzegovina, as well as neighbouring States, particularly Serbia, to capture Mr. Stanković and to sanction those who facilitated his escape.

The Office worked to strengthen the capacity of national authorities to handle the remaining war crimes cases. To that end, it engaged in dialogue with its counterparts throughout the former Yugoslavia. It also supported training, the development of best practices and information exchanges.

The Office continued to support national prosecutions by facilitating access to investigative material and evidence from Tribunal case files, as well as its database. In addition, the "liaison prosecutors" project funded by the European Union was a key mechanism for strengthening working relationships between the State Prosecutor's Offices in Bosnia and Herzegovina, Croatia and the War Crimes Prosecutor's Office in Serbia.

The Registry

The Registry provided operational support to the Chambers and the Office of the Prosecutor, assisted the defence, and provided diplomatic and administrative support for the Tribunal. It also managed the UN Detention Unit, the Victims and Witnesses Section, the legal aid office and the interpretation and translation service. The Immediate Office of the Registrar supported the Registrar in his role as focal point for diplomatic relations, and maintained contact with embassies, Member States, the United Nations and other international organizations, including relations with the host State. The Office also negotiated agreements for the enforcement of the Tribunal's sentences with States, thereby ensuring that persons convicted by the Tribunal were transferred to serve their sentences. Efforts were made to raise the awareness of Member States regarding the lack of sufficient enforcement capacity and the ensuing risk to a successful completion of the Tribunal's mandate.

Following the adoption of Security Council resolution 1966(2010) [YUN 2010, p. 1306], in which the Council established the International Residual Mechanism for Criminal Tribunals, the Office was involved in the arrangements necessary for the commencement of the Mechanism's operations. Under the direction of the UN Office of Legal Affairs, the two International Tribunals worked jointly to develop a budget proposal for the biennium 2012–2013, a proposal for an information security and access regime for the archives of the Tribunals and the Mechanism, and the Rules of Procedure and Evidence for the Mechanism.

The Tribunal's Communications Service managed major media events, such as the arrest of Ratko Mladić, which brought about increased interest from the media, victims, the diplomatic community, academics and the general public. The outreach programme intensified its efforts to bring the Tribunal closer to the communities in the former Yugoslavia. It issued a publication entitled "Assessing the Legacy of the ICTY" in languages of the region. The programme expanded its reach to the region and international audiences through the Tribunal's accounts on YouTube and Twitter. The Tribunal's website continued to be a key strategic communications tool. In May, the Tribunal's website recorded 400,000 page views—the site's highest-ever monthly total since its launch in 2008.

Financing

2010–2011 biennium

The Secretary-General's second performance report on the ICTY budget for the 2010–2011 biennium [A/66/555], submitted in response to General Assembly resolution 65/253 [YUN 2010, p. 1297], reflected an increase of $6,960,500 gross (a decrease of $3,797,400 net) as compared with the revised appropriation for that biennium of $320,511,800 gross ($289,810,000 net). The Assembly was requested to revise the appropriation for 2010–2011 to the ICTY Special Account to $327,472,300 gross ($286,012,600 net).

In December [A/66/600], the Advisory Committee on Administrative and Budgetary Questions (ACABQ) recommended that the General Assembly approve the final appropriation proposed by the Secretary-General.

2012–2013 biennium

In September [A/66/386 & Corr.1], the Secretary-General submitted ICTY resource requirements for the 2012–2013 biennium, which before recosting amounted to $280,158,300 gross ($249,637,000 net) and reflected a decrease in real terms of $40,353,500 gross or 12.6 per cent ($40,173,000 net or 13.9 per cent) compared to the revised appropriation for 2010–2011. ACABQ, in December [A/66/600], recommended approval of those requirements, bearing in mind its observations and recommendations.

In December [A/66/605], the Secretary-General submitted revised estimates for the ICTY proposed budget for 2012–2013, arising from the effect of changes in rates of exchange and inflation, which after recosting amounted to $287,594,000 gross. ACABQ found no objections to the revised estimates and transmitted them to the General Assembly for consideration [A/66/7/Add.22].

GENERAL ASSEMBLY ACTION

On 24 December [meeting 93], the General Assembly, on the recommendation of the Fifth (Administrative and Budgetary) Committee [A/66/630], adopted **resolution 66/239** without vote [agenda item 145].

Financing of the International Tribunal for the Prosecution of Persons Responsible for Serious Violations of International Humanitarian Law Committed in the Territory of the Former Yugoslavia since 1991

The General Assembly,

I

Second performance report on the budget, for the biennium 2010–2011, of the International Tribunal for the Former Yugoslavia

Having considered the second performance report of the Secretary-General on the budget, for the biennium 2010–2011, of the International Tribunal for the Prosecution of Persons Responsible for Serious Violations of International Humanitarian Law Committed in the Territory of the Former Yugoslavia since 1991 and the related report of the Advisory Committee on Administrative and Budgetary Questions,

Recalling its resolution 47/235 of 14 September 1993 on the financing of the International Tribunal for the Former Yugoslavia and its subsequent resolutions thereon, the latest of which were resolutions 64/240 of 24 December 2009 and 65/253 of 24 December 2010,

1. *Takes note* of the second performance report of the Secretary-General on the budget, for the biennium 2010–2011, of the International Tribunal for the Former Yugoslavia and the related report of the Advisory Committee on Administrative and Budgetary Questions;

2. *Endorses* the conclusions and recommendations contained in section IV.B of the report of the Advisory Committee on Administrative and Budgetary Questions;

3. *Resolves* that, for the biennium 2010–2011, the amount of 320,511,800 United States dollars gross (289,810,000 dollars net) approved in its resolution 65/253 for the financing of the Tribunal shall be adjusted by the amount of 6,960,500 dollars gross (a decrease of 3,797,400 dollars net), for a total amount of 327,472,300 dollars gross (286,012,600 dollars net);

II

Budget for the biennium 2012–2013 of the International Tribunal for the Former Yugoslavia

Having considered the reports of the Secretary-General on the financing of the International Tribunal for the Former Yugoslavia for the biennium 2012–2013 and on the revised estimates arising from the effects of changes in rates of exchange and inflation,

Having also considered the related reports of the Advisory Committee on Administrative and Budgetary Questions,

1. *Takes note* of the reports of the Secretary-General on the financing of the International Tribunal for the Former Yugoslavia for the biennium 2012–2013 and on the revised estimates arising from the effects of changes in rates of exchange and inflation;

2. *Notes with appreciation* the support of the Government of the Netherlands for the work of the Tribunal;

3. *Endorses* the conclusions and recommendations contained in the related reports of the Advisory Committee on Administrative and Budgetary Questions, subject to the provisions of the present resolution;

4. *Recognizes* the critical importance of retaining highly skilled and experienced staff members with relevant institutional memory in order to successfully complete the trials and meet the targets set out in the completion strategy of the Tribunal;

5. *Commends* the Secretary-General for innovative solutions in applying the Staff Regulations and Rules of the United Nations for staff retention purposes;

6. *Reaffirms* paragraph 5 of its resolution 63/256 of 24 December 2008 and paragraph 6 of section II of its

resolution 64/239 of 24 December 2009, and requests the Secretary-General to utilize his existing authority under the existing contractual framework to offer contracts to staff, taking into account the needs of the Tribunal;

7. *Requests* the Secretary-General to continue to provide guidance to the Tribunal on all matters relating to the recruitment and administration of human resources;

8. *Encourages* the Secretary-General to exercise due diligence in applying staff rule 12.3 on exceptions to the Staff Rules in the context of the decisions on retention of the staff members in the Tribunal, and requests the Secretary-General to ensure that exceptions granted to the Tribunal based on the existing legislative framework shall not constitute a precedent for other United Nations entities;

9. *Requests* the Secretary-General to provide greater clarity on temporary posts and positions funded through general temporary assistance funds in his next report;

10. *Decides* to appropriate to the Special Account for the International Tribunal for the Prosecution of Persons Responsible for Serious Violations of International Humanitarian Law Committed in the Territory of the Former Yugoslavia since 1991 a total amount of 281,036,100 dollars gross (250,814,300 dollars net) for the biennium 2012–2013, as detailed in the annex to the present resolution;

11. *Also decides* that the financing of the appropriation for the biennium 2012–2013 under the Special Account shall take into account the estimated income of 299,500 dollars for the biennium, which shall be set off against the aggregate amount of the appropriation;

12. *Further decides* that the total assessment for 2012 under the Special Account, amounting to 147,328,800 dollars, shall consist of:

(*a*) 140,368,300 dollars, being half of the estimated appropriation approved for the biennium 2012–2013, after taking into account 149,750 dollars, which is half of the estimated income for the biennium of 299,500 dollars;

(*b*) 6,960,500 dollars, being the increase in the final appropriation for the biennium 2010–2011 approved by the General Assembly in paragraph 3 of section I above;

13. *Decides* to apportion the amount of 73,664,400 dollars gross (60,730,000 dollars net) among Member States in accordance with the scale of assessments applicable to the regular budget of the United Nations for 2012;

14. *Also decides* to apportion the amount of 73,664,400 dollars gross (60,730,000 dollars net) among Member States in accordance with the scale of assessments applicable to peacekeeping operations of the United Nations for 2012;

15. *Further decides* that, in accordance with the provisions of its resolution 973(X) of 15 December 1955, there shall be set off against the apportionment among Member States, as provided for in paragraphs 13 and 14 above, their respective share in the Tax Equalization Fund of the estimated staff assessment income of 25,868,800 dollars approved for the Tribunal for 2012.

ANNEX

Financing for the biennium 2012–2013 of the International Tribunal for the Prosecution of Persons Responsible for Serious Violations of International Humanitarian Law Committed in the Territory of the Former Yugoslavia since 1991

	Gross	Net
	(United States dollars)	
Estimated appropriation for the biennium 2012–2013	282,887,000	252,227,300
Revised estimates: effect of changes in rates of exchange and inflation	4,707,000	3,952,200
Recommendations of the Advisory Committee on Administrative and Budgetary Questions	—	—
Recommendations of the Fifth Committee	(6,557,900)	(5,365,200)
Estimated initial appropriation for the biennium 2012–2013	281,036,100	250,814,300
Less:		
Estimated income for the biennium 2012–2013	(299,500)	(299,500)
TOTAL assessment for 2012	**147,328,800**	**121,460,000**
Comprising:		
(a) Requirements representing half of the estimated appropriation for the biennium 2012–2013, after taking into account 149,750 dollars, which is half of the estimated income for the biennium 2012–2013 of 299,500 dollars	140,368,300	125,257,400
(b) Requirements arising from the final appropriation for the biennium 2010–2011	6,960,500	(3,797,400)
Of which:		
Contributions assessed on Member States in accordance with the scale of assessments applicable to the regular budget of the United Nations for 2012	73,664,400	60,730,000
Contributions assessed on Member States in accordance with the scale of assessments applicable to peacekeeping operations of the United Nations for 2012	73,664,400	60,730,000

On 24 December, the General Assembly decided that the agenda item on ICTY financing would remain for consideration during its resumed sixty-sixth (2012) session (**decision 66/557**).

International Tribunal for Rwanda

In 2011, the International Criminal Tribunal for Rwanda (ICTR), established by Security Council resolution 955(1994) [YUN 1994, p. 299] and based in Arusha, United Republic of Tanzania, delivered six Trial Chamber judgements and six Appeals Chamber judgements.

The efforts of the Office of the Prosecutor resulted in the arrest of one fugitive, who was transferred to the Tribunal in June. The Security Council adopted four resolutions—1995(2011), 2006(2011), 2013(2011) and 2029(2011)—addressing, among other issues, the reappointment of the Prosecutor, the extension of the terms of office of permanent and ad litem judges, and the eligibility and powers of ad litem judges.

In May [S/2011/317] and November [S/2011/731], the ICTR President reported on progress made in implementing the completion strategy. Addressing the Security Council on 7 December [S/PV.6678], the President said that all judgements projected for completion during the preceding six months were delivered and that the final multi-accused trial judgement would be delivered by the end of the year. Trial work was expected to be finished by mid-2012 and appeals work was on track to be completed by the end of 2014. One case remained in the evidence phase and was expected to finish by early 2012. Judgement would be rendered in the three remaining single-accused cases, all of which were projected to be delivered in the first half of 2012. Nine fugitives remained at large, and the Tribunal depended on the cooperation of Member States, especially those in the Great Lakes region, for their tracking, arrest and transfer.

The activities of ICTR were covered in two reports to the Security Council and the General Assembly, for the periods of 1 July 2010 to 30 June 2011 [A/66/209-S/2011/472] and 1 July 2011 to 30 June 2012 [A/67/253-S/2012/594]. The Assembly took note of the 2010/2011 report on 11 November (**decision 66/511**).

The Chambers

The Chambers were composed of 12 permanent judges and 10 ad litem judges at the end of June. Five permanent judges sat in the two Trial Chambers, while seven permanent judges sat in the Appeals Chamber.

New arrests

Bernard Munyagishari, wanted by the Tribunal on charges of genocide and crimes against humanity, was arrested in the Democratic Republic of the Congo on 25 May and transferred to Arusha on 14 June. He made his initial appearance before the Tribunal on 20 June, where he pleaded not guilty to the five counts against him.

Ongoing cases, trials and appeals

On 29 March, Trial Chamber III delivered its judgement in the case of Jean-Baptiste Gatete, a director in the Rwandan Ministry of Women and Family Affairs and former *bourgmestre* of Murambi commune (Byumba prefecture) [YUN 2002, p. 1285], sentencing him to life imprisonment for genocide and extermination as a crime against humanity. During the trial, 49 witnesses were heard over 30 trial days.

On 17 May, Trial Chamber II delivered a judgement in the "Military II" trial [YUN 2006, p. 1497]. The case involved four accused: François-Xavier Nzuwonemeye, former Commander of the Reconnaissance Battalion of the Rwandan army; Augustin Bizimungu, former Chief of Staff of the Rwandan army; Augustin Ndindiliyimana, former Chief of Staff of the *Gendarmerie nationale*; and Innocent Sagahutu, former Commander of Squadron A, Reconnaissance Battalion of the Rwandan army. Mr. Ndindiliyimana was sentenced to time already served and was ordered to be released immediately. Mr. Bizimungu was sentenced to 30 years' imprisonment, while Mr. Nzuwonemeye and Mr. Sagahutu were each sentenced to 20 years' imprisonment. The Chamber heard 217 witnesses over the course of 393 trial days.

On 24 June, Trial Chamber II delivered its judgement in the "Butare" case [YUN 1999, p. 1222 & YUN 2001, p. 1208]. The trial involved six accused: Pauline Nyiramasuhuko, former Minister of Family and Women's Development; Arsène Shalom Ntahobali, alleged leader of an Interahamwe group in Butare in April 1994; Sylvain Nsabimana, prefect of Butare from 19 April to 17 June 1994; Alphonse Nteziryayo, prefect of Butare from 17 June to July 1994; Joseph Kanyabashi, former *bourgmestre* of Ngoma commune in Butare prefecture; and Elie Ndayambaje, former *bourgmestre* of Muganza commune in Butare prefecture. The Chamber convicted the six of various crimes, including genocide and crimes against humanity, sentencing Ms. Nyiramasuhuko, Mr. Ntahobali and Mr. Ndayambaje to life imprisonment, Mr. Nsabimana to 25 years' imprisonment, Mr. Kanyabashi to 35 years' imprisonment, and Mr. Nteziryayo to 30 years' imprisonment. During the trial, the Chamber heard 189 witnesses over the course of 714 trial days.

On 30 September, Trial Chamber II delivered its judgement in the "Government II" case [YUN 2003, p. 1321]. The trial involved four Rwandan ministers during the genocide: Casimir Bizimungu, Justin Mugenzi, Prosper Mugiraneza and Jérôme-Clément Bicamumpaka. Messrs. Mugenzi and Mugiraneza were convicted of conspiracy to commit genocide and direct and public incitement to commit genocide, and were sentenced to 30 years of imprisonment. Messrs. Bizimungu and Bicamumpaka were acquitted on all counts, and their immediate release was ordered. In the course of the trial, the Chamber heard 171 witnesses over 404 trial days.

On 17 November, Trial Chamber III delivered its judgement in the case of Grégoire Ndahimana, a former *bourgmestre* of Kivumu commune in Kibuye prefecture. The Chamber sentenced Mr. Ndahimana to imprisonment for 15 years after finding him guilty of genocide and extermination as a crime against humanity. During the proceedings, the Chamber heard 45 witnesses and issued 14 written decisions. Mr. Ndahimana was arrested in August 2009 in the Democratic Republic of the Congo and made his initial appearance on 28 September 2009, when he pleaded not guilty to all counts [YUN 2009, p. 1288].

On 21 December 2011, Trial Chamber III rendered its judgement in the Karemera et al. trial against Édouard Karemera, former Vice-President of the Mouvement républicain national pour le développement et la démocratie (MRDN) and Minister of the Interior of the Interim Government, and Matthieu Ngirumpatse, former National Party Chairman of MRND and Chairman of its Executive Bureau. They were convicted of genocide, direct and public incitement to commit genocide, extermination, rape and sexual assault as crimes against humanity, and murder as causing violence to life, health and physical or mental well-being. Each was sentenced to life imprisonment. The Chamber heard 153 witnesses over 374 trial days. The third accused, Joseph Nziroera, former National Secretary of MRND, had died in custody [YUN 2010, p. 1300].

On 1 April, the Appeals Chamber reversed some of Colonel Tharcisse Renzaho's convictions while affirming convictions for genocide and murder as a crime against humanity and a serious violation of article 3 common to the Geneva Conventions and of Additional Protocol II thereto. The Chamber also affirmed Mr. Renzaho's sentence. The trial of Colonel Renzaho, former prefect of Kigali-ville, charged with six counts of genocide, complicity in genocide, crimes against humanity and violations of the Geneva Conventions and Additional Protocol II, began on 8 January 2007 [YUN 2007, p. 1343]. He was sentenced to life imprisonment on 14 July 2009 [YUN 2009, p. 1289].

In its judgement of 1 April 2011, the Appeals Chamber affirmed the conviction and sentence of Tharcisse Muvunyi. Mr. Muvunyi, a former lieutenant-colonel stationed at the École des sous-officiers in Butare, was convicted in 2006 of direct and public incitement to commit genocide and sentenced to 15 years' imprisonment [YUN 2006, p. 1495]. His retrial took place in 2009 and related to one allegation of the indictment, namely incitement to commit genocide [YUN 2009, p. 1290].

The Appeals Chamber on 28 September rendered its judgement in the case of Yussuf Munyakazi, and affirmed his convictions and sentence after hearing the parties' appeals on 28 March. Mr. Munyakazi, a businessman and former leader of a militia group in Cyangugu prefecture [YUN 2004, p. 1286], was convicted in 2010 of genocide and extermination as a crime against humanity and sentenced to 25 years of imprisonment [YUN 2010, p. 1298].

The Appeals Chamber on 28 September rendered its judgement in the case of Ephrem Setako: it affirmed his convictions, entered an additional conviction for serious violations of article 3 common to the Geneva Conventions and of Additional Protocol II thereto, and affirmed the sentence. Mr. Setako, a former senior official of the Ministry of Defence [YUN 2004, p. 1286] was convicted in 2010 of genocide, extermination as a crime against humanity and serious violations of article 3 common to the Geneva Conventions and of Additional Protocol II thereto and was sentenced to 25 years of imprisonment [YUN 2010, p. 1299].

On 14 December, the Appeals Chamber reversed the conviction of Dominique Ntawukulilyayo for ordering genocide, while affirming his conviction for aiding and abetting genocide. The Chamber set aside his sentence and imposed a new sentence of 20 years of imprisonment. In 2010, the Trial Chamber had convicted Mr. Ntawukulilyayo, a former sub-prefect in Butare prefecture, of genocide, sentencing him to 25 years' imprisonment [YUN 2010, p. 1299]. His appeal was heard on 26 September 2011.

From 30 March to 1 April, the Appeals Chamber heard appeals brought by Théoneste Bagosora, the former *Directeur de cabinet* in the Ministry of Defence, and Anatole Nsengiyumva, the former Commander of the Gisenyi Operational Sector, with regard to the trial judgement rendered by Trial Chamber I on 18 December 2008 [YUN 2008, p. 1417]. The Appeals Chamber rendered its judgement on 14 December 2011. It affirmed Mr. Bagosora's convictions for genocide, murder, extermination, persecution, rape and other inhumane acts as crimes against humanity and as serious violations of article 3 common to the Geneva Conventions and of Additional Protocol II thereto. The Chamber reversed his convictions for certain killings and set aside the finding that he was responsible for ordering certain crimes, finding him liable as a superior instead. In addition, the Chamber reversed a number of his convictions for murder and for other inhumane acts as crimes against humanity. As a consequence, the Chamber set aside his sentence of life imprisonment and imposed a sentence of 35 years of imprisonment. In respect of Mr. Nsengiyumva, the Appeals Chamber affirmed his convictions for genocide, extermination and persecution as crimes against humanity, and as serious violations of Article 3 common to the Geneva Conventions and of Additional Protocol II thereto in relation to certain killings. The Chamber reversed his convictions for other killings as well as his convictions for murder as a crime against humanity. In addition, the Chamber set aside the finding that he was responsible for ordering certain killings, finding him liable as a superior instead. The Chamber considered that the reversal of nearly all of his convictions called for a revision of his life sentence and entered a new sentence of 15 years of imprisonment.

In the case of Aloys Ntabakuze, the former commander of a para-commando battalion of the Rwandan army, the Appeals Chamber heard his appeal on 27 September, since his counsel was unavailable for the scheduled hearing of his appeal from 30 March to 1 April. Mr. Ntabakuze had been sentenced to life imprisonment on 18 December 2008 [YUN 2008, p. 1417].

In the case of Gaspard Kanyarukiga, a former businessman, who was convicted on 1 November 2010 of genocide and extermination as a crime against humanity and sentenced to 30 years of imprisonment [YUN 2010, p. 1299], the Appeals Chamber heard the parties' appeals on 14 December 2011. Mr. Kanyarukiga was arrested and transferred to the Tribunal in 2004 on charges of genocide, complicity in genocide, conspiracy to commit genocide and extermination as a crime against humanity [YUN 2004, p. 1286].

The Appeals Chamber on 15 December heard the parties in the case of Ildephonse Hategekimana, the former commander of the Ngoma Military Camp in Butare, who on 6 December 2010 was convicted of genocide, murder and rape as crimes against humanity and sentenced to life imprisonment [YUN 2010, p. 1299].

On 29 June 2011, a Chamber referred the case against Jean Uwinkindi, apprehended in Uganda in 2010 and transferred to the Tribunal [YUN 2010, p. 1298], to the courts of Rwanda. Another Chamber deferred hearing the referral applications of fugitives Charles Sikubwabo and Fulgence Kayishema until the accused were arrested or until a final decision was rendered in the Uwinkindi case.

On 27 July, the Tribunal transferred Emmanuel Rukundo [YUN 2010, p. 1300] to Mali to serve the remainder of his sentence.

Judges of the Court

Extension of terms of office and ad litem judges

General Assembly action. On 14 January, the General Assembly, following up on Security Council resolution 1955(2010) [YUN 2010, p. 1302], authorized three ICTR judges to complete their cases and temporarily increased the number of ad litem judges to a maximum of 12, in order to allow the Tribunal to complete existing trials or conduct additional ones (**decision 65/412**).

ICTR requests. On 20 May [A/65/855-S/2011/329], the Secretary-General transmitted to the Security Council and General Assembly Presidents a letter of 5 May from the ICTR President, Dennis Byron, related to filling the position of ICTR President. Owing to the forthcoming resignation of two judges and the redeployment of four, the Tribunal would be left without any Arusha-based permanent judges. The President therefore requested amendments to the Statute of the Tribunal in order to allow the President to be a member of the Appeals Chamber and to be based in The Hague. As an alternative, if it was decided that the President should continue to be a member of one of the Trial Chambers and to be based in Arusha, the Statute could be amended to allow an ad litem judge to be eligible for election as President. A second request was that the current President be permitted to work part-time at the Tribunal and simultaneously engage in another occupation from 1 September, since he had been appointed as President of the Caribbean Court of Justice and would be sworn in on 1 September. The President intended to resign from the Tribunal upon the delivery of the judgement in the Karemera et al. case around December.

ICTR report. In a May assessment report to the Security Council [S/2011/317], the ICTR President noted that one permanent and one ad litem judge would demit office at the end of May when the "Military II" judgement was delivered. Another permanent judge and an ad litem judge would demit office when the Karemera et al. and Bizimungu et al. judgements were delivered. That left four permanent judges and nine ad litem judges. All four permanent judges were assigned to the Appeals Chamber after the completion of their cases. In those circumstances, without some adjustment to the rules which required that the Office of President be held by a permanent judge of the Trial Chambers, there was no one eligible to hold office as of early 2012. The Tribunal had therefore asked that the Council approve its request that an ad litem judge might be elected Vice-President with provision to become President on the deployment of the President to the Appeals Chamber or, alternatively, allow the President to be a member of the Appeals Chamber.

SECURITY COUNCIL ACTION

On 6 July [meeting 6573], the Security Council unanimously adopted **resolution 1995(2011)**. The draft [S/2011/410] was submitted by Portugal.

The Security Council,

Taking note of the letter dated 20 May 2011 from the Secretary-General to the President of the Security Council attaching a letter dated 5 May 2011 from the President of the International Criminal Tribunal for Rwanda ("the International Tribunal"),

Recalling its resolutions 955(1994) of 8 November 1994, 1503(2003) of 28 August 2003 and 1534(2004) of 26 March 2004 and its previous resolutions concerning the International Tribunal,

Recalling also its resolution 1966(2010) of 22 December 2010 establishing the International Residual Mechanism for Criminal Tribunals ("the Mechanism") and requesting the International Tribunal to take all possible measures to expeditiously complete all its remaining work no later than 31 December 2014, prepare its closure and ensure a smooth transition to the Mechanism,

Recalling further that the branch of the Mechanism for the International Criminal Tribunal for Rwanda shall commence functioning on 1 July 2012,

Taking note of the assessments by the International Tribunal in its completion strategy report,

Noting that, upon the completion of the cases to which they are assigned, four permanent judges will be redeployed from the Trial Chambers to the Appeals Chamber and two permanent judges will leave the International Tribunal,

Noting also the concerns expressed by the President and Prosecutor of the International Tribunal about staffing, and reaffirming that staff retention is essential for the timely completion of the work of the International Tribunal,

Urging the International Tribunal to take all possible measures to complete its work expeditiously as requested in resolution 1966(2010),

Acting under Chapter VII of the Charter of the United Nations,

1. *Decides* that, notwithstanding article 13, paragraph 1, and article 12 quater, paragraph 2 (*a*), of the statute of the International Tribunal, ad litem judges may be eligible for election as, and may vote in the election of, the President of the International Tribunal;

2. *Decides also*, in this regard, that, notwithstanding article 12 quater, paragraph 2, of the statute of the International Tribunal, an ad litem judge elected as President of the International Tribunal may exercise the same powers as a permanent judge, which will not alter his or her status or give rise to any additional allowances or benefits other than those which already exist, and will effect no changes of the current terms and conditions of service as an ad litem judge;

3. *Decides further* that, notwithstanding article 12 quater, paragraph 2, of the statute of the International Tribunal, an ad litem judge elected as Vice-President of the International Tribunal may act as President when required to do so under the statute or the Rules of Procedure and Evidence, which will not alter his or her status or give rise to any additional allowances or benefits other than those which already exist, and will effect no changes of the current terms and conditions of service as an ad litem judge;

4. *Decides*, in the light of the exceptional circumstances, that, notwithstanding article 12 bis, paragraph 3, of the statute of the International Tribunal, Judge Dennis Byron may work part-time and engage in another judicial occupation from 1 September 2011 until the completion of the case to which he is assigned, takes note of the intention of the International Tribunal to complete the case by December 2011, and underscores that this exceptional authorization shall not be considered as establishing a precedent. The President of the International Tribunal shall have the responsibility to ensure that this arrangement is compatible with the independence and impartiality of the judge, does not give rise to conflicts of interest and does not delay the delivery of the judgement;

5. *Reaffirms* the necessity of trial of persons indicted by the International Tribunal and reiterates its call upon all States, especially the States of the Great Lakes region, to intensify cooperation with and render all necessary assistance to the International Tribunal, and, in particular, calls upon relevant States to increase their efforts to bring Mr. Félicien Kabuga, Mr. Augustin Bizimana, Mr. Protais Mpiranya and other indictees of the International Tribunal to justice;

6. *Reiterates* the importance of the International Tribunal being adequately staffed to complete its work expeditiously, calls upon relevant United Nations bodies to intensify cooperation with the Secretariat and the Registrar of the International Tribunal and to take a flexible approach in order to find practicable solutions to address this issue as the International Tribunal approaches the completion of its work, and at the same time calls upon the International Tribunal to renew its efforts to focus on its core functions;

7. *Commends* States that have accepted the relocation of acquitted persons or convicted persons who have completed serving their sentences to their territories, and calls upon other States in a position to do so to cooperate with and render all necessary assistance to the International Tribunal in the relocation of acquitted persons and convicted persons who have completed serving their sentences;

8. *Decides* to remain seized of the matter.

Nomination for reappointment. By a letter of 7 September to the Security Council [S/2011/561], the Secretary-General requested the Council to reappoint Hassan Bubacar Jallow as Prosecutor, effective 15 September, for a four-year term, subject to an earlier termination in view of the expectation that the Tribunal would complete its work before the expiry of the four-year term.

SECURITY COUNCIL ACTION

On 14 September [meeting 6612], the Security Council unanimously adopted **resolution 2006(2011)**. The draft [S/2011/567] was submitted by Portugal.

The Security Council,

Recalling its resolution 1774(2007) adopted on 14 September 2007,

Having regard to article 15 of the statute of the International Criminal Tribunal for Rwanda,

Having considered the nomination by the Secretary-General of Mr. Hassan Bubacar Jallow for reappointment as Prosecutor of the International Tribunal,

Recalling that in its resolution 1966(2010) of 22 December 2010 it called upon the International Tribunal to take all possible measures to expeditiously complete all its remaining work as provided for in that resolution no later than 31 December 2014,

Decides to reappoint Mr. Hassan Bubacar Jallow as Prosecutor of the International Criminal Tribunal for Rwanda, notwithstanding the provisions of article 15, paragraph 4, of the statute of the International Tribunal related to the length of office of the Prosecutor, for a term with effect from 15 September 2011 until 31 December 2014, which is subject to an earlier termination by the Security Council upon the completion of the work of the International Tribunal.

ICTR request. On 30 September [S/2011/609], the Secretary-General transmitted to the Security Council a 26 September letter from the ICTR President, requesting permission for Judge Bakhtiyar Tuzmukhamedov to work part-time at ICTR and to engage simultaneously in another judicial occupation from 28 September to 31 December. During that period he would complete his duties at the Russian Constitutional Court. Judge Tuzmukhamedov intended to resume full-time work at the Tribunal thereafter, in order to complete the Nzabonimana case. The Secretary-General noted that the judge's term of office would expire on 31 December, and that the ICTR President would seek permission for the judge to continue serving at the Tribunal beyond that date and might request his redeployment to the Tribunal's Appeals Chamber.

SECURITY COUNCIL ACTION

On 14 October [meeting 6632], the Security Council unanimously adopted **resolution 2013(2011)**. The draft [S/2011/636] was submitted by Portugal.

The Security Council,

Taking note of the letter dated 30 September 2011 from the Secretary-General to the President of the Security Council attaching a letter dated 26 September 2011 from the President of the International Criminal Tribunal for Rwanda ("the International Tribunal"),

Recalling its resolutions 955(1994) of 8 November 1994, 1503(2003) of 28 August 2003 and 1534(2004) of 26 March 2004 and its previous resolutions concerning the International Tribunal,

Recalling also its resolution 1966(2010) of 22 December 2010 establishing the International Residual Mechanism for Criminal Tribunals ("the Mechanism") and requesting the International Tribunal to take all possible measures to expeditiously complete all its remaining work no later than 31 December 2014, prepare its closure and ensure a smooth transition to the Mechanism,

Noting that, upon the completion of the cases to which they are assigned, four permanent judges will be redeployed from the Trial Chambers to the Appeals Chamber and two permanent judges will leave the International Tribunal,

Urging the International Tribunal to take all possible measures to complete its work expeditiously as requested in resolution 1966(2010),

Acting under Chapter VII of the Charter of the United Nations,

1. *Decides*, in the light of the exceptional circumstances, that, notwithstanding article 12 bis, paragraph 3, of the statute of the International Tribunal, Judge Bakhtiyar Tuzmukhamedov may work part-time and engage in another judicial occupation until 31 December 2011, and takes note of Judge Tuzmukhamedov's commitment to ensuring timely delivery of judgement in the two cases in which he is currently involved;

2. *Underscores* that this exceptional authorization shall not be considered as establishing a precedent. The President of the International Tribunal shall have the responsibility to ensure that this arrangement is compatible with the independence and impartiality of the judge, does not give rise to conflicts of interest and does not delay the delivery of the judgement;

3. *Decides* to remain seized of the matter.

ICTR requests for extension. On 16 December [A/66/620-S/2011/780], the Secretary-General transmitted to the Security Council and the General Assembly a 26 November letter from the ICTR President requesting the extension of the terms of office of four permanent judges and seven ad litem judges until 30 June 2012 or until the completion of the cases to which they were assigned.

On 20 December [A/66/625-S/2011/781], the Secretary-General transmitted to the Council and the Assembly a letter of 13 December from the ICTR President, requesting the extension of the term of office of an ad litem judge until 30 June 2012 or until the completion of the cases to which she was assigned.

SECURITY COUNCIL ACTION

On 21 December [meeting 6694], the Security Council unanimously adopted **resolution 2029(2011)**. The draft [S/2011/787] was submitted by Portugal.

The Security Council,

Taking note of the letters dated 16 and 20 December 2011 from the Secretary-General to the President of the Security Council attaching letters dated 26 November and 13 December 2011, respectively, from the President of the International Criminal Tribunal for Rwanda ("the International Tribunal"),

Recalling its resolutions 955(1994) of 8 November 1994, 1503(2003) of 28 August 2003 and 1534(2004) of 26 March 2004 and its previous resolutions concerning the International Tribunal,

Recalling also its resolution 1966(2010) of 22 December 2010 establishing the International Residual Mechanism for Criminal Tribunals ("the Mechanism") and requesting the International Tribunal to take all possible measures to expeditiously complete all its remaining work no later than 31 December 2014, prepare its closure and ensure a smooth transition to the Mechanism,

Recalling further that the branch of the Mechanism for the International Criminal Tribunal for Rwanda shall commence functioning on 1 July 2012,

Taking note of the assessments by the International Tribunal in its completion strategy report, and the updated trial and appeals schedule,

Noting that, upon the completion of the cases to which they are assigned, three permanent judges will be redeployed from the Trial Chambers to the Appeals Chamber, and two ad litem judges will leave the International Tribunal,

Noting also the concerns expressed by the President and Prosecutor of the International Tribunal about staffing, and reaffirming that staff retention is essential for the timely completion of the work of the International Tribunal,

Noting with concern that the International Tribunal continues to face problems in the relocation of acquitted persons and convicted persons who have completed serving their sentences,

Urging the International Tribunal to take all possible measures to complete its work expeditiously as requested in resolution 1966(2010),

Acting under Chapter VII of the Charter of the United Nations,

1. *Decides* to extend the term of office of the following permanent judges at the International Tribunal, who are members of the Trial Chambers, until 30 June 2012

or until the completion of the trials to which they are assigned, if sooner:
—Sir Charles Michael Dennis Byron (Saint Kitts and Nevis)
—Ms. Khalida Rachid Khan (Pakistan)
—Mr. William H. Sekule (United Republic of Tanzania)
—Mr. Bakhtiyar Tuzmukhamedov (Russian Federation);

2. *Decides also* to extend the term of office of the following ad litem judges at the International Tribunal, who are members of the Trial Chambers, until 30 June 2012 or until the completion of the trials to which they are assigned, if sooner:
—Ms. Florence Rita Arrey (Cameroon)
—Ms. Solomy Balungi Bossa (Uganda)
—Mr. Robert Fremr (Czech Republic)
—Mr. Vagn Joensen (Denmark)
—Mr. Gberdao Gustave Kam (Burkina Faso)
—Mr. Lee Gacuiga Muthoga (Kenya)
—Mr. Seon Ki Park (Republic of Korea)
—Mr. Mparany Mamy Richard Rajohnson (Madagascar);

3. *Reiterates* the importance of the International Tribunal being adequately staffed to complete its work expeditiously, and calls upon relevant United Nations bodies to intensify cooperation with the Secretariat and the Registrar of the International Tribunal and to take a flexible approach in order to find practicable solutions to address this issue as the International Tribunal approaches the completion of its work, and at the same time calls upon the International Tribunal to renew its efforts to focus on its core functions;

4. *Urges* all States, especially States where fugitives are suspected to be at large, to intensify further their cooperation with and render all necessary assistance to the International Tribunal, in particular to achieve the arrest and surrender of all remaining fugitives as soon as possible;

5. *Commends* States that have accepted the relocation of acquitted persons or convicted persons who have completed serving their sentences to their territories, and reiterates its call upon other States in a position to do so to cooperate with and render all necessary assistance to the International Tribunal in the relocation of acquitted persons and convicted persons who have completed serving their sentences;

6. *Decides* to remain seized of the matter.

On 24 December, the Assembly decided that the agenda item on ICTR would remain for consideration during its resumed sixty-sixth (2012) session (**decision 66/557**).

Office of the Prosecutor

The Office of the Prosecutor focused its efforts on the completion of the ongoing trials, the commencement of one new trial and the preparation of another from the two recently arrested fugitives, the transfer of cases of fugitives to national jurisdictions and the preservation of evidence in respect of three top-level fugitives: Félicien Kabuga, Protais Mpiranya and Augustin Bizimana. The Office intensified tracking efforts to arrest the remaining fugitives, conducted final and interlocutory appeals, managed archives and records to be transferred to the Residual Mechanism and provided assistance to national prosecuting authorities on cases being investigated or prosecuted.

Rigorous tracking efforts led to the arrest of the fugitive Bernard Munyagishari on 25 May by the Democratic Republic of the Congo (DRC) in cooperation with officers from the ICTR tracking team. Efforts continued for the arrest of the remaining nine fugitives—the majority of whom were believed to be in the DRC—and especially of the three top-level fugitives earmarked for trial at the Tribunal.

In conjunction with his efforts to strengthen international cooperation between Member States in the region and ICTR, the Prosecutor held consultations with the Executive Secretary of the International Conference on the Great Lakes Region. Noting that progress on the Félicien Kabuga file remained slow, the Prosecutor urged Kenya to expedite work on his tracking and arrest.

In the framework of implementing the ICTR referral strategy, the Prosecutor visited a number of European countries in April and held discussions with senior officials to encourage their Governments to consider accepting cases for trial from the Tribunal. The Office noted that there had been a positive signal for international cooperation against impunity and for accountability at the highest levels. Several Member States had enhanced their efforts to bring to trial, within their national jurisdictions, the Rwandan suspects appearing on the International Criminal Police Organization (INTERPOL) wanted list. The Office provided mutual legal assistance and information to national prosecuting authorities for the prosecution of those suspects. As a result, requests for information from the Office's extensive database had increased substantially.

The Registry

The Registry supported the judicial process by servicing the Tribunal's other organs and the defence, as well as by seeking support from States, international organizations and other stakeholders in the conduct of proceedings. It maintained high-level diplomatic contacts with Member States, international organizations and non-governmental organizations. Rwanda continued to cooperate with the Tribunal by facilitating the flow of witnesses from Kigali to Arusha and by providing documents for use in trial proceedings.

The issue of the relocation of persons acquitted by the Tribunal continued to be a matter of concern. Three acquitted persons remained in Arusha, under the protection of the Tribunal, without proper immigration status as they awaited relocation to a safe country. The challenge to their relocation was the result of the absence of a formal mechanism to secure the support of Member States to accept them within their territories. The Tribunal considered the resettlement of persons acquitted by an international tribunal to be a fundamental expression of the rule of law and was concerned about the consequences of failing to fulfil that obligation. That view was shared by the Office of the United Nations High Commissioner for Refugees (UNHCR) in a UNHCR-ICTR expert meeting (Arusha, April). Participants concluded that the Security Council was where the plight of the acquitted persons should be addressed, and that the Tribunal had no other choice but to call upon the Council to find a sustainable solution.

The External Relations and Strategic Planning Section was successful in raising voluntary contributions to the Trust Fund, enabling the Tribunal to carry on its capacity-building and outreach activities. Those activities formed an important part of the Tribunal's mandate and legacy and were a vital tool for bridging the information gap between the Tribunal and the people of Rwanda.

The Information and Documentation Centre in Kigali and 10 additional provincial information centres across Rwanda played a key role in information dissemination, communication and access to the jurisprudence of the Tribunal.

The Tribunal undertook capacity-building activities for about 700 legal professionals in Rwanda, with the aim of strengthening the Rwandan justice sector in areas such as investigation, witness protection, evidence and information management, and advocacy skills. Those activities sought to equip the Rwandan judiciary with the tools for taking up cases that might be referred from the Tribunal. The Tribunal conducted online legal research training for law students and two similar trainings for members of the Rwandan judiciary at the Institute for Legal Practice and Development and the Huye Intermediate Court. The Tribunal also organized training and workshops to strengthen the capacity of the Rwandan judiciary and raise awareness of the work of the Tribunal among the Rwandan public.

The Court Management Section provided support services to the judicial process, including provision of real-time transcripts of proceedings, support for site visits to Rwanda, certification of witness statements, depositions and video-link hearings from various countries. The Section conducted training sessions for representatives of various African countries, including demonstrations of the Tribunal's system for the instantaneous production of transcripts. It also conducted training sessions to strengthen the institutional capacity of the judicial sector in Rwanda. In preparation for the transition to the Residual Mechanism, the Section contributed to drafting the policies and guidelines for the records and archives to be transferred and managed by the Mechanism. It also worked on the redaction and digitization of the collection of audiovisual recordings of the Tribunal's proceedings.

Bernard Munyagishari, arrested in the DRC on 25 May, was transferred to the United Nations Detention Facility on 14 June. As at 30 June, the population of inmates at the Facility was 36 detained persons (12 detainees and 24 convicted persons). The International Committee of the Red Cross visited the Facility on 15 June and interviewed detainees; it commended the Facility's management for accomplishing its goals, particularly the good condition of the detention.

Financing

2010–2011 biennium

In response to General Assembly resolution 65/252 [YUN 2010, p. 1303], the Secretary-General in November submitted the second performance report on the ICTR budget for the 2010–2011 biennium [A/66/557 & Corr.1], which reflected a decrease in requirements of $722,600 gross ($1,635,600 net) as compared to the revised appropriation for the biennium. The General Assembly was requested to revise the appropriation for 2010–2011 to the Special Account for ICTR to $257,081,500 gross ($233,691,800 net).

ACABQ, in December [A/66/600], recommended approval of that appropriation.

2012–2013 biennium

In September [A/66/368 & Corr.1], the Secretary-General presented resource requirements for ICTR for the 2012–2013 biennium, which before recosting amounted to $174,318,200 gross ($157,938,900 net), reflecting a decrease in real terms of $83,485,900 gross or 32.4 per cent ($77,388,500 net or 32.9 per cent), compared to the revised appropriation for the 2010–2011 biennium.

ACABQ, on 9 December [A/66/600], recommended approval of those requirements.

In December [A/66/605], the Secretary-General presented revised estimates to the proposed programme budget for the 2012–2013 biennium, arising from the recosting of the effect of changes in rates of exchange and inflation, which would amount to $181,777,100 gross.

ACABQ, in December [A/66/7/Add.22], stated that it had no objection to the revised estimates.

GENERAL ASSEMBLY ACTION

On 24 December [meeting 93], the General Assembly, on the recommendation of the Fifth Committee [A/66/629], adopted **resolution 66/238** without vote [agenda item 144].

Financing of the International Criminal Tribunal for the Prosecution of Persons Responsible for Genocide and Other Serious Violations of International Humanitarian Law Committed in the Territory of Rwanda and Rwandan Citizens Responsible for Genocide and Other Such Violations Committed in the Territory of Neighbouring States between 1 January and 31 December 1994

The General Assembly,

I
Second performance report on the budget, for the biennium 2010–2011, of the International Criminal Tribunal for Rwanda

Having considered the second performance report of the Secretary-General on the budget, for the biennium 2010–2011, of the International Criminal Tribunal for the Prosecution of Persons Responsible for Genocide and Other Serious Violations of International Humanitarian Law Committed in the Territory of Rwanda and Rwandan Citizens Responsible for Genocide and Other Such Violations Committed in the Territory of Neighbouring States between 1 January and 31 December 1994, and the related report of the Advisory Committee on Administrative and Budgetary Questions,

Recalling its resolution 49/251 of 20 July 1995 on the financing of the International Criminal Tribunal for Rwanda and its subsequent resolutions thereon, the latest of which were resolutions 64/239 of 24 December 2009 and 65/252 of 24 December 2010,

1. *Takes note* of the second performance report of the Secretary-General on the budget, for the biennium 2010–2011, of the International Criminal Tribunal for Rwanda and the related report of the Advisory Committee on Administrative and Budgetary Questions;

2. *Endorses* the conclusions and recommendations contained in section III.B of the report of the Advisory Committee on Administrative and Budgetary Questions;

3. *Resolves* that, for the biennium 2010–2011, the amount of 257,804,100 United States dollars gross (235,327,400 dollars net) approved in its resolution 65/252 for the financing of the Tribunal shall be adjusted by the amount of 722,600 dollars gross (1,635,600 dollars net), for a total amount of 257,081,500 dollars gross (233,691,800 dollars net);

II
Budget of the International Criminal Tribunal for Rwanda for the biennium 2012–2013

Having considered the reports of the Secretary-General on the financing of the International Criminal Tribunal for Rwanda for the biennium 2012–2013 and on the revised estimates arising from the effects of changes in rates of exchange and inflation,

Having also considered the related reports of the Advisory Committee on Administrative and Budgetary Questions,

1. *Takes note* of the reports of the Secretary-General on the financing of the International Criminal Tribunal for Rwanda for the biennium 2012–2013 and on the revised estimates arising from the effects of changes in rates of exchange and inflation;

2. *Notes with appreciation* the support of the Government of the United Republic of Tanzania for the work of the Tribunal;

3. *Endorses* the conclusions and recommendations contained in the reports of the Advisory Committee on Administrative and Budgetary Questions, subject to the provisions of the present resolution;

4. *Recognizes* the critical importance of retaining highly skilled and experienced staff members with relevant institutional memory in order to successfully complete the trials and meet the targets set out in the completion strategy of the Tribunal;

5. *Commends* the Secretary-General for innovative solutions in applying the Staff Regulations and Rules of the United Nations for staff retention purposes;

6. *Reaffirms* paragraph 5 of its resolution 63/256 of 24 December 2008 and paragraph 6 of section II of its resolution 64/239, and requests the Secretary-General to utilize his existing authority under the existing contractual framework to offer contracts to staff, taking into account the needs of the Tribunal;

7. *Requests* the Secretary-General to continue to provide guidance to the Tribunal on all matters related to the recruitment and administration of human resources;

8. *Encourages* the Secretary-General to exercise due diligence in applying staff rule 12.3 on exceptions to the Staff Rules in the context of the decisions on retention of the staff members in the Tribunal, and requests the Secretary-General to ensure that exceptions granted to the Tribunal based on the existing legislative framework shall not constitute a precedent for other United Nations entities;

9. *Decides* to appropriate to the Special Account for the International Criminal Tribunal for the Prosecution of Persons Responsible for Genocide and Other Serious Violations of International Humanitarian Law Committed in the Territory of Rwanda and Rwandan Citizens Responsible for Genocide and Other Such Violations Committed in the Territory of Neighbouring States between 1 January and 31 December 1994 a total amount of 171,623,100 dollars gross (159,535,800 dollars net) for the biennium 2012–2013, as detailed in the annex to the present resolution;

10. *Also decides* that the total assessment for 2012 under the Special Account, amounting to 85,088,950 dollars, shall consist of:

(*a*) 85,811,550 dollars, being half of the estimated appropriation approved for the biennium 2012–2013;

(*b*) 722,600 dollars, being the decrease in the final appropriation for the biennium 2010–2011 approved by the General Assembly in paragraph 3 of section I above;

11. *Further decides* to apportion the amount of 42,544,475 dollars gross (39,066,150 dollars net) among Member States in accordance with the scale of assessments applicable to the regular budget of the United Nations for 2012;

12. *Decides* to apportion the amount of 42,544,475 dollars gross (39,066,150 dollars net) among Member States in accordance with the scale of assessments applicable to peacekeeping operations of the United Nations for 2012;

13. *Also decides* that, in accordance with the provisions of its resolution 973(X) of 15 December 1955, there shall be set off against the apportionment among Member States, as provided for in paragraphs 11 and 12 above, their respective share in the Tax Equalization Fund of the estimated staff assessment income of 6,956,650 dollars approved for the Tribunal for 2012;

ANNEX

Financing for the biennium 2012–2013 of the International Criminal Tribunal for the Prosecution of Persons Responsible for Genocide and Other Serious Violations of International Humanitarian Law Committed in the Territory of Rwanda and Rwandan Citizens Responsible for Genocide and Other Such Violations Committed in the Territory of Neighbouring States between 1 January and 31 December 1994

	Gross	Net
	(United States dollars)	
Estimated appropriation for the biennium 2012–2013	183,324,900	166,527,700
Revised estimates: effects of changes in rates of exchange and inflation	(1,547,800)	2,794,300
Recommendations of the Advisory Committee on Administrative and Budgetary Questions	—	—
Recommendations of the Fifth Committee	(10,154,000)	(9,786,200)
Estimated initial appropriation for the biennium 2012–2013	171,623,100	159,535,800
TOTAL assessment for 2012	**85,088,950**	**78,132,300**
Comprising:		
(a) Requirements representing half of the estimated appropriation for the biennium 2012–2013	85,811,550	79,767,900
(b) Requirements arising from the final appropriation for the biennium 2010–2011	(722,600)	(1,635,600)
Of which:		
Contributions assessed on Member States in accordance with the scale of assessments applicable to the regular budget of the United Nations for 2012	42,544,475	39,066,150
Contributions assessed on Member States in accordance with the scale of assessments applicable to peacekeeping operations of the United Nations for 2012	42,544,475	39,066,150

On 24 December, the General Assembly decided that the agenda item on ICTR financing would remain for consideration during its resumed sixty-sixth (2012) session (**decision 66/557**).

Functioning of the Tribunals

Implementation of completion strategy

ICTY

In response to Security Council resolution 1534(2004) [YUN 2004, p. 1292], the ICTY President reported in May [S/2011/316] and November [S/2011/716] on progress made in implementing the ICTY completion strategy.

In the May report, the President noted that the Tribunal faced unprecedented challenges, but also achieved unprecedented advancement in implementing its completion strategy. It conducted proceedings in nine trials concurrently by doubling up judges and staff so that they were working on more than one case at a time. The Tribunal had taken all measures possible to expedite its trials without sacrificing due process. Over the years, the Tribunal had continually kept its procedures under review and had introduced a variety of reforms to improve its work. Those reforms included the use of e-Court and e-Filing, amendments to the Rules of Procedure and Evidence, and case management techniques. Nevertheless, the pace of trials and appeals continued to be affected by staffing shortages and the loss of highly experienced staff members. Despite resolutions by the General Assembly and the Security Council on the issue of staff retention, the problem persisted. Without practical and effective staff retention measures, the Council should expect the estimates for the completion of the core work of the Tribunal to continue to be revised.

The Tribunal had transferred all low- and mid-level accused from its trial docket in accordance with Security Council resolution 1503(2003) [YUN 2003, p. 1330]. The Prosecutor, with the assistance of the Organization for Security and Cooperation in Europe (OSCE), continued to monitor the progress of referred proceedings ongoing in the region.

As at 15 November, two persons indicted by the Tribunal were at the pretrial stage, 16 persons were on trial and 17 persons were in appeal proceedings. With the arrest of Ratko Mladić and Goran Hadžić, there were no outstanding fugitives. The Tribunal had concluded proceedings against 126 of the 161 persons it indicted. Appeals against six trial judgements were pending before the Appeals Chamber. The Tribunal continued its efforts to ensure a smooth transition to the Residual Mechanism and continued to pursue a number of legacy and capacity-building projects.

The Joint Archives Strategy Working Group held two meetings (The Hague, 8–9 February and Arusha, 27–29 September). At the meetings, representatives from both Tribunals, the UN Archives and Records Management Section and the UN Office of Legal Affairs discussed the information security and access regime for the records of the Tribunals and the Residual Mechanism, and the steps needed to transfer the archives and records management function to the Mechanism.

ICTR

In response to Security Council resolution 1534(2004) [YUN 2004, p. 1292], the ICTR President submitted reports in May [S/2011/317] and November [S/2011/731] that assessed progress made in implementing the ICTR completion strategy.

Despite staffing challenges, the Tribunal was at or close to completion of all trial work. Because of the progress made on the major multi-accused cases, the remaining workload, including completing trials and delivering trial judgements in six cases involving seven accused, was expected to be completed by mid-2012. The Tribunal continued to realize gains from increased efficiencies in trial management. Two major multi-accused trial judgements involving 10 accused were delivered on or before the projected date. The Trial Chambers were preparing for delivery of the last multi-accused judgement before the end of the year, in line with projections.

Serious challenges, however, continued to plague the implementation of the completion strategy. Staff attrition had been severe in relation to trials and the investigative support that they depended on. Owing to the early abolition of posts, the Prosecution Division and the Information and Evidence Support Section had seen substantial staff losses. Key staff members continued to depart, including nearly one third of Chambers legal staff, who had left for more stable employment.

In the light of Security Council resolution 1966(2010) [YUN 2010, p. 1306], the Office of the Prosecutor had, in consultation with the ICTY Office of the Prosecutor, been engaged in ensuring a smooth transition to the Residual Mechanism, working out its projected staffing and its budget and aligning the Tribunal's archiving strategy with the projected takeover of the management of archives by the Mechanism in July 2012.

International Residual Mechanism

The Security Council established the International Residual Mechanism for Criminal Tribunals by resolution 1966(2010) [YUN 2010, p. 1306], with the mandate to execute the residual functions of ICTY and ICTR, following the closure of those entities. The Mechanism had two branches: the one for ICTR was scheduled to commence functioning on 1 July 2012 and the one for ICTY on 1 July 2013.

The Mechanism would begin carrying out the residual functions of the Tribunals during the 2012–2013 biennium. In view of the substantially reduced nature of those functions, the Mechanism would be a small structure. As the Mechanism would coexist with the two Tribunals during the 2012–2013 biennium, the Mechanism and the Tribunals would share resources and provide mutual support, particularly through common services and the use of the double-hatting of staff. The Mechanism would initially pursue two main objectives: the commencement of operations on the basis of a coordinated transition of functions and operations of the Tribunals; and the implementation of the residual functions as mandated by the Security Council.

Election of judges. On 23 June [A/66/143], the Secretary-General requested the inclusion of an agenda item entitled "International Residual Mechanism for Criminal Tribunals" in the provisional agenda of the General Assembly's sixty-sixth session.

On 20 October [S/2011/659], the Secretary-General forwarded to the Security Council the 37 nominations received for judges of the Mechanism from Member States. He recalled that, according to the statute of the Mechanism, annexed to Security Council resolution 1966(2010), the Mechanism should have a roster of 25 independent judges. The judges should only be present at the seats of the branches of the Mechanism as necessary. The terms and conditions of service of the judges for each day on which they exercised their functions should be those of the judges ad hoc of the International Court of Justice.

On 16 November [A/66/564], the Security Council transmitted to the General Assembly a list of 36 candidates established by the Council.

On 30 November [A/66/571/Rev.1], the Secretary-General transmitted the list of candidates to the General Assembly. A note containing the curricula vitae of the candidates was transmitted to the Assembly on 6 December [A/66/572].

On 20 December, the General Assembly elected 25 judges of the International Residual Mechanism for Criminal Tribunals for a four-year term of office beginning on 1 July 2012 (**decision 66/416**).

Financing

2012–2013 biennium. In November [A/66/537 & Corr.1], the Secretary-General presented resource requirements for the International Residual Mechanism for Criminal Tribunals for the 2012–2013 biennium, which, before recosting, amounted to $50,434,400 gross ($46,827,900 net). The staffing for the Mechanism would consist of 97 posts: 67 posts would be established in the biennium 2012–2013, with the functions and responsibilities of the remaining 30 posts covered by staff of ICTY and ICTR under a double-hatting arrangement.

ACABQ, in December [A/66/600], recommended the approval of the proposed budget for the 2012–2013 biennium; the approval of the establishment of 67 posts during that biennium; and the appropriation of an amount of $50,434,400 gross ($46,827,900 net), before recosting.

In December [A/66/605], the Secretary-General presented revised estimates, which would amount to $53,793,300 gross.

ACABQ, on 15 December [A/66/7/Add.22], stated that it had no objection to the revised estimates arising from the recosting of the effect of changes in rates of exchange and inflation.

GENERAL ASSEMBLY ACTION

On 24 December [meeting 93], the General Assembly, on the recommendation of the Fifth Committee [A/66/631], adopted **resolution 66/240 A** without vote [agenda items 129, 144 & 145].

International Residual Mechanism for Criminal Tribunals

The General Assembly,

Having considered the reports of the Secretary-General on the budget, for the biennium 2012–2013, for the International Residual Mechanism for Criminal Tribunals and on the revised estimates arising from the effect of changes in rates of exchange and inflation,

Having also considered the related reports of the Advisory Committee on Administrative and Budgetary Questions,

Recalling Security Council resolution 1966(2010) of 22 December 2010 regarding the establishment of the International Residual Mechanism for Criminal Tribunals, comprising a branch for the International Criminal Tribunal for the Prosecution of Persons Responsible for Genocide and Other Serious Violations of International Humanitarian Law Committed in the Territory of Rwanda and Rwandan Citizens Responsible for Genocide and Other Such Violations Committed in the Territory of Neighbouring States between 1 January and 31 December 1994, which shall commence functioning on 1 July 2012, and a branch for the International Tribunal for the Prosecution of Persons Responsible for Serious Violations of International Humanitarian Law Committed in the Territory of the Former Yugoslavia since 1991, which shall commence functioning on 1 July 2013,

1. *Takes note* of the reports of the Secretary-General on the budget, for the biennium 2012–2013, of the International Residual Mechanism for Criminal Tribunals and on the revised estimates arising from the effects of changes in rates of exchange and inflation;

2. *Endorses* the conclusions and recommendations contained in the reports of the Advisory Committee on Administrative and Budgetary Questions, subject to the provisions of the present resolution;

3. *Encourages* the Secretary-General to enhance efforts to transfer cases of the Mechanism to national jurisdiction;

4. *Recalls* paragraph 76 of the report of the Advisory Committee on Administrative and Budgetary Questions, and requests the Secretary-General to report on lessons learned on the use of the "double-hatting" arrangement in the context of the second performance report on the programme budget for the biennium;

5. *Requests* the Secretary-General to submit to the General Assembly, no later than at the second part of its resumed sixty-sixth session, a report providing detailed information on a comprehensive project management plan for the construction, in Arusha, United Republic of Tanzania, of the proposed new facilities for the archives of the Mechanism, including programmatic and functional requirements, a conceptual design and key milestones from design to construction to occupation;

6. *Decides* to appropriate an initial amount of 3 million United States dollars for the overall construction of the proposed new facilities for the archives;

7. *Authorizes* the expenditures, from within the amount appropriated in paragraph 6 above, to cover only expenses related to the conceptual design phase of the proposed new facilities for the archives;

8. *Decides* to review the project requirements in the context of the consideration of the report requested in paragraph 5 above;

9. *Requests* the Secretary-General to ensure the full involvement of the Overseas Property Management Unit of the Office of Central Support Services of the Secretariat in all phases of implementation of the project;

10. *Decides* that the staffing for the continuous activities of the Mechanism shall comprise 67 posts for the biennium 2012–2013, as set out in table 3 of the report of the Secretary-General;

11. *Also decides* that the expenses of the Mechanism shall be met through additional resources on the basis of assessed contributions and that such expenses shall be financed through a separate special account;

12. *Further decides* to appropriate to the Special Account for the International Residual Mechanism for Criminal Tribunals a total amount of 49,771,700 dollars gross (47,325,100 dollars net) for the biennium 2012–2013, to include the amount reflected in paragraph 6 above, as detailed in the annex to the present resolution;

13. *Decides* that the total assessment for 2012 under the Special Account shall amount to 24,885,850 dollars, being half of the estimated appropriation approved for the biennium 2012–2013;

14. *Also decides* to apportion the amount of 12,442,925 dollars gross (11,831,275 dollars net) among Member States in accordance with the scale of assessments applicable to the regular budget of the United Nations for 2012;

15. *Further decides* to apportion the amount of 12,442,925 dollars gross (11,831,275 dollars net) among Member States in accordance with the scale of assessments applicable to peacekeeping operations of the United Nations for 2012;

16. *Decides* that, in accordance with the provisions of its resolution 973(X) of 15 December 1955, there shall be set off against the apportionment among Member States, as provided for in paragraphs 14 and 15 above, their respective share in the Tax Equalization Fund of the estimated staff assessment income of 1,223,300 dollars approved for the Mechanism for 2012.

ANNEX

Financing for the biennium 2012–2013 of the International Residual Mechanism for Criminal Tribunals

	Gross	Net
	(United States dollars)	
Estimated appropriation for the biennium 2012–2013	55,051,400	51,198,800
Revised estimates: effects of changes in rates of exchange and inflation	(1,258,100)	(20,500)
Recommendations of the Advisory Committee on Administrative and Budgetary Questions	—	—
Recommendations of the Fifth Committee	(4,021,600)	(3,853,200)
Estimated initial appropriation for the biennium 2012–2013	49,771,700	47,325,100
TOTAL assessment for 2012	**24,885,850**	**23,662,550**
Of which:		
Contributions assessed on Member States in accordance with the scale of assessments applicable to the regular budget of the United Nations for 2012	12,442,925	11,831,275
Contributions assessed on Member States in accordance with the scale of assessments applicable to peacekeeping operations of the United Nations for 2012	12,442,925	11,831,275

On 24 December, the General Assembly decided that the agenda item on "International residual mechanism for criminal tribunals" would remain for consideration during its resumed sixty-sixth (2012) session (**decision 66/557**).

International Criminal Court

In 2011, the International Criminal Court (ICC) carried out investigations in the Central African Republic, Côte d'Ivoire, the Democratic Republic of the Congo (DRC), Darfur (the Sudan), Kenya, the Libyan Arab Jamahiriya and Uganda. The Court, based at The Hague, was established by the Rome Statute of the International Criminal Court [YUN 1998, p. 1209] as a permanent institution with jurisdiction over persons accused of the most serious crimes of international concern (genocide, crimes against humanity, war crimes and the crime of aggression). Reports covering ICC activities during the year [A/66/309, A/67/308] were submitted to the General Assembly. As at 31 December, 120 countries had ratified the Rome Statute.

On 26 February, by **resolution 1970(2011)** (see p. 267), the Security Council referred the situation in the Libyan Arab Jamahiriya since 15 February 2011 to the ICC Prosecutor.

In June, arrest warrants were issued against Libyan leader Muammar Mohammed Abu Minyar Qadhafi, his son Saif al-Islam Qadhafi, a Libyan Government Spokesman, and Abdullah Al-Senussi, Director of Military Intelligence, for crimes against humanity. In October, an arrest warrant was issued against Laurent Gbagbo, former President of Côte d'Ivoire, for the crimes against humanity of murder, rape and other forms of sexual violence, persecution and other inhumane acts. As at 31 July, 12 arrest warrants were outstanding: one in the situation in the DRC, four in the situation in Darfur, four in the situation in Uganda, and three in the situation in Libya. On 12 December, the Assembly of States Parties to the Rome Statute elected Ms. Fatou B. Bensouda as the Court's new Prosecutor for a nine-year term.

Assembly of States Parties

The Assembly of States Parties to the Rome Statute of the International Criminal Court adopted six resolutions at its tenth session (New York, 12–21 December) [ICC-ASP/10/20].

In a resolution on cooperation [ICC-ASP/10/Res.2], the Assembly stressed the importance of cooperation of States and non-States Parties with the Court, as well as the need for the ratification process of the Rome Statute to be matched by national implementation of the ensuing obligations.

An amendment to rule 4 of the Rules of Procedure and Evidence [ICC-ASP/10/Res.1] aimed at strengthening the Presidency of the Court and increasing efficiency of the judicial proceedings by having the Presidency decide on the assignment of judges to divisions.

A resolution on reparations [ICC-ASP/10/Res.3] requested the Court to establish coherent principles to guide the issuance of individual orders for reparations. The resolution underlined that, as the freezing and identification of assets of the convicted person were of paramount importance for reparations, the Court should take all possible measures to that end, including effective communication with relevant States.

A resolution on the Court's permanent premises [ICC-ASP/10/Res.6] reiterated the intention of the project to remain within the proposed €190 million budget, also emphasizing the role of the Oversight Committee in the permanent premises project. A resolution on strengthening the ICC and the Assembly of States Parties [ICC-ASP/10/Res.5] addressed, among other issues, cooperation, complementarity, victims and affected communities and the Trust Fund for Victims. The Assembly approved appropriations totalling €111,000,000, with €108,800,000 for the budget and €2,200,000 to replenish the Contingency Fund [ICC-ASP/10/Res.4]. Furthermore, the Assembly approved a staffing level of 766.

Election of Prosecutor. On 12 December, the Assembly of States Parties elected Ms. Fatou B. Bensouda (The Gambia) as the Court's new Prosecutor for a nine-year term starting from 16 June 2012. Her curriculum vitae was detailed in a note of 9 December [ICC-ASP/10/38/Add.1].

The Chambers

The judicial activities of the Court were conducted by the Chambers, which consisted of 18 judges, organized in three divisions: the Appeals Division, the Trial Division and the Pre-Trial Division. The Pre-Trial Chambers played an important role in the first phase of judicial proceedings.

On 12 May, Pre-Trial Chamber I issued a decision informing the Security Council and the Assembly of States Parties regarding the visit of Omar Hassan Ahmad Al Bashir, the President of the Sudan, to Djibouti, noting that the country had an obligation to cooperate with the Court in enforcing arrest warrants. In 2009, the Court had issued an arrest warrant for President Al Bashir for war crimes and crimes against humanity [YUN 2009, pp. 261 & 1300]. On 12 and 13 December 2011, Pre-Trial Chamber I issued two decisions, concerning Malawi and Chad, in which it found that the two States parties had failed to cooperate with the Court owing to their failure to arrest and surrender Mr. Al Bashir to the Court while he was present on their territory. Finding that customary international law created an exception to Head-of-State immunity when international courts sought a Head of State's arrest for the commission of international crimes, the Chamber reiterated that States parties were under the obligation to arrest and surrender Mr. Al Bashir to the Court if he was on their territory.

Communications. On 17 May [S/2011/318], the Secretary-General transmitted to the Security Council a notification of the "Decision informing the United Nations Security Council and the Assembly of the States Parties to the Rome Statute about Omar Al-Bashir's recent visit to Djibouti", issued by the Court's Pre-Trial Chamber I on 12 May.

On 1 August [A/65/919], Norway transmitted to the Secretary-General resolution RC/Res.3, entitled "Strengthening the enforcement of sentences", adopted at the Review Conference of the Rome Statute of the International Criminal Court (Kampala, Uganda, 31 May–11 June 2010) [YUN 2010, p. 1316].

New arrests, warrants and summonses

On 8 March, Pre-Trial Chamber II issued summonses to appear for William Samoei Ruto, a suspended Minister of Higher Education, Science and Technology, Henry Kiprono Kosgey, a member of Parliament and Chairman of the Orange Democratic Movement (ODM), and Joshua Arap Sang, the head of operations at Kass FM in Nairobi, for their alleged roles in committing crimes against humanity in connection with the post-election violence in Kenya in 2007 and 2008. All three accused were members of ODM, one of the two political parties of Kenya's ruling coalition. The three suspects voluntarily appeared before Pre-Trial Chamber II on 7 April. The confirmation of charges hearing was held from 1 to 8 September, when the Chamber considered the charges, namely, three counts of crimes against humanity (murder, forcible transfer of population and persecution).

Also on 8 March, Pre-Trial Chamber II issued summonses to appear for Francis Kirimi Muthaura, Head of Public Service and Secretary to the Cabinet, Uhuru Muigai Kenyatta, Deputy Prime Minister and Minister for Finance, and Mohammed Hussein Ali, Chief Executive of the Postal Corporation, for their alleged roles in committing crimes against humanity in connection with the post-election violence in Kenya in 2007 and 2008. All three accused were members of the Party of National Unity, one of the two political parties of Kenya's ruling coalition. The three suspects voluntarily appeared before Pre-Trial Chamber II on 8 April. The confirmation of charges hearing was held from 21 September to 5 October, when the Chamber considered the charges of five counts of crimes against humanity (murder, forcible transfer of population, rape, persecution and other inhumane acts).

In a letter of 4 March [S/2011/116] to the Secretary-General and the Security Council, Kenya requested a deferral of the Court's proceedings relating to Kenya under article 16 of the Rome Statute. Kenya expressed its concern that the naming of six individuals by the Prosecutor of the Court as bearing the greatest responsibility for the post-election violence had slowed down the implementation of the new Constitution and the reform process, and interfered with the delicate political climate.

In a letter of 23 March [S/2011/201], Kenya requested the Security Council to hold an open meeting to further consider its request for deferral. The deferral would greatly enhance the country's ability to complete its reform programme, including putting in place a local tribunal, in keeping with its primary responsibility to investigate and prosecute cases in accordance with the Rome Statute.

On 31 March, Kenya filed an application pursuant to article 19 of the Rome Statute challenging the admissibility of both cases before the Court. Pre-Trial Chamber II rejected the application on 30 May, considering that the application did not provide concrete evidence of ongoing national proceedings with respect to the persons subject of the proceedings at the Court. On 30 August, the Appeals Chamber, by majority, rejected the appeal of Kenya against the decision of Pre-Trial Chamber II of 30 May on the admissibility of the cases.

On 27 June, Pre-Trial Chamber I issued arrest warrants against Libyan leader Muammar Mohammed Abu Minyar Qadhafi, his son Saif al-Islam Qadhafi, Government Spokesman, and Abdullah Al-Senussi, Director of Military Intelligence, for two counts of crimes against humanity (murder and persecution) allegedly committed since 15 February 2011. Pre-Trial Chamber I found that there were reasonable grounds to believe that Muammar Qadhafi, in coordination with his inner circle, conceived and orchestrated a plan to deter and quell, by all means, civilian demonstrations against the regime. The warrants of arrest followed the investigation into the situation in Libya opened by the Prosecutor on 3 March pursuant to Security Council resolution 1970(2011) (see p. 267), by which the Council referred the situation to the Prosecutor.

On 22 November, Pre-Trial Chamber I terminated the proceedings against Muammar Qadhafi upon receipt of a death certificate from the Libyan authorities. The following day, the Chamber was informed of the arrest of Saif al-Islam Qadhafi in Libya. On 6 December, the Chamber decided to seek information from the Libyan authorities on a number of issues, including the arrest and surrender of Saif al-Islam Qadhafi, his legal representation and his state of health.

On 3 October, Pre-Trial Chamber III authorized the Prosecutor to start an investigation in Côte d'Ivoire with respect to crimes committed since 28 November 2010. On 25 October, the Prosecutor presented an application for an arrest warrant against Laurent Gbagbo, former President of Côte d'Ivoire. On 23 November, the Chamber issued a warrant against him for the crimes against humanity of murder, rape and other forms of sexual violence, persecution and other inhumane acts committed in Côte d'Ivoire between 16 December 2010 and 12 April 2011. Mr. Gbagbo was surrendered to the Court on 30 November and his first court appearance took place on 5 December.

On 2 December, the Prosecutor presented an application for an arrest warrant against Abdel Raheem Muhammad Hussein, Minister of National Defense of the Sudan.

Ongoing cases, trials and appeals

In the trial against Thomas Lubanga Dyilo (situation in the DRC), Trial Chamber I on 23 February refused the defence application to stay the proceedings as an abuse of the process. The trial resumed on 21 March and the defence concluded its presentation on 18 April. On 20 May, the Chamber ordered the closing of the presentation of evidence stage. The prosecution and the defence submitted their closing briefs on 1 June and 15 July, respectively. The closing statements of the prosecution, the defence and the legal representatives of victims were heard on 25 and 26 August.

In the case against Germain Katanga and Mathieu Ngudjolo Chui, two former leaders of armed groups active in the Ituri region (situation in the DRC), Mr. Katanga presented his case between 24 March and 12 July and called 17 witnesses to testify, including three witnesses in common with the second accused. The defence case of Mr. Ngudjolo was presented from 15 August to 11 November, during which time 12 witnesses were called to testify and the defence tendered 132 items of evidence. Both accused testified during the presentation of their defence case.

Following his arrest in 2010 [YUN 2010, p. 1317], Callixte Mbarushimana, the alleged Executive Secretary of the Forces démocratiques de libération du Rwanda (situation in the DRC), was transferred on 25 January 2011 to the Court's Detention Centre in The Hague. His initial appearance before the Court took place on 28 January. During the confirmation of charges hearing, which was held from 16 to 21 September, 32 victims were authorized to participate in the proceedings. On 16 December, Pre-Trial Chamber I, by majority, declined to confirm the charges against Mr. Mbarushimana. It found that the prosecution had not provided sufficient evidence to establish that the suspect was individually responsible for the crimes with which he was charged. The majority accordingly decided to release Mr. Mbarushimana from custody. On 20 December, the Appeals Chamber rejected the prosecution's appeal against the release. Mr. Mbarushimana was subsequently released.

In the case against Jean-Pierre Bemba Gombo (situation in the Central African Republic), as at 31 July, the prosecution had presented 25 of its 40 planned witnesses.

In the case against Abdallah Banda Abakaer Nourain, alleged to be the former Commander-in-Chief of the Justice and Equality Movement, and Saleh Mohammed Jerbo Jamus, alleged to be the former Chief-of-Staff of the Sudan Liberation Army-Unity (situation in Darfur), Pre-Trial Chamber I, on 7 March, confirmed three charges of war crimes (violence to life, intentionally directing attacks against a peacekeeping mission and pillaging) in relation to an attack on peacekeepers of the African Union Mission in the Sudan on 29 September 2007 [YUN 2007, p. 255]. On 16 March, the ICC President referred the case to the newly constituted Trial Chamber IV. On 16 May, the parties filed a joint submission stating that the accused would contest only certain specified issues. As at 31 May, 89 victims had been authorized to participate through their legal representatives in the proceedings. On 28 September, Trial Chamber IV decided that, following the agreement reached between the parties as to facts and evidence, the trial would only proceed on the basis of the contested issues.

Communication. On 12 April [S/2011/236], the Secretary-General transmitted to the Security Council notification of the "Decision on the Confirmation of Charges" issued by the Court's Pre-Trial Chamber I on 7 March in the case of The Prosecutor v. Abdallah Banda Abakaer Nourain and Saleh Mohammed Jerbo Jamus. The case was one of four arising out of the referral by the Council, in its resolution 1593(2005) [YUN 2005, p. 324], of the situation in Darfur since 1 July 2002 to the ICC Prosecutor.

Office of the Prosecutor

Investigations

The Office of the Prosecutor continued investigations into the situations in the Central African Republic, the DRC, Darfur (the Sudan), Kenya and Uganda. The Prosecutor opened two new investigations in the Libyan Arab Jamahiriya and Côte d'Ivoire.

During the period 1 August 2010 to 31 July 2011, the Office carried out 14 missions to five countries, including for screening potential witnesses and following up on new information, in relation to its investigation into the situation in the Central African Republic.

Regarding the DRC, the Office conducted 16 missions to five countries with regard to the cases of Thomas Lubanga Dyilo, Germain Katanga and Mathieu Ngudjolo Chui, and 34 missions to 10 countries relating to the case of the Kivu provinces.

On the situation in Darfur, the Office conducted 16 missions to 9 countries. The information collected indicated that crimes against humanity, war crimes and genocide continued to be committed.

On the situation in Kenya, the Office conducted 71 missions to 14 countries.

The Office continued to gather information on crimes allegedly committed by the Lord's Resistance Army (LRA) and to promote action to implement warrants against the top LRA leadership, carrying out three missions to three countries in relation to the situation in Uganda. Crimes allegedly committed by LRA under Joseph Kony's leadership throughout the year included a substantial number of killings and abductions across the DRC, Southern Sudan and the Central African Republic. Since early 2008, the LRA was reported to have killed more than 2,000 people, abducted more than 2,500 and displaced well over 300,000 in the DRC. During the same period, more than 120,000 people were displaced, at least 450 killed and more than 800 abducted in Southern Sudan and the Central African Republic. The Office also continued gathering and analysing information related to alleged crimes committed by the Ugandan armed forces, and encouraged the Ugandan authorities to conduct proceedings in relation to both parties to the conflict.

On the situation in Libya, the Office conducted 28 missions to 11 countries. Following the Security Council referral (see p. 1261), the Office conducted a factual and legal analysis covering issues of jurisdiction, admissibility and the interests of justice. As a result of the analysis, the Office on 3 March determined that the statutory criteria for opening an investigation had been met.

On the situation in Côte d'Ivoire, the Prosecutor on 3 October received authorization from the Pre-Trial Chamber to open an investigation into the alleged crimes committed in the country.

The Prosecutor, Luis Moreno-Ocampo, briefed the Security Council on 4 May on Libya [S/PV.6528], on 8 June on the Sudan [S/PV.6548], on 2 November on Libya [S/PV.6647] and on 15 December on the Sudan [S/PV.6688]. On 15 December, presenting the status of the investigation in the situation in Darfur, the Prosecutor highlighted the lack of cooperation by the Government of the Sudan and the lack of national proceedings against those responsible for the crimes, in violation of Security Council resolution 1593(2005) [YUN 2005, p. 324].

Preliminary examinations

The Office of the Prosecutor continued to monitor information on crimes potentially falling within the jurisdiction of the Court, analysing communications received from various sources. Between 1 August 2010 and 30 June 2011, the Office received 419 communications relating to article 15 of the Rome Statute. The Office also conducted preliminary examinations, including in Afghanistan, Colombia, Georgia, Guinea, Honduras, Nigeria, Palestine and the Republic of Korea.

The Registry

The Registry provided judicial and administrative support to all organs of the Court and carried out its responsibilities concerning victims, witnesses, defence and outreach. The Registry sought to develop understanding and awareness of ICC and its activities by strengthening the Court's public information capacity for outreach services in countries where the Court was active. It provided security, administrative and logistical support to the Court's investigations.

On 13 June, the Registry concluded a memorandum of understanding with the United Nations concerning the provision of support services and facilities by the UN Office at Nairobi to the Registry in connection with its activities in Kenya.

International cooperation

Regular contact between ICC and the United Nations continued to be instrumental in facilitating cooperation. On 17 March, the President of the Court met with the Administrator of the United Nations Development Programme and discussed the synergies between the United Nations and the Court in supporting the capacity of States to prosecute serious crimes. On 9 May, the President met with the United Nations High Commissioner for Human Rights and discussed various forms of cooperation between the two organizations in ensuring accountability for Rome Statute crimes. The President also met with the heads of UN missions in several countries to discuss issues of mutual interest.

The annual round table between the United Nations and the Court took place in New York on 8 and 9 December. Issues including the disclosure of UN documents to the Court and cooperation with the defence teams were discussed. The Office of the Prosecutor conducted a series of lessons-learned discussions with departments of the UN Secretariat with regard to situations under investigation.

ICC increased its cooperation and engagement with the League of Arab States. Court representatives, Government delegations, legal experts and media representatives attended a regional conference on ICC (Doha, Qatar, 24–25 May) organized by Qatar and the League of Arab States in cooperation with the Court. The conference was the first major event of its kind in the Middle East aimed at providing information on the workings of ICC and its legal framework. Speakers included the President, Registrar and Prosecutor of the Court, as well as leading Arab experts on international criminal justice. In September, the Court organized a seminar in Tunisia, with the support of the International Organization of la Francophonie and France, to increase the understanding of the Rome Statute in the Maghreb and the Middle East.

The Court continued to communicate closely with the African Union (AU). On 18 and 19 July, at AU headquarters in Addis Ababa, Ethiopia, ICC officials and more than 50 participants representing 15 African States participated in a seminar on the technical aspects of the Rome Statute and Court practice, jointly organized by the AU and the Court. Presentations on ICC structure and governing principles were followed by candid discussions about the role of the Court within the international justice system, the relationship between regional and international organizations and the relationship between peace and justice.

ICC also continued to provide detention services and other related assistance to the Special Court for Sierra Leone in its trial of Charles Taylor in The Hague.

The Court welcomed the adoption by the European Union (EU) on 21 March of a Council Decision replacing the Union's previous Common Position on the Court. The EU continued to provide technical, financial and other forms of support to the Court.

ICC continued to develop its bilateral exchanges and arrangements for cooperation with States, especially with respect to analysis and investigative activities, asset tracking and freezing, victim and witness protection, arrest operations, the enforcement of sentences and the provisional release of accused persons pending trial. ICC officials met regularly with representatives of States, international organizations and civil society to update them on the Court's work, raise awareness about the Rome Statute system and discuss issues of mutual interest.

Report of Secretary-General. Pursuant to General Assembly resolution 65/12 [YUN 2010, p. 1315], the Secretary-General submitted a report [A/66/333] on expenses incurred and reimbursement received by the United Nations in connection with assistance provided to ICC. From 1 July 2010 to 30 June 2011, the United Nations provided facilities and services in the amount of $772,952. Facilities and services included satellite communications, conference and related services, costs for staff who worked exclusively on matters pertaining to the Court, field security and library services.

Chapter III

International legal questions

In 2011, the International Law Commission (ILC) continued to examine topics relating to the progressive development and codification of international law. It adopted a set of 18 draft articles on the effects of armed conflicts on treaties, a set of 67 draft articles on the responsibility of international organizations and the Guide to Practice on Reservations to Treaties. It reconstituted its study groups on treaties over time and on the most-favoured-nation clause, and the working group on the long-term programme of work. ILC also established working groups on reservations to treaties and on methods of work. In December, the General Assembly took note of the set of articles on the responsibility of international organizations and the set of articles on the effects of armed conflicts on treaties, and commended them to the attention of Governments.

The Ad Hoc Committee established by the General Assembly in resolution 51/210 continued to elaborate a draft comprehensive convention on international terrorism—an issue also addressed by the Assembly's Sixth (Legal) Committee. The Secretary-General in June reported on measures taken by States, UN system entities and intergovernmental organizations to implement the 1994 General Assembly Declaration on Measures to Eliminate International Terrorism. In December, the Assembly condemned all acts, methods and practices of terrorism as criminal and unjustifiable, and called on Member States to implement the United Nations Global Counter-Terrorism Strategy.

The United Nations Commission on International Trade Law (UNCITRAL) adopted the UNCITRAL Model Law on Public Procurement, which updated the 1994 UNCITRAL Model Law on Procurement of Goods, Construction and Services, as well as "The UNCITRAL Model Law on Cross-Border Insolvency: the Judicial Perspective", a text designed to provide information and guidance for judges on cross-border related insolvency issues. It continued its work on public procurement, arbitration and conciliation, online dispute resolution, insolvency law and security interests, and considered future work in the areas of electronic commerce and microfinance. The Commission approved the establishment of an UNCITRAL Regional Centre for Asia and the Pacific in the Republic of Korea.

The Special Committee on the Charter of the United Nations and on the Strengthening of the Role of the Organization considered, among other subjects, proposals relating to the maintenance of international peace and security, with a view to strengthening the Organization, and the implementation of Charter provisions on assistance to third States affected by the application of sanctions.

The Committee on Relations with the Host Country addressed a number of issues raised by permanent missions to the United Nations, including those related to activities to assist members of the UN community, delays in issuing visas, the security of missions and their personnel, and transportation and parking.

During 2011, the United Nations provided rule-of-law assistance in over 150 Member States, including in the areas of development, conflict and peacebuilding.

Legal aspects of international political relations

International Law Commission

The 34-member International Law Commission (ILC) held its sixty-third session in Geneva in two parts (26 April–3 June and 4 July–12 August) [A/66/10]. During the second part, the International Law Seminar held its forty-seventh session, which was attended by 26 young academics and diplomats from all regions of the world. They observed ILC meetings, attended specially arranged lectures and participated in working groups on specific topics.

ILC carried out its work with the assistance of various working groups and a drafting committee. On the topic of reservations to treaties, ILC had before it the comments and observations received from Governments on the provisional version of the Guide to Practice on Reservations to Treaties, adopted by the Commission at its sixty-second session [YUN 2010, p. 1324]. The Commission established a working group to proceed with the finalization of the text of the guidelines constituting the Guide to Practice. On the basis of the recommendations of the working group, the Commission adopted the Guide to Practice on Reservations to Treaties. The Commission recommended that the General Assembly take note of the Guide and ensure its widest possible dissemination. The Commission also adopted a recommendation to the Assembly on mechanisms of assistance in relation to reservations.

The Commission adopted a set of 67 draft articles, together with commentaries thereto, on the responsibility of international organizations (see p. 1268), and recommended to the Assembly that it take note of the draft articles and that it consider, at a later stage, the elaboration of a convention on the basis of the draft articles. As to the effects of armed conflicts on treaties (see p. 1275), the Commission adopted a set of 18 draft articles and an annex containing an indicative list of treaties, the subject matter of which implied that they continued in operation during armed conflict, together with commentaries on the effects of armed conflicts on treaties. The Committee recommended to the Assembly that it take note of the draft articles and consider, at a later stage, the elaboration of a convention on based on them.

In relation to the topic of immunity of State officials from foreign criminal jurisdiction (see p. 1278), the debate revolved around issues relating to methodology, possible exceptions to immunity and questions of procedure.

Regarding the expulsion of aliens (see p. 1278), ILC considered expulsion proceedings and the legal consequences of expulsion. ILC referred seven draft articles on those issues to the Drafting Committee, as well as a draft article on expulsion in connection with extradition, as revised by the Special Rapporteur. On the topic of protection of persons in the event of disasters (see p. 1279), the Commission provisionally adopted six draft articles, together with commentaries, dealing with humanitarian principles in disaster response, human dignity, human rights, the role of the affected State, the duty of the affected State to seek assistance and the consent of the affected State to external assistance. On the obligation to extradite or prosecute (*aut dedere aut judicare*) (see p. 1279), the Commission considered the fourth report of the Special Rapporteur addressing the question of sources of the obligation to extradite or prosecute, focusing on treaties and custom, and concerning which three draft articles were proposed.

The Commission reconstituted the Study Group on Treaties over Time, which continued its work on the aspects of the topic relating to subsequent agreements and practice (see p. 1279). ILC also reconstituted the Study Group on the most-favoured-nation clause (see p. 1280).

The Commission held a discussion on peaceful settlement of disputes on the basis of a working paper [A/CN.4/641]. The Planning Group established by the Commission reconstituted the Working Group on the Long-term Programme of Work. The Commission endorsed the inclusion of the following topics in its long-term programme of work: formation and evidence of customary international law; protection of the atmosphere; provisional application of treaties; the fair and equitable treatment standard in international investment law; and protection of the environment in relation to armed conflicts. The Planning Group also established a Working Group on Methods of Work. ILC decided that its sixty-fourth session would be held in Geneva from 7 May to 1 June and from 2 July to 3 August 2012.

Topical summary report. Pursuant to Assembly resolution 65/26 [YUN 2010, p. 1327], the Secretariat prepared a topical summary [A/CN.4/638] of the debate held on the report of the Commission at the Assembly's sixty-fifth (2010) session.

Assistance to special rapporteurs. On 7 December [A/C.6/66/SR.26], the Secretariat of the Commission provided to the Sixth (Legal) Committee of the General Assembly an oral report on assistance to the Commission's special rapporteurs.

Casual vacancies. On 28 April, the Commission elected Concepción Escobar Hernández (Spain) to fill the vacancy occasioned by the death of Paula Escarameia (Portugal). On 17 May, the Commission elected Mohammed Bello Adoke (Nigeria) to fill the vacancy occasioned by the resignation of Bayo Ojo (Nigeria).

Election of members. In June and August, the Secretary-General submitted to the General Assembly a list of candidates nominated by Member States for election to ILC [A/66/88 & Add.1–3] and their curricula vitae [A/66/90 & Add.1,2], respectively.

On 17 October, by **decision 66/506**, the Assembly requested the Secretary-General to issue a consolidated list of candidates for the election of ILC members, incorporating new information provided subsequent to the 1 June deadline for submitting candidatures. The Secretary-General submitted that list on 17 October [A/66/514].

On 17 November, by **decision 66/413**, the Assembly elected 34 members of the Commission for a five-year term of office beginning on 1 January 2012.

Reservations to treaties

ILC, at its sixty-third session [A/66/10], considered the seventeenth report on reservations to treaties [A/CN.4/647] of Special Rapporteur Alain Pellet (France), addressing the question of reservations dialogue, as well as an addendum to the report [A/CN.4/647/Add.1], which considered the issue of assistance in the resolution of disputes concerning reservations and contained a draft introduction to the Guide to Practice on Reservations to Treaties. The Commission also had before it the comments and observations received from Governments on the provisional version of the Guide [A/CN.4/639 & Add.1], adopted by the Commission at its sixty-second session [YUN 2010, p. 1324].

The Commission established a Working Group on Reservations to Treaties to finalize the Guide to Practice on Reservations to Treaties. The Commission also referred to the Working Group a draft recommendation or conclusions on the reservations dialogue, contained in the Special Rapporteur's report, and a draft recommendation on technical assistance and assistance in the settlement of disputes concerning reservations, contained in the addendum. On the basis of the recommendations of the Working Group, the Commission adopted the guidelines and commentaries constituting the Guide to Practice on Reservations to Treaties, including an introduction and an annex setting out conclusions and a recommendation of the Commission on the reservations dialogue. The Commission recommended to the General Assembly that it take note of the Guide and ensure its dissemination. Although some members expressed doubts about proposing a specific mechanism of assistance in relation to reservations to treaties, the Commission entrusted the Working Group with the task of considering the draft recommendation on the subject proposed by the Special Rapporteur. It subsequently adopted a recommendation to the Assembly on mechanisms of assistance in relation to reservations.

Responsibility of international organizations

ILC [A/66/10] had before it the eighth report on responsibility of international organizations [A/CN.4/640] by Special Rapporteur Giorgio Gaja (Italy), which surveyed the comments made by States and international organizations on the draft articles on the responsibility of international organizations adopted on first reading at the sixty-first ILC session [YUN 2009, p. 1306]. The Commission also had before it the comments and information received from Governments [A/CN.4/636 & Add.1,2] and international organizations [A/CN.4/637 & Add.1] on the draft articles adopted on first reading.

On 28 April, the Commission referred draft articles 1 to 18 to the Drafting Committee with the instruction that the Committee begin the second reading of the articles, taking into account the comments of Governments and international organizations, the Rapporteur's proposals and the debate in the plenary on the Rapporteur's report. On 6 May, it referred draft articles 19 to 66 to the Drafting Committee. On 3 June, it considered the report of the Drafting Committee [A/CN.4/L.778] and adopted the set of draft articles on the responsibility of international organizations on second reading. On 5 August, it adopted the commentaries to the draft articles. On 8 August, the Commission recommended to the General Assembly that it take note of the draft articles in a resolution and annex them to the resolution; and that it consider elaborating a convention on the basis of the draft articles.

GENERAL ASSEMBLY ACTION

On 9 December [meeting 82], the General Assembly, on the recommendation of the Sixth Committee [A/66/473], adopted **resolution 66/100** without vote [agenda item 81].

Responsibility of international organizations

The General Assembly,

Having considered chapter V of the report of the International Law Commission on the work of its sixty-third session, which contains the draft articles on the responsibility of international organizations,

Noting that the International Law Commission decided to recommend to the General Assembly that it take note of the draft articles on the responsibility of international organizations in a resolution and annex the draft articles to that resolution, and that it consider, at a later stage, the elaboration of a convention on the basis of the draft articles,

Emphasizing the continuing importance of the codification and progressive development of international law, as referred to in Article 13, paragraph 1 (*a*), of the Charter of the United Nations,

Noting that the subject of responsibility of international organizations is of major importance in the relations of States and international organizations,

Taking note of the comments of Governments and the discussion in the Sixth Committee at the sixty-sixth session of the General Assembly on this topic,

1. *Welcomes* the conclusion of the work of the International Law Commission on responsibility of international organizations and its adoption of the draft articles and a detailed commentary on the subject;

2. *Expresses its appreciation* to the International Law Commission for its continuing contribution to the codification and progressive development of international law;

3. *Takes note* of the articles on the responsibility of international organizations, presented by the International Law Commission, the text of which is annexed to the present resolution, and commends them to the attention of Governments and international organizations without prejudice to the question of their future adoption or other appropriate action;

4. *Decides* to include in the provisional agenda of its sixty-ninth session an item entitled "Responsibility of international organizations", with a view to examining, inter alia, the question of the form that might be given to the articles.

ANNEX

Responsibility of international organizations

PART ONE

Introduction

Article 1

Scope of the present articles

1. The present articles apply to the international responsibility of an international organization for an internationally wrongful act.

2. The present articles also apply to the international responsibility of a State for an internationally wrongful act in connection with the conduct of an international organization.

Article 2
Use of terms

For the purposes of the present articles:

(a) "International organization" means an organization established by a treaty or other instrument governed by international law and possessing its own international legal personality. International organizations may include as members, in addition to States, other entities;

(b) "Rules of the organization" means, in particular, the constituent instruments, decisions, resolutions and other acts of the international organization adopted in accordance with those instruments, and established practice of the organization;

(c) "Organ of an international organization" means any person or entity which has that status in accordance with the rules of the organization;

(d) "Agent of an international organization" means an official or other person or entity, other than an organ, who is charged by the organization with carrying out, or helping to carry out, one of its functions, and thus through whom the organization acts.

PART TWO
The internationally wrongful act of an international organization

Chapter I
General principles

Article 3
Responsibility of an international organization for its internationally wrongful acts

Every internationally wrongful act of an international organization entails the international responsibility of that organization.

Article 4
Elements of an internationally wrongful act of an international organization

There is an internationally wrongful act of an international organization when conduct consisting of an action or omission:

(a) Is attributable to that organization under international law; and

(b) Constitutes a breach of an international obligation of that organization.

Article 5
Characterization of an act of an international organization as internationally wrongful

The characterization of an act of an international organization as internationally wrongful is governed by international law.

Chapter II
Attribution of conduct to an international organization

Article 6
Conduct of organs or agents of an international organization

1. The conduct of an organ or agent of an international organization in the performance of functions of that organ or agent shall be considered an act of that organization under international law, whatever position the organ or agent holds in respect of the organization.

2. The rules of the organization apply in the determination of the functions of its organs and agents.

Article 7
Conduct of organs of a State or organs or agents of an international organization placed at the disposal of another international organization

The conduct of an organ of a State or an organ or agent of an international organization that is placed at the disposal of another international organization shall be considered under international law an act of the latter organization if the organization exercises effective control over that conduct.

Article 8
Excess of authority or contravention of instructions

The conduct of an organ or agent of an international organization shall be considered an act of that organization under international law if the organ or agent acts in an official capacity and within the overall functions of that organization, even if the conduct exceeds the authority of that organ or agent or contravenes instructions.

Article 9
Conduct acknowledged and adopted by an international organization as its own

Conduct which is not attributable to an international organization under articles 6 to 8 shall nevertheless be considered an act of that organization under international law if and to the extent that the organization acknowledges and adopts the conduct in question as its own.

Chapter III
Breach of an international obligation

Article 10
Existence of a breach of an international obligation

1. There is a breach of an international obligation by an international organization when an act of that international organization is not in conformity with what is required of it by that obligation, regardless of the origin or character of the obligation concerned.

2. Paragraph 1 includes the breach of any international obligation that may arise for an international organization towards its members under the rules of the organization.

Article 11
International obligation in force for an international organization

An act of an international organization does not constitute a breach of an international obligation unless the organization is bound by the obligation in question at the time the act occurs.

Article 12
Extension in time of the breach of an international obligation

1. The breach of an international obligation by an act of an international organization not having a continuing character occurs at the moment when the act is performed, even if its effects continue.

2. The breach of an international obligation by an act of an international organization having a continuing character extends over the entire period during which the act continues and remains not in conformity with that obligation.

3. The breach of an international obligation requiring an international organization to prevent a given event occurs when the event occurs and extends over the entire period during which the event continues and remains not in conformity with that obligation.

Article 13
Breach consisting of a composite act

1. The breach of an international obligation by an international organization through a series of actions and omissions defined in aggregate as wrongful occurs when the action or omission occurs which, taken with the other actions or omissions, is sufficient to constitute the wrongful act.

2. In such a case, the breach extends over the entire period starting with the first of the actions or omissions of the series and lasts for as long as these actions or omissions are repeated and remain not in conformity with the international obligation.

Chapter IV
Responsibility of an international organization in connection with the act of a State or another international organization

Article 14
Aid or assistance in the commission of an internationally wrongful act

An international organization which aids or assists a State or another international organization in the commission of an internationally wrongful act by the State or the latter organization is internationally responsible for doing so if:

(*a*) The former organization does so with knowledge of the circumstances of the internationally wrongful act; and

(*b*) The act would be internationally wrongful if committed by that organization.

Article 15
Direction and control exercised over the commission of an internationally wrongful act

An international organization which directs and controls a State or another international organization in the commission of an internationally wrongful act by the State or the latter organization is internationally responsible for that act if:

(*a*) The former organization does so with knowledge of the circumstances of the internationally wrongful act; and

(*b*) The act would be internationally wrongful if committed by that organization.

Article 16
Coercion of a State or another international organization

An international organization which coerces a State or another international organization to commit an act is internationally responsible for that act if:

(*a*) The act would, but for the coercion, be an internationally wrongful act of the coerced State or international organization; and

(*b*) The coercing international organization does so with knowledge of the circumstances of the act.

Article 17
Circumvention of international obligations through decisions and authorizations addressed to members

1. An international organization incurs international responsibility if it circumvents one of its international obligations by adopting a decision binding member States or international organizations to commit an act that would be internationally wrongful if committed by the former organization.

2. An international organization incurs international responsibility if it circumvents one of its international obligations by authorizing member States or international organizations to commit an act that would be internationally wrongful if committed by the former organization and the act in question is committed because of that authorization.

3. Paragraphs 1 and 2 apply whether or not the act in question is internationally wrongful for the member States or international organizations to which the decision or authorization is addressed.

Article 18
Responsibility of an international organization member of another international organization

Without prejudice to articles 14 to 17, the international responsibility of an international organization that is a member of another international organization also arises in relation to an act of the latter under the conditions set out in articles 61 and 62 for States that are members of an international organization.

Article 19
Effect of this Chapter

This Chapter is without prejudice to the international responsibility of the State or international organization which commits the act in question, or of any other State or international organization.

Chapter V
Circumstances precluding wrongfulness

Article 20
Consent

Valid consent by a State or an international organization to the commission of a given act by another international organization precludes the wrongfulness of that act in relation to that State or the former organization to the extent that the act remains within the limits of that consent.

Article 21
Self-defence

The wrongfulness of an act of an international organization is precluded if and to the extent that the act constitutes a lawful measure of self-defence under international law.

Article 22
Countermeasures

1. Subject to paragraphs 2 and 3, the wrongfulness of an act of an international organization not in conformity with an international obligation towards a State or another international organization is precluded if and to the extent that the act constitutes a countermeasure taken in accordance with the substantive and procedural conditions required by international law, including those set forth in Chapter II of Part Four for countermeasures taken against another international organization.

2. Subject to paragraph 3, an international organization may not take countermeasures against a responsible member State or international organization unless:

(*a*) The conditions referred to in paragraph 1 are met;

(b) The countermeasures are not inconsistent with the rules of the organization; and

(c) No appropriate means are available for otherwise inducing compliance with the obligations of the responsible State or international organization concerning cessation of the breach and reparation.

3. Countermeasures may not be taken by an international organization against a member State or international organization in response to a breach of an international obligation under the rules of the organization unless such countermeasures are provided for by those rules.

Article 23
Force majeure

1. The wrongfulness of an act of an international organization not in conformity with an international obligation of that organization is precluded if the act is due to force majeure, that is, the occurrence of an irresistible force or of an unforeseen event, beyond the control of the organization, making it materially impossible in the circumstances to perform the obligation.

2. Paragraph 1 does not apply if:

(a) The situation of force majeure is due, either alone or in combination with other factors, to the conduct of the organization invoking it; or

(b) The organization has assumed the risk of that situation occurring.

Article 24
Distress

1. The wrongfulness of an act of an international organization not in conformity with an international obligation of that organization is precluded if the author of the act in question has no other reasonable way, in a situation of distress, of saving the author's life or the lives of other persons entrusted to the author's care.

2. Paragraph 1 does not apply if:

(a) The situation of distress is due, either alone or in combination with other factors, to the conduct of the organization invoking it; or

(b) The act in question is likely to create a comparable or greater peril.

Article 25
Necessity

1. Necessity may not be invoked by an international organization as a ground for precluding the wrongfulness of an act not in conformity with an international obligation of that organization unless the act:

(a) Is the only means for the organization to safeguard against a grave and imminent peril an essential interest of its member States or of the international community as a whole, when the organization has, in accordance with international law, the function to protect the interest in question; and

(b) Does not seriously impair an essential interest of the State or States towards which the international obligation exists, or of the international community as a whole.

2. In any case, necessity may not be invoked by an international organization as a ground for precluding wrongfulness if:

(a) The international obligation in question excludes the possibility of invoking necessity; or

(b) The organization has contributed to the situation of necessity.

Article 26
Compliance with peremptory norms

Nothing in this Chapter precludes the wrongfulness of any act of an international organization which is not in conformity with an obligation arising under a peremptory norm of general international law.

Article 27
Consequences of invoking a circumstance precluding wrongfulness

The invocation of a circumstance precluding wrongfulness in accordance with this Chapter is without prejudice to:

(a) Compliance with the obligation in question, if and to the extent that the circumstance precluding wrongfulness no longer exists;

(b) The question of compensation for any material loss caused by the act in question.

PART THREE

Content of the international responsibility of an international organization

Chapter I

General principles

Article 28
Legal consequences of an internationally wrongful act

The international responsibility of an international organization which is entailed by an internationally wrongful act in accordance with the provisions of Part Two involves legal consequences as set out in this Part.

Article 29
Continued duty of performance

The legal consequences of an internationally wrongful act under this Part do not affect the continued duty of the responsible international organization to perform the obligation breached.

Article 30
Cessation and non-repetition

The international organization responsible for the internationally wrongful act is under an obligation:

(a) To cease that act, if it is continuing;

(b) To offer appropriate assurances and guarantees of non-repetition, if circumstances so require.

Article 31
Reparation

1. The responsible international organization is under an obligation to make full reparation for the injury caused by the internationally wrongful act.

2. Injury includes any damage, whether material or moral, caused by the internationally wrongful act of an international organization.

Article 32
Relevance of the rules of the organization

1. The responsible international organization may not rely on its rules as justification for failure to comply with its obligations under this Part.

2. Paragraph 1 is without prejudice to the applicability of the rules of an international organization to the relations between the organization and its member States and organizations.

Article 33
Scope of international obligations set out in this Part

1. The obligations of the responsible international organization set out in this Part may be owed to one or more States, to one or more other organizations, or to the international community as a whole, depending in particular on the character and content of the international obligation and on the circumstances of the breach.

2. This Part is without prejudice to any right, arising from the international responsibility of an international organization, which may accrue directly to any person or entity other than a State or an international organization.

Chapter II
Reparation for injury

Article 34
Forms of reparation

Full reparation for the injury caused by the internationally wrongful act shall take the form of restitution, compensation and satisfaction, either singly or in combination, in accordance with the provisions of this Chapter.

Article 35
Restitution

An international organization responsible for an internationally wrongful act is under an obligation to make restitution, that is, to re-establish the situation which existed before the wrongful act was committed, provided and to the extent that restitution:

(a) Is not materially impossible;

(b) Does not involve a burden out of all proportion to the benefit deriving from restitution instead of compensation.

Article 36
Compensation

1. The international organization responsible for an internationally wrongful act is under an obligation to compensate for the damage caused thereby, insofar as such damage is not made good by restitution.

2. The compensation shall cover any financially assessable damage, including loss of profits insofar as it is established.

Article 37
Satisfaction

1. The international organization responsible for an internationally wrongful act is under an obligation to give satisfaction for the injury caused by that act insofar as it cannot be made good by restitution or compensation.

2. Satisfaction may consist in an acknowledgement of the breach, an expression of regret, a formal apology or another appropriate modality.

3. Satisfaction shall not be out of proportion to the injury and may not take a form humiliating to the responsible international organization.

Article 38
Interest

1. Interest on any principal sum due under this Chapter shall be payable when necessary in order to ensure full reparation. The interest rate and mode of calculation shall be set so as to achieve that result.

2. Interest runs from the date when the principal sum should have been paid until the date the obligation to pay is fulfilled.

Article 39
Contribution to the injury

In the determination of reparation, account shall be taken of the contribution to the injury by wilful or negligent action or omission of the injured State or international organization or of any person or entity in relation to whom reparation is sought.

Article 40
Ensuring the fulfilment of the obligation to make reparation

1. The responsible international organization shall take all appropriate measures in accordance with its rules to ensure that its members provide it with the means for effectively fulfilling its obligations under this Chapter.

2. The members of a responsible international organization shall take all the appropriate measures that may be required by the rules of the organization in order to enable the organization to fulfil its obligations under this Chapter.

Chapter III
Serious breaches of obligations under peremptory norms of general international law

Article 41
Application of this Chapter

1. This Chapter applies to the international responsibility which is entailed by a serious breach by an international organization of an obligation arising under a peremptory norm of general international law.

2. A breach of such an obligation is serious if it involves a gross or systematic failure by the responsible international organization to fulfil the obligation.

Article 42
Particular consequences of a serious breach of an obligation under this Chapter

1. States and international organizations shall cooperate to bring to an end through lawful means any serious breach within the meaning of article 41.

2. No State or international organization shall recognize as lawful a situation created by a serious breach within the meaning of article 41, nor render aid or assistance in maintaining that situation.

3. Article 42 is without prejudice to the other consequences referred to in this Part and to such further consequences that a breach to which this Chapter applies may entail under international law.

Part Four
The implementation of the international responsibility of an international organization

Chapter I
Invocation of the responsibility of an international organization

Article 43
Invocation of responsibility by an injured State or international organization

A State or an international organization is entitled as an injured State or an injured international organization to invoke the responsibility of another international organization if the obligation breached is owed to:

(a) That State or the former international organization individually;

(b) A group of States or international organizations including that State or the former international organization, or the international community as a whole, and the breach of the obligation:

  (i) Specially affects that State or that international organization; or

  (ii) Is of such a character as radically to change the position of all the other States and international organizations to which the obligation is owed with respect to the further performance of the obligation.

Article 44
Notice of claim by an injured State or international organization

1. An injured State or international organization which invokes the responsibility of another international organization shall give notice of its claim to that organization.

2. The injured State or international organization may specify in particular:

(a) The conduct that the responsible international organization should take in order to cease the wrongful act, if it is continuing;

(b) What form reparation should take in accordance with the provisions of Part Three.

Article 45
Admissibility of claims

1. An injured State may not invoke the responsibility of an international organization if the claim is not brought in accordance with any applicable rule relating to the nationality of claims.

2. When the rule of exhaustion of local remedies applies to a claim, an injured State or international organization may not invoke the responsibility of another international organization if any available and effective remedy has not been exhausted.

Article 46
Loss of the right to invoke responsibility

The responsibility of an international organization may not be invoked if:

(a) The injured State or international organization has validly waived the claim;

(b) The injured State or international organization is to be considered as having, by reason of its conduct, validly acquiesced in the lapse of the claim.

Article 47
Plurality of injured States or international organizations

Where several States or international organizations are injured by the same internationally wrongful act of an international organization, each injured State or international organization may separately invoke the responsibility of the international organization for the internationally wrongful act.

Article 48
Responsibility of an international organization and one or more States or international organizations

1. Where an international organization and one or more States or other international organizations are responsible for the same internationally wrongful act, the responsibility of each State or organization may be invoked in relation to that act.

2. Subsidiary responsibility may be invoked insofar as the invocation of the primary responsibility has not led to reparation.

3. Paragraphs 1 and 2:

(a) Do not permit any injured State or international organization to recover, by way of compensation, more than the damage it has suffered;

(b) Are without prejudice to any right of recourse that the State or international organization providing reparation may have against the other responsible States or international organizations.

Article 49
Invocation of responsibility by a State or an international organization other than an injured State or international organization

1. A State or an international organization other than an injured State or international organization is entitled to invoke the responsibility of another international organization in accordance with paragraph 4 if the obligation breached is owed to a group of States or international organizations, including the State or organization that invokes responsibility, and is established for the protection of a collective interest of the group.

2. A State other than an injured State is entitled to invoke the responsibility of an international organization in accordance with paragraph 4 if the obligation breached is owed to the international community as a whole.

3. An international organization other than an injured international organization is entitled to invoke the responsibility of another international organization in accordance with paragraph 4 if the obligation breached is owed to the international community as a whole and safeguarding the interest of the international community as a whole underlying the obligation breached is within the functions of the international organization invoking responsibility.

4. A State or an international organization entitled to invoke responsibility under paragraphs 1 to 3 may claim from the responsible international organization:

(a) Cessation of the internationally wrongful act, and assurances and guarantees of non-repetition in accordance with article 30; and

(b) Performance of the obligation of reparation in accordance with Part Three, in the interest of the injured State or international organization or of the beneficiaries of the obligation breached.

5. The requirements for the invocation of responsibility by an injured State or international organization under articles 44, 45, paragraph 2, and 46 apply to an invocation of responsibility by a State or international organization entitled to do so under paragraphs 1 to 4.

Article 50
Scope of this Chapter

This Chapter is without prejudice to the entitlement that a person or entity other than a State or an international organization may have to invoke the international responsibility of an international organization.

Chapter II
Countermeasures

Article 51
Object and limits of countermeasures

1. An injured State or an injured international organization may only take countermeasures against an international organization which is responsible for an internationally wrongful act in order to induce that organization to comply with its obligations under Part Three.
2. Countermeasures are limited to the non-performance for the time being of international obligations of the State or international organization taking the measures towards the responsible international organization.
3. Countermeasures shall, as far as possible, be taken in such a way as to permit the resumption of performance of the obligations in question.
4. Countermeasures shall, as far as possible, be taken in such a way as to limit their effects on the exercise by the responsible international organization of its functions.

Article 52
Conditions for taking countermeasures by members of an international organization

1. Subject to paragraph 2, an injured State or international organization which is a member of a responsible international organization may not take countermeasures against that organization unless:
  (a) The conditions referred to in article 51 are met;
  (b) The countermeasures are not inconsistent with the rules of the organization; and
  (c) No appropriate means are available for otherwise inducing compliance with the obligations of the responsible international organization concerning cessation of the breach and reparation.
2. Countermeasures may not be taken by an injured State or international organization which is a member of a responsible international organization against that organization in response to a breach of an international obligation under the rules of the organization unless such countermeasures are provided for by those rules.

Article 53
Obligations not affected by countermeasures

1. Countermeasures shall not affect:
  (a) The obligation to refrain from the threat or use of force as embodied in the Charter of the United Nations;
  (b) Obligations for the protection of human rights;
  (c) Obligations of a humanitarian character prohibiting reprisals;
  (d) Other obligations under peremptory norms of general international law.
2. An injured State or international organization taking countermeasures is not relieved from fulfilling its obligations:
  (a) Under any dispute settlement procedure applicable between it and the responsible international organization;
  (b) To respect any inviolability of organs or agents of the responsible international organization and of the premises, archives and documents of that organization.

Article 54
Proportionality of countermeasures

Countermeasures must be commensurate with the injury suffered, taking into account the gravity of the internationally wrongful act and the rights in question.

Article 55
Conditions relating to resort to countermeasures

1. Before taking countermeasures, an injured State or international organization shall:
  (a) Call upon the responsible international organization, in accordance with article 44, to fulfil its obligations under Part Three;
  (b) Notify the responsible international organization of any decision to take countermeasures and offer to negotiate with that organization.
2. Notwithstanding paragraph 1 (b), the injured State or international organization may take such urgent countermeasures as are necessary to preserve its rights.
3. Countermeasures may not be taken and, if already taken, must be suspended without undue delay if:
  (a) The internationally wrongful act has ceased; and
  (b) The dispute is pending before a court or tribunal which has the authority to make decisions binding on the parties.
4. Paragraph 3 does not apply if the responsible international organization fails to implement the dispute settlement procedures in good faith.

Article 56
Termination of countermeasures

Countermeasures shall be terminated as soon as the responsible international organization has complied with its obligations under Part Three in relation to the internationally wrongful act.

Article 57
Measures taken by States or international organizations other than an injured State or organization

This Chapter does not prejudice the right of any State or international organization, entitled under article 49, paragraphs 1 to 3, to invoke the responsibility of another international organization, to take lawful measures against that organization to ensure cessation of the breach and reparation in the interest of the injured State or organization or of the beneficiaries of the obligation breached.

PART FIVE

Responsibility of a State in connection with the conduct of an international organization

Article 58
Aid or assistance by a State in the commission of an internationally wrongful act by an international organization

1. A State which aids or assists an international organization in the commission of an internationally wrongful act by the latter is internationally responsible for doing so if:

(a) The State does so with knowledge of the circumstances of the internationally wrongful act; and

(b) The act would be internationally wrongful if committed by that State.

2. An act by a State member of an international organization done in accordance with the rules of the organization does not as such engage the international responsibility of that State under the terms of article 58.

Article 59
Direction and control exercised by a State over the commission of an internationally wrongful act by an international organization

1. A State which directs and controls an international organization in the commission of an internationally wrongful act by the latter is internationally responsible for that act if:

(a) The State does so with knowledge of the circumstances of the internationally wrongful act; and

(b) The act would be internationally wrongful if committed by that State.

2. An act by a State member of an international organization done in accordance with the rules of the organization does not as such engage the international responsibility of that State under the terms of article 59.

Article 60
Coercion of an international organization by a State

A State which coerces an international organization to commit an act is internationally responsible for that act if:

(a) The act would, but for the coercion, be an internationally wrongful act of the coerced international organization; and

(b) The coercing State does so with knowledge of the circumstances of the act.

Article 61
Circumvention of international obligations of a State member of an international organization

1. A State member of an international organization incurs international responsibility if, by taking advantage of the fact that the organization has competence in relation to the subject matter of one of the State's international obligations, it circumvents that obligation by causing the organization to commit an act that, if committed by the State, would have constituted a breach of the obligation.

2. Paragraph 1 applies whether or not the act in question is internationally wrongful for the international organization.

Article 62
Responsibility of a State member of an international organization for an internationally wrongful act of that organization

1. A State member of an international organization is responsible for an internationally wrongful act of that organization if:

(a) It has accepted responsibility for that act towards the injured party; or

(b) It has led the injured party to rely on its responsibility.

2. Any international responsibility of a State under paragraph 1 is presumed to be subsidiary.

Article 63
Effect of this Part

This Part is without prejudice to the international responsibility of the international organization which commits the act in question, or of any State or other international organization.

PART SIX

General provisions

Article 64
Lex specialis

These articles do not apply where and to the extent that the conditions for the existence of an internationally wrongful act or the content or implementation of the international responsibility of an international organization, or of a State in connection with the conduct of an international organization, are governed by special rules of international law. Such special rules of international law may be contained in the rules of the organization applicable to the relations between an international organization and its members.

Article 65
Questions of international responsibility not regulated by these articles

The applicable rules of international law continue to govern questions concerning the responsibility of an international organization or a State for an internationally wrongful act to the extent that they are not regulated by these articles.

Article 66
Individual responsibility

These articles are without prejudice to any question of the individual responsibility under international law of any person acting on behalf of an international organization or a State.

Article 67
Charter of the United Nations

These articles are without prejudice to the Charter of the United Nations.

Effects of armed conflict on treaties

ILC [A/66/10] had before it two notes by Special Rapporteur Lucius Caflisch (Switzerland) on the recommendations to be made to the General Assembly about the draft articles on the effects of armed conflicts on treaties [A/CN.4/644], and on draft article 5 on the application of rules on treaty interpretation and the annex to the draft articles [A/CN.4/645].

In May, the Commission considered the report of the Drafting Committee [A/CN.4/L.777 & Corr.1] and adopted the set of 18 draft articles on the effects of armed conflicts on treaties, on second reading, together with the commentaries to those draft articles. In accordance with its Statute, the Commission submitted the draft articles to the General Assembly. In August, the Commission recommended to the Assembly that it take note of the draft articles in a resolution and annex them to the resolution, and to consider, at a later stage, the elaboration of a convention on the basis of the draft articles.

GENERAL ASSEMBLY ACTION

On 9 December [meeting 82], the General Assembly, on the recommendation of the Sixth Committee [A/66/473], adopted **resolution 66/99** without vote [agenda item 81].

Effects of armed conflicts on treaties

The General Assembly,

Having considered chapter VI of the report of the International Law Commission on the work of its sixty-third session, which contains the draft articles on the effects of armed conflicts on treaties,

Noting that the International Law Commission decided to recommend to the General Assembly that it take note of the draft articles on the effects of armed conflicts on treaties in a resolution and annex the draft articles to that resolution, and that it consider, at a later stage, the elaboration of a convention on the basis of the draft articles,

Emphasizing the continuing importance of the codification and progressive development of international law, as referred to in Article 13, paragraph 1 (*a*), of the Charter of the United Nations,

Noting that the subject of the effects of armed conflicts on treaties is of major importance in the relations of States,

1. *Welcomes* the conclusion of the work of the International Law Commission on the effects of armed conflicts on treaties and its adoption of the draft articles and a detailed commentary on the subject;

2. *Expresses its appreciation* to the International Law Commission for its continuing contribution to the codification and progressive development of international law;

3. *Takes note* of the articles on the effects of armed conflicts on treaties, presented by the International Law Commission, the text of which is annexed to the present resolution, and commends them to the attention of Governments without prejudice to the question of their future adoption or other appropriate action;

4. *Decides* to include in the provisional agenda of its sixty-ninth session an item entitled "Effects of armed conflicts on treaties" with a view to examining, inter alia, the question of the form that might be given to the articles.

ANNEX
Effects of armed conflicts on treaties
PART ONE
Scope and definitions
Article 1
Scope

The present articles apply to the effects of armed conflict on the relations of States under a treaty.

Article 2
Definitions

For the purposes of the present articles:

(*a*) "Treaty" means an international agreement concluded between States in written form and governed by international law, whether embodied in a single instrument or in two or more related instruments and whatever its particular designation, and includes treaties between States to which international organizations are also parties;

(*b*) "Armed conflict" means a situation in which there is resort to armed force between States or protracted resort to armed force between governmental authorities and organized armed groups.

PART TWO
Principles
Chapter I
Operation of treaties in the event of armed conflicts
Article 3
General principle

The existence of an armed conflict does not ipso facto terminate or suspend the operation of treaties:

(*a*) As between States parties to the conflict;

(*b*) As between a State party to the conflict and a State that is not.

Article 4
Provisions on the operation of treaties

Where a treaty itself contains provisions on its operation in situations of armed conflict, those provisions shall apply.

Article 5
Application of rules on treaty interpretation

The rules of international law on treaty interpretation shall be applied to establish whether a treaty is susceptible to termination, withdrawal or suspension in the event of an armed conflict.

Article 6
Factors indicating whether a treaty is susceptible to termination, withdrawal or suspension

In order to ascertain whether a treaty is susceptible to termination, withdrawal or suspension in the event of an armed conflict, regard shall be had to all relevant factors, including:

(*a*) The nature of the treaty, in particular its subject matter, its object and purpose, its content and the number of parties to the treaty; and

(*b*) The characteristics of the armed conflict, such as its territorial extent, its scale and intensity, its duration and, in the case of non-international armed conflict, also the degree of outside involvement.

Article 7
Continued operation of treaties resulting from their subject matter

An indicative list of treaties, the subject matter of which involves an implication that they continue in operation, in whole or in part, during armed conflict, is to be found in the annex to the present articles.

Chapter II
Other provisions relevant to the operation of treaties

Article 8
Conclusion of treaties during armed conflict

1. The existence of an armed conflict does not affect the capacity of a State party to that conflict to conclude treaties in accordance with international law.

2. States may conclude agreements involving termination or suspension of a treaty or part of a treaty that is operative between them during situations of armed conflict, or may agree to amend or modify the treaty.

Article 9
Notification of intention to terminate or withdraw from a treaty or to suspend its operation

1. A State intending to terminate or withdraw from a treaty to which it is a Party, or to suspend the operation of that treaty, as a consequence of an armed conflict shall notify the other State Party or States Parties to the treaty, or its depositary, of such intention.

2. The notification takes effect upon receipt by the other State Party or States Parties, unless it provides for a subsequent date.

3. Nothing in the preceding paragraphs shall affect the right of a Party to object within a reasonable time, in accordance with the terms of the treaty or other applicable rules of international law, to the termination of or withdrawal from the treaty, or suspension of its operation.

4. If an objection has been raised in accordance with paragraph 3, the States concerned shall seek a solution through the means indicated in Article 33 of the Charter of the United Nations.

5. Nothing in the preceding paragraphs shall affect the rights or obligations of States with regard to the settlement of disputes insofar as they have remained applicable.

Article 10
Obligations imposed by international law independently of a treaty

The termination of or the withdrawal from a treaty, or the suspension of its operation, as a consequence of an armed conflict, shall not impair in any way the duty of any State to fulfil any obligation embodied in the treaty to which it would be subject under international law independently of that treaty.

Article 11
Separability of treaty provisions

Termination, withdrawal from or suspension of the operation of a treaty as a consequence of an armed conflict shall, unless the treaty otherwise provides or the Parties otherwise agree, take effect with respect to the whole treaty except where:

(a) The treaty contains clauses that are separable from the remainder of the treaty with regard to their application;

(b) It appears from the treaty or is otherwise established that acceptance of those clauses was not an essential basis of the consent of the other Party or Parties to be bound by the treaty as a whole; and

(c) Continued performance of the remainder of the treaty would not be unjust.

Article 12
Loss of the right to terminate or withdraw from a treaty or to suspend its operation

A State may no longer terminate or withdraw from a treaty or suspend its operation as a consequence of an armed conflict if, after becoming aware of the facts:

(a) It shall have expressly agreed that the treaty remains in force or continues in operation; or

(b) It must by reason of its conduct be considered as having acquiesced in the continued operation of the treaty or in its maintenance in force.

Article 13
Revival or resumption of treaty relations subsequent to an armed conflict

1. Subsequent to an armed conflict, the States Parties may regulate, on the basis of agreement, the revival of treaties terminated or suspended as a consequence of the armed conflict.

2. The resumption of the operation of a treaty suspended as a consequence of an armed conflict shall be determined in accordance with the factors referred to in article 6.

Part Three
Miscellaneous

Article 14
Effect of the exercise of the right to self-defence on a treaty

A State exercising its inherent right of individual or collective self-defence in accordance with the Charter of the United Nations is entitled to suspend in whole or in part the operation of a treaty to which it is a Party insofar as that operation is incompatible with the exercise of that right.

Article 15
Prohibition of benefit to an aggressor State

A State committing aggression within the meaning of the Charter of the United Nations and resolution 3314(XXIX) of the General Assembly of the United Nations shall not terminate or withdraw from a treaty or suspend its operation as a consequence of an armed conflict that results from the act of aggression if the effect would be to the benefit of that State.

Article 16
Decisions of the Security Council

The present articles are without prejudice to relevant decisions taken by the Security Council in accordance with the Charter of the United Nations.

Article 17
Rights and duties arising from the laws of neutrality

The present articles are without prejudice to the rights and duties of States arising from the laws of neutrality.

Article 18
Other cases of termination, withdrawal or suspension

The present articles are without prejudice to the termination, withdrawal or suspension of treaties as a consequence of, inter alia: (a) a material breach; (b) supervening impossibility of performance; or (c) a fundamental change of circumstances.

Annex

Indicative list of treaties referred to in article 7

(a) Treaties on the law of armed conflict, including treaties on international humanitarian law;

(b) Treaties declaring, creating or regulating a permanent regime or status or related permanent rights, including treaties establishing or modifying land and maritime boundaries;

(c) Multilateral law-making treaties;

(d) Treaties on international criminal justice;

(e) Treaties of friendship, commerce and navigation and agreements concerning private rights;

(f) Treaties for the international protection of human rights;

(g) Treaties relating to the international protection of the environment;

(h) Treaties relating to international watercourses and related installations and facilities;

(i) Treaties relating to aquifers and related installations and facilities;

(j) Treaties which are constituent instruments of international organizations;

(k) Treaties relating to the international settlement of disputes by peaceful means, including resort to conciliation, mediation, arbitration and judicial settlement;

(l) Treaties relating to diplomatic and consular relations.

Immunity of State officials

The Commission [A/66/10] considered the second [YUN 2010, p. 1325] and third [A/CN.4/646] reports on immunity of State officials from foreign criminal jurisdiction by Special Rapporteur Roman Anatolevich Kolodkin (Russian Federation). The second report reviewed and presented the substantive issues concerning and implicated by the scope of immunity of a State official from foreign criminal jurisdiction, while the third report addressed the procedural aspects, focusing on questions concerning the timing of consideration of immunity, its invocation and waiver.

The Special Rapporteur noted that since ILC began its consideration of the topic, the question of immunity of a State official had continued to be considered, both in practice, as new judicial decisions were rendered, and in academia. Regarding the second report, members acknowledged the political ramifications of the topic, as well as its impact on international relations. Some members agreed broadly with the report's conclusions. Other members expressed concern that the report presented certain biased conclusions, failing to take into consideration trends in international law concerning, in particular, the question of grave crimes under international law. Some members were of the view that the Commission should establish a working group to consider the questions raised in the discussions, as well as how to proceed with the topic.

Concerning the third report, it was generally considered that the analysis made in the report was convincing and the extrapolations drawn were logical. Some members stated that the debate concerning the second report highlighted the fact that there were a number of basic issues that needed to be resolved. As a consequence of those issues—including the scope of immunity *ratione personae* in the case where grave international crimes had been committed—some of the conclusions were problematic. Some members noted that their concerns raised in regard to the second report, including the seemingly absolutist and expansive approach to immunity, remained. Members cautioned that there was a risk to the reputation of the Commission if there was a greater tilt towards State interests; ILC would not be in a position to find the necessary balance between the old law—based on an absolute conception of sovereignty—and the new expectation of the international community in favour of accountability. Others preferred a balance between legitimate interests of sovereign States and the concern for accountability. Some members noted that the Commission had no cause to be concerned about risking its reputation since it was part of its functioning to balance different legitimate considerations and not let itself be disproportionately swayed by any one of them.

Expulsion of aliens

The Commission [A/66/10] had before it the second addendum to the sixth report of Special Rapporteur Maurice Kamto (Cameroon) on the expulsion of aliens [A/CN.4/625/Add.2] and the Special Rapporteur's seventh report [A/CN.4/642]. The issuance of the addendum completed the consideration of the expulsion proceedings, including the implementation of the expulsion decision, appeals against the expulsion decision, the determination of the State of destination and the protection of human rights in the transit State. The addendum also considered the legal consequences of expulsion, notably the protection of the property rights and similar interests of aliens subject to expulsion, the question of the existence of a right of return in the case of unlawful expulsion, and the responsibility of the expelling State as a result of an unlawful expulsion, including the question of diplomatic protection. The addendum also contained the last of the draft articles that the Special Rapporteur intended to propose.

Following a debate in plenary, the Commission referred to the Drafting Committee seven draft articles on the issues dealt with in the report and the addendum, as well as a draft article on expulsion in connection with extradition, as revised by the Special Rapporteur during the sixty-second session [YUN 2010, p. 1324].

The seventh report reviewed recent developments relevant to the topic and proposed a restructured summary of the draft articles. The Commission referred the summary to the Drafting Committee.

On 11 August, ILC took note of an interim report by the chairman of the Drafting Committee informing the Commission of the progress of work on the set of draft articles, which were being finalized with a view to being submitted to the Commission's sixty-fourth (2012) session for adoption on first reading.

Protection of persons in the event of disasters

ILC [A/66/10] considered the fourth report on the protection of persons in the event of disasters [A/CN.4/643 & Corr.1] by Special Rapporteur Eduardo Valencia-Ospina (Colombia). Proposals for three further draft articles were made in the report: draft articles 10 on the duty of the affected State to seek assistance where its national response capacity was exceeded; 11 on the duty of the affected State not to arbitrarily withhold its consent to external assistance; and 12 on the right to offer assistance in the international community.

The Special Rapporteur recalled that in his third report [YUN 2010, p. 1325] he had proposed a provision on the principle of the consent of the affected State. He sought to build on that proposal in the fourth report. The broad concept of protection proposed by the Special Rapporteur since his first report called for the recognition of the tensions underlying the link between protection and the principles of respect for territorial sovereignty and non-interference in the internal affairs of the affected States.

Following a debate in plenary, the Commission referred draft articles 10 to 12, as proposed by the Special Rapporteur, to the Drafting Committee. The Commission provisionally adopted six draft articles, together with commentaries, including draft articles 6 to 9, of which it had taken note at its sixty-second session [YUN 2010, p. 1325], dealing with humanitarian principles in disaster response, human dignity, human rights and the role of the affected State, respectively; and draft articles 10 and 11, dealing with the duty of the affected State to seek assistance and with the question of the consent of the affected State to external assistance.

Obligation to extradite or prosecute

The Commission [A/66/10] considered the fourth report of Special Rapporteur Zdzislaw Galicki (Poland) on the obligation to extradite or prosecute (*aut dedere aut judicare*) [A/CN.4/648]. It addressed the question of sources of the obligation to extradite or prosecute, focusing on treaties and custom.

The Special Rapporteur proposed that the former article 2 (Use of terms) be replaced with a new draft article 2 on the duty to cooperate, in order to underscore that the duty to cooperate was overarching in the appreciation of the obligation to extradite or prosecute. In light of the variety and differentiation of provisions concerning the obligation, he considered it useful to propose the addition of another paragraph to draft article 3 on treaty as a source of the obligation to extradite or prosecute. Having considered the various issues implicated, the Rapporteur proposed draft article 4 on international custom as a source of the obligation *aut dedere aut judicare*.

ILC members noted that the topic had implications for other aspects of the law, including questions of prosecutorial discretion, questions of asylum, the law on extradition, the immunity of State officials from criminal jurisdiction, peremptory norms of international law, and universal jurisdiction, which posed problems in terms of the direction to be taken and what needed to be achieved. Moreover, concerns were expressed about the draft articles as proposed and the analysis on which they were based. It was noted that the methodology of separately treating the main sources of international law—treaties and customary law—and proposing two separate draft articles was conceptually problematic; the focus should be on the obligation to extradite or prosecute and how treaties and custom evidenced the rule, rather than on treaties or custom as the "source" of the obligation; there was no need for a draft article to demonstrate that there was a rule in a treaty or under custom. Other sources would help inform the nature, scope and content of the obligation.

Treaties over time

The Commission [A/66/10] reconstituted the Study Group on Treaties over Time, and the Group continued its work on the subsequent agreements and practice. It first completed its consideration of the introductory report by its chairman on the relevant jurisprudence of the International Court of Justice and of arbitral tribunals of ad hoc jurisdiction by examining the question of possible modifications of a treaty by subsequent agreements and practice as well as the relation of subsequent agreements and practice to formal amendment procedures. The Group considered that no conclusions should be drawn at that stage on the matters covered in the introductory report.

The Study Group began its consideration of the second report by its chairman on the jurisprudence under special regimes relating to subsequent agreements and practice by focusing on certain conclusions contained therein. In the light of the discussions, the chairman reformulated the text of nine preliminary conclusions relating to issues such as reliance by adjudicatory bodies on the general rule of treaty interpretation, different approaches to treaty interpretation, and various aspects concerning subsequent agreements and practice as a means of treaty interpretation.

Most-favoured-nation clause

ILC reconstituted the Study Group on the Most-Favoured-Nation Clause (MFN) [A/66/10], which held a discussion on the interpretation and application of MFN clauses in investment agreements, as well as a framework of questions prepared to provide an overview of issues that might need to be considered in the context of the Group's work. The Group reaffirmed the need to study further the question of MFN in relation to trade in services and investment agreements, as well as the relationship between MFN, fair and equitable treatment, and national treatment standards.

The Commission took note of the oral report of the co-chairmen of the Study Group on 8 August.

GENERAL ASSEMBLY ACTION

On 9 December [meeting 82], the General Assembly, on the recommendation of the Sixth Committee [A/66/473], adopted **resolution 66/98** without vote [agenda item 81].

Report of the International Law Commission on the work of its sixty-third session

The General Assembly,

Having considered the report of the International Law Commission on the work of its sixty-third session,

Emphasizing the importance of furthering the progressive development and codification of international law as a means of implementing the purposes and principles set forth in the Charter of the United Nations and in the Declaration on Principles of International Law concerning Friendly Relations and Cooperation among States in accordance with the Charter of the United Nations,

Recognizing the desirability of referring legal and drafting questions to the Sixth Committee, including topics that might be submitted to the International Law Commission for closer examination, and of enabling the Sixth Committee and the Commission to enhance further their contribution to the progressive development and codification of international law,

Recalling the need to keep under review those topics of international law which, given their new or renewed interest for the international community, may be suitable for the progressive development and codification of international law and therefore may be included in the future programme of work of the International Law Commission,

Recalling also the role of Member States in submitting proposals for new topics for the consideration of the International Law Commission, and noting in this regard the recommendation of the Commission that such proposals be accompanied by a statement of reasons,

Reaffirming the importance for the successful work of the International Law Commission of the information provided by Member States concerning their views and practice,

Recognizing the importance of the work of the special rapporteurs of the International Law Commission,

Welcoming the holding of the International Law Seminar, and noting with appreciation the voluntary contributions made to the United Nations Trust Fund for the International Law Seminar,

Acknowledging the importance of facilitating the timely publication of the *Yearbook of the International Law Commission* and of eliminating the backlog,

Stressing the usefulness of focusing and structuring the debate on the report of the International Law Commission in the Sixth Committee in such a manner that conditions are provided for concentrated attention to each of the main topics dealt with in the report and for discussions on specific topics,

Wishing to enhance further, in the context of the revitalization of the debate on the report of the International Law Commission, the interaction between the Sixth Committee as a body of governmental representatives and the Commission as a body of independent legal experts, with a view to improving the dialogue between the two bodies,

Welcoming initiatives to hold interactive debates, panel discussions and question time in the Sixth Committee, as envisaged in resolution 58/316 of 1 July 2004 on further measures for the revitalization of the work of the General Assembly,

1. *Takes note* of the report of the International Law Commission on the work of its sixty-third session;

2. *Expresses its appreciation* to the International Law Commission for the work accomplished at its sixty-third session;

3. *Recommends* that the International Law Commission continue its work on the topics in its current programme, taking into account the comments and observations of Governments, whether submitted in writing or expressed orally in debates in the Sixth Committee;

4. *Commends* the International Law Commission for the completion of its work on the draft articles on the responsibility of international organizations, the draft articles on the effects of armed conflicts on treaties, and the Guide to Practice on Reservations to Treaties;

5. *Decides* that the consideration of chapter IV of the report of the International Law Commission on the work of its sixty-third session, dealing with the topic "Reservations to treaties", shall be continued at the sixty-seventh session of the General Assembly, during the consideration of the report of the Commission on the work of its sixty-fourth session;

6. *Draws the attention* of Governments to the importance for the International Law Commission of having their views on the various aspects of the topics on the agenda of the Commission, in particular on all the specific issues identified in chapter III of its report, regarding:

(*a*) Immunity of State officials from foreign criminal jurisdiction;

(*b*) Expulsion of aliens;

(*c*) Protection of persons in the event of disasters;

(*d*) The obligation to extradite or prosecute (*aut dedere aut judicare*);

(*e*) Treaties over time;

(*f*) The most-favoured-nation clause;

7. *Takes note* of paragraphs 365 to 369 of the report of the International Law Commission and, in particular, of the inclusion of the topics "Formation and evidence of customary international law", "Protection of the atmosphere", "Provisional application of treaties", "The fair and equitable

treatment standard in international investment law" and "Protection of the environment in relation to armed conflicts" in the long-term programme of work of the Commission, and also takes note of the respective comments made by Member States;

8. *Invites* the International Law Commission to continue to give priority to, and work towards the conclusion of, the topics "Immunity of State officials from foreign criminal jurisdiction" and "The obligation to extradite or prosecute (*aut dedere aut judicare*)";

9. *Takes note* of the oral report by the Secretariat on assistance to special rapporteurs of the International Law Commission and of paragraph 400 of the report of the Commission, and requests the Secretary-General to continue his efforts to identify concrete options for support for the work of special rapporteurs, additional to those provided under General Assembly resolution 56/272 of 27 March 2002;

10. *Also takes note* of paragraphs 370 to 388 of the report of the International Law Commission, and in this regard welcomes the work of the Commission during its sixty-third session to improve its methods of work relating to the role of the special rapporteurs, the study groups, the Drafting Committee, the Planning Group, the preparation of commentaries to draft articles, the final form of the work undertaken on a specific topic, the Commission's report and the relationship with the Sixth Committee;

11. *Welcomes*, in this regard, in particular, the decision of the International Law Commission to define a tentative schedule for the development of any new topic, to periodically review the attainment of annual targets, and to discuss a preliminary plan for the next annual session at the end of each session, and invites the Commission to make such information available to Member States;

12. *Decides* to revert to the consideration of the recommendation contained in paragraph 388 of the report of the International Law Commission during the sixty-seventh session of the General Assembly;

13. *Invites* the International Law Commission to continue taking measures to enhance its efficiency and productivity and to consider making proposals to Member States to that end;

14. *Encourages* the International Law Commission to continue taking cost-saving measures at its future sessions, without prejudice to the efficiency and effectiveness of its work;

15. *Takes note* of paragraphs 389 to 391 and 413 to 415 of the report of the International Law Commission and, while acknowledging the exceptional character of its short duration, decides that the next session of the Commission shall be held at the United Nations Office at Geneva from 7 May to 1 June and from 2 July to 3 August 2012, and requests the Secretariat to present options on how to secure earlier dates for the sessions of the Commission to ensure optimal working conditions for the Commission and the timely publication of its report to the General Assembly;

16. *Stresses* the desirability of further enhancing the dialogue between the International Law Commission and the Sixth Committee at the sixty-seventh session of the General Assembly, and in this context encourages, inter alia, the continued practice of informal consultations in the form of discussions between the members of the Sixth Committee and the members of the Commission attending the sixty-seventh session of the Assembly;

17. *Encourages* delegations, during the debate on the report of the International Law Commission, to adhere as far as possible to the structured work programme agreed to by the Sixth Committee and to consider presenting concise and focused statements;

18. *Encourages* Member States to consider being represented at the level of legal adviser during the first week in which the report of the International Law Commission is discussed in the Sixth Committee (International Law Week) to enable high-level discussions on issues of international law;

19. *Requests* the International Law Commission to continue to pay special attention to indicating in its annual report, for each topic, any specific issues on which expressions of views by Governments, either in the Sixth Committee or in written form, would be of particular interest in providing effective guidance for the Commission in its further work;

20. *Takes note* of paragraphs 418 to 422 of the report of the International Law Commission with regard to cooperation and interaction with other bodies, and encourages the Commission to continue the implementation of articles 16 (*e*), 25 and 26 of its statute in order to further strengthen cooperation between the Commission and other bodies concerned with international law, having in mind the usefulness of such cooperation;

21. *Notes* that consulting with national organizations and individual experts concerned with international law may assist Governments in considering whether to make comments and observations on drafts submitted by the International Law Commission and in formulating their comments and observations;

22. *Reaffirms* its previous decisions concerning the indispensable role of the Codification Division of the Office of Legal Affairs of the Secretariat in providing assistance to the International Law Commission, including in the preparation of memorandums and studies on topics on the agenda of the Commission;

23. *Approves* the conclusions reached by the International Law Commission in paragraph 402 of its report, and reaffirms its previous decisions concerning the documentation and summary records of the Commission;

24. *Welcomes* the efforts of the Secretariat to include on a trial basis the provisional summary records on the website relating to the work of the International Law Commission, encourages their immediate inclusion as soon as the electronic versions are received by the secretariat of the Commission, and looks forward to the institutionalization of this practice;

25. *Takes note* of paragraphs 403 to 405 of the report of the International Law Commission, and stresses the need to expedite the preparation of the summary records of the Commission;

26. *Also takes note* of paragraphs 406 to 409 of the report of the International Law Commission, stresses the value of the *Yearbook of the International Law Commission*, and requests the Secretary-General to ensure its timely publication in all official languages;

27. *Further takes note* of paragraph 410 of the report of the International Law Commission, expresses its appreciation to Governments that have made voluntary contributions to the trust fund on the backlog relating to the *Yearbook of the International Law Commission*, and encourages further contributions to the fund;

28. *Welcomes* the continuous efforts of the Codification Division to maintain and improve the website relating to the work of the International Law Commission;

29. *Expresses the hope* that the International Law Seminar will continue to be held in connection with the sessions of the International Law Commission and that an increasing number of participants representing the principal legal systems of the world, including in particular those from developing countries, will be given the opportunity to attend the Seminar, as well as delegates to the Sixth Committee, and appeals to States to continue to make urgently needed voluntary contributions to the United Nations Trust Fund for the International Law Seminar;

30. *Requests* the Secretary-General to provide the International Law Seminar with adequate services, including interpretation, as required, and encourages him to continue considering ways to improve the structure and content of the Seminar;

31. *Underlines the importance* of the records and topical summary of the debate in the Sixth Committee for the deliberations of the International Law Commission and, in this regard, requests the Secretary-General to forward to the Commission, for its attention, the records of the debate on the report of the Commission at the sixty-sixth session of the General Assembly, together with such written statements as delegations may circulate in conjunction with their oral statements, and to prepare and distribute a topical summary of the debate, following established practice;

32. *Requests* the Secretariat to circulate to States, as soon as possible after the conclusion of the session of the International Law Commission, chapter II of its report containing a summary of the work of that session, chapter III containing the specific issues on which the views of Governments would be of particular interest to the Commission and the draft articles adopted on either first or second reading by the Commission;

33. *Also requests* the Secretariat to make the complete report of the International Law Commission available as soon as possible after the conclusion of the session of the Commission for the consideration of Member States with due anticipation and no later than the prescribed time limit for reports in the General Assembly;

34. *Encourages* the International Law Commission to continue considering ways in which specific issues on which the views of Governments would be of particular interest to the Commission could be framed so as to help Governments to have a better appreciation of the issues on which responses are required;

35. *Recommends* that the debate on the report of the International Law Commission at the sixty-seventh session of the General Assembly commence on 29 October 2012.

International State relations and international law

Nationality of natural persons in relation to the succession of States

Pursuant to resolution 63/118 [YUN 2008, p. 1440], the Secretariat issued a July note and a later addendum [A/66/178 & Add.1] on the nationality of natural persons in relation to the succession of States, which contained the comments of 16 Governments on the issue. The Sixth Committee considered the item on 17 October [A/C.6/66/SR.15] and 9 November [A/C.6/66/SR.29]. ILC had submitted to the General Assembly in 1999 [YUN 1999, p. 1230] a set of draft articles on nationality of natural persons in relation to the succession of States, recommending that they be adopted by the Assembly in the form of a declaration. The Assembly considered the item at its fifty-fifth (2000) [YUN 2000, p. 1242], fifty-ninth (2004) [YUN 2004, p. 1302] and sixty-third (2008) [YUN 2008, p. 1439] sessions.

GENERAL ASSEMBLY ACTION

On 9 December [meeting 82], the General Assembly, on the recommendation of the Sixth Committee [A/66/469], adopted **resolution 66/92** without vote [agenda item 77].

Nationality of natural persons in relation to the succession of States

The General Assembly,

Having examined the item entitled "Nationality of natural persons in relation to the succession of States",

Recalling its resolution 54/112 of 9 December 1999, in which it decided to consider at its fifty-fifth session the draft articles on nationality of natural persons in relation to the succession of States prepared by the International Law Commission,

Recalling also its resolution 55/153 of 12 December 2000, the annex to which contains the articles on nationality of natural persons in relation to the succession of States,

Recalling further its resolutions 59/34 of 2 December 2004 and 63/118 of 11 December 2008,

Taking into consideration the comments and observations of Governments and the discussions held in the Sixth Committee at the fifty-ninth, sixty-third and sixty-sixth sessions of the General Assembly on the question of nationality of natural persons in relation to the succession of States, with a view, in particular, to preventing the occurrence of statelessness as a result of a succession of States, as well as on the advisability of elaborating a legal instrument on this question,

Taking note, in this regard, of the efforts made at the regional level towards the elaboration of a legal instrument on the avoidance of statelessness in relation to State succession,

1. *Reiterates its invitation* to Governments to take into account, as appropriate, the provisions of the articles contained in the annex to resolution 55/153, in dealing with issues of nationality of natural persons in relation to the succession of States;

2. *Once again encourages* States to consider, as appropriate, at the regional or subregional levels, the elaboration of legal instruments regulating questions of nationality of natural persons in relation to the succession of States, with a view, in particular, to preventing the occurrence of statelessness as a result of a succession of States;

3. *Emphasizes* the value of the articles in providing guidance to the States dealing with issues of nationality of natural persons in relation to the succession of States, in particular concerning the avoidance of statelessness;

4. *Decides* that, upon the request of any State, it will revert to the question of nationality of natural persons in relation to the succession of States at an appropriate time, in the light of the development of State practice in these matters.

Law of transboundary aquifers

In response to General Assembly resolution 63/124 [YUN 2008, p. 1433], the Secretary-General transmitted to the Assembly a June report and later addendum [A/66/116 & Add.1] on the law of transboundary aquifers. The report contained the comments and observations of 26 Governments and the League of Arab States on the draft articles on the law of transboundary aquifers. The Sixth Committee considered the item on 18 October [A/C.6/66/SR.16] and 9 November [A/C.6/66/SR.29]. ILC had submitted the draft articles to the Assembly in 2008 [YUN 2008, p. 1433], recommending that the States concerned make arrangements for the management of their transboundary aquifers on the basis of the principles enunciated in the articles and consider at a later stage the elaboration of a convention based upon them.

GENERAL ASSEMBLY ACTION

On 9 December [meeting 82], the General Assembly, on the recommendation of the Sixth Committee [A/66/477], adopted **resolution 66/104** without vote [agenda item 85].

The law of transboundary aquifers

The General Assembly,

Recalling its resolution 63/124 of 11 December 2008, in which it took note of the draft articles on the law of transboundary aquifers formulated by the International Law Commission,

Noting the major importance of the subject of the law of transboundary aquifers in the relations of States and the need for reasonable and proper management of transboundary aquifers, a vitally important natural resource, through international cooperation,

Emphasizing the continuing importance of the codification and progressive development of international law, as referred to in Article 13, paragraph 1 (*a*), of the Charter of the United Nations,

Taking note of the comments of Governments and the discussions in the Sixth Committee at its sixty-third and sixty-sixth sessions on this topic,

1. *Further encourages* the States concerned to make appropriate bilateral or regional arrangements for the proper management of their transboundary aquifers, taking into account the provisions of the draft articles annexed to its resolution 63/124;

2. *Encourages* the International Hydrological Programme of the United Nations Educational, Scientific and Cultural Organization, whose contribution was noted in resolution 63/124, to offer further scientific and technical assistance to the States concerned;

3. *Decides* to include in the provisional agenda of its sixty-eighth session the item entitled "The law of transboundary aquifers" and, in the light of written comments of Governments, as well as views expressed in the debates of the Sixth Committee held at its sixty-third and sixty-sixth sessions, to continue to examine, inter alia, the question of the final form that might be given to the draft articles.

Principle of universal jurisdiction

In response to General Assembly resolution 65/33 [YUN 2010, p. 1330], the Secretary-General issued a June report and a later addendum [A/66/93 & Add.1] on the scope and application of the principle of universal jurisdiction, on the basis of comments and observations received from 19 Member States and 6 observers.

Working Group. Pursuant to resolution 65/33, the Sixth Committee, on 3 October, established a working group to discuss the scope and application of the principle of universal jurisdiction. The Working Group held three meetings (13–14 and 20 October). The Chair of the Working Group delivered an oral report to the Sixth Committee on 21 October [A/C.6/66/SR.17].

GENERAL ASSEMBLY ACTION

On 9 December [meeting 82], the General Assembly, on the recommendation of the Sixth Committee [A/66/476], adopted **resolution 66/103** without vote [agenda item 84].

The scope and application of the principle of universal jurisdiction

The General Assembly,

Reaffirming its commitment to the purposes and principles of the Charter of the United Nations, to international law and to an international order based on the rule of law, which is essential for peaceful coexistence and cooperation among States,

Recalling its resolutions 64/117 of 16 December 2009 and 65/33 of 6 December 2010,

Taking into account the comments and observations of Governments and observers and the discussions held in the Sixth Committee at the sixty-fourth, sixty-fifth and sixty-sixth sessions of the General Assembly, on the scope and application of universal jurisdiction,

Recognizing the diversity of views expressed by States and the need for further consideration towards a better understanding of the scope and application of universal jurisdiction,

Reiterating its commitment to fighting impunity, and noting the views expressed by States that the legitimacy and credibility of the use of universal jurisdiction are best ensured by its responsible and judicious application consistent with international law,

1. *Takes note with appreciation* of the report of the Secretary-General prepared on the basis of comments and observations of Governments and relevant observers;

2. *Decides* that the Sixth Committee shall continue its consideration of the scope and application of universal jurisdiction, without prejudice to the consideration of this topic and related issues in other forums of the United Nations, and for this purpose decides to establish, at its sixty-seventh session, a working group of the Sixth Committee to continue to undertake a thorough discussion of the scope and application of universal jurisdiction;

3. *Invites* Member States and relevant observers, as appropriate, to submit, before 30 April 2012, information and observations on the scope and application of universal jurisdiction, including, where appropriate, information on the relevant applicable international treaties, their domestic legal rules and judicial practice, and requests the Secretary-General to prepare and submit to the General Assembly, at its sixty-seventh session, a report based on such information and observations;

4. *Decides* that the Working Group shall be open to all Member States and that relevant observers to the General Assembly will be invited to participate in the work of the Working Group;

5. *Also decides* to include in the provisional agenda of its sixty-seventh session the item entitled "The scope and application of the principle of universal jurisdiction".

Law of treaties

The 1969 Vienna Convention on the Law of Treaties [YUN 1969, p. 730], which entered into force in 1980 [YUN 1980, p. 1141], had 111 parties as at 31 December 2011.

Special missions

The General Assembly in 1969, by resolution 2530(XXIV) [YUN 1969, p. 750], adopted the Convention on Special Missions and its Optional Protocol on the compulsory settlement of disputes. The Convention, which entered into force in 1985, had 38 States parties as at 31 December 2011. The Optional Protocol, which also entered into force in 1985, had 17 States parties.

Treaties involving international organizations

The 1975 Vienna Convention on the Representation of States in their Relations with International Organizations of a Universal Character [YUN 1975, p. 879], which would enter into force when ratified by 35 parties, had 34 States parties as at 31 December 2011.

The 1986 Vienna Convention on the Law of Treaties between States and International Organizations or between International Organizations [YUN 1986, p. 1006] had 41 parties, including 12 international organizations. It would enter into force when ratified by 35 States.

Succession of States

The 1978 Vienna Convention on Succession of States in Respect of Treaties [YUN 1978, p. 951], which entered into force in 1996 [YUN 1996, p. 1214], had 22 States parties as at 31 December 2011.

The 1983 Vienna Convention on Succession of States in Respect of State Property, Archives and Debts [YUN 1983, p. 1119], which would enter into force when ratified by 15 parties, had 7 States parties.

Jurisdictional immunities of States and their properties

The General Assembly, by resolution 59/38 [YUN 2004, p. 1304], adopted the Convention on Jurisdictional Immunities of States and Their Properties. As at 31 December, the Convention had 13 States parties. The Convention would enter into force when ratified by 30 parties.

International terrorism

Convention on international terrorism

Ad Hoc Committee. In accordance with General Assembly resolution 65/341 [YUN 2010, p. 1331], the Ad Hoc Committee established by Assembly resolution 51/210 [YUN 1996, p. 1208] held its fifteenth session (New York, 11–15 April) [A/66/37] to continue, within the framework of a working group of the Sixth Committee, the elaboration of a draft comprehensive convention on international terrorism.

The Ad Hoc Committee held informal consultations on the draft comprehensive convention, and on the question of convening a high-level conference under UN auspices to formulate a joint organized response of the international community to terrorism in all its forms and manifestations. Delegations reiterated their support of the principle of concluding work on and adopting the draft comprehensive convention by consensus. Concerning the outstanding issues surrounding the draft convention, several delegations reiterated that the convention should contain a definition of terrorism that would provide a clear distinction between acts of terrorism covered by the convention and the legitimate struggle of peoples in the exercise of their right to self-determination or under foreign occupation. Some delegations stated that the convention should address terrorism in all its forms and manifestations, including State terrorism, and that activities undertaken by the armed forces of States not regulated by international humanitarian law should also fall within its scope. Some delegations considered that it might be necessary to revisit the definition of terrorism contained in draft article 2, in order to appropriately address those issues.

On the proposed convening of a high-level conference, Egypt, as sponsor delegation, reiterated its 1999 proposal concerning the convening of an international conference under UN auspices to formulate a joint organized response to terrorism in all its forms and manifestations. The proposed conference would aim at adopting an action plan and providing a forum to address all issues related to the fight against terrorism, including the conditions conducive to its spread and a discussion on the definition of terrorism. Egypt recalled that the proposal had been supported by the Movement of Non-Aligned Countries, the Organization of the Islamic Conference, the African Union and the League of Arab States. Egypt further stressed that the issue should be discussed on its own merits and, although not mutually exclusive, should not be linked to the discussions on the draft comprehensive convention.

At the conclusion of its session on 15 April, the Ad Hoc Committee recommended that the Sixth Committee, at the General Assembly's sixty-sixth (2011) session, establish a working group with a view to finalizing the draft convention and continue to discuss the agenda item on the question of convening a highlevel conference.

Working Group. Pursuant to General Assembly resolution 65/34 [YUN 2010, p. 1331] and as recommended by the Ad Hoc Committee (see above), the Sixth Committee, on 3 October, established a working group to finalize the draft convention and to discuss convening a high-level conference. The Working Group held four meetings, on 17 and 19 October, and on 1 November, as well as informal consultations. On 4 November, the Chair of the Working Group provided an oral report on the Group's work and the results of the informal consultations [A/C.6/66/SR.28].

Measures to eliminate international terrorism

In accordance with General Assembly resolution 50/53 [YUN 1995, p. 1330], the Secretary-General issued his annual report in June and a later addendum [A/66/96 & Add.1] on measures taken by 32 Member States, 4 UN system entities and 5 international organizations to implement the 1994 Declaration on Measures to Eliminate International Terrorism, adopted by the Assembly in resolution 49/60 [YUN 1994, p. 1293]. The report listed 33 international instruments pertaining to terrorism, and provided information on workshops and training courses on combating terrorism by one international organization.

During the twentieth session of the Commission on Crime Prevention and Criminal Justice (Vienna, 11–15 April and 12–13 December) [E/2011/30 & Add.1], the role of the United Nations in coordinating multilateral efforts to counter terrorism was highlighted as being essential to maximizing synergies, avoiding duplication and ensuring a holistic approach in line with the United Nations Global Counter-Terrorism Strategy [YUN 2006, p. 65]. The need for strengthened partnerships and cooperation with all actors, including UN entities (the Counter-Terrorism Executive Directorate and the Counter-Terrorism Implementation Task Force) and international, regional and subregional organizations was stressed. The importance of a criminal justice response based on the international legal instruments against terrorism and respect for the rule of law and for human rights was emphasized, as well as the importance of international and regional cooperation in criminal matters and national and regional action to counter terrorism. Other issues raised included money-laundering, financing of terrorism, hostage-taking, financial intelligence units, cybercrime, the definition of terrorism and self-determination. The Commission had before it a report of the Secretary-General on assistance in implementing the universal conventions and protocols related to terrorism [E/CN.15/2011/4].

GENERAL ASSEMBLY ACTION

On 9 December [meeting 82], the General Assembly, on the recommendation of the Sixth Committee [A/66/478], adopted **resolution 66/105** without vote [agenda item 109].

Measures to eliminate international terrorism

The General Assembly,

Guided by the purposes and principles of the Charter of the United Nations,

Reaffirming, in all its aspects, the United Nations Global Counter-Terrorism Strategy adopted on 8 September 2006, enhancing the overall framework for the efforts of the international community to effectively counter the scourge of terrorism in all its forms and manifestations, and recalling the first and second biennial review of the Strategy, on 4 and 5 September 2008 and on 8 September 2010, respectively, and the debates that were held on those occasions,

Recalling the Declaration on the Occasion of the Fiftieth Anniversary of the United Nations,

Recalling also the United Nations Millennium Declaration,

Recalling further the 2005 World Summit Outcome, and reaffirming in particular the section on terrorism,

Recalling the Declaration on Measures to Eliminate International Terrorism, contained in the annex to General Assembly resolution 49/60 of 9 December 1994, and the Declaration to Supplement the 1994 Declaration on Measures to Eliminate International Terrorism, contained in the annex to Assembly resolution 51/210 of 17 December 1996,

Recalling also all General Assembly resolutions on measures to eliminate international terrorism and Security Council resolutions on threats to international peace and security caused by terrorist acts,

Convinced of the importance of the consideration of measures to eliminate international terrorism by the General Assembly as the universal organ having competence to do so,

Deeply disturbed by the persistence of terrorist acts, which have been carried out worldwide,

Reaffirming its strong condemnation of the heinous acts of terrorism that have caused enormous loss of human life, destruction and damage, including those which prompted the adoption of General Assembly resolution 56/1 of 12 September 2001, as well as Security Council resolutions 1368(2001) of 12 September 2001, 1373(2001) of 28 September 2001 and 1377(2001) of 12 November 2001, and those that have occurred since,

Reaffirming also its strong condemnation of the atrocious and deliberate attacks that have occurred against United Nations offices in various parts of the world,

Affirming that States must ensure that any measure taken to combat terrorism complies with all their obligations under international law and must adopt such measures in accordance with international law, in particular international human rights, refugee and humanitarian law,

Stressing the need to strengthen further international cooperation among States and among international organizations and agencies, regional organizations and arrangements and the United Nations in order to prevent, combat and eliminate terrorism in all its forms and manifestations, wherever and by whomsoever committed, in accordance with the principles of the Charter, international law and the relevant international conventions,

Noting the role of the Security Council Committee established pursuant to resolution 1373(2001) concerning counter-terrorism in monitoring the implementation of that resolution, including the taking of the necessary financial, legal and technical measures by States and the ratification or acceptance of the relevant international conventions and protocols,

Mindful of the need to enhance the role of the United Nations and the relevant specialized agencies in combating international terrorism and of the proposals of the Secretary-General to enhance the role of the Organization in this respect,

Mindful also of the essential need to strengthen international, regional and subregional cooperation aimed at enhancing the national capacity of States to prevent and effectively suppress international terrorism in all its forms and manifestations,

Reiterating its call upon States to review urgently the scope of the existing international legal provisions on the prevention, repression and elimination of terrorism in all its forms and manifestations, with the aim of ensuring that there is a comprehensive legal framework covering all aspects of the matter,

Emphasizing that tolerance and dialogue among civilizations and the enhancement of interfaith and intercultural understanding are among the most important elements in promoting cooperation and success in combating terrorism, and welcoming the various initiatives to this end,

Reaffirming that no terrorist act can be justified in any circumstances,

Recalling Security Council resolution 1624(2005) of 14 September 2005, and bearing in mind that States must ensure that any measure taken to combat terrorism complies with their obligations under international law, in particular international human rights, refugee and humanitarian law,

Taking note of recent developments and initiatives at the international, regional and subregional levels to prevent and suppress international terrorism, including those of the African Union, the Asia-Pacific Economic Cooperation, the Association of Southeast Asian Nations, the Bali Counter-Terrorism Process, the Central American Integration System, the Collective Security Treaty Organization, the Common Market for Eastern and Southern Africa, the Conference on Interaction and Confidence-building Measures in Asia, the Cooperation Council for the Arab States of the Gulf, the Council of Europe, the East African Community, the Economic Community of West African States, the Euro-Mediterranean Partnership, the European Free Trade Association, the European Union, the Global Counterterrorism Forum, the Group of Eight, the Intergovernmental Authority on Development, the International Civil Aviation Organization, the International Maritime Organization, the League of Arab States, the Movement of Non-Aligned Countries, the North Atlantic Treaty Organization, the Organization for Economic Cooperation and Development, the Organization for Security and Cooperation in Europe, the Organization of American States, the Organization of Islamic Cooperation, the Pacific Islands Forum, the Regional Forum of the Association of Southeast Asian Nations, the Shanghai Cooperation Organization, the Southern African Development Community and the World Customs Organization,

Noting regional efforts to prevent, combat and eliminate terrorism in all its forms and manifestations, wherever and by whomsoever committed, including through the elaboration of, and adherence to, regional conventions,

Recalling its decision in resolutions 54/110 of 9 December 1999, 55/158 of 12 December 2000, 56/88 of 12 December 2001, 57/27 of 19 November 2002, 58/81 of 9 December 2003, 59/46 of 2 December 2004, 60/43 of 8 December 2005, 61/40 of 4 December 2006, 62/71 of 6 December 2007, 63/129 of 11 December 2008, 64/118 of 16 December 2009 and 65/34 of 6 December 2010 that the Ad Hoc Committee established by General Assembly resolution 51/210 should address, and keep on its agenda, the question of convening a high-level conference under the auspices of the United Nations to formulate a joint organized response of the international community to terrorism in all its forms and manifestations,

Recalling also the Final Document of the Fifteenth Summit Conference of Heads of State and Government of the Movement of Non-Aligned Countries, adopted in Sharm el-Sheikh, Egypt, on 16 July 2009, which reiterated the collective position of the Movement of Non-Aligned Countries on terrorism and reaffirmed its previous initiative calling for an international summit conference under the auspices of the United Nations to formulate a joint organized response of the international community to terrorism in all its forms and manifestations, as well as other relevant initiatives,

Aware of its resolutions 57/219 of 18 December 2002, 58/187 of 22 December 2003, 59/191 of 20 December 2004, 60/158 of 16 December 2005, 61/171 of 19 December 2006, 62/159 of 18 December 2007, 63/185 of 18 December 2008, 64/168 of 18 December 2009 and 65/221 of 21 December 2010,

Having examined the report of the Secretary-General, the report of the Ad Hoc Committee and the oral report of the Chair of the Working Group established by the Sixth Committee at the sixty-sixth session of the Assembly,

1. *Strongly condemns* all acts, methods and practices of terrorism in all its forms and manifestations as criminal and unjustifiable, wherever and by whomsoever committed;

2. *Calls upon* all Member States, the United Nations and other appropriate international, regional and subregional organizations to implement the United Nations Global Counter-Terrorism Strategy, as well as the resolutions relating to the first and second biennial review of the Strategy, in all its aspects at the international, regional, subregional and national levels without delay, including by mobilizing resources and expertise;

3. *Recalls* the pivotal role of the General Assembly in following up the implementation and the updating of the Strategy, looks forward to the third biennial review and in this regard recalls its invitation to the Secretary-General to contribute to the future deliberations of the Assembly, and requests the Secretary-General when doing so to provide information on relevant activities within the Secretariat to ensure overall coordination and coherence in the counter-terrorism efforts of the United Nations system;

4. *Reiterates* that criminal acts intended or calculated to provoke a state of terror in the general public, a group of persons or particular persons for political purposes are in any circumstances unjustifiable, whatever the considerations of a political, philosophical, ideological, racial, ethnic, religious or other nature that may be invoked to justify them;

5. *Reiterates its call upon* all States to adopt further measures in accordance with the Charter of the United Nations and the relevant provisions of international law, including international standards of human rights, to prevent terrorism and to strengthen international cooperation in combating terrorism and, to that end, to consider in particular the implementation of the measures set out in paragraphs 3 (*a*) to (*f*) of General Assembly resolution 51/210;

6. *Also reiterates its call upon* all States, with the aim of enhancing the efficient implementation of relevant legal instruments, to intensify, as and where appropriate, the exchange of information on facts related to terrorism and, in so doing, to avoid the dissemination of inaccurate or unverified information;

7. *Reiterates its call upon* States to refrain from financing, encouraging, providing training for or otherwise supporting terrorist activities;

8. *Expresses concern* at the increase in incidents of kidnapping and hostage-taking with demands for ransom and/or political concessions by terrorist groups, and expresses the need to address this issue;

9. *Urges* States to ensure that their nationals or other persons and entities within their territory that wilfully provide or collect funds for the benefit of persons or entities who commit, or attempt to commit, facilitate or participate in the commission of terrorist acts are punished by penalties consistent with the grave nature of such acts;

10. *Reminds* States of their obligations under relevant international conventions and protocols and Security Council resolutions, including Council resolution 1373(2001), to ensure that perpetrators of terrorist acts are brought to justice;

11. *Reaffirms* that international cooperation as well as actions by States to combat terrorism should be conducted in conformity with the principles of the Charter, international law and relevant international conventions;

12. *Recalls* the adoption of the International Convention for the Suppression of Acts of Nuclear Terrorism, the Amendment to the Convention on the Physical Protection of Nuclear Material, the Protocol of 2005 to the Convention for the Suppression of Unlawful Acts against the Safety of Maritime Navigation and the Protocol of 2005 to the Protocol for the Suppression of Unlawful Acts against the Safety of Fixed Platforms Located on the Continental Shelf, and urges all States to consider, as a matter of priority, becoming parties to these instruments;

13. *Urges* all States that have not yet done so to consider, as a matter of priority and in accordance with Security Council resolution 1373(2001) and Council resolution 1566(2004) of 8 October 2004, becoming parties to the relevant conventions and protocols as referred to in paragraph 6 of General Assembly resolution 51/210, as well as the International Convention for the Suppression of Terrorist Bombings, the International Convention for the Suppression of the Financing of Terrorism, the International Convention for the Suppression of Acts of Nuclear Terrorism and the Amendment to the Convention on the Physical Protection of Nuclear Material, and calls upon all States to enact, as appropriate, the domestic legislation necessary to implement the provisions of those conventions and protocols, to ensure that the jurisdiction of their courts enables them to bring to trial the perpetrators of terrorist acts and to cooperate with and provide support and assistance to other States and relevant international and regional organizations to that end;

14. *Urges* States to cooperate with the Secretary-General and with one another, as well as with interested intergovernmental organizations, with a view to ensuring, where appropriate within existing mandates, that technical and other expert advice is provided to those States requiring and requesting assistance in becoming parties to and implementing the conventions and protocols referred to in paragraph 13 above;

15. *Notes with appreciation and satisfaction* that, consistent with the call contained in paragraphs 12 and 13 of General Assembly resolution 65/34, a number of States became parties to the relevant conventions and protocols referred to therein, thereby realizing the objective of wider acceptance and implementation of those conventions;

16. *Reaffirms* the Declaration on Measures to Eliminate International Terrorism and the Declaration to Supplement the 1994 Declaration on Measures to Eliminate International Terrorism, and calls upon all States to implement them;

17. *Calls upon* all States to cooperate to prevent and suppress terrorist acts;

18. *Urges* all States and the Secretary-General, in their efforts to prevent international terrorism, to make the best use of the existing institutions of the United Nations;

19. *Notes with appreciation* the contribution agreement to launch the United Nations Counter-Terrorism Centre signed between the United Nations and Saudi Arabia on 19 September 2011, established within the Counter-Terrorism Implementation Task Force;

20. *Requests* the Terrorism Prevention Branch of the United Nations Office on Drugs and Crime in Vienna to continue its efforts to enhance, through its mandate, the ca-

pabilities of the United Nations in the prevention of terrorism, and recognizes, in the context of the United Nations Global Counter-Terrorism Strategy and Security Council resolution 1373(2001), its role in assisting States in becoming parties to and implementing the relevant international conventions and protocols relating to terrorism, including the most recent among them, and in strengthening international cooperation mechanisms in criminal matters related to terrorism, including through national capacity-building;

21. *Welcomes* the current efforts by the Secretariat to prepare the third edition of the publication *International Instruments related to the Prevention and Suppression of International Terrorism* in all official languages;

22. *Invites* regional intergovernmental organizations to submit to the Secretary-General information on the measures they have adopted at the regional level to eliminate international terrorism, as well as on intergovernmental meetings held by those organizations;

23. *Notes* the progress made in the elaboration of the draft comprehensive convention on international terrorism during the meetings of the Ad Hoc Committee established by General Assembly resolution 51/210 and of the Working Group established by the Sixth Committee during the sixty-sixth session of the Assembly, and welcomes continuing efforts to that end;

24. *Decides* that the Sixth Committee, at the sixty-seventh session of the General Assembly, will establish a working group with a view to finalizing the draft comprehensive convention on international terrorism and continuing to discuss the item included in its agenda by Assembly resolution 54/110 concerning the question of convening a high-level conference under the auspices of the United Nations;

25. *Also decides* to reconvene the Ad Hoc Committee in 2013, as appropriate, on dates to be decided at the sixty-seventh session of the General Assembly, in order to, on an expedited basis, continue to elaborate the draft comprehensive convention on international terrorism and continue to discuss the item included in its agenda by Assembly resolution 54/110 concerning the question of convening a high-level conference under the auspices of the United Nations;

26. *Encourages* all Member States to redouble their efforts during the intersessional period towards resolving any outstanding issues;

27. *Decides* to include in the provisional agenda of its sixty-seventh session the item entitled "Measures to eliminate international terrorism".

On 28 July, the Economic and Social Council, by **resolution 2011/31** (see p. 1204), recommended to the General Assembly the adoption of a draft resolution on technical assistance for implementing the international conventions and protocols related to counter-terrorism. The General Assembly adopted **resolution 66/178** (see p. 1204) on that topic on 19 December.

On 24 December, the Assembly decided that the agenda item on the United Nations Global Counter-Terrorism Strategy would remain for consideration during its resumed sixty-sixth (2012) session (**decision 66/557**).

Terrorist attacks on internationally protected persons

Communications. In a 7 April letter [A/65/946], Saudi Arabia informed the Secretary-General that its diplomatic missions in Iran had recently been attacked repeatedly.

In identical letters of 11 October [A/66/513-S/2011/633] to the Secretary-General and the General Assembly and Security Council Presidents, Iran rejected allegations by the United States that it was involved in an assassination plot targeting a foreign diplomat in Washington, D.C.

In identical letters of 12 October [A/66/517-S/2011/649] to the Assembly and Council Presidents, the Secretary-General transmitted a 12 October letter from the United States alleging a recently disrupted conspiracy to assassinate in Washington, D.C., the Ambassador of Saudi Arabia to the United States and to carry out additional follow-on attacks inside the United States and against other countries. The United States maintained that it had confirmed information that the conspiracy was conceived, sponsored and directed by elements of the Iranian Government.

In a 14 October letter [S/2011/640] to the Secretary-General and the Council President, Qatar, acting in its capacity as Chair of the Arab Group, transmitted a statement adopted by the Council of the League of Arab States at its extraordinary session (Cairo, 13 October) regarding the alleged attempt to assassinate the Saudi Ambassador to the United States.

Saudi Arabia, in a 14 October letter [A/66/553] to the Secretary-General, expressed its concern and outrage about the alleged plot against its Ambassador to the United States.

In a 4 November letter [A/66/546-S/2011/696] to the Secretary-General, Iran rejected and denied the involvement of any of its officials or organs in the alleged plot against the Saudi Ambassador.

In a 15 November letter [A/66/561] to the Assembly President, Iran expressed its concerns about the draft resolution entitled "Terrorist attacks on internationally protected persons" [A/66/L.8], which referred to the alleged plot against the Saudi Ambassador.

GENERAL ASSEMBLY ACTION

On 18 November [meeting 61], the General Assembly, on the recommendation of the Sixth Committee [A/66/L.8 & Add.1], adopted **resolution 66/12** by recorded vote (106-9-40) [agenda item 118].

Terrorist attacks on internationally protected persons

The General Assembly,

Guided by the purposes and principles of the Charter of the United Nations, and reaffirming its role under the Charter, including on questions related to international peace and security,

Recalling the United Nations Global Counter-Terrorism Strategy, contained in General Assembly resolution 60/288 of 8 September 2006, as well as Assembly resolutions 62/272 of 5 September 2008 and 64/297 of 8 September 2010 which reaffirmed the Strategy,

Recalling also the Convention on the Prevention and Punishment of Crimes against Internationally Protected Persons, including Diplomatic Agents,

Renewing its unwavering commitment to strengthening international cooperation to prevent and combat terrorism in all its forms and manifestations,

Convinced that respect for the principles and rules of international law governing diplomatic and consular relations is a basic prerequisite for the normal conduct of relations among States and for the fulfilment of the purposes and principles of the Charter,

Concerned at the failure to respect the inviolability of diplomatic and consular missions and representatives,

Noting the note verbale dated 7 April 2011 from the Permanent Mission of Saudi Arabia to the United Nations addressed to the Secretary-General regarding hostile actions committed against diplomatic missions in the Islamic Republic of Iran, and recalling the obligations of States regarding the protection, security and safety of diplomatic missions, consulates and personnel on their territories,

Emphasizing the duty of States to take all appropriate measures required by international law in a timely manner, including measures of a preventive nature, and to bring offenders to justice,

Noting the letter dated 14 October 2011 from the Permanent Representative of Saudi Arabia to the United Nations addressed to the Secretary-General regarding a disrupted plot to assassinate the Ambassador of Saudi Arabia to the United States of America, and noting also the statement of the Gulf Cooperation Council of 12 October 2011 and of the Council of the League of Arab States of 13 October 2011,

Noting also the letter dated 11 October 2011 from the Permanent Representative of the United States of America to the United Nations addressed to the Secretary-General reporting an Iranian plot,

Noting further the letter dated 11 October 2011, from the Permanent Representative of the Islamic Republic of Iran to the United Nations addressed to the Secretary-General, the President of the General Assembly and the President of the Security Council,

Alarmed by the new and recurring acts of violence against diplomatic and consular representatives, which endanger or take innocent lives and seriously impede the normal work of such representatives and officials,

Deeply concerned by the plot to assassinate the Ambassador of Saudi Arabia to the United States of America,

1. *Reiterates its strong and unequivocal condemnation* of terrorism in all its forms and manifestations, committed by whomever, wherever and for whatever purposes, as it constitutes one of the most serious threats to international peace and security;

2. *Strongly condemns* acts of violence against diplomatic and consular missions and representatives, as well as against missions and representatives of international intergovernmental organizations and officials of such organizations, and emphasizes that such acts can never be justified;

3. *Deplores* the plot to assassinate the Ambassador of Saudi Arabia to the United States of America;

4. *Encourages* all States to take additional steps to prevent, on their territories, the planning, financing, sponsorship or organization or commission of similar terrorist acts and to deny safe haven to those who plan, finance, support or commit such terrorist acts;

5. *Calls upon* the Islamic Republic of Iran to comply with all of its obligations under international law, including the Convention on the Prevention and Punishment of Crimes against Internationally Protected Persons, including Diplomatic Agents, particularly with respect to its obligations to provide law enforcement assistance, and to cooperate with States seeking to bring to justice all those who participated in the planning, sponsoring, organization and attempted execution of the plot to assassinate the Ambassador of Saudi Arabia to the United States of America.

RECORDED VOTE ON RESOLUTION 66/12:

In favour: Albania, Algeria, Andorra, Australia, Austria, Bahamas, Bahrain, Barbados, Belgium, Belize, Bosnia and Herzegovina, Botswana, Bulgaria, Cameroon, Canada, Central African Republic, Chad, Colombia, Costa Rica, Côte d'Ivoire, Croatia, Cyprus, Czech Republic, Denmark, Djibouti, Dominica, Dominican Republic, Egypt, El Salvador, Estonia, Ethiopia, Fiji, Finland, France, Gabon, Germany, Greece, Haiti, Honduras, Hungary, Iceland, Ireland, Israel, Italy, Jamaica, Japan, Jordan, Kuwait, Latvia, Lebanon, Liberia, Lithuania, Luxembourg, Malaysia, Maldives, Malta, Marshall Islands, Mauritania, Mexico, Micronesia, Monaco, Mongolia, Montenegro, Morocco, Netherlands, New Zealand, Norway, Oman, Palau, Panama, Papua New Guinea, Philippines, Poland, Portugal, Qatar, Republic of Korea, Republic of Moldova, Romania, Rwanda, Saint Kitts and Nevis, Saint Lucia, Samoa, San Marino, Saudi Arabia, Senegal, Slovakia, Slovenia, Solomon Islands, Somalia, South Sudan, Spain, Sudan, Sweden, the former Yugoslav Republic of Macedonia, Timor-Leste, Tonga, Tunisia, Turkey, Uganda, Ukraine, United Arab Emirates, United Kingdom, United Republic of Tanzania, United States, Vanuatu, Yemen.

Against: Armenia, Bolivia, Cuba, Democratic People's Republic of Korea, Ecuador, Iran, Nicaragua, Venezuela, Zambia.

Abstaining: Antigua and Barbuda, Argentina, Bangladesh, Benin, Bhutan, Brazil, Brunei Darussalam, Chile, China, Comoros, Gambia, Grenada, Guatemala, Guinea, Guyana, India, Indonesia, Kazakhstan, Kenya, Kyrgyzstan, Liechtenstein, Myanmar, Nepal, Niger, Nigeria, Pakistan, Paraguay, Peru, Russian Federation, Saint Vincent and the Grenadines, Serbia, Singapore, South Africa, Sri Lanka, Switzerland, Thailand, Trinidad and Tobago, Turkmenistan, Uruguay, Viet Nam.

Diplomatic relations

Protection of diplomatic and consular missions and representatives

As at 31 December, the States parties to the following conventions relating to the protection of diplomatic and consular relations numbered: 187 States parties to the 1961 Vienna Convention on Diplomatic Relations [YUN 1961, p. 512], 51 parties to the Optional Protocol concerning the acquisition of nationality [ibid., p. 516] and 67 parties to the Optional Protocol concerning the compulsory settlement of disputes [ibid.].

The 1963 Vienna Convention on Consular Relations [YUN 1963, p. 510] had 173 parties, the Optional Protocol concerning acquisition of nationality [ibid., p. 512] had 39, and the Optional Protocol concerning the compulsory settlement of disputes [ibid.] had 50. Parties to the 1973 Convention on the Prevention and Punishment of Crimes against Internationally Protected Persons, including Diplomatic Agents [YUN 1973, p. 775] numbered 173.

Communication. In identical letters dated 19 March to the Secretary-General and the Security Council President [A/65/792-S/2011/159], Lebanon transmitted a complaint against the Libyan Arab Jamahiriya, which allegedly directed groups under its control to storm the Lebanese Embassy in Tripoli.

Treaties and agreements

UN registration and publication of treaties

During 2011, the United Nations received 1,529 treaties and 919 actions for registration. In accordance with Article 102 of the Charter of the United Nations and relevant General Assembly regulations, 1,394 treaties and 786 subsequent actions were registered with the Secretariat. Registered treaties and actions included those submitted prior to 2011 but not registered at the time of submission due to defects in the submission, as well as treaties and actions deposited with the Secretary-General.

The United Nations published 12 issues of the *Monthly Statement of Treaties and International Agreements* and 65 volumes of the *United Nations Treaty Series* (UNTS), incorporating the texts of treaties registered or filed and recorded and related subsequent actions in the original languages, with translations into English and French, as appropriate. The United Nations Treaty Collection website, which contained published UNTS volumes, the *League of Nations Treaty Series*, the *Treaty Handbook*, *Multilateral Treaties Deposited with the Secretary-General*, the *Summary of Practice of the Secretary-General as Depositary of Multilateral Treaties*, the *Final Clauses of Multilateral Treaties Handbook,* the Treaty Event publications, information on capacity-building training and a range of materials on treaty law and practice, generated over 3.4 million page views.

The 2011 Treaty Event: Towards Universal Participation and Implementation (New York, 20–22 and 26–27 September) resulted in 88 treaty actions undertaken by 57 States with respect to 38 treaties deposited with the Secretary-General.

Multilateral treaties deposited with the Secretary-General

The United Nations received 939 treaty actions—including signatures, ratifications, acceptances, approvals, accessions, declarations, reservations, objections and notifications—for deposit with the Secretary-General, resulting in the issuance of 1,748 depositary notifications.

The *United Nations Treaty Series* and the regularly updated status of multilateral treaties deposited with the Secretary-General were available on the Internet at the UN Treaty Collection website.

The Secretary-General was performing depositary functions for 616 multilateral treaties.

The following new protocol was deposited with the Secretary-General in 2011:

Optional Protocol to the Convention on the Rights of the Child on a communications procedure, adopted in New York on 19 December.

The following multilateral treaties and protocols deposited with the Secretary-General came into force in 2011:

International Tropical Timber Agreement, adopted in Geneva on 27 January 2006 and which entered into force on 7 December 2011;

International Convention on Arrest of Ships, adopted in Geneva on 12 March 1999 and which entered into force on 14 September 2011; and

Additional Protocol to the Convention on the Contract for the International Carriage of Goods by Road (CMR) concerning the Electronic Consignment Note, adopted in Geneva on 20 February 2008 and which entered into force on 5 June 2011.

Advice and capacity-building in treaty law and practice

Advice and assistance on treaty law and practice were provided to Member States, the specialized agencies, the regional commissions, UN bodies, treaty bodies and other entities. Two seminars on treaty law and practice were conducted at UN Headquarters for legal advisors from Member States and other officials. A regional capacity-building seminar on treaty law and practice and the domestic implementation of human rights treaty obligations (Cartagena de Indias, Colombia, 1–2 November) was attended by 35 participants from 19 countries. A capacity-building workshop on treaty law and practice (Minsk, Belarus, 16–17 November) was attended by 124 participants from 6 countries.

International economic law

In 2011, international economic law continued to be considered by the United Nations Commission on International Trade Law (UNCITRAL) and by the Sixth Committee of the General Assembly.

Commission on International Trade Law

At its forty-fourth session (Vienna, 27 June–8 July) [A/66/17], UNCITRAL adopted the UNCITRAL Model Law on Public Procurement, which updated the 1994 UNCITRAL Model Law on Procurement of Goods, Construction and Services [YUN 1994, p. 1328]. The Commission recommended that States use the Model Law in assessing their public procurement legal regime and give favourable consideration to the Model Law when enacting or revising their laws. The Commission also adopted "The UNCITRAL Model Law on Cross-Border Insolvency: the Judicial Perspective" [A/CN.9/732], a text designed to provide information and guidance for judges on cross-border related insolvency issues.

The Commission considered the status of the conventions and model laws emanating from its work and the status of the 1958 Convention on the Recognition and Enforcement of Foreign Arbitral Awards (the New York Convention) [YUN 1958, p. 390], on the basis of a Secretariat note [A/CN.9/723] and further information from the Secretariat. The Commission also considered a bibliography of writings relating to its work [A/CN.9/722]. UNCITRAL continued its work on public procurement, cross-border insolvency, arbitration and conciliation, online dispute resolution, insolvency law, security interests, electronic commerce and microfinance. It also reviewed the implementation of the New York Convention and technical assistance activities. (See headings below for details.)

Procurement

UNCITRAL [A/66/17] had before it the draft revised text of the Model Law on Public Procurement resulting from the nineteenth session of Working Group I (Procurement), with an accompanying note by the Secretariat [A/CN.9/729 & Add.1–8]; a compilation of comments from Governments on the draft Model Law received by the Secretariat before the forty-fourth session of the Commission [A/CN.9/730 & Add.1,2]; a working draft of the Guide to Enactment to accompany the draft Model Law [A/CN.9/731 & Add.1–9 & A/CN.9/WG.I/WP.77 & Add.19]; and the reports on the nineteenth (Vienna, 1–5 November 2010) [A/CN.9/713] and twentieth (New York, 14–18 March 2011) [A/CN.9/718] sessions of the Working Group.

On 1 July, the Commission adopted the UNCITRAL Model Law on Public Procurement; requested the Secretary-General to disseminate the text of the Model Law to Governments and other bodies; recommended that States use the Model Law in assessing their public procurement legal regime and give favourable consideration to the Model Law when enacting or revising their laws; and requested States to support the promotion and implementation of the Model Law. UNCITRAL requested the Secretariat to prepare a study on possible future work in the area of public-private partnerships and privately financed infrastructure projects for consideration by the Commission at a future session. The topic could include many aspects, including public procurement.

Working Group I (Procurement), at its twentieth session (see above), commenced work on the elaboration of proposals for a Guide to the Enactment of the UNCITRAL Model Law on Public Procurement.

GENERAL ASSEMBLY ACTION

On 9 December [meeting 82], the General Assembly, on the recommendation of the Sixth Committee [A/66/471], adopted **resolution 66/95** without vote [agenda item 79].

United Nations Commission on International Trade Law Model Law on Public Procurement

The General Assembly,

Recalling its resolution 2205(XXI) of 17 December 1966, by which it established the United Nations Commission on International Trade Law with the purpose of furthering the progressive harmonization and unification of the law of international trade in the interests of all peoples, in particular those of developing countries,

Noting that procurement constitutes a significant portion of public expenditure in most States,

Recalling its resolution 49/54 of 9 December 1994 recommending the use of the United Nations Commission on International Trade Law Model Law on Procurement of Goods, Construction and Services,

Observing that the 1994 Model Law, which has become an important international benchmark in procurement law reform, sets out procedures aimed at achieving competition, transparency, fairness, economy and efficiency in the procurement process,

Observing also that, despite the widely recognized value of the 1994 Model Law, new issues and practices have arisen since its adoption that have justified revision of the text,

Recognizing that at its thirty-seventh session, in 2004, the Commission agreed that the 1994 Model Law would benefit from being updated to reflect new practices, in particular those resulting from the use of electronic communications in public procurement, and the experience gained in the use of the 1994 Model Law as a basis for law reform, not departing, however, from the basic principles behind it and not modifying the provisions whose usefulness had been proved,

Noting that the revisions to the 1994 Model Law were the subject of due deliberation and extensive consultations with Governments and interested international organizations, and that thus it can be expected that the revised Model Law, to be called the "United Nations Commission on International Trade Law Model Law on Public Procurement", would be acceptable to States with different legal, social and economic systems,

Noting also that the revised Model Law is expected to contribute significantly to the establishment of a harmonized and modern legal framework for public procurement that promotes economy, efficiency and competition in procurement and, at the same time, fosters integrity, confidence, fairness and transparency in the procurement process,

Convinced that the revised Model Law will significantly assist all States, in particular developing countries and countries with economies in transition, in enhancing their existing procurement laws and formulating procurement laws where none presently exist, and will lead to the development of harmonious international economic relations and increased economic development,

1. *Expresses its appreciation* to the United Nations Commission on International Trade Law for developing and adopting the draft United Nations Commission on International Trade Law Model Law on Public Procurement;

2. *Requests* the Secretary-General to transmit the text of the Model Law to Governments and other interested bodies;

3. *Recommends* that all States use the Model Law in assessing their legal regimes for public procurement and give favourable consideration to the Model Law when they enact or revise their laws;

4. *Calls for* closer cooperation and coordination among the Commission and other international organs and organizations, including regional organizations, active in the field of procurement law reform, in order to avoid undesirable duplication of efforts and inconsistent, incoherent or conflicting results in the modernization and harmonization of public procurement law;

5. *Endorses* the efforts and initiatives of the secretariat of the Commission aimed at increasing the coordination of, and cooperation on, legal activities concerned with public procurement reform.

Insolvency law

UNCITRAL, at its 2011 session [A/66/17], heard a report on the Ninth Multinational Judicial Colloquium (Singapore, 12–13 March). The colloquium, organized jointly by the Commission, the International Association of Restructuring, Insolvency and Bankruptcy Professionals (INSOL International) and the World Bank, was attended by approximately 80 judges from 44 States. It discussed issues of cross-border insolvency coordination and cooperation, including in the context of enterprise groups, as well as the draft text of the UNCITRAL Model Law on Cross-Border Insolvency: the Judicial Perspective, the preparation of which was widely supported as a valuable source of information on current issues and practice.

The Commission considered the revised version of the draft judicial materials on the UNCITRAL Model Law on Cross-Border Insolvency [A/CN.9/732 & Add.1-3], the comments from Governments [A/CN.9/733 & Add.1] and the report of the thirty-ninth session of Working Group V (Insolvency Law) (Vienna, 6–10 December 2010) [A/CN.9/715].

The Commission, on 1 July, adopted the UNCITRAL Model Law on Cross-Border Insolvency: the Judicial Perspective. It authorized the Secretariat to edit and finalize the text in the light of the deliberations of the Commission; requested the Secretariat to establish a mechanism for updating the Judicial Perspective on an ongoing basis in the same flexible manner as it was developed; requested the Secretary-General to publish, including electronically, the text of the Judicial Perspective, as periodically updated/amended, and to transmit it to Governments with the request that the text be made available to relevant authorities; and recommended that the Judicial Perspective be given due consideration by judges, insolvency practitioners and others involved in cross-border insolvency proceedings.

Working Group V, at its fortieth session (Vienna, 31 October–4 November) [A/CN.9/738], discussed the provision of guidance on the interpretation and application of selected concepts of the UNCITRAL Model Law on Cross-Border Insolvency relating to "centre of main interests"; and directors' responsibilities and liabilities in insolvency and pre-insolvency cases.

GENERAL ASSEMBLY ACTION

On 9 December [meeting 82], the General Assembly, on the recommendation of the Sixth Committee [A/66/471], adopted **resolution 66/96** without vote [agenda item 79].

United Nations Commission on International Trade Law Model Law on Cross-Border Insolvency: The Judicial Perspective

The General Assembly,

Recalling its resolution 2205(XXI) of 17 December 1966, by which it established the United Nations Commission on International Trade Law with the purpose of furthering the progressive harmonization and unification of the law of international trade in the interests of all peoples, in particular those of developing countries,

Noting that, where individuals and enterprises conduct their businesses on a global basis and have assets and interests in more than one State, the efficient conduct of the insolvency of those individuals and enterprises requires cross-border cooperation in, and coordination of, the supervision and administration of those assets and affairs,

Considering that the United Nations Commission on International Trade Law Model Law on Cross-Border Insolvency contributes significantly to the establishment of a harmonized legal framework for effectively administering cross-border insolvency and facilitating cooperation and coordination,

Acknowledging that familiarity with cooperation and coordination in cross-border insolvency cases and how the Model Law may be implemented in practice is not widespread,

Convinced that providing readily accessible information on the interpretation of and current practice with respect to the Model Law for reference and use by judges in insolvency proceedings has the potential to promote wider use and understanding of the Model Law and facilitate cross-border judicial cooperation and coordination, avoiding unnecessary delay and costs,

Noting with satisfaction the completion and adoption on 1 July 2011 of the United Nations Commission on International Trade Law Model Law on Cross-Border Insolvency: The Judicial Perspective by the Commission at its forty-fourth session,

Noting that the preparation of the Model Law on Cross-Border Insolvency: The Judicial Perspective was the subject of consultation with Governments, judges and other insolvency professionals,

1. *Expresses its appreciation* to the United Nations Commission on International Trade Law for the completion and adoption of the United Nations Commission on International Trade Law Model Law on Cross-Border Insolvency: The Judicial Perspective;

2. *Requests* the establishment by the Secretariat of the United Nations of a mechanism for updating the Model Law on Cross-Border Insolvency: The Judicial Perspective on an ongoing basis in the same flexible manner as that in which it was developed, ensuring that it maintains a neutral tone and continues to meet its stated purpose;

3. *Requests* the Secretary-General to publish, including electronically, the text of the Model Law on Cross-Border Insolvency: The Judicial Perspective, as updated or amended from time to time in accordance with paragraph 2 of the present resolution, and to transmit it to Governments with the request that the text be made available to relevant authorities so that it becomes widely known and available;

4. *Recommends* that the Model Law on Cross-Border Insolvency: The Judicial Perspective be given due consideration, as appropriate, by judges, insolvency practitioners and other stakeholders involved in cross-border insolvency proceedings;

5. *Also recommends* that all States consider the implementation of the United Nations Commission on International Trade Law Model Law on Cross-Border Insolvency.

Arbitration and conciliation

UNCITRAL [A/66/17] considered the reports of Working Group II (Arbitration and Conciliation) on its fifty-third (Vienna, 4–8 October 2010) [A/CN.9/712] and fifty-fourth (New York, 7–11 February [A/CN.9/717] sessions.

The Commission noted the progress made by the Working Group regarding the preparation of a legal standard on transparency in treaty-based investor-State arbitration. The Group had considered matters of content, form and applicability of the legal standard on transparency to both future and existing investment treaties. It was confirmed that the question of applicability of the legal standard on transparency to existing investment treaties was part of the mandate of the Working Group. The Commission reiterated its commitment regarding the importance of ensuring transparency in investor-State arbitration.

The Commission noted that, following consultations between the secretariats of UNCITRAL and the United Nations Conference on Trade and Development (UNCTAD), the latter had submitted a proposal [A/CN.9/734] on the question of mediation in the context of settlement of investor-State disputes. The Commission agreed that the proposal was worthy of further consideration. It was suggested that conciliation and mediation with respect to the settlement of treaty-based investor-State disputes should be considered as a topic for future work by the Working Group.

At its fifty-fifth session (Vienna, 3–7 October) [A/CN.9/736], Working Group II continued the preparation of a legal standard on transparency in treaty-based investor-State arbitration.

Implementation of the 1958 New York Convention

UNCITRAL, at its forty-fourth session [A/66/17], was informed that the Secretariat was conducting two complementary projects aimed at monitoring the legislative implementation of the 1958 Convention on the Recognition and Enforcement of Foreign Arbitral Awards (the New York Convention) [YUN 1958, p. 390]. One project related to the publication on the UNCITRAL website of information contributed by States on their legislative implementation of the Convention. UNCITRAL urged States to continue providing the Secretariat with accurate information to ensure that the data published on the Commission's website remained current. The other project related to the preparation of a guide on the Convention, which was being carried out by the Secretariat in close cooperation with international legal scholars George Bermann and Emmanuel Gaillard, who had established research teams to work on the project. UNCITRAL requested the Secretariat to pursue its efforts in that regard.

Online dispute resolution

UNCITRAL [A/66/17] noted that Working Group III (Online Dispute Resolution) had, at its twenty-second session (Vienna, 13–17 December 2010) [A/CN.9/716], commenced its deliberations on the preparation of legal standards, in particular procedural rules on online dispute resolution for cross-border electronic transactions, and continued its work at its twenty-third session (New York, 23–27 May 2011) [A/CN.9/721]. The Commission also noted that, in addition to the procedural rules, the Working Group had requested the Secretariat to prepare documentation for its next session addressing the issues of guidelines for neutrals and for online dispute resolution providers, substantive legal principles for resolving disputes, and a cross-border enforcement mechanism.

The Commission took note of a concern raised that, given that online dispute resolution was a somewhat novel subject for UNCITRAL and that it related at least in part to transactions involving consumers, the Working Group should adopt a prudent approach in its deliberations, bearing in mind the Commission's direction that the Working Group's work should be carefully designed not to affect the rights of consumers. The Commission reaffirmed the Working Group's mandate relating to cross-border electronic transactions, including business-to-business and business-to-consumer transactions. It decided that, while the Working Group should be free to interpret that mandate as covering consumer-to-consumer transactions and to elaborate possible rules governing consumer-to-consumer relationships, it should be particularly mindful of the need not to displace consumer protection legislation.

At its twenty-fourth session (Vienna, 14–18 November) [A/CN.9/739], the Working Group discussed draft procedural rules on online dispute resolution for cross-border electronic transactions.

Security interests

UNCITRAL [A/66/17] considered the reports of Working Group VI (Security Interests) on the work of its eighteenth (Vienna, 8–12 November 2010) [A/CN.9/714] and nineteenth (New York, 11–15 April 2011) [A/CN.9/719] sessions. Noting the progress made by the Working Group in preparing a text on the registration of security rights in movable assets and the guidance needed by a number of States, the Commission requested the Working Group to submit the text for final approval and adoption at the Commission's forty-fifth (2012) session.

The Commission requested the Secretariat to proceed with the preparation, in cooperation with the World Bank and outside experts, of a joint set of principles on effective secured transactions regimes. Such efforts would be aimed at preparing a text that would be approved by the Commission and the World Bank, and could include consultations and meetings with experts from the public and private sector.

The Commission approved the paper "Comparison and analysis of major features of international instruments relating to secured transactions" [A/CN.9/720], prepared jointly by the Permanent Bureau of the Hague Conference on Private International Law, the International Institute for the Unification of Private Law (Unidroit) and the UNCITRAL secretariat, and requested that it be given the widest possible dissemination.

At its twentieth session (Vienna, 12–16 December) [A/CN.9/740], the Working Group continued its work on a text on the registration of security rights in movable assets.

Electronic commerce

UNCITRAL [A/66/17] considered a Secretariat note on current and possible future work on electronic commerce [A/CN.9/728 & Add.1], which summarized the discussions that had taken place at a colloquium on electronic commerce (New York, 14–16 February). Broad consensus was expressed on the desirability of reconvening Working Group IV (Electronic Commerce). In particular, it was noted that the past work of UNCITRAL in that area had contributed significantly to the advancement of the use of electronic communications in international trade; a long lapse in Working Group meetings might erode that leadership, as well as prevent UNCITRAL from updating and complementing legal standards in that rapidly evolving field. The Commission agreed that Working Group IV should be convened to undertake work in the field of electronic transferable records.

Working Group IV began work on electronic transferable records at its forty-fifth session (Vienna, 10–14 October) [A/CN.9/737].

Microfinance

UNCITRAL [A/66/17] considered a Secretariat note on legal and regulatory issues surrounding microfinance [A/CN.9/727], summarizing the proceedings of an international colloquium on microfinance (Vienna, 12–13 January). The colloquium highlighted that, although initiatives to address issues related to microfinance had been successfully carried out in a number of countries, there was no coherent set of global legal and regulatory measures that could serve as a standard for countries wishing to legislate in accordance with international best practice. Subjects indicated included cross-border funding; secured transactions in microfinance to enhance the availability of credit, in particular to small and medium-sized enterprises or clients lacking sufficient capital or access to other kinds of credit; use of electronic money, or "e-money"; and dispute resolution mechanisms to address complaints of microfinance users.

The Commission took note of the Secretariat's involvement in a UN inter-agency mechanism for the promotion of inclusive finance, and of the fact that UNCITRAL was the only participant therein focusing on the legal and regulatory aspects of microfinance. The Secretariat was encouraged to continue its participation in that initiative.

The Commission agreed to include microfinance as an item for future UNCITRAL work and to further consider that matter at its 2012 session. To assist the Commission in defining the areas where work was needed, UNCITRAL requested the Secretariat to circulate to all States a short questionnaire regarding their experience with the establishment of a legislative and regulatory framework for microfinance, including any obstacles they might have encountered, for consideration by the Commission at its next session.

Case law on UNCITRAL texts

The Commission [A/66/17] considered a Secretariat note on the promotion of ways and means of ensuring a uniform interpretation and application of UNCITRAL legal texts [A/CN.9/726], which provided information on the current status of the case law on UNCITRAL texts (CLOUT) system and an update on work undertaken by the Secretariat on digests of case law relating to the 1980 United Nations Convention on Contracts for the International Sale of Goods (United Nations Sales Convention) [YUN 1980, p. 1131] and the Model Law on International Commercial Arbitration (Model Law on Arbitration) [YUN 1985, p. 1192].

The Commission noted the continuing work under the CLOUT system. As at 6 May, 107 issues of compiled case-law abstracts from the CLOUT system had been prepared for publication, dealing with 1,055 cases relating mainly to the United Nations Sales Convention and the Model Law on Arbitration. The Commission noted the increase in the number of abstracts on the UNCITRAL Model Law on Cross-Border Insolvency [YUN 1997, p. 1377] and on the New York Convention [YUN 1958, p. 390], as well as the publication of abstracts related to the 1974 Convention on the Limitation Period in the International Sale of Goods [YUN 1974, p. 853]. The Secretariat was encouraged to continue its efforts to extend the composition and vitality of the network of contributors to the CLOUT system. A meeting of national correspondents was held on 7 July and discussed, among other issues, the revised digest of case law on the United Nations Sales Convention and the advanced work on the digest on the Model Law on Arbitration.

Technical cooperation and assistance

UNCITRAL [A/66/17] considered a Secretariat note [A/CN.9/724] describing technical cooperation and assistance activities undertaken since 2010. The Commission took note of the strategic framework for technical assistance suggested by the Secretariat and endorsed its priority lines of action, which included stressing a regional and subregional approach to achieve economies of scale and to complement regional integration initiatives; promoting the universal adoption of those international trade law texts enjoying wide acceptance, namely the New York Convention [YUN 1958, p. 390] and the United Nations Sales Convention [YUN 1980, p. 1131]; and disseminating information on recently adopted treaties to foster their early adoption and entry into force.

The Commission approved the establishment of an UNCITRAL Regional Centre for Asia and the Pacific in the Republic of Korea and expressed its gratitude to that country for its generous contribution to the related pilot project.

Coordination and cooperation

UNCITRAL [A/66/17] considered a Secretariat note [A/CN.9/725] providing information on the activities of other international organizations active in the field of international trade law in which the UNCITRAL Secretariat had participated since 2010. The Commission noted that, pursuant to General Assembly resolution 65/21 [YUN 2010, p. 1344], the Secretariat had engaged in a dialogue with a number of organizations, including the European Union, the Hague Conference on Private International Law (the Hague Conference), the Organization for Economic Cooperation and Development, the UNCTAD-led Inter-Agency Cluster on Trade and Productive Capacity of the United Nations System Chief Executives Board for Coordination, Unidroit, the World Bank and the World Intellectual Property Organization. The Secretariat principally participated in expert groups, working groups and plenary meetings of those organizations to share information and expertise and avoid duplication of work. The Commission reiterated the importance of coordination work by UNCITRAL as the core legal body in the UN system in the field of international trade law.

UNCITRAL, on 5 July, commended the use of the 2010 revision of the Uniform Rules for Demand Guarantees, approved by the International Chamber of Commerce, in transactions involving demand guarantees.

Future work

UNCITRAL approved the holding of its forty-fifth session in New York from 18 June to 6 July 2012. It also approved the schedule of meetings for its working groups up to and after its forty-fifth session.

GENERAL ASSEMBLY ACTION

On 9 December [meeting 82], the General Assembly, on the recommendation of the Sixth Committee [A/66/471], adopted **resolution 66/94** without vote [agenda item 79].

Report of the United Nations Commission on International Trade Law on the work of its forty-fourth session

The General Assembly,

Recalling its resolution 2205(XXI) of 17 December 1966, by which it established the United Nations Commission on International Trade Law with a mandate to further the progressive harmonization and unification of the law of international trade and in that respect to bear in mind the interests of all peoples, in particular those of developing countries, in the extensive development of international trade,

Reaffirming its belief that the progressive modernization and harmonization of international trade law, in reducing or removing legal obstacles to the flow of international trade, especially those affecting developing countries, would contribute significantly to universal economic cooperation among all States on a basis of equality, equity, common interest and respect for the rule of law, to the elimination of discrimination in international trade and, thereby, to peace, stability and the well-being of all peoples,

Having considered the report of the Commission,

Reiterating its concern that activities undertaken by other bodies in the field of international trade law without adequate coordination with the Commission might lead to undesirable duplication of efforts and would not be in keeping with the aim of promoting efficiency, consistency and coherence in the unification and harmonization of international trade law,

Reaffirming the mandate of the Commission, as the core legal body within the United Nations system in the field of international trade law, to coordinate legal activities in this field, in particular to avoid duplication of efforts, including among organizations formulating rules of international trade, and to promote efficiency, consistency and coherence in the modernization and harmonization of international trade law, and to continue, through its secretariat, to maintain close cooperation with other international organs and organizations, including regional organizations, active in the field of international trade law,

1. *Takes note with appreciation* of the report of the United Nations Commission on International Trade Law;

2. *Commends* the Commission for the finalization and adoption of the United Nations Commission on International Trade Law Model Law on Public Procurement and the United Nations Commission on International Trade Law Model Law on Cross-Border Insolvency: The Judicial Perspective;

3. *Takes note with interest* of the progress made by the Commission in its work on the preparation of legal standards on transparency in treaty-based investor-State arbitration, online dispute resolution for cross-border electronic transactions and electronic commerce, in particular at the colloquium held in February 2011, the interpretation and application of selected concepts of the United Nations Commission on International Trade Law Model Law on Cross-Border Insolvency relating to centre of main interests, and a draft text on the registration of security rights in movable assets;

4. *Welcomes* the decisions of the Commission to prepare a guide to enactment of the Model Law on Public Procurement, in as efficient and practical a manner as possible, and a study on possible future work of the Commission in the area of public-private partnerships and privately financed infrastructure projects, to undertake work in the field of electronic transferable records, to prepare, in cooperation with the World Bank, draft principles on effective secured transactions regimes, within existing resources and without utilizing working group resources, and to include microfinance as an item for the future work of the Commission and to further consider that matter at its next session, in 2012;

5. *Notes with appreciation* the decision of the Commission to commend the use of the 2010 revision of the Uniform Rules for Demand Guarantees, published by the International Chamber of Commerce, as appropriate, in transactions involving demand guarantees;

6. *Also notes with appreciation* the progress made in the ongoing project of the Commission on monitoring the implementation of the Convention on the Recognition and Enforcement of Foreign Arbitral Awards, done in New York on 10 June 1958, and the decision of the Commission to request the Secretariat to pursue its efforts towards the preparation of a guide on the Convention;

7. *Endorses* the efforts and initiatives of the Commission, as the core legal body within the United Nations system in the field of international trade law, aimed at increasing coordination of and cooperation on legal activities of international and regional organizations active in the field of international trade law and at promoting the rule of law at the national and international levels in this field, and in this regard appeals to relevant international and regional organizations to coordinate their legal activities with those of the Commission, to avoid duplication of efforts and to promote efficiency, consistency and coherence in the modernization and harmonization of international trade law;

8. *Notes with appreciation* the significant progress in the Commission's coordination and cooperation activities in the field of security interests and in particular the approval by the Commission of a paper prepared jointly by the Permanent Bureau of the Hague Conference on Private International Law and the secretariats of the Commission and the International Institute for the Unification of Private Law, with the assistance of outside experts, entitled "Comparison and analysis of major features of international instruments relating to secured transactions", as well as the request that it be given the widest possible dissemination, including as a United Nations sales publication, with proper recognition of the contribution of the Permanent Bureau of the Hague Conference on Private International Law and the secretariat of the International Institute for the Unification of Private Law;

9. *Notes* the agreement of the Commission that a coordinated approach to the matter of the law applicable to the proprietary effects of assignments of receivables is in the interest of all States and its request to the Secretariat to cooperate closely with the European Commission with a view to ensuring a coordinated approach to the matter, taking into account the approach followed in the United Nations Convention on the Assignment of Receivables in International Trade and the *UNCITRAL Legislative Guide on Secured Transactions*;

10. *Reaffirms* the importance, in particular for developing countries, of the work of the Commission concerned with technical cooperation and assistance in the field of international trade law reform and development, and in this connection:

(*a*) Welcomes the initiatives of the Commission towards expanding, through its secretariat, its technical cooperation and assistance programme, and in that respect encourages the Secretary-General to seek partnerships with State and non-State actors to increase awareness about the work of the Commission and facilitate the effective implementation of legal standards resulting from its work;

(*b*) Expresses its appreciation to the Commission for carrying out technical cooperation and assistance activities and for providing assistance with legislative drafting in the field of international trade law, and draws the attention of the Secretary-General to the limited resources that are made available in this field;

(c) Takes note with interest of the comprehensive approach to technical cooperation and assistance, based on the strategic framework for technical assistance suggested by the Secretariat to promote universal adoption of the texts of the Commission and to disseminate information on recently adopted texts;

(d) Expresses its appreciation to the Governments whose contributions enabled the technical cooperation and assistance activities to take place, and appeals to Governments, the relevant bodies of the United Nations system, organizations, institutions and individuals to make voluntary contributions to the United Nations Commission on International Trade Law Trust Fund for Symposia and, where appropriate, for the financing of special projects, and otherwise to assist the secretariat of the Commission in carrying out technical cooperation and assistance activities, in particular in developing countries;

(e) Reiterates its appeal to the United Nations Development Programme and other bodies responsible for development assistance, such as the World Bank and regional development banks, as well as to Governments in their bilateral aid programmes, to support the technical cooperation and assistance programme of the Commission and to cooperate and coordinate their activities with those of the Commission, in the light of the relevance and importance of the work and programmes of the Commission for the promotion of the rule of law at the national and international levels and for the implementation of the United Nations development agenda, including the achievement of the Millennium Development Goals;

11. *Calls upon* Member States, non-member States, observer organizations and the Secretariat to apply the rules of procedure and methods of work of the Commission, taking into account the summary of conclusions as reproduced in annex III to the report on the work of its forty-third session, with a view to ensuring the high quality of the work of the Commission and international acceptability of its instruments, and in this regard recalls its previous resolutions related to this matter;

12. *Welcomes* the decision by the Commission to establish, subject to the relevant rules and regulations of the United Nations and the internal approval process in the Office of Legal Affairs of the Secretariat, a Regional Centre for Asia and the Pacific, in the Republic of Korea, as a novel yet important first step for the Commission in reaching out and providing technical assistance to developing countries in the region, it being understood that the establishment of a regional presence would have to rely entirely on extrabudgetary resources, including but not limited to voluntary contributions from States, expresses its appreciation to the Government of the Republic of Korea for its generous contribution to the pilot project, and requests the Secretary-General to keep the General Assembly informed of developments regarding the establishment of such regional centres, including the Regional Centre for Asia and the Pacific in the Republic of Korea and, in particular, their funding and budgetary situation;

13. *Appeals* to Governments, the relevant bodies of the United Nations system, organizations, institutions and individuals to make voluntary contributions to the trust fund established to provide travel assistance to developing countries that are members of the Commission, at their request and in consultation with the Secretary-General, in order to enable renewal of the provision of that assistance and to increase expert representation from developing countries at sessions of the Commission and its working groups, necessary to build local expertise and capacities in the field of international trade law in those countries to facilitate the development of international trade and the promotion of foreign investment;

14. *Decides*, in order to ensure full participation of all Member States in the sessions of the Commission and its working groups, to continue, in the competent Main Committee during the sixty-sixth session of the General Assembly, its consideration of granting travel assistance to the least developed countries that are members of the Commission, at their request and in consultation with the Secretary-General;

15. *Endorses* the conviction of the Commission that the implementation and effective use of modern private law standards on international trade are essential for advancing good governance, sustained economic development and the eradication of poverty and hunger and that the promotion of the rule of law in commercial relations should be an integral part of the broader agenda of the United Nations to promote the rule of law at the national and international levels, including through the Rule of Law Coordination and Resource Group, supported by the Rule of Law Unit in the Executive Office of the Secretary-General;

16. *Welcomes*, in this regard, the panel discussion on the role of the Commission in the promotion of the rule of law in conflict and post-conflict societies, held during the forty-fourth session of the Commission, and takes note of the particular relevance of the instruments and resources of the Commission for creating an environment of sustainable economic activity conducive to post-conflict reconstruction and preventing societies from sliding back into conflict;

17. *Takes note* of the views expressed by the Commission at the end of the panel discussion that, owing to a lack of sufficient resources, innovative ways need to be found for the early engagement of the instruments and resources of the Commission in post-conflict recovery operations of the United Nations and other donors, and that awareness needs to be increased of the fact that the Commission deals also with the basic building blocks for commercial activity and thus makes a real and immediate contribution in societies emerging from conflict;

18. *Reiterates its request* to the Secretary-General, in conformity with General Assembly resolutions on documentation-related matters, which, in particular, emphasize that any invitation to limit, where appropriate, the length of documents should not adversely affect either the quality of the presentation or the substance of the documents, to bear in mind the particular characteristics of the mandate and functions of the Commission in the progressive development and codification of international trade law when implementing page limits with respect to the documentation of the Commission;

19. *Requests* the Secretary-General to continue providing summary records of the meetings of the Commission, including committees of the whole established by the Commission for the duration of its annual session, relating to the formulation of normative texts, and encourages the Commission to discuss the matter at its next session, on the basis of a report to be prepared by the Secretariat;

20. *Reaffirms* the need to ensure the broadest possible participation in meetings of the Commission, and in this connection notes the existing rationale for the historical alternating pattern of sites for meetings of the Commission, that is, the proportionate distribution of travel costs among delegations, the global influence and presence of the Commission and the needs of developing countries, many of which do not have representation in Vienna, also notes the agreement of the Commission that every effort should be made to identify alternatives to abolishing the alternating pattern of meetings that would achieve a similar result, and in this respect encourages Member States, jointly with the Secretariat, to continue to review current working practices to achieve increased efficiency, and with a view to identifying budgetary savings;

21. *Stresses* the importance of promoting the use of texts emanating from the work of the Commission for the global unification and harmonization of international trade law, and to this end urges States that have not yet done so to consider signing, ratifying or acceding to conventions, enacting model laws and encouraging the use of other relevant texts;

22. *Welcomes* the preparation of digests of case law relating to the texts of the Commission, such as a digest of case law relating to the United Nations Convention on Contracts for the International Sale of Goods, a digest of case law relating to the United Nations Commission on International Trade Law Model Law on International Commercial Arbitration, and a digest of case law relating to the Model Law on Cross-Border Insolvency, with the aim of assisting in the dissemination of information on those texts and promoting their use, enactment and uniform interpretation.

Other questions

Rule of law at the national and international levels

In August, pursuant to General Assembly resolution 65/32 [YUN 2010, p. 1347], the Secretary-General submitted his third annual report [A/66/133] on strengthening and coordinating UN rule-of-law activities, which illustrated achievements and challenges in strengthening the rule of law at the national and international levels over the preceding year and highlighted progress towards a more comprehensive and coordinated UN approach in support of national priorities and plans. The Secretary-General noted that the Rule of Law Coordination and Resource Group, chaired by the Deputy Secretary-General and supported by the Rule of Law Unit, continued to drive the Organization towards more strategic and effective rule-of-law assistance by ensuring greater overall quality, coordination and coherence of engagement.

The United Nations was providing rule-of-law assistance to over 150 Member States. Three or more UN entities engaged in rule-of-law activities in at least 70 countries, and five or more entities in over 35 countries. Evidence supported the trend towards more joint and comprehensive initiatives by key operational rule-of-law entities, particularly in conflict and post-conflict settings, where there were 17 peace operations with rule-of-law mandates. Coordination and coherence efforts continued to reach out to the over 40 UN actors involved in rule-of-law activities. The third annual system-wide meeting (New York, 10 June) brought the UN system together to examine ways to strengthen joint programming on the rule of law. Participants reviewed tools and practices for measuring rule-of-law development and the impact of assistance. They considered the UN-Women report *Progress of the World's Women: In Pursuit of Justice* with a view to exploring system-wide implementation of its recommendations. From 11 to 15 July, the United Nations Rule of Law Coordination and Resource Group, in partnership with United Nations System Staff College, piloted the *UN Unified Rule of Law Training* course at the United Nations Campus in Turin, Italy.

The Secretary-General said that the General Assembly high-level event on the rule of law in 2012 would be an opportunity to renew the commitment to the universal adherence to and implementation of the rule of law and to take stock of progress. In view of that opportunity, he recommended that Member States support the United Nations in enhancing coherence, coordination and effectiveness of its assistance, and consider ways in which the international community could enhance and better coordinate its efforts to strengthen the rule of law, including through an international policy forum on the rule of law.

GENERAL ASSEMBLY ACTION

On 9 December [meeting 82], the General Assembly, on the recommendation of the Sixth Committee [A/66/475], adopted **resolution 66/102** without vote [agenda item 83].

The rule of law at the national and international levels

The General Assembly,

Recalling its resolution 65/32 of 6 December 2010,

Reaffirming its commitment to the purposes and principles of the Charter of the United Nations and international law, which are indispensable foundations of a more peaceful, prosperous and just world, and reiterating its determination to foster strict respect for them and to establish a just and lasting peace all over the world,

Reaffirming that human rights, the rule of law and democracy are interlinked and mutually reinforcing and that they belong to the universal and indivisible core values and principles of the United Nations,

Reaffirming also the need for universal adherence to and implementation of the rule of law at both the national and international levels and its solemn commitment to an international order based on the rule of law and international law, which, together with the principles of justice, is essential for peaceful coexistence and cooperation among States,

Convinced that the advancement of the rule of law at the national and international levels is essential for the realization of sustained economic growth, sustainable development, the eradication of poverty and hunger and the protection of all human rights and fundamental freedoms, and acknowledging that collective security depends on effective cooperation, in accordance with the Charter and international law, against transnational threats,

Reaffirming the duty of all States to refrain in their international relations from the threat or use of force in any manner inconsistent with the purposes and principles of the United Nations and to settle their international disputes by peaceful means in such a manner that international peace and security, and justice, are not endangered, in accordance with Chapter VI of the Charter, and calling upon States that have not yet done so to consider accepting the jurisdiction of the International Court of Justice in accordance with its Statute,

Convinced that the promotion of and respect for the rule of law at the national and international levels, as well as justice and good governance, should guide the activities of the United Nations and of its Member States,

Recalling paragraph 134 (*e*) of the 2005 World Summit Outcome,

1. *Takes note* of the annual report of the Secretary-General on strengthening and coordinating United Nations rule of law activities;

2. *Reaffirms* the role of the General Assembly in encouraging the progressive development of international law and its codification, and reaffirms further that States shall abide by all their obligations under international law;

3. *Reaffirms also* the imperative of upholding and promoting the rule of law at the international level in accordance with the principles of the Charter;

4. *Welcomes* the dialogue initiated by the Rule of Law Coordination and Resource Group and the Rule of Law Unit with Member States on the topic "Promoting the rule of law at the international level", and calls for the continuation of this dialogue with a view to fostering the rule of law at the international level;

5. *Stresses* the importance of adherence to the rule of law at the national level and the need to strengthen support to Member States, upon their request, in the domestic implementation of their respective international obligations through enhanced technical assistance and capacity-building, based on greater coordination and coherence within the United Nations system and among donors, and reiterates its call for greater evaluation of the effectiveness of such activities, including possible measures to improve the effectiveness of those capacity-building activities;

6. *Calls*, in this context, for dialogue to be enhanced among all stakeholders with a view to placing national perspectives at the centre of rule of law assistance in order to strengthen national ownership;

7. *Calls upon* the United Nations system to systematically address, as appropriate, aspects of the rule of law in relevant activities, including the participation of women in rule of law-related activities, recognizing the importance of the rule of law to virtually all areas of United Nations engagement;

8. *Expresses full support* for the overall coordination and coherence role of the Rule of Law Coordination and Resource Group within the United Nations system within existing mandates, supported by the Rule of Law Unit in the Executive Office of the Secretary-General, under the leadership of the Deputy Secretary-General;

9. *Requests* the Secretary-General to submit, in a timely manner, his next annual report on United Nations rule of law activities, in accordance with paragraph 5 of its resolution 63/128 of 11 December 2008;

10. *Recognizes* the importance of restoring confidence in the rule of law as a key element of transitional justice;

11. *Encourages* the Secretary-General and the United Nations system to accord high priority to rule of law activities;

12. *Invites* the International Court of Justice, the United Nations Commission on International Trade Law and the International Law Commission to continue to comment, in their respective reports to the General Assembly, on their current roles in promoting the rule of law;

13. *Invites* the Rule of Law Coordination and Resource Group and the Rule of Law Unit to continue to interact with Member States on a regular basis, in particular in informal briefings;

14. *Stresses* the need to provide the Rule of Law Unit with the necessary funding and staff in order to enable it to carry out its tasks in an effective and sustainable manner, and urges the Secretary-General and Member States to continue to support the functioning of the Unit;

15. *Recalls* its decision to convene a high-level meeting of the General Assembly on the topic "The rule of law at the national and international levels" during the high-level segment of its sixty-seventh session, and decides that the organizational arrangements for the high-level meeting should be as follows:

(*a*) The high-level meeting will be held as a one-day plenary on Monday, 24 September 2012;

(*b*) The President of the General Assembly, the Secretary-General, the President of the International Court of Justice, the President of the Security Council, the United Nations High Commissioner for Human Rights, the Administrator of the United Nations Development Programme, the Executive Director of the United Nations Office on Drugs and Crime, the Chair of the International Law Commission, Member States and observers, as well as a limited number of representatives of non-governmental organizations active in the field of the rule of law, will be invited to speak at the plenary;

(*c*) The President of the General Assembly shall draw up a list of representatives of non-governmental organizations in consultative status with the Economic and Social Council who will participate in the high-level meeting;

(*d*) The President of the General Assembly shall draw up a list of representatives of civil society organizations, including non-governmental organizations active in the field of the rule of law and, taking into account the principle of equitable geographical representation, submit the list to Member States for consideration on a no-objection basis, for participation in the high-level meeting;

16. *Decides* that the high-level meeting will result in a concise outcome document, and requests the President of the General Assembly to produce a draft text, in consulta-

tion with Member States, and to convene inclusive informal consultations at an appropriate date in order to enable sufficient consideration and agreement by Member States prior to the meeting;

17. *Requests* the President of the General Assembly, in consultation with Member States, to finalize the organizational arrangements of the meetings, including the list of speakers for the plenary, taking into account the length of the high-level meeting, the level of representation, equitable geographical representation and the need to ensure that all listed speakers will have the opportunity to speak;

18. *Requests* the Secretary-General to submit a report for the consideration of Member States in preparation for the high-level meeting, no later than March 2012;

19. *Decides* to include in the provisional agenda of its sixty-seventh session the item entitled "The rule of law at the national and international levels";

20. *Invites* Member States as well as the Secretary-General to suggest possible sub-topics for future Sixth Committee debates for inclusion in the forthcoming annual report, with a view to assisting the Sixth Committee in choosing future sub-topics.

Strengthening the role of the United Nations

Special Committee on United Nations Charter

In accordance with General Assembly resolution 65/31 [YUN 2010, p. 1350], the Special Committee on the Charter of the United Nations and on the Strengthening of the Role of the Organization, at its sixty-sixth session (New York, 28 February–4 March; 7, 9 March) [A/66/33], considered proposals relating to the maintenance of international peace and security; the peaceful settlement of disputes; working methods of the Committee and identification of new subjects; and the status of the publications *Repertory of Practice of United Nations Organs* and *Repertoire of the Practice of the Security Council*.

Regarding the maintenance of international peace and security, the Committee considered the question of the implementation of the Charter provisions relating to assistance to third States affected by sanctions. Several delegations reaffirmed that sanctions remained an important tool for maintaining and restoring international peace and security. The sanctions regimes adopted by the Security Council had demonstrated that sanctions could be applied in a targeted way so as to substantially minimize the possibility of adverse consequences to civilian populations as well as to third States.

Delegations emphasized that sanctions should be introduced only after all means of peaceful settlement had been exhausted and their effects had been thoroughly considered. They should not be applied preventively in instances of violation of international law; sanctions should be imposed only when international peace and security were threatened or an act of aggression was carried out. Sanctions should have a specified time frame, be subject to periodic review and be lifted as soon as their objectives were achieved. Concern was expressed over the imposition of unilateral sanctions in violation of international law and the right to development. The role of the General Assembly should be strengthened in relation to sanctions.

Several delegations noted that none of the sanctions committees had been approached by Member States with regard to special economic problems arising from the implementation of sanctions since 2003. They also noted that in 2010, neither the Assembly nor the Economic and Social Council had found it necessary to take any action relating to that matter. Therefore, the question of assistance to third States affected by the application of sanctions was no longer relevant, should not be a matter of priority for the Special Committee and did not merit further discussion. For other delegations, the consideration of the issue was of a preventive nature and therefore should continue to be considered by the Committee; any proposal submitted on that matter should be considered on a priority basis. The fact that no State had required assistance in the matter should not imply that the subject no longer merited discussion.

Some delegations stated that although the introduction by the Security Council of targeted sanctions and improved working methods with regard to the application of sanctions had helped to avoid the unintended effects of sanctions, the possibility of such effects remained. The view was expressed that the issue of establishing mechanisms for assisting affected States, including special funds for economic assistance, merited further consideration. It was also stated that the Council should continue to pay attention to the humanitarian effects of sanctions before applying them. The Special Committee considered a revised working paper submitted by the Libyan Arab Jamahiriya on the strengthening of certain principles concerning the application of sanctions contained in the Committee's 2002 report [YUN 2002, p. 1329].

The Special Committee considered a further revised working paper entitled "Strengthening of the role of the Organization and enhancing its effectiveness", submitted by Cuba in 2009 [YUN 2009, p. 1321]. Cuba indicated that the proposal had been before the Committee for several years and had been revised in 2009, in the light of comments made by delegations. The Working Group of the Whole recommended the working paper for adoption but the Committee decided not to adopt it.

The Special Committee discussed Libya's revised proposal on strengthening the role of the United Nations in the maintenance of international peace and security [YUN 1998, p. 1233]. Libya indicated that it was not aware of any suggestions or amendments to the revised working paper and called upon delegations to study the document further.

The Special Committee considered the revised working paper submitted by Belarus and the Russian Federation in 2005 [YUN 2005, p. 1445], in which it was recommended that an advisory opinion be requested from the International Court of Justice (ICJ) as to the legal consequences of the resort to the use of force by States without prior authorization by the Security Council, except in the exercise of the right to self-defence. The Russian Federation said that such an advisory opinion would address lacunae in the UN Charter, which did not contain detailed provisions regarding the use of force; the contemporary political situation required additional interpretation of Charter provisions. An advisory opinion would contribute to strengthening the implementation of the *jus cogens* principle of the non-use of force or the threat of force and clarify the notion of "armed attack" in the light of the provisions of the Charter. Some representatives stated that the proposal would contribute to preventing subjective unilateral interpretations by States of the provisions of the Charter. It was noted that the proposal would clarify in which situations States' resort to the use of force without prior Council authorization, except for self-defence, would be unlawful. Others maintained that the issue of the use of force had been adequately addressed in the Charter and, consequently, that the proposal for an advisory opinion could not be supported. The Committee should stop considering the proposal, as it had not been able to reach consensus on the issue after many years of discussion. The Committee decided to keep the proposal on its agenda.

Venezuela announced that it had revised the working paper entitled "Special mechanism for the study on the functional relationship of the General Assembly, the Economic and Social Council, with the Security Council", and introduced a revised version entitled "Open-ended working group to study the proper implementation of the Charter of the United Nations with respect to the functional relationship of its organs" [A/AC.182/L.130]. Some delegations expressed support for the proposal and maintained that the Special Committee was a proper forum to consider it. Others maintained that the responsibilities of the principal UN organs were amply defined in the Charter, and that the resources of the Committee should be used in a more productive manner.

During the general exchange of views on the item entitled "Peaceful settlement of disputes", some delegations reiterated that, in accordance with the mandate of the Special Committee, the item should remain on its agenda. The central role of ICJ in the peaceful settlement of disputes and its contribution to maintaining global security was emphasized. The importance of a free choice of means in peaceful dispute settlement was highlighted.

Delegations commended ongoing Secretariat efforts to update the *Repertory of Practice of United Nations Organs* and the *Repertoire of the Practice of the Security Council* and reduce the backlog in the preparation of those publications. Concerning the *Repertory*, the backlog with respect to volumes II, IV and VI had been eliminated and the Secretariat would submit five volumes for translation and publication. The situation with respect to the backlog in volume III, however, remained unchanged. A number of studies for Supplement 10, covering the period from 2000 to 2009, had been completed; some other studies for the Supplement were under preparation or review. With regard to the *Repertoire*, in the previous year, the Secretariat had worked on the fourteenth and fifteenth Supplements, covering the period from 2000 to 2007; initiated work on the sixteenth Supplement, covering the years 2008 and 2009; and laid the groundwork for the seventeenth Supplement, which would cover the years 2010 and 2011. The Special Committee recommended that the General Assembly call on the Secretary-General to continue efforts to update the two publications and make them available in all language versions; and call for voluntary contributions to the trust funds for updating the *Repertoire* and eliminating the backlog of the *Repertory*.

Regarding the identification of new subjects, the Special Committee discussed the proposal by Ghana on including a new subject entitled "Principles and practical measures/mechanisms for strengthening and ensuring more effective cooperation between the United Nations and regional organizations on the maintenance of international peace and security in areas of conflict prevention and resolution and post-conflict peacebuilding and peacekeeping, consistent with Chapter VIII of the Charter of the United Nations".

Reports of Secretary-General. In response to General Assembly resolution 65/31 [YUN 2010, p. 1350], the Secretary-General submitted a July report [A/66/213] on implementation of the provisions of the Charter related to assistance to third States affected by the application of sanctions. The report highlighted operational changes that occurred due to the shift in focus in the Security Council and its sanctions committees towards targeted sanctions; recent developments concerning the activities of the Assembly and the Economic and Social Council in the area of assistance to such States; and Secretariat arrangements related to assistance to third States affected by the application of sanctions.

Also in response to General Assembly resolution 65/31, the Secretary-General reported in July [A/66/201] on progress made in updating the *Repertory of Practice of United Nations Organs* and *Repertoire of the Practice of the Security Council*.

With respect to the *Repertory*, the Secretary-General concluded that the Assembly might wish to note the progress made in the preparation of *Repertory* studies and their posting on the Internet in English, French and Spanish; consider the recommendations of the Special Committee—including the increased use of the UN internship programme, expanded cooperation with academic institutions for the preparation of the studies and the sponsoring, on a voluntary basis and with no cost to the United Nations, of associate experts to assist in updating the publication; note the progress made towards the elimination of the backlog through the use of the trust fund; and encourage States to make additional contributions to it.

With regard to the *Repertoire*, the Secretary-General concluded that the Assembly might wish to note the progress made towards updating the publication and posting it in electronic form in all language versions on the UN website; call for voluntary contributions to the trust fund for the updating of the *Repertoire*; note the enhancement of the *Repertoire* website; and note the support of Germany in sponsoring an associate expert to assist in the preparation of the *Repertoire* and encourage other States to consider providing such assistance.

GENERAL ASSEMBLY ACTION

On 9 December [meeting 82], the General Assembly, on the recommendation of the Sixth Committee [A/66/474], adopted **resolution 66/101** without vote [agenda item 82].

Report of the Special Committee on the Charter of the United Nations and on the Strengthening of the Role of the Organization

The General Assembly,

Recalling its resolution 3499(XXX) of 15 December 1975, by which it established the Special Committee on the Charter of the United Nations and on the Strengthening of the Role of the Organization, and its relevant resolutions adopted at subsequent sessions,

Recalling also its resolution 47/233 of 17 August 1993 on the revitalization of the work of the General Assembly,

Recalling further its resolution 47/62 of 11 December 1992 on the question of equitable representation on and increase in the membership of the Security Council,

Taking note of the report of the Open-ended Working Group on the Question of Equitable Representation on and Increase in the Membership of the Security Council and Other Matters related to the Security Council,

Recalling the elements relevant to the work of the Special Committee contained in its resolution 47/120 B of 20 September 1993,

Recalling also its resolution 51/241 of 31 July 1997 on the strengthening of the United Nations system and its resolution 51/242 of 15 September 1997, entitled "Supplement to an Agenda for Peace", by which it adopted the texts on coordination and the question of sanctions imposed by the United Nations, which are annexed to that resolution,

Concerned about the special economic problems confronting certain States arising from the carrying out of preventive or enforcement measures taken by the Security Council against other States, and taking into account the obligation of Members of the United Nations under Article 49 of the Charter of the United Nations to join in affording mutual assistance in carrying out the measures decided upon by the Council,

Recalling the right of third States confronted with special economic problems of that nature to consult the Security Council with regard to a solution of those problems, in accordance with Article 50 of the Charter,

Recalling also that the International Court of Justice is the principal judicial organ of the United Nations, and reaffirming its authority and independence,

Mindful of the adoption of the revised working papers on the working methods of the Special Committee,

Taking note of the report of the Secretary-General entitled "*Repertory of Practice of United Nations Organs* and *Repertoire of the Practice of the Security Council*",

Taking note also of paragraphs 106 to 110, 176 and 177 of the 2005 World Summit Outcome,

Mindful of the decision of the Special Committee in which it expressed its readiness to engage, as appropriate, in the implementation of any decisions that might be taken at the high-level plenary meeting of the sixtieth session of the General Assembly in September 2005 that concerned the Charter and any amendments thereto,

Recalling the provisions of its resolutions 50/51 of 11 December 1995, 51/208 of 17 December 1996, 52/162 of 15 December 1997, 53/107 of 8 December 1998, 54/107 of 9 December 1999, 55/157 of 12 December 2000, 56/87 of 12 December 2001, 57/25 of 19 November 2002, 58/80 of 9 December 2003 and 59/45 of 2 December 2004,

Recalling also its resolution 64/115 of 16 December 2009 and the document entitled "Introduction and implementation of sanctions imposed by the United Nations" annexed thereto,

Having considered the report of the Special Committee on the work of its session held in 2011,

Noting with appreciation the work done by the Special Committee to encourage States to focus on the need to prevent and to settle peacefully their disputes which are likely to endanger the maintenance of international peace and security,

1. *Takes note* of the report of the Special Committee on the Charter of the United Nations and on the Strengthening of the Role of the Organization;

2. *Decides* that the Special Committee shall hold its next session from 21 to 28 February and on 1 March 2012;

3. *Requests* the Special Committee, at its session in 2012, in accordance with paragraph 5 of General Assembly resolution 50/52 of 11 December 1995:

(*a*) To continue its consideration of all proposals concerning the question of the maintenance of international peace and security in all its aspects in order to strengthen the role of the United Nations and, in this context, to consider other proposals relating to the maintenance of international peace and security already submitted or which may be submitted to the Special Committee at its session in 2012;

(*b*) To continue to consider, on a priority basis and in an appropriate substantive manner and framework, the question of the implementation of the provisions of the Charter of the United Nations related to assistance to third States affected by the application of sanctions under Chapter VII of the Charter based on all of the related reports of the Secretary-General and the proposals submitted on the question;

(c) To keep on its agenda the question of the peaceful settlement of disputes between States;

(d) To consider, as appropriate, any proposal referred to it by the General Assembly in the implementation of the decisions of the high-level plenary meeting of the sixtieth session of the Assembly in September 2005 that concern the Charter and any amendments thereto;

(e) To continue to consider, on a priority basis, ways and means of improving its working methods and enhancing its efficiency with a view to identifying widely acceptable measures for future implementation;

4. *Invites* the Special Committee, at its session in 2012, to continue to identify new subjects for consideration in its future work with a view to contributing to the revitalization of the work of the United Nations;

5. *Notes* the readiness of the Special Committee to provide, within its mandate, such assistance as may be sought at the request of other subsidiary bodies of the General Assembly in relation to any issues before them;

6. *Requests* the Special Committee to submit a report on its work to the General Assembly at its sixty-seventh session;

7. *Recognizes* the important role of the International Court of Justice, the principal judicial organ of the United Nations, in adjudicating disputes among States and the value of its work, as well as the importance of having recourse to the Court in the peaceful settlement of disputes, takes note, consistent with Article 96 of the Charter, of the Court's advisory jurisdiction that may be requested by the General Assembly, the Security Council or other authorized organs of the United Nations and the specialized agencies, and requests the Secretary-General to distribute, in due course, the advisory opinions requested by the principal organs of the United Nations as official documents of the United Nations;

8. *Commends* the Secretary-General for the progress made in the preparation of studies of the *Repertory of Practice of United Nations Organs*, including the increased use of the internship programme of the United Nations and further expanded cooperation with academic institutions for this purpose, as well as the progress made towards updating the *Repertoire of the Practice of the Security Council*;

9. *Notes with appreciation* the contributions made by Member States to the trust fund for the updating of the *Repertoire*, as well as the trust fund for the elimination of the backlog in the *Repertory*;

10. *Reiterates its call for* voluntary contributions to the trust fund for the updating of the *Repertoire*, voluntary contributions to the trust fund for the elimination of the backlog in the *Repertory* so as to further support the Secretariat in carrying out the effective elimination of that backlog, as well as the sponsoring, on a voluntary basis, and with no cost to the United Nations, of associate experts to assist in the updating of the two publications;

11. *Calls upon* the Secretary-General to continue his efforts towards updating the two publications and making them available electronically in all their respective language versions and to continue to address, in particular, the backlog in the preparation of volume III of the *Repertory*;

12. *Reiterates* the responsibility of the Secretary-General for the quality of the *Repertory* and the *Repertoire*, and, with regard to the *Repertoire*, calls upon the Secretary-General to continue to follow the modalities outlined in paragraphs 102 to 106 of the report of the Secretary-General of 18 September 1952;

13. *Requests* the Secretary-General to submit to the General Assembly, at its sixty-seventh session, a report on both the *Repertory* and the *Repertoire*;

14. *Also requests* the Secretary-General to brief the Special Committee at its next session on the information referred to in paragraph 11 of his report on the implementation of the provisions of the Charter related to assistance to third States affected by the application of sanctions;

15. *Further requests* the Secretary-General to submit to the General Assembly, at its sixty-seventh session, under the item entitled "Report of the Special Committee on the Charter of the United Nations and on the Strengthening of the Role of the Organization", a report on the implementation of the provisions of the Charter related to assistance to third States affected by the application of sanctions;

16. *Decides* to include in the provisional agenda of its sixty-seventh session the item entitled "Report of the Special Committee on the Charter of the United Nations and on the Strengthening of the Role of the Organization".

UN Programme for the teaching and study of international law

In response to General Assembly resolution 65/25 [YUN 2010, p. 1352], the Secretary-General submitted an October report [A/66/505] on the United Nations Programme of Assistance in the Teaching, Study, Dissemination and Wider Appreciation of International Law, which covered implementation of the Programme in 2011. Activities included the holding of the forty-seventh session of the International Law Seminar (Geneva, 4–22 July) and the convening of the International Law Fellowship Programme (The Hague, 4 July–12 August), in which fellows—nine men and 11 women—from 21 countries participated.

Lectures, seminars and study visits were organized by the UN Office of Legal Affairs (OLA). The Office organized regional courses in international law, including a regional course for African lawyers (Addis Ababa, 7–25 February), which was attended by 32 participants. The United Nations Audiovisual Library of International Law was created in response to the increasing demand for international law training; it could be accessed free of charge on the Internet. The Library had been accessed by users in 191 Member States. It offered more than 220 lectures by eminent international law scholars and practitioners on a broad range of subjects relating to international law. OLA worked on the substantive preparation of numerous legal publications, and maintained 21 websites.

The United Nations Treaty Collection website was further upgraded to offer various opportunities for legal research through the integration of a broad range of search and retrieval tools. Information on published volumes of the *United Nations Treaty Series*, subsequent treaty actions and the issuance of related publications was disseminated on the website and through e-mail. In addition, the treaty database entitled "Status of multilateral treaties deposited with the Secretary-General", including its online version, was updated daily and made available to view and download. The website also provided information on training seminars, the annual treaty event and special events, as well as electronic versions of OLA publications.

The report also described the legal publications issued during the year, outlined administrative and financial implications of UN participation in the Programme of Assistance in 2011 and provided guidelines and recommendations for the execution of the Programme for the 2012–2013 biennium.

The Advisory Committee on the Programme held its forty-sixth session on 7 October.

GENERAL ASSEMBLY ACTION

On 9 December [meeting 82], the General Assembly, on the recommendation of the Sixth Committee [A/66/472], adopted **resolution 66/97** without vote [agenda item 80].

United Nations Programme of Assistance in the Teaching, Study, Dissemination and Wider Appreciation of International Law

The General Assembly,

Recalling its resolution 2099(XX) of 20 December 1965, in which it established the United Nations Programme of Assistance in the Teaching, Study, Dissemination and Wider Appreciation of International Law to contribute towards a better knowledge of international law as a means of strengthening international peace and security and promoting friendly relations and cooperation among States,

Reaffirming that the Programme of Assistance is a core activity of the United Nations and that it has provided the foundation for the efforts of the United Nations to promote a better knowledge of international law for nearly half a century,

Reaffirming also that the increasing demand for international law training and dissemination activities creates new challenges for the Programme of Assistance,

Recognizing the importance of the Programme of Assistance effectively reaching its beneficiaries, including with regard to languages, while bearing in mind limitations on available resources,

Taking note with appreciation of the report of the Secretary-General on the implementation of the Programme of Assistance and the views of the Advisory Committee on the Programme of Assistance, which are contained in that report,

Noting with concern the reduction in the programme budget for the biennium 2010–2011 for fellowships for the benefit of developing countries indicated in the report of the Secretary-General, notwithstanding its resolutions 64/113 of 16 December 2009 and 65/25 of 6 December 2010,

Considering that international law should occupy an appropriate place in the teaching of legal disciplines at all universities,

Convinced that States, international and regional organizations, universities and institutions should be encouraged to give further support to the Programme of Assistance and to increase their activities to promote the teaching, study, dissemination and wider appreciation of international law, in particular those activities which are of special benefit to persons from developing countries,

Reaffirming that in the conduct of the Programme of Assistance it would be desirable to use as far as possible the resources and facilities made available by Member States, international and regional organizations, universities, institutions and others,

Reaffirming also the hope that, in appointing lecturers for the seminars to be held within the framework of the fellowship programmes in international law, account would be taken of the need to secure the representation of major legal systems and balance among various geographical regions,

1. *Approves* the guidelines and recommendations contained in section III of the report of the Secretary-General, in particular those designed to strengthen and revitalize the United Nations Programme of Assistance in the Teaching, Study, Dissemination and Wider Appreciation of International Law in response to the increasing demand for international law training and dissemination activities;

2. *Authorizes* the Secretary-General to carry out, in 2012 and 2013, the activities specified in his report, in accordance with the guidelines and recommendations contained therein, including the provision of:

(*a*) A number of fellowships, to be determined in the light of the overall resources for the Programme of Assistance and to be awarded to qualified candidates from developing countries, to attend the International Law Fellowship Programme in The Hague in 2012 and 2013;

(*b*) A number of fellowships, to be determined in the light of the overall resources for the Programme of Assistance and to be awarded to qualified candidates from developing countries, to attend regional courses in international law in 2012 and 2013;

and to finance the above activities from provisions in the regular budget as well as, when necessary, from voluntary financial contributions for these fellowships, which would be received as a result of the requests set out in paragraphs 18 to 20 below;

3. *Also authorizes* the Secretary-General to award a minimum of one scholarship in 2012 and 2013 under the Hamilton Shirley Amerasinghe Memorial Fellowship on the Law of the Sea, subject to the availability of voluntary contributions made for this fellowship, and in this regard calls upon States, intergovernmental organizations, international financial institutions, donor agencies, non-governmental organizations and natural and juridical persons to make voluntary contributions specifically for this fellowship;

4. *Further authorizes* the Secretary-General to continue and further develop the United Nations Audiovisual Library of International Law as a major contribution to the teaching and dissemination of international law around the world and to continue to finance this activity from provisions in the regular budget as well as, when necessary, from volun-

tary financial contributions, which would be received as a result of the requests set out in paragraphs 18 and 19 below;

5. *Expresses its appreciation* to the Secretary-General for the efforts to strengthen, expand and enhance the international law training and dissemination activities within the framework of the Programme of Assistance in 2011;

6. *Requests* the Secretary-General to consider admitting, for participation in the various components of the Programme of Assistance, candidates from countries willing to bear the entire cost of such participation;

7. *Also requests* the Secretary-General to provide to the programme budget for the next and future bienniums the necessary resources for the Programme of Assistance to ensure the continued effectiveness and further development of the Programme, in particular the organization of regional courses in international law on a regular basis and the viability of the United Nations Audiovisual Library of International Law;

8. *Recognizes* the importance of the United Nations legal publications prepared by the Office of Legal Affairs of the Secretariat, and strongly encourages their continued publication in various formats, including hard copy publications, which are essential for developing countries;

9. *Welcomes* the efforts undertaken by the Office of Legal Affairs to bring up to date the United Nations legal publications, and, in particular, commends the Codification Division of the Office of Legal Affairs for its desktop publishing initiative, which has greatly enhanced the timely issuance of its legal publications and has made possible the preparation of legal training materials;

10. *Encourages* the Office of Legal Affairs to continue to maintain and expand its websites listed in the annex to the report of the Secretary-General as an invaluable tool for the dissemination of international law materials as well as for advanced legal research;

11. *Encourages* the use of interns and research assistants for the preparation of materials for the United Nations Audiovisual Library of International Law;

12. *Welcomes* the training and technical assistance activities in international law undertaken by the Office of Legal Affairs within the framework of the Programme of Assistance, as described in the report of the Secretary-General, and encourages the continuation of such activities within available resources;

13. *Commends* the Codification Division for the cost-saving measures undertaken with regard to the International Law Fellowship Programme to maintain the number of fellowships available for this comprehensive international law training programme;

14. *Expresses its appreciation* to The Hague Academy of International Law for the valuable contribution it continues to make to the Programme of Assistance, which has enabled candidates under the International Law Fellowship Programme to attend and participate in the Fellowship Programme in conjunction with the Academy courses;

15. *Notes with appreciation* the contributions of The Hague Academy to the teaching, study, dissemination and wider appreciation of international law, and calls upon Member States and interested organizations to give favourable consideration to the appeal of the Academy for a continuation of support and a possible increase in their financial contributions, to enable the Academy to carry out its activities, particularly those relating to the summer courses, regional courses and programmes of the Centre for Studies and Research in International Law and International Relations;

16. *Welcomes* the efforts of the Codification Division to revitalize and conduct regional courses in international law as an important training activity;

17. *Expresses its appreciation* to Ethiopia and Thailand for offering to host regional courses in international law in 2012 and to Mexico for offering to host a regional course in international law in 2013, subject to adequate funding from the overall resources referred to in paragraph 2 above;

18. *Requests* the Secretary-General to continue to publicize the Programme of Assistance and periodically to invite Member States, universities, philanthropic foundations and other interested national and international institutions and organizations, as well as individuals, to make voluntary contributions towards the financing of the Programme or otherwise to assist in its implementation and possible expansion;

19. *Reiterates its request* to Member States and interested organizations, institutions and individuals to make voluntary contributions, inter alia, for the International Law Fellowship Programme and the United Nations Audiovisual Library of International Law, and expresses its appreciation to those Member States, institutions and individuals that have made voluntary contributions for this purpose;

20. *Urges*, in particular, all Governments to make voluntary contributions for the regional courses in international law organized by the Codification Division as an important complement to the International Law Fellowship Programme, thus alleviating the burden on prospective host countries and making it possible to conduct the regional courses on a regular basis;

21. *Decides* to appoint twenty-five Member States, six from African States, five from Asia-Pacific States, three from Eastern European States, five from Latin American and Caribbean States and six from Western European and other States, as members of the Advisory Committee on the Programme of Assistance for a period of four years beginning on 1 January 2012;

22. *Requests* the Secretary-General, following consultations with the Advisory Committee on the Programme of Assistance, to submit recommendations regarding the execution of the Programme of Assistance in subsequent years;

23. *Decides* to include in the provisional agenda of its sixty-seventh session the item entitled "United Nations Programme of Assistance in the Teaching, Study, Dissemination and Wider Appreciation of International Law".

Host country relations

At five meetings held in New York (3 February, 31 March, 22 July, 7 October, 2 November), the 19-member Committee on Relations with the Host Country considered the following aspects of relations between the UN diplomatic community and the United States, the host country: host country activities to assist members of the UN community; entry visas issued by the host country; the question of the security of missions and the safety of personnel; transportation, the use of motor vehicles, parking and related issues; and other matters. The recommendations and conclusions on those items, approved by the Committee at its 2 November meeting, were incorporated into its report [A/66/26]. The Committee expressed appreciation for the host country's efforts to maintain appropriate conditions for delegations and missions accredited to the United Nations and anticipated that all issues raised at its meetings would be settled in a spirit of cooperation and in accordance with international law.

Noting the importance of the observance of privileges and immunities, the Committee emphasized the need to solve, through negotiations, problems that might arise in that regard for the normal functioning of accredited delegations and missions. It urged the host country to continue to take appropriate action, such as the training of police, security, customs and border control officers, with a view to maintaining respect for diplomatic privileges and immunities. In case of violations, the Committee urged the host country to ensure that such cases were investigated and remedied, in accordance with applicable law. Considering that the security of missions and the safety of their personnel were indispensable for their effective functioning, the Committee appreciated the host country's efforts to that end and anticipated that the host country would continue to take all measures necessary to prevent any interference with the missions' functioning.

The Committee noted the problems experienced by some missions in connection with the implementation of the Parking Programme for Diplomatic Vehicles, in force since 2002 [YUN 2002, p. 1338]. It would remain seized of the matter to ensure its proper implementation in a manner that was fair, non-discriminatory, effective and therefore consistent with international law. It also requested that the host country continue to bring to the attention of New York City officials reports about other problems experienced by permanent missions or their staff, in order to improve the conditions for their functioning and to promote compliance with international norms concerning diplomatic privileges and immunities.

The Committee anticipated that the host country would enhance its efforts to ensure the issuance, in a timely manner, of entry visas to representatives of Member States to travel to New York on official UN business, and noted that a number of delegations had requested shortening the time frame applied by the host country for issuance of entry visas, since the existing time frame posed difficulties for the full-fledged participation of Member States in UN meetings. The Committee urged the host country to remove the remaining travel restrictions for personnel of certain missions and staff members of the Secretariat of certain nationalities. It also stressed the importance of permanent missions, their personnel and Secretariat personnel meeting their financial obligations.

The Committee expressed concern over the decision by JPMorgan Chase Bank to close all bank accounts held by permanent missions by 31 March, and welcomed the host country's efforts to facilitate the opening of bank accounts for permanent missions with other financial institutions.

The Committee reiterated its appreciation to the representative of the United States Mission in charge of host country affairs, to the Host Country Affairs Section of the United States Mission to the United Nations and the Office of Foreign Missions, as well as to those local entities, in particular the New York City Commission for the United Nations, Consular Corps and Protocol, that contributed to its efforts to help accommodate the needs, interests and requirements of the diplomatic community and to promote mutual understanding between the diplomatic community and the people of the City of New York.

Communications. The Committee had before it a letter from Iran addressed to the Chair of the Committee on Relations with the Host Country [A/AC.154/401] regarding denials of entry visas to three high-ranking Iranian officials for attending UN meetings. It also had before it a response from the host country addressed to the Chair of the Committee [A/AC.154/402], stating that visas were issued promptly in the vast majority of cases, provided that complete applications were submitted sufficiently in advance.

Also before the Committee was a letter from Iran [A/AC.154/403] informing the Chair of the Committee that the request for an entry visa for a member of the Iranian delegation to the second session of the Preparatory Committee for the United Nations Conference on the Arms Trade Treaty had not been issued. Owing to the delay, the member of the delegation was unable to attend the meeting, which was to begin on 28 February.

GENERAL ASSEMBLY ACTION

On 9 December [meeting 82], the General Assembly, on the recommendation of the Sixth Committee [A/66/482], adopted **resolution 66/108** without vote [agenda item 166].

Report of the Committee on Relations with the Host Country

The General Assembly,

Having considered the report of the Committee on Relations with the Host Country,

Recalling Article 105 of the Charter of the United Nations, the Convention on the Privileges and Immunities of the United Nations, the Agreement between the United Nations and the United States of America regarding the Headquarters of the United Nations and the responsibilities of the host country,

Recalling also that, in accordance with paragraph 7 of General Assembly resolution 2819(XXVI) of 15 December

1971, the Committee should consider, and advise the host country on, issues arising in connection with the implementation of the Agreement between the United Nations and the United States of America regarding the Headquarters of the United Nations,

Recognizing that effective measures should continue to be taken by the competent authorities of the host country, in particular to prevent any acts violating the security of missions and the safety of their personnel,

1. *Endorses* the recommendations and conclusions of the Committee on Relations with the Host Country contained in paragraph 39 of its report;

2. *Considers* that the maintenance of appropriate conditions for the normal work of the delegations and the missions accredited to the United Nations and the observance of their privileges and immunities, which is an issue of great importance, are in the interest of the United Nations and all Member States, and requests the host country to continue to solve, through negotiations, problems that might arise and to take all measures necessary to prevent any interference with the functioning of missions; and urges the host country to continue to take appropriate action, such as training of police, security, customs and border control officers, with a view to maintaining respect for diplomatic privileges and immunities and if violations occur to ensure that such cases are properly investigated and remedied, in accordance with applicable law;

3. *Notes* the problems experienced by some permanent missions in connection with the implementation of the Parking Programme for Diplomatic Vehicles, and notes that the Committee shall remain seized of the matter, with a view to continuing to maintain the proper implementation of the Parking Programme in a manner that is fair, non-discriminatory, effective and therefore consistent with international law;

4. *Requests* the host country to consider removing the remaining travel restrictions imposed by it on staff of certain missions and staff members of the Secretariat of certain nationalities, and in this regard notes the long-standing positions of affected States, of the Secretary-General and of the host country;

5. *Notes* the concerns expressed by some delegations concerning the denial and delay of entry visas to representatives of Member States;

6. *Also notes* that the Committee anticipates that the host country will continue to enhance its efforts to ensure the issuance of entry visas, in a timely manner, to representatives of Member States, pursuant to article IV, section 11, of the Agreement between the United Nations and the United States of America regarding the Headquarters of the United Nations to travel to New York on United Nations business, and that the Committee anticipates that the host country will continue to enhance efforts, including visa issuance, to facilitate the participation of representatives of Member States in other United Nations meetings, as appropriate;

7. *Further notes* that a number of delegations have requested shortening the time frame applied by the host country for issuance of entry visas to representatives of Member States, since this time frame poses difficulties for the full-fledged participation of Member States in United Nations meetings;

8. *Notes* the concerns over the decision by JPMorgan Chase Bank to close all bank accounts held by Permanent Missions to the United Nations by 31 March 2011, and welcomes the efforts of the host country to facilitate the opening of bank accounts for permanent missions with other financial institutions;

9. *Expresses its appreciation* for the efforts made by the host country, and hopes that the issues raised at the meetings of the Committee will continue to be resolved in a spirit of cooperation and in accordance with international law;

10. *Affirms* the importance of the Committee being in a position to fulfil its mandate and meet on short notice to deal with urgent and important matters concerning the relations between the United Nations and the host country, and in that connection requests the Secretariat and the Committee on Conferences to accord priority to requests from the Committee on Relations with the Host Country for conference-servicing facilities for meetings of that Committee that must be held while the General Assembly and its Main Committees are meeting, without prejudice to the requirements of those bodies and on an "as available" basis;

11. *Requests* the Secretary-General to remain actively engaged in all aspects of the relations of the United Nations with the host country;

12. *Requests* the Committee to continue its work in conformity with General Assembly resolution 2819(XXVI);

13. *Decides* to include in the provisional agenda of its sixty-seventh session the item entitled "Report of the Committee on Relations with the Host Country".

Chapter IV
Law of the sea

In 2011, the United Nations continued to promote universal acceptance of the 1982 United Nations Convention on the Law of the Sea and its two implementing Agreements on the implementation of Part XI of the Convention and on the conservation and management of straddling fish stocks and highly migratory fish stocks, respectively.

The three institutions created by the Convention—the International Seabed Authority, the International Tribunal for the Law of the Sea and the Commission on the Limits of the Continental Shelf—held sessions during the year.

Convention on the Law of the Sea

Signatures and ratifications

In 2011, Thailand ratified the United Nations Convention on the Law of the Sea, bringing the number of parties to 162. The Convention, which was adopted by the Third United Nations Conference on the Law of the Sea in 1982 [YUN 1982, p. 178], entered into force on 16 November 1994 [YUN 1994, p. 1301].

Meeting of States Parties

The twenty-first Meeting of States Parties to the Convention (New York, 13–17 June) [SPLOS/231] discussed the 2010 activities of the International Tribunal for the Law of the Sea [YUN 2010, p. 1371]; took note of the report of the Tribunal for 2010 [SPLOS/222]; took action on a number of Tribunal-related financial and administrative issues, including the performance report for 2009–2010 [SPLOS/224] and the report of the external auditor for the financial period 2009–2010 [SPLOS/223]; elected seven members of the Tribunal; and adopted decisions on the workload of the Commission on the Limits of the Continental Shelf [SPLOS/229] and on the adjustment mechanism for the remuneration of members of the Tribunal [SPLOS/230]. Also discussed were the activities of the International Seabed Authority (see p. 1323) and the Commission on the Limits of the Continental Shelf (see p. 1325) during the previous 12 months, as well as the Secretary-General's report [A/66/70/Add.2] submitted under article 319 of the Convention (see p. 1325).

Special Meeting. As a vacancy had occurred in the Commission on the Limits of the Continental Shelf—owing to the death of Kensaku Tamaki (Japan) on 5 April—a Special Meeting of States Parties to the Convention was convened (New York, 11 August) [SPLOS/237] to elect one member to the Commission. The Meeting had before it the list of candidates nominated by States parties [SPLOS/233] and the curriculum vitae of the candidate nominated by Japan [SPLOS/234]. Following the balloting, Tetsuro Urabe (Japan) was elected for the remainder of his predecessor's five-year term, which would end on 15 June 2012.

Agreement relating to the Implementation of Part XI of the Convention

During 2011, the number of parties to the 1994 Agreement relating to the Implementation of Part XI of the Convention (governing exploitation of seabed resources beyond national jurisdiction), adopted by General Assembly resolution 48/263 [YUN 1994, p. 1301], reached 141, with Thailand acceding to the treaty during the year. The Agreement, which entered into force on 28 July 1996 [YUN 1996, p. 1215], sought to address certain difficulties with the seabed mining provisions contained in Part XI of the Convention, which had been raised primarily by the industrialized countries. The Agreement was to be interpreted and applied together with the Convention as a single instrument and, in the event of any inconsistency between the Agreement and Part XI of the Convention, the provisions of the Agreement would prevail. Any ratification of or accession to the Convention after 28 July 1994 represented consent to be bound by the Agreement. Parties to the Convention prior to the Agreement's adoption had to deposit a separate instrument of ratification of or accession to the Agreement.

Agreement relating to conservation and management of straddling fish stocks and highly migratory fish stocks

As at 31 December, the number of parties to the 1995 Agreement for the Implementation of the Provisions of the United Nations Convention on the Law of the Sea of 10 December 1982 relating to the Conservation and Management of Straddling Fish Stocks and Highly Migratory Fish Stocks [YUN 1995, p. 1334] remained at 78. Referred to as the Fish Stocks Agreement, it entered into force in 2001 [YUN 2001, p. 1232].

Report of Secretary-General. Pursuant to General Assembly resolution 65/38 [YUN 2010, p. 1357], the Secretary-General reported in August [A/66/307] on actions taken by States and regional fisheries management organizations and arrangements in response to Assembly resolutions 61/105 [YUN 2006, p. 1543] and 64/72 [YUN 2009, p. 1331] on sustainable fisheries. The report reviewed the impact of bottom fisheries on vulnerable marine ecosystems and the long-term sustainability of deep-sea fish stocks; addressed actions taken by States and regional fisheries management organizations, as well as arrangements to address the impact of bottom fisheries on vulnerable marine ecosystems and the long-term sustainability of deep-sea fish stocks; and discussed activities of the Food and Agriculture Organization of the United Nations (FAO) to promote the regulation of bottom fisheries and the protection of vulnerable marine ecosystems. The Secretary-General observed that States and regional fisheries management organizations or arrangements had made substantial progress in implementing the relevant General Assembly resolutions. All such organizations or arrangements with competence to regulate bottom fisheries had adopted measures and taken action to implement the resolutions. In some instances, new fishing areas had been effectively closed; in others, fishing activity had been essentially limited to relatively small fishing areas under certain conditions and regulations. Many States had adopted measures for areas within and beyond national jurisdiction to complement those measures. Some States had also adopted measures for vessels fishing in areas where there was no regional fisheries management organization or there were no interim measures in place. The General Assembly resolutions, as well as the 2008 FAO International Guidelines for the Management of Deep-sea Fisheries on the High Seas [YUN 2008, p. 1488], provided the tools necessary to protect vulnerable marine ecosystems from adverse impacts due to bottom fishing and to ensure the long-term sustainability of deep-sea fish stocks. Although significant actions had been taken, implementation of the resolutions was uneven and further efforts were needed.

Workshop on sustainable fisheries. Pursuant to General Assembly resolution 64/72 [YUN 2009, p. 1331], a workshop on sustainable fisheries (New York, 15–16 September) [A/66/566] addressed the impacts of bottom fishing on vulnerable marine ecosystems and the long-term sustainability of deep-sea fish stocks.

GENERAL ASSEMBLY ACTION

On 6 December [meeting 76], the General Assembly adopted **resolution 66/68** [draft: A/66/L.22 & Add.1] without vote [agenda item 76 (*b*)].

Sustainable fisheries, including through the 1995 Agreement for the Implementation of the Provisions of the United Nations Convention on the Law of the Sea of 10 December 1982 relating to the Conservation and Management of Straddling Fish Stocks and Highly Migratory Fish Stocks, and related instruments

The General Assembly,

Reaffirming its annual resolutions on sustainable fisheries, including resolution 65/38 of 7 December 2010, and other relevant resolutions,

Recalling the relevant provisions of the United Nations Convention on the Law of the Sea ("the Convention"), and bearing in mind the relationship between the Convention and the 1995 Agreement for the Implementation of the Provisions of the United Nations Convention on the Law of the Sea of 10 December 1982 relating to the Conservation and Management of Straddling Fish Stocks and Highly Migratory Fish Stocks ("the Agreement"),

Welcoming the recent ratifications of and accessions to the Agreement and the fact that a growing number of States, entities referred to in the Convention and in article 1, paragraph 2 (*b*), of the Agreement, and subregional and regional fisheries management organizations and arrangements, have taken measures, as appropriate, towards the implementation of the provisions of the Agreement,

Welcoming also the work of the Food and Agriculture Organization of the United Nations and its Committee on Fisheries and the 2005 Rome Declaration on Illegal, Unreported and Unregulated Fishing, adopted on 12 March 2005, and recognizing that the Code of Conduct for Responsible Fisheries of the Food and Agriculture Organization of the United Nations ("the Code") and other related instruments, including its international plans of action, set out principles and global standards of behaviour for responsible practices for conservation of fisheries resources and the management and development of fisheries,

Welcoming further the outcomes, including the decisions and recommendations, of the twenty-ninth session of the Committee on Fisheries, held in Rome from 31 January to 4 February 2011,

Noting with concern that effective management of marine capture fisheries has been made difficult in some areas by unreliable information and data caused by, inter alia, unreported and misreported fish catch and fishing effort and that this lack of accurate data contributes to overfishing in some areas,

Recognizing the significant contribution of sustainable fisheries to food security, income, wealth and poverty alleviation for present and future generations,

Welcoming in this regard the decision of the Committee on Fisheries at its twenty-ninth session that the Food and Agriculture Organization of the United Nations should develop a new international instrument on small-scale fisheries that would draw on relevant existing instruments, complementing the Code, and that should be voluntary in nature and focus on the needs of developing countries,

Recognizing the urgent need for action at all levels to ensure the long-term sustainable use and management of fisheries resources through the wide application of the precautionary approach and ecosystem approaches,

Expressing concern over the current and projected adverse effects of climate change on food security and the sustainability of fisheries, and noting in that regard the work of the Intergovernmental Panel on Climate Change, the Food and Agriculture Organization of the United Nations and the United Nations Environment Programme,

Deploring the fact that fish stocks, including straddling fish stocks and highly migratory fish stocks, in many parts of the world are overfished or subject to sparsely regulated and heavy fishing efforts, as a result of, inter alia, illegal, unreported and unregulated fishing, inadequate flag State control and enforcement, including monitoring, control and surveillance measures, inadequate regulatory measures, harmful fisheries subsidies and overcapacity, as well as inadequate port State control, as highlighted in the report of the Food and Agriculture Organization of the United Nations, *The State of World Fisheries and Aquaculture 2010*,

Expressing its support for the ongoing negotiations in the World Trade Organization to strengthen disciplines on subsidies in the fisheries sector, including through the prohibition of certain forms of fisheries subsidies that contribute to overcapacity and overfishing,

Concerned that a limited number of States have taken measures to implement, individually and through regional fisheries management organizations and arrangements, the International Plan of Action for the Management of Fishing Capacity adopted by the Food and Agriculture Organization of the United Nations,

Recalling the International Plan of Action to Prevent, Deter and Eliminate Illegal, Unreported and Unregulated Fishing adopted by the Food and Agriculture Organization of the United Nations,

Particularly concerned that illegal, unreported and unregulated fishing constitutes a serious threat to fish stocks and marine habitats and ecosystems, to the detriment of sustainable fisheries as well as the food security and the economies of many States, particularly developing States,

Concerned that some operators increasingly take advantage of the globalization of fishery markets to trade fishery products stemming from illegal, unreported and unregulated fishing and make economic profits from those operations, which constitutes an incentive for them to pursue their activities,

Recognizing that effective deterrence and combating of illegal, unreported and unregulated fishing has significant financial and other resource implications,

Recognizing also the duty provided in the Convention, the Agreement to Promote Compliance with International Conservation and Management Measures by Fishing Vessels on the High Seas ("the Compliance Agreement"), the Agreement and the Code for flag States to exercise effective control over fishing vessels flying their flag, and vessels flying their flag which provide support to fishing vessels, to ensure that the activities of such fishing and support vessels do not undermine the effectiveness of conservation and management measures taken in accordance with international law and adopted at the national, subregional, regional or global levels,

Recognizing further the importance of adequately regulating, monitoring and controlling trans-shipment at sea to contribute to combating illegal, unreported and unregulated fishing activities,

Acknowledging the convening by the Food and Agriculture Organization of the United Nations of the Technical Consultation on Flag State Performance, in Rome from 2 to 6 May 2011, and noting the resumed session of the Technical Consultation, to be held in Rome from 5 to 9 March 2012,

Noting the obligation of all States, in accordance with international law, as reflected in the relevant provisions of the Convention, to cooperate in the conservation and management of living marine resources, and recognizing the importance of coordination and cooperation at the global, regional, subregional as well as national levels in the areas, inter alia, of marine scientific research, data collection, information-sharing, capacity-building and training for the conservation, management and sustainable development of living marine resources,

Welcoming the holding of the third joint meeting of the five regional fisheries management organizations with competence to regulate highly migratory species, in San Diego, United States of America, from 12 to 14 July 2011,

Acknowledging the importance of ocean data buoy systems moored in areas beyond national jurisdiction to sustainable development, promoting safety at sea and limiting human vulnerability to natural disasters, due to their use in weather and marine forecasts, fisheries management, tsunami forecasts and climate prediction, and expressing concern that most damage to ocean data buoys, such as moored buoys and tsunameters, frequently results from actions taken by some fishing operations which render the buoys inoperable,

Welcoming, in this regard, the adoption of measures by States, individually or through regional fisheries management organizations and arrangements, to protect ocean data buoy systems from the impacts of fishing activities,

Recognizing the need for States, individually and through regional fisheries management organizations and arrangements, to continue to develop and implement, consistent with international law, effective port State measures to combat overfishing and illegal, unreported and unregulated fishing, the critical need for cooperation with developing States to build their capacity, and the importance of cooperation between the Food and Agriculture Organization of the United Nations and the International Maritime Organization in this regard,

Noting with satisfaction the recent ratification of, accessions to and approval of the Agreement on Port State Measures to Prevent, Deter and Eliminate Illegal, Unreported and Unregulated Fishing of the Food and Agriculture Organization of the United Nations,

Welcoming the decision of the Committee on Fisheries at its twenty-ninth session that the Food and Agriculture Organization of the United Nations should form an open-ended working group or similar mechanism to draft terms of reference for the ad hoc working group envisioned in article 21 of the Agreement on Port State Measures to Prevent, Deter and Eliminate Illegal, Unreported and Unregulated Fishing,

Welcoming also the convening of the third Global Fisheries Enforcement Training Workshop, in Maputo from 28 February to 4 March 2011,

Concerned that marine pollution from all sources constitutes a serious threat to human health and safety, endangers fish stocks, marine biodiversity and marine and coastal habitats and has significant costs to local and national economies,

Recognizing that marine debris is a global transboundary pollution problem and that, due to the many different types and sources of marine debris, different approaches to their prevention and removal are necessary,

Noting that the contribution of sustainable aquaculture to global fish supplies continues to respond to opportunities in developing countries to enhance local food security and poverty alleviation and, together with the efforts of other aquaculture-producing countries, will make a significant contribution to meeting future demands in fish consumption, bearing in mind article 9 of the Code,

Reaffirming the importance of sustainable aquaculture to food security, and concerned about the potential effects of genetically engineered aquatic fish species on the health and sustainability of wild fish stocks,

Welcoming the approval by the Committee on Fisheries at its twenty-ninth session of Technical Guidelines on Aquaculture Certification,

Noting the publication in 2011 by the Food and Agriculture Organization of the United Nations of Technical Guidelines on the Use of Wild Fish as Feed in Aquaculture,

Calling attention to the particular vulnerabilities of small island developing States, other developing coastal States and subsistence fishing communities whose livelihoods, economic development and food security are heavily dependent on sustainable fisheries and will suffer disproportionately if sustainable fisheries are negatively affected,

Calling attention also to the circumstances affecting fisheries in many developing States, in particular African States and small island developing States, and recognizing the urgent need for capacity-building, including the transfer of marine technology and in particular fisheries-related technology, to enhance the ability of such States to exercise their rights in order to realize the benefits from fisheries resources and fulfil their obligations under international instruments,

Recognizing the need for appropriate measures to minimize by-catch, waste, discards, including high-grading, loss of fishing gear and other factors which adversely affect the sustainability of fish stocks and, consequently, can also have harmful effects on the economies and food security of small island developing States, other developing coastal States, and subsistence fishing communities,

Welcoming the endorsement by the Committee on Fisheries at its twenty-ninth session of the International Guidelines on By-catch Management and Reduction of Discards,

Recognizing the need to further integrate ecosystem approaches into fisheries conservation and management and, more generally, the importance of applying ecosystem approaches to the management of human activities in the ocean, and noting in this regard the Reykjavik Declaration on Responsible Fisheries in the Marine Ecosystem, the work of the Food and Agriculture Organization of the United Nations related to guidelines for the implementation of the ecosystem approach to fisheries management and the importance of this approach to relevant provisions of the Agreement and the Code, as well as decision VII/11 and other relevant decisions of the Conference of the Parties to the Convention on Biological Diversity,

Recognizing also the economic and cultural importance of sharks in many countries, the biological importance of sharks in the marine ecosystem as key predatory species, the vulnerability of certain shark species to overexploitation, the fact that some are threatened with extinction, the need for measures to promote the long-term conservation, management and sustainable use of shark populations and fisheries, and the relevance of the International Plan of Action for the Conservation and Management of Sharks, adopted by the Food and Agriculture Organization of the United Nations in 1999, in providing guidance on the development of such measures,

Reaffirming its support for the initiative of the Food and Agriculture Organization of the United Nations and relevant subregional and regional fisheries management organizations and arrangements on the conservation and management of sharks, and noting with concern that basic data on shark stocks and harvests continue to be lacking, that only a small number of countries have implemented the International Plan of Action for the Conservation and Management of Sharks, and that not all regional fisheries management organizations and arrangements have adopted conservation and management measures for directed shark fisheries and for the regulation of by-catch of sharks from other fisheries,

Welcoming science-based measures taken by States to conserve and sustainably manage sharks, and noting in this respect management measures taken by coastal States, including limits on catch or fishing effort, technical measures, including by-catch reduction measures, sanctuaries, closed seasons and monitoring, control and surveillance,

Recognizing the importance of marine species occupying low trophic levels in the ecosystem and for food security, and the need to ensure their long-term sustainability,

Expressing concern over continued incidental mortality, in fishing operations, of seabirds, particularly albatrosses and petrels, as well as other marine species, including sharks, fin-fish species, marine mammals and marine turtles, while recognizing considerable efforts by States and through various regional fisheries management organizations and arrangements to reduce incidental mortality as a result of by-catch,

I

Achieving sustainable fisheries

1. *Reaffirms* the importance it attaches to the long-term conservation, management and sustainable use of the living marine resources of the world's oceans and seas and the obligations of States to cooperate to this end, in accordance with international law, as reflected in the relevant provisions of the Convention, in particular the provisions on cooperation set out in Part V and Part VII, section 2, of the Convention, and where applicable, the Agreement;

2. *Encourages* States to give due priority to the implementation of the Plan of Implementation of the World Summit on Sustainable Development ("Johannesburg Plan of Implementation") in relation to achieving sustainable fisheries, especially restoring depleted stocks to levels that can produce maximum sustainable yield on an urgent basis and, where possible, not later than 2015;

3. *Emphasizes* the importance of addressing the sustainable development of fisheries in the context of the

United Nations Conference on Sustainable Development, to be held in Rio de Janeiro, Brazil, from 20 to 22 June 2012, and recognizing the significant contribution of fisheries to the three pillars of sustainable development;

4. *Urges* States, either directly or through appropriate subregional, regional or global organizations or arrangements, to intensify efforts to assess and address, as appropriate, the impacts of global climate change on the sustainability of fish stocks and the habitats that support them, in particular the most affected ones;

5. *Emphasizes* the obligations of flag States to discharge their responsibilities, in accordance with the Convention and the Agreement, to ensure compliance by vessels flying their flag with the conservation and management measures adopted and in force with respect to fisheries resources on the high seas;

6. *Calls upon* all States that have not done so, in order to achieve the goal of universal participation, to become parties to the Convention, which sets out the legal framework within which all activities in the oceans and seas must be carried out, taking into account the relationship between the Convention and the Agreement;

7. *Calls upon* all States, directly or through regional fisheries management organizations and arrangements, to apply widely, in accordance with international law and the Code, the precautionary approach and ecosystem approaches to the conservation, management and exploitation of fish stocks, and also calls upon States parties to the Agreement to implement fully the provisions of article 6 of the Agreement as a matter of priority;

8. *Encourages* States to increase their reliance on scientific advice in developing, adopting and implementing conservation and management measures, and to increase their efforts, including through international cooperation, to promote science for conservation and management measures that apply, in accordance with international law, the precautionary approach and ecosystem approaches to fisheries management, enhancing understanding of ecosystem approaches, in order to ensure the long-term conservation and sustainable use of living marine resources, and in this regard encourages the implementation of the Strategy for Improving Information on Status and Trends of Capture Fisheries of the Food and Agriculture Organization of the United Nations as a framework for the improvement and understanding of fishery status and trends;

9. *Calls upon* all States, directly or through regional fisheries management organizations and arrangements, to apply stock-specific precautionary reference points, as described in annex II to the Agreement and in the Code, to ensure that populations of harvested stocks and, where necessary, associated or dependent species, are maintained at or restored to sustainable levels, and to use these reference points for triggering conservation and management action;

10. *Encourages* States to apply the precautionary approach and ecosystem approaches in adopting and implementing conservation and management measures addressing, inter alia, by-catch, pollution and overfishing, and protecting habitats of specific concern, taking into account existing guidelines developed by the Food and Agriculture Organization of the United Nations;

11. *Also encourages* States to enhance or develop observer programmes, individually or through regional fisheries management organizations or arrangements, in order to improve data collection on, inter alia, target and by-catch species, which could also assist monitoring, control and surveillance tools, and to take into account standards, forms of cooperation and other existing structures for such programmes as described in article 25 of the Agreement and article 5 of the Code;

12. *Calls upon* States and regional fisheries management organizations and arrangements to collect and, where appropriate, report to the Food and Agriculture Organization of the United Nations required catch and effort data, and fishery-related information, in a complete, accurate and timely way, including for straddling fish stocks and highly migratory fish stocks within and beyond areas under national jurisdiction, discrete high seas fish stocks, and by-catch and discards; and, where they do not exist, to establish processes to strengthen data collection and reporting by members of regional fisheries management organizations and arrangements, including through regular reviews of member compliance with such obligations, and, when such obligations are not met, require the member concerned to rectify the problem, including through the preparation of plans of action with timelines;

13. *Invites* States and regional fisheries management organizations and arrangements to cooperate with the Food and Agriculture Organization of the United Nations in the implementation and further development of the Fisheries Resources Monitoring System initiative;

14. *Reaffirms* paragraph 10 of resolution 61/105 of 8 December 2006, and calls upon States, including through regional fisheries management organizations or arrangements, to urgently adopt measures to fully implement the International Plan of Action for the Conservation and Management of Sharks for directed and non-directed shark fisheries, based on the best available scientific information, through, inter alia, limits on catch or fishing effort, by requiring that vessels flying their flag collect and regularly report data on shark catches, including species-specific data, discards and landings, undertaking, including through international cooperation, comprehensive stock assessments of sharks, reducing shark by-catch and by-catch mortality and, where scientific information is uncertain or inadequate, not increasing fishing effort in directed shark fisheries until measures have been established to ensure the long-term conservation, management and sustainable use of shark stocks and to prevent further declines of vulnerable or threatened shark stocks;

15. *Calls upon* States to take immediate and concerted action to improve the implementation of and compliance with existing regional fisheries management organization or arrangement and national measures that regulate shark fisheries and incidental catch of sharks, in particular those measures which prohibit or restrict fisheries conducted solely for the purpose of harvesting shark fins and, where necessary, to consider taking other measures, as appropriate, such as requiring that all sharks be landed with each fin naturally attached;

16. *Calls upon* regional fisheries management organizations with the competence to regulate highly migratory species to strengthen or establish precautionary, science-based conservation and management measures, as appropriate, for sharks taken in fisheries within their convention

areas consistent with the International Plan of Action for the Conservation and Management of Sharks;

17. *Welcomes* the decision of the Committee on Fisheries of the Food and Agriculture Organization of the United Nations at its twenty-ninth session that the Organization should prepare a report on the extent of implementation of the International Plan of Action for the Conservation and Management of Sharks, and requests the Organization also to report on the challenges being faced by its member States in implementing that instrument and paragraph 14 of the present resolution;

18. *Urges* States to eliminate barriers to trade in fish and fisheries products which are not consistent with their rights and obligations under the World Trade Organization agreements, taking into account the importance of the trade in fish and fisheries products, particularly for developing countries;

19. *Urges* States and relevant international and national organizations to provide for the participation of small-scale fishery stakeholders in related policy development and fisheries management strategies in order to achieve long-term sustainability for such fisheries, consistent with the duty to ensure the proper conservation and management of fisheries resources;

20. *Encourages* States, either directly or through competent and appropriate subregional, regional or global organizations and arrangements, to analyse, as appropriate, the impact of fishing for marine species occupying low trophic levels;

21. *Invites* the Food and Agriculture Organization of the United Nations to consider the potential effects of genetically engineered fish species on the health and sustainability of wild fish stocks and to provide guidance, consistent with the Code, on minimizing harmful impacts in this regard;

II

Implementation of the 1995 Agreement for the Implementation of the Provisions of the United Nations Convention on the Law of the Sea of 10 December 1982 relating to the Conservation and Management of Straddling Fish Stocks and Highly Migratory Fish Stocks

22. *Calls upon* all States, and entities referred to in the Convention and in article 1, paragraph 2 (*b*), of the Agreement, that have not done so to ratify or accede to the Agreement and in the interim to consider applying it provisionally;

23. *Calls upon* States parties to the Agreement to effectively implement, as a matter of priority, the provisions of the Agreement through their domestic legislation and through regional fisheries management organizations and arrangements in which they participate;

24. *Emphasizes* the importance of those provisions of the Agreement relating to bilateral, subregional and regional cooperation in enforcement, and urges continued efforts in this regard;

25. *Urges* States parties to the Agreement, in accordance with article 21, paragraph 4, thereof to inform, either directly or through the relevant subregional or regional fisheries management organization or arrangement, all States whose vessels fish on the high seas in the same subregion or region of the form of identification issued by those States parties to officials duly authorized to carry out boarding and inspection functions in accordance with articles 21 and 22 of the Agreement;

26. *Also urges* States parties to the Agreement, in accordance with article 21, paragraph 4, thereof, to designate an appropriate authority to receive notifications pursuant to article 21 and to give due publicity to such designation through the relevant subregional or regional fisheries management organization or arrangement;

27. *Invites* regional fisheries management organizations and arrangements which have not yet done so to adopt procedures for high seas boarding and inspection that are consistent with articles 21 and 22 of the Agreement;

28. *Calls upon* States, individually and, as appropriate, through subregional and regional fisheries management organizations and arrangements with competence over discrete high seas fish stocks, to adopt the necessary measures to ensure the long-term conservation, management and sustainable use of such stocks in accordance with the Convention and consistent with the Code and the general principles set forth in the Agreement;

29. *Invites* States to assist developing States in enhancing their participation in regional fisheries management organizations or arrangements, including by facilitating access to fisheries for straddling fish stocks and highly migratory fish stocks, in accordance with article 25, paragraph 1 (*b*), of the Agreement, taking into account the need to ensure that such access benefits the developing States concerned and their nationals;

30. *Invites* States and international financial institutions and organizations of the United Nations system to provide assistance according to Part VII of the Agreement, including, if appropriate, the development of special financial mechanisms or instruments to assist developing States, in particular the least developed among them and small island developing States, to enable them to develop their national capacity to exploit fishery resources, including developing their domestically flagged fishing fleet, value-added processing and the expansion of their economic base in the fishing industry, consistent with the duty to ensure the proper conservation and management of fisheries resources;

31. *Notes with appreciation* the contributions made by States to the Assistance Fund established under Part VII of the Agreement, and encourages States, intergovernmental organizations, international financial institutions, national institutions and non-governmental organizations, as well as natural and juridical persons, to make further voluntary financial contributions to the Fund;

32. *Notes with satisfaction* that the Food and Agriculture Organization of the United Nations and the Division for Ocean Affairs and the Law of the Sea of the Office of Legal Affairs of the Secretariat ("the Division") have taken measures to publicize the availability of assistance through the Assistance Fund, and encourages the Organization and the Division to continue their efforts in this regard;

33. *Encourages* accelerated progress by States, individually and, as appropriate, through subregional and regional fisheries management organizations and arrangements, regarding the recommendations of the Review Conference on the Agreement, held in New York from 22 to 26 May 2006, and the identification of emerging priorities;

34. *Encourages* States, individually and, as appropriate, through subregional and regional fisheries management organizations and arrangements, to consider implementing, as appropriate, the recommendations of the resumed Review Conference, held in New York from 24 to 28 May 2010;

35. *Reaffirms its request* that the Food and Agriculture Organization of the United Nations initiate arrangements with States for the collection and dissemination of data on fishing in the high seas by vessels flying their flag at the subregional and regional levels where no such arrangements exist;

36. *Also reaffirms its request* that the Food and Agriculture Organization of the United Nations revise its global fisheries statistics database to provide information on straddling fish stocks, highly migratory fish stocks and discrete high seas fish stocks on the basis of where the catch is taken;

III

Related fisheries instruments

37. *Emphasizes* the importance of the effective implementation of the provisions of the Compliance Agreement, and urges continued efforts in this regard;

38. *Calls upon* all States and other entities referred to in article X, paragraph 1, of the Compliance Agreement that have not yet become parties to that Agreement to do so as a matter of priority and, in the interim, to consider applying it provisionally;

39. *Urges* States and subregional and regional fisheries management organizations and arrangements to implement and promote the application of the Code within their areas of competence;

40. *Urges* States to develop and implement, as a matter of priority, national and, as appropriate, regional plans of action to put into effect the international plans of action of the Food and Agriculture Organization of the United Nations;

41. *Encourages* the development of best practice guidelines for safety at sea in connection with marine fisheries by the competent international organizations;

42. *Also encourages* widespread participation at the diplomatic conference convened by the International Maritime Organization in South Africa in 2012 for the purpose of adopting an agreement on the implementation of the Torremolinos Protocol of 1993 relating to the Torremolinos International Convention for the Safety of Fishing Vessels, 1977;

IV

Illegal, unreported and unregulated fishing

43. *Emphasizes once again its serious concern* that illegal, unreported and unregulated fishing remains one of the greatest threats to marine ecosystems and continues to have serious and major implications for the conservation and management of ocean resources, as well as the food security and the economies of many States, particularly developing States, and renews its call upon States to comply fully with all existing obligations and to combat such fishing and urgently to take all necessary steps to implement the International Plan of Action to Prevent, Deter and Eliminate Illegal, Unreported and Unregulated Fishing;

44. *Urges* States to exercise effective control over their nationals, including beneficial owners, and vessels flying their flag, in order to prevent and deter them from engaging in illegal, unreported and unregulated fishing activities or supporting vessels engaging in illegal, unreported and unregulated fishing activities, including those vessels listed by regional fisheries management organizations or arrangements as engaged in those activities, and to facilitate mutual assistance to ensure that such actions can be investigated and proper sanctions imposed;

45. *Also urges* States to take effective measures, at the national, subregional, regional and global levels, to deter the activities, including illegal, unreported and unregulated fishing, of any vessel which undermines conservation and management measures that have been adopted by subregional and regional fisheries management organizations and arrangements in accordance with international law;

46. *Calls upon* States not to permit vessels flying their flag to engage in fishing on the high seas or in areas under the national jurisdiction of other States, unless duly authorized by the authorities of the States concerned and in accordance with the conditions set out in the authorization, and to take specific measures, including deterring the reflagging of vessels by their nationals, in accordance with the relevant provisions of the Convention, the Agreement and the Compliance Agreement, to control fishing operations by vessels flying their flag;

47. *Urges* States, individually and collectively through regional fisheries management organizations and arrangements, to develop appropriate processes to assess the performance of States with respect to implementing the obligations regarding fishing vessels flying their flag set out in relevant international instruments;

48. *Encourages* States within the Food and Agriculture Organization of the United Nations to continue the work of the Technical Consultation on Flag State Performance with regard to the draft criteria for flag State performance, assessing flag State performance and possible actions in accordance with international law to encourage compliance, and assistance to developing countries to improve their performance as flag States;

49. *Reaffirms* the need to strengthen, where necessary, the international legal framework for intergovernmental cooperation, in particular at the subregional and regional levels, in the management of fish stocks and in combating illegal, unreported and unregulated fishing, in a manner consistent with international law, and for States and entities referred to in the Convention and in article 1, paragraph 2 (*b*), of the Agreement to collaborate in efforts to address these types of fishing activities;

50. *Urges* regional fisheries management organizations and arrangements to further coordinate measures for combating illegal, unreported and unregulated fishing activities, such as through the development of a common list of vessels identified as engaged in illegal, unreported and unregulated fishing or the mutual recognition of the illegal, unreported and unregulated vessel lists established by each organization or arrangement;

51. *Reaffirms its call upon* States to take all necessary measures consistent with international law, without prejudice to a State's sovereignty over ports in its territory and to reasons of force majeure or distress, including the pro-

hibition of vessels from accessing their ports followed by a report to the flag State concerned, when there is clear evidence that they are or have been engaged in or have supported illegal, unreported and unregulated fishing, or when they refuse to give information either on the origin of the catch or on the authorization under which the catch has been made;

52. *Reaffirms* paragraph 48 of resolution 65/38 with regard to eliminating illegal, unreported and unregulated fishing by vessels flying "flags of convenience" and requiring that a "genuine link" be established between States and fishing vessels flying their flags, and urges States operating open registry to effectively control all fishing vessels flying their flag, as required by international law, or otherwise stop open registry for fishing vessels;

53. *Recognizes* the need for enhanced port State measures to combat illegal, unreported and unregulated fishing, and urges States to cooperate, in particular at the regional level and through subregional and regional fisheries management organizations and arrangements, to adopt all necessary port measures, consistent with international law taking into account article 23 of the Agreement, and to further promote the development and application of standards at the regional level;

54. *Encourages*, in this regard, States and regional economic integration organizations that have not yet done so to consider ratifying, accepting, approving or acceding to the Agreement on Port State Measures to Prevent, Deter and Eliminate Illegal, Unreported and Unregulated Fishing with a view to its early entry into force;

55. *Encourages* strengthened collaboration between the Food and Agriculture Organization of the United Nations and the International Maritime Organization, taking into account the respective competencies, mandates and experience of the two organizations, to combat illegal, unreported and unregulated fishing, particularly in improving the implementation of flag State responsibilities and port State measures;

56. *Encourages* States, with respect to vessels flying their flag, and port States, to make every effort to share data on landings and catch quotas, and in this regard encourages regional fisheries management organizations and arrangements to consider developing open databases containing such data for the purpose of enhancing the effectiveness of fisheries management;

57. *Calls upon* States to take all necessary measures to ensure that vessels flying their flag do not engage in trans-shipment of fish caught by fishing vessels engaged in illegal, unreported and unregulated fishing, through adequate regulation, monitoring and control of trans-shipment of fish at sea, including through additional national measures applicable to vessels flying their flag to prevent such trans-shipment;

58. *Urges* States, individually and through regional fisheries management organizations and arrangements, to adopt and implement internationally agreed market-related measures in accordance with international law, including principles, rights and obligations established in World Trade Organization agreements, as called for in the International Plan of Action to Prevent, Deter and Eliminate Illegal, Unreported and Unregulated Fishing;

59. *Encourages* information-sharing regarding emerging market- and trade-related measures by States and other relevant actors with appropriate international forums, given the potential implications of these measures for all States, consistent with the established plan of work of the Committee on Fisheries, and taking into account the Technical Guidelines for Responsible Fish Trade of the Food and Agriculture Organization of the United Nations;

60. *Notes* the concerns about possible connections between international organized crime and illegal fishing in certain regions of the world, and encourages States, including through the appropriate international forums and organizations, to study the causes and methods of and contributing factors to illegal fishing to increase knowledge and understanding of those possible connections, and to make the findings publicly available, and in this regard takes note of the study issued by the United Nations Office on Drugs and Crime on transnational organized crime in the fishing industry, bearing in mind the distinct legal regimes and remedies under international law applicable to illegal fishing and international organized crime;

V

Monitoring, control and surveillance and compliance and enforcement

61. *Calls upon* States, in accordance with international law, to strengthen implementation of or, where they do not exist, adopt comprehensive monitoring, control and surveillance measures and compliance and enforcement schemes individually and within those regional fisheries management organizations or arrangements in which they participate, in order to provide an appropriate framework for promoting compliance with agreed conservation and management measures, and further urges enhanced coordination among all relevant States and regional fisheries management organizations and arrangements in these efforts;

62. *Encourages* further work by competent international organizations, including the Food and Agriculture Organization of the United Nations and subregional and regional fisheries management organizations and arrangements, to develop guidelines on flag State control of fishing vessels;

63. *Urges* States, individually and through relevant regional fisheries management organizations and arrangements, to establish mandatory vessel monitoring, control and surveillance systems, in particular to require that vessel monitoring systems be carried by all vessels fishing on the high seas as soon as practicable, recalling that paragraph 62 of resolution 63/112 of 5 December 2008 urged that large-scale fishing vessels be required to carry vessel monitoring systems no later than December 2008, and to share information on fisheries enforcement matters;

64. *Calls upon* States, individually and through regional fisheries management organizations or arrangements, to strengthen or establish, consistent with national and international law, positive or negative lists of vessels fishing within the areas covered by relevant regional fisheries management organizations and arrangements in order to promote compliance with conservation and management measures and to identify products from illegal, unreported and unregulated catches, and encourages improved coordination among all States and regional fisheries management

organizations and arrangements in sharing and using this information, taking into account the forms of cooperation with developing States as set out in article 25 of the Agreement;

65. *Encourages* the Food and Agriculture Organization of the United Nations, in cooperation with States, regional economic integration organizations, the International Maritime Organization and, as appropriate, regional fisheries management organizations and arrangements, to expedite efforts to develop and manage a comprehensive global record, including with a unique vessel identifier system;

66. *Requests* States and relevant international bodies to develop, in accordance with international law, more effective measures to trace fish and fishery products to enable importing States to identify fish or fishery products caught in a manner that undermines international conservation and management measures agreed in accordance with international law, taking into account the special requirements of developing States and the forms of cooperation with developing States as set out in article 25 of the Agreement, and at the same time to recognize the importance of market access, in accordance with provisions 11.2.4, 11.2.5 and 11.2.6 of the Code, for fish and fishery products caught in a manner that is in conformity with such international measures;

67. *Requests* States to take the necessary measures, consistent with international law, to help to prevent fish and fishery products caught in a manner that undermines applicable conservation and management measures adopted in accordance with international law from entering international trade;

68. *Invites* the Food and Agriculture Organization of the United Nations to report on the state of progress in the development of best practice guidelines for catch documentation schemes and traceability, for inclusion in the report of the Secretary-General on fisheries to the General Assembly at its sixty-seventh session;

69. *Encourages* States to establish and undertake cooperative surveillance and enforcement activities in accordance with international law to strengthen and enhance efforts to ensure compliance with conservation and management measures, and prevent and deter illegal, unreported and unregulated fishing;

70. *Urges* States, directly and through regional fisheries management organizations or arrangements, to develop and adopt effective monitoring, control and surveillance measures for trans-shipment, as appropriate, in particular at-sea trans-shipment, in order to, inter alia, monitor compliance, collect and verify fisheries data, and to prevent and suppress illegal, unreported and unregulated fishing activities, in accordance with international law and, in parallel, to encourage and support the Food and Agriculture Organization of the United Nations in studying the current practices of trans-shipment and produce a set of guidelines for this purpose;

71. *Expresses its appreciation* for financial contributions from States to improve the capacity of the existing voluntary International Monitoring, Control and Surveillance Network for Fisheries-Related Activities, and encourages States to join and actively participate in the Network and to consider supporting, when appropriate, its transformation in accordance with international law into an international unit with dedicated resources to further assist Network members, taking into account the forms of cooperation with developing States as set out in article 25 of the Agreement;

VI

Fishing overcapacity

72. *Calls upon* States to commit themselves to urgently reducing the capacity of the world's fishing fleets to levels commensurate with the sustainability of fish stocks, through the establishment of target levels and plans or other appropriate mechanisms for ongoing capacity assessment, while avoiding the transfer of fishing capacity to other fisheries or areas in a manner that undermines the sustainable management of fish stocks, including those areas where fish stocks are overexploited or in a depleted condition, and recognizing in this context the legitimate rights of developing States to develop their fisheries for straddling fish stocks and highly migratory fish stocks consistent with article 25 of the Agreement, article 5 of the Code, and paragraph 10 of the International Plan of Action for the Management of Fishing Capacity of the Food and Agriculture Organization of the United Nations;

73. *Reiterates its call upon* States, individually and through regional fisheries management organizations and arrangements, to ensure that the urgent actions required in the International Plan of Action for the Management of Fishing Capacity are undertaken expeditiously and that its implementation is facilitated without delay;

74. *Invites* the Food and Agriculture Organization of the United Nations to report on the state of progress in the implementation of the International Plan of Action for the Management of Fishing Capacity, as provided for in paragraph 48 of the Plan of Action;

75. *Calls upon* States individually and, as appropriate, through subregional and regional fisheries management organizations and arrangements with competence to regulate highly migratory species, urgently to address global fishing capacity for tunas, inter alia, in a way that recognizes the legitimate rights of developing States, in particular small island developing States, to participate in and benefit from such fisheries, taking into account the recommendations of the Joint Tuna Regional Fisheries Management Organizations International Workshop on rfmo Management of Tuna Fisheries, held in Brisbane, Australia, from 29 June to 1 July 2010 and the recommendations of the third joint meeting of tuna regional fisheries management organizations and arrangements, in July 2011;

76. *Encourages* those States which are cooperating to establish subregional and regional fisheries management organizations and arrangements, taking into account the best scientific information available as well as the precautionary approach, to exercise voluntary restraint of fishing effort levels in those areas that will come under the regulation of the future organizations and arrangements until adequate regional conservation and management measures are adopted and implemented, taking into account the need to ensure the long-term conservation, management and sustainable use of the relevant fish stocks and to prevent significant adverse impacts on vulnerable marine ecosystems;

77. *Urges* States to eliminate subsidies that contribute to overfishing and overcapacity and to illegal, unreported

and unregulated fishing, including by accelerating work to complete World Trade Organization negotiations on fisheries subsidies in accordance with the 2001 Doha Ministerial Declaration to clarify and improve and the 2005 Hong Kong Ministerial Declaration to strengthen disciplines on fisheries subsidies, taking into account the importance of the fisheries sector to developing countries;

VII

Large-scale pelagic drift-net fishing

78. *Expresses concern* that, despite the adoption of General Assembly resolution 46/215 of 20 December 1991, the practice of large-scale pelagic drift-net fishing still exists and remains a threat to living marine resources;

79. *Urges* States, individually and through regional fisheries management organizations and arrangements, to adopt effective measures, or strengthen existing measures, to implement and enforce the provisions of resolution 46/215 and subsequent resolutions on large-scale pelagic drift-net fishing in order to eliminate the use of large-scale pelagic drift nets in all seas and oceans, which means that efforts to implement resolution 46/215 should not result in the transfer to other parts of the world of drift nets that contravene the resolution;

80. *Also urges* States, individually and through regional fisheries management organizations and arrangements, to adopt effective measures, or strengthen existing measures, to implement and enforce the present global moratorium on the use of large-scale pelagic drift nets on the high seas, and calls upon States to ensure that vessels flying their flag that are duly authorized to use large-scale drift nets in waters under their national jurisdiction do not use such gear for fishing while on the high seas;

81. *Reaffirms* the request in paragraph 6 of resolution 46/215 for the submission of information to the Secretary-General, and requests the Secretary-General to include this information in his report to the General Assembly at its sixty-seventh session;

VIII

Fisheries by-catch and discards

82. *Urges* States, subregional and regional fisheries management organizations and arrangements and other relevant international organizations that have not done so to take action, including with consideration of the interests of developing coastal States and, as appropriate, subsistence fishing communities, to reduce or eliminate by-catch, catch by lost or abandoned gear, fish discards and post-harvest losses, including juvenile fish, consistent with international law and relevant international instruments, including the Code, and in particular to consider measures including, as appropriate, technical measures related to fish size, mesh size or gear, discards, closed seasons and areas and zones reserved for selected fisheries, particularly artisanal fisheries, the establishment of mechanisms for communicating information on areas of high concentration of juvenile fish, taking into account the importance of ensuring the confidentiality of such information, and support for studies and research that will reduce or eliminate by-catch of juvenile fish, and to ensure that these measures are implemented so as to optimize their effectiveness;

83. *Calls upon* States, either individually, collectively or through regional management organizations and arrangements, to further study, develop and adopt effective management measures, taking into account the best available scientific information on fishing methods, including fish aggregating devices, to minimize by-catch;

84. *Urgently calls upon* States, subregional and regional fisheries management organizations and arrangements and, where appropriate, other relevant international organizations to develop and implement effective management measures to reduce the incidence of catch of non-target species, including the utilization of selective fishing gear, where appropriate;

85. *Calls upon* States, subregional and regional fisheries management organizations and arrangements to adopt or improve measures to assess the impact of their fisheries on species caught as by-catch and to improve the comprehensiveness and accuracy of information and reporting on incidental catch of species caught as by-catch, including through adequate observer coverage and the use of modern technologies, and to provide assistance to developing States to meet data collection and reporting obligations;

86. *Requests* States and regional fisheries management organizations and arrangements, as appropriate, to strengthen or establish data-collection programmes to obtain reliable estimates of shark, marine turtle, fin-fish, marine mammal and sea bird by-catch, and to promote further research on selective fishing gear and practices and on the use of appropriate by-catch mitigation measures;

87. *Encourages* States and entities referred to in the Convention and in article 1, paragraph 2 (*b*), of the Agreement to give due consideration to participation, as appropriate, in subregional and regional instruments and organizations with mandates to conserve non-target species taken incidentally in fishing operations;

88. *Encourages* States to strengthen, if necessary, the capacity of those subregional and regional fisheries management organizations and arrangements in which they participate to ensure the adequate conservation of non-target species taken incidentally in fishing operations, taking into consideration best practices for non-target species management, and to expedite their ongoing efforts in this regard;

89. *Requests* States and regional fisheries management organizations and arrangements urgently to implement, as appropriate, the measures recommended in the 2004 Guidelines to Reduce Sea Turtle Mortality in Fishing Operations and the International Plan of Action for Reducing Incidental Catch of Seabirds in Longline Fisheries of the Food and Agriculture Organization of the United Nations in order to prevent the decline of sea turtles and seabird populations by minimizing by-catch and increasing post-release survival in their fisheries, including through research and development of gear and bait alternatives, promoting the use of available by-catch mitigation technology, and establishing and strengthening data-collection programmes to obtain standardized information to develop reliable estimates of the by-catch of these species;

90. *Also requests* States and regional fisheries management organizations and arrangements to take urgent action to reduce the by-catch of seabirds, including albatrosses and petrels, in fisheries by adopting and implementing conservation measures consistent with the 2009 best practices

technical guidelines of the Food and Agriculture Organization of the United Nations to support implementation of the International Plan of Action for Reducing Incidental Catch of Seabirds in Longline Fisheries and taking into account the work of the Agreement on the Conservation of Albatrosses and Petrels and of organizations such as the Commission for the Conservation of Antarctic Marine Living Resources;

IX

Subregional and regional cooperation

91. *Urges* coastal States and States fishing on the high seas, in accordance with the Convention, the Agreement and other relevant instruments, to pursue cooperation in relation to straddling fish stocks and highly migratory fish stocks, either directly or through appropriate subregional or regional fisheries management organizations or arrangements, to ensure the effective conservation and management of such stocks;

92. *Urges* States fishing for straddling fish stocks and highly migratory fish stocks on the high seas, and relevant coastal States, where a subregional or regional fisheries management organization or arrangement has the competence to establish conservation and management measures for such stocks, to give effect to their duty to cooperate by becoming members of such an organization or participants in such an arrangement, or by agreeing to apply the conservation and management measures established by such an organization or arrangement, or to otherwise ensure that no vessel flying their flag is authorized to access the fisheries resources to which regional fisheries management organizations and arrangements or conservation and management measures established by such organizations or arrangements apply;

93. *Invites*, in this regard, subregional and regional fisheries management organizations and arrangements to ensure that all States having a real interest in the fisheries concerned may become members of such organizations or participants in such arrangements, in accordance with the Convention, the Agreement and the Code;

94. *Encourages* relevant coastal States and States fishing on the high seas for a straddling fish stock or a highly migratory fish stock, where there is no subregional or regional fisheries management organization or arrangement to establish conservation and management measures for such stocks, to cooperate to establish such an organization or enter into another appropriate arrangement to ensure the conservation and management of such stocks, and to participate in the work of the organization or arrangement;

95. *Urges* all signatory States and other States whose vessels fish within the area of the Convention on the Conservation and Management of Fishery Resources in the South-East Atlantic Ocean for fishery resources covered by that Convention to become parties to that Convention as a matter of priority and, in the interim, to ensure that vessels flying their flags fully comply with the measures adopted;

96. *Welcomes* the recent ratification of the South Indian Ocean Fisheries Agreement and encourages signatory States and States having a real interest to become parties to it, and urges those States to agree on and implement interim measures, including measures in accordance with paragraphs 80 and 83 to 87 of resolution 61/105 and paragraphs 117, 119, 120, 122 and 123 of resolution 64/72 of 4 December 2009, to ensure the conservation and management of the fisheries resources and their marine ecosystems and habitats in the area to which that Agreement applies until such time as that Agreement enters into force;

97. *Takes note* of recent efforts at the regional level to promote responsible fishing practices, including combating illegal, unreported and unregulated fishing;

98. *Welcomes* the recent ratifications of and accession to the Convention on the Conservation and Management of High Seas Fishery Resources in the South Pacific Ocean, and encourages further ratifications, accessions, acceptances and approvals of that Convention with a view to its early entry into force;

99. *Encourages* States, regional economic integration organizations and the entities referred to in article 1, paragraph 2 (*b*), of the Convention on the Conservation and Management of High Seas Fishery Resources in the South Pacific Ocean that participated in the negotiation of that Convention to fully implement the voluntary interim measures that have been adopted to give effect to paragraphs 80 and 83 to 87 of resolution 61/105 until that Convention has entered into force and conservation and management measures have been adopted;

100. *Also encourages* States, regional economic integration organizations and the entities referred to in article 1, paragraph 2 (*b*), of the Convention on the Conservation and Management of High Seas Fishery Resources in the South Pacific Ocean that participated in the negotiation of that Convention to fully implement the voluntary interim measures that have been adopted and to voluntarily restrain fishing effort and catches to avoid overexploitation of certain pelagic fisheries resources in the area to which that Convention will apply until it has entered into force and conservation and management measures have been adopted, and to take into account the scientific advice given by the Science Working Group in the adoption of future interim measures that should apply to certain pelagic fisheries resources before the entry into force of that Convention, and further calls for full and accurate reporting of catches in accordance with the interim measures;

101. *Notes with satisfaction* the conclusion of negotiations to establish a regional fisheries management organization in the North Pacific, and encourages participating States to implement fully interim voluntary measures adopted in accordance with paragraphs 80 and 83 to 87 of resolution 61/105 and paragraphs 117, 119, 120, 122 and 123 of resolution 64/72;

102. *Takes note* of the ongoing efforts of the members of the Indian Ocean Tuna Commission to strengthen the functioning of the Commission so that it can more effectively discharge its mandate, and invites the Food and Agriculture Organization of the United Nations to provide members of the Commission with the necessary assistance to this end;

103. *Encourages* signatory States and States having a real interest to become parties to the Convention for the Strengthening of the Inter-American Tropical Tuna Commission Established by the 1949 Convention between the United States of America and the Republic of Costa Rica;

104. *Welcomes* the recent approval of the 2007 Amendment to the Convention on Future Multilateral

Cooperation in the Northwest Atlantic Fisheries by some Contracting Parties to that Convention, and encourages the Contracting Parties that have not yet done so to approve the Amendment with a view to its early entry into effect;

105. *Urges* further efforts by regional fisheries management organizations and arrangements, as a matter of priority, in accordance with international law, to strengthen and modernize their mandates and the measures adopted by such organizations or arrangements, and to implement modern approaches to fisheries management, as reflected in the Agreement and other relevant international instruments, relying on the best scientific information available and application of the precautionary approach and incorporating an ecosystem approach to fisheries management and biodiversity considerations, including the conservation and management of ecologically related and dependent species and protection of their habitats, where these aspects are lacking, to ensure that they effectively contribute to long-term conservation and management and sustainable use of living marine resources, and welcomes those regional fisheries management organizations and arrangements that have taken steps in this direction;

106. *Calls upon* regional fisheries management organizations with the competence to conserve and manage highly migratory fish stocks that have not yet adopted effective conservation and management measures in line with the best scientific information available to conserve and manage stocks falling under their mandate to do so urgently;

107. *Urges* States to strengthen and enhance cooperation among existing and developing regional fisheries management organizations and arrangements in which they participate, including increased communication and further coordination of measures, such as through the holding of joint consultations, and to strengthen integration, coordination and cooperation by such regional fisheries management organizations and arrangements with other relevant fisheries organizations, regional seas arrangements and other relevant international organizations;

108. *Urges* the five regional fisheries management organizations with competence to manage highly migratory species to continue to take measures to implement the Course of Actions adopted at the second joint meeting of tuna regional fisheries management organizations and arrangements and to consider the recommendations of the third joint meeting of tuna regional fisheries management organizations and arrangements;

109. *Invites* States and regional fisheries management organizations and arrangements with competence to manage straddling fish stocks to share experiences and good practices, for example by considering organizing joint meetings, where appropriate;

110. *Urges* regional fisheries management organizations and arrangements to improve transparency and to ensure that their decision-making processes are fair and transparent, rely on the best scientific information available, incorporate the precautionary approach and ecosystem approaches, address participatory rights, including through, inter alia, the development of transparent criteria for allocating fishing opportunities which reflects, where appropriate, the relevant provisions of the Agreement, taking due account, inter alia, of the status of the relevant stocks and the respective interests in the fishery;

111. *Welcomes* the 2010 performance review of the South East Atlantic Fisheries Organization and the 2011 performance review of the Northwest Atlantic Fisheries Organization, and the fact that a number of regional fisheries management organizations and arrangements have completed performance reviews, and encourages the implementation, as appropriate, of the recommendations of their respective reviews as a matter of priority;

112. *Urges* States, through their participation in regional fisheries management organizations and arrangements that have not done so, to undertake, on an urgent basis, performance reviews of those regional fisheries management organizations and arrangements, initiated either by the organization or arrangement itself or with external partners, including in cooperation with the Food and Agriculture Organization of the United Nations, using transparent criteria based on the provisions of the Agreement and other relevant instruments, and taking into account the best practices of regional fisheries management organizations or arrangements and, as appropriate, any set of criteria developed by States or other regional fisheries management organizations or arrangements, and encourages that such performance reviews include some element of independent evaluation and propose means for improving the functioning of the regional fisheries management organization or arrangement, as appropriate;

113. *Encourages* regional fisheries management organizations and arrangements to make the results of those performance reviews publicly available and to discuss the results jointly, and furthermore to consider undertaking performance reviews on a regular basis;

114. *Urges* States to cooperate, taking into account those performance reviews, to develop best practice guidelines for regional fisheries management organizations and arrangements and to apply, to the extent possible, those guidelines to organizations and arrangements in which they participate;

115. *Encourages* the development of regional guidelines for States to use in establishing sanctions for non-compliance by vessels flying their flag and by their nationals, to be applied in accordance with national law, that are adequate in severity for effectively securing compliance, deterring further violations and depriving offenders of the benefits deriving from their illegal activities, as well as in evaluating their systems of sanctions to ensure that they are effective in securing compliance and deterring violations;

X

Responsible fisheries in the marine ecosystem

116. *Urges* States, individually or through regional fisheries management organizations and arrangements, to enhance their efforts to apply an ecosystem approach to fisheries, taking into account paragraph 30 (*d*) of the Johannesburg Plan of Implementation;

117. *Encourages* States, individually or through regional fisheries management organizations and arrangements and other relevant international organizations, to work to ensure that fisheries and other ecosystem data collection is performed in a coordinated and integrated manner, facilitating incorporation into global observation initiatives, where appropriate;

118. *Calls upon* States and regional fisheries management organizations or arrangements, working in cooperation with other relevant organizations, including the Food and Agriculture Organization of the United Nations, the Intergovernmental Oceanographic Commission and the World Meteorological Organization, to adopt, as appropriate, measures to protect ocean data buoy systems moored in areas beyond national jurisdiction from actions that impair their operation;

119. *Encourages* States to increase scientific research on the marine ecosystem in accordance with international law;

120. *Calls upon* States, the Food and Agriculture Organization of the United Nations and other specialized agencies, subregional and regional fisheries management organizations and arrangements, where appropriate, and other appropriate intergovernmental bodies, to cooperate in achieving sustainable aquaculture, including through information exchange, developing equivalent standards on such issues as aquatic animal health and human health and safety concerns, assessing the potential positive and negative impacts of aquaculture, including socioeconomics, on the marine and coastal environment, including biodiversity, and adopting relevant methods and techniques to minimize and mitigate adverse effects, and in this regard encourages the implementation of the 2007 Strategy and Outline Plan for Improving Information on Status and Trends of Aquaculture of the Food and Agriculture Organization of the United Nations, as a framework for the improvement and understanding of aquaculture status and trends;

121. *Calls upon* States to take action immediately, individually and through regional fisheries management organizations and arrangements, and consistent with the precautionary approach and ecosystem approaches, to continue implementing the 2008 International Guidelines for the Management of Deep-Sea Fisheries in the High Seas of the Food and Agriculture Organization of the United Nations ("the Guidelines") in order to sustainably manage fish stocks and protect vulnerable marine ecosystems, including seamounts, hydrothermal vents and cold water corals, from destructive fishing practices, recognizing the immense importance and value of deep-sea ecosystems and the biodiversity they contain;

122. *Reaffirms* the importance of paragraphs 80 to 90 of resolution 61/105 and paragraphs 113 to 127 of resolution 64/72 addressing the impacts of bottom fishing on vulnerable marine ecosystems and the long-term sustainability of deep-sea fish stocks and the actions called for in those resolutions, and emphasizes the need for full implementation by all States and relevant regional fisheries management organizations and arrangements of their commitments under those paragraphs on an urgent basis;

123. *Recalls* that nothing in the paragraphs of resolutions 61/105 and 64/72 and the present resolution addressing the impacts of bottom fishing on vulnerable marine ecosystems prejudices the sovereign rights of coastal States over their continental shelf or the exercise of the jurisdiction of coastal States with respect to their continental shelf under international law as reflected in the Convention, in particular article 77 thereof;

124. *Notes in this regard* the adoption by coastal States of conservation measures regarding their continental shelf to address the impacts of bottom fishing on vulnerable marine ecosystems, as well as their efforts to ensure compliance with those measures;

125. *Welcomes* the important progress made by States, regional fisheries management organizations and arrangements and those States participating in negotiations in establishing a regional fisheries management organization or arrangement competent to regulate bottom fisheries to implement paragraphs 80 and 83 to 87 of resolution 61/105 and paragraphs 113, 117 and 119 to 124 of resolution 64/72 and address the impacts of bottom fishing on vulnerable marine ecosystems;

126. *Also welcomes* the substantial ongoing work of the Food and Agriculture Organization of the United Nations related to the management of deep-sea fisheries in the high seas and the protection of vulnerable marine ecosystems, and urges States and regional fisheries management organizations and arrangements to ensure that their actions in sustainably managing deep-sea fisheries and implementing paragraphs 80 and 83 to 87 of resolution 61/105 and paragraphs 119, 120 and 122 to 124 of resolution 64/72 are consistent with the Guidelines;

127. *Takes note* of the report of the Food and Agriculture Organization of the United Nations workshop on the implementation of the Guidelines, held in Busan, Republic of Korea, from 10 to 12 May 2010;

128. *Welcomes* the convening by the Secretary-General, pursuant to paragraph 128 of resolution 64/72, of the workshop to discuss implementation of paragraphs 80 and 83 to 87 of resolution 61/105 and paragraphs 117 and 119 to 127 of resolution 64/72, addressing the impacts of bottom fishing on vulnerable marine ecosystems and the long-term sustainability of deep-sea fish stocks, held in New York on 15 and 16 September 2011;

129. *Considers*, on the basis of the review carried out in accordance with paragraph 129 of resolution 64/72, that despite the progress made, the urgent actions called for in the relevant paragraphs of resolutions 61/105 and 64/72 have not been fully implemented in all cases, and in this regard further actions in accordance with the precautionary approach, ecosystem approaches and international law and consistent with the Guidelines are needed to strengthen the continued implementation, and in this regard calls upon States, through regional fisheries management organizations and arrangements with the competence to regulate bottom fisheries, States participating in negotiations to establish such organizations or arrangements and flag States to take the following urgent actions regarding bottom fishing in areas beyond national jurisdiction:

(*a*) To strengthen procedures for carrying out assessments to take into account individual, collective and cumulative impacts, and for making the assessments publicly available, recognizing that doing so can support transparency and capacity-building globally;

(*b*) To establish and improve procedures to ensure that assessments are updated when new conditions or information so require;

(*c*) To establish and improve procedures for evaluating, reviewing and revising, on a regular basis, assessments based on best available science and management measures;

(*d*) To establish mechanisms to promote and enhance compliance with applicable measures related to the protection of vulnerable marine ecosystems, adopted in accordance with international law;

130. *Notes* that not all impact assessments have been made publicly available, and calls upon States, consistent with domestic law, and regional fisheries management organizations and arrangements to publish all assessments without delay;

131. *Recognizes* that different types of marine scientific research, including seabed mapping carried out in different parts of the oceans, have resulted in identification of areas where vulnerable marine ecosystems occur and in the adoption of conservation and management measures to prevent significant adverse impacts on such ecosystems, including the closure of areas to bottom fishing in accordance with paragraph 119 (*b*) of resolution 64/72;

132. *Encourages*, in this regard, regional fisheries management organizations and arrangements with the competence to manage bottom fisheries, States participating in negotiations to establish such organizations or arrangements and flag States to consider the results available from marine scientific research, including those obtained from seabed mapping programmes concerning the identification of areas containing vulnerable marine ecosystems, and to adopt conservation and management measures to prevent significant adverse impacts from bottom fishing on such ecosystems, consistent with the Guidelines, or to close such areas to bottom fishing until such conservation and management measures are adopted, as well as to continue to undertake further marine scientific research, for the above-mentioned purposes, in accordance with international law as reflected in Part XIII of the Convention;

133. *Encourages* States, regional fisheries management organizations and arrangements and States participating in negotiations to establish such organizations or arrangements to undertake further research on deep-sea species and ecosystems and assessments of fishing activities on target and non-target species, consistent with the Guidelines and in accordance with the Convention, including Part XIII of the Convention;

134. *Recognizes in particular* the special circumstances and requirements of developing States and the specific challenges they may face in giving full effect to certain technical aspects of the Guidelines, and that implementation by such States of paragraphs 83 to 87 of resolution 61/105, paragraph 119 of resolution 64/72, paragraph 129 of the present resolution and the Guidelines should proceed in a manner that gives full consideration to section 6 of the Guidelines on special requirements of developing countries;

135. *Invites* the Food and Agriculture Organization of the United Nations, in facilitating implementation by States and regional fisheries management organizations and arrangements of the Guidelines, to consider undertaking the following work as part of its ongoing programme for deep-sea fisheries:

(*a*) To compile, clarify the use of and make available technical guidance on encounter protocols and related mitigation measures, including encounter thresholds and move-on distances;

(*b*) To develop guidance on the application of criteria for identifying vulnerable marine ecosystems contained in the Guidelines;

(*c*) To develop guidance for conducting assessments, including addressing risk assessment on individual, collective and cumulative impacts, and to promote better standardization of such assessments;

(*d*) To support and facilitate work on deep-sea high seas stock assessments to ensure that such fisheries are sustainable;

(*e*) To continue its work in creating a global database on information on vulnerable marine ecosystems;

136. *Also invites* the Food and Agriculture Organization of the United Nations to consider convening a meeting of scientists from regional fisheries management organizations and arrangements with the competence to manage bottom fishing and States to examine impact assessments, in order to propose best practices, as well as standards for implementation of such assessments, including addressing risk assessment;

137. *Decides* to conduct a further review in 2015 of the actions taken by States and regional fisheries management organizations and arrangements in response to paragraphs 117 and 119 to 127 of resolution 64/72 and paragraphs 121, 126 and 129 to 136 of the present resolution, with a view to ensuring effective implementation of the measures therein and to make further recommendations, where necessary;

138. *Encourages* accelerated progress to establish criteria on the objectives and management of marine protected areas for fisheries purposes, and in this regard welcomes the proposed work of the Food and Agriculture Organization of the United Nations to develop technical guidelines in accordance with the Convention and the Code on the design, implementation and testing of marine protected areas for such purposes, and urges coordination and cooperation among all relevant international organizations and bodies;

139. *Notes in this regard* the adoption at the tenth meeting of the Conference of the Parties to the Convention on Biological Diversity, held in Nagoya, Japan, from 18 to 29 October 2010, of a new Strategic Plan for Biodiversity 2011–2020;

140. *Urges* all States to implement the 1995 Global Programme of Action for the Protection of the Marine Environment from Land-based Activities and to accelerate activity to safeguard the marine ecosystem, including fish stocks, against pollution and physical degradation;

141. *Acknowledges* the serious environmental impacts on the marine environment caused by abandoned, lost or otherwise discarded fishing gear, and encourages States to take action to reduce such gear, noting the recommendations of the 2009 report by the United Nations Environment Programme and the Food and Agriculture Organization of the United Nations;

142. *Reaffirms* the importance it attaches to paragraphs 77 to 81 of resolution 60/31 of 29 November 2005 concerning the issue of lost, abandoned or discarded fishing gear and related marine debris and the adverse impacts such debris and derelict fishing gear have on, inter alia, fish stocks, habitats and other marine species, and urges accelerated progress by States and regional fisheries management organizations and arrangements in implementing those paragraphs of the resolution;

143. *Encourages* further studies, including by the Food and Agriculture Organization of the United Nations, on

the impacts of underwater noise on fish stocks and fishing catch rates, as well as associated socioeconomic effects;

144. *Calls upon* States, including through regional fisheries management organizations and arrangements, to play an active role in global efforts to conserve and sustainably use living marine resources, so as to contribute to marine biological diversity;

145. *Encourages* States, either individually or through regional fisheries management organizations and arrangements, as appropriate, to identify any spawning and nursery areas for fish stocks under their jurisdiction or competence and, where required, to adopt science-based measures to conserve such stocks during these critical life stages;

XI

Capacity-building

146. *Reiterates* the crucial importance of cooperation by States directly or, as appropriate, through the relevant subregional and regional organizations, and by other international organizations, including the Food and Agriculture Organization of the United Nations through its FishCode programme, including through financial and/or technical assistance, in accordance with the Agreement, the Compliance Agreement, the Code and its associated international plans of action, to increase the capacity of developing States to achieve the goals and implement the actions called for in the present resolution;

147. *Welcomes* the work of the Food and Agriculture Organization of the United Nations in developing guidance on the strategies and measures required for the creation of an enabling environment for small-scale fisheries, and encourages studies for creating possible alternative livelihoods for coastal communities;

148. *Encourages* increased capacity-building and technical assistance by States, international financial institutions and relevant intergovernmental organizations and bodies for fishers, in particular small-scale fishers, in developing countries, and in particular small island developing States, consistent with environmental sustainability, in recognition of the fact that food security and livelihoods may depend on fisheries;

149. *Encourages* the international community to enhance the opportunities for sustainable development in developing countries, in particular the least developed countries, small island developing States and coastal African States, by encouraging greater participation of those States in authorized fisheries activities being undertaken within areas under their national jurisdiction, in accordance with the Convention, by distant-water fishing nations in order to achieve better economic returns for developing countries from their fisheries resources within areas under their national jurisdiction and an enhanced role in regional fisheries management, as well as by enhancing the ability of developing countries to develop their own fisheries, as well as to participate in high seas fisheries, including access to such fisheries, in conformity with international law, in particular the Convention and the Agreement, and taking into account article 5 of the Code;

150. *Requests* distant-water fishing nations, when negotiating access agreements and arrangements with developing coastal States, to do so on an equitable and sustainable basis and to take into account their legitimate expectation to fully benefit from the sustainable use of the natural resources of their exclusive economic zones, to ensure that vessels flying their flag comply with the laws and regulations of the developing coastal States adopted in accordance with international law and to give greater attention to fish processing and fish-processing facilities within the national jurisdiction of the developing coastal State to assist the realization of the benefits from the development of fisheries resources and also to the transfer of technology and assistance for monitoring, control and surveillance and compliance and enforcement within areas under the national jurisdiction of the developing coastal State providing fisheries access, taking into account the forms of cooperation set out in article 25 of the Agreement and article 5 of the Code;

151. *Encourages* States, individually and through regional fisheries management organizations and arrangements, to provide greater assistance and to promote coherence in such assistance for developing States in designing, establishing and implementing relevant agreements, instruments and tools for the conservation and sustainable management of fish stocks, including in designing and strengthening their domestic regulatory fisheries policies and those of regional fisheries management organizations or arrangements in their regions, and the enhancement of research and scientific capabilities through existing funds, such as the Assistance Fund under Part VII of the Agreement, bilateral assistance, regional fisheries management organizations and arrangements assistance funds, the FishCode programme, the World Bank's global programme on fisheries and the Global Environment Facility;

152. *Encourages* States to provide technical and financial support to developing countries to address their special requirements and challenges in implementing the Guidelines;

153. *Calls upon* States to promote, through continuing dialogue and the assistance and cooperation provided in accordance with articles 24 to 26 of the Agreement, further ratifications of or accessions to the Agreement by seeking to address, inter alia, the issue of lack of capacity and resources that might stand in the way of developing States becoming parties;

154. *Notes with appreciation* the compilation prepared by the Secretariat of the needs of developing States for capacity-building and assistance in the conservation and management of straddling fish stocks and highly migratory fish stocks and the sources of available assistance for developing States to address such needs;

155. *Encourages* States, regional fisheries management organizations and arrangements and other relevant bodies to assist developing States in the implementation of the actions called for in paragraphs 80 and 83 to 87 of resolution 61/105 and paragraphs 113, 117 and 119 to 124 of resolution 64/72;

156. *Urges* States and regional economic integration organizations, individually and through regional fisheries management organizations and arrangements, to mainstream efforts to assist developing States, in particular the least developed and small island developing States, with other relevant international development strategies with a view to enhancing international coordination to enable them to develop their national capacity to exploit fishery resources, consistent with the duty to ensure the conserva-

tion and management of those resources, and in this regard requests the Secretary-General to fully mobilize and coordinate the agencies, funds and programmes of the United Nations system, including at the level of the regional economic commissions, within their respective mandates;

157. *Requests* States and regional fisheries management organizations to develop strategies to further assist developing States, in particular the least developed and small island developing States, in fully realizing the benefits from the catch of straddling fish stocks and highly migratory fish stocks and in strengthening regional efforts to sustainably conserve and manage such stocks, and in this regard, to make available such information;

XII

Cooperation within the United Nations system

158. *Requests* the relevant parts of the United Nations system, international financial institutions and donor agencies to support increased enforcement and compliance capabilities for regional fisheries management organizations and their member States;

159. *Invites* the Food and Agriculture Organization of the United Nations to continue its cooperative arrangements with United Nations agencies on the implementation of the international plans of action and to report to the Secretary-General, for inclusion in his annual report on sustainable fisheries, on priorities for cooperation and coordination in this work;

XIII

Activities of the Division for Ocean Affairs and the Law of the Sea

160. *Expresses its appreciation* to the Secretary-General for the report on the actions taken by States and regional fisheries management organizations and arrangements in response to paragraphs 80 and 83 to 87 of resolution 61/105 and paragraphs 113 to 117 and 119 to 127 of resolution 64/72 on sustainable fisheries, addressing the impacts of bottom fishing on vulnerable marine ecosystems and the long-term sustainability of deep-sea fish stocks, prepared by the Division, as well as for the other activities of the Division, which reflect the high standard of assistance provided to Member States by the Division;

161. *Requests* the Secretary-General to continue to carry out the responsibilities and functions entrusted to him by the Convention, the Agreement and the related resolutions of the General Assembly and to ensure the allocation of appropriate resources to the Division for the performance of its activities under the approved budget for the Organization;

XIV

Sixty-seventh session of the General Assembly

162. *Requests* the Secretary-General to bring the present resolution to the attention of all States, relevant intergovernmental organizations, the organizations and bodies of the United Nations system, subregional and regional fisheries management organizations and relevant non-governmental organizations, and to invite them to provide the Secretary-General with information relevant to the implementation of the present resolution;

163. *Also requests* the Secretary-General to submit to the General Assembly at its sixty-seventh session a report on sustainable fisheries, including through the 1995 Agreement for the Implementation of the Provisions of the United Nations Convention on the Law of the Sea of 10 December 1982 relating to the Conservation and Management of Straddling Fish Stocks and Highly Migratory Fish Stocks, and related instruments, taking into account information provided by States, relevant specialized agencies, in particular the Food and Agriculture Organization of the United Nations, and other appropriate organs, organizations and programmes of the United Nations system, subregional and regional organizations and arrangements for the conservation and management of straddling fish stocks and highly migratory fish stocks, as well as other relevant intergovernmental bodies and non-governmental organizations, and consisting, inter alia, of elements provided in relevant paragraphs in the present resolution;

164. *Notes* the desire to further improve the efficiency of and the effective participation of delegations in the informal consultations concerning the annual General Assembly resolution on sustainable fisheries, decides that the informal consultations on this resolution will be held in a single round of consultations in November for a period of six days, and invites States to submit text proposals for inclusion in the resolution to the Coordinator of the informal consultations no later than four weeks before the start of the consultations;

165. *Decides* to include in the provisional agenda of its sixty-seventh session, under the item entitled "Oceans and the law of the sea", the sub-item entitled "Sustainable fisheries, including through the 1995 Agreement for the Implementation of the Provisions of the United Nations Convention on the Law of the Sea of 10 December 1982 relating to the Conservation and Management of Straddling Fish Stocks and Highly Migratory Fish Stocks, and related instruments", and to consider the possibility of including this sub-item in future provisional agendas on a biennial basis.

Institutions created by the Convention

International Seabed Authority

Through the International Seabed Authority, established by the United Nations Convention on the Law of the Sea and the 1994 Implementation Agreement [YUN 1994, p. 1301], States organized and conducted exploration of the resources of the seabed and ocean floor and subsoil beyond the limits of national jurisdiction. In 2011, the Authority, which had 162 members as at 31 May, held its seventeenth session (Kingston, Jamaica, 11–22 July) [ISBA/17/A/10]. Its subsidiary bodies, namely, the Assembly, the Council, the Legal and Technical Commission and the Finance Committee, also met during the session.

The Assembly considered the annual report of the Authority's Secretary-General [ISBA/17/A/2], which reviewed the Authority's work since the fourteenth session and assessed the status of and prospects for deep seabed mining. The work programme for 2011–2013 focused on the supervision of contracts for exploration and award of new contracts; development of the regulatory regime for activities in the Area (the seabed and ocean floor and subsoil beyond the limits of national jurisdiction); monitoring of trends and developments relating to deep seabed mining activities, including world metal market conditions and metal prices, trends and prospects; collection and assessment of data from prospecting and exploration, and analysis of the results; and promotion of marine scientific research in the Area. There were eight contractors for exploration for polymetallic nodules. The rules, regulations and procedures of the Authority contained requirements relating to the relationship between the Authority and contractors. The regulations were supplemented by recommendations issued by the Legal and Technical Commission. Each year, the Commission reviewed and evaluated the annual reports provided by contractors. In 2010, the Commission expressed concerns about the reporting of financial expenditure by contractors and about the quality of environmental data provided by contractors.

The Authority's Council [ISBA/17/C/21] approved applications [ISBA/17/C/14-17] for plans of work submitted by four entities for exploration in the Area. Following their approval, the plans of work were prepared in the form of contracts. The four new contractors would join the eight contractors already at work in the international deep-sea area. The Council was unable to complete its work on draft regulations for prospecting and exploration for cobalt-rich ferromanganese crusts in the Area, reaching agreement on all provisions except those dealing with certificate of sponsorship (regulation 11), total area covered by application (regulation 12), fee for application (regulation 21) and size of area and relinquishment (regulation 27).

The Council also considered a proposal for an environmental management plan for the Clarion-Clipperton Zone [ISBA/17/LTC/7], submitted by the Legal and Technical Commission. The plan provided for the establishment of nine areas of particular environmental interest intended to protect the biodiversity and ecosystem structure and functioning of the Zone from the potential impacts of seabed mining. The Council adopted a decision [ISBA/17/C/19] relating to the environmental management plan for the Zone that stressed the precautionary approach, as called for by the Regulations on Prospecting and Exploration for Polymetallic Nodules in the Area.

The Assembly adopted a decision on financial and budgetary matters [ISBA/17/A/5]; decided to convene a special meeting during its eighteenth (2012) session to commemorate the thirtieth anniversary of the opening for signature of the United Nations Convention on the Law of the Sea [ISBA/17/A/8]; and took note of the 11 February advisory opinion [ISBA/17/C/6] of the Seabed Disputes Chamber of the International Tribunal for the Law of the Sea on the responsibilities and obligations of States sponsoring persons and entities with respect to activities in the Area [ISBA/17/A/9].

The Legal and Technical Commission [ISBA/17/C/13] noted the need to make adjustments to the Regulations on Prospecting and Exploration for Polymetallic Nodules in the Area to bring them into line with the Regulations on Prospecting and Exploration for Polymetallic Sulphides in the Area with respect to best environmental practices and the protection of biodiversity. The Commission suggested that the Authority prepare model legislation to assist sponsoring States in fulfilling their obligations as outlined in the 11 February advisory opinion of the Seabed Disputes Chamber. The Commission should consider the suggestion made by the Disputes Chamber to create mechanisms to compensate for damage when neither the contractor nor the sponsoring State was responsible. Addressing the annual reports of the eight contractors, the Commission said that progress was needed in technology-related issues, particularly with respect to the mining and metallurgical processing of nodules.

The Finance Committee [ISBA/17/A/3] authorized the Secretary-General to make an advance payment of up to $30,000 from the interest accrued from the Endowment Fund for Marine Scientific Research in the Area to supplement the Voluntary Trust Fund for the participation of members of the Finance Committee and the Legal and Technical Commission from developing countries, which amounted to $20,231 as at 30 June. The balance of the Endowment Fund was $3,355,015 as at 30 June. The Fund supported the participation of scientists from developing countries in approved programmes.

As at 31 December, the 1998 Protocol on the Privileges and Immunities of the International Seabed Authority [YUN 1998, p. 1226], which entered into force in 2003 [YUN 2003, p. 1353], had 33 parties. Guyana and Ireland acceded to it during the year.

International Tribunal for the Law of the Sea

The International Tribunal for the Law of the Sea held its thirty-first (14–25 March) and thirty-second (26 September–7 October) sessions in Hamburg, Germany [SPLOS/241].

The Seabed Disputes Chamber on 1 February delivered an advisory opinion in the case *Responsibilities and obligations of States sponsoring persons and entities with respect to activities in the Area (Request for Advisory Opinion submitted to the Seabed Disputes Chamber).*

The Tribunal met to deal with the *Dispute concerning delimitation of the maritime boundary between Bangladesh and Myanmar in the Bay of Bengal (Bangladesh/Myanmar)*. The dispute concerned the delimitation of the maritime boundary between the two countries in the Bay of Bengal with respect to the territorial sea, the exclusive economic zone and the continental shelf. The parties presented their oral statements at 15 public sittings held from 8 to 24 September.

The Tribunal met to deal with *The M/V "Louisa" Case (Saint Vincent and the Grenadines v. Spain)*, regarding a research vessel. Saint Vincent and the Grenadines in 2010 had instituted proceedings before the Tribunal against Spain in a dispute concerning the arrest of the *M/V Louisa* by Spanish authorities in 2006. Saint Vincent and the Grenadines submitted a memorial on 10 June 2011; Spain submitted a counter-memorial on 12 December. The time limits for filing the reply and the rejoinder were extended to 10 February and 10 April 2012, respectively.

On 4 July, Panama instituted proceedings before the Tribunal in a dispute with Guinea Bissau, *The M/V "Virginia G" Case (Panama/Guinea-Bissau)*, concerning the oil tanker *Virginia G*, arrested by the Guinea Bissau authorities in 2009. The President of the Tribunal issued orders on 18 August, 30 September and 23 December. By the latter, the President extended the time limits for the submission of the memorial by Panama and the counter-memorial by Guinea-Bissau to 23 January and 11 June 2012, respectively.

On 21 February, Mauritius requested the President of the Tribunal to appoint three arbitrators in the arbitral proceedings instituted under annex VII to the Convention for the settlement of the dispute between Mauritius and the United Kingdom concerning the "marine protected area" related to the Chagos Archipelago. The President held consultations with the parties in March, and subsequently chose three arbitrators.

The Tribunal devoted part of its two sessions to the consideration of legal and judicial matters. It examined legal issues of relevance to its jurisdiction, its Rules and its judicial procedures, and exchanged views on recent developments concerning the law of the sea.

As at 31 December, the Agreement on the Privileges and Immunities of the International Tribunal for the Law of the Sea, which was adopted by the seventh Meeting of States Parties to the Convention in 1997 [YUN 1997, p. 1361] and entered into force in 2001 [YUN 2001, p. 1235], had 40 parties.

Communication. In a note of 6 June [SPLOS/226], Germany presented information on its financial support for the Tribunal in the budget years 1997–2010.

Commission on the Limits of the Continental Shelf

The Commission on the Limits of the Continental Shelf, established in 1997 [YUN 1997, p. 1362], held its twenty-seventh (7 March–21 April) [CLCS/70 & Corr.1] and twenty-eighth (1 August–9 September) [CLCS/72] sessions in New York.

At its twenty-seventh session, the Commission received presentations of submissions from Denmark in respect of the Faroe-Rockall Plateau Region, from Mozambique and from Maldives. Its subcommissions, which examined submissions made by coastal States in accordance with the Convention on the Law of the Sea, considered those made by Japan, Suriname and Uruguay, as well as that made by France in respect of the areas of the French Antilles and the Kerguelen Islands; that made by the Philippines in respect of the Benham Rise region; and the joint submission by Mauritius and Seychelles in respect of the Mascarene Plateau. The subcommissions established to consider the submission made by Suriname and the joint submission made by Mauritius and Seychelles in respect of the Mascarene Plateau submitted their recommendations to the Commission. The Commission adopted the "Recommendations of the Commission on the Limits of the Continental Shelf in regard to the submission made by Indonesia in respect of the area North West of Sumatra on 16 June 2008", which had been introduced at the previous session; the "Recommendations of the Commission on the Limits of the Continental Shelf in regard to the joint submission made by Mauritius and Seychelles concerning the Mascarene Plateau region on 1 December 2008"; and the "Recommendations of the Commission on the Limits of the Continental Shelf in regard to the submission made by Suriname on 5 December 2008". The Commission established two new subcommissions to consider the submissions made by Uruguay and by the Philippines in respect of the Benham Rise region.

At its twenty-eighth session, the Commission continued to examine data and other materials submitted by France in respect of the areas of the French Antilles and the Kerguelen Islands, Japan, the Philippines in respect of the Benham Rise region, and Uruguay. The Commission received presentations of the submissions made by Bangladesh and Madagascar. It established a subcommission to examine the submission made by the Cook Islands in respect of the Manihiki Plateau.

Other developments related to the Convention

Pursuant to article 319 of the United Nations Convention on the Law of the Sea [YUN 1982, p. 237] and to General Assembly resolution 65/37 A [YUN 2010, p. 1373], the Secretary-General in August submitted his annual report on the oceans and the law of the sea [A/66/70/Add.2], which covered developments and issues relating to ocean affairs and the law of the sea, including implementation of the resolution. The report reviewed developments regarding the Convention and its implementing Agreements with regard to State practice, maritime claims and the delimitation of maritime zones; bodies established by the Convention; developments relating to international shipping; people at sea; maritime security; the conservation and management of marine living resources; and marine biological diversity, among other issues. It also addressed the crossover between climate change and oceans.

The Secretary-General noted that in many countries the pace of economic and social development had resulted in greater pressure on marine living and non-living resources. Many coastal States were turning increasingly to the oceans and seas for additional supplies of food, minerals and energy, in particular oil and gas, but also clean renewable energy, such as geothermal, tidal and wave energy. Adopting a precautionary approach, ecosystem-based mitigation and adaptation strategies, and sound management would help to ensure that key components of marine ecosystems remained resilient to the cumulative impacts of those pressures.

Delineating and delimiting maritime jurisdictions and exercise of sovereignty, and sovereign rights in accordance with international law, were crucial for the rule of law in the oceans and for ensuring that States would benefit from the use of ocean resources. States had made progress in that regard by establishing precise boundaries of maritime zones, including lines of delimitation.

Many coastal States had made submissions to the Commission on the Limits of the Continental Shelf with regard to the outer limits of their continental shelves beyond 200 nautical miles. At the same time, progress was needed with regard to the resolution of disputes concerning maritime boundary delimitation, in particular those disputes with potential to become sources of tension and conflict. Other issues included the surge in acts of piracy and armed robbery at sea, especially off the coast of Somalia, and the smuggling and trafficking of drugs and people by sea, which was increasingly resulting in loss of lives.

Further pursuant to General Assembly resolution 65/37 A, the Secretary-General in March submitted a report [A/66/70] on environmental impact assessments undertaken with respect to planned activities in areas beyond national jurisdiction, including capacity-building needs, on the basis of information provided by States and international organizations. The report also contained information on activities carried out by relevant organizations since the previous report [YUN 2009, p. 1346], including with regard to the scientific, technical, economic, legal, environmental and socio-economic aspects of the conservation and sustainable use of marine biodiversity beyond areas of national jurisdiction.

The report reviewed activities in the areas of marine science and technology; fishing activities and developments related to marine living resources, including illegal, unreported and unregulated fishing; shipping activities; waste disposal; land-based activities; mineral exploration and exploitation; research on, and exploitation of, marine genetic resources; management tools; governance; and possible options and approaches to promote international cooperation and coordination, among others.

The Secretary-General recalled that at the high-level events of the General Assembly in September 2010 [YUN 2010, p. 1030], Governments had renewed their commitments to the sustainable management of biodiversity and ecosystems that contributed to achieving food security and eradicating hunger. Global and regional organizations and entities had taken encouraging steps towards the conservation and sustainable use of marine biodiversity beyond areas of national jurisdiction, including through cooperative mechanisms. Yet the cumulative impacts of human uses and human-induced environmental changes—such as climate change and ocean acidification—continued to take their toll on vital marine ecosystems. Further actions and cooperative mechanisms were necessary to understand and address the impacts of various sectors on marine biodiversity beyond areas of national jurisdiction. Owing to the specificities of areas beyond national jurisdiction in terms of governance, legal regime and geographical and ecological conditions, global guidance was necessary on ways to adapt and implement management tools commonly used within national jurisdiction.

The General Assembly, through its Ad Hoc Open-ended Informal Working Group to study issues relating to the conservation and sustainable use of marine biological diversity beyond areas of national jurisdiction (see p. 1328), was the only global institution with a multidisciplinary and cross-sectoral perspective and competence on all issues related to marine biodiversity beyond areas of national jurisdiction. It was, therefore, uniquely placed to review progress, identify what additional actions might be required and galvanize the necessary political commitments.

Communication. In a letter dated 18 July [A/65/912], Germany transmitted the conclusions of the Chair of the International Conference on Arctic Science, International Law and Climate Protection: Legal Aspects of Marine Science in the Arctic Ocean (Berlin, 17–18 March).

Assessment of global marine environment

Pursuant to General Assembly resolution 65/37 A [YUN 2010, p. 1373], the Ad Hoc Working Group of the Whole on the Regular Process for Global Reporting and Assessment of the State of the Marine Environment, including Socioeconomic Aspects ("the Regular Process"), at its first meeting (New York, 14–18 February) [A/65/759], issued recommendations to the General Assembly on the first global integrated assessment of the state of the marine environment, including socioeconomic aspects. It recommended that the Group of Experts established by resolution 65/37 A explore means of leveraging systems to manage the information that comprised the foundation of the global marine assessment and report its findings for the consideration of the Working Group at its next meeting. Workshops organized under UN auspices should be a key mechanism by which the first global marine assessment would be accomplished and States could enhance their assessment capacity. The secretariat of the Regular Process should inventory capacity-building for assessments and types of experts for workshops, and report thereon at the next meeting of the Working Group. States should appoint a pool of experts to support the work of the Group of Experts in the preparation of the first global marine assessment. States should provide comments by 30 April on the possible outline for the first global integrated assessment of the state of the marine environment, including socioeconomic aspects. The Group of Experts should provide revised versions of those draft documents, reflecting the comments of States, to the secretariat for discussion and adoption at the next meeting of the Working Group. Representatives of 75 Member States, 15 intergovernmental organizations and other bodies, and 10 non-governmental organizations (NGOs) attended the meeting.

The General Assembly, by **decision 65/545** of 15 March, requested the Ad Hoc Working Group to report on its first meeting.

GENERAL ASSEMBLY ACTION

On 4 April [meeting 84], the General Assembly adopted **resolution 65/37 B** [draft: A/65/L.65] without vote [agenda item 74 (a)].

Oceans and the law of the sea

B

The General Assembly,

Having considered the report of the first meeting of the Ad Hoc Working Group of the Whole on the Regular Process for Global Reporting and Assessment of the State of the Marine Environment, including Socio-economic Aspects ("the Regular Process"),

Recognizing the work done by the Group of Experts on the Regular Process, and welcoming their contribution to moving the Regular Process forward,

1. *Endorses* the recommendations of the Ad Hoc Working Group of the Whole on the Regular Process;
2. *Requests* the Secretary-General to explore, in consultation with the Group of Experts on the Regular Process, the establishment of appropriate means to address the communication requirements of the Regular Process, having in mind the need to avoid duplication of efforts, and to report on the findings as soon as practicable;
3. *Requests* the secretariat of the Regular Process, with the assistance of the Group of Experts, to inventory, on a preliminary basis, capacity-building for assessments and types of experts for workshops and to report on these issues at the next meeting of the Ad Hoc Working Group of the Whole;
4. *Requests* the Secretary-General, upon the request of the Group of Experts and in line with paragraph 211 of resolution 65/37 A of 7 December 2010, to facilitate the use of appropriate data handling and information schemes within the United Nations system, drawing on the experiences, existing systems and support of other United Nations specialized agencies and programmes;
5. *Invites* States to provide comments on the possible outline for the first global integrated assessment of the state of the marine environment, including socio-economic aspects, the draft criteria for the appointment of experts and the draft guidelines for workshops by 30 April 2011, and requests the Group of Experts to prepare, by 30 May 2011, revised versions of those draft documents so as to reflect the comments of States, for further discussion and adoption at the next meeting of the Ad Hoc Working Group of the Whole;
6. *Requests* the Group of Experts, in consultation with the secretariat of the Regular Process and with the assistance of the members of UN-Oceans, to explore means of leveraging existing systems to manage the information that comprises the foundation of the global marine assessment and to report its findings by 30 May 2011 for the consideration of the Ad Hoc Working Group of the Whole at its next meeting;
7. *Requests* the Secretary-General to convene within existing resources the second meeting of the Ad Hoc Working Group of the Whole on 27 and 28 June 2011 to address outstanding issues identified in the report of the first meeting of the Ad Hoc Working Group of the Whole, with a view to enabling the first cycle of the first global integrated assessment to proceed, and to provide recommendations to the General Assembly for consideration at its sixty-sixth session.

The Ad Hoc Working Group of the Whole, at its second meeting (New York, 27–28 June) [A/66/189], submitted to the General Assembly for adoption the criteria for appointment of experts and the guidelines for workshops to assist the Regular Process. It recommended that its next meeting be convened in the first half of 2012. It also recommended that workshops be organized in order to inform the first cycle of the Regular Process.

Communication. On 28 October [A/66/587], Chile transmitted the summary of a workshop

(Santiago, 3–15 September) held under UN auspices in support of the first phase of the first assessment cycle of the regular process for global reporting and assessment of the state of the marine environment, including socioeconomic aspects.

Marine biological resources

The Ad Hoc Open-ended Informal Working Group to study issues relating to the conservation and sustainable use of marine biological diversity beyond areas of national jurisdiction, established pursuant to General Assembly resolution 59/24 [YUN 2004, p. 1333] held a meeting (New York, 31 May–3 June) [A/66/119] to provide recommendations to the Assembly, as requested in resolution 65/37 A [YUN 2010, p. 1373].

The Working Group recommended that the Assembly initiate a process with a view to ensuring that the legal framework for the conservation and sustainable use of marine biodiversity in areas beyond national jurisdiction effectively addressed those issues by identifying gaps and ways forward, including through the implementation of existing instruments and the possible development of a multilateral agreement under the United Nations Convention on the Law of the Sea. Such a process would address the conservation and sustainable use of marine biodiversity in areas beyond national jurisdiction; marine genetic resources, including questions on the sharing of benefits; measures such as area-based management tools, including marine protected areas; and environmental impact assessments, capacity-building and the transfer of marine technology. The process would take place in the Working Group and in intersessional workshops. The Secretary-General should convene a meeting of the Working Group in 2012.

United Nations Open-ended Informal Consultative Process

Pursuant to General Assembly resolution 65/37 A [YUN 2010, p. 1373], the twelfth meeting of the United Nations Open-ended Informal Consultative Process on Oceans and the Law of the Sea (New York, 20–24 June) [A/66/186] focused its discussions on "Contributing to the assessment, in the context of the United Nations Conference on Sustainable Development, of progress to date and the remaining gaps in the implementation of the outcomes of the major summits on sustainable development and addressing new and emerging challenges". The meeting was attended by representatives of 88 States, 17 intergovernmental organizations and other bodies and 12 NGOs. The meeting had before it a report of the Secretary-General [A/66/70/Add.1] on the implementation of resolution 65/37 A aimed at facilitating those discussions, and which concluded that despite efforts undertaken by the international community, the negative impacts of human activities on the oceans and seas were increasingly visible.

Participants heard presentations from experts and held plenary and panel discussions on sustainable development, oceans and the law of the sea; progress made and remaining gaps in the implementation of the outcomes of the major summits on sustainable development; new and emerging challenges for the sustainable development and use of oceans and seas; and "the road to Rio+20 and beyond". Participants further considered interagency cooperation and coordination, as well as issues that could benefit from attention in the future work of the General Assembly on oceans and the law of the sea.

The report was transmitted to the Co-Chairs of the Bureau for the Preparatory Process of the United Nations Conference on Sustainable Development, to be held in Rio de Janeiro, Brazil, in 2012.

Piracy

The International Maritime Organization (IMO) during the year issued guidelines to assist in the investigation of the crimes of piracy and armed robbery against ships [MSC.1/Circ.140]; revised interim guidance to shipowners, ship operators and shipmasters on the use of privately contracted armed security personnel on board ships in the High Risk Area (an area bounded by Suez and the Strait of Hormuz to the North, 10°S and 78°E) [MSC.1/Circ.1405/Rev.1]; revised interim recommendations for flag States regarding the use of privately contracted armed security personnel on board ships in the High Risk Area [MSC.1/Circ.1406/Rev.1]; and interim recommendations for port and coastal States regarding the use of privately contracted armed security personnel on board ships in the High Risk Area [MSC.1/Circ.1408]. IMO issued Best Management Practices to Deter Piracy off the Coast of Somalia and in the Arabian Sea Area [MSC.1/Circ.1337, annex 2], and on 20 May adopted a resolution on the implementation of best management practice guidance [MSC 89/25/Add.4, annex 29], which addressed piracy at sea. IMO also issued an annual report [MSC.4/Circ.169] on acts of piracy and armed robbery against ships in 2010, including a regional analysis.

The Security Council addressed piracy by **resolutions 1976(2011)** of 11 April (see p. 244), **2015(2011)** of 24 October (see p. 247), **2018(2011)** of 31 October (see p. 137) and **2020(2011)** of 22 November (see p. 250).

Division for Ocean Affairs and the Law of the Sea

During 2011, the Division for Ocean Affairs and the Law of the Sea of the Office of Legal Affairs continued to fulfil its role as the substantive unit of the

UN Secretariat responsible for reviewing and monitoring all developments related to the law of the sea and ocean affairs, as well as for the implementation of the United Nations Convention on the Law of the Sea and related General Assembly resolutions.

The Division maintained its Geographic Information System services in support of the Commission on the Limits of the Continental Shelf as well as in the performance of the depositary functions of the Secretary-General under the Convention in relation to charts and lists of geographical coordinates of points.

Capacity-building activities carried out by the Division included the management of fellowship programmes, trust funds and training or seminar events. The twenty-fourth Hamilton Shirley Amerasinghe Memorial Fellowship on the Law of the Sea, established in 1981 [YUN 1981, pp. 130 & 139], was awarded to Sri Asih Roza Nova of Indonesia. The Division also administered the United Nations-Nippon Foundation of Japan Fellowship Programme, which provided capacity-building opportunities to developing States through a nine-month research fellowship in partnership with more than 40 leading academic institutions worldwide. Individuals from 10 States took advantage of the Fellowship Programme in 2011. Since its inception in 2004, the Programme had made 70 awards to individuals from 54 States.

GENERAL ASSEMBLY ACTION

On 24 December [meeting 93], the General Assembly adopted **resolution 66/231** [draft: A/66/L.21 & Add.1] by recorded vote (134-1-6) [agenda item 76 (*a*)].

Oceans and the law of the sea

The General Assembly,

Recalling its annual resolutions on the law of the sea and on oceans and the law of the sea, including resolutions 65/37 A of 7 December 2010 and 65/37 B of 4 April 2011, and other relevant resolutions concerning the United Nations Convention on the Law of the Sea ("the Convention"),

Having considered the report of the Secretary-General, the recommendations of the Ad Hoc Open-ended Informal Working Group to study issues relating to the conservation and sustainable use of marine biological diversity beyond areas of national jurisdiction ("the Ad Hoc Open-ended Informal Working Group") and the reports on the work of the United Nations Open-ended Informal Consultative Process on Oceans and the Law of the Sea ("the Informal Consultative Process") at its twelfth meeting, on the twenty-first Meeting of States Parties to the Convention, and on the work of the Ad Hoc Working Group of the Whole on the Regular Process for Global Reporting and Assessment of the State of the Marine Environment, including Socioeconomic Aspects ("the Regular Process"),

Noting with satisfaction the upcoming thirtieth anniversary of the opening for signature of the Convention on 10 December 1982 at Montego Bay, Jamaica, and recognizing the pre-eminent contribution provided by the Convention to the strengthening of peace, security, cooperation and friendly relations among all nations in conformity with the principles of justice and equal rights and to the promotion of the economic and social advancement of all peoples of the world, in accordance with the purposes and principles of the United Nations as set forth in the Charter of the United Nations, as well as to the sustainable development of the oceans and seas,

Emphasizing the universal and unified character of the Convention, and reaffirming that the Convention sets out the legal framework within which all activities in the oceans and seas must be carried out and is of strategic importance as the basis for national, regional and global action and cooperation in the marine sector, and that its integrity needs to be maintained, as recognized also by the United Nations Conference on Environment and Development in chapter 17 of Agenda 21,

Recognizing the important contribution of sustainable development and management of the resources and uses of the oceans and seas to the achievement of international development goals, including those contained in the United Nations Millennium Declaration,

Conscious that the problems of ocean space are closely interrelated and need to be considered as a whole through an integrated, interdisciplinary and intersectoral approach, and reaffirming the need to improve cooperation and coordination at the national, regional and global levels, in accordance with the Convention, to support and supplement the efforts of each State in promoting the implementation and observance of the Convention, and the integrated management and sustainable development of the oceans and seas,

Reiterating the essential need for cooperation, including through capacity-building and transfer of marine technology, to ensure that all States, especially developing countries, in particular the least developed countries and small island developing States, as well as coastal African States, are able both to implement the Convention and to benefit from the sustainable development of the oceans and seas, as well as to participate fully in global and regional forums and processes dealing with oceans and law of the sea issues,

Emphasizing the need to strengthen the ability of competent international organizations to contribute, at the global, regional, subregional and bilateral levels, through cooperation programmes with Governments, to the development of national capacity in marine science and the sustainable management of the oceans and their resources,

Recalling that marine science is important for eradicating poverty, contributing to food security, conserving the world's marine environment and resources, helping to understand, predict and respond to natural events and promoting the sustainable development of the oceans and seas, by improving knowledge, through sustained research efforts and the evaluation of monitoring results, and applying such knowledge to management and decision-making,

Reiterating its deep concern at the serious adverse impacts on the marine environment and biodiversity, in particular on vulnerable marine ecosystems and their physical and biogenic structure, including coral reefs, cold water habitats, hydrothermal vents and seamounts, of certain human activities,

Emphasizing the need for the safe and environmentally sound recycling of ships,

Expressing deep concern at the adverse economic, social and environmental impacts of the physical alteration and destruction of marine habitats that may result from land-based and coastal development activities, in particular those land reclamation activities that are carried out in a manner that has a detrimental impact on the marine environment,

Reiterating its serious concern at the current and projected adverse effects of climate change on the marine environment and marine biodiversity, and emphasizing the urgency of addressing this issue,

Expressing concern that climate change continues to increase the severity and incidence of coral bleaching throughout tropical seas and weakens the ability of reefs to withstand ocean acidification, which could have serious and irreversible negative effects on marine organisms, particularly corals, as well as to withstand other pressures, including overfishing and pollution,

Reiterating its deep concern at the vulnerability of the environment and the fragile ecosystems of the polar regions, including the Arctic Ocean and the Arctic ice cap, particularly affected by the projected adverse effects of climate change,

Recognizing the need for a more integrated and ecosystem-based approach to, further study of and the promotion of measures for enhanced cooperation, coordination and collaboration relating to the conservation and sustainable use of marine biodiversity beyond areas of national jurisdiction,

Recognizing also that the realization of the benefits of the Convention could be enhanced by international cooperation, technical assistance and advanced scientific knowledge, as well as by funding and capacity-building,

Recognizing further that hydrographic surveys and nautical charting are critical to the safety of navigation and life at sea, environmental protection, including the protection of vulnerable marine ecosystems, and the economics of the global shipping industry, and encouraging further efforts towards electronic charting, which not only provides significantly increased benefits for safe navigation and management of ship movement, but also provides data and information that can be used for sustainable fisheries activities and other sectoral uses of the marine environment, the delimitation of maritime boundaries and environmental protection, and noting the entry into force of amendments to the International Convention for the Safety of Life at Sea, 1974, on requirements for ships on international voyages to carry an electronic chart display information system,

Recognizing that ocean data buoys deployed and operated in accordance with international law are critical for saving lives by detecting storm surges and tsunamis and for improving understanding of weather, climate and ecosystems, and reiterating its serious concern at intentional and unintentional damage to such buoys,

Emphasizing that underwater archaeological, cultural and historical heritage, including shipwrecks and watercraft, holds essential information on the history of humankind and that such heritage is a resource that needs to be protected and preserved,

Noting with concern the continuing problem of transnational organized crime committed at sea, including illicit traffic in narcotic drugs and psychotropic substances, the smuggling of migrants and trafficking in persons, and threats to maritime safety and security, including piracy, armed robbery at sea, smuggling and terrorist acts against shipping, offshore installations and other maritime interests, and noting the deplorable loss of life and adverse impact on international trade, energy security and the global economy resulting from such activities,

Recognizing that fibre-optic submarine cables transmit most of the world's data and communications and, hence, are vitally important to the global economy and the national security of all States, conscious that these cables are susceptible to intentional and accidental damage from shipping and other activities, and that the maintenance, including the repair, of these cables is important, noting that these matters have been brought to the attention of States at various workshops and seminars, and conscious of the need for States to adopt national laws and regulations to protect submarine cables and render their wilful damage or damage by culpable negligence punishable offences,

Noting the importance of the delineation of the outer limits of the continental shelf beyond 200 nautical miles and that it is in the broader interest of the international community that coastal States with a continental shelf beyond 200 nautical miles submit information on the outer limits of the continental shelf beyond 200 nautical miles to the Commission on the Limits of the Continental Shelf ("the Commission"), and welcoming the submissions to the Commission by a considerable number of States Parties on the outer limits of their continental shelf beyond 200 nautical miles, that the Commission has continued to fulfil its role, including of making recommendations to coastal States, and that the summaries of recommendations are being made publicly available,

Noting also that many coastal States Parties have submitted preliminary information indicative of the outer limits of the continental shelf beyond 200 nautical miles, as provided for in the decision of the eighteenth Meeting of States Parties to the Convention regarding the workload of the Commission and the ability of States, particularly developing States, to fulfil the requirements of article 4 of annex II to the Convention, as well as the decision contained in SPLOS/72, paragraph (*a*),

Noting further that some coastal States may continue to face particular challenges in relation to preparing and presenting submissions to the Commission,

Noting that financial and technical assistance may be sought by developing countries for activities in relation to preparing and presenting submissions to the Commission, including through the voluntary trust fund established by resolution 55/7 of 30 October 2000 for the purpose of facilitating the preparation of submissions to the Commission for developing States, in particular the least developed countries and small island developing States, and compliance with article 76 of the Convention, as well as other accessible international assistance,

Recognizing the importance of the trust funds established by resolution 55/7 in facilitating the participation of members of the Commission from developing States in the meetings of the Commission and in fulfilling the requirements of article 4 of annex II to the Convention, while noting with appreciation the recent contributions made to them,

Reaffirming the importance of the work of the Commission for coastal States and for the international community,

Recognizing the significant workload of the Commission in view of the large number of submissions already received and a number of submissions yet to be received, which places additional demands and challenges on its members and the secretariat as provided by the Secretary-General of the United Nations through the Division for Ocean Affairs and the Law of the Sea of the Office of Legal Affairs of the Secretariat ("the Division"), and acknowledging the decision of the twenty-first Meeting of States Parties to the Convention regarding the workload of the Commission,

Noting with concern the projected timetable of the work of the Commission on the submissions already received by it and those yet to be received and, in this regard, the consequences of the duration of the sessions of the Commission and the meetings of its subcommissions,

Recognizing significant inequities and difficulties for States arising out of the projected timetable, including with respect to retaining expertise, when there is a considerable delay between preparation of submissions and their consideration by the Commission,

Recognizing also the need to take action to ensure that the Commission can perform its functions under the Convention expeditiously, efficiently and effectively, and maintain its high level of quality and expertise,

Recalling its decision, in resolutions 57/141 of 12 December 2002 and 58/240 of 23 December 2003, to establish a regular process under the United Nations for global reporting and assessment of the state of the marine environment, including socioeconomic aspects, both current and foreseeable, building on existing regional assessments, as recommended by the World Summit on Sustainable Development, and noting the need for cooperation among all States to this end,

Recalling also its decisions, in paragraphs 202, 203 and 209 of resolution 65/37 A, regarding the Regular Process, as established under the United Nations and accountable to the General Assembly,

Recalling further that the Division has been designated to provide secretariat support to the Regular Process, including its established institutions,

Recognizing the importance and the contribution of the work of the Informal Consultative Process established by resolution 54/33 of 24 November 1999 to facilitate the annual review of developments in ocean affairs by the General Assembly,

Noting the responsibilities of the Secretary-General under the Convention and related resolutions of the General Assembly, in particular resolutions 49/28 of 6 December 1994, 52/26 of 26 November 1997, 54/33 and 65/37 A and 65/37 B, and in this context the substantial increase in activities of the Division, in particular in view of the growing number of requests to the Division for additional outputs and servicing of meetings, its increasing capacity-building activities, the need for enhanced support and assistance to the Commission and the role of the Division in inter-agency coordination and cooperation,

Reaffirming the importance of the work of the International Seabed Authority ("the Authority") in accordance with the Convention and the Agreement relating to the Implementation of Part XI of the United Nations Convention on the Law of the Sea of 10 December 1982 ("the Part XI Agreement"),

Reaffirming also the importance of the work of the International Tribunal for the Law of the Sea ("the Tribunal") in accordance with the Convention,

I

Implementation of the Convention and related agreements and instruments

1. *Reaffirms* its annual resolutions on the law of the sea and on oceans and the law of the sea, including resolutions 65/37 A and 65/37 B, and other relevant resolutions concerning the Convention;

2. *Also reaffirms* the unified character of the Convention and the vital importance of preserving its integrity;

3. *Calls upon* all States that have not done so, in order to achieve the goal of universal participation, to become parties to the Convention and the Part XI Agreement;

4. *Calls upon* States that have not done so, in order to achieve the goal of universal participation, to become parties to the Agreement for the Implementation of the Provisions of the United Nations Convention on the Law of the Sea of 10 December 1982 relating to the Conservation and Management of Straddling Fish Stocks and Highly Migratory Fish Stocks ("the Fish Stocks Agreement");

5. *Calls upon* States to harmonize their national legislation with the provisions of the Convention and, where applicable, relevant agreements and instruments, to ensure the consistent application of those provisions and to ensure also that any declarations or statements that they have made or make when signing, ratifying or acceding to the Convention do not purport to exclude or to modify the legal effect of the provisions of the Convention in their application to the State concerned and to withdraw any such declarations or statements;

6. *Calls upon* States Parties to the Convention that have not yet done so to deposit with the Secretary-General charts or lists of geographical coordinates, as provided for in the Convention, preferably using generally accepted and the most recent geodetic datums;

7. *Urges* all States to cooperate, directly or through competent international bodies, in taking measures to protect and preserve objects of an archaeological and historical nature found at sea, in conformity with the Convention, and calls upon States to work together on such diverse challenges and opportunities as the appropriate relationship between salvage law and scientific management and conservation of underwater cultural heritage, increasing technological abilities to discover and reach underwater sites, looting and growing underwater tourism;

8. *Notes* the recent deposit of instruments of ratification and acceptance of the 2001 Convention on the Protection of the Underwater Cultural Heritage, calls upon States that have not yet done so to consider becoming parties to that Convention, and notes in particular the rules annexed to that Convention, which address the relationship between salvage law and scientific principles of management, conservation and protection of underwater cultural heritage among Parties, their nationals and vessels flying their flag;

II
Capacity-building

9. *Emphasizes* that capacity-building is essential to ensure that States, especially developing countries, in particular the least developed countries and small island developing States, as well as coastal African States, are able to fully implement the Convention, benefit from the sustainable development of the oceans and seas and participate fully in global and regional forums on ocean affairs and the law of the sea;

10. *Emphasizes also* the need for international cooperation for capacity-building, including cross-sectoral cooperation, at national, regional and global levels, to address, in particular, gaps in capacity-building in ocean affairs and the law of the sea, including marine science;

11. *Calls for* capacity-building initiatives to take into account the needs of developing countries, and calls upon States, international organizations and donor agencies to make efforts to ensure the sustainability of such initiatives;

12. *Calls upon* donor agencies and international financial institutions to keep their programmes systematically under review to ensure the availability in all States, particularly in developing States, of the economic, legal, navigational, scientific and technical skills necessary for the full implementation of the Convention and the objectives of the present resolution, as well as the sustainable development of the oceans and seas nationally, regionally and globally, and in so doing to bear in mind the interests and needs of landlocked developing States;

13. *Encourages* intensified efforts to build capacity for developing countries, in particular for the least developed countries and small island developing States, as well as coastal African States, to improve hydrographic services and the production of nautical charts, including electronic charts, as well as the mobilization of resources and building of capacity with support from international financial institutions and the donor community;

14. *Calls upon* States and international financial institutions, including through bilateral, regional and global cooperation programmes and technical partnerships, to continue to strengthen capacity-building activities, in particular in developing countries, in the field of marine scientific research by, inter alia, training personnel to develop and enhance relevant expertise, providing the necessary equipment, facilities and vessels and transferring environmentally sound technologies;

15. *Also calls upon* States and international financial institutions, including through bilateral, regional and global cooperation programmes and technical partnerships, to strengthen capacity-building activities in developing countries, in particular least developed countries and small island developing States, to develop their maritime administration and appropriate legal frameworks to establish or enhance the necessary infrastructure, legislative and enforcement capabilities to promote effective compliance with, and implementation and enforcement of, their responsibilities under international law;

16. *Emphasizes* the need to focus on strengthening South-South cooperation as an additional way to build capacity and as a cooperative mechanism to further enable countries to set their own priorities and needs;

17. *Recognizes* the importance of the work of the International Maritime Law Institute of the International Maritime Organization as a centre of education and training of Government legal advisers, mainly from developing States, confirms its effective capacity-building role in the field of international law, and urges States, intergovernmental organizations and financial institutions to make voluntary financial contributions to the budget of the Institute;

18. *Also recognizes* the importance of the World Maritime University of the International Maritime Organization as a centre for maritime education and research, confirms its effective capacity-building role in the field of maritime transportation, policy, administration, management, safety, security and environmental protection, as well as its role in the international exchange and transfer of knowledge, and urges States, intergovernmental organizations and other bodies to make voluntary financial contributions to the University;

19. *Welcomes* ongoing activities for capacity-building so as to address maritime security and safety needs and the protection of the marine environment of developing States, and encourages States and international financial institutions to provide additional funding for capacity-building programmes, including for transfer of technology, including through the International Maritime Organization and other competent international organizations;

20. *Recognizes* the considerable need to provide sustained capacity-building assistance, including on financial and technical aspects, by relevant international organizations and donors to developing States, with a view to further strengthening their capacity to take effective measures against the multiple facets of international criminal activities at sea, in line with the relevant international instruments, including the United Nations Convention against Transnational Organized Crime and the Protocols thereto;

21. *Also recognizes* the need to build the capacity of developing States to raise awareness of and support the implementation of improved waste management practices, noting the particular vulnerability of small island developing States to the impact of marine pollution from land-based sources and marine debris;

22. *Further recognizes* the importance of assisting developing States, in particular the least developed countries and small island developing States, as well as coastal African States, in implementing the Convention, and urges States, intergovernmental organizations and agencies, national institutions, non-governmental organizations and international financial institutions, as well as natural and juridical persons, to make voluntary financial or other contributions to the trust funds, as referred to in resolutions 55/7, 57/141 and 64/71 of 4 December 2009, established for this purpose;

23. *Acknowledges* the importance of capacity-building for developing States, in particular the least developed countries and small island developing States, as well as coastal African States, for the protection of the marine environment and the conservation and sustainable use of marine resources;

24. *Recognizes* that promoting the voluntary transfer of technology is an essential aspect of building capacity in marine science;

25. *Encourages* States to use the Criteria and Guidelines on the Transfer of Marine Technology adopted by

the Assembly of the Intergovernmental Oceanographic Commission of the United Nations Educational, Scientific and Cultural Organization at its twenty-second session, in 2003, and recalls the important role of the secretariat of that Commission in the implementation and promotion of the Criteria and Guidelines;

26. *Notes with satisfaction* the efforts of the Division to compile information on capacity-building initiatives, requests the Secretary-General to continue to regularly update such information provided by States, international organizations and donor agencies and include it in his annual report to the General Assembly, invites States, international organizations and donor agencies to submit such information to the Secretary-General for this purpose, and requests the Division to post the information on capacity-building initiatives from the annual report of the Secretary-General on the website of the Division in an easily accessible manner so as to facilitate the matching of capacity-building needs with opportunities;

27. *Calls upon* States to continue to assist developing States, and especially the least developed countries and small island developing States, as well as coastal African States, at the bilateral and, where appropriate, multilateral levels, in the preparation of submissions to the Commission regarding the establishment of the outer limits of the continental shelf beyond 200 nautical miles, including the assessment of the nature and extent of the continental shelf of a coastal State, and recalls that coastal States can make requests to the Commission for scientific and technical advice in the preparation of data for their submissions, in accordance with article 3 of annex II to the Convention;

28. *Calls upon* the Division to continue to disseminate information on relevant procedures related to the trust fund established for the purpose of facilitating the preparation of submissions to the Commission and to continue its dialogue with potential beneficiaries with a view to providing financial support to developing countries for activities to facilitate their submissions in accordance with the requirements of article 76 of the Convention and with the Rules of Procedure and the Scientific and Technical Guidelines of the Commission;

29. *Requests* the Secretary-General, in cooperation with States and relevant international organizations and institutions, to continue to support training and other activities to assist developing States in the preparation and presentation of their submissions to the Commission;

30. *Notes with appreciation* the contribution of the Division to capacity-building activities at the national and regional level;

31. *Invites* Member States and others in a position to do so to support the capacity-building activities of the Division, including, in particular, the training and other activities to assist developing States in the preparation of their submissions to the Commission and also invites Member States and others in a position to do so to contribute to the trust fund established by the Secretary-General for the Office of Legal Affairs to support the promotion of international law, and expresses its appreciation to those who have contributed;

32. *Recognizes with appreciation* the important contribution of the Hamilton Shirley Amerasinghe Memorial Fellowship on the Law of the Sea to the capacity-building of developing countries and the promotion of the law of the sea, notes that the twenty-fourth award, in 2011, was made possible thanks to the generous contributions of Member States, further notes that the fellowship fund balance continues to be at a very low level, reiterates therefore its serious concern regarding the continued lack of resources, appeals urgently to Member States and others in a position to do so to contribute generously to the further development of the Fellowship to ensure that it is awarded every year, and takes due note of the inclusion by the Secretary-General of the Fellowship on the list of trust funds for the United Nations Pledging Conference for Development Activities;

33. *Also recognizes with appreciation* the important contribution that the United Nations-Nippon Foundation of Japan Fellowship Programme which, relying on its network of more than 40 host institutions, has awarded 70 fellowships to individuals from 54 Member States since 2005, and held from 10 to 16 July 2011 its third regional alumni meeting, in Nairobi, has made to human resources development for developing Member States in the field of ocean affairs and the law of the sea and related disciplines and the promotion of holistic and cross-sectoral approaches, emphasizing the integration of physical and social sciences and promoting interlinkages among alumni and between their organizations;

34. *Further recognizes with appreciation* the funding set aside by the Global Environment Facility for projects relating to oceans and marine biodiversity;

III

Meetings of States Parties

35. *Welcomes* the report of the twenty-first Meeting of States Parties to the Convention and of the special meeting held on 11 August 2011 for the purpose of electing one member of the Commission;

36. *Requests* the Secretary-General to convene the twenty-second Meeting of States Parties to the Convention, in New York from 4 to 11 June 2012, and to provide full conference services, including documentation, as required;

IV

Peaceful settlement of disputes

37. *Notes with satisfaction* the continued and significant contribution of the Tribunal to the settlement of disputes by peaceful means in accordance with Part XV of the Convention, and underlines the important role and authority of the Tribunal concerning the interpretation or application of the Convention and the Part XI Agreement;

38. *Pays tribute* to the important and long-standing role of the International Court of Justice with regard to the peaceful settlement of disputes concerning the law of the sea;

39. *Notes* that States parties to an international agreement related to the purposes of the Convention may submit to, inter alia, the Tribunal or the International Court of Justice any dispute concerning the interpretation or application of that agreement submitted in accordance with that agreement, and notes also the possibility, provided for in the Statutes of the Tribunal and the Court, to submit disputes to a chamber;

40. *Encourages* States Parties to the Convention that have not yet done so to consider making a written decla-

ration choosing from the means set out in article 287 of the Convention for the settlement of disputes concerning the interpretation or application of the Convention and the Part XI Agreement, bearing in mind the comprehensive character of the dispute settlement mechanism provided for in Part XV of the Convention;

V

The Area

41. *Encourages* progress on the finalization of the regulations for prospecting and exploration for cobalt-rich ferromanganese crusts in the Area, and reiterates the importance of the ongoing elaboration by the Authority, pursuant to article 145 of the Convention, of rules, regulations and procedures to ensure the effective protection of the marine environment, for, inter alia, the protection and conservation of the natural resources of the Area, and for the prevention of damage to the flora and fauna of the marine environment from harmful effects that may arise from activities in the Area;

42. *Acknowledges* the activities undertaken by the Authority for the dissemination of the advisory opinion on the responsibilities and obligations of States sponsoring persons and entities with respect to activities in the Area, issued by the Seabed Disputes Chamber of the Tribunal on 1 February 2011, at the request of the Council of the Authority, pursuant to article 191 of the Convention;

43. *Notes* the importance of the responsibilities entrusted to the Authority by articles 143 and 145 of the Convention, which refer to marine scientific research and protection of the marine environment, respectively;

VI

Effective functioning of the Authority and the Tribunal

44. *Appeals* to all States Parties to the Convention to pay their assessed contributions to the Authority and to the Tribunal in full and on time, and also appeals to States Parties in arrears with their contributions to fulfil their obligations without delay;

45. *Urges* all States Parties to the Convention to attend the sessions of the Authority, and calls upon the Authority to continue to pursue all options, including making concrete recommendations on the issue of dates, in order to improve attendance in Kingston and to ensure global participation;

46. *Calls upon* States that have not done so to consider ratifying or acceding to the Agreement on the Privileges and Immunities of the Tribunal and to the Protocol on the Privileges and Immunities of the Authority;

47. *Emphasizes* the importance of the Tribunal's rules and staff regulations in promoting the recruitment of a geographically representative staff in the Professional and higher categories, and welcomes the actions taken by the Tribunal in observance of those rules and regulations;

48. *Takes note with appreciation* of the advisory opinion on the responsibilities and obligations of States sponsoring persons and entities with respect to activities in the Area, issued by the Seabed Disputes Chamber of the Tribunal on 1 February 2011, at the request of the Council of the Authority, pursuant to article 191 of the Convention;

VII

The continental shelf and the work of the Commission

49. *Recalls* that, in accordance with article 76, paragraph 8, of the Convention, information on the limits of the continental shelf beyond 200 nautical miles from the baselines from which the breadth of the territorial sea is measured shall be submitted by the coastal State to the Commission set up under annex II to the Convention on the basis of equitable geographical representation, that the Commission shall make recommendations to coastal States on matters related to the establishment of the outer limits of their continental shelf, and that the limits of the shelf established by a coastal State on the basis of these recommendations shall be final and binding;

50. *Also recalls* that, in accordance with article 77, paragraph 3, of the Convention, the rights of the coastal State over the continental shelf do not depend on occupation, effective or notional, or on any express proclamation;

51. *Notes with satisfaction* that a considerable number of States Parties to the Convention have submitted information to the Commission regarding the establishment of the outer limits of the continental shelf beyond 200 nautical miles, in conformity with article 76 of the Convention and article 4 of annex II to the Convention, taking into account the decision of the eleventh Meeting of States Parties to the Convention contained in SPLOS/72, paragraph (*a*);

52. *Also notes with satisfaction* that a considerable number of States Parties to the Convention have submitted to the Secretary-General, pursuant to the decision of the eighteenth Meeting of States Parties to the Convention, preliminary information indicative of the outer limits of the continental shelf beyond 200 nautical miles and a description of the status of preparation and intended date of submission in accordance with the requirements of article 76 of the Convention and with the Rules of Procedure and the Scientific and Technical Guidelines of the Commission;

53. *Further notes with satisfaction* the progress in the work of the Commission and that it is giving current consideration to a number of submissions that have been made regarding the establishment of the outer limits of the continental shelf beyond 200 nautical miles;

54. *Notes with satisfaction* that the Commission, taking into account the decision of the eighteenth Meeting of States Parties to the Convention, has compiled lists of websites of organizations, data/information portals and data holders where general information and publicly available scientific and technical data can be accessed that may be relevant to the preparation of submissions, and has made this information available on its website;

55. *Takes note* of the recommendations made by the Commission on the submissions of a number of coastal States, and welcomes the fact that summaries of recommendations are being made publicly available;

56. *Notes* that the consideration by the Commission of submissions by coastal States in accordance with article 76 of and annex II to the Convention is without prejudice to the application of other parts of the Convention by States Parties;

57. *Notes with concern* that the heavy workload of the Commission, owing to the considerable number of submis-

sions, places additional demands on and challenges before its members and the secretariat as provided by the Division, and in that regard emphasizes the need to ensure that the Commission can perform its functions expeditiously, efficiently and effectively and maintain its high level of quality and expertise;

58. *Takes note* of the decision of the twenty-first Meeting of States Parties to the Convention regarding the workload of the Commission, in which, among other measures, the Commission is requested to consider, in coordination with the Secretariat, as from 16 June 2012, within the existing resources made available to the Secretariat, that the Commission, and its subcommissions meeting simultaneously as far as possible, meet in New York for up to twenty-six weeks but not less than an intended minimum of twenty-one weeks a year for a period of five years, distributed in such a way that the Commission determines to be the most effective, and that no two sessions be sequential;

59. *Welcomes* the decision of the twenty-first Meeting of States Parties to the Convention to review the measures proposed in paragraph 1 of the decision at the twenty-sixth Meeting of States Parties to the Convention, with a view to assessing progress in reducing the projected timeline in the workload of the Commission;

60. *Reiterates* the duty of States under the Convention, whose experts are serving on the Commission, to defray the expenses of the experts they have nominated while in performance of Commission duties, and urges these States to do their utmost to ensure the full participation of those experts in the work of the Commission, including the meetings of subcommissions, in accordance with the Convention;

61. *Requests* the Secretary-General to continue to take appropriate measures, within overall existing resource levels, to further strengthen the capacity of the Division, serving as the secretariat of the Commission, in order to ensure enhanced support and assistance to the Commission and its subcommissions in their consideration of submissions, as required by paragraph 9 of annex III to the Rules of Procedure of the Commission, in particular its human resources, taking into account the need for simultaneous work on several submissions;

62. *Urges* the Secretary-General to continue to provide all necessary secretariat services to the Commission in accordance with article 2, paragraph 5, of annex II to the Convention;

63. *Requests* the Secretary-General to take appropriate and timely measures to ensure secretariat services for the Commission and its subcommissions for the extended duration of time requested in the decision of the twenty-first Meeting of States Parties to the Convention;

64. *Also requests* the Secretary-General, consequently, to allocate appropriate and sufficient resources to the Division to provide adequate services and assistance to the Commission in view of the increase in the number of its working weeks, including through the establishment of additional posts to reinforce the geographic information system, legal and administrative support to the Commission by the Division;

65. *Expresses its appreciation* to States that have made contributions to the voluntary trust fund established by resolution 55/7 for the purpose of facilitating the preparation of submissions to the Commission and to the voluntary trust fund also established by that resolution for the purpose of defraying the cost of participation of the members of the Commission from developing States in the meetings of the Commission, and encourages States to make additional contributions to these funds;

66. *Approves* the convening by the Secretary-General of the twenty-ninth and thirtieth sessions of the Commission, in New York from 19 March to 27 April 2012 and from 30 July to 10 August 2012, respectively, with full conference services, including documentation, for the plenary parts of these sessions, as well as any resumed twenty-ninth and thirtieth sessions as may be required by the Commission, and requests the Secretary-General to make every effort to meet these requirements within overall existing resources, on the understanding that the following periods of the twenty-ninth session will be used for the technical examinations of submissions at the Geographic Information System laboratories and other technical facilities of the Division: 19 March to 5 April 2012 and 23 to 27 April 2012;

67. *Expresses its firm conviction* about the importance of the work of the Commission, carried out in accordance with the Convention, including with respect to the participation of coastal States in relevant proceedings concerning their submissions, and recognizes the continued need for active interaction between coastal States and the Commission;

68. *Expresses its appreciation* to States that have exchanged views in order to increase understanding of issues, including expenditures involved, arising from the application of article 76 of the Convention, thus facilitating the preparation of submissions by States, in particular developing States, to the Commission, and encourages States to continue exchanging views;

69. *Notes* the considerable number of submissions yet to be considered by the Commission, and in this regard stresses the urgent need for States Parties to the Convention to take appropriate and prompt steps that will allow the Commission to consider the increased number of submissions in a timely, efficient and effective manner;

70. *Requests* the Secretary-General, in cooperation with Member States, to continue supporting workshops or symposiums on scientific and technical aspects of the establishment of the outer limits of the continental shelf beyond 200 nautical miles, taking into account the need to strengthen capacity-building for developing countries in preparing their submissions, and takes note of the workshop held by the Government of Angola from 16 to 20 May 2011 in Luanda for this purpose;

VIII

Maritime safety and security and flag State implementation

71. *Encourages* States to ratify or accede to international agreements addressing the safety and security of navigation, as well as maritime labour, and to adopt the necessary measures consistent with the Convention and other relevant international instruments aimed at implementing and enforcing the rules contained in those agreements, and emphasizes the need for capacity-building for and assistance to developing States;

72. *Recognizes* that the legal regimes governing maritime safety and maritime security may have common and mutually reinforcing objectives that may be interrelated and could benefit from synergies, and encourages States to take this into account in their implementation;

73. *Emphasizes* the need for further efforts to promote a culture of safety and security in the shipping industry and to address the shortage of adequately trained personnel, and urges the establishment of more centres to provide the required education and training;

74. *Emphasizes also* that safety and security measures should be implemented with minimal negative effects on seafarers and fishers, especially in relation to their working conditions;

75. *Notes* the 2010 amendments to the International Convention on Standards of Training, Certification and Watchkeeping for Seafarers, 1978, and to the Standards of Training, Certification and Watchkeeping for Seafarers Code, otherwise known as the Manila amendments, and invites States that have not yet done so to ratify or accede to that Convention, as well as the International Convention on Standards of Training, Certification and Watchkeeping for Fishing Vessel Personnel, 1995;

76. *Invites* States that have not yet done so to ratify or accede to the Maritime Labour Convention, 2006, the Work in Fishing Convention, 2007 (No. 188) and the Seafarers' Identity Documents Convention (Revised), 2003 (No. 185), of the International Labour Organization and to effectively implement those Conventions, and emphasizes the need to provide to States, at their request, technical cooperation and assistance in that regard;

77. *Welcomes* ongoing cooperation between the Food and Agriculture Organization of the United Nations, the International Maritime Organization and the International Labour Organization relating to the safety of fishers and fishing vessels, underlines the urgent need for continued work in that area, and takes note of the approval by the International Maritime Organization of the Guidelines to Assist Competent Authorities in the Implementation of Part B of the Code of Safety for Fishermen and Fishing Vessels, the Voluntary Guidelines for the Design, Construction and Equipment of Small Fishing Vessels, and the Safety Recommendations for Decked Fishing Vessels of Less than 12 Metres in Length and Undecked Fishing Vessels, which were subsequently forwarded for approval to the Food and Agriculture Organization of the United Nations and the International Labour Organization;

78. *Encourages* continued cooperation between the parties to the Basel Convention on the Control of Transboundary Movements of Hazardous Wastes and Their Disposal and the International Maritime Organization on regulations on the prevention of pollution from ships;

79. *Encourages* States to consider becoming parties to the 2010 Protocol to the 1996 International Convention on Liability and Compensation for Damage in Connection with the Carriage of Hazardous and Noxious Substances by Sea;

80. *Recalls* that all actions taken to combat threats to maritime security must be in accordance with international law, including the principles embodied in the Charter and the Convention;

81. *Recognizes* the crucial role of international cooperation at the global, regional, subregional and bilateral levels in combating, in accordance with international law, threats to maritime security, including piracy, armed robbery at sea, terrorist acts against shipping, offshore installations and other maritime interests, through bilateral and multilateral instruments and mechanisms aimed at monitoring, preventing and responding to such threats, the enhanced sharing of information among States relevant to the detection, prevention and suppression of such threats, and the prosecution of offenders with due regard to national legislation, and the need for sustained capacity-building to support such objectives;

82. *Notes* that piracy affects the entire range of vessels engaged in maritime activities;

83. *Emphasizes* the importance of promptly reporting incidents to enable accurate information on the scope of the problem of piracy and armed robbery against ships and, in the case of armed robbery against ships, by affected vessels to the coastal State, underlines the importance of effective information-sharing with States potentially affected by incidents of piracy and armed robbery against ships, and takes note of the important role of the International Maritime Organization;

84. *Urges* all States, in cooperation with the International Maritime Organization, to actively combat piracy and armed robbery at sea by adopting measures, including those relating to assistance with capacity-building through training of seafarers, port staff and enforcement personnel in the prevention, reporting and investigation of incidents, bringing the alleged perpetrators to justice, in accordance with international law, and by adopting national legislation, as well as providing enforcement vessels and equipment and guarding against fraudulent ship registration;

85. *Encourages* States to ensure effective implementation of international law applicable to combating piracy, as reflected in the Convention, and calls upon States to take appropriate steps under their national law to facilitate, in accordance with international law, the apprehension and prosecution of those who are alleged to have committed acts of piracy, including the financing or facilitation of such acts, also taking into account other relevant instruments that are consistent with the Convention;

86. *Expresses grave concern* at the threats posed by piracy and armed robbery at sea to the safety and welfare of seafarers and other persons;

87. *Invites* all States, the International Maritime Organization, the International Labour Organization and other relevant international organizations and agencies to adopt or recommend, as appropriate, measures to protect the interest and welfare of seafarers and fishers who are victims of pirates, after their release from captivity, including their post-incident care and reintegration into society;

88. *Takes note* of the ongoing cooperation between the International Maritime Organization, the United Nations Office on Drugs and Crime and the Division with respect to the compilation of national legislation on piracy, and notes that copies of national legislation received by the Secretariat have been placed on the website of the Division;

89. *Encourages* continued national, bilateral and trilateral initiatives as well as regional cooperative mechanisms, in accordance with international law, to address piracy, including the financing or facilitation of acts of piracy,

and armed robbery at sea in the Asian region, and calls upon other States to give immediate attention to adopting, concluding and implementing cooperation agreements at the regional level on combating piracy and armed robbery against ships;

90. *Reiterates its serious concern* regarding continued incidents of piracy and armed robbery at sea off the coast of Somalia, expresses alarm in particular at the hijacking of vessels, supports the recent efforts to address this problem at the global and regional levels, notes the adoption by the Security Council of resolutions 1816(2008) of 2 June 2008, 1838(2008) of 7 October 2008, 1846(2008) of 2 December 2008, 1851(2008) of 16 December 2008, 1897(2009) of 30 November 2009, 1918(2010) of 27 April 2010, 1950(2010) of 23 November 2010, 1976(2011) of 11 April 2011 and 2015(2011) of 24 October 2011, as well as the statement by the President of the Security Council of 25 August 2010, and also notes that the authorization in resolution 1816(2008), and the provisions in resolutions 1838(2008), 1846(2008), 1851(2008), 1897(2009) and 1950(2010) apply only to the situation in Somalia and do not affect the rights, obligations or responsibilities of Member States under international law, including any rights or obligations under the Convention, with respect to any other situation, and underscores, in particular, the fact that they are not to be considered as establishing customary international law;

91. *Notes with appreciation* the report of the Secretary-General of 15 June 2011, prepared pursuant to the request of the Security Council in resolution 1976(2011);

92. *Notes* the continued efforts within the Contact Group on Piracy off the Coast of Somalia, following the adoption of Security Council resolution 1851(2008), including the establishment under the Contact Group of Working Group 5 on the financial aspects of Somali piracy to focus on and coordinate efforts to disrupt the pirate enterprise ashore, and commends contributions of all States in the efforts to fight piracy off the coast of Somalia;

93. *Recognizes* the primary role of the Transitional Federal Government of Somalia in combating piracy and armed robbery against ships, acknowledges the importance of a comprehensive and sustainable settlement of the situation in Somalia, and emphasizes the need to address the underlying causes of piracy and to assist Somalia and States in the region in strengthening institutional capacity to fight piracy, including the financing or facilitation of acts of piracy, and armed robbery against ships off the coast of Somalia and to bring to justice those involved in such acts;

94. *Notes* the approval by the International Maritime Organization of guidelines to assist in the investigation of the crimes of piracy and armed robbery against ships, revised interim guidance to shipowners, ship operators and shipmasters on the use of privately contracted armed security personnel on board ships in the high risk area, revised interim recommendations for flag States regarding the use of privately contracted armed security personnel on board ships in the high risk area and interim recommendations for port and coastal States regarding the use of privately contracted armed security personnel on board ships in the high risk area;

95. *Also notes* the issuance by the International Maritime Organization of Best Management Practices to Deter Piracy off the Coast of Somalia and in the Arabian Sea Area, developed by the industry, and notes the adoption on 20 May 2011 by the International Maritime Organization of the resolution on the implementation of best management practice guidance;

96. *Recalls* the adoption on 29 January 2009 of the Code of Conduct concerning the Repression of Piracy and Armed Robbery against Ships in the Western Indian Ocean and the Gulf of Aden (Djibouti Code of Conduct) under the auspices of the International Maritime Organization, the establishment of the International Maritime Organization Djibouti Code Trust Fund, a multi-donor trust fund initiated by Japan, and the ongoing activities for the implementation of the Code of Conduct;

97. *Urges* States to ensure the full implementation of resolution A.1026(26), adopted on 2 December 2009 by the Assembly of the International Maritime Organization, on acts of piracy and armed robbery against ships in waters off the coast of Somalia;

98. *Calls upon* States that have not yet done so to become parties to the Convention for the Suppression of Unlawful Acts against the Safety of Maritime Navigation and the Protocol for the Suppression of Unlawful Acts against the Safety of Fixed Platforms Located on the Continental Shelf, notes the entry into force on 28 July 2010 of the 2005 Protocol to the Convention for the Suppression of Unlawful Acts against the Safety of Maritime Navigation and of the 2005 Protocol to the 1988 Protocol for the Suppression of Unlawful Acts against the Safety of Fixed Platforms Located on the Continental Shelf, invites States that have not yet done so to consider becoming parties to those Protocols, and urges States parties to take appropriate measures to ensure the effective implementation of those instruments through the adoption of legislation, where appropriate;

99. *Calls upon* States to effectively implement the International Ship and Port Facility Security Code and the amendments to the International Convention for the Safety of Life at Sea, and to work with the International Maritime Organization to promote safe and secure shipping while ensuring freedom of navigation;

100. *Notes* the approval by the Maritime Safety Committee of the International Maritime Organization of the user guide to chapter XI-2 of the International Convention for the Safety of Life at Sea and to the International Ship and Port Facility Security Code;

101. *Urges* all States, in cooperation with the International Maritime Organization, to improve the protection of offshore installations by adopting measures related to the prevention, reporting and investigation of acts of violence against installations, in accordance with international law, and by implementing such measures through national legislation to ensure proper and adequate enforcement;

102. *Emphasizes* the progress in regional cooperation, including the efforts of littoral States, on the enhancement of safety, security and environmental protection in the Straits of Malacca and Singapore, and the effective functioning of the Cooperative Mechanism on safety of navigation and environmental protection to promote dialogue and facilitate close cooperation between the littoral States, user States, shipping industry and other stakeholders in line with article 43 of the Convention, notes with appreciation the convening of the fourth Cooperation Fo-

rum, in Malaysia on 10 and 11 October 2011, the fourth Project Coordination Committee Meeting, in Malaysia on 12 October 2011, and the seventh Aids to Navigation Fund Committee Meeting, in Malaysia on 17 and 18 October 2011, the three events being key pillars of the Cooperative Mechanism, notes with appreciation the important role of the Information Sharing Centre of the Regional Cooperation Agreement on Combating Piracy and Armed Robbery against Ships in Asia, based in Singapore, and calls upon States to give immediate attention to adopting, concluding and implementing cooperation agreements at the regional level;

103. *Recognizes* that some transnational organized criminal activities threaten legitimate uses of the oceans and endanger the lives of people at sea;

104. *Notes* that transnational organized criminal activities are diverse and may be interrelated in some cases and that criminal organizations are adaptive and take advantage of the vulnerabilities of States, in particular coastal and small island developing States in transit areas, and calls upon States and relevant intergovernmental organizations to increase cooperation and coordination at all levels to detect and suppress the smuggling of migrants and trafficking in persons, in accordance with international law;

105. *Recognizes* the importance of enhancing international cooperation at all levels to fight transnational organized criminal activities, including illicit traffic in narcotic drugs and psychotropic substances, within the scope of the United Nations instruments against illicit drug trafficking, as well as the smuggling of migrants and trafficking in persons and criminal activities at sea falling within the scope of the United Nations Convention against Transnational Organized Crime;

106. *Calls upon* States that have not yet done so to consider becoming parties to the Protocol against the Smuggling of Migrants by Land, Sea and Air, supplementing the United Nations Convention against Transnational Organized Crime, the Protocol against the Illicit Manufacturing of and Trafficking in Firearms, Their Parts and Components and Ammunition, supplementing the United Nations Convention against Transnational Organized Crime, and the Protocol to Prevent, Suppress and Punish Trafficking in Persons, Especially Women and Children, supplementing the United Nations Convention against Transnational Organized Crime, and to take appropriate measures to ensure their effective implementation;

107. *Calls upon* States to ensure freedom of navigation, the safety of navigation and the rights of transit passage, archipelagic sea lanes passage and innocent passage in accordance with international law, in particular the Convention;

108. *Welcomes* the work of the International Maritime Organization relating to the protection of shipping lanes of strategic importance and significance, and in particular in enhancing safety, security and environmental protection in straits used for international navigation, and calls upon the International Maritime Organization, States bordering straits and user States to continue their cooperation to keep such straits safe, secure and environmentally protected and open to international navigation at all times, consistent with international law, in particular the Convention;

109. *Calls upon* user States and States bordering straits used for international navigation to continue to cooperate by agreement on matters relating to navigational safety, including safety aids for navigation, and the prevention, reduction and control of pollution from ships, and welcomes developments in this regard;

110. *Calls upon* States that have accepted the amendments to regulation XI-1/6 of the International Convention for the Safety of Life at Sea, 1974, to implement the Code of International Standards and Recommended Practices for a Safety Investigation into a Marine Casualty or Marine Incident, which took effect on 1 January 2010;

111. *Calls upon* States that have not yet done so to consider becoming members of the International Hydrographic Organization, and urges all States to work with that Organization to increase the coverage of hydrographic information on a global basis to enhance capacity-building and technical assistance and to promote safe navigation, particularly through the production and use of accurate electronic navigational charts, especially in areas used for international navigation, in ports and where there are vulnerable or protected marine areas;

112. *Encourages* States to continue their efforts in the implementation of all areas of the Action Plan for the Safety of Transport of Radioactive Material, approved by the Board of Governors of the International Atomic Energy Agency in March 2004;

113. *Notes* that cessation of the transport of radioactive materials through the regions of small island developing States is an ultimate desired goal of small island developing States and some other countries, and recognizes the right of freedom of navigation in accordance with international law; that States should maintain dialogue and consultation, in particular under the auspices of the International Atomic Energy Agency and the International Maritime Organization, with the aim of improved mutual understanding, confidence-building and enhanced communication in relation to the safe maritime transport of radioactive materials; that States involved in the transport of such materials are urged to continue to engage in dialogue with small island developing States and other States to address their concerns; and that these concerns include the further development and strengthening, within the appropriate forums, of international regulatory regimes to enhance safety, disclosure, liability, security and compensation in relation to such transport;

114. *Acknowledges*, in the context of paragraph 113 above, the potential environmental and economic impacts of maritime incidents and accidents on coastal States, in particular those related to the transport of radioactive materials, and emphasizes the importance of effective liability regimes in that regard;

115. *Encourages* States to draw up plans and to establish procedures to implement the Guidelines on Places of Refuge for Ships in Need of Assistance adopted by the International Maritime Organization on 5 December 2003;

116. *Invites* States that have not yet done so to consider becoming parties to the Nairobi International Convention on the Removal of Wrecks, 2007;

117. *Requests* States to take appropriate measures with regard to ships flying their flag or of their registry to address hazards that may be caused by wrecks and drifting or sunken cargo to navigation or the marine environment;

118. *Calls upon* States to ensure that masters on ships flying their flag take the steps required by relevant instruments to provide assistance to persons in distress at sea, and urges States to cooperate and to take all necessary measures to ensure the effective implementation of the amendments to the International Convention on Maritime Search and Rescue and to the International Convention for the Safety of Life at Sea relating to the delivery of persons rescued at sea to a place of safety, as well as of the associated Guidelines on the Treatment of Persons Rescued at Sea;

119. *Recognizes* that all States must fulfil their search and rescue responsibilities and the ongoing need for the International Maritime Organization and other relevant organizations to assist, in particular, developing States both to increase their search and rescue capabilities, including through the establishment of additional rescue coordination centres and regional sub-centres, and to take effective action to address, to the extent feasible, the issue of unseaworthy ships and small craft within their national jurisdiction;

120. *Welcomes* the ongoing work of the International Maritime Organization in relation to disembarkation of persons rescued at sea, and notes in this regard the need to implement all relevant international instruments;

121. *Notes* the adoption by the International Maritime Organization on 2 December 2010 of revised guidelines on the prevention of access by stowaways and the allocation of responsibilities to seek the successful resolution of stowaway cases;

122. *Calls upon* States to continue to cooperate in developing comprehensive approaches to international migration and development, including through dialogue on all their aspects;

123. *Also calls upon* States to take measures to protect fibre-optic submarine cables and to fully address issues relating to these cables, in accordance with international law, as reflected in the Convention;

124. *Encourages* greater dialogue and cooperation among States and the relevant regional and global organizations through workshops and seminars on the protection and maintenance of fibre-optic submarine cables to promote the security of such critical communications infrastructure;

125. *Encourages* the adoption by States of laws and regulations addressing the breaking or injury of submarine cables or pipelines beneath the high seas done wilfully or through culpable negligence by a ship flying its flag or by a person subject to its jurisdiction, in accordance with international law, as reflected in the Convention;

126. *Affirms* the importance of maintenance, including the repair, of submarine cables, undertaken in conformity with international law, as reflected in the Convention;

127. *Reaffirms* that flag, port and coastal States all bear responsibility for ensuring the effective implementation and enforcement of international instruments relating to maritime security and safety, in accordance with international law, in particular the Convention, and that flag States have primary responsibility that requires further strengthening, including through increased transparency of ownership of vessels;

128. *Urges* flag States without an effective maritime administration and appropriate legal frameworks to establish or enhance the necessary infrastructure, legislative and enforcement capabilities to ensure effective compliance with, and implementation and enforcement of, their responsibilities under international law, in particular the Convention, and, until such action is taken, to consider declining the granting of the right to fly their flag to new vessels, suspending their registry or not opening a registry, and calls upon flag and port States to take all measures consistent with international law necessary to prevent the operation of substandard vessels;

129. *Recognizes* that international shipping rules and standards adopted by the International Maritime Organization in respect of maritime safety, efficiency of navigation and the prevention and control of marine pollution, complemented by best practices of the shipping industry, have led to a significant reduction in maritime accidents and pollution incidents, encourages all States to participate in the Voluntary International Maritime Organization Member State Audit Scheme, and notes the decision of the International Maritime Organization on a phased-in introduction of the Audit Scheme as an institutionalized process;

130. *Welcomes* the work of the International Maritime Organization to develop a mandatory code for ships operating in polar waters ("Polar Code"), and encourages States and competent international organizations and bodies to support continued efforts to finalize the Polar Code within the agreed framework, with an entry into force as soon as possible;

131. *Recognizes* that maritime safety can also be improved through effective port State control, the strengthening of regional arrangements and increased coordination and cooperation among them, and increased information-sharing, including among safety and security sectors;

132. *Encourages* flag States to take appropriate measures sufficient to achieve or maintain recognition by intergovernmental arrangements that recognize satisfactory flag State performance, including, as appropriate, satisfactory port State control examination results on a sustained basis, with a view to improving quality shipping and furthering flag State implementation of relevant instruments under the International Maritime Organization as well as relevant goals and objectives of the present resolution;

IX

Marine environment and marine resources

133. *Emphasizes once again* the importance of the implementation of Part XII of the Convention in order to protect and preserve the marine environment and its living marine resources against pollution and physical degradation, and calls upon all States to cooperate and take measures consistent with the Convention, directly or through competent international organizations, for the protection and preservation of the marine environment;

134. *Notes* the work of the Intergovernmental Panel on Climate Change, including its findings on the acidification of oceans, and in this regard encourages States and competent international organizations and other relevant institutions, individually and in cooperation, to urgently pursue further research on ocean acidification, especially programmes of observation and measurement, noting in particular paragraph 4 of decision IX/20 adopted at the ninth meeting of the Conference of the Parties to

the Convention on Biological Diversity, held in Bonn, Germany, from 19 to 30 May 2008, and the continued work of the Convention on Biological Diversity, and to increase national, regional and international efforts to address levels of ocean acidity and the negative impact of such acidity on vulnerable marine ecosystems, particularly coral reefs;

135. *Encourages* States, individually or in collaboration with relevant international organizations and bodies, to enhance their scientific activity to better understand the effects of climate change on the marine environment and marine biodiversity and develop ways and means of adaptation, taking into account, as appropriate, the precautionary approach and ecosystem approaches;

136. *Encourages* States that have not yet done so to become parties to international agreements addressing the protection and preservation of the marine environment and its living marine resources against the introduction of harmful aquatic organisms and pathogens and marine pollution from all sources, including the dumping of wastes and other matter, and other forms of physical degradation, as well as agreements that provide for preparedness for, response to and cooperation on pollution incidents and that include provisions on liability and compensation for damage resulting from marine pollution, and to adopt the necessary measures consistent with international law, including the Convention, aimed at implementing and enforcing the rules contained in those agreements;

137. *Encourages* States, directly or through competent international organizations, to consider the further development and application, as appropriate and consistent with international law, including the Convention, of environmental impact assessment processes covering planned activities under their jurisdiction or control that may cause substantial pollution of or significant and harmful changes to the marine environment, and also encourages the communication of the reports of the results of such assessments to the competent international organizations in accordance with the Convention;

138. *Encourages* States that have not done so to become parties to regional seas conventions addressing the protection and preservation of the marine environment;

139. *Encourages* States, in accordance with international law, including the Convention and other relevant instruments, either bilaterally or regionally, to jointly develop and promote contingency plans for responding to pollution incidents, as well as other incidents that are likely to have significant adverse effects on the marine environment and biodiversity;

140. *Recognizes* the importance of improving understanding of the impact of climate change on oceans and seas;

141. *Welcomes* the activities of the United Nations Environment Programme relating to marine debris carried out in cooperation with relevant United Nations bodies and organizations, notes the holding of the Fifth International Marine Debris Conference, organized by the United States of America and the United Nations Environment Programme, in Honolulu, United States of America, from 20 to 25 March 2011, and encourages States to further develop partnerships with industry and civil society to raise awareness of the extent of the impact of marine debris on the health and productivity of the marine environment and consequent economic loss;

142. *Urges* States to integrate the issue of marine debris into national strategies dealing with waste management in the coastal zone, ports and maritime industries, including recycling, reuse, reduction and disposal, and to encourage the development of appropriate economic incentives to address this issue, including the development of cost-recovery systems that provide an incentive to use port reception facilities and discourage ships from discharging marine debris at sea, and support for measures to prevent, reduce and control pollution from any source, including land-based sources, such as community-based coastal and waterway clean-up and monitoring activities, and encourages States to cooperate regionally and subregionally to identify potential sources and coastal and oceanic locations where marine debris aggregates, and to develop and implement joint prevention and recovery programmes for marine debris;

143. *Notes* the work of the International Maritime Organization to prevent pollution by garbage from ships, and welcomes the adoption of amendments to annex V to the International Convention for the Prevention of Pollution from Ships, 1973, as modified by the Protocol of 1978 relating thereto, on the prevention of pollution by garbage from ships;

144. *Welcomes* the entry into force on 1 August 2011 of amendments regarding special requirements for the use or carriage of oils in the Antarctic area to annex I to the International Convention for the Prevention of Pollution from Ships, 1973, as modified by the Protocol of 1978 relating thereto, on the prevention of pollution by oil from ships, which prohibit the carriage in bulk as cargo or carriage and use as fuel of heavy grade oils in the Antarctic area;

145. *Encourages* States that have not yet done so to become parties to the Protocol of 1997 (Annex VI-Regulations for the Prevention of Air Pollution from Ships) to the International Convention for the Prevention of Pollution from Ships, 1973, as modified by the Protocol of 1978 relating thereto, and the 1996 Protocol to the Convention on the Prevention of Marine Pollution by Dumping of Wastes and Other Matter, 1972 ("the London Protocol"), and furthermore to ratify or accede to the International Convention for the Control and Management of Ships' Ballast Water and Sediments, 2004, thereby facilitating its early entry into force;

146. *Notes* the ongoing work of the International Maritime Organization in accordance with its resolution on International Maritime Organization policies and practices related to the reduction of greenhouse gas emissions from ships;

147. *Urges* States to cooperate in correcting the shortfall in port waste reception facilities in accordance with the action plan to address the inadequacy of port waste reception facilities developed by the International Maritime Organization;

148. *Recognizes* that most of the pollution load of the oceans emanates from land-based activities and affects the most productive areas of the marine environment, and calls upon States as a matter of priority to implement the Global Programme of Action for the Protection of the Marine Environment from Land-based Activities and to take all appropriate measures to fulfil the commit-

ments of the international community embodied in the Beijing Declaration on Furthering the Implementation of the Global Programme of Action;

149. *Notes* that the third intergovernmental review of the Global Programme of Action for the Protection of the Marine Environment from Land-based Activities will be held in Manila on 25 and 26 January 2012;

150. *Expresses its concern* regarding the spreading of hypoxic dead zones in oceans as a result of eutrophication fuelled by riverine run-off of fertilizers, sewage outfall and reactive nitrogen resulting from the burning of fossil fuels and resulting in serious consequences for ecosystem functioning, and calls upon States to enhance their efforts to reduce eutrophication and, to this effect, to continue to cooperate within the framework of relevant international organizations, in particular the Global Programme of Action;

151. *Calls upon* all States to ensure that urban and coastal development projects and related land-reclamation activities are carried out in a responsible manner that protects the marine habitat and environment and mitigates the negative consequences of such activities;

152. *Notes* the second and third sessions of the Intergovernmental Negotiating Committee to prepare a global legally binding instrument on mercury, held in Chiba, Japan, from 24 to 28 January 2011 and Nairobi from 31 October to 4 November 2011, respectively, pursuant to the agreement of the twenty-fifth session of the United Nations Environment Programme Governing Council/Global Ministerial Environment Forum;

153. *Welcomes* the continued work of States, the United Nations Environment Programme and regional organizations in the implementation of the Global Programme of Action, and encourages increased emphasis on the link between fresh water, the coastal zone and marine resources in the implementation of international development goals, including those contained in the United Nations Millennium Declaration, and of the time-bound targets in the Plan of Implementation of the World Summit on Sustainable Development ("Johannesburg Plan of Implementation"), in particular the target on sanitation, and the Monterrey Consensus of the International Conference on Financing for Development;

154. *Recalls* the resolution of the thirtieth Consultative Meeting of Contracting Parties to the Convention on the Prevention of Marine Pollution by Dumping of Wastes and Other Matter, 1972 ("the London Convention") and the third Meeting of Contracting Parties to the London Protocol, held from 27 to 31 October 2008, on the regulation of ocean fertilization, in which the Contracting Parties agreed, inter alia, that the scope of the London Convention and Protocol includes ocean fertilization activities and that, given the present state of knowledge, ocean fertilization activities other than for legitimate scientific research should not be allowed, and that scientific research proposals should be assessed on a case-by-case basis using an assessment framework to be developed by the scientific groups under the London Convention and Protocol, and also agreed that, to this end, such other activities should be considered as contrary to the aims of the London Convention and Protocol and should not currently qualify for any exemption from the definition of dumping in article III, paragraph 1 (*b*), of the London Convention and article 1, paragraph 4.2, of the London Protocol;

155. *Also recalls* the resolution of the thirty-second Consultative Meeting of Contracting Parties to the London Convention and the fifth Meeting of Contracting Parties to the London Protocol, held from 11 to 15 October 2010, on the Assessment Framework for Scientific Research Involving Ocean Fertilization;

156. *Further recalls* decision IX/16 C adopted at the ninth meeting of the Conference of the Parties to the Convention on Biological Diversity, in which the Conference of the Parties, inter alia, bearing in mind the ongoing scientific and legal analysis occurring under the auspices of the London Convention and Protocol requested parties and urged other Governments, in accordance with the precautionary approach, to ensure that ocean fertilization activities were not carried out until there was an adequate scientific basis on which to justify such activities, including an assessment of associated risks, and that a global, transparent and effective control and regulatory mechanism was in place for those activities, with the exception of small-scale scientific research studies within coastal waters, and stated that such studies should be authorized only if justified by the need to gather specific scientific data, should be subject to a thorough prior assessment of the potential impacts of the research studies on the marine environment, should be strictly controlled and should not be used for generating and selling carbon offsets or for any other commercial purposes, and notes decision X/29, adopted at the tenth meeting of the Conference of the Parties to the Convention on Biological Diversity, held in Nagoya, Japan, from 18 to 29 October 2010, in which the Conference of the Parties requested parties to implement decision IX/16 C;

157. *Reaffirms* paragraph 119 of resolution 61/222 of 20 December 2006 regarding ecosystem approaches and oceans, including the proposed elements of an ecosystem approach, means to achieve implementation of an ecosystem approach and requirements for improved application of an ecosystem approach, and in this regard:

(*a*) Notes that continued environmental degradation in many parts of the world and increasing competing demands require an urgent response and the setting of priorities for management actions aimed at conserving ecosystem integrity;

(*b*) Notes that ecosystem approaches to ocean management should be focused on managing human activities in order to maintain and, where needed, restore ecosystem health to sustain goods and environmental services, provide social and economic benefits for food security, sustain livelihoods in support of international development goals, including those contained in the Millennium Declaration, and conserve marine biodiversity;

(*c*) Recalls that States should be guided in the application of ecosystem approaches by a number of existing instruments, in particular the Convention, which sets out the legal framework for all activities in the oceans and seas, and its implementing Agreements, as well as other commitments, such as those contained in the Convention on Biological Diversity and the World Summit on Sustainable Development call for the application of an ecosystem approach by 2010, and in this context encourages States to enhance their efforts towards applying such an approach;

(*d*) Encourages States to cooperate and coordinate their efforts and take, individually or jointly, as appropriate, all measures, in conformity with international law, including the Convention and other applicable instruments, to address impacts on marine ecosystems within and beyond areas of national jurisdiction, taking into account the integrity of the ecosystems concerned;

158. *Encourages* competent organizations and bodies that have not yet done so to incorporate an ecosystem approach into their mandates, as appropriate, in order to address impacts on marine ecosystems;

159. *Invites* States, in particular those States with advanced technology and marine capabilities, to explore prospects for improving cooperation with, and assistance to, developing States, in particular least developed countries and small island developing States, as well as coastal African States, with a view to better integrating into national policies and programmes sustainable and effective development in the marine sector;

160. *Encourages* the competent international organizations, the United Nations Development Programme, the World Bank and other funding agencies to consider expanding their programmes within their respective fields of competence for assistance to developing countries and to coordinate their efforts, including in the allocation and application of Global Environment Facility funding;

161. *Notes* the information compiled by the Secretariat in relation to the assistance available to and measures that may be taken by developing States, in particular the least developed countries and small island developing States, as well as coastal African States, to realize the benefits of sustainable and effective development of marine resources and uses of the oceans, as provided by States and competent international organizations and global and regional funding agencies, and urges them to provide information for the annual report of the Secretary-General and for incorporation on the website of the Division;

162. *Encourages* States that have not yet done so to consider ratifying or acceding to the Hong Kong International Convention for the Safe and Environmentally Sound Recycling of Ships, 2009, to facilitate its early entry into force;

163. *Takes note* of the role of the Basel Convention in protecting the marine environment against the adverse effects which may result from such wastes;

164. *Notes with concern* the potential for serious environmental consequences resulting from oil spill incidents, urges States, consistent with international law, to cooperate, directly or through competent international organizations, and share best practices, in the fields of protection of the marine environment, human health and safety, prevention, emergency response and mitigation, and encourages the undertaking of scientific research, including marine scientific research, to better understand the consequences of marine oil spills;

X

Marine biodiversity

165. *Reaffirms* its central role relating to the conservation and sustainable use of marine biological diversity beyond areas of national jurisdiction, notes the work of States and relevant intergovernmental organizations and bodies on those issues, and invites them to contribute to its consideration of these issues within the areas of their respective competence;

166. *Welcomes* the meeting of the Ad Hoc Open-ended Informal Working Group, convened in New York from 31 May to 3 June 2011 in accordance with paragraph 163 of resolution 65/37 A, and endorses its recommendations;

167. *Decides*, accordingly, to initiate within the Ad Hoc Open-ended Informal Working Group the process provided for in paragraph 1 (*a*) of the recommendations of the Working Group, that the process will address the issues identified in paragraph 1 (*b*) of the recommendations and in the fashion described in that paragraph, and that the process will take place: (i) in the Ad Hoc Open-ended Informal Working Group; and (ii) in the format of intersessional workshops as described in paragraph 1 (*c*) of the recommendations;

168. *Requests* the Secretary-General, consequently, noting paragraph 73 of resolution 59/24 of 17 November 2004, to convene meetings of the Ad Hoc Open-ended Informal Working Group in accordance with paragraph 167 of the present resolution and paragraphs 79 and 80 of resolution 60/30 of 29 November 2005, and in this regard to convene, with full conference services, a meeting of the Ad Hoc Open-ended Informal Working Group, to take place from 7 to 11 May 2012, to provide recommendations to the General Assembly at its sixty-seventh session, and requests the Secretary-General to make every effort to meet the requirement for full conference services within existing resources;

169. *Recognizes* the abundance and diversity of marine genetic resources and their value in terms of the benefits, goods and services they can provide;

170. *Also recognizes* the importance of research on marine genetic resources for the purpose of enhancing the scientific understanding, potential use and application, and enhanced management of marine ecosystems;

171. *Encourages* States and international organizations, including through bilateral, regional and global cooperation programmes and partnerships, to continue in a sustainable and comprehensive way to support, promote and strengthen capacity-building activities, in particular in developing countries, in the field of marine scientific research, taking into account, in particular, the need to create greater taxonomic capabilities;

172. *Notes* the work under the Jakarta Mandate on Marine and Coastal Biological Diversity and the Convention on Biological Diversity elaborated programme of work on marine and coastal biological diversity, and, while reiterating the central role of the General Assembly relating to the conservation and sustainable use of marine biological diversity beyond areas of national jurisdiction, notes the work done by the Conference of the Parties to the Convention on Biological Diversity;

173. *Reaffirms* the need for States, individually or through competent international organizations, to urgently consider ways to integrate and improve, based on the best available scientific information and the precautionary approach and in accordance with the Convention and related agreements and instruments, the management of risks to the marine biodiversity of seamounts, cold water corals, hydrothermal vents and certain other underwater features;

174. *Calls upon* States and international organizations to urgently take further action to address, in accordance with international law, destructive practices that have adverse

impacts on marine biodiversity and ecosystems, including seamounts, hydrothermal vents and cold water corals;

175. *Calls upon* States to strengthen, in a manner consistent with international law, in particular the Convention, the conservation and management of marine biodiversity and ecosystems and national policies in relation to marine protected areas;

176. *Reaffirms* the need for States to continue and intensify their efforts, directly and through competent international organizations, to develop and facilitate the use of diverse approaches and tools for conserving and managing vulnerable marine ecosystems, including the possible establishment of marine protected areas, consistent with international law, as reflected in the Convention, and based on the best scientific information available, and the development of representative networks of any such marine protected areas by 2012;

177. *Notes* the work of States, relevant intergovernmental organizations and bodies, including the Convention on Biological Diversity, in the assessment of scientific information on and compilation of ecological criteria for the identification of marine areas that require protection, in light of the objective of the World Summit on Sustainable Development to develop and facilitate the use of diverse approaches and tools, such as ecosystem approaches and the establishment of marine protected areas consistent with international law, as reflected in the Convention, and based on scientific information, including representative networks, by 2012;

178. *Encourages* States to further progress towards the 2012 target for the establishment of marine protected areas, including representative networks, and calls upon States to further consider options to identify and protect ecologically or biologically significant areas, consistent with international law and on the basis of the best available scientific information;

179. *Recalls* that the Conference of the Parties to the Convention on Biological Diversity, at its ninth meeting, adopted scientific criteria for identifying ecologically or biologically significant marine areas in need of protection in open-ocean waters and deep-sea habitats and scientific guidance for selecting areas to establish a representative network of marine protected areas, including in open-ocean waters and deep-sea habitats, and further recalls that the Food and Agriculture Organization of the United Nations has developed guidance for the identification of vulnerable marine ecosystems through the International Guidelines for the Management of Deep-sea Fisheries in the High Seas;

180. *Acknowledges* the Micronesia Challenge, the Eastern Tropical Pacific Seascape project, the Caribbean Challenge and the Coral Triangle Initiative, which in particular seek to create and link domestic marine protected areas to better facilitate ecosystem approaches, and reaffirms the need for further international cooperation, coordination and collaboration in support of such initiatives;

181. *Reiterates its support* for the International Coral Reef Initiative, takes note of the International Coral Reef Initiative General Meeting, held in Saint-Denis, Réunion, from 12 to 15 December 2011, and supports the work under the Jakarta Mandate on Marine and Coastal Biological Diversity and the elaborated programme of work on marine and coastal biological diversity related to coral reefs;

182. *Encourages* States and relevant international institutions to improve efforts to address coral bleaching by, inter alia, improving monitoring to predict and identify bleaching events, supporting and strengthening action taken during such events and improving strategies to manage reefs to support their natural resilience and enhance their ability to withstand other pressures, including ocean acidification;

183. *Encourages* States to cooperate, directly or through competent international bodies, in exchanging information in the event of accidents involving vessels on coral reefs and in promoting the development of economic assessment techniques for both restoration and non-use values of coral reef systems;

184. *Emphasizes* the need to mainstream sustainable coral reef management and integrated watershed management into national development strategies, as well as into the activities of relevant United Nations agencies and programmes, international financial institutions and the donor community;

185. *Notes* that ocean noise is a potential threat to living marine resources, affirms the importance of sound scientific studies in addressing this matter, encourages further research, studies and consideration of the impacts of ocean noise on living marine resources, and requests the Division to continue to compile the peer-reviewed scientific studies it receives from Member States and intergovernmental organizations pursuant to paragraph 107 of resolution 61/222 and, as appropriate, to make them, or references and links to them, available on its website;

XI

Marine science

186. *Calls upon* States, individually or in collaboration with each other or with competent international organizations and bodies, to continue to strive to improve understanding and knowledge of the oceans and the deep sea, including, in particular, the extent and vulnerability of deep sea biodiversity and ecosystems, by increasing their marine scientific research activities in accordance with the Convention;

187. *Encourages*, in that regard, relevant international organizations and other donors to consider supporting the Endowment Fund of the International Seabed Authority in order to promote the conduct of collaborative marine scientific research in the international seabed area by supporting the participation of qualified scientists and technical personnel from developing countries in relevant programmes, initiatives and activities;

188. *Invites* all relevant organizations, funds, programmes and bodies within the United Nations system, in consultation with interested States, to coordinate relevant activities with regional and national marine scientific and technological centres in small island developing States, as appropriate, to ensure the more effective achievement of their objectives in accordance with relevant United Nations small island developing States development programmes and strategies;

189. *Takes note with appreciation* of the work of the Intergovernmental Oceanographic Commission, with the advice of the Advisory Body of Experts on the Law of the Sea, on the development of procedures for the implemen-

tation of Parts XIII and XIV of the Convention, and also takes note of the ongoing review of the Advisory Body of Experts by an open-ended working group with representatives from member States;

190. *Notes with appreciation* the work of the Advisory Body of Experts, including its work in cooperation with the Division, on the practice of member States related to marine scientific research and transfer of marine technology within the framework of the Convention;

191. *Also notes with appreciation* the issuance of the revised publication entitled *Marine Scientific Research: A guide to the implementation of the relevant provisions of the United Nations Convention on the Law of the Sea* in December 2010, and requests the Secretariat to make efforts to publish the guide in all official languages of the United Nations;

192. *Notes* the contribution of the Census of Marine Life to marine biodiversity research, including through its report entitled "First Census of Marine Life 2010: Highlights of a Decade of Discovery";

193. *Stresses* the importance of increasing the scientific understanding of the oceans-atmosphere interface, including through participation in ocean observing programmes and geographic information systems, such as the Global Ocean Observing System, sponsored by the Intergovernmental Oceanographic Commission, the United Nations Environment Programme, the World Meteorological Organization and the International Council for Science, particularly considering their role in monitoring and forecasting climate change and variability and in the establishment and operation of tsunami warning systems;

194. *Takes note with appreciation* of the progress made by the Intergovernmental Oceanographic Commission and Member States towards the establishment of regional and national tsunami warning and mitigation systems, welcomes the continued collaboration of the United Nations and other intergovernmental organizations in this effort, and encourages Member States to establish and sustain their national warning and mitigation systems, within a global, ocean-related multi-hazard approach, as necessary, to reduce loss of life and damage to national economies and strengthen the resilience of coastal communities to natural disasters;

195. *Stresses* the need for continued efforts in developing mitigation and preparedness measures for natural disasters, particularly following tsunami events caused by earthquakes, such as the 11 March 2011 event in Japan;

196. *Notes* the 2011 report of the Intergovernmental Oceanographic Commission and the World Meteorological Organization, entitled "Ocean data buoy vandalism—incidence, impact and responses";

197. *Urges* States to take necessary action and to cooperate in relevant organizations, including the Food and Agriculture Organization of the United Nations, the Intergovernmental Oceanographic Commission and the World Meteorological Organization, to address damage to ocean data buoys deployed and operated in accordance with international law, including through education and outreach about the importance and purpose of these buoys, and by strengthening these buoys against such damage, and increasing reporting of such damage;

XII

Regular Process for Global Reporting and Assessment of the State of the Marine Environment, including Socioeconomic Aspects

198. *Reiterates* the need to strengthen the regular scientific assessment of the state of the marine environment in order to enhance the scientific basis for policymaking;

199. *Welcomes* the meetings of the Ad Hoc Working Group of the Whole on the Regular Process for Global Reporting and Assessment of the State of the Marine Environment, including Socioeconomic Aspects, convened in New York from 14 to 18 February 2011 in accordance with paragraph 203 of resolution 65/37 A and on 27 and 28 June 2011 in accordance with paragraph 7 of resolution 65/37 B;

200. *Endorses* the recommendations adopted by the Ad Hoc Working Group of the Whole at its second meeting;

201. *Reaffirms* the principles guiding the Regular Process and the objective and scope of its first cycle (2010–2014) as agreed upon at the first meeting of the Ad Hoc Working Group of the Whole in 2009;

202. *Adopts* the criteria for the appointment of experts and the guidelines for workshops to assist the Regular Process;

203. *Takes note* of the draft terms of reference and working methods for the Group of Experts of the Ad Hoc Working Group of the Whole on the Regular Process for Global Reporting and Assessment of the State of the Marine Environment, including Socioeconomic Aspects, the report on communication requirements and data and information management for the Regular Process and the report on the preliminary inventory of capacity-building for assessments and types of experts for workshops;

204. *Requests* the Secretary-General to bring the preliminary inventory of capacity-building for assessments to the attention of Member States, heads of the specialized agencies, funds and programmes of the United Nations and other relevant intergovernmental organizations engaged in activities relating to capacity-building for assessment of the state of the marine environment, including socioeconomic aspects, as well as funding institutions, and invite their contribution to the preliminary inventory on existing opportunities and arrangements for capacity-building for assessments;

205. *Welcomes* the establishment by the Ad Hoc Working Group of the Whole of the Bureau to put into practice the decisions and guidance of the Ad Hoc Working Group of the Whole during the intersessional period, such as approving the assignments of members of the pool of experts to work on drafting or to review drafts, and approving arrangements proposed by the Group of Experts for peer review;

206. *Decides* that the Bureau shall be composed of fifteen Member States (three Member States from each regional group) and that at least one co-chair and a quorum of five Member States, one per regional group, shall be considered as the minimum requirement for the Bureau to perform its functions;

207. *Recommends* that workshops be organized at the earliest possible opportunity in order to inform the first cycle of the Regular Process and welcomes the first of those workshops, held in Santiago from 13 to 15 September 2011,

takes note of its report and invites other States to host such workshops, and in this regard notes with appreciation the offer made by China to host a workshop for the Eastern and South-Eastern Asian Seas, which is planned for the end of February 2012, and the offer made by Belgium to host a workshop for the North Atlantic, the Baltic Sea, the Mediterranean Sea and the Black Sea in March 2012;

208. *Requests* the Secretary-General to convene the third meeting of the Ad Hoc Working Group of the Whole from 23 to 27 April 2012 with a view to enabling the first cycle of the first global integrated assessment to proceed, and to provide recommendations to the General Assembly at its sixty-seventh session;

209. *Takes note* of the ongoing work of States aimed at the finalization of the possible outline for the first global integrated assessment of the state of the marine environment, including socioeconomic aspects, which would be further considered by the Ad Hoc Working Group of the Whole at its next meeting;

210. *Recalls* that the Regular Process, as established under the United Nations, is accountable to the General Assembly and is an intergovernmental process guided by international law, including the Convention and other applicable international instruments, and takes into account relevant Assembly resolutions;

211. *Emphasizes* that the first cycle of the Regular Process has begun and that the deadline for the first integrated assessment is 2014;

212. *Notes* that the first phase of the first cycle of the Regular Process (2010–2012) will provide for the preparation of key questions to be answered by the first integrated assessment, at all regional levels, to ensure an effective science-policy relationship and the participation of all relevant stakeholders, in particular local experts, in defining specific objectives and scope of the assessments;

213. *Invites* the Intergovernmental Oceanographic Commission, the United Nations Environment Programme, the International Maritime Organization and the Food and Agriculture Organization of the United Nations, and other competent United Nations specialized agencies, as appropriate, to continue to provide technical and scientific support to the Regular Process;

214. *Requests* the secretariat of the Regular Process to convene at least one meeting of the Group of Experts, as appropriate and subject to the availability of resources, prior to the next meeting of the Ad Hoc Working Group of the Whole;

215. *Notes with appreciation* the support provided by the Division to the Regular Process, and notes also with appreciation the technical and logistical support of the United Nations Environment Programme and the Intergovernmental Oceanographic Commission;

216. *Requests* the Secretary-General to promptly take appropriate measures, by mobilizing all available extrabudgetary and existing resources, including through the redeployment of staff, to further strengthen the capacity of the Division, in particular its human resources, serving as the secretariat of the Regular Process, including in the context of the programme budget for the current biennium and the proposed programme budget for the biennium 2012–2013;

217. *Notes with appreciation* the contributions made to the voluntary trust fund for the purpose of supporting the operations of the first five-year cycle of the Regular Process, expresses its serious concern regarding the limited resources available in the trust fund, and urges Member States, international financial institutions, donor agencies, intergovernmental organizations, non-governmental organizations and natural and juridical persons to make financial contributions to those funds established pursuant to paragraph 183 of resolution 64/71 and to make other contributions to the Regular Process;

XIII
Regional cooperation

218. *Notes* that there have been a number of initiatives at the regional level, in various regions, to further the implementation of the Convention, takes note in that context of the Caribbean-focused Assistance Fund, which is intended to facilitate, mainly through technical assistance, the voluntary undertaking of maritime delimitation negotiations between Caribbean States, takes note once again of the Fund for Peace: Peaceful Settlement of Territorial Disputes, established by the General Assembly of the Organization of American States in 2000 as a primary mechanism, given its broader regional scope, for the prevention and resolution of pending territorial, land border and maritime boundary disputes, and calls upon States and others in a position to do so to contribute to these funds;

219. *Notes with appreciation* efforts at the regional level to further the implementation of the Convention and respond, including through capacity-building, to issues related to maritime safety and security, the conservation and sustainable use of living marine resources, the protection and preservation of the marine environment and the conservation and sustainable use of marine biodiversity;

220. *Invites* States and international organizations to enhance their cooperation to better protect the marine environment, and in this respect welcomes the memorandum of understanding for enhanced cooperation, concluded between the Commission for the Protection of the Marine Environment of the North-East Atlantic, the North East Atlantic Fisheries Commission, the International Seabed Authority and the International Maritime Organization;

221. *Recognizes* the results of the International Polar Year, 2007–2008, with particular emphasis on new knowledge about the linkages between environmental change in the polar regions and global climate systems, encourages States and scientific communities to strengthen their cooperation in this respect, and notes the International Polar Year "From Knowledge to Action" Conference to be held in Montreal, Canada, from 22 to 27 April 2012;

222. *Welcomes* regional cooperation, and in this regard notes the Pacific Oceanscape Framework as an initiative to enhance cooperation among coastal States in the Pacific island region to foster marine conservation and sustainable development;

223. *Notes with appreciation* the various cooperative efforts displayed by States at the regional and subregional levels, and in this regard welcomes initiatives such as the Integrated Assessment and Management of the Gulf of Mexico Large Marine Ecosystem;

224. *Notes* the twenty-fifth anniversary of the Zone of Peace and Cooperation of the South Atlantic;

XIV

Open-ended Informal Consultative Process on Oceans and the Law of the Sea

225. *Welcomes* the report on the work of the Informal Consultative Process at its twelfth meeting, which focused on contributing to the assessment, in the context of the United Nations Conference on Sustainable Development, of progress to date and the remaining gaps in the implementation of the outcomes of the major summits on sustainable development and addressing new and emerging challenges;

226. *Recognizes* the role of the Informal Consultative Process as a unique forum for comprehensive discussions on issues related to oceans and the law of the sea, consistent with the framework provided by the Convention and chapter 17 of Agenda 21, and that the perspective of the three pillars of sustainable development should be further enhanced in the examination of the selected topics;

227. *Welcomes* the work of the Informal Consultative Process and its contribution to improving coordination and cooperation between States and strengthening the annual debate of the General Assembly on oceans and the law of the sea by effectively drawing attention to key issues and current trends, emphasizes the timeliness of this year's topic, and in this regard encourages States to consider the 2012 United Nations Conference on Sustainable Development as an opportunity to consider measures to implement internationally agreed goals and commitments relating to the conservation and sustainable use of the marine environment and its resources;

228. *Also welcomes* efforts to improve and focus the work of the Informal Consultative Process, and in that respect recognizes the primary role of the Informal Consultative Process in integrating knowledge, the exchange of opinions among multiple stakeholders and coordination among competent agencies, and enhancing awareness of topics, including emerging issues, while promoting the three pillars of sustainable development, and recommends that the Informal Consultative Process devise a transparent, objective and inclusive process for the selection of topics and panellists so as to facilitate the work of the General Assembly during informal consultations concerning the annual resolution on oceans and the law of the sea;

229. *Recalls* the need to strengthen and improve the efficiency of the Informal Consultative Process, and encourages States, intergovernmental organizations and programmes to provide guidance to the Co-Chairs to this effect, particularly before and during the preparatory meeting for the Informal Consultative Process;

230. *Also recalls* that a further review of the effectiveness and utility of the Informal Consultative Process will be undertaken by the General Assembly at its sixty-seventh session;

231. *Requests* the Secretary-General to convene, in accordance with paragraphs 2 and 3 of resolution 54/33, the thirteenth meeting of the Informal Consultative Process, in New York from 29 May to 1 June 2012, to provide it with the necessary facilities for the performance of its work and to arrange for support to be provided by the Division, in cooperation with other relevant parts of the Secretariat, as appropriate;

232. *Expresses its continued serious concern* regarding the lack of resources available in the voluntary trust fund established by resolution 55/7 for the purpose of assisting developing countries, in particular least developed countries, small island developing States and landlocked developing States, in attending the meetings of the Informal Consultative Process, and urges States to make additional contributions to the trust fund;

233. *Decides* that those representatives from developing countries who are invited by the Co-Chairs, in consultation with Governments, to make presentations during the meetings of the Informal Consultative Process shall receive priority consideration in the disbursement of funds from the voluntary trust fund established by resolution 55/7 in order to cover the costs of their travel, and shall also be eligible to receive daily subsistence allowance subject to the availability of funds after the travel costs of all other eligible representatives from those countries mentioned in paragraph 232 above have been covered;

234. *Recalls* its decision in resolution 65/37 A that, in its deliberations on the report of the Secretary-General on oceans and the law of the sea, the Informal Consultative Process will focus its discussions at its thirteenth meeting on marine renewable energies;

XV

Coordination and cooperation

235. *Encourages* States to work closely with and through international organizations, funds and programmes, as well as the specialized agencies of the United Nations system and relevant international conventions, to identify emerging areas of focus for improved coordination and cooperation and how best to address these issues;

236. *Encourages* bodies established by the Convention to strengthen coordination and cooperation, as appropriate, in fulfilling their respective mandates;

237. *Requests* the Secretary-General to bring the present resolution to the attention of heads of intergovernmental organizations, the specialized agencies, funds and programmes of the United Nations engaged in activities relating to ocean affairs and the law of the sea, as well as funding institutions, and underlines the importance of their constructive and timely input for the report of the Secretary-General on oceans and the law of the sea and of their participation in relevant meetings and processes;

238. *Welcomes* the work done by the secretariats of relevant United Nations specialized agencies, programmes, funds and bodies and the secretariats of related organizations and conventions to enhance inter-agency coordination and cooperation on ocean issues, including through UN-Oceans, the inter-agency coordination mechanism on ocean and coastal issues within the United Nations system;

239. *Invites* the Joint Inspection Unit to review UN-Oceans and to submit a report thereon to the General Assembly for its consideration, and requests UN-Oceans to submit to the Assembly draft terms of reference for its work, to be considered by the Assembly at its sixty-seventh session with a view to reviewing the mandate of UN-Oceans and enhancing transparency and reporting of its activities to Member States;

240. *Encourages* continued updates to Member States by UN-Oceans regarding its priorities and initiatives, in particular with respect to the proposed participation in UN-Oceans;

XVI

Activities of the Division for Ocean Affairs and the Law of the Sea

241. *Expresses its appreciation* to the Secretary-General for the annual comprehensive report on oceans and the law of the sea, prepared by the Division, as well as for the other activities of the Division, which reflect the high standard of assistance provided to Member States by the Division;

242. *Notes with satisfaction* the third observance by the United Nations of World Oceans Day on 8 June 2011, recognizes with appreciation the efforts deployed by the Division in organizing its celebration, and invites the Division to continue to promote and facilitate international cooperation on the law of the sea and ocean affairs in the context of the future observance of World Oceans Day, as well as through its participation in other events such as the World Expo to be held in Yeosu, Republic of Korea, in 2012;

243. *Requests* the Secretary-General to continue to carry out the responsibilities and functions entrusted to him in the Convention and by the related resolutions of the General Assembly, including resolutions 49/28 and 52/26, and to ensure the allocation of appropriate resources to the Division for the performance of its activities under the approved budget for the Organization;

244. *Also requests* the Secretary-General to continue the publication activities of the Division, in particular through the publication of *The Law of the Sea: A Select Bibliography* and the *Law of the Sea Bulletin*;

XVII

Commemoration of the thirtieth anniversary of the opening for signature of the Convention

245. *Decides* to devote two days of plenary meetings at its sixty-seventh session, on 10 and 11 December 2012, to the consideration of the item entitled "Oceans and the law of the sea" and the commemoration of the thirtieth anniversary of the opening for signature of the Convention, including special recognition of the crucial role played by Ambassador Arvid Pardo of Malta and, in particular, his visionary speech delivered on 1 November 1967 before the General Assembly, leading to the adoption of the Convention, and encourages Member States and observers to be represented at the highest possible level;

246. *Invites* States Parties to the Convention to commemorate at their twenty-second meeting the thirtieth anniversary of the opening for signature of the Convention;

247. *Welcomes* the decision of the Assembly of the International Seabed Authority to convene a special meeting during its eighteenth session to commemorate the thirtieth anniversary of the opening for signature of the Convention;

248. *Requests* the Secretary-General to organize, as appropriate, activities to mark this occasion, and invites States, United Nations agencies, funds and programmes, intergovernmental and non-governmental organizations and other relevant bodies, in accordance with the practices of the United Nations, to support these activities, as appropriate;

XVIII

Sixty-seventh session of the General Assembly

249. *Requests* the Secretary-General to prepare a report for consideration by the General Assembly at its sixty-seventh session on developments and issues relating to ocean affairs and the law of the sea, including the implementation of the present resolution, in accordance with resolutions 49/28, 52/26 and 54/33, and to make the section of the report related to the topic that is the focus of the thirteenth meeting of the Informal Consultative Process available at least six weeks in advance of the meeting of the Informal Consultative Process;

250. *Emphasizes* the critical role of the annual report of the Secretary-General, which integrates information on developments relating to the implementation of the Convention and the work of the Organization, its specialized agencies and other institutions in the field of ocean affairs and the law of the sea at the global and regional levels, and as a result constitutes the basis for the annual consideration and review of developments relating to ocean affairs and the law of the sea by the General Assembly as the global institution having the competence to undertake such a review;

251. *Notes* that the report referred to in paragraph 249 above will also be submitted to States Parties pursuant to article 319 of the Convention regarding issues of a general nature that have arisen with respect to the Convention;

252. *Also notes* the desire to further improve the efficiency of and effective participation of delegations in the informal consultations concerning the annual General Assembly resolution on oceans and the law of the sea, decides that the period of the informal consultations on that resolution should not exceed a maximum of two weeks in total and that the consultations should be scheduled in such a way that the Division has sufficient time to produce the report referred to in paragraph 249 above, and invites States to submit text proposals for inclusion in the resolution to the Coordinator of the informal consultations at the earliest possible date;

253. *Decides* to include in the provisional agenda of its sixty-seventh session the item entitled "Oceans and the law of the sea".

ANNEX

Recommendations of the Ad Hoc Open-ended Informal Working Group to study issues relating to the conservation and sustainable use of marine biological diversity beyond areas of national jurisdiction

The Ad Hoc Open-ended Informal Working Group, having met from 31 May to 3 June 2011 in accordance with paragraph 163 of General Assembly resolution 65/37 A of 7 December 2010, recommends that:

(*a*) A process be initiated, by the General Assembly, with a view to ensuring that the legal framework for the conservation and sustainable use of marine biodiversity in areas beyond national jurisdiction effectively addresses those issues by identifying gaps and ways forward, including through the implementation of existing instruments and the possible development of a multilateral agreement under the United Nations Convention on the Law of the Sea;

(*b*) This process address the conservation and sustainable use of marine biodiversity in areas beyond national jurisdiction, in particular, together and as a whole, marine genetic resources, including questions on the sharing of benefits, measures such as area-based management tools, including marine protected areas, and environmental impact assessments, capacity-building and the transfer of marine technology;

(c) This process take place: (i) in the existing Working Group; and (ii) in the format of intersessional workshops aimed at improving understanding of the issues and clarifying key questions as an input to the work of the Working Group;

(d) The mandate of the Working Group be reviewed and, as appropriate, amended, with a view to undertaking the tasks entrusted by the present recommendations;

(e) The Secretary-General be requested to convene a meeting of the Working Group in 2012 to make progress on all issues under examination within the Working Group and to provide recommendations to the General Assembly at its sixty-seventh session.

RECORDED VOTE ON RESOLUTION 66/231:

In favour: Afghanistan, Albania, Algeria, Andorra, Antigua and Barbuda, Argentina, Armenia, Australia, Austria, Bahamas, Bahrain, Bangladesh, Barbados, Belarus, Belgium, Benin, Bosnia and Herzegovina, Botswana, Brazil, Brunei Darussalam, Bulgaria, Burkina Faso, Cameroon, Canada, Chile, China, Colombia, Comoros, Congo, Costa Rica, Côte d'Ivoire, Croatia, Cuba, Cyprus, Czech Republic, Denmark, Djibouti, Egypt, Estonia, Fiji, Finland, France, Germany, Ghana, Greece, Grenada, Guatemala, Honduras, Hungary, Iceland, India, Indonesia, Iraq, Ireland, Italy, Jamaica, Japan, Jordan, Kazakhstan, Kenya, Kuwait, Kyrgyzstan, Lao People's Democratic Republic, Latvia, Lebanon, Liberia, Libya, Liechtenstein, Lithuania, Luxembourg, Madagascar, Malaysia, Maldives, Mali, Malta, Marshall Islands, Mauritius, Mexico, Micronesia, Monaco, Mongolia, Montenegro, Morocco, Myanmar, Namibia, Nepal, Netherlands, New Zealand, Nicaragua, Nigeria, Norway, Oman, Pakistan, Palau, Panama, Peru, Philippines, Poland, Portugal, Qatar, Republic of Korea, Republic of Moldova, Romania, Russian Federation, Saint Vincent and the Grenadines, Samoa, San Marino, Saudi Arabia, Serbia, Sierra Leone, Singapore, Slovakia, Slovenia, Solomon Islands, South Africa, Spain, Sri Lanka, Sudan, Sweden, Switzerland, Thailand, the former Yugoslav Republic of Macedonia, Tonga, Trinidad and Tobago, Tunisia, Ukraine, United Arab Emirates, United Kingdom, United Republic of Tanzania, United States, Uruguay, Viet Nam, Yemen, Zambia.

Against: Turkey.

Abstaining: Bolivia, Dominican Republic, Ecuador, El Salvador, Ethiopia, Venezuela.

On 24 December (**decision 66/557**), the General Assembly decided that the agenda item on oceans and the law of the sea would remain for consideration during its sixty-sixth (2012) resumed session.

PART FIVE

Institutional, administrative and budgetary questions

Chapter I
United Nations restructuring and institutional matters

In 2011, the General Assembly continued efforts to strengthen UN coherence system-wide by streamlining institutional arrangements for consolidating governance of UN system operational activities for development. In that regard, the Secretary-General, in February, appointed nine experts to the Evaluation Management Group for the independent evaluation of lessons learned from the "Delivering as one" pilots.

The Ad Hoc Working Group on the Revitalization of the General Assembly focused on the Assembly's working methods, its role and relationship to other principal UN organs, the implementation of Assembly resolutions on revitalization, the selection and appointment of the Secretary-General, and the strengthening of the institutional memory of the Office of the Assembly President. The Assembly resumed its sixty-fifth session in January, and opened its sixty-sixth session on 13 September. It held high-level meetings on youth; AIDS; prevention and control of non-communicable diseases; addressing desertification, land degradation and drought in the context of sustainable development and poverty eradication; as well as a commemorative meeting on the tenth anniversary of the Durban Declaration and Programme of Action adopted at the 2001 World Conference against Racism, Racial Discrimination, Xenophobia and Related Intolerance. The Assembly granted observer status to a number of international and regional organizations to participate in its work.

The Security Council held 225 formal meetings to deal with regional conflicts, peacekeeping operations and other issues related to the maintenance of international peace and security.

In addition to its organizational and substantive sessions, the Economic and Social Council held a special high-level meeting with the Bretton Woods institutions (the Word Bank Group and the International Monetary Fund), the World Trade Organization and the United Nations Conference on Trade and Development.

The Committee for Programme and Coordination considered the annual overview report of the UN System Chief Executives Board for Coordination, while the Assembly considered a number of reports by the Secretary-General on cooperation activities between the United Nations and regional organizations.

In July, a new State, the Republic of South Sudan, became a Member of the Organization, bringing its membership to 193 States.

Restructuring matters

Programme of reform

UN system-wide coherence

Delivering as one. In response to General Assembly resolution 64/289 [YUN 2010, p. 1396], the Secretary-General, by a February note [A/65/737 & Add.1], appointed nine experts to the Evaluation Management Group for the independent evaluation of lessons learned from the "Delivering as one" pilots, covering all aspects of the initiative. The original mandate was contained in Assembly resolution 62/208 [YUN 2007, p. 877], in which the Assembly encouraged the Secretary-General to support countries in their evaluation of efforts to improve coherence, coordination and harmonization in the UN development system, and emphasized the need for an independent evaluation of lessons learned from such efforts. The names of the experts were attached in an annex.

The Evaluation Management Group would oversee the conduct of the evaluation, ensure its design, and manage the evaluation process, including the identification and selection of the evaluation team. It would also ensure the independence of the evaluation and the compliance of the final product with the highest evaluation standards.

Also responding to resolution 64/289, the Secretariat, in a September note [A/66/384], informed that the independent evaluation should inform the preparation of the quadrennial comprehensive policy review, to be conducted in 2012. The preparation of the report would require extensive data collection, analysis and stakeholder consultations at the country, regional and headquarters levels in 2011 and during the first half of 2012. The Chair of the Evaluation Management Group would report to the Assembly by August 2012.

Institutional arrangements for gender issues. In July, the Secretary-General submitted a report [A/66/120] on strengthening the institutional arrangements for support of gender equality and the empowerment of women. The report summarized progress in the implementation of Assembly resolution 64/289 [YUN 2010, p. 1396], establishing the United Nations Entity for Gender Equality and the Empowerment of Women, known as UN-Women, including progress with regard to general principles; governance of the entity; administration and human resources; financing; and transitional arrangements.

The Secretary-General noted that UN-Women had made excellent progress in putting in place the necessary administrative frameworks and consolidating its staff resources, especially at its headquarters. In January, the "Vision and 100-day action plan" setting out the core principles and priorities for the building of a strong organization was launched, and in June, the Executive Board of UN-Women endorsed its 2011–2013 strategic plan. The completion of the alignment process at Headquarters was imminent and the senior management team had been appointed. While UN-Women had initiated the consolidation and strengthening of its field office structure, it had yet to fully establish its presence on the ground. With further progress in that area, UN-Women would be able to provide, through its normative support functions and operational activities, guidance and technical support on the empowerment and rights of women, gender equality and gender mainstreaming to all Member States, across all levels of development and in all regions, at their request. The mobilization of resources for achieving its goals remained a challenge. Those resources were critical if UN-Women was to deliver on the expectations of stakeholders. The availability of projected contributions would send a clear signal of political will and commitment of support to the realization of gender equality and the empowerment of women. The Secretary-General noted that while the components of an effective coordination and accountability framework were being put in place, further elaboration of the role of UN-Women in leading, coordinating and promoting the accountability of the UN work for gender equality was needed in order for the framework to become fully effective.

Accountability architecture

In accordance with resolution 64/259 [YUN 2010, p. 1404], the Joint Inspection Unit (JIU) submitted a report [JIU/REP/2011/5] on accountability frameworks in the UN system. The objective of the report was to map out and assess the various accountability frameworks in the UN system and to identify gaps. The report also analysed those UN system organizations without a stand-alone formal accountability framework document and identified good/best practices in developing and implementing accountability frameworks/components of accountability. The report identified 17 benchmarks for measuring a robust accountability framework based on transparency and a culture of accountability. Measurement of implementation of the framework would need to test whether the benchmarks were being implemented effectively and efficiently and assess their impacts.

The report found that seven UN organizations possessed a stand-alone formal accountability framework (the International Labour Organization, the United Nations, the United Nations Development Programme, the United Nations Population Fund, the United Nations Children's Fund, the United Nations Office for Project Services, and the World Health Organization). Three Secretariat entities (the Economic Commission for Europe, the United Nations Environment Programme and the Office of the United Nations High Commissioner for Refugees) possessed a programme level accountability framework. Other UN system organizations had varying degrees of key components of accountability, several of them with strong internal control systems. The study identified a gap between the staff's and management's perceptions of the strength of the culture of accountability. The review concluded that transparency and a culture of accountability were necessary for the framework to be implemented. A number of recommendations were made, including that those organizations without stand-alone accountability systems should develop such systems as a matter of priority.

In March [A/65/788], the Secretary-General transmitted to the General Assembly a JIU report [JIU/REP/2010/4] entitled "Review of enterprise risk management in the United Nations system: benchmarking framework" [YUN 2010, p. 1054]. The objective of the study was to review enterprise risk management (ERM) policies, practices and experience in the UN system, and identify best practices and lessons learned. Overall, UN system organizations were found to be at the beginning stages of ERM adoption and implementation. Progress was slow and depended on ad hoc decisions rather than a formal plan. Many organizations were either preparing policy and framework documents or undertaking pilot exercises. Some were comparatively advanced in ERM, but their implementation of it remained immature. Several organizations had yet to consider ERM.

Reasons for the slow progress included a lack of collective understanding and commitment by senior management; lack of a formal implementation plan; uncertainty about how to implement and integrate ERM into organizational processes; lack of a governance structure to support implementation; and the pressure of competing reform initiatives. While it was necessary to adjust to the nature of each organization, there was also a need for a common approach to ensure system-wide coherence on ERM; the identification and management of cross-cutting risks; the avoidance of duplication; and the optimal use of scarce resources. The inspectors identified 10 benchmarks for successful ERM implementation in UN organizations. It was recommended that the first nine be adopted and implemented as a package by the executive head of each organization, while benchmark 10 should be discussed and adopted at the level of the United Nations Chief Executives Board for Coordination (CEB). It was also recommended that governing bodies exercise their oversight role regarding the adoption of the ERM benchmarks.

In August [A/65/788/Add.1], the Secretary-General transmitted to the Assembly his comments and those of the CEB on the JIU report.

Strengthening of UN system

In 2011, the General Assembly continued consideration of the agenda item on strengthening the United Nations system. It had before it a JIU report [A/66/380] on transparency in the selection and appointment of senior managers in the UN Secretariat (see p. 1443).

On 24 December, by **decision 66/557**, the Assembly decided that the item on strengthening the United Nations system would remain for consideration during its resumed sixty-sixth (2012) session. It also decided that the item on United Nations reform: measures and proposals would remain for consideration during that session.

UN central role in global governance

In October, responding to General Assembly resolution 65/94 [YUN 2010, p. 1407], the Secretary-General submitted a report [A/66/506] on global economic governance and development. The report focused on the link between global economic governance and development in the aftermath of the world financial and economic crisis, as well as on the role of the UN system with respect to economic governance more broadly, touching on its relationship with the Group of Twenty (G20) and regional institutions. It described the main features of the current system, outlined the different options proposed by Member States to address perceived gaps in the existing framework, and made recommendations for strengthening the international framework of global economic cooperation in support of development. The report concluded that there was a need for enhanced coordination, cooperation, coherence and effective policymaking across the entire UN system, and consideration should be given to various proposals made in that regard. Member States should consider the best ways to balance effectiveness with inclusiveness and representation. Measures should be considered to enhance the functioning and working methods of relevant UN organs (especially the Economic and Social Council) and their subsidiary machinery, improve coordination and efficiency at the inter-agency and operational levels and enhance engagement with non-State actors. The performance of UN organs and bodies should be periodically reviewed and, when necessary, reformed. Efforts should be made to ensure predictable and consistent engagement between the G20 and the United Nations.

On 16 December [A/66/PV.88], in a statement delivered on his behalf, the Assembly President stated that global economic governance suffered from serious shortcomings in legitimacy, efficiency and coherence. He called on the Assembly to give careful consideration to the findings and conclusions of the Secretary-General's report, and pointed out that a central issue was strengthening coordination, cooperation, coherence and effective policymaking across the UN system. Other topics highlighted included enhancing the functioning and working methods of UN organs and periodically reviewing their performance; strengthening coordination among all the major informal groups dealing with the global economic and financial system, the United Nations and other multilateral organizations; ensuring the participation of developing countries in the major institutions of global economic governance; and incorporating regional arrangements into the architecture of global governance.

On 24 December, by **decision 66/557**, the Assembly decided that the sub-item on the central role of the UN system in global governance would remain for consideration during its resumed sixty-sixth (2012) session.

Institutional matters

Admission to UN of new Member

In 2011, a new State, the Republic of South Sudan, was admitted to the United Nations, bringing the total membership to 193. Its application for UN membership [A/65/900-S/2011/418] was submitted on 9 July.

Admission of South Sudan

SECURITY COUNCIL ACTION

On 13 July [meeting 6582], the Security Council, acting on the recommendation of the Committee on the Admission of New Members [S/2011/420], adopted **resolution 1999(2011)** without vote.

The Security Council,
Having examined the application of the Republic of South Sudan for admission to membership in the United Nations,
Recommends to the General Assembly that the Republic of South Sudan be admitted to membership in the United Nations.

Following the adoption of the resolution, the Council President made statement **S/PRST/2011/14** on behalf of the Council:

The Security Council has decided to recommend to the General Assembly that the Republic of South Sudan be admitted as a Member of the United Nations. On behalf of the members of the Council, I wish to extend my congratulations to the Republic of South Sudan on this historic occasion.

The Council notes with great satisfaction the Republic of South Sudan's solemn commitment to uphold the purposes and principles of the Charter of the United Nations and to fulfil all the obligations contained therein.

We look forward to the Republic of South Sudan joining us as a Member of the United Nations and to working closely with its representatives.

On the same day [A/65/905], the Council requested the Secretary-General to transmit the resolution to the General Assembly.

GENERAL ASSEMBLY ACTION

On 14 July [meeting 108], the General Assembly adopted **resolution 65/308** [draft: A/65/L.84 & Add.1] without vote [agenda item 114].

Admission of the Republic of South Sudan to membership in the United Nations

The General Assembly,

Having received the recommendation of the Security Council of 13 July 2011 that the Republic of South Sudan should be admitted to membership in the United Nations,

Having considered the application for membership of the Republic of South Sudan,

Decides to admit the Republic of South Sudan to membership in the United Nations.

On 24 December, the Assembly decided that the item on the admission of new members would remain for consideration at its resumed sixty-sixth (2012) session (**decision 66/557**).

General Assembly

Revitalization of the work of the General Assembly

In response to General Assembly resolution 64/301 [YUN 2010, p. 1407], the Secretary-General submitted a February report [A/65/712] on the revitalization of the work of the Assembly. The report presented an updated inventory of the provisions of Assembly resolutions on revitalization addressed to the Secretariat for implementation that had not been implemented, with an indication of the constraints and reasons behind any lack of implementation, for consideration by the Ad Hoc Working Group (see below).

In July [A/65/902], in response to Assembly resolution 58/316 [YUN 2004, p. 1374], the Secretary-General submitted a report on the revitalization of the work of the Assembly, which outlined the draft programme of work of the plenary and five of the Assembly's six Main Committees for its sixty-sixth (2011) session.

An addendum to the report [A/65/902/Add.1] contained the status of documentation for that session as at 3 August 2011.

Ad Hoc Working Group report. As requested in Assembly resolution 64/301 [YUN 2010, p. 1407], the Ad Hoc Working Group on the Revitalization of the General Assembly submitted an August report [A/65/909] summarizing its activities and presenting recommendations for further progress. The Working Group held six meetings and conducted its work programme through general discussion and exchange of views on all issues related to revitalization and thematic meetings. The thematic meetings focused on implementation of Assembly resolutions on revitalization; the Assembly working methods, including operational and technical issues such as the voting system; its role and authority and its relationship to the other principal UN organs and groups outside the United Nations; its role and responsibility in the selection and appointment of the Secretary-General; and strengthening the institutional memory of the Office of the Assembly President.

Communication. On 8 September [A/65/945], Finland transmitted to the Assembly President the report of the high-level retreat it had organized entitled "Towards a stronger General Assembly" (Tarrytown, New York, United States, 16–17 June), with the aim of contributing to the revitalization of the Assembly's work.

GENERAL ASSEMBLY ACTION

On 12 September [meeting 118], the General Assembly adopted **resolution 65/315** [draft: A/65/909] without vote [agenda item 118].

Revitalization of the work of the General Assembly

The General Assembly,

Reaffirming its previous resolutions relating to the revitalization of its work, including resolutions 46/77 of 12 December 1991, 47/233 of 17 August 1993, 48/264 of 29 July 1994, 51/241 of 31 July 1997, 52/163 of 15 December 1997, 55/14 of 3 November 2000, 55/285 of 7 September 2001, 56/509 of 8 July 2002, 57/300 of 20 December 2002, 57/301 of 13 March 2003, 58/126 of 19 December 2003, 58/316 of 1 July 2004, 59/313 of 12 September 2005, 60/286 of 8 September 2006, 61/292 of 2 August 2007, 62/276 of 15 September 2008, 63/309 of 14 September 2009 and 64/301 of 13 September 2010,

Stressing the importance of the implementation of resolutions of the General Assembly on the revitalization of its work, and noting with concern their lack of implementation and impact on the authority, effectiveness and efficiency of the Assembly,

Recognizing the role of the General Assembly in addressing issues of peace and security, in accordance with the Charter of the United Nations,

Reaffirming the role and authority of the General Assembly on global matters of concern to the international community, including global governance, as set out in the Charter,

Welcoming the decision of the President of the General Assembly to designate "Reaffirming the central role of the United Nations in global governance" as the theme of the general debate at its sixty-fifth session,

Recognizing the need to further enhance the role, authority, effectiveness and efficiency of the General Assembly,

Noting the important role and the activities of the Office of the President of the General Assembly,

Reiterating that the revitalization of the work of the General Assembly is a critical component of the overall reform of the United Nations,

1. *Welcomes* the report of the Ad Hoc Working Group on the Revitalization of the General Assembly;

2. *Decides* to establish, at its sixty-sixth session, an ad hoc working group on the revitalization of the work of the General Assembly, open to all Member States:

(*a*) To identify further ways to enhance the role, authority, effectiveness and efficiency of the Assembly, inter alia, by building on previous resolutions and evaluating the status of their implementation;

(*b*) To submit a report thereon to the Assembly at its sixty-sixth session;

3. *Also decides* that the Ad Hoc Working Group shall continue its review of the inventory of General Assembly resolutions on revitalization, based on the updated annex to the report of the Ad Hoc Working Group submitted at the sixty-third session, and requests the Secretary-General to submit an update on the provisions of the Assembly resolutions on revitalization addressed to the Secretariat for implementation that have not been implemented, with an indication of the constraints and reasons behind any lack of implementation, for further consideration by the Ad Hoc Working Group at the sixty-sixth session;

Role and authority of the General Assembly

4. *Reaffirms* the role and authority of the General Assembly, including on questions relating to international peace and security, in accordance with Articles 10 to 14 and 35 of the Charter of the United Nations, where appropriate, using the procedures set forth in rules 7 to 10 of the rules of procedure of the Assembly which enable swift and urgent action by the Assembly, bearing in mind that the Security Council has primary responsibility for the maintenance of international peace and security in accordance with Article 24 of the Charter;

5. *Stresses* the need for the General Assembly to actively undertake its role and effectively respond, in a timely manner, to emerging challenges and current events of common concern to the international community;

6. *Welcomes* the holding of thematic debates on current issues of critical importance to the international community and their interactive inclusive character, and invites the President of the General Assembly to continue this practice and to consult with Member States on the possibilities for achieving, where appropriate, results-oriented outcomes in such debates;

7. *Recognizes* the importance and benefit of a continuing interaction between the General Assembly and international or regional forums and organizations dealing with global matters of concern to the international community in the perspective of the revitalization of the work of the Assembly;

8. *Welcomes* the continued practice of holding periodic informal briefings by the Secretary-General on his priorities, travels and most recent activities, including his participation in international meetings and events organized outside the United Nations, and encourages him to continue with this practice;

9. *Stresses* the importance of ensuring increased cooperation, coordination and exchange of information among the principal organs, and welcomes the holding of regular meetings of the President of the General Assembly at its sixty-fifth session with the Secretary-General and the Presidents of the Security Council and the Economic and Social Council, as well as with the Chairs of subsidiary bodies, and briefings to Member States on the outcomes of these meetings on a regular basis, and encourages the continuation of such practice;

10. *Welcomes* the improvements that have been made in the quality of the annual reports of the Security Council to the General Assembly, encourages the Council to make further improvements as necessary, and takes note of the holding of informal meetings of the President of the Council with all Member States before the preparation of the report;

11. *Notes* that, in accordance with Article 15 and Article 24, paragraph 3, of the Charter, the Security Council shall submit to the General Assembly an annual report and, when necessary, special reports for its consideration;

12. *Recognizes* that non-implementation of various General Assembly resolutions, in particular those adopted by consensus, may diminish the role and authority of the Assembly, and underlines the important role and responsibility of Member States in their implementation;

Working methods

13. *Welcomes* the substantial discussion undertaken and the decision adopted on 20 December 2010 by the Second Committee of the General Assembly at the sixty-fifth session aimed at rationalizing and streamlining its agenda and improving its working methods;

14. *Requests* that the General Assembly and its Main Committees, at the sixty-sixth session, in consultation with Member States, continue consideration of and make proposals for the further biennialization, triennialization, clustering and elimination of items on the agenda of the Assembly, taking into account the relevant recommendations of the Ad Hoc Working Group, including through the introduction of a sunset clause, with the clear consent of the sponsoring State or States;

15. *Encourages* each Main Committee to discuss its working methods at the sixty-sixth session, and invites the Chairs of the Main Committees, at the sixty-sixth session, to brief the Ad Hoc Working Group, as appropriate, on the discussions on the working methods;

16. *Notes with appreciation* that the high-level meetings held at the United Nations give more visibility to very important topics, while mindful of the need to facilitate full participation of all Member States and to preserve the integrity of the general debate in September, and invites the Secretary-General, the President of the General Assembly and the Chairs of the Main Committees, in consultation with Member States, to enhance the coordination of the scheduling of high-level meetings with a view to optimizing the number and distribution of such events;

17. *Encourages* Member States, United Nations bodies and the Secretariat to consult on the consolidation of documentation in order to avoid duplication of work and to exercise the fullest possible discipline in striving for concise resolu-

tions, reports and other documentation, inter alia, by referring to previous documents rather than repeating actual content;

18. *Stresses* the importance of further enhancing public and media awareness of the work and decisions of the General Assembly, including through their timely issuance and distribution in all official languages;

19. *Decides* that the Ad Hoc Working Group shall remain apprised of options for more time-effective, efficient and secure balloting, reiterating the need to ascertain the credibility, reliability and confidentiality of the balloting process, and requests the Secretariat to submit an update in case of any new technological developments, on the understanding that the adoption of any new balloting system in the future will require a decision of the plenary of the General Assembly;

Selection and appointment of the Secretary-General and other executive heads

20. *Reaffirms its commitment* to continue, in the Ad Hoc Working Group, in accordance with the provisions of Article 97 of the Charter, its consideration of the revitalization of the role of the General Assembly in the selection and appointment of the Secretary-General, and calls for the full implementation of all relevant resolutions, including resolutions 11(I) of 24 January 1946, 51/241, 60/286, in particular paragraphs 17 to 22 of the annex thereto, and 64/301;

21. *Takes note* of the recommendation contained in the report of the Joint Inspection Unit on the selection and conditions of service of executive heads in the United Nations system organizations proposing that the General Assembly conduct hearings or meetings with candidates running for the post of Secretary-General of the United Nations;

22. *Recognizes* that the process of selecting and appointing the Secretary-General differs from the process used with regard to other executive heads in the United Nations system, given the role of the Security Council in accordance with Article 97 of the Charter, and re-emphasizes the need for the process of selection of the Secretary-General to be transparent and inclusive of all Member States;

Strengthening the institutional memory of the Office of the President of the General Assembly

23. *Welcomes* the views expressed by the President of the General Assembly to the Ad Hoc Working Group on the strengthening of the institutional memory of the Office of the President of the Assembly and its relationship with the Secretariat;

24. *Also welcomes* the periodic briefings by the President of the General Assembly at its sixty-fifth session to Member States on his recent activities, including official travels, and encourages the continuation of such practice;

25. *Notes* that the activities of the President of the General Assembly have increased markedly in recent years, recalls provisions regarding support for the Office of the President of the General Assembly in previous resolutions, expresses continued interest in seeking ways to further support the Office, in accordance with existing procedures, in particular rule 153 of the rules of procedure of the General Assembly, and in this context looks forward to the submission by the Secretary-General of his proposals pursuant to paragraph 10 of resolution 64/301;

26. *Requests* the Secretary-General, at the sixty-sixth session, to report on the funding and staffing of the Office of the President of the General Assembly, including on any technical, logistical, protocol-related or financial questions;

27. *Notes* the concerns raised on the protocol arrangements in place for the President of the General Assembly, and requests the Secretary-General to further endeavour to ensure, within agreed resources, that the President is provided with proper protocol and security services and adequate office space, with a view to enabling the President to carry out his or her functions in a manner commensurate with the dignity and stature of the Office;

28. *Emphasizes* the need to ensure, within agreed resources, that the Office of the President of the General Assembly is allocated dedicated staff within the Secretariat with responsibility for coordinating the transition between Presidents, managing interactions between the President of the Assembly and the Secretary-General and the retention of institutional memory, and requests the outgoing Presidents of the Assembly to brief their successors on the lessons learned and best practices;

29. *Notes with appreciation* the contributions of Member States to the Trust Fund in support of the Office of the President of the General Assembly, and invites Member States to continue to contribute to the Fund.

On 24 December, the Assembly decided that the item on the revitalization of its work would remain for consideration during its resumed sixty-sixth (2012) session (**decision 66/557**).

Assembly sessions and meetings

The General Assembly met throughout 2011. It resumed and concluded its sixty-fifth session and held the major part of its sixty-sixth session. The sixty-fifth session resumed in plenary meetings on 14 January and closed on 12 September. The sixty-sixth session opened on 13 September and continued until its suspension on 23 December.

The Assembly held high-level meetings on youth (25–26 July) (see p. 1035); HIV/AIDS (8–10 June) (see p. 1135); the prevention and control of non-communicable diseases (19–20 September) (see p. 1146); addressing desertification, land degradation and drought in the context of sustainable development and poverty eradication (20 September) (see p. 982); as well as a high-level meeting to commemorate the tenth anniversary of the Durban Declaration and Programme of Action (22 September) (see p. 652).

Resumed sixty-fifth (2011) session

On 25 March, the General Assembly decided that the commemorative meeting on the occasion of the International Day of Remembrance of the Victims of Slavery and the Transatlantic Slave Trade (25 March) would include, without setting a precedent, a statement on behalf of the Caribbean Community, a statement by Ruth Simmons, President of Brown University, and some cultural presentations (**decision 65/546**).

On 18 April, the Assembly approved the list of civil society representatives drawn up by its President for participation in the high-level meeting on a comprehensive review of the progress achieved in realizing the Declaration of Commitment on HIV/AIDS and the Political Declaration on HIV/AIDS, to be convened from 8 to 10 June (**decision 65/547**).

On 20 May, the Assembly decided that the opening plenary meeting of the 2011 comprehensive review of the progress achieved in realizing the Declaration of Commitment on HIV/AIDS and the Political Declaration on HIV/AIDS would be held on 8 June, on the understanding that such arrangements in no way created a precedent for the scheduling of future plenary meetings of the Assembly (**decision 65/548**).

On 28 July, the Assembly approved the list of civil society representatives drawn up by its President for participation in its high-level meeting on the Prevention and Control of Non-communicable Diseases (19–20 September) (**decision 65/549**).

Sixty-sixth (2011) session

By **decision 66/501** of 13 September, the Assembly authorized a number of subsidiary bodies to meet in New York during the main part of its sixty-sixth (2011) session.

On 16 September, by **decision 66/502**, the Assembly adopted a number of provisions concerning the organization of the sixty-sixth session [A/66/250 & Add.1].

On 31 October, the Assembly decided to invite Gordon Brown, former Prime Minister of the United Kingdom, to make a statement during the plenary meeting devoted to the launch of the International Year of Cooperatives, 2012 (**decision 66/508**).

Credentials

The Credentials Committee, at its meetings on 14 September and 20 October [A/66/360 & Add.1], had before it memorandums by the Secretary-General indicating that 17 and 129 Member States, respectively, had submitted the formal credentials of their representatives. Information concerning the representatives of 47 other Member States had also been communicated.

The Committee adopted resolutions accepting the credentials received, and recommended draft resolutions to the General Assembly for adoption. On 16 September [A/66/PV.2] and 26 October [A/66/PV.43], the Assembly, by resolutions 66/1 A and B approved the Committee's first and second reports, respectively.

GENERAL ASSEMBLY ACTION

On 16 September [meeting 2], the General Assembly adopted **resolution 66/1 A** [draft: A/66/360] by recorded vote (114-17-15) [agenda item 3 (*b*)].

**Credentials of representatives
to the sixty-sixth session of the General Assembly**

The General Assembly,

Having considered the report of the Credentials Committee and the recommendation contained therein,

Approves the report of the Credentials Committee.

RECORDED VOTE ON RESOLUTION 66/1 A:

In favour: Afghanistan, Andorra, Argentina, Armenia, Australia, Austria, Azerbaijan, Bahrain, Bangladesh, Belgium, Belize, Benin, Bosnia and Herzegovina, Botswana, Brazil, Brunei Darussalam, Bulgaria, Burkina Faso, Canada, Cape Verde, Chad, Chile, China, Colombia, Costa Rica, Côte d'Ivoire, Croatia, Cyprus, Czech Republic, Denmark, Djibouti, Egypt, Estonia, Ethiopia, Fiji, Finland, France, Gabon, Gambia, Georgia, Germany, Greece, Guatemala, Honduras, Hungary, Iceland, India, Iran, Iraq, Ireland, Israel, Italy, Jamaica, Japan, Jordan, Kazakhstan, Kuwait, Latvia, Lebanon, Liechtenstein, Lithuania, Luxembourg, Madagascar, Malaysia, Maldives, Malta, Mauritius, Mexico, Monaco, Mongolia, Montenegro, Morocco, Netherlands, New Zealand, Norway, Oman, Panama, Paraguay, Peru, Philippines, Poland, Portugal, Qatar, Republic of Korea, Republic of Moldova, Romania, Russian Federation, Saint Lucia, San Marino, Senegal, Serbia, Singapore, Slovakia, Slovenia, South Sudan, Spain, Sri Lanka, Sudan, Sweden, Switzerland, Syrian Arab Republic, Thailand, the former Yugoslav Republic of Macedonia, Timor-Leste, Togo, Tunisia, Turkey, Ukraine, United Arab Emirates, United Kingdom, United States, Vanuatu, Viet Nam, Yemen.

Against: Angola, Bolivia, Cuba, Democratic Republic of the Congo, Ecuador, Equatorial Guinea, Kenya, Lesotho, Malawi, Namibia, Nicaragua, South Africa, Swaziland, United Republic of Tanzania, Venezuela, Zambia, Zimbabwe.

Abstaining: Algeria, Antigua and Barbuda, Cameroon, Dominican Republic, El Salvador, Indonesia, Mali, Mauritania, Nepal, Saint Vincent and the Grenadines, Saudi Arabia, Suriname, Trinidad and Tobago, Uganda, Uruguay.

On 26 October, by **resolution 66/1 B**, the Assembly approved the second report of the Credentials Committee.

Agenda

During the resumed sixty-fifth (2011) session, the General Assembly, by **decision 65/503 B**, decided to include additional items in the agenda of that session to be considered directly in plenary and to reopen consideration of a number of items and sub-items. The Assembly also decided to include an additional item, entitled "Question of equitable representation on and increase in the membership of the Security Council and other matters related to the Security Council" on the agenda of its sixty-sixth (2011) session (**decision 65/554**).

The Assembly deferred consideration of the following items and included them in the draft agenda of its sixty-sixth (2011) session: question of the Comorian island of Mayotte (**decision 65/553**); the situation in the occupied territories of Azerbaijan (**decision 65/552**); follow-up to the recommendations on administrative management and internal oversight of the Independent Inquiry Committee into the United Nations Oil-for-Food Programme (**decision 65/555**); and financing of the United Nations Mission in East Timor (**decision 65/556**).

On 12 September, the Assembly, on the proposal of its President, decided to include in the draft agenda of its sixty-sixth (2011) session an item entitled "Implementation of the Declaration of Commitment on HIV/AIDS and the Political Declarations on HIV and AIDS" (**decision 65/551**).

On the recommendation of the General Committee [A/66/250 & Add.1], the Assembly, by **decision 66/503 A**, adopted the agenda [A/66/251 & Add.1,2] and the allocation of items [A/66/252 & Add.1,2] for its sixty-sixth (2011) session. The Assembly included in the agenda of that session the item "Question of the Comorian island of Mayotte", on the understanding that there would be no consideration of the item by the Assembly; and the items entitled "Observer status for the West African Economic and Monetary Union in the General Assembly" and "Follow-up to the Fourth United Nations Conference on the Least Developed Countries", the latter to be considered in plenary meeting. It also decided to consider the sub-items entitled "Appointment of members and alternate members of the United Nations Staff Pension Committee" and "Appointment of members of the International Civil Service Commission" and to allocate them to the Fifth Committee. The Assembly, on 24 December, decided to retain 85 items for consideration during its resumed sixty-sixth (2012) session (**decision 66/557**).

On 16 September, the Assembly deferred consideration of the item entitled "Question of the Malagasy islands of Glorieuses, Juan de Nova, Europa and Bassas da India" and included it in the provisional agenda of its sixty-seventh (2012) session (**decision 66/503 A**).

On 2 December, the Assembly included in the provisional agenda of its sixty-seventh (2012) session the items entitled "Role of science and technology in the context of international security and disarmament" (**decision 66/515**) and "Missiles" (**decision 66/516**). On the same date, the Assembly included in the provisional agenda of its sixty-eighth (2013) session the items entitled "Review of the implementation of the Declaration on the Strengthening of International Security" (**decision 66/514**) and "Transparency and confidence-building measures in outer space activities" (**decision 66/517**).

On 24 December, the Assembly decided that the item entitled "Implementation of the resolutions of the United Nations" would remain for consideration at its resumed sixty-sixth (2012) session (**decision 66/557**).

Programme of work of Assembly Committees

The General Assembly, on 2 December, approved the proposed programme of work and timetable of the First (Disarmament and International Security) Committee for 2012 (**decision 66/519**). On 9 December, it approved the proposed programme of work and timetable of the Fourth (Special Political and Decolonization) Committee (**decision 66/523**) and noted the provisional programme of work adopted by the Sixth (Legal) Committee (**decision 66/525**) for the sixty-seventh (2012) session. On 19 December and 22 December, respectively, it approved the programme of work of the Third (Social, Humanitarian and Cultural) Committee (**decision 66/540**) and of the Second (Economic and Financial) Committee (**decision 66/551**) for the sixty-seventh (2012) session.

Security Council

Review of Security Council membership and related matters

On 12 September, by **decision 65/554**, the General Assembly decided to continue intergovernmental negotiations on Security Council reform in informal plenary at its sixty-sixth (2011) session, building on progress achieved during its sixty-fifth session, as well as on the positions of and proposals by Member States, while noting the initiatives and efforts of the Assembly President and the Chair of the intergovernmental negotiations, including the preparation of a text reflecting the positions and proposals submitted by Member States, with a view to an early comprehensive reform of the Council. It also decided to convene the Open-ended Working Group on the Question of Equitable Representation on and Increase in the Membership of the Security Council and Other Matters Related to the Security Council during its sixty-sixth (2011) session and to include in the agenda of that session the item entitled "Question of equitable representation on and increase in the membership of the Security Council and other matters related to the Security Council".

On 24 December, by **decision 66/557**, the Assembly decided that the agenda item on the equitable representation on and increase in the membership of the Security Council and related matters would remain for consideration at its resumed sixty-sixth (2012) session.

Security Council sessions

During 2011, the Security Council held 225 formal meetings, adopted 66 resolutions and issued 22 presidential statements. It considered 48 questions (see APPENDIX IV). The President made 74 statements to the press on behalf of Council members. Monthly assessments of the Council's work in 2011 were issued by the successive Council Presidents [S/2011/254, S/2011/401, S/2011/506, S/2011/507, S/2011/508, S/2011/509, S/2011/525, S/2011/784, S/2011/796, S/2012/24, S/2012/282, S/2012/359]. The Council held an open debate on its working methods on 30 November [S/PV.6672].

In a 1 September note [A/66/300], the Secretary-General, in accordance with Article 12, paragraph 2 of the UN Charter and with the consent of the Council, notified the General Assembly of 86 matters relative to the maintenance of peace and security that were being dealt with by the Council since his previous annual notification [YUN 2010, p. 1411]. Items subject to deletion in 2011, which would remain on the list of items of which the Council was seized for one additional year, were recorded in document [S/2011/10/Add.9]. The Assembly took note of the Secretary-General's notification on 8 November (**decision 66/509**).

On 8 November, the Assembly took note of the Council's report for the period from 1 August 2010 to 31 July 2011 [A/66/2 & Corr.1] (**decision 66/510**).

On 24 December, the Assembly decided that the item on the Council's report would remain for consideration during its resumed sixty-sixth (2012) session (**decision 66/557**).

Economic and Social Council

Strengthening of the Economic and Social Council

In a June note [A/65/866], the General Assembly President transmitted to the Assembly the final report and recommendations on the review of the implementation of Assembly resolution 61/16 on the strengthening of the Economic and Social Council [YUN 2006, p. 1589]. The report was based on the views expressed by Member States during informal consultations of the Assembly, held on 7 and 15 March and 4 April. Among the recommendations were that the Assembly might consider: inviting UN specialized agencies, including international financial and trade organizations, civil society organizations, the private sector and academia, to participate in the Council's high-level meetings and events; requesting the Council to have a closer relationship with funds and programmes, including through more frequent and substantive joint meetings, to discuss issues of common interest; encouraging the Development Cooperation Forum to continue engaging all stakeholders in its work; and requesting the Council to enhance its coordination role vis-à-vis UN system specialized agencies and regional commissions to contribute to the preparatory process for the annual ministerial review. The Assembly should request that the Council urge its functional commissions and other subsidiary bodies to contribute to the annual ministerial review, and invite the Secretary-General to present such contributions in his report on the role of the Council in the integrated and coordinated follow-up to major UN conferences and summits in the economic, social and related fields. The Council should continue to mainstream the achievement of the Millennium Development Goals (MDGs) [YUN 2000, p. 51] throughout its work and activities and provide regular reports and assessments of its activities and those of Member States and other actors. The Council and the Peacebuilding Commission should be requested to organize additional joint meetings to discuss issues of common interest. The Assembly should review implementation of resolution 61/16 in 2013.

GENERAL ASSEMBLY ACTION

On 29 June [meeting 105], the General Assembly adopted **resolution 65/285** [draft: A/65/L.81] without vote [agenda items 13 & 115].

Review of the implementation of General Assembly resolution 61/16 on the strengthening of the Economic and Social Council

The General Assembly,

Recalling the 2005 World Summit Outcome,

Recalling also its resolution 61/16 of 20 November 2006 on the strengthening of the Economic and Social Council,

1. *Takes note* of the report of the President of the General Assembly on the review of the implementation of General Assembly resolution 61/16 on the strengthening of the Economic and Social Council;

2. *Encourages* Member States, the Economic and Social Council, the regional commissions and other entities of the United Nations system to consider the recommendations contained in the report;

3. *Decides* to review further the implementation of resolution 61/16 at its sixty-seventh session.

Council sessions and meetings

The Economic and Social Council held its organizational session for 2011 on 18 January and 15–18 February; a resumed organizational session on 26–27 April and 18 and 26 May; its special high-level meeting with the Bretton Woods institutions (the World Bank Group and the International Monetary Fund), the World Trade Organization (WTO) and the United Nations Conference on Trade and Development (UNCTAD) on 10 and 11 March; its substantive session from 4 July to 29 July; and its resumed substantive session on 6, 24 and 27 October, and 5 December in New York. The Council's work for 2011 was covered in its report to the General Assembly [A/66/3/Rev.1]. During the year, the Council adopted 44 resolutions and 83 decisions [E/2011/99].

On 18 January, the Council elected its Bureau (a President and four Vice-Presidents) for 2011 (see APPENDIX III) and adopted the agenda of its organizational session [E/2011/2 & Add.1 & Corr.1].

On 15 February, the Council approved the provisional agenda and documentation of its 2011 substantive session (**decision 2011/203**), and decided on the working arrangements for that session (**decision 2011/205). On 4 July, the Council adopted the agenda of its 2011 substantive session [E/2011/100 & Corr.1], approved the programme of work and list of documents for that session [E/2011/L.12 & E/2011/L.11], and approved the requests for hearings from non-governmental organizations (NGOs) [E/2011/127] (**decision 2011/214**).

The General Assembly, by **decision 66/557** of 24 December, decided that the item on the report of the Economic and Social Council would remain for consideration during its resumed sixty-sixth (2012) session.

Themes of Council segments and meetings

On 15 February, the Economic and Social Council decided that the operational activities segment of its substantive session should be devoted to the progress on and implementation of General Assembly resolutions 62/208 [YUN 2007, p. 877], 63/232 [YUN 2008, p. 962], 64/220 [YUN 2009, p. 852] and 65/177 [YUN 2010, p. 865] and Economic and Social Council resolutions 2008/2 [YUN 2008, p. 959], 2009/1 [YUN 2009, p. 847] and 2010/22 [YUN 2010, p. 862] concerning operational activities for development of the UN system (**decision 2011/206**), and that the high-level meeting with the Bretton Woods institutions, WTO and UNCTAD would be held in New York on 10 and 11 March (**decision 2011/202**).

On 26 April, by **decision 2011/210**, the Council decided that the theme for the humanitarian affairs segment of its 2011 substantive session would be "Working in partnership to strengthen coordination of humanitarian assistance in a changing world"; and that it would convene two panels on: preparing for the future: predictable, effective, flexible and adequate humanitarian financing and its accountable use to meet the evolving needs and challenges in the delivery of humanitarian assistance; and strengthening resilience, preparedness and capacities for humanitarian response. On the same date, it decided that the theme for the item on regional cooperation of its substantive session would be "Regional cooperation as a catalyst for development: examples from the regions" (**decision 2011/209**). The Council also decided that the event to discuss transition from relief to development would be held on 19 July under the title "The role of the United Nations and the international community in supporting the capacity of the Government of South Sudan to manage the transition". It would consist of one panel discussion and have no negotiated outcome (**decision 2011/212**).

Also on 26 April (**decision 2011/208**), the Council adopted the following themes for its multi-year annual ministerial review for the period 2012–2014: "Promoting productive capacity, employment and decent work to eradicate poverty in the context of inclusive, sustainable and equitable economic growth at all levels for achieving the Millennium Development Goals" (2012); "Science, technology and innovation, and the potential of culture, for promoting sustainable development and achieving the Millennium Development Goals" (2013); and "Addressing ongoing and emerging challenges for meeting the Millennium Development Goals in 2015 and for sustaining development gains in the future" (2014).

Work programme

On 15 February, the Economic and Social Council took note of the questions to be included in its programme of work for 2012 [E/2011/1], and the list of documents for each agenda item (**decision 2011/204**).

On 22 July, the Council, on the recommendation of the Committee on Conferences [E/2011/128], approved the provisional calendar of conferences and meetings in the economic, social and related fields for 2012 and 2013 [E/2011/L.10] (**decision 2011/220**).

Coordination, monitoring and cooperation

Institutional mechanisms

CEB activities

In its annual overview report for 2011–2012 [E/2012/67], the United Nations System Chief Executives Board for Coordination (CEB) highlighted its key system-wide policy, and operational and management activities undertaken to advance a coherent UN system response to intergovernmental mandates and priorities. It also highlighted the main activities of the three CEB pillars—the High-level Committee on Programmes, the High-level Committee on Management and the United Nations Development Group—in promoting inter-agency cooperation on matters of system-wide concern. The report also highlighted major activities carried out under the aegis of CEB to enhance system-wide coherence and coordination of the UN system in support of and in conformity with intergovernmental mandates.

In successive sessions, CEB reflected on system-wide contributions to the preparations for the United Nations Conference on Sustainable Development (see p. 799) and considered elements of the broader global development agenda, including key dimensions of a greener, fairer and more sustainable globalization. Through its subsidiary machinery, it addressed major management and administrative issues for improving the coordination and compatibility of administrative processes across UN system organizations. In terms of operational activities, a top priority of the UN system continued to be supporting country efforts to accelerate the achievement of the MDGs through the United Nations Development Assistance Frameworks, including in countries in crisis and in transition. Particular emphasis continued to be given to the simplification and harmonization of business practices, strengthening leadership and improving knowledge management. In addition, CEB took further steps to enhance coherence and coordination among its subsidiary machinery by improving information exchanges, enhancing thematic collaboration and deepening joint programmatic activities.

CEB noted that the 2010 High-level Plenary Meeting on the MDGs [YUN 2010, p. 813] had resulted in a global action agenda for reaching the goals by 2015, and recommitted all actors to accelerating progress towards that end. The meeting's outcome document provided the strategic guidance for the work of the UN system in supporting the achievement of the MDGs. On behalf of CEB, the United Nations Development Group continued to support country efforts to accelerate achievement of the MDGs through implementation of the Acceleration Framework and the United Nations Development Assistance Frameworks. The Acceleration Framework supported the design and implementation of national strategies aimed at achieving the MDGs.

CEB held two regular sessions in 2011: the first in Nairobi (1 April) [CEB/2011/1] and the second in New York (28 October) [CEB/2011/2]. Its principal subsidiary bodies met as follows: the High-level Committee on Management, twenty-first (Paris, 8–9 March) [CEB/2011/3] and twenty-second (Washington, D.C., 26–27 September) [CEB/2011/5] sessions; and the High-level Committee on Programmes, twenty-first (New York, 3–4 March) [CEB/2011/4] and twenty-second (New York, 15–16 September) [CEB/2011/6] sessions.

CEB report

CPC consideration. The Committee for Programme and Coordination (CPC) [A/66/16] considered the CEB annual overview report for 2010/11 [YUN 2010, p. 1412].

CPC recommended that the General Assembly bring to the attention of the Secretary-General, in his capacity as Chair of CEB, the need for the Board to continue to act in accordance with its mandate of enhancing system-wide coordination in conformity with the intergovernmental mandates of its member organizations. It also recommended that the Secretary-General be requested to report to the Assembly on the occurrence of direct and substantive dialogue between CEB and Member States, in accordance with paragraph 4 of resolution 64/289 [ibid., p. 1396], in order to enhance the Board's transparency and accountability. The Committee further recommended that the Assembly take note of the Secretary-General's efforts concerning change management and requested that he ensure that the focus of those efforts was the effective and efficient implementation of mandates approved by intergovernmental organs. It also noted CEB's role in the preparations for the United Nations Conference on Sustainable Development (see p. 799), and recommended that the Assembly request the Secretary-General to report on the challenges and opportunities for the UN system resulting from that global event. It reiterated that any criteria and methodology for the comprehensive evaluation of the eight "Delivering as one" pilot projects should first be approved by the Assembly and that UN support for those projects should not prejudice the outcome of the intergovernmental deliberations on system-wide coherence. The Committee also reiterated its recommendation that the Assembly bring to the attention of the Secretary-General the need to continue to better address the issue of increasing the participation of developing countries and economies in transition in the Organization's procurement processes. The Assembly should request the Secretary-General to ensure that projects funded by the High-level Committee on Management Plan of Action were implemented in accordance with relevant provisions of the Assembly resolutions concerning administrative and budgetary matters, as well as the UN financial regulations and rules. It recommended continuous cooperation between CEB, the International Civil Service Commission and JIU and encouraged CEB to strengthen that cooperation through more frequent participation of JIU and the Commission in the meetings of the High-level Committees on Management and on Programmes and the United Nations Development Group.

The Economic and Social Council took note of the CEB annual overview report for 2010/11 on 22 July (**decision 2011/219**).

Programme coordination

The Committee for Programme and Coordination held its organizational meeting (28 April) and its fifty-first session (6 June–1 July) in New York [A/66/16].

CPC considered questions related to the 2010–2011 programme budget (see p. 1375) and the 2012–2013 proposed programme budget and strategic framework (see p. 1382). It also considered strengthening the role of evaluation and the application of evaluation findings on programme design, delivery and policy directives; programme evaluation of the Department of Economic and Social Affairs; and the triennial review of the implementation of CEB recommendations made at its forty-eight session [YUN 2008, p. 1527] on the in-depth evaluation of political affairs (see p. 1405); the CEB annual overview report for 2010–2011 (see p. 1360); the Secretary-General's report on the New Partnership for Africa's Development (see p. 891); and JIU reports.

The Economic and Social Council took note of the CPC report on 22 July (**decision 2011/219**).

Other matters

Follow-up to international conferences

On 22 July, by **decision 2011/216**, the Economic and Social Council, recalling its decision 2010/252 [YUN 2010, p. 1414] on the role of the Council in the integrated and coordinated implementation of and follow-up to the outcomes of major UN conferences and summits, and in the light of relevant General Assembly resolutions, including resolution 61/16 [YUN 2006, p. 1589], requested the Secretary-General to prepare a note containing recommendations on the periodicity and scope of future reports on the topic for consideration at its 2012 substantive session.

On 24 December, by **decision 66/557**, the Assembly decided that the agenda item on the integrated and coordinated implementation of and follow-up to the outcomes of the major UN conferences and summits in the economic, social and related fields would remain for consideration during its resumed sixty-sixth (2012) session.

UN and other organizations

Cooperation with organizations

International Organization of la Francophonie

The Secretary-General, in his consolidated report on cooperation between the United Nations and regional and other organizations [YUN 2010, p. 1414], reported on cooperation between the United Nations and the International Organization of la Francophonie.

GENERAL ASSEMBLY ACTION

On 14 January [meeting 74], the General Assembly adopted **resolution 65/263** [draft: A/65/L.26/Rev.1 & Add.1] without vote [agenda item 122 (*l*)].

Cooperation between the United Nations
and the International Organization
of la Francophonie

The General Assembly,

Recalling its resolutions 33/18 of 10 November 1978, 50/3 of 16 October 1995, 52/2 of 17 October 1997, 54/25 of 15 November 1999, 56/45 of 7 December 2001, 57/43 of 21 November 2002, 59/22 of 8 November 2004, 61/7 of 20 October 2006 and 63/236 of 22 December 2008, as well as its decision 53/453 of 18 December 1998,

Recalling also its resolutions 61/266 of 16 May 2007 and 63/306 of 9 September 2009 on multilingualism,

Considering that the International Organization of la Francophonie, which is made up of seventy-two States Members of the United Nations, representing more than one third of the members of the General Assembly, is promoting multilateral cooperation in areas of common interest,

Bearing in mind the Articles of the Charter of the United Nations which encourage the promotion of the purposes and principles of the United Nations through regional cooperation,

Bearing in mind also that, according to the Charter of la Francophonie adopted on 23 November 2005 at the Ministerial Conference of la Francophonie, held in Antananarivo, the objectives of the International Organization of la Francophonie are to assist in the establishment and development of democracy, the prevention, management and settlement of conflicts, support for the rule of law and for human rights, the intensification of dialogue between cultures and civilizations, the establishment of closer ties among peoples through mutual knowledge, the strengthening of their solidarity through multilateral cooperation activities with a view to promoting the growth of their economies, and the promotion of education and training,

Welcoming the steps taken by the International Organization of la Francophonie to strengthen its ties with the organizations of the United Nations system and with international and regional organizations with a view to attaining its objectives,

Affirming the importance of a balanced and effective multilateral system that is representative of today's world, one that is based upon a strong and renewed United Nations,

Noting with satisfaction the commitment of the International Organization of la Francophonie to multilateral cooperation for peace, democratic governance and the rule of law, economic governance and solidarity, the environment, sustainable development, and climate change,

Noting with satisfaction also the commitments made at the High-level Plenary Meeting of the General Assembly on the Millennium Development Goals, held in New York from 20 to 22 September 2010, and reaffirmed by the Heads of State and Government of countries using French as a common language at the thirteenth Summit of la Francophonie, held in Montreux, Switzerland, from 22 to 24 October 2010, and their determination to work together to bring about, through targeted action, added value in these areas,

Having considered the report of the Secretary-General on the implementation of resolution 63/236,

Noting with satisfaction the substantial progress achieved in cooperation between the United Nations, the specialized agencies and other United Nations bodies and programmes and the International Organization of la Francophonie,

Convinced that strengthening cooperation between the United Nations and the International Organization of la Francophonie serves the purposes and principles of the United Nations,

Noting the desire of the two organizations to consolidate, develop and strengthen the ties that exist between them in the political, economic, social and cultural fields,

1. *Takes note* of the report of the Secretary-General, and welcomes the strengthened and fruitful cooperation

between the United Nations and the International Organization of la Francophonie;

2. *Notes with satisfaction* that, in accordance with the declaration adopted by Heads of State and Government of countries using French as a common language at the thirteenth Summit of la Francophonie, the International Organization of la Francophonie participates actively in the work of the United Nations whose purposes, as set forth in its Charter, include to achieve international cooperation in solving international problems of an economic, social, cultural or humanitarian character and to be a centre for harmonizing the actions of nations in the attainment of common ends;

3. *Notes with great satisfaction* the recent strengthening of cooperation between the United Nations and the International Organization of la Francophonie in the area of human rights, and commends the initiatives taken by the International Organization of la Francophonie in the areas of crisis and conflict prevention, the promotion of peace, support for democracy and the rule of law, in accordance with the commitments set forth in the Bamako Declaration on an African Common Position on the Illicit Proliferation, Circulation and Trafficking of Small Arms and Light Weapons and reaffirmed at the Ministerial Conference of la Francophonie on Conflict Prevention and Human Security, held on 13 and 14 May 2006 in Saint Boniface, Canada;

4. *Welcomes* the genuine contribution of the International Organization of la Francophonie, in cooperation with the United Nations, in Haiti, the Comoros, Côte d'Ivoire, Burundi, Madagascar, the Niger, the Democratic Republic of the Congo, Guinea, the Central African Republic and Chad;

5. *Also welcomes* the cooperation between the United Nations and the International Organization of la Francophonie, with the participation of other regional and subregional organizations, as well as non-governmental organizations, in the fields of early warning and crisis and conflict prevention, and encourages the pursuit of this initiative with a view to formulating practical recommendations to facilitate the establishment of relevant operational mechanisms, where necessary;

6. *Further welcomes* the new impetus given to the participation of States members of the International Organization of la Francophonie in peacekeeping operations, while recalling that it is up to the United Nations to preserve the multilingualism of these operations, and draws attention to the strengthened cooperation between the International Organization of la Francophonie and the Department of Peacekeeping Operations of the Secretariat with a view to increasing the number of French-speaking personnel in United Nations peacekeeping operations;

7. *Encourages* the continuation of efforts by the States members of the International Organization of la Francophonie and by the Organization itself, taking into account the authority of the Secretary-General of the United Nations, to increase the supply of French-speaking civilian and military contingents on missions to francophone countries and to build their capacities, including access by French-speaking personnel to leadership positions in peacekeeping operations in francophone countries;

8. *Welcomes* the participation of the International Organization of la Francophonie in the Peacebuilding Commission's work on Burundi, the Central African Republic and Guinea-Bissau, and strongly encourages the International Organization of la Francophonie and the Peacebuilding Commission to continue to cooperate actively;

9. *Notes with satisfaction* the continued collaboration between the United Nations and the International Organization of la Francophonie in the area of electoral monitoring and assistance, and encourages the strengthening of cooperation between the two Organizations in that area;

10. *Expresses its appreciation* to the Secretary-General for including the International Organization of la Francophonie in the periodic meetings he holds with heads of regional organizations, and invites him to continue to do so, taking into account the role played by the International Organization of la Francophonie in conflict prevention and support for democracy and the rule of law;

11. *Welcomes* the fact that the thirteenth Summit of la Francophonie led to a concrete commitment by States members of the International Organization of la Francophonie to take action by pursuing efforts aimed at:

(*a*) Mobilizing with a view to achieving the Millennium Development Goals, in particular with regard to education;

(*b*) Taking into account the needs of the most vulnerable States, in particular in the areas of sustainable development, food security, the environment and biodiversity;

(*c*) Reforming financial regulations and the international monetary system;

(*d*) Combating cross-cutting threats which compromise international peace and sustainability;

12. *Invites* the specialized agencies, funds and programmes of the United Nations system, as well as the regional commissions, including the Economic Commission for Africa, to collaborate to this end with the Secretary-General of la Francophonie by identifying new synergies in favour of development, in particular in the areas of poverty elimination, energy, sustainable development, education, training and the development of new information technologies, in particular with a view to meeting the Millennium Development Goals;

13. *Expresses its gratitude* to the International Organization of la Francophonie for the steps it has taken in recent years to promote cultural and linguistic diversity and dialogue between cultures and civilizations;

14. *Welcomes* the establishment of the United Nations Entity for Gender Equality and the Empowerment of Women (UN-Women), and encourages the International Organization of la Francophonie to work in synergy with UN-Women in the spirit of the Francophone Declaration on Violence against Women adopted on 1 March 2010;

15. *Expresses its appreciation* to the Secretary-General of the United Nations and the Secretary-General of la Francophonie for their sustained efforts to strengthen cooperation and coordination between the two Organizations, thereby serving their mutual interests in the political, economic, social and cultural fields;

16. *Welcomes* the involvement of the countries that use French as a common language, particularly through the International Organization of la Francophonie, in the preparation for, conduct of and follow-up to international conferences organized under the auspices of the United Nations;

17. *Also welcomes* the high-level meetings held periodically between the Secretariat of the United Nations and the Secretariat of the International Organization of la Francophonie, and requests the Secretary-General of the United Nations, acting in cooperation with the Secretary-General of la Francophonie, to encourage the holding of periodic meetings between their representatives in order to promote the exchange of information, coordination of activities and identification of new areas of cooperation;

18. *Invites* the Secretary-General of the United Nations to take the steps necessary, in consultation with the Secretary-General of la Francophonie, to continue to promote cooperation between the two Organizations;

19. *Requests* the Secretary-General to submit to the General Assembly at its sixty-seventh session a report on the implementation of the present resolution;

20. *Decides* to include in the provisional agenda of its sixty-seventh session the sub-item entitled "Cooperation between the United Nations and the International Organization of la Francophonie".

African Union

The Secretary-General, in his consolidated report on cooperation between the United Nations and regional and other organizations [YUN 2010, p. 111], reported on cooperation between the African Union (AU) and the United Nations.

In a February report [A/65/716-S/2011/54], submitted in response to General Assembly resolution 63/310 [YUN 2009, p. 106], the Secretary-General presented the review of the ten-year capacity-building programme for the African Union. The report covered support provided by UN departments and programmes, funds and agencies to the implementation of the ten-year capacity-building programme; coordination and consultation mechanisms; findings; and recommendations and observations. The review found tremendous support for the ten-year capacity-building programme, although its full potential and benefits had yet to be achieved. One of the main difficulties was the divergence of views among the stakeholders as to what constituted "capacity-building" in the context of the framework. Since the signing of the declaration, a full-fledged programme had yet to be established in the form of a body of activities to be undertaken towards meeting its objectives. In the absence of such a programme, it had not been easy to make targeted interventions in support of the development needs of AU institutions. Adopting a programme with targets would help to further strengthen the Commission's leadership vis-à-vis the implementation of the ten-year capacity-building programme. There was a need also to enhance engagement with the regional economic communities as part of the AU building block strategy, especially in the area of development, including in the fields of energy, water and infrastructure, in addition to ongoing cooperation in the area of peace and security. The absence of a well-defined programme of work for the ten-year capacity-building programme, compounded by the absence of resources, had adversely affected implementation efforts. The Secretary-General called upon all partners and stakeholders, including Member States, to support the mobilization of resources for UN entities involved in the implementation of the programme, in particular the secretariat of the Regional Coordination Mechanism.

GENERAL ASSEMBLY ACTION

On 18 April [meeting 86], the General Assembly adopted **resolution 65/274** [draft: A/65/L.68 & Add.1] without vote [agenda item 122 (*a*)].

Cooperation between the United Nations and the African Union

The General Assembly,

Having considered the report of the Secretary-General on cooperation between the United Nations and regional and other organizations,

Recalling the provisions of Chapter VIII of the Charter of the United Nations, as well as its resolutions 55/218 of 21 December 2000, 56/48 of 7 December 2001, 57/48 of 21 November 2002, 59/213 of 20 December 2004, 61/296 of 17 September 2007 and 63/310 of 14 September 2009,

Recalling also the principles enshrined in the Constitutive Act of the African Union adopted in 2000 in Lomé,

Recalling further the decisions and declarations adopted by the Assembly of the African Union at all its ordinary and extraordinary sessions,

Welcoming the adoption of the framework for the ten-year capacity-building programme for the African Union set out in the declaration on enhancing United Nations-African Union cooperation, signed in Addis Ababa on 16 November 2006 by the Secretary-General and the Chair of the African Union Commission, which highlights the key areas for cooperation between the African Union and the United Nations,

Acknowledging the decision of the Peace and Security Council of the African Union at its sixty-eighth meeting, held on 14 December 2006, on the establishment of a coordination and consultation mechanism between the Peace and Security Council of the African Union and the United Nations Security Council, welcoming the June 2007 agreement to hold joint meetings at least once a year, noting that such meetings offer an important platform for dialogue, in this regard welcoming the fourth consultative meeting between members of the United Nations Security Council and the Peace and Security Council of the African Union, held at United Nations Headquarters on 9 July 2010, and welcoming also the first joint consultative meeting between the Peace and Security Council of the African Union and the Peacebuilding Commission, held on 8 July 2010,

Recalling the adoption, at the fourth ordinary session of the Assembly of the African Union, of the African Union Non-Aggression and Common Defence Pact, as an instrument to reinforce cooperation among States members of the African Union in the areas of defence and security and, in particular, to contribute to the work of the Peace and Security Council of the African Union and its cooperation with the United Nations,

Welcoming, while taking into account the role of the General Assembly, the statements by the President of the Security Council of 19 November 2004 on the institutional relationship with the African Union, of 28 March 2007 on the relationship between the United Nations and regional organizations, in particular the African Union, in the maintenance of international peace and security and of 18 March 2009 on peace and security in Africa, as well as Council resolution 1809(2008) of 16 April 2008 and all subsequent related resolutions,

Welcoming also the efforts to enhance cooperation between the peace and security structure of the United Nations and the peace and security architecture of the African Union in the realms of conflict prevention and resolution, early warning, mediation, crisis management, peacekeeping, security sector reform and post-conflict peacebuilding in Africa, including efforts to implement the African Union Framework for Postconflict Reconstruction and Development,

Acknowledging the significant contribution made by the African Union towards preventing and combating terrorism, and noting the centrality of the international partnership and cooperation among the African Union, the relevant United Nations organs and the wider international community in the global fight against terrorism,

Recognizing the need to enhance the strategic relationship between the United Nations and the African Union, as a basis for a more effective partnership embodying the principles of mutual respect when addressing issues of mutual concern,

Welcoming the efforts of the African Union and the United Nations, together with other international partners, to provide effective support for peacekeeping missions undertaken in accordance with Chapter VIII of the Charter of the United Nations by regional organizations, in particular the African Union, with reference to start-up funding, equipment, logistics and long-term capacity-building, as reflected in Security Council resolution 1809(2008),

Noting that, on the occasion of the special session of the Assembly of Heads of State and Government of the African Union on the consideration and resolution of conflicts in Africa, held in Tripoli on 31 August 2009, the Heads of State and Government of the African Union adopted the Tripoli Declaration on the Elimination of Conflicts in Africa and the Promotion of Sustainable Peace and the Plan of Action and declared 2010 as the Year of Peace and Security on the Continent, under the general slogan "Make peace happen", and commending the efforts being made by the African Union and various partners in this regard,

Bearing in mind the United Nations Declaration on the New Partnership for Africa's Development, recalled in various relevant resolutions adopted since 2002,

Recognizing the pivotal need to bring Africa into the mainstream of the global economy and to strengthen the global partnership to address the special development needs of Africa, in particular the eradication of poverty, and in this regard welcoming the political declaration adopted on 22 September 2008, on the occasion of the high-level meeting on the theme "Africa's development needs: state of implementation of various commitments, challenges and the way forward", and reaffirming the importance of its implementation and the responsibilities of the States members of the African Union and of the United Nations in this regard, as well as the implementation of the New Partnership for Africa's Development,

Stressing the need to extend the scope of cooperation between the United Nations and the African Union in the area of combating the illegal exploitation of natural resources in Africa,

Emphasizing the importance of the effective, coordinated and integrated implementation of the United Nations Millennium Declaration, the Doha Development Agenda, the Monterrey Consensus of the International Conference on Financing for Development, the Doha Declaration on Financing for Development: outcome document of the Follow-up International Conference on Financing for Development to Review the Implementation of the Monterrey Consensus, the Plan of Implementation of the World Summit on Sustainable Development ("Johannesburg Plan of Implementation") and the 2005 World Summit Outcome,

Noting the adoption of the Revised African Maritime Transport Charter by the Assembly of the African Union at its fifteenth ordinary session, held in Kampala from 25 to 27 July 2010, as an instrument that can help to enhance international trade and development,

Emphasizing the importance of the 1995 World Summit for Social Development, at which the Copenhagen Declaration on Social Development was adopted, the 1995 Fourth World Conference on Women and the outcomes of the twenty-third special session of the General Assembly entitled "Women 2000: gender equality, development and peace for the twenty-first century", and stressing the importance for all Member States of the full and effective implementation of the Beijing Declaration and Platform for Action and the Programme of Action of the International Conference on Population and Development,

Recalling the African Union Convention on Preventing and Combating Corruption and the Protocol to the African Charter on Human and Peoples' Rights on the Rights of Women in Africa, both adopted in Maputo on 11 July 2003,

Recommitting to improving the effectiveness of development assistance, including the fundamental principles of ownership, alignment, harmonization, managing for results and mutual accountability, and calling for a continuing dialogue to improve the effectiveness of aid, including the full implementation of the Accra Agenda for Action by countries and organizations that commit to it,

Acknowledging the contribution of the United Nations Office to the African Union in Addis Ababa in strengthening coordination and cooperation between the United Nations and the African Union in the areas of peace and security, and recognizing the efforts made to consolidate the Office so as to enhance its performance in view of the expanding scope for cooperation between the United Nations and the African Union in those areas,

Convinced that strengthening cooperation between the United Nations and the African Union will contribute to the advancement of the principles of the Charter of the United Nations, the principles of the Constitutive Act of the African Union and the development of Africa,

1. *Takes note with appreciation* of the report of the Secretary-General, calls for the implementation of the declaration on enhancing United Nations-African Union cooperation and the framework for the ten-year capacity-

building programme for the African Union, and in this regard takes note of the report of the Secretary-General on the review of the ten-year capacity-building programme for the African Union, and requests the Secretary-General to continue to take appropriate measures to strengthen the capacity of the Secretariat and to implement its mandate with respect to meeting the special needs of Africa in accordance with the established United Nations procedures;

2. *Recalls* that the Security Council has the primary responsibility for the maintenance of international peace and security, and requests the United Nations system to intensify its assistance to the African Union, as appropriate, in strengthening the African peace and security architecture, including the institutional and operational capacity of its Peace and Security Council, and in coordinating with other international partners when needed;

3. *Emphasizes* the need to pursue the ongoing measures to improve the effectiveness and efficiency of cooperation between the United Nations and the African Union, and in this regard welcomes the establishment of the United Nations Office to the African Union in Addis Ababa, integrating the United Nations Liaison Office to the African Union, and also welcomes the appointment of an Assistant Secretary-General to head the Office with a view to intensifying, improving and better coordinating United Nations engagement with the African Union in existing and emerging areas of cooperation in peace and security and political and humanitarian affairs, and recommends speedy implementation to ensure the adequate handling of the responsibilities related to coordinating the United Nations system in those areas, including implementing relevant aspects of the ten-year capacity-building programme, in order to enhance the strategic and operational partnership between the United Nations and the African Union and its subregions;

4. *Welcomes* the establishment of the United Nations Regional Office for Central Africa, and encourages the Regional Office and the United Nations Office for West Africa to deepen their relationships with the Economic Community of Central African States and the Economic Community of West African States, respectively, in order to further strengthen United Nations-African Union cooperation;

5. *Recognizes* the need to enhance the predictability, sustainability and flexibility of financing for regional organizations, including the African Union, when they undertake peacekeeping operations under a United Nations mandate, and notes the determination of the Security Council to continue working on this issue in accordance with its responsibilities under the Charter of the United Nations;

6. *Welcomes* the report of the Secretary-General on support to African Union peacekeeping operations authorized by the United Nations and the related statement by the President of the Security Council of 22 October 2010 as important steps towards the further strengthening of the partnership between the Security Council and the Peace and Security Council of the African Union;

7. *Notes with appreciation* the ongoing efforts of the African Union to address the issue of the protection of civilians in armed conflict and in the context of peacekeeping operations, and encourages the African Union to continue those efforts;

8. *Welcomes* the launching, in New York on 25 September 2010, of the United Nations-African Union Joint Task Force on Peace and Security as an important framework for furthering the strategic partnership on peace and security between the Secretariat and the African Union Commission, and calls for the full implementation of the agreed terms of reference of the Task Force;

9. *Stresses* the urgent need for the United Nations and the African Union to develop close cooperation and concrete programmes aimed at addressing the problems posed by landmines, illicit trafficking in small arms and light weapons and transnational organized crime, in particular trafficking in persons and drugs, within the framework of the relevant declarations and resolutions adopted by the two organizations;

10. *Calls upon* the United Nations system, the African Union and the international community to intensify their cooperation in the global fight against terrorism through the implementation of the relevant international and regional treaties and protocols and, in particular, the African Plan of Action adopted in Algiers on 14 September 2002, as well as their support for the operation of the African Centre for Studies and Research on Terrorism, inaugurated in Algiers in October 2004;

11. *Calls upon* the United Nations system to intensify its efforts, in collaboration with the African Union, in combating the illegal exploitation of natural resources, in particular in conflict areas, in accordance with relevant resolutions and decisions of the United Nations and the African Union;

12. *Also calls upon* the United Nations system to continue its support for the African Union and its member States in their efforts to implement the internationally agreed development goals, including the Millennium Development Goals, and requests the Secretary-General and the international community to fulfil the commitments that they undertook during the high-level event on the Millennium Development Goals, held in New York on 25 September 2008, and the High-level Plenary Meeting of the General Assembly on the Millennium Development Goals, held in New York from 20 to 22 September 2010;

13. *Urges* the organizations of the United Nations system to coordinate closely with the African Union Commission and its structures relating to the New Partnership for Africa's Development, in particular through the Regional Coordination Mechanism, in order to enhance overall coordination, monitoring and evaluation of all development programmes and projects of all international development stakeholders;

14. *Stresses* the need for closer cooperation and coordination between the United Nations system and the African Union, in accordance with the Cooperation Agreement and other relevant memorandums of understanding between the two organizations, in particular in the implementation of the commitments contained in the United Nations Millennium Declaration and the 2005 World Summit Outcome and as regards achieving the internationally agreed development goals, including the Millennium Development Goals, at the national, subregional and regional levels;

15. *Urges* the United Nations system to increase its support for Africa in the implementation of the declaration of the extraordinary summit meeting of the Assembly of Heads of State and Government of the Organization of African Unity on HIV/AIDS, malaria, tuberculosis and other related infectious diseases, held in Abuja in April 2001, and to extend that support until 2015 to coincide with the date

envisaged for the achievement of the Millennium Development Goals, and in the implementation of the Declaration of Commitment on HIV/AIDS, so as to eradicate or control the spread of those diseases, inter alia, through sound capacity-building in human resources;

16. *Invites* the United Nations system to enhance its support for African countries in their efforts to implement the Johannesburg Plan of Implementation and to support efforts aimed at strengthening cooperation among the African Union Commission, the African Development Bank and the Economic Commission for Africa to address the development challenges of Africa, including the efforts for the eradication of mother-to-child transmission of HIV/AIDS, as decided by the Assembly of the African Union at its fifteenth ordinary session, held in Kampala from 25 to 27 July 2010;

17. *Notes* the establishment on 11 October 2010 of a joint secretariat for the African Union Commission, the African Development Bank and the Economic Commission for Africa, to be based at the headquarters of the Economic Commission in Addis Ababa, to enhance coherence, cooperation and information-sharing, as well as to build stronger links among the departments and divisions of the three institutions in support of the development agenda of Africa;

18. *Encourages* the United Nations to take special measures, as appropriate, to address the challenges of poverty eradication through the United Nations agencies, funds and programmes, noting the importance of addressing, inter alia, debt cancellation, enhanced official development assistance, increases in flows of foreign direct investment and voluntary transfer of technology, the World Food Programme, the agriculture partnership to combat hunger, universal primary education initiatives, gender equality programmes, improved maternal health programmes and HIV/AIDS education;

19. *Encourages* the deepening of collaboration between the United Nations and the African Union, recalling the African Union Framework for Post-conflict Reconstruction and Development and the efforts of the Peacebuilding Commission to enhance international support for African countries on the agenda of the Commission, and reiterates the need for enhanced coordination and consultations between the Commission and the African Union on assistance for countries emerging from conflict;

20. *Invites* the Secretary-General to request all relevant United Nations agencies, funds and programmes to intensify their efforts to support cooperation with the African Union, including through the implementation of the protocols to the Constitutive Act of the African Union and the Treaty establishing the African Economic Community, and, in cooperation with other international partners, to assist in harmonizing the programmes of the African Union with those of the African regional economic communities with a view to enhancing regional economic cooperation and integration;

21. *Encourages* the United Nations system to effectively support the efforts of the African Union by urging the international community to strive for the successful and timely completion of the Doha round of trade negotiations, including negotiations aimed at substantial improvements in areas such as trade-related measures, including market access, to promote sustainable growth in Africa;

22. *Calls upon* the United Nations system to accelerate the implementation of the Plan of Action contained in the document entitled "A world fit for children", adopted on 10 May 2002 at the twenty-seventh special session of the General Assembly on children, and to provide assistance, as appropriate, to the African Union and its member States in this regard, welcomes the ongoing efforts of the African Union to ensure the protection of the rights of children, and in this regard recalls the adoption of the Call for accelerated action on the implementation of the Plan of Action towards Africa Fit for Children (2008–2012);

23. *Calls upon* the United Nations system and the African Union to develop a coherent and effective strategy, including through joint programmes and activities, for the promotion and protection of human rights in Africa, within the framework of the implementation of regional and international treaties, resolutions and plans of action adopted by the two organizations;

24. *Requests* the United Nations system to cooperate with the African Union and its member States in the implementation of appropriate policies for the promotion of the culture of democracy, including the effective application of the African Charter on Democracy, Elections and Governance, as well as the promotion of good governance, respect for human rights and the rule of law, and the strengthening of democratic institutions, and in this regard notes that the sixteenth ordinary session of the Assembly of the African Union, held on 30 and 31 January 2011, had as its theme "Towards greater unity and integration through shared values";

25. *Urges* the United Nations system to continue to implement General Assembly resolutions 58/149 of 22 December 2003 and 63/149 of 18 December 2008 on assistance to refugees, returnees and displaced persons in Africa and to effectively support African countries in their efforts to incorporate the problems of refugees into national and regional development plans, and in this regard recalls the Plan of Action for the implementation of the outcome of the 2009 Special Summit of Heads of State and Government of the African Union on Refugees, Returnees and Internally Displaced Persons in Africa, and the adoption of the African Union Convention for the Protection and Assistance of Internally Displaced Persons in Africa, adopted on 23 October 2009;

26. *Welcomes and supports* the ongoing efforts of the African Union to support gender equality, the empowerment of women and social development, and recalls in this regard the declaration of the African Women's Decade by the Assembly of the African Union in February 2009, and the African Union Gender Policy, the Social Policy Framework for Africa and the Windhoek Declaration on Social Development, adopted by the Executive Council of the African Union in January 2009;

27. *Welcomes* the creation of the United Nations Entity for Gender Equality and the Empowerment of Women (UN-Women) and the appointment of an Under-Secretary-General for UN-Women;

28. *Encourages* the United Nations to work with the African Union and its partners to ensure more effective implementation of the relevant Security Council resolutions and statements by the President of the Council relating to women and peace and security, including resolutions 1325(2000) of 31 October 2000, 1820(2008) of 19 June

2008, 1888(2009) of 30 September 2009, 1889(2009) of 5 October 2009 and 1960(2010) of 16 December 2010;

29. *Recalls* its resolution 63/250 of 24 December 2008 on human resources management, and urges the Secretary-General to encourage the United Nations system to work, within existing rules and regulations, towards ensuring the effective and equitable representation of African men and women at senior and policy levels at the respective headquarters of its organizations and in their regional fields of operation;

30. *Encourages* the United Nations and the African Union to pursue joint initiatives for partnerships in Africa through, inter alia, the United Nations Office to the African Union, the Office of the Special Adviser on Africa and the United Nations Office for Partnerships;

31. *Takes note* of the comprehensive report on "Africa's development needs: state of implementation of various commitments, challenges and the way forward", including recommendations, submitted by the Secretary-General to the General Assembly pursuant to paragraph 39 of its resolution 63/1 of 22 September 2008, and in this regard looks forward to the formulation, by the end of the sixty-seventh session of the Assembly, of a mechanism to review the full and timely implementation of all commitments related to the development of Africa, building on existing mechanisms, to ensure that Member States remain seized of the issue of addressing the special development needs of Africa;

32. *Calls upon* the Secretary-General and the Chair of the African Union Commission, working in collaboration, to review every two years the progress made in the cooperation between the two organizations, and requests the Secretary-General to include the results of the review in his next report;

33. *Requests* the Secretary-General to report to the General Assembly at its sixty-seventh session on the implementation of the present resolution.

Inter-Parliamentary Union and national parliaments

On 1 June [A/66/87], Namibia transmitted to the Secretary-General the text of four resolutions adopted at the 124th Assembly of the Inter-Parliamentary Union (Panama City, Panama, 15–20 April). The resolutions related to transparency and accountability in the funding of political parties and election campaigns; providing a sound legislative framework aimed at preventing electoral violence, improving election monitoring and ensuring the smooth transition of power; strengthening democratic reform in emerging democracies, including in North Africa and the Middle East; and the role of parliaments in ensuring sustainable development through the management of natural resources, agricultural production and demographic change.

On 24 December, the Assembly decided that the item on interaction between the United Nations, national parliaments and the Inter-Parliamentary Union would remain for consideration during its resumed sixty-sixth (2012) session (**decision 66/557**).

Shanghai Cooperation Organization

On 28 June [A/65/895], China transmitted to the Secretary-General the Astana Declaration of the tenth anniversary of the Shanghai Cooperation Organization, signed by the Presidents of China, Kazakhstan, Kyrgyzstan, the Russian Federation, Tajikistan, and Uzbekistan at the meeting of the Council of the Heads of State of the Shanghai Cooperation Organization (Astana, Kazakhstan, 15 June).

Caribbean Community

In identical letters of 12 August [A/65/937-S/2011/516], the Secretary-General transmitted to the Security Council and General Assembly Presidents the joint statement adopted by the participants of the Sixth General Meeting between the United Nations system and the Caribbean Community and its associated institutions (Georgetown, Guyana, 28–29 July), which reviewed actions taken following the Fifth General Meeting [YUN 2009, p. 331].

Pacific Islands Forum

The Secretary-General, in his consolidated report on cooperation between the United Nations and regional and other organizations [YUN 2010, p. 1414], reported on cooperation between the United Nations and the Pacific Islands Forum.

GENERAL ASSEMBLY ACTION

On 12 September [meeting 118], the General Assembly adopted **resolution 65/316** [draft: A/65/L.90 & Add.1] without vote [agenda item 122 (*t*)].

Cooperation between the United Nations and the Pacific Islands Forum

The General Assembly,

Recalling its resolutions 49/1 of 17 October 1994, 59/20 of 8 November 2004, 61/48 of 4 December 2006 and 63/200 of 19 December 2008,

Welcoming the ongoing efforts towards closer cooperation between the United Nations and the Pacific Islands Forum and its associated institutions, and affirming the value of considering ways to further strengthen this cooperation,

Recognizing the fortieth anniversary of the establishment of the Pacific Islands Forum in 1971, and noting the key role the Forum continues to play in promoting sustainable development, environmental protection, good governance and peace and security in the Pacific through regional cooperation, including through the implementation of the Pacific Plan which was endorsed by leaders of the Forum in 2005,

Welcoming the first-ever participation by a Secretary-General of the United Nations at a Pacific Islands Forum, during the forty-second Forum, held on 7 and 8 September 2011, in Auckland, New Zealand, as well as his preceding visits to Australia, Kiribati and Solomon Islands, and taking note of the joint statement issued by Forum leaders and the Secretary-General,

Having considered the report of the Secretary-General on cooperation between the United Nations and regional and other organizations,

1. *Takes note* of the report of the Secretary-General, in particular paragraphs 116 to 123 on cooperation between the United Nations and the Pacific Islands Forum, and encourages further such cooperation;

2. *Welcomes* the commitment by Pacific Islands Forum leaders and the Secretary-General to enhanced high-level dialogue between the members of the Pacific Islands Forum and the United Nations, including meetings between the Secretary-General and Forum leaders at regular intervals;

3. *Invites* the Secretary-General to consider ways to promote and expand cooperation and coordination with Pacific Islands Forum members and the Forum secretariat, particularly in the areas identified in the joint statement issued by Forum leaders and the Secretary-General on 7 September 2011;

4. *Requests* the Secretary-General to submit to the General Assembly at its sixty-seventh session a report on the implementation of the present resolution;

5. *Decides* to include in the provisional agenda of its sixty-seventh session the sub-item entitled "Cooperation between the United Nations and the Pacific Islands Forum".

Other cooperation

Cooperation with the private sector

In August [A/66/320], the Secretary-General submitted a report on enhanced cooperation between the United Nations and all relevant partners, in particular the private sector. He noted that the past few years had seen significant progress in bringing the voice of the private sector into the work of the Organization and in developing innovative forms of collaboration that built upon key lessons learned. In order to ensure that the United Nations was at the forefront of efforts to more effectively leverage the contributions of the private sector in achieving development objectives, a more strategic and harmonized approach was needed. Attention was also required to ensure that recommendations were implemented in alignment with the values of the United Nations and its Member States and to strengthen the Organization's ability to collaborate effectively with the private sector towards achieving UN goals.

The report included a discussion of the concept of partnerships; Member States and partnerships; developments at the system level; trends at the level of agencies, funds and programmes; addressing key operational challenges; as well as recommendations and conclusions.

Participation in UN work

European Union

General Assembly consideration. On 3 May [A/65/PV.88], the General Assembly considered the status of the European Union's (EU) participation in the work of the United Nations. It adopted resolution 65/276 (see below), which allowed EU representatives to present the positions of EU to the Assembly; make interventions during sessions; and be invited to participate in the general debate of the Assembly. It also permitted EU communications relating to the Assembly's sessions and work to be circulated directly as documents of the Assembly, relevant meeting or conference. EU representatives were not allowed to vote, co-sponsor draft resolutions or decisions, or put forward candidates. The Secretary-General was requested to inform the Assembly on implementation of the modalities set out in the annex to the resolution during its sixty-fifth (2011) session.

GENERAL ASSEMBLY ACTION

On 3 May [meeting 88], the General Assembly adopted **resolution 65/276** [draft: A/65/L.64/Rev.1, as orally revised] by recorded vote (180-0-2) [agenda item 120].

Participation of the European Union in the work of the United Nations

The General Assembly,

Bearing in mind the role and authority of the General Assembly as a principal organ of the United Nations and the importance of its effectiveness and efficiency in fulfilling its functions under the Charter of the United Nations,

Recognizing that the current interdependent international environment requires the strengthening of the multilateral system in accordance with the purposes and principles of the United Nations and the principles of international law,

Recognizing also the importance of cooperation between the United Nations and regional organizations, as well as the benefits to the United Nations of such cooperation,

Acknowledging that it is for each regional organization to define the modalities of its external representation,

Recalling its resolution 3208(XXIX) of 11 October 1974, by which it granted observer status to the European Economic Community,

Recalling also that, consistent with the relevant legal provisions, the European Union has replaced the European Community and is a party to many instruments concluded under the auspices of the United Nations and an observer or participant in the work of several specialized agencies and bodies of the United Nations,

Noting that the States members of the European Union have entrusted the external representation of the European Union, previously performed by the representatives of the member State holding the rotating Presidency of the Council of the European Union, to the following institutional representatives: the President of the European Council, the High Representative of the Union for Foreign Affairs and Security Policy, the European Commission, and European Union delegations, which have assumed the role of acting on behalf of the European Union in the exercise of the competences conferred by its member States,

Mindful of the modalities for the participation of observer States and entities, and other observers in the work of the United Nations, as set out in the respective resolutions,

1. *Reaffirms* that the General Assembly is an intergovernmental body whose membership is limited to States that are Members of the United Nations;

2. *Decides* to adopt the modalities set out in the annex to the present resolution for the participation of the representatives of the European Union, in its capacity as observer, in the sessions and work of the General Assembly and its committees and working groups, in international meetings and conferences convened under the auspices of the Assembly and in United Nations conferences;

3. *Recognizes* that, following a request on behalf of a regional organization that has observer status in the General Assembly and whose member States have agreed arrangements that allow that organization's representatives to speak on behalf of the organization and its member States, the Assembly may adopt modalities for the participation of that regional organization's representatives, such as those set out in the annex to the present resolution;

4. *Requests* the Secretary-General to inform the General Assembly during its sixty-fifth session on the implementation of the modalities set out in the annex to the present resolution.

Annex

Participation of the European Union in the work of the United Nations

1. In accordance with the present resolution, the representatives of the European Union, in order to present positions of the European Union and its member States as agreed by them, shall be:

(a) Allowed to be inscribed on the list of speakers among representatives of major groups, in order to make interventions;

(b) Invited to participate in the general debate of the General Assembly, in accordance with the order of precedence as established in the practice for participating observers and the level of participation;

(c) Permitted to have its communications relating to the sessions and work of the General Assembly and to the sessions and work of all international meetings and conferences convened under the auspices of the Assembly and of United Nations conferences, circulated directly, and without intermediary, as documents of the Assembly, meeting or conference;

(d) Also permitted to present proposals and amendments orally as agreed by the States members of the European Union; such proposals and amendments shall be put to a vote only at the request of a Member State;

(e) Allowed to exercise the right of reply regarding positions of the European Union as decided by the presiding officer; such right of reply shall be restricted to one intervention per item.

2. The representatives of the European Union shall be ensured seating among the observers.

3. The representatives of the European Union shall not have the right to vote, to co-sponsor draft resolutions or decisions, or to put forward candidates.

4. A precursory explanation or recall of the present resolution shall be made only once by the President of the General Assembly at the start of each session.

RECORDED VOTE ON RESOLUTION 65/276:

In favour: Afghanistan, Albania, Algeria, Andorra, Angola, Antigua and Barbuda, Argentina, Armenia, Australia, Austria, Bahamas, Bahrain, Bangladesh, Barbados, Belarus, Belgium, Belize, Benin, Bhutan, Bolivia, Bosnia and Herzegovina, Botswana, Brazil, Brunei Darussalam, Bulgaria, Burkina Faso, Burundi, Cambodia, Cameroon, Canada, Cape Verde, Central African Republic, Chad, Chile, China, Colombia, Comoros, Congo, Costa Rica, Croatia, Cuba, Cyprus, Czech Republic, Democratic People's Republic of Korea, Democratic Republic of the Congo, Denmark, Djibouti, Dominica, Dominican Republic, Ecuador, Egypt, El Salvador, Equatorial Guinea, Eritrea, Estonia, Ethiopia, Fiji, Finland, France, Gabon, Gambia, Georgia, Germany, Ghana, Greece, Grenada, Guatemala, Guinea, Guinea-Bissau, Guyana, Haiti, Honduras, Hungary, Iceland, India, Indonesia, Iran, Iraq, Ireland, Israel, Italy, Jamaica, Japan, Jordan, Kazakhstan, Kenya, Kuwait, Kyrgyzstan, Lao People's Democratic Republic, Latvia, Lebanon, Lesotho, Liberia, Liechtenstein, Lithuania, Luxembourg, Madagascar, Malawi, Malaysia, Maldives, Mali, Malta, Marshall Islands, Mauritania, Mauritius, Mexico, Micronesia, Monaco, Mongolia, Montenegro, Morocco, Mozambique, Myanmar, Namibia, Nepal, Netherlands, New Zealand, Nicaragua, Niger, Nigeria, Norway, Oman, Pakistan, Palau, Panama, Papua New Guinea, Paraguay, Peru, Philippines, Poland, Portugal, Qatar, Republic of Korea, Republic of Moldova, Romania, Russian Federation, Saint Kitts and Nevis, Saint Lucia, Saint Vincent and the Grenadines, Samoa, San Marino, Sao Tome and Principe, Saudi Arabia, Senegal, Serbia, Seychelles, Sierra Leone, Singapore, Slovakia, Slovenia, Solomon Islands, South Africa, Spain, Sudan, Suriname, Swaziland, Sweden, Switzerland, Tajikistan, Thailand, the former Yugoslav Republic of Macedonia, Timor-Leste, Togo, Tonga, Trinidad and Tobago, Tunisia, Turkey, Turkmenistan, Tuvalu, Uganda, Ukraine, United Arab Emirates, United Kingdom, United Republic of Tanzania, United States, Uruguay, Uzbekistan, Viet Nam, Yemen, Zambia.

Against: None.

Abstaining: Syrian Arab Republic, Zimbabwe.

Note by Secretary-General. Pursuant to Assembly resolution 65/276 (see above), in a June note [A/65/856], the Secretary-General informed the Assembly of the modalities that applied to EU participation, in its capacity as observer, in the sessions and work of the Assembly, including its committees and working groups; in international meetings and conferences convened under the Assembly's auspices; and in UN conferences.

Observer status

Union of South American Nations

In June [A/66/144], Guyana requested the inclusion in the agenda of the General Assembly's sixty-sixth session of an item on observer status for the Union of South American Nations (UNASUR). An explanatory memorandum informed that UNASUR, as a regional organization, was dedicated to the promotion of regional integration and the strengthening of the international presence of the region. Its participation in the consolidation of a world community fully adhered to the purposes and principles enshrined in the UN Charter.

Guyana noted that UNASUR would initiate a mutually beneficial institutional dialogue with the United Nations, promote coherence of efforts and open avenues for cooperation in a wide spectrum of areas. Observer status would assist UNASUR in fostering regional initiatives aimed at integration among its Member States.

GENERAL ASSEMBLY ACTION

On 9 December [meeting 82], the General Assembly, on the recommendation of the Sixth (Legal) Committee [A/66/484], adopted **resolution 66/109** without vote [agenda item 168].

Observer status for the Union of South American Nations in the General Assembly

The General Assembly,

Wishing to promote cooperation between the United Nations and the Union of South American Nations,

1. *Decides* to invite the Union of South American Nations to participate in the sessions and the work of the General Assembly in the capacity of observer;

2. *Requests* the Secretary-General to take the necessary action to implement the present resolution.

International Renewable Energy Agency

On 11 July [A/66/145], the United Arab Emirates requested the inclusion in the agenda of the General Assembly's sixty-sixth session of an item on observer status for the International Renewable Energy Agency (IRENA). An explanatory memorandum recalled that IRENA performed its activities to promote peace and international cooperation, in conformity with UN policies that furthered sustainable development. IRENA also complemented global and sectoral mandates and strategies of the United Nations and its departments, programmes and agencies. There was clear potential for close cooperation between the United Nations and IRENA. Identifying synergies and coordinating activities would ensure efficient use of resources and coherence in addressing major challenges such as fighting climate change, alleviating poverty and promoting sustainable development by tapping into the potential that renewable energy offered. IRENA was a fully committed global partner with expertise that could help address those challenges.

GENERAL ASSEMBLY ACTION

On 9 December [meeting 82], the General Assembly, on the recommendation of the Sixth Committee [A/66/485], adopted **resolution 66/110** without vote [agenda item 169].

Observer status for the International Renewable Energy Agency in the General Assembly

The General Assembly,

Wishing to promote cooperation between the United Nations and the International Renewable Energy Agency,

1. *Decides* to invite the International Renewable Energy Agency to participate in the sessions and the work of the General Assembly in the capacity of observer;

2. *Requests* the Secretary-General to take the necessary action to implement the present resolution.

Central European Initiative

On 13 July [A/66/191], Italy, Montenegro, Serbia and Ukraine requested the inclusion in the agenda of the General Assembly's sixty-sixth session of an item on observer status for the Central European Initiative. An explanatory memorandum recalled that the Initiative cooperated with a number of UN specialized entities in science and technology. Through its various funds and cooperation instruments, the Initiative had financed and supported projects on a number of other issues that were in line with the MDGs [YUN 2000, p. 51], such as combating poverty, and improving child and maternal health.

GENERAL ASSEMBLY ACTION

On 9 December [meeting 82], the General Assembly, on the recommendation of the Sixth Committee [A/66/486], adopted **resolution 66/111** without vote [agenda item 170].

Observer status for the Central European Initiative in the General Assembly

The General Assembly,

Wishing to promote cooperation between the United Nations and the Central European Initiative,

1. *Decides* to invite the Central European Initiative to participate in the sessions and the work of the General Assembly in the capacity of observer;

2. *Requests* the Secretary-General to take the necessary action to implement the present resolution.

Intergovernmental Authority on Development

On 5 August [A/66/193], Ethiopia requested the inclusion in the agenda of the General Assembly's sixty-sixth session of an item on observer status for the Intergovernmental Authority on Development (IGAD). An explanatory memorandum recalled that in 1996, the Authority's Assembly of Heads of State and Government revitalized IGAD, which was first established in 1986 as the Intergovernmental Authority on Drought and Development [YUN 1986, p. 665]. Since then, IGAD had cooperated closely with the AU, the United Nations and its agencies, and concluded cooperation agreements with other multilateral organizations. It had become imperative for IGAD, with its ever-increasing engagements in areas of peace and development in the subregion, to take part in the work of UN conferences and committees relevant to its mandate and shared mission with the United Nations.

GENERAL ASSEMBLY ACTION

On 9 December [meeting 82], the General Assembly, on the recommendation of the Sixth Committee [A/66/488], adopted **resolution 66/112** without vote [agenda item 172].

Observer status for the Intergovernmental Authority on Development in the General Assembly

The General Assembly,

Wishing to promote cooperation between the United Nations and the Intergovernmental Authority on Development,

1. *Decides* to invite the Intergovernmental Authority on Development to participate in the sessions and the work of the General Assembly in the capacity of observer;
2. *Requests* the Secretary-General to take the necessary action to implement the present resolution.

West African Economic and Monetary Union

On 26 October [A/66/232], Togo requested the inclusion in the agenda of the General Assembly's sixty-sixth session of an item on observer status for the West African Economic and Monetary Union (WAEMU). An explanatory memorandum stated that WAEMU had already obtained permanent observer status with the Economic and Social Council, the United Nations Conference on Trade and Development and a number of bodies of the World Trade Organization in Geneva. Established in 1994, WAEMU had experience in the policies of competition and, in that regard, was involved with the work of the Organization for the Harmonization of Business Law in Africa. The promotion of peace and security in the West African subregion was the new area of activity of the Union. Observer status would open the way to increased inter-institutional dialogue which would be beneficial to both organizations and would facilitate the coordination of efforts and cooperation in specific areas. It would also help WAEMU to encourage integration initiatives among its members.

GENERAL ASSEMBLY ACTION

On 9 December [meeting 82], the General Assembly, on the recommendation of the Sixth Committee [A/66/550], adopted **resolution 66/113** without vote [agenda item 175].

Observer status for the West African Economic and Monetary Union in the General Assembly

The General Assembly,

Wishing to promote cooperation between the United Nations and the West African Economic and Monetary Union,

1. *Decides* to invite the West African Economic and Monetary Union to participate in the sessions and the work of the General Assembly in the capacity of observer;
2. *Requests* the Secretary-General to take the necessary action to implement the present resolution.

Cooperation Council of Turkic-speaking States

On 2 May [A/66/141], Azerbaijan, Kazakhstan, Kyrgyzstan and Turkey requested the inclusion in the agenda of the General Assembly's sixty-sixth session of an item on observer status for the Cooperation Council of Turkic-speaking States. An explanatory memorandum recalled that the Cooperation Council, as an intergovernmental organization dedicated to strengthening peace and stability, enhancing dialogue, promoting cooperation and disclosing the potential for common development among its member States, fully adhered to the purposes and principles enshrined in the UN Charter. By promoting deeper relations and solidarity among Turkic-speaking countries, it served as a new regional instrument for enriching international cooperation in the Central Asian and Caucasian regions. The granting of observer status would initiate a mutually beneficial institutional dialogue between itself and the United Nations, bring about coherence of efforts and open avenues for cooperation in specific areas.

On 9 December, the Assembly deferred a decision on the request for observer status for the Cooperation Council of Turkic-speaking States to its sixty-seventh (2012) session (**decision 66/527**).

International Emergency Management Organization

On 20 May [A/66/142], the former Yugoslav Republic of Macedonia requested the inclusion in the agenda of the General Assembly's sixty-sixth session of an item on observer status for the International Emergency Management Organization (IEMO). An explanatory memorandum indicated that IEMO, established in 2006 [YUN 2006, p. 1606], had as its objective the strengthening of resilience to emergencies, as well as working for recovery from neglected crises. Its principal activity consisted of mobilizing under-mobilized resources in support of the UN system, through a large arrangement of about 750 emergency-related entities called the Global Prevention Network. IEMO also worked for the diffusion of emergency prevention in support of the MDGs.

In a 14 September meeting [A/BUR/66/SR.1] of the General Committee on the organization of the Assembly's sixty-sixth session, the former Yugoslav Republic of Macedonia withdrew its proposal of the item and indicated that the Secretary-General had been informed of that decision by a 5 September letter from the Permanent Representative. The Committee took note of the withdrawal of the item.

United Cities and Local Governments

On 19 July [A/66/192], Turkey requested the inclusion in the agenda of the General Assembly's sixty-sixth session of an item on observer status for the United Cities and Local Governments (UCLG). An explanatory memorandum stated that UCLG was the world organization of local and regional authorities. With members in 140 countries, it represented the interests of the group before the international community and promoted exchange and innovation among its members, while fostering solidarity and development cooperation. UCLG enjoyed a unique status as a world organization of local authorities, and was convinced that it was in the interest of the United Nations to promote cooperation between itself and local authorities in the era of urbanization.

In a 14 November report [A/66/487], the Assembly's Sixth Committee reported that it had concluded consideration of the item on 9 November without taking action.

On 9 December, the Assembly took note of the Sixth Committee's report regarding observer status for UCLG (**decision 66/528**).

International Conference of Asian Political Parties

On 10 August [A/66/198], Cambodia, Japan, Nepal, the Philippines, the Republic of Korea and Viet Nam requested the inclusion in the agenda of the General Assembly's sixty-sixth session of an item on observer status for the International Conference of Asian Political Parties (ICAPP). An explanatory memorandum indicated that ICAPP was launched in 2000 to build bridges of political cooperation and to establish networks of mutual benefit among mainstream political parties in Asia, both ruling and in opposition.

ICAPP would play a key role not only in Asia's inevitable movement to build an Asian community but in the global quest for a more peaceful and prosperous world, and in forging cooperation between the United Nations and the political parties not only of Asia but also of Latin America and Africa.

On 9 December, the Assembly deferred a decision on the request for observer status for ICAPP to the Assembly's sixty-seventh (2012) session (**decision 66/530**).

Parliamentary Assembly of Turkic-speaking Countries

On 12 August [A/66/196], Azerbaijan requested the inclusion in the agenda of the General Assembly's sixty-sixth session of an item on observer status for the Parliamentary Assembly of Turkic-speaking Countries (TURKPA). An explanatory memorandum recalled that TURKPA, established in 2008, was an inter-parliamentary organization established to develop inter-parliamentary cooperation among its members (Azerbaijan, Kazakhstan, Kyrgyzstan, Turkey), promote political dialogue and create a favourable political climate for elaborating and implementing various initiatives aimed at safeguarding regional and global security.

Granting observer status to TURKPA would institutionalize cooperation, enhance the interaction between the two organizations and assist its efforts to encourage regional initiatives.

In a 14 November report [A/66/489], the Assembly's Sixth Committee reported that it had concluded consideration of the item on 9 November without taking action.

On 9 December, the Assembly took note of the Sixth Committee's report regarding observer status for TURKPA (**decision 66/529**).

Intergovernmental organizations

On 29 July, the Economic and Social Council granted observer status to the intergovernmental organization International Anti-Corruption Academy on a continuing basis, without the right to vote, in its deliberations on questions within the scope of its activities (**decision 2011/269**).

Non-governmental organizations

Committee on NGOs

The Committee on Non-Governmental Organizations held its 2011 regular session (31 January–9 February and 3 March) [E/2011/32 (Part I)] and its resumed session (16–24 May and 16 June) [E/2011/32 (Part II)] in New York. At both sessions, the Committee considered the strengthening of the Non-Governmental Organizations Branch of the Department of Economic and Social Affairs of the Secretariat and the General voluntary trust fund in support of the United Nations Non-Governmental Organizations Informal Regional Network; reviewed its methods of work relating to the implementation of Economic and Social Council resolution 1996/31 [YUN 1996, p. 1360], including the process of accreditation of non-governmental organization (NGO) representatives, and Council decision 1995/304 [YUN 1995, p. 1445]; and considered special reports and complaints by Member States.

At its regular session, the Committee considered 352 applications for consultative status, including applications deferred from its 1999–2010 sessions. It recommended 112 applications for consultative status, deferred consideration of 216, took note of one NGO that had withdrawn its application and closed consideration without prejudice of 23 applications. The Committee also had before it 10 requests for reclassification of consultative status, of which it recommended five. It considered one deferred request for reclassification and recommended the reclassification. It considered seven requests for change of name; it took note of six and deferred consideration of one to its next (2012) session. The Committee also took note of 212 quadrennial reports and heard 13 representatives from the 27 NGOs attending the session.

On 25 July, the Council granted consultative status to 111 organizations; reclassified three from special to general consultative status and another three from roster to special consultative status. It took note of the request of one NGO to withdraw its application, the request of six NGOs for change of name, and the quadrennial reports submitted by 212 NGOs for the reporting period 2006–2009 and seven for reporting periods earlier than 2006–2009. It noted that the Committee had closed consideration of 23 applications after failure to respond to queries by Committee members (**decision 2011/227**).

On the same day, the Council suspended for one year the consultative status of 102 NGOs with outstanding quadrennial reports and requested the Secretary-General to advise them of its decision (**decision 2011/230**) and withdrew the consultative status of 61 NGOs with continued outstanding quadrennial reports and requested the Secretary-General to advise them accordingly (**decision 2011/232**).

On 29 July, the Council took note of the Committee's report on its 2011 regular session (**decision 2011/273**).

At its resumed session in May and June, the Committee considered 333 applications for consultative status. It recommended 146 applications, deferred 154 for further consideration, recommended not to grant consultative status to one and closed consideration of 32 applications. It also took note of one NGO that had withdrawn its application. The Committee recommended granting three requests for reclassification, and took note of eight requests for change of name and 154 quadrennial reports, including 15 reports of organizations that had been suspended in 2010 and whose consultative status had been reinstated upon receipt of the outstanding quadrennial reports. The Committee heard 28 representatives out of 34 NGOs and recommended seven draft decisions for action by the Council.

On 25 July, the Council granted consultative status to 146 NGOs, reclassified two from special to general consultative status and one from roster to special consultative status, and noted the withdrawal of its application by one NGO. It also noted that the Committee had recommended not to grant consultative status to one NGO and had taken note of the name change of eight NGOs and of the quadrennial reports of 154 organizations for the period 2006–2009 and earlier (**decision 2011/228**).

On the same date, the Council reinstated the consultative status of 16 NGOs that had submitted their outstanding quadrennial reports (**decision 2011/231**) and granted special consultative status to three NGOs (**decisions 2011/224, 2011/225** and **2011/226**). Also on 25 July, the Council decided to close without prejudice its consideration of the applications for consultative status submitted by 32 NGOs after they had failed to respond, despite three reminders over the course of two consecutive sessions of the Committee, to queries posed to them by members of the Committee (**decision 2011/229**).

On 29 July, the Council requested the Committee to resume its consideration of the application for consultative status of one NGO at its 2012 regular session (**decision 2011/272**).

The Council took note of the Committee's report on its resumed 2011 session (**decision 2011/234**), decided that the Committee's 2012 regular session would be held from 30 January to 8 February and on 17 February, and its resumed session from 21 to 30 May and on 8 June, and approved the provisional agenda for that session (**decision 2011/233**).

On 22 December, the General Assembly decided on arrangements for accreditation and participation in the United Nations Conference on Sustainable Development (see p. 799) and its preparatory process of relevant NGOs and other major groups (**decision 66/544A**).

Chapter II

United Nations financing and programming

During 2011, the financial situation of the United Nations was generally positive, despite the global financial climate. By year's end, aggregate assessments had decreased to $11.7 billion, compared to $12.5 billion in 2010. Total unpaid assessments were higher, with $454 million for the regular budget and $2.6 billion for peacekeeping operations, up from $351 million and $2.5 billion in 2010. Cash balances were lower, with $94 million available for the regular budget, while debt owed to Member States decreased to $529 million. The number of Member States paying their regular budget assessments in full increased to 143.

In December, the General Assembly adopted final budget appropriations for the 2010–2011 biennium, increasing the amount of $5,367,234,700 approved in 2010 to $5,416,433,700, and increasing income estimates by $8,308,000 to $601,279,800. It also adopted revised budget appropriations for the 2012–2013 biennium totalling $5,152,299,600.

The Committee on Contributions continued to review the methodology for preparing the scale of assessments of Member States' contributions to the UN budget and to encourage the payment of arrears through the multi-year payment process. The General Assembly continued to review the efficiency of the administrative and financial functioning of the Organization, including its financial management practices. During the year, the Secretary-General transmitted reports to the Assembly on the status of implementation of the International Public Accounting Standards, the work of the Independent Audit Advisory Committee and the administration of trust funds.

Financial situation

The overall UN financial situation in 2011 was generally positive, despite the global financial climate. In October [A/66/521], the Secretary-General reported that unpaid assessed contributions remained concentrated among a few Member States, particularly for the regular budget, the international tribunals and the capital master plan (CMP). As at 5 October, aggregate assessments stood at $10.5 billion (compared to $12.3 billion in 2010). That amount included assessments for the regular budget ($2,415 million), the two international tribunals ($286 million), peacekeeping ($7,433 million) and a fixed amount for the CMP ($341 million). Meanwhile, for 10 active missions, payment of troop obligations was broadly current up to June 2011 for contingent-owned equipment. Debt to Member States providing troops and equipment to peacekeeping operations at the end of 2011 was expected to be some $448 million.

As at 5 October, unpaid assessments for the regular budget, peacekeeping and the tribunals totalled $4.2 billion, which included $3.3 billion for peacekeeping (compared to $3.2 billion at 5 October 2010); $867 million for the regular budget ($80 million more than in 2010); and $56 million for the tribunals ($6 million more than in 2010). Member States that had paid their regular budget assessments in full as at 5 October 2011 numbered 131, which was 12 more than at 5 October 2010.

In his end-of-year review of the financial situation [A/66/521/Add.1], the Secretary-General noted that the performance of the four main indicators of the Organization's financial health reflected improvement as compared to 31 December 2010: aggregate assessments were lower at $11.7 billion (compared to $12.5 billion in 2010), due to a $1.0 billion decrease for peacekeeping operations (from $9,671 million to $8,651 million), and assessments for the regular budget and the international tribunals increased.

Unpaid assessments were higher for the regular budget at $454 million, up from $351 million in 2010, and $2.6 billion for peacekeeping operations, slightly up from just under $2.5 billion in 2010. Outstanding assessments for the two tribunals remained the same as in 2010 at $27 million. Cash balances were lower with $94 million available for the regular budget; and debt owed to Member States was $529 million. The number of Member States paying their regular budget assessments in full was 143, five more than in 2010.

On 24 December, the Assembly decided that the agenda item on improving the financial situation of the United Nations would remain for consideration at its resumed sixty-sixth (2012) session (**decision 66/557**).

UN budget

Budget for 2010–2011

Final appropriations

In 2011, the General Assembly adopted final budget appropriations for the 2010–2011 biennium, increasing the amount of $5,367,234,700 approved in resolution 65/260 A [YUN 2010, p. 1425] by $49,199,000 to $5,416,433,700 and increasing income estimates by $8,308,000 to $601,279,800.

Report of Secretary-General. In his second performance report on the 2010–2011 programme budget [A/66/578 & Corr.1], the Secretary-General provided estimates of anticipated final expenditures and income for the biennium, based on actual expenditures for the first 21 months, projections for the last three months, changes in inflation and exchange rates, and cost-of-living adjustments.

The anticipated final level of expenditures and income represented a net increase of $40.9 million, reflecting projected additional requirements of $139.7 million due to changes in exchange ($103.7 million) and inflation rates ($11.9 million), and commitments ($24.1 million) entered into under the provisions of Assembly resolution 64/246 [YUN 2009, p. 1409], and reduced requirements of $98.8 million due to variations in posts costs and adjustments to other objects of expenditure ($90.5 million) and an increase in income ($8.3 million).

The projected expenditure for the biennium was estimated at $5,416.4 million gross—an increase of $49.2 million compared with the revised appropriation of $5,367.2 million approved in 2010. The projected income was estimated at $601.3 million—an increase of $8.3 million compared with the revised income estimate of $593 million.

The Advisory Committee on Administrative and Budgetary Questions (ACABQ), in December [A/66/611], recommended that the Secretary-General explore and analyse additional options for addressing the different aspects of the recosting methodology, including the practice of recosting the programme budget four times in the biennial budget cycle; report on alternative options for the recosting methodology, with an analysis of the risks and resource requirements of each option; and submit the report separately from the performance report for the Assembly's consideration at its sixty-seventh (2013) session. It also recommended that the Assembly approve the revised estimates for the 2010–2011 biennium, as set out in the performance report.

GENERAL ASSEMBLY ACTION

On 24 December [meeting 93], the General Assembly, on the recommendation of the Fifth (Administrative and Budgetary) Committee [A/66/636], adopted **resolution 66/245 A** and **B** without vote [agenda item 133].

Programme budget for the biennium 2010–2011

A

FINAL BUDGET APPROPRIATIONS FOR THE BIENNIUM 2010–2011

The General Assembly

1. *Takes note* of the second performance report of the Secretary-General on the programme budget for the biennium 2010–2011, and endorses the observations and recommendations contained in the related report of the Advisory Committee on Administrative and Budgetary Questions;

2. *Resolves* that, for the biennium 2010–2011:

(*a*) The amount of 5,367,234,700 United States dollars appropriated by it in its resolution 65/260 A of 24 December 2010 shall be increased by 49,199,000 dollars, as follows:

Section		Amount approved in resolution 65/260 A	Increase/ (decrease)	Final appropriations
		(United States dollars)		
Part I.	**Overall policymaking, direction and coordination**			
1.	Overall policymaking, direction and coordination	101,770,300	6,280,500	108,050,800
2.	General Assembly and Economic and Social Council affairs and conference management	672,835,300	16,409,200	689,244,500
	TOTAL, part I	774,605,600	22,689,700	797,295,300
Part II.	**Political affairs**			
3.	Political affairs	1,313,276,700	(3,814,800)	1,309,461,900
4.	Disarmament	22,134,800	393,400	22,528,200
5.	Peacekeeping operations	112,903,800	(3,911,500)	108,992,300
6.	Peaceful uses of outer space	8,023,000	634,100	8,657,100
	TOTAL, part II	1,456,338,300	(6,698,800)	1,449,639,500
Part III.	**International justice and law**			
7.	International Court of Justice	46,605,800	(30,900)	46,574,900
8.	Legal affairs	45,396,500	978,900	46,375,400
	TOTAL, part III	92,002,300	948,000	92,950,300
Part IV.	**International cooperation for development**			
9.	Economic and social affairs	159,110,900	(684,100)	158,426,800
10.	Least developed countries, landlocked developing countries and small island developing States	7,406,100	(121,800)	7,284,300
11.	United Nations support for the New Partnership for Africa's Development	12,641,000	(2,461,900)	10,179,100
12.	Trade and development	136,629,800	10,840,900	147,470,700

Section		Amount approved in resolution 65/260 A	Increase/ (decrease)	Final appropriations
		(United States dollars)		
13.	International Trade Centre UNCTAD/WTO	31,793,300	4,464,200	36,257,500
14.	Environment	14,211,300	673,600	14,884,900
15.	Human settlements	20,564,700	1,701,000	22,265,700
16.	International drug control, crime and terrorism prevention and criminal justice	39,191,100	3,674,300	42,865,400
37.	United Nations Entity for Gender Equality and the Empowerment of Women (UN-Women)	6,957,100	(479,100)	6,478,000
	TOTAL, part IV	**428,505,300**	**17,607,100**	**446,112,400**
Part V.	**Regional cooperation for development**			
17.	Economic and social development in Africa	123,662,500	(11,306,600)	112,355,900
18.	Economic and social development in Asia and the Pacific	98,326,800	2,320,400	100,647,200
19.	Economic development in Europe	65,547,100	6,427,100	71,974,200
20.	Economic and social development in Latin America and the Caribbean	110,129,900	7,991,800	118,121,700
21.	Economic and social development in Western Asia	63,298,400	1,788,300	65,086,700
22.	Regular programme of technical cooperation	52,246,200	(2,615,300)	49,630,900
	TOTAL, part V	**513,210,900**	**4,605,700**	**517,816,600**
Part VI.	**Human rights and humanitarian affairs**			
23.	Human rights	141,191,400	8,084,400	149,275,800
24.	International protection, durable solutions and assistance to refugees	83,717,500	(18,100)	83,699,400
25.	Palestine refugees	43,712,400	4,697,100	48,409,500
26.	Humanitarian assistance	29,399,900	96,800	29,496,700
	TOTAL, part VI	**298,021,200**	**12,860,200**	**310,881,400**
Part VII.	**Public information**			
27.	Public information	184,996,600	246,800	185,243,400
	TOTAL, part VII	**184,996,600**	**246,800**	**185,243,400**
Part VIII.	**Common support services**			
28A.	Office of the Under-Secretary-General for Management	26,126,100	375,500	26,501,600
28B.	Office of Programme Planning, Budget and Accounts	38,552,500	(1,253,300)	37,299,200
28C.	Office of Human Resources Management	74,614,600	221,700	74,836,300
28D.	Office of Central Support Services	174,871,100	1,936,800	176,807,900
28E.	Administration, Geneva	126,778,700	15,013,900	141,792,600
28F.	Administration, Vienna	39,127,000	1,380,400	40,507,400
28G.	Administration, Nairobi	29,136,300	(200,700)	28,935,600
29.	Office of Information and Communications Technology	72,120,000	(684,800)	71,435,200
	TOTAL, part VIII	**581,326,300**	**16,789,500**	**598,115,800**
Part IX.	**Internal oversight**			
30.	Internal oversight	38,925,000	(3,769,200)	35,155,800
	TOTAL, part IX	**38,925,000**	**(3,769,200)**	**35,155,800**
Part X.	**Jointly financed administrative activities and special expenses**			
31.	Jointly financed administrative activities	11,993,400	(1,459,400)	10,534,000
32.	Special expenses	114,134,100	(3,935,600)	110,198,500
	TOTAL, part X	**126,127,500**	**(5,395,000)**	**120,732,500**
Part XI.	**Capital expenditures**			
33.	Construction, alteration, improvement and major maintenance	60,326,800	480,200	60,807,000
	TOTAL, part XI	**60,326,800**	**480,200**	**60,807,000**
Part XII.	**Safety and security**			
34.	Safety and security	238,447,700	(6,892,900)	231,554,800
	TOTAL, part XII	**238,447,700**	**(6,892,900)**	**231,554,800**
Part XIII.	**Development Account**			
35.	Development Account	23,651,300	—	23,651,300
	TOTAL, part XIII	**23,651,300**	**—**	**23,651,300**
Part XIV.	**Staff assessment**			
36.	Staff assessment	550,749,900	(4,272,300)	546,477,600
	TOTAL, part XIV	**550,749,900**	**(4,272,300)**	**546,477,600**
	GRAND TOTAL	**5,367,234,700**	**49,199,000**	**5,416,433,700**

(b) The Secretary-General shall be authorized to transfer credits between sections of the budget, with the concurrence of the Advisory Committee on Administrative and Budgetary Questions;

(c) In addition to the appropriations approved under subparagraph (a) above, an amount of 75,000 dollars shall be appropriated for each year of the biennium 2010–2011 from the accumulated income of the Library Endowment Fund for the purchase of books, periodicals, maps and library equipment and for such other expenses of the Library at the Palais des Nations in Geneva as are in accordance with the objects and provisions of the endowment.

B

FINAL INCOME ESTIMATES FOR THE BIENNIUM 2010–2011

The General Assembly

Resolves that, for the biennium 2010–2011:

(a) The estimates of income of 592,971,800 United States dollars approved by it in its resolution 65/260 B of 24 December 2010 shall be increased by 8,308,000 dollars, as follows:

Income section	Amount approved in resolution 65/260 B	Increase/ (decrease)	Final estimates
	(United States dollars)		
1. Income from staff assessment	555,041,000	(5,617,400)	549,423,600
TOTAL, income section 1	555,041,000	(5,617,400)	549,423,600
2. General income	40,487,800	10,210,500	50,698,300
3. Services to the public	(2,557,000)	3,714,900	1,157,900
TOTAL, income sections 2 and 3	37,930,800	13,925,400	51,856,200
GRAND TOTAL	592,971,800	8,308,000	601,279,800

(b) The income from staff assessment shall be credited to the Tax Equalization Fund in accordance with the provisions of General Assembly resolution 973(X) of 15 December 1955;

(c) Direct expenses of the United Nations Postal Administration, services to visitors, catering and related services, garage operations, television services and the sale of publications not provided for under the budget appropriations shall be charged against the income derived from those activities.

Also on 24 December, the Assembly, by **decision 66/557**, decided that the agenda item on the programme budget for the 2010–2011 biennium would remain for consideration during its resumed sixty-sixth (2012) session.

Questions relating to the 2010–2011 programme budget

The Fifth Committee considered special subjects related to the 2010–2011 programme budget concerning estimates in respect of special political missions, good offices and other political initiatives authorized by the General Assembly and/or the Security Council (see below). Other subjects considered included revised estimates resulting from the entry into force of the International Convention for the Protection of All Persons from Enforced Disappearance (see p. 634), conditions of service and compensation for officials, other than Secretariat officials, serving the General Assembly, and standards of accommodation for air travel (see p. 1448). In addition, on 18 May, the Secretary-General submitted a consolidated report on the changes to the biennial programme plan as reflected in the 2010–2011 programme budget and the 2012–2013 proposed programme budget [A/66/82].

Revised estimates in respect of matters of which the Security Council was seized

In February [A/65/328/Add.6 & Corr.1], the Secretary-General submitted proposed resource requirements for the period 1 January to 31 December 2011 for two special political missions: the United Nations Office in Burundi (BNUB) and the United Nations Representative on the International Advisory and Monitoring Board (IAMB) of the Development Fund for Iraq, totalling $23,127,800. In March [A/65/602/Add.1], ACABQ recommended that the General Assembly approve the resources requested for BNUB and the UN Representative on the IAMB, subject to the Committee's recommendations.

In May [A/65/328/Add.7], the Secretary-General submitted proposed resource requirements for 2011 for two additional special political missions: the Panel of Experts on the Libyan Arab Jamahiriya and the United Nations Representative to the Geneva International Discussions, in the amount of $3,595,800, which ACABQ recommended that the Assembly approve, subject to its recommendations [A/65/602/Add.2].

GENERAL ASSEMBLY ACTION

On 4 April [meeting 84], the General Assembly, on the recommendation of the Fifth Committee [A/65/646/Add.2], adopted **resolution 65/268** without vote [agenda item 129].

Special subjects relating to the programme budget for the biennium 2010–2011

The General Assembly,

I

Revised estimates resulting from the entry into force of the International Convention for the Protection of All Persons from Enforced Disappearance

Having considered the report of the Secretary-General on revised estimates resulting from the entry into force of the International Convention for the Protection of All Persons from Enforced Disappearance and the related report of the Advisory Committee on Administrative and Budgetary Questions,

1. *Takes note* of the report of the Secretary-General;
2. *Endorses* the conclusions and recommendations contained in the report of the Advisory Committee on Administrative and Budgetary Questions, subject to the provisions of the present resolution;

3. *Decides* to establish one P-4 post and one General Service (Other level) post under section 23 (Human rights) of the programme budget for the biennium 2010–2011 effective 1 April 2011;

4. *Also decides* that an additional amount of 815,625 United States dollars (at initial 2010–2011 rates), comprising 529,400 dollars under section 2 (General Assembly and Economic and Social Council affairs and conference management), 236,800 dollars under section 23 (Human rights), 25,500 dollars under section 28E (Administration, Geneva), and 23,925 dollars under section 36 (Staff assessment), to be offset by a corresponding amount under income section 1 (Income from staff assessment), should be met from within the resources already appropriated under the programme budget for the biennium 2010–2011;

5. *Requests* the Secretary-General to report on the above, as necessary, in the context of the second performance report on the programme budget for the biennium 2010–2011;

II

Estimates in respect of special political missions, good offices and other political initiatives authorized by the General Assembly and/or the Security Council: United Nations Office in Burundi and United Nations Representative on the International Advisory and Monitoring Board of the Development Fund for Iraq

Recalling its resolution 64/244 A of 24 December 2009, section VI of its resolution 64/245 of 24 December 2009, section IV of its resolution 64/260 of 29 March 2010, section XIII of its resolution 65/259 of 24 December 2010 and its resolution 65/260 A of 24 December 2010,

Having considered the report of the Secretary-General entitled "Estimates in respect of special political missions, good offices and other political initiatives authorized by the General Assembly and/or the Security Council: United Nations Office in Burundi and United Nations Representative on the International Advisory and Monitoring Board" and the related report of the Advisory Committee on Administrative and Budgetary Questions,

1. *Takes note* of the report of the Secretary-General;

2. *Endorses* the conclusions and recommendations contained in the report of the Advisory Committee on Administrative and Budgetary Questions, subject to the provisions of the present resolution;

3. *Underscores* the need for a smooth transition from the United Nations Integrated Office in Burundi to the United Nations Office in Burundi;

4. *Takes note* of paragraphs 21, 26 and 32 (*a*) of the report of the Advisory Committee on Administrative and Budgetary Questions;

5. *Approves* the budget for the United Nations Office in Burundi in the amount of 23,989,700 dollars gross (22,145,800 dollars net) for the period from 1 January to 31 December 2011;

6. *Also approves* the budget for the United Nations Representative on the International Advisory and Monitoring Board in the amount of 24,600 dollars gross (24,600 dollars net) for the period from 1 January to 30 June 2011, and notes that the requirements for the Representative will be accommodated from within the overall appropriation for special political missions and reported to the General Assembly in the context of the second performance report on the programme budget for the biennium 2010–2011;

7. *Decides* to appropriate, under the provisions of its resolution 41/213 of 19 December 1986, the amount of 7,504,600 dollars under section 3 (Political affairs) and 624,800 dollars under section 36 (Staff assessment), to be offset by an equivalent amount under income section 1 (Income from staff assessment) of the programme budget for the biennium 2010–2011, taking into consideration the amount of 14,641,200 dollars already approved for the United Nations Integrated Office in Burundi (the predecessor mission);

8. *Also decides* to utilize the unencumbered balance for the United Nations Integrated Office in Burundi to offset part of the additional appropriation required for the United Nations Office in Burundi for the period from 1 January to 31 December 2011, and requests the Secretary-General to meet the additional requirements for the United Nations Office in Burundi from the overall appropriation for special political missions, and to report thereon in the context of the second performance report on the programme budget for the biennium 2010–2011;

III

Conditions of service and compensation for officials, other than Secretariat officials, serving the General Assembly: full-time members of the International Civil Service Commission and the Chair of the Advisory Committee on Administrative and Budgetary Questions

Recalling its resolution 35/221 of 17 December 1980, section VII of its resolution 55/238 of 23 December 2000 and its resolution 58/266 of 23 December 2003,

Recalling also its resolution 3357(XXIX) of 18 December 1974, by which the General Assembly recognized that the salaries and allowances of the Chair and Vice-Chair of the International Civil Service Commission should be established separately from those of the staff of organizations for which the Commission has the power to recommend or determine such salaries and allowances and that the remuneration and status of the Chair and Vice-Chair should be such as to permit them to speak on equal terms with executive heads,

Having considered the report of the Secretary-General entitled "Conditions of service and compensation for officials, other than Secretariat officials, serving the General Assembly: full-time members of the International Civil Service Commission and the Chair of the Advisory Committee on Administrative and Budgetary Questions", as well as the related report of the Advisory Committee on Administrative and Budgetary Questions,

1. *Takes note* of the report of the Secretary-General;

2. *Endorses* the conclusions and recommendations contained in the report of the Advisory Committee on Administrative and Budgetary Questions, subject to the provisions of the present resolution;

3. *Takes note* of paragraph 12 of the report of the Advisory Committee on Administrative and Budgetary Questions;

4. *Decides* to discontinue the use of the consumer price index as the basis for annual adjustments to the annual net compensation of the Chair and Vice-Chair of the International Civil Service Commission and of the Chair of the Advisory Committee on Administrative and Budgetary Questions;

5. *Also decides* that the annual net compensation of the Chairs of the International Civil Service Commission and the Advisory Committee on Administrative and Budgetary Questions shall be set at 224,833 dollars, including the special allowance, with retroactive effect from 1 January 2011, and that the pensionable remuneration shall be adjusted accordingly to 279,283 dollars;

6. *Further decides* that the annual net compensation of the Vice-Chair of the International Civil Service Commission shall be set at 214,833 dollars, with retroactive effect from 1 January 2011, and that the pensionable remuneration shall be adjusted accordingly to 264,320 dollars;

7. *Decides* that, effective 1 January 2012, the annual net compensation of the three officials shall be subject to a cost-of-living adjustment equivalent to the annual change in the midpoint net base salary of the most senior officials in the Secretariat, namely the Under-Secretaries-General and Assistant Secretaries-General;

8. *Also decides* to review every four years the other elements of the conditions of service of the three officials, including the special allowances for the Chairs of the International Civil Service Commission and the Advisory Committee on Administrative and Budgetary Questions, the education grant, the installation grant and the survivor's benefit, with the next review to be conducted at the sixty-eighth session of the General Assembly;

9. *Recalls* rule 157 of the rules of procedure of the General Assembly, and decides that, on an exceptional basis and without setting a precedent for other agenda items, the Secretary-General shall henceforth submit reports on the conditions of service of the Chair and Vice-Chair of the International Civil Service Commission and of the Chair of the Advisory Committee on Administrative and Budgetary Questions directly to the Assembly;

IV

Standards of accommodation for air travel

Recalling its resolution 42/214 of 21 December 1987, section IV, paragraph 14, of its resolution 53/214 of 18 December 1998, section IV of its resolution 60/255 of 8 May 2006, section XV of its resolution 62/238 of 22 December 2007, section II of its resolution 63/268 of 7 April 2009 and its decision 57/589 of 18 June 2003,

Having considered the report of the Secretary-General on standards of accommodation for air travel, the report of the United Nations System Chief Executives Board for Coordination on the feasibility of harmonizing standards of travel and the related report of the Advisory Committee on Administrative and Budgetary Questions,

Having also considered the report of the Joint Inspection Unit entitled "Review of travel arrangements within the United Nations system" and the note by the Secretary-General transmitting his comments and those of the United Nations System Chief Executives Board for Coordination thereon,

1. *Takes note* of the report of the Secretary-General;

2. *Endorses* the conclusions and recommendations contained in the report of the Advisory Committee on Administrative and Budgetary Questions, subject to the provisions of the present resolution;

3. *Regrets* that the Secretary-General has not presented the comprehensive report mentioned in section II, paragraph 3, of its resolution 63/268, based on a review by the United Nations System Chief Executives Board for Coordination and specific proposals, with a view to harmonizing standards of travel for staff of the United Nations common system, indicating the measures that can be implemented under the authority of the Secretary-General, as well as those that will require the approval of the General Assembly;

4. *Recognizes* the need for efficient and effective air travel to effectively implement the mandates of the United Nations through the facilitation of direct contacts;

5. *Requests* the Secretary-General to improve, as a matter of urgency, the management of air travel in the United Nations and to pursue a more effective and efficient utilization of resources for air travel, including through the implementation of the measures outlined in the annex to the present resolution;

6. *Also requests* the Secretary-General to ensure that the procurement process for all air travel management services contracts is conducted in full compliance with the general procurement principles set out in financial regulation 5.12, namely: (*a*) best value for money; (*b*) fairness, integrity and transparency; (*c*) effective international competition; and (*d*) the interest of the United Nations, and to ensure that the procurement process includes the option of awarding a contract to multiple vendors to allow for greater competition among the selected vendors;

7. *Stresses* the importance of effective coordination among United Nations entities in harmonizing the standards and practices of acquiring air travel services, and encourages the Secretary-General, in his capacity as Chair of the United Nations System Chief Executives Board for Coordination, to promote the sharing of best practices with respect to air travel across the United Nations system;

8. *Notes* the increase in exceptions authorized by the Secretary-General in accordance with resolution 42/214, and requests the Secretary-General to make every effort to better govern the granting of such exceptions;

9. *Decides* to extend to the Deputy Secretary-General the entitlements regarding official travel accorded to the Secretary-General in paragraph 2 of General Assembly resolution 42/214;

10. *Requests* the Secretary-General, in the context of a more effective and efficient utilization of resources for air travel, to present proposals to the General Assembly at the first part of its resumed sixty-sixth session on the conditions under which staff members below the level of Assistant Secretary-General may travel in business class;

11. *Notes with concern* the lack of consolidated and comprehensive data on air travel across the United Nations system, and stresses the need for such information to be provided to the General Assembly in the context of the programme budget;

12. *Requests* the Secretary-General to entrust the Office of Internal Oversight Services of the Secretariat to conduct a comprehensive audit of all air travel activities and related practices, including: (*a*) the implementation of all provisions contained in the present resolution; (*b*) the delegation of authority by the Secretary-General for the granting of exceptions for air travel; (*c*) processes related to bidding on air travel services in the United Nations and their procurement; and (*d*) the identification of all expenditures

on air travel, using the most recent data available, for the programme budget, including special political missions, for peacekeeping operations, and for lump-sum payments to eligible staff members, and to carry out a cost-benefit analysis for this option and to submit the findings of the audit and the analysis to the General Assembly at the first part of its resumed sixty-seventh session;

13. *Also requests* the Secretary-General to report to the General Assembly at the main part of its sixty-sixth session on the projected total expenditure on air travel under the regular budget, by budget section, including payments under lump-sum schemes, for the biennium 2010–2011, with corresponding data for the bienniums 2008–2009 and 2006–2007;

14. *Further requests* the Secretary-General to report to the General Assembly at the first part of its resumed sixty-sixth session on the implementation of the present resolution, including the measures set out in the annex, and on practical steps taken to enhance the effective and efficient utilization of resources for air travel in the United Nations;

15. *Decides* to consider, at the first part of its resumed sixty-sixth session, the issue of a system for allowing United Nations staff to provide data on frequent flyer miles accrued as a result of official air travel.

ANNEX

Measures for the effective and efficient utilization of resources for air travel in the United Nations

1. The delegation to the Under-Secretary-General for Management, or any other senior management official, of the Secretary-General's authority to grant exceptions for air travel shall be done with a formal non-transferable letter of appointment.

2. In addition, the Secretary-General is requested:

(*a*) To make a proposal for a mechanism to allow for the effective tracking of all costs associated with commercial air travel in the Secretariat, including with regard to peacekeeping operations, special political missions and lump-sum payments to eligible staff members, and to maximize cost efficiencies in the purchase of air tickets and other services related to air travel, benefiting from best practices, including, but not limited to, those set out in the present resolution;

(*b*) To promote greater coordination across the United Nations system on air travel matters, including by leveraging the experiences of existing bodies, such as the Inter-Agency Travel Network;

(*c*) To implement, as a matter of priority, the planned enterprise resource planning/Umoja travel module to facilitate and better regulate all travel activities undertaken by the United Nations, including the collection of data necessary for negotiating global deals with airlines and airline alliances;

(*d*) To introduce a set of clear and comprehensive guidelines to better regulate the authorization of upgrades in the class of air travel on an exceptional basis, inter alia, in the case of a medical condition, restricting such upgrades to business class at the highest, without prejudice to instances of medical emergency, taking into account the opinion of the Director of the Medical Services Division of the Secretariat, which was reiterated in the position paper adopted by all medical directors in the United Nations common system in 2007, that there is no substantive difference between business class and first class in terms of the safety of an individual with a medical condition;

(*e*) To update the administrative instruction on official travel, taking into account, inter alia, the relevant resolutions of the General Assembly and recent developments in air travel, such as new products introduced by air carriers and new classes of air travel, and to include provisions instructing staff (*a*) to collect and, where possible, use frequent flyer miles to fund official travel; (*b*) to not use frequent flyer miles accrued as a result of official travel for personal travel; and (*c*) where possible, to purchase tickets at least two weeks in advance of travel;

(*f*) To continue exploring, in the context of section II, paragraph 3, of General Assembly resolution 63/268 of 7 April 2009, all possible options, including various tools for enhancing the effective and efficient utilization of resources for air travel across the United Nations system, including forecasting and planning, making online and early bookings, using advance-purchase discount tickets, using frequent flyer miles accumulated by staff members from official travel to purchase and upgrade tickets where appropriate, making alternative arrangements for the procurement of air travel utilizing the collective purchasing power of the United Nations and making the most effective use possible of the lump-sum scheme, where applicable;

(*g*) To ensure that the Travel and Transportation Section properly performs its contract management role by monitoring the performance of air travel vendors and their full compliance with contract provisions, including the provision of all information requested by United Nations management entities and oversight bodies.

On 30 June [meeting 106], the General Assembly, on the recommendation of the Fifth Committee [A/65/646/Add.3], adopted **resolution 65/288** without vote [agenda item 129].

Estimates in respect of special political missions, good offices and other political initiatives authorized by the General Assembly and/or the Security Council

The General Assembly,

Recalling its resolution 64/244 A of 24 December 2009, section VI of its resolution 64/245, also of 24 December 2009, section IV of its resolution 64/260 of 29 March 2010, section XIII of its resolution 65/259 of 24 December 2010, its resolution 65/260 A, also of 24 December 2010 and section II of its resolution 65/268 of 4 April 2011,

Having considered the report of the Secretary-General entitled "Estimates in respect of special political missions, good offices and other political initiatives authorized by the General Assembly and/or the Security Council: Panel of Experts on the Libyan Arab Jamahiriya and the United Nations Representative to the Geneva International Discussions" and the related report of the Advisory Committee on Administrative and Budgetary Questions,

1. *Takes note* of the report of the Secretary-General;

2. *Endorses* the conclusions and recommendations contained in the report of the Advisory Committee on Administrative and Budgetary Questions;

3. *Decides* to approve the budget for the Panel of Experts on the Libyan Arab Jamahiriya for the period from 1 June to 31 December 2011 in the amount of 1,693,500 United States dollars gross (1,670,400 dollars net);

4. *Also decides* to approve the budget for the United Nations Representative to the Geneva International Discussions for the period from 1 May to 31 December 2011 in the amount of 1,590,600 dollars gross (1,469,000 dollars net);

5. *Further decides* that the resources for the activities of the Panel of Experts on the Libyan Arab Jamahiriya and the United Nations Representative to the Geneva International Discussions will be absorbed within the overall appropriation approved for special political missions for the biennium 2010–2011, and requests the Secretary-General to report thereon in the context of his second performance report on the programme budget for the biennium 2010–2011.

Budget for 2012–2013

Introducing the proposed programme budget for the 2012–2013 biennium [A/66/6] before the Fifth Committee on 27 October, the Secretary-General said that the proposed budget, which amounted to approximately $5.2 billion before recosting, represented a 3.2 per cent decrease ($170.2 million) over the 2010–2011 programme budget. Adjustment to the staffing table would result in a net decrease of 44 posts. Priorities for the 2012–2013 biennium included promotion of sustained economic growth and sustainable development; maintenance of international peace and security; development of Africa; promotion of human rights; effective coordination of humanitarian assistance; promotion of justice and international law; disarmament; and drug control, crime prevention and combating international terrorism in all its forms and manifestations. In conjunction with the reallocation of resources and the implementation of efficiency measures, the programme budget also reflected continued focus on the implementation of the Regulations and Rules Governing Programme Planning [ST/SGB/2000/8] and on the issues of categorization and quantification of outputs. Based on a review of outputs delivered in 2010–2011, some 1,792 outputs would be discontinued in 2012–2013. Other areas to be addressed included administrative and financial arrangements at the United Nations Office at Nairobi; the provision of training with a view to strengthening the Organization's human resources capacity, developing mechanisms to encourage and support mobility and expand staff training and leadership development; activities related to monitoring and evaluation; and information technology.

The Secretary-General noted that, although the budget had been prepared against the backdrop of global financial austerity and uncertainty, managers had not focused solely on technical and mechanical questions, but had taken decisions based on how best to perform the Organization's mandates. They had been given full discretion to review their business processes and find the optimal approach to funding their operations. Information and communications technology would play a key role in meeting the expectations of Member States and would generate substantial efficiencies once deployed. The Organization remained fully committed to implementing an enterprise resource planning (ERP) system (see p. 1420) and the International Public Sector Accounting Standards (IPSAS) (see p. 1402). He added that he would continue to update and improve the way the Organization operated, including through the change management team established earlier in the year under the direction of the Deputy Secretary-General.

The Committee for Programme and Coordination (CPC) considered the proposed programme budget at its 2011 session (6 June–1 July) [A/66/16], including the 2012–2013 strategic framework [A/65/6/Rev.1] and the Secretary-General's consolidated report on the changes to the biennial programme plan as reflected in the 2010–2011 programme budget and the 2012–2013 proposed programme budget [A/66/82].

CPC recommended that the Assembly approve the changes to the 2012–2013 biennial programme, subject to certain modifications.

Limited budgetary discretion

In response to General Assembly resolution 64/260 [YUN 2010, p. 1437], the Secretary-General submitted a November report [A/66/570] on the implementation of Assembly resolution 60/283 [YUN 2006, p. 1580] on limited budgetary discretion, which was applied on an experimental basis during the 2006–2007 and 2008–2009 bienniums, and extended to the 2010–2011 biennium. That discretion authorized the Secretary-General to enter into commitments up to $20 million in each biennium to meet the Organization's evolving needs. He reported that use of the limited budgetary discretion over the previous three bienniums had covered activities related to organizational management requirements such as influenza pandemic preparedness, fire code compliance, the start-up of the ERP system, requirements relating to the administration of justice system, and natural or man-made events. On the basis of that experience and how it had provided him with the ability to carry out his managerial responsibilities more effectively, the Secretary-General proposed to establish the limited budgetary mechanism with some modification.

In December [A/66/7/Add.18], noting that the Secretary-General's proposal did not present any new rationale in support of the proposed modifications to the limited budgetary discretionary authority and that clearer criteria for determining the activities to be funded through limited budgetary discretion would ensure a more consistent approach to its utilization, ACABQ recommended that the mechanism be continued on an experimental basis under the existing arrangements for the 2012–2013 biennium.

On 24 December, the General Assembly deferred consideration of the reports of the Secretary-General and ACABQ on limited budgetary discretion until its resumed sixty-sixth (2012) session (**decision 66/556 A**).

GENERAL ASSEMBLY ACTION

On 24 December [meeting 93], the General Assembly, on the recommendation of the Fifth Committee [A/66/637], adopted **resolution 66/246** without vote [agenda item 134].

Questions relating to the proposed programme budget for the biennium 2012–2013

The General Assembly,

Recalling its resolutions 60/283 of 7 July 2006, 64/243 of 24 December 2009 and 64/260 of 29 March 2010,

Reaffirming its resolutions 41/213 of 19 December 1986, 42/211 of 21 December 1987, 45/248 B, section VI, of 21 December 1990, 55/231 of 23 December 2000, 56/253 of 24 December 2001, 58/269 and 58/270 of 23 December 2003, 59/276, section XI, of 23 December 2004, 61/263 of 4 April 2007, 62/236 of 22 December 2007, 63/262 and 63/266 of 24 December 2008, 64/243, 64/260, and 65/262 of 24 December 2010,

Reaffirming also the respective mandates of the Advisory Committee on Administrative and Budgetary Questions and the Committee for Programme and Coordination in the consideration of the proposed programme budget,

Reaffirming further the role of the General Assembly, through the Fifth Committee, in carrying out a thorough analysis and approval of posts and financial resources, as well as of human resources policies,

Recognizing that late payments of assessed contributions, bearing in mind the special situation of certain countries, adversely affect the financial situation of the Organization,

Having considered the proposed programme budget for the biennium 2012–2013, the report of the Secretary-General on revised estimates relating to the proposed programme budget for the biennium 2012–2013 under section 1, Overall policymaking, direction and coordination, and section 37, Staff assessment, related to the strengthening of the Office of the Director General, United Nations Office at Nairobi, the report of the Independent Audit Advisory Committee on the proposed programme budget for the Office of Internal Oversight Services for the biennium 2012–2013, the seventh progress report of the Secretary-General on the implementation of projects financed from the Development Account, the fourth progress report of the Secretary-General on the adoption of the International Public Sector Accounting Standards by the United Nations, the report of the Board of Auditors on the progress in the implementation of the International Public Sector Accounting Standards, the report of the Secretary-General on enterprise information and communications technology initiatives for the United Nations Secretariat, the third progress report of the Secretary-General on the Umoja enterprise resource planning project, the report of the Secretary-General on limited budgetary discretion and the related reports of the Advisory Committee on Administrative and Budgetary Questions,

Having also considered chapter II, section A, of the report of the Committee for Programme and Coordination on its fifty-first session and the consolidated report of the Secretary-General on the changes to the biennial programme plan as reflected in the programme budget for the biennium 2010–2011 and the proposed programme budget for the biennium 2012–2013,

Having further considered the report of the Office of Internal Oversight Services on the review of the organizational framework of the public information function of the Secretariat and the report of the Secretary-General on progress on the implementation of the recommendations of the report of the Office of Internal Oversight Services on the efficiency of the implementation of the mandate of the Office of the United Nations High Commissioner for Human Rights,

Having considered the reports of the Joint Inspection Unit entitled "Review of management and administration in the United Nations Office on Drugs and Crime", "Policies and procedures for the administration of trust funds in the United Nations system organizations" and "Preparedness of United Nations system organizations for the International Public Sector Accounting Standards" and the notes by the Secretary-General transmitting his comments and those of the United Nations System Chief Executives Board for Coordination thereon,

1. *Reaffirms* that the Fifth Committee is the appropriate Main Committee of the General Assembly entrusted with responsibilities for administrative and budgetary matters, and reaffirms the role of the Fifth Committee in carrying out a thorough analysis and approving human and financial resources and policies, with a view to ensuring full, effective and efficient implementation of all mandated programmes and activities and the implementation of policies in this regard;

2. *Also reaffirms* the role of the Committee for Programme and Coordination as the main subsidiary organ of the General Assembly and the Economic and Social Council for planning, programming and coordination;

3. *Further reaffirms* rule 153 of its rules of procedure;

4. *Reaffirms* the Regulations and Rules Governing Programme Planning, the Programme Aspects of the Budget, the Monitoring of Implementation and the Methods of Evaluation;

5. *Also reaffirms* the Financial Regulations and Rules of the United Nations;

6. *Endorses* the conclusions and recommendations of the Committee for Programme and Coordination as contained in chapter II, section A, of its report;

7. *Also endorses* the conclusions and recommendations contained in the reports of the Advisory Committee on Administrative and Budgetary Questions, subject to the provisions of the present resolution;

Policy/cross-cutting issues

8. *Reaffirms* the established budgetary procedures and methodologies, based on its resolutions 41/213 and 42/211;

9. *Also reaffirms* that no changes to the budget methodology, to established budgetary procedures and practices or

to the financial regulations may be implemented without prior review and approval by the General Assembly, in accordance with established budgetary procedures;

10. *Reiterates* the need for Member States to participate fully in the budget preparation process, from its early stages and throughout the process;

11. *Emphasizes* the importance of providing the consistent and timely information necessary to enable Member States to make well-informed decisions;

12. *Stresses* that all Member States should fulfil their financial obligations as set out in the Charter of the United Nations on time, in full and without conditions;

Results-based budgeting

13. *Also stresses* that results-based budgeting and results-based management are mutually supportive management tools and that improved implementation of results-based budgeting enhances both management and accountability in the Secretariat, and encourages the Secretary-General to continue his efforts in this regard;

14. *Reaffirms* paragraph 28 of resolution 55/231, and stresses the importance of adequate training to ensure the full implementation of results-based budgeting;

Human resources, vacancy rates and staffing

15. *Regrets* the delays in the recruitment of staff for the Umoja enterprise resource planning project, including of its Project Director, resulting from internal processes, and in this regard requests the Secretary-General to redouble his efforts to fill all the approved posts, taking into account existing regulations and rules regarding recruitment in the Secretariat, and to report thereon to the General Assembly at its sixty-seventh session;

16. *Recalls* paragraph 31 of resolution 64/243, and expresses serious concern about the lack of progress by the Secretary-General in developing a comprehensive succession plan for the Organization, including, inter alia, for the language services, and in this regard reiterates its requests for the Secretary-General to formulate a strategy on succession planning for all departments of the Secretariat and to report thereon to the General Assembly at its sixty-seventh session;

17. *Decides* not to approve any of the cuts in posts and non-post resources proposed by the Secretary-General in parts IV and V of the proposed programme budget for the biennium 2012–2013;

18. *Decides* that the staffing table for the biennium 2012–2013 shall be as set out in the annex to the present resolution;

19. *Reaffirms* that the vacancy rate is a tool for budgetary calculations and should not be used to achieve budgetary savings;

20. *Decides* that a vacancy rate of 4.7 per cent for General Service staff shall be used as a basis for the calculation of the budget for the biennium 2012–2013;

Training

21. *Requests* the Secretary-General, using the resources allocated for training in the present resolution, to increase training opportunities for staff throughout the Secretariat, including for duty stations and regional commissions, and in this context stresses that equal training opportunities should be available for all staff, in accordance with their functions and categories;

22. *Stresses* that the largest possible share of resources provided for training purposes should be directed towards the preparation and delivery of training and that ancillary costs, including associated travel, should be minimized;

23. *Recalls* paragraph 112 of the report of the Advisory Committee on Administrative and Budgetary Questions, and requests the Secretary-General to assess how training programmes and objectives contribute to mandate implementation and organizational goals;

Conference services and publications

24. *Emphasizes* the importance of ensuring that there is no discriminatory treatment among the principal organs of the United Nations and the Main Committees and subsidiary bodies and that they are provided with adequate and quality conference servicing and support;

Non-post resources

25. *Decides* to reduce non-post resources by 17 million United States dollars, excluding parts IV and V of the proposed budget for the biennium 2012–2013;

Consultants and contractual services

26. *Requests* the Secretary-General to continue to ensure that, in future programme budget proposals, requests for consultants and experts are clearly and separately identified in the programme narratives;

Recosting

27. *Decides* to defer consideration of post-related recosting for inflation and exchange rate projections to the first performance report on the budget for the biennium 2012–2013, in order to ensure appropriation of post-related costs in line with actual expenditure experience;

Extrabudgetary resources

28. *Stresses* that all extrabudgetary posts must be administered and managed with the same rigour as regular budget posts;

29. *Also stresses* that the use of extrabudgetary resources shall be consistent with the policies, aims and activities of the Organization, and reiterates its request to the Secretary-General to provide information on the financial and human resource implications of the use of extrabudgetary resources in the Organization in his next proposed programme budget;

PART I

Overall policymaking, direction and coordination

Section 1
Overall policymaking, direction and coordination

30. *Stresses* the importance of strengthened accountability in the Organization and of ensuring greater accountability of the Secretary-General to Member States, inter alia, for the effective and efficient implementation of legislative mandates and the use of human and financial resources;

31. *Recalls* paragraph I.6 of the report of the Advisory Committee on Administrative and Budgetary Questions, and decides to establish one post at the D-1 level to head the Rule of Law Unit and to retain the P-5 post;

Chapter II: United Nations financing and programming

Office of the President of the General Assembly

32. *Requests* the Secretary-General to submit, in the context of the proposed programme budget for the biennium 2014–2015, proposals to review the budget allocation to the Office of the President of the General Assembly in accordance with existing procedures;

Office of the Director General, United Nations Office at Nairobi

33. *Takes note* of paragraphs 8 and 9 of the report of the Advisory Committee on Administrative and Budgetary Questions, and decides to establish one P-4 and two Local level posts in the Office of the Director General, United Nations Office at Nairobi;

Section 2
General Assembly and Economic and Social Council affairs and conference management

34. *Decides* to decrease the non-post resources allocated to the Department for General Assembly and Conference Management by 10 million dollars;

35. *Reiterates its request* to the Secretary-General to improve the on-time submission of documents and to institute measures to hold author departments accountable for the late submission of documents;

36. *Recalls* paragraph I.58 of the report of the Advisory Committee on Administrative and Budgetary Questions, decides not to implement the proposals of the Secretary-General on summary records, and also decides to allocate 10 million dollars for the purpose of summary records;

37. *Also recalls* paragraph I.72 of the report of the Advisory Committee on Administrative and Budgetary Questions, and requests the Secretary-General to take all the necessary measures to maximize the use of workload-sharing among duty stations, in respect of translation services, without compromising the quality of the services;

38. *Requests* the Secretary-General to ensure that all duty stations are given equal treatment in respect of the application of modern technologies;

39. *Emphasizes* the paramount importance of ensuring the equality of the six official languages of the United Nations;

PART II
Political affairs

Section 3
Political affairs

40. *Takes note* of paragraph II.7 of the report of the Advisory Committee on Administrative and Budgetary Questions, and decides not to abolish one P-4 post and one General Service (Other level) post, under subprogramme 4 (Decolonization);

Peacebuilding Support Office

41. *Recalls* paragraph II.30 of the report of the Advisory Committee on Administrative and Budgetary Questions, and decides to establish two P-4 posts for the Peacebuilding Support Office;

Office of the Register of Damage Caused by the Construction of the Wall in the Occupied Palestinian Territory

42. *Takes note* of paragraph II.36 of the report of the Advisory Committee on Administrative and Budgetary Questions, and decides to increase by 306,000 dollars the level of non-post resources of the Office of the Register of Damage Caused by the Construction of the Wall in the Occupied Palestinian Territory;

Section 4
Disarmament

43. *Requests* the Secretary-General to continue to provide the United Nations regional centres for peace and disarmament with the necessary resources to discharge their mandates;

Section 5
Peacekeeping operations

44. *Also requests* the Secretary-General to make further concrete efforts to ensure proper representation of troop-contributing countries in the Department of Peacekeeping Operations and the Department of Field Support, taking into account their contribution to United Nations peacekeeping;

Section 6
Peaceful uses of outer space

45. *Notes* the review of the organizational structure of the Office for Outer Space Affairs and the United Nations Platform for Space-based Information for Disaster Management and Emergency Response (UN-SPIDER) programme, and requests the Secretary-General to ensure that the consolidation of the organizational structure will enhance effectiveness and efficiency without undermining the implementation by the Office of its mandate;

PART III
International justice and law

Section 7
International Court of Justice

46. *Emphasizes* the importance of proceeding expeditiously with the renovation of the Great Hall of Justice in the Peace Palace at The Hague;

Section 8
Legal affairs

47. *Recalls* paragraph III.25 of the report of the Advisory Committee on Administrative and Budgetary Questions, notes that publications are a means for the Organization to implement its mandates, and in this regard encourages the Secretary-General to enhance the use of appropriate technology, to focus on areas of interest to Member States and to explore options for cost recovery as appropriate;

48. *Decides* to increase non-post resources by 274,200 dollars in order to provide sufficient funding for servicing the work of the United Nations Commission on International Trade Law for fourteen weeks and to retain the rotation scheme between Vienna and New York;

49. *Takes note* of paragraph III.23 of the report of the Advisory Committee on Administrative and Budgetary Questions, and decides to approve 2,451,800 dollars for travel and related costs for representatives and staff of the International Law Commission;

PART IV
International cooperation for development

50. *Requests* the Secretary-General to intensify his efforts to mobilize adequate resources from all sources to support the mandates related to sections 10 and 11 of the programme budget during the biennium 2012–2013;

51. *Reaffirms* its resolutions 57/7 of 4 November 2002 and 57/300 of 20 December 2002, by which it established the Office of the Special Adviser on Africa, and its resolution 56/227 of 24 December 2001, by which it established the Office of the High Representative for the Least Developed Countries, Landlocked Developing Countries and Small Island Developing States;

52. *Recalls* paragraph IV.29 of the report of the Advisory Committee on Administrative and Budgetary Questions, strongly reaffirms the relevant provisions of its resolutions 62/236, 63/260 of 24 December 2008, 64/243, and 66/8 of 11 November 2011 in this regard, and requests the Secretary-General to implement the provisions pertaining to the Office of the Special Adviser on Africa and the Office of the High Representative for the Least Developed Countries, Landlocked Developing Countries and Small Island Developing States in those resolutions accordingly, in full and without delay;

Section 11
United Nations support for the New Partnership for Africa's Development

53. *Also recalls* that the development of Africa is an established priority of the United Nations, and reaffirms its commitment to address the special needs of Africa;

54. *Further recalls* its resolution 57/300 and other resolutions calling for the strengthening of mechanisms to support the New Partnership for Africa's Development;

Section 12
Trade and development

55. *Encourages* the Secretary-General to broaden the efforts of the United Nations Conference on Trade and Development in supporting the strengthening of regional economic integration in Africa by providing, within the allocation to the Conference, technical assistance and capacity-building in the areas of trade, customs and infrastructure, including the strengthening of statistical capacity;

Section 16
International drug control, crime and terrorism prevention and criminal justice

56. *Recalls* paragraph 83 of resolution 64/243, and requests the Secretary-General to strengthen the provision of technical assistance to the United Nations Office on Drugs and Crime through the West Africa Coast Initiative in order to support the implementation of a regional action plan to address the growing problem of illicit drug trafficking, organized crime and drug abuse in West Africa;

57. *Also recalls* paragraph 84 of resolution 64/243, profoundly regrets the delays experienced by the Secretary-General in opening a programme office of the United Nations Office on Drugs and Crime in Barbados to collaborate with the Caribbean Community in such areas as corruption, drug trafficking, international judicial cooperation and the promotion of firearms control, and requests the Secretary-General to urgently open the office;

PART V
Regional cooperation for development

58. *Emphasizes* the important contribution that regional commissions are making towards the implementation of the development agenda and other mandates given to them arising from the outcome of the Millennium Summit, the Conference on the World Financial and Economic Crisis and Its Impact on Development and other major United Nations conferences and summits in the economic, social and related fields;

59. *Requests* the Secretary-General to ensure that the resource requirements of the commissions are allocated in such a way as to enable them to fully implement their mandates and contribute to the implementation of development priorities and mandates of the Organization;

Section 18
Economic and social development in Africa

60. *Decides* to increase the grant to the African Institute for Economic Development and Planning to 2.6 million dollars per biennium;

Section 22
Economic and social development in Western Asia

61. *Takes note* of paragraphs V.84 and V.85 of the report of the Advisory Committee on Administrative and Budgetary Questions, and decides to establish one post at the D-1 level for the Chief of the Division for Women, under subprogramme 6; one post at the D-1 level for the Chief of the Emerging Trends and Conflict-related Issues Division, under subprogramme 7; and one P-5 post for the Chief of the Governance, Instability and Development Section, under subprogramme 7;

PART VI
Human rights and humanitarian affairs

Section 24
Human rights

62. *Decides* to reclassify one P-5 post to the D-1 level, under subprogramme 4, and requests the Secretary-General to designate capacity to support the universal periodic review and to report thereon in the context of the performance report;

63. *Stresses* the importance of having detailed and comprehensive information on the utilization of extrabudgetary resources for the activities of the Office of the United Nations High Commissioner for Human Rights;

Section 25
International protection, durable solutions and assistance to refugees

64. *Recalls* paragraph VI.32 of the report of the Advisory Committee on Administrative and Budgetary Questions, and in this regard stresses the importance of sharing lessons learned and best practices with other parts of the Organization;

Section 26
Palestine refugees

65. *Reaffirms* its resolution 3331 B(XXIX) of 17 December 1974, stating that expenses for salaries of international staff in the service of the United Nations Relief and Works Agency for Palestine Refugees in the Near East, which would otherwise be a charge on voluntary contributions, should be financed by the regular budget of the United Nations for the duration of the Agency's mandate;

66. *Notes with appreciation* the valuable work done by the United Nations Relief and Works Agency for Palestine Refugees in the Near East, and expresses concern about the significant reduction in the total resources for the Agency over the past ten years while its overall workload and responsibilities have continued to increase;

PART VII
Public information
Section 28
Public information

67. *Stresses* the importance of publishing United Nations information materials and translating important documents into languages other than United Nations official languages, with a view to reaching the widest possible spectrum of audiences and extending the United Nations message to all the corners of the world in order to strengthen international support for the activities of the Organization;

68. *Requests* the Secretary-General to continue to expand the scope of press releases in addition to the existing languages in order to widen the United Nations message, assuring their comprehensiveness and up-to-date nature and ensuring their accuracy;

69. *Recalls* paragraph VII.16 of the report of the Advisory Committee on Administrative and Budgetary Questions, commends the Secretary-General on his outreach efforts to the general public, particularly youth, through enhanced use of new media technologies, and stresses that more traditional means of communication, such as radio and print media, remain an important part of the efforts to ensure that the message of the Organization is effectively promoted, particularly in developing countries;

70. *Requests* the Secretary-General to promote public awareness of and to mobilize support for the work of the United Nations at the local level through all possible means of communications, including publications, the broadcasting of news and the network of United Nations information centres, bearing in mind that information in local languages has the strongest impact on local populations;

71. *Recognizes* the vital role of the United Nations information centres in promoting awareness about the United Nations, and requests the Secretary-General to continue to make efforts to mobilize resources for the effective functioning of United Nations information centres in developing countries;

72. *Welcomes* the initiatives to modernize the Dag Hammarskjöld Library, including through the acquisition of technical solutions for upgrading and customizing current information management systems and digitizing United Nations parliamentary documents dating from 1946, as measures that serve to enhance and modernize the storage and retrieval of United Nations documents and to preserve the institutional memory of the Organization;

73. *Decides* to convert the general temporary assistance position in the Russian News Centre to an established post at the P-3 level, with a view to ensuring the same level of support in this language as in the other official languages of the United Nations;

74. *Also decides* to reclassify one P-2 post to the P-3 level in the Chinese Unit and one P-3 post to the P-4 level as head of the Kiswahili Unit of United Nations Radio;

75. *Further decides* to establish two P-3 posts, two P-2 posts and one General Service (Other level) post in the Kiswahili Unit of United Nations Radio and one P-3 post and two P-2 posts in the Portuguese Unit of United Nations Radio;

76. *Stresses* the importance of an open, transparent and all-inclusive United Nations, decides to approve the live webcasting, and subsequent web storage, of all the formal meetings of its six Main Committees, and in this regard approves 835,500 dollars to cover all related costs;

77. *Requests* the Secretary-General to clearly identify the level of resources related to public information activities for special conferences in future budget presentations under this section;

PART VIII
Common support services
Section 29A
Office of the Under-Secretary-General for Management

Umoja enterprise resource planning project

78. *Expresses serious concern* about the potential escalation of costs of the Umoja enterprise resource planning project, and requests the Secretary-General to ensure its implementation without further delay;

79. *Requests* the Secretary-General to ensure by all means that the project costs are brought back within the approved budget;

80. *Reiterates its request* to the Secretary-General to make every effort to avoid budget increases through sound project management practices and to ensure that the Umoja project is completed within the budget as approved in its resolution 64/243;

81. *Underlines* that the overall qualitative and quantitative benefits related to the Umoja project, which were identified in the first and second progress reports, remain valid, regrets the delay in the realization of those benefits, and requests the Secretary-General to make all efforts to maximize them;

82. *Stresses* the centrality of the leadership and oversight of the Secretary-General and of senior management, as well as of the commitment of all departments to completing the Umoja project, in order to avoid a recurrence of the mistakes and delays in its implementation to date and thereby their negative implications for the Organization;

83. *Requests* the Secretary-General to ensure full accountability for the delays, the lack of responsiveness of management to the needs of the Umoja project and other factors that have contributed to delays in its implementation and the projected budget overrun, and to include this information in his fourth annual progress report;

84. *Expresses serious concern* about the governance crisis in the Umoja project, and reaffirms its decision to designate the Under-Secretary-General for Management as the Chair of the Steering Committee for the project;

85. *Stresses* the need for a simple and operationally effective information and communications technology governance structure with clear lines of authority and accountability;

86. *Emphasizes* that the Umoja enterprise resource planning project should be viewed primarily as a business project driven by business process demands;

87. *Decides* that the Umoja Project Director will report solely and directly to the Under-Secretary-General for Management and that the Umoja project team and administration of the project budget will be placed within the Department of Management;

88. *Reiterates* that successful implementation of the Umoja project requires the full support and commitment of senior management, as well as close and continuous engagement with key stakeholders, and calls upon the Secretary-General to ensure this through his performance management and accountability mechanism;

89. *Stresses* the supportive role of the Office of Information and Communications Technology, and requests in this regard that the Chief Information Technology Officer provide full cooperation and support to the Project Director;

90. *Expresses its concern* that no specific information has been shared with Member States concerning the related costs and activities of the Umoja project, and requests the Secretary-General to include such information in his next progress report and to make every effort to fully implement such activities within the approved budget level of each department;

91. *Approves* commitment authority for the Umoja project for one year at maintenance level, and requests the Secretary-General to submit to the General Assembly at the main part of its sixty-seventh session a revised comprehensive proposal for funding the project during the biennium 2012–2013;

92. *Requests* the Secretary-General to update Member States through regular informal briefings to the Fifth Committee at the first and second parts of the resumed sessions of the General Assembly, as well as by submitting annual progress reports, on all aspects of the implementation of the Umoja project, including its current status, significant activities carried out since the previous report and risk analysis information outlining any risks identified, actions to be taken, status and trends, and to update the relevant information on the Umoja project website on a regular basis;

93. *Requests* the Advisory Committee on Administrative and Budgetary Questions to request the Board of Auditors to conduct a comprehensive audit of the implementation of the Umoja project and to report annually to the General Assembly starting at the main part of its sixty-seventh session;

Section 29B
Office of Programme Planning, Budget and Accounts

94. *Recalls* paragraph VIII.33 of the report of the Advisory Committee on Administrative and Budgetary Questions, notes the measures undertaken by the Office of Programme Planning, Budget and Accounts to improve the efficiency of its services, and urges the Secretary-General to intensify his efforts and to report thereon in the context of his next budget submission;

95. *Takes note* of the observations and endorses the recommendations contained in the reports of the Board of Auditors and the Joint Inspection Unit on progress in the implementation of the International Public Sector Accounting Standards and on preparedness of United Nations system organizations for the International Public Sector Accounting Standards, respectively;

96. *Requests* the Secretary-General to ensure that the implementation of the International Public Sector Accounting Standards at the United Nations is completed no later than 2014, and reaffirms that the enterprise resource planning system will serve as the backbone for implementation by the United Nations of the Standards;

97. *Stresses* the importance of benefiting from the experience and guidance of the early implementers and of ensuring that the United Nations is adequately prepared for its transition to the International Public Sector Accounting Standards;

98. *Requests* the Secretary-General to exercise strict oversight over the implementation of the International Public Sector Accounting Standards project to ensure prudent stewardship of project resources and to establish clear lines of reporting and effective mechanisms for the rapid resolution of issues on a day-to-day basis;

99. *Also requests* the Secretary-General to continue to ensure that the General Assembly is kept informed, on an annual basis, of the progress in implementing the International Public Sector Accounting Standards by 2014, including milestones and deliverables, outstanding activities and utilization of resources, as well as to ensure full realization of the benefits associated with the implementation of the Standards;

Section 29C
Office of Human Resources Management

100. *Takes note* of paragraph VIII.40 of the report of the Advisory Committee on Administrative and Budgetary Questions, and decides to increase by 50 per cent the non-post resources available for outreach, under component 2, strategic planning and staffing;

Section 29H
Office of Information and Communications Technology

101. *Underlines* the importance of information and communications technology in meeting the growing demands of the Organization as it becomes increasingly reliant on its information and communications technology infrastructure;

102. *Also underlines* the importance of information and communications technology in strengthening oversight and accountability and in increasing the availability of accurate and timely information to support decision-making;

103. *Stresses* the need for strengthened accountability and clearer lines of authority to ensure a more efficient and effective Office of Information and Communications Technology;

104. *Takes note* of paragraph 122 of the report of the Advisory Committee on Administrative and Budgetary Questions, decides in this regard to place the Office of Information and Communications Technology under the Department of Management, also decides that the Chief Information Technology Officer will report accordingly to the Head of the Department of Management, and further

decides to place the budget of the Office within the budget of the Department of Management;

105. *Also takes note* of paragraphs 89, 99, 107, 117 and 118 of the report of the Advisory Committee on Administrative and Budgetary Questions, requests the Secretary-General to implement initiative 1, Improve enterprise information and communications technology management, and initiative 4, Create a resilient information and communications technology infrastructure, decides not to approve additional funding for the implementation of these initiatives, and also decides not to approve initiative 2, Leverage knowledge through information and communications technology, and initiative 3, Enhance information and communications technology service delivery;

106. *Requests* the Secretary-General to submit any future funding proposals for major information and communications technology projects for consideration by the General Assembly only after the full implementation of the Umoja enterprise resource planning project;

107. *Requests* the Advisory Committee on Administrative and Budgetary Questions to request the Board of Auditors to audit and evaluate the handling of information and communications technology affairs in the Secretariat, including the Office of Information and Communications Technology, and to report thereon to the General Assembly at the main part of its sixty-seventh session;

PART IX
Internal oversight
Section 31
Internal oversight

108. *Takes note* of paragraph IX.6 of the report of the Advisory Committee on Administrative and Budgetary Questions, and decides to establish the post of Assistant Secretary-General in the Office of Internal Oversight Services;

109. *Reaffirms* paragraph 130 of its resolution 64/243, and takes note of paragraph IX.12 of the report of the Advisory Committee on Administrative and Budgetary Questions;

PART X
Jointly financed administrative activities and special expenses
Section 32
Jointly financed administrative activities

Joint Inspection Unit

110. *Recalls* paragraph X.16 of the report of the Advisory Committee on Administrative and Budgetary Questions, and authorizes an amount of 100,000 dollars for the Joint Inspection Unit for requirements related to consultants, while urging the Unit to make greater use of its secretariat and the available expertise within the United Nations common system in providing such specialized advice and technical services to the inspectors;

United Nations System Chief Executives Board for Coordination, including the International Public Sector Accounting Standards project

111. *Also recalls* paragraph X.24 of the report of the Advisory Committee on Administrative and Budgetary Questions, and requests the Secretary-General, in his capacity as the Chair of the United Nations System Chief Executives Board for Coordination, to consult all the participating organizations on consolidating the secretariat of the Board at United Nations Headquarters in New York and to report thereon to the General Assembly at its sixty-seventh session;

PART XI
Capital expenditures
Section 34
Construction, alteration, improvement and major maintenance

112. *Decides* to reduce the overall requirements for construction, alteration, improvement and major maintenance by 6.9 million dollars, and requests the Secretary-General to prioritize between the projects proposed in order to ensure the security of staff, delegates and other personnel at all duty stations;

PART XII
Safety and security
Section 35
Safety and security

113. *Requests* the Secretary-General to review the appropriateness of the use of private security personnel, particularly in situations in which they are the only option available to provide safety and security for staff, and also requests the Secretary-General to report thereon to the General Assembly at its sixty-seventh session;

PART XIII
Development Account
Section 36
Development Account

114. *Decides* to appropriate an additional 6 million dollars for the Development Account;

Limited budgetary discretion

115. *Recalls* section III of resolution 60/283, and decides to extend its provisions until 30 April 2012, pending a decision at the first part of the resumed sixty-sixth session of the General Assembly.

ANNEX
Staffing table for the biennium 2012–2013

Category	Number of posts
Professional and above	
Deputy Secretary-General	1
Under-Secretary-General	33
Assistant Secretary-General	29
D-2	105
D-1	287
P-5	845
P-4/3	2,787
P-2/1	543
SUBTOTAL	**4,630**
General Service	
Principal level	281
Other level	2,733
SUBTOTAL	**3,014**
Other	
Security Service	320
Local level	2,024
Field Service	129
National Officer	79
Trades and Crafts	140
SUBTOTAL	**2,692**
TOTAL	**10,336**

Appropriations

In his proposed programme budget for the 2012–2013 biennium [A/66/6], the Secretary-General recommended expenditures of $5,343.8 million, general income of $52.6 million, and staff assessment income of $559 million (an increase of $4 million), resulting in a net budget estimate of $4,732.2 million, or a 0.9 per cent real decrease from the 2010–2011 budget.

Extrabudgetary resources for the 2012–2013 biennium were estimated at $12,441.6 million, comprising $425 million for support activities, $2,538.9 million for substantive activities and $9,477.7 million for operational activities.

ACABQ, in its first report on the proposed 2012–2013 programme budget [A/66/7 & Corr.1], agreed with the overall budget proposed by the Secretary-General; made recommendations regarding posts and other objects of expenditure; and noted that the overall level of resources would be affected by the submission of proposals for special political missions and by the decisions taken on the separate reports with financial implications. The Committee further noted that issues foreseen during the preparation of the proposed programme budget could have been included in the Secretary-General's proposals; expressed concern that the piecemeal approach did not provide it with the full information required for it to be able to render advice to the Assembly on the proposed programme budget; and made recommendations on the preparation and content of future proposed programme budgets, such as the inclusion of more information on the status and results of major reform initiatives, the demonstrable impact of efficiency measures being undertaken and the conclusions drawn from monitoring and evaluation activities.

In December [A/66/614], the Secretary-General recommended revised estimates to reflect the updated projections for inflation and the effect of the evolution of operational rates of exchange in 2011 on the proposed 2012–2013 programme budget. The recosted level of expenditure amounted to $5,387.3 million, while income was revised to $542.6 million.

Also in December [A/66/605], the Secretary-General recommended revised estimates in the amount of $181.8 million for the International Criminal Tribunal for Rwanda, $287.6 million for the International Tribunal for the Former Yugoslavia, and $53,793 for the International Residual Mechanism for Criminal Tribunals.

ACABQ, in its twenty-third report on the 2012–2013 programme budget [A/66/7/Add.22], had no objection to the revised estimates in the two reports and transmitted them to the General Assembly for consideration.

GENERAL ASSEMBLY ACTION

On 24 December [meeting 93], the General Assembly, on the recommendation of the Fifth Committee [A/66/637], adopted **resolution 66/248 A** to **C** without vote [agenda item 134].

Programme budget for the biennium 2012–2013

A

BUDGET APPROPRIATIONS FOR THE BIENNIUM 2012–2013

The General Assembly

Resolves that, for the biennium 2012–2013:

1. Appropriations totalling 5,152,299,600 United States dollars are hereby approved for the following purposes:

Section		Amount (United States dollars)
Part I.	**Overall policymaking, direction and coordination**	
1.	Overall policymaking, direction and coordination	105,133,800
2.	General Assembly and Economic and Social Council affairs and conference management	616,654,500
	SUBTOTAL	**721,788,300**
Part II.	**Political affairs**	
3.	Political affairs	1,193,700,800
4.	Disarmament	22,422,000
5.	Peacekeeping operations	109,725,100
6.	Peaceful uses of outer space	8,001,400
	SUBTOTAL	**1,333,849,300**
Part III.	**International justice and law**	
7.	International Court of Justice	47,766,400
8.	Legal affairs	45,388,700
	SUBTOTAL	**93,155,100**
Part IV.	**International cooperation for development**	
9.	Economic and social affairs	148,979,300
10.	Least developed countries, landlocked developing countries and small island developing States	7,264,900
11.	United Nations support for the New Partnership for Africa's Development	12,587,700

Section		Amount (United States dollars)
12.	Trade and development	136,524,600
13.	International Trade Centre	41,337,700
14.	Environment	13,925,500
15.	Human settlements	20,631,500
16.	International drug control, crime and terrorism prevention and criminal justice	40,902,200
17.	UN-Women	14,482,300
	SUBTOTAL	**436,635,700**
Part V.	**Regional cooperation for development**	
18.	Economic and social development in Africa	138,308,300
19.	Economic and social development in Asia and the Pacific	98,654,500
20.	Economic development in Europe	65,247,200
21.	Economic and social development in Latin America and the Caribbean	110,256,000
22.	Economic and social development in Western Asia	62,646,700
23.	Regular programme of technical cooperation	57,779,600
	SUBTOTAL	**532,892,300**
Part VI.	**Human rights and humanitarian affairs**	
24.	Human rights	154,315,400
25.	International protection, durable solutions and assistance to refugees	95,507,100
26.	Palestine refugees	47,377,700
27.	Humanitarian assistance	29,374,000
	SUBTOTAL	**326,574,200**
Part VII.	**Public information**	
28.	Public information	179,092,100
	SUBTOTAL	**179,092,100**
Part VIII.	**Common support services**	
29.	Management and support services	600,210,000
	SUBTOTAL	**600,210,000**
Part IX.	**Internal oversight**	
31.	Internal oversight	38,254,200
	SUBTOTAL	**38,254,200**
Part X.	**Jointly financed administrative activities and special expenses**	
32.	Jointly financed administrative activities	10,762,400
33.	Special expenses	120,456,700
	SUBTOTAL	**131,219,100**
Part XI.	**Capital expenditures**	
34.	Construction, alteration, improvement and major maintenance	64,886,900
	SUBTOTAL	**64,886,900**
Part XII.	**Safety and security**	
35.	Safety and security	213,412,400
	SUBTOTAL	**213,412,400**
Part XIII.	**Development Account**	
36.	Development Account	29,243,200
	SUBTOTAL	**29,243,200**
Part XIV.	**Staff assessment**	
37.	Staff assessment	451,086,800
	SUBTOTAL	**451,086,800**
	TOTAL	**5,152,299,600**

2. The Secretary-General shall be authorized to transfer credits between sections of the budget, with the concurrence of the Advisory Committee on Administrative and Budgetary Questions;

3. In addition to the appropriations approved under paragraph 1 above, an amount of 75,000 dollars is appropriated for each year of the biennium 2012–2013 from the accumulated income of the Library Endowment Fund for the purchase of books, periodicals, maps and library equipment and for such other expenses of the Library at the Palais des Nations in Geneva as are in accordance with the objects and provisions of the endowment.

B

INCOME ESTIMATES FOR THE BIENNIUM 2012–2013

The General Assembly

Resolves that, for the biennium 2012–2013:

1. Estimates of income other than assessments on Member States totalling 507,751,200 United States dollars are approved as follows:

Income section		Amount (United States dollars)
1.	Income from staff assessment	455,366,000
2.	General income	52,500,600
3.	Services to the public	(115,400)
	Total	**507,751,200**

2. The income from staff assessment shall be credited to the Tax Equalization Fund in accordance with the provisions of General Assembly resolution 973(X) of 15 December 1955;

3. Direct expenses of the United Nations Postal Administration, services to visitors, the sale of statistical products, catering operations and related services, garage operations, television services and the sale of publications not provided for under the budget appropriations shall be charged against the income derived from those activities.

C

FINANCING OF APPROPRIATIONS FOR THE YEAR 2012

The General Assembly

Resolves that, for the year 2012:

1. Budget appropriations consisting of 2,576,149,800 United States dollars, being half of the appropriation of 5,152,299,600 dollars approved for the biennium 2012–2013 by the General Assembly in paragraph 1 of resolution A above, plus 49,199,000 dollars, being the net increase in revised appropriations for the biennium 2010–2011 approved by the Assembly in its resolution 66/245 A of 24 December 2011, shall be financed in accordance with regulations 3.1 and 3.2 of the Financial Regulations and Rules of the United Nations, as follows:

(*a*) 40,118,000 dollars, consisting of 26,192,600 dollars, being half of the estimated income other than staff assessment income approved for the biennium 2012–2013 under resolution B above, plus 13,925,400 dollars, being the increase in income other than staff assessment income for the biennium 2010–2011 approved by the Assembly in its resolution 66/245 B of 24 December 2011;

(*b*) 2,585,230,800 dollars, being the assessment on Member States in accordance with its resolution 64/248 of 24 December 2009 on the scale of assessments for the apportionment of the expenses of the United Nations;

2. There shall be set off against the assessment on Member States, in accordance with the provisions of General Assembly resolution 973(X) of 15 December 1955, their respective share in the Tax Equalization Fund in the total amount of 222,065,600 dollars, consisting of:

(*a*) 227,683,000 dollars, being half of the estimated staff assessment income approved for the biennium 2012–2013 in resolution B above;

(*b*) Offset by 5,617,400 dollars, being the decrease in income from staff assessment for the biennium 2010–2011 approved by the Assembly in its resolution 66/245 B.

Also on 24 December, the Assembly decided that the item on the 2012–2013 proposed programme budget would remain for consideration during its resumed sixty-sixth (2012) session **(decision 66/557)**.

Other questions relating to the programme budget

The Fifth Committee considered a number of special subjects relating to the 2012–2013 programme budget, among them, revised estimates resulting from resolutions and decisions adopted by the Economic and Social Council at its substantive sessions of 2011; revised estimates resulting from resolutions and decisions adopted by the Human Rights Council; estimates in respect of special political missions, good offices and other political initiatives authorized by the General Assembly and/or the Security Council; the effects of changes in rates of exchange and inflation; the contingency fund; unforeseen and extraordinary expenses; and the Working Capital Fund (see sections below).

Other subjects concerned the emergency management framework (see p. 1419); transitional measures on financial reporting by the Office of the United Nations High Commissioner for Refugees (see p. 1403); request for a subvention to the United Nations Institute for Disarmament Research (see p. 540); administrative expenses of the United Nations Joint Staff Pension Fund (see p. 1448); UNCTAD/International Trade Centre/WTO (see p. 909); construction of additional office facilities at the Economic Commission for Africa in Addis Ababa and at the United Nations Office at Nairobi (see p. 1427) and the strategic heritage plan of the United Nations Office at Geneva (see p. 1426); administrative and financial implications of the decisions and recommendations contained in the 2011 report of the International Civil Service Commission (ICSC) (see p. 1428); financial implications of the administration of justice at the United Nations (see p. 1448); and the gross budgets for the Joint Inspection Unit, ICSC, the United Nations System Chief Executives Board for Coordination, and the UN Department of Safety and Security.

Chapter II: United Nations financing and programming

GENERAL ASSEMBLY ACTION

On 24 December [meeting 93], the General Assembly, on the recommendation of the Fifth Committee [A/66/637], adopted **resolution 66/247** without vote [agenda item 134].

Special subjects relating to the proposed programme budget for the biennium 2012–2013

The General Assembly,

I

Revised estimates under section 29D, Office of Central Support Services, and section 30, Office of Information and Communications Technology, of the proposed programme budget for the biennium 2012–2013 relating to the organizational resilience management system: emergency management framework

Having considered the report of the Secretary-General on revised estimates under section 29D, Office of Central Support Services, and section 30, Office of Information and Communications Technology, of the proposed programme budget for the biennium 2012–2013 relating to the organizational resilience management system: emergency management framework and the related report of the Advisory Committee on Administrative and Budgetary Questions,

1. *Takes note* of the report of the Secretary-General;

2. *Endorses* the conclusions and recommendations contained in the report of the Advisory Committee on Administrative and Budgetary Questions, subject to the provisions of the present resolution;

3. *Takes note* of paragraphs 32 (*a*) and (*c*) of the report of the Advisory Committee on Administrative and Budgetary Questions;

4. *Also takes note* of the organizational resilience management system approach, on the understanding that the follow-up report to be submitted to the General Assembly at its sixty-seventh session will present a complete picture of the comprehensive emergency management framework, in accordance with the provisions of paragraphs 6 and 11 of section II of its resolution 64/260 of 29 March 2010;

5. *Regrets* the lack of coordination in the Secretariat which led to delays in submitting the proposal requested in paragraph 11 of resolution 64/260;

6. *Decides* not to use the contingency fund to finance the proposals contained in the report of the Secretary-General, and in this regard requests the Secretary-General to strictly observe its resolutions 41/213 of 19 December 1986 and 42/211 of 21 December 1987 regarding the use of the contingency fund;

7. *Decides* to approve the extension of the lease of the secondary data centre in Piscataway, New Jersey, United States of America, for thirty months beyond 31 December 2011 and the procurement of software to maintain emergency preparedness plans and the staff accounting system, and further decides not to approve additional resources in this regard;

II

Transitional measures concerning financial reporting by the Office of the United Nations High Commissioner for Refugees under the International Public Sector Accounting Standards

Having considered the report of the United Nations High Commissioner for Refugees on transitional measures concerning financial reporting by the Office of the United Nations High Commissioner for Refugees under the International Public Sector Accounting Standards and the related report of the Advisory Committee on Administrative and Budgetary Questions,

1. *Takes note* of the report of the United Nations High Commissioner for Refugees;

2. *Endorses* the conclusions and recommendations contained in the report of the Advisory Committee on Administrative and Budgetary Questions;

3. *Authorizes* the Office of the United Nations High Commissioner for Refugees to apply mutatis mutandis the Financial Regulations and Rules of the United Nations to the accounting processes and financial reporting of its voluntary funds, for the sole purpose of the timely implementation by the Office of the International Public Sector Accounting Standards;

III

Revised estimates resulting from resolutions and decisions adopted by the Economic and Social Council at its substantive session of 2011

Having considered the report of the Secretary-General on revised estimates resulting from resolutions and decisions adopted by the Economic and Social Council at its substantive session of 2011 and the related report of the Advisory Committee on Administrative and Budgetary Questions,

1. *Takes note* of the report of the Secretary-General;

2. *Endorses* the conclusions and recommendations contained in the report of the Advisory Committee on Administrative and Budgetary Questions;

IV

Request for a subvention to the United Nations Institute for Disarmament Research resulting from the recommendations of the Board of Trustees of the Institute on the programme of work of the Institute for 2012–2013

Recalling section IV of its resolution 60/248 of 23 December 2005,

Having considered the note by the Secretary-General on the request for a subvention to the United Nations Institute for Disarmament Research resulting from the recommendations of the Board of Trustees of the Institute on the programme of work of the Institute for 2012–2013 and the related report of the Advisory Committee on Administrative and Budgetary Questions,

1. *Takes note* of the note by the Secretary-General;

2. *Endorses* the conclusions and recommendations contained in the report of the Advisory Committee on Administrative and Budgetary Questions;

3. *Approves* the request for a subvention to the Institute of 577,800 United States dollars (before recosting) for

the biennium 2012–2013 from the regular budget of the United Nations, on the understanding that no additional provision would be required under section 4, Disarmament, of the proposed programme budget for the biennium 2012–2013;

V

Administrative expenses of the United Nations Joint Staff Pension Fund and transitional measures concerning the financial reporting of the Fund under the International Public Sector Accounting Standards

Recalling its resolutions 55/224 of 23 December 2000, 57/286 of 20 December 2002, 59/269 of 23 December 2004, 61/240 of 22 December 2006, 62/241 of 22 December 2007 and 63/252 of 24 December 2008, section II of its resolution 64/245 of 24 December 2009 and its resolution 65/249 of 24 December 2010,

Having considered the report of the United Nations Joint Staff Pension Board on the administrative expenses of the United Nations Joint Staff Pension Fund and transitional measures concerning the financial reporting of the Fund under the International Public Sector Accounting Standards, the report of the Secretary-General on the administrative and financial implications arising from the report of the Board and the related report of the Advisory Committee on Administrative and Budgetary Questions,

1. *Endorses* the conclusions and recommendations contained in the report of the Advisory Committee on Administrative and Budgetary Questions, subject to the provisions of the present resolution;

2. *Encourages* the Secretary-General to continue to ensure, through consultations with the United Nations Joint Staff Pension Fund, that posts in the Fund are announced as widely as possible, inter alia on the Inspira website, as appropriate;

3. *Approves* the revised estimate of 154,545,700 dollars for the biennium 2010–2011 for the administration of the Fund;

4. *Also approves* expenses, chargeable directly to the Fund, totalling 173,412,600 dollars net for the biennium 2012–2013;

5. *Further approves* the amount of 20,688,300 dollars as the United Nations share of the cost of the administrative expenses of the Fund for the biennium 2012–2013, of which 13,240,500 dollars represents the share of the regular budget and the balance of 7,447,800 dollars represents the share of the United Nations funds and programmes;

6. *Approves* the reduction of 1,035,600 dollars in the United Nations share of the cost of the administrative expenses of the central secretariat of the Fund under section 1, Overall policymaking, direction and coordination, of the proposed programme budget for the biennium 2012–2013;

7. *Authorizes* the United Nations Joint Staff Pension Board to supplement the voluntary contributions to the Emergency Fund for the biennium 2012–2013 by an amount not to exceed 200,000 dollars;

8. *Authorizes* the United Nations Joint Staff Pension Fund to continue to apply mutatis mutandis the Financial Regulations and Rules of the United Nations to its accounting processes and financial reporting in a manner that allows the Fund to be compliant with the International Public Sector Accounting Standards by 1 January 2012;

9. *Recalls* its resolution 65/249;

VI

International Trade Centre

Having considered the programme budget proposals for the International Trade Centre for the biennium 2012–2013 and the related report of the Advisory Committee on Administrative and Budgetary Questions,

1. *Endorses* the conclusions and recommendations contained in the report of the Advisory Committee on Administrative and Budgetary Questions, subject to the provisions of the present resolution;

2. *Takes note* of paragraph 11 of the report of the Advisory Committee on Administrative and Budgetary Questions, and decides that the temporary position of Associate Graphic Designer (P-2) shall continue to be funded as general temporary assistance;

3. *Decides* to approve resources in the amount of 41,337,700 dollars (the United Nations share equivalent to 38,072,000 Swiss francs at the exchange rate of 0.921 Swiss francs to 1 dollar) proposed for the biennium 2012–2013 under section 13, International Trade Centre, of the proposed programme budget for the biennium 2012–2013;

VII

Construction of additional office facilities at the United Nations Office at Nairobi and the Economic Commission for Africa in Addis Ababa and strategic heritage plan of the United Nations Office at Geneva

Recalling its resolution 56/270 of 27 March 2002, section IV of its resolution 58/272 of 23 December 2003, sections IX and X of its resolution 62/238 of 22 December 2007, section I of its resolution 63/263 of 24 December 2008, its resolution 64/243 of 24 December 2009 and section III of its resolution 65/259 of 24 December 2010,

Having considered the reports of the Secretary-General on the construction of additional office facilities at the United Nations Office at Nairobi, on progress in the construction of additional office facilities at the Economic Commission for Africa in Addis Ababa and on the strategic heritage plan of the United Nations Office at Geneva, as well as the related report of the Advisory Committee on Administrative and Budgetary Questions,

1. *Takes note* of the reports of the Secretary-General;

2. *Endorses* the conclusions and recommendations contained in the report of the Advisory Committee on Administrative and Budgetary Questions, subject to the provisions of the present resolution;

3. *Requests* the Secretary-General, through the Office of Central Support Services, to take into account lessons learned and best practices from past construction projects in implementing future construction projects, in particular to draw from the experience and the know-how acquired from large capital projects, including the capital master plan;

4. *Also requests* the Secretary-General to ensure that major capital expenditure projects are not implemented simultaneously in order to prevent the need to finance them at the same time;

5. *Recalls* paragraph 15 of the report of the Advisory Committee on Administrative and Budgetary Questions, and expresses concern that an estimated expenditure of 734,000 dollars from the contingency provision has arisen, owing to an error by the architecture and construction management consultant, which has resulted in a substantial

depletion of the budgeted contingency, thereby increasing the risk to the Economic Commission for Africa project;

6. *Reiterates its request* to the Secretary-General that the renovation phase of the strategic heritage plan not start before the General Assembly has taken a decision on this matter and the capital master plan has been completed;

7. *Requests* the Secretary-General to submit to the General Assembly at its sixty-eighth session in the context of the proposed programme budget for the biennium 2014–2015 a detailed implementation plan and cost analysis based on the medium-term option, with fully developed explanations of the composition and calculation of the costs, as well as the basis for assumptions that underpin the estimates and relevant supporting data, and a prioritized list of tasks highlighting essential items that need renovation for health and safety reasons, without prejudice to any decisions to be made by the General Assembly on this matter;

8. *Also requests* the Secretary-General to include, as a potential complement to assessed contributions by Member States for the realization of the strategic heritage plan, options for voluntary funding sources, public or private, in line with the rules and regulations of the United Nations;

9. *Decides* to approve general temporary assistance in the amount of 810,600 dollars under section 29E, Administration, Geneva, of the proposed programme budget for the biennium 2012–2013 to provide for one P-4 Architect and one P-4 Engineer, as well as the additional requirement of 2.8 million dollars for contractual services in relation to the development of the detailed project implementation and phasing plan under section 34, Construction, alteration, improvement and major maintenance;

10. *Also decides* to approve an amount of 74,000 dollars under section 37, Staff assessment, to be offset by an equivalent amount under Income section 1, Income from staff assessment, of the proposed programme budget for the biennium 2012–2013;

VIII

Revised estimates resulting from resolutions and decisions adopted by the Human Rights Council at its sixteenth, seventeenth and eighteenth sessions and its fifteenth, sixteenth and seventeenth special sessions

Having considered the report of the Secretary-General on revised estimates resulting from resolutions and decisions adopted by the Human Rights Council at its sixteenth, seventeenth and eighteenth sessions and its fifteenth, sixteenth and seventeenth special sessions and the related report of the Advisory Committee on Administrative and Budgetary Questions,

1. *Takes note* of the report of the Secretary-General;

2. *Endorses* the conclusions and recommendations contained in the report of the Advisory Committee on Administrative and Budgetary Questions;

3. *Welcomes* the establishment of the Office of the President of the Human Rights Council;

IX

Estimates in respect of special political missions, good offices and other political initiatives authorized by the General Assembly and/or the Security Council

Having considered the reports of the Secretary-General on the estimates in respect of special political missions, good offices and other political initiatives authorized by the General Assembly and/or the Security Council and on the request for a subvention to the Special Court for Sierra Leone, as well as the related reports of the Advisory Committee on Administrative and Budgetary Questions,

1. *Takes note* of the reports of the Secretary-General;

2. *Endorses* the conclusions and recommendations contained in the reports of the Advisory Committee on Administrative and Budgetary Questions, subject to the provisions of the present resolution;

3. *Reiterates* the need for greater transparency in the presentation of resources for travel and consultancies so that the General Assembly can make well-informed decisions regarding the resource requirements for special political missions;

4. *Requests* the Secretary-General to make additional efforts to ensure that support sought in the form of consultancies is not already available in-house or in situ;

5. *Regrets* the late introduction of the reports on the estimates in respect of special political missions, good offices and other political initiatives authorized by the General Assembly and/or the Security Council;

6. *Takes note* of paragraphs 57, 64, 82, 109, 112, 115, 138, 162 and 245 of the report of the Advisory Committee on Administrative and Budgetary Questions;

7. *Decides* to reduce the 2012 budget for the United Nations Integrated Peacebuilding Office in the Central African Republic by 350,000 dollars;

8. *Also decides* to reduce the 2012 budget for the Cameroon-Nigeria Mixed Commission by 250,000 dollars;

9. *Approves* the total amount of 583,383,800 dollars for the budgets of the twenty-nine special political missions authorized by the General Assembly and/or the Security Council listed in table 1 of the report of the Secretary-General;

10. *Also approves* a charge totalling 583,383,800 dollars net against the provision for special political missions requested in section 3, Political affairs, of the proposed programme budget for the biennium 2012–2013;

11. *Authorizes* the Secretary-General to enter into commitments in an amount not to exceed 16 million dollars for the United Nations Support Mission in Libya;

12. *Also authorizes* the Secretary-General to enter into commitments in an amount not to exceed 9,066,400 dollars for the subvention for the Special Court for Sierra Leone;

X

Administrative and financial implications of the decisions and recommendations contained in the report of the International Civil Service Commission for 2011

Having considered the statement submitted by the Secretary-General in accordance with rule 153 of the rules of procedure of the General Assembly on the administrative and financial implications of the decisions and recommendations contained in the report of the International Civil Service Commission for 2011 and the related report of the Advisory Committee on Administrative and Budgetary Questions,

1. *Recalls* its resolution 66/235 of 24 December 2011;

2. *Takes note* of the statement submitted by the Secretary-General;

3. *Endorses* the conclusions and recommendations contained in the report of the Advisory Committee on Administrative and Budgetary Questions;

XI

Financial implications of the administration of justice at the United Nations

Recalling its resolution 66/237 of 24 December 2011 on the administration of justice at the United Nations,

1. *Decides* to approve an additional amount of 7,078,700 dollars, at 2012–2013 rates, in the proposed programme budget for the biennium 2012–2013, reflecting an increase comprising 2,178,600 dollars under section 1, Overall policymaking, direction and coordination, 557,600 dollars under section 8, Legal affairs, 402,600 dollars under section 19, Economic and social development in Asia and the Pacific, 299,400 dollars under section 29A, Office of the Under-Secretary-General for Management, 689,200 dollars under section 29C, Office of Human Resources Management, 649,700 dollars under section 29D, Office of Central Support Services, 868,200 dollars under section 29E, Administration, Geneva, and 695,000 dollars under section 29G, Administration, Nairobi, and an increase of 738,400 dollars under section 37, Staff assessment, to be offset by a corresponding amount under income section 1, Income from staff assessment;

2. *Also decides* that the additional amount of 7,078,700 dollars would represent a charge against the contingency fund for the biennium 2012–2013;

XII

Effects of changes in rates of exchange and inflation

Having considered the report of the Secretary-General on the revised estimates resulting from changes in rates of exchange and inflation and the related report of the Advisory Committee on Administrative and Budgetary Questions,

Takes note of the revised estimates arising from recosting due to changes in the rates of exchange and inflation;

XIII

Contingency fund

Notes that a balance of 13,762,500 dollars remains in the contingency fund;

XIV

Joint Inspection Unit

Approves the gross budget for the Joint Inspection Unit for the biennium 2012–2013 in the amount of 12,743,200 dollars;

XV

International Civil Service Commission

Also approves the gross budget for the International Civil Service Commission for the biennium 2012–2013 in the amount of 17,546,300 dollars;

XVI

United Nations System Chief Executives Board for Coordination

Notes the gross budget for the United Nations System Chief Executives Board for Coordination for the biennium 2012–2013 in the amount of 5,380,700 dollars;

XVII

Gross jointly financed budget of the Department of Safety and Security

Approves the gross jointly financed budget of the Department of Safety and Security for the biennium 2012–2013 in the amount of 244,536,400 dollars, broken down as follows:

(*a*) Field Security Operations: 215,032,200 dollars;

(*b*) Security and Safety Services at the United Nations Office at Vienna: 29,504,200 dollars.

Revised estimates resulting from Economic and Social Council action

In an October report [A/66/510], the Secretary-General submitted estimates of $572,900 in additional requirements for the 2012–2013 programme budget, all of which could be absorbed, resulting from Economic and Social Council **resolutions 2011/14** (see p. 946), **2011/23** (see p. 931) and **2011/24** (see p. 967), and **decisions 2011/258** (see p. 1173) and **2011/268** (see p. 900).

In October [A/66/7/Add.9], ACABQ stated that it had no objection to the recommendations proposed in the Secretary-General's report.

Revised estimates resulting from Human Rights Council action

In a 5 December report [A/66/586], the Secretary-General submitted revised estimated requirements relating to the proposed 2012–2013 programme budget, totalling $13,261,800, arising from resolutions and decisions adopted by the Human Rights Council at its sixteen, seventeenth and eighteenth regular sessions and its fifteenth, sixteenth and seventeenth special sessions held in 2011 (see p. 603). The amount would be considered in the context of the contingency fund for the 2012–2013 biennium.

In December [A/66/7/Add.20], ACABQ recommended approval of the Secretary-General's proposals, subject to the Committee's observations and recommendations.

Financing of unforeseen and extraordinary expenses

Pursuant to General Assembly resolution 65/281 (see p. 607), the Secretary-General submitted a November report [A/66/558 & Corr.1] outlining options for providing adequate financing to fund unforeseen and extraordinary expenses arising from Human Rights Council resolutions and decisions for consideration by the Assembly. Three possible options included: a provision for financing urgent independent commissions of inquiry and/or fact-finding missions in the additional amount of $2 million under the 2012–2013 programme budget; establishment of a reserve fund in the amount of $2 million per biennium for financing such commissions or missions; and access to resources under Assembly resolution 64/246 [YUN 2009, p. 1409] on unforeseen and extraordinary expenses, which could be amended to include commitment authority for urgent requirements in the area of human rights within a limit of $2 million per biennium or by increasing the existing limit from $8 to $9 million.

In its seventeenth report [A/66/7/Add.16] on the 2012–2013 proposed programme budget, ACABQ recommended that the Assembly maintain the current procedure for meeting unforeseen and extraordinary requirements not related to peace and security, and request the Secretary-General to report on the utilization of the procedure to the Assembly at its sixty-eighth (2013) session.

On 24 December, the Assembly, by decision **66/556 A**, deferred consideration of the reports of the Secretary-General and ACABQ until its resumed sixty-sixth (2012) session.

Revised estimates in respect of matters of which the Security Council was seized

In November [A/66/354 & Corr.1], as a result of action taken or expected to be taken by the General Assembly and/or the Security Council, the Secretary-General submitted proposed resource requirements for the period up to 31 December 2012 for 30 special political missions, which was estimated at $617,620,600 net ($662,260,500 gross). Six addenda [A/66/354/Add.1–6] to the report were issued.

ACABQ, in its thirteenth report on the 2012–2013 proposed programme budget [A/66/7/Add.12], recommended that the Assembly approve the resources requested by the Secretary-General, subject to the Committee's observations and recommendations.

Review of funding and backstopping arrangements for special political missions

Pursuant to section XIII of General Assembly resolution 65/259 [YUN 2010, p. 1433], the Secretary-General submitted an October report [A/66/340] on the review of current funding and backstopping arrangements for special political missions, which found that, given the evolution of the role of those missions over the past decade, the funding arrangements and their associated requirements for backstopping them were inadequate in three respects. The biennial programme budget was not the optimal vehicle for funding special political missions; start-up and expansion of the missions were impeded by the lack of well-defined mechanisms to finance them between conferral of a mandate and approval of a budget; and much of the backstopping capacity that missions needed to draw upon was provided by the Department of Peacekeeping Operations, the Department of Field Support and the Global Service Centre, which were not funded from the programme budget. The report presented a number of options for consideration by the General Assembly that could address those challenges.

ACABQ, in its twenty-second report on the 2012–2013 proposed programme budget [A/66/7/Add.21], recommended that the Assembly establish a special and separate account for funding special political missions that would be budgeted, funded and reported upon on an annual basis with a financial period of 1 July to 30 June; authorize special political missions, with the prior concurrence of the Advisory Committee and in accordance with a decision of the Assembly or the Security Council, to access up to $25 million from the Peacekeeping Reserve Fund for the start-up or expansion phase of field-based special political missions, and up to $25 million in strategic deployment stocks in advance of the corresponding budget appropriation; and make the support account available to all departments and offices to fund their variable backstopping requirements in relation to the field-based special political missions and confirm the responsibility to support special political missions, while maintaining the existing arrangements for the financing of the support account and the Global Service Centre.

On 24 December, the Assembly deferred consideration of the reports of the Secretary-General and ACABQ on the review of arrangements for funding and backstopping special political missions until its sixty-seventh (2012) session (**decision 66/556 A**).

Contingency fund

The contingency fund, established by General Assembly resolution 41/213 [YUN 1986, p. 1024], accommodated additional expenditures relating to each biennium that derived from legislative mandates not provided for in the proposed programme budget or from revised estimates. Guidelines for its use were annexed to Assembly resolution 42/211 [YUN 1987, p. 1098].

The Fifth Committee considered the Secretary-General's December report [A/C.5/66/13] containing a consolidated statement of all programme budget implications and revised estimates falling under the guidelines for the use of the fund. The consolidated amount of $34,601,700 would be within the approved level of the fund; an available balance of $5,876,500 would remain in the fund.

ACABQ, in its twenty-fourth report [A/66/7/Add.23] on the 2012–2013 proposed programme budget, pointed out that the additional requirements would deplete the fund by some 85 per cent before the biennium had started, and was of the view that some of those requirements could have been included in the

2012–2013 programme budget. It recommended that the Secretary-General analyse the way in which the fund was utilized, and in future make every effort to incorporate additional requirements into the initial budget proposals.

Unforeseen and extraordinary expenses

Under the terms of General Assembly resolution 64/246 [YUN 2009, p. 1409], the Secretary-General was authorized, with the prior concurrence of ACABQ, to enter into commitments to meet unforeseen and extraordinary expenses arising either during or subsequent to the 2010–2011 biennium, without reverting to the Assembly for approval.

GENERAL ASSEMBLY ACTION

On 24 December [meeting 93], the General Assembly, on the recommendation of the Fifth Committee [A/66/637], adopted **resolution 66/249** without vote [agenda item 134].

Unforeseen and extraordinary expenses for the biennium 2012–2013

The General Assembly

1. *Authorizes* the Secretary-General, with the prior concurrence of the Advisory Committee on Administrative and Budgetary Questions and subject to the Financial Regulations and Rules of the United Nations and the provisions of paragraph 3 below, to enter into commitments in the biennium 2012–2013 to meet unforeseen and extraordinary expenses arising either during or subsequent to the biennium, provided that the concurrence of the Advisory Committee shall not be necessary for:

(*a*) Such commitments not exceeding a total of 8 million United States dollars in any one year of the biennium 2012–2013 as the Secretary-General certifies relate to the maintenance of peace and security;

(*b*) Such commitments as the President of the International Court of Justice certifies relate to expenses occasioned by:
  (i) The designation of ad hoc judges (Statute of the International Court of Justice, Article 31), not exceeding a total of 200,000 dollars;
  (ii) The calling of witnesses and the appointment of experts (Statute, Article 50) and the appointment of assessors (Statute, Article 30), not exceeding a total of 50,000 dollars;
  (iii) The maintenance in office for the completion of cases of judges who have not been re-elected (Statute, Article 13, paragraph 3), not exceeding a total of 40,000 dollars;
  (iv) The payment of pensions and travel and removal expenses of retiring judges and travel and removal expenses and installation grants of members of the Court (Statute, Article 32, paragraph 7), not exceeding a total of 410,000 dollars;
  (v) The work of the Court or its Chambers away from The Hague (Statute, Article 22), not exceeding a total of 25,000 dollars;

(*c*) Such commitments not exceeding a total of 1 million dollars in the biennium 2012–2013 as the Secretary-General certifies are required for security measures pursuant to section XI, paragraph 6, of General Assembly resolution 59/276 of 23 December 2004;

2. *Resolves* that the Secretary-General shall report to the Advisory Committee on Administrative and Budgetary Questions and to the General Assembly at its sixty-seventh and sixty-eighth sessions all commitments made under the provisions of the present resolution, together with the circumstances relating thereto, and shall submit supplementary estimates to the Assembly in respect of such commitments;

3. *Decides* that, for the biennium 2012–2013, if a decision of the Security Council results in the need for the Secretary-General to enter into commitments relating to the maintenance of peace and security in an amount exceeding 10 million dollars in respect of the decision, that matter shall be brought to the General Assembly, or, if the Assembly is suspended or not in session, a resumed or special session of the Assembly shall be convened by the Secretary-General to consider the matter.

Working Capital Fund

In December, the General Assembly established the Working Capital Fund for the 2012–2013 biennium at $150 million, the same level as for the 2010–2011 biennium [YUN 2009, p. 1409]. As in the past, the Fund was to be used to finance appropriations, pending the receipt of assessed contributions, to pay for unforeseen and extraordinary expenses, as well as for miscellaneous self-liquidating purchases and advance insurance premiums, and to enable the Tax Equalization Fund to meet current commitments pending the accumulation of credits.

GENERAL ASSEMBLY ACTION

On 24 December [meeting 93], the General Assembly, on the recommendation of the Fifth Committee [A/66/637], adopted **resolution 66/250** without vote [agenda item 134].

Working Capital Fund for the biennium 2012–2013

The General Assembly
Resolves that:

1. The Working Capital Fund shall be established for the biennium 2012–2013 in the amount of 150 million United States dollars;

2. Member States shall make advances to the Working Capital Fund in accordance with the scale of assessments adopted by the General Assembly for contributions of Member States to the budget for the year 2012;

3. There shall be set off against this allocation of advances:

(a) Credits to Member States resulting from transfers made in 1959 and 1960 from the surplus account to the Working Capital Fund in an adjusted amount of 1,025,092 dollars;

(b) Cash advances paid by Member States to the Working Capital Fund for the biennium 2010–2011 in accordance with General Assembly resolution 64/247 of 24 December 2009;

4. Should the credits and advances paid by any Member State to the Working Capital Fund for the biennium 2010–2011 exceed the amount of that Member State's advance under the provisions of paragraph 2 above, the excess shall be set off against the amount of the contributions payable by the Member State in respect of the biennium 2012–2013;

5. The Secretary-General is authorized to advance from the Working Capital Fund:

(a) Such sums as may be necessary to finance budgetary appropriations pending the receipt of contributions; sums so advanced shall be reimbursed as soon as receipts from contributions are available for that purpose;

(b) Such sums as may be necessary to finance commitments that may be duly authorized under the provisions of the resolutions adopted by the General Assembly, in particular resolution 66/249 of 24 December 2011 relating to unforeseen and extraordinary expenses; the Secretary-General shall make provision in the budget estimates for reimbursing the Working Capital Fund;

(c) Such sums as may be necessary to continue the revolving fund to finance miscellaneous self-liquidating purchases and activities, which, together with net sums outstanding for the same purpose, do not exceed 200,000 dollars; advances in excess of 200,000 dollars may be made with the prior concurrence of the Advisory Committee on Administrative and Budgetary Questions;

(d) With the prior concurrence of the Advisory Committee on Administrative and Budgetary Questions, such sums as may be required to finance payments of advance insurance premiums where the period of insurance extends beyond the end of the biennium in which payment is made; the Secretary-General shall make provision in the budget estimates of each biennium, during the life of the related policies, to cover the charges applicable to each biennium;

(e) Such sums as may be necessary to enable the Tax Equalization Fund to meet current commitments pending the accumulation of credits; such advances shall be repaid as soon as credits are available in the Tax Equalization Fund;

6. Should the provision in paragraph 1 above prove inadequate to meet the purposes normally related to the Working Capital Fund, the Secretary-General is authorized to utilize, in the biennium 2012–2013, cash from special funds and accounts in his custody, under the conditions approved by the General Assembly in its resolution 1341(XIII) of 13 December 1958, or the proceeds of loans authorized by the Assembly.

Contributions

According to the Secretary-General's report on improving the financial situation of the United Nations [A/66/521/Add.1], unpaid assessed contributions to the UN budget at the end of 2011 totalled $454 million (compared to $351 million in 2010); outstanding peacekeeping arrears totalled $2.6 billion (compared to $2.5 billion in 2010); and total unpaid assessments to the international tribunals remained at $27 million.

The number of Member States paying their regular budget assessment in full increased to 143 (compared to 138 at the end of 2010).

Assessments

The Committee on Contributions, at its seventy-first session (New York, 6–24 June) [A/66/11], considered a number of issues related to the payment of assessments, including a review of the methodology for preparing the scale of assessments for the period 2013–2015, multi-year payment plans and the application of Article 19 of the Charter. The Committee decided to hold its seventy-second session from 4 to 29 June 2012. On its working methods, the Committee decided that consideration could be given in future to exploring options for increasing interaction of members in between the holding of regular sessions, including online training and other interactive mechanisms for follow-up on various issues, and on arrangements for increasing the online availability of restricted documents.

The General Assembly took action on the Committee's recommendations in October (see below).

Application of Article 19

Committee on Contributions. The Committee on Contributions [A/66/11] reviewed requests for exemption under Article 19, whereby a Member would lose its vote in the General Assembly if the amount of its arrears should equal or exceed the amount of contributions due from it for the preceding two full years. The Committee noted the Members' written and oral presentations and evaluated them against their payment records and economic and political circumstances.

Having reviewed requests from six Member States, the Committee determined that the failure of the Central African Republic, the Comoros, Guinea-Bissau, Liberia, Sao Tome and Principe and Somalia to pay the full minimum amount of their arrears necessary to avoid the application of Article 19 was due to conditions beyond their control and recommended that they be allowed to vote until the end of the sixty-sixth session of the Assembly. The Committee urged the Central African Republic, which had made a sizeable payment in 2010, to implement the multi-year payment plan system and Sao Tome and Principe, which had made no payment since 2002, to pay amounts slightly in excess of its current annual assessments. It urged the

Comoros and Guinea-Bissau to submit a multi-year payment plan and to ensure that their payments, to the extent possible, exceeded the level of their annual contributions. Noting the regular payments made by Liberia under its payment plan, in amounts well above its annual assessments, the Committee expressed its appreciation for the exemplary and continuing efforts of Liberia to pay its arrears.

Reports of Secretary-General. During the year, the Secretary-General reported to the Assembly on payments made by certain Member States to reduce their level of arrears below that specified in Article 19, so that they could vote in the Assembly. As at 11 January [A/65/691], 18 Member States were below the gross amount assessed for the preceding two full years (2009–2010). By a series of letters from January to May [A/65/691/Add.1–11], that number was reduced to six and remained there through 9 September [A/66/350].

GENERAL ASSEMBLY ACTION

On 11 October [meeting 32], the General Assembly, on the recommendation of the Fifth Committee [A/66/492], adopted **resolution 66/4** without vote [agenda item 138].

Scale of assessments for the apportionment of the expenses of the United Nations: requests under Article 19 of the Charter

The General Assembly,

Having considered chapter V of the report of the Committee on Contributions on its seventy-first session,

Reaffirming the obligation of Member States under Article 17 of the Charter of the United Nations to bear the expenses of the Organization as apportioned by the General Assembly,

1. *Reaffirms* its role in accordance with the provisions of Article 19 of the Charter of the United Nations and the advisory role of the Committee on Contributions in accordance with rule 160 of the rules of procedure of the General Assembly;

2. *Also reaffirms* its resolution 54/237 C of 23 December 1999;

3. *Requests* the Secretary-General to continue to bring to the attention of Member States the deadline specified in resolution 54/237 C, including through an early announcement in the *Journal of the United Nations* and through direct communication;

4. *Urges* all Member States requesting exemption under Article 19 of the Charter to submit as much information as possible in support of their requests and to consider submitting such information in advance of the deadline specified in resolution 54/237 C so as to enable the collation of any additional detailed information that may be necessary;

5. *Agrees* that the failure of the Central African Republic, the Comoros, Guinea-Bissau, Liberia, Sao Tome and Principe and Somalia to pay the full minimum amount necessary to avoid the application of Article 19 of the Charter was due to conditions beyond their control;

6. *Decides* that the Central African Republic, the Comoros, Guinea-Bissau, Liberia, Sao Tome and Principe and Somalia shall be permitted to vote in the General Assembly until the end of its sixty-sixth session.

Multi-year payment plans

Pursuant to General Assembly resolutions 57/4 B [YUN 2002, p. 1385] and 64/248 [YUN 2009, p. 1412], the Secretary-General submitted a March report [A/66/69] providing information on the payment plans/schedules submitted by Liberia and Sao Tome and Principe, and on the status of their implementation as at 31 December 2010. Under the plans, each year a Member State would pay for the current year's assessments and a part of its arrears, so as to eliminate the arrears within six years. In 2010, although Liberia had not submitted a revised multi-year payment plan, it continued to make payments during the year, while Sao Tome and Principe fell below the level foreseen for the period from 2002 to 2009 in its payment schedule. The Secretary-General recommended that the Assembly encourage Member States with significant arrears to consider submitting a multi-year payment plan.

The Committee on Contributions [A/66/11] noted Liberia's intention to complete its commitments by 2013. Recalling the successful implementation of the plans of five other States in prior years, the Committee concluded that the system of multi-year payment plans continued to be a viable means in assisting Member States to reduce their unpaid assessed contributions and to demonstrate their commitment to meeting their financial obligations. The Committee noted that no new multi-year payment plans had been submitted for several years.

Other matters related to payment of assessed contributions

Scale methodology

Pursuant to General Assembly resolution 58/1 B [YUN 2003, p. 1424], the Committee on Contributions [A/66/11] continued to review the different elements of the methodology for preparing future scales of assessments, focusing on elements relating to income measures; conversion rates; base period; low per capita income adjustment; debt burden adjustment; minimum (floor) and maximum (ceiling) assessment rates; annual recalculation; and large scale-to-scale increases in rates of assessments. It explored the use of exponential functions in the scale methodology and found no technical merit in their use, which would move the scale of assessments away from the principle of capacity to pay.

With regard to income measure, the Committee recommended that the scale continue to be based on the most current, comprehensive and comparable gross national income data available and that the Assembly encourage States to submit the required statistical information under the 1993 System of National Accounts [YUN 1993, p. 1112], and where available, based on gross national disposable income, so that more comprehensive information could be used to measure capacity to pay. It also recommended that, whether a long or short base period was used, once it was chosen, it should be maintained for as long as possible. In the absence of other factors, there was no rationale for changing the current combined approach based on both the three-year and the six-year periods. The Committee also decided to continue to consider the questions of debt-burden adjustment, annual recalculation, and the feasibility of the application of systematic measures of transitional relief for Member States facing large scale-to-scale increases in their assessment rates.

On 24 December, the Assembly decided that the item on the scale of assessments for the apportionment of the expenses of the United Nations would remain for consideration during its resumed sixty-sixth (2012) session (**decision 66/557**).

Accounts and auditing

The General Assembly, at its resumed sixty-fifth (2011) session, considered the report of the Board of Auditors on UN peacekeeping operations for the period 1 July 2009 to 30 June 2010 [A/65/5 (Vol. II)] and the related ACABQ report [A/65/782], together with the Secretary-General's report on the implementation of the Board's recommendations [A/65/719].

On 30 June, the Assembly, in **resolution 65/243 B**, endorsed the Board's recommendations (see p. 74).

Board of Auditors reports. The Assembly, at its sixty-sixth session, had before it the reports of the Board of Auditors on the financial report and audited financial statements of the voluntary funds administered by the United Nations High Commissioner for Refugees (UNHCR)] [A/66/5/Add.5] (see p. 1132) and on the capital master plan (CMP) [A/66/5 (Vol. V)] (see p. 1425) for the year ended 31 December 2010; the Secretary-General's September report [A/66/324] on the implementation of the recommendations of the Board of Auditors contained in its report on CMP for the year ended 31 December 2010; and a July note [A/66/139], submitted pursuant to resolution 52/212 B [YUN 2002, p. 1288] transmitting the report of the Board of Auditors on the implementation of its recommendations relating to the 2008–2009 biennium and covering the accounts of 15 organizations. The comments and recommendations of ACABQ on those reports were contained in its reports of 26 September [A/66/377] and 2 December [A/66/7/Add.11].

On 4 April, the Assembly, in **resolution 65/269** (see p. 1421), took note of the Board's report on CMP and endorsed the conclusions and recommendations of ACABQ.

GENERAL ASSEMBLY ACTION

On 24 December [meeting 93], the General Assembly, on the recommendation of the Fifth Committee [A/66/626], adopted **resolution 66/232 A** without vote [agenda item 131].

Financial reports and audited financial statements, and reports of the Board of Auditors

The General Assembly,

Recalling its resolutions 64/227 of 22 December 2009, 64/268 of 24 June 2010, 65/243 A of 24 December 2010 and 65/243 B of 30 June 2011,

Having considered the financial report and audited financial statements and the report of the Board of Auditors on the voluntary funds administered by the United Nations High Commissioner for Refugees for the year ended 31 December 2010, the note by the Secretary-General transmitting to the General Assembly the letter dated 12 July 2011 from the Chair of the Board of Auditors transmitting the report of the Board on the implementation of its recommendations relating to the biennium 2008–2009 and the related report of the Advisory Committee on Administrative and Budgetary Questions,

1. *Accepts* the financial report and audited financial statements and the report and audit opinion of the Board of Auditors on the voluntary funds administered by the United Nations High Commissioner for Refugees for the year ended 31 December 2010;
2. *Approves* the recommendations of the Board of Auditors;
3. *Takes note* of the note by the Secretary-General transmitting to the General Assembly the letter dated 12 July 2011 from the Chair of the Board of Auditors transmitting the report of the Board on the implementation of its recommendations relating to the biennium 2008–2009;
4. *Endorses* the observations and recommendations contained in the report of the Advisory Committee on Administrative and Budgetary Questions;
5. *Commends* the Board of Auditors for the continued high quality of its report and the streamlined format thereof;
6. *Also commends* the Board of Auditors for its identification of common reasons for the lack of full implementation of the recommendations, as well as for good practices in relation to the implementation and follow-up of its reports;
7. *Invites* the Office of the United Nations High Commissioner for Refugees (UNHCR) to resume its efforts to develop, as a matter of priority, a simple organization-wide risk management approach without imposing onerous burdens on country operations;
8. *Acknowledges* the improvements made by the Office of the United Nations High Commissioner for Refugees (UNHCR) to implement the recommendations of the Board of Auditors, notes the concerns of the Board about the significant deficiencies found in the Office of the United Nations High Commissioner for Refugees (UNHCR) in matters relating to internal control and the management of assets, requests the Office of the United Nations High Commis-

sioner for Refugees (UNHCR) to continue to implement the recommendations of the Board, and encourages the Office of the United Nations High Commissioner for Refugees (UNHCR) to expeditiously develop an action plan with a time frame to address the concerns and systemic problems previously identified by the Board;

9. *Reiterates* the need to strengthen administrative and institutional measures to address the root causes of recurring issues and to minimize the ageing of the previous recommendations of the Board of Auditors;

10. *Recalls* paragraph 4 of the report of the Advisory Committee on Administrative and Budgetary Questions, and requests the Office of the United Nations High Commissioner for Refugees (UNHCR) to ensure that any future arrangements provide for a sound and reliable internal audit;

11. *Requests* the Advisory Committee on Administrative and Budgetary Questions to request the Board of Auditors to report on the internal audit arrangements in line with paragraph 1 (*d*) of the annex to the Financial Regulations and Rules of the United Nations;

12. *Emphasizes* that the implementation of the International Public Sector Accounting Standards is a tool for establishing better accountability and financial management, and requests the Secretary-General and the Office of the United Nations High Commissioner for Refugees (UNHCR) to ensure the arrangements necessary to realize the maximum benefits of the implementation of the Standards;

13. *Notes with concern*, in this regard, the reservations expressed by the Board of Auditors about the Office of the United Nations High Commissioner for Refugees (UNHCR) completing the preparations necessary for the successful implementation of the International Public Sector Accounting Standards in 2012, and requests the Office of the United Nations High Commissioner for Refugees (UNHCR) to ensure the further intensification of its efforts so that its financial statements are fully compliant with the implementation requirements of the Standards within the scheduled time frame;

14. *Reiterates its request* to the Secretary-General and the executive heads of the funds and programmes of the United Nations to ensure the full implementation of the recommendations of the Board of Auditors and the related recommendations of the Advisory Committee on Administrative and Budgetary Questions in a prompt and timely manner, to continue to hold programme managers accountable for the non-implementation of the recommendations and to effectively address the root causes of the problems highlighted by the Board;

15. *Reiterates its request* to the Secretary-General to provide in his reports on the implementation of the recommendations of the Board of Auditors on the accounts of the United Nations, as well as on the financial statements of its funds and programmes, a full explanation for the delays in the implementation of the recommendations of the Board, in particular those which have not yet been fully implemented that are two or more years old;

16. *Also reiterates its request* to the Secretary-General to continue to indicate an expected time frame for the implementation of the recommendations of the Board of Auditors and the priorities for their implementation, including the office holders to be held accountable and measures taken in that regard;

17. *Requests* the Secretary-General and the executive heads of the funds and programmes of the United Nations to consider, where they have not done so, exploring web-based follow-up systems, in line with lessons learned and best practices, to track the recommendations of the Board of Auditors, including the updated status of their acceptance, implementation and impact.

On the same date, the Assembly decided that the item on voluntary funds administered by the United Nations High Commissioner for Refugees would remain for consideration during its resumed sixty-sixth (2012) session (**decision 66/557**).

Financial management practices
International Public Sector Accounting Standards

In September, the Secretary-General submitted the fourth progress report [A/66/379] on the adoption of the International Public Sector Accounting Standards (IPSAS) by the United Nations. The report provided an update on IPSAS implementation since the third progress report in 2010 [YUN 2010, p. 1444] and covered the period from 1 August 2010 to 31 August 2011. The General Assembly adopted IPSAS in 2006 by resolution 60/283 [YUN 2006, p. 1580].

The Secretary-General indicated that the system-wide IPSAS project team continued to provide guidance and technical support to UN system organizations during and after IPSAS implementation. The team was in the process of comparing the 2010 financial statements of IPSAS implementers and preparing technical issue papers to address common diversity issues. The team's role had been extended until the end of 2013, with the presumption of continuation until 2015. An independent review of system-wide IPSAS-related activities would be conducted before the end of 2013, with a reassessment of the way forward, including a decision on resource requirements and the issue of institutionalization. Nine UN system organizations had implemented IPSAS as at 31 December 2010, and 14 others were in the process of implementation. All organizations projected to implement IPSAS from 2011 to 2014 had reported to be on track with their project timelines.

The first set of IPSAS-compliant financial statements for the period ending June 2014, for peacekeeping operations, and December 2014, for other UN Secretariat operations, had to be delivered by September 2014 and March 2015, respectively. Several challenges needed to be met in order to remain on track with those targets. A risk management strategy was established to address challenges and mitigate or eliminate the risks identified. Contingency plans were formulated and commissioned, in some cases, to further strengthen the strategy. Revised Financial Regulations and Rules would be presented for General Assembly approval in 2012 in order to meet the target date of 1 July 2013 for field missions.

Board of Auditors report. In a July note [A/66/151], the Secretary-General transmitted to the General Assembly a report of the Board of Auditors on progress in IPSAS implementation as at 30 June 2011, which indicated that there were a number of critical risks to achieving IPSAS implementation on time. Urgent and effective action was needed to address those risks. The Board stated that there should be no further deferment of the deadlines. Clear and effective organizational accountability and risk management frameworks that aligned both the appropriate accountability and authority against those managers responsible for delivering the core services and mandates of their organizations were needed. The Board concluded with a number of specific recommendations addressed to UN peacekeeping operations, and to all entities, including the United Nations and peacekeeping operations.

JIU report. In August [A/66/308], the Secretary-General submitted a Joint Inspection Unit (JIU) report on the preparedness of UN system organizations for IPSAS that provided an overview of the transition to and implementation status of IPSAS in UN system organizations and how the process was being carried out by each organization, with a focus on identifying best practices and possible risks. Of the 22 organizations reviewed, one had received a favourable opinion from its external auditor on its IPSAS-compliant 2008 and 2009 financial statements, and eight had introduced IPSAS by the original 2010 target date; two expected to implement IPSAS in 2011, nine in 2012, and two in 2014. The review demonstrated that the adoption of IPSAS was beginning to have a major impact well beyond accounting; however, many organizations underestimated the concerted efforts and resources required and failed to undertake initial preparedness and risk assessments. Successful transition to IPSAS hinged on strong senior management support and engagement, dedicated intra-departmental task forces and the adoption of a project management approach. The report identified and addressed a number of risks for consideration by executive heads to ensure a successful transition to IPSAS. The Board recommended that executive heads ensure implementation of 16 best practices as identified in the report. The Secretary-General submitted his comments and those of the United Nations System Chief Executives Board for Coordination (CEB) on the JIU report [A/66/308/Add.1].

ACABQ report. In November [A/66/536], ACABQ recognized the progress made towards IPSAS implementation by the United Nations, along with efforts for strengthening oversight, enhancing risk management and engaging with oversight bodies. It recommended that all entities be requested to expedite full implementation of the Board's recommendations and that the General Assembly take note of the Secretary-General's plan to present proposals for amendments to the Financial Regulations and Rules at the Assembly's sixty-seventh (2012) session. While recognizing the need to plan for contingencies as recommended by the Board of Auditors, ACABQ remained concerned by the extent of the manual workarounds and planned temporary adaptations to existing systems, and by the unsustainable nature of those solutions. The approach envisaged presented risks that significant resources might be devoted to implementing temporary solutions not sufficiently robust to ensure successful implementation and take vital resources away from the implementation of the ERP (Umoja) project. To mitigate those risks, the Secretary-General should exercise strict oversight over the IPSAS implementation project, ensure prudent stewardship of project resources, and establish clear lines of reporting and mechanisms for the rapid resolution of issues on a day-to-day basis. ACABQ expected the Secretary-General to develop a benefits realization plan as recommended by the Board of Auditors, and encouraged him to develop a business culture focused on improved performance and effectiveness as the Organization prepared for its IPSAS transition.

Transitional measures. In a September note [A/66/352], the Secretary-General transmitted to the General Assembly a report of the United Nations High Commissioner for Refugees (UNHCR) on transitional measures concerning financial reporting under IPSAS standards, which requested the Assembly to authorize UNHCR to apply mutatis mutandis the Financial Regulations and Rules to its voluntary funds accounting processes and financial reporting in a manner that would allow it to be IPSAS-compliant as of 1 January 2012. ACABQ had no objections to that request [A/66/376].

On 24 December, in Part VIII of resolution 66/246 (see p. 1383), the General Assembly endorsed the recommendations contained in the reports of the Board of Auditors and JIU and requested the Secretary-General to ensure that IPSAS implementation was completed no later than 2014. In section II of resolution 66/247 (see p. 1393), the Assembly authorized the UNHCR financial reporting request.

Review of UN administrative and financial functioning

In 2011, the General Assembly continued its consideration of the efficiency of the administrative and financial functioning of the United Nations. To that end, the Secretary-General issued a report on the Independent Audit Advisory Committee (see p. 1404) and transmitted to the Assembly a JIU report on the audit function in the UN system (see p. 1407).

On 24 December, the Assembly decided that the agenda item on the review of the efficiency of UN administrative and financial functioning would remain for consideration during its resumed sixty-sixth (2012) session (**decision 66/557**).

Independent Audit Advisory Committee

Pursuant to General Assembly resolution 61/275 [YUN 2007, p. 1471], the Secretary-General submitted an August report [A/66/299] on the activities of the Independent Audit Advisory Committee, established in 2007 to serve in an expert advisory capacity and assist the Assembly in fulfilling its oversight responsibilities [YUN 2007, p. 1471]. The report covered the period from 1 August 2010 to 31 July 2011, in which the Committee held four sessions, and summarized developments since its first annual report in 2008 [YUN 2008, p. 1562]. It also contained an overview of the Committee's sessions, the status of its recommendations and its workplan for 2012, as well as the Committee's comments on the status of the recommendations of UN oversight bodies; risk management procedures and the UN internal control framework; effectiveness, efficiency and impact of the audit activities and other functions of the Office of Internal Oversight Services (OIOS); financial reporting; coordination among UN oversight bodies; and cooperation and access.

During the reporting period, the Committee submitted three reports to the General Assembly on the OIOS 2012–2013 proposed programme budget [A/66/85]; the OIOS budget under the support account for peacekeeping operations for the period 1 July 2011 to 30 June 2012 [A/65/734]; and the Committee's 2010 annual report [YUN 2010, p. 1445]. As at 30 June, the Committee had made a total of 82 recommendations in its reports. Ten of the recommendations were before the Assembly; of the remaining 72 recommendations, 15 had been deferred by the Assembly to subsequent sessions, 43 had been implemented and 14 were in the process of being implemented.

The Assembly, in section II of **resolution 66/236** of 24 December (see p. 1407), endorsed the recommendations of the Independent Audit Advisory Committee.

Administration of trust funds

In September [A/66/348], the Secretary-General transmitted to the General Assembly the JIU report on policies and procedures for the administration of trust funds in UN system organizations [YUN 2010, p. 1445], which reviewed policies, rules and regulations for the management and administration of those funds, as well as major trends in their overall volume and use. The Secretary-General submitted his comments and those of CEB on the report [A/66/348/Add.1].

Programme planning

On 2, 9, 19 and 22 December, the General Assembly took note, respectively, of the reports of the First (Disarmament and International Security) Committee [A/66/422] (**decision 66/520**), Fourth (Special Political and Decolonization) Committee [A/66/436] (**decision 66/524**), Sixth (Legal) Committee [A/66/480] (**decision 66/526**), Third (Social, Humanitarian and Cultural) Committee [A/66/466] (**decision 66/541**) and Second (Economic and Financial) Committee [A/66/451] (**decision 66/552**).

GENERAL ASSEMBLY ACTION

On 11 November [meeting 58], the General Assembly, on the recommendation of the Fifth Committee [A/66/525], adopted **resolution 66/8** without vote [agenda item 135].

Programme planning

The General Assembly,

Recalling its resolutions 37/234 of 21 December 1982, 38/227 A of 20 December 1983, 41/213 of 19 December 1986, 55/234 of 23 December 2000, 56/253 of 24 December 2001, 57/282 of 20 December 2002, 58/268 and 58/269 of 23 December 2003, 59/275 of 23 December 2004, 60/257 of 8 May 2006, 61/235 of 22 December 2006, 62/224 of 22 December 2007 and 65/244 of 24 December 2010,

Recalling also the terms of reference of the Committee for Programme and Coordination, as outlined in the annex to Economic and Social Council resolution 2008(LX) of 14 May 1976,

Having considered the report of the Committee for Programme and Coordination on the work of its fifty-first session,

1. *Reaffirms* the role of the Committee for Programme and Coordination as the main subsidiary organ of the General Assembly and the Economic and Social Council for planning, programming and coordination;

2. *Re-emphasizes* the role of the plenary and the Main Committees of the General Assembly in reviewing and taking action on the appropriate recommendations of the Committee for Programme and Coordination relevant to their work, in accordance with regulation 4.10 of the Regulations and Rules Governing Programme Planning, the Programme Aspects of the Budget, the Monitoring of Implementation and the Methods of Evaluation;

3. *Stresses* that setting the priorities of the United Nations is the prerogative of the Member States, as reflected in legislative mandates;

4. *Also stresses* the need for Member States to participate fully in the budget preparation process, from its early stages and throughout the process;

5. *Recalls* paragraph 131 of the report of the Committee for Programme and Coordination, and reaffirms the provisions of General Assembly resolutions 62/236 of 22 December 2007, 63/260 of 24 December 2008, 64/243 of 24 December 2009 and 65/244 of 24 December 2010 concerning the appointment of the Under-Secretary-General and Special Adviser on Africa, and in this regard reiterates its request to the Secretary-General to abide by those mandates;

6. *Endorses* the conclusions and recommendations of the Committee for Programme and Coordination on evaluation, on the annual overview report of the United Nations System Chief Executives Board for Coordination for 2010/11 and on United Nations system support for the New Partnership for Africa's Development.

On 24 December, the Assembly decided that the item on programme planning would remain for consideration during its resumed sixty-sixth (2012) session (**decision 66/557**).

Programme performance

Evaluation

OIOS reports to CPC. The Secretary-General transmitted to the Committee for Programme and Coordination (CPC) OIOS evaluation reports on strengthening the role of evaluation and the application of evaluation findings on programme design, delivery and policy directives [A/66/71]; the programme evaluation of the Department of Economic and Social Affairs [E/AC.51/2011/2]; and the triennial review of the implementation of recommendations made by CPC at its forty-eighth session on the in-depth evaluation of political affairs: field special political missions led by the Department of Political Affairs but supported by the Department of Field Support [E/AC.51/2011/3].

CPC comments and recommendations on those reports were contained in the report on its 2011 session [A/66/16].

By **decision 2011/219** of 22 July, the Economic and Social Council took note of the CPC report.

Chapter III

Administrative and staff matters

In 2011, the United Nations General Assembly and its subsidiary bodies examined issues of managerial reform and oversight, including the work of the Office of Internal Oversight, the Independent Audit Advisory Committee and the Joint Inspection Unit (JIU). It approved the recommendations of those bodies for improving internal controls, accountability mechanisms and organizational efficiency. The Assembly further reviewed the recommendations of the Committee on Conferences on meetings management and the utilization of conference services and facilities; the impact of the capital master plan (CMP) on meetings services and facilities; and matters related to translation and interpretation. The Assembly requested the Secretary-General to propose a review of conference servicing, with a view to identifying innovative ideas, potential synergies and other cost-saving measures. The Assembly also requested the Secretary-General to implement two out of the four initiatives on information and communications technology (ICT) identified in his June report thereon—namely, to improve enterprise ICT management and to create a resilient ICT infrastructure. Despite delays in implementation, the enterprise resource planning project Umoja was entering its second phase in delivering the remaining functionality.

There was significant progress in the implementation of the CMP for the renovation of the UN Secretariat building and plans for the building's reoccupation were at an advanced stage. The Secretary-General also submitted the results of a study on progress in preparing the strategic heritage plan for the Palais des Nations in Geneva, whose deterioration had reached a crucial point. An eight-year medium-term multiphased renovation option was recommended.

The Assembly, on the recommendation of the Security Council, reappointed Mr. Ban Ki-moon as Secretary-General of the United Nations for a five-year term beginning on 1 January 2012 and ending on 31 December 2016.

The International Civil Service Commission reviewed the conditions of service for staff of the common system and the Assembly adopted its recommendations on matters such as performance management, the education grant methodology, the base/floor salary scale, and a revised rest and recuperation framework for staff in non-family duty stations. As far as safety and security, UN personnel continued to be subject to violent attacks, although the Secretary-General reported a reduction in the number of affected staff in the previous year. As for UN security management, new policies on evacuation, relocation and alternate work modalities were developed, as well as a new policy on security clearances.

Regarding human resources management, the Secretary-General forwarded to the Assembly a number of JIU reports on inter-agency staff and work/life balance; selection and appointment of senior managers in the Secretariat; and the adoption of occupational safety and health policies as part of the UN-system medical service. Ethics issues addressed included conflict of interest of personnel in the exercise of their functions, and the disciplinary actions taken by the Organization against personnel who had broken ethics rules.

The Organization continued to execute the new system of administration of justice. Calls were made for the entry into force of the code of conduct for judges of the United Nations Dispute Tribunal and the United Nations Appeals Tribunals, and for a mechanism for handling complaints against judges.

Administrative matters

Managerial reform and oversight

Procurement

In a 2011 note [JIU/NOTE/2011/1], the Joint Inspection Unit (JIU) transmitted the report of its study of procurement reform in the UN system. The study assessed the efficiency, effectiveness, transparency and coherence of procurement policies, practices and reform initiatives, and identified potential good practices and areas for improvement. It covered procurement strategy development; the supply chain management approach; sustainable procurement; procurement from developing countries; ethics management; vendor sanctioning and procurement challenge mechanisms; a common coding system; risk management; monitoring, reporting and performance management; and inter-agency coordination and collaboration. JIU found that procurement needed to be considered as a profession and recognized as an important function on par with others. It needed to be structured, and resources provided in keeping with its importance. The number and professional qualifications of procurement staff were important in ensuring effective procurement processes. JIU made 18 recommendations for implementation by organizations. Annexed to the note was a table identifying recommendations for each organization reviewed.

Oversight

Internal oversight

OIOS report. In August, the Office of Internal Oversight Services (OIOS) submitted to the General Assembly a report [A/66/286 (Part I)] on its activities from 1 July 2010 to 30 June 2011. The oversight of peacekeeping activities was covered in a separate report [A/66/286 (Part II)]. During the reporting period, OIOS issued 323 oversight reports, including seven to the Assembly, and 65 closure reports. The reports included 1,702 recommendations to improve internal controls, accountability mechanisms and organizational efficiency and effectiveness. Of those, 398 were classified as critical to the Organization. The recommendations were aimed at cost savings, recovery of overpayments, efficiency gains and other improvements. The financial implications of the OIOS recommendations issued during the period amounted to approximately $19.7 million.

An addendum to the report [A/66/286 (Part I)/Add.1] provided an assessment of the status of implementation of the recommendations; an analysis of open recommendations; and a breakdown of those with financial implications related to unnecessary or excess expenditures, losses and opportunities for future cost avoidance. As at 30 June, programme managers had implemented 806 (50 per cent) of all recommendations issued between 1 July 2010 and 31 May 2011, and 165 (42 per cent) of the critical recommendations issued during the same period.

Other OIOS reports submitted to the Assembly in 2011 dealt with programme evaluation of the United Nations Mission in the Sudan [A/65/752] (see p. 210); thematic evaluation of cooperation between the Department of Peacekeeping Operations/Department of Field Support and regional organizations [A/65/762] (see p. 60); the preliminary report [A/65/765] (see p. 59) on the implementation of the pilot project designated by the General Assembly in resolution 63/287 [YUN 2009, p. 84]; triennial review of the implementation of recommendations by the Committee for Programme and Coordination at its forty-eighth session on the evaluation of political affairs [E/AC.51/2011/3]; strengthening the role of evaluation and the application of evaluation findings on programme design, delivery and policy directives [A/66/71]; programme evaluation of the Department of Economic and Social Affairs [E/AC.51/2011/2]; and review of the organizational framework of the public information function of the Secretariat [A/66/180] (see p. 590).

UN system audit function. In April [A/66/73], the Secretary-General transmitted the report of JIU on the audit function of the UN system organizations. JIU reported significant progress in enhancing the audit function at UN organizations in the past 10 years in response to demands for higher scrutiny, transparency and accountability. There was improvement in the scope, coverage and effectiveness of audit activity, but the audit function still lacked system-wide coherence and coordination. Many organizations needed to improve independence, capabilities, resources and processes to overcome performance gaps and bring the value delivered closer in line with stakeholder expectations. The review identified the following challenges and constraints faced by internal audit/oversight heads: the follow-up and implementation of audit recommendations; ensuring adequate audit resources; auditing the "One United Nations" initiative; coordination with other oversight bodies; and the need for independence and objectivity. Additional constraints were related to the authority, centralization/decentralization, structure, planning, reporting and quality assessment of internal audit activity and the performance and competence of internal auditors. Other challenges were the lack of accountability and sanctions against those responsible for the non-implementation of recommendations.

The report contained 18 recommendations for enhancing the efficiency and effectiveness of the audit function in the UN system organizations. Regarding the internal audit/oversight function, recommendations focused on the periodic review of the authority and responsibility of internal auditors; ways to improve the independence and status of the function; ensuring the competency and professional quality of audit staff; the risk-based needs assessment and work planning process; the review of audit resources; the accountability, transparency and comprehensiveness of internal auditors' reporting; the follow-up systems on implementation of recommendations; and assessment of the internal audit function. Recommendations regarding external auditors focused on the review of their performance/mandate; competitiveness, the need for rotation and diversification of the selection process; the timeliness and accountability of the reporting process; and the role of external auditors in implementation of the single audit principle. The last four recommendations concerned the audit/oversight committees, including their mandate/scope; their composition and selection; and the independence, transparency and accountability of their reporting.

In September [A/66/73/Add.1], the Secretary-General transmitted to the Assembly his comments and those of the United Nations System Chief Executives Board for Coordination (CEB) on the JIU report.

GENERAL ASSEMBLY ACTION

On 24 December [meeting 93], the General Assembly, on the recommendation of the Fifth (Administrative and Budgetary) Committee [A/66/643], adopted **resolution 66/236** without vote [agenda items 132 & 142].

Report of the Office of Internal Oversight Services on its activities

The General Assembly,

I

Activities of the Office of Internal Oversight Services

Recalling its resolutions 48/218 B of 29 July 1994, 54/244 of 23 December 1999, 59/272 of 23 December 2004, 60/259 of 8 May 2006, 63/265 of 24 December 2008, 63/287 of 30 June 2009, 64/232 of 22 December 2009, 64/263 of 29 March 2010 and 65/250 of 24 December 2010,

Having considered the report of the Office of Internal Oversight Services on its activities for the period from 1 July 2010 to 30 June 2011, as well as the report of the Joint Inspection Unit entitled "The audit function in the United Nations system" and the related note by the Secretary-General transmitting his comments and those of the United Nations System Chief Executives Board for Coordination thereon,

1. *Reaffirms* its primary role in the consideration of and action taken on reports submitted to it;

2. *Also reaffirms* its oversight role and the role of the Fifth Committee in administrative and budgetary matters;

3. *Further reaffirms* the independence and the separate and distinct roles of the internal and external oversight mechanisms;

4. *Recalls* that the Office of Internal Oversight Services of the Secretariat shall exercise operational independence relating to the performance of its internal oversight functions, under the authority of the Secretary-General, in accordance with the relevant resolutions;

5. *Encourages* United Nations internal and external oversight bodies to further enhance the level of their cooperation with one another, such as through joint work planning sessions, without prejudice to the independence of each;

6. *Takes note* of the report of the Office of Internal Oversight Services on its activities for the period from 1 July 2010 to 30 June 2011;

7. *Requests* the Secretary-General to ensure that all relevant resolutions pertaining to the work of the Office of Internal Oversight Services are brought to the attention of the relevant managers;

8. *Also requests* the Secretary-General to ensure that all relevant resolutions, including resolutions of a cross-cutting nature, are brought to the attention of relevant managers, and that the Office of Internal Oversight Services also takes those resolutions into account in the conduct of its activities;

9. *Encourages* the Office of Internal Oversight Services to continue its efforts aimed at enhancing its audit, investigation, inspection and evaluation functions;

10. *Recalls* paragraphs 7 and 8 of its resolution 64/263, and in this regard requests the Secretary-General to entrust the Office of Internal Oversight Services with comprehensively defining and compiling key oversight terms related to the work of the Office in close consultation with relevant departments and offices, including the Department of Management and the Office of Legal Affairs of the Secretariat, bearing in mind existing definitions used by the Board of Auditors and the Joint Inspection Unit, and taking into account the views of the Independent Audit Advisory Committee;

11. *Encourages* the Office of Internal Oversight Services to continue to identify in its analysis in future annual reports general trends and strategic challenges over time regarding internal oversight in the United Nations, including an update on all critical recommendations and taking into account the risk category and the target date for implementation and the office concerned that is to be held accountable for such implementation;

12. *Requests* the Secretary-General to implement outstanding and recurring accepted recommendations of the Office of Internal Oversight Services dealing with issues that are systemic in nature;

13. *Notes with concern* the status of implementation of recommendations contained in the report of the Office of Internal Oversight Services on its activities for the period from 1 July 2010 to 30 June 2011;

14. *Requests* the Secretary-General to encourage all programme managers to increase their efforts to fully implement the accepted recommendations of the Office of Internal Oversight Services;

15. *Also requests* the Secretary-General to ensure the full implementation of the accepted recommendations of the Office of Internal Oversight Services, including those relating to cost avoidance, recovery of overpayments, efficiency gains and other improvements, in a prompt and timely manner and to provide detailed justifications in cases where recommendations of the Office are not accepted;

16. *Notes* the role of the Management Committee in monitoring closely the implementation of the recommendations of oversight bodies, and stresses the importance of follow-up with programme managers to ensure the full implementation of those recommendations in a prompt and timely manner;

17. *Welcomes* the efforts undertaken to reduce the high number of vacant posts in the Office of Internal Oversight Services, in particular at the senior levels;

18. *Reaffirms its concern* over the continuing vacancies in the Office of Internal Oversight Services, and in this regard reiterates its requests to the Secretary-General to make every effort to fill vacancies in the Office at all levels as a matter of priority, in accordance with the relevant provisions governing recruitment in the United Nations;

19. *Recognizes* the efforts and initiatives of the Office of Internal Oversight Services undertaken to strengthen internal oversight, including the improvement of internal controls, accountability mechanisms, and organizational efficiency and effectiveness, as well as improvements in the monitoring of its recommendations, in accordance with its given mandate, and encourages the Office to continue its efforts in this regard;

20. *Reaffirms* paragraph 12 of its resolution 64/263;

21. *Requests* the Secretary-General to entrust the Office of Internal Oversight Services with submitting to the General Assembly no later than the main part of its sixty-seventh session a proposal on the dissemination and distribution of internal audit reports, including the parameters and modalities, and in full consultation with key stakeholders, including the Department of Management,

the Office of Legal Affairs and the Independent Audit Advisory Committee;

22. *Takes note* of paragraph 28 of the report of the Office of Internal Oversight Services, and decides that the Office shall continue its current procedures for reporting to the General Assembly;

23. *Reaffirms* that the Board of Auditors and the Joint Inspection Unit shall continue to be provided with copies of all reports produced by the Office of Internal Oversight Services, requests that these be made available within one month of their finalization, and emphasizes the need for comments by the Board and the Unit, as appropriate;

II

Activities of the Independent Audit Advisory Committee

Recalling its resolution 61/275 of 29 June 2007,

Having considered the annual report of the Independent Audit Advisory Committee on its activities for the period from 1 August 2010 to 31 July 2011,

1. *Notes with appreciation* the work of the Independent Audit Advisory Committee;

2. *Reaffirms* the terms of reference of the Independent Audit Advisory Committee, as contained in the annex to resolution 61/275;

3. *Recalls* paragraph 5 of its resolution 61/275, and in that regard emphasizes the role of the Independent Audit Advisory Committee in ensuring the operational independence of the Office of Internal Oversight Services;

4. *Encourages* United Nations oversight bodies to continue sharing experience, knowledge, best practices and lessons learned with the Independent Audit Advisory Committee, in order for the Committee to better conduct its roles and responsibilities under its terms of reference, without prejudice to the respective mandates of United Nations oversight bodies;

5. *Recalls* paragraph 6 of its resolution 64/263, and in this regard:

(*a*) Decides to keep under review observations, comments and recommendations contained in paragraphs 19, 20 (*d*), 21, 24, 42 and 43 of the annex to the report of the Independent Audit Advisory Committee on its activities for the period from 1 August 2008 to 31 July 2009;

(*b*) Requests the Secretary-General to ensure that the annual reports of the Office of Internal Oversight Services include a brief description of any impairment of its independence;

6. *Endorses* the observations, comments and recommendations contained in paragraphs 14, 17, 18, 20, 26, 31, 37, 40, 42, 44 and 50 of the annual report of the Independent Audit Advisory Committee, and requests the Secretary-General to ensure their full implementation, taking into account the provisions of the resolutions of the General Assembly relevant to the work of the Office of Internal Oversight Services.

On the same date, the Assembly decided that the item on the report on OIOS activities would remain for consideration during its resumed sixty-sixth (2012) session (**decision 66/557**).

External oversight

Joint Inspection Unit

At its resumed sixty-fifth session, the General Assembly had before it the annual report of the Joint Inspection Unit (JIU) for 2010 and its programme of work for 2011 [YUN 2010, p. 1454].

Note by Secretary-General. In response to resolution 64/262 [YUN 2010, p. 1452], the Secretary-General submitted a note [A/65/718] on the support provided by CEB member organizations to JIU for the preparation and completion of reports. The CEB secretariat circulated all JIU reports of system-wide concern to UN system organizations and compiled the comments it received. In 2010, the CEB secretariat prepared comments in response to seven JIU reports. Those comments, which reflected the overall consensus of the UN system, were subsequently issued as UN documents. The CEB secretariat maintained dialogue with the Unit on preparing the annual JIU programme of work and ensuring the smooth preparation of JIU reports. It also participated in the first meeting of focal points, organized by JIU in September 2010, which provided an opportunity for CEB to share the mechanisms for report production and encourage participating agencies to respond to requests for comments.

GENERAL ASSEMBLY ACTION

On 4 April [meeting 84], the General Assembly, on the recommendation of the Fifth Committee [A/65/796], adopted **resolution 65/270** without vote [agenda item 135].

Report of the Joint Inspection Unit for 2010 and programme of work for 2011

The General Assembly,

Reaffirming its previous resolutions on the Joint Inspection Unit, in particular resolutions 31/192 of 22 December 1976, 50/233 of 7 June 1996, 54/16 of 29 October 1999, 55/230 of 23 December 2000, 56/245 of 24 December 2001, 57/284 A and B of 20 December 2002, 58/286 of 8 April 2004, 59/267 of 23 December 2004, 60/258 of 8 May 2006, 61/238 of 22 December 2006, 61/260 of 4 April 2007, 62/226 of 22 December 2007, 62/246 of 3 April 2008, 63/272 of 7 April 2009 and 64/262 of 29 March 2010,

Reiterating that the impact of the work of the Unit on the cost-effectiveness of activities within the United Nations system is a shared responsibility of the Member States, the Unit and the secretariats of the participating organizations,

Reaffirming the commitment by the Unit, the legislative organs and the secretariats of the participating organizations to implement a system of follow-up to the recommendations of the Unit, as set out in resolution 54/16,

Reaffirming also the statute of the Unit and the unique role of the Unit as the only external and independent system-wide inspection, evaluation and investigation body,

Having considered the report of the Unit for 2010 and programme of work for 2011 and the note by the Secretary-General,

1. *Recalls* its resolutions 61/260, 62/246, 63/272 and 64/262;
2. *Takes note with appreciation* of the report of the Joint Inspection Unit for 2010 and programme of work for 2011;
3. *Takes note* of the note by the Secretary-General;
4. *Affirms* that oversight is a shared responsibility of Member States, the organizations and the internal and external oversight bodies;
5. *Reiterates its request* to the Unit, in line with its mandate, to continue to focus its work and reports on system-wide issues of interest and relevance to the participating organizations and the States Members of the United Nations and to provide advice on ways to ensure the avoidance of duplication and overlap and more efficient and effective use of resources in implementing the mandates of the Organization;
6. *Stresses* the need for the Unit to continuously update and improve its medium- and long-term strategy for 2010–2019, taking into account the dynamics and challenges of the environment in which it undertakes its activities;
7. *Reiterates its request* to the Secretary-General contained in paragraph 15 of its resolution 64/262, in the light of the ongoing development of the medium- and long-term strategy for 2010–2019, to reflect the appropriate resource requirements associated with the implementation of the relevant portions of the strategy, in the context of the proposed programme budgets, including those relevant to the biennium 2012–2013;
8. *Invites* the Unit to report to the General Assembly on the reform process, and the progress achieved therein, and to present new assessments on options for enhancing the effectiveness of its work, and requests the Secretary-General to report to the Assembly on any related implications;
9. *Welcomes* the efforts undertaken by the Unit to achieve greater effectiveness and efficiency in its working methods, and encourages the Unit to further intensify its efforts in this regard by, inter alia, increasing the use of Junior Professional Officers to assist with the workload of the Unit;
10. *Reiterates its request* to the Unit to continue to focus its reports on important priority items, identifying concrete managerial, administrative and programming questions aimed at providing the General Assembly and other legislative organs of participating organizations with practical and action-oriented recommendations;
11. *Also reiterates its request* to the Unit to issue its reports well in advance of meetings of the legislative organs of participating organizations so that the reports can be thoroughly and effectively utilized in their deliberations;
12. *Stresses* the importance of optimizing the capacity of the Unit in order to allow it to complete its reports in a timely manner, in accordance with its programme of work, and requests the Unit, during its preparation of future annual programmes of work, to optimize the number of projects therein through prioritization, by taking into account the ongoing and foreseeable processes of the legislative organs of the participating organizations as well as the number of projects carried over from previous programmes of work;
13. *Requests* the Unit to improve its future programmes of work so that Member States can easily trace the progress of each project in future annual reports;
14. *Reiterates its request* to the executive heads of the participating organizations to fully comply with the statutory procedures for consideration of the reports of the Unit and, in particular, to submit their comments, including information on what they intend to do regarding the recommendations of the Unit, to distribute reports in time for their consideration by legislative organs and to provide information on the steps to be taken to implement those recommendations accepted by the legislative organs and the executive heads of participating organizations;
15. *Notes* the difficulties that the Unit encountered in 2010 in obtaining relevant information and data from the United Nations Secretariat for the preparation of the report mandated by the General Assembly, and reiterates its request to the Secretary-General and the other executive heads of the participating organizations to fully assist the Unit with the timely provision of all information requested by it pursuant to article 6.2 of the statute of the Unit and all relevant resolutions of the Assembly;
16. *Reiterates its invitation* to the legislative organs of the participating organizations to fully consider, discuss and take concrete action in a timely manner on the relevant recommendations issued by the Unit, including follow-up, as appropriate, taking into account the provisions of paragraph 4 of its resolution 50/233;
17. *Requests* the Secretary-General, in his capacity as Chair of the United Nations System Chief Executives Board for Coordination, to expedite the implementation of the present resolution, including through the expected provision of support to the Unit by the secretariats of the participating organizations in the preparation of its reports, notes and confidential letters, and through the consideration of and action on the recommendations of the Unit in the light of pertinent resolutions of the General Assembly, and to report to the Assembly on an annual basis on the results achieved;
18. *Welcomes and urges* further strengthening of the interaction between the Unit and focal points identified by the participating organizations regarding the work of the Unit, including discussion of the consideration of and action by the participating organizations on the recommendations of the Unit;
19. *Welcomes* the efforts made by the Unit to advance the development and implementation of the web-based follow-up system;
20. *Notes* the ongoing progress in the development of a web-based follow-up system to track the recommendations of the Unit, including the status of acceptance, implementation and impact;
21. *Authorizes* the Secretary-General to enter into commitments in the amount of 71,300 United States dollars under the programme budget for the biennium 2010–2011 for the development of the web-based follow-up system, and requests him to report on expenditures in the context of the second performance report;
22. *Invites* other participating organizations of the Unit to make every possible effort to contribute to the cost-sharing arrangement of the web-based follow-up system in 2011;
23. *Invites* the Unit to include in its annual report information on the status of the development and implementation of the web-based follow-up system;

24. *Requests* the Unit to make every effort to ensure that future funding requests are made in the context of the established regular budget cycle;

25. *Requests* the Secretary-General to invite all relevant oversight bodies to explore the possibility of utilizing the web-based follow-up system to enhance coordination, taking into account their different mandates and status;

26. *Welcomes* the coordination of the Unit with the Board of Auditors and the Office of Internal Oversight Services of the Secretariat, and encourages those bodies to continue sharing experiences, knowledge, best practices and lessons learned with other United Nations audit and oversight bodies, as well as with the Independent Audit Advisory Committee, with a view to avoiding overlap or duplication and achieving further synergy, cooperation, effectiveness and efficiency, without prejudice to the respective mandates of the oversight bodies.

JIU activities. In its annual report to the Assembly [A/66/34], JIU reviewed its activities in 2011, during which it issued 11 reports: review of the medical service in the UN system [JIU/REP/2011/1]; transparency in the selection and appointment of senior managers in the UN Secretariat [JIU/REP/2011/2]; South-South and triangular cooperation in the UN system [JIU/REP/2011/3]; multilingualism in UN system organizations—status of implementation [JIU/REP/2011/4]; accountability frameworks in the UN system [JIU/REP/2011/5]; business continuity in the UN system [JIU/REP/2011/6]; the investigation function in the UN system [JIU/REP/2011/7]; review of management and administration in the United Nations Educational, Scientific and Cultural Organization [JIU/REP/2011/8]; information and communications technology governance in UN system organizations [JIU/REP/2011/9]; staff-management relations within the United Nations [JIU/REP/2011/10]; and evaluation of the scope, organization, effectiveness and approach of the work of the United Nations in mine action [JIU/REP/2011/11]. JIU also issued a note on procurement reforms in the UN system [JIU/NOTE/2011/1].

JIU had requested participating organizations to provide information on all 371 recommendations issued between 2008 and 2010, and had received information from all but two organizations—UN-Habitat and the World Meteorological Organization. An analysis of data concerning the 128 recommendations contained in single-organization reports and notes issued in 2008, 2009 and 2010 showed, as at 31 December 2011, a 61 per cent acceptance rate. An analysis of the data for the 243 recommendations contained in system-wide reports and notes issued between the same period showed an improved rate of acceptance of 55 per cent, compared to previous reporting periods. The data on recommendations approved or accepted showed lower rates of implementation. At the end of 2011, the data for single-organization reports and notes showed that 42 per cent of recommendations were implemented and 35 per cent were in progress. No information on implementation status was received for the remaining 19 per cent of recommendations accepted. The implementation of accepted or approved recommendations in system-wide and multi-organization reports and notes issued in 2008, 2009 and 2010 showed a positive variance, with 53 per cent of the recommendations implemented, and 29 per cent in progress. The overall implementation rate for that period increased by 9 per cent. The rate of recommendations for which implementation had not started stood at 6 per cent. No information was received on the status of implementation for 13 per cent of accepted recommendations.

Appointment of JIU members. On 16 June [A/66/106 & Add.1], the Secretary-General noted that at its sixty-sixth session, the General Assembly would need to fill the vacancies resulting from the expiry of the term of office, in December 2012, of six JIU members.

On 11 October [A/66/509 & Corr.1], the Secretary-General noted that due to the resignation of one JIU member in early September, it would be necessary for the Assembly to fill a further JIU membership vacancy, also during its sixty-sixth session. On 20 December [A/66/621], the President of the General Assembly submitted to the Assembly a candidate for that post, who would serve for a five-year term beginning on 1 January 2012. Annexed to the note were letters of endorsement for the candidate from the Secretary-General and the President of the Economic and Social Council.

On 24 December, the Assembly decided that the items on the JIU and on the appointment of its members would remain for consideration during its resumed sixty-sixth (2012) session (**decision 66/557**).

Oil-for-food programme

On 12 September (**decision 65/555**), the Assembly deferred consideration of the item entitled "Follow-up to the recommendations on administrative management and internal oversight of the Independent Inquiry Committee into the United Nations Oil-for-Food Programme" [YUN 2005, p. 1475] and included it in the draft agenda of its sixty-sixth (2011) session.

On 24 December (**decision 66/557**), the Assembly decided that the item would remain for consideration during its resumed sixty-sixth (2012) session.

Conference management

Committee on Conferences

The Committee on Conferences held its organizational session on 30 March, and its substantive session from 6 to 12 September [A/66/32]. It had before it the draft biennial calendar of conferences and meetings for 2012 and 2013 [A/AC.172/2011/L.2], and considered requests for changes to the 2011 calendar [A/AC.172/2011/2]. The Committee discussed meetings management, including the utilization of conference-servicing resources and facilities and the impact of the implementation of the capital master plan (CMP) on meetings held at Headquarters; integrated global management; matters related to documentation and publications; and matters related to translation and interpretation. (The Committee's deliberations and recommendations on those matters are detailed in the sections below.)

The Committee considered the Secretary-General's report on the pattern of conferences (see below). It also recommended that the General Assembly authorize nine bodies, listed in a letter of 6 September from the Committee Chair [A/66/346], to meet in New York during the main part of the Assembly's sixty-sixth (2011) session.

The Assembly, on 13 September, authorized those bodies to meet (**decision 66/501**).

Report of Secretary-General. In response to Assembly resolution 65/245 [YUN 2010, p. 1457], the Secretary-General submitted a July report on the pattern of conferences [A/66/118 & Corr.1], which addressed the items on the Committee's agenda and contained a number of recommendations to address those issues.

ACABQ report. In October [A/66/397], the Advisory Committee on Administrative and Budgetary Questions (ACABQ) commented on the Secretary-General's report. ACABQ recognized the necessity of a measure proposed by the Secretary-General to include in new legislative mandates all relevant information related to meetings and documentation so the Secretariat could fully assess conference-servicing needs. It was of the opinion that the proposal should be considered by the Assembly, bearing in mind the rules of procedure for dealing with decisions with programme budget implications. Regarding the decreasing utilization rate of the Economic Commission for Africa conference centre, ACABQ called upon the Secretary-General to formulate a more competitive pricing structure and an appropriate marketing strategy. ACABQ also reiterated its recommendation that the Secretary-General broaden efforts to secure extrabudgetary funding for training activities related to all six official languages, particularly following the successful use of traineeship programmes in New York and Vienna to enhance the pool of qualified professionals in language combinations identified as problematic or critical for succession planning.

Use of conference services and facilities

The Committee on Conferences [A/66/32] noted that starting in 2011, statistical data on all meetings held at the four duty stations considered in the report—New York, Geneva, Vienna and Nairobi—as well as away from established headquarters was being recorded in a harmonized manner. The overall utilization factor for all four duty stations in 2010 was 85 per cent (86 per cent in 2009). To improve the utilization factor, the Chair proposed reducing the impact of foreseeable cancellations by providing advance notice to the Meetings Management Section not later than one week before the session; reducing the meeting blocks to two hours when it was anticipated that less time would be required, thus releasing some of the resources; and adjusting the programme of work based on past practice and actual utilization of conference services. Regarding the provision of interpretation services to meetings of bodies entitled to meet "as required", the Committee noted that a comparative analysis showed a slight decrease in the provision of services in New York from 95 per cent in 2009 to 94 per cent in 2010. The Committee noted that in 2010 the meetings of all Nairobi-based bodies were held at the United Nations Office at Nairobi, in conformity with the headquarters rule, but that the utilization rate of the conference centre at the Economic Commission for Africa had decreased to 70 per cent, owing to increased competition in local and regional markets. The Commission therefore undertook a marketing strategy to increase the centre's occupancy rate.

Impact of CMP on conference services

The Committee [A/66/32] noted that the Department for General Assembly and Conference Management (DGACM) continued to work closely with the CMP secretariat on the renovation of the rooms in the conference building in order to minimize disruptions to the intergovernmental process. The projected completion date had been revised to December 2012. A study would be conducted to determine the cost implications of the Department's request for additional seating in the General Assembly Hall, and the findings would be submitted to the Assembly for review. In the meantime, the Department was liaising with the Facilities and Commercial Services Division of the Department of Management to meet the current demand for seating. To facilitate flexible working arrangements, the Department provided some 700 Mobile Office licences to language staff, secretaries of committees and conference officers. Answering queries from delegations, a Secretariat representative said that as a result of an analysis of security standards conducted under the CMP, it had become necessary to increase the distance between conference rooms and roads outside the UN complex, necessitating some redesign of the large conference rooms, in consultation with the Department.

Integrated global management

Achieving the objectives of the DGACM integrated global management initiative continued to be a high priority for the Department. The Committee [A/66/32] noted that initiatives such as annual coordination meetings of UN conference managers and quarterly videoconferences involving all four duty stations had contributed to the harmonization of policies and practices and to greater sharing of the workload. Furthermore, wider implementation of the proximity rule for the assignment of conference personnel to meetings held away from their home duty stations had resulted in the most efficient use of resources. With regard to the major information technology projects launched in the past few years, progress continued to be made on "project 1" (gData), which aimed to provide management with a reliable statistical data reporting system in order to compare key performance indicators both over time and across duty stations. "Project 2" (gMeets) was in production at all four duty stations and undergoing phase II of maintenance and enhancements. "Project 3" (gDoc), the development of which was being steered by a governance board comprised of users from Headquarters and the UN Office at Geneva, proposed to achieve a common document submission module that would include harmonized slotting and forecasting. A Secretariat representative noted that it was difficult to quantify financial savings arising out of integrated global management, which had not been part of the original mandate given by the General Assembly. Nevertheless, the Secretariat would seek to provide details on savings, especially with regard to enforcement of the proximity rule. Information on efficiency gains and qualitative improvements in services provided to Member States would also be detailed.

Documentation

The Committee [A/66/32] was informed that the documentation slotting system was being implemented at all four duty stations, and DGACM was implementing word limits and deadlines for reports from the Secretariat. The Assembly mandate called for pre-session documents to be submitted for processing 10 weeks before a session and distributed six weeks before, which required the Department to complete the editing, referencing and translation of documents simultaneously within a four-week period, an inefficient system that duplicated work. Changing the rules to require documents to be issued four weeks before a session would allow for sequential processing within a six-week period, thus ensuring cost efficiencies, enhancing quality and reducing overall processing time. Delegations expressed the view that increasing the time allotted to the Department to process documents would ensure better use of the available resources, and that the savings generated by the change would depend on a decreased reliance on temporary assistance, resulting from sequential, rather than parallel, processing of documents. As the Committee was unable to reach a consensus on the Secretariat's proposed change in the document-processing schedule, it referred the question to the Fifth Committee for consideration.

The Committee also discussed paper-smart meetings and digital audio files as alternatives to printed official records. It noted the arrangements to conduct the upcoming United Nations Conference on Sustainable Development (Rio+20) in a paper-smart fashion, representing a fundamental shift in the provision of conference services. Similarly, innovations in digital audio files presented an opportunity to provide meetings records at considerably less cost than the traditional six-language printed versions. Digital records were proposed to complement the one-language written summary records or unedited transcripts. The Committee concluded that there would be further discussions in the Fifth Committee.

Translation and interpretation

The Committee [A/66/32] considered matters related to translation and interpretation. It noted that recruitment of qualified language professionals continued to be a challenge. OHRM had agreed to several measures proposed by DGACM to facilitate the recruitment of language staff for short-term contracts. Additionally, the Department's succession planning programme sought to foster internships in language services and provide additional training to candidates who showed promising results in the competitive examinations. However, dedicated resources for outreach and training activities were still not in place. Responding to queries from delegations, a Secretariat representative said that fifteen competitive examinations would be administered in the coming year, notice of which would be publicized around the world. It was hoped that the internship programme would help increase the number of qualified candidates. The Department was seeking to simplify the recruitment methods without compromising standards, including holding exams on a predictable rather than an ad hoc basis and testing for several types of job categories at the same time. As a result of an appeal to all Member States in 2008 to initiate contact with universities with relevant language programmes—an invitation that remained open—memorandums of understanding were signed with three Arabic-language universities. The Department gave priority to recruiting from all regions of the world, so it employed creative methods, such as combining home leave with outreach activities. Following from the first pan-African conference on training conference interpreters, translators and public service interpreters, an interpreter training programme was established in Nairobi, in collaboration with the European Union, and a memorandum of understanding signed with the University of Nairobi.

GENERAL ASSEMBLY ACTION

On 24 December [meeting 93], the General Assembly, on the recommendation of the Fifth Committee [A/66/642], adopted **resolution 66/233** without vote [agenda item 137].

Pattern of conferences

The General Assembly,

Recalling its relevant resolutions, including resolutions 40/243 of 18 December 1985, 41/213 of 19 December 1986, 43/222 A to E of 21 December 1988, 51/211 A to E of 18 December 1996, 52/214 of 22 December 1997, 53/208 A to E of 18 December 1998, 54/248 of 23 December 1999, 55/222 of 23 December 2000, 56/242 of 24 December 2001, 56/254 D of 27 March 2002, 56/262 of 15 February 2002, 56/287 of 27 June 2002, 57/283 A of 20 December 2002, 57/283 B of 15 April 2003, 58/250 of 23 December 2003, 59/265 of 23 December 2004, 60/236 A of 23 December 2005, 60/236 B of 8 May 2006, 61/236 of 22 December 2006, 62/225 of 22 December 2007, 63/248 of 24 December 2008, 63/284 of 30 June 2009, 64/230 of 22 December 2009 and 65/245 of 24 December 2010,

Reaffirming its resolution 42/207 C of 11 December 1987, in which it requested the Secretary-General to ensure the equal treatment of the official languages of the United Nations,

Having considered the report of the Committee on Conferences for 2011 and the relevant report of the Secretary-General,

Having also considered the report of the Advisory Committee on Administrative and Budgetary Questions,

Reaffirming the provisions relating to conference services in its resolutions on multilingualism, in particular resolution 65/311 of 19 July 2011,

I

Calendar of conferences and meetings

1. *Welcomes* the report of the Committee on Conferences for 2011;
2. *Approves* the draft calendar of conferences and meetings of the United Nations for 2012 and 2013, as submitted by the Committee on Conferences, taking into account the observations of the Committee and subject to the provisions of the present resolution;
3. *Authorizes* the Committee on Conferences to make any adjustments to the calendar of conferences and meetings for 2012 and 2013 that may become necessary as a result of actions and decisions taken by the General Assembly at its sixty-sixth session;
4. *Notes with satisfaction* that the Secretariat has taken into account the arrangements referred to in General Assembly resolutions 53/208 A, 54/248, 55/222, 56/242, 57/283 B, 58/250, 59/265, 60/236 A, 61/236, 62/225, 63/248, 64/230 and 65/245 concerning Orthodox Good Friday and the official holidays of Eid al-Fitr and Eid al-Adha, and requests all intergovernmental bodies to observe those decisions when planning their meetings;
5. *Requests* the Secretary-General to ensure that any modification to the calendar of conferences and meetings is implemented strictly in accordance with the mandate of the Committee on Conferences and other relevant resolutions of the General Assembly;
6. *Invites* Member States to include in new legislative mandates adequate information on the modalities for the organization of conferences or meetings;
7. *Recalls* rule 153 of its rules of procedure, and requests the Secretary-General to include the modalities of conferences in resolutions involving expenditure, with a view to mobilizing conference services and documentation in the most efficient and cost-effective manner possible;

II

A. Utilization of conference-servicing resources

1. *Reaffirms* the practice that, in the use of conference rooms, priority must be given to the meetings of Member States;
2. *Calls upon* the Secretary-General and Member States to adhere to the guidelines and procedures contained in the administrative instruction for the authorization of the use of United Nations premises for meetings, conferences, special events and exhibits;
3. *Emphasizes* that such meetings, conferences, special events and exhibits must be consistent with the purposes and principles of the United Nations;
4. *Notes* that the overall utilization factor at the four main duty stations in 2010 was 85 per cent, as compared with 86 per cent in 2009 and 85 per cent in 2008, which is above the established benchmark of 80 per cent;
5. *Welcomes* the steps taken by those bodies that have adjusted their programmes of work in order to achieve the optimum utilization of conference-servicing resources, and requests the Committee on Conferences to continue consultations with the secretariats and bureaux of bodies that underutilize their conference-servicing resources;
6. *Recognizes* that late starts and unplanned early endings seriously affect the utilization factor of the bodies owing to the amount of time lost, and invites the secretariats and bureaux of bodies to pay adequate attention to avoiding late starts and unplanned early endings;
7. *Notes* that the percentage of meetings held by the bodies entitled to meet "as required" that were provided with interpretation services in New York in 2010 was 94 per cent, as compared with 95 per cent in 2009, and requests the Secretary-General to continue to impress upon such bodies the need to strive to optimize the utilization of the conference services provided and to report on the provision of conference services to those bodies through the Committee on Conferences;
8. *Reiterates its request* to intergovernmental bodies to review their meeting entitlements and to plan and adjust their programmes of work on the basis of their actual utilization of conference-servicing resources in order to improve their efficient use of conference services;
9. *Recognizes* the importance of meetings of regional and other major groupings of Member States for the smooth functioning of the sessions of intergovernmental

bodies, requests the Secretary-General to ensure that, as far as possible, all requests for conference services for the meetings of regional and other major groupings of Member States are met, and requests the Secretariat to inform the requesters as early as possible about the availability of conference services, including interpretation, as well as about any changes that might occur before the holding of meetings;

10. *Notes* that the percentage of meetings held by regional and other major groupings of Member States that were provided with interpretation services at the four main duty stations was 84 per cent in 2010, as compared with 79 per cent in 2009, and requests the Secretary-General to continue to employ innovative means to address the difficulties experienced by Member States owing to the lack of conference services for some meetings of regional and other major groupings of Member States and to report thereon to the General Assembly through the Committee on Conferences;

11. *Once again urges* intergovernmental bodies to spare no effort at the planning stage to take into account the meetings of regional and other major groupings of Member States, to make provision for such meetings in their programmes of work and to notify conference services, well in advance, of any cancellations so that unutilized conference-servicing resources may, to the extent possible, be reassigned to meetings of regional and other major groupings of Member States;

12. *Notes with satisfaction* that, in accordance with several resolutions of the General Assembly, including resolution 65/245, section II.A, paragraph 10, in conformity with the headquarters rule, all meetings of Nairobi-based United Nations bodies were held in Nairobi in 2010, and requests the Secretary-General to report thereon to the Assembly at its sixty-seventh session through the Committee on Conferences;

13. *Notes with concern* the decrease in the utilization rate of the conference centre of the Economic Commission for Africa, and recognizes the ongoing promotional efforts and initiatives of the Commission;

14. *Requests* the Secretary-General to continue to explore means to increase the utilization of the conference centre of the Economic Commission for Africa and to report thereon, including on the impact of the initiatives of the Commission, to the General Assembly at its sixty-seventh session;

15. *Recognizes* the proactive efforts of the Secretary-General to identify ways to enhance efficiencies and effectiveness in conference services;

16. *Requests* the Secretary-General to propose, at its sixty-seventh session, a comprehensive review of conference servicing highlighting any duplications and redundancies, with a view to identifying innovative ideas, potential synergies and other cost-saving measures, without compromising the quality of its services;

17. *Reiterates its request* to the Committee on Conferences to consult with those bodies that have consistently utilized less than the applicable benchmark figure of their allocated resources of the past three sessions, with a view to making appropriate recommendations in order to achieve the optimum utilization of conference-servicing resources, and urges the secretariats and bureaux of bodies that underutilize their conference-servicing resources to work more closely with the Department for General Assembly and Conference Management of the Secretariat and to consider changes to their programmes of work, as appropriate, including adjustments based on previous patterns of recurring agenda items, with a view to making improvements in their utilization factors;

B. Impact of the capital master plan, strategy IV (phased approach), on meetings held at Headquarters during its implementation

1. *Requests* the Secretary-General to ensure that the implementation of the capital master plan, including the temporary relocation of conference-servicing staff to swing spaces, will not compromise the quality of conference services provided to Member States in the six official languages and the equal treatment of the language services, which should be provided with equally favourable working conditions and resources, with a view to receiving the maximum quality of services;

2. *Requests* all meeting requesters and organizers to liaise closely with the Department for General Assembly and Conference Management on all matters related to the scheduling of meetings to allow maximum predictability in coordinating activities at Headquarters during the construction period;

3. *Requests* the Committee on Conferences to keep the matter under constant review, and requests the Secretary-General to report regularly to the Committee on matters pertaining to the calendar of conferences and meetings of the United Nations during the construction period;

4. *Requests* the Secretary-General to continue to provide adequate information technology support for conference services, within the existing resources of the Department for General Assembly and Conference Management, in order to ensure their seamless operation throughout the implementation of the capital master plan;

5. *Notes* that, for the duration of the implementation of the capital master plan, a part of the conference-servicing staff and information technology resources of the Department for General Assembly and Conference Management has been temporarily relocated to swing spaces, and requests the Secretary-General to continue to provide adequate support, within the existing resources of the Department, to ensure continued maintenance of the information technology facilities of the Department, implementation of the global information technology initiative and delivery of high-quality conference services;

6. *Requests* the Secretary-General to consult with Member States on initiatives that affect the utilization of conference services and conference facilities;

III

Integrated global management

1. *Notes* the progress made in the implementation of the global information technology project, aimed at integrating, across duty stations, information technology into meetings management and documentation-processing systems, and the global approach to harmonizing standards and information technology and sharing good practices and technological achievements among conference services at the four main duty stations;

2. *Notes with appreciation* the efforts of the Secretary-General, using in-house capacity, to improve the utilization of conference services, in particular through the implementation of the project on the Electronic Meetings Planning and Resource Allocation System (e-Meets) and the interpreters assignment programme (e-APG module)

("project 2"), and requests the Secretary-General to report to the General Assembly at its sixty-seventh session on other efforts to that end;

3. *Requests* the Secretary-General to ensure the full implementation of the project on global documentation management ("project 3") and to report thereon to the General Assembly at its sixty-seventh session;

4. *Notes* the initiatives undertaken in the context of integrated global management aimed at streamlining procedures, achieving economies of scale and improving the quality of conference services, and in this regard stresses the importance of ensuring equal treatment of conference-servicing staff, as well as the principle of equal grade for equal work at the four main duty stations;

5. *Emphasizes* that the major goals of the Department for General Assembly and Conference Management are to provide high-quality documents in a timely manner in all official languages, in accordance with established regulations, as well as high-quality conference services to Member States at all duty stations, and to achieve those aims as efficiently and cost-effectively as possible, in accordance with the relevant resolutions of the General Assembly;

6. *Notes* that the pool of language professionals at duty stations is uneven in terms of language combinations, and requests the Secretary-General to develop recruitment, subcontracting and outreach policies that take full account of these imbalances;

7. *Requests* the Secretary-General to ensure that all language services are given equal treatment and are provided with equally favourable working conditions and resources, with a view to achieving the maximum quality of services, with full respect for the specificities of the six official languages and taking into account their respective workloads;

8. *Reiterates* the need for the Secretary-General to ensure the compatibility of technologies used in all duty stations and to ensure that they are user-friendly in all official languages;

9. *Also reiterates* that the satisfaction of Member States is a key performance indicator in conference management and conference services;

10. *Requests* the Secretary-General to continue to ensure that measures taken by the Department for General Assembly and Conference Management to seek the evaluation by Member States of the quality of the conference services provided to them, as a key performance indicator of the Department, provide equal opportunities to Member States to present their evaluations in the six official languages of the United Nations and are in full compliance with relevant resolutions of the General Assembly, and requests the Secretary-General to report to the Assembly, through the Committee on Conferences, on progress made in this regard;

11. *Also requests* the Secretary-General to continue to explore best practices and techniques in client satisfaction evaluations and to report on a regular basis to the General Assembly on the results achieved;

12. *Welcomes* the efforts made by the Department for General Assembly and Conference Management to seek the evaluation by Member States of the quality of the conference services provided to them, and requests the Secretary-General to continue to explore innovative ways to systematically capture and analyse feedback from Member States and committee Chairs and Secretaries on the quality of conference services and to report thereon to the General Assembly through the Committee on Conferences;

13. *Requests* the Secretary-General to keep the General Assembly apprised of progress made in integrated global management;

14. *Notes with concern* that the Secretary-General did not include in his report on the pattern of conferences information about the financial savings achieved through the implementation of the integrated global management projects, as requested in section III, paragraph 4, of its resolution 63/248, in section III, paragraph 12, of its resolution 64/230 and in section III, paragraph 14, of its resolution 65/245, and reiterates its request that the Secretary-General redouble his efforts to include this information in his next report on the pattern of conferences;

15. *Notes* the undertakings of the Secretary-General described in paragraph 25 of his report, and requests him to continue to assess the conference management efficiency and accountability mechanisms across the four main duty stations and to report thereon to the General Assembly at its sixty-seventh session;

16. *Also notes* the flextime pilot project initiated by the United Nations Office at Vienna, stresses that the rules and regulations of the United Nations governing human resources issues should be applied uniformly during the implementation of the pilot project, and requests the Secretary-General to report to the General Assembly at its sixty-seventh session on the evaluation of the pilot project, including a recommendation on whether the project should be continued at the United Nations Office at Vienna and further implemented at other duty stations;

17. *Takes note* of paragraph 11 of the report of the Advisory Committee on Administrative and Budgetary Questions, welcomes the proximity rule as an efficient approach, where feasible, to servicing meetings away from duty stations, and in this regard requests the Secretary-General to rigorously apply the proximity rule to those meetings that are applicable without jeopardizing the quality of the services and to report thereon to the substantive session of the Committee on Conferences in 2012;

IV

Matters related to documentation and publications

1. *Emphasizes* the paramount importance of the equality of the six official languages of the United Nations;

2. *Reaffirms* its decision in section IV of its resolution 64/230 that all reports adopted by the Working Group on the Universal Periodic Review of the Human Rights Council shall be issued as documents in all official languages of the United Nations in a timely manner before their consideration by the Council, in accordance with General Assembly resolutions 36/117 A of 10 December 1981, 51/211 A to E, 52/214, 53/208 A to E and 59/265, and requests the Secretary-General to ensure the support necessary to that effect and to report to the General Assembly thereon at its sixty-seventh session;

3. *Reiterates with concern its request* that the Secretary-General ensure that the rules concerning the simultaneous distribution of documents in all six official languages be strictly respected as regards both the distribution of printed copies and the posting of parliamentary documentation on

the Official Document System and the United Nations website, in keeping with section III, paragraph 5, of its resolution 55/222;

4. *Reaffirms* that the Fifth Committee is the appropriate Main Committee of the General Assembly entrusted with responsibilities for administrative and budgetary matters;

5. *Stresses* that matters related to conference management, including documentation, fall within the purview of the Fifth Committee;

6. *Reiterates* the importance of the timely issuance of documents for the Fifth Committee;

7. *Acknowledges* that a multipronged approach is required to find a solution to the perennial difficulties of the late issuance of documents for the Fifth Committee;

8. *Recognizes* the work done by the interdepartmental task force on documentation chaired by the Department for General Assembly and Conference Management in positively addressing the problem of issuance of documents for the Fifth Committee;

9. *Encourages* the Chairs of the Fifth Committee and the Advisory Committee on Administrative and Budgetary Questions to continue to promote cooperation between the two bodies in the sphere of documentation;

10. *Welcomes* the continued efforts of the task force to shepherd the submission of documents by the author departments of the Secretariat;

11. *Notes* that accurate, timely and consistent information provided by the Secretariat to the Fifth Committee during its informal consultations facilitates the decision-making process in the Committee;

12. *Notes with satisfaction* that all documents submitted on time and within the word limit were processed by the Department for General Assembly and Conference Management within four weeks, and encourages the Secretary-General to sustain that level of performance;

13. *Reaffirms* its decision in section III, paragraph 9, of its resolution 59/265 that the issuance of documents in all six official languages on planning, budgetary and administrative matters requiring urgent consideration by the General Assembly shall be accorded priority;

14. *Reiterates its request* that the Secretary-General direct all departments of the Secretariat to include the following elements in their reports:

(*a*) A summary of the report;

(*b*) Consolidated conclusions, recommendations and other proposed actions;

(*c*) Relevant background information;

15. *Also reiterates its request* that all documents submitted to legislative organs by the Secretariat and intergovernmental and expert bodies for consideration and action have conclusions and recommendations in bold print;

16. *Notes with concern* that only 52 per cent of the author departments reached the compliance rate of 90 per cent in the timely submission of their reports to the Department for General Assembly and Conference Management, and requests the Secretary-General to enforce the slotting system more rigorously through a dedicated focus, such as the interdepartmental task force on documentation, and to report thereon to the General Assembly at its sixty-seventh session;

17. *Urges* author departments to fully adhere to deadlines in meeting the goal of 90 per cent submission compliance, and requests the Secretary-General to ensure that documents submitted late do not adversely affect the issuance of documents submitted on time and in compliance with set guidelines;

18. *Reiterates its request* in section IV, paragraph 16, of its resolution 65/245 that the Secretary-General provide information on the waiver process for documents that are submitted over the word limit;

19. *Welcomes* the interactions between the Department for General Assembly and Conference Management and the author departments on waiver management, and requests the Secretary-General to ensure continuous efforts in this regard and to report thereon to the General Assembly at its sixty-seventh session;

20. *Notes* that the effects of workload-sharing in the context of global document management remain minimal, and requests the Secretary-General to continue to seek ways to promote workload-sharing among the four duty stations and to report thereon to the General Assembly at its sixty-seventh session;

21. *Emphasizes* the role of Member States and their intergovernmental bodies in determining the policies of conference management;

22. *Stresses* that proposals to change such policies are to be approved by Member States in their relevant intergovernmental bodies;

23. *Notes* the concept of "paper-smart" meetings, and requests the Secretary-General to submit to the General Assembly a report defining in detail this emerging concept, clearly identifying the appropriate technologies for its effective implementation, including the technological benchmark and procurement needs, including those related to the provision of technological support to Member States, business continuity plans, human resources implications and training needs at the four duty stations, bearing in mind the need for document and data security, as well as proper archiving;

24. *Requests* the Secretary-General to include in the report requested in paragraph 23 above the lessons learned from the meetings that will implement the paper-smart concept on a trial basis with the full consent of the relevant intergovernmental bodies;

25. *Notes* that the Official Document System is the official digital repository of the United Nations;

26. *Requests* the Secretary-General to complete the task of uploading all important older United Nations documents onto the United Nations website in all six official languages on a priority basis so that these archives are also available to Member States through that medium;

27. *Also requests* the Secretary-General to report to the General Assembly at its sixty-seventh session on a detailed time frame for the digitization of all important older United Nations documents, including parliamentary documents, and on options for expediting this process within existing resources;

28. *Notes* the pilot project undertaken by the Committee on the Peaceful Uses of Outer Space at the United Nations Office at Vienna to transition to digital recordings of meetings in the six official languages of the Organization as a cost-saving measure;

29. *Emphasizes* that the further expansion of this measure would require consideration, including of its legal, financial and human resources implications, by the General Assembly and full compliance with the relevant resolutions of the Assembly, and requests the Secretary-General to report thereon and on the evaluation of the pilot project mentioned above to the Assembly at its sixty-seventh session;

V

Matters related to translation and interpretation

1. *Requests* the Secretary-General to redouble his efforts to ensure the highest quality of interpretation and translation services in all six official languages;

2. *Also requests* the Secretary-General to continue to seek evaluation by Member States of the quality of the conference services provided to them, including through the language-specific informational meetings held twice a year, and to ensure that such measures provide equal opportunities to Member States to present their evaluations in the six official languages of the United Nations and that they are in full compliance with the relevant resolutions of the General Assembly;

3. *Reiterates its request* that the Secretary-General ensure that the terminology used in the translation and interpretation services reflects the latest linguistic norms and terminology of the official languages in order to ensure the highest quality;

4. *Reaffirms* section V, paragraph 4, of its resolution 65/245, and reiterates its request that the Secretary-General, when recruiting temporary assistance in the language services, including through the use of international or local contracts, as appropriate, ensure that all language services are given equal treatment and are provided with equally favourable working conditions and resources, with a view to achieving maximum quality of their services, with full respect for the specificities of each of the six official languages and taking into account their respective workloads;

5. *Notes with appreciation* the measures taken by the Secretariat to fill current vacancies in the language services at the United Nations Office at Nairobi, reiterates its request that the Secretary-General consider further measures aimed at decreasing the vacancy rates in Nairobi, and requests that the Secretary-General report thereon to the General Assembly at its sixty-seventh session;

6. *Requests* the Secretary-General to hold competitive examinations for the recruitment of language staff sufficiently in advance in order to fill current and future vacancies in the language services in a timely manner and to inform the General Assembly at its sixty-seventh session of efforts in this regard;

7. *Also requests* the Secretary-General to continue to improve the quality of translation of documents into the six official languages, giving particular significance to the accuracy of translation;

8. *Further requests* the Secretary-General to increase the proportion of translation done contractually, with a view to achieving, inter alia, further efficiencies where this mode of delivery yields a final product that is of comparable quality to in-house translation, and to report thereon to the General Assembly at its sixty-seventh session;

9. *Reiterates its request* that the Secretary-General provide, at all duty stations, adequate staff at the appropriate level, with a view to ensuring appropriate quality control for external translation, with due consideration of the principle of equal grade for equal work;

10. *Requests* the Secretary-General to report to the General Assembly at its sixty-seventh session on the experience, lessons learned and best practices of the main duty stations in performing quality control of contractual translations, including on requirements relating to the number and appropriate level of the staff needed to carry out this function;

11. *Encourages* the Secretary-General to establish globally standardized performance indicators and costing models aimed at a more cost-effective strategy for the in-house processing of documents, and requests the Secretary-General to submit such information to the General Assembly at its sixty-seventh session;

12. *Notes with appreciation* the measures taken by the Secretary-General, in accordance with its resolutions, to address, inter alia, the issue of the replacement of retiring staff in the language services, and requests the Secretary-General to maintain and intensify those efforts, including the strengthening of cooperation with institutions that train language specialists, in order to meet the needs in the six official languages of the United Nations;

13. *Notes* the need for energetic measures to avoid a disruptive shortage of applicants and a high turnover rate in the language career fields, and requests the Secretary-General to use the appropriate means to improve the internship programme, including through partnerships with organizations that promote the official languages of the United Nations;

14. *Also notes*, in this regard, that recent efforts have led to the signing of two memorandums of understanding with two universities in Africa, and that no memorandums of understanding have been signed with Latin American institutions;

15. *Requests* the Secretary-General to make further concerted efforts to promote outreach programmes, such as traineeships and internships, and to introduce innovative methods to increase awareness of the programmes, including through partnerships with Member States, relevant international organizations and language institutions in all regions, in particular to close the wide gap in Africa and Latin America, and to report to the General Assembly thereon at its sixty-seventh session;

16. *Requests* the Department for General Assembly and Conference Management, in cooperation with the Office of Human Resources Management, to continue to increase its efforts to raise awareness among all Member States about opportunities for employment and internships in the language services at the four main duty stations;

17. *Notes with appreciation* the positive experience with traineeships at Headquarters and at the United Nations Office at Vienna in training young professionals in and attracting them to the translation and interpretation services of the United Nations, while enhancing the pool of qualified language professionals in language combinations that are critical for succession-planning purposes, and requests the Secretary-General to develop the initiative further, to extend it to all duty stations and to report thereon to the General Assembly at its sixty-seventh session;

18. *Notes* that the consolidated lists of individuals and entities subject to sanctions, according to the sanctions committees of the Security Council, have not yet been translated into all six official languages, reiterates its recommendation that the Informal Working Group on Documentation and Other Procedural Questions of the Security Council look further into the practices related to the issuance of these consolidated lists, including their translation, and requests the Secretary-General to report thereon at its sixty-seventh session.

On the same date, the Assembly decided that the item "Pattern of conferences" would remain for consideration during its resumed sixty-sixth (2012) session (**decision 66/557**).

UN information systems

Information and communications technology

Report of Secretary-General. In response to General Assembly resolutions 65/259 [YUN 2010, p. 1429], 63/262 [YUN 2008, p. 1592], 63/269 [YUN 2009, p. 1438] and 64/243 [ibid., p. 1395], the Secretary-General, in a June report [A/66/94], provided an update on the status of implementation of the Secretariat's information and communications technology (ICT) strategy [YUN 2008, p. 1589], information on the development of a unified ICT disaster recovery plan and business continuity approach, and information on how to address critical institutional needs and improve the effective and efficient delivery of the Secretariat's ICT programmes. The Secretary-General proposed four integrated, Organization-wide, high-impact enterprise ICT initiatives expected to bring significant qualitative and quantitative benefits to the Organization; enhance the role of ICT as a strategic enabler for UN mandates and substantive programmes; and provide the Organization with overarching ICT management capabilities and an infrastructure for implementing—in a more streamlined and efficient manner—strategic programmes and improvements, including future knowledge management and service delivery initiatives.

The initiative to "Improve enterprise ICT management" would rationalize local ICT management structures, minimize fragmentation of the Secretariat's ICT environment and create cross-cutting ICT functions to prevent future fragmentation. By the end of the 2012–2013 biennium, standards for ICT functions and jobs, as well as sourcing rules, would be defined and new ICT career paths created across the Organization. All Secretariat ICT units would be reviewed and recommendations presented for organizational changes in ICT units. A management framework for measuring the performance of ICT units and resources would be established and made operational Secretariat-wide, along with a central repository of ICT personnel.

The initiative to "Leverage knowledge through ICT" intended to create an integrated knowledge management environment in the Secretariat through, among other objectives, the creation of enterprise-wide platforms; the enhancement of analysis and decision-making support capabilities; the facilitation of knowledge-sharing; and the improvement of management policies and processes and accessibility and usability of information.

The initiative to "Enhance ICT service delivery" proposed a shift towards an enterprise ICT service model in which the common ICT needs of the various organizational units would be addressed through regional service centres (one each in the Americas, Europe, the Middle East, Africa, Asia), thus reducing local ICT service capacity at duty stations.

The initiative to "Create a resilient ICT infrastructure" would involve the transition towards a model consisting of only two enterprise data centres to host enterprise systems: the enterprise data centre at the United Nations Logistics Base at Brindisi, Italy and the secondary data centre in Valencia, Spain. Local data centres would continue to exist but their scope would decrease significantly. The initiative would enhance ICT and substantive performance by enabling secure and reliable access to data and systems throughout the Secretariat, while improving productivity and agility at reduced costs.

It was estimated that $42,822,500 would be required in the 2012–2013 biennium for implementation of the four initiatives.

ACABQ report. In its November report [A/66/7/Add.1], ACABQ recommended that the Secretary-General reprioritize and reduce the scope of the activities envisaged for the 2012–2013 biennium under each of the four enterprise ICT initiatives and identify the features that could be postponed without cutting short or negatively impacting ongoing activities or compromising return on investments already made.

General Assembly action. The Assembly, in **resolution 66/246** of 24 December (see p. 1383), requested the Secretary-General to implement the initiatives to "Improve enterprise ICT management" and to "Create a resilient ICT infrastructure". It did not approve additional funding for those activities and decided not to approve the initiatives to "Leverage knowledge through ICT" and to "Enhance ICT service delivery".

Comprehensive emergency management framework

Report of Secretary-General. In October [A/66/516], the Secretary-General, as requested in resolution 64/260 [YUN 2010, p. 1437], described a comprehensive emergency management framework based on the organizational resilience management system approach, outlined the outcome of a pilot organizational management system in the Secretariat, and presented an example of its practical application at the secondary data centre in Piscataway, New Jersey. The system integrated emergency planning and preparedness, as well as organizational crisis response, recovery, reconstitution and the return to normal business.

The Secretary-General proposed that the Organization procure specialized software to allow for automated maintenance of all information contained in preparedness plans, thereby avoiding time-intensive manual updating and duplication of the same information in different plan documents. Additional resource requirements for those proposals for the 2012–2013 biennium were estimated in the amount of $3,141,300.

ACABQ report. ACABQ, in its November report [A/66/7/Add.10], was of the view that the proposed organizational resilience management system could not be regarded as comprehensive because the full scope of its application had not yet been determined and the full amount of resources required for its operation was not yet known. On the understanding that a follow-up report—to be submitted to the Assembly at its sixty-seventh (2012) session—would present a complete picture of the scope of the system and related resource requirements, ACABQ recommended that the Assembly approve the organizational resilience management system approach as the emergency management framework and appropriate $3,141,300 for the 2012–2013 biennium.

General Assembly action. On 24 December, in section I of **resolution 66/247** (see p. 1393), the Assembly endorsed the ACABQ conclusions and recommendations relating to the Secretary-General's report and approved the extension of the lease of the secondary data centre in Piscataway, for thirty months beyond 31 December 2011, and the procurement of software to maintain emergency preparedness plans and the staff accounting system. It did not approve additional resources in that regard.

Enterprise resource planning

Report of Secretary-General. As requested in General Assembly resolution 64/243, the Secretary-General, in September, submitted his third progress report [A/66/381] on the Umoja (enterprise resource planning) project [YUN 2008, p. 1591], an organizational transformation designed to enable high-quality and cost-effective service delivery anywhere in the world in support of evolving UN mandates. According to the Secretary-General, Umoja had achieved significant progress since its initial funding in 2009 [YUN 2009, p. 1439]. It had re-engineered hundreds of existing administrative processes across the Secretariat, and it was at a critical point as it transitioned from the design phase to the build phase. The timeline contained in the second progress report [YUN 2010, p. 1462] needed to be adjusted. The implementation of Umoja functionality, projected for the end of 2015, was subject to delays due to lateness in the procurement of the enterprise resource planning software; the need for a wide-scale analysis of existing operations in order to transition the Organization to the future operating model; cultural and institutional changes that proved more complex than anticipated; additional time spent in the design phase; more time spent on educating and gaining acceptance from the Organization owners and end-users; and more time spent on the hiring of UN staff and subject experts. To address those delays and accelerate progress, a number of steps were taken, including changes to Umoja's governance to better manage project implementation. The Umoja Steering Committee had adopted a phased approach; the first phase, referred to as Umoja Foundation, would include functionality to support the International Public Sector Accounting Standards requirements. It would pilot in January 2013 and deploy by clusters across the Organization through December 2014. The second phase, called Umoja Extension, would deliver the remaining comprehensive functionality and be deployed by December 2015. Human resources and budget formulation functions, which were part of Umoja Extension, would be built at the same time as Umoja Foundation, given their importance to the Organization and the urgency for replacing existing processes and systems. The deployment of those two functions would commence in 2014. The design phase for the rest of Umoja Extension would commence in 2013 and move to a building phase in 2014. The overall level of projected expenditure for Umoja for the 2012–2013 biennium was estimated at $117,373,500.

ACABQ report. In November [A/66/7/Add.1], ACABQ submitted its comments on the report.

General Assembly action. On 24 December, in PART VIII, Section 29A of **resolution 66/246** (see p. 1383), the Assembly requested the Secretary-General to ensure the implementation of the Umoja enterprise resource planning project without further delay; to bring project costs back within the approved budget; and to include in his fourth annual report information on all factors that had contributed to delays in the project's implementation and the projected budget overrun. The Assembly decided that the Project Director would report solely to the Under-Secretary-General for Management and that the Umoja project team and budget administration would be placed within the Department of Management. It approved commitment authority for the project for one year at maintenance level, and requested the Secretary-General to submit, in 2012, a revised comprehensive proposal for funding the project during the 2012–2013 biennium.

International cooperation in informatics

In accordance with Economic and Social Council resolution 2010/38 [YUN 2010, p. 1463], the Secretary-General submitted a May report [E/2011/101] on international cooperation in the field of informatics. The Secretariat and the Ad Hoc Open-ended Working Group on Informatics continued to collaborate with regard to website tools and to maintain a shared responsibility for the creation and maintenance of web pages and document updates. With guidance from the Working Group, the Secretariat expanded efforts to more fully utilize collaboration tools to meet the needs of the General Assembly Committees. The delegate website (www.un.int) provided content in English and French from the Secretariat's Intranet site iSeek, as well as links to other information created especially for delegates. The Office of Information and Communications Technology (OICT) provided website hosting services and a standard web content management system for 62 permanent missions. It continued to provide e-mail services to permanent missions by supporting 1,200 e-mail accounts on four dedicated servers at Headquarters. OICT also supported the Internet Café for delegates (ICT resource centre), located in the North Lawn Conference Building. DGACM launched the e-Subscription portal http://undocs.org to meet the needs of Member States to learn immediately about the release of any document on the Official Document System (ODS) that was relevant to their national interests.

On 29 July, the Economic and Social Council took note of the Secretary-General's report on international cooperation in the field of informatics (**decision 2011/271**).

UN premises and property

Capital master plan

Implementation of CMP

In February [A/65/725], ACABQ provided its comments and recommendations on the Secretary-General's eighth annual progress report on the capital master plan (CMP) [YUN 2010, p. 1463], his proposals for financing the associated costs for 2011 from within the approved CMP budget [ibid., p. 1464], the report of the Board of Auditors on CMP for the year ended 31 December 2009 [ibid.], and the related Secretary-General's report on the implementation of the Board of Auditors' recommendations [ibid.].

GENERAL ASSEMBLY ACTION

On 4 April [meeting 84], the General Assembly, on the recommendation of the Fifth Committee [A/65/646/Add.2], adopted **resolution 65/269** without vote [agenda item 129].

Capital master plan

The General Assembly,

Recalling its resolutions 54/249 of 23 December 1999, 55/238 of 23 December 2000, 56/234 and 56/236 of 24 December 2001 and 56/286 of 27 June 2002, section II of its resolution 57/292 of 20 December 2002, its resolution 59/295 of 22 June 2005, section II of its resolution 60/248 of 23 December 2005, its resolutions 60/256 of 8 May 2006, 60/282 of 30 June 2006, 61/251 of 22 December 2006 and 62/87 of 10 December 2007, section II.B of its resolution 63/248 of 24 December 2008, its resolutions 63/270 of 7 April 2009 and 64/228 of 22 December 2009 and its decisions 58/566 of 8 April 2004 and 65/543 of 24 December 2010,

Recognizing the importance of ensuring that persons with disabilities have access to the physical environment on an equal basis with others,

Having considered the eighth annual progress report of the Secretary-General on the implementation of the capital master plan, the report of the Secretary-General on proposals for financing the associated costs required for the year 2011 from within the approved budget for the capital master plan, the report of the Board of Auditors on the capital master plan for the year ended 31 December 2009, the report of the Secretary-General on the implementation of the recommendations of the Board of Auditors contained in its report on the capital master plan for the year ended 31 December 2009, the relevant sections of the annual report of the Office of Internal Oversight Services for the period from 1 July 2009 to 30 June 2010 and the related report of the Advisory Committee on Administrative and Budgetary Questions,

1. *Takes note* of the eighth annual progress report of the Secretary-General on the implementation of the capital master plan, the report of the Secretary-General on proposals for financing the associated costs required for the year 2011 from within the approved budget for the capital master plan, the report of the Board of Auditors on the capital master plan for the year ended 31 December 2009, the report of the Secretary-General on the implementation of the recommendations of the Board of Auditors contained in its report on the capital master plan for the year ended 31 December 2009, and the relevant sections of the annual report of the Office of Internal Oversight Services for the period from 1 July 2009 to 30 June 2010;

2. *Reaffirms* the oversight role of the Fifth Committee in administrative and budgetary matters;

3. *Stresses* the importance of effective oversight, transparency and accountability in the management of the project;

4. *Also stresses* the special role of the host country Government with regard to support for United Nations Headquarters, in New York;

5. *Notes* the benefits, including economic ones, accruing to host countries from the presence of the United Nations, and the costs incurred;

6. *Recalls* the current practices of Governments of host countries with regard to support for United Nations headquarters and United Nations bodies located in their territories;

7. *Reaffirms* paragraphs 31 through 34 of its resolution 61/251;

8. *Recalls* paragraph 10 of its resolution 61/251 and paragraph 37 of its resolution 62/87, and reaffirms that any scope options in addition to those already approved by the General Assembly shall be submitted by the Secretary-General to the Assembly for its consideration and approval;

9. *Endorses* the conclusions and recommendations contained in the report of the Advisory Committee on Administrative and Budgetary Questions, subject to the provisions of the present resolution;

10. *Accepts* the report of the Board of Auditors on the capital master plan for the year ended 31 December 2009;

11. *Approves* the recommendations of the Board of Auditors contained in its report;

12. *Notes with concern* the findings of the Board of Auditors as contained in its report, and emphasizes the importance of the full implementation of the recommendations of the Board;

I

Eighth annual progress report

13. *Reiterates its request* that the Secretary-General make every effort to avoid budget increases through sound project management practices and to ensure by all means that the capital master plan is completed within the budget as approved in its resolution 61/251, and to report thereon in the context of his ninth annual progress report;

Schedule

14. *Recalls* paragraph 7 of the report of the Advisory Committee on Administrative and Budgetary Questions, and reiterates its request that the Secretary-General make every effort to finish the project in accordance with the schedule approved in its resolution 62/87;

15. *Requests* the Secretary-General to ensure full accountability for delays, and all factors contributing to delays, in the implementation of the capital master plan and the budget overrun, and to include this information in his ninth annual progress report;

16. *Reiterates its request* to the Secretary-General to continue to update the Member States through regular informal briefings, besides submitting annual progress reports, on all aspects of the implementation of the capital master plan, including the current status, significant activities carried out since the previous report and risk analysis information outlining any risks identified, action to be taken, status and trends, and to update the relevant information on its website on a regular basis;

17. *Requests* the Secretary-General to include, in his ninth annual progress report, information on lessons learned in the implementation of the capital master plan and how they are being utilized to improve the current and future planning and implementation of the capital master plan;

18. *Also requests* the Secretary-General to ensure that the process of the relocation of Secretariat staff from office swing space is carried out in the most effective and timely manner, taking full advantage of the lessons learned during the capital master plan project, and in this regard requests him to prepare well in advance detailed office plans of the Secretariat Building in order to avoid delays and any potential additional costs;

19. *Reaffirms its support* for the timely deconstruction and removal of the temporary North Lawn Building upon the completion of the Headquarters renovation work;

Value engineering

20. *Encourages* the Secretary-General to continue finding efficiency gains and cost reductions throughout the implementation of the capital master plan;

21. *Emphasizes* that the value engineering exercise shall not undermine the quality, durability and sustainability of the materials used, the original design of Headquarters or the commitment of the project to the highest standards for the safety, health and well-being of staff and delegations, in particular with regard to the handling of asbestos;

22. *Regrets* that the Secretary-General did not provide detailed information on the value engineering exercise as requested in paragraph 6 of section I of its resolution 64/228;

23. *Notes* that the Board of Auditors was unable to provide any assurance as to the actual efficiency of value engineering in terms of cost reduction, and that such measures are instrumental in bringing costs back on budget, and in this regard requests the Secretary-General to reassess the merits of value engineering, and to include detailed information thereon in his next annual progress report;

Procurement and sustainability

24. *Reaffirms* paragraphs 36 to 38 of its resolution 61/251, on the importance of transparency in the procurement process, and requests the Secretary-General to ensure that the construction manager takes them fully into account when subcontracting and to report, in the context of his ninth annual progress report, on the specific steps taken and progress achieved in the context of increasing procurement opportunities for vendors from developing countries and countries with economies in transition in the implementation of the capital master plan;

25. *Reaffirms once again* paragraph 38 of its resolution 61/251, and requests the Secretary-General to ensure that procurement activities conducted by the construction manager in the implementation of the capital master plan are in compliance with United Nations rules, regulations and procedures and General Assembly resolutions governing United Nations procurement activities, as well as ethics policies, including post-employment restrictions, and that the relevant provisions are taken fully into account by the construction manager when subcontracting;

26. *Reaffirms* paragraph 13 of section I of its resolution 63/270;

27. *Reiterates its request* to the Secretary-General in its resolutions 61/276 of 29 June 2007 and 62/269 of 20 June 2008, and requests the Secretary-General to continue to explore additional innovative ways to promote procurement from developing countries and countries with economies in transition and to identify obstacles preventing their participation in United Nations procurement contracts and to report on concrete measures taken in this regard;

28. *Notes* that the action plan prepared by the construction manager to promote procurement opportunities for contractors and vendors from developing countries and countries with economies in transition has not led to a significant increase in the value of contracts awarded to contractors and vendors from developing countries and countries with economies in transition;

29. *Requests* the Secretary-General to continue to review all expression of interest notices and invitations to bid issued by the construction manager in order to ensure that their contents fully comply with the relevant resolutions of the General Assembly and do not unduly restrict the diversification of the origin of vendors;

30. *Notes* that some measures taken to avoid delays in the capital master plan procurement process, in particular the ex post facto review of contracts, carry the risk of a negative impact in terms of internal controls, and requests

the Secretary-General to ensure that the procurement processes are in full compliance with the Financial Regulations and Rules of the United Nations;

31. *Recalls* that, in accordance with article 5 of the United Nations general conditions of contract, the terms of any subcontract shall be subject to and conform to the provisions of the general conditions of contract;

32. *Requests* the Secretary-General to continue to exercise his authority to undertake, in respect of the subcontractors directly involved in the provision of goods and services to the Organization on behalf of the capital master plan construction manager, a thorough review of their qualifications and the identities of the principals involved, and also requests the Secretary-General to provide prior written approval and clearance for the use of such subcontractors, as required in article 5 of the general conditions of contract, so as to ensure the integrity, fairness and transparency of the procurement process;

33. *Also requests* the Secretary-General to continue to post and regularly update the list of subcontractors approved by the United Nations on the capital master plan website and to include information on the implementation of article 5 of the general conditions of contract, including the procedure for review and approval of subcontractors by the United Nations, in future progress reports on the implementation of the capital master plan;

Security

34. *Authorizes* the implementation of the security enhancements, as reflected in paragraph 6 of the report of the Advisory Committee on Administrative and Budgetary Questions, estimated to amount to 100 million United States dollars;

35. *Recognizes* the efforts of the host country to improve the safety and security of United Nations Headquarters, as well as its financial contribution to the security enhancements;

36. *Notes* that the funding provided by the host country will cover all costs related to the security enhancements, including design, construction, delay, swing space rent where applicable, contingencies and any other costs;

37. *Decides* that all costs related to the security enhancements, including any associated costs resulting from the delay in the capital master plan as a result of the implementation of the security enhancements, will not result in additional assessments on Member States, without prejudice to the costs related to the regular maintenance of such enhancements, which shall be part of the regular budget after the completion of the capital master plan;

38. *Reaffirms* that the General Assembly has the sole prerogative of deciding on any changes to the capital master plan project, budget and implementation strategy, as approved in its resolutions, notes that the Secretary-General did not seek the approval of the General Assembly for the security enhancements, and expresses concern that the completion of the project as approved in its resolution 62/87 will be delayed as a result of the security enhancements;

39. *Stresses* the importance of the timely sharing by the Secretary-General with the General Assembly of information regarding the capital master plan;

40. *Expresses concern* that the Secretary-General did not provide to the General Assembly detailed information regarding security enhancements;

41. *Requests* the Secretary-General to provide, in the context of his next annual progress report, comprehensive information on the implementation of the security enhancements;

Donations and artwork

42. *Recalls* paragraph 8 of the report of the Advisory Committee on Administrative and Budgetary Questions, and in this regard reaffirms the relevant provisions of its resolutions, in particular resolution 63/270, relating to donations for the capital master plan, and reiterates that the donation policy should not be restrictive and that it should be in full conformity with the international and intergovernmental character of the Organization as well as with the Financial Regulations and Rules of the United Nations and without prejudice to the scope, specifications and design of the project;

43. *Requests* the Secretary-General to ensure that works of art, masterpieces and other gifts are handled appropriately during all the stages of the capital master plan, and also requests him to cooperate with those Member States that wish to take care of their gifts of works of art, masterpieces and other items during the renovation period;

Parking

44. *Recalls* paragraphs 30 to 33 of section I of its resolution 63/270, expresses concern about the issue of the availability of parking spaces to the Member States in the garage of the United Nations complex, and the limitations imposed on Member States in this regard, including those related to night-time parking, reiterates its request that the total number of parking spaces available to the Member States before the implementation of the capital master plan be retained upon its completion and that every effort be made to maintain that number during the implementation of the capital master plan, and looks forward, in this context, to information on the review of the options in the forthcoming annual progress report;

Health and safety

45. *Reaffirms its commitment* to the safety, security, health and well-being of staff, delegations, visitors and tourists at the United Nations, and requests the Secretary-General to ensure that concrete safeguards for the achievement of those objectives are in place and are part of the standard operating procedures throughout the implementation of the capital master plan;

46. *Requests* the Secretary-General to continue to make provisions for appropriate health and wellness facilities and improved physical accessibility for persons with disabilities;

Accessibility

47. *Also requests* the Secretary-General to continue providing specific information, in the context of his next annual progress report, about the measures taken to eliminate physical, communication or technical barriers to persons with disabilities at United Nations Headquarters within the framework of the capital master plan, in particular regarding improvement in terms of the accessibility of interpretation booths;

48. *Further requests* the Secretary-General to ensure that measures to be taken in the context of the capital master plan, including the security enhancements, in applying

building, fire and safety codes of the host city do not violate the provisions of the Convention on the Rights of Persons with Disabilities, especially those relating to accessibility, and also reiterates its request to the Secretary-General to report on this subject in future annual progress reports;

Oversight

49. *Reaffirms* the importance of oversight with respect to the implementation of the capital master plan, and requests the Board of Auditors and all other relevant oversight bodies to continue to report to the General Assembly annually on the capital master plan;

50. *Requests* the Secretary-General to continue to develop and implement a comprehensive internal control framework for the capital master plan to mitigate and effectively address all possible risks, to ensure full compliance and responsiveness on the part of management to the specific requirements of the project, to avoid any delays in the implementation of any aspect of the project and to ensure full compliance with United Nations rules and procedures and General Assembly resolutions governing procurement;

Advisory Board

51. *Notes with appreciation* the establishment of the Advisory Board of the United Nations Capital Master Plan, and encourages it to continue its work;

52. *Requests* the Secretary-General to provide, in his annual progress report on the capital master plan, information about the activities of the Advisory Board, including any observations, recommendations or any other aspects or developments of the project deemed important by the Board, as well as any additional comments that the Secretary-General may wish to provide;

Ninth annual progress report

53. *Requests* the Secretary-General to continue to report on the status of the project, the schedule, the projected completion cost, the status of contributions, the working capital reserve and the letter of credit in his ninth annual progress report, as well as to include therein the information requested in the present resolution;

II

Associated costs

54. *Reiterates its decision* that the approved associated costs will be financed from within the budget approved for the capital master plan;

55. *Notes* the anticipated cash flow problem over the long term;

56. *Takes note* of paragraph 15 of the report of the Advisory Committee on Administrative and Budgetary Questions, and in this regard requests the Secretary-General to exhaust all possible options for absorbing the associated costs from within the overall budget approved for the capital master plan, including through cost efficiency measures, in order to avoid any additional financial burden on Member States, and to report thereon to the General Assembly, in the context of his ninth annual progress report on the capital master plan, at the main part of its sixty-sixth session;

57. *Requests* the Secretary-General to make every effort to ensure that furniture in good condition is reused and to report thereon to the General Assembly in the context of his ninth annual progress report;

58. *Takes note* of paragraph 20 of the report of the Advisory Committee, decides to approve eleven general temporary assistance positions, and requests the Secretary-General to report thereon in the context of his ninth annual progress report;

59. *Also takes note* of paragraph 29 of the report of the Advisory Committee, and requests the Secretary-General to make every effort to absorb the associated costs for 2011 from within the overall budget approved for the capital master plan in a total amount of 58,871,305 dollars (net), broken down as follows:

(a) 628,600 dollars for the Department for General Assembly and Conference Management;
(b) 190,080 dollars for the Department of Public Information;
(c) 51,350,750 dollars for the Office of Central Support Services;
(d) 199,400 dollars for the Office of Information and Communications Technology;
(e) 534,555 dollars for construction, alteration, improvement and major maintenance activities at Headquarters;
(f) 5,967,920 dollars for the Department of Safety and Security;

60. *Authorizes* the Secretary-General to enter into commitments in an amount of up to 286,300 dollars, and requests him to report on expenditures in the context of his next report on proposals for financing the associated costs.

Report of Secretary-General. Pursuant to Assembly resolutions 57/292 [YUN 2002, p. 1375] and 65/269 (see p. 1421), the Secretary-General submitted, in October [A/66/527], the ninth progress report on the implementation of CMP. Since the previous report [YUN 2010, p. 1463], significant progress had been achieved, including replacement of the curtain wall in the Secretariat Building, the abatement of asbestos and the removal of obsolete materials, the construction of an electrical vault in the basements, coordination with participating Member States regarding donations for particular rooms, and the award of guaranteed maximum price contracts for additional aspects of the project. In addition, the Conference Building was redesigned to take into account enhanced security upgrades following discussions with and the receipt of funding from the host country. Plans were at an advanced stage for the reoccupation of the Secretariat Building.

Three years into the project, the Organization remained within reach of its completion with a variance of no more than 4 per cent above the original budget. The infrastructure and Secretariat portions of the project would be completed approximately on schedule, and the Conference and the General Assembly buildings would be completed about one year behind schedule. Actual expenditure for the project, as at 1 October 2011, amounted to $1,586.2 million.

In an addendum submitted in October [A/66/527/Add.1], in accordance with resolution 65/269, the Secretary-General provided an update of the status of activities associated with CMP, including historical expenditure to 2010, forecasted expenditure for 2011 and estimated resource requirements for 2012–2013. The resources required for associated costs for the period from 2008 to 2013 were estimated at $146,806,000. For 2012, the estimated resource requirements amounted to $46,322,200. Taking into account the estimated balance of unutilized funds of $34,957,100 against the amounts approved for the period 2008–2011, the net additional requirements for 2012 amounted to $11,365,100.

General Assembly action. On 24 December, the Assembly authorized the continued utilization in 2012 of the unspent balance of the funding for associated costs approved in 2011 to allow the Secretary-General to continue the activities planned for 2012. It also decided to consider, in the first part of its resumed sixty-sixth (2012) session, the Secretary-General's proposals for financing the associated costs required for 2012 from within the approved CMP budget (**decision 66/555**).

Review of CMP

Report of OIOS. In July [A/66/179], OIOS submitted a report on its audit of CMP procurement and contract management, including change orders, in accordance with General Assembly resolution 63/270 [YUN 2009, p. 1442]. The audit assessed the adequacy and effectiveness of the key controls over procurement and contract management activities. OIOS noted that the CMP Office had established an internal control structure for reviewing and evaluating guaranteed maximum price proposals; however, controls over the procurement of trade contracts by the construction manager, Skanska, needed improvement to ensure the transparency and fairness of the procurement process. There was also a delay in setting up the Post-Award Review Committee to conduct the technical review of change orders and the compliance review of contract amendments. Coupled with the slow review process, the delay contributed to a large backlog of cases for the Committee to review and a need to reconsider the current working arrangements to ensure the Committee's relevance to ex post facto control. It took the CMP Office between 29 and 174 days to approve the change orders under review. In addition, the reasons for initiating change orders were not adequately explained; the fundamental question of why change occurred and who was accountable could not be answered, and there were high numbers of change orders on some contracts.

OIOS issued eight recommendations to the CMP Office and the Office of Central Support Services for further strengthening internal controls, all of which were accepted by both offices.

Report of Board of Auditors. In its report on CMP for the year ended 31 December 2010 [A/66/5 (Vol. V)], the Board of Auditors concluded that the project was entering a critical phase, where the flexibility to manage unexpected problems and pressures on cost and time was greatly reduced. It was clear the project would be delivered late, as its completion date had slipped from mid-2013 to mid-2014. The General Assembly and Conference Buildings were projected to be delayed by a year, and there was the potential for scope reductions to the planned work on the Dag Hammarskjöld Library and South Annex Buildings. The cost forecast was $79 million (4 per cent) over-budget, and there were risks that, if not mitigated, could increase the delays and costs. The cost forecast did not include an estimate for all change orders until project completion and there was no provision for the most likely costs of identified risks. The full cost for renting temporary swing space also needed to be assessed and reflected in the cost forecast. There was a lack of a workable design solution in the Dag Hammarskjöld Library and South Annex Buildings. The CMP lacked effective control over the volume of changes to the project and continued to experience a large number of changes driven by the end occupiers and incomplete designs. The handover from the CMP Office to the Facilities Management Service was another critical risk area.

Of the 20 recommendations the Board made in its report for the year ended 31 December 2009 [YUN 2010, p. 1464], 9 (45 per cent) were fully implemented, 5 (25 per cent) were under implementation, 5 (25 per cent) were not implemented—of which 3 were superseded by new recommendations—and 1 (5 per cent) had been overtaken by events. The Board reiterated the recommendations from its previous report that had not been superseded or overtaken by events, but had not yet been fully implemented.

The Board recommended that the CMP Office strengthen its approach to forecasting future costs by including a robustly calculated and auditable estimate for the cost of all change orders until project completion and by allowing for the most likely costs of identified risks. The Administration should review the situation regarding the Dag Hammarskjöld Library and South Annex Buildings and decide on a way forward. It should also resolve the situation arising from CMP-associated costs; establish effective change control governance to minimize occupier-driven changes; and monitor, on a quarterly basis, the commissioning arrangements between the Facilities Management Service and the CMP Office.

Report of Secretary-General. In accordance with General Assembly resolution 48/216 B [YUN 1993, p. 1207], the Secretary-General, in a September report [A/66/324], provided additional information in response to the Board of Auditors' recommendations contained in its report on CMP for the year ended 31 December 2010 (see above).

ACABQ report. In a report submitted in December [A/66/7/Add.11], ACABQ submitted its comments and recommendations on the Secretary-General's ninth progress report on CMP and his report on proposals for financing associated costs for 2012 from within the approved CMP budget; the report of the Board of Auditors on CMP for the year ended 31 December 2010; and the related report of the Secretary-General on implementation of the Board's recommendations (see p. 1425).

General Assembly action. On 24 December, the Assembly decided to defer, until the first part of its resumed sixty-sixth (2012) session, consideration of the report of the Board of Auditors on CMP for the year ended 31 December 2010; the associated Secretary-General's report on implementation of the Board's recommendations; the Secretary-General's ninth progress report on CMP and his report on proposals for financing associated costs for 2012; the ACABQ report on CMP; and the OIOS report on the audit of CMP procurement and contract management, including change orders (**decision 66/556A**).

On the same date, the Assembly deferred consideration of the agenda item on CMP until its resumed sixty-sixth (2012) session (**decision 66/557**).

Headquarters accommodation needs

Report of Secretary-General. Responding to General Assembly resolution 60/282 [YUN 2006, p. 1667], the Secretary-General submitted the feasibility study [A/66/349] on a new building on the North Lawn in the context of the projected accommodation needs of UN Headquarters and participating funds and programmes (the United Nations Joint Staff Pension Fund, the United Nations Development Programme, the United Nations Population Fund and the United Nations Office for Project Services) from 2014 to 2034. The study addressed factors such as security, architectural, host city and community issues that had not been incorporated into the Secretary-General's preceding business analysis [YUN 2006, p. 1666]. A motivating factor for the study was the forthcoming expiration of the office space leases of the United Nations Development Corporation buildings one and two. Those leases would expire at the end of March 2018, with the option to extend until the end of March 2023, but no renewal options beyond that date. The study indicated that in 2014, an additional 1.62 million square feet (150,500 square metres) would be required to complement the existing office accommodations provided in the Organization's compound. That requirement would increase to 1.81 million square feet (168,150 square metres) in 2023 and to 1.88 million square feet (174,660 square metres) in 2034. Those estimates assumed that between 2023 and 2034, the United Nations would proactively implement "alternative workplace strategies", achieving 20 per cent efficiency gains and thereby reducing the need for additional office space for the designated time period. The study considered and compared a newly constructed building on the North Lawn with other long-term approaches to real estate with respect to four primary categories/options: build on campus (new North Lawn building); buy an existing building off campus; lease space off campus; and construct a building off campus.

On 15 July, the Governor of the State of New York signed legislation authorizing New York City to transfer part of the Robert Moses Playground, south of 42nd Street and east of First Avenue, to the United Nations Development Corporation to construct on that land a building that should not be higher than the Secretariat Building, with no more than 900,000 square feet of floor area. Should Member States decide to proceed, incorporating either a "lease-to-own" or similar arrangement that would result in the United Nations owning such a building, that would be seen as a decision to build off campus and would preclude following up on other major approaches.

The study also pointed to advantages for the United Nations in constructing on the North Lawn. The Assembly was requested to provide guidance to the Secretariat as to any further reporting on the options available for meeting long-term space requirements at Headquarters.

ACABQ report. In its October report [A/66/7/Add.3], ACABQ recommended that the Secretary-General reassess the issues and present a detailed analysis of the costs, benefits and risks of each option no later than at the second part of its resumed sixty-sixth (2012) session.

General Assembly action. On 24 December, the Assembly deferred until the first part of its resumed sixty-sixth (2012) session consideration of the Secretary-General's report on the feasibility study on the UN Headquarters accommodation needs for 2014–2034 (**decision 66/556A**).

Additional office/conference facilities

Geneva. In August [A/66/279], the Secretary-General reported on progress made in preparing the strategic heritage plan for the Palais des Nations in Geneva, as requested by the General Assembly in resolution 64/243 [YUN 2009, p. 1395]. The preliminary study, conducted in 2009, highlighted the maintenance challenges at the Palais des Nations resulting from normal deterioration over the past 70 years of use. Building upon the results of that study, a conceptual engineering and architectural study was initiated in August 2010, and the consultant's report submitted in February 2011. The study established that the state of the buildings of the Palais des Nations was undermining the efforts of the UN Office at Geneva not only to ensure the safety and security of its users but also to deliver its mandated services. Throughout the years, energy and maintenance demands had increased steadily owing to the age of the facilities. Even if limited timely corrective actions were taken, they would not prevent those costs from growing exponentially. Three project implementation options were identified: a fast-track (approximately 5-year) implementation; a phased implementation over a medium-term (approximately 8-year) period; and a phased implementation over a long-term (approximately 13-year) period. The eight-year, medium-term, multiphased renovation was the recommended option, as it would result in the lowest cost and be the least disruptive. With regard to next steps, the report proposed that in 2012, a project management team could prepare the documentation for securing a programme management firm to develop, during the course of 2013, an overall project implementation and phasing plan inclusive of financial implications. The estimated cost of that action amounted to $4,069,700 for the 2012–2013 biennium. In June, Switzerland, the host country, indicated that it would participate in the renovation through a voluntary contribution of up to a maximum of 50 million Swiss francs.

Nairobi. In a September report [A/66/336] on the construction of additional office facilities at the United Nations Office at Nairobi (UNON), the Secretary-General reported that construction of the new UNON office facility finished on time and substantial completion was achieved at the end of December 2010. According to the original schedule, internal office partitioning work was to commence in early 2011, and occupation of the new facility completed by June, but the actual rate of work resulted in the completion of internal partitioning by March, which allowed for occupancy of the building earlier than anticipated. The United Nations Environment Programme moved into the new facility in January and the first half of February, and the United Nations Human Settlements Programme (UN-Habitat) during February and March. Inauguration of the office, presided over by the Secretary-General and the President of Kenya, took place on 31 March.

The total cost of the project remained at $25,252,200, as approved by the General Assembly in 2009 [YUN 2009, p. 1451], however, the final cost would be determined at the time of issuance of the final payments in June 2012.

Addis Ababa. Also in September [A/66/351], the Secretary-General reported on progress in the construction of additional office facilities at the Economic Commission for Africa (ECA) in Addis Ababa, in response to Assembly resolution 65/259 [YUN 2010, p. 1429]. As at June, the project was 30 per cent complete, while about 50 per cent of the contracted time had elapsed. The disparity was mainly due to a shortage of cement. ECA was working with the contractor to accelerate the construction process in order to complete the project by the end of August 2012. The project team was working on selection of the finishing materials and collaborating with the host Government to avoid future delays owing to importation restrictions. The latest cost plan for the project amounted to $15,333,224.

ACABQ report. ACABQ comments and recommendations regarding the Secretary-General's reports were contained in an October report [A/66/7/Add.3].

General Assembly action. The General Assembly, in Section VII of **resolution 66/247** of 24 December (see p. 1393), took note of the Secretary-General's reports and endorsed the ACABQ conclusions and recommendations thereon. It expressed concern that the estimated expenditure of $734,000 for the contingency provision for the ECA facilities had arisen, owing to an error by the architecture and construction management consultant, and that this had resulted in a depletion of the budgeted contingency, thereby increasing the risk to the ECA project. It reiterated its request to the Secretary-General that the strategic heritage plan for the Palais des Nations not start before the Assembly had taken a decision on the matter and the CMP was completed. The Assembly requested the Secretary-General to submit at its sixty-eighth (2013) session, in the context of the proposed programme budget for the 2014–2015 biennium, a detailed plan and cost analysis based on the medium-term option for the strategic heritage plan project, including a prioritized list highlighting essential items that needed renovation for health and safety reasons. He should also include, towards realization of the strategic heritage plan, options for voluntary funding sources. The Assembly approved $810,600 to provide for an architect and an engineer, and $2.8 million for contractual services in relation to developing the project implementation and phasing plan.

Staff matters

Appointment of Secretary-General

In June, Mr. Ban Ki-moon of the Republic of Korea was reappointed Secretary-General of the United Nations for a five-year term beginning on 1 January 2012 and ending on 31 December 2016.

Nomination

On 7 June [A/65/234], Kuwait informed the General Assembly President that the Group of Asian States, at a meeting on 6 June, had decided to endorse the re-election of Secretary-General Ban Ki-moon for a second term. The endorsement reflected the Group's appreciation for Mr. Ban's work and leadership over the past four-and-a half years. It was their hope that he would continue to serve at the helm of the United Nations.

In accordance with rule 15 of the General Assembly rules of procedure, the Group requested that an item entitled "Appointment of the Secretary-General of the United Nations" be included in the agenda of the Assembly's resumed sixty-fifth (2011) session, for consideration in plenary.

On 15 June, the Assembly decided to include the item in the agenda [A/65/251/Add.3].

SECURITY COUNCIL ACTION

On 17 June [meeting 6556], the Security Council held a closed meeting and adopted **resolution 1987(2011)** by acclamation.

The Security Council,

Having considered the question of the recommendation for the appointment of the Secretary-General of the United Nations,

Recommends to the General Assembly that Mr. Ban Ki-moon be appointed Secretary-General of the United Nations for a second term of office from 1 January 2012 to 31 December 2016.

On the same date [A/65/865], the Council President informed the Assembly President of the Council's recommendation concerning the appointment of the Secretary-General of the United Nations.

GENERAL ASSEMBLY ACTION

On 21 June [meeting 101], the General Assembly adopted **resolution 65/282** [draft: A/65/L.80] without vote [agenda item 163].

Appointment of the Secretary-General of the United Nations

The General Assembly,

Having considered the recommendation contained in Security Council resolution 1987(2011) of 17 June 2011,

Expressing its appreciation for the effective and dedicated service rendered to the United Nations by Mr. Ban Ki-moon during his first term of office,

Appoints Mr. Ban Ki-moon Secretary-General of the United Nations for a second term of office beginning on 1 January 2012 and ending on 31 December 2016.

Conditions of service

International Civil Service Commission

The International Civil Service Commission (ICSC), a 15-member body established in 1974 by General Assembly resolution 3357(XXIX) [YUN 1974, p. 875] to regulate and coordinate the conditions of service and the salaries and allowances of the UN common system, held its seventy-second (New York, 22 March–1 April) and seventy-third (Paris, 18–29 July) sessions to consider, in addition to organizational matters, the conditions of service applicable to Professional and General Service categories of staff, locally recruited staff, and staff in the field. ICSC deliberations, recommendations and decisions were detailed in its annual report to the Assembly [A/66/30 & Corr.1,2] (see sections below on specific issues).

In an October statement [A/66/394 & Corr.1], the Secretary-General summarized the administrative and financial implications of the ICSC decisions and recommendations: additional net requirements of $15,200 for the 2010–2011 biennium programme budget, and reduced net requirements of $3,275,400 for the proposed 2012–2013 biennium programme budget. Factored into those requirements were a 2.5 per cent increase to the level of mobility, hardship and non-removal allowances, including additional non-family hardship allowance; changes to the hardship reclassification system; reduced requirements for danger pay; implementation of the 2010 place-to-place survey result; and the base/floor salary scale. The Secretary-General also described additional net requirements of $217,000 and $15,000 for the proposed 2012–2013 biennium budgets of the International Criminal Tribunal for Rwanda and the International Tribunal for the Former Yugoslavia, respectively; reduced net requirements of $2,504,700 and $5,338,400, respectively, for peacekeeping operations for the financial periods 2011–2012 and 2012–2013; and additional net requirements of $41,000 and $82,000, respectively, for the support account for peacekeeping operations for the financial periods 2011–2012 and 2012–2013.

In an October report [A/66/7/Add.4 & Corr.1], the Advisory Committee on Administrative and Budgetary Questions (ACABQ) stated that it had no objection to the Secretary-General's approach.

The Assembly, in section X of **resolution 66/247** of 24 December (see p. 1393), took note of the Secretary-General's statement and endorsed the conclusions and recommendations of ACABQ.

Conditions of service applicable to both categories of staff

Mobility and hardship scheme

ICSC [A/66/30 & Corr.1,2] reviewed the mobility/hardship scheme. It decided that each organization should determine how to best administer the payment of the mobility and hardship elements and requested its secretariat to assess the impact of the revised scheme on mobility in 2015. ICSC defined "H" category duty stations as headquarters and similarly designated locations where the United Nations had no developmental or humanitarian assistance programmes, or locations in European Union countries. The secretariat would review all "H" category and all field duty stations in which common system organizations maintained humanitarian or developmental activities to determine their correct classification, and report to the Commission at its seventy-fourth (2012) session. It agreed to maintain the following aspects of the mobility-hardship scheme: the current modalities for payment of mobility allowance for service in "H" and "A" duty stations; the existing relativities between the amounts applicable to the grade-level groupings; the existing relativities for single and dependency rates; the approach to reviewing, every three years, the amounts payable under the scheme; and the five-year ceiling on the payment of the mobility allowance, except in the case of staff members who remained at the same duty station on the request of the Organization or for compelling humanitarian reasons, who would be permitted payment of the full mobility allowance for a maximum of one additional year.

ICSC decided to discontinue hazard pay and introduce danger pay on the basis of the revised criteria, effective 1 January 2012, which was annexed to its report. The revised hardship classification system—to be established in a confidential manner by the ICSC secretariat and Working Group for the Review of Conditions of Life and Work in Field Duty Stations—would also take effect on that day. ICSC granted a 2.5 per cent increase for the hardship allowance, the mobility allowance and the non-removal allowance, to be implemented on 1 January 2012. The revised allowances were annexed to its report. It further decided to adjust the additional non-family hardship element for staff serving in non-family duty stations by the same percentage as the hardship, mobility and non-removal allowances, for implementation on 1 January 2012.

The Commission decided to establish, effective 1 January 2012, the level of danger pay for internationally recruited staff at $1,600 per month; to apply, effective 1 January 2012, the danger pay modalities set out in annex II of its report; to request its secretariat to study the methodology for establishing the level of danger pay for locally recruited staff and report thereon at its seventy-fifth (2012) session; to review the levels of danger pay for internationally recruited staff every three years; and to establish, pending a review and as an interim measure, the level of danger pay at the rate of 25 per cent of the net midpoint of the applicable local General Service salary scale, and to make adjustments as salary scales were revised.

Education grant

In response to a Chief Executives Board for Coordination (CEB) request, ICSC [A/66/30 & Corr.1,2] addressed the issue of the minimum eligibility age requirement for receipt of the education grant. The request was driven by the HarmoS-Konkordat, a Swiss inter-cantonal agreement on the harmonization of compulsory education, which came into effect on 1 August 2009. One of the expected changes was the extension of compulsory education to children four years of age. The change applied to public schools only and did not affect private educational institutions. Accordingly, an amendment to the current minimum eligibility age for receipt of the grant was proposed so as to exceptionally allow common system organizations to lower the minimum eligibility age for receipt of the education grant from five years of age if laws at specific locations mandated an earlier start of formal education.

ICSC recommended to the General Assembly that for the school year in progress on 1 January 2012, the current eligibility requirements for the receipt of the education grant should be amended to set the minimum age at five years of age or older at the beginning of the school year or when the child reached the age of five within three months of the beginning of the school year. Exceptionally, a lower minimum eligibility age could be accepted for those educational institutions which, by virtue of law, required an earlier start of formal education. Common system organizations should be invited to amend the minimum eligibility age requirement accordingly in order to harmonize the grant eligibility criteria.

Performance management

As requested by the General Assembly in resolution 63/251 [YUN 2008, p. 1601], ICSC [A/66/30 & Corr.1,2] reviewed a refined version of the performance management framework, first set out in 1997 [YUN 1997, p. 1465] and updated at its seventy-first (2010) session. The framework emphasized the need for staff to work in a supportive and trusting environment and to have a clear understanding of what was expected of them if they were to be engaged and motivated. The framework outlined certain "enablers" for organizations to consider putting in place if performance management was to be successfully implemented, including a results-oriented culture in which staff understood what they should be doing and were given the opportunity to make decisions about their work; a system of governance under which staff were managed respectfully through fair and transparent processes; a comprehensive communication strategy; and useful, reliable data backed up by appropriate technology. The framework outlined ways of rewarding staff, including proposed guidelines for the use of merit steps. ICSC approved the revised framework, which was annexed to its report.

ICSC decided to submit the revised framework to the Assembly for approval and to consider the use of merit steps at a future session.

Pensionable remuneration

ICSC [A/66/30 & Corr.1,2] reviewed the pensionable remuneration. The review revealed some inconsistencies and presented recommendations in order to bring the common scale of staff assessment closer in line with outside taxes and reflect the effect of the one-to-one interim adjustment procedure on the machine scale; compare the United States and United Nations income replacement ratios; reduce the income inversion phenomenon; improve the income replacement ratios of the United Nations Joint Staff Pension Fund, considering the fact that the comparison had revealed higher-income replacement ratios under the United States scheme; harmonize components of the pensionable remuneration among common system organizations in order to bring them in line with article 54 of the Pension Fund Regulations; reaffirm that double taxation was a misconception; and initiate the review of small pensions.

ICSC requested its secretariat to continue its review of pensionable remuneration in accordance with a two-phase workplan. Phase I would entail the development of a methodology for comparing rates, and Phase II would involve the overall review of pensionable remuneration methodologies. The establishment of a working group would be considered to conduct the review and make recommendations on the methodologies used in determining the pensionable remuneration scales of the Professional and General Service categories. Initial proposals would be submitted to the Commission in 2012. Upon review by the Commission, the issue would be reviewed again by the Pension Board in 2012 and finalized by the Commission in 2013.

With respect to the non-pensionable component, the Commission decided that no changes would be presently introduced; however, the issue would be included in the overall review of pensionable remuneration. Regarding the service differential, the Commission took note of the decision of the Chief Executive Officer of the Pension Fund to request that the Rome-based organizations stop the practice of making service differential pensionable, pending a review of that issue during the next comprehensive salary survey in Rome in 2012.

Conditions of service of staff in the Professional and higher categories

Post adjustment

ICSC [A/66/30 & Corr.1,2] reviewed the operation of the post adjustment classification system, designed to measure cost-of-living through periodic place-to-place surveys of all duty stations. On the results of the surveys, it considered the recommendations of the Advisory Committee on Post Adjustment Questions from its thirty-third session, in January. The estimated financial implications, based on the implementation of the survey results effective 1 April 2011, totalled approximately $7.5 million per year.

ICSC approved the results of the 2010 place-to-place surveys for Geneva, London, Madrid, Montreal, Paris, Rome, Vienna and Washington, D.C., and decided that they should be taken into account in determining their respective post adjustment classification with effect from 1 April. Additional place-to-place surveys should be conducted for Bulgaria, Hungary, Poland and Romania in the current round of surveys.

Base/floor salary scale and review of staff assessment rates

The concept of the base/floor salary scale was introduced by the General Assembly in resolution 44/198 [YUN 1989, p. 886] and took effect on 1 July 1990. The scale was set by reference to the General Schedule salary scale of the comparator civil service in Washington, D.C. Periodic adjustments were made on the basis of a comparison of net base salaries of UN officials at the midpoint of the scale (P-4, step VI, at the dependency rate) with the corresponding salaries of their counterparts in the United States federal civil service.

ICSC [A/66/30 & Corr.1,2] was informed that, as a result of a pay freeze, the gross levels of the comparator's General Schedule would not be adjusted between 1 January 2011 and 31 December 2012. Despite the pay freeze, the change in the federal tax rates resulted in an increase of the reference comparator pay level in net terms, which amounted to 0.13 per cent as compared with the 2010 level.

ICSC recommended for approval, with effect from 1 January 2012, the revised base/floor salary scale for the Professional and higher categories, adjusted by 0.13 per cent by increasing the base salary and commensurately reducing post adjustment multiplier points; and the revised rates of staff assessment used in conjunction with gross base salaries for the Professional and higher categories of staff. The revised rates would be calculated and added to the net dependency rates of salaries to determine the corresponding gross salary levels. The staff assessment amounts for single staff would be computed by subtracting the net single rate from the gross salary at each grade and step in the salary scale. The revised salary scale and staff assessment rates were annexed to the Commission's report. ICSC also decided that the staff assessment rates used in conjunction with gross salaries should be reviewed every three years and revised as appropriate.

Evolution of the net remuneration margin

ICSC [A/66/30 & Corr.1,2] continued to review the relationship between the net remuneration of UN staff in the Professional and higher categories in New York (grades P-1 to D-2) and that of the United States federal civil service employees in comparable positions in Washington, D.C., referred to as "the margin". The Commission was informed that the margin for the calendar year 2011 was estimated at 114.2, with its five-year average (2007–2011) standing at 114.0.

Icsc drew the Assembly's attention to the fact that the average margin level for the past five years (2007–2011), estimated at 114.0, was below the desirable midpoint of 115. It requested its Chair to update the margin estimate on the basis of the actual post adjustment multiplier, as necessary.

Based on updated information that the actual post adjustment multiplier for New York for the period from August to December 2011 would be 65.7 (as opposed to 61.3 for January through July 2011), the Chair reported that the margin between the net remuneration of United Nations staff in New York and that of the United States federal civil service in Washington, D.C., for the period covering 2011, stood at 114.9. He also noted that the average margin level for the past five years (2007–2011) amounted to 114.1. Details of the updated comparison of average net remuneration, by equivalent grades, were annexed to the Commission's report.

Identification of the highest paid national civil service

Icsc [A/66/30 & Corr.1,2] conducted compensation comparisons under the Noblemaire principle, intended to determine the highest-paid national civil service, which could potentially replace the current comparator of the UN common system. Ten national civil services (Australia, Belgium, Canada, France, Germany, Netherlands, Norway, Republic of Korea, Spain, United Kingdom) were selected for the study. Icsc noted the abbreviated scope of the initial phase of the Noblemaire study. It pointed out that the use of only cash elements of compensation limited the number of grades and jobs covered by the comparisons, and simple averages and proxy indicators used to adjust the remuneration levels by differences in cost of living could have impacted the results. Some reservations were expressed as to the accuracy of some of the job matches established for the salary comparisons. Icsc further acknowledged the economic background of the study, noting that national civil services were reacting in different ways to the ongoing financial crisis. It therefore decided that it would not be opportune to proceed with phase II of the Noblemaire study at that time, and that because the comparison result showed that the current comparator paid the highest level of cash compensation and the percentage differences with other civil services seemed too large to be offset by other compensation elements, the current comparator would be retained. Icsc would carry out another study to determine the highest-paid national civil service no later than the next Noblemaire study, scheduled for 2016.

Diversity in UN common system

As requested by the General Assembly in resolution 64/231 [YUN 2009, p. 1455], Icsc had before it an examination of diversity policies in common system organizations. It was informed that organizations had implemented policies for creating diversified workforces. Those policies focused on gender parity, employment of persons with disabilities, HIV/AIDS awareness in the workplace and geographical balance. The secretariat reported in some detail on geographical balance in the larger organizations of the common system, whose governing bodies had shown increasing interest in the progress being made in terms of geographical balance.

Icsc [A/66/30 & Corr.1,2] decided to inform the Assembly of the status of geographical distribution in the common system organizations and of actions being taken by them and their governing bodies to achieve geographical balance; to study recruitment policies with a view to recommending to organizations measures that would be more favourable to diversity; and to revert to the diversity discussion at a later date.

Conditions of service of General Service and other locally recruited categories

General service salary survey methodologies

Icsc [A/66/30 & Corr.1,2] reviewed the two proposed methodologies for conducting surveys of best prevailing conditions for employment at headquarters and non-headquarters duty stations, referred to as "methodology I" and "methodology II", respectively. The review looked at the inclusion of national civil service employers as a requirement under the headquarters methodology; the application of the methodologies to similarly situated labour markets; the periodicity of surveys; the review and approval of surveys; the non-pensionable component; parastatal employers; and salary scales in multiple duty stations within a single country.

Among the Committee's decisions on these topics was that the ministry of foreign affairs, or its equivalent, should be used in the surveys as the employer representing the respective national civil service. In anticipation of situations where that was not possible, it agreed on contingency procedures to identify alternative civil service employers. On the periodicity of surveys, excluding exceptional circumstances, surveys under methodology I would be every 8 to 10 years, while surveys under methodology II would be every five years. Regarding in-country salary scales, the Committee decided that the normal practice should be to apply a single salary scale to all duty stations within a single country, but that the responsible agency might decide on separate salary scales where justified. Decisions also pertained to the categorization of duty stations under the two survey methodologies, such as that methodology I should include, in addition to the eight headquarters duty stations, Bonn, Brussels, Copenhagen, The Hague, Tokyo and Washington, D.C.

ICSC reviewed the option to use vendor-provided salary movement data to complete the surveys if, owing to participation problems, the normal minimum number of employers could not be surveyed. It decided that the use of salary movement data from two vendors, averaged and adjusted for the gross to net relationship based on the tax regulations at the duty station, would be permitted under circumstances that differed according to the type of survey methodology being applied, but generally occurred when the normal minimum required number of employers could not be surveyed. The results of the analysis of the data from the surveyed employers would be weighted by the number of employers surveyed, and the salary movement data weighted by the number of employers short of the normal required minimum to determine the final adjustment to be applied to the salary scales.

ICSC reviewed further issues common to both methodologies, including benchmark jobs, quantification of minor in-kind benefits, and quantification of meal and motor vehicle benefits; issues pertaining to methodologies I and II separately; and the schedule for the next round of surveys under methodology I. It approved the revised methodologies I and II, effective 1 January 2012, and approved the schedule for the next round of surveys under methodology I.

Conditions of service in the field

ICSC [A/66/30 & Corr.1,2] decided to promulgate, effective 1 January 2012, a revised set of criteria for the granting of rest and recuperation travel, and the corresponding frequencies of travel, as shown in a framework annexed to its report. It recommended to the General Assembly that the period of authorized absence on rest and recuperation, as stipulated in the approved framework, be amended from five consecutive working days to five consecutive calendar days, plus approved travel time. ICSC approved the list of unified special operations living allowance rates for non-family duty stations, also annexed to its report, which would take effect on 1 January 2012 for staff assigned to a new administrative place of assignment between 1 January and 30 June 2012. For existing staff, the new unified rates would become effective 1 July 2012. It delegated the decision on the location-specific special operations living allowance amounts for new non-family duty stations and their promulgation to its Chair during the transitional period, until 30 June 2016. It also requested organizations to consult the Chair on all policy issues related to the rates.

ICSC delegated to its Chair the authority to decide when to declare a duty station non-family, after consultation with its Working Group for the Review of Conditions of Life and Work in Field Duty Stations. It also decided that the Chair might designate a duty station as a non-family duty station for the purposes of the additional hardship allowance for service in non-family duty stations. That would apply to those duty stations where the United Nations Department of Safety and Security decided that for reasons of safety and security all eligible dependents were restricted from being present at the duty station for a period of six months or longer. The additional hardship allowance was payable to internationally recruited staff assigned to non-family duty stations.

GENERAL ASSEMBLY ACTION

On 24 December [meeting 93], the General Assembly, on the recommendation of the Fifth Committee [A/66/644], adopted **resolution 66/235 A** without vote [agenda item 141].

United Nations common system: report of the International Civil Service Commission

The General Assembly,

Recalling its resolutions 44/198 of 21 December 1989, 51/216 of 18 December 1996, 52/216 of 22 December 1997, 53/209 of 18 December 1998, 55/223 of 23 December 2000, 56/244 of 24 December 2001, 57/285 of 20 December 2002, 58/251 of 23 December 2003, 59/268 of 23 December 2004, 60/248 of 23 December 2005, 61/239 of 22 December 2006, 62/227 of 22 December 2007, 63/251 of 24 December 2008, 64/231 of 22 December 2009 and 65/248 of 24 December 2010,

Having considered the report of the International Civil Service Commission for 2011,

Reaffirming its commitment to a single, unified United Nations common system as the cornerstone for the regulation and coordination of the conditions of service of the common system,

Reiterating the importance of maintaining and strengthening the salaries, allowances and personnel standards of the organizations of the United Nations common system,

Convinced that the United Nations common system constitutes the best instrument through which to secure staff with the highest standards of efficiency, competence and integrity for the international civil service, as stipulated in the Charter of the United Nations,

1. *Takes note with appreciation* of the work of the International Civil Service Commission;
2. *Takes note* of the report of the Commission for 2011;
3. *Encourages* the Commission to continue to coordinate and regulate the conditions of service of staff of the organizations of the United Nations common system, bearing in mind the limitations imposed by Member States on their national civil services;
4. *Reaffirms* the role of the General Assembly in approving conditions of service and entitlements for all staff serving in the organizations of the United Nations common

system, bearing in mind articles 10 and 11 of the statute of the Commission;

5. *Recalls* articles 10 and 11 of the statute of the Commission, and reaffirms the central role of the Commission in regulating and coordinating conditions of service and entitlements for all staff serving in the organizations of the United Nations common system;

A. Conditions of service applicable to both categories of staff

1. Mobility and hardship scheme

1. *Recognizes* the hardship conditions under which staff members are often required to perform their official duties and the disruption that operationally required mobility may impose on staff;

2. *Endorses* the decisions of the Commission relating to the mobility and hardship scheme as contained in paragraph 38 of its report;

3. *Reaffirms* the importance of mobility as a means of developing a more versatile, multi-skilled and experienced international civil service that is capable of fulfilling complex mandates, and requests the Commission to provide an overview of the different existing mobility schemes in the organizations of the United Nations common system;

4. *Takes note* of the decisions of the Commission contained in paragraph 47 of its report and annex III thereto, and decides, with effect from 1 January 2012, that a 2.5 per cent increase shall be granted for the hardship, mobility and non-removal allowances, while the additional non-family hardship elements for staff serving in non-family duty stations shall be adjusted by the same percentage;

5. *Also takes note* of the conclusions of the Commission with respect to the establishment of danger pay as contained in paragraph 59 of its report;

6. *Further takes note* of paragraph 56 of the report of the Commission regarding the United Nations system-wide financial implications of the establishment of danger pay;

2. Performance management

Recalling its resolutions 51/216 and 63/251,

Recognizing the differing organizational strategies and cultures prevailing in the United Nations common system, and considering that a flexible approach to performance management would be desirable,

1. *Welcomes with appreciation* the work of the Commission with regard to the performance management framework, which would assist organizations of the United Nations common system in securing and retaining staff of the highest standard of efficiency, competency and integrity as stipulated in the Charter;

2. *Notes* that the Commission will continue its work on rewards and incentives, and requests it to take the lead in analysing new approaches in human resources management;

3. *Approves* the performance management framework contained in annex IV to the report of the Commission, which should be taken into account by the organizations of the United Nations common system in furthering their policies on this matter, and requests the Commission to report to the General Assembly at its sixty-eighth session on the implementation by the organizations of measures taken in response to the recommendations of the Commission;

4. *Recalls* paragraph 90 of the report of the Commission, notes the intention of the Commission to consider the use of merit steps, and requests the Commission to report on its conclusion to the General Assembly at its sixty-seventh session;

3. Education grant methodology

1. *Endorses*, with effect from the school year in progress on 1 January 2012, the amendment to the current eligibility requirements for the receipt of the education grant, as contained in paragraph 96 (*a*) of the report of the Commission;

2. *Invites* the governing bodies of the organizations of the United Nations common system to harmonize the education grant eligibility criteria with respect to the minimum age, as specified in paragraph 96 (*a*) of the report of the Commission;

B. Conditions of service of staff in the Professional and higher categories

1. Post adjustment matters

Recalls paragraphs 103 and 123 of the report of the Commission and paragraph 2 of section I.A of its resolution 51/216, and requests the Commission to explore the feasibility and suitability of possible measures to reflect in the administration of the post adjustment system the pay freeze of the comparator civil service; to determine whether the implementation of such measures falls under its authority; to exercise such authority, as appropriate; and to report thereon to the General Assembly at its sixty-seventh session;

2. Base/floor salary scale

Recalling its resolution 44/198, by which it established a floor net salary level for staff in the Professional and higher categories by reference to the corresponding base net salary levels of officials in comparable positions serving at the base city of the comparator civil service (the United States federal civil service),

1. *Approves*, with effect from 1 January 2012, as recommended by the Commission in paragraph 120 (*a*) of its report, the revised base/floor salary scale of gross and net salaries for staff in the Professional and higher categories, as contained in annex V.A to the report;

2. *Also approves*, with effect from 1 January 2012, as recommended by the Commission in paragraph 120 (*b*) of its report, the revised rates of staff assessment used in conjunction with gross base salaries for the Professional and higher categories of staff, as contained in annex V.B to the report;

3. *Endorses* the decision of the Commission, stated in paragraph 121 of its report, to review the staff assessment rates used in conjunction with gross salaries every three years, for revision as appropriate;

3. Evolution of the margin

Recalling section I.B of its resolution 51/216 and the standing mandate from the General Assembly, in which the Commission is requested to continue its review of the relationship between the net remuneration of United Nations staff in the Professional and higher categories in New York and that of the comparator civil service (the United States federal civil service) employees in comparable positions in Washington, D.C. (referred to as "the margin"),

1. *Reaffirms* that the range of 110 to 120 for the margin between the net remuneration of officials in the Professional and higher categories of the United Nations in New York and officials in comparable positions in the comparator civil service should continue to apply, on the understanding that the margin would be maintained at a level around the desirable midpoint of 115 over a period of time;

2. *Notes* that the margin between net remuneration of the United Nations staff in grades P-1 to D-2 in New York and that of officials in comparable positions in the United States federal civil service in Washington, D.C., for the period from 1 January to 31 December 2011 is estimated at 114.9 and that the average margin level for the past five years (2007–2011) stands at 114.1;

4. Identification of the highest paid national civil service

Takes note of the decision of the Commission contained in paragraph 106 of its report to terminate its current Noblemaire study to identify the highest paid national civil service and to undertake the next study in 2016;

5. Diversity in the United Nations common system

1. *Notes* the status of geographical distribution in the organizations of the United Nations common system and actions being taken by the organizations to achieve equitable geographical balance;

2. *Endorses* the decision of the Commission to conduct studies on recruitment policies and to revert to discussing the issue with recommended measures that would be more favourable to diversity;

3. *Requests* the Commission, when preparing proposals on measures for diversity in the United Nations common system, to bear in mind that the paramount consideration in the employment of staff is professional qualifications, which are key to the capacities of the organizations to deliver on their mandates;

C. Conditions of service in the field

1. Harmonization of the conditions of service of staff of the organizations of the United Nations common system serving in non-family duty stations

1. *Recalls* section C of its resolution 65/248, and requests the Commission, in the context of its annual report, to report to the General Assembly on the implementation of its decisions regarding the harmonization of the conditions of service in non-family duty stations during the transition period;

2. *Requests* the Commission and the Secretary-General, as Chair of the United Nations System Chief Executives Board for Coordination, to give due regard to the process of timely implementation of its decisions on the harmonization of the conditions of service of staff of the organizations of the United Nations common system serving in non-family duty stations;

2. Rest and recuperation framework

Recalling paragraph 19 of section C of its resolution 65/248, requesting the Commission to regulate the rest and recuperation framework,

Approves, with effect from 1 January 2012, the revised set of criteria for the granting of rest and recuperation travel and the corresponding frequencies of travel as contained in paragraph 238 and annex VIII of the report of the Commission.

On the same date, the Assembly decided that the item on the United Nations common system would remain for consideration during its resumed sixty-sixth (2012) session (**decision 66/557**).

Other remuneration issues

Conditions of service and compensation for non-Secretariat officials

Compensation of members of ICSC and Chair of ACABQ

ACABQ report. In March [A/65/767], ACABQ recommended that the General Assembly approve the recommendations contained in the Secretary-General's 2010 report [YUN 2010, p. 1473] in respect of the annual compensation of the Chair and Vice-Chair of ICSC and the Chair of ACABQ. It also recommended that the Assembly consider establishing an automatic mechanism for adjusting the compensation of those three officials, which would provide a clear guideline for compensation relativity.

General Assembly action. The General Assembly, in section III of **resolution 65/268** of 4 April (see p. 1378), decided to set the annual net compensation of the Chairs of ICSC and ACABQ at $224,833, and that of the Vice-chair of ICSC at $214,833, with retroactive effect from 1 January 2011. Effective 1 January 2012, the annual compensation of the three officials should be subject to a cost-of-living adjustment equivalent to the annual change in the midpoint net base salary of the most senior officials in the Secretariat, and their other conditions of service would be reviewed every four years.

Review of pension schemes for international judges

Pursuant to resolution 65/258 [YUN 2010, p. 1472], the Secretary-General reviewed [A/66/617] the pension schemes for members of the International Court of Justice (ICJ) and judges of the International Tribunal for the Former Yugoslavia (ICTY) and International Criminal Tribunal for Rwanda (ICTR). The study included surveys on the benefits of judges throughout the world; the development of alternative retirement benefit designs; determination of the various, but related actuarial costs; and an actuarial costing of existing liabilities for current judges. It analysed the judges' current retirement benefits and presented options for defined-benefit and defined-contribution pension schemes, as well as a proposal for a mechanism that could be used to determine retirement pension benefit rights accrued prior to serving in the Court or the two Tribunals. The Secretary-General presented recommendations and financial implications and noted that the next review of the conditions of service and compensation for ICJ members and ICTY/ICTR judges would take place at the sixty-eighth (2013) session of the General Assembly.

Staff safety and security

In response to General Assembly resolution 65/132 [YUN 2010, p. 1474], the Secretary-General submitted a September report [A/66/345] on the safety and security of UN and associated personnel. The UN security management system had responsibility for over 150,000 personnel in more than 170 countries. In 2010, 24 UN personnel lost their lives in security incidents, compared to 45 in 2009. Five lost their lives as a result of violence and 19 others were killed in safety-related incidents. A total of 232 personnel were injured (compared to 190 in 2009), 68 as the result of violence and 164 in safety-related incidents. Among the 19 personnel killed and 164 injured in safety-related incidents, 16 died and 147 were injured because of road traffic accidents. Of all the UN personnel affected by security incidents, 99 per cent were based in the field. Internationally recruited personnel continued to be disproportionately more affected by security incidents than locally recruited personnel. Female personnel were disproportionately more affected by robbery, crimes at residences, aggravated assault, sexual assault and harassment than their male counterparts. As for location, UN personnel were most affected by security incidents in Afghanistan, the Darfur region of the Sudan and Somalia. In 2010, the earthquake in Haiti [YUN 2010, p. 907] killed 102 UN staff members. That catastrophe represented the first instance of mass casualties affecting the United Nations due to a natural disaster.

Twelve UN personnel were abducted in eight countries in 2010. Of the 12 abductions, nine were financially motivated. One protracted hostage situation lasted for three months, while all the others ended within hours or days. Some 239 personnel were affected by robberies, 35 by break-ins to their residences, while 64 were subjected to aggravated assault, and 227 to acts of intimidation and harassment. UN personnel detained or arrested stood at 211, 89 per cent of whom were locally recruited. Of all detentions, 24 per cent (50 cases) were considered to be job-related, in that the personnel were detained in the course of, or in connection with, their official duties. Most of those cases were resolved and the detained personnel released within hours, days or weeks; in only three cases was the United Nations denied access to a detainee and given no reasons for the arrest.

To advance the strategic vision of the UN security management system, the security phase system was abolished on 1 January 2011, and in line with the security risk management approach, the security level system was introduced, which enabled security managers to adopt a wider range of measures to address risks and support UN programmes and activities. To support the new approach, the Department of Safety and Security developed new policies on evacuation, relocation and alternate work modalities. A new policy on security clearances and a computer-based system were developed to facilitate the process of submitting and obtaining security clearances. In response to concerns about the impact of road safety hazards on UN personnel and others, the Department drafted a road safety policy.

The Department re-examined the recommendations of the Independent Panel on Safety and Security of United Nations Personnel and Premises Worldwide, and conducted pilot tests of three initiatives to strengthen host country collaboration on security issues, focusing on host country agreements, liaison committees and model security agreements. The pilot tests showed that those initiatives were not feasible and would not adequately address the root issues regarding host country collaboration. The Inter-Agency Security Management Network agreed to explore a more holistic approach to strengthening collaboration with host country authorities.

GENERAL ASSEMBLY ACTION

On 15 December [meeting 86], the General Assembly adopted **resolution 66/117** [draft: A/66/L.26 & Add.1] without vote [agenda item 70].

Safety and security of humanitarian personnel and protection of United Nations personnel

The General Assembly,

Reaffirming its resolution 46/182 of 19 December 1991 on the strengthening of the coordination of humanitarian emergency assistance of the United Nations,

Recalling all relevant resolutions on safety and security of humanitarian personnel and protection of United Nations personnel, including its resolution 65/132 of 15 December 2010, as well as Security Council resolution 1502(2003) of 26 August 2003 and relevant statements by the President of the Council,

Recalling also all Security Council resolutions and presidential statements and reports of the Secretary-General to the Council on the protection of civilians in armed conflict,

Recalling further all relevant provisions of international law, including international humanitarian law and human rights law, as well as all relevant treaties,

Reaffirming the need to promote and ensure respect for the principles and rules of international law, including international humanitarian law,

Reaffirming also the principles of neutrality, humanity, impartiality and independence for the provision of humanitarian assistance,

Recalling that primary responsibility under international law for the security and protection of humanitarian personnel and United Nations and associated personnel lies with the Government hosting a United Nations operation conducted under the Charter of the United Nations or its agreements with relevant organizations,

Expressing its appreciation to those Governments which respect the internationally agreed principles on the protection of humanitarian and United Nations personnel, while expressing concern over the lack of respect for these principles in some areas,

Urging all parties involved in armed conflicts, in compliance with international humanitarian law, in particular their obligations under the Geneva Conventions of 12 August 1949 and the obligations applicable to them under the Additional Protocols thereto of 8 June 1977, to ensure the security and protection of all humanitarian personnel and United Nations and associated personnel,

Welcoming the fact that the number of States parties to the Convention on the Safety of United Nations and Associated Personnel, which entered into force on 15 January 1999, has continued to rise, the number now having reached eighty-nine, mindful of the need to promote the universality of the Convention, and welcoming the entry into force on 19 August 2010 of the Optional Protocol to the Convention on the Safety of United Nations and Associated Personnel, which expands the scope of legal protection under the Convention,

Deeply concerned by the dangers and security risks faced by humanitarian personnel and United Nations and associated personnel at the field level, as they operate in increasingly complex contexts, as well as the continuous erosion, in many cases, of respect for the principles and rules of international law, in particular international humanitarian law,

Stressing the importance of fully respecting the obligations relating to the use of vehicles and premises of humanitarian personnel and United Nations and associated personnel as defined by relevant international instruments, as well as the obligations relating to distinctive emblems recognized in the Geneva Conventions,

Commending the courage and commitment of those who take part in humanitarian operations, often at great personal risk, especially locally recruited staff,

Noting that about one per cent of United Nations system personnel have been affected by significant security incidents, and noting the substantial reduction in the number of United Nations personnel killed or injured by violence in 2010, while noting with concern the increase in the number of United Nations personnel killed or injured by violence in the first half of 2011,

Expressing profound regret at the deaths of and violent acts against international and national humanitarian personnel and United Nations and associated personnel involved in the provision of humanitarian assistance, and strongly deploring the casualties among such personnel in complex humanitarian emergencies, in particular in armed conflicts and in post-conflict situations,

Expressing deep concern at the deep and long-lasting impacts of attacks and threats against humanitarian personnel and United Nations and associated personnel,

Strongly condemning acts of murder and other forms of violence, rape and sexual assault and all forms of violence committed in particular against women and children, and intimidation, armed robbery, abduction, hostage-taking, kidnapping, harassment and illegal arrest and detention to which those participating in humanitarian operations are exposed, as well as attacks on humanitarian convoys and acts of destruction and looting of property,

Expressing deep concern that the occurrence of attacks and threats against humanitarian personnel and United Nations and associated personnel is a factor that increasingly restricts the provision of assistance and protection to populations in need,

Affirming the need for States to ensure that perpetrators of attacks committed on their territory against humanitarian personnel and United Nations and associated personnel do not operate with impunity, and that the perpetrators of such acts are brought to justice, as provided for by national laws and obligations under international law,

Recalling the inclusion of attacks intentionally directed against personnel involved in a humanitarian assistance or peacekeeping mission in accordance with the Charter as a war crime in the Rome Statute of the International Criminal Court, and noting the role that the Court can play in appropriate cases in bringing to justice those responsible for serious violations of international humanitarian law,

Reaffirming the need to ensure adequate levels of safety and security for United Nations personnel and associated humanitarian personnel, including locally recruited staff, which constitutes an underlying duty of the Organization, and mindful of the need to promote and enhance security consciousness within the organizational culture of the United Nations and a culture of accountability at all levels, as well as to continue to promote awareness of and sensitivity to national and local cultures and laws,

Gravely concerned at the high number of accidents and resulting casualties among United Nations and associated personnel, and conscious of the importance of road safety in ensuring the continuity of United Nations humanitarian operations and preventing casualties among civilians and United Nations and associated personnel, and in this regard regretting the loss of civilian life as a result of such incidents,

Noting the importance of reinforcing close collaboration between the United Nations and the host country on contingency planning, information exchange and risk assessment in the context of good mutual cooperation on issues relating to the security of United Nations and associated personnel,

1. *Welcomes* the report of the Secretary-General on safety and security of United Nations and associated personnel;

2. *Urges* all States to make every effort to ensure the full and effective implementation of the relevant principles and rules of international law, including international humanitarian law, human rights law and refugee law related to the safety and security of humanitarian personnel and United Nations personnel;

3. *Strongly urges* all States to take the necessary measures to ensure the safety and security of humanitarian personnel and United Nations and associated personnel and to respect and ensure respect for the inviolability of United Nations premises, which are essential to the continuation and successful implementation of United Nations operations;

4. *Calls upon* all Governments and parties in complex humanitarian emergencies, in particular in armed conflicts and in post-conflict situations, in countries in which humanitarian personnel are operating, in conformity with the relevant provisions of international law and national laws, to cooperate fully with the United Nations and other humanitarian agencies and organizations and to ensure the safe and unhindered access of humanitarian personnel and delivery of supplies and equipment, in order to allow those personnel to perform efficiently their task of assisting the

affected civilian population, including refugees and internally displaced persons;

5. *Calls upon* all States to consider becoming parties to and to respect fully their obligations under the relevant international instruments;

6. *Also calls upon* all States to consider becoming parties to the Rome Statute of the International Criminal Court;

7. *Further calls upon* all States to consider becoming parties to the Optional Protocol to the Convention on the Safety of United Nations and Associated Personnel, and urges States parties to put in place appropriate national legislation, as necessary, to enable its effective implementation;

8. *Calls upon* all States, all parties involved in armed conflict and all humanitarian actors to respect the principles of neutrality, humanity, impartiality and independence for the provision of humanitarian assistance;

9. *Expresses deep concern* over the continuing threats and deliberate targeting of and the disturbing trend of politically or criminally motivated attacks against the safety and security of humanitarian personnel and United Nations and associated personnel;

10. *Welcomes* the contribution of female United Nations and associated personnel in United Nations humanitarian operations, expresses concern that in some cases these personnel are relatively more exposed to certain forms of crime and acts of intimidation and harassment, and strongly urges the United Nations system and Member States to take appropriate action for their safety and security;

11. *Strongly condemns* all threats and acts of violence against humanitarian personnel and United Nations and associated personnel, reaffirms the need to hold accountable those responsible for such acts, strongly urges all States to take stronger action to ensure that any such acts committed on their territory are investigated fully and to ensure that the perpetrators of such acts are brought to justice in accordance with national laws and obligations under international law, and urges States to end impunity for such acts;

12. *Calls upon* all States to comply fully with their obligations under international humanitarian law, including as provided by the Geneva Convention relative to the Protection of Civilian Persons in Time of War of 12 August 1949, in order to respect and protect civilians, including humanitarian personnel, in territories subject to their jurisdiction;

13. *Also calls upon* all States to provide adequate and prompt information in the event of the arrest or detention of humanitarian personnel or United Nations and associated personnel, so as to afford them the necessary medical assistance and to allow independent medical teams to visit and examine the health of those detained, and urges them to take the necessary measures to ensure the speedy release of those who have been arrested or detained in violation of the relevant conventions referred to in the present resolution and applicable international humanitarian law;

14. *Calls upon* all other parties involved in armed conflict to refrain from abducting, taking hostage or kidnapping humanitarian personnel or United Nations and associated personnel or detaining them in violation of the relevant conventions referred to in the present resolution and applicable international humanitarian law, and speedily to release, without harm or requirement of concession, any abductee or detainee;

15. *Requests* the Secretary-General to take the necessary measures to promote full respect for the human rights, privileges and immunities of United Nations and other personnel carrying out activities in fulfilment of the mandate of a United Nations operation, and also requests the Secretary-General to seek the inclusion, in negotiations of headquarters and other mission agreements concerning United Nations and associated personnel, of the applicable conditions contained in the Convention on the Privileges and Immunities of the United Nations, the Convention on the Privileges and Immunities of the Specialized Agencies and the Convention on the Safety of United Nations and Associated Personnel;

16. *Recommends* that the Secretary-General continue to seek the inclusion of, and that host countries include, key provisions of the Convention on the Safety of United Nations and Associated Personnel, among others, those regarding the prevention of attacks against members of the operation, the establishment of such attacks as crimes punishable by law and the prosecution or extradition of offenders, in future as well as, if necessary, in existing status-of-forces, status-of-mission, host country and other related agreements negotiated between the United Nations and those countries, mindful of the importance of the timely conclusion of such agreements, and encourages further efforts in this regard;

17. *Reaffirms* the obligation of all humanitarian personnel and United Nations and associated personnel to respect and, where required, observe the national laws of the country in which they are operating, in accordance with international law and the Charter of the United Nations;

18. *Stresses* the importance of ensuring that humanitarian personnel and United Nations and associated personnel are aware of and sensitive to national and local customs and traditions in their countries of assignment and communicate clearly their purpose and objectives to local populations;

19. *Requests* the Secretary-General to continue to take the necessary measures to ensure that United Nations and other personnel carrying out activities in fulfilment of the mandate of a United Nations operation are properly informed about and operate in conformity with the minimum operating security standards and relevant codes of conduct and are properly informed about the conditions under which they are called upon to operate and the standards that they are required to meet, including those contained in relevant national laws and international law, and that adequate training in security, human rights law and international humanitarian law is provided so as to enhance their security and effectiveness in accomplishing their functions, and reaffirms the necessity for all other humanitarian organizations to provide their personnel with similar support;

20. *Also requests* the Secretary-General to continue, in coordination with Member States, to take the necessary measures to ensure that all United Nations premises and assets, including staff residences, are compliant with the United Nations minimum operating security standards and other relevant United Nations security standards;

21. *Welcomes* the ongoing efforts of the Secretary-General to ensure that all United Nations personnel receive adequate safety and security training, stresses the need to continue to improve training so as to enhance cultural awareness and knowledge of relevant law, including international humanitarian law, prior to their deployment to the field, and reaffirms the necessity for all other humanitarian organizations to provide their personnel with similar support;

22. *Also welcomes* the efforts of the Secretary-General to provide counselling and support services to United Nations personnel affected by safety and security incidents, and emphasizes the importance of making available stress management, mental health and related services for United Nations personnel throughout the system, and encourages all humanitarian organizations to provide their personnel with similar support;

23. *Notes with appreciation* the ongoing measures taken by the Secretary-General and the United Nations system to enhance road safety, including through improved training and initiatives to promote road safety so as to reduce incidents caused by road hazards, and requests the Secretary-General to continue the collection and analysis of data and to report on road incidents, including civilian casualties resulting from road accidents;

24. *Welcomes* the progress made towards further enhancing the security management system of the United Nations and supports the focus on enabling the United Nations system to deliver its mandates, programmes and activities by effectively managing the risks to which personnel are exposed, and encourages the United Nations and other relevant humanitarian actors to include as part of their risk-management strategy the building of good relations and trust with national and local governments and the promotion of acceptance by local communities and all relevant actors;

25. *Encourages* the Secretary-General to continue developing enabling procedures that facilitate the deployment of suitably qualified United Nations security personnel and that strengthen the ability of the United Nations to deploy its personnel;

26. *Requests* the Secretary-General, inter alia through the Inter-Agency Security Management Network, to continue the increased cooperation and collaboration among United Nations departments, organizations, funds and programmes and affiliated international organizations, including between their headquarters and field offices, in the planning and implementation of measures aimed at improving staff security, training and awareness, and calls upon all relevant United Nations departments, organizations, funds and programmes and affiliated international organizations to support those efforts;

27. *Calls upon* all relevant actors to make every effort to support in their public statements a favourable environment for the safety and security of humanitarian personnel and United Nations and associated personnel;

28. *Emphasizes* the need to pay particular attention to the safety and security of locally recruited humanitarian personnel, who are particularly vulnerable to attacks and who account for the majority of casualties, including in cases of kidnapping, harassment, banditry and intimidation, requests the Secretary-General to keep under review the relevant United Nations safety and security policy, operational and administrative arrangements related to locally recruited personnel, and calls upon the United Nations and humanitarian organizations to ensure that their personnel are adequately consulted on, informed about and trained in the relevant security measures, plans and initiatives of their respective organizations, which should be in line with applicable national laws and international law;

29. *Notes with appreciation* the progress reported in implementing the recommendations of the Independent Panel on Safety and Security of United Nations Personnel and Premises Worldwide, including the revision of the accountability framework, requests the continued implementation of the recommendations, and looks forward to the report of the Secretary-General on safety and security, including on refinements and innovations, as appropriate, for the development of the security management system, to be submitted to the General Assembly at its sixty-seventh session;

30. *Requests* the Department of Safety and Security of the Secretariat to further strengthen the analysis of threats and to continue to improve and implement an effective, modern and flexible information management capacity in support of analytical and operational requirements, including the ongoing system-wide analysis of best practices and information on the range and scope of safety and security incidents involving humanitarian personnel and United Nations and associated personnel, including attacks against them, in order to make objective and evidence-based decisions on how to reduce the risks arising in the context of United Nations related operations;

31. *Welcomes* the work of the Secretary-General in enhancing security collaboration with host Governments, including efforts to support United Nations designated officials with regard to collaboration with host Government authorities on staff safety and security;

32. *Stresses* that the effective functioning at the country level of security operations requires a unified capacity for policy, standards, coordination, communication, compliance and threat and risk assessment, and notes the benefits thereof to United Nations and associated personnel, including those achieved by the Department of Safety and Security since its establishment;

33. *Recognizes* the steps taken by the Secretary-General thus far, as well as the need for continued efforts to enhance coordination and cooperation, at both the headquarters and the field levels, between the United Nations and other humanitarian and non-governmental organizations on matters relating to the safety and security of humanitarian personnel and United Nations and associated personnel, with a view to addressing mutual security concerns in the field, taking into account relevant national and local initiatives in this regard, inter alia, those derived from the "Saving Lives Together" framework, encourages collaborative initiatives to address security training needs, invites Member States to consider increasing support to those initiatives, and requests the Secretary-General to report on steps taken in this regard;

34. *Underlines* the urgent need to allocate adequate and predictable resources to the safety and security of United Nations personnel, through regular and extrabudgetary resources, including through the consolidated appeals process, and encourages all States to contribute to the Trust Fund for Security of Staff Members of the United Nations System, inter alia, with a view to reinforcing the efforts of the Department of Safety and Security to meet its mandate and responsibilities to enable the safe delivery of programmes;

35. *Also underlines* the need for better coordination between the United Nations and host Governments, in accordance with the relevant provisions of international law and national laws, on the use and deployment of essential equipment required to provide for the safety and security of

United Nations personnel and associated personnel working in the delivery of humanitarian assistance by United Nations organizations;

36. *Recalls* the essential role of telecommunications resources in facilitating the safety of humanitarian personnel and United Nations and associated personnel, calls upon States to consider acceding to or ratifying the Tampere Convention on the Provision of Telecommunication Resources for Disaster Mitigation and Relief Operations of 18 June 1998, which entered into force on 8 January 2005, and urges them to facilitate and expedite, consistent with their national laws and international obligations applicable to them, the use of communications equipment in such operations, inter alia, by limiting and, whenever possible, expeditiously lifting the restrictions placed on the use of communications equipment by United Nations and associated personnel;

37. *Requests* the Secretary-General to submit to the General Assembly at its sixty-seventh session a comprehensive and updated report on the safety and security of humanitarian personnel and protection of United Nations personnel and on the implementation of the present resolution.

Revised security management framework

The General Assembly, in Part XII of **resolution 66/246** of 24 December (see p. 1383), requested the Secretary-General to review the appropriateness of the use of private security personnel, particularly in situations in which they were the only option available to provide safety and security for staff, and to report thereon at its sixty-seventh (2012) session.

Other staff matters

Human resources management

Inter-agency staff mobility and work/life balance

JIU report. In a September note [A/66/355], the Secretary-General transmitted a JIU report entitled "Inter-agency staff mobility and work/life balance in the organizations of the United Nations system". The review examined the policies and mechanisms regulating staff mobility and work/life balance from a system-wide perspective and provided participating organizations and their respective governing organs with an independent assessment.

The inspectors found that the mandates, size, operational needs and activities of the UN system organizations were very different; there were highly mobile entities coexisting with others where staff mobility was not a major concern. There was no one mobility scheme that fit all organizations. Data showed that inter-agency mobility was generally insignificant; driven by the needs of individual staff, not the consequence of a planned strategy or proactive actions taken by organizations. One of the most important hurdles to overcome in order to promote mobility was the difficulty of accompanying expatriate spouses being unable to continue their careers due to legal restrictions imposed by host countries on accessing their local labour markets.

JIU recommended that CEB, through its High-Level Committee on Management, agree on the contents and use across the UN system of one legal instrument to regulate staff mobility among UN organizations, and define the responsibilities of those organizations with regard to the financial liabilities of staff movement; develop system-wide standards for collecting, monitoring and reporting staff mobility data; and elaborate a plan of action for developing one set of common staff regulations and rules applicable to the whole UN common system. The executive heads of UN common system organizations should review their internal staff mobility and/or staff rotation schemes from a system-wide perspective in order to make them supportive, consistent and coherent with inter-agency mobility initiatives. Executive heads should review their internal rules with a view to opening all vacant posts to all UN staff members, and CEB should elaborate an inter-agency common system policy for new contracts and the induction of new staff joining any common system organization, with a view to developing a common system culture. In addition, the legislative bodies of the UN organizations should bring to the attention of host countries the need to facilitate access to local labour markets for staff spouses.

As to work/life balance, some of the most popular options provided by all organizations were flexi-time, maternity, paternity and family leave. The inspectors considered that the work/life balance options available across the system covered reasonably well the needs of staff for enhanced flexibility at work. The issue, in their view, was not the choice of options but rather how they were implemented. JIU recommended that the executive heads of UN organizations should periodically assess the performance of work/life balance programmes, including a cost-benefit analysis, as part of their regular reporting.

Note by Secretary-General. In another September note [A/66/355/Add.1], the Secretary-General conveyed to the General Assembly his comments and those of CEB on the JIU report (see above). Agencies noted that the majority of the JIU recommendations were being acted upon by entities tasked with human resource responsibilities.

Staff composition

Report of Secretary-General. In accordance with Assembly resolution 65/247 [YUN 2010, p. 1480] concerning human resources management, the Secretary-General submitted a September report [A/66/347], which presented a demographic analysis of the composition of the Secretariat staff for the period 1 July

2010 to 30 June 2011. The global staff of the Secretariat as at 30 June totalled 43,747. That number comprised all categories of staff holding permanent/probationary, fixed-term and temporary contracts recruited internationally and locally from 186 Member States. All Secretariat staff were employed in four entity groups—departments/offices, regional commissions, tribunals and field operations. Field offices of the Office for the Coordination of Humanitarian Affairs, the United Nations Office on Drugs and Crime and other departments/offices were included in their respective departments/offices. Field operations referred to peacekeeping missions and certain special political missions. Non-field operations comprised 20,256 staff members (46.3 per cent) and field operations 23,491 (53.7 per cent). By category, the staff was distributed as follows: 26,992 General Service and related categories (62 per cent); 12,214 Professional and higher categories (28 per cent); and 4,541 Field Service (10 per cent). Staff were appointed under one of three appointment types: permanent/probationary (6,835), fixed term (34,614) and temporary (2,298). The overall percentage of female staff was 33 per cent (14,417 of 43,747), and the average age for all staff was 42.3 years.

As at 30 June, 2,049 Secretariat staff were subject to the system of desirable ranges. Under that system, 20 countries were unrepresented, 56 underrepresented, 109 within range and 7 overrepresented.

ACABQ report. In October [A/66/511 & Corr.1], ACABQ expressed concern that some 40 per cent of the posts subject to the system of geographic ranges were not encumbered by staff having geographic status. The Committee urged the Secretary-General to ensure that the recruitment of candidates was carried out in accordance with the established recruitment procedures, and requested him to provide, in his report on human resources management to be considered at the sixty-seventh (2012) session of the General Assembly, comprehensive information on measures taken to address the high number of posts encumbered by staff having no geographic status.

Ethics in the UN system

Conflict of interest

Report of Secretary-General. In response to Assembly resolution 65/247 [YUN 2010, p. 1480], the Secretary-General submitted a June report on personal conflict of interest [A/66/98]. The Organization therefore managed conflict of interest using the following three-step approach: identification/disclosure of the conflict; detailed review of the conflict; and implementation or recommendation of the best remedial measures to resolve the conflict.

The Organization's regulatory and policy framework addressed a range of conflict of interest situations. The tools of that framework allowed for proactive (e.g., disclosure) and retroactive (e.g., disciplinary measures) conflict identification and management. To prevent possible harm to the Organization's reputation and/or assets, proactive identification was preferable; as such harm might not necessarily be rectified through the available retroactive mechanisms. Consequently, the regulated areas of conflict of interest remained subject to various proactive reporting or disclosure obligations. Conflicts of interest falling within the scope of the financial disclosure programme were subject to annual disclosure obligations by certain categories of staff. The Assembly might therefore also wish to consider the Secretary-General's report on the activities of the Ethics Office (see below), which addressed aspects of the financial disclosure programme.

ACABQ report. In October [A/66/511 & Corr.1], ACABQ underlined the importance for all staff members to act in a manner compatible with their status as international civil servants and encouraged the Secretary-General to ensure that staff members abided by the applicable regulatory framework, in accordance with the relevant provisions of the Charter. It also underscored the importance of the financial disclosure programme as a means of mitigating the risk of personal conflicts of interest.

Ethics Office

Report of Secretary-General. As requested by the Assembly in resolution 60/254 [YUN 2006, p. 1633], the Secretary-General submitted an August report [A/66/319 & Corr.1] on the activities of the Ethics Office between 1 August 2010 and 31 July 2011. The Office received 766 requests for its services, a 78 per cent increase compared to the average for the preceding three reporting periods. Those requests covered ethics advice (70 per cent); protection from retaliation (7 per cent); training (7 per cent); office alerted (5 per cent); coherence (4 per cent); procurement due diligence (3 per cent); general information (3 per cent); and standard setting and policy input (2 per cent). The majority of requests continued to emanate from offices and personnel based in New York (43 per cent), but there was a 9 per cent increase in requests from outside Headquarters, notably from peacekeeping missions and the UN Offices at Geneva, Vienna and Nairobi.

The Office handled 531 requests for ethics advice and guidance, subdivided as follows: 122 related to outside activities (23 per cent); 112 to employment-related concerns (21 per cent); 109 to allegations of misconduct (21 per cent); 77 to other conflicts of interest (15 per cent); 53 to personal investments and assets (10 per cent); 54 to gifts and hospitality (10 per cent); and 4 to post-employment restrictions (1 per cent). The category "allegations of misconduct" experienced a significant rise from 34 to 109 requests, representing an increase of 220 per cent. The Ethics Office received 55 requests related to protection against retaliation, a 56 per cent increase. Preliminary review assessments were warranted in 14 of the 55 requests. Of those, the Office concluded its review of 11 cases. One case was referred for investigation, and while it was determined that there was no prima facie case of retaliation in 9 of the remaining 10 cases, the request for protection in the tenth case was withdrawn by the complainant. The preliminary review process continued in regard to the remaining three cases.

Under the financial disclosure programme, 4,065 staff members were required to file, including 1,244 new entrants. A total of 4,031 staff members (99.2 per cent) complied with their filing obligations. The Ethics Office implemented additional procedures to support compliance with programme requirements.

To ensure the long-term performance and stability of the UN financial disclosure programme, the Secretary-General recommended that the external review arrangement be maintained, and that a new information technology platform for the programme be created to allow for the leveraging of newer technologies, thereby enhancing system capacity and programme performance and ensuring robust data security protection. The General Assembly was therefore requested to appropriate $398,300 under section 1, Overall policymaking, direction and coordination.

ACABQ report. In October [A/66/511 & Corr.1], ACABQ supported the Secretary-General's recommendations to maintain the external vendor as the review function of the financial disclosure programme and to develop a new information technology platform, but considered that the related costs could be covered in the resources for the Office requested by the Secretary-General. It therefore recommended against the appropriation of additional funds and that the amount instead be absorbed and reported in the performance report for the 2012–2013 biennium.

Disciplinary matters

Reports of Secretary-General. As requested in General Assembly resolution 59/287 [YUN 2005, p. 1474], the Secretary-General submitted, in July [A/66/135], a report on the practice of the Secretary-General in disciplinary matters and possible criminal behaviour, from 1 July 2010 to 30 June 2011. The report showed that 123 cases of misconduct were received by the Office of Human Resources Management (OHRM), subdivided as follows: 60 related to staff based at Headquarters and offices away from Headquarters; and 63 to field staff. Of those, 25 related to fraud/misrepresentation, 23 to financial disclosure, 16 to computer-related misconduct, 14 to assault, both verbal and physical, 13 to theft/misappropriation, 7 to abuse of authority/harassment/discrimination, 3 to sexual abuse and sexual exploitation, 3 to the violation of local laws, and 2 to outside activities. Seventeen cases were categorized as "Other".

A total of 271 cases were completed, 14 by dismissal. Of the others, 93 were completed by other disciplinary measures; 80 were closed with no measures; 38 were not pursued; 26 by separation of the staff member after referral of the case to OHRM prior to the completion of the disciplinary process; 19 by administrative measures; and 1 by other means. Eight cases involving credible allegations of criminal conduct by UN officials or experts on mission were referred to Member States. The Secretary-General was not aware of any action taken in respect of such cases by the Member States concerned.

ACABQ report. In October [A/66/511 & Corr.1], ACABQ, in its comments and recommendations on the report, said that it expected the Secretary-General to ensure that disciplinary measures were imposed in a fully consistent manner and in proportion to the seriousness of the misconduct and/or criminal behaviour.

Also in July [A/66/174 & Add.1], the Secretary-General reported on the criminal accountability of UN officials and experts on mission (see p. 83).

General Assembly action. The Assembly, in **resolution 66/93** of 9 December (see p. 84), urged States to take all measures to ensure that crimes by UN officials and experts on mission did not go unpunished, and to consider establishing jurisdiction over crimes committed by their nationals while serving as UN officials or experts on mission.

GENERAL ASSEMBLY ACTION

On 24 December [meeting 93], the General Assembly, on the recommendation of the Fifth Committee [A/66/627], adopted **resolution 66/234** without vote [agenda item 139].

Human resources management

The General Assembly,

Recalling its resolutions 49/222 A and B of 23 December 1994 and 20 July 1995, 51/226 of 3 April 1997, 52/219 of 22 December 1997, 52/252 of 8 September 1998, 53/221 of 7 April 1999, 55/258 of 14 June 2001, 57/305 of 15 April 2003, 59/266 of 23 December 2004, 60/1 of 16 September 2005, 60/238 of 23 December 2005, 60/254 of 8 May 2006, 60/260 of 8 May 2006, 61/244 of 22 December 2006, 62/238, section XXI, of 22 December 2007, 62/248 of 3 April 2008, 63/250 of 24 December 2008, 63/271 of 7 April 2009 and 65/247 of 24 December 2010, and its decisions 64/546 of 22 December 2009 and 64/548 A of 24 December 2009,

Recalling also its resolutions 52/226 A and B of 31 March 1998, 54/14 of 29 October 1999, 58/296 of 18 June 2004, 59/287 of 13 April 2005, 60/266 of 30 June 2006, 61/246 of 22 December 2006, 61/276, section VIII, of 29 June 2007 and 62/269 of 20 June 2008, as well as its other relevant resolutions and decisions,

Having considered the relevant reports of the Secretary-General on human resources management submitted to the General Assembly and the related reports of the Advisory Committee on Administrative and Budgetary Questions,

Having also considered the report of the Joint Inspection Unit on inter-agency staff mobility and work-life balance in the organizations of the United Nations system, as well as the note by the Secretary-General transmitting his comments and those of the United Nations System Chief Executives Board for Coordination thereon,

Reaffirming that the staff of the United Nations is an invaluable asset of the Organization, and commending its contribution to furthering the purposes and principles of the United Nations,

Emphasizing the fundamental importance of human resources management reform in the United Nations as a contribution to the strengthening of the international civil service,

1. *Endorses* the conclusions and recommendations contained in the reports of the Advisory Committee on Administrative and Budgetary Questions, subject to the provisions of the present resolution;

2. *Expresses serious concern* that progress towards the goal of 50/50 gender balance in the United Nations system, especially at senior and policymaking levels, in conformity with Article 101, paragraph 3, of the Charter of the United Nations, has been slow;

3. *Reiterates its requests* to the Secretary-General to increase his efforts to attain and monitor the goal of gender parity in the Secretariat, in particular at senior levels, and in this context to ensure that women, especially those from developing countries and countries with economies in transition, are appropriately represented within the Secretariat, and to report thereon to the General Assembly at its sixty-seventh session;

4. *Reiterates* that the Secretary-General has to ensure that the highest standards of efficiency, competence and integrity serve as the paramount consideration in the employment of staff, with due regard to the principle of equitable geographical distribution, in accordance with Article 101, paragraph 3, of the Charter;

5. *Reiterates its request* to the Secretary-General to continue his ongoing efforts to ensure the attainment of equitable geographical distribution in the Secretariat and to also ensure as wide a geographical distribution of staff as possible in all departments, offices and levels, including at the Director and higher levels, of the Secretariat, and in that regard reiterates its request contained in paragraph 64 of resolution 65/247;

6. *Urges* the Secretary-General to ensure that the recruitment of candidates is carried out in accordance with the established recruitment procedures, including through the use of the national competitive recruitment examination roster, which has been replaced by the young professionals programme;

7. *Recalls* paragraph 7 of the report of the Advisory Committee on Administrative and Budgetary Questions, and requests the Secretary-General to address the problem of the high number of posts subject to the system of geographical ranges not encumbered by staff having geographical status;

8. *Stresses* that the Secretary-General should not recur to the practice of temporarily filling posts in the Professional and higher categories with General Service staff members who have not passed the General Service to Professional category examination other than on an exceptional basis, and requests the Secretary-General to ensure that temporary occupation of such posts by the General Service staff shall not exceed a period of one year, effective 1 January 2013, and to report thereon, including on the rationale for such practice, to the General Assembly every two years, starting at its sixty-seventh session;

9. *Takes note* of paragraph 8 of the report of the Advisory Committee on Administrative and Budgetary Questions referred to in paragraph 7 above, reiterates section VII of resolution 65/247, and looks forward to the report of the Secretary-General on human resources management, which should include, inter alia, details on the implementation of that resolution, to be submitted to the General Assembly at its sixty-seventh session;

10. *Welcomes* the launch of the online reporting tool entitled "HR Insight", and requests the Secretary-General to ensure that the information provided on the portal is systematically developed and periodically updated;

11. *Requests* the Secretary-General, in the context of his report on the activities of the Ethics Office to be submitted during the main part of the sixty-seventh session of the General Assembly, to provide information on his efforts to address and mitigate personal conflicts of interest, and in this regard requests him to propose measures such as the extension to other staff categories of the financial disclosure programme and post-employment restrictions;

12. *Decides* that staff regulation 1.2 (*m*) shall be amended to read:

"A conflict of interest occurs when, by act or omission, a staff member's personal interests interfere with the performance of his or her official duties and responsibilities or with the integrity, independence and impartiality required by the staff member's status as an international civil servant. When an actual or possible conflict of interest does arise, the conflict shall be disclosed by staff members to their head of office, mitigated by the Organization and resolved in favour of the interests of the Organization";

13. *Welcomes* the significant efforts made by the Ethics Office towards the implementation of the financial disclosure programme, and requests the Secretary-General to ensure full compliance by staff in fulfilling their financial disclosure requirements;

14. *Decides* to absorb the amount of 398,300 United States dollars for the development of the information technology platform within the amount of 3,880,100 dollars allocated to the Ethics Office in the regular budget for the biennium 2012–2013;

15. *Recognizes* the work of the Joint Inspection Unit, and in this regard takes note of the report of the Unit on interagency staff mobility and work-life balance in the organizations of the United Nations system;

16. *Requests* the Secretary-General, in his capacity as Chair of the United Nations System Chief Executives

Board for Coordination, to expedite the conclusion of a revised version of the inter-agency agreement on inter-organization movement and to ensure its utilization by all organizations of the United Nations common system;

17. *Recalls* section C, paragraph 13, of its resolution 65/248 of 24 December 2010;

18. *Also recalls* section II, paragraph 34, of its resolution 65/247, and looks forward to its consideration of a comprehensive proposal on a mobility policy at its sixty-seventh session.

On the same date, the Assembly decided that the item on human resources management would remain for consideration during its resumed sixty-sixth (2012) session (**decision 66/557**).

Selection and appointment of senior managers in UN Secretariat

JIU report. In September [A/66/380], the Secretary-General transmitted to the General Assembly the JIU report on transparency in the selection and appointment of senior managers in the UN Secretariat, prepared in response to resolution 64/259 [YUN 2010, p. 1404]. The objective of the study was to review the effectiveness, coherence, timeliness and transparency of the current processes of selection and appointment of senior managers in the Secretariat (Deputy Secretary-General, Under-Secretaries-General, Assistant Secretaries-General), and provide recommendations for enhanced transparency.

JIU noted that the concern was not with the selection process as outlined in the Secretary-General's report on accountability [ibid., p. 1403], but with its implementation, which was seen as opaque, raising questions as to how it actually worked. Both JIU and the Member States recognized the Secretary-General's discretionary power in making senior manager appointments, but the inspectors expressed the view that such authority did not mean he could avoid the established process; discretionary authority should not be used to avoid transparency. The challenge was to strike a balance between providing enough information to Member States so they were confident the process was open and fair without compromising the privacy of the candidates and jeopardizing the confidentiality of the deliberative process of either the interview panels or the Secretary-General.

JIU established a set of guidelines with procedural approaches for enhancing transparency, according to which vacancy announcements should be issued for all positions, except for special envoys and personal advisers, and sent to all Member States and UN agencies, funds and programmes with at least one month's notice. Merit should be the primary criteria in the selection of senior managers and Member States were responsible for putting forward fully qualified candidates for the Secretary-General to consider. A website should be set up to convey information on senior appointments to Member States and potential candidates. Basic screening to filter out candidates who did not satisfy mandatory eligibility criteria should be performed by the OHRM or its equivalent. Once a short list was determined, all information provided by those candidates should be vetted by OHRM or its equivalent before the candidate list could be forwarded by the interview panel to the Secretary-General for decision.

JIU recommended that the Assembly direct the Executive Office of the Secretary-General to set up and maintain on a monthly basis a dedicated website conveying to Member States and potential candidates specific information on senior appointments; and endorse the recommended JIU guidelines and direct the Secretary-General to follow them in selecting and appointing senior managers, in tandem with the process outlined in the accountability report.

Review of UN system medical service

JIU report. In September [A/66/327], the Secretary-General transmitted a JIU report entitled "Review of the Medical Service in the United Nations system". The review assessed the manner in which UN medical services were provided, managed, supported and monitored, with a view to proposing improvements, especially in the context of the UN strategic movement towards mobility and increased field presence, and particularly for staff deployed at hardship duty stations. The report elaborated on the implications of the endorsement by the CEB High-Level Committee on Management (HLCM) of the proposal submitted by the United Nations Medical Directors Working Group for the adoption of an Occupational Safety and Health (OSH) policy, and its recommendation that all organizations adopt an individual OSH policy.

The report concluded that the Secretary-General should, in the light of the HLCM recommendation, modify the mandate/role of the United Nations Chief Medical Director and the Medical Services Division (MSD). OSH and medical services should remain independent from other administrative/organizational units and report either directly to the Chief Executive Officer or to their appointed representative. To ensure effective coordination and implementation, the adoption of OSH policies would require the centralization of distinct OSH services under one umbrella at both the organizational and system-wide levels.

The report looked at medical services in the field, which were deemed inadequate, and it described the functions of the respective service providers and their interaction with MSD, the United Nations Medical Directors Working Group and the United Nations Department of Safety and Security. The issue of accountability in field medical services was also raised, for although MSD was supposed to have a supervisory role, it had no input with regard to field unit budgets and workplans, or in the performance management process of other service providers.

JIU drew attention to the need to improve the overall coordination of UN medical/OHS services, as the absence of a relevant system-wide mechanism and fragmented lines of authority were hampering service-level optimization. With a view to facilitating the implementation of OSH policies, JIU called for the establishment of a United Nations Network on Occupational Safety and Health (UNNOSH), modelled on the Inter-Agency Security Management Network, established to address security-related issues. The proposed new coordinating body would monitor the implementation of UNNOSH policies, practices and procedures, and thereby support HLCM in its comprehensive review of issues pertaining to the entire UN occupational safety and health structure.

The review contained seven recommendations, including that legislative bodies of UN system organizations should adopt appropriate standards with regard to OSH issues, taking into account and ensuring compatibility with emerging modifications to the Minimum Operating Safety and Security Standards; and that the General Assembly should mandate the Secretary-General to create UNNOSH, which should be headed by the United Nations Chief Medical Director.

Multilingualism

In 2011, the General Assembly considered multilingualism, including the Secretary-General's 2010 report [YUN 2010, p. 1485].

GENERAL ASSEMBLY ACTION

On 19 July [meeting 109], the General Assembly adopted **resolution 65/311** [draft: A/65/L.85 & Add.1] without vote [agenda item 121].

Multilingualism

The General Assembly,

Recognizing that the United Nations pursues multilingualism as a means of promoting, protecting and preserving diversity of languages and cultures globally,

Recognizing also that genuine multilingualism promotes unity in diversity and international understanding, and recognizing the importance of the capacity to communicate to the peoples of the world in their own languages, including in formats accessible to persons with disabilities,

Stressing the need for strict observance of the resolutions and rules establishing language arrangements for the different bodies and organs of the United Nations,

Emphasizing the importance of multilingualism in the activities of the United Nations, including those linked to public relations and information,

Recalling its resolution 47/135 of 18 December 1992, by which it adopted the Declaration on the Rights of Persons Belonging to National or Ethnic, Religious and Linguistic Minorities, and the International Covenant on Civil and Political Rights, in particular article 27 thereof, concerning the rights of persons belonging to ethnic, religious or linguistic minorities,

Recalling also its resolutions 2(I) of 1 February 1946, 2480 B(XXIII) of 21 December 1968, 42/207 C of 11 December 1987, 50/11 of 2 November 1995, 52/23 of 25 November 1997, 54/64 of 6 December 1999, 56/262 of 15 February 2002, 59/309 of 22 June 2005, 63/306 of 9 September 2009, 64/266 of 21 May 2010, 65/107 B of 10 December 2010, 65/245 of 24 December 2010 and 65/247 of 24 December 2010,

1. *Takes note* of the report of the Secretary-General;
2. *Calls upon* the Secretary-General to continue to develop the informal network of focal points in order to support his activities;
3. *Emphasizes* the paramount importance of the equality of the six official languages of the United Nations;
4. *Underlines* the need for full implementation of the resolutions establishing language arrangements for the official languages of the United Nations and the working languages of the Secretariat;
5. *Requests* the Secretary-General to ensure that all language services are given equal treatment and are provided with equally favourable working conditions and resources, with a view to achieving maximum quality of those services, with full respect for the specificities of the six official languages, and in that regard recalls section D, paragraph 11, of its resolution 54/248 of 23 December 1999;
6. *Reiterates its request* to the Secretary-General to complete the task of uploading all important older United Nations documents onto the United Nations website in all six official languages on a priority basis, so that those archives are also available to Member States through that medium;
7. *Reiterates* that all content-providing offices in the Secretariat should continue their efforts to translate into all official languages all English-language materials and databases posted on the United Nations website in the most practical, efficient and cost-effective manner;
8. *Requests* the Secretary-General to continue to ensure, through the provision of documentation services and meeting and publishing services under conference management, including high-quality translation and interpretation, effective multilingual communication among representatives of Member States in intergovernmental organs and members of expert bodies of the United Nations equally in all the official languages of the United Nations;
9. *Stresses* the importance of providing United Nations information, technical assistance and training materials, whenever possible, in the local languages of the beneficiary countries;
10. *Acknowledges* the measures undertaken by the Secretary-General, in accordance with its resolutions, to address the issue of the replacement of retiring staff in the language services, and requests the Secretary-General to maintain and intensify those efforts, including through the strengthening of cooperation with institutions that train language specialists to meet the need in the six official languages of the United Nations;

11. *Notes with satisfaction* the willingness of the Secretariat to encourage staff members, in meetings with interpretation services, to use any of the six official languages of which they have a command;

12. *Reiterates its request* to the Secretary-General to ensure that the rules concerning the simultaneous distribution of documents in all six official languages are strictly respected as regards both the distribution of printed copies and the posting of parliamentary documentation on the Official Document System and the United Nations website, in keeping with section III, paragraph 5, of its resolution 55/222 of 23 December 2000;

13. *Emphasizes* the importance of:

(a) Making appropriate use of all the official languages of the United Nations in all the activities of the Department of Public Information of the Secretariat, with the aim of eliminating the disparity between the use of English and the use of the five other official languages;

(b) Ensuring the full and equitable treatment of all the official languages of the United Nations in all the activities of the Department of Public Information;

and, in this regard, reaffirms its request to the Secretary-General to ensure that the Department has appropriate staffing capacity in all the official languages of the United Nations to undertake all its activities;

14. *Requests* the Secretary-General to continue his efforts to ensure that, in accordance with their income-generating nature, guided tours at United Nations Headquarters are consistently available, in particular, in all six official languages of the United Nations;

15. *Encourages* the Secretary-General to strengthen his efforts to develop and maintain multilingual United Nations websites, from within existing resources, including efforts to keep the Secretary-General's web page up to date in all the official languages of the United Nations;

16. *Reaffirms* the need to achieve full parity among the six official languages on United Nations websites;

17. *Also reaffirms* that the United Nations website is an essential tool for Member States, the media, educational institutions, the general public and non-governmental organizations, and reiterates the continued need for efforts by the Department of Public Information to maintain and improve it;

18. *Further reaffirms* its request to the Secretary-General to ensure, while maintaining an up-to-date and accurate website, the adequate distribution of financial and human resources within the Department of Public Information allocated to the United Nations website among all official languages, with full respect for the specificities of the six official languages;

19. *Notes with concern* that the multilingual development and enrichment of the United Nations website in several official languages has improved at a much slower rate than expected, and in this regard requests the Department of Public Information, in coordination with content-providing offices, to improve the actions taken to achieve parity among the six official languages on the United Nations website, in particular by expediting the filling of current vacant posts in some sections;

20. *Requests* the Department of Public Information, in cooperation with the Office of Information and Communications Technology of the Secretariat, to continue its efforts to ensure that technological infrastructures and supportive applications fully support Latin, non-Latin and bidirectional scripts in order to enhance the equality of all official languages on the United Nations website;

21. *Welcomes* the cooperative arrangements undertaken by the Department of Public Information with academic institutions in order to increase the number of web pages available in some official languages, and requests the Secretary-General, in coordination with content-providing offices, to extend these cooperative arrangements, in a cost-effective manner, to all the official languages of the United Nations, bearing in mind the necessity of adherence to United Nations standards and guidelines;

22. *Urges* the Secretariat to keep iSeek up to date in the two working languages of the Secretariat, to continue its efforts to implement iSeek at all duty stations and to develop and implement cost-neutral measures to provide Member States with secure access to the information currently accessible only on the Intranet of the Secretariat;

23. *Notes with appreciation* the work carried out by the United Nations information centres, including the United Nations Regional Information Centre, in favour of the publication of United Nations information materials and the translation of important documents into languages other than the official languages of the United Nations, with a view to reaching the widest possible audience and extending the United Nations message to all corners of the world in order to strengthen international support for the activities of the Organization, and encourages United Nations information centres to continue their multilingual activities in the interactive and proactive aspects of their work, especially by arranging seminars and debates to further the spread of information and the understanding and exchange of views regarding United Nations activities at the local level;

24. *Recalls* its resolution 65/247, in particular paragraphs 26 and 54 (f) thereof, in which it reaffirmed the need to respect the equality of the two working languages of the Secretariat, reaffirmed the use of additional working languages in specific duty stations, as mandated, and, in that regard, requested the Secretary-General to ensure that vacancy announcements specified the need for either of the working languages of the Secretariat, unless the functions of the post required a specific working language;

25. *Also recalls* section II, paragraph 17, of its resolution 61/244 of 22 December 2006, in which it acknowledged that the interaction of the United Nations with the local population in the field was essential and that language skills constituted an important element of the selection and training processes and therefore affirmed that a good command of the official language(s) spoken in the country of residence should be taken into account as an additional asset during those processes;

26. *Further recalls* its resolution 64/266, in which it endorsed the proposals, recommendations and conclusions of the Special Committee on Peacekeeping Operations;

27. *Takes note* of section II.D.1 of the report of the Secretary-General, requests the Secretary-General to continue his ongoing efforts in this regard, and further recalls its resolution 64/266 without prejudice to Article 101 of the Charter of the United Nations;

28. *Urges* the Secretariat to translate all peacekeeping training documents into the six official languages of the United Nations, within existing resources, to ensure that all Member States can use them;

29. *Stresses* that the employment of staff shall continue to be carried out in strict accordance with Article 101 of the Charter and in line with the relevant provisions of General Assembly resolutions;

30. *Invites* the Secretary-General to ensure compliance with the requirement for United Nations staff to have the ability to use one of the working languages of the Secretariat, and encourages the Secretary-General to further implement resolution 2480 B(XXIII);

31. *Also invites* the Secretary-General to take the appropriate measures to consider the linguistic specificities mentioned in vacancy announcements during the composition of interview panels for the employment of United Nations staff;

32. *Stresses* that the promotion of staff in the Professional and higher categories shall be carried out in strict accordance with Article 101 of the Charter and in line with the provisions of resolution 2480 B(XXIII) and the relevant provisions of resolution 55/258 of 14 June 2001;

33. *Encourages* United Nations staff members to continue actively to use existing training facilities to acquire and enhance their proficiency in one or more of the official languages of the United Nations;

34. *Notes with interest* the cost-neutral initiatives of the Secretariat to produce publications in several languages, increase the volume of translated publications and encourage a multilingual acquisition policy for the libraries of the United Nations, and requests the Secretariat to continue those initiatives;

35. *Reaffirms* that linguistic diversity is an important element of cultural diversity, stresses the importance of the full and effective implementation of the Convention on the Protection and Promotion of the Diversity of Cultural Expressions, which entered into force on 18 March 2007, and recalls the Recommendation concerning the Promotion and Use of Multilingualism and Universal Access to Cyberspace of 15 October 2003;

36. *Welcomes* the activities of the United Nations Educational, Scientific and Cultural Organization, Member States, the entities of the United Nations system and all other participating bodies aimed at fostering respect for and the promotion and protection of all languages, in particular endangered ones, linguistic diversity and multilingualism;

37. *Requests* the Secretary-General to submit to the General Assembly at its sixty-seventh session a comprehensive report on the full implementation of its resolutions on multilingualism;

38. *Decides* to include in the provisional agenda of its sixty-seventh session the item entitled "Multilingualism".

JIU report. JIU assessed the status of the implementation of multilingualism across the UN system organizations. Its 2011 report [JIU/REP/2011/4] reviewed key dimensions of multilingualism, analysing its rationale and policy implications, and identifying measures to foster its implementation. The research covered conference services, recruitment, training, outreach and institutional partnerships, among others.

JIU found that few UN system organizations had a formal policy on multilingualism. The trend towards "monolingualism" was far from decreasing, with the "hegemonic" use of one language, English, over the other five UN languages, for the sake of pragmatism. Executive heads of organizations did not always lead by example, or ensure effective monitoring, controls and compliance regarding the parity of the six official languages and the equal treatment of the working languages within secretariats, including the use of additional working languages in specific duty stations. The role of the Coordinator for Multilingualism was not well known. Challenges faced by the interpretation and translation services included a shortage of professional language staff, a problem of succession planning, and related issues regarding the Language Competitive Examination (LCE) and roster management of successful LCE candidates. The inspectors identified positive and encouraging actions in several organizations, but generally determined that the piecemeal and fragmented approach across the system should be replaced by a "One UN policy on Multilingualism". JIU made 15 recommendations, four of which were addressed to the legislative bodies of the organizations and 11 to their executive heads.

The recommendations for executive heads included that they should appoint a senior official as coordinator for multilingualism, tasked with proposing action plans for the implementation of multilingualism, with the assistance of an internal network of focal points within their respective organization, and regularly report on progress to their legislative bodies; develop a common understanding of the differences between "official" and "working" languages as a basis for better coordinating the use of languages and promoting multilingualism across the UN system; take measures to eliminate the imbalance in the use of the working languages within secretariats, and require all staff to develop their language skills so as to acquire good knowledge of at least a second working language; and regularly assess users' needs and formulate strategies to enhance the implementation of multilingualism through the involvement of their respective coordinators for multilingualism and related network of focal points.

Legislative organs, when creating new institutional bodies that would require the provision of conference services, should plan for the budgetary resources associated with the resulting additional workload, in particular for translation and interpretation.

Protection from sexual exploitation and abuse

Report of Secretary-General. As requested by General Assembly resolution 57/306 [YUN 2003, p. 1237], the Secretary-General submitted a February report [A/65/742] on special measures for protection from sexual exploitation and abuse, in which he presented data on such allegations in the UN system during 2010. Information from 43 UN entities indicated that 116 allegations were made, a marked decline from the 154 reported in 2009. Five entities reported having received one or more allegations, and 38 reported having received none. Allegations of sexual exploitation and abuse against UN Secretariat staff members were conveyed to OIOS for investigation; investigations of alleged misconduct by military personnel were governed under the revised model memorandum of understanding between troop-contributing countries and the Secretariat, as approved by Assembly resolution 61/267 B [YUN 2007, p. 69]; and investigations of allegations in the separately administered UN funds and programmes were conducted by their respective investigative units.

The majority of cases (85 out of 116, or 73 per cent) involved personnel deployed in peacekeeping and special political missions supported by the Department of Field Support (see p. 58). A cause for concern was the number of allegations involving the abuse of minors (30 out of 85, or 35 per cent), or the non-consensual sexual abuse of persons above the age of 18 or of persons for whom age could not be ascertained (13 out of 85, or 16 per cent). Therefore, in 2010, 51 per cent of reported allegations were of the most egregious forms of sexual exploitation and abuse. The proportion of allegations involving civilian personnel (33 out of 85, or 39 per cent) continued to increase over the figures reported in 2008 (27 out of 83, or 33 per cent) and 2009 (38 out of 112, or 34 per cent). For allegations reported in 2010, investigations had been completed in 38 per cent of cases. Fifty-five per cent of the allegations reported were substantiated. In terms of referrals, 35 cases were forwarded to Member States, 15 of which indicated that they intended to investigate or appoint an officer to conduct an investigation in coordination with the United Nations. The results of investigations were shared in five out of those 15 cases. In four out of those five cases the allegations were considered unsubstantiated, while in the fifth case disciplinary action was taken.

Of the 31 cases involving personnel other than those in peacekeeping and special political missions, 58 per cent had been investigated as at 31 December 2010, 39 per cent of which were substantiated and forwarded to the relevant offices for action. One staff member of the Office for the Coordination of Humanitarian Affairs was reprimanded, while cases against two United Nations Development Programme staff, two personnel affiliated with the United Nations High Commissioner for Refugees, and four personnel affiliated with the United Nations Relief and Works Agency for Palestine Refugees in the Near East were found to be unsubstantiated. Another case at the Agency was closed due to the resignation of the staff member before the investigation could be initiated. At the World Food Programme, one case was unsubstantiated and another forwarded to the competent human resources service for action. The remaining 13 allegations, or 42 per cent of the caseload, were either still being investigated or pending investigation at the end of the reporting period.

The report described measures taken to strengthen UN standards of conduct related to sexual exploitation and abuse. It noted that the Task Force on Protection from Sexual Exploitation and Abuse had conducted a global review of protection from sexual exploitation and abuse by UN and other international personnel, the results of which indicated that although progress had been made in establishing policies, it was not translating into adequate managerial and staff understanding and acceptance of those policies. With few exceptions, Headquarters were not giving clear directives to staff in the field or supporting directives with sufficient guidance and training, and managers were not being held accountable. Consistent with those findings, a task force was established under the direction of the Inter-Agency Standing Committee with a two-year mandate focused on supporting field activities to institutionalize protection from sexual exploitation and abuse in their respective organizations.

ACABQ report. Commenting on the Secretary-General's report, ACABQ [A/65/743] noted the reduced number of allegations of sexual exploitation and abuse involving peacekeeping personnel and commended the joint efforts of the Secretary-General and troop- and police-contributing countries, however, given the importance of the issue, the Committee emphasized the need for sustained efforts in that regard.

The General Assembly, in part V of **resolution 65/289** (see p. 78) of 30 June, took note of the Secretary-General's report.

UN Joint Staff Pension Fund

As at 31 December, the United Nations Joint Staff Pension Fund (UNJSPF) had 120,774 active participants compared to 121,138 at the end of 2010 [YUN 2010, p. 1486]. The number of periodic payments in awards increased from 63,830 to 65,387: 23,147 full retirement benefits; 14,405 early retirement benefits; 7,161 deferred retirement benefits; 10,212 widow benefits; 784 widower benefits; 1,238 disability benefits; 8,401 child benefits; and 39 secondary dependants' benefits. The payroll for benefits in payments for 2011 increased to $2 billion, representing a 7.7 per cent increase over the 2010 figure. The total expenditure for benefits, administration and investment costs of $2.2 billion exceeded contribution income by some $66 million. Contribution income increased by approximately 5.5 per cent, from approximately $2 billion to $2.1 billion. The market value of the Fund's assets decreased by some 6.2 per cent, from $40.3 billion to $37.8 billion.

The Fund was administered by the 33-member United Nations Joint Staff Pension Board (UNJSPB), which held its fifty-eighth session in 2011 (Geneva, 11–15 July) [A/67/9].

Administrative and financial matters

In August [A/66/266 & Corr.1], UNJSPB submitted a report on the administrative expenses of the Fund and transitional measures concerning the Fund's financial reporting under the International Public Sector Accounting Standards (IPSAS). The report contained the UNJSPF revised budget for the 2010–2011 biennium, which indicated a reduction in appropriations amounting to $21,772,800. The revised appropriations would therefore amount to $154,545,700, divided into administrative costs ($80,478,500), investment costs ($71,289,000), audit costs ($2,532,900) and Board expenses ($245,300). Of that amount, $133,037,000 would be apportioned to the Fund and $21,508,700 would be chargeable to the United Nations under the cost-sharing arrangement.

The report also contained budget estimates for the 2012–2013 biennium, which amounted to $194,164,000 (after recosting) for administrative costs ($98,407,600), investment costs ($92,938,200), audit costs ($2,613,800) and Pension Board expenses ($204,400). Of this amount, $173,260,600 would be apportioned to the Fund and $20,903,400 charged to the United Nations. The report provided for 227 continuing established posts, 17 temporary posts, seven newly established posts and the reclassification of one post.

The Board recommended that the General Assembly approve the revised appropriations and budget estimates, as well as the interim measure concerning the Fund's financial reporting pending the adoption of IPSAS by the Board in 2012.

Report of Secretary-General. In September [A/C.5/66/2], the Secretary-General informed the General Assembly that the appropriations required under the regular budget for the 2012–2013 biennium, arising from the Board's recommendations, would reflect a reduction in the amount of $897,900 after applying revised distribution rates.

ACABQ report. In its October report [A/66/7/Add.2], ACABQ recommended approval of the Board's proposals, taking into account the adjustment reflected in the report of the Secretary-General. It also indicated that it had no objection to the proposed transitional measures concerning the adoption of IPSAS in January 2012.

General Assembly action. The Assembly, in section V of **resolution 66/247** of 24 December (see p. 1393), approved the revised estimate of $154,545,700 for the UNJSPF for 2010–2011. It also approved expenses, chargeable directly to the Fund, totalling $173,412,600 for 2012–2013. An amount of $20,688,300 would comprise the UN share of the Fund's administrative expenses for 2012–2013, of which $13,240,500 represented the regular budget share and $7,447,800 the share of the UN funds and programmes.

Travel-related matters

At its resumed sixty-fifth (2011) session, the General Assembly considered the Secretary-General's report on standards of accommodation for air travel; the CEB report on the feasibility of harmonizing standards of air travel and the related ACABQ report; the JIU report entitled "Review of travel arrangements within the United Nations system"; and the Secretary-General's note transmitting his comments and those of CEB thereon [YUN 2010, p. 1488].

The Assembly, in section IV of **resolution 65/268** of 4 April (see p. 1378), decided to extend to the Deputy Secretary-General the entitlements regarding official travel accorded to the Secretary-General. It further asked the Secretary-General to present, at its resumed sixty-sixth (2012) session, proposals on the conditions under which staff members below the level of Assistant Secretary-General could travel in business class; entrust OIOS to conduct a comprehensive audit of all air-travel activities and related practices; and report to the main part of its sixty-sixth (2011) session on the projected total expenditure on air travel for the 2010–2011 biennium, with corresponding data for the two previous bienniums. It also decided to consider, in 2012, a system for allowing UN staff to provide data on frequent flyer miles accrued as a result of official air travel. Annexed to the resolution were measures for the effective utilization of resources for air travel in the United Nations.

Administration of justice

Report of Secretary-General. In August [A/66/275 & Corr.1], the Secretary-General submitted a report on the administration of justice at the United Nations. The report recalled that by resolutions 61/261 [YUN 2007, p. 1525], 62/228 [ibid., p. 1528] and 63/253 [YUN 2008, p. 1637], the Assembly had established a new system of justice for Secretariat staff that became operational on 1 July 2009. The Secretary-General described the accomplishments of the new system during the reporting period from 1 July 2010 to 31 May 2011. The processing of cases through all phases of the formal system continued to demonstrate a marked improvement in efficiency. The Management Evaluation Unit received 390 requests for review and closed or resolved 281 matters, and the Office of Staff Legal Assistance resolved approximately one third of the more than 850 cases for which it was responsible.

The offices representing the Secretary-General before the United Nations Dispute Tribunal handled cases resulting in 195 judgements, and the Office of Legal Affairs handled cases resulting in 90 judgements of the United Nations Appeals Tribunal. The success and productivity of the system had resulted in serious strains upon the financial and human resources of the offices and units that serviced it. There was a need for significant strengthening in a number of key areas in order to maintain the current pace of work and continue to implement all of the Assembly's mandates for the new system. The Secretary-General therefore requested, under the proposed 2012–2013 programme budget, additional resources amounting to $8,657,900 (before recosting) and approval of the establishment, reclassification or continuation of posts at a range of levels. In his consideration of issues relevant to the General Assembly's review of the statutes of the Tribunals, as called for in resolution 65/251 [YUN 2010, p. 1491], the Secretary-General presented proposed amendments to certain articles of the statutes, with a view to enhancing the Tribunals' functioning.

ACABQ report. In October [A/66/7/Add.6], ACABQ recommended approval of the Secretary-General's proposals.

General Assembly action. The Assembly, in section XI of **resolution 66/247** (see p. 1393) of 24 December, approved an additional amount of $7,078,700 in the proposed 2012–2013 programme budget.

Report of Internal Justice Council. In July [A/66/158], the Internal Justice Council transmitted to the Assembly its views and conclusion from monitoring the second year of the new justice system. The report examined the draft code of conduct for judges and a complaints mechanism to enforce it; the Tribunals, including the registries; the Office of Administration of Justice; the Office of Staff Legal Assistance; the Internal Justice Council; the Management Evaluation Unit; and proposed amendments to the statutes of the Tribunals.

The Council was satisfied with the functioning of the new system, yet it was convinced that the shortage of resources was a growing threat which, if not addressed, could plague the new system with the problems and delays it sought to avoid. The successful functioning of the system to date was due to the commitment and work of the judges of the two Tribunals, the staff of the registries, lawyers representing management and staff, and the team in the Office of Administration of Justice, among others, but that level of commitment was unsustainable in the long run. If the necessary resources were made available, however, the new system would continue to improve.

The Council recommended that the Assembly establish a complaints panel, comprising the Chairperson and the two "distinguished external jurist" members of the Internal Justice Council, to hear and determine any complaints that a judge had breached the code of conduct or was otherwise unfit to occupy judicial office within the internal justice system; appoint three additional permanent full-time judges to the United Nations Dispute Tribunal to replace the ad litem judges when the terms of the ad litem judges expired; and amend the provisions of the United Nations Dispute Tribunal statute to provide for two part-time judges, rather than two half-time judges.

Letter from Presidents of the Tribunals. In a 23 September letter to the General Assembly President [A/66/399], the Presidents of the United Nations Appeals Tribunal and the United Nations Dispute Tribunal expressed their concern to the General Assembly regarding recommendations on the procedure for the amendment of the Tribunals' rules of procedure, as contained in the reports of the Secretary-General and Internal Justice Council (see above). The judges recalled that articles of the statutes of both Tribunals stipulated that they should establish their own rules of procedure through a process whereby amendments were adopted by the Tribunals, applied provisionally and submitted to the Assembly for approval. Because the process proposed by the Secretary-General, by which the Tribunals would have to consult with parties appearing before them, would raise a number of practical difficulties, the judges considered that they should continue to discharge the functions entrusted to them, under their respective statutes, regarding amendments to the rules.

Letter from President of Dispute Tribunal. In a 5 October letter to the General Assembly President [A/66/507], the President of the Dispute Tribunal conveyed the concern of the Tribunal's judges regarding recommendations contained in the reports of the Secretary-General and Internal Justice Council. Annexed to the letter were observations responding to the proposed amendments to the Tribunal's statute on the suspensory effect of appeals of interlocutory orders; jurisdiction of the Dispute Tribunal over acts and omissions by independent entities in connection with the performance of their operational mandates; the redaction of names of staff identified in judgements; and audio recordings of oral hearings. The mechanism for addressing complaints against judges and the recourse mechanisms for non-staff personnel were also addressed. Generally, they considered it to be premature to propose fundamental changes to the statute based on two years' experience.

Letter from Chair of Sixth Committee. On 4 November [A/C.5/66/9], the Assembly President transmitted to the Chair of the Fifth Committee a 1 November letter from the Chair of the Sixth (Legal) Committee regarding the agenda item entitled

"Administration of justice at the United Nations". The Sixth Committee Chair conveyed the Committee's concern about the expiration of the terms of office of three ad litem judges of the United Nations Dispute Tribunal by the end of 2011, which would reduce their number by half and might thereby result in a backlog and delays in the handling of cases and, in turn, raise concerns regarding due process. In considering the amendments to the statutes of the Tribunals proposed in the above reports, delegations were of the view that the proposals concerning appeals to interlocutory orders should not be taken up at that time but should be re-examined in the course of a future review of the statutes. Delegations felt it was premature to envisage any amendment to the statute of the Dispute Tribunal with regard to the question of the jurisdiction of the Tribunal over acts and omissions by independent entities, rather, more time should be allowed for practice to develop. They considered it unnecessary to amend the statute of the Dispute Tribunal regarding the redaction of names, and were unconvinced of the necessity to amend the statute of the Appeals Tribunal for the provision of a mechanism for the dismissal of inadmissible cases. They expressed support, however, for proposals that an extension of the deadline for management evaluation be allowed by the Dispute Tribunal in exceptional circumstances, and to extend the deadline for filing appeals with the Appeals Tribunal from 45 to 60 days.

On the question of redress mechanisms for non-staff personnel, delegations proposed that the Secretary-General be requested to elaborate further his proposal concerning an expedited arbitration procedure, and to include in future reports information on how that mechanism, if adopted, would apply to the different categories of non-staff personnel that would be covered by it, and how it would be operationalized. As to categories of non-staff personnel not covered by the arbitration procedure, it was proposed that the Secretary-General should provide information on measures to assist such individuals in addressing disputes that might arise. Concerning the establishment of a mechanism for addressing complaints against judges, delegations were of the opinion that the Assembly should request further study of the issue.

Office of Ombudsman and Mediation Services

Report of Secretary-General. The Secretary-General, as requested by the General Assembly in resolution 65/251 [YUN 2010, p. 1491], reported in August [A/66/224] on the activities of the integrated Office of the Ombudsman and Mediation Services for 2010. The Office had conducted a preliminary assessment of its impact and effectiveness. The assessment found that decentralization had provided the Office with better access to its constituencies and enabled it to provide in-person intervention at the field level, which was the most effective means for conflict resolution. The Office had been able to develop a greater understanding of regional dynamics, and the Mediation Service had provided staff and managers with an additional alternative tool for resolving workplace disputes. Budgetary, however, constraints made it difficult for regional ombudsmen to travel within their respective areas, including in the deep field, to provide in-person intervention for the resolution of conflicts or festering issues, and for the Office to deploy rapid response ombudsmen and mediation teams as needed.

During the reporting period, the case volume relating to staff members in the UN Secretariat increased by 70 per cent, and the overall case volume by 35 per cent, due in large part to the availability of on-site services provided by the ombudsmen in the regional branches. The primary areas of concern for visitors who used ombudsmen services were job and career; interpersonal relationships; and compensation and benefits. The Mediation Service also witnessed an increase in its caseload, with several complex and sensitive mediations leading to successful resolutions. The primary areas of concern for parties seeking assistance were job and career; legal; regulatory; financial and compliance matters; and evaluative relationships.

The Secretary-General requested $918,400 (before recosting) in additional resources for the Office.

ACABQ report. In October [A/66/7/Add.6], ACABQ conveyed its comments and recommendations on the Secretary-General's report.

GENERAL ASSEMBLY ACTION

On 24 December [meeting 93], the General Assembly, on the recommendation of the Fifth Committee [A/66/628], adopted **resolution 66/237** without vote [agenda item 143].

Administration of justice at the United Nations

The General Assembly,

Recalling section XI of its resolution 55/258 of 14 June 2001, its resolutions 57/307 of 15 April 2003, 59/266 of 23 December 2004, 59/283 of 13 April 2005, 61/261 of 4 April 2007, 62/228 of 22 December 2007, 63/253 of 24 December 2008, 64/233 of 22 December 2009 and 65/251 of 24 December 2010, as well as its decisions 63/531 of 11 December 2008 and 65/513 of 6 December 2010,

Having considered the reports of the Secretary-General on administration of justice at the United Nations and on the activities of the Office of the United Nations Ombudsman and Mediation Services, the report of the Internal Justice Council on administration of justice at the United Nations, the letter dated 4 November 2011 from the President of the General Assembly to the Chair of the Fifth Committee and the related report of the Advisory Committee on Administrative and Budgetary Questions,

1. *Takes note* of the reports of the Secretary-General on administration of justice at the United Nations and on the activities of the Office of the United Nations Ombudsman and Mediation Services;

2. *Reaffirms* its resolutions 61/261, 62/228, 63/253, 64/233 and 65/251 regarding the establishment of the new system of administration of justice;

3. *Endorses* the conclusions and recommendations contained in the report of the Advisory Committee on Administrative and Budgetary Questions, subject to the provisions of the present resolution;

I

System of administration of justice

4. *Notes with appreciation* the achievements produced since the inception of the new system of administration of justice in regard to both the disposal of the backlog and the addressing of new cases, despite the numerous difficulties faced during the implementation of the new system of administration of justice;

5. *Acknowledges* the evolving nature of the new system of administration of justice and the need to carefully monitor its implementation to ensure that it remains within the parameters set out by the General Assembly;

6. *Stresses* that all elements of the new system of administration of justice must work in accordance with the Charter of the United Nations and the legal and regulatory framework approved by the General Assembly;

7. *Emphasizes* the importance of the principle of judicial independence in the system of administration of justice;

8. *Reaffirms* its decision, contained in paragraph 4 of resolution 61/261, to establish a new, independent, transparent, professionalized, adequately resourced and decentralized system of administration of justice consistent with the relevant rules of international law and the principles of the rule of law and due process to ensure respect for the rights and obligations of staff members and the accountability of managers and staff members alike;

9. *Also reaffirms* that, in accordance with paragraph 28 of resolution 63/253, the United Nations Dispute Tribunal and the United Nations Appeals Tribunal shall not have any powers beyond those conferred under their respective statutes;

10. *Affirms* that recourse to general principles of law and the Charter by the Tribunals is to take place within the context of and consistent with their statutes and the relevant General Assembly resolutions, regulations, rules and administrative issuances;

11. *Requests* the Secretary-General to make every effort to institutionalize good management practices in order to address the underlying factors that give rise to disputes in the workplace;

12. *Stresses* the importance of ensuring access for all staff members to the new system of administration of justice, regardless of their duty station;

13. *Invites* all who are involved in the implementation and functioning of the system of administration of justice, including managers and staff members, to recognize that the system of administration of justice has been made possible by contributions from the Member States aiming to ensure that it has a positive impact on staff-management relations and improves the performance of both staff and managers;

14. *Recalls* paragraph 46 of its resolution 65/251 and paragraphs 247 to 293 of the report of the Secretary-General on administration of justice at the United Nations, and requests the Secretary-General to submit to the General Assembly, for consideration at the main part of its sixty-seventh session, an updated report on issues relevant to its review of the statutes of the Tribunals;

II

Informal system

15. *Recognizes* that the informal system of administration of justice is an efficient and effective option for staff who seek redress of grievances;

16. *Reaffirms* that the informal resolution of conflict is a crucial element of the system of administration of justice, emphasizes that all possible use should be made of the informal system in order to avoid unnecessary litigation, and in this regard requests the Secretary-General to recommend to the General Assembly at its sixty-seventh session additional measures to encourage recourse to informal resolution of disputes and to avoid unnecessary litigation;

17. *Takes note* of the reference in paragraph 5 of the report of the Advisory Committee on Administrative and Budgetary Questions to a "culture of litigation", endorses the remainder of the paragraph, and stresses the importance of developing a culture of dialogue and amicable resolution of dispute through the informal system;

18. *Recalls* paragraph 18 of its resolution 65/251 regarding the establishment of a single integrated and decentralized Office of the Ombudsman for the United Nations Secretariat, funds and programmes, and acknowledges that progress has been made in this regard;

19. *Requests* the Secretary-General to work with the United Nations funds and programmes in order to finalize, as early as possible, revised terms of reference for the Office of the United Nations Ombudsman and Mediation Services that reflect the responsibility of the United Nations Ombudsman for the oversight of the entire Office and enhance the coordination among the three pillars of the Office, and to submit to the General Assembly at the main part of its sixty-seventh session a report thereon;

20. *Recalls* paragraph 29 of resolution 65/251, welcomes the information provided informally by the Office of the United Nations Ombudsman and Mediation Services on the financial and administrative implications resulting from settlements reached through informal dispute resolution, and requests the Office to provide to the General Assembly at its sixty-seventh session another informal briefing on such implications;

21. *Welcomes* the recommendations made by the Office of the United Nations Ombudsman and Mediation Services to address systemic and cross-cutting issues, and requests the Secretary-General to submit to the General Assembly at the main part of its sixty-seventh session a report containing his views on the recommendations;

22. *Also welcomes* the establishment, in 2010, of the seven regional offices of the United Nations Ombudsman and Mediation Services in Bangkok, Geneva, Nairobi, Santiago and Vienna and in the peacekeeping missions in the Democratic Republic of the Congo and the Sudan, and their initial positive impact;

III

Formal system

23. *Takes note* of paragraph 7 of the report of the Advisory Committee on Administrative and Budgetary Questions, and requests the Secretary-General to explore all possible ways to bring about more coherent representation and efficient use of resources, taking into account the specificities of representation of the Secretary-General at the Tribunals, and to report thereon at the main part of its sixty-seventh session;

24. *Stresses* the need for the construction of fully equipped courtrooms for the Tribunals, and requests the Secretary-General to provide functional courtrooms with adequate facilities, as a matter of urgency;

25. *Emphasizes* that the formal system of administration of justice must be adequately resourced with regard to posts, travel, hearing/conference rooms, videoconferencing, sound recording, communications systems and up-to-date computer hardware and software;

26. *Notes* the important role played by the Office of Staff Legal Assistance in providing legal assistance to staff members in an independent and impartial manner, and also notes that the Office currently represents staff members in cases before the Dispute Tribunal in New York, Geneva and Nairobi and before the Appeals Tribunal;

27. *Decides* that, pending further consideration of this issue by the General Assembly at its sixty-seventh session, the role of the Office of Staff Legal Assistance shall continue to be that of assisting staff members and their volunteer representatives in processing claims through the formal system of administration of justice, including representation, within the financial parameters agreed upon in the present resolution;

28. *Also decides* to revert, at its sixty-seventh session, to the issue of the mandate, scope and functioning of the Office of Staff Legal Assistance, and in this regard requests the Secretary-General to submit, after consultation with the Internal Justice Council and other relevant bodies, a comprehensive report proposing different options for the representation of staff members before the internal Tribunals, taking into account all relevant resolutions and reports, including the letters of the Sixth Committee to the Fifth Committee, and the relevant recommendations of the Advisory Committee on Administrative and Budgetary Questions contained in its report, including a detailed proposal for a mandatory staff-funded mechanism, reflecting, if necessary, the implications of the different proposals, for consideration by both the Fifth Committee and the Sixth Committee, in their respective capacities, at the sixty-seventh session;

29. *Recalls* article 2 of the statute of the United Nations Dispute Tribunal, and affirms that an action instituted against the Secretary-General under the statute is an action against the Secretary-General as the Chief Administrative Officer of the United Nations, responsible for administrative decisions taken by or on behalf of the Organization by staff appointed by the Secretary-General;

30. *Also recalls* article 7 of the statute of the Dispute Tribunal and article 6 of the statute of the United Nations Appeals Tribunal, and requests both Tribunals to review their procedures with regard to the dismissal of manifestly inadmissible cases;

31. *Decides* to amend article 7, paragraph 1 (*c*), of the statute of the Appeals Tribunal to extend the deadline for filing appeals of Dispute Tribunal judgements from 45 days to 60 days and to establish a 30-day deadline for filing appeals of interlocutory orders;

32. *Recalls* paragraph 54 of resolution 62/228, and decides that the time limit for completing management evaluations may be extended by the Dispute Tribunal for a period of up to fifteen days in exceptional circumstances when both parties to a dispute agree;

33. *Also recalls* paragraph 28 of resolution 63/253, reaffirms article 10, paragraphs 5 (*b*) and 7, of the statute of the Dispute Tribunal, endorses the practice under the previous United Nations Administrative Tribunal to limit awards in any one case normally to a total of no more than two years net base salary for compensation and in exceptional cases to no more than three years net base salary, and reaffirms the requirement in article 10, paragraph 5 (*b*), that in all cases where the Dispute Tribunal orders the payment of a compensation higher than two years net pay, the Tribunal must provide clear and well-documented reasons for that decision;

34. *Requests* the Secretary-General to provide the General Assembly at the main part of its sixty-seventh session with a report on the practice of tribunals in other international organizations and in Member States comparable to the Dispute Tribunal and the Appeals Tribunal regarding the awarding of exemplary or punitive damages, including their practice with regard to awards for moral damages, emotional distress, procedural irregularities and violations of due process;

35. *Recalls* article 11, paragraph 3, of the statute of the Dispute Tribunal, and affirms that judgements of the Dispute Tribunal, including judgements, orders or rulings, imposing financial obligations on the Organization are not executable until the expiry of the time provided for appeal in the statute of the Appeals Tribunal or, if an appeal has been filed in accordance with the statute of the Appeals Tribunal, until the Appeals Tribunal has completed action on such appeal in accordance with articles 10 and 11 of its statute;

36. *Also recalls* article 7 of the statute of the Dispute Tribunal and article 6 of the statute of the Appeals Tribunal, and encourages the Tribunals to continue and expand, as appropriate, their practice of consultation in the process for developing amendments to their rules of procedure;

37. *Further recalls* section I, paragraph 5, of its resolution 53/221 of 7 April 1999, in which it underlined its full respect for the prerogatives and responsibilities of the Secretary-General under the Charter, and reaffirms that the resolutions of the General Assembly and the decisions of the International Civil Service Commission are binding on the Secretary-General and on the Organization;

38. *Requests* the Secretary-General to submit to the General Assembly at the main part of its sixty-seventh session a report providing:

(*a*) A proposal for implementing the proposed mechanism for expedited arbitration procedures for individual contractors and consultants provided in annex II to the report of the Secretary-General on administration of justice, including the cost implications for various aspects of the proposal;

(b) An analysis of the policy and financial implications in the event that individual contractors and consultants covered by the proposed expedited arbitration procedures were to be permitted access to mediation under the informal system;

39. *Also requests* the Secretary-General to submit to the General Assembly at the main part of its sixty-seventh session a report on access to the system of administration of justice for different categories of non-staff personnel who are not covered under the dispute resolution mechanism proposed in annex II of the report on administration of justice;

40. *Further requests* the Secretary-General to include in the report requested in paragraph 39 above information on measures to be made available with regard to the informal and formal aspects of the system of administration of justice in order to assist such non-staff personnel to address disputes that may arise;

41. *Recalls* paragraph 89 of the report of the Advisory Committee on Administrative and Budgetary Questions, and requests the Secretary-General to include in his report on administration of justice, to be submitted to the General Assembly at its sixty-seventh session, information on the concrete measures taken to enforce accountability in cases where contested decisions have resulted in awards of compensation to staff;

IV

Financial implications and cost-sharing arrangements

42. *Takes note* of paragraphs 19 to 21 of the report of the Advisory Committee on Administrative and Budgetary Questions, decides to extend the mandate for the three ad litem judges of the Dispute Tribunal for one year, subject to review and possible extension for a further year, and also decides to approve, under general temporary assistance, three Legal Officer (P-3), two General Service (Other level) and one General Service (Local level) positions to support the ad litem judges for the same period;

43. *Requests* the Secretary-General to make every effort to expedite the finalization of an agreement on a cost-sharing arrangement for the totality of the internal justice system and to report thereon, including on the expected reimbursement of approximately 6.8 million United States dollars from the participating United Nations entities, to the General Assembly at the main part of its sixty-seventh session;

V

Other issues

44. *Also requests* the Secretary-General to submit to the General Assembly at the main part of its sixty-seventh session a report providing proposals and analysis for a mechanism for addressing possible misconduct of judges, as well as additional views or analysis with regard to the proposals contained in the reports of the Secretary-General on administration of justice at the United Nations and in the reports of the Internal Justice Council, as well as other proposals, including a proposal for a new mechanism for addressing such misconduct, consisting of one jurist from the highest judicial tribunal drawn from one Member State from each of the five geographical regions appointed or elected by the General Assembly to serve when and as needed;

45. *Stresses* that the Internal Justice Council can help to ensure independence, professionalism and accountability in the system of administration of justice, and requests the Secretary-General to entrust the Council with including the views of both the Dispute Tribunal and the Appeals Tribunal in its annual reports;

46. *Requests* the Secretary-General to submit to the General Assembly at the main part of its sixty-seventh session, in consultation with the Internal Justice Council and other relevant bodies, a report providing his recommendations and analysis regarding the proposal in the report of the Council to the General Assembly at its sixty-fifth session on a code of conduct for legal representation;

47. *Also requests* the Secretary-General to provide the reports requested in paragraphs 14, 16, 19, 21, 23, 28, 34, 38, 39, 43, 44 and 46 above in a single comprehensive report on administration of justice to be submitted to the General Assembly at the main part of its sixty-seventh session;

48. *Invites* the Sixth Committee to consider the legal aspects of the report to be submitted by the Secretary-General, without prejudice to the role of the Fifth Committee as the Main Committee entrusted with responsibilities for administrative and budgetary matters.

On the same date, the Assembly decided that the agenda item on the administration of justice would remain for consideration during its resumed sixty-sixth (2012) session (**decision 66/557**).

UN Dispute and Appeals Tribunals

Appointment of judges

On 28 January (**decision 65/414**), the General Assembly appointed Ms. Mary Faherty (Ireland) as a judge of the United Nations Appeals Tribunal for a term of office beginning on 28 January 2011 and ending on 30 June 2016, as a result of the resignation of Ms. Rose Boyko [YUN 2010, p. 1491].

The Secretary-General transmitted a 4 May letter [A/65/853] of the Internal Justice Council recommending the reappointment of two out of the three ad litem judges serving on the United Nations Dispute Tribunal—Judge Jean-François Cousin (France) and Judge Nkemdilim Amelia Izuako (Nigeria)—to serve for a further six months. The Council did not recommend any candidates to fill the vacancy created by Judge Marilyn Kaman (United States), who was unable to be considered for reappointment for the additional six months.

On 27 May [A/65/233], the Secretary-General requested that an additional sub-item entitled "Appointment of ad litem judges of the United Nations Dispute Tribunal" be included in the agenda of the General Assembly's resumed sixty-fifth (2011) session. This would allow for consideration, on the recommendation of the Internal Justice Council, of the reappointment and extension for six months of ad litem judges whose terms would expire on 30 June.

On 29 June (**decision 65/419**), the Assembly extended the terms of office of the two ad litem judges for an additional six months beginning 1 July 2011.

On 24 December (**decision 66/557**), the Assembly decided that the agenda items on the appointment of judges of the United Nations Dispute Tribunal and the United Nations Appeals Tribunal would remain on the agenda of its resumed sixty-sixth (2012) session.

Code of conduct for judges

The Internal Justice Council, in its July report [A/66/158], noted that it had submitted the draft code of conduct for judges of the United Nations Dispute Tribunal and the United Nations Appeals Tribunal to the Secretary-General for transmission to the General Assembly at its sixty-fifth (2010) session [YUN 2010, p. 1489]; however, the Assembly did not consider the code at that session. The Council noted that there was an urgent need for the code to come into force, particularly because complaints against judges had been received by the Council, and the code would be the basis for determining whether they had merit once a complaints mechanism was put in place.

In December, by resolution 66/106 (see below), the General Assembly approved the code of conduct for the judges of the Tribunals, the text of which was annexed to the resolution.

GENERAL ASSEMBLY ACTION

On 9 December [meeting 82], the General Assembly, on the recommendation of the Sixth Committee [A/66/481], adopted **resolution 66/106** without vote [agenda item 143].

Code of conduct for the judges of the United Nations Dispute Tribunal and the United Nations Appeals Tribunal

The General Assembly,

Recalling its resolution 62/228 of 22 December 2007, in which it decided that the Internal Justice Council should draft a code of conduct for the judges of the United Nations Dispute Tribunal and the United Nations Appeals Tribunal, for consideration by the General Assembly,

Recalling also the invitation, made in the relevant resolutions, to the Sixth Committee to consider the legal aspects of the administration of justice at the United Nations, without prejudice to the role of the Fifth Committee as the Main Committee entrusted with responsibilities for administrative and budgetary matters,

Having considered the reports of the Internal Justice Council submitted to the General Assembly at its sixty-fifth and sixty-sixth sessions, which contain in the annexes thereto the draft text of a code of conduct for the judges of the Tribunals,

Expressing its appreciation to the Internal Justice Council for preparing the draft code of conduct for the judges,

Approves the code of conduct for the judges of the United Nations Dispute Tribunal and the United Nations Appeals Tribunal, as set out in the annex to the present resolution.

ANNEX

Code of conduct for the judges of the United Nations Dispute Tribunal and the United Nations Appeals Tribunal

Preamble

Whereas the Charter of the United Nations affirms, inter alia, the determination of Member States to establish conditions under which justice can be maintained to achieve international cooperation in promoting and encouraging respect for human rights and fundamental freedoms without any discrimination,

Whereas the Universal Declaration of Human Rights recognizes as fundamental the principle that everyone is entitled in full equality to a fair and public hearing by an independent and impartial tribunal, in the determination of rights and obligations,

Whereas this right is endorsed and elaborated upon in a range of important international human rights instruments, including the International Covenant on Civil and Political Rights,

Whereas the General Assembly, in paragraph 4 of its resolution 61/261 of 4 April 2007, decided to establish an independent, transparent, professionalized, adequately resourced and decentralized system of administration of justice consistent with the relevant rules of international law and the principles of the rule of law and due process to ensure respect for the rights and obligations of staff members and the accountability of managers and staff members alike,

Whereas the fair resolution of employment grievances will contribute to efficiency in the work carried out by the United Nations and enhance the integrity of the Organization,

Whereas public confidence in the internal justice system and in the moral authority and integrity of the United Nations Dispute Tribunal and the United Nations Appeals Tribunal is of the utmost importance within the working environment of the United Nations,

Whereas it is essential that judges, individually and collectively, respect and honour judicial office as a public trust, and strive to enhance and maintain confidence in the internal justice system,

And whereas the Basic Principles on the Independence of the Judiciary are designed to secure and promote the independence of judicial bodies, and can provide guidance for the internal administration of justice,

The following values and principles are adopted to establish standards for the conduct of the judges of the United Nations Dispute Tribunal and the United Nations Appeals Tribunal, to provide guidance to those judges and also to assist the staff and management of the United Nations to better understand and support the work of the United Nations Dispute Tribunal and the United Nations Appeals Tribunal within the United Nations:

1. Independence

(*a*) Judges must uphold the independence and integrity of the internal justice system of the United Nations and must act independently in the performance of their duties, free of any inappropriate influences, inducements, pressures or threats from any party or quarter;

(*b*) In order to protect the institutional independence of the Tribunals, judges must take all reasonable steps to ensure that no person, party, institution or State interferes, directly or indirectly, with the Tribunals;

2. Impartiality

(a) Judges must act without fear, favour, or prejudice in all matters that they adjudicate;

(b) Judges must ensure that their conduct at all times maintains the confidence of all in the impartiality of the Tribunals;

(c) Judges must recuse themselves from a case if:
  (i) They have a conflict of interest;
  (ii) It may reasonably appear to a properly informed person that they have a conflict of interest;
  (iii) They have personal knowledge of disputed evidentiary facts concerning the proceedings;

(d) Judges must not recuse themselves on insubstantial grounds. Judges must provide reasons when they decide an application for recusal;

(e) Judges must disclose to the parties in good time any matter that could reasonably be perceived to give rise to an application for recusal in a particular matter;

(f) Judges must not participate in the determination of a case in which any member of their family is a litigant or represents a litigant, or in the outcome of which any member of their family has a significant interest;

(g) In order to determine whether they should recuse themselves from any matter, judges must be aware of their personal and fiduciary financial interests and shall, as far as reasonably possible, make efforts to be informed about the financial interests of members of their immediate family;

(h) (i) Judges must not directly or indirectly negotiate or accept any remuneration, income, compensation, gift, advantage or privilege that is incompatible with judicial office or that can reasonably be perceived either as a reward or as likely to influence them in favour of a particular party;
  (ii) Judges may receive a token gift, decoration, award or benefit that does not result in the incompatibility or reasonable perception referred to in subparagraph (h) (i) above;

(i) Judges must not engage in financial, political or business dealings or activities, including fund-raising activities, that are inconsistent with, and reflect adversely upon, the independence and impartiality required by their status as judges, that may reasonably be perceived to exploit the judge's judicial position, or that are in any other way incompatible with judicial office in the United Nations;

3. Integrity

(a) Judges must be of high moral character and always, and not only in the discharge of their duties, act honourably and in accordance with the values and principles set out in the present Code;

(b) Judges at all times, including periods when they are not on official business, must comply with the law of the country in which they live, work or visit;

(c) Judges must inform the presiding judge of their Tribunal should they suffer from an illness or other condition that might threaten the performance of their duties;

4. Propriety

(a) Judges must exhibit and promote high standards of judicial conduct to reinforce confidence in the integrity of the administration of justice at the United Nations;

(b) Save in the discharge of judicial office, judges must not comment publicly on the merits of any case pending before the Tribunals or make any comment that might reasonably be expected to affect the outcome of such proceedings or impair the manifest fairness of the process;

(c) Judges are bound by professional duties of confidentiality with regard to deliberations with judicial colleagues and confidential information acquired in the course of their duties;

(d) Judges, like other citizens, are entitled to freedom of expression, belief, association and assembly, but must exercise these freedoms with due regard to the values and principles set out in the present Code;

(e) Judges must not use or lend the prestige of judicial office to advance the private interests of the judge, a member of the judge's family or anyone else, nor shall judges convey the impression that anyone is in a position to influence them improperly;

(f) In their personal relations with individual staff members who are parties, legal representatives and others who appear regularly in the Tribunal presided over by them, judges must avoid situations which might give rise to the reasonable apprehension of favouritism or partiality;

(g) Full-time judges of the United Nations Dispute Tribunal must not practise law, but may give informal advice to family members, friends, charitable organizations and the like without remuneration;

(h) Judges should use their best endeavours to foster collegiality in the Tribunals. In so doing they must act courteously and respect the dignity of others, including members of the Tribunal staff;

(i) Judges may form or join associations of judges;

(j) Subject to the proper and effective performance of judicial duties, a judge may engage in any lawful activity as long as it does not bring the judicial office in the United Nations into disrepute in the mind of reasonable members of the community;

5. Transparency

Judges must observe the principle of open justice, namely that justice must be seen to be done, and take reasonable steps to ensure that this principle is honoured in the manner in which cases before the Tribunals are handled;

6. Fairness in the conduct of proceedings

(a) Judges must resolve disputes by making findings of fact and applying the appropriate law in fair proceedings. This includes the duty to:
  (i) Observe the letter and spirit of the *audi alteram partem* ("hear the other side") rule;
  (ii) Remain manifestly impartial;
  (iii) Publish reasons for any decision;

(b) Judges must not conduct themselves in a manner that is racist, sexist or otherwise discriminatory. They must uphold and respect the principles set out in the Charter of the United Nations, the Universal Declaration of Human Rights and the International Covenant on Civil and Political Rights. Judges must not by word or conduct unfairly discriminate against any individual or group of individuals, or abuse the power and authority vested in them;

(c) Judges must not permit Tribunal staff or legal representatives appearing before the Tribunals, or others under their direction or control, to act in a manner that is racist, sexist or otherwise discriminatory;

(d) Judges have a duty to protect witnesses and parties from harassment and bullying during Tribunal proceedings;

(e) When conducting judicial proceedings, judges must act courteously to legal representatives, parties, witnesses, Tribunal staff, judicial colleagues and the public, and require them to act courteously;

7. Competence and diligence

(a) Judges must perform all assigned judicial duties, including tasks relevant to the judicial office or the operation of the Tribunals, diligently and dispose of judicial work promptly in an efficient and professional manner;

(b) Judges must give judgement or rulings in a case promptly. Judgements should be given no later than three months from the end of the hearing or the close of pleadings or, in the case of the United Nations Appeals Tribunal, from the end of the session in which the matter is decided, unless there are exceptional circumstances;

(c) Judges must cooperate with any formal inquiry into their conduct in office;

(d) Judges must not engage in conduct that is prejudicial to the effective and expeditious administration of justice or the work of the Tribunal;

(e) When engaged in the administration of justice, judges must attend chambers during their normal working hours, as determined by the members of the Tribunal, and attend hearings and deliberations of the Tribunal during stipulated hours, unless they have a good reason not to do so. Judges must inform the presiding judge of the Tribunal in advance if they need to be absent. If they are to be absent for longer than three days, they must obtain the approval of the presiding judge of their Tribunal;

(f) Judges must respect and comply with the reasonable administrative requests of the presiding judge of the Tribunal of which they are members;

(g) Judges must take reasonable steps to maintain the necessary level of professional competence and to keep themselves informed about relevant developments in international administrative and employment law, as well as international human rights norms;

(h) Judges' judicial duties must take precedence over other duties and activities.

Mechanism for handling complaints against judges

The Secretary-General, in his August report on the administration of justice [A/66/275], noted the absence of a mechanism for handling complaints made against judges of the Tribunals. He therefore proposed that the General Assembly, as an interim measure and pending its decision on a permanent mechanism, might wish to authorize the Internal Justice Council to investigate complaints against judges, including any complaints that had already arisen, and to provide a report and recommendations on those complaints to the Assembly for action, as appropriate. As for a possible permanent mechanism, the Secretary-General proposed that when an allegation regarding the misconduct or incapacity of a judge was made, it would be reported to the President of the Tribunal in question, who would investigate the claim, first determining an appropriate investigative process and subsequently appointing a panel of specialists to conduct the investigation. The findings of the investigation would be reviewed by the entire Tribunal, with the exception of the judge under investigation, and the matter reported to the Assembly if it was found to be of sufficient severity to warrant the removal of the judge. An alternative would be an amendment to the terms of reference of the Internal Justice Council to provide it with the responsibility to investigate and make recommendations regarding any complaint against a judge of the Tribunals and, where allegations were determined to be well founded, to recommend appropriate sanctions.

The Assembly, in section V of resolution 66/237 of 24 December (see p. 1450), requested the Secretary-General to submit proposals and analysis for a complaints mechanism at the main part of its sixty-seventh (2012) session.

Amendments to rules of procedure

In June [A/66/86 & Add.1], the Secretary-General informed the General Assembly of amendments adopted by the United Nations Dispute Tribunal to article 19 (Case management) of its rules of procedure [YUN 2009, p. 1476]. He also reported amendments adopted by the United Nations Appeals Tribunal to article 9 (Answers), paragraph 4, and article 4 (Panels), paragraph 2 of its rules of procedure [ibid., p. 1481]. The rules, as amended, were to apply provisionally until approved by the Assembly.

In December, by resolution 66/107 (see below), the General Assembly decided not to approve the amendment to article 19 (Case management). Those amendments which it did approve were annexed to the resolution.

GENERAL ASSEMBLY ACTION

On 9 December [meeting 82], the General Assembly, on the recommendation of the Sixth Committee [A/66/481], adopted **resolution 66/107** without vote [agenda item 143].

Amendments to the rules of procedure of the United Nations Appeals Tribunal

The General Assembly,

Recalling its resolution 63/253 of 24 December 2008, in which it adopted the statutes of the United Nations Dispute Tribunal and the United Nations Appeals Tribunal, as set out in annexes I and II to that resolution,

Recalling also article 7, paragraph 1, of the statute of the United Nations Dispute Tribunal and article 6, paragraph 1, of the statute of the United Nations Appeals Tribunal,

Recalling further article 37, paragraphs 1 and 2, of the rules of procedure of the United Nations Dispute Tribunal, as well as article 32, paragraphs 1 and 2, of the rules of procedure of the United Nations Appeals Tribunal,

Having considered the report of the Secretary-General,

1. *Approves* the amendments to the rules of procedure of the United Nations Appeals Tribunal, as set out in the annex to the present resolution;

2. *Decides* not to approve the amendment to article 19 (Case management) of the rules of procedure of the United Nations Dispute Tribunal contained in annex I of document A/66/86 and adopted by the Tribunal on 14 December 2010 in accordance with article 37, paragraph 1, of the rules of procedure.

Annex
Amendments to the rules of procedure of the United Nations Appeals Tribunal

Article 4
Panels

2. When the President or any two judges sitting on a particular case consider that the case so warrants, the case shall be heard by the whole Appeals Tribunal. If there is a tie in the voting by the judges of the whole Appeals Tribunal, the President shall have a casting vote.

Article 9
Answers, cross-appeals and answers to cross-appeals

4. Within 45 days of notification of the appeal, a party answering the appeal may file a cross-appeal, accompanied by a brief which shall not exceed 15 pages, with the Appeals Tribunal stating the relief sought and the grounds of the cross-appeal. The cross-appeal may not add new claims.

6. The provisions of article 9.1 to 9.3 and 9.5 apply, mutatis mutandis, to a cross-appeal and answer to a cross-appeal.

Article 18 bis
Case management

1. The President may, at any time, either on a motion of a party or of his or her own volition, issue any order which appears to be appropriate for the fair and expeditious management of the case and to do justice to the parties.

2. If, before the opening date of the session during which the case is to be considered, the appellant informs the Appeals Tribunal, in writing, with notice to the respondent, that he or she wishes to discontinue the proceedings, the President may order the case to be removed from the register.

3. If an action has become devoid of purpose and there is no longer any need to adjudicate it, the President may, at any time, of his or her own volition, after having informed the parties of that intention and, if applicable, received their observations, adopt a reasoned order.

4. The President may designate a judge or a panel of judges to issue any order within the purview of the present article.

Article 19
Adoption and issuance of judgements

2. Judgements shall be issued in writing and shall state the reasons, facts and law on which they are based. Summary judgements may be issued at any time, even when the Appeals Tribunal is not in session. They shall be adopted by panels of three judges designated by the President.

Appendices

Appendix I

Roster of the United Nations

(There were 193 Member States as at 31 December 2011.)

Member State	Date of admission	Member State	Date of admission	Member State	Date of admission
Afghanistan	19 Nov. 1946	Democratic Republic of the Congo[4]	20 Sep. 1960	Latvia	17 Sep. 1991
Albania	14 Dec. 1955			Lebanon	24 Oct. 1945
Algeria	8 Oct. 1962	Denmark	24 Oct. 1945	Lesotho	17 Oct. 1966
Andorra	28 July 1993	Djibouti	20 Sep. 1977	Liberia	2 Nov. 1945
Angola	1 Dec. 1976	Dominica	18 Dec. 1978	Libyan Arab Jamahiriya	14 Dec. 1955
Antigua and Barbuda	11 Nov. 1981	Dominican Republic	24 Oct. 1945	Liechtenstein	18 Sep. 1990
Argentina	24 Oct. 1945	Ecuador	21 Dec. 1945	Lithuania	17 Sep. 1991
Armenia	2 Mar. 1992	Egypt[5]	24 Oct. 1945	Luxembourg	24 Oct. 1945
Australia	1 Nov. 1945	El Salvador	24 Oct. 1945	Madagascar	20 Sep. 1960
Austria	14 Dec. 1955	Equatorial Guinea	12 Nov. 1968	Malawi	1 Dec. 1964
Azerbaijan	2 Mar. 1992	Eritrea	28 May 1993	Malaysia[8]	17 Sep. 1957
Bahamas	18 Sep. 1973	Estonia	17 Sep. 1991	Maldives	21 Sep. 1965
Bahrain	21 Sep. 1971	Ethiopia	13 Nov. 1945	Mali	28 Sep. 1960
Bangladesh	17 Sep. 1974	Fiji	13 Oct. 1970	Malta	1 Dec. 1964
Barbados	9 Dec. 1966	Finland	14 Dec. 1955	Marshall Islands	17 Sep. 1991
Belarus[1]	24 Oct. 1945	France	24 Oct. 1945	Mauritania	27 Oct. 1961
Belgium	27 Dec. 1945	Gabon	20 Sep. 1960	Mauritius	24 Apr. 1968
Belize	25 Sep. 1981	Gambia	21 Sep. 1965	Mexico	7 Nov. 1945
Benin	20 Sep. 1960	Georgia	31 July 1992	Micronesia (Federated States of)	17 Sep. 1991
Bhutan	21 Sep. 1971	Germany[6]	18 Sep. 1973		
Bolivia	14 Nov. 1945	Ghana	8 Mar. 1957	Monaco	28 May 1993
Bosnia and Herzegovina[2]	22 May 1992	Greece	25 Oct. 1945	Mongolia	27 Oct. 1961
Botswana	17 Oct. 1966	Grenada	17 Sep. 1974	Montenegro[2]	28 June 2006
Brazil	24 Oct. 1945	Guatemala	21 Nov. 1945	Morocco	12 Nov. 1956
Brunei Darussalam	21 Sep. 1984	Guinea	12 Dec. 1958	Mozambique	16 Sep. 1975
Bulgaria	14 Dec. 1955	Guinea-Bissau	17 Sep. 1974	Myanmar	19 Apr. 1948
Burkina Faso	20 Sep. 1960	Guyana	20 Sep. 1966	Namibia	23 Apr. 1990
Burundi	18 Sep. 1962	Haiti	24 Oct. 1945	Nauru	14 Sep. 1999
Cambodia	14 Dec. 1955	Honduras	17 Dec. 1945	Nepal	14 Dec. 1955
Cameroon	20 Sep. 1960	Hungary	14 Dec. 1955	Netherlands	10 Dec. 1945
Canada	9 Nov. 1945	Iceland	19 Nov. 1946	New Zealand	24 Oct. 1945
Cape Verde	16 Sep. 1975	India	30 Oct. 1945	Nicaragua	24 Oct. 1945
Central African Republic	20 Sep. 1960	Indonesia[7]	28 Sep. 1950	Niger	20 Sep. 1960
Chad	20 Sep. 1960	Iran (Islamic Republic of)	24 Oct. 1945	Nigeria	7 Oct. 1960
Chile	24 Oct. 1945	Iraq	21 Dec. 1945	Norway	27 Nov. 1945
China	24 Oct. 1945	Ireland	14 Dec. 1955	Oman	7 Oct. 1971
Colombia	5 Nov. 1945	Israel	11 May 1949	Pakistan	30 Sep. 1947
Comoros	12 Nov. 1975	Italy	14 Dec. 1955	Palau	15 Dec. 1994
Congo	20 Sep. 1960	Jamaica	18 Sep. 1962	Panama	13 Nov. 1945
Costa Rica	2 Nov. 1945	Japan	18 Dec. 1956	Papua New Guinea	10 Oct. 1975
Côte d'Ivoire	20 Sep. 1960	Jordan	14 Dec. 1955	Paraguay	24 Oct. 1945
Croatia[2]	22 May 1992	Kazakhstan	2 Mar. 1992	Peru	31 Oct. 1945
Cuba	24 Oct. 1945	Kenya	16 Dec. 1963	Philippines	24 Oct. 1945
Cyprus	20 Sep. 1960	Kiribati	14 Sep. 1999	Poland	24 Oct. 1945
Czech Republic[3]	19 Jan. 1993	Kuwait	14 May 1963	Portugal	14 Dec. 1955
Democratic People's Republic of Korea	17 Sep. 1991	Kyrgyzstan	2 Mar. 1992	Qatar	21 Sep. 1971
		Lao People's Democratic Republic	14 Dec. 1955		

Member State	Date of admission	Member State	Date of admission	Member State	Date of admission
Republic of Korea	17 Sep. 1991	Solomon Islands	19 Sep. 1978	Turkey	24 Oct. 1945
Republic of Moldova	2 Mar. 1992	Somalia	20 Sep. 1960	Turkmenistan	2 Mar. 1992
Romania	14 Dec. 1955	South Africa	7 Nov. 1945	Tuvalu	5 Sep. 2000
Russian Federation[9]	24 Oct. 1945	South Sudan[10]	14 July 2011	Uganda	25 Oct. 1962
Rwanda	18 Sep. 1962	Spain	14 Dec. 1955	Ukraine	24 Oct. 1945
Saint Kitts and Nevis	23 Sep. 1983	Sri Lanka	14 Dec. 1955	United Arab Emirates	9 Dec. 1971
Saint Lucia	18 Sep. 1979	Sudan	12 Nov. 1956	United Kingdom of Great Britain and Northern Ireland	24 Oct. 1945
Saint Vincent and the Grenadines	16 Sep. 1980	Suriname	4 Dec. 1975		
		Swaziland	24 Sep. 1968		
Samoa	15 Dec. 1976	Sweden	19 Nov. 1946	United Republic of Tanzania[11]	14 Dec. 1961
San Marino	2 Mar. 1992	Switzerland	10 Sep. 2002		
Sao Tome and Principe	16 Sep. 1975	Syrian Arab Republic[5]	24 Oct. 1945	United States of America	24 Oct. 1945
Saudi Arabia	24 Oct. 1945	Tajikistan	2 Mar. 1992	Uruguay	18 Dec. 1945
Senegal	28 Sep. 1960	Thailand	16 Dec. 1946	Uzbekistan	2 Mar. 1992
Serbia[2]	1 Nov. 2000	The former Yugoslav Republic of Macedonia[2]	8 Apr. 1993	Vanuatu	15 Sep. 1981
Seychelles	21 Sep. 1976			Venezuela (Bolivarian Republic of)	15 Nov. 1945
Sierra Leone	27 Sep. 1961	Timor-Leste	27 Sep. 2002		
Singapore[8]	21 Sep. 1965	Togo	20 Sep. 1960	Viet Nam	20 Sep. 1977
Slovakia[3]	19 Jan. 1993	Tonga	14 Sep. 1999	Yemen[12]	30 Sep. 1947
Slovenia[2]	22 May 1992	Trinidad and Tobago	18 Sep. 1962	Zambia	1 Dec. 1964
		Tunisia	12 Nov. 1956	Zimbabwe	25 Aug. 1980

Notes

[1] On 19 September 1991, the Byelorussian Soviet Socialist Republic informed the United Nations that it had changed its name to Belarus.

[2] The Socialist Federal Republic of Yugoslavia was an original Member of the United Nations, the Charter having been signed on its behalf on 26 June 1945 and ratified 19 October 1945, until its dissolution following the establishment and subsequent admission, as new Members, of Bosnia and Herzegovina, the Republic of Croatia, the Republic of Slovenia, the former Yugoslav Republic of Macedonia, and the Federal Republic of Yugoslavia. The Republic of Bosnia and Herzegovina, the Republic of Croatia and the Republic of Slovenia were admitted as Members of the United Nations on 22 May 1992. On 8 April 1993, the General Assembly decided to admit as a Member of the United Nations the state provisionally referred to for all purposes within the United Nations as "the former Yugoslav Republic of Macedonia", pending settlement of the difference that had arisen over its name. The Federal Republic of Yugoslavia was admitted as a Member of the United Nations on 1 November 2000. On 12 February 2003, it informed the United Nations that it had changed its name to Serbia and Montenegro, effective 4 February 2003. In a letter dated 3 June 2006, the President of the Republic of Serbia informed the Secretary-General that the membership of Serbia and Montenegro was being continued by the Republic of Serbia following Montenegro's declaration of independence from Serbia on 3 June 2006. On 28 June 2006, Montenegro was accepted as a United Nations Member State by the General Assembly.

[3] Czechoslovakia, an original Member of the United Nations from 24 October 1945, changed its name to the Czech and Slovak Federal Republic on 20 April 1990. It was dissolved on 1 January 1993 and succeeded by the Czech Republic and Slovakia, both of which became Members of the United Nations on 19 January 1993.

[4] The Republic of Zaire informed the United Nations that, effective 17 May 1997, it had changed its name to the Democratic Republic of the Congo.

[5] Egypt and Syria, both of which became Members of the United Nations on 24 October 1945, joined together—following a plebiscite held in those countries on 21 February 1958—to form the United Arab Republic. On 13 October 1961, Syria, having resumed its status as an independent State, also resumed its separate membership in the United Nations; it changed its name to the Syrian Arab Republic on 14 September 1971. The United Arab Republic continued as a Member of the United Nations and reverted to the name Egypt on 2 September 1971.

[6] Through accession of the German Democratic Republic to the Federal Republic of Germany on 3 October 1990, the two German States (both of which had become Members of the United Nations on 18 September 1973) united to form one sovereign State. As from that date, the Federal Republic of Germany has acted in the United Nations under the designation Germany.

[7] On 20 January 1965, Indonesia informed the Secretary-General that it had decided to withdraw from the United Nations. On 19 September 1966, it notified the Secretary-General of its decision to resume participation in the activities of the United Nations. On 28 September 1966, the General Assembly took note of that decision, and the President invited the representatives of Indonesia to take their seats in the Assembly.

[8] On 16 September 1963, Sabah (North Borneo), Sarawak and Singapore joined with the Federation of Malaya (which became a Member of the United Nations on 17 September 1957) to form Malaysia. On 9 August 1965, Singapore became an independent State; on 21 September 1965, it became a Member of the United Nations.

[9] The Union of Soviet Socialist Republics was an original Member of the United Nations from 24 October 1945. On 24 December 1991, the President of the Russian Federation informed the Secretary-General that the membership of the USSR in all United Nations organs was being continued by the Russian Federation.

[10] The Republic of South Sudan formally seceded from Sudan on 9 July 2011 as a result of an internationally monitored referendum held in January 2011, and was admitted as a new Member State by the United Nations General Assembly on 14 July 2011.

[11] Tanganyika was admitted to the United Nations on 14 December 1961, Zanzibar on 16 December 1963. Following ratification, on 26 April 1964, of the Articles of Union between Tanganyika and Zanzibar, the two States became represented as a single Member: the United Republic of Tanganyika and Zanzibar; it changed its name to the United Republic of Tanzania on 1 November 1964.

[12] Yemen was admitted to the United Nations on 30 September 1947, Democratic Yemen on 14 December 1967. On 22 May 1990, the two countries merged and were thereafter represented as one Member of the United Nations under the designation Yemen.

Appendix II

Charter of the United Nations and Statute of the International Court of Justice

Charter of the United Nations

NOTE: The Charter of the United Nations was signed on 26 June 1945, in San Francisco, at the conclusion of the United Nations Conference on International Organization, and came into force on 24 October 1945. The Statute of the International Court of Justice is an integral part of the Charter.

Amendments to Articles 23, 27 and 61 of the Charter were adopted by the General Assembly on 17 December 1963 and came into force on 31 August 1965. A further amendment to Article 61 was adopted by the General Assembly on 20 December 1971 and came into force on 24 September 1973. An amendment to Article 109, adopted by the General Assembly on 20 December 1965, came into force on 12 June 1968.

The amendment to Article 23 enlarges the membership of the Security Council from 11 to 15. The amended Article 27 provides that decisions of the Security Council on procedural matters shall be made by an affirmative vote of nine members (formerly seven) and on all other matters by an affirmative vote of nine members (formerly seven), including the concurring votes of the five permanent members of the Security Council.

The amendment to Article 61, which entered into force on 31 August 1965, enlarges the membership of the Economic and Social Council from 18 to 27. The subsequent amendment to that Article, which entered into force on 24 September 1973, further increases the membership of the Council from 27 to 54.

The amendment to Article 109, which relates to the first paragraph of that Article, provides that a General Conference of Member States for the purpose of reviewing the Charter may be held at a date and place to be fixed by a two-thirds vote of the members of the General Assembly and by a vote of any nine members (formerly seven) of the Security Council. Paragraph 3 of Article 109, which deals with the consideration of a possible review conference during the tenth regular session of the General Assembly, has been retained in its original form in its reference to a "vote of any seven members of the Security Council", the paragraph having been acted upon in 1955 by the General Assembly, at its tenth regular session, and by the Security Council.

WE THE PEOPLES OF THE UNITED NATIONS DETERMINED

to save succeeding generations from the scourge of war, which twice in our lifetime has brought untold sorrow to mankind, and

to reaffirm faith in fundamental human rights, in the dignity and worth of the human person, in the equal rights of men and women and of nations large and small, and

to establish conditions under which justice and respect for the obligations arising from treaties and other sources of international law can be maintained, and

to promote social progress and better standards of life in larger freedom,

AND FOR THESE ENDS

to practice tolerance and live together in peace with one another as good neighbours, and

to unite our strength to maintain international peace and security, and

to ensure, by the acceptance of principles and the institution of methods, that armed force shall not be used, save in the common interest, and

to employ international machinery for the promotion of the economic and social advancement of all peoples,

HAVE RESOLVED TO COMBINE OUR EFFORTS TO ACCOMPLISH THESE AIMS

Accordingly, our respective Governments, through representatives assembled in the city of San Francisco, who have exhibited their full powers found to be in good and due form, have agreed to the present Charter of the United Nations and do hereby establish an international organization to be known as the United Nations.

Chapter I
PURPOSES AND PRINCIPLES

Article 1

The Purposes of the United Nations are:

1. To maintain international peace and security, and to that end: to take effective collective measures for the prevention and removal of threats to the peace, and for the suppression of acts of aggression or other breaches of the peace, and to bring about by peaceful means, and in conformity with the principles of justice and international law, adjustment or settlement of international disputes or situations which might lead to a breach of the peace;

2. To develop friendly relations among nations based on respect for the principle of equal rights and self-determination of peoples, and to take other appropriate measures to strengthen universal peace;

3. To achieve international co-operation in solving international problems of an economic, social, cultural or humanitarian character, and in promoting and encouraging respect for human rights and for fundamental freedoms for all without distinction as to race, sex, language or religion; and

4. To be a centre for harmonizing the actions of nations in the attainment of these common ends.

Article 2

The Organization and its Members, in pursuit of the Purposes stated in Article 1, shall act in accordance with the following Principles:

1. The Organization is based on the principle of the sovereign equality of all its Members.
2. All Members, in order to ensure to all of them the rights and benefits resulting from membership, shall fulfil in good faith the obligations assumed by them in accordance with the present Charter.
3. All Members shall settle their international disputes by peaceful means in such a manner that international peace and security, and justice, are not endangered.
4. All Members shall refrain in their international relations from the threat or use of force against the territorial integrity or political independence of any state, or in any other manner inconsistent with the Purposes of the United Nations.
5. All Members shall give the United Nations every assistance in any action it takes in accordance with the present Charter, and shall refrain from giving assistance to any state against which the United Nations is taking preventive or enforcement action.
6. The Organization shall ensure that states which are not Members of the United Nations act in accordance with these Principles so far as may be necessary for the maintenance of international peace and security.
7. Nothing contained in the present Charter shall authorize the United Nations to intervene in matters which are essentially within the domestic jurisdiction of any state or shall require the Members to submit such matters to settlement under the present Charter; but this principle shall not prejudice the application of enforcement measures under Chapter VII.

Chapter II
MEMBERSHIP

Article 3

The original Members of the United Nations shall be the states which, having participated in the United Nations Conference on International Organization at San Francisco or having previously signed the Declaration by United Nations of 1 January 1942, sign the present Charter and ratify it in accordance with Article 110.

Article 4

1. Membership in the United Nations is open to all other peace-loving states which accept the obligations contained in the present Charter and, in the judgment of the Organization, are able and willing to carry out these obligations.
2. The admission of any such state to membership in the United Nations will be effected by a decision of the General Assembly upon the recommendation of the Security Council.

Article 5

A Member of the United Nations against which preventive or enforcement action has been taken by the Security Council may be suspended from the exercise of the rights and privileges of membership by the General Assembly upon the recommendation of the Security Council. The exercise of these rights and privileges may be restored by the Security Council.

Article 6

A Member of the United Nations which has persistently violated the Principles contained in the present Charter may be expelled from the Organization by the General Assembly upon the recommendation of the Security Council.

Chapter III
ORGANS

Article 7

1. There are established as the principal organs of the United Nations: a General Assembly, a Security Council, an Economic and Social Council, a Trusteeship Council, an International Court of Justice, and a Secretariat.
2. Such subsidiary organs as may be found necessary may be established in accordance with the present Charter.

Article 8

The United Nations shall place no restrictions on the eligibility of men and women to participate in any capacity and under conditions of equality in its principal and subsidiary organs.

Chapter IV
THE GENERAL ASSEMBLY

Composition

Article 9

1. The General Assembly shall consist of all the Members of the United Nations.
2. Each Member shall have not more than five representatives in the General Assembly.

Functions and Powers

Article 10

The General Assembly may discuss any questions or any matters within the scope of the present Charter or relating to the powers and functions of any organs provided for in the present Charter, and, except as provided in Article 12, may make recommendations to the Members of the United Nations or to the Security Council or both on any such questions or matters.

Article 11

1. The General Assembly may consider the general principles of co-operation in the maintenance of international peace and security, including the principles governing disarmament and the regulation of armaments, and may make recommendations with regard to such principles to the Members or to the Security Council or to both.
2. The General Assembly may discuss any questions relating to the maintenance of international peace and security brought before it by any Member of the United Nations, or by the Security Council, or by a state which is not a Member of the United Nations in accordance with Article 35, paragraph 2, and, except as provided in Article 12, may make recommendations with regard to any such questions to the state or states concerned or to the Security Council or to both. Any such question on which action is necessary shall be referred to the Security Council by the General Assembly either before or after discussion.
3. The General Assembly may call the attention of the Security Council to situations which are likely to endanger international peace and security.
4. The powers of the General Assembly set forth in this Article shall not limit the general scope of Article 10.

Article 12

1. While the Security Council is exercising in respect of any dispute or situation the functions assigned to it in the present Charter, the General Assembly shall not make any recommendation with regard to that dispute or situation unless the Security Council so requests.

2. The Secretary-General, with the consent of the Security Council, shall notify the General Assembly at each session of any matters relative to the maintenance of international peace and security which are being dealt with by the Security Council and shall similarly notify the General Assembly, or the Members of the United Nations if the General Assembly is not in session, immediately the Security Council ceases to deal with such matters.

Article 13

1. The General Assembly shall initiate studies and make recommendations for the purpose of:
   a. promoting international co-operation in the political field and encouraging the progressive development of international law and its codification;
   b. promoting international co-operation in the economic, social, cultural, educational and health fields, and assisting in the realization of human rights and fundamental freedoms for all without distinction as to race, sex, language or religion.

2. The further responsibilities, functions and powers of the General Assembly with respect to matters mentioned in paragraph 1 (b) above are set forth in Chapters IX and X.

Article 14

Subject to the provisions of Article 12, the General Assembly may recommend measures for the peaceful adjustment of any situation, regardless of origin, which it deems likely to impair the general welfare or friendly relations among nations, including situations resulting from a violation of the provisions of the present Charter setting forth the Purposes and Principles of the United Nations.

Article 15

1. The General Assembly shall receive and consider annual and special reports from the Security Council; these reports shall include an account of the measures that the Security Council has decided upon or taken to maintain international peace and security.

2. The General Assembly shall receive and consider reports from the other organs of the United Nations.

Article 16

The General Assembly shall perform such functions with respect to the international trusteeship system as are assigned to it under Chapters XII and XIII, including the approval of the trusteeship agreements for areas not designated as strategic.

Article 17

1. The General Assembly shall consider and approve the budget of the Organization.

2. The expenses of the Organization shall be borne by the Members as apportioned by the General Assembly.

3. The General Assembly shall consider and approve any financial and budgetary arrangements with specialized agencies referred to in Article 57 and shall examine the administrative budgets of such specialized agencies with a view to making recommendations to the agencies concerned.

Voting

Article 18

1. Each member of the General Assembly shall have one vote.

2. Decisions of the General Assembly on important questions shall be made by a two-thirds majority of the members present and voting. These questions shall include: recommendations with respect to the maintenance of international peace and security, the election of the non-permanent members of the Security Council, the election of the members of the Economic and Social Council, the election of the members of the Trusteeship Council in accordance with paragraph 1 (c) of Article 86, the admission of new Members to the United Nations, the suspension of the rights and privileges of membership, the expulsion of Members, questions relating to the operation of the trusteeship system, and budgetary questions.

3. Decisions on other questions, including the determination of additional categories of questions to be decided by a two thirds majority, shall be made by a majority of the members present and voting.

Article 19

A Member of the United Nations which is in arrears in the payment of its financial contributions to the Organization shall have no vote in the General Assembly if the amount of its arrears equals or exceeds the amount of the contributions due from it for the preceding two full years. The General Assembly may, nevertheless, permit such a Member to vote if it is satisfied that the failure to pay is due to conditions beyond the control of the Member.

Procedure

Article 20

The General Assembly shall meet in regular annual sessions and in such special sessions as occasion may require. Special sessions shall be convoked by the Secretary-General at the request of the Security Council or of a majority of the Members of the United Nations.

Article 21

The General Assembly shall adopt its own rules of procedure. It shall elect its President for each session.

Article 22

The General Assembly may establish such subsidiary organs as it deems necessary for the performance of its functions.

Chapter V

THE SECURITY COUNCIL

Composition

Article 23[1]

1. The Security Council shall consist of fifteen Members of the United Nations. The Republic of China, France, the Union of Soviet Socialist Republics, the United Kingdom of Great Britain and Northern Ireland and the United States of America shall be permanent members of the Security Council. The General Assembly shall elect ten other Members of the United Nations to be non-permanent members of the Security Council, due regard being specially paid, in the first instance to the contribution of Members of the United Nations to the maintenance of international peace and security and to the other purposes of the Organization, and also to equitable geographical distribution.

2. The non-permanent members of the Security Council shall be elected for a term of two years. In the first election of the non-permanent members after the increase of the membership of the Security Council from eleven to fifteen, two of the four additional members shall be chosen for a term of one year. A retiring member shall not be eligible for immediate re-election.

3. Each member of the Security Council shall have one representative.

Functions and Powers

Article 24

1. In order to ensure prompt and effective action by the United Nations, its Members confer on the Security Council primary responsibility for the maintenance of international peace and security, and agree that in carrying out its duties under this responsibility the Security Council acts on their behalf.

2. In discharging these duties the Security Council shall act in accordance with the Purposes and Principles of the United Nations. The specific powers granted to the Security Council for the discharge of these duties are laid down in Chapters VI, VII, VIII and XII.

3. The Security Council shall submit annual and, when necessary, special reports to the General Assembly for its consideration.

Article 25

The Members of the United Nations agree to accept and carry out the decisions of the Security Council in accordance with the present Charter.

Article 26

In order to promote the establishment and maintenance of international peace and security with the least diversion for armaments of the world's human and economic resources, the Security Council shall be responsible for formulating, with the assistance of the Military Staff Committee referred to in Article 47, plans to be submitted to the Members of the United Nations for the establishment of a system for the regulation of armaments.

Voting

Article 27 [2]

1. Each member of the Security Council shall have one vote.
2. Decisions of the Security Council on procedural matters shall be made by an affirmative vote of nine members.
3. Decisions of the Security Council on all other matters shall be made by an affirmative vote of nine members including the concurring votes of the permanent members; provided that, in decisions under Chapter VI, and under paragraph 3 of Article 52, a party to a dispute shall abstain from voting.

Procedure

Article 28

1. The Security Council shall be so organized as to be able to function continuously. Each member of the Security Council shall for this purpose be represented at all times at the seat of the Organization.

2. The Security Council shall hold periodic meetings at which each of its members may, if it so desires, be represented by a member of the government or by some other specially designated representative.

3. The Security Council may hold meetings at such places other than the seat of the Organization as in its judgment will best facilitate its work.

Article 29

The Security Council may establish such subsidiary organs as it deems necessary for the performance of its functions.

Article 30

The Security Council shall adopt its own rules of procedure, including the method of selecting its President.

Article 31

Any Member of the United Nations which is not a member of the Security Council may participate, without vote, in the discussion of any question brought before the Security Council whenever the latter considers that the interests of that Member are specially affected.

Article 32

Any Member of the United Nations which is not a member of the Security Council or any state which is not a Member of the United Nations, if it is a party to a dispute under consideration by the Security Council, shall be invited to participate, without vote, in the discussion relating to the dispute. The Security Council shall lay down such conditions as it deems just for the participation of a state which is not a Member of the United Nations.

Chapter VI
PACIFIC SETTLEMENT OF DISPUTES

Article 33

1. The parties to any dispute, the continuance of which is likely to endanger the maintenance of international peace and security, shall, first of all, seek a solution by negotiation, enquiry, mediation, conciliation, arbitration, judicial settlement, resort to regional agencies or arrangements, or other peaceful means of their own choice.

2. The Security Council shall, when it deems necessary, call upon the parties to settle their dispute by such means.

Article 34

The Security Council may investigate any dispute, or any situation which might lead to international friction or give rise to a dispute, in order to determine whether the continuance of the dispute or situation is likely to endanger the maintenance of international peace and security.

Article 35

1. Any Member of the United Nations may bring any dispute, or any situation of the nature referred to in Article 34, to the attention of the Security Council or of the General Assembly.

2. A state which is not a Member of the United Nations may bring to the attention of the Security Council or of the General Assembly any dispute to which it is a party if it accepts in advance, for the purposes of the dispute, the obligations of pacific settlement provided in the present Charter.

3. The proceedings of the General Assembly in respect of matters brought to its attention under this Article will be subject to the provisions of Articles 11 and 12.

Article 36

1. The Security Council may, at any stage of a dispute of the nature referred to in Article 33 or of a situation of like nature, recommend appropriate procedures or methods of adjustment.

2. The Security Council should take into consideration any procedures for the settlement of the dispute which have already been adopted by the parties.

3. In making recommendations under this Article the Security Council should also take into consideration that legal disputes should as a general rule be referred by the parties to the International Court of Justice in accordance with the provisions of the Statute of the Court.

Article 37

1. Should the parties to a dispute of the nature referred to in Article 33 fail to settle it by the means indicated in that Article, they shall refer it to the Security Council.

2. If the Security Council deems that the continuance of the dispute is in fact likely to endanger the maintenance of international peace and security, it shall decide whether to take action under Article 36 or to recommend such terms of settlement as it may consider appropriate.

Article 38

Without prejudice to the provisions of Articles 33 to 37, the Security Council may, if all the parties to any dispute so request, make recommendations to the parties with a view to a pacific settlement of the dispute.

Chapter VII

ACTION WITH RESPECT TO THREATS TO THE PEACE, BREACHES OF THE PEACE, AND ACTS OF AGGRESSION

Article 39

The Security Council shall determine the existence of any threat to the peace, breach of the peace, or act of aggression and shall make recommendations, or decide what measures shall be taken in accordance with Articles 41 and 42, to maintain or restore international peace and security.

Article 40

In order to prevent an aggravation of the situation, the Security Council may, before making the recommendations or deciding upon the measures provided for in Article 39, call upon the parties concerned to comply with such provisional measures as it deems necessary or desirable. Such provisional measures shall be without prejudice to the rights, claims or position of the parties concerned. The Security Council shall duly take account of failure to comply with such provisional measures.

Article 41

The Security Council may decide what measures not involving the use of armed force are to be employed to give effect to its decisions, and it may call upon the Members of the United Nations to apply such measures. These may include complete or partial interruption of economic relations and of rail, sea, air, postal, telegraphic, radio and other means of communication, and the severance of diplomatic relations.

Article 42

Should the Security Council consider that measures provided for in Article 41 would be inadequate or have proved to be inadequate, it may take such action by air, sea or land forces as may be necessary to maintain or restore international peace and security. Such action may include demonstrations, blockade, and other operations by air, sea, or land forces of Members of the United Nations.

Article 43

1. All Members of the United Nations, in order to contribute to the maintenance of international peace and security, undertake to make available to the Security Council, on its call and in accordance with a special agreement or agreements, armed forces, assistance and facilities, including rights of passage, necessary for the purpose of maintaining international peace and security.

2. Such agreement or agreements shall govern the numbers and types of forces, their degree of readiness and general location, and the nature of the facilities and assistance to be provided.

3. The agreement or agreements shall be negotiated as soon as possible on the initiative of the Security Council. They shall be concluded between the Security Council and Members or between the Security Council and groups of Members and shall be subject to ratification by the signatory states in accordance with their respective constitutional processes.

Article 44

When the Security Council has decided to use force it shall, before calling upon a Member not represented on it to provide armed forces in fulfilment of the obligations assumed under Article 43, invite that Member, if the Member so desires, to participate in the decisions of the Security Council concerning the employment of contingents of that Member's armed forces.

Article 45

In order to enable the United Nations to take urgent military measures, Members shall hold immediately available national air-force contingents for combined international enforcement action. The strength and degree of readiness of these contingents and plans for their combined action shall be determined, within the limits laid down in the special agreement or agreements referred to in Article 43, by the Security Council with the assistance of the Military Staff Committee.

Article 46

Plans for the application of armed force shall be made by the Security Council with the assistance of the Military Staff Committee.

Article 47

1. There shall be established a Military Staff Committee to advise and assist the Security Council on all questions relating to the Security Council's military requirements for the maintenance of international peace and security, the employment and command of forces placed at its disposal, the regulation of armaments, and possible disarmament.

2. The Military Staff Committee shall consist of the Chiefs of Staff of the permanent members of the Security Council or their representatives. Any Member of the United Nations not permanently represented on the Committee shall be invited by the Committee to be associated with it when the efficient discharge of the Committee's responsibilities requires the participation of that Member in its work.

3. The Military Staff Committee shall be responsible under the Security Council for the strategic direction of any armed forces placed at the disposal of the Security Council. Questions relating to the command of such forces shall be worked out subsequently.

4. The Military Staff Committee, with the authorization of the Security Council and after consultation with appropriate regional agencies, may establish regional sub-committees.

Article 48

1. The action required to carry out the decisions of the Security Council for the maintenance of international peace and security shall be taken by all the Members of the United Nations or by some of them, as the Security Council may determine.

2. Such decisions shall be carried out by the Members of the United Nations directly and through their action in the appropriate international agencies of which they are members.

Article 49

The Members of the United Nations shall join in affording mutual assistance in carrying out the measures decided upon by the Security Council.

Article 50

If preventive or enforcement measures against any state are taken by the Security Council, any other state, whether a Member of the United Nations or not, which finds itself confronted with special economic problems arising from the carrying out of those measures shall have the right to consult the Security Council with regard to a solution of those problems.

Article 51

Nothing in the present Charter shall impair the inherent right of individual or collective self-defence if an armed attack occurs against a Member of the United Nations, until the Security Council has taken measures necessary to maintain international peace and security. Measures taken by Members in the exercise of this right of self-defence shall be immediately reported to the Security Council and shall not in any way affect the authority and responsibility of the Security Council under the present Charter to take at any time such action as it deems necessary in order to maintain or restore international peace and security.

Chapter VIII

REGIONAL ARRANGEMENTS

Article 52

1. Nothing in the present Charter precludes the existence of regional arrangements or agencies for dealing with such matters relating to the maintenance of international peace and security as are appropriate for regional action, provided that such arrangements or agencies and their activities are consistent with the Purposes and Principles of the United Nations.

2. The Members of the United Nations entering into such arrangements or constituting such agencies shall make every effort to achieve pacific settlement of local disputes through such regional arrangements or by such regional agencies before referring them to the Security Council.

3. The Security Council shall encourage the development of pacific settlement of local disputes through such regional arrangements or by such regional agencies either on the initiative of the states concerned or by reference from the Security Council.

4. This Article in no way impairs the application of Articles 34 and 35.

Article 53

1. The Security Council shall, where appropriate, utilize such regional arrangements or agencies for enforcement action under its authority. But no enforcement action shall be taken under regional arrangements or by regional agencies without the authorization of the Security Council, with the exception of measures against any enemy state, as defined in paragraph 2 of this Article, provided for pursuant to Article 107 or in regional arrangements directed against renewal of aggressive policy on the part of any such state, until such time as the Organization may, on request of the Governments concerned, be charged with the responsibility for preventing further aggression by such a state.

2. The term enemy state as used in paragraph 1 of this Article applies to any state which during the Second World War has been an enemy of any signatory of the present Charter.

Article 54

The Security Council shall at all times be kept fully informed of activities undertaken or in contemplation under regional arrangements or by regional agencies for the maintenance of international peace and security.

Chapter IX

INTERNATIONAL ECONOMIC AND SOCIAL CO-OPERATION

Article 55

With a view to the creation of conditions of stability and well-being which are necessary for peaceful and friendly relations among nations based on respect for the principle of equal rights and self-determination of peoples, the United Nations shall promote:
 a. higher standards of living, full employment, and conditions of economic and social progress and development;
 b. solutions of international economic, social, health, and related problems; and international cultural and educational co-operation; and
 c. universal respect for, and observance of, human rights and fundamental freedoms for all without distinction as to race, sex, language, or religion.

Article 56

All Members pledge themselves to take joint and separate action in co-operation with the Organization for the achievement of the purposes set forth in Article 55.

Article 57

1. The various specialized agencies, established by intergovernmental agreement and having wide international responsibilities, as defined in their basic instruments, in economic, social, cultural, educational, health, and related fields, shall be brought into relationship with the United Nations in accordance with the provisions of Article 63.

2. Such agencies thus brought into relationship with the United Nations are hereinafter referred to as specialized agencies.

Article 58

The Organization shall make recommendations for the coordination of the policies and activities of the specialized agencies.

Article 59

The Organization shall, where appropriate, initiate negotiations among the states concerned for the creation of any new specialized agencies required for the accomplishment of the purposes set forth in Article 55.

Article 60

Responsibility for the discharge of the functions of the Organization set forth in this Chapter shall be vested in the General Assembly and, under the authority of the General Assembly, in the Economic and Social Council, which shall have for this purpose the powers set forth in Chapter X.

Chapter X
THE ECONOMIC AND SOCIAL COUNCIL

Composition

Article 61 [3]

1. The Economic and Social Council shall consist of fifty-four Members of the United Nations elected by the General Assembly.

2. Subject to the provisions of paragraph 3, eighteen members of the Economic and Social Council shall be elected each year for a term of three years. A retiring member shall be eligible for immediate re-election.

3. At the first election after the increase in the membership of the Economic and Social Council from twenty-seven to fifty-four members, in addition to the members elected in place of the nine members whose term of office expires at the end of that year, twenty-seven additional members shall be elected. Of these twenty-seven additional members, the term of office of nine members so elected shall expire at the end of one year, and of nine other members at the end of two years, in accordance with arrangements made by the General Assembly.

4. Each member of the Economic and Social Council shall have one representative.

Functions and Powers

Article 62

1. The Economic and Social Council may make or initiate studies and reports with respect to international economic, social, cultural, educational, health, and related matters and may make recommendations with respect to any such matters to the General Assembly, to the Members of the United Nations, and to the specialized agencies concerned.

2. It may make recommendations for the purpose of promoting respect for, and observance of, human rights and fundamental freedoms for all.

3. It may prepare draft conventions for submission to the General Assembly, with respect to matters falling within its competence.

4. It may call, in accordance with the rules prescribed by the United Nations, international conferences on matters falling within its competence.

Article 63

1. The Economic and Social Council may enter into agreements with any of the agencies referred to in Article 57, defining the terms on which the agency concerned shall be brought into relationship with the United Nations. Such agreements shall be subject to approval by the General Assembly.

2. It may co-ordinate the activities of the specialized agencies through consultation with and recommendations to such agencies and through recommendations to the General Assembly and to the Members of the United Nations.

Article 64

1. The Economic and Social Council may take appropriate steps to obtain regular reports from the specialized agencies. It may make arrangements with the Members of the United Nations and with the specialized agencies to obtain reports on the steps taken to give effect to its own recommendations and to recommendations on matters falling within its competence made by the General Assembly.

2. It may communicate its observations on these reports to the General Assembly.

Article 65

The Economic and Social Council may furnish information to the Security Council and shall assist the Security Council upon its request.

Article 66

1. The Economic and Social Council shall perform such functions as fall within its competence in connection with the carrying out of the recommendations of the General Assembly.

2. It may, with the approval of the General Assembly, perform services at the request of Members of the United Nations and at the request of specialized agencies.

3. It shall perform such other functions as are specified elsewhere in the present Charter or as may be assigned to it by the General Assembly.

Voting

Article 67

1. Each member of the Economic and Social Council shall have one vote.

2. Decisions of the Economic and Social Council shall be made by a majority of the members present and voting.

Procedure

Article 68

The Economic and Social Council shall set up commissions in economic and social fields and for the promotion of human rights, and such other commissions as may be required for the performance of its functions.

Article 69

The Economic and Social Council shall invite any Member of the United Nations to participate, without vote, in its deliberations on any matter of particular concern to that Member.

Article 70

The Economic and Social Council may make arrangements for representatives of the specialized agencies to participate, without vote, in its deliberations and in those of the commissions established by it, and for its representatives to participate in the deliberations of the specialized agencies.

Article 71

The Economic and Social Council may make suitable arrangements for consultation with non-governmental organizations which are concerned with matters within its competence. Such arrangements may be made with international organizations and, where appropriate, with national organizations after consultation with the Member of the United Nations concerned.

Article 72

1. The Economic and Social Council shall adopt its own rules of procedure, including the method of selecting its President.
2. The Economic and Social Council shall meet as required in accordance with its rules, which shall include provision for the convening of meetings on the request of a majority of its members.

Chapter XI
DECLARATION REGARDING NON-SELF-GOVERNING TERRITORIES

Article 73

Members of the United Nations which have or assume responsibilities for the administration of territories whose peoples have not yet attained a full measure of self-government recognize the principle that the interests of the inhabitants of these territories are paramount, and accept as a sacred trust the obligation to promote to the utmost, within the system of international peace and security established by the present Charter, the well-being of the inhabitants of these territories and, to this end:

a. to ensure, with due respect for the culture of the peoples concerned, their political, economic, social, and educational advancement, their just treatment, and their protection against abuses;
b. to develop self-government, to take due account of the political aspirations of the peoples, and to assist them in the progressive development of their free political institutions, according to the particular circumstances of each territory and its peoples and their varying stages of advancement;
c. to further international peace and security;
d. to promote constructive measures of development, to encourage research, and to co-operate with one another and, when and where appropriate, with specialized international bodies with a view to the practical achievement of the social, economic, and scientific purposes set forth in this Article; and
e. to transmit regularly to the Secretary-General for information purposes, subject to such limitation as security and constitutional considerations may require, statistical and other information of a technical nature relating to economic, social, and educational conditions in the territories for which they are respectively responsible other than those territories to which Chapters XII and XIII apply.

Article 74

Members of the United Nations also agree that their policy in respect of the territories to which this Chapter applies, no less than in respect of their metropolitan areas, must be based on the general principle of good-neighbourliness, due account being taken of the interests and well-being of the rest of the world, in social, economic, and commercial matters.

Chapter XII
INTERNATIONAL TRUSTEESHIP SYSTEM

Article 75

The United Nations shall establish under its authority an international trusteeship system for the administration and supervision of such territories as may be placed thereunder by subsequent individual agreements. These territories are hereinafter referred to as trust territories.

Article 76

The basic objectives of the trusteeship system, in accordance with the Purposes of the United Nations laid down in Article 1 of the present Charter, shall be:

a. to further international peace and security;
b. to promote the political, economic, social, and educational advancement of the inhabitants of the trust territories, and their progressive development towards self-government or independence as may be appropriate to the particular circumstances of each territory and its peoples and the freely expressed wishes of the peoples concerned, and as may be provided by the terms of each trusteeship agreement;
c. to encourage respect for human rights and for fundamental freedoms for all without distinction as to race, sex, language, or religion, and to encourage recognition of the interdependence of the peoples of the world; and
d. to ensure equal treatment in social, economic, and commercial matters for all Members of the United Nations and their nationals, and also equal treatment for the latter in the administration of justice, without prejudice to the attainment of the foregoing objectives and subject to the provisions of Article 80.

Article 77

1. The trusteeship system shall apply to such territories in the following categories as may be placed thereunder by means of trusteeship agreements:

a. territories now held under mandate;
b. territories which may be detached from enemy states as a result of the Second World War; and
c. territories voluntarily placed under the system by states responsible for their administration.

2. It will be a matter for subsequent agreement as to which territories in the foregoing categories will be brought under the trusteeship system and upon what terms.

Article 78

The trusteeship system shall not apply to territories which have become Members of the United Nations, relationship among which shall be based on respect for the principle of sovereign equality.

Article 79

The terms of trusteeship for each territory to be placed under the trusteeship system, including any alteration or amendment, shall be agreed upon by the states directly concerned, including the mandatory power in the case of territories held under mandate by a Member of the United Nations, and shall be approved as provided for in Articles 83 and 85.

Article 80

1. Except as may be agreed upon in individual trusteeship agreements, made under Articles 77, 79 and 81, placing each territory under the trusteeship system, and until such agreements have been concluded, nothing in this Chapter shall be construed in or of itself to alter in any manner the rights whatsoever of any states or any peoples or the terms of existing international instruments to which Members of the United Nations may respectively be parties.
2. Paragraph 1 of this Article shall not be interpreted as giving grounds for delay or postponement of the negotiation and conclusion of agreements for placing mandated and other territories under the trusteeship system as provided for in Article 77.

Article 81

The trusteeship agreement shall in each case include the terms under which the trust territory will be administered and designate the authority which will exercise the administration of the trust territory. Such authority, hereinafter called the administering authority, may be one or more states or the Organization itself.

Article 82

There may be designated, in any trusteeship agreement, a strategic area or areas which may include part or all of the trust territory to which the agreement applies, without prejudice to any special agreement or agreements made under Article 43.

Article 83

1. All functions of the United Nations relating to strategic areas, including the approval of the terms of the trusteeship agreements and of their alteration or amendment, shall be exercised by the Security Council.
2. The basic objectives set forth in Article 76 shall be applicable to the people of each strategic area.
3. The Security Council shall, subject to the provisions of the trusteeship agreements and without prejudice to security considerations, avail itself of the assistance of the Trusteeship Council to perform those functions of the United Nations under the trusteeship system relating to political, economic, social, and educational matters in the strategic areas.

Article 84

It shall be the duty of the administering authority to ensure that the trust territory shall play its part in the maintenance of international peace and security. To this end the administering authority may make use of volunteer forces, facilities, and assistance from the trust territory in carrying out the obligations towards the Security Council undertaken in this regard by the administering authority, as well as for local defence and the maintenance of law and order within the trust territory.

Article 85

1. The functions of the United Nations with regard to trusteeship agreements for all areas not designated as strategic, including the approval of the terms of the trusteeship agreements and of their alteration or amendment, shall be exercised by the General Assembly.
2. The Trusteeship Council, operating under the authority of the General Assembly, shall assist the General Assembly in carrying out these functions.

Chapter XIII
THE TRUSTEESHIP COUNCIL

Composition

Article 86

1. The Trusteeship Council shall consist of the following Members of the United Nations:
    a. those Members administering trust territories;
    b. such of those Members mentioned by name in Article 23 as are not administering trust territories; and
    c. as many other Members elected for three-year terms by the General Assembly as may be necessary to ensure that the total number of members of the Trusteeship Council is equally divided between those Members of the United Nations which administer trust territories and those which do not.
2. Each member of the Trusteeship Council shall designate one specially qualified person to represent it therein.

Functions and Powers

Article 87

The General Assembly and, under its authority, the Trusteeship Council, in carrying out their functions, may:
a. consider reports submitted by the administering authority;
b. accept petitions and examine them in consultation with the administering authority;
c. provide for periodic visits to the respective trust territories at times agreed upon with the administering authority; and
d. take these and other actions in conformity with the terms of the trusteeship agreements.

Article 88

The Trusteeship Council shall formulate a questionnaire on the political, economic, social, and educational advancement of the inhabitants of each trust territory, and the administering authority for each trust territory within the competence of the General Assembly shall make an annual report to the General Assembly upon the basis of such questionnaire.

Voting

Article 89

1. Each member of the Trusteeship Council shall have one vote.
2. Decisions of the Trusteeship Council shall be made by a majority of the members present and voting.

Procedure

Article 90

1. The Trusteeship Council shall adopt its own rules of procedure, including the method of selecting its President.
2. The Trusteeship Council shall meet as required in accordance with its rules, which shall include provision for the convening of meetings on the request of a majority of its members.

Article 91

The Trusteeship Council shall, when appropriate, avail itself of the assistance of the Economic and Social Council and of the specialized agencies in regard to matters with which they are respectively concerned.

Chapter XIV
THE INTERNATIONAL COURT OF JUSTICE

Article 92

The International Court of Justice shall be the principal judicial organ of the United Nations. It shall function in accordance with the annexed Statute, which is based upon the Statute of the Permanent Court of International Justice and forms an integral part of the present Charter.

Article 93

1. All Members of the United Nations are *ipso facto* parties to the Statute of the International Court of Justice.
2. A state which is not a Member of the United Nations may become a party to the Statute of the International Court of Justice on conditions to be determined in each case by the General Assembly upon the recommendation of the Security Council.

Article 94

1. Each Member of the United Nations undertakes to comply with the decision of the International Court of Justice in any case to which it is a party.

2. If any party to a case fails to perform the obligations incumbent upon it under a judgment rendered by the Court, the other party may have recourse to the Security Council, which may, if it deems necessary, make recommendations or decide upon measures to be taken to give effect to the judgment.

Article 95

Nothing in the present Charter shall prevent Members of the United Nations from entrusting the solution of their differences to other tribunals by virtue of agreements already in existence or which may be concluded in the future.

Article 96

1. The General Assembly or the Security Council may request the International Court of Justice to give an advisory opinion on any legal question.

2. Other organs of the United Nations and specialized agencies, which may at any time be so authorized by the General Assembly, may also request advisory opinions of the Court on legal questions arising within the scope of their activities.

Chapter XV
THE SECRETARIAT

Article 97

The Secretariat shall comprise a Secretary-General and such staff as the Organization may require. The Secretary-General shall be appointed by the General Assembly upon the recommendation of the Security Council. He shall be the chief administrative officer of the Organization.

Article 98

The Secretary-General shall act in that capacity in all meetings of the General Assembly, of the Security Council, of the Economic and Social Council, and of the Trusteeship Council, and shall perform such other functions as are entrusted to him by these organs. The Secretary-General shall make an annual report to the General Assembly on the work of the Organization.

Article 99

The Secretary-General may bring to the attention of the Security Council any matter which in his opinion may threaten the maintenance of international peace and security.

Article 100

1. In the performance of their duties the Secretary-General and the staff shall not seek or receive instructions from any government or from any other authority external to the Organization. They shall refrain from any action which might reflect on their position as international officials responsible only to the Organization.

2. Each Member of the United Nations undertakes to respect the exclusively international character of the responsibilities of the Secretary-General and the staff and not to seek to influence them in the discharge of their responsibilities.

Article 101

1. The staff shall be appointed by the Secretary-General under regulations established by the General Assembly.

2. Appropriate staffs shall be permanently assigned to the Economic and Social Council, the Trusteeship Council, and, as required, to other organs of the United Nations. These staffs shall form a part of the Secretariat.

3. The paramount consideration in the employment of the staff and in the determination of the conditions of service shall be the necessity of securing the highest standards of efficiency, competence, and integrity. Due regard shall be paid to the importance of recruiting the staff on as wide a geographical basis as possible.

Chapter XVI
MISCELLANEOUS PROVISIONS

Article 102

1. Every treaty and every international agreement entered into by any Member of the United Nations after the present Charter comes into force shall as soon as possible be registered with the Secretariat and published by it.

2. No party to any such treaty or international agreement which has not been registered in accordance with the provisions of paragraph 1 of this Article may invoke that treaty or agreement before any organ of the United Nations.

Article 103

In the event of a conflict between the obligations of the Members of the United Nations under the present Charter and their obligations under any other international agreement, their obligations under the present Charter shall prevail.

Article 104

The Organization shall enjoy in the territory of each of its Members such legal capacity as may be necessary for the exercise of its functions and the fulfilment of its purposes.

Article 105

1. The Organization shall enjoy in the territory of each of its Members such privileges and immunities as are necessary for the fulfilment of its purposes.

2. Representatives of the Members of the United Nations and officials of the Organization shall similarly enjoy such privileges and immunities as are necessary for the independent exercise of their functions in connection with the Organization.

3. The General Assembly may make recommendations with a view to determining the details of the application of paragraphs 1 and 2 of this Article or may propose conventions to the Members of the United Nations for this purpose.

Chapter XVII
TRANSITIONAL SECURITY ARRANGEMENTS

Article 106

Pending the coming into force of such special agreements referred to in Article 43 as in the opinion of the Security Council enable it to begin the exercise of its responsibilities under Article 42, the parties to the Four-Nation Declaration, signed at Moscow, 30 October 1943, and France, shall, in accordance with the provisions of paragraph 5 of that Declaration, consult with one another and as occasion requires with other Members of the United Nations with a view to such joint action on behalf of the Organization as may be necessary for the purpose of maintaining international peace and security.

Article 107

Nothing in the present Charter shall invalidate or preclude action, in relation to any state which during the Second World War has been an enemy of any signatory to the present Charter, taken or authorized as a result of that war by the Governments having responsibility for such action.

Chapter XVIII
AMENDMENTS

Article 108

Amendments to the present Charter shall come into force for all Members of the United Nations when they have been adopted by a vote of two thirds of the members of the General Assembly and ratified in accordance with their respective constitutional processes by two thirds of the Members of the United Nations, including all the permanent members of the Security Council.

Article 109[4]

1. A General Conference of the Members of the United Nations for the purpose of reviewing the present Charter may be held at a date and place to be fixed by a two-thirds vote of the members of the General Assembly and by a vote of any nine members of the Security Council. Each Member of the United Nations shall have one vote in the conference.

2. Any alteration of the present Charter recommended by a two-thirds vote of the conference shall take effect when ratified in accordance with their respective constitutional processes by two thirds of the Members of the United Nations including all the permanent members of the Security Council.

3. If such a conference has not been held before the tenth annual session of the General Assembly following the coming into force of the present Charter, the proposal to call such a conference shall be placed on the agenda of that session of the General Assembly, and the conference shall be held if so decided by a majority vote of the members of the General Assembly and by a vote of any seven members of the Security Council.

Chapter XIX
RATIFICATION AND SIGNATURE

Article 110

1. The present Charter shall be ratified by the signatory states in accordance with their respective constitutional pro-cesses.

2. The ratifications shall be deposited with the Government of the United States of America, which shall notify all the signatory states of each deposit as well as the Secretary-General of the Organization when he has been appointed.

3. The present Charter shall come into force upon the deposit of ratifications by the Republic of China, France, the Union of Soviet Socialist Republics, the United Kingdom of Great Britain and Northern Ireland and the United States of America, and by a majority of the other signatory states. A protocol of the ratifications deposited shall thereupon be drawn up by the Government of the United States of America which shall communicate copies thereof to all the signatory states.

4. The states signatory to the present Charter which ratify it after it has come into force will become original Members of the United Nations on the date of the deposit of their respective ratifications.

Article 111

The present Charter, of which the Chinese, French, Russian, English, and Spanish texts are equally authentic, shall remain deposited in the archives of the Government of the United States of America. Duly certified copies thereof shall be transmitted by that Government to the Governments of the other signatory states.

IN FAITH WHEREOF the representatives of the Governments of the United Nations have signed the present Charter.

DONE at the city of San Francisco the twenty-sixth day of June, one thousand nine hundred and forty-five.

NOTES

[1]Amended text of Article 23, which came into force on 31 August 1965. The text of Article 23 before it was amended read as follows:
1. The Security Council shall consist of eleven Members of the United Nations. The Republic of China, France, the Union of Soviet Socialist Republics, the United Kingdom of Great Britain and Northern Ireland and the United States of America shall be permanent members of the Security Council. The General Assembly shall elect six other Members of the United Nations to be non-permanent members of the Security Council, due regard being specially paid in the first instance to the contributions of Members of the United Nations to the maintenance of international peace and security and to the other purposes of the Organization, and also to equitable geographical distribution.
2. The non-permanent members of the Security Council shall be elected for a term of two years. In the first election of the non-permanent members, however, three shall be chosen for a term of one year. A retiring member shall not be eligible for immediate re-election.
3. Each member of the Security Council shall have one representative.

[2]Amended text of Article 27, which came into force on 31 August 1965. The text of Article 27 before it was amended read as follows:
1. Each member of the Security Council shall have one vote.
2. Decisions of the Security Council on procedural matters shall be made by an affirmative vote of seven members.
3. Decisions of the Security Council on all other matters shall be made by an affirmative vote of seven members including the concurring votes of the permanent members; provided that, in decisions under Chapter VI, and under paragraph 3 of Article 52, a party to a dispute shall abstain from voting.

[3] Amended text of Article 61, which came into force on 24 September 1973. The text of Article 61 as previously amended on 31 August 1965 read as follows:
1. The Economic and Social Council shall consist of twenty-seven Members of the United Nations elected by the General Assembly.
2. Subject to the provisions of paragraph 3, nine members of the Economic and Social Council shall be elected each year for a term of three years. A retiring member shall be eligible for immediate re-election.
3. At the first election after the increase in the membership of the Economic and Social Council from eighteen to twenty-seven members, in addition to the members elected in place of the six members whose term of office expires at the end of that year, nine additional members shall be elected. Of these nine additional members, the term of office of three members so elected shall expire at the end of one year, and of three other members at the end of two years, in accordance with arrangements made by the General Assembly.
4. Each member of the Economic and Social Council shall have one representative.

[4] Amended text of Article 109, which came into force on 12 June 1968. The text of Article 109 before it was amended read as follows:
1. A General Conference of the Members of the United Nations for the purpose of reviewing the present Charter may be held at a date and place to be fixed by a two-thirds vote of the members of the General Assembly and by a vote of any seven members of the Security Council. Each Member of the United Nations shall have one vote in the conference.
2. Any alteration of the present Charter recommended by a two-thirds vote of the conference shall take effect when ratified in accordance with their respective constitutional processes by two thirds of the Members of the United Nations including all the permanent members of the Security Council.
3. If such a conference has not been held before the tenth annual session of the General Assembly following the coming into force of the present Charter, the proposal to call such a conference shall be placed on the agenda of that session of the General Assembly, and the conference shall be held if so decided by a majority vote of the members of the General Assembly and by a vote of any seven members of the Security Council.

Statute of the International Court of Justice

Article 1

The International Court of Justice established by the Charter of the United Nations as the principal judicial organ of the United Nations shall be constituted and shall function in accordance with the provisions of the present Statute.

Chapter I
ORGANIZATION OF THE COURT

Article 2

The Court shall be composed of a body of independent judges, elected regardless of their nationality from among persons of high moral character, who possess the qualifications required in their respective countries for appointment to the highest judicial offices, or are jurisconsults of recognized competence in international law.

Article 3

1. The Court shall consist of fifteen members, no two of whom may be nationals of the same state.
2. A person who for the purposes of membership in the Court could be regarded as a national of more than one state shall be deemed to be a national of the one in which he ordinarily exercises civil and political rights.

Article 4

1. The members of the Court shall be elected by the General Assembly and by the Security Council from a list of persons nominated by the national groups in the Permanent Court of Arbitration, in accordance with the following provisions.
2. In the case of Members of the United Nations not represented in the Permanent Court of Arbitration, candidates shall be nominated by national groups appointed for this purpose by their governments under the same conditions as those prescribed for members of the Permanent Court of Arbitration by Article 44 of the Convention of The Hague of 1907 for the pacific settlement of international disputes.
3. The conditions under which a state which is a party to the present Statute but is not a Member of the United Nations may participate in electing the members of the Court shall, in the absence of a special agreement, be laid down by the General Assembly upon recommendation of the Security Council.

Article 5

1. At least three months before the date of the election, the Secretary-General of the United Nations shall address a written request to the members of the Permanent Court of Arbitration belonging to the states which are parties to the present Statute, and to the members of the national groups appointed under Article 4, paragraph 2, inviting them to undertake, within a given time, by national groups, the nomination of persons in a position to accept the duties of a member of the Court.
2. No group may nominate more than four persons, not more than two of whom shall be of their own nationality. In no case may the number of candidates nominated by a group be more than double the number of seats to be filled.

Article 6

Before making these nominations, each national group is recommended to consult its highest court of justice, its legal faculties and schools of law, and its national academies and national sections of international academies devoted to the study of law.

Article 7

1. The Secretary-General shall prepare a list in alphabetical order of all the persons thus nominated. Save as provided in Article 12, paragraph 2, these shall be the only persons eligible.
2. The Secretary-General shall submit this list to the General Assembly and to the Security Council.

Article 8

The General Assembly and the Security Council shall proceed independently of one another to elect the members of the Court.

Article 9

At every election, the electors shall bear in mind not only that the persons to be elected should individually possess the qualifications required, but also that in the body as a whole the representation of the main forms of civilization and of the principal legal systems of the world should be assured.

Article 10

1. Those candidates who obtain an absolute majority of votes in the General Assembly and in the Security Council shall be considered as elected.
2. Any vote of the Security Council, whether for the election of judges or for the appointment of members of the conference envisaged in Article 12, shall be taken without any distinction between permanent and non-permanent members of the Security Council.
3. In the event of more than one national of the same state obtaining an absolute majority of the votes both of the General Assembly and of the Security Council, the eldest of these only shall be considered as elected.

Article 11

If, after the first meeting held for the purpose of the election, one or more seats remain to be filled, a second and, if necessary, a third meeting shall take place.

Article 12

1. If, after the third meeting, one or more seats still remain unfilled, a joint conference consisting of six members, three appointed by the General Assembly and three by the Security Council, may be formed at any time at the request of either the General Assembly or the Security Council, for the purpose of choosing by the vote of an absolute majority one name for each seat still vacant, to submit to the General Assembly and the Security Council for their respective acceptance.
2. If the joint conference is unanimously agreed upon any person who fulfils the required conditions, he may be included in its list, even though he was not included in the list of nominations referred to in Article 7.
3. If the joint conference is satisfied that it will not be successful in procuring an election, those members of the Court who have already been elected shall, within a period to be fixed by the Security Council, proceed to fill the vacant seats by selection from among those candidates who have obtained votes either in the General Assembly or in the Security Council.
4. In the event of an equality of votes among the judges, the eldest judge shall have a casting vote.

Article 13

1. The members of the Court shall be elected for nine years and may be re-elected; provided, however, that of the judges elected at the first election, the terms of five judges shall expire at the end of three years and the terms of five more judges shall expire at the end of six years.

2. The judges whose terms are to expire at the end of the above-mentioned initial periods of three and six years shall be chosen by lot to be drawn by the Secretary-General immediately after the first election has been completed.

3. The members of the Court shall continue to discharge their duties until their places have been filled. Though replaced, they shall finish any cases which they may have begun.

4. In the case of the resignation of a member of the Court, the resignation shall be addressed to the President of the Court for transmission to the Secretary-General. This last notification makes the place vacant.

Article 14

Vacancies shall be filled by the same method as that laid down for the first election, subject to the following provision: the Secretary-General shall, within one month of the occurrence of the vacancy, proceed to issue the invitations provided for in Article 5, and the date of the election shall be fixed by the Security Council.

Article 15

A member of the Court elected to replace a member whose term of office has not expired shall hold office for the remainder of his predecessor's term.

Article 16

1. No member of the Court may exercise any political or administrative function, or engage in any other occupation of a professional nature.

2. Any doubt on this point shall be settled by the decision of the Court.

Article 17

1. No member of the Court may act as agent, counsel, or advocate in any case.

2. No member may participate in the decision of any case in which he has previously taken part as agent, counsel, or advocate for one of the parties, or as a member of a national or international court, or of a commission of enquiry, or in any other capacity.

3. Any doubt on this point shall be settled by the decision of the Court.

Article 18

1. No member of the Court can be dismissed unless, in the unanimous opinion of the other members, he has ceased to fulfil the required conditions.

2. Formal notification thereof shall be made to the Secretary-General by the Registrar.

3. This notification makes the place vacant.

Article 19

The members of the Court, when engaged on the business of the Court, shall enjoy diplomatic privileges and immunities.

Article 20

Every member of the Court shall, before taking up his duties, make a solemn declaration in open court that he will exercise his powers impartially and conscientiously.

Article 21

1. The Court shall elect its President and Vice-President for three years; they may be re-elected.

2. The Court shall appoint its Registrar and may provide for the appointment of such other officers as may be necessary.

Article 22

1. The seat of the Court shall be established at The Hague. This, however, shall not prevent the Court from sitting and exercising its functions elsewhere whenever the Court considers it desirable.

2. The President and the Registrar shall reside at the seat of the Court.

Article 23

1. The Court shall remain permanently in session, except during the judicial vacations, the dates and duration of which shall be fixed by the Court.

2. Members of the Court are entitled to periodic leave, the dates and duration of which shall be fixed by the Court, having in mind the distance between The Hague and the home of each judge.

3. Members of the Court shall be bound, unless they are on leave or prevented from attending by illness or other serious reasons duly explained to the President, to hold themselves permanently at the disposal of the Court.

Article 24

1. If, for some special reason, a member of the Court considers that he should not take part in the decision of a particular case, he shall so inform the President.

2. If the President considers that for some special reason one of the members of the Court should not sit in a particular case, he shall give him notice accordingly.

3. If in any such case the member of the Court and the President disagree, the matter shall be settled by the decision of the Court.

Article 25

1. The full Court shall sit except when it is expressly provided otherwise in the present Statute.

2. Subject to the condition that the number of judges available to constitute the Court is not thereby reduced below eleven, the Rules of the Court may provide for allowing one or more judges, according to circumstances and in rotation, to be dispensed from sitting.

3. A quorum of nine judges shall suffice to constitute the Court.

Article 26

1. The Court may from time to time form one or more chambers, composed of three or more judges as the Court may determine, for dealing with particular categories of cases; for example, labour cases and cases relating to transit and communications.

2. The Court may at any time form a chamber for dealing with a particular case. The number of judges to constitute such a chamber shall be determined by the Court with the approval of the parties.

3. Cases shall be heard and determined by the chambers provided for in this Article if the parties so request.

Article 27

A judgment given by any of the chambers provided for in Articles 26 and 29 shall be considered as rendered by the Court.

Article 28

The chambers provided for in Articles 26 and 29 may, with the consent of the parties, sit and exercise their functions elsewhere than at The Hague.

Article 29

With a view to the speedy dispatch of business, the Court shall form annually a chamber composed of five judges which, at the request of the parties, may hear and determine cases by summary procedure. In addition, two judges shall be selected for the purpose of replacing judges who find it impossible to sit.

Article 30

1. The Court shall frame rules for carrying out its functions. In particular, it shall lay down rules of procedure.
2. The Rules of the Court may provide for assessors to sit with the Court or with any of its chambers, without the right to vote.

Article 31

1. Judges of the nationality of each of the parties shall retain their right to sit in the case before the Court.
2. If the Court includes upon the Bench a judge of the nationality of one of the parties, any other party may choose a person to sit as judge. Such person shall be chosen preferably from among those persons who have been nominated as candidates as provided in Articles 4 and 5.
3. If the Court includes upon the Bench no judge of the nationality of the parties, each of these parties may proceed to choose a judge as provided in paragraph 2 of this Article.
4. The provisions of this Article shall apply to the case of Articles 26 and 29. In such cases, the President shall request one or, if necessary, two of the members of the Court forming the chamber to give place to the members of the Court of the nationality of the parties concerned, and, failing such, or if they are unable to be present, to the judges specially chosen by the parties.
5. Should there be several parties in the same interest, they shall, for the purpose of the preceding provisions, be reckoned as one party only. Any doubt upon this point shall be settled by the decision of the Court.
6. Judges chosen as laid down in paragraphs 2, 3 and 4 of this Article shall fulfil the conditions required by Articles 2, 17 (paragraph 2), 20, and 24 of the present Statute. They shall take part in the decision on terms of complete equality with their colleagues.

Article 32

1. Each member of the Court shall receive an annual salary.
2. The President shall receive a special annual allowance.
3. The Vice-President shall receive a special allowance for every day on which he acts as President.
4. The judges chosen under Article 31, other than members of the Court, shall receive compensation for each day on which they exercise their functions.
5. These salaries, allowances, and compensation shall be fixed by the General Assembly. They may not be decreased during the term of office.
6. The salary of the Registrar shall be fixed by the General Assembly on the proposal of the Court.
7. Regulations made by the General Assembly shall fix the conditions under which retirement pensions may be given to members of the Court and to the Registrar, and the conditions under which members of the Court and the Registrar shall have their travelling expenses refunded.
8. The above salaries, allowances, and compensation shall be free of all taxation.

Article 33

The expenses of the Court shall be borne by the United Nations in such a manner as shall be decided by the General Assembly.

Chapter II
COMPETENCE OF THE COURT

Article 34

1. Only states may be parties in cases before the Court.
2. The Court, subject to and in conformity with its Rules, may request of public international organizations information relevant to cases before it, and shall receive such information presented by such organizations on their own initiative.
3. Whenever the construction of the constituent instrument of a public international organization or of an international convention adopted thereunder is in question in a case before the Court, the Registrar shall so notify the public international organization concerned and shall communicate to it copies of all the written proceedings.

Article 35

1. The Court shall be open to the states parties to the present Statute.
2. The conditions under which the Court shall be open to other states shall, subject to the special provisions contained in treaties in force, be laid down by the Security Council, but in no case shall such conditions place the parties in a position of inequality before the Court.
3. When a state which is not a Member of the United Nations is a party to a case, the Court shall fix the amount which that party is to contribute towards the expenses of the Court. This provision shall not apply if such state is bearing a share of the expenses of the Court.

Article 36

1. The jurisdiction of the Court comprises all cases which the parties refer to it and all matters specially provided for in the Charter of the United Nations or in treaties and conventions in force.
2. The states parties to the present Statute may at any time declare that they recognize as compulsory *ipso facto* and without special agreement, in relation to any other state accepting the same obligation, the jurisdiction of the Court in all legal disputes concerning:
   a. the interpretation of a treaty;
   b. any question of international law;
   c. the existence of any fact which, if established, would constitute a breach of an international obligation;
   d. the nature or extent of the reparation to be made for the breach of an international obligation.
3. The declarations referred to above may be made unconditionally or on condition of reciprocity on the part of several or certain states, or for a certain time.
4. Such declarations shall be deposited with the Secretary-General of the United Nations, who shall transmit copies thereof to the parties to the Statute and to the Registrar of the Court.
5. Declarations made under Article 36 of the Statute of the Permanent Court of International Justice and which are still in force shall be deemed, as between the parties to the present Statute, to be acceptances of the compulsory jurisdiction of the International Court of Justice for the period which they still have to run and in accordance with their terms.
6. In the event of a dispute as to whether the Court has jurisdiction, the matter shall be settled by the decision of the Court.

Article 37

Whenever a treaty or convention in force provides for reference of a matter to a tribunal to have been instituted by the League of Nations, or to the Permanent Court of International Justice, the matter shall, as between the parties to the present Statute, be referred to the International Court of Justice.

Article 38

1. The Court, whose function is to decide in accordance with international law such disputes as are submitted to it, shall apply:
   a. international conventions, whether general or particular, establishing rules expressly recognized by the contesting states;
   b. international custom, as evidence of a general practice accepted as law;
   c. the general principles of law recognized by civilized nations;
   d. subject to the provisions of Article 59, judicial decisions and the teachings of the most highly qualified publicists of the various nations, as subsidiary means for the determination of rules of law.
2. This provision shall not prejudice the power of the Court to decide a case *ex aequo et bono*, if the parties agree thereto.

Chapter III
PROCEDURE

Article 39

1. The official languages of the Court shall be French and English. If the parties agree that the case shall be conducted in French, the judgment shall be delivered in French. If the parties agree that the case shall be conducted in English, the judgment shall be delivered in English.
2. In the absence of an agreement as to which language shall be employed, each party may, in the pleadings, use the language which it prefers; the decision of the Court shall be given in French and English. In this case the Court shall at the same time determine which of the two texts shall be considered as authoritative.
3. The Court shall, at the request of any party, authorize a language other than French or English to be used by that party.

Article 40

1. Cases are brought before the Court, as the case may be, either by the notification of the special agreement or by a written application addressed to the Registrar. In either case the subject of the dispute and the parties shall be indicated.
2. The Registrar shall forthwith communicate the application to all concerned.
3. He shall also notify the Members of the United Nations through the Secretary-General, and also any other states entitled to appear before the Court.

Article 41

1. The Court shall have the power to indicate, if it considers that circumstances so require, any provisional measures which ought to be taken to preserve the respective rights of either party.
2. Pending the final decision, notice of the measures suggested shall forthwith be given to the parties and to the Security Council.

Article 42

1. The parties shall be represented by agents.
2. They may have the assistance of counsel or advocates before the Court.
3. The agents, counsel, and advocates of parties before the Court shall enjoy the privileges and immunities necessary to the independent exercise of their duties.

Article 43

1. The procedure shall consist of two parts: written and oral.
2. The written proceedings shall consist of the communication to the Court and to the parties of memorials, counter-memorials and, if necessary, replies; also all papers and documents in support.
3. These communications shall be made through the Registrar, in the order and within the time fixed by the Court.
4. A certified copy of every document produced by one party shall be communicated to the other party.
5. The oral proceedings shall consist of the hearing by the Court of witnesses, experts, agents, counsel, and advocates.

Article 44

1. For the service of all notices upon persons other than the agents, counsel, and advocates, the Court shall apply direct to the government of the state upon whose territory the notice has to be served.
2. The same provision shall apply whenever steps are to be taken to procure evidence on the spot.

Article 45

The hearing shall be under the control of the President or, if he is unable to preside, of the Vice-President; if neither is able to preside, the senior judge present shall preside.

Article 46

The hearing in Court shall be public, unless the Court shall decide otherwise, or unless the parties demand that the public be not admitted.

Article 47

1. Minutes shall be made at each hearing and signed by the Registrar and the President.
2. These minutes alone shall be authentic.

Article 48

The Court shall make orders for the conduct of the case, shall decide the form and time in which each party must conclude its arguments, and make all arrangements connected with the taking of evidence.

Article 49

The Court may, even before the hearing begins, call upon the agents to produce any document or to supply any explanations. Formal note shall be taken of any refusal.

Article 50

The Court may, at any time, entrust any individual, body, bureau, commission, or other organization that it may select, with the task of carrying out an enquiry or giving an expert opinion.

Article 51

During the hearing any relevant questions are to be put to the witnesses and experts under the conditions laid down by the Court in the rules of procedure referred to in Article 30.

Article 52

After the Court has received the proofs and evidence within the time specified for the purpose, it may refuse to accept any further oral or written evidence that one party may desire to present unless the other side consents.

Article 53

1. Whenever one of the parties does not appear before the Court, or fails to defend its case, the other party may call upon the Court to decide in favour of its claim.
2. The Court must, before doing so, satisfy itself, not only that it has jurisdiction in accordance with Articles 36 and 37, but also that the claim is well founded in fact and law.

Article 54

1. When, subject to the control of the Court, the agents, counsel, and advocates have completed their presentation of the case, the President shall declare the hearing closed.
2. The Court shall withdraw to consider the judgment.
3. The deliberations of the Court shall take place in private and remain secret.

Article 55

1. All questions shall be decided by a majority of the judges present.
2. In the event of an equality of votes, the President or the judge who acts in his place shall have a casting vote.

Article 56

1. The judgment shall state the reasons on which it is based.
2. It shall contain the names of the judges who have taken part in the decision.

Article 57

If the judgment does not represent in whole or in part the unanimous opinion of the judges, any judge shall be entitled to deliver a separate opinion.

Article 58

The judgment shall be signed by the President and by the Registrar. It shall be read in open court, due notice having been given to the agents.

Article 59

The decision of the Court has no binding force except between the parties and in respect of that particular case.

Article 60

The judgment is final and without appeal. In the event of dispute as to the meaning or scope of the judgment, the Court shall construe it upon the request of any party.

Article 61

1. An application for revision of a judgment may be made only when it is based upon the discovery of some fact of such a nature as to be a decisive factor, which fact was, when the judgment was given, unknown to the Court and also the party claiming revision, always provided that such ignorance was not due to negligence.
2. The proceedings for revision shall be opened by a judgment of the Court expressly recording the existence of the new fact, recognizing that it has such a character as to lay the case open to revision, and declaring the application admissible on this ground.
3. The Court may require previous compliance with the terms of the judgment before it admits proceedings in revision.
4. The application for revision must be made at latest within six months of the discovery of the new fact.
5. No application for revision may be made after the lapse of ten years from the date of the judgment.

Article 62

1. Should a state consider that it has an interest of a legal nature which may be affected by the decision in the case, it may submit a request to the Court to be permitted to intervene.
2. It shall be for the Court to decide upon this request.

Article 63

1. Whenever the construction of a convention to which states other than those concerned in the case are parties is in question, the Registrar shall notify all such states forthwith.
2. Every state so notified has the right to intervene in the proceedings; but if it uses this right, the construction given by the judgment will be equally binding upon it.

Article 64

Unless otherwise decided by the Court, each party shall bear its own costs.

Chapter IV
ADVISORY OPINIONS

Article 65

1. The Court may give an advisory opinion on any legal question at the request of whatever body may be authorized by or in accordance with the Charter of the United Nations to make such a request.
2. Questions upon which the advisory opinion of the Court is asked shall be laid before the Court by means of a written request containing an exact statement of the question upon which an opinion is required, and accompanied by all documents likely to throw light upon the question.

Article 66

1. The Registrar shall forthwith give notice of the request for an advisory opinion to all states entitled to appear before the Court.
2. The Registrar shall also, by means of a special and direct communication, notify any state entitled to appear before the Court or international organization considered by the Court, or, should it not be sitting, by the President, as likely to be able to furnish information on the question, that the Court will be prepared to receive, within a time limit to be fixed by the President, written statements, or to hear, at a public sitting to be held for the purpose, oral statements relating to the question.
3. Should any such state entitled to appear before the Court have failed to receive the special communication referred to in paragraph 2 of this Article, such state may express a desire to submit a written statement or to be heard; and the Court will decide.
4. States and organizations having presented written or oral statements or both shall be permitted to comment on the statements made by other states or organizations in the form, to the extent, and within the time limits which the Court, or, should

it not be sitting, the President, shall decide in each particular case. Accordingly, the Registrar shall in due time communicate any such written statements to states and organizations having submitted similar statements.

Article 67

The Court shall deliver its advisory opinions in open court, notice having been given to the Secretary-General and to the representatives of Members of the United Nations, of other states and of international organizations immediately concerned.

Article 68

In the exercise of its advisory functions the Court shall further be guided by the provisions of the present Statute which apply in contentious cases to the extent to which it recognizes them to be applicable.

Chapter V
AMENDMENT

Article 69

Amendments to the present Statute shall be effected by the same procedure as is provided by the Charter of the United Nations for amendments to that Charter, subject however to any provisions which the General Assembly upon recommendation of the Security Council may adopt concerning the participation of states which are parties to the present Statute but are not Members of the United Nations.

Article 70

The Court shall have power to propose such amendments to the present Statute as it may deem necessary, through written communications to the Secretary-General, for consideration in conformity with the provisions of Article 69.

Appendix III

Structure of the United Nations

General Assembly

The General Assembly is composed of all Member States of the United Nations.

SESSIONS

Resumed sixty-fifth session: 14 January–12 September
Sixty-sixth session: 13 September–24 December (suspended)

OFFICERS
Resumed sixty-fifth session
President: Joseph Deiss (Switzerland)
Vice-Presidents: Afghanistan, Belarus, Botswana, China, Ecuador, Equatorial Guinea, France, Gambia, Indonesia, Luxembourg, Mauritania, Nicaragua, Pakistan, Russian Federation, Senegal, Sudan, Suriname, United Arab Emirates, United Kingdom, United States

Sixty-sixth session
President: Nassir Abdulaziz Al-Nasser (Qatar)[1]
Vice-Presidents[2]: Australia, Austria, Benin, Bolivia, Chad, China, Fiji, France, Haiti, Hungary, Iran, Kuwait, Liberia, Malawi, Mauritius, Morocco, Republic of Korea, Russian Federation, United Kingdom, United States, Uruguay

The Assembly has four types of committees: (1) Main Committees, (2) procedural committees, (3) standing committees, (4) subsidiary and ad hoc bodies. In addition, it convenes conferences to deal with specific subjects.

Main Committees

By resolution 47/233, the General Assembly rationalized its Committee structure as follows:
Disarmament and International Security Committee (First Committee), Special Political and Decolonization Committee (Fourth Committee), Economic and Financial Committee (Second Committee), Social, Humanitarian and Cultural Committee (Third Committee), Administrative and Budgetary Committee (Fifth Committee), Legal Committee (Sixth Committee).

The General Assembly may constitute other committees, on which all Member States of the United Nations have the right to be represented.

OFFICERS OF THE MAIN COMMITTEES
Resumed sixty-fifth session

Fourth Committee[3]
Chairperson: Chitsaka Chipaziwa (Zimbabwe)
Vice-Chairpersons: Radoslaw Flisiuk (Poland), David Windsor (Australia), Marcela Zamora (Costa Rica)
Rapporteur: Mohammad Wali Naeemi (Afghanistan)

Fifth Committee[3]
Chairperson: Gert Rosenthal (Guatemala)
Vice-Chairpersons: Muhammad Irfan Soomro (Pakistan), Ioana Sanda Stoica (Romania), Josiel Motumisi Tawana (South Africa)
Rapporteur: Nicole Mannion (Ireland)

Sixty-sixth session[4]

First Committee
Chairperson: Jarmo Viinanen (Finland)
Vice-Chairpersons: Amr Aljowaily (Egypt), Mohammad Almutairi (Kuwait), Ayesha Borland (Belize)
Rapporteur: Archil Gheghechkori (Georgia)

Fourth Committee
Chairperson: Simona Mirela Miculescu (Romania)
Vice-Chairpersons: Jim Kelly (Ireland), Mansor Ciss (Senegal), María Waleska Vivas Mendoza (Bolivaria)
Rapporteur: Hasan Abulhasan (Kuwait)

Second Committee
Chairperson: Abulkalam Abdul Momen (Bangladesh)
Vice-Chairpersons: Denis Zdorov (Belarus), Philippe Donckel (Luxembourg), Bitrus Vandy Yohanna (Nigeria)
Rapporteur: Raymond Landveld (Suriname)

Third Committee
Chairperson: Hussein Haniff (Malaysia)
Vice-Chairpersons: Donnette Critchlow (Guyana), Carolina Popovici (Republic of Moldova), Luca Zelioli (Italy)
Rapporteur: Kadra Ahmed Hassan (Djibouti)

Fifth Committee
Chairperson: Michel Tommo Monthé (Cameroon)
Vice-Chairpersons: Paul Ballantyne (New Zealand), Jelena Plakalović (Serbia), Mariam Saif Abdulla Al-Shamisi (United Arab Emirates)
Rapporteur: Noel González Segura (Mexico)

Sixth Committee
Chairperson: Hernán Salinas Burgos (Chile)
Vice-Chairpersons: Petr Válek (Czech Republic), Ceta Noland (Netherlands), Mattanee Kaewpanya (Thailand)
Rapporteur: Jacqueline K. Moseti (Kenya)

Procedural committees

General Committee
The General Committee consists of the President of the General Assembly, as Chairperson, the 21 Vice-Presidents and the Chairpersons of the six Main Committees.

Credentials Committee
The Credentials Committee consists of nine members appointed by the General Assembly on the proposal of the President.

Resumed sixty-fifth session
Bahamas, China, Finland, Gabon, Guatemala, Kenya, Russian Federation, Singapore, United States

Sixty-sixth session[5]
China, Costa Rica, Egypt, Italy, Maldives, Panama, Russian Federation, Senegal, United States

Standing committees

The two standing committees consist of experts appointed in their individual capacity for three-year terms.

Advisory Committee on Administrative and Budgetary Questions (ACABQ)
To serve until 31 December 2011: Aïcha Afifi (Morocco), Renata Archini (Italy), Vladimir A. Iosifov (Russian Federation), Alejandro Torres Lépori (Argentina), David Traystman (United States)[6]
To serve until 31 December 2012: Jasminka Dinić (Croatia), Collen V. Kelapile (Botswana), Stafford Oliver Neil (Jamaica), Mohammad Mustafa Tal (Jordan), Nonye Udo (Nigeria)
To serve until 31 December 2013: Namgya C. Khampa (India), Peter Maddens (Belgium), Carlos Ruiz Massieu (Mexico), Richard Moon (United Kingdom), Akira Sugiyama (Japan), Zhang Wanhai (China)

Structure of the United Nations

On 11 November 2011 (dec. 66/405), the General Assembly appointed the following persons for a three-year term beginning on 1 January 2012 to fill vacancies occurring on 31 December 2011: Pavel Chernikov (Russian Federation), Dietrich Lingenthal (Germany), Bruno Nunes Brant (Brazil), Jean Christian Obame (Gabon), David Traystman (United States).

Committee on Contributions

To serve until 31 December 2011: Patrick Haughey (United Kingdom)[7], Hae-yun Park (Republic of Korea), Gönke Roscher (Germany), Sun Xudong (China)[7], Courtney H. Williams (Jamaica)
To serve until 31 December 2012: Andrzej T. Abraszewski (Poland), Meshal al-Mansour (Kuwait), Elmi Ahmed Dualeh (Somalia), Ihor V. Humenny (Ukraine), Lisa Spratt (United States), Shigeki Sumi (Japan)
To serve until 31 December 2013: Joseph Acakpo-Satchivi (Benin), Gordon Eckersley (Australia), Bernardo Greiver del Hoyo (Uruguay), Juan Ndong Mbomio Mangue (Equatorial Guinea), Pedro Luis Pedroso (Cuba), Thomas Schlesinger (Austria)

On 11 November 2011 (dec. 66/406 A), the General Assembly appointed the following persons for a three-year term beginning on 1 January 2012 to fill the vacancies occurring on 31 December 2011: NneNne Iwuji-Eme (United Kingdom), Nikolay Lozinskiy (Russian Federation), Park Hae-yun (Republic of Korea), Gönke Roscher (Germany), Henrique da Silveira Sardinha Pinto (Brazil), Sun Xudong (China).

Subsidiary and ad hoc bodies

The following is a list of subsidiary and ad hoc bodies functioning in 2011, including the number of members, dates of meetings/sessions in 2011, document numbers of reports (which generally provide specific information on membership) and relevant decision numbers pertaining to elections.

Ad Hoc Committee on the Administration of Justice at the United Nations

Session: Did not meet in 2011
Membership: Open to all Member States of the United Nations or member States of the specialized agencies or of IAEA

Ad Hoc Committee on Criminal Accountability of United Nations Officials and Experts on Mission

Session: Did not meet in 2011
Membership: Open to all Member States of the United Nations or member States of the specialized agencies or of IAEA

Ad Hoc Committee established by General Assembly resolution 51/210 of 17 December 1996

Session: Fifteenth, New York, 11–15 April
Chairperson: Rohan Perera (Sri Lanka)
Membership: Open to all Member States of the United Nations or members of the specialized agencies or of IAEA
Report: A/66/37

Ad Hoc Committee on the Indian Ocean

Meeting: Four hundred and fifty-fourth, New York, 14 July
Chairperson: Palitha T. B. Kohona (Sri Lanka)
Membership: 43
Report: A/66/29

Advisory Board on Disarmament Matters

Sessions: Fifty-fifth, New York, 23–25 February; fifty-sixth, Geneva, 29 June–1 July
Chairperson: Olga Pellicer (Mexico)
Membership: 15 (plus 1 ex-officio member)
Report: A/66/125

Advisory Committee on the United Nations Programme of Assistance in the Teaching, Study, Dissemination and Wider Appreciation of International Law

Session: Forty-sixth, New York, 7 October
Chairperson: Ken Kanda (Ghana)
Membership: 25
Report: A/66/505

Board of Auditors

Sessions: Sixty-fifth (regular), New York, 12 July; forty-first (special), New Dehli, India, 3–6 December
Chairperson: Liu Jiayi (China)
Membership: 3
Decision: GA 66/408

Committee on Conferences

Sessions: New York, 20 April (organizational); 6 September (substantive)
Chairperson: Woinshet Tadesse Woldegiorgis (Ethiopia)
Membership: 21
Report: A/66/32
Decisions: GA 65/405 B, GA 66/414 A

Committee on the Exercise of the Inalienable Rights of the Palestinian People

Meetings: Throughout the year
Chairperson: Abdou Salam Diallo (Senegal)
Membership: 24
Report: A/66/35

Committee on Information

Session: Thirty-third, New York, 27 April–6 May
Chairperson: Eduardo Ulibarri (Costa Rica)
Membership: 113
Report: A/66/21

Committee on the Peaceful Uses of Outer Space

Session: Fifty-fourth, Vienna, 1–10 June
Chairperson: Dumitru-Dorin Prunariu (Romania)
Membership: 70
Report: A/66/20

Committee for Programme and Coordination (CPC)

Sessions: Fifty-first, New York, 28 April (organizational); 6 June–1 July (substantive)
Chairperson: Gastón Lasarte (Uruguay)
Membership: 30
Report: A/66/16
Decisions: GA 65/404 B, GA 66/411 A

Committee on Relations with the Host Country

Meetings: New York, 3 February, 31 March, 22 July, 7 October and 2 November
Chairperson: Minas Hadjimichael (Cyprus)
Membership: 19 (including the United States as host country)
Report: A/66/26

Committee for the United Nations Population Award

Chairperson: Maged A. Abdelaziz (Egypt)
Membership: 10 (plus the Secretary-General and the UNFPA Executive Director as ex-officio members)
Report: A/66/263

Disarmament Commission

Sessions: New York, 28 March (organizational); 4–22 April (substantive)
Chairperson: Hamid Al-Bayati (Iraq)
Membership: All Member States of the United Nations
Report: A/66/42

High-level Committee on South-South Cooperation

Session: Did not meet in 2011
Membership: All Member States of the United Nations

Human Rights Council

Sessions: Fifteenth (special), 25 February; sixteenth (special), 29 April; seventeenth (special), 22 August; eighteenth (special), 2 December; sixteenth (regular), 28 February–25 March; seventeenth (regular), 30 May–17 June; eighteenth (regular), 12–30 September, all in Geneva

Presidents: Sihasak Phuangketkeow (Thailand) (until June), Laura Dupuy Lasserre (Uruguay) (from June)
Membership: 47
Reports: A/66/53, A/66/53/Add.1, A/66/53/Add.1/Corr.1, A/66/53/Add.2, A/66/53/Add.2/Corr.1
Decision: GA 65/415

Independent Audit Advisory Committee

Sessions: Thirteenth, 15–17 February; fourteenth, 12–13 April; fifteenth, 11–13 July; sixteenth, 12–14 December, all in New York
Chairperson: David M. Walker (United States)
Membership: 5
Reports: A/66/299, A/67/259
Decision: GA 66/409

International Civil Service Commission (ICSC)

Sessions: Seventy-second, New York, 22 March–1 April; seventy-third, Paris, 18–29 July
Chairperson: Kingston P. Rhodes (Sierra Leone)
Membership: 15
Reports: A/66/30, A/66/30/Add.1, A/66/30/Corr.2

ADVISORY COMMITTEE ON POST ADJUSTMENT QUESTIONS

Session: Thirty-third, New York, 24–31 January
Chairperson: Wolfgang Stöckl (Germany)
Membership: 6

International Law Commission

Session: Sixty-third, Geneva, 26 April–3 June, 4 July–12 August
Chairperson: Maurice Kamto (Cameroon)
Membership: 34
Reports: A/66/10 & Add.1
Decision: GA 66/413

Investments Committee

Chairperson: William J. McDonough (United States)
Membership: 9 (plus ad hoc members)
Decision: GA 66/407

Joint Advisory Group on the International Trade Centre UNCTAD/WTO

Session: Forty-fifth, Geneva, 30 June–1 July
Chairperson: Darlington Mwape (Zambia)
Membership: Open to all member States of UNCTAD and all member States of WTO
Report: ITC/AG(XLV)/242

Joint Inspection Unit (JIU)

Chairperson: M. Mounir Zahran (Egypt)
Membership: 11
Report: A/66/34
Decision: GA 66/417 A

Office of the United Nations High Commissioner for Refugees (UNHCR)

EXECUTIVE COMMITTEE OF THE HIGH COMMISSIONER'S PROGRAMME

Session: Sixty-second, Geneva, 3–7 October
Chairperson: Hisham Badr (Egypt)
Membership: 85
Report: A/66/12/Add.1
Decision: ESC 2011/201 B
High Commissioner: António Guterres (Portugal)

Panel of External Auditors

Meeting: Fifty-second, New Delhi, India, 5–6 December
Membership: Members of the UN Board of Auditors and the appointed external auditors of the specialized agencies and IAEA

Special Committee on the Charter of the United Nations and on the Strengthening of the Role of the Organization

Meetings: New York, 28 February, 4 and 9 March
Chairperson: María Rubiales de Chamorro (Nicaragua)
Membership: Open to all Member States of the United Nations
Report: A/66/33

Special Committee to Investigate Israeli Practices Affecting the Human Rights of the Palestinian People and Other Arabs of the Occupied Territories

Chairperson: Palitha T. B. Kohona (Sri Lanka)
Membership: 3
Report: A/66/370

Special Committee on Peacekeeping Operations

Session: New York, 22 February–18 March, 9 May
Chairperson: U. Joy Ogwu (Nigeria)
Membership: 147
Report: A/65/19

Special Committee on the Situation with regard to the Implementation of the Declaration on the Granting of Independence to Colonial Countries and Peoples

Session: New York, 24 February and 31 March (first part); 13, 20, 21 and 23–24 June (second part)
Chairperson: Francisco Carrión-Mena (Ecuador)
Membership: 29
Report: A/66/23

United Nations Commission on International Trade Law (UNCITRAL)

Session: Forty-fourth, Vienna, 27 June–8 July
Chairperson: Salim Moollan (Mauritius)
Membership: 60
Report: A/66/17

United Nations Conciliation Commission for Palestine

Membership: 3
Report: A/66/296

United Nations Conference on Trade and Development (UNCTAD)

Session: Did not meet in 2011
Membership: Open to all Member States of the United Nations or member States of the specialized agencies or of IAEA
Secretary-General of UNCTAD: Supachai Panitchpakdi (Thailand)

TRADE AND DEVELOPMENT BOARD

Sessions: Fifty-eighth (annual), 12–23 September; fifty-eighth (resumed), 28 September; fifty-second, fifty-third, fifty-fourth (executive), 11–12 and 14 April, 27–28 June and 11 July, 28–29 November, all in Geneva
Presidents: Mothae Anthony Maruping (Lesotho) (fifty-eighth annual and fifty-fourth executive sessions), Luis Manuel Piantini Munnigh (Domincan Republic) (fifty-second and fifty-third executive sessions)
Membership: Open to all member States of UNCTAD
Reports: TD/B/58/9, TD/B/EX(52)/2, TD/B/EX(53)/8, TD/B/EX(54)/2

INVESTMENT, ENTERPRISE AND DEVELOPMENT COMMISSION

Session: Third, Geneva, 2–6 May
Chairperson: Kenichi Suganuma (Japan)
Membership: Open to all member States of UNCTAD
Report: TD/B/C.II/15

TRADE AND DEVELOPMENT COMMISSION

Session: Third, Geneva, 6–10 June
Chairperson: Tom Mboya Okeyo (Kenya)
Membership: Open to all member States of UNCTAD
Report: TD/B/C.I/21

INTERGOVERNMENTAL GROUP OF EXPERTS ON COMPETITION LAW AND POLICY

Session: Eleventh, Geneva, 19–21 July
Chairperson: Theodor Thanner (Austria)
Membership: Open to all member States of UNCTAD
Report: TD/B/C.I/CLP/12

WORKING PARTY ON THE STRATEGIC FRAMEWORK AND THE PROGRAMME BUDGET

Sessions: Fifty-eighth, 14–15 and 29 March; fifty-ninth, 5–7 September; sixtieth, 21–23 and 29 November, all in Geneva

Chairpersons: Karolina Frischkopf (Switzerland) (fifty-eighth), Wang Dawei (China) (fifty-ninth), Andrei Popov (Belarus) (sixtieth)
Membership: Open to all member States of UNCTAD
Reports: TD/B/WP/230, TD/B/WP/236, TD/B/WP/238

United Nations Entity for Gender Equality and the Empowerment of Women (UN-Women)

EXECUTIVE BOARD

Sessions: New York, 27–30 June (annual); first (regular), 24–26 January; first (resumed regular), 21 March and 8 April; second (regular), 5–7 December
President: U. Joy Ogwu (Nigeria)
Executive Director: Michelle Bachelet (Chile)
Membership: 41
Reports: UNW/2011/10, UNW/2011/8 & Add.1, UNW/2012/2

United Nations Environment Programme (UNEP)

GOVERNING COUNCIL

Session: Twenty-sixth/Global Ministerial Environment Forum, Nairobi, 21–24 February
Presidents: Oliver Dulić (Serbia), Henri Djombo (Congo) (acting President)
Membership: 57
Report: A/66/25
Decision: GA 66/412
Executive Director of UNEP: Achim Steiner (Germany/Brazil)

United Nations Human Settlements Programme (UN-Habitat)

GOVERNING COUNCIL

Session: Twenty-third, Nairobi, 11–15 April
President: Clifford Everald Warmington (Jamica)
Membership: 58
Report: A/66/8
Decision: ESC 2011/201 A & B
Executive Director of UN-Habitat: Joan Clos (Spain)

United Nations Institute for Disarmament Research (UNIDIR)

BOARD OF TRUSTEES

Sessions: Fifty-fifth, New York, 23–25 February; fifty-sixth, Geneva, 29 June–1 July
Chairperson: Olga Pellicer (Mexico)
Membership: 14 (plus 1 ex-officio member)
Report: A/66/125
Director of UNIDIR: Theresa Hitchens (United States)

United Nations Institute for Training and Research (UNITAR)

BOARD OF TRUSTEES

Sessions: Fiftieth, Geneva, 31 January–1 February; fifty-first, Brazzaville, Congo, 21–22 November
Chairperson: Henri Lopes (Congo)
Membership: 16
Reports: UNITAR/BT/50/2, UNITAR/BT/51/5
Executive Director of UNITAR: Carlos Lopes (Guinea Bissau)

United Nations Joint Staff Pension Board

Session: Fifty-eighth, Geneva, 11–15 July
Chairperson: Nana Yaa Nikoi (Ghana)
Membership: 33
Report: A/67/9
Chief Executive Officer: Bernard Cochemé (France)

United Nations Relief and Works Agency for Palestine Refugees in the Near East (UNRWA)

ADVISORY COMMISSION OF UNRWA

Meeting: Dead Sea, Jordan, 22 June
Chairperson: Fahed Abd Al-Muhsen Al-Zeid (Saudi Arabia)
Membership: 24
Report: A/66/13

WORKING GROUP ON THE FINANCING OF UNRWA

Meetings: New York, 15 and 30 September, 6 October
Chairperson: Ertuğrul Apakan (Turkey)
Membership: 9
Report: A/66/520
Commissioner-General of UNRWA: Filippo Grandi (Italy)

United Nations Scientific Committee on the Effects of Atomic Radiation

Session: Fifty-eighth, Vienna, 23–27 May
Chairperson: Wolfgang Weiss (Germany)
Membership: 21
Report: A/66/46

United Nations Staff Pension Committee

Membership: 8
Decision: GA 66/410 A

United Nations University (UNU)

COUNCIL OF THE UNITED NATIONS UNIVERSITY

Session: Fifty-eighth, Bruges, Belgium, 28 November–1 December
Chairperson: Juan Ramón de la Fuente (Mexico)
Membership: 24 (plus 3 ex-officio members and the UNU Rector)
Report: E/2011/129
Rector of the University: Konrad Osterwalder (Switzerland)

United Nations Voluntary Fund for Indigenous Populations

BOARD OF TRUSTEES

Session: Twenty-fourth, Geneva, 7–11 February
Chairperson: Dalee Sambo Dorough (United States)
Membership: 5
Report: A/67/221

United Nations Voluntary Fund for Victims of Torture

BOARD OF TRUSTEES

Sessions: Thirty-fourth, Geneva, 31 January–4 February
Chairperson: Mercedes Doretti (Argentina)
Membership: 5
Report: A/66/276

United Nations Voluntary Trust Fund on Contemporary Forms of Slavery

BOARD OF TRUSTEES

Session: Sixteenth, Geneva, 28 November–5 December
Chairperson: Virginia Herrera Murillo (Costa Rica)
Membership: 5
Report: A/67/269

Security Council

The Security Council consists of 15 Member States of the United Nations (five permanent members and ten non-permanent members), in accordance with the provisions of Article 23 of the United Nations Charter as amended in 1965.

MEMBERS

Permanent members: China, France, Russian Federation, United Kingdom, United States

Non-permanent members: Bosnia and Herzegovina, Brazil, Colombia, Gabon, Germany, India, Lebanon, Nigeria, Portugal, South Africa

On 21 and 24 October 2011 (dec. 66/402), the General Assembly elected Azerbaijan, Guatemala, Morocco, Pakistan and Togo for a two-year term beginning on 1 January 2012, to replace Bosnia and Herzegovina, Brazil, Gabon, Lebanon and Nigeria, whose terms of office expired on 31 December 2011.

PRESIDENT

The presidency of the Council rotates monthly, according to the English alphabetical listing of its Member States. The following served as President during 2011:

Month	Member	Representative
January	Bosnia and Herzegovina	Ivan Barbalić
February	Brazil	Maria Luiza Ribeiro Viotti
March	China	Li Baodong
April	Colombia	Néstor Osori
May	France	Gérard Araud
June	Gabon	Nelson Messone
July	Germany	Peter Wittig
August	India	Hardeep Singh Puri
September	Lebanon	Nawaf Salam
October	Nigeria	U. Joy Ogwu, Viola Onwuliri
November	Portugal	José Filipe Moraes Cabral
December	Russian Federation	Vitaly Churkin

Military Staff Committee

The Military Staff Committee consists of the chiefs of staff of the permanent members of the Security Council or their representatives. It meets fortnightly.

Standing committees

Each of the three standing committees of the Security Council is composed of representatives of all Council members:

Committee of Experts (to examine the provisional rules of procedure of the Council and any other matters entrusted to it by the Council),
Committee on the Admission of New Members,
Committee on Council Meetings Away from Headquarters.

Subsidiary bodies

Counter-Terrorism Committee (CTC)

Chairperson: Hardeep Singh Puri (India)

United Nations Compensation Commission

Governing Council

Sessions: Seventy-first and seventy-second, Geneva, 5–7 April and 11–13 October
President: Reinhard Schweppe (Germany)
Reports: S/2011/284, S/2011/639

1540 Committee

Chairperson: Baso Sangqu (South Africa)

International Tribunal for the former Yugoslavia (ICTY)

President: Patrick Robinson (Jamaica)
Under-Secretary-General, Prosecutor: Serge Brammertz (Belgium)
Assistant Secretary-General, Registrar: John Hocking (Australia)

International Criminal Tribunal for Rwanda (ICTR)

Presidents: Judge Dennis Byron (Saint Kitts and Nevis), Khalida Rachid Khan (Pakistan)
Under-Secretary-General, Prosecutor: Hassan Bubacar Jallow (Gambia)
Assistant Secretary-General, Registrar: Adama Dieng (Senegal)

Advisory Subsidiary body

Peacebuilding Commission (PBC)[8]

Organizational Committee

Session: Fifth, New York, 26 January
Chairperson: Eugène-Richard Gasana (Rwanda)
Membership: 31
Report: A/66/675-S/2012/70
Decisions: GA 66/415, ESC 2011/201 E

Peacekeeping operations

United Nations Truce Supervision Organization (UNTSO)

Head of Mission, Chief of Staff: Major General Robert Mood (Norway) (until February), Major General Juha Kilpia (Finland) (from March)

United Nations Military Observer Group in India and Pakistan (UNMOGIP)

Chief Military Observer: Major General Raul Gloodtdofsky Fernandez (Uruguay)

United Nations Peacekeeping Force in Cyprus (UNFICYP)

Special Representative of the Secretary-General and Head of Mission: Lisa M. Buttenheim (United States)
Force Commander: Major General Chao Liu (China)

United Nations Disengagement Observer Force (UNDOF)

Head of Mission, Force Commander: Major General Natalio C. Ecarma (Philippines)

United Nations Interim Force in Lebanon (UNIFIL)

Force Commander: Major General Alberto Asarta Cuevas (Spain)

United Nations Mission for the Referendum in Western Sahara (MINURSO)

Special Representative of the Secretary-General and Head of Mission: Hany Abdel-Aziz (Egypt)
Force Commander: Major General Jingmin Zhao (China) (until April), Major General Abdul Hafiz (Bangladesh) (from July)

United Nations Interim Administration Mission in Kosovo (UNMIK)

Special Representative of the Secretary-General and Head of Mission: Lamberto Zannier (Italy) (until June), Farid Zarif (Afghanistan) (from October)
OSCE Head of Mission in Kosovo: Werner Almhofer (Austria)
Deputy Special Representative of the Secretary-General: Robert E. Sorenson (United States)

United Nations Organization Stabilization Mission in the Democratic Republic of the Congo (MONUSCO)

Special Representative of the Secretary-General and Head of Mission: Roger A. Meece (United States)
Deputy Special Representative of the Secretary-General: Fidèle Sarassoro (Côte d'Ivoire)
Force Commander: Lieutenant General Chander Prakash Wadhwa (India)

United Nations Mission in Liberia (UNMIL)

Special Representative of the Secretary-General and Head of Mission: Ellen Margrethe Løj (Denmark)
Deputy Special Representative for Recovery and Governance: Moustapha Soumaré (Mali)
Deputy Special Representative for Rule of Law: Henrietta Joy Abena Nyarko Mensa-Bonsu (Ghana) (until October), Louis M. Aucoin (United States) (from December)
Force Commander: Major General Muhammad Khalid (Pakistan)

United Nations Operation in Côte d'Ivoire (UNOCI)

Special Representative of the Secretary-General and Head of Mission: Choi Young-jin (Republic of Korea) (until August), Albert Gerard (Bert) Koenders (Netherlands) (from September)
Principal Deputy Special Representative: Abou Moussa (Chad) (until March), Arnauld Antoine Akodjènou (Benin) (from June)
Deputy Special Representative: Ndolamb Ngokwey (Democratic Republic of the Congo) (until June), Arnauld Antoine Akodjènou (Benin) (from June)
Force Commander: Major General Abdul Hafiz (Bangladesh) (until March), Major General Gnakoudè Béréna (Togo) (from March)

United Nations Stabilization Mission in Haiti (MINUSTAH)

Special Representative of the Secretary-General and Head of Mission: Edmond Mulet (Guatemala) (until May), Mariano Fernández Amunátegui (Chile) (from June)
Principal Deputy Special Representative: Kevin Kennedy (United States)
Deputy Special Representative: Nigel Fisher (Canada) (ad interim)
Force Commander: Major General Luiz Guilherme Paul Cruz (Brazil) (until March), Major General Luiz Eduardo Ramos Pereira (Brazil) (from April)

United Nations Mission in the Sudan (UNMIS)[9]

Special Representative of the Secretary-General and Head of Mission: Haile Menkerios (South Africa)
Deputy Special Representative: Jasbir Singh Lidder (India)
Force Commander: Major General Moses Bisong Obi (Nigeria)
Police Commissioner: Rajesh Dewan (India) (until February), Klaus Dieter-Tietz (Germany) (from February)

United Nations Mission in South Sudan (UNMISS)[10]

Special Representative of the Secretary-General and Head of Mission: Hilde Johnson (Norway)
Deputy Special Representative and Resident and Humanitarian Coordinator: Lise Grande (United States) (ad interim)
Force Commander: Major General Moses Bisong Obi (Nigeria)
Police Commissioner (Officer-in-Charge): Klaus Dieter Tietz

United Nations Integrated Mission in Timor-Leste (UNMIT)

Special Representative of the Secretary-General and Head of Mission: Ameerah Haq (Bangladesh)
Deputy Special Representative for Governance Support, Development and Humanitarian Coordination: Finn Reske-Nielsen (Denmark)
Deputy Special Representative for Security Sector Support and Rule of Law: Shigeru Mochida (Japan)
Police Commissioner: Luis Carrilho (Portugal)

African Union-United Nations Hybrid Operation in Darfur (UNAMID)

AU-UN Joint Special Representative for Darfur and Head of Mission: Ibrahim Gambari (Nigeria)
Deputy Joint Special Representative for Operations and Management: Mohamed Yonis (Somalia)
Force Commander: Lieutenant General Patrick Nyamvumba (Rwanda)
Police Commissioner: Major General Michael Fryer (South Africa)

United Nations Interim Security Force for Abyei (UNISFA)[11]

Head of Mission and Force Commander: Lieutenant General Tadesse Werede Tesfay (Ethiopia)

Political, peacebuilding and other missions

United Nations Political Office for Somalia (UNPOS)

Special Representative of the Secretary-General and Head of UNPOS: Augustine P. Mahiga (Tanzania)
Deputy Special Representative of the Secretary-General for Somalia: Christian R. Manahl (Austria) (from February)

United Nations Integrated Peace-building Office in Guinea-Bissau (UNIOGBIS)

Special Representative of the Secretary-General and Head of UNIOGBIS: Joseph Mutaboba (Rwanda)
Deputy Special Representative: Gana Fofang (Cameroon)

Office of the United Nations Special Coordinator for the Middle East (UNSCO)

Special Coordinator for the Middle East Peace Process and Personal Representative of the Secretary-General to the Palestine Liberation Organization and the Palestinian Authority: Robert H. Serry (Netherlands)
Deputy Special Coordinator for the Middle East Peace Process: Maxwell Gaylard (Australia)

United Nations Integrated Peacebuilding Office in the Central African Republic (BINUCA)

Special Representative of the Secretary-General and Head of BINUCA: Sahle-Work Zewde (Ethiopia) (until March), Margaret Vogt (Nigeria) (since May)
Deputy Special Representative: Bo Schack (Denmark)

Office of the United Nations Special Coordinator of the Secretary-General for Lebanon (UNSCOL)

Special Coordinator of the Secretary-General for Lebanon: Michael C. Williams (United Kingdom)
Deputy Special Coordinator: Robert Watkins (Canada)

Office of the Special Representative of the Secretary-General for West Africa (UNOWA)

Special Representative of the Secretary-General: Said Djinnit (Algeria)

United Nations Assistance Mission in Afghanistan (UNAMA)

Special Representative of the Secretary-General and Head of Mission: Staffan de Mistura (Sweden)
Deputy Special Representative: Robert Watkins (Canada) (until July), Michael Keating (United Kingdom) (from July)
Deputy Special Representative (Political Affairs): Martin Kobler (Germany) (until August), Wolfgang Weisbrod-Weber (Germany) (from October) (ad interim)

United Nations Assistance Mission for Iraq (UNAMI)

Special Representative of the Secretary-General and Head of Mission: Ad Melkert (Netherlands) (until August), Martin Kobler (Germany) (from October)
Deputy Special Representative for Political, Electoral and Constitutional Support: Jerzy Skuratowicz (Poland), György Busztin (Hungary) (from December)
Deputy Special Representative for Humanitarian, Reconstruction and Development Affairs: Christine McNab (Sweden)

United Nations Integrated Peacebuilding Office in Sierra Leone (UNIPSIL)

Executive Representative of the Secretary-General: Michael von der Schulenburg (Germany)

United Nations Office in Burundi (BNUB)[12]

Special Representative of the Secretary-General and Head of BNUB: Karin Landgren (Sweden)
Deputy Special Representative: Rosine Sori-Coulibaly (Burkina Faso) (from May)

United Nations Mission in Nepal (UNMIN)[13]

Representative of the Secretary-General and Head of Mission: Karin Landgren (Sweden)

United Nations Regional Centre for Preventive Diplomacy for Central Asia (UNRCCA)

Special Representative of the Secretary-General and Head of UNRCCA: Miroslav Jenča (Slovakia)

Economic and Social Council

The Economic and Social Council consists of 54 Member States of the United Nations, elected by the General Assembly, each for a three-year term, in accordance with the provisions of Article 61 of the United Nations Charter as amended in 1965 and 1973.

MEMBERS

To serve until 31 December 2011: Côte d'Ivoire, Estonia, France, Germany, Guatemala, Guinea-Bissau, India, Japan, Malta, Mauritius, Morocco, Namibia, Peru, Saint Kitts and Nevis, Saudi Arabia, Spain, Switzerland, Venezuela

To serve until 31 December 2012: Argentina, Bahamas, Bangladesh, Canada, Chile, Comoros, Egypt, Ghana, Iraq, Italy, Mongolia, Netherlands, Philippines, Rwanda, Slovakia, Ukraine, United States, Zambia

To serve until 31 December 2013: Australia, Bulgaria, Cameroon, China, Ecuador, Finland, Gabon, Latvia, Malawi, Mexico, Nicaragua, Pakistan, Qatar, Republic of Korea, Russian Federation, Senegal, Switzerland, United Kingdom

On 24 October 2011 (dec. 66/403), the General Assembly elected Bulgaria, the Netherlands and Switzerland as members of the Economic and Social Council for the remainder of the terms of office of Hungary, Belgium and Norway, respectively, beginning on 1 January 2012. At the same meeting, the General Assembly elected the following for a three-year term of office beginning on 1 January 2012 to fill vacancies occurring on 31 December 2011: Côte d'Ivoire, Estonia, France, Germany, Guatemala, Guinea-Bissau, India, Japan, Malta, Mauritius, Morocco, Namibia, Peru, Saint Kitts and Nevis, Saudi Arabia, Spain, Switzerland and Venezuela.

SESSIONS

Organizational session: New York, 18 January, 15–18 February
Resumed organizational session: New York, 26–27 April, 18 and 26 May
Special high-level meeting with the Bretton Woods institutions, WTO and UNCTAD: New York, 10–11 March
Substantive session: Geneva, 4–29 July
Resumed substantive session: New York, 6, 24 and 27 October, 5 December

OFFICERS

President: Lazarous Kapambwe (Zambia)
Vice-Presidents: Abdulkalam Abdul Momen (Bangladesh), Miloš Koterec (Slovakia), Gonzalo Gutiérrez Reinel (Peru), Jan Grauls (Belgium)

Subsidiary and other related organs

SUBSIDIARY ORGANS

The Economic and Social Council may, at each session, set up committees or working groups, of the whole or of limited membership, and refer to them any item on the agenda for study and report.

Other subsidiary organs reporting to the Council consist of functional commissions, regional commissions, standing committees, expert and ad hoc bodies.

The inter-agency United Nations System Chief Executives Board for Coordination also reports to the Council.

Functional commissions

Commission on Crime Prevention and Criminal Justice

Sessions: Twentieth, Vienna, 11–15 April and 12–13 December
Chairperson: John Barrett (Canada)
Membership: 40
Report: E/2011/30 & Add.1
Decision: ESC 2011/201 B, D & E

Commission on Narcotic Drugs

Session: Fifty-fourth, Vienna, 21–25 March and 12–13 December
Chairperson: Veronika Kuchynová Smigolová (Czech Republic)
Membership: 53
Report: E/2011/28 & Add.1
Decision: ESC 2011/201 B & D

Commission on Population and Development

Session: Forty-fourth, New York, 11–15 April
Chairperson: Brian Bowler (Malawi)
Membership: 47
Report: E/2011/25
Decision: ESC 2011/201 B & C

Commission on Science and Technology for Development

Session: Fourteenth, Geneva, 23–27 May
Intersessional panel: 15–17 December
Chairperson: Sherry Ayittey (Ghana)
Membership: 43
Report: E/2011/31
Decision: ESC 2011/201 A, B & D

Commission for Social Development

Session: Forty-ninth, New York, 9–18 February
Chairperson: Jorge Valero (Venezuela)
Membership: 46
Report: E/2011/26 & Corr.1
Decision: ESC 2011/201 B & E

Commission on the Status of Women

Session: Fifty-fifth, New York, 22 February–4 March and 14 March
Chairperson: Garen Nazarian (Armenia)
Membership: 45
Report: E/2011/27
Decision: ESC 2011/201 B & C

Commission on Sustainable Development

Session: Nineteeth, New York, 2–13 May
Chairperson: László Borbély (Romania)
Membership: 53
Report: E/2011/29
Decision: ESC 2011/201 B & D

Statistical Commission

Session: Forty-second, New York, 22–25 February
Chairperson: Ali bin Mahboob Al-Raisi (Oman)
Membership: 24
Report: E/2011/24
Decision: ESC 2011/201 B

United Nations Forum on Forests

Session: Ninth, New York, 24 January–4 February
Chairperson: Arvids Ozols (Latvia)
Membership: Open to all Member States of the United Nations and members of the specialized agencies
Report: E/2011/42

Regional commissions

Economic Commission for Africa (ECA)

Session: The forty-fourth session of the Commission/Fourth Joint Annual Meetings of the AU and ECA Conference of Ministers, Addis Ababa, Ethiopia, 28–29 March
Chairperson: Kerfalla Yansane (Guinea)
Membership: 53

Structure of the United Nations

Economic Commission for Europe (ECE)
Session: Sixty-fourth, 29–31 March
Chairperson: Herman De Croo (Belgium)
Membership: 56
Report: E/2011/37

Economic Commission for Latin America and the Caribbean (ECLAC)
Session: Did not meet in 2011
Membership: 44 members, 9 associate members

Economic and Social Commission for Asia and the Pacific (ESCAP)
Session: Sixty-seventh, Bangkok, Thailand, 19–25 May
Chairperson: Sarath Amunugama (Sri Lanka)
Membership: 53 members, 9 associate members
Report: E/2011/39

Economic and Social Commission for Western Asia (ESCWA)
Session: Did not meet in 2011
Membership: 14

Standing committees

Committee on Non-Governmental Organizations
Sessions: New York, 31 January–9 February and 3 March (regular); 16–24 May and 16 June (resumed)
Chairperson: Aydan Karamanoğlu (Turkey)
Membership: 19
Report: E/2011/32 (Part I & II)

Committee for Programme and Coordination (CPC)
Sessions: Fifty-first, New York, 28 April (organizational); 6 June–1 July (substantive)
Chairperson: Gastón Lasarte (Uruguay)
Membership: 34
Report: A/66/16
Decision: ESC 2011/201 B & D

Expert bodies

Committee of Experts on International Cooperation in Tax Matters
Session: Seventh, Geneva, 24–28 October
Chairperson: Armando Lara Yaffar (Mexico)
Membership: 25
Report: E/2011/45

Committee for Development Policy
Session: Thirteenth, New York, 21–25 March
Chairperson: Frances Stewart (United Kingdom)
Membership: 24
Report: E/2011/33 & Corr.1

Committee on Economic, Social and Cultural Rights
Sessions: Forty-sixth and forty-seventh, Geneva, 2–20 May and 14 November–2 December
Chairpersons: Ibrahim Salama (temporary), Ariranga Govindasamy Pillay (Mauritius)
Membership: 18
Report: E/2012/22

Committee of Experts on Public Administration
Session: Tenth, New York, 4–8 April
Chairperson: Luis F. Aguilar Villanueva (Mexico)
Membership: 24
Report: E/2011/44

Committee of Experts on the Transport of Dangerous Goods and on the Globally Harmonized System of Classification and Labelling of Chemicals
Session: Did not meet in 2011
Membership: 66

Intergovernmental Working Group of Experts on International Standards of Accounting and Reporting
Session: Twenty-eighth, Geneva, 12–14 October
Chairperson: Damir Kaufman (Croatia)
Membership: 34
Report: TD/B/C.II/ISAR/61
Decision: ESC 2011/201 B, C & D

Permanent Forum on Indigenous Issues
Session: Tenth, New York, 16–27 May
Chairperson: Mirna Cunningham (Nicaragua)
Membership: 16
Report: E/2011/43 & Corr.1

United Nations Group of Experts on Geographical Names
Session: Twenty-sixth, Vienna, 2–6 May
Chairperson: Helen Kerfoot (Canada)
Membership: Representatives of the 24 geographical/linguistic divisions of the Group of Experts
Report: E/2011/119

Ad hoc body

United Nations System Chief Executives Board for Coordination (CEB)
Sessions: First, Nairobi, 1 April; second, New York, 28 October
Chairperson: Secretary-General Ban Ki-moon (Republic of Korea)
Membership: 29
Reports: CEB/2011/1, CEB/2011/2

Other related bodies

Joint United Nations Programme on Human Immunodeficiency Virus/Acquired Immunodeficiency Syndrome (UNAIDS)
PROGRAMME COORDINATING BOARD

Meetings: Twenty-eighth and twenty-ninth, Geneva, 21–23 June and 13–15 December
Chairperson: María Isabel Rodriguez (El Salvador)
Membership: 22
Reports: UNAIDS/PCB(28)/11.14, UNAIDS/PCB(28)/11.15
Decision: ESC 2011/201 B & E
Executive Director of UNAIDS: Michel Sidibé (Mali)

United Nations Children's Fund (UNICEF)
EXECUTIVE BOARD

Sessions: First and second (regular), 8–11 February and 12–15 September; (annual), 20–23 June, all in New York
President: Sanja Štiglic (Slovenia)
Membership: 36
Report: E/2011/34/Rev.1
Decision: ESC 2011/201 B
Executive Director of UNICEF: Anthony Lake (United States)

United Nations Development Programme (UNDP)/ United Nations Population Fund (UNFPA)/ United Nations Office for Project Services (UNOPS)
EXECUTIVE BOARD

Sessions: First and second (regular), 31 January–3 February and 6–9 September; (annual), 6–17 June, all in New York
President: Edita Hrdá (Czech Republic)
Membership: 36
Report: E/2011/35
Decision: ESC 2011/201 B
Administrator of UNDP: Helen Clark (New Zealand)
Associate Administrator: Rebeca Grynspan (Costa Rica)
Executive Director of UNFPA: Babatunde Osotimehin (Nigeria)
Executive Director of UNOPS: Jan Mattsson (Sweden)

UNITED NATIONS CAPITAL DEVELOPMENT FUND (UNCDF)
The UNDP/UNFPA/UNOPS Executive Board acts as the Executive Board of the Fund.
Managing Director: Helen Clark (UNDP Administrator)
Report: DP/2011/28

UNITED NATIONS VOLUNTEERS (UNV)
Report: DP/2012/12

United Nations Research Institute for Social Development (UNRISD)

BOARD

Session: Forty-ninth, Geneva, 4–5 April
Chairpersons: Lourdes Arizpe (Mexico) (until October), Maureen O'Neil (Canada) (from October)
Membership: 12
Reports: Board/11/3, Board/12/3
Decision: ESC 2011/278
Director of UNRISD: Sarah Cook (United Kingdom)

United Nations Interregional Crime and Justice Research Institute (UNICRI)

BOARD OF TRUSTEES

Membership: 7 (plus 4 ex-officio members)
Director of UNICRI: Jonathan Lucas (Seychelles)

United Nations System Staff College (UNSSC)

BOARD OF GOVERNORS

Chairperson: Susanna Malcorra (Argentina)
Membership: 9 (plus 3 ex-officio members)
Director: Carlos Lopes (Guinea Bissau)

World Food Programme (WFP)

EXECUTIVE BOARD

Sessions: First and second (regular), 14–16 February and 14–17 November; (annual), 6–9 June, all in Rome
Presidents: Agnes van Ardenne (Netherlands) (first regular and annual sessions), James Alexander Harvey (second regular session)
Membership: 36
Report: E/2012/36
Decision: ESC 2011/201 D & E
Executive Director of WFP: Josette Sheeran (United States)

Trusteeship Council

The Trusteeship Council suspended operation on 1 November 1994, following the independence on 1 October 1994 of Palau, the last remaining United Nations trust territory. The General Assembly, in resolution 60/1 of 16 September 2005, considering that the Council no longer met and had no remaining functions, decided that Chapter XIII of the United Nations Charter and references to the Council in Chapter XII should be deleted.

International Court of Justice

Judges of the Court

The International Court of Justice consists of 15 Judges elected for nine-year terms by the General Assembly and the Security Council.

Judge	Country of nationality	End of term
Hisashi Owada, President[14]	Japan	2021
Peter Tomka, Vice-President[14]	Slovakia	2021
Xue Hanqin[14]	China	2021
Abdul G. Koroma[15]	Sierra Leone	2012
Awn Shawkat Al-Khasawneh	Jordan	2018
Joan E. Donoghue	United States	2015
Bruno Simma[15]	Germany	2012
Ronny Abraham	France	2018
Kenneth Keith	New Zealand	2015
Bernardo Sepúlveda Amor	Mexico	2015
Mohamed Bennouna	Morocco	2015
Leonid Skotnikov	Russian Federation	2015
Antônio Augusto Cançado Trindade	Brazil	2018
Abdulqawi Ahmed Yusuf	Somalia	2018
Christopher Greenwood	United Kingdom	2018

Registrar: Philippe Couvreur (Belgium)
Deputy Registrar: Thérèse de Saint Phalle (United States/France)

Chamber of Summary Procedure

Members: Hisashi Owada, Peter Tomka, Abdul G. Koroma, Bernardo Sepúlveda Amor, Bruno Simma
Substitute members: Leonid Skotnikov, Christopher Greenwood

Parties to the Court's Statute

All Member States of the United Nations are ipso facto parties to the Statute of the International Court of Justice.

States accepting the compulsory jurisdiction of the Court

Declarations made by the following States, several with reservations, accepting the Court's compulsory jurisdiction (or made under the Statute of the Permanent Court of International Justice and deemed to be an acceptance of the jurisdiction of the International Court), were in force at the end of 2010:

Australia, Austria, Barbados, Belgium, Botswana, Bulgaria, Cambodia, Cameroon, Canada, Costa Rica, Côte d'Ivoire, Cyprus, Democratic Republic of the Congo, Denmark, Djibouti, Dominica, Dominican Republic, Egypt, Estonia, Finland, Gambia, Georgia, Germany, Guinea, Guinea-Bissau, Haiti, Honduras, Hungary, India, Ireland, Japan, Kenya, Lesotho, Liberia, Liechtenstein, Luxembourg, Madagascar, Malawi, Malta, Mauritius, Mexico, Netherlands, New Zealand, Nicaragua, Nigeria, Norway, Pakistan, Panama, Paraguay, Peru, Philippines, Poland, Portugal, Senegal, Slovakia, Somalia, Spain, Sudan, Suriname, Swaziland, Sweden, Switzerland, Togo, Uganda and Uruguay.

United Nations organs and specialized and related agencies authorized to request advisory opinions from the Court

Authorized by the United Nations Charter to request opinions on any legal question: General Assembly, Security Council
Authorized by the General Assembly in accordance with the Charter to request opinions on legal questions arising within the scope of their activities: Economic and Social Council, Trusteeship Council, Interim Committee of the General Assembly, ILO, FAO, UNESCO, ICAO, WHO, World Bank, IFC, IDA, IMF, ITU, WMO, IMO, WIPO, IFAD, UNIDO, IAEA

Committees of the Court

BUDGETARY AND ADMINISTRATIVE COMMITTEE
Members: Hisashi Owada (Chairperson), Peter Tomka, Kenneth Keith, Bernardo Sepúlveda Amor, Mohamed Bennouna, Abdulqawi Ahmed Yusuf, Christopher Greenwood
LIBRARY COMMITTEE
Members: Bruno Simma (Chairperson), Ronny Abraham, Mohamed Bennouna, Antônio Augusto Cançado Trindade
RULES COMMITTEE
Members: Awn Shawkat Al-Khasawneh (Chairperson), Ronny Abraham, Kenneth Keith, Leonid Skotnikov, Antônio Augusto Cançado Trindade, Christopher Greenwood

Other United Nations-related bodies

The following bodies are not subsidiary to any principal organ of the United Nations, but were established by an international treaty instrument or arrangement sponsored by the United Nations and are thus related to the Organization and its work. These bodies, often referred to as "Treaty organs", are serviced by the United Nations Secretariat and may be financed in part or wholly from the Organization's regular budget, as authorized by the General Assembly, to which most of them report annually.

Committee on the Elimination of Discrimination against Women (CEDAW)

Sessions: Forty-eighth, Geneva, 17 January–4 February; forty-ninth, New York, 11–29 July; fiftieth, Geneva, 3–21 October
Chairperson: Silvia Pimentel (Brazil)
Membership: 23
Reports: A/66/38, A/67/38

Committee on the Elimination of Racial Discrimination (CERD)

Sessions: Seventy-eighth, Geneva, 14 February–11 March; seventy-ninth, Geneva, 8 August–2 September
Chairperson: Anwar Kemal (Pakistan)
Membership: 18
Report: A/66/18

Committee on the Protection of the Rights of All Migrant Workers and Members of Their Families

Sessions: Fourteenth, 4–8 April; fifteenth, 12–23 September, all in Geneva
Chairperson: Abdelhamid El Jamri (Morocco)
Membership: 14
Reports: A/66/48, A/67/48

Committee on the Rights of the Child

Sessions: Fifty-sixth, fifty-seventh and fifty-eighth, Geneva, 17 January–4 February, 30 May–17 June, 19 September–7 October
Chairperson: Jean Zermatten (Switzerland)
Membership: 18
Report: A/67/41

Committee against Torture

Sessions: Forty-sixth, 9 May–3 June; forty-seventh, 31 October–25 November, all in Geneva
Chairperson: Claudio Grossman (Chile)
Membership: 10
Reports: A/66/44, A/67/44

Conference on Disarmament

Meetings: Geneva, 24 January–1 April, 16 May–1 July, 2 August–16 September
Presidents: Canada, Chile, China, Colombia, the Democratic People's Republic of Korea and Cuba[16] (successively)
Membership: 65
Report: A/66/27

Human Rights Committee

Sessions: 101st, New York, 14 March–1 April; 102nd, Geneva, 11–29 July; 103rd, Geneva, 17 October–4 November
Chairperson: Zonke Zanele Majodina (South Africa)
Membership: 18
Reports: A/66/40 (Vol. I), A/67/40 (Vol. I)

International Narcotics Control Board (INCB)

Sessions: 100th, 31 January–4 February; 101st, 2–13 May; 102nd, 24 October–11 November, all in Vienna
President: Hamid Ghodse (Iran)
Membership: 13
Report: E/INCB/2011/1
Decision: ESC 2011/201 B

Principal members of the United Nations Secretariat

Secretariat

Secretary-General: Ban Ki-moon
Deputy Secretary-General: Asha-Rose Migiro

Executive Office of the Secretary-General

Under-Secretary-General, Chef de Cabinet: Vijay Nambiar
Assistant Secretary-General, Deputy Chef de Cabinet: Kim Won-soo
Assistant Secretary-General for Policy Planning: Robert C. Orr

Office of Internal Oversight Services

Under-Secretary-General: Carman L. Lapointe

Office of Legal Affairs

Under-Secretary-General, Legal Counsel: Patricia O'Brien
Assistant Secretary-General: D. Stephen Mathias

Department of Political Affairs

Under-Secretary-General: B. Lynn Pascoe
Assistant Secretary-General: Tayé-Brook Zerihoun

Office for Disarmament Affairs

Under-Secretary-General, High Representative: Sergio Duarte

Department of Peacekeeping Operations

Under-Secretary-General: Alain Le Roy (until October), Hervé Ladsous (from October)
Assistant Secretaries-General: Atul Khare (until May), Edmond Mulet (from June)
Assistant Secretary-General, Military Adviser: Lieutenant General Babacar Gaye

Department of Field Support

Under-Secretary-General: Susana Malcorra
Assistant Secretary-General: Anthony Banbury

Office for the Coordination of Humanitarian Affairs

Under-Secretary-General for Humanitarian Affairs, Emergency Relief Coordinator: Valerie Amos
Assistant Secretary-General, Deputy Emergency Relief Coordinator: Catherine Bragg

Department of Economic and Social Affairs

Under-Secretary-General: Sha Zukang
Assistant Secretary-General for Economic Development: Jomo Kwame Sundaram
Assistant Secretary-General for Policy Coordination and Inter-Agency Affairs: Thomas Stelzer

Department for General Assembly and Conference Management

Under-Secretary-General: Muhammad Shaaban
Assistant Secretary-General: Franz Baumann

Department of Public Information

Under-Secretary-General for Communications and Public Information and Coordinator for Multilingualism: Kiyotaka Akasaka

Department of Safety and Security

Under-Secretary-General: Gregory B. Starr

Department of Management

Under-Secretary-General: Angela Kane

OFFICE OF PROGRAMME PLANNING, BUDGET AND ACCOUNTS
Assistant Secretary-General, Controller: Jun Yamazaki (until September), María Eugenia Casar (from September)

OFFICE OF HUMAN RESOURCES MANAGEMENT
Assistant Secretary-General: Catherine Pollard

OFFICE OF CENTRAL SUPPORT SERVICES
Assistant Secretary-General: Warren Sach

CAPITAL MASTER PLAN PROJECT
Assistant Secretary-General, Executive Director: Michael Adlerstein

Office of Information and Communications Technology
Assistant Secretary-General, Chief Information Technology Officer: Choi Soon-Hong

Office of the United Nations Ombudsman
Assistant Secretary-General, Ombudsman: Johnston Barkat

Peacebuilding Support Office
Assistant Secretary-General: Judy Cheng-Hopkins

United Nations Joint Staff Pension Fund
Assistant Secretary-General, Chief Executive Officer: Bernard G. Cochemé

Economic Commission for Africa
Under-Secretary-General, Executive Secretary: Abdoulie Janneh

Economic Commission for Europe
Under-Secretary-General, Executive Secretary: Ján Kubiš

Economic Commission for Latin America and the Caribbean
Under-Secretary-General, Executive Secretary: Alicia Bárcena Ibarra

Economic and Social Commission for Asia and the Pacific
Under-Secretary-General, Executive Secretary: Noeleen Heyzer

Economic and Social Commission for Western Asia
Under-Secretary-General, Executive Secretary: Rima Khalaf

United Nations Office at Geneva
Under-Secretary-General, Director-General of the United Nations Office at Geneva: Sergei Ordzhonikidze (until March), Kassym-Jomart Tokayev (from March)

United Nations Office at Vienna
Under-Secretary-General, Director-General of the United Nations Office at Vienna and Executive Director of the United Nations Office on Drugs and Crime: Yury Fedotov

United Nations Office at Nairobi
Under-Secretary-General, Director-General of the United Nations Office at Nairobi: Achim Steiner[17] (until May), Sahle-Work Zewde[17] (from May)

International Court of Justice Registry
Assistant Secretary-General, Registrar: Philippe Couvreur

Secretariats of subsidiary organs, special representatives and other related bodies

Counter-Terrorism Committee Executive Directorate (CTED)
Assistant Secretary-General, Executive Director: Michael Smith

International Civil Service Commission
Under-Secretary-General, Chairperson: Kingston Papie Rhodes
Assistant Secretary-General, Vice-Chairperson: Wolfgang Stöckl

International Trade Centre UNCTAD/WTO
Executive Director: Patricia Francis

Joint United Nations Programme on HIV/AIDS
Under-Secretary-General, Executive Director: Michel Sidibé
Under-Secretary-General, Special Adviser to the Secretary-General, Special Envoy for HIV/AIDS in Asia and the Pacific: Nafis Sadik
Assistant Secretary-General, Deputy Executive Director: Paul De Lay
Assistant Secretary-General, Deputy Executive Director, Management and Governance: Jan Beagle
Assistant Secretary-General, Special Envoy for HIV/AIDS in Africa: Elizabeth Mataka
Assistant Secretary-General, Special Envoy for HIV/AIDS in the Caribbean: John Edward Green (from November)

Office of the Administration of Justice
Executive Director: Andrei Terekhov

Office of the High Representative for the Least Developed Countries, Landlocked Developing Countries and Small Island Developing States
Under-Secretary-General, High Representative: Cheick Sidi Diarra

Office of the Secretary-General's Special Envoy for Malaria
Assistant Secretary-General, Special Envoy: Ray Chambers

Office of the Special Adviser to the Secretary-General on Africa
Under-Secretary-General, Special Adviser: Cheick Sidi Diarra

Office of the Special Adviser of the Secretary-General for Myanmar
Under-Secretary-General, Special Adviser: Vijay Nambiar

Office of the Special Representative of the Secretary-General for Children and Armed Conflict
Under-Secretary-General, Special Representative: Radhika Coomaraswamy

Office of the Special Adviser of the Secretary-General on the Prevention of Genocide
Under-Secretary-General, Special Adviser: Francis Deng

Office of the Special Representative of the Secretary-General for West Africa
Under-Secretary-General, Special Representative: Said Djinnit

Office of the United Nations High Commissioner for Refugees
Under-Secretary-General, High Commissioner: António Manuel de Oliveira Guterres
Assistant Secretary-General, Deputy High Commissioner: Alexander Aleinikoff
Assistant Secretary-General, Assistant High Commissioner (Protection): Erika Feller
Assistant Secretary-General, Assistant High Commissioner (Operations): Janet Lim

Office of the United Nations High Commissioner for Human Rights
Under-Secretary-General, High Commissioner: Navanethem Pillay
Assistant Secretary-General, Deputy High Commissioner: Kyung-wha Kang
Assistant Secretary-General (New York Office): Ivan Šimonović

Office of the United Nations Special Coordinator for the Middle East
Under-Secretary-General, Special Coordinator for the Middle East Peace Process and Personal Representative of the Secretary-General to the Palestine Liberation Organization and the Palestinian Authority: Robert H. Serry
Deputy Special Coordination: Maxwell Gaylard

Office of the Special Representative of the Secretary-General for Violence against Children
Assistant Secretary-General, Special Representative: Marta Santos Pais

Structure of the United Nations

Personal Envoy of the Secretary-General for the Greece-FYROM Talks
Under-Secretary-General, Personal Envoy: Matthew Nimetz

Personal Envoy of the Secretary-General for Western Sahara
Under-Secretary-General, Personal Envoy: Christopher Ross

Personal Representative of the Secretary-General on the Border Controversy between Guyana and Venezuela
Under-Secretary-General: Norman Girvan

Secretary-General's High-level Coordinator for compliance by Iraq with its obligations regarding the repatriation or return of all Kuwaiti and third country nationals or their remains, as well as the return of all Kuwaiti property, including archives seized by Iraq
Under-Secretary-General, High-Level Coordinator: Gennady P. Tarasov

Senior UN System Coordinator for Avian and Human Influenza
Assistant Secretary-General, Senior UN System Coordinator: David Nabarro

Special Advisers to the Secretary-General
Under-Secretary-General, Special Advisers: Joseph V. Reed, Iqbal Riza

Special Adviser to the Secretary-General on Cyprus
Under-Secretary-General, Special Adviser: Alexander Downer

Special Adviser to the Secretary-General on Innovative Financing for Development
Under-Secretary-General, Special Adviser: Philippe Douste-Blazy

Special Adviser of the Secretary-General on Legal Issues related to Piracy off the Coast of Somalia
Special Adviser: Jack Lang

Special Adviser to the Secretary-General and Mediator in the border dispute between Equatorial Guinea and Gabon
Under-Secretary-General, Special Adviser: Nicolas Michel

Special Envoy of the Secretary-General for the implementation of Security Council resolution 1559(2004)
Under-Secretary-General, Special Envoy: Terje Roed-Larsen

Special Representative of the Secretary-General on Food Security and Nutrition
Special Representative: David Nabarro

Special Representative on Sexual Violence in Conflict
Under-Secretary-General, Special Representative: Margot Wallström

Special Representative of the Secretary-General on Migration
Under-Secretary-General, Special Representative: Peter Sutherland

Special Representative of Secretary-General on the issue of human rights, transnational corporations and other business enterprises
Under-Secretary-General, Special Representative: John Ruggie

Special Representative of the Secretary-General for the Sudan[18]
Under-Secretary-General, Special Representative: Haile Menkerios
Assistant Secretary-General, Principal Deputy Special Representative: Jasbir Singh Lidder (until January)

Special Envoy of the Secretary-General for the Sudan and South Sudan[18]
Under-Secretary-General, Special Envoy: Haile Menkerios (from July)

Special Court for Sierra Leone
Under-Secretary-General, Prosecutor: Brenda Hollis
Assistant Secretary-General, Registrar: Binta Mansaray

Special Tribunal for Lebanon
Under-Secretary-General, Prosecutor: Daniel Bellemare
Assistant Secretary-General, Registrar: Herman von Hebel

Staff-Management Coordination Committee[19]
Assistant Secretary-General, President: Veronica Luard

United Nations Alliance of Civilizations
Under-Secretary-General, High Representative: Jorge Sampaio

United Nations Children's Fund
Under-Secretary-General, Executive Director: Anthony Lake
Assistant Secretaries-General, Deputy Executive Directors, External Relations: Hilde Frafjord Johnson, Rima Salah
Assistant Secretaries-General, Deputy Executive Directors, Programmes: Saad Houry, Geeta Rao
Assistant Secretary-General, Deputy Executive Director, Management: Martin Mogwanja

United Nations Compensation Commission
Assistant Secretary-General, Executive Secretary: Mojtaba Kazazi

United Nations Conference on Trade and Development
Under-Secretary-General, Secretary-General of UNCTAD: Supachai Panitchpakdi
Assistant Secretary-General, Deputy Secretary-General: Petko Draganov

United Nations Convention on Biological Diversity
Assistant Secretary-General, Executive Secretary: Ahmed Djoghlaf

United Nations Convention to Combat Desertification
Assistant Secretary-General, Executive Secretary: Luc Gnacadja

United Nations Development Programme
Under-Secretary-General, Administrator: Helen Clark
Under-Secretary-General, Associate Administrator: Rebeca Grynspan
Assistant Administrator and Director, Bureau for Crisis Prevention and Recovery: Jordan Ryan
Assistant Administrator and Director, Bureau of External Relations and Advocacy[20]: Sigrid Kaag
Assistant Administrator and Director, Bureau of Management: Akiko Yuge
Assistant Administrator and Director, Bureau for Development Policy: Olav Kjørven
Assistant Administrator and Regional Director, Africa: Tegegnework Gettu
Assistant Administrator and Regional Director, Arab States: Amat Al Alim Alsoswa
Assistant Administrator and Regional Director, Asia and the Pacific: Ajay Chhibber
Assistant Administrator and Regional Director, Europe and the Commonwealth of Independent States: Kori Udovički
Assistant Administrator and Regional Director, Latin America and the Caribbean: Heraldo Muñoz

United Nations Environment Programme
Under-Secretary-General, Executive Director: Achim Steiner
Assistant Secretary-General, Deputy Executive Director: Angela Cropper, Amina Mohamed
Assistant Secretary-General, Executive Secretary United Nations Framework Convention on Climate Change: Christiana Figueres

United Nations Global Compact
Executive Director: Georg Kell

United Nations Human Settlements Programme (UN-Habitat)
Under-Secretary-General, Executive Director: Joan Clos
Assistant Secretary-General, Deputy Executive Director: Inga Björk-Klevby (until October), Aisa Kirabo Kacyira (from October)

United Nations Institute for Training and Research
Assistant Secretary-General, Executive Director: Carlos Lopes

United Nations International School
Assistant Secretary-General, Special Representative: Michael Adlerstein

United Nations Office for Disaster Risk Reduction
Assistant Secretary-General, Special Representative: Margareta Wahlström

United Nations Office for Project Services
Assistant Secretary-General, Executive Director: Jan Mattsson

United Nations Office for Partnerships
Executive Director (Officer-in-Charge): Roland Rich

United Nations Office of the Special Envoy to Haiti
Special Envoy: William J. Clinton
Deputy Special Envoy: Paul Farmer

United Nations Office on Sport for Development and Peace
Under-Secretary-General, Special Adviser: Wilfried Lemke

United Nations Population Fund
Under-Secretary-General, Executive Director: Babatunde Osotimehin
Assistant Secretary-General, Deputy Executive Director (Management): Mari Simonen
Assistant Secretary-General, Deputy Executive Director (Programme): Purnima Mane

United Nations Relief and Works Agency for Palestine Refugees in the Near East
Under-Secretary-General, Commissioner-General: Filippo Grandi
Assistant Secretary-General, Deputy Commissioner-General: Margot B. Ellis

United Nations University
Under-Secretary-General, Rector: Konrad Osterwalder

World Food Programme
Under-Secretary-General, Executive Director: Josette Sheeran
Assistant Secretary-General, Deputy Executive Director: Amir Mahmoud Abdulla
Assistant Secretary-General, Deputy Executive Director for Hunger Solutions: Sheila Sisulu

Notes

[1] Elected on 22 June 2011 (General Assembly dec. 65/416).
[2] Elected on 22 June 2011 (General Assembly dec. 65/418 A & B).
[3] One of the Main Committees that met during the resumed session.
[4] Elected on 22 June 2011 (General Assembly dec. 65/417).
[5] Appointed on 13 September 2011 (General Assembly dec. 66/401).
[6] Appointed on 23 July 2011 (General Assembly dec. 65/406 B) to fill the vacancy created by the resignation of Susan McLurg.
[7] Appointed on 15 March 2011 (General Assembly dec. 65/407 B) to fill the vacancies created by the resignations of Richard Moon and Wu Gang.
[8] Also an advisory subsidiary body of the General Assembly.
[9] Mandate ended on 9 July 2011 (Security Council res. 1997(2011)).
[10] Established on 9 July 2011 as a successor mission to UNMIS (Security Council res. 1996(2011)).
[11] Established on 27 June 2011 (Security Council res. 1990(2011)).
[12] Established as a successor office to the United Nations Integrated Office in Burundi (BINUB) by Security Council resolution 1959(2010) to be operational on 1 January 2011.
[13] Mandate ended on 15 January 2011 pursuant Security Council resolution 1939(2010).
[14] Re-elected on 10 November 2011 for a term of office beginning on 6 February 2012 after the expiration of their previous mandate (General Assembly dec. 66/404 A).
[15] On 10 November 2011 and 13 December 2011, the General Assembly and the Security Council elected, independently of one another, Giorgio Gaja (Italy) and Julia Sebutinde (Uganda), respectively, for a term of office beginning on 6 February 2012 to replace the vacancies occurring on the expiration of the terms of office of Abdul G. Koroma (Sierra Leone) and Bruno Simma (Germany) (General Assembly dec. 66/404A).
[16] Cuba and the Democratic People's Republic of Korea switched the order in which they served as President, according to agreement reached at the 1227th plenary meeting of the Conference on Disarmament.
[17] By its resolution 64/243, the General Assembly decided to establish a dedicated post of Director-General of the United Office at Nairobi starting from 1 May 2015. Until then, the Executive Director of the United Nations Environment Programme served also as the Director-General of the United Office at Nairobi. Mr. Steiner was the last person to cover both positions and Ms. Zewde was the first person to be appointed to the newly created position.
[18] On 29 July 2011, Mr. Menkerios, who had been serving as Special Representative of the Secretary-General for the Sudan, was appointed Special Envoy of the Secretary-General for the Sudan and South Sudan.
[19] Dissolved as of 1 October 2011 and renamed Staff-Management Committee.
[20] Formerly known as the Partnerships Bureau.

Appendix IV

Agendas of the United Nations principal organs in 2011

This appendix lists the items on the agendas of the General Assembly, the Security Council and the Economic and Social Council during 2011. For the Assembly, the column headed "*Allocation*" indicates the assignment of each item to plenary meetings or committees.

General Assembly
Agenda items considered at the resumed sixty-fifth session
(14 January–12 September 2011) [decision 65/544, A/65/49 (Vol. II)]

Item No.	Title	Allocation
9.	Report of the Economic and Social Council.	Plenary
10.	Implementation of the Declaration of Commitment on HIV/AIDS and the Political Declaration on HIV/AIDS.	Plenary
12.	2001–2010: Decade to Roll Back Malaria in Developing Countries, Particularly in Africa.	Plenary
13.	Integrated and coordinated implementation of and follow-up to the outcomes of the major United Nations conferences and summits in the economic, social and related fields.	Plenary
14.	Global Agenda for Dialogue among Civilizations.	Plenary
15.	Culture of peace.	Plenary
20.	Sustainable development:	Plenary, 2nd
	(*i*) Harmony with Nature.	
26.	Agriculture development and food security.	2nd
29.	Report of the Security Council.	Plenary
30.	Report of the Peacebuilding Commission.	Plenary
33.	Prevention of armed conflict.	Plenary
34.	Protracted conflicts in the GUAM area and their implications for international peace, security and development.	Plenary
36.	The situation in the Middle East.	Plenary
37.	Question of Palestine.	Plenary
38.	The situation in Afghanistan.	Plenary
39.	The situation in the occupied territories of Azerbaijan.	Plenary
40.	Question of the Comorian island of Mayotte.	Plenary
42.	The situation in Central America: progress in fashioning a region of peace, freedom, democracy and development.	Plenary
43.	Question of Cyprus.	Plenary
44.	Armed aggression against the Democratic Republic of the Congo.	Plenary
45.	Question of the Falkland Islands (Malvinas).	Plenary
46.	The situation of democracy and human rights in Haiti.	Plenary
47.	Armed Israeli aggression against the Iraqi nuclear installations and its grave consequences for the established international system concerning the peaceful uses of nuclear energy, the non-proliferation of nuclear weapons and international peace and security.	Plenary
48.	Consequences of the Iraqi occupation of and aggression against Kuwait.	Plenary
51.	United Nations Relief and Works Agency for Palestine Refugees in the Near East.	4th
53.	Comprehensive review of the whole question of peacekeeping operations in all their aspects.	4th
60.	Permanent sovereignty of the Palestinian people in the Occupied Palestinian Territory, including East Jerusalem, and of the Arab population in the occupied Syrian Golan over their natural resources.	2nd
62.	New Partnership for Africa's Development: progress in implementation and international support.	Plenary
63.	Report of the Human Rights Council.	Plenary, 3rd
66.	Elimination of racism, racial discrimination, xenophobia and related intolerance.	3rd
69.	Strengthening of the coordination of humanitarian and disaster relief assistance of the United Nations, including special economic assistance.	Plenary
107.	Measures to eliminate international terrorism.	6th
108.	Report of the Secretary-General on the work of the Organization.	Plenary
109.	Report of the Secretary-General on the Peacebuilding Fund.	Plenary
112.	Elections to fill vacancies in subsidiary organs and other elections:	Plenary
	(*a*) Election of seven members of the Committee for Programme and Coordination;	
	(*b*) Election of fifteen members of the Human Rights Council.	
113.	Appointments to fill vacancies in subsidiary organs and other appointments:	Plenary, 5th
	(*f*) Appointment of members of the Committee on Conferences.	
114.	Admission of new Members to the United Nations.	Plenary
115.	Follow-up to the outcome of the Millennium Summit.	Plenary

Item No.	Title	Allocation
116.	Follow-up to the commemoration of the two-hundredth anniversary of the abolition of the transatlantic slave trade.	Plenary
117.	Implementation of the resolutions of the United Nations.	Plenary
118.	Revitalization of the work of the General Assembly.	Plenary, 1st, 4th, 2nd, 3rd, 5th, 6th
119.	Question of equitable representation on and increase in the membership of the Security Council and related matters.	Plenary
120.	Strengthening of the United Nations system.	Plenary
121.	Multilingualism.	Plenary
122.	Cooperation between the United Nations and regional and other organizations: (a) Cooperation between the United Nations and the African Union; (b) Cooperation between the United Nations and the Asian-African Legal Consultative Organization; (i) Cooperation between the United Nations and the Economic Community of Central African States; (l) Cooperation between the United Nations and the International Organization of la Francophonie; (n) Cooperation between the United Nations and the Latin American Economic System; (q) Cooperation between the United Nations and the Organization for Security and Cooperation in Europe; (r) Cooperation between the United Nations and the Organization of American States; (t) Cooperation between the United Nations and the Pacific Islands Forum; (w) Cooperation between the United Nations and the Southern African Development Community.	Plenary
123.	Follow-up to the recommendations on administrative management and internal oversight of the Independent Inquiry Committee into the United Nations Oil-for-Food Programme.	Plenary
125.	International Criminal Tribunal for the Prosecution of Persons Responsible for Genocide and Other Serious Violations of International Humanitarian Law Committed in the Territory of Rwanda and Rwandan Citizens Responsible for Genocide and Other Such Violations Committed in the Territory of Neighbouring States between 1 January and 31 December 1994.	Plenary
126.	International Tribunal for the Prosecution of Persons Responsible for Serious Violations of International Humanitarian Law Committed in the Territory of the Former Yugoslavia since 1991.	Plenary
127.	Financial reports and audited financial statements, and reports of the Board of Auditors.	5th
128.	Review of the efficiency of the administrative and financial functioning of the United Nations.	5th
129.	Programme budget for the biennium 2010–2011.	5th
130.	Programme planning.	Plenary, 1st, 4th, 2nd, 3rd, 5th, 6th
131.	Improving the financial situation of the United Nations.	5th
132.	Pattern of conferences.	5th
133.	Scale of assessments for the apportionment of the expenses of the United Nations.	5th
134.	Human resources management.	5th
135.	Joint Inspection Unit.	5th
136.	United Nations common system.	5th
137.	United Nations pension system.	5th
138.	Administrative and budgetary coordination of the United Nations with the specialized agencies and the International Atomic Energy Agency.	5th
139.	Report on the activities of the Office of Internal Oversight Services.	5th
140.	Administration of justice at the United Nations.	5th, 6th
141.	Financing of the International Criminal Tribunal for the Prosecution of Persons Responsible for Genocide and Other Serious Violations of International Humanitarian Law Committed in the Territory of Rwanda and Rwandan Citizens Responsible for Genocide and Other Such Violations Committed in the Territory of Neighbouring States between 1 January and 31 December 1994.	5th
142.	Financing of the International Tribunal for the Prosecution of Persons Responsible for Serious Violations of International Humanitarian Law Committed in the Territory of the Former Yugoslavia since 1991.	5th
143.	Administrative and budgetary aspects of the financing of the United Nations peacekeeping operations.	5th
144.	Financing of the United Nations Mission in the Central African Republic and Chad.	5th
145.	Financing of the United Nations Operation in Côte d'Ivoire.	5th
146.	Financing of the United Nations Peacekeeping Force in Cyprus.	5th
147.	Financing of the United Nations Organization Mission in the Democratic Republic of the Congo.	5th
148.	Financing of the United Nations Organization Stabilization Mission in the Democratic Republic of the Congo.	5th
149.	Financing of the United Nations Mission in East Timor.	5th
150.	Financing of the United Nations Integrated Mission in Timor-Leste.	5th
151.	Financing of the United Nations Mission in Ethiopia and Eritrea.	5th
152.	Financing of the United Nations Observer Mission in Georgia.	5th
153.	Financing of the United Nations Stabilization Mission in Haiti.	5th
154.	Financing of the United Nations Interim Administration Mission in Kosovo.	5th

Agendas of the United Nations principal organs in 2011

Item No.	Title	Allocation
155.	Financing of the United Nations Mission in Liberia.	5th
156.	Financing of the United Nations peacekeeping forces in the Middle East.	5th
157.	Financing of the United Nations Mission in the Sudan.	5th
158.	Financing of the United Nations Mission for the Referendum in Western Sahara.	5th
159.	Financing of the African Union-United Nations Hybrid Operation in Darfur.	5th
160.	Financing of the activities arising from Security Council resolution 1863(2009).	5th
162.	Follow-up to the high-level meeting held on 24 September 2010: revitalizing the work of the Conference on Disarmament and taking forward multilateral disarmament negotiations.	Plenary, 1st

Agenda of the sixty-sixth session, first part
(13 September–24 December 2010) [A/66/49 (Vol. I), Annex I]

Item No.	Title	Allocation
1.	Opening of the session by the President of the General Assembly.	Plenary
2.	Minute of silent prayer or meditation.	Plenary
3.	Credentials of representatives to the sixty-sixth session of the General Assembly: (a) Appointment of the members of the Credentials Committee; (b) Report of the Credentials Committee.	Plenary
4.	Election of the President of the General Assembly.	Plenary
5.	Election of the officers of the Main Committees.	1st, 4th, 2nd, 3rd, 5th, 6th
6.	Election of the Vice-Presidents of the General Assembly.	Plenary
7.	Organization of work, adoption of the agenda and allocation of items: reports of the General Committee.	Plenary
8.	General debate.	Plenary
A.	**Promotion of sustained economic growth and sustainable development in accordance with the relevant resolutions of the General Assembly and recent United Nations conferences**	
9.	Report of the Economic and Social Council.	Plenary
10.	Implementation of the Declaration of Commitment on HIV/AIDS and the Political Declarations on HIV/AIDS.	Plenary
11.	Sport for peace and development: (a) Building a peaceful and better world through sport and the Olympic ideal.	Plenary
12.	Global road safety crisis.	Plenary
13.	2001–2010: Decade to Roll Back Malaria in Developing Countries, Particularly in Africa.	Plenary
14.	Integrated and coordinated implementation of and follow-up to the outcomes of the major United Nations conferences and summits in the economic, social and related fields.	Plenary
15.	Culture of peace.	Plenary
16.	Information and communications technologies for development.	2nd
17.	Macroeconomic policy questions: (a) International trade and development; (b) International financial system and development; (c) External debt sustainability and development; (d) Commodities.	2nd
18.	Follow-up to and implementation of the outcome of the 2002 International Conference on Financing for Development and the 2008 Review Conference.	Plenary, 2nd
19.	Sustainable development: (a) Implementation of Agenda 21, the Programme for the Further Implementation of Agenda 21 and the outcomes of the World Summit on Sustainable Development; (b) Follow-up to and implementation of the Mauritius Strategy for the Further Implementation of the Programme of Action for the Sustainable Development of Small Island Developing States; (c) International Strategy for Disaster Reduction; (d) Protection of global climate for present and future generations of humankind; (e) Implementation of the United Nations Convention to Combat Desertification in Those Countries Experiencing Serious Drought and/or Desertification, Particularly in Africa; (f) Convention on Biological Diversity; (g) Report of the Governing Council of the United Nations Environment Programme on its twenty-sixth session; (h) Harmony with Nature; (i) Sustainable mountain development; (j) Promotion of new and renewable sources of energy.	Plenary, 2nd
20.	Implementation of the outcome of the United Nations Conference on Human Settlements (Habitat II) and strengthening of the United Nations Human Settlements Programme (UN-Habitat).	2nd
21.	Globalization and interdependence: (a) Role of the United Nations in promoting development in the context of globalization and interdependence; (b) Science and technology for development; (c) Development cooperation with middle-income countries.	2nd

Item No.	Title	Allocation
22.	Groups of countries in special situations: (a) Follow-up to the Fourth United Nations Conference on the Least Developed Countries; (b) Specific actions related to the particular needs and problems of landlocked developing countries: outcome of the International Ministerial Conference of Landlocked and Transit Developing Countries and Donor Countries and International Financial and Development Institutions on Transit Transport Cooperation.	2nd
23.	Eradication of poverty and other development issues: (a) Implementation of the Second United Nations Decade for the Eradication of Poverty (2008–2017); (b) Women in development; (c) Human resources development.	2nd
24.	Operational activities for development: (a) Operational activities for development of the United Nations system; (b) South-South cooperation for development.	2nd
25.	Agriculture development and food security.	2nd
26.	Towards global partnerships.	2nd
27.	Social development: (a) Implementation of the outcome of the World Summit for Social Development and of the twenty-fourth special session of the General Assembly; (b) Social development, including questions relating to the world social situation and to youth, ageing, disabled persons and the family; (c) Follow-up to the International Year of Older Persons: Second World Assembly on Ageing.	Plenary, 3rd
28.	Advancement of women: (a) Advancement of women; (b) Implementation of the outcome of the Fourth World Conference on Women and of the twenty-third special session of the General Assembly.	3rd
29.	People's empowerment and a peace-centric development model.	2nd

B. Maintenance of international peace and security

Item No.	Title	Allocation
30.	Report of the Security Council.	Plenary
31.	Report of the Peacebuilding Commission.	Plenary
32.	Support by the United Nations system of the efforts of Governments to promote and consolidate new or restored democracies.	Plenary
33.	The role of diamonds in fuelling conflict.	Plenary
34.	Prevention of armed conflict: (a) Strengthening the role of mediation in the peaceful settlement of disputes, conflict prevention and resolution.	Plenary
35.	Protracted conflicts in the GUAM area and their implications for international peace, security and development.	Plenary
36.	The situation in the Middle East.	Plenary
37.	Question of Palestine.	Plenary
38.	The situation in Afghanistan.	Plenary
39.	The situation in the occupied territories of Azerbaijan.	Plenary
40.	Question of the Comorian island of Mayotte.	Plenary
41.	Necessity of ending the economic, commercial and financial embargo imposed by the United States of America against Cuba.	Plenary
42.	The situation in Central America: progress in fashioning a region of peace, freedom, democracy and development.	Plenary
43.	Question of Cyprus.	Plenary
44.	Armed aggression against the Democratic Republic of the Congo.	Plenary
45.	Question of the Falkland Islands (Malvinas).	Plenary
46.	The situation of democracy and human rights in Haiti.	Plenary
47.	Armed Israeli aggression against the Iraqi nuclear installations and its grave consequences for the established international system concerning the peaceful uses of nuclear energy, the non-proliferation of nuclear weapons and international peace and security.	Plenary
48.	Consequences of the Iraqi occupation of and aggression against Kuwait.	Plenary
49.	Assistance in mine action.	4th
50.	Effects of atomic radiation.	4th
51.	International cooperation in the peaceful uses of outer space.	4th
52.	United Nations Relief and Works Agency for Palestine Refugees in the Near East.	4th
53.	Report of the Special Committee to Investigate Israeli Practices Affecting the Human Rights of the Palestinian People and Other Arabs of the Occupied Territories.	4th
54.	Comprehensive review of the whole question of peacekeeping operations in all their aspects.	4th
55.	Questions relating to information.	4th
56.	Information from Non-Self-Governing Territories transmitted under Article 73 e of the Charter of the United Nations.	4th
57.	Economic and other activities which affect the interests of the peoples of the Non-Self-Governing Territories.	4th

Agendas of the United Nations principal organs in 2011

Item No.	Title	Allocation
58.	Implementation of the Declaration on the Granting of Independence to Colonial Countries and Peoples by the specialized agencies and the international institutions associated with the United Nations.	4th
59.	Offers by Member States of study and training facilities for inhabitants of Non-Self-Governing Territories.	4th
60.	Implementation of the Declaration on the Granting of Independence to Colonial Countries and Peoples.	4th
61.	Permanent sovereignty of the Palestinian people in the Occupied Palestinian Territory, including East Jerusalem, and of the Arab population in the occupied Syrian Golan over their natural resources.	2nd
62.	Report of the United Nations High Commissioner for Refugees, questions relating to refugees, returnees and displaced persons and humanitarian questions.	3rd

C. Development of Africa

63.	New Partnership for Africa's Development: progress in implementation and international support: (a) New Partnership for Africa's Development: progress in implementation and international support; (b) Causes of conflict and the promotion of durable peace and sustainable development in Africa.	Plenary

D. Promotion of human rights

64.	Report of the Human Rights Council.	Plenary, 3rd
65.	Promotion and protection of the rights of children: (a) Promotion and protection of the rights of children; (b) Follow-up to the outcome of the special session on children.	3rd
66.	Rights of indigenous peoples: (a) Rights of indigenous peoples; (b) Second International Decade of the World's Indigenous People.	3rd
67.	Elimination of racism, racial discrimination, xenophobia and related intolerance: (a) Elimination of racism, racial discrimination, xenophobia and related intolerance; (b) Comprehensive implementation of and follow-up to the Durban Declaration and Programme of Action.	Plenary, 3rd
68.	Right of peoples to self-determination.	3rd
69.	Promotion and protection of human rights: (a) Implementation of human rights instruments; (b) Human rights questions, including alternative approaches for improving the effective enjoyment of human rights and fundamental freedoms; (c) Human rights situations and reports of special rapporteurs and representatives; (d) Comprehensive implementation of and follow-up to the Vienna Declaration and Programme of Action.	3rd

E. Effective coordination of humanitarian assistance efforts

70.	Strengthening of the coordination of humanitarian and disaster relief assistance of the United Nations, including special economic assistance: (a) Strengthening of the coordination of emergency humanitarian assistance of the United Nations; (b) Assistance to the Palestinian people; (c) Special economic assistance to individual countries or regions.	Plenary
71.	Assistance to survivors of the 1994 genocide in Rwanda, particularly orphans, widows and victims of sexual violence.	Plenary

F. Promotion of justice and international law

72.	Report of the International Court of Justice.	Plenary
73.	Report of the International Criminal Tribunal for the Prosecution of Persons Responsible for Genocide and Other Serious Violations of International Humanitarian Law Committed in the Territory of Rwanda and Rwandan Citizens Responsible for Genocide and Other Such Violations Committed in the Territory of Neighbouring States between 1 January and 31 December 1994.	Plenary
74.	Report of the International Tribunal for the Prosecution of Persons Responsible for Serious Violations of International Humanitarian Law Committed in the Territory of the Former Yugoslavia since 1991.	Plenary
75.	Report of the International Criminal Court.	Plenary
76.	Oceans and the law of the sea: (a) Oceans and the law of the sea; (b) Sustainable fisheries, including through the 1995 Agreement for the Implementation of the Provisions of the United Nations Convention on the Law of the Sea of 10 December 1982 relating to the Conservation and Management of Straddling Fish Stocks and Highly Migratory Fish Stocks, and related instruments.	Plenary
77.	Nationality of natural persons in relation to the succession of States.	6th
78.	Criminal accountability of United Nations officials and experts on mission.	6th
79.	Report of the United Nations Commission on International Trade Law on the work of its forty-fourth session.	6th
80.	United Nations Programme of Assistance in the Teaching, Study, Dissemination and Wider Appreciation of International Law.	6th
81.	Report of the International Law Commission on the work of its sixty-third session.	6th
82.	Report of the Special Committee on the Charter of the United Nations and on the Strengthening of the Role of the Organization.	6th
83.	The rule of law at the national and international levels.	6th
84.	The scope and application of the principle of universal jurisdiction.	6th
85.	The law of transboundary aquifers.	6th

Item No.	Title	Allocation

G. Disarmament

86. Report of the International Atomic Energy Agency. — Plenary
87. Reduction of military budgets: — 1st
    (a) Reduction of military budgets;
    (b) Objective information on military matters, including transparency of military expenditures.
88. Prohibition of the development and manufacture of new types of weapons of mass destruction and new systems of such weapons: report of the Conference on Disarmament. — 1st
89. Implementation of the Declaration of the Indian Ocean as a Zone of Peace. — 1st
90. African Nuclear-Weapon-Free Zone Treaty. — 1st
91. Verification in all its aspects, including the role of the United Nations in the field of verification. — 1st
92. Review of the implementation of the Declaration on the Strengthening of International Security. — 1st
93. Developments in the field of information and telecommunications in the context of international security. — 1st
94. Establishment of a nuclear-weapon-free zone in the region of the Middle East. — 1st
95. Conclusion of effective international arrangements to assure non-nuclear-weapon States against the use or threat of use of nuclear weapons. — 1st
96. Prevention of an arms race in outer space. — 1st
97. Role of science and technology in the context of international security and disarmament. — 1st
98. General and complete disarmament: — 1st
    (a) Notification of nuclear tests;
    (b) Follow-up to nuclear disarmament obligations agreed to at the 1995 and 2000 Review Conferences of the Parties to the Treaty on the Non-Proliferation of Nuclear Weapons;
    (c) Treaty on the South-East Asia Nuclear-Weapon-Free Zone (Bangkok Treaty);
    (d) Prohibition of the dumping of radioactive wastes;
    (e) Towards an arms trade treaty: establishing common international standards for the import, export and transfer of conventional arms;
    (f) Problems arising from the accumulation of conventional ammunition stockpiles in surplus;
    (g) Transparency in armaments;
    (h) Regional disarmament;
    (i) Conventional arms control at the regional and subregional levels;
    (j) Confidence building measures in the regional and subregional context;
    (k) Assistance to States for curbing the illicit traffic in small arms and light weapons and collecting them;
    (l) Relationship between disarmament and development;
    (m) Observance of environmental norms in the drafting and implementation of agreements on disarmament and arms control;
    (n) Promotion of multilateralism in the area of disarmament and non-proliferation;
    (o) Nuclear disarmament;
    (p) Implementation of the Convention on the Prohibition of the Development, Production, Stockpiling and Use of Chemical Weapons and on Their Destruction;
    (q) Towards a nuclear-weapon-free world: accelerating the implementation of nuclear disarmament commitments;
    (r) Reducing nuclear danger;
    (s) Measures to prevent terrorists from acquiring weapons of mass destruction;
    (t) The illicit trade in small arms and light weapons in all its aspects;
    (u) Treaty banning the production of fissile material for nuclear weapons or other nuclear explosive devices;
    (v) Transparency and confidence-building measures in outer space activities;
    (w) United action towards the total elimination of nuclear weapons;
    (x) Follow-up to the advisory opinion of the International Court of Justice on the *Legality of the Threat or Use of Nuclear Weapons*;
    (y) Missiles.
99. Review and implementation of the Concluding Document of the Twelfth Special Session of the General Assembly: — 1st
    (a) United Nations Regional Centre for Peace and Disarmament in Africa;
    (b) United Nations regional centres for peace and disarmament;
    (c) United Nations Regional Centre for Peace, Disarmament and Development in Latin America and the Caribbean;
    (d) Convention on the Prohibition of the Use of Nuclear Weapons;
    (e) United Nations Regional Centre for Peace and Disarmament in Asia and the Pacific;
    (f) Regional confidence-building measures: activities of the United Nations Standing Advisory Committee on Security Questions in Central Africa.
100. Review of the implementation of the recommendations and decisions adopted by the General Assembly at its tenth special session: — 1st
    (a) Report of the Conference on Disarmament;
    (b) Report of the Disarmament Commission.

Agendas of the United Nations principal organs in 2011

Item No.	Title	Allocation
101.	The risk of nuclear proliferation in the Middle East.	1st
102.	Convention on Prohibitions or Restrictions on the Use of Certain Conventional Weapons Which May Be Deemed to Be Excessively Injurious or to Have Indiscriminate Effects.	1st
103.	Strengthening of security and cooperation in the Mediterranean region.	1st
104.	Comprehensive Nuclear-Test-Ban Treaty.	1st
105.	Convention on the Prohibition of the Development, Production and Stockpiling of Bacteriological (Biological) and Toxin Weapons and on Their Destruction.	1st
106.	Revitalizing the work of the Conference on Disarmament and taking forward multilateral disarmament negotiations.	1st

H. Drug control, crime prevention and combating international terrorism in all its forms and manifestations

107.	Crime prevention and criminal justice.	3rd
108.	International drug control.	3rd
109.	Measures to eliminate international terrorism.	6th

I. Organizational, administrative and other matters

110.	Report of the Secretary-General on the work of the Organization.	Plenary
111.	Report of the Secretary-General on the Peacebuilding Fund.	Plenary
112.	Notification by the Secretary-General under Article 12, paragraph 2, of the Charter of the United Nations.	Plenary
113.	Elections to fill vacancies in principal organs:	Plenary
	(a) Election of five non-permanent members of the Security Council;	
	(b) Election of eighteen members of the Economic and Social Council;	
	(c) Election of five members of the International Court of Justice.	
114.	Elections to fill vacancies in subsidiary organs and other elections:	Plenary
	(a) Election of twenty members of the Committee for Programme and Coordination;	
	(b) Election of the members of the International Law Commission;	
	(c) Election of twenty-nine members of the Governing Council of the United Nations Environment Programme;	
	(d) Election of two members of the Organizational Committee of the Peacebuilding Commission.	
115.	Appointments to fill vacancies in subsidiary organs and other appointments:	Plenary, 5th
	(a) Appointment of members of the Advisory Committee on Administrative and Budgetary Questions;	
	(b) Appointment of members of the Committee on Contributions;	
	(c) Confirmation of the appointment of members of the Investments Committee;	
	(d) Appointment of a member of the Board of Auditors;	
	(e) Appointment of members of the Independent Audit Advisory Committee;	
	(f) Appointment of members of the Committee on Conferences;	
	(g) Appointment of members of the Joint Inspection Unit;	
	(h) Approval of the appointment of the United Nations High Commissioner for Human Rights;	
	(i) Appointment of the judges of the United Nations Dispute Tribunal;	
	(j) Appointment of the judges of the United Nations Appeals Tribunal;	
	(k) Appointment of members and alternate members of the United Nations Staff Pension Committee;	
	(l) Appointment of members of the International Civil Service Commission.	
116.	Admission of new Members to the United Nations.	Plenary
117.	Follow-up to the outcome of the Millennium Summit.	Plenary
118.	The United Nations Global Counter-Terrorism Strategy.	Plenary
119.	Follow-up to the commemoration of the two-hundredth anniversary of the abolition of the transatlantic slave trade.	Plenary
120.	Implementation of the resolutions of the United Nations.	Plenary
121.	Revitalization of the work of the General Assembly.	Plenary, 1st, 4th, 2nd, 3rd, 5th, 6th
122.	Question of equitable representation on and increase in the membership of the Security Council and related matters.	Plenary
123.	Strengthening of the United Nations system:	Plenary
	(a) Strengthening of the United Nations system;	
	(b) Central role of the United Nations system in global governance.	
124.	United Nations reform: measures and proposals.	Plenary
125.	Follow-up to the recommendations on administrative management and internal oversight of the Independent Inquiry Committee into the United Nations Oil-for-Food Programme.	Plenary
126.	Global health and foreign policy.	Plenary
127.	International Criminal Tribunal for the Prosecution of Persons Responsible for Genocide and Other Serious Violations of International Humanitarian Law Committed in the Territory of Rwanda and Rwandan Citizens Responsible for Genocide and Other Such Violations Committed in the Territory of Neighbouring States between 1 January and 31 December 1994.	Plenary

Item No.	Title	Allocation
128.	International Tribunal for the Prosecution of Persons Responsible for Serious Violations of International Humanitarian Law Committed in the Territory of the Former Yugoslavia since 1991.	Plenary
129.	International residual mechanism for criminal tribunals.	Plenary, 5th
130.	Interaction between the United Nations, national parliaments and the Inter-Parliamentary Union.	Plenary
131.	Financial reports and audited financial statements, and reports of the Board of Auditors: (a) United Nations peacekeeping operations; (b) Voluntary funds administered by the United Nations High Commissioner for Refugees; (c) Capital master plan.	5th
132.	Review of the efficiency of the administrative and financial functioning of the United Nations.	5th
133.	Programme budget for the biennium 2010–2011.	5th
134.	Proposed programme budget for the biennium 2012–2013.	5th
135.	Programme planning.	Plenary, 1st, 4th, 2nd, 3rd, 5th, 6th
136.	Improving the financial situation of the United Nations.	5th
137.	Pattern of conferences.	5th
138.	Scale of assessments for the apportionment of the expenses of the United Nations.	5th
139.	Human resources management.	5th
140.	Joint Inspection Unit.	5th
141.	United Nations common system.	5th
142.	Report on the activities of the Office of Internal Oversight Services.	5th
143.	Administration of justice at the United Nations.	5th
144.	Financing of the International Criminal Tribunal for the Prosecution of Persons Responsible for Genocide and Other Serious Violations of International Humanitarian Law Committed in the Territory of Rwanda and Rwandan Citizens Responsible for Genocide and Other Such Violations Committed in the Territory of Neighbouring States between 1 January and 31 December 1994.	5th
145.	Financing of the International Tribunal for the Prosecution of Persons Responsible for Serious Violations of International Humanitarian Law Committed in the Territory of the Former Yugoslavia since 1991.	5th
146.	Administrative and budgetary aspects of the financing of the United Nations peacekeeping operations.	5th
147.	Financing of the United Nations Interim Security Force for Abyei.	5th
148.	Financing of the United Nations Mission in the Central African Republic and Chad.	5th
149.	Financing of the United Nations Operation in Côte d'Ivoire.	5th
150.	Financing of the United Nations Peacekeeping Force in Cyprus.	5th
151.	Financing of the United Nations Organization Mission in the Democratic Republic of the Congo.	5th
152.	Financing of the United Nations Organization Stabilization Mission in the Democratic Republic of the Congo.	5th
153.	Financing of the United Nations Mission in East Timor.	5th
154.	Financing of the United Nations Integrated Mission in Timor-Leste.	5th
155.	Financing of the United Nations Mission in Ethiopia and Eritrea.	5th
156.	Financing of the United Nations Observer Mission in Georgia.	5th
157.	Financing of the United Nations Stabilization Mission in Haiti.	5th
158.	Financing of the United Nations Interim Administration Mission in Kosovo.	5th
159.	Financing of the United Nations Mission in Liberia.	5th
160.	Financing of the United Nations peacekeeping forces in the Middle East: (a) United Nations Disengagement Observer Force; (b) United Nations Interim Force in Lebanon.	5th
161.	Financing of the United Nations Mission in South Sudan.	5th
162.	Financing of the United Nations Mission in the Sudan.	5th
163.	Financing of the United Nations Mission for the Referendum in Western Sahara.	5th
164.	Financing of the African Union-United Nations Hybrid Operation in Darfur.	5th
165.	Financing of the activities arising from Security Council resolution 1863(2009).	5th
166.	Report of the Committee on Relations with the Host Country.	6th
167.	Observer status for the Cooperation Council of Turkic-speaking States in the General Assembly.	6th
168.	Observer status for the Union of South American Nations in the General Assembly.	6th
169.	Observer status for the International Renewable Energy Agency in the General Assembly.	6th
170.	Observer status for the Central European Initiative in the General Assembly.	6th
171.	Observer status for the United Cities and Local Governments in the General Assembly.	6th
172.	Observer status for the Intergovernmental Authority on Development in the General Assembly.	6th
173.	Observer status for the Parliamentary Assembly of Turkic-speaking Countries in the General Assembly.	6th
174.	Observer status for the International Conference of Asian Political Parties in the General Assembly.	6th
175.	Observer status for the West African Economic and Monetary Union in the General Assembly.	6th

Agendas of the United Nations principal organs in 2011

Security Council
Questions considered during 2011

Title

The situation in the Middle East, including the Palestinian question.
The situation in the Middle East.
The situation in Cyprus.
The situation concerning Western Sahara.
The situation in Timor-Leste.
United Nations peacekeeping operations.
The situation in Liberia.
The situation in Somalia.
The situation in Bosnia and Herzegovina.
Security Council resolutions 1160(1998), 1199(1998), 1203(1998), 1239(1999) and 1244(1999).
International Tribunal for the Prosecution of Persons Responsible for Serious Violations of International Humanitarian Law Committed in the Territory of the Former Yugoslavia since 1991.
International Criminal Tribunal for the Prosecution of Persons Responsible for Genocide and Other Serious Violations of International Humanitarian Law Committed in the Territory of Rwanda and Rwandan Citizens Responsible for Genocide and Other Such Violations Committed in the Territory of Neighbouring States between 1 January 1994 and 31 December 1994.
The question concerning Haiti.
The situation in Burundi.
The situation in Afghanistan.
The situation in Sierra Leone.
The situation in the Great Lakes region.
The situation concerning the Democratic Republic of the Congo.
The situation in the Central African Republic.
Children and armed conflict.
The situation in Guinea-Bissau.
Protection of civilians in armed conflict.
Women and peace and security.
Briefing by the President of the International Court of Justice.
Briefing by the Chairman-in-Office of the Organization for Security and Cooperation in Europe.
Meeting of the Security Council with the troop- and police-contributing countries [UNFICYP, UNDOF, UNIFIL, MINURSO, MONUSCO, UNMIL, UNOCI, MINUSTAH, UNMIS, UNMIT, UNAMID].
Threats to international peace and security caused by terrorist acts.
Briefings by Chairmen of subsidiary bodies of the Security Council.
The situation in Côte d'Ivoire.
Security Council mission.
The promotion and strengthening of the rule of law in the maintenance of international peace and security.
Central African region.
Non-proliferation of weapons of mass destruction.
Reports of the Secretary-General on the Sudan.
Post-conflict peacebuilding.
The situation concerning Iraq.
Threats to international peace and security.
Non-proliferation.
Peace consolidation in West Africa.
Non-proliferation/Democratic People's Republic of Korea.
Letter dated 22 November 2006 from the Secretary-General addressed to the President of the Security Council.
Maintenance of international peace and security [the interdependence between security and development; impact of HIV/AIDS epidemic on international peace and security; impact of climate change; conflict prevention; moving forward with security sector reform: prospects and challenges in Africa; new challenges to international peace and security and conflict prevention].
The situation in Chad, the Central African Republic and the subregion.
Peace and security in Africa.
Cooperation between the United Nations and regional and subregional organizations in maintaining international peace and security.
Letter dated 18 December 2010 from the Permanent Representative of the Russian Federation to the United Nations addressed to the President of the Security Council.
The situation in Libya.
Letter dated 6 February 2011 from the Permanent Representative of Cambodia to the United Nations addressed to the President of the Security Council.

Other matters considered during 2011

Title

Items relating to Security Council documentation and working methods and procedure.
Annual report of the Security Council to the General Assembly.
International Court of Justice [election of five members].
Admission of new Members.

Economic and Social Council

Agenda of the organizational and resumed organizational session for 2011
(18 January, 15–18 February, 26 and 27 April, 18 and 26 May)

Item No. *Title*

1. Election of the Bureau.
2. Adoption of the agenda and other organizational matters.
3. Basic programme of work of the Council.
4. Elections, nominations, confirmations and appointments.

Agenda of the substantive and resumed substantive sessions of 2011
(4–29 July, 6, 24 and 27 October and 5 December)

Item No. *Title*

1. Adoption of the agenda and other organizational matters.

High-level segment

2. High-level segment:
   (a) High-level policy dialogue with international financial and trade institutions;
   (b) Annual ministerial review:
       Implementing the internationally agreed goals and commitments in regard to education;
   (c) Thematic discussion:
       Current global and national trends and challenges and their impact on education.

Operational activities segment

3. Operational activities of the United Nations for international development cooperation:
   (a) Follow-up to policy recommendations of the General Assembly and the Council;
   (b) Reports of the Executive Boards of the United Nations Development Programme/United Nations Population Fund, the United Nations Children's Fund, the United Nations Entity for Gender Equality and the Empowerment of Women and the World Food Programme;
   (c) South-South cooperation for development.

Coordination segment

4. The role of the United Nations system in implementing the ministerial declaration of the high-level segment of the 2010 substantive session of the Economic and Social Council.
6. Implementation of and follow-up to major United Nations conferences and summits:
   (a) Follow-up to the International Conference on Financing for Development.
7. Coordination, programme and other questions:
   (a) Reports of coordination bodies;
   (e) Mainstreaming a gender perspective into all policies and programmes in the United Nations system.

Humanitarian affairs segment

5. Special economic, humanitarian and disaster relief assistance.

General segment

6. Implementation of and follow-up to major United Nations conferences and summits:
   (b) Review and coordination of the implementation of the Programme of Action for the Least Developed Countries for the Decade 2001–2010.
7. Coordination, programme and other questions:
   (a) Reports of coordination bodies;
   (b) Proposed programme budget for the biennium 2012–2013;
   (c) International cooperation in the field of informatics;
   (d) Long-term programme of support for Haiti;
   (f) African countries emerging from conflict;
   (g) Joint United Nations Programme on HIV/AIDS (UNAIDS);
   (h) Calendar of conferences and meetings in the economic, social and related fields.
8. Implementation of General Assembly resolutions 50/227, 52/12 B, 57/270 B and 60/265.
9. Implementation of the Declaration on the Granting of Independence to Colonial Countries and Peoples by the specialized agencies and the international institutions associated with the United Nations.

Item No.	Title

10. Regional cooperation:
11. Economic and social repercussions of the Israeli occupation on the living conditions of the Palestinian people in the Occupied Palestinian Territory, including East Jerusalem, and the Arab population in the occupied Syrian Golan.
12. Non-governmental organizations.
13. Economic and environmental questions:
    - (a) Sustainable development;
    - (b) Science and technology for development;
    - (c) Statistics;
    - (d) Human settlements;
    - (e) Environment;
    - (f) Population and development;
    - (g) Public administration and development;
    - (h) International cooperation in tax matters;
    - (i) United Nations Forum on Forests;
    - (j) Assistance to third States affected by the application of sanctions;
    - (k) Cartography;
    - (l) Women and development;
    - (m) Transport of dangerous goods.
14. Social and human rights questions:
    - (a) Advancement of women;
    - (b) Social development;
    - (c) Crime prevention and criminal justice;
    - (d) Narcotic drugs;
    - (e) United Nations High Commissioner for Refugees;
    - (f) Comprehensive implementation of the Durban Declaration and Programme of Action;
    - (g) Human rights;
    - (h) Permanent Forum on Indigenous Issues;
    - (i) Genetic privacy and non-discrimination.
15. United Nations research and training institutes.

Appendix V

United Nations information centres and services
(as at December 2014)

ACCRA. United Nations Information Centre
Gamal Abdel Nasser/Liberia Roads
(P.O. Box GP 2339)
Accra, Ghana
Serving: Ghana, Sierra Leone

ALGIERS. United Nations Information Centre
41 Rue Mohamed Khoudi, El Biar
El Biar, 16030 El Biar, Alger
(Boîte Postale 444, Hydra-Alger 16035)
Algiers, Algeria
Serving: Algeria

ANKARA. United Nations Information Centre
Birlik Mahallesi, 415. Cadde No. 11
06610 Cankaya
Ankara, Turkey
Serving: Turkey

ANTANANARIVO. United Nations Information Centre
159, Rue Damantsoa, Amkorahotra
(Boîte Postale, 1348)
Antananarivo, Madagascar
Serving: Madagascar

ASUNCIÓN. United Nations Information Centre
Avda. Mariscal López esq. Guillermo Saraví
Edificio Naciones Unidas
(Casilla de Correo 1107)
Asunción, Paraguay
Serving: Paraguay

BEIRUT. United Nations Information Centre/
United Nations Information Service,
Economic and Social Commission
for Western Asia
UN House, Riad El-Solh Square
(P.O. Box 11-8575-4656)
Beirut, Lebanon
Serving: Jordan, Kuwait, Lebanon,
Syrian Arab Republic, ESCWA

BOGOTÁ. United Nations Information Centre
Calle 100 No. 8A-55, Piso 10
Edificio World Trade Center-Torre "C"
(Apartado Aéro 058964)
Bogotá 2, Colombia
Serving: Colombia, Ecuador, Venezuela

BRAZZAVILLE. United Nations Information Centre
Avenue Foch, Case Ortf 15
(Boîte Postale 13210)
Brazzaville, Congo
Serving: Congo

BRUSSELS. Regional United Nations Information Centre
Résidence Palace
Rue de la Loi/Wetstraat 155
Quartier Rubens, Block C2
1040 Brussels, Belgium
Serving: Andorra, Belgium, Cyprus, Denmark, Finland, France, Germany, Greece, Holy See, Iceland, Ireland, Italy, Luxembourg, Malta, Monaco, Netherlands, Norway, Portugal, San Marino, Spain, Sweden, United Kingdom, European Union

BUENOS AIRES. United Nations Information Centre
Junín 1940, 1er piso
1113 Buenos Aires, Argentina
Serving: Argentina, Uruguay

BUJUMBURA. United Nations Information Centre
13 Avenue de la Révolution
(Boîte Postale 2160)
Bujumbura, Burundi
Serving: Burundi

CAIRO. United Nations Information Centre
1 Osiris Street, Garden City
(P.O. Box 262)
Cairo, Egypt
Serving: Egypt, Saudi Arabia

CANBERRA. United Nations Information Centre
Level 1, 7 National Circuit, Barton, ACT 2600
(P.O. Box 5366, Kingston, ACT 2604)
Canberra, Australia
Serving: Australia, Fiji, Kiribati, Nauru, New Zealand, Samoa, Tonga, Tuvalu, Vanuatu

COLOMBO. United Nations Information Centre
202/204 Bauddhaloka Mawatha
(P.O. Box 1505, Colombo)
Colombo 7, Sri Lanka
Serving: Sri Lanka

DAKAR. United Nations Information Centre
Parcelle N° 20
Route du King Fahd (ex. Méridien Président)
en face Hôtel AZUR
(Boîte Postale 154)
Dakar, Senegal
Serving: Cape Verde, Côte d'Ivoire, Gambia, Guinea-Bissau, Mauritania, Senegal

DAR ES SALAAM. United Nations Information Centre
182 Mzinga Way, Oysterbay
(P.O. Box 9224)
Dar es Salaam, United Republic of Tanzania
Serving: United Republic of Tanzania

DHAKA. United Nations Information Centre
IDB Bhaban (8th floor)
Sher-e-Banglanagar
(G.P.O. Box 3658, Dhaka-1000)
Dhaka-1207, Bangladesh
Serving: Bangladesh

GENEVA. United Nations Information Service
United Nations Office at Geneva
Palais des Nations
1211 Geneva 10, Switzerland
Serving: Switzerland

HARARE. United Nations Information Centre
Sanders House (2nd floor), cnr. First Street
Jason Moyo Avenue
(P.O. Box 4408)
Harare, Zimbabwe
Serving: Zimbabwe

ISLAMABAD. United Nations Information Centre
Serena Business Complex (2nd floor)
Sector G-5/1
Khayaban e Suhrawardy
(P.O. Box 1107)
Islamabad, Pakistan
Serving: Pakistan

JAKARTA. United Nations Information Centre
Menara Thamrin Building (3A floor)
Jalan MH Thamrin, Kav. 3
Jakarta 10250, Indonesia
Serving: Indonesia

KATHMANDU. United Nations Information Centre
Harihar Bhavan Pulchowk
(P.O. Box 107, UN House)
Kathmandu, Nepal
Serving: Nepal

KHARTOUM. United Nations Information Centre
United Nations Compound House #7, Blk 5
Gamma'a Avenue
(P.O. Box 1992)
Khartoum, Sudan
Serving: Somalia, Sudan

United Nations information centres and services

LAGOS. United Nations Information Centre
17 Alfred Rewane Road
(formely Kingsway Road), Ikoyi
(P.O. Box 1068)
Lagos, Nigeria
 Serving: Nigeria

LA PAZ. United Nations Information Centre
Calle 14 esq. S. Bustamante
Edificio Metrobol II, Calacoto
(Apartado Postal 9072)
La Paz, Bolivia
 Serving: Bolivia

LIMA. United Nations Information Centre
Av. Perez Aranibar 750, Magdalena
(P.O. Box 14-0199)
Lima 17, Peru
 Serving: Peru

LOMÉ. United Nations Information Centre
468, Angle rue Atime
Avenue de la Libération
(Boîte Postale 911)
Lomé, Togo
 Serving: Benin, Togo

LUSAKA. United Nations Information Centre
Revenue House (Ground floor)
Kalambo Roads
(P.O. Box 32905, Lusaka 10101)
Lusaka, Zambia
 Serving: Malawi, Swaziland, Zambia

MANAMA. United Nations Information Centre
United Nations House
Bldg. 69, Road 1901, Block 319
(P.O. Box 26004, Manama)
Manama, Bahrain
 Serving: Bahrain, Qatar, United Arab Emirates

MANILA. United Nations Information Centre
GC Corporate Plaza
(ex Jaka II Building) (5th floor)
150 Legaspi Street, Legaspi Village
(P.O. Box 7285 ADC (DAPO)
1300 Domestic Road Pasay City, Makati City
1229 Metro Manila, Philippines
 Serving: Papua New Guinea, Philippines, Solomon Islands

MASERU. United Nations Information Centre
United Nations Road, UN House
(P.O. Box 301, Maseru 100)
Maseru, Lesotho
 Serving: Lesotho

MEXICO CITY. United Nations Information Centre
Montes Urales 440 (3rd floor)
Colonia Lomas de Chapultepec
Mexico City, D.F. 11000, Mexico
 Serving: Cuba, Dominican Republic, Mexico

MOSCOW. United Nations Information Centre
9 Leontievsky Pereulok
Moscow 125009, Russian Federation
 Serving: Russian Federation

NAIROBI. United Nations Information Centre
United Nations Office, Gigiri
(P.O. Box 67578-00200)
Nairobi, Kenya
 Serving: Kenya, Seychelles, Uganda

NEW DELHI. United Nations Information Centre
55 Lodi Estate
New Delhi 110 003, India
 Serving: Bhutan, India

OUAGADOUGOU. United Nations Information Centre
14 Avenue de la Grande Chancellerie
Secteur no. 4
(Boîte Postale 135 Ouagadougou 01)
Ouagadougou, Burkina Faso
 Serving: Burkina Faso, Chad, Mali, Niger

PANAMA CITY. United Nations Information Centre
UN House Bldg 128 (1st floor)
Ciudad del Saber, Clayton
(P.O. Box 0819-01082)
Panama City, Panama
 Serving: Panama

PORT OF SPAIN. United Nations Information Centre
2nd floor, Bretton Hall, 16 Victoria Avenue
(P.O. Box 130)
Port of Spain, Trinidad and Tobago
 Serving: Antigua and Barbuda, Aruba, Bahamas, Barbados, Belize, Dominica, Grenada, Guyana, Jamaica, Netherlands Antilles, Saint Kitts and Nevis, Saint Lucia, Saint Vincent and the Grenadines, Suriname, Trinidad and Tobago

PRAGUE. United Nations Information Centre
Zelezna 24
110 00 Prague 1, Czech Republic
 Serving: Czech Republic

PRETORIA. United Nations Information Centre
Metropark Building, 351 Francis Baard Street
(P.O. Box 12677), Tramshed
Pretoria, South Africa 0126
 Serving: South Africa

RABAT. United Nations Information Centre
13 Avenue Ahmed Balafrej
(Boîte postale 601), Casier ONU, Rabat-Chellah
Rabat, Morocco
 Serving: Morocco

RIO DE JANEIRO. United Nations Information Centre
Palácio Itamaraty
Av. Marechal Floriano 196
20080-002 Rio de Janeiro RJ, Brazil
 Serving: Brazil

SANA'A. United Nations Information Centre
Street 5, Off Albawnya Area
Handhel Zone, beside Handhal Mosque
(P.O. Box 237), Sana'a, Yemen
 Serving: Yemen

TEHRAN. United Nations Information Centre
No. 8, Shahrzad Blvd. Darrous
(P.O. Box 15875-4557)
Tehran, Iran
 Serving: Iran

TOKYO. United Nations Information Centre
UNU Building (8th floor)
53–70 Jingumae 5-Chome
Shibuya-Ku, Tokyo 150-0001, Japan
 Serving: Japan

TRIPOLI. United Nations Information Centre
Khair Aldeen Baybers Street
Hay El-Andalous
(P.O. Box 286, Hay El-Andalous)
Tripoli, Libya
 Serving: Libya

TUNIS. United Nations Information Centre
41 Bis, Av. Louis Braille, Cité El Khadra
(Boîte postale 863)
1003 Tunis, Tunisia
 Serving: Tunisia

VIENNA. United Nations Information Service, United Nations Office at Vienna
Vienna International Centre
Wagramer Strasse 5
(P.O. Box 500, A-1400 Vienna)
A-1220 Vienna, Austria
 Serving: Austria, Hungary, Slovakia, Slovenia

WARSAW. United Nations Information Centre
ul. Piękna 19
00-549 Warszawa, Poland
 Serving: Poland

WASHINGTON, D.C. United Nations Information Centre
1775 K Street, N.W., Suite 400
Washington, D.C. 20006
United States of America
 Serving: United States of America

WINDHOEK. United Nations Information Centre
UN House
38–44 Stein Street, Klein
(Private Bag 13351)
Windhoek, Namibia
 Serving: Namibia

YANGON. United Nations Information Centre
6 Natmauk Road
Tamwe Township
(P.O. Box 230)
Yangon, Myanmar
 Serving: Myanmar

YAOUNDÉ. United Nations Information Centre
Immeuble Tchinda
Rue 2044, Derrière camp SIC TSINGA
(Boîte postale 836)
Yaoundé, Cameroon
 Serving: Cameroon, Central African Republic, Gabon

NOTE: For more information on UNICS, please visit the website: unic.un.org.

Appendix VI

Intergovernmental organizations related to the United Nations

(respective heads as at December 2011)

International Atomic Energy Agency (IAEA)
Vienna International Centre
P.O. Box 100, A-1400 Vienna, Austria
　Telephone: (43) (1) 2600-0
　Fax: (43) (1) 2600-7
　E-mail: official.mail@iaea.org
　Internet: www.iaea.org
　Director General: Yukiya Amano (Japan)

IAEA Office at the United Nations
One United Nations Plaza, Room DC1-1155
New York, NY 10017, U.S.A.
　Telephone: (1) (212) 963-6010/6011
　Fax: (1) (917) 367-4046
　E-mail: iaeany@un.org

International Labour Organization (ILO)
4, route des Morillons
CH-1211 Geneva 22, Switzerland
　Telephone: (41) (22) 799-6111
　Fax: (41) (22) 798-8685
　E-mail: ilo@ilo.org
　Internet: www.ilo.org
　Director General: Guy Ryder
　(United Kingdom)

ILO Office at the United Nations
One Dag Hammarskjöld Plaza
885 Second Avenue, 30th floor
New York, NY 10017, U.S.A.
　Telephone: (1) (212) 697-0150
　Fax: (1) (212) 697-5218
　E-mail: newyork@ilo.org

Food and Agriculture Organization of the United Nations (FAO)
Viale delle Terme di Caracalla
00153 Rome, Italy
　Telephone: (39) (06) 57051
　Fax: (39) (06) 570 53152
　E-mail: fao-hq@fao.org
　Internet: www.fao.org
　Director General: José Graziano da Silva
　(Brazil)

FAO Office at the United Nations
One United Nations Plaza, Room DC1-1125
New York, NY 10017, U.S.A.
　Telephone: (1) (212) 963-6036
　Fax: (1) (212) 963-5425
　E-mail: FAO-LON@fao.org

United Nations Educational, Scientific and Cultural Organization (UNESCO)
UNESCO House
7, place de Fontenoy
75352 Paris 07-SP, France
　Telephone: (33) (0) (1) 45-68-10-00
　E-mail: info@unesco.org
　Internet: www.unesco.org
　Director General: Irina Bokova
　(Bulgaria)

UNESCO Office at the United Nations
Two United Nations Plaza, Room DC2-900
New York, NY 10017, U.S.A.
　Telephone: (1) (212) 963-5995
　Fax: (1) (212) 963-8014
　E-mail: newyork@unesco.org

World Health Organization (WHO)
Avenue Appia, 20
CH-1211 Geneva 27, Switzerland
　Telephone: (41) (22) 791-2111
　Fax: (41) (22) 791-3111
　E-mail: info@who.int
　Internet: www.who.int
　Director General: Dr. Margaret Chan
　(China)

WHO Office at the United Nations
One Dag Hammarskjöld Plaza
885 Second Avenue, 26th floor
New York, NY 10017, U.S.A.
　Telephone: (1) (646) 626-6060
　Fax: (1) (646) 626-6080
　E-mail: wun@whoun.org

World Bank (IBRD, IDA and IFC)
1818 H Street, N.W.
Washington, D.C. 20433, U.S.A.
　Telephone: (1) (202) 473-1000
　Fax: (1) (202) 477-6391
　Internet: www.worldbank.org
　President: Jim Yong Kim
　(United States)

Office of the Special Representative to the United Nations
One Dag Hammarskjöld Plaza
885 Second Avenue, 26th floor
New York, NY 10017, U.S.A.
　Telephone: (1) (212) 355-5112
　Fax: (1) (212) 355-4523

International Monetary Fund (IMF)
700 19th Street, N.W.
Washington, D.C. 20431, U.S.A.
　Telephone: (1) (202) 623-7000
　Fax: (1) (202) 623-4661
　E-mail: publicaffairs@imf.org
　Internet: www.imf.org
　Managing Director: Christine Lagarde
　(France)

IMF Office at the United Nations
One Dag Hammarskjöld Plaza
885 Second Avenue, 26th floor
New York, NY 10017, U.S.A.
　Telephone: (1) (212) 317-4720
　Fax: (1) (212) 317-4733

International Civil Aviation Organization (ICAO)
999 University Street
Montreal, Quebec, H3C 5H7, Canada
　Telephone: (1) (514) 954-8219
　Fax: (1) (514) 954-6077
　E-mail: icaohq@icao.int
　Internet: www.icao.int
　Secretary-General: Raymond Benjamin
　(France)

Universal Postal Union (UPU)
Weltpost Strasse, 4
Case Postale 312
3000 Berne 15, Switzerland
　Telephone: (41) (31) 350-3111
　Fax: (41) (31) 350-3110
　E-mail: info@upu.int
　Internet: www.upu.int
　Director General: Bishar Abdirahman Hussein (Kenya)

International Telecommunication Union (ITU)
Place des Nations
CH-1211 Geneva 20, Switzerland
　Telephone: (41) (22) 730-5111
　Fax: (41) (22) 733-7256
　E-mail: itumail@itu.int
　Internet: www.itu.int
　Secretary-General: Houlin Zhao (China)

World Meteorological Organization (WMO)
7 bis, avenue de la Paix
Case postale 2300
CH-1211 Geneva 2, Switzerland

Intergovernmental organizations

Telephone: (41) (22) 730-8111
Fax: (41) (22) 730-8181
E-mail: wmo@wmo.int
Internet: www.wmo.int
President: David Grimes (Canada)
Secretary-General: Michel Jarraud (France)

WMO Office at the United Nations
866 United Nations Plaza, Room A-302
New York, NY 10017, U.S.A.
Telephone: (1) (212) 963-9444
Fax: (1) (917) 367-6997
E-mail: nyliaison@wmo.int

International Maritime Organization (IMO)
4, Albert Embankment
London SE1 7SR, United Kingdom
Telephone: (44) (207) 735-7611
Fax: (44) (207) 587-3210
E-mail: info@imo.org
Internet: www.imo.org
Secretary-General: Koji Sekimizu (Japan)

World Intellectual Property Organization (WIPO)
34, chemin des Colombettes
CH-1211 Geneva 20, Switzerland
Telephone: (41) (22) 338-9111
Fax: (41) (22) 733-5428
E-mail: wipo.mail@wipo.int
Internet: www.wipo.int
Director General: Francis Gurry (Australia)

WIPO Office at the United Nations
Two United Nations Plaza, Room DC2-2525
New York, NY 10017, U.S.A.
Telephone: (1) (212) 963-6813
Fax: (1) (212) 963-4801
E-mail: wipo@un.org

International Fund for Agricultural Development (IFAD)
Via Paolo di Dono, 44
00142 Rome, Italy
Telephone: (39) (06) 54591
Fax: (39) (06) 504 3463
E-mail: ifad@ifad.org
Internet: www.ifad.org
President: Kanayo F. Nwanze (Nigeria)

IFAD Office at the United Nations
Two United Nations Plaza, Rooms DC2-1128/1129
New York, NY 10017, U.S.A.
Telephone: (1) (212) 963-0546
Fax: (1) (212) 963-2787
E-mail: ifad@un.org

United Nations Industrial Development Organization (UNIDO)
Vienna International Centre
Wagramer Strasse, 5
P.O. Box 300, A-1400 Vienna, Austria
Telephone: (43) (1) 26026-0
Fax: (43) (1) 269-2669
E-mail: unido@unido.org
Internet: www.unido.org
Director General: LI Yong (China)

UNIDO Office in New York
One United Nations Plaza, Room DC1-1118
New York, NY 10017, U.S.A.
Telephone: (1) (212) 963-6890/6885
Fax: (1) (212) 963-7904
E-mail: office.newyork@unido.org

World Trade Organization (WTO)
Centre William Rappard
Rue de Lausanne, 154
CH-1211 Geneva 21, Switzerland
Telephone: (41) (22) 739-5111
Fax: (41) (22) 731-4206
E-mail: enquiries@wto.org
Internet: www.wto.org
Director General: Roberto Azevêdo (Brazil)

World Tourism Organization (UNWTO)
Capitan Haya, 42
28020 Madrid, Spain
Telephone: (34) (91) 567-8100
Fax: (34) (91) 571-3733
E-mail: omt@unwto.org
Internet: www.unwto.org
Secretary-General: Taleb Rifai (Jordan)

Preparatory Commission for the Comprehensive Nuclear-Test-Ban Treaty Organization (CTBTO)
Vienna International Centre
P.O. Box 1200
A-1400 Vienna, Austria
Telephone: (43) (1) 26030
Fax: (43) (1) 26030 5823
E-mail: info@ctbto.org
Internet: www.ctbto.org
Executive Secretary: Lassina Zerbo (Burkina Faso)

Organization for the Prohibition of Chemical Weapons (OPCW)
Johan de Wittlaan 32
2517 JR-The Hague
The Netherlands
Telephone: (31) (70) 416 3300
Fax: (31) (70) 306 3535
E-mail: media@opcw.org
Internet: www.opcw.org
Director General: Ahmet Üzümcü (Turkey)

NOTE: For more information on liaison, regional, subregional and country offices maintained by any of these organizations, please visit their respective websites.

Indices

Subject index

BOLD CAPITAL LETTERS are used for main subject entries (e.g. **DEVELOPMENT**) and chapter topics (e.g. **DISARMAMENT**), as well as country names (e.g. **AFGHANISTAN**), region names (e.g. **AFRICA**) and principal UN organs (e.g. **GENERAL ASSEMBLY**).

CAPITAL LETTERS are used to highlight major issues (e.g. POVERTY), as well as the names of territories (e.g. MONTSERRAT), subregions (e.g. CENTRAL AMERICA), specialized agencies (e.g. WORLD HEALTH ORGANIZATION) and regional commissions (e.g. ECONOMIC COMMISSION FOR AFRICA).

Regular text is used for single and cross-reference entries (e.g. disabled persons, transport).

An asterisk (*) preceding a page number or range of page numbers indicates the presence of a text, reproduced in full, of a General Assembly, Security Council or Economic and Social Council resolution or decision, or a Security Council presidential statement.

United Nations bodies are listed alphabetically and may also appear under related entries.

A

Abkhazia *see* Georgia
administration, UN *see* institutional, administrative and budgetary questions
AFGHANISTAN
  humanitarian assistance 887–888
  human rights 763
  political and security questions *310–351
    Al-Qaida Sanctions Committee *350–351
    children and armed conflict 335–336
    International Security Assistance Force (ISAF) *331–335
    sanctions *336–351
    situation in Afghanistan *320–329
    terrorist attacks 329
    United Nations Assistance Mission in Afghanistan (UNAMA) 331
AFRICA *see also* Economic Commission for Africa (ECA); humanitarian assistance; human rights; *specific regions and countries by name*
  admission of South Sudan to UN membership 201
  African Union, cooperation with 92–93
  African Union Mission in Somalia (AMISOM) 89, 93, 233–236, 238–239, 243, 250, 255–256, *260–261, 265, 759
  African Union-United Nations Hybrid Operation in Darfur (UNAMID) *230–232
  arms embargo, Democratic Republic of the Congo *110–114
  assessment missions, West Africa 135–136, 138–139
  Cameroon-Nigeria Mixed Commission 186–188
  children and armed conflict
    Central African Republic 127–128
    Central African Republic and Chad 130–131
    Darfur 229
    Democratic Republic of the Congo 114
    Somalia 254
    Sudan and South Sudan 209–210
  conflict prevention and resolution 90–91
  cooperation with African Union 92–93
  crime prevention and criminal justice, United Nations African Institute for the Prevention of Crime and Treatment of Offenders 1196–1198
  disarmament
    Standing Committee on Security Questions in Central Africa *543–545
    United Nations Regional Centre for Peace and Disarmament in Africa *546–547
  economic recovery and development *891–899
    African countries emerging from conflict *898–899
    Commission for Social Development 896
    New Partnership for Africa's Development (NEPAD) *891–898, 939
    Republic of South Sudan *899
  elections
    Côte d'Ivoire *140–145, 154
    Liberia 167
  Group of Experts
    Côte d'Ivoire, sanctions *156–160
    Democratic Republic of the Congo, arms embargo *110–114
  Horn of Africa *189–266
    Darfur *217–230
    Eritrea *261–265
    Eritrea-Ethiopia *265–266
    political and security questions *189–266
    Somalia *233–261
    Sudan and South Sudan *189–232
  humanitarian assistance *881–887
    Central Africa and Great Lakes region 881–883
    Horn of Africa *884–887
    North Africa 887
    West Africa 883–884
  human rights *641–642, 649, 754–761
    Burundi 754
    Côte d'Ivoire 754–757

Democratic Republic of the Congo 757
Guinea 757–758
Human Rights Council special session and follow-up, Libya 758–759
Libya 758–759
Somalia 759–760
South Sudan 761
Sudan 760–761
Tunisia 761
ICC Prosecutor activities
   Darfur 226–227
   Libyan Arab Jamahiriya 287–288
international drug control 1186
International Year for People of African Descent 649
Kampala Accord, Somalia *237–243
legislative elections
   Côte d'Ivoire 154
   Liberia 167
Lord's Resistance Army (LRA) *99–102
North Africa *266–296
   Libyan Arab Jamahiriya *266–287
   political and security questions *266–296
   Western Sahara *289–296
nuclear-weapon-free zones *517
Office of the Special Adviser on Africa 97
Panel of Experts, Liberia, sanctions *168–171
peace, promotion of 90–97
Peacebuilding Commission
   Burundi 120
   Central African Republic 126–127
   Guinea 188–189
   Guinea-Bissau 185–186
   Liberia 171
   Sierra Leone 178–179
peacekeeping capacities 93
piracy
   Gulf of Guinea *136–139
   Somalia *243–254
political and security questions *87–296
   Burundi *117–120
   Cameroon–Nigeria 186–188
   Central Africa and Great Lakes region *97–133
   Central African Republic *121–128
   Central African Republic and Chad *128–132
   Côte d'Ivoire *140–162
   Darfur *217–230
   Democratic Republic of the Congo *102–117
   Egypt 296
   Eritrea *261–265
   Eritrea–Ethiopia *265–266
   Guinea 188–189
   Guinea-Bissau *180–186
   Horn of Africa *189–266
   Liberia *162–174
   Libyan Arab Jamahiriya *266–287
   Mauritius–United Kingdom 296
   North Africa *266–296
   Rwanda *132–133
   Sierra Leone *174–180
   Somalia *233–261
   Sudan and South Sudan *189–232
   Tunisia 296
   Uganda 132
   West Africa *133–189
   Western Sahara *289–296
promotion of peace in *90–97
refugees and displaced persons *1121–1124
regional economic and social activities *938–944
sanctions
   Côte d'Ivoire *155–160
   Darfur *227–229
   Eritrea *262–265
   Liberia *167–171
   Libyan Arab Jamahiriya 288–289
   Somalia *254–259
Security Council mission to Africa 91–92
Special Court for Sierra Leone *179–180
Standing Advisory Committee on Security Questions, UNOCA 99
Subregional Centre for Human Rights and Democracy in Central Africa *641–642
United Nations Integrated Peacebuilding Office in the Central African Republic (BINUCA) 128
United Nations Integrated Peacebuilding Office in Guinea-Bissau (UNIOGBIS) 186
United Nations Integrated Peacebuilding Office in Sierra Leone (UNIPSIL) 179
United Nations Interim Security Force for Abyei (UNISFA) *215–232
United Nations Mission for the Referendum in Western Sahara (MINURSO) *293–296
United Nations Mission in Ethiopia and Eritrea (UNMEE) *265–266
United Nations Mission in Liberia (UNMIL) 166–167, *172–174
United Nations Mission in South Sudan (UNMISS) *213–215
United Nations Mission in the Central African Republic and Chad (MINURCAT) *131–132
United Nations Mission in the Sudan (UNMIS) *210–213
United Nations Office for West Africa 139–140
United Nations Office in Burundi (BNUB) 120
United Nations Office to the African Union 92–93
United Nations Operation in Côte d'Ivoire (UNOCI) *160–162
United Nations Organization Stabilization Mission in the Democratic Republic of the Congo (MONUSCO) *114–117
United Nations Political Office for Somalia (UNPOS) 259–260
United Nations Regional Office for Central Africa (UNOCA) 97–99
United Nations Support Mission in Libya (UNSMIL) 289
West Africa *133–189
   assessment missions
      on piracy in Gulf of Guinea 138–139
      to Sahel region 135–136
   Cameroon–Nigeria 186–188
   Côte d'Ivoire *140–162
   Guinea 188–189
   Guinea-Bissau *180–186
   Liberia *162–174
   piracy and armed robbery *136–139

Subject index

political and security questions *133–189
  regional issues *133–140
  Sierra Leone *174–180
  United Nations Office for West Africa (UNOWA) 139–140
African Union Mission in Somalia (AMISOM) 89, 93, 233–236, 238–239, 243, 250, 255–256, *260–261, 265, 759
African Union Pledging Conference 885
African Union-United Nations Hybrid Operation in Darfur (UNAMID) 64, *230–232
AGEING PERSONS *1024–1029
  Madrid Plan of Action *1027–1029
  open-ended Working Group on Ageing 1027
AGRICULTURE see food; humanitarian assistance; nutrition
AIDS see HIV/AIDS
AMERICAN SAMOA
  decolonization, under review for 567
AMERICAS see also Caribbean; Central America; Economic Commission for Latin America and the Caribbean (ECLAC); specific regions and countries by name
  human rights 761–763
    Bolivia 761–762
    Colombia 762
    Guatemala 762
    Haiti 762–763
  international drug control 1186–1187
    Central America and the Caribbean 1186
    North America 1186
    South America 1186–1187
  political and security questions *297–309
    Central America 297–298
    Cuba–United States, embargo *308–309
    Guatemala 297–298
    Haiti 297
    Honduras 298
    Nicaragua–Costa Rica 298
  refugees and displaced persons 1127–1128
AMISOM see African Union Mission in Somalia (AMISOM)
ANGUILLA
  decolonization, under review for 567–568
ARMENIA
  political and security questions, with Azerbaijan 392
  arms and weapons see disarmament
ASIA AND THE PACIFIC see also Economic and Social Commission for Asia and the Pacific (ESCAP); landlocked developing countries; specific country names
  disarmament, United Nations Regional Centre for Peace and Disarmament in Asia and the Pacific *547–548
  humanitarian assistance 887–890
    Afghanistan 887–888
    Flood Rapid Response Plan 889
    Iraq 888
    Occupied Palestinian Territory 888
    Pakistan 888–889
    Philippines 889
    Sri Lanka 889
    Yemen 890
  human rights *763–778
    Afghanistan 763
    Cambodia 763–764
    Democratic People's Republic of Korea *764–768
    Iran *768–771
    Kyrgyzstan 771–772
    Myanmar *772–776
    Nepal 776–777
    Yemen 777–778
  International Conference of Asian Political Parties 1373
  international drug control 1187–1188
    East and South-East Asia 1187
    South Asia 1187
    West Asia 1187
  nuclear-weapon-free zones *518–519
    Central Asia 518
    South-East Asia *518–519
    Treaty on South-East Asia Nuclear-Weapon-Free Zone (Bangkok Treaty) *518–519
  political and security questions *310–376
    Afghanistan *310–351
    Democratic People's Republic of Korea *368–369
    The Greater Tunb, Lesser Tunb and Abu Musa 376
    India–Pakistan 375
    Iran *369–372
    Iraq *351–359
    Iraq–Kuwait 360–362
    Nepal *372
    Pakistan 375
    Sri Lanka 375
    Thailand–Cambodia 375–376
    Timor–Leste *362–368
    United Arab Emirates–Iran 376
  refugees and displaced persons 1128–1129
  regional economic and social activities *944–950
  atomic radiation, effects of *580–589
AZERBAIJAN
  political and security questions, with Armenia 392

B

bacteriological (biological) weapons, disarmament *520–522
BELARUS
  human rights 778
BELIZE
  humanitarian assistance *890–891
BERMUDA
  decolonization, under review for 568
BINUB see United Nations Integrated Office in Burundi (BINUB)
BINUCA see United Nations Integrated Peacebuilding Office in the Central African Republic (BINUCA)
BNUB see United Nations Office in Burundi (BNUB)
BOLIVIA
  human rights 761–762
BOSNIA AND HERZEGOVINA
  political and security questions *377–384
    civilian aspects, implementation of Peace Agreement *378–384
    displaced persons, return of 380
    economic reform 380
    European Union Force (EUFOR) 383
    European Union Police Mission (EUPM) 383–384
    judicial reform 380
    media development 380

military and police aspects 383–384
Office of High Representative *378–384
public administration reform 380
refugees, return of 380
return of refugees and displaced persons 380
BRITISH VIRGIN ISLANDS
decolonization, under review for 568–569
budget, UN see institutional, administrative and budgetary questions
BURUNDI
human rights 754
Peacebuilding Commission 120
political and security developments *117–120
United Nations Office in Burundi (BNUB) 120

C

CAMBODIA
human rights 763–764
CAMEROON–NIGERIA
Cameroon-Nigeria Mixed Commission 186–188
political and security questions 186–188
CARIBBEAN see also Caribbean Community; Economic Commission for Latin America and the Caribbean (ECLAC); Latin America and the Caribbean; specific country names
humanitarian assistance, Haiti 890
Caribbean Community (CARICOM) 300–301
CARICOM see Caribbean Community (CARICOM)
CARTOGRAPHY *967–969
CAYMAN ISLANDS
decolonization, under review for 569
CDP see Committee for Development Policy
CEDAW see Committee on the Elimination of Discrimination against Women (CEDAW)
CENTRAL AFRICA AND GREAT LAKES REGION *97–133
see also specific country names
Burundi *117–120
Central Africa and Great Lakes region *97–102
Central African Republic *121–128
Central African Republic and Chad *128–132
Democratic Republic of the Congo *102–117
humanitarian assistance 881–883
Central African Republic 881
Chad 881–882
Democratic Republic of Congo 882
Namibia 882
South Sudan 882–883
Sudan 883
Uganda 883
Zimbabwe 883
Lord's Resistance Army (LRA) *99–102
political and security questions *97–133
Burundi *117–120
Central Africa and Great Lakes region *97–102
Central African Republic *121–128
Central African Republic and Chad *128–132
Democratic Republic of the Congo *102–117
Lord's Resistance Army (LRA) *99–102
Rwanda *132–133
Standing Advisory Committee on Security Questions 99
Uganda 132

United Nations Regional Office for Central Africa (UNOCA) 97–99
Rwanda *132–133
Uganda 132
United Nations Regional Office for Central Africa (UNOCA) 97–99
CENTRAL AFRICAN REPUBLIC see also Central African Republic and Chad
children and armed conflict 127–128
Peacebuilding Commission 126–127
political and security questions *121–128
United Nations Integrated Peacebuilding Office in the Central African Republic (BINUCA) 128
CENTRAL AFRICAN REPUBLIC AND CHAD *128–132
children and armed conflict 130–131
political and security questions *128–132
United Nations Mission in the Central African Republic and Chad (MINURCAT) *131–132
CENTRAL AMERICA see also Economic Commission for Latin America and the Caribbean (ECLAC); specific country names
humanitarian assistance *890–891
Belize *890–891
Costa Rica *890–891
Declaration of Comalapa *890–891
Economic Commission for Latin America and the Caribbean (ECLAC) *890–891
El Salvador *890–891
Guatemala *890–891
Honduras *890–891
Nicaragua *890–891
Panama *890–891
Tropical Depression E-12 *890–891
political and security questions 297–298
Guatemala 297–298
Honduras 298
Nicaragua–Costa Rica 298
CENTRAL AMERICA AND THE CARIBBEAN
international drug control 1186
CENTRAL ASIA
nuclear-weapon-free zones 518
CHAD see Central African Republic and Chad; Chad–Sudan
CHAD–SUDAN
children and armed conflict 233
political and security questions 232–233
chemical weapons *522–524
Organization for Prohibition of Chemical Weapons (OPCW) 524
Chernobyl disaster
special economic assistance 900
CHILDREN see also United Nations Children's Fund (UNICEF); youth; specific country names
abuse, protection from 1107
basic education and gender equality 1107
economic and social questions *1101–1111
Follow-up to 2002 General Assembly special session on children 1101–1102
HIV/AIDS 1107
humanitarian action 1107–1108
human rights *740–745
children and armed conflict *741–745

Subject index

rights of children working and/or living on the street 741
sale of children, child prostitution and child pornography 740–741
violence against children 740
United Nations Children's Fund (UNICEF) 1101, 1103–1111
violence, protection from 1107
young child survival and development 1106
CIVIL AND POLITICAL RIGHTS see human rights
COLOMBIA
human rights 762
colonies and colonialism see decolonization
Commission on Crime Prevention and Criminal Justice (CCPCJ) 1170, 1188–1189
Commission on Narcotic Drugs (CND) 1170, 1174–1176
Commission on Science and Technology for Development *810–814
Commission for Social Development 896, 1020–1021
Commission on Sustainable Development (CSD) 797–798
Committee for Development Policy (CDP) 826
Committee for Programme and Coordination (CPC) 1361–1362
Committee on the Elimination of Discrimination against Women (CEDAW) *1090–1091
Comprehensive Nuclear-Test-Ban Treaty (CTBT) 493–498
conference see specific conferences by main part of title
conventional weapons see disarmament
conventions see main part of the title
coral reefs *989–991
COSTA RICA
humanitarian assistance *890–891
CÔTE D'IVOIRE
elections *140–145, 154
Group of Experts on Côte d'Ivoire, sanctions *156–160
humanitarian assistance 884
human rights 754–757
legislative elections 154
political and security questions *140–162
post-electoral situation *140–145
sanctions *155–160
United Nations Operation in Côte d'Ivoire (UNOCI) *160–162
Counter-Terrorism Centre *54–55
Counter-Terrorism Committee 53–54
covenants see human rights
CRIME PREVENTION AND CRIMINAL JUSTICE see drug abuse and control; terrorism
criminal justice see international crime prevention and criminal justice
CTBT see Comprehensive Nuclear-Test-Ban Treaty (CTBT)
CUBA–UNITED STATES *308–309
cultural development *1042–1051
Alliance of Civilizations 1046–1047
International Day of Friendship *1047
interreligious and intercultural understanding *1044–1046
Olympic Truce and ideal *1047–1049
peace, culture of *1042–1047
sport for peace and development *1047–1049
cultural issues see social policy and cultural issues

CYPRUS
human rights 778–779
political and security questions *392–400
good offices mission 393–394
United Nations Peacekeeping Force in Cyprus (UNFICYP) *394–400

D

DARFUR
African Union-United Nations Hybrid Operation in Darfur (UNAMID) *230–232
children and armed conflict 229
ICC Prosecutor, activities of 226–227
political and security questions *217–230
sanctions *227–229
Declaration of Comalapa *890–891
decolonization *553–577
American Samoa 567
Anguilla 567–568
Bermuda 568
British Virgin Islands 568–569
Caribbean regional seminar 553–554
Cayman Islands 569
Decade for the Eradication of Colonialism 553–554
Declaration on Granting of Independence to Colonial Countries and Peoples *554–556
international organizations, implementation of Declaration *556–560
dissemination of information *574–576
economic and other activities affecting NSGTs *572–574
Falkland Islands (Malvinas) 560–561
Gibraltar 561
Guam 569–570
information
dissemination of *574–576
on territories *575–576
island Territories *564–572
military activities and arrangements in colonial countries 572
Montserrat 570
New Caledonia *561–563
Pitcairn 570
Puerto Rico 560
Saint Helena 571
study and training facilities for inhabitants of NSGTs *576
support to NSGTs *556–558
Territories under review *560–572
Tokelau *563–564
Turks and Caicos Islands 571
United States Virgin Islands 572
visiting missions 576–577
Western Sahara 564
DEMOCRATIC PEOPLE'S REPUBLIC OF KOREA
human rights *764–768
political and security questions *368–369
2010 naval ship sinking 369
non-proliferation *368–369
DEMOCRATIC REPUBLIC OF THE CONGO
arms embargo *110–114

children and armed conflict 114
Group of Experts, arms embargo *110–114
human rights 757
political and security questions *102–117
United Nations Organization Stabilization Mission in the Democratic Republic of the Congo (MONUSCO) *114–117

DEVELOPING COUNTRIES *see* landlocked developing countries; small island developing States

DEVELOPMENT *see also* economic and social questions; social policy and cultural issues; international finance; United Nations Conference on Trade and Development (UNCTAD); United Nations Development Programme (UNDP); *specific country names*
and disarmament *483–485
Commission on Science and Technology for Development *810–814
Commission for Social Development 896, 1020–1021
Commission on Sustainable Development (CSD) 797–798
Committee for Development Policy (CDP) 826
Development Account 853
international finance and *914–932
operational activities for *838–860
policy and international economic cooperation *789–837
policy and public administration *821–825
population and development 956
science and technology for *810–821
sustainable *797–805
United Nations Conference on Sustainable Development, preparatory process for *799–802, 972

diamonds, conflict 42–43
disabled persons *see* persons with disabilities

DISARMAMENT *478–550 *see also* non-proliferation; nuclear disarmament; terrorism
Advisory Board on Disarmament Matters 485
Africa *543–547
anti-personnel mines *532–533
arms race in outer space, prevention of *538–539
Asia and the Pacific, United Nations Regional Centre for Peace and Disarmament in *547–548
bacteriological (biological) weapons 520, *521–522
chemical weapons 520, *522–524
cluster munitions 532
Comprehensive Programme of Disarmament 482
Conference on Disarmament *480–482
  follow-up to high-level meeting *481–482
conventional weapons *524–538
  anti-personnel mines *532–533
  arms trade treaty 524
  assistance to States for curbing illicit small arms traffic *527–528
  cluster munitions 532
  excessively injurious conventional weapons *529–532
  illicit trade in small arms, United Nations Programme of Action on *525–529
  light weapons *524–529
  military expenditures, transparency of *535–537
  Mine Ban Convention *532–533
  national legislation *535
  practical disarmament 533
  problems arising from accumulation of surplus ammunition stockpiles *528–529
  small arms *524–529
  stockpile management, small arms *528–529
  transparency *533–538
  United Nations Programme of Action on illicit trade in small arms *525–529
  United Nations Register of Conventional Arms, transparency *534–535
  verification 538
Convention on excessively injurious conventional weapons and Protocols *529–532
  Annual Conference of States Parties *530–532
  Fourth Review Conference of High Contracting Parties to CCW 529–530
  Group of Governmental Experts 529
  Protocol II on Mines, Booby-traps and other Devices *530–532
  Protocol V on explosive remnants of war 530
Convention on Prohibition of Development, Production, Stockpiling and Use of Chemical Weapons and on Their Destruction *522–524
Convention on Prohibition of Development, Production and Stockpiling of Bacteriological (Biological) and Toxin Weapons and on Their Destruction *521–522
disarmament and development *483–485
disarmament information programme 541
environmental norms, observance of *539–540
excessively injurious conventional weapons *529–532
fellowships, training and advisory services 541
Latin America and the Caribbean, United Nations Regional Centre for Peace, Disarmament and Development in *548–550
light weapons *524–529
Mine Ban Convention *532–533
multilateral disarmament agreements 482–483
nuclear *see* nuclear disarmament; nuclear-weapon-free zones
Organization for Prohibition of Chemical Weapons (OPCW) 524
practical disarmament 533
Preparatory Committee, Convention on Prohibition of Development, Production and Stockpiling of Bacteriological (Biological) and Toxin Weapons and on Their Destruction *521–522
regional disarmament *541–550
  Africa *543–547
  Asia and the Pacific, United Nations Regional Centre for Peace and Disarmament in *547–548
  confidence-building measures in regional and subregional context *543
  Latin America and the Caribbean, United Nations Regional Centre for Peace, Disarmament and Development in *548–550
  Standing Committee on Security Questions in Central Africa *543–545
Register of Conventional Arms, transparency *534–535
relationship between disarmament and development *484–485
safeguards, IAEA * 513–516

Subject index   1519

science and technology and 540
small arms *524–529
Standing Committee on Security Questions in Central Africa *543–545
stockpile management, small arms *528–529
studies, research and training 540–541
transparency *533–538
United Nations, role in disarmament *483–485
United Nations Disarmament Commission *479–480
United Nations Disarmament Information Programme 541
United Nations Institute for Disarmament Research (UNIDIR) 540
United Nations Office for Disarmament Affairs (UNODA) *479
United Nations Programme of Action on illicit trade in small arms *525–529
United Nations Register of Conventional Arms, transparency *534–535
verification 538

DISASTERS AND DISASTER RESPONSE
drought in Horn of Africa region *885–886
Fukushima Daiichi incident 479, 516, 551, 587, 963, 964
humanitarian assistance *869–879, *887–891
Hyogo Framework for Action 877
International Strategy for Disaster Reduction *876–878, 948
natural disasters and refugees 920
Pakistan, floods 888–889
Philippines, Tropical Storm Washi 889
protection of persons 1279
Tropical Depression E-12 *890–891
discrimination see human rights
displaced persons see refugees and displaced persons

DJIBOUTI
humanitarian assistance 886
DPRK see Democratic People's Republic of Korea
DRC see Democratic Republic of the Congo

DRUG ABUSE AND CONTROL
Africa 1186
Americas 1186–1187
   Central America and the Caribbean 1186
   North America 1186
   South America 1186–1187
Asia 1187–1188
   East and South-East Asia 1187
   South Asia 1187
   West Asia 1187
Commission on Crime Prevention and Criminal Justice (CCPCJ) 1170
Commission on Narcotic Drugs (CND) 1170, 1174–1176
conventions 1183–1188
cooperation against world drug problem *1176–1183
demand reduction and drug abuse 1175–1176
driving, drug-affected 1175
economic and social questions *1174–1188
Europe 1188
HIV, zero new infections of 1176
international cooperation *1176–1183
International Narcotics Control Board (INCB) 1170, 1185–1188
Oceania 1188
Paris Pact initiative 1175
regional cooperation 1183
United Nations Office on Drugs and Crime (UNODC) *1170–1174
world drug situation 1186–1188

E

East and South-East Asia
   international drug control 1187
EAST TIMOR see Timor-Leste
ECA see Economic Commission for Africa (ECA)
ECE see Economic Commission for Europe (ECE)
ECLAC see Economic Commission for Latin America and the Caribbean (ECLAC)
ECONOMIC COMMISSION FOR AFRICA (ECA) *938–944
   African Institute for Economic Development and Planning (IDEP) 942
   African Union Conference of Ministers of Economy and Finance 938
   climate change 939–940
   Conference of African Ministers of Finance, Planning and Economic Development 938
   construction of office facilities 944
   development planning and administration *942–943
   economic trends 938
   Europe-Africa fixed link through Strait of Gibraltar *941–942
   food security and sustainable development 939–940
   gender and women in development 942
   governance and public administration 940
   information and science and technology for development 940
   infrastructure and trade, regional integration *940–942
   macroeconomic analysis, finance and economic development 939
   New Partnership for Africa's Development (NEPAD) 939
   programme and organizational questions 944
   programme of work 2012–2013 944
   social development 943–944
   statistics 943
   subregional development activities 942
ECONOMIC COMMISSION FOR EUROPE (ECE) 951–954
   activities 951–954
   economic cooperation and integration 953
   economic trends 951
   energy 952–953
   environment 953
   housing and land management 953
   reform 954
   statistics 953–954
   timber 952
   trade 951
   transport 952
ECONOMIC COMMISSION FOR LATIN AMERICA AND THE CARIBBEAN (ECLAC) *890–891, 954–958
   activities 954–958
   economic trends 954
   environment and human settlements 956–957
   global economy, regional integration and cooperation 954–955

macroeconomic policies and growth 955
mainstreaming gender in regional development 955
natural resources and infrastructure 957
population and development 956
production and innovation 955
public administration 956
social development and equality 955
statistics and economic projections 957
subregional activites 957–958
economic, social and cultural rights see human rights
ECONOMIC AND SOCIAL COMMISSION FOR ASIA AND THE PACIFIC (ESCAP) *944–950
activities *945–950
disaster risk reduction 948
energy security and sustainable use of energy 946–947
environment and development 946–947
information and communications technology 947
least developed and landlocked developing countries 945
macroeconomic policy, poverty reduction and development 945
policy issues, economic trends 945
programme and organizational questions 950
social development 948
statistics *948–950
technical cooperation 950
trade and investment 945–946
transport 946
trends, economic 944–945
United Nations Asian and Pacific Centre for Agricultural Engineering and Machinery (UNAPCAEM) 945
ECONOMIC AND SOCIAL COMMISSION FOR WESTERN ASIA (ESCWA) 958–962
activities 958–962
Beijing Platform for Action in the Arab countries after fifteen years: Beijing+15 *960–961
conflict mitigation and development *961–962
economic development and integration 959
economic trends 958
ICT for regional integration 959
social development 959
statistics 959–960
sustainable development, natural resources management for 958–959
women, advancement of 960–961
ECONOMIC AND SOCIAL COUNCIL *1359–1360
see also economic and social questions
ECONOMIC AND SOCIAL QUESTIONS *789–1224
see also specific regional commissions and economic and social topics
African economic recovery and development *891–899
agriculture development and food security *1162–1169
cartography *967–969
Chernobyl, special economic assistance 900
children *1101–1111
Committee for Development Policy (CDP) *821–823
country and regional programmes, UNDP 844–845
crime prevention and criminal justice 1188–1214
crisis prevention and recovery, UNDP 846–847
cultural development *1042–1051
Alliance of Civilizations 1046–1047

International Day of Friendship *1047
interreligious and intercultural understanding *1044–1046
Olympic Truce and ideal *1047–1049
peace, culture of *1042–1047
sport for peace and development *1047–1049
democratic governance, UNDP 846
Department of Economic and Social Affairs (DESA) 853–854
developing countries, economic and technical cooperation among *859–860
development
operational activities for *838–860
technical cooperation through UNDP 843–853
Development Account 853
development policy and international economic cooperation *789–837
development policy and public administration *821–825
drug control *1174–1188
Economic and Social Council, operational activities segment 838–839
energy 847, *963–966
environment *970–994
food and agriculture *1160–1169
geographical names, standardization of 968–969
global geospatial information management *967–968
groups of countries in special situations *825–837
landlocked developing countries *834–837
least developed countries (LDCs) *826–832
small island developing States *832–834
Haiti, special economic assistance 899–900
health 1134–1160
Human Development Report 844
human resources development *1051–1056
education 1056
United Nations Institute for Training and Research (UNITAR) *1053–1056
United Nations System Staff College *1055–1056
United Nations University (UNU) 1055
human settlements *994–1001
international crime prevention and criminal justice 1188–1214
international drug control *1174–1188
international economic relations *789–821
Agenda 21 798–799
agricultural technology for development 802–804
Central America, sustainable tourism and sustainable development *805
Commission on Science and Technology for Development *810–814
Commission on Sustainable Development (CSD) 797–798
Decade for the Eradication of Poverty *806–809
empowerment and development *797
empowerment of the poor, legal 809
globalization and interdependence *792–793
global partnerships *794–796
happiness and well-being 796
high-level segment of Economic and Social Council 791
human security 797

Subject index 1521

Johannesburg Plan of Implementation 798–799
middle-income countries, development cooperation with *793
Millennium Development Goals (MDGs) 809
partnerships, development through *793–796
poverty, eradication of *805–809
Programme for the Further Implementation of Agenda 21 798–799
science and technology for development *810–821
Second United Nations Decade for the Eradication of Poverty *805–809
sustainable development *797–805
sustainable tourism *804–805
International Year of Family Farming *1168–1169
Kazakhstan, special economic assistance *900–901
landlocked developing countries *834–837
least developed countries (LDCs) *826–832
  Fourth United Nations Conference on Least Developed Countries *827–832
  Istanbul Declaration 828
  list *826–827
  Programme of Action for the Least Developed Countries 828–829
  Review of the Programme of Action (2001–2010) 827
  smooth transition strategy for countries graduating from list of least developed countries *826–827
Myanmar, assistance to, UNDP 845
natural resources 966–967
New Partnership for Africa's Development (NEPAD) *891–898
nutrition 1169
operational activities for development *838–860
population 1002–1012
poverty reduction and MDG achievement, UNDP 846
public administration *823–825
refugees and displaced persons *1112–1133
resident coordinator system 841
Rio Conventions 977
science and technology for development *810–821
small island developing States *832–834
social policy *1013–1042
  ageing persons *1024–1029
  Commission for Social Development 1020–1021
  cooperatives in social development *1023–1024
  family *1039–1042
  International Year of the Family *1039–1042
  International Year of Youth 1035
  persons with disabilities *1029–1032
  recovery from economic and financial crisis *1018–1020
  Report on world social situation 1022–1023
  social development *1013–1024
  social inclusion *1021–1022
  social integration *1021–1022
  youth *1032–1039
South-South cooperation *859–860
special economic assistance *891–901
  African economic recovery and development *891–899
  Chernobyl 900
  Haiti 899–900
  Kazakhstan *900–901

standardization of geographical names 968–969
Standing Committee on Nutrition 1169
statistics 1215–1224
system-wide activities *838–843
technical cooperation 843–860
United Nations Capital Development Fund 860
United Nations Democracy Fund 855
United Nations Fund for International Partnerships 855
United Nations Development Programme, technical cooperation through 843–853
United Nations University Food and Nutrition Programme for Human and Social Development (UNU-FNP) 1169
United Nations Office for Partnerships 854–855
United Nations Regional Cartographic Conference for Asia and the Pacific 969
United Nations Volunteers (UNV) *857–859
UN-Water 966–967
water resources 966–967
women *1057–1100
EDUCATION
basic education and gender equality 1107
human resources development 1056
human rights *645–648
  Follow-up to the International Year of Human Rights Learning *647–648
  United Nations Declaration on Human Rights Education and Training *645–647
women, education and training of women 1068–1070
EGYPT
political and security questions 296
EL SALVADOR
humanitarian assistance *890–891
ENERGY *963–966
environment and 847
International Atomic Energy Agency (IAEA) *963–965
new and renewable sources of energy *965–966
nuclear energy *963–965
ENVIRONMENT *970–994 see also United Nations Environment Programme (UNEP)
Africa, convention to combat desertification *981–983
air pollution, convention on 980
the atmosphere 984–985
Basel Convention 983–984
biodiversity 974, *981
biological diversity, convention on *980–981
chemical munitions dumped at sea, waste from 991
Conference of Parties to UNFCCC 977
convention on air pollution 980
convention on biological diversity *980–981
convention on climate change *977–979
convention to combat desertification *981–983
coral reefs *989–991
Environment Management Group (EMG) 973
forests 985–986
Global Environment Facility (GEF) 976–977
Global Programme of Action for the Protection of the Marine Environment from Land-based Activities 974
green economy 971
harmony with nature *993–994

Intergovernmental Panel on Climate Change (IPCC), 984–985
International conventions and mechanisms *977–991
International Year of Forests 986
Joint Liaison Group of the Rio Conventions 977
Kyoto Protocol to the Convention 977
marine ecosystems 974, *989–991
Montreal Protocol on Substances that Deplete the Ozone Layer 979–980
mountains *986–989
oil slick on Lebanese shores *991–993
Preparatory Committee for the United Nations Conference on Sustainable Development 972
Rotterdam Convention 984
Stockholm Convention 984
sustainable mountain development *986–989
terrestrial ecosystems *985–989
United Nations Decade on Biodiversity *981
United Nations Conference on Sustainable Development 971–972
United Nations Environment Programme (UNEP) *970–976
United Nations Forum on Forests (UNFF) 985–986
United Nations Framework Convention on Climate Change (UNFCCC), 977
Vienna Convention for the Protection of the Ozone Layer 979–980
ERITREA
political and security questions *261–265
sanctions *262–265
ERITREA–ETHIOPIA *265–266
political and security questions *265–266
United Nations Mission in Ethiopia and Eritrea (UNMEE) *265–266
ESCAP see Economic and Social Commission for Asia and the Pacific (ESCAP)
ESCWA see Economic and Social Commission for Western Asia (ESCWA)
EUROPE AND THE MEDITERRANEAN see also Economic Commission for Europe; specific regions and countries by name
human rights 778–779
    Belarus 778
    Cyprus 778–779
international drug control 1188
political and security questions *377–401
    Armenia and Azerbaijan 392
    Bosnia and Herzegovina *377–384
    Cyprus *392–400
    European Union Force (EUFOR) 383
    European Union Police Mission (EUPM) 383–384
    European Union Rule of Law Mission in Kosovo (EULEX) 386–387
    The former Yugoslav Republic of Macedonia (FYROM) 389
    Georgia *389–392
    Kosovo *384–389
    Kosovo Force (KFOR) 389
    Mediterranean region, strengthening of security and cooperation in *400–401
    Organization for Democracy and Economic Development 401
    United Nations Interim Administration Mission (UNMIK) *387–389
    United Nations Observer Mission in Georgia (UNOMIG) *391–392
    United Nations Peacekeeping Force in Cyprus (UNFICYP) *394–400
refugees and displaced persons 1130–1131
European Union, participation in UN work *1369–1370

F

FALKLAND ISLANDS (MALVINAS), decolonization 560–561
FAO, see Food and Agriculture Organization of the United Nations (FAO)
female genital mutilation 1007
financial and administrative matters see international finance; international trade; legal questions
fissile material *490–491
Flood Rapid Response Plan, humanitarian assistance 889
FOOD see also nutrition; Food and Agriculture Organization of the United Nations (FAO); World Food Programme (WFP)
aid *1160–1162
food and commodity markets, price volatility in *1167–1168
food security *1162–1169
International Year of Quinoa *1168
FOOD AND AGRICULTURE ORGANIZATION OF THE UNITED NATIONS 1162
food security *1162–1169
bottom fisheries 1309
THE FORMER YUGOSLAV REPUBLIC OF MACEDONIA (FYROM) 389
THE FORMER YUGOSLAVIA see International Tribunal for the Former Yugoslavia
Fukushima Daiichi incident 479, 516, 551, 587, 963, 964

G

gender issues see women
GENERAL ASSEMBLY *1354–1358
genocide, convention on, *636–638
GEORGIA
IDPs and refugees *390–392
appointment of Special Representative 391
political and security questions *389–392
United Nations Observer Mission in Georgia (UNOMIG) *391–392
GIBRALTAR decolonization 561
global counter-terrorism strategy *54–55
GREAT LAKES REGION see Central Africa and Great Lakes region
GUAM decolonization 569–570
GUATEMALA
humanitarian assistance *890–891
human rights 762
International Commission against Impunity in Guatemala (CICIG) 297–298
political and security questions 297–298
GUINEA 188–189
human rights 757–758
Peacebuilding Commission 188–189
political and security questions 188–189
GUINEA-BISSAU *180–186
Peacebuilding Commission 185–186

political and security questions *180–186
United Nations Integrated Peacebuilding Office in Guinea-Bissau (UNIOGBIS) 186

H

HAITI
 ad hoc advisory group 301
 cholera outbreak 301
 humanitarian assistance 890
 human rights 762–763
 political and security questions *297–308
 special economic assistance 899–900
 United Nations Stabilization Mission in Haiti (MINUSTAH) *305–308
HEALTH 1134–1145 *see also* HIV/AIDS
 AIDS prevention and control 1134–1145
 fertility, reproductive health and development 1003–1004
 global public health 1157–1159
 health statistics 1216
 HIV/AIDS 1134–1145
 Joint United Nations Programme on HIV/AIDS (UNAIDS) 1143–1145
 malaria 1153–1157
 non-communicable diseases 1145–1152
 older persons, health of 729
 reproductive health and rights 1006–1007
 road safety 1159–1160
 Roll Back Malaria initiative 1153–1157
 tobacco 1152–1153
 women and 1070–1071
 World AIDS Day 1145
Herzegovina *see* Bosnia and Herzegovina
HIV/AIDS
 children 1107
 human rights 728
 Joint United Nations Programme on HIV/AIDS (UNAIDS) 1011, 1143–1145
 refugees and displaced persons 1119–1120
 women 1070
HONDURAS
 humanitarian assistance *890–891
 political and security questions 298
HORN OF AFRICA *see also specific country names*
 Chad–Sudan 232–233
 Darfur *217–230
 Eritrea *261–265
 Eritrea–Ethiopia *265–266
 humanitarian assistance *884–887
 political and security questions *189–266
 Somalia *233–261
 Sudan and South Sudan *189–232
human immunodeficiency virus/acquired immunodeficiency syndrome (HIV/AIDS) *see* HIV/AIDS
HUMANITARIAN ASSISTANCE *861–891 *see also* disasters and disaster response; refugees and displaced persons
 Africa *881–887
 Asia 887–890
 Central Africa and Great Lakes region 881–883
 Central America *890–891
 Central Emergency Response Fund (CERF) *865–869
 consolidated appeals 881–891
 coordination *861–865
 disaster response *869–879
  international cooperation *869–876
  UN-SPIDER programme *873
 Global Platform for Disaster Risk Reduction 877
 Horn of Africa *884–887
 humanitarian affairs segment of Economic and Social Council *861–865
 Hyogo Framework for Action 877
 International Strategy for Disaster Reduction *876–878
 Latin America and the Caribbean *890–891
 military and civil response *878–879
 mine action *879–881
 North Africa 887
 Office for the Coordination of Humanitarian Affairs (OCHA) 418, 423, 861, 865, 869, 973–974
 strengthening of coordination of emergency humanitarian assistance of the United Nations *861–869
 West Africa 883–884
HUMAN RESOURCES DEVELOPMENT *1051–1056
 education 1056
 UN Institute for Training and Research (UNITAR) *1053–1056
 United Nations System Staff College *1055–1056
 United Nations University (UNU) 1055
HUMAN RIGHTS *603–785 *see also* racism and racial discrimination; *specific rights*
 adequate housing, right to 726–727
 advisory services and technical cooperation 640–641
 Africa 754–761
  Burundi 754
  Côte d'Ivoire 754–757
  Democratic Republic of the Congo 757
  Guinea 757–758
  Libya 758–759
  Somalia 759–760
  Sudan 760–761
  South Sudan 761
  Tunisia 761
 Americas 761–763
  Bolivia 761–762
  Colombia 762
  Guatemala 762
  Haiti 762–763
 arbitrary detention 698
 Asia *763–778
  Afghanistan 763
  Cambodia 763–764
  Democratic People's Republic of Korea *764–768
  Iran 768–771
  Kyrgyzstan 771–772
  Myanmar *772–776
  Nepal 776–777
  Yemen 777–778
 capital punishment 691
 children *740–745
  children and armed conflict *741–745
  children working and/or living on the street, rights of 741

sale of children, child prostitution and child pornography 740–741
violence against children 740
civil and political rights *651–704
Committee against Torture 637–638
Committee on Economic, Social and Cultural Rights 621
Committee on the Elimination of Racial Discrimination 619
Committee on the Rights of Persons with Disabilities 633
Committee on the Rights of the Child 638–639
complaint procedure 613–614
conventions see instruments of human rights
country situations *753–785
cultural rights *730–733
defenders, human rights *663–665
democratic and equitable international order *710–712
development, right to *704–720
disabilities, persons with 749
disappearance of persons 691–692
diversity, cultural *731–733
economic, social and cultural rights 704–752
education *645–648
    Follow-up to the International Year of Human Rights Learning *647–648
    United Nations Declaration on Human Rights Education and Training *645–647
education, right to 733–734
environmental and scientific concerns 734–735
Europe and the Mediterranean 778–779
    Belarus 778
    Cyprus 778
extralegal executions 692–693
Follow-up to 1993 World Conference 649
Follow-up to the International Year of Human Rights Learning *647–648
food, right to *721–726
foreign debt 715–716
forensic genetics 735
freedom of religion or belief *674–680
gender equality, see women; children; education; population
gender identity 703–704
genocide prevention 636
genetic privacy 735
globalization *712–715
health, right to 727–730
HIV/AIDS 728
human rights and international solidarity 709
Human Rights Council *603–614
    complaint procedure 613–614
    Council sessions *603–604
    election of members 604
    Human Rights Council Advisory Committee 613
    Libyan Arab Jamahiriya, suspension and restoration of membership rights of *604–606
    report of Human Rights Council *604
    review of work and functioning *606–611
    universal periodic review 611–613
    work of the Council *606–611
human rights treaty body system *636–638

indigenous peoples *749–752
    expert mechanism 750–751
    expert meetings and conferences *752
    Permanent Forum on Indigenous Issues 751
    Voluntary Fund for Indigenous Populations 751
    Voluntary Fund for International Decade 751
instruments of human rights *617–638
    child, convention on the rights of the *622–632
    civil and political rights, covenant on 620
    discrimination
        racial discrimination, convention against 619–620
        women, convention on elimination of discrimination against 621
    economic, social and cultural rights, covenant on *620–621
    effective implementation of international human rights instruments 618–619
    enforced disappearance, convention for protection from *634–635
    genocide, convention on 636
    migrant workers, convention on 633
    persons with disabilities, convention on rights of *633–634
    prevention of genocide 636
    protection from enforced disappearance, convention for *634–635
    torture, convention against 621–622
    treaty body system *636–638
    women, convention on elimination discrimination against 621
internally displaced persons (IDPs) *745–748
international cooperation *638–640
International Year for People of African Descent 649
maternal mortality 728–729
mercenaries *682–685
Middle East *779–785
    Syrian Arab Republic 779
    Territories occupied by Israel 782–785
migrants, protection of *666–671
minorities, discrimination against *671–674
missing persons 692
national institutions for the promotion and protection of human rights *642–644
nature of all human rights and fundamental freedoms *616–617
non-repatriation of funds of illicit origin 719–720
North Africa, migrants fleeing political unrest in *667–671
Office of High Commissioner for Human Rights (OHCHR) 614–616
    composition of staff 615–616
    joint workplan 616
older persons, health of 729
Palestinians, right of self-determination *681–682
peace, right to 703
persons with disabilities 749
poverty, extreme 720–721
prevention, role of 616
promotion of human rights *603–649
protection of human rights *650–752
racism and racial discrimination *651–663

contemporary forms of racism *659–663
follow-up to 2001 World Conference *651–659
General Assembly high-level meeting *652–653
sports and combating discrimination *654–659
regional arrangements *641–642
reprisals for cooperation with human rights bodies 665–666
rule of law, democracy and human rights *685–690
   administration of justice 685
   electoral processes *687–689
   expression, freedom of 689–690
   independence of judges and lawyers 686–687
   peaceful assembly and association, freedom of 691
   right to the truth 685–686
   transitional justice 685
   truth, justice, reparation and non-recurrence 686
self-determination, right to *680–685
sexual orientation and gender identity 703–704
slavery and related issues 735–737
   fund on slavery 735
   permanent memorial *736–737
   transatlantic slave trade 736–737
Social Forum 720
special procedures, protection of human rights 650–651
strengthening action to promote human rights *638–640
Subregional Centre for Human Rights and Democracy in Central Africa *641–642
terrorism *698–703
torture and cruel treatment *693–697
toxic wastes 734–735
traditional values 703
trafficking in women and girls 739–740
transnational corporations 716–717
unilateral coercive measures *717–719
United Nations Declaration on Human Rights Education and Training *645–647
violence against women 737–739
Voluntary Fund 641
Voluntary Fund for torture victims 694
vulnerable groups *737–752
water and sanitation 729–730
women 737–740
World Down Syndrome Day *648–649
Human Rights Council *603–614
HUMAN SETTLEMENTS *994–1001
   African Ministerial Conference on Housing and Urban Development 995
   crime prevention 996
   equitable access 997
   gender equality 994–995
   global housing 997
   Habitat III 996
   natural disaster risk reduction 997
   Occupied Palestinian Territory 995
   pro-poor housing 995
   public spaces 995
   United Nations Human Settlements Programme (UN-Habitat) *994–1001
   urban youth development 995–996
   World Urban Forum 995

I

IAEA *see* International Atomic Energy Agency (IAEA)
IAMB *see* International Advisory and Monitoring Board for Iraq (IAMB)
ICC *see* International Criminal Court (ICC)
ICJ *see* International Court of Justice (ICJ)
ICSC *see* International Civil Service Commission (ICSC)
ICTR *see* International Criminal Tribunal for Rwanda (ICTR)
ICTY *see* International Tribunal for the Former Yugoslavia (ICTY)
IFAD *see* International Fund for Agricultural Development (IFAD)
ILC *see* International Law Commission (ILC)
INCB *see* International Narcotics Control Board (INCB)
INDIA–PAKISTAN 375
Indian Ocean
   Declaration of Indian Ocean as a Zone of Peace *552–553
indigenous peoples
   expert mechanism 750–751
   expert meetings and conferences *752
   human rights *749–752
   Permanent Forum on Indigenous Issues 751
   Voluntary Fund for Indigenous Populations 751
   Voluntary Fund for International Decade 751
INFORMATION
   accessibility 591–592
   Committee on Information 590
   Department of Public Information (DPI) *590–599
   multilingualism 591–592
   oversight activities 590
   UN information centres (UNICs) *592–599
   UN website, multilingualism and accessibility 591–592
   video and photo services 592
INSTITUTIONAL, ADMINISTRATIVE AND BUDGETARY QUESTIONS 1351–1457
   accounts and auditing 1401–1404
      administration of trust funds 1404
      financial management practices 1402–1403
      International Public Sector Accounting Standards 1402–1403
      Independent Audit Advisory Committee 1404
   administrative and staff matters *1406–1457
      appointment of Secretary-General *1427–1428
      conditions of service 1428–1435
      conference management *1411–1419
      disciplinary matters *1441–1443
      education grant 1429
      ethics 1440–1441
      human resources management 1439–1443
      inter-agency staff mobility and work/life balance 1439
      International Civil Service Commission (ICSC) 1430–1434
      international judges, review of pension schemes for 1434
      justice, administration of *1448–1453
      managerial reform and oversight *1406–1411
      mobility and hardship scheme 1428–1429
      multilingualism *1444–1446
      nomination for Secretary-General *1427–1428

Office of Ombudsman and Mediation Services *1450–1453
pensionable remuneration 1430
performance management 1429
review of UN system medical service 1443–1444
safety and security of staff *1435–1439
selection and appointment of senior managers in UN Secretariat 1443
sexual exploitation and abuse, protection from 1446–1447
staff composition 1439–1440
travel-related matters 1448
United Nations Dispute and Appeals Tribunals 1453–1457
UN information systems 1419–1421
United Nations Network on Occupational Safety and Health (UNNOSH) 1444
United Nations Joint Staff Pension Fund 1447–1448
UN premises and property *1421–1427
budget 1375–1399
appropriations 1390–1392
budget for 2010–2011
contingency fund 1397–1398
financing of unforeseen and extraordinary expenses *1396–1397
funding and backstopping arrangements for special political missions 1397
limited budgetary discretion 1382–1390
unforeseen and extraordinary expenses 1398
Working Capital Fund 1398–1399
Central European Initiative, participation in UN work *1371
conference management *1411–1419
contributions 1399–1401
assessments 1399–1401
multi-year payment plans 1400
scale methodology 1400–1401
cooperation with organizations *1362–1370
African Union *1364–1368
Caribbean Community 1368
International Organization of la Francophonie *1362–1364
Inter-Parliamentary Union and national parliaments 1368
Pacific Islands Forum *1368–1369
Shanghai Cooperation Organization 1368
coordination, monitoring and cooperation 1360–1362
Economic and Social Council *1359–1360
financial situation 1375
financing and programming 1375–1405
gender issues, institutional arrangements for 1352
General Assembly *1354–1358
institutional matters *1353–1360
intergovernmental organizations 1373
International Renewable Energy Agency *1371
NGOs, committee on 1373–1374
non-governmental organizations 1373–1374
observer status *1370–1373
other organizations, UN and *1362–1374
participation in UN work 1369–1374
private sector, cooperation with 1369
programme planning 1404–1405

performance, evaluation 1405
performance, programme 1405
restructuring matters 1351–1353
Security Council 1358–1359
South Sudan, new United Nations Member *1353–1354
Intergovernmental Authority on Development (IGAD) 885
Intergovernmental Panel on Climate Change (IPCC) 984–985
Intergovernmental Working Group of Experts on International Standards of Accounting and Reporting (ISAR) 931
internally displaced persons (IDPs) *745–748, 861, 881, 1113, 1119, 1121, 1126
International Advisory and Monitoring Board for Iraq 356–357
INTERNATIONAL ATOMIC ENERGY AGENCY (IAEA)
nuclear energy *963–965
safeguards *513–516
International Civil Service Commission (ICSC)
compensation of members of 1434
INTERNATIONAL COURT OF JUSTICE (ICJ) 1227–1241
advisory proceedings 1240
composition 1240–1241
contentious proceedings 1228–1240
election of judges 1240–1241
functioning and organization 1240–1241
judicial work 1227–1240
Judgments 1227
Trust Fund to Assist States in the Settlement of Disputes 1241
INTERNATIONAL CRIME PREVENTION AND CRIMINAL JUSTICE, see crime prevention
Africa, United Nations African crime prevention institute 1196–1198
child justice reform 1213–1214
children, protection in digital age 1209
civilian private security services 1212
Commission on Crime Prevention and Criminal Justice (CCPCJ) 1188–1189
corruption 1203
Crime Prevention and Criminal Justice Programme network 1196–1198
crime prevention programme 1190–1198
cultural property, trafficking in 1199–1201
cybercrime 1211–1212
data collection 1198
drugs, trafficking of fraudulent medicines 1203
economic fraud and identity-related crime 1208–1209
endangered species, trafficking in 1201–1203
Follow-up to the Twelfth United Nations Crime Congress 1189–1190
fraud and identity-related crime 1208–1209
fraudulent medicines, trafficking of 1203
illicit financial flows 1205–1208
international cooperation 1192
medications, trafficking of fraudulent medicines 1203
organized crime, transnational 1198–1214
piracy 1212–1213
rule of law, strengthening 1214
standards and norms, United Nations 1213
technical cooperation 1192–1196

Subject index

terrorism 1203–1205
trafficking
    in cultural property 1199–1201
    in endangered species 1201–1203
    of fraudulent medicines 1203
    in persons 1199
UN Convention against transnational organized crime 1198–1199
United Nations African crime prevention institute 1196–1198
United Nations Convention against Corruption 1203
United Nations Interregional Crime and Justice Research Institute 1196

INTERNATIONAL CRIMINAL COURT (ICC) 1261–1265
Chambers 1261–1263
international cooperation 1264–1265
ongoing cases 1263
investigations 1263–1264
Office of the Prosecutor 1263–1264
Registry 1264

INTERNATIONAL CRIMINAL TRIBUNAL FOR RWANDA (ICTR) *1249–1258
Chambers *1250–1255
judges of the Court *1252–1255
Office of the Prosecutor 1255
ongoing cases 1250–1252
Registry 1255–1256

INTERNATIONAL ECONOMIC RELATIONS *789–821
Agenda 21 798–799
agricultural technology for development 802–804
empowerment of the poor, legal 809
globalization and interdependence *792–793
global partnerships *794–796
human security 797
middle-income countries, development cooperation with *793
Millennium Development Goals (MDGs) 809
partnerships, development through *793–796
people's empowerment and development *796–797
poverty, eradication of *805–809
science and technology for development *810–821
sustainable development *797–805
sustainable tourism *804–805

INTERNATIONAL FINANCE *914–932 see also development; United Nations Conference on Trade and Development (UNCTAD)
accounting, International Standards of Accounting and Reporting 931
ad hoc panel of experts *929–930
Committee of Experts on International Cooperation in Tax Matters *931–932
competition law and policy 930–931
developing countries, debt situation of *917–921
development and *914–932
external debt sustainability and development *917–921
financing for development *921–930
follow-up to conference on world financial and economic crisis *929–930
group of experts, competition law and policy 930–931
International Standards of Accounting and Reporting 931

recovering from world financial and economic crisis *929
Special high-level meeting of the Economic and Social Council *921–927
tax matters, international cooperation in *931–932
International Fund for Agricultural Development (IFAD) 1240

INTERNATIONAL LAW see treaties and agreements
INTERNATIONAL LAW COMMISSION (ILC) *1266–1282
aliens, expulsion of 1278–1279
armed conflict, effects on treaties *1275–1278
disasters, protection of persons in event of 1279
immunity of state officials 1278
most-favoured-nation clause *1280
obligation to extradite or prosecute 1279
reservations to treaties 1267–1268
responsibility of international organizations *1268–1278
treaties over time *1279–1280
international legal questions see legal questions
International Narcotics Control Board (INCB) 1170, 1185–1188

INTERNATIONAL PEACE AND SECURITY *33–86 see also peacekeeping operations; political and security questions; terrorism
aftermath of conflict, civilian capacity in 44–45
civilians, protection in armed conflict 49–50
conflict prevention 42–43
Declaration of Indian Ocean as a Zone of Peace *552–553
democracies, support for 551–552
development, security and *40–42
diamonds, conflict 42–43
diplomacy, preventive *37–42
disarmament, demobilization and reintegration (DDR) 45–46
dispute mediation and settlement *35–39
Indian Ocean *552–553
maintenance of international peace and security *33–43
mediation and settlement of disputes *35–39
Organizational Committee, Peacebuilding Commission 48
Peacebuilding Commission, rule of law 47–48
Peacebuilding Fund 48
peacemaking and peacebuilding *43–48 see also peacekeeping operations
post-conflict stabilization and peacebuilding *43–44
promotion of international peace and security *33–52
responsibility to protect 49
roster of 2011 political missions and offices 50–52
rule of law 46–47
special political missions 50–52
terrorism *52–56 see also terrorism
threats to *52–56 see also terrorism
international terrorism see terrorism

INTERNATIONAL TRADE *902–914 see also United Nations Conference on Trade and Development (UNCTAD)
coercive economic measures *913–914
commodities *910–913
    cocoa 912–913

Common Fund for Commodities 913
individual commodities 912–913
sugar 913
tropical timber 913
multilateral trading system *902–905
United Nations Conference on Trade and Development (UNCTAD) 905–909
INTERNATIONAL TRANSPORT *932–936
INTERNATIONAL TRIBUNAL FOR THE FORMER YUGOSLAVIA (ICTY) *1242–1249
Chambers *1242–1246
judges of the Court *1244–1246
Office of the Prosecutor 1246–1247
ongoing cases 1243–1244
Registry 1247
INTERNATIONAL TRIBUNALS AND COURTS *1242–1265
see also International Criminal Court (ICC); International Criminal Tribunal for Rwanda (ICTR); International Tribunal for the Former Yugoslavia (ICTY)
functioning of the Tribunals *1258–1261
International Criminal Court (ICC) 1261–1265
International Residual Mechanism 1259
International Tribunal for Rwanda (ICTR) *1249–1258
International Tribunal for the Former Yugoslavia (ICTY) *1242–1249
International Year for People of African Descent 649
International Year of Family Farming *1168–1169
IPCC see Intergovernmental Panel on Climate Change (IPCC)
IRAN
human rights *768–771, *769–771
non-proliferation *369–372
political and security questions *369–372
Sanctions Committee, non-proliferation 371–372
IRAQ
children and armed conflict 358
humanitarian assistance 888
non-proliferation and disarmament obligations 357
political and security questions *351–359
post-development fund mechanism 356–357
United Nations Assistance Mission for Iraq (UNAMI) 356
United Nations Oil-for-Food Programme 358–359
IRAQ–KUWAIT
Kuwaiti property 360–361
missing persons 360–361
political and security questions 360–362
POWs 360–361
UN Compensation Commission and Fund 361–362
ISAR see Intergovernmental Working Group of Experts on International Standards of Accounting and Reporting (ISAR)
Islamic Republic of Iran see Iran
islands see small island developing States
ISLAND TERRITORIES decolonization *564–572
ISRAEL see Middle East; Palestine; Territories occupied by Israel
Occupied Palestinian Territory *403–434

J

Joint United Nations Programme on HIV/AIDS (UNAIDS) 1143–1145

K

KAZAKHSTAN
special economic assistance *900–901
KENYA
humanitarian assistance 886–887
KOSOVO
political and security questions *384–389
European Union Rule of Law Mission in Kosovo (EULEX) 386–387
Kosovo Force (KFOR) 389
United Nations Interim Administration Mission in Kosovo (UNMIK) *387–389
KYRGYZSTAN
human rights 771–772

L

LANDLOCKED DEVELOPING COUNTRIES
economic and social questions *834–837
LATIN AMERICA AND THE CARIBBEAN see also Americas; Caribbean; Central America; Economic Commission for Latin America and the Caribbean (ECLAC); specific country names
disarmament, United Nations Regional Centre for Peace, Disarmament and Development in Latin America and Caribbean *548–550
humanitarian assistance
Caribbean 890
Central America *890–891
regional economic and social activities 954–958
LAW OF THE SEA *1308–1349 see also landlocked developing countries; small island developing States
assessment of global marine environment 1327–1328
Commission on the Limits of the Continental Shelf 1325
Division for Ocean Affairs and the Law of the Sea 1328–1348
fish stocks, agreement relating to conservation and management of *1308–1323
institutions created by the Convention 1323–1325
International Seabed Authority 1323–1324
International Tribunal for the Law of the Sea 1324–1325
marine biological resources 1328
meeting of States Parties 1308
piracy 1328
signatures and ratifications 1308
United Nations Convention on the Law of the Sea *1308–1323
United Nations Open-ended Informal Consultative Process 1328
LEAST DEVELOPED COUNTRIES (LDCs) *826–832
economic and social questions *826–832
Fourth United Nations Conference on Least Developed Countries *827–832
Istanbul Declaration 828
list *826–827
Programme of Action for the Least Developed Countries for the Decade 2001–2010 827
smooth transition strategy for countries graduating from list of least developed countries *826–827
Trade and Development Board (TDB) action *829
LEBANON see also Middle East
political and security questions *455–467
Special Tribunal for Lebanon 466–467

Subject index

United Nations Interim Force in Lebanon (UNIFIL) *464–466
LEGAL QUESTIONS *1227–1348
  Convention on Special Missions and its Optional Protocol 1284
  diplomatic relations 1289–1290
  economic law, international *1290–1298
    arbitration and conciliation 1293
    case law 1295
    coordination and cooperation 1295
    electronic commerce 1294
    future work 1295
    insolvency law *1292–1293
    microfinance 1294
    online dispute resolution 1293–1294
    procurement *1291–1292
    security interests 1294
    technical cooperation and assistance 1295
    United Nations Commission on International Trade Law (UNCITRAL) *1291–1298
  host country relations *1305–1307
  International Court of Justice (ICJ) 1227–1241
  International Law Commission (ILC) *1266–1282
    aliens, expulsion of 1278–1279
    armed conflict, effects on treaties *1275–1278
    disasters, protection of persons in event of 1279
    immunity of state officials 1278
    most-favoured-nation clause *1280
    obligation to extradite or prosecute 1279
    reservations to treaties 1267–1268
    responsibility of international organizations *1268–1278
    treaties over time *1279–1280
  international legal questions *1266–1307
  international State relations and international law *1282–1289
  international tribunals and court *1242–1265
    functioning of the Tribunals *1258–1261
    International Criminal Court (ICC) 1261–1265
    International Residual Mechanism 1259
    International Tribunal for Rwanda (ICTR) *1249–1258
    International Tribunal for the Former Yugoslavia (ICTY) *1242–1249
  jurisdictional immunities of states and their properties 1284
  law of the sea *1308–1349
  legal aspects of international political relations *1266–1290
  nationality of natural persons in relation to succession of States *1282–1283
  political relations, legal aspects of *1266–1290
  protection of diplomatic and consular missions and representatives 1289–1290
  rule of law at the national and international levels *1298–1300
  Special Committee on United Nations Charter *1300–1305
  special missions 1284
  strengthening role of United Nations *1300–1305
  succession of States 1284
  terrorism, international *1284–1289
  transboundary aquifers, law of *1283
  treaties and agreements 1290
    advice and capacity-building in treaty law and practice 1290
    international organizations 1284
    law of treaties 1284
    multilateral treaties deposited with Secretary-General 1290
    UN registration and publication of treaties 1290
  universal jurisdiction, principle of *1283–1284
  UN Programme for teaching and study of international law *1303–1305
  Vienna Convention on the Law of Treaties 1284
LIBERIA
  humanitarian assistance 884
  political and security questions *162–174
    elections 167
    legislative elections 167
    Panel of Experts, sanctions *168–171
    Peacebuilding Commission 171
    presidential and legislative elections 167
    sanctions *167–171
    United Nations Mission in Liberia (UNMIL) 166–167, *172–174
LIBYAN ARAB JAMAHIRIYA
  human rights 758–759
  humanitarian assistance 887
  Human Rights Council, suspension and restoration of membership rights of *604–606
  ICC Prosecutor activities 287–288
  political and security questions *266–287
  sanctions 288–289
  United Nations Support Mission for Libya (UNSMIL) 289

M

MACEDONIA see The former Yugoslav Republic of Macedonia
malaria *1153–1157
management see Institutional, Administrative and Budgetary Questions
maritime law see law of the sea
MAURITIUS–UNITED KINGDOM 296
  political and security questions 296
MIDDLE EAST see also Middle East Peace Process; Palestine; specific country names
  human rights *779–785
    Follow-up to 2009 Fact-Finding Mission on Gaza Conflict 784–785
    Follow-up to 2010 fact-finding mission on humanitarian flotilla incident 785
    Occupied Syrian Golan 784
    Syrian Arab Republic *779–782
    Territories occupied by Israel 782–785
  political and security questions *402–477
    Lebanon *455–467
    Palestine *434–455
    Syrian Arab Republic *468–477
    United Nations Truce Supervision Organization (UNTSO) 477
  refugees and displaced persons 1129
Middle East Peace Process *403–434 see also Palestine
  diplomatic efforts *403–434
  economic and social situation *428–433

Fourth Geneva Convention *433–434
human rights of the Palestinian people and other Arabs of the Occupied Territories *424–428
Israeli settlements *417–420
Jerusalem *420–421
Occupied Palestinian Territory *403–434
Panel of Inquiry on 2010 flotilla incident 412–413
peaceful settlement of the question of Palestine *413–417
permanent sovereignty over natural resources *431–433
Special Committee to Investigate Israeli Practices Affecting Human Rights *421–428
migrant persons *see* refugees and displaced persons
MONTSERRAT
decolonization, under review for 570
MONUSCO *see* United Nations Organization Stabilization Mission in the Democratic Republic of the Congo (MONUSCO)
munitions *see* disarmament; weapons
MYANMAR
human rights *772–776

N

natural resources 966–967
NEPAD *see* New Partnership for Africa's Development (NEPAD)
NEPAL *see also* United Nations Mission in Nepal (UNMIN)
human rights 776–777
political and security questions *372
NEW CALEDONIA
decolonization *561–563
New Partnership for Africa's Development (NEPAD) *891–898
NICARAGUA *see also* Nicaragua–Costa Rica
humanitarian assistance *890–891
NICARAGUA–COSTA RICA 298
NIGER
humanitarian assistance 884
NIGERIA
Cameroon-Nigeria Mixed Commission 186–187
terrorist attack 56
non-governmental organizations 1373–1374
non-proliferation *500–520
Conference on Disarmament *509–510
Democratic People's Republic of Korea 513
Hague Code of Conduct against Ballistic Missile Proliferation 506
Iran 513–514
Middle East *514–515
missiles 505–506
multilateralism in disarmament and non-proliferation *511–512
nuclear-weapon-free zones (NWFZs) 517–520
radioactive waste *516–517
safeguards, IAEA 513–516
Syrian Arab Republic 515–516
Treaty on the Non-Proliferation of Nuclear Weapons (NPT) *500–505
weapons of mass destruction (WMDs) *506–511
Security Council Committee on *506–509
terrorism and *510–511

Non-Self-Governing Territories (NSGTs) *see* decolonization
NORTH AFRICA *266–296 *see also specific country names*
NORTH AMERICA
international drug control 1186
nuclear disarmament *485–500
accelerating implementation of nuclear disarmament commitments *495–497
Comprehensive Nuclear-Test-Ban Treaty (CTBT) 493–498
conference on facilitating entry into force of CTBT *494–497
Preparatory Commission for CTBT Organization 497–498
Conference on Disarmament *487–490
Convention on the Prohibition of the Use of Nuclear Weapons *499–500
fissile material *490–491
ICJ advisory opinion *498–499
reduction of nuclear danger *486–487
security assurances *492–493
nuclear energy *see* energy
nuclear-weapon-free zones (NWFZs) 517–520
Africa *517
African Nuclear-Weapon-Free Zone Treaty *517
Asia *518–519
Central Asia 518
South-East Asia *518–519
Treaty on South-East Asia Nuclear-Weapon-Free Zone (Bangkok Treaty) *518–519
Latin America and the Caribbean 519
Middle East *519–520
South Pacific 520
nutrition *see also* food; humanitarian assistance
Standing Committee on Nutrition 1169
United Nations University Food and Nutrition Programme for Human and Social Development (UNU-FNP) 1169

O

OCCUPIED PALESTINIAN TERRITORY *403–434 *see also* Middle East; Palestine
humanitarian assistance 888
Occupied Syrian Golan
human rights 784
OCHA *see* humanitarian assistance
OHCHR *see* human rights
OUTER SPACE
Committee on the Peaceful Uses of Outer Space *577–586
Legal Subcommittee 581–582
Scientific and Technical Subcommittee 578–581
International Day of Human Space Flight *577
International Space Weather Initiative 580–581
political and security questions *577–586
scientific and technical issues 579–581
space-based disaster management and emergency response (UN-SPIDER) 580
treaties 582
UNISPACE III recommendations 577
United Nations Programme on Space Applications 578–579
UN system coordination *582–586

Subject index

P

PAKISTAN
 humanitarian assistance 888–889
PALESTINE see also Middle East; Middle East Peace Process
 assistance to Palestinians *438–455
  Committee on the Exercise of the Inalienable Rights of the Palestinian People *434–438
  displaced persons *450–451
  Division for Palestinian Rights *436–437
  human rights of the Palestinian people and other Arabs of the Occupied Territories *424–426
  management capacity *448–450
  Occupied Palestinian Territory *403–434
  Palestinian women *451–454
  peaceful settlement of the question of Palestine *413–417
  political and security questions *434–455
  property rights *454–455
  Special Committee to Investigate Israeli Practices Affecting Human Rights *421–428
  special information programme *437–438
  UNCTAD assistance to Palestinians *439–442
  United Nations Relief and Works Agency for Palestine Refugees in the Near East (UNRWA) *442–450
PANAMA
 humanitarian assistance *890–891
PEACEBUILDING *43–48
 Peacebuilding Commission 47–48
 Peacebuilding Fund 48
PEACEKEEPING OPERATIONS *57–86 see also specific country and mission names
 2011 operations 62–63
  Africa 62
  Americas 62
  Asia 62
  Europe and the Mediterranean 62
  Middle East 62–63
  roster 63–64
 complex peacekeeping operations, strategies for 59–60
 comprehensive review of peacekeeping *61–62
 conduct and discipline 58–59
 cooperation
  with regional organizations 60
  with troop- and police-contributing countries 60
 criminal accountability of UN staff and experts on mission *83–86
 cross-cutting issues 78–82
 financial and administrative aspects of 65–86
  accounts and auditing 74–75
  air operations, financing 73
  asset management 76–77
  audited statements 74–75
  Board of Auditors, reports of 74–75
  closed missions, funds for 73–74
  contingent-owned equipment, reimbursement for *75–76
  cross-cutting issues 78–82
  financial performance 65
  financing 65–77
  management of peacekeeping assets 76–77
  oversight activities 61
  peacekeeping support account 65–66
  personnel matters *83–86
  reimbursement issues *75–76
  restructuring issues 77–83
  staff *83–86
  support account 65–66
  UN police capacities 83
 general aspects of UN peacekeeping 58–61
 global field support strategy, restructuring issues 78–83
 operational capacity 59
 police capacities, restructuring issues 83
 safety and security 58
 Security Council Working Group on Peacekeeping Operations 61
 sexual exploitation and abuse in UN peacekeeping operations 58–59
 Special Committee on Peacekeeping Operations *61–62
 strengthening capacity to manage and sustain operations 66–72
 United Nations Logistics Base 76–77
 women in peacekeeping 60
persons with disabilities
 convention on the rights of *633–634
 equalization of opportunities *1030–1032
 World Programme of Action *1029–1030
THE PHILIPPINES
 humanitarian assistance 889
POLITICAL AND SECURITY QUESTIONS *31–599 see also Africa; Americas; Asia and the Pacific; decolonization; disarmament; Europe; information; international peace and security; outer space; peacekeeping operations; terrorism; specific regions and country names
 Afghanistan *310–351
 Africa *87–296
 Americas *297–309
 Armenia and Azerbaijan 392
 arms see disarmament
 Asia and the Pacific *310–376
 atomic radiation, effects of *586–589
 Bosnia and Herzegovina *377–384
 Burundi *117–120
 Cameroon–Nigeria 186–188
 Central Africa and Great Lakes region *97–133
 Central African Republic *121–128
 Central African Republic and Chad *128–132
 Central America 297–298
 Chad–Sudan 232–233
 Côte d'Ivoire *140–162
 Cyprus *392–400
 Darfur *217–230
 Democratic People's Republic of Korea *368–369
 Democratic Republic of the Congo *102–117
 disarmament *478–550
 Egypt 296
 Eritrea *261–265
 Eritrea–Ethiopia *265–266
 Europe and the Mediterranean *377–401
 Georgia *389–392

Guinea 188–189
Guinea-Bissau *180–186
Haiti *297–308
Horn of Africa *189–266
India–Pakistan 375
information and information security *589–599
Iran *369–372
Iraq *351–359
Iraq–Kuwait 360–362
Kosovo *384–389
Lebanon *455–467
Liberia *162–174
Libyan Arab Jamahiriya *266–287
Mauritius–United Kingdom 296
Middle East *402–477
Nepal *372
North Africa *266–296
Pakistan 375
Palestine *434–455
Rwanda *132–133
Sierra Leone *174–180
Somalia *233–261
Sri Lanka 375
Sudan and South Sudan *189–232
Syrian Arab Republic *468–477
Thailand–Cambodia 375–376
the former Yugoslav Republic of Macedonia 389
Timor-Leste *362–368
Tunisia 296
Uganda 132
United Arab Emirates–Iran 376
United Nations Department of Public Information (DPI) *590–599
West Africa *133–189
Western Sahara 289–296
political missions, special see specific mission names
POPULATION 1002–1012
   Commission on Population and Development 1002–1004
   country and intercountry programmes 1007–1009
   fertility, reproductive health and development 1003–1004
   gender equality and women's empowerment 1007
   General Assembly informal thematic debate 1004
   Global Forum on Migration and Development 1004
   International Conference on Population and Development (ICPD) 1002
   international migration and development 1004–1005
   Joint United Nations Programme on HIV/AIDS 1011
   reproductive health and rights 1006–1007
   United Nations Population Fund (UNFPA) 1005–1011
   United Nations Population Division 1011–1012
POVERTY
   eradication of *805–809
   General Assembly high-level meeting addressing desertification, land degradation and drought in the context of sustainable development and poverty eradication 982
   women *1061–1068
public information see information
PUERTO RICO
   decolonization 560

R

racism and racial discrimination *651–663 see also human rights
   contemporary forms of racism *659–663
   follow-up to 2001 World Conference *651–659
   General Assembly high-level meeting *652–653
   sports and combating discrimination *654–659
   united against racism, racial discrimination, xenophobia and related intolerance *653
REFUGEES AND DISPLACED PERSONS
   Africa, regional activities *1121–1124
   Americas 1127–1128
   Asia and the Pacific 1128–1129
   community services 1120
   economic and social questions *1112–1133
   Europe 1130–1131
   global needs assessment 1133
   HIV/AIDS 1119–1120
   host countries, role of 1120
   inspections 1125
   international instruments 1121
   Middle East and North Africa 1129
   natural disasters 1120
   Office of the United Nations High Commissioner for Refugees (UNHCR) *1112–1133
   partnerships and coordination 1131
   policy development and cooperation 1131–1133
   populations of concern 1118–1119
   programme policy *1112–1117
   protection and assistance 1117–1121
   protracted situations and durable solutions 1121
   regional activities *1121–1125
   staff security 1120–1121
   United Nations Minimum Operating Security Standards (MOSS) 1119
   women 1119
REGIONAL ECONOMIC AND SOCIAL ACTIVITIES *937–962 see also specific regions and regional commissions
rights see human rights
rule of law 46–47
   European Rule of Law Mission in Kosovo (EULEX) 386–387
   strengthening 1214
RWANDA *132–133 see also International Criminal Tribunal for Rwanda (ICTR)
   assistance to survivors of 1994 genocide, particularly orphans, widows and victims of sexual violence *132–133
   International Criminal Tribunal for Rwanda (ICTR) *1249–1258
   political and security questions *132–133

S

SAINT HELENA, decolonization 571
science and technology for development
   Commission on Science and Technology for Development *810–814
   economic and social questions *810–821
   Follow-up to World Summit on the Information Society *815–818
   information and communication technologies *814–821

Subject index

  Inter-Agency Round Table on Communication for Development 814
  Internet governance *817
  public policy pertaining to the Internet 814
SECRETARIAT, UNITED NATIONS see United Nations
security see political and security questions
SECURITY COUNCIL 1358–1359
  review of Security Council membership and related matters 1358
  sessions 1358–1359
SIERRA LEONE
  military guard force, withdrawal of *180
  Peacebuilding Commission 178–179
  political and security questions *174–180
  Special Court for Sierra Leone *179–180
  United Nations Integrated Peacebuilding Office in Sierra Leone (UNIPSIL) 179
slavery and related issues 735–737
  Fund on Slavery 735
  transatlantic slave trade *736–737
small island developing States *832–834
  Commission on Sustainable Development consideration 832
  economic and social questions *832–834
  Mauritius Strategy for the Further Implementation of the Programme of Action for the Sustainable Development of Small Island Developing States *833–834
SOCIAL POLICY AND CULTURAL ISSUES *1013–1042
  ageing persons *1024–1029
  Commission for Social Development 1020–1021
  cooperatives in social development *1023–1024
  family *1039–1042
  International Year of the Family *1039–1042
  International Year of Youth 1035
  persons with disabilities *1029–1032
  recovery from economic and financial crisis *1018–1020
  Report on world social situation 1022–1023
  social development *1013–1024
  social inclusion *1021–1022
  social integration *1021–1022
  World Elder Abuse Awareness Day *1025–1027
  World Programme of Action for Youth *1032–1039
  youth *1032–1039
SOMALIA
  African Union Mission in Somalia (AMISOM) *260–261
  children and armed conflict 254
  humanitarian assistance 887
  human rights 759–760
  Kampala Accord *237–243
  piracy *243–254
  political and security questions *233–261
  sanctions *254–259
  United Nations Political Office for Somalia (UNPOS) 259–260
SOUTH AMERICA
  international drug control 1186–1187
SOUTH ASIA
  international drug control 1187
SOUTH-EAST ASIA
  nuclear-weapon-free zones (NWFZs) *518–519

SOUTHERN AFRICA see specific country names
SOUTH SUDAN see also Sudan and South Sudan
  economic recovery and development *899
  human rights 761
  new United Nations Member *1353–1354
  United Nations Mission in South Sudan (UNMISS) 64, 193,*197–200, 203–204, 208, *213–215
space see outer space
SRI LANKA
  children and armed conflict 375
  humanitarian assistance 889
  political and security questions 375
staff of United Nations see institutional, administrative and budgetary questions
STATISTICS 1215–1224
  agricultural statistics 1218
  business registers 1218
  capacity-building 1222–1223
  coordination and integration of statistical programmes 1221
  demographic statistics 1215–1217
  development indicators 1223
  economic statistics 1217–1220
  education statistics 1216
  energy statistics 1218–1219
  environmental-economic accounting 1220–1221
  environment statistics 1220
  follow-up to Economic and Social Council policy decisions 1223
  Fundamental Principles of Official Statistics 1222
  gender statistics 1216–1217
  global geospatial information management 1224
  health statistics 1216
  human development statistics 1221–1222
  integrated economic statistics 1219–1220
  International Comparison Programme 1219
  inventory of global statistical standards 1224
  measurement of economic performance and social progress 1224
  national accounts 1217–1218
  national quality assurance frameworks 1223
  natural resources statistics 1220–1221
  population and housing censuses 1215–1216
  price statistics 1219
  regional statistical development 1223
  short-term economic indicators 1220
  standards on data and metadata exchange (SDMX) 1222
  Statistical Commission 1215–1224
  tourism statistics 1219
  Western Asia, regional statistical development 1223
  World Statistics Day 1224
SUDAN AND SOUTH SUDAN *189–232 see also African Union-United Nations Hybrid Operation in Darfur (UNAMID); Darfur
  admission of South Sudan to UN membership 201
  children and armed conflict 209–210
  Darfur *217–230
  human rights 760–761
  political and security questions *189–232
  United Nations Interim Security Force for Abyei (UNISFA) *215–232

United Nations Mission in South Sudan (UNMISS) *213–215
United Nations Mission in the Sudan (UNMIS) 200, *210–213
sustainable development *797–805 *see also* development

SYRIAN ARAB REPUBLIC
human rights *779–782
political and security questions *468–477
    The Syrian Golan *471–477
    United Nations Disengagement Observer Force (UNDOF) 474–477

T

TDB *see* Trade and Development Board (TDB)
technical cooperation *see* development
TERRORISM *52–56
  Afghanistan 55
  anniversary of 2001 terrorist attacks 56
  attacks in 2011 55–56
  Belarus 56
  Burundi 55
  Counter-Terrorism Committee (CTC) 53–54
  global counter-terrorism strategy *54–55
  international peace and security *52–56
  Iraq 55
  Israel 55
  Lebanon 55
  legal questions, international terrorism *1284–1289
    attacks on internationally protected persons *1288–1289
    convention on 1284–1285
  measures to eliminate international terrorism 53–54
  Morocco 55
  Nigeria 56
  Norway 56
  Pakistan 56
  Russian Federation 56
  Somalia 56
  Sudan 56
  Syria 56
  United Nations Counter-Terrorism Centre *54–55

THE FORMER YUGOSLAV REPUBLIC OF MACEDONIA 389

TIMOR-LESTE
political and security questions *362–368
    United Nations Integrated Mission in Timor-Leste (UNMIT) *366–368
    United Nations Mission in East Timor (UNAMET) 366
TOKELAU, decolonization *563–564
trade *see* international trade
Trade and Development Board (TDB) 905–906
trafficking
  in cultural property 1199–1201
  in endangered species 1201–1203
  of fraudulent medicines 1203
  in persons 1199
transport *932–936
  Chemicals, Globally Harmonized System of Classification and Labelling of *933–936
  dangerous goods, transport of *933–936
  maritime transport 932–933

TREATIES AND AGREEMENTS *see specific name of treaty or agreement*
Tunisia
  human rights 761
  political and security questions 296
TURKS AND CAICOS ISLANDS
  decolonization, under review for 571

U

UGANDA 132
UNAMA *see* United Nations Assistance Mission in Afghanistan (UNAMA)
UNAMI *see* United Nations Assistance Mission for Iraq (UNAMI)
UNAMID *see* African Union-United Nations Hybrid Operation in Darfur (UNAMID)
UNCTAD *see* United Nations Conference on Trade and Development (UNCTAD)
UNDOF *see* United Nations Disengagement Observer Force (UNDOF)
UNDP *see* United Nations Development Programme (UNDP)
UNEP *see* United Nations Environment Programme (UNEP)
UNFF *see* United Nations Forum on Forests (UNFF)
UNFICYP *see* United Nations Peacekeeping Force in Cyprus (UNFICYP)
UNFPA *see* United Nations Population Fund (UNFPA)
UN-Habitat *see* United Nations Human Settlements Programme
UNHCR *see* Office of the United Nations High Commissioner for Refugees (UNHCR)
UNICEF *see* United Nations Children's Fund (UNICEF)
UNIFIL *see* United Nations Interim Force in Lebanon (UNIFIL)
UNIOGBIS *see* United Nations Integrated Peacebuilding Office in Guinea-Bissau (UNIOGBIS)
UNIPSIL *see* United Nations Integrated Peacebuilding Office in Sierra Leone (UNIPSIL)
UNITAR *see* United Nations Institute for Training and Research (UNITAR)
UNITED NATIONS *see* Economic and Social Council; General Assembly; institutional, administrative and budgetary questions; International Court of Justice (ICJ); Security Council
  budget *see* institutional, administrative and budgetary questions
United Nations Assistance Mission for Iraq (UNAMI) 51, 356
United Nations Assistance Mission in Afghanistan (UNAMA) 50, 331
United Nations Children's Fund (UNICEF) 1101
  basic education and gender equality 1107
  Ethics Office 1108
  Gender equality 1105, 1107
  HIV/AIDS 1107
  humanitarian action 1107–1108
  International Public Sector Accounting Standards (IPSAS) 1110–1111
  joint programming 1105
  policy advocacy and partnerships for children's rights 1107
  programme policies 1103–1105
  programmes
    by region 1105–1106
    by sector 1106–1108

Subject index 1535

protection of children from violence, exploitation and abuse 1107
young child survival and development 1106
United Nations Conference on Trade and Development (UNCTAD) *439–442, 905
  subsidiary bodies 906–908
  Trade and Development Board 905–906
  UNCTAD/World Trade Organization International Trade Centre (ITC) 908–909
United Nations Development Programme (UNDP) 843–853
  audit reports 851–852
  budget 850–851
  country and regional programmes 844–845
  crisis prevention and recovery 846–847
  democratic governance 846
  energy and the environment 847
  Ethics Office 852
  financial and administrative matters 849–853
  gender equality 847
  Human Development Report 844
  information disclosure, audit reports 852
  monitoring and evaluation 848–849
  Myanmar, assistance to 845
  operational activities 844–847
  poverty reduction and MDG achievement 846
  programme results 845–847
  programming arrangements 847–849
  revised rules of procedure 843
  technical cooperation through 843–853
  UNDP/UNFPA activities 843–844
  UNDP/UNFPA/UNOPS Executive Board 843–844
United Nations Disengagement Observer Force (UNDOF) 63, 474–477
United Nations Entity for Gender Equality and the Empowerment of Women (UN-Women) 1082, *1093–1100
United Nations Environment Programme (UNEP) *970–976
  biodiversity 974
  chemicals and waste 972
  cooperation with UN Scientific Committee on the Effects of Atomic Radiation 976
  emergencies, environmental 973–974
  Environment Management Group (EMG) 973
  Global Programme of Action for the Protection of the Marine Environment from Land-based Activities 974
  governance, work programme and budget 974–975
  Governing Council/Global Ministerial Environment Forum (GC/GMEF) *970–976
  green economy 971
  international environmental governance 971–972
  marine and coastal ecosystems 974
  ministerial consultations 971–972
  monitoring and assessment 972
  programme areas 972–974
  South-South cooperation 973
  sustainable consumption and production 972–973
  trust funds, work programme and budget 975
  United Nations Conference on Sustainable Development, preparatory process for 972
  UN system coordination and cooperation 973
  UNEP/UN-Habitat cooperation 973
  waste management 972
  Year Book 976
United Nations Forum on Forests (UNFF) 985–986
United Nations High Commissioner for Refugees (UNHCR) *1112–1133
United Nations Human Settlements Programme (UN-Habitat) *994–1001
United Nations Institute for Training and Research (UNITAR) *1053–1056
United Nations Integrated Mission in Timor-Leste (UNMIT) *366–368
United Nations Integrated Office in Burundi (BINUB) 50, 59, 117, 120
United Nations Integrated Peacebuilding Office in Guinea-Bissau (UNIOGBIS) 51–52, 186
United Nations Integrated Peacebuilding Office in Sierra Leone (UNIPSIL) 51, 179
United Nations Integrated Peacebuilding Office in the Central African Republic (BINUCA) 50–51, 87, 121–124, 128
United Nations Interim Administration Mission in Kosovo (UNMIK) 63, *387–389
United Nations Interim Force in Lebanon (UNIFIL) *464–466
United Nations Interim Security Force for Abyei (UNISFA) 64, *195–196, *201–209
United Nations Mission for the Referendum in Western Sahara (MINURSO) 63, *293–296
United Nations Mission in Liberia (UNMIL) 63, 166–167, *172–174
United Nations Mission in Nepal (UNMIN) 51, *372
United Nations Mission in South Sudan (UNMISS) 64, 193, 197–200, 203–204, 208, *213–215
United Nations Mission in the Sudan (UNMIS) 64, 200, *210–213
United Nations Observer Mission in Georgia (UNOMIG) *391–392
United Nations Office for Disarmament Affairs (UNODA) 479
United Nations Office for Project Services (UNPOS) 856–857
United Nations Office for West Africa (UNOWA) 50, 139–140
United Nations Office in Burundi (BNUB) 50, 52, 87, 117–118, 120
United Nations Office on Drugs and Crime (UNODC) *1170–1174
United Nations Operation in Côte d'Ivoire (UNOCI) 63–64, *146–153, *160–162
United Nations Organization Stabilization Mission in the Democratic Republic of the Congo (MONUSCO) *114–117
United Nations Peacekeeping Force in Cyprus (UNFICYP) 63, *394–400
United Nations Platform for Space-based Information for Disaster Management and Emergency Response (UN-SPIDER) 580, *873
United Nations Political Office for Somalia (UNPOS) 50, 259–260
United Nations Population Fund (UNFPA) 1002
United Nations Relief and Works Agency for Palestine Refugees in the Near East (UNRWA) *442–450
United Nations Security Council *see* Security Council
United Nations Statistical Commission *see* statistics

United Nations Support Mission in Libya (UNSMIL) 52, *280–283, *285–286
United Nations Truce Supervision Organization (UNTSO) 63, 477
United Nations University Food and Nutrition Programme for Human and Social Development (UNU-FNP) 1169
United Nations University (UNU) 1055
UNITED STATES VIRGIN ISLANDS, decolonization 572
UNMIK see United Nations Interim Administration Mission in Kosovo (UNMIK)
UNMIL see United Nations Mission in Liberia (UNMIL)
UNMIN see United Nations Mission in Nepal (UNMIN)
UNMIS see United Nations Mission in the Sudan (UNMIS)
UNMISS see United Nations Mission in South Sudan (UNMISS)
UNMIT see United Nations Integrated Mission in Timor-Leste (UNMIT)
UNOCI see United Nations Operation in Côte d'Ivoire (UNOCI)
UNODA see United Nations Office for Disarmament Affairs (UNODA)
UNODC see United Nations Office on Drugs and Crime (UNODC)
UNOMIG see United Nations Observer Mission in Georgia (UNOMIG)
UNOWA see United Nations Office for West Africa (UNOWA)
UNRWA see United Nations Relief and Works Agency for Palestine Refugees in the Near East (UNRWA)
UN-SPIDER see United Nations Platform for Space-based Information for Disaster Management and Emergency Response (UN-SPIDER)
UNTSO see United Nations Truce Supervision Organization (UNTSO)
UNU see United Nations University (UNU)
UNU-FNP see United Nations University Food and Nutrition Programme for Human and Social Development (UNU-FNP)
UN-Water 966–967

W

water resources 966–967
weapons see disarmament; weapons of mass destruction (WMDs)
weapons of mass destruction (WMDs) see also disarmament; terrorism
  non-proliferation of *506–511
WEST AFRICA see also Cameroon; Côte d'Ivoire; Guinea-Bissau; Mauritius; Sierra Leone; specific country names
  humanitarian assistance 883–884
    Côte d'Ivoire and neighbouring countries 884
    Liberia 884
    Niger 884
  political and security questions *133–189
    assessment missions
      on piracy 138–139
      to Sahel region 135–136
    Cameroon–Nigeria 186–188
    Côte d'Ivoire *140–162
    Guinea 188–189
    Guinea-Bissau *180–186
    Liberia *162–174
    piracy and armed robbery *136–139
    regional issues *133–140
    Sierra Leone *174–180

United Nations Office for West Africa (UNOWA) 139–140
West African Economic and Monetary Union see specific country names
WESTERN ASIA see also Economic and Social Commission for Western Asia
  international drug control 1187
  regional economic and social activities 958–962
WESTERN SAHARA see also United Nations Mission for the Referendum in Western Sahara (MINURSO)
  decolonization 564
  political and security questions *289–296
  United Nations Mission for the Referendum in Western Sahara (MINURSO) *293–296
WFP see World Food Programme (WFP)
WMDs see weapons of mass destruction (WMDs)
WOMEN *1057–1100
  advancement of *1080–1082
  armed conflict and *1075–1077
  climate change policies and 1083
  Commission on the Status of Women (CSW) 1092–1093
  Committee on the Elimination of Discrimination against Women (CEDAW) *1090–1091
  Convention on the Elimination of Discrimination against Women *1090–1091
  critical areas of concern *1061–1090
  development, women in *1061–1066
  education and training of 1068–1070
  environment and 1082–1083
  follow-up to the Fourth World Conference and Beijing+5 *1057–1090
  gender equality and sustainable development 1082–1083
  the girl child *1083–1090
  International Day of the Girl Child *1089–1090
  health 1070–1071
  HIV/AIDS 1070
  human rights of 1082
  indigenous women, violence against 1075
  maternal mortality 1070–1071
  migrant workers, violence against women *1071–1075
  Palestinian women 1082
  peace and security *1075–1077
  political participation *1077–1080
  poverty *1061–1068
  power, women in *1077–1080
  refugees and displaced persons 1119
  rural areas, women in *1066–1068
  United Nations Entity for Gender Equality and the Empowerment of Women (UN-Women) 1082, *1093–1100
  UN machinery *1090–1100
  violence against *1071–1075
World Down Syndrome Day *648–649
World Food Programme (WFP)
  activities 1160–1161
  administrative and financial matters *1161–1162
World Health Organization (WHO)
  global public health *1157–1159
  malaria *1153–1156
  road safety 1159–1160
  tobacco 1152–1153
World Water Day 966
World Water Week 966

Y

YEMEN
    humanitarian assistance 890
    human rights 777–778
YOUTH *see also* children; United Nations Children's Fund (UNICEF)
    social policy *1032–1039
        high-level meeting on youth *1035–1039
        International Year of Youth 1035
        World Programme of Action for Youth *1032–1039

Index of resolutions and decisions
(For dates of sessions please refer to Appendix III.)

Resolution No.	Page	Resolution No.	Page	Resolution No.	Page	Resolution No.	Page
General Assembly		65/310	61	66/17	414	66/71	582
Sixty-fifth session		65/311	1444	66/18	420	66/72	444
65/37 B	1327	65/312	1036	66/19	472	66/73	450
65/243 B	74	65/313	929	66/20	536	66/74	445
65/254 B	131	65/314	927	66/21	509	66/75	454
65/256 B	306	65/315	1354	66/22	552	66/76	426
65/257 B	211	65/316	1368	66/23	517	66/77	433
65/263	1362	Decision No.	Page	66/24	589	66/78	419
65/264	869	65/404 B	1483	66/25	519	66/79	424
65/265	605	65/405 B	1483	66/26	492	66/80	473
65/266	1161	65/406 B	1494	66/27	538	66/81 A	593
65/267	1035	65/407 B	1494	66/28	500	66/81 B	593
65/268	1378	65/412	1252	66/29	532	66/82	575
65/269	1421	65/413 A	1244	66/30	484	66/83	572
65/270	1409	65/413 B	1245	66/31	540	66/84	558
65/271	577	65/414	1453	66/32	511	66/85	576
65/272	449	65/415	604, 1484	66/33	502	66/86	293
65/273	1153	65/416	1494	66/34	527	66/87	561
65/274	1364	65/417	1494	66/35	523	66/88	563
65/275	1047	65/418 A	1494	66/36	541	66/89 A	564
65/276	1369	65/418 B	1494	66/37	542	66/89 B	564
65/277	1135	65/419	1454	66/38	543	66/90	574
65/278	94	65/503 B	1357	66/39	534	66/91	554
65/279	652	65/545	1327	66/40	495	66/92	1282
65/280	829	65/546	736, 1356	66/41	535	66/93	84
65/281	607	65/547	1135, 1357	66/42	528	66/94	1295
65/282	1428	65/548	1135, 1357	66/43	518	66/95	1291
65/283	35	65/549	1146, 1357	66/44	491	66/96	1292
65/284	892	65/550	1162	66/45	502	66/97	1304
65/285	1359	65/551	1143, 1358	66/46	498	66/98	1280
65/286	826	65/552	392, 1357	66/47	525	66/99	1276
65/287	390	65/553	1357	66/48	486	66/100	1268
65/288	1381	65/554	1357, 1358	66/49	504	66/101	1302
65/289	78	65/555	359, 1358, 1411	66/50	510	66/102	1298
65/290	66	65/556	366, 1358	66/51	488	66/103	1283
65/291	76	*Sixty-sixth session*		66/52	516	66/104	1283
65/292	76	Resolution No.	Page	66/53	545	66/105	1285
65/293	73	66/1 A	1357	66/54	549	66/106	1454
65/294	160	66/1 B	1357	66/55	544	66/107	1456
65/295	398	66/2	1146	66/56	548	66/108	1306
65/296	115	66/3	653	66/57	499	66/109	1371
65/297	366	66/4	1400	66/58	547	66/110	1371
65/298	265	66/5	1047	66/59	480	66/111	1371
65/299	391	66/6	308	66/60	479	66/112	1372
65/300	387	66/7	964	66/61	514	66/113	1372
65/301	172	66/8	1404	66/62	530	66/114	736
65/302	475	66/9	890	66/63	400	66/115	1157
65/303	464	66/10	54	66/64	494	66/116	1043
65/304	294	66/11	606	66/65	521	66/117	1435
65/305	230	66/12	1288	66/66	482	66/118	440
65/306	260	66/13	320	66/67	857	66/119	866
65/307	878	66/14	435	66/68	1309	66/120	885
65/308	1354	66/15	436	66/69	879	66/121	1033
65/309	796	66/16	437	66/70	587	66/122	1021

Index of resolutions and decisions

Resolution No.	Page	Resolution No.	Page	Resolution No.	Page	Decision No.	Page
66/123	1023	66/185	903	66/246	1383	66/537	615, 620, 622, 636, 666, 687, 690, 693, 694, 715, 721, 726, 727, 733, 735, 739, 745
66/124	1029	66/186	913	66/247	1393		
66/125	1014	66/187	915	66/248 A	1390		
66/126	1041	66/188	1167	66/248 B	1390		
66/127	1025	66/189	917	66/248 C	1390	66/538	649
66/128	1072	66/190	910	66/249	1398	66/539	1189, 1198
66/129	1066	66/191	924	66/250	1398	66/540	1358
66/130	1078	66/192	991	66/251	116	66/541	1404
66/131	1091	66/193	901	*Decision No.*	*Page*	66/542	791, 905, 912, 917, 921
66/132	1058	66/194	989	66/401	1494	66/543	986
66/133	1114	66/195	803	66/402	1486	66/544 A	802, 1374
66/134	1116	66/196	805	66/403	1488	66/545	825
66/135	1123	66/197	799	66/404 A	1241, 1494	66/546	827
66/136	604	66/198	833	66/405	1483	66/547	809
66/137	645	66/199	877	66/406 A	1483	66/548	843
66/138	623	66/200	979	66/407	1484	66/549	860
66/139	1102	66/201	982	66/408	1483	66/550	860
66/140	1084	66/202	981	66/409	1484	66/551	1358
66/141	627	66/203	975	66/410 A	1485	66/552	1404
66/142	752	66/204	993	66/411 A	1483	66/553	826
66/143	660	66/205	986	66/412	1485	66/554	855
66/144	654	66/206	966	66/413	1267, 1484,	66/555	1425
66/145	680	66/207	999	66/414 A	1483	66/556 A	1383, 1397, 1426
66/146	681	66/208	1049	66/415	48, 1486	66/557	43, 48, 110, 117, 132, 162, 174, 213, 215, 217, 232, 261, 266, 296, 297, 305, 308, 359, 362, 366, 368, 388, 392, 394, 400, 401, 417, 466, 477, 552, 561, 736, 763, 799, 832, 869, 901, 1044, 1049, 1133, 1143, 1228, 1246, 1249, 1255, 1258, 1261, 1288, 1348, 1353, 1354, 1356, 1358, 1359, 1360, 1362, 1368, 1375, 1378, 1392, 1401, 1402, 1404, 1405, 1409, 1411, 1419, 1426, 1434, 1443, 1453, 1454
66/147	683	66/209	825	66/416	1259		
66/148	621	66/210	792	66/417 A	1484		
66/149	648	66/211	812	66/501	1357, 1412		
66/150	694	66/212	793	66/502	1357		
66/151	616	66/213	830	66/503 A	1358		
66/152	638	66/214	834	66/504	653		
66/153	636	66/215	806	66/505	3		
66/154	731	66/216	1062	66/506	1267		
66/155	705	66/217	1051	66/507	1228		
66/156	717	66/218	842	66/508	1023, 1357		
66/157	639	66/219	859	66/509	1359		
66/158	723	66/220	1163	66/510	1359		
66/159	710	66/221	1168	66/511	1250		
66/160	635	66/222	1168	66/512	1242		
66/161	713	66/223	794	66/513	538		
66/162	641	66/224	797	66/514	43, 1358	**Security Council**	
66/163	688	66/225	431	66/515	540, 1358	*Resolution No.*	*Page*
66/164	664	66/226	1045	66/516	506, 1358	1967(2011)	141
66/165	746	66/227	873	66/517	539, 1358	1968(2011)	142
66/166	672	66/228	132	66/518	524	1969(2011)	363
66/167	678	66/229	633	66/519	1358	1970(2011)	267
66/168	675	66/230	773	66/520	1404	1971(2011)	180
66/169	643	66/231	1329	66/521	62	1972(2011)	255
66/170	1089	66/232 A	1401	66/522	561	1973(2011)	271
66/171	700	66/233	1414	66/523	1358	1974(2011)	312
66/172	667	66/234	1441	66/524	1404	1975(2011)	144
66/173	647	66/235 A	1432	66/525	1358	1976(2011)	244
66/174	765	66/236	1407	66/526	1404	1977(2011)	506
66/175	769	66/237	1450	66/527	1372	1978(2011)	192
66/176	781	66/238	1256	66/528	1373	1979(2011)	290
66/177	1205	66/239	1248	66/529	1373	1980(2011)	157
66/178	1204	66/240 A	1259	66/530	1373	1981(2011)	147
66/179	1189	66/241 A	216	66/531	1014, 1023	1982(2011)	228
66/180	1199	66/242 A	162	66/532	738	1983(2011)	39
66/181	1192	66/243 A	214	66/533	686	1984(2011)	370
66/182	1197	66/244	213	66/534	740, 1084	1985(2011)	368
66/183	1178	66/245 A	1376	66/535	651	1986(2011)	395
66/184	818	66/245 B	1376	66/536	681	1987(2011)	1428

Resolution No.	Page	Decision No.	Page	Resolution No.	Page	Decision No.	Page
1988(2011)	337	2011/201 A	1485, 1488	2011/29	1039	2011/245	1215
1989(2011)	341	2011/202	921, 1360	2011/30	1189	2011/246	971
1990(2011)	195	2011/203	1359	2011/31	1204	2011/247	1004
1991(2011)	105	2011/204	1360	2011/32	1205	2011/248	986
1992(2011)	148	2011/205	1360	2011/33	1209	2011/249	985
1993(2011)	1245	2011/206	838, 1360	2011/34	1172	2011/250	985
1994(2011)	474	2011/207	900	2011/35	1208	2011/251	969
1995(2011)	1252	*Resumed organizational session, 2011*		2011/36	1201	2011/252	825
1996(2011)	197			2011/37	1019	2011/253	932
1997(2011)	200	Resolution No.	Page	2011/38	922	2011/254	1091
1998(2011)	742	2011/2	823	2011/39	930	2011/255	1020
1999(2011)	1353	2011/3	961	2011/40	556	2011/256	1189
2000(2011)	149	2011/4	960	2011/41	428	2011/257	1189
2001(2011)	354	Decision No.	Page	2011/42	1199	2011/258	1173, 1396
2002(2011)	256	2011/201 B	1484, 1485, 1488, 1489, 1491	2011/43	899	2011/259	1173, 1174, 1189
2003(2011)	220			Decision No.	Page		
2004(2011)	461			2011/214	1360	2011/260	1175
2005(2011)	176	2011/201 C	1488, 1489	2011/215	838, 843, 1005, 1103, 1160	2011/261	1175
2006(2011)	1253	2011/208	791, 1360			2011/262	1186
2007(2011)	1246	2011/209	937, 1360	2011/216	1362	2011/263	1116
2008(2011)	164	2011/210	861, 1360	2011/217	1162	2011/264	621
2009(2011)	280	2011/211	900	2011/218	791, 1162	2011/265	704
2010(2011)	239	2011/212	861, 1360	2011/219	1361, 1362, 1405	2011/266	751, 1075
2011(2011)	332	2011/213	937			2011/267	751
2012(2011)	302	*Substantive session, 2011*		2011/220	1360	2011/268	301, 900, 1396
2013(2011)	1254	Resolution No.	Page	2011/221	1055		
2014(2011)	373	2011/5	1094	2011/222	953	2011/269	1203, 1373
2015(2011)	247	2011/6	1080	2011/223	937, 938	2011/270	1162
2016(2011)	283	2011/7	840	2011/224	1374	2011/271	1421
2017(2011)	284	2011/8	862	2011/225	1374	2011/272	1374
2018(2011)	137	2011/9	829	2011/226	1374	2011/273	1374
2019(2011)	380	2011/10	1056	2011/227	1374	2011/274	832
2020(2011)	250	2011/11	1054	2011/228	1374	2011/275	814
2021(2011)	112	2011/12	941	2011/229	1374	2011/276	969
2022(2011)	286	2011/13	942	2011/230	1374	2011/277	751
2023(2011)	263	2011/14	946	2011/231	1374	*Resumed substantive session, 2011*	
2024(2011)	205	2011/15	948	2011/232	1374		
2025(2011)	169	2011/16	815	2011/233	1374	Resolution No.	Page
2026(2011)	397	2011/17	810	2011/234	1374	2011/44	832
2027(2011)	118	2011/18	452	2011/235	810, 1070	Decision No.	Page
2028(2011)	475	2011/19	1144	2011/236	810	2011/201 D	1488, 1489, 1490
2029(2011)	1254	2011/20	822	2011/237	810		
2030(2011)	183	2011/21	999	2011/238	810	2011/201 E	1486, 1488, 1489, 1490
2031(2011)	124	2011/22	824	2011/239	810		
2032(2011)	206	2011/23	931	2011/240	810	2011/278	1490
Economic and Social Council		2011/24	967	2011/241	1092	2011/279	621
Organizational session, 2011		2011/25	933	2011/242	735		
Resolution No.	Page	2011/26	896	2011/243	798		
2011/1	1161	2011/27	1031	2011/244	798		
		2011/28	1028				

Index of Security Council presidential statements

Number	Subject	Date	Page
S/PRST/2011/1	Letter dated 22 November 2006 from the Secretary-General addressed to the President of the Security Council	14 January 2011	372
S/PRST/2011/2	Post-conflict peacebuilding: institution-building	21 January 2011	44
S/PRST/2011/3	Reports of the Secretary-General on the Sudan	9 February 2011	190
S/PRST/2011/4	Maintenance of international peace and security: the interdependence between security and development	11 February 2011	41
S/PRST/2011/5	Threats to international peace and security caused by terrorist acts	28 February 2011	350
S/PRST/2011/6	The situation in Somalia	10 March 2011	234
S/PRST/2011/7	The question concerning Haiti	6 April 2011	300
S/PRST/2011/8	Reports of the Secretary-General on the Sudan	21 April 2011	191
S/PRST/2011/9	Threats to international peace and security caused by terrorist acts	2 May 2011	52
S/PRST/2011/10	The situation in Somalia	11 May 2011	236
S/PRST/2011/11	The situation concerning the Democratic Republic of the Congo	18 May 2011	103
S/PRST/2011/12	Reports of the Secretary-General on the Sudan	3 June 2011	193
S/PRST/2011/13	The situation in Somalia	24 June 2011	237
S/PRST/2011/14	Admission of new Members to the United Nations (Republic of South Sudan)	13 July 2011	1353
S/PRST/2011/15	Maintenance of international peace and security: impact of climate change	20 July 2011	978
S/PRST/2011/16	The situation in the Middle East	3 August 2011	469
S/PRST/2011/17	United Nations peacekeeping operations	26 August 2011	57
S/PRST/2011/18	Maintenance of international peace and security: conflict prevention	22 September 2011	38
S/PRST/2011/19	Maintenance of international peace and security: moving forward with security sector reform— prospects and challenges in Africa	12 October 2011	34
S/PRST/2011/20	Women and peace and security	28 October 2011	1076
S/PRST/2011/21	Central African region	14 November 2011	100
S/PRST/2011/22	The situation in Afghanistan	19 December 2011	330

Recent volumes of the *Yearbook of the United Nations* may be
obtained through bookstores worldwide, as well as ordered from:

United Nations Publications
300 East 42nd Street
New York, New York 10017
United States of America

e-mail: **publications@un.org**
website: **un.org/publications**

All volumes of the *Yearbook of the United Nations* from the 1946–47 edition (Vol. 1) to the 2011 edition (Vol. 65) can be accessed in full online on the *Yearbook* website: **unyearbook.un.org**.